P9-CLR-924
3 9082 08468 8772

The STRONGEST STRONG'S

EXHAUSTIVE CONCORDANCE OF THE BIBLE

About the Authors

Dr. James Strong (LL.D., S.T.D.) devoted 35 years of his life to the creation of his concordance. *Strong's Exhaustive Concordance of the Bible* was first published in the 1890s and has been acclaimed an indispensable reference work of Bible students and scholars ever since. Dr. Strong was professor of exegetical theology at Drew Theological Seminary from 1868 to 1893.

John R. Kohlenberger III is a specialist in the application of computers to Bible-related reference projects. He has taught at Multnomah School of Bible and Western Seminary in Portland and has produced *The NIV Interlinear Hebrew-English Old Testament*, the *Zondervan NIV Exhaustive Concordance*, and *The NRSV Concordance, Unabridged.*

James A. Swanson, associate editor, is a specialist in applying database management to biblical studies and has degrees in theology and ministry. He has taught at Multnomah Bible College and is coeditor with John R. Kohlenberger III on several Old and New Testament language concordances. He is also author of the ground-breaking *Dictionary of Biblical Languages With Semantic Domains: Hebrew and Aramaic.*

The STRONGEST STRONG'S EXHAUSTIVE CONCORDANCE OF THE BIBLE

JAMES STRONG, LL.D., S.T.D.

FULLY REVISED AND CORRECTED BY
John R. Kohlenberger III *and* James A. Swanson

GRAND RAPIDS, MICHIGAN 49530

We want to hear from you. Please send your comments about this book to us in care of the address below. Thank you.

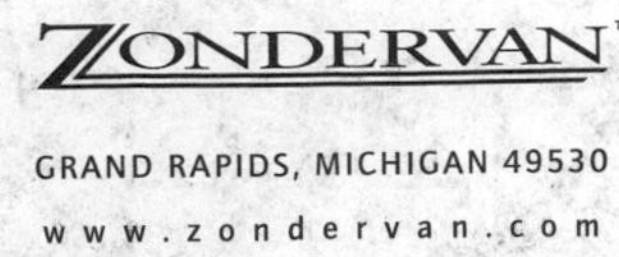

GRAND RAPIDS, MICHIGAN 49530

www.zondervan.com

ZONDERVAN™

The Strongest Strong's Exhaustive Concordance of the Bible

Requests for information should be addressed to:

Zondervan, *Grand Rapids, Michigan 49530*

Library of Congress Cataloging-in-Publication Data

Strong, James, 1822–1894.
The strongest Strong's exhaustive concordance of the Bible / James Strong. —21st century ed., fully rev. and corrected / by John R. Kohlenberger III and James A. Swanson.
p. cm.
ISBN 0-310-23343-7
1. Bible—Concordances, English. 2. Hebrew language—Dictionaries—English. 3. Greek language, Biblical—Dictionaries—English. I. Kohlenberger, John R. II. Swanson, James A., 1952– . III. Strong, James, 1822–1894. Exhaustive concordance of the Bible. IV. Title.
BS425 .S8 2001
220.5'2033—dc21 2001026577

This edition printed on acid-free paper.

Printed in the United States of America

01 02 03 04 05 06 07 08 / ❖ DW / 10 9 8 7 6 5 4 3 2

CONTENTS

DEDICATION

This concordance is dedicated to the memory of

Dr. James Strong

1822–1894

PREFACE

A BRIEF HISTORY OF THE STRONGEST STRONG'S EXHAUSTIVE CONCORDANCE PROJECT

The King James Version was published in 1611. Its first multilingual concordance, Robert Young's *Analytical Concordance to the Bible*, appeared 268 years later. It took forty years of manual labor. In 1894, James Strong's *Exhaustive Concordance to the Bible* joined Young's. It too involved nearly three decades of labor. The Revised Standard Version was completed in 1952, and its first multilingual concordance was issued in 1988: *Eerdmans' Analytical Concordance to the Revised Standard Version*, edited by Richard E. Whitaker. The New American Standard was published in 1971. *The New American Standard Exhaustive Concordance of the Bible* (Holman) appeared in 1981, a project that involved more than ten years and seventy contributors under the general editorship of Robert L. Thomas. Between 1979 and 1999, a team of scholars and computer analysts produced ten concordances to the New International Version. The data developed over a twenty-year period for The NIV Concordance Project form the foundation for *The Strongest Strong's Exhaustive Concordance.*

Within two years of its inception in October of 1979, and just three years after the release of the New International Version itself, The NIV Concordance Project created *The NIV Complete Concordance* (Zondervan, 1981, retitled *The New International Bible Concordance* in 1999). The following year, 1982, saw the release of *The NIV Handy Concordance*, which is also printed in millions of NIV Bibles as the NIV "Mini" or "Standard" Concordance. (Anglicized Editions of these two *Concordances* were prepared and published by Hodder and Stoughton in 1983 and 1985, respectively.) A further abridgment, known in-house as the NIV "Micro" Concordance, was also made in 1982 and is published only in NIV Bibles.

Work on *The NIV Exhaustive Concordance* began in 1983, pairing editors Edward W. Goodrick and John R. Kohlenberger III with computer analysts Dennis B. Thomas and Barbara Perz. Proofreaders James Swanson and Donald Potts put in so many hours on the project that they were named associate editors. The analysts developed software that would assist the editors to manually interrelate or "match up" the NIV to the Hebrew, Aramaic, and Greek originals. The primary focus of this "match-up" process was on the identification of the lexical or root form of each Hebrew, Aramaic, and Greek word and on the description of the interrelation of each word of the original with each word of the NIV. The "match-up" process and its several levels of proofreading took six years—from 1983 through 1989.

The database that resulted from this process contains nearly 900,000 lines, each of which has five fields of data. Thus, the database contains nearly 4,500,000 items of information that required at least ten million editorial decisions. This database, dubbed the "Portland Index" after its place of origin, can be read in either the order of the NIV or the order of the original languages. Since its completion in 1990, it has been featured in all of Zondervan's Bible software. Following Ed Goodrick's untimely passing in 1992, Kohlenberger and Swanson continued refining the Portland Index and used it to produce several other multilingual concordances, including *The Exhaustive Concordance to the Greek New Testament* (Zondervan, 1995), *The Greek-English Concordance to the New Testament* (Zondervan, 1997), *The Hebrew-English Concordance to the Old Testament* (Zondervan, 1998), and the second edition of *The NIV Exhaustive Concordance*, with expanded and enhanced dictionary-indexes (Zondervan, 1999).

Work on *The Strongest Strong's Exhaustive Concordance* began in 1998. Working from a public-domain database of the 1894 edition of Strong's Concordance provided by Scott Musser, computer analyst Ed van der Maas developed a program to compare and merge the contents of the Portland Index with Strong's analysis. Jim Swanson spent a year working through the resulting files verse-by-verse to resolve conflicts between the two analyses of the Bible. Meanwhile, working with June Gunden and her colleagues at Peachtree Editorial and Proofreading, John Kohlenberger developed the first electronic edition of the Cambridge Paragraph Bible of 1873, the best modern edition of the King James Version. John applied this KJV database to Jim's analyzed files and spent a year enhancing and correcting the Strong's edition of the Portland Index and converting the enhanced dictionary-indexes of *The NIV Exhausive Concordance* into the order of Strong's numbering system.

As a result, *The Strongest Strong's Exhaustive Concordance* is the most thoroughly analyzed and most accurate concordance ever produced for the King James Version.

ACKNOWLEDGMENTS

The Strongest Strong's Exhaustive Concordance was conceived of and championed by Jack Kuhatschek, Executive Editor, Zondervan Publishing House. It truly would not have been done without his involvement. Stan Gundry, Vice President and Editor-in-Chief, Zondervan Publishing House, was always there to make decisions and to provide encouragement and support. Senior Editor Verlyn D. Verbrugge worked through all the proofs with his insightful attention to detail.

Scott Musser provided the original public-domain database that served as the starting point of the project. Ed van der Maas developed the programming to merge the NIV data of the Portland Index with the KJV data from Strong. Tim Hare of Telios Systems wrote the programming that created the main concordance and the KJV indexes for the dictionaries. Brent Knopf wrote the programming to convert the related words indexes from G/K numbers to Strong numbers.

June Gunden and her colleagues at Peachtree Editorial and Proofreading did an excellent job of reading the Cambridge Paragraph Bible of 1873 against the KJV text used to produce *The Strongest Strong's Exhaustive Concordance*. Special thanks to Dr. Donald Brake of Multnomah Biblical Seminary for loaning us his personal copy of this rare Bible.

As always, we must thank our families for their patience, encouragement, and support. John Kohlenberger thanks his wife, Carolyn, and children, Sarah and Joshua. Jim Swanson thanks his wife, Sandi, and children, Jonathan, David, and Natanya.

INTRODUCTION

Dr. James Strong (1822–1894) was professor of exegetical theology at Drew Theological Seminary from 1868 to 1893. During his quarter century at Drew, his most important publication was considered to be the massive 10-volume *Cyclopaedia of Biblical, Theological, and Ecclesiastical Literature* (1867–1881), coedited with John McClintock. But today few would doubt his most important publication to be *The Exhaustive Concordance to the Bible*, still a best-seller more than a century after its initial publication in 1894.

The Exhaustive Concordance remains a monument to Strong's brilliant design and excellent editing, especially considering that all of its hundreds of thousands of contexts and thousands of dictionary entries were researched, collated, and typeset by hand without the benefit of computers! But with advances in biblical scholarship and the assistance of computer technology, even Strong's *Concordance* can be significantly improved. This introduction will first explain the nature of Bible concordances, then list the unique features of Strong's *Concordance*, and then detail the new and improved features of *The Strongest Strong's Exhaustive Concordance.*

Bible Concordances in General

A concordance is an index to a book. It is usually arranged in alphabetical order and shows the location of each word in the book. In addition, it often supplies several words of the context in which each word is found.

There are two kinds of Bible concordances for the nonspecialist: those that deal only with the English text of the Bible version on which they are based, and those that also deal with the Hebrew, Aramaic, and Greek texts from which the Bible version was translated.

Examples of English-only concordances are *Cruden's Complete Concordance* for the King James Version and the *NIV Complete Concordance.* The best-known examples of multilingual concordances are Young's *Analytical Concordance* and Strong's *Exhaustive Concordance*, both based on the King James Version (KJV).

An *analytical* concordance is organized in English alphabetical order and shows a complete index of all the different words of a given translation (with the exception of the most common articles, conjunctions, prepositions, and pronouns, such as *a, and, to,* and *he*). Each entry is subdivided according to the Hebrew, Aramaic, or Greek words that underlie the English. Each reference in these subdivisions is listed with a brief context. The analytical concordance also contains index-lexicons of biblical language vocabulary, showing the various English words that translate them.

An *exhaustive* concordance by definition should contain every reference to every word of the Bible version on which it is based. An exhaustive concordance is organized in English alphabetical order, indexes every word of the Bible, and lists every single biblical reference in which that word appears. For all but the most common words (which are indexed by reference only), a context is also given with each reference.

Strong's *Exhaustive Concordance* in Particular

Strong's *Concordance* went beyond the mere listing of words and references to give "exhaustive" a whole new meaning in biblical reference books.

In Strong's *Concordance* the relationship of the English to the original languages is indicated by a numbering system that was originally devised for his *Concordance.* Strong made a list of the Hebrew and "Chaldee" (Aramaic) words used in the Old Testament and of the Greek words used in the New. To each word he assigned a number, indicating its alphabetical order. This number appears at the end of most context lines to indicate the word the English translates. By consulting the dictionaries in the back of Strong's *Concordance*, the user can match numbers in order to identify the biblical word, to see its "root" definition, and to find its range of translation in the KJV.

Improvements in *The Strongest Strong's*

An exhaustive word index to the KJV and a simple guide to the relation of the English Bible to the original languages, Strong's *Concordance* has remained unsurpassed for more than a century. However, advances in biblical scholarship and computer technology, as well as shortcomings in Strong's methodology, have made a new edition desirable and even necessary. Earlier "new" or "expanded" editions of Strong did little other than minor corrections or resetting the original in new type or adding features not intrinsic to the concordance. The *Strongest Strong's Exhaustive Concordance* rebuilt the original from the ground up. Using a gentle pun based on his name, we seek to honor and improve on the strengths of Strong's innovative excellence.

First, we started with the best modern edition of KJV: the Cambridge Paragraph Bible of 1873, edited by F. H. A. Scrivener. Dr. Scrivener was commissioned by Cambridge University Press to create a standardized edition of the KJV to eliminate all of the errors and inconsistencies that had crept into the text in two and a half centuries of printing. Dr. Scrivener spent seven years comparing at least fifteen early editions and all the important editions of the eighteenth and nineteenth centuries in order to conform all matters of italicizing, punctuation and spelling to the exacting standards of the late nineteenth century, while following closely the principles evident in the first editions of 1611. To this standard *The Strongest Strong's* conforms meticulously.

Second, our contexts reflect the KJV text more accurately. As just mentioned, they follow the spelling and punctuation of the 1873 edition with computer-verified accuracy. But beyond that, we also include all the italics of the 1873 edition. The KJV translators used italic type to show English words that were supplied in translation, but did not directly translate a word in the original Hebrew, Aramaic, or Greek. Because Strong's *Concordance* shows the relationship between the original languages and the English, it is extremely significant to show these italicized words and phrases. In the 1873 edition of the KJV, 34,712 words are italicized, but only *The Strongest Strong's* shows italics in the contexts.

Third, our contexts reflect the relationship of the original languages and the English far more exhaustively than the original edition. Since most of Strong's contexts index a single word with a single number, the user gets the wrong impression that the KJV is a word-for-word, one-to-one translation. But the translators often translated single words with phrases, phrases with single words, and phrases with idiomatic phrases. *The Strongest Strong's* uses bold type and multiple Strong numbers to indicate tens of thousands of multi-word translation not indexed in any other edition.

Fourth, Strong's dictionaries are flawed by a methodology of the nineteenth century that has come to be called the "root fallacy." He assumed that biblical words could be defined by the sum of their parts. But just as we do not think that a *pineapple* is an apple that grows on a pine tree or that a *butterfly* is a fly that likes butter, so we should not use this methodology to define biblical words as was so common in the nineteenth and even the twentieth centuries. Our dictionaries are based on the latest dictionaries, lexicons, and word study books, reflecting great advances in biblical scholarship.

Fifth, the indexes in Strong's dictionaries do not list KJV words by their exact spelling, often making it more difficult to find the exact concordance entries. Our indexes are generated from the same database that generated the concordance, so the indexed words are spelled exactly as in the KJV. And, as an added feature, each word has a statistic indicating the number of times it translates any Hebrew, Aramaic, or Greek word in the KJV. No other edition of Strong's has these features.

Sixth, as one would expect with such an enormous work done over so many years and involving so many people, there are errors in Strong's concordance and dictionaries. For example, under the heading RED, the references in Acts 7:36 and Hebrews 11:29 have the number *2281* at the end of the context lines; however, this is the number for the Greek word for "sea," not "red." Even the "new" and "corrected" editions repeat this error. *The Strongest Strong's* goes farther than any other edition in correcting the generally excellent work of the original editor.

Seventh, as a bonus feature, *The Strongest Strong's* contains an updated edition of the other most significant KJV reference book: *Nave's Topical Bible.* Our edition, called *Nave's Topical Bible Reference System*, has all the features and references of the original, but does not print out the text of the KJV for selected references. No other edition of Strong's or Nave's has half of the information combined in *The Strongest Strong's.*

FEATURES OF THE STRONGEST STRONG'S EXHAUSTIVE CONCORDANCE

The Strongest Strong's is divided into four major sections: (1) the Main Concordance, (2) the Index of Articles, Conjunctions, Particles, Prepositions, and Pronouns, (3) the Biblical Language Dictionary-Indexes, and (4) the Nave's Topical Bible Reference System.

THE MAIN CONCORDANCE

Below is a typical entry from the Main Concordance:

AARON (319) [AARON'S, AARONITES]

Ex	4:14	and he said, Is not **A** the Levite thy brother?	175
	4:27	the LORD said to **A,** "Go into the wilderness	175

The heading consists of:

(1) the indexed word (AARON);
(2) the frequency count in parentheses (319);
(3) the list of related words (AARON'S, AARONITES).

The context lines consist of:

(1) the book-chapter-verse reference;
(2) the context for the indexed word;
(3) the number key to the Dictionary-Index.

HEADINGS

There are three kinds of headings: (1) KJV word headings, (2) KJV Index references, and (3) "See" references.

KJV Word Headings

The 1873 Edition of the KJV contains 790,915 total words (in the 66 canonical books), with a unique vocabulary of 12,858. *The Strongest Strong's* is an exhaustive alphabetic index to every word of the KJV.

The simplest heading is composed of the KJV word and its frequency count, for example:

ABBA (3)

The frequency count lists the total number of times the word appears in the KJV, which is also the number of contexts listed in the concordance. *The Strongest Strong's* is the first exhaustive KJV concordance to provide this information.

The headings show the indexed words exactly as they are spelled in the KJV. In a few instances a word occurs both as a compound word and as a hyphenated word, as in the case of "Beth-lehem," the OT spelling, and "Bethlehem," the NT spelling. For these words, both forms appear in the heading and the contexts are all organized under that heading:

BETHLEHEM, BETH-LEHEM (39)

If the English word occurs in other forms or spellings, these words appear in square brackets following the frequency count:

ABASE (4) [ABASED, ABASING]

ABASED (4) [ABASING]

ABASING (1) [ABASED]

Rather than listing all related words after each indexed word, the editors chose one indexed word to act as the "group heading." All related words are listed after the group heading, and each of the related word headings points back to the group heading. In the example above, ABASE serves as the group heading for ABASED and ABASING.

The headings also group together words that share common elements. For example:

HEART (830) [BROKEN-HEARTED, FAINTHEARTED, HARDHEARTED, HEART'S, HEARTED, HEARTS, MERRYHEARTED, STOUTHEARTED, TENDERHEARTED]

In addition to studying related words, these lists also allow *The Strongest Strong's* to be used with any edition of the KJV. Most of the differences among the countless settings and printings of the KJV are found in italics, punctuation, and spelling. Italics and punctuation do not affect a concordance, but spelling certainly does. Use the related words lists to find all forms and spelling variations of any word. For example, the past tense of "fetch" is not only spelled "fetched," but also "fet" and "fetcht." In the 1873 edition of the KJV (as in the 1611 edition), "more" is also spelled "moe" and "mo."

KJV Index References

Forty-seven words occur a total of 383,541 times—nearly half the bulk of the KJV! These words are exhaustively indexed in their own section: the Index of Articles, Conjunctions, Particles, Prepositions, and Pronouns (see page xiii). These words are also represented by headings in the Main Concordance, with a message referring to this special index:

A (8718) [AN] See Index of Articles, Etc.

"See" References

The King James or Authorized Version has been the dominant English Bible translation from the early seventeenth century to the latter half of the twentieth century. Because of this, the KJV has had profound impact on the language of the Church. Similarly in the last half of the twentieth century, new Bible translations and biblical reference books began to impact the language of the Church. *The Strongest Strong's* includes nearly 1,100 "see" references to 1,500 proper names and key words that are spelled differently in modern versions from the KJV:

CAESAR; CAESAR'S See CESAR; CESAR'S

HOLY SPIRIT See also HOLY GHOST

SINFUL NATURE See CARNAL; FLESH

CONTEXT LINES

Concordances are word indexes. At the very least, they index the book, chapter, and verse in which these words are located. Most concordances also show each word within a brief phrase or clause: a context. This gives the user a better idea of the use of the word and helps to locate a specific verse that contains that word.

The purpose of context lines in a concordance is merely to help the reader recognize or find a specific verse in the Bible. For word study—or any kind of Bible study—the context offered by a concordance is rarely enough to go on. Nevertheless, sometimes a short sentence or a whole verse fits on one line, as in the case of John 11:35: "Jesus wept." Under the heading PRAISE, *The Strongest Strong's* was able to present almost the entirety of Psalm 150 on thirteen consecutive lines!

Taken by themselves, context lines can and do misrepresent the teaching of Scripture by omitting key words. "There is no God" is a context taken straight from Psalm 14:1. Of course the Bible does not teach this; it is what "the fool hath said in his heart"! Similarly, a context for Leviticus 24:16 might read "the LORD, shall be put to death" while the text actually says "he that is born in the land, when he blasphemeth the name of the LORD, shall be put to death."

Great care has been taken by the editors, programmers, and proofreaders of *The Strongest Strong's* to create contexts that are informative and accurate. But the reader should always check word contexts by looking them up in the KJV itself. "The Wicked Bible," a KJV edition of 1631, accidentally omitted the word "not" from the seventh commandment, for which the printers were fined 300 pounds sterling! Though there are no such fines for misleading contexts, the editors are still deeply concerned that *The Strongest Strong's* be used discerningly.

Bible Translating and Concordance Making

Traduttore traditore, "the translator is a traitor," is an ancient proverb oft quoted in books about Bible translations. To a degree this proverb is true, for no translation can perfectly bring over all the meaning and nuances of one language into another. Because no two languages share identical grammar and an identical range of word meanings, not even the best-intentioned word-for-word translation can claim to perfectly represent the original.

If the translator is a traitor, the concordance maker must be a partner in crime. For no multilingual concordance can perfectly represent both the English and biblical language texts it indexes. It can perfectly represent the vocabulary of the English text, for it needs only to list the location of each of its words. In this respect a concordance is either absolutely right or absolutely wrong. But when a concordance attempts to display the relationship between the English text and the biblical languages, it falls heir to the same difficulties that face the Bible translator.

Much of Bible translation involves one-to-one relationships. More often than not, אֱלֹהִים (Strong number 430) is translated "God," Ἰησοῦς (*2424*) is "Jesus," and ἀγαπάω (*25*) is "love." This part of translating and concordance making is easy.

Often, however, more than one word is needed in English to render a word in the originals. For example, the Greek word τεκνίον (*5040*) is "little child" or "little children" twelve times in the KJV. Conversely, one English word can translate several words from the originals. The simple preposition "before" translates two Hebrew words (3807.1+6440) 958 times.

Sometimes, because of differences in idiom, it takes several English words to translate two or more words from the original languages. This is called "dynamic equivalence" or "functional equivalence." For example, the famous KJV expletive "God forbid!" translates one word in Hebrew and two words in Greek—neither of which has either "God" or "forbid" as part of its "literal" meaning! Nevertheless, "God forbid!" is the *functional* equivalent of the Greek and Hebrew phrases.

Multilingual concordances of the past, following the lead of the original Strong's *Concordance*, have tended to display the relationship between English and the original languages as if it were almost always one-to-one. Scan a few columns of Strong's *Concordance*, and you see context after context presenting one indexed word followed by one number. Over the years, this has lent support to the misconception that the KJV is an absolutely "literal," word-for-word translation. However, the original preface to the KJV stated, "We have not tied our selves to an uniformity of phrasing, or to an identity of words, as some peradventure would wish that we had done."

The Strongest Strong's, by means of two different typefaces in the context line and a greatly enhanced use of Strong's numbering system, shows more fully than any previous KJV concordance the interrelation of the English text and the biblical languages.

Context Lines: Word-for-Word Translation

The simplest context line presents four items of information. First, the location of the indexed word by book, chapter, and verse. Second, the context line. Third, within the context line, the indexed word is abbreviated by its first letter and is *usually* in bold type. Fourth, a number at the right margin indicates the Hebrew, Aramaic, or Greek word the indexed word translates. For example, under the heading AARON on page 1:

Ex 4:14 and he said, Is not **A** the Levite thy brother? 175
4:27 the LORD said to **A**, "Go into the wilderness 175

Note that the book abbreviation is not repeated in the second reference. Book abbreviations are repeated at the top of new columns (see columns 2 and 3, page 1). A complete list of KJV book abbreviations appears at the beginning of the Main Concordance.

The numbering system indicates which biblical language is translated. Hebrew and Aramaic words are represented by numbers in normal "roman" type, from 1 through 8674. Greek word numbers are in italics, from *1* through *5624*.

After compiling his original word list, Strong added two Hebrew words and two Greek words. To keep them in order he added an apostrophe or prime symbol to the preceding number. So when you see 1699' and 6211' at the end of OT contexts, be sure to match the number *and* the symbol in the Hebrew-Aramaic dictionary-index. Though added to the Greek numbering system, Strong did not use words *2312'* and *2526'* in the concordance.

Strong also did not include the Hebrew and Aramaic articles, conjunctions, prepositions, and pronouns that attach to words as prefixes and suffixes, though he regularly refers to these terms in his dictionaries. Because of the far more exhaustive analysis of *The Strongest Strong's*, we added these fifty forms to Strong's list. But since we did not want to change his numbering system, we added decimals to his numbers. The first two additions involve the first letter of the Hebrew and Aramaic alphabet, so the first entries in the Hebrew-Aramaic dictionary-index are now 0.1 and 0.2.

Because *The Strongest Strong's* shows the italics of the KJV in its contexts, if an indexed word is italicized in the KJV, it is bold and italic in the context. For example, in Mark 5:24 *Jesus* is italicized: the KJV translators supplied the name for clarity, though it was not in the Greek. Appropriately, the context in *The Strongest Strong's* is:

5:24 And ***J*** went with him; and much people NIG

Note the abbreviation "NIG" instead of a number at the end of the context line. This indicates the word *Jesus* is "Not in Greek." The abbreviation "NIH" (Not in Hebrew [Aramaic]) is used in the OT.

Context Lines: Multiple-Word Translation

One English Word—Multiple Original Words. When the indexed word translates more than one word from the original, this is indicated by an appropriate number of Strong numbers at the end of the line. This is especially true of numbers. "Twelve," for example, always translates a combination of two Hebrew or Aramaic words in the OT, though it is one-to-one in the NT:

Nu 1:44 the princes of Israel, being **t** men: 6240+8147

Mk 3:14 And he ordained **t**, that they should be with *1427*

The original Strong's usually shows multiple numbers for such numerals (though some "new" editions do not), but rarely shows multiple numbers for the more than 14,000 times that KJV translators used this multi-word translation technique.

Multiple-word Translation. As mentioned above, the Greek word τεκνίον (*5040*) is translated "little child" or "little children" twelve times in the KJV. If you were to look up the word "little" in any edition of Strong's and look at the context for 1 John 2:1, you would find the word abbreviated by its first letter with the number *5040* at the end of the line. However, if you looked up the word "children" you would find the same thing:

1Jo 2: 1 My *l* children, these things write *5040*

1Jo 2: 1 My little *c*, these things write I *5040*

In these examples, it would appear that the Greek word number *5040* meant only "little" or "children," depending on which entry you looked up first. Nothing in the context line would inform you that Greek word *5040* actually means "little children."

The Strongest Strong's has solved the problem of indicating such multiple-word translations by putting *all* the words in bold type. Here is the same example of 1 John 2:1, under the headings "little" and "children":

1Jn 2: 1 My **l children**, these *things* write I unto *5040*

1Jn 2: 1 My **little c**, these *things* write I unto you, *5040*

If more than one English word is used to render several words from the original, the typefaces and the Strong numbers show all the words involved in this multiple-word translation. Such is the case of "with child" in Matthew 1:18, as indexed under CHILD:

Mt 1: 18 **with c** of the Holy Ghost. *1064+1722+2192*

The use of multiple Strong numbers and bold type, first introduced in *The NIV Exhaustive Concordance*, show at a glance all the words involved in more than 44,000 instances of multiple-word translation in English and in more than 14,000 instances of multiple-word translation of the original languages. For these conventions alone, *The Strongest Strong's* is truly the most exhaustive concordance to the KJV.

Context Lines: "Substitution" Translation

Bible translators often substitute nouns for pronouns and pronouns for nouns for clarity. For example, Matthew 9:10 reads "as Jesus sat at meat in the house, behold, . . ." "Jesus" here translates Greek word *846*, which is not the proper name Ἰησοῦς (*2424*), but the pronoun αὐτός, "he." Such "substitutionary" translations are common and acceptable in Bible translations, but other concordances treat them as if they were one-to-one translations.

The Strongest Strong's indicates substitutionary translation by attaching a raised "S" to the bolded letter:

Mt 9: 10 as **J**^{S} sat at meat in the house, behold, *846*

The KJV is not unique in using substitutionary translation. *The Strongest Strong's* is unique in displaying it.

Context Lines: "Not in Hebrew" and "Not in Greek"

Because modern English and ancient Hebrew, Aramaic, and Greek do not have identical rules of grammar and style, translators must often add words for the sake of clarity. For example, Mark 16:9 begins, "Now when Jesus was risen early. . . ." Other editions of Strong have no number at the end of this context line under the entry JESUS because there is no Greek word for "Jesus" in this verse; it was supplied by the translators to give a subject to the verb.

The Strongest Strong's indicates KJV words that are not in the originals by using the code NIH, "Not In Hebrew," for both the Hebrew and Aramaic of the Old Testament and NIG, "Not In Greek," for the New. Under the heading ABRAHAM, we find, for example:

Ge 21: 33 ***A*** planted a grove in Beer-sheba, and NIH

Ac 7: 8 and so ***A*** begat Isaac, and circumcised him NIG

As in the case of Mark 16:9, these proper names were supplied for clarity, for the benefit of the reader.

Context Lines: Shaded Background

Because most editions of the KJV produced today have the words of Jesus in red letter, all contexts that contain words of Jesus are highlighted with a shaded background.

THE INDEX OF ARTICLES, CONJUNCTIONS, PARTICLES, PREPOSITIONS, AND PRONOUNS

The Main Concordance indexes 407,296 references to 12,811 KJV words. The Index of Articles, Conjunctions, Particles, Prepositions, and Pronouns indexes 383,541 references to 47 KJV words.

The format of the Index of Articles, Etc. is very simple. Each of the 47 words has its own heading, followed by a frequency count. For example:

A (8718)

The 47 words of this section are indexed without contexts, since providing contexts would be of little benefit to the reader and would double the size of *The Strongest Strong's*! Book, chapter, and verse references appear in biblical order. Each book starts a new paragraph and is set in bold print for easy location.

THE BIBLICAL LANGUAGE DICTIONARY-INDEXES

At the end of each context line in the Main Concordance is a code or a Strong number, describing the relationship of the KJV to the original languages. Two Biblical Language Dictionary-Indexes list all of the words that are found in the Hebrew, Aramaic, and Greek texts from which the KJV was translated. These lists are in the alphabetical order of each of the languages, which is also the order of the Strong numbering system.

Note that in keeping with some reference works of the nineteenth century, Strong merged Hebrew and Aramaic (or "Chaldee") into one list. All major reference works of the twentieth century treat these as two separate languages. Further, he also alphabetized the letters שׂ and שׁ as though they were the same character, though again all major reference works since have treated them as distinct. In order to preserve Strong's numbering system, *The Strongest Strong's* retained his sorting conventions.

The Dictionary-Indexes to *The Strongest Strong's* have three features not found in the indexes or dictionaries of any other KJV concordance. First, for all but sixteen highly frequent words, *The Strongest Strong's* lists all the KJV words and phrases that translate each word of the original, showing multiple-word translation and substitution translation. Second, *The Strongest Strong's* sorts the KJV word indexes according to their frequency and provides the exact number of times these words and phrases are used in the KJV. Third, the KJV words and phrases indexed are in their exact textual spelling, so the user can locate its heading in the Main Concordance without any further cross-referencing.

The entry for Greek word *25* can serve as an example for most features of both Dictionary-Indexes:

> ***26*** ἀγάπη, ***agapē***, n. GK: *27* [→ *25*]. love, in the NT usually the active love of God for his Son and his people, and the active love his people are to have for God, each other, and even enemies; love feast, the common meal shared by Christians in connection with church meetings:– love [85], charity [27], charitably (+*2596*) [1], dear [1], feasts of charity [1], love's [1]

The entry begins with the Strong number, in bold type for easy location. Next is the lexical form or dictionary form of the Greek word, followed by its transliteration (in bold italics), the part of speech (abbreviated), the Goodrick/Kohlenberger number, and related words (listed by Strong number in square brackets, see below for more on related words).

The transliteration follows the system used in Zondervan's *New International Dictionary of New Testament Theology* and *New International Dictionary of Old Testament Theology and Exegesis.* A complete transliteration and pronunication guide, as well as a list of abbreviations, appears before each index.

The Goodrick/Kohlenberger or G/K numbering system was developed for *The NIV Exhaustive Concordance.* Since it takes into account thousands of words and word forms not in Strong's system, the G/K numbering system is widely used in modern reference books. For those who wish to consult these more up-to-date and thorough resources, the G/K number (or numbers) is included for every entry in both Dictionary-Indexes.

The six heading elements are concluded by a period. Following the period is an essential definition for the word as it is used in the NT. These definitions can be as brief as one or two words. In the case of hundreds of theologically and culturally significant words, like ἀγάπη, the definition functions as a concise expository dictionary. In the case of a proper name, like "Bethlehem," the definition will include the possible meaning of the name in the originals: "*house of bread;* poss. *temple [house] of Lakhmu.*"

The definition ends with a colon and a dash (:–). Following this symbol is a list of all the ways in which the word is translated in the KJV, in descending order of frequency. If two words (or phrases) have the same frequency, they are listed in alphabetical order. Following the KJV word is its frequency count, in square brackets. Word *3588* (the article ὁ), which occurs almost 20,000 times in the NT, and fifteen highly-frequent Hebrew words are not indexed exhaustively, but their most frequent KJV equivalents are listed. These sixteen entries end with an asterisk (*).

One-to-one translations are indicated by one KJV word, as in the case of the first and last KJV words in the example above. Multiple-word translations are indicated in two ways: by multiple KJV words and/or multiple Strong numbers. The next-to-the-last word, "feasts of charity [1]," indicates a multiple-word KJV translation. If you look up "charity" and "feasts" in the Main Concordance, you will find the following contexts under Jude 1:12:

> Jude 1:12 These are spots in your **feasts of c** when they 26
>
> Jude 1:12 These are spots in your **f of charity** when 26

Under both headings, the phrase "feasts of charity" is shown to be the definition of Greek word *26.* (Multiple-word translation is described above on pages xii-xiii.)

When a KJV word or phrase translates more than one word of the original, the Strong number of the additional word (or words) precedes the frequency count in parentheses. This is seen in entry *26* in "charitably (+*2596*) [1]."

"Substitution" translation (see above, page xiii) is noted with a raised "s," as in the Main Concordance. The example on page xiii cited a substitute translation of word *846* by the word "Jesus" in Mt 9:10. The corresponding index in the entry for word *846* is "Jesus^{S} [1]."

Related Words

One popular element of Strong's original dictionaries has been intentionally omitted in *The Strongest Strong's.* Following the majority of nineteenth century scholarship, Strong attempted to explain the meaning of each word by referring to its alleged "root" meaning. Though popularized in many other dated reference books like Vine's *Expository Dictionary of New Testament Words*, this practice has been largely abandoned by modern scholars, who often label it the "root fallacy."

In his original entry on Hebrew word 3563, Strong explains:

> *koce* . . . [is] from an unused root mean. to *hold* together; a *cup* (as a container), often fig. a *lot* (as if a potion); also some unclean bird, prob. an *owl* (perh.from the cup-like cavity of its eye)

In his attempt to relate the "unused root meaning" to both "cup" and "owl," he stretches for an explanation that would apply to almost any animal with an eyeball, since all eyeballs are set in cup-like cavities!

Modern scholars understand that word 3563 is actually two completely different words, one meaning "cup" and the other "owl." Though spelled identically in Hebrew, in other related ancient languages they have different spellings. This is seen in the KJV word "cleave," which means both "stick together" (Ge 2:24) and "cut apart" (Zec 14:4). Though spelled the same in the KJV, in Old English the two meanings had separate spellings: *clifan* and *cleofan* respectively. One should not attempt to relate the meanings of these separate words, just as Strong should not have in thousands of cases.

Instead of attempting such speculative analysis and perpetuating the root fallacy, the Dictionary-Indexes of *The Strongest Strong's* list all biblical words that are related by common elements. The arrow symbol (→) points to a word or a list of words that share common elements with the word in the entry. These related words lists are provided to allow the user to do more thorough word studies. These studies, however, should be done carefully with more attention paid to contextual definitions than fanciful etymologies.

Dictionary Definition versus KJV Translation

The original dictionaries in Strong's *Concordance* often give a single "root" definition for each word. This is often misunderstood as the *only* definition or the "literal" meaning of the word and can be misused to criticize other valid translations of the word—even in the KJV itself! The entry for ποιέω (*4160*) lists 76 different KJV words and phrases that translate this common word, yet Strong's original dictionary simply defines this word as "to *make* or *do*." Either the KJV translators were wrong in 96% of their definitions or there is more to the meaning of ποιέω than "to *make* or *do*"!

The KJV translations that follow the definition are listed in order from most used to least used. They represent careful choices the KJV translators made to render each word accurately and understandably in its context. But they also represent the translators' express principle not to tie themselves to "a uniformity of phrasing or identity of words." The KJV translations list is a good indicator of the range of a word's meaning in seventeenth-century English, as the dictionary definition is a good summary of meaning in modern English. Use these resources together, not in opposition.

For further and more detailed word studies, there are a wide variety of resources available that are keyed to Strong's numbering system.

On a basic level, there is the popular but dated *Expository Dictionary of Biblical Words* (Nelson), indexed to Strong numbers. More up-to-date and superior in methodology and OT word studies is Zondervan's *New International Encyclopedia of Bible Words*, edited by Larry Richards and indexed to G/K numbers.

On an intermediate level, there is *The NIV Theological Dictionary of New Testament Words* (Zondervan), edited by Verlyn D. Verbrugge from the four-volume *New International Dictionary of New Testament Theology* (Zondervan), edited by Colin Brown. This excellent tool gives important information for the most theologically significant words of the NT. It is keyed to G/K numbers, but also has indexes to convert G/K to Strong and Strong to G/K. For the OT, *The Theological Wordbook of the Old Testament* (Moody) uses its own numbering system, but does have a key to Strong numbers.

On an advanced level the four-volume *New International Dictionary of New Testament Theology* (Zondervan), edited by Colin Brown, and the five-volume *New International Dictionary of Old Testament Theology and Exegesis*, edited by Willem VanGemeren, are outstanding resources for deeper research. Both have English indexes and indexes to Greek and Hebrew words spelled in the same transliteration system used in *The Strongest Strong's*. The *NIDOTTE* is also keyed to G/K numbers and has an index to Strong's numbers.

Less conservative, but excellent in scholarship, are the three-volume *Theological Lexicon of the New Testament* (Hendrickson) by Ceslas Spicq and the *Theological Lexicon of the Old Testament* (Hendrickson) edited by Jenni and Westermann. Both of these sets are keyed to Strong's numbers and to a variety of more advanced resources for students of biblical languages.

NAVE'S TOPICAL BIBLE REFERENCE SYSTEM

Just as Strong's *Exhaustive Concordance* is the best and most popular concordance to the KJV, so *Nave's Topical Bible* is the best and most popular conceptual index to the KJV—and *The Strongest Strong's Exhaustive Concordance* is the best edition of both of these indispensable resources!

The original edition of *Nave's Topical Bible* fills 1464 pages, but most of that space is used by the KJV verse text, which is printed in full for many of the biblical references. Without this Bible text, and with 500 new headings and many other enhancements, all of the other content of *Nave's Topical Bible* fits in just 162 pages in *The Strongest Strong's*! Because it does not include the Bible text of the original, we have titled this section *Nave's Topical Bible Reference System.*

What is a Topical Bible?

A Topical Bible combines the most useful features of a Bible Handbook, a Bible Dictionary, and a Bible Concordance. Like a Bible Handbook, this Topical Bible introduces the reader to each book of the Bible and surveys its contents. Like a Bible Dictionary, this Topical Bible is an alphabetically organized presentation of biblical and extrabiblical information on Bible people, places, events, and objects. Like a Concordance, this Topical Bible indexes the Scriptures with thousands of biblical references and biblical text samplings.

Nave's Topical Bible Reference System is also much more than these other general reference works. A Bible Handbook offers only selected comments on the biblical text; *Nave's Topical Bible Reference System* offers a thorough survey of most biblical topics, people, places, and events. A Bible Dictionary cites a handful of biblical texts to document its articles; *Nave's Topical Bible Reference System* cites more than 100,000 verses. A Bible Concordance is limited to the vocabulary of the Bible it indexes; *Nave's Topical Bible Reference System* is based on the vocabulary of the NIV and the KJV, the two best-selling English translations today.

How to Use *Nave's Topical Bible Reference System*

Nave's Topical Bible Reference System offers quick and easy access to more than 7,000 biblical topics. Simply look up any subject, person, place, or book of the Bible in alphabetical order. There you will find a concise summary of biblical insights, well documented with Scripture references.

Entry Headings

The following shows the two types of headings used in *Nave's Topical Bible Reference System*:

ABIJAH (*[my] father is Yahweh*).

ABI *See Abijah, 7.*

ABIA, ABIAH *See Abijah, 1 & 3.*

Proper and place names are indexed according to NIV spelling. When KJV spelling differs, as in the case of "Abi," "Abia," and "Abijah," those spellings are listed in "See" references that specify both the entry word and the subdivision of the entry. The definition of the name follows in parentheses and italics. When sources disagree on the definitions, these differences are listed and documented:

ASA (possibly *healer* BDB; *myrtle* KB).

The abbreviations are explained on the example page 1548.

Sometimes an entry heading contains only a cross reference to another article. This is often the case of KJV terms, such as:

WINEBIBBER *See Drunkard; Drunkenness; Wine.*

The Entry Proper

An entry can be as simple as:

JAGUR. A town of Judah (Jos 15:21).

or as complex as JESUS THE CHRIST, which fills 12 columns with 454 paragraphs of information including 84 primary subdivisions, 20 secondary subdivisions, 43 cross references to 68 topics, and more than 4,100 biblical references.

Subdivisions. Short articles appear as single paragraphs. Longer articles are usually subdivided to one or two levels.

Proper names that refer to more than one person or place are subdivided by numbered paragraphs. For example, there are three listings for Abel; thirty-one for Zechariah. More than 3,000 proper name subdivisions are identified.

Primary subdivisions are set flush left in bold print. Secondary subdivisions are indented, italicized, and followed by a dash:

JESUS THE CHRIST
Death of:
Purpose of His Death—

Biblical References. More than 100,000 biblical references are indexed in the entries, but no biblical text is printed out. This is the main difference between the full sized and compact editions of the NIV Nave's Topical Bibles.

The ampersand symbol (&) and "w" (with) are used to indicate closely related texts, often New Testament citations of the Old and parallel passages, as in this example from JESUS THE CHRIST; Head of the Church:

(Ps 118:22-23, w Mt 21:42-43, & Mk 12:10; Isa 28:16, w Eph 2:2-22, & 1Pe 2:6; Lk 20:17-18, w 1Pe 2:7; Jn 15:1-8; 1Co 3:11; Eph 1:22-23; 4:15; 5:23-32; Col 1:18; 2:10, 19; 3:11; Rev 2:2-28; 3:1, 7; 22:16).

The biblical citations index and illustrate the information of the entries. *Nave's Topical Bible Reference System* is an index to the Bible, not a substitute for the Bible. Always look up each reference in the Bible itself. Read the whole context in order to see how the text functions in the KJV or in any other translation. The easiest way to misinterpret the Bible is to study its texts out of their contexts. The editors have taken great care to select only relevant texts, but we strongly encourage users not only to double check our work, but to double check your own insights.

Cross References. More than 3,700 cross references to 6,100 entries are set in italics:

See Jesus the Christ, Second Coming; Millennium.

Entry headings are separated by semicolons; entry subdivisions follow commas.

How to Use *Nave's Topical Bible Reference System* With *The Strongest Strong's*

Nave's Topical Bible Reference System and *The Strongest Strong's* are made for each other. The *Concordance* provides an exhaustive index of every word in the KJV, listed in alphabetical order, and an exhaustive index of the relationship of the KJV to the original biblical languages. *Nave's Topical Bible Reference System* provides a biblical index that is organized by subjects, is not limited to KJV vocabulary, and is arranged by thematic development rather than by biblical order. Together these works provide endless access to the riches of God's Word.

Exhaustive KJV Word Studies

The Strongest Strong's indexes every reference to every KJV word. *Nave's Topical Bible Reference System*, while not exhaustive in its treatment of KJV vocabulary, does list every person and place in the KJV, subdivided by individual people and locations.

When you want to study any KJV word in full, begin with *The Strongest Strong's*. Look up the word exactly as it is spelled in the KJV. *The Strongest Strong's* also gives you complete listings of related KJV words you can work through. Then check the same words in *Nave's Topical Bible Reference System* for insights from its analysis and cross references.

Thorough Synonym Studies

While working through any entry in *Nave's Topical Bible Reference System*, you will notice that the verses cited regularly contain key words that are synonymns of the entry heading. This is one major advantage of the Topical Bible over the Concordance. For example, the entry on Truth contains the synonymns "faithful," "faithfulness," "just," "love," and "right." The Strongest Strong's indexes 235 verses on "truth" and another 127 on its related words. When you add the five synonymns identified in *Nave's Topical Bible Reference System*, you get another 864 references—and that does not even count their related words!

IN CONCLUSION

To Ralph Waldo Emerson, "A foolish consistency is the hobgoblin of little minds." To the editors of the *The Strongest Strong's Exhaustive Concordance*, there is no such thing as a foolish consistency in a biblical reference book. Every effort has been made by the editors, programmers, and proofreaders to make the *The Strongest Strong's* consistent and error-free. Strong's and Young's *Concordances* have each been through more than two dozen revisions, and we realize that our work has not been perfect either.

If you find anything that appears to be an error, write to The KJV Concordance Project, c/o Zondervan, 5300 Patterson Avenue, S.E., Grand Rapids, MI 49530.

THE STRONGEST STRONG'S EXHAUSTIVE CONCORDANCE

FEATURES OF THE MAIN CONCORDANCE

KJV WORD HEADING
The indexed word as spelled in the KJV (see the introduction, pages x, xi).

FREQUENCY COUNT
Total number of occurrences in the KJV (see the introduction, page xi).

RELATED WORD LIST
Other spellings and related words in the KJV (see the introduction, page xi).

ACCEPT (25) [ACCEPTABLE, ACCEPTABLY, ACCEPTANCE, ACCEPTATION, ACCEPTED]

Ex 22:11 the owner of it shall **a** *thereof,* and he shall 3947

STRONG NUMBER
Refers to the biblical-language dictionary-indexes; one- to four-digit normal "roman" type is Hebrew or Aramaic; *italic* is Greek (see the introduction, pages xii–xiv).

ITALIC TYPEFACE
Indicates words that are italicized in the KJV (see the introduction, pages x, xii).

INDEXED WORD
Abbreviated by its first letter, usually in **bold** type.

BIBLICAL REFERENCE
See the abbreviations table below.

ADDITIONAL STRONG NUMBER(S)
Indicates more than one Hebrew, Aramaic, or Greek word is represented by the KJV translation (see the introduction, pages xii, xiii).

Ge 32:20 peradventure he will **a** of me. 5375+6440

BOLD TYPEFACE
In addition to the indexed word, indicates multiple-word translation (introduction, pages xii, xiii).

Eph 1: 6 wherein he hath **made** us **a** in the beloved: *5487*

NIG OR NIH
"Not in Greek" and "Not in Hebrew/ Aramaic" indicates the indexed word was supplied for clarity in translation (see the introduction, pages xii, xiii).

Ge 41:25 God hath shewed Pharaoh what he is **a** to NIH

SHADED BACKGROUND
Contexts containing the words of Jesus, printed in red letter in most editions of the KJV, are highlighted with a shaded background (see the introduction, page xiii).

Lk 4:24 No prophet is **a** in his own country. *1884*

KJV INDEX REFERENCES
Refers to an index of highly frequent words (see the introduction, page xi).

A (8718) [AN] See Index of Articles, Etc.

"SEE" REFERENCES
Cross-references key words from various edtions of the KJV and from modern translations and reference books to KJV vocabulary (see the introduction, page xi).

ABYSS See BOTTOMLESS

ACHBOR See ACBOR

ABBREVIATIONS FOR THE BOOKS OF THE BIBLE

Ge .... Genesis	1Ch ..... 1 Chronicles	La ...... Lamentations	Hag .... Haggai	Eph .... Ephesians	2Pe.......... 2 Peter
Ex........... Exodus	2Ch ..... 2 Chronicles	Eze .... Ezekiel	Zec .... Zechariah	Php ...... Philippians	1Jn............ 1 John
Lev......... Leviticus	Ezr .... Ezra	Da........... Daniel	Mal .... Malachi	Col......... Colossians	2Jn............ 2 John
Nu .... Numbers	Ne......... Nehemiah	Hos .... Hosea	Mt.......... Matthew	1Th ... 1 Thessalonians	3Jn............ 3 John
Dt...... Deuteronomy	Est .... Esther	Joel .... Joel	Mk .... Mark	2Th ... 2 Thessalonians	Jude .... Jude
Jos .... Joshua	Job .... Job	Am .... Amos	Lk .... Luke	1Ti......... 1 Timothy	Rev......... Revelation
Jdg .... Judges	Ps .... Psalms	Ob.......... Obadiah	Jn............. John	2Ti......... 2 Timothy	
Ru .... Ruth	Pr .... Proverbs	Jnh .... Jonah	Ac .... Acts	Tit .... Titus	
1Sa........ 1 Samuel	Ecc .... Ecclesiastes	Mic .... Micah	Ro .... Romans	Phm........ Philemon	Other Abbreviations
2Sa........ 2 Samuel	SS... Song of Solomon	Na.......... Nahum	1Co..... 1 Corinthians	Heb .... Hebrews	S..... Epistle subscript
1Ki.......... 1 Kings	Isa............ Isaiah	Hab....... Habakkuk	2Co..... 2 Corinthians	Jas .... James	T .... Psalm title
2Ki.......... 2 Kings	Jer.......... Jeremiah	Zep .... Zephaniah	Gal .... Galatians	1Pe .... 1 Peter	

THE STRONGEST STRONG'S EXHAUSTIVE CONCORDANCE

A

A (8718) [AN] See Index of Articles, Etc.

AARON (319) [AARON'S, AARONITES]

Ex 4:14 and he said, Is not **A** the Levite thy brother? 175
4:27 the LORD said to **A**, Go into the wilderness 175
4:28 Moses told **A** all the words of the LORD 175
4:29 Moses and **A** went and gathered together all 175
4:30 **A** spake all the words which the LORD had 175
5: 1 afterward Moses and **A** went in, and 175
5: 4 Wherefore do ye, Moses and **A**, let 175
5:20 they met Moses and **A**, who stood in 175
6:13 the LORD spake unto Moses and unto **A**, 175
6:20 to wife; and she bare him **A** and Moses: 175
6:23 **A** took him Elisheba, daughter of 175
6:26 *These are* that **A** and Moses, to whom 175
6:27 from Egypt: *these are* that Moses and **A**. 175
7: 1 and **A** thy brother shall be thy prophet. 175
7: 2 and **A** thy brother shall speak unto Pharaoh, 175
7: 6 and **A** did as the LORD commanded them, 175
7: 7 **A** fourscore and three years old, when they 175
7: 8 the LORD spake unto Moses and unto **A**, 175
7: 9 then thou shalt say unto **A**, Take thy rod, and 175
7:10 And Moses and **A** went in unto Pharaoh, and 175
7:10 and **A** cast down his rod before Pharaoh, and 175
7:19 Say unto **A**, Take thy rod, and stretch out 175
7:20 Moses and **A** did so, as the LORD 175
8: 5 the LORD spake unto Moses, Say unto **A**, 175
8: 6 **A** stretched out his hand over the waters of 175
8: 8 Pharaoh called for Moses and **A**, and said, 175
8:12 Moses and **A** went out from Pharaoh: and 175
8:16 Say unto **A**, Stretch out thy rod, and 175
8:17 for **A** stretched out his hand with his rod, 175
8:25 Pharaoh called for Moses and for **A**, and 175
9: 8 the LORD said unto Moses and unto **A**, 175
9:27 called for Moses and **A**, and said unto them, 175
10: 3 Moses and **A** came in unto Pharaoh, and 175
10: 8 and **A** were brought again unto Pharaoh: 175
10:16 Pharaoh called for Moses and **A** in haste; 175
11:10 and **A** did all these wonders before Pharaoh: 175
12: 1 unto Moses and **A** in the land of Egypt, 175
12:28 the LORD had commanded Moses and **A**, 175
12:31 And he called for Moses and **A** by night, and 175
12:43 the LORD said unto Moses and **A**, This *is* 175
12:50 as the LORD commanded Moses and **A**, so 175
15:20 the sister of **A**, took a timbrel in her hand; 175
16: 2 against Moses and **A** in the wilderness: 175
16: 6 and **A** said unto all the children of Israel, 175
16: 9 Moses spake unto **A**, Say unto all 175
16:10 as **A** spake unto the whole congregation of 175
16:33 Moses said unto **A**, Take a pot, and put an 175
16:34 so **A** laid it up before the Testimony, to be 175
17:10 **A**, and Hur went up *to* the top of the hill. 175
17:12 **A** and Hur stayed up his hands, the one on 175
18:12 **A** came, and all the elders of Israel, to eat 175
19:24 thou shalt come up, thou, and **A** with thee: 175
24: 1 thou, and **A**, Nadab, and Abihu, and 175
24: 9 **A**, Nadab, and Abihu, and seventy of 175
24:14 behold, **A** and Hur *are* with you: if any man 175
27:21 **A** and his sons shall order it from evening to 175
28: 1 take thou unto thee **A** thy brother, and his 175
28: 1 *even* **A**, Nadab and Abihu, Eleazar and 175
28: 2 thou shalt make holy garments for **A** thy 175
28: 4 they shall make holy garments for **A** thy 175
28:12 **A** shall bear their names before the LORD 175
28:29 **A** shall bear the names of the children of 175
28:30 **A** shall bear the judgment of the children of 175
28:35 it shall be upon **A** to minister: and his sound 175
28:38 that **A** may bear the iniquity of the holy 175
Ex 28:41 And thou shalt put them upon **A** thy brother, 175
28:43 they shall be upon **A**, and upon his sons, 175
29: 4 **A** and his sons thou shalt bring unto the door 175
29: 5 put upon **A** the coat, and the robe of 175
29: 9 **A** and his sons, and put the bonnets on them: 175
29: 9 and thou shalt consecrate **A** and his sons. 175
29:10 **A** and his sons shall put their hands upon 175
29:15 **A** and his sons shall put their hands upon 175
29:19 **A** and his sons shall put their hands upon 175
29:20 put *it* upon the tip of the *right* ear of **A**, and 175
29:21 sprinkle *it* upon **A**, and upon his garments, 175
29:24 And thou shalt put all in the hands of **A**, and 175
29:27 *even* of *that* which *is* for **A**, and of *that* 175
29:29 the holy garments of **A** shall be his sons' 175
29:32 **A** and his sons shall eat the flesh of the ram, 175
29:35 thus shalt thou do unto **A**, and to his sons, 175
29:44 I will sanctify also both **A** and his sons, 175
30: 7 **A** shall burn thereon sweet incense every 175
30: 8 when **A** lighteth the lamps at even, he shall 175
30:10 **A** shall make an atonement upon the horns 175
30:19 For **A** and his sons shall wash their hands 175
30:30 thou shalt anoint **A** and his sons, and 175
31:10 the holy garments for **A** the priest, and 175
32: 1 people gathered themselves together unto **A**, 175
32: 2 **A** said unto them, Break off the golden 175
32: 3 *were* in their ears, and brought *them* unto **A**. 175
32: 5 when **A** saw *it*, he built an altar before it; 175
32: 5 **A** made proclamation, and said, To morrow 175
32:21 Moses said unto **A**, What did this people 175
32:22 **A** said, Let not the anger of my lord wax hot: 175
32:25 (for **A** had made them naked unto *their* 175
32:35 because they made the calf, which **A** made. 175
34:30 when **A** and all the children of Israel saw 175
34:31 **A** and all the rulers of the congregation 175
35:19 *place*, the holy garments for **A** the priest, 175
38:21 by the hand of Ithamar, son to **A** the priest. 175
39: 1 and made the holy garments for **A**; 175
39:27 coats *of* fine linen *of* woven work for **A**, 175
39:41 and the holy garments for **A** the priest, 175
40:12 thou shalt bring **A** and his sons unto the door 175
40:13 thou shalt put upon **A** the holy garments, 175
40:31 Moses and **A** and his sons washed their 175
Lev 1: 7 the sons of **A** the priest shall put fire upon 175
3:13 the sons of **A** shall sprinkle the blood thereof 175
6: 9 Command **A** and his sons, saying, This *is* 175
6:14 the sons of **A** shall offer it before 175
6:16 the remainder thereof shall **A** and his sons 175
6:18 All the males among the children of **A** shall 175
6:20 This *is* the offering of **A** and of his sons, 175
6:25 Speak unto **A** and to his sons, saying, This *is* 175
7:10 and dry, shall all the sons of **A** have, 175
7:33 He among the sons of **A**, that offereth 175
7:34 have given them unto **A** the priest and 175
7:35 This *is the portion* of the anointing of **A**, and 175
8: 2 Take **A** and his sons with him, and 175
8: 6 Moses brought **A** and his sons, and 175
8:14 **A** and his sons laid their hands upon 175
8:18 **A** and his sons laid their hands upon 175
8:22 **A** and his sons laid their hands upon 175
8:30 sprinkled *it* upon **A**, *and* upon his garments, 175
8:30 sanctified **A**, *and* his garments, and his sons, 175
8:31 Moses said unto **A** and to his sons, Boil 175
8:31 **A** and his sons shall eat it. 175
8:36 So **A** and his sons did all things which 175
9: 1 *that* Moses called **A** and his sons, and 175
9: 2 he said unto **A**, Take thee a young calf for a 175
9: 7 Moses said unto **A**, Go unto the altar, and 175
9: 8 **A** therefore went unto the altar, and slew 175
9: 9 the sons of **A** brought the blood unto him: 175
9:21 the right shoulder **A** waved *for* a wave 175
9:22 **A** lift up his hand towards the people, and 175
9:23 **A** went into the tabernacle of 175
10: 1 Nadab and Abihu, the sons of **A**, took either 175
10: 3 Moses said unto **A**, This *is it* that 175
10: 3 I will be glorified. And **A** held his peace. 175
10: 4 the sons of Uzziel the uncle of **A**, and 175
10: 6 Moses said unto **A**, and unto Eleazar and 175
10: 8 And the LORD spake unto **A**, saying, 175
10:12 Moses spake unto **A**, and unto Eleazar and 175
Lev 10:16 Ithamar the sons of **A** which were left *alive*, 175
10:19 **A** said unto Moses, Behold, *this* day have 175
11: 1 And the LORD spake unto Moses and to **A**, 175
13: 1 the LORD spake unto Moses and **A**, 175
13: 2 then he shall be brought unto **A** the priest, or 175
14:33 the LORD spake unto Moses and unto **A**, 175
15: 1 And the LORD spake unto Moses and to **A**, 175
16: 1 Moses after the death of the two sons of **A**, 175
16: 2 said unto Moses, Speak unto **A** thy brother, 175
16: 3 Thus shall **A** come into the holy *place*: with 175
16: 6 **A** shall offer *his* bullock of the sin offering, 175
16: 8 **A** shall cast lots upon the two goats; one lot 175
16: 9 **A** shall bring the goat upon which 175
16:11 **A** shall bring the bullock of the sin offering, 175
16:21 **A** shall lay both his hands upon the head of 175
16:23 **A** shall come into the tabernacle of 175
17: 2 Speak unto **A**, and unto his sons, and unto all 175
21: 1 Speak unto the priests the sons of **A**, and 175
21:17 Speak unto **A**, saying, Whosoever *he be* of 175
21:21 hath a blemish, of the seed of **A** the priest, 175
21:24 Moses told *it* unto **A**, and to his sons, and 175
22: 2 Speak unto **A** and to his sons, that they 175
22: 4 What man soever of the seed of **A** *is* a leper, 175
22:18 Speak unto **A**, and to his sons, and unto all 175
24: 3 shall **A** order it from the evening unto 175
Nu 1: 3 and **A** shall number them by their armies. 175
1:17 **A** took these men which are expressed by 175
1:44 which Moses and **A** numbered, and 175
2: 1 the LORD spake unto Moses and unto **A**, 175
3: 1 These also *are* the generations of **A** and 175
3: 2 these *are* the names of the sons of **A**; 175
3: 3 These *are* the names of the sons of **A**, 175
3: 4 priest's office in the sight of **A** their father. 175
3: 6 and present them before **A** the priest, 175
3: 9 thou shalt give the Levites unto **A** and to his 175
3:10 thou shalt appoint **A** and his sons, and 175
3:32 Eleazar the son of **A** the priest *shall be* chief 175
3:38 *shall be* Moses, and **A** and his sons, 175
3:39 **A** numbered at the commandment of 175
3:48 is *to be* redeemed, unto **A** and to his sons. 175
3:51 money of them that were redeemed unto **A** 175
4: 1 the LORD spake unto Moses and unto **A**, 175
4: 5 **A** shall come, and his sons, and they shall 175
4:15 when **A** and his sons have made an end of 175
4:16 *to* the office of Eleazar the son of **A** 175
4:17 the LORD spake unto Moses and unto **A**, 175
4:19 they approach unto the most holy *things*: **A** 175
4:27 At the appointment of **A** and his sons shall 175
4:28 the hand of Ithamar the son of **A** the priest. 175
4:33 under the hand of Ithamar the son of **A** 175
4:34 Moses and **A** and the chief of 175
4:37 **A** did number according to 175
4:41 **A** did number according to 175
4:45 **A** numbered according to the word of 175
4:46 whom Moses and **A** and the chief of Israel 175
6:23 Speak unto **A** and unto his sons, saying, 175
7: 8 under the hand of Ithamar the son of **A** 175
8: 2 Speak unto **A**, and say unto him, When thou 175
8: 3 **A** did so; he lighted the lamps thereof over 175
8:11 **A** shall offer the Levites before the LORD 175
8:13 And thou shalt set the Levites before **A**, and 175
8:19 I have given the Levites *as* a gift to **A** and 175
8:20 **A**, and all the congregation of the children of 175
8:21 **A** offered them *as* an offering before 175
8:21 **A** made an atonement for them to cleanse 175
8:22 the tabernacle of the congregation before **A**, 175
9: 6 before Moses and before **A** on that day: 175
10: 8 the sons of **A**, the priests, shall blow with 175
12: 1 and **A** spake against Moses because 175
12: 4 unto Moses, and unto **A**, and unto Miriam, 175
12: 5 of the tabernacle, and called **A** and Miriam: 175
12:10 **A** looked upon Miriam, and behold, *she was* 175
12:11 **A** said unto Moses, Alas, my lord, I beseech 175
13:26 to **A**, and to all the congregation of 175
14: 2 murmured against Moses and against **A**: 175
14: 5 **A** fell on their faces before all the assembly 175
14:26 the LORD spake unto Moses and unto **A**, 175
15:33 sticks brought him unto Moses and **A**, 175
16: 3 together against Moses and against **A**, 175

A

Nu 16:11 and what *is* **A**, that ye murmur against him? 175
16:16 thou, and they, and **A**, to morrow: 175
16:17 thou also, and **A**, each *of you* his censer. 175
16:18 of the congregation with Moses and **A**. 175
16:20 the LORD spake unto Moses and unto **A**, 175
16:37 Speak unto Eleazar the son of **A** the priest, 175
16:40 no stranger, which *is* not of the seed of **A**, 175
16:41 murmured against Moses and against **A**, 175
16:42 was gathered against Moses and against **A**, 175
16:43 **A** came before the tabernacle of 175
16:46 Moses said unto **A**, Take a censer, and 175
16:47 **A** took as Moses commanded, and ran into 175
16:50 **A** returned unto Moses unto the door of 175
17: 6 and the rod of **A** *was* among their rods. 175
17: 8 the rod of **A** for the house of Levi was 175
18: 1 the LORD said unto **A**, Thou and thy sons 175
18: 8 the LORD spake unto **A**, Behold, I also 175
18:20 the LORD spake unto **A**, Thou shalt have 175
18:28 the LORD'S heave offering to **A** the priest. 175
19: 1 the LORD spake unto Moses and unto **A**, 175
20: 2 together against Moses and against **A**. 175
20: 6 **A** went from the presence of the assembly 175
20: 8 **A** thy brother, and speak ye unto the rock 175
20:10 **A** gathered the congregation together before 175
20:12 the LORD spake unto Moses and **A**, 175
20:23 spake unto Moses and **A** in mount Hor, 175
20:24 **A** shall be gathered unto his people: for he 175
20:25 Take **A** and Eleazar his son, and bring them 175
20:26 strip **A** of his garments, and put them upon 175
20:26 and **A** shall be gathered *unto his people*, and 175
20:28 Moses stripped **A** of his garments, and 175
20:28 and **A** died there in the top of the mount: 175
20:29 when all the congregation saw that **A** was 175
20:29 they mourned for **A** thirty days, *even* all 175
25: 7 the son of Eleazar, the son of **A** the priest, 175
25:11 the son of Eleazar, the son of **A** the priest, 175
26: 1 and unto Eleazar the son of **A** the priest, 175
26: 9 and against **A** in the company of Korah, 175
26:59 and she bare unto Amram **A** and Moses, and 175
26:60 unto **A** was born Nadab, and Abihu, Eleazar, 175
26:64 whom Moses and **A** the priest numbered, 175
27:13 thy people, as **A** thy brother was gathered. 175
33: 1 their armies under the hand of Moses and **A**. 175
33:38 **A** the priest went up into mount Hor at 175
33:39 **A** *was* an hundred and twenty and 175
Dt 9:20 the LORD was very angry with **A** to have 175
9:20 and I prayed for **A** also the same time. 175
10: 6 there **A** died, and there he was buried; 175
32:50 as **A** thy brother died in mount Hor, and 175
Jos 21: 4 the children of **A** the priest, *which were* of 175
21:10 Which the children of **A**, *being* of 175
21:13 Thus they gave to the children of **A** 175
21:19 All the cities of the children of **A**, the priests, 175
24: 5 I sent Moses also and **A**, and I plagued 175
24:33 Eleazar the son of **A** died; and they buried 175
Jdg 20:28 the son of Eleazar, the son of **A**, 175
1Sa 12: 6 *It is* the LORD that advanced Moses and **A**, 175
12: 8 then the LORD sent Moses and **A**, 175
1Ch 6: 3 of Amram; **A**, and Moses, and Miriam. 175
6: 3 The sons also of **A**; Nadab, and Abihu, 175
6:49 **A** and his sons offered upon the altar of 175
6:50 And these *are* the sons of **A**; Eleazar his son, 175
6:54 of the sons of **A**, of the families of 175
6:57 to the sons of **A** they gave the cities of 175
15: 4 And David assembled the children of **A**, and 175
23:13 The sons of Amram; **A** and Moses: and 175
23:13 **A** was separated, that he should sanctify 175
23:28 **A** for the service of the house of 175
23:32 the charge of the sons of **A** their brethren, 175
24: 1 Now *these are* the divisions of the sons of **A**. 175
24: 1 The sons of **A**; Nadab, and Abihu, Eleazar, 175
24:19 to their manner, under **A** their father, 175
24:31 sons of **A** in the presence of David the king, 175
2Ch 13: 9 the sons of **A**, and the Levites, and 175
13:10 *are* the sons of **A**, and the Levites *wait* upon 175
26:18 the LORD, but to the priests the sons of **A**, 175
29:21 he commanded the priests the sons of **A** to 175
31:19 Also of the sons of **A** the priests, *which were* 175
35:14 the priests the sons of **A** *were busied* in 175
35:14 and for the priests the sons of **A**. 175
Ezr 7: 5 son of Eleazar, the son of **A** the chief priest: 175
Ne 10:38 the priest the son of **A** shall be with 175
12:47 sanctified *them* unto the children of **A**. 175
Ps 77:20 like a flock by the hand of Moses and **A**. 175
99: 6 Moses and **A** among his priests, and 175
105:26 his servant; *and* **A** whom he had chosen. 175
106:16 in the camp, *and* **A** the saint of the LORD. 175
115:10 O house of **A**, trust in the LORD: he *is* their 175
115:12 house of Israel; he will bless the house of **A**. 175
118: 3 Let the house of **A** now say, that his mercy 175
135:19 of Israel: bless the LORD, O house of **A**: 175
Mic 6: 4 I sent before thee Moses, **A**, and Miriam. 175
Lk 1: 5 and his wife *was* of the daughters of **A**, and *2*
Ac 7:40 Saying unto **A**, Make us gods to go before us: *2*
Heb 5: 4 but he that is called of God, as *was* **A**. *2*
7:11 and not be called after the order of **A**? *2*

AARON'S (31) [AARON]

Ex 6:25 Eleazar **A** son took him *one* of the daughters 175
7:12 but **A** rod swallowed up their rods. 175
28: 1 and Abihu, Eleazar and Ithamar, **A** sons. 175
28: 3 that they may make **A** garments to 175
28:30 they shall be upon **A** heart, when he goeth in 175
28:38 it shall be upon **A** forehead, that Aaron may 175
28:40 for **A** sons thou shalt make coats, and 175
29:26 thou shalt take the breast of the ram of **A** 175
29:28 it shall be **A** and his sons' by a 175+3807.1
Lev 1: 5 and the priests, **A** sons, shall bring the blood, 175
1: 8 the priests, **A** sons, shall lay the parts, 175
1:11 the priests, **A** sons, shall sprinkle his blood 175
2: 2 he shall bring it to **A** sons the priests: and 175
2: 3 of the meat offering *shall be* **A** 175+3807.1
2:10 left of the meat offering *shall be* **A** 175+3807.1
3: 2 **A** sons the priests shall sprinkle the blood 175
3: 5 **A** sons shall burn it on the altar upon 175
Lev 3: 8 **A** sons shall sprinkle the blood thereof round 175
7:31 but the breast shall be **A** and his sons'. 175
8:12 he poured of the anointing oil upon **A** head, 175
8:13 Moses brought **A** sons, and put coats upon 175
8:23 put *it* upon the tip of **A** right ear, and 175
8:24 he brought **A** sons, and Moses put of 175
8:27 he put all upon **A** hands, and upon his sons' 175
9:12 **A** sons presented unto him the blood, 175
9:18 **A** sons presented unto him the blood, 175
24: 9 it shall be **A** and his sons'; and 175+3807.1
Nu 17: 3 thou shalt write **A** name upon the rod of 175
17:10 Bring **A** rod again before the Testimony, 175
Ps 133: 2 that ran down upon the beard, *even* **A** beard: 175
Heb 9: 4 and **A** rod that budded, and the tables of *2*

AARONITES (2) [AARON]

1Ch 12:27 Jehoiada *was* the leader of the **A**, and 175
27:17 the son of Kemuel: of the **A**, Zadok: 175

ABADDON (1)

Rev 9:11 *pit*, whose name in the Hebrew tongue *is* **A**, *3*

ABAGTHA (1)

Est 1:10 Harbona, Bigtha, and **A**, Zethar, and Carcas, 5

ABANA (1)

2Ki 5:12 *Are* not **A** and Pharpar, rivers of Damascus, 71

ABARIM (4) [IJE-ABARIM]

Nu 27:12 Get thee up into this mount **A**, and see 5682
33:47 pitched in the mountains of **A**, before 5682
33:48 they departed from the mountains of **A**, 5682
Dt 32:49 Get thee up into this mountain **A**, 5682

ABASE (4) [ABASED, ABASING]

Job 40:11 behold every one *that is* proud, and **a** him. 8213
Isa 31: 4 nor **a** himself for the noise of them: 6031
Eze 21:26 *him that is* low, and **a** *him that is* high. 8213
Da 4:37 and those that walk in pride he *is* able to **a**. 8214

ABASED (4) [ABASING]

Mt 23:12 whosoever shall exalt himself shall be **a**; *5013*
Lk 14:11 For whosoever exalteth himself shall be **a**; *5013*
18:14 every one that exalteth himself shall be **a**; *5013*
Php 4:12 I know both *how* to be **a**, and I know *how* *5013*

ABASING (1) [ABASED]

2Co 11: 7 Have I committed an offence in **a** myself *5013*

ABATED (6)

Ge 8: 3 and fifty days the waters were **a**. 2637
8: 8 to see if the waters were **a** from off the face 7043
8:11 Noah knew that the waters were **a** from off 7043
Lev 27:18 and it shall be **a** from thy estimation. 1639
Dt 34: 7 his eye was not dim, nor his natural force **a**. 5127
Jdg 8: 3 their anger was **a** toward him, when he had 7503

ABBA (3)

Mk 14:36 And he said, **A**, Father, all *things are* possible *5*
Ro 8:15 Spirit of adoption, whereby we cry, **A**, Father. *5*
Gal 4: 6 of his Son into your hearts, crying, **A**, Father. *5*

ABDA (2)

1Ki 4: 6 Adoniram the son of **A** *was* over 5653
Ne 11:17 **A** the son of Shammua, the son of Galal, 5653

ABDEEL (1)

Jer 36:26 Shelemiah the son of **A**, to take Baruch 5655

ABDI (3)

1Ch 6:44 of Kishi, the son of **A**, the son of Malluch, 5660
2Ch 29:12 Kish the son of **A**, and Azariah the son of 5660
Ezr 10:26 and Jehiel, and **A**, and Jeremoth, and Eliah. 5660

ABDIEL (1)

1Ch 5:15 Ahi the son of **A**, the son of Guni, chief of 5661

ABDON (8)

Jos 21:30 with her suburbs, **A** with her suburbs, 5658
Jdg 12:13 after him **A** the son of Hillel, a Pirathonite, 5658
12:15 **A** the son of Hillel the Pirathonite died, 5658
1Ch 6:74 with her suburbs, and **A** with her suburbs, 5658
8:23 And **A**, and Zichri, and Hanan, 5658
8:30 his firstborn son **A**, and Zur, and Kish, and 5658
9:36 his firstborn son **A**, then Zur, and Kish, 5658
2Ch 34:20 **A** the son of Micah, and Shaphan 5658

ABED-NEGO (15) [AZARIAH]

Da 1: 7 of Meshach; and to Azariah, of **A**. 5664
2:49 and he set Shadrach, Meshach, and **A**, 5665
3:12 of Babylon, Shadrach, Meshach, and **A**; 5665
3:13 to bring Shadrach, Meshach, and **A**. 5665
3:14 *Is it* true, O Shadrach, Meshach, and **A**, 5665
3:16 and **A**, answered and said to the king, 5665
3:19 against Shadrach, Meshach, and **A**: 5665
3:20 **A**, *and* to cast *them* into the burning fiery 5665
3:22 that took up Shadrach, Meshach, and **A**. 5665
3:23 three men, Shadrach, Meshach, and **A**, 5665
3:26 spake, and said, Shadrach, Meshach, and **A**, 5665
3:26 *hither*. Then Shadrach, Meshach, and **A**, 5665
3:28 Meshach, and **A**, who hath sent his angel, 5665
3:29 Meshach, and **A**, shall be cut in pieces, and 5665
3:30 Meshach, and **A**, in the province of 5665

ABEL (16) [ABEL-BETH-MAACHAH]

Ge 4: 2 she again bare his brother **A**. And Abel was 1893
4: 2 **A** was a keeper of sheep, but Cain was a 1893
4: 4 **A**, he also brought of the firstlings of his 1893
4: 4 the LORD had respect unto **A** and to his 1893
4: 8 Cain talked with **A** his brother: and it came 1893
4: 8 that Cain rose up against **A** his brother, and 1893
4: 9 said unto Cain, Where *is* **A** thy brother? 1893
4:25 appointed me another seed instead of **A**, 1893
1Sa 6:18 even unto the great *stone of* **A**, 59
2Sa 20:14 he went through all the tribes of Israel unto **A**, 59
20:15 and besieged him in **A** of Beth-maachah, 59
20:18 They shall surely ask *counsel* at **A**: 59
Mt 23:35 from the blood of righteous **A** unto the blood of *6*
Lk 11:51 From the blood of **A** unto the blood of *6*
Heb 11: 4 By faith **A** offered unto God a more excellent *6*
12:24 that speaketh better *things* than *that of* **A**. *6*

ABEL-BETH-MAACHAH (2) [BETH-MAACHAH]

1Ki 15:20 and Dan, and **A**, and all Cinneroth, 59
2Ki 15:29 **A**, and Janoah, and Kedesh, and Hazor, and 59

ABEL-MAIM (1)

2Ch 16: 4 and **A**, and all the store cities of Naphtali. 66

ABEL-MEHOLAH (3)

Jdg 7:22 *and* to the border of **A**, unto Tabbath. 65
1Ki 4:12 beneath Jezreel, from Beth-shean to **A**, 65
19:16 Elisha the son of Shaphat of **A** shalt thou 65

ABEL-MIZRAIM (1) [MIZRAIM]

Ge 50:11 wherefore the name of it was called **A**, 67

ABEL-SHITTIM (1) [SHITTIM]

Nu 33:49 from Beth-jesimoth *even* unto **A** in the plains 63

ABEZ (1)

Jos 19:20 And Rabbith, and Kishion, and **A**, 77

ABHOR (19) [ABHORRED, ABHORREST, ABHORRETH, ABHORRING]

Lev 26:11 amongst you: and my soul shall not **a** you. 1602
26:15 or if your soul **a** my judgments, so that *ye* 1602
26:30 of your idols, and my soul shall **a** you. 1602
26:44 neither will I **a** them, to destroy them 1602
Dt 7:26 detest it, and thou shalt **utterly a** it; 8581+8581
23: 7 Thou shalt not **a** an Edomite; for he *is* thy 8581
23: 7 thou shalt not **a** an Egyptian; because 8581
1Sa 27:12 **made** his people Israel **utterly to a** 887+887
Job 9:31 the ditch, and mine own clothes shall **a** me. 8581
30:10 They **a** me, they flee far from me, and 8581
42: 6 Wherefore I **a** *myself*, and repent in dust 3988
Ps 5: 6 the LORD will **a** the bloody and 8581
119:163 I hate and **a** lying: *but* thy law do I love. 8581
Pr 24:24 shall the people curse, nations shall **a** him: 2194
Jer 14:21 Do not **a** *us*, for thy name's sake, do not 5006
Am 5:10 and they **a** him that speaketh uprightly. 8581
6: 8 I **a** the excellency of Jacob, and hate his 8374
Mic 3: 9 that **a** judgment, and pervert all equity. 8581
Ro 12: 9 **A** *that which is* evil; cleave to *that which is* *655*

ABHORRED (16) [ABHOR]

Ex 5:21 you have **made** our savour **to be a** in 887
Lev 20:23 all these *things*, and therefore I **a** them. 6973
26:43 and because their soul **a** my statutes. 1602
Dt 32:19 when the LORD saw *it*, he **a** *them*, 5006
1Sa 2:17 for men **a** the offering of the LORD. 5006
2Sa 16:21 all Israel shall hear that thou art **a** of thy 887
1Ki 11:25 mischief that Hadad *did*: and he **a** Israel, 6973
Job 19:19 All my inward friends **a** me: and 8581
Ps 22:24 For he hath not despised nor **a** the affliction 8262
78:59 *this*, he was wroth, and greatly **a** Israel: 3988
89:38 thou hast cast off and **a**, thou hast been 3988
106:40 insomuch that he **a** his own inheritance. 8581
Pr 22:14 he that is **a** of the LORD shall fall therein. 2194
La 2: 7 cast off his altar, he hath **a** his sanctuary, 5010
Eze 16:25 hast **made** thy beauty **to be a**, and 8581
Zec 11: 8 soul lothed them, and their soul also **a** me. 973

ABHORREST (2) [ABHOR]

Isa 7:16 the land that thou **a** shall be forsaken of 6973
Ro 2:22 thou that **a** idols, dost thou commit *948*

ABHORRETH (5) [ABHOR]

Job 33:20 So that his life **a** bread, and his soul dainty 2092
Ps 10: 3 blesseth the covetous, *whom* the LORD **a**. 5006
36: 4 in a way *that is* not good; he **a** not evil. 3988
107:18 Their soul **a** all *manner of* meat; and 8581
Isa 49: 7 to him whom the nation **a**, to a servant of 8581

ABHORRING (1) [ABHOR]

Isa 66:24 and they shall be an **a** unto all flesh. 1860

ABI (1)

2Ki 18: 2 His mother's name also *was* **A**, the daughter 21

ABIA (4)

1Ch 3:10 **A** his son, Asa his son, Jehoshaphat his son, 29
Mt 1: 7 and Roboam begat **A**; and Abia begat Asa; *7*
1: 7 and Roboam begat Abia; and **A** begat Asa; *7*
Lk 1: 5 priest named Zacharias, of the course of **A**: *7*

ABIAH (4)

1Sa 8: 2 was Joel; and the name of his second, **A**: 29
1Ch 2:24 **A** Hezron's wife bare him Ashur the father of 29
6:28 sons of Samuel; the firstborn Vashni, and **A**. 29
7: 8 Jerimoth, and **A**, and Anathoth, and Alameth. 29

ABIALBON (1)

2Sa 23:31 **A** the Arbathite, Azmaveth the Barhumite, 45

ABIASAPH (1)

Ex 6:24 the sons of Korah; Assir, and Elkanah, and **A**: 23

ABIATHAR (30) [ABIATHAR'S]

1Sa 22:20 named **A**, escaped, and fled after David. 54
22:21 **A** shewed David that Saul had slain 54
22:22 David said unto **A**, I knew *it* that day, when 54
23: 6 when **A** the son of Ahimelech fled to David *to* 54
23: 9 he said to **A** the priest, Bring hither the ephod. 54
30: 7 David said to **A** the priest, Ahimelech's son, 54
30: 7 And **A** brought thither the ephod to David. 54

2Sa 8:17 and Ahimelech the son of **A**, *were* the priests; 54
15:24 **A** went up, until all the people had done 54
15:27 Ahimaaz thy son, and Jonathan the son of **A**. 54
15:29 **A** carried the ark of God again *to* Jerusalem: 54
15:35 not there with thee Zadok and **A** the priests? 54
15:35 thou shalt tell *it* to Zadok and **A** the priests. 54
17:15 said Hushai unto Zadok and to **A** the priests, 54
19:11 king David sent to Zadok and to **A** the priests, 54
20:25 *was* scribe: and Zadok and **A** *were* the priests: 54
1Ki 1: 7 Joab the son of Zeruiah, and with **A** the priest: 54
1:19 **A** the priest, and Joab the captain of the host: 54
1:25 and the captains of the host, and **A** the priest; 54
1:42 behold, Jonathan the son of **A** the priest came: 54
2:22 for **A** the priest, and for Joab the son of 54
2:26 unto **A** the priest said the king, Get thee *to* 54
2:27 So Solomon thrust out **A** from being priest 54
2:35 the priest did the king put in the room of **A**. 54
4: 4 the host: and Zadok and **A** *were* the priests: 54
1Ch 15:11 And David called for Zadok and **A** the priests, 54
18:16 and Abimelech the son of **A**, *were* the priests; 54
24: 6 Ahimelech the son of **A**, and *before* the chief 54
27:34 *was* Jehoiada the son of Benaiah, and **A**: 54
Mk 2:26 house of God in the days of **A** the high priest, *8*

ABIATHAR'S (1) [ABIATHAR]
2Sa 15:36 Zadok's *son*, and Jonathan **A** *son;* and 54+3807.1

ABIB (6)
Ex 13: 4 *This* day came ye out in the month **A**. 24
23:15 in the time appointed of the month **A**; 24
34:18 commanded thee, in the time of the month **A**: 24
34:18 for in the month **A** thou camest out from 24
Dt 16: 1 Observe the month of **A**, and keep 24
16: 1 for in the month of **A** the LORD thy God 24

ABIDA (1) [ABIDAH]
1Ch 1:33 and Epher, and Henoch, and **A**, and Eldaah. 28

ABIDAH (1) [ABIDA]
Ge 25: 4 and Epher, and Hanoch, and **A**, and Eldaah. 28

ABIDAN (5)
Nu 1:11 Of Benjamin; **A** the son of Gideoni. 27
2:22 the captain of the sons of Benjamin *shall be* **A** 27
7:60 On the ninth day **A** the son of Gideoni, 27
7:65 this *was* the offering of **A** the son of Gideoni. 27
10:24 of Benjamin *was* **A** the son of Gideoni. 27

ABIDE (81) [ABIDETH, ABIDING, ABODE, ABODEST]
Ge 19: 2 Nay; but we will **a** in the street **all night**. 3885
22: 5 his young men, **A** you here with the ass; 3427
24:55 Let the damsel **a** with us *a few* days, at 3427
29:19 should give her to another man: **a** with me. 3427
44:33 let thy servant **a** instead of the lad **a** 3427
Ex 16:29 **a** ye every man in his place, let no man go 3427
Lev 8:35 Therefore shall ye **a** *at* the door of 3427
19:13 not **a** with thee **all night** until the morning. 3885
Nu 22: 5 of the earth, and they **a** over against me: 3427
31:19 do ye **a** without the camp seven days: 2583
31:23 Every thing that may **a** the fire, 935+871.1
35:25 he shall **a** in it unto the death of the high 3427
Dt 3:19 shall **a** in your cities which I have given 3427
Jos 18: 5 Judah shall **a** in their coast on the south, 5975
18: 5 the house of Joseph shall **a** in their coasts 5975
Ru 2: 8 from hence, but **a** here **fast** by my maidens: 1692
1Sa 1:22 before the LORD, and there **a** for ever. 3427
5: 7 The ark of the God of Israel shall not **a** 3427
19: 2 and **a** in a secret place, and hide thyself: 3427
22: 5 Gad said unto David, **A** not in the hold; 3427
22:23 **A** thou with me, fear not: for he that 3427
30:21 whom they had **made** also **to a** at the brook 3427
2Sa 11:11 The ark, and Israel, and Judah, **a** in tents; 3427
15:19 return to thy place, and **a** with the king: 3427
16:18 choose, his will I be, and with him will I **a**. 3427
1Ki 8:13 a settled place for thee to **a in** for ever. 3427
2Ch 25:19 **a** now at home; why shouldest thou meddle 3427
32:10 ye trust, that ye **a** in the siege in Jerusalem? 3427
Job 24:13 the ways thereof, nor **a** in the paths thereof. 3427
38:40 *their* dens, *and* **a** in the covert to lie in wait? 3427
39: 9 be willing to serve thee, or **a** by thy crib? 3885
Ps 15: 1 LORD, who shall **a** in thy tabernacle? 1481
61: 4 I will **a** in thy tabernacle for ever: I will 1481
61: 7 He shall **a** before God for ever: O prepare 3427
91: 1 shall **a** under the shadow of the Almighty. 3885
Pr 7:11 and stubborn; her feet **a** not in her house: 7931
19:23 *he that hath it* shall **a** satisfied; he shall not 3885
Ecc 8:15 for that shall **a with** him of his labour 3867
Jer 10:10 the nations shall not be **able to a** his 3557
42:10 If ye will still **a** in this land, then will I 3427
49:18 saith the LORD, no man shall **a** there, 3427
49:33 there shall no man **a** there, nor *any* son of 3427
50:40 *so* shall no man **a** there, neither shall any 3427
Hos 3: 3 unto her, Thou shalt **a** for me many days; 3427
3: 4 For the children of Israel shall **a** many days 3427
11: 6 the sword shall **a** on his cities, and 2342
Joel 2:11 *is* great and very terrible; and who can **a** it? 3557
Mic 5: 4 of the LORD his God; and they shall **a**: 3427
Na 1: 6 who can **a** in the fierceness of his anger? 6965
Mal 3: 2 who *may* **a** the day of his coming? and 3557
Mt 10:11 in it is worthy; and there **a** till ye go thence. *3306*
Mk 6:10 there **a** till ye depart from that place. *3306*
Lk 9: 4 ye enter into, there **a**, and thence depart. *3306*
19: 5 for to day I must **a** at thy house. *3306*
24:29 they constrained him, saying, **A** with us: *3306*
Jn 12:46 believeth on me should not **a** in darkness. *3306*
14:16 that he may **a** with you for ever; *3306*
15: 4 **A** in me, and I in you. As the branch cannot *3306*
15: 4 bear fruit of itself, except it **a** in the vine; *3306*
15: 4 no more can ye, except ye **a** in me. *3306*
15: 6 If a man **a** not in me, he is cast forth as a *3306*
15: 7 If ye **a** in me, and my words abide in you, *3306*
15: 7 If ye abide in me, and my words **a** in you, *3306*
15:10 my commandments, ye shall **a** in my love; *3306*
Jn 15:10 Father's commandments, and **a** in his love. *3306*
Ac 15:34 Notwithstanding it pleased Silas to **a** there *1961*
16:15 and **a** *there*. And she constrained us. *3306*
20:23 saying that bonds and afflictions **a** me. *3306*
27:31 to the soldiers, Except these **a** in the ship, *3306*
1Co 3:14 If any *man's* work **a** which he hath built *3306*
7: 8 It is good for them if they **a** even as I. *3306*
7:20 Let every man **a** in the same calling *3306*
7:24 wherein he is called, therein **a** with God. *3306*
7:40 But she is happier if she so **a**, after my *3306*
16: 6 And it may be that I will **a**, yea, and *3887*
Php 1:24 Nevertheless to **a** in the flesh *is* more *1961*
1:25 I know that I shall **a** and continue with you *3306*
1Ti 1: 3 As I besought thee to **a** *still* at Ephesus, *4357*
1Jn 2:24 Let *that* therefore **a** in you, which ye have *3306*
2:27 as it hath taught you, ye shall **a** in him. *3306*
2:28 And now, little children, **a** in him; that, *3306*

ABIDETH (30) [ABIDE]
Nu 31:23 all that **a** not the fire ye shall make go 935+871.1
2Sa 16: 3 unto the king, Behold, he **a** at Jerusalem: 3427
Job 39:28 She dwelleth and **a** on the rock, upon 3885
Ps 49:12 Nevertheless man *being* in honour **a** not: 3885
55:19 and afflict them, even he that **a** of old. 3427
119:90 thou hast established the earth, and it **a**. 5975
125: 1 *which* cannot be removed, *but* **a** for ever. 3427
Pr 15:31 The ear that heareth the reproof of life **a** 3885
Ecc 1: 4 generation cometh: but the earth **a** for ever. 5975
Jer 21: 9 He that **a** in this city shall die by the sword, 3427
Jn 3:36 not see life; but the wrath of God **a** on him. *3306*
8:35 And the servant **a** not in the house for ever: *3306*
8:35 in the house for ever: *but* the son **a** ever. *3306*
12:24 fall into the ground and die, it **a** alone: *3306*
12:34 We have heard out of the law that Christ **a** *3306*
15: 5 He that **a** in me, and I in him, the same *3306*
1Co 13:13 And now **a** faith, hope, charity, these three; *3306*
2Ti 2:13 If we believe not, *yet* he **a** faithful: *3306*
Heb 7: 3 unto the Son of God; **a** a priest continually. *3306*
1Pe 1:23 word of God, which liveth and **a** for ever. *3306*
1Jn 2: 6 He that saith *he* **a** in him ought himself also *3306*
2:10 He that loveth his brother **a** in the light, and *3306*
2:14 and the word of God **a** in you, and ye have *3306*
2:17 but he that doeth the will of God **a** for ever. *3306*
2:27 which ye have received of him **a** in you, *3306*
3: 6 Whosoever **a** in him sinneth not: *3306*
3:14 He that loveth not *his* brother **a** in death. *3306*
3:24 And hereby we know that he **a** in us, by *3306*
2Jn 1: 9 and **a** not in the doctrine of Christ, hath not *3306*
1: 9 He that **a** in the doctrine of Christ, he hath *3306*

ABIDING (9) [ABIDE]
Nu 24: 2 he saw Israel **a** *in his tents* according to 7931
Jdg 16: 9 lying in wait, **a** with her in the chamber. 3427
16:12 *there were* liers in wait **a** in the chamber. 3427
1Sa 26:19 for they have driven me out *this* day from **a** 5596
1Ch 29:15 earth *are* as a shadow, and *there is* none **a** 4723
Lk 2: 8 **in** the same **country** shepherds **a** in the field, *63*
Jn 5:38 And ye have not his word **a** in you: *3306*
Ac 16:12 and we were in that city **a** certain days. *1304*
1Jn 3:15 that no murderer hath eternal life **a** in him. *3306*

ABIEL (3)
1Sa 9: 1 the son of **A**, the son of Zeror, the son of 22
14:51 and Ner the father of Abner *was* the son of **A**. 22
1Ch 11:32 of the brooks of Gaash, **A** the Arbathite, 22

ABIEZER, ABI-EZER (7) [ABI-EZRITE, ABI-EZRITES]
Jos 17: 2 for the children of **A**, and for the children of 44
Jdg 6:34 blew a trumpet; and **A** was gathered after him. 44
8: 2 of Ephraim better than the vintage of **A**? 44
2Sa 23:27 **A** the Anethothite, Mebunnai the Hushathite, 44
1Ch 7:18 bare Ishod, and **A**, and Mahalah. 44
11:28 son of Ikkesh the Tekoite, **A** the Antothite, 44
27:12 The ninth *captain* for the ninth month *was* **A** 44

ABI-EZRITE (1) [ABI-EZER]
Jdg 6:11 in Ophrah, that *pertained* unto Joash the **A**: 33

ABI-EZRITES (2) [ABI-EZER]
Jdg 6:24 unto this day it *is* yet in Ophrah of the **A**. 33
8:32 of Joash his father, in Ophrah of the **A**. 33

ABIGAIL (17)
1Sa 25: 3 man *was* Nabal; and the name of his wife **A**: 26
25:14 one of the young men told **A**, Nabal's wife, 26
25:18 **A** made haste, and took two hundred loaves, 26
25:23 when **A** saw David, she hasted, and 26
25:32 David said to **A**, Blessed *be* the LORD God 26
25:36 **A** came to Nabal; and behold, he held a feast 26
25:39 David sent and communed with **A**, to take her 26
25:40 when the servants of David were come to **A** to 26
25:42 And **A** hasted, and rose, and rode upon an ass, 26
27: 3 and **A** the Carmelitess, Nabal's wife. 26
30: 5 and **A** the wife of Nabal the Carmelite. 26
2Sa 2: 2 and **A** Nabal's wife the Carmelite. 26
3: 3 Chileab, of **A** the wife of Nabal the Carmelite; 26
17:25 that went in to **A** the daughter of Nahash, 26
1Ch 2:16 Whose sisters *were* Zeruiah, and **A**. And 26
2:17 **A** bare Amasa: and the father of Amasa *was* 26
3: 1 the second Daniel, of **A** the Carmelitess: 26

ABIHAIL (6)
Nu 3:35 families of Merari *was* Zuriel the son of **A**: 32
1Ch 2:29 And the name of the wife of Abishur *was* **A**, 32
5:14 These *are* the children of **A** the son of Huri, 32
2Ch 11:18 *and* **A** the daughter of Eliab the son of Jesse; 32
Est 2:15 the daughter of **A** the uncle of Mordecai, 32
9:29 the daughter of **A**, and Mordecai the Jew, 32

ABIHU (12)
Ex 6:23 bare him Nadab, and **A**, Eleazar, and Ithamar. 30
24: 1 and **A**, and seventy of the elders of Israel; 30
24: 9 and **A**, and seventy of the elders of Israel: 30
28: 1 Nadab and **A**, Eleazar and Ithamar, 30
Lev 10: 1 Nadab and **A**, the sons of Aaron, took either 30
Nu 3: 2 the firstborn, and **A**, Eleazar, and Ithamar. 30
3: 4 Nadab and **A** died before the LORD, 30
26:60 was born Nadab, and **A**, Eleazar, and Ithamar. 30
26:61 Nadab and **A** died, when they offered strange 30
1Ch 6: 3 Nadab, and **A**, Eleazar, and Ithamar. 30
24: 1 Nadab, and **A**, Eleazar, and Ithamar. 30
24: 2 But Nadab and **A** died before their father, and 30

ABIHUD (1)
1Ch 8: 3 sons of Bela were, Addar, and Gera, and **A**, 31

ABIJAH (20) [ABIJAM]
1Ki 14: 1 At that time **A** the son of Jeroboam fell sick. 29
1Ch 24:10 The seventh to Hakkoz, the eighth to **A**, 29
2Ch 11:20 which bare him **A**, and Attai, and Ziza, and 29
11:22 Rehoboam made **A** the son of Maachah 29
12:16 of David: and **A** his son reigned in his stead. 29
13: 1 king Jeroboam *began* **A** to reign over Judah. 29
13: 2 And there was war between **A** and Jeroboam. 29
13: 3 **A** set the battle in array with an army of 29
13: 4 **A** stood up upon mount Zemaraim, which *is* 29
13:15 and all Israel before **A** and Judah. 29
13:17 **A** and his people slew them *with* a great 29
13:19 **A** pursued after Jeroboam, and took cities 29
13:20 recover strength again in the days of **A**: 29
13:21 **A** waxed mighty, and married fourteen wives, 29
13:22 the rest of the acts of **A**, and his ways, and 29
14: 1 So **A** slept with his fathers, and they buried 29
29: 1 his mother's name *was* **A**, the daughter of 29
Ne 10: 7 Meshullam, **A**, Mijamin, 29
12: 4 Iddo, Ginnetho, **A**, 29
12:17 Of **A**, Zichri; of Miniamin, of Moadiah, Piltai; 29

ABIJAM (5) [ABIJAH]
1Ki 14:31 And **A** his son reigned in his stead. 38
15: 1 the son of Nebat reigned **A** over Judah. 38
15: 7 Now the rest of the acts of **A**, and all that he 38
15: 7 And there was war between **A** and Jeroboam. 38
15: 8 **A** slept with his fathers; and they buried him 38

ABILENE (1)
Lk 3: 1 of Trachonitis, and Lysanias the tetrarch of **A**, *9*

ABILITY (7) [ABLE]
Lev 27: 8 according to his **a** that vowed shall 3027+5381
Ezr 2:69 They gave after their **a** unto the treasure of 3581
Ne 5: 8 We after our **a** have redeemed our brethren 1767
Da 1: 4 such as *had* **a** in them to stand in the king's 3581
Mt 25:15 to every man according to his several **a**; *1411*
Ac 11:29 the disciples, every man according to his **a**, *2141*
1Pe 4:11 *let him do it* as of the **a** which God giveth: *2479*

ABIMAEL (2)
Ge 10:28 And Obal, and **A**, and Sheba, 39
1Ch 1:22 And Ebal, and **A**, and Sheba, 39

ABIMELECH (65) [ABIMELECH'S]
Ge 20: 2 and **A** king of Gerar sent, and took Sarah. 40
20: 3 But God came to **A** in a dream by night, and 40
20: 4 **A** had not come near her; and he said, Lord, 40
20: 8 Therefore **A** rose early in the morning, and 40
20: 9 Then **A** called Abraham, and said unto him, 40
20:10 And **A** said unto Abraham, What sawest thou, 40
20:14 **A** took sheep, and oxen, and menservants, 40
20:15 And **A** said, Behold, my land *is* before thee: 40
20:17 God healed **A**, and his wife, and 40
20:18 closed up all the wombs of the house of **A**, 40
21:22 that **A** and Phichol the chief captain of his 40
21:25 Abraham reproved **A** because of a well of 40
21:26 **A** said, I wot not who hath done this thing: 40
21:27 took sheep and oxen, and gave *them* unto **A**; 40
21:29 **A** said unto Abraham, What *mean* these seven 40
21:32 **A** rose up, and Phichol the chief captain of his 40
26: 1 Isaac went unto **A** king of the Philistims unto 40
26: 8 that **A** king of the Philistims looked out at a 40
26: 9 **A** called Isaac, and said, Behold, of a surety 40
26:10 **A** said, What *is* this thou hast done unto us? 40
26:11 **A** charged all *his* people, saying, He that 40
26:16 **A** said unto Isaac, Go from us; for thou art 40
26:26 **A** went to him from Gerar, and Ahuzzath *one* 40
Jdg 8:31 also bare him a son, whose name he called **A**. 40
9: 1 **A** the son of Jerubbaal went to Shechem unto 40
9: 3 their hearts inclined to follow **A**; for they said, 40
9: 4 wherewith **A** hired vain and light persons, 40
9: 6 house of Millo, and went, and made **A** king, 40
9:16 in that ye have made **A** king, and if ye have 40
9:18 upon one stone, and have made **A**, 40
9:19 *then* rejoice ye in **A**, and let him also rejoice 40
9:20 let fire come out from **A**, and devour the men 40
9:20 and from the house of Millo, and devour **A**. 40
9:21 and dwelt there, for fear of **A** his brother. 40
9:22 When **A** had reigned three years over Israel, 40
9:23 God sent an evil spirit between **A** and the men 40
9:23 men of Shechem dealt treacherously with **A**: 40
9:24 and their blood be laid upon **A** their brother, 40
9:25 along *that* way by them: and it was told **A**. 40
9:27 their god, and did eat and drink, and cursed **A**. 40
9:28 Who *is* **A**, and who *is* Shechem, that we 40
9:29 were under my hand; then would I remove **A**. 40
9:29 he said to **A**, Increase thine army, and 40
9:31 he sent messengers unto **A** privily, saying, 40
9:34 **A** rose up, and all the people that *were* with 40
9:35 **A** rose up, and the people that *were* with him, 40
9:38 thy mouth, wherewith thou saidst, Who *is* **A**, 40
9:39 the men of Shechem, and fought with **A**. 40
9:40 **A** chased him, and he fled before him, and 40
9:41 **A** dwelt at Arumah: and Zebul thrust out Gaal 40
9:42 went out *into* the field; and they told **A**. 40
9:44 And **A**, and the company that *was* with him, 40
9:45 And **A** fought against the city all that day; and 40
9:47 it was told **A**, that all the men of the tower of 40
9:48 And **A** gat him up *to* mount Zalmon, he and 40
9:48 **A** took an axe in his hand, and cut down a 40

Jdg 9:49 and followed **A**, and put *them* to the hold, and 40
9:50 went **A** to Thebez, and encamped against 40
9:52 **A** came unto the tower, and fought against it, 40
9:55 when the men of Israel saw that **A** was dead, 40
9:56 Thus God rendered the wickedness of **A**, 40
10: 1 after **A** there arose to defend Israel Tola 40
2Sa 11:21 Who smote **A** the son of Jerubbesheth? did 40
1Ch 18:16 and **A** the son of Abiathar, *were* the priests; 40
Ps 34: T when he changed his behaviour before **A**; 40

ABIMELECH'S (2) [ABIMELECH]
Ge 21:25 which **A** servants had violently taken away. 40
Jdg 9:53 cast a piece of a millstone upon **A** head, 40

ABINADAB (13)
1Sa 7: 1 and brought it into the house of **A** in the hill, 41
16: 8 Jesse called **A**, and made him pass before 41
17:13 and next unto him **A**, and the third Shammah. 41
31: 2 and **A**, and Malchishua, Saul's sons. 41
2Sa 6: 3 brought it out of the house of **A** that *was* in 41
6: 3 Uzzah and Ahio, the sons of **A**, drave the new 41
6: 4 they brought it out of the house of **A** which 41
1Ki 4:11 The son of **A**, *in* all the region of Dor; 41
1Ch 2:13 and **A** the second, and Shimma the third, 41
8:33 and Malchishua, and **A**, and Eshbaal. 41
9:39 and Malchishua, and **A**, and Eshbaal. 41
10: 2 and **A**, and Malchishua, the sons of Saul. 41
13: 7 of God in a new cart out of the house of **A**: 41

ABINOAM (4)
Jdg 4: 6 called Barak the son of **A** out of 42
4:12 they shewed Sisera that Barak the son of **A** 42
5: 1 and Barak the son of **A** on that day, 42
5:12 and lead thy captivity captive, thou son of **A**. 42

ABIRAM (11)
Nu 16: 1 the son of Levi, and Dathan and **A**, the sons 48
16:12 Moses sent to call Dathan and **A**, the sons of 48
16:24 about the tabernacle of Korah, Dathan, and **A**. 48
16:25 Moses rose up and went unto Dathan and **A**; 48
16:27 of Korah, Dathan, and **A**, on every side: 48
16:27 Dathan and **A** came out, and stood *in* the door 48
26: 9 sons of Eliab; Nemuel, and Dathan, and **A**. 48
26: 9 This *is that* Dathan and **A**, *which were* famous 48
Dt 11: 6 what he did unto Dathan and **A**, the sons of 48
1Ki 16:34 he laid the foundation thereof in **A** his 48
Ps 106:17 up Dathan, and covered the company of **A**. 48

ABISHAG (5)
1Ki 1: 3 found **A** a Shunammite, and brought her to 49
1:15 **A** the Shunammite ministered unto the king. 49
2:17 that he give me **A** the Shunammite to wife. 49
2:21 Let **A** the Shunammite be given to Adonijah 49
2:22 why dost thou ask **A** the Shunammite for 49

ABISHAI (25)
1Sa 26: 6 and to **A** the son of Zeruiah, brother to Joab, 52
26: 6 And **A** said, I will go down with thee. 52
26: 7 So David and **A** came to the people by night: 52
26: 8 said **A** to David, God hath delivered thine 52
26: 9 David said to **A**, Destroy him not: for who 52
2Sa 2:18 of Zeruiah there, Joab, and **A**, and Asahel: 52
2:24 Joab also and **A** pursued after Abner: and 52
3:30 So Joab and **A** his brother slew Abner, 52
10:10 he delivered into the hand of **A** his brother, 52
10:14 *then* fled they *also* before **A**, and entered *into* 52
16: 9 Then said **A** the son of Zeruiah unto the king, 52
16:11 And David said to **A**, and to all his servants, 52
18: 2 a third part under the hand of **A** the son of 52
18: 5 the king commanded Joab and **A** and Ittai, 52
18:12 hearing the king charged thee and **A** and Ittai, 52
19:21 But **A** the son of Zeruiah answered and said, 52
20: 6 David said to **A**, Now shall Sheba the son of 52
20:10 **A** his brother pursued after Sheba the son of 52
21:17 But **A** the son of Zeruiah succoured him, and 52
23:18 **A**, the brother of Joab, the son of Zeruiah, 52
1Ch 2:16 of Zeruiah; **A**, and Joab, and Asahel, three. 52
11:20 **A** the brother of Joab, he was chief of 52
18:12 Moreover **A** the son of Zeruiah slew of 52
19:11 he delivered unto the hand of **A** his brother, 52
19:15 they likewise fled before **A** his brother, and 52

ABISHALOM (2)
1Ki 15: 2 name *was* Maachah, the daughter of **A**. 53
15:10 name *was* Maachah, the daughter of **A**. 53

ABISHUA (5)
1Ch 6: 4 Eleazar begat Phinehas, Phinehas begat **A**, 50
6: 5 And **A** begat Bukki, and Bukki begat Uzzi, 50
6:50 Eleazar his son, Phinehas his son, **A** his son, 50
8: 4 And **A**, and Naaman, and Ahoah, 50
Ezr 7: 5 The son of **A**, the son of Phinehas, the son of 50

ABISHUR (2)
1Ch 2:28 And the sons of Shammai; Nadab, and **A**. 51
2:29 And the name of the wife of **A** *was* Abihail, 51

ABITAL (2)
2Sa 3: 4 and the fifth, Shephatiah the son of **A**; 37
1Ch 3: 3 The fifth, Shephatiah of **A**: the sixth, 37

ABITUB (1)
1Ch 8:11 And of Hushim he begat **A**, and Elpaal. 36

ABIUD (2)
Mt 1:13 And Zorobabel begat **A**; and Abiud begat *10*
1:13 and **A** begat Eliakim; and Eliakim begat Azor; *10*

ABJECTS (1)
Ps 35:15 *yea*, the **a** gathered themselves together 5222

ABLE (160) [ABILITY]
Ge 13: 6 the land was not **a to bear** them, that they 5375
15: 5 tell the stars, if thou be **a** to number them: 3201
33:14 and the children be **a to endure**, 7272+3807.1
Ex 10: 5 that *one* cannot be **a** to see the earth: 3201
18:18 thou art not **a** to perform it thyself alone. 3201
18:21 shalt provide out of all the people **a** men, 2428
18:23 *so*, then thou shalt be **a** to endure, 3201
18:25 Moses chose **a** men out of all Israel, and 2428
40:35 Moses was not **a** to enter into the tent of 3201
Lev 5: 7 if he be not **a** to bring a lamb, then he shall 1767
5:11 if he be not **a to bring** two 3027+5381
12: 8 if she be not **a to bring a** 1767+3027+4672
14:22 such as he is **a to get**; 3027+5381
14:31 *Even* such as he is **a to get**, the one 3027+5381
14:32 whose **hand is** not **a to get** *that* 3027+5381
25:26 be **a** to redeem it; 1767+3027+5381+3509.1
25:28 if he be not **a** to restore *it* to 1767+3027+4672
25:49 or if he be **a**, he may redeem himself. 3027+5381
Nu 1: 3 all that *are* **a** *to* go forth *to* war in Israel: NIH
1:20 upward, all that *were* **a** *to* go forth *to* war; NIH
1:22 upward, all that *were* **a** *to* go forth *to* war; NIH
1:24 upward, all that *were* **a** *to* go forth *to* war; NIH
1:26 upward, all that *were* **a** *to* go forth *to* war; NIH
1:28 upward, all that *were* **a** *to* go forth *to* war; NIH
1:30 upward, all that *were* **a** *to* go forth *to* war; NIH
1:32 upward, all that *were* **a** *to* go forth *to* war; NIH
1:34 upward, all that *were* **a** *to* go forth *to* war; NIH
1:36 upward, all that *were* **a** *to* go forth *to* war; NIH
1:38 upward, all that *were* **a** *to* go forth *to* war; NIH
1:40 upward, all that *were* **a** *to* go forth *to* war; NIH
1:42 upward, all that *were* **a** *to* go forth *to* war; NIH
1:45 all that *were* **a** *to* go forth *to* war in Israel; NIH
11:14 I am not **a** to bear all this people alone, 3201
13:30 for we are **well a to overcome** it. 3201+3201
13:31 We be not **a** to go up against the people; 3201
14:16 Because the LORD was not **a** to bring this 3201
22:11 peradventure I shall be **a** to overcome 3201
22:37 am I not **a** indeed to promote thee to 3201
26: 2 all that *are* **a** *to* go *to* war in Israel. NIH
Dt 1: 9 I am not **a** to bear you myself alone: 3201
7:24 there shall no man *be* **a** *to* stand before thee, NIH
9:28 Because the LORD was not **a** to bring 3201
11:25 There shall no man *be* **a** *to* stand before NIH
14:24 for thee, so that thou art not **a** to carry it; 3201
16:17 Every man *shall give* as he is **a**, 3027+4979
Jos 1: 5 There shall not any man *be* **a** *to* stand before NIH
14:12 I shall *be* **a** *to* drive them out, as the LORD NIH
23: 9 no man hath *been* **a** *to* stand before you unto NIH
Jdg 8: 3 what was I **a** to do in comparison of you? 3201
1Sa 6:20 Who is **a** to stand before this holy LORD 3201
17: 9 If he be **a** to fight with me, and *to* kill me, 3201
17:33 Thou art not **a** to go against this Philistine 3201
1Ki 3: 9 for who is **a** to judge this thy *so* great a 3201
9:21 whom the children of Israel also were not **a** 3201
2Ki 3:21 they gathered all that *were* **a** *to* put on NIH
18:23 if thou be **a** on thy part to set riders upon 3201
18:29 for he shall not be **a** to deliver you out of 3201
1Ch 5:18 men **a** *to* bear buckler and sword, and NIH
9:13 **very a** men *for* the work of the service of 2428
26: 8 **a** men for strength for the service, 2428
29:14 that we should be **a** to offer *so* 3581
2Ch 2: 6 who is **a** to build him a house, 3581+6113
7: 7 was not **a** to receive the burnt offerings, 3201
20: 6 so that none is **a to withstand** thee? 3320+5973
20:37 that they were not **a** to go to Tarshish. 6113
25: 5 thousand choice *men*, **a** *to* go forth *to* war, NIH
25: 9 The LORD **is a** to give thee much more 3426
32:13 **any ways a** to deliver their lands out 3201+3201
32:14 that your God should be **a** to deliver you 3201
32:15 kingdom was **a** to deliver his people out of 3201
Ezr 10:13 and *we are* not **a** to stand without, 3581
Ne 4:10 so that we are not **a** to build the wall. 3201
Job 41:10 him up: who then is **a** to stand before me? NIH
Ps 18:38 I have wounded them that they were not **a** 3201
21:11 *which* they are not **a** *to perform*. 3201
36:12 are cast down, and shall not be **a** to rise. 3201
40:12 that I am not **a** to look *up*; they are moe 3201
Pr 27: 4 but who is **a to stand** before envy? 5975
Ecc 8:17 to know *it*, yet shall he not be **a** to find *it*. 3201
Isa 36: 8 if thou be **a** on thy part to set riders upon 3201
36:14 for he shall not be **a** to deliver you. 3201
47:11 upon thee; thou shalt not be **a** to put it off: 3201
47:12 if so be thou shalt be **a** to profit, if so 3201
Jer 10:10 the nations shall not be **a to abide** his 3557
11:11 which they shall not be **a** to escape; 3201
49:10 and he shall not be **a** to hide himself: 3201
La 1:14 *from whom* I am not **a** to rise up. 3201
Eze 7:19 their gold shall not be **a** to deliver them in 3201
33:12 neither shall the righteous be **a** to live for 3201
46: 5 for the lambs **as** he shall be **a** to give, 3027
46:11 to the lambs **as** he is **a** to give, and a hin of 3027
Da 2:26 Art thou **a** to make known unto me 3546
3:17 our God whom we serve *is* **a** to deliver us 3202
4:18 **a** to make known unto me 3202
4:18 thou *art* **a**; for the spirit of the holy gods *is* 3546
4:37 those that walk in pride he *is* **a** to abase. 3202
6:20 **a** to deliver thee from the lions? 3202
Am 7:10 the land is not **a** to bear all his words. 3201
Zep 1:18 Neither their silver nor their gold shall be **a** 3201
Mt 3: 9 that God is **a** of these stones to raise up *1410*
9:28 Believe ye that I am **a** to do this? *1410*
10:28 kill the body, but are not **a** to kill the soul: *1410*
10:28 rather fear him which is **a** to destroy both *1410*
19:12 He that is **a** to receive *it*, let him receive *it*. *1410*
20:22 Are ye **a** to drink *of* the cup that I shall *1410*
20:22 *with?* They say unto him, We are **a**. *1410*
22:46 And no *man* was **a** to answer him a word, *1410*
26:61 I am **a** to destroy the temple of God, and *1410*
Mk 4:33 word unto them, as they were **a** to hear *it*. *1410*
Lk 1:20 thou shalt be dumb, and not **a** to speak, *1410*
3: 8 That God is **a** of these stones to raise up *1410*
12:26 then be not **a** *to do that thing which is* least, *1410*
13:24 will seek to enter in, and shall not be **a**. *2480*
14:29 is not **a** to finish *it*, all that behold *it* begin *2480*
14:30 man began to build, and was not **a** to finish. *2480*
14:31 consulteth whether he be **a** with ten *1415*
21:15 which all your adversaries shall not be **a** to *1410*
Jn 10:29 no *man* is **a** to pluck *them* out of my *1410*
21: 6 now they were not **a** to draw it for *2480*
Ac 6:10 And they were not **a** to resist the wisdom *2480*
15:10 which neither our fathers nor we were **a** to *2480*
20:32 which is **a** to build *you* up, and to give you *1410*
25: 5 said he, which among you are **a**, go down *1415*
Ro 4:21 he had promised, he was **a** also to perform. *1415*
8:39 shall be **a** to separate us from the love of *1410*
11:23 for God is **a** to graff them in again. *1415*
14: 4 holden up: for God is **a** to make him stand. *1415*
15:14 **a** also to admonish one another. *1410*
1Co 3: 2 for hitherto ye were not **a** *to bear it*, neither *1410*
3: 2 not able *to bear it*, neither yet now are ye **a**. *1410*
6: 5 not one that shall be **a** to judge between his *1410*
10:13 you to be tempted above that you are **a**; *1410*
10:13 way to escape, that ye may be **a** to bear *it*. *1410*
2Co 1: 4 that we may be **a** to comfort them which *1410*
3: 6 Who also hath **made** us **a** ministers of *2427*
9: 8 And God *is* **a** to make all grace abound *1415*
Eph 3:18 May be **a** to comprehend with all saints *1840*
3:20 Now unto him that is **a** to do exceeding *1410*
6:11 that ye may be **a** to stand against the wiles *1410*
6:13 that ye may be **a** to withstand in the evil *1410*
6:16 wherewith ye shall be **a** to quench all *1410*
Php 3:21 according to the working whereby he is **a** *1410*
2Ti 1:12 I am persuaded that he is **a** to keep that *1415*
2: 2 who shall be **a** to teach others also. *2425*
3: 7 never **a** to come to the knowledge of *1410*
3:15 which are **a** to make thee wise unto *1410*
Tit 1: 9 that he may be **a** by sound doctrine both to *1415*
Heb 2:18 he is **a** to succour them that are tempted. *1410*
5: 7 tears unto him that was **a** to save him from *1410*
7:25 Wherefore he is **a** also to save them to *1410*
11:19 Accounting that God *was* **a** to raise *him* up, *1415*
Jas 1:21 which is **a** to save your souls. *1410*
3: 2 *and* **a** also to bridle the whole body. *1415*
4:12 who is **a** to save and to destroy: *1410*
2Pe 1:15 **a** after my decease to have these *things* *4160*
Jude 1:24 Now unto him that is **a** to keep you from *1410*
Rev 5: 3 under the earth, was **a** to open the book, *1410*
6:17 wrath is come; and who shall be **a** to stand? *1410*
13: 4 the beast? who is **a** to make war with him? *1410*
15: 8 and no *man* was **a** to enter into the temple, *1410*

ABNER (62) [ABNER'S]
1Sa 14:50 and the name of the captain of his host *was* **A**, 74
14:51 and Ner the father of **A** *was* the son of Abiel. 74
17:55 he said unto **A**, the captain of the host, Abner, 74
17:55 he said unto Abner, the captain of the host, **A**, 74
17:55 **A** said, *As* thy soul liveth, O king, I cannot 74
17:57 **A** took him, and brought him before Saul with 74
20:25 **A** sat by Saul's side, and David's place was 74
26: 5 and **A** the son of Ner, the captain of his host: 74
26: 7 but **A** and the people lay round about him. 74
26:14 to **A** the son of Ner, saying, Answerest thou 74
26:14 son of Ner, saying, Answerest thou not, **A**? 74
26:14 **A** answered and said, Who *art* thou *that* criest 74
26:15 David said to **A**, *Art* not thou a *valiant* man? 74
2Sa 2: 8 But **A** the son of Ner, captain of Saul's host, 74
2:12 **A** the son of Ner, and the servants of 74
2:14 **A** said to Joab, Let the young men now arise, 74
2:17 **A** was beaten, and the men of Israel, before 74
2:19 Asahel pursued after **A**; and in going he 74
2:19 right hand nor to the left from following **A**. 74
2:20 **A** looked behind him, and said, *Art* thou 74
2:21 **A** said to him, Turn thee aside to thy right 74
2:22 **A** said again to Asahel, Turn thee aside from 74
2:23 wherefore **A** with the hinder end of the spear 74
2:24 Joab also and Abishai pursued after **A**: and 74
2:25 gathered themselves together after **A**, 74
2:26 **A** called to Joab, and said, Shall the sword 74
2:29 **A** and his men walked all that night through 74
2:30 Joab returned from following **A**: and when he 74
3: 6 that **A** made himself strong for the house of 74
3: 7 *Ish-bosheth* said to **A**, Wherefore hast thou 74
3: 8 was **A** very wroth for the words of 74
3: 9 So do God to **A**, and more also, except, as 74
3:11 he could not answer **A** a word again, because 74
3:12 **A** sent messengers to David on his behalf, 74
3:16 said **A** unto him, Go, return. And he returned. 74
3:17 **A** had communication with the elders of 74
3:19 **A** also spake in the ears of Benjamin: and 74
3:19 **A** went also to speak in the ears of David in 74
3:20 So **A** came to David to Hebron, and 74
3:20 David made **A** and the men that *were* with 74
3:21 **A** said unto David, I will arise and go, and 74
3:21 David sent **A** away; and he went in peace. 74
3:22 **A** *was* not with David in Hebron; for he had 74
3:23 **A** the son of Ner came to the king, and 74
3:24 behold, **A** came unto thee; why *is* it *that* thou 74
3:25 Thou knowest **A** the son of Ner, that he came 74
3:26 out from David, he sent messengers after **A**, 74
3:27 when **A** was returned *to* Hebron, Joab took 74
3:28 for ever from the blood of **A** the son of Ner: 74
3:30 So Joab and Abishai his brother slew **A**, 74
3:31 gird you with sackcloth, and mourn before **A**. 74
3:32 they buried **A** in Hebron: and the king lift up 74
3:32 lift up his voice, and wept at the grave of **A**; 74
3:33 the king lamented over **A**, and said, Died 74
3:33 over Abner, and said, Died **A** as a fool dieth? 74
3:37 it was not of the king to slay **A** the son of Ner. 74
4: 1 when Saul's son heard that **A** was dead in 74
4:12 and buried *it* in the sepulchre of **A** in Hebron. 74
1Ki 2: 5 unto **A** the son of Ner, and unto Amasa 74
2:32 not knowing *thereof, to wit*, **A** the son of Ner, 74
1Ch 26:28 **A** the son of Ner, and Joab the son of Zeruiah, 74
27:21 of Benjamin, Jaasiel the son of **A**: 74

ABNER'S (1) [ABNER]
2Sa 2:31 of **A** men, *so that* three hundred and 74

ABOARD (1)
Ac 21: 2 unto Phenicia, we **went a**, and set forth. *1910*

A

Ex 30: 3 the sides thereof **round a**, and the horns 5439
30: 3 shalt make unto it a crown *of* gold **round a**. 5439
32:28 there fell of the people that day **a** three 3509.1
37: 2 and made a crown *of* gold to it **round a**. 5439
37:11 made thereunto a crown *of* gold **round a**. 5439
37:12 a border of a handbreadth **round a**; 5439
37:12 of gold for the border thereof **round a**. 5439
37:26 the sides thereof **round a**, and the horns of 5439
37:26 he made unto it a crown *of* gold **round a**. 5439
38:16 All the hangings of the court **round a** *were* 5439
38:20 and of the court **round a**, *were of* brass. 5439
38:31 the sockets of the court **round a**, and 5439
38:31 and all the pins of the court **round a**. 5439
39:23 *with* a band **round a** the hole, *that* it should 5439
39:25 **round a** between the pomegranates; 5439
39:26 **round a** the hem of the robe to minister *in;* 5439
40: 8 thou shalt set up the court **round a**, and 5439
40:33 he reared up the court **round a** 5439
Lev 1: 5 sprinkle the blood **round a** upon the altar 5439
1:11 shall sprinkle his blood **round a** upon 5439
3: 2 sprinkle the blood upon the altar **round a**. 5439
3: 8 the blood thereof **round a** upon the altar. 5439
3:13 the blood thereof upon the altar **round a**. 5439
6: 5 Or all *that* **a** which he hath sworn falsely; NIH
7: 2 the blood thereof shall he sprinkle **round a** 5439
8:15 put *it* upon the horns of the altar **round a** 5439
8:19 sprinkled the blood upon the altar **round a**. 5439
8:24 sprinkled the blood upon the altar **round a**. 5439
9:12 which he sprinkled **round a** upon the altar. 5439
9:18 which he sprinkled upon the altar **round a**, 5439
14:41 the house to be scraped within **round a**, 5439
16:18 put *it* upon the horns of the altar **round a**. 5439
25:31 **round a** them shall be counted as the fields 5439
25:44 *shall be* of the heathen that *are* **round a** 5439
Nu 1:50 and shall encamp **round a** the tabernacle. 5439
1:53 the Levites shall pitch **round a** 5439
2: 2 far off **a** the tabernacle of the congregation 5439
3:26 by the altar **round a**, and the cords of it for 5439
3:37 the pillars of the court **round a**, and 5439
4: 4 of the congregation, **a** the most holy *things:* NIH
4:14 wherewith they minister **a** it, *even* 5921
4:26 by the tabernacle and by the altar **round a**, 5439
4:32 the pillars of the court **round a**, and 5439
11: 8 *And* the people **went a**, and gathered *it,* and 7751
11:24 and set them **round a** the tabernacle. 5439
11:31 **round a** the camp, and as it were two 5439
11:32 abroad for themselves **round a** the camp. 5439
16:24 Get you up from **a** the tabernacle of Korah, 5439
16:34 all Israel that *were* **round a** them fled at 5439
16:49 beside them that died **a** the matter of 5921
22: 4 company lick up all *that are* **round a** us, 5439
32:33 *even* the cities of the country **round a**. 5439
34:12 your land with the coasts thereof **round a**. 5439
35: 2 suburbs for the cities **round a** them. 5439
35: 4 and outward a thousand cubits **round a**. 5439
Dt 6:14 gods of the people which *are* **round a** you; 5439
12:10 rest from all your enemies **round a**, 4480+5439
13: 7 gods of the people which *are* **round a** you, 5439
17:14 like as all the nations that *are* **a** me; 5439
21: 2 cities which *are* **round a** him that is slain: 5439
25:19 rest from all thine enemies **round a**, 4480+5439
31:21 I know their imagination which they **go a**, 6213
32:10 he **led** him **a**, he instructed him, he kept 5437
Jos 2: 5 it came to pass **a** *the time* of shutting of NIH
3: 4 and it, **a** two thousand cubits by measure: 3509.1
4:13 **A** forty thousand prepared for war passed 3509.1
6: 3 men of war, *and* **go round a** the city once. 5362
6:11 compassed the city, **going a** *it* once: 5362
6:15 that they rose early **a** the dawning of 3509.1
7: 3 *but* let **a** two or three thousand men go up 3509.1
7: 4 So there went up thither of the people **a** 3509.1
7: 5 the men of Ai smote of them **a** thirty and 3509.1
8:12 he took **a** five thousand men, and 3509.1
10:13 and hasted not to go down **a** a whole day. 3509.1
11: 6 for to morrow **a** this time will I deliver 3509.1
15:12 Judah **round a** according to their families. 5439
16: 6 the border **went a** eastward *unto* 5437
18:20 by the coasts thereof **round a**, according to 5439
19: 8 all the villages that *were* **round a** these 5439
21:11 with the suburbs thereof **round a** it. 5439
21:42 every one with their suburbs **round a** them: 5439
21:44 the LORD gave them rest **round a**, 5439
23: 1 from all their enemies **round a**, 4480+5439
Jdg 2:12 of the gods of the people that *were* **round a** 5439
2:14 the hands of their enemies **round a**, 4480+5439
3:29 they slew *of* Moab at that time **a** ten 3509.1
7:21 they stood every man in his place **round a** 5439
8:10 **a** fifteen thousand *men,* all that were left 3509.1
8:26 beside the chains that *were* **a** their camels' 871.1
9:49 died also, **a** a thousand men and women. 3509.1
16:27 *there were* upon the roof **a** three thousand 3509.1
17: 2 **a** which thou cursedst, and spakest of also NIH
19:22 **beset** the house **round a**, *and* beat at 5437
20: 5 **beset** the house **round a** upon me by night, 5437
20:29 And Israel set liers in wait **round a** Gibeah. 5439
20:31 Gibeah in the field, **a** thirty men of Israel. 3509.1
20:39 kill of the men of Israel **a** thirty persons: 3509.1
20:43 they **inclosed** the Benjamites **round a**, 3803
Ru 1: 4 and they dwelled there **a** ten years. 3509.1
1:19 that all the city was moved **a** them, and 5921
2:17 and it was **a** an ephah of barley. 3509.1
1Sa 1:20 when the time was **come a** after 8622+3807.1
4: 2 they slew of the army in the field **a** four 3509.1
4:20 **a** the time of her death the *women* that 3509.1
5: 8 the God of Israel be **carried a** *unto* Gath. 5437
5: 8 they **carried** the ark of the God of Israel **a** 5437
5: 9 it was *so,* that after they had **carried** it **a**, 5437
5:10 They have **brought a** the ark of the God of 5437
9:13 you up; for **a** *this* time ye shall find him. 3509.1
9:16 To morrow **a** *this* time I will send thee **a** 3509.1
9:22 were bidden, which *were* **a** thirty persons. 3509.1
9:26 it came to pass **a** the spring of the day, 3509.1
13:15 present with him, **a** six hundred men. 3509.1
14: 2 the people that *were* with him *were* **a** six 3509.1
14:14 armourbearer made, was **a** twenty men, 3509.1

1Sa 14:21 into the camp *from the country* **round a**, 5439
15:12 is **gone a**, and passed on, and gone down *to* 5437
15:27 as Samuel **turned a** to go away, he laid 5437
17:42 when the Philistine **looked a**, and 5027
20:12 when I have sounded my father **a** to 3509.1
21: 5 *been* kept from us **a** these three days, 3509.1
22: 2 there were with him **a** four hundred men. 3509.1
22: 6 and all his servants *were* standing **a** him;) 5921
22: 7 Saul said unto his servants that stood **a** him, 5921
22:17 the king said unto the footmen that stood **a** 5921
23:13 *which were* **a** six hundred, arose and 3509.1
23:26 **compassed** David and his men **round a** 5849
25:13 there went up after David **a** four hundred 3509.1
25:38 it came to pass **a** ten days *after,* that 3509.1
26: 5 and the people pitched **round a** him. 5439
26: 7 but Abner and the people lay **round a** him. 5439
31: 9 into the land of the Philistines **round a**, 5439
2Sa 3:12 *be* with thee, to **bring a** all Israel unto thee. 5437
4: 5 came **a** the heat of the day to the house of 3509.1
5: 9 David built **round a** from Millo and 5439
7: 1 rest **round a** from all his enemies; 4480+5439
14:20 To **fetch a** *this* form of speech hath thy 5437
18:15 men that bare Joab's armour **compassed a** 5437
20:26 Ira also the Jairite was a chief ruler **a** 3807.1
22: 6 The sorrows of hell **compassed** me **a**; 5437
22:12 he made darkness pavilions **round a** him, 5439
24: 6 and they came to Dan-jaan, and **a** to Zidon, 5439
1Ki 2: 5 of war upon his girdle that *was* **a** his loins, 871.1
2:15 howbeit the kingdom is **turned a**, and 5437
3: 1 and the wall of Jerusalem **round a**. 5439
4:24 had peace on all sides **round a** him. 4480+5439
4:31 and his fame was in all nations **round a**. 5439
5: 3 the wars which were **a** him **on every side**, 5437
6: 5 of the house he built chambers **round a**, 5439
6: 5 *against* the walls of the house **round a**, 5439
6: 5 the oracle: and he made chambers **round a**: 5439
6: 6 the house he made narrowed rests **round a**, 5439
6:29 carved all the walls of the house **round a** 4524
7:12 the great court **round a** *was with* three 5439
7:15 twelve cubits did **compass** either of them **a**. 5437
7:18 two rows **round a** upon the one network, 5439
7:20 *in* rows **round a** upon the other chapiter. 5439
7:23 *it was* round **a**ll **a**, and his height *was* five 5439
7:23 thirty cubits did **compass** it **round a**. 5437+5439
7:24 **round a** *there were* knops **compassing** 5437+5439
7:24 ten in a cubit, compassing the sea **round a**: 5439
7:36 of every one, and additions **round a**. 5439
8:14 the king **turned** his face **a**, and blessed all 5437
18:32 he made a trench **a** the altar, as great as 5439
18:35 the water ran **round a** the altar; and 5439
19: 2 of one of them *by* to morrow **a** *this* time. 3509.1
20: 6 servants unto thee to morrow **a** *this* time, 3509.1
22: 6 **a** four hundred men, and said unto them, 3509.1
22:36 the host **a** the going down of the sun, 3509.1
2Ki 1: 8 girt *with* a girdle of leather **a** his loins. 871.1
3:25 howbeit the slingers **went a** *it,* and smote it. 5437
4:16 he said, **A** this season, according to 3807.1
6:14 came by night, and **compassed** the city **a**. 5362
6:17 and chariots of fire **round a** Elisha. 5439
7: 1 To morrow **a** *this* time *shall* a measure of 3509.1
7:18 shall be to morrow **a** *this* time in the gate 3509.1
8:21 the Edomites which **compassed** him **a**, 5437
11: 7 watch of the house of the LORD **a** the king. 413
11: 8 ye shall compass the king **round a**, 5439
11:11 his weapons in his hand, **round a** the king, 5439
17:15 *went* after the heathen that *were* **round a** 5439
23: 5 and in the **places round a** Jerusalem; 4524
25: 1 and they built forts against it **round a**. 5439
25: 4 Chaldees *were* against the city **round a**:) 5439
25:10 down the walls of Jerusalem **round a**. 5439
25:17 pomegranates upon the chapiter **round a**, 5439
1Ch 4:33 all their villages that *were* **round a** 5439
6:55 and the suburbs thereof **round a** it. 5439
9:27 they lodged **round a** the house of God, 5439
10: 9 into the land of the Philistines **round a**, 5439
11: 8 he built the city **round a**, even from Millo 5439
11: 8 city round about, even from Millo **round a**: 5439
15:22 he instructed **a** the song, because he *was* 871.1
18:17 of David *were* chief **a** the king. 3027+3807.1
22: 9 rest from all his enemies **round a**: 4480+5439
28:12 of all the chambers **round a**, of 5439
2Ch 2: 9 for the house which I am **a** to build *shall be* NIH
4: 2 line of thirty cubits did compass it **round a**. 5439
4: 3 which did compass it **round a**: 5439+5439
4: 3 ten in a cubit, compassing the sea **round a**. 5439
13:13 **caused** an ambushment to come **a** 5437
14: 7 **make a** *them* walls, and towers, gates, and 5437
14:14 they smote all the cities **round a** Gerar; 5439
15:15 the LORD gave them rest **round a**. 4480+5439
17: 9 **went a** throughout all the cities of Judah, 5437
17:10 of the lands that *were* **round a** Judah, 5439
18:31 Therefore they compassed **a** him to fight: 5921
18:34 **a** the time of the sun going down he died. 3807.1
20:30 for his God gave him rest **round a**. 4480+5439
23: 2 they **went a** in Judah, and gathered 5437
23: 7 Levites shall compass the king **round a**, 5439
23:10 and the temple, by the king **round a**. 5439
26: 6 built cities **a** Ashdod, and among 871.1
33:14 compassed **a** Ophel, and raised it up **a** 3807.1
34: 6 unto Naphtali, with their mattocks **round a**. 5439
Ezr 1: 6 all *they that were* **a** them strengthened their 5439
10:15 son of Tikvah were employed **a** this *matter:* 5921
Ne 5:17 us from among the heathen that *are* **a** us. 5439
6:16 all the heathen that *were* **a** us saw *these* 5439
12:28 both out of the plain country **round a** 5439
12:29 builded them villages **round a** Jerusalem. 5439
13:21 said unto them, Why lodge ye **a** the wall? 5048
Job 1: 5 the days of *their* feasting were **gone a**, 5362
1:10 Hast not thou made a hedge **a** him, and 1157
1:10 **a** his house, and about all that he hath on 1157
1:10 and **a** all that he hath on every side? 1157
8:17 His roots are wrapped **a** the heap, *and* 5921
10: 8 and fashioned me together **round a**; 5439
11:18 thou shalt dig *a thee, and* thou shalt take thy NIH

Job 16:13 His archers **compass** me **round a**, he 5437
19:12 and encamp **round a** my tabernacle. 5439
20:23 *When* he is **a** to fill his belly, *God* shall 3807.1
22:10 Therefore snares *are* **round a** thee, and 5439
29: 5 yet with me, *when* my children *were* **a** me; 5439
30:18 it **bindeth** me **a** as the collar of my coat. 247
37:12 it is turned **round a** by his counsels: 4524
40:22 the willows of the brook **compass** him **a**. 5437
41:14 of his face? his teeth *are* terrible **round a**. 5439
Ps 3: 6 have set *themselves* against me **round a**. 5439
7: 7 congregation of the people **compass** thee **a**: 5437
17: 9 my deadly enemies, *who* **compass** me **a**. 5362
18: 5 The sorrows of hell **compassed** me **a**: 5437
18:11 his pavilion **round a** him *were* dark waters 5439
27: 6 lifted up above mine enemies **round a** me: 5439
32: 7 thou shalt **compass** me **a** *with* songs of 5437
32:10 in the LORD, mercy shall **compass** him **a**. 5437
34: 7 encampeth **round a** them that fear him, 5439
40:12 innumerable evils have **compassed** me **a**: 661
44:13 and a derision to them that are **round a** us. 5439
48:12 **Walk a** Zion, and go round about her: 5437
48:12 Walk about Zion, and **go round a** her: 5362
49: 5 iniquity of my heels shall **compass** me **a**? 5437
50: 3 it shall be very tempestuous **round a** him. 5439
55:10 night they **go a** it upon the walls thereof: 5437
59: 6 a noise like a dog, and **go round a** the city. 5437
59:14 a noise like a dog, and **go round a** the city. 5437
73: 6 pride **compasseth** them **a as a chain**; 6059
76:11 let all that be **round a** him bring presents 5439
78:28 of their camp, **round a** their habitations. 5439
79: 3 they shed like water **round a** Jerusalem; 5439
79: 4 and derision to them that are **round a** us. 5439
88:17 They **came round a** me daily like water; 5437
88:17 like water; they **compassed** me **a** together. 5362
89: 7 to be had in reverence of all them that are **a** 5439
89: 8 or *to* thy faithfulness **round a** thee? 5439
97: 2 Clouds and darkness *are* **round a** him: 5439
97: 3 and burneth up his enemies **round a**. 5439
109: 3 They **compassed** me **a** also *with* words of 5437
118:10 All nations **compassed** me **a**: but in 5437
118:11 They **compassed** me **a**; yea, 5437
118:11 me about; yea, they **compassed** me **a**: 5437
118:12 They **compassed** me **a** like bees; they are 5437
125: 2 *As* the mountains *are* **round a** Jerusalem, 5439
125: 2 the LORD *is* **round a** his people from 5439
128: 3 thy children like olive plants **round a** thy 5439
139:11 even the night *shall be* light **a** me. 1157
140: 9 *for* the head of those that **compass** me **a**, 4524
142: 7 the righteous shall **compass** me **a**; for thou 3803
Pr 1: 9 unto thy head, and chains **a** thy neck. 3807.1
3: 3 bind them **a** thy neck; write them upon 5921
6:21 upon thine heart, *and* tie them **a** thy neck. 5921
20:19 He that **goeth a** *as* a talebearer revealeth 1980
Ecc 1: 6 the south, and **turneth a** unto the north; 5437
1: 6 it **whirleth a continually**, and 1980+5437+5437
2:20 Therefore I **went a** to cause my heart to 5437
12: 5 and the mourners **go a** the streets: 5437
SS 3: 2 **go a** the city in the streets and in the broad 5437
3: 3 The watchmen that **go a** the city found me: 5437
3: 7 threescore valiant *men are* **a** it, of 5439
5: 7 The watchmen that **went a** the city found 5437
7: 2 thy belly *is like* a heap of wheat **set a** with 5473
Isa 3:18 of *their* tinkling ornaments **a** *their feet,* NIH
15: 8 For the cry is **gone round a** the borders of 5362
23:16 Take a harp, **go a** the city, thou harlot that 5437
26:20 thy chambers, and shut thy doors **a** thee: 1157
28:27 is a cart wheel **turned a** upon the cummin; 5437
29: 3 against thee **round a**, 1754+1886.1+3509.1
42:25 it hath set him on fire **round a**, 4480+5439
49:18 Lift up thine eyes **round a**, and behold: 5439
50:11 that **compass** *yourselves* **a** with sparks: 247
60: 4 Lift up thine eyes **round a**, and see: 5439
Jer 1:15 against all the walls thereof **round a**, and 5439
2:36 Why **gaddest** thou **a** *so* much to change thy 235
4:17 a field, are they against her **round a**; 4480+5439
6: 3 shall pitch *their* tents against her **round a**; 5439
12: 9 the birds **round a** *are* against her; 5439
14:18 the priest **go a** into a land that they know 5503
17:26 from the places **a** Jerusalem, and from 5439
21:14 and it shall devour all things **round a** it. 5439
25: 9 against all these nations **round a**, and 5439
31:22 How long wilt thou **go a**, O thou 2559
31:39 hill Gareb, and shall **compass a** to Goath. 5437
32:44 in the places **a** Jerusalem, and in the cities 5439
33:13 in the places **a** Jerusalem, and in the cities 5439
41:14 carried away captive from Mizpah **cast a** 5437
46: 5 fear *was* **round a**, saith the LORD. 4480+5439
46:14 for the sword shall devour **round a** thee. 5439
48:17 All ye that are **a** him, bemoan him; and 5439
48:39 and a dismaying to all them **a** him. 5439
49: 5 of hosts, from all those that be **a** thee; 5439
50:14 in array against Babylon **round a**: 5439
50:15 Shout against her **round a**: she hath given 5439
50:29 that bend the bow, camp against it **round a**; 5439
50:32 and it shall devour all **round a** him. 5439
51: 2 they shall be against her **round a**. 4480+5439
52: 4 against it, and built forts against it **round a**. 5439
52: 7 the Chaldeans *were* by the city **round a**:) 5439
52:14 down all the walls of Jerusalem **round a**. 5439
52:22 pomegranates upon the chapiters **round a**, 5439
52:23 the network *were* an hundred **round a**. 5439
La 1:17 *that* his adversaries *should be* **round a** him. 5439
2: 3 a flaming fire, *which* devoureth **round a**. 5439
2:22 *in* a solemn day my terrors **round a**, 4480+5439
3: 7 He hath hedged me **a**, that I cannot get out: 1157
Eze 1: 4 a brightness *was* **a** it, and out of the midst 5439
1:18 their rings *were* full *of* eyes **round a** them 5439
1:27 as the appearance of fire **round a** within it, 5439
1:27 of fire, and it had brightness **round a**. 5439
1:28 the appearance of the brightness **round a**. 5439
4: 2 and set *battering* rams against it **round a**. 5439
5: 2 take a third *part, and* smite **a** it with a knife: 5439
5: 5 and countries *that are* **round a** her. 5439
5: 6 than the countries that *are* **round a** her: 5439
5: 7 more than the nations that *are* **round a** you, 5439

ABODE (69) [ABIDE]
Ge 29:14 And he **a** with him the space of a month. 3427
49:24 his bow **a** in strength, and the arms of his 3427
Ex 24:16 the glory of the LORD **a** upon mount 7931
40:35 because the cloud **a** thereon, and the glory 7931
Nu 9:17 in the place where the cloud **a**, there 7931
9:18 as long as the cloud **a** upon the tabernacle 7931
9:20 of the LORD they **a in** their **tents**, 2583
9:21 when the cloud **a** from even unto 1961
9:22 the children of Israel **a in** their **tents**, and 2583
11:35 *unto* Hazeroth; and **a** at Hazeroth. 1961
20: 1 the people **a** in Kadesh; and Miriam died 3427
22: 8 and the princes of Moab **a** with Balaam. 3427
25: 1 Israel **a** in Shittim, and the people begun to 3427
Dt 1:46 So ye **a** in Kadesh many days, 3427
1:46 according unto the days that ye **a** *there*. 3427
3:29 So we **a** in the valley over against 3427
9: 9 I **a** in the mount forty days and forty nights, 3427
Jos 2:22 unto the mountain, and **a** there three days, 3427
5: 8 that they **a** in their places in the camp, 3427
8: 9 **a** between Beth-el and Ai, on the west side 3427
Jdg 5:17 Gilead **a** beyond Jordan: and why did Dan 7931
5:17 on the sea shore, and **a** in his breaches. 7931
11:17 would not consent: and Israel **a** in Kadesh. 3427
19: 4 retained him; and he **a** with him three days: 3427
20:47 and **a** in the rock Rimmon four months. 3427
21: 2 **a** there till even before God, and lift up 3427
1Sa 1:23 So the woman **a**, and gave her son suck 3427
7: 2 to pass, while the ark **a** in Kirjath-jearim, 3427
13:16 with them, **a** in Gibeah of Benjamin: 3427
22: 6 (now Saul **a** in Gibeah under a tree in 3427
23:14 David **a** in the wilderness in strong holds, 3427
23:18 David **a** in the wood, and Jonathan went to 3427
23:25 a rock, and **a** in the wilderness of Maon. 3427
25:13 and two hundred **a** by the stuff. 3427
26: 3 David **a** in the wilderness, and he saw that 3427
30:10 for two hundred **a** *behind*, which were so 5975
2Sa 1: 1 and David had **a** two days in Ziklag; 3427
11:12 So Uriah **a** in Jerusalem that day, and 3427
15: 8 For thy servant vowed a vow while I **a** at 3427
1Ki 17:19 where he **a**, and laid him upon his own bed. 3427
2Ki 19:27 I know thy **a**, and thy going out, and 3427
Ezr 8:15 and there **a** we **in tents** three days: 2583
8:32 came *to* Jerusalem, and **a** there three days. 3427
Isa 37:28 I know thy **a**, and thy going out, and thy 3427
Jer 38:28 So Jeremiah **a** in the court of the prison 3427
Mt 17:22 And while they **a** in Galilee, Jesus said unto *390*
Lk 1:56 And Mary **a** with her about three months, *3306*
8:27 neither **a** in *any* house, but in the tombs. *3306*
21:37 **a** in the mount that is called *the mount* of *835*
Jn 1:32 from heaven like a dove, and it **a** upon him. *3306*
1:39 where he dwelt, and **a** with him that day: *3306*
4:40 tarry with them: and he **a** there two days. *3306*
7: 9 these *words* unto them, he **a** *still* in Galilee. *3306*
8:44 and **a** not in the truth, because there is no *2476*
10:40 John at first baptized; and there he **a**. *3306*
11: 6 he **a** two days *still* in the *same* place where *3306*
14:23 come unto him, and make *our* **a** with him. *3438*
Ac 1:13 where **a** both Peter, and James, and John, *2650*
12:19 down from Judea to Cesarea, and *there* **a**. *1304*
14: 3 **a** they speaking boldly in the Lord, *1304*
14:28 And there they **a** long time with *1304*
17:14 but Silas and Timotheus **a** there **still**. *5278*
18: 3 same craft, he **a** with them, and wrought: *3306*
20: 3 And *there* **a** three months: and when *4160*
20: 6 Troas in five days; where we **a** seven days. *1304*
21: 7 the brethren, and **a** with them one day. *3306*
21: 8 was *one* of the seven; and **a** with him. *3306*
Gal 1:18 to see Peter, and **a** with him fifteen days. *1961*
2Ti 4:20 Erastus **a** at Corinth: but Trophimus have I *3306*

ABODEST (1) [ABIDE]
Jdg 5:16 Why **a** thou among the sheepfolds, to hear 3427

ABOLISH (1) [ABOLISHED]
Isa 2:18 And the idols he shall utterly **a**. 2498

ABOLISHED (5) [ABOLISH]
Isa 51: 6 and my righteousness shall not be **a**. 2865
Eze 6: 6 be cut down, and your works may be **a**. 4229
2Co 3:13 stedfastly look to the end of that which is **a**: *2673*
Eph 2:15 Having **a** in his flesh the enmity, *even* *2673*
2Ti 1:10 who hath **a** death, and hath brought life and *2673*

ABOMINABLE (23) [ABOMINATION]
Lev 7:21 or any **a** unclean *thing*, and eat of the flesh 8263
11:43 Ye shall not **make** yourselves **a** with any 8262
18:30 that *ye* commit not *any one* of *these* **a** 8441
19: 7 if it be eaten at all on the third day, it *is* **a**; 6292
20:25 ye shall not **make** your souls **a** by beast, 8262
Dt 14: 3 Thou shalt not eat any **a** *thing*. 8441
1Ch 21: 6 for the king's word was **a** to Joab. 8581
2Ch 15: 8 put away the **a idols** out of all the land of 8251
Job 15:16 How much more **a** and filthy *is* man, 8581
Ps 14: 1 They are corrupt, they have **done a** works, 8581
53: 1 Corrupt are they, and have **done a** iniquity: 8581
Isa 14:19 thou art cast out of thy grave like an **a** 8581
65: 4 and broth of **a** *things is in* their vessels; 6292
Jer 16:18 carcases of their detestable and **a things**. 8441
44: 4 Oh, do not this **a** thing that I hate. 8441
Eze 4:14 neither came there **a** flesh into my mouth. 6292
8:10 **a** beasts, and all the idols of the house of 8263
16:52 that thou hast committed more **a** than they: 8581
Mic 6:10 the wicked, and the scant measure *that is* **a**? 2194
Na 3: 6 I will cast **a filth** upon thee, and make thee 8251
Tit 1:16 but in works they deny *him*, being **a**, and *947*
1Pe 4: 3 revellings, banquetings, and **a** idolatries: *111*
Rev 21: 8 and the **a**, and murderers, and *948*

ABOMINABLY (1) [ABOMINATION]
1Ki 21:26 he did very **a** in following idols, 8581

ABOMINATION (76) [ABOMINABLE, ABOMINABLY, ABOMINATIONS]
Ge 43:32 for that *is* an **a** unto the Egyptians. 8441
46:34 for every shepherd *is* an **a** unto 8441
Ex 8:26 for we shall sacrifice the **a** of the Egyptians 8441
8:26 shall we sacrifice the **a** of the Egyptians 8441
Lev 7:18 it shall be an **a**, and the soul that eateth of it 6292
11:10 *is* in the waters, they *shall be* an **a** unto you: 8263
11:11 They shall be even an **a** unto you: ye shall 8263
11:11 but you shall have their carcases in **a**. 8262
11:12 in the waters, that *shall be* an **a** unto you. 8263
11:13 these *are they which* ye shall have in **a** 8262
11:13 they shall not be eaten, they *are* an **a**: 8263
11:20 going upon *all* four, *shall be* an **a** unto you. 8263
11:23 have four feet, *shall be* an **a** unto you. 8263
11:41 that creepeth upon the earth *shall be* an **a**; 8263
11:42 them ye shall not eat; for they *are* an **a**. 8263
18:22 with mankind, as with womankind: it *is* **a**. 8441
20:13 both of them have committed an **a**: 8441
Dt 7:25 for it *is* an **a** to the LORD thy God. 8441
7:26 Neither shalt thou bring an **a** into thine 8441
12:31 for every **a** to the LORD, which he hateth, 8441
13:14 *that* such **a** is wrought among you; 8441
17: 1 for that *is* an **a** unto the LORD thy God. 8441
17: 4 *that* such **a** is wrought in Israel: 8441
18:12 For all that do these *things are* an **a** unto 8441
22: 5 that do so *are* **a** unto the LORD thy God. 8441
23:18 for even both these *are* **a** unto the LORD 8441
24: 4 is defiled; for that *is* **a** before the LORD: 8441
25:16 *are* an **a** unto the LORD thy God. 8441
27:15 or molten image, an **a** unto the LORD, 8441
1Sa 13: 4 *that* Israel also was **had in a** with 887
1Ki 11: 5 and after Milcom the **a** of the Ammonites. 8251
11: 7 the **a** of Moab, in the hill that *is* before 8251
11: 7 the **a** of the children of Ammon. 8251
2Ki 23:13 for Ashtoreth the **a** of the Zidonians, 8251
23:13 and for Chemosh the **a** of the Moabites, and 8251
23:13 for Milcom the **a** of the children of 8441
Ps 88: 8 thou hast made me an **a** unto them: 8441
Pr 3:32 For the froward *is* **a** to the LORD: but 8441
6:16 LORD hate: yea, seven *are* an **a** unto him: 8441
8: 7 and wickedness *is* an **a** to my lips. 8441
11: 1 A false balance *is* **a** to the LORD: but 8441
11:20 *They that are* of a froward heart *are* **a** unto 8441
12:22 Lying lips *are* **a** to the LORD: but 8441
13:19 but *it is* **a** to fools to depart from evil. 8441
15: 8 The sacrifice of the wicked *is* an **a** to 8441
15: 9 The way of the wicked *is* an **a** unto 8441
15:26 The thoughts of the wicked *are* an **a** to 8441
16: 5 Every one *that is* proud in heart *is* an **a** to 8441
16:12 *It is* an **a** to kings to commit wickedness: 8441
17:15 even they both *are* **a** to the LORD. 8441
20:10 both of them *are* alike **a** to the LORD. 8441
20:23 Divers weights *are* an **a** unto the LORD; 8441
21:27 The sacrifice of the wicked *is* **a**: how much 8441
24: 9 *is* sin: and the scorner *is* an **a** to men. 8441
28: 9 hearing the law, even his prayer *shall be* **a**. 8441
29:27 An unjust man is an **a** to the just: and 8441
29:27 *he that is* upright in the way *is* **a** to 8441
Isa 1:13 incense *is* an **a** unto me; the new moons 8441
41:24 of nought: an **a** *is he that* chooseth you. 8441
44:19 and shall I make the residue thereof an **a**? 8441
66:17 swine's flesh, and the **a**, and the mouse, 8263
Jer 2: 7 my land, and made mine heritage an **a**. 8441
6:15 they ashamed when they had committed **a**? 8441
8:12 they ashamed when they had committed **a**? 8441
32:35 that *they* should do this **a**, to cause Judah to 8441
Eze 16:50 were haughty, and committed **a** before me: 8441
18:12 up his eyes to the idols, hath committed **a**, 8441
22:11 one hath committed **a** with his neighbour's 8441
33:26 ye work **a**, and ye defile every one his 8441
Da 11:31 they shall place the **a** that maketh desolate. 8251
12:11 the **a** that maketh desolate set up, 8251
Mal 2:11 an **a** is committed in Israel and 8441
Mt 24:15 therefore shall see the **a** of desolation, *946*
Mk 13:14 But when ye shall see the **a** of desolation, *946*
Lk 16:15 amongst men is **a** in the sight of God. *946*
Rev 21:27 neither *whatsoever* worketh **a**, or *maketh* a *946*

ABOMINATIONS (76) [ABOMINATION]
Lev 18:26 and shall not commit any of these **a**; 8441
18:27 (For all these **a** have the men of the land 8441
18:29 For whosoever shall commit any of these **a**, 8441
Dt 18: 9 thou shalt not learn to do after the **a** of 8441
18:12 of these **a** the LORD thy God doth drive 8441
20:18 they teach you not to do after all their **a**, 8441
29:17 ye have seen their **a**, and their idols, wood 8251
32:16 *gods*, with **a** provoked they him to anger. 8441
1Ki 14:24 they did according to all the **a** of 8441
2Ki 16: 3 the fire, according to the **a** of the heathen, 8441
21: 2 after the **a** of the heathen, whom 8441
21:11 Manasseh king of Judah hath done these **a**, 8441
23:24 all the **a** that were spied in the land of 8251
2Ch 28: 3 burnt his children in the fire after the **a** of 8441
33: 2 the LORD, like unto the **a** of the heathen, 8441
34:33 Josiah took away all the **a** out of all 8441
36: 8 his **a** which he did, and that which was 8441
36:14 transgressed very much after all the **a** of 8441
Ezr 9: 1 *doing* according to their **a**, *even* of 8441
9:11 of the people of the lands, with their **a**, 8441
9:14 join in affinity with the people of these **a**? 8441
Pr 26:25 him not: for *there are* seven **a** in his heart. 8441
Isa 66: 3 and their soul delighteth in their **a**. 8251
Jer 4: 1 if thou wilt put away thine **a** out of my 8251
7:10 say, We are delivered to do all these **a**? 8441
7:30 they have set their **a** in the house which is 8251
13:27 *and* thine **a** on the hills in the fields. 8251
32:34 they set their **a** in the house, which is called 8251
44:22 because of the **a** which ye have committed; 8441
Eze 5: 9 do any more the like, because of all thine **a**. 8441
5:11 with all thine **a**, therefore will I also 8441
6: 9 which they have committed in all their **a**. 8441
6:11 Alas for all the evil **a** of the house of Israel: 8441
7: 3 and will recompense upon thee all thine **a**. 8441
Eze 7: 4 and thine **a** shall be in the midst of thee: 8441
7: 8 and will recompense thee for all thine **a**. 8441
7: 9 and thine **a** *that* are in the midst of thee; 8441
7:20 they made the images of their **a** *and* of their 8441
8: 6 *even* the great **a** that the house of Israel 8441
8: 6 thee yet again, *and* thou shalt see great*er* **a**. 8441
8: 9 and behold the wicked **a** that they do here. 8441
8:13 *and* thou shalt see great*er* **a** that they do. 8441
8:15 *and* thou shalt see greater **a** than these. 8441
8:17 commit the **a** which they commit here? 8441
9: 4 that cry for all the **a** that be done in 8441
11:18 and all the **a** thereof from thence. 8441
11:21 heart of their detestable things and their **a**, 8441
12:16 that they may declare all their **a** among 8441
14: 6 and turn away your faces from all your **a**. 8441
16: 2 of man, cause Jerusalem to know her **a**, 8441
16:22 in all thine **a** and thy whoredoms thou hast 8441
16:36 with all the idols of thy **a**, and by the blood 8441
16:43 not commit *this* lewdness above all thine **a**. 8441
16:47 after their ways, nor done after their **a**: 8441
16:51 thou hast multiplied thine **a** more than they, 8441
16:51 hast justified thy sisters in all thine **a** which 8441
16:58 Thou hast borne thy lewdness and thine **a**, 8441
18:13 he hath done all these **a**; he shall surely die; 8441
18:24 doeth according to all the **a** that the wicked 8441
20: 4 cause them to know the **a** of their fathers: 8441
20: 7 Cast ye away every man the **a** of his eyes, 8251
20: 8 they did not every man cast away the **a** of 8251
20:30 and commit ye whoredom after their **a**? 8251
22: 2 yea, thou shalt shew her all her **a**. 8441
23:36 yea, declare unto them their **a**; 8441
33:29 of all their **a** which they have committed. 8441
36:31 own sight for your iniquities and for your **a**. 8441
43: 8 name by their **a** that they have committed: 8441
44: 6 of Israel, let it suffice you of all your **a**, 8441
44: 7 broken my covenant because of all your **a**. 8441
44:13 and their **a** which they have committed. 8441
Da 9:27 for the overspreading of **a** he *shall* make *it* 8251
Hos 9:10 and *their* **a** were according as they loved. 8251
Zec 9: 7 and his **a** from between his teeth: 8251
Rev 17: 4 having a golden cup in her hand full of **a** and *946*
17: 5 THE MOTHER OF HARLOTS AND **A** OF *946*

ABOUND (19) [ABOUNDED, ABOUNDETH, ABOUNDING, ABUNDANCE, ABUNDANT, ABUNDANTLY]
Pr 28:20 A faithful man shall **a** with blessings: but 7227
Mt 24:12 And because iniquity shall **a**, the love of *4129*
Ro 5:20 the law entered, that the offence might **a**. *4121*
5:20 sin abounded, grace did **much more a**: *5248*
6: 1 Shall we continue in sin, that grace may **a**? *4121*
15:13 peace in believing, that ye may **a** in hope, *4052*
2Co 1: 5 For as the sufferings of Christ **a** in us, so *4052*
8: 7 as ye **a** in every *thing*, *in* faith, and *4052*
8: 7 love to us, *see* that ye **a** in this grace also. *4052*
9: 8 And God *is* able to **make** all grace **a** *4052*
9: 8 in all *things*, may **a** to every good work: *4052*
Php 1: 9 that your love may **a** yet more and more in *4052*
4:12 *how* to be abased, and I know *how* to **a**: *4052*
4:12 to be hungry, both to **a** and to suffer need. *4052*
4:17 I desire fruit that *may* **a** to your account. *4121*
4:18 But I have all, and **a**: I am full, *4052*
1Th 3:12 and **a** in love one towards another, *4052*
4: 1 *so* ye would **a** more *and more*. *4052*
2Pe 1: 8 For if these *things* be in you, and **a**, *4121*

ABOUNDED (5) [ABOUND]
Ro 3: 7 For if the truth of God hath *more* **a** through *4052*
5:15 one man, Jesus Christ, hath **a** unto many. *4052*
5:20 But where sin **a**, grace did much more *4121*
2Co 8: 2 their deep poverty **a** unto the riches of their *4052*
Eph 1: 8 Wherein he hath **a** toward us in all wisdom *4052*

ABOUNDETH (3) [ABOUND]
Pr 29:22 and a furious man **a** in transgression. 7227
2Co 1: 5 in us, so our consolation also **a** by Christ. *4052*
2Th 1: 3 every one of you all towards each other **a**; *4121*

ABOUNDING (3) [ABOUND]
Pr 8:24 when *there were* no fountains **a** with water. 3513
1Co 15:58 always **a** in the work of the Lord, *4052*
Col 2: 7 been taught, **a** therein with thanksgiving. *4052*

ABOUT (632)
Ge 23:17 that *were* in all the borders **round a**, 5439
35: 5 upon the cities that *were* **round a** them, 5439
37: 7 your sheaves **stood round a**, and 5437
38:24 it came to pass **a** three months after, 3509.1
39:11 it came to pass **a** this time, that *Joseph* 3509.1
41:25 God hath shewed Pharaoh what he *is* **a** to NIH
41:28 What God *is* **a** to do he sheweth unto NIH
41:42 fine linen, and put a gold chain **a** his neck; 5921
41:48 of the field, which *was* **round a** every city, 5439
42:24 he **turned** himself **a** from them, and wept; 5437
46:34 Thy servants' **trade** hath been **a cattle** 376+4735
Ex 7:24 all the Egyptians digged **round a** the river 5439
9:18 to morrow **a** *this* time I will cause it to 3509.1
11: 4 **A** midnight will I go out into the midst of 3509.1
12:37 **a** six hundred thousand on foot *that were* 3509.1
13:18 God **led** the people **a**, *through* the way of 5437
16:13 in the morning the dew lay **round a** 5439
19:12 shalt set bounds unto the people **round a**, 5439
19:23 **Set bounds a** the mount, and sanctify it. 1379
25:11 make upon it a crown *of* gold **round a**. 5439
25:24 and make thereto a crown *of* gold **round a**. 5439
25:25 unto it a border of a handbreadth **round a**, 5439
25:25 crown to the border thereof **round a**. 5439
27:17 All the pillars **round a** the court *shall be* 5439
28:32 of woven work **round a** the hole of it, 5439
28:33 and of scarlet, **round a** the hem thereof; 5439
28:33 and bells of gold between them **round a**: 5439
28:34 upon the hem of the robe **round a**. 5439
29:16 and sprinkle *it* **round a** upon the altar. 5439
29:20 sprinkle the blood upon the altar **round a**. 5439

Eze 5: 7 of the nations that *are* **round a** you; 5439
5:12 a third *part* shall fall by the sword **round a** 5439
5:14 among the nations that *are* **round a** thee, 5439
5:15 unto the nations that *are* **round a** thee, 5439
6: 5 I will scatter your bones **round a** your 5439
6:13 be among their idols **round a** their altars, 5439
8:10 pourtrayed upon the wall **round a**. 5439+5439
8:16 and the altar, *were* **a** five and twenty men, 3509.1
10:12 and the wheels, *were* full *of* eyes **round a**, 5439
11:12 of the heathen that *are* **round a** you. 5439
12:14 every wind all that *are* **a** him to help him, 5439
16:10 and I **girded** thee **a** with fine linen, 2280
16:37 I will even gather them **round a** 4480+5439
16:57 all *that are* **round a** her, the daughters of 5439
16:57 which despise thee **round a**. 4480+5439
23:24 and shield and helmet **round a**: 5439
27:11 thine army *were* upon thy walls **round a**, 5439
27:11 their shields upon thy walls **round a**; 5439
28:24 grieving thorn of all *that are* **round a** them, 5439
28:26 that despise them **round a** them; 4480+5439
31: 4 with her rivers running **round a** his plants, 5439
32:22 his graves *are* **a** him: all of them slain, 5439
32:23 and her company is **round a** her grave: 5439
32:24 and all her multitude **round a** her grave, 5439
32:25 her graves *are* **round a** him: all of them 5439
32:26 her graves *are* **round a** him: all of them 5439
34:26 and the **places round a** my hill a blessing; 5439
36: 4 of the heathen that *are* **round a**; 4480+5439
36: 7 Surely the heathen that *are* **a** you, 4480+5439
36:36 the heathen that are left **round a** you shall 5439
37: 2 caused me to pass by them **round a**: 5439+5439
40: 5 on the outside of the house **round a**, 5439+5439
40:14 post of the court **round a** the gate. 5439+5439
40:16 their posts within the gate **round a**, 5439+5439
40:16 windows *were* **round a** inward: 5439+5439
40:17 made for the court **round a**: 5439+5439
40:25 and in the arches thereof **round a**, 5439+5439
40:29 and in the arches thereof **round a**: 5439+5439
40:30 the arches **round a** *were* five and 5439+5439
40:33 in the arches thereof **round a**: 5439+5439
40:36 and the windows to it **round a**: 5439+5439
40:43 a hand broad, fastened **round a**: 5439+5439
41: 5 **round a** the house on every side. 5439+5439
41: 6 for the side chambers **round a**, 5439+5439
41: 7 a **winding a** still upward to the side 5437
41: 7 for the **winding a** of the house *went* still 5437
41: 7 *went* still upward **round a** the house: 5439+5439
41: 8 also the height of the house **round a**: 5439+5439
41:10 cubits **round a** the house on every side. 5439
41:11 that was left *was* five cubits **round a**. 5439+5439
41:12 *was* five cubits thick **round a**, 5439+5439
41:16 the galleries **round a** on their three *stories*, 5439
41:16 cieled with wood **round a**, and 5439+5439
41:17 by all the wall **round a** within 5439+5439
41:19 made through all the house **round a**. 5439+5439
42:15 the east, and measured it **round a**. 5439+5439
42:16 with the measuring reed **round a**. 5439
42:17 with the measuring reed **round a**. 5439
42:19 He **turned a** to the west side, *and* 5437
42:20 it had a wall **round a**, five hundred 5439+5439
43:12 thereof **round a** *shall be* most holy. 5439+5439
43:13 the edge thereof **round a** *shall be* a span: 5439
43:17 the border **a** it *shall be* half a cubit; and 5439
43:17 the bottom thereof *shall be* a cubit **a**; and 5439
43:20 of the settle, and upon the border **round a**: 5439
45: 1 *be* holy in all the borders thereof **round a**. 5439
45: 2 five hundred *in breadth,* square **round a**; 5439
45: 2 fifty cubits **round a** *for* the suburbs thereof. 5439
46:23 *there was* a row *of building* **round a** in 5439
46:23 **round a** them four, and *it was* made *with* 5439
46:23 boiling places under the rows **round a**. 5439
47: 2 **led** me **a** the way without unto the utter 5437
48:35 *It was* **round a** eighteen thousand 5439
Da 5: 7 *have* a chain of gold **a** his neck, and 5922
5:16 *have* a chain of gold **a** thy neck, and 5922
5:29 *put* a chain of gold **a** his neck, and made a 5922
5:31 *being* **a** threescore and two year old. 3509.4
9:16 *are become* a reproach to all *that are* **a** us. 5439
9:21 touched me **a** the time of the evening 3509.1
Hos 7: 2 now their own doings have **beset** them **a**; 5437
11:12 Ephraim **compasseth** me **a** with lies, and 5437
Joel 3:11 gather yourselves together **round a**: 4480+5439
3:12 I sit to judge all the heathen **round a**. 4480+5439
Am 3:11 An adversary *there shall be* even **round a** 5439
Jnh 2: 3 the seas; and the floods **compassed** me **a**: 5437
2: 5 The waters **compassed** me **a**, *even* to 661
2: 5 the depth **closed** me **round a**, the weeds 5437
2: 5 the weeds *were* **wrapt a** my head. 2280
2: 6 the earth *with* her bars *was* **a** me for ever: 1157
Na 3: 8 *that had* the waters **round a** it, 5439
Hab 1: 4 for the wicked doth **compass a** 3803
Zec 2: 5 will be unto her a wall of fire **round a**, and 5439
7: 7 and the cities thereof **round a** her, 5439
9: 8 I will **encamp a** mine house because of 2583
12: 2 of trembling unto all the people **round a**, 5439
12: 6 they shall devour all the people **round a**, 5439
14:14 the wealth of all the heathen **round a** shall 5439
Mt 1:11 **a the time** they were carried away to *1909*
3: 4 and a leathern girdle **a** his loins; *4012*
3: 5 and all the **region round a** Jordan, *4066*
4:23 And Jesus **went a** all Galilee, teaching in *4013*
8:18 Now when Jesus saw great multitudes **a** *4012*
9:22 But Jesus **turned** him **a**, and when he saw *1994*
9:35 And Jesus **went a** all the cities and villages, *4013*
14:21 And they that had eaten were **a** five *5616*
14:35 they sent out into all that **country round a**, *4066*
18: 6 that a millstone were hanged **a** his neck, *1909*
20: 3 And he went out **a** the third hour, and *4012*
20: 5 Again he went out **a** the sixth and *4012*
20: 6 And **a** the eleventh hour he went out, and *4012*
20: 9 And when they came that *were hired* **a** *4012*
21:33 and hedged it **round a**, and digged a *4060*
27:46 And **a** the ninth hour Jesus cried with a *4012*
Mk 1: 6 and with a girdle of a skin **a** his loins; *4012*
1:28 throughout all the **region round a** Galilee. *4066*

Mk 2: 2 *them*, no, not so much as **a** the door: *4314*
3: 5 And when he had **looked round a** on them *4017*
3: 8 and they **a** Tyre and Sidon, a great *4012*
3:32 And *the* multitude sat **a** him, and they said *4012*
3:34 And he looked **round a** on them which sat *2945*
3:34 round about on them which sat **a** him, *4012*
4:10 they that were **a** him with the twelve asked *4012*
5:13 into the sea, (they were **a** two thousand,) *5613*
5:30 **turned** him **a** in the press, and said, *1994*
5:32 And he **looked round a** to see her that had *4017*
6: 6 And he went **round a** the villages, *2945*
6:36 that they may go into the country **round a**, *2945*
6:44 And they that did eat *of* the loaves were **a** *5616*
6:48 **a** the fourth watch of the night he cometh *4012*
6:55 ran through that whole **region round a**, *4066*
6:55 began to **carry a** in beds those that were *4064*
8: 9 And they that had eaten were **a** four *5613*
8:33 But when he had **turned a** and looked on *1994*
9: 8 when they had **looked round a**, *4017*
9:14 he saw a great multitude **a** them, and *4012*
9:42 that a millstone were hanged **a** his neck, *4012*
10:23 And Jesus **looked round a**, and saith unto *4017*
11:11 when he had **looked round a** upon all *4017*
12: 1 and **set** a hedge **a** *it*, and digged *a place for* *4060*
14:51 having a linen cloth cast **a** *his* naked *body*; *1909*
15:17 a crown of thorns, and **put** *it* **a** his *head*, *4060*
Lk 1:56 And Mary abode with her **a** three months, *5616*
1:65 And fear came on all that **dwelt round a** *4039*
2: 9 the glory of the Lord **shone round a** them: *4034*
2:37 And she *was* a widow of **a** fourscore and *5613*
2:49 wist ye not that I must be **a** my Father's *1722*
3: 3 And he came into all the **country a** Jordan, *4066*
3:23 And Jesus himself began *to be* **a** thirty *5616*
4:14 of him through all the **region round a**. *4066*
4:37 into every place of the **country round a**. *4066*
6:10 And **looking round a** upon them all, *4017*
7: 9 and turned him **a**, and said unto the people NIG
7:17 and throughout all the **region round a**. *4066*
8:37 **country** of the Gadarenes **round a** *4066*
8:42 **a** twelve years of age, and she lay a dying. *5613*
9:12 go into the towns and country **round a**, *2945*
9:14 For they were **a** five thousand men. And he *5616*
9:28 And it came to pass **a** an eight days after *5616*
10:40 But Martha was cumbered **a** much serving, *4012*
10:41 art careful and troubled **a** many *things*: *4012*
12:35 Let your loins be **girded a**, and *your* lights *4024*
13: 8 year also, till I shall dig **a** it, and dung *it*: *4012*
17: 2 a millstone were **hanged a** his neck, *4029*
19:43 that thine enemies shall **cast** a trench **a** *4016*
22:41 And he was withdrawn from them **a** a *5616*
22:49 When they which were **a** him saw what *4012*
22:59 And **a** the space of one hour after another *5616*
23:44 And it was **a** the sixth hour, and there was a *5616*
24:13 which was from Jerusalem **a** threescore NIG
Jn 1:39 him that day: for it was **a** the tenth hour. *5613*
3:25 John's disciples and the Jews **a** purifying. *4012*
4: 6 on the well: *and* it was **a** the sixth hour. *5616*
6:10 men sat down, *in* number **a** five thousand. *5616*
6:19 So when they had rowed **a** five and twenty *5613*
7:14 **Now a** the midst of the feast Jesus *1161+2235*
7:19 keepeth the law? Why **go** ye **a** to kill me? *2212*
7:20 Thou hast a devil: who **goeth a** to kill thee? *2212*
10:24 Then **came** the Jews **round a** him, and *2944*
11:18 nigh unto Jerusalem, **a** fifteen furlongs off: *5613*
11:44 and his face was **bound a** with a napkin. *4019*
19:14 of the passover, and **a** the sixth hour: *5616*
19:39 and aloes, **a** an hundred pound *weight*. *5616*
20: 7 And the napkin, that was **a** his head, *1909*
21:20 Then Peter, **turning a**, seeth the disciple *1994*
Ac 1:15 (the number of names together were **a** an *5613*
2:10 and in the parts of Libya **a** Cyrene, and *2596*
2:41 the same day there were added *unto them* **a** *5616*
3: 3 and John **a to** go into the temple, *3195*
4: 4 the number of the men was **a** five thousand. *5616*
5: 7 And it was **a** the space of three hours after, *5613*
5:16 *out* of the cities **round a** unto Jerusalem, *4038*
5:36 of men, **a** four hundred, joined themselves: *5616*
9: 3 suddenly there **shined round a** him a light *4015*
9:29 the Grecians: but they **went a** to slay him. *2021*
10: 3 **a** the ninth hour of the day, *5616*
10: 9 Peter went up upon the house to pray **a** *4012*
10:38 who **went a** doing good, and healing all *1330*
11:19 arose **a** Stephen travelled as far as Phenice, *1909*
12: 1 Now **a** that time Herod the king stretched *2596*
12: 8 **Cast** thy garment **a** thee, and follow me. *4016*
13:11 he **went a** seeking *some* to lead him by *4013*
13:18 And **a** the time of forty years suffered he *5613*
13:20 And after that he gave *unto them* judges **a** *5613*
14: 6 and *unto* the **region that lieth round a**: *4066*
14:20 as the disciples **stood round a** him, *2944*
15: 2 unto the apostles and elders **a** this question. *4012*
18:14 And when Paul was *now* **a to** open *his* *3195*
19: 7 And all the men were **a** twelve. *5616*
19:23 time there arose no small stir **a** *that* way. *4012*
19:34 all with one voice **a** the space of two hours *5613*
20: 3 wait for him, as he was **a to** sail into Syria, *3195*
21:31 And as *they* **went a** to kill him, *2212*
22: 6 and was come nigh unto Damascus **a** noon, *4012*
22: 6 from heaven a great light **round a** me. *4012*
24: 6 Who also hath **gone a** to profane *3985*
25: 7 came down from Jerusalem **stood round a**, *4026*
25:15 **A** whom, when I was at Jerusalem, *4012*
25:24 ye see this *man*, **a** whom all the multitude *4012*
26:13 **shining round a** me and them which *4034*
26:21 me in the temple, and **went a** to kill *me*. *3987*
27:27 **a** midnight the shipmen deemed that they *2596*
27:30 And as the shipmen were **a** to flee out of *2212*
Ro 4:19 when he was **a** an hundred year old, *4225*
10: 3 **going a** to establish their own *2212*
15:19 and **round a** unto Illyricum, *2945*
1Co 9: 5 Have we not power to **lead a** a sister, *4013*
9:13 Do ye not know that they which minister **a** NIG
2Co 4:10 Always **bearing a** in the body the dying of *4064*
Eph 4:14 and **carried a** with every wind of doctrine, *4064*
6:14 having your loins **girt a** with truth, and *4024*

1Ti 5:13 *be* idle, **wandering a** from house to house; *4022*
6: 4 but doting **a** questions and strifes of words, *4012*
2Ti 2:14 that *they* **strive** not **a words** to no profit, *3054*
Tit 3: 9 and contentions, and strivings **a** the **law**; *3544*
Heb 8: 5 God when he was **a to** make the tabernacle: *3195*
9: 4 the ark of the covenant overlaid **round a** *3840*
11:30 after they were **compassed a** seven days. *2944*
11:37 they **wandered a** in sheepskins and *4022*
12: 1 Wherefore seeing we also are **compassed a** *4029*
13: 9 Be not **carried a** with divers and *4064*
Jas 3: 3 obey us; and we **turn a** their whole body. *3329*
3: 4 *yet* are they **turned a** with a very small *3329*
1Pe 5: 8 the devil, as a roaring lion, **walketh a**, *4043*
Jude 1: 7 and Gomorrha, and the cities **a** them, *4012*
1: 9 the devil he disputed **a** the body of Moses, *4012*
1:12 *they are* without water, **carried a** of winds; *4064*
Rev 1:13 and girt **a** the paps with a golden girdle. *4314*
4: 3 *there was* a rainbow **round a** the throne, *2943*
4: 4 And **round a** the throne *were* four and *2943*
4: 6 of the throne, and **round a** the throne, *2945*
4: 8 beasts had each of them six wings **a** *him*; *2943*
5:11 I heard the voice of many angels **round a** *2943*
7:11 And all the angels stood **round a** *2945*
7:11 and *a* the elders and the four beasts, and NIG
8: 1 there was silence in heaven **a** the space of *5613*
10: 4 had uttered their voices, I was **a to** write: *3195*
16:21 *every stone* **a** the weight of a talent: *5613*
20: 9 and **compassed** the camp of the saints **a**, *2944*

ABOVE (223)

Ge 1: 7 waters which *were* **a** the firmament: 4480+5921
1:20 fowl *that* may fly **a** the earth in the open 5921
3:14 thou *art* cursed **a** all cattle, and above every 4480
3:14 all cattle, and **a** every beast of the field; 4480
6:16 shalt thou finish it **a**; 4480+4605+1886.5+3807.1
7:17 the ark, and it was lift up **a** the earth. 4480+5921
27:39 the earth, and of the dew of heaven from **a**; 5920
28:13 the LORD stood **a** it, and said, 5921
48:22 given to thee one portion **a** thy brethren, 5921
49:25 thee *with* blessings of heaven **a**, 4480+5920
49:26 The blessings of thy father have prevailed **a** 5921
Ex 18:11 wherein they dealt proudly *he was* **a** them. 5921
19: 5 ye shall be a peculiar treasure unto me **a** all 4480
20: 4 *of any thing* that *is* in heaven **a**, 4480+4605
25:21 seat **a** upon the ark; 4480+4605+1886.5+3807.1
25:22 I will commune with thee from **a** the mercy 5921
26:14 **a** of badgers' skins. 4480+4605+1886.5+3807.1
26:24 they shall be coupled together **a** the head of 5921
28:27 against *the other* coupling thereof, **a** 4480+4605
28:28 that *it* may be **a** the curious girdle of 5921
29:13 the caul *that is* **a** the liver, and the two 5921
29:22 the caul **a** the liver, and the two kidneys, NIH
30:14 from twenty years old and **a**, shall 4605+1886.5
36:19 skins **a** *that*. 4480+4605+1886.5+3807.1
39:20 against the *other* coupling thereof, **a** 4480+4605
39:21 that *it* might be **a** the curious girdle of 5921
40:19 of the tent **a** upon it; 4480+4605+1886.5+3807.1
40:20 seat **a** upon the ark: 4480+4605+1886.5+3807.1
Lev 3: 4 the caul **a** the liver, with the kidneys, 5921
3:10 the caul **a** the liver, with the kidneys, 5921
3:15 the caul **a** the liver, with the kidneys, 5921
4: 9 the caul **a** the liver, with the kidneys, 5921
7: 4 the caul *that is* **a** the liver, with the kidneys, 5921
8:16 the caul **a** the liver, and the two kidneys, NIH
8:25 the caul **a** the liver, and the two kidneys, NIH
9:10 and the caul **a** the liver of the sin offering, 4480
9:19 and the kidneys, and the caul **a** the liver: NIH
11:21 which have legs **a** their feet, 4480+4605+3807.1
27: 7 if *it be* from sixty years old and **a**; 4605+1886.5
Nu 3:49 money of them that were **over and a** 5736+5921
4:25 that *is* **a** upon it, 4480+4605+1886.5+3807.1
12: 3 **a** all the men which *were* upon the face of 4480
16: 3 lift you up yourselves **a** the congregation of 5921
Dt 4:39 the LORD he *is* God in heaven **a**, 4480+4605
5: 8 *of any thing* that *is* in heaven **a**, 4480+4605
7: 6 **a** all people that *are* upon the face of 4480
7:14 Thou shalt be blessed **a** all people: 4480
10:15 *even* you **a** all people, as *it is* this day. 4480
14: 2 **a** all the nations that *are* upon the earth. 4480
17:20 That his heart be not lifted up **a** his 4480
25: 3 beat him **a** these *with* many stripes, then 5921
26:19 to make thee high **a** all nations which he 5921
28: 1 set thee on high **a** all nations of the earth: 5921
28:13 thou shalt be **a** only, and 4605+1886.5+3807.1
28:43 *is* within thee shall get up **a** thee very high; 5921
30: 5 thee good, and multiply thee **a** thy fathers. 4480
Jos 2:11 he *is* God in heaven **a**, and in earth 4480+4605
3:13 that come down from **a**; 4605+1886.5+3807.1
3:16 came down from **a** stood 4605+1886.5+3807.1
Jdg 5:24 Blessed **a** women shall Jael the wife of 4480
5:24 blessed shall she be **a** women in the tent. 4480
1Sa 2:29 honourest thy sons **a** me, to make 4480
2Sa 22:17 He sent from **a**, he took me; he drew me 4791
22:49 thou also hast lifted me up on high **a** them 4480
1Ki 7: 3 *it was* covered with cedar **a** upon 4480+4605
7:11 **a** *were* costly stones, 4480+4605+1886.5+3807.1
7:20 two pillars *had pomegranates* also **a**, 4480+4605
7:25 the sea *was set* **a** 4480+4605+1886.5+3807.1
7:29 upon the ledges *there was* a base **a**: 4480+4605
7:31 the chapiter and **a** *was* a cubit: 4605+1886.5
8: 7 the staves thereof **a**. 4480+4605+1886.5+3807.1
8:23 in heaven **a**, or on earth beneath, 4480+4605
14: 9 hast done evil **a** all that were before thee: 4480
14:22 **a** all that their fathers had done. 4480
16:30 of the LORD **a** all that *were* before him. 4480
2Ki 21:11 hath done wickedly **a** all that the Amorites 4480
25:28 set his throne **a** the throne of 4480+5921
1Ch 5: 2 For Judah prevailed **a** his brethren, and of 871.1
16:25 he also *is* to be feared **a** all gods. 5921
23:27 twenty years old and **a**: 4605+1886.5+3807.1
27: 6 mighty among the thirty, and **a** the thirty: 5921
29: 3 my God, **over and a** 4480+4605+1886.5+3807.1
29:11 and *thou* art **exalted** as head **a** all. 5375
2Ch 2: 5 *is* great: for great *is* our God **a** all gods. 4480
4: 4 the sea *was set* **a** 4480+4605+1886.5+3807.1

2Ch 5: 8 the staves thereof a. 4480+4605+1886.5+3807.1
11:21 the daughter of Absalom a all his wives 4480
24:20 which stood a the people, and 4480+5921
25: 5 them from twenty years old and a, 4605+1886.5
34: 4 the images, that *were* on high a 4480+5921
Ne 3:28 From a the horse gate repaired the priests, 5921
7: 2 *was* a faithful man, and feared God a many. 4480
8: 5 (for he was a all the people;) and 4480+5921
9: 5 which *is* exalted a all blessing and praise. 5921
12:37 at the going up of the wall, a 4480+5921
12:39 from a the gate of Ephraim, and above 5921
12:39 a the old gate, and above the fish gate, and 5921
12:39 a the fish gate, and the tower of Hananeel, 5921
Est 2:17 the king loved Esther a all the women, and 4480
3: 1 set his seat a all the princes that *were* 4480+5921
5:11 how he had advanced him a the princes and 5921
Job 3: 4 let not God regard it from a, neither let 4605
18:16 a shall his branch be cut off. 4480+4605
28:18 for the price of wisdom *is* a rubies. 4480
31: 2 what portion of God *is there* from a? 4480+4605
31:28 should have denied the God *that is* a. 4480+4605
Ps 8: 1 who hast set thy glory a the heavens. 5921
10: 5 thy judgments *are* far a out of his sight: 4791
18:16 He sent from a, he took me, he drew me 4791
18:48 thou liftest me up a those that rise up 4480
27: 6 now shall mine head be lifted up a mine 5921
45: 7 thee *with* the oil of gladness a thy fellows. 4480
50: 4 He shall call to the heavens from a, and 5920
57: 5 Be thou exalted, O God, a the heavens; 5921
57: 5 the heavens; *let* thy glory *be* a all the earth. 5921
57:11 Be thou exalted, O God, a the heavens: 5921
57:11 the heavens: *let* thy glory *be* a all the earth. 5921
78:23 he had commanded the clouds from a, 4605
95: 3 *is* a great God, and a great King a all gods. 5921
96: 4 to be praised: he *is* to be feared a all gods. 5921
97: 9 For thou, LORD, *art* High a all the earth: 5921
97: 9 all the earth: thou art exalted far a all gods. 5921
99: 2 in Zion; and he *is* high a all the people. 5921
103:11 For as the heaven is high a the earth, *so* 5921
104: 6 the waters stood a the mountains. 5921
108: 4 For thy mercy *is* great a the heavens: 4480+5921
108: 5 Be thou exalted, O God, a the heavens: and 5921
108: 5 the heavens: and thy glory a all the earth. 5921
113: 4 The LORD *is* high a all nations, *and* 5921
113: 4 all nations, *and* his glory a the heavens. 5921
119:127 Therefore I love thy commandments a 4480
119:127 above gold; yea, a fine gold. 4480
135: 5 *is* great, and *that* our Lord *is* a all gods. 4480
136: 6 To him that stretched out the earth a 5921
137: 6 if I prefer not Jerusalem a my chief joy. 5921
138: 2 for thou hast magnified thy word a all thy 5921
144: 7 Send thine hand from a; rid me, and 4791
148: 4 and ye waters that *be* a the heavens. 4480+5921
148:13 his glory *is* a the earth and heaven. 5921
Pr 8:28 When he established the clouds a: 4480+4605
15:24 The way of life *is* a to 4605+1886.5+3807.1
31:10 for her price *is* far a rubies. 4480
Ecc 2: 7 small cattle a all that were in Jerusalem 4480
3:19 that a man hath no preeminence a a beast: 4480
Isa 2: 2 and *shall be* exalted a the hills; 4480
6: 2 A it stood the seraphims: each one 4480+4605
7:11 or in the height a. 4605+1886.5+3807.1
14:13 exalt my throne a the stars of God: 4480+4605
14:14 I will ascend a the heights of the clouds; 5921
45: 8 from a, and let the skies pour down 4605
Jer 4:28 and the heavens a be black: 4480+4605
15: 8 Their widows are increased to me a 4480
17: 9 The heart *is* deceitful a all *things*, and 4480
31:37 If heaven a can be 4480+4605+1886.5+3807.1
35: 4 which *was* a the chamber of 4480+4605
52:32 set his throne a the throne of 4480+4605
La 1:13 From a hath he sent fire into my bones, and 4791
Eze 1:22 over their heads a. 4480+4605+1886.5+3807.1
1:26 a the firmament that *was* over their 4480+4605
1:26 of a man a upon it. 4480+4605+1886.5+3807.1
10: 1 in the firmament that *was* a the head of 5921
10:19 *was* over them a. 4480+4605+1886.5+3807.1
11:22 *was* over them a. 4480+4605+1886.5+3807.1
16:43 thou shalt not commit *this* lewdness a all 5921
29:15 neither shall it exalt itself any more a 5921
31: 5 Therefore his height was exalted a all 4480
37: 8 skin covered them a: 4480+4605+1886.5+3807.1
41:17 To *that* a the door, even unto 4480+5921
41:20 From the ground unto a the door 4480+5921
Da 6: 3 this Daniel was preferred a the presidents 5922
11: 5 he shall be strong a him, and 5921
11:36 magnify himself a every god, and 5921
11:37 any god: for he shall magnify himself a all. 5921
Am 2: 9 yet I destroyed his fruit from a, and 4605
Mic 4: 1 and *it shall be* exalted a the hills; 4480
Na 3:16 Thou hast multiplied thy merchants a 4480
Mt 10:24 The disciple is not a *his* master, nor 5228
10:24 above *his* master, nor the servant a his lord. 5228
Lk 3:20 Added yet this a all, that he shut up John in 1909
6:40 The disciple is not a his master: but 5228
13: 2 Galileans were sinners a all the Galileans, 3844
13: 4 think ye that they were sinners a all men 3844
Jn 3:31 He that cometh from a is above all: he that 509
3:31 He that cometh from above is a all: he that 1883
3:31 he that cometh from heaven is a all. 1883
6:13 which remained over and a unto them that 4052
8:23 Ye are from beneath; I am from a: 507
19:11 except it were given thee from a: 509
Ac 2:19 And I will shew wonders in heaven a, and 507
4:22 For the man was a forty years old, 4183
26:13 a the brightness of the sun, shining round 5228
Ro 10: 6 (that is, to bring Christ down *from* a:) NIG
14: 5 One man esteemeth one day a another: 3844
1Co 4: 6 not to think *of men* a *that* which is written, 5228
10:13 who will not suffer you to be tempted a that 5228
15: 6 he was seen of a five hundred brethren at 1883
2Co 1: 8 we were pressed out of measure, a strength, 5228
11:23 in stripes a measure, in prisons more 5234
12: 2 I knew a man in Christ a fourteen years 4253
12: 6 lest any *man* should think of me a *that* 5228
2Co 12: 7 And lest I should be exalted a measure 5229
12: 7 lest I should be exalted a measure. 5229
Gal 1:14 And profited in the Jews' religion a many 5228
4:26 But Jerusalem which is a is free, which is 507
Eph 1:21 Far a all principality, and power, and 5231
3:20 do exceeding abundantly a all that we ask 5228
4: 6 who *is* a all, and through all, and in you all. 1909
4:10 also that ascended up far a all heavens, 5231
6:16 A all, taking the shield of faith, 1909
Php 2: 9 given him a name which is a every name: 5228
Col 3: 1 with Christ, seek those *things* which are a, 507
3: 2 Set your affection on *things* a, not on *things* 507
3:14 And a all these *things put on* charity, 1909
2Th 2: 4 exalteth himself a all that is called God, 1909
Phm 1:16 but a a servant, a brother beloved, 5228
Heb 1: 9 anointed thee *with* the oil of gladness a 3844
10: 8 A when he said, Sacrifice and offering and 511
Jas 1:17 good gift and every perfect gift is from a, 509
3:15 This wisdom descendeth not from a, but 509
3:17 But the wisdom that is from a is first pure, 509
5:12 But a all *things*, my brethren, swear not, 4253
1Pe 4: 8 And a all *things* have fervent charity 4253
3Jn 1: 2 I wish a all *things* that thou mayest prosper 4012

ABRAHAM (231) [ABRAHAM'S, ABRAM, ABRAM'S]

Ge 17: 5 be called Abram, but thy name shall be A; 85
17: 9 God said unto A, Thou shalt keep my 85
17:15 And God said unto A, *As for* Sarai thy wife, 85
17:17 Then A fell upon his face, and laughed, and 85
17:18 A said unto God, O that Ishmael might live 85
17:22 talking with him, and God went up from A. 85
17:23 A took Ishmael his son, and all that were born 85
17:24 A *was* ninety years old and nine, when he was 85
17:26 In the selfsame day was A circumcised, and 85
18: 6 And A hastened into the tent unto Sarah, and 85
18: 7 A ran unto the herd, and fetcht a calf tender 85
18:11 Now A and Sarah *were* old *and* well stricken 85
18:13 the LORD said unto A, Wherefore did Sarah 85
18:16 A went with them to bring them on the way. 85
18:17 Shall I hide from A *that thing* which I do; 85
18:18 Seeing that A shall surely become a great and 85
18:19 that the LORD may bring upon A that which 85
18:22 but A stood yet before the LORD. 85
18:23 A drew near, and said, Wilt thou also destroy 85
18:27 A answered and said, Behold now, I have 85
18:33 as soon as he had left communing with A: 85
18:33 with Abraham: and A returned unto his place. 85
19:27 A gat up early in the morning to the place 85
19:29 that God remembered A, and sent Lot out of 85
20: 1 A journeyed from thence toward the south 85
20: 2 A said of Sarah his wife, She *is* my sister: 85
20: 9 Then Abimelech called A, and said unto him, 85
20:10 Abimelech said unto A, What sawest thou, 85
20:11 A said, Because I thought, Surely the fear of 85
20:14 gave *them* unto A, and restored him Sarah his 85
20:17 So A prayed unto God: and God healed 85
21: 2 and bare A a son in his old age, 85
21: 3 A called the name of his son that was born 85
21: 4 A circumcised his son Isaac being eight days 85
21: 5 A *was* an hundred years old, when his son 85
21: 7 And she said, Who would have said unto A, 85
21: 8 A made a great feast the *same* day that Isaac 85
21: 9 which she had born unto A, mocking. 85
21:10 Wherefore she said unto A, Cast out this 85
21:12 God said unto A, Let it not be grievous in thy 85
21:14 A rose up early in the morning, and 85
21:22 the chief captain of his host spake unto A, 85
21:24 And A said, I will swear. 85
21:25 A reproved Abimelech because of a well of 85
21:27 A took sheep and oxen, and gave *them* unto 85
21:28 A set seven ewe lambs of the flock by 85
21:29 Abimelech said unto A, What *mean* these 85
21:33 *A* planted a grove in Beer-sheba, and NIH
21:34 A sojourned in the Philistines' land many 85
22: 1 that God did tempt A, and said unto him, 85
22: 1 did tempt Abraham, and said unto him, A: 85
22: 3 A rose up early in the morning, and 85
22: 4 Then on the third day A lift up his eyes, and 85
22: 5 A said unto his young men, Abide you here 85
22: 6 A took the wood of the burnt offering, and 85
22: 7 And Isaac spake unto A his father, and said, 85
22: 8 A said, My son, God will provide himself a 85
22: 9 A built an altar there, and laid the wood in 85
22:10 A stretched forth his hand, and took the knife 85
22:11 him out of heaven, and said, A, Abraham: 85
22:11 him out of heaven, and said, Abraham, A: 85
22:13 A lifted up his eyes, and looked, and 85
22:13 A went and took the ram, and offered him up 85
22:14 A called the name of that place Jehovah-jireh: 85
22:15 the angel of the LORD called unto A out of 85
22:19 So A returned unto his young men, and 85
22:19 to Beer-sheba; and A dwelt at Beer-sheba. 85
22:20 that it was told A, saying, Behold, Milcah, 85
23: 2 A came to mourn for Sarah, and to weep for 85
23: 3 A stood up from before his dead, and 85
23: 5 the children of Heth answered A, saying unto 85
23: 7 A stood up, and bowed himself to the people 85
23:10 Ephron the Hittite answered A in the audience 85
23:12 A bowed down himself before the people of 85
23:14 And Ephron answered A, saying unto him, 85
23:16 A hearkened unto Ephron; and 85
23:16 A weighed to Ephron the silver, which he had 85
23:18 Unto A for a possession in the presence of 85
23:19 A buried Sarah his wife in the cave of 85
23:20 were made sure unto A for a possession of a 85
24: 1 And A was old, *and* well stricken in age: and 85
24: 1 and the LORD had blessed A in all things. 85
24: 2 A said unto his eldest servant of his house that 85
24: 6 A said unto him, Beware thou that thou bring 85
24: 9 the servant put his hand under the thigh of A 85
24:12 O LORD God of my master A, I pray thee, 85
24:12 and shew kindness unto my master A. 85
24:27 Blessed *be* the LORD God of my master A, 85
24:42 and said, O LORD God of my master A, 85
Ge 24:48 and blessed the LORD God of my master A, 85
25: 1 again A took a wife, and her name *was* 85
25: 5 And A gave all that he had unto Isaac. 85
25: 6 which A had, Abraham gave gifts, and 85
25: 6 A gave gifts, and sent them away from Isaac 85
25: 8 A gave up the ghost, and died in a good old 85
25:10 The field which A purchased of the sons of 85
25:10 there was A buried, and Sarah his wife. 85
25:11 it came to pass after the death of A, that God 85
25:12 the Egyptian, Sarah's handmaid, bare unto A: 85
25:19 of Isaac, Abraham's son: A begat Isaac: 85
26: 1 the first famine that was in the days of A. 85
26: 3 I will perform the oath which I sware unto A 85
26: 5 Because that A obeyed my voice, and kept my 85
26:15 had digged in the days of A his father, 85
26:18 which they had digged in the days of A his 85
26:18 had stopped them after the death of A: 85
26:24 and said, I *am* the God of A thy father: 85
28: 4 And give thee the blessing of A, to thee, and 85
28: 4 thou art a stranger, which God gave unto A. 85
28:13 I *am* the LORD God of A thy father, and 85
31:42 the God of A, and the fear of Isaac, had been 85
31:53 The God of A, and the God of Nahor, the God 85
32: 9 O God of my father A, and God of my father 85
35:12 the land which I gave A and Isaac, to thee I 85
35:27 *is* Hebron, where A and Isaac sojourned. 85
48:15 before whom my fathers A and Isaac did 85
48:16 and the name of my fathers A and Isaac; 85
49:30 which A bought with the field of Ephron 85
49:31 There they buried A and Sarah his wife; 85
50:13 which A bought with the field for a 85
50:24 this land unto the land which he sware to A, 85
Ex 2:24 God remembered his covenant with A, 85
3: 6 the God of A, the God of Isaac, and the God 85
3:15 the God of A, the God of Isaac, and the God 85
3:16 the God of A, of Isaac, and of Jacob, 85
4: 5 the God of A, the God of Isaac, and the God 85
6: 3 I appeared unto A, unto Isaac, and unto Jacob, 85
6: 8 the which I did swear to give it to A, 85
32:13 Remember A, Isaac, and Israel, thy servants, 85
33: 1 unto the land which I sware unto A, to Isaac, 85
Lev 26:42 also my covenant with A will I remember; 85
Nu 32:11 shall see the land which I sware unto A, 85
Dt 1: 8 A, Isaac, and Jacob, to give unto them and 85
6:10 to A, to Isaac, and to Jacob, to give thee great 85
9: 5 sware unto thy fathers, A, Isaac, and Jacob. 85
9:27 Remember thy servants, A, Isaac, and Jacob; 85
29:13 unto thy fathers, to A, to Isaac, and to Jacob. 85
30:20 to A, to Isaac, and to Jacob, to give them. 85
34: 4 This *is* the land which I sware unto A, 85
Jos 24: 2 the father of A, and the father of Nachor: 85
24: 3 I took your father A from the *other* side of 85
1Ki 18:36 said, LORD God of A, Isaac, and of Israel, 85
2Ki 13:23 because of his covenant with A, Isaac, and 85
1Ch 1:27 Abram; the same *is* A. 85
1:28 The sons of A; Isaac, and Ishmael. 85
1:34 A begat Isaac. The sons of Isaac; Esau and 85
16:16 *Even of the covenant* which he made with A, 85
29:18 O LORD God of A, Isaac, and of Israel, 85
2Ch 20: 7 gavest it to the seed of A thy friend for ever? 85
30: 6 turn again unto the LORD God of A, Isaac, 85
Ne 9: 7 the Chaldees, and gavest him the name of A; 85
Ps 47: 9 *even* the people of the God of A: 85
105: 6 O ye seed of A his servant, ye children of 85
105: 9 Which *covenant* he made with A, and his oath 85
105:42 his holy promise, *and* A his servant. 85
Isa 29:22 who redeemed A, concerning the house of 85
41: 8 whom I have chosen, the seed of A my friend. 85
51: 2 Look unto A your father, and unto Sarah *that* 85
63:16 though A be ignorant of us, and 85
Jer 33:26 *any* of his seed *to be* rulers over the seed of A, 85
Eze 33:24 saying, A was one, and he inherited the land: 85
Mic 7:20 the truth to Jacob, *and* the mercy to A, 85
Mt 1: 1 Jesus Christ, the son of David, the son of A. *11*
1: 2 A begat Isaac; and Isaac begat Jacob; and *11*
1:17 So all the generations from A to David *are* *11*
3: 9 within yourselves, We have A to *our* father: *11*
3: 9 of these stones to raise up children unto A. *11*
8:11 and shall sit down with A, and Isaac, and *11*
22:32 I am the God of A, and the God of Isaac, and *11*
Mk 12:26 I *am* the God of A, and the God of Isaac, and *11*
Lk 1:55 to our fathers), to A, and to his seed for ever. *11*
1:73 The oath which he sware to our father A, *11*
3: 8 within yourselves, We have A to *our* father: *11*
3: 8 of these stones to raise up children unto A. *11*
3:34 was *the son* of Isaac, which was *the son* of A, *11*
13:16 ought not this *woman*, being a daughter of A, *11*
13:28 when ye shall see A, and Isaac, and Jacob, *11*
16:23 and seeth A afar off, and Lazarus in his *11*
16:24 And he cried and said, Father A, have mercy *11*
16:25 But A said, Son, remember that thou in thy *11*
16:29 A saith unto him, They have Moses and *11*
16:30 And he said, Nay, father A: but if one went *11*
19: 9 this house, forsomuch as he also is a son of A. *11*
20:37 when he calleth the Lord the God of A, and *11*
Jn 8:39 and said unto him, A is our father. *11*
8:39 ye would do the works of A. *11*
8:40 which I have heard of God: this did not A. *11*
8:52 A is dead, and the prophets; and thou sayest, *11*
8:53 Art thou greater than our father A, which is *11*
8:56 Your father A rejoiced to see my day: and *11*
8:57 not yet fifty years old, and hast thou seen A? *11*
8:58 verily, I say unto you, Before A was, I am. *11*
Ac 3:13 The God of A, and of Isaac, and of Jacob, *11*
3:25 God made with our fathers, saying unto A, *11*
7: 2 The God of glory appeared unto our father A, *11*
7: 8 and so A begat Isaac, and circumcised him NIG
7:16 laid in the sepulchre that A bought for a sum *11*
7:17 which God had sworn to A, the people grew *11*
7:32 the God of A, and the God of Isaac, and *11*
13:26 children of the stock of A, and *11*
Ro 4: 1 What shall we say then that A our father, *11*
4: 2 For if A were justified by works, he hath *11*
4: 3 A believed God, and it was counted unto him *11*
4: 9 for we say that faith was reckoned to A for *11*

Ro 4:12 walk in the steps of *that* faith of our father **A**, *11*
4:13 *was* not to **A**, or to his seed, through the law, *11*
4:16 but to that also which is of the faith of **A**; *11*
9: 7 Neither, because they are the seed of **A**, *11*
11: 1 of the seed of **A**, *of* the tribe of Benjamin. *11*
2Co 11:22 so *am* I. Are they the seed of **A**? so *am* I. *11*
Gal 3: 6 Even as **A** believed God, and it was accounted *11*
3: 7 are of faith, the same are the children of **A**. *11*
3: 8 preached before the gospel unto **A**, *saying*, In *11*
3: 9 which be of faith are blessed with faithful **A**. *11*
3:14 That the blessing of **A** might come on *11*
3:16 Now to **A** and his seed were the promises *11*
3:18 of promise: but God gave *it* to **A** by promise. *11*
4:22 For it is written, that **A** had two sons, the one *11*
Heb 2:16 *of* angels; but he took on *him* the seed of **A**. *11*
6:13 For when God made promise to **A**, because *11*
7: 1 who met **A** returning from the slaughter of *11*
7: 2 To whom also **A** gave a tenth *part* of all; *11*
7: 4 the patriarch **A** gave the tenth of the spoils. *11*
7: 5 though they come out of the loins of **A**: *11*
7: 6 is not counted from them received tithes of **A**, *11*
7: 9 who receiveth tithes, payed tithes in **A**. *11*
11: 8 By faith **A**, when he was called to go out into *11*
11:17 By faith **A**, when he was tried, offered up *11*
Jas 2:21 Was not **A** our father justified by works, *11*
2:23 **A** believed God, and it was imputed unto him *11*
1Pe 3: 6 *Even* as Sara obeyed **A**, calling him lord: *11*

ABRAHAM'S (19) [ABRAHAM]

Ge 17:23 every male among the men of **A** house; 85
20:18 house of Abimelech, because of Sarah **A** wife. 85
21:11 the thing was very grievous in **A** sight 85
22:23 eight Milcah did bear to Nahor, **A** brother. 85
24:15 son of Milcah, the wife of Nahor, **A** brother, 85
24:34 And he said, I *am* **A** servant. 85
24:52 that, when **A** servant heard their words, 85
24:59 and her nurse, and **A** servant, and his men. 85
25: 7 these *are* the days of the years of **A** life which 85
25:12 **A** son, whom Hagar the Egyptian, 85
25:19 And these *are* the generations of Isaac, **A** son: 85
26:24 and multiply thy seed for my servant **A** sake. 85
28: 9 had Mahalath the daughter of Ishmael **A** son, 85
1Ch 1:32 Now the sons of Keturah, **A** concubine: 85
Lk 16:22 and was carried by the angels into **A** bosom: *11*
Jn 8:33 We be **A** seed, and were never in bondage to *11*
8:37 I know that ye are **A** seed; but ye seek to kill *11*
8:39 Jesus saith unto them, If ye were **A** children, *11*
Gal 3:29 then are ye **A** seed, and heirs according to *11*

ABRAM (54) [ABRAHAM]

Ge 11:26 and begat **A**, Nahor, and Haran. 87
11:27 Terah begat **A**, Nahor, and Haran; and 87
11:29 **A** and Nahor took them wives: the name of 87
11:31 Terah took **A** his son, and Lot the son of 87
12: 1 Now the LORD had said unto **A**, Get thee 87
12: 4 So **A** departed, as the LORD had spoken 87
12: 4 **A** *was* seventy and five years old when he 87
12: 5 **A** took Sarai his wife, and Lot his brother's 87
12: 6 **A** passed through the land unto the place of 87
12: 7 And the LORD appeared unto **A**, and said, 87
12: 9 **A** journeyed, going on still toward the south. 87
12:10 and **A** went down into Egypt to sojourn there; 87
12:14 to pass, that, when **A** was come into Egypt, 87
12:16 he entreated **A** well for her sake: and he had 87
12:18 Pharaoh called **A**, and said, What *is* this *that* 87
13: 1 And **A** went up out of Egypt, he, and his wife, 87
13: 2 **A** *was* very rich in cattle, in silver, and 87
13: 4 there **A** called on the name of the LORD. 87
13: 5 which went with **A**, had flocks, and herds, and 87
13: 8 **A** said unto Lot, Let there be no strife, I pray 87
13:12 **A** dwelled in the land of Canaan, and 87
13:14 the LORD said unto **A**, after that Lot was 87
13:18 **A** removed his tent, and came and dwelt in 87
14:13 one that had escaped, and told **A** the Hebrew; 87
14:13 of Aner: and these *were* confederate with **A**. 87
14:14 when **A** heard that his brother was taken 87
14:19 and said, Blessed *be* **A** of the most high God, 87
14:21 the king of Sodom said unto **A**, Give me 87
14:22 **A** said to the king of Sodom, I have lift up 87
14:23 lest thou shouldest say, I have made **A** rich: 87
15: 1 word of the LORD came unto **A** in a vision, 87
15: 1 unto Abram in a vision, saying, Fear not, **A**: 87
15: 2 **A** said, Lord GOD, what wilt thou give me, 87
15: 3 **A** said, Behold, to me thou hast given no 87
15:11 down upon the carcases, **A** drove them away. 87
15:12 was going down, a deep sleep fell upon **A**; 87
15:13 he said unto **A**, Know of a surety that thy seed 87
15:18 day the LORD made a covenant with **A**, 87
16: 2 Sarai said unto **A**, Behold now, the LORD 87
16: 2 And **A** hearkened to the voice of Sarai. 87
16: 3 after **A** had dwelt ten years in the land of 87
16: 3 and gave her to her husband **A** to be his wife. 87
16: 5 Sarai said unto **A**, My wrong *be* upon thee: 87
16: 6 **A** said unto Sarai, Behold, thy maid *is* in thy 87
16:15 Hagar bare **A** a son: and Abram called his 87
16:15 **A** called his son's name, which Hagar bare, 87
16:16 **A** *was* fourscore and six years old, 87
16:16 six years old, when Hagar bare Ishmael to **A**. 87
17: 1 when **A** was ninety years old and nine, 87
17: 1 the LORD appeared to **A**, and said unto him, 87
17: 3 **A** fell on his face: and God talked with him, 87
17: 5 Neither shall thy name any more be called **A**, 87
1Ch 1:27 **A**; the same *is* Abraham. 87
Ne 9: 7 who didst choose **A**, and broughtest him forth 87

ABRAM'S (7) [ABRAHAM]

Ge 11:29 the name of **A** wife *was* Sarai; and the name 87
11:31 and Sarai his daughter in law, his son **A** wife; 87
12:17 with great plagues because of Sarai **A** wife. 87
13: 7 there was a strife between the herdmen of **A** 87
14:12 they took Lot, **A** brother's son, who dwelt in 87
16: 1 Now Sarai **A** wife bare him no *children*: and 87
16: 3 Sarai **A** wife took Hagar her maid 87

ABROAD (80)

Ge 10:18 the families of the Canaanites **spread a**. 6327
11: 4 lest we be **scattered a** upon the face of 6327
11: 8 So the LORD **scattered** them **a** from 6327
11: 9 from thence did the LORD **scatter** them **a** 6327
15: 5 he brought him forth **a**, and said, 2351+1886.5
19:17 they had brought them forth **a**, 2351+1886.5
28:14 thou shalt **spread a** to the west, and to 6555
Ex 5:12 So the people were **scattered a** throughout 6327
9:29 I will **spread a** my hands unto the LORD; 6566
9:33 **spread a** his hands unto the LORD: 6566
12:46 of the flesh **a** out of the house; 2351+1886.5
21:19 walk **a** upon his staff, then 2351+871.1+1886.1
40:19 he **spread a** the tent over the tabernacle, 6566
Lev 13: 7 if the scab **spread much a** in 6581+6581
13:12 if a leprosy **break out a** in the skin, 6524+6524
13:22 if it **spread much a** in the skin, then 6581+6581
13:27 *and* if it be **spread much a** in 6581+6581
14: 8 and shall **tarry a** out of his tent seven days. 3427
18: 9 *whether she be* born at home, or born **a**, 2351
Nu 11:32 they **spread** *them* **all a** for 7849+7849
Dt 23:10 shall he go **a** out of the camp, 2351+4480
23:12 the camp, whither thou shalt go forth **a**: 2351
23:13 it shall be, when thou wilt ease thyself **a**, 2351
24:11 Thou shalt stand **a**, and the man to whom 2351
24:11 bring out the pledge **a** unto thee. 2351+1886.5
32:11 **spreadeth a** her wings, taketh them, 6566
Jdg 12: 9 *whom* he sent **a**, and took in thirty 2351+1886.5
12: 9 took in thirty daughters from **a** for his sons. 2351
1Sa 9:26 both of them, he and Samuel, **a**. 2351+1886.5
30:16 behold *they were* **spread a** upon all 5203
2Sa 22:43 mire of the street, *and* did **spread** them **a**. 7554
1Ki 2:42 walkest **a** any whither, that thou shalt surely NIH
2Ki 4: 3 **a** of all thy neighbours, 2351+4480+1886.1
1Ch 13: 2 us send **a** unto our brethren **every where**, 6555
14:13 again **spread** themselves **a** in the valley. 6584
2Ch 26: 8 his name **spread a** even to the entering in 1980
26:15 his name spread **far a**; 4480+5704+7350+3807.1
29:16 the Levites took *it*, to carry *it* out **a** 2351+1886.5
31: 5 as soon as the commandment **came a**, 6555
Ne 1: 8 I will **scatter** you **a** among the nations: 6327
Est 1:17 For *this* deed of the queen shall **come a** 3318
3: 8 There is a certain people **scattered a** and 6340
Job 4:11 and the stout lion's whelps are **scattered a**. 6504
15:23 He **wandereth a** for bread, *saying*, Where 5074
40:11 **Cast a** the rage of thy wrath: and 6327
Ps 41: 6 he goeth **a**, he telleth *it*. 2351+1886.1+3807.1
77:17 sent out a sound: thine arrows also **went a**. 1980
Pr 5:16 Let thy fountains be dispersed **a**, 2351+1886.5
Isa 24: 1 and **scattereth a** the inhabitants thereof. 6327
28:25 doth he not **cast a** the fitches, and 6327
44:24 that **spreadeth a** the earth by myself; 7554
Jer 6:11 I *will* pour *it* out upon the children **a**, and 2351
La 1:20 **a** the sword bereaveth, at home *there* 2351+4480
Eze 34:21 scattered them **a**; 413+2351+1886.1+1886.5
Zec 1:17 through prosperity shall yet be **spread a**; 6327
2: 6 for I have **spread** you **a** as the four winds 6566
Mt 9:26 And the fame hereof **went a** into all that *1831*
9:31 **spread a** his **fame** in all that country. *1310*
9:36 they fainted, and were **scattered a**, *4496*
12:30 he that gathereth not with me **scattereth a**. *4650*
26:31 the sheep of the flock shall be **scattered a**. *1287*
Mk 1:28 And immediately his fame **spread a** *1831*
1:45 publish *it* much, and to **blaze a** the matter, *1310*
4:22 kept secret, but that it should come **a**. *1519+5318*
6:14 heard *of him*; (for his name was **spread a**:) *5318*
Lk 1:65 all these sayings were **noised a** throughout *1255*
2:17 **made known a** the saying which was told *1232*
5:15 *much* the more **went** there a fame **a** of him: *1330*
8:17 that shall not be known and come **a**. *1519+5318*
Jn 11:52 the children of God that were **scattered a**. *1287*
21:23 Then **went** this saying **a** among *1831*
Ac 2: 6 Now when this **was noised a**, *1096+3588+5456*
8: 1 they were all **scattered a** throughout *1289*
8: 4 Therefore they that were **scattered a** went *1289*
11:19 Now they which were **scattered a** upon *1289*
Ro 5: 5 the love of God is **shed a** in our hearts by *1632*
16:19 For your obedience is **come a** unto all *men*. I *864*
2Co 9: 9 (As it is written, He hath **dispersed a**; *4650*
1Th 1: 8 place your faith to God-ward is **spread a**; *1831*
Jas 1: 1 tribes which are **scattered a**, *1290+1722+3588*

ABRONAH See EBRONAH

ABSALOM (104) [ABSALOM'S]

2Sa 3: 3 **A** the son of Maacah the daughter of Talmai 53
13: 1 that **A** the son of David had a fair sister, 53
13:20 **A** her brother said unto her, Hath Amnon thy 53
13:22 **A** spake unto his brother Amnon neither good 53
13:22 for **A** hated Amnon, because he had forced his 53
13:23 that **A** had sheepshearers in Baal-hazor, 53
13:23 and **A** invited all the king's sons. 53
13:24 **A** came to the king, and said, Behold now, 53
13:25 the king said to **A**, Nay, my son, let us not all 53
13:26 said **A**, If not, I pray thee, let my brother 53
13:27 **A** pressed him, that he let Amnon and all 53
13:28 Now **A** had commanded his servants, saying, 53
13:29 the servants of **A** did unto Amnon as Absalom 53
13:29 the servants of Absalom did unto Amnon as **A** 53
13:30 **A** hath slain all the king's sons, and there is 53
13:32 for by the appointment of **A** *this* hath been 53
13:34 **A** fled. And the young man that kept 53
13:37 **A** fled, and went to Talmai, the son of 53
13:38 So **A** fled, and went to Geshur, and was there 53
13:39 *soul of* king David longed to go forth unto **A**: 53
14: 1 perceived that the king's heart *was* toward **A**. 53
14:21 go therefore, bring the young man **A** again. 53
14:23 went to Geshur, and brought **A** *to* Jerusalem. 53
14:24 So **A** returned to his own house, and saw not 53
14:25 to be so much praised as **A** for his beauty: 53
14:27 unto **A** there were born three sons, and 53
14:28 So **A** dwelt two full years in Jerusalem, and 53
14:29 Therefore **A** sent for Joab, to have sent him to 53
14:31 came to **A** unto *his* house, and said unto him, 53
2Sa 14:32 **A** answered Joab, Behold, I sent unto thee, 53
14:33 when he had called for **A**, he came to 53
14:33 ground before the king: and the king kissed **A**. 53
15: 1 that **A** prepared him chariots and horses, and 53
15: 2 **A** rose up early, and stood beside the way of 53
15: 2 **A** called unto him, and said, Of what city *art* 53
15: 3 **A** said unto him, See, thy matters *are* good 53
15: 4 **A** said moreover, Oh that I were made judge 53
15: 6 on this manner did **A** to all Israel that came to 53
15: 6 so **A** stole the hearts of the men of Israel. 53
15: 7 that **A** said unto the king, I pray thee, let me 53
15:10 **A** sent spies throughout all the tribes of Israel, 53
15:10 then ye shall say, **A** reigneth in Hebron. 53
15:11 with **A** went two hundred men out of 53
15:12 **A** sent *for* Ahithophel the Gilonite, 53
15:12 for the people increased continually with **A**. 53
15:13 The hearts of the men of Israel are after **A**. 53
15:14 us flee; for we shall not *else* escape from **A**: 53
15:31 Ahithophel *is* among the conspirators with **A**. 53
15:34 and say unto **A**, I will be thy servant, O king; 53
15:37 *into* the city, and **A** came *into* Jerusalem. 53
16: 8 the kingdom into the hand of **A** thy son: 53
16:15 And **A**, and all the people the men of Israel, 53
16:16 the Archite, David's friend, was come unto **A**, 53
16:16 that Hushai said unto **A**, God save the king, 53
16:17 **A** said to Hushai, *Is* this thy kindness to thy 53
16:18 Hushai said unto **A**, Nay; but whom 53
16:20 said **A** to Ahithophel, Give counsel among 53
16:21 Ahithophel said unto **A**, Go in unto thy 53
16:22 So they spread **A** a tent upon the top of 53
16:22 **A** went in unto his father's concubines in 53
16:23 of Ahithophel both with David and with **A**. 53
17: 1 Moreover Ahithophel said unto **A**, Let me 53
17: 4 the saying pleased **A** well, and all the elders 53
17: 5 said **A**, Call now Hushai the Archite also, 53
17: 6 when Hushai was come to **A**, Absalom spake 53
17: 6 come to Absalom, **A** spake unto him, saying, 53
17: 7 Hushai said unto **A**, The counsel that 53
17: 9 is a slaughter among the people that follow **A**. 53
17:14 **A** and all the men of Israel said, The counsel 53
17:14 that the LORD might bring evil upon **A**. 53
17:15 Thus and thus did Ahithophel counsel **A** and 53
17:18 Nevertheless a lad saw them, and told **A**: but 53
17:24 **A** passed over Jordan, he and all the men of 53
17:25 **A** made Amasa captain of the host instead of 53
17:26 So Israel and **A** pitched *in* the land of Gilead. 53
18: 5 for my sake with the young man, *even* with **A**. 53
18: 5 gave all the captains charge concerning **A**. 53
18: 9 **A** met the servants of David. And Absalom 53
18: 9 **A** rode upon a mule, and the mule went under 53
18:10 and said, Behold, I saw **A** hanged in an oak. 53
18:12 Beware *that* none *touch* the young man **A**. 53
18:14 and thrust them through the heart of **A**, 53
18:15 Joab's armour compassed about and smote **A**, 53
18:17 they took **A**, and cast him into a great pit in 53
18:18 Now **A** in his lifetime had taken and reared up 53
18:29 And the king said, *Is* the young man **A** safe? 53
18:32 said unto Cushi, *Is* the young man **A** safe? 53
18:33 as he went, thus he said, O my son **A**, my son, 53
18:33 O my son Absalom, my son, my son **A**! 53
18:33 God I had died for thee, O **A**, my son, my son. 53
19: 1 the king weepeth and mourneth for **A**. 53
19: 4 O my son **A**, O Absalom, my son, my son. 53
19: 4 O my son Absalom, O **A**, my son, my son. 53
19: 6 that if **A** had lived, and all we had died *this* 53
19: 9 and now he is fled out of the land for **A**. 53
19:10 **A**, whom we anointed over us, is dead in 53
20: 6 the son of Bichri do us more harm than *did* **A**: 53
1Ki 1: 6 goodly *man*; and *his mother* bare him after **A**. 53
2: 7 to me when I fled because of **A** thy brother. 53
2:28 after Adonijah, though he turned not after **A**. 53
1Ch 3: 2 **A** the son of Maachah the daughter of Talmai 53
2Ch 11:20 after her he took Maachah the daughter of **A**; 53
11:21 Rehoboam loved Maachah the daughter of **A** 53
Ps 3: T Psalm of David, when he fled from **A** his son. 53

ABSALOM'S (5) [ABSALOM]

2Sa 13: 4 unto him, I love Tamar, my brother **A** sister. 53
13:20 So Tamar remained desolate in her brother **A** 53
14:30 it on fire. And **A** servants set the field on fire. 53
17:20 when **A** servants came to the woman to 53
18:18 and it is called unto this day, **A** place. 53

ABSENCE (2) [ABSENT]

Lk 22: 6 him unto them **in the a of** the multitude. *817*
Php 2:12 presence only, but now much more in my **a**, *666*

ABSENT (11) [ABSENCE]

Ge 31:49 and thee, when we are **a** one from another. 5641
1Co 5: 3 I verily, as **a** in body, but present in spirit, *548*
2Co 5: 6 home in the body, we are **a** from the Lord: *1553*
5: 8 and willing rather to be **a** from the body, *1553*
5: 9 we labour, that, whether present or **a**, *1553*
10: 1 among you, but being **a** am bold toward you: *548*
10:11 as we are in word by letters when we are **a**, *548*
13: 2 being **a** now I write to them which *548*
13:10 Therefore I write these *things* being **a**, *548*
Php 1:27 whether I come and see you, or *else* be **a**, *548*
Col 2: 5 For though I be **a** in the flesh, yet am I with *548*

ABSTAIN (6) [ABSTINENCE]

Ac 15:20 that *they* **a** from pollutions of idols, and *568*
15:29 That *ye* **a from** meats offered to idols, and *568*
1Th 4: 3 that ye should **a** from fornication: *568*
5:22 **A** from all appearance of evil. *568*
1Ti 4: 3 to marry, *and commanding* to **a from** meats, *568*
1Pe 2:11 and pilgrims, **a from** fleshly lusts, *568*

ABSTINENCE (1) [ABSTAIN]

Ac 27:21 But after long **a** Paul stood *forth* in the midst *776*

ABUNDANCE (68) [ABOUND]

Dt 28:47 gladness of heart, for the **a** of all *things*; 7230
33:19 for they shall suck *of* the **a** of the seas, and 8228

1Sa 1:16 for out of the **a** of my complaint and 7230
2Sa 12:30 brought forth the spoil of the city in great **a**. 7235
1Ki 1:19 slain oxen and fat cattle and sheep in **a**, 7230
1:25 slain oxen and fat cattle and sheep in **a**, 7230
10:10 there came no more such **a** of 7230+3807.1
10:27 sycomore trees that *are* in the vale, for **a**. 7230
18:41 and drink; for *there is* a sound of **a** of rain. 1995
1Ch 22: 3 David prepared iron in **a** for the nails for 7230
22: 3 the joinings; and brass in **a** without weight; 7230
22: 4 Also cedar trees in **a**: for 369+4557
22:14 and iron without weight; for it is in **a**: 7230
22:15 *there are* workmen with thee in **a**, 7230
29: 2 *of* precious stones, and marble stones in **a**. 7230
29:21 and sacrifices in **a** for all Israel: 7230
2Ch 1:15 the sycomore trees that *are* in the vale for **a**. 7230
2: 9 Even to prepare me timber in **a**: for 7230
4:18 Solomon made all these vessels in great **a**: 7230
9: 1 and gold in **a**, and precious stones: 7230
9: 9 spices great **a**, and precious stones: 7230+3807.1
9:27 trees that *are* in the low plains in **a**. 7230
11:23 he gave them victual in **a**. And he desired 7230
14:15 carried away sheep and camels in **a**, and 7230
15: 9 for they fell to him out of Israel in **a**, 7230
17: 5 and he had riches and honour in **a**. 7230
18: 1 Jehoshaphat had riches and honour in **a**, 7230
18: 2 Ahab killed sheep and oxen for him in **a**, 7230
20:25 they found among them in **a** both riches 7230
24:11 did day by day, and gathered money in **a**. 7230
29:35 also the burnt offerings *were* in **a**, with 7230
31: 5 the children of Israel **brought in a** 7235
32: 5 of David, and made darts and shields in **a**. 7230
32:29 and possessions of flocks and herds in **a**: 7230
Ne 9:25 and oliveyards, and fruit trees **in a**: 7230+3807.1
Est 1: 7 royal wine **in a**, according to the state of 7227
Job 22:11 canst not see; and **a** of waters cover thee. 8229
36:31 judgeth he the people; he giveth meat in **a**. 4342
38:34 the clouds, that **a** of waters may cover thee? 8229
Ps 37:11 shall delight themselves in the **a** of peace. 7230
52: 7 trusted in the **a** of his riches, *and* 7230
72: 7 **a** of peace so long as the moon endureth. 7230
105:30 Their land **brought forth** frogs **in a**, in 8317
Ecc 5:10 nor he that loveth **a** *with* increase: 1995
5:12 the **a** of the rich will not suffer him to 7647
Isa 7:22 for the **a** of milk *that they* shall give he 7230
15: 7 Therefore the **a** they have gotten, and 3502
47: 9 *and* for the great **a** of thine enchantments. 6109
60: 5 the **a** of the sea shall be converted unto 1995
66:11 and be delighted with the **a** of her glory. 2123
Jer 33: 6 will reveal unto them the **a** of peace and 6283
Eze 16:49 **a** of idleness was in her and in her 7962
26:10 By reason of the **a** of his horses their dust 8229
Zec 14:14 gold, and silver, and apparel, in great **a**. 7230
Mt 12:34 speak good *things?* for out of the **a** of *4051*
13:12 shall be given, and he shall **have** *more* **a**: *4052*
25:29 hath shall be given, and he shall **have a**: *4052*
Mk 12:44 For all *they* did cast in of their **a**; *4052*
Lk 6:45 for of the **a** of the heart his mouth speaketh. *4051*
12:15 for a man's life consisteth not in the **a** of *4052*
21: 4 For all these have of their **a** cast in unto *4052*
Ro 5:17 much more they which receive **a** of grace *4050*
2Co 8: 2 How that in a great trial of affliction the **a** *4050*
8:14 *that* now at *this* time your **a** *may be* **a** *4051*
8:14 that their **a** also may be *a supply* for your *4051*
8:20 that no *man* should blame us in this **a** which *100*
12: 7 measure through the **a** of the revelations, *5236*
Rev 18: 3 waxed rich through the **a** of her delicacies. *1411*

ABUNDANT (13) [ABOUND]
Ex 34: 6 longsuffering, and **a** in goodness and truth, 7227
Isa 56:12 shall be as this day, *and* much more **a**. 3499
Jer 51:13 **a** in treasures, thine end is come, *and* 7227
1Co 12:23 upon these we bestow **more a** honour; *4055*
12:23 our uncomely *parts* have **more a** *4055*
12:24 having given **more a** honour to that *part* *4055*
2Co 4:15 that the **a** grace might through *4121*
7:15 And his inward affection is **more a** toward *4056*
9:12 is **a** also by many thanksgivings unto God; *4052*
11:23 in labours **more a**, in stripes above *4056*
Php 1:26 That your rejoicing may be *more* **a** in Jesus *4052*
1Ti 1:14 And the grace of our Lord was **exceeding a** *5250*
1Pe 1: 3 which according to his **a** mercy hath *4183*

ABUNDANTLY (32) [ABOUND]
Ge 1:20 Let the waters **bring forth a** 8317+8318
1:21 which the waters **brought forth a**, 8317
8:17 that they may **breed a** in the earth, and 8317
9: 7 **bring forth a** in the earth, and 8317
Ex 1: 7 **increased a**, and multiplied, and 8317
8: 3 the river shall **bring forth** frogs **a**, 8317
Nu 20:11 the water came out **a**, and the congregation 7227
1Ch 12:40 and oil, and oxen, and sheep **a**: 7230+3807.1
22: 5 David prepared **a** before his death. 7230+3807.1
22: 8 Thou hast shed blood **a**, and 7230+3807.1
2Ch 31: 5 and the tithe of all *things* brought they in **a**. 7230
Job 12: 6 into whose hand God bringeth **a**. NIH
36:28 the clouds do drop *and* distil upon man **a**. *7227*
Ps 36: 8 They shall be **a satisfied** with the fatness of 7301
65:10 *Thou* **waterest** the ridges thereof **a**: 7301
132:15 I will **a bless** her provision: I will 1288+1288
145: 7 They shall **a utter** the memory of thy great 5042
SS 5: 1 O friends; drink, yea, **drink a**, O beloved. 7937
Isa 15: 3 every one shall howl, weeping **a**. 3381
35: 2 It shall **blossom a** and rejoice even 6524+6524
55: 7 and to our God, for he will **a** pardon. 7235
Jn 10:10 and that they might have *it more* **a**. *4053*
1Co 15:10 but I laboured **more a than** they all: *4054*
2Co 1:12 in the world, and **more a** to you-wards. *4056*
2: 4 the love which I have **more a** unto you. *4056*
10:15 by you according to our rule **a**, *1519+4050*
12:15 though the **more a** I love you, the less I be *4056*
Eph 3:20 do exceeding **a** above all that we ask *1537+4053*
1Th 2:17 endeavoured the **more a** to see your face *4056*
Tit 3: 6 Which he shed on us **a** through Jesus Christ *4146*
Heb 6:17 willing **more a** to shew unto the heirs of *4054*
2Pe 1:11 an entrance shall be ministered unto you **a** *4146*

ABUSE (3) [ABUSED, ABUSERS, ABUSING]
1Sa 31: 4 and thrust me through, and **a** me. 5953
1Ch 10: 4 lest these uncircumcised come and **a** me. 5953
1Co 9:18 that *I* **a** not my power in the gospel. *2710*

ABUSED (1) [ABUSE]
Jdg 19:25 and **a** her all the night until the morning: 5953

ABUSERS (1) [ABUSE]
1Co 6: 9 nor **a** of themselves **with mankind**, *733*

ABUSING (1) [ABUSE]
1Co 7:31 as not **a** *it*: for the fashion of this world *2710*

ABYSS See BOTTOMLESS

ACBOR See ACHBOR

ACCAD (1)
Ge 10:10 Erech, and **A**, and Calneh, in the land of 390

ACCEPT (25) [ACCEPTABLE, ACCEPTABLY, ACCEPTANCE, ACCEPTATION, ACCEPTED, ACCEPTEST, ACCEPTETH, ACCEPTING]
Ge 32:20 peradventure he will **a** of me. 5375+6440
Ex 22:11 the owner of it shall **a** *thereof*, and he shall 3947
Lev 26:41 then **a** of the punishment of their iniquity: 7521
26:43 they shall **a** of the punishment of their 7521
Dt 33:11 his substance, and **a** the work of his hands: 7521
1Sa 26:19 thee up against me, let him **a** an offering: 7306
2Sa 24:23 unto the king, The LORD thy God **a** thee. 7521
Job 13: 8 Will ye **a** his person? will ye contend for 5375
13:10 reprove you, if ye do secretly **a** persons. 5375
32:21 Let me not, I pray you, **a** *any* man's person, 5375
42: 8 for him will I **a**: lest *I* deal with you 5375+6440
Ps 20: 3 all thy offerings, and **a** thy burnt sacrifice. 1878
82: 2 and **a** the persons of the wicked? 5375
119:108 **A**, I beseech thee, the freewill offerings of 7521
Pr 18: 5 *It is* not good to **a** the person of the wicked, 5375
Jer 14:10 therefore the LORD doth not **a** them; 7521
14:12 and an oblation, I will not **a** them: 7521
Eze 20:40 there will I **a** them, and there will I require 7521
20:41 I will **a** you with *your* sweet savour, when I 7521
43:27 and I will **a** you, saith the Lord GOD. 7521
Am 5:22 I will not **a** *them*: neither will I regard 7521
Mal 1: 8 he be pleased with thee, or **a** thy person? 5375
1:10 neither will I **a** an offering at your hand. 7521
1:13 should I **a** this of your hand? saith 7521
Ac 24: 3 We **a** *it* always, and in all places, most noble *588*

ACCEPTABLE (23) [ACCEPT]
Lev 22:20 ye not offer: for it shall not be **a** for you. 7522
Dt 33:24 let him be **a** to his brethren, and let him dip 7521
Ps 19:14 be **a** in thy sight, O LORD, 7522+3807.1
69:13 *is* unto thee, O LORD, *in* an **a** time: 7522
Pr 10:32 The lips of the righteous know what is **a**: 7522
21: 3 judgment *is* more **a** to the LORD than 977
Ecc 12:10 The Preacher sought to find out **a** words: 2656
Isa 49: 8 In an **a** time have I heard thee, and in a day 7522
58: 5 call this a fast, and an **a** day to the LORD? 7522
61: 2 To proclaim the **a** year of the LORD, and 7522
Jer 6:20 your burnt offerings *are* not **a**, nor your 7522
Da 4:27 let my counsel be **a** unto thee, and break off 8232
Lk 4:19 To preach the **a** year of the Lord. *1184*
Ro 12: 1 holy, **a** unto God, *which is* your reasonable *2101*
12: 2 *that* good, and **a**, and perfect, will of God. *2101*
14:18 in these *things* serveth Christ *is* **a** to God, *2101*
15:16 the offering up of the Gentiles might be **a**, *2144*
Eph 5:10 Proving what is **a** unto the Lord. *2101*
Php 4:18 a sacrifice **a**, well pleasing to God. *1184*
1Ti 2: 3 and **a** in the sight of God our Saviour; *587*
5: 4 for that is good and **a** before God. *587*
1Pe 2: 5 **a** to God by Jesus Christ. *2144*
2:20 *it*, ye take it patiently, this *is* **a** with God. *5485*

ACCEPTABLY (1) [ACCEPT]
Heb 12:28 whereby we may serve God **a** with *2102*

ACCEPTANCE (1) [ACCEPT]
Isa 60: 7 they shall come up with **a** on mine altar, 7522

ACCEPTATION (2) [ACCEPT]
1Ti 1:15 *This is* a faithful saying, and worthy of all **a**, *594*
4: 9 *This is* a faithful saying and worthy of all **a**. *594*

ACCEPTED (29) [ACCEPT]
Ge 4: 7 If thou doest well, *shalt thou* not be **a**? and 7613
19:21 I have **a** thee concerning this thing, 5375+6440
Ex 28:38 that they may be **a** before the LORD. 7522
Lev 1: 4 it shall be **a** for him to make atonement for 7521
7:18 it shall not be **a**, neither shall it be imputed 7521
10:19 should it have been **a** in the sight of 3190
19: 7 third day, it *is* abominable; it shall not be **a**. 7521
22:21 or sheep, it shall be perfect to be **a**; 7522
22:23 but for a vow it shall not be **a**. 7521
22:25 *be* in them: they shall not be **a** for you. 7521
22:27 thenceforth it shall be **a** for an offering 7521
23:11 sheaf before the LORD, to be **a** for you: 7522
1Sa 18: 5 he was **a** in the sight of all the people, and 3190
25:35 to thy voice, and have **a** thy person. 5375
Est 10: 3 and **a** of the multitude of his brethren, 7521
Job 42: 9 the LORD also **a** Job. 5375+6440
Isa 56: 7 their sacrifices *shall be* **a** upon mine altar; 7522
Jer 37:20 I pray thee, be **a** before thee, 5307
42: 2 our supplication be **a** before thee, and 5307
Lk 4:24 No prophet is **a** in his own country. *1184*
Ac 10:35 and worketh righteousness, is **a** with him. *1184*
Ro 15:31 I have for Jerusalem may be **a** of the saints; *2144*
2Co 5: 9 or absent, we may be **a** of him. *2101*
6: 2 I have heard thee in a time **a**, and in the day *1184*
6: 2 behold, now *is* the **a** time; behold, now *is* *2144*
8:12 *it is* **a** according to that a man hath, *and* *2144*
8:17 For indeed he **a** the exhortation; but *1209*

2Co 11: 4 or another gospel, which ye have not **a**, *1209*
Eph 1: 6 wherein he hath **made** us **a** in the beloved: *5487*

ACCEPTEST (1) [ACCEPT]
Lk 20:21 neither **a** thou the person *of any*, but *2983*

ACCEPTETH (4) [ACCEPT]
Job 34:19 *How much less to him* that **a** not 5375
Ecc 9: 7 a merry heart; for God now **a** thy works. 7521
Hos 8:13 and eat *it; but* the LORD **a** them not; 7521
Gal 2: 6 God **a** no man's person:) for they who *2983*

ACCEPTING (1) [ACCEPT]
Heb 11:35 and others were tortured, not **a** deliverance; *4327*

ACCESS (3)
Ro 5: 2 By whom also we have **a** by faith into this *4318*
Eph 2:18 For through him we both have **a** by one *4318*
3:12 and **a** with confidence by the faith of him. *4318*

ACCESSORIES See FURNITURE

ACCHO (1)
Jdg 1:31 did Asher drive out the inhabitants of **A**, 5910

ACCIDENTALLY See UNAWARES

ACCO See ACCHO

ACCOMPANIED (4) [ACCOMPANY]
Ac 10:23 and certain brethren from Joppa **a** him. *4905*
11:12 Moreover these six brethren **a** me, *2064+4862*
20: 4 And there **a** him into Asia Sopater of *4902*
20:38 no more. And they **a** him unto the ship. *4311*

ACCOMPANY (1) [ACCOMPANIED, ACCOMPANYING]
Heb 6: 9 and *things* that **a** salvation, though we thus *2192*

ACCOMPANYING (1) [ACCOMPANY]
2Sa 6: 4 which *was* at Gibeah, **a** the ark of God: 5973

ACCOMPLISH (13) [ACCOMPLISHED, ACCOMPLISHING, ACCOMPLISHMENT]
Lev 22:21 offerings unto the LORD to **a** *his* vow, 6381
1Ki 5: 9 receive *them*: and thou shalt **a** my desire, 6213
Job 14: 6 till he shall **a**, as a hireling, his day. 7521
Ps 64: 6 out iniquities; they **a** a diligent search: 8552
Isa 55:11 it shall **a** that which I please, and it shall 6213
Jer 44:25 ye will **surely a** your vows, and 6965+6965
Eze 6:12 thus will I **a** my fury upon them. 3615
7: 8 upon thee, and **a** mine anger upon thee: 3615
13:15 Thus will I **a** my wrath upon the wall, and 3615
20: 8 to **a** my anger against them in the midst of 3615
20:21 to **a** my anger against them in 3615
Da 9: 2 that *he* would **a** seventy years in 4390
Lk 9:31 spake of his decease which he should **a** at *4137*

ACCOMPLISHED (26) [ACCOMPLISH]
2Ch 36:22 by the mouth of Jeremiah might be **a**, 3615
Est 2:12 so were the days of their purifications **a**, 4390
Job 15:32 It shall be **a** before his time, and his branch 4390
Pr 13:19 The desire **a** is sweet to the soul: but *it is* 1961
Isa 40: 2 cry unto her, that her warfare is **a**, that her 4390
Jer 25:12 come to pass, when seventy years are **a**, 4390
25:34 and of your dispersions are **a**. 4390
29:10 That after seventy years be **a** at Babylon I 4390
39:16 and they shall be *a* in that day before thee. NIH
La 4:11 The LORD hath **a** his fury; he hath poured 3615
4:22 The punishment of thine iniquity is **a**, 8552
Eze 4: 6 when thou hast **a** them, lie again on thy 3615
5:13 Thus shall mine anger be **a**, and I will 3615
5:13 in my zeal, when I have **a** my fury in them. 3615
Da 11:36 and shall prosper till the indignation be **a**: 3615
12: 7 when *he* shall have **a** to scatter the power of 3615
Lk 1:23 soon as the days of his ministration were **a**, *4130*
2: 6 the days were **a** that she should be *4130*
2:21 And when eight days were **a** for *4130*
2:22 according to the law of Moses were **a**, *4130*
12:50 and how am I straitened till it be **a**! *5055*
18:31 concerning the Son of man shall be **a**. *5055*
22:37 that this that is written must yet be **a** in me, *5055*
Jn 19:28 Jesus knowing that all *things* were now **a**, *5055*
Ac 21: 5 And when we had **a** *those* days, *1822*
1Pe 5: 9 knowing that the same afflictions are **a** in *2005*

ACCOMPLISHING (1) [ACCOMPLISH]
Heb 9: 6 the first tabernacle, **a** the service *of God*. *2005*

ACCOMPLISHMENT (1) [ACCOMPLISH]
Ac 21:26 to signify the **a** of the days of purification, *1604*

ACCORD (16) [ACCORDING, ACCORDINGLY]
Lev 25: 5 **That which groweth of it own a** of thy 5599
Jos 9: 2 with Joshua and with Israel, *with* one **a**. 6310
Ac 1:14 These all continued **with one a** in prayer *3661*
2: 1 they were all **with one a** in one place. *3661*
2:46 continuing daily **with one a** in the temple, *3661*
4:24 they lift up their voice to God **with one a**, *3661*
5:12 they were all **with one a** in Solomon's *3661*
7:57 their ears, and ran upon him **with one a**, *3661*
8: 6 And the people **with one a** gave heed unto *3661*
12:10 the city; which opened to them **of his own a**: *844*
12:20 but they came **with one a** to him, and, *3661*
15:25 good unto us, being assembled **with one a**, *3661*
18:12 the Jews made insurrection **with one a** *3661*
19:29 they rushed **with one a** into the theatre. *3661*
2Co 8:17 **of his own a** he went unto you. *830*
Php 2: 2 the same love, *being* of **one a**, of one mind. *4861*

ACCORDING (793) [ACCORD]
Ge 6:22 **a to** all that God commanded him, so 3509.1
7: 5 Noah did **a unto** all that the LORD 3509.1

Dt 33: 9 neither did he a his brethren, nor knew his 5234
Ps 51: 3 For I a my transgressions: and my sin is 3045
Pr 3: 6 In all thy ways a him, and he shall direct 3045
Isa 33:13 and ye that are near, a my might. 3045
61: 9 all that see them shall a them, that they are 5234
63:16 be ignorant of us, and Israel a us not: 5234
Jer 3:13 Only a thine iniquity, that thou hast 3045
14:20 We a, O LORD, our wickedness, and 3045
24: 5 will I a them that are carried away captive 5234
Da 11:39 whom he shall a and increase with glory: 5234
Hos 5:15 till they a their offence, and seek my face: 816
1Co 14:37 let him a that the things that I write unto 1921
16:18 therefore a ye them that are such. 1921
2Co 1:13 things unto you, than what you read or a; 1921
1:13 and I trust you shall a even to the end; 1921

ACKNOWLEDGED (3) [ACKNOWLEDGE]
Ge 38:26 Judah a them, and said, She hath been more 5234
Ps 32: 5 I a my sin unto thee, and mine iniquity 3045
2Co 1:14 As also you have a us in part, that we are 1921

ACKNOWLEDGEMENT (1) [ACKNOWLEDGE]
Col 2: 2 to the a of the mystery of God and of 1922

ACKNOWLEDGETH (1) [ACKNOWLEDGE]
1Jn 2:23 but he that a the Son hath the [Father] [also.] NIG

ACKNOWLEDGING (3) [ACKNOWLEDGE]
2Ti 2:25 give them repentance to the a of the truth; 1922
Tit 1: 1 the a of the truth which is after godliness, 1922
Phm 1: 6 a of every good thing which is in you in 1922

ACQUAINT (1) [ACQUAINTANCE, ACQUAINTED, ACQUAINTING]
Job 22:21 A now thyself with him, and be at peace: 5532

ACQUAINTANCE (11) [ACQUAINT]
2Ki 12: 5 priests take it to them, every man of his a: 4378
12: 7 therefore receive no more money of your a, 4378
Job 19:13 and mine a are verily estranged from me. 3045
42:11 all they that had been of his a before, and 3045
Ps 31:11 my neighbours, and a fear to mine a: 3045
55:13 a man mine equal, my guide, and mine a. 3045
88: 8 Thou hast put away mine a far from me; 3045
88:18 put far from me, and mine a into darkness. 3045
Lk 2:44 sought him among their kinsfolk and a. 1110
23:49 And all his a, and the women that followed 1110
Ac 24:23 that he should forbid none of his a to 2398

ACQUAINTED (2) [ACQUAINT]
Ps 139: 3 my lying down, and art a with all my ways. 5532
Isa 53: 3 of men; a man of sorrows, and a with grief: 3045

ACQUAINTING (1) [ACQUAINT]
Ecc 2: 3 unto wine, (yet a mine heart with wisdom) 5090

ACQUIT (2)
Job 10:14 and thou wilt not a me from mine iniquity. 5352
Na 1: 3 will not at all a the wicked: 5352+5352

ACRE (1) [ACRES]
1Sa 14:14 within as it were a half a of land, 4618

ACRES (1) [ACRE]
Isa 5:10 ten a of vineyard shall yield one bath, and 6776

ACSAH See ACHSA; ACHSAH

ACSHAPH See ACHSHAPH

ACT (4) [ACTIONS, ACTIVITY, ACTS]
Isa 28:21 and bring to pass his a, his strange act. 5656
28:21 and bring to pass his act, his strange a. 5656
59: 6 and the a of violence is in their hands. 6467
Jn 8: 4 was taken in adultery, in the very a. 1888

ACTIONS (1) [ACT]
1Sa 2: 3 of knowledge, and by him a are weighed. 5949

ACTIVITY (1) [ACT]
Ge 47: 6 if thou knowest any man of a amongst 2428

ACTS (66) [ACT]
Dt 11: 3 his miracles, and his a, which he did in 4639
11: 7 your eyes have seen all the great a of 4639
Jdg 5:11 rehearse the righteous a of the LORD, 6666
5:11 even the righteous a towards 6666
1Sa 12: 7 of all the righteous a of the LORD, 6666
2Sa 23:20 of Kabzeel, who had done many a, 6467
1Ki 10: 6 that I heard in mine own land of thy a 1697
11:41 the rest of the a of Solomon, and all that he 1697
11:41 are they not written in the book of the a of 1697
14:19 the rest of the a of Jeroboam, how he 1697
14:29 Now the rest of the a of Rehoboam, and 1697
15: 7 Now the rest of the a of Abijam, and 1697
15:23 The rest of all the a of Asa, and all his 1697
15:31 Now the rest of the a of Nadab, and all that 1697
16: 5 Now the rest of the a of Baasha, and 1697
16:14 Now the rest of the a of Elah, and all that 1697
16:20 Now the rest of the a of Zimri, and 1697
16:27 Now the rest of the a of Omri which he did, 1697
22:39 Now the rest of the a of Ahab, and all that 1697
22:45 Now the rest of the a of Jehoshaphat, and 1697
2Ki 1:18 Now the rest of the a of Ahaziah which he 1697
8:23 the rest of the a of Joram, and all that he 1697
10:34 Now the rest of the a of Jehu, and all that 1697
12:19 the rest of the a of Joash, and all that he 1697
13: 8 Now the rest of the a of Jehoahaz, and 1697
13:12 the rest of the a of Joash, and all that he 1697
14:15 Now the rest of the a of Jehoash which he 1697
14:18 the rest of the a of Amaziah, are they not 1697
14:28 Now the rest of the a of Jeroboam, and 1697
15: 6 the rest of the a of Azariah, and all that he 1697
2Ki 15:11 the rest of the a of Zachariah, behold, 1697
15:15 the rest of the a of Shallum, and 1697
15:21 the rest of the a of Menahem, and all that 1697
15:26 the rest of the a of Pekahiah, and all that he 1697
15:31 the rest of the a of Pekah, and all that he 1697
15:36 Now the rest of the a of Jotham, and all that 1697
16:19 Now the rest of the a of Ahaz which he did, 1697
20:20 the rest of the a of Hezekiah, and all his 1697
21:17 Now the rest of the a of Manasseh, and 1697
21:25 Now the rest of the a of Amon which he 1697
23:19 did to them according to all the a that he 4639
23:28 Now the rest of the a of Josiah, and all that 1697
24: 5 Now the rest of the a of Jehoiakim, and 1697
1Ch 11:22 man of Kabzeel, who had done many a; 6467
29:29 Now the a of David the king, first and last, 1697
2Ch 9: 5 which I heard in mine own land of thine a, 1697
9:29 Now the rest of the a of Solomon, first and 1697
12:15 Now the a of Rehoboam, first and last, are 1697
13:22 the rest of the a of Abijah, and his ways, 1697
16:11 behold, the a of Asa, first and last, lo, 1697
20:34 Now the rest of the a of Jehoshaphat, first 1697
25:26 Now the rest of the a of Amaziah, first and 1697
26:22 Now the rest of the a of Uzziah, first and 1697
27: 7 Now the rest of the a of Jotham, and all his 1697
28:26 Now the rest of his a and of all his ways, 1697
32:32 Now the rest of the a of Hezekiah, and 1697
33:18 Now the rest of the a of Manasseh, and 1697
35:26 Now the rest of the a of Josiah, and 1697
36: 8 Now the rest of the a of Jehoiakim, and 1697
Est 10: 2 all the a of his power and of his might, and 4639
Ps 103: 7 his a unto the children of Israel. 5949
106: 2 Who can utter the mighty a of 1369
145: 4 to another, and shall declare thy mighty a. 1369
145: 6 shall speak of the might of thy terrible a: 3372
145:12 known to the sons of men his mighty a, 1369
150: 2 Praise him for his mighty a: praise him 1369

ACTS OF RIGHTEOUSNESS See ALMS

ACZIB See ACHZIB

ADADAH (1)
Jos 15:22 And Kinah, and Dimonah, and A, 5735

ADAH (8)
Ge 4:19 the name of the one was A, and the name of 5711
4:20 A bare Jabal: he was the father of such as 5711
4:23 his wives, A and Zillah, Hear my voice; 5711
36: 2 A the daughter of Elon the Hittite, and 5711
36: 4 A bare to Esau Eliphaz; and 5711
36:10 Eliphaz the son of A the wife of Esau, 5711
36:12 these were the sons of A Esau's wife. 5711
36:16 the land of Edom; these were the sons of A. 5711

ADAIAH (9)
2Ki 22: 1 was Jedidah, the daughter of A of Boscath. 5718
1Ch 6:41 son of Ethni, the son of Zerah, the son of A, 5718
8:21 A, and Beraiah, and Shimrath, the sons of 5718
9:12 A the son of Jeroham, the son of Pashur, 5718
2Ch 23: 1 Maaseiah the son of A, and Elishaphat 5718
Ezr 10:29 and A, Jashub, and Sheal, and Ramoth. 5718
10:39 And Shelemiah, and Nathan, and A, 5718
Ne 11: 5 of Hazaiah, the son of A, the son of Joiarib, 5718
11:12 A the son of Jeroham, the son of Pelaliah, 5718

ADALIA (1)
Est 9: 8 And Poratha, and A, and Aridatha, 118

ADAM (30) [ADAM'S]
Ge 2:19 brought them unto A to see what he would 120
2:19 whatsoever A called every living creature, 120
2:20 A gave names to all cattle, and to the fowl of 120
2:20 for A there was not found a help meet for 120
2:21 God caused a deep sleep to fall upon A, 120
2:23 A said, This is now bone of my bones, and 120
3: 8 A and his wife hid themselves from 120
3: 9 the LORD God called unto A, and 120
3:17 unto A he said, Because thou hast hearkened 120
3:20 A called his wife's name Eve; because 120
3:21 Unto A also and to his wife did the LORD 120
4: 1 A knew Eve his wife; and she conceived, 120
4:25 A knew his wife again; and she bare a son, 120
5: 1 This is the book of the generations of A. 120
5: 2 blessed them, and called their name A, in 120
5: 3 And A lived an hundred and thirty years, and 120
5: 4 the days of A after he had begotten Seth 120
5: 5 all the days that A lived were nine hundred 120
Dt 32: 8 when he separated the sons of A, 120
Jos 3:16 from the city A, that is beside Zaretan: 121
1Ch 1: 1 A, Sheth, Enosh, 121
Job 31:33 If I covered my transgressions as A, by 120
Lk 3:38 which was the son of A, which was the son of 76
Ro 5:14 Nevertheless death reigned from A to Moses, 76
1Co 15:22 For as in A all die, even so in Christ shall all 76
15:45 The first man A was made a living soul; 76
15:45 the last A was made a quickening spirit. 76
1Ti 2:13 For A was first formed, then Eve. 76
2:14 And A was not deceived, but the woman 76
Jude 1:14 And Enoch also, the seventh from A, 76

ADAM'S (1) [ADAM]
Ro 5:14 sinned after the similitude of A transgression, 76

ADAMAH (1)
Jos 19:36 And A, and Ramah, and Hazor, 128

ADAMANT (2)
Eze 3: 9 As an a harder than flint have I made thy 8068
Zec 7:12 Yea, they made their hearts as an a stone, 8068

ADAMI (1)
Jos 19:33 and A, Nekeb, and Jabneel, unto Lakum; 129

ADAR (10)
Jos 15: 3 went up to A, and fetched a compass to 146
Ezr 6:15 finished on the third day of the month A, 144
Est 3: 7 to the twelfth month, that is, the month A. 143
3:13 which is the month A, and to take the spoil 143
8:12 of the twelfth month, which is the month A. 143
9: 1 in the twelfth month, that is, the month A, 143
9:15 on the fourteenth day also of the month A, 143
9:17 On the thirteenth day of the month A; and 143
9:19 made the fourteenth day of the month A a 143
9:21 keep the fourteenth day of the month A, 143

ADBEEL (2)
Ge 25:13 Nebajoth; and Kedar, and A, and Mibsam, 110
1Ch 1:29 Nebajoth; then Kedar, and A, and Mibsam, 110

ADD (33) [ADDED, ADDETH, ADDITION, ADDITIONS]
Ge 30:24 The LORD shall a to me another son. 3254
Lev 5:16 holy thing, and shall a the fifth part thereto, 3254
6: 5 shall a the fifth part more thereto, and 3254
27:13 he shall a a fifth part thereof unto thy 3254
27:15 he shall a the fifth part of the money of thy 3254
27:19 he shall a the fifth part of the money of thy 3254
27:27 and shall a a fifth part of it thereto: 3254
27:31 he shall a thereto the fifth part thereof. 3254
Nu 5: 7 a unto it the fifth part thereof, and give it 3254
35: 6 to them ye shall a forty and two cities. 5414
Dt 4: 2 Ye shall not a unto the word which I 3254
12:32 thou shalt not a thereto, nor diminish from 3254
19: 9 shalt thou a three cities moe for thee, 3254
29:19 of mine heart, to a drunkenness to thirst: 5595
2Sa 24: 3 Now the LORD thy God a unto 3254
1Ki 12:11 with a heavy yoke, I will a to your yoke: 3254
12:14 your yoke heavy, and I will a to your yoke: 3254
2Ki 20: 6 I will a unto thy days fifteen years; and 3254
1Ch 22:14 have I prepared; and thou mayest a thereto. 3254
2Ch 10:14 made your yoke heavy, but I will a thereto: 3254
28:13 already, ye intend to a more to our sins 3254
Ps 69:27 A iniquity unto their iniquity: and let them 5414
Pr 3: 2 long life, and peace, shall they a to thee. 3254
30: 6 A thou not unto his words, lest he reprove 3254
Isa 29: 1 a ye year to year; let them kill sacrifices. 5595
30: 1 not of my Spirit, that they may a sin to sin: 5595
38: 5 behold, I will a unto thy days fifteen years. 3254
Mt 6:27 Which of you by taking thought can a one 4369
Lk 12:25 which of you with taking thought can a 4369
Php 1:16 supposing to a affliction to my bonds: 2018
2Pe 1: 5 giving all diligence, a to your faith virtue; 2023
Rev 22:18 If any man shall a unto these things, God 2007
22:18 a unto him the plagues that are written in 2007

ADDAN (1)
Ezr 2:59 Tel-harsa, Cherub, A, and Immer: 135

ADDAR (1) [HAZAR-ADDAR]
1Ch 8: 3 sons of Bela were, A, and Gera, and Abihud, 146

ADDED (16) [ADD]
Dt 5:22 he a no more. And he wrote them in two 3254
1Sa 12:19 for we have a unto all our sins this evil, 3254
Jer 36:32 there were a besides unto them many like 3254
45: 3 for the LORD hath a grief to my sorrow; 3254
Da 4:36 and excellent majesty was a unto me. 3255
Mt 6:33 and all these things shall be a unto you. 4369
Lk 3:20 A yet this above all, that he shut up John in 4369
12:31 and all these things shall be a unto you. 4369
19:11 And as they heard these things, he a and 4369
Ac 2:41 the same day there were a unto them about 4369
2:47 And the Lord a to the church daily such as 4369
5:14 And believers were the more a to the Lord, 4369
11:24 and much people was a unto the Lord. 4369
Gal 2: 6 somewhat in conference a nothing to me: 4323
3:15 no man disannulleth, or a thereto. 1928
3:19 It was a because of transgressions, till 4369

ADDER (4) [ADDER'S]
Ge 49:17 an a in the path, that biteth the horse heels, 8207
Ps 58: 4 they are like the deaf a that stoppeth her 6620
91:13 Thou shalt tread upon the lion and a: 6620
Pr 23:32 biteth like a serpent, and stingeth like an a. 6848

ADDER'S (1) [ADDER]
Ps 140: 3 like a serpent; a poison is under their lips. 5919

ADDETH (3) [ADD]
Job 34:37 For he a rebellion unto his sin, he clappeth 3254
Pr 10:22 it maketh rich, and he a no sorrow with it. 3254
16:23 his mouth, and a learning to his lips. 3254

ADDI (1)
Lk 3:28 which was the son of A, which was the son of 78

ADDICTED (1)
1Co 16:15 that they have a themselves to the ministry 5021

ADDITION (1) [ADD]
1Ki 7:30 undersetters molten, at the side of every a. 3914

ADDITIONS (2) [ADD]
1Ki 7:29 and oxen were certain a made of thin work. 3914
7:36 proportion of every one, and a round about. 3914

ADDON (1)
Ne 7:61 Tel-haresha, Cherub, A, and Immer: 114

ADER (1)
1Ch 8:15 And Zebadiah, and Arad, and A, 5738

ADIEL (3)
1Ch 4:36 Asaiah, and A, and Jesimiel, and Benaiah, 5717
9:12 Maasiai the son of A, the son of Jahzerah, 5717
27:25 treasures was Azmaveth the son of A: 5717

Ge 18:10 I will certainly return unto thee a to 3509.1
18:14 a to the time of life, and Sarah shall have 3509.1
18:21 have done altogether a to the cry of it, 3509.1
21:23 a to the kindness that I have done unto 3509.1
25:13 by their names, a to their generations: 3807.1
25:16 twelve princes a to their nations. 3807.1
27: 8 obey my voice a to that which I 3807.1
27:19 I have done a as thou badest me: 3509.1
30:34 I would it might be a to thy word. 3509.1
33:14 a as the cattle that goeth before me and 3807.1
34:12 I will give a as ye shall say unto me: 834+3509.1
36:40 a to their families, after their places, 3807.1
36:43 a to their habitations in the land of their 3807.1
39:17 she spake unto him a to these words, 3509.1
40: 5 each man a to the interpretation of his 3509.1
41:11 we dreamed each man a to 3509.1
41:12 each man a to his dream he did interpret. 3509.1
41:40 a unto thy word shall all my people be 5921
41:54 to come, a as Joseph had said: 834+3509.1
43: 7 we told him a to the tenor of these words: 5921
43:33 the firstborn a to his birthright, and 3509.1
43:33 and the youngest a to his youth: 3509.1
44: 2 he did a to the word that Joseph had 3509.1
44: 7 that thy servants should do a to this thing: 3509.1
44:10 Now also let it be a unto your words: 3509.1
45:21 a to the commandment of Pharaoh, and 5921
47:12 with bread, a to their families. 6310+3807.1
49:28 every one a to his blessing he blessed 3509.1
50: 6 thy father, a as he made thee swear. 834+3509.1
50:12 his sons did unto him a as he commanded 3651
Ex 6:16 of the sons of Levi a to their generations; 3807.1
6:17 Libni, and Shimi, a to their families. 3807.1
6:19 these are the families of Levi a to their 3807.1
6:25 fathers of the Levites a to their families. 3807.1
6:26 from the land of Egypt a to their armies. 5921
8:10 he said, Be it a to thy word: that thou 3509.1
8:13 the LORD did a to the word of Moses; 3509.1
8:31 the LORD did a to the word of Moses; 3509.1
12: 3 a to the house of their fathers, a lamb for 3807.1
12: 4 house take it a to the number of the souls; 871.1
12: 4 every man a to his eating shall 6310+3807.1
12:21 and take you a lamb a to your families, 3807.1
12:25 a as he hath promised, that ye shall 834+3509.1
12:35 the children of Israel did a to the word of 3509.1
16:16 Gather of it every man a to his 6310+3807.1
16:16 every man, a to the number of your persons; NIH
16:18 gathered every man a to his eating. 6310+3807.1
16:21 every man a to his eating: 6310+3509.1
17: 1 a to the commandment of the LORD, and 5921
21:22 a as the woman's husband will lay 834+3509.1
21:31 a to this judgment shall it be done unto 3509.1
22:17 he shall pay money a to the dowry of 3509.1
24: 4 a to the twelve tribes of Israel. 3807.1
25: 9 A to all that I shew thee, after the pattern 3509.1
25:35 a to the six branches that proceed out of 3807.1
26:30 thou shalt rear up the tabernacle a to 3509.1
28: 8 be of the same, a to the work thereof; 3509.1
28:10 rest on the other stone, a to their birth. 3509.1
28:21 twelve, a to their names, like 5921
28:21 one with his name shall they be a to 3807.1
29:35 a to all things which I have commanded 3509.1
29:41 shalt do thereto a to the meat offering of 3509.1
29:41 a to the drink offering thereof, for a 3509.1
30:37 you shall not make to yourselves a to 871.1
31:11 sweet incense for the holy place: a to all 3509.1
32:28 the children of Levi did a to the word of 3509.1
36: 1 a to all that the LORD had commanded. 3807.1
37:21 a to the six branches going out of it. 3807.1
37:29 a to the work of the apothecary. NIH
38:21 a to the commandment of Moses, 5921
39: 5 was of the same, a to the work thereof; 3509.1
39:14 the stones were a to the names of 5921
39:14 twelve, a to their names, like 5921
39:14 one with his name, a to the twelve tribes. 3807.1
39:32 the children of Israel did a to all that 3509.1
39:42 A to all that the LORD commanded 3509.1
40:16 a to all that the LORD commanded him, 3509.1
Lev 4: 3 If the priest that is anointed do sin a to 3807.1
4:35 a to the offerings made by fire unto 5921
5:10 for a burnt offering, a to the manner: 3509.1
5:12 a to the offerings made by fire unto 5921
9:16 and offered it a to the manner. 3509.1
10: 7 And they did a to the word of Moses. 3509.1
12: 2 a to the days of the separation for her 3509.1
25:15 A to the number of years after the jubile 871.1
25:15 a unto the number of years of the fruits he 871.1
25:16 A to the multitude of years thou 6310+3807.1
25:16 a to the fewness of years thou shalt 6310+3807.1
25:16 for a to the number of the years of the fruits NIH
25:50 the price of his sale shall be a unto 871.1
25:50 a to the time of a hired servant shall it be 3509.1
25:51 a unto them he shall give again 6310+3807.1
25:52 a unto his years shall he give him 6310+3509.1
26:21 moe plagues upon you a to your sins. 3509.1
27: 8 a to his ability that vowed shall 834+5921+6310
27:16 thy estimation shall be a to 6310+3807.1
27:17 a to thy estimation it shall stand. 3509.1
27:18 the money a to the years that remain, 5921+6310
27:25 all thy estimations shall be a to the shekel 871.1
27:27 he shall redeem it a to thine estimation, 871.1
27:27 then it shall be sold a to thy estimation. 871.1
Nu 1:18 a to the number of the names, from twenty 871.1
1:20 a to the number of the names, by their 871.1
1:22 a to the number of the names, by their 871.1
1:24 a to the number of the names, from twenty 871.1
1:26 a to the number of the names, from twenty 871.1
1:28 a to the number of the names, from twenty 871.1
1:30 a to the number of the names, from twenty 871.1
1:32 a to the number of the names, from twenty 871.1
1:34 a to the number of the names, from twenty 871.1
1:36 a to the number of the names, from twenty 871.1
1:38 a to the number of the names, from twenty 871.1
1:40 a to the number of the names, from twenty 871.1
1:42 a to the number of the names, from twenty 871.1
1:54 the children of Israel did a to all that 3509.1
Nu 2:10 of the camp of Reuben a to their armies: 3807.1
2:18 of the camp of Ephraim a to their armies: 3807.1
2:34 the children of Israel did a to all that 3509.1
2:34 a to the house of their fathers. 5921
3:16 Moses numbered them a to the word of 5921
3:20 These are the families of the Levites a to 3807.1
3:22 a to the number of all the males, from a 871.1
3:34 a to the number of all the males, from a 871.1
3:51 to his sons, a to the word of the LORD, 5921
4:31 a to all their service in the tabernacle of 3807.1
4:33 a to all their service, in the tabernacle of 3807.1
4:37 Aaron did number a to the commandment 5921
4:41 Aaron did number a to the commandment 5921
4:45 Aaron numbered a to the word of 5921
4:49 A to the commandment of the LORD they 5921
4:49 every one a to his service, and according to 5921
4:49 to his service, and a to his burden: 5921
6:21 a to the vow which he vowed, 6310+3509.1
7: 5 to every man a to his service. 6310+3509.1
7: 7 sons of Gershon, a to their service: 6310+3509.1
7: 8 of Merari, a unto their service, 6310+3509.1
8: 4 a unto the pattern which the LORD had 3509.1
8:20 did to the Levites a unto all that 3509.1
9: 3 a to all the rites of it, and according to all 3509.1
9: 3 a to all the ceremonies thereof, shall ye 3509.1
9: 5 a to all that the LORD commanded 3509.1
9:12 a to all the ordinances of the passover 3509.1
9:14 a to the ordinance of the passover, and 3509.1
9:14 a to the manner thereof, so shall he do: 3509.1
9:20 a to the commandment of the LORD they 5921
9:20 a to the commandment of the LORD they 5921
10:13 they first took their journey a to 5921
10:14 of the children of Judah a to their armies: 3807.1
10:18 of Reuben set forward a to their armies: 3807.1
10:22 of Ephraim set forward a to their armies: 3807.1
10:28 of the children of Israel a to their armies, 3807.1
14:17 a as thou hast spoken, saying, 834+3509.1
14:19 the iniquity of this people a unto 3509.1
14:20 I have pardoned a to thy word: 3509.1
14:29 a to your whole number, from twenty 3807.1
15:12 A to the number that ye shall prepare, so 3509.1
15:12 ye do to every one a to their number. 3509.1
15:24 a to the manner, and one kid of the goats 3509.1
17: 2 take of every one of them a rod a to 3807.1
17: 2 of all their princes a to the house of their 3807.1
17: 6 a to their fathers' houses, even twelve 3807.1
18:16 a to thine estimation, for the money of five 871.1
23:23 a to this time it shall be said of Jacob and 3509.1
24: 2 he saw Israel abiding in his tents a to 3807.1
26:18 a to those that were numbered of them, 3807.1
26:22 These are the families of Judah a to those 3807.1
26:25 These are the families of Issachar a to 3807.1
26:27 a to those that were numbered of them, 3807.1
26:37 a to those that were numbered of them, 3807.1
26:43 a to those that were numbered of them, 3807.1
26:47 a to those that were numbered of them; 3807.1
26:50 These are the families of Naphtali a to 3807.1
26:53 an inheritance a to the number of names. 871.1
26:54 a to those that were numbered of 6310+3807.1
26:55 a to the names of the tribes of their 3807.1
26:56 A to the lot shall the possession 5921+6310
29: 6 a unto their manner, for a sweet savour, 3509.1
29:18 for the lambs, shall be a to their number, 871.1
29:21 for the lambs, shall be a to their number, 871.1
29:24 for the lambs, shall be a to their number, 871.1
29:27 for the lambs, shall be a to their number, 871.1
29:30 for the lambs, shall be a to their number, 871.1
29:33 for the lambs, shall be a to their number, 871.1
29:37 for the lambs, shall be a to their number, 871.1
29:40 Moses told the children of Israel a to all 3509.1
30: 2 he shall do a to all that proceedeth out of 3509.1
33: 2 Moses wrote their goings out a to their 3807.1
33: 2 these are their journeys a to their goings 3807.1
33:54 a to the tribes of your fathers ye shall 3807.1
34:14 of Reuben a to the house of their fathers, 3807.1
34:14 the tribe of the children of Gad a to 3807.1
35: 8 a to his inheritance which he 6310+3509.1
35:24 the revenger of blood a to these judgments: 5921
36: 5 of Israel a to the word of the LORD, 5921
Dt 1: 3 a unto all that the LORD had given him 3509.1
1:30 a to all that he did for you in Egypt 3509.1
1:41 a to all that the LORD our God 3509.1
1:46 a unto the days that ye abode there. 3509.1
3:24 that can do a to thy works, and 3509.1
3:24 to thy works, and a to thy might? 3509.1
4:34 a to all that the LORD your God did for 3509.1
9:10 on them was written a to all the words, 3509.1
10: 4 a to the first writing, the ten 3509.1
10: 9 a as the LORD thy God promised 834+3509.1
10:10 a to the first time, forty days and 3509.1
12:15 a to the blessing of the LORD thy God 3509.1
16:10 a as the LORD thy God hath 834+3509.1
16:17 a to the blessing of the LORD thy God 3509.1
17:10 thou shalt do a to the sentence, 5921+6310
17:10 thou shalt observe to do a to all that they 3509.1
17:11 A to the sentence of the law which 5921+6310
17:11 a to the judgment which they shall tell thee, 5921
18:16 A to all that thou desiredst of the LORD 3509.1
23:23 a as thou hast vowed unto 834+3509.1
24: 8 do a to all that the priests 834+3509.1
25: 2 before his face, a to his fault, 1767+3509.1
26:13 a to all thy commandments which thou 3509.1
26:14 have done a to all that thou hast 3509.1
29:21 a to all the curses of the covenant that are 3509.1
30: 2 shalt obey his voice a to all that I 3509.1
31: 5 that ye may do unto them a unto all 3509.1
32: 8 he set the bounds of the people a to 3807.1
34: 5 land of Moab, a to the word of the LORD. 5921
Jos 1: 7 that thou mayest observe to do a to all 3509.1
1: 8 that thou mayest observe to do a to all 3509.1
1:17 A as we hearkened unto Moses in all 3509.1
2:21 she said, A unto your words, so be it. 3509.1
4: 5 a unto the number of the tribes of 3807.1
4: 8 a to the number of the tribes of 3807.1
4:10 a to all that Moses commanded Joshua: 3509.1
Jos 7:14 ye shall be brought a to your tribes: 3807.1
7:14 shall come a to the families thereof; 3807.1
8: 8 a to the commandment of the LORD 3509.1
8:27 a unto the word of the LORD which he 3509.1
8:34 a to all that is written in the book of 3509.1
10:32 a to all that he had done to Libnah. 3509.1
10:35 a to all that he had done to Lachish. 3509.1
10:37 a to all that he had done to Eglon; 3509.1
11:23 a to all that the LORD said unto Moses; 3509.1
11:23 Israel a to their divisions by their tribes. 3509.1
12: 7 for a possession a to their divisions; 3509.1
13:15 of Reuben inheritance a to their families. 3807.1
13:24 even unto the children of Gad a to their 3807.1
15:12 of Judah round about a to their families. 3807.1
15:13 a to the commandment of the LORD to 413
15:20 the children of Judah a to their families. 3807.1
16: 5 the border of the children of Ephraim a to 3807.1
17: 4 Therefore a to the commandment of 413
18: 4 it a to the inheritance of them; 6310+3807.1
18:10 the children of Israel a to their divisions. 3509.1
18:11 of Benjamin came up a to their families: 3807.1
18:20 thereof round about, a to their families. 3807.1
18:21 a to their families were Jericho, 3807.1
18:28 children of Benjamin a to their families. 3807.1
19: 1 the children of Simeon a to their families: 3807.1
19: 8 the children of Simeon a to their families. 3807.1
19:10 children of Zebulun a to their families: 3807.1
19:16 children of Zebulun a to their families, 3807.1
19:17 for the children of Issachar a to their 3807.1
19:23 children of Issachar a to their families, 3807.1
19:24 the children of Asher a to their families. 3807.1
19:31 the children of Asher a to their families, 3807.1
19:32 even for the children of Naphtali a to 3807.1
19:39 children of Naphtali a to their families, 3807.1
19:40 of the children of Dan a to their families. 3807.1
19:48 of the children of Dan a to their families, 3807.1
19:50 A to the word of the LORD they gave him 5921
21:33 All the cities of the Gershonites a to their 3807.1
21:44 a to all that he sware unto their fathers: 3509.1
22: 9 a to the word of the LORD by the hand of 5921
24: 5 a to that which I did amongst them: 3509.1
Jdg 8:35 a to all the goodness which he had 3509.1
9:16 have done unto him a to the deserving of 3509.1
11:10 if we do not so a to thy words. 3509.1
11:36 do to me a to that which hath proceeded 3509.1
11:39 who did with her a to his vow which he had NIH
20:10 a to all the folly that they have wrought 3509.1
21:23 took them wives, a to their number, 3807.1
Ru 3: 6 a to all that her mother in law bade her. 3509.1
1Sa 2:35 that shall do a to that which is in my 3509.1
6: 4 a to the number of the lords of NIH
6:18 a to the number of all the cities of NIH
8: 8 A to all the works which they have done 3509.1
13: 8 a to the set time that Samuel had 3807.1
14: 7 behold, I am with thee a to thy heart. 3509.1
17:23 and spake a to the same words: 3509.1
23:20 come down a to all the desire of thy soul 3807.1
25: 9 they spake to Nabal a to all those words 3509.1
25:30 a to all the good that he hath spoken 3509.1
2Sa 3:39 the doer of evil a to his wickedness. 3509.1
7:17 A to all these words, and according to all 3509.1
7:17 a to all this vision, so did Nathan speak 3509.1
7:21 thy word's sake, and a to thine own heart, 3509.1
7:22 a to all that we have heard with our ears. 871.1
9:11 A to all that my lord the king hath 3509.1
14:20 a to the wisdom of an angel of God, 3509.1
22:21 The LORD rewarded me a to my 3509.1
22:21 a to the cleanness of my hands hath he 3509.1
22:25 recompensed me a to my righteousness; 3509.1
22:25 a to my cleanness in his eye sight. 3509.1
24:19 David, a to the saying of Gad, went up as 3509.1
1Ki 2: 6 Do therefore a to thy wisdom, and let not 3509.1
3: 6 a as he walked before thee in truth, 834+3509.1
3:12 Behold, I have done a to thy word: lo, 3509.1
4:28 officers were, every man a to his charge. 3509.1
5: 6 servants a to all that thou shalt appoint: 3509.1
5:10 cedar trees and fir trees a to all his desire. NIH
6: 3 a to the breadth of the house; 5921+6440
6:38 and a to all the fashion of it. 3807.1
7: 9 a to the measures of hewed stones, 3509.1
7:36 a to the proportion of every one, and 3509.1
8:32 to give him a to his righteousness. 3509.1
8:39 do, and give to every man a to his ways, 3509.1
8:43 do a to all that the stranger calleth to thee 3509.1
8:56 people Israel, a to all that he promised: 3509.1
9: 4 to do a to all that I have commanded 3509.1
9:11 and with gold, a to all his desire,) 3807.1
11:37 thou shalt reign a to all that thy soul 871.1
12:24 to depart, a to the word of the LORD. 3509.1
13: 5 a to the sign which the man of God had 3509.1
13:26 slain him, a to the word of the LORD, 3509.1
14:18 for him, a to the word of the LORD, 3509.1
14:24 they did a to all the abominations of 3509.1
15:29 a unto the saying of the LORD, 3509.1
16:12 of Baasha, a to the word of the LORD, 3509.1
16:34 a to the word of the LORD, which he 3509.1
17: 1 rain these years, but a to my word. 6310+3807.1
17: 5 and did a unto the word of the LORD: 3509.1
17:15 and did a to the saying of Elijah: 3509.1
17:16 a to the word of the LORD, which he 3509.1
18:31 a to the number of the tribes of the sons 3509.1
20: 4 said, My lord, O king, a to thy saying, 3509.1
21:26 a to all things as did the Amorites, 3509.1
22:38 a unto the word of the LORD which he 3509.1
22:53 a unto all that his father had done. 3509.1
2Ki 1:17 So he died a to the word of the LORD 3509.1
2:22 a to the saying of Elisha which he spake. 3509.1
4:16 About this season, a to the time of life, 3509.1
4:17 had said unto her, a to the time of life. 3509.1
4:44 left thereof, a to the word of the LORD. 3509.1
5:14 a to the saying of the man of God: 3509.1
6:18 he smote them with blindness a to 3509.1
7:16 for a shekel, a to the word of the LORD. 3509.1
9:26 cast him into the plat of ground, a to 3509.1
10:17 a to the saying of the LORD, which he 3509.1

2Ki 10:30 hast done unto the house of Ahab **a to** all 3509.1
11: 9 the captains over the hundreds did **a to** all 3509.1
14: 3 he did **a to** all *things* as Joash his father 3509.1
14: 6 **a unto** that which is written in the book 3509.1
14:25 **a to** the word of the LORD God of 3509.1
15: 3 **a to** all that his father Amaziah had done; 3509.1
15:34 he did **a to** all that his father Uzziah had 3509.1
16: 3 **a to** the abominations of the heathen, 3509.1
16:10 of it, **a to** all the workmanship thereof. 3807.1
16:11 Urijah the priest built an altar **a to** all that 3509.1
16:16 **a to** all that king Ahaz commanded. 3509.1
17:13 **a to** all the law which I commanded your 3509.1
18: 3 **a to** all that David his father did. 3509.1
21: 8 only if they will observe to do **a to** all 3509.1
21: 8 **a to** all the law that my servant Moses 3807.1
22:13 to do **a unto** all that which is written 3509.1
23:16 **a to** the word of the LORD which 3509.1
23:19 did to them **a to** all the acts that he had 3509.1
23:25 all his might, **a to** all the law of Moses; 3509.1
23:32 **a to** all that his fathers had done. 3509.1
23:35 he taxed the land to give the money **a to** 5921
23:35 of every one **a to** his taxation, to give *it* 3509.1
23:37 **a to** all that his fathers had done. 3509.1
24: 2 destroy it, **a to** the word of the LORD, 3509.1
24: 3 the sins of Manasseh, **a to** all that he did; 3509.1
24: 9 **a to** all that his father had done. 3509.1
24:19 **a to** all that Jehoiakim had done. 3509.1
1Ch 6:19 these *are* the families of the Levites **a to** 3807.1
6:32 waited on their office **a to** their order. 3509.1
6:49 **a to** all that Moses the servant of God had 3509.1
9: 9 **a to** their generations, nine hundred and 3807.1
11: 3 **a to** the word of the LORD by Samuel. 3509.1
11:10 **a to** the word of the LORD concerning 3509.1
12:23 Saul to him, **a to** the word of the LORD. 3509.1
15:15 as Moses commanded **a to** the word of 3509.1
16:40 *to do* **a to** all that is written in the law of 3807.1
17:15 **A to** all these words, and according to all 3509.1
17:15 **a to** all this vision, so did Nathan speak 3509.1
17:17 hast regarded me **a to** the estate of a man 3509.1
17:19 servant's sake, and **a to** thine own heart, 3509.1
17:20 **a to** all that we have heard with our ears. 871.1
23:11 one reckoning, **a to** *their* father's house. 3807.1
23:31 **a to** the order commanded unto them, 3509.1
24: 3 **a to** their offices in their service. 3807.1
24: 4 eight among the sons of Ithamar **a to** 3807.1
24:19 **a to** their manner, under Aaron their 3509.1
25: 1 the number of the workmen **a to** their 3807.1
25: 2 which prophesied **a to** the order of the king. 5921
25: 6 **a to** the king's order *to* Asaph, Jeduthun, 5921
26:13 **a to** the house of their fathers, for every 3807.1
26:31 **a to** the generations of his fathers. 3807.1
28:15 **a to** the use of every candlestick. 3509.1
2Ch 3: 4 *it was* **a to** the breadth of the house, 5921+6440
3: 8 the length whereof *was* **a to** 5921+6440
4: 7 he made ten candlesticks of gold **a to** 3509.1
6:23 by giving him **a to** his righteousness. 3509.1
6:30 unto every man **a unto** all his ways, 3509.1
6:33 do **a to** all that the stranger calleth to thee 3509.1
7:17 do **a to** all that I have commanded thee, 3509.1
7:18 **a as** I have covenanted with David 834+3509.1
8:13 offering **a to** the commandment of 3509.1
8:14 **a to** the order of David his father, 3509.1
17:14 these *are* the numbers of them **a to** 3807.1
23: 8 all Judah did **a to** all *things* that Jehoiada 3509.1
24: 6 *a to the commandment* of Moses the servant NIH
25: 5 **a to** the houses of *their* fathers, 3807.1
26: 4 **a to** all that his father Amaziah did. 3509.1
26:11 **a to** the number of their account by 871.1
27: 2 **a to** all that his father Uzziah did: 3509.1
29: 2 **a to** all that David his father had done. 3509.1
29:15 came, **a to** the commandment of the king, 3509.1
29:25 **a to** the commandment of David, and 871.1
30: 6 and **a to** the commandment of the king, 3509.1
30:16 **a to** the law of Moses the man of God: 3509.1
30:19 though *he be* not *cleansed* **a to** 3509.1
31: 2 every man **a to** his service, 6310+3509.1
31:16 service in their charges **a to** their courses; 3509.1
32:25 Hezekiah rendered not again **a to** 3509.1
33: 8 **a to** the whole law and the statutes and 3807.1
34:32 Jerusalem did **a to** the covenant of God, 3509.1
35: 4 **a to** the writing of David king of Israel, 871.1
35: 4 and **a to** the writing of Solomon his son. 871.1
35: 5 stand in the holy *place* **a to** the divisions 3807.1
35: 6 that *they* may do **a to** the word of 3509.1
35:10 **a to** the king's commandment. 3509.1
35:12 that they might give **a to** the divisions of 3807.1
35:13 they roasted the passover with fire **a to** 3509.1
35:15 **a to** the commandment of David, and 3509.1
35:16 **a to** the commandment of king Josiah. 3509.1
35:26 **a to** that which was written in the law of 3509.1
Ezr 3: 4 **a to the custom**, as the duty of every day 3509.1
3: 7 **a to** the grant that they had of Cyrus king 3509.1
6: 9 **a to** the appointment of the priests which 3509.4
6:13 their companions, **a to** that which 6903+3807.2
6:14 finished *it*, **a to** the commandment of 4481
6:14 **a to** the commandment of Cyrus, and 4481
6:17 **a to** the number of the tribes of Israel. 3807.2
7: 6 **a to** the hand of the LORD his God 3509.1
7: 9 **a to** the good hand of his God upon him. 3509.1
7:14 **a to** the law of thy God which *is* in thine 871.2
9: 1 *doing* **a to** their abominations, *even* of 3509.1
10: 3 **a to** the counsel of my lord, and of those 871.1
10: 3 our God; and let it be done **a to** the law. 3509.1
10: 5 swear that *they* should do **a to** this word. 3509.1
10: 8 **a to** the counsel of the princes and 3509.1
Ne 2: 8 **a to** the good hand of my God upon me. 3509.1
5:12 that *they* should do **a to** this promise. 3509.1
5:13 And the people did **a to** this promise. 3509.1
5:19 *a to* all that I have done for this people. NIH
6: 6 mayest be their king, **a to** these words. 3509.1
6: 7 now shall it be reported to the king **a to** 3509.1
6:14 and Sanballat **a to** these their works, 3509.1
8:18 a solemn assembly, **a unto** the manner. 3509.1
9:27 **a to** thy manifold mercies thou gavest 3509.1
9:28 many times didst thou deliver them **a to** 3509.1
Ne 12:24 **a to** the commandment of David the man 871.1
12:45 **a to** the commandment of David, *and* 3509.1
13:22 spare me **a to** the greatness of thy mercy. 3509.1
13:24 but **a to** the language of each people. 3509.1
Est 1: 7 in abundance, **a to** the state of the king. 3509.1
1: 8 the drinking *was* **a to** the law; none did 3509.1
1: 8 that *they* should do **a to** every man's 3509.1
1:15 *we* do unto the queen Vashti **a to** law, 3509.1
1:21 the king did **a to** the word of Memucan: 3509.1
1:22 into every province **a to** the writing 3509.1
1:22 that it should be published **a to** 3509.1
2:12 **a to** the manner of the women, (for so 3509.1
2:18 and gave gifts, **a to** the state of the king. 3509.1
3:12 there was written **a to** all that Haman had 3509.1
3:12 of every province **a to** the writing thereof, 3509.1
4:16 unto the king, which *is* not **a to** the law: 3509.1
4:17 did **a to** all that Esther had commanded 3509.1
8: 9 it was written **a to** all that Mordecai 3509.1
8: 9 *unto* every province **a to** the writing 3509.1
8: 9 to the Jews **a to** their writing, and 3509.1
8: 9 to their writing, and **a to** their language. 3509.1
9:13 to morrow also **a unto** *this* day's decree, 3509.1
9:27 that they would keep these two days **a to** 3509.1
9:27 and **a to** their *appointed* time every year; 3509.1
9:31 *appointed*, **a as** Mordecai the Jew 834+3509.1
Job 1: 5 offered burnt offerings *a to* the number of NIH
20:18 **a to** *his* substance *shall* the restitution *be*, 3509.1
33: 6 Behold, I *am* **a to** thy wish in God's 3509.1
34:11 cause every man to find **a to** *his* ways. 3509.1
34:33 *Should it be* **a to** thy **mind**? he will 4480+5973
36:27 they pour down rain **a to** the vapour 3807.1
42: 9 **a as** the LORD commanded them: 834+3509.1
Ps 7: 8 **a to** my righteousness, and according to 3509.1
7: 8 and **a to** mine integrity *that is* in me. 3509.1
7:17 I will praise the LORD **a to** his 3509.1
18:20 The LORD rewarded me **a to** my 3509.1
18:20 **a to** the cleanness of my hands hath he 3509.1
18:24 recompensed me **a to** my righteousness, 3509.1
18:24 **a to** the cleanness of my hands in his 3509.1
20: 4 Grant thee **a to** thine own heart, and 3509.1
25: 7 **a to** thy mercy remember thou me for thy 3509.1
28: 4 Give them **a to** their deeds, and 3509.1
28: 4 **a to** the wickedness of their endeavours: 3509.1
33:22 be upon us, **a as** we hope in thee. 834+3509.1
35:24 LORD my God, **a to** thy righteousness; 3509.1
48:10 **A to** thy name, O God, so *is* thy praise 3509.1
51: 1 O God, **a to** thy lovingkindness: 3509.1
51: 1 **a unto** the multitude of thy tender 3509.1
62:12 for thou renderest to *every* man **a to** his 3509.1
69:16 turn unto me **a to** the multitude of thy 3509.1
74: 5 *A man* was famous **a as** he had lifted up 3509.1
78:72 So he fed them **a to** the integrity of his 3509.1
79:11 **a to** the greatness of thy power: 3509.1
90:11 even **a to** thy fear, *so is* thy wrath. 3509.1
90:15 Make us glad **a to** the days *wherein* thou 3509.1
103:10 nor rewarded us **a to** our iniquities. 3509.1
106:45 **a to** the multitude of his mercies. 3509.1
109:26 my God: O save me **a to** thy mercy: 3509.1
119: 9 by taking heed *thereto* **a to** thy word. 3509.1
119:25 the dust: quicken thou me **a to** thy word. 3509.1
119:28 strengthen thou me **a unto** thy word. 3509.1
119:41 *even* thy salvation, **a to** thy word. 3509.1
119:58 be merciful unto me **a to** thy word. 3509.1
119:65 thy servant, O LORD, **a unto** thy word. 3509.1
119:76 **a to** thy word unto thy servant. 3509.1
119:91 They continue *this* day **a to** thine 3807.1
119:107 quicken me, O LORD, **a unto** thy word. 3509.1
119:116 Uphold me **a unto** thy word, that I may 3509.1
119:124 Deal with thy servant **a unto** thy mercy, 3509.1
119:149 Hear my voice **a unto** thy 3509.1
119:149 quicken me **a to** thy judgment. 3509.1
119:154 deliver me: quicken me **a to** thy word. 3807.1
119:156 quicken me **a to** thy judgments. 3509.1
119:159 O LORD, **a to** thy lovingkindness. 3509.1
119:169 give me understanding **a to** thy word. 3509.1
119:170 before thee: deliver me **a to** thy word. 3509.1
150: 2 praise him **a to** his excellent greatness. 3509.1
Pr 12: 8 A man shall be commended **a to** 6310+3807.1
24:12 shall *not* he render to *every* man **a to** his 3509.1
24:29 I will render to the man **a to** his work. 3509.1
26: 4 Answer not a fool **a to** his folly, lest thou 3509.1
26: 5 Answer a fool **a to** his folly, lest he be 3509.1
Ecc 1: 6 the wind returneth *again* **a to** his circuits. 5921
8:14 it happeneth **a to** the work of the wicked; 3509.1
8:14 happeneth **a to** the work of the righteous: 3509.1
Isa 8:20 if they speak not **a to** this word, *it is* 3509.1
9: 3 they joy before thee **a to** the joy in 3509.1
10:26 **a to** the slaughter of Midian at the rock 3509.1
21:16 **a to** the years of a hireling, and all 3509.1
23:15 seventy years, **a to** the days of one king: 3509.1
27: 7 is he slain **a to** the slaughter of them that 3509.1
44:13 figure of a man, **a to** the beauty of a man; 3509.1
59:18 **A to** *their* deeds, accordingly he 5921+3509.1
63: 7 **a to** all that the LORD hath 5921+3509.1
63: 7 which he hath bestowed on them **a to** his 3509.1
63: 7 **a to** the multitude of his 3509.1
Jer 2:28 for *a to* the number of thy cities are thy NIH
3:15 I will give you pastors **a to** mine heart, 3509.1
11: 4 do them, **a to** all which I command you: 3509.1
11:13 For *a to* the number of thy cities were thy NIH
11:13 *a to* the number of the streets of Jerusalem NIH
13: 2 **a to** the word of the LORD, and put *it* 3509.1
17:10 even to give every man **a to** his ways, *and* 3509.1
17:10 his ways, *and* **a to** the fruit of his doings. 3509.1
21: 2 be that the LORD will deal with us **a to** 3509.1
21:14 I will punish you **a to** the fruit of your 3509.1
25:14 I will recompense them **a to** their deeds, 3509.1
25:14 and **a to** the works of their own hands. 3509.1
26:20 against this land **a to** all the words of 3509.1
27:12 king of Judah **a to** all these words, 3509.1
31:32 Not **a to** the covenant that I made with 3509.1
32: 8 the prison **a to** the word of the LORD, 3509.1
32:11 *both* that which was sealed *a to* the law and NIH
32:19 to give every one **a to** his ways, and 3509.1
32:19 his ways, and **a to** the fruit of his doings: 3509.1
Jer 35:10 done **a to** all that Jonadab our father 3509.1
35:18 done **a unto** all that he hath commanded 3509.1
36: 8 Baruch the son of Neriah did **a to** all that 3509.1
38:27 he told them **a to** all these words that 3509.1
40: 3 and done **a as** he hath said: 834+3509.1
42: 4 the LORD your God **a to** your words; 3509.1
42: 5 if we do not even **a to** all things *for* 3509.1
42:20 **a unto** all that the LORD our God shall 3509.1
50:21 do **a to** all that I have commanded thee. 3509.1
50:29 recompense her **a to** her work; 3509.1
50:29 **a to** all that she hath done, do unto her: 3509.1
52: 2 **a to** all that Jehoiakim had done. 3509.1
La 3:32 yet will he have compassion **a to** 3509.1
3:64 O LORD, **a to** the work of their hands. 3509.1
Eze 4: 4 *a to* the number of the days that thou shalt NIH
4: 5 **a to** the number of the days, 3807.1
4: 9 *a to* the number of the days that thou shalt NIH
5: 7 neither have done **a to** the judgments of 3509.1
7: 3 will judge thee **a to** thy ways, and 3509.1
7: 8 I will judge thee **a to** thy ways, and 3509.1
7: 9 I will recompense thee **a to** thy ways and 3509.1
7:27 and **a to** their deserts will I judge them; 871.1
8: 4 **a to** the vision that I saw in the plain. 3509.1
14: 4 that cometh **a to** the multitude of his idols; 871.1
18:24 doeth **a to** all the abominations that 3509.1
18:30 O house of Israel, every one **a to** his 3509.1
20:44 not **a to** your wicked ways, nor according 3509.1
20:44 nor **a to** your corrupt doings, O ye house 3509.1
23:24 they shall judge thee **a to** their judgments. 871.1
24:14 **a to** thy ways, and according to thy 3509.1
24:14 **a to** thy doings, shall they judge thee, 3509.1
24:24 **a to** all that he hath done shall ye do: and 3509.1
25:14 shall do in Edom **a to** mine anger and 3509.1
25:14 to mine anger and **a to** my fury; 3509.1
35:11 I will even do **a to** thine anger, and 3509.1
35:11 **a to** thine envy which thou hast used out 3509.1
36:19 **a to** their way and according to their 3509.1
36:19 and **a to** their doings I judged them. 3509.1
39:24 **A to** their uncleanness and according to 3509.1
39:24 **a to** their transgressions have I done unto 3509.1
40:24 the arches thereof **a to** these measures. 3509.1
40:28 he measured the south gate **a to** these 3509.1
40:29 the arches thereof, **a to** these measures: 3509.1
40:32 he measured the gate **a to** these measures. 3509.1
40:33 arches thereof, *were* **a to** these measures: 3509.1
40:35 and measured *it* **a to** these measures; 3509.1
42:11 all their goings out *were* both **a to** their 3509.1
42:11 to their fashions, and **a to** their doors. 3509.1
42:12 **a to** the doors of the chambers that *were* 3509.1
43: 3 *it was* **a to** the appearance of the vision 3509.1
43: 3 *even* **a to** the vision that I saw when I 3509.1
44:24 *and* they shall judge it **a to** my judgments: 871.1
45: 8 to the house of Israel **a to** their tribes. 3807.1
45:25 **a to** the sin offering, according to 3509.1
45:25 **a to** the burnt offering, and according to 3509.1
45:25 **a to** the meat offering, and according to 3509.1
45:25 to the meat offering, and **a to** the oil. 3509.1
46: 7 for the lambs **a as** his hand shall 834+3509.1
47:10 their fish shall be **a to** their kinds, as 3807.1
47:12 it shall bring forth new fruit **a to** his 3807.1
47:13 whereby ye shall inherit the land **a to** 3807.1
47:21 So shall ye divide this land unto you **a to** 3807.1
Da 4: 8 **a to** the name of my god, and in whom *is* 3509.4
4:35 he doeth **a to** his will in the army of 3509.4
6: 8 **a to** the law of the Medes and Persians, 3509.4
6:12 **a to** the law of the Medes and Persians, 3509.4
8: 4 but he did **a to** his will, and became great. 3509.1
9:16 O Lord, **a to** all thy righteousness, 3509.1
11: 3 *with* great dominion, and do **a to** his will. 3509.1
11: 4 nor **a to** his dominion which he ruled: 3509.1
11:16 he that cometh against him shall do **a to** 3509.1
11:36 the king shall do **a to** his will; and 3509.1
Hos 3: 1 **a to** the love of the LORD toward 3509.1
9:10 *their* abominations were **a as** they loved. 3509.1
10: 1 **a to** the multitude of his fruit he hath 3509.1
10: 1 **a to** the goodness of his land they have 3509.1
12: 2 and *will* punish Jacob **a to** his ways; 3509.1
12: 2 **a to** his doings will he recompense him. 3509.1
13: 2 *and* idols **a to** their own understanding, 3509.1
13: 6 **A to** their pasture, so were they filled; 3509.1
Jnh 3: 3 **a to** the word of the LORD. 3509.1
Mic 7:15 **A to** the days of thy coming out of 3509.1
Hab 3: 9 *a to* the oaths of the tribes, *even* thy word. NIH
Hag 2: 5 *A to* the word that I covenanted with you NIH
Zec 1: 6 **a to** our ways, and according to our 3509.1
1: 6 **a to** our doings, so hath he dealt with us. 3509.1
5: 3 shall be cut off *as* on this *side* **a to** it; 3644
5: 3 shall be cut off *as* on that *side* **a to** it. 3644
Mal 2: 9 **a as** ye have not kept my 834+6310+3509.1
Mt 2:16 **a to** the time which he had diligently *2596*
9:29 saying, **A to** your faith be it unto you. *2596*
16:27 he shall reward every man **a to** his works. *2596*
25:15 to every man **a to** his several ability; and *2596*
Mk 7: 5 Why walk not thy disciples **a to** *2596*
Lk 1: 9 **A to** the custom of the priest's office, *2596*
1:38 of the Lord; be it unto me **a to** thy word. *2596*
2:22 And when the days of her purification **a to** *2596*
2:24 And to offer a sacrifice **a to** that which is *2596*
2:29 thy servant depart in peace, **a to** thy word: *2596*
2:39 all *things* **a to** the law of the Lord, *2596*
5:14 for thy cleansing, **a as** Moses commanded, *2531*
12:47 prepared not *himself*, neither did **a to** his *4314*
23:56 rested the sabbath day **a to** *2596*
Jn 7:24 Judge not **a to** the appearance, but *2596*
18:31 Take ye him, and judge him **a to** your law. *2596*
Ac 2:30 that of the fruit of his loins, **a to** the flesh, *2596*
4:35 distribution was made unto every man **a as** *2530*
7:44 that *he* should make it **a to** the fashion that *2596*
11:29 the disciples, every man **a to** his ability, *2531*
13:23 Of this *man's* seed hath God **a to** *his* *2596*
22: 3 taught **a to** the perfect manner of the law of *2596*
22:12 one Ananias, a devout man **a to** the law, *2596*
24: 6 and would have judged **a to** our law. *2596*
Ro 1: 3 which was made of the seed of David **a to** *2596*
1: 4 **a to** the Spirit of holiness, by *2596*

Ro 2: 2 **a to** truth against them which commit such *2596*
2: 6 Who will render to every *man* **a to** his *2596*
2:16 of men by Jesus Christ **a** to my gospel. *2596*
4:18 **a to** that which was spoken, So shall thy *2596*
8:27 he maketh intercession for the saints **a to** *2596*
8:28 to them who are *the* called **a to** *his* purpose. *2596*
9: 3 for my brethren, my kinsmen **a to** the flesh: *2596*
9:11 that the purpose of God **a to** election might *2596*
10: 2 have a zeal of God, but not **a to** knowledge. *2596*
11: 5 at *this* present time also there is a remnant **a** *2596*
11: 8 (**A as** it is written, God hath given them *2531*
12: 3 **a as** God hath dealt to every man *5613*
12: 6 gifts differing **a to** the grace that is given to *2596*
12: 6 *let us prophesy* **a to** the proportion of faith; *2596*
15: 5 one towards another **a to** Christ Jesus: *2596*
16:25 is of power to stablish you **a to** my gospel, *2596*
16:25 **a to** the revelation of the mystery, *2596*
16:26 **a to** the commandment of the everlasting *2596*
1Co 1:31 That, **a as** it is written, He that glorieth, *2531*
3: 8 man shall receive his own reward **a to** *2596*
3:10 **A to** the grace of God which is given unto *2596*
15: 3 how that Christ died for our sins **a to** *2596*
15: 4 that he rose *again* the third day **a to** *2596*
2Co 1:17 that I purpose, do I purpose **a to** the flesh, *2596*
4:13 **a as** it is written, I believed, *and* therefore *2596*
5:10 **a to** that he hath done, whether *it be* good *4314*
8:12 *it is* accepted **a to that** a man hath, *1437+2526*
8:12 a man hath, *and* not **a to that** he hath not. *2526*
9: 7 Every man **a as** he purposeth in *his* heart, *2531*
10: 2 which think of us as if we walked **a to** *2596*
10:13 **a to** the measure of the rule which God *2596*
10:15 that *we* shall be enlarged by you **a to** our *2596*
11:15 whose end shall be **a to** their works. *2596*
13:10 **a to** the power which the Lord hath given *2596*
Gal 1: 4 **a to** the will of God and our Father: *2596*
2:14 not uprightly **a to** the truth of the gospel, *4314*
3:29 and heirs **a to** the promise. *2596*
6:16 And as many as walk **a** to this rule, peace *be* NIG
Eph 1: 4 **A as** he hath chosen us in him before *2531*
1: 5 **a to** the good pleasure of his will, *2596*
1: 7 of sins, **a to** the riches of his grace; *2596*
1: 9 **a to** his good pleasure which he had *2596*
1:11 being predestinated **a to** the purpose of him *2596*
1:19 **a to** the working of his mighty power, *2596*
2: 2 Wherein in time past ye walked **a to** *2596*
2: 2 **a to** the prince of the power of the air, *2596*
3: 7 **a to** the gift of the grace of God given unto *2596*
3:11 **A to** the eternal purpose which he purposed *2596*
3:16 grant you, **a to** the riches of his glory, *2596*
3:20 or think, **a to** the power that worketh in us, *2596*
4: 7 But unto every one of us is given grace **a to** *2596*
4:16 **a to** the effectual working in the measure of *2596*
4:22 which is corrupt **a to** the deceitful lusts; *2596*
6: 5 to *them that are your* masters **a to** the flesh, *2596*
Php 1:20 **A to** my earnest expectation and *my* hope, *2596*
3:21 **a to** the working whereby he is able even to *2596*
4:19 But my God shall supply all your need **a to** *2596*
Col 1:11 **a to** his glorious power, unto all patience *2596*
1:25 **a to** the dispensation of God which is given *2596*
1:29 I also labour, striving **a to** his working, *2596*
3:22 obey in all *things your* masters **a to** *2596*
2Th 1:12 **a to** the grace of our God and the Lord *2596*
1Ti 1:11 **A to** the glorious gospel of the blessed *2596*
1:18 **a to** the prophecies which went before on *2596*
6: 3 and to the doctrine which is **a to** godliness; *2596*
2Ti 1: 1 **a to** the promise of life which is in Christ *2596*
1: 8 of the gospel **a to** the power of God; *2596*
1: 9 not **a to** our works, but according to his *2596*
1: 9 but **a to** his own purpose and grace, *2596*
2: 8 *was* raised from the dead **a to** my gospel: *2596*
4:14 the Lord reward him **a to** his works: *2596*
Tit 1: 1 **a to** the faith of God's elect, and *2596*
1: 3 which is committed unto me **a to** *2596*
3: 5 but **a to** his mercy he saved us, by *2596*
3: 7 we should be made heirs **a to** the hope of *2596*
Heb 2: 4 gifts of the Holy Ghost, **a to** his own will? *2596*
7: 5 to take tithes of the people **a to** the law, *2596*
8: 4 there are priests that offer gifts **a to** the law: *2596*
8: 5 saith *he, that* thou make all *things* **a to** *2596*
8: 9 Not **a to** the covenant that I made with their *2596*
9:19 every precept to all the people **a to** the law, *2596*
Jas 2: 8 If ye fulfil the royal law **a to** the scripture, *2596*
1Pe 1: 2 Elect **a to** the foreknowledge of God *2596*
1: 3 which **a to** his abundant mercy hath *2596*
1:14 not **fashioning** yourselves **a to** the former *4964*
1:17 who without respect of persons judgeth **a to** *2596*
3: 7 dwell with *them* **a to** knowledge, *2596*
4: 6 that they might be judged **a to** men in *2596*
4: 6 in the flesh, but live **a to** God in the spirit. *2596*
4:19 Wherefore let them that suffer **a to** the will *2596*
2Pe 1: 3 **A as** his divine power hath given unto us *5613*
2:22 But it is happened unto them **a** to the true NIG
3:13 Nevertheless we, **a to** his promise, look for *2596*
3:15 even as our beloved brother Paul also **a to** *2596*
1Jn 5:14 that, if we ask any *thing* **a to** his will, *2596*
Rev 2:23 I will give unto every one of you **a to** your *2596*
18: 6 and double unto her double **a to** her works: *2596*
20:12 were written in the books, **a to** their works. *2596*
20:13 they were judged every man **a to** their *2596*
21:17 *a to* the measure of a man, that is, NIG
22:12 to give every man **a as** his work shall be. *5613*

ACCORDINGLY (1) [ACCORD]

Isa 59:18 **a** he will repay, fury to his 5921+3509.1

ACCOUNT (17) [ACCOUNTED, ACCOUNTING, ACCOUNTS]

2Ki 12: 4 *the* **a**, the money that every man is set at, NIH
1Ch 27:24 neither was the number put in the **a** of 4557
2Ch 26:11 according to the number of their **a** by 6486
Job 33:13 for he **giveth** not **a** of any of his matters. 6030
Ps 144: 3 the son of man, that thou **makest a** of him? 2803
Ecc 7:27 *counting* one by one, to find out the **a**: 2808
Mt 12:36 they shall give **a** thereof in the day of *3056*
Mt 18:23 which would take **a** of his servants. *3056*
Lk 16: 2 give an **a** of thy stewardship; for thou *3056*
Ac 19:40 we may give an **a** of this concourse. *3056*
Ro 14:12 every one of us shall give **a** of himself to *3056*
1Co 4: 1 Let a man so **a** of us, as of the ministers of *3049*
Php 4:17 but I desire fruit that *may* abound to your **a**. *3056*
Phm 1:18 or oweth *thee* ought, **put** that **on** mine **a**; *1677*
Heb 13:17 as they that must give **a**, that they may do it *3056*
1Pe 4: 5 Who shall give **a** to him that is ready to *3056*
2Pe 3:15 And **a** *that* the longsuffering of our Lord *is* *2233*

ACCOUNTED (12) [ACCOUNT]

Dt 2:11 Which also were **a** giants, as the Anakims; 2803
2:20 (That also was **a** a land of giants: 2803
1Ki 10:21 it was nothing **a** of in the days of Solomon. 2803
2Ch 9:20 it was *not* any thing **a** of in the days of 2803
Ps 22:30 it shall be **a** to the Lord for a generation. 5608
Isa 2:22 in his nostrils: for wherein is he *to be* **a** of? 2803
Mk 10:42 Ye know that they which are **a** to rule over *1380*
Lk 20:35 But they which shall be **a worthy** to obtain *2661*
21:36 that ye may be **a worthy** to escape all these *2661*
22:24 which of them should be **a** the greatest. *1380*
Ro 8:36 we are **a** as sheep for the slaughter. *3049*
Gal 3: 6 and it was **a** to him for righteousness. *3049*

ACCOUNTING (1) [ACCOUNT]

Heb 11:19 **A** that God *was* able to raise *him* up, *3049*

ACCOUNTS (1) [ACCOUNT]

Da 6: 2 that the princes might give **a** unto them, 2942

ACCURSED (20) [CURSE]

Dt 21:23 (for he that is hanged *is* **a** of God;) that thy 7045
Jos 6:17 the city shall be **a**, *even* it, and all that *are* 2764
6:18 any wise keep *yourselves* from the **a thing**, 2764
6:18 lest ye **make** *yourselves* **a**, when ye take of 2763
6:18 when ye take of the **a thing**, and make 2764
7: 1 Israel committed a trespass in the **a thing**: 2764
7: 1 of the tribe of Judah, took of the **a thing**: 2764
7:11 for they have even taken of the **a thing**, and 2764
7:12 before their enemies, because they were **a**: 2764
7:12 except ye destroy the **a** from amongst you. 2764
7:13 *There is* an **a thing** in the midst of thee, 2764
7:13 until ye take away the **a thing** from among 2764
7:15 *that* he that is taken with the **a thing** shall 2764
22:20 of Zerah commit a trespass in the **a thing**, 2764
1Ch 2: 7 of Israel, who transgressed in the **thing a**. 2764
Isa 65:20 *being* an hundred years old shall be **a**. 7043
Ro 9: 3 For I could wish that myself were **a** from *331*
1Co 12: 3 by the Spirit of God calleth Jesus **a**: *331*
Gal 1: 8 we have preached unto you, let him be **a**. *331*
1: 9 you than that ye have received, let him be **a**. *331*

ACCUSATION (10) [ACCUSE]

Ezr 4: 6 wrote they *unto him* an **a** against 7855
Mt 27:37 And set up over his head his **a** written, *156*
Mk 15:26 And the superscription of his **a** was written *156*
Lk 6: 7 that they might find an **a against** him. *2724*
19: 8 **taken** any *thing* from any *man* **by false a**, *4811*
Jn 18:29 said, What **a** bring you against this man? *2724*
Ac 25:18 brought none **a** of *such things* as I supposed: *156*
1Ti 5:19 Against an elder receive not an **a**, but *2724*
2Pe 2:11 bring not railing **a** against them before *2920*
Jude 1: 9 durst not bring against *him* a railing **a**, but *2920*

ACCUSE (16) [ACCUSATION, ACCUSED, ACCUSER, ACCUSERS, ACCUSETH, ACCUSING]

Pr 30:10 **A** not a servant unto his master, lest he 3960
Mt 12:10 on the sabbath days? that they might **a** him. *2723*
Mk 3: 2 on the sabbath day; that they might **a** him. *2723*
Lk 3:14 violence to no man, neither **a** *any* **falsely**; *4811*
11:54 out of his mouth, that they might **a** him. *2723*
23: 2 And they began to **a** him, saying, We found *2723*
23:14 *touching those things* whereof ye **a** him: *2723*
Jn 5:45 Do not think that I will **a** you to the Father: *2723*
8: 6 that they might have to **a** him. *2723*
Ac 24: 2 *forth*, Tertullus began to **a** *him*, saying, *2723*
24: 8 of all these *things*, whereof we **a** him. *2723*
24:13 prove *the things* whereof they now **a** me. *2723*
25: 5 are able, go down with *me*, and **a** this man, *2723*
25:11 be none *of these things* whereof these **a** me, *2723*
28:19 not that I had ought to **a** my nation of. *2723*
1Pe 3:16 they may be ashamed that **falsely a** your *1908*

ACCUSED (14) [ACCUSE]

Da 3: 8 Chaldeans came near, and **a** the Jews. 399+7170
6:24 they brought those men which had **a** 399+7170
Mt 27:12 And when he was **a** of the chief priests and *2723*
Mk 15: 3 And the chief priests **a** him of many *things*: *2723*
Lk 16: 1 the same was **a** unto him that he had wasted *1225*
23:10 and scribes stood and vehemently **a** him. *2723*
Ac 22:30 certainty wherefore he was **a** of the Jews, *2723*
23:28 known the cause wherefore they **a** him, *1458*
23:29 Whom I perceived to be **a** of questions of *1458*
25:16 before that he which is **a** have the accusers *2723*
26: 2 all *the things* whereof I am **a** of the Jews: *1458*
26: 7 king Agrippa, I am **a** of the Jews. *1458*
Tit 1: 6 having faithful children not **a** of riot *1722+2724*
Rev 12:10 which **a** them before our God day and *2723*

ACCUSER (1) [ACCUSE]

Rev 12:10 for the **a** of our brethren is cast down, *2725*

ACCUSERS (8) [ACCUSE]

Jn 8:10 unto her, Woman, where are those thine **a**? *2725*
Ac 23:30 gave commandment to *his* **a** also to say *2725*
23:35 said he, when thine **a** are also come. *2725*
24: 8 Commanding his **a** to come unto thee: *2725*
25:16 before that he which is accused have the **a** *2725*
25:18 Against whom when the **a** stood *up*, they *2725*
2Ti 3: 3 trucebreakers, **false a**, incontinent, fierce, *1228*
Tit 2: 3 not **false a**, not given to much wine, *1228*

ACCUSETH (1) [ACCUSE]

Jn 5:45 there is *one* that **a** you, *even* Moses, *2723*

ACCUSING (1) [ACCUSE]

Ro 2:15 and *their* thoughts the mean while **a** or *2723*

ACCUSTOMED (1) [CUSTOM]

Jer 13:23 may ye also do good, that are **a to** do evil. 3928

ACELDAMA (1)

Ac 1:19 **A**, that is to say, The field of blood. *184*

ACHAIA (11)

Ac 18:12 And when Gallio was the deputy of **A**, *882*
18:27 And when he was disposed to pass into **A**, *882*
19:21 he had passed through Macedonia and **A**, *882*
Ro 15:26 **A** to make a certain contribution for the poor *882*
16: 5 who is the firstfruits of **A** unto Christ. *882*
1Co 16:15 that it is the firstfruits of **A**, and *that* they *882*
2Co 1: 1 with all the saints which are in all **A**: *882*
9: 2 of Macedonia, that **A** was ready a year ago; *882*
11:10 stop me of this boasting in the regions of **A**. *882*
1Th 1: 7 to all that believe in Macedonia and **A**. *882*
1: 8 of the Lord not only in Macedonia and **A**, *882*

ACHAICUS (2)

1Co 16:17 coming of Stephanas and Fortunatus and **A**: *883*
16: S and Fortunatus, and **A**, and Timotheus. *883*

ACHAN (6) [ACHAR]

Jos 7: 1 for **A**, the son of Carmi, the son of Zabdi, 5912
7:18 **A**, the son of Carmi, the son of Zabdi, 5912
7:19 Joshua said unto **A**, My son, give, I pray 5912
7:20 **A** answered Joshua, and said, Indeed I have 5912
7:24 took **A** the son of Zerah, and the silver, and 5912
22:20 Did not **A** the son of Zerah commit a 5912

ACHAR (1) [ACHAN]

1Ch 2: 7 **A**, the troubler of Israel, who transgressed 5917

ACHAZ (2) [AHAZ]

Mt 1: 9 and Joatham begat **A**; and Achaz begat *881*
1: 9 Joatham begat Achaz; and **A** begat Ezekias; *881*

ACHBOR (7)

Ge 36:38 Baal-hanan the son of **A** reigned in his 5907
36:39 Baal-hanan the son of **A** died, and 5907
2Ki 22:12 **A** the son of Michaiah, and Shaphan 5907
22:14 Ahikam, and **A**, and Shaphan, and Asahiah, 5907
1Ch 1:49 Baal-hanan the son of **A** reigned in his 5907
Jer 26:22 *namely*, Elnathan the son of **A**, and 5907
36:12 Elnathan the son of **A**, and Gemariah 5907

ACHIM (2)

Mt 1:14 and Sadoc begat **A**; and Achim begat Eliud; *885*
1:14 and Sadoc begat Achim; and **A** begat Eliud; *885*

ACHISH (21)

1Sa 21:10 fear of Saul, and went to **A** the king of Gath. 397
21:11 the servants of **A** said unto him, *Is* not this 397
21:12 and was sore afraid of **A** the king of Gath. 397
21:14 said **A** unto his servants, Lo, you see 397
27: 2 six hundred men that *were* with him unto **A**, 397
27: 3 David dwelt with **A** at Gath, he and his men, 397
27: 5 David said unto **A**, If I have now found 397
27: 6 **A** gave him Ziklag that day: wherefore 397
27: 9 the apparel, and returned, and came to **A**. 397
27:10 **A** said, Whither have ye made a road to day? 397
27:12 **A** believed David, saying, He hath made his 397
28: 1 **A** said unto David, Know thou assuredly, 397
28: 2 David said to **A**, Surely thou shalt know 397
28: 2 **A** said to David, Therefore will I make thee 397
29: 2 his men passed on in the rereward with **A**. 397
29: 3 What *do* these Hebrews *here?* And **A** said 397
29: 6 **A** called David, and said unto him, Surely, 397
29: 8 David said unto **A**, But what have I done? 397
29: 9 **A** answered and said to David, I know that 397
1Ki 2:39 away unto **A** son of Maachah king of Gath. 397
2:40 and went to Gath to **A** to seek his servants: 397

ACHMETHA (1)

Ezr 6: 2 there was found at **A**, in the palace that *is* in 307

ACHOR (5)

Jos 7:24 and they brought them *unto* the valley of **A**. 5911
7:26 was called, The valley of **A**, unto this day. 5911
15: 7 went up toward Debir from the valley of **A**, 5911
Isa 65:10 the valley of **A** a place for the herds to lie 5911
Hos 2:15 and the valley of **A** for a door of hope: 5911

ACHSAH (5)

Jos 15:16 to him will I give **A** my daughter to wife. 5915
15:17 and he gave him **A** his daughter to wife. 5915
Jdg 1:12 to him will I give **A** my daughter to wife. 5915
1:13 and he gave him **A** his daughter to wife. 5915
1Ch 2:49 of Gibea: and the daughter of Caleb *was* **A**. 5915

ACHSHAPH (3)

Jos 11: 1 to the king of Shimron, and to the king of **A**, 407
12:20 of Shimron-meron, one; the king of **A**, one; 407
19:25 was Helkath, and Hali, and Beten, and **A**, 407

ACHZIB (4)

Jos 15:44 Keilah, and **A**, and Mareshah; nine cities 392
19:29 thereof are at the sea from the coast to **A**: 392
Jdg 1:31 nor of Ahlab, nor of **A**, nor of Helbah, nor of 392
Mic 1:14 the houses of **A** *shall be* a lie to the kings of 392

ACKNOWLEDGE (16) [ACKNOWLEDGED, ACKNOWLEDGEMENT, ACKNOWLEDGETH, ACKNOWLEDGING]

Dt 21:17 he shall **a** the son of the hated *for* 5234

ADIN (4)
Ezr 2:15 The children of **A**, four hundred fifty and 5720
8: 6 Of the sons also of **A**; Ebed the son of 5720
Ne 7:20 The children of **A**, six hundred fifty and 5720
10:16 Adonijah, Bigvai, **A**, 5720

ADINA (1)
1Ch 11:42 **A** the son of Shiza the Reubenite, a captain 5721

ADINO (1)
2Sa 23: 8 the captains; the same *was* **A** the Eznite: 5722

ADITHAIM (1)
Jos 15:36 and **A**, and Gederah, and Gederothaim; 5723

ADJURE (5) [ADJURED]
1Ki 22:16 How many times shall I **a** thee that thou tell 7650
2Ch 18:15 How many times shall I **a** thee that thou say 7650
Mt 26:63 said unto him, I **a** thee by the living God, *1844*
Mk 5: 7 I **a** thee by God, that thou torment me not. *3726*
Ac 19:13 We **a** you by Jesus whom Paul preacheth. *3726*

ADJURED (2) [ADJURE]
Jos 6:26 Joshua **a** *them* at that time, saying, 7650
1Sa 14:24 for Saul had **a** the people, saying, Cursed *be* 422

ADLAI (1)
1Ch 27:29 in the valleys *was* Shaphat the son of **A**: 5724

ADMAH (5)
Ge 10:19 Gomorrah, and **A**, and Zeboim, even unto 126
14: 2 Shinab king of **A**, and Shemeber king of 126
14: 8 the king of **A**, and the king of Zeboiim, and 126
Dt 29:23 of Sodom, and Gomorrah, **A**, and Zeboim, 126
Hos 11: 8 how shall I make thee as **A**? *how* shall I set 126

ADMATHA (1)
Est 1:14 Shethar, **A**, Tarshish, Meres, Marsena, *and* 133

ADMINISTERED (2) [ADMINISTRATION]
2Co 8:19 which is **a** by us to the glory of the same *1247*
8:20 us in this abundance which is **a** by us: *1247*

ADMINISTRATION (1) [ADMINISTERED, ADMINISTRATIONS]
2Co 9:12 For the **a** of this service not only supplieth *1248*

ADMINISTRATIONS (1) [ADMINISTRATION]
1Co 12: 5 And there are differences of **a**, but the same *1248*

ADMIRATION (2) [ADMIRED]
Jude 1:16 *words,* **having** *men's* persons **in a** *2296+4383*
Rev 17: 6 when I saw her, I wondered *with* great **a**. *2295*

ADMIRED (1) [ADMIRATION]
2Th 1:10 and to be **a** in all them that believe (because *2296*

ADMONISH (3) [ADMONISHED, ADMONISHING, ADMONITION]
Ro 15:14 all knowledge, able also to **a** one another. *3560*
1Th 5:12 and are over you in the Lord, and **a** you; *3560*
2Th 3:15 not as an enemy, but **a** *him* as a brother. *3560*

ADMONISHED (5) [ADMONISH]
Ecc 4:13 and foolish king, who will no more be **a**. 2094
12:12 further, by these, my son, be **a**: of making 2094
Jer 42:19 know certainly that I have **a** you *this* day. 5749
Ac 27: 9 the fast was now already past, Paul **a** *them,* *3867*
Heb 8: 5 **a of God** when he was about to make *5537*

ADMONISHING (1) [ADMONISH]
Col 3:16 and **a** one another in psalms and hymns and *3560*

ADMONITION (3) [ADMONISH]
1Co 10:11 and they are written for our **a**, upon whom *3559*
Eph 6: 4 them up in the nurture and **a** of the Lord. *3559*
Tit 3:10 *is* a heretick after the first and second **a**, *3559*

ADNA (2)
Ezr 10:30 **A**, and Chelal, Benaiah, Maaseiah, 5733
Ne 12:15 Of Harim, **A**; of Meraioth, Helkai; 5733

ADNAH (2)
1Ch 12:20 **A**, and Jozabad, and Jediael, and Michael, 5734
2Ch 17:14 **A** the chief, and with him mighty *men* of 5734

ADO (1)
Mk 5:39 unto them, Why **make** ye *this* **a**, and weep? *2350*

ADONI-BEZEK (3)
Jdg 1: 5 they found **A** in Bezek: and they fought 137
1: 6 **A** fled; and they pursued after him, and 137
1: 7 **A** said, Threescore and ten kings, 137

ADONIJAH (26)
2Sa 3: 4 the fourth, **A** the son of Haggith; and 138
1Ki 1: 5 **A** the son of Haggith exalted himself, 138
1: 7 the priest: and they following **A** helped *him.* 138
1: 8 which *belonged* to David, were not with **A**. 138
1: 9 **A** slew sheep and oxen and fat cattle by 138
1:11 Hast thou not heard that **A** the son of 138
1:13 sit upon my throne? why then doth **A** reign? 138
1:18 now behold, **A** reigneth; and now, my lord 138
1:24 **A** shall reign after me, and he shall sit upon 138
1:25 drink before him, and say, God save king **A**. 138
1:41 **A** and all the guests that *were* with him 138
1:42 **A** said *unto him,* Come in; for thou *art* a 138
1:43 Jonathan answered and said to **A**, Verily our 138
1:49 all the guests that *were* with **A** were afraid, 138
1:50 **A** feared because of Solomon, and arose, 138
1:51 Behold, **A** feareth king Solomon: 138
2:13 **A** the son of Haggith came to Bath-sheba 138
1Ki 2:19 unto king Solomon, to speak unto him for **A**. 138
2:21 Let Abishag the Shunammite be given to **A** 138
2:22 thou ask Abishag the Shunammite for **A**? 138
2:23 if **A** have not spoken this word against his 138
2:24 he promised, **A** shall be put to death *this* day. 138
2:28 for Joab had turned after **A**, though he turned 138
1Ch 3: 2 of Geshur: the fourth, **A** the son of Haggith: 138
2Ch 17: 8 **A**, and Tobijah, and Tob-adonijah, Levites; 138
Ne 10:16 **A**, Bigvai, Adin, 138

ADONIKAM (3)
Ezr 2:13 The children of **A**, six hundred sixty and six. 140
8:13 of the last sons of **A**, whose names *are* these, 140
Ne 7:18 The children of **A**, six hundred threescore 140

ADONIRAM (2)
1Ki 4: 6 and **A** the son of Abda *was* over the tribute. 141
5:14 months at home: and **A** *was* over the levy. 141

ADONI-ZEDEK (2)
Jos 10: 1 when **A** king of Jerusalem had heard how 139
10: 3 Wherefore **A** king of Jerusalem sent unto 139

ADOPTION (5)
Ro 8:15 but ye have received the Spirit of **a**, *5206*
8:23 waiting for the **a**, *to wit,* the redemption of *5206*
9: 4 to whom pertaineth the **a**, and the glory, *5206*
Gal 4: 5 that we might receive the **a of sons**. *5206*
Eph 1: 5 **a of children** by Jesus Christ to himself, *5206*

ADORAIM (1)
2Ch 11: 9 And **A**, and Lachish, and Azekah, 115

ADORAM (2)
2Sa 20:24 **A** *was* over the tribute: and Jehoshaphat 151
1Ki 12:18 king Rehoboam sent **A**, who *was* over 151

ADORN (2) [ADORNED, ADORNETH, ADORNING]
1Ti 2: 9 that women **a** themselves in modest *2885*
Tit 2:10 that they may **a** the doctrine of God our *2885*

ADORNED (4) [ADORN]
Jer 31: 4 thou shalt again be **a** *with* thy tabrets, and 5710
Lk 21: 5 how it was **a** with goodly stones and gifts, *2885*
1Pe 3: 5 who trusted in God, **a** themselves, being in *2885*
Rev 21: 2 prepared as a bride **a** for her husband. *2885*

ADORNETH (1) [ADORN]
Isa 61:10 and as a bride **a** *herself* **with** her jewels. 5710

ADORNING (2) [ADORN]
1Pe 3: 3 Whose **a** let it not be that outward *adorning* *2889*
3: 3 Whose adorning let it not be that outward **a** NIG

ADRAMMELECH (3)
2Ki 17:31 Sepharvites burnt their children in fire to **A** 152
19:37 that **A** and Sharezer *his sons* smote him with 152
Isa 37:38 that **A** and Sharezer his sons smote him with 152

ADRAMYTTIUM (1)
Ac 27: 2 And entering into a ship of **A**, we launched, *98*

ADRIA (1)
Ac 27:27 as we were driven up and down in **A**, *99*

ADRIATIC See ADRIA

ADRIEL (2)
1Sa 18:19 that she was given unto **A** the Meholathite 5741
2Sa 21: 8 whom she brought up for **A** the son of 5741

ADULLAM (8) [ADULLAMITE]
Jos 12:15 king of Libnah, one; the king of **A**, one; 5725
15:35 Jarmuth, and **A**, Socoh, and Azekah, 5725
1Sa 22: 1 departed thence, and escaped to the cave **A**: 5725
2Sa 23:13 in the harvest time unto the cave of **A**: 5725
1Ch 11:15 to the rock to David, into the cave of **A**; 5725
2Ch 11: 7 And Beth-zur, and Shoco, and **A**, 5725
Ne 11:30 Zanoah, **A**, and *in* their villages, *at* Lachish, 5725
Mic 1:15 he shall come unto **A** the glory of Israel. 5725

ADULLAMITE (3) [ADULLAM]
Ge 38: 1 turned in to a certain **A**, whose name *was* 5726
38:12 to Timnath, he and his friend Hirah the **A**. 5726
38:20 sent the kid by the hand of his friend the **A**, 5726

ADULTERER (3) [ADULTERY]
Lev 20:10 the **a** and the adulteress shall surely be put 5003
Job 24:15 The eye also of the **a** waiteth for 5003
Isa 57: 3 the seed of the **a** and the whore. 5003

ADULTERERS (9) [ADULTERY]
Ps 50:18 with him, and hast been partaker with **a**. 5003
Jer 9: 2 for they *be* all **a**, an assembly of 5003
23:10 For the land is full *of* **a**; for because 5003
Hos 7: 4 They *are* all **a**, as an oven heated by 5003
Mal 3: 5 against the **a**, and against false swearers, 5003
Lk 18:11 unjust, **a**, or even as this publican. *3432*
1Co 6: 9 nor idolaters, nor **a**, nor effeminate, *3432*
Heb 13: 4 but whoremongers and **a** God will judge. *3432*
Jas 4: 4 Ye **a** and adulteresses, know ye not that *3432*

ADULTERESS (5) [ADULTERY]
Lev 20:10 and the **a** shall surely be put to death. 5003
Pr 6:26 and the **a** will hunt for the precious life. 376+802
Hos 3: 1 a woman beloved of *her* friend, yet an **a**, 5003
Ro 7: 3 to another man, she shall be called an **a**: *3428*
7: 3 so that she is no **a**, though she be married to *3428*

ADULTERESSES (3) [ADULTERY]
Eze 23:45 they shall judge them after the manner of **a**, 5003
Eze 23:45 because they *are* **a**, and blood *is* in their 5003
Jas 4: 4 Ye adulterers and **a**, know ye not that *3428*

ADULTERIES (5) [ADULTERY]
Jer 13:27 I have seen thine **a**, and thy neighings, 5004
Eze 23:43 said I unto *her that was* old *in* **a**, Will they 5004
Hos 2: 2 and her **a** from between her breasts; 5005
Mt 15:19 murders, **a**, fornications, thefts, *3430*
Mk 7:21 evil thoughts, **a**, fornications, murders, *3430*

ADULTEROUS (4) [ADULTERY]
Pr 30:20 Such *is* the way of an **a** woman; she eateth, 5003
Mt 12:39 and **a** generation seeketh after a sign; *3428*
16: 4 and **a** generation seeketh after a sign; *3428*
Mk 8:38 and of my words in this **a** and *3428*

ADULTERY (40) [ADULTERER, ADULTERERS, ADULTERESS, ADULTERESSES, ADULTERIES, ADULTEROUS]
Ex 20:14 Thou shalt not **commit a**. 5003
Lev 20:10 the man that **committeth a** with *another* 5003
20:10 *even he* that **committeth a** with his 5003
Dt 5:18 Neither shalt thou **commit a**. 5003
Pr 6:32 *But* whoso **committeth a** with a woman 5003
Jer 3: 8 Israel **committed a** I had put her away, 5003
3: 9 **committed a** with stones and with stocks. 5003
5: 7 they then **committed a**, and 5003
7: 9 **commit a**, and swear falsely, and 5003
23:14 *they* **commit a**, and walk in lies: 5003
29:23 have **committed a** with their neighbours' 5003
Eze 16:32 *But as* a wife that **committeth a**, 5003
23:37 That they have **committed a**, and blood *is* 5003
23:37 with their idols have they **committed a**, 5003
Hos 4: 2 killing, and stealing, and **committing a**, 5003
4:13 and your spouses shall **commit a**. 5003
4:14 nor your spouses when they **commit a**: 5003
Mt 5:27 them of old time, Thou shalt not **commit a**: *3431*
5:28 **committed a** with her already in his heart. *3431*
5:32 of fornication, causeth her to **commit a**: *3429*
5:32 marry her that is divorced **committeth a**. *3429*
19: 9 and shall marry another, **committeth a**: *3429*
19: 9 her *which is* put away doth **commit a**. *3429*
19:18 Thou shalt not **commit a**, Thou shalt not *3431*
Mk 10:11 marry another, **committeth a** against her. *3429*
10:12 be married to another, she **committeth a**. *3429*
10:19 Do not **commit a**, Do not kill, Do not steal, *3431*
Lk 16:18 and marrieth another, **committeth a**: *3431*
16:18 put away from *her* husband **committeth a**. *3431*
18:20 Do not **commit a**, Do not kill, Do not steal, *3431*
Jn 8: 3 brought unto him a woman taken in **a**; *3430*
8: 4 Master, this woman was taken in **a**, in *3431*
Ro 2:22 that sayest *a man* should not **commit a**, *3431*
2:22 not commit adultery, dost thou **commit a**? *3431*
13: 9 For *this,* Thou shalt not **commit a**, *3431*
Gal 5:19 which are *these;* **A**, fornication, *3430*
Jas 2:11 Do not **commit a**, said also, Do not kill. *3431*
2:11 Now if thou **commit** no **a**, yet *if* thou kill, *3431*
2Pe 2:14 Having eyes full of **a** and that cannot cease *3428*
Rev 2:22 them that **commit a** with her into great *3431*

ADUMMIM (2)
Jos 15: 7 that *is* before the going up to **A**, 131
18:17 which *is* over against the going up of **A**, and 131

ADVANCED (4)
1Sa 12: 6 *It is* the LORD that **a** Moses and Aaron, 6213
Est 3: 1 **a** him, and set his seat above all the princes 5375
5:11 how he had **a** him above the princes and 5375
10: 2 of Mordecai, where*unto* the king **a** him, 1431

ADVANTAGE (4) [ADVANTAGED, ADVANTAGETH]
Job 35: 3 For thou saidst, What **a** will it be unto thee? 5532
Ro 3: 1 What **a** then hath the Jew? or what profit *is* *4053*
2Co 2:11 Lest Satan should **get an a** of us: for we are *4122*
Jude 1:16 *men's* persons in admiration because of **a**. *5622*

ADVANTAGED (1) [ADVANTAGE]
Lk 9:25 For what is a man **a**, if he gain the whole *5623*

ADVANTAGETH (1) [ADVANTAGE]
1Co 15:32 what **a** it me, if the dead rise not? *3786*

ADVENTURE (2) [ADVENTURED]
Dt 28:56 which would not **a** to set the sole of her 5254
Ac 19:31 desiring *him* that *he* would not **a** himself *1325*

ADVENTURED (1) [ADVENTURE]
Jdg 9:17 **a** his life far, and delivered you out of 7993

ADVERSARIES (36) [ADVERSARY]
Ex 23:22 and an adversary unto thine **a**. 6887
Dt 32:27 lest their **a** should behave themselves 6862
32:43 will render vengeance to his **a**, and will be 6862
Jos 5:13 said unto him, *Art* thou for us, or for our **a**? 6862
1Sa 2:10 The **a** of the LORD shall be broken to 7378
2Sa 19:22 that ye should *this* day be **a** unto me? 7854
Ezr 4: 1 Now *when* the **a** of Judah and 6862
Ne 4:11 our **a** said, They shall not know, 6862
Ps 38:20 also that render evil for good are mine **a**; 7853
69:19 my dishonour: mine **a** *are* all before thee. 6887
71:13 *and* consumed that are **a** to my soul; 7853
81:14 and turned my hand against their **a**. 6862
89:42 Thou hast set up the right hand of his **a**; 6862
109: 4 For my love they are my **a**: but I *give* 7853
109:20 *Let* this *be* the reward of mine **a** from 7853
109:29 Let mine **a** be clothed with shame, and 7853
Isa 1:24 I will ease me of mine **a**, and avenge me of 6862
9:11 Therefore the LORD shall set up the **a** of 6862
11:13 and the **a** of Judah shall be cut off: 6887
59:18 accordingly he will repay, fury to his **a**, 6862
63:18 our **a** have trodden down thy sanctuary. 6862
64: 2 to boil, to make thy name known to thine **a**, 6862

A

Jer 30:16 all thine **a**, every one of them, shall go into 6862
46:10 that *he* may avenge him of his **a**: 6862
50: 7 their **a** said, We offend not, because they 6862
La 1: 5 Her **a** are the chief, her enemies prosper; 6862
1: 7 the **a** saw her, *and* did mock at her 6862
1:17 *that* his **a** *should be* round about him: 6862
2:17 he hath set up the horn of thine **a**. 6862
Mic 5: 9 Thine hand shall be lift up upon thine **a**, 6862
Na 1: 2 the LORD will take vengeance on his **a**, 6862
Lk 13:17 And when he had said these *things*, all his **a** *480*
21:15 which all your **a** shall not be able to gainsay *480*
1Co 16: 9 is opened unto me, and *there are* many **a**. *480*
Php 1:28 And in nothing terrified by *your* **a**: which is *480*
Heb 10:27 fiery indignation, which shall devour the **a**. *5227*

ADVERSARY (22) [ADVERSARIES]

Ex 23:22 and an **a** unto thine adversaries. 6696
Nu 22:22 stood in the way for an **a** against him. 7854
1Sa 1: 6 her **a** also provoked her sore, for to make 6869
29: 4 to battle, lest in the battle he be an **a** to us: 7854
1Ki 5: 4 *so that there is* neither **a** nor evil occurrent. 7854
11:14 the LORD stirred up an **a** unto Solomon, 7854
11:23 God stirred him up *another* **a**, Rezon 7854
11:25 he was an **a** to Israel all the days of 7854
Est 7: 6 **a** and enemy *is* this wicked Haman. 376+6862
Job 31:35 and *that* mine **a** had written a book. 376+7379
Ps 74:10 O God, how long shall the **a** reproach? 6862
Isa 50: 8 *is* mine **a**? let him come near to me. 1167+4941
La 1:10 The **a** hath spread out his hand upon all her 6862
2: 4 *he* stood *with* his right hand as an **a**, and 6862
4:12 would not have believed that the **a** and 6862
Am 3:11 An **a** *there shall be* even round about 6862
Mt 5:25 Agree with thine **a** quickly, whiles thou art *476*
5:25 lest at any time the **a** deliver thee to *476*
Lk 12:58 When thou goest with thine **a** to *476*
18: 3 unto him, saying, Avenge me of mine **a**. *476*
1Ti 5:14 give none occasion to the **a** to speak *480*
1Pe 5: 8 because your **a** the devil, as a roaring lion, *476*

ADVERSITIES (2) [ADVERSITY]

1Sa 10:19 who himself saved you out of all your **a** 7451
Ps 31: 7 my trouble; thou hast known my soul in **a**; 6869

ADVERSITY (10) [ADVERSITIES]

2Sa 4: 9 who hath redeemed my soul out of all **a**, 6869
2Ch 15: 6 of city: for God did vex them with all **a**. 6869
Ps 10: 6 not be moved: for *I shall* never *be* in **a**. 7451
35:15 in mine **a** they rejoiced, and 6761
94:13 mayest give him rest from the days of **a**, 7451
Pr 17:17 at all times, and a brother is born for **a**. 6869
24:10 *If* thou faint in the day of **a**, thy strength *is* 6869
Ecc 7:14 be joyful, but in the day of **a** consider: 7451
Isa 30:20 *though* the Lord give you the bread of **a**, 6862
Heb 13: 3 bound with *them; and* them which **suffer a**, *2558*

ADVERTISE (2)

Nu 24:14 I will **a** thee what this people shall do to thy 3289
Ru 4: 4 I thought to **a** thee, saying, Buy *it* 241+1540

ADVICE (9) [ADVISE]

Jdg 19:30 of it, **take a**, and speak *your minds.* 5779
20: 7 of Israel; give here your **a** and counsel. 1697
1Sa 25:33 blessed *be* thy **a**, and blessed *be* thou, 2940
2Sa 19:43 that our **a** should not be first had in 1697
2Ch 10: 9 What **a give** ye that we may return answer 3289
10:14 answered them after the **a** of the young 6098
25:17 Amaziah king of Judah **took a**, and sent to 3289
Pr 20:18 by counsel: and with **good a** make war. 8458
2Co 8:10 And herein I give *my* **a**: for this is *1106*

ADVISE (3) [ADVICE, ADVISED, ADVISEMENT]

2Sa 24:13 now **a**, and see what answer I shall return 3045
1Ki 12: 6 How do you **a** that *I* may answer this 3289
1Ch 21:12 **a** thyself what word I shall bring again to 7200

ADVISED (2) [ADVISE]

Pr 13:10 but with the **well a** *is* wisdom. 3289
Ac 27:12 the more part **a** to depart thence also, *1012+5087*

ADVISEMENT (1) [ADVISE]

1Ch 12:19 for the lords of the Philistines upon **a** sent 6098

ADVOCATE (1)

1Jn 2: 1 any *man* sin, we have an **a** with the Father, *3875*

AENEAS (2)

Ac 9:33 And there he found a certain man named **A**, *132*
9:34 And Peter said unto him, **A**, Jesus Christ *132*

AENON (1)

Jn 3:23 And John also was baptizing in **A** near to *137*

AFAR (51) [FAR]

Ge 22: 4 up his eyes, and saw the place **a off**. 4480+7350
37:18 when they saw him **a off**, even 4480+7350
Ex 2: 4 his sister stood **a off**, to wit what 4480+7350
20:18 *it,* they removed, and stood **a off**. 4480+7350
20:21 the people stood **a off**, and 4480+7350
24: 1 elders of Israel; and worship ye **a off**. 4480+7350
33: 7 **a off** from the camp, and called it 7368
Nu 9:10 or *be* in a journey **a off**, yet he shall keep 7350
1Sa 26:13 and stood on the top of a hill **a off**; 4480+7350
2Ki 2: 7 and stood to view **a off**: 4480+7350
4:25 when the man of God saw her **a off**, 4480+5048
Ezr 3:13 noise was heard **a off**. 4480+5704+7350+3807.1
Ne 12:43 of Jerusalem was heard **even a off**. 4480+7350
Job 2:12 when they lift up their eyes **a off**, 4480+7350
36: 3 I will fetch my knowledge from **a**, and 7350
36:25 may see it; man may behold *it* **a off**. 4480+7350
39:25 he smelleth the battle **a off**, 4480+7350
39:29 the prey, *and* her eyes behold **a off**. 4480+7350
Ps 10: 1 Why standest thou **a off**, O LORD? 7350+871.1
38:11 and my kinsmen stand **a off**. 4480+7350
65: 5 and of them that are **a off** *upon* the sea: 7350
138: 6 but the proud he knoweth **a off**. 4480+4801
139: 2 thou understandest my thought **a off**. 4480+7350
Pr 31:14 she bringeth her food from **a**. 4801
Isa 23: 7 her own feet shall carry her **a off** to 4480+7350
49: 1 unto me; and hearken, ye people, from **a**; 7350
59:14 and justice standeth **a off**: 4480+7350
66:19 *to* Tubal, and Javan, *to* the isles **a off**, 7350
Jer 23:23 the LORD, and not a God **a off**? 4480+7350
30:10 I *will* save thee from **a**, and thy seed from 7350
31:10 declare *it* in the isles **a off**, and say, 4480+4801
46:27 I *will* save thee from **a off**, and thy seed 7350
51:50 remember the LORD **a off**, and 4480+7350
Mic 4: 3 and rebuke strong nations **a off**; 5704+7350
Mt 26:58 But Peter followed him **a** off unto the high *3113*
27:55 And many women were there beholding **a** *3113*
Mk 5: 6 But when he saw Jesus **a off**, he ran and *3113*
11:13 And seeing a fig tree **a off** having leaves, *3113*
14:54 And Peter followed him **a** off, even into *3113*
15:40 There were also women looking on **a** off: *3113*
Lk 16:23 and seeth Abraham **a off**, and *575+3113*
17:12 ten men *that were* lepers, which stood **a off**: *4207*
18:13 standing **a off**, would not lift up so much as *3113*
22:54 priest's house. And Peter followed **a off**. *3113*
23:49 stood **a off**, beholding these *things.* *575+3113*
Ac 2:39 and to all that are **a off**, *1519+3112*
Eph 2:17 preached peace to you which were **a off**, *3112*
Heb 11:13 but having seen them **a off**, and *4207*
Rev 18:10 Standing **a off** for the fear of her *575+3113*
18:15 shall stand **a off** for the fear of her *575+3113*
18:17 as many as trade by sea, stood **a off**, *575+3113*

AFFAIRS (8)

1Ch 26:32 matter pertaining to God, and **a** of the king. 1697
Ps 112: 5 lendeth: he will guide his **a** with discretion. 1697
Da 2:49 over the **a** of the province of Babylon: 5673
3:12 set over the **a** of the province of Babylon, 5673
Eph 6:21 But that ye also may know my **a**, *and* *2596+3588*
6:22 that ye might know our **a**, and *that* he *3588+4012*
Php 1:27 or *else* be absent, I may hear of your **a**, *4012*
2Ti 2: 4 entangleth himself with the **a** of *this* life; *4230*

AFFECT (2) [AFFECTED, AFFECTETH]

Gal 4:17 They **zealously a** you, *but* not well; yea, *2206*
4:17 would exclude you, that you might **a** them. *2206*

AFFECTED (2) [AFFECT]

Ac 14: 2 **made** their minds **evil a** against *2559*
Gal 4:18 But *it is* good to be **zealously a** always in a *2206*

AFFECTETH (1) [AFFECT]

La 3:51 Mine eye **a** mine heart because of all 5953

AFFECTION (6) [AFFECTIONATELY, AFFECTIONED, AFFECTIONS]

1Ch 29: 3 I have **set** my **a** to the house of my God, 7521
Ro 1:31 **without natural a**, implacable, unmerciful: *794*
2Co 7:15 And his **inward a** is more abundant toward *4698*
Col 3: 2 **Set** your **a on** *things* above, not on *things* *5426*
3: 5 fornication, uncleanness, **inordinate a**, *3806*
2Ti 3: 3 **Without natural a**, trucebreakers, *794*

AFFECTIONATELY (1) [AFFECTION]

1Th 2: 8 So being **a desirous** of you, we were *2442*

AFFECTIONED (1) [AFFECTION]

Ro 12:10 *Be* **kindly a** one to another with brotherly *5387*

AFFECTIONS (2) [AFFECTION]

Ro 1:26 this cause God gave them up unto vile **a**: *3806*
Gal 5:24 Christ's have crucified the flesh with the **a** *3804*

AFFINITY (3)

1Ki 3: 1 Solomon **made a** with Pharaoh king of 2859
2Ch 18: 1 in abundance, and **joined a** with Ahab. 2859
Ezr 9:14 **join in a** with the people of these 2859

AFFIRM (3) [AFFIRMED]

Ro 3: 8 and as some **a** that we say,) *5346*
1Ti 1: 7 neither what they say, nor whereof they **a**. *1226*
Tit 3: 8 these *things* I will that thou **a constantly**, *1226*

AFFIRMED (3) [AFFIRM]

Lk 22:59 of one hour after another **confidently a**, *1340*
Ac 12:15 But she **constantly a** that it was *even* so. *1340*
25:19 *which was* dead, whom Paul **a** to be alive. *5335*

AFFLICT (36) [AFFLICTED, AFFLICTEST, AFFLICTION, AFFLICTIONS]

Ge 15:13 and they shall **a** them four hundred years; 6031
31:50 If thou shalt **a** my daughters, or if thou 6031
Ex 1:11 taskmasters to **a** them with their burdens. 6031
22:22 Ye shall not **a** any widow, or 6031
22:23 If thou **a** them **in any wise**, and they 6031+6031
Lev 16:29 ye shall **a** your souls, and do no work *at all,* 6031
16:31 ye shall **a** your souls, *by a* statute for ever. 6031
23:27 ye shall **a** your souls, and offer an offering 6031
23:32 a sabbath of rest, and ye shall **a** your souls: 6031
Nu 24:24 shall **a** Asshur, and shall afflict Eber, and 6031
24:24 shall **a** Eber, and he also shall perish for 6031
29: 7 and ye shall **a** your souls: 6031
30:13 and every binding oath to **a** the soul, 6031
Jdg 16: 5 that we may bind him to **a** him: 6031
16: 6 wherewith thou mightest be bound to **a** 6031
16:19 she began to **a** him, and his strength went 6031
2Sa 7:10 neither shall the children of wickedness **a** 6031
1Ki 11:39 I will for this **a** the seed of David, but 6031
2Ch 6:26 turn from their sin, when thou dost **a** them; 6031
Ezr 8:21 that we might **a** ourselves before our God, 6031
Job 37:23 and *in* plenty of justice: he will not **a**. 6031
Ps 44: 2 *how* thou didst **a** the people, and cast them 7489
55:19 God shall hear, and **a** them, even he that 6031
89:22 upon him; nor the son of wickedness **a** him. 6031
94: 5 thy people, O LORD, and **a** thine heritage. 6031
143:12 and destroy all them that **a** my soul: 6887
Isa 9: 1 afterward did **more grievously a** *her by* 3513
51:23 I will put it into the hand of them that **a** 3013
58: 5 a day for a man to **a** his soul? *is it* to bow 6031
64:12 thou hold thy peace, and **a** us very sore? 6031
Jer 31:28 to throw down, and to destroy, and to **a**; 7489
La 3:33 For he doth not **a** willingly nor grieve 6031
Am 5:12 they **a** the just, they take a bribe, and 6887
6:14 they shall **a** you from the entering in of 3905
Na 1:12 I have afflicted thee, I will **a** thee no more. 6031
Zep 3:19 at that time I *will* undo all that **a** thee: 6031

AFFLICTED (55) [AFFLICT]

Ex 1:12 the more they **a** them, the more they 6031
Lev 23:29 For whatsoever soul *it be* that shall not be **a** 6031
Nu 11:11 Wherefore hast thou **a** thy servant? 7489
Dt 26: 6 and **a** us, and laid upon us hard bondage: 6031
Ru 1:21 against me, and the Almighty hath **a** me? 7489
2Sa 22:28 the **a** people thou wilt save: but thine eyes 6041
1Ki 2:26 thou hast been **a** in all where*in* my father 6031
2:26 afflicted in all where*in* my father was **a**. 6031
2Ki 17:20 **a** them, and delivered them into the hand of 6031
Job 6:14 To him that is **a** pity *should be shewed* 4523
30:11 Because he hath loosed my cord, and **a** me, 6031
34:28 unto him, and he heareth the cry of the **a**. 6041
Ps 18:27 For thou wilt save the **a** people; but 6041
22:24 nor abhorred the affliction of the **a**; 6041
25:16 mercy upon me; for I *am* desolate and **a**. 6041
82: 3 fatherless: do justice to the **a** and needy. 6041
88: 7 and thou hast **a** *me with* all thy waves. 6031
88:15 I *am* **a** and ready to die from *my* youth *up:* 6041
90:15 to the days *wherein* thou hast **a** us, 6031
102: T A Prayer of the **a**, when he is 6041
107:17 because of their iniquities, are **a**. 6031
116:10 therefore have I spoken: I was greatly **a**: 6031
119:67 Before I was **a** I went astray: but now have 6031
119:71 *It is* good for me that I have been **a**; that I 6031
119:75 and *that* thou *in* faithfulness hast **a** me. 6031
119:107 I am **a** very much: quicken me, O LORD, 6031
129: 1 Many a time have they **a** me from my 6887
129: 2 Many a time have they **a** me from my 6887
140:12 LORD will maintain the cause of the **a**, 6041
Pr 15:15 All the days of the **a** *are* evil: but *he that is* 6041
22:22 he *is* poor: neither oppress the **a** in the gate: 6041
26:28 A lying tongue hateth *those that are* **a** by it; 1790
31: 5 pervert the judgment of any of the **a**. 1121+6040
Isa 9: 1 when at the first he **lightly a** the land of 7043
49:13 his people, and will have mercy upon his **a**. 6041
51:21 thou **a**, and drunken, but not with wine: 6041
53: 4 esteem him stricken, smitten of God, and **a**. 6031
53: 7 He was oppressed, and he was **a**, yet he 6031
54:11 O thou **a**, tossed with tempest, *and* 6041
58: 3 *wherefore* have we **a** our soul, and 6031
58:10 soul to the hungry, and satisfy the **a** soul; 6031
60:14 The sons also of them that **a** thee shall 6031
63: 9 In all their affliction he was **a**, and 6862
La 1: 4 her virgins *are* **a**, and she *is* in bitterness. 3013
1: 5 for the LORD hath **a** her for the multitude 3013
1:12 wherewith the LORD hath **a** *me* in the day 3013
Mic 4: 6 her that is driven out, and *her* that I have **a**; 7489
Na 1:12 Though I have **a** thee, I will afflict thee no 6031
Zep 3:12 I will also leave in the midst of thee an **a** 6041
Mt 24: 9 Then shall they deliver you up to be **a**, and *2347*
2Co 1: 6 And whether we be **a**, *it is* for your *2346*
1Ti 5:10 the saints' feet, if she have relieved the **a**, *2346*
Heb 11:37 being destitute, **a**, tormented; *2346*
Jas 4: 9 Be **a**, and mourn, and weep: let your *5003*
5:13 Is any among you **a**? let him pray. Is any *2553*

AFFLICTEST (1) [AFFLICT]

1Ki 8:35 and turn from their sin, when thou **a** them: 6031

AFFLICTION (75) [AFFLICT]

Ge 16:11 because the LORD hath heard thy **a**. 6040
29:32 Surely the LORD hath looked upon my **a**; 6040
31:42 God hath seen mine **a** and the labour of my 6040
41:52 caused me to be fruitful in the land of my **a**. 6040
Ex 3: 7 I have surely seen the **a** of my people 6040
3:17 I will bring you up out of the **a** of Egypt 6040
4:31 that he had looked upon their **a**, then 6040
Dt 16: 3 bread therewith, *even* the bread of **a**; 6040
26: 7 looked on our **a**, and our labour, and 6040
1Sa 1:11 if thou wilt indeed look on the **a** of thine 6040
2Sa 16:12 be that the LORD will look on mine **a**, 5771
1Ki 22:27 feed him with bread of **a** and with water of 3906
22:27 with bread of affliction and with water of **a**, 3906
2Ki 14:26 For the LORD saw the **a** of Israel, *that it* 6040
2Ch 18:26 feed him with bread of **a** and with water of 3906
18:26 with bread of affliction and with water of **a**, 3906
20: 9 cry unto thee in our **a**, then thou wilt hear 6869
33:12 when he was in **a**, he besought the LORD 6887
Ne 1: 3 captivity there in the province *are* in great **a** 7451
9: 9 didst see the **a** of our fathers in Egypt, and 6040
Job 5: 6 Although **a** cometh not forth of the dust, 205
10:15 of confusion; therefore see thou mine **a**; 6040
30:16 the days of **a** have taken hold upon me. 6040
30:27 and rested not: the days of **a** prevented me. 6040
36: 8 in fetters, *and* be holden in cords of **a**; 6040
36:15 He delivereth the poor in his **a**, and 6040
36:21 for this hast thou chosen rather than **a**. 6040
Ps 22:24 For he hath not despised nor abhorred the **a** 6039
25:18 Look upon mine **a** and my pain; and 6040
44:24 *and* forgettest our **a** and our oppression? 6040
66:11 us into the net; thou laidst **a** upon our loins. 4157
88: 9 Mine eye mourneth by reason of **a**: 6040
106:44 Nevertheless he regarded their **a**, when he 6862
107:10 of death, *being* bound in **a** and iron; 6040
107:39 low through oppression, **a**, and sorrow. 7451
107:41 Yet setteth he the poor on high from **a**, and 6040
119:50 This *is* my comfort in my **a**: for thy word 6040
119:92 I should then have perished in mine **a**. 6040
119:153 Consider mine **a**, and deliver me: for I do 6040
Isa 30:20 the bread of adversity, and the water of **a**, 3906

Isa 48:10 I have chosen thee in the furnace of **a**. 6040
63: 9 In all their **a** he was afflicted, and the angel 6869
Jer 4:15 and publisheth **a** from mount Ephraim. 205
15:11 in the time of evil, and in the time of **a**. 6869
16:19 my fortress, and my refuge in the day of **a**, 6869
30:15 Why criest thou for thine **a**? thy sorrow *is* 7667
48:16 *is* near to come, and his **a** hasteth fast. 7451
La 1: 3 Judah is gone into captivity because of **a**, 6040
1: 7 Jerusalem remembered in the days of her **a** 6040
1: 9 O LORD, behold my **a**: for the enemy 6040
3: 1 I *am* the man *that* hath seen **a** by the rod of 6040
3:19 Remembering mine **a** and my misery, 6040
Hos 5:15 my face: in their **a** they will seek me early. 6862
Am 6: 6 but they are not grieved for the **a** of Joseph. 7667
Ob 1:13 thou shouldest not have looked on their **a** in 7451
Jnh 2: 2 I cried by reason of mine **a** unto 6869
Na 1: 9 **a** shall not rise up the second time. 6869
Hab 3: 7 I saw the tents of Cushan in **a**: *and* 205
Zec 1:15 and they helped forward the **a**. 7451
8:10 that went out or came in because of the **a**: 6862
10:11 he shall pass through the sea *with* **a**, and 6869
Mk 4:17 when **a** or persecution ariseth for *2347*
13:19 For *in* those days shall be **a**, such as was *2347*
Ac 7:11 the land of Egypt and Canaan, and great **a**: *2347*
7:34 I have seen the **a** of my people which is in *2561*
2Co 2: 4 For out of much **a** and anguish of heart I *2347*
4:17 For our light **a**, which is but for a moment, *2347*
8: 2 How that in a great trial of **a** the abundance *2347*
Php 1:16 supposing to add **a** to my bonds: *2347*
4:14 that ye did communicate with my **a**. *2347*
1Th 1: 6 having received the word in much **a**, *2347*
3: 7 we were comforted over you in all our **a** *2347*
Heb 11:25 Choosing rather to **suffer a with** the people *4778*
Jas 1:27 visit the fatherless and widows in their **a**, *2347*
5:10 for an example of **suffering a**, and *2552*

AFFLICTIONS (13) [AFFLICT]
Ps 34:19 Many *are* the **a** of the righteous: but 7451
132: 1 LORD, remember David, *and* all his **a**: 6031
Ac 7:10 And delivered him out of all his **a**, and *2347*
20:23 saying that bonds and **a** abide me. *2347*
2Co 6: 4 in **a**, in necessities, in distresses, *2347*
Col 1:24 fill up that which is behind of the **a** of *2347*
1Th 3: 3 That no *man* should be moved by these **a**: *2347*
2Ti 1: 8 be thou **partaker of** the **a** of the gospel *4777*
3:11 Persecutions, **a**, which came unto me at *3804*
4: 5 But watch thou in all *things*, **endure a**, *2553*
Heb 10:32 ye endured a great fight of **a**; *3804*
10:33 a gazingstock both by reproaches and **a**; *2347*
1Pe 5: 9 knowing that the same **a** are accomplished *3804*

AFFORDING (1)
Ps 144:13 garners *may be* full, **a** all manner of store: 6329

AFFRIGHT (1) [AFFRIGHTED]
2Ch 32:18 on the wall, to **a** them, and to trouble them; 3372

AFFRIGHTED (9) [AFFRIGHT]
Dt 7:21 Thou shalt not be **a** at them: for the LORD 6206
Job 18:20 as they that went before were **a**. 270+8178
39:22 He mocketh at fear, and is not **a**; 2865
Isa 21: 4 My heart panted, fearfulness **a** me: 1204
Jer 51:32 burnt with fire, and the men of war are **a**. 926
Mk 16: 5 in a long white garment; and they were **a**. *1568*
16: 6 And he saith unto them, Be not **a**: Ye seek *1568*
Lk 24:37 But they were terrified and **a**, and *1719*
Rev 11:13 and the remnant were **a**, and gave glory to *1719*

AFOOT (2) [FOOT]
Mk 6:33 and ran **a** thither out of all cities, and *3979*
Ac 20:13 had he appointed, minding himself to **go a**. *3978*

AFORE (7) [AFOREHAND, AFORETIME]
2Ki 20: 4 **a** Isaiah was gone out *into* the middle court, 3808
Ps 129: 6 which withereth **a** it groweth up: 6927
Isa 18: 5 For **a** the harvest, when the bud is 6440+3807.1
Eze 33:22 was upon me in the evening, **a** 6440+3807.1
Ro 1: 2 (Which he had **promised a** by his prophets *4279*
9:23 which he had **a prepared** unto glory, *4282*
Eph 3: 3 the mystery; (as I **wrote a** in few *words*, *4270*

AFOREHAND (1) [AFORE]
Mk 14: 8 she is **come a** to anoint my body to *4301*

AFORETIME (7) [AFORE]
Ne 13: 5 where **a** they laid the meat 6440+3807.1
Job 17: 6 the people; and **a** I was *as* a tabret. 6440+3807.1
Isa 52: 4 My people went down **a** 7223+871.1+1886.1
Jer 30:20 Their children also shall be as **a**, and 6924
Da 6:10 before his God, as he did **a**. 1836+4481+6928
Jn 9:13 They brought to the Pharisees him that **a** *4218*
Ro 15: 4 For whatsoever *things* were **written a** were *4270*

AFRAID (193) [FEAR]
Ge 3:10 and I was **a**, because I *was* naked; 3372
18:15 saying, I laughed not; for she was **a**. 3372
20: 8 in their ears: and the men were sore **a**. 3372
28:17 he was **a**, and said, How dreadful *is* this 3372
31:31 and said to Laban, Because I was **a**: 3372
32: 7 Jacob was greatly **a** and distressed: and 3372
42:28 their heart failed *them*, and they were **a**, 2729
42:35 saw the bundles of money, they were **a**. 3372
43:18 the men were **a**, because they were brought 3372
Ex 3: 6 hid his face; for he was **a** to look upon God. 3372
14:10 marched after them; and they were sore **a**: 3372
15:14 The people shall hear, *and* be **a**: 7264
34:30 and they were **a** to come nigh him. 3372
Lev 26: 6 shall lie down, and none shall **make** *you* **a**: 2729
Nu 12: 8 were ye not **a** to speak against my servant 3372
22: 3 Moab was sore **a** of the people, because 1481
Dt 1:17 you shall not be **a** of the face of man; 1481
1:29 unto you, Dread not, neither be **a** of them. 3372
2: 4 dwell in Seir; and they shall be **a** of you: 3372
5: 5 for ye were **a** by reason of the fire, and 3372
Dt 7:18 Thou shalt not be **a** of them: *but* shalt well 3372
7:19 do unto all the people of whom thou *art* **a**. 3373
9:19 For I was **a** of the anger and 3025
18:22 thou shalt not be **a** of him. 1481
20: 1 a people more than thou, be not **a** of them: 3372
28:10 of the LORD; and they shall be **a** of thee. 3372
28:60 diseases of Egypt, which thou wast **a** of; 3025
31: 6 a good courage, fear not, nor be **a** of them: 6206
Jos 1: 9 be not **a**, neither be thou dismayed: 6206
9:24 we were sore **a** of our lives because of you, 3372
11: 6 said unto Joshua, Be not **a** because of them: 3372
Jdg 7: 3 saying, Whosoever *is* fearful and **a**, let him 2730
Ru 3: 8 that the man was **a**, and turned himself: 2729
1Sa 4: 7 the Philistines were **a**, for they said, God is 3372
7: 7 heard *it*, they were **a** of the Philistines. 3372
17:11 they were dismayed, and greatly **a**. 3372
17:24 the man, fled from him, and were sore **a**. 3372
18:12 Saul was **a** of David, because the LORD 3372
18:15 himself very wisely, he was **a** of him. 1481
18:29 Saul was yet the more **a** of David; and 3372
21: 1 Ahimelech was **a** at the meeting of David, 2729
21:12 and was sore **a** of Achish the king of Gath. 3372
23: 3 unto him, Behold, we *be* **a** here in Judah: 3373
28: 5 he was **a**, and his heart greatly trembled. 3372
28:13 the king said unto her, Be not **a**: for what 3372
28:20 was sore **a**, because of the words of 3372
31: 4 armourbearer would not; for he was sore **a**: 3372
2Sa 1:14 How wast thou not **a** to stretch forth thine 3372
6: 9 David was **a** of the LORD that day, 3372
14:15 *it is* because the people have **made** me **a**: 3372
17: 2 and weak handed, and will **make** him **a**: 2729
22: 5 the floods of ungodly men **made** me **a**; 1204
22:46 and they shall be **a** out of their close places. 2296
1Ki 1:49 the guests that *were* with Adonijah were **a**, 2729
2Ki 1:15 be not **a** of him. And he arose, and 3372
10: 4 they were exceedingly **a**, and said, Behold, 3372
19: 6 Be not **a** of the words which thou hast 3372
25:26 *to* Egypt: for they were **a** of the Chaldees. 3372
1Ch 10: 4 armourbearer would not; for he was sore **a**. 3372
13:12 David was **a** of God that day, saying, 3372
21:30 for he was **a** because of the sword of 1204
2Ch 20:15 Be not **a** nor dismayed by reason of this 3372
32: 7 be not **a** nor dismayed for the king of 3372
Ne 2: 2 but sorrow of heart. Then I was very sore **a**, 3372
4:14 the rest of the people, Be not ye **a** of them: 3372
6: 9 For they all **made** us **a**, saying, Their hands 3372
6:13 that I should be **a**, and do so, and sin, and 3372
Est 7: 6 Haman was **a** before the king and 1204
Job 3:25 and *that* which I was **a** of is come unto me. 3025
5:21 neither shalt thou be **a** of destruction when 3372
5:22 neither shalt thou be **a** of the beasts of 3372
6:21 ye see *my* casting down, and are **a**. 3372
9:28 I am **a** of all my sorrows, I know that thou 3025
11:19 shalt lie down, and none shall **make** *thee* **a**; 2729
13:11 Shall not his excellency **make** you **a**? 1204
13:21 from me: and let not thy dread **make** me **a**. 1204
15:24 Trouble and anguish shall **make** him **a**; 1204
18:11 Terrors shall **make** him **a** on every side, 1204
19:29 Be ye **a** of the sword: for wrath *bringeth* 1481
21: 6 Even when I remember I am **a**, and 926
23:15 when I consider, I am **a** of him. 6342
32: 6 wherefore I was **a**, and durst not shew you 2119
33: 7 Behold, my terror shall not **make** thee **a**, 1204
39:20 Canst thou **make** him **a** as a grasshopper? 7493
41:25 he raiseth up *himself*, the mighty are **a**: 1481
Ps 3: 6 I will not be **a** of ten thousands of people, 3372
18: 4 and the floods of ungodly men **made** me **a**. 1204
18:45 and be **a** out of their close places. 2727
27: 1 strength of my life; of whom shall I be **a**? 6342
49:16 Be not thou **a** when one is made rich, 3372
56: 3 *What* time I am **a**, I will trust in thee. 3372
56:11 I will not be **a** what man can do unto me. 3372
65: 8 in the uttermost parts are **a** at thy tokens: 3372
77:16 O God, the waters saw thee; they were **a**: 2342
83:15 and **make** them **a** with thy storm. 926
91: 5 Thou shalt not be **a** for the terror by night; 3372
112: 7 He shall not be **a** of evil tidings: his heart is 3372
112: 8 His heart *is* established, he shall not be **a**, 3372
119:120 fear of thee; and I am **a** of thy judgments. 3372
Pr 3:24 When thou liest down, thou shalt not be **a**: 6342
3:25 Be not **a** of sudden fear, neither of 3372
31:21 She is not **a** of the snow for her household: 3372
Ecc 12: 5 Also *when* they shall be **a** of *that which is* 3372
Isa 8:12 neither fear ye their fear, nor be **a**. 6206
10:24 dwellest in Zion, be not **a** of the Assyrian: 3372
10:29 Ramah is **a**; Gibeah of Saul is fled. 2729
12: 2 *is* my salvation; I will trust, and not be **a**: 6342
13: 8 they shall be **a**: pangs and sorrows shall take 926
17: 2 lie down, and none shall **make** *them* **a**. 2729
19:16 it shall be **a** and fear because of the shaking 2729
19:17 mention thereof shall be **a** in himself, 6342
20: 5 they shall be **a** and ashamed of Ethiopia 2865
31: 4 he will not be **a** of their voice, nor abase 2865
31: 9 his princes shall be **a** of the ensign, 2865
33:14 The sinners in Zion are **a**; fearfulness hath 6342
37: 6 Be not **a** of the words that thou hast heard, 3372
40: 9 lift *it* up, be not **a**; say unto the cities of 3372
41: 5 the ends of the earth were **a**, drew near, and 2729
44: 8 Fear ye not, neither be **a**: have not I told 7297
51: 7 of men, neither be ye **a** of their revilings. 2865
51:12 that thou shouldest be **a** of a man *that* shall 3372
57:11 of whom hast thou been **a** or feared, 1672
Jer 1: 8 Be not **a** of their faces: for I *am* with thee to 3372
2:12 O ye heavens, at this, and be **horribly a**, 8175
10: 5 Be not **a** of them; for they cannot do evil, 3372
26:21 when Urijah heard *it*, he was **a**, and fled, 3372
30:10 and be quiet, and none shall **make** *him* **a**. 2729
36:16 they were **a** both one and other, and 6342
36:24 Yet they were not **a**, nor rent their 6342
38:19 I am **a** of the Jews that are fallen to 1672
39:17 the hand of the men of whom thou *art* **a**. 3016
41:18 for they were **a** of them, because 3372
42:11 Be not **a** of the king of Babylon, of whom 3372
42:11 of the king of Babylon, of whom ye *are* **a**; 3373
42:11 be not **a** of him, saith the LORD: 3372
Jer 42:16 the famine, whereof ye were **a**, shall follow 1672
46:27 and at ease, and none shall **make** *him* **a**. 2729
Eze 2: 6 thou, son of man, be not **a** of them, 3372
2: 6 neither be **a** of their words, though briers 3372
2: 6 be not **a** of their words, nor be dismayed at 3372
27:35 their kings shall be **sore a**, they shall 8175+8178
30: 9 in ships to **make** the careless Ethiopians **a**, 2729
32:10 and their kings shall be horribly **a** for thee, 8175
34:28 dwell safely, and none shall **make** *them* **a**. 2729
39:26 safely in their land, and none **made** *them* **a**. 2729
Da 4: 5 I saw a dream which **made** me **a**, and 1763
8:17 he came, I was **a**, and fell upon my face: 1204
Joel 2:22 Be not **a**, ye beasts of the field: for 3372
Am 3: 6 blown in the city, and the people not be **a**? 2729
Jnh 1: 5 the mariners were **a**, and cried every man 3372
1:10 were the men **exceedingly a**, 1419+3372+3374
Mic 4: 4 his fig tree; and none shall **make** *them* **a**: 2729
7:17 they shall be **a** of the LORD our God, and 6342
Na 2:11 the lion's whelp, and none **made** *them* **a**? 2729
Hab 2:17 *which* **made** them **a**, because of men's 2865
3: 2 I have heard thy speech, *and* was **a**: 3372
Zep 3:13 and lie down, and none shall **make** *them* **a**. 2729
Mal 2: 5 he feared me, and was **a** before my name. 2865
Mt 2:22 of his father Herod, he was **a** to go thither: *5399*
14:27 saying, Be of good cheer; it is I, be not **a**. *5399*
14:30 he saw the wind boisterous, he was **a**; *5399*
17: 6 *it*, they fell on their face, and were sore **a**. *5399*
17: 7 touched them, and said, Arise, and be not **a**. *5399*
25:25 And I was **a**, and went and hid thy talent in *5399*
28:10 Then said Jesus unto them, Be not **a**: go tell *5399*
Mk 5:15 and in his right mind: and they were **a**. *5399*
5:36 of the synagogue, Be not **a**, only believe. *5399*
6:50 Be of good cheer: it is I; be not **a**. *5399*
9: 6 wist not what to say; for they were **sore a**. *1630*
9:32 not *that* saying, and were **a** to ask him. *5399*
10:32 and as they followed, they were **a**. *5399*
16: 8 they any *thing* to any *man*; for they were **a**. *5399*
Lk 2: 9 about them: and they were sore **a**. *5399+5401*
8:25 And they being **a** wondered, saying one to *5399*
8:35 and in his right mind: and they were **a**. *5399*
12: 4 Be not **a** of them that kill the body, and *5399*
24: 5 And as they were **a**, and bowed down *their* *1719*
Jn 6:19 nigh unto the ship: and they were **a**. *5399*
6:20 But he saith unto them, It is I; be not **a**. *5399*
14:27 your heart be troubled, neither let it be **a**. *1168*
19: 8 heard that saying, he was the more **a**; *5399*
Ac 9:26 but they were all **a** of him, and believed not *5399*
10: 4 he was **a**, and said, What is it, Lord? *1719*
18: 9 Be not **a**, but speak, and hold not thy peace: *5399*
22: 9 with me saw indeed the light, and were **a**; *1719*
22:29 and the chief captain also was **a**, after he *5399*
Ro 13: 3 Wilt thou then not be **a** of the power? *5399*
13: 4 But if thou do *that which is* evil, be **a**; *5399*
Gal 4:11 I am **a** of you, lest I have bestowed upon *5399*
Heb 11:23 they were not **a** of the king's *5399*
1Pe 3: 6 do well, and are not **a** with any amazement. *5399*
3:14 happy *are ye*: and be not **a** of their terror, *5399*
2Pe 2:10 they are not **a** to speak evil of dignities. *5141*

AFRESH (1) [FRESH]
Heb 6: 6 they **crucify** to themselves the Son of God **a**, *388*

AFTER (1180) [AFTERWARD, AFTERWARDS, HEREAFTER]
Ge 1:11 *and* the fruit tree yielding fruit **a** his kind, 3807.1
1:12 *and* herb yielding seed **a** his kind, and 3807.1
1:12 whose seed *was* in itself, **a** his kind: 3807.1
1:21 **a** their kind, and every winged fowl after 3807.1
1:21 and every winged fowl **a** his kind: 3807.1
1:24 bring forth the living creature **a** his kind, 3807.1
1:24 and beast of the earth **a** his kind: 3807.1
1:25 God made the beast of the earth **a** his 3807.1
1:25 cattle **a** their kind, and every thing that 3807.1
1:25 every thing that creepeth upon the earth **a** his 3807.1
1:26 make man in our image, **a** our likeness: 3509.1
4:17 of the city, **a** the name of his son, Enoch. 3509.1
5: 3 *a son* in his own likeness, **a** his image; 3509.1
5: 4 the days of Adam **a** he had begotten Seth 310
5: 7 Seth lived **a** he begat Enos eight hundred 310
5:10 Enos lived **a** he begat Cainan eight hundred 310
5:13 Cainan lived **a** he begat Mahalaleel eight 310
5:16 Mahalaleel lived **a** he begat Jared eight 310
5:19 Jared lived **a** he begat Enoch eight hundred 310
5:22 Enoch walked with God **a** he begat 310
5:26 Methuselah lived **a** he begat Lamech seven 310
5:30 Lamech lived **a** he begat Noah five hundred 310
6: 4 also **a** that, when the sons of God came in 310
6:20 Of fowls **a** their kind, and of cattle after 3807.1
6:20 after their kind, and of cattle **a** their kind, 3807.1
6:20 of every creeping thing of the earth **a** his 3807.1
7:10 it came to pass **a** seven days, that 3807.1
7:14 every beast **a** his kind, and all the cattle 3807.1
7:14 all the cattle **a** their kind, and 3807.1
7:14 that creepeth upon the earth **a** his kind, 3807.1
7:14 every fowl **a** his kind, every bird of every 3807.1
8: 3 **a** the end of the hundred and fifty days 4480
8:19 **a** their kinds, went forth out of the ark. 3807.1
9: 9 covenant with you and with your seed **a** you; 310
9:28 Noah lived **a** the flood three hundred and 310
10: 1 and unto them were sons born **a** the flood. 310
10: 5 every one **a** his tongue, after their 3807.1
10: 5 **a** their families, in their nations. 3807.1
10:20 **a** their families, after their tongues, 3807.1
10:20 **a** their tongues, in their countries, *and* 3807.1
10:31 **a** their families, after their tongues, 3807.1
10:31 **a** their tongues, in their lands, after their 3807.1
10:31 in their lands, **a** their nations. 3807.1
10:32 **a** their generations, in their nations: 3807.1
10:32 the nations divided in the earth **a** the flood. 310
11:10 and begat Arphaxad two years **a** the flood: 310
11:11 Shem lived **a** he begat Arphaxad five 310
11:13 Arphaxad lived **a** he begat Salah four 310
11:15 Salah lived **a** he begat Eber four hundred 310
11:17 Eber lived **a** he begat Peleg four hundred 310

Ge 11:19 And Peleg lived **a** he begat Reu two hundred 310
11:21 And Reu lived **a** he begat Serug two hundred 310
11:23 Serug lived **a** he begat Nahor two hundred 310
11:25 Nahor lived **a** he begat Terah an hundred 310
13:14 **a** that Lot was separated from him, Lift up 310
14:17 the king of Sodom went out to meet him **a** 310
15: 1 **A** these things the word of the LORD came 310
16: 3 **a** Abram had dwelt ten years in 4480+7093
16:13 Have I also here looked **a** him that seeth me? 310
17: 7 thy seed **a** thee in their generations for an 310
17: 7 to be a God unto thee, and to thy seed **a** thee. 310
17: 8 I will give unto thee, and to thy seed **a** thee, 310
17: 9 and thy seed **a** thee in their generations. 310
17:10 between me and you and thy seed **a** thee; 310
17:19 *and* with his seed **a** him. 310
18: 5 ye your hearts; **a** *that* you shall pass on: 310
18:11 it ceased to be with Sarah **a** the manner of 3509.1
18:12 **A** I am waxed old shall I have pleasure, 310
18:19 his children and his household **a** him, 310
18:25 That be far from thee to do **a** this manner, 3509.1
19: 6 the door unto them, and shut the door **a** him, 310
19:31 in unto us **a** the manner of all the earth: 3509.1
22: 1 it came to pass **a** these things, that God did 310
22:20 it came to pass **a** these things, that it was told 310
23:19 **a** this, Abraham buried Sarah his wife in 310
24:55 *few* days, at the least ten; **a** *that* she shall go. 310
24:67 Isaac was comforted **a** his mother's *death.* 310
25:11 And it came to pass **a** the death of Abraham, 310
25:26 **a** that came his brother out, and his hand 310
26:18 for the Philistims had stopped them **a** 310
26:18 he called their names **a** the names by 3509.1
31:23 and pursued **a** him seven days' journey; 310
31:30 thou sore longedst **a** thy father's house, 3807.1
31:36 that thou hast *so* hotly pursued **a** me? 310
32:29 Wherefore *is* it *that* thou dost ask **a** my 3807.1
33: 2 and Leah and her children **a**, and Rachel and 314
33: 7 **a** came Joseph near and Rachel, and 310
35: 5 and they did not pursue **a** the sons of Jacob. 310
35:12 and to thy seed **a** thee will I give the land. 310
36:40 **a** their places, by their names; 3807.1
37:17 Joseph went **a** his brethren, and found them 310
38:24 it came to pass about three months **a**, that it 4480
39: 7 it came to pass **a** these things, that his 310
39:19 **A** this manner did thy servant to me; 3509.1
40: 1 it came to pass **a** these things, *that* the butler 310
40:13 **a** the former manner when thou wast his 3509.1
41: 3 seven other kine came up **a** them out of 310
41: 6 blasted with the east wind sprang up **a** them. 310
41:19 seven other kine came up **a** them, poor and 310
41:23 with the east wind, sprung up **a** them: 310
41:27 ill favoured kine that came up **a** them *are* 310
41:30 there shall arise **a** them seven years of 310
44: 4 said unto his steward, Up, follow **a** the men; 310
45:15 and **a** that his brethren talked with him. 310
45:23 to his father he sent **a** this manner; 3509.1
48: 1 it came to pass **a** these things, that *one* told 310
48: 4 will give this land to thy seed **a** thee *for* an 310
48: 6 which thou begettest **a** them, shall be thine, 310
48: 6 shall be called **a** the name of their brethren 5921
50:14 to bury his father, **a** he had buried his father. 310
Ex 3:20 midst thereof: and **a** that he will let you go. 310
5:19 *that* they *were* in evil *case,* **a** it was said, 3807.1
7:25 **a** *that* the LORD had smitten the river. 310
10:14 locusts as they, neither **a** them shall be such. 310
11: 8 **a** that I will go out. And he went out from 310
14: 4 Pharaoh's heart, that he shall follow **a** them; 310
14: 8 and he pursued **a** the children of Israel: 310
14: 9 the Egyptians pursued **a** them (all the horses 310
14:10 and behold, the Egyptians marched **a** them; 310
14:23 went in **a** them to the midst of the sea, 310
14:28 of Pharaoh that came into the sea **a** them; 310
15:20 all the women went out **a** her with timbrels 310
16: 1 **a** their departing out of the land of Egypt. 3807.1
17: 1 **a** their journeys, according to 3807.1
18: 2 Moses' wife, **a** he had sent her *back,* 310
21: 9 he shall deal with her **a** the manner of 3509.1
23: 2 cause to decline **a** many to wrest *judgment:* 310
23:24 nor serve them, nor do **a** their works: 3509.1
25: 9 ***a*** the pattern of the tabernacle, and NIH
25:40 look that thou make *them* **a** their pattern, 871.1
28:15 **a** the work of the ephod thou shalt make 3509.1
28:43 statute for ever unto him and his seed **a** him. 310
29:29 garments of Aaron shall be his sons' **a** him, 310
30:12 of the children of Israel **a** their number, 3807.1
30:13 half a shekel **a** the shekel of the sanctuary: 871.1
30:24 of cassia five hundred *shekels,* **a** the shekel 871.1
30:25 an ointment compound ***a*** the art of NIH
30:32 *any other* like it, **a** the composition of it: 871.1
30:35 a confection ***a*** the art of the apothecary, NIH
32: 4 **a** he had made it a molten calf: 2050.1
33: 8 man *at* his tent door, and looked **a** Moses, 310
34:15 they go a whoring **a** their gods, and 310
34:16 their daughters go a whoring **a** their gods, 310
34:16 make thy sons go a whoring **a** their gods. 310
34:27 for **a** the tenor of these words I have made 5921
37:19 **made a the fashion of almonds** in one 8246
38:24 **a** the shekel of the sanctuary. 871.1
38:25 **a** the shekel of the sanctuary: 871.1
38:26 half a shekel, **a** the shekel of the sanctuary, 871.1
Lev 5:15 **a** the shekel of the sanctuary, for a trespass 871.1
11:14 And the vulture, and the kite **a** his kind; 3807.1
11:15 Every raven **a** his kind; 3807.1
11:16 and the cuckow, and the hawk **a** his kind, 3807.1
11:19 the heron **a** her kind, and the lapwing, 3807.1
11:22 the locust **a** his kind, and the bald locust 3807.1
11:22 the bald locust **a** his kind, and the beetle 3807.1
11:22 the beetle **a** his kind, and the grasshopper 3807.1
11:22 his kind, and the grasshopper **a** his kind. 3807.1
11:29 the mouse, and the tortoise **a** his kind, 3807.1
13: 7 **a** that he hath been seen of the priest for his 310
13:35 if the scall spread much in the skin **a** his 310
13:55 shall look on the plague, **a** *that* it is washed: 310
13:56 the plague *be* somewhat dark **a** the washing 310
14: 8 **a** *that* he shall come into the camp, and 310
14:43 **a** *that* he hath taken away the stones, and 310

Lev 14:43 **a** he hath scraped the house, and after it is 310
14:43 hath scraped the house, and **a** it is plaistered; 310
14:48 in the house, **a** the house was plaistered: 310
15:28 seven days, and **a** *that* she shall be clean. 310
16: 1 the LORD spake unto Moses **a** the death of 310
17: 7 **a** whom they have gone a whoring. 310
18: 3 **A** the doings of the land of Egypt, 3509.1
18: 3 **a** the doings of the land of Canaan, 3509.1
19:31 neither seek **a** wizards, to be defiled by 413
20: 5 cut him off, and all that go a whoring **a** him, 310
20: 6 the soul that turneth **a** such as have familiar 413
20: 6 **a** wizards, to go a whoring after them, I will 413
20: 6 after wizards, to go a whoring **a** them, I will 310
23:11 on the morrow **a** the sabbath the priest shall NIH
23:15 ye shall count unto you from the morrow **a** NIH
23:16 Even unto the morrow **a** the seventh sabbath NIH
25:15 According to the number of years **a** 310
25:29 he may redeem it within a whole year **a** it is 5704
25:46 as an inheritance for your children **a** you, 310
25:48 **A** *that* he is sold he may be redeemed again; 310
26:33 and will draw out a sword **a** you: 310
27: 3 of silver, **a** the shekel of the sanctuary. 871.1
27:18 if he sanctify his field **a** the jubile, then 310
Nu 1: 1 in the second year **a** they were come out 3807.1
1: 2 **a** their families, by the house of their 3807.1
1:18 they declared their pedigrees **a** their 5921
1:20 *by* their generations, **a** their families, 3807.1
1:22 *by* their generations, **a** their families, 3807.1
1:24 *by* their generations, **a** their families, 3807.1
1:26 *by* their generations, **a** their families, 3807.1
1:28 *by* their generations, **a** their families, 3807.1
1:30 *by* their generations, **a** their families, 3807.1
1:32 *by* their generations, **a** their families, 3807.1
1:34 *by* their generations, **a** their families, 3807.1
1:36 *by* their generations, **a** their families, 3807.1
1:38 *by* their generations, **a** their families, 3807.1
1:40 *by* their generations, **a** their families, 3807.1
1:42 **a** their families, by the house of their 3807.1
1:47 the Levites **a** the tribe of their fathers 3807.1
2:34 set forward, every one **a** their families, 3807.1
3:15 Number the children of Levi **a** the house 3807.1
3:47 **a** the shekel of the sanctuary shalt thou 871.1
3:50 five *shekels,* **a** the shekel of the sanctuary: 871.1
4: 2 **a** their families, by the house of their 3807.1
4:15 **a that**, the sons of Kohath 310+3651+2050.1
4:29 thou shalt number them **a** their families, 3807.1
4:34 sons of the Kohathites **a** their families, 3807.1
4:34 and **a** the house of their fathers, 3807.1
4:44 Even those that were numbered of them **a** 3807.1
4:46 **a** their families, and after the house of 3807.1
4:46 and **a** the house of their fathers, 3807.1
6:19 **a** *the hair of* his separation is shaven: 310
6:20 and **a** *that* the Nazarite may drink wine. 310
6:21 so he must do **a** the law of his separation. 5921
7:13 **a** the shekel of the sanctuary; 871.1
7:19 **a** the shekel of the sanctuary; 871.1
7:25 **a** the shekel of the sanctuary; 871.1
7:31 **a** the shekel of the sanctuary; 871.1
7:37 **a** the shekel of the sanctuary; 871.1
7:43 **a** the shekel of the sanctuary; 871.1
7:49 **a** the shekel of the sanctuary; 871.1
7:55 **a** the shekel of the sanctuary; 871.1
7:61 **a** the shekel of the sanctuary; 871.1
7:67 **a** the shekel of the sanctuary; 871.1
7:73 **a** the shekel of the sanctuary; 871.1
7:79 **a** the shekel of the sanctuary; 871.1
7:85 four hundred *shekels,* **a** the shekel of 871.1
7:86 **a** the shekel of the sanctuary: 871.1
7:88 dedication of the altar, **a** *that* it was anointed. 310
8:15 **a that** shall the Levites go in to do 310+3651
8:22 **a** that went the Levites in to do their service 310
9: 1 in the first month of the second year **a** 3807.1
9:17 then **a** that the children of Israel journeyed: 310
12:14 and **a** *that* let her be received in *again.* 310
13:25 searching of the land **a** forty days. 4480+7093
14:34 **A** the number of the days *in* which ye 871.1
15:13 shall do these *things* **a this manner**, 3602
15:39 that ye seek not **a** your own heart and 310
15:39 own eyes, **a** which ye use to go a whoring: 310
16:29 if they be visited **a** the visitation of all men; NIH
18:16 **a** the shekel of the sanctuary, which *is* 871.1
25: 8 he went **a** the man of Israel into the tent, 310
25:13 he shall have it, and his seed **a** him, *even* 310
26: 1 it came to pass **a** the plague, that the LORD 310
26:12 The sons of Simeon **a** their families: 3807.1
26:15 The children of Gad **a** their families: 3807.1
26:20 the sons of Judah **a** their families were, 3807.1
26:23 *Of* the sons of Issachar **a** their families: 3807.1
26:26 *Of* the sons of Zebulun **a** their families: 3807.1
26:28 The sons of Joseph **a** their families *were* 3807.1
26:35 These *are* the sons of Ephraim **a** their 3807.1
26:37 These *are* the sons of Joseph **a** their 3807.1
26:38 The sons of Benjamin **a** their families: 3807.1
26:41 These *are* the sons of Benjamin **a** their 3807.1
26:42 These *are* the sons of Dan **a** their 3807.1
26:42 These *are* the families of Dan **a** their 3807.1
26:44 *Of* the children of Asher **a** their families: 3807.1
26:48 *Of* the sons of Naphtali **a** their families: 3807.1
26:57 numbered of the Levites **a** their families: 3807.1
27:21 who shall ask *counsel* for him **a** 871.1
28:24 **A** this **manner** ye shall offer daily, 3509.1
28:26 **a** your weeks *be out,* ye shall have a holy 871.1
29:18 according to their number, **a** the manner: 3509.1
29:21 according to their number, **a** the manner: 3509.1
29:24 according to their number, **a** the manner: 3509.1
29:27 according to their number, **a** the manner: 3509.1
29:30 according to their number, **a** the manner: 3509.1
29:33 according to their number, **a** the manner: 3509.1
29:37 according to their number, **a** the manner: 3509.1
30:15 if he shall any ways make them void **a** *that* 310
32:15 For if ye turn away from **a** him, he will yet 310
32:42 and called it Nobah, **a** his own name. 871.1
33: 3 on the morrow **a** the passover the children NIH
33:38 in the fortieth year **a** the children of Israel 3807.1
35:28 **a** the death of the high priest the slayer shall 310

Dt 1: 4 **A** he had slain Sihon the king of 310
1: 8 to give unto them and to their seed **a** them. 310
3:11 the breadth of it, **a** the cubit of a man. 871.1
3:14 called them **a** his own name, 5921
4:37 therefore he chose their seed **a** them, and 310
4:40 with thy children **a** thee, and that thou 310
4:45 of Israel, **a** they came forth out of Egypt, 871.1
4:46 **a** they were come forth out of Egypt: 871.1
6:14 Ye shall not go **a** other gods, of the gods of 310
8:19 walk **a** other gods, and serve them, and 310
9: 4 **a** that the LORD thy God hath cast them 871.1
10:15 he chose their seed **a** them, *even* you above 310
11: 4 sea to overflow them as they pursued **a** you, 310
11:28 to go **a** other gods, which ye have not 310
12: 8 Ye shall not do **a** all *the things* that we do 3509.1
12:15 all thy gates, whatsoever thy soul **lusteth a**, 185
12:20 eat flesh, whatsoever thy soul **lusteth a**. 185
12:21 in thy gates whatsoever thy soul **lusteth a**. 185
12:25 well with thee, and with thy children **a** thee, 310
12:28 and with thy children **a** thee for ever, 310
12:30 **a** that they be destroyed from before thee; 310
12:30 that thou inquire not **a** their gods, saying, 3807.1
13: 2 saying, Let us go **a** other gods, which thou 310
13: 4 Ye shall walk **a** the LORD your God, and 310
14:13 and the kite, and the vulture **a** his kind, 3807.1
14:14 And every raven **a** his kind, 3807.1
14:15 and the cuckow, and the hawk **a** his kind, 3807.1
14:18 the heron **a** her kind, and the lapwing, 3807.1
14:26 money for whatsoever thy soul **lusteth a**, 183
16:13 **a** that thou hast gathered in thy corn and 871.1
18: 9 thou shalt not learn to do **a** 3509.1
20:18 That they teach you not to do **a** all their 3509.1
21:13 **a that** thou shalt go in unto her, and 310+3651
22: 2 it shall be with thee until thy brother **seek a** 1875
24: 4 her again to be his wife, **a** that she is defiled; 310
24: 9 **a** that ye were come forth out of Egypt. 871.1
28:14 *to* the left, to go **a** other gods to serve them. 310
29:22 your children that shall rise up **a** you, 310+4480
31:16 go a whoring **a** the gods of the strangers of 310
31:27 and how much more **a** my death? 310
31:29 For I know that **a** my death ye will utterly 310
Jos 1: 1 Now **a** the death of Moses the servant of 310
2: 5 pursue **a** them quickly; for ye shall overtake 310
2: 7 the men pursued **a** them the way to Jordan 310
2: 7 as soon as they which pursued **a** them were 310
3: 2 it came to pass **a** three days, that 4480+7097
3: 3 ye shall remove from your place, and go **a** it. 310
5: 4 by the way, **a** they came out of Egypt. 871.1
5:11 of the land on the **morrow a** the passover, 4283
5:12 the manna ceased on the **morrow a** they 4283
6: 9 the rereward came **a** the ark, *the priests* 310
6:13 the rereward came **a** the ark of the LORD, 310
6:15 compassed the city **a** the same manner 3509.1
7:25 **a** they had stoned them with stones. 2050.1
8: 6 (For they will come out **a** us) till we have 310
8:16 in Ai were called *together* to pursue **a** them: 310
8:16 they pursued **a** Joshua, and were drawn 310
8:17 in Ai or Beth-el, that went not out **a** Israel: 310
8:17 they left the city open, and pursued **a** Israel. 310
9:16 it came to pass at the end of three days **a** 310
10:14 there was no day like that before it or **a** it, 310
10:19 *but* pursue **a** your enemies, and smite 310
13:23 of the children of Reuben **a** their families, 3807.1
13:28 of the children of Gad **a** their families, 3807.1
19:47 Dan, **a** the name of Dan their father. 3509.1
20: 5 if the avenger of blood pursue **a** him, then 310
22:27 and you, and our generations **a** us, 310
23: 1 it came to pass **a** long time **a** that 310
24: 6 the Egyptians pursued **a** your fathers with 310
24:20 consume you, **a** that he hath done you good. 310
24:29 it came to pass **a** these things, that Joshua 310
Jdg 1: 1 Now **a** the death of Joshua it came to pass, 310
1: 6 and they pursued **a** him, and caught him, and 310
2:10 there arose another generation **a** them, 310
2:17 they went a whoring **a** other gods, and 310
3:22 the haft also went in **a** the blade; and the fat 310
3:28 he said unto them, Follow **a** me: for 310
3:28 they went down **a** him, and took the fords of 310
3:31 **a** him was Shamgar the son of Anath, 310
4:14 mount Tabor, and ten thousand men **a** him. 310
4:16 Barak pursued **a** the chariots, and after 310
4:16 **a** the host, unto Harosheth of the Gentiles: 310
5:14 **a** thee, Benjamin, among thy people; out of 310
6:34 **a** trumpet; and Abi-ezer was gathered **a** him. 310
6:35 all Manasseh; who also was gathered **a** him: 310
7:23 all Manasseh, and pursued **a** the Midianites. 310
8: 5 I am pursuing **a** Zebah and Zalmunna, 310
8:12 he pursued **a** them, and took the two kings of 310
8:27 all Israel went thither a whoring **a** it: 310
8:33 went a whoring **a** Baalim, and 310
10: 1 **a** Abimelech there arose to defend Israel 310
10: 3 **a** him arose Jair, a Gileadite, and 310
12: 8 **a** him Ibzan of Beth-lehem judged Israel. 310
12:11 And **a** him Elon, a Zebulonite, judged Israel; 310
12:13 **a** him Abdon the son of Hillel, a Pirathonite, 310
13:11 went **a** his wife, and came to the man, and 310
13:18 Why askest thou thus **a** my name, 3807.1
14: 8 **a** a time he returned to take her, and 4480
15: 1 it came to pass **within a while a**, 3117+4480
15: 7 I be avenged of you, and **a** *that* I will cease. 310
16:22 to grow *again* **a** he was shaven. 834+3509.1
18: 7 **a** the manner of the Zidonians, quiet and 3509.1
18:29 **a** the name of Dan their father, who was 871.1
19: 3 her husband arose, and went **a** her, to speak 310
20:45 pursued hard **a** them unto Gidom, and 310
Ru 1:15 unto her gods: return thou **a** thy sister in law. 310
1:16 *or* to return from **following a** thee: 310
2: 2 glean ears of corn **a** *him* in whose sight I 310
2: 3 came, and gleaned in the field **a** the reapers: 310
2: 7 gather **a** the reapers amongst the sheaves: 310
2: 9 field that they do reap, and go thou **a** them: 310
2:18 gave to her that she had reserved **a** she was 4480
4: 4 to redeem *it* besides thee; and I *am* **a** thee. 310
1Sa 1: 9 So Hannah rose up **a** *they* had eaten in 310
1: 9 had eaten in Shiloh, and **a** *they* had drunk. 310

1Sa 1:20 when the time was come about a Hannah 2050.1
5: 9 it was *so,* that a they had carried it about, 310
6:12 the lords of the Philistines went a them unto 310
7: 2 all the house of Israel lamented a 310
8: 3 but turned aside a lucre, and took bribes, and 310
10: 5 A that thou shalt come to the hill of God, 310
11: 5 Saul came a the herd out of the field; 310
11: 7 Whosoever cometh not forth a Saul and 310
11: 7 cometh not forth after Saul and a Samuel, 310
12:21 *should ye go* a vain *things,* which cannot 310
13: 4 the people were called together a Saul *to* 310
13:14 the LORD hath sought him a man a his 3509.1
14:12 said unto his armourbearer, Come up a me: 310
14:13 upon his feet, and his armourbearer a him: 310
14:13 and his armourbearer slew a him. 310
14:22 even they also followed hard a them in 310
14:36 Let us go down a the Philistines by night, 310
14:37 of God, Shall I go down a the Philistines? 310
15:31 So Samuel turned again a Saul; and 310
17:27 the people answered him a this manner, 3509.1
17:30 and spake a the same manner: 3509.1
17:30 the people answered him again a 3509.1
17:35 I went out a him, and smote him, and 310
17:53 returned from chasing a the Philistines, 310
18:30 it came to pass, a they went forth, 1767+4480
20:37 Jonathan cried a the lad, and said, *Is* not 310
20:38 Jonathan cried a the lad, Make speed, haste, 310
22:20 named Abiathar, escaped, and fled a David. 310
23:25 when Saul heard *that,* he pursued a David *in* 310
23:28 Wherefore Saul returned from pursuing a 310
24: 8 and cried a Saul, saying, My lord the king. 310
24:14 A whom is the king of Israel come out? 310
24:14 a whom dost thou pursue? after a dead dog, 310
24:14 dost thou pursue? a a dead dog, after a flea. 310
24:14 dost thou pursue? after a dead dog, a a flea. 310
24:21 that thou wilt not cut off my seed a me, and 310
25:13 there went up a David about four hundred 310
25:19 Go on before me; behold, I come a you. 310
25:38 it came to pass about ten days *a,* that NIH
25:42 damsels of hers that went a her; 7272+3807.1
25:42 and she went a the messengers of David, and 310
26: 3 he saw that Saul came a him into 310
26:18 Wherefore doth my lord thus pursue a his 310
30: 8 saying, Shall I pursue a this troop? 310
2Sa 1: 1 Now it came to pass a the death of Saul, 310
1: 6 and horsemen **followed hard** a him. 1692
1:10 I was sure that he could not live a *that* he 310
2: 1 it came to pass a this, that David inquired of 310
2:19 Asahel pursued a Abner; and in going he 310
2:24 Joab also and Abishai pursued a Abner: and 310
2:25 gathered themselves together a Abner, 310
2:28 stood still, and pursued a Israel no more, 310
3:26 out from David, he sent messengers a Abner, 310
5:13 of Jerusalem, a he was come from Hebron: 310
7:12 with thy fathers, I will set up thy seed a thee, 310
8: 1 a this it came to pass, that David smote 310
10: 1 it came to pass a this, that the king of 310
11: 1 it came to pass, a the year was expired, 3807.1
11: 3 David sent and inquired a the woman. 3807.1
12:28 I take the city, and it be called a my name. 5921
13: 1 it came to pass a this, that Absalom the son 310
13:17 *woman* out from me, and bolt the door a her. 310
13:18 brought her out, and bolted the door a her. 310
13:23 it came to pass a two full years, 3807.1
14:26 two hundred shekels a the king's weight. 871.1
15: 1 it came to pass a this, that Absalom 310+4480
15: 7 it came to pass a forty years, 4480+7093
15:13 The hearts of the men of Israel are a 310
15:16 and all his household a him. 7272+871.1
15:17 all the people a him, and tarried *in* a 7272+871.1
15:18 six hundred men which came a him 7272+871.1
17: 1 I will arise and pursue a David *this* night: 310
17: 6 Ahithophel hath spoken a this manner: 3509.1
17: 6 shall we do a his saying? if not; speak thou. NIH
17:21 it came to pass, a they were departed, 310
18:16 the people returned from pursuing a Israel: 310
18:18 he called the pillar a his own name: and 5921
18:22 let me, I pray thee, also run a Cushi. 310
20: 2 So every man of Israel went up from a 310
20: 6 pursue a him, lest he get him fenced cities, 310
20: 7 there went out a him Joab's men, and 310
20: 7 to pursue a Sheba the son of Bichri. 310
20:10 Abishai his brother pursued a Sheba the son 310
20:11 and he that *is* for David, *let him go* a Joab. 310
20:13 all the people went on a Joab, to pursue after 310
20:13 to pursue a Sheba the son of Bichri. 310
20:14 were gathered together, and went also a him. 310
21: 1 in the days of David three years, year a year; 310
21:14 And a that God was intreated for the land. 310
21:18 it came to pass a this, that there was again a 310
23: 4 out of the earth by clear shining a rain. 4480
23: 9 a him *was* Eleazar the son of Dodo 310
23:10 the people returned a him only to spoil. 310
23:11 a him *was* Shammah the son of Agee 310
24:10 David's heart smote him a that he had 310
1Ki 1: 6 and *his mother* bare him a Absalom. 310
1:13 Assuredly Solomon thy son shall reign a me, 310
1:14 I also will come in a thee, and confirm thy 310
1:17 Assuredly Solomon thy son shall reign a me, 310
1:20 sit on the throne of my lord the king a him. 310
1:24 Adonijah shall reign a me, and he shall sit 310
1:27 sit on the throne of my lord the king a him? 310
1:30 Assuredly Solomon thy son shall reign a me, 310
1:35 ye shall come up a him, that he may come 310
1:40 all the people came up a him, and the people 310
2:28 for Joab had turned a Adonijah, though he 310
2:28 though he turned not a Absalom. 310
3:12 neither a thee shall any arise like unto thee. 310
3:18 it came to pass the third day a **that** I was 3807.1
6: 1 eightieth year a the children of Israel 3807.1
7:11 a the measures of hewed stones, and 3509.1
7:31 the mouth thereof *was* round a the work of NIH
7:37 A this *manner* he made the ten bases: 3509.1
9:21 Their children that were left a them in 310
11: 2 *for* surely they will turn away your heart a 310
1Ki 11: 4 *that* his wives turned away his heart a other 310
11: 5 For Solomon went a Ashtoreth the goddess 310
11: 5 a Milcom the abomination of 310
11: 6 went not fully a the LORD, as *did* David 310
11:10 that *he* should not go a other gods: 310
11:15 a he had smitten every male in Edom; 2050.1
12:14 spake to them a the counsel of the young 3509.1
13:14 went a the man of God, and found him 310
13:23 a he had eaten bread, and after he had drunk, 310
13:23 after he had eaten bread, and a he had drunk, 310
13:31 it came to pass, a he had buried him, that he 310
13:33 A this thing Jeroboam returned not from his 310
15: 4 to set up his son a him, and to establish 310
16:24 a the name of Shemer, owner of the hill, 5921
17: 7 it came to pass a a while, that 4480+7093
17:13 a make for thee and for thy 314+871.1+1886.1
17:17 it came to pass a these things, *that* the son of 310
18: 1 it came to pass a many days, that the word NIH
18:28 cut themselves a their manner with 3509.1
19:11 a the wind an earthquake; *but* the LORD 310
19:12 a the earthquake a fire; *but* the LORD *was* 310
19:12 in the fire: and a the fire a still small voice. 310
19:20 ran a Elijah, and said, Let me, I pray thee, 310
19:21 and went a Elijah, and ministered unto him. 310
20:15 a them he numbered all the people, *even* all 310
21: 1 it came to pass a these things, *that* Naboth 310
2Ki 1: 1 Moab rebelled against Israel a the death of 310
5:20 I will run a him, and take somewhat of him. 310
5:21 So Gehazi followed a Naaman. And when 310
5:21 And when Naaman saw *him* running a him, 310
6:24 it came to pass a this, that Ben-hadad king of 310
7:14 the king sent a the host of the Syrians, 310
7:15 they went a them unto Jordan: and lo, all 310
8: 2 and did a the saying of the man of God: 3509.1
9:25 and thou rode together a Ahab his father, 310
9:27 Jehu followed a him, and said, Smite him 310
10:29 Israel to sin, Jehu departed not from a them, 310
14:17 a the death of Jehoash son of Jehoahaz king 310
14:19 they sent a him to Lachish, and slew him 310
14:22 a that the king slept with his fathers. 310
17:15 *went* a the heathen that *were* round about 310
17:33 a the manner of the nations whom they 3509.1
17:34 Unto this day they do a the former 3509.1
17:34 neither do they a their statutes, or 3509.1
17:34 or a their ordinances, or after the law and 3509.1
17:34 or a the law and commandment which 3509.1
17:40 but they did a their former manner. 3509.1
18: 5 that a him was none like him among all 310
21: 2 a the abominations of the heathen, 3509.1
23: 3 to walk a the LORD, and to keep his 310
23:25 neither a him arose there *any* like him. 310
25: 5 the army of the Chaldees pursued a the king, 310
1Ch 2:24 a that Hezron was dead in Caleb-ephratah, 310
5: 1 the genealogy is not to be reckoned a 3807.1
5:25 went a whoring a the gods of the people of 310
6:31 of the LORD, a that the ark had rest. 4480
7: 4 a the house of their fathers, 3807.1
7: 9 the **number** of them, a their **genealogy** by 3187
8: 8 country of Moab, a he had sent them away; 4480
9:25 *were* to come a seven days from time to 3807.1
10: 2 the Philistines followed hard a Saul, and 310
10: 2 followed hard after Saul, and a his sons; 310
11:12 a him *was* Eleazar the son of Dodo, 310
14:14 God said unto him, Go not up a them; 310
15:13 that we sought him not a the due order. 3509.1
17:11 that I will raise up thy seed a thee, 310
18: 1 Now a this it came to pass, that David smote 310
19: 1 Now it came to pass a this, that Nahash 310
20: 1 to pass, that a the year was expired, 6256+3807.1
20: 4 it came to pass a this, that there arose war at 310
23:24 These *were* the sons of Levi a the house 3807.1
24:30 These *were* the sons of the Levites a 3807.1
27: 1 Now the children of Israel a their 3807.1
27: 7 brother of Joab, and Zebadiah his son a him: 310
27:34 a Ahithophel *was* Jehoiada the son of 310
28: 8 leave *it* for an inheritance for your children a 310
29:14 willingly a this *sort?* for all *things come* 3509.1
29:21 on the **morrow** a that day, *even* a thousand 4283
2Ch 1:12 neither shall there any a thee have the like. 310
2:17 a the numbering where*with* David his father 310
3: 3 The length *by* cubits a the first measure 871.1
4:20 that they should burn a the manner before 3509.1
8: 8 who were left a them in the land, 310
8:13 Even a a certain rate every day, offering 871.1
10: 5 Come again unto me a three days. 5750
10:14 answered them a the advice of the young 3509.1
11:16 a them out of all the tribes of Israel such as 310
11:20 a her he took Maachah the daughter of 310
13: 9 have made you priests a **the manner of** 3509.1
13:19 Abijah pursued a Jeroboam, and took cities 310
17: 4 and not a the doings of Israel. 3509.1
18: 2 a *certain* years he went down to Ahab to 7093
18:19 one spake saying a **this manner**, and 3602
18:19 and another saying a **that manner**. 3602
20: 1 It came to pass a this also, *that* the children 310
20:35 a this did Jehoshaphat king of Judah join 310
21:18 a all this the LORD smote him in his 310
21:19 of time, a the end of two years, 6256+3509.1
22: 4 for they were his counsellers a the death of 310
22: 5 He walked also a their counsel, and 871.1
23:21 a **that** they had slain Athaliah with 2050.1
24: 4 it came to pass a this, *that* Joash was minded 310
24:17 Now a the death of Jehoiada came 310
25:14 a that Amaziah was come from the slaughter 310
25:15 Why hast thou **sought** a the gods of 1875
25:20 because they **sought** a the gods of Edom. 1875
25:25 a the death of Joash son of Jehoahaz king of 310
25:27 Now a the time that Amaziah did turn away 4480
25:27 they sent to Lachish a him, and slew him 310
26: 2 a that the king slept with his fathers. 310
26:17 Azariah the priest went in a him, and 310
28: 3 burnt his children in the fire a 3509.1
30:16 they stood in their place a their manner, 3509.1
31: 2 the priests and the Levites a their courses, 5921
32: 1 A these things, and the establishment 310
2Ch 32: 9 A this did Sennacherib king of Assyria send 310
33:14 Now a this he built a wall without the city of 310
34: 3 he began to seek a the God of David his 3807.1
34:21 to do a all that is written in this book. 3509.1
34:31 to walk a the LORD, and to keep his 310
35: 4 a your courses, according to the writing 3509.1
35: 5 *a* the division of the families of the Levites. NIH
35:20 A all this, when Josiah had prepared 310
36:14 transgressed very much a all 3509.1
Ezr 2:61 the Gileadite, and was called a their name: 5921
2:69 They gave a their ability unto the treasure 3509.1
3:10 a the ordinance of David king of Israel. 5921
5: 4 said we unto them a **this manner**, What are 3660
5:12 a that our fathers had provoked the God of 4481
7: 1 Now a these things, in the reign of 310
7:18 and gold, *that* do a the will of your God. 3509.4
7:25 thou, Ezra, a the wisdom of thy God, 3509.4
9:10 O our God, what shall we say a this? 310
9:13 a all that is come upon us for our evil deeds, 310
10:16 a the house of their fathers, and all of 3807.1
Ne 3:16 A him repaired Nehemiah the son of Azbuk, 310
3:17 A him repaired the Levites, Rehum the son 310
3:18 A him repaired their brethren, Bavai the son 310
3:20 A him Baruch the son of Zabbai earnestly 310
3:21 A him repaired Meremoth the son of Urijah 310
3:22 a him repaired the priests, the men of 310
3:23 A him repaired Benjamin and Hashub over 310
3:23 A him repaired Azariah the son of Maaseiah 310
3:24 A him repaired Binnui the son of Henadad 310
3:25 the prison. A him Pedaiah the son of Parosh. 310
3:27 A them the Tekoites repaired another piece, 310
3:29 A them repaired Zadok the son of Immer 310
3:29 A him repaired also Shemaiah the son of 310
3:30 A him repaired Hananiah the son of 310
3:30 A him repaired Meshullam the son of 310
3:31 A him repaired Malchiah the goldsmith's 310
4:13 I even set the people a *their* families with 3807.1
5: 8 We a our ability have redeemed our 3509.1
6: 4 Yet they sent unto me four times a this 3509.1
6: 4 and I answered them a the same manner. 3509.1
7:63 *to* wife, and was called a their name. 5921
9:28 a they had rest, they did evil again before 3509.1
10:34 a the houses of our fathers, at times 3807.1
11: 8 a him Gabbai, Sallai, nine hundred twenty 310
12:32 a them went Hoshaiah, and half of 310
12:38 thanks went over against *them,* and I a them, 310
13: 6 a certain days obtained I *leave* of 7093+3807.1
13:19 charged that they should not be opened till a 310
Est 1:22 to every people a their language, 3509.1
2: 1 A these things, when the wrath of king 310
2:12 a **that** she had been twelve 1961+4480+7093
3: 1 A these things did king Ahasuerus promote 310
3:12 and *to* every people a their language; 3509.1
8: 9 *unto* every people a their language, and 3509.1
9:26 Wherefore they called these days Purim a 5921
Job 3: 1 A this opened Job his mouth, and cursed his 310
10: 6 That thou inquirest a mine iniquity, and 3807.1
10: 6 mine iniquity, and searchest a my sin? 3807.1
18:20 They that come a *him* shall be astonied at 314
19:26 *though* a my skin *worms* destroy this *body,* 310
21: 3 and a that I have spoken, mock on. 310
21:21 For what pleasure hath he in his house a 310
21:33 every man shall draw a him, as *there are* 310
29:22 A my words they spake not again; and 310
30: 5 (they cried a them as *after* a thief;) 5921
30: 5 (they cried after them as a a thief;) NIH
31: 7 mine heart walked a mine eyes, and *if any* 310
37: 4 A it a voice roareth: he thundereth with 310
39: 8 and he searcheth a every green thing. 310
39:10 or will he harrow the valleys a thee? 310
41:32 He maketh a path to shine a him; *one* would 310
42: 7 that a the LORD had spoken these words 310
42: 8 lest *I* deal with you a *your* folly, in that ye NIH
42:16 A this lived Job an hundred and forty years, 310
Ps 4: 2 will ye love vanity, *and* **seek** a leasing? 1245
10: 4 will not seek a *God:* God *is* not *in* all his NIH
16: 4 *a* another *god:* their drink offerings of blood NIH
27: 4 I desired of the LORD, that will I **seek** a; 1245
28: 4 give them a the work of their hands; 3509.1
35: 4 and put to shame that **seek** a my soul: 1245
38:12 They also that **seek** a my life lay snares *for* 1245
40:14 confounded together that **seek** a my soul to 1245
42: 1 As the hart panteth a the water brooks, so 5921
42: 1 so panteth my soul a thee, O God. 413
49:11 they call *their* lands a their own names. 5921
49:17 his glory shall not descend a him. 310
51: T a he had gone in to Bath-sheba. 834+3509.1
54: 3 against me, and oppressors **seek** a my soul: 1245
63: 8 My soul followeth hard a thee: thy right 310
68:25 the players on instruments *followed* a; 310
70: 2 and confounded that **seek** a my soul: 1245
78:34 they returned and **inquired early** a God. 7836
86:14 of violent *men* have **sought** a my soul; 1245
103:10 He hath not dealt with us a our sins; 3509.1
104:21 The young lions roar a *their* prey, and 3807.1
110: 4 Thou *art* a priest for ever a the order of 5921
119:40 Behold, I have longed a thy precepts: 3807.1
119:85 pits for me, which *are* not a thy law. 3509.1
119:88 Quicken me a thy lovingkindness; so 3509.1
119:150 They draw nigh that **follow** a mischief: 7291
143: 6 my soul *thirsteth* a thee, as a thirsty land. 3807.1
144:12 polished a the similitude of a palace: NIH
Pr 2: 3 if thou criest a knowledge, *and* liftest up 3807.1
6:25 **Lust** not a her beauty in thine heart; 2530
7:22 He goeth a her straightway, as an ox goeth 310
15: 9 he loveth him that **followeth** a 7291
20: 7 his integrity: his children *are* blessed a him. 310
20:25 *which is* holy, and a vows to make inquiry. 310
21:21 He that **followeth** a righteousness and 7291
28:19 he that **followeth** a vain *persons* shall have 7291
Ecc 1:11 are to come with *those* that shall come a. 314
2:12 for what *can* the man *do* that cometh a 310
2:18 I should leave it unto the man that shall be a 310
3:22 shall bring him to see what shall be a him? 310
4:16 they also that **come** a shall not rejoice in 314

A

Ecc 6:12 for who can tell a man what shall be **a** him 310
7:14 to the end that man should find nothing **a** 310
9: 3 they live, and **a** that *they go* to the dead. 310
10:14 what shall be **a** him, who can tell him? 310+4480
11: 1 for thou shalt find it **a** many days. 871.1
12: 2 nor the clouds return **a** the rain: 310
SS 1: 4 Draw me, we will run **a** thee: the king hath 310
Isa 1:23 one loveth gifts, and **followeth a** rewards: 7291
5:17 shall the lambs feed **a** their manner, and 3509.1
10:24 staff against thee, **a** the manner of Egypt. 871.1
10:26 so shall he lift it up **a** the manner of Egypt. 871.1
11: 3 he shall not judge **a** the sight of his eyes, 3807.1
11: 3 neither reprove **a** the hearing of his ears: 3807.1
23:15 **a** the end of seventy years shall Tyre sing 4480
23:17 it shall come to pass **a** the end of seventy 4480
24:22 and **a** many days shall they be visited. 4480
43:10 no God formed, neither shall there be **a** me. 310
44:13 maketh it **a** the figure of a man, 3509.1
45:14 they shall come **a** thee, in chains they shall 310
49:20 **a** thou hast lost the other, shall say again in NIH
51: 1 to me, ye that **follow a** righteousness, 7291
65: 2 way *that was* not good, **a** their own thoughts; 310
Jer 2: 2 when thou wentest **a** me in the wilderness, 310
2: 5 have walked **a** vanity, and are become vain? 310
2: 8 and walked **a** *things that* do not profit. 310
2:23 I am not polluted, I have not gone **a** Baalim? 310
2:25 I have loved strangers, and **a** them will I go. 310
3: 7 I said **a** she had done all these *things*, Turn 310
3:17 neither shall they walk any more **a** 310
5: 8 every one neighed **a** his neighbour's wife. 413
7: 6 neither walk **a** other gods to your hurt: 310
7: 9 and walk **a** other gods whom ye know not; 310
8: 2 **a** whom they have walked, and whom they 310
9:14 have walked **a** the imagination of their own 310
9:14 **a** Baalim, which their fathers taught them: 310
9:16 I will send a sword **a** them, till I have 310
9:22 as the handful **a** the harvestman, and 310+4480
11:10 and they went **a** other gods to serve them: 310
12: 6 yea, they have called a multitude **a** thee: 310
12:15 **a** that I have plucked them out, I will return, 310
13: 6 it came to pass **a** many days, that 4480+7093
13: 9 **A this manner** will I mar the pride of 3602
13:10 walk **a** other gods, to serve them, and 310
16:11 have walked **a** other gods, and have served 310
16:12 ye walk every one **a** the imagination of his 310
16:16 **a** will I send for many hunters, and 310
18:12 we will walk **a** our own devices, and we will 310
23:17 they say *unto* every one that walketh **a** 871.1
24: 1 **a** that Nebuchadrezzar king of Babylon had 310
25: 6 go not **a** other gods to serve them, and 310
25:26 and the king of Sheshach shall drink **a** them. 310
28:12 **a** that Hananiah the prophet had broken 310
29: 2 (**A** that Jeconiah the king, and the queen, and 310
29:10 That **a** seventy years be 6310+3807.1
30:17 This *is* Zion, whom no man **seeketh a**. 1875
30:18 the palace shall remain **a** the manner 5921
31:19 Surely **a** that I was turned, I repented; and 310
31:19 **a** that I was instructed, I smote upon *my* 310
31:33 **A** those days, saith the LORD, I will put 310
32:18 into the bosom of their children **a** them: 310
32:39 good of them, and of their children **a** them: 310
34: 8 **a** that the king Zedekiah had made a 310
35:15 go not **a** other gods to serve them, and 310
36:27 **a** the king had burnt the roll, and 310
39: 5 the Chaldeans' army pursued **a** them, and 310
40: 1 **a** that Nebuzar-adan the captain of the guard 310
41: 4 it came to pass the second day **a** *he* had 3807.1
41:16 **a** *that* he had slain Gedaliah the son of 310
42: 7 it came to pass **a** ten days, that 4480+7093
42:16 shall follow close **a** you there in Egypt; 310
49:37 I will send the sword **a** them, till I have 310
50:21 waste and utterly destroy **a** them, saith 310
51:46 **a** that in *another* year *shall come* a rumour, 310
52: 8 the army of the Chaldeans pursued **a** 310
Eze 5: 2 and I will draw out a sword **a** them. 310
5:12 and I will draw out a sword **a** them. 310
6: 9 their eyes, which go a whoring **a** their idols: 310
7:27 I will do unto them **a** their way, and 4480
9: 5 Go ye **a** him through the city, and smite: 310
11:12 have done **a** the manners of the heathen 3509.1
11:21 *as for them* whose heart walketh **a** the heart 413
12:14 and I will draw out the sword **a** them. 310
16:23 it came to pass **a** all thy wickedness, (woe, 310
16:47 Yet hast thou not walked **a** their ways, 871.1
16:47 their ways, nor done **a** their abominations: 871.1
20:16 for their heart went **a** their idols. 310
20:24 and their eyes were **a** their fathers' idols. 310
20:30 Are ye polluted **a** the manner of your 871.1
20:30 commit ye whoredom **a** their abominations? 310
23:15 **a** the manner of the Babylonians of NIH
23:30 thou hast gone a whoring **a** the heathen, 310
23:45 they shall judge them **a the manner** of 4941
23:45 **a the manner** of *women* that shed blood; 4941
23:48 that all women may be taught not to do **a** 3509.1
29:16 when they shall look **a** them: 310
33:20 I will judge you every one **a** his ways. 3509.1
33:31 *but* their heart goeth **a** their covetousness. 310
34: 6 and none did search or seek **a** *them*. NIH
36:11 I will settle you **a** your old estates, and 3509.1
38: 8 **A** many days thou shalt be visited: in 4480
39:14 **a** the end of seven months shall they 4480
39:26 **A** that they have borne their shame, and 2050.1
40: 1 in the fourteenth year **a** that the city was 310
40:21 the arches thereof were **a** the measure of 3509.1
40:22 *were* **a** the measure of the gate that 3509.1
40:24 **A that** he brought me toward the south, 2050.1
41: 5 **A** he measured the wall of the house, 2050.1
43:13 these *are* the measures of the altar **a** 871.1
44:10 which went astray away from me **a** their 310
44:26 **a** he is cleansed, they shall reckon unto him 310
45:11 the measure thereof shall be **a** the homer. 413
46:12 and **a** his going forth *one* shall shut the gate. 310
46:17 of liberty; **a**, it shall return to the prince: 2050.1
46:19 **A**, he brought me through the entry, 2050.1
48:31 the gates of the city *shall be* **a** the names of 5921

Da 2:39 **a** thee shall arise another kingdom inferior to 870
3:29 no other God that can deliver **a** this **sort**. 3509.4
4:26 **a** that thou shalt have known that 4481
7: 6 **A** this I beheld, and lo another, like a 870
7: 7 **A** this I saw in the night visions, and behold, 870
7:24 another shall rise **a** them; and he shall be 311
8: 1 **a** that which appeared unto me at the first. 310
9:26 **a** threescore and two weeks shall Messiah be 310
11:13 shall certainly come **a** certain years with a 7093
11:18 **A this** shall he turn his face unto the isles, 2050.1
11:23 **a** the league *made* with him he shall work 4480
Hos 2: 5 for she said, I will go **a** my lovers, that give 310
2: 7 she shall **follow a** her lovers, but she shall 7291
2:13 and she went **a** her lovers, and forgat me, 310
5: 8 cry aloud *at* Beth-aven, **a** thee, O Benjamin. 310
5:11 he willingly walked **a** the commandment. 310
6: 2 **A** two days will he revive us: in the third 4480
7: 4 *who* ceaseth from raising **a** *he* hath kneaded 4480
11:10 They shall walk **a** the LORD: he shall roar 310
12: 1 on wind, and **followeth a** the east wind: 7291
Joel 2: 2 ever the like, neither shall be any more **a** it, 310
Am 2: 4 to err, **a** the which their fathers have walked: 310
2: 7 That pant **a** the dust of the earth on 5921
4: 4 *and* your tithes **a** three years: 3807.1
4:10 I have sent among you the pestilence **a** 871.1
7: 1 *it was* the latter growth **a** the king's 310
Zec 2: 8 **A** the glory hath he sent me unto the nations 310
6: 6 the white go forth **a** them; and 310+413
7:14 thus the land was desolate **a** them, that no 310
Mt 1:12 And **a** they were brought to Babylon, *3326*
3:11 but he that cometh **a** me is mightier than I, *3694*
5: 6 which do hunger and thirst **a** righteousness: NIG
5:28 **lust a** her hath committed adultery with her *1937*
6: 9 **A this manner** therefore pray ye: *3779*
6:32 **a** all these *things* do the Gentiles **seek**): *1934*
10:38 and followeth **a** me, is not worthy of me. *3694*
12:39 and adulterous generation **seeketh a** a sign; *1934*
15:12 were offended, **a** they heard *this* saying? NIG
15:23 saying, Send her away; for she crieth **a** us. *3693*
16: 4 and adulterous generation **seeketh a** a sign; *1934*
16:24 If any *man* will come **a** me, let him deny *3694*
17: 1 And **a** six days Jesus taketh Peter, James, *3326*
18:32 Then his lord, **a** that he had called him, NIG
23: 3 and do; but do not ye **a** their works: *2596*
24:29 Immediately **a** the tribulation of those days *3326*
25:19 **A** a long time the lord of those servants *3326*
26: 2 Ye know that **a** two days is *the feast of* *3326*
26:32 But **a** I am risen *again*, I will go *3326+3588*
26:73 And **a** a while came unto *him* they that *3326*
27:31 And **a** that they had mocked him, they took *3753*
27:53 And came out of the graves **a** his *3326*
27:63 yet alive, **A** three days I will rise *again*. *3326*
Mk 1: 7 There cometh one mightier than I **a** me, *3694*
1:14 Now **a** that John was put in prison, *3326+3588*
1:17 Come ye **a** me, and I will make you to *3694*
1:20 with the hired servants, and went **a** him. *3694*
1:36 they that were with him **followed a** him. *2614*
2: 1 And again he entered into Capernaum **a** *1223*
4:28 then the ear, **a that** the full corn in the ear. *1534*
8:12 Why doth this generation **seek a** a sign? *1934*
8:25 **A that** he put *his* hands again upon his *1534*
8:31 and be killed, and **a** three days rise again. *3326*
8:34 unto them, Whosoever will come **a** me, *3694*
9: 2 And **a** six days Jesus taketh with *him* Peter, *3326*
9:31 and **a** that he is killed, he shall rise the third NIG
12:34 And no *man* **a that** durst ask him *any* *3765*
13:24 But in those days, **a** that tribulation, the sun *3326*
14: 1 **A** two days was *the feast of* the passover, *3326*
14:28 But **a** that I am risen, I will go before *3326+3588*
14:70 And a little **a**, they that stood by said again *3326*
16:12 **A** that he appeared in another form unto *3326*
16:14 them which had seen him **a** he was risen. NIG
16:19 So then **a** the Lord had spoken unto *3326+3588*
Lk 1:24 And **a** those days his wife Elisabeth *3326*
1:59 him Zacharias, **a** the name of his father. *1909*
2:27 to do for him **a** the custom of the law, *2596*
2:42 they went up to Jerusalem **a** the custom of *2596*
2:46 *that* **a** three days they found him in *3326*
5:27 And **a** these *things* he went forth, and saw a *3326*
6: 1 to pass on the **second** sabbath **a the first**, *1207*
7:11 And it came to pass the *day* **a**, *1722+1836+3588*
9:23 If any *man* will come **a** me, let him deny *3694*
9:28 And it came to pass about an eight days **a** *3326*
10: 1 **A** these *things* the Lord appointed other *3326*
12: 4 and **a** that have no more that *they* can do. *3326*
12: 5 which **a** *he* hath killed hath power to *3326+3588*
12:30 *things* do the nations of the world **seek a**: *1934*
13: 9 **a that** thou shalt cut it down. *1519+3195+3588*
14:27 and come **a** me, cannot be my disciple. *3694*
14:29 **a** he hath laid the foundation, and is not *2443*
15: 4 and go **a** that which is lost, until he find it? *1909*
15:13 And not many days **a** the younger son *3326*
17:23 see there: **go** not **a** *them*, nor follow *them*. *565*
19:14 and sent a message **a** him, saying, *3694*
20:40 And **a that** they durst not ask him any *3765*
21: 8 draweth near: go ye not therefore **a** them. *3694*
21:26 *for* **looking a** those *things* which are *4329*
22:20 Likewise also the cup **a** supper, saying, *3326*
22:58 And **a** a little while another saw him, and *3326*
22:59 And about the **space** of one hour **a** another *1339*
23:26 laid the cross, that *he* might bear *it* **a** Jesus. *3693*
23:55 **followed a**, and beheld the sepulchre, and *2628*
Jn 1:15 He that cometh **a** me is preferred before *3694*
1:27 who coming **a** me is preferred before me, *3694*
1:30 **A** me cometh a man which is preferred *3694*
1:35 Again the next day **a** John stood, and two of NIG
2: 6 **a the manner** of the purifying of the Jews, *2596*
2:12 **A** this he went down to Capernaum, he, and *3326*
3:22 **A** these *things* came Jesus and his disciples *3326*
4:43 Now **a** two days he departed thence, and *3326*
5: 1 **A** this there was a feast of the Jews; and *3326*
5: 4 first **a** the troubling of the water stepped in, *3326*
6: 1 **A** these *things* Jesus went over the sea of *3326*
6:23 eat bread, **a** that the Lord had given thanks:) NIG
7: 1 **A** these *things* Jesus walked in Galilee: *3326*

Jn 8:15 Ye judge **a** the flesh; I judge no *man*. *2596*
11: 7 Then **a** that saith he to *his* disciples, Let us *3326*
11:11 and **a** that he saith unto them, Our friend *3326*
12:19 behold, the world is gone **a** him. *3694*
13: 5 **A that**, he poureth water into a bason, and *1534*
13:12 So **a** he had washed their feet, and *3753*
13:27 And **a** the sop Satan entered into him. *3326*
19:28 **A** this, Jesus knowing that all *things* were *3326*
19:38 And **a** this Joseph of Arimathea, being a *3326*
20:26 And **a** eight days again his disciples were *3326*
21: 1 **A** these *things* Jesus shewed himself again *3326*
21:14 **a** that he was risen from the dead. NIG
Ac 1: 2 **a** that he through the Holy Ghost had given NIG
1: 3 **a** his passion by many infallible *3326+3588*
1: 8 **a** that the Holy Ghost is come upon you: NIG
3:24 from Samuel and those that **follow a**, *2517*
5: 4 and **a** it was sold, was it not in thine own NIG
5: 7 it was about the **space** of three hours **a**, *1292*
5:37 **A** this *man* rose up Judas of Galilee in *3326*
5:37 and drew away much people **a** him: *3694*
7: 5 and to his seed **a** him, when *as yet* he had *3326*
7: 7 and **a** that shall they come forth, and *3326*
7:36 **a** that he had shewed wonders and signs in NIG
7:45 Which also our fathers that **came a** brought *1237*
9:23 And **a that** many days were fulfilled, *5613*
10:24 And the morrow **a** they entered into NIG
10:37 **a** the baptism which John preached; *3326*
10:41 with him **a** he rose from the dead. *3326+3588*
12: 4 intending **a** Easter to bring him forth to *3326*
13:15 And **a** the reading of the law and *3326*
13:20 And **a** that he gave *unto them* judges about *3326*
13:22 **a** mine own heart, which shall fulfil *2596*
13:25 not *he*. But behold, there cometh *one* **a** me, *3326*
13:36 **a** he had served his own generation by NIG
14:24 And **a** they had passed throughout Pisidia, NIG
15: 1 *said*, Except ye be circumcised **a** NIG
15:13 And **a** they had held their peace, *3326+3588*
15:16 **A** this I will return, and will build again *3326*
15:17 That the residue of men might **seek a** *1567*
15:23 they wrote *letters* by them **a this manner**; *3592*
15:33 And **a** they had tarried *there* a space, NIG
15:36 And some days **a** Paul said unto Barnabas, *3326*
16: 7 **A** they were come to Mysia, they assayed to NIG
16:10 And **a** he had seen the vision, *5613*
17:27 if haply they might **feel a** him, and *5584*
18: 1 **A** these *things* Paul departed from Athens, *3326*
18:18 And Paul **a** *this* tarried *there* yet a good NIG
18:23 And **a** he had spent some time *there*, he NIG
19: 4 believe on him which should come **a** him, *3326*
19:21 **A** these *things* were ended, Paul purposed *5613*
19:21 saying, **A** I have been there, *3326+3588*
20: 1 And **a** the uproar was ceased, Paul *3326+3588*
20: 6 And we sailed away from Philippi **a** *3326*
20:18 **a what manner** I have been with you at all *4459*
20:29 that **a** my departing shall grievous wolves *3326*
20:30 *things*, to draw away disciples **a** them. *3694*
21: 1 that **a** we were gotten from them, and NIG
21:15 And **a** those days we took up our carriages, *3326*
21:21 neither to walk **a** the customs. NIG
21:36 For the multitude of the people followed **a**, NIG
22:29 **a** he knew that he was a Roman, and NIG
23: 3 for sittest thou to judge me **a** the law, and *2596*
23:25 And he wrote a letter **a** this manner: *4023*
24: 1 And **a** five days Ananias the high priest *3326*
24:10 **a** that the governor had beckoned unto him NIG
24:14 that **a** the way which they call heresy, so *2596*
24:17 Now **a** many years I came to bring alms to *1223*
24:24 And **a** certain days, when Felix came with *3326*
24:27 But **a** two years Porcius Festus came into *4137*
25: 1 **a** three days he ascended from Cesarea to *3326*
25:13 And **a** certain days king Agrippa and *1230*
25:26 O king Agrippa, that, **a** examination had, NIG
26: 5 that **a** the most straitest sect of our religion *2596*
27:14 But not long **a** there arose against it a *3326*
27:21 But **a** long abstinence Paul stood *5119+5225*
28: 6 but **a** they had looked a great while, and NIG
28:11 And **a** three months we departed in a ship *3326*
28:13 and **a** one day the south wind blew, and *3326*
28:17 that **a** three days Paul called the chief of *3326*
28:25 **a** that Paul had spoken one word, NIG
Ro 2: 5 But **a** thy hardness and impenitent heart *2596*
3:11 there is none that seeketh **a** God. *1567*
5:14 even over them that had not sinned **a** *1909*
6:19 I speak **a the manner of men** because of *442*
7:22 For I delight in the law of God **a** the inward *2596*
8: 1 in Christ Jesus who walk not **a** the flesh, *2596*
8: 1 walk not after the flesh, but **a** the Spirit. *2596*
8: 4 who walk not **a** the flesh, but after *2596*
8: 4 walk not after the flesh, but **a** the Spirit. *2596*
8: 5 For they that are **a** the flesh do mind *2596*
8: 5 they *that are* **a** the Spirit the *things* of *2596*
8:12 not to the flesh, to live **a** the flesh. *2596*
8:13 For if ye live **a** the flesh, ye shall die: but *2596*
9:30 which followed not **a** righteousness, NIG
9:31 which followed **a** the law of righteousness, NIG
10:20 manifest unto them that **asked** not **a** me. *1905*
14:19 follow **a** the *things* which make for peace, NIG
1Co 1:21 For **a that** in the wisdom of God the world *1894*
1:22 a sign, and the Greeks **seek a** wisdom: *2212*
1:26 how that not many wise *men* **a** the flesh, *2596*
7: 7 his proper gift of God, one **a this manner**, *3779*
7: 7 one after this manner, and another **a that**. *3779*
7:40 is happier if she so abide, **a** my judgment: *2596*
10: 6 to the intent we should not **lust a** evil *1938*
10:18 Behold Israel **a** the flesh: are not they *2596*
11:25 **A the same manner** also *he took* the cup, *5615*
12:28 **a that** miracles, then gifts of healings, *1899*
14: 1 **Follow a** charity, and desire spiritual *gifts*, *1377*
15: 6 **A that**, he was seen of above five hundred *1899*
15: 7 **A that**, he was seen of James; then of all *1899*
15:32 If **a the manner of** men I have fought with *2596*
2Co 5:16 Wherefore henceforth know we no *man* **a** *2596*
5:16 though we have known Christ **a** the flesh, *2596*
7: 9 for ye were made sorry **a a** godly **manner**, *2596*
7:11 *thing*, that ye sorrowed **a a** godly **sort**, *2596*

2Co 9:14 which **long a** you for the exceeding grace *1971*
10: 3 walk in the flesh, we do not war **a** the flesh: *2596*
10: 7 Do ye look on *things* **a** the outward *2596*
11:17 I speak *it* not **a** the Lord, but as *it were* *2596*
11:18 Seeing that many glory **a** the flesh, I will *2596*
Gal 1:11 which was preached of me is not **a** man. *2596*
1:18 Then **a** three years I went up to Jerusalem *3326*
2: 1 Then fourteen years **a** I went up again to *1223*
2:14 livest **a the manner of Gentiles**, and not as *1483*
3:15 Brethren, I speak **a the manner** of men; *2596*
3:17 which was four hundred and thirty years **a**, *3326*
3:25 But **a** that faith is come, we are no longer NIG
4: 9 **a** that ye have known God, or rather are NIG
4:23 of the bondwoman was born **a** the flesh; *2596*
4:29 he that was born **a** the flesh persecuted him *2596*
4:29 persecuted him that was *born* **a** the Spirit, *2596*
Eph 1:11 all *things* **a** the counsel of his own will: *2596*
1:13 In whom ye also *trusted*, **a** that ye heard NIG
1:13 in whom also **a** that ye believed, ye were NIG
1:15 **a** I heard of your faith in the Lord Jesus, and NIG
4:24 which **a** God is created in righteousness *2596*
Php 1: 8 how *greatly* I **long a** you all in the bowels *1971*
2:26 For he **longed a** you all, and *was* full of *1971*
3:12 I follow **a**, if that I may apprehend *that* for NIG
Col 2: 8 and vain deceit, **a** the tradition of men, *2596*
2: 8 **a** the rudiments of the world, and not after *2596*
2: 8 rudiments of the world, and not **a** Christ. *2596*
2:22 **a** the commandments and doctrines of *2596*
3:10 **a** the image of him that created him: *2596*
1Th 2: 2 But even **a** that we had suffered before, and NIG
2Th 2: 9 *Even him*, whose coming is **a** the working *2596*
3: 6 not **a** the tradition which he received of us. *2596*
1Ti 5:15 For some are already turned aside **a** Satan. *3694*
5:24 to judgment; and some *men* they **follow a**. *1872*
6:10 which while some **coveted a**, they have *3713*
6:11 these *things*; and follow **a** righteousness, NIG
2Ti 4: 3 **a** their own lusts shall they heap to *2596*
Tit 1: 1 the acknowledging of the truth which is **a** *2596*
1: 4 *mine* own son **a** the common faith: *2596*
3: 4 But **a** that the kindness and love of God our *3753*
3:10 A man *that is* a heretick **a** the first and *3326*
Heb 3: 5 of those *things* which were to be spoken **a**; NIG
4: 7 saying in David, To day, **a** so long a time; *3326*
4:11 lest any *man* fall **a** the same example of *1722*
5: 6 a priest for ever **a** the order of Melchisedec. *2596*
5:10 Called of God a high priest **a** the order of *2596*
6:15 And so, **a** he had patiently endured, NIG
6:20 made a high priest for ever **a** the order of *2596*
7: 2 and **a that** also King of Salem, which is, *1899*
7:11 should rise **a** the order of Melchisedec, *2596*
7:11 and not be called **a** the order of Aaron? *2596*
7:15 for that **a** the similitude of Melchisedec *2596*
7:16 not **a** the law of a carnal commandment, *2596*
7:16 but **a** the power of an endless life. *2596*
7:17 Thou *art* a priest for ever **a** the order of *2596*
7:21 Thou *art* a priest for ever **a** the order of *2596*
8:10 make with the house of Israel **a** those days, *3326*
9: 3 And **a** the second vail, the tabernacle which *3326*
9:17 For a testament *is* of force **a** *men* are dead: *1909*
9:27 men once to die, but **a** this the judgment: *3326*
10:12 But this *man*, **a** he had offered one sacrifice NIG
10:15 for to us: for **a** that *he* had said before, *3326+3588*
10:16 that I will make with them **a** those days, *3326*
10:26 For if we sin wilfully **a** that *we* have *3326+3588*
10:32 in which, **a** ye were illuminated, ye endured NIG
10:36 that, **a** ye have done the will of God, NIG
11: 8 he should **a** receive for an inheritance, *3195*
11:30 **a** they were compassed about seven days. NIG
12:10 few days chastened *us* **a** their own pleasure; *2596*
Jas 3: 9 which are made **a** the similitude of God. *2596*
1Pe 3: 5 For **a this manner** in the old time the holy *3779*
5:10 **a** that ye have suffered a while, make you NIG
2Pe 1:15 **a** my decease to have these *things* always NIG
2: 6 making *them* an ensample unto those that **a** *3195*
2:10 But chiefly them that walk **a** the flesh in *3694*
2:20 For if **a** they have escaped the pollutions of NIG
2:21 **a** they have known *it*, to turn from the holy NIG
3: 3 days scoffers, walking **a** their own lusts, *2596*
2Jn 1: 6 is love, that we walk **a** his commandments. *2596*
3Jn 1: 6 forward on their journey **a** a godly **sort**, *516*
Jude 1: 7 and going **a** a strange flesh, are set forth for *3694*
1:11 **ran greedily a** the error of Balaam for *1632*
1:16 complainers, walking **a** their own lusts; *2596*
1:18 who should walk **a** their own ungodly lusts. *2596*
Rev 4: 1 **A** this I looked, and behold, a door *was* *3326*
7: 1 And **a** these *things* I saw four angels *3326*
7: 9 **A** this I beheld, and lo, a great multitude, *3326*
11:11 And **a** three days and a half the spirit of life *3326*
12:15 of his mouth water as a flood **a** the woman, *3694*
13: 3 and all the world wondered **a** the beast. *3694*
15: 5 And **a** that I looked, and behold, the temple *3326*
18: 1 And **a** these *things* I saw another angel *3326*
18:14 And the fruits that thy soul **lusted a** are *1939*
19: 1 And **a** these *things* I heard a great voice of *3326*
20: 3 and **a** that he must be loosed a little season. *3326*

AFTERNOON (1)

Jdg 19: 8 they tarried until **a**, and 3117+5186+1886.1

AFTERWARD (64) [AFTER]

Ge 10:18 **a** were the families of the Canaanites spread 310
15:14 **a** shall they come out with great 310+3651
32:20 before me, and **a** I will see his face; 310+3651
38:30 **a** came out his brother, that had the scarlet 310
Ex 5: 1 **a** Moses and Aaron went in, and 310
34:32 **a** all the children of Israel came nigh: 310+3651
Lev 14:19 and **a** he shall kill the burnt offering: 310
14:36 **a** the priest shall go in to see 310+3651
16:26 in water, and **a** come into the camp. 310+3651
16:28 and **a** he shall come into the camp. 310+3651
22: 7 shall **a** eat of the holy *things*; because it *is* 310
Nu 5:26 **a** shall cause the woman to drink the water. 310
12:16 **a** the people removed from Hazeroth, and 310
19: 7 **a** he shall come into the camp, and the priest 310
31: 2 **a** shalt thou be gathered unto thy people. 310
31:24 be clean, and **a** ye shall come into the camp. 310
32:22 **a** ye shall return, and be guiltless before 310
Dt 17: 7 **a** the hands of all the people. 314+871.1+1886.1
24:21 of thy vineyard, thou shalt not glean *it* **a**: 310
Jos 2:16 be returned: and **a** may ye go your way. 310
8:34 **a** he read all the words of the law, 310+3651
10:26 **a** Joshua smote them, and slew them, 310+3651
24: 5 I did amongst them: and **a** I brought you out. 310
Jdg 1: 9 **a** the children of Judah went down to fight 310
7:11 **a** shall thine hands be strengthened to go 310
16: 4 it came to pass **a**, that he loved a woman in 310
19: 5 *with* a morsel of bread, and **a** go your way. 310
1Sa 24: 5 it came to pass **a**, that David's heart 310+3651
24: 8 David also rose **a**, and went out of 310+3651
2Sa 3:28 **a** when David heard *it*, he said, 310+3651+4480
1Ch 2:21 **a** Hezron went in to the daughter of Machir 310
2Ch 35:14 **a** they made ready for themselves, and 310
Ezr 3: 5 **a** *offered* the continual burnt offering, 310+3651
Ne 6:10 **A** I came *unto* the house of Shemaiah 2050.1
Ps 73:24 with thy counsel, and **a** receive me *to* glory. 310
Isa 1:26 **a** thou shalt be called, The city of 310+3651
9: 1 **a** did more grievously afflict *her by* the way 314
Jer 21: 7 **a**, saith the LORD, I will deliver 310+3651
49: 6 **a** I will bring again the captivity of 310+3651
Eze 41: 1 **A** he brought me to the temple, and 2050.1
43: 1 **A** he brought me to the gate, *even* 2050.1
47: 1 **A** he brought me again unto the door of 2050.1
47: 5 **A** he measured a thousand; *and it was* a 2050.1
Da 8:27 **a** I rose up, and did the king's business; 2050.1
Hos 3: 5 **A** shall the children of Israel return, and 310
Joel 2:28 it shall come to pass **a**, that I will pour 310+3651
Mt 4: 2 and forty nights, he was **a** a hungred. *5306*
21:29 I will not: but **a** he repented, and went. *5306*
21:32 and ye, when ye had seen *it*, repented not **a**, *5306*
25:11 **A** came also the other virgins, saying, Lord, *5306*
Mk 4:17 **a**, when affliction or persecution ariseth for *1534*
16:14 **A** he appeared unto the eleven as they sat at *5306*
Lk 4: 2 and when they were ended, he **a** hungered. *5306*
8: 1 And it came to pass **a**, that he *1722+2517+3588*
17: 8 and **a** thou shalt eat and drink? *3326+3778*
18: 4 but **a** he said within himself, *3326+3778*
Jn 5:14 **A** Jesus findeth him in the temple, *3326+3778*
Ac 13:21 **And a** they desired a king: and God gave *2547*
1Co 15:23 **a** they that are Christ's at his coming. *1899*
15:46 *is* natural; *and* **a** *that which is* spiritual. *1899*
Heb 4: 8 he not **a** have spoken of another day. *3326+3778*
12:11 nevertheless **a** it yieldeth the peaceable *5306*
12:17 For ye know how that **a**, when he would *3347*
Jude 1: 5 **a** destroyed them that believed not. *1208*

AFTERWARDS (15) [AFTER]

Ge 30:21 **a** she bare a daughter, and called her name 310
Ex 11: 1 **a** he will let you go hence: 310+3651
Dt 13: 9 to death, and **a** the hand of all the people. 314
1Sa 9:13 *and* **a** they eat that be bidden. 310+3651
Job 18: 2 an end of words? mark, and **a** we will speak. 310
Pr 20:17 but **a** his mouth shall be filled *with* gravel. 310
24:27 thyself in the field; and **a** build thine house. 310
28:23 **a** shall find more favour than he that 310
29:11 his mind: but a wise *man* keepeth it in *till* **a**. 268
Jer 34:11 **a** they turned, and caused the servants 310+3651
46:26 **a** it shall be inhabited, as *in* the days 310+3651
Eze 11:24 **A** the spirit took me up, and brought me 2050.1
Jn 13:36 follow me now; but thou shalt follow me **a**. *5306*
Gal 1:21 **A** I came into the regions of Syria and *1899*
3:23 shut up unto the faith which should **a** be *3195*

AGABUS (2)

Ac 11:28 And there stood up one of them named **A**, and *13*
21:10 down from Judea a certain prophet, named **A**. *13*

AGAG (8) [AGAGITE]

Nu 24: 7 his king shall be higher than **A**, and 90
1Sa 15: 8 he took **A** the king of the Amalekites alive, 90
15: 9 Saul and the people spared **A**, and the best of 90
15:20 and have brought **A** the king of Amalek, and 90
15:32 Bring you hither to me **A** the king of 90
15:32 **A** came unto him delicately. And Agag said, 90
15:32 **A** said, Surely the bitterness of death is past. 90
15:33 Samuel hewed **A** in pieces before the LORD 90

AGAGITE (5) [AGAG]

Est 3: 1 Haman the son of Hammedatha the **A**, 91
3:10 it unto Haman the son of Hammedatha the **A**, 91
8: 3 to put away the mischief of Haman the **A**, 91
8: 5 by Haman the son of Hammedatha the **A**, 91
9:24 the **A**, the enemy of all the Jews, 91

AGAIN (672)

Ge 4: 2 she **a** bare his brother Abel. And Abel was 3254
4:25 Adam knew his wife **a**; and she bare a son, 5750
8:10 and **a** he sent forth the dove out of the ark; 3254
8:12 which returned not **a** unto him any more. 3254
8:21 I will not **a** curse the ground any more for 3254
8:21 neither will I **a** smite any more every *thing* 3254
14:16 also **brought a** his brother Lot, and 7725
15:16 fourth generation they shall **come** hither **a**: 7725
18:29 he spake unto him **yet a**, and said, 3254+5750
19: 9 they said **a**, *This one fellow* came in to NIH
22: 5 go yonder and worship, and **come a** to you. 7725
24: 5 **must** I **needs bring** thy son **a** unto 7725+7725
24: 6 thou that thou **bring** not my son thither **a**. 7725
24: 8 my oath: only **bring** not my son thither **a**. 7725
24:20 ran **a** unto the well to draw *water*, and 5750
25: 1 **a** Abraham took a wife, and her name *was* 3254
26:18 Isaac digged **a** the wells of water, 7725
28:15 and will **bring** thee **a** into this land; 7725
28:21 So that I **come a** to my father's house in 7725
29: 3 **put** the stone **a** upon the well's mouth in 7725
29:33 she conceived **a**, and bare a son; and said, 5750
29:34 she conceived **a**, and bare a son; and said, 5750
29:35 she conceived **a**, and bare a son: and 5750
30: 7 Bilhah Rachel's maid conceived **a**, and 5750
30:19 Leah conceived **a**, and bare Jacob the sixth 5750
Ge 30:31 for me, I will **a** feed *and* keep thy flock: 7725
35: 9 God appeared unto Jacob **a**, when he came 5750
37:14 well with the flocks; and **bring** me word **a**. 7725
37:22 their hands, to deliver him to his father **a**. 7725
38: 4 she conceived **a**, and bare a son; and 5750
38: 5 she **yet a** conceived, and bare a son; 3254+5750
38:26 my son. And he knew her **a** no more. 3254
40:21 **restored** the chief butler unto his butlership **a** 7725
42:24 returned to them **a**, and communed with NIH
42:37 my hand, and I will **bring** him to thee **a**. 7725
43: 2 said unto them, **Go a**, buy us a little food. 7725
43:12 the money that was **brought a** in the mouth 7725
43:12 of your sacks, **carry** *it* **a** in your hand; 7725
43:13 your brother, and arise, **go a** unto the man: 7725
43:21 we have **brought** it **a** in our hand. 7725
44: 8 we **brought a** unto thee out of the land of 7725
44:25 father said, **Go a**, *and* buy us a little food. 7725
46: 4 I will also surely bring thee up **a**: and NIH
48:21 **bring** you **a** unto the land of your fathers. 7725
50: 5 and bury my father, and I will **come a**. 7725
Ex 4: 7 he said, **Put** thine hand into thy bosom **a**. 7725
4: 7 he **put** his hand into his bosom **a**; and 7725
4: 7 behold, it was **turned a** as his *other* flesh. 7725
10: 8 and Aaron were **brought a** unto Pharaoh: 7725
10:29 spoken well, I will see thy face **a** no more. 3254
14:13 ye shall see them **a** no more for ever. 3254
14:26 that the waters may **come a** upon 7725
15:19 the LORD **brought a** the waters of the sea 7725
21:19 If he **rise a**, and walk abroad upon his staff, 6965
23: 4 shalt **surely bring** it **back** to him **a**. 7725+7725
24:14 ye here for us, until we **come a** unto you: 7725
33:11 he **turned a** into the camp: but his servant 7725
34:35 Moses **put** the vail upon his face **a**, until he 7725
Lev 13: 6 the priest shall look on him **a** the seventh 8145
13: 7 he shall be seen of the priest **a**: 8145
13:16 Or if the raw flesh **turn a**, and be changed 7725
14:39 the priest shall **come a** the seventh day, 7725
14:43 if the plague **come a**, and break out in 7725
20: 2 **A**, thou shalt say to the children of Israel, 2050.1
24:20 in a man, so shall it be done to him **a**. NIH
25:48 After *that* he is sold he may be redeemed **a**; NIH
25:51 **give a** the price of his redemption out of 7725
25:52 unto his years shall he **give** *him* **a** 7725
26:26 they shall **deliver** *you* your bread **a** by 7725
Nu 11: 4 the children of Israel also wept **a**, and said, 7725
12:14 and after *that* let her be received in **a**. NIH
12:15 journeyed not till Miriam was brought in **a**. NIH
17:10 **Bring** Aaron's rod **a** before the Testimony, 7725
22: 8 *this* night, and I will **bring** you word **a**, 7725
22:15 Balak sent yet **a** princes, more, and 3254
22:25 foot against the wall: and he smote her **a**. 3254
22:34 if it displease thee, I will **get** me **back a**. 7725
23:16 and said, **Go a** unto Balak, and say thus. 7725
32:15 he will yet **a** leave them in the wilderness; 3254
33: 7 **turned a** unto Pi-hahiroth, which *is* before 7725
35:32 that he should **come a** to dwell in the land, 7725
Dt 1:22 **bring** us word **a** by what way we must go 7725
1:25 unto us, and **brought** us word **a**, and said, 7725
5:30 Go say to them, **Get** you into your tents **a**. 7725
13:16 be a heap for ever; it shall not be built **a**. 5750
15: 3 Of a foreigner thou mayest exact *it* **a**: but NIH
18:16 Let me not hear **a** the voice of the LORD 3254
22: 1 thou shalt **in any case bring** them **a** 7725+7725
22: 2 after it, and thou shalt **restore** it to him **a**. 7725
22: 4 **surely** help him to **lift** *them* **up a**. 6965+6965
23:11 sun is down, he shall come into the camp **a**. NIH
24: 4 her away, may not take her **a** to be his wife, 7725
24:13 **In any case** thou shalt **deliver** him the pledge **a** 7725+7725
24:19 in the field, thou shalt not go **a** to fetch it: 7725
24:20 thou shalt not go over the boughs **a**: 310
28:68 the LORD shall **bring** thee *into* Egypt **a** 7725
28:68 unto thee, Thou shalt see it no more **a**: 5750
30: 9 for the LORD will **a** rejoice over thee for 7725
33:11 of them that hate him, that they rise **not a**. 4480
Jos 5: 2 circumcise **a** the children of Israel 7725
8:21 they **turned a**, and slew the men of Ai. 7725
14: 7 I **brought** him word **a** as it *was* in mine 7725
18: 4 of them; and they shall come **a** to me. NIH
18: 8 the land, and describe it, and **come a** to me, 7725
18: 9 and came **a** to Joshua to the host at Shiloh. NIH
22:28 that we may say **a**, Behold the pattern of NIH
22:32 of Israel, and **brought** them word **a**. 7725
Jdg 3:12 the children of Israel did evil **a** in the sight 3254
3:19 he himself **turned a** from the quarries that 7725
4: 1 the children of Israel **a** did evil in the sight 3254
4:20 **A** he said unto her, Stand *in* the door of 2050.1
6:18 And he said, I will tarry until thou **come a**. 7725
8: 9 saying, When I **come a** in peace, I will 7725
8:33 that the children of Israel **turned a**, and 7725
9:37 Gaal spake **a** and said, See there 3254+5750
10: 6 the children of Israel did evil **a** in the sight 3254
11: 8 Therefore we **turn a** to thee now, that thou 7725
11: 9 If ye **bring** me *home* **a** to fight against 7725
11:13 therefore **restore** those *lands* **a** peaceably. 7725
11:14 Jephthah sent messengers **a** unto 3254+5750
13: 1 the children of Israel did evil **a** in the sight 3254
13: 8 God which thou didst send come **a** unto us, 5750
13: 9 the angel of God came **a** unto the woman as 5750
15:19 his spirit **came a**, and he revived: 7725
16:22 head began to grow **a** after he was shaven. NIH
19: 3 speak friendly unto her, *and* to **bring** her **a**, 7725
19: 7 law urged him: therefore he lodged there **a** 7725
20:22 set *their* battle **a** in array in the place where 3254
20:23 Shall I go *up* **a** to battle against the children 3254
20:25 children of Israel **a** eighteen thousand men; 5750
20:28 Shall I **yet a** go out to battle against 3254+5750
20:41 when the men of Israel turned **a**, the men of NIH
20:48 the men of Israel **turned a** upon 7725
21:14 Benjamin **came a** at that time; and 7725
Ru 1:11 Naomi said, **Turn a**, my daughters: why 7725
1:12 **Turn a**, my daughters, go *your way*; for I 7725
1:14 they lift up their voice, and wept **a**: and 5750
1:21 the LORD hath **brought** me *home* **a** 7725
4: 3 that is **come a** out of the country of Moab, 7725

1Sa 3: 5 he said, I called not; lie down **a**. And he 7725
3: 6 the LORD called yet **a**, Samuel. 3254
3: 6 I called not, my son; lie down **a**. 7725
3: 8 the LORD called Samuel **a** the third time. 3254
3:21 the LORD appeared **a** in Shiloh: for 3254
4: 5 *with* a great shout, so that the earth **rang a**. 1949
5: 3 took Dagon, and **set** him in his place **a**. 7725
5:11 let it **go a** to his own place, that it slay us 7725
6:21 The Philistines have **brought a** the ark of 7725
9: 8 the servant answered Saul **a**, and said, 3254
15:25 pardon my sin, and **turn a** with me, 7725
15:30 and before Israel, and **turn a** with me, 7725
15:31 So Samuel **turned a** after Saul; and 7725
16:10 **A**, Jesse made seven of his sons to pass 2050.1
17:30 the people answered him **a** after the former 7725
19: 8 there was war **a**: and David went out, and 3254
19:15 Saul sent the messengers **a** to see David, NIH
19:21 Saul sent messengers **a** the third time, and 3254
20:17 Jonathan **caused** David to swear **a**, because 3254
23: 4 David inquired of the LORD yet **a**. 3254
23:23 and **come** ye **a** to me with the certainty, and 7725
25:12 **went a**, and came and told him all those 7725
27: 4 *to* Gath: and he sought no more **a** for him. 3254
29: 4 fellow return, that he may **go a** to his place, 7725
30:12 he had eaten, his spirit **came a** to him: 7725
2Sa 1: 9 He said unto me **a**, Stand, I pray thee, 2050.1
2:22 Abner said **a** to Asahel, Turn thee 3254+5750
3:11 he could not answer Abner a word **a**, 5750
3:26 which **brought** him **a** from the well of 7725
3:34 And all the people wept **a** over him. 3254
5:22 the Philistines came up yet **a**, and 3254
6: 1 **A**, David gathered together all 5750+2050.1
12:23 can I bring him back **a**? I shall go to him, 5750
14:13 in that the king doth not **fetch** *home* **a** his 7725
14:14 which cannot be gathered up **a**; neither doth NIH
14:21 **bring** the young man Absalom **a**. 7725
14:29 when he sent **a** the second time, he would 5750
15: 8 **bring** me **a indeed** *to* Jerusalem, 7725+7725
15:25 he will **bring** me **a**, and shew me *both* it, 7725
15:29 Abiathar **carried** the ark of God **a** *to* 7725
16:19 **a**, whom should I serve? *should I* not *serve* 8145
18:22 said Ahimaaz the son of Zadok **yet a** 3254+5750
19:24 departed until the day he came **a** in peace. NIH
19:30 forasmuch as my lord the king is come **a** in NIH
19:37 Let thy servant, I pray thee, **turn back a**, 7725
20:10 bowels to the ground, and strake him not **a**; 8138
21:15 Moreover the Philistines had **yet** war **a** with 5750
21:18 that there was **a** a battle with the Philistines 5750
21:19 there was **a** a battle in Gob with 5750
22:38 **turned** not **a** until I had consumed them. 7725
24: 1 **a** the anger of the LORD was kindled 3254
1Ki 1:45 thence rejoicing, so that the city **rang a**. 1949
2:30 Benaiah **brought** the king word **a**, saying, 7725
2:41 from Jerusalem *to* Gath, and was **come a**. 7725
8:33 shall **turn a** to thee, and confess thy name, 7725
8:34 **bring** them **a** unto the land which thou 7725
12: 5 yet *for* three days, then **come a** to me. 7725
12:12 saying, **Come** to me **a** the third day. 7725
12:20 all Israel heard that Jeroboam was **come a**, 7725
12:21 to **bring** the kingdom **a** to Rehoboam 7725
12:27 shall the heart of this people **turn a** unto 7725
12:27 and **go a** to Rehoboam king of Judah. 7725
13: 4 so that he could not **pull** it **in a** to him. 7725
13: 6 that my hand may be **restored** me **a**. 7725
13: 6 the king's hand was **restored** him **a**, and 7725
13: 9 nor **turn a** by the *same* way that thou 7725
13:17 nor **turn a** to go by the way that thou 7725
13:33 made **a** of the lowest of the people priests 7725
17:21 let this child's soul **come** into him **a**. 7725
17:22 the soul of the child **came** into him **a**, and 7725
18:37 and *that* thou hast turned their heart back **a**. 322
18:43 *is* nothing. And he said, **Go a** seven times. 7725
19: 6 he did eat and drink, and laid him down **a**. 7725
19: 7 the angel of the LORD **came a** the second 7725
19:20 he said unto him, Go **back a**: for what have 7725
20: 5 the messengers **came a**, and said, 7725
20: 9 and **brought** him word **a**. 7725
2Ki 1: 6 **turn a** unto the king that sent you, and 7725
1:11 **A** also he sent unto him another captain of 7725
1:13 he sent **a** a captain of the third fifty with his 7725
2:18 when they **came a** to him, (for he tarried at 7725
4:22 I may run to the man of God, and **come a**. 7725
4:29 answer him not **a**: and lay my staff upon NIH
4:31 Wherefore he **went a** to meet him, and 7725
4:38 Elisha **came a** to Gilgal: and *there was* a 7725
4:43 He said **a**, Give the people, that they may 2050.1
5:10 thy flesh shall **come a** to thee, and 7725
5:14 his flesh **came a** like unto the flesh of a 7725
5:26 man turned **a** from his chariot to meet thee? NIH
7: 8 went and hid *it*; and **came a**, and 7725
9:18 came to them, but he **cometh** not **a**. 7725
9:20 came even unto them, and **cometh** not **a**: 7725
9:36 Wherefore they **came a**, and told him. 7725
13:25 Jehoash the son of Jehoahaz took **a** out of 7725
19: 9 he sent messengers **a** unto Hezekiah, 7725
19:30 of Judah shall *yet* **a** take root downward, 3254
20: 5 **Turn a**, and tell Hezekiah the captain of 7725
21: 3 For he built *up* **a** the high places which 7725
22: 9 and **brought** the king word **a**, and said, 7725
22:20 And they **brought** the king word **a**. 7725
24: 7 the king of Egypt came not **a** any more out 3254
1Ch 13: 3 And let us **bring a** the ark of our God to us: 5437
14:13 the Philistines yet **a** spread 3254+5750
14:14 Therefore David inquired **a** of God; and 5750
20: 5 there was war **a** with the Philistines; and 5750
20: 6 yet **a** there was war at Gath, where was a 5750
21:12 advise thyself what word I shall **bring a** to 7725
21:27 he **put up** his sword **a** into the sheath 7725
2Ch 6:25 **bring** them **a** unto the land which thou 7725
10: 5 **Come a** unto me after three days. 7725
10:12 saying, **Come a** to me on the third day. 7725
11: 1 that *he* might **bring** the kingdom **a** to 7725
12:11 **brought** them **a** into the guard chamber. 7725
13:20 Neither did Jeroboam recover strength **a** in 5750
18:18 **A** he said, Therefore hear the word of 2050.1
2Ch 18:32 they turned back **a** from pursuing him. NIH
19: 4 he went out **a** through the people from 7725
20:27 of them, to **go a** to Jerusalem with joy; 7725
24:11 and took it, and **carried** it to his place **a**. 7725
24:19 to them, to **bring** them **a** unto the LORD; 7725
25:10 to go home **a**: wherefore their anger was NIH
28:11 me therefore, and **deliver** the captives **a**, 7725
28:17 For **a** the Edomites had come and 5750
30: 6 **turn a** unto the LORD God of Abraham, 7725
30: 9 For if ye **turn a** unto the LORD, 7725
30: 9 so that *they shall* **come a** into this land: 7725
32:25 Hezekiah **rendered** not **a** according to 7725
33: 3 For he built **a** the high places which 7725
33:13 **brought** him **a** *to* Jerusalem into his 7725
34:16 brought the king word back **a**, saying, 5750
34:28 the same. So they **brought** the king word **a**. 7725
Ezr 2: 1 **came a** unto Jerusalem and Judah, 7725
4:13 the walls set up **a**, *then* will they not pay NIH
4:16 if this city be builded **a**, and the walls NIH
6: 5 brought **a** unto the temple which *is* at NIH
6:21 which were **come a** out of captivity, and 7725
9:14 Should we **a** break thy commandments, and 7725
Ne 7: 6 **came a** to Jerusalem and to Judah, 7725
8:17 **come a** out of the captivity made booths, 7725
9:28 they had rest, they did evil **a** before thee: 7725
9:29 that *thou* mightest **bring** them **a** unto thy 7725
13: 9 thither **brought** I **a** the vessels of the house 7725
13:21 if ye **do** *so* **a**, I will lay hands on you. 8138
Est 4:10 **A** Esther spake unto Hatach, and 2050.1
6:12 Mordecai **came a** to the king's gate. 7725
7: 2 the king said **a** unto Esther on the second 1571
8: 3 And Esther spake yet **a** before the king, and 3254
Job 2: 1 **A** there was a day when the sons of God 2050.1
6:29 yea, return **a**, my righteousness *is* in it. 5750
10: 9 and wilt thou **bring** me into dust **a**? 7725
10:16 **a** thou shewest thyself marvellous upon me. 7725
12:14 it cannot be built **a**: he shutteth up a man, NIH
12:23 the nations, and straiteneth them **a**. NIH
14: 7 that it will sprout **a**, and that the tender 5750
14:14 shall he live **a**? all the days of my appointed NIH
20:15 down riches, and he shall vomit them up **a**: NIH
29:22 After my words they spake not **a**; and 8138
34:15 and man shall **turn a** unto dust. 7725
Ps 18:37 neither did I **turn a** till they were 7725
37:21 The wicked borroweth, and **payeth** not **a**: 7999
60: 1 been displeased; O **turn** thyself to us **a**. 7725
68:22 The Lord said, I will **bring a** from Bashan, 7725
68:22 I will **bring** *my people* **a** from the depths of 7725
71:20 shalt quicken me **a**, and shalt bring me up 7725
71:20 shalt bring me up **a** from the depths of 7725
78:39 wind that passeth away, and **cometh** not **a**. 7725
80: 3 **Turn** us **a**, O God, and cause thy face to 7725
80: 7 **Turn** us **a**, O God *of* hosts, and cause thy 7725
80:19 **Turn** us **a**, O LORD God *of* hosts, 7725
85: 6 Wilt thou not revive us **a**: that thy people 7725
85: 8 to his saints: but let them not turn **a** to folly. NIH
104: 9 *that* they **turn** not **a** to cover the earth. 7725
107:26 *to* the heaven, they go down **a** *to* the depths: NIH
107:39 **A**, they are minished and brought low 2050.1
126: 1 When the LORD **turned a** the captivity of 7725
126: 4 **Turn a** our captivity, O LORD, as 7725
126: 6 shall **doubtless come a** with rejoicing, 935+935
140:10 into deep pits, *that* they **rise** not **up a**. 6965
Pr 2:19 None that go *unto* her return **a**, neither take NIH
3:28 Go, and **come a**, and to morrow I will give; 7725
19:17 that which he hath given will he **pay** him **a**. 7999
19:19 deliver *him*, yet thou must **do** *it* **a**. 3254+5750
19:24 will not so much as **bring** it to his mouth **a**. 7725
23:35 shall I awake? I will seek it **yet a**. 3254+5750
24:16 *man* falleth seven *times*, and riseth up **a**: but NIH
26:15 it grieveth him to **bring** it **a** to his mouth. 7725
Ecc 1: 6 the wind returneth **a** according to his NIH
1: 7 rivers come, thither they **return a**. 1980+7725
3:20 all are of the dust, and all **turn** to dust **a**. 7725
4: 4 **A**, I considered all travail, and every right 2050.1
4:11 **A**, if two lie together, then they have heat: 1571
8:14 **a**, there be wicked *men*, to whom it 2050.1
Isa 7:10 Moreover the LORD spake **a** unto Ahaz, 3254
8: 5 The LORD spake also unto me **a**, 3254+5750
10:20 shall no more **a** stay upon him that smote 5750
11:11 *that* the Lord shall **set** his hand **a** the second 3254
24:20 upon it; and it shall fall, and not rise **a**. 3254
37:31 house of Judah shall **a** take root downward, 3254
38: 8 I will **bring a** the shadow of the degrees, 7725
46: 8 **bring** *it* **a** to mind, O ye transgressors. 7725
49: 5 to **bring** Jacob **a** to him, Though Israel be 7725
49:20 hast lost the other, shall say **a** in thine ears, 5750
51:22 of my fury; thou shalt no more drink it **a**: 5750
52: 8 when the LORD shall **bring a** Zion. 7725
Jer 3: 1 another man's, shall he return unto her **a**? 5750
3: 1 yet **return a** to me, saith the LORD. 7725
12:15 will **bring** them **a**, every man to his 7725
15:19 will I **bring** thee **a**, *and* thou shalt stand 7725
16:15 I will **bring** them **a** into their land that I 7725
18: 4 so he made it **a** another vessel, as seemed 7725
19:11 that cannot be made whole **a**: 5750
23: 3 and will **bring** them **a** to their folds; 7725
24: 4 **A** the word of the LORD came unto me, 2050.1
24: 6 and I will **bring** them **a** to this land: 7725
25: 5 **Turn** ye **a** now every one from his evil 7725
27:16 now shortly be **brought a** from Babylon: 7725
28: 3 Within two full years *will* I **bring a** into 7725
28: 4 I *will* **bring a** to this place Jeconiah the son 7725
28: 6 to **bring a** the vessels of the LORD'S 7725
29:14 I will **bring** you **a** into the place whence I 7725
30: 3 that I will **bring a** the captivity of my 7725
30:18 I *will* **bring a** the captivity of Jacob's tents, 7725
31: 4 **A** I will build thee, and thou shalt be built, 5750
31: 4 thou shalt **a** be adorned *with* thy tabrets, 5750
31:16 they shall **come a** from the land of 7725
31:17 that *thy* children shall **come a** to their own 7725
31:21 **turn a**, O virgin of Israel, turn again to 7725
31:21 O virgin of Israel, **turn a** to these thy cities, 7725
31:23 when I shall **bring a** their captivity; 7725
32:15 vineyards shall be possessed **a** in this land. 5750
Jer 32:37 I will **bring** them **a** unto this place, and 7725
33:10 **A** there shall be heard in this place, which 5750
33:12 **A** in this place, *which is* desolate without 5750
33:13 shall the flocks pass **a** under the hands of 5750
36:28 Take thee **a** another roll, and write in it all 7725
37: 8 the Chaldeans shall **come a**, and 7725
41:16 whom he had **brought a** from Gibeon: 7725
46:16 let us **go a** to our own people, and to 7725
48:47 Yet will I **bring a** the captivity of Moab in 7725
49: 6 afterward I will **bring a** the captivity of 7725
49:39 *that* I will **bring a** the captivity of Elam, 7725
50:19 I will **bring** Israel **a** to his habitation, and 7725
La 3:40 try our ways, and **turn a** to the LORD. 7725
Eze 3:20 **A**, When a righteous *man* doth turn from 2050.1
4: 6 lie **a** on thy right side, and thou shalt bear 8145
5: 4 take of them **a**, and cast them into the midst 5750
7: 7 and not the **sounding a** of the mountains. 1906
8: 6 **turn** thee yet **a**, *and* thou shalt see great*er* 7725
8:13 **Turn** thee yet **a**, *and* thou shalt see great*er* 7725
8:15 **turn** thee yet **a**, *and* thou shalt see greater 7725
11:14 **A** the word of the LORD came unto me, 2050.1
12:26 **A** the word of the LORD came to me, 2050.1
14:12 The word of the LORD came **a** to me, 2050.1
16: 1 **A** the word of the LORD came unto me, 2050.1
16:53 When I shall **bring a** their captivity, 7725
16:53 *will I bring* **a** the captivity of thy captives in NIH
18: 1 the word of the LORD came unto me **a**, 2050.1
18:27 **A**, when the wicked *man* turneth away 2050.1
21: 8 **A** the word of the LORD came unto me, 2050.1
21:18 The word of the LORD came unto me **a**, 2050.1
23: 1 The word of the LORD came **a** unto me, 2050.1
24: 1 **A** in the ninth year, in the tenth month, 2050.1
25: 1 The word of the LORD came **a** unto me, 2050.1
26:21 yet shalt thou never be found **a**, saith 5750
27: 1 The word of the LORD came **a** unto me, 2050.1
28: 1 The word of the LORD came **a** unto me, 2050.1
28:20 **A** the word of the LORD came unto me, 2050.1
29:14 I will **bring a** the captivity of Egypt, and 7725
30: 1 The word of the LORD came **a** unto me, 2050.1
33: 1 **A** the word of the LORD came unto me, 2050.1
33:14 **A**, when I say unto the wicked, 2050.1
33:15 **give a** that he had robbed, walk in 7999
34: 4 neither have ye **brought a** that which was 7725
34:16 **bring a** that which was driven away, and 7725
37: 4 **A** he said unto me, Prophesy upon these 2050.1
37:15 The word of the LORD came **a** unto me, 2050.1
39:25 Now will I **bring a** the captivity of Jacob, 7725
39:27 When I have **brought** them **a** from 7725
47: 1 Afterward he **brought** me **a** unto the door 7725
47: 4 **A** he measured a thousand, and 2050.1
47: 4 **A** he measured a thousand, and 2050.1
Da 2: 7 They answered **a** and said, Let the king tell 8579
9:25 the street shall be built **a**, and the wall, 7725
10:18 there **came a** and touched me *one* like 3254
Hos 1: 6 she conceived **a**, and bare a daughter. 5750
Joel 3: 1 when I shall **bring a** the captivity of Judah 7725
Am 7: 8 I will not **a** pass by them any more: 3254
7:13 prophesy not **a** any more *at* Beth-el: for it *is* 3254
8: 2 I will not **a** pass by them any more. 3254
8:14 they shall fall, and **never** rise up **a**. 3808+5750
9:14 I will **bring a** the captivity of my people of 7725
Jnh 2: 4 yet I will look **a** toward thy holy temple. 3254
Mic 7:19 He will **turn a**, he will have compassion 7725
Zep 3:20 At that time will I bring you **a**, even in NIH
Hag 2:20 **a** the word of the LORD came unto 8145
Zec 2: 1 I lift up mine eyes **a**, and looked, and 2050.1
2:12 the holy land, and shall choose Jerusalem **a**. 5750
4: 1 the angel that talked with me **came a**, and 7725
4:12 I answered **a**, and said unto him, What *be* 8145
8: 1 **A** the word of the LORD of hosts came 2050.1
8:15 So **a** have I thought in these days to do well 7725
10: 6 and I will bring them **a** to place them; NIH
10: 9 shall live with their children, and **turn a**. 7725
10:10 I will **bring** them **a** also out of the land of 7725
12: 6 Jerusalem shall be inhabited **a** in her own 5750
Mal 2:13 this have ye done **a**, covering the altar of 8145
Mt 2: 8 when ye have found *him*, **bring** me **word a**, *518*
4: 7 Jesus said unto him, It is written **a**, *3825*
4: 8 **A**, the devil taketh him *up* into an *3825*
5:33 **A**, ye have heard that it hath been said by *3825*
7: 2 ye mete, it shall be **measured** to you **a**. *488*
7: 6 under their feet, and turn **a** and rent you. NIG
11: 4 **shew** John **a** *those things* which ye do hear *518*
13:44 **A**, the kingdom of heaven is like unto *3825*
13:45 **A**, the kingdom of heaven is like unto a *3825*
13:47 **A**, the kingdom of heaven is like unto a net, *3825*
16:21 and be killed, and be raised **a** the third day. NIG
17: 9 the Son of man be **risen a** from the dead. *450*
17:23 the third day he shall be raised **a**. And they NIG
18:19 **A** I say unto you, That if two of you shall *3825*
19:24 And **a** I say unto you, It is easier for a *3825*
20: 5 **A** he went out about the sixth and *3825*
20:19 crucify *him*: and the third day he shall **rise a**. *450*
21:36 **A**, he sent other servants more than the first: *3825*
22: 1 and spake unto them **a** by parables, *3825*
22: 4 **A**, he sent forth other servants, saying, *3825*
26:32 But after I am risen **a**, I will go before you NIG
26:42 He went away **a** the second time, and *3825*
26:43 And he came and found them asleep **a**: *3825*
26:44 and went away **a**, and prayed the third time, *3825*
26:52 unto him, **Put up a** thy sword into his place: *654*
26:72 And **a** he denied with an oath, I do not *3825*
27: 3 **brought a** the thirty pieces of silver to *654*
27:50 when he had cried **a** with a loud voice, *3825*
27:63 was yet alive, After three days I will rise **a**. NIG
Mk 2: 1 And **a** he entered into Capernaum after *3825*
2:13 And he went forth **a** by the sea side; and *3825*
3: 1 And he entered **a** into the synagogue; and *3825*
3:20 And *the* multitude cometh together **a**, so *3825*
4: 1 And he began **a** to teach by the sea side: *3825*
5:21 And when Jesus was passed over **a** by ship *3825*
7:31 And **a**, departing from the coasts of Tyre *3825*
8:13 entering into the ship **a** departed to *3825*
8:25 After that he put *his* hands **a** upon his eyes, *3825*
8:31 and be killed, and after three days **rise a**. *450*

Mk 10: 1 and the people resort unto him **a**; and, as he 3825
10: 1 and, as he was wont, he taught them **a**. 3825
10:10 And in the house his disciples asked him **a** 3825
10:24 But Jesus answereth **a**, and saith unto them, 3825
10:32 And he took **a** the twelve, and began to tell 3825
10:34 kill him: and the third day he shall **rise a**. 450
11:27 And they come **a** to Jerusalem: and as he 3825
12: 4 And **a** he sent unto them another servant; 3825
12: 5 And **a** he sent another; and him they killed, 3825
13:16 **a** for to take up his garment. 1519+3588+3694
14:39 And **a** he went away, and prayed, and 3825
14:40 when he returned, he found them asleep **a**, 3825
14:61 **A** the high priest asked him, and said unto 3825
14:69 And a maid saw him **a**, and began to say to 3825
14:70 And he denied *it* **a**. And a little after, 3825
14:70 they that stood by said **a** to Peter, 3825
15: 4 And Pilate asked him **a**, saying, 3825
15:12 And Pilate answered and said **a** unto them, 3825
15:13 And they cried out **a**, Crucify him. 3825
Lk 2:34 set for the fall and **rising a** of many in Israel; 386
2:45 they **turned back a** to Jerusalem, 5290
4:20 and he **gave** *it* **a** to the minister, and 591
6:30 that taketh away thy *goods* **ask** *them* not **a**. 523
6:34 also lend to sinners, to **receive** as much **a**. 618
6:35 do good, and lend, **hoping for** nothing **a**; 560
6:38 mete withal it shall be **measured** to you **a**. 488
8:37 went *up* into the ship, and returned *back* **a**. NIG
8:55 And her spirit **came a**, and she arose 1994
9: 8 that one of the old prophets was **risen a**. 450
9:19 *say*, that one of the old prophets is **risen a**. 450
9:39 **and** it teareth him that he foameth **a**, and 2532
9:42 the child, and **delivered** him **a** to his father. 591
10: 6 rest upon it: if not, it shall **turn** to you **a**. 344
10:17 And the seventy returned **a** with joy, saying, NIG
10:35 when I **come a**, I will repay thee. 1880
13:20 And **a** he said, Whereunto shall I liken 3825
14: 6 And they could not **answer** him **a** to these 470
14:12 lest they also **bid** thee **a**, and a recompence 479
15:24 For this my son was dead, and is **alive a**; 326
15:32 for this thy brother was dead, and is **alive a**; 326
17: 4 and seven times in a day **turn a** to thee, 1994
18:33 to death: and the third day he shall **rise a**. 450
20:11 And **a** he sent another servant: and 4369
20:12 And **a** he sent a third: and they wounded 4369
23:11 in a gorgeous robe, and **sent** him **a** to Pilate. 375
23:20 willing to release Jesus, spake **a** to *them*. 3825
24: 7 and be crucified, and the third day **rise a**. 450
Jn 1:35 **A** the next day *after* John stood, and two of 3825
3: 3 I say unto thee, Except a man be born **a**, 509
3: 7 not that I said unto thee, Ye must be born **a**. 509
4: 3 He left Judea, and departed **a** into Galilee. 3825
4:13 drinketh of this water shall thirst **a**: 3825
4:46 So Jesus came **a** into Cana of Galilee, 3825
4:54 This *is* **a** the second miracle *that* Jesus did, 3825
6:15 he departed **a** into a mountain himself 3825
6:39 but should raise it up **a** at the last day. NIG
8: 2 And early in the morning he came **a** into 3825
8: 8 And **a** he stooped down, and wrote on 3825
8:12 Then spake Jesus **a** unto them, saying, I am 3825
8:21 Then said Jesus **a** unto them, I go my way, 3825
9:15 Then **a** the Pharisees also asked him how 3825
9:17 They say unto the blind man **a**, What sayest 3825
9:24 Then **a** called they the man that was 1208+1537
9:26 Then said they to him **a**, What did he to 3825
9:27 wherefore would you hear *it* **a**? will ye also 3825
10: 7 Then said Jesus unto them **a**, Verily, verily, 3825
10:17 I lay down my life, that I might take it **a**. 3825
10:18 lay it down, and I have power to take it **a**. 3825
10:19 **a** among the Jews for these sayings. 3825
10:31 Then the Jews took up stones **a** to stone 3825
10:39 Therefore they sought **a** to take him: but 3825
10:40 And went away **a** beyond Jordan into 3825
11: 7 he to *his* disciples, Let us go into Judea **a**. 3825
11: 8 to stone thee; and goest thou thither **a**? 3825
11:23 Jesus saith unto her, Thy brother shall **rise a**. 450
11:24 I know that he shall **rise a** in the resurrection 450
11:38 **a** groaning in himself cometh to the grave. 3825
12:22 and **a** Andrew and Philip tell Jesus. 3825
12:28 I have both glorified *it*, and will glorify *it* **a**. 3825
12:39 not believe, because that Esaias said **a**, 3825
13:12 and was set down **a**, he said unto them, 3825
14: 3 I will come **a**, and receive you unto myself; 3825
14:28 unto you, I go away, and come **a** unto you. NIG
16:16 and **a**, a little while, and ye shall see me, 3825
16:17 and **a**, a little while, and ye shall see me: 3825
16:19 and **a**, a little while, and ye shall see me? 3825
16:22 but I will see you **a**, and your heart shall 3825
16:28 **a**, I leave the world, and go to the Father. 3825
18: 7 Then asked he them **a**, Whom seek ye? 3825
18:27 Peter then denied **a**: and immediately 3825
18:33 Pilate entered into the judgment hall **a**, 3825
18:38 he went out **a** unto the Jews, and saith unto 3825
18:40 Then cried they all **a**, saying, Not this *man*, 3825
19: 4 Pilate therefore went forth **a**, and 3825
19: 9 And went **a** into the judgment hall, and 3825
19:37 And **a** another scripture saith, They shall 3825
20: 9 that he must **rise a** from the dead. 450
20:10 Then the disciples went away **a** unto their 3825
20:21 Then said Jesus to them **a**, Peace *be* unto 3825
20:26 And after eight days **a** his disciples were 3825
21: 1 After these *things* Jesus shewed himself **a** 3825
21:16 He saith to him **a** the second time, Simon, 3825
Ac 1: 6 wilt thou at this time **restore a** the kingdom 600
7:26 and would have set them at one **a**, saying, NIG
7:39 and in their hearts turned *back* **a** into Egypt, NIG
10:15 And *the* voice *spake* unto him **a** the second 3825
10:16 the vessel was received up **a** into heaven. 3825
11: 9 But *the* voice answered me **a** from 1208+1537
11:10 and all were drawn up **a** into heaven. 3825
13:33 in that he hath **raised up** Jesus **a**; 450
13:37 whom God raised **a**, saw no corruption. NIG
14:21 they returned **a** to Lystra, and *to* Iconium, NIG
15:16 and will **build a** the tabernacle of David, 456
15:16 and I will **build a** the ruins thereof, and 456
15:36 Let us **go a** and visit our brethren in every 1994
Ac 17: 3 have suffered, and **risen a** from the dead; 450
17:32 We will hear thee **a** of this *matter*. 3825
18:21 but I will return **a** unto you, if God will. 3825
20:11 When he therefore was come up **a**, and NIG
21: 6 we took ship; and they returned home **a**. NIG
22:17 pass that, when I was **come a** to Jerusalem, 5290
27:28 they sounded **a**, and found *it* fifteen 3825
Ro 4:25 and was raised **a** for our justification. NIG
8:15 not received the spirit of bondage **a** to fear; 3825
8:34 that is risen **a**, who is even at the right hand NIG
10: 7 (that is, to **bring up** Christ **a** from the dead.) 321
11:23 for God is able to graff them in **a**. 3825
11:35 and it shall be recompensed unto him **a**? NIG
15:10 And **a** *he* saith, Rejoice, *ye* Gentiles, 3825
15:11 And **a**, Praise the Lord, all ye Gentiles; and 3825
15:12 And **a** Esaias saith, There shall be a root of 3825
1Co 3:20 And **a**, The Lord knoweth the thoughts of 3825
7: 5 to fasting and prayer, and come together **a**, 3825
12:21 nor **a** the head to the feet, I have no need of 3825
15: 4 that he rose **a** the third day according to NIG
2Co 1:16 and to come **a** out of Macedonia unto you, 3825
2: 1 that *I* would not come **a** to you in 3825
3: 1 Do we begin **a** to commend ourselves? or 3825
5:12 For we commend not ourselves **a** unto you, 3825
5:15 unto him which died for them, and rose **a**. NIG
10: 7 let him of himself think this **a**, that, as he *is* 3825
11:16 I say **a**, Let no *man* think me a fool; 3825
12:19 **A**, think you that we excuse ourselves unto 3825
12:21 *And* lest, when I come **a**, my God will 3825
13: 2 and to all other, that, if I come **a**, I will not 3825
Gal 1: 9 As we said before, so say I now **a**, If any 3825
1:17 into Arabia, and returned **a** unto Damascus. 3825
2: 1 Then fourteen years after I went up **a** to 3825
2:18 For if I build **a** the *things* which I 3825
4: 9 how turn ye **a** to the weak and 3825
4: 9 whereunto ye desire **a** to be in bondage? 509
4:19 of whom I travail in birth **a** until Christ be 3825
5: 1 be not entangled **a** with the yoke of 3825
5: 3 For I testify **a** to every man that is 3825
Php 1:26 Jesus Christ for me by my coming to you **a**. 3825
2:28 that, when ye see him **a**, ye may rejoice, 3825
4: 4 in the Lord alway: *and* **a** I say, Rejoice. 3825
4:10 at the last your care of me hath **flourished a**; 330
4:16 ye sent once and **a** unto my necessity. 1364
1Th 2:18 come unto you, even I Paul, once and **a**; 1364
3: 9 For what thanks can we **render** to God **a** for 467
4:14 For if we believe that Jesus died and **rose a**, 450
Tit 2: 9 *them* well in all *things;* not **answering a**; 483
Phm 1:12 Whom I have **sent a**: thou therefore 375
Heb 1: 5 And **a**, I will be to him a Father, and 3825
1: 6 And **a**, when he bringeth in 3825
2:13 And **a**, I will put my trust in him. 3825
2:13 And **a**, Behold, I, and the children which 3825
4: 5 And in this *place* **a**, If they shall enter into 3825
4: 7 **A** he limiteth a certain day, saying in 3825
5:12 ye have need that *one* teach you **a** which *be* 3825
6: 1 not laying **a** the foundation of repentance 3825
6: 6 fall away, to renew *them* **a** unto repentance; 3825
10: 3 *is* a remembrance **a** *made* of sins every year. NIG
10:30 And **a**, The Lord shall judge his people. 3825
11:35 received their dead **raised to life a**: 386+1537
13:20 that **brought a** from the dead our Lord 321
Jas 5:18 And he prayed **a**, and the heaven gave rain, 3825
1Pe 1: 3 **begotten** us **a** unto a lively hope by 313
1:23 Being **born a**, not of corruptible seed, but 313
2:23 Who, when he was reviled, **reviled** not **a**; 486
2Pe 2:20 they are **a** entangled therein, and overcome, 3825
2:22 The dog *is* **turned** to his own vomit **a**; 1994
1Jn 2: 8 **A**, a new commandment I write unto you, 3825
Rev 10: 8 I heard from heaven spake unto me **a**, 3825
10:11 Thou must prophesy **a** before many 3825
19: 3 And **a** they said, Alleluia. And her smoke 1208
20: 5 But the rest of the dead **lived** not **a** until 326

AGAINST (1667)

Ge 4: 8 that Cain rose up **a** Abel his brother, and 413
14:15 he divided himself **a** them, he and 5921
15:10 and laid each piece one **a** another: 7125
16:12 his hand *will be* **a** every man, and 871.1
16:12 every man, and every man's hand **a** him; 871.1
20: 6 I also withheld thee from sinning **a** me: 3807.1
21:16 sat her down over **a** *him* a good way off, 5048
21:16 she sat over **a** *him*, and lift up her voice, 5048
30: 2 Jacob's anger was kindled **a** Rachel: and 871.1
32:25 when he saw that he prevailed not **a** him, 3807.1
34:30 they shall gather themselves together **a** me, 5921
37:18 they **conspired a** him to slay him. 5230
39: 9 do this great wickedness, and sin **a** God? 3807.1
40: 2 Pharaoh was wroth **a** two *of* his officers, 5921
40: 2 **a** the chief of the butlers, and against 5921
40: 2 of the butlers, and **a** the chief of the bakers. 5921
41:36 *that* food shall be for store to the land **a** 3807.1
42:22 unto you, saying, Do not sin **a** the child; 871.1
42:36 Benjamin *away:* all these things are **a** me. 5921
43:18 that he may seek occasion **a** us, and fall 5921
43:25 they made ready the present **a** Joseph came 5704
44:18 and let not thine anger burn **a** thy servant: 871.1
50:20 as for you, ye thought evil **a** me; *but* 5921
Ex 1:10 fight **a** us, and *so* get them up out of 871.1
4:14 the anger of the LORD was kindled **a** 871.1
7:15 thou shalt stand by the river's brink **a** he 5921
8:12 of the frogs which he had brought **a** 3807.1
9:17 As yet exaltest thou thyself **a** my people, 871.1
10:16 I have sinned **a** the LORD your God, 3807.1
10:16 against the LORD your God, and **a** you. 3807.1
11: 7 **a** any of the children of Israel shall not **a** 3807.1
11: 7 **a** dog move his tongue, **a** man or beast: 3807.1
12:12 **a** all the gods of Egypt I will execute 871.1
14: 2 and the sea, **over a** Baal-zephon: 6440
14: 5 and of his servants was turned **a** the people, 413
14:25 for the LORD fighteth for them **a** 871.1
14:27 the Egyptians fled **a** it; and the LORD 7125
15: 7 hast overthrown them that **rose up a** thee: 6965
15:24 And the people murmured **a** Moses, saying, 5921
16: 2 of the children of Israel murmured **a** Moses 5921
Ex 16: 7 for that he heareth your murmurings **a** 5921
16: 7 and what *are* we, that ye murmur **a** us? 5921
16: 8 your murmurings which ye murmur **a** him: 5921
16: 8 your murmurings *are* not **a** us, but 5921
16: 8 *are* not against us, but **a** the LORD. 5921
17: 3 the people murmured **a** Moses, and said, 5921
19:11 be ready **a** the third day: for the third day 3807.1
19:15 unto the people, Be ready **a** the third day: 3807.1
20:16 Thou shalt not bear false witness **a** thy 871.1
23:29 and the beast of the field multiply **a** thee. 5921
23:33 in thy land, lest they make thee sin **a** me: 3807.1
25:27 Over **a** the border shall the rings be for 5980
25:37 that they may give light over **a** it. 5676+6440
26:17 *be* in one board, set in order one **a** another: 413
26:35 the candlestick **over a** the table on the side 5227
28:27 the forepart thereof, **over a** 5980+3807.1
32:10 that my wrath may wax hot **a** them, and 871.1
32:11 why doth thy wrath wax hot **a** thy people, 871.1
32:12 and repent of *this* evil **a** thy people. 3807.1
32:33 Whosoever hath sinned **a** me, him will I 3807.1
37:14 **Over a** the border were the rings, 5980+3807.1
39:20 of it, over **a** the *other* coupling thereof, 5980
40:24 **over a** the table, on the side of 5227
Lev 4: 2 If a soul shall sin through ignorance **a** any 4480
4: 2 not to be done, and shall do **a** any of them: 4480
4:13 they have done somewhat **a** any of 4480
4:14 which they have sinned **a** it, is known, then 5921
4:22 done somewhat through ignorance **a** any of 4480
4:27 while he doeth somewhat **a** *any of* 4480
5:19 hath certainly trespassed **a** the LORD. 3807.1
6: 2 commit a trespass **a** the LORD, and 871.1
17:10 I will even set my face **a** *that* soul that 871.1
19:16 neither shalt thou stand **a** the blood of thy 5921
19:18 nor **bear any grudge a** the children of thy 5201
20: 3 I will set my face **a** that man, and will cut 871.1
20: 5 I will set my face **a** that man, and 871.1
20: 5 **a** his family, and will cut him off, and all 871.1
20: 6 I will even set my face **a** that soul, and 871.1
26:17 I will set my face **a** you, and ye shall be 871.1
26:40 with their trespass which they trespassed **a** 871.1
Nu 5: 6 to do a trespass **a** the LORD, and 871.1
5: 7 give *it* unto *him* **a** whom he hath 3807.1
5:12 go aside, and commit a trespass **a** him, 871.1
5:13 be defiled, and *there be* no witness **a** her, 871.1
5:27 and have done trespass **a** her husband, 871.1
8: 2 light **over a** the candlestick. 413+4136+6440
8: 3 thereof **over a** the candlestick, 413+4136+6440
10: 9 if ye go *to* war in your land **a** the enemy 5921
10:21 *the other* did set up the tabernacle **a** they 5704
11:18 Sanctify yourselves **a** to morrow, and 3807.1
11:33 the wrath of the LORD was kindled **a** 871.1
12: 1 and Aaron spake **a** Moses because 871.1
12: 8 were ye not afraid to speak **a** my servant 871.1
12: 9 the anger of the LORD was kindled **a** 871.1
13:31 We be not able to go up **a** the people; 413
14: 2 all the children of Israel murmured **a** Moses 5921
14: 2 murmured against Moses and **a** Aaron: 5921
14: 9 Only rebel not ye **a** the LORD, 871.1
14:27 evil congregation, which murmur **a** me? 5921
14:27 of Israel, which they murmur **a** me. 5921
14:29 and upward, which have murmured **a** me, 5921
14:35 that are gathered together **a** me: 5921
14:36 made all the congregation to murmur **a** 5921
16: 3 they gathered themselves together **a** Moses 5921
16: 3 together against Moses and **a** Aaron, 5921
16:11 all thy company *are* gathered together **a** 5921
16:11 and what *is* Aaron, that ye murmur **a** him? 5921
16:19 Korah gathered all the congregation **a** them 5921
16:38 The censers of these sinners **a** their own 871.1
16:41 of the children of Israel murmured **a** Moses 5921
16:41 murmured against Moses and **a** Aaron, 5921
16:42 when the congregation was gathered **a** 5921
16:42 was gathered against Moses and **a** Aaron, 5921
17: 5 of Israel, whereby they murmur **a** you. 5921
17:10 to be kept for a token **a** the rebels; 3807.1
20: 2 they gathered themselves together **a** Moses 5921
20: 2 together against Moses and **a** Aaron. 5921
20:18 lest I come out **a** thee with the sword. 7125
20:20 Edom came out **a** him with much people, 7125
20:24 ye rebelled **a** my word at the water of 854
21: 1 he fought **a** Israel, and took *some* of them 871.1
21: 5 the people spake **a** God, and 871.1
21: 5 people spake against God, and **a** Moses, 871.1
21: 7 for we have spoken **a** the LORD, and 871.1
21: 7 spoken against the LORD, and **a** thee; 871.1
21:23 and went out **a** Israel into the wilderness: 7125
21:23 and he came *to* Jahaz, and fought **a** Israel. 871.1
21:26 who had fought **a** the former king of 871.1
21:33 Og the king of Bashan went out **a** them, 7125
22: 5 the earth, and they abide **over a** me: 4136+4480
22:22 stood in the way for an adversary **a** him. 3807.1
22:25 and crusht Balaam's foot **a** the wall: 413
22:34 not that thou stoodest in the way **a** me: 7125
23:23 Surely *there is* no enchantment **a** Jacob, 871.1
23:23 neither *is there* any divination **a** Israel: 871.1
24:10 Balak's anger was kindled **a** Balaam, and 413
25: 3 the anger of the LORD was kindled **a** 871.1
25: 4 hang them up before the LORD **a** the sun, 5048
26: 9 who strove **a** Moses and against Aaron in 5921
26: 9 and **a** Aaron in the company of Korah, 5921
26: 9 of Korah, when they strove **a** the LORD: 5921
27: 3 **a** the LORD in the company of Korah; 5921
27:14 For ye **rebelled a** my commandment in 4784
30: 9 have bound their souls, shall stand **a** her. 5921
31: 3 let them go **a** the Midianites, and avenge 5921
31: 7 they warred **a** the Midianites, as 5921
31:16 to commit trespass **a** the LORD in 871.1
32:13 the LORD'S anger was kindled **a** Israel, 871.1
32:23 behold, ye have sinned **a** the LORD: 3807.1
35:30 one witness shall not testify **a** *any* person 871.1
Dt 1: 1 in the plain **over a** the Red *sea*, between 4136
1:26 rebelled **a** the commandment of the LORD 854
1:41 unto me, We have sinned **a** the LORD, 3807.1
1:43 rebelled **a** the commandment of the LORD, 854
1:44 came out **a** you, and chased you, as bees 7125

A

Dt 2:15 For indeed the hand of the LORD was a 871.1
2:19 when thou comest nigh over a the children 4136
2:32 Sihon came out a us, he and all his people, 7125
3: 1 Og the king of Bashan came out a us, he 7125
3:29 So we abode in the valley over a 4136
4:26 and earth to witness a you this day, 871.1
4:46 side Jordan, in the valley over a Beth-peor, 4136
5:20 Neither shalt thou bear false witness a thy 871.1
6:15 of the LORD thy God be kindled a thee, 871.1
7: 4 will the anger of the LORD be kindled a 871.1
8:19 I testify a you this day that ye shall surely 871.1
9: 7 ye have been rebellious a the LORD. 5973
9:16 ye had sinned a the LORD your God, 3807.1
9:19 wherewith the LORD was wroth a you to 5921
9:23 you rebelled a the commandment of 854
9:24 You have been rebellious a the LORD 5973
11:17 then the LORD'S wrath be kindled a you, 871.1
11:30 which dwell in the champaign over a 4136
15: 9 thine eye be evil a thy poor brother, and 871.1
15: 9 he cry unto the LORD a thee, and it be sin 5921
19:11 rise up a him, and smite him mortally that 5921
19:15 One witness shall not rise up a a man for 871.1
19:16 If a false witness rise up a any man to 871.1
19:16 man to testify a him that which is wrong; 871.1
19:18 and hath testified falsely a his brother; 871.1
20: 1 When thou goest out to battle a thine 5921
20: 3 you approach this day unto battle a your 5921
20: 4 to fight for you a your enemies, to save 5973
20:10 thou comest nigh unto a city to fight a it, 5921
20:12 will make war a thee, then thou shalt 5973
20:18 so should ye sin a the LORD your God. 3807.1
20:19 a long time, in making war a it to take it, 5921
20:19 the trees thereof by forcing an axe a them: 4480
20:20 thou shalt build bulwarks a the city that 5921
21:10 When thou goest forth to war a thine 5921
22:14 give occasions of speech a her, and 3807.1
22:17 he hath given occasions of speech a her, NIH
22:26 for as when a man riseth a his neighbour, 5921
23: 4 they hired a thee Balaam the son of Beor of 5921
23: 9 When the host goeth forth a thine enemies, 5921
24:15 lest he cry a thee unto the LORD, and 5921
28: 7 rise up a thee to be smitten before thy face: 5921
28: 7 they shall come out a thee one way, and flee 413
28:25 thou shalt go out one way a them, and 413
28:48 which the LORD shall send a thee, 871.1
28:49 The LORD shall bring a nation a thee 5921
29: 7 came out a us unto battle, and we smote 7125
29:20 and his jealousy shall smoke a that man, 871.1
29:27 the anger of the LORD was kindled a this 871.1
30:19 and earth to record this day a you, 871.1
31:17 my anger shall be kindled a them in that 871.1
31:19 that this song may be a witness for me a 871.1
31:21 that this song shall testify a them 6440+3807.1
31:26 that it may be there for a witness a thee. 871.1
31:27 ye have been rebellious a the LORD; 5973
31:28 call heaven and earth to record a them. 871.1
32:49 land of Moab, that is over a Jericho; 5921+6440
32:51 Because ye trespassed a me among 871.1
33:11 smite through the loins of them that rise a NIH
34: 1 top of Pisgah, that is over a Jericho. 5921+6440
34: 6 in the land of Moab, over a Beth-peor: 4136
Jos 1:18 Whosoever he be that doth rebel a thy 854
3:16 and the people passed over right a Jericho. 5048
5:13 there stood a man over a him with 5048+3807.1
7: 1 the anger of the LORD was kindled a 871.1
7:13 say, Sanctify yourselves a to morrow: 3807.1
7:20 Indeed I have sinned a the LORD God 3807.1
8: 3 and all the people of war, to go up a Ai: NIH
8: 4 Behold, ye shall lie in wait a the city, 693
8: 5 when they come out a us, as at the first, 7125
8:14 the men of the city went out a Israel to 7125
8:14 liers in ambush a him behind the city. 3807.1
8:22 the other issued out of the city a them; so 7125
8:33 half of them over a mount Gerizim, 413+4136
8:33 and half of them over a mount Ebal; 4136
9: 1 in all the coasts of the great sea over a 4136
9:18 all the congregation murmured a 5921
10: 5 before Gibeon, and made war a it. 5921
10: 6 in the mountains are gathered together a us. 413
10:21 none moved his tongue a any of 3807.1
10:25 do to all your enemies a whom ye fight. 854
10:29 unto Libnah, and fought a Libnah: 5973
10:31 and encamped a it, and fought against it: 5921
10:31 and encamped against it, and fought a it: 871.1
10:34 they encamped a it, and fought against it: 5921
10:34 they encamped against it, and fought a it: 5921
10:36 unto Hebron; and they fought a it: 5921
10:38 Israel with him, to Debir; and fought a it: 5921
11: 5 at the waters of Merom, to fight a Israel. 5973
11: 7 a them by the waters of Merom suddenly; 5921
11:20 that they should come a Israel in battle, that 7125
18:17 which is over a the going up of Adummim, 5227
18:18 passed along toward the side over a Arabah 4136
19:47 the children of Dan went up to fight a 5973
22:11 built an altar over a the land of Canaan, 4136
22:12 together at Shiloh, to go up to war a them. 5921
22:16 ye have committed a the God of Israel, 871.1
22:16 that ye might rebel this day a the LORD? 871.1
22:18 seeing ye rebel to day a the LORD, 871.1
22:19 rebel not a the LORD, nor rebel against 871.1
22:19 rebel not against the LORD, nor rebel a us, 854
22:22 or if in transgression a the LORD, 871.1
22:29 God forbid that we should rebel a 871.1
22:31 ye have not committed this trespass a 871.1
22:33 and did not intend to go up a them in battle, 5921
23:16 shall the anger of the LORD be kindled a 871.1
24: 9 arose and warred a Israel, and sent and 871.1
24:11 the men of Jericho fought a you, 871.1
24:22 Ye are witnesses a yourselves that ye have 871.1
Jdg 1: 1 Who shall go up for us a the Canaanites 413
1: 1 the Canaanites first, to fight a them? 871.1
1: 3 my lot, that we may fight a the Canaanites; 871.1
1: 5 they fought a him, and they slew 871.1
1: 8 Now the children of Judah had fought a 871.1
1: 9 Judah went down to fight a the Canaanites, 871.1

Jdg 1:10 Judah went a the Canaanites that dwelt in 413
1:11 from thence he went a the inhabitants of 413
1:22 of Joseph, they also went up a Beth-el: NIH
2:14 the anger of the LORD was hot a Israel, 871.1
2:15 the hand of the LORD was a them for 871.1
2:20 the anger of the LORD was hot a Israel; 871.1
3: 8 the anger of the LORD was hot a Israel, 871.1
3:10 his hand prevailed a Chushan-rishathaim. 5921
3:12 Eglon the king of Moab a Israel, 5921
4:24 prevailed a Jabin the king of Canaan, 5921
5:14 Out of Ephraim was there a root of them a 871.1
5:20 the stars in their courses fought a Sisera. 5973
5:23 to the help of the LORD a the mighty. 871.1
6: 2 the hand of Midian prevailed a Israel: and 5921
6: 3 of the east, even they came up a them; 5921
6: 4 they encamped a them, and destroyed 5921
6:31 Joash said unto all that stood a him, Will ye 5921
6:32 saying, Let Baal plead a him, because 871.1
6:39 Let not thine anger be hot a me, and I will 871.1
7: 2 lest Israel vaunt themselves a me, saying, 5921
7:22 the LORD set every man's sword a his 871.1
7:24 Come down a the Midianites, and 7125
9:18 ye are risen up a my father's house this 5921
9:31 and behold, they fortify the city a thee. 5921
9:33 the people that is with him come out a thee, 413
9:34 they laid wait a Shechem in four 5921
9:43 and he rose up a them, and smote them. 5921
9:45 Abimelech fought a the city all that day; 871.1
9:50 and encamped a Thebez, and took it. 871.1
9:52 fought a it, and went hard unto the door of 871.1
10: 7 the anger of the LORD was hot a Israel, 871.1
10: 9 passed over Jordan to fight also a Judah, 871.1
10: 9 a Benjamin, and against the house of 871.1
10: 9 and a the house of Ephraim; 871.1
10:10 We have sinned a thee, both because 3807.1
10:18 What man is he that will begin to fight a 871.1
11: 4 that the children of Ammon made war a 5973
11: 5 the children of Ammon made war a Israel, 5973
11: 8 fight a the children of Ammon, and be our 871.1
11: 9 If ye bring me home again to fight a 871.1
11:12 that thou art come a me to fight in my land? 413
11:20 and pitched in Jahaz, and fought a Israel. 5973
11:25 did he ever strive a Israel, or did he ever 5973
11:25 against Israel, or did he ever fight a them, 871.1
11:27 Wherefore I have not sinned a thee, but 3807.1
11:27 but thou doest me wrong to war a me: 871.1
11:32 the children of Ammon to fight a them; 871.1
12: 1 Wherefore passedst thou over to fight a 871.1
12: 1 passed over a the children of Ammon, and 413
12: 3 come up unto me this day, to fight a me? 871.1
14: 4 that he sought an occasion a the Philistines: 4480
14: 5 behold, a young lion roared a him. 7125
15:10 of Judah said, Why are ye come up a us? 5921
15:14 unto Lehi, the Philistines shouted a him: 7125
16: 5 by what means we may prevail a him, 3807.1
18: 9 they said, Arise, that we may go up a them: 5921
19: 2 his concubine played the whore a him, and 5921
19:10 and departed, and came over a Jebus, 5227
20: 5 the men of Gibeah rose a me, and beset 5921
20: 9 will do to Gibeah; we will go up by lot a it; 5921
20:11 So all the men of Israel were gathered a 413
20:14 to go out to battle a the children of Israel. 5973
20:18 Which of us shall go up first to the battle a 5973
20:19 up in the morning, and encamped a Gibeah. 5921
20:20 the men of Israel went out to battle a 5973
20:20 in array to fight a them at Gibeah. 854
20:23 Shall I go up again to battle a the children 5973
20:23 And the LORD said, Go up a him.) 413
20:24 the children of Israel came near a 413
20:25 Benjamin went forth a them out of Gibeah 7125
20:28 Shall I yet again go out to battle a 5973
20:30 the children of Israel went up a the children 413
20:30 put themselves in array a Gibeah, as at other 413
20:31 the children of Benjamin went out a 7125
20:34 there came a Gibeah ten thousand 4480+5048
20:43 trode them down with ease over a Gibeah 5227
Ru 1:13 the hand of the LORD is gone out a me. 871.1
1:21 seeing the LORD hath testified a me, and 871.1
1Sa 2:25 If one man sin a another, the judge shall 3807.1
2:25 if a man sin a the LORD, who shall 3807.1
3:12 In that day I will perform a Eli all things 413
4: 1 Now Israel went out a the Philistines to 7125
4: 2 the Philistines put themselves in array a 7125
5: 9 the hand of the LORD was a the city with 871.1
7: 6 said there, We have sinned a the LORD. 3807.1
7: 7 the lords of the Philistines went up a Israel. 413
7:10 the Philistines drew near to battle a Israel: 871.1
7:13 the hand of the LORD was a 871.1
9:14 behold, Samuel came out a them, for to go 7125
11: 1 came up, and encamped a Jabesh-gilead: 5921
12: 3 here I am: witness a me before 871.1
12: 5 The LORD is witness a you, and 871.1
12: 9 the king of Moab, and they fought a them. 871.1
12:12 king of the children of Ammon came a you, 5921
12:14 not rebel a the commandment of 854
12:15 rebel a the commandment of the LORD, 854
12:15 shall the hand of the LORD be a you, 871.1
12:15 be against you, as it was a your fathers. 871.1
12:23 God forbid that I should sin a the LORD 3807.1
14: 5 was situate northward over a Michmash, 4136
14: 5 and the other southward over a Gibeah. 4136
14:20 every man's sword was a his fellow, and 871.1
14:33 Behold, the people sin a the LORD, 3807.1
14:34 sin not a the LORD in eating with 3807.1
14:47 fought a all his enemies on every side, 871.1
14:47 a Moab, and against the children of 871.1
14:47 a the children of Ammon, and 871.1
14:47 a Edom, and against the kings of Zobah, 871.1
14:47 a the kings of Zobah, and against 871.1
14:47 the kings of Zobah, and a the Philistines: 871.1
14:52 there was sore war a the Philistines all 5921
15: 7 comest to Shur, that is over a Egypt. 5921+6440
15:18 and fight a them until they be consumed. 871.1
17: 2 and set the battle in array a the Philistines. 7125
17: 9 if I prevail a him, and kill him, then 3807.1

1Sa 17:21 had put the battle in array, army a army. 7125
17:28 Eliab's anger was kindled a David, and 871.1
17:33 Thou art not able to go a this Philistine to 413
17:35 when he arose a me, I caught him by his 5921
17:55 when Saul saw David go forth a 7125
18:21 that the hand of the Philistines may be a 871.1
19: 4 Let not the king sin a his servant, 871.1
19: 4 the king sin against his servant, a David; 871.1
19: 4 because he hath not sinned a thee, and 3807.1
19: 5 then wilt thou sin a innocent blood, 871.1
20:30 Saul's anger was kindled a Jonathan, and 871.1
22: 8 That all of you have conspired a me, and 5921
22: 8 my son hath stirred up my servant a me, 5921
22:13 Why have ye conspired a me, thou and 5921
22:13 that he should rise a me, to lie in wait, as at 413
23: 1 the Philistines fight a Keilah, and they rob 871.1
23: 3 if we come to Keilah a the armies of 413
23: 9 that Saul secretly practised mischief a him; 5921
23:28 after David, and went a the Philistines: 7125
24: 6 to stretch forth mine hand a him, 871.1
24: 7 and suffered them not to rise a Saul. 413
24:10 I will not put forth mine hand a my lord; 871.1
24:11 mine hand, and I have not sinned a thee; 3807.1
25:17 for evil is determined a our master, and 413
25:17 against our master, and a all his household: 5921
25:20 David and his men came down a her; 7125
25:22 morning light any that pisseth a the wall. 871.1
25:34 morning light any that pisseth a the wall. 871.1
26: 9 for who can stretch forth his hand a 871.1
26:11 forth mine hand a the LORD'S anointed: 871.1
26:19 If the LORD have stirred thee up a me, 871.1
26:23 I would not stretch forth mine hand a 871.1
27:10 A the south of Judah, and against the south 5921
27:10 a the south of the Jerahmeelites, and 5921
27:10 and a the south of the Kenites. 413
28:15 for the Philistines make war a me, and 871.1
29: 8 that I may not go fight a the enemies of my 871.1
30:23 delivered the company that came a us into 5921
31: 1 Now the Philistines fought a Israel: and 871.1
31: 3 the battle went sore a Saul, and the archers 413
2Sa 1:16 for thy mouth hath testified a thee, saying, 871.1
3: 8 which a Judah do shew kindness this day 3807.1
5:23 upon them over a the mulberry trees. 4136+4480
6: 7 the anger of the LORD was kindled a 871.1
8:10 because he had fought a Hadadezer, and 871.1
10: 9 that the front of the battle was a him before 413
10: 9 and put them in array a the Syrians: 7125
10:10 that he might put them in array a 7125
10:13 with him, unto the battle a the Syrians: 871.1
10:17 the Syrians set themselves in array a David, 7125
11:23 Surely the men prevailed a us, and 5921
11:25 make thy battle more strong a the city, and 413
12: 5 David's anger was greatly kindled a 871.1
12:11 I will raise up evil a thee out of thine own 5921
12:13 unto Nathan, I have sinned a the LORD. 3807.1
12:26 Joab fought a Rabbah of the children of 871.1
12:27 I have fought a Rabbah, and have taken 871.1
12:28 and encamp a the city, and take it: 5921
12:29 to Rabbah, and fought a it, and took it. 871.1
14: 7 the whole family is risen a thine handmaid, 5921
14:13 hast thou thought such a thing a the people 5921
16:13 Shimei went along on the hill's side over a 5980
17:21 for thus hath Ahithophel counselled a you. 5921
18: 6 So the people went out into the field a 7125
18:12 yet would I not put forth mine hand a 413
18:13 have wrought falsehood a mine own life: 871.1
18:13 wouldest have set thyself a me. 4480+5048
18:28 that lift up their hand a my lord the king. 871.1
18:31 thee this day of all them that rose up a thee. 5921
18:32 all that rise a thee to do thee hurt, be as 5921
20:15 they cast up a bank a the city, and it stood in 413
20:21 hath lift up his hand a the king, 871.1
20:21 up his hand against the king, even a David: 871.1
21: 5 that devised a us that we should be 3807.1
21:15 with him, and fought a the Philistines: 3898
22:40 them that rose up a me hast thou subdued NIH
22:49 up on high above them that rose up a me: NIH
23: 8 he lift up his spear a eight hundred, 5921
23:18 he lift up his spear a three hundred, and 5921
24: 1 anger of the LORD was kindled a Israel, 871.1
24: 1 he moved David a them to say, Go, 871.1
24: 4 Notwithstanding the king's word prevailed a 413
24: 4 against Joab, and a the captains of the host. 5921
24:17 be a me, and against my father's house. 871.1
24:17 be against me, and a my father's house. 871.1
1Ki 2:23 if Adonijah have not spoken this word a 871.1
6: 5 a the wall of the house he built chambers 5921
6: 5 a the walls of the house round about, NIH
6:10 then he built chambers a all the house, 5921
7: 4 and light was a light in three ranks. 413
7: 5 and light was a light in three ranks. 413+4136
7:20 a the belly which was by 5980+3807.1
7:39 side of the house eastward over a the south. 4136
8:31 If any man trespass a his neighbour, and NIH
8:33 because they have sinned a thee, and 3807.1
8:35 no rain, because they have sinned a thee; 3807.1
8:44 If thy people go out to battle a their enemy, 5921
8:46 If they sin a thee, (for there is no man 3807.1
8:50 forgive thy people that have sinned a 3807.1
8:50 wherein they have transgressed a thee, 871.1
11:26 even he lift up his hand a the king. 871.1
11:27 this was the cause that he lift up his hand a 871.1
12:19 So Israel rebelled a the house of David 871.1
12:21 were warriors, to fight a the house of Israel, 5973
12:24 nor fight a your brethren the children of 5973
13: 2 he cried a the altar in the word of 5921
13: 4 which had cried a the altar in Beth-el, 5921
13: 4 which he put forth a him, dried up, so 5921
13:32 word of the LORD a the altar in Beth-el, 5921
13:32 a all the houses of the high places which 5921
14:10 from Jeroboam him that pisseth a the wall, 871.1
14:25 that Shishak king of Egypt came up a 5921
15:17 Baasha king of Israel went up a Judah, and 5921
15:20 the hosts which he had a the cities of Israel, 5921
15:27 of the house of Issachar, conspired a him; 5921

1Ki 16: 1 came to Jehu the son of Hanani **a** Baasha, 5921
16: 7 came the word of the LORD **a** Baasha, 413
16: 7 **a** his house, even for all the evil that he did 413
16: 9 conspired **a** him, as he was in Tirzah, 5921
16:11 he left him not one that pisseth **a** a wall, 871.1
16:12 which he spake **a** Baasha by Jehu 413
16:15 the people were encamped **a** Gibbethon, 5921
16:22 the people that followed Omri prevailed **a** 854
20: 1 and besieged Samaria, and warred **a** it. 871.1
20:12 And they set themselves in array **a** the city. 5921
20:22 year the king of Syria will come up **a** thee. 5921
20:23 let us fight **a** them in the plain, and surely we 854
20:25 we will fight **a** them in the plain, and 854
20:26 and went up to Aphek, to fight **a** Israel. 5973
20:27 and were all present, and went **a** them: 7125
20:29 they pitched one **over a** the other seven 5227
21:10 before him, to **bear witness a** him, saying, 5749
21:13 the men of Belial **witnessed a** him, 5749
21:13 even **a** Naboth, in the presence of NIH
21:21 will cut off from Ahab him that pisseth **a** 871.1
22: 6 Shall I go **a** Ramoth-gilead to battle, or 5921
22:15 shall we go **a** Ramoth-gilead to battle, or 413
22:32 they turned aside to fight **a** him: and 5921
22:35 the king was stayed up in his chariot **a** 5227
2Ki 1: 1 Moab rebelled **a** Israel after the death of 871.1
3: 5 that the king of Moab rebelled **a** the king 871.1
3: 7 The king of Moab hath rebelled **a** me: 871.1
3: 7 wilt thou go with me **a** Moab to battle? 413
3:21 the kings were come up to fight **a** them, 871.1
3:27 there was great indignation **a** Israel: and 5921
5: 7 and see how he seeketh a quarrel **a** me. 3807.1
6: 8 the king of Syria warred **a** Israel, and 871.1
7: 6 the king of Israel hath hired **a** us the kings 5921
8:28 **a** Hazael king of Syria in Ramoth-gilead; 5973
8:29 when he fought **a** Hazael king of Syria. 854
9: 8 I will cut off from Ahab him that pisseth **a** 871.1
9:14 the son of Nimshi conspired **a** Joram. 413
9:21 they went out **a** Jehu, and met him in 7125
10: 9 I conspired **a** my master, and slew him: 5921
12:17 went up, and fought **a** Gath, and took it: 5921
13: 3 the anger of the LORD was kindled **a** 871.1
13:12 his might wherewith he fought **a** Amaziah 5973
14:19 Now they made a conspiracy **a** him in 5921
15:10 Shallum the son of Jabesh conspired **a** him, 5921
15:19 And Pul the king of Assyria came **a** 5921
15:25 conspired **a** him, and smote him in 5921
15:30 a conspiracy **a** Pekah the son of Remaliah, 5921
15:37 In those days the LORD began to send **a** 871.1
16: 7 of the king of Israel, which rise up **a** me. 5921
16: 9 for the king of Assyria went up **a** Damascus, 413
16:11 Urijah the priest made it **a** king Ahaz came 5704
17: 3 **A** him came up Shalmaneser king of 5921
17: 7 that the children of Israel had sinned **a** 3807.1
17: 9 that were not right **a** the LORD their God, 5921
17:13 Yet the LORD testified **a** Israel, and 871.1
17:13 **a** Judah, by all the prophets, and by all 871.1
17:15 his testimonies which he testified **a** them; 871.1
18: 7 he rebelled **a** the king of Assyria, and 871.1
18: 9 king of Assyria came up **a** Samaria, 5921
18:13 come up **a** all the fenced cities of Judah, 5921
18:17 Hezekiah with a great host **a** Jerusalem. NIH
18:20 dost thou trust, that thou rebellest **a** me? 871.1
18:25 Am I now come up without the LORD **a** 5921
18:25 to me, Go up **a** this land, and destroy it. 5921
19: 8 found the king of Assyria warring **a** 5921
19: 9 Behold, he is come out to fight **a** thee: 854
19:20 That which thou hast prayed to me **a** 413
19:22 **a** whom hast thou exalted thy voice, and 5921
19:22 on high? even **a** the Holy One of Israel. 5921
19:27 and thy coming in, and thy rage **a** me. 413
19:28 Because thy rage **a** me and thy tumult is 413
19:32 before it with shield, nor cast a bank **a** it. 5921
21:23 And the servants of Amon conspired **a** him, 5921
21:24 all them that had conspired **a** king Amon; 5921
22:13 wrath of the LORD that is kindled **a** us, 871.1
22:17 my wrath shall be kindled **a** this place, 871.1
22:19 when thou heardest what I spake **a** this 5921
22:19 **a** the inhabitants thereof, that they should 5921
23:17 that thou hast done **a** the altar of Beth-el. 5921
23:26 wherewith his anger was kindled **a** Judah, 871.1
23:29 **a** the king of Assyria to the river Euphrates: 5921
23:29 king Josiah went **a** him; and he slew him at 7125
24: 1 then he turned and rebelled **a** him. 871.1
24: 2 the LORD sent **a** him bands of 871.1
24: 2 and sent them **a** Judah to destroy it, 871.1
24:10 king of Babylon came up **a** Jerusalem, NIH
24:11 Nebuchadnezzar king of Babylon came **a** 5921
24:20 that Zedekiah rebelled **a** the king of 871.1
25: 1 **a** Jerusalem, and pitched against it; 5921
25: 1 against Jerusalem, and pitched **a** it; 5921
25: 1 and they built forts **a** it round about. 5921
25: 4 (now the Chaldees were **a** the city round 5921
1Ch 5:11 the children of Gad dwelt over **a** them, 5048
5:20 they were helped **a** them, and the Hagarites 5921
5:25 they transgressed **a** the God of their 871.1
8:32 their brethren in Jerusalem, **over a** them. 5048
9:38 brethren at Jerusalem, over **a** their brethren. 5973
10: 1 Now the Philistines fought **a** Israel; and 871.1
10: 3 the battle went sore **a** Saul, and the archers 5921
10:13 which he committed **a** the LORD, 871.1
10:13 even **a** the word of the LORD, which he 5921
11:11 he lift up his spear **a** three hundred slain by 5921
11:20 for lifting up his spear **a** three hundred, 5921
12:19 when he came with the Philistines **a** Saul to 5921
12:21 they helped David **a** the band of the rovers: 5921
13:10 the anger of the LORD was kindled **a** 871.1
14: 8 heard of it, and went out **a** them. 6440+3807.1
14:10 saying, Shall I go up **a** the Philistines? 5921
14:14 upon them **over a** the mulberry trees. 4136+4480
18:10 because he had fought **a** Hadarezer, and 871.1
19:10 Now when Joab saw that the battle was set **a** 413
19:10 and put them in array **a** the Syrians. 7125
19:11 they set themselves in array **a** the children 7125
19:17 upon them, and set the battle in array **a** them. 413
19:17 So when David had put the battle in array **a** 7125

1Ch 21: 1 Satan stood up **a** Israel, and 5921
21: 4 Nevertheless the king's word prevailed **a** 5921
24:31 These likewise cast lots over **a** their 5980
24:31 even the principal fathers over **a** their 5980
25: 8 **a** ward, as well the small as 5980+3807.1
26:12 having wards one **a** another, 5980+3807.1
26:16 of the going up, ward **a** ward. 5980+3807.1
27:24 because there fell wrath for it **a** Israel; 5921
2Ch 4:10 right side of the east end, over **a** the south. 4136
6:22 If a man sin **a** his neighbour, and an oath 3807.1
6:24 because they have sinned **a** thee; 3807.1
6:26 no rain, because they have sinned **a** thee; 3807.1
6:34 If thy people go out to war **a** their enemies 5921
6:36 If they sin **a** thee, (for there is no man 3807.1
6:39 forgive thy people which have sinned **a** 3807.1
8: 3 went to Hamath-zobah, and prevailed **a** it. 5921
9:29 in the visions of Iddo the seer **a** Jeroboam 5921
10:19 Israel rebelled **a** the house of David unto 871.1
11: 1 to fight **a** Israel, that he might bring 5973
11: 4 shall not go up, nor fight **a** your brethren: 5973
11: 4 and returned from going **a** Jeroboam. 413
12: 2 king of Egypt came up **a** Jerusalem, 5921
12: 2 they had transgressed **a** the LORD, 871.1
12: 9 So Shishak king of Egypt came up **a** 5921
13: 3 Jeroboam also set the battle in array **a** him 5973
13: 6 is risen up, and hath rebelled **a** his lord. 5921
13: 7 have strengthened themselves **a** Rehoboam 5921
13:12 with sounding trumpets to cry alarm **a** you. 5921
13:12 fight ye not **a** the LORD God of your 5973
14: 9 there came out **a** them Zerah the Ethiopian 413
14:10 Asa went out **a** him, and they set 6440+3807.1
14:11 and in thy name we go **a** this multitude. 5921
14:11 art our God; let not man prevail **a** thee. 5973
16: 1 Asa Baasha king of Israel came up **a** Judah, 5921
16: 4 sent the captains of his armies **a** the cities of 413
17: 1 his stead, and strengthened himself **a** Israel. 5921
17:10 so that they made no war **a** Jehoshaphat. 5973
18:22 and the LORD hath spoken evil **a** thee. 5921
18:34 in his chariot **a** the Syrians until the even: 5227
19:10 them that they trespass not **a** the LORD, 3807.1
20: 1 came **a** Jehoshaphat to battle. 5921
20: 2 There cometh a great multitude **a** thee from 5921
20:12 for we have no might **a** this great 6440+3807.1
20:12 this great company that cometh **a** us; 5921
20:16 To morrow go ye down **a** them: behold, 5921
20:17 to morrow go out **a** them: 6440+3807.1
20:22 the LORD set ambushments **a** the children 5921
20:22 mount Seir, which were come **a** Judah; 3807.1
20:23 Moab stood up **a** the inhabitants of mount 5921
20:29 the LORD fought **a** the enemies of Israel. 5973
20:37 of Mareshah prophesied **a** Jehoshaphat, 5921
21:16 Moreover the LORD stirred up **a** Jehoram 5921
22: 5 **a** Hazael king of Syria at Ramoth-gilead: 5921
22: 7 he went out with Jehoram **a** Jehu the son of 413
24:19 the LORD; and they testified **a** them: 871.1
24:21 they conspired **a** him, and stoned him with 5921
24:23 that the host of Syria came up **a** him: 5921
24:24 So they executed judgment **a** Joash. NIH
24:25 his own servants conspired **a** him for 5921
24:26 these are they that conspired **a** him; 5921
25:10 their anger was greatly kindled **a** Judah, 871.1
25:15 of the LORD was kindled **a** Amaziah, 871.1
25:27 they made a conspiracy **a** him in Jerusalem; 5921
26: 6 he went forth and warred **a** the Philistines, 871.1
26: 7 God helped him **a** the Philistines, and 5921
26: 7 **a** the Arabians that dwelt in Gur-baal, and 5921
26:13 to help the king **a** the enemy. 5921
26:16 for he transgressed **a** the LORD his God, 871.1
27: 5 of the Ammonites, and prevailed **a** them. 5921
28:10 with you, sins **a** the LORD your God? 3807.1
28:12 stood up **a** them that came from the war, 5921
28:13 for whereas we have offended **a** 5921
28:13 is great, and there is fierce wrath **a** Israel. 5921
28:19 and transgressed sore **a** the LORD. 871.1
28:22 did he trespass yet more **a** the LORD: 871.1
30: 7 which trespassed **a** the LORD God of 871.1
32: 1 encamped **a** the fenced cities, and 5921
32: 2 that he was purposed to fight **a** Jerusalem, 5921
32: 9 (but he himself laid siege **a** Lachish, and 5921
32:16 his servants spake yet more **a** the LORD 5921
32:16 LORD God, and **a** his servant Hezekiah. 5921
32:17 God of Israel, and to speak **a** him, saying, 5921
32:19 they spake **a** the God of Jerusalem, 413
32:19 as **a** the gods of the people of the earth, 5921
33:24 his servants conspired **a** him, and slew him 5921
33:25 all them that had conspired **a** king Amon; 5921
34:27 when thou heardest his words **a** this place, 5921
34:27 **a** the inhabitants thereof, and 5921
35:20 Necho king of Egypt came up to fight **a** 871.1
35:20 by Euphrates: and Josiah went out **a** him. 7125
35:21 I come not **a** thee this day, but against 5921
35:21 but **a** the house wherewith I have war: 413
36: 6 **A** him came up Nebuchadnezzar king of 5921
36:13 he also rebelled **a** king Nebuchadnezzar, 871.1
36:16 until the wrath of the LORD arose **a** his 871.1
Ezr 4: 5 hired counsellers **a** them, to frustrate their 5921
4: 6 wrote they unto him an accusation **a** 5921
4: 8 Shimshai the scribe wrote a letter **a** 5922
4:19 of old time hath made insurrection **a** kings, 5922
7:23 for why should there be wrath **a** the realm 5922
8:22 horsemen to help us **a** the enemy in 4480
8:22 and his wrath is **a** all them that forsake him. 5921
10: 2 We have trespassed **a** our God, and 871.1
Ne 1: 6 of Israel, which we have sinned **a** thee: 3807.1
1: 7 We have dealt very corruptly **a** thee, and 3807.1
2:19 thing that ye do? will ye rebel **a** the king? 5921
3:10 son of Harumaph, even **over a** his house. 5048
3:16 unto the place **over a** the sepulchres of 5048
3:19 another piece **over a** the going up to 4480+5048
3:23 and Hashub **over a** their house. 5048
3:25 Palal the son of Uzai, **over a** 4480+5048
3:26 unto the place **over a** the water gate toward 5048
3:27 **over a** the great tower that lieth out, 4480+5048
3:28 every one **over a** his house. 5048+3807.1
3:29 Zadok the son of Immer **over a** his house. 5048

Ne 3:30 the son of Berechiah **over a** his chamber. 5048
3:31 **over a** the gate Miphkad, and to the going 5048
4: 8 together to come and to fight **a** Jerusalem, 871.1
4: 9 set a watch **a** them day and night, because 5921
5: 1 and of their wives **a** their brethren the Jews. 413
5: 7 And I set a great assembly **a** them. 5921
6:12 but that he pronounced this prophecy **a** me: 5921
7: 3 and every one to be **over a** his house. 5048
9:10 for thou knewest that they dealt proudly **a** 5921
9:26 rebelled **a** thee, and cast thy law behind 871.1
9:26 slew thy prophets which testified **a** them to 871.1
9:29 testifiedst **a** them, that thou mightest bring 871.1
9:29 sinned **a** thy judgments, (which if a man 871.1
9:30 testifiedst **a** them by thy spirit in thy 871.1
9:34 wherewith thou didst testify **a** them. 871.1
12: 9 their brethren, were **over a** them in 5048+3807.1
12:24 with their brethren **over a** them, 5048+3807.1
12:24 the man of God, ward **over a** ward, 5980+3807.1
12:37 the fountain gate, which was **over a** them, 5048
12:38 of them that gave thanks went **over a** them, 4136
13: 2 and with water, but hired Balaam **a** them, 5921
13:15 I testified **a** them in the day wherein they NIH
13:21 I testified **a** them, and said unto them, 871.1
13:27 to transgress **a** our God in marrying 871.1
Est 2: 1 she had done, and what was decreed **a** her. 5921
3:14 that they should be ready **a** that day. 3807.1
5: 1 the king's house, **over a** the king's house: 5227
5: 1 royal house, **over a** the gate of the house. 5227
5: 9 he was full of indignation **a** Mordecai. 5921
6:13 thou shalt not prevail **a** him, but 3807.1
7: 7 for he saw that there was evil determined **a** 413
8: 3 his device that he had devised **a** the Jews. 5921
8:13 that the Jews should be ready **a** that day 3807.1
9:24 had devised **a** the Jews to destroy them, and 5921
9:25 which he devised **a** the Jews, should return 5921
Job 2: 3 although thou movedst me **a** him, 871.1
6: 4 of God do set themselves in array **a** me. NIH
7:20 why hast thou set me as a mark **a** thee, so 3807.1
8: 4 If thy children have sinned **a** him, and 3807.1
9: 4 who hath hardened himself **a** him, and 413
10:17 Thou renewest thy witnesses **a** me, and 5048
10:17 upon me; changes and war are **a** me. 5973
11: 5 God would speak, and open his lips **a** thee; 5973
13:26 For thou writest bitter things **a** me, and 5921
14:20 Thou **prevailest** for ever **a** him, and 8630
15: 6 and not I; yea, thine own lips testify **a** thee. 871.1
15:13 That thou turnest thy spirit **a** God, and 413
15:24 they shall **prevail a** him, as a king ready to 8630
15:25 For he stretcheth out his hand **a** God, and 413
15:25 and strengtheneth himself **a** the Almighty. 413
16: 4 I could heap up words **a** you, and 5921
16: 8 which is a witness **a** me: and my leanness NIH
16:10 they have gathered themselves together **a** 5921
17: 8 the innocent shall stir up himself **a** 5921
18: 9 the heel, and the robber shall prevail **a** him. 5921
19: 5 If indeed ye will magnify yourselves **a** me, 5921
19: 5 against me, and plead **a** me my reproach: 5921
19:11 He hath also kindled his wrath **a** me, and 5921
19:12 raise up their way **a** me, and encamp round 5921
19:18 despised me; I arose, and they spake **a** me. 871.1
19:19 and they whom I loved are turned **a** me. 871.1
20:27 and the earth shall rise up **a** him. 3807.1
21:27 the devices which ye wrongfully imagine **a** 5921
23: 6 Will he plead **a** me with his great power? 5978
24:13 They are of those that **rebel a** the light; 4775
27: 7 he that riseth up **a** me as the unrighteous. NIH
30:12 they raise up **a** me the ways of their 5921
30:21 with thy strong hand thou opposest thyself **a** NIH
31:21 If I have lift up my hand **a** the fatherless, 5921
31:38 If my land cry **a** me, or that the furrows 5921
32: 2 **a** Job was his wrath kindled, because 871.1
32: 3 Also **a** his three friends was his wrath 871.1
32:14 Now he hath not directed his words **a** me: 413
33:10 Behold, he findeth occasions **a** me, 5921
33:13 Why dost thou strive **a** him? for he giveth 413
34: 6 Should I lie **a** my right? my wound is 5921
34:29 whether it be done **a** a nation, or against a 5921
34:29 it be done against a nation, or **a** a man only: 5921
34:37 and multiplieth his words **a** God. 3807.1
35: 6 If thou sinnest, what doest thou **a** him? or 871.1
38:23 Which I have reserved **a** the time of 3807.1
38:23 of trouble, **a** the day of battle and war? 3807.1
39:16 She is **hardened a** her young ones, 7188
39:23 The quiver rattleth **a** him, the glittering 5921
42: 7 My wrath is kindled **a** thee, and against thy 871.1
42: 7 kindled against thee, and **a** thy two friends: 871.1
Ps 2: 2 **a** the LORD, and against his anointed, 5921
2: 2 the LORD, and **a** his anointed, saying, 5921
3: 1 many are they that rise up **a** me. 5921
3: 6 that have set themselves **a** me round about. 5921
5:10 for they have rebelled **a** thee. 871.1
7:13 he ordaineth his arrows **a** the persecutors. 3807.1
10: 8 his eyes are privily set **a** the poor. 3807.1
13: 4 mine enemy say, I have **prevailed a** him; 3201
15: 3 nor taketh up a reproach **a** his neighbour. 5921
15: 5 to usury, nor taketh reward **a** the innocent. 5921
17: 7 trust in thee from those that rise up **a** them. NIH
18:39 subdued under me those that **rose up a** me. 6965
18:48 thou liftest me up above those that rise up **a** NIH
21:11 For they intended evil **a** thee: 5921
21:12 arrows upon thy strings **a** the face of them. 5921
27: 3 Though a host should encamp **a** me, 5921
27: 3 though war should rise **a** me, in this will I 5921
27:12 for false witnesses are risen up **a** me, and 871.1
31:13 while they took counsel together **a** me, 5921
31:18 and contemptuously **a** the righteous. 5921
34:16 The face of the LORD is **a** them that do 871.1
35: 1 with me: fight **a** them that fight against me. 854
35: 1 with me: fight against them that fight **a** me. NIH
35: 3 and stop the way **a** them that persecute me: 7125
35:15 abjects gathered themselves together **a** me, 5921
35:20 they devise deceitful matters **a** them that 5921
35:21 they opened their mouth wide **a** me, and 5921
35:26 dishonour that magnify themselves **a** me. 5921
36:11 Let not the foot of pride come **a** me, and NIH

Ps 37: 1 neither be thou envious **a** the workers of 871.1
37:12 The wicked plotteth **a** the just, and 3807.1
38:16 they magnify *themselves* **a** me. 5921
41: 4 heal my soul; for I have sinned **a** thee. 3807.1
41: 7 All that hate me whisper together **a** me: 5921
41: 7 against me: **a** me do they devise my hurt. 5921
41: 9 eat *of* my bread, hath lift up *his* heel **a** me. 5921
43: 1 and plead my cause **a** an ungodly nation: 4480
44: 5 will we tread them under that rise up **a** us. NIH
50: 7 O Israel, and I will testify **a** thee: 871.1
50:20 Thou sittest *and* speakest **a** thy brother; 871.1
51: 4 **A** thee, thee only, have I sinned, and 3807.1
53: 5 the bones of him that encampeth **a** thee: NIH
54: 3 For strangers are risen up **a** me, and 5921
55:12 hated me *that* did magnify *himself* **a** me; 5921
55:18 in peace from the battle *that was* **a** me: 3807.1
55:20 He hath put forth his hands **a** such as be at 871.1
56: 2 for *they be* many that fight **a** me, O thou 3807.1
56: 5 all their thoughts *are* **a** me for evil. 5921
59: 1 defend me from them that rise up **a** me. NIH
59: 3 the mighty are gathered **a** me; not *for* my 5921
62: 3 How long will ye imagine mischief **a** a 5921
65: 3 Iniquities prevail **a** me: *as for* our 4480
69:12 They that sit in the gate speak **a** me; and 871.1
71:10 For mine enemies speak **a** me; and 3807.1
73: 9 They set their mouth **a** the heavens, and 871.1
73:15 I should offend **a** the generation of thy NIH
74: 1 *why* doth thine anger smoke **a** the sheep of 871.1
74:23 the tumult of those that rise up **a** thee NIH
78:17 they sinned yet more **a** him by provoking 3807.1
78:19 Yea, they spake **a** God; they said, Can God 871.1
78:21 so a fire was kindled **a** Jacob, and 871.1
78:21 and anger also came up **a** Israel; 871.1
79: 8 O remember not **a** us former iniquities: 3807.1
80: 4 how long wilt thou be angry **a** the prayer 871.1
81:14 and turned my hand **a** their adversaries. 5921
83: 3 They have taken crafty counsel **a** thy 5921
83: 3 and consulted **a** thy hidden ones. 5921
83: 5 *one* consent: they are confederate **a** thee: 5921
86:14 the proud are risen **a** me, and 5921
91:12 lest thou dash thy foot **a** a stone. 871.1
92:11 *my desire* of the wicked that rise up **a** me. 5921
94:16 Who will rise up for me **a** the evildoers? *or* 5973
94:16 who will stand up for me **a** the workers of 5973
94:21 They gather themselves together **a** the soul 5921
102: 8 they that are mad **a** me are sworn against NIH
102: 8 they that are mad against me are sworn **a** 871.1
105:28 it dark; and they rebelled not **a** his word. 854
106:26 Therefore he lifted up his hand **a** them, 3807.1
106:40 wrath of the LORD kindled **a** his people, 871.1
107:11 Because they rebelled **a** the words of God, NIH
109: 2 the mouth of the deceitful are opened **a** me: 5921
109: 2 they have spoken **a** me *with* a lying tongue. 854
109: 3 of hatred; and fought **a** me without a cause. NIH
109:20 and of them that speak evil **a** my soul. 5921
119:11 in mine heart, that I might not sin **a** thee. 3807.1
119:23 Princes also did sit *and* speak **a** me: *but* 871.1
119:69 The proud have forged a lie **a** me: *but* I will 5921
124: 2 was on our side, when men rose up **a** us: 5921
124: 3 when their wrath was kindled **a** us: 871.1
129: 2 yet they have not prevailed **a** me. 3807.1
137: 9 and dasheth thy little ones **a** the stones. 413
138: 7 thou shalt stretch forth thine hand **a** 5921
139:20 For they speak **a** thee wickedly, *and* NIH
139:21 am not I grieved with those that rise up **a** NIH
Pr 3:29 Devise not evil **a** thy neighbour, seeing he 5921
8:36 he that sinneth **a** me wrongeth his own soul: NIH
14:35 but his wrath is **a** him that causeth shame. NIH
17:11 a cruel messenger shall be sent **a** him. 871.1
19: 3 and his heart fretteth **a** the LORD. 5921
20: 2 *whoso* provoketh him to anger sinneth **a** his NIH
21:30 nor counsel **a** the LORD. 5048+3807.1
21:31 The horse *is* prepared **a** the day of battle: 3807.1
24: 1 Be not thou envious **a** evil men, 871.1
24:15 O wicked *man*, **a** the dwelling of 3807.1
24:28 Be not a witness **a** thy neighbour without 871.1
25:18 A man that beareth false witness **a** his 871.1
30:31 and a king, **a** whom *there is* no rising up. 5973
Ecc 4:12 if one **prevail a** him, two shall withstand 8630
7:14 God also hath set the one **over a** 5980+3807.1
8:11 Because sentence *a* an evil work is not NIH
9:14 there came a great king **a** it, and besieged it, 413
9:14 besieged it, and built great bulwarks **a** it: 5921
10: 4 If the spirit of the ruler rise up **a** thee, 5921
Isa 1: 2 up children, and they have rebelled **a** me. 871.1
2: 4 nation shall not lift up sword **a** nation, 413
3: 5 the child shall behave himself proudly **a** 871.1
3: 5 the ancient, and the base **a** the honourable. 871.1
3: 8 and their doings *are* **a** the LORD, 413
3: 9 of their countenance doth witness **a** them; 871.1
5:25 anger of the LORD kindled **a** his people, 871.1
5:25 and he hath stretched forth his hand **a** them, 5921
5:30 in that day they shall roar **a** them like 5921
7: 1 went up *towards* Jerusalem to war **a** it, but 5921
7: 1 to war against it, but could not prevail **a** it. 5921
7: 5 have taken evil counsel **a** thee, saying, 5921
7: 6 Let us go up **a** Judah, and vex it, and let us 871.1
9:11 shall set up the adversaries of Rezin **a** him, 5921
9:21 *and* they together *shall be* **a** Judah. For all 5921
10: 6 I will send him **a** a hypocritical nation, and 871.1
10: 6 **a** the people of my wrath will I give him a 5921
10:15 Shall the axe boast itself **a** him that heweth 5921
10:15 shall the saw magnify itself **a** him that 5921
10:15 as if the rod should shake *itself* **a** them that NIH
10:24 shall lift up his staff **a** thee, after 5921
10:32 he shall shake his hand **a** the mount of NIH
13:17 Behold, I will stir up the Medes **a** them, 5921
14: 4 That thou shalt take up this proverb **a** 5921
14: 8 art laid down, no feller is come up **a** us. 5921
14:22 For I will rise up **a** them, saith the LORD 5921
19: 2 I will set the Egyptians **a** the Egyptians: 871.1
19: 2 they shall fight every one **a** his brother, 871.1
19: 2 his brother, and every one **a** his neighbour; 871.1
19: 2 city **a** city, *and* kingdom against kingdom. 871.1
19: 2 city against city, *and* kingdom **a** kingdom. 871.1

Isa 19:17 of hosts, which he hath determined **a** it. 5921
20: 1 and fought **a** Ashdod, and took it; 871.1
23: 8 Who hath taken this counsel **a** Tyre, 5921
23:11 the LORD hath given a commandment **a** 413
25: 4 of the terrible ones *is* as a storm *a* the wall. NIH
27: 4 set the briers *and* thorns **a** me in battle? NIH
29: 3 I will camp **a** thee round about, and will lay 5921
29: 3 will lay siege **a** thee *with* a mount, and 5921
29: 3 *with* a mount, and I will raise forts **a** thee. 5921
29: 7 the multitude of all the nations that fight **a** 5921
29: 7 even all that fight **a** her and her munition, NIH
29: 8 all the nations be, that fight **a** mount Zion. 5921
31: 2 will arise **a** the house of the evildoers, and 5921
31: 2 and **a** the help of them that work iniquity. 5921
31: 4 of shepherds is called forth **a** him, 5921
32: 6 and to utter error **a** the LORD, 413
36: 1 *that* Sennacherib king of Assyria came up **a** 5921
36: 5 dost thou trust, that thou rebellest **a** me? 871.1
36:10 am I now come up without the LORD **a** 5921
36:10 unto me, Go up **a** this land, and destroy it. 413
37: 8 found the king of Assyria warring **a** 5921
37:21 Whereas thou hast prayed to me **a** 413
37:23 **a** whom hast thou exalted *thy* voice, and 5921
37:23 eyes on high? *even* **a** the Holy One of Israel. 413
37:28 and thy coming in, and thy rage **a** me. 413
37:29 Because thy rage **a** me, and thy tumult, 413
37:33 before it *with* shields, nor cast a bank **a** it. 5921
41:11 all they that were incensed **a** thee shall be 871.1
41:12 they that war **a** thee shall be as nothing, and NIH
42:13 yea, roar; he shall prevail **a** his enemies. 5921
42:24 the LORD, he **a** whom we have sinned? 3807.1
43:27 and thy teachers have transgressed **a** me. 871.1
45:24 all that are incensed **a** him shall be 871.1
54:15 whosoever shall gather together **a** thee shall 854
54:17 No weapon *that* is formed **a** thee shall 5921
54:17 every tongue *that* shall rise **a** thee in 854
57: 4 **A** whom do ye sport yourselves? 5921
57: 4 **a** whom make ye a wide mouth, *and* 5921
59:12 before thee, and our sins testify **a** us: 871.1
59:13 In transgressing and lying **a** the LORD, 871.1
59:19 the LORD shall lift up a standard **a** him. 871.1
63:10 to be their enemy, *and* he fought **a** them. 871.1
66:24 of the men that have transgressed **a** me: 871.1
Jer 1:15 **a** all the walls thereof round about, and 5921
1:15 round about, and **a** all the cities of Judah. 5921
1:16 I will utter my judgments **a** them touching NIH
1:18 and brasen walls **a** the whole land, 5921
1:18 **a** the kings of Judah, against the princes 3807.1
1:18 **a** the princes thereof, against the priests 3807.1
1:18 **a** the priests thereof, and against 3807.1
1:18 and **a** the people of the land. 3807.1
1:19 they shall fight **a** thee; but they shall not 413
1:19 they shall not prevail **a** thee; for I *am* 3807.1
2: 8 the pastors also transgressed **a** me, and 871.1
2:29 ye all have transgressed **a** me, saith 871.1
3:13 that thou hast transgressed **a** the LORD 871.1
3:25 for we have sinned **a** the LORD our 3807.1
4:12 now also will I give sentence **a** them. 854
4:16 behold, publish **a** Jerusalem, *that* watchers 5921
4:16 give out their voice **a** the cities of Judah. 5921
4:17 of a field, are they **a** her round about; 5921
4:17 because she hath been rebellious **a** me, 854
5:11 Judah have dealt very treacherously **a** me, 871.1
6: 3 they shall pitch *their* tents **a** her round 5921
6: 4 Prepare ye war **a** her; arise, and let us go up 5921
6: 6 down trees, and cast a mount **a** Jerusalem: 5921
6:23 set in array as men for war **a** thee, 5921
8:14 because we have sinned **a** the LORD. 3807.1
8:18 *When* I would comfort myself **a** sorrow, 5921
11:17 planted thee, hath pronounced evil **a** thee, 5921
11:17 which they have done **a** themselves to 3807.1
11:19 I knew not that they had devised devices **a** 5921
12: 8 me as a lion in the forest; it crieth out **a** me: 5921
12: 9 the birds round about *are* **a** her; 5921
12:14 Thus saith the LORD **a** all mine evil 5921
13:14 I will dash them one **a** another, even 413
14: 7 though our iniquities testify **a** us, 871.1
14: 7 are many; we have sinned **a** thee. 3807.1
14:20 of our fathers: for we have sinned **a** thee. 3807.1
15: 6 therefore will I stretch out my hand **a** thee, 5921
15: 8 I have brought upon them **a** the mother of 5921
15:20 they shall fight **a** thee, but they shall not 413
15:20 but they shall not prevail **a** thee: 3807.1
16:10 LORD pronounced all this great evil **a** us? 5921
16:10 what *is* our sin that we have committed **a** 3807.1
18: 8 If that nation, **a** whom I have pronounced, 5921
18:11 I frame evil **a** you, and devise a device 5921
18:11 evil against you, and devise a device **a** you: 5921
18:18 and let us devise devices **a** Jeremiah; 5921
18:23 thou knowest all their counsel **a** me to slay 5921
19:15 all the evil that I have pronounced **a** it, 5921
20:10 we shall prevail **a** him, and we shall take 3807.1
21: 2 king of Babylon maketh war **a** us; 5921
21: 4 wherewith ye fight **a** the king of Babylon, NIH
21: 4 **a** the Chaldeans, which besiege you without NIH
21: 5 I myself will fight **a** you with an 854
21:10 For I have set my face **a** this city for evil, 871.1
21:13 Behold, I *am* **a** thee, O inhabitant of 413
21:13 which say, Who shall come down **a** us? 5921
22: 7 I will prepare destroyers **a** thee, every one 5921
23: 2 of Israel **a** the pastors that feed my people; 5921
23:30 I *am* **a** the prophets, saith the LORD, 5921
23:31 Behold, I *am* **a** the prophets, saith 5921
23:32 I *am* **a** them that prophesy false dreams, 5921
25: 9 will bring them **a** this land, and against 5921
25: 9 **a** the inhabitants thereof, and against all 5921
25: 9 **a** all these nations round about, and 5921
25:13 all my words which I have pronounced **a** it, 5921
25:13 which Jeremiah hath prophesied **a** all 5921
25:30 Therefore prophesy thou **a** them all these 413
25:30 as they that tread *the grapes*, **a** all 413
26: 9 all the people were gathered **a** Jeremiah in 413
26:11 for he hath prophesied **a** this city, as ye have 413
26:12 The LORD sent me to prophesy **a** this 413
26:12 **a** this city all the words that ye have heard. 413

Jer 26:13 of the evil that he hath pronounced **a** you. 5921
26:19 the evil which he had pronounced **a** them? 5921
26:19 Thus *might* we procure great evil **a** our 5921
26:20 who prophesied **a** this city and against this 5921
26:20 **a** this land according to all the words of 5921
27:13 as the LORD hath spoken **a** the nation that 413
28: 8 before thee of old prophesied both **a** many 413
28: 8 **a** great kingdoms, of war, and of evil, and 5921
28:16 thou hast taught rebellion **a** the LORD. 413
29:32 he hath taught rebellion **a** the LORD. 5921
31:20 for since I spake **a** him, I do earnestly 871.1
31:39 the measuring line shall yet go forth **over a** 5048
32:24 that fight **a** it, because of the sword, and 5921
32:29 that fight **a** this city, shall come and set fire 5921
33: 8 whereby they have sinned **a** me, and 3807.1
33: 8 whereby they have transgressed **a** me. 871.1
34: 1 fought **a** Jerusalem, and against all 5921
34: 1 and **a** all the cities thereof, saying, 5921
34: 7 When the king of Babylon's army fought **a** 5921
34: 7 **a** all the cities of Judah that were left, 5921
34: 7 were left, **a** Lachish, and against Azekah: 413
34: 7 were left, against Lachish, and **a** Azekah: 413
34:22 they shall fight **a** it, and take it, and burn it 5921
35:17 all the evil that I have pronounced **a** them: 5921
36: 2 words that I have spoken unto thee **a** Israel, 5921
36: 2 **a** Judah, and against all the nations, 5921
36: 2 against Judah, and **a** all the nations, 5921
36: 7 the fury that the LORD hath pronounced **a** 413
36:31 all the evil that I have pronounced **a** them; 413
37: 8 fight **a** this city, and take it, and burn it 5921
37:10 army of the Chaldeans that fight **a** you, 854
37:18 What have I offended **a** thee, or 3807.1
37:18 or **a** thy servants, or against this people, 3807.1
37:18 or against thy servants, or **a** this people, 3807.1
37:19 The king of Babylon shall not come **a** you, 5921
37:19 shall not come against you, nor **a** this land? 5921
38: 5 for the king *is* not *he that* can do *any* thing **a** 854
38:22 set thee on, and have prevailed **a** thee: 3807.1
39: 1 of Babylon and all his army **a** Jerusalem, 413
40: 3 because ye have sinned **a** the LORD, 3807.1
43: 3 Baruch the son of Neriah setteth thee on **a** 871.1
44: 7 Wherefore commit ye *this* great evil **a** your 413
44:11 I will set my face **a** you for evil, and to cut 871.1
44:23 because ye have sinned **a** the LORD, 3807.1
44:29 my words shall surely stand **a** you for evil: 5921
46: 1 to Jeremiah the prophet **a** the Gentiles; 5921
46: 2 **A** Egypt, against the army of 3807.1
46: 2 **a** the army of Pharaoh-necho king of 5921
46:12 for the mighty *man* hath stumbled **a** 871.1
46:22 come **a** her with axes, as hewers of wood. 3807.1
47: 1 to Jeremiah the prophet **a** the Philistines, 413
47: 7 seeing the LORD hath given it a charge **a** 413
47: 7 against Ashkelon, and **a** the sea shore? 413
48: 1 **A** Moab thus saith the LORD of hosts, 3807.1
48: 2 in Heshbon they have devised evil **a** it; 5921
48:26 for he magnified *himself* **a** the LORD: 5921
48:42 he hath magnified *himself* **a** the LORD. 5921
49:14 and come **a** her, and rise up to the battle. 5921
49:19 of Jordan **a** the habitation of the strong: 413
49:20 of the LORD, that he hath taken **a** Edom; 413
49:20 that he hath purposed **a** the inhabitants of 413
49:30 king of Babylon hath taken counsel **a** you, 5921
49:30 and hath conceived a purpose **a** you. 5921
49:34 **a** Elam in the beginning of the reign of 413
50: 1 The word that the LORD spake **a** Babylon 413
50: 1 **a** the land of the Chaldeans by Jeremiah 413
50: 3 of the north there cometh up a nation **a** her, 5921
50: 7 because they have sinned **a** the LORD, 3807.1
50: 9 cause to come up **a** Babylon an assembly of 5921
50: 9 they shall set *themselves* in array **a** her; 3807.1
50:14 Put *yourselves* in array **a** Babylon round 5921
50:14 for she hath sinned **a** the LORD. 3807.1
50:15 Shout **a** her round about: she hath given her 5921
50:21 Go up **a** the land of Merathaim, 5921
50:21 *even* **a** it, and against the inhabitants of 5921
50:21 against it, and **a** the inhabitants of Pekod: 413
50:24 because thou hast striven **a** the LORD. 871.1
50:26 Come **a** her from the utmost border, 3807.1
50:29 Call together the archers **a** Babylon: all ye 413
50:29 that bend the bow, camp **a** it round about; 5921
50:29 for she hath been proud **a** the LORD, 413
50:29 the LORD, **a** the Holy One of Israel. 413
50:31 Behold, I *am* **a** thee, *O thou* most proud, 413
50:42 put in array, like a man to the battle, **a** thee, 5921
50:45 of the LORD, that he hath taken **a** Babylon; 413
50:45 that he hath purposed **a** the land of 413
51: 1 I *will* raise up **a** Babylon, and against them 5921
51: 1 **a** them that dwell in the midst of them that 413
51: 1 dwell in the midst of them that rise up **a** me, NIH
51: 2 for in the day of trouble they shall be **a** her 5921
51: 3 **A** *him that* bendeth let the archer bend his 413
51: 3 **a** *him that* lifteth himself up in his 413
51: 5 though their land was filled *with* sin **a** 4480
51:11 for his device *is* **a** Babylon, to destroy it; 5921
51:12 done that which he spake **a** the inhabitants of 413
51:14 and they shall lift up a shout **a** thee. 5921
51:25 Behold, I *am* **a** thee, O destroying mountain, 413
51:27 the nations, prepare the nations **a** her, 5921
51:27 call together **a** her the kingdoms of Ararat, 5921
51:27 and Ashchenaz; appoint a captain **a** her; 5921
51:28 Prepare **a** her the nations with the kings of 5921
51:29 the LORD shall be performed **a** Babylon, 5921
51:46 and violence in the land, ruler **a** a ruler. 5921
51:60 *even* all these words that are written **a** 413
51:62 O LORD, thou hast spoken **a** this place, 413
52: 3 that Zedekiah rebelled **a** the king of 871.1
52: 4 **a** Jerusalem, and pitched against it, and 5921
52: 4 pitched **a** it, and built forts against it round 5921
52: 4 against it, and built forts **a** it round about. 5921
La 1:13 into my bones, and it prevaileth **a** them: 871.1
1:15 he hath called an assembly **a** me to crush 5921
1:18 for I have rebelled **a** his commandment: NIH
2: 3 he burned **a** Jacob like a flaming fire, 871.1
2:16 enemies have opened their mouth **a** thee: 5921
3: 3 Surely **a** me is he turned; he turneth his 871.1

La 3: 3 he turneth his hand **a** *me* all the day. NIH
3: 5 He hath builded **a** me, and compassed *me* 5921
3:46 our enemies have opened their mouths **a** us. 5921
3:60 *and* all their imaginations **a** me. 3807.1
3:61 O LORD, *and* all their imaginations **a** me; 5921
3:62 The lips of those that rose up **a** me, and NIH
3:62 and their device **a** me all the day. 5921
5:22 utterly rejected us; thou art very wroth **a** us. 5921
Eze 1:20 wheels were lifted up **over a** them: 5980+3807.1
1:21 wheels were lifted up **over a** them: 5980+3807.1
2: 3 to a rebellious nation that hath rebelled **a** 871.1
2: 3 and their fathers have transgressed **a** me, 871.1
3: 8 I have made thy face strong **a** their 5980+3807.1
3: 8 forehead strong **a** their foreheads. 5980+3807.1
3:13 the noise of the wheels **over a** 5980+3807.1
4: 2 lay siege **a** it, and build a fort against it, 5921
4: 2 build a fort **a** it, and cast a mount against it; 5921
4: 2 build a fort against it, and cast a mount **a** it; 5921
4: 2 set the camp also **a** it, and set *battering* 5921
4: 2 and set *battering* rams **a** it round about. 5921
4: 3 and set thy face **a** it, and it shall be besieged, 413
4: 3 be besieged, and thou shalt lay siege **a** it. 5921
4: 7 *be* uncovered, and thou shalt prophesy **a** it. 5921
5: 8 *am* **a** thee, and will execute judgments in 5921
6: 2 mountains of Israel, and prophesy **a** them, 413
11: 4 Therefore prophesy **a** them, prophesy, 5921
13: 2 prophesy **a** the prophets of Israel that 413
13: 8 seen lies, therefore behold, I *am* **a** you, 413
13:17 set thy face **a** the daughters of thy people, 413
13:17 their own heart; and prophesy thou **a** them, 5921
13:20 Behold, I *am* **a** your pillows, where*with* ye 413
14: 8 I will set my face **a** that man, and 871.1
14:13 when the land sinneth **a** me by 3807.1
15: 7 I will set my face **a** them; they shall go out 871.1
15: 7 the LORD, when I set my face **a** them. 871.1
16:37 I will even gather them round about **a** thee, 5921
16:40 They shall also bring up a company **a** thee, 5921
16:44 useth proverbs shall use *this* proverb **a** thee, 5921
17:15 he rebelled **a** him in sending his 871.1
17:20 his trespass that he hath trespassed **a** me. 871.1
19: 8 the nations set **a** him on every side from 5921
20: 8 they rebelled **a** me, and would not hearken 871.1
20: 8 to accomplish my anger **a** them in 871.1
20:13 the house of Israel rebelled **a** me in 871.1
20:21 Notwithstanding the children rebelled **a** 871.1
20:21 to accomplish my anger **a** them in 871.1
20:27 in that they have committed a trespass **a** 871.1
20:38 the rebels, and them that transgress **a** me: 871.1
20:46 and prophesy **a** the forest of the south field; 413
21: 2 and prophesy **a** the land of Israel, 413
21: 3 I *am* **a** thee, and will draw forth my sword 413
21: 4 shall my sword go forth out of his sheath **a** 413
21:15 I have set the point of the sword **a** all their 5921
21:22 to appoint *battering* rams **a** the gates, 5921
21:31 I will blow **a** thee in the fire of my wrath, 5921
22: 3 and maketh idols **a** herself to defile *herself*. 5921
23:22 Behold, I will raise up thy lovers **a** thee, 5921
23:22 and I will bring them **a** thee on every side; 5921
23:24 they shall come **a** thee *with* chariots, 5921
23:24 *which* shall set **a** thee buckler and shield 5921
23:25 I will set my jealousy **a** thee, and they shall 871.1
24: 2 the king of Babylon set himself **a** Jerusalem 413
25: 2 set thy face **a** the Ammonites, and 413
25: 2 the Ammonites, and prophesy **a** them; 5921
25: 3 Because thou saidst, Aha, **a** my sanctuary, 413
25: 3 **a** the land of Israel, when it was desolate; 413
25: 3 **a** the house of Judah, when they went into 413
25: 6 rejoiced in heart with all thy despite **a** 413
25:12 Because that Edom hath dealt **a** the house 3807.1
26: 2 because that Tyrus hath said **a** Jerusalem, 5921
26: 3 Behold, I *am* **a** thee, O Tyrus, and 5921
26: 3 will cause many nations to come up **a** thee, 5921
26: 8 he shall make a fort **a** thee, and cast a 5921
26: 8 cast a mount **a** thee, and lift up the buckler 5921
26: 8 against thee, and lift up the buckler **a** thee. 5921
26: 9 he shall set engines of war **a** thy walls, and 871.1
27:30 shall cause their voice to be heard **a** thee, 5921
28: 7 they shall draw their swords **a** the beauty of 5921
28:21 set thy face **a** Zidon, and prophesy against it, 413
28:21 thy face against Zidon, and prophesy **a** it, 5921
28:22 Behold, I *am* **a** thee, O Zidon; and I will be 5921
29: 2 set thy face **a** Pharaoh king of Egypt, and 5921
29: 2 and prophesy **a** him, and against all Egypt: 5921
29: 2 and prophesy against him, and **a** all Egypt: 5921
29: 3 Behold, I *am* **a** thee, Pharaoh king of 5921
29:10 I *am* **a** thee, and against thy rivers, and I will 413
29:10 **a** thy rivers, and I will make the land of 413
29:18 his army to serve a great service **a** Tyrus: 413
29:18 for the service that he had served **a** it: 5921
29:20 *for* his labour wherewith he served **a** it, 871.1
30:11 they shall draw their swords **a** Egypt, and 5921
30:22 I *am* **a** Pharaoh king of Egypt, and will break 413
33:30 the children of thy people still are talking **a** 871.1
34: 2 prophesy **a** the shepherds of Israel, 5921
34:10 Behold, I *am* **a** the shepherds; and I will 413
35: 2 set thy face **a** mount Seir, and 5921
35: 2 face against mount Seir, and prophesy **a** it, 5921
35: 3 I *am* **a** thee, and I will stretch out mine hand 413
35: 3 I will stretch out mine hand **a** thee, and 5921
35:11 thou hast used out of thy hatred **a** them; 871.1
35:12 thou hast spoken **a** the mountains of Israel, 5921
35:13 Thus with your mouth ye have boasted **a** 5921
35:13 and have multiplied your words **a** me: 5921
36: 2 Because the enemy hath said **a** you, Aha, 5921
36: 5 have I spoken **a** the residue of the heathen, 5921
36: 5 residue of the heathen, and **a** all Idumea, 5921
38: 2 Son of man, set thy face **a** Gog, the land of 413
38: 2 and Tubal, and prophesy **a** him, 5921
38: 3 Behold, I *am* **a** thee, O Gog, the chief prince 413
38: 8 **a** the mountains of Israel, which have been 5921
38:16 thou shalt come up **a** my people of Israel, 5921
38:16 latter days, and I will bring thee **a** my land, 5921
38:17 that *I* would bring thee **a** them? 5921
38:18 when Gog shall come **a** the land of Israel, 5921
38:21 I will call *for* a sword **a** him throughout all 5921
Eze 38:21 every man's sword shall be **a** his brother. 871.1
38:22 I will plead **a** him with pestilence and 854
39: 1 thou son of man, prophesy **a** Gog, and say, 5921
39: 1 Behold, I *am* **a** thee, O Gog, the chief prince 413
39:23 because they trespassed **a** me, therefore 871.1
39:26 whereby they have trespassed **a** me, 871.1
40:13 *was* five and twenty cubits, door **a** door. 5048
40:18 **over a** the length of the gates *was* 5980+3807.1
40:23 the gate of the inner court *was* **over a** 5048
41:15 **over a** the separate place which *was* 413+6440
41:16 on their three *stories*, **over a** the door, 5048
42: 1 chamber that *was* **over a** the separate place, 5048
42: 3 **Over a** the twenty *cubits* which *were* for 5048
42: 3 **over a** the pavement which *was* for 5048
42: 3 *was* gallery **a** gallery in three *stories*. 413+6440
42: 7 the wall that *was* without **over a** 5980+3807.1
42:10 **over a** the separate place, and over 413+6440
42:10 and **over a** the building. 413+6440
44:12 therefore have I lift up mine hand **a** them, 5921
45: 6 **over a** the oblation of the holy 5980+3807.1
45: 7 the length *shall be* **over a** one of 5980+3807.1
46: 9 he came in, but shall go forth **over a** it. 5226
47:20 the border, till *a man* come **over a** Hamath. 5227
48:13 **over a** the border of the priests, 5980+3807.1
48:15 that are left in the breadth **over a** 5921+6440
48:18 the residue in length **over a** 5980+3807.1
48:18 it shall be **over a** the oblation of 5980+3807.1
48:21 **over a** the five and twenty thousand 413+6440
48:21 westward **over a** the five and 5921+6440
48:21 **over a** the portions for the prince: 5980+3807.1
Da 3:19 the form of his visage was changed **a** 5922
3:29 which speak any thing amiss **a** the God of 5922
5: 5 wrote over **a** the candlestick upon 6903
5: 6 and his knees smote one **a** another. 3807.2
5:23 hast lifted up thyself **a** the Lord of heaven; 5922
6: 4 princes sought to find occasion **a** Daniel 3807.2
6: 5 We shall not find any occasion **a** this 3807.2
6: 5 except we find *it* **a** him concerning the law 5922
7:21 war with the saints, and prevailed **a** them; 3807.2
7:25 he shall speak *great* words **a** 6655+3807.2
8: 7 he was moved with choler **a** him, and 413
8:12 a host was given *him* **a** the daily *sacrifice* 5921
8:25 he shall also stand up **a** the Prince of 5921
9: 7 of their trespass that they have trespassed **a** 871.1
9: 8 because we have sinned **a** thee. 3807.1
9: 9 though we have rebelled **a** him; 871.1
9:11 of God, because we have sinned **a** him. 3807.1
9:12 which he spake **a** us, and against our judges 5921
9:12 against us, and **a** our judges that judged us, 5921
11: 2 he shall stir up all **a** the realm of Grecia. 854
11: 7 and shall deal **a** them, and shall prevail: 871.1
11:14 in those times there shall many stand up **a** 5921
11:16 he that cometh **a** him shall do according to 413
11:24 he shall **forecast** his devices **a** the strong 2803
11:25 his courage **a** the king of the south with a 5921
11:25 for they shall forecast devices **a** him. 5921
11:28 his heart *shall be* **a** the holy covenant; and 5921
11:30 For *the* ships of Chittim shall come **a** him: 871.1
11:30 and have indignation **a** the holy covenant: 5921
11:32 such as do wickedly **a** the covenant shall he NIH
11:36 shall speak marvellous *things* **a** the God of 5921
11:40 the king of the north shall come **a** him like 5921
Hos 4: 7 they were increased, so they sinned **a** me: 3807.1
5: 7 They have dealt treacherously **a** 871.1
6: 7 there have they dealt treacherously **a** me. 871.1
7:13 because they have transgressed **a** me: 871.1
7:13 yet they have spoken lies **a** me. 5921
7:14 for corn and wine, *and* they rebel **a** me. 871.1
7:15 yet do they imagine mischief **a** me. 413
8: 1 *He shall come* as an eagle **a** the house of 5921
8: 1 my covenant, and trespassed **a** my law. 5921
8: 5 cast *thee* off; mine anger is kindled **a** them: 871.1
10: 9 the battle in Gibeah **a** the children of 5921
10:10 *the* people shall be gathered **a** them, 5921
13:16 for she hath rebelled **a** her God: 871.1
Joel 3:19 for the violence **a** the children of Judah, NIH
Am 1: 8 and I will turn mine hand **a** Ekron: 5921
3: 1 word that the LORD hath spoken **a** you, 5921
3: 1 **a** the whole family which I brought up 5921
5: 1 Hear ye this word which I take up **a** you, 5921
5: 9 That strengtheneth the spoiled **a** the strong, 5921
5: 9 so that the spoiled shall come **a** the fortress. 5921
6:14 behold, I *will* raise up **a** you a nation, 5921
7: 9 I will rise **a** the house of Jeroboam with 5921
7:10 Amos hath conspired **a** thee in the midst of 5921
7:16 Prophesy not **a** Israel, and drop not *thy* 5921
7:16 and drop not *thy word* **a** the house of Isaac. 5921
Ob 1: 1 Arise ye, and let us rise up **a** her in battle. 5921
1: 7 have deceived thee, *and* prevailed **a** thee; 3807.1
1:10 For *thy* violence **a** thy brother Jacob shame NIH
Jnh 1: 2 go to Nineveh, *that* great city, and cry **a** it; 5921
1:13 sea wrought, and was tempestuous **a** them. 5921
Mic 1: 2 let the Lord GOD be witness **a** you, 871.1
2: 3 Behold, **a** this family do I devise an evil, 5921
2: 4 In that day shall *one* take up a parable **a** 5921
3: 5 their mouths, they even prepare war **a** him. 5921
4: 3 nation shall not lift up a sword **a** nation, 413
4:11 Now also many nations are gathered **a** thee, 5921
5: 1 he hath laid siege **a** us: they shall smite 5921
5: 5 shall we raise **a** him seven shepherds, and 5921
6: 3 wherein have I wearied thee? testify **a** me. 871.1
7: 6 the daughter riseth up **a** her mother, 871.1
7: 6 the daughter in law **a** her mother in law; 871.1
7: 8 Rejoice not **a** me, O mine enemy: when I 3807.1
7: 9 because I have sinned **a** him, until he 3807.1
Na 1: 9 What do ye imagine **a** the LORD? he *will* 413
1:11 that imagineth evil **a** the LORD, a wicked 5921
2: 4 they shall **justle** one **a**nother in the broad 8264
2:13 Behold, I *am* **a** thee, saith the LORD of 413
3: 5 Behold, I *am* **a** thee, saith the LORD of 413
Hab 2: 6 Shall not all these take up a parable **a** him, 5921
2: 6 and a taunting proverb **a** him, and say, 3807.1
2:10 off many people, and *hast* sinned **a** thy soul. NIH
3: 8 Was the LORD displeased **a** the rivers? 871.1
3: 8 *was* thine anger **a** the rivers? *was* thy wrath 871.1
Hab 3: 8 *was* thy wrath **a** the sea, that thou didst 871.1
Zep 1:16 the trumpet and alarm **a** the fenced cities, 5921
1:16 the fenced cities, and **a** the high towers. 5921
1:17 because they have sinned **a** the LORD: 3807.1
2: 5 the word of the LORD *is* **a** you; 5921
2: 8 and magnified *themselves* **a** their border. 5921
2:10 magnified *themselves* **a** the people of 5921
2:13 he will stretch out his hand **a** the north, 5921
3:11 wherein thou hast transgressed **a** me: 871.1
Zec 1:12 **a** which thou hast had indignation these NIH
7:10 let none of you imagine evil **a** his brother in NIH
8:10 for I set all men every one **a** his neighbour. 871.1
8:17 let none of you imagine evil in your hearts **a** NIH
9:13 O Zion, **a** thy sons, O Greece, and 5921
10: 3 Mine anger was kindled **a** the shepherds, 5921
12: 2 when they shall be in the siege both **a** 5921
12: 2 siege both against Judah *and* **a** Jerusalem. 5921
12: 3 of the earth be gathered together **a** it. 5921
12: 7 do not magnify *themselves* **a** Judah. 5921
12: 9 all the nations that come **a** Jerusalem. 5921
13: 7 **a** my shepherd, and against the man *that is* 5921
13: 7 and **a** the man *that is* my fellow, 5921
14: 2 For I will gather all nations **a** Jerusalem to 413
14: 3 LORD go forth, and fight **a** those nations, 871.1
14:12 all the people that have fought **a** Jerusalem; 5921
14:13 his hand shall rise up **a** the hand of his 5921
14:16 **a** Jerusalem shall even go up from year to 5921
Mal 1: 4 The people **a** whom the LORD hath NIH
2:10 why do we deal treacherously every man **a** 871.1
2:14 **a** whom thou hast dealt treacherously: 871.1
2:15 let none deal treacherously **a** the wife of 871.1
3: 5 I will be a swift witness **a** the sorcerers, 871.1
3: 5 **a** the adulterers, and against false swearers, 871.1
3: 5 **a** false swearers, and against those that 871.1
3: 5 **a** those that oppress the hireling in *his* 871.1
3:13 Your words have been stout **a** me, saith 5921
3:13 What have we spoken so much **a** thee? 5921
Mt 4: 6 lest at any time thou dash thy foot **a** a *4314*
5:11 shall say all manner of evil **a** you falsely, *2596*
5:23 that thy brother hath ought **a** thee; *2596*
10: 1 he gave them power **a** unclean spirits, NIG
10:18 for a testimony **a** them and the Gentiles. NIG
10:21 children shall **rise up a** *their* parents, *1881*
10:35 For I am come to set a man at variance **a** *2596*
10:35 and the daughter **a** her mother, and *2596*
10:35 the daughter in law **a** her mother in law. *2596*
12:14 went out, and held a council **a** him, *2596*
12:25 Every kingdom divided **a** itself is brought *2596*
12:25 or house divided **a** itself shall not stand: *2596*
12:26 cast out Satan, he is divided **a** himself; *1909*
12:30 He that is not with me is **a** me; and he that *2596*
12:31 the blasphemy **a** the *Holy* Ghost shall not be NIG
12:32 And whosoever speaketh a word **a** the Son *2596*
12:32 but whosoever speaketh **a** the Holy Ghost, *2596*
16:18 and the gates of hell shall not **prevail a** it. *2729*
18:15 Moreover if thy brother shall trespass **a** *1519*
18:21 how oft shall my brother sin **a** me, and I *1519*
20:11 murmured **a** the goodman of the house, *2596*
20:24 moved with indignation **a** the two brethren. *4012*
21: 2 Go into the village **over a** you, and *561*
23:13 for ye shut up the kingdom of heaven **a** *1715*
24: 7 For nation shall rise **a** nation, and *1909*
24: 7 against nation, and kingdom **a** kingdom: *1909*
26:55 Are ye come out as **a** a thief with swords *1909*
26:59 all the council, sought false witness **a** Jesus, *2596*
26:62 what *is it which* these **witness a** thee? *2649*
27: 1 elders of the people took counsel **a** Jesus to *2596*
27:13 not how many *things* they **witness a** thee? *2649*
27:61 the other Mary, sitting **over a** the sepulchre. *561*
Mk 3: 6 took counsel with the Herodians **a** him, *2596*
3:24 And if a kingdom be divided **a** itself, *1909*
3:25 And if a house be divided **a** itself, *1909*
3:26 And if Satan rise up **a** himself, and *1909*
3:29 But he that shall blaspheme **a** the Holy *1519*
6:11 dust under your feet for a testimony **a** them. NIG
6:19 Therefore Herodias **had a quarrel a** him, *1758*
9:40 For he that is not **a** us is on our part. *2596*
10:11 marry another, committeth adultery **a** her. *1909*
11: 2 Go your way into the village **over a** you: *2713*
11:25 forgive, if ye have ought **a** any: *2596*
12:12 that he had spoken the parable **a** them: *4314*
12:41 And Jesus sat **over a** the treasury, and *2713*
13: 3 the mount of Olives **over a** the temple, *2713*
13: 8 For nation shall rise **a** nation, and *1909*
13: 8 against nation, and kingdom **a** kingdom: *1909*
13: 9 kings for my sake, for a testimony **a** them. NIG
13:12 and children shall rise up **a** *their* parents, *1909*
14: 5 to the poor. And they **murmured a** her. *1690*
14:48 as **a** a thief, with swords and *with* staves to *1909*
14:55 all the council sought for witness **a** Jesus to *2596*
14:56 For many bare false witness **a** him, but *2596*
14:57 and bare false witness **a** him, saying, *2596*
14:60 what *is it which* these **witness a** thee? *2649*
15: 4 behold how many *things* they **witness a** *2649*
15:39 which stood **over a** him, saw that he *1537+1727*
Lk 2:34 and for a sign which shall be **spoken a**; *483*
4:11 lest at any time thou dash thy foot **a** a *4314*
5:30 and Pharisees murmured **a** his disciples, *4314*
6: 7 that they might find an **accusation a** him. *2724*
6:49 **a** which the stream did **beat vehemently**, *4366*
7:30 lawyers rejected the counsel of God **a** *1519*
8:26 of the Gadarenes, which is **over a** Galilee. *495*
9: 5 dust from your feet for a testimony **a** them. *1909*
9:50 *him* not: for he that is not **a** us is for us. *2596*
10:11 which cleaveth on us, we do **wipe off a** you: *631*
11:17 Every kingdom divided **a** itself is brought *1909*
11:17 and a house *divided* **a** a house falleth. *1909*
11:18 If Satan also be divided **a** himself, *1909*
11:23 He that is not with me is **a** me: and he that *2596*
12:10 And whosoever shall speak a word **a** *1519*
12:10 unto him that blasphemeth **a** the Holy *1519*
12:52 three **a** two, and two against three. *1909*
12:52 three against two, and two **a** three. *1909*
12:53 The father shall be divided **a** the son, and *1909*
12:53 against the son, and the son **a** the father; *1909*

A

Lk 12:53 the mother **a** the daughter, and the daughter *1909*
12:53 and the daughter **a** the mother; *1909*
12:53 the mother in law **a** her daughter in law, *1909*
12:53 the daughter in law **a** her mother in law. *1909*
14:31 to **make war a** another king, *1519+4171+4820*
14:31 that cometh **a** him with twenty thousand? *1909*
15:18 I have sinned **a** heaven, and before thee, *1519*
15:21 I have sinned **a** heaven, and in thy sight, *1519*
17: 3 If thy brother trespass **a** thee, rebuke him; *1519*
17: 4 And if he trespass **a** thee seven times in a *1519*
19:30 Go ye into the village **over a** *you;* in *2713*
20:19 that he had spoken this parable **a** them. *4314*
21:10 Nation shall rise **a** nation, and *1909*
21:10 against nation, and kingdom **a** kingdom: *1909*
22:52 as **a** a thief, with swords and staves? *1909*
22:53 ye stretched forth no hands **a** me: *1909*
22:65 *things* blasphemously spake they **a** him. *1519*
Jn 12: 7 **a** the day of my burying hath she kept this. *1519*
13:18 bread with me hath lift up his heel **a** me. *1909*
13:29 Buy *those things* that we have need of **a** *1519*
18:29 What accusation bring you **a** this man? *2596*
19:11 Thou couldest have no power *at all* **a** me, *2596*
19:12 maketh himself a king **speaketh a** *483*
Ac 4:14 with them, they could **say** nothing **a** *it.* *471*
4:26 the rulers were gathered together **a** *2596*
4:26 together against the Lord, and **a** his Christ. *2596*
4:27 For of a truth **a** thy holy child Jesus, *1909*
5:39 lest haply ye be found even to **fight a God**. *2314*
6: 1 there arose a murmuring of the Grecians **a** *4314*
6:11 him speak blasphemous words **a** Moses, *1519*
6:11 words against Moses, and **a** God. NIG
6:13 speak blasphemous words **a** this holy place, *2596*
8: 1 **a** the church which was at Jerusalem; *1909*
9: 1 and slaughter **a** the disciples of the Lord, *1519*
9: 5 *it is* hard for thee to kick **a** the pricks. *4314*
9:29 Lord Jesus, and disputed **a** the Grecians: *4314*
13:45 **spake a** those *things* which were spoken by *483*
13:50 and raised persecution **a** Paul and *1909*
13:51 But they shook off the dust of their feet **a** *1909*
14: 2 made their minds evil affected **a** *2596*
16:22 And the multitude rose up together **a** them: *2596*
18:12 **made insurrection** with one accord **a** Paul, *2721*
19:16 and prevailed **a** them, so that *they* fled out *2596*
19:36 then that these *things* **cannot be spoken a**, *368*
19:38 have a matter **a** any *man,* the law is open, *4314*
20:15 and came the next *day* **over a** Chios; *481*
21:28 that teacheth all *men* every where **a** *2596*
22:24 he might know wherefore they **cried** so **a** *2019*
23: 9 hath spoken to him, let us not **fight a God**. *2313*
23:30 to say before thee what *they had* **a** him. *4314*
24: 1 who informed the governor **a** Paul. *2596*
24:19 and object, if they had ought **a** me. *4314*
25: 2 the chief of the Jews informed him **a** Paul, *2596*
25: 3 And desired favour **a** him, that he would *2596*
25: 7 laid many and grievous complaints **a** Paul, *2596*
25: 8 Neither **a** the law of the Jews, *1519*
25: 8 neither **a** the temple, nor *yet* against Cesar, *1519*
25: 8 neither against the temple, nor *yet* **a** Cesar, *1519*
25:15 *me,* desiring *to have* judgment **a** him. *2596*
25:16 himself concerning the crime laid **a** *him.* NIG
25:18 **A** whom when the accusers stood *up,* they *4012*
25:19 But had certain questions **a** him of their *4314*
25:27 not withal to signify the crimes *laid* **a** him. *2596*
26:10 were put to death, I gave my **voice a** *them.* *5586*
26:11 and being exceedingly **mad a** them, *1693*
26:14 *it is* hard for thee to kick **a** the pricks. *4314*
27: 7 and scarce were come **over a** Cnidus, *2596*
27: 7 we sailed under Crete, **over a** Salmone; *2596*
27:14 But not long after there arose **a** it a *2596*
28:17 though I have committed nothing **a** *1727*
28:19 But when the Jews **spake a** *it,* I was *483*
28:22 we know that every where it is **spoken a**. *483*
Ro 1:18 is revealed from heaven **a** all ungodliness *1909*
1:26 the natural use into that which is **a** nature: *3844*
2: 2 to truth **a** them which commit such *things.* *1909*
2: 5 up unto thyself wrath **a** the day of wrath *1722*
4:18 Who **a** hope believed in hope, that he might *3844*
7:23 **warring a** the law of my mind, and *497*
8: 7 Because the carnal mind *is* enmity **a** God: *1519*
8:31 *things? If* God *be* for us, who *can be* **a** us? *2596*
9:20 O man, who art thou that **repliest a** God? *470*
11: 2 how he maketh intercession to God **a** *2596*
11:18 **Boast** not **a** the branches: but if thou boast, *2620*
1Co 4: 6 that no one of you be puffed up for one **a** *2596*
6: 1 Dare any of you, having a matter **a** another, *4314*
6:18 he that committeth fornication sinneth **a** his *1519*
8:12 But when ye sin so **a** the brethren, and *1519*
8:12 their weak conscience, ye sin **a** Christ. *1519*
9:17 but if **a** my **will**, a dispensation *of the gospel* *210*
2Co 10: 2 wherewith I think to be bold **a** some, *1909*
10: 5 every high thing that exalteth itself **a** *2596*
13: 8 For we can do nothing **a** the truth, but *2596*
Gal 3:21 *Is* the law then **a** the promises of God? *2596*
5:17 For the flesh lusteth **a** the Spirit, and *2596*
5:17 against the Spirit, and the Spirit **a** the flesh: *2596*
5:23 **a** such there is no law. *2596*
Eph 6:11 that ye may be able to stand **a** the wiles of *4314*
6:12 For we wrestle not **a** flesh and blood, but *4314*
6:12 against flesh and blood, but **a** principalities, *4314*
6:12 blood, but against principalities, **a** powers, *4314*
6:12 **a** the rulers of the darkness of this world, *4314*
6:12 **a** spiritual wickedness in high *places.* *4314*
Col 2:14 handwriting of ordinances that was **a** us, *2596*
3:13 if any *man* have a quarrel **a** any: *4314*
3:19 love *your* wives, and be not bitter **a** them. *4314*
1Ti 5:11 for when they have *begun to* **wax wanton a** *2691*
5:19 **A** an elder receive not an accusation, but *2596*
6:19 a good foundation **a** the time to come, *1519*
2Ti 1:12 I have committed unto *him* **a** that day. *1519*
Heb 12: 3 such contradiction of sinners **a** himself, *1519*
12: 4 not yet resisted unto blood, striving **a** sin. *4314*
Jas 2:13 no mercy; and mercy **rejoiceth a** judgment. *2620*
3:14 glory not, and lie *not* **a** the truth. *2596*
5: 3 the rust of them shall be a witness **a** you, *1519*
5: 9 Grudge not one **a** another, brethren, lest ye *2596*
1Pe 2:11 from fleshly lusts, which war **a** the soul; *2596*
2:12 whereas they **speak a** you as evildoers, *2635*
3:12 the face of the Lord *is* **a** them that do evil. *1909*
2Pe 2:11 bring not railing accusation **a** them before *2596*
3: 7 reserved unto fire **a** the day of judgment *1519*
3Jn 1:10 **prating a** us with malicious words: *5396*
Jude 1: 9 durst not **bring a** *him* a railing accusation, *2018*
1:15 which ungodly sinners have spoken **a** him. *2596*
Rev 2: 4 Nevertheless I have *somewhat* **a** thee, *2596*
2:14 But I have a few *things* **a** thee, because *2596*
2:16 will fight **a** them with the sword of my *3326*
2:20 Notwithstanding I have a few *things* **a** thee, *2596*
11: 7 the bottomless *pit* shall make war **a** them, *3326*
12: 7 Michael and his angels fought **a** the dragon; *2596*
13: 6 And he opened his mouth in blasphemy **a** *4314*
19:19 gathered together to make war **a** him that *3326*
19:19 him that sat on the horse, and **a** his army. *3326*

AGAR (2) [HAGAR]
Gal 4:24 which gendereth to bondage, which is **A**. *28*
4:25 For *this* **A** is mount Sinai in Arabia, and *28*

AGATE (3) [AGATES]
Ex 28:19 third row a ligure, an **a**, and an amethyst. 7618
39:12 third row, a ligure, an **a**, and an amethyst. 7618
Eze 27:16 and fine linen, and coral, and **a**. 3539

AGATES (1) [AGATE]
Isa 54:12 I will make thy windows *of* **a**, and thy gates 3539

AGE (42) [AGED, AGES]
Ge 15:15 thou shalt be buried in a good **old a**. 7872
18:11 and Sarah *were* old *and* well stricken in **a**; 3117
21: 2 and bare Abraham a son in his **old a**, 2208
21: 7 for I have born *him* a son in his **old a**. 2208
24: 1 Abraham was old, *and* well stricken in **a**: 3117
25: 8 died in a good **old a**, an old man, and 7872
37: 3 because he *was* the son of his **old a**: 2208
44:20 and a child of *his* **old a**, a little one; 2208
47:28 **whole a** of Jacob was an 2416+3117+8141
48:10 Now the eyes of Israel were dim for **a**, *so* 2207
Nu 8:25 from the **a** of fifty years they shall cease 1121
Jos 23: 1 that Joshua waxed old *and* stricken in **a**. 3117
23: 2 said unto them, I am old *and* stricken in **a**: 3117
Jdg 8:32 the son of Joash died in a good **old a**, 7872
Ru 4:15 of *thy* life, and a nourisher of thine **old a**: 7872
1Sa 2:33 thine house shall die **in the flower of** their **a**. 376
1Ki 14: 4 for his eyes were set by reason of his **a**. 7869
15:23 Nevertheless in the time of his **old a** he was 2209
1Ch 23: 3 Now the Levites were numbered from the **a** 1121
23:24 from the **a** of twenty years and upward. 1121
29:28 he died in a good **old a**, full of days, riches, 7872
2Ch 36:17 old man, or **him that stooped for a**: 3486
Job 5:26 Thou shalt come to *thy* grave in a **full a**, 3624
8: 8 of the former **a**, and prepare *thyself* to 1755
11:17 *thine* **a** shall be clearer than the noonday; 2465
30: 2 profit me, in whom **old a** was perished? 3624
Ps 39: 5 and mine **a** *is* as nothing before thee: 2465
71: 9 Cast me not off in the time of **old a**; 2209
92:14 They shall still bring forth fruit in **old a**; 7872
Isa 38:12 Mine **a** is departed, and is removed from 1755
46: 4 *even* to *your* **old a** I *am* he; and *even* to 2209
Zec 8: 4 man with his staff in his hand for very **a**. 3117
Mk 5:42 for she was *of the* **a** of twelve years. NIG
Lk 1:36 she hath also conceived a son in her **old a**: *1094*
2:36 of Aser: she was of a great **a**, *1722+2250+4260*
3:23 himself began *to be* about thirty **years of a**, *2094*
8:42 about twelve **years of a**, and she lay a *2094*
Jn 9:21 he is of **a**; ask him: he shall speak for *2244*
9:23 Therefore said his parents, He is of **a**; *2244*
1Co 7:36 if she **pass the flower of** *her* **a**, *1510+5230*
Heb 5:14 meat belongeth to *them that are* of **full a**, *5046*
11:11 of a child when *she* was past **a**, *2244+2540*

AGED (9) [AGE]
2Sa 19:32 Now Barzillai was a very **a man**, 2204
Job 12:20 and taketh *away* the understanding of the **a**. 2205
15:10 *are* both the grayheaded and **very a men**, 3453
29: 8 and the **a** arose, *and* stood *up.* 3453
32: 9 neither do the **a** understand judgment. 2205
Jer 6:11 be taken, the **a** with *him that is* full of days. 2205
Tit 2: 2 That the **a men** be sober, grave, temperate, *4246*
2: 3 The **a women** likewise, *that they be* in *4247*
Phm 1: 9 *thee,* being such a one as Paul the **a**, *4246*

AGEE (1)
2Sa 23:11 after him *was* Shammah the son of **A** 89

AGES (4) [AGE]
Eph 2: 7 That in the **a** to come he might shew *165*
3: 5 Which in other **a** was not made known unto *1074*
3:21 the church by Christ Jesus throughout all **a**, *1074*
Col 1:26 the mystery which hath been hid from **a** *165*

AGO (13)
1Sa 9:20 for thine asses that were lost three days **a**, 3117
2Ki 19:25 Hast thou not heard **long a** 4480+7350+3807.1
Ezr 5:11 that was builded these many years **a**, 4481+6928
Isa 22:11 unto him that fashioned it **long a**. 4480+7350
37:26 Hast thou not heard **long a**, 4480+7350+3807.1
Mt 11:21 Sidon they would have repented **long a** in *3819*
Mk 9:21 How **long** is it **a** since this came unto him? *5550*
Lk 10:13 they had a **great while a** repented, sitting in *3819*
Ac 10:30 Four days **a** I was fasting until this hour; *575*
15: 7 know how that **a good while a** *575+744+2250*
2Co 8:10 to do, but also to be forward **a year a**. *575+4070*
9: 2 that Achaia was ready **a year a**; *575+4070*
12: 2 a man in Christ above fourteen years **a**, NIG

AGONE (1)
1Sa 30:13 left me, because three days **a** I fell sick. NIH

AGONY (1)
Lk 22:44 And being in an **a** he prayed more earnestly: *74*

AGREE (7) [AGREED, AGREEMENT, AGREETH]
Mt 5:25 **A with** thine adversary quickly, *2132*
18:19 That if two of you shall **a** on earth as *4856*
20:13 didst not thou **a with** me for a penny? *4856*
Mk 14:59 so did their witness **a together**. *1510+2470*
Ac 15:15 And to this **a** the words of the prophets; *4856*
1Jn 5: 8 and the blood: and *these* three **a** in one. *1510*
Rev 17:17 to fulfil his will, and to **a**, *1106+1520+4160*

AGREED (8) [AGREE]
Am 3: 3 Can two walk together, except they be **a**? 3259
Mt 20: 2 And when he had **a** with the labourers for a *4856*
Mk 14:56 but *their* witness **a** not **together**. *1510+2470*
Jn 9:22 for the Jews had **a** already, that if any *man* *4934*
Ac 5: 9 How *is it* that ye have **a together** to tempt *4856*
5:40 And to him they **a**: and when they had *3982*
23:20 The Jews have **a** to desire thee that thou *4934*
28:25 And when they **a not** among *800+1510*

AGREEMENT (6) [AGREE]
2Ki 18:31 Make *an* **a** with me *by* a present, and NIH
Isa 28:15 with death, and with hell are we at **a**; 2374
28:18 and your **a** with hell shall not stand; 2380
36:16 Make *an* **a** with me *by* a present, and NIH
Da 11: 6 come to the king of the north to make an **a**: 4339
2Co 6:16 And what **a** hath the temple of God with *4783*

AGREETH (2) [AGREE]
Mk 14:70 art a Galilean, and thy speech **a** *thereto.* *3662*
Lk 5:36 the piece that was *taken* out of the new **a** *4856*

AGRIPPA (12)
Ac 25:13 And after certain days king **A** and *67*
25:22 Then **A** said unto Festus, I would also hear *67*
25:23 when **A** was come, and Bernice, with great *67*
25:24 King **A**, and all men which are here present *67*
25:26 and specially before thee, O king **A**, that, *67*
26: 1 Then **A** said unto Paul, Thou art permitted to *67*
26: 2 king **A**, because I shall answer for myself this *67*
26: 7 For which hope's sake, king **A**, I am accused *67*
26:19 Whereupon, O king **A**, I was not disobedient *67*
26:27 King **A**, believest thou the prophets? I know *67*
26:28 Then **A** said unto Paul, Almost thou *67*
26:32 Then said **A** unto Festus, This man might *67*

AGROUND (1) [GROUND]
Ac 27:41 where two seas met, they **ran** the ship **a**; *2027*

AGUE (1)
Lev 26:16 consumption, and the **burning a**, that shall 6920

AGUR (1)
Pr 30: 1 The words of **A** the son of Jakeh, *even* 94

AH (18) [AHA]
Ps 35:25 say in their hearts, **A**, so would we have it: 1889
Isa 1: 4 **A** sinful nation, a people laden with 1945
1:24 of hosts, the mighty One of Israel, **A**, 1945
Jer 1: 6 said I, **A**, Lord GOD, behold, I cannot 162
4:10 (Then said I, **A**, Lord GOD! surely thou 162
14:13 said I, **A** Lord GOD! behold, the prophets 162
22:18 not lament for him, *saying,* **A** my brother! 1945
22:18 or, **A** sister! they shall not lament for him, 1945
22:18 shall not lament for him, *saying,* **A** lord! 1945
22:18 for him, *saying,* Ah lord! or, **A** his glory. 1945
32:17 **A** Lord GOD! behold, thou hast made 162
34: 5 and they will lament thee, *saying,* **A** lord! 1945
Eze 4:14 said I, **A** Lord GOD, behold, my soul *hath* 162
9: 8 my face, and cried, and said, **A** Lord GOD, 162
11:13 *with* a loud voice, and said, **A** Lord GOD, 162
20:49 said I, **A** Lord GOD, they say of me, Doth 162
21:15 **a**, *it is* made bright, *it is* wrapt up for 253
Mk 15:29 wagging their heads, and saying, **A**, *3758*

AHA (10) [AH, HA]
Ps 35:21 *and* said, **A**, aha, our eye hath seen *it.* 1889
35:21 *and* said, Aha, **a**, our eye hath seen *it.* 1889
40:15 of their shame that say unto me, **A**, aha! 1889
40:15 of their shame that say unto me, Aha, **a**! 1889
70: 3 for a reward of their shame that say, **A**, aha. 1889
70: 3 a reward of their shame that say, Aha, **a**. 1889
Isa 44:16 saith, **A**, I am warm, I have seen the fire: 1889
Eze 25: 3 Because thou saidst, **A**, against my 1889
26: 2 that Tyrus hath said against Jerusalem, **A**, 1889
36: 2 the enemy hath said against you, **A**, 1889

AHAB (92) [AHAB'S]
1Ki 16:28 and **A** his son reigned in his stead. 256
16:29 eighth year of Asa king of Judah *began* **A** 256
16:29 **A** the son of Omri reigned over Israel in 256
16:30 **A** the son of Omri did evil in the sight of 256
16:33 **A** made a grove; and Ahab did more to 256
16:33 **A** did more to provoke the LORD God of 256
17: 1 said unto **A**, *As* the LORD God of Israel 256
18: 1 third year, saying, Go, shew thyself unto **A**; 256
18: 2 Elijah went to shew himself unto **A**. 256
18: 3 **A** called Obadiah, which *was* the governor 256
18: 5 **A** said unto Obadiah, Go into the land, 256
18: 6 **A** went one way by himself, and 256
18: 9 deliver thy servant into the hand of **A**, 256
18:12 *so* when I come and tell **A**, and he cannot 256
18:16 So Obadiah went to meet **A**, and told him: 256
18:16 and told him: and **A** went to meet Elijah. 256
18:17 it came to pass, when **A** saw Elijah, 256
18:17 when Ahab saw Elijah, that **A** said unto him, 256
18:20 So **A** sent unto all the children of Israel, and 256
18:41 And Elijah said unto **A**, Get thee up, eat and 256
18:42 So **A** went up to eat and to drink. And Elijah 256
18:44 he said, Go up, say unto **A**, Prepare *thy* 256
18:45 great rain. And **A** rode, and went to Jezreel. 256
18:46 and ran before **A** to the entrance of Jezreel. 256
19: 1 **A** told Jezebel all that Elijah had done, and 256
20: 2 he sent messengers to **A** king of Israel into 256

1Ki 20:13 there came a prophet unto **A** king of Israel, 256
20:14 **A** said, By whom? And he said, Thus saith 256
20:34 *said* **A**, I will send thee away with *this* NIH
21: 1 hard by the palace of **A** king of Samaria. 256
21: 2 **A** spake unto Naboth, saying, Give me thy 256
21: 3 Naboth said to **A**, The LORD forbid it me, 256
21: 4 **A** came into his house heavy and displeased 256
21:15 and was dead, that Jezebel said to **A**, Arise, 256
21:16 to pass, when **A** heard that Naboth was dead, 256
21:16 that **A** rose up to go down to the vineyard of 256
21:18 Arise, go down to meet **A** king of Israel, 256
21:20 **A** said to Elijah, Hast thou found me, 256
21:21 will cut off from **A** *him that* pisseth against 256
21:24 Him that dieth of **A** in the city the dogs shall 256
21:25 (But there was none like unto **A**, which did 256
21:27 it came to pass, when **A** heard those words, 256
21:29 Seest thou how **A** humbleth himself before 256
22:20 Who shall persuade **A**, that he may go up 256
22:39 Now the rest of the acts of **A**, and all that he 256
22:40 So **A** slept with his fathers; and Ahaziah his 256
22:41 Judah in the fourth year of **A** king of Israel. 256
22:49 said Ahaziah the son of **A** unto Jehoshaphat, 256
22:51 Ahaziah the son of **A** *began* to reign over 256
2Ki 1: 1 rebelled against Israel after the death of **A**. 256
3: 1 Now Jehoram the son of **A** *began* to reign 256
3: 5 it came to pass, when **A** was dead, that 256
8:16 in the fifth year of Joram the son of **A** king 256
8:18 of the kings of Israel, as did the house of **A**: 256
8:18 for the daughter of **A** was his wife: and 256
8:25 In the twelfth year of Joram the son of **A** 256
8:27 And he walked in the way of the house of **A**, 256
8:27 sight of the LORD, as *did* the house of **A**: 256
8:27 for he *was* the son in law of the house of **A**. 256
8:28 he went with Joram the son of **A** to the war 256
8:29 down to see Joram the son of **A** in Jezreel, 256
9: 7 thou shalt smite the house of **A** thy master, 256
9: 8 For the whole house of **A** shall perish: and 256
9: 8 I will cut off from **A** *him that* pisseth against 256
9: 9 I will make the house of **A** like the house of 256
9:25 and thou rode together after **A** his father, 256
9:29 in the eleventh year of Joram the son of **A** 256
10: 1 **A** had seventy sons in Samaria. And Jehu 256
10:10 LORD spake concerning the house of **A**: 256
10:11 that remained of the house of **A** in Jezreel, 256
10:17 he slew all that remained unto **A** in Samaria, 256
10:18 and said unto them, **A** served Baal a little; 256
10:30 hast done unto the house of **A** according to 256
21: 3 and made a grove, as did **A** king of Israel; 256
21:13 and the plummet of the house of **A**: 256
2Ch 18: 1 in abundance, and joined affinity with **A**. 256
18: 2 after *certain* years he went down to **A** to 256
18: 2 **A** killed sheep and oxen for him in 256
18: 3 **A** king of Israel said unto Jehoshaphat king 256
18:19 Who shall entice **A** king of Israel, that he 256
21: 6 kings of Israel, like as did the house of **A**: 256
21: 6 for he had the daughter of **A** to wife: and 256
21:13 like to the whoredoms of the house of **A**, and 256
22: 3 also walked in the ways of the house of **A**: 256
22: 4 the sight of the LORD, like the house of **A**: 256
22: 5 went with Jehoram the son of **A** king of 256
22: 6 down to see Jehoram the son of **A** at Jezreel, 256
22: 7 had anointed to cut off the house of **A**. 256
22: 8 executing judgment upon the house of **A**, 256
Jer 29:21 of **A** the son of Kolaiah, and of Zedekiah, 256
29:22 LORD make thee like Zedekiah and like **A**, 256
Mic 6:16 all the works of the house of **A**, and ye walk 256

AHAB'S (2) [AHAB]

1Ki 21: 8 So she wrote letters in **A** name, and 256
2Ki 10: 1 to them that brought up **A** *children*, saying, 256

AHARAH (1)

1Ch 8: 1 Ashbel the second, and **A** the third, 315

AHARHEL (1)

1Ch 4: 8 and the families of **A** the son of Harum. 316

AHASAI (1)

Ne 11:13 the son of **A**, the son of Meshillemoth, 273

AHASBAI (1)

2Sa 23:34 Eliphelet the son of **A**, the son of 308

AHASUERUS (30) [AHASUERUS']

Ezr 4: 6 in the reign of **A**, in the beginning of his 325
Est 1: 1 Now it came to pass in the days of **A**, (this *is* 325
1: 1 (this *is* **A** which reigned, from India even 325
1: 2 when the king **A** sat on the throne of his 325
1: 9 *in* the royal house which *belonged* to king **A**. 325
1:10 that served in the presence of **A** the king, 325
1:15 of the king **A** by the chamberlains? 325
1:16 that *are* in all the provinces of the king **A**. 325
1:17 The king **A** commanded Vashti the queen to 325
1:19 That Vashti come no *more* before king **A**; 325
2: 1 when the wrath of king **A** was appeased, 325
2:12 maid's turn was come to go in to king **A**, 325
2:16 So Esther was taken unto king **A** into his 325
2:21 and sought to lay hand on the king **A**. 325
3: 1 After these things did king **A** promote 325
3: 6 *were* throughout the whole kingdom of **A**, 325
3: 7 in the twelfth year of king **A**, they cast Pur, 325
3: 8 Haman said unto king **A**, There is a certain 325
3:12 in the name of king **A** was it written, and 325
6: 2 who sought to lay hand on the king **A**. 325
7: 5 the king **A** answered and said unto Esther 325
8: 1 On that day did the king **A** give the house of 325
8: 7 the king **A** said unto Esther the queen and 325
8:12 Upon one day in all the provinces of king **A**, 325
9: 2 throughout all the provinces of the king **A**, 325
9:20 that *were* in all the provinces of the king **A**, 325
9:30 and seven provinces of the kingdom of **A**, 325
10: 1 the king **A** laid a tribute upon the land, and 325
10: 3 For Mordecai the Jew *was* next unto king **A**, 325
Da 9: 1 In the first year of Darius the son of **A**, 325

AHASUERUS' (1) [AHASUERUS]

Est 8:10 he wrote in the king **A** name, and sealed *it* 325

AHAVA (3)

Ezr 8:15 them together to the river that runneth to **A**; 163
8:21 Then I proclaimed a fast there, at the river **A**, 163
8:31 we departed from the river of **A** on 163

AHAZ (42) [ACHAZ]

2Ki 15:38 his father: and **A** his son reigned in his stead. 271
16: 1 **A** the son of Jotham king of Judah *began* to 271
16: 2 Twenty years old *was* **A** when he *began* to 271
16: 5 they besieged **A**, but could not overcome 271
16: 7 So **A** sent messengers to Tiglath-pileser king 271
16: 8 **A** took the silver and gold that was found *in* 271
16:10 king **A** went *to* Damascus to meet 271
16:10 king **A** sent to Urijah the priest the fashion 271
16:11 to all that king **A** had sent from Damascus: 271
16:11 Urijah the priest made *it* against king **A** 271
16:15 king **A** commanded Urijah the priest, saying, 271
16:16 according to all that king **A** commanded. 271
16:17 And king **A** cut off the borders of the bases, 271
16:19 Now the rest of the acts of **A** which he did, 271
16:20 **A** slept with his fathers, and was buried with 271
17: 1 In the twelfth year of **A** king of Judah *began* 271
18: 1 *that* Hezekiah the son of **A** king of Judah 271
20:11 by which it had gone down in the dial of **A**. 271
23:12 *were* on the top of the upper chamber of **A**, 271
1Ch 3:13 **A** his son, Hezekiah his son, Manasseh his 271
8:35 *were*, Pithon, and Melech, and Tarea, and **A**. 271
8:36 **A** begat Jehoadah; and Jehoadah begat 271
9:41 and Melech, and Tahrea, *and* **A**. NIH
9:42 **A** begat Jarah; and Jarah begat Alemeth, 271
2Ch 27: 9 of David: and **A** his son reigned in his stead. 271
28: 1 **A** *was* twenty years old when he *began* to 271
28:16 At that time did king **A** send unto the kings 271
28:19 Judah low because of **A** king of Israel; 271
28:21 For **A** took away a portion *out* of the house 271
28:22 more against the LORD: this *is that* king **A**. 271
28:24 **A** gathered together the vessels of the house 271
28:27 **A** slept with his fathers, and they buried him 271
29:19 which king **A** in his reign did cast away in 271
Isa 1: 1 Jotham, **A**, *and* Hezekiah, kings of Judah. 271
7: 1 it came to pass in the days of **A** the son of 271
7: 3 Go forth now to meet **A**, thou, and 271
7:10 Moreover the LORD spake again unto **A**, 271
7:12 **A** said, I will not ask, neither will I tempt 271
14:28 In the year that king **A** died was this burden. 271
38: 8 which is gone down in the sun dial of **A**, 271
Hos 1: 1 Jotham, **A**, *and* Hezekiah, kings of Judah, 271
Mic 1: 1 **A**, *and* Hezekiah, kings of Judah, which he 271

AHAZIAH (37)

1Ki 22:40 and **A** his son reigned in his stead. 274
22:49 said **A** the son of Ahab unto Jehoshaphat, 274
22:51 **A** the son of Ahab *began* to reign over Israel 274
2Ki 1: 2 **A** fell down through a lattice in his upper 274
1:18 Now the rest of the acts of **A** which he did, 274
8:24 of David: and **A** his son reigned in his stead. 274
8:25 **A** the son of Jehoram king of Judah *begin* to 274
8:26 twenty years old *was* **A** when he *began* to 274
8:29 **A** the son of Jehoram king of Judah went 274
9:16 **A** king of Judah was come down to see 274
9:21 king of Israel and **A** king of Judah went out, 274
9:23 fled, and said to **A**, *There is* treachery, 274
9:23 and said to Ahaziah, *There is* treachery, O **A**. 274
9:27 when **A** the king of Judah saw *this*, he fled 274
9:29 son of Ahab *began* **A** to reign over Judah. 274
10:13 Jehu met with the brethren of **A** king of 274
10:13 they answered, We *are* the brethren of **A**; 274
11: 1 when Athaliah the mother of **A** saw that her 274
11: 2 the daughter of king Joram, sister of **A**, 274
11: 2 took Joash the son of **A**, and stale him from 274
12:18 Jehoram, and **A**, his fathers, kings of Judah, 274
13: 1 twentieth year of Joash the son of **A** king of 274
14:13 the son of Jehoash the son of **A**, 274
1Ch 3:11 Joram his son, **A** his son, Joash his son, 274
2Ch 20:35 of Judah join himself with **A** king of Israel, 274
20:37 Because thou hast joined thyself with **A**, 274
22: 1 the inhabitants of Jerusalem made **A** his 274
22: 1 So **A** the son of Jehoram king of Judah 274
22: 2 two years old *was* **A** when he *began* to reign, 274
22: 7 the destruction of **A** was of God by coming 274
22: 8 the sons of the brethren of **A**, that ministered 274
22: 8 that ministered to **A**, he slew them. 274
22: 9 he sought **A**: and they caught him, (for he 274
22: 9 So the house of **A** had no power to keep still 274
22:10 when Athaliah the mother of **A** saw that her 274
22:11 took Joash the son of **A**, and stole him from 274
22:11 the priest, (for she was the sister of **A**,) 274

AHBAN (1)

1Ch 2:29 *was* Abihail, and she bare him **A**, and Molid. 257

AHER (1)

1Ch 7:12 children of Ir, *and* Hushim, the sons of **A**. 313

AHI (2)

1Ch 5:15 **A** the son of Abdiel, the son of Guni, 277
7:34 **A**, and Rohgah, Jehubbah, and Aram. 277

AHIAH (4)

1Sa 14: 3 And **A**, the son of Ahitub, Ichabod's brother, 281
14:18 Saul said unto **A**, Bring hither the ark of 281
1Ki 4: 3 Elihoreph and **A**, the sons of Shisha, scribes; 281
1Ch 8: 7 Naaman, and **A**, and Gera, he removed them, 281

AHIAM (2)

2Sa 23:33 **A** the son of Sharar the Hararite, 279
1Ch 11:35 **A** the son of Sacar the Hararite, Eliphal 279

AHIAN (1)

1Ch 7:19 **A**, and Shechem, and Likhi, and Aniam. 291

AHIEZER (6)

Nu 1:12 Of Dan; **A** the son of Ammishaddai. 295
2:25 the captain of the children of Dan *shall be* **A** 295
7:66 On the tenth day **A** the son of Ammishaddai, 295
7:71 this *was* the offering of **A** the son of 295
10:25 over his host *was* **A** the son of 295
1Ch 12: 3 The chief *was* **A**, then Joash, the sons of 295

AHIHUD (2)

Nu 34:27 the children of Asher, **A** the son of Shelomi. 282
1Ch 8: 7 he removed them, and begat Uzza, and **A**. 284

AHIJAH (20)

1Ki 11:29 that the prophet **A** the Shilonite found him in 281
11:30 **A** caught the new garment that *was* on him, 281
12:15 which the LORD spake by **A** the Shilonite 281
14: 2 behold, there *is* **A** the prophet, which told 281
14: 4 went *to* Shiloh, and came *to* the house of **A**. 281
14: 4 **A** could not see; for his eyes were set by 281
14: 5 the LORD said unto **A**, Behold, the wife of 281
14: 6 *so*, when **A** heard the sound of her feet, 281
14:18 which he spake by the hand of his servant **A** 281
15:27 Baasha the son of **A**, of the house of 281
15:29 which he spake by his servant **A** 281
15:33 son of **A** to reign over all Israel in Tirzah, 281
21:22 like the house of Baasha the son of **A**, for 281
2Ki 9: 9 and like the house of Baasha the son of **A**: 281
1Ch 2:25 and Bunah, and Oren, and Ozem, *and* **A**. 281
11:36 Hepher the Mecherathite, **A** the Pelonite, 281
26:20 **A** *was* over the treasures of the house of 281
2Ch 9:29 in the prophecy of **A** the Shilonite, and in 281
10:15 which he spake by the hand of **A** 281
Ne 10:26 And **A**, Hanan, Anan, 281

AHIKAM (20)

2Ki 22:12 **A** the son of Shaphan, and Achbor the son of 296
22:14 **A**, and Achbor, and Shaphan, and Asahiah, 296
25:22 over them he made Gedaliah the son of **A**, 296
2Ch 34:20 **A** the son of Shaphan, and Abdon the son of 296
Jer 26:24 Nevertheless the hand of **A** the son of 296
39:14 committed him unto Gedaliah the son of **A** 296
40: 5 to Gedaliah the son of **A** the son of Shaphan, 296
40: 6 went Jeremiah unto Gedaliah the son of **A** to 296
40: 7 Gedaliah the son of **A** governor in the land, 296
40: 9 Gedaliah the son of **A** the son of Shaphan 296
40:11 Gedaliah the son of **A** the son of Shaphan; 296
40:14 Gedaliah the son of **A** believed them not. 296
40:16 Gedaliah the son of **A** said unto Johanan 296
41: 1 came unto Gedaliah the son of **A** to Mizpah; 296
41: 2 smote Gedaliah the son of **A** the son of 296
41: 6 unto them, Come to Gedaliah the son of **A**. 296
41:10 had committed to Gedaliah the son of **A**: 296
41:16 after *that* he had slain Gedaliah the son of **A**, 296
41:18 Nethaniah had slain Gedaliah the son of **A**, 296
43: 6 Gedaliah the son of **A** the son of Shaphan, 296

AHILUD (5)

2Sa 8:16 and Jehoshaphat the son of **A** *was* recorder; 286
20:24 and Jehoshaphat the son of **A** *was* recorder: 286
1Ki 4: 3 Jehoshaphat the son of **A**, the recorder. 286
4:12 Baana the son of **A**; *to him pertained* 286
1Ch 18:15 and Jehoshaphat the son of **A**, recorder. 286

AHIMAAZ (15)

1Sa 14:50 wife *was* Ahinoam, the daughter of **A**: 290
2Sa 15:27 **A** thy son, and Jonathan the son of Abiathar. 290
15:36 **A** Zadok's *son*, and Jonathan Abiathar's *son*; 290
17:17 Now Jonathan and **A** stayed by En-rogel; 290
17:20 they said, Where *is* **A** and Jonathan? 290
18:19 said **A** the son of Zadok, Let me now run, 290
18:22 said **A** the son of Zadok yet again to Joab, 290
18:23 **A** ran *by* the way of the plain, and 290
18:27 *is* like the running of **A** the son of Zadok. 290
18:28 **A** called, and said unto the king, All is well. 290
18:29 **A** answered, When Joab sent the king's 290
1Ki 4:15 **A** *was* in Naphtali; he also took Basmath 290
1Ch 6: 8 Ahitub begat Zadok, and Zadok begat **A**, 290
6: 9 **A** begat Azariah, and Azariah begat 290
6:53 Zadok his son, **A** his son. 290

AHIMAN (4)

Nu 13:22 where **A**, Sheshai, and Talmai, the children 289
Jos 15:14 Sheshai, and **A**, and Talmai, the children of 289
Jdg 1:10 and they slew Sheshai, and **A**, and Talmai. 289
1Ch 9:17 and Talmon, and **A**, and their brethren: 289

AHIMELECH (16) [AHIMELECH'S]

1Sa 21: 1 Then came David to Nob to **A** the priest: and 288
21: 1 **A** was afraid at the meeting of David, and 288
21: 2 David said unto **A** the priest, The king hath 288
21: 8 David said unto **A**, And is there not here 288
22: 9 Jesse coming to Nob, to **A** the son of Ahitub: 288
22:11 the king sent to call **A** the priest, the son of 288
22:14 **A** answered the king, and said, And who *is* 288
22:16 **A**, thou, and all thy father's house. 288
22:20 And one of the sons of **A** the son of Ahitub, 288
23: 6 when Abiathar the son of **A** fled to David *to* 288
26: 6 answered David and said to **A** the Hittite, 288
2Sa 8:17 and **A** the son of Abiathar, *were* the priests; 288
1Ch 24: 3 of Eleazar, and **A** of the sons of Ithamar, 288
24: 6 **A** the son of Abiathar, and *before* the chief 288
24:31 **A**, and the chief of the fathers of the priests 288
Ps 52: T unto him, David is come to the house of **A**. 288

AHIMELECH'S (1) [AHIMELECH]

1Sa 30: 7 **A** son, I pray thee, bring me hither 288

AHIMOTH (1)

1Ch 6:25 And the sons of Elkanah; Amasai, and **A**. 287

AHINADAB (1)

1Ki 4:14 **A** the son of Iddo *had* Mahanaim: 292

AHINOAM (7)
1Sa 14:50 the name of Saul's wife *was* **A**, the daughter 293
25:43 David also took **A** of Jezreel; and they were 293
27: 3 **A** the Jezreelitess, and Abigail 293
30: 5 **A** the Jezreelitess, and Abigail the wife of 293
2Sa 2: 2 **A** the Jezreelitess, and Abigail Nabal's wife 293
3: 2 firstborn was Amnon, of **A** the Jezreelitess; 293
1Ch 3: 1 the firstborn Amnon, of **A** the Jezreelitess; 293

AHIO (6)
2Sa 6: 3 Uzzah and **A**, the sons of Abinadab, 283
6: 4 the ark of God: and **A** went before the ark. 283
1Ch 8:14 And **A**, Shashak, and Jeremoth, 283
8:31 And Gedor, and **A**, and Zacher. 283
9:37 and **A**, and Zechariah, and Mikloth. 283
13: 7 of Abinadab: and Uzza and **A** drave the cart. 283

AHIRA (5)
Nu 1:15 Of Naphtali; **A** the son of Enan. 299
2:29 of Naphtali *shall be* **A** the son of Enan. 299
7:78 On the twelfth day **A** the son of Enan, 299
7:83 this *was* the offering of **A** the son of Enan. 299
10:27 children of Naphtali *was* **A** the son of Enan. 299

AHIRAM (1) [AHIRAMITES]
Nu 26:38 of **A**, the family of the Ahiramites: 297

AHIRAMITES (1) [AHIRAM]
Nu 26:38 of Ahiram, the family of the **A**: 298

AHISAMACH (3)
Ex 31: 6 the son of **A**, of the tribe of Dan: 294
35:34 *both* he, and Aholiab, the son of **A**, of 294
38:23 son of **A**, of the tribe of Dan, an engraver, 294

AHISHAHAR (1)
1Ch 7:10 and Zethan, and Tharshish, and **A**. 300

AHISHAR (1)
1Ki 4: 6 **A** *was* over the household: and 301

AHITHOPHEL (20)
2Sa 15:12 Absalom sent *for* **A** the Gilonite, 302
15:31 **A** *is* among the conspirators with Absalom. 302
15:31 turn the counsel of **A** into foolishness. 302
15:34 mayest thou for me defeat the counsel of **A**. 302
16:15 came *to* Jerusalem, and **A** with him. 302
16:20 said Absalom to **A**, Give counsel among you 302
16:21 **A** said unto Absalom, Go in unto thy father's 302
16:23 the counsel of **A**, which he counselled in 302
16:23 so *was* all the counsel of **A** both with David 302
17: 1 Moreover **A** said unto Absalom, Let me now 302
17: 6 **A** hath spoken after this manner: 302
17: 7 The counsel that **A** hath given *is* not good at 302
17:14 the Archite *is* better than the counsel of **A**. 302
17:14 appointed to defeat the good counsel of **A**, 302
17:15 Thus and thus did **A** counsel Absalom and 302
17:21 for thus hath **A** counselled against you. 302
17:23 when **A** saw that his counsel was not 302
23:34 Eliam the son of **A** the Gilonite, 302
1Ch 27:33 **A** *was* the king's counseller: and Hushai 302
27:34 after **A** *was* Jehoiada the son of Benaiah, 302

AHITUB (15)
1Sa 14: 3 And Ahiah, the son of **A**, Ichabod's brother, 285
22: 9 coming to Nob, to Ahimelech the son of **A**: 285
22:11 the son of **A**, and all his father's house, 285
22:12 Saul said, Hear now, thou son of **A**. And he 285
22:20 one of the sons of Ahimelech the son of **A**, 285
2Sa 8:17 Zadok the son of **A**, and Ahimelech the son 285
1Ch 6: 7 begat Amariah, and Amariah begat **A**, 285
6: 8 **A** begat Zadok, and Zadok begat Ahimaaz, 285
6:11 begat Amariah, and Amariah begat **A**, 285
6:12 **A** begat Zadok, and Zadok begat Shallum, 285
6:52 his son, Amariah his son, **A** his son, 285
9:11 of Zadok, the son of Meraioth, the son of **A**, 285
18:16 Zadok the son of **A**, and Abimelech the son 285
Ezr 7: 2 of Shallum, the son of Zadok, the son of **A**, 285
Ne 11:11 of Zadok, the son of Meraioth, the son of **A**, 285

AHLAB (1)
Jdg 1:31 nor of **A**, nor of Achzib, nor of Helbah, 303

AHLAI (2)
1Ch 2:31 Sheshan. And the children of Sheshan; **A**. 304
11:41 Uriah the Hittite, Zabad the son of **A**, 304

AHOAH (1)
1Ch 8: 4 And Abishua, and Naaman, and **A**, 265

AHOHITE (5)
2Sa 23: 9 *was* Eleazar the son of Dodo the **A**, 266+1121
23:28 Zalmon the **A**, Maharai the Netophathite, 266
1Ch 11:12 the **A**, who *was one* of the three mighties. 266
11:29 Sibbecai the Hushathite, Ilai the **A**, 266
27: 4 course of the second month *was* Dodai an **A**, 266

AHOLAH (5)
Eze 23: 4 the names of them *were* **A** the elder, and 170
23: 4 Samaria *is* **A**, and Jerusalem Aholibah. 170
23: 5 And **A** played the harlot when she was mine; 170
23:36 of man, wilt thou judge **A** and Aholibah? 170
23:44 so went they in unto **A** and unto Aholibah, 170

AHOLIAB (5)
Ex 31: 6 I, behold, I have given with him **A**, the son 171
35:34 *both* he, and **A**, the son of Ahisamach, of 171
36: 1 wrought Bezaleel and **A**, and every wise 171
36: 2 Moses called Bezaleel and **A**, and every 171
38:23 with him *was* **A**, son of Ahisamach, of 171

AHOLIBAH (6)
Eze 23: 4 *were* Aholah the elder, and **A** her sister: 172
23: 4 Samaria *is* Aholah, and Jerusalem **A**. 172
23:11 when her sister **A** saw *this*, she was more 172
23:22 Therefore, O **A**, thus saith the Lord GOD; 172
23:36 Son of man, wilt thou judge Aholah and **A**? 172
23:44 so went they in unto Aholah and unto **A**, 172

AHOLIBAMAH (8)
Ge 36: 2 **A** the daughter of Anah the daughter of 173
36: 5 **A** bare Jeush, and Jaalam, and Korah: 173
36:14 these were the sons of **A**, the daughter of 173
36:18 these *are* the sons of **A** Esau's wife; 173
36:18 these *were* the dukes *that came* of **A** 173
36:25 Dishon, and **A** the daughter of Anah. 173
36:41 Duke **A**, duke Elah, duke Pinon, 173
1Ch 1:52 Duke **A**, duke Elah, duke Pinon, 173

AHUMAI (1)
1Ch 4: 2 begat Jahath; and Jahath begat **A**, and Lahad. 267

AHUZAM (1)
1Ch 4: 6 Naarah bare him **A**, and Hepher, and 275

AHUZZAM See AHUZAM

AHUZZATH (1)
Ge 26:26 **A** *one* of his friends, and Phichol the chief 276

AHZAI See AHASAI

AI (36) [HAI]
Jos 7: 2 Joshua sent men from Jericho *to* **A**, 5857
7: 2 And the men went up and viewed **A**. 5857
7: 3 or three thousand men go up and smite **A**; 5857
7: 4 and they fled before the men of **A**. 5857
7: 5 the men of **A** smote of them about thirty 5857
8: 1 of war with thee, and arise, go up to **A**: 5857
8: 1 I have given into thy hand the king of **A**, 5857
8: 2 thou shalt do to **A** and her king as thou 5857
8: 3 all the people of war, to go up *against* **A**: 5857
8: 9 abode between Beth-el and **A**, on the west 5857
8: 9 and Ai, on the west side of **A**: 5857
8:10 the elders of Israel, before the people *to* **A**. 5857
8:11 the city, and pitched on the north side of **A**: 5857
8:11 *there was* a valley between them and **A**. 5857
8:12 to lie in ambush between Beth-el and **A**, 5857
8:14 when the king of **A** saw *it*, that they hasted 5857
8:16 all the people that *were* in **A** were called 5857
8:17 there was not a man left in **A** or Beth-el, 5857
8:18 out the spear that *is* in thy hand toward **A**; 5857
8:20 when the men of **A** looked behind them, 5857
8:21 they turned again, and slew the men of **A**. 5857
8:23 the king of **A** they took alive, and 5857
8:24 slaying all the inhabitants of **A** in the field, 5857
8:24 that all the Israelites returned *unto* **A**, and 5857
8:25 twelve thousand, *even* all the men of **A**. 5857
8:26 utterly destroyed all the inhabitants of **A**. 5857
8:28 Joshua burnt **A**, and made it a heap for 5857
8:29 the king of **A** he hanged on a tree until 5857
9: 3 Joshua had done unto Jericho and to **A**, 5857
10: 1 had heard how Joshua had taken **A**, 5857
10: 1 her king, so he had done to **A** and her king; 5857
10: 2 because it *was* greater than **A**, and all 5857
12: 9 the king of **A**, which *is* beside Beth-el, one; 5857
Ezr 2:28 The men of Beth-el and **A**, two hundred 5857
Ne 7:32 The men of Beth-el and **A**, an hundred 5857
Jer 49: 3 Howl, O Heshbon, for **A** is spoiled: cry, 5857

AIAH (6)
Ge 36:24 the children of Zibeon; both **A**, and Anah: 345
2Sa 3: 7 whose name *was* Rizpah, the daughter of **A**: 345
21: 8 the two sons of Rizpah the daughter of **A**, 345
21:10 Rizpah the daughter of **A** took sackcloth, 345
21:11 told David what Rizpah the daughter of **A**, 345
1Ch 1:40 And the sons of Zibeon; **A**, and Anah. 345

AIATH (1)
Isa 10:28 He is come to **A**, he is passed to Migron; 5857

AIDED (1)
Jdg 9:24 **a** him in the killing of his 853+2388+3027

AIJA (1)
Ne 11:31 and **A**, and Beth-el, and *in* their villages, 5857

AIJALON (8)
Jos 19:42 And Shaalabbin, and **A**, and Jethlah, 357
21:24 **A** with her suburbs, Gath-rimmon with her 357
Jdg 1:35 Amorites would dwell in mount Heres in **A**, 357
12:12 was buried in **A** in the country of Zebulun. 357
1Sa 14:31 the Philistines that day from Michmash to **A**: 357
1Ch 6:69 **A** with her suburbs, and Gath-rimmon with 357
8:13 heads of the fathers of the inhabitants of **A**, 357
2Ch 11:10 Zorah, and **A**, and Hebron, which *are* in 357

AIJELETH (1)
Ps 22: T To the chief Musician upon **A** Shahar, 365

AILED (1) [AILETH]
Ps 114: 5 What **a** thee, O thou sea, that thou 3807.1

AILETH (7) [AILED]
Ge 21:17 said unto her, **What a** thee, Hagar? 4100+3807.1
Jdg 18:23 and said unto Micah, What **a** thee, 3807.1
18:24 *is* this *that* ye say unto me, What **a** thee? 3807.1
1Sa 11: 5 What **a** the people that they weep? 3807.1
2Sa 14: 5 the king said unto her, What **a** thee? 3807.1
2Ki 6:28 the king said unto her, What **a** thee? 3807.1
Isa 22: 1 What **a** thee now, that thou art wholly 3807.1

AIN (5)
Nu 34:11 Shepham *to* Riblah, on the east side of **A**; 5871
Jos 15:32 and Shilhim, and **A**, and Rimmon: 5871
19: 7 **A**, Remmon, and Ether, and Ashan; 5871
21:16 **A** with her suburbs, and Juttah with her 5871
1Ch 4:32 **A**, Rimmon, and Tochen, and Ashan, 5871

AIR (39)
Ge 1:26 over the fowl of the **a**, and over the cattle, 8064
1:28 over the fowl of the **a**, and over every 8064
1:30 to every fowl of the **a**, and to every *thing* 8064
2:19 beast of the field, and every fowl of the **a**; 8064
2:20 to the fowl of the **a**, and to every beast of 8064
6: 7 the creeping thing, and the fowls of the **a**; 8064
7: 3 Of fowls also of the **a** by sevens, the male 8064
9: 2 upon every fowl of the **a**, upon all that 8064
Dt 4:17 of any winged fowl that flieth in the **a**, 8064
28:26 shall be meat unto all fowls of the **a**, 8064
1Sa 17:44 I will give thy flesh unto the fowls of the **a**, 8064
17:46 Philistines this day unto the fowls of the **a**, 8064
2Sa 21:10 suffered neither the birds of the **a** to rest on 8064
1Ki 14:11 in the field shall the fowls of the **a** eat: 8064
16: 4 his in the fields shall the fowls of the **a** eat. 8064
21:24 in the field shall the fowls of the **a** eat. 8064
Job 12: 7 the fowls of the **a**, and they shall tell thee: 8064
28:21 and kept close from the fowls of the **a**. 8064
41:16 that no **a** can come between them. 7307
Ps 8: 8 The fowl of the **a**, and the fish of the sea, 8064
Pr 30:19 The way of an eagle in the **a**; the way of a 8064
Ecc 10:20 for a bird of the **a** shall carry the voice, and 8064
Mt 6:26 Behold the fowls of the **a**: for they sow not, *3772*
8:20 and the birds of the **a** *have* nests; *3772*
13:32 so that the birds of the **a** come and lodge in *3772*
Mk 4: 4 and the fowls of the **a** came and devoured it *3772*
4:32 that the fowls of the **a** may lodge under *3772*
Lk 8: 5 and the fowls of the **a** devoured it. *3772*
9:58 have holes, and birds of the **a** *have* nests; *3772*
13:19 the fowls of the **a** lodged in the branches of *3772*
Ac 10:12 and creeping things, and fowls of the **a**. *3772*
11: 6 and creeping things, and fowls of the **a**. *3772*
22:23 *off their* clothes, and threw dust into the **a**, *109*
1Co 9:26 so fight I, not as one that beateth the **a**: *109*
14: 9 what is spoken? for ye shall speak into the **a**. *109*
Eph 2: 2 according to the prince of the power of the **a**, *109*
1Th 4:17 them in the clouds, to meet the Lord in the **a**: *109*
Rev 9: 2 the **a** were darkened by reason of the smoke *109*
16:17 seventh angel poured out his vial into the **a**; *109*

AJALON (2)
Jos 10:12 and thou, Moon, in the valley of **A**. 357
2Ch 28:18 **A**, and Gederoth, and Shocho with 357

AKAN (1)
Ge 36:27 Ezer *are* these; Bilhan, and Zaavan, and **A**. 6130

AKELDAMA See ACELDAMA

AKIM See ACHIM

AKKAD See ACCAD

AKKUB (8)
1Ch 3:24 **A**, and Johanan, and Dalaiah, and Anani, 6126
9:17 **A**, and Talmon, and Ahiman, and 6126
Ezr 2:42 the children of **A**, the children of Hatita, 6126
2:45 the children of Hagabah, the children of **A**, 6126
Ne 7:45 the children of **A**, the children of Hatita, 6126
8: 7 Bani, and Sherebiah, Jamin, **A**, Shabbethai, 6126
11:19 **A**, Talmon, and their brethren that kept 6126
12:25 Obadiah, Meshullam, Talmon, **A**, 6126

AKRABBIM (2)
Nu 34: 4 shall turn from the south to the ascent of **A**, 6137
Jdg 1:36 the Amorites *was* from the going up to **A**, 6137

ALABASTER (3)
Mt 26: 7 having an **a box** of very precious ointment, *211*
Mk 14: 3 there came a woman having an **a box** of *211*
Lk 7:37 brought an **a box** of ointment, *211*

ALAMETH (1)
1Ch 7: 8 Jerimoth, and Abiah, and Anathoth, and **A**. 5964

ALAMMELECH (1)
Jos 19:26 **A**, and Amad, and Misheal; and reacheth to 487

ALAMOTH (2)
1Ch 15:20 and Benaiah, with psalteries on **A**; 5961
Ps 46: T for the sons of Korah, A Song upon **A**. 5961

ALARM (10)
Nu 10: 5 When ye blow an **a**, then the camps that lie 8643
10: 6 When you blow an **a** the second time, then 8643
10: 6 they shall blow an **a** for their journeys. 8643
10: 7 shall blow, but you shall not **sound an a**. 7321
10: 9 then ye shall **blow an a** with the trumpets; 7321
2Ch 13:12 his priests with sounding trumpets to **cry a** 7321
Jer 4:19 the sound of the trumpet, the **a** of war. 8643
49: 2 that I will cause an **a** of war to be heard in 8643
Joel 2: 1 and **sound an a** in my holy mountain: 7321
Zep 1:16 the trumpet and **a** against the fenced cities, 8643

ALAS (20)
Nu 12:11 **A**, my lord, I beseech thee, lay not the sin 994
24:23 he took up his parable, and said, **A**, 188
Jos 7: 7 Joshua said, **A**, O Lord GOD, 162
Jdg 6:22 the LORD, Gideon said, **A**, O Lord GOD! 162
11:35 he rent his clothes, and said, **A**, my daughter, 162
1Ki 13:30 mourned over him, *saying*, **A**, my brother. 1945
2Ki 3:10 the king of Israel said, **A**, that the LORD 162
6: 5 he cried, and said, **A**, master, for it *was* 162
6:15 unto him, **A**, my master, how shall we do? 162
Jer 30: 7 **A**! for that day *is* great, so that none *is* like 1945
Eze 6:11 **A** for all the evil abominations of the house 253
Joel 1:15 **A** for the day! for the day of the LORD *is* 162
Am 5:16 and they shall say in all the highways, **A**! 1930
5:16 **a**! and they shall call the husbandman to 1930
Rev 18:10 saying, **A**, alas, *that* great city Babylon, *3759*

Rev 18:10 saying, Alas, **a**, *that* great city Babylon, *3759*
18:16 And saying, **A**, alas, *that* great city, *3759*
18:16 And saying, Alas, **a**, *that* great city, *3759*
18:19 cried, weeping and wailing, saying, **A**, alas, *3759*
18:19 cried, weeping and wailing, saying, Alas, **a**, *3759*

ALBEIT (2)
Eze 13: 7 The LORD saith *it;* **a** I have not spoken? 2050.1
Phm 1:19 I will repay *it:* **a** I do not say to thee how *2443*

ALEMETH (3)
1Ch 6:60 **A** with her suburbs, and Anathoth with her 5964
8:36 Jehoadah begat **A**, and Azmaveth, and 5964
9:42 Jarah begat **A**, and Azmaveth, and Zimri; 5964

ALEXANDER (6)
Mk 15:21 the father of **A** and Rufus, to bear his cross. *223*
Ac 4: 6 and **A**, and as many as were of the kindred *223*
19:33 And they drew **A** out of the multitude, *223*
19:33 And **A** beckoned with the hand, and *223*
1Ti 1:20 Of whom is Hymeneus and **A**; whom I have *223*
2Ti 4:14 **A** the coppersmith did me much evil: *223*

ALEXANDRIA (3) [ALEXANDRIANS]
Ac 18:24 born **at A**, an eloquent man, *and* mighty in *221*
27: 6 And there the centurion found a ship of **A** *222*
28:11 three months we departed in a ship of **A**, *222*

ALEXANDRIANS (1) [ALEXANDRIA]
Ac 6: 9 and **A**, and of them of Cilicia and of Asia, *221*

ALGUM (3) [ALMUG]
2Ch 2: 8 fir trees, and **a trees**, out of Lebanon: 418
9:10 brought **a** trees and precious stones. 418
9:11 the king made *of* the **a** trees terraces to 418

ALIAH (1)
1Ch 1:51 duke Timnah, duke **A**, duke Jetheth, 5933

ALIAN (1)
1Ch 1:40 **A**, and Manahath, and Ebal, Shephi, and 5935

ALIEN (5) [ALIENATE, ALIENATED, ALIENS]
Ex 18: 3 he said, I have been an **a** in a strange land: 1616
Dt 14:21 may eat it; or thou mayest sell *it* unto an **a**: 5237
Job 19:15 me for a stranger: I am an **a** in their sight. 5237
Ps 69: 8 and an **a** unto my mother's children. 5237
Isa 61: 5 the sons of the **a** *shall be* your plowmen 5236

ALIENATE (1) [ALIEN]
Eze 48:14 nor **a** the firstfruits of the land: 5674

ALIENATED (7) [ALIEN]
Eze 23:17 with them, and her mind was **a** from them. 3363
23:18 my mind was **a** from her, like as my mind 3363
23:18 like as my mind was **a** from her sister. 5361
23:22 from whom thy mind is **a**, and I will bring 5361
23:28 the hand *of them* from whom thy mind is **a**: 5361
Eph 4:18 being **a** from the life of God through *526*
Col 1:21 that were sometime **a** and enemies in *your* *526*

ALIENS (3) [ALIEN]
La 5: 2 is turned to strangers, our houses to **a**. 5237
Eph 2:12 being **a** from the commonwealth of Israel, *526*
Heb 11:34 in fight, turned to flight the armies of the **a**. *245*

ALIKE (11) [LIKE]
Dt 12:22 and the clean shall eat of them **a**. 3162
15:22 and the clean *person shall eat it* **a**, 3162
1Sa 30:24 that tarrieth by the stuff: they shall part **a**. 3162
Job 21:26 They shall lie down **a** in the dust, and 3162
Ps 33:15 He fashioneth their hearts **a**; he considereth 3162
139:12 and the light *are* both **a** *to thee*. 3509.1
Pr 20:10 both of them *are* **a** abomination to 1571
27:15 rainy day and a contentious woman are **a**. 7737
Ecc 9: 2 All *things come* **a** to all: *there is* one 834+3509.1
11: 6 whether they both *shall be* **a** good. 259+3509.1
Ro 14: 5 another esteemeth every day **a**. Let every NIG

ALIVE (88) [LIVE]
Ge 6:19 into the ark, to **keep** *them* **a** with thee; 2421
6:20 *sort* shall come unto thee, to **keep** *them* **a**. 2421
7: 3 to **keep** seed **a** upon the face of all 2421
7:23 Noah only remained **a**, and *they that were* NIH
12:12 they will kill me, but they will **save** thee **a**. 2421
43: 7 of our kindred, saying, *Is* your father yet **a**? 2416
43:27 the old man of whom ye spake? *Is* he yet **a**? 2416
43:28 our father *is* in good health, he *is* yet **a**. 2416
45:26 Joseph *is* yet **a**, and he *is* governor over all 2416
45:28 *It is* enough; Joseph my son *is* yet **a**: 2416
46:30 I have seen thy face, because thou *art* yet **a**. 2416
50:20 as *it is* this day, to **save** much people **a**. 2421
Ex 1:17 but **saved** the men children **a**. 2421
1:18 and have **saved** the men children **a**? 2421
1:22 and every daughter ye shall **save a**. 2421
4:18 *are* in Egypt, and see whether they be yet **a**. 2416
22: 4 If the theft be certainly found in his hand **a**, 2416
Lev 10:16 the sons of Aaron which were left **a**, saying, NIH
14: 4 for him that is to be cleansed two birds **a** 2416
16:10 shall be presented **a** before the LORD, 2416
26:36 *upon* them that are left **a** of you I will send a NIH
Nu 16:33 went down **a** into the pit, and the earth 2416
21:35 his people, until there was none left him **a**: 8300
22:33 now also I had slain thee, and **saved** her **a**. 2421
31:15 unto them, Have ye **saved** all the women **a**? 2421
31:18 by lying with him, **keep a** for yourselves. 2421
Dt 4: 4 your God *are* **a** every one of you *this* day. 2416
5: 3 *even* us, who *are* all of us here **a** *this* day. 2416
6:24 that he might **preserve** us **a**, as *it is at* this 2421
20:16 thou shalt **save a** nothing that breatheth: 2421
31:27 behold, while I am yet **a** with you *this* day, 2416
32:39 I kill, and I **make a**; I wound, and I heal: 2421
Jos 2:13 *that* ye will **save a** my father, and 2421
6:25 Joshua **saved** Rahab the harlot **a**, and her 2421
8:23 the king of Ai they took **a**, and brought him 2416
14:10 the LORD hath **kept** me **a**, as he said, 2421
Jdg 8:19 if ye had **saved** them **a**, I would not slay 2421
21:14 **saved a** of the women of Jabesh-gilead: 2421
1Sa 2: 6 The LORD killeth, and **maketh a**: 2421
15: 8 he took Agag the king of the Amalekites **a**, 2416
27: 9 **left** neither man nor woman **a**, and 2421
27:11 David **saved** neither man nor woman **a**, 2421
2Sa 8: 2 to death, and *with* one full line to **keep a**. 2421
12:18 Behold, while the child was *yet* **a**, 2416
12:21 and weep for the child, *while it was* **a**; 2416
12:22 While the child *was* yet **a**, I fasted and 2416
18:14 while he *was* yet **a** in the midst of the oak. 2416
1Ki 18: 5 find grass to **save** the horses and mules **a**, 2421
20:18 they be come out for peace, take them **a**; 2416
20:18 they be come out for war, take them **a**. 2416
20:32 And he said, *Is* he yet **a**? he *is* my brother. 2416
21:15 for money: for Naboth is not **a**, but dead. 2416
2Ki 5: 7 and said, *Am* I God, to kill and to **make a**, 2421
7: 4 if they **save** us **a**, we shall live; and if they 2421
7:12 we shall catch them **a**, and get into the city. 2416
10:14 he said, Take them **a**. And they took them 2416
10:14 they took them **a**, and slew them at the pit 2416
2Ch 25:12 *other* ten thousand *left* **a** did the children of 2416
Ps 22:29 and none can **keep a** his own soul. 2421
30: 3 thou hast **kept** me **a**, that I should not go 2421
33:19 from death, and to **keep** them **a** in famine. 2421
41: 2 LORD will preserve him, and **keep** him **a**; 2421
Pr 1:12 Let us swallow them up **a** as the grave; and 2416
Ecc 4: 2 dead more than the living which are yet **a**. 2416
Jer 49:11 fatherless children, I will **preserve** *them* **a**; 2421
Eze 7:13 although they were yet **a**: 2416+871.1+1886.1
13:18 will ye **save** the souls **a** *that come* unto 2421
13:19 and to **save** the souls that should not live, 2421
18:27 is lawful and right, he shall **save** his soul **a**. 2421
Da 5:19 whom he would he **kept a**; and whom he 2418
Mt 27:63 while he was yet **a**, After three days I will *2198*
Mk 16:11 when they had heard that he was **a**, and *2198*
Lk 15:24 For this my son was dead, and is **a again**; *326*
15:32 for this thy brother was dead, and is **a again**; *326*
24:23 a vision of angels, which said that he was **a**. *2198*
Ac 1: 3 To whom also he shewed himself **a** after *2198*
9:41 the saints and widows, presented her **a**. *2198*
20:12 And they brought the young man **a**, and *2198*
25:19 *was* dead, whom Paul affirmed to be **a**. *2198*
Ro 6:11 **a** unto God through Jesus Christ our Lord. *2198*
6:13 as *those that are* **a** from the dead, and *2198*
7: 9 For I was **a** without the law once: but *2198*
1Co 15:22 even so in Christ shall all be **made a**. *2227*
1Th 4:15 that we which are **a** *and* remain unto *2198*
4:17 Then we which are **a** *and* remain shall be *2198*
Rev 1:18 and behold, I am **a** for evermore, Amen; *2198*
2: 8 and the last, which was dead, and is **a**; *2198*
19:20 *These* both were cast **a** into a lake of fire *2198*

ALL (5621)
Ge 1:26 over **a** the earth, and over every creeping 3605
1:29 which *is* upon the face of **a** the earth, and 3605
2: 1 earth were finished, and **a** the host of them. 3605
2: 2 he rested on the seventh day from **a** his 3605
2: 3 that in it he had rested from **a** his work 3605
2:20 Adam gave names to **a** cattle, and to 3605
3:14 thou *art* cursed above **a** cattle, and 3605
3:14 dust shalt thou eat **a** the days of thy life: 3605
3:17 in sorrow shalt thou eat *of* it **a** the days of 3605
3:20 because she was the mother of **a** living. 3605
4:21 he was the father of **a** such as handle 3605
5: 5 **a** the days that Adam lived were nine 3605
5: 8 **a** the days of Seth were nine hundred 3605
5:11 **a** the days of Enos were nine hundred 3605
5:14 **a** the days of Cainan were nine hundred 3605
5:17 **a** the days of Mahalaleel were eight 3605
5:20 **a** the days of Jared were nine hundred sixty 3605
5:23 **a** the days of Enoch were three hundred 3605
5:27 **a** the days of Methuselah were nine 3605
5:31 **a** the days of Lamech were seven hundred 3605
6: 2 they took them wives of **a** which they 3605
6:12 for **a** flesh had corrupted his way upon 3605
6:13 The end of **a** flesh is come before me; 3605
6:17 to destroy **a** flesh, wherein *is* the breath of 3605
6:19 of every living *thing* of **a** flesh, two of 3605
6:21 take thou unto thee of **a** food that is eaten, 3605
6:22 according to **a** that God commanded him, 3605
7: 1 Come thou and **a** thy house into the ark; 3605
7: 3 to keep seed alive upon the face of **a** 3605
7: 5 Noah did according unto **a** that the LORD 3605
7:11 the same day were **a** the fountains of 3605
7:14 **a** the cattle after their kind, and 3605
7:15 two and two of **a** flesh, wherein *is* 3605
7:16 went in, went in male and female of **a** flesh, 3605
7:19 **a** the high hills, that *were* under the whole 3605
7:21 And **a** flesh died that moved upon the earth, 3605
7:22 **A** in whose nostrils *was* the breath of life, 3605
7:22 of life, of **a** that *was* in the dry *land*, died. 3605
8: 1 **a** the cattle that *was* with him in the ark: 3605
8:17 of **a** flesh, *both* of fowl, and of cattle, and 3605
9: 2 upon **a** that moveth *upon* the earth, and 3605
9: 2 the earth, and upon **a** the fishes of the sea; 3605
9: 3 *even* as the green herb have I given you **a** 3605
9:10 from **a** that go out of the ark, to every beast 3605
9:11 neither shall **a** flesh be cut off any more by 3605
9:15 and every living creature of **a** flesh; 3605
9:15 no more become a flood to destroy **a** flesh. 3605
9:16 every living creature of **a** flesh that *is* upon 3605
9:17 and **a** flesh that *is* upon the earth. 3605
9:29 **a** the days of Noah were nine hundred and 3605
10:21 the father of **a** the children of Eber, 3605
10:29 and Jobab: **a** these *were* the sons of Joktan. 3605
11: 6 *is* one, and they have **a** one language; 3605
11: 8 from thence upon the face of **a** the earth: 3605
11: 9 there confound the language of **a** the earth: 3605
11: 9 them abroad upon the face of **a** the earth. 3605
12: 3 in thee shall **a** families of the earth be 3605
12: 5 **a** their substance that they had gathered, 3605
12:20 him away, and his wife, and **a** that he had. 3605
13: 1 and **a** that he had, and Lot with him, 3605
13:10 his eyes, and beheld **a** the plain of Jordan, 3605
13:11 Lot chose him **a** the plain of Jordan; and 3605
13:15 For **a** the land which thou seest, to thee will 3605
14: 3 **A** these were joined together in the vale of 3605
14: 7 smote **a** the country of the Amalekites, and 3605
14:11 they took **a** the goods of Sodom and 3605
14:11 and **a** their victuals, and went their way. 3605
14:16 he brought back **a** the goods, and 3605
14:20 into thy hand. And he gave him tithes of **a**. 3605
15:10 he took unto him **a** these, and divided them 3605
16:12 he shall dwell in the presence of **a** his 3605
17: 8 **a** the land of Canaan, for an everlasting 3605
17:23 **a** that were born in his house, and all that 3605
17:23 and **a** that were bought with his money, 3605
17:27 **a** the men of his house, born in the house, 3605
18:18 **a** the nations of the earth shall be blessed in 3605
18:25 Shall not the Judge of **a** the earth do right? 3605
18:26 then I will spare **a** the place for their sakes. 3605
18:28 wilt thou destroy **a** the city for *lack of* five? 3605
19: 2 **tarry a night**, and wash your feet, and 3885
19: 2 but we will **abide** in the street **a night**. 3885
19: 4 young, **a** the people from every quarter: 3605
19:17 behind thee, neither stay thou in **a** the plain; 3605
19:25 **a** the plain, and all the inhabitants of 3605
19:25 **a** the inhabitants of the cities, and 3605
19:28 toward **a** the land of the plain, and beheld, 3605
19:31 in unto us after the manner of **a** the earth: 3605
20: 7 shalt surely die, thou, and **a** that *are* thine. 3605
20: 8 called **a** his servants, and told all these 3605
20: 8 and told **a** these things in their ears: 3605
20:16 unto **a** that *are* with thee, and with all *other:* 3605
20:16 and with **a** *other:* thus she was reproved. 3605
20:18 For the LORD had fast closed up **a** 3605
21: 6 *so that* **a** that hear will laugh with me. 3605
21:12 in **a** that Sarah hath said unto thee, 3605
21:22 God *is* with thee in **a** that thou doest: 3605
22:18 in thy seed shall **a** the nations of the earth 3605
23:10 *even* of **a** that went in *at* the gate of his city, 3605
23:17 **a** the trees that *were* in the field, 3605
23:17 that *were* in **a** the borders round about, 3605
23:18 before **a** that went in *at* the gate of his city. 3605
24: 1 LORD had blessed Abraham in **a things**. 3605
24: 2 of his house that ruled over **a** that he had, 3605
24:10 for **a** the goods of his master *were* in his 3605
24:20 to draw *water*, and drew for **a** his camels. 3605
24:36 and unto him hath he given **a** that he hath. 3605
24:54 that *were* with him, and **tarried a night**; 3885
24:66 the servant told Isaac **a** things that he had 3605
25: 4 **A** these *were* the children of Keturah. 3605
25: 5 Abraham gave **a** that he had unto Isaac. 3605
25:18 he died in the presence of **a** his brethren. 3605
25:25 came out red, **a over** like a hairy garment; 3605
26: 3 I will give **a** these countries, and I will 3605
26: 4 will give unto thy seed **a** these countries; 3605
26: 4 in thy seed shall **a** the nations of the earth 3605
26:11 Abimelech charged **a** *his* people, saying, 3605
26:15 For **a** the wells which his father's servants 3605
27:33 I have eaten of **a** before thou camest, and 3605
27:37 **a** his brethren have I given to him for 3605
28:11 **tarried** there **a night**, because the sun was 3885
28:14 in thy seed shall **a** the families of the earth 3605
28:15 will keep thee in **a** *places* whither thou 3605
28:22 of **a** that thou shalt give me I will surely 3605
29: 3 thither were **a** the flocks gathered: and 3605
29: 8 until **a** the flocks be gathered together, and 3605
29:13 And he told Laban **a** these things. 3605
29:22 Laban gathered together **a** the men of 3605
30:32 I will pass through **a** thy flock to day, 3605
30:32 removing from thence **a** the speckled and 3605
30:32 **a** the brown cattle among the sheep, and 3605
30:35 **a** the she goats that were speckled and 3605
30:35 **a** the brown amongst the sheep, and 3605
30:40 and **a** the brown in the flock of Laban; 3605
31: 1 Jacob hath taken away **a** that *was* our 3605
31: 1 of our father's hath he gotten **a** this glory. 3605
31: 6 ye know that with **a** my power I have 3605
31: 8 thy wages; then **a** the cattle bare speckled: 3605
31: 8 thy hire; then bare **a** the cattle ringstraked. 3605
31:12 **a** the rams which leap upon the cattle *are* 3605
31:12 for I have seen **a** that Laban doeth unto 3605
31:16 For **a** the riches which God hath taken from 3605
31:18 he carried away **a** his cattle, and all his 3605
31:18 **a** his goods which he had gotten, the cattle 3605
31:21 So he fled with **a** that he had; and he rose 3605
31:34 Laban searched **a** the tent, but found *them* 3605
31:37 Whereas thou hast searched **a** my stuff, 3605
31:37 what hast thou found of **a** thy household 3605
31:43 *are* my cattle, and **a** that thou seest *is* mine: 3605
31:54 and **tarried a night** in the mount. 3885
32:10 I am not worthy of the least of **a** 3605
32:10 of **a** the truth, which thou hast shewed unto 3605
32:19 and **a** that followed the droves, saying, 3605
33: 8 What meanest thou by **a** this drove which I 3605
33:13 them one day, **a** the flock will die. 3605
34:19 he *was* more honourable than **a** the house 3605
34:24 unto Shechem his son hearkened **a** that 3605
34:24 **a** that went out of the gate of his city. 3605
34:25 upon the city boldly, and slew **a** the males. 3605
34:29 **a** their wealth, and all their little ones, and 3605
34:29 **a** their little ones, and their wives took they 3605
34:29 and spoiled even **a** that *was* in the house. 3605
35: 2 his household, and to **a** that *were* with him, 3605
35: 4 they gave unto Jacob **a** the strange gods 3605
35: 4 **a** *their* earrings which *were* in their ears; NIH
35: 6 he and **a** the people that *were* with him. 3605
36: 6 **a** the persons of his house, and his cattle, 3605
36: 6 and **a** his beasts, and all his substance, 3605
36: 6 and all his beasts, and **a** his substance, 3605
37: 3 Now Israel loved Joseph more than **a** his 3605
37: 4 father loved him more than **a** his brethren, 3605
37:35 **a** his sons and all his daughters rose up to 3605
37:35 and **a** his daughters rose up to comfort him; 3605
39: 3 *that* the LORD made **a** that he did to 3605

A

Ge 39: 4 and **a** *that* he had he put into his hand. 3605
39: 5 over **a** that he had, that the LORD blessed 3605
39: 5 the blessing of the LORD was upon **a** that 3605
39: 6 he left **a** that he had in Joseph's hand; and 3605
39: 8 he hath committed **a** that he hath to my 3605
39:22 hand **a** the prisoners that *were* in the prison; 3605
40:17 in the uppermost basket *there was* of **a** 3605
40:20 that he made a feast unto **a** his servants: 3605
41: 8 and called for **a** the magicians of Egypt, 3605
41: 8 of Egypt, and **a** the wise men thereof: 3605
41:19 such as I never saw in **a** the land of Egypt 3605
41:29 great plenty throughout **a** the land of Egypt: 3605
41:30 **a** the plenty shall be forgotten in the land of 3605
41:35 let them gather **a** the food of those good 3605
41:37 and in the eyes of **a** his servants. 3605
41:39 Forasmuch as God hath shewed thee **a** this, 3605
41:40 according unto thy word shall **a** my people 3605
41:41 I have set thee over **a** the land of Egypt. 3605
41:43 he made him *ruler* over **a** the land of Egypt. 3605
41:44 up his hand or foot in **a** the land of Egypt. 3605
41:45 Joseph went out over **a** the land of Egypt. NIH
41:46 and went throughout **a** the land of Egypt. 3605
41:48 he gathered up **a** the food of the seven 3605
41:51 *said he,* hath made me forget **a** my toil, and 3605
41:51 forget all my toil, and **a** my father's house. 3605
41:54 the dearth was in **a** lands; but in all the land 3605
41:54 but in **a** the land of Egypt there was bread. 3605
41:55 when **a** the land of Egypt was famished, 3605
41:55 Pharaoh said unto **a** the Egyptians, Go unto 3605
41:56 the famine was over **a** the face of the earth: 3605
41:56 Joseph opened **a** the storehouses, and 3605
41:57 **a** countries came into Egypt to Joseph for 3605
41:57 that the famine was *so* sore in **a** lands. 3605
42: 6 he *it was* that sold to **a** the people of 3605
42:11 We *are* **a** one man's sons; we *are* true *men,* 3605
42:17 he **put** them **a together** into ward three days. 622
42:29 and told him **a** that befell unto them; 3605
42:36 ye will take Benjamin *away:* **a** these things 3605
45: 1 Joseph could not refrain himself before **a** 3605
45: 8 lord of **a** his house, and a ruler throughout 3605
45: 8 and a ruler throughout **a** the land of Egypt. 3605
45: 9 God hath made me lord of **a** Egypt: 3605
45:10 and thy herds, and **a** that thou hast: 3605
45:11 and thy household, and **a** that thou hast, 3605
45:13 you shall tell my father of **a** my glory in 3605
45:13 glory in Egypt, and of **a** that you have seen; 3605
45:15 Moreover he kissed **a** his brethren, and 3605
45:20 for the good of **a** the land of Egypt *is* yours. 3605
45:22 To **a** of them he gave each man changes of 3605
45:26 he *is* governor over **a** the land of Egypt. 3605
45:27 they told him **a** the words of Joseph, 3605
46: 1 Israel took his journey with **a** that he had, 3605
46: 6 into Egypt, Jacob, and **a** his seed with him: 3605
46: 7 **a** his seed brought he with him into Egypt. 3605
46:15 **a** the souls of his sons and his daughters 3605
46:22 born to Jacob: **a** the souls *were* fourteen. 3605
46:25 these unto Jacob: **a** the souls *were* seven. 3605
46:26 **A** the souls that came with Jacob into 3605
46:26 **a** the souls *were* threescore and six; 3605
46:27 **a** the souls of the house of Jacob, 3605
46:32 and their herds, and **a** that they have. 3605
47: 1 and their herds, and **a** that they have, 3605
47:12 and **a** his father's household, *with* bread, 3605
47:13 *there was* no bread in **a** the land; for 3605
47:13 *a* the land of Canaan fainted by reason of NIH
47:14 Joseph gathered up **a** the money that was 3605
47:15 **a** the Egyptians came unto Joseph, and 3605
47:17 he fed them with bread for **a** their cattle for 3605
47:20 Joseph bought **a** the land of Egypt for 3605
48:15 the God which fed me **a** my **life long** 4480+5750
48:16 The Angel which redeemed me from **a** evil, 3605
49:28 **A** these *are* the twelve tribes of Israel: and 3605
50: 7 with him went up **a** the servants of 3605
50: 7 and **a** the elders of the land of Egypt, 3605
50: 8 **a** the house of Joseph, and his brethren, 3605
50:14 **a** that went up with him to bury his father, 3605
50:15 will certainly requite us **a** the evil which we 3605
Ex 1: 5 **a** the souls that came *out of* the loins of 3605
1: 6 and **a** his brethren, and all that generation. 3605
1: 6 and all his brethren, and **a** that generation. 3605
1:14 and in **a manner** of service in the field: 3605
1:14 **a** their service, wherein they made them 3605
1:22 Pharaoh charged **a** his people, saying, 3605
3:15 *is* my memorial unto **a generations**. 1755+1755
3:20 smite Egypt with **a** my wonders which I 3605
4:19 for **a** the men are dead which sought thy 3605
4:21 see that thou do **a** *those* wonders before 3605
4:28 Moses told Aaron **a** the words of 3605
4:28 **a** the signs which he had commanded him. 3605
4:29 gathered together **a** the elders of 3605
4:30 Aaron spake **a** the words which the LORD 3605
5:12 **a** the land of Egypt to gather stubble 3605
5:23 hast thou **delivered** thy people **at a.** 5337+5337
6:29 speak thou unto Pharaoh king of Egypt **a** 3605
7: 2 Thou shalt speak **a** that I command thee: 3605
7:19 and upon **a** their pools of water, 3605
7:19 *that* there may be blood throughout **a** 3605
7:20 **a** the waters that *were* in the river were 3605
7:21 there was blood throughout **a** the land of 3605
7:24 **a** the Egyptians digged round about 3605
8: 2 I will smite **a** thy borders with frogs: 3605
8: 4 upon thy people, and upon **a** thy servants. 3605
8:16 that it may become lice throughout **a** 3605
8:17 **a** the dust of the land became lice 3605
8:17 became lice throughout **a** the land of Egypt. 3605
8:24 and into **a** the land of Egypt: 3605
9: 4 there shall nothing die of **a** *that is* 3605
9: 6 the morrow, and **a** the cattle of Egypt died: 3605
9: 9 it shall become small dust in **a** the land of 3605
9: 9 upon beast, throughout **a** the land of Egypt. 3605
9:11 the magicians, and upon **a** the Egyptians. 3605
9:14 For I will at this time send **a** my plagues 3605
9:14 that *there is* none like me in **a** the earth. 3605
9:16 may be declared throughout **a** the earth. 3605
9:19 thy cattle, and **a** that thou hast in the field; 834

Ex 9:22 that there may be hail in **a** the land of 3605
9:24 such as there was none like it in **a** the land 3605
9:25 the hail smote throughout **a** the land of 3605
9:25 all the land of Egypt **a** that *was* in the field, 3605
10: 6 the houses of **a** thy servants, and the houses 3605
10: 6 and the houses of **a** the Egyptians; 3605
10:12 of the land, *even* **a** that the hail hath left. 3605
10:13 an east wind upon the land **a** that day, 3605
10:13 upon the land all that day, and **a** *that* night; 3605
10:14 the locusts went up over **a** the land of 3605
10:14 and rested in **a** the coasts of Egypt: 3605
10:15 **a** the fruit of the trees which the hail had 3605
10:15 of the field, through **a** the land of Egypt. 3605
10:19 there remained not one locust in **a** 3605
10:22 there was a thick darkness in **a** the land of 3605
10:23 **a** the children of Israel had light in their 3605
11: 5 **a** the firstborn in the land of Egypt shall 3605
11: 5 the mill; and **a** the firstborn of beasts. 3605
11: 6 there shall be a great cry throughout **a** 3605
11: 8 **a** these thy servants shall come down unto 3605
11: 8 thee out, and **a** the people that follow thee: 3605
11:10 Aaron did **a** these wonders before Pharaoh: 3605
12: 3 Speak ye unto **a** the congregation of Israel, 3605
12: 9 nor **sodden at a** with water, but roast 1310+1311
12:12 will smite **a** the firstborn in the land of 3605
12:12 against **a** the gods of Egypt I will execute 3605
12:20 in **a** your habitations shall ye eat 3605
12:21 Moses called for **a** the elders of Israel, 3605
12:29 that at midnight the LORD smote **a** 3605
12:29 in the dungeon; and **a** the firstborn of cattle. 3605
12:30 he, and **a** his servants, and all 3605
12:30 and all his servants, and **a** the Egyptians; 3605
12:33 in haste; for they said, We *be* **a** dead *men.* 3605
12:41 *that* **a** the hosts of the LORD went out 3605
12:42 **a** the children of Israel in their generations. 3605
12:47 **A** the congregation of Israel shall keep it. 3605
12:48 let **a** his males be circumcised, and then 3605
12:50 Thus did **a** the children of Israel; as 3605
13: 2 Sanctify unto me **a** the firstborn, 3605
13: 7 be leaven seen with thee in **a** thy quarters. 3605
13:12 That thou shalt set apart unto the LORD **a** 3605
13:13 **a** the firstborn of man amongst thy children 3605
13:15 that the LORD slew **a** the firstborn in 3605
13:15 I sacrifice to the LORD **a** that openeth 3605
13:15 but **a** the firstborn of my children I redeem. 3605
14: 4 upon Pharaoh, and upon **a** his host; 3605
14: 7 **a** the chariots of Egypt, and captains over 3605
14: 9 the Egyptians pursued after them (**a** 3605
14:17 upon **a** his host, upon his chariots, and 3605
14:20 that the one came not near the other **a** 3605
14:21 go *back* by a strong east wind **a** *that* night, 3605
14:23 *even* **a** Pharaoh's horses, his chariots, and 3605
14:28 **a** the host of Pharaoh that came into the sea 3605
15:15 **a** the inhabitants of Canaan shall melt 3605
15:20 **a** the women went out after her with 3605
15:26 his commandments, and keep **a** his statutes, 3605
16: 1 **a** the congregation of the children of Israel 3605
16: 6 Aaron said unto **a** the children of Israel, 3605
16: 9 Say unto **a** the congregation of the children 3605
16:22 **a** the rulers of the congregation came and 3605
17: 1 **a** the congregation of the children of Israel 3605
18: 1 heard of **a** that God had done for Moses, 3605
18: 8 Moses told his father in law **a** that 3605
18: 8 **a** the travail that had come upon them by 3605
18: 9 Jethro rejoiced for **a** the goodness which 3605
18:11 that the LORD *is* greater than **a** gods: 3605
18:12 Aaron came, and **a** the elders of Israel, 3605
18:14 when Moses' father in law saw **a** that he 3605
18:14 **a** the people stand by thee from morning 3605
18:21 Moreover thou shalt provide out of **a** 3605
18:22 let them judge the people at **a** seasons: and 3605
18:23 **a** this people shall also go to their place in 3605
18:24 his father in law, and did **a** that he had said. 3605
18:25 Moses chose able men out of **a** Israel, and 3605
18:26 they judged the people at **a** seasons: 3605
19: 5 a peculiar treasure unto me above **a** people: 3605
19: 5 above all people: for **a** the earth *is* mine: 3605
19: 7 laid before their faces **a** these words which 3605
19: 8 **a** the people answered together, and said, 3605
19: 8 **A** that the LORD hath spoken we will do. 3605
19:11 the sight of **a** the people upon mount Sinai. 3605
19:16 that **a** the people that *was* in the camp 3605
20: 1 And God spake **a** these words, saying, 3605
20: 9 days shalt thou labour, and do **a** thy work: 3605
20:11 **a** that in them *is,* and rested the seventh 3605
20:18 **a** the people saw the thunderings, and 3605
20:24 in **a** places where I record my name I will 3605
22: 9 For **a** manner of trespass, *whether it be* for 3605
22:23 they **cry at a** unto me, I will surely 6817+6817
22:26 **at a take** thy neighbour's raiment
to pledge, 2254+2254
23:13 in **a** *things* that I have said unto you be 3605
23:17 Three times in the year **a** thy males shall 3605
23:22 obey his voice, and do **a** that I speak; 3605
23:27 will destroy **a** the people to whom thou 3605
23:27 I will make **a** thine enemies turn their backs 3605
24: 3 told the people **a** the words of the LORD, 3605
24: 3 words of the LORD, and **a** the judgments: 3605
24: 3 **a** the people answered *with* one voice, and 3605
24: 3 **A** the words which the LORD hath said 3605
24: 4 Moses wrote **a** the words of the LORD, 3605
24: 7 **A** that the LORD hath said will we do, 3605
24: 8 made with you concerning **a** these words. 3605
25: 9 According to **a** that I shew thee, *after* 3605
25: 9 and the pattern of **a** the instruments thereof, 3605
25:22 of **a** *things* which I will give thee in 3605
25:36 **a** it *shall be* one beaten work *of* pure gold. 3605
25:39 gold shall he make it, with **a** these vessels. 3605
26: 8 the eleven curtains *shall be* **a** of one NIH
26:17 thus shalt thou make for **a** the boards of 3605
27: 3 **a** the vessels thereof thou shalt make *of* 3605
27:17 **A** the pillars round about the court *shall be* 3605
27:19 **A** the vessels of the tabernacle in all 3605
27:19 All the vessels of the tabernacle in **a** 3605
27:19 **a** the pins thereof, and all the pins of 3605

Ex 27:19 **a** the pins of the court, *shall be of* brass. 3605
28: 3 thou shalt speak unto **a** *that are* wise 3605
28:31 thou shalt make the robe of the ephod **a** of 3632
28:38 of Israel shall hallow in **a** their holy gifts; 3605
29:12 pour **a** the blood beside the bottom of 3605
29:13 thou shalt take **a** the fat that covereth 3605
29:24 thou shalt put **a** in the hands of Aaron, and 3605
29:35 according to **a** *things* which I have 3605
30:27 the table and **a** his vessels, and 3605
30:28 the altar of burnt offering with **a** his 3605
31: 3 and in **a** *manner of* workmanship, 3605
31: 5 to work in **a** *manner of* workmanship. 3605
31: 6 in the hearts of **a** that are wise hearted I 3605
31: 6 that they may make **a** that I have 3605
31: 7 **a** the furniture of the tabernacle, 3605
31: 8 the pure candlestick with **a** his furniture, 3605
31: 9 the altar of burnt offering with **a** his 3605
31:11 **a** that I have commanded thee shall they 3605
32: 3 **a** the people brake off the golden earrings 3605
32:13 **a** this land that I have spoken of will I give 3605
32:26 **a** the sons of Levi gathered themselves 3605
33: 8 *that* **a** the people rose up, and stood every 3605
33:10 **a** the people saw the cloudy pillar stand *at* 3605
33:10 **a** the people rose up and worshipped, 3605
33:16 from **a** the people that *are* upon the face of 3605
33:19 I will make **a** my goodness pass before 3605
34: 3 neither let any man be seen throughout **a** 3605
34:10 before **a** thy people I will do marvels, 3605
34:10 such as have not been done in **a** the earth, 3605
34:10 **a** the people among which thou *art* shall see 3605
34:19 **A** that openeth the matrix *is* mine; and 3605
34:20 **A** the firstborn of thy sons thou shalt 3605
34:23 Thrice in the year shall **a** your men children 3605
34:30 and **a** the children of Israel saw Moses, 3605
34:31 **a** the rulers of the congregation returned 3605
34:32 afterward **a** the children of Israel came 3605
34:32 he gave them in commandment **a** that 3605
35: 1 Moses gathered **a** the congregation of 3605
35: 4 Moses spake unto **a** the congregation of 3605
35:10 make **a** that the LORD hath commanded; 3605
35:13 and **a** his vessels, and the shewbread, 3605
35:16 and **a** his vessels, the laver and his foot, 3605
35:20 **a** the congregation of the children of Israel 3605
35:21 for **a** his service, and for the holy garments. 3605
35:22 and rings, and tablets, **a** jewels of gold: 3605
35:25 **a** the women that were wise hearted did 3605
35:26 **a** the women whose heart stirred them up 3605
35:29 them willing to bring for **a** *manner of* work, 3605
35:31 and in **a** *manner of* workmanship; 3605
35:35 to work **a** *manner of* work, of the engraver, 3605
36: 1 understanding to know how to work **a** 3605
36: 1 according to **a** that the LORD had 3605
36: 3 they received of Moses **a** the offering, 3605
36: 4 **a** the wise *men,* that wrought all the work 3605
36: 4 all the wise *men,* that wrought **a** the work 3605
36: 7 For the stuff *they had* was sufficient for **a** 3605
36: 9 four cubits: the curtains *were* **a** of one size. 3605
36:22 thus did he make for **a** the boards of 3605
37:22 **a** of it *was* one beaten work *of* pure gold. 3605
37:24 gold made he it, and **a** the vessels thereof. 3605
38: 3 he made **a** the vessels of the altar, the pots, 3605
38: 3 **a** the vessels thereof made he *of* brass. 3605
38:16 **A** the hangings of the court round about 3605
38:17 **a** the pillars of the court *were* filleted *with* 3605
38:20 **a** the pins of the tabernacle, and of 3605
38:22 made **a** that the LORD commanded 3605
38:24 **A** the gold that was occupied for the work 3605
38:24 **a** the work of the holy *place,* even the gold 3605
38:30 grate for it, and **a** the vessels of the altar, 3605
38:31 **a** the pins of the tabernacle, and all the pins 3605
38:31 and **a** the pins of the court round about. 3605
39:22 of the ephod *of* woven work, **a** of blue. 3632
39:32 Thus was **a** the work of the tabernacle of 3605
39:32 the children of Israel did according to **a** that 3605
39:33 the tent, and **a** his furniture, his taches, 3605
39:36 *and* **a** the vessels thereof, and 3605
39:37 **a** the vessels thereof, and the oil for light, 3605
39:39 and **a** his vessels, the laver and his foot, 3605
39:40 **a** the vessels of the service of 3605
39:42 According to **a** that the LORD 3605
39:42 so the children of Israel made **a** the work. 3605
39:43 Moses did look upon **a** the work, and 3605
40: 9 **a** that *is* therein, and shalt hallow it, and 3605
40: 9 shalt hallow it, and **a** the vessels thereof: 3605
40:10 and **a** his vessels, and sanctify the altar: 3605
40:16 according to **a** that the LORD commanded 3605
40:36 the children of Israel went onward in **a** 3605
40:38 in the sight of **a** the house of Israel, 3605
40:38 house of Israel, throughout **a** their journeys. 3605
Lev 1: 9 the priest shall burn **a** on the altar, *to be* a 3605
1:13 the priest shall bring *it* **a**, and burn *it* upon 3605
2: 2 oil thereof, with **a** the frankincense thereof; 3605
2:13 with **a** thine offerings thou shalt offer salt. 3605
2:16 oil thereof, with **a** the frankincense thereof: 3605
3: 3 and **a** the fat that *is* upon the inwards, 3605
3: 9 and **a** the fat that *is* upon the inwards, 3605
3:14 and **a** the fat that *is* upon the inwards, 3605
3:16 a sweet savour: **a** the fat *is* the LORD'S. 3605
3:17 generations throughout **a** your dwellings, 3605
4: 7 shall pour **a** the blood of the bullock at 3605
4: 8 he shall take off from it **a** the fat of 3605
4: 8 and **a** the fat that *is* upon the inwards, 3605
4:11 **a** his flesh, with his head, and with his legs, 3605
4:18 shall pour out **a** the blood at the bottom of 3605
4:19 he shall take **a** his fat from him, and burn *it* 3605
4:26 he shall burn **a** his fat upon the altar, as 3605
4:30 shall pour out **a** the blood thereof at 3605
4:31 he shall take away **a** the fat thereof, as 3605
4:34 shall pour out **a** the blood thereof at 3605
4:35 he shall take away **a** the fat thereof, as 3605
6: 3 in any of **a** *these* that a man doeth, sinning 3605
6: 5 Or **a** *that* about which he hath sworn 3605
6: 7 it shall be forgiven him for any *thing* of **a** 3605
6: 9 of the burning upon the altar **a** night unto 3605
6:15 **a** the frankincense which *is* upon the meat 3605

Lev 6:18 **A** the males among the children of Aaron 3605
6:29 **A** the males among the priests shall eat 3605
7: 3 he shall offer of it **a** the fat thereof; 3605
7: 9 **a** the meat offering that is baken in 3605
7: 9 **a** *that is* dressed in the fryingpan, and in 3605
7:10 and dry, shall **a** the sons of Aaron have, 3605
7:18 offerings be **eaten at a** on the third day, 398+398
7:19 the flesh, **a** that be clean shall eat thereof. 3605
8: 3 gather thou **a** the congregation together 3605
8:10 the tabernacle and **a** that *was* therein, 3605
8:11 anointed the altar and **a** his vessels, 3605
8:16 he took **a** the fat that *was* upon the inwards, 3605
8:25 **a** the fat that *was* upon the inwards, and 3605
8:27 he put **a** upon Aaron's hands, and upon his 3605
8:36 his sons did **a** things which the LORD 3605
9: 5 **a** the congregation drew near and 3605
9:23 the glory of the LORD appeared unto **a** 3605
9:24 *which* when **a** the people saw, they 3605
10: 3 and before **a** the people I will be glorified. 3605
10: 6 and lest wrath come upon **a** the people: 3605
10:11 that *ye* may teach the children of Israel **a** 3605
11: 2 eat among **a** the beasts that *are* on the earth. 3605
11: 9 These shall ye eat of **a** that *are* in 3605
11:10 **a** that have not fins nor scales in the seas, 3605
11:10 of **a** that move in the waters, and of any 3605
11:20 **A** fowls that creep, going upon *all* four, 3605
11:20 All fowls that creep, going upon **a** four, NIH
11:21 flying creeping thing that goeth upon ***a*** four, NIH
11:23 **a** *other* flying creeping things, which have 3605
11:27 among **a** *manner of* beasts that go on *all* 3605
11:27 among all *manner of* beasts that go on ***a*** NIH
11:31 These *are* unclean to you among **a** that 3605
11:34 Of **a** meat which may be eaten, *that* on 3605
11:34 **a** drink that may be drunk in every *such* 3605
11:42 whatsoever goeth upon ***a*** four, or NIH
11:42 whatsoever hath more feet among **a** 3605
13:12 the leprosy cover **a** the skin of *him that* 3605
13:13 *if* the leprosy have covered **a** his flesh, 3605
13:13 the plague: it is **a** turned white: he *is* clean. 3605
13:46 **A** the days wherein the plague *shall be* in 3605
14: 8 shave off **a** his hair, and wash *himself* in 3605
14: 9 *that* he shall shave **a** his hair off his head 3605
14: 9 even **a** his hair he shall shave off: 3605
14:36 that **a** that *is* in the house be not *made* 3605
14:45 and **a** the morter of the house; 3605
14:46 Moreover he that goeth into the house **a** 3605
14:54 This *is* the law for **a** *manner of* plague of 3605
15:16 he shall wash **a** his flesh in water, and 3605
15:24 if any man **lie with** her at **a**, 854+7901+7901
15:24 **a** the bed whereon he lieth shall be unclean. 3605
15:25 **a** the days of the issue of her uncleanness 3605
15:26 Every bed whereon she lieth **a** the days of 3605
16: 2 that he come not at **a** times into the holy 3605
16:16 of their transgressions in **a** their sins: 3605
16:17 and for **a** the congregation of Israel. 3605
16:21 confess over him **a** the iniquities of 3605
16:21 **a** their transgressions in all their sins, 3605
16:21 all their transgressions in **a** their sins, 3605
16:22 the goat shall bear upon him **a** their 3605
16:29 do no work *at a, whether it be* one of your NIH
16:30 *that* ye may be clean from **a** your sins 3605
16:33 and for **a** the people of the congregation. 3605
16:34 of Israel for **a** their sins once a year. 3605
17: 2 unto **a** the children of Israel, and say unto 3605
17:14 for *it is* the life of **a** flesh; the blood of it *is* 3605
17:14 for the life of **a** flesh *is* the blood thereof: 3605
18:24 **a** these the nations are defiled which I cast 3605
18:27 (For **a** these abominations have the men of 3605
19: 2 Speak unto **a** the congregation of 3605
19: 7 if it be **eaten at a** on the third day, it *is* 398+398
19:13 **abide** with thee **a night** until the morning. 3885
19:20 not **at a redeemed**, nor freedom 6299+6299
19:23 shall have planted **a** *manner of* trees for 3605
19:24 in the fourth year **a** the fruit thereof shall 3605
19:37 Therefore shall ye observe **a** my statutes, 3605
19:37 and **a** my judgments, and do them: 3605
20: 5 him off, and **a** that go a whoring after him, 3605
20:22 Ye shall therefore keep **a** my statutes, and 3605
20:22 and **a** my judgments, and do them: 3605
20:23 for they committed **a** these *things*, and 3605
21:24 his sons, and unto **a** the children of Israel. 3605
22: 3 Whosoever *he be* of **a** your seed among 3605
22:18 unto **a** the children of Israel, and say unto 3605
22:18 that will offer his oblation for **a** his vows, 3605
22:18 his vows, and for **a** his freewill offerings, 3605
23: 3 sabbath of the LORD in **a** your dwellings. 3605
23:14 your generations in **a** your dwellings. 3605
23:21 **a** your dwellings throughout your 3605
23:31 your generations in **a** your dwellings. 3605
23:38 beside **a** your vows, and beside all your 3605
23:38 and beside **a** your freewill offerings, 3605
23:42 **a** that are Israelites born shall dwell in 3605
24:14 let **a** that heard *him* lay their hands upon his 3605
24:14 and let **a** the congregation stone him. 3605
24:16 **a** the congregation shall certainly stone 3605
25: 7 shall **a** the increase thereof be meat. 3605
25: 9 the trumpet sound throughout **a** your land. 3605
25:10 proclaim liberty throughout ***a*** the land unto NIH
25:10 *all* the land unto **a** the inhabitants thereof: 3605
25:24 in **a** the land of your possession ye shall 3605
26:14 and will not do **a** these commandments; 3605
26:15 so that *ye* will not do **a** my commandments, 3605
26:18 if ye will not yet for **a** this hearken unto me, NIH
26:27 if ye will not for **a** this hearken unto me, NIH
26:44 yet for **a** that, when they be in the land of NIH
27: 9 **a** that *any man* giveth of such unto 3605
27:10 if he shall **at a change** beast for 4171+4171
27:13 if he will **at a redeem** it, then 1350+1350
27:25 **a** thy estimations shall be according to 3605
27:28 devote unto the LORD of **a** that he hath, 3605
27:30 **a** the tithe of the land, *whether* of the seed 3605
27:31 if a man will **at a redeem** *ought* of 1350+1350
27:33 if he **change** it **at a**, then both it and 4171+4171
Nu 1: 2 Take ye the sum of **a** the congregation of 3605
1: 3 **a** that *are able to* go forth *to* war in Israel: 3605

Nu 1:18 they assembled **a** the congregation together 3605
1:20 upward, **a** that *were able to* go forth *to* war; 3605
1:22 upward, **a** that *were able to* go forth *to* war; 3605
1:24 upward, **a** that *were able to* go forth *to* war; 3605
1:26 upward, **a** that *were able to* go forth *to* war; 3605
1:28 upward, **a** that *were able to* go forth *to* war; 3605
1:30 upward, **a** that *were able to* go forth *to* war; 3605
1:32 upward, **a** that *were able to* go forth *to* war; 3605
1:34 upward, **a** that *were able to* go forth *to* war; 3605
1:36 upward, **a** that *were able to* go forth *to* war; 3605
1:38 upward, **a** that *were able to* go forth *to* war; 3605
1:40 upward, **a** that *were able to* go forth *to* war; 3605
1:42 upward, **a** that *were able to* go forth *to* war; 3605
1:45 So were **a** those that were numbered of 3605
1:45 **a** that *were able to* go forth *to* war in Israel; 3605
1:46 Even **a** they that were numbered were six 3605
1:50 over **a** the vessels thereof, and over all 3605
1:50 and over **a** *things* that *belong* to it: 3605
1:50 the tabernacle, and **a** the vessels thereof; 3605
1:54 the children of Israel did according to **a** that 3605
2: 9 **A** that were numbered in the camp of Judah 3605
2:16 **A** that were numbered in the camp of 3605
2:24 **A** that were numbered of the camp of 3605
2:31 **A** they that were numbered in the camp of 3605
2:32 **a** those that were numbered of the camps 3605
2:34 the children of Israel did according to **a** that 3605
3: 8 they shall keep **a** the instruments of 3605
3:12 **a** the firstborn that openeth the matrix 3605
3:13 Because **a** the firstborn *are* mine; *for* on 3605
3:13 *for* on the day that I smote **a** the firstborn in 3605
3:13 I hallowed unto me **a** the firstborn in Israel, 3605
3:22 according to the number of **a** the males, 3605
3:26 and the cords of it for **a** the service thereof. 3605
3:28 In the number of **a** the males, from a month 3605
3:31 and the hanging, and **a** the service thereof. 3605
3:34 according to the number of **a** the males, 3605
3:36 **a** the vessels thereof, and all that serveth 3605
3:36 vessels thereof, and **a** that serveth thereto, 3605
3:39 **A** that were numbered of the Levites, 3605
3:39 **a** the males from a month old and upward, 3605
3:40 Number **a** the firstborn of the males of 3605
3:41 instead of **a** the firstborn among 3605
3:41 the cattle of the Levites instead of **a** 3605
3:42 **a** the firstborn among the children of Israel. 3605
3:43 **a** the firstborn males by the number of 3605
3:45 Take the Levites instead of **a** the firstborn 3605
4: 3 fifty years old, **a** that enter into the host, 3605
4: 9 and **a** the oil vessels thereof, 3605
4:10 **a** the vessels thereof within a covering of 3605
4:12 they shall take **a** the instruments of 3605
4:14 they shall put upon it **a** the vessels thereof, 3605
4:14 and the basons, **a** the vessels of the altar; 3605
4:15 **a** the vessels of the sanctuary, as the camp 3605
4:16 *and* the oversight of **a** the tabernacle, and 3605
4:16 of **a** that therein *is*, in the sanctuary, and 3605
4:23 **a** that enter in to perform the service, to do 3605
4:26 **a** the instruments of their service, and all 3605
4:26 their service, and **a** that is made for them: 3605
4:27 his sons shall be **a** the service of the sons of 3605
4:27 in **a** their burdens, and in all their service: 3605
4:27 in all their burdens, and in **a** their service: 3605
4:27 ye shall appoint unto them in charge **a** their 3605
4:31 according to **a** their service in 3605
4:32 with **a** their instruments, and with all their 3605
4:32 their instruments, and with **a** their service: 3605
4:33 according to **a** their service, in 3605
4:37 **a** that *might* do service in the tabernacle of 3605
4:41 of **a** that *might* do service in the tabernacle 3605
4:46 **A** those that were numbered of the Levites, 3605
5: 9 every offering of **a** the holy *things* of 3605
5:30 the priest shall execute upon her **a** this law. 3605
6: 4 **A** the days of his separation shall he eat 3605
6: 5 **A** the days of the vow of his separation 3605
6: 6 **A** the days that he separateth *himself* unto 3605
6: 8 **A** the days of his separation he *is* holy unto 3605
7: 1 sanctified it, and **a** the instruments thereof, 3605
7: 1 both the altar and **a** the vessels thereof, and 3605
7:85 **a** the silver vessels *weighed* two thousand 3605
7:86 **a** the gold of the spoons *was* an hundred 3605
7:87 **A** the oxen for the burnt offering *were* 3605
7:88 **a** the oxen for the sacrifice of the peace 3605
8: 7 let them shave **a** their flesh, and let them 3605
8:16 *even instead of* the firstborn of **a** 3605
8:17 For **a** the firstborn of the children of Israel 3605
8:18 I have taken the Levites for **a** the firstborn 3605
8:20 **a** the congregation of the children of Israel, 3605
8:20 did to the Levites according unto **a** that 3605
9: 3 according to **a** the rites of it, and 3605
9: 3 according to **a** the ceremonies thereof, 3605
9: 5 according to **a** that the LORD commanded 3605
9:12 according to **a** the ordinances of 3605
10: 3 **a** the assembly shall assemble themselves 3605
10:25 *which was* the rereward of **a** the camps 3605
11: 6 *there is* nothing at **a**, beside *this* manna, 3605
11:11 that *thou* layest the burden of **a** this people 3605
11:12 Have I conceived **a** this people? have I 3605
11:13 Whence should I have flesh to give unto **a** 3605
11:14 I am not able to bear **a** this people alone, 3605
11:22 shall **a** the fish of the sea be gathered 3605
11:29 would God that **a** the LORD'S people 3605
11:32 the people stood up **a** that day, and all *that* 3605
11:32 **a** *that* night, and all the next day, and 3605
11:32 **a** the next day, and they gathered 3605
11:32 they **spread** *them* **a abroad** for 7849+7849
12: 3 above **a** the men which *were* upon the face 3605
12: 7 *is* not so, who *is* faithful in **a** mine house. 3605
13: 3 **a** those men *were* heads of the children of 3605
13:26 to **a** the congregation of the children of 3605
13:26 unto **a** the congregation, and shewed them 3605
13:32 **a** the people that we saw in it *are* men of a 3605
14: 1 **a** the congregation lifted up their voice, 3605
14: 2 **a** the children of Israel murmured against 3605
14: 5 Aaron fell on their faces before **a** 3605
14: 7 they spake unto **a** the company of 3605
14:10 **a** the congregation bade stone them with 3605

Nu 14:10 congregation before **a** the children of Israel. 3605
14:11 for **a** the signs which I have shewed among 3605
14:15 Now *if* thou shalt kill ***a*** this people as one NIH
14:21 **a** the earth shall be filled *with* the glory of 3605
14:22 Because **a** *those* men which have seen my 3605
14:29 **a** that were numbered of you, according to 3605
14:35 I will surely do it unto **a** this evil 3605
14:36 made **a** the congregation to murmur against 3605
14:39 Moses told these sayings unto **a** 3605
15:13 **A** that are born of the country shall do these 3605
15:22 and not observed **a** these commandments, 3605
15:23 *Even* **a** that the LORD hath commanded 3605
15:24 that **a** the congregation shall offer one 3605
15:25 the priest shall make an atonement for **a** 3605
15:26 it shall be forgiven **a** the congregation of 3605
15:26 seeing **a** the people were in ignorance. 3605
15:33 and Aaron, and unto **a** the congregation. 3605
15:35 **a** the congregation shall stone him with 3605
15:36 **a** the congregation brought him without 3605
15:39 remember **a** the commandments of 3605
15:40 do **a** my commandments, and be holy unto 3605
16: 3 seeing **a** the congregation *are* holy, 3605
16: 5 spake unto Korah and unto **a** his company, 3605
16: 6 you censers, Korah, and **a** his company; 3605
16:10 **a** thy brethren the sons of Levi with thee: 3605
16:11 **a** thy company *are* gathered together 3605
16:16 and **a** thy company before the LORD, 3605
16:19 Korah gathered **a** the congregation against 3605
16:19 the glory of the LORD appeared unto **a** 3605
16:22 O God, the God of the spirits of **a** flesh, 3605
16:22 wilt thou be wroth with **a** the congregation? 3605
16:26 lest ye be consumed in **a** their sins. 3605
16:28 LORD hath sent me to do **a** these works; 3605
16:29 If these *men* die the common death of **a** 3605
16:29 if they be visited after the visitation of **a** 3605
16:30 with **a** that *appertain* unto them, and 3605
16:31 as he had made an end of speaking **a** these 3605
16:32 **a** the men that *appertained* unto Korah, and 3605
16:32 *appertained* unto Korah, and **a** *their* goods. 3605
16:33 They, and **a** that *appertained* to them, 3605
16:34 **a** Israel that *were* round about them fled at 3605
16:41 on the morrow **a** the congregation of 3605
17: 2 of **a** their princes according to the house of 3605
17: 9 Moses brought out **a** the rods from before 3605
17: 9 the LORD unto **a** the children of Israel: 3605
17:12 Behold, we die, we perish, we **a** perish. 3605
18: 3 and the charge of **a** the tabernacle: 3605
18: 4 for **a** the service of the tabernacle: 3605
18: 8 **a** the hallowed *things* of the children of 3605
18:11 with **a** the wave offerings of the children of 3605
18:12 **A** the best of the oil, and all the best of 3605
18:12 **a** the best of the wine, and of the wheat, 3605
18:15 Every thing that openeth the matrix in **a** 3605
18:19 **A** the heave offerings of the holy *things*, 3605
18:21 I have given the children of Levi **a** the tenth 3605
18:28 offering unto the LORD of **a** your tithes, 3605
18:29 Out of **a** your gifts ye shall offer every 3605
18:29 of **a** the best thereof, *even* the hallowed *part* 3605
19:14 **a** that come into the tent, and all that *is* in 3605
19:14 come into the tent, and **a** that *is* in the tent, 3605
19:18 upon **a** the vessels, and upon the persons 3605
20:14 Thou knowest **a** the travail that hath 3605
20:27 Hor in the sight of **a** the congregation. 3605
20:29 when **a** the congregation saw that Aaron 3605
20:29 thirty days, *even* **a** the house of Israel. 3605
21:23 Sihon gathered **a** his people together, and 3605
21:25 Israel took **a** these cities: and Israel dwelt 3605
21:25 Israel dwelt in **a** the cities of the Amorites, 3605
21:25 in Heshbon, and in **a** the villages thereof. 3605
21:26 taken **a** his land out of his hand, *even* unto 3605
21:33 he, and **a** his people, to the battle *at* Edrei. 3605
21:34 thy hand, and **a** his people, and his land; 3605
21:35 smote him, and his sons, and **a** his people, 3605
22: 2 Balak the son of Zippor saw **a** that Israel 3605
22: 4 Now shall *this* company lick up **a** *that are* 3605
22:38 have I now **any power at a** to say 3201+3201
23: 6 he, and **a** the princes of Moab. 3605
23:13 part of them, and shalt not see them **a**: 3605
23:25 Neither **curse** them **at a**, nor bless 5344+5344
23:25 them at all, nor **bless** them **at a**. 1288+1288
23:26 saying, **A** that the LORD speaketh, that I 3605
24:17 and destroy **a** the children of Sheth. 3605
25: 4 Take **a** the heads of the people, and 3605
25: 6 in the sight of **a** the congregation of 3605
26: 2 Take the sum of **a** the congregation of 3605
26: 2 **a** that *are able to* go *to* war in Israel. 3605
26:43 **A** the families of the Shuhamites, 3605
26:62 **a** males from a month old and upward: 3605
27: 2 before the princes and **a** the congregation, 3605
27:16 the God of the spirits of **a** flesh, 3605
27:19 the priest, and before **a** the congregation; 3605
27:20 that **a** the congregation of the children of 3605
27:21 and **a** the children of Israel with him, 3605
27:21 of Israel with him, even **a** the congregation. 3605
27:22 the priest, and before **a** the congregation: 3605
29:40 to **a** that the LORD commanded Moses. 3605
30: 2 he shall do according to **a** that proceedeth 3605
30: 4 **a** her vows shall stand, and every bond 3605
30: 6 if she **had at a** a husband, 1961+1961+3807.1
30:11 **a** her vows shall stand, and every bond 3605
30:14 he establisheth **a** her vows, or all her bonds, 3605
30:14 or **a** her bonds, which *are* upon her: 3605
31: 4 throughout **a** the tribes of Israel, shall ye 3605
31: 7 and they slew **a** the males. 3605
31: 9 the children of Israel took ***a*** the women of NIH
31: 9 took the spoil of **a** their cattle, and all their 3605
31: 9 and **a** their flocks, and all their goods. 3605
31: 9 and all their flocks, and **a** their goods. 3605
31:10 they burnt **a** their cities wherein they dwelt, 3605
31:10 and **a** their goodly castles, with fire. 3605
31:11 they took **a** the spoil, and all the prey, 3605
31:11 and **a** the prey, *both* of men and of beasts. 3605
31:13 and **a** the princes of the congregation, 3605
31:15 Have ye saved **a** the women alive? 3605
31:18 **a** the women children, that have not known 3605

Nu 31:20 purify **a** *your* raiment, and all that is made 3605
31:20 **a** that is made of skins, and all work of 3605
31:20 **a** work of goats' *hair,* and all things made 3605
31:20 of goats' *hair,* and **a** things made of wood. 3605
31:23 **a** that abideth not the fire ye shall make go 3605
31:27 to battle, and between **a** the congregation: 3605
31:30 of **a** *manner of* beasts, and give them unto 3605
31:35 thirty and two thousand persons in **a**, 3605
31:51 the gold of them, *even* **a** wrought jewels. 3605
31:52 **a** the gold of the offering that they offered 3605
32:13 until **a** the generation, that had done evil in 3605
32:15 and ye shall destroy **a** this people. 3605
32:21 will go **a** of you armed over Jordan before 3605
32:26 our wives, our flocks, and **a** our cattle, 3605
33: 3 a high hand in the sight of **a** the Egyptians. 3605
33: 4 For the Egyptians buried **a** *their* firstborn, 3605
33:52 ye shall drive out **a** the inhabitants of 3605
33:52 destroy **a** their pictures, and destroy all 3605
33:52 destroy **a** their molten images, and quite 3605
33:52 and quite pluck down **a** their high places: 3605
35: 3 and for their goods, and for **a** their beasts. 3605
35: 7 *So* **a** the cities which ye shall give to 3605
35:29 your generations in **a** your dwellings. 3605
Dt 1: 1 **a** Israel on *this* side Jordan in 3605
1: 3 according unto **a** that the LORD had given 3605
1: 7 unto **a** *the places* nigh thereunto, in 3605
1:18 I commanded you at that time **a** the things 3605
1:19 we went *through* **a** that great and terrible 3605
1:30 according to **a** that he did for you in Egypt 3605
1:31 bear his son, in **a** the way that ye went, 3605
1:41 according to **a** that the LORD our God 3605
2: 7 blessed thee in **a** the works of thy hand: 3605
2:14 until **a** the generation of the men of war 3605
2:16 when **a** the men of war were consumed and 3605
2:32 he and **a** his people, to fight *at* Jahaz. 3605
2:33 smote him, and his sons, and **a** his people. 3605
2:34 we took **a** his cities at that time, and 3605
2:36 the LORD our God delivered **a** unto us: 3605
3: 1 he and **a** his people, to battle *at* Edrei. 3605
3: 2 **a** his people, and his land, into thy hand; 3605
3: 3 the king of Bashan, and **a** his people: 3605
3: 4 we took **a** his cities at that time, there was 3605
3: 4 threescore cities, **a** the region of Argob, 3605
3: 5 **A** these cities *were* fenced *with* high walls, 3605
3: 7 **a** the cattle, and the spoil of the cities, 3605
3:10 **A** the cities of the plain, and all Gilead, and 3605
3:10 **a** Gilead, and all Bashan, unto Salchah and 3605
3:10 all Gilead, and **a** Bashan, unto Salchah and 3605
3:13 the rest of Gilead, and **a** Bashan, *being* 3605
3:13 **a** the region of Argob, with all Bashan, 3605
3:13 all the region of Argob, with **a** Bashan, 3605
3:14 Jair the son of Manasseh took **a** the country 3605
3:18 of Israel, **a** *that are* meet for the war. 3605
3:21 Thine eyes have seen **a** that the LORD 3605
3:21 shall the LORD do unto **a** the kingdoms 3605
4: 3 for **a** the men that followed Baal-peor, 3605
4: 6 which shall hear **a** these statutes, and say, 3605
4: 7 as the LORD our God *is* in **a** *things that* 3605
4: 8 and judgments *so* righteous as **a** this law, 3605
4: 9 lest they depart from thy heart **a** the days of 3605
4:10 that they may learn to fear me **a** the days 3605
4:19 and the stars, *even* **a** the host of heaven, 3605
4:19 unto **a** nations under the whole heaven. 3605
4:29 thou shalt find *him,* if thou seek him with **a** 3605
4:29 him with all thy heart and with **a** thy soul. 3605
4:30 **a** these things are come upon thee, *even* in 3605
4:34 according to **a** that the LORD your God 3605
4:49 **a** the plain on *this* side Jordan eastward, 3605
5: 1 Moses called **a** Israel, and said unto them, 3605
5: 3 *even* us, who *are* **a** of us here alive *this* day. 3605
5:13 days thou shalt labour, and do **a** thy work: 3605
5:22 These words the LORD spake unto **a** your 3605
5:23 *even* **a** the heads of your tribes, and 3605
5:26 For who *is there of* **a** flesh, that hath heard 3605
5:27 hear **a** that the LORD our God shall say: 3605
5:27 speak thou unto us **a** that the LORD our 3605
5:28 they have well *said* **a** that they have 3605
5:29 and keep **a** my commandments always, 3605
5:31 I will speak unto thee **a** 3605
5:33 You shall walk in **a** the ways which 3605
6: 2 to keep **a** his statutes and 3605
6: 2 and thy son's son, **a** the days of thy life; 3605
6: 5 thou shalt love the LORD thy God with **a** 3605
6: 5 and with **a** thy soul, and with all thy might. 3605
6: 5 and with all thy soul, and with **a** thy might. 3605
6:11 houses full *of* **a** good *things,* which thou 3605
6:19 To cast out **a** thine enemies from before 3605
6:22 upon Pharaoh, and upon **a** his household, 3605
6:24 the LORD commanded us to do **a** these 3605
6:25 if we observe to do **a** these commandments 3605
7: 6 above **a** people that *are* upon the face of 3605
7: 7 for ye *were* the fewest of **a** people: 3605
7:14 Thou shalt be blessed above **a** people: 3605
7:15 the LORD will take away from thee **a** 3605
7:15 will lay them upon **a** *them* that hate thee. 3605
7:16 thou shalt consume **a** the people which 3605
7:18 God did unto Pharaoh, and unto **a** Egypt; 3605
7:19 shall the LORD thy God do unto **a** 3605
8: 1 **A** the commandments which I command 3605
8: 2 thou shalt remember **a** the way which 3605
8:13 and **a** that thou hast is multiplied; 3605
8:19 if thou **do at a forget** the LORD 7911+7911
9:10 on them *was written* according to **a** 3605
9:18 because of **a** your sins which ye sinned, 3605
10:12 to walk in **a** his ways, and to love him, and 3605
10:12 to serve the LORD thy God with **a** thy 3605
10:12 God with all thy heart and with **a** thy soul, 3605
10:14 the earth *also,* with **a** that therein *is.* 3605
10:15 *even* you above **a** people, as *it is* this day. 3605
11: 3 the king of Egypt, and unto **a** his land; 3605
11: 6 **a** the substance that *was* in their possession, 3605
11: 6 in their possession, in the midst of **a** Israel: 3605
11: 7 your eyes have seen **a** the great acts of 3605
11: 8 Therefore shall ye keep **a** 3605
11:13 to serve him with **a** your heart and with all 3605

Dt 11:13 with all your heart and with **a** your soul, 3605
11:22 For if ye shall diligently keep **a** these 3605
11:22 to walk in **a** his ways, and to cleave unto 3605
11:23 will the LORD drive out **a** these nations 3605
11:25 the dread of you upon **a** the land that ye 3605
11:32 ye shall observe to do **a** the statutes and 3605
12: 1 **a** the days that ye live upon the earth. 3605
12: 2 Ye shall utterly destroy **a** the places, 3605
12: 5 out of **a** your tribes to put his name there, 3605
12: 7 ye shall rejoice in **a** that you put your hand 3605
12: 8 Ye shall not do after **a** *the things* that we do 3605
12:10 *when* he giveth you rest from **a** your 3605
12:11 thither shall ye bring **a** that I command 3605
12:11 **a** your choice vows which ye vow unto 3605
12:14 there thou shalt do **a** that I command thee. 3605
12:15 mayest kill and eat flesh in **a** thy gates, 3605
12:18 God in **a** that thou puttest thine hands unto. 3605
12:28 hear **a** these words which I command thee, 3605
13: 3 the LORD your God with **a** your heart 3605
13: 3 with all your heart and with **a** your soul. 3605
13: 9 and afterwards the hand of **a** the people. 3605
13:11 **a** Israel shall hear, and fear, and shall do no 3605
13:15 and **a** that *is* therein, and the cattle thereof, 3605
13:16 thou shalt gather **a** the spoil of it into 3605
13:16 **a** the spoil thereof every whit, for 3605
13:18 to keep **a** his commandments which I 3605
14: 2 above **a** the nations that *are* upon the earth. 3605
14: 9 These ye shall eat of **a** that *are* in 3605
14: 9 **a** that have fins and scales shall ye eat: 3605
14:11 *Of* **a** clean birds ye shall eat. 3605
14:20 *But of* **a** clean fowls ye may eat. 3605
14:22 Thou shalt truly tithe **a** the increase of thy 3605
14:28 **a** the tithe of thine increase the same year, 3605
14:29 **a** the work of thine hand which thou doest. 3605
15: 5 to observe to do **a** these commandments 3605
15:10 thy God shall bless thee in **a** thy works, 3605
15:10 and in **a** that thou puttest thine hand unto. 3605
15:18 the LORD thy God shall bless thee in **a** 3605
15:19 **A** the firstling males that come of thy herd 3605
16: 3 of the land of Egypt **a** the days of thy life. 3605
16: 4 seen with thee in **a** thy coast seven days; 3605
16: 4 at even, **remain a night** until the morning. 3885
16:15 the LORD thy God shall bless thee in **a** 3605
16:15 in **a** the works of thine hands, therefore 3605
16:16 Three times in a year shall **a** thy males 3605
16:18 officers shalt thou make thee in **a** thy gates, 3605
17: 7 and afterward the hands of **a** the people. 3605
17:10 thou shalt observe to do according to **a** that 3605
17:13 **a** the people shall hear, and fear, and do no 3605
17:14 like as **a** the nations that *are* about me; 3605
17:19 he shall read therein **a** the days of his life: 3605
17:19 to keep **a** the words of this law and 3605
18: 1 priests the Levites, *and* **a** the tribe of Levi, 3605
18: 5 God hath chosen him out of **a** thy tribes, 3605
18: 6 come from any of thy gates out of **a** Israel, 3605
18: 6 come with **a** the desire of his mind unto 3605
18: 7 as **a** his brethren the Levites *do,* which 3605
18:12 For **a** that do these *things are* an 3605
18:16 According to **a** that thou desiredst of 3605
18:18 he shall speak unto them **a** that I shall 3605
19: 8 give thee **a** the land which he promised to 3605
19: 9 If thou shalt keep **a** these commandments 3605
20:11 *that* **a** the people that is found therein shall 3605
20:14 and the cattle, and **a** that is in the city, 3605
20:14 that is in the city, *even* **a** the spoil thereof, 3605
20:15 Thus shalt thou do unto **a** the cities *which* 3605
20:18 That they teach you not to do after **a** their 3605
21: 6 **a** the elders of that city, *that are* next unto 3605
21:14 thou shalt not **sell her at a** for 4376+4376
21:17 by giving him a double portion of **a** that he 3605
21:21 **a** the men of his city shall stone him with 3605
21:21 and **a** Israel shall hear, and fear. 3605
21:23 His body shall not **remain a night** upon 3885
22: 3 with a lost *thing* of thy brother's, which he 3605
22: 5 for **a** that do so *are* abomination unto 3605
22:19 he may not put her away **a** his days. 3605
22:29 he may not put her away **a** his days. 3605
23: 6 nor their prosperity **a** thy days for ever. 3605
23:20 the LORD thy God may bless thee in **a** 3605
24: 8 do according to **a** that the priests 3605
24:19 bless thee in **a** the work of thine hands. 3605
25:16 For **a** that do such *things, and* all that do 3605
25:16 do such *things, and* **a** that do unrighteously, 3605
25:18 *even* **a** that were feeble behind thee, 3605
25:19 thee rest from **a** thine enemies round about, 3605
26: 2 That thou shalt take of the first of **a** 3605
26:12 When thou hast made an end of tithing **a** 3605
26:13 according to **a** thy commandments which 3605
26:14 have done according to **a** that thou hast 3605
26:16 keep and do them with **a** thine heart, 3605
26:16 with all thine heart, and with **a** thy soul. 3605
26:18 that *thou* shouldest keep **a** his 3605
26:19 to make thee high above **a** nations which he 3605
27: 1 Keep **a** the commandments which I 3605
27: 3 thou shalt write upon them **a** the words of 3605
27: 8 thou shalt write upon the stones **a** 3605
27: 9 the priests the Levites spake unto **a** Israel, 3605
27:14 say unto **a** the men of Israel *with* a loud 3605
27:15 putteth *it* in a secret *place.* And **a** 3605
27:16 And **a** the people shall say, Amen. 3605
27:17 And **a** the people shall say, Amen. 3605
27:18 the way. And **a** the people shall say, Amen. 3605
27:19 widow. And **a** the people shall say, Amen. 3605
27:20 And **a** the people shall say, Amen. 3605
27:21 *of* beast. And **a** the people shall say, Amen. 3605
27:22 And **a** the people shall say, Amen. 3605
27:23 in law. And **a** the people shall say, Amen. 3605
27:24 And **a** the people shall say, Amen. 3605
27:25 And **a** the people shall say, Amen. 3605
27:26 Cursed *be* he that confirmeth not **a** NIH
27:26 do them. And **a** the people shall say, Amen. 3605
28: 1 to do **a** his commandments which I 3605
28: 1 thee on high above **a** nations of the earth: 3605
28: 2 **a** these blessings shall come on thee, and 3605
28: 8 and in **a** that thou settest thine hand unto; 3605

Dt 28:10 **a** people of the earth shall see that thou art 3605
28:12 and to bless **a** the work of thine hand: 3605
28:15 to observe to do **a** his commandments and 3605
28:15 that **a** these curses shall come upon thee, 3605
28:20 in **a** that thou settest thine hand unto for to 3605
28:25 shalt be removed into **a** the kingdoms of 3605
28:26 thy carcase shall be meat unto **a** fowls of 3605
28:32 fail *with longing* for them **a** the day long: 3605
28:33 The fruit of thy land, and **a** thy labours, 3605
28:37 among **a** nations whither the LORD shall 3605
28:40 Thou shalt have olive trees throughout **a** 3605
28:42 **A** thy trees and fruit of thy land shall 3605
28:45 Moreover **a** these curses shall come upon 3605
28:47 of heart, for the abundance of **a** *things;* 3605
28:48 in want of **a** *things:* and he shall put a yoke 3605
28:52 he shall besiege thee in **a** thy gates, 3605
28:52 thou trustedst, throughout **a** thy land: 3605
28:52 he shall besiege thee in **a** thy gates 3605
28:52 thee in all thy gates throughout **a** thy land, 3605
28:55 enemies shall distress thee in **a** thy gates. 3605
28:57 for she shall eat them for want of **a** *things* 3605
28:58 If thou wilt not observe to do **a** the words 3605
28:60 Moreover he will bring upon thee **a** 3605
28:64 the LORD shall scatter thee among **a** 3605
29: 2 Moses called unto **a** Israel, and said unto 3605
29: 2 Ye have seen **a** that the LORD did before 3605
29: 2 unto **a** his servants, and unto all his land; 3605
29: 2 unto all his servants, and unto **a** his land; 3605
29: 9 that ye may prosper *in* **a** that ye do. 3605
29:10 Ye stand *this* day **a** of you before 3605
29:10 and your officers, *with* **a** the men of Israel, 3605
29:20 **a** the curses that are written in this book 3605
29:21 him unto evil out of **a** the tribes of Israel, 3605
29:21 according to **a** the curses of the covenant 3605
29:24 Even **a** nations shall say, Wherefore hath 3605
29:27 to bring upon it **a** the curses that are written 3605
29:29 that *we* may do **a** the words of this law. 3605
30: 1 when **a** these things are come upon thee, 3605
30: 1 thou shalt call *them* to mind among **a** 3605
30: 2 shalt obey his voice according to **a** that I 3605
30: 2 with **a** thine heart, and with all thy soul; 3605
30: 2 with all thine heart, and with **a** thy soul; 3605
30: 3 and gather thee from **a** the nations, 3605
30: 6 to love the LORD thy God with **a** thine 3605
30: 6 and with **a** thy soul, that thou mayest live. 3605
30: 7 the LORD thy God will put **a** these curses 3605
30: 8 do **a** his commandments which I command 3605
30:10 the LORD thy God with **a** thine heart, 3605
30:10 with all thine heart, and with **a** thy soul. 3605
31: 1 and spake these words unto **a** Israel. 3605
31: 5 that ye may do unto them according unto **a** 3605
31: 7 said unto him in the sight of **a** Israel, 3605
31: 9 the LORD, and unto **a** the elders of Israel. 3605
31:11 When **a** Israel is come to appear before 3605
31:11 thou shalt read this law before **a** Israel in 3605
31:12 and observe to do **a** the words of this law: 3605
31:18 I will surely hide my face in that day for **a** 3605
31:28 Gather unto me **a** the elders of your tribes, 3605
31:30 Moses spake in the ears of **a** 3605
32: 4 for **a** his ways *are* judgment: a God of truth 3605
32:27 and the LORD hath not done **a** this. 3605
32:44 spake **a** the words of this song in the ears of 3605
32:45 Moses made an end of speaking **a** these 3605
32:45 end of speaking all these words to **a** Israel: 3605
32:46 Set your hearts unto **a** the words which I 3605
32:46 to observe to do, **a** the words of this law. 3605
33: 3 the people; **a** his saints *are* in thy hand: 3605
33:12 *the LORD* shall cover him **a** the day long, 3605
34: 1 the LORD shewed him **a** the land of 3605
34: 2 **a** Naphtali, and the land of Ephraim, and 3605
34: 2 Manasseh, and **a** the land of Judah, unto 3605
34:11 In **a** the signs and the wonders, which 3605
34:11 and to **a** his servants, and to all his land, 3605
34:11 and to all his servants, and to **a** his land, 3605
34:12 in **a** *that* mighty hand, and in all the great 3605
34:12 in **a** the great terror which Moses shewed in 3605
34:12 Moses shewed in the sight of **a** Israel. 3605
Jos 1: 2 go over this Jordan, thou, and **a** this people, 3605
1: 4 **a** the land of the Hittites, and unto the great 3605
1: 5 *to* stand before thee **a** the days of thy life: 3605
1: 7 observe to do according to **a** the law, 3605
1: 8 to do according to **a** that is written therein: 3605
1:14 **a** the mighty *men* of valour, and help them; 3605
1:16 **A** that thou commandest us we will do, and 3605
1:17 as we hearkened unto Moses in **a** 3605
1:18 will not hearken unto thy words in **a** that 3605
2: 3 for they be come to search out **a** 3605
2: 9 that **a** the inhabitants of the land faint 3605
2:13 **a** that they have, and deliver our lives from 3605
2:18 thy brethren, and **a** thy father's household, 3605
2:22 the pursuers sought *them* throughout **a** 3605
2:23 and told him **a** *things* that befell them: 3605
2:24 hath delivered into our hands **a** the land; 3605
2:24 for even **a** the inhabitants of the country do 3605
3: 1 he and **a** the children of Israel, and 3605
3: 7 to magnify thee in the sight of **a** Israel, 3605
3:11 *even* the Lord of **a** the earth passeth over 3605
3:13 the Lord of **a** the earth, shall rest in 3605
3:15 (for Jordan overfloweth **a** his banks all 3605
3:15 (for Jordan overfloweth all his banks **a** 3605
3:17 **a** the Israelites passed over on dry *ground,* 3605
3:17 **a** the people were passed clean over Jordan. 3605
4: 1 when **a** the people were clean passed over 3605
4:10 according to **a** that Moses commanded 3605
4:11 when **a** the people were clean passed over, 3605
4:14 magnified Joshua in the sight of **a** Israel; 3605
4:14 as they feared Moses, **a** the days of his life. 3605
4:18 flowed over **a** his banks, as *they did* before. 3605
4:24 That **a** the people of the earth might know 3605
5: 1 to pass, when **a** the kings of the Amorites, 3605
5: 1 **a** the kings of the Canaanites, which *were* 3605
5: 4 **A** the people that came out of Egypt, 3605
5: 4 *that were* males, *even* **a** the men of war, 3605
5: 5 Now **a** the people that came out were 3605
5: 5 **a** the people *that were* born in 3605

Jos 5: 6 till **a** the people *that were* men of war, 3605
5: 8 when they had done circumcising **a** 3605
6: 3 **a** *ye* men of war, *and* go round about 3605
6: 5 **a** the people shall shout *with* a great shout; 3605
6:17 *even* it, and **a** that *are* therein, to 3605
6:17 she and **a** that *are* with her in the house, 3605
6:19 **a** the silver, and gold, and vessels of brass 3605
6:21 they utterly destroyed **a** that *was* in the city, 3605
6:22 and **a** that she hath, as ye sware unto her. 3605
6:23 and her brethren, and **a** that she had; 3605
6:23 they brought out **a** her kindred, and 3605
6:24 the city with fire, and **a** that *was* therein: 3605
6:25 her father's household, and **a** that she had; 3605
6:27 his fame was *noised* throughout **a** 3605
7: 3 said unto him, Let not **a** the people go up; 3605
7: 3 *and* make not **a** the people to labour thither; 3605
7: 7 **at a brought** this people **over** 5674+5674
7: 9 **a** the inhabitants of the land shall hear *of it*, 3605
7:15 be burnt with fire, he and **a** that he hath: 3605
7:23 unto **a** the children of Israel, and laid them 3605
7:24 Joshua, and **a** Israel with him, took Achan 3605
7:24 his sheep, and his tent, and **a** that he had: 3605
7:25 **a** Israel stoned him *with* stones, and 3605
8: 1 take **a** the people of war with thee, 3605
8: 3 So Joshua arose, and **a** the people of war, 3605
8: 4 very far from the city, but be ye **a** ready: 3605
8: 5 I, and **a** the people that *are* with me, 3605
8:11 **a** the people, *even the people* of war that 3605
8:13 *even* **a** the host that *was* on the north of 3605
8:14 he and **a** his people, at a time appointed, 3605
8:15 **a** Israel *made as if they* were beaten before 3605
8:16 **a** the people that *were* in Ai were called 3605
8:21 **a** Israel saw that the ambush had taken 3605
8:24 when Israel had made an end of slaying **a** 3605
8:24 *when* they were **a** fallen on the edge of 3605
8:24 that **a** the Israelites returned *unto* Ai, and 3605
8:25 *so* it was, *that* **a** that fell that day, both of 3605
8:25 twelve thousand, *even* **a** the men of Ai. 3605
8:26 until *he* had utterly destroyed **a** 3605
8:33 **a** Israel, and their elders, and officers, and 3605
8:34 afterward he read **a** the words of the law, 3605
8:34 according to **a** that is written in the book of 3605
8:35 There was not a word of **a** that Moses 3605
8:35 which Joshua read not before **a** 3605
9: 1 when **a** the kings which *were* on *this* side 3605
9: 1 in **a** the coasts of the great sea over against 3605
9: 5 **a** the bread of their provision was dry *and* 3605
9: 9 the fame of him, and **a** that he did in Egypt, 3605
9:10 **a** that he did to the two kings of 3605
9:11 **a** the inhabitants of our country spake to us, 3605
9:18 **a** the congregation murmured against 3605
9:19 **a** the princes said unto all the congregation, 3605
9:19 all the princes said unto **a** the congregation, 3605
9:21 drawers of water unto **a** the congregation; 3605
9:24 his servant Moses to give you **a** the land, 3605
9:24 to destroy **a** the inhabitants of the land from 3605
10: 2 and **a** the men thereof *were* mighty. 3605
10: 5 they and **a** their hosts, and 3605
10: 6 for **a** the kings of the Amorites that dwell in 3605
10: 7 he, and **a** the people of war with him, and 3605
10: 7 with him, and **a** the mighty *men* of valour. 3605
10: 9 *and* went up from Gilgal **a** night. 3605
10:15 And Joshua returned, and **a** Israel with him, 3605
10:21 **a** the people returned to the camp to Joshua 3605
10:24 that Joshua called for **a** the men of Israel, 3605
10:25 for thus shall the LORD do to **a** your 3605
10:28 them, and **a** the souls that *were* therein; 3605
10:29 **a** Israel with him, *unto* Libnah, and 3605
10:30 and **a** the souls that *were* therein; 3605
10:31 **a** Israel with him, unto Lachish, and 3605
10:32 and **a** the souls that *were* therein, 3605
10:32 according to **a** that he had done to Libnah. 3605
10:34 passed unto Eglon, and **a** Israel with him; 3605
10:35 **a** the souls that *were* therein he utterly 3605
10:35 according to **a** that he had done to Lachish. 3605
10:36 and **a** Israel with him, unto Hebron; 3605
10:37 **a** the cities thereof, and all the souls that 3605
10:37 and **a** the souls that *were* therein; 3605
10:37 according to **a** that he had done to Eglon; 3605
10:37 it utterly, and **a** the souls that *were* therein; 3605
10:38 and **a** Israel with him, to Debir; 3605
10:39 the king thereof, and **a** the cities thereof; 3605
10:39 utterly destroyed **a** the souls that *were* 3605
10:40 So Joshua smote **a** the country of the hills, 3605
10:40 and of the springs, and **a** their kings: 3605
10:40 but utterly destroyed **a** that breathed, 3605
10:41 **a** the country of Goshen, even unto Gibeon. 3605
10:42 **a** these kings and their land did Joshua take 3605
10:43 And Joshua returned, and **a** Israel with him, 3605
11: 4 they and **a** their hosts with them, 3605
11: 5 when **a** these kings were met together, 3605
11: 6 will I deliver them up **a** slain before Israel: 3605
11: 7 and **a** the people of war with him, 3605
11:10 for Hazor beforetime *was* the head of **a** 3605
11:11 they smote **a** the souls that *were* therein 3605
11:12 **a** the cities of those kings, and all the kings 3605
11:12 **a** the kings of them, did Joshua take, and 3605
11:14 **a** the spoil of these cities, and the cattle, 3605
11:15 he left nothing undone of **a** that the LORD 3605
11:16 So Joshua took **a** that land, the hills, and all 3605
11:16 **a** the south *country*, and all the land of 3605
11:16 south *country*, and **a** the land of Goshen, 3605
11:17 **a** their kings he took, and smote them, and 3605
11:18 Joshua made war a long time with **a** those 3605
11:19 of Gibeon: **a** *other* they took in battle. 3605
11:21 from **a** the mountains of Judah, and 3605
11:21 and from **a** the mountains of Israel: 3605
11:23 according to **a** that the LORD said unto 3605
12: 1 mount Hermon, and **a** the plain on the east: 3605
12: 5 and in Salcah, and in **a** Bashan, 3605
12:24 of Tirzah, one: **a** the kings thirty and one. 3605
13: 2 **a** the borders of the Philistines, and 3605
13: 2 borders of the Philistines, and **a** Geshuri, 3605
13: 4 **a** the land of the Canaanites, and 3605
13: 5 and **a** Lebanon, *toward* the sunrising, 3605

Jos 13: 6 **A** the inhabitants of the hill country from 3605
13: 6 *and* **a** the Sidonians, them will I drive out 3605
13: 9 and **a** the plain of Medeba unto Dibon; 3605
13:10 **a** the cities of Sihon king of the Amorites, 3605
13:11 **a** mount Hermon, and all Bashan unto 3605
13:11 mount Hermon, and **a** Bashan unto Salcah; 3605
13:12 **A** the kingdom of Og in Bashan, 3605
13:16 of the river, and **a** the plain by Medeba; 3605
13:17 and **a** her cities that *are* in the plain; 3605
13:21 **a** the cities of the plain, and all 3605
13:21 **a** the kingdom of Sihon king of 3605
13:25 **a** the cities of Gilead, and half the land of 3605
13:30 their coast was from Mahanaim, **a** Bashan, 3605
13:30 **a** the kingdom of Og king of Bashan, and 3605
13:30 **a** the towns of Jair, which *are* in Bashan, 3605
15:32 **a** the cities *are* twenty and nine, with their 3605
15:46 **a** that *lay* near Ashdod, with their villages: 3605
16: 9 **a** the cities with their villages. 3605
17:16 **a** the Canaanites that dwell in the land of 3605
19: 8 **a** the villages that *were* round about these 3605
20: 9 These were the cities appointed for **a** 3605
21:19 **A** the cities of the children of Aaron, 3605
21:26 **A** the cities *were* ten with their suburbs for 3605
21:33 **A** the cities of the Gershonites according to 3605
21:39 Jazer with her suburbs; four cities in **a**. 3605
21:40 So **a** the cities for the children of Merari by 3605
21:41 **A** the cities of the Levites within 3605
21:42 round about them: thus *were* **a** these cities. 3605
21:43 the LORD gave unto Israel **a** the land 3605
21:44 according to **a** that he sware unto their 3605
21:44 there stood not a man of **a** their enemies 3605
21:44 the LORD delivered **a** their enemies into 3605
21:45 unto the house of Israel; **a** came to pass. 3605
22: 2 Ye have kept **a** that Moses the servant of 3605
22: 2 have obeyed my voice in **a** that I 3605
22: 5 to walk in **a** his ways, and to keep his 3605
22: 5 to serve him with **a** your heart and with all 3605
22: 5 with all your heart and with **a** your soul. 3605
22:14 of each chief house a prince throughout **a** 3605
22:20 wrath fell on **a** the congregation of Israel? 3605
23: 1 Israel from **a** their enemies round about, 3605
23: 2 Joshua called for **a** Israel, *and* for their 3605
23: 3 ye have seen **a** that the LORD your God 3605
23: 3 your God hath done unto **a** these nations 3605
23: 4 with **a** the nations that I have cut off, 3605
23: 6 to do **a** that is written in the book of the law 3605
23:14 *this* day I am going the way of **a** the earth: 3605
23:14 ye know in **a** your hearts and in all your 3605
23:14 know in all your hearts and in **a** your souls, 3605
23:14 that not one thing hath failed of **a** the good 3605
23:14 **a** are come to pass unto you, *and* not one 3605
23:15 *that* as **a** good things are come upon you, 3605
23:15 shall the LORD bring upon you **a** evil 3605
24: 1 Joshua gathered **a** the tribes of Israel to 3605
24: 2 Joshua said unto **a** the people, Thus saith 3605
24: 3 led him throughout **a** the land of Canaan, 3605
24:17 preserved us in **a** the way wherein we went, 3605
24:17 among **a** the people through whom we 3605
24:18 the LORD drave out from before us **a** 3605
24:27 Joshua said unto **a** the people, Behold, this 3605
24:27 for it hath heard **a** the words of the LORD 3605
24:31 Israel served the LORD **a** the days of 3605
24:31 **a** the days of the elders that overlived 3605
24:31 which had known **a** the works of 3605
Jdg 1:25 but they let go the man and **a** his family. 3605
2: 4 these words unto **a** the children of Israel, 3605
2: 7 the people served the LORD **a** the days of 3605
2: 7 **a** the days of the elders that outlived 3605
2: 7 who had seen **a** the great works of 3605
2:10 also **a** that generation were gathered unto 3605
2:18 of their enemies **a** the days of the judge: 3605
3: 1 *even* as many *of Israel* as had not known **a** 3605
3: 3 **a** the Canaanites, and the Sidonians, and 3605
3:19 **a** that stood by him went out from him. 3605
3:29 **a** lusty, and all men of valour; 3605
3:29 all lusty, and **a** men of valour; 3605
4:13 Sisera gathered together **a** his chariots, 3605
4:13 and **a** the people that *were* with him, 3605
4:15 and **a** *his* chariots, and all *his* host, 3605
4:15 and all *his* chariots, and **a** *his* host, 3605
4:16 **a** the host of Sisera fell upon the edge of 3605
5:31 So let **a** thine enemies perish, O LORD: 3605
6: 9 and out of the hand of **a** that oppressed you, 3605
6:13 be with us, why then is **a** this befallen us? 3605
6:13 where *be* **a** his miracles which our fathers 3605
6:31 Joash said unto **a** that stood against him, 3605
6:33 **a** the Midianites and the Amalekites and 3605
6:35 he sent messengers throughout **a** Manasseh; 3605
6:37 *it be* dry upon **a** the earth *beside*, then 3605
6:39 upon **a** the ground let there be dew. 3605
6:40 and there was dew on **a** the ground. 3605
7: 1 **a** the people that *were* with him, rose up 3605
7: 6 **a** the rest of the people bowed down upon 3605
7: 7 let **a** the *other* people go every man unto his 3605
7: 8 he sent **a** *the rest of* Israel every man 376+3605
7:12 **a** the children of the east lay along in 3605
7:14 hath God delivered Midian, and **a** the host. 3605
7:18 I and **a** that *are* with me, then blow ye 3605
7:18 trumpets also on every side of **a** the camp, 3605
7:21 and **a** the host ran, and cried, and fled. 3605
7:22 his fellow, even throughout **a** the host: 3605
7:23 out of **a** Manasseh, and pursued after 3605
7:24 Gideon sent messengers throughout **a** 3605
7:24 **a** the men of Ephraim gathered themselves 3605
8:10 about fifteen thousand *men*, **a** that were left 3605
8:10 of **a** the hosts of the children of the east: 3605
8:12 and Zalmunna, and discomfited **a** the host. 3605
8:27 **a** Israel went thither a whoring after it: 3605
8:34 the hands of **a** their enemies on every side: 3605
8:35 according to **a** the goodness which he had 3605
9: 1 with **a** the family of the house of his 3605
9: 2 in the ears of **a** the men of Shechem, 3605
9: 2 either that **a** the sons of Jerubbaal, 3605
9: 3 of **a** the men of Shechem all these words: 3605
9: 3 of all the men of Shechem **a** these words: 3605

Jdg 9: 6 **a** the men of Shechem gathered together, 3605
9: 6 **a** the house of Millo, and went, and 3605
9:14 said **a** the trees unto the bramble, 3605
9:25 they robbed **a** that came along *that* way by 3605
9:34 **a** the people that *were* with him, by night, 3605
9:44 the two *other* companies ran upon **a** 3605
9:45 Abimelech fought against the city **a** that 3605
9:46 when **a** the men of the tower of Shechem 3605
9:47 that **a** the men of the tower of Shechem 3605
9:48 he and **a** the people that *were* with him; 3605
9:49 **a** the people likewise cut down every man 3605
9:49 that **a** the men of the tower of Shechem 3605
9:51 thither fled **a** the men and women, and 3605
9:51 **a** they of the city, and shut *it* to them, and 3605
9:53 and **a to brake** his skull. 7533
9:57 **a** the evil of the men of Shechem did God 3605
10: 8 **a** the children of Israel that *were* on 3605
10:18 he shall be head over **a** the inhabitants of 3605
11: 8 be our head over **a** the inhabitants of 3605
11:11 Jephthah uttered **a** his words before 3605
11:20 Sihon gathered **a** his people together, and 3605
11:21 and **a** his people into the hand of Israel, 3605
11:21 Israel possessed **a** the land of the Amorites, 3605
11:22 they possessed **a** the coasts of 3605
11:26 in **a** the cities that *be* along by the coasts of 3605
12: 4 Jephthah gathered together **a** the men of 3605
13:13 Of **a** that I said unto the woman let her 3605
13:14 nor eat any unclean *thing*: **a** that I 3605
13:23 neither would he have shewed us **a** these 3605
14: 3 of thy brethren, or among **a** my people, 3605
16: 2 laid wait for him **a** night in the gate of 3605
16: 2 were quiet **a** the night, saying, In 3605
16: 3 bar and **a**, and put *them* upon his shoulders, NIH
16:17 That he told her **a** his heart, and said unto 3605
16:18 when Delilah saw that he had told her **a** his 3605
16:18 for he hath shewed me **a** his heart. 3605
16:27 **a** the lords of the Philistines *were* there; 3605
16:30 he bowed *himself* with **a** *his* might; and NIH
16:30 and upon **a** the people that *were* therein. 3605
16:31 and **a** the house of his father came down, 3605
18: 1 **a** *their* inheritance had not fallen unto them NIH
18:31 **a** the time that the house of God was in 3605
19: 6 **tarry a night**, and let thine heart be merry. 3885
19: 9 towards evening, I pray you **tarry a night**: 3885
19:13 to one of *these* places to **lodge a night**, 3885
19:20 howsoever *let* **a** thy wants *lie* upon me; 3605
19:25 abused her **a** the night until the morning: 3605
19:29 and sent her into **a** the coasts of Israel. 3605
19:30 it was so, that **a** that saw it said, There was 3605
20: 1 **a** the children of Israel went out, and 3605
20: 2 the chief of **a** the people, *even* of all 3605
20: 2 all the people, *even* of **a** the tribes of Israel, 3605
20: 6 sent her throughout **a** the country of 3605
20: 7 Behold, ye *are* **a** children of Israel; 3605
20: 8 **a** the people arose as one man, saying, 3605
20:10 hundred throughout **a** the tribes of Israel, 3605
20:10 according to **a** the folly that they have 3605
20:11 So **a** the men of Israel were gathered 3605
20:12 the tribes of Israel sent men through **a** 3605
20:16 Among **a** this people *there were* seven 3605
20:17 that drew sword: **a** these *were* men of war. 3605
20:25 thousand men; **a** these drew the sword. 3605
20:26 **a** the children of Israel, and all the people, 3605
20:26 **a** the people, went up, and came *unto* 3605
20:33 **a** the men of Israel rose up out of their 3605
20:34 ten thousand chosen men out of **a** Israel, 3605
20:35 an hundred men: **a** these drew the sword. 3605
20:37 smote **a** the city with the edge of the sword. 3605
20:44 thousand men; **a** these *were* men of valour. 3605
20:46 So that **a** which fell that day of Benjamin 3605
20:46 the sword; **a** these *were* men of valour. 3605
20:48 as the beast, and **a** that came to hand: 3605
20:48 also they set on fire **a** the cities that they 3605
21: 5 Who *is there* among **a** the tribes of Israel 3605
Ru 1:19 that **a** the city was moved about them, and 3605
2:11 **a** that thou hast done unto thy mother in 3605
2:21 until they have ended **a** my harvest. 3605
3: 5 **A** that thou sayest unto me I will do. 3605
3: 6 did according to **a** that her mother in law 3605
3:11 I will do to thee **a** that thou requirest: 3605
3:11 for **a** the city of my people doth know that 3605
3:16 she told her **a** that the man had done to her. 3605
4: 7 for to confirm **a** things; 3605
4: 9 *unto* **a** the people, Ye *are* witnesses *this* 3605
4: 9 that I have bought **a** that *was* Elimelech's, 3605
4: 9 **a** that *was* Chilion's and Mahlon's, of 3605
4:11 **a** the people that *were* in the gate, and 3605
1Sa 1: 4 to **a** her sons and her daughters, portions: 3605
1:11 I will give him unto the LORD **a** the days 3605
1:21 the man Elkanah, and **a** his house, went up 3605
2:14 **a** that the fleshhook brought up the priest 3605
2:14 So they did in Shiloh unto **a** the Israelites 3605
2:22 and heard **a** that his sons did unto all Israel; 3605
2:22 and heard all that his sons did unto **a** Israel; 3605
2:23 for I hear of your evil dealings by **a** this 3605
2:28 did I choose him out of **a** the tribes of Israel 3605
2:28 did I give unto the house of thy father **a** 3605
2:29 make yourselves fat with the chiefest of **a** 3605
2:32 in **a** *the wealth* which *God* shall give Israel: 3605
2:33 **a** the increase of thine house shall die in 3605
3:12 In that day I will perform against Eli **a** 3605
3:17 if thou hide *any* thing from me of **a** 3605
3:20 **a** Israel from Dan even to Beer-sheba knew 3605
4: 1 the word of Samuel came to **a** Israel. 3605
4: 5 **a** Israel shouted *with* a great shout, so 3605
4: 8 with **a** the plagues in the wilderness. 3605
4:13 into the city, and told *it*, **a** the city cried out. 3605
5: 8 gathered **a** the lords of the Philistines unto 3605
5:11 gathered together **a** the lords of 3605
5:11 a deadly destruction throughout **a** the city; 3605
6: 4 for one plague *was* on you **a**, and on your 3605
6:18 *according to* the number of **a** the cities of 3605
7: 2 **a** the house of Israel lamented after 3605
7: 3 Samuel spake unto **a** the house of Israel, 3605
7: 3 If ye do return unto the LORD with **a** your 3605

1Sa 7: 5 Gather **a** Israel to Mizpeh, and I will pray 3605
7:13 the Philistines **a** the days of Samuel. 3605
7:15 Samuel judged Israel **a** the days of his life. 3605
7:16 Mizpeh, and judged Israel in **a** those places. 3605
8: 4 **a** the elders of Israel gathered themselves 3605
8: 5 now make us a king to judge us like **a** 3605
8: 7 Hearken unto the voice of the people in **a** 3605
8: 8 According to **a** the works which they have 3605
8:10 Samuel told **a** the words of the LORD 3605
8:20 That we also may be like **a** the nations; and 3605
8:21 Samuel heard **a** the words of the people, 3605
9: 6 **a** that he saith cometh surely to pass: 3605
9:19 and will tell thee **a** that *is* in thine heart. 3605
9:20 on whom *is* **a** the desire of Israel? *Is it* not 3605
9:20 *it* not on thee, and on **a** thy father's house? 3605
9:21 my family the least of **a** the families of 3605
10: 9 and **a** those signs came to pass that day. 3605
10:11 when **a** that knew him beforetime saw that 3605
10:18 out of the hand of **a** kingdoms, *and* of them 3605
10:19 who himself saved you out of **a** your 3605
10:20 when Samuel had caused **a** the tribes of 3605
10:24 Samuel said to **a** the people, See ye him 3605
10:24 that *there is* none like him among **a** 3605
10:24 **a** the people shouted, and said, God save 3605
10:25 Samuel sent **a** the people away, every man 3605
11: 1 **a** the men of Jabesh said unto Nahash, 3605
11: 2 that *I* may thrust out **a** your right eyes, and 3605
11: 2 and lay it *for* a reproach upon **a** Israel. 3605
11: 3 that we may send messengers unto **a** 3605
11: 4 **a** the people lift up their voices, and wept. 3605
11: 7 sent *them* throughout **a** the coasts of Israel 3605
11:10 ye shall do with us **a** that seemeth good 3605
11:15 **a** the people went *to* Gilgal; and there they 3605
11:15 and **a** the men of Israel rejoiced greatly. 3605
12: 1 Samuel said unto **a** Israel, Behold, I have 3605
12: 1 I have hearkened unto your voice in **a** that 3605
12: 7 of **a** the righteous acts of the LORD, 3605
12:18 **a** the people greatly feared the LORD and 3605
12:19 **a** the people said unto Samuel, Pray for thy 3605
12:19 for we have added unto **a** our sins *this* evil, 3605
12:20 ye have done **a** this wickedness: yet turn 3605
12:20 but serve the LORD with **a** your heart; 3605
12:24 and serve him in truth with **a** your heart: 3605
13: 3 blew the trumpet throughout **a** the land, 3605
13: 4 **a** Israel heard say *that* Saul had smitten a 3605
13: 7 and **a** the people followed him trembling. 3605
13:19 smith found throughout **a** the land of Israel: 3605
13:20 **a** the Israelites went down *to* 3605
14: 7 said unto him, Do **a** that *is* in thine heart: 3605
14:15 in the field, and among **a** the people: 3605
14:20 **a** the people that *were* with him assembled 3605
14:22 Likewise **a** the men of Israel which had hid 3605
14:25 And **a** *they of* the land came to a wood; and 3605
14:34 **a** the people brought every man his ox with 3605
14:38 ye near hither, **a** the chief of the people: 3605
14:39 *there was* not *a man* among **a** the people 3605
14:40 said he unto **a** Israel, Be ye on one side, 3605
14:47 fought against **a** his enemies on every side, 3605
14:52 there was sore war against the Philistines **a** 3605
15: 3 utterly destroy **a** that they have, and 3605
15: 6 for ye shewed kindness to **a** the children of 3605
15: 8 utterly destroyed **a** the people with the edge 3605
15: 9 **a** *that was* good, and would not utterly 3605
15:11 and he cried unto the LORD **a** night. 3605
16:11 said unto Jesse, Are here **a** *thy* children? 8552
17:11 **a** Israel heard those words of the Philistine, 3605
17:19 and they, and **a** the men of Israel, 3605
17:24 **a** the men of Israel, when they saw 3605
17:46 that **a** the earth may know that there is a 3605
17:47 **a** this assembly shall know that the LORD 3605
18: 5 he was accepted in the sight of **a** 3605
18: 6 that the women came out of **a** cities of 3605
18:14 David behaved himself wisely in **a** his 3605
18:16 **a** Israel and Judah loved David, because 3605
18:22 delight in thee, and **a** his servants love thee: 3605
18:30 more wisely than **a** the servants of Saul; 3605
19: 1 to **a** his servants, that they should kill 3605
19: 5 the LORD wrought a great salvation for **a** 3605
19: 7 and Jonathan shewed him **a** those things. 3605
19:18 and told him **a** that Saul had done to him. 3605
19:24 lay down naked **a** that day and all *that* 3605
19:24 down naked all that day and **a** *that* night. 3605
20: 6 If thy father **at a miss** me, then say, 6485+6485
20: 6 for *there is* a yearly sacrifice there for **a** 3605
22: 1 **a** his father's house heard *it*, they went 3605
22: 4 they dwelt with him **a** the while that David 3605
22: 6 **a** his servants *were* standing about him;) 3605
22: 7 *and* make you **a** captains of thousands, and 3605
22: 8 That **a** of you have conspired against me, 3605
22:11 the son of Ahitub, and **a** his father's house, 3605
22:11 and they came **a** of them to the king. 3605
22:14 *so* faithful among **a** thy servants as David, 3605
22:15 his servant, *nor* to **a** the house of my father: 3605
22:15 for thy servant knew nothing of **a** this, less 3605
22:16 thou, and **a** thy father's house. 3605
22:22 I have occasioned *the death* of **a** 3605
23: 8 Saul called **a** the people together to war, 3605
23:20 come down according to **a** the desire of thy 3605
23:23 take knowledge of **a** the lurking places 3605
23:23 that I will search him out throughout **a** 3605
24: 2 three thousand chosen men out of **a** Israel, 3605
25: 1 **a** the Israelites were gathered together, and 3605
25: 6 and peace *be unto* **a** that thou hast. 3605
25: 7 **a** the while they were in Carmel. 3605
25: 9 they spake to Nabal according to **a** those 3605
25:12 and came and told him **a** those sayings. 3605
25:16 **a** the while we were with them keeping 3605
25:17 our master, and against **a** his household: 3605
25:21 Surely in vain have I kept **a** that this *fellow* 3605
25:21 that nothing was missed of **a** that *pertained* 3605
25:22 if I leave of **a** that *pertain* to him by 3605
25:28 evil hath not been found in thee **a** thy days. NIH
25:30 **a** the good that he hath spoken concerning 3605
26:12 for they *were* **a** asleep; because a deep 3605
26:24 and let him deliver me out of **a** tribulation. 3605

1Sa 27:11 *will be* his manner **a** the while he dwelleth 3605
28: 3 **a** Israel had lamented him, and buried him 3605
28: 4 Saul gathered **a** Israel together, and 3605
28:20 Saul fell straightway **a along** on 4393+6967
28:20 for he had eaten no bread **a** the day, nor all 3605
28:20 eaten no bread all the day, nor **a** the night. 3605
29: 1 Now the Philistines gathered together **a** 3605
30: 6 the soul of **a** the people was grieved, 3605
30: 8 overtake *them*, and without fail recover **a**. NIH
30:16 behold *they were* spread abroad upon **a** 3605
30:16 of **a** the great spoil that they had taken out 3605
30:18 David recovered **a** that the Amalekites had 3605
30:19 they had taken to them: David recovered **a**. 3605
30:20 David took **a** the flocks and the herds, 3605
30:22 answered **a** the wicked men and *men* of 3605
30:31 to **a** the places where David himself and 3605
31: 6 and his armourbearer, and **a** his men, 3605
31:12 **A** the valiant men arose, and went all night, 3605
31:12 and went **a** night, and took the body of Saul 3605
2Sa 1:11 and likewise **a** the men that *were* with him: 3605
2: 9 and over Benjamin, and over **a** Israel. 3605
2:28 **a** the people stood still, and pursued after 3605
2:29 his men walked **a** that night through 3605
2:29 went *through* **a** Bithron, and they came *to* 3605
2:30 when he had gathered **a** the people 3605
2:32 Joab and his men went **a** night, and they 3605
3:12 with thee, to bring about **a** Israel unto thee. 3605
3:18 and out of the hand of **a** their enemies. 3605
3:19 in Hebron **a** that seemed good to Israel, 3605
3:21 will gather **a** Israel unto my lord the king, 3605
3:21 that thou mayest reign over **a** that thine 3605
3:23 **a** the host that *was* with him were come, 3605
3:25 coming in, and to know **a** that thou doest. 3605
3:29 head of Joab, and on **a** his father's house; 3605
3:31 to **a** the people that *were* with him, 3605
3:32 the grave of Abner; and **a** the people wept. 3605
3:34 And **a** the people wept again over him. 3605
3:35 when **a** the people came to cause David to 3605
3:36 **a** the people took notice *of it*, and it pleased 3605
3:36 the king did, pleased **a** the people. 3605
3:37 For **a** the people and all Israel understood 3605
3:37 **a** Israel understood that day that it was not 3605
4: 1 and **a** the Israelites were troubled. 3605
4: 7 gat them away through the plain **a** night. 3605
4: 9 who hath redeemed my soul out of **a** 3605
5: 1 came **a** the tribes of Israel to David unto 3605
5: 3 So **a** the elders of Israel came to the king to 3605
5: 5 and three years over **a** Israel and Judah. 3605
5:17 **a** the Philistines came up to seek David; 3605
6: 1 David gathered together **a** the chosen *men* 3605
6: 2 went with **a** the people that *were* with him 3605
6: 5 **a** the house of Israel played before 3605
6: 5 **a** *manner of instruments made of* fir wood, 3605
6:11 blessed Obed-edom, and **a** his household. 3605
6:12 **a** that *pertaineth* unto him, because of 3605
6:14 David danced before the LORD with **a** *his* 3605
6:15 **a** the house of Israel brought up the ark of 3605
6:19 he dealt among **a** the people, *even* among 3605
6:19 a flagon *of wine*. So **a** the people departed 3605
6:21 before thy father, and before **a** his house, 3605
7: 1 him rest round about from **a** his enemies; 3605
7: 3 to the king, Go, do **a** that *is* in thine heart; 3605
7: 7 In **a** *the places* wherein I have walked with 3605
7: 7 **a** the children of Israel spake I a word with 3605
7: 9 have cut off **a** thine enemies out of thy 3605
7:11 have caused thee to rest from **a** thine 3605
7:17 According to **a** these words, and 3605
7:17 according to **a** this vision, so did Nathan 3605
7:21 hast thou done **a** these great things, 3605
7:22 according to **a** that we have heard with our 3605
8: 4 David houghed **a** the chariot *horses*, but 3605
8: 9 David had smitten **a** the host of Hadadezer, 3605
8:11 gold that he had dedicated of **a** nations 3605
8:14 throughout **a** Edom put he garrisons, and 3605
8:14 **a** they of Edom became David's servants. 3605
8:15 David reigned over **a** Israel; and David 3605
8:15 and justice unto **a** his people. 3605
9: 7 will restore thee **a** the land of Saul thy 3605
9: 9 I have given unto thy master's son **a** that 3605
9: 9 all that pertained to Saul and to **a** his house. 3605
9:11 According to **a** that my lord the king hath 3605
9:12 **a** that dwelt in the house of Ziba *were* 3605
10: 7 and **a** the host *of* the mighty *men*. 3605
10: 9 he chose of **a** the choice *men* of Israel, and 3605
10:17 he gathered **a** Israel together, and 3605
10:19 when **a** the kings *that were* servants to 3605
11: 1 and his servants with him, and **a** Israel; 3605
11: 9 king's house with **a** the servants of his lord, 3605
11:18 told David **a** the things concerning the war; 3605
11:22 shewed David **a** that Joab had sent him for. 3605
12:12 I will do this thing before **a** Israel, and 3605
12:16 and went in, and lay **a night** upon the earth. 3885
12:29 David gathered **a** the people together, and 3605
12:31 thus did he unto **a** the cities of the children 3605
12:31 and **a** the people returned *unto* Jerusalem. 3605
13: 9 Amnon said, Have out **a** men from me. 3605
13:21 when king David heard of **a** these things, 3605
13:23 and Absalom invited **a** the king's sons. 3605
13:25 Nay, my son, let us not **a** now go, 3605
13:27 and **a** the king's sons go with him. 3605
13:29 **a** the king's sons arose, and every man gat 3605
13:30 Absalom hath slain **a** the king's sons, and 3605
13:31 **a** his servants stood *by* with their clothes 3605
13:32 have slain **a** the young men the king's sons; 3605
13:33 to think *that* **a** the king's sons are dead: 3605
13:36 king also and **a** his servants wept very sore. 3605
14:19 *Is not* the hand of Joab with thee in **a** this? 3605
14:19 he put **a** these words in the mouth of thine 3605
14:20 to know **a** *things* that *are* in the earth. 3605
14:25 in **a** Israel there was none to be so 3605
15: 6 on this manner did Absalom to **a** Israel that 3605
15:10 Absalom sent spies throughout **a** the tribes 3605
15:14 David said unto **a** his servants that *were* 3605
15:16 went forth, and **a** his household after him. 3605
15:17 **a** the people after him, and tarried *in* a 3605

2Sa 15:18 **a** his servants passed on beside him; and 3605
15:18 and **a** the Cherethites, and all the Pelethites, 3605
15:18 and **a** the Pelethites, and all the Gittites, 3605
15:18 and all the Pelethites, and **a** the Gittites, 3605
15:22 **a** his men, and all the little ones that *were* 3605
15:22 and **a** the little ones that *were* with him. 3605
15:23 **a** the country wept *with* a loud voice, and 3605
15:23 a loud voice, and **a** the people passed over: 3605
15:23 **a** the people passed over, toward the way of 3605
15:24 and **a** the Levites *were* with him, 3605
15:24 until **a** the people had done passing out of 3605
15:30 **a** the people that *was* with him covered 3605
16: 4 thine *are* **a** that *pertained* unto 3605
16: 6 and at **a** the servants of king David: 3605
16: 6 **a** the people and all the mighty *men were* 3605
16: 6 **a** the mighty *men were* on his right hand 3605
16: 8 The LORD hath returned upon thee **a** 3605
16:11 and to **a** his servants, Behold, my son, 3605
16:14 **a** the people that *were* with him, 3605
16:15 and **a** the people the men of Israel, 3605
16:18 this people, and **a** the men of Israel, choose, 3605
16:21 **a** Israel shall hear that thou art abhorred of 3605
16:21 shall the hands of **a** that *are* with thee be 3605
16:22 father's concubines in the sight of **a** Israel. 3605
16:23 *was* **a** the counsel of Ahithophel both with 3605
17: 2 **a** the people that *are* with him shall flee; 3605
17: 3 I will bring back **a** the people unto thee: 3605
17: 3 the man whom thou seekest *is* as if **a** 3605
17: 3 *so* **a** the people shall be *in* peace. 3605
17: 4 Absalom well, and **a** the elders of Israel. 3605
17:10 for **a** Israel knoweth that thy father *is* a 3605
17:11 Therefore I counsel *that* **a** Israel be 3605
17:12 of **a** the men that *are* with him there shall 3605
17:13 shall **a** Israel bring ropes to that city, and 3605
17:14 Absalom and **a** the men of Israel said, 3605
17:16 and **a** the people that *are* with him. 3605
17:22 **a** the people that *were* with him, and 3605
17:24 he and **a** the men of Israel with him. 3605
18: 4 **a** the people came out by hundreds and 3605
18: 5 **a** the people heard when the king gave all 3605
18: 5 all the people heard when the king gave **a** 3605
18: 8 scattered over the face of **a** the country: 3605
18:17 and **a** Israel fled every one to his tent. 3605
18:28 and said unto the king, **A is well**. 7965
18:31 *this* day of **a** them that rose up against thee. 3605
18:32 **a** that rise against thee to do *thee* hurt, 3605
19: 2 *turned* into mourning unto **a** the people: 3605
19: 5 Thou hast shamed *this* day the faces of **a** 3605
19: 6 **a** we had died *this* day, then it had pleased 3605
19: 7 that *will be* worse unto thee than **a** the evil 3605
19: 8 they told unto **a** the people, saying, Behold, 3605
19: 8 **a** the people came before the king: 3605
19: 9 **a** the people were at strife throughout all 3605
19: 9 all the people were at strife throughout **a** 3605
19:11 seeing the speech of **a** Israel is come to 3605
19:14 he bowed the heart of **a** the men of Judah, 3605
19:14 the king, Return thou, and **a** thy servants. 3605
19:20 I am come the first *this* day of **a** the house 3605
19:28 For **a** *of* my father's house were but dead 3605
19:30 said unto the king, Yea, let him take **a**, 3605
19:39 **a** the people went over Jordan. And when 3605
19:40 **a** the people of Judah conducted the king, 3605
19:41 **a** the men of Israel came to the king, and 3605
19:41 and **a** David's men with him, over Jordan? 3605
19:42 **a** the men of Judah answered the men of 3605
19:42 have we **eaten at a** of the king's *cost?* 398+398
20: 7 **a** the mighty *men*: and they went out of 3605
20:12 when the man saw that **a** the people stood 3605
20:13 **a** the people went on after Joab, to pursue 3605
20:14 he went through **a** the tribes of Israel unto 3605
20:14 and *to* Beth-maachah, and **a** the Berites: 3605
20:15 **a** the people that *were* with Joab battered 3605
20:22 the woman went unto **a** the people in her 3605
20:23 Now Joab *was* over **a** the host of Israel: and 3605
21: 9 they fell **a** seven together, and were put to NIH
21:14 they performed **a** that the king commanded. 3605
22: 1 him out of the hand of **a** his enemies, 3605
22:23 For **a** his judgments *were* before me: and 3605
22:31 he *is* a buckler to **a** them that trust in him. 3605
23: 5 ordered in **a** *things*, and sure: 3605
23: 5 for *this is* **a** my salvation, and all *my* desire, 3605
23: 5 for *this is* all my salvation, and **a** *my* desire, 3605
23: 6 *the sons of* Belial *shall be* **a** of them as 3605
23:39 Uriah the Hittite: thirty and seven *in* **a**. 3605
24: 2 Go now through **a** the tribes of Israel, 3605
24: 7 *to* **a** the cities of the Hivites, and of 3605
24: 8 So when they had gone through **a** the land, 3605
24:23 **A** *these things* did Araunah, *as* a king, 3605
1Ki 1: 3 damsel throughout **a** the coasts of Israel, 3605
1: 9 called **a** his brethren the king's sons, and 3605
1: 9 and **a** the men of Judah the king's servants: 3605
1:19 hath called **a** the sons of the king, and 3605
1:20 O king, the eyes of **a** Israel *are* upon thee, 3605
1:25 hath called **a** the king's sons, and 3605
1:29 that hath redeemed my soul out of **a** 3605
1:39 **a** the people said, God save king Solomon. 3605
1:40 **a** the people came up after him, and 3605
1:41 **a** the guests that *were* with him heard *it* as 3605
1:49 **a** the guests that *were* with Adonijah were 3605
2: 2 I go the way of **a** the earth: be thou strong 3605
2: 3 that thou mayest prosper *in* **a** that thou 3605
2: 4 to walk before me in truth with **a** their heart 3605
2: 4 with all their heart and with **a** their soul, 3605
2:15 *that* **a** Israel set their faces on me, that *I* 3605
2:26 thou hast been afflicted in **a** wherein my 3605
2:44 Thou knowest **a** the wickedness which 3605
3:13 among the kings like unto thee **a** thy days. 3605
3:15 and made a feast to **a** his servants. 3605
3:28 **a** Israel heard of the judgment which 3605
4: 1 So king Solomon was king over **a** Israel. 3605
4: 7 Solomon had twelve officers over **a** Israel, 3605
4:10 and **a** the land of Hepher: 3605
4:11 son of Abinadab, *in* **a** the region of Dor; 3605
4:12 and Megiddo, and **a** Beth-shean, 3605
4:21 Solomon reigned over **a** kingdoms from 3605

1Ki 4:21 and served Solomon **a** the days of his life. 3605
4:24 For he had dominion over **a** *the region* on 3605
4:24 over **a** the kings on *this* side the river: 3605
4:24 he had peace on **a** sides round about him. 3605
4:25 even to Beer-sheba, **a** the days of Solomon. 3605
4:27 for **a** that came unto king Solomon's table, 3605
4:30 of **a** the children of the east country, 3605
4:30 east country, and **a** the wisdom of Egypt. 3605
4:31 For he was wiser than **a** men; than Ethan 3605
4:31 and his fame was in **a** nations round about. 3605
4:34 there came of **a** people to hear the wisdom 3605
4:34 from **a** kings of the earth, which had heard 3605
5: 6 according to **a** that thou shalt appoint: 3605
5: 8 I will do **a** thy desire concerning timber of 3605
5:10 and fir trees *according to* **a** his desire. 3605
5:13 king Solomon raised a levy out of **a** Israel; 3605
6:10 *then* he built chambers against **a** the house, 3605
6:12 keep **a** my commandments to walk in them; 3605
6:18 **a** *was* cedar; there was no stone seen. 3605
6:22 with gold, until *he* had finished **a** the house: 3605
6:29 he carved **a** the walls of the house round 3605
6:38 was the house finished throughout **a** 3605
6:38 and according to **a** the fashion of it. 3605
7: 1 thirteen years, and he finished **a** his house. 3605
7: 5 **a** the doors and posts *were* square, *with* 3605
7: 9 **A** these *were of* costly stones, according to 3605
7:14 and cunning to work **a** works in brass. 3605
7:14 to king Solomon, and wrought **a** his work. 3605
7:23 *it was* round **a about**, and his height *was* 5439
7:25 and **a** their hinder parts *were* inward. 3605
7:33 and their spokes, *were* **a** molten. 3605
7:37 **a** of them had one casting, one measure, 3605
7:40 So Hiram made an end of doing **a** the work 3605
7:45 **a** these vessels, which Hiram made to king 3605
7:47 Solomon left **a** the vessels *unweighed,* 3605
7:48 Solomon made **a** the vessels that *pertained* 3605
7:51 So was ended **a** the work that king 3605
8: 1 of Israel, and **a** the heads of the tribes, 3605
8: 2 **a** the men of Israel assembled themselves 3605
8: 3 **a** the elders of Israel came, and the priests 3605
8: 4 **a** the holy vessels that *were* in 3605
8: 5 and **a** the congregation of Israel, 3605
8:14 and blessed **a** the congregation of Israel: 3605
8:14 (and **a** the congregation of Israel stood;) 3605
8:16 I chose no city out of **a** the tribes of Israel 3605
8:22 the presence of **a** the congregation of Israel, 3605
8:23 that walk before thee with **a** their heart: 3605
8:38 *made* by any man, *or* by **a** thy people Israel, 3605
8:39 knowest the hearts of **a** the children of 3605
8:40 That they may fear thee **a** the days that they 3605
8:43 do according to **a** that the stranger calleth 3605
8:43 that **a** people of the earth may know thy 3605
8:48 *so* return unto thee with **a** their heart, and 3605
8:48 with **a** their soul, in the land of their 3605
8:50 **a** their transgressions wherein they have 3605
8:52 to hearken unto them in **a** that they call for 3605
8:53 For thou didst separate them from among **a** 3605
8:54 had made an end of praying **a** this prayer 3605
8:55 blessed **a** the congregation of Israel *with* **a** 3605
8:56 according to **a** that he promised: 3605
8:56 there hath not failed one word of **a** his good 3605
8:58 to walk in **a** his ways, and to keep his 3605
8:59 his people Israel **at a times**, 3117+3117+871.1
8:60 That **a** the people of the earth may know 3605
8:62 the king, and **a** Israel with him, 3605
8:63 **a** the children of Israel dedicated the house 3605
8:65 and **a** Israel with him, a great congregation, 3605
8:66 glad of heart for **a** the goodness that 3605
9: 1 **a** Solomon's desire which he was pleased 3605
9: 4 to do according to **a** that I have 3605
9: 6 *But* if you shall **at a turn** from following 7725
9: 7 a proverb and a byword among **a** people: 3605
9: 9 hath the LORD brought upon them **a** this 3605
9:11 and with gold, according to **a** his desire,) 3605
9:19 **a** the cities of store that Solomon had, 3605
9:19 and in **a** the land of his dominion. 3605
9:20 *And* **a** the people that were left of 3605
10: 2 she communed with him of **a** that was in 3605
10: 3 Solomon told her **a** her questions: there was 3605
10: 4 when the queen of Sheba had seen **a** 3605
10:13 gave unto the queen of Sheba **a** her desire, 3605
10:15 *of* **a** the kings of Arabia, and *of* 3605
10:21 **a** king Solomon's drinking vessels *were of* 3605
10:21 **a** the vessels of the house of the forest of 3605
10:23 So king Solomon exceeded **a** the kings of 3605
10:24 **a** the earth sought to Solomon, to hear his 3605
10:29 so for **a** the kings of the Hittites, and for 3605
11: 8 And likewise did he for **a** his strange wives, 3605
11:13 Howbeit I will not rend away **a** 3605
11:16 months did Joab remain there with **a** Israel, 3605
11:25 he was an adversary to Israel **a** the days of 3605
11:28 he made him ruler over **a** the charge of 3605
11:32 the city which I have chosen out of **a** 3605
11:34 I will make him prince **a** the days of his life 3605
11:37 thou shalt reign according to **a** that thy soul 3605
11:38 if thou wilt hearken unto **a** that I command 3605
11:41 and **a** that he did, and his wisdom, 3605
11:42 in Jerusalem over **a** Israel *was* forty years. 3605
12: 1 for **a** Israel were come *to* Shechem to make 3605
12: 3 and **a** the congregation of Israel came, 3605
12:12 **a** the people came to Rehoboam the third 3605
12:16 So when **a** Israel saw that the king 3605
12:18 **a** Israel stoned him with stones, that he 3605
12:20 when **a** Israel heard that Jeroboam was 3605
12:20 and made him king over **a** Israel: 3605
12:21 he assembled **a** the house of Judah, with 3605
12:23 unto **a** the house of Judah and Benjamin, 3605
13:11 told him **a** the works that the man of God 3605
13:32 against **a** the houses of the high places 3605
14: 8 and who followed me with **a** his heart, 3605
14: 9 hast done evil above **a** that were before 3605
14:10 *a man* taketh away dung, till it be **a gone**. 8552
14:13 **a** Israel shall mourn for him, and bury him: 3605
14:18 **a** Israel mourned for him, according to 3605
14:21 did choose out of **a** the tribes of Israel, 3605
1Ki 14:22 above **a** that their fathers had done. 3605
14:24 they did according to **a** the abominations of 3605
14:26 of the king's house; he even took away **a**: 3605
14:26 he took away **a** the shields of gold which 3605
14:29 of the acts of Rehoboam, and **a** that he did, 3605
14:30 and Jeroboam **a** *their* days. 3605
15: 3 he walked in **a** the sins of his father, 3605
15: 5 he commanded him **a** the days of his life, 3605
15: 6 and Jeroboam **a** the days of his life. 3605
15: 7 rest of the acts of Abijam, and **a** that he did, 3605
15:12 removed **a** the idols that his fathers had 3605
15:14 was perfect with the LORD **a** his days. 3605
15:16 and Baasha king of Israel **a** their days. 3605
15:18 Asa took **a** the silver and the gold that were 3605
15:20 and Abel-beth-maachah, and **a** Cinneroth, 3605
15:20 all Cinneroth, with **a** the land of Naphtali. 3605
15:22 made a proclamation **throughout a** Judah; 3605
15:23 The rest of **a** the acts of Asa, and all his 3605
15:23 **a** his might, and all that he did, and 3605
15:23 **a** that he did, and the cities which he built, 3605
15:27 and **a** Israel laid siege to Gibbethon. 3605
15:29 *that* he smote **a** the house of Jeroboam; 3605
15:31 rest of the acts of Nadab, and **a** that he did, 3605
15:32 and Baasha king of Israel **a** their days. 3605
15:33 of Ahijah to reign over **a** Israel in Tirzah, 3605
16: 7 even for **a** the evil that he did in the sight of 3605
16:11 *that* he slew **a** the house of Baasha: 3605
16:12 Thus did Zimri destroy **a** the house of 3605
16:13 For **a** the sins of Baasha, and the sins of 3605
16:14 rest of the acts of Elah, and **a** that he did, 3605
16:16 wherefore **a** Israel made Omri, the captain 3605
16:17 **a** Israel with him, and they besieged Tirzah. 3605
16:25 and did worse than **a** that *were* before him. 3605
16:26 For he walked in **a** the way of Jeroboam 3605
16:30 the LORD above **a** that *were* before him. 3605
16:33 **a** the kings of Israel that were before him. 3605
18: 5 unto **a** fountains of water, and unto all 3605
18: 5 all fountains of water, and unto **a** brooks: 3605
18: 5 mules alive, that we leese not **a** the beasts. 4480
18:19 gather to me **a** Israel unto mount Carmel, 3605
18:20 So Ahab sent unto **a** the children of Israel, 3605
18:21 Elijah came unto **a** the people, and said, 3605
18:24 **a** the people answered and said, It is well 3605
18:30 Elijah said unto **a** the people, Come near 3605
18:30 **a** the people came near unto him. And he 3605
18:36 *that* I have done **a** these things at thy word. 3605
18:39 when **a** the people saw *it*, they fell on their 3605
19: 1 Ahab told Jezebel **a** that Elijah had done, 3605
19: 1 withal how he had slain **a** the prophets with 3605
19:18 **a** the knees which have not bowed unto 3605
20: 1 Ben-hadad the king of Syria gathered **a** his 3605
20: 4 to thy saying, I *am* thine, and **a** that I have. 3605
20: 7 the king of Israel called **a** the elders of 3605
20: 8 **a** the elders and all the people said unto 3605
20: 8 the elders and **a** the people said unto him, 3605
20: 9 **A** that thou didst send for to thy servant at 3605
20:10 handfuls for **a** the people that follow me. 3605
20:13 Hast thou seen **a** this great multitude? 3605
20:15 after them he numbered **a** the people, 3605
20:15 *even* **a** the children of Israel, *being* seven 3605
20:27 and were **a** present, and went against them: NIH
20:28 will I deliver **a** this great multitude into 3605
21:26 according to **a** *things* as did the Amorites, 3605
22:10 and **a** the prophets prophesied before them. 3605
22:12 **a** the prophets prophesied so, saying, Go up 3605
22:17 I saw **a** Israel scattered upon the hills, 3605
22:19 **a** the host of heaven standing by him on his 3605
22:22 I will be a lying spirit in the mouth of **a** his 3605
22:23 spirit in the mouth of **a** these thy prophets, 3605
22:28 If thou **return at a** in peace, 7725+7725
22:39 **a** that he did, and the ivory house which he 3605
22:39 he made, and **a** the cities that he built, 3605
22:43 he walked in **a** the ways of Asa his father; 3605
22:53 according unto **a** that his father had done. 3605
2Ki 3: 6 the same time, and numbered **a** Israel. 3605
3:19 stop **a** wells of water, and mar every good 3605
3:21 when **a** the Moabites heard that the kings 3605
3:21 they gathered **a** that *were able to* put on 3605
3:25 they stopped **a** the wells of water, and 3605
3:25 wells of water, and felled **a** the good trees: 3605
4: 3 borrow thee vessels abroad of **a** thy 3605
4: 4 shalt pour out into **a** those vessels, and 3605
4:13 thou hast been careful for us with **a** this 3605
5:12 better than **a** the waters of Israel? 3605
5:15 he and **a** his company, and came, and 3605
5:15 now I know that *there is* no God in **a** 3605
5:21 the chariot to meet him, and said, *Is* **a** well? NIH
5:22 he said, **A** *is* well. My master hath sent me, NIH
6:24 that Ben-hadad king of Syria gathered **a** his 3605
7:13 they *are* as **a** the multitude of Israel that are 3605
7:13 *I say,* they *are even* as **a** the multitude of 3605
7:15 **a** the way *was* full *of* garments and vessels, 3605
8: 4 **a** the great *things* that Elisha hath done. 3605
8: 6 Restore **a** that *was* hers, and all the fruits of 3605
8: 6 **a** the fruits of the field since the day that 3605
8:21 over to Zair, and **a** the chariots with him: 3605
8:23 rest of the acts of Joram, and **a** that he did, 3605
9: 5 Jehu said, Unto which of **a** us? And he said, 3605
9: 7 the blood of **a** the servants of the LORD, 3605
9:11 *one* said unto him, *Is* **a** well? NIH
9:14 he and **a** Israel, because of Hazael king of 3605
10: 5 and will do **a** that thou shalt bid us; 3605
10: 9 stood, and said to **a** the people, Ye *be* 3605
10: 9 and slew him: but who slew **a** these? 3605
10:11 So Jehu slew **a** that remained of the house 3605
10:11 **a** his great *men*, and his kinsfolks, and 3605
10:17 he slew **a** that remained unto Ahab in 3605
10:18 Jehu gathered **a** the people together, and 3605
10:19 call unto me **a** the prophets of Baal, 3605
10:19 of Baal, **a** his servants, and all his priests; 3605
10:19 of Baal, all his servants, and **a** his priests; 3605
10:21 Jehu sent through **a** Israel: and all 3605
10:21 **a** the worshippers of Baal came, so 3605
10:22 Bring forth vestments for **a** the worshippers 3605
10:30 Ahab according to **a** that *was* in mine heart, 3605
2Ki 10:31 the LORD God of Israel with **a** his heart: 3605
10:32 Hazael smote them in **a** the coasts of Israel; 3605
10:33 **a** the land of Gilead, the Gadites, and 3605
10:34 of Jehu, and **a** that he did, and all his might, 3605
10:34 of Jehu, and all that he did, and **a** his might, 3605
11: 1 she arose and destroyed **a** the seed royal. 3605
11: 7 two parts of **a** you that go forth on 3605
11: 9 **a** *things* that Jehoiada the priest 3605
11:14 **a** the people of the land rejoiced, and 3605
11:18 **a** the people of the land went *into* the house 3605
11:19 and the guard, and **a** the people of the land; 3605
11:20 **a** the people of the land rejoiced, and 3605
12: 2 **a** his days where*in* Jehoiada the priest 3605
12: 4 **A** the money of the dedicated *things* that is 3605
12: 4 **a** the money that cometh into any man's 3605
12: 9 the priests that kept the door put therein **a** 3605
12:12 for **a** that was laid out for the house to 3605
12:18 Jehoash king of Judah took **a** the hallowed 3605
12:18 **a** the gold that was found in the treasures of 3605
12:19 rest of the acts of Joash, and **a** that he did, 3605
13: 3 Ben-hadad the son of Hazael, **a** *their* days. 3605
13: 8 and **a** that he did, and his might, 3605
13:11 he departed not from **a** the sins of 3605
13:12 **a** that he did, and his might where*with* he 3605
13:22 Hazael king of Syria oppressed Israel **a** 3605
14: 3 he did according to **a** *things* as Joash his 3605
14:14 he took **a** the gold and silver, and all 3605
14:14 **a** the vessels that were found *in* the house 3605
14:21 **a** the people of Judah took Azariah, which 3605
14:24 he departed not from **a** the sins of 3605
14:28 **a** that he did, and his might, how he 3605
15: 3 according to **a** that his father Amaziah had 3605
15: 6 of the acts of Azariah, and **a** that he did, 3605
15:16 **a** that *were* therein, and the coasts thereof 3605
15:16 **a** the women therein that were with child 3605
15:18 he departed not **a** his days from the sins of 3605
15:20 *even* of **a** the mighty *men* of wealth, 3605
15:21 of the acts of Menahem, and **a** that he did, 3605
15:26 acts of Pekahiah, and **a** that he did, behold, 3605
15:29 **a** the land of Naphtali, and carried them 3605
15:31 the acts of Pekah, and **a** that he did, behold, 3605
15:34 he did according to **a** that his father Uzziah 3605
15:36 rest of the acts of Jotham, and **a** that he did, 3605
16:10 according to **a** the workmanship thereof. 3605
16:11 the priest built an altar according to **a** 3605
16:15 with the burnt offering of **a** the people of 3605
16:15 sprinkle upon it **a** the blood of the burnt 3605
16:15 and **a** the blood of the sacrifice: 3605
16:16 according to **a** that king Ahaz commanded. 3605
17: 5 the king of Assyria came up throughout **a** 3605
17: 9 they built them high places in **a** their cities, 3605
17:11 there they burnt incense in **a** the high 3605
17:13 by **a** the prophets, *and by* all the seers, 3605
17:13 all the prophets, *and by* **a** the seers, saying, 3605
17:13 according to **a** the law which I commanded 3605
17:16 they left **a** the commandments of 3605
17:16 worshipped **a** the host of heaven, and 3605
17:20 the LORD rejected **a** the seed of Israel, 3605
17:22 For the children of Israel walked in **a** 3605
17:23 as he had said by **a** his servants 3605
17:39 he shall deliver you out of the hand of **a** 3605
18: 3 according to **a** that David his father did. 3605
18: 5 that after him was none like him among **a** 3605
18:12 **a** that Moses the servant of the LORD 3605
18:13 up against **a** the fenced cities of Judah, 3605
18:15 Hezekiah gave *him* **a** the silver that was 3605
18:21 *is* Pharaoh king of Egypt unto **a** that trust 3605
18:33 **delivered at a** his land out of 5337+5337
18:35 Who *are they* among **a** the gods of 3605
19: 4 It may be the LORD thy God will hear **a** 3605
19:11 the kings of Assyria have done to **a** lands, 3605
19:15 thou alone, of **a** the kingdoms of the earth; 3605
19:19 that **a** the kingdoms of the earth may know 3605
19:24 with the sole of my feet have I dried up **a** 3605
19:35 behold, they *were* **a** dead corpses. 3605
20:13 shewed them **a** the house of his precious 3605
20:13 **a** the house of his armour, and all that was 3605
20:13 and **a** that was found in his treasures: 3605
20:13 nothing in his house, nor in **a** his dominion, 3605
20:15 **A** *the things* that *are* in mine house have 3605
20:17 that **a** that *is* in thine house, and *that* which 3605
20:20 **a** his might, and how he made a pool, and 3605
21: 3 worshipped **a** the host of heaven, and 3605
21: 5 he built altars for **a** the host of heaven in 3605
21: 7 which I have chosen out of **a** tribes of 3605
21: 8 to **a** that I have commanded them, 3605
21: 8 according to **a** the law that my servant 3605
21:11 hath done wickedly above **a** that 3605
21:14 a prey and a spoil to **a** their enemies; 3605
21:17 and **a** that he did, and his sin that he sinned, 3605
21:21 he walked in **a** the way that his father 3605
21:24 the people of the land slew **a** them that had 3605
22: 2 walked in **a** the way of David his father, 3605
22:13 for me, and for the people, and for **a** Judah, 3605
22:13 to do according unto **a** that which is written 3605
22:16 *even* **a** the words of the book which 3605
22:17 that they might provoke me to anger with **a** 3605
22:20 thine eyes shall not see **a** the evil which I 3605
23: 1 they gathered unto him **a** the elders of 3605
23: 2 **a** the men of Judah and all the inhabitants 3605
23: 2 **a** the inhabitants of Jerusalem with him, 3605
23: 2 and **a** the people, both small and great: 3605
23: 2 he read in their ears **a** the words of 3605
23: 3 his statutes with **a** *their* heart and all *their* 3605
23: 3 statutes with all *their* heart and **a** *their* soul, 3605
23: 3 And **a** the people stood to the covenant. 3605
23: 4 **a** the vessels that were made for Baal, 3605
23: 4 for the grove, and for **a** the host of heaven: 3605
23: 5 to the planets, and to **a** the host of heaven. 3605
23: 8 he brought **a** the priests out of the cities of 3605
23:19 **a** the houses also of the high places that 3605
23:19 did to them according to **a** the acts that he 3605
23:20 he slew **a** the priests of the high places that 3605
23:21 the king commanded **a** the people, saying, 3605
23:22 nor *in* **a** the days of the kings of Israel, 3605

2Ki 23:24 **a** the abominations that were spied in 3605
23:25 that turned to the LORD with **a** his heart, 3605
23:25 with **a** his soul, and with all his might, 3605
23:25 with all his soul, and with **a** his might, 3605
23:25 his might, according to **a** the law of Moses; 3605
23:26 of **a** the provocations that Manasseh had 3605
23:28 rest of the acts of Josiah, and **a** that he did, 3605
23:32 according to **a** that his fathers had done. 3605
23:37 according to **a** that his fathers had done. 3605
24: 3 of Manasseh, according to **a** that he did; 3605
24: 5 of the acts of Jehoiakim, and **a** that he did, 3605
24: 7 **a** that pertained to the king of Egypt. 3605
24: 9 according to **a** that his father had done. 3605
24:13 he carried out thence **a** the treasures of 3605
24:13 cut in pieces **a** the vessels of gold which 3605
24:14 he carried away **a** Jerusalem, and all 3605
24:14 **a** the princes, and all the mighty *men* of 3605
24:14 and **a** the mighty *men* of valour, 3605
24:14 and **a** the craftsmen and smiths: 3605
24:16 **a** the men of might, *even* seven thousand, 3605
24:16 **a** *that were* strong *and* apt for war, 3605
24:19 according to **a** that Jehoiakim had done. 3605
25: 1 he, and **a** his host, against Jerusalem, and 3605
25: 4 **a** the men of war *fled* by night *by* the way 3605
25: 5 and **a** his army were scattered from him. 3605
25: 9 **a** the houses of Jerusalem, and every great 3605
25:10 **a** the army of the Chaldees, that *were with* 3605
25:14 **a** the vessels of brass wherewith they 3605
25:16 the brass of **a** these vessels was without 3605
25:17 upon the chapiter round about, **a** *of* brass: 3605
25:23 And when **a** the captains of the armies, they 3605
25:26 **a** the people, both small and great, and 3605
25:29 he did eat bread continually before him **a** 3605
25:30 rate for every day, **a** the days of his life. 3605
1Ch 1:23 and Jobab. **A** these *were* the sons of Joktan. 3605
1:33 Eldaah. **A** these *are* the sons of Keturah. 3605
2: 4 and Zerah. **A** the sons of Judah *were* five. 3605
2: 6 and Calcol, and Dara: five of them in **a**. 3605
2:23 **A** these *belonged to* the sons of Machir 3605
3: 9 *These were* **a** the sons of David, beside 3605
4:27 neither did **a** their family multiply, like to 3605
4:33 **a** their villages that *were* round about 3605
5:10 they dwelt in their tents throughout **a** 3605
5:16 her towns, and in **a** the suburbs of Sharon, 3605
5:17 **A** these were reckoned by genealogies in 3605
5:20 into their hand, and **a** that *were* with them: 3605
6:48 **a** *manner of* service of the tabernacle of 3605
6:49 *were appointed* for **a** the work of the *place* 3605
6:49 according to **a** that Moses the servant of 3605
6:60 **A** their cities throughout their families *were* 3605
7: 3 and Joel, Ishiah, five: **a** of them chief *men.* 3605
7: 5 their brethren among **a** the families of 3605
7: 5 reckoned in **a** by their genealogies 3605
7: 8 Alameth. **A** these *are* the sons of Becher. 3605
7:11 **A** these the sons of Jediael, by the heads of 3605
7:40 **A** these *were* the children of Asher, 3605
8:38 and Hanan. **A** these *were* the sons of Azel. 3605
8:40 fifty. **A** these *are* of the sons of Benjamin. 3605
9: 1 So **a** Israel were reckoned by genealogies; 3605
9: 9 **A** these men *were* chief of the fathers in 3605
9:22 **A** these which were chosen to be porters in 3605
9:29 **a** the instruments of the sanctuary, and 3605
10: 6 three sons, and **a** his house died together. 3605
10: 7 when **a** the men of Israel that *were* in 3605
10:11 when **a** Jabesh-gilead heard all that 3605
10:11 when all Jabesh-gilead heard **a** that 3605
10:12 **a** the valiant men, and took away the body 3605
11: 1 **a** Israel gathered themselves to David unto 3605
11: 3 Therefore came **a** the elders of Israel to 3605
11: 4 David and **a** Israel went *to* Jerusalem, 3605
11:10 *and* with **a** Israel, to make him king, 3605
12:15 when it had overflown **a** his banks; 3605
12:15 they put to flight **a** *them of* the valleys, 3605
12:21 for they *were* **a** mighty *men* of valour, 3605
12:32 **a** their brethren *were* at their 3605
12:33 expert in war, with **a** instruments of war, 3605
12:37 with **a** *manner of* instruments of war for 3605
12:38 **A** these men of war, that could keep rank, 3605
12:38 to make David king over **a** Israel: 3605
12:38 **a** the rest also of Israel *were of* one heart to 3605
13: 2 David said unto **a** the congregation of 3605
13: 2 that are left in **a** the land of Israel, and 3605
13: 4 **a** the congregation said that *they* would do 3605
13: 4 for the thing was right in the eyes of **a** 3605
13: 5 So David gathered **a** Israel together, 3605
13: 6 And David went up, and **a** Israel, to Baalah, 3605
13: 8 **a** Israel played before God with all *their* 3605
13: 8 all Israel played before God with **a** *their* 3605
13:14 the house of Obed-edom, and **a** that he had. 3605
14: 8 that David was anointed king over **a** Israel, 3605
14: 8 **a** the Philistines went up to seek David. 3605
14:17 the fame of David went out into **a** lands; 3605
14:17 the LORD brought the fear of him upon **a** 3605
15: 3 David gathered **a** Israel together to 3605
15:27 **a** the Levites that bare the ark, and 3605
15:28 Thus **a** Israel brought up the ark of 3605
16: 9 talk you of **a** his wondrous works. 3605
16:14 our God; his judgments *are* in **a** the earth. 3605
16:23 Sing unto the LORD, **a** the earth; 3605
16:24 his marvellous works among **a** nations. 3605
16:25 he also *is* to be feared above **a** gods. 3605
16:26 For **a** the gods of the people *are* idols: but 3605
16:30 Fear before him, **a** the earth: the world also 3605
16:32 let the fields rejoice, and **a** that *is* therein. 3605
16:36 **a** the people said, Amen, and praised 3605
16:40 *to do* according to **a** that is written in 3605
16:43 **a** the people departed every man to his 3605
17: 2 said unto David, Do **a** that *is* in thine heart; 3605
17: 6 Wheresoever I have walked with **a** Israel, 3605
17: 8 have cut off **a** thine enemies from before 3605
17:10 Moreover I will subdue **a** thine enemies. 3605
17:15 According to **a** these words, and 3605
17:15 according to **a** this vision, so did Nathan 3605
17:19 own heart, hast thou done **a** this greatness, 3605
17:19 in making known **a** *these* great things. 3605
1Ch 17:20 according to **a** that we have heard with our 3605
18: 4 David also houghed **a** the chariot *horses,* 3605
18: 9 **a** the host of Hadarezer king of Zobah; 3605
18:10 *with him* **a** *manner of* vessels of gold and 3605
18:11 the gold that he brought from **a** *these* 3605
18:13 **a** the Edomites became David's servants. 3605
18:14 So David reigned over **a** Israel, and 3605
18:14 and justice among **a** his people. 3605
19: 8 and **a** the host *of* the mighty *men.* 3605
19:10 he chose out of **a** the choice of Israel, and 3605
19:17 he gathered **a** Israel, and passed over 3605
20: 3 dealt David with **a** the cities of the children 3605
20: 3 and **a** the people returned *to* Jerusalem. 3605
21: 3 the king, *are* they not **a** my lord's servants? 3605
21: 4 went throughout **a** Israel, and came *to* 3605
21: 5 **a** *they of* Israel were a thousand thousand 3605
21:12 destroying throughout **a** the coasts of Israel. 3605
21:23 the wheat for the meat offering; I give *it* **a**. 3605
22: 5 and of glory throughout **a** countries: 3605
22: 9 I will give him rest from **a** his enemies 3605
22:15 **a** *manner of* cunning *men* for every *manner* 3605
22:17 David also commanded **a** the princes of 3605
23: 2 he gathered together **a** the princes of Israel, 3605
23:28 in the purifying of **a** holy *things,* and 3605
23:29 and for **a** *manner of* measure and size; 3605
23:31 to offer **a** burnt sacrifices unto the LORD 3605
25: 5 **A** these *were* the sons of Heman the king's 3605
25: 6 **A** these *were* under the hands of their father 3605
25: 7 *even* **a** that were cunning, was two hundred 3605
26: 8 **A** these of the sons of Obed-edom: they 3605
26:11 **a** the sons and brethren of Hosah *were* 3605
26:26 his brethren *were* over **a** the treasures of 3605
26:28 **a** that Samuel the seer, and Saul the son of 3605
26:30 westward in **a** the business of the LORD, 3605
27: 1 went out month by month throughout **a** 3605
27: 3 Of the children of Perez *was* the chief of **a** 3605
27:31 **A** these *were* the rulers of the substance 3605
28: 1 David assembled **a** the princes of Israel, 3605
28: 1 the stewards over **a** the substance and 3605
28: 1 mighty *men,* and with **a** the valiant men, 3605
28: 4 **a** the house of my father to be king over 3605
28: 4 he liked me to make *me* king over **a** Israel: 3605
28: 5 of **a** my sons, (for the LORD hath given 3605
28: 8 in the sight of **a** Israel the congregation of 3605
28: 8 seek for **a** the commandments of 3605
28: 9 for the LORD searcheth **a** hearts, and 3605
28: 9 understandeth **a** the imaginations of 3605
28:12 the pattern of **a** that he had by the spirit, 3605
28:12 of **a** the chambers round about, of 3605
28:13 for **a** the work of the service of the house of 3605
28:13 for **a** the vessels of service in the house of 3605
28:14 for **a** instruments of all manner of service; 3605
28:14 of **a manner of service**; 5656+5656+2050.1
28:14 *silver also* for **a** instruments of silver by 3605
28:14 for **a** instruments of every kind of service: 3605
28:19 **A** *this, said David,* the LORD made me 3605
28:19 upon me, *even* **a** the works of *this* pattern. 3605
28:20 until *thou* hast finished **a** the work for 3605
28:21 *even they shall be with thee* for **a** 3605
28:21 *there shall be* with thee for **a** *manner of* 3605
28:21 **a** the people *will be* wholly at thy 3605
29: 1 Furthermore David the king said unto **a** 3605
29: 2 Now I have prepared with **a** my might for 3605
29: 2 **a** *manner of* precious stones, and 3605
29: 3 above **a** *that* I have prepared for the holy 3605
29: 5 for **a** *manner of* work *to be made* by 3605
29:10 the LORD before **a** the congregation: 3605
29:11 for **a** *that is* in the heaven and in the earth *is* 3605
29:11 and *thou* art exalted as head above **a**. 3605
29:12 *come* of thee, and thou reignest over **a**; 3605
29:12 to make great, and to give strength unto **a**. 3605
29:14 willingly after this *sort?* for **a** *things come* 3605
29:15 and sojourners, as *were* **a** our fathers: 3605
29:16 **a** this store that we have prepared to build 3605
29:16 *cometh* of thine hand, and *is* **a** thine own. 3605
29:17 I have willingly offered **a** these *things:* 3605
29:19 to do **a** *these things,* and to build the palace, 3605
29:20 David said to **a** the congregation, 3605
29:20 **a** the congregation blessed the LORD God 3605
29:21 and sacrifices in abundance for **a** Israel: 3605
29:23 and prospered; and **a** Israel obeyed him. 3605
29:24 And **a** the princes, and the mighty *men,* and 3605
29:24 and **a** the sons likewise of king David, 3605
29:25 exceedingly in the sight of **a** Israel, 3605
29:26 Thus David the son of Jesse reigned over **a** 3605
29:30 With **a** his reign and his might, and 3605
29:30 and over **a** the kingdoms of the countries. 3605
2Ch 1: 2 Solomon spake unto **a** Israel, to 3605
1: 2 and to every governor in **a** Israel, 3605
1: 3 and **a** the congregation with him, 3605
1:17 brought they out *horses* for **a** the kings of 3605
2: 5 *is* great: for great *is* our God above **a** gods. 3605
2:17 Solomon numbered **a** the strangers that 3605
4: 4 and **a** their hinder parts *were* inward. 3605
4:16 and the fleshhooks, and **a** their instruments, 3605
4:18 Thus Solomon made **a** these vessels in 3605
4:19 Solomon made **a** the vessels that *were for* 3605
5: 1 Thus **a** the work that Solomon made for 3605
5: 1 Solomon brought in ***a*** *the things* that David NIH
5: 1 and the gold, and **a** the instruments, 3605
5: 2 of Israel, and **a** the heads of the tribes, 3605
5: 3 Wherefore **a** the men of Israel assembled 3605
5: 4 **a** the elders of Israel came; and the Levites 3605
5: 5 **a** the holy vessels that *were* in 3605
5: 6 **a** the congregation of Israel that were 3605
5:11 **a** the priests that were present were 3605
5:12 **a** of them of Asaph, of Heman, 3605
6: 3 and **a** the congregation of Israel stood. 3605
6: 5 **a** the tribes of Israel to build a house *in,* 3605
6:12 the presence of **a** the congregation of Israel, 3605
6:13 kneeled *down* upon his knees before **a** 3605
6:14 that walk before thee with **a** their hearts: 3605
6:29 or of **a** thy people Israel, when every one 3605
6:30 render unto every man according unto **a** his 3605
6:33 do according to **a** that the stranger calleth 3605
2Ch 6:33 that **a** people of the earth may know thy 3605
6:38 If they return to thee with **a** their heart and 3605
6:38 with **a** their soul in the land of their 3605
7: 3 when **a** the children of Israel saw how 3605
7: 4 **a** the people offered sacrifices before 3605
7: 5 **a** the people dedicated the house of God. 3605
7: 6 trumpets before them, and **a** Israel stood. 3605
7: 8 **a** Israel with him, a very great 3605
7:11 **a** that came into Solomon's heart to make 3605
7:17 do according to **a** that I have commanded 3605
7:20 a proverb and a byword among **a** nations. 3605
7:22 hath he brought **a** this evil upon them. 3605
8: 4 **a** the store cities, which he built in Hamath. 3605
8: 6 **a** the store cities that Solomon had, and all 3605
8: 6 **a** the chariot cities, and the cities of 3605
8: 6 **a** that Solomon desired to build in 3605
8: 6 and throughout **a** the land of his dominion. 3605
8: 7 *As for* **a** the people that were left of 3605
8:16 Now **a** the work of Solomon was prepared 3605
9: 1 she communed with him of **a** that was in 3605
9: 2 Solomon told her **a** her questions: and 3605
9:12 king Solomon gave to the queen of Sheba **a** 3605
9:14 **a** the kings of Arabia and governors of 3605
9:20 **a** the drinking vessels of king Solomon 3605
9:20 **a** the vessels of the house of the forest of 3605
9:22 king Solomon passed **a** the kings of 3605
9:23 **a** the kings of the earth sought the presence 3605
9:26 he reigned over **a** the kings from the river 3605
9:28 horses out of Egypt, and out of **a** lands. 3605
9:30 Solomon reigned in Jerusalem over **a** Israel 3605
10: 1 for *to* Shechem were **a** Israel come to make 3605
10: 3 So Jeroboam and **a** Israel came and 3605
10:12 **a** the people came to Rehoboam on 3605
10:16 when **a** Israel saw that the king would not 3605
10:16 own house. So **a** Israel went to their tents. 3605
11: 3 to **a** Israel in Judah and Benjamin, saying, 3605
11:13 the Levites that *were* in **a** Israel resorted to 3605
11:13 Israel resorted to him out of **a** their coasts. 3605
11:16 after them out of **a** the tribes of Israel such 3605
11:21 the daughter of Absalom above **a** his wives 3605
11:23 dispersed of **a** his children throughout all 3605
11:23 dispersed of all his children throughout **a** 3605
12: 1 law of the LORD, and **a** Israel with him. 3605
12: 9 the treasures of the king's house; he took **a**: 3605
12:13 had chosen out of **a** the tribes of Israel, 3605
13: 4 said, Hear me, *thou* Jeroboam, and **a** Israel; 3605
13:15 and **a** Israel before Abijah and Judah. 3605
14: 5 Also he took away out of **a** the cities of 3605
14: 8 **a** these *were* mighty *men* of valour. 3605
14:14 they smote **a** the cities round about Gerar; 3605
14:14 they spoiled **a** the cities; for there was 3605
15: 2 ye me, Asa, and **a** Judah and Benjamin; 3605
15: 5 great vexations *were* upon **a** the inhabitants 3605
15: 6 for God did vex them with **a** adversity. 3605
15: 8 put away the abominable idols out of **a** 3605
15: 9 he gathered **a** Judah and Benjamin, and 3605
15:12 God of their fathers with **a** their heart 3605
15:12 with all their heart and with **a** their soul; 3605
15:15 **a** Judah rejoiced at the oath: for they had 3605
15:15 for they had sworn with **a** their heart, and 3605
15:17 nevertheless the heart of Asa was perfect **a** 3605
16: 4 and **a** the store cities of Naphtali. 3605
16: 6 Asa the king took **a** Judah; and they carried 3605
17: 2 he placed forces in **a** the fenced cities of 3605
17: 5 **a** Judah brought to Jehoshaphat presents; 3605
17: 9 went about throughout **a** the cities of Judah, 3605
17:10 the fear of the LORD fell upon **a** 3605
17:19 put in the fenced cities throughout **a** Judah. 3605
18: 9 and **a** the prophets prophesied before them. 3605
18:11 **a** the prophets prophesied so, saying, Go up 3605
18:16 I did see **a** Israel scattered upon 3605
18:18 **a** the host of heaven standing on his right 3605
18:21 be a lying spirit in the mouth of **a** his 3605
18:27 by me. And he said, Hearken, **a** ye people. 3605
19: 5 he set judges in the land throughout **a** 3605
19:11 Amariah the chief priest *is* over you in **a** 3605
19:11 the house of Judah, for **a** the king's matters: 3605
20: 3 and proclaimed a fast throughout **a** Judah. 3605
20: 4 even out of **a** the cities of Judah they came 3605
20: 6 rulest *not* thou over **a** the kingdoms of 3605
20:13 **a** Judah stood before the LORD, 3605
20:15 **a** Judah, and ye inhabitants of Jerusalem, 3605
20:18 **a** Judah and the inhabitants of Jerusalem 3605
20:29 the fear of God was on **a** the kingdoms of 3605
21: 2 **a** these *were* the sons of Jehoshaphat king 3605
21: 4 slew **a** his brethren with the sword, and 3605
21: 9 his princes, and **a** *his* chariots with him: 3605
21:14 and thy wives, and **a** thy goods: 3605
21:17 carried away **a** the substance that was 3605
21:18 after **a** this the LORD smote him in his 3605
22: 1 Arabians to the camp had slain **a** the eldest. 3605
22: 9 who sought the LORD with **a** his heart. 3605
22:10 destroyed **a** the seed royal of the house of 3605
23: 2 gathered the Levites out of **a** the cities of 3605
23: 3 **a** the congregation made a covenant with 3605
23: 5 **a** the people *shall be* in the courts of 3605
23: 6 **a** the people shall keep the watch of 3605
23: 8 **a** Judah did according to all *things* that 3605
23: 8 all Judah did according to **a** *things* that 3605
23:10 he set **a** the people, every man having his 3605
23:13 **a** the people of the land rejoiced, and 3605
23:16 between **a** the people, and between 3605
23:17 **a** the people went *to* the house of Baal, 3605
23:20 **a** the people of the land, and brought down 3605
23:21 **a** the people of the land rejoiced: and 3605
24: 2 LORD **a** the days of Jehoiada the priest. 3605
24: 5 gather of **a** Israel money to repair the house 3605
24: 7 also **a** the dedicate *things* of the house of 3605
24:10 **a** the princes and all the people rejoiced, 3605
24:10 all the princes and **a** the people rejoiced, 3605
24:14 LORD continually **a** the days of Jehoiada. 3605
24:23 destroyed **a** the princes of the people from 3605
24:23 sent **a** the spoil of them unto the king of 3605
25: 5 throughout **a** Judah and Benjamin: 3605
25: 7 *to wit, with* **a** the children of Ephraim. 3605

2Ch 25:12 the rock, that they a were broken in pieces. 3605
25:24 he took a the gold and the silver, and all 3605
25:24 a the vessels that were found in the house 3605
26: 1 a the people of Judah took Uzziah, who 3605
26: 4 according to a that his father Amaziah did. 3605
26:14 Uzziah prepared for them throughout a 3605
26:20 a the priests, looked upon him, and behold, 3605
27: 2 according to a that his father Uzziah did: 3605
27: 7 of Jotham, and a his wars, and his ways, 3605
28: 6 in one day, which were a valiant men; 3605
28:14 before the princes and a the congregation. 3605
28:15 with the spoil clothed a that were naked 3605
28:15 and carried a the feeble of them upon asses, 3605
28:23 they were the ruin of him, and of a Israel. 3605
28:26 Now the rest of his acts and of a his ways, 3605
29: 2 according to a that David his father had 3605
29:16 brought out a the uncleanness that they 3605
29:18 We have cleansed a the house of 3605
29:18 with a the vessels thereof, and 3605
29:18 shewbread table, with a the vessels thereof. 3605
29:19 Moreover a the vessels, which king Ahaz 3605
29:24 the altar, to make an atonement for a Israel: 3605
29:24 the sin offering should be made for a Israel. 3605
29:28 a the congregation worshipped, and 3605
29:28 a this continued until the burnt offering was 3605
29:29 a that were present with him bowed 3605
29:32 a these were for a burnt offering to 3605
29:34 that they could not flay a the burnt 3605
29:36 Hezekiah rejoiced, and a the people, that 3605
30: 1 Hezekiah sent to a Israel and Judah, and 3605
30: 2 and a the congregation in Jerusalem, 3605
30: 4 pleased the king and a the congregation. 3605
30: 5 to make proclamation throughout a Israel, 3605
30: 6 his princes throughout a Israel and Judah, 3605
30:14 a the altars for incense took they away, and 3605
30:22 Hezekiah spake comfortably unto a 3605
30:25 a the congregation of Judah, with 3605
30:25 a the congregation that came out of Israel, 3605
31: 1 Now when a this was finished, all Israel 3605
31: 1 a Israel that were present went out to 3605
31: 1 and the altars out of a Judah and Benjamin, 3605
31: 1 until they had utterly destroyed them a. NIH
31: 1 all. Then a the children of Israel returned, 3605
31: 5 honey, and of a the increase of the field; 3605
31: 5 the tithe of a things brought they in 3605
31:18 to the genealogy of a their little ones, 3605
31:18 their daughters, through a the congregation: 3605
31:19 to give portions to a the males among 3605
31:19 to a that were reckoned by genealogies 3605
31:20 thus did Hezekiah throughout a Judah, and 3605
31:21 he did it with a his heart, and prospered. 3605
32: 4 who stopt a the fountains, and the brook 3605
32: 5 and built up a the wall that was broken, and 3605
32: 7 nor for a the multitude that is with him: 3605
32: 9 against Lachish, and a his power with him,) 3605
32: 9 unto a Judah that were at Jerusalem, 3605
32:13 my fathers have done unto a the people of 3605
32:14 Who was there among a the gods of those 3605
32:21 which cut off a the mighty men of valour, 3605
32:22 from the hand of a other, and guided them 3605
32:23 that he was magnified in the sight of a 3605
32:27 and for a manner of pleasant jewels; 3605
32:28 stalls for a manner of beasts, and cotes for 3605
32:30 And Hezekiah prospered in a his works. 3605
32:31 that he might know a that was in his heart. 3605
32:33 a Judah and the inhabitants of Jerusalem 3605
33: 3 worshipped a the host of heaven, and 3605
33: 5 he built altars for a the host of heaven in 3605
33: 7 which I have chosen before a the tribes of 3605
33: 8 that they will take heed to do a that I have 3605
33:14 put captains of war in a the fenced cities of 3605
33:15 a the altars that he had built in the mount of 3605
33:19 a his sin, and his trespass, and the places 3605
33:22 for Amon sacrificed unto a the carved 3605
33:25 the people of the land slew a them that had 3605
34: 7 cut down a the idols throughout all the land 3605
34: 7 cut down all the idols throughout a the land 3605
34: 9 of a the remnant of Israel, and of all Judah 3605
34: 9 of Israel, and of a Judah and Benjamin; 3605
34:12 a that could skill of instruments of musick. 3605
34:13 were overseers of a that wrought the work 3605
34:16 A that was committed to thy servants, 3605
34:21 to do after a that is written in this book. 3605
34:24 even a the curses that are written in 3605
34:25 that they might provoke me to anger with a 3605
34:28 neither shall thine eyes see a the evil that I 3605
34:29 gathered together a the elders of Judah and 3605
34:30 a the men of Judah, and the inhabitants of 3605
34:30 and a the people, great and small: 3605
34:30 he read in their ears a the words of 3605
34:31 with a his heart, and with all his soul, 3605
34:31 with all his heart, and with a his soul, 3605
34:32 he caused a that were present in Jerusalem 3605
34:33 Josiah took away a the abominations out of 3605
34:33 a the countries that pertained to 3605
34:33 made a that were present in Israel to serve, 3605
34:33 And a his days they departed not from 3605
35: 3 said unto the Levites that taught a Israel, 3605
35: 7 a for the passover offerings, for all that 3605
35: 7 all for the passover offerings, for a that 3605
35:13 divided them speedily among a the people. 3605
35:16 So a the service of the LORD was 3605
35:18 neither did a the kings of Israel keep such a 3605
35:18 a Judah and Israel that were present, and 3605
35:20 After a this, when Josiah had prepared 3605
35:24 a Judah and Jerusalem mourned for Josiah. 3605
35:25 a the singing men and the singing women 3605
36:14 Moreover a the chief of the priests, and 3605
36:14 transgressed very much after a 3605
36:17 for age: he gave them a into his hand. 3605
36:18 a the vessels of the house of God, great 3605
36:18 his princes; a these he brought to Babylon. 3605
36:19 burnt a the palaces thereof with fire, and 3605
36:19 and destroyed a the goodly vessels thereof. 3605
36:22 that he made a proclamation throughout a 3605
2Ch 36:23 A the kingdoms of the earth hath 3605
36:23 Who is there among you of a his people? 3605
Ezr 1: 1 that he made a proclamation throughout a 3605
1: 2 hath given me a the kingdoms of the earth; 3605
1: 3 Who is there among you of a his people? 3605
1: 5 with a them whose spirit God had raised, 3605
1: 6 a they that were about them strengthened 3605
1: 6 beside a that was willingly offered. 3605
1:11 A the vessels of gold and of silver were 3605
1:11 A these did Sheshbazzar bring up with 3605
2:42 of Shobai, in a an hundred thirty and nine. 3605
2:58 A the Nethinims, and the children of 3605
2:70 in their cities, and a Israel in their cities. 3605
3: 5 of a the set feasts of the LORD that were 3605
3: 8 a they that were come out of the captivity 3605
3:11 a the people shouted with a great shout, 3605
4: 5 a the days of Cyrus king of Persia, 3605
4:20 which have ruled over a countries beyond 3606
5: 7 written thus: Unto Darius the king, a peace. 3606
6:12 his name to dwell there destroy a kings 3606
6:17 for a sin offering for a Israel, twelve he 3606
6:20 a of them were pure, and killed 3605
6:20 killed the passover for a the children of 3605
6:21 a such as had separated themselves unto 3605
7: 6 the king granted him a his request, 3605
7:13 that a they of the people of Israel, and 3606
7:16 a the silver and gold that thou canst find in 3606
7:16 gold that thou canst find in a the province 3606
7:21 do make a decree to a the treasurers which 3606
7:25 which may judge a the people that are 3606
7:25 a such as know the laws of thy God; 3606
7:28 and before a the king's mighty princes. 3605
8:20 a of them were expressed by name. 3605
8:21 for our little ones, and for a our substance. 3605
8:22 The hand of our God is upon a them for 3605
8:22 his wrath is against a them that forsake 3605
8:25 his lords, and a Israel there present, had 3605
8:34 and a the weight was written at that time. 3605
8:35 twelve bullocks for a Israel, ninety and 3605
8:35 a this was a burnt offering unto 3605
9:13 after a that is come upon us for our evil 3605
10: 3 with our God to put away a the wives, 3605
10: 5 the chief priests, the Levites, and a Israel, 3605
10: 7 Jerusalem unto a the children of 3605
10: 8 a his substance should be forfeited, and 3605
10: 9 a the men of Judah and Benjamin gathered 3605
10: 9 a the people sat in the street of the house of 3605
10:12 a the congregation answered and said with 3605
10:14 Let now our rulers of a the congregation 3605
10:14 let a them which have taken strange wives 3605
10:16 a of them by their names, were separated, 3605
10:17 they made an end with a the men that had 3605
10:44 A these had taken strange wives: and 3605
Ne 4: 6 a the wall was joined together unto the half 3605
4: 8 conspired a of them together to come and 3605
4:12 From a places whence ye shall return unto 3605
4:15 that we returned a of us to the wall, 3605
4:16 the rulers were behind a the house of 3605
5:13 a the congregation said, Amen, and 3605
5:16 a my servants were gathered thither unto 3605
5:18 once in ten days store of a sorts of wine: 3605
5:18 yet for a this required not I the bread of NIH
5:19 according to a that I have done for this 3605
6: 9 For they a made us afraid, saying, 3605
6:16 that when a our enemies heard thereof, and 3605
6:16 a the heathen that were about us saw these 3605
7:60 A the Nethinims, and the children of 3605
7:73 the people, and the Nethinims, and a Israel, 3605
8: 1 a the people gathered themselves together 3605
8: 2 and a that could hear with understanding, 3605
8: 3 the ears of a the people were attentive unto 3605
8: 5 Ezra opened the book in the sight of a 3605
8: 5 (for he was above a the people;) and 3605
8: 5 when he opened it, a the people stood up: 3605
8: 6 a the people answered, Amen, Amen, 3605
8: 9 taught the people, said unto a the people, 3605
8: 9 For a the people wept, when they heard 3605
8:11 So the Levites stilled a the people, saying, 3605
8:12 a the people went their way to eat, and 3605
8:13 the chief of the fathers of a the people, 3605
8:15 and proclaim in a their cities, 3605
8:17 a the congregation of them that were come 3605
9: 2 separated themselves from a strangers, 3605
9: 5 which is exalted above a blessing and 3605
9: 6 with a their host, the earth, and all things 3605
9: 6 a things that are therein, the seas, and 3605
9: 6 a that is therein, and thou preservest them 3605
9: 6 that is therein, and thou preservest them a; 3605
9:10 on a his servants, and on all the people of 3605
9:10 and on a the people of his land: 3605
9:25 and possessed houses full of a goods, 3605
9:32 let not a the trouble seem little before thee, 3605
9:32 and on our fathers, and on a thy people, 3605
9:33 Howbeit thou art just in a that is brought 3605
9:38 because of a this we make a sure covenant, 3605
10:28 a they that had separated themselves from 3605
10:29 do a the commandments of the LORD our 3605
10:33 and for a the work of the house of our God. 3605
10:35 the firstfruits of a fruit of all trees, year by 3605
10:35 the firstfruits of all fruit of a trees, year by 3605
10:37 the fruit of a manner of trees, of wine and 3605
10:37 have the tithes in a the cities of our tillage. 3605
11: 2 the people blessed a the men, that willingly 3605
11: 6 A the sons of Perez that dwelt at Jerusalem 3605
11:18 A the Levites in the holy city were two 3605
11:20 the Levites, were in a the cities of Judah, 3605
11:24 was at the king's hand in a matters 3605
12:27 sought the Levites out of a their places, 3605
12:47 a Israel in the days of Zerubbabel, and 3605
13: 3 that they separated from Israel a the mixed 3605
13: 6 in a this time was not I at Jerusalem: for in 3605
13: 8 I cast forth a the household stuff of Tobiah 3605
13:12 brought a Judah the tithe of the corn and 3605
13:15 grapes, and figs, and a manner of burdens, 3605
13:16 a manner of ware, and sold on the sabbath 3605
Ne 13:18 did not our God bring a this evil upon us, 3605
13:20 sellers of a kind of ware lodged without 3605
13:26 and God made him king over a Israel: 3605
13:27 hearken unto you to do a this great evil, 3605
13:30 Thus cleansed I them from a strangers, and 3605
Est 1: 3 he made a feast unto a his princes and 3605
1: 5 the king made a feast unto a the people that 3605
1: 8 the king had appointed to a the officers of 3605
1:13 was the king's manner towards a that knew 3605
1:16 also to a the princes, and to all the people 3605
1:16 to a the people that are in all the provinces 3605
1:16 to all the people that are in a the provinces 3605
1:17 queen shall come abroad unto a women, 3605
1:18 Media say this day unto a the king's 3605
1:20 shall be published throughout a his empire, 3605
1:20 a the wives shall give to their husbands 3605
1:22 For he sent letters into a the king's 3605
2: 3 let the king appoint officers in a 3605
2: 3 that they may gather together a the fair 3605
2:15 Esther obtained favour in the sight of a 3605
2:17 the king loved Esther above a the women, 3605
2:17 favour in his sight more than a the virgins; 3605
2:18 the king made a great feast unto a his 3605
3: 1 set his seat above a the princes that were 3605
3: 2 a the king's servants, that were in 3605
3: 6 wherefore Haman sought to destroy a 3605
3: 8 dispersed among the people in a 3605
3: 8 their laws are diverse from a people; 3605
3:12 there was written according to a that 3605
3:13 the letters were sent by posts into a 3605
3:13 a Jews, both young and old, little children 3605
3:14 province was published unto a people, 3605
4: 1 When Mordecai perceived a that was done, 3605
4: 7 Mordecai told him of a that had happened 3605
4:11 A the king's servants, and the people of 3605
4:13 in the king's house, more than a the Jews. 3605
4:16 gather together a the Jews that are present 3605
4:17 did according to a that Esther had 3605
5:11 a the things wherein the king had promoted 3605
5:13 Yet a this availeth me nothing, so long as I 3605
5:14 Zeresh his wife and a his friends unto him, 3605
6:10 let nothing fail of a that thou hast spoken. 3605
6:13 a his friends every thing that had befallen 3605
8: 5 Jews which are in a the king's provinces: 3605
8: 9 it was written according to a that Mordecai 3605
8:11 a the power of the people and province that 3605
8:12 Upon one day in a the provinces of king 3605
8:13 province was published unto a people, 3605
9: 2 a the provinces of the king Ahasuerus, 3605
9: 2 for the fear of them fell upon a people. 3605
9: 3 a the rulers of the provinces, and 3605
9: 4 his fame went out throughout a 3605
9: 5 Thus the Jews smote a their enemies with 3605
9:20 sent letters unto a the Jews that were in all 3605
9:20 sent letters unto all the Jews that were in a 3605
9:24 the Agagite, the enemy of a the Jews, 3605
9:26 Therefore for a the words of this letter, and 3605
9:27 upon a such as joined themselves unto 3605
9:29 Mordecai the Jew, wrote with a authority, 3605
9:30 he sent the letters unto a the Jews, to 3605
10: 2 a the acts of his power and of his might, 3605
10: 3 and speaking peace to a his seed. 3605
Job 1: 3 that this man was the greatest of a the men 3605
1: 5 according to the number of them a: 3605
1:10 and about a that he hath on every side? 3605
1:11 touch a that he hath, and he will curse thee 3605
1:12 Behold, a that he hath is in thy power; 3605
1:22 In a this Job sinned not, nor charged God 3605
2: 4 a that a man hath will he give for his life. 3605
2:10 In a this did not Job sin with his lips. 3605
2:11 Now when Job's three friends heard of a 3605
4:14 which made a my bones to shake. 7230
8:13 So are the paths of a that forget God; and 3605
9:28 I am afraid of a my sorrows, I know that 3605
12: 9 Who knoweth not in a these that the hand 3605
12:10 living thing, and the breath of a mankind. 3605
13: 1 mine eye hath seen a this, mine ear hath 3605
13: 4 of lies, ye are a physicians of no value. 3605
13:27 and lookest narrowly unto a my paths; 3605
14:14 shall he live again? a the days of my 3605
15:20 The wicked man travaileth with pain a his 3605
16: 2 such things: miserable comforters are ye a. 3605
16: 7 thou hast made desolate a my company. 3605
17: 7 and a my members are as a shadow. 3605
17:10 as for you a, do you return, and come now: 3605
19:19 A my inward friends abhorred me: and 3605
20:26 A darkness shall be hid in his secret places: 3605
24:24 they are taken out of the way as a other, 3605
27: 3 A the while my breath is in me, and 3605
27:12 a ye yourselves have seen it; why then 3605
28: 3 searcheth out a perfection, the stones of 3605
28:21 Seeing it is hid from the eyes of a living, 3605
29:19 and the dew lay a night upon my branch. 3885
30:23 and to the house appointed for a living. 3605
31: 4 not he see my ways, and count a my steps? 3605
31:12 and would root out a mine increase. 3605
33: 1 my speeches, and hearken to a my words. 3605
33:11 feet in the stocks, he marketh a my paths. 3605
33:29 a these things worketh God oftentimes with 3605
34:15 A flesh shall perish together, and man shall 3605
34:19 for they a are the work of his hands. 3605
34:21 the ways of man, and he seeth a his goings. 3605
36:19 no, not gold, nor a the forces of strength. 3605
37: 7 every man; that a men may know his work. 3605
38: 7 and a the sons of God shouted for joy? 3605
38:18 of the earth? declare if thou knowest it a. 3605
40:20 where a the beasts of the field play. 3605
41:34 He beholdeth a high things: he is a king 3605
41:34 he is a king over a the children of pride. 3605
42:11 came there unto him a his brethren, and 3605
42:11 a his sisters, and all they that had been of 3605
42:11 a they that had been of his acquaintance 3605
42:11 comforted him over a the evil that 3605
42:15 in a the land were no women found so 3605
Ps 2:12 blessed are a they that put their trust in 3605

Ps 3: 7 for thou hast smitten **a** mine enemies *upon* 3605
5: 5 thy sight: thou hatest **a** workers of iniquity. 3605
5:11 let **a** those that put their trust in thee 3605
6: 6 **a** the night make I my bed to swim; 3605
6: 7 it waxeth old because of **a** mine enemies. 3605
6: 8 Depart from me, **a** ye workers of iniquity; 3605
6:10 Let **a** mine enemies be ashamed and 3605
7: 1 save me from **a** them that persecute me, 3605
8: 1 how excellent *is* thy name in **a** the earth! 3605
8: 6 thou hast put **a** *things* under his feet: 3605
8: 7 **A** sheep and oxen, yea, and the beasts of 3605
8: 9 how excellent *is* thy name in **a** the earth! 3605
9: 1 I will shew forth **a** thy marvellous works. 3605
9:14 That I may shew forth **a** thy praise in 3605
9:17 into hell, *and* **a** the nations that forget God. 3605
10: 4 will not seek *after God:* God *is* not *in* **a** his 3605
10: 5 *as for* **a** his enemies, he puffeth at them. 3605
12: 3 The LORD shall cut off **a** flattering lips, 3605
14: 3 They are **a** gone aside, they are *all* together 3605
14: 3 they are *a* together become filthy: NIH
14: 4 Have **a** the workers of iniquity no 3605
16: 3 *to* the excellent, in whom *is* **a** my delight. 3605
18: T him from the hand of **a** his enemies, 3605
18:22 For **a** his judgments *were* before me, and 3605
18:30 he *is* **a** buckler to **a** those that trust in him. 3605
19: 4 Their line is gone out through **a** the earth, 3605
20: 3 Remember **a** thy offerings, and accept thy 3605
20: 4 to thine own heart, and fulfil **a** thy counsel. 3605
20: 5 the LORD fulfil **a** thy petitions. 3605
21: 8 Thine hand shall find out **a** thine enemies: 3605
22: 7 **A** they that see me laugh me to scorn: 3605
22:14 like water, and **a** my bones are out of joint: 3605
22:17 I may tell **a** my bones: they look *and* 3605
22:23 **a** ye the seed of Jacob, glorify him; and 3605
22:23 and fear him, **a** ye the seed of Israel. 3605
22:27 **A** the ends of the world shall remember and 3605
22:27 **a** the kindreds of the nations shall worship 3605
22:29 **A** *they that be* fat upon earth shall eat and 3605
22:29 **a** they that go down to the dust shall bow 3605
23: 6 mercy shall follow me **a** the days of my 3605
25: 5 my salvation; on thee do I wait **a** the day. 3605
25:10 **A** the paths of the LORD *are* mercy and 3605
25:18 and my pain; and forgive **a** my sins. 3605
25:22 O God, out of **a** his troubles. 3605
26: 7 and tell of **a** thy wondrous works. 3605
27: 4 house of the LORD **a** the days of my life, 3605
31:11 I was a reproach among **a** mine enemies, 3605
31:23 O love the LORD, **a** ye his saints: *for* 3605
31:24 your heart, **a** ye that hope in the LORD. 3605
32: 3 my bones waxed old through my roaring **a** 3605
32:11 shout for joy, **a** *ye that are* upright in heart. 3605
33: 4 *is* right; and **a** his works *are done* in truth. 3605
33: 6 **a** the host of them by the breath of his 3605
33: 8 Let **a** the earth fear the LORD: let all 3605
33: 8 let **a** the inhabitants of the world stand in 3605
33:11 his heart to **a generations**. 1755+1755+2050.1
33:13 he beholdeth **a** the sons of men. 3605
33:14 looketh upon **a** the inhabitants of the earth. 3605
33:15 hearts alike; he considereth **a** their works. 3605
34: 1 I will bless the LORD at **a** times: 3605
34: 4 and delivered me from **a** my fears. 3605
34: 6 and saved him out of **a** his troubles. 3605
34:17 and delivereth them out of **a** their troubles. 3605
34:19 the LORD delivereth him out of them **a**. 3605
34:20 He keepeth **a** his bones: not one of them is 3605
35:10 **A** my bones shall say, LORD, who *is* like 3605
35:28 *and* of thy praise **a** the day long. 3605
38: 6 I go mourning **a** the day long. 3605
38: 9 Lord, **a** my desire *is* before thee; and 3605
38:12 and imagine deceits **a** the day long. 3605
39: 8 Deliver me from **a** my transgressions: 3605
39:12 *and* a sojourner, as **a** my fathers *were*. 3605
40:16 Let **a** those that seek thee rejoice and 3605
41: 3 thou wilt make **a** his bed in his sickness. 3605
41: 7 **A** that hate me whisper together against 3605
42: 7 **a** thy waves and thy billows are gone over 3605
44: 8 In God we boast **a** the day long, and 3605
44:17 **A** this is come upon us; yet have we not 3605
44:22 for thy sake are we killed **a** the day long; 3605
45: 8 **A** thy garments *smell of* myrrh, and aloes, 3605
45:13 The king's daughter *is* **a** glorious within: 3605
45:16 whom thou mayest make princes in **a** 3605
45:17 in **a generations**: 1755+1755+3605+2050.1
47: 1 O clap *your* hands, **a** ye people; shout unto 3605
47: 2 *he is* **a** great King over **a** the earth. 3605
47: 7 For God *is* the King of **a** the earth: sing ye 3605
49: 1 Hear this, **a** ye people; give ear, all ye 3605
49: 1 give ear, **a** ye inhabitants of the world: 3605
49:11 places to **a generations**; 1755+1755+2050.1
50:11 I know **a** the fowls of the mountains: and 3605
51: 9 my sins, and blot out **a** mine iniquities. 3605
52: 4 Thou lovest **a** devouring words, O thou 3605
54: 7 For he hath delivered me out of **a** trouble: 3605
56: 5 **a** their thoughts *are* against me for evil. 3605
57: 2 unto God that performeth *a things* for me. NIH
57: 5 *let* thy glory *be* above **a** the earth. 3605
57:11 *let* thy glory *be* above **a** the earth. 3605
59: 5 God of Israel, awake to visit **a** the heathen: 3605
59: 8 thou shalt have **a** the heathen in derision. 3605
62: 3 ye shall be slain **a** of you: as a bowing wall 3605
62: 8 Trust in him at **a** times; ye people, pour out 3605
64: 8 **a** that see them shall flee away. 3605
64: 9 **a** men shall fear, and shall declare the work 3605
64:10 and **a** the upright in heart shall glory. 3605
65: 2 hearest prayer, unto thee shall **a** flesh come. 3605
65: 5 *who art* the confidence of **a** the ends of 3605
66: 1 Make a joyful noise unto God, **a** ye lands: 3605
66: 4 **A** the earth shall worship thee, and 3605
66:16 **a** ye that fear God, and I will declare what 3605
67: 2 thy saving health among **a** nations. 3605
67: 3 O God; let **a** the people praise thee. 3605
67: 5 O God; let **a** the people praise thee. 3605
67: 7 and **a** the ends of the earth shall fear him. 3605
69:19 mine adversaries *are* **a** before thee. 3605
70: 4 Let **a** those that seek thee rejoice and 3605

Ps 71: 8 thy praise *and with* thy honour **a** the day. 3605
71:15 *and* thy salvation **a** the day; 3605
71:24 talk of thy righteousness **a** the day long: 3605
72: 5 **throughout a generations**. 1755+1755
72:11 Yea, **a** kings shall fall down before him: 3605
72:11 down before him: **a** nations shall serve him. 3605
72:17 in him: **a** nations shall call him blessed. 3605
73:14 For **a** the day long have I been plagued, and 3605
73:27 thou hast destroyed **a** them that go a 3605
73:28 that *I* may declare **a** thy works. 3605
74: 3 *even* **a** *that* the enemy hath done wickedly 3605
74: 8 they have burnt up **a** the synagogues of 3605
74:17 Thou hast set **a** the borders of the earth: 3605
75: 3 and **a** the inhabitants thereof *are* dissolved: 3605
75: 8 **a** the wicked of the earth shall wring *them* 3605
75:10 **A** the horns of the wicked also will I cut 3605
76: 9 to save **a** the meek of the earth. 3605
76:11 let **a** that be round about him bring presents 3605
77:12 I will meditate also of **a** thy work, and 3605
78:14 a cloud, and **a** the night with a light of fire. 3605
78:32 For **a** this they sinned still, and believed not 3605
78:38 anger away, and did not stir up **a** his wrath. 3605
78:51 smote **a** the firstborn in Egypt; the chief of 3605
79:13 thy praise to **a generations**. 1755+1755+2050.1
80:12 that **a** they which pass by the way do pluck 3605
82: 5 **a** the foundations of the earth are out of 3605
82: 6 and **a** of you *are* children of the most High. 3605
82: 8 the earth: for thou shalt inherit **a** nations. 3605
83:11 **a** their princes as Zebah, and as Zalmunna: 3605
83:18 *art* the most High over **a** the earth. 3605
85: 2 of thy people, thou hast covered **a** their sin. 3605
85: 3 Thou hast taken away **a** thy wrath: 3605
85: 5 anger to **a generations**? 1755+1755+2050.1
86: 5 plenteous in mercy unto **a** them that call 3605
86: 9 **A** nations whom thou hast made shall come 3605
86:12 O Lord my God, with **a** my heart: 3605
87: 2 of Zion more than **a** the dwellings of Jacob. 3605
87: 7 *shall be there:* **a** my springs *are* in thee. 3605
88: 7 thou hast afflicted *me with* **a** thy waves. 3605
89: 1 to **a generations**. 1755+1755+2050.1
89: 4 thy throne to **a generations**. 1755+1755+2050.1
89: 7 to be had in reverence of **a** them that are 3605
89:16 In thy name shall they rejoice **a** the day: 3605
89:40 Thou hast broken down **a** his hedges; 3605
89:41 **A** that pass by the way spoil him: he is a 3605
89:42 thou hast made **a** his enemies to rejoice. 3605
89:47 wherefore hast thou made **a** men in vain? 3605
89:50 bosom *the reproach of* **a** the mighty people; 3605
90: 1 place in **a generations**. 1755+1755+2050.1
90: 9 For **a** our days are passed away in thy 3605
90:14 that we may rejoice and be glad **a** our days. 3605
91:11 over thee, to keep thee in **a** thy ways. 3605
92: 7 when **a** the workers of iniquity do flourish; 3605
92: 9 **a** the workers of iniquity shall be scattered. 3605
94: 4 **a** the workers of iniquity boast themselves? 3605
94:15 and **a** the upright in heart shall follow it. 3605
95: 3 a great God, and a great King above **a** gods. 3605
96: 1 sing unto the LORD, **a** the earth. 3605
96: 3 the heathen, his wonders among **a** people. 3605
96: 4 be praised: he *is* to be feared above **a** gods. 3605
96: 5 For **a** the gods of the nations *are* idols: but 3605
96: 9 of holiness: fear before him, **a** the earth. 3605
96:12 Let the field be joyful, and **a** that *is* therein: 3605
96:12 shall **a** the trees of the wood rejoice 3605
97: 6 and **a** the people see his glory. 3605
97: 7 Confounded be **a** they that serve graven 3605
97: 7 of idols: worship him, **a** ye gods. 3605
97: 9 LORD, *art* High above **a** the earth: 3605
97: 9 the earth: thou art exalted far above **a** gods. 3605
98: 3 **a** the ends of the earth have seen 3605
98: 4 a joyful noise unto the LORD, **a** the earth: 3605
99: 2 in Zion; and he *is* high above **a** the people. 3605
100: 1 a joyful noise unto the LORD, **a** ye lands. 3605
100: 5 *endureth* to **a generations**. 1755+1755+2050.1
101: 8 I will early destroy **a** the wicked of 3605
101: 8 that *I* may cut off **a** wicked doers from 3605
102: 8 Mine enemies reproach me **a** the day; *and* 3605
102:12 unto **a generations**. 1755+1755+2050.1
102:15 and **a** the kings of the earth thy glory. 3605
102:24 years *are* throughout **a generations**. 1755+1755
102:26 yea, **a** of them shall wax old like a garment; 3605
103: 1 **a** that is within me, *bless* his holy name. 3605
103: 2 O my soul, and forget not **a** his benefits: 3605
103: 3 Who forgiveth **a** thine iniquities; 3605
103: 3 thine iniquities; who healeth **a** thy diseases; 3605
103: 6 and judgment for **a** that are oppressed. 3605
103:19 the heavens; and his kingdom ruleth over **a**. 3605
103:21 Bless ye the LORD, **a** ye his hosts; 3605
103:22 **a** his works in all places of his dominion: 3605
103:22 all his works in **a** places of his dominion: 3605
104:20 wherein **a** the beasts of the forest do creep 3605
104:24 in wisdom hast thou made them **a**: the earth 3605
104:27 These wait **a** upon thee; that *thou* mayest 3605
105: 2 unto him: talk ye of **a** his wondrous works. 3605
105: 7 our God: his judgments *are* in **a** the earth. 3605
105:21 of his house, and ruler of **a** his substance: 3605
105:31 sorts *of flies, and* lice in **a** their coasts. 3605
105:35 And did eat up **a** the herbs in their land, and 3605
105:36 He smote also **a** the firstborn in their land, 3605
105:36 in their land, the chief of **a** their strength. 3605
106: 2 *who* can shew forth **a** his praise? 3605
106: 3 *and* he that doeth righteousness at **a** times. 3605
106:31 **a generations** for evermore. 1755+1755+2050.1
106:46 He made them also to be pitied of **a** those 3605
106:48 let **a** the people say, Amen. Praise ye 3605
107:18 Their soul abhorreth **a** manner *of* meat; and 3605
107:42 rejoice: and **a** iniquity shall stop her mouth. 3605
108: 5 and thy glory above **a** the earth. 3605
109:11 Let the extortioner catch **a** that he hath; and 3605
111: 2 sought out of **a** them that have pleasure 3605
111: 7 judgment; **a** his commandments *are* sure. 3605
111:10 a good understanding have **a** they that do 3605
113: 4 The LORD *is* high above **a** nations, *and* 3605
116:11 I said in my haste, **A** men *are* liars. 3605
116:12 What shall I render unto the LORD *for* **a** 3605

Ps 116:14 now in the presence of **a** his people. 3605
116:18 now in the presence of **a** his people, 3605
117: 1 O praise the LORD, **a** ye nations: 3605
117: 1 all ye nations: praise him, **a** ye people. 3605
118:10 **A** nations compassed me about: but in 3605
119: 6 when I have respect unto **a** thy 3605
119:13 With my lips have I declared **a** 3605
119:14 of thy testimonies, as *much as* in **a** riches. 3605
119:20 *that it hath* unto thy judgments at **a** times. 3605
119:63 I *am* a companion of **a** *them* that fear thee, 3605
119:86 **A** thy commandments *are* faithful: 3605
119:90 *is* unto **a generations**: 1755+1755+2050.1
119:91 to thine ordinances: for **a** *are* thy servants. 3605
119:96 I have seen an end of **a** perfection: *but* 3605
119:97 I thy law! it *is* my meditation **a** the day. 3605
119:99 I have more understanding than **a** my 3605
119:118 Thou hast trodden down **a** them that err 3605
119:119 Thou puttest away **a** the wicked of the earth 3605
119:128 Therefore I esteem **a** *thy* precepts 3605
119:128 precepts concerning **a** *things* to be right; 3605
119:151 and **a** thy commandments *are* truth. 3605
119:168 for **a** my ways *are* before thee. 3605
119:172 for **a** thy commandments *are* righteousness. 3605
121: 7 The LORD shall preserve thee from **a** 3605
128: 5 thou shalt see the good of Jerusalem **a** 3605
129: 5 Let them **a** be confounded and turned back 3605
130: 8 he shall redeem Israel from **a** his iniquities. 3605
132: 1 remember David, *and* **a** his afflictions: 3605
134: 1 the LORD, **a** ye servants of the LORD, 3605
135: 5 *is* great, and *that* our Lord *is* above **a** gods. 3605
135: 6 and in earth, in the seas, and **a** deep places. 3605
135: 9 upon Pharaoh, and upon **a** his servants. 3605
135:11 of Bashan, and **a** the kingdoms of Canaan: 3605
135:13 throughout **a generations**. 1755+1755+2050.1
136:25 Who giveth food to **a** flesh: for his mercy 3605
138: 2 for thou hast magnified thy word above **a** 3605
138: 4 **A** the kings of the earth shall praise thee, 3605
139: 3 and art acquainted *with* **a** my ways. 3605
139:16 in thy book **a** *my members* were written, 3605
143: 5 the days of old; I meditate on **a** thy works; 3605
143:12 and destroy **a** them that afflict my soul: 3605
144:13 **a manner of store**: 413+2177+2177+4480
145: 9 The LORD *is* good to **a**: and his tender 3605
145: 9 and his tender mercies *are* over **a** his works. 3605
145:10 **A** thy works shall praise thee, O LORD; 3605
145:13 thy dominion *endureth* throughout **a** 3605
145:14 The LORD upholdeth **a** that fall, and 3605
145:14 and raiseth up **a** those that be bowed down. 3605
145:15 The eyes of **a** wait upon thee; and 3605
145:17 The LORD *is* righteous in **a** his ways, and 3605
145:17 in all his ways, and holy in **a** his works. 3605
145:18 The LORD *is* nigh unto **a** them that call 3605
145:18 upon him, to **a** that call upon him in truth. 3605
145:20 The LORD preserveth **a** them that love 3605
145:20 love him: but **a** the wicked will he destroy. 3605
145:21 let **a** flesh bless his holy name for ever and 3605
146: 6 and earth, the sea, and **a** that therein is: 3605
146:10 O Zion, unto **a generations**. 1755+1755+2050.1
147: 4 the stars; he calleth them **a** *by their* names. 3605
148: 2 Praise ye him, **a** his angels: praise ye him, 3605
148: 2 all his angels: praise ye him, **a** his hosts. 3605
148: 3 and moon: praise him, **a** ye stars of light. 3605
148: 7 from the earth, ye dragons, and **a** deeps: 3605
148: 9 Mountains, and **a** hills; fruitful trees, and 3605
148: 9 all hills; fruitful trees, and **a** cedars: 3605
148:10 Beasts, and **a** cattle; creeping things, and 3605
148:11 Kings of the earth, and **a** people; princes, 3605
148:11 princes, and **a** judges of the earth: 3605
148:14 of his people, the praise of **a** his saints; 3605
149: 9 this honour have **a** his saints. Praise ye 3605
Pr 1:13 We shall find **a** precious substance, 3605
1:14 thy lot among us; let us **a** have one purse: 3605
1:25 ye have set at nought **a** my counsel, and 3605
1:30 of my counsel: they despised **a** my reproof. 3605
3: 5 Trust in the LORD with **a** thine heart; and 3605
3: 6 In **a** thy ways acknowledge him, and 3605
3: 9 and with the firstfruits of **a** thine increase: 3605
3:15 **a** the things thou canst desire are not to be 3605
3:17 of pleasantness, and **a** her paths *are* peace. 3605
4: 7 and with **a** thy getting get understanding. 3605
4:22 that find them, and health to **a** their flesh. 3605
4:23 Keep thy heart with **a** diligence; for out of 3605
4:26 thy feet, and let **a** thy ways be established. 3605
5:14 I was almost in **a** evil in the midst of 3605
5:19 let her breasts satisfy thee at **a** times; and 3605
5:21 the LORD, and he pondereth **a** his goings. 3605
6:31 he shall give **a** the substance of his house. 3605
8: 8 **A** the words of my mouth *are* in 3605
8: 9 They *are* **a** plain to him that understandeth, 3605
8:11 **a** the things that may be desired are not to 3605
8:16 and nobles, *even* **a** the judges of the earth. 3605
8:36 own soul: **a** they that hate me love death. 3605
10:12 stirreth up strifes: but love covereth **a** sins. 3605
14:23 In **a** labour there is profit: but the talk of 3605
15:15 **A** the days of the afflicted *are* evil: but 3605
16: 2 **A** the ways of a man *are* clean in his own 3605
16: 4 The LORD hath made **a** *things* for 3605
16:11 **a** the weights of the bag *are* his work. 3605
17:17 A friend loveth at **a** times, and a brother is 3605
18: 1 seeketh *and* intermeddleth with **a** wisdom. 3605
19: 7 **A** the brethren of the poor do hate him: 3605
20: 8 scattereth *away* **a** evil with his eyes. 3605
20:27 searching **a** the inward parts of the belly. 3605
21:26 He coveteth greedily **a** the day long: but 3605
22: 2 the LORD *is* the Maker of them **a**. 3605
23:17 *be thou* in the fear of the LORD **a** the day 3605
24: 4 shall the chambers be filled *with* **a** precious 3605
24:31 it was **a** grown over with thorns, *and* 3605
26:10 The great *God* that formed **a** *things* both 3605
28: 5 they that seek the LORD understand **a** 3605
29:11 A fool uttereth **a** his mind: but a wise *man* 3605
29:12 hearken to lies, **a** his servants *are* wicked. 3605
30: 4 who hath established **a** the ends of 3605
30:27 yet go they forth **a** of them by bands; 3605
31: 8 of **a** such as are appointed to destruction. 3605

Pr 31:12 him good and not evil a the days of her life. 3605
31:21 for a her household are clothed with 3605
31:29 done virtuously, but thou excellest them a. 3605
Ecc 1: 2 the Preacher, vanity of vanities; a is vanity. 3605
1: 3 What profit hath a man of a his labour 3605
1: 7 A the rivers run into the sea; yet the sea is 3605
1: 8 A things are full of labour; man cannot 3605
1:13 search out by wisdom concerning a things 3605
1:14 I have seen a the works that are done under 3605
1:14 behold, a is vanity and vexation of spirit. 3605
1:16 have gotten more wisdom than a they that 3605
2: 3 which they should do under the heaven a 4557
2: 5 I planted trees in them of a kind of fruits: 3605
2: 7 small cattle above a that were in Jerusalem 3605
2: 8 **musical instruments**, and that **of a sorts.** 7705+7705
2: 9 increased more than a that were before me 3605
2:10 for my heart rejoiced in a my labour: 3605
2:10 and this was my portion of a my labour. 3605
2:11 I looked on a the works that my hands had 3605
2:11 a was vanity and vexation of spirit, and 3605
2:14 also that one event happeneth to them a. 3605
2:16 is, in the days to come shall a be forgotten. 3605
2:17 for a is vanity and vexation of spirit. 3605
2:18 I hated a my labour which I had taken 3605
2:19 yet shall he have rule over a my labour 3605
2:20 of a the labour which I took under the sun. 3605
2:22 For what hath man of a his labour, and 3605
2:23 For a his days are sorrows, and his travail 3605
3:13 drink, and enjoy the good of a his labour, 3605
3:19 yea, they have a one breath; so that a man 3605
3:19 preeminence above a beast: for a is vanity. 3605
3:20 A go unto one place; all are of the dust, and 3605
3:20 a are of the dust, and all turn to dust again. 3605
3:20 all are of the dust, and a turn to dust again. 3605
4: 1 considered a the oppressions that are done 3605
4: 4 I considered a travail, and every right work, 3605
4: 8 yet is there no end of a his labour; 3605
4:15 I considered a the living which walk under 3605
4:16 There is no end of a the people, even of all 3605
4:16 even of a that have been before them: 3605
5: 9 Moreover the profit of the earth is for a: 3605
5:16 that in a points as he came, so shall he go: 3605
5:17 A his days also he eateth in darkness, and 3605
5:18 to enjoy the good of a his labour that he 3605
5:18 taketh under the sun a the days of his life, 4557
6: 2 that he wanteth nothing for his soul of a 3605
6: 6 he seen no good: do not a go to one place? 3605
6: 7 A the labour of man is for his mouth, and 3605
6:12 a the days of his vain life which he 4557
7: 2 for that is the end of a men; and the living 3605
7:15 A things have I seen in the days of my 3605
7:18 that feareth God shall come forth of them a. 3605
7:21 Also take no heed unto a words that are 3605
7:23 A this have I proved by wisdom: I said, 3605
7:28 a woman among a those have I not found. 3605
8: 9 A this have I seen, and applied my heart 3605
8:17 I beheld a the work of God, that a man 3605
9: 1 For a this I considered in my heart even to 3605
9: 1 in my heart even to declare a this, 3605
9: 1 or hatred by a that is before them. 3605
9: 2 A things come alike to all: there is one 3605
9: 2 All things come alike to a: there is one 3605
9: 3 This is an evil among a things that are done 3605
9: 3 the sun, that there is one event unto a: 3605
9: 4 For to him that is joined to a the living 3605
9: 9 lovest a the days of the life of thy vanity, 3605
9: 9 thee under the sun, a the days of thy vanity: 3605
9:11 but time and chance happeneth to them a. 3605
10:19 but money answereth a things. 3605
11: 5 not the works of God who maketh a. 3605
11: 8 man live many years, and rejoice in them a; 3605
11: 8 shall be many. A that cometh is vanity. 3605
11: 9 that for a these things God will bring thee 3605
12: 4 a the daughters of musick shall be brought 3605
12: 8 of vanities, saith the Preacher; a is vanity. 3605
SS 1:13 he shall **lie a night** betwixt my breasts. 3885
3: 6 with a powders of the merchant? 3605
3: 8 They a hold swords, being expert in war: 3605
4: 4 a shields of mighty men. 3605
4: 7 Thou art a fair, my love; there is no spot in 3605
4:10 the smell of thine ointments than a spices! 3605
4:14 and cinnamon, with a trees of frankincense; 3605
4:14 myrrh and aloes, with a the chief spices: 3605
7:13 at our gates are a manner of pleasant fruits, 3605
8: 7 if a man would give a the substance of his 3605
Isa 1:25 away thy dross, and take away a thy tin: 3605
2: 2 the hills; and a nations shall flow unto it. 3605
2:13 upon a the cedars of Lebanon, that are high 3605
2:13 lifted up, and upon a the oaks of Bashan, 3605
2:14 upon a the high mountains, and upon all 3605
2:14 upon a the hills that are lifted up, 3605
2:16 upon a the ships of Tarshish, and upon all 3605
2:16 of Tarshish, and upon a pleasant pictures. 3605
4: 5 for upon a the glory shall be a defence. 3605
5:25 For a this his anger is not turned away, but 3605
5:28 arrows are sharp, and a their bows bent, 3605
7:19 shall rest a of them in the desolate valleys, 3605
7:19 and upon a thorns, and upon all bushes. 3605
7:19 and upon all thorns, and upon a bushes. 3605
7:24 a the land shall become briers and thorns. 3605
7:25 on a hills that shall be digged with 3605
8: 7 even the king of Assyria, and a his glory: 3605
8: 7 he shall come up over a his channels, and 3605
8: 7 all his channels, and go over a his banks: 3605
8: 9 and give ear, a ye of far countries: 3605
8:12 to a them to whom this people shall say, 3605
9: 9 And a the people shall know, even Ephraim 3605
9:12 For a this his anger is not turned away, but 3605
9:17 For a this his anger is not turned away, but 3605
9:21 For a this his anger is not turned away, but 3605
10: 4 For a this his anger is not turned away, but 3605
10:14 that are left, have I gathered a the earth; 3605
10:23 in the midst of a the land. 3605
11: 9 They shall not hurt nor destroy in a my 3605

Isa 12: 5 this is known in a the earth. 3605
13: 7 Therefore shall a hands be faint, and 3605
14: 9 for thee, even a the chief ones of the earth; 3605
14: 9 it hath raised up from their thrones a 3605
14:10 A they shall speak and say unto thee, 3605
14:18 A the kings of the nations, even all of them, 3605
14:18 of the nations, even a of them, lie in glory, 3605
14:26 this is the hand that is stretched out upon a 3605
15: 2 on a their heads shall be baldness, and 3605
16:14 be contemned, with a that great multitude; 3605
18: 3 A ye inhabitants of the world, and 3605
18: 6 a the beasts of the earth shall winter upon 3605
19: 8 a they that cast angle into the brooks shall 3605
19:10 a that make sluces and ponds for fish. 3605
21: 2 a the sighing thereof have I made to cease. 3605
21: 9 a the graven images of her gods he hath 3605
21:16 and a the glory of Kedar shall fail: 3605
22: 3 A thy rulers are fled together, they are 3605
22: 3 a that are found in thee are bound together, 3605
22:24 they shall hang upon him a the glory of his 3605
22:24 and the issue, a vessels of small quantity, 3605
22:24 of cups, even to a the vessels of flagons. 3605
23: 9 to stain the pride of a glory, and to bring 3605
23: 9 to bring into contempt a the honourable of 3605
23:17 shall commit fornication with a 3605
24: 7 a the merryhearted do sigh. 3605
24:11 a joy is darkened, the mirth of the land is 3605
25: 6 make unto a people a feast of fat things, 3605
25: 7 the face of the covering cast over a people, 3605
25: 7 and the vail that is spread over a nations. 3605
25: 8 will wipe away tears from off a faces; 3605
25: 8 shall he take away from off a the earth: 3605
26:12 for thou also hast wrought a our works in 3605
26:14 and made a their memory to perish. 3605
26:15 thou hadst removed it far unto a the ends of 3605
27: 9 and this is a the fruit to take away his sin; 3605
27: 9 when he maketh a the stones of the altar as 3605
28: 8 For a tables are full of vomit and filthiness, 3605
28:24 Doth the plowman plow a day to sow? 3605
29: 7 the multitude of a the nations that fight 3605
29: 7 even a that fight against her and 3605
29: 8 so shall the multitude of a the nations be, 3605
29:11 the vision of a is become unto you as 3605
29:20 and a that watch for iniquity are cut off: 3605
30: 5 They were a ashamed of a people that 3605
30:18 blessed are a they that wait for him. 3605
31: 3 fall down, and they a shall fail together. 3605
32:13 upon a the houses of joy in the joyous city: 3605
32:20 Blessed are ye that sow beside a waters, 3605
34: 1 let the earth hear, and **a that is therein**; 4393
34: 1 and **a things** that come forth of it. 3605
34: 2 the indignation of the LORD is upon a 3605
34: 2 and his fury upon a their armies: 3605
34: 4 a the host of heaven shall be dissolved, 3605
34: 4 a their host shall fall down, as the leaf 3605
34:12 be there, and a her princes shall be nothing. 3605
36: 1 up against a the defenced cities of Judah, 3605
36: 6 is Pharaoh king of Egypt to a that trust in 3605
36:20 Who are they amongst a the gods of these 3605
37:11 done to a lands by destroying them utterly; 3605
37:16 thou alone, of a the kingdoms of the earth: 3605
37:17 hear a the words of Sennacherib, 3605
37:18 the kings of Assyria have laid waste a 3605
37:20 that a the kingdoms of the earth may know 3605
37:25 with the sole of my feet have I dried up a 3605
37:36 behold, they were a dead corpses. 3605
38:13 that, as a lion, so will he break a my bones: 3605
38:15 himself hath done it: I shall go softly a my 3605
38:16 and in a these things is the life of my spirit: 3605
38:17 for thou hast cast a my sins behind thy 3605
38:20 a the days of our life in the house of 3605
39: 2 a the house of his armour, and all that was 3605
39: 2 and a that was found in his treasures: 3605
39: 2 nothing in his house, nor in a his dominion, 3605
39: 4 A that is in mine house have they seen: 3605
39: 6 that a that is in thine house, and that which 3605
40: 2 of the LORD'S hand double for a her sins. 3605
40: 5 and a flesh shall see it together: 3605
40: 6 A flesh is grass, and all the goodliness 3605
40: 6 a the goodliness thereof is as the flower of 3605
40:17 A nations before him are as nothing; and 3605
40:26 he calleth them a by names by 3605
41:11 a they that were incensed against thee shall 3605
41:29 Behold, they are a vanity; their works are 3605
42:10 go down to the sea, and **a that is therein**; 4393
42:15 and hills, and dry up a their herbs; 3605
42:22 they are a of them snared in holes, and 3605
43: 9 Let a the nations be gathered together, and 3605
43:14 have brought down a their nobles, and 3605
44: 9 They that make a graven image are a of 3605
44:11 Behold, a his fellows shall be ashamed: and 3605
44:11 let them a be gathered together, let them 3605
44:24 I am the LORD that maketh a things; that 3605
44:28 and shall perform a my pleasure: 3605
45: 7 create evil: I the LORD do a these things. 3605
45:12 and a their host have I commanded. 3605
45:13 and I will direct a his ways: 3605
45:16 and also confounded, a of them: 3605
45:22 and be ye saved, a the ends of the earth: 3605
45:24 a that are incensed against him shall be 3605
45:25 In the LORD shall a the seed of Israel be 3605
46: 3 and a the remnant of the house of Israel, 3605
46:10 shall stand, and I will do a my pleasure: 3605
48: 6 Thou hast heard, see a this; and will not ye 3605
48:14 A ye, assemble yourselves, and hear; 3605
49: 9 and their pastures shall be in a high places. 3605
49:11 I will make a my mountains a way, and 3605
49:18 a these gather themselves together, and 3605
49:18 thou shalt surely clothe thee with them a, 3605
49:26 a flesh shall know that I the LORD am thy 3605
50: 2 Is my hand **shortened at a**, that it 7114+7114
50: 9 lo, they a shall wax old as a garment; 3605
50:11 Behold, a ye that kindle a fire, 3605
51: 3 he will comfort a her waste places; and 3605
51:18 There is none to guide her among a 3605

Isa 51:18 hand of a the sons that she hath brought up. 3605
51:20 they lie at the head of a the streets, as a 3605
52:10 his holy arm in the eyes of a the nations; 3605
52:10 a the ends of the earth shall see 3605
53: 6 A we like sheep have gone astray; we have 3605
53: 6 hath laid on him the iniquity of us a. 3605
54:12 a thy borders of pleasant stones. 3605
54:13 a thy children shall be taught of 3605
55:12 a the trees of the field shall clap their 3605
56: 7 be called a house of prayer for a people. 3605
56: 9 A ye beasts of the field, come to devour, 3605
56: 9 to devour, yea, a ye beasts in the forest. 3605
56:10 they are a ignorant, they are all dumb dogs, 3605
56:10 they are a dumb dogs, they cannot bark; 3605
56:11 they a look to their own way, every one for 3605
57:13 the wind shall carry them a away; 3605
58: 3 you find pleasure, and exact a your labours. 3605
59:11 We roar a like bears, and mourn sore like 3605
60: 4 a they gather themselves together, 3605
60: 6 and Ephah; a they from Sheba shall come: 3605
60: 7 A the flocks of Kedar shall be gathered 3605
60:14 a they that despised thee shall bow 3605
60:21 Thy people also shall be a righteous: 3605
61: 2 of our God; to comfort a that mourn; 3605
61: 9 a that see them shall acknowledge them, 3605
61:11 praise to spring forth before a the nations. 3605
62: 2 thy righteousness, and a kings thy glory: 3605
63: 3 my garments, and I will stain a my raiment. 3605
63: 7 according to a that the LORD hath 3605
63: 9 In a their affliction he was afflicted, and 3605
63: 9 and carried them a the days of old. 3605
64: 6 we are a as an unclean thing, and all our 3605
64: 6 and a our righteousnesses are as filthy rags; 3605
64: 6 we a do fade as a leaf; and our iniquities, 3605
64: 8 and we a are the work of thine hand. 3605
64: 9 see, we beseech thee, we are a thy people. 3605
64:11 and a our pleasant things are laid waste. 3605
65: 2 I have spread out mine hands a the day 3605
65: 5 in my nose, a fire that burneth a the day. 3605
65: 8 that I may not destroy them a. 3605
65:12 and ye shall a bow down to the slaughter: 3605
65:25 They shall not hurt nor destroy in a my 3605
66: 2 For a those things hath mine hand made, 3605
66: 2 a those things have been, saith the LORD: 3605
66:10 and be glad with her, a ye that love her: 3605
66:10 for joy with her, a ye that mourn for her: 3605
66:16 by his sword will the LORD plead with a 3605
66:18 that I will gather a nations and tongues; 3605
66:20 they shall bring a your brethren for an 3605
66:20 the LORD out of a nations upon horses, 3605
66:23 shall a flesh come to worship before me, 3605
66:24 they shall be an abhorring unto a flesh. 3605
Jer 1: 7 for thou shalt go to a that I shall send thee, 3605
1:14 forth upon a the inhabitants of the land. 3605
1:15 I will call a the families of the kingdoms of 3605
1:15 and against a the walls thereof round about, 3605
1:15 and against a the cities of Judah. 3605
1:16 against them touching a their wickedness, 3605
1:17 speak unto them a that I command thee: 3605
2: 3 a that devour him shall offend; evil shall 3605
2: 4 and a the families of the house of Israel: 3605
2:24 a they that seek her will not weary 3605
2:29 ye a have transgressed against me, saith 3605
2:34 found it by secret search, but upon a these. 3605
3: 7 I said after she had done a these things, 3605
3: 8 when for a the causes whereby backsliding 3605
3:10 yet for a this her treacherous sister Judah 3605
3:17 a the nations shall be gathered unto it, 3605
4:24 and a the hills moved lightly. 3605
4:25 and a the birds of the heavens were fled. 3605
4:26 a the cities thereof were broken down at 3605
5:16 an open sepulchre, they are a mighty men. 3605
5:19 Wherefore doth the LORD our God a 3605
6:15 nay, they were not **at a ashamed**, 954+954
6:28 They are a grievous revolters, walking with 3605
6:28 are brass and iron; they are a corrupters. 3605
7: 2 the word of the LORD, a ye of Judah, 3605
7:10 We are delivered to do a these 3605
7:13 because ye have done a these works, 3605
7:15 as I have cast out a your brethren, even 3605
7:23 walk ye in a the ways that I have 3605
7:25 I have even sent unto you a my servants 3605
7:27 Therefore thou shalt speak a these words 3605
8: 2 the moon, and a the host of heaven, 3605
8: 3 death shall be chosen rather than life by a 3605
8: 3 which remain in a the places whither I have 3605
8:12 nay, they were not **at a ashamed**, 954+954
8:16 have devoured the land, and **a that is in** it; 4393
9: 2 for they be a adulterers, an assembly of 3605
9:25 that I will punish a them which are 3605
9:26 and a that are in the utmost corners, 3605
9:26 for a these nations are uncircumcised, and 3605
9:26 a the house of Israel are uncircumcised in 3605
10: 7 forasmuch as among a the wise men of 3605
10: 7 in a their kingdoms, there is none like unto 3605
10: 9 they are a the work of cunning men. 3605
10:16 for he is the former of a things; and 3605
10:20 is spoiled, and a my cords are broken: 3605
10:21 and a their flocks shall be scattered. 3605
11: 4 according to a which I command you: 3605
11: 6 Proclaim a these words in the cities of 3605
11: 8 I will bring upon them a the words of this 3605
11:12 they shall not **save** them **at a** in 3467+3467
12: 1 wherefore are a they happy that deal very 3605
12: 9 come ye, assemble a the beasts of the field, 3605
12:12 The spoilers are come upon a high places 3605
12:14 Thus saith the LORD against a mine evil 3605
13:13 I will fill a the inhabitants of this land, 3605
13:13 and a the inhabitants of Jerusalem, 3605
13:19 Judah shall be carried away captive a of it, 3605
14:22 for thou hast made a these things. 3605
15: 4 I will cause them to be removed into a 3605
15:13 that for a thy sins, even in all thy borders. 3605
15:13 that for all thy sins, even in a thy borders. 3605
16:10 when thou shalt shew this people a these 3605

A

Jer 16:10 Wherefore hath the LORD pronounced **a** 3605
16:15 from **a** the lands whither he had driven 3605
16:17 For mine eyes *are* upon **a** their ways: 3605
17: 3 *and* **a** thy treasures to the spoil, 3605
17: 3 places for sin, throughout **a** thy borders. 3605
17: 9 The heart *is* deceitful above **a** *things,* and 3605
17:13 **a** that forsake thee shall be ashamed, and 3605
17:19 go out, and in **a** the gates of Jerusalem; 3605
17:20 **a** Judah, and all the inhabitants of 3605
17:20 and **a** the inhabitants of Jerusalem, 3605
18:23 thou knowest **a** their counsel against me to 3605
19: 8 and hiss because of **a** the plagues thereof. 3605
19:13 of **a** the houses upon whose roofs they have 3605
19:13 burnt incense unto **a** the host of heaven, 3605
19:14 LORD'S house; and said to **a** the people, 3605
19:15 upon **a** her towns all the evil that I have 3605
19:15 upon all her towns **a** the evil that I have 3605
20: 4 thee a terror to thyself, and to **a** thy friends: 3605
20: 4 I will give **a** Judah into the hand of the king 3605
20: 5 Moreover I will deliver **a** the strength of 3605
20: 5 **a** the labours thereof, and all the precious 3605
20: 5 **a** the precious things thereof, and all 3605
20: 5 **a** the treasures of the kings of Judah will I 3605
20: 6 **a** that dwell in thine house shall go into 3605
20: 6 be buried there, thou, and **a** thy friends, 3605
20:10 **A** my familiars watched for my halting, 3605
21: 2 with us according to **a** his wondrous works, 3605
21:14 and it shall devour **a things** round about it. 3605
22:20 the passages: for **a** thy lovers are destroyed. 3605
22:22 The wind shall eat up **a** thy pastors, and 3605
22:22 and confounded for **a** thy wickedness. 3605
23: 3 will gather the remnant of my flock out of **a** 3605
23: 8 from **a** countries whither I had driven them; 3605
23: 9 because of the prophets; **a** my bones shake; 3605
23:14 they are **a** of them unto me as Sodom, and 3605
23:15 is profaneness gone forth into **a** the land. 3605
23:32 they shall not **profit** this people **at a**, 3276+3276
24: 9 I will deliver them to be removed into **a** 3605
24: 9 in **a** places whither I shall drive them. 3605
25: 1 **a** the people of Judah in the fourth year of 3605
25: 2 prophet spake unto **a** the people of Judah, 3605
25: 2 to **a** the inhabitants of Jerusalem, saying, 3605
25: 4 the LORD hath sent unto you **a** his 3605
25: 9 and take **a** the families of the north, 3605
25: 9 against **a** these nations round about, and 3605
25:13 I will bring upon that land **a** my words 3605
25:13 *even* **a** that is written in this book, which 3605
25:13 which Jeremiah hath prophesied against **a** 3605
25:15 cause **a** the nations, to whom I send thee, 3605
25:17 made **a** the nations to drink, unto whom 3605
25:19 and his princes, and **a** his people; 3605
25:20 **a** the mingled people, and all the kings of 3605
25:20 **a** the kings of the land of Uz, and all 3605
25:20 **a** the kings of the land of the Philistines, 3605
25:22 **a** the kings of Tyrus, and all the kings of 3605
25:22 **a** the kings of Zidon, and the kings of 3605
25:23 and **a** *that are* in the utmost corners, 3605
25:24 **a** the kings of Arabia, and all the kings of 3605
25:24 **a** the kings of the mingled people that 3605
25:25 **a** the kings of Zimri, and all the kings of 3605
25:25 **a** the kings of Elam, and all the kings of 3605
25:25 of Elam, and **a** the kings of the Medes, 3605
25:26 **a** the kings of the north, far and near, 3605
25:26 and **a** the kingdoms of the world, 3605
25:29 for I *will* call for a sword upon **a** 3605
25:30 Therefore prophesy thou against them **a** 3605
25:30 as they that tread *the grapes,* against **a** 3605
25:31 with the nations, he *will* plead with **a** flesh; 3605
26: 2 and speak unto **a** the cities of Judah, 3605
26: 2 **a** the words that I command thee to speak 3605
26: 6 will make this city a curse to **a** the nations 3605
26: 7 **a** the people heard Jeremiah speaking these 3605
26: 8 **a** that the LORD had commanded *him* to 3605
26: 8 *him* to speak unto **a** the people, 3605
26: 8 and the prophets and **a** the people took him, 3605
26: 9 **a** the people were gathered against 3605
26:11 unto the princes and to **a** the people, 3605
26:12 Then spake Jeremiah unto **a** the princes and 3605
26:12 unto all the princes and to **a** the people, 3605
26:12 against this city **a** the words that ye have 3605
26:15 you to speak **a** these words in your ears. 3605
26:16 **a** the people unto the priests and to 3605
26:17 spake to **a** the assembly of the people, 3605
26:18 spake to **a** the people of Judah, saying, 3605
26:19 and **a** Judah put him at all to death? 3605
26:19 and all Judah **put** him **at a to death**? 4191+4191
26:20 against this land according to **a** the words 3605
26:21 with **a** his mighty *men,* and all the princes, 3605
26:21 with all his mighty *men,* and **a** the princes, 3605
27: 6 now have I given **a** these lands into 3605
27: 7 **a** nations shall serve him, and his son, and 3605
27:12 king of Judah according to **a** these words, 3605
27:16 I spake to the priests and to **a** this people, 3605
27:20 and **a** the nobles of Judah and Jerusalem; 3605
28: 1 presence of the priests and of **a** the people, 3605
28: 3 place **a** the vessels of the LORD'S house, 3605
28: 4 with **a** the captives of Judah, that went into 3605
28: 5 in the presence of **a** the people that stood in 3605
28: 6 **a** that is carried away captive, 3605
28: 7 thine ears, and in the ears of **a** the people. 3605
28:11 Hananiah spake in the presence of **a** 3605
28:11 **a** nations within the space of two full years. 3605
28:14 I have put a yoke of iron upon the neck of **a** 3605
29: 1 to **a** the people whom Nebuchadnezzar had 3605
29: 4 unto **a** that are carried away captives, 3605
29:13 find *me,* when ye shall search for me with **a** 3605
29:14 I will gather you from **a** the nations, and 3605
29:14 from **a** the places whither I have driven 3605
29:16 of **a** the people that dwelleth in this city, 3605
29:18 will deliver them to be removed to **a** 3605
29:18 among **a** the nations whither I have driven 3605
29:20 word of the LORD, **a** *ye of* the captivity, 3605
29:22 of them shall be taken up a curse by **a** 3605
29:25 unto **a** the people that *are* at Jerusalem, 3605
29:25 the priest, and to **a** the priests, saying, 3605

Jer 29:31 Send to **a** them of the captivity, saying, 3605
30: 2 Write thee **a** the words that I have spoken 3605
30: 6 and **a** faces are turned into paleness? 3605
30:11 though I make a full end of **a** nations 3605
30:14 **A** thy lovers have forgotten thee; they seek 3605
30:16 Therefore **a** they that devour thee shall be 3605
30:16 **a** thine adversaries, every one of them, 3605
30:16 **a** that prey upon thee will I give for a prey. 3605
30:20 and I will punish **a** that oppress them. 3605
31: 1 will I be the God of **a** the families of Israel, 3605
31:12 they shall not sorrow **any more at a**. 3254+5750
31:24 *in* **a** the cities thereof together, 3605
31:34 for they shall **a** know me, from the least of 3605
31:37 I will also cast off **a** the seed of Israel for 3605
31:37 the seed of Israel for **a** that they have done, 3605
31:40 **a** the fields unto the brook of Kidron, 3605
32:12 before **a** the Jews that sat in the court of 3605
32:19 for thine eyes *are* open upon **a** the ways of 3605
32:23 they have done nothing of **a** that thou 3605
32:23 thou hast caused **a** this evil to come upon 3605
32:27 I *am* the LORD, the God of **a** flesh: 3605
32:32 Because of **a** the evil of the children of 3605
32:37 I *will* gather them out of **a** countries, 3605
32:42 Like as I have brought **a** this great evil 3605
32:42 will I bring upon them **a** the good that I 3605
33: 5 for **a** whose wickedness I have hid my face 3605
33: 8 I will cleanse them from **a** their iniquity, 3605
33: 8 I will pardon **a** their iniquities, 3605
33: 9 an honour before **a** the nations of the earth, 3605
33: 9 which shall hear **a** the good that I do unto 3605
33: 9 and tremble for **a** the goodness and 3605
33: 9 for **a** the prosperity that I procure unto it. 3605
33:12 without beast, and in **a** the cities thereof, 3605
34: 1 **a** his army, and all the kingdoms of 3605
34: 1 **a** the kingdoms of the earth of his 3605
34: 1 **a** the people, fought against Jerusalem, and 3605
34: 1 and against **a** the cities thereof, saying, 3605
34: 6 Jeremiah the prophet spake **a** these words 3605
34: 7 against **a** the cities of Judah that were left, 3605
34: 8 with **a** the people which *were* at Jerusalem, 3605
34:10 *Now* when **a** the princes, and all the people, 3605
34:10 *Now* when all the princes, and **a** the people, 3605
34:17 I will make you to be removed into **a** 3605
34:19 the priests, and **a** the people of the land, 3605
35: 3 **a** his sons, and the whole house of 3605
35: 7 but **a** your days ye shall dwell in tents; 3605
35: 8 our father in **a** that he hath charged us, 3605
35: 8 to drink no wine **a** our days, we, our wives, 3605
35:10 done according to **a** that Jonadab our father 3605
35:15 I have sent also unto you **a** my servants 3605
35:17 upon **a** the inhabitants of Jerusalem all 3605
35:17 upon all the inhabitants of Jerusalem **a** 3605
35:18 kept **a** his precepts, and done according 3605
35:18 done according unto **a** that he hath 3605
36: 2 write therein **a** the words that I have spoken 3605
36: 2 against Judah, and against **a** the nations, 3605
36: 3 **a** the evil which I purpose to do unto them; 3605
36: 4 Baruch wrote from the mouth of Jeremiah **a** 3605
36: 6 also thou shalt read them in the ears of **a** 3605
36: 8 Baruch the son of Neriah did according to **a** 3605
36: 9 the LORD *to* **a** the people in Jerusalem, 3605
36: 9 *to* **a** the people that came from the cities of 3605
36:10 in the ears of **a** the people. 3605
36:11 had heard out of the book **a** the words of 3605
36:12 lo, **a** the princes sat there, *even* Elishama 3605
36:12 the son of Hananiah, and **a** the princes. 3605
36:13 Michaiah declared unto them **a** the words 3605
36:14 Therefore **a** the princes sent Jehudi the son 3605
36:16 Now it came to pass when they had heard **a** 3605
36:16 We will surely tell the king of **a** these 3605
36:17 How didst thou write **a** these words at his 3605
36:18 He pronounced **a** these words unto me with 3605
36:20 and told **a** the words in the ears of the king. 3605
36:21 in the ears of **a** the princes which stood 3605
36:23 until **a** the roll was consumed in the fire 3605
36:24 nor any of his servants that heard **a** these 3605
36:28 write in it **a** the former words that were in 3605
36:31 **a** the evil that I have pronounced against 3605
36:32 **a** the words of the book which Jehoiakim 3605
37:21 until **a** the bread in the city were spent. 3605
38: 1 that Jeremiah had spoken unto **a** the people, 3605
38: 4 the hands of **a** the people, in speaking such 3605
38: 9 these men have done evil in **a** that they 3605
38:22 **a** the women that are left in the king of 3605
38:23 So they *shall* bring out **a** thy wives and thy 3605
38:27 came **a** the princes unto Jeremiah, and 3605
38:27 he told them according to **a** these words 3605
39: 1 and **a** his army against Jerusalem, 3605
39: 3 **a** the princes of the king of Babylon came 3605
39: 3 with **a** the residue of the princes of the king 3605
39: 4 **a** the men of war, then they fled, and 3605
39: 6 also the king of Babylon slew **a** the nobles 3605
39:13 and **a** the king of Babylon's princes; 3605
40: 1 **a** that were carried away captive of 3605
40: 4 behold, **a** the land *is* before thee: whither it 3605
40: 7 *Now* when **a** the captains of the forces 3605
40:11 Likewise when **a** the Jews that *were* in 3605
40:11 in Edom, and that *were* in **a** the countries, 3605
40:12 Even **a** the Jews returned out of all places 3605
40:12 Even all the Jews returned out of **a** places 3605
40:13 **a** the captains of the forces that *were* in 3605
40:15 that **a** the Jews which are gathered unto 3605
41: 3 Ishmael also slew **a** the Jews that were with 3605
41: 6 weeping **a along as** he **went**: 1980+1980
41: 9 Now the pit wherein Ishmael had cast **a** 3605
41:10 Ishmael carried away captive **a** the residue 3605
41:10 and **a** the people that remained in Mizpah, 3605
41:11 **a** the captains of the forces that *were* with 3605
41:11 heard of **a** the evil that Ishmael the son of 3605
41:12 they took **a** the men, and went to fight with 3605
41:13 *that* when **a** the people which *were* with 3605
41:13 **a** the captains of the forces that *were* with 3605
41:14 So **a** the people that Ishmael had carried 3605
41:16 **a** the captains of the forces that *were* with 3605
41:16 **a** the remnant of the people whom he had 3605

Jer 42: 1 **a** the captains of the forces, and 3605
42: 1 **a** the people from the least even unto 3605
42: 2 LORD thy God, *even* for **a** this remnant; 3605
42: 5 if we do not even according to **a** things *for* 3605
42: 8 **a** the captains of the forces which *were* 3605
42: 8 **a** the people from the least even to 3605
42:17 So shall it be with **a** the men that set their 3605
42:20 according unto **a** that the LORD our God 3605
43: 1 **a** the people all the words of the LORD 3605
43: 1 **a** the words of the LORD their God, 3605
43: 1 had sent him to them, *even* **a** these words; 3605
43: 2 **a** the proud men, saying unto Jeremiah, 3605
43: 4 **a** the captains of the forces, and all 3605
43: 4 the captains of the forces, and **a** the people, 3605
43: 5 **a** the captains of the forces, took all 3605
43: 5 of the forces, took **a** the remnant of Judah, 3605
43: 5 that were returned from **a** nations, 3605
44: 1 **a** the Jews which dwell in the land of 3605
44: 2 Ye have seen **a** the evil that I have brought 3605
44: 2 and upon **a** the cities of Judah; 3605
44: 4 Howbeit I sent unto you **a** my servants 3605
44: 8 a reproach among **a** the nations of 3605
44:11 against you for evil, and to cut off **a** Judah. 3605
44:12 they shall **a** be consumed, *and* fall in 3605
44:15 **a** the men which knew that their wives had 3605
44:15 **a** the women that stood *by,* a great 3605
44:15 even **a** the people that dwelt in the land of 3605
44:18 we have wanted **a** *things,* and have been 3605
44:20 Jeremiah said unto **a** the people, to 3605
44:20 to **a** the people which had given him *that* 3605
44:24 Moreover Jeremiah said unto **a** the people, 3605
44:24 to **a** the women, Hear the word of 3605
44:24 **a** Judah that *are* in the land of Egypt: 3605
44:26 **a** Judah that dwell in the land of Egypt; 3605
44:26 of any man of Judah in **a** the land of Egypt, 3605
44:27 **a** the men of Judah that *are* in the land of 3605
44:28 **a** the remnant of Judah, that are gone into 3605
45: 5 for behold, I *will* bring evil upon **a** flesh, 3605
45: 5 thy life will I give unto thee for a prey in **a** 3605
46:25 even Pharaoh, and ***a*** them that trust in him: NIH
46:28 for I will make a full end of **a** the nations 3605
47: 2 overflow the land, and **a that is therein**; 4393
47: 2 and **a** the inhabitants of the land shall howl. 3605
47: 4 Because of the day that cometh to spoil **a** 3605
48:17 **A** ye that are about him, bemoan him; and 3605
48:17 **a** ye that know his name, say, How is 3605
48:24 upon **a** the cities of the land of Moab, far 3605
48:31 for Moab, and I will cry out for **a** Moab; 3605
48:37 upon **a** the hands *shall be* cuttings, and 3605
48:38 generally upon **a** the housetops of Moab, 3605
48:39 and a dismaying to **a** them about him. 3605
49: 5 of hosts, from **a** those that be about thee; 3605
49:13 **a** the cities thereof shall be perpetual 3605
49:17 and shall hiss at **a** the plagues thereof. 3605
49:26 **a** the men of war shall be cut off in that 3605
49:29 and **a** their vessels, and their camels; 3605
49:32 I will scatter into **a** winds them *that are* in 3605
49:32 I will bring their calamity from **a** sides 3605
49:36 will scatter them towards **a** those winds; 3605
50: 7 **A** that found them have devoured them: 3605
50:10 **a** that spoil her shall be satisfied, saith 3605
50:13 be astonished, and hiss at **a** her plagues. 3605
50:14 **a** ye that bend the bow, shoot at her, 3605
50:21 do according to **a** that I have commanded 3605
50:27 Slay **a** her bullocks; let them go down to 3605
50:29 **a** ye that bend the bow, camp against it 3605
50:29 according to **a** that she hath done, do unto 3605
50:30 **a** her men of war shall be cut off in that 3605
50:32 and it shall devour **a** round about him. 3605
50:33 **a** that took them captives held them fast; 3605
50:37 upon **a** the mingled people that *are* in 3605
51: 3 young men; destroy ye utterly **a** her host. 3605
51: 7 that made **a** the earth drunken: 3605
51:19 for he *is* the former of **a** *things:* and 3605
51:24 to **a** the inhabitants of Chaldea all their evil 3605
51:24 to all the inhabitants of Chaldea **a** their evil 3605
51:25 the LORD, which destroyest **a** the earth: 3605
51:28 **a** the rulers thereof, and all the land of his 3605
51:28 and **a** the land of his dominion. 3605
51:47 and **a** her slain shall fall in the midst of her. 3605
51:48 and the earth, and **a** that *is* therein, 3605
51:49 at Babylon shall fall the slain of **a** the earth. 3605
51:52 through **a** her land the wounded shall 3605
51:60 So Jeremiah wrote in a book **a** the evil that 3605
51:60 *even* **a** these words that are written against 3605
51:61 and shalt see, and shalt read **a** these words; 3605
52: 2 according to **a** that Jehoiakim had done. 3605
52: 4 he and **a** his army, against Jerusalem, and 3605
52: 7 **a** the men of war fled, and went forth out of 3605
52: 8 and **a** his army was scattered from him. 3605
52:10 he slew also **a** the princes of Judah in 3605
52:13 **a** the houses of Jerusalem, and all 3605
52:13 **a** the houses of the great *men,* burnt he with 3605
52:14 **a** the army of the Chaldeans, that *were* with 3605
52:14 brake down **a** the walls of Jerusalem round 3605
52:17 and carried **a** the brass of them to Babylon. 3605
52:18 **a** the vessels of brass wherewith they 3605
52:20 the brass of **a** these vessels was without 3605
52:22 upon the chapiters round about, **a** *of* brass. 3605
52:23 **a** the pomegranates upon the network *were* 3605
52:30 **a** the persons *were* four thousand and 3605
52:33 he did continually eat bread before him **a** 3605
52:34 the day of his death, **a** the days of his life. 3605
La 1: 2 among **a** her lovers she hath none to 3605
1: 2 **a** her friends have dealt treacherously with 3605
1: 3 **a** her persecutors overtook her between 3605
1: 4 **a** her gates are desolate: her priests sigh: 3605
1: 6 from the daughter of Zion **a** her beauty is 3605
1: 7 of her miseries **a** her pleasant things that 3605
1: 8 **a** that honoured her despise her, because 3605
1:10 out his hand upon **a** her pleasant things: 3605
1:11 **A** her people sigh, they seek bread; 3605
1:12 *Is it* nothing to you, **a** ye that pass by? 3605
1:13 hath made me desolate *and* faint **a** the day. 3605
1:15 The Lord hath trodden under foot **a** my 3605

La 1:18 pray you, **a** people, and behold my sorrow: 3605
1:21 **a** mine enemies have heard of my trouble; 3605
1:22 Let **a** their wickedness come before thee; 3605
1:22 as thou hast done unto me for **a** my 3605
2: 2 The Lord hath swallowed up **a** 3605
2: 3 He hath cut off in *his* fierce anger **a** 3605
2: 4 slew **a** *that were* pleasant to the eye, in 3605
2: 5 he hath swallowed up **a** her palaces: 3605
2:15 **A** that pass by clap *their* hands at thee; 3605
2:16 **A** thine enemies have opened their mouth 3605
3: 3 he turneth his hand *against me* **a** the day. 3605
3:14 I was a derision to **a** my people; *and* 3605
3:14 to all my people; *and* their song **a** the day. 3605
3:34 To crush under his feet **a** the prisoners of 3605
3:46 **A** our enemies have opened their mouths 3605
3:51 because of **a** the daughters of my city. 3605
3:60 Thou hast seen **a** their vengeance *and* 3605
3:60 *and* **a** their imaginations against me. 3605
3:61 *and* **a** their imaginations against me; 3605
3:62 and their device against me **a** the day. 3605
4:12 and **a** the inhabitants of the world, 3605
Eze 3: 7 for **a** the house of Israel *are* impudent 3605
3:10 **a** my words that I shall speak unto thee 3605
5: 4 *for* thereof shall a fire come forth into **a** 3605
5: 9 the like, because of **a** thine abominations. 3605
5:10 of thee will I scatter into **a** the winds. 3605
5:11 thou hast defiled my sanctuary with **a** thy 3605
5:11 with **a** thine abominations, therefore will I 3605
5:12 I will scatter a third *part* into **a** the winds, 3605
5:14 about thee, in the sight of **a** that pass by. 3605
6: 6 In **a** your dwelling places the cities shall be 3605
6: 9 have committed in **a** their abominations. 3605
6:11 Alas for **a** the evil abominations of 3605
6:13 in **a** the tops of the mountains, and 3605
6:13 they did offer sweet savour to **a** their idols. 3605
6:14 toward Diblath, in **a** their habitations: 3605
7: 3 will recompense upon thee **a** thine 3605
7: 8 will recompense thee for **a** thine 3605
7:12 for wrath *is* upon **a** the multitude thereof. 3605
7:14 blown the trumpet, even to make **a** ready; 3605
7:14 for my wrath *is* upon **a** the multitude 3605
7:16 **a** of them mourning, every one for his 3605
7:17 **A** hands shall be feeble, and all knees shall 3605
7:17 and **a** knees shall be weak *as* water. 3605
7:18 shame *shall be* upon **a** faces, and 3605
7:18 all faces, and baldness upon **a** their heads. 3605
8:10 and **a** the idols of the house of Israel, 3605
9: 4 that cry for **a** the abominations that be done 3605
9: 8 *wilt* thou destroy **a** the residue of Israel in 3605
11:15 and **a** the house of Israel wholly, 3605
11:18 they shall take away **a** the detestable things 3605
11:18 **a** the abominations thereof from thence. 3605
11:25 I spake unto them of the captivity **a** 3605
12:10 **a** the house of Israel that *are* among them. 3605
12:14 I will scatter toward every wind **a** that *are* 3605
12:14 *are* about him to help him, and **a** his bands; 3605
12:16 that they may declare **a** their abominations 3605
12:19 may be desolate from **a that is therein,** 4393
12:19 of the violence of **a** them that dwell therein. 3605
13:18 Woe to *the women* that sew pillows to **a** 3605
14: 3 I be **inquired of at a** by them? 1875+1875
14: 5 they are **a** estranged from me through their 3605
14: 6 turn away your faces from **a** your 3605
14:11 neither be polluted any more with **a** their 3605
14:22 *even* concerning **a** that I have brought upon 3605
14:23 done without cause **a** that I have done in it, 3605
16: 4 *thee;* thou wast not **salted at a,** 4414+4414
16: 4 not salted at all, nor **swaddled at a.** 2853+2853
16:22 in **a** thine abominations and thy whoredoms 3605
16:23 it came to pass after **a** thy wickedness, 3605
16:30 seeing thou doest **a** these *things,* the work 3605
16:33 They give gifts to **a** whores: but thou givest 3605
16:33 thou givest thy gifts to **a** thy lovers, and 3605
16:36 with **a** the idols of thy abominations, and 3605
16:37 Behold therefore, I will gather **a** thy lovers, 3605
16:37 **a** *them* that thou hast loved, with all *them* 3605
16:37 with **a** *them* that thou hast hated; 3605
16:37 that they may see **a** thy nakedness. 3605
16:43 hast fretted me in **a** these *things;* behold 3605
16:43 *this* lewdness above **a** thine abominations. 3605
16:47 corrupted more than they in **a** thy ways. 3605
16:51 hast justified thy sisters in **a** thine 3605
16:54 mayest be confounded in **a** that thou hast 3605
16:57 **a** *that are* round about her, the daughters of 3605
16:63 when I am pacified toward thee for **a** that 3605
17: 9 it shall wither *in* **a** the leaves of her spring, 3605
17:18 hath done **a** these *things,* he shall not 3605
17:21 **a** his fugitives with all his bands shall fall 3605
17:21 all his fugitives with **a** his bands shall fall 3605
17:21 remain shall be scattered towards **a** winds: 3605
17:23 under it shall dwell **a** fowl of every wing; 3605
17:24 **a** the trees of the field shall know that I 3605
18: 4 Behold, **a** souls *are* mine; as the soul of 3605
18:13 he hath done **a** these abominations; he shall 3605
18:14 that seeth **a** his father's sins which he hath 3605
18:19 *and* hath kept **a** my statutes, and hath done 3605
18:21 if the wicked will turn from **a** his sins that 3605
18:21 keep **a** my statutes, and do that which is 3605
18:22 **A** his transgressions that he hath 3605
18:23 Have I **any pleasure at a** that 2654+2654
18:24 doeth according to **a** the abominations that 3605
18:24 **A** his righteousness that he hath done shall 3605
18:28 turneth away from **a** his transgressions that 3605
18:30 turn *yourselves* from **a** your transgressions; 3605
18:31 Cast away from you **a** your transgressions, 3605
20: 6 and honey, which *is* the glory of **a** lands: 3605
20:15 and honey, which *is* the glory of **a** lands; 3605
20:26 through *the fire* **a** that openeth the womb, 3605
20:28 **a** the thick trees, and they offered there 3605
20:31 ye pollute yourselves with **a** your idols, 3605
20:32 cometh into your mind shall not **be at a,** 1961
20:40 there shall **a** the house of Israel, 3605
20:40 of Israel, **a** of them in the land, serve me: 3605
20:40 of your oblations, with **a** your holy *things.* 3605
20:43 **a** your doings, wherein ye have been 3605

Eze 20:43 for **a** your evils that ye have committed. 3605
20:47 **a** faces from the south to the north shall be 3605
20:48 **a** flesh shall see that I the LORD have 3605
21: 4 against **a** flesh from the south *to* the north: 3605
21: 5 That **a** flesh may know that I the LORD 3605
21: 7 **a** hands shall be feeble, and every spirit 3605
21: 7 and **a** knees shall be weak *as* water: 3605
21:12 it *shall be* upon **a** the princes of Israel: 3605
21:15 I have set the point of the sword against **a** 3605
21:24 that in **a** your doings your sins do appear; 3605
22: 2 thou shalt shew her **a** her abominations. 3605
22: 4 the heathen, and a mocking to **a** countries. 3605
22:18 **a** they *are* brass, and tin, and iron, and lead, 3605
22:19 Because ye are **a** become dross, 3605
23: 6 and rulers, **a** of them desirable young men, 3605
23: 7 *with* **a** them *that were* the chosen men of 3605
23: 7 of Assyria, and with **a** *on* whom she doted: 3605
23: 7 with **a** their idols she defiled herself. 3605
23:12 **a** of them desirable young men. 3605
23:15 their heads, **a** of them princes to look to, 3605
23:23 **a** the Chaldeans, Pekod, and Shoa, and 3605
23:23 Shoa, and Koa, *and* **a** the Assyrians with them: 3605
23:23 **a** of them desirable young men, captains 3605
23:23 renowned, **a** of them riding upon horses. 3605
23:29 shall take *away* **a** thy labour, and 3605
23:48 that **a** women may be taught not to do after 3605
24:24 according to **a** that he hath done shall ye 3605
25: 6 rejoiced in heart with **a** thy despite against 3605
25: 8 the house of Judah *is* like unto **a** 3605
26:11 his horses shall he tread down **a** thy streets: 3605
26:16 **a** the princes of the sea shall come down 3605
26:17 which cause their terror *to be* on **a** that 3605
27: 5 They have made **a** thy *ship* boards of fir 3605
27: 9 **a** the ships of the sea with their mariners 3605
27:12 reason of the multitude of **a** *kind of* riches; 3605
27:18 of thy making, for the multitude of **a** riches; 3605
27:21 Arabia, and **a** the princes of Kedar, 3605
27:22 they occupied in thy fairs with chief of **a** 3605
27:22 and with **a** precious stones, and gold. 3605
27:24 *were* thy merchants in **a sorts of things,** 4360
27:27 **a** thy men of war, that *are* in thee, and in all 3605
27:27 in **a** thy company which *is* in the midst of 3605
27:29 And **a** that handle the oar, the mariners, *and* 3605
27:29 the mariners, *and* **a** the pilots of the sea, 3605
27:34 **a** thy company in the midst of thee shall 3605
27:35 **A** the inhabitants of the isles shall be 3605
28:18 in the sight of **a** them that behold thee. 3605
28:19 **A** they that know thee among the people 3605
28:24 nor *any* grieving thorn of **a** *that are* round 3605
28:26 when I have executed judgments upon **a** 3605
29: 2 prophesy against him, and against **a** Egypt: 3605
29: 4 **a** the fish of thy rivers shall stick unto thy 3605
29: 5 thee and **a** the fish of thy rivers: 3605
29: 6 **a** the inhabitants of Egypt shall know that I 3605
29: 7 thou didst break, and rent **a** their shoulder: 3605
29: 7 and madest **a** their loins to be at a stand. 3605
30: 5 **a** the mingled people, and Chub, and 3605
30: 8 and *when* **a** her helpers shall be destroyed. 3605
30:12 **a that is therein,** by the hand of strangers: 4393
31: 4 sent out her little rivers unto **a** the trees of 3605
31: 5 Therefore his height was exalted above **a** 3605
31: 6 **A** the fowls of heaven made their nests in 3605
31: 6 under his branches did **a** the beasts of 3605
31: 6 and under his shadow dwelt **a** great nations. 3605
31: 9 so that **a** the trees of Eden, that *were* in 3605
31:12 and in **a** the valleys his branches are fallen, 3605
31:12 his boughs are broken by **a** the rivers of 3605
31:12 **a** the people of the earth are gone down 3605
31:13 Upon his ruin shall **a** the fowls of 3605
31:13 **a** the beasts of the field shall be upon his 3605
31:14 To the end that none of **a** the trees by 3605
31:14 stand up in their height, **a** that drink water: 3605
31:14 for they are **a** delivered unto death, to 3605
31:15 and **a** the trees of the field fainted for him. 3605
31:16 **a** the trees of Eden, the choice and best of 3605
31:16 and best of Lebanon, **a** that drink water, 3605
31:18 This *is* Pharaoh and **a** his multitude, 3605
32: 4 will cause **a** the fowls of the heaven to 3605
32: 8 **A** the bright lights of heaven will I make 3605
32:12 to fall, the terrible of the nations, **a** of them: 3605
32:12 **a** the multitude thereof shall be destroyed. 3605
32:13 I will destroy also **a** the beasts thereof from 3605
32:15 when I shall smite **a** them that dwell 3605
32:16 *even* for Egypt, and for **a** her multitude, 3605
32:20 the sword: draw her and **a** her multitudes. 3605
32:22 Asshur *is* there and **a** her company: 3605
32:22 **a** of them slain, fallen by the sword: 3605
32:23 **a** of them slain, fallen by the sword, 3605
32:24 and **a** her multitude round about her grave, 3605
32:24 **a** of them slain, fallen by the sword, 3605
32:25 the midst of the slain with **a** her multitude: 3605
32:25 **a** of them uncircumcised, slain by 3605
32:26 *is* Meshech, Tubal, and **a** her multitude: 3605
32:26 **a** of them uncircumcised, slain by 3605
32:29 *is* Edom, her kings, and **a** her princes, 3605
32:30 the north, **a** of them, and all the Zidonians, 3605
32:30 the north, all of them, and **a** the Zidonians, 3605
32:31 shall be comforted over **a** his multitude, 3605
32:31 and **a** his army slain by the sword, 3605
32:32 *even* Pharaoh and **a** his multitude, saith 3605
33:13 **a** his righteousnesses shall not be 3605
33:29 of **a** their abominations which they have 3605
34: 5 they became meat to **a** the beasts of 3605
34: 6 My sheep wandered through **a** 3605
34: 6 my flock was scattered upon **a** the face of 3605
34:12 will deliver them out of **a** places where 3605
34:13 and in **a** the inhabited places of the country. 3605
34:21 and pusht **a** the diseased with your horns, 3605
35: 8 in thy valleys, and in **a** thy rivers, shall they 3605
35:12 *that* I have heard **a** thy blasphemies which 3605
35:15 O mount Seir, and **a** Idumea, *even* all of it: 3605
35:15 O mount Seir, and all Idumea, *even* **a** of it: 3605
36: 5 of the heathen, and against **a** Idumea, 3605
36: 5 possession with the joy of **a** *their* heart, 3605
36:10 **a** the house of Israel, *even* all of it: 3605

Eze 36:10 all the house of Israel, *even* **a** of it: 3605
36:24 gather you out of **a** countries, and 3605
36:25 from **a** your filthiness, and from all your 3605
36:25 and from **a** your idols, will I cleanse you. 3605
36:29 I will also save you from **a** your 3605
36:33 have cleansed you from **a** your iniquities, 3605
36:34 whereas it lay desolate in the sight of **a** that 3605
37:16 *for* **a** the house of Israel his companions: 3605
37:22 and one king shall be king to them **a**: 3605
37:22 into two kingdoms **any more at a**: 5750+5750
37:23 I will save them out of **a** their dwelling 3605
37:24 and they **a** shall have one shepherd: 3605
38: 4 and **a** thine army, horses and horsemen, 3605
38: 4 **a** of them clothed with all sorts *of armour,* 3605
38: 4 all of them clothed with **a sorts** *of armour,* 4358
38: 4 and shields, **a** of them handling swords: 3605
38: 5 **a** of them *with* shield and helmet: 3605
38: 6 Gomer, and **a** his bands; the house of 3605
38: 6 *of* the north quarters, and **a** his bands: 3605
38: 7 **a** thy company that are assembled unto 3605
38: 8 and they shall dwell safely **a** of them. 3605
38: 9 **a** thy bands, and many people with thee. 3605
38:11 **a** of them dwelling without walls, and 3605
38:13 with **a** the young lions thereof, shall say 3605
38:15 **a** of them riding upon horses, a great 3605
38:20 **a** creeping things that creep upon the earth, 3605
38:20 **a** the men that *are* upon the face of 3605
38:21 against him throughout **a** my mountains, 3605
39: 4 **a** thy bands, and the people that *is* with 3605
39:11 shall they bury Gog and **a** his multitude: 3605
39:13 **a** the people of the land shall bury *them;* 3605
39:18 of bullocks, **a** of them fatlings of Bashan. 3605
39:20 with mighty *men,* and *with* **a** men of war, 3605
39:21 **a** the heathen shall see my judgment that I 3605
39:23 their enemies: so fell they **a** by the sword. 3605
39:26 **a** their trespasses whereby they have 3605
40: 4 set thine heart upon **a** that I shall shew thee; 3605
40: 4 declare **a** that thou seest to the house of 3605
41:17 by **a** the wall round about within 3605
41:19 *it was* made through **a** the house round 3605
42:11 **a** their goings out *were* both according to 3605
43:11 if they be ashamed of **a** that they have 3605
43:11 **a** the forms thereof, and all the ordinances 3605
43:11 **a** the ordinances thereof, and all the forms 3605
43:11 **a** the forms thereof, and all the laws 3605
43:11 the forms thereof, and **a** the laws thereof: 3605
43:11 and **a** the ordinances thereof, and do them. 3605
44: 5 hear with thine ears **a** that I say unto thee 3605
44: 5 **a** the ordinances of the house of 3605
44: 5 of the LORD, and **a** the laws thereof; 3605
44: 6 let it suffice you of **a** your abominations, 3605
44: 7 because of **a** your abominations. 3605
44:14 for **a** the service thereof, and for all that 3605
44:14 and for **a** that shall be done therein. 3605
44:24 and my statutes in **a** mine assemblies; 3605
44:30 the first of **a** the firstfruits of all *things,* 3605
44:30 the first of all the firstfruits of **a** *things,* 3605
44:30 of all *things,* and every oblation of **a**, 3605
45: 1 This *shall be* holy in **a** the borders thereof 3605
45:16 **A** the people of the land shall give this 3605
45:17 in the sabbaths in **a** solemnities of 3605
45:22 for **a** the people of the land a bullock *for* **a** 3605
47:12 on that side, shall grow **a** trees for meat, 3605
48:13 **a** the length *shall be* five and 3605
48:19 shall serve it out of **a** the tribes of Israel. 3605
48:20 **A** the oblation *shall be* five and 3605
Da 1: 4 skilful in **a** wisdom, and cunning in 3605
1:15 fatter in flesh than **a** the children which did 3605
1:17 and skill in **a** learning and wisdom: 3605
1:17 Daniel had understanding in **a** visions and 3605
1:19 among them **a** was found none like Daniel, 3605
1:20 *in* **a** matters of wisdom *and* understanding, 3605
1:20 he found them ten times better than **a** 3605
1:20 *and* astrologers that *were* in **a** his realm. 3605
2:12 commanded to destroy **a** the wise *men* of 3606
2:38 and hath made thee ruler over them **a**. 3606
2:39 which shall bear rule over **a** the earth. 3606
2:40 subdueth **a** *things:* and as iron that breaketh 3606
2:40 all *things:* and as iron that breaketh **a** these, 3606
2:44 in pieces and consume **a** these kingdoms, 3606
2:48 chief of the governors over **a** the wise *men* 3606
3: 2 and **a** the rulers of the provinces, 3606
3: 3 and **a** the rulers of the provinces, 3606
3: 5 psaltery, dulcimer, and **a** kinds of musick, 3606
3: 7 when **a** the people heard the sound of 3606
3: 7 sackbut, psaltery, and **a** kinds of musick, 3606
3: 7 **a** the people, the nations, and 3606
3:10 and dulcimer, and **a** kinds of musick, 3606
3:15 and dulcimer, and **a** kinds of musick, 3606
4: 1 unto **a** people, nations, and languages, that 3606
4: 1 languages, that dwell in **a** the earth; 3606
4: 6 Therefore made I a decree to bring in **a** 3606
4:11 the sight thereof to the end of **a** the earth: 3606
4:12 fruit thereof much, and in it *was* meat for **a**: 3606
4:12 boughs thereof, and **a** flesh was fed of it. 3606
4:18 forasmuch as **a** the wise *men* of my 3606
4:20 and the sight thereof to **a** the earth; 3606
4:21 fruit thereof much, and in it *was* meat for **a**; 3606
4:28 **A** this came upon the king 3606
4:35 **a** the inhabitants of the earth *are* reputed as 3606
4:37 **a** whose works *are* truth, and his ways 3606
5: 8 came in **a** the king's wise *men:* but 3606
5:19 **a** people, nations, and languages, trembled 3606
5:22 thine heart, though thou knewest **a** this; 3606
5:23 thy breath *is,* and whose *are* **a** thy ways, 3606
6: 7 **A** the presidents of the kingdom, 3606
6:24 brake **a** their bones in pieces or ever they 3606
6:25 king Darius wrote unto **a** people, nations, 3606
6:25 languages, that dwell in **a** the earth; 3606
7: 7 it *was* diverse from **a** the beasts that *were* 3606
7:14 that **a** people, nations, and languages, 3606
7:16 stood *by,* and asked him the truth of **a** this. 3606
7:19 which was diverse from **a** the others, 3606
7:23 which shall be diverse from **a** kingdoms, 3606
7:27 and **a** dominions shall serve and obey him. 3606

A

Da 9: 6 our fathers, and to **a** the people of the land. 3605
9: 7 unto **a** Israel, *that are* near, and *that are* far 3605
9: 7 through **a** the countries whither thou hast 3605
9:11 Yea, **a** Israel have transgressed thy law, 3605
9:13 law of Moses, **a** this evil is come upon us: 3605
9:14 for the LORD our God *is* righteous in **a** 3605
9:16 O Lord, according to **a** thy righteousness, 3605
9:16 thy people *are become* a reproach to **a** *that* 3605
10: 3 neither did I **anoint** myself **at a**, till 5480+5480
11: 2 the fourth shall be far richer than *they* **a**: 3605
11: 2 shall stir up **a** against the realm of Grecia. 3605
11:37 for he shall magnify himself above **a**. 3605
11:43 and over **a** the precious *things* of Egypt: 3605
12: 7 **a** these *things* shall be finished. 3605
Hos 2:11 I will also cause **a** her mirth to cease, 3605
2:11 and her sabbaths, and **a** her solemn feasts. 3605
5: 2 though I *have been* a rebuker of them **a**. 3605
7: 2 hearts *that* I remember **a** their wickedness: 3605
7: 4 They *are* **a** adulterers, as an oven heated by 3605
7: 6 their baker sleepeth **a** the night; *in* 3605
7: 7 They are **a** hot as an oven, and 3605
7: 7 their judges; **a** their kings are fallen: 3605
7:10 LORD their God, nor seek him for **a** this. 3605
9: 4 **a** that eat thereof shall be polluted: 3605
9: 8 the prophet *is* a snare of a fowler in **a** his 3605
9:15 **A** their wickedness *is* in Gilgal, for there I 3605
9:15 them no more: **a** their princes *are* revolters. 3605
10:14 and **a** thy fortresses shall be spoiled, 3605
11: 7 the most High, none **at a** would exalt *him*. 3162
12: 8 *in* **a** my labours they shall find none 3605
13: 2 **a** of it the work of the craftsmen: 3605
13:10 where *is any other* that may save thee in **a** 3605
13:15 he shall spoil the treasure of **a** pleasant 3605
14: 2 Take away **a** iniquity, and receive *us* 3605
Joel 1: 2 and give ear, **a** ye inhabitants of the land. 3605
1: 5 howl, **a** ye drinkers of wine, because of 3605
1:12 *even* **a** the trees of the field, are withered: 3605
1:13 come, **lie a night** in sackcloth, ye ministers 3885
1:14 **a** the inhabitants of the land *into* the house 3605
1:19 the flame hath burnt **a** the trees of the field. 3605
2: 1 let **a** the inhabitants of the land tremble: 3605
2: 6 **a** faces shall gather blackness. 3605
2:12 turn ye *even* to me with **a** your heart, and 3605
2:28 that I will pour out my spirit upon **a** flesh; 3605
3: 2 I will also gather **a** nations, and will bring 3605
3: 4 and Zidon, and **a** the coasts of Palestine? 3605
3: 9 wake up the mighty *men*, let **a** the men of 3605
3:11 **a** ye heathen, and gather yourselves 3605
3:12 for there will I sit to judge **a** the heathen 3605
3:18 **a** the rivers of Judah shall flow *with* waters, 3605
Am 1:11 did cast off **a** pity, and his anger did tear NIH
2: 3 will slay **a** the princes thereof with him, 3605
3: 2 You only have I known of **a** the families of 3605
3: 2 I will punish you for **a** your iniquities. 3605
3: 5 and have **taken** nothing **at a**? 3920+3920
4: 6 you cleanness of teeth in **a** your cities, 3605
4: 6 and want of bread in **a** your places: 3605
5:16 Wailing *shall be* in **a** streets; and they shall 3605
5:16 and they shall say in **a** the highways, Alas! 3605
5:17 in **a** vineyards *shall be* wailing: for I will 3605
6: 8 I deliver up the city with **a that is therein**. 4393
7:10 the land is not able to bear **a** his words. 3605
8:10 and **a** your songs into lamentation; 3605
8:10 I will bring up sackcloth upon **a** loins, and 3605
9: 1 cut them in the head, **a** of them; and I will 3605
9: 5 and **a** that dwell therein shall mourn: 3605
9: 9 I will sift the house of Israel among **a** 3605
9:10 **A** the sinners of my people shall die by 3605
9:12 of **a** the heathen, which are called by my 3605
9:13 drop sweet wine, and **a** the hills shall melt. 3605
Ob 1: 7 **A** the men of thy confederacy have brought 3605
1:15 For the day of the LORD *is* near upon **a** 3605
1:16 *so* shall **a** the heathen drink continually, 3605
Jnh 2: 3 **a** thy billows and thy waves passed over 3605
Mic 1: 2 Hear, **a** ye people; hearken, O earth, and 3605
1: 2 hearken, O earth, and **a that therein is**: 4393
1: 5 For the transgression of Jacob *is* **a** this, and 3605
1: 7 **a** the graven images thereof shall be beaten 3605
1: 7 **a** the hires thereof shall be burnt with 3605
1: 7 and **a** the idols thereof will I lay desolate: 3605
1:10 ye *it* not at Gath, **weep** ye not **at a**: 1058+1058
2:12 I will surely assemble, O Jacob, **a** of thee; 3605
3: 7 yea, they shall **a** cover their lips; for *there* 3605
3: 9 that abhor judgment, and pervert **a** equity. 3605
4: 5 For **a** people will walk every one in 3605
5: 9 and **a** thine enemies shall be cut off. 3605
5:11 and throw down **a** thy strong holds: 3605
6:16 **a** the works of the house of Ahab, and 3605
7: 2 they **a** lie in wait for blood; they hunt every 3605
7:16 and be confounded at **a** their might: 3605
7:19 thou wilt cast **a** their sins into the depths of 3605
Na 1: 3 will not **at a acquit** *the wicked*: 5352+5352
1: 4 maketh it dry, and drieth up **a** the rivers: 3605
1: 5 yea, the world, and **a** that dwell therein. 3605
2: 9 *and* glory out of **a** the pleasant furniture. 3605
2:10 much pain *is* in **a** loins, and the faces of 3605
2:10 the faces of them **a** gather blackness. 3605
3: 1 it *is* **a** full *of* lies *and* robbery; the prey 4392
3: 7 *that* **a** they that look upon thee shall flee 3605
3:10 dashed in pieces at the top of **a** the streets: 3605
3:10 and **a** her great *men* were bound in chains. 3605
3:12 **A** thy strong holds *shall be like* fig trees 3605
3:19 **a** that hear the bruit of thee shall clap 3605
Hab 1: 9 They shall come **a** for violence: their faces 3605
1:15 They take up **a** of them with the angle, 3605
2: 5 gathereth unto him **a** nations, and 3605
2: 5 all nations, and heapeth unto him **a** people: 3605
2: 6 Shall not **a** these take up a parable against 3605
2: 8 **a** the remnant of the people shall spoil thee; 3605
2: 8 *of* the city, and *of* **a** that dwell therein. 3605
2:17 *of* the city, and *of* **a** that dwell therein. 3605
2:19 and *there is* no breath at **a** in the midst of it. 3605
2:20 let **a** the earth keep silence before him. 3605
Zep 1: 2 I will utterly consume **a** *things* from off 3605
1: 4 and upon **a** the inhabitants of Jerusalem; 3605

Zep 1: 8 **a** such as are clothed with strange apparel. 3605
1: 9 In the same day also will I punish **a** those 3605
1:11 for **a** the merchant people are cut down; 3605
1:11 cut down; **a** they that bear silver are cut off. 3605
1:18 riddance of **a** them that dwell in the land. 3605
2: 3 ye the LORD, **a** ye meek of the earth, 3605
2:11 for he will famish **a** the gods of the earth; 3605
2:11 his place, *even* **a** the isles of the heathen. 3605
2:14 the midst of her, **a** the beasts of the nations: 3605
3: 7 rose early, *and* corrupted **a** their doings. 3605
3: 8 mine indignation, *even* **a** my fierce anger: 3605
3: 8 for **a** the earth shall be devoured with 3605
3: 9 that they may **a** call upon the name of 3605
3:11 In that day shalt thou not be ashamed for **a** 3605
3:14 be glad and rejoice with **a** the heart, 3605
3:19 at that time I *will* undo **a** that afflict thee: 3605
3:20 and a praise among **a** people of the earth, 3605
Hag 1:11 and upon **a** the labour of the hands. 3605
1:12 with **a** the remnant of the people, 3605
1:14 the spirit of **a** the remnant of the people; 3605
2: 4 be strong, **a** ye people of the land, saith 3605
2: 7 I will shake **a** nations, and the desire of all 3605
2: 7 and the desire of **a** nations shall come: 3605
2:17 with hail *in* **a** the labours of your hands; 3605
Zec 1:11 **a** the earth sitteth still, and is at rest. 3605
2:13 Be silent, O **a** flesh, before the LORD: 3605
4: 2 and behold, a candlestick **a** of gold, 3605
5: 6 This *is* their resemblance through **a** 3605
6: 5 standing before the Lord of **a** the earth. 3605
7: 5 Speak unto **a** the people of the land, and 3605
7: 5 did ye **at a fast** *unto* me, *even* to me? 6684+6684
7:14 I scattered them with a whirlwind among **a** 3605
8:10 for I set **a** men every one against his 3605
8:12 of this people to possess **a** these *things*. 3605
8:17 for **a** these *are things* that I hate, saith 3605
8:23 take hold out of **a** languages of the nations, 3605
9: 1 the eyes of man, as of **a** the tribes of Israel, 3605
10:11 and **a** the deeps of the river shall dry up: 3605
11:10 which I had made with **a** the people. 3605
12: 2 of trembling unto **a** the people round about, 3605
12: 3 Jerusalem a burdensome stone for **a** people: 3605
12: 3 **a** that burden themselves with it shall be 3605
12: 3 though **a** the people of the earth be 3605
12: 6 they shall devour **a** the people round about, 3605
12: 9 *that* I will seek to destroy **a** the nations that 3605
12:14 **A** the families that remain, every family 3605
13: 8 to pass, *that* in **a** the land, saith the LORD, 3605
14: 2 For I will gather **a** nations against 3605
14: 5 God shall come, *and* **a** the saints with thee. 3605
14: 9 the LORD shall be king over **a** the earth: 3605
14:10 **A** the land shall be turned as a plain from 3605
14:12 **a** the people that have fought against 3605
14:14 the wealth of **a** the heathen round about 3605
14:15 of **a** the beasts that shall be in these tents, 3605
14:16 *that* every one that is left of **a** the nations 3605
14:17 *that* whoso will not come up of *a* NIH
14:19 the punishment of **a** nations that come not 3605
14:21 **a** they that sacrifice shall come and take of 3605
Mal 2: 9 and base before **a** the people, 3605
2:10 Have we not **a** one father? hath not one 3605
3:10 Bring ye **a** the tithes into the storehouse, 3605
3:12 **a** nations shall call you blessed: for ye shall 3605
4: 1 **a** the proud, yea, and all that do wickedly, 3605
4: 1 all the proud, yea, and **a** that do wickedly, 3605
4: 4 commanded unto him in Horeb for **a** Israel, 3605
Mt 1:17 So **a** the generations from Abraham to *3956*
1:22 Now **a** this was done, that it might be *3650*
2: 3 he was troubled, and **a** Jerusalem with him. *3956*
2: 4 And when he had gathered **a** the chief *3956*
2:16 slew **a** the children that were in Bethlehem, *3956*
2:16 and in **a** the coasts thereof, from two years *3956*
3: 5 and **a** Judea, and all the region round about *3956*
3: 5 and **a** the region round about Jordan, *3956*
3:15 for thus it becometh us to fulfil **a** *3956*
4: 8 sheweth him **a** the kingdoms of the world, *3956*
4: 9 unto him, **A** these *things* will I give thee, *3956*
4:23 And Jesus went about **a** Galilee, *1722+3650*
4:23 and healing **a** *manner of* sickness and *3956*
4:23 and **a** *manner of* disease among the people. *3956*
4:24 And his fame went throughout **a** Syria: and *3650*
4:24 they brought unto him **a** sick people that *3956*
5:11 shall say **a manner** of evil against you *3956*
5:15 it giveth light unto **a** that are in the house. *3956*
5:18 wise pass from the law, till **a** be fulfilled. *3956*
5:34 But I say unto you, Swear not **at a**; *3654*
6:29 That even Solomon in **a** his glory was not *3956*
6:32 (For after **a** these *things* do the Gentiles *3956*
6:32 knoweth that ye have need of **a** these *things*. *537*
6:33 and **a** these *things* shall be added unto you. *3956*
7:12 Therefore **a** *things* whatsoever ye would *3956*
8:16 with *his* word, and healed **a** that were sick: *3956*
9:26 And the fame hereof went abroad into **a** *3650*
9:31 spread abroad his fame in **a** that country. *3650*
9:35 And Jesus went about **a** the cities and *3956*
10: 1 and to heal **a** *manner of* sickness and *3956*
10: 1 *of* sickness and **a** *manner of* disease. *3956*
10:22 And ye shall be hated of **a** *men* for my *3956*
10:30 But the very hairs of your head are **a** *3956*
11:13 For **a** the prophets and the law prophesied *3956*
11:27 **A** *things* are delivered unto me of my *3956*
11:28 **a** *ye* that labour and are heavy laden, and I *3956*
12:15 followed him, and he healed them **a**, *3956*
12:23 And **a** the people were amazed, and said, *3956*
12:31 **A** *manner of* sin and blasphemy shall be *3956*
13:32 Which indeed is the least of **a** seeds: but *3956*
13:34 **A** these *things* spake Jesus unto *3956*
13:41 they shall gather out of his kingdom **a** *3956*
13:44 joy thereof goeth and selleth **a** that he hath, *3956*
13:46 went and sold **a** that he had, and bought it. *3956*
13:51 Have ye understood **a** these *things?* They *3956*
13:56 And his sisters, are they not **a** with us? *3956*
13:56 Whence then hath this *man* **a** these *things?* *3956*
14:20 And they did **a** eat, and were filled: and *3956*
14:35 they sent out into **a** that country round *3650*
14:35 and brought unto him **a** that were diseased; *3956*

Mt 15:37 And they did **a** eat, and were filled: and *3956*
17:11 truly shall first come, and restore **a** *things*. *3956*
18:25 and **a** that he had, and payment to be made. *3956*
18:26 patience with me, and I will pay thee **a**. *3956*
18:29 patience with me, and I will pay thee **a**. *3956*
18:31 and told unto their lord **a** that was done. *3956*
18:32 I forgave thee **a** that debt, because *3956*
18:34 till he should pay **a** that was due unto him. *3956*
19:11 **A** *men* cannot receive this saying, *3956*
19:20 **A** these *things* have I kept from my youth *3956*
19:26 but with God **a** *things* are possible. *3956*
19:27 we have forsaken **a**, and followed thee; *3956*
20: 6 Why stand ye here **a** the day idle? *3650*
21: 4 **A** this was done, that it might be fulfilled *3650*
21:10 **a** the city was moved, saying, Who is this? *3956*
21:12 and cast out **a** them that sold and bought in *3956*
21:22 And **a** *things*, whatsoever ye shall ask in *3956*
21:26 the people; for **a** hold John as a prophet. *3956*
21:37 But last *of* **a** he sent unto them his son, NIG
22: 4 fatlings *are* killed, and **a** *things are* ready: *3956*
22:10 gathered together **a** as many as they found, *3956*
22:27 And last of **a** the woman died also. *3956*
22:28 she be of the seven? for they **a** had her. *3956*
22:37 Thou shalt love the Lord thy God with **a** *3650*
22:37 and with **a** thy soul, and with all thy mind. *3650*
22:37 and with all thy soul, and with **a** thy mind. *3650*
22:40 On these two commandments hang **a** *3650*
23: 3 **A** therefore whatsoever they bid you *3956*
23: 5 But **a** their works they do for to be seen of *3956*
23: 8 *even* Christ; and **a** ye are brethren. *3956*
23:20 sweareth by it, and by **a** *things* thereon. *3956*
23:27 of dead *men's* bones, and of **a** uncleanness. *3956*
23:35 That upon you may come **a** the righteous *3956*
23:36 **A** these *things* shall come upon this *3956*
24: 2 See ye not **a** these *things?* verily I say unto *3956*
24: 6 for **a** *these things* must come to pass, but *3956*
24: 8 **A** these *are* the beginning of sorrows. *3956*
24: 9 ye shall be hated of **a** nations for my *3956*
24:14 **a** the world for a witness unto all nations; *3650*
24:14 all the world for a witness unto **a** nations; *3956*
24:30 then shall **a** the tribes of the earth mourn, *3956*
24:33 when ye shall see **a** these *things*, know that *3956*
24:34 not pass, till **a** these *things* be fulfilled. *3956*
24:39 until the flood came, and took *them* **a** away; *537*
24:47 That he shall make him ruler over **a** his *3956*
25: 5 they **a** slumbered and slept. *3956*
25: 7 Then **a** those virgins arose, and *3956*
25:31 and **a** the holy angels with him, then *3956*
25:32 And before him shall be gathered **a** nations: *3956*
26: 1 when Jesus had finished **a** these sayings, *3956*
26:27 gave *it* to them, saying, Drink ye **a** of it; *3956*
26:31 **A** ye shall be offended because of me this *3956*
26:33 Though **a** *men* shall be offended because *3956*
26:35 Likewise also said **a** the disciples. *3956*
26:52 for **a** they that take the sword shall perish *3956*
26:56 But **a** this was done, that the scriptures of *3650*
26:56 Then **a** the disciples forsook him, and fled. *3956*
26:59 chief priests, and elders, and **a** the council, *3650*
26:70 But he denied before *them* **a**, saying, *3956*
27: 1 **a** the chief priests and elders of the people *3956*
27:22 *They* **a** say unto him, Let him be crucified. *3956*
27:25 Then answered **a** the people, and said, *3956*
27:45 over **a** the land unto the ninth hour. *3956*
28: 9 behold, Jesus met them, saying, *A* hail. NIG
28:11 shewed unto the chief priests **a** the *things* *537*
28:18 **A** power is given unto me in heaven and *3956*
28:19 Go ye therefore, and teach **a** nations, *3956*
28:20 Teaching them to observe **a** *things* *3956*
Mk 1: 5 And there went out unto him **a** the land of *3956*
1: 5 were **a** baptized of him in the river *of* *3956*
1:27 And they were **a** amazed, insomuch that *3956*
1:28 **a** the region round about Galilee. *3650*
1:32 they brought unto him **a** that were diseased, *3956*
1:33 And **a** the city was gathered together at *3650*
1:37 they said unto him, **A** *men* seek for thee. *3956*
1:39 in their synagogues throughout **a** Galilee, *3650*
2:12 up the bed, and went forth before *them* **a**; *3956*
2:12 insomuch that *they* were **a** amazed, and *3956*
2:13 and **a** the multitude resorted unto him, and *3956*
3:28 **A** sins shall be forgiven unto the sons of *3956*
4:11 **a** *these things* are done in parables: *3956*
4:13 and how *then* will ye know **a** parables? *3956*
4:31 is less than **a** the seeds that be in the earth: *3956*
4:32 and becometh greater than **a** herbs, and *3956*
4:34 he expounded **a** *things* to his disciples. *3956*
5:12 And **a** the devils besought him, saying, *3956*
5:20 had done for him: and **a** *men* did marvel. *3956*
5:26 and had spent **a** that she had, *3956*
5:33 down before him, and told him **a** the truth. *3956*
5:40 But when he had put *them* **a** out, he taketh *537*
6:30 told him **a** *things*, both what they had done, *3956*
6:33 and ran afoot thither out of **a** cities, and *3956*
6:39 And he commanded them to make **a** sit *3956*
6:41 the two fishes divided he among *them* **a**. *3956*
6:42 And they did **a** eat, and were filled. *3956*
6:50 For they **a** saw him, and were troubled. *3956*
7: 3 For the Pharisees, and **a** the Jews, *3956*
7:14 And when he had called **a** the people unto *3956*
7:19 out into the draught, purging **a** meats? *3956*
7:23 **A** these evil *things* come from within, and *3956*
7:37 saying, He hath done **a** *things* well: *3956*
9:12 and restoreth **a** *things;* and how it is written *3956*
9:15 And straightway **a** the people, when they *3956*
9:23 **a** *things are* possible to him that believeth. *3956*
9:35 *the same* shall be last of **a**, and servant of *3956*
9:35 *same* shall be last of all, and servant of **a**. *3956*
10:20 **a** these have I observed from my youth. *3956*
10:27 for with God **a** *things* are possible. *3956*
10:28 Lo, we have left **a**, and have followed thee. *3956*
10:44 will be the chiefest, shall be servant of **a**. *3956*
11:11 when he had looked round about upon **a** *3956*
11:17 My house shall be called of **a** nations *3956*
11:18 **a** the people was astonished at his doctrine. *3956*
11:32 for **a** *men* counted John, that he was a *537*
12:22 left no seed: last of **a** the woman died also. *3956*

Mk 12:28 Which is the first commandment of a? 3956
12:29 The first of a the commandments is, Hear, 3956
12:30 thou shalt love the Lord thy God with a 3650
12:30 and with a thy soul, and with all thy mind, 3650
12:30 and with a thy mind, and with all thy 3650
12:30 with all thy mind, and with a thy strength: 3650
12:33 And to love him with a the heart, and 3650
12:33 and with a the understanding, and with all 3650
12:33 and with a the soul, and with all 3650
12:33 and with a the strength, and to love his 3650
12:33 is more than a whole burnt offerings and 3956
12:43 than a they which have cast into 3956
12:44 For a they did cast in of their abundance; 3956
12:44 she of her want did cast in a that she had, 3956
12:44 cast in all that she had, even a her living. 3650
13: 4 what shall be the sign when a these things 3956
13:10 must first be published among a nations. 3956
13:13 And ye shall be hated of a men for my 3956
13:23 behold, I have foretold you a things. 3956
13:30 shall not pass, till a these things be done. 3956
13:37 And what I say unto you I say unto a, 3956
14:23 he gave it to them: and they a drank of it. 3956
14:27 A ye shall be offended because of me this 3956
14:29 Although a shall be offended, yet will not I. 3956
14:31 thee in any wise. Likewise also said they a. 3956
14:36 a things are possible unto thee; 3956
14:50 And they a forsook him, and fled. 3956
14:53 with him were assembled a the chief priests 3956
14:55 a the council sought for witness against 3650
14:64 And they a condemned him to be guilty of 3956
16:15 Go ye into a the world, and preach 537
Lk 1: 3 having had perfect understanding of a 3956
1: 6 walking in a the commandments and 3956
1:48 from henceforth a generations shall call me 3956
1:63 His name is John. And they marvelled a. 3956
1:65 And fear came on a that dwelt round about 3956
1:65 a these sayings were noised abroad 3956
1:65 throughout a the hill country of Judea. 3650
1:66 And a they that heard them laid them up in 3956
1:71 and from the hand of a that hate us; 3956
1:75 before him, a the days of our life. 3956
2: 1 that a the world should be taxed. 3956
2: 3 And a went to be taxed, every one into his 3956
2:10 of great joy, which shall be to a people. 3956
2:18 And a they that heard it wondered at those 3956
2:19 But Mary kept a these things, and 3956
2:20 praising God for a the things that they had 3956
2:31 hast prepared before the face of a people; 3956
2:38 spake of him to a them that looked for 3956
2:39 And when they had performed a things 537
2:47 And a that heard him were astonished at his 3956
2:51 his mother kept a these sayings in her heart. 3956
3: 3 And he came into a the country about 3956
3: 6 And a flesh shall see the salvation of God. 3956
3:15 and a men mused in their hearts of John, 3956
3:16 John answered, saying unto them a, I indeed 537
3:19 and for a the evils which Herod had done, 3956
3:20 Added yet this above a, that he shut up 3956
3:21 Now when a the people were baptized, 537
4: 5 shewed unto him a the kingdoms of 3956
4: 6 A this power will I give thee, and the glory 537
4: 7 therefore wilt worship me, a shall be thine. 3956
4:13 And when the devil had ended a 3956
4:14 there went out a fame of him through a 3650
4:15 in their synagogues, being glorified of a. 3956
4:20 And the eyes of a them that were in 3956
4:22 And a bare him witness, and wondered at 3956
4:25 when great famine was throughout a 3956
4:28 And a they in the synagogue, when they 3956
4:36 And they were a amazed, and spake among 3956
4:40 a they that had any sick with divers 3956
5: 5 we have toiled a the night, and have taken 3650
5: 9 was astonished, and a that were with him, 3956
5:11 brought their ships to land, they forsook a, 537
5:26 And they were a amazed, 537
5:28 And he left a, rose up, and followed him. 537
6:10 And looking round about upon them a, 3956
6:12 and continued a night in prayer to God. 1273
6:17 a great multitude of people out of a Judea 3956
6:19 went virtue out of him, and healed them a. 3956
6:26 when a men shall speak well of you: 3956
7: 1 Now when he had ended a his sayings in 3956
7:16 And there came a fear on a: 537
7:17 of him went forth throughout a Judea, 3650
7:17 and throughout a the region round about. 3956
7:18 And the disciples of John shewed him of a 3956
7:29 And a the people that heard him, and 3956
7:35 But wisdom is justified of a her children. 3956
8:40 for they were a waiting for him. 3956
8:43 which had spent a her living upon 3650
8:45 When a denied, Peter and they that were 3956
8:47 she declared unto him before a the people 3956
8:52 And a wept, and bewailed her: but he said, 3956
8:54 And he put them a out, and took her by 3956
9: 1 them power and authority over a devils, 3956
9: 7 Now Herod the tetrarch heard of a that was 3956
9:10 told him a that they had done. 3745
9:13 should go and buy meat for a this people. 3956
9:15 And they did so, and made them a sit down. 537
9:17 And they did eat, and were a filled: and 3956
9:23 And he said to them a, If any man will 3956
9:43 And they were a amazed at the mighty 3956
9:43 But while they wondered every one at a 3956
9:48 for he that is least among you a, the same 3956
10:19 and over a the power of the enemy: 3956
10:22 A things are delivered to me of my Father: 3956
10:27 Thou shalt love the Lord thy God with a 3650
10:27 and with a thy soul, and with all thy 3650
10:27 and with a thy strength, and with all thy 3650
10:27 with all thy strength, and with a thy mind; 3650
11:22 he taketh from him a his armour wherein 3833
11:41 and behold, a things are clean unto you. 3956
11:42 tithe mint and rue and a manner of herbs, 3956
11:50 That the blood of a the prophets, which was 3956
12: 1 he began to say unto his disciples first of a, NIG

Lk 12: 7 But even the very hairs of your head are a 3956
12:18 and there will I bestow a my fruits and 3956
12:27 that Solomon in a his glory was not arrayed 3956
12:30 For a these things do the nations of 3956
12:31 and a these things shall be added unto you. 3956
12:41 thou this parable unto us, or even to a? 3956
12:44 that he will make him ruler over a that he 3956
13: 2 were sinners above a the Galileans, 3956
13: 3 except ye repent, ye shall a likewise perish. 3956
13: 4 think ye that they were sinners above a 3956
13: 5 except ye repent, ye shall a likewise perish. 3956
13:17 And when he had said these things, a his 3956
13:17 a the people rejoiced for all the glorious 3956
13:17 all the people rejoiced for a the glorious 3956
13:27 depart from me, a ye workers of iniquity. 3956
13:28 and Isaac, and Jacob, and a the prophets, 3956
14:17 Come; for a things are now ready. 3956
14:18 And they a with one consent began to make 3956
14:29 is not able to finish it, a that behold it begin 3956
14:33 whosoever he be of you that forsaketh not a 3956
15: 1 Then drew near unto him a the publicans 3956
15:13 after the younger son gathered a together, 537
15:14 And when he had spent a, there arose a 3956
15:31 art ever with me, and a that I have is thine. 3956
16:14 heard a these things: and they derided him. 3956
16:26 And besides a this, between us and 3956
17:10 when ye shall have done a those things 3956
17:27 and the flood came, and destroyed them a. 537
17:29 from heaven, and destroyed them a. 537
18:12 in the week, I give tithes of a that I possess. 3956
18:21 A these have I kept from my youth up. 3956
18:22 Yet lackest thou one thing: sell a that thou 3956
18:28 Then Peter said, Lo, we have left a, 3956
18:31 a things that are written by the prophets 3956
18:43 and a the people, when they saw it, gave 3956
19: 7 And when they saw it, they a murmured, 537
19:37 praise God with a loud voice for a 3956
19:48 for a the people were very attentive to hear 537
20: 6 we say, Of men; a the people will stone us: 3956
20:32 Last of a the woman died also. 3956
20:38 but of the living: for a live unto him. 3956
20:40 they durst not ask him any question at a. NIG
20:45 Then in the audience of a the people he 3956
21: 3 poor widow hath cast in more than they a: 3956
21: 4 For a these have of their abundance cast in 537
21: 4 she of her penury hath cast in a the living 537
21:12 But before a these, they shall lay their hands 537
21:15 which a your adversaries shall not be able 3956
21:17 And ye shall be hated of a men for my 3956
21:22 that a things which are written may be 3956
21:24 shall be led away captive into a nations: 3956
21:29 Behold the fig tree, and a the trees; 3956
21:32 shall not pass away, till a be fulfilled. 3956
21:35 For as a snare shall it come on a them that 3956
21:36 a these things that shall come to pass, 3956
21:38 And a the people came early in 3956
22:70 Then said they a, Art thou then the Son of 3956
23: 5 up the people, teaching throughout a Jewry, 3650
23:18 And they cried out a at once, saying, 3826
23:44 there was a darkness over a the earth until 3650
23:48 And a the people that came together to that 3956
23:49 And a his acquaintance, and the women 3956
24: 9 and told a these things unto the eleven, and 3956
24: 9 things unto the eleven, and to a the rest. 3956
24:14 And they talked together of a these things 3956
24:19 and word before God and a the people: 3956
24:21 and beside a this, to day is the third day 3956
24:25 slow of heart to believe a that the prophets 3956
24:27 beginning at Moses and a the prophets, 3956
24:27 he expounded unto them in a the scriptures 3956
24:44 yet with you, that a things must be fulfilled, 3956
24:47 be preached in his name among a nations, 3956
Jn 1: 3 A things were made by him; and 3956
1: 7 that a men through him might believe. 3956
1:16 And of his fulness have a we received, and 3956
2:15 he drove them a out of the temple, and 3956
2:24 unto them, because he knew a men, 3956
3:26 same baptizeth, and a men come to him. 3956
3:31 He that cometh from above is above a: 3956
3:31 he that cometh from heaven is above a. 3956
3:35 and hath given a things into his hand. 3956
4:25 when he is come, he will tell us a things. 3956
4:29 which told me a things that ever I did: 3956
4:39 He told me a that ever I did. 3956
4:45 having seen a the things that he did at 3956
5:20 sheweth him a things that himself doeth: 3956
5:22 hath committed a judgment unto the Son: 3956
5:23 That a men should honour the Son, even as 3956
5:28 in the which a that are in the graves shall 3956
6:37 A that the Father giveth me shall come to 3956
6:39 that of a which he hath given me I should 3956
6:45 And they shall be a taught of God. 3956
7:21 I have done one work, and ye a marvel. 3956
8: 2 and a the people came unto him; 3956
10: 8 A that ever came before me are thieves and 3956
10:29 which gave them me, is greater than a; 3956
10:41 a things that John spake of this man were 3956
11:48 him thus alone, a men will believe on him: 3956
11:49 unto them, Ye know nothing at a, 3756+3762
12:32 from the earth, will draw a men unto me. 3956
13: 3 Jesus knowing that the Father had given a 3956
13:10 every whit: and ye are clean, but not a. 3956
13:11 therefore said he, Ye are not a clean. 3956
13:18 I speak not of you a: I know whom I have 3956
13:35 By this shall a men know that ye are my 3956
14:26 he shall teach you a things, and bring all 3956
14:26 and bring a things to your remembrance, 3956
15:15 for a things that I have heard of my Father I 3956
15:21 But a these things will they do unto you for 3956
16:13 is come, he will guide you into a truth: 3956
16:15 A things that the Father hath are mine: 3956
16:30 Now are we sure that thou knowest a 3956
17: 2 As thou hast given him power over a flesh, 3956
17: 7 Now they have known that a things 3956
17:10 And a mine are thine, and thine are mine; 3956

Jn 17:21 That they a may be one; as thou, Father, 3956
18: 4 knowing a things that should come upon 3956
18:38 saith unto them, I find in him no fault at a. NIG
18:40 Then cried they a again, saying, Not this 3956
19:11 Thou couldest have no power at a against NIG
19:28 Jesus knowing that a things were now 3956
21:11 and for a there were so many, yet was not 5118
21:17 thou knowest a things; thou knowest that I 3956
Ac 1: 1 of a that Jesus began both to do and teach, 3956
1: 8 and in a Judea, and in Samaria, and 3956
1:14 These a continued with one accord in 3956
1:18 in the midst, and a his bowels gushed out. 3956
1:19 And it was known unto a the dwellers at 3956
1:21 us a the time that the Lord Jesus went in 3956
1:24 which knowest the hearts of a men, shew 3956
2: 1 they were a with one accord in one place. 537
2: 2 it filled a the house where they were sitting. 3650
2: 4 And they were a filled with the Holy Ghost, 537
2: 7 And they were a amazed and marvelled, 3956
2: 7 are not a these which speak Galileans? 3956
2:12 And they were a amazed, and were in 3956
2:14 of Judea, and a ye that dwell at Jerusalem, 537
2:17 I will pour out of my Spirit upon a flesh: 3956
2:32 God raised up, whereof we a are witnesses. 3956
2:36 Therefore let a the house of Israel know 3956
2:39 to your children, and to a that are afar off, 3956
2:44 And a that believed were together, 3956
2:44 were together, and had a things common; 537
2:45 parted them to a men, as every man had 3956
2:47 and having favour with a the people. 3650
3: 9 And a the people saw him walking and 3956
3:11 a the people ran together unto them in 3956
3:16 perfect soundness in the presence of you a. 3956
3:18 had shewed by the mouth of a his prophets, 3956
3:21 a things, which God hath spoken by 3956
3:21 a his holy prophets since the world began. 3956
3:22 him shall ye hear in a things whatsoever he 3956
3:24 and a the prophets from Samuel and 3956
3:25 And in thy seed shall a the kindreds of 3956
4:10 Be it known unto you a, and to all 3956
4:10 unto you all, and to a the people of Israel, 3956
4:16 manifest to a them that dwell in Jerusalem; 3956
4:18 commanded them not to speak at a nor 2527
4:21 for a men glorified God for that which was 3956
4:23 and reported a that the chief priests and 3745
4:24 and earth, and the sea, and a that in them is: 3956
4:29 that with a boldness they may speak thy 3956
4:31 and they were a filled with the Holy Ghost, 537
4:32 was his own; but they had a things common. 537
4:33 and great grace was upon them a. 3956
5: 5 great fear came on a them that heard these 3956
5:11 And great fear came upon a the church, and 3650
5:12 they were a with one accord in Solomon's 537
5:17 rose up, and a they that were with him, 3956
5:20 speak in the temple to the people a 3956
5:21 and a the senate of the children of Israel, 3956
5:23 The prison truly found we shut with a 3956
5:34 had in reputation among a the people, and 3956
5:36 and a, as many as obeyed him, 3956
5:37 and a, even as many as obeyed him, 3956
6:15 And a that sat in the council, 537
7:10 And delivered him out of a his afflictions, 3956
7:10 him governor over Egypt and a his house. 3650
7:11 Now there came a dearth over a the land of 3650
7:14 his father Jacob to him, and a his kindred, 3956
7:22 And Moses was learned in a the wisdom of 3956
7:50 Hath not my hand made a these things? 3956
8: 1 they were a scattered abroad throughout 3956
8:10 To whom they a gave heed, from the least 3956
8:27 who had the charge of a her treasure, and 3956
8:37 If thou believest with a thine heart, 3650
8:40 passing through he preached in a the cities, 3956
9:14 chief priests to bind a that call on thy name. 3956
9:21 But a that heard him were amazed, and 3956
9:26 but they were a afraid of him, and 3956
9:31 Then had the churches rest throughout a 3650
9:32 as Peter passed throughout a quarters, he 3956
9:35 And a that dwelt at Lydda and Saron saw 3956
9:39 and a the widows stood by him weeping, 3956
9:40 But Peter put them a forth, 3956
9:42 And it was known throughout a Joppa; and 3650
10: 2 and one that feared God with a his house, 3956
10: 8 And when he had declared a these things 537
10:12 Wherein were a manner of fourfooted 3956
10:22 of good report among a the nation of 3650
10:33 therefore are we a here present before God, 3956
10:33 to hear a things that are commanded thee of 3956
10:36 peace by Jesus Christ: (he is Lord of a:) 3956
10:37 which was published throughout a Judea, 3650
10:38 healing a that were oppressed of the devil; 3956
10:39 And we are witnesses of a things which he 3956
10:41 Not to a the people, but unto witnesses 3956
10:43 To him give a the prophets witness, 3956
10:44 the Holy Ghost fell on a them which heard 3956
11:10 and a were drawn up again into heaven. 537
11:14 and a thy house shall be saved. 3956
11:23 of God, was glad, and exhorted them a, 3956
11:28 be great dearth throughout a the world: 3650
12:11 from a the expectation of the people of 3956
13:10 O full of a subtilty and all mischief, 3956
13:10 O full of all subtilty and a mischief, 3956
13:10 of the devil, thou enemy of a righteousness, 3956
13:22 own heart, which shall fulfil a my will. 3956
13:24 of repentance to a the people of Israel. 3956
13:29 And when they had fulfilled a that was 537
13:39 And by him a that believe are justified 3956
13:39 a things, from which ye could not be 3956
13:49 was published throughout a the region. 3650
14:15 and the sea, and a things that are therein: 3956
14:16 Who in times past suffered a nations to 3956
14:27 they rehearsed a that God had done with 3745
15: 3 they caused great joy unto a the brethren. 3956
15: 4 they declared a things that God had done 3745
15:12 Then a the multitude kept silence, and 3956
15:17 and a the Gentiles, upon whom my name is 3956

A

Ac 15:17 saith the Lord, who doeth a these *things.* 3956
15:18 Known unto God are a his works from 3956
16: 3 for they knew a that his father was a Greek. 537
16:26 and immediately a the doors were opened, 3956
16:28 Do thyself no harm: for we are a here. 537
16:32 of the Lord, and to a that were in his house. 3956
16:33 was baptized, he and a his, straightway. 3956
16:34 rejoiced, believing in God with a his **house**. 3832
17: 5 and set a the city on an uproar, and NIG
17: 7 these a do contrary to the decrees of Cesar, 3956
17:11 in that they received the word with a 3956
17:15 for to come to him **with a speed**, 5030+5613
17:21 (For a the Athenians and strangers which 3956
17:22 I perceive that in a *things* ye are too 3956
17:24 that made the world and a *things* therein, 3956
17:25 needed any *thing*, seeing he giveth to a life, 3956
17:25 giveth to all life, and breath, and a *things;* 3956
17:26 And hath made of one blood a nations of 3956
17:26 men for to dwell on a the face of the earth, 3956
17:30 now commandeth a men every where to 3956
17:31 *whereof* he hath given assurance unto a 3956
18: 2 that Claudius had commanded a Jews to 3956
18: 8 believed on the Lord with a his house; 3650
18:17 Then a the Greeks took Sosthenes, 3956
18:21 I must **by a means** keep *this* feast that 3843
18:23 and went over a the country of Galatia and NIG
18:23 in order, strengthening a the disciples. 3956
19: 7 And a the men were about twelve. 3956
19:10 that a they which dwelt in Asia heard 3956
19:17 And this was known to a the Jews and 3956
19:17 and fear fell on them a, and the name of 3956
19:19 and burned *them* before a *men:* and 3956
19:26 but almost throughout a Asia, this Paul 3956
19:27 whom a Asia and the world worshippeth. 3650
19:34 a with one voice about the space of two 3956
20:18 manner I have been with you at a seasons, 3956
20:19 Serving the Lord with a humility of mind, 3956
20:25 And now behold, I know that ye a, 3956
20:26 that I *am* pure from the blood of a *men.* 3956
20:27 to declare unto you a the counsel of God. 3956
20:28 unto yourselves, and to a the flock, 3956
20:32 to give you an inheritance among a them 3956
20:35 I have shewed you a *things,* how that so 3956
20:36 he kneeled down, and prayed with them a. 3956
20:37 And *they* a wept sore, and fell on Paul's 3956
20:38 Sorrowing most *of* a for the words which he NIG
21: 5 *our way;* and *they* a brought us on our way, 3956
21:18 unto James; and a the elders were present. 3956
21:20 and they are a zealous of the law: 3956
21:21 that thou teachest a the Jews which are 3956
21:24 a may know that *those things,* whereof they 3956
21:27 stirred up a the people, and laid hands on 3956
21:28 that teacheth a *men* every where against 3956
21:30 And a the city was moved, and the people 3650
21:31 the band, that a Jerusalem was in an uproar. 3650
22: 3 zealous towards God, as ye a are this day. 3956
22: 5 me witness, and a the estate of the elders: 3956
22:10 there it shall be told thee of a *things* which 3956
22:12 having a good report of a the Jews which 3956
22:15 For thou shalt be his witness unto a men of 3956
22:30 chief priests and a their council to appear, 3650
23: 1 I have lived in a good conscience before 3956
24: 3 and **in a places**, most noble Felix, 3837
24: 3 most noble Felix, with a thankfulness. 3956
24: 5 a mover of sedition among a the Jews 3956
24: 8 of a these *things,* whereof we accuse him. 3956
24:14 believing a *things* which are written in 3956
25: 8 have I offended any *thing at* a. NIG
25:24 and a men which are here present with us, 3956
25:24 ye see this *man,* about whom a 3956
26: 2 a *the things* whereof I am accused of 3956
26: 3 *I know* thee to be expert in a customs and 3956
26: 4 own nation at Jerusalem, know a the Jews; 3956
26:14 And when we were a fallen to the earth, 3956
26:20 and throughout a the coasts of Judea, and 3956
26:29 but also a that hear me this day, were both 3956
27:20 no small tempest lay on *us,* a hope that we 3956
27:24 God hath given thee a them that sail with 3956
27:33 Paul besought *them* a to take meat, saying, 537
27:35 gave thanks to God in presence of *them* a: 3956
27:36 Then were they a of good cheer, and 3956
27:37 And we were in a in the ship two hundred 3956
27:44 to pass, that *they* escaped a safe to land. 3956
28:30 and received a that came in unto him, 3956
28:31 with a confidence, no man forbidding him. 3956
Ro 1: 5 for obedience to the faith among a nations, 3956
1: 7 To a that be in Rome, beloved of God, 3956
1: 8 my God through Jesus Christ for you a, 3956
1:18 revealed from heaven against a ungodliness 3956
1:29 Being filled with a unrighteousness, 3956
3: 9 and Gentiles, that *they* are a under sin; 3956
3:12 They are a gone out of the way, they are 3956
3:19 a the world may become guilty before God. 3956
3:22 God *which is* by faith of Jesus Christ unto a 3956
3:22 unto all and upon a them that believe: 3956
3:23 For a have sinned, and come short of 3956
4:11 that he might be the father of a them that 3956
4:16 to the end the promise might be sure to a 3956
4:16 faith of Abraham; who is the father of us a, 3956
5:12 and so death passed upon a men, for that all 3956
5:12 passed upon all men, for that a have sinned: 3956
5:18 *came* upon a men to condemnation; 3956
5:18 *came* upon a men unto justification of life. 3956
7: 8 wrought in me a *manner of* concupiscence. 3956
8:28 And we know that a *things* work together 3956
8:32 his own Son, but delivered him up for us a, 3956
8:32 not with him also freely give us a *things?* 3956
8:36 For thy sake we are killed a the day long; 3650
8:37 in a these *things* we are more than 3956
9: 5 the flesh Christ *came,* who is over a, 3956
9: 6 For they *are* not a Israel, which are of 3956
9: 7 the seed of Abraham, *are they* a children: 3956
9:17 might be declared throughout a the earth. 3956
10:12 for the same Lord over a *is* rich unto all 3956
10:12 for the same Lord over all *is* rich unto a 3956
Ro 10:16 But they have not a obeyed the gospel. 3956
10:18 their sound went into a the earth, and 3956
10:21 A day **long** have I stretched forth my hands 3650
11:26 And so a Israel shall be saved: as it is 3956
11:32 For God hath concluded *them* a in unbelief, 3956
11:32 that he might have mercy upon a. 3956
11:36 *are* a *things:* to whom *be* glory for ever. 3956
12: 4 and a members have not the same office: 3956
12:17 Provide *things* honest in the sight of a men. 3956
12:18 as lieth in you, live peaceably with a men. 3956
13: 7 Render therefore to a *their* dues: tribute to 3956
14: 2 For one believeth that *he* may eat a *things:* 3956
14:10 for we shall a stand before the judgment 3956
14:20 A *things* indeed *are* pure; but *it is* evil for 3956
15:11 And again, Praise the Lord, a ye Gentiles; 3956
15:11 all ye Gentiles; and laud him, a ye people. 3956
15:13 Now the God of hope fill you with a joy 3956
15:14 full of goodness, filled with a knowledge, 3956
15:33 Now the God of peace *be* with you a. 3956
16: 4 but also a the churches of the Gentiles. 3956
16:15 and a the saints which are with them. 3956
16:19 For your obedience is come abroad unto a 3956
16:24 of our Lord Jesus Christ *be* with you a. 3956
16:26 made known to a nations for the obedience 3956
1Co 1: 2 with a that in every place call upon 3956
1: 5 in a utterance, and *in* all knowledge; 3956
1: 5 in all utterance, and *in* a knowledge; 3956
1:10 that ye a speak the same *thing,* and 3956
2:10 for the Spirit searcheth a *things,* yea, 3956
2:15 But he that is spiritual judgeth a *things,* yet 3956
3:21 *man* glory in men. For a *things* are yours; 3956
3:22 or *things* to come; a are yours; 3956
4:13 *are* the offscouring of a *things* unto this 3956
6:12 A *things* are lawful unto me, but all *things* 3956
6:12 unto me, but a *things* are not expedient: 3956
6:12 a *things* are lawful for me, but I will not be 3956
7: 7 For I would that a men were even as I 3956
7:17 let him walk. And so ordain I in a churches. 3956
8: 1 we know that we a have knowledge. 3956
8: 6 of whom *are* a *things,* and we in him; 3956
8: 6 by whom *are* a *things,* and we by him. 3956
9:12 suffer a *things,* lest we should hinder 3956
9:19 For though I be free from a *men,* yet have I 3956
9:19 yet have I made myself servant unto a, 3956
9:22 I am made a *things* to all *men,* that I might 3956
9:22 I am made all *things* to a *men,* that I might 3956
9:22 *men,* that I might **by a means** save some. 3843
9:24 ye not that they which run in a race run a, 3956
9:25 a *things.* Now they *do it* to obtain a 3956
10: 1 how that a our fathers were under 3956
10: 1 the cloud, and a passed through the sea; 3956
10: 2 And were a baptized unto Moses in 3956
10: 3 And did a eat the same spiritual meat; 3956
10: 4 And did a drink the same spiritual drink: 3956
10:11 Now a these *things* happened unto them for 3956
10:17 for we are a partakers of *that* one bread. 3956
10:23 A *things* are lawful for me, but all *things* 3956
10:23 for me, but a *things* are not expedient: 3956
10:23 a *things* are lawful for me, but all *things* 3956
10:23 are lawful for me, but a *things* edify not. 3956
10:31 whatsoever ye do, do a to the glory of God. 3956
10:33 Even as I please a *men* in all *things,* not 3956
10:33 Even as I please all *men* in a *things,* not 3956
11: 2 that ye remember me in a *things,* and 3956
11: 5 **even a one as if** she were 846+1520+2532+3588
11:12 also by the woman; but a *things* of God. 3956
11:18 For **first of a**, when ye come together in 4412
12: 6 it is the same God which worketh a in all. 3956
12: 6 it is the same God which worketh all in a. 3956
12:11 But a these worketh *that* one and 3956
12:12 and a the members of *that* one body, 3956
12:13 For by one Spirit are we a baptized into one 3956
12:13 have been a made to drink into one Spirit. 3956
12:19 And if they were a one member, 3956
12:26 a the members suffer with *it;* or 3956
12:26 a the members rejoice with *it.* 3956
12:29 *Are* a apostles? *are* all prophets? *are* all 3956
12:29 *are* a prophets? *are* all teachers? *are* all 3956
12:29 *are* a teachers? *are* all workers of miracles? 3956
12:29 *are* all teachers? *are* a workers of miracles? 3956
12:30 Have a the gifts of healing? do all speak 3956
12:30 do a speak with tongues? do all interpret? 3956
12:30 do all speak with tongues? do a interpret? 3956
13: 2 and understand a mysteries, and 3956
13: 2 understand all mysteries, and a knowledge; 3956
13: 2 and though I have a faith, so that *I* could 3956
13: 3 And though I bestow a my goods to feed 3956
13: 7 Beareth a *things,* believeth all *things,* 3956
13: 7 Beareth all *things,* believeth a *things,* 3956
13: 7 *things,* hopeth a *things,* endureth all *things.* 3956
13: 7 *things,* hopeth all *things,* endureth a *things.* 3956
14: 5 I would that ye a spake with tongues, but 3956
14:18 I speak with tongues more than you a: 3956
14:21 and yet **for a that** will they not hear me, 3779
14:23 and a speak with tongues, and there come 3956
14:24 But if a prophesy, and there come in one 3956
14:24 or *one* unlearned, he is convinced of a, 3956
14:24 he is convinced of all, he is judged of a: 3956
14:26 Let a *things* be done unto edifying. 3956
14:31 For ye may a prophesy one by one, that all 3956
14:31 that a may learn, and all may be comforted. 3956
14:31 that all may learn, and a may be comforted. 3956
14:33 but of peace, as in a churches of the saints. 3956
14:40 Let a *things* be done decently and in order. 3956
15: 3 For I delivered unto you first *of* a that NIG
15: 7 was seen of James; then of a the apostles. 3956
15: 8 And last of a he was seen of me also, as of 3956
15:10 but I laboured more abundantly than they a: 3956
15:19 in Christ, we are of a men most miserable. 3956
15:22 For as in Adam a die, even so in Christ 3956
15:22 even so in Christ shall a be made alive, 3956
15:24 when he shall have put down a rule and 3956
15:24 down all rule and a authority and power. 3956
15:25 till he hath put a enemies under his feet. 3956
15:27 For he hath put a *things* under his feet. 3956
1Co 15:27 a *things* are put under *him, it is* manifest 3956
15:27 which did put a *things* under him. 3956
15:28 And when a *things* shall be subdued unto 3956
15:28 unto him that put a *things* under him, 3956
15:28 *things* under him, that God may be a in all. 3956
15:28 *things* under him, that God may be all in a. 3956
15:29 for the dead, if the dead rise not **at a**? 3654
15:39 A flesh *is* not the same flesh: but *there is* 3956
15:51 We shall not a sleep, but we shall all be 3956
15:51 not all sleep, but we shall a be changed, 3956
16:12 *his* will was not **at a** to come at this time; 3843
16:14 Let a your *things* be done with charity. 3956
16:20 A the brethren greet you. Greet ye one 3956
16:24 My love *be* with you a in Christ Jesus. 3956
2Co 1: 1 with a the saints which are in all Achaia: 3956
1: 1 with all the saints which are in a Achaia: 3650
1: 3 of mercies, and the God of a comfort; 3956
1: 4 Who comforteth us in a our tribulation, 3956
1:20 For a the promises of God in him *are* yea, 3745
2: 3 having confidence in you a, that my joy is 3956
2: 3 in you all, that my joy is *the joy* of you a. 3956
2: 5 in part: that I may not overcharge you a. 3956
2: 9 of you, whether ye be obedient in a *things.* 3956
3: 2 in our hearts, known and read of a men: 3956
3:18 But we a, with open face beholding as in a 3956
4:15 For a *things are* for your sakes, that 3956
5:10 For we must a appear before the judgment 3956
5:14 that if one died for a, then were all dead: 3956
5:14 that if one died for all, then were a dead: 3956
5:15 And *that* he died for a, that they which live 3956
5:17 behold, a *things* are become new. 3956
5:18 And a *things are* of God, who hath 3956
6: 4 But in a *things* approving ourselves as 3956
6:10 and *yet* possessing a *things.* 3956
7: 1 let us cleanse ourselves from a filthiness of 3956
7: 4 I am exceeding joyful in a our tribulation. 3956
7:11 In a *things* ye have approved yourselves to 3956
7:13 because his spirit was refreshed by you a. 3956
7:14 but as we spake a *things* to you in truth, 3956
7:15 he remembereth the obedience of you a, 3956
7:16 that I have confidence in you in a *things.* 3956
8: 7 and *in* a diligence, and *in* your love to us, 3956
8:18 whose praise *is* in the gospel throughout a 3956
9: 8 And God *is* able to make a grace abound 3956
9: 8 always having a sufficiency in all *things,* 3956
9: 8 always having all sufficiency in a *things,* 3956
9:11 Being enriched in every *thing* to a 3956
9:13 distribution unto them, and unto a *men;* 3956
10: 6 And having in a readiness to revenge a 3956
11: 6 made manifest among you in a *things.* 3956
11: 9 in a *things* I have kept myself from being 3956
11:28 upon me daily, the care of a the churches. 3956
12:12 were wrought among you in a patience, 3956
12:19 but *we do* a *things,* dearly beloved, for your 3956
13: 2 and to a other, that, if I come again, I will 3956
13:13 A the saints salute you. 3956
13:14 of the Holy Ghost, *be* with you a. 3956
Gal 1: 2 And a the brethren which are with me, 3956
2:14 I said unto Peter before *them* a, If thou, 3956
3: 8 *saying,* In thee shall a nations be blessed. 3956
3:10 Cursed *is* every one that continueth not in a 3956
3:22 But the scripture hath concluded a under 3956
3:26 For ye are a the children of God by faith in 3956
3:28 nor female: for ye are a one in Christ Jesus. 3956
4: 1 from a servant, though he be lord of a; 3956
4:12 I *am* as ye *are:* ye have **not** injured me **at a**. 3762
4:26 above is free, which is the mother of us a. 3956
5:14 For a the law is fulfilled in one word, 3956
6: 6 unto him that teacheth in a good *things.* 3956
6:10 let us do good unto a *men,* especially unto 3956
Eph 1: 3 who hath blessed us with a spiritual 3956
1: 8 Wherein he hath abounded toward us in a 3956
1:10 gather together in one a *things* in Christ, 3956
1:11 a *things* after the counsel of his own will: 3956
1:15 the Lord Jesus, and love unto a the saints, 3956
1:21 Far above a principality, and power, and 3956
1:22 And hath put a *things* under his feet, and 3956
1:22 gave him *to be* the head over a *things* to 3956
1:23 the fulness of him that filleth a in all. 3956
1:23 the fulness of him that filleth all in a. 3956
2: 3 Among whom also we a had our 3956
2:21 In whom a the building fitly framed 3956
3: 8 *who am* less than the least of a saints, 3956
3: 9 And to make a *men* see what *is* 3956
3: 9 who created a *things* by Jesus Christ: 3956
3:18 May be able to comprehend with a saints 3956
3:19 that ye might be filled with a the fulness of 3956
3:20 exceeding abundantly above a that we ask 3956
3:21 church by Christ Jesus throughout a ages, 3956
4: 2 With a lowliness and meekness, with 3956
4: 6 One God and Father of a, who *is* above all, 3956
4: 6 who *is* above a, and through all, and in you 3956
4: 6 *is* above all, and through a, and in you all. 3956
4: 6 *is* above all, and through all, and in you a. 3956
4:10 also that ascended up far above a heavens, 3956
4:10 all heavens, that he might fill a *things.*) 3956
4:13 Till we a come in the unity of the faith, and 3956
4:15 may grow *up* into him *in* a *things,* which is 3956
4:19 to work a uncleanness with greediness. 3956
4:31 Let a bitterness, and wrath, and anger, and 3956
4:31 be put away from you, with a malice: 3956
5: 3 and a uncleanness, or covetousness, 3956
5: 9 (For the fruit of the Spirit *is* in a goodness 3956
5:13 But a *things* that are reproved are made 3956
5:20 Giving thanks always for a *things* unto God 3956
6:13 in the evil day, and having done a, to stand. 537
6:16 Above a, taking the shield of faith, 3956
6:16 wherewith ye shall be able to quench a 3956
6:18 Praying always with a prayer and 3956
6:18 watching thereunto with a perseverance 3956
6:18 and supplication for a saints; 3956
6:21 shall make known to you a *things:* 3956
6:24 Grace *be* with a them that love our Lord 3956
Php 1: 1 to a the saints in Christ Jesus which are at 3956
1: 4 Always in every prayer of mine for you a 3956

Php 1: 7 as it is meet for me to think this of you a, 3956
1: 7 the gospel, ye a are partakers of my grace. 3956
1: 8 how greatly I long after you a in the bowels 3956
1: 9 and more in knowledge and in a judgment; 3956
1:13 bonds in Christ are manifest in a the palace, 3650
1:13 in all the palace, and in a other places; 3956
1:20 but that with a boldness, as always, so 3956
1:25 continue with you a for your furtherance 3956
2:14 Do a things without murmurings and 3956
2:17 of your faith, I joy, and rejoice with you a. 3956
2:21 For a seek their own, not the things which 3956
2:26 For he longed after you a, and was full of 3956
2:29 therefore in the Lord with a gladness; 3956
3: 8 and I count a things but loss for 3956
3: 8 for whom I have suffered the loss of a 3956
3:21 able even to subdue a things unto himself. 3956
4: 5 Let your moderation be known unto a men. 3956
4: 7 which passeth a understanding, shall keep 3956
4:12 in a things I am instructed both to be full 3956
4:13 I can do a things through Christ which 3956
4:18 But I have a, and abound: I am full, 3956
4:19 But my God shall supply a your need 3956
4:22 A the saints salute you, chiefly they that are 3956
4:23 of our Lord Jesus Christ be with you a. 3956
Col 1: 4 of the love which ye have to a the saints, 3956
1: 6 is come unto you, as it is in a the world; 3956
1: 9 with the knowledge of his will in a wisdom 3956
1:10 walk worthy of the Lord unto a pleasing, 3956
1:11 Strengthened with a might, according to his 3956
1:11 unto a patience and longsuffering with 3956
1:16 For by him were a things created, that are 3956
1:16 a things were created by him, and for him: 3956
1:17 And he is before a things, and by him all 3956
1:17 all things, and by him a things consist. 3956
1:18 that in a things he might have 3956
1:19 Father that in him should a fulness dwell; 3956
1:20 by him to reconcile a things unto himself; 3956
1:28 and teaching every man in a wisdom; 3956
2: 2 unto a riches of the full assurance of 3956
2: 3 In whom are hid a the treasures of wisdom 3956
2: 9 For in him dwelleth a the fulness of 3956
2:10 which is the head of a principality and 3956
2:13 with him, having forgiven you a trespasses; 3956
2:19 from which a the body by joints and 3956
2:22 Which a are to perish with the using;) 3956
3: 8 But now you also put off a these; anger, 3956
3:11 bond nor free: but Christ is a, and in all. 3956
3:11 bond nor free: but Christ is all, and in a. 3956
3:14 And above a these things put on charity, 3956
3:16 of Christ dwell in you richly in a wisdom; 3956
3:17 or deed, do a in the name of the Lord Jesus, 3956
3:20 obey your parents in a things: for this is 3956
3:22 obey in a things your masters according to 3956
4: 7 A my state shall Tychicus declare unto you, 3956
4: 9 They shall make known unto you a things 3956
4:12 and complete in a the will of God. 3956
1Th 1: 2 We give thanks to God always for you a, 3956
1: 7 So that ye were ensamples to a that believe 3956
2:15 please not God, and are contrary to a men: 3956
3: 7 we were comforted over you in a our 3956
3: 9 for a the joy wherewith we joy for your 3956
3:12 towards a men, even as we do towards you: 3956
3:13 of our Lord Jesus Christ with a his saints. 3956
4: 6 that the Lord is the avenger of a such, 3956
4:10 And indeed ye do it towards a the brethren 3956
4:10 all the brethren which are in a Macedonia: 3650
5: 5 Ye are a the children of light, and 3956
5:14 support the weak, be patient toward a men. 3956
5:15 both among yourselves, and to a men. 3956
5:21 Prove a things; hold fast that which is 3956
5:22 Abstain from a appearance of evil. 3956
5:26 Greet a the brethren with a holy kiss. 3956
5:27 this epistle be read unto a the holy brethren. 3956
2Th 1: 3 the charity of every one of you a towards 3956
1: 4 and faith in a your persecutions and 3956
1:10 and to be admired in a them that believe 3956
1:11 fulfil a the good pleasure of his goodness, 3956
2: 4 exalteth himself above a that is called God, 3956
2: 9 is after the working of Satan with a power 3956
2:10 And with a deceivableness of 3956
2:12 That they a might be damned who believed 3956
3: 2 and wicked men: for a men have not faith. 3956
3:11 working not at a, but are busybodies. 3367
3:16 himself give you peace always by a means. 3956
3:16 by all means. The Lord be with you a. 3956
3:18 of our Lord Jesus Christ be with you a. 3956
1Ti 1:15 and worthy of a acceptation, 3956
1:16 Christ might shew forth a longsuffering, 3956
2: 1 I exhort therefore that, first of a, 3956
2: 1 and giving of thanks, be made for a men; 3956
2: 2 For kings, and for a that are in authority; 3956
2: 2 and peaceable life in a godliness and 3956
2: 4 Who will have a men to be saved, and 3956
2: 6 Who gave himself a ransom for a, to be 3956
2:11 Let the woman learn in silence with a 3956
3: 4 having his children in subjection with a 3956
3:11 not slanderers, sober, faithful in a things. 3956
4: 8 godliness is profitable unto a things, having 3956
4: 9 faithful saying and worthy of a acceptation. 3956
4:10 living God, who is the Saviour of a men, 3956
4:15 to them; that thy profiting may appear to a. 3956
5: 2 the younger as sisters, with a purity. 3956
5:20 Them that sin rebuke before a, that others 3956
6: 1 their own masters worthy of a honour, 3956
6:10 For the love of money is the root of a evil: 3956
6:13 who quickeneth a things, and before Christ 3956
6:17 who giveth us richly a things to enjoy; 3956
2Ti 1:15 that a they which are in Asia be turned 3956
2: 7 the Lord give thee understanding in a 3956
2:10 Therefore I endure a things for the elects' 3956
2:24 but be gentle unto a men, apt to teach, 3956
3: 9 for their folly shall be manifest unto a men, 3956
3:11 but out of them a the Lord delivered me. 3956
3:12 a that will live godly in Christ Jesus shall 3956
3:16 A scripture is given by inspiration of God, 3956

2Ti 3:17 throughly furnished unto a good works. 3956
4: 2 exhort with a longsuffering and doctrine. 3956
4: 5 But watch thou in a things, endure 3956
4: 8 unto a them also that love his appearing. 3956
4:16 man stood with me, but a men forsook me: 3956
4:17 and that a the Gentiles might hear: 3956
4:21 and Linus, and Claudia, and a the brethren. 3956
Tit 1:15 Unto the pure a things are pure: but 3956
2: 7 In a things shewing thyself a pattern of 3956
2: 9 to please them well in a things; not 3956
2:10 but shewing a good fidelity; 3956
2:10 doctrine of God our Saviour in a things. 3956
2:11 bringeth salvation hath appeared to a men, 3956
2:14 that he might redeem us from a iniquity, 3956
2:15 and exhort, and rebuke with a authority. 3956
3: 2 gentle, shewing a meekness unto all men. 3956
3: 2 gentle, shewing all meekness unto a men. 3956
3:15 A that are with me salute thee. Greet them 3956
3:15 us in the faith. Grace be with you a. Amen. 3956
Phm 1: 5 toward the Lord Jesus, and toward a saints; 3956
Heb 1: 2 whom he hath appointed heir of a things, 3956
1: 3 upholding a things by the word of his 3956
1: 6 And let a the angels of God worship him. 3956
1:11 and they a shall wax old as doth a garment; 3956
1:14 Are they not a ministering spirits, sent forth 3956
2: 8 Thou hast put a things in subjection under 3956
2: 8 For in that he put a in subjection under 3956
2: 8 But now we see not yet a things put under 3956
2:10 for whom are a things, and by whom are all 3956
2:10 by whom are a things, in bringing many 3956
2:11 and they who are sanctified are a of one: 3956
2:15 were a their lifetime subject to bondage. 3956
2:17 Wherefore in a things it behoved him to be 3956
3: 2 as also Moses was faithful in a his house. 3650
3: 4 some man; but he that built a things is God. 3956
3: 5 And Moses verily was faithful in a his 3650
3:16 howbeit not a that came out of Egypt by 3956
4: 4 And God did rest the seventh day from a 3956
4:13 but a things are naked and opened unto 3956
4:15 was in a points tempted like as we are, yet 3956
5: 9 salvation unto a them that obey him; 3956
6:16 confirmation is to them an end of a strife. 3956
7: 2 whom also Abraham gave a tenth part of a; 3956
7: 7 And without a contradiction the less is 3956
8: 5 saith he, that thou make a things according 3956
8:11 for a shall know me, from the least to 3956
9: 3 tabernacle which is called the holiest of a; 40+40
9: 8 that the way into the holiest of a was not yet NIG
9:17 otherwise it is of no strength at a whilst 3379
9:19 to a the people according to the law, 3956
9:19 sprinkled both the book, and a the people, 3956
9:21 and a the vessels of the ministry. 3956
9:22 And almost a things are by the law purged 3956
10:10 of the body of Jesus Christ once for a. 2178
11:13 These a died in faith, not having received 3956
11:39 And these a, having obtained a good report 3956
12: 8 whereof a are partakers, then are ye 3956
12:14 Follow peace with a men, and holiness, 3956
12:23 and to God the Judge of a, and to the spirits 3956
13: 4 Marriage is honourable in a, and the bed 3956
13:18 in a things willing to live honestly. 3956
13:24 Salute a them that have the rule over you, 3956
13:24 have the rule over you, and a the saints. 3956
13:25 Grace be with you a. Amen. 3956
Jas 1: 2 count it a joy when ye fall into divers 3956
1: 5 that giveth to a men liberally, and 3956
1: 8 A double minded man is unstable in a his 3956
1:21 Wherefore lay apart a filthiness and 3956
2:10 yet offend in one point, he is guilty of a. 3956
3: 2 For in many things we offend a. If any man 537
4:16 in your boastings: a such rejoicing is evil. 3956
5:12 But above a things, my brethren, swear not, 3956
1Pe 1:15 so be ye holy in a manner of conversation; 3956
1:24 For a flesh is as grass, and all the glory of 3956
1:24 a the glory of man as the flower of grass. 3956
2: 1 Wherefore laying aside a malice, and 3956
2: 1 and a guile, and hypocrisies, and envies, 3956
2: 1 and envies, and a evil speakings, 3956
2:17 Honour a men. Love the brotherhood. 3956
2:18 be subject to your masters with a fear; 3956
3: 8 Finally, be ye a of one mind, 3956
4: 7 But the end of a things is at hand: be ye 3956
4: 8 And above a things have fervent charity 3956
4:11 that God in a things may be glorified 3956
5: 5 a of you be subject one to another, and 3956
5: 7 Casting a your care upon him; for he careth 3956
5:10 But the God of a grace, who hath called us 3956
5:14 Peace be with you a that are in Christ 3956
2Pe 1: 3 given unto us a things that pertain unto life 3956
1: 5 And beside this, giving a diligence, add to 3956
3: 4 a things continue as they were from 3956
3: 9 but that a should come to repentance. 3956
3:11 then that a these things shall be dissolved, 3956
3:11 what manner of persons ought ye to be in a NIG
3:16 As also in a his epistles, speaking in them 3956
1Jn 1: 5 God is light, and in him is no darkness at a. 3762
1: 7 Christ his Son cleanseth us from a sin. 3956
1: 9 and to cleanse us from a unrighteousness. 3956
2:16 For a that is in the world, the lust of 3956
2:19 made manifest that they were not a of us. 3956
2:20 from the Holy One, and ye know a things. 3956
2:27 as the same anointing teacheth you of a 3956
3:20 than our heart, and knoweth a things. 3956
5:17 A unrighteousness is sin: and there is a sin 3956
2Jn 1: 1 but also a they that have known the truth; 3956
3Jn 1: 2 I wish above a things that thou mayest 3956
1:12 Demetrius hath good report of a men, and 3956
Jude 1: 3 when I gave a diligence to write unto you 3956
1:15 To execute judgment upon a, and 3956
1:15 to convince a that are ungodly among them 3956
1:15 a their ungodly deeds which they have 3956
1:15 of a their hard speeches which ungodly 3956
Rev 1: 2 of Jesus Christ, and of a things that he saw. 3745
1: 7 and a kindreds of the earth shall wail 3956
2:23 a the churches shall know that I am he 3956

Rev 3:10 which shall come upon a the world, to try 3650
4:11 for thou hast created a things, and for thy 3956
5: 6 spirits of God sent forth into a the earth. 3956
5:13 and a that are in them, heard I saying, 3956
7: 4 four thousand of a the tribes of the children 3956
7: 9 of a nations, and kindreds, and people, and 3956
7:11 And a the angels stood round about 3956
7:17 God shall wipe away a tears from their 3956
8: 3 that he should offer it with the prayers of a 3956
8: 7 burnt up, and a green grass was burnt up. 3956
11: 6 and to smite the earth with a plagues, 3956
12: 5 who was to rule a nations with a rod of 3956
13: 3 and a the world wondered after the beast. 3650
13: 7 and power was given him over a kindreds, 3956
13: 8 And a that dwell upon the earth shall 3956
13:12 And he exerciseth a the power of the first 3956
13:16 And he causeth a, both small and great, 3956
14: 8 she made a nations drink of the wine of 3956
15: 4 for a nations shall come and worship before 3956
18: 3 For a nations have drunk of the wine of 3956
18:12 and a thyine wood, and all manner vessels 3956
18:12 and a manner vessels of ivory, and 3956
18:12 a manner vessels of most precious wood, 3956
18:14 and a things which were dainty and goodly 3956
18:14 shalt find them no more at a. 3361+3756+3765
18:17 and a the company in ships, 3956
18:19 wherein were made rich a that had ships in 3956
18:21 and shall be found no more at a. 3364
18:22 shall be heard no more at a in thee; 3364
18:22 shall be heard no more at a in thee; 3364
18:23 of a candle shall shine no more at a in thee; 3364
18:23 of the bride shall be heard no more at a in 3364
18:23 for by thy sorceries were a nations 3956
18:24 and of a that were slain upon the earth. 3956
19: 5 a ye his servants, and ye that fear him, 3956
19:17 saying to a the fowls that fly in the midst of 3956
19:18 and the flesh of a men, both free and bond, 3956
19:21 and a the fowls were filled with their flesh. 3956
21: 4 And God shall wipe away a tears from their 3956
21: 5 throne said, Behold, I make a things new. 3956
21: 7 He that overcometh shall inherit a things; 3956
21: 8 and sorcerers, and idolaters, and a liars, 3956
21:19 with a manner of precious stones. 3956
21:25 And the gates of it shall not be shut at a by 3364
22:21 of our Lord Jesus Christ be with you a. 3956

ALLAMMELECH See ALAMMELECH

ALLEGING (1)

Ac 17: 3 Opening and a, that Christ must needs have 3908

ALLEGORY (1)

Gal 4:24 Which things are an a: for these are the two 238

ALLELUIA (4)

Rev 19: 1 voice of much people in heaven, saying, A; 239
19: 3 And again they said, A. And her smoke rose 239
19: 4 God that sat on the throne, saying, Amen; A. 239
19: 6 the voice of mighty thunderings, saying, A: 239

ALLIED (1)

Ne 13: 4 the house of our God, was a unto Tobiah: 7138

ALLON (2)

Jos 19:33 from A to Zaanannim, and Adami, Nekeb, 438
1Ch 4:37 the son of A, the son of Jedaiah, the son of 438

ALLON BACUTH See ALLON-BACHUTH

ALLON-BACHUTH (1)

Ge 35: 8 an oak: and the name of it was called A. 439

ALLOW (3) [ALLOWANCE, ALLOWED, ALLOWETH]

Lk 11:48 Truly ye bear witness that ye a the deeds of 4909
Ac 24:15 which they themselves also a, 4327
Ro 7:15 For that which I do I a not: for what I 1097

ALLOWANCE (2) [ALLOW]

2Ki 25:30 his a was a continual allowance given him of 737
25:30 his allowance was a continual a given him of 737

ALLOWED (1) [ALLOW]

1Th 2: 4 But as we were a of God to be put in trust 1381

ALLOWETH (1) [ALLOW]

Ro 14:22 not himself in that thing which he a. 1381

ALLURE (2)

Hos 2:14 I will a her, and bring her into 6601
2Pe 2:18 they a through the lusts of the flesh, 1185

ALMIGHTY (57) [MIGHT]

Ge 17: 1 and said unto him, I am the A God; 7706
28: 3 God A bless thee, and make thee fruitful, 7706
35:11 God said unto him, I am God A: be fruitful 7706
43:14 God A give you mercy before the man, 7706
48: 3 God A appeared unto me at Luz in the land 7706
49:25 by the A, who shall bless thee with 7706
Ex 6: 3 by the name of God A, but by my name 7706
Nu 24: 4 which saw the vision of the A, falling into a 7706
24:16 which saw the vision of the A, falling into a 7706
Ru 1:20 for the A hath dealt very bitterly with me. 7706
1:21 against me, and the A hath afflicted me? 7706
Job 5:17 despise not thou the chastening of the A: 7706
6: 4 For the arrows of the A are within me, 7706
6:14 but he forsaketh the fear of the A. 7706
8: 3 or doth the A pervert justice? 7706
8: 5 and make thy supplication to the A; 7706
11: 7 canst thou find out the A unto perfection? 7706
13: 3 Surely I would speak to the A, and I desire 7706
15:25 and strengtheneth himself against the A. 7706
21:15 What is the A, that we should serve him? 7706

A

Job 21:20 and he shall drink of the wrath of the A. 7706
22: 3 Is it any pleasure to the A, that thou art 7706
22:17 from us: and what can the A do for them? 7706
22:23 If thou return to the A, thou shalt be built 7706
22:25 the A shall be thy defence, and thou shalt 7706
22:26 then shalt thou have thy delight in the A, 7706
23:16 my heart soft, and the A troubleth me: 7706
24: 1 seeing times are not hidden from the A, 7706
27: 2 and the A, who hath vexed my soul; 7706
27:10 Will he delight himself in the A? will he 7706
27:11 that which is with the A will I not conceal. 7706
27:13 which they shall receive of the A. 7706
29: 5 When the A was yet with me, when my 7706
31: 2 what inheritance of the A from on high? 7706
31:35 my desire is, that the A would answer me, 7706
32: 8 the inspiration of the A giveth them 7706
33: 4 and the breath of the A hath given me life. 7706
34:10 from the A, that he should commit iniquity. 7706
34:12 neither will the A pervert judgment. 7706
35:13 not hear vanity, neither will the A regard it. 7706
37:23 Touching the A, we cannot find him out: 7706
40: 2 Shall he that contendeth with the A instruct 7706
Ps 68:14 When the A scattered kings in it, it was 7706
91: 1 shall abide under the shadow of the A. 7706
Isa 13: 6 it shall come as a destruction from the A. 7706
Eze 1:24 as the voice of the A, the voice of speech, 7706
10: 5 as the voice of the A God when he 7706
Joel 1:15 as a destruction from the A shall it come. 7706
2Co 6:18 my sons and daughters, saith the Lord A. 3841
Rev 1: 8 which was, and which is to come, the A. 3841
4: 8 saying, Holy, holy, holy, Lord God A, 3841
11:17 O Lord God A, which art, and wast, and 3841
15: 3 and marvellous are thy works, Lord God A; 3841
16: 7 Lord God A, true and righteous are thy 3841
16:14 to the battle of that great day of God A. 3841
19:15 of the fierceness and wrath of A God. 3841
21:22 for the Lord God A and the Lamb are 3841

ALMODAD (2)

Ge 10:26 Joktan begat A, and Sheleph, and 486
1Ch 1:20 Joktan begat A, and Sheleph, and 486

ALMON (1)

Jos 21:18 with her suburbs, and A with her suburbs; 5960

ALMOND (2) [ALMONDS]

Ecc 12: 5 the a tree shall flourish, and 8247
Jer 1:11 And I said, I see a rod of an a tree. 8247

ALMON-DIBLATHAIM (2)

Nu 33:46 from Dibon-gad, and encamped in A. 5963
33:47 they removed from A, and pitched in 5963

ALMONDS (8) [ALMOND]

Ge 43:11 little honey, spices, and myrrh, nuts, and a: 8247
Ex 25:33 Three bowls made like unto a, with a knop 8246
25:33 three bowls made like a in the other 8246
25:34 shall be four bowls made like unto a, 8246
37:19 Three bowls made after the fashion of a 8246
37:19 Three bowls made like a in another branch, 8246
37:20 candlestick were four bowls made like a, 8246
Nu 17: 8 and bloomed blossoms, and yielded a. 8247

ALMOST (11)

Ex 17: 4 shall I do unto this people? they be a 4592+5750
Ps 73: 2 as for me, my feet were a gone; 4592+3509.1
94:17 my soul had a dwelt in silence. 4592+3509.1
119:87 They had a consumed me upon 4592+3509.1
Pr 5:14 I was a in all evil in the midst of 4592+3509.1
Ac 13:44 And the next sabbath day came a the whole 4975
19:26 but a throughout all Asia, this Paul hath 4975
21:27 And when the seven days were a ended, 3195
26:28 A thou persuadest me to be a 1722+3641
26:29 that hear me this day, were both a, 1722+3641
Heb 9:22 And a all things are by the law purged with 4975

ALMS (13) [ALMSDEEDS]

Mt 6: 1 Take heed that ye do not your a before 1654
6: 2 Therefore when thou doest thine a, do not 1654
6: 3 But when thou doest a, let not thy left hand 1654
6: 4 That thine a may be in secret: and 1654
Lk 11:41 But rather give a of such things as you 1654
12:33 Sell that ye have, and give a; 1654
Ac 3: 2 to ask a of them that entered into 1654
3: 3 about to go into the temple, asked an a. 1654
3:10 sat for a at the Beautiful gate of the temple: 1654
10: 2 which gave much a to the people, and 1654
10: 4 thine a are come up for a memorial before 1654
10:31 thine a are had in remembrance in the sight 1654
24:17 Now after many years I came to bring a to 1654

ALMSDEEDS (1) [ALMS]

Ac 9:36 full of good works and a which she did. 1654

ALMUG (3) [ALGUM]

1Ki 10:11 brought in from Ophir great plenty of a 484
10:12 the king made of the a trees pillars for 484
10:12 there came no such a trees, nor were seen 484

ALOES (5)

Nu 24: 6 as the trees of lign a which the LORD hath 174
Ps 45: 8 and a, and cassia, out of the ivory palaces, 174
Pr 7:17 my bed with myrrh, a, and cinnamon. 174
SS 4:14 myrrh and a, with all the chief spices: 174
Jn 19:39 and brought a mixture of myrrh and a, 250

ALONE (108)

Ge 2:18 not good that the man should be a; 905+3807.1
32:24 Jacob was left a; and there wrestled 905+3807.1
42:38 his brother is dead, and he is left a: 905+3807.1
44:20 he a is left of his mother, and 905+3807.1
Ex 14:12 saying, Let us a, that we may serve 2308+4480
18:14 why sittest thou thyself a, and all 905+3807.1
18:18 art not able to perform it thyself a. 905+3807.1
Ex 24: 2 Moses a shall come near 905+3807.1
32:10 Now therefore let me a, that my wrath may 3240
Lev 13:46 he shall dwell a; without the camp shall his 910
Nu 11:14 am not able to bear all this people a, 905+3807.1
11:17 that thou bear it not thyself a. 905+3807.1
23: 9 lo, the people shall dwell a, and 910+3807.1
Dt 1: 9 I am not able to bear you myself a: 905+3807.1
1:12 How can I myself a bear your 905+3807.1
9:14 Let me a, that I may destroy them, and 7503
32:12 So the LORD a did lead him, and there was 910
33:28 Israel then shall dwell in safety a: 910
Jos 22:20 and that man perished not a in his iniquity. 259
Jdg 3:20 which he had for himself a. 905+2050.2+3807.1
11:37 let me a two months, that I may go up and 7503
1Sa 21: 1 art thou a, and no man with thee? 905+3807.1
2Sa 16:11 now may this Benjamite do it? let him a, 3240
18:24 looked, and behold a man running a. 905+3807.1
18:25 the king said, If he be a, there is 905+3807.1
18:26 said, Behold another man running a. 905+3807.1
1Ki 11:29 and they two were a in the field: 905+3807.1
2Ki 4:27 the man of God said, Let her a; for her soul 7503
19:15 thou art the God, even thou a, of all 905+3807.1
23:18 he said, Let him a; let no man move his 3240
23:18 So they let his bones a, with the bones of 4422
1Ch 29: 1 whom a God hath chosen, is yet young and 259
Ezr 6: 7 Let the work of this house of God a; let 7662
Ne 9: 6 Thou, even thou, art LORD a; thou 905+3807.1
Est 3: 6 scorn to lay hands on Mordecai a; 905+3807.1
Job 1:15 and I only am escaped a to tell thee. 905+3807.1
1:16 and I only am escaped a to tell thee. 905+3807.1
1:17 and I only am escaped a to tell thee. 905+3807.1
1:19 and I only am escaped a to tell thee. 905+3807.1
7:16 let me a; for my days are vanity. 2308
7:19 nor let me a till I swallow down my spittle? 7503
9: 8 Which a spreadeth out the heavens, 905+3807.1
10:20 cease then, and let me a, that I may 4480+7896
13:13 let me a, that I may speak, and let come on 4480
15:19 Unto whom a the earth was given, 905+3807.1
31:17 Or have eaten my morsel myself a, 3807.1
Ps 83:18 whose name a is JEHOVAH, 905+3807.1
86:10 wondrous things: thou art God a. 905+3807.1
102: 7 and am as a sparrow a upon the housetop. 909
136: 4 To him who a doeth great wonders: 905+3807.1
148:13 for his name a is excellent; his glory 905+3807.1
Pr 9:12 if thou scornest, thou a shalt bear it. 905+3807.1
Ecc 4: 8 There is one a, and there is not a second; NIH
4:10 woe to him that is a when he falleth; for he 259
4:11 have heat: but how can one be warm a? NIH
Isa 2:11 a shall be exalted in that day. 905+3807.1
2:17 a shall be exalted in that day. 905+3807.1
5: 8 that they may be placed a in 905+3807.1
14:31 and none shall be a in his appointed times. 909
37:16 thou art the God, even thou a, of all 905+3807.1
44:24 that stretcheth forth the heavens a; 905+3807.1
49:21 Behold, I was left a; these, 905+3807.1
51: 2 for I called him a, and blessed him, and 259
63: 3 I have trodden the winepress a; 905+3807.1
Jer 15:17 nor rejoiced; I sat a because of thy hand: 910
49:31 have neither gates nor bars, which dwell a. 910
La 3:28 He sitteth a and keepeth silence, because 910
Da 10: 7 I Daniel a saw the vision: for 905+3807.1
10: 8 Therefore I was left a, and saw this 905+3807.1
Hos 4:17 Ephraim is joined to idols: let him a. 3240
8: 9 gone up to Assyria, a wild ass a by himself: 909
Mt 4: 4 Man shall not live by bread a, but by every 3441
14:23 the evening was come, he was there a. 3441
15:14 Let them a: they be blind leaders of 863
18:15 tell him his fault between thee and him a: 3441
Mk 1:24 Saying, Let us a; what have we to do with 1436
4:10 And when he was a, they that were about 2651
4:34 and when they were a, he expounded 2398+2596
6:47 the midst of the sea, and he a on the land. 3441
14: 6 And Jesus said, Let her a; why trouble you 863
15:36 a reed, and gave him to drink, saying, Let a; 863
Lk 4: 4 That man shall not live by bread a, but 3441
4:34 Saying, Let us a; what have we to do with 1436
5:21 Who can forgive sins, but God a? 3441
6: 4 it is not lawful to eat but for the priests a? 3441
9:18 And it came to pass, as he was a 2596+3441
9:36 the voice was past, Jesus was found a. 3441
10:40 care that my sister hath left me to serve a? 3441
13: 8 Lord, let it a this year also, till I shall dig 863
Jn 6:15 departed again into a mountain himself a. 3441
6:22 but that his disciples were gone away a; 3441
8: 9 and Jesus was left a, and the woman 3441
8:16 for I am not a, but I and the Father that sent 3441
8:29 the Father hath not left me a; for I do 3441
11:48 If we let him thus a, all men will believe on 863
12: 7 Then said Jesus, Let her a: against the day 863
12:24 fall into the ground and die, it abideth a: 3441
16:32 every man to his own, and shall leave me a: 3441
16:32 and yet I am not a, because the Father is 3441
17:20 Neither pray I for these a, but for them also 3440
Ac 5:38 Refrain from these men, and let them a: 1439
19:26 that not a at Ephesus, but 3440
Ro 4:23 Now it was not written for his sake a, that it 3440
11: 3 and I am left a, and they seek my life. 3441
Gal 6: 4 then shall he have rejoicing in himself a, 3441
1Th 3: 1 we thought it good to be left at Athens a; 3441
Heb 9: 7 But into the second went the high priest a 3441
Jas 2:17 if it hath not works, is dead, being a. 1438+2596

ALONG (30)

Ex 2: 5 her maidens walked a by the river's side; 5921
9:23 hail, and the fire ran a upon the ground; 1980
Nu 21:22 but we will go a by the king's high way, 1980
34: 3 wilderness of Zin a by the coast of Edom, 5921
Dt 2:27 I will go a by the high way, I will neither 1980
Jos 10:10 chased them a the way that goeth up to NIH
15: 3 passed a to Zin, and ascended up on 5674
15: 3 passed a to Hezron, and went up to Adar, 5674
15: 6 and passed a by the north of Beth-arabah; 5674
15:10 passed a unto the side of mount Jearim, 5674
15:11 passed a to mount Baalah, and went out 5674
16: 2 passeth a unto the borders of Archi to 5674
Jos 17: 7 the border went a on the right hand unto NIH
18:18 passed a toward the side over against 5674
18:19 the border passed a to the side of 5674
19:13 from thence passeth on a on the east to 5674
Jdg 7:12 all the children of the east lay a in 5307
7:13 it fell, and overturned it, that the tent lay a. 5307
9:25 they robbed all that came a that way by 5674
9:37 another company come a by 1870+4480
11:18 they went a through the wilderness, and 1980
11:26 in all the cities that be a by the coasts of 5921
20:37 the liers in wait drew themselves a, and 4900
1Sa 6:12 and went a the highway, lowing as they 1980
28:20 Saul fell straightway all a on 4393+6967
2Sa 3:16 her husband went with her a weeping 1980
16:13 Shimei went a on the hill's side over 1980
2Ki 11:11 of the temple, a by the altar and the temple. NIH
2Ch 23:10 a by the altar and the temple, by the king NIH
Jer 41: 6 weeping all a as he went: 1980+1980

ALOOF (1)

Ps 38:11 my friends stand a from my sore; 4480+5048

ALOTH (1)

1Ki 4:16 the son of Hushai was in Asher and in A: 1175

ALOUD (19) [LOUD]

Ge 45: 2 he wept a: and 1065+5414+6963+871.1
1Ki 18:27 and said, Cry a: 1419+6963+871.1
Ezr 3:12 shouted a for 6963+7311+8643+871.1+3807.1
Job 19: 7 not heard: I cry a, but there is no judgment. 7768
Ps 51:14 my tongue shall sing a of thy 7442
55:17 and at noon, will I pray, and cry a: 1993
59:16 I will sing a of thy mercy in the morning: 7442
81: 1 Sing a unto God our strength: make a 7442
132:16 and her saints shall shout a for joy. 7442+7444
149: 5 in glory: let them sing a upon their beds. 7442
Isa 24:14 the LORD, they shall cry a from the sea. 6670
54: 1 break forth into singing, and cry a, 6670
58: 1 Cry a, spare not, lift up thy voice 1627+871.1
Da 3: 4 a herald cried a, To you it is 2429+871.2
4:14 He cried a, and said thus, Hew down 2429+871.2
5: 7 The king cried a to bring in 2429+871.2
Hos 5: 8 cry a at Beth-aven, after thee, O Benjamin. 7321
Mic 4: 9 Now why dost thou cry out a? is 7321+7452
Mk 15: 8 And the multitude crying a began to desire 310

ALPHA (4)

Rev 1: 8 I am A and Omega, the beginning and 1
1:11 Saying, I am A and Omega, the first and 1
21: 6 I am A and Omega, the beginning and the end. 1
22:13 I am A and Omega, the beginning and the end, 1

ALPHEUS (5)

Mt 10: 3 James the son of A, and Lebbeus, 256
Mk 2:14 he saw Levi the son of A sitting at 256
3:18 and James the son of A, and Thaddeus, and 256
Lk 6:15 James the son of A, and Simon called 256
Ac 1:13 James the son of A, and Simon Zelotes, and 256

ALREADY (31) [READY]

Ex 1: 5 seventy souls: for Joseph was in Egypt a. NIH
2Ch 28:13 LORD a, ye intend to add more to our sins NIH
Ne 5: 5 a: neither is it in our power to redeem them; NIH
Ecc 1:10 it hath been a of old time, which was 3528
2:12 the king? even that which hath been a done. 3528
3:15 that which is to be hath a been; and God 3528
4: 2 Wherefore I praised the dead which are a 3528
6:10 That which hath been is named a, and it is 3528
Mal 2: 2 yea, I have cursed them a, because ye do NIH
Mt 5:28 committed adultery with her a in his heart. 2235
17:12 That Elias is come a, and they knew him 2235
Mk 15:44 And Pilate marvelled if he were a dead: 2235
Lk 12:49 the earth; and what will I, if it be a kindled? 2235
Jn 3:18 but he that believeth not is condemned a, 2235
4:35 the fields; for they are white a to harvest. 2235
9:22 for the Jews had agreed a, that if any man 2235
9:27 I have told you a, and ye did not hear: 2235
11:17 that he had lien in the grave four days a. 2235
19:33 and saw that he was dead a, they brake not 2235
Ac 11:11 immediately there were three men a come 1824
27: 9 because the fast was now a past, Paul 2235
1Co 5: 3 but present in spirit, have judged a, 2235
2Co 12:21 I shall bewail many which have sinned a, 4258
Php 3:12 Not as though I had a attained, either were 2235
3:12 had already attained, either were a perfect: 2235
3:16 Nevertheless, whereto we have a attained, NIG
2Th 2: 7 For the mystery of iniquity doth a work: 2235
1Ti 5:15 For some are a turned aside after Satan. 2235
2Ti 2:18 saying that the resurrection is past a; 2235
1Jn 4: 3 and even now a is it in the world. 2235
Rev 2:25 But that which ye have a hold fast till I NIG

ALSO (1768)

Ge 1:16 to rule the night: he made the stars a. 2050.1
2: 9 the tree of life a in the midst of the garden, NIH
3: 6 and gave a unto her husband with her; 1571
3:18 Thorns a and thistles shall it bring forth 2050.1
3:21 Unto Adam a and to his wife did 2050.1
3:22 take a of the tree of life, and eat, and 1571
4: 4 he a brought of the firstlings of his flock 1571
4:22 Zillah, she a bare Tubal-cain, an instructor 1571
4:26 to Seth, to him a there was born a son; and 1571
6: 3 strive with man, for that he a is flesh: 1571
6: 4 a after that, when the sons of God came in 1571
6:11 The earth a was corrupt before God, and 2050.1
7: 3 Of fowls a of the air by sevens, the male 1571
8: 2 The fountains a of the deep and 2050.1
8: 8 A he sent forth a dove from him, to see if 2050.1
10:21 Unto Shem a, the father of all 2050.1
12:15 The princes a of Pharaoh saw her, and 2050.1
13: 5 Lot a, which went with Abram, had flocks, 1571
13:16 then shall thy seed a be numbered. 1571
14: 7 a the Amorites, that dwelt in 1571
14:16 a brought again his brother Lot, and 1571

Ge 14:16 and the women a, and the people. 1571
15:14 a that nation, whom they shall serve, will I 1571
16:13 Have I a here looked after him that seeth 1571
17:16 will bless her, and give thee a son a of her: 1571
18:12 I have pleasure, my lord being old a? 2050.1
18:23 Wilt thou a destroy the righteous with 637
18:24 wilt thou a destroy and not spare the place 637
19:34 let us make him drink wine this night a; 1571
19:35 made their father drink wine that night a: 1571
19:38 she a bare a son, and called his name 1571
20: 4 Lord, wilt thou slay a a righteous nation? 1571
20: 6 for I a withheld thee from sinning against 1571
21:13 a of the son of the bondwoman will I make 1571
22:20 she hath a born children unto thy brother 1571
22:24 she bare a Tebah, and Gaham, and 1571
24:14 Drink, and I will give thy camels drink a: 1571
24:19 she said, I will draw *water* for thy camels a, 1571
24:44 and I will a draw for thy camels: 1571
24:46 Drink, and I will give thy camels drink a: 1571
24:46 I drank, and she made the camels drink a. 1571
24:53 he gave a to her brother and to her 2050.1
26:21 digged another well, and strove for that a: 1571
27:31 he a had made savoury meat, and brought *it* 1571
27:34 Bless me, *even* me a, O my father. 1571
27:38 bless me, *even* me a, O my father. 1571
27:45 why should I be deprived a of you both *in* 1571
29:27 we will give thee this a for the service 1571
29:28 he gave him Rachel his daughter to wife a. NIH
29:30 he went in a unto Rachel, and he loved also 1571
29:30 he loved a Rachel more than Leah, and 1571
29:33 he hath therefore given me this *son* a: 1571
30: 3 that I may a have children by her. 1571
30: 6 hath a heard my voice, and hath given me a 1571
30:15 thou take away my son's mandrakes a? 1571
30:30 shall I provide for mine own house a? 1571
31:15 and hath quite devoured a our money. 1571
32: 6 a he cometh to meet thee, and four hundred 1571
32:18 lord Esau: and behold, a he *is* behind us. 1571
33: 7 Leah a with her children came near, and 1571
35:17 Fear not; thou shalt have this son a. 1571
37: 7 and lo, my sheaf arose, and a stood upright; 1571
38:10 the LORD: wherefore he slew him a. 1571
38:11 for he said, Lest peradventure he die a, 1571
38:22 a the men of the place said, *that* there was 1571
38:24 a, behold, she *is* with child by whoredom. 1571
40:15 here a have I done nothing that they should 1571
40:16 I a *was* in my dream, and behold, 637
42:22 therefore, behold, a his blood is required. 1571
43: 8 both we, and thou, *and* a our little ones. 1571
43:13 Take a your brother, and arise, go again 2050.1
44: 9 and we a will be my lord's bondmen. 1571
44:10 Now a *let* it *be* according unto your words: 1571
44:16 and *he* a with whom the cup is found. 1571
44:29 if ye take this a from me, and 1571
45:20 A regard not your stuff; for the good of 2050.1
46: 4 I will a surely bring thee up *again:* and 1571
46:34 even until now, both we, *and* a our fathers: 1571
47: 3 *are* shepherds, both we, *and* a our fathers. 1571
47:18 my lord a had our herds of cattle; 2050.1
48:11 and lo, God hath shewed me a thy seed. 1571
48:19 I know *it:* he a shall become a people, and 1571
48:19 become a people, and he a shall be great: 1571
50:18 his brethren a went and fell down before 1571
50:23 a of Machir the son of Manasseh were 1571
Ex 1:10 they join a unto our enemies, and 1571
2:19 a drew water enough for us, and 1571
3: 9 I have a seen the oppression wherewith 1571
4: 9 if they will not believe a these two signs, 1571
4:14 a, behold, he cometh forth to meet thee: 1571
6: 4 I have a established my covenant with 1571
6: 5 I have a heard the groaning of the children 1571
7:11 Pharaoh a called the wise men and 1571
7:11 they a did in like manner with their 1571
7:23 neither did he set his heart to this a. 1571
8:21 and a the ground whereon they *are.* 1571
8:32 Pharaoh hardened his heart at this time a, 1571
10:24 be stayed: let your little ones a go with you. 1571
10:25 Thou must give us a sacrifices and 1571
10:26 Our cattle a shall go with us; there shall not 1571
12:32 A take your flocks and your herds, as ye 1571
12:32 ye have said, and be gone; and bless me a. 1571
12:38 a mixed multitude went up a with them; 1571
15: 4 his chosen captains a are drowned in 2050.1
18:23 all this people shall a go to their place in 1571
19:22 let the priests a, which come near to 1571
21: 6 he shall a bring him to the door, or 2050.1
21:29 and his owner a shall be put to death. 1571
21:35 of it; and the dead *ox* a they shall divide. 1571
23: 9 A thou shalt not oppress a stranger: for ye 2050.1
24:11 a they saw God, and did eat and drink. 2050.1
25:23 Thou shalt a make a table *of* shittim 2050.1
29:15 Thou shalt a take one ram; and Aaron and 2050.1
29:22 A thou shalt take of the ram the fat and 2050.1
29:44 I will sanctify a both Aaron and his sons, 2050.1
30:18 Thou shalt a make a laver *of* brass, and 2050.1
30:18 his foot a *of* brass, to wash *withal:* and NIH
30:23 Take thou a unto thee principal spices, 2050.1
31:13 Speak thou a unto the children of Israel, 2050.1
33:12 and thou hast a found grace in my sight. 1571
33:17 I will do this thing a that thou hast spoken: 1571
35:14 The candlestick a for the light, and his 2050.1
37:12 A he made thereunto a border of a 2050.1
37:26 a he made unto it a crown *of* gold round 2050.1
Lev 5: 2 he a shall be unclean, and guilty. 2050.1
7:16 on the morrow a the remainder of it shall 2050.1
8: 8 a he put in the breastplate the Urim and 2050.1
8: 9 a upon the mitre, *even* upon his forefront, 2050.1
9: 4 A a bullock and a ram for peace 2050.1
9:18 He slew a the bullock and the ram *for* a 2050.1
11:29 These a *shall be* unclean unto you among 2050.1
11:40 he a that beareth the carcase of it shall 2050.1
13:18 The flesh a, in which, *even* in the skin 2050.1
13:38 If a man a or a woman have in the skin of 2050.1
13:47 The garment a that the plague of leprosy 2050.1
14: 9 a he shall wash his flesh in water, and 2050.1
Lev 15:18 The woman a with whom man shall lie 2050.1
15:20 every *thing* a that she sitteth upon shall 2050.1
18:19 A thou shalt not approach unto a woman 2050.1
18:28 That the land spue not you out a, when ye 2050.1
20:13 If a man a lie with mankind, as he lieth 2050.1
20:27 A man a or woman that hath a familiar 2050.1
22:12 If the priest's daughter a be *married* unto 2050.1
23:27 A on the tenth *day* of this seventh month 389
23:39 A in the fifteenth day of the seventh month, 389
26:16 I a will do this unto you; I will even appoint 637
26:22 I will a send wild beasts among you, 2050.1
26:24 will I a walk contrary unto you, and 637
26:28 Then I will walk contrary unto you a in 2050.1
26:39 a in the iniquities of their fathers shall they 637
26:40 that a they have walked contrary unto me; 637
26:41 *And that* I a have walked contrary unto 637
26:42 a my covenant with Isaac, and also my 637
26:42 a my covenant with Abraham will I 637
26:43 The land a shall be left of them, and 2050.1
Nu 3: 1 These a *are* the generations of Aaron and 2050.1
4:22 Take a the sum of the sons of Gershon, 1571
6:17 the priest shall offer a his meat offering, 2050.1
9: 2 Let the children of Israel a keep 2050.1
10:10 A in the day of your gladness, and in your 2050.1
11: 4 the children of Israel a wept again, 1571+2050.1
11:10 kindled greatly; Moses a was displeased. 2050.1
12: 2 hath he not spoken a by us? And 1571
15:15 and a for the stranger that sojourneth 2050.1
16:10 with thee: and seek ye the priesthood a? 1571
16:17 a, and Aaron, each *of you* his censer. 2050.1
16:34 they said, Lest the earth swallow us up a. NIH
18: 2 thy brethren a *of* the tribe of Levi, the tribe 1571
18: 3 the altar, that neither they, nor you a, die. 1571
18: 8 I a have given thee the charge of mine 2050.1
18:28 Thus you a shall offer a heave offering 1571
20:11 the congregation drank, and their beasts a. NIH
22:19 I pray you, tarry ye a here *this* night, 1571
22:33 surely now a I had slain thee, and saved her 1571
24:12 Spake I not a to thy messengers which thou 1571
24:18 Seir a shall be a possession for his 2050.1
24:24 afflict Eber, and he a shall perish for ever. 1571
24:25 to his place: and Balak a went his way. 1571
27:13 thou a shalt be gathered unto thy people, 2050.1
28:26 A in the day of the firstfruits, when ye 2050.1
30: 3 If a woman a vow a vow unto 2050.1
31: 8 Balaam a the son of Beor they slew with 2050.1
33: 4 upon their gods a the LORD executed 2050.1
35: 2 ye shall give a unto the Levites suburbs for NIH
Dt 1:37 A the LORD was angry with me for your 1571
1:37 Thou a shalt not go in thither. 1571
2: 6 ye shall a buy water of them for money, 1571
2:11 Which a were accounted giants, as 637
2:12 The Horims a dwelt in Seir beforetime; 2050.1
2:20 (That a was accounted a land of giants: 637
3: 3 our God delivered into our hands Og a, 1571
3:17 The plain a, and Jordan, and the coast 2050.1
3:20 *until* they a possess the land which 1571
7:13 he will a bless the fruit of thy womb, and 2050.1
8: 5 Thou shalt a consider in thine heart, that, 2050.1
9: 8 A in Horeb ye provoked the LORD to 2050.1
9:19 LORD hearkened unto me at that time a. 1571
9:20 and I prayed for Aaron a the same time. 1571
10:10 LORD hearkened unto me at that time a, 1571
10:14 thy God, the earth a, with all that therein *is.* NIH
15:17 a unto thy maidservant thou shalt do 637
18: 4 The firstfruit a of thy corn, of thy wine, and NIH
20: 6 let him a go and return unto his house, NIH
23:12 Thou shalt have a place a without 2050.1
26:13 a have given them unto the Levite, and 1571
28:51 which a shall not leave thee *either* corn, NIH
28:61 A every sickness, and every plague, 1571
29:15 and a with *him* that *is* not here with us 2050.1
31: 2 a the LORD hath said unto me, 2050.1
32:24 I will a send the teeth of beasts upon 2050.1
32:25 the suckling a with the man of gray hairs. NIH
33:28 wine; a his heavens shall drop down dew. 637
Jos 1:15 they a have possessed the land which 1571
2:12 that ye will a shew kindness unto my 1571
7:11 they have a transgressed my covenant 1571
7:11 have a stolen, and dissembled also, and 1571
7:11 dissembled a, and they have put *it* even 1571
10:30 the LORD delivered it a, and the king 1571
10:39 as he had done a to Libnah, and to her 2050.1
13: 3 and the Ekronites; a the Avites: 2050.1
13:22 Balaam a the son of Beor, the soothsayer, 2050.1
15:19 a south land; give me a springs of water. 2050.1
17: 1 There was a a lot for the tribe of 2050.1
17: 2 There was a *a lot* for the rest of 2050.1
17: 9 the coast of Manasseh a *was* on the north 2050.1
19:30 Ummah a, and Aphek, and Rehob: 2050.1
20: 1 The LORD a spake unto Joshua, saying, 2050.1
22: 7 when Joshua sent them away a unto their 1571
24: 5 I sent Moses a and Aaron, and I plagued 2050.1
24:18 *therefore* will we a serve the LORD; 1571
Jdg 1:15 a south land; give me a springs of water. 2050.1
1:18 A Judah took Gaza with the coast thereof, 2050.1
1:22 of Joseph, they a went up *against* Beth-el: 1571
2: 3 Wherefore I a said, I will not drive them 1571
2:10 a all that generation were gathered unto 1571
2:21 I a will not henceforth drive out any from 1571
3:22 the haft a went in after the blade; and 1571
3:31 with an ox goad: and he a delivered Israel. 1571
5: 4 the clouds a dropped water. 1571
5:15 with Deborah; even Issachar, *and* a Barak: 3651
6:35 who a was gathered after him: 1571
7:18 blow ye the trumpets a on every side of all 1571
8: 9 he spake a unto the men of Penuel, saying, 1571
8:22 and thy son, and thy son's son a: 1571
8:31 she a bare him a son, whose name he called 1571
9: 2 remember a that I *am* your bone and NIH
9:19 in Abimelech, and let him a rejoice in you: 1571
9:49 all the men of the tower of Shechem died a, 1571
10: 9 passed over Jordan to fight a against Judah, 1571
10:10 forsaken our God, and a served Baalim. NIH
10:12 The Zidonians a, and the Amalekites, and 2050.1
Jdg 15: 5 a the standing corn, with the vineyards *and* 5704
17: 2 spakest of a in mine ears, behold, the silver 1571
19:10 his concubine a *was* with him. 2050.1
19:16 at even, which *was* a of mount Ephraim; 376
19:19 there is bread and wine a for me, and 2050.1
20:48 a they set on fire all the cities that they 1571
Ru 1: 5 and Chilion died a both of them; 1571
1:12 *if* I should have a husband a to night, and 1571
1:12 also to night, and should a bear sons; 1571
1:17 the LORD do so to me, and more a, 3541
2:16 let fall a *some* of the handfuls of purpose 1571
2:21 the Moabitess said, He said unto me a, 1571
3:15 A he said, Bring the vail that *thou hast* 2050.1
4: 5 thou must buy *it* a of Ruth the Moabitess, 854
1Sa 1: 6 her adversary a provoked her sore, for to 1571
1:28 Therefore a I have lent him to the LORD; 1571
2:15 A before they burnt the fat, the priest's 1571
2:26 both with the LORD, and a with men. 1571
3:12 when I begin, I will a make an end. 2050.1
3:17 God do so to thee, and more a, if thou hide 3541
4:17 there hath been a a great slaughter among 1571
4:17 thy two sons a, Hophni and Phinehas, 1571
8: 8 served other gods, so do they a unto thee. 1571
8:20 That we a may be like all the nations; and 1571
10:11 son of Kish? *Is* Saul a among the prophets? 1571
10:12 a proverb, *Is* Saul a among the prophets? 1571
10:26 Saul a went home to Gibeah; and 1571
12:14 a the king that reigneth over you continue 1571
13: 4 *that* Israel a was had in abomination with 1571
14:15 they a trembled, and the earth quaked: 1571
14:21 even they a *turned* to be with the Israelites 1571
14:22 even they a followed hard after them in 1571
14:44 Saul answered, God do so and more a: 2050.1
15: 1 Samuel a said unto Saul, The LORD 2050.1
15:23 he hath a rejected thee from *being* king. 2050.1
15:29 a the Strength of Israel will not lie nor 1571
17:38 a he armed him with a coat *of mail.* 2050.1
18: 5 and a in the sight of Saul's servants. 1571
19:11 Saul a sent messengers unto David's 2050.1
19:20 messengers of Saul, and they a prophesied. 1571
19:21 again the third time, and they prophesied a. 1571
19:22 went he a to Ramah, and came to a great 1571
19:23 the Spirit of God was upon him a, and 1571
19:24 he stript off his clothes a, and 1571
19:24 they say, *Is* Saul a among the prophets? 1571
20:15 a thou shalt not cut off thy kindness from NIH
22:17 because their hand a *is* with David, and 1571
23:17 and that a Saul my father knoweth. 1571
23:25 Saul a and his men went to seek *him.* 2050.1
24: 8 David a rose afterward, and went out of 2050.1
25:13 and David a girded on his sword: 1571
25:22 more a do God unto the enemies of David, 3541
25:43 David a took Ahinoam of Jezreel; and 2050.1
25:43 and they were a both of them his wives. 1571
26:25 do great things, and a shalt still prevail. 1571
28:19 Moreover the LORD will a deliver Israel 1571
28:19 the LORD a shall deliver the host of Israel 1571
28:22 hearken thou a unto the voice of thine 1571
30:21 whom they had made a to abide at 2050.1
2Sa 1: 4 many of the people a are fallen and dead; 1571
1: 4 and Saul and Jonathan his son are dead a. 1571
1:18 (A he bade *them* teach the children of 2050.1
2: 2 his two wives a, Ahinoam the Jezreelitess, 1571
2: 6 I a will requite you this kindness, because 1571
2: 7 a the house of Judah have anointed me king 1571
2:24 Joab a and Abishai pursued after Abner: 2050.1
3: 9 So do God to Abner, and more a, except, 3541
3:12 saying a, Make thy league with me, and NIH
3:19 Abner a spake in the ears of Benjamin: 1571
3:19 Abner went a to speak in the ears of David 1571
3:35 and more a, if I taste bread, or ought else, 3588
4: 2 (for Beeroth a was reckoned to Benjamin: 1571
5: 2 A in time past, when Saul was king over us, 1571
5:15 Ibhar a, and Elishua, and Nepheg, and 2050.1
5:18 The Philistines a came and 2050.1
7:11 A the LORD telleth thee that he will 2050.1
7:19 thou hast spoken a of thy servant's house 1571
8: 3 David smote a Hadadezer, the son of 2050.1
8:11 Which a king David did dedicate unto 1571
10:14 *then* fled they a before Abishai, and NIH
11:12 Tarry here to day a, and to morrow I will 1571
11:17 of David; and Uriah the Hittite died a. 1571
11:21 Thy servant Uriah the Hittite is dead a. 1571
11:24 and thy servant Uriah the Hittite is dead a. 1571
12:13 The LORD a hath put away thy sin; 1571
12:14 the child a that is born unto thee shall 1571
13:36 the king a and all his servants wept very 1571
14: 7 he slew; and we will destroy the heir a: 1571
15:19 the Gittite, Wherefore goest thou a with us? 1571
15:19 for thou *art* a stranger, and a an exile. 1571
15:21 or life, even there a will thy servant be. NIH
15:23 the king a *himself* passed over the brook 2050.1
15:24 lo Zadok a, and all the Levites *were* with 1571
15:27 The king said a unto Zadok the priest, *Art* 2050.1
15:34 so *will* I now a *be* thy servant: 2050.1
17: 5 Call now Hushai the Archite a, and let us 1571
17:10 he a *that is* valiant, whose heart *is* as 1571
18: 2 I will surely go forth with you myself a. 1571
18:22 let me, I pray thee, a run after Cushi. 1571
18:26 And the king said, He a bringeth tidings. 1571
19:13 God do so to me, and more a, if thou 3254+3541
19:40 the king, and a half the people of Israel. 1571
19:43 and we have a more *right* in David than ye: 1571
20:14 gathered together, and went a after him. 637
20:26 Ira a the Jairite was a chief ruler about 1571
21:20 *in* number; and he a was born to the giant. 1571
22:10 He bowed the heavens a, and came down; 2050.1
22:20 He brought me forth a into a large place: 2050.1
22:24 I was a upright before him, and have kept 2050.1
22:36 Thou hast a given me the shield of thy 2050.1
22:41 Thou hast a given me the necks of mine 2050.1
22:44 Thou a hast delivered me from 2050.1
22:49 thou a hast lifted me up on high above 2050.1
23:20 he went down a and slew a lion in 2050.1
1Ki 1: 6 he a *was* a very goodly *man;* and 1571

A

1Ki 1:14 I **a** will come in after thee, and 2050.1
1:22 the king, Nathan the prophet **a** came in. 2050.1
1:33 The king **a** said unto them, Take with you 2050.1
1:46 **a** Solomon sitteth on the throne of 1571
1:48 **a** thus said the king, Blessed *be* the LORD 1571
2:5 Moreover thou knowest **a** what Joab 1571
2:22 ask for him the kingdom **a**; for he *is* mine 2050.1
2:23 God do so to me, and **more a**, 3254
3:13 I have **a** given thee *that* which thou hast not 1571
3:18 that this woman was delivered **a**: 1571
4:13 to him ***a*** *pertained* the region of Argob, NIH
4:15 he **a** took Basmath the daughter of 1571
4:28 Barley **a** and straw for the horses and 2050.1
4:33 he spake **a** of beasts, and of fowl, and 2050.1
6:22 **a** the whole altar that *was* by the oracle 2050.1
6:32 The two doors **a** *were* of olive tree; and 2050.1
6:33 So **a** made he for the door of the temple 2050.1
7:2 He built **a** the house of the forest of 2050.1
7:8 Solomon made **a** a house for Pharaoh's 2050.1
7:20 the two pillars *had pomegranates* **a** above, 1571
7:31 **a** upon the mouth of it *were* gravings with 1571
8:24 thou spakest **a** with thy mouth, and 2050.1
9:21 whom the children of Israel **a** were not 2050.1
10:11 the navy **a** of Hiram, that brought gold 1571
10:12 harps **a** and psalteries for singers: 2050.1
12:14 my father **a** chastised you with whips, but NIH
13:5 The altar **a** *was* rent, and the ashes poured 2050.1
13:11 the king, them they told **a** to their father. 2050.1
13:18 I *am* a prophet **a** as thou *art;* and an angel 1571
13:24 by it, the lion **a** stood by the carcase. 2050.1
14:23 For they **a** built them high places, and 1571
14:24 there were **a** sodomites in the land: *and* 1571
15:13 **a** Maachah his mother, even her he 1571
16:7 **a** by the hand of the prophet Jehu the son of 1571
16:16 hath conspired, and hath **a** slain the king: 1571
17:20 hast thou **a** brought evil upon the widow 1571
18:35 and he filled the trench **a** *with* water. 1571
19:2 So let the gods do *to me,* and more **a**, 3541
20:3 thy wives **a** and thy children, *even* 2050.1
20:10 said, The gods do so unto me, and more **a**, 3541
21:19 Hast thou killed, and **a** taken possession? 1571
21:23 And of Jezebel **a** spake the LORD, saying, 1571
22:22 Thou shalt persuade *him,* and prevail **a**: 1571
2Ki 1:11 Again **a** he sent unto him another captain 2050.1
2:13 He took up **a** the mantle of Elijah that fell 2050.1
2:14 when he **a** had smitten the waters, they 2050.1
3:18 he will deliver the Moabites **a** into your 2050.1
5:1 he was **a** a mighty *man* in valour, *but* 2050.1
6:31 he said, God do so and more **a** to me, if 3541
7:4 if we sit still here, we die **a**. Now 2050.1
7:8 and carried thence **a**, and went and hid *it.* NIH
8:1 it shall **a** come upon the land seven years. 1571
9:27 and said, Smite him **a** in the chariot. 1571
10:2 and horses, a fenced city **a**, and armour; 2050.1
10:5 the elders **a**, and the bringers up *of* 2050.1
11:17 between the king **a** and the people. 2050.1
13:6 and there remained the grove **a** in Samaria.) 1571
16:14 he brought **a** the brasen altar, which *was* 2050.1
17:19 **A** Judah kept not the commandments of 1571
18:2 His mother's name **a** *was* Abi, 2050.1
21:11 and hath made Judah **a** to sin with his idols: 1571
22:19 I **a** have heard *thee,* saith the LORD. 1571
23:5 them **a** that burnt incense unto Baal, 2050.1
23:19 all the houses **a** of the high places that *were* 1571
23:27 I will remove Judah **a** out of my sight, 1571
24:4 **a** *for* the innocent blood that he shed: for he 1571
1Ch 1:14 The Jebusite **a**, and the Amorite, and 2050.1
1:21 Hadoram **a**, and Uzal, and Diklah, 2050.1
1:51 Hadad died **a**. And the dukes of Edom 2050.1
2:9 The sons **a** of Hezron, that were born 2050.1
2:26 Jerahmeel had **a** another wife, 2050.1
2:49 She bare **a** Shaaph the father of 2050.1
3:6 Ibhar **a**, and Elishama, and Eliphelet, 2050.1
3:18 Malchiram **a**, and Pedaiah, and Shenazar, 2050.1
6:3 The sons **a** of Aaron; Nadab, and Abihu, 2050.1
6:48 Their brethren **a** the Levites *were* 2050.1
6:67 *they gave* **a** Gezer with her suburbs, 2050.1
6:79 Kedemoth **a** with her suburbs, and 2050.1
7:10 The sons **a** of Jediael; Bilhan: and 2050.1
7:12 Shuppim **a**, and Huppim, the children of 2050.1
7:25 **a** Resheph, and Telah his son, and 2050.1
7:28 Shechem **a** and the towns thereof, 2050.1
8:13 Beriah **a**, and Shema, who *were* heads of 2050.1
8:18 Ishmerai **a**, and Jezliah, and Jobab, 2050.1
8:32 these **a** dwelt with their brethren in 637
9:29 *Some* of them **a** *were* appointed to 2050.1
9:38 they **a** dwelt with their brethren at 2050.1
10:13 **a** for asking *counsel* of *one that had* a 1571
11:10 These **a** *are* the chief of the mighty *men* 2050.1
11:22 **a** he went down and slew a lion in a pit in 2050.1
11:26 **A** The valiant *men* of the armies *were,* 2050.1
12:38 all the rest **a** of Israel *were of* one heart to 1571
13:2 with them **a** *to* the priests and Levites *which* NIH
15:27 David **a** *had* upon him an ephod of linen. 2050.1
16:6 Benaiah **a** and Jahaziel the priests with 2050.1
16:25 he **a** *is* to be feared above all gods. 2050.1
16:30 the world **a** shall be stable, that it be not 637
16:38 Obed-edom **a** the son of Jeduthun and 2050.1
17:9 **A** I will ordain a place for my people 2050.1
17:17 for thou hast **a** spoken of thy servant's NIH
18:4 David **a** houghed all the chariot *horses,* 2050.1
18:11 Them **a** king David dedicated unto 1571
20:2 **and** he brought **a** exceeding much spoil 2050.1
20:6 *each foot:* and he **a** was the son of the giant. 1571
21:23 lo, I give *thee* the oxen **a** for burnt offerings, NIH
22:4 **A** cedar trees in abundance: for 2050.1
22:14 timber **a** and stone have I prepared; and 2050.1
22:17 David **a** commanded all the princes of 2050.1
23:26 **a** unto the Levites; *they* shall no *more* carry 1571
24:30 The sons **a** of Mushi; Mahli, and Eder, 2050.1
26:6 **A** unto Shemaiah his son were sons born, 2050.1
26:10 **A** Hosah, of the children of Merari, 2050.1
27:4 and *of* his course *was* Mikloth **a** the ruler: 2050.1
27:30 Over the camels **a** *was* Obil 2050.1
27:32 **A** Jonathan David's uncle *was* a 2050.1
1Ch 28:13 **A** for the courses of the priests and 2050.1
28:14 *silver* **a** for all instruments of silver by NIH
28:15 the candlestick, and ***a*** *for* the lamps thereof, NIH
28:17 **A** pure gold *for* the fleshhooks, and 2050.1
28:21 **a** the princes and all the people *will be* 2050.1
29:9 David the king **a** rejoiced *with* great joy. 1571
29:17 I know **a**, my God, that thou triest 2050.1
2Ch 2:8 Send me **a** cedar trees, fir trees, and 2050.1
2:14 **a** to grave any *manner of* graving, and 2050.1
3:7 He overlaid **a** the house, the beams, 2050.1
3:12 the other wing *was* five cubits **a**, joining to NIH
3:15 **A** he made before the house two pillars of 2050.1
4:2 **A** he made a molten sea of ten cubits 2050.1
4:6 He made **a** ten lavers, and put five on 2050.1
4:8 He made **a** ten tables, and placed *them* in 2050.1
4:14 He made **a** bases and lavers made he 2050.1
4:16 The pots **a**, and the shovels, and 2050.1
4:19 the golden altar **a**, and the tables 2050.1
5:6 **A** king Solomon, and all the congregation 2050.1
5:12 **A** the Levites *which were* the singers, all 2050.1
7:6 the Levites **a** with instruments of musick 2050.1
7:8 **A** at the same time Solomon kept 2050.1
8:5 **A** he built Beth-horon the upper, and 2050.1
8:14 the porters **a** by their courses at every 2050.1
9:4 his cupbearers **a**, and their apparel; and 2050.1
9:10 the servants **a** of Huram, and the servants 1571
12:5 have I **a** left you in the hand of Shishak. 637
12:9 he carried away **a** the shields of gold 2050.1
12:12 and **a** in Judah things went well. 1571
13:2 His mother's name **a** *was* Michaiah 2050.1
13:3 Jeroboam **a** set the battle in array against 2050.1
13:11 the *shew*bread **a** *set they* in order upon 2050.1
14:5 **A** he took away out of all the cities of 2050.1
14:15 They smote **a** the tents of cattle, 1571+2050.1
15:16 **a** *concerning* Maachah the mother of Asa 1571
17:7 **A** in the third year of his reign he sent to 2050.1
17:11 **A** *some* of the Philistines brought 2050.1
18:21 shalt entice *him,* and thou shalt **a** prevail: 1571
19:11 **a** the Levites *shall be* officers before you. 2050.1
20:1 It came to pass after this **a**, *that* 2050.1
21:4 and *divers* **a** of the princes of Israel. 1571
21:10 The same time **a** did Libnah revolt from 227
21:13 **a** hast slain thy brethren of thy father's 1571
21:17 king's house, and his sons **a**, and his wives; 1571
22:2 His mother's name **a** *was* Athaliah 2050.1
22:3 He **a** walked in the ways of the house of 1571
22:5 He walked **a** after their counsel, and 1571
23:13 **a** the singers with instruments of musick, 2050.1
23:18 **A** Jehoiada appointed the offices of 2050.1
24:1 His mother's name **a** *was* Zibiah of 2050.1
24:7 **a** all the dedicate *things* of the house of 1571
24:12 **a** such as wrought iron and brass to mend 1571
24:20 the LORD, he hath **a** forsaken you. 2050.1
25:6 He hired **a** an hundred thousand mighty 2050.1
25:24 the hostages **a**, and returned *to* Samaria. 2050.1
26:3 His mother's name **a** *was* Jecoliah of 2050.1
26:10 **A** he built towers in the desert, and 2050.1
26:10 husbandmen **a**, and vinedressers in NIH
26:20 yea, himself hasted **a** to go out, because 2050.1
27:1 His mother's name **a** *was* Jerushah, 2050.1
27:5 He fought **a** with the king of 2050.1
28:2 and made **a** molten images for Baalim. 1571
28:4 He sacrificed **a** and burnt incense in 2050.1
28:5 he was **a** delivered into the hand of the king 1571
28:8 took **a** away much spoil from them, and 1571
28:18 The Philistines **a** had invaded the cities of 2050.1
28:18 Gimzo **a** and the villages thereof: 2050.1
29:7 **A** they have shut up the doors of the porch, 1571
29:22 they killed **a** the lambs, and 2050.1
29:27 the song of the LORD began ***a*** with NIH
29:35 **a** the burnt offerings *were* in abundance, 1571
30:1 wrote letters **a** to Ephraim and Manasseh, 1571
30:12 **A** in Judah the hand of God was to give 1571
31:1 Benjamin, in Ephraim **a** and Manasseh, 2050.1
31:3 *He appointed* **a** the king's portion of his 2050.1
31:6 they **a** brought in the tithe of oxen and 1571
31:19 **A** of the sons of Aaron the priests, 2050.1
32:5 **A** he strengthened himself, and built up 2050.1
32:17 He wrote **a** letters to rail on the LORD 2050.1
32:28 Storehouses **a** for the increase of corn, 2050.1
32:30 This same Hezekiah **a** stopped the upper 2050.1
33:4 **A** he built altars in the house of 2050.1
33:6 **a** he observed times, and 2050.1
33:19 His prayer **a**, and *how God* was intreated 2050.1
34:13 **A** *they were* over the bearers of burdens, 2050.1
34:27 I have even heard *thee* **a**, saith the LORD. 1571
35:9 Conaniah **a**, and Shemaiah and 2050.1
36:7 Nebuchadnezzar **a** carried of the vessels 2050.1
36:13 he **a** rebelled against king Nebuchadnezzar, 1571
36:22 his kingdom, and *put it* **a** in writing, saying, 1571
Ezr 1:1 his kingdom, and *put it* **a** in writing, saying, 1571
1:7 **A** Cyrus the king brought forth 2050.1
3:4 They kept **a** the feast of tabernacles, as it 2050.1
3:7 They gave money **a** unto the masons, and 2050.1
4:20 There have been mighty kings **a** over 2050.3
5:10 We asked their names **a**, to certify 638+2050.3
5:14 the vessels **a** of gold and silver of the house 638
6:5 **a** let the golden and silver vessels of 638
6:11 **A** I have made a decree, that whosoever 2050.3
7:19 The vessels **a** that *are* given thee for 2050.3
7:24 **A** *we* certify you, that *touching* any of 2050.3
8:6 Of the sons **a** of Adin; Ebed the son of 2050.1
8:14 Of the sons **a** of Bigvai; Uthai, and 2050.1
8:16 chief *men;* **a** for Joiarib, and for Elnathan, 2050.1
8:20 **A** of the Nethinims, whom David and 2050.1
8:27 **A** twenty basons of gold, of a thousand 2050.1
8:28 the vessels *are* holy **a**; and the silver and 2050.1
8:35 ***A*** the children of those that had been carried NIH
10:4 we **a** *will be* with thee: be of good 2050.1
10:23 **A** of the Levites; Jozabad, and Shimei, 2050.1
10:24 Of the singers **a**; Eliashib: and of 2050.1
10:28 Of the sons **a** of Bebai; Jehohanan, 2050.1
Ne 1:3 the wall of Jerusalem **a** *is* broken down, 2050.1
2:6 unto me, (the queen **a** sitting by him,) 2050.1
2:18 as **a** the king's words that he had spoken 637
Ne 3:3 who ***a*** laid the beams thereof, and set up NIH
3:8 Next unto him **a** repaired Hananiah 2050.1
3:29 After him repaired **a** Shemaiah the son of 2050.1
5:3 *Some* **a** there were that said, We *have* 2050.1
5:4 There were **a** that said, We have 2050.1
5:9 **A** I said, It *is* not good that ye do: ought 2050.1
5:11 **a** the hundredth *part* of the money, and 2050.1
5:13 **A** I shook my lap, and said, So God shake 1571
5:16 Yea **a** I continued in the work of this 2050.1
5:18 **a** fowls were prepared for me, and 2050.1
6:7 thou hast **a** appointed prophets to preach of 1571
6:19 **A** they reported his good deeds before me, 1571
7:61 these *were* they which went up ***a*** from NIH
8:7 **A** Jeshua, and Bani, and Sherebiah, 2050.1
8:18 **A** day by day, from the first day unto 2050.1
9:13 Thou camest down **a** upon mount Sinai, 2050.1
9:20 Thou gavest **a** thy good spirit to instruct 2050.1
9:23 Their children **a** multipliedst thou as 2050.1
9:37 **a** they have dominion over our bodies, 2050.1
10:32 **A** we made ordinances for us, to charge 2050.1
10:36 **A** the firstborn of our sons, and of our 2050.1
11:1 the rest of the people **a** cast lots, to bring 2050.1
11:15 **A** of the Levites: Shemaiah the son of 2050.1
11:22 The overseer **a** of the Levites at 2050.1
11:31 The children **a** of Benjamin from Geba 2050.1
12:9 **A** Bakbukiah and Unni, their brethren, 2050.1
12:10 Joiakim **a** begat Eliashib, and 2050.1
12:22 **a** the priests, to the reign of Darius 2050.1
12:29 **A** from the house of Gilgal, and out of 2050.1
12:43 **A** that day they offered great sacrifices, 2050.1
12:43 the wives **a** and the children rejoiced: so 1571
13:15 as **a** wine, grapes, and figs, and all *manner* 637
13:16 There dwelt men of Tyre **a** therein, which 2050.1
13:22 *concerning* this **a**, and spare me according 1571
13:23 In those days **a** saw I Jews *that* had married 1571
Est 1:9 **A** Vashti the queen made a feast for 1571
1:16 ***a*** to all the princes, and to all the people that NIH
2:8 that Esther was brought ***a*** unto the king's NIH
3:11 The silver *is* given to thee, the people **a**, 2050.1
4:8 **A** he gave him the copy of the writing of 2050.1
4:16 I **a** and my maidens will fast likewise; and 1571
5:12 to morrow *am* I invited unto her **a** with 1571
7:8 Will he force the queen **a** before me in 1571
7:9 said before the king, Behold **a**, 1571
8:8 Write ye **a** for the Jews, as it liketh you, 2050.1
9:13 morrow **a** according unto *this* day's decree, 1571
9:15 on the fourteenth day **a** of the month Adar, 1571
Job 1:3 His substance **a** was seven thousand 2050.1
1:6 and Satan came **a** among them. 1571
1:16 there came **a** another, and said, 2050.1
1:17 there came **a** another, and said, 2050.1
1:18 there came **a** another, and said, Thy sons 2050.1
2:1 Satan came **a** among them to present 1571
5:25 Thou shalt know **a** that thy seed *shall be* 2050.1
7:1 *are not* his days **a** like the days of a 2050.1
9:11 he passeth on **a**, but I perceive him not. 2050.1
9:20 I *am* perfect, it shall **a** prove me perverse. 2050.1
11:11 he seeth wickedness **a**; will he not then 2050.1
11:19 **A** thou shalt lie down, and none shall 2050.1
12:15 **a** he sendeth them out, and they overturn 2050.1
13:2 What ye know, *the same* do I know **a**. I *am* 1571
13:16 He **a** *shall be* my salvation: for a hypocrite 1571
13:27 Thou puttest my feet **a** in the stocks, and 2050.1
14:2 he fleeth **a** as a shadow, and 2050.1
16:4 I **a** could speak as ye *do:* if your soul were 1571
16:12 he hath **a** taken *me* by my neck, and 2050.1
16:17 in mine hands: **a** my prayer is pure. 2050.1
16:19 **A** now, behold my witness *is* in heaven, 1571
17:6 He hath made me **a** a byword of 2050.1
17:7 Mine eye **a** is dim by reason of sorrow, 2050.1
17:9 The righteous **a** shall hold on his way, 2050.1
19:11 He hath **a** kindled his wrath against me, 2050.1
20:9 The eye **a** *which* saw him shall *see him* 2050.1
22:28 Thou shalt **a** decree a thing, and it shall 2050.1
24:15 The eye **a** of the adulterer waiteth for 2050.1
24:22 He draweth **a** the mighty with his power: 2050.1
30:11 they have **a** let loose the bridle before me. 2050.1
30:31 My harp **a** is *turned* to mourning, and 2050.1
31:28 This **a** *were* an iniquity *to be punished by* 1571
32:3 **A** against his three friends was his wrath 2050.1
32:10 Hearken to me; I **a** will shew mine opinion. 637
32:17 *I said,* I will answer **a** my part, I also will 637
32:17 also my part, I **a** will shew mine opinion. 637
33:6 God's stead: I **a** am formed out of the clay. 1571
33:19 He is chastened **a** with pain upon his bed, 2050.1
36:1 Elihu **a** proceeded, and said, 2050.1
36:10 He openeth **a** their ear to discipline, and 2050.1
36:29 **A** can *any* understand the spreadings of 518+637
36:33 the cattle **a** concerning the vapour. 637
37:1 At this **a** my heart trembleth, and is moved 637
37:11 **A** by watering he wearieth the thick cloud: 637
39:30 Her young ones **a** suck up blood: and 2050.1
40:8 Wilt thou **a** disannul my judgment? wilt thou 637
40:14 will I **a** confess unto thee that thine own 1571
42:9 the LORD **a** accepted Job. 2050.1
42:10 **a** the LORD gave Job twice as much as 2050.1
42:11 every man **a** gave him a piece of money, 2050.1
42:13 He had **a** seven sons and three daughters. 2050.1
Ps 1:3 his leaf **a** shall not wither; and 2050.1
5:11 let them **a** that love thy name be joyful in 2050.1
6:3 My soul is **a** sore vexed: but thou, 2050.1
7:13 He hath **a** prepared for him 2050.1
9:9 The LORD **a** will be a refuge for 2050.1
16:7 my reins **a** instruct me *in* the night seasons. 637
16:9 glory rejoiceth: my flesh **a** shall rest in hope. 637
18:7 the foundations **a** of the hills moved and 2050.1
18:9 He bowed the heavens **a**, and came down: 2050.1
18:13 The LORD **a** thundered in the heavens, 2050.1
18:19 He brought me forth **a** into a large place; 2050.1
18:23 I was **a** upright before him, and I kept 2050.1
18:35 Thou hast **a** given me the shield of thy 2050.1
18:40 Thou hast **a** given me the necks of mine 2050.1
19:10 sweeter **a** than honey and the honeycomb. 2050.1
19:13 Keep back thy servant **a** from 1571
26:1 I have trusted **a** in the LORD; *therefore* 2050.1

Ps 27: 7 have mercy a upon me, and answer me. 2050.1
28: 9 feed them a, and lift them up for ever. 2050.1
29: 6 He maketh them a to skip like a calf; 2050.1
35: 3 Draw out a the spear, and stop *the way* 2050.1
37: 4 Delight thyself a in the LORD; and 2050.1
37: 5 a in him; and he shall bring *it* to pass. 2050.1
38:10 the light of mine eyes, it a is gone from me. 1571
38:12 They a that seek after my life lay snares 2050.1
38:20 They a that render evil for good are mine 2050.1
40: 2 He brought me up a out of a horrible pit, 2050.1
45:10 forget a thine own people, and 2050.1
52: 6 The righteous a shall see, and fear, and 2050.1
55:10 mischief a and sorrow *are* in the midst of 2050.1
60: 7 Ephraim a *is* the strength of mine head; 2050.1
62:12 A unto thee, O Lord, *belongeth* mercy: 2050.1
65: 8 They a that dwell in the uttermost parts 2050.1
65:13 the valleys a are covered over with corn; 2050.1
65:13 with corn; they shout for joy, they a sing. 637
68: 1 let them a that hate him flee before him. 2050.1
68: 8 the heavens a dropped at the presence of 637
68:18 yea, *for* the rebellious a, that the LORD 2050.1
69:11 I made sackcloth a my garment; and 2050.1
69:21 They gave me a gall for my meat; and 2050.1
69:31 *This* a shall please the LORD better 2050.1
69:36 The seed a of his servants shall inherit it: 2050.1
71:18 Now a when I am old and grayheaded, 1571
71:19 Thy righteousness a, O God, *is* very high, 2050.1
71:22 I will a praise thee with the psaltery, 1571
71:24 My tongue a shall talk of thy righteousness 1571
72: 8 He shall have dominion a from sea to sea, 2050.1
72:12 the poor a, and *him* that hath no helper. 2050.1
72:15 prayer a shall be made for him 2050.1
74:16 The day *is* thine, the night a *is* thine: 637
75:10 All the horns of the wicked a will I cut 2050.1
76: 2 In Salem a is his tabernacle, and 2050.1
77:12 I will meditate a of all thy work, and 2050.1
77:16 they were afraid: the depths a were troubled. 637
77:17 out a sound: thine arrows a went abroad. 637
78:14 In the daytime a he led them with a 2050.1
78:16 He brought streams a out of the rock, and 2050.1
78:20 streams overflowed; can he give bread a? 1571
78:21 and anger a came up against Israel; 1571
78:27 He rained flesh a upon them as dust, and 2050.1
78:46 He gave a their increase unto 2050.1
78:48 He gave up their cattle a to the hail, and 2050.1
78:55 He cast out the heathen a before them, 2050.1
78:62 He gave his people over a unto 2050.1
78:70 He chose David a his servant, and 2050.1
81:16 He should have fed them a with the finest 2050.1
83: 8 Assur a is joined with them: they have 1571
84: 6 make it a well; the rain a filleth the pools. 1571
89: 5 thy faithfulness a in the congregation of 637
89:11 The heavens *are* thine, the earth a *is* thine: 637
89:21 mine arm a shall strengthen him. 637
89:25 I will set his hand a in the sea, and 2050.1
89:27 A I will make him *my* firstborn, higher than 637
89:29 His seed a will I make *to endure* for ever, 2050.1
89:43 Thou hast a turned the edge of his sword, 637
92:11 Mine eye a shall see *my desire* on mine 2050.1
93: 1 the world a is stablished, *that* it cannot be 637
95: 4 the earth: the strength of the hills *is* his a. 2050.1
96:10 the world a shall be established *that* it shall 637
99: 4 The king's strength a loveth judgment; 2050.1
105:23 Israel a came *into* Egypt; and 2050.1
105:33 He smote their vines a and their fig trees; 2050.1
105:36 He smote a all the firstborn in their land, 2050.1
105:37 He brought them forth a with silver and 2050.1
106: 9 He rebuked the Red sea a, and it was 2050.1
106:16 They envied Moses a in the camp, *and* 2050.1
106:27 To overthrow their seed a among 2050.1
106:28 They joined themselves a unto Baal-peor, 2050.1
106:32 They angered *him* a at the waters of 2050.1
106:42 Their enemies a oppressed them, and 2050.1
106:46 He made them a to be pitied of all those 2050.1
107:32 Let them exalt him a in the congregation 2050.1
107:38 He blesseth them a, so that they are 2050.1
108: 8 Ephraim a *is* the strength of mine head; 2050.1
109: 3 They compassed me about a *with* words 2050.1
109:10 let them seek *their bread* a out of their 2050.1
109:25 I became a a reproach unto them: 2050.1
119: 3 They a do no iniquity: they walk in his 637
119:23 Princes a did sit *and* speak against me: *but* 1571
119:24 Thy testimonies a *are* my delight *and* 1571
119:41 Let thy mercies come a *unto* me, 2050.1
119:46 I will speak of thy testimonies a before 2050.1
119:48 My hands a will I lift up unto thy 2050.1
132:12 their children a shall sit upon thy throne for 1571
132:16 I will a clothe her priests with salvation: 2050.1
139:17 How precious a are thy thoughts unto me, 2050.1
141: 5 for yet my prayer a *shall be* in their 2050.1
145:19 a will hear their cry, and will save them. 2050.1
148: 6 He hath a stablished them for ever and 2050.1
148:14 He a exalteth the horn of his people, 2050.1
Pr 1:26 I a will laugh at your calamity; I will mock 1571
4: 4 He taught me a, and said unto me, 2050.1
9: 2 her wine; she hath a furnished her table. 637
11:25 he that watereth shall be watered a himself. 1571
17:26 A to punish the just *is* not good, *nor* to 1571
18: 3 *then* cometh a contempt, and 1571
18: 9 He a that is slothful in his work *is* brother 1571
19: 2 A, *that* the soul *be* without knowledge, *it is* 1571
21:13 he a shall cry himself, but shall not be 1571
23:23 a wisdom, and instruction, and NIH
23:28 She a lieth in wait as *for* a prey, and 637
24:23 These *things* a *belong* to the wise. *It is* not 1571
25: 1 These *are* a proverbs of Solomon, 1571
26: 4 to his folly, lest thou a be like unto him. 1571
28:16 understanding *is* a a great oppressor: 2050.1
30:31 a he goat a; and a king, against whom *there* 176
31:15 She riseth a while *it is* yet night, and 2050.1
31:28 her husband a, and he praiseth her. NIH
Ecc 1: 5 The sun a ariseth, and the sun goeth 2050.1
1:17 I perceived that this a *is* vexation of spirit. 1571
2: 1 enjoy pleasure: and behold, this a *is* vanity. 1571
2: 7 a I had great possessions of great and 1571

Ecc 2: 8 I gathered me a silver and gold, and 1571
2: 9 a my wisdom remained with me. 637
2:14 I myself perceived a that one event 1571
2:15 I said in my heart, that this a *is* vanity. 1571
2:19 myself wise under the sun. This *is* a vanity. 1571
2:21 This a *is* vanity and a great evil. 1571
2:23 taketh not rest in the night. This *is* a vanity. 1571
2:24 This a I saw, that it *was* from the hand of 1571
2:26 This a *is* vanity and vexation of spirit. 1571
3:11 a he hath set the world in their heart, so that 1571
3:13 a that every man should eat and drink, and 1571
4: 4 This *is* a vanity and vexation of spirit. 1571
4: 8 This *is* a vanity, yea, it *is* a sore travail. 1571
4:14 whereas a *he that is* born in his kingdom 1571
4:16 they a that come after shall not rejoice in 1571
4:16 Surely this a *is* vanity and vexation of 1571
5: 7 many words *there are* a *divers* vanities: 2050.1
5:10 abundance *with* increase: this *is* a vanity. 1571
5:16 this a *is* a sore evil, *that* in all points as he 1571
5:17 All his days a he eateth in darkness, and 1571
5:19 Every man a to whom God hath given 1571
6: 3 with good, and a *that* he have no burial; 1571
6: 9 this *is* a vanity and vexation of spirit. 1571
7: 6 of the fool: this a *is* vanity. 1571+2050.1
7:14 God a hath set the one over against 1571
7:18 yea, a from this withdraw not thine hand: 1571
7:21 A take no heed unto all words that are 1571
7:22 For oftentimes a thine own heart knoweth 1571
8:10 where they had so done: this *is* a vanity. 1571
8:14 of the righteous: I said that this a *is* vanity. 1571
8:16 (for a *there is that* neither day nor night 1571
9: 3 a the heart of the sons of men is full *of* evil, 1571
9: 6 A their love, and their hatred, and 1571
9:12 For man a knoweth not his time: as 1571
9:13 This wisdom have I seen a under the sun, 1571
10: 3 Yea a, when he that is a fool walketh by 1571
10:14 A fool a is full of words: a man cannot 2050.1
11: 2 Give a portion to seven, and a to eight; 1571
12: 5 A *when* they shall be afraid of *that which is* 1571
SS 1:16 yea, pleasant: a our bed *is* green. 637
7: 8 now a thy breasts shall be as clusters of 2050.1
Isa 2: 7 Their land a is full *of* silver and gold, 2050.1
2: 7 their land is a full *of* horses, neither *is* 2050.1
2: 8 Their land a is full *of* idols; they worship 2050.1
5: 2 midst of it, and a made a winepress therein: 1571
5: 6 I will a command the clouds that they 2050.1
6: 1 In the year that king Uzziah died I saw a 2050.1
6: 8 A I heard the voice of the Lord, saying, 2050.1
7:13 weary men, but will ye weary my God a? 1571
7:20 the feet: and it shall a consume the beard. 1571
8: 5 The LORD spake a unto me again, 2050.1
11: 6 The wolf a shall dwell with the lamb, and 2050.1
11:13 The envy a of Ephraim shall depart, and 2050.1
12: 2 *my* song; he a is become my salvation. 2050.1
13: 3 I have a called my mighty ones for mine 1571
13:16 Their children a shall be dashed to pieces 2050.1
13:18 *Their* bows a shall dash the young men to 2050.1
14:10 unto thee, Art thou a become weak as we? 1571
14:13 I will sit a upon the mount of 2050.1
14:23 I will a make it a possession for 2050.1
17: 3 The fortress a shall cease from Ephraim, 2050.1
19: 8 The fishers a shall mourn, and all they 2050.1
19:13 they have a seduced Egypt, *even they that* NIH
21:12 The morning cometh, and a the night: 1571
22: 9 Ye have seen a the breaches of the city of 2050.1
22:11 Ye made a a ditch between the two walls 2050.1
23:12 *to* Chittim; there a shalt thou have no rest. 1571
24: 5 The earth a is defiled under 2050.1
26:12 for thou a hast wrought all our works in us. 1571
26:21 the earth a shall disclose her blood, and 2050.1
28: 7 they a have erred through wine, and 1571
28:17 Judgment a will I lay to the line, and 2050.1
28:29 This a cometh forth from the LORD of 1571
29:19 The meek a shall increase *their* joy in 2050.1
29:24 They a that erred in spirit shall come to 2050.1
30: 5 nor profit, but a shame, and a a reproach. 1571
30:22 Ye shall defile a the covering of thy 2050.1
31: 2 Yet he a *is* wise, and will bring evil, and 1571
31: 5 defending a he will deliver *it;* and 2050.1
32: 4 The heart a of the rash shall understand 2050.1
32: 7 The instruments a of the churl *are* evil: 2050.1
33: 2 our salvation a in the time of trouble. 637
34: 3 Their slain a shall be cast out, and 2050.1
34:11 the owl a and the raven shall dwell in it: 2050.1
34:14 The wild beasts of the desert shall a meet 2050.1
34:14 the shrich owl a shall rest there, and find for 389
34:15 there shall the vultures a be gathered, 389
38:22 Hezekiah a had said, What *is* the sign that 2050.1
40:24 he shall a blow upon them, and they shall 1571
44:19 a I have baked bread upon the coals 2050.1
45:16 be ashamed, and a confounded, all of them: 1571
46:11 yea, I have spoken *it,* I will a bring it to pass; 637
46:11 it to pass; I have purposed *it,* I will a do it. 637
48:12 I *am* he; I *am* the first, I a *am* the last. 637
48:13 Mine hand a hath laid the foundation of 637
48:19 Thy seed a had been as the sand, and 2050.1
48:21 he clave the rock a, and the waters 2050.1
49: 6 I will a give thee for a light to 2050.1
49: 7 and arise, princes a shall worship, 2050.1
56: 6 A the sons of the stranger, that join 2050.1
57: 8 Behind the doors a and the posts hast 2050.1
57:15 holy *place,* with him a *that is* of a contrite 2050.1
57:18 I will lead him a, and restore comforts 2050.1
60:14 The sons a of them that afflicted thee 2050.1
60:16 Thou shalt a suck the milk of 2050.1
60:17 I will a make thy officers peace, and 2050.1
60:21 Thy people a *shall be* all righteous: 2050.1
62: 3 Thou shalt a be a crown of glory in 2050.1
66: 4 I a will choose their delusions, and 1571
66:21 I will a take of them for priests *and* 1571
Jer 1: 3 It came a in the days of Jehoiakim 2050.1
2: 8 the pastors a transgressed against me, and 2050.1
2:16 A the children of Noph and 1571
2:33 hast thou a taught the wicked ones thy 1571
2:34 A in thy skirts is found the blood of 1571

Jer 2:36 thou a shalt be ashamed of Egypt, as thou 1571
3: 6 The LORD said a unto me in the days of 2050.1
3: 8 but went and played the harlot a. 1571
4:12 now a will I give sentence against them. 1571
6:14 They have healed a the hurt of 2050.1
6:17 A I set watchmen over you, 2050.1
7:27 thou shalt a call unto them; but they will 2050.1
9:16 I will scatter them a among the heathen, 2050.1
10: 5 do evil, neither a *is it* in them to do good. 1571
13:23 *then* may ye a do good, that are accustomed 1571
14: 5 the hind a calved in the field, and 1571
16: 1 The word of the LORD came a unto me, 2050.1
16: 8 Thou shalt not a go *into* the house of 2050.1
19: 5 They have built a the high places of Baal, 2050.1
20: 1 who *was* a chief governor in the house of 2050.1
23:14 I have seen a in the prophets of Jerusalem 2050.1
23:14 they strengthen a the hands of evildoers, 2050.1
25:14 kings shall serve themselves of them a: 1571
26:20 there was a a man that prophesied in 1571
27: 6 the beasts of the field have I given him a to 1571
27:12 I spake a to Zedekiah king of Judah 2050.1
27:16 A I spake to the priests and to all this 2050.1
28:14 I have given him the beasts of the field a. 1571
29:24 *Thus* shalt thou a speak to Shemaiah 2050.1
30:19 I will a glorify them, and they shall not 2050.1
30:20 Their children a shall be as aforetime, 2050.1
31:36 the seed of Israel a shall cease from being a 1571
31:37 I will a cast off all the seed of Israel for all 1571
33:21 *Then* may a my covenant be broken with 1571
35:15 I have sent a unto you all my servants 2050.1
36: 6 a thou shalt read them in the ears of all 1571
38:25 to death; a what the king said unto thee: 2050.1
39: 6 a the king of Babylon slew all the nobles 2050.1
40: 5 *he said,* Go back a to Gedaliah the son of 2050.1
41: 3 Ishmael a slew all the Jews that were 2050.1
43:13 He shall break a the images of 2050.1
46:21 A her hired men *are* in the midst of her like 1571
46:21 for they a are turned back, *and* are fled 1571
48: 2 A thou shalt be cut down, O Madmen; 1571
48: 7 and in thy treasures, thou shalt a be taken: 1571
48: 8 the valley a shall perish, and the plain 2050.1
48:26 Moab a shall wallow in his vomit, and 2050.1
48:26 in his vomit, and he a shall be in derision. 1571
48:34 for the waters a of Nimrim shall be 1571
49:17 A Edom shall be a desolation: every one 2050.1
50:24 thou art a taken, O Babylon, and thou wast 1571
50:24 a caught, because thou hast striven against 1571
51:22 With thee a will I break in pieces man 2050.1
51:23 I will a break in pieces with thee 2050.1
52:10 he slew a all the princes of Judah 1571+2050.1
52:17 A the pillars of brass that *were* in 2050.1
52:18 The caldrons a, and the shovels, and 2050.1
52:22 The second pillar a and the pomegranates 2050.1
52:25 He took a out of the city an eunuch, 2050.1
La 2: 9 the law *is* no *more;* her prophets a find no 1571
3: 8 A when I cry and shout, he shutteth out my 1571
3:16 He hath a broken my teeth with gravel 2050.1
4:21 the cup a shall pass through unto thee: 1571
Eze 1: 5 A out of the midst thereof *came* 2050.1
1:10 they four a had the face of an eagle. 2050.1
3:13 *I heard* a the noise of the wings of 2050.1
3:21 is warned; a thou hast delivered thy soul. 2050.1
4: 1 Thou a, son of man, take thee a tile, and 2050.1
4: 2 set the camp a against it, and set *battering* 2050.1
4: 4 Lie thou a upon thy left side, and lay 2050.1
4: 9 Take thou a unto thee wheat, and barley, 2050.1
4:11 Thou shalt drink a water by measure, 2050.1
5: 3 Thou shalt a take thereof a few in 2050.1
5:11 will I a diminish *thee;* neither shall mine 1571
7: 2 A, thou son of man, thus saith the Lord 2050.1
7:18 They shall a gird *themselves* with 2050.1
7:22 My face will I turn a from them, and 2050.1
7:24 I will a make the pomp of the strong to 2050.1
8:13 He said a unto me, Turn thee yet again, 2050.1
8:18 Therefore will I a deal in fury: mine eye 2050.1
9: 1 He cried a in mine ears *with* a loud voice, 2050.1
9:10 *as for* me a, mine eye shall not spare, 1571
10:16 the same wheels a turned not from beside 1571
10:17 *these* lift up themselves a: for the spirit of NIH
10:19 the wheels a *were* besides them, and 2050.1
12: 1 The word of the LORD a came unto me, 2050.1
12:13 My net a will I spread upon him, and 2050.1
13:21 Your kerchiefs a will I tear, and 2050.1
16:10 I clothed thee a with broidered work, and 2050.1
16:11 I decked thee a *with* ornaments, and I put 2050.1
16:17 Thou hast a taken thy fair jewels of my 2050.1
16:19 My meat a which I gave thee, fine flour, 2050.1
16:24 *That* thou hast a built unto thee an 2050.1
16:26 Thou hast a committed fornication with 2050.1
16:28 Thou hast played the whore a with 2050.1
16:39 And I will a give thee into their hand, 2050.1
16:39 they shall strip thee a of thy clothes, and 2050.1
16:40 They shall a bring up a company against 2050.1
16:41 and thou a shalt give no hire any more. 1571
16:43 I a will recompense thy way upon *thine* 1571
16:52 Thou a, which hast judged thy sisters, 1571
16:52 be thou confounded a, and bear thy shame, 1571
17: 5 He took a of the seed of the land, and 2050.1
17: 7 There was a another great eagle with 2050.1
17:13 he hath a taken the mighty of the land: 2050.1
17:22 I will a take of the highest branch of 2050.1
18: 4 so a the soul of the son *is* mine: 2050.1
19: 4 The nations a heard of him; he was taken 2050.1
20:12 Moreover a I gave them my sabbaths, to be 1571
20:15 Yet a I lifted up my hand unto them in 1571
20:23 I lifted up mine hand unto them a in 1571
20:25 Wherefore I gave them a statutes *that were* 1571
20:28 there a they made their sweet savour, and 2050.1
20:39 hereafter a, if ye will not hearken unto me: NIH
21: 9 a sword is sharpened, and a furbished: 1571
21:17 I will a smite mine hands together, 1571+2050.1
21:19 A, thou son of man, appoint thee two 2050.1
23:26 They shall a strip thee out of thy clothes, 2050.1
23:35 therefore bear thou a thy lewdness and thy 1571
23:37 have a caused their sons, whom they bare 1571

A

Eze 24: 3 on a pot, set *it* on, and **a** pour water into it: 1571
24: 5 burn **a** the bones under it, *and* make it boil 1571
24:15 **A** the word of the LORD came unto me, 2050.1
24:25 **A**, thou son of man, *shall it* not *be* in 2050.1
25:13 I will **a** stretch out mine hand upon 2050.1
26: 4 I will **a** scrape her dust from her, and 2050.1
27:19 Dan **a** and Javan going to and 2050.1
30: 6 They **a** that uphold Egypt shall fall; and 2050.1
30:10 I will **a** make the multitude of Egypt to 2050.1
30:13 I will **a** destroy the idols, and I will cause 2050.1
30:18 At Tehaphnehes **a** the day shall be 2050.1
31:17 They **a** went down into hell with him unto 1571
32: 6 I will **a** water with thy blood the land 2050.1
32: 9 I will **a** vex the hearts of many people, 2050.1
32:13 I will destroy **a** all the beasts thereof from 2050.1
32:17 It came to pass **a** in the twelfth year, 2050.1
33:30 **A**, thou son of man, the children of thy 2050.1
36: 1 **A**, thou son of man, prophesy unto 2050.1
36:26 A new heart **a** will I give you, and a new 2050.1
36:29 I will **a** save you from all your 2050.1
36:33 I will **a** cause *you* to dwell in the cities, 2050.1
37:24 they shall **a** walk in my judgments, and 2050.1
37:27 My tabernacle **a** shall be with them: yea, 2050.1
38:10 It shall **a** come to pass, *that* at the same 2050.1
39:16 **a** the name of the city *shall be* Hamonah. 1571
40: 8 He measured **a** the porch of the gate 2050.1
40:12 The space **a** before the little chambers 2050.1
40:14 He made **a** posts *of* threescore cubits, 2050.1
40:42 whereupon **a** they laid the instruments 2050.1
41: 8 I saw **a** the height of the house round 2050.1
41:14 **A** the breadth of the face of the house, 2050.1
43:21 Thou shalt take the bullock **a** of the sin 2050.1
43:25 they shall **a** prepare a young bullock, and 2050.1
44:30 ye shall **a** give unto the priest the first of 2050.1
45: 5 shall **a** the Levites, the ministers of 2050.1
47:20 The west side **a** *shall be* the great sea 2050.1
Da 6:22 **a** before thee, O king, have I done no hurt. 638
7: 6 the beast had **a** four heads; and 2050.3
8:25 through his policy **a** he shall cause craft 2050.1
8:25 he shall **a** stand up against the Prince of 2050.1
10: 6 His body **a** *was* like the beryl, and 2050.1
11: 1 **A** I in the first year of Darius the Mede, 2050.1
11: 8 shall **a** carry captives *into* Egypt their gods, 1571
11:14 **a** the robbers of thy people shall exalt 2050.1
11:17 He shall **a** set his face to enter with 2050.1
11:22 yea **a**, the prince of the covenant. 1571
11:41 He shall enter **a** into the glorious land, 2050.1
11:42 He shall stretch forth his hand **a** upon 2050.1
Hos 2:11 I will **a** cause all her mirth to cease, 2050.1
3: 3 be for *another* man: so *will* I **a** *be* for thee. 1571
4: 3 the fishes of the sea **a** shall be taken away. 1571
4: 5 the prophet **a** shall fall with thee *in* 1571
4: 6 rejected knowledge, I will **a** reject thee, 2050.1
4: 6 law of thy God, I will **a** forget thy children. 1571
5: 5 their iniquity; Judah **a** shall fall with them. 1571
6:11 **A**, O Judah, he hath set a harvest for thee, 1571
7:11 Ephraim **a** is like a silly dove, 2050.1
8: 6 For from Israel *was* it **a**: the workman 2050.1
9:12 woe **a** to them when I depart from them! 1571
10: 6 It shall be **a** carried unto Assyria *for* a 1571
10: 8 The high places **a** of Aven, the sin of 2050.1
11: 3 I taught Ephraim **a** to go, taking them by 2050.1
12: 2 The LORD hath **a** a controversy with 2050.1
12:10 I have **a** spoken by the prophets, and 2050.1
Joel 1:12 the palm tree **a**, and the apple tree, NIH
1:20 The beasts of the field cry **a** unto thee: 1571
2:12 Therefore **a** now, saith the LORD, turn ye 1571
2:29 **a** upon the servants and upon 1571
3: 2 I will **a** gather all nations, and will bring 2050.1
3: 6 The children **a** of Judah and the children 2050.1
3:16 The LORD **a** shall roar out of Zion, and 2050.1
Am 1: 5 I will break **a** the bar of Damascus, and 2050.1
2:10 **A** I brought you up from the land of 2050.1
3:14 him I will **a** visit the altars of Beth-el: 2050.1
4: 6 I **a** have given you cleanness of teeth in all 1571
4: 7 **a** I have withholden the rain from you, 1571
7: 6 This **a** shall not be, saith the Lord GOD. 1571
7:12 **A** Amaziah said unto Amos, O thou seer, 2050.1
9:14 they shall **a** make gardens, and eat 2050.1
Jnh 4:11 and their left hand; and *a* much cattle? NIH
Mic 3: 3 Who **a** eat the flesh of my people, and 2050.1
4:11 Now **a** many nations are gathered against 2050.1
5:13 Thy graven images **a** will I cut off, and 2050.1
6:13 Therefore **a** will I make *thee* sick in smiting 1571
7:12 *In* that day **a** he shall come even to thee NIH
Na 3:10 her young children **a** were dashed in pieces 1571
3:11 Thou **a** shalt be drunken: thou shalt be hid, 1571
3:11 thou **a** shalt seek strength because of 1571
Hab 1: 8 Their horses **a** are swifter than 2050.1
2: 5 Yea **a**, because he transgresseth *by* wine, 637
2:15 thy bottle to *him*, and makest *him* drunken **a**, 637
2:16 drink thou **a**, and let thy foreskin be 1571
Zep 1: 4 I will **a** stretch out mine hand upon 2050.1
1: 9 In the same day **a** will I punish all those 2050.1
1:13 they shall **a** build houses, but not inhabit 2050.1
2:12 Ye Ethiopians **a**, ye *shall be* slain by my 1571
3:12 I will **a** leave in the midst of thee an 2050.1
Zec 3: 7 thou shalt **a** judge my house, and shalt also 1571
3: 7 shalt **a** keep my courts, and I will give thee 1571
4: 9 his hands shall **a** finish *it;* and thou shalt 2050.1
8: 6 should it **a** be marvellous in my eyes? 1571
8:21 to seek the LORD of hosts: I will go **a**. 1571
9: 2 Hamath **a** shall border thereby; Tyrus, and 1571
9: 5 Gaza **a** *shall see it*, and be very sorrowful, 2050.1
9:11 *As for* thee **a**, by the blood of thy covenant 1571
10:10 I will bring them again **a** out of the land 2050.1
11: 8 Three shepherds **a** I cut off in one month; 2050.1
11: 8 lothed them, and their soul **a** abhorred me. 1571
12: 7 The LORD **a** shall save the tents of 2050.1
13: 2 **a** I will cause the prophets and the unclean 1571
14:14 Judah **a** shall fight at Jerusalem; and 1571
Mal 1:13 Ye said **a**, Behold, what a weariness *is it!* 2050.1
2: 9 Therefore have I **a** made you contemptible 1571
Mt 2: 8 that **I** may come and worship him **a**. *2504*
3:10 And now **a** the axe is laid unto the root of *2532*

Mt 5:39 on thy right cheek, turn to him the other **a**. *2532*
5:40 *away* thy coat, let him have *thy* cloke **a**. *2532*
6:14 your heavenly Father will **a** forgive you: *2532*
6:21 your treasure is, there will your heart be **a**. *2532*
10: 4 and Judas Iscariot, who **a** betrayed him. *2532*
10:32 him will **I** confess **a** before my Father *2504*
10:33 him will **I a** deny before my Father which *2504*
12:45 so shall it be **a** unto this wicked generation. *2532*
13:22 He **a** that received seed among the thorns is *1161*
13:23 and understandeth *it;* which **a** beareth fruit, *1211*
13:26 forth fruit, then appeared the tares **a**. *2532*
13:29 the tares, ye root up **a** the wheat with them. NIG
15: 3 Why do you **a** transgress *2532*
15:16 Are ye **a** yet without understanding? *2532*
16: 1 The Pharisees **a** with the Sadducees came, *2532*
16:18 And **I** say **a** unto thee, That thou art Peter, *2504*
17:12 Likewise shall **a** the Son of man suffer of *2532*
18:33 Shouldest not thou **a** have had compassion *2532*
18:35 So likewise shall my heavenly Father do *a* NIG
19: 3 The Pharisees **a** came unto him, *2532*
19:28 ye **a** shall sit upon twelve thrones, *2532*
20: 4 Go ye **a** into the vineyard, and *2532*
20: 7 saith unto them, Go ye **a** into the vineyard; *2532*
21:21 but **a if** ye shall say unto this mountain, *2579*
21:24 said unto them, **I a** will ask you one thing, *2504*
22:26 Likewise the second **a**, and the third, *2532*
22:27 And last of all the woman died **a**. *2532*
23:26 that the outside of them may be clean **a**. *2532*
23:28 ye **a** outwardly appear righteous unto men, *2532*
24:27 so shall **a** the coming of the Son of man be. *2532*
24:37 so shall **a** the coming of the Son of man be. *2532*
24:39 so shall **a** the coming of the Son of man be. *2532*
24:44 Therefore be ye **a** ready: for in such an *2532*
25:11 Afterward came **a** the other virgins, saying, *2532*
25:17 *had received* two, he **a** gained other two. *2532*
25:22 He **a** that had received two talents came *2532*
25:41 Then shall he say **a** unto them on the left *2532*
25:44 Then shall they **a** answer him, saying, *2532*
26:13 *there* shall **a** *this*, that this *woman* hath *2532*
26:35 deny thee. Likewise **a** said all the disciples. *2532*
26:69 saying, Thou **a** wast with Jesus of Galilee. *2532*
26:71 This *fellow* was **a** with Jesus of Nazareth. *2532*
26:73 said to Peter, Surely thou **a** art *one* of them; *2532*
27:41 Likewise **a** the chief priests mocking *him*, *2532*
27:44 The thieves **a**, which were crucified with *2532*
27:57 who **a** himself was Jesus' disciple: *2532*
Mk 1:19 who **a** *were* in the ship mending *their* nets. *2532*
1:38 the next towns, that I may preach **there a**: *2546*
2:15 and sinners **sat a together with** Jesus and *4873*
2:21 No *man* **a** seweth a piece of new cloth on *2532*
2:26 and gave **a** to them which were with him? *2532*
2:28 Therefore the Son of man is Lord **a** of *2532*
3:19 And Judas Iscariot, which **a** betrayed him. *2532*
4:36 And there were **a** with him other little *2532*
5:16 with the devil, and *a* concerning the swine. NIG
7:18 Are ye so without understanding **a**? *2532*
8: 7 and commanded to set them **a** before *them.* *2532*
8:34 the people unto *him* **with** his disciples **a**, *4862*
8:38 of him **a** shall the Son of man be ashamed, *2532*
11:25 that your Father **a** which is in heaven may *2532*
11:29 **I** will **a** ask of you one question, and *2504*
12: 6 he sent him **a** last unto them, saying, *2532*
12:22 left no seed: last of all the woman died **a**. *2532*
14: 9 *this* **a** that she hath done shall be spoken of *2532*
14:31 thee in any wise. Likewise **a** said they all. *2532*
14:67 *And* thou **a** wast with Jesus of Nazareth. *2532*
15:31 Likewise **a** the chief priests mocking said *2532*
15:40 There were **a** women looking on afar off: *2532*
15:41 (Who **a**, when he was in Galilee, *2532*
15:43 which **a** waited for the kingdom of God, *2532*
Lk 1: 3 It seemed good to **me a**, having had perfect *2504*
1:35 **a** *that* holy thing which shall be born of *2532*
1:36 she hath **a** conceived a son in her old age: *2532*
2: 4 And Joseph **a** went up from Galilee, out of *2532*
2:35 sword shall pierce through thy own soul **a**,) *2532*
3: 9 And now **a** the axe is laid unto the root of *2532*
3:12 Then came **a** publicans to be baptized, and *2532*
3:21 *that* Jesus **a** being baptized, and praying, *2532*
4:23 in Capernaum, do **a** here in thy country. *2532*
4:41 And devils **a** came out of many, crying out, *2532*
4:43 the kingdom of God to other cities **a**: *2532*
5:10 And so *was* **a** James, and John, *the* sons of *2532*
5:36 And he spake **a** a parable unto them; No *2532*
5:39 No *man* **a** having drunk old *wine* *2532*
6: 4 and gave **a** to them that were with him; *2532*
6: 5 That the Son of man is Lord **a** of *2532*
6: 6 And it came to pass **a** on another sabbath, *2532*
6:13 chose twelve, whom **a** he named apostles; *2532*
6:14 Simon, (whom he **a** named Peter,) and *2532*
6:16 and Judas Iscariot, which **a** was the traitor. *2532*
6:29 thee on the *one* cheek offer **a** the other; *2532*
6:29 thy cloke forbid not *to take thy* coat **a**. *2532*
6:31 should do to you, do ye **a** to them likewise. *2532*
6:32 for sinners **a** love those that love them. *2532*
6:33 have ye? for sinners **a** do *even* the same. *2532*
6:34 for sinners **a** lend to sinners, to receive as *2532*
6:36 merciful, as your Father **a** is merciful. *2532*
7: 8 For I **a** am a man set under authority, *2532*
7:49 Who is this that forgiveth sins **a**? *2532*
8:36 They **a** which saw *it* told them by what *2532*
9:61 And another **a** said, Lord, I will follow *2532*
10: 1 *things* the Lord appointed other seventy **a**, *2532*
10:39 which **a** sat at Jesus' feet, and heard his *2532*
11: 1 us to pray, as John **a** taught his disciples. *2532*
11: 4 for we **a** forgive every one *that is* indebted *2532*
11:18 If Satan **a** be divided against himself, *2532*
11:30 shall **a** the Son of man be to this *2532*
11:34 is single, thy whole body **a** is full of light; *2532*
11:34 *eye* is evil, thy body **a** *is* full of darkness. *2532*
11:40 *is* without make that *which is* within **a**? *2532*
11:45 Master, thus saying thou reproachest us **a**. *2532*
11:46 And he said, Woe unto you **a**, *ye* lawyers! *2532*
11:49 Therefore **a** said the wisdom of God, I will *2532*
12: 8 **A** I say unto you, Whosoever shall confess *1161*
12: 8 him shall the Son of man **a** confess before *2532*

Lk 12:34 your treasure is, there will your heart be **a**. *2532*
12:40 Be ye therefore ready **a**: for the Son of man *2532*
12:54 And he said **a** to the people, When ye see a *2532*
13: 6 He spake **a** this parable; A certain *man* had *1161*
13: 8 Lord, let it alone this year **a**, till I shall dig *2532*
14:12 Then said he **a** to him that bade him, *2532*
14:12 lest they **a** bid thee again, and *2532*
14:26 and sisters, yea, and his own life **a**, *2532*
16: 1 And he said **a** unto his disciples, There was *2532*
16:10 in *that which is* least is faithful **a** in much: *2532*
16:10 he that is unjust in the least is unjust **a** in *2532*
16:14 And the Pharisees **a**, who were covetous, *2532*
16:22 the rich *man* **a** died, and was buried; *2532*
16:28 lest they **a** come into this place of torment. *2532*
17:24 so shall **a** the Son of man be in his day. *2532*
17:26 shall it be **a** in the days of the Son of man. *2532*
17:28 Likewise **a** as it was in the days of Lot; *2532*
18:15 And they brought unto him **a** infants, *2532*
19: 9 forsomuch as he **a** is a son of Abraham. *2532*
19:19 likewise to him, Be thou **a** over five cities. *2532*
20: 3 said unto them, **I** will **a** ask you one thing; *2504*
20:11 and they beat **him a**, and entreated *him* *2548*
20:12 and they wounded him **a**, and cast *him* out. *2532*
20:31 took her; and in like manner the seven **a**: *2532*
20:32 Last of all the woman died **a**. *2532*
21: 2 And he saw **a** a certain poor widow casting *2532*
22:20 Likewise **a** the cup after supper, saying, *2532*
22:24 And there was **a** a strife among them, *2532*
22:39 of Olives; and his disciples **a** followed him. *2532*
22:56 and said, This *man* was **a** with him. *2532*
22:58 saw him, and said, Thou art **a** of them. *2532*
22:59 Of a truth this *fellow* **a** was with him: *2532*
22:68 And if I **a** ask *you*, you will not answer me, *2532*
23: 7 who himself **a** was at Jerusalem at that *2532*
23:27 which **a** bewailed and lamented him. *2532*
23:32 And there were **a** two other, malefactors, *2532*
23:35 And the rulers **a** with them derided *him*, *2532*
23:36 And the soldiers **a** mocked him, coming to *2532*
23:38 And a superscription **a** was written over *2532*
23:51 who **a** himself waited for the kingdom of *2532*
23:55 And the women **a**, which came with him *2532*
24:22 certain women *a* of our company made us NIG
24:23 that *they* had **a** seen a vision of angels, *2532*
Jn 3:23 And John **a** was baptizing in Aenon near to *2532*
4:45 at the feast: for they **a** went unto the feast. *2532*
5:18 but said **a** that God was his Father, *2532*
5:19 he doeth, these **a** doeth the Son likewise. *2532*
5:27 given him authority to execute judgment **a**, *2532*
6:24 neither his disciples, they **a** took shipping, *2532*
6:36 That ye **a** have seen me, and believe not. *2532*
6:67 Jesus unto the twelve, Will ye **a** go away? *2532*
7: 3 that thy disciples **a** may see the works that *2532*
7:10 then went he **a** up unto the feast, *2532*
7:47 them the Pharisees, Are ye **a** deceived? *2532*
7:52 and said unto him, Art thou **a** of Galilee? *2532*
8:17 It is **a** written in your law, that *2532*
8:19 ye should have known my Father **a**. *2532*
9:15 Then again the Pharisees **a** asked him how *2532*
9:27 hear *it* again? will ye **a** be his disciples? *2532*
9:40 and said unto him, Are we blind **a**? *2532*
10:16 **them a** I must bring, and they shall hear *2548*
11:16 unto *his* fellow-disciples, Let us **a** go, *2532*
11:33 **and** the Jews **a** weeping which came with *2532*
11:52 that **a** he should gather together in one *2532*
12: 9 but that they might see Lazarus **a**, *2532*
12:10 that they might put Lazarus **a** to death; *2532*
12:18 For this cause the people **a** met him, *2532*
12:26 where I am, there shall **a** my servant be: *2532*
12:42 Nevertheless among the *chief* rulers **a** *2532*
13: 9 my feet only, but **a** *my* hands and *my* head. *2532*
13:14 ye **a** ought to wash one another's feet. *2532*
13:32 in him, God shall **a** glorify him in himself, *2532*
13:34 have loved you, that ye **a** love one another. *2532*
14: 1 ye believe in God, believe **a** in me. *2532*
14: 3 that where I am, *there* ye may be **a**. *2532*
14: 7 ye should have known my Father **a**: *2532*
14:12 on me, the works that I do shall **he** do **a**; *2548*
14:19 ye see me: because I live, ye shall live **a**. *2532*
15:20 persecuted me, they will **a** persecute you; *2532*
15:20 kept my saying, they will keep yours **a**. *2532*
15:23 He that hateth me hateth my Father **a**. *2532*
15:27 And ye **a** shall bear witness, because *2532*
17: 1 thy Son, that thy Son **a** may glorify thee: *2532*
17:18 **even** *so* have **I a** sent them into the world. *2504*
17:19 that they **a** might be sanctified through *2532*
17:20 for them **a** which shall believe on me *2532*
17:21 and I in thee, that they **a** may be one in us: *2532*
17:24 Father, I will that **they a**, whom thou hast *2548*
18: 2 And Judas **a**, which betrayed him, knew *2532*
18: 5 I am *he.* And Judas **a**, which betrayed him, *2532*
18:17 Art not thou **a** *one* of this man's disciples? *2532*
18:25 Art not thou **a** *one* of his disciples? *2532*
19:23 to every soldier a part; and *a his* coat: NIG
19:39 And there came **a** Nicodemus, which at *2532*
20: 8 Then went in **a** *that* other disciple, *2532*
21: 3 They say unto him, We **a** go with thee. *2532*
21:20 which **a** leaned on his breast at supper, and *2532*
21:25 And there are **a** many other *things* which *2532*
Ac 1: 3 To whom **a** he shewed himself alive after *2532*
1:11 Which **a** said, Ye men of Galilee, *2532*
2:22 the midst of you, as ye yourselves **a** know: *2532*
2:26 moreover **a** my flesh shall rest in hope: *2532*
3:17 ignorance ye did *it*, as *did* **a** your rulers. *2532*
5: 2 his wife **a** being privy *to it*, and brought a *2532*
5:16 There came **a** a multitude *out* of the cities *2532*
5:32 and *so is* **a** the Holy Ghost, whom God hath *1161*
5:37 **he a** perished; and all, *even* as many as *2548*
7:45 Which **a** our fathers that came after brought *2532*
8:13 Then Simon himself believed **a**: and *2532*
8:19 Saying, Give **me a** this power, that on *2504*
9:32 down **a** to the saints which dwelt at Lydda. *2532*
10:26 saying, Stand up; **I** myself **a** am a man. *2504*
10:45 that on the Gentiles **a** was poured out *2532*
11: 1 Gentiles had **a** received the word of God. *2532*
11:18 Then hath God **a** to the Gentiles granted *2532*

Ac 11:30 Which **a** they did, and sent it to the elders *2532*
12: 3 he proceeded further to take Peter **a**. *2532*
13: 5 and they had **a** John to *their* minister. *2532*
13: 9 Then Saul, (who **a** *is called* Paul,) *2532*
13:22 to whom **a** he gave testimony, and said, *2532*
13:33 as it is **a** written in the second psalm, *2532*
13:35 Wherefore he saith **a** in another *psalm,* *2532*
14: 1 of the Jews and ***a*** of the Greeks believed. NIG
14: 5 and ***a*** of the Jews with their rulers, to use NIG
14:15 why do ye these *things?* We **a** are men of *2532*
15:27 who shall **a** tell *you* the same *things* by *2532*
15:32 and Silas, being prophets **a** themselves, *2532*
15:35 Paul **a** and Barnabas continued in Antioch, *1161*
15:35 the word of the Lord, with many others **a**. *2532*
17: 6 the world upside down are come hither **a**; *2532*
17:12 **a** of honourable women which were *2532*
17:13 they came **thither a**, and stirred up *2546*
17:28 as certain **a** of your own poets have said, *2532*
17:28 poets have said, For we are **a** his offspring. *2532*
19:17 the Jews and Greeks **a** dwelling at Ephesus; *5037*
19:19 Many **a** of them which used curious arts *1161*
19:21 After I have been there, I must **a** see Rome. *2532*
19:27 **a** that the temple of the great goddess *2532*
20:21 and ***a*** to the Greeks, repentance toward NIG
20:30 **A** of your own selves shall men arise, *2532*
21:13 **a** to die at Jerusalem for the name of *2532*
21:16 There went with us **a** *certain* of *2532*
21:24 but *that* thou thyself **a** walkest orderly, and *2532*
21:28 further brought Greeks **a** into the temple, *2532*
22: 5 As **a** the high priest doth bear me witness, *2532*
22: 5 from whom **a** I received letters unto *2532*
22:20 I **a** was standing by, and consenting unto *2532*
22:29 and the chief captain **a** was afraid, after he *1161*
23:11 so must thou bear witness **a** at Rome. *2532*
23:30 gave commandment to *his* accusers **a** to say *2532*
23:33 the governor, presented Paul **a** before him. *2532*
23:35 said he, when thine accusers are **a** come. *2532*
24: 6 Who **a** hath gone about to profane *2532*
24: 9 And the Jews **a** assented, saying that these *2532*
24:15 which they themselves **a** allow, *2532*
24:26 He hoped **a** that money should have *260+2532*
25:22 unto Festus, I would **a** hear the man myself. *2532*
25:24 both at Jerusalem, and ***a*** here, crying that he NIG
26:10 Which *thing* I **a** did in Jerusalem: and *2532*
26:26 these *things,* before whom **a** I speak freely: *2532*
26:29 but **a** all that hear me this day, were both *2532*
27:10 of the lading and ship, but **a** of our lives. *2532*
27:12 the more part advised to depart **thence a**, *2547*
27:36 of good cheer, and they **a** took *some* meat. *2532*
28: 9 So when this was done, others **a**, which had *2532*
28:10 Who **a** honoured us with many honours; *2532*
Ro 1: 6 Among whom are ye **a** *the* called of Jesus *2532*
1:13 that I might have some fruit among you **a**, *2532*
1:15 the gospel to you that are at Rome **a**. *2532*
1:16 to the Jew first, and ***a*** to the Greek. NIG
1:24 Wherefore God **a** gave them up to *2532*
1:27 And likewise **a** the men, leaving the natural *2532*
2: 9 of the Jew first, and ***a*** of the Gentile; NIG
2:10 to the Jew first, and ***a*** to the Gentile: NIG
2:12 without law shall **a** perish without law: *2532*
2:15 their conscience **a bearing witness**, and *4828*
3: 7 why yet am **I a** judged as a sinner? *2504*
3:29 *is he* not **a** of the Gentiles? Yes, of *2532*
3:29 also of the Gentiles? Yes, of the Gentiles **a**: *2532*
4: 6 Even as David **a** describeth the blessedness *2532*
4: 9 or upon the uncircumcision **a**? *2532*
4:11 might be imputed unto them **a**: *2532*
4:12 who **a** walk in the steps of *that* faith of our *2532*
4:16 to that **a** which is of the faith of Abraham; *2532*
4:21 he had promised, he was able **a** to perform. *2532*
4:24 But for us **a**, to whom it shall be imputed, *2532*
5: 2 By whom **a** we have access by faith into *2532*
5: 3 not only *so,* but we glory in tribulations **a**: *2532*
5:11 we **a** joy in God through our Lord Jesus *2532*
5:15 But not as the offence, so **a** *is* the free gift. *2532*
6: 4 so we **a** should walk in newness of life. *2532*
6: 5 we shall be **a** *in the likeness of his* *235+2532*
6: 8 we believe that we shall **a** live with him: *2532*
6:11 Likewise reckon ye **a** yourselves to be dead *2532*
7: 4 ye **a** are become dead to the law by *2532*
8:11 **a** quicken your mortal bodies by his Spirit *2532*
8:17 *him,* that we may be **a** glorified together. *2532*
8:21 Because the creature itself **a** shall be *2532*
8:23 And not only *they,* but ourselves **a**, *2532*
8:26 Likewise the Spirit **a** helpeth our *2532*
8:29 he **a** did predestinate *to be* conformed to *2532*
8:30 he did predestinate, them he **a** called: *2532*
8:30 and whom he called, them he **a** justified: *2532*
8:30 and whom he justified, them he **a** glorified. *2532*
8:32 how shall he not with him **a** freely give us *2532*
8:34 of God, who **a** maketh intercession for us. *2532*
9: 1 my conscience **a bearing** me **witness** in *4828*
9:10 but when Rebecca **a** had conceived by one, *2532*
9:24 not of the Jews only, but **a** of the Gentiles? *2532*
9:25 As he saith **a** in Osee, I will call *them* my *2532*
9:27 Esaias **a** crieth concerning Israel, *1161*
11: 1 For I **a** am an Israelite, of the seed of *2532*
11: 5 at *this* present time **a** there is a remnant *2532*
11:16 the lump *is* **a** *holy:* and if the root *be* holy, *2532*
11:21 *take heed* lest he **a** spare **not** thee. *3761*
11:22 otherwise thou **a** shalt be cut off. *2532*
11:23 And they **a**, if they bide not still in unbelief, *2532*
11:31 *Even* so have these **a** now not believed, *2532*
11:31 that through your mercy they **a** may obtain *2532*
13: 5 only for wrath, but **a** for conscience sake. *2532*
13: 6 For for this cause pay you tribute **a**: *2532*
15: 7 as Christ **a** received us, to the glory of God. *2532*
15:14 And I myself **a** am persuaded of you, *2532*
15:14 my brethren, that ye **a** are full of goodness, *2532*
15:14 able **a** to admonish one another. *2532*
15:22 For which cause **a** I have been much *2532*
15:27 is **a** to minister unto them in carnal *things.* *2532*
16: 2 been a succourer of many, and of myself **a**. NIG
16: 4 but **a** all the churches of the Gentiles. *2532*
16: 7 who **a** were in Christ before me. *2532*

1Co 1: 8 Who shall **a** confirm you unto the end, *2532*
1:16 And I baptized **a** the household of *2532*
2:13 Which *things* **a** we speak, not in the words *2532*
4: 8 did reign, that we **a** might reign with you. *2532*
5:12 For what have I to do to judge them **a** that *2532*
6:14 and will ***a*** raise up us by his own power. NIG
7: 3 and likewise **a** the wife unto the husband. *2532*
7: 4 likewise **a** the husband hath not power of *2532*
7:22 likewise **a** he that is called, *being* free, *2532*
7:34 There is difference ***a*** between a wife and a NIG
7:40 and I think **a** that *I* have the Spirit of God. *2504*
9: 8 as a man? or saith not the law the same **a**? *2532*
10: 6 not lust after evil *things,* as **they a** lusted. *2548*
10: 9 as some of them **a** tempted, and *2532*
10:10 as some of them **a** murmured, and *2532*
10:13 will with the temptation **a** make a way to *2532*
11: 1 followers of me, even as **I a** *am* of Christ. *2504*
11: 6 woman be not covered, let her **a** be shorn: *2532*
11:12 *even* so *is* the man **a** by the woman; *2532*
11:19 For there must be **a** heresies among you, *2532*
11:23 the Lord *that* which **a** I delivered unto you, *2532*
11:25 After the same manner **a** *he took* the cup, *2532*
12:12 being many, are one body: so **a** *is* Christ. *2532*
13:12 then shall I know even as **a** I am known. *2532*
14:15 and will pray with the understanding **a**: *2532*
14:15 and I will sing with the understanding **a**. *2532*
14:19 that *by my voice* I might teach others **a**, *2532*
14:34 to be under obedience, as **a** saith the law. *2532*
15: 1 which **a** you have received, and wherein ye *2532*
15: 2 By which **a** ye are saved, if ye keep in *2532*
15: 3 unto you first *of all* that which I **a** received, *2532*
15: 8 And last of all he was seen of **me a**, as of *2504*
15:14 our preaching vain, and your faith *is* **a** vain. *2532*
15:18 Then they **a** which are fallen asleep in *2532*
15:21 by man *came* **a** the resurrection of the dead. *2532*
15:28 shall the Son **a** himself be subject unto him *2532*
15:40 *There are* **a** celestial bodies, and *2532*
15:42 So **a** *is* the resurrection of the dead. It is *2532*
15:48 the earthy, such *are they* **a** *that are* earthy: *2532*
15:48 such *are they* **a** *that are* heavenly. *2532*
15:49 we shall **a** bear the image of the heavenly. *2532*
16: 4 And if it be meet that I go **a**, they shall go *2504*
16:10 he worketh the work of the Lord, as **I a** *do.* *2504*
2Co 1: 5 so our consolation **a** aboundeth by Christ. *2532*
1: 6 of the same sufferings which we **a** suffer: *2532*
1: 7 so *shall ye be* **a** of the consolation. *2532*
1:11 You **a** helping together by prayer for us, *2532*
1:14 As **a** you have acknowledged us in part, *2532*
1:14 even as ye **a** *are* ours in the day of the Lord *2532*
1:22 Who hath **a** sealed us, and given the earnest *2532*
2: 9 For to this end **a** did I write, that I might *2532*
2:10 To whom ye forgive any *thing,* I *forgive* **a**: *2532*
3: 6 Who **a** hath made us able ministers of *2532*
4:10 that the life **a** of Jesus might be made *2532*
4:11 that the life **a** of Jesus might be made *2532*
4:13 we **a** believe, and therefore speak; *2532*
4:14 the Lord Jesus shall raise up us **a** by Jesus, *2532*
5: 5 who **a** hath given unto us the earnest of *2532*
5:11 I trust **a** are made manifest in your *2532*
6: 1 workers together *with him,* beseech *you* **a** *2532*
6:13 as unto *my* children,) be ye **a** enlarged. *2532*
8: 6 he would **a** finish in you the same grace *2532*
8: 6 would also finish in you the same grace **a**. *2532*
8: 7 to us, *see* that ye abound in this grace **a**. *2532*
8:10 only to do, but **a** to be forward a year ago. *2532*
8:11 *there may be* a performance **a** out of that *2532*
8:14 that their abundance **a** may be *a supply* for *2532*
8:19 who was **a** chosen of the churches to travel *2532*
8:21 sight of the Lord, but **a** in the sight of men. *2532*
9: 6 soweth sparingly shall reap **a** sparingly; *2532*
9: 6 he which soweth bountifully shall reap **a** *2532*
9:12 is abundant **a** by many thanksgivings unto *2532*
10:11 such *will we be* **a** in deed when we are *2532*
10:14 for we are come as far as to you **a** in *2532*
11:15 **if** his ministers **a** be transformed as *1499*
11:18 many glory after the flesh, **I** will glory **a**. *2504*
11:21 is bold, (I speak foolishly,) **I** am bold **a**. *2504*
13: 4 For we **a** are weak in him, but we shall live *2532*
13: 9 and this **a** we wish, *even* your perfection. *2532*
Gal 2: 1 with Barnabas, and took Titus with *me* **a**. *2532*
2:10 the same which I **a** was forward to do. *2532*
2:13 insomuch that Barnabas **a** was carried away *2532*
2:17 we ourselves **a** are found sinners, *is* *2532*
5:21 as I have **a** told *you* in time past, *2532*
5:25 live in the Spirit, let us **a** walk in the Spirit. *2532*
6: 1 considering thyself, lest thou **a** be tempted. *2532*
6: 7 a man soweth, that shall he **a** reap. *2532*
Eph 1:11 In whom **a** we have obtained an *2532*
1:13 In whom ye **a** *trusted,* after that ye heard *2532*
1:13 in whom **a** after that ye believed, ye were *2532*
1:15 Wherefore **I a**, after I heard of your faith in *2504*
1:21 this world, but **a** in that which is to come: *2532*
2: 3 Among whom **a** we all had our *2532*
2:22 In whom you **a** are builded together for a *2532*
4: 9 that he **a** descended first into the lower *2532*
4:10 He that descended is the same **a** that *2532*
5: 2 as Christ **a** hath loved us, and hath given *2532*
5:25 even as Christ **a** loved the church, and *2532*
6: 9 knowing that your Master **a** is in heaven; *2532*
6:21 But that ye **a** may know my affairs, *and* *2532*
Php 1:15 of envy and strife; and some **a** of good will: *2532*
1:20 now **a** Christ shall be magnified in my *2532*
1:29 believe on him, but **a** to suffer for his sake; *2532*
2: 4 but every man **a** on the *things* of others. *2532*
2: 5 be in you, which *was* **a** in Christ Jesus: *2532*
2: 9 Wherefore God **a** hath highly exalted him, *2532*
2:18 *For* the same *cause* **a** do ye joy, and *2532*
2:19 that **I a** may be of good comfort, when I *2504*
2:24 But I trust in the Lord that I **a** myself shall *2532*
2:27 and not on him only, but on me **a**, lest I *2532*
3: 4 Though I *might* **a** have confidence in *2532*
3:12 which **a** I am apprehended of Christ Jesus. *2532*
3:20 from whence **a** we look for the Saviour, *2532*
4: 3 **And** I intreat thee **a**, true yokefellow, *2532*
4: 3 with Clement **a**, and *with* other my *2532*

Php 4:10 wherein ye were **a** careful, but ye lacked *2532*
4:15 Now ye Philippians know **a**, that in *2532*
Col 1: 6 and bringeth forth fruit, as *it doth* **a** in you, *2532*
1: 7 As ye **a** learned of Epaphras our dear *2532*
1: 8 Who **a** declared unto us your love in *2532*
1: 9 For this cause we **a**, since the day we heard *2532*
1:29 Whereunto I **a** labour, striving according to *2532*
2:11 In whom **a** ye are circumcised with *2532*
2:12 wherein **a** you are risen with *him* through *2532*
3: 4 then shall ye **a** appear with him in glory. *2532*
3: 7 In the which ye **a** walked sometime, *2532*
3: 8 But now you **a** put off all *these;* anger, *2532*
3:13 even as Christ forgave you, so **a** *do* ye. *2532*
3:15 to the which **a** ye are called in one body; *2532*
4: 1 knowing that ye **a** have a Master in heaven. *2532*
4: 3 Withal praying **a** for us, that God would *2532*
4: 3 of Christ, for which I am **a** in bonds: *2532*
4:16 cause that it be read **a** in the church of *2532*
1Th 1: 5 but **a** in power, and in the Holy Ghost, and *2532*
1: 8 **a** in every place your faith to God-ward is *2532*
2: 8 but **a** our own souls, because ye were dear *2532*
2:10 and God ***a***, how holily and justly and NIG
2:13 For this cause **a** thank we God without *2532*
2:13 which effectually worketh **a** in you that *2532*
2:14 for ye **a** have suffered like *things* of your *2532*
3: 6 greatly to see us, as we **a** *to see* you: *2532*
4: 6 as we **a** have forewarned you and testified. *2532*
4: 8 who hath **a** given unto us his holy Spirit. *2532*
4:14 them **a** which sleep in Jesus will God bring *2532*
5:11 and edify one another, even as **a** ye do. *2532*
5:24 *is* he that calleth you, who **a** will do *it.* *2532*
2Th 1: 5 the kingdom of God, for which ye **a** suffer: *2532*
1:11 Wherefore **a** we pray always for you, *2532*
1Ti 2: 9 In like manner **a**, that women adorn *2532*
3:10 And let these **a** first be proved; then *2532*
5:13 not only idle, but tattlers **a** and busybodies, *2532*
5:20 rebuke before all, that others **a** may fear. *2532*
5:25 Likewise **a** the good works *of some* are *2532*
6:12 whereunto thou art **a** called, and *2532*
2Ti 1: 5 and I am persuaded that in thee **a**. *2532*
1:12 For the which cause I **a** suffer these *things:* *2532*
2: 2 who shall be able to teach others **a**. *2532*
2: 5 And if a man **a** strive for masteries, *yet* is *2532*
2:10 that they may **a** obtain the salvation which *2532*
2:11 For if we be dead with *him,* we shall **a** live *2532*
2:12 we shall **a** reign with *him:* if we deny *him,* *2532*
2:12 *him:* if we deny *him,* **he a** will deny us: *2548*
2:20 and of silver, but **a** of wood and of earth; *2532*
2:22 Flee **a** youthful lusts: but *1161*
3: 1 This know **a**, that in the last days perilous *1161*
3: 8 so do these **a** resist the truth: *2532*
3: 9 be manifest unto all *men,* as theirs **a** was. *2532*
4: 8 but unto all them **a** that love his appearing. *2532*
4:15 Of whom be thou ware **a**; for he hath *2532*
Tit 3: 3 For we ourselves **a** were sometimes foolish, *2532*
3:14 And let ours **a** learn to maintain good *2532*
Phm 1: 9 and now **a** a prisoner of Jesus Christ. *2532*
1:21 knowing that thou wilt **a** do more than I *2532*
1:22 But withal prepare me **a** a lodging: for I *2532*
Heb 1: 2 all *things,* by whom **a** he made the worlds; *2532*
2: 4 God **a bearing** *them* **witness**, both with *4901*
2:14 he **a** himself likewise took part of the same; *2532*
3: 2 as **a** Moses *was faithful* in all his house. *2532*
4:10 he **a** hath ceased from his own works, *2532*
5: 2 for that he himself **a** is compassed with *2532*
5: 3 so **a** for himself, to offer for sins. *2532*
5: 5 So **a** Christ glorified not himself to be *2532*
5: 6 As he saith **a** in another *place,* Thou *art* a *2532*
7: 2 To whom **a** Abraham gave a tenth *part* of *2532*
7: 2 and after that **a** King of Salem, which is, *2532*
7: 9 And as *I* may so say, Levi **a**, who receiveth *2532*
7:12 there is made of necessity a change **a** of *2532*
7:25 Wherefore he is able **a** to save them to *2532*
8: 3 that this *man* have somewhat **a** to offer. *2532*
8: 6 by how much **a** he is the mediator of a *2532*
9: 1 Then verily the first *covenant* had **a** *2532*
9:16 For where a testament *is,* there must **a** of NIG
10:15 *Whereof* the Holy Ghost **a** is a witness to *2532*
11:11 Through faith **a** Sara herself received *2532*
11:19 from whence **a** he received him in a figure. *2532*
11:32 *of* David **a**, and Samuel, and *of* *5037*
12: 1 Wherefore seeing we **a** are compassed *2532*
12:26 I shake not the earth only, but **a** heaven. *2532*
13: 3 as being yourselves **a** in the body. *2532*
13:12 Wherefore Jesus **a**, that he might sanctify *2532*
Jas 1:11 **a** shall the rich *man* fade away in his ways. *2532*
2: 2 there come in **a** a poor *man* in vile raiment; *2532*
2:11 Do not commit adultery, said **a**, Do not kill. *2532*
2:19 the devils **a** believe, and tremble. *2532*
2:25 Likewise **a** was not Rahab the harlot *2532*
2:26 is dead, so faith without works is dead **a**. *2532*
3: 2 *and* able **a** to bridle the whole body. *2532*
3: 4 Behold **a** the ships, which though they be *2532*
5: 8 Be ye **a** patient; stablish your hearts: for *2532*
1Pe 2: 5 Ye **a**, as lively stones, are built *up* a *2532*
2: 6 Wherefore **a** it is contained in the scripture, *2532*
2: 8 whereunto **a** they were appointed. *2532*
2:18 to the good and gentle, but **a** to the froward. *2532*
2:21 because Christ **a** suffered for us, leaving us *2532*
3: 1 they **a** may without the word be won by *2532*
3: 5 manner in the old time the holy women **a**, *2532*
3:18 For Christ **a** hath once suffered for sins, *2532*
3:19 By which **a** he went and preached unto *2532*
3:21 **a** now save us (not the putting away of *2532*
4: 6 the gospel preached **a** to *them that are* dead, *2532*
4:13 ye may be glad **a** with exceeding joy. *2532*
5: 1 who am **a an elder**, and a witness of *4850*
5: 1 **and a** a partaker of the glory that shall be *2532*
2Pe 1:19 We have **a** a more sure word of prophecy; *2532*
2: 1 But there were false prophets **a** among *2532*
3:10 the earth **a** and the works that are therein *2532*
3:15 even as our beloved brother Paul **a** *2532*
3:16 As **a** in all *his* epistles, speaking in them of *2532*
3:16 as *they do* **a** the other scriptures, *2532*
3:17 know *these things* before, beware lest ye **a**, NIG

1Jn 1: 3 that ye **a** may have fellowship with us: *2532*
2: 2 but **a** for *the sins of* the whole world. *2532*
2: 6 that saith *he* abideth in him ought himself **a** *2532*
2:23 *acknowledgeth the Son hath the Father* **a**. NIG
2:24 ye **a** shall continue in the Son, and in *2532*
3: 4 Whosoever committeth sin transgresseth **a** *2532*
4:11 loved us, we ought **a** to love one another. *2532*
4:21 That he who loveth God love his brother **a**. *2532*
5: 1 begat loveth him **a** that is begotten of him. *2532*
2Jn 1: 1 but **a** all they that have known the truth; *2532*
3Jn 1:12 yea, and we **a** bear record; and ye know that NIG
Jude 1: 8 Likewise **a** these *filthy* dreamers defile *2532*
1:14 And Enoch **a**, the seventh from Adam, *2532*
Rev 1: 7 see him, and they **a** which pierced him: NIG
1: 9 who **a** am your brother, and companion in *2532*
2: 6 deeds of the Nicolaitans, which **I a** hate. *2504*
2:15 So hast thou **a** them that hold the doctrine *2532*
3:10 **I a** will keep thee from the hour of *2504*
3:21 *even* as **I a** overcame, and am set down *2504*
6:11 until their fellowservants **a** and their *2532*
11: 8 and Egypt, where **a** our Lord was crucified. *2532*
14:17 is in heaven, he **a** having a sharp sickle. *2532*

ALTAR (378) [ALTARS]

Ge 8:20 Noah builded an **a** unto the LORD; and 4196
8:20 and offered burnt offerings on the **a**. 4196
12: 7 there builded he an **a** unto the LORD, 4196
12: 8 there he builded an **a** unto the LORD, and 4196
13: 4 Unto the place of the **a**, which he had made 4196
13:18 and built there an **a** unto the LORD. 4196
22: 9 Abraham built an **a** there, and laid 4196
22: 9 and laid him on the **a** upon the wood. 4196
26:25 he builded an **a** there, and called upon 4196
33:20 he erected there an **a**, and called it 4196
35: 1 make there an **a** unto God, that appeared 4196
35: 3 I will make there an **a** unto God, 4196
35: 7 he built there an **a**, and called the place 4196
Ex 17:15 Moses built an **a**, and called the name of it 4196
20:24 An **a** of earth thou shalt make unto me, and 4196
20:25 if thou wilt make me an **a** of stone, 4196
20:26 shalt thou go up by steps unto mine **a**, 4196
21:14 thou shalt take him from mine **a**, that he 4196
24: 4 builded an **a** under the hill, and 4196
24: 6 and half of the blood he sprinkled on the **a**. 4196
27: 1 thou shalt make an **a** *of* shittim wood, 4196
27: 1 five cubits broad; the **a** shall be foursquare: 4196
27: 5 thou shalt put it under the compass of the **a** 4196
27: 5 the net may be even to the midst of the **a**. 4196
27: 6 thou shalt make staves for the **a**, staves of 4196
27: 7 staves shall be upon the two sides of the **a**, 4196
28:43 when they come near unto the **a** to minister 4196
29:12 put *it* upon the horns of the **a** with thy 4196
29:12 all the blood beside the bottom of the **a**. 4196
29:13 *is* upon them, and burn *them* upon the **a**. 4196
29:16 and sprinkle *it* round about upon the **a**. 4196
29:18 thou shalt burn the whole ram upon the **a**: 4196
29:20 sprinkle the blood upon the **a** round about. 4196
29:21 shalt take of the blood that *is* upon the **a**, 4196
29:25 burn *them* upon the **a** for a burnt offering, 4196
29:36 thou shalt cleanse the **a**, when thou hast 4196
29:37 thou shalt make an atonement for the **a**, 4196
29:37 sanctify it; and it shall be an **a** most holy: 4196
29:37 whatsoever toucheth the **a** shall be holy. 4196
29:38 *is that* which thou shalt offer upon the **a**; 4196
29:44 tabernacle of the congregation, and the **a**: 4196
30: 1 thou shalt make an **a** to burn incense upon: 4196
30:18 tabernacle of the congregation and the **a**, 4196
30:20 when they come near to the **a** to minister, 4196
30:27 and his vessels, and the **a** of incense, 4196
30:28 the **a** of burnt offering with all his vessels, 4196
31: 8 with all his furniture, and the **a** of incense, 4196
31: 9 the **a** of burnt offering with all his furniture, 4196
32: 5 when Aaron saw *it*, he built an **a** before it; 4196
35:15 the incense **a** and his staves, and 4196
35:16 The **a** of burnt offering with his brasen 4196
37:25 he made the incense **a** *of* shittim wood: 4196
38: 1 he made the **a** of burnt offering *of* shittim 4196
38: 3 he made all the vessels of the **a**, the pots, 4196
38: 4 he made for the **a** a brasen grate of network 4196
38: 7 staves into the rings on the sides of the **a**, 4196
38: 7 it withal; he made *the* **a** hollow with boards. NIH
38:30 and the brasen **a**, and the brasen grate for it, 4196
38:30 grate for it, and all the vessels of the **a**, 4196
39:38 the golden **a**, and the anointing oil, and 4196
39:39 The brasen **a**, and his grate of brass, his 4196
40: 5 thou shalt set the **a** of gold for the incense 4196
40: 6 thou shalt set the **a** of the burnt offering 4196
40: 7 the tent of the congregation and the **a**, 4196
40:10 thou shalt anoint the **a** of the burnt offering, 4196
40:10 and all his vessels, and sanctify the **a**: 4196
40:10 the altar: and it shall be an **a** most holy. 4196
40:26 he put the golden **a** in the tent of 4196
40:29 he put the **a** of burnt offering *by* the door of 4196
40:30 the tent of the congregation and the **a**, 4196
40:32 when they came near unto the **a**, 4196
40:33 court round about the tabernacle and the **a**, 4196
Lev 1: 5 sprinkle the blood round about upon the **a** 4196
1: 7 of Aaron the priest shall put fire upon the **a**, 4196
1: 8 that *is* on the fire which *is* upon the **a**: 4196
1: 9 the priest shall burn all on the **a**, *to be* a 4196
1:11 he shall kill it on the side of the **a** 4196
1:11 sprinkle his blood round about upon the **a**. 4196
1:12 that *is* on the fire which *is* upon the **a**: 4196
1:13 shall bring *it* all, and burn *it* upon the **a**: 4196
1:15 the priest shall bring it unto the **a**, and 4196
1:15 and wring off his head, and burn *it* on the **a**; 4196
1:15 shall be wrung out at the side of the **a**: 4196
1:16 cast it beside the **a** on the east part, by 4196
1:17 the priest shall burn it upon the **a**, upon 4196
2: 2 shall burn the memorial of it upon the **a**, 4196
2: 8 unto the priest, he shall bring it unto the **a**. 4196
2: 9 and shall burn *it* upon the **a**: 4196
2:12 they shall not be burnt on the **a** for a sweet 4196
3: 2 sprinkle the blood upon the **a** round about. 4196
3: 5 Aaron's sons shall burn it on the **a** upon 4196

Lev 3: 8 the blood thereof round about upon the **a**. 4196
3:11 the priest shall burn it upon the **a**: *it is* 4196
3:13 the blood thereof upon the **a** round about. 4196
3:16 the priest shall burn them upon the **a**: *it is* 4196
4: 7 the **a** of sweet incense before the LORD, 4196
4: 7 at the bottom of the **a** of the burnt offering, 4196
4:10 the priest shall burn them upon the **a** of 4196
4:18 horns of the **a** which *is* before the LORD, 4196
4:18 at the bottom of the **a** of the burnt offering, 4196
4:19 all his fat from him, and burn *it* upon the **a**. 4196
4:25 put *it* upon the horns of the **a** of burnt 4196
4:25 at the bottom of the **a** of burnt offering. 4196
4:26 he shall burn all his fat upon the **a**, as 4196
4:30 put *it* upon the horns of the **a** of burnt 4196
4:30 all the blood thereof at the bottom of the **a**. 4196
4:31 the priest shall burn *it* upon the **a** for a 4196
4:34 put *it* upon the horns of the **a** of burnt 4196
4:34 all the blood thereof at the bottom of the **a**; 4196
4:35 the priest shall burn them upon the **a**, 4196
5: 9 of the sin offering upon the side of the **a**; 4196
5: 9 shall be wrung out at the bottom of the **a**: 4196
5:12 a memorial thereof, and burn *it* on the **a**, 4196
6: 9 of the burning upon the **a** all night unto 4196
6: 9 and the fire of the **a** shall be burning in it. 4196
6:10 consumed with the burnt offering on the **a**, 4196
6:10 and he shall put them besides the **a**. 4196
6:12 the fire upon the **a** shall be burning in it; 4196
6:13 The fire shall ever be burning upon the **a**; 4196
6:14 offer it before the LORD, before the **a**. 4196
6:15 shall burn *it upon* the **a** *for* a sweet savour, 4196
7: 2 shall he sprinkle round about upon the **a**. 4196
7: 5 the priest shall burn them upon the **a** *for* an 4196
7:31 the priest shall burn the fat upon the **a**: but 4196
8:11 he sprinkled thereof upon the **a** seven 4196
8:11 anointed the **a** and all his vessels, both 4196
8:15 put *it* upon the horns of the **a** round about 4196
8:15 purified the **a**, and poured the blood at 4196
8:15 and poured the blood at the bottom of the **a**, 4196
8:16 their fat, and Moses burned *it* upon the **a**. 4196
8:19 Moses sprinkled the blood upon the **a** 4196
8:21 and Moses burnt the whole ram upon the **a**: 4196
8:24 Moses sprinkled the blood upon the **a** 4196
8:28 burnt *them* on the **a** upon the burnt 4196
8:30 of the blood which *was* upon the **a**, and 4196
9: 7 Go unto the **a**, and offer thy sin offering, 4196
9: 8 Aaron therefore went unto the **a**, and 4196
9: 9 put *it* upon the horns of the **a**, and poured 4196
9: 9 poured out the blood at the bottom of the **a**: 4196
9:10 of the sin offering, he burnt upon the **a**; 4196
9:12 which he sprinkled round about upon the **a**. 4196
9:13 and the head: and he burnt *them* upon the **a**. 4196
9:14 *them* upon the burnt offering on the **a**. 4196
9:17 a handful thereof, and burnt *it* upon the **a**, 4196
9:18 which he sprinkled upon the **a** round about, 4196
9:20 the breasts, and he burnt the fat upon the **a**: 4196
9:24 consumed upon the **a** the burnt offering and 4196
10:12 and eat it without leaven beside the **a**: 4196
14:20 and the meat offering upon the **a**: 4196
16:12 of fire from off the **a** before the LORD, 4196
16:18 he shall go out unto the **a** that *is* before 4196
16:18 put *it* upon the horns of the **a** round about. 4196
16:20 and the **a**, he shall bring the live goat: 4196
16:25 of the sin offering shall he burn upon the **a**. 4196
16:33 for the **a**, and he shall make an atonement 4196
17: 6 **a** of the LORD *at* the door of 4196
17:11 I have given it to you upon the **a** to make 4196
21:23 nor come nigh unto the **a**, because he hath a 4196
22:22 fire of them upon the **a** unto the LORD. 4196
Nu 3:26 by the **a** round about, and the cords of it for 4196
4:11 upon the golden **a** they shall spread a cloth 4196
4:13 they shall take away the ashes from the **a**, 4196
4:14 and the basons, all the vessels of the **a**; 4196
4:26 by the tabernacle and by the **a** round about, 4196
5:25 before the LORD, and offer it upon the **a**: 4196
5:26 burn *it* upon the **a**, and afterward shall 4196
7: 1 both the **a** and all the vessels thereof, and 4196
7:10 the princes offered *for* dedicating of the **a** 4196
7:10 princes offered their offering before the **a**. 4196
7:11 on *his* day, for the dedicating of the **a**. 4196
7:84 This *was* the dedication of the **a**, in the day 4196
7:88 This *was* the dedication of the **a**, after *that* 4196
16:38 them broad plates *for* a covering of the **a**: 4196
16:39 made broad *plates for* a covering of the **a**: 4196
16:46 put fire therein from off the **a**, and put on 4196
18: 3 nigh the vessels of the sanctuary and the **a**, 4196
18: 5 of the sanctuary, and the charge of the **a**: 4196
18: 7 your priest's office for every thing of the **a**, 4196
18:17 thou shalt sprinkle their blood upon the **a**, 4196
23: 2 Balaam offered on *every* **a** a bullock and 4196
23: 4 I have offered upon *every* **a** a bullock and 4196
23:14 and offered a bullock and a ram on *every* **a**. 4196
23:30 and offered a bullock and a ram on *every* **a**. 4196
Dt 12:27 upon the **a** of the LORD thy God: 4196
12:27 out upon the **a** of the LORD thy God, 4196
16:21 near unto the **a** of the LORD thy God, 4196
26: 4 set it down before the **a** of the LORD thy 4196
27: 5 there shalt thou build an **a** unto the LORD 4196
27: 5 unto the LORD thy God, an **a** of stones: 4196
27: 6 Thou shalt build the **a** of the LORD thy 4196
33:10 and whole *burnt sacrifice* upon thine **a**. 4196
Jos 8:30 Joshua built an **a** unto the LORD God of 4196
8:31 an **a** of whole stones, over which no *man* 4196
9:27 for the **a** of the LORD, *even* unto this day, 4196
22:10 the half tribe of Manasseh built there an **a** 4196
22:10 there an altar by Jordan, a great **a** to see to. 4196
22:11 the half tribe of Manasseh have built an **a** 4196
22:16 in that ye have builded you an **a**, that ye 4196
22:19 in building you an **a** beside the altar of 4196
22:19 in building you an altar beside the **a** of 4196
22:23 That we have built us an **a** to turn from 4196
22:26 Let us now prepare to build us an **a**, 4196
22:28 Behold the pattern of the **a** of the LORD, 4196
22:29 to build an **a** for burnt offerings, for meat 4196
22:29 besides the **a** of the LORD our God that *is* 4196
22:34 the children of Gad called the **a** *Ed*: for it 4196

Jdg 6:24 Gideon built an **a** there unto the LORD, 4196
6:25 throw down the **a** of Baal that thy father 4196
6:26 build an **a** unto the LORD thy God upon 4196
6:28 the **a** of Baal was cast down, and the grove 4196
6:28 the second bullock was offered upon the **a** 4196
6:30 because he hath cast down the **a** of Baal, 4196
6:31 because *one* hath cast down his **a**. 4196
6:32 because he hath thrown down his **a**. 4196
13:20 went up toward heaven from off the **a**, 4196
13:20 the LORD ascended in the flame of the **a**. 4196
21: 4 built there an **a**, and offered burnt offerings 4196
1Sa 2:28 to offer upon mine **a**, to burn incense, 4196
2:33 *whom* I shall not cut off from mine **a**, 4196
7:17 and there he built an **a** unto the LORD. 4196
14:35 Saul built an **a** unto the LORD: the same 4196
14:35 the same was the first **a** that he built unto 4196
2Sa 24:18 rear an **a** unto the LORD in 4196
24:21 of thee, to build an **a** unto the LORD, 4196
24:25 David built there an **a** unto the LORD, 4196
1Ki 1:50 went, and caught hold on the horns of the **a**. 4196
1:51 he hath caught hold on the horns of the **a**, 4196
1:53 and they brought him down from the **a**. 4196
2:28 and caught hold on the horns of the **a**. 4196
2:29 of the LORD; and behold, *he is* by the **a**. 4196
3: 4 offerings did Solomon offer up on that **a**. 4196
6:20 and *so* covered the **a** *which was of* cedar. 4196
6:22 also the whole **a** that *was* by the oracle he 4196
7:48 the **a** of gold, and the table *of* gold, 4196
8:22 Solomon stood before the **a** of the LORD 4196
8:31 the oath come before thine **a** in this house: 4196
8:54 he arose from before the **a** of the LORD, 4196
8:64 the brasen **a** that *was* before the LORD 4196
9:25 peace offerings upon the **a** which he built 4196
9:25 he burnt incense upon **the a** that *was* 2050.2
12:32 he offered upon the **a** (so did he in Beth-el,) 4196
12:33 So he offered upon the **a** which he had 4196
12:33 he offered upon the **a**, and burnt incense. 4196
13: 1 Jeroboam stood by the **a** to burn incense. 4196
13: 2 he cried against the **a** in the word of 4196
13: 2 and said, O **a**, altar, thus saith the LORD; 4196
13: 2 and said, O altar, **a**, thus saith the LORD; 4196
13: 3 the **a** *shall be* rent, and the ashes that *are* 4196
13: 4 which had cried against the **a** in Beth-el, 4196
13: 4 that he put forth his hand from the **a**, 4196
13: 5 The **a** also *was* rent, and the ashes poured 4196
13: 5 and the ashes poured out from the **a**, 4196
13:32 of the LORD against the **a** in Beth-el, 4196
16:32 he reared up an **a** for Baal *in* the house of 4196
18:26 And they leapt upon the **a** which was made. 4196
18:30 he repaired the **a** of the LORD that was 4196
18:32 *with* the stones he built an **a** in the name of 4196
18:32 he made a trench about the **a**, as great as 4196
18:35 the water ran round about the **a**; and 4196
2Ki 11:11 the temple, *along* by the **a** and the temple. 4196
12: 9 a hole in the lid of it, and set it beside the **a**, 4196
16:10 and saw an **a** that *was* at Damascus: 4196
16:10 to Urijah the priest the fashion of the **a**, 4196
16:11 Urijah the priest built an **a** according to all 4196
16:12 come from Damascus, the king saw the **a**: 4196
16:12 the king approached to the **a**, and 4196
16:13 blood of his peace offerings, upon the **a**. 4196
16:14 he brought also the brasen **a**, which *was* 4196
16:14 from between the **a** and the house of 4196
16:14 and put it on the north side of the **a**. 4196
16:15 Upon the great **a** burn the morning burnt 4196
16:15 the brasen **a** shall be for me to inquire *by*. 4196
18:22 Ye shall worship before this **a** in 4196
23: 9 not up to the **a** of the LORD in Jerusalem, 4196
23:15 Moreover the **a** that *was* at Beth-el, *and* 4196
23:15 both that **a** and the high place he brake 4196
23:16 and burnt *them* upon the **a**, and polluted it, 4196
23:17 that thou hast done against the **a** of Beth-el. 4196
1Ch 6:49 his sons offered upon the **a** of the burnt 4196
6:49 on the **a** of incense, *and were appointed* for 4196
16:40 **a** of the burnt offering continually morning 4196
21:18 set up an **a** unto the LORD in 4196
21:22 that I may build an **a** therein unto 4196
21:26 David built there an **a** unto the LORD, 4196
21:26 heaven by fire upon the **a** of burnt offering. 4196
21:29 and the **a** of the burnt offering, 4196
22: 1 this *is* the **a** of the burnt offering for Israel. 4196
28:18 for the **a** of incense refined gold by weight; 4196
2Ch 1: 5 Moreover the brasen **a**, that Bezaleel 4196
1: 6 Solomon went up thither to the brasen **a** 4196
4: 1 Moreover he made an **a** of brass, 4196
4:19 the golden **a** also, and the tables whereon 4196
5:12 stood *at* the east *end* of the **a**, and 4196
6:12 he stood before the **a** of the LORD in 4196
6:22 the oath come before thine **a** in this house; 4196
7: 7 the brasen **a** which Solomon had made was 4196
7: 9 for they kept the dedication of the **a** seven 4196
8:12 unto the LORD on the **a** of the LORD, 4196
15: 8 renewed the **a** of the LORD, that *was* 4196
23:10 *along* by the **a** and the temple, by the king 4196
26:16 to burn incense upon the **a** of incense. 4196
26:19 of the LORD, from beside the incense **a**. 4196
29:18 the **a** of burnt offering, with all the vessels 4196
29:19 they *are* before the **a** of the LORD. 4196
29:21 to offer *them* on the **a** of the LORD. 4196
29:22 the blood, and sprinkled *it* on the **a**: 4196
29:22 they sprinkled the blood upon the **a**: 4196
29:22 and they sprinkled the blood upon the **a**. 4196
29:24 reconciliation with their blood upon the **a**, 4196
29:27 to offer the burnt offering upon the **a**. 4196
32:12 Ye shall worship before one **a**, and 4196
33:16 he repaired the **a** of the LORD, and 4196
35:16 to offer burnt offerings upon the **a** of 4196
Ezr 3: 2 and builded the **a** of the God of Israel, 4196
3: 3 they set the **a** upon his bases; for fear *was* 4196
7:17 offer them upon the **a** of the house of your 4056
Ne 10:34 to burn upon the **a** of the LORD our God, 4196
Ps 26: 6 so will I compass thine **a**, O LORD: 4196
43: 4 will I go unto the **a** of God, unto God my 4196
51:19 then shall they offer bullocks upon thine **a**. 4196
118:27 with cords, *even* unto the horns of the **a**. 4196

Isa 6: 6 he had taken with the tongs from off the **a**: 4196
19:19 In that day shall there be an **a** to 4196
27: 9 when he maketh all the stones of the **a** as 4196
36: 7 Ye shall worship before this **a**? 4196
56: 7 sacrifices *shall be* accepted upon mine **a**; 4196
60: 7 shall come up with acceptance on mine **a**, 4196
La 2: 7 The Lord hath cast off his **a**, he hath 4196
Eze 8: 5 northward at the gate of the **a** this image of 4196
8:16 between the porch and the **a**, *were* about 4196
9: 2 they went in, and stood beside the brasen **a**. 4196
40:46 the keepers of the charge of the **a**: 4196
40:47 and the **a** *that was* before the house. 4196
41:22 The **a** *of* wood *was* three cubits high, and 4196
43:13 these *are* the measures of the **a** after 4196
43:13 and this *shall be* the higher place of the **a**. 4196
43:15 So the **a** *shall be* four cubits; and from 2025
43:15 from the **a** and upward *shall be* four horns. 741
43:16 the **a** *shall be* twelve *cubits* long, twelve 741
43:18 These *are* the ordinances of the **a** in the day 4196
43:22 they shall cleanse the **a**, as they did cleanse 4196
43:26 Seven days shall they purge the **a** and 4196
43:27 shall make your burnt offerings upon the **a**, 4196
45:19 upon the four corners of the settle of the **a**, 4196
47: 1 side of the house, at the south *side* of the **a**. 4196
Joel 1:13 howl, ye ministers of the **a**: come, lie all 4196
2:17 weep between the porch and the **a**, and 4196
Am 2: 8 upon clothes laid to pledge by every **a**, 4196
3:14 the horns of the **a** shall be cut off, and 4196
9: 1 I saw the Lord standing upon the **a**: and 4196
Zec 9:15 like bowls, *and* as the corners of the **a**. 4196
14:20 house shall be like the bowls before the **a**. 4196
Mal 1: 7 *Ye* offer polluted bread upon mine **a**; and 4196
1:10 do ye kindle *fire on* mine **a** for nought. 4196
2:13 covering the **a** of the LORD *with* tears, 4196
Mt 5:23 Therefore if thou bring thy gift to the **a**, and *2379*
5:24 Leave there thy gift before the **a**, and *2379*
23:18 And, Whosoever shall swear by the **a**, it is *2379*
23:19 the gift, or the **a** that sanctifieth the gift? *2379*
23:20 Whoso therefore shall swear by the **a**, *2379*
23:35 ye slew between the temple and the **a**. *2379*
Lk 1:11 on the right side of the **a** of incense. *2379*
11:51 which perished between the **a** and *2379*
Ac 17:23 I found an **a** with this inscription, *1041*
1Co 9:13 they which wait at the **a** are partakers with *2379*
9:13 wait at the altar are partakers with the **a**? *2379*
10:18 eat *of* the sacrifices partakers of the **a**? *2379*
Heb 7:13 of which no *man* gave attendance at the **a**. *2379*
13:10 We have an **a**, whereof they have no right *2379*
Jas 2:21 he had offered Isaac his son upon the **a**? *2379*
Rev 6: 9 I saw under the **a** the souls of them that *2379*
8: 3 And another angel came and stood at the **a**, *2379*
8: 3 the golden **a** which was before the throne. *2379*
8: 5 and filled it with fire of the **a**, and cast *it* *2379*
9:13 horns of the golden **a** which is before God, *2379*
11: 1 and the **a**, and them that worship therein. *2379*
14:18 And another angel came out from the **a**, *2379*
16: 7 And I heard another out of the **a** say, *2379*

ALTARS (55) [ALTAR]

Ex 34:13 ye shall destroy their **a**, break their images, 4196
Nu 3:31 the **a**, and the vessels of the sanctuary 4196
23: 1 Build me here seven **a**, and prepare me here 4196
23: 4 I have prepared seven **a**, and I have offered 4196
23:14 and built seven **a**, and offered a bullock and 4196
23:29 Build me here seven **a**, and prepare me here 4196
Dt 7: 5 ye shall destroy their **a**, and break down 4196
12: 3 you shall overthrow their **a**, and break their 4196
Jdg 2: 2 of this land; you shall throw down their **a**: 4196
1Ki 19:10 thrown down thine **a**, and slain thy 4196
19:14 thrown down thine **a**, and slain thy 4196
2Ki 11:18 his **a** and his images brake they in pieces 4196
11:18 slew Mattan the priest of Baal before the **a**. 4196
18:22 and whose **a** Hezekiah hath taken away, 4196
21: 3 he reared up **a** for Baal, and made a grove, 4196
21: 4 he built **a** in the house of the LORD, 4196
21: 5 he built **a** for all the host of heaven in 4196
23:12 the **a** that *were* on the top of the upper 4196
23:12 the **a** which Manasseh had made in the two 4196
23:20 the high places that *were* there upon the **a**, 4196
2Ch 14: 3 For he took away the **a** of the strange *gods*, 4196
23:17 brake his **a** and his images in pieces, and 4196
23:17 slew Mattan the priest of Baal before the **a**. 4196
28:24 he made him **a** in every corner of 4196
30:14 and took away the **a** that *were* in Jerusalem, 4196
30:14 all the **a for incense** took they away, and 6999
31: 1 and the **a** out of all Judah and Benjamin, 4196
32:12 taken away his high places and his **a**, 4196
33: 3 he reared up **a** for Baalim, and 4196
33: 4 Also he built **a** in the house of the LORD, 4196
33: 5 he built **a** for all the host of heaven in 4196
33:15 all the **a** that he had built in the mount of 4196
34: 4 they brake down the **a** of Baalim in his 4196
34: 5 burnt the bones of the priests upon their **a**, 4196
34: 7 when he had broken down the **a** and 4196
Ps 84: 3 *even* thine **a**, O LORD of hosts, my King, 4196
Isa 17: 8 he shall not look to the **a**, the work of his 4196
36: 7 and whose **a** Hezekiah hath taken away, 4196
65: 3 and burneth incense upon **a of brick**; 3843
Jer 11:13 have ye set up **a** to *that* shameful thing, 4196
11:13 *even* **a** to burn incense unto Baal. 4196
17: 1 of their heart, and upon the horns of your **a**; 4196
17: 2 Whilst their children remember their **a** and 4196
Eze 6: 4 your **a** shall be desolate, and your images 4196
6: 5 will scatter your bones round about your **a**. 4196
6: 6 that your **a** may be laid waste and 4196
6:13 be among their idols round about their **a**, 4196
Hos 8:11 Because Ephraim hath made many **a** to sin, 4196
8:11 altars to sin, **a** shall be unto him to sin. 4196
10: 1 of his fruit he hath increased the **a**; 4196
10: 2 he shall break down their **a**, he shall spoil 4196
10: 8 and the thistle shall come up on their **a**; 4196
12:11 their **a** *are* as heaps in the furrows of 4196
Am 3:14 upon him I will also visit the **a** of Beth-el: 4196
Ro 11: 3 thy prophets, and digged down thine **a**; *2379*

AL-TASCHITH (4)

Ps 57: T the chief Musician, **A**, Michtam of David, 516
58: T the chief Musician, **A**, Michtam of David. 516
59: T the chief Musician, **A**, Michtam of David; 516
75: T **A**, A Psalm *or* Song of Asaph. 516

ALTER (4) [ALTERED, ALTERETH]

Lev 27:10 He shall not **a** it, nor change it, a good for a 2498
Ezr 6:11 a decree, that whosoever shall **a** this word, 8133
6:12 that shall put to their hand to **a** *and* 8133
Ps 89:34 nor **a** the thing that is gone out of my lips. 8138

ALTERED (2) [ALTER]

Est 1:19 the Persians and the Medes, that it be not **a**, 5674
Lk 9:29 the fashion of his countenance was **a**, and *2087*

ALTERETH (2) [ALTER]

Da 6: 8 of the Medes and Persians, which **a** not. 5709
6:12 of the Medes and Persians, which **a** not. 5709

ALTHOUGH (16) [THOUGH]

Ex 13:17 the land of the Philistines, **a** that *was* near; 3588
Jos 22:17 **a** there was a plague in the congregation 2050.1
2Sa 23: 5 **A** my house *be* not so with God; yet he 3588
23: 5 and all *my* desire, **a** he make *it* not to grow. 3588
1Ki 20: 5 **A** I have sent unto thee, saying, 3588
Est 7: 4 **a** the enemy could not countervail 3588
Job 2: 3 **a** thou movedst me against him, 2050.1
5: 6 **A** affliction cometh not forth of the dust, 3588
35:14 **A** thou sayest thou shalt not see him, 637+3588
Jer 31:32 **a** I was a husband unto them, saith 2050.1
Eze 7:13 which is sold, **a** they were yet alive: 2050.1
11:16 **A** I have cast them far off among 3588
11:16 **a** I have scattered them among 3588
Hab 3:17 **A** the fig tree shall not blossom, 3588
Mk 14:29 **A** all shall be offended, yet *will* not I. *1487+2532*
Heb 4: 3 **a** the works were finished from *2543*

ALTOGETHER (29) [TOGETHER]

Ge 18:21 see whether they have done **a** according to 3617
Ex 11: 1 he shall surely thrust you out hence **a**. 3617
19:18 mount Sinai was **a** on a smoke, because 3605
Nu 16:13 except thou **make** thyself **a a prince** 8323+8323
23:11 behold, thou hast **blessed** *them* **a**. 1288+1288
24:10 **a blessed** *them* these three times. 1288+1288
30:14 if her husband **a hold** his **peace** at 2790+2790
Dt 16:20 That which is **a just** shalt thou 6664+6664
2Ch 12:12 from him, that *he* would not destroy *him* **a**: 3617
Est 4:14 For if thou **a holdest** thy **peace** at 2790+2790
Job 13: 5 O that you would **a hold** your **peace**, 2790+2790
27:12 have seen *it;* why then are ye thus **a vain**? 1892
Ps 19: 9 of the LORD *are* true *and* righteous **a**. 3162
39: 5 verily every man at his best state *is* **a** 3605
50:21 thou thoughtest that I **was a** *such a* 1961+1961
53: 3 is gone back, they are **a** become filthy; 3162
62: 9 the balance, they *are* **a** *lighter* than vanity. 3162
139: 4 *but* lo, O LORD, thou knowest it **a**. 3605
SS 5:16 yea, he *is* **a** lovely. This *is* my beloved, and 3605
Isa 10: 8 For he saith, *Are* not my princes **a** kings? 3162
Jer 5: 5 these have **a** broken the yoke, *and* burst 3162
10: 8 they are **a** brutish and foolish: 259+871.1
15:18 wilt thou **be a** unto me as a liar, *and* 1961+1961
30:11 will not **leave** thee **a unpunished**. 5352+5352
49:12 thou he *that* shall **a go unpunished**? 5352+5352
Jn 9:34 Thou wast **a** born in sins, and dost thou *3650*
Ac 26:29 were both almost, and **a** such as I *1722+4183*
1Co 5:10 Yet not **a** with the fornicators of this world, *3843*
9:10 Or saith he *it* **a** for our sakes? For our *3843*

ALUSH (2)

Nu 33:13 departed from Dophkah, and encamped in **A**. 442
33:14 they removed from **A**, and encamped at 442

ALVAH (1)

Ge 36:40 duke Timnah, duke **A**, duke Jetheth, 5933

ALVAN (1)

Ge 36:23 **A**, and Manahath, and Ebal, Shepho, and 5935

ALWAY (23) [ALWAYS]

Ex 25:30 set upon the table shewbread before me **a**. 8548
Nu 9:16 So it was **a**: the cloud covered it *by day,* 8548
Dt 11: 1 and his commandments **a**. 3117+3605+1886.1
28:33 and crushed **a**: 3117+3605+1886.1
2Sa 9:10 master's son shall eat bread **a** at my table. 8548
1Ki 11:36 **a** before me in Jerusalem, 3117+3605+1886.1
2Ki 8:19 him to give to him **a** 3117+3605+1886.1
Job 7:16 I loathe *it;* I would not live **a**: 5769+3807.1
Ps 9:18 For the needy shall not **a** be 5331+3807.1
119:112 heart to perform thy statutes **a**, 5769+3807.1
Pr 28:14 Happy *is* the man that feareth **a**: but he that 8548
Mt 28:20 and lo, I am with you **a**, *even* *2250+3588+3956*
Jn 7: 6 is not yet come: but your time is **a** ready. *3842*
Ac 10: 2 alms to the people, and prayed to God **a**. *1275*
Ro 11:10 may not see, and bow down their back **a**. *1275*
2Co 4:11 For we which live are **a** delivered unto death *104*
6:10 As sorrowful, yet **a** rejoicing; as poor, *104*
Php 4: 4 Rejoice in the Lord **a**: *and* again I say, *3842*
Col 4: 6 Let your speech *be* **a** with grace, *3842*
1Th 2:16 they might be saved, to fill up their sins **a**: *3842*
2Th 2:13 But we are bound to give thanks **a** to God *3842*
Tit 1:12 said, The Cretians *are* **a** liars, evil beasts, *104*
Heb 3:10 and said, They do **a** err in *their* heart; *104*

ALWAYS (62) [ALWAY]

Ge 6: 3 spirit shall not **a** strive with man, 5769+3807.1
Ex 27:20 for the light, to cause the lamp to burn **a**. 8548
28:38 it shall be **a** upon his forehead, that they 8548
Dt 5:29 all my commandments **a**, 3117+3605+1886.1
6:24 our God, for our good **a**, 3117+3605+1886.1
11:12 the eyes of the LORD thy God *are* **a** upon 8548
14:23 fear the LORD thy God **a**. 3117+3605+1886.1
1Ch 16:15 Be ye mindful **a** of his covenant; 5769+3807.1
2Ch 18: 7 prophesied good unto me, but **a** evil: 3117+3605
Job 27:10 will he **a** call upon God? 3605+6256+871.1
32: 9 Great men are not **a** wise: neither do NIH
Ps 10: 5 His ways are **a** grievous; 3605+871.1
16: 8 I have set the LORD **a** before me: because 8548
103: 9 He will not **a** chide: neither will he 5331+3807.1
Pr 5:19 and be thou ravisht **a** with her love. 8548
8:30 rejoicing **a** before him; 3605+6256+871.1
Ecc 9: 8 Let thy garments be **a** white; 3605+6256+871.1
Isa 57:16 for ever, neither will I be **a** wroth: 5331+3807.1
Jer 20:17 and her womb *to be* **a** great *with me.* 5769
Eze 38: 8 of Israel, which have been **a** waste: 8548
Mt 18:10 That in heaven their angels do **a** *1223+3956*
26:11 For ye have the poor **a** with you; but me ye *3842*
26:11 always with you; but me ye have not **a**. *3842*
Mk 5: 5 And **a**, night and day, he was in *1275*
14: 7 For ye have the poor with you **a**, and *3842*
14: 7 may do them good: but me ye have not **a**. *3842*
Lk 18: 1 them *to this end,* that *men* ought **a** to pray, *3842*
21:36 ye therefore, and pray **a**, *1722+2540+3956*
Jn 8:29 for I do **a** those *things* that please him. *3842*
11:42 And I knew that thou hearest me **a**: but *3842*
12: 8 For the poor **a** ye have with you; but me ye *3842*
12: 8 ye have with you; but me ye have not **a**. *3842*
18:20 in the temple, whither the Jews **a** resort; *3842*
Ac 2:25 I foresaw the Lord **a** before my face, *1223+3956*
7:51 and ears, ye do **a** resist the Holy Ghost: *104*
24: 3 We accept *it* **a**, and in all places, *3839*
24:16 to have **a** a conscience void of offence *1275*
Ro 1: 9 I make mention of you, **a** in my prayers, *3842*
1Co 1: 4 I thank my God **a** on your behalf, for *3842*
15:58 **a** abounding in the work of the Lord, *3842*
2Co 2:14 which **a** causeth us to triumph in Christ, *3842*
4:10 **A** bearing about in the body the dying of *3842*
5: 6 Therefore *we are* **a** confident, knowing *3842*
9: 8 **a** having all sufficiency in all *things,* may *3842*
Gal 4:18 But *it is* good to be zealously affected **a** in *3842*
Eph 5:20 Giving thanks **a** for all *things* unto God and *3842*
6:18 Praying **a** with all prayer and *1722+2540+3956*
Php 1: 4 **A** in every prayer of mine for you all *3842*
1:20 as **a**, *so* now also Christ shall be magnified *3842*
2:12 my beloved, as ye have **a** obeyed, *3842*
Col 1: 3 of our Lord Jesus Christ, praying **a** for you, *3842*
4:12 **a** labouring fervently for you in prayers, *3842*
1Th 1: 2 We give thanks to God **a** for you all, *3842*
3: 6 that ye have good remembrance of us **a**, *3842*
2Th 1: 3 We are bound to thank God **a** for you, *3842*
1:11 Wherefore also we pray **a** for you, that our *3842*
3:16 give you peace **a** by all means. *1223+3956*
Phm 1: 4 making mention of thee **a** in my prayers, *3842*
Heb 9: 6 the priests went **a** into the first tabernacle, *1275*
1Pe 3:15 *be* ready **a** to *give* an answer to every *man* *104*
2Pe 1:12 **a** in remembrance of these *things,* though ye *104*
1:15 to have these *things* **a** in remembrance. *1539*

AM (874) [BE]

Ge 4: 9 I know not: **A** I my brother's keeper? NIH
15: 1 I **a** thy shield, *and* thy exceeding great NIH
15: 7 I **a** the LORD that brought thee out of Ur NIH
17: 1 and said unto him, I **a** the Almighty God; NIH
18:12 After I **a** waxed old shall I have pleasure, NIH
18:13 Shall I of a surety bear *a child,* which **a** old? NIH
18:27 unto the Lord, which **a** *but* dust and ashes: NIH
22: 1 Abraham: and he said, Behold, *here* I **a**. NIH
22: 7 he said, Here **a** I, my son. And he said, NIH
22:11 Abraham, Abraham: and he said, Here **a** I. NIH
23: 4 I **a** a stranger and a sojourner with you: NIH
24:24 I **a** the daughter of Bethuel the son of NIH
24:34 And he said, I **a** Abraham's servant. NIH
25:22 and she said, If *it be* so, why **a** I thus? NIH
25:30 with that same red *pottage;* for I **a** faint: NIH
25:32 Esau said, Behold, I **a** at the point to die: NIH
26:24 and said, I **a** the God of Abraham thy father: NIH
26:24 for I **a** with thee, and will bless thee, and NIH
27: 1 and he said unto him, Behold, *here* **a** I. NIH
27: 2 he said, Behold now, I **a** old, I know not NIH
27:11 *is* a hairy man, and I **a** a smooth man: NIH
27:18 and he said, Here **a** I; who *art* thou, my son? NIH
27:19 said unto his father, I **a** Esau thy firstborn; NIH
27:24 thou my very son Esau? And he said, I **a**. NIH
27:32 And he said, I **a** thy son, thy firstborn Esau. NIH
27:46 I **a** weary of my life because of NIH
28:13 I **a** the LORD God of Abraham thy father, NIH
28:15 I **a** with thee, and will keep thee in all NIH
30: 2 he said, *A* I in God's stead, who hath NIH
30:13 Leah said, Happy **a** I, for the daughters will NIH
31:11 a dream, *saying,* Jacob: And I said, Here **a** I. NIH
31:13 I **a** the God of Beth-el, where thou NIH
32:10 I **a** not worthy of the least of all the mercies, NIH
32:10 this Jordan; and now I **a** become two bands. NIH
35:11 God said unto him, I **a** God Almighty: NIH
37:13 unto them. And he said to him, Here **a** I. NIH
38:25 By the man, whose these *are,* **a** I with child: NIH
41:44 I **a** Pharaoh, and without thee shall no man NIH
43:14 I be bereaved of my children, I **a** bereaved. NIH
45: 3 Joseph said unto his brethren, I **a** Joseph; NIH
45: 4 he said, I **a** Joseph your brother, whom ye NIH
46: 2 said, Jacob, Jacob. And he said, Here **a** I. NIH
46: 3 And he said, I **a** God, the God of thy father: NIH
49:29 I **a** *to be* gathered unto my people: NIH
50:19 Fear not: for **a** I in the place of God? NIH
Ex 3: 4 said, Moses, Moses. And he said, Here **a** I. NIH
3: 6 Moreover he said, I **a** the God of thy father, NIH
3: 8 I **a** come down to deliver them out of NIH
3:11 Moses said unto God, Who **a** I, that I should NIH
3:14 God said unto Moses, I **A** THAT I AM: 1961
3:14 God said unto Moses, I AM THAT I **A**: 1961
3:14 of Israel, I **A** hath sent me unto you. 1961
3:19 I **a** sure that the king of Egypt will not let NIH
4:10 O my Lord, I **a** not eloquent, neither NIH
4:10 I **a** slow of speech, and of a slow tongue. NIH
6: 2 and said unto him, I **a** the LORD: NIH
6: 6 I **a** the LORD, and I will bring you out NIH
6: 7 ye shall know that I **a** the LORD your NIH
6: 8 give it you *for* an heritage: I **a** the LORD. NIH

A

Ex 6:12 hear me, who a of uncircumcised lips? NIH
6:29 spake unto Moses, saying, I a the LORD: NIH
6:30 I a of uncircumcised lips, and how shall NIH
7: 5 the Egyptians shall know that I a NIH
7:17 In this thou shalt know that I a the LORD: NIH
8:22 to the end thou mayest know that I a NIH
9:29 As soon as I a gone out of the city, NIH
10: 2 that ye may know how that I a the LORD. NIH
12:12 I will execute judgment: I a the LORD. NIH
14: 4 that the Egyptians may know that I a NIH
14:18 the Egyptians shall know that I a NIH
15:26 for I a the LORD that healeth thee. NIH
16:12 ye shall know that I a the LORD your NIH
18: 6 I thy father in law Jethro a come unto thee, NIH
20: 2 I a the LORD thy God, which have NIH
20: 5 for I the LORD thy God a a jealous God, NIH
22:27 unto me, that I will hear; for I a gracious. NIH
29:46 they shall know that I a the LORD their NIH
29:46 amongst them: I a the LORD their God. NIH
31:13 that *ye* may know that I a the LORD that NIH
Lev 8:35 that ye die not: for so I a commanded. NIH
10:13 made by fire: for so I a commanded. NIH
11:44 For I a the LORD your God: ye shall NIH
11:44 and ye shall be holy; for I a holy: NIH
11:45 For I a the LORD that bringeth you up out NIH
11:45 ye shall therefore be holy, for I a holy. NIH
18: 2 say unto them, I a the LORD your God. NIH
18: 4 to walk therein: I a the LORD your God. NIH
18: 5 he shall live in them: I a the LORD. NIH
18: 6 to uncover *their* nakedness: I a the LORD. NIH
18:21 the name of thy God: I a the LORD. NIH
18:30 I a the LORD your God. NIH
19: 2 be holy: for I the LORD your God a holy. NIH
19: 3 my sabbaths: I a the LORD your God. NIH
19: 4 molten gods: I a the LORD your God. NIH
19:10 and stranger: I a the LORD your God. NIH
19:12 the name of thy God: I a the LORD. NIH
19:14 but shalt fear thy God: I a the LORD. NIH
19:16 the blood of thy neighbour: I a the LORD. NIH
19:18 thy neighbour as thyself: I a the LORD. NIH
19:25 increase thereof: I a the LORD your God. NIH
19:28 print any marks upon you: I a the LORD. NIH
19:30 reverence my sanctuary: I a the LORD. NIH
19:31 defiled by them: I a the LORD your God. NIH
19:32 old man, and fear thy God: I a the LORD. NIH
19:34 the land of Egypt: I a the LORD your God. NIH
19:36 I a the LORD your God, which brought NIH
19:37 and do them: I a the LORD. NIH
20: 7 be ye holy: for I a the LORD your God. NIH
20: 8 I a the LORD which sanctify you. NIH
20:24 I a the LORD your God, which have NIH
20:26 for I the LORD a holy, and have severed NIH
21: 8 I the LORD, which sanctify you, a holy. NIH
21:12 oil of his God *is* upon him: I a the LORD. NIH
22: 2 which they hallow unto me: I a the LORD. NIH
22: 3 cut off from my presence: I a the LORD. NIH
22: 8 to defile *himself* therewith: I a the LORD. NIH
22:30 none of it until the morrow: I a the LORD. NIH
22:31 and do them: I a the LORD. NIH
22:32 of Israel: I a the LORD which hallow you, NIH
22:33 of Egypt, to be your God: I a the LORD. NIH
23:22 to the stranger: I a the LORD your God. NIH
23:43 the land of Egypt: I a the LORD your God. NIH
24:22 own country: for I a the LORD your God. NIH
25:17 fear thy God: for I a the LORD your God. NIH
25:38 I a the LORD your God, which brought NIH
25:55 the land of Egypt: I a the LORD your God. NIH
26: 1 down unto it: for I a the LORD your God. NIH
26: 2 reverence my sanctuary: I a the LORD. NIH
26:13 I a the LORD your God, which brought NIH
26:44 with them: for I a the LORD their God. NIH
26:45 that *I* might be their God: I a the LORD. NIH
Nu 3:13 beast: mine they shall be: I a the LORD. NIH
3:41 thou shalt take the Levites for me (I a NIH
3:45 the Levites shall be mine: I a the LORD. NIH
10:10 before your God: I a the LORD your God. NIH
11:14 I a not able to bear all this people alone, NIH
11:21 amongst whom I a, *are* six hundred NIH
15:41 I a the LORD your God, which brought NIH
15:41 to be your God: I a the LORD your God. NIH
18:20 I a thy part and thine inheritance among NIH
22:30 the ass said unto Balaam, A not I thine ass, NIH
22:37 a I not able indeed to promote thee to NIH
22:38 said unto Balak, Lo, I a come unto thee: NIH
Dt 1: 9 I a not able to bear you myself alone: NIH
1:42 not up, neither fight; for I a not among you; NIH
5: 6 I a the LORD thy God, which brought thee NIH
5: 9 for I the LORD thy God a a jealous God, NIH
26: 3 that I a come unto the country which NIH
29: 6 that ye might know that I a the LORD NIH
31: 2 I a an hundred and twenty years old *this* NIH
31:27 while I a yet alive with you *this* day, NIH
32:39 *even* I, a he, and *there is* no god with me: NIH
Jos 5:14 *as* captain of the host of the LORD a I now NIH
14:10 I a *this* day fourscore and five years old. NIH
14:11 As yet I a *as* strong *this* day as *I was* in NIH
17:14 portion to inherit, seeing I a a great people, NIH
23: 2 said unto them, I a old *and* stricken in age: NIH
23:14 *this* day I a going the way of all the earth: NIH
Jdg 4:19 a little water to drink; for I a thirsty. NIH
6:10 I said unto you, I a the LORD your God; NIH
6:15 and I a the least in my father's house. NIH
8: 5 and I a pursuing after Zebah and Zalmunna, NIH
9: 2 remember also that I a your bone and NIH
13:11 spakest unto the woman? And he said, I a. NIH
17: 9 I a a Levite of Beth-lehem-judah, and I go NIH
18: 4 and hath hired me, and I a his priest. 1961
19:18 the side of mount Ephraim; from thence a I: NIH
19:18 I a *now* going *to* the house of the LORD; NIH
Ru 1:12 go *your way;* for I a too old to have a NIH
2:10 knowledge of me, seeing I a a stranger? NIH
3: 9 she answered, I a Ruth thine handmaid: NIH
3:12 And now it is true that I a *thy* near kinsman: NIH
4: 4 to redeem *it* besides thee; and I a after thee. NIH
1Sa 1: 8 a not I better to thee than ten sons? NIH
1Sa 1:15 my lord, I a a woman of a sorrowful spirit: NIH
1:26 I a the woman that stood by thee here, NIH
3: 4 called Samuel: and he answered, Here a I. NIH
3: 5 he ran unto Eli, and said, Here a I; for thou NIH
3: 6 and went to Eli, and said, Here a I; NIH
3: 8 he arose and went to Eli, and said, Here a I; NIH
3:16 my son. And he answered, Here a I. NIH
4:16 I a he that came out of the army, and I fled NIH
9:19 answered Saul, and said, I a the seer: NIH
9:21 and said, A not I a Benjamite, NIH
12: 2 I a old and grayheaded; and behold, NIH
12: 3 here I a: witness against me before NIH
14: 7 behold, I a with thee according to thy heart. NIH
16: 2 say, I a come to sacrifice to the LORD. NIH
16: 5 I a come to sacrifice unto the LORD: NIH
17: 8 a not I a Philistine, and you servants to NIH
17:43 the Philistine said unto David, A I a dog, NIH
17:58 *I* a the son of thy servant Jesse NIH
18:18 David said unto Saul, Who a I? and what *is* NIH
18:23 seeing that I a a poor man, and NIH
22:12 And he answered, Here I a, my lord. NIH
28:15 Saul answered, I a sore distressed; for NIH
30:13 he said, I a a young man of Egypt, NIH
2Sa 1: 3 Out of the camp of Israel a I escaped. NIH
1: 7 called unto me. And I answered, Here a I. NIH
1: 8 And I answered him, I a an Amalekite. NIH
1:13 I a the son of a stranger, an Amalekite. NIH
1:26 I a distressed for thee, my brother Jonathan: NIH
2:20 *Art* thou Asahel? And he answered, I a. NIH
3: 8 of Ish-bosheth, and said, A I a dog's head, NIH
3:39 I a *this* day weak, though anointed king; NIH
7:18 and he said, Who a I, O Lord GOD? NIH
9: 8 look upon such a dead dog as I a? NIH
11: 5 sent and told David, and said, I a with child. NIH
14: 5 I a indeed a widow woman, and NIH
14:15 that I a come to speak of this thing unto my NIH
14:32 to say, Wherefore a I come from Geshur? NIH
15:26 behold, *here* a I, let him do to me as NIH
19:20 I a come the first *this* day of all the house of NIH
19:22 for do not I know that I a *this* day king over NIH
19:35 I a *this* day fourscore years old: *and* can I NIH
20:17 I a *he*. Then she said unto him, NIH
20:19 I a *one of them that are* peaceable *and* NIH
24:14 David said unto Gad, I a in a great strait: NIH
1Ki 3: 7 I a *but* a little child: I know not *how* to go NIH
8:20 I a risen up in the room of David my father, NIH
13:14 that camest from Judah? And he said, I a. NIH
13:18 I a a prophet also as thou *art;* and an angel NIH
13:31 When I a dead, then bury me in NIH
14: 6 for I a sent to thee *with* heavy *tidings*. NIH
17:12 behold, I a gathering two sticks, that I may NIH
18: 8 I a: go, tell thy lord, Behold, Elijah *is here*. NIH
18:12 come to pass, *as soon as* I a gone from thee, NIH
18:36 *that* I a thy servant, and *that* I have done all NIH
19: 4 my life; for I a not better than my fathers. NIH
19:10 I, *even* I only, a left; and they seek my life, NIH
19:14 I, *even* I only, a left; and they seek my life, NIH
20: 4 to thy saying, I a thine, and all that I have. NIH
20:13 and thou shalt know that I a the LORD. NIH
20:28 and ye shall know that I a the LORD. NIH
22: 4 I a as thou *art,* my people as thy people, my NIH
22:34 carry me out of the host; for I a wounded. NIH
2Ki 2:10 *nevertheless,* if thou see me *when I* a taken NIH
3: 7 I a as thou *art,* my people as thy people, *and* NIH
5: 7 and said, A I God, to kill and to make alive, NIH
16: 7 saying, I a thy servant and thy son: NIH
18:25 A I now come up without the LORD NIH
19:23 With the multitude of my chariots I a come NIH
21:12 I a bringing *such* evil upon Jerusalem and NIH
1Ch 17:16 said, Who a I, O LORD God, and what *is* NIH
21:13 David said unto Gad, I a in a great strait: NIH
29:14 who a I, and what *is* my people, that we NIH
2Ch 2: 6 who a I then, that I should build him a NIH
2: 9 for the house which I a about to build *shall* NIH
6:10 for I a risen up in the room of David my NIH
6:10 a set on the throne of Israel, as the LORD NIH
18: 3 I a as thou *art,* and my people as thy people; NIH
18:33 carry me out of the host; for I a wounded. NIH
35:23 Have me away; for I a sore wounded. NIH
Ezr 9: 6 I a ashamed and blush to lift up my face to NIH
Ne 6: 3 I a doing a great work, so that I cannot NIH
6:11 *being* as I a, would go into the temple to NIH
Est 5:12 to morrow a I invited unto her also with NIH
Job 1:15 and I only a escaped alone to tell thee. NIH
1:16 and I only a escaped alone to tell thee. NIH
1:17 and I only a escaped alone to tell thee. NIH
1:19 and I only a escaped alone to tell thee. NIH
7: 3 So a I made to possess months of vanity, NIH
7: 4 I a full *of* tossings to and fro unto NIH
7: 8 *more:* thine eyes *are* upon me, and I a not. NIH
7:12 A I a sea, or a whale, that thou settest a NIH
7:20 against thee, so that I a a burden to myself? 1961
9:20 *if I say,* I a perfect, it shall also prove me NIH
9:28 I a afraid of all my sorrows, I know that NIH
9:32 as I a, *that* I should answer him, *and* NIH
10: 7 Thou knowest that I a not wicked; and NIH
10:15 *I* a full of confusion; therefore see thou NIH
11: 4 doctrine *is* pure, and I a clean in thine eyes. 1961
12: 3 as well as you; I a not inferior to you: NIH
12: 4 I a *as* one mocked of his neighbour, 1961
13: 2 do I know also. I a not inferior unto you. NIH
16: 6 and *though* I forbear, what a I eased? NIH
19: 7 I cry out *of* wrong, but I a not heard: NIH
19:10 destroyed me on every side, and I a gone: NIH
19:15 me for a stranger: I a an alien in their sight. 1961
19:20 and I a escaped with the skin of my teeth. NIH
21: 6 Even when I remember I a afraid, and NIH
23:15 Therefore a I troubled at his presence: NIH
23:15 when I consider, I a afraid of him. NIH
30: 9 now a I their song, yea, I am their byword. 1961
30: 9 now am I their song, yea, I a their byword. 1961
30:19 and I a become like dust and ashes. NIH
30:29 I a a brother to dragons, and a companion 1961
32: 6 and said, I a young, and ye *are* very old; NIH
32:18 For I a full *of* matter, the spirit within me NIH
Job 33: 6 I a according to thy wish in God's stead: NIH
33: 6 God's stead: I also a formed out of the clay. NIH
33: 9 I a clean without transgression, I *am* NIH
33: 9 clean without transgression, I a innocent; NIH
34: 5 For Job hath said, I a righteous: and NIH
40: 4 Behold, I a vile; what shall I answer thee? NIH
Ps 6: 2 mercy upon me, O LORD; for I a weak: NIH
6: 6 I a weary with my groaning; all the night NIH
13: 4 those that trouble me rejoice when I a NIH
17: 3 I a purposed *that* my mouth shall not NIH
22: 2 and in the night season, and a not silent. NIH
22: 6 I a a worm, and no man; a reproach of men, NIH
22:14 I a poured out like water, and all my bones NIH
25:16 upon me; for I a desolate and afflicted. NIH
28: 7 my heart trusted in him, and I a helped: NIH
31: 9 upon me, O LORD, for I a in trouble: NIH
31:12 I a forgotten as a dead man out of mind: NIH
31:12 man out of mind: I a like a broken vessel. 1961
31:22 my haste, I a cut off from before thine eyes: NIH
35: 3 say unto my soul, I a thy salvation. NIH
37:25 I have been young, and *now* a old; yet have NIH
38: 6 I a troubled; I am bowed down greatly; I go NIH
38: 6 I am troubled; I a bowed down greatly; I go NIH
38: 8 I a feeble and sore broken: I have roared by NIH
38:17 For I a ready to halt, and my sorrow *is* NIH
39: 4 what it *is; that* I may know how frail I a. NIH
39:10 I a consumed by the blow of thine hand. NIH
39:12 for I a a stranger with thee, *and* a sojourner, NIH
40:12 that I a not able to look *up;* they are moe NIH
40:17 I a poor and needy; *yet* the Lord thinketh NIH
46:10 Be still, and know that I a God: I will be NIH
50: 7 testify against thee: I a God, *even* thy God. NIH
52: 8 I a like a green olive tree in the house of NIH
56: 3 *What* time I a afraid, I will trust in thee. NIH
69: 2 I a come into deep waters, where the floods NIH
69: 3 I a weary of my crying: my throat is dried: NIH
69: 8 I a become a stranger unto my brethren, and NIH
69:17 thy face from thy servant; for I a in trouble: NIH
69:20 broken my heart; and I a full of heaviness: NIH
69:29 I a poor and sorrowful: let thy salvation, NIH
70: 5 I a poor and needy: make haste unto me, NIH
71: 7 I a as a wonder unto many; but thou *art* my 1961
71:18 Now also when I a old and grayheaded, NIH
73:23 Nevertheless I a continually with thee: NIH
77: 4 I a *so* troubled that I cannot speak. NIH
81:10 I a the LORD thy God, which brought thee NIH
86: 1 O LORD, hear me: for I a poor and needy. NIH
86: 2 Preserve my soul; for I a holy: O thou my NIH
88: 4 I a counted with them that go down into NIH
88: 4 the pit: I a as a man *that hath* no strength: 1961
88: 8 *I* a shut up, and I cannot come forth. NIH
88:15 I a afflicted and ready to die from *my* youth NIH
88:15 *up: while* I suffer thy terrors I a distracted. NIH
102: 2 face from me in the day *when* I a in trouble; NIH
102: 6 I a like a pelican of the wilderness: I am NIH
102: 6 the wilderness: I a like an owl of the desert. 1961
102: 7 a as a sparrow alone upon the housetop. 1961
102:11 that declineth; and I a withered like grass. NIH
109:22 For I a poor and needy, and my heart is NIH
109:23 I a gone like the shadow when it declineth: NIH
109:23 I a tossed up and down as the locust. NIH
116:16 Oh LORD, truly I a thy servant; I *am* thy NIH
116:16 I a thy servant, *and* the son of thy NIH
119:19 I a a stranger in the earth: hide not thy NIH
119:63 I a a companion of all *them* that fear thee, NIH
119:83 For I a become like a bottle in the smoke; NIH
119:94 I a thine, save me; for I have sought thy NIH
119:107 I a afflicted very much: quicken me, NIH
119:120 fear of thee; and I a afraid of thy judgments. NIH
119:125 I a thy servant; give me understanding, NIH
119:141 I a small and despised: *yet* do not I forget NIH
120: 7 I a *for* peace: but when I speak, they *are* for NIH
139:14 for I a fearfully and wonderfully made: NIH
139:18 the sand: when I awake, I a still with thee. NIH
139:21 a not I grieved with those that rise up NIH
142: 6 unto my cry; for I a brought very low: NIH
143:12 them that afflict my soul: for I a thy servant. NIH
Pr 8:14 I a understanding; I have strength. NIH
20: 9 made my heart clean, I a pure from my sin? NIH
26:19 his neighbour, and saith, A not I in sport? NIH
30: 2 Surely I a more brutish than *any* man, and NIH
Ecc 1:16 Lo, I a come to great estate, and have gotten NIH
SS 1: 5 I a black, but comely, O ye daughters of NIH
1: 6 because I a black, because the sun hath NIH
2: 1 I a the rose of Sharon, *and* the lily of NIH
2: 5 comfort me with apples: for I a sick of love. NIH
2:16 My beloved *is* mine, and I a his: he feedeth NIH
5: 1 I a come into my garden, my sister, NIH
5: 8 that ye tell him, that I a sick of love. NIH
6: 3 I a my beloved's, and my beloved *is* mine: NIH
7:10 I a my beloved's, and his desire *is* towards NIH
8:10 I a a wall, and my breasts like towers: then NIH
Isa 1:11 I a full *of* the burnt offerings of rams, and NIH
1:14 a trouble unto me; I a weary to bear *them*. NIH
6: 5 for I a undone; because I *am* a man of NIH
6: 5 because I a a man of unclean lips, and NIH
6: 8 go for us? Then I said, Here a I; send me. NIH
10:13 done *it,* and by my wisdom; for I a prudent: NIH
19:11 I a the son of the wise, the son of ancient NIH
21: 8 and I a set in my ward whole nights: NIH
29:12 I pray thee: and he saith, I a not learned. NIH
33:24 the inhabitant shall not say, I a sick: NIH
36:10 a I now come up without the LORD NIH
37:24 By the multitude of my chariots a I come up NIH
38:10 I a deprived of the residue of my years. NIH
38:14 O LORD, I a oppressed; undertake for me. NIH
41: 4 the first, and with the last; I a he. NIH
41:10 Fear thou not; for I a with thee: be not NIH
41:10 be not dismayed; for I a thy God: I will NIH
42: 8 I a the LORD: that *is* my name: and NIH
43: 3 For I a the LORD thy God, the Holy One NIH
43: 5 for I a with thee: I will bring thy seed from NIH
43:10 and believe me, and understand that I a he: NIH
43:11 I, *even* I, a the LORD; and beside me *there* NIH
43:12 saith the LORD, that I a God. NIH

Isa 43:13 Yea, before the day *was* I **a** he; and *there is* NIH
43:15 I **a** the LORD, your Holy One, the creator NIH
43:25 **a** he that blotteth out thy transgressions for NIH
44: 5 One shall say, I **a** the LORD'S; and NIH
44: 6 I **a** the first, and I *am* the last; and besides NIH
44: 6 I *am* the first, and I **a** the last; and besides NIH
44:16 saith, Aha, I **a** warm, I have seen the fire: NIH
44:24 I **a** the LORD that maketh all *things;* that NIH
45: 3 call *thee* by thy name, **a** the God of Israel. NIH
45: 5 I **a** the LORD, and *there is* none else, NIH
45: 6 I **a** the LORD, and *there is* none else. NIH
45:18 I **a** the LORD; and *there is* none else. NIH
45:22 for I **a** God, and *there is* none else. NIH
46: 4 *even* to *your* old age I **a** he; and *even* to NIH
46: 9 for I **a** God, and *there is* none else; *I am* NIH
46: 9 *I* **a** God, and *there is* none like me, NIH
47: 8 in thine heart, I **a**, and none else besides me; NIH
47:10 in thine heart, I **a**, and none else besides me. NIH
48:12 I **a** he; I *am* the first, I also *am* the last. NIH
48:12 I *am* he; I **a** the first, I also *am* the last. NIH
48:12 I *am* he; I *am* the first, I also **a** the last. NIH
48:16 from the time that it was, there **a** I: NIH
48:17 I **a** the LORD thy God which teacheth thee NIH
49:21 **a** desolate, a captive, and removing to and NIH
49:23 and thou shalt know that I **a** the LORD: NIH
49:26 all flesh shall know that I the LORD **a** thy NIH
51:12 I, *even* I, **a** he that comforteth you: who *art* NIH
51:15 I **a** the LORD thy God, that divided NIH
52: 6 *they shall know* in that day that I **a** he that NIH
56: 3 let the eunuch say, Behold, I **a** a dry tree. NIH
58: 9 Here I **a**. If thou take away from the midst NIH
60:16 thou shalt know that I the LORD **a** thy NIH
65: 1 I **a** sought of *them that* asked not *for me:* I NIH
65: 1 *me:* I **a** found of *them that* sought me not: NIH
65: 5 not near to me; for I **a** holier than thou. NIH
Jer 1: 6 behold, I cannot speak: for I **a** a child. NIH
1: 7 LORD said unto me, Say not, I **a** a child: NIH
1: 8 for I **a** with thee to deliver thee, saith NIH
1:19 for I **a** with thee, saith the LORD, NIH
2:23 How canst thou say, I **a** not polluted, I have NIH
2:35 Yet thou sayest, Because I **a** innocent, NIH
3:12 for I **a** merciful, saith the LORD, *and* I will NIH
3:14 saith the LORD; for I **a** married unto you: NIH
4:19 I **a** pained *at* my very heart; my heart NIH
6:11 Therefore I **a** full *of* the fury of the LORD; NIH
6:11 of the LORD; I **a** weary with holding in: NIH
8:21 For the hurt of the daughter of my people **a** NIH
8:21 I **a** black; astonishment hath taken hold on NIH
9:24 that I **a** the LORD which exercise NIH
15: 6 and destroy thee; I **a** weary with repenting. NIH
15:16 for I **a** called by thy name, O LORD God NIH
15:20 for I **a** with thee to save thee and to deliver NIH
20: 7 I **a** in derision daily, every one mocketh 1961
21:13 Behold, I **a** against thee, O inhabitant of NIH
23: 9 I **a** like a drunken man, and like a man 1961
23:23 *A* I a God at hand, saith the LORD, and NIH
23:30 I **a** against the prophets, saith the LORD, NIH
23:31 Behold, I **a** against the prophets, saith NIH
23:32 I **a** against them that prophesy false dreams, NIH
24: 7 a heart to know me, that I **a** the LORD: NIH
26:14 As for me, behold, I **a** in your hand: do with NIH
29:23 even I know, and **a** a witness, saith NIH
30:11 For I **a** with thee, saith the LORD, to save NIH
31: 9 for I **a** a father to Israel, and Ephraim *is* my 1961
32:27 Behold, I **a** the LORD, the God of all NIH
36: 5 commanded Baruch, saying, I **a** shut up; NIH
38:19 I **a** afraid of the Jews that are fallen to NIH
42:11 for I **a** with you to save you, and to deliver NIH
46:28 for I **a** with thee; for I will make a full end NIH
50:31 Behold, I **a** against thee, *O thou* most proud, NIH
51:25 Behold, I **a** against thee, O destroying NIH
La 1:11 and consider; for I **a** become vile. NIH
1:14 *from whom* I **a** not able to rise up. NIH
1:20 Behold, O LORD; for I **a** in distress: my NIH
3: 1 I **a** the man *that* hath seen affliction by NIH
3:54 over mine head; *then* I said, I **a** cut off. NIH
3:63 and their rising up; I **a** their musick. NIH
Eze 5: 8 **a** against thee, and will execute judgments NIH
6: 7 and ye shall know that I **a** the LORD. NIH
6: 9 because I **a** broken with their whorish heart, NIH
6:10 they shall know that I **a** the LORD, *and* NIH
6:13 shall ye know that I **a** the LORD, NIH
6:14 and they shall know that I **a** the LORD. NIH
7: 4 and ye shall know that I **a** the LORD. NIH
7: 9 ye shall know that I **a** the LORD that NIH
7:27 and they shall know that I **a** the LORD. NIH
11:10 and ye shall know that I **a** the LORD. NIH
11:12 ye shall know that I **a** the LORD: for ye NIH
12:11 Say, I **a** your sign: like as I have done, so NIH
12:15 they shall know that I **a** the LORD, when I NIH
12:16 and they shall know that I **a** the LORD. NIH
12:20 and ye shall know that I **a** the LORD. NIH
12:25 For I **a** the LORD: I will speak, and NIH
13: 8 seen lies, therefore behold, I **a** against you, NIH
13: 9 and ye shall know that I **a** the Lord GOD. NIH
13:14 and ye shall know that I **a** the LORD. NIH
13:20 Behold, I **a** against your pillows, NIH
13:21 and ye shall know that I **a** the LORD. NIH
13:23 and ye shall know that I **a** the LORD. NIH
14: 8 and ye shall know that I **a** the LORD. NIH
15: 7 ye shall know that I **a** the LORD, when I NIH
16:62 and thou shalt know that I **a** the LORD: NIH
16:63 when I **a** pacified toward thee for all that NIH
20: 5 saying, I **a** the LORD your God; NIH
20: 7 idols of Egypt: I **a** the LORD your God. NIH
20:12 that *they* might know that I **a** the LORD NIH
20:19 I **a** the LORD your God; walk in my NIH
20:20 that *ye* may know that I **a** the LORD your NIH
20:26 to the end that they might know that I **a** NIH
20:38 and ye shall know that I **a** the LORD. NIH
20:42 ye shall know that I **a** the LORD, when I NIH
20:44 ye shall know that I **a** the LORD, when I NIH
21: 3 I **a** against thee, and will draw forth my NIH
22:16 and thou shalt know that I **a** the LORD. NIH
22:26 my sabbaths, and I **a** profaned among them. NIH
Eze 23:49 and ye shall know that I **a** the Lord GOD. NIH
24:24 ye shall know that I **a** the Lord GOD. NIH
24:27 and they shall know that I **a** the LORD. NIH
25: 5 and ye shall know that I **a** the LORD. NIH
25: 7 and thou shalt know that I **a** the LORD. NIH
25:11 and they shall know that I **a** the LORD. NIH
25:17 they shall know that I **a** the LORD, when I NIH
26: 3 Behold, I **a** against thee, O Tyrus, and NIH
26: 6 and they shall know that I **a** the LORD. NIH
27: 3 thou hast said, I **a** of perfect beauty. NIH
28: 2 thou hast said, I **a** a God, I sit *in* the seat of NIH
28: 9 say before him that slayeth thee, I **a** God? NIH
28:22 Behold, I **a** against thee, O Zidon; and I will NIH
28:22 they shall know that I **a** the LORD, when I NIH
28:23 and they shall know that I **a** the LORD. NIH
28:24 they shall know that I **a** the Lord GOD. NIH
28:26 they shall know that I **a** the LORD their NIH
29: 3 Behold, I **a** against thee, Pharaoh king of NIH
29: 6 of Egypt shall know that I **a** the LORD, NIH
29: 9 and they shall know that I **a** the LORD: NIH
29:10 I **a** against thee, and against thy rivers, and NIH
29:16 but they shall know that I **a** the Lord GOD. NIH
29:21 and they shall know that I **a** the LORD. NIH
30: 8 they shall know that I **a** the LORD, when I NIH
30:19 and they shall know that I **a** the LORD. NIH
30:22 I **a** against Pharaoh king of Egypt, and NIH
30:25 they shall know that I **a** the LORD, when I NIH
30:26 and they shall know that I **a** the LORD. NIH
32:15 shall they know that I **a** the LORD. NIH
33:29 shall they know that I **a** the LORD, when I NIH
34:10 Behold, I **a** against the shepherds; and I will NIH
34:27 and shall know that I **a** the LORD, NIH
34:30 that I the LORD their God **a** with them, NIH
34:31 *are* men, *and* I **a** your God, saith the Lord NIH
35: 3 I **a** against thee, and I will stretch out mine NIH
35: 4 and thou shalt know that I **a** the LORD. NIH
35: 9 and ye shall know that I **a** the LORD. NIH
35:12 thou shalt know that I **a** the LORD, *and* NIH
35:15 and they shall know that I **a** the LORD. NIH
36: 9 I **a** for you, and I will turn unto you, and NIH
36:11 and ye shall know that I **a** the LORD. NIH
36:23 the heathen shall know that I **a** the LORD, NIH
36:38 and they shall know that I **a** the LORD. NIH
37: 6 and ye shall know that I **a** the LORD. NIH
37:13 ye shall know that I **a** the LORD, when I NIH
38: 3 Behold, I **a** against thee, O Gog, the chief NIH
38:23 and they shall know that I **a** the LORD. NIH
39: 1 Behold, I **a** against thee, O Gog, the chief NIH
39: 6 and they shall know that I **a** the LORD. NIH
39: 7 the heathen shall know that I **a** the LORD, NIH
39:22 So the house of Israel shall know that I **a** NIH
39:27 a sanctified in them in the sight of many NIH
39:28 shall they know that I **a** the LORD their NIH
44:28 I **a** their inheritance: and ye shall give them NIH
44:28 no possession in Israel: I **a** their possession. NIH
Da 9:22 I **a** now come forth to give thee skill and NIH
9:23 I **a** come to shew *thee;* for thou *art* greatly NIH
10:11 for unto thee **a** I now sent. And when he had NIH
10:12 were heard, and I **a** come for thy words. NIH
10:14 Now I **a** come to make thee understand NIH
10:20 when I **a** gone forth, lo, the prince of Grecia NIH
Hos 2: 2 she *is* not my wife, neither **a** I her husband: NIH
11: 9 for I **a** God, and not man; the Holy One in NIH
12: 8 Ephraim said, Yet I **a** become rich, I have NIH
12: 9 I *that* **a** the LORD thy God from the land NIH
13: 4 Yet I **a** the LORD thy God from the land NIH
14: 8 I **a** like a green fir tree. From me is thy fruit NIH
Joel 2:27 ye shall know that I **a** in the midst of Israel, NIH
2:27 *that* I **a** the LORD your God, and NIH
3:10 into spears: let the weak say, I **a** strong. NIH
3:17 So shall ye know that I **a** the LORD your NIH
Am 2:13 Behold, I **a** pressed under you, as a cart is NIH
Jnh 1: 9 he said unto them, I **a** a Hebrew; and I fear NIH
2: 4 I said, I **a** cast out of thy sight; yet I will NIH
Mic 3: 8 truly I **a** full *of* power by the spirit of NIH
7: 1 for I **a** as when they have gathered 1961
Na 2:13 Behold, I **a** against thee, saith the LORD NIH
3: 5 Behold, I **a** against thee, saith the LORD NIH
Hab 2: 1 and what I shall answer when I **a** reproved. NIH
Zep 2:15 her heart, I **a**, and *there is* none beside me: NIH
Hag 1:13 I **a** with you, saith the LORD. NIH
2: 4 for I **a** with you, saith the LORD of hosts: NIH
Zec 1:14 I **a** jealous for Jerusalem and for Zion *with* a NIH
1:15 I **a** very sore displeased with the heathen NIH
1:16 I **a** returned to Jerusalem with mercies: NIH
8: 3 I **a** returned unto Zion, and will dwell in NIH
10: 6 for I **a** the LORD their God, and will hear NIH
11: 5 Blessed *be* the LORD; for I **a** rich: NIH
13: 5 he shall say, I **a** no prophet, I *am* a NIH
13: 5 I *am* no prophet, I **a** a husbandman; NIH
Mal 1:14 Lord a corrupt *thing:* for I **a** a great King, NIH
3: 6 For I **a** the LORD, I change not; therefore NIH
Mt 3:11 than I, whose shoes I **a** not worthy to bear: *1510*
3:17 my beloved Son, in whom I **a** well pleased. NIG
5:17 Think not that I **a** come to destroy the law, NIG
5:17 I **a** not come to destroy, but to fulfil. NIG
8: 8 I **a** not worthy that thou shouldest come *1510*
8: 9 For I **a** a man under authority, *1510*
9:13 for I **a** not come to call *the* righteous, but NIG
9:28 Believe ye that I **a** able to do this? NIG
10:34 Think not that I **a** come to send peace on NIG
10:35 For I **a** come to set a man at variance NIG
11:29 of me; for I **a** meek and lowly in heart: *1510*
15:24 I **a** not sent but unto the lost sheep of NIG
16:13 Whom do men say that I the Son of man **a**? *1510*
16:15 saith unto them, But whom say ye that I **a**? *1510*
17: 5 my beloved Son, in whom I **a** well pleased; NIG
18:20 in my name, there **a** I in the midst of them. *1510*
20:15 Is thine eye evil, because I **a** good? *1510*
20:22 to be baptized *with* the baptism that I **a** NIG
20:23 be baptized *with* the baptism that I **a** NIG
22:32 I **a** the God of Abraham, and the God of *1510*
24: 5 shall come in my name, saying, I **a** Christ; *1510*
26:32 But after I **a** risen *again,* I will go before NIG
26:61 I **a** able to destroy the temple of God, and NIG
Mt 27:24 I **a** innocent of the blood of this just *1510*
27:43 have him: for he said, I **a** the Son of God. *1510*
28:20 and lo, I **a** with you alway, *even* unto *1510*
Mk 1: 7 the latchet of whose shoes I **a** not worthy to *1510*
1:11 my beloved Son, in whom I **a** well pleased. NIG
8:27 unto them, Whom do men say that I **a**? *1510*
8:29 saith unto them, But whom say ye that I **a**? *1510*
10:38 be baptized *with* the baptism that I **a** NIG
10:39 *with* the baptism that I **a** baptized *withal* NIG
12:26 I **a** the God of Abraham, and the God of NIG
13: 6 saying, I **a** *Christ;* and shall deceive many. *1510*
14:28 But after that I **a** risen, I will go before you NIG
14:62 And Jesus said, I **a**: and ye shall see *1510*
Lk 1:18 for I **a** an old man, and my wife well *1510*
1:19 I **a** Gabriel, that stand in the presence of *1510*
1:19 and **a** sent to speak unto thee, and to shew NIG
3:16 the latchet of whose shoes I **a** not worthy to *1510*
3:22 my beloved Son; in thee I **a** well pleased. NIG
4:43 to other cities also: for therefore **a** I sent. NIG
5: 8 from me; for I **a** a sinful man, O Lord. *1510*
7: 6 for I **a** not worthy that thou shouldest enter *1510*
7: 8 For I also **a** a man set under authority, *1510*
9:18 saying, Whom say the people that I **a**? *1510*
9:20 said unto them, But whom say ye that I **a**? *1510*
12:49 I **a** come to send fire on the earth; and NIG
12:50 how **a** I straitened till it be accomplished! NIG
12:51 Suppose ye that I **a** come to give peace on NIG
15:19 And **a** no more worthy to be called thy *1510*
15:21 and **a** no more worthy to be called thy son. *1510*
16: 3 I cannot dig; to beg I **a** ashamed. NIG
16: 4 I **a** resolved what to do, that, when I am put NIG
16: 4 that, when I **a** put out of the stewardship, NIG
16:24 my tongue; for I **a** tormented in this flame. NIG
18:11 that I **a** not as other men *are,* extortioners, *1510*
21: 8 I **a** *Christ;* and the time draweth near: *1510*
22:27 but I **a** among you as he that serveth. *1510*
22:33 Lord, I **a** ready to go with thee, both into *1510*
22:58 also of them. And Peter said, Man, I **a** not. *1510*
22:70 And he said unto them, Ye say that I **a**. *1510*
Jn 1:20 but confessed, I **a** not the Christ. *1510*
1:21 And he saith, I **a** not. Art thou *that* prophet? *1510*
1:23 I **a** the voice of one crying in NIG
1:27 whose shoe's latchet I **a** not worthy to *1510*
1:31 therefore **a** I come baptizing with water. NIG
3:28 I **a** not the Christ, but that I am sent before *1510*
3:28 not the Christ, but that I **a** sent before him. *1510*
4: 9 drink of me, which **a** a woman of Samaria? *1510*
4:26 saith unto her, I that speak unto thee **a** *he.* *1510*
5: 7 but while I **a** coming, another steppeth NIG
5:43 I **a** come in my Father's name, and NIG
6:35 Jesus said unto them, I **a** the bread of life: *1510*
6:41 I **a** the bread which came down from *1510*
6:48 I **a** *that* bread of life. *1510*
6:51 I **a** the living bread which came down from *1510*
7:28 both know me, and ye know whence I **a**: *1510*
7:28 and I **a** not come of myself, but he that sent NIG
7:29 for I **a** from him, and he hath sent me. *1510*
7:33 Yet a little while **a** I with you, and *then* I go *1510*
7:34 and shall not find *me:* and where I **a**, *1510*
7:36 and shall not find *me:* and where I **a**, *1510*
8:12 saying, I **a** the light of the world: *1510*
8:16 for I **a** not alone, but I and the Father that *1510*
8:18 I **a** *one* that bear witness of myself, and *1510*
8:23 Ye are from beneath; I **a** from above: *1510*
8:23 ye are of this world; I **a** not of this world. *1510*
8:24 for if ye believe not that I **a** *he,* ye shall die *1510*
8:28 then shall ye know that I **a** *he,* and *that* I do *1510*
8:58 I say unto you, Before Abraham was, I **a**. *1510*
9: 5 As long as I **a** in the world, I am the light of *1510*
9: 5 I am in the world, I **a** the light of the world. *1510*
9: 9 *said,* He is like him: *but* he said, I **a** *he.* *1510*
9:39 For judgment I **a** come into this world, NIG
10: 7 I say unto you, I **a** the door of the sheep. *1510*
10: 9 I **a** the door: by me if any *man* enter in, *1510*
10:10 I **a** come that they might have life, and NIG
10:11 I **a** the good shepherd: the good shepherd *1510*
10:14 I **a** the good shepherd, and know my *sheep,* *1510*
10:14 and know my *sheep,* and **a** known of mine. NIG
10:36 because I said, I **a** the Son of God? *1510*
11:15 And I **a** glad for your sakes that I was not NIG
11:25 unto her, I **a** the resurrection, and the life: *1510*
12:26 and where I **a**, there shall also my servant *1510*
12:46 I **a** come a light into the world, NIG
13:13 and Lord: and ye say well; for *so* I **a**. *1510*
13:19 is come to pass, ye may believe that I **a** *he.* *1510*
13:33 yet a little while I **a** with you. *1510*
14: 3 that where I **a**, *there* ye may be also. *1510*
14: 6 I **a** the way, the truth, and the life: *1510*
14:10 Believest thou not that I **a** in the Father, *1510*
14:11 Believe me that I **a** in the Father, and NIG
14:20 At that day ye shall know that I **a** in my NIG
15: 1 I **a** the true vine, and my Father is *1510*
15: 5 I **a** the vine, ye *are* the branches: He that *1510*
16:28 from the Father, and **a** come into the world: NIG
16:32 and *yet* I **a** not alone, because the Father is *1510*
17:10 thine are mine; and I **a** glorified in them. NIG
17:11 And *now* I **a** no more in the world, but *1510*
17:14 of the world, even as I **a** not of the world. *1510*
17:16 of the world, even as I **a** not of the world. *1510*
17:24 thou hast given me, be with me where I **a**; *1510*
18: 5 I **a** *he.* And Judas also, which betrayed him, *1510*
18: 6 said unto them, I **a** *he,* they went backward, *1510*
18: 8 I have told you that I **a** *he:* if therefore *1510*
18:17 of this man's disciples? He saith, I **a** not. *1510*
18:25 He denied *it,* and said, I **a** not. *1510*
18:35 Pilate answered, **A** I a Jew? Thine own *1510*
18:37 Jesus answered, Thou sayest that I **a** a king. *1510*
19:21 but that he said, I **a** King of the Jews. *1510*
20:17 for I **a** not yet ascended to my Father: NIG
Ac 7:32 *Saying,* I **a** the God of thy fathers, the God NIG
7:34 and **a** come down to deliver them. NIG
9: 5 Lord said, I **a** Jesus whom thou persecutest: *1510*
9:10 And he said, Behold, I **a** *here,* Lord. NIG
10:21 and said, Behold, I **a** he whom ye seek: *1510*
10:26 saying, Stand up; I myself also **a** a man. *1510*

Ac 13:25 *his* course, he said, Whom think ye that I **a**? *1510*
13:25 I **a** not *he.* But behold, there cometh *one* *1510*
13:25 whose shoes of *his* feet I **a** not worthy to *1510*
18: 6 blood *be* upon your own heads; I **a** clean: NIG
18:10 For I **a** with thee, and no *man* shall set on *1510*
20:26 that I **a** pure from the blood of all *men.* NIG
21:13 for I **a** ready not to be bound only, but *2192*
21:39 I **a** a man *which am* a Jew of Tarsus, *1510*
21:39 I am a man *which* **a** a Jew of Tarsus, NIG
22: 3 I **a** verily a man *which am* a Jew, born in *1510*
22: 3 I am verily a man *which* **a** a Jew, born in NIG
22: 8 And he said unto me, I **a** Jesus of Nazareth, *1510*
23: 6 Men *and* brethren, I **a** a Pharisee, the son of *1510*
23: 6 resurrection of the dead I **a** called in NIG
24:21 Touching the resurrection of the dead I **a** NIG
26: 2 *the things* whereof I **a** accused of the Jews: NIG
26: 6 **a** judged for the hope of the promise made NIG
26: 7 king Agrippa, I **a** accused of the Jews. NIG
26:15 he said, I **a** Jesus whom thou persecutest. *1510*
26:25 But he said, I **a** not mad, most noble Festus; NIG
26:26 for I **a** persuaded that none of these *things* NIG
26:29 both almost, and altogether such as I **a**, *1510*
27:23 angel of God, whose I **a**, and whom I serve, *1510*
28:20 that for the hope of Israel I **a** bound with NIG
Ro 1:14 I **a** debtor both to the Greeks, and to *1510*
1:15 I **a** ready to preach the gospel to you that NIG
1:16 For I **a** not ashamed of the gospel of Christ: NIG
3: 7 why yet **a** I also judged as a sinner? NIG
7:14 is spiritual: but I **a** carnal, sold under sin. *1510*
7:24 O wretched man that I **a**! who shall deliver NIG
8:38 For I **a** persuaded, that neither death, NIG
11: 1 For I also **a** an Israelite, of the seed of *1510*
11: 3 and I **a** left alone, and they seek my life. NIG
11:13 inasmuch as I **a** the apostle of the Gentiles, *1510*
14:14 I know, and **a** persuaded by the Lord Jesus, NIG
15:14 And I myself also **a** persuaded of you, NIG
15:29 And I **a** sure that, when I come unto you, NIG
16:19 is come abroad unto all *men.* I **a** glad NIG
1Co 1:12 that every one of you saith, I **a** of Paul; *1510*
3: 4 For while one saith, I **a** of Paul; and *1510*
3: 4 I am of Paul; and another, I *a* of Apollos; NIG
4: 4 by myself; yet **a** I not hereby justified: NIG
9: 1 **A** I not an apostle? am I not free? have I *1510*
9: 1 **a** I not free? have I not seen Jesus Christ *1510*
9: 2 unto others, yet doubtless I **a** to you: *1510*
9:22 I **a** made all *things* to all *men,* that I might NIG
10:30 why **a** I evil spoken of for *that for* which I NIG
11: 1 followers of me, even as I also *a* of Christ. NIG
12:15 the foot shall say, Because I **a** not the hand, *1510*
12:15 I am not the hand, I **a** not of the body; *1510*
12:16 Because I **a** not the eye, I am not of *1510*
12:16 I am not the eye, I **a** not of the body; *1510*
13: 1 I **a** become *as* sounding brass, or a tinkling NIG
13: 2 and have no charity, I **a** nothing. *1510*
13:12 then shall I know even as also I **a** known. NIG
15: 9 For I **a** the least of the apostles, that am not *1510*
15: 9 that **a** not meet to be called an apostle, *1510*
15:10 But by the grace of God I **a** what I am: and *1510*
15:10 But by the grace of God I am what I **a**: and *1510*
16:17 I **a** glad of the coming of Stephanas and NIG
2Co 7: 4 I **a** filled with comfort, I am exceeding NIG
7: 4 I **a** exceeding joyful in all our tribulation. NIG
7:14 any *thing* to him of you, I **a** not ashamed; NIG
10: 1 who in presence *a* base among you, but NIG
10: 1 but being absent **a** bold toward you: NIG
10: 2 bold when I **a** present with *that* confidence, NIG
11: 2 For I **a** jealous over you with godly NIG
11:21 is bold, (I speak foolishly,) I **a** bold also. NIG
11:22 so **a** I. Are they Israelites? so *am* I. Are they NIG
11:22 so **a** I. Are they the seed of Abraham? so *am* NIG
11:22 *am* I. Are they the seed of Abraham? so *a* I. NIG
11:23 (I speak as a fool) I *a* more; in labours more NIG
11:29 Who is weak, and I **a** not weak? who is NIG
12:10 for when I **a** weak, then am I strong. NIG
12:10 for when I am weak, then **a** I strong. *1510*
12:11 I **a** become a fool in glorying; ye have NIG
12:11 for *in* nothing **a** I behind the very chiefest NIG
12:14 the third *time* I **a** ready to come to you; *2192*
13: 1 This *is* the third *time* I **a** coming to you. NIG
Gal 2:19 For I through the law **a** dead to the law, NIG
2:20 I **a** crucified with Christ: nevertheless I live; NIG
4:11 I **a** afraid of you, lest I have bestowed upon NIG
4:12 be as I *a*; for I *am* as ye *are:* ye have not NIG
4:12 be as I *am;* for I *a* as ye *are:* ye have not NIG
4:16 **A** I therefore become your enemy, because NIG
4:18 and not only when I **a** present with you. NIG
Eph 3: 8 *who* **a** less than the least of all saints, NIG
6:20 For which I **a** an ambassador in bonds: NIG
Php 1:17 knowing that I **a** set for the defence of NIG
1:23 For I **a** in a strait betwixt two, having a NIG
3:12 which also I **a** apprehended of Christ Jesus. NIG
4:11 for I have learned, in whatsoever *state* I **a**, *1510*
4:12 in all *things* I **a** instructed both to be full NIG
4:18 I **a** full, having received of Epaphroditus NIG
Col 1:23 whereof I Paul **a** made a minister; NIG
1:25 Whereof I **a** made a minister, according to NIG
2: 5 yet **a** I with you in the spirit, joying and *1510*
4: 3 of Christ, for which I **a** also in bonds: NIG
1Ti 1:15 world to save sinners; of whom I **a** chief. *1510*
2: 7 Whereunto I **a** ordained a preacher, and NIG
2Ti 1: 5 and I **a** persuaded that in thee also. NIG
1:11 Whereunto I **a** appointed a preacher, and NIG
1:12 these *things:* nevertheless I **a** not ashamed: NIG
1:12 I **a** persuaded that he is able to keep that NIG
4: 6 For I **a** now ready to be offered, and NIG
Jas 1:13 say when he is tempted, I **a** tempted of God: NIG
1Pe 1:16 it is written, Be ye holy; for I **a** holy. *1510*
5: 1 who **a** also an elder, and a witness of NIG
2Pe 1:13 it meet, as long as I **a** in this tabernacle, *1510*
1:17 my beloved Son, in whom I **a** well pleased. NIG
Rev 1: 8 I **a** Alpha and Omega, the beginning and *1510*
1: 9 who also **a** your brother, and companion in NIG
1:11 Saying, I **a** Alpha and Omega, the first and *1510*
1:17 unto me, Fear not; I **a** the first and the last: *1510*
1:18 I **a** he that liveth, and was dead; and behold, NIG
Rev 1:18 and behold, I **a** alive for evermore, Amen; *1510*
2:23 all the churches shall know that I **a** he *1510*
3:17 I **a** rich, and increased with goods, and *1510*
3:21 **a** set down with my Father in his throne. NIG
18: 7 and **a** no widow, and shall see no sorrow. *1510*
19:10 I **a** thy fellowservant, and of thy brethren *1510*
21: 6 I **a** Alpha and Omega, the beginning and *1510*
22: 9 for I **a** thy fellowservant, and of thy *1510*
22:13 I **a** Alpha and Omega, the beginning and *1510*
22:16 I **a** the root and the offspring of David, *and* *1510*

AMAD (1)
Jos 19:26 Alammelech, and **A**, and Misheal; and 6008

AMAL (1)
1Ch 7:35 Zophah, and Imna, and Shelesh, and **A**. 6000

AMALEK (24) [AMALEKITE, AMALEKITES]
Ge 36:12 Esau's son; and she bare to Eliphaz **A**: 6002
36:16 Duke Korah, duke Gatam, *and* duke **A**: 6002
Ex 17: 8 came **A**, and fought with Israel in 6002
17: 9 us out men, and go out, fight with **A**: 6002
17:10 Moses had said to him, and fought with **A**: 6002
17:11 when he let down his hand, **A** prevailed. 6002
17:13 Joshua discomfited **A** and his people with 6002
17:14 the remembrance of **A** from under heaven. 6002
17:16 war with **A** from generation *to* generation. 6002
Nu 24:20 when he looked on **A**, he took up his 6002
24:20 and said, **A** *was* the first of the nations; 6002
Dt 25:17 Remember what **A** did unto thee by 6002
25:19 the remembrance of **A** from under heaven; 6002
Jdg 3:13 unto him the children of Ammon and **A**, 6002
5:14 *was there* a root of them against **A**; 6002
1Sa 15: 2 I remember *that* which **A** did to Israel, 6002
15: 3 Now go and smite **A**, and utterly destroy all 6002
15: 5 Saul came to a city of **A**, and laid wait in 6002
15:20 have brought Agag the king of **A**, and 6002
28:18 nor executedst his fierce wrath upon **A**, 6002
2Sa 8:12 of **A**, and of the spoil of Hadadezer, son of 6002
1Ch 1:36 and Gatam, Kenaz, and Timna, and **A**. 6002
18:11 and from the Philistines, and from **A**. 6002
Ps 83: 7 Gebal, and Ammon, and **A**; the Philistines 6002

AMALEKITE (3) [AMALEK]
1Sa 30:13 young man of Egypt, servant to an **A**; 376+6003
2Sa 1: 8 *art* thou? And I answered him, I *am* an **A**. 6003
1:13 I *am* the son of a stranger, an **A**. 6003

AMALEKITES (24) [AMALEK]
Ge 14: 7 smote all the country of the **A**, and also 6003
Nu 13:29 The **A** dwell in the land of the south: and 6003
14:25 (Now the **A** and the Canaanites dwelt in 6003
14:43 For the **A** and the Canaanites *are* there 6003
14:45 the **A** came down, and the Canaanites 6003
Jdg 6: 3 and the **A**, and the children of the east, 6002
6:33 all the Midianites and the **A** and 6002
7:12 the Midianites and the **A** and all 6002
10:12 the **A**, and the Maonites, did oppress you; 6002
12:15 the land of Ephraim, in the mount of the **A**. 6003
1Sa 14:48 smote the **A**, and delivered Israel out of 6002
15: 6 depart, get you down from among the **A**, 6003
15: 6 So the Kenites departed from among the **A**. 6002
15: 7 Saul smote the **A** from Havilah *until* thou 6002
15: 8 he took Agag the king of the **A** alive, and 6002
15:15 They have brought them from the **A**: 6003
15:18 Go and utterly destroy the sinners the **A**, 6002
15:20 and have utterly destroyed the **A**. 6002
15:32 you hither to me Agag the king of the **A**. 6002
27: 8 the Geshurites, and the Gezrites, and the **A**: 6003
30: 1 that the **A** had invaded the south, and 6003
30:18 David recovered all that the **A** had carried 6002
2Sa 1: 1 was returned from the slaughter of the **A**, 6002
1Ch 4:43 they smote the rest of the **A** that were 6002

AMAM (1)
Jos 15:26 **A**, and Shema, and Moladah, 538

AMANA (1)
SS 4: 8 look from the top of **A**, from the top of 549

AMARIAH (16)
1Ch 6: 7 Meraioth begat **A**, and Amariah begat 568
6: 7 begat Amariah, and **A** begat Ahitub, 568
6:11 Azariah begat **A**, and Amariah begat Ahitub, 568
6:11 Azariah begat Amariah, and **A** begat Ahitub, 568
6:52 Meraioth his son, **A** his son, Ahitub his son, 568
23:19 Jeriah the first, **A** the second, Jahaziel 568
24:23 the sons *of Hebron;* Jeriah *the first,* **A** 568
2Ch 19:11 **A** the chief priest *is* over you in all matters 568
31:15 Jeshua, and Shemaiah, **A**, and Shecaniah, 568
Ezr 7: 3 The son of **A**, the son of Azariah, the son of 568
10:42 Shallum, **A**, *and* Joseph. 568
Ne 10: 3 Pashur, **A**, Malchijah, 568
11: 4 the son of Zechariah, the son of **A**, the son of 568
12: 2 **A**, Malluch, Hattush, 568
12:13 Of Ezra, Meshullam; of **A**, Jehohanan; 568
Zep 1: 1 the son of **A**, the son of Hizkiah, 568

AMASA (16)
2Sa 17:25 Absalom made **A** captain of the host 6021
17:25 which **A** *was* a man's son, whose name *was* 6021
19:13 say ye to **A**, *Art* thou not *of* my bone, and 6021
20: 4 said the king to **A**, Assemble me the men of 6021
20: 5 So **A** went to assemble *the men of* Judah: 6021
20: 8 which *is* in Gibeon, **A** went before them. 6021
20: 9 Joab said to **A**, *Art* thou in health, 6021
20: 9 Joab took **A** by the beard with the right 6021
20:10 **A** took no heed to the sword that *was* in 6021
20:12 **A** wallowed in blood in the midst of 6021
20:12 he removed **A** out of the highway *into* 6021
1Ki 2: 5 unto **A** the son of Jether, whom he slew, 6021
2:32 the host of Israel, and **A** the son of Jether, 6021
1Ch 2:17 Abigail bare **A**: and the father of Amasa 6021
2:17 the father of **A** *was* Jether the Ishmeelite. 6021
2Ch 28:12 son of Shallum, and **A** the son of Hadlai, 6021

AMASAI (5)
1Ch 6:25 And the sons of Elkanah; **A**, and Ahimoth. 6022
6:35 the son of Mahath, the son of **A**, 6022
12:18 the spirit came upon **A**, *who was* chief of 6022
15:24 **A**, and Zechariah, and Benaiah, and 6022
2Ch 29:12 Mahath the son of **A**, and Joel the son of 6022

AMASHAI (1)
Ne 11:13 **A** the son of Azareel, the son of Ahasai, 6023

AMASHSAI See AMASHAI

AMASIAH (1)
2Ch 17:16 next him *was* **A** the son of Zichri, 6007

AMAZED (21) [AMAZEMENT]
Ex 15:15 the dukes of Edom shall be **a**; the mighty 926
Jdg 20:41 turned *again,* the men of Benjamin were **a**: 926
Job 32:15 They were **a**, they answered no more: 2865
Isa 13: 8 they shall be **a** one at another; their faces 8539
Eze 32:10 I will **make** many people **a** at thee, and 8074
Mt 12:23 And all the people were **a**, and said, Is this *1839*
19:25 disciples heard *it,* they were exceedingly **a**, *1605*
Mk 1:27 And they were all **a**, insomuch that *they* *2284*
2:12 insomuch that *they* were all **a**, and *1839*
6:51 they were sore **a** in themselves beyond *1839*
9:15 were **greatly a**, and running to *him* saluted *1568*
10:32 and they were **a**; and as they followed, *2284*
14:33 and began to be **sore a**, and to be very *1568*
16: 8 for they trembled and were **a**: *1611*
Lk 2:48 And when they saw him, they were **a**: and *1605*
4:36 And they were all **a**, and spake among *2285*
5:26 And they were all **a**, *1611+2983*
9:43 And they were all **a** at the mighty power of *1605*
Ac 2: 7 And they were all **a** and marvelled, *1839*
2:12 And they were all **a**, and were in doubt, *1839*
9:21 But all that heard *him* were **a**, and said; *1839*

AMAZEMENT (2) [AMAZED]
Ac 3:10 and **a** at that which had happened unto him. *1611*
1Pe 3: 6 as ye do well, and are not afraid *with* any **a**. *4423*

AMAZIAH (40) [OZIAS]
2Ki 12:21 of David: and **A** his son reigned in his stead. 558
13:12 his might where*with* he fought against **A** 558
14: 1 reigned **A** the son of Joash king of Judah. 558
14: 8 **A** sent messengers to Jehoash, the son of 558
14: 9 Jehoash the king of Israel sent to **A** king of 558
14:11 **A** would not hear. Therefore Jehoash king of 558
14:11 **A** king of Judah looked one another *in* 558
14:13 Jehoash king of Israel took **A** king of Judah, 558
14:15 and how he fought with **A** king of Judah, 558
14:17 **A** the son of Joash king of Judah lived after 558
14:18 the rest of the acts of **A**, *are* they not written 558
14:21 and made him king instead of his father **A**. 558
14:23 In the fifteenth year of **A** the son of Joash 558
15: 1 Azariah son of **A** king of Judah to reign. 558
15: 3 according to all that his father **A** had done; 558
1Ch 3:12 **A** his son, Azariah his son, Jotham his son, 558
4:34 and Jamlech, and Joshah the son of **A**, 558
6:45 the son of **A**, the son of Hilkiah, 558
2Ch 24:27 And **A** his son reigned in his stead. 558
25: 1 **A** *was* twenty and five years old *when* he 558
25: 5 Moreover **A** gathered Judah together, and 558
25: 9 **A** said to the man of God, But what *shall we* 558
25:10 **A** separated them, to wit, the army that was 558
25:11 **A** strengthened himself, and led forth his 558
25:13 the soldiers of the army which **A** sent back, 558
25:14 after that **A** was come from the slaughter of 558
25:15 anger of the LORD was kindled against **A**, 558
25:17 **A** king of Judah took advice, and sent to 558
25:18 Joash king of Israel sent to **A** king of Judah, 558
25:20 **A** would not hear; for it *came* of God, that *he* 558
25:21 *both* he and **A** king of Judah, 558
25:23 Joash the king of Israel took **A** king of 558
25:25 **A** the son of Joash king of Judah lived after 558
25:26 Now the rest of the acts of **A**, first and last, 558
25:27 Now after the time that **A** did turn away 558
26: 1 made him king in the room of his father **A**. 558
26: 4 according to all that his father **A** did. 558
Am 7:10 **A** *the* priest of Beth-el sent to Jeroboam king 558
7:12 Also **A** said unto Amos, O thou seer, go, 558
7:14 and said to **A**, I *was* no prophet, 558

AMBASSADOR (4) [AMBASSADORS, AMBASSAGE]
Pr 13:17 into mischief: but a faithful **a** *is* health. 6735
Jer 49:14 an **a** *is* sent unto the heathen, 6735
Ob 1: 1 an **a** is sent among the heathen, Arise ye, 6735
Eph 6:20 For which I am an **a** in bonds: that therein I *4243*

AMBASSADORS (8) [AMBASSADOR]
Jos 9: 4 went and **made as if** they had been **a**, and 6737
2Ch 32:31 Howbeit in *the business of* the **a** of 3887
35:21 he sent **a** to him, saying, What have I to do 4397
Isa 18: 2 That sendeth **a** by the sea, even in vessels 6735
30: 4 were at Zoan, and his **a** came to Hanes. 4397
33: 7 the **a** of peace shall weep bitterly. 4397
Eze 17:15 he rebelled against him in sending his **a** 4397
2Co 5:20 *Now* then we are **a** for Christ, as though *4243*

AMBASSAGE (1) [AMBASSADOR]
Lk 14:32 he sendeth an **a**, and desireth conditions of *4242*

AMBER (3)
Eze 1: 4 out of the midst thereof as the colour of **a**, 2830
1:27 I saw as the colour of **a**, as the appearance 2830
8: 2 of brightness, as the colour of **a**. 2830

AMBUSH (7) [AMBUSHES, AMBUSHMENT, AMBUSHMENTS]
Jos 8: 2 lay thee an **a** for the city behind it. 693
8: 7 ye shall rise up from the **a**, and seize upon 693
8: 9 they went to **lie in a**, and abode between 3993
8:12 set them to **lie in a** between Beth-el and Ai, 693
8:14 he wist not that *there were* **liers in a** against 693
8:19 the **a** arose quickly out of their place, and 693
8:21 all Israel saw that the **a** had taken the city, 693

AMBUSHES (1) [AMBUSH]
Jer 51:12 set up the watchmen, prepare the **a**: 693

AMBUSHMENT (2) [AMBUSH]
2Ch 13:13 Jeroboam caused an **a** to come about 3993
13:13 before Judah, and the **a** *was* behind them. 3993

AMBUSHMENTS (1) [AMBUSH]
2Ch 20:22 the LORD set **a** against the children of 693

AMEN (78)
Nu 5:22 to rot: And the woman shall say, **A**, amen. 543
5:22 to rot: And the woman shall say, Amen, **a**. 543
Dt 27:15 And all the people shall answer and say, **A**. 543
27:16 his mother. And all the people shall say, **A**. 543
27:17 And all the people shall say, **A**. 543
27:18 of the way. And all the people shall say, **A**. 543
27:19 and widow. And all the people shall say, **A**. 543
27:20 And all the people shall say, **A**. 543
27:21 *of* beast. And all the people shall say, **A**. 543
27:22 his mother. And all the people shall say, **A**. 543
27:23 in law. And all the people shall say, **A**. 543
27:24 And all the people shall say, **A**. 543
27:25 And all the people shall say, **A**. 543
27:26 to do them. And all the people shall say, **A**. 543
1Ki 1:36 of Jehoiada answered the king, and said, **A**: 543
1Ch 16:36 the people said, **A**, and praised the LORD. 543
Ne 5:13 **A**, and praised the LORD. 543
8: 6 **A**, Amen, with lifting up their hands: 543
8: 6 Amen, **A**, with lifting up their hands: 543
Ps 41:13 and to everlasting. **A**, and Amen. 543
41:13 and to everlasting. Amen, and **A**. 543
72:19 earth be filled *with* his glory; **A**, and Amen. 543
72:19 earth be filled *with* his glory; Amen, and **A**. 543
89:52 *be* the LORD for evermore. **A**, and Amen. 543
89:52 *be* the LORD for evermore. Amen, and **A**. 543
106:48 let all the people say, **A**. Praise ye 543
Jer 28: 6 Even the prophet Jeremiah said, **A**: 543
Mt 6:13 and the power, and the glory, for ever. **A**. *281*
28:20 *even* unto the end of the world. **A**. *281*
Mk 16:20 the word with signs following. **A**. *281*
Lk 24:53 in the temple, praising and blessing God. **A**. *281*
Jn 21:25 contain the books that should be written. **A**. *281*
Ro 1:25 than the Creator, who is blessed for ever. **A**. *281*
9: 5 who is over all, God blessed for ever. **A**. *281*
11:36 *are* all *things*: to whom *be* glory for ever. **A**. *281*
15:33 Now the God of peace *be* with you all. **A**. *281*
16:20 of our Lord Jesus Christ *be* with you. **A**. *281*
16:24 of our Lord Jesus Christ *be* with you all. **A**. *281*
16:27 *be* glory through Jesus Christ for ever. **A**. *281*
1Co 14:16 the unlearned say **A** at thy giving of thanks, *281*
16:24 My love *be* with you all in Christ Jesus. **A**. *281*
2Co 1:20 and in him **A**, unto the glory of God by us. *281*
13:14 of the Holy Ghost, *be* with you all. **A**. *281*
Gal 1: 5 To whom *be* glory for ever and ever. **A**. *281*
6:18 our Lord Jesus Christ *be* with your spirit. **A**. *281*
Eph 3:21 throughout all ages, world without end. **A**. *281*
6:24 love our Lord Jesus Christ in sincerity. **A**. *281*
Php 4:20 our Father *be* glory for ever and ever. **A**. *281*
4:23 of our Lord Jesus Christ *be* with you all. **A**. *281*
Col 4:18 Remember my bonds. Grace *be* with you. **A**. *281*
1Th 5:28 of our Lord Jesus Christ *be* with you. **A**. *281*
2Th 3:18 of our Lord Jesus Christ *be* with you all. **A**. *281*
1Ti 1:17 *be* honour and glory for ever and ever. **A**. *281*
6:16 whom *be* honour and power everlasting. **A**. *281*
6:21 concerning the faith. Grace *be* with thee. **A**. *281*
2Ti 4:18 to whom *be* glory for ever and ever. **A**. *281*
4:22 *be* with thy spirit. Grace *be* with you. **A**. *281*
Tit 3:15 love us in the faith. Grace *be* with you all. **A**. *281*
Phm 1:25 our Lord Jesus Christ *be* with your spirit. **A**. *281*
Heb 13:21 to whom *be* glory for ever and ever. **A**. *281*
13:25 Grace *be* with you all. **A**. *281*
1Pe 4:11 be praise and dominion for ever and ever. **A**. *281*
5:11 *be* glory and dominion for ever and ever. **A**. *281*
5:14 *be* with you all that are in Christ Jesus. **A**. *281*
2Pe 3:18 To him *be* glory both now and for ever. **A**. *281*
1Jn 5:21 keep yourselves from idols. **A**. *281*
2Jn 1:13 The children of thy elect sister greet thee. **A**. *281*
Jude 1:25 dominion and power, both now and ever. **A**. *281*
Rev 1: 6 *be* glory and dominion for ever and ever. **A**. *281*
1: 7 earth shall wail because of him. Even so, **A**. *281*
1:18 and behold, I am alive for evermore, **A**; and *281*
3:14 These *things* saith the **A**, the faithful and *281*
5:14 And the four beasts said, **A**. And the four *281*
7:12 Saying, **A**: Blessing, and glory, and wisdom, *281*
7:12 might, *be* unto our God for ever and ever. **A**. *281*
19: 4 God that sat on the throne, saying, **A**; *281*
22:20 come quickly. **A**. Even so, come, Lord Jesus. *281*
22:21 of our Lord Jesus Christ *be* with you all. **A**. *281*

AMEND (5) [AMENDS]
Jer 7: 3 **A** your ways and your doings, and I will 3190
7: 5 For if you **throughly a** your ways 3190+3190
26:13 Therefore now **a** your ways and 3190
35:15 **a** your doings, and go not after other gods 3190
Jn 4:52 them the hour when he **began to a**. *2192+2866*

AMENDS (1) [AMEND]
Lev 5:16 he shall **make a** for the harm that he hath 7999

AMERCE (1)
Dt 22:19 they shall **a** him in an hundred *shekels* of 6064

AMETHYST (3)
Ex 28:19 the third row a ligure, an agate, and an **a**. 306
39:12 the third row, a ligure, an agate, and an **a**. 306
Rev 21:20 the eleventh, a jacinth; the twelfth, an **a**. *271*

AMI (1)
Ezr 2:57 of Pochereth of Zebaim, the children of **A**. 532

AMIABLE (1)
Ps 84: 1 How **a** *are* thy tabernacles, O LORD of 3039

AMINADAB (3)
Mt 1: 4 And Aram begat **A**; and Aminadab begat *284*
1: 4 and **A** begat Naasson; and Naasson begat *284*
Lk 3:33 Which was *the son* of **A**, which was *the son* *284*

AMISS (4) [MISS]
2Ch 6:37 we have **done a**, and have dealt wickedly; 5753
Da 3:29 which speak **any thing a** against the God 7960
Lk 23:41 our deeds: but this *man* hath done nothing **a**. *824*
Jas 4: 3 Ye ask, and receive not, because ye ask **a**, *2560*

AMITTAI (2)
2Ki 14:25 the son of **A**, the prophet, which *was* of 573
Jnh 1: 1 the LORD came unto Jonah the son of **A**, 573

AMMAH (1) [METHEG-AMMAH]
2Sa 2:24 down when they were come to the hill of **A**, 522

AMMI (1) [LO-AMMI]
Hos 2: 1 Say ye unto your brethren, **A**; 5971+2967.1

AMMIEL (6)
Nu 13:12 Of the tribe of Dan, **A** the son of Gemalli. 5988
2Sa 9: 4 house of Machir, the son of **A**, in Lo-debar. 5988
9: 5 of Machir, the son of **A**, from Lo-debar. 5988
17:27 Machir the son of **A** of Lo-debar, and 5988
1Ch 3: 5 four, of Bath-shua the daughter of **A**: 5988
26: 5 **A** the sixth, Issachar the seventh, 5988

AMMIHUD (10)
Nu 1:10 of Ephraim; Elishama the son of **A**: 5989
2:18 of Ephraim *shall be* Elishama the son of **A**. 5989
7:48 On the seventh day Elishama the son of **A**, 5989
7:53 *was* the offering of Elishama the son of **A**. 5989
10:22 over his host *was* Elishama the son of **A**. 5989
34:20 children of Simeon, Shemuel the son of **A**. 5989
34:28 children of Naphtali, Pedahel the son of **A**. 5989
2Sa 13:37 to Talmai, the son of **A**, king of Geshur. 5989
1Ch 7:26 Laadan his son, **A** his son, Elishama his 5989
9: 4 Uthai the son of **A**, the son of Omri, the son 5989

AMMINADAB (13)
Ex 6:23 daughter of **A**, sister of Naashon, to wife; 5992
Nu 1: 7 Of Judah; Nahshon the son of **A**. 5992
2: 3 Nahshon the son of **A** *shall be* captain of 5992
7:12 the first day was Nahshon the son of **A**, 5992
7:17 *was* the offering of Nahshon the son of **A**. 5992
10:14 over his host *was* Nahshon the son of **A**. 5992
Ru 4:19 And Hezron begat Ram, and Ram begat **A**, 5992
4:20 **A** begat Nahshon, and Nahshon begat 5992
1Ch 2:10 Ram begat **A**; and Amminadab begat 5992
2:10 **A** begat Nahshon, prince of the children of 5992
6:22 **A** his son, Korah his son, Assir his son, 5992
15:10 **A** the chief, and his brethren an hundred 5992
15:11 and Joel, Shemaiah, and Eliel, and **A**, 5992

AMMI-NADIB (1)
SS 6:12 my soul made me *like* the chariots of **A**. 5993

AMMISHADDAI (5)
Nu 1:12 Of Dan; Ahiezer the son of **A**. 5996
2:25 of Dan *shall be* Ahiezer the son of **A**. 5996
7:66 On the tenth day Ahiezer the son of **A**, 5996
7:71 *was* the offering of Ahiezer the son of **A**. 5996
10:25 and over his host *was* Ahiezer the son of **A**. 5996

AMMIZABAD (1)
1Ch 27: 6 the thirty: and *in* his course *was* **A** his son. 5990

AMMON (91) [AMMONITE, AMMONITES, AMMONITESS]
Ge 19:38 the same *is* the father of the children of **A** 5983
Nu 21:24 unto Jabbok, *even* unto the children of **A**: 5983
21:24 for the border of the children of **A** *was* 5983
Dt 2:19 comest nigh over against the children of **A**, 5983
2:19 land of the children of **A** *any* possession; 5983
2:37 Only unto the land of the children of **A** 5983
3:11 *is* it not in Rabbath of the children of **A**? 5983
3:16 *which is* the border of the children of **A**; 5983
Jos 12: 2 *which is* the border of the children of **A**; 5983
13:10 unto the border of the children of **A**; 5983
13:25 and half the land of the children of **A**, 5983
Jdg 3:13 And he gathered unto him the children of **A** 5983
10: 6 the gods of the children of **A**, and the gods 5983
10: 7 and into the hands of the children of **A**. 5983
10: 9 Moreover the children of **A** passed over 5983
10:11 from the children of **A**, and from 5983
10:17 the children of **A** were gathered together, 5983
10:18 begin to fight against the children of **A**? 5983
11: 4 that the children of **A** made war against 5983
11: 5 that when the children of **A** made war 5983
11: 6 that we may fight with the children of **A**. 5983
11: 8 fight against the children of **A**, and be our 5983
11: 9 again to fight against the children of **A**, 5983
11:12 unto the king of the children of **A**, 5983
11:13 the king of the children of **A** answered unto 5983
11:14 again unto the king of the children of **A**: 5983
11:15 of Moab, nor the land of the children of **A**: 5983
11:27 the children of Israel and the children of **A**. 5983
11:28 Howbeit the king of the children of **A** 5983
11:29 he passed over *unto* the children of **A**. 5983
11:30 deliver the children of **A** into mine hands, 5983
Jdg 11:31 I return in peace from the children of **A**, 5983
11:32 the children of **A** to fight against them; 5983
11:33 Thus the children of **A** were subdued 5983
11:36 of thine enemies, *even* of the children of **A**. 5983
12: 1 thou over to fight against the children of **A**, 5983
12: 2 were at great strife with the children of **A**; 5983
12: 3 passed over against the children of **A**, and 5983
1Sa 12:12 king of the children of **A** came against you, 5983
14:47 against the children of **A**, and 5983
2Sa 8:12 of the children of **A**, and of the Philistines, 5983
10: 1 that the king of the children of **A** died, and 5983
10: 2 came *into* the land of the children of **A**. 5983
10: 3 the princes of the children of **A** said unto 5983
10: 6 when the children of **A** saw that they stank 5983
10: 6 the children of **A** sent and hired the Syrians 5983
10: 8 the children of **A** came out, and put 5983
10:10 put *them* in array against the children of **A**. 5983
10:11 if the children of **A** be too strong for thee, 5983
10:14 when the children of **A** saw that the Syrians 5983
10:14 So Joab returned from the children of **A**, 5983
10:19 feared to help the children of **A** any more. 5983
11: 1 they destroyed the children of **A**, and 5983
12: 9 him with the sword of the children of **A**. 5983
12:26 fought against Rabbah of the children of **A**, 5983
12:31 he unto all the cities of the children of **A**. 5983
17:27 of Nahash of Rabbah of the children of **A**, 5983
1Ki 11: 7 the abomination of the children of **A**. 5983
11:33 Milcom the god of the children of **A**, and 5983
2Ki 23:13 the abomination of the children of **A**, 5983
24: 2 bands of the children of **A**, and sent them 5983
1Ch 18:11 from the children of **A**, and from 5983
19: 1 that Nahash the king of the children of **A** 5983
19: 2 into the land of the children of **A** to Hanun, 5983
19: 3 the princes of the children of **A** said to 5983
19: 6 when the children of **A** saw that they had 5983
19: 6 the children of **A** sent a thousand talents of 5983
19: 7 the children of **A** gathered themselves 5983
19: 9 the children of **A** came out, and put 5983
19:11 in array against the children of **A**. 5983
19:12 if the children of **A** be too strong for thee, 5983
19:15 when the children of **A** saw that the Syrians 5983
19:19 Syrians help the children of **A** any more. 5983
20: 1 wasted the country of the children of **A**, 5983
20: 3 with all the cities of the children of **A**. 5983
2Ch 20: 1 the children of **A**, and with them *other* 5983
20:10 the children of **A** and Moab and 5983
20:22 set ambushments against the children of **A**, 5983
20:23 For the children of **A** and Moab stood up 5983
27: 5 the children of **A** gave him the same year 5983
27: 5 So much did the children of **A** pay unto 5983
Ne 13:23 wives of Ashdod, **of A**, *and* of Moab: 5984
Ps 83: 7 Gebal, and **A**, and Amalek; the Philistines 5983
Isa 11:14 and the children of **A** shall obey them. 5983
Jer 9:26 the children of **A**, and Moab, and all *that* 5983
25:21 Edom, and Moab, and the children of **A**, 5983
49: 6 again the captivity of the children of **A**, 5983
Da 11:41 Moab, and the chief of the children of **A**. 5983
Am 1:13 three transgressions of the children of **A**, 5983
Zep 2: 8 and the revilings of the children of **A**, 5983
2: 9 the children of **A** as Gomorrah, *even* 5983

AMMONITE (9) [AMMON]
Dt 23: 3 An **A** or Moabite shall not enter into 5984
1Sa 11: 1 Nahash the **A** came up, and 5984
11: 2 Nahash the **A** answered them, On this 5984
2Sa 23:37 Zelek the **A**, Naharai the Beerothite, 5984
1Ch 11:39 Zelek the **A**, Naharai the Berothite, 5984
Ne 2:10 and Tobiah the servant, the **A**, 5984
2:19 the **A**, and Geshem the Arabian, 5984
4: 3 Now Tobiah the **A** *was* by him, and he said, 5984
13: 1 that the **A** and the Moabite should not come 5984

AMMONITES (23) [AMMON]
Dt 2:20 and the **A** call them Zamzummims; 5984
1Sa 11:11 and slew the **A** until the heat of the day: 5983
1Ki 11: 1 **A**, Edomites, Zidonians, *and* Hittites; 5984
11: 5 and after Milcom the abomination of the **A**. 5984
2Ch 20: 1 and with them *other* beside the **A**, 5984
26: 8 the **A** gave gifts to Uzziah: and his name 5984
27: 5 fought also with the king of the **A**, 1121+5983
Ezr 9: 1 the Jebusites, the **A**, the Moabites, 5984
Ne 4: 7 and the **A**, and the Ashdodites, 5984
Jer 27: 3 to the king of the **A**, and to the king 1121+5983
40:11 among the **A**, and in Edom, and 1121+5983
40:14 **A** hath sent Ishmael the son of 1121+5983
41:10 and departed to go over to the **A**. 1121+5983
41:15 with eight men, and went to the **A**. 1121+5983
49: 1 Concerning the **A**, thus saith 1121+5983
49: 2 war to be heard in Rabbah of the **A**; 1121+5983
Eze 21:20 may come to Rabbath of the **A**, 1121+5983
21:28 the Lord GOD concerning the **A**, 1121+5983
25: 2 set thy face against the **A**, 1121+5983
25: 3 say unto the **A**, Hear the word of 1121+5983
25: 5 the **A** a couching place for flocks: 1121+5983
25:10 Unto the men of the east with the **A**, 1121+5983
25:10 that the **A** may not be remembered 1121+5983

AMMONITESS (4) [AMMON]
1Ki 14:21 And his mother's name *was* Naamah an **A**. 5984
14:31 his mother's name *was* Naamah an **A**. 5984
2Ch 12:13 And his mother's name *was* Naamah an **A**. 5984
24:26 Zabad the son of Shimeath an **A**, and 5984

AMNON (25) [AMNON'S]
2Sa 3: 2 his firstborn was **A**, of Ahinoam 550
13: 1 and **A** the son of David loved her. 550
13: 2 **A** was *so* vexed, that he fell sick for his 550
13: 2 **A** thought it hard for him to do any thing to 550
13: 3 **A** had a friend, whose name *was* Jonadab, 550
13: 4 **A** said unto him, I love Tamar, my brother 550
13: 6 So **A** lay down, and made himself sick: and 550
13: 6 **A** said unto the king, I pray thee, let Tamar 550
13: 9 **A** said, Have out all men from me. And they 550
13:10 **A** said unto Tamar, Bring the meat *into* 550

2Sa 13:10 brought *them* into the chamber to **A** her 550
13:15 **A** hated her exceedingly; so that the hatred 550
13:15 And **A** said unto her, Arise, be gone. 550
13:20 unto her, Hath **A** thy brother been with thee? 550
13:22 Absalom spake unto his brother **A** neither 550
13:22 for Absalom hated **A**, because he had forced 550
13:26 I pray thee, let my brother **A** go with us. 550
13:27 that he let **A** and all the king's sons go with 550
13:28 and when I say unto you, Smite **A**; 550
13:29 the servants of Absalom did unto **A** as 550
13:32 men the king's sons; for **A** only is dead: 550
13:33 the king's sons are dead: for **A** only is dead. 550
13:39 for he was comforted concerning **A**, 550
1Ch 3: 1 the firstborn **A**, of Ahinoam the Jezreelitess; 550
4:20 the sons of Shimon *were*, **A**, and Rinnah, 550

AMNON'S (3) [AMNON]

2Sa 13: 7 Go now *to* thy brother **A** house, and 550
13: 8 So Tamar went *to* her brother **A** house; and 550
13:28 Mark ye now when **A** heart is merry with 550

AMOK (2)

Ne 12: 7 Sallu, **A**, Hilkiah, Jedaiah. These *were* 5987
12:20 Of Sallai, Kallai; of **A**, Eber; 5987

AMON (19)

1Ki 22:26 carry him back unto **A** the governor of 526
2Ki 21:18 of Uzza: and **A** his son reigned in his stead. 526
21:19 **A** *was* twenty and two years old when he 526
21:23 And the servants of **A** conspired against him, 526
21:24 all them that had conspired against king **A**; 526
21:25 Now the rest of the acts of **A** which he did, 526
1Ch 3:14 **A** his son, Josiah his son. 526
2Ch 18:25 carry him back to **A** the governor of the city, 526
33:20 and **A** his son reigned in his stead. 526
33:21 **A** *was* two and twenty years old when he 526
33:22 for **A** sacrificed unto all the carved images 526
33:23 but **A** trespassed more and more. 526
33:25 all them that had conspired against king **A**; 526
Ne 7:59 of Pochereth Zebaim, the children of **A**. 526
Jer 1: 2 days of Josiah the son of **A** king of Judah, 526
25: 3 year of Josiah the son of **A** king of Judah, 526
Zep 1: 1 in the days of Josiah the son of **A**, king of 526
Mt 1:10 and Manasses begat **A**; and Amon begat *300*
1:10 Manasses begat Amon; and **A** begat Josias; *300*

AMONG (859) [AMONGST]

Ge 17:10 Every man *child* **a** you shall be 3807.1
17:12 eight days old shall be circumcised **a** you, 3807.1
17:23 every male **a** the men of Abraham's house; 871.1
23: 6 thou *art* a mighty prince **a** us: in 8432+871.1
30:32 all the brown cattle **a** the sheep, and 871.1
30:32 and the spotted and speckled **a** the goats: 871.1
30:41 that they might conceive **a** the rods. 871.1
34:22 if every male **a** us be circumcised, 3807.1
34:30 Ye have troubled me to make me to stink **a** 871.1
35: 2 Put away the strange gods that *are* **a** 8432+871.1
36:30 of Hori, **a** their dukes in the land of Seir. 3807.1
40:20 and of the chief baker **a** his servants. 8432+871.1
42: 5 the sons of Israel came to buy *corn* **a** 8432+871.1
Ex 2: 5 when she saw the ark **a** the flags, 8432+871.1
7: 5 bring out the children of Israel from **a** 8432
12:49 the stranger that sojourneth **a** you. 8432+871.1
13: 2 whatsoever openeth the womb **a** 871.1
15:11 *is* like unto thee, O LORD, **a** the gods? 871.1
28: 1 with him, from **a** the children of Israel, 8432
30:13 every one that passeth **a** them that are 5921
30:14 Every one that passeth **a** them that are 5921
34:10 all the people **a** which thou *art* shall 7130+871.1
35:10 every wise hearted **a** you shall come, and 871.1
36: 8 every wise hearted *man* **a** them that 871.1
Lev 6:18 All the males **a** the children of Aaron shall 871.1
6:29 All the males **a** the priests shall eat thereof: 871.1
7: 6 Every male **a** the priests shall eat thereof: 871.1
7:33 He **a** the sons of Aaron, that offereth 4480
7:34 unto his sons by a statute for ever from **a** 854
11: 2 These *are* the beasts which ye shall eat **a** all 4480
11: 3 cheweth cud, **a** the beasts, 871.1
11:13 ye shall have in abomination **a** the fowls; 4480
11:27 **a** all *manner of* beasts that go on *all* four, 871.1
11:29 These also *shall be* unclean unto you **a** 871.1
11:31 These *are* unclean to you **a** all that creep: 871.1
11:42 whatsoever hath more feet **a** all creeping 3807.1
15:31 defile my tabernacle that *is* **a** them. 8432+871.1
16:16 that remaineth **a** them in the midst of their 854
16:29 or a stranger that sojourneth **a** you: 8432+871.1
17: 4 that man shall be cut off from **a** his people: 7130
17: 8 or of the strangers which sojourn **a** 8432+871.1
17: 9 even that man shall be cut off **from a** his 4480
17:10 or of the strangers that sojourn **a** 8432+871.1
17:10 and will cut him off from **a** his people. 7130
17:12 that sojourneth **a** you eat blood. 8432+871.1
17:13 or of the strangers that sojourn **a** 8432+871.1
18:26 any stranger that sojourneth **a** you: 8432+871.1
18:29 *them* shall be cut off from **a** their people. 7130
19: 8 that soul shall be cut off **from a** his people. 4480
19:16 and down *as* a talebearer **a** thy people: 871.1
20: 3 and will cut him off from **a** his people; 7130
20: 5 with Molech, from **a** their people. 7130
20: 6 and will cut him off from **a** his people. 7130
20:14 that there be no wickedness **a** you. 8432+871.1
20:18 both of them shall be cut off from **a** their 7130
21: 1 There shall none be defiled for the dead **a** 871.1
21: 4 *being* a chief man **a** his people, to profane 871.1
21:10 And *he that is* the high priest **a** his brethren, 4480
21:15 Neither shall he profane his seed **a** his 871.1
22: 3 Whosoever *he be* of all your seed **a** your 3807.1
22:32 be hallowed **a** the children of Israel: 8432+871.1
23:29 he shall be cut off **from a** his people. 4480
23:30 the same soul will I destroy from **a** his 7130
24:10 went out **a** the children of Israel: 8432+871.1
25:33 possession **a** the children of Israel. 8432+871.1
25:45 of the strangers that do sojourn **a** you, 5973
26:12 I will walk **a** you, and will be your 8432+871.1
Lev 26:22 I will also send wild beasts **a** you, which 871.1
26:25 I will send the pestilence **a** you; 8432+871.1
26:33 I will scatter you **a** the heathen, and 871.1
26:38 ye shall perish **a** the heathen, and the land 871.1
Nu 1:47 fathers were not numbered **a** them. 8432+871.1
1:49 neither take the sum of them **a** 8432+871.1
2:33 the Levites were not numbered **a** 8432+871.1
3:12 I have taken the Levites from **a** the children 8432
3:12 openeth the matrix **a** the children of Israel: 4480
3:41 instead of all the firstborn **a** the children of 871.1
3:41 **a** the cattle of the children of Israel. 871.1
3:42 all the firstborn **a** the children of Israel. 871.1
3:45 of all the firstborn **a** the children of Israel, 871.1
4: 2 Take the sum of the sons of Kohath from **a** 8432
4:18 of the Kohathites from **a** the Levites: 8432
5:21 a curse and an oath **a** thy people, 8432+871.1
5:27 shall be a curse **a** her people. 7130+871.1
8: 6 Take the Levites from **a** the children of 8432
8:14 Thus shalt thou separate the Levites from **a** 8432
8:16 For they *are* wholly given unto me from **a** 8432
8:19 to his sons from **a** the children of Israel, 8432
8:19 that there be no plague **a** the children of 871.1
9: 7 season **a** the children of Israel? 8432+871.1
9:13 even the same soul shall be cut off **from a** 4480
9:14 if a stranger shall sojourn **a** you, and 854
11: 1 the fire of the LORD burnt **a** them, and 871.1
11: 3 the fire of the LORD burnt **a** them. 871.1
11: 4 the mixt multitude that *was* **a** them 7130+871.1
11:20 despised the LORD which *is* **a** you, 7130+871.1
12: 6 If there be a prophet **a** you, *I* the LORD NIH
13: 2 ye send a man, every one a ruler **a** them. 871.1
14:11 signs which I have shewed **a** them? 7130+871.1
14:13 up this people in thy might from **a** them;) 7130
14:14 that thou LORD *art* **a** this people, 7130+871.1
14:42 Go not up, for the LORD *is* not **a** 7130+871.1
15:14 or whosoever *be* **a** you in your 8432+871.1
15:23 and henceforward **a** your generations; 3807.1
15:26 the stranger that sojourneth **a** them; 8432+871.1
15:29 the stranger that sojourneth **a** them. 8432+871.1
15:30 that soul shall be cut off from **a** his people. 7130
16: 3 of them, and the LORD *is* **a** them: 8432+871.1
16:21 Separate yourselves from **a** this 8432
16:33 and they perished from **a** the congregation. 8432
16:45 Get you up from **a** this congregation, that I 8432
16:47 behold, the plague was begun **a** the people: 871.1
17: 6 the rod of Aaron *was* **a** their rods. 8432+871.1
18: 6 the Levites from **a** the children of Israel: 8432
18:20 shalt thou have any part **a** them: 8432+871.1
18:20 inheritance **a** the children of Israel. 8432+871.1
18:23 that **a** the children of Israel they 8432+871.1
18:24 **A** the children of Israel they shall 8432+871.1
19:10 the stranger that sojourneth **a** them, 8432+871.1
19:20 that soul shall be cut off from **a** 8432
21: 6 the LORD sent fiery serpents **a** 871.1
23: 9 and shall not be reckoned **a** the nations. 871.1
23:21 and the shout of a king *is* **a** them. 871.1
25:11 he was zealous for my sake **a** them, 8432+871.1
25:14 prince of a chief house **a** the Simeonites. 3807.1
26:62 for they were not numbered **a** 8432+871.1
26:62 given them **a** the children of Israel. 8432+871.1
26:64 **a** these there was not a man of them whom 871.1
27: 4 our father be done away from **a** his family, 8432
27: 4 **a** the brethren of our father. 8432+871.1
27: 7 inheritance **a** their father's brethren; 8432+871.1
31:16 there was a plague **a** the congregation of 871.1
31:17 therefore kill every male **a** the little ones, 871.1
32:30 they shall have possessions **a** you in 8432+871.1
33: 4 which the LORD had smitten **a** them: 871.1
33:54 **divide** the land by lot for **an inheritance a** 5157
35: 6 *a* the cities which ye shall give unto NIH
35:15 and for the sojourner **a** them: 8432+871.1
35:34 for I the LORD dwell **a** 8432+871.1
Dt 1:13 known **a** your tribes, and I will make 3807.1
1:15 over tens, and officers **a** your tribes. 3807.1
1:42 neither fight; for I *am* not **a** you; 7130+871.1
2:14 of war were wasted out from **a** the host, 7130
2:15 to destroy them from **a** the host, until they 7130
2:16 and dead from **a** the people, 7130
4: 3 thy God hath destroyed them from **a** you. 7130
4:27 the LORD shall scatter you **a** the nations, 871.1
4:27 ye shall be left few in number **a** 871.1
6:15 thy God *is* a jealous God **a** you) 7130+871.1
7:14 shall not be male or female barren **a** you, 871.1
7:14 female barren among you, or **a** your cattle. 871.1
7:20 thy God will send the hornet **a** them, 871.1
7:21 for the LORD thy God *is* **a** you, 7130+871.1
13: 1 If there arise **a** you a prophet, or 7130+871.1
13:11 such wickedness as this is **a** you. 7130+871.1
13:13 are gone out from **a** you, and 7130
13:14 such abomination is wrought **a** you; 7130+871.1
15: 4 Save when there shall be no poor **a** you; 871.1
15: 7 If there be **a** you a poor man of one of thy 871.1
16:11 and the widow, that *are* **a** you, 7130+871.1
17: 2 If there be found **a** you, within any 7130+871.1
17: 7 So thou shalt put the evil away from **a** you. 7130
17:15 *one* from **a** thy brethren shalt thou set king 7130
18: 2 have no inheritance **a** their brethren: 7130+871.1
18:10 There shall not be found **a** you *any one* 871.1
18:18 I will raise them up a Prophet from **a** their 7130
19:19 so shalt thou put the evil away from **a** you. 7130
19:20 no more any such evil **a** you. 7130+871.1
21: 9 the *guilt of* innocent blood from **a** you, 7130
21:11 seest **a** the captives a beautiful woman, 871.1
21:21 so shalt thou put evil away from **a** you; and 7130
22:21 so shalt thou put evil away from **a** you. 7130
22:24 so thou shalt put away evil from **a** you. 7130
23:10 If there be **a** you any man, that is not clean 871.1
23:16 He shall dwell with thee, *even* **a** 7130+871.1
24: 7 and thou shalt put evil away from **a** you. 7130
26:11 and the stranger that *is* **a** you. 7130+871.1
28:37 **a** all nations whither the LORD shall lead 871.1
28:54 *So that* the man *that is* tender **a** you, and 871.1
28:56 The tender and delicate *woman* **a** you, 871.1
28:64 the LORD shall scatter thee **a** all people, 871.1
28:65 **a** these nations shalt thou find no ease, 871.1
Dt 29:17 stone, silver and gold, which *were* **a** them:) 5973
29:18 Lest there should be **a** you man, or woman, 871.1
29:18 lest there should be **a** you a root that 871.1
30: 1 thou shalt call *them* to mind **a** all 871.1
32:26 remembrance of them to cease **from a** men: 4480
32:34 with me, *and* sealed up **a** my treasures? 871.1
32:46 all the words which I testify **a** you *this* day, 871.1
32:51 Because ye trespassed against me **a** 8432+871.1
Jos 3: 5 the LORD will do wonders **a** you. 7130+871.1
3:10 know that the living God *is* **a** you, 7130+871.1
4: 6 That this may be a sign **a** you, 7130+871.1
7:13 take away the accursed thing from **a** you. 7130
7:21 When I saw **a** the spoils a goodly 871.1
8: 9 lodged that night **a** the people. 8432+871.1
8:33 the stranger, as he that was **born a** them; 249
8:35 that were conversant **a** them. 7130+871.1
9: 7 Peradventure ye dwell **a** us; 7130+871.1
9:16 and *that* they dwelt **a** them. 7130+871.1
9:22 far from you; when ye dwell **a** us? 7130+871.1
10: 1 peace with Israel, and were **a** them; 7130+871.1
13:13 the Maachathites dwell **a** 7130+871.1
13:22 the sword **a** them that were slain by them. 413
14: 3 he gave none inheritance **a** them. 8432+871.1
14:15 which *Arba was* a great man **a** 871.1
15:13 gave a part **a** the children of Judah, 8432+871.1
16: 9 **a** the inheritance of the children of 8432+871.1
16:10 the Canaanites dwell **a** 7130+871.1
17: 4 us an inheritance **a** our brethren. 8432+871.1
17: 4 **a** the brethren of their father. 8432+871.1
17: 6 had an inheritance **a** his sons: 8432+871.1
17: 9 these cities of Ephraim *are* **a** 8432+871.1
18: 2 there remained **a** the children of Israel 871.1
18: 4 Give out **from a** you three men for *each* 3807.1
18: 7 the Levites have no part **a** you; 7130+871.1
19:49 to Joshua the son of Nun **a** them: 8432+871.1
20: 4 give him a place, that he may dwell **a** them. 5973
20: 9 the stranger that sojourneth **a** them, 8432+871.1
22: 7 unto the *other* half thereof gave Joshua **a** 5973
22:14 of their fathers **a** the thousands of Israel. 3807.1
22:19 and take possession **a** us: 8432+871.1
22:31 we perceive that the LORD *is* **a** us, 8432+871.1
23: 7 That ye come not **a** these nations, these 871.1
23:12 *even* these that remain **a** you, and shall make 854
24:17 **a** all the people through whom we passed: 871.1
24:23 *said he,* the strange gods which *are* **a** 7130+871.1
Jdg 1:16 and they went and dwelt **a** the people. 854
1:29 Canaanites dwelt in Gezer **a** them. 7130+871.1
1:30 the Canaanites dwelt **a** them, and 7130+871.1
1:32 the Asherites dwelt **a** 7130+871.1
1:33 he dwelt **a** the Canaanites, 7130+871.1
3: 5 the children of Israel dwelt **a** 7130+871.1
5: 8 or spear seen **a** forty thousand in Israel? 871.1
5: 9 that offered themselves willingly **a** 871.1
5:13 have dominion over the nobles *a* the people: NIH
5:14 after thee, Benjamin, **a** thy people; out of 871.1
5:16 Why abodest thou **a** the sheepfolds, to hear 996
10:16 they put away the strange gods from **a** 7130
12: 4 Ye Gileadites *are* fugitives of Ephraim **a** 8432
12: 4 *and* **a** the Manassites. 8432+871.1
14: 3 *Is there* never a woman **a** the daughters of 871.1
14: 3 of thy brethren, or **a** all my people, 871.1
18: 1 unto them **a** the tribes of Israel. 8432+871.1
18:25 Let not thy voice be heard **a** us, lest angry 5973
20:12 wickedness *is* this that is done **a** you? 871.1
20:16 **A** all this people *there were* seven hundred 4480
21: 5 Who *is there* **a** all the tribes of Israel that 4480
21:12 they found **a** the inhabitants of 4480
Ru 2:15 Let her glean even **a** the sheaves, and 996
4:10 the dead be not cut off from **a** his brethren, 5973
1Sa 2: 8 to set *them* **a** princes, and to make them 5973
4: 3 that when it cometh **a** us, it may 7130+871.1
4:17 there hath been also a great slaughter **a** 871.1
6: 6 when he had wrought wonderfully **a** them, 871.1
7: 3 the strange gods and Ashtaroth from **a** you, 8432
9: 2 *there was* not **a** the children of Israel a 4480
9:22 made them sit **in** the chiefest place **a** them 871.1
10:10 and he prophesied **a** them. 8432+871.1
10:11 he prophesied **a** the prophets, then 5973
10:11 son of Kish? *Is* Saul also **a** the prophets? 871.1
10:12 a proverb, *Is* Saul also **a** the prophets? 871.1
10:22 Behold, he hath hid himself **a** the stuff. 413
10:23 when he stood **a** the people, he was 8432+871.1
10:24 that *there is* none like him **a** all the people? 871.1
14:15 the host, in the field, and **a** all the people: 871.1
14:30 a much greater slaughter **a** the Philistines? 871.1
14:34 Disperse yourselves **a** the people, and 871.1
14:39 *there was* not *a man* **a** all the people *that* 4480
15: 6 get you down from **a** the Amalekites, 8432
15: 6 So the Kenites departed from **a** 8432
15:33 so shall thy mother be childless **a** women. 4480
16: 1 for I have provided me a king **a** his sons. 871.1
17:12 the man went **a** men *for* an old man in 871.1
19:24 they say, *Is* Saul also **a** the prophets? 871.1
22:14 *so* faithful **a** all thy servants as David, 871.1
31: 9 *in* the house of their idols, and **a** the people. 854
2Sa 6:19 he dealt **a** all the people, *even* among 3807.1
6:19 *even* **a** the whole multitude of Israel, 3807.1
15:31 Ahithophel *is* **a** the conspirators with 871.1
16:20 Give counsel **a** you what we shall do. 3807.1
17: 9 There is a slaughter **a** the people that 871.1
19:28 yet didst thou set thy servant **a** them that 871.1
22:50 **a** the heathen, and I will sing praises unto 871.1
23: 8 that sat in the seat, chief **a** the captains; NIH
23:18 the son of Zeruiah, *was* chief **a** three. NIH
23:18 and slew them, and had the name **a** three. 871.1
23:22 and had the name **a** three mighty *men.* 871.1
1Ki 3:13 that there shall not be any **a** the kings like 871.1
5: 6 for thou knowest that *there is* not **a** us any 871.1
6:13 I will dwell **a** the children of Israel, 8432+871.1
7:51 did he put **a** the treasures of the house of 871.1
8:53 For thou didst separate them **from a** all 4480
9: 7 be a proverb and a byword **a** all people: 871.1
11:20 household **a** the sons of Pharaoh. 8432+871.1
14: 7 Forasmuch as I exalted thee from **a** 8432
21: 9 a fast, and set Naboth on high **a** the people: NIH

1Ki 21:12 a fast, and set Naboth on high a the people. NIH
2Ki 4:13 I dwell a mine own people. 8432+871.1
9: 2 make him arise up from a his brethren, and 8432
11: 2 stale him from a the king's sons which 8432
17:25 therefore the LORD sent lions a them, 871.1
17:26 therefore he hath sent lions a them, 871.1
18: 5 that after him was none like him a all 871.1
18:35 Who are they a all the gods of 871.1
20:15 there is nothing a my treasures that I have 871.1
23: 9 unleavened bread a their brethren. 8432+871.1
1Ch 7: 5 their brethren a all the families of 3807.1
11:20 he slew them, and had a name a the three. 871.1
11:24 and had the name a the three mighties. 871.1
11:25 he was honourable a the thirty, but 4480
12: 1 they were a the mighty men, helpers of 871.1
12: 4 a mighty man a the thirty, and over 871.1
16: 8 make known his deeds a the people. 871.1
16:24 Declare his glory a the heathen; 871.1
16:24 his marvellous works a all nations. 871.1
16:31 let men say a the nations, The LORD 871.1
18:14 and justice a all his people. 3807.1
21: 6 Benjamin counted he not a them: 8432+871.1
23: 6 David divided them into courses a 3807.1
24: 4 A the sons of Eleazar there were sixteen 3807.1
24: 4 eight a the sons of Ithamar according to 3807.1
26:12 A these were the divisions of the porters, 3807.1
26:12 even a the chief men, having wards one 3807.1
26:19 These are the divisions of the porters a 3807.1
26:19 sons of Kore, and a the sons of Merari. 3807.1
26:30 were officers a them of Israel on this side 5921
26:31 A the Hebronites was Jerijah the chief, 3807.1
26:31 even a the Hebronites, according to 3807.1
26:31 there were found a them mighty men of 871.1
27: 6 who was mighty a the thirty, and above NIH
28: 4 a the sons of my father he liked me to 871.1
2Ch 5: 1 put he a the treasures of the house of God. 871.1
6: 5 a all the tribes of Israel to build a house in, 4480
7:13 or if I send pestilence a my people; 871.1
7:20 to be a proverb and a byword a all nations. 871.1
11:22 the chief, to be ruler a his brethren: 871.1
20:25 they found a them in abundance both 871.1
22:11 stole him from a the king's sons that were 8432
24:16 they buried him in the city of David a 5973
24:23 the princes of the people from a the people, 4480
26: 6 cities about Ashdod, and a the Philistines. 871.1
28:15 with the spoil clothed all that were naked a NIH
31:19 to give portions to all the males a 871.1
31:19 to all that were reckoned by genealogies a 871.1
32:14 Who was there a all the gods of those 871.1
33:11 which took Manasseh a the thorns, and 871.1
33:19 they are written a the sayings of the seers. 5921
35:13 divided them speedily a all the people. 3807.1
36:23 Who is there a you of all his people? 871.1
Ezr 1: 3 Who is there a you of all his people? 871.1
2:62 These sought their register a those that were NIH
2:65 there were a them two hundred singing 3807.1
10:18 a the sons of the priests there were found 4480
Ne 1: 8 I will scatter you abroad a the nations: 871.1
4:11 till we come in the midst a them, and 8432
5:17 besides those that came unto us from a 4480
6: 6 It is reported a the heathen, and 871.1
7:64 These sought their register a those that were NIH
9:17 of thy wonders that thou didst a them; 5973
10:34 we cast the lots a the priests, the Levites, NIH
11:17 Bakbukiah the second a his brethren, and 4480
13:26 a many nations was there no king like him, 871.1
Est 1:19 let it be written a the laws of the Persians 871.1
3: 8 dispersed a the people in all the provinces of 996
4: 3 there was great mourning a the Jews, and 3807.1
9:21 To stablish this a them, that they should 5921
9:28 of Purim should not fail from a the Jews, 8432
10: 3 great a the Jews, and accepted of 3807.1
Job 1: 6 and Satan came also a them. 8432+871.1
2: 1 Satan came also a them to present 8432+871.1
2: 8 and he sat down a the ashes. 8432+871.1
15:19 and no stranger passed a them. 8432+871.1
17:10 for I cannot find one wise man a you. 871.1
18:19 He shall neither have son nor nephew a his 871.1
28:10 He cutteth out rivers a the rocks; and 871.1
30: 5 They were driven forth from a men, 1460
30: 7 A the bushes they brayed; under the nettles 996
33:23 with him, an interpreter, one a a thousand, 4480
34: 4 let us know a ourselves what is good. 996
36:14 die in youth, and their life is a the unclean. 871.1
39:25 He saith a the trumpets, Ha, ha; and 1767+871.1
41: 6 of him? shall they part him a the merchants? 996
42:15 their father gave them inheritance a 8432+871.1
Ps 9:11 in Zion: declare a the people his doings. 871.1
12: 1 for the faithful fail from a the children of 4480
18:49 a the heathen, and sing praises unto thy 871.1
21:10 and their seed from a the children of men. 4480
22:18 They part my garments a them, and 3807.1
22:28 and he is the governor a the nations. 871.1
31:11 I was a reproach a all mine enemies, but 4480
31:11 especially a my neighbours, and a fear to 3807.1
35:18 I will praise thee a much people. 871.1
44:11 and hast scattered us a the heathen. 871.1
44:14 Thou makest us a byword a the heathen, 871.1
44:14 a shaking of the head a the people. 871.1
45: 9 Kings' daughters were a thy honourable 871.1
45:12 even the rich a the people shall intreat thy NIH
46:10 I will be exalted a the heathen, I will be 871.1
55:15 is in their dwellings, and a them. 7130+871.1
57: 4 My soul is a lions: and I lie even 8432+871.1
57: 4 and I lie even a them that are set on fire, NIH
57: 9 I will praise thee, O Lord, a the people: 871.1
57: 9 I will sing unto thee a the nations. 871.1
67: 2 upon earth, thy saving health a all nations. 871.1
68:13 Though ye have lien a the pots, yet shall ye 996
68:17 the Lord is a them, as in Sinai, in the holy 871.1
68:18 that the LORD God might dwell a them. NIH
68:25 a them were the damsels playing with 8432
74: 9 neither is there a us any that knoweth how 854
77:14 thou hast declared thy strength a 871.1
78:45 He sent divers sorts of flies a them, 871.1

Ps 78:49 and trouble, by sending evil angels a them. NIH
78:60 of Shiloh, the tent which he placed a men; 871.1
79:10 let him be known a the heathen in our 871.1
80: 6 and our enemies laugh a themselves. 3807.1
82: 1 of the mighty; he judgeth a the gods. 7130+871.1
86: 8 A the gods there is none like unto thee, 871.1
88: 5 Free a the dead, like the slain that lie in 871.1
89: 6 who a the sons of the mighty can be 871.1
94: 8 Understand, ye brutish a the people: and 871.1
96: 3 Declare his glory a the heathen, 871.1
96: 3 the heathen, his wonders a all people. 871.1
96:10 Say a the heathen that the LORD 871.1
99: 6 Moses and Aaron a his priests, and 871.1
99: 6 Samuel a them that call upon his name; 871.1
104:10 into the valleys, which run a the hills. 996
104:12 which sing a the branches. 996+4480
105: 1 make known his deeds a the people. 871.1
105:27 They shewed his signs a them, 871.1
105:37 there was not one feeble person a their 871.1
106:27 To overthrow their seed also a the nations, 871.1
106:35 were mingled a the heathen, and 871.1
106:47 our God, and gather us from a the heathen, 4480
108: 3 I will praise thee, O LORD, a the people: 871.1
108: 3 I will sing praises unto thee a the nations. 871.1
109:30 I will praise him a the multitude. 8432+871.1
110: 6 He shall judge a the heathen, he shall fill 871.1
126: 2 said they a the heathen, The LORD hath 871.1
136:11 brought out Israel from a them: for his 8432
Pr 1:14 Cast in thy lot a us; let us all have 8432+871.1
6:19 and he that soweth discord a brethren. 996
7: 7 beheld a the simple ones, I discerned 871.1
7: 7 the simple ones, I discerned a the youths, 871.1
14: 9 at sin: but a the righteous there is favour. 996
15:31 reproof of life abideth a the wise. 7130+871.1
17: 2 shall have part of the inheritance a 8432+871.1
23:28 and increaseth the transgressors a men. 871.1
27:22 in a mortar a wheat with a pestle, 8432+871.1
30:14 off the earth, and the needy from a men. NIH
30:30 A lion which is strongest a beasts, and 871.1
31:23 when he sitteth a the elders of the land. 5973
Ecc 6: 1 under the sun, and it is common a men: 5921
7:28 one man a a thousand have I found; but 4480
7:28 but a woman a all those have I not found. 871.1
9: 3 This is an evil a all things that are done 871.1
9:17 more than the cry of him that ruleth a 871.1
SS 1: 8 If thou know not, O thou fairest a women, 871.1
2: 2 As the lily a thorns, so is my love among 996
2: 2 among thorns, so is my love a the daughters. 996
2: 3 As the apple tree a the trees of the wood, 871.1
2: 3 of the wood, so is my beloved a the sons. 996
2:16 and I am his: he feedeth a the lilies. 871.1
4: 2 beareth twins, and none is barren a them. 871.1
4: 5 roes that are twins, which feed a the lilies. 871.1
5: 9 another beloved, O thou fairest a women? 871.1
5:10 and ruddy, the chiefest a ten thousand. 4480
6: 1 thy beloved gone, O thou fairest a women? 871.1
6: 3 my beloved is mine: he feedeth a the lilies. 871.1
6: 6 and there is not one barren a them. 871.1
Isa 2: 4 he shall judge a the nations, and shall rebuke 996
4: 3 even every one that is written a the living 3807.1
8:15 many a them shall stumble, and fall, and 871.1
8:16 the testimony, seal the law a my disciples. 871.1
10:16 Lord of hosts, send a his fat ones leanness; 871.1
12: 4 his name, declare his doings a the people, 871.1
24:13 in the midst of the land a the people, 8432+871.1
29:19 the poor a men shall rejoice in the Holy One NIH
33:14 Who a us shall dwell with the devouring 3807.1
39: 4 there is nothing a my treasures that I have 871.1
42:23 Who a you will give ear to this? who will 871.1
43: 9 who a them can declare this, and shew us 871.1
43:12 when there was no strange god a you: 871.1
44: 4 they shall spring up as a the grass, 996+871.1
44:14 which he strengtheneth for himself a 871.1
48:14 which a them hath declared these things? 871.1
50:10 Who is a you that feareth the LORD, 871.1
51:18 There is none to guide her a all the sons 4480
57: 6 A the smooth stones of the stream is thy 871.1
61: 9 their seed shall be known a the Gentiles, 871.1
61: 9 and their offspring a the people: 8432+871.1
65: 4 Which remain a the graves, and lodge in 871.1
66:19 I will set a sign a them, and I will send 871.1
66:19 they shall declare my glory a the Gentiles. 871.1
Jer 3:19 How shall I put thee a the children, and 871.1
4: 3 up your fallow ground, and sow not a thorns. 413
5:26 For a my people are found wicked men: 871.1
6:15 therefore they shall fall a them that fall: 871.1
6:18 and know, O congregation, what is a them. 871.1
6:27 for a tower and a fortress a my people, 871.1
8:12 therefore shall they fall a them that fall: 871.1
8:17 I will send serpents, cockatrices, a you, 871.1
9:16 I will scatter them also a the heathen, 871.1
10: 7 forasmuch as a all the wise men of 871.1
11: 9 A conspiracy is found a the men of Judah, 871.1
11: 9 and a the inhabitants of Jerusalem. 871.1
12:14 pluck out the house of Judah from a them. 8432
14:22 Are there any a the vanities of the Gentiles 871.1
18:13 Ask ye now a the heathen, who hath heard 871.1
24:10 the famine, and the pestilence, a them, 871.1
25:16 because of the sword that I will send a them. 996
25:27 of the sword which I will send a you. 996
29:18 a all the nations whither I have driven 871.1
29:32 he shall not have a man to dwell a 8432+871.1
31: 7 and shout a the chief of the nations: 871.1
37: 4 came in and went out a the people: 8432+871.1
37:10 there remained but wounded men a them, 871.1
39:14 him home: so he dwelt a the people. 8432+871.1
40: 1 a all that were carried away captive 8432+871.1
40: 5 and dwell with him a the people: 8432+871.1
40: 6 dwelt with him a the people that 8432+871.1
40:11 a the Ammonites, and in Edom, and 871.1
41: 8 ten men were found a them that said unto 871.1
41: 8 and slew them not a their brethren. 8432+871.1
44: 8 a reproach a all the nations of the earth? 871.1
46:18 Surely as Tabor is a the mountains, and 871.1
48:27 was he found a thieves? for since thou 871.1

Jer 49:15 I will make thee small a the heathen, and 871.1
49:15 among the heathen, and despised a men. 871.1
50: 2 Declare ye a the nations, and publish, and 871.1
50:23 how is Babylon become a desolation a 871.1
50:46 and the cry is heard a the nations. 871.1
51:27 blow the trumpet a the nations, prepare 871.1
51:41 how is Babylon become an astonishment a 871.1
La 1: 1 she that was great a the nations, and 871.1
1: 1 and princess a the provinces, how is she 871.1
1: 2 a all her lovers she hath none to comfort 4480
1: 3 she dwelleth a the heathen, she findeth no 871.1
1:17 Jerusalem is as a menstruous woman a them. 996
2: 9 her king and her princes are a the Gentiles: 871.1
4:15 they said a the heathen, They shall no 871.1
4:20 Under his shadow we shall live a 871.1
Eze 1: 1 as I was a the captives by the river 8432+871.1
1:13 it went up and down a the living creatures; 996
2: 5 there hath been a prophet a them. 8432+871.1
2: 6 with thee, and thou dost dwell a scorpions: 413
3:15 remained there astonished a them 8432+871.1
3:25 and thou shalt not go out a them: 8432+871.1
4:13 Israel eat their defiled bread a the Gentiles, 871.1
5:14 a reproach a the nations that are round 871.1
6: 8 that shall escape the sword a the nations, 871.1
6: 9 a the nations whither they shall be carried 871.1
6:13 when their slain men shall be a their 8432+871.1
9: 2 man a them was clothed with linen, 8432+871.1
11: 1 a whom I saw Jaazaniah the son of 8432+871.1
11: 9 and will execute judgments a you. 871.1
11:16 Although I have cast them far off a 871.1
11:16 although I have scattered them a 871.1
12:10 the house of Israel that are a them. 8432+871.1
12:12 the prince that is a them shall bear 8432+871.1
12:15 when I shall scatter them a the nations, and 871.1
12:16 a the heathen whither they come; 871.1
13:19 will ye pollute me a my people for handfuls 413
15: 2 than a branch which is a the trees of 871.1
15: 6 As the vine tree a the trees of the forest, 871.1
16:14 thy renown went forth a the heathen for 871.1
18:18 did that which is not good a his 8432+871.1
19: 2 she lay down a lions, she nourished her 996
19: 2 nourished her whelps a young lions. 8432+871.1
19: 6 he went up and down a the lions, 8432+871.1
19:11 her stature was exalted a the thick 996+5921
20: 9 a whom they were, in whose sight I 8432+871.1
20:23 that I would scatter them a the heathen, 871.1
20:38 I will purge out from a you the rebels, and 4480
22:15 I will scatter thee a the heathen, and 871.1
22:26 and I am profaned a them. 8432+871.1
22:30 I sought for a man a them, that should 4480
23:10 she became famous a women; for they 3807.1
25:10 may not be remembered a the nations. 871.1
27:24 and made of cedar, a thy merchandise. 871.1
27:36 The merchants a the people shall hiss at 871.1
28:19 All they that know thee a the people shall 871.1
28:25 from the people a whom they are scattered, 871.1
29:12 her cities a the cities that are laid 8432+871.1
29:12 I will scatter the Egyptians a the nations, 871.1
30:23 I will scatter the Egyptians a the nations, 871.1
30:26 I will scatter the Egyptians a the nations, 871.1
30:26 and disperse them a the countries; 871.1
31: 3 and his top was a the thick boughs. 996
31:10 hath shot up his top a the thick boughs, 413+996
31:14 neither shoot up their top a the thick 413+996
31:18 and in greatness a the trees of Eden? 871.1
32: 9 when I shall bring thy destruction a 871.1
32:21 The strong a the mighty shall speak to him NIH
33: 6 and take any person from a them, 4480
33:33 that a prophet hath been a them. 8432+871.1
34:12 he is a his sheep that are scattered; 8432+871.1
34:24 my servant David a prince a them; 8432+871.1
36:19 I scattered them a the heathen, and 871.1
36:21 which the house of Israel had profaned a 871.1
36:22 which ye have profaned a the heathen, 871.1
36:23 which was profaned a the heathen, 871.1
36:24 For I will take you from a the heathen, and 4480
36:30 no more reproach of famine a the heathen. 871.1
37:21 I will take the children of Israel from a 996
39: 6 a them that dwell carelessly in the isles: 871.1
39:21 I will set my glory a the heathen, and 871.1
39:28 which caused them to be led into captivity a 413
40:46 these are the sons of Zadok a the sons of 4480
44: 9 of any stranger that is a the children 8432+871.1
47:22 to the strangers that sojourn a you, 8432+871.1
47:22 which shall beget children a you: 8432+871.1
47:22 born in the country a the children of Israel; 871.1
47:22 with you a the tribes of Israel. 8432+871.1
Da 1: 6 Now a these were of the children of Judah, 871.1
1:19 a them all was found none like Daniel, 4480
4:35 of heaven, and a the inhabitants of the earth: NIH
7: 8 there came up a them another little horn, 997
11:24 he shall scatter a them the prey, and spoil, 3807.1
11:33 they that understand a the people shall 3807.1
Hos 5: 9 a the tribes of Israel have I made known 871.1
7: 7 there is none a them that calleth unto me. 871.1
7: 8 he hath mixed himself a the people; 871.1
8: 8 now shall they be a the Gentiles as a vessel 871.1
8:10 Yea, though they have hired a the nations, 871.1
9:17 and they shall be wanderers a the nations. 871.1
10:14 Therefore shall a tumult arise a thy people, 871.1
13:15 Though he be fruitful a his brethren, an east 996
Joel 2:17 wherefore should they say a the people, 871.1
2:19 I will no more make you a reproach a 871.1
2:25 my great army which I sent a you. 871.1
3: 2 whom they have scattered a the nations, 871.1
3: 9 Proclaim ye this a the Gentiles; 871.1
Am 1: 1 who was a the herdmen of Tekoa, 871.1
2:16 he that is courageous a the mighty shall 871.1
4:10 I have sent a you the pestilence after 871.1
9: 9 I will sift the house of Israel a all nations, 871.1
Ob 1: 1 an ambassador is sent a the heathen, 871.1
1: 2 I have made thee small a the heathen: 871.1
1: 4 though thou set thy nest a the stars, 996
Mic 3:11 and say, Is not the LORD a us? 7130+871.1
4: 3 he shall judge a many people, and 996

Mic 5: 2 *though thou* be little **a** the thousands of 871.1
5: 8 the remnant of Jacob shall be **a** 871.1
5: 8 people as a lion **a** the beasts of the forest, 871.1
5: 8 as a young lion **a** the flocks of sheep: 871.1
7: 2 *there is* none upright **a** men: they all lie in 871.1
Na 3: 8 populous No, that was situate **a** the rivers, 871.1
Hab 1: 5 Behold ye **a** the heathen, and regard, and 871.1
Zep 3:20 and a praise **a** all people of the earth, 871.1
Hag 2: 3 Who *is* left **a** you that saw this house in her 871.1
2: 5 so my spirit remaineth **a** you: 8432+871.1
Zec 1: 8 he stood **a** the myrtle trees that *were* in 996
1:10 the man that stood **a** the myrtle trees 996
1:11 of the LORD that stood **a** the myrtle trees, 996
3: 7 I will give thee places to walk **a** these that 996
7:14 I scattered them with a whirlwind **a** all 5921
8:13 *that* as ye were a curse **a** the heathen, 871.1
10: 9 I will sow them **a** the people: and they 871.1
12: 6 of Judah like a hearth of fire **a** the wood, 871.1
12: 8 he that is feeble **a** them at that day shall be 871.1
14:13 tumult from the LORD shall be **a** them; 871.1
Mal 1:10 Who *is there* even **a** you that would shut 871.1
1:11 my name *shall be* great **a** the Gentiles; 871.1
1:11 for my name *shall be* great **a** the heathen, 871.1
1:14 and my name *is* dreadful **a** the heathen. 871.1
Mt 2: 6 art not the least **a** the princes of Juda: *1722*
4:23 and all *manner of* disease **a** the people. *1722*
9:35 and every disease **a** the people. *1722*
11:11 **A** *them that are* born of women there hath *1722*
12:11 unto them, What man shall there be **a** you, *1537*
13: 7 And some fell **a** thorns; and the thorns *1909*
13:22 He also that received seed **a** the thorns is he *1519*
13:25 and sowed tares **a** the wheat, *303+3319*
13:32 it is the greatest **a** herbs, and becometh a NIG
13:49 and sever the wicked from **a** the just, *3319*
16: 7 And they reasoned **a** themselves, saying, *1722*
16: 8 why reason ye **a** yourselves, because *1722*
20:26 But it shall not be so **a** you: but *1722*
20:26 but whosoever will be great **a** you, let him *1722*
20:27 And whosoever will be chief **a** you, let him *1722*
21:38 they said **a** themselves, This is the heir; *1722*
23:11 But he that is greatest **a** you shall be your NIG
26: 5 *day*, lest there be an uproar **a** the people. *1722*
27:35 They parted my garments **a** them, and NIG
27:56 **A** which was Mary Magdalene, and *1722*
28:15 this saying is commonly reported **a** *3844*
Mk 1:27 insomuch that *they* questioned **a** *4314*
4: 7 And some fell **a** thorns, and the thorns grew *1519*
4:18 And these are they which are sown **a** *1519*
5: 3 Who had *his* dwelling **a** the tombs; *1722*
6: 4 and **a** his own kin, and in his own house. *1722*
6:41 and the two fishes divided he **a** *them* all. NIG
8:16 And they reasoned **a** themselves, saying, *4314*
8:19 When I brake the five loaves **a** five *1519*
8:20 And when the seven **a** four thousand, *1519*
9:33 What *was it that* ye disputed **a** yourselves *4314*
9:34 for by the way they had disputed **a** *4314*
10:26 saying **a** themselves, Who then can be *4314*
10:43 But so shall it not be **a** you: but *1722*
10:43 but whosoever will be great **a** you, shall be *1722*
13:10 And the gospel must first be published **a** all *1519*
15:31 mocking said **a** themselves with the scribes, *4314*
15:40 **a** whom was Mary Magdalene, and *1722*
16: 3 And they said **a** themselves, Who shall roll *4314*
Lk 1: 1 things which are most surely believed **a** us, *1722*
1:25 on *me*, to take away my reproach **a** men. *1722*
1:28 *is* with thee: blessed *art* thou **a** women. *1722*
1:42 Blessed *art* thou **a** women, and blessed *is* *1722*
2:44 and they sought him **a** *their* kinsfolk and *1722*
4:36 and spake **a** themselves, saying, What a *4314*
7:16 That a great prophet is risen up **a** us; *1722*
7:28 **A** *those that are* born of women there is not *1722*
8: 7 And some fell **a** thorns; and *1722+3319*
8:14 And that which fell **a** thorns are they, *1519*
9:46 Then there arose a reasoning **a** them, which *1722*
9:48 for he that is least **a** you all, the same shall *1722*
10: 3 I send you forth as lambs **a** wolves. *1722+3319*
10:30 and **fell a** thieves, which stripped him of his *4045*
10:36 was neighbour unto him that fell **a** *1519*
19: 2 which was *the* **chief a** the **publicans**, and *754*
19:39 And some of the Pharisees **from a** *575*
20:14 they reasoned **a** themselves, saying, This is *4314*
22:17 said, Take this, and divide *it* **a** yourselves: *1519*
22:23 And they began to inquire **a** themselves, *4314*
22:24 And there was also a strife **a** them, which *1722*
22:26 but he that is greatest **a** you, let him be as *1722*
22:27 but I am **a** you as he that serveth. *1722+3319*
22:37 And he was reckoned **a** the transgressors: *3326*
22:55 Peter sat down **a** them. *1722+3319*
24: 5 Why seek ye the living **a** the dead? *3326*
24:47 be preached in his name **a** all nations, *1519*
Jn 1:14 and dwelt **a** us, (and we beheld his glory, *1722*
1:26 but there standeth one **a** you, whom ye *3319*
6: 9 small fishes: but what are they **a** so many? *1519*
6:43 said unto them, Murmur not **a** yourselves. *3326*
7:12 And there was much murmuring **a** *1722*
7:35 Then said the Jews **a** themselves, *4314*
7:35 will he go unto the **dispersed a** *1290*
7:43 So there was a division **a** the people *1722*
8: 7 said unto them, He that is without sin **a** you, NIG
9:16 And there was a division **a** them. *1722*
10:19 again **a** the Jews for these sayings. *1722*
11:54 walked no more openly **a** the Jews; *1722*
11:56 and spake **a** themselves, as they stood in *3326*
12:19 The Pharisees therefore said **a** themselves, *4314*
12:20 And there were certain Greeks **a** them that *1537*
12:42 Nevertheless **a** the *chief* rulers also many *1537*
15:24 If I had not done **a** them the works which *1722*
16:17 Then said *some* of his disciples **a** *4314*
16:19 Do ye inquire **a** yourselves of that I said, *3326*
19:24 They said therefore **a** themselves, Let us *4314*
19:24 They **parted** my raiment **a** them, and *1266*
21:23 Then went this saying abroad **a** *1519*
Ac 1:21 that the Lord Jesus went in and out **a** us, *1909*
2:22 a man approved of God **a** you by miracles *1519*
3:23 shall be destroyed **from a** the people. *1537*

Ac 4:12 other name under heaven given **a** men, *1722*
4:15 of the council, they conferred **a** themselves, *4314*
4:17 But that it spread no further **a** the people, *1519*
4:34 Neither was there any **a** them that lacked: *1722*
5:12 and wonders wrought **a** the people; *1722*
5:34 had in reputation **a** all the people, and NIG
6: 3 look ye out **a** you seven men of honest *1537*
6: 8 great wonders and miracles **a** the people. *1722*
10:22 of good report **a** all the nation of the Jews, *5259*
12:18 there was no small stir **a** the soldiers, *1722*
13:26 and whosoever **a** you feareth God, *1722*
14:14 and ran in **a** the people, crying out, *1519*
15: 7 a good while ago God made choice **a** us, *1722*
15:12 wonders God had wrought **a** the Gentiles *1722*
15:19 which **from a** the Gentiles are turned to *575*
15:22 and Silas, chief *men* **a** the brethren: *1722*
17:33 So Paul departed from **a** them. *3319*
17:34 **a** the which *was* Dionysius the Areopagite, *1722*
18:11 teaching the word of God **a** them. *1722*
20:25 **a** whom I have gone preaching *1722*
20:29 shall grievous wolves enter **in a** you, *1519*
20:32 to give you an inheritance **a** all them which *1722*
21:19 had wrought **a** the Gentiles by his ministry. *1722*
21:21 that thou teachest all the Jews which are **a** *2596*
21:34 one *thing*, some another, **a** the multitude: *1722*
23:10 and to take him by force from **a** them, and *3319*
24: 5 a mover of sedition **a** all the Jews NIG
24:21 this one voice, that I cried standing **a** them, *1722*
25: 5 said he, which **a** you are able, go down *1722*
25: 6 And when he had tarried **a** them more than *1722*
26: 3 and questions which are **a** the Jews: *2596*
26: 4 which was at the first **a** mine own nation at *1722*
26:18 inheritance **a** them which are sanctified by *1722*
27:22 shall be no loss of *any man's* life **a** you, *1537*
28: 4 they said **a** themselves, No doubt this man *4314*
28:25 And when they agreed not **a** themselves, *4314*
28:29 and had great reasoning **a** themselves. *1722*
Ro 1: 5 for obedience to the faith **a** all nations, *1722*
1: 6 **A** whom are ye also *the* called of Jesus *1722*
1:13 that I might have some fruit **a** you also, *1722*
1:13 among you also, even as **a** other Gentiles. *1722*
2:24 For the name of God is blasphemed **a** *1722*
12: 3 given unto me, to every *man* that is **a** you, *1722*
15: 9 For this cause I will confess to thee **a** *1722*
16: 7 who are of note **a** the apostles, *1722*
1Co 1:10 and *that* there be no divisions **a** you; *1722*
1:11 of Chloe, that there are contentions **a** you. *1722*
2: 2 For I determined not to know any *thing* **a** *1722*
2: 6 Howbeit we speak wisdom **a** *them that are* *1722*
3: 3 for whereas *there is* **a** you envying, and *1722*
3:18 If any *man* **a** you seemeth to be wise in this *1722*
5: 1 commonly *that there is* fornication **a** you, *1722*
5: 2 this deed might be taken away from **a** you. *3319*
5:13 Therefore put away **from a** yourselves *that* *1537*
6: 7 therefore there is utterly a fault **a** you, *1722*
11:18 I hear that there be divisions **a** you; *1722*
11:19 For there must be also heresies **a** you, *1722*
11:19 *are* approved may be made manifest **a** you. *1722*
11:30 this cause many *are* weak and sickly **a** you, *1722*
15:12 how say some **a** you that there is no *1722*
2Co 1:19 who was preached **a** you by us, *even* by me *1722*
6:17 Wherefore come out from **a** them, and *3319*
10: 1 who in presence *am* base **a** you, but *1722*
11: 6 we *have been* throughly made manifest **a** *1519*
11:26 perils in the sea, *in* perils **a** false brethren; *1722*
12:12 apostle were wrought **a** you in all patience, *1722*
12:21 my God will humble *me* **a** you, and *that* I *4314*
Gal 1:16 that I might preach him **a** the heathen; *1722*
2: 2 *that* gospel which I preach **a** the Gentiles, *1722*
3: 1 been evidently set forth, crucified **a** you? *1722*
3: 5 you the Spirit, and worketh miracles **a** you, *1722*
Eph 2: 3 **A** whom also we all had our conversation *1722*
3: 8 that *I* should preach **a** the Gentiles *1722*
Php 2:15 **a** whom ye shine as lights in the world; *1722*
Col 1:27 of the glory of this mystery **a** the Gentiles; *1722*
1Th 1: 5 as ye know what manner of *men* we were **a** *1722*
2: 7 But we were gentle **a** you, *even* as a *1722+3319*
2:10 unblameably we behaved ourselves **a** you NIG
5:12 to know them which labour **a** you, and *1722*
5:13 work's sake. *And* be at peace **a** yourselves. *1722*
5:15 *is* good, both **a** yourselves, and to all *men*. *1519*
2Th 1:10 (because our testimony **a** you was believed) *1909*
3: 7 for we behaved not ourselves disorderly **a** *1722*
3:11 *are* some which walk **a** you disorderly, *1722*
2Ti 2: 2 And *the things* that thou hast heard of me **a** *1223*
Heb 5: 1 For every high priest taken **from a** men is *1537*
Jas 1:26 If any *man* **a** you seem to be religious, and *1722*
4: 1 whence *come* wars and fightings **a** you? *1722*
5:13 Is any **a** you afflicted? let him pray. Is any *1722*
5:14 Is any sick **a** you? let him call for the elders *1722*
1Pe 2:12 Having your conversation honest **a** *1722*
4: 8 And above all *things* have fervent charity **a** *1519*
5: 1 The elders which are **a** you I exhort, *1722*
5: 2 Feed the flock of God which is **a** you, *1722*
2Pe 2: 1 But there were false prophets also **a** *1722*
2: 1 even as there shall be false teachers **a** you, *1722*
2: 8 (For *that* righteous *man* dwelling **a** them, *1722*
3Jn 1: 9 who **loveth to have** the **preeminence a** *5383*
Jude 1:15 to convince all *that are* ungodly **a** them of *4012*
Rev 2:13 who was slain **a** you, where Satan dwelleth. *3844*
7:15 he that sitteth on the throne shall dwell **a** *1909*
14: 4 These were redeemed **from a** men, *being* *575*

AMONGST (59) [AMONG]

Ge 3: 8 God **a** the trees of the garden. 8432+871.1
23: 9 possession of a buryingplace **a** you. 8432+871.1
23:10 Ephron dwelt **a** the children of Heth: 8432+871.1
24: 3 of the Canaanites, **a** whom I dwell: 7130+871.1
30:33 *is* not speckled and spotted **a** the goats, 871.1
30:33 amongst the goats, and brown **a** the sheep, 871.1
30:35 all the brown **a** the sheep, and gave *them* 871.1
34:30 **a** the Canaanites and the Perizzites: 871.1
47: 6 thou knowest *any* man of activity **a** them, 871.1
Ex 9:20 He that feared the word of the LORD **a** 4480
10: 2 and my signs which I have done **a** them; 871.1
12:31 *and* get you forth from **a** my people, 8432
13:13 all the firstborn of man **a** thy children shalt 871.1
17: 7 Is the LORD **a** us, or not? 7130+871.1
25: 8 that I may dwell **a** them. 8432+871.1
29:45 I will dwell **a** the children of Israel, 8432+871.1
29:46 of Egypt, that I may dwell **a** them: 8432+871.1
30:12 that there be no plague **a** them, when *thou* 871.1
31:14 that soul shall be cut off from **a** his people. 7130
32:25 naked unto *their* shame **a** their enemies:) 871.1
34: 9 let my Lord, I pray thee, go **a** us; 7130+871.1
34:19 every firstling **a** thy cattle, *whether* ox or NIH
35: 5 Take ye from **a** you an offering unto 854
Lev 19:34 you shall be unto you as **one born a** you, 249
26:11 I will set my tabernacle **a** you: and 8432+871.1
Nu 11:21 **a** whom I *am, are* six hundred 7130+871.1
15:29 *both for* him that is born **a** the children of 871.1
25: 7 saw *it*, he rose up from **a** the congregation, 8432
Dt 14: 6 *and* cheweth the cud **a** the beasts: 871.1
31:16 whither they go *to be* **a** them, and 7130+871.1
31:17 because our God *is* not **a** us? 7130+871.1
Jos 7:11 and they have put *it* even **a** their own stuff. 871.1
7:12 except ye destroy the accursed from **a** you. 7130
23: 7 these nations, these that remain **a** you; 854
24: 5 to *that* which I did **a** them: 7130+871.1
Ru 2: 7 and gather after the reapers **a** the sheaves: 871.1
1Ch 4:23 and those that **dwelt a** plants and hedges: 3427
Job 34:37 he clappeth *his hands* **a** us, and 996
Pr 23:20 Be not **a** winebibbers; amongst riotous 871.1
23:20 **a** riotous eaters of flesh: 871.1
Isa 5:27 None *shall be* weary nor stumble **a** them; 871.1
29:14 I will proceed to do a marvellous work **a** NIH
33:14 who **a** us shall dwell *with* everlasting 3807.1
36:20 Who *are they* **a** all the gods of these lands, 871.1
41:28 even **a** them, and *there was* no counseller, 4480
Jer 32:20 this day, and in Israel, and **a** *other* men; 871.1
Eze 35:11 I will make myself known **a** them, when I 871.1
Mk 12: 7 But those husbandmen said **a** themselves, *4314*
Lk 16:15 for that which is highly esteemed **a** men is *1722*
Jn 6:52 The Jews therefore strove **a** themselves, *4314*
Ro 8:29 that he might be the firstborn **a** many *1722*
11:17 wert graffed in **a** them, and with *them* *1722*
1Co 5: 1 as is not so much as named **a** the Gentiles, *1722*
6: 5 Is it so, that there is not a wise *man* **a** you? *1722*
2Co 10:12 and **comparing** themselves **a** themselves, *4793*
Eph 5: 3 let it not be once named **a** you, *1722*
Col 4:16 And when *this* epistle is read **a** you, *3844*
Jas 3: 6 so is the tongue **a** our members, that it *1722*
3:13 and endued with knowledge **a** you? *1722*

AMORITE (14) [AMORITES]

Ge 10:16 the Jebusite, and the **A**, and the Girgashite, 567
14:13 for he dwelt in the plain of Mamre the **A**, 567
48:22 which I took out of the hand of the **A** with 567
Ex 33: 2 the **A**, and the Hittite, and the Perizzite, 567
34:11 I drive out before thee the **A**, and 567
Nu 32:39 and dispossessed the **A** which *was* in it. 567
Dt 2:24 I have given into thy hand Sihon the **A**, 567
Jos 9: 1 the Hittite, and the **A**, the Canaanite, 567
11: 3 *to* the **A**, and the Hittite, and the Perizzite, 567
1Ch 1:14 Jebusite also, and the **A**, and the Girgashite, 567
Eze 16: 3 thy father *was* an **A**, and thy mother a 567
16:45 mother *was* a Hittite, and your father an **A**. 567
Am 2: 9 Yet destroyed I the **A** before them, 567
2:10 the wilderness, to possess the land of the **A**. 567

AMORITES (73) [AMORITE]

Ge 14: 7 and also the **A**, that dwelt in Hazezon-tamar. 567
15:16 for the iniquity of the **A** *is* not yet full. 567
15:21 the **A**, and the Canaanites, and 567
Ex 3: 8 the **A**, and the Perizzites, and the Hivites, 567
3:17 the **A**, and the Perizzites, and the Hivites, 567
13: 5 and the **A**, and the Hivites, and the Jebusites, 567
23:23 and bring thee in unto the **A**, and the Hittites, 567
Nu 13:29 and the Hittites, and the Jebusites, and the **A**, 567
21:13 that cometh out of the coasts of the **A**: 567
21:13 border of Moab, between Moab and the **A**. 567
21:21 sent messengers unto Sihon king of the **A**, 567
21:25 Israel dwelt in all the cities of the **A**, 567
21:26 *was* the city of Sihon the king of the **A**, 567
21:29 into captivity unto Sihon king of the **A**. 567
21:31 Thus Israel dwelt in the land of the **A**. 567
21:32 and drove out the **A** that *were* there. 567
21:34 him as thou didst unto Sihon king of the **A**, 567
22: 2 Zippor saw all that Israel had done to the **A**. 567
32:33 the kingdom of Sihon king of the **A**, and 567
Dt 1: 4 After he had slain Sihon the king of the **A**, 567
1: 7 go *to* the mount of the **A**, and unto all 567
1:19 saw *by* the way of the mountain of the **A**, 567
1:20 Ye are come unto the mountain of the **A**, 567
1:27 to deliver us into the hand of the **A**, 567
1:44 the **A**, which dwelt in that mountain, came 567
3: 2 him as thou didst unto Sihon king of the **A**, 567
3: 8 the **A** the land that *was* on *this* side Jordan, 567
3: 9 call Sirion; and the **A** call it Shenir;) 567
4:46 in the land of Sihon king of the **A**, 567
4:47 of Og king of Bashan, two kings of the **A**, 567
7: 1 the **A**, and the Canaanites, and the Perizzites, 567
20:17 and the **A**, the Canaanites, and the Perizzites, 567
31: 4 kings of the **A**, and unto the land of them, 567
Jos 2:10 what you did unto the two kings of the **A**, 567
3:10 the Girgashites, and the **A**, and the Jebusites. 567
5: 1 it came to pass, when all the kings of the **A**, 567
7: 7 to deliver us into the hand of the **A**, 567
9:10 And all that he did to the two kings of the **A**, 567
10: 5 Therefore the five kings of the **A**, the king of 567
10: 6 for all the kings of the **A** that dwell in 567
10:12 up the **A** before the children of Israel, 567
12: 2 Sihon king of the **A**, who dwelt in Heshbon, 567
12: 8 the **A**, and the Canaanites, the Perizzites, 567
13: 4 unto Aphek, to the borders of the **A**: 567
13:10 all the cities of Sihon king of the **A**, 567
13:21 all the kingdom of Sihon king of the **A**, 567
24: 8 I brought you into the land of the **A**, 567
24:11 the **A**, and the Perizzites, and the Canaanites, 567
24:12 before you, *even* the two kings of the **A**; 567

Jos 24:15 or the gods of the **A**, in whose land ye dwell: 567
24:18 even the **A** which dwelt in the land: 567
Jdg 1:34 the **A** forced the children of Dan into 567
1:35 the **A** would dwell in mount Heres in 567
1:36 the coast of the **A** *was* from the going up to 567
3: 5 **A**, and Perizzites, and Hivites, and Jebusites: 567
6:10 fear not the gods of the **A**, in whose land ye 567
10: 8 on the *other* side Jordan in the land of the **A**, 567
10:11 from the **A**, from the children of Ammon, 567
11:19 sent messengers unto Sihon king of the **A**, 567
11:21 so Israel possessed all the land of the **A**, 567
11:22 they possessed all the coasts of the **A**, 567
11:23 the **A** from before his people Israel, 567
1Sa 7:14 there was peace between Israel and the **A**. 567
2Sa 21: 2 of Israel, but of the remnant of the **A**; 567
1Ki 4:19 *in* the country of Sihon king of the **A**, and 567
9:20 *And* all the people *that* were left of the **A**, 567
21:26 according to all *things* as did the **A**, 567
2Ki 21:11 hath done wickedly above all that the **A** did, 567
2Ch 8: 7 the **A**, and the Perizzites, and the Hivites, 567
Ezr 9: 1 the Moabites, the Egyptians, and the **A**. 567
Ne 9: 8 the **A**, and the Perizzites, and the Jebusites, 567
Ps 135:11 Sihon king of the **A**, and Og king of Bashan, 567
136:19 Sihon king of the **A**: for his mercy *endureth* 567

AMOS (8)
Am 1: 1 The words of **A**, who was among 5986
7: 8 LORD said unto me, **A**, what seest thou? 5986
7:10 **A** hath conspired against thee in the midst 5986
7:11 For thus **A** saith, Jeroboam shall die by 5986
7:12 Also Amaziah said unto **A**, O thou seer, go, 5986
7:14 answered **A**, and said to Amaziah, I *was* no 5986
8: 2 he said, **A**, what seest thou? And I said, 5986
Lk 3:25 which was *the son* of **A**, which was *the son* *301*

AMOUNTING (1)
2Ch 3: 8 it with fine gold, ***a*** to six hundred talents. NIH

AMOZ (13)
2Ki 19: 2 to Esai the prophet the son of **A**. 531
19:20 Isaiah the son of **A** sent to Hezekiah, saying, 531
20: 1 the prophet Isaiah the son of **A** came to him, 531
2Ch 26:22 did Isaiah the prophet, the son of **A**, write. 531
32:20 the prophet Isaiah the son of **A**, prayed and 531
32:32 the son of **A**, *and* in the book of the kings of 531
Isa 1: 1 The vision of Isaiah the son of **A**, which he 531
2: 1 The word that Isaiah the son of **A** saw 531
13: 1 which Isaiah the son of **A** did see. 531
20: 2 spake the LORD by Isaiah the son of **A**, 531
37: 2 unto Isaiah the prophet the son of **A**. 531
37:21 Then Isaiah the son of **A** sent unto Hezekiah, 531
38: 1 Isaiah the prophet the son of **A** came unto 531

AMPHIPOLIS (1)
Ac 17: 1 Now when they had passed through **A** and *295*

AMPLIAS (1)
Ro 16: 8 Greet **A** my beloved in the Lord. *291*

AMPLIATUS See AMPLIAS

AMRAM (14) [AMRAM'S, AMRAMITES]
Ex 6:18 **A**, and Izhar, and Hebron, and Uzziel: 6019
6:20 **A** took him Jochebed his father's sister to 6019
6:20 the years of the life of **A** *were* an hundred 6019
Nu 3:19 **A**, and Izehar, Hebron, and Uzziel. 6019
26:58 of the Korahites. And Kohath begat **A**. 6019
26:59 she bare unto **A** Aaron and Moses, and 6019
1Ch 1:41 **A**, and Eshban, and Ithran, and Cheran. 2566
6: 2 **A**, Izhar, and Hebron, and Uzziel. 6019
6: 3 the children of **A**; Aaron, and Moses, and 6019
6:18 the sons of Kohath *were*, **A**, and Izhar, and 6019
23:12 **A**, Izhar, Hebron, and Uzziel, four. 6019
23:13 The sons of **A**; Aaron and Moses: and 6019
24:20 sons of Levi *were these:* Of the sons of **A**; 6019
Ezr 10:34 Of the sons of Bani; Maadai, **A**, and Uel, 6019

AMRAM'S (1) [AMRAM]
Nu 26:59 the name of **A** wife *was* Jochebed, 6019

AMRAMITES (2) [AMRAM]
Nu 3:27 of Kohath *was* the family of the **A**, and 6020
1Ch 26:23 Of the **A**, *and* the Izharites, the Hebronites, 6020

AMRAPHEL (2)
Ge 14: 1 it came to pass in the days of **A** king of 569
14: 9 **A** king of Shinar, and Arioch king of Ellasar; 569

AMZI (2)
1Ch 6:46 The son of **A**, the son of Bani, the son of 557
Ne 11:12 the son of Pelaliah, the son of **A**, the son of 557

AN (1267) [A] See Index of Articles, Etc.

ANAB (2)
Jos 11:21 from **A**, and from all the mountains of 6024
15:50 And **A**, and Eshtemoh, and Anim, 6024

ANAH (12)
Ge 36: 2 Aholibamah the daughter of **A** the daughter 6034
36:14 the daughter of **A**, daughter of Zibeon, 6034
36:18 *came* of Aholibamah the daughter of **A**, 6034
36:20 Lotan, and Shobal, and Zibeon, and **A**, 6034
36:24 the children of Zibeon; both Aiah, and **A**: 6034
36:24 this *was that* **A** that found the mules in 6034
36:25 the children of **A** *were* these; Dishon, and 6034
36:25 Dishon, and Aholibamah the daughter of **A**. 6034
36:29 duke Shobal, duke Zibeon, duke **A**, 6034
1Ch 1:38 and **A**, and Dishon, and Ezer, and Dishan. 6034
1:40 And the sons of Zibeon; Aiah, and **A**. 6034
1:41 The sons of **A**; Dishon. And the sons of 6034

ANAHARATH (1)
Jos 19:19 And Hapharaim, and Shion, and **A**, 588

ANAIAH (2)
Ne 8: 4 **A**, and Urijah, and Hilkiah, and Maaseiah, 6043
10:22 Pelatiah, Hanan, **A**, 6043

ANAK (9) [ANAKIMS]
Nu 13:22 Sheshai, and Talmai, the children of **A**, 6061
13:28 moreover we saw the children of **A** there. 6061
13:33 the sons of **A**, *which come* of the giants: 6061
Dt 9: 2 Who can stand before the children of **A**! 6061
Jos 15:13 *even* the city of Arba the father of **A**, 6061
15:14 Caleb drove thence the three sons of **A**, 6061
15:14 and Ahiman, and Talmai, the children of **A**. 6061
21:11 gave them the city of Arbah the father of **A**, 6061
Jdg 1:20 and he expelled thence the three sons of **A**. 6061

ANAKIMS (9) [ANAK]
Dt 1:28 moreover we have seen the sons of the **A** 6062
2:10 a people great, and many, and tall, as the **A**; 6062
2:11 also were accounted giants, as the **A**; 6062
2:21 people great, and many, and tall, as the **A**; 6062
9: 2 people great and tall, the children of the **A**, 6062
Jos 11:21 cut off the **A** from the mountains, 6062
11:22 There was none of the **A** left in the land of 6062
14:12 for thou heardest in that day how the **A** 6062
14:15 which *Arba was* a great man among the **A**. 6062

ANAKITE See ANAKIMS

ANAMIM (2)
Ge 10:13 and **A**, and Lehabim, and Naphtuhim, 6047
1Ch 1:11 and **A**, and Lehabim, and Naphtuhim, 6047

ANAMITES See ANAMIM

ANAMMELECH (1)
2Ki 17:31 children in fire to Adrammelech and **A**, 6048

ANAN (1)
Ne 10:26 And Ahijah, Hanan, **A**, 6052

ANANI (1)
1Ch 3:24 and Johanan, and Dalaiah, and **A**, seven. 6054

ANANIAH (2)
Ne 3:23 son of Maaseiah the son of **A** by his house. 6055
11:32 *And at* Anathoth, Nob, **A**, 6055

ANANIAS (11)
Ac 5: 1 But a certain man named **A**, with Sapphira *367*
5: 3 But Peter said, **A**, why hath Satan filled *367*
5: 5 And **A** hearing these words fell down, and *367*
9:10 a certain disciple at Damascus, named **A**; *367*
9:10 and to him said the Lord in a vision, **A**. *367*
9:12 And hath seen in a vision a man named **A** *367*
9:13 Then **A** answered, Lord, I have heard by *367*
9:17 And **A** went his way, and entered into *367*
22:12 And one **A**, a devout man according to *367*
23: 2 And the high priest **A** commanded them that *367*
24: 1 And after five days **A** the high priest *367*

ANATH (2) [BETH-ANATH]
Jdg 3:31 after him was Shamgar the son of **A**, 6067
5: 6 In the days of Shamgar the son of **A**, in 6067

ANATHEMA (1)
1Co 16:22 Lord Jesus Christ, let him be **a**, Maran-atha. *331*

ANATHOTH (16)
Jos 21:18 **A** with her suburbs, and Almon with her 6068
1Ki 2:26 Get thee *to* **A**, unto thine own fields; 6068
1Ch 6:60 with her suburbs, and **A** with her suburbs. 6068
7: 8 Jerimoth, and Abiah, and **A**, and Alameth. 6068
Ezr 2:23 The men of **A**, an hundred twenty and 6068
Ne 7:27 The men of **A**, an hundred twenty and 6068
10:19 Hariph, **A**, Nebai, 6068
11:32 *And at* **A**, Nob, Ananiah, 6068
Isa 10:30 cause *it* to be heard unto Laish, O poor **A**. 6068
Jer 1: 1 of the priests that *were* in **A** in the land of 6068
11:21 thus saith the LORD of the men of **A**, 6068
11:23 for I will bring evil upon the men of **A**, 6068
29:27 why hast thou not reproved Jeremiah of **A**, 6069
32: 7 saying, Buy thee my field that *is* in **A**: 6068
32: 8 Buy my field, I pray thee, that *is* in **A**, 6068
32: 9 that *was* in **A**, and weighed him the money, 6068

ANATHOTHITE See ANETHOTHITE; ANETOTHITE

ANCESTORS (1)
Lev 26:45 sakes remember the covenant of their **a**, 7223

ANCHOR (1) [ANCHORS]
Heb 6:19 Which *hope* we have as an **a** of the soul, *45*

ANCHORS (3) [ANCHOR]
Ac 27:29 they cast four **a** out of the stern, and *45*
27:30 they would have cast **a** out of the foreship, *45*
27:40 And when they had taken up the **a**, *45*

ANCIENT (26) [ANCIENTS]
Dt 33:15 And for the chief things of the **a** mountains, 6924
Jdg 5:21 them away, *that* **a** river, the river Kishon. 6917
2Ki 19:25 *and* of **a** times that I have formed it? 6924
1Ch 4:22 and Jashubi-lehem. And *these are* **a** things. 6267
Ezr 3:12 *who were* **a men** that had seen the first 2205
Job 12:12 With the **a** *is* wisdom; and *in* length of days 3453
Ps 77: 5 the days of old, the years of **a times**. 5769
Pr 22:28 Remove not the **a** landmark, which thy 5769
Isa 3: 2 and the prophet, and the prudent, and the **a**, 2205
3: 5 shall behave himself proudly against the **a**, 2205
9:15 The **a** and honourable, he *is* the head; and 2205
19:11 *am* the son of the wise, the son of **a** kings? 6924
23: 7 joyous *city*, whose antiquity *is* of **a** days? 6924
37:26 *and* of **a** times, that I have formed it? 6924
44: 7 for me, since I appointed the **a** people? 5769
45:21 who hath declared this from **a time**? 6924
46:10 from **a times** *the things* that are not *yet* 6924
47: 6 upon the **a** hast thou very heavily laid thy 2205
51: 9 awake, as *in* the **a** days, *in* the generations 6924
Jer 5:15 it *is* a mighty nation, it *is* an **a** nation, 4480+5769
18:15 to stumble in their ways *from* the **a** paths, 5769
Eze 9: 6 they began at the **a** men which *were* before 2205
36: 2 even the **a** high places are ours in 5769
Da 7: 9 were cast *down*, and the **A** of days did sit, 6268
7:13 came to the **A** of days, and they brought 6268
7:22 Until the **A** of days came, and 6268

ANCIENTS (10) [ANCIENT]
1Sa 24:13 As saith the proverb of the **a**, 6931
Ps 119:100 I understand more than the **a**, because 2205
Isa 3:14 into judgment with the **a** of his people, 2205
24:23 in Jerusalem, and before his **a** gloriously. 2205
Jer 19: 1 *take* of the **a** of the people, and of 2205
19: 1 of the people, and of the **a** of the priests; 2205
Eze 7:26 from the priest, and counsel from the **a**. 2205
8:11 seventy men of the **a** of the house of Israel, 2205
8:12 hast thou seen what the **a** of the house of 2205
27: 9 The **a** of Gebal and the wise *men* thereof 2205

AND (51713) See Index of Articles, Etc.

ANDREW (13)
Mt 4:18 Simon called Peter, and **A** his brother, *406*
10: 2 who is called Peter, and **A** his brother; *406*
Mk 1:16 and **A** his brother casting a net into the sea: *406*
1:29 they entered into the house of Simon and **A**, *406*
3:18 And **A**, and Philip, and Bartholomew, and *406*
13: 3 James and John and **A** asked him privately, *406*
Lk 6:14 and **A** his brother, James and John, Philip *406*
Jn 1:40 and followed him, was **A**, Simon Peter's *406*
1:44 was of Bethsaida, the city of **A** and Peter. *406*
6: 8 One of his disciples, **A**, Simon Peter's *406*
12:22 Philip cometh and telleth **A**: and *406*
12:22 and again **A** and Philip tell Jesus. *406*
Ac 1:13 James, and John, and **A**, Philip, and Thomas, *406*

ANDRONICUS (1)
Ro 16: 7 Salute **A** and Junia, my kinsmen, and *408*

ANEM (1)
1Ch 6:73 with her suburbs, and **A** with her suburbs: 6046

ANER (3)
Ge 14:13 brother of Eshcol, and brother of **A**: 6063
14:24 went with me, **A**, Eshcol, and Mamre; 6063
1Ch 6:70 **A** with her suburbs, and Bileam with her 6063

ANETHOTHITE (1) [ANETOTHITE]
2Sa 23:27 Abiezer the **A**, Mebunnai the Hushathite, 6069

ANETOTHITE (1) [ANETHOTHITE]
1Ch 27:12 for the ninth month *was* Abiezer the **A**, 6069

ANGEL (201) [ANGEL'S, ANGELS, ANGELS', ARCHANGEL]
Ge 16: 7 the **a** of the LORD found her by a 4397
16: 9 the **a** of the LORD said unto her, 4397
16:10 the **a** of the LORD said unto her, I will 4397
16:11 the **a** of the LORD said unto her, Behold, 4397
21:17 the **a** of God called to Hagar out of heaven, 4397
22:11 the **a** of the LORD called unto him out of 4397
22:15 the **a** of the LORD called unto Abraham 4397
24: 7 he shall send his **a** before thee, and 4397
24:40 will send his **a** with thee, and prosper thy 4397
31:11 the **a** of God spake unto me in a dream, 4397
48:16 The **A** which redeemed me from all evil, 4397
Ex 3: 2 the **a** of the LORD appeared unto him in a 4397
14:19 the **a** of God, which went before the camp 4397
23:20 Behold, I send an **A** before thee, to keep 4397
23:23 For mine **A** shall go before thee, and 4397
32:34 behold, mine **A** shall go before thee: 4397
33: 2 I will send an **a** before thee; and I will drive 4397
Nu 20:16 sent an **a**, and hath brought us forth out of 4397
22:22 the **a** of the LORD stood in the way for an 4397
22:23 the ass saw the **a** of the LORD standing in 4397
22:24 the **a** of the LORD stood in a path of 4397
22:25 when the ass saw the **a** of the LORD, she 4397
22:26 the **a** of the LORD went further, and 4397
22:27 when the ass saw the **a** of the LORD, she 4397
22:31 he saw the **a** of the LORD standing in 4397
22:32 the **a** of the LORD said unto him, 4397
22:34 Balaam said unto the **a** of the LORD, 4397
22:35 the **a** of the LORD said unto Balaam, 4397
Jdg 2: 1 an **a** of the LORD came up from Gilgal to 4397
2: 4 when the **a** of the LORD spake these 4397
5:23 Curse ye Meroz, said the **a** of the LORD, 4397
6:11 there came an **a** of the LORD, and 4397
6:12 the **a** of the LORD appeared unto him, 4397
6:20 the **a** of God said unto him, Take the flesh 4397
6:21 the **a** of the LORD put forth the end of 4397
6:21 the unleavened *cakes*. Then the **a** of 4397
6:22 when Gideon perceived that he *was* an **a** of 4397
6:22 I have seen an **a** of the LORD face to face. 4397
13: 3 the **a** of the LORD appeared unto 4397
13: 6 *was* like the countenance of an **a** of God, 4397
13: 9 the **a** of God came again unto the woman as 4397
13:13 the **a** of the LORD said unto Manoah, 4397
13:15 Manoah said unto the **a** of the LORD, 4397
13:16 the **a** of the LORD said unto Manoah, 4397
13:16 For Manoah knew not that he *was* an **a** of 4397
13:17 Manoah said unto the **a** of the LORD, 4397
13:18 the **a** of the LORD said unto him, Why 4397
13:19 *the* **a** did wondrously; and Manoah and NIH

Jdg 13:20 that the **a** of the LORD ascended in 4397
13:21 the **a** of the LORD did no more appear to 4397
13:21 Manoah knew that he *was* an **a** of 4397
1Sa 29: 9 thou *art* good in my sight, as an **a** of God: 4397
2Sa 14:17 for as an **a** of God, so *is* my lord the king to 4397
14:20 according to the wisdom of an **a** of God, 4397
19:27 but my lord the king *is* as an **a** of God: 4397
24:16 when the **a** stretched out his hand *upon* 4397
24:16 said to the **a** that destroyed the people, *It is* 4397
24:16 the **a** of the LORD was by 4397
24:17 when he saw the **a** that smote the people, 4397
1Ki 13:18 an **a** spake unto me by the word of 4397
19: 5 an **a** touched him, and said unto him, Arise 4397
19: 7 the **a** of the LORD came again the second 4397
2Ki 1: 3 the **a** of the LORD said to Elijah 4397
1:15 the **a** of the LORD said unto Elijah, 4397
19:35 that the **a** of the LORD went out, and 4397
1Ch 21:12 the **a** of the LORD destroying throughout 4397
21:15 God sent an **a** unto Jerusalem to destroy it: 4397
21:15 said to the **a** that destroyed, *It is* enough, 4397
21:15 the **a** of the LORD stood by 4397
21:16 saw the **a** of the LORD stand between 4397
21:18 the **a** of the LORD commanded Gad to 4397
21:20 Ornan turned back, and saw the **a**; and 4397
21:27 the LORD commanded the **a**; and he put 4397
21:30 of the sword of the **a** of the LORD. 4397
2Ch 32:21 the LORD sent an **a**, which cut off all 4397
Ps 34: 7 The **a** of the LORD encampeth round 4397
35: 5 and let the **a** of the LORD chase *them.* 4397
35: 6 and let the **a** of the LORD persecute them. 4397
Ecc 5: 6 neither say thou before the **a**, that it *was* an 4397
Isa 37:36 the **a** of the LORD went forth, and 4397
63: 9 and the **a** of his presence saved them: 4397
Da 3:28 who hath sent his **a**, and delivered his 4398
6:22 My God hath sent his **a**, and hath shut 4398
Hos 12: 4 he had power over *the* **a**, and prevailed: 4397
Zec 1: 9 And the **a** that talked with me said unto me, 4397
1:11 they answered the **a** of the LORD that 4397
1:12 the **a** of the LORD answered and said, 4397
1:13 the LORD answered the **a** that talked with 4397
1:14 So the **a** that communed with me said unto 4397
1:19 I said unto the **a** that talked with me, 4397
2: 3 the **a** that talked with me went forth, and 4397
2: 3 and another **a** went out to meet him, 4397
3: 1 priest standing before the **a** of the LORD, 4397
3: 3 filthy garments, and stood before the **a**. 4397
3: 5 And the **a** of the LORD stood *by.* 4397
3: 6 the **a** of the LORD protested unto Joshua, 4397
4: 1 the **a** that talked with me came again, and 4397
4: 4 and spake to the **a** that talked with me, 4397
4: 5 the **a** that talked with me answered and 4397
5: 5 the **a** that talked with me went forth, and 4397
5:10 said I to the **a** that talked with me, 4397
6: 4 and said unto the **a** that talked with me, 4397
6: 5 the **a** answered and said unto me, These *are* 4397
12: 8 as the **a** of the LORD before them. 4397
Mt 1:20 *the* **a** of the Lord appeared unto him in a 32
1:24 sleep did as the **a** of the Lord had bidden him, 32
2:13 *the* **a** of the Lord appeareth to Joseph in a 32
2:19 an **a** of the Lord appeareth in a dream to 32
28: 2 for *the* **a** of the Lord descended from heaven, 32
28: 5 And the **a** answered and said unto the women, 32
Lk 1:11 And there appeared unto him an **a** of the Lord 32
1:13 But the **a** said unto him, Fear not, Zacharias: 32
1:18 And Zacharias said unto the **a**, Whereby shall 32
1:19 And the **a** answering said unto him, I am 32
1:26 And in the sixth month the **a** Gabriel was sent 32
1:28 And the **a** came in unto her, and said, Hail, 32
1:30 And the **a** said unto her, Fear not, Mary: 32
1:34 Then said Mary unto the **a**, How shall this be, 32
1:35 And the **a** answered and said unto her, 32
1:38 to thy word. And the **a** departed from her. 32
2: 9 *the* **a** of the Lord came upon them, and 32
2:10 And the **a** said unto them, Fear not: 32
2:13 And suddenly there was with the **a** a 32
2:21 named of the **a** before he was conceived in 32
22:43 And there appeared an **a** unto him from 32
Jn 5: 4 For an **a** went down at a *certain* season into 32
12:29 it thundered: others said, An **a** spake to him. 32
Ac 5:19 But *the* **a** of the Lord by night opened 32
6:15 saw his face as it had been the face of an **a**. 32
7:30 an **a** of the Lord in a flame of fire in a bush. 32
7:35 a deliverer by the hand of the **a** which 32
7:38 the **a** which spake to him in the mount Sina, 32
8:26 And *the* **a** of the Lord spake unto Philip, 32
10: 3 an **a** of God coming in to him, and 32
10: 7 And when the **a** which spake unto Cornelius 32
10:22 was warned from God by a holy **a** to send for 32
11:13 And he shewed us how he had seen an **a** in his 32
12: 7 *the* **a** of the Lord came upon *him,* and a light 32
12: 8 And the **a** said unto him, Gird thyself, and 32
12: 9 not that it was true which was done by the **a**; 32
12:10 and forthwith the **a** departed from him. 32
12:11 that the Lord hath sent his **a**, and 32
12:15 that it was *even* so. Then said they, It is his **a**. 32
12:23 And immediately *the* **a** of the Lord smote 32
23: 8 there is no resurrection, neither **a** nor spirit: 32
23: 9 but if a spirit or an **a** hath spoken to him, 32
27:23 For there stood by me this night *the* **a** of God, 32
2Co 11:14 for Satan himself is transformed into an **a** of 32
Gal 1: 8 But though we, or an **a** from heaven, 32
4:14 but received me as an **a** of God, *even* as 32
Rev 1: 1 and signified *it* by his **a** unto his servant John: 32
2: 1 Unto the **a** of the church of Ephesus write; 32
2: 8 And unto the **a** of the church in Smyrna write; 32
2:12 And to the **a** of the church in Pergamos write; 32
2:18 And unto the **a** of the church in Thyatira 32
3: 1 And unto the **a** of the church in Sardis write; 32
3: 7 And to the **a** of the church in Philadelphia 32
3:14 And unto the **a** of the church of 32
5: 2 And I saw a strong **a** proclaiming with a loud 32
7: 2 And I saw another **a** ascending from the east, 32
8: 3 And another **a** came and stood at the altar, 32
8: 5 And the **a** took the censer, and filled it with 32
8: 7 The first **a** sounded, and there followed hail NIG

Rev 8: 8 And the second **a** sounded, and as *it were* a 32
8:10 And the third **a** sounded, and there fell a great 32
8:12 And the fourth **a** sounded, and the third *part* 32
8:13 heard an **a** flying through the midst of heaven, 32
9: 1 And the fifth **a** sounded, and I saw a star fall 32
9:11 *which is* the **a** of the bottomless *pit,* whose 32
9:13 And the sixth **a** sounded, and I heard a voice 32
9:14 Saying to the sixth **a** which had the trumpet, 32
10: 1 And I saw another mighty **a** come down from 32
10: 5 And the **a** which I saw stand upon the sea and 32
10: 7 But in the days of the voice of the seventh **a**, 32
10: 8 the hand of the **a** which standeth upon the sea 32
10: 9 And I went unto the **a**, and said unto him, 32
11: 1 and the **a** stood, saying, Rise, and measure 32
11:15 And the seventh **a** sounded; and there were 32
14: 6 And I saw another **a** fly in the midst of 32
14: 8 And there followed another **a**, saying, 32
14: 9 And *the* third **a** followed them, saying with a 32
14:15 And another **a** came out of the temple, 32
14:17 And another **a** came out of the temple which 32
14:18 And another **a** came out from the altar, 32
14:19 And the **a** thrust in his sickle into the earth, 32
16: 3 And the second **a** poured out his vial upon 32
16: 4 And the third **a** poured out his vial upon 32
16: 5 And I heard the **a** of the waters say, Thou art 32
16: 8 And the fourth **a** poured out his vial upon 32
16:10 And the fifth **a** poured out his vial upon 32
16:12 And the sixth **a** poured out his vial upon 32
16:17 And the seventh **a** poured out his vial into 32
17: 7 And the **a** said unto me, Wherefore didst thou 32
18: 1 And after these *things* I saw another **a** come 32
18:21 And a mighty **a** took up a stone like a great 32
19:17 And I saw an **a** standing in the sun; and 32
20: 1 And I saw an **a** come down from heaven, 32
21:17 *to* the measure of a man, that is, of *the* **a**. 32
22: 6 the Lord God of the holy prophets sent his **a** 32
22: 8 I fell down to worship before the feet of the **a** 32
22:16 I Jesus have sent mine **a** to testify unto you 32

ANGEL'S (2) [ANGEL]

Rev 8: 4 ascended up before God out of the **a** hand. 32
10:10 And I took the little book out of the **a** hand, 32

ANGELS (93) [ANGEL]

Ge 19: 1 there came two **a** to Sodom at even; and 4397
19:15 the **a** hastened Lot, saying, Arise, take thy 4397
28:12 behold the **a** of God ascending and 4397
32: 1 went on his way, and the **a** of God met him. 4397
Job 4:18 and his **a** he charged with folly: 4397
Ps 8: 5 thou hast made him a little lower than the **a**, 430
68:17 *are* twenty thousand, *even* thousands of **a**: 8136
78:49 trouble, *by* sending evil **a** *among them.* 4397
91:11 For he shall give his **a** charge over thee, 4397
103:20 Bless the LORD, ye his **a**, that excel in 4397
104: 4 Who maketh his **a** spirits; his ministers a 4397
148: 2 Praise ye him, all his **a**: praise ye him, 4397
Mt 4: 6 He shall give his **a** charge concerning thee: 32
4:11 and behold, **a** came and ministered unto him. 32
13:39 the end of the world; and the reapers are *the* **a**. 32
13:41 The Son of man shall send forth his **a**, and 32
13:49 the **a** shall come forth, and sever the wicked 32
16:27 come in the glory of his Father with his **a**: 32
18:10 That in heaven their **a** do always behold 32
22:30 but are as *the* **a** of God in heaven. 32
24:31 And he shall send his **a** with a great sound of 32
24:36 not the **a** of heaven, but my Father only. 32
25:31 and all the holy **a** with him, then shall he sit 32
25:41 prepared for the devil and his **a**: 32
26:53 give me more than twelve legions of **a**? 32
Mk 1:13 wild beasts; and the **a** ministered unto him. 32
8:38 in the glory of his Father with the holy **a**. 32
12:25 but are as *the* **a** which are in heaven. 32
13:27 And then shall he send his **a**, and shall gather 32
13:32 not the **a** which are in heaven, neither the Son, 32
Lk 2:15 as the **a** were gone away from them into 32
4:10 He shall give his **a** charge over thee, to keep 32
9:26 and *in his* Father's, and of the holy **a**. 32
12: 8 Son of man also confess before the **a** of God: 32
12: 9 men shall be denied before the **a** of God. 32
15:10 there is joy in the presence of the **a** of God 32
16:22 was carried by the **a** into Abraham's bosom: 32
20:36 for they are **equal unto** *the* **a**; and are 2465
24:23 saying, that *they* had also seen a vision of **a**, 32
Jn 1:51 and the **a** of God ascending and 32
20:12 And seeth two **a** in white sitting, the one at 32
Ac 7:53 have received the law by the disposition of **a**, 32
Ro 8:38 nor life, nor **a**, nor principalities, nor powers, 32
1Co 4: 9 unto the world, and to **a**, and to men. 32
6: 3 Know ye not that we shall judge **a**? how much 32
11:10 to have power on *her* head because of the **a**. 32
13: 1 I speak with the tongues of men and of **a**, 32
Gal 3:19 *it was* ordained by **a** in the hand of a 32
Col 2:18 in a voluntary humility and worshipping of **a**, 32
2Th 1: 7 be revealed from heaven with his mighty **a**, 32
1Ti 3:16 justified in the Spirit, seen of **a**, preached unto 32
5:21 and the Lord Jesus Christ, and the elect **a**, 32
Heb 1: 4 Being made so much better than the **a**, as he 32
1: 5 For unto which of the **a** said he at any time, 32
1: 6 And let all the **a** of God worship him. 32
1: 7 And of the **a** he saith, Who maketh his angels 32
1: 7 Who maketh his **a** spirits, and his ministers a 32
1:13 But to which of the **a** said he at any time, 32
2: 2 For if the word spoken by **a** was stedfast, and 32
2: 5 For unto *the* **a** hath he not put in subjection 32
2: 7 Thou madest him a little lower than the **a**; 32
2: 9 who was made a little lower than the **a**, 32
2:16 For verily he took not on *him the nature of* **a**; 32
12:22 and to an innumerable company of **a**, 32
13: 2 for thereby some have entertained **a** 32
1Pe 1:12 which *things the* **a** desire to look into. 32
3:22 **a** and authorities and powers being made 32
2Pe 2: 4 For if God spared not the **a** that sinned, but 32
2:11 Whereas **a**, which are greater in power and 32
Jude 1: 6 And the **a** which kept not their first estate, but 32
Rev 1:20 The seven stars are the **a** of the seven 32

Rev 3: 5 his name before my Father, and before his **a**. 32
5:11 I heard the voice of many **a** round about 32
7: 1 And after these *things* I saw four **a** standing 32
7: 2 and he cried with a loud voice to the four **a**, 32
7:11 And all the **a** stood round about the throne, 32
8: 2 And I saw the seven **a** which stood before 32
8: 6 And the seven **a** which had the seven 32
8:13 the other voices of the trumpet of the three **a**, 32
9:14 Loose the four **a** which are bound in the great 32
9:15 And the four **a** were loosed, which were 32
12: 7 Michael and his **a** fought against the dragon; 32
12: 7 the dragon; and the dragon fought and his **a**, 32
12: 9 the earth, and his **a** were cast *out* with him. 32
14:10 and brimstone in the presence of the holy **a**, 32
15: 1 seven **a** having the seven last plagues; 32
15: 6 And the seven **a** came out of the temple, 32
15: 7 **a** seven golden vials full of the wrath of God, 32
15: 8 till the seven plagues of the seven **a** were 32
16: 1 voice out of the temple saying to the seven **a**, 32
17: 1 And there came one of the seven **a** which had 32
21: 9 And there came unto me one of the seven **a** 32
21:12 and at the gates twelve **a**, and names written 32

ANGELS' (1) [ANGEL]

Ps 78:25 Man did eat **a** food: he sent them meat to 47

ANGER (234) [ANGERED, ANGRY]

Ge 27:45 Until thy brother's **a** turn away from thee, 639
30: 2 Jacob's **a** was kindled against Rachel: and 639
44:18 and let not thine **a** burn against thy servant: 639
49: 6 for in their **a** they slew a man, and in their 639
49: 7 Cursed *be* their **a**, for *it was* fierce; and 639
Ex 4:14 the **a** of the LORD was kindled against 639
11: 8 And he went out from Pharaoh in a great **a**. 639
32:19 Moses' **a** waxed hot, and he cast the tables 639
32:22 Let not the **a** of my lord wax hot: 639
Nu 11: 1 the LORD heard *it;* and his **a** was kindled; 639
11:10 and the **a** of the LORD was kindled greatly; 639
12: 9 the **a** of the LORD was kindled against 639
22:22 God's **a** was kindled because he went: and 639
22:27 Balaam's **a** was kindled, and he smote 639
24:10 Balak's **a** was kindled against Balaam, and 639
25: 3 the **a** of the LORD was kindled against 639
25: 4 that the fierce **a** of the LORD may be 639
32:10 the LORD'S **a** was kindled the same time, 639
32:13 the LORD'S **a** was kindled against Israel, 639
32:14 to augment yet the fierce **a** of the LORD 639
Dt 4:25 the LORD thy God, to **provoke** him **to a**: 3707
6:15 lest the **a** of the LORD thy God be kindled 639
7: 4 will the **a** of the LORD be kindled against 639
9:18 sight of the LORD, to **provoke** him **to a**. 3707
9:19 For I was afraid of the **a** and hot displeasure, 639
13:17 may turn from the fierceness of his **a**, 639
29:20 then the **a** of the LORD and his jealousy 639
29:23 which the LORD overthrew in his **a**, and 639
29:24 what *meaneth* the heat of this great **a**? 639
29:27 the **a** of the LORD was kindled against this 639
29:28 LORD rooted them out of their land in **a**, 639
31:17 my **a** shall be kindled against them in that 639
31:29 to **provoke** him **to a** through the work of 3707
32:16 with abominations **provoked** they him **to a**. 3707
32:21 they have **provoked** me **to a** with their 3707
32:21 I will **provoke** them **to a** with a foolish 3707
32:22 For a fire is kindled in my **a**, and shall burn 639
Jos 7: 1 the **a** of the LORD was kindled against 639
7:26 LORD turned from the fierceness of his **a**. 639
23:16 shall the **a** of the LORD be kindled against 639
Jdg 2:12 unto them, and **provoked** the LORD **to a**. 3707
2:14 the **a** of the LORD was hot against Israel, 639
2:20 the **a** of the LORD was hot against Israel; 639
3: 8 Therefore the **a** of the LORD was hot 639
6:39 Let not thine **a** be hot against me, and I will 639
8: 3 their **a** was abated toward him, when he 7307
9:30 of Gaal the son of Ebed, his **a** was kindled. 639
10: 7 the **a** of the LORD was hot against Israel, 639
14:19 his **a** was kindled, and he went up *to* his 639
1Sa 11: 6 those tidings, and his **a** was kindled greatly. 639
17:28 and Eliab's **a** was kindled against David, and 639
20:30 Then Saul's **a** was kindled against Jonathan, 639
20:34 So Jonathan arose from the table in fierce **a**, 639
2Sa 6: 7 the **a** of the LORD was kindled against 639
12: 5 David's **a** was greatly kindled against 639
24: 1 again the **a** of the LORD was kindled 639
1Ki 14: 9 to **provoke** me **to a**, and hast cast me 3707
14:15 their groves, **provoking** the LORD **to a**. 3707
15:30 **provoked** the LORD God of Israel **to a**. 3707
16: 2 to sin, to **provoke** me **to a** with their sins; 3707
16: 7 in **provoking** him **to a** with the work of his 3707
16:13 **provoking** the LORD God of Israel **to a** 3707
16:26 to **provoke** the LORD God of Israel **to a** 3707
16:33 **provoke** the LORD God of Israel **to a** 3707
21:22 wherewith thou hast **provoked** *me* **to a**, 3707
22:53 **provoked to a** the LORD God of Israel, 3707
2Ki 13: 3 the **a** of the LORD was kindled against 639
17:11 wicked things to **provoke** the LORD **to a**: 3707
17:17 sight of the LORD, to **provoke** him **to a**. 3707
21: 6 sight of the LORD, to **provoke** *him* **to a**. 3707
21:15 have **provoked** me **to a**, since the day their 3707
22:17 that they might **provoke** me **to a** with all 3707
23:19 had made to **provoke** *the LORD* **to a**, 3707
23:26 where*with* his **a** was kindled against Judah, 639
24:20 For through the **a** of the LORD it came to 639
1Ch 13:10 the **a** of the LORD was kindled against 639
2Ch 25:10 to go home *again:* wherefore their **a** was 639
25:10 and they returned home in great **a**. 639
25:15 Wherefore the **a** of the LORD was kindled 639
28:25 **provoked to a** the LORD God of his 3707
33: 6 sight of the LORD, to **provoke** him **to a**. 3707
34:25 that *they* might **provoke** me **to a** with all 3707
Ne 4: 5 for they have **provoked** *thee* **to a** before 3707
9:17 slow to **a**, and of great kindness, and 639
Est 1:12 king very wroth, and his **a** burned in him. 2534
Job 9: 5 know not: which overturneth them in his **a**. 639
9:13 *If* God will not withdraw his **a**, the proud 639
18: 4 He teareth himself in his **a**: shall the earth be 639

Job 21:17 *God* distributeth sorrows in his **a**. 639
35:15 because *it is* not *so,* he hath visited *in* his **a**; 639
Ps 6: 1 O LORD, rebuke me not in thine **a**, 639
7: 6 Arise, O LORD, in thine **a**, lift up thyself 639
21: 9 them as a fiery oven in the time of thine **a**: 6440
27: 9 *far* from me; put not thy servant away in **a**: 639
30: 5 For his **a** *endureth but* a moment; in his 639
37: 8 Cease from **a**, and forsake wrath: fret not 639
38: 3 soundness in my flesh because of thine **a**; 2195
56: 7 in *thine* **a** cast down the people, O God. 639
69:24 and let thy wrathful **a** take hold of them. 639
74: 1 *why* doth thine **a** smoke against the sheep of 639
77: 9 hath he in **a** shut up his tender mercies? 639
78:21 and **a** also came up against Israel; 639
78:38 many a time turned he his **a** away, and 639
78:49 He cast upon them the fierceness of his **a**, 639
78:50 He made a way to his **a**; he spared not their 639
78:58 For they **provoked** him **to a** with their high 3707
85: 3 turned *thyself* from the fierceness of thine **a**. 639
85: 4 and cause thine **a** towards us to cease. 3708
85: 5 wilt thou draw out thine **a** to all generations? 639
90: 7 For we are consumed by thine **a**, and by thy 639
90:11 Who knoweth the power of thine **a**? 639
103: 8 gracious, slow to **a**, and plenteous in mercy. 639
103: 9 neither will he keep *his* **a** for ever. NIH
106:29 Thus they **provoked** *him* **to a** with their 3707
145: 8 slow to **a**, and of great mercy. 639
Pr 15: 1 away wrath: but grievous words stir up **a**. 639
15:18 but *he that is* slow to **a** appeaseth strife. 639
16:32 *He that is* slow to **a** *is* better than the mighty; 639
19:11 The discretion of a man deferreth his **a**; and 639
20: 2 *whoso* **provoketh** him **to a** sinneth *against* 5674
21:14 A gift in secret pacifieth **a**: and a reward in 639
22: 8 reap vanity: and the rod of his **a** shall fail. 5678
27: 4 Wrath *is* cruel, and **a** *is* outrageous; but 639
Ecc 7: 9 for **a** resteth in the bosom of fools. 3708
Isa 1: 4 **provoked** the Holy One of Israel **unto a**, 5006
5:25 Therefore is the **a** of the LORD kindled 639
5:25 For all this his **a** is not turned away, but 639
7: 4 for the fierce **a** of Rezin with Syria, and 639
9:12 For all this his **a** is not turned away, but 639
9:17 For all this his **a** is not turned away, but 639
9:21 For all this his **a** is not turned away, but 639
10: 4 For all this his **a** is not turned away, but 639
10: 5 the rod of mine **a**, and the staff in their hand 639
10:25 shall cease, and mine **a** in their destruction. 639
12: 1 thine **a** is turned away, and thou comfortedst 639
13: 3 have also called my mighty ones for mine **a**, 639
13: 9 cruel both *with* wrath and fierce **a**, to lay 639
13:13 of hosts, and in the day of his fierce **a**. 639
14: 6 he that ruled the nations in **a**, *is* persecuted, 639
30:27 burning *with* his **a**, and the burden *thereof is* 639
30:30 with the indignation of *his* **a**, and *with* 639
42:25 he hath poured upon him the fury of his **a**, 639
48: 9 For my name's sake will I defer mine **a**, and 639
63: 3 for I will tread them in mine **a**, and 639
63: 6 And I will tread down the people in mine **a**, 639
65: 3 A people that **provoketh** me **to a** 3707
66:15 to render his **a** with fury, and his rebuke with 639
Jer 2:35 am innocent, surely his **a** shall turn from me. 639
3: 5 Will he reserve *his* **a** for ever? will he keep NIH
3:12 I will not cause mine **a** to fall upon you: 6440
3:12 the LORD, *and* I will not keep **a** for ever. NIH
4: 8 for the fierce **a** of the LORD is not turned 639
4:26 presence of the LORD, *and* by his fierce **a**. 639
7:18 other gods, that *they* may **provoke** me **to a**. 3707
7:19 Do they **provoke** me **to a**? saith 3707
7:20 mine **a** and my fury *shall be* poured out upon 639
8:19 Why have they **provoked** me **to a** with 3707
10:24 not in thine **a**, lest thou bring me to nothing. 639
11:17 **provoke** me **to a** in offering incense unto 3707
12:13 because of the fierce **a** of the LORD. 639
15:14 for a fire is kindled in mine **a**, *which* shall 639
17: 4 for ye have kindled a fire in mine **a**, 639
18:23 deal *thus* with them in the time of thine **a**. 639
21: 5 even in **a**, and in fury, and in great wrath. 639
23:20 The **a** of the LORD shall not return, 639
25: 6 **provoke** me not **to a** with the works of 3707
25: 7 that *ye* might **provoke** me **to a** with 3707
25:37 because of the fierce **a** of the LORD. 639
25:38 of the oppressor, and because of his fierce **a**. 639
30:24 The fierce **a** of the LORD shall not return, 639
32:29 unto other gods, to **provoke** me **to a**. 3707
32:30 **provoked** me **to a** with the work of their 3707
32:31 hath been to me *as a* **provocation of** mine **a** 639
32:32 which they have done to **provoke** me **to a**, 3707
32:37 whither I have driven them in mine **a**, and 639
33: 5 whom I have slain in mine **a** and in my fury, 639
36: 7 for great *is* the **a** and the fury that 639
42:18 As mine **a** and my fury hath been poured 639
44: 3 they have committed to **provoke** me **to a**, 3707
44: 6 my fury and mine **a** was poured forth, 639
49:37 *even* my fierce **a**, saith the LORD; 639
51:45 his soul from the fierce **a** of the LORD. 639
52: 3 For through the **a** of the LORD it came to 639
La 1:12 hath afflicted *me* in the day of his fierce **a**. 639
2: 1 the daughter of Zion with a cloud in his **a**, 639
2: 1 not his footstool in the day of his **a**! 639
2: 3 He hath cut off in *his* fierce **a** all the horn of 639
2: 6 hath despised in the indignation of his **a** 639
2:21 thou hast slain *them* in the day of thine **a**; 639
2:22 that in the day of the LORD'S **a** none 639
3:43 Thou hast covered with **a**, and persecuted us: 639
3:66 destroy them in **a** from under the heavens of 639
4:11 he hath poured out his fierce **a**, and 639
4:16 The **a** of the LORD hath divided them; 6440
Eze 5:13 Thus shall mine **a** be accomplished, and 639
5:15 when I shall execute judgments in thee in **a** 639
7: 3 I will send mine **a** upon thee, and will judge 639
7: 8 and accomplish mine **a** upon thee: 639
8:17 and have returned to **provoke** me **a**: 3707
13:13 shall be an overflowing shower in mine **a**, 639
16:26 thy whoredoms, to **provoke** me **to a**. 3707
20: 8 to accomplish my **a** against them in 639
20:21 to accomplish my **a** against them in 639
Eze 22:20 to melt *it;* so will I gather *you* in mine **a** and 639
25:14 they shall do in Edom according to mine **a** 639
35:11 I will even do according to thine **a**, and 639
43: 8 wherefore I have consumed them in mine **a**. 639
Da 9:16 let thine **a** and thy fury be turned away from 639
11:20 shall be destroyed, neither in **a**, nor in battle. 639
Hos 8: 5 cast *thee* off; mine **a** is kindled against them: 639
11: 9 I will not execute the fierceness of mine **a**, 639
12:14 Ephraim **provoked** *him* **to a** most bitterly: 3707
13:11 I gave thee a king in mine **a**, and took *him* 639
14: 4 for mine **a** is turned away from him. 639
Joel 2:13 slow to **a**, and of great kindness, and 639
Am 1:11 his **a** did tear perpetually, and he kept his 639
Jnh 3: 9 and repent, and turn away from his fierce **a**, 639
4: 2 slow to **a**, and of great kindness, and 639
Mic 5:15 I will execute vengeance in **a** and fury upon 639
7:18 he retaineth not his **a** for ever, because 639
Na 1: 3 The LORD *is* slow to **a**, and great in power, 639
1: 6 and who can abide in the fierceness of his **a**? 639
Hab 3: 8 *was* thine **a** against the rivers? *was* thy wrath 639
3:12 thou didst thresh the heathen in **a**. 639
Zep 2: 2 before the fierce **a** of the LORD come upon 639
2: 2 before the day of the LORD'S **a** come upon 639
2: 3 ye shall be hid in the day of the LORD'S **a**. 639
3: 8 them mine indignation, *even* all my fierce **a**: 639
Zec 10: 3 Mine **a** was kindled against the shepherds, 639
Mk 3: 5 he had looked round about on them with **a**, *3709*
Ro 10:19 *and* by a foolish nation I will **a** you. *3949*
Eph 4:31 and **a**, and clamour, and evil speaking, *3709*
Col 3: 8 But now you also put off all *these;* **a**, wrath, *3709*
3:21 provoke not your children *to* **a**, lest they be NIG

ANGERED (1) [ANGER]

Ps 106:32 They **a** *him* also at the waters of strife, so 7107

ANGLE (2)

Isa 19: 8 all they that cast **a** into the brooks shall 2443
Hab 1:15 They take up all of them with the **a**, 2443

ANGRY (44) [ANGER]

Ge 18:30 he said *unto him,* Oh let not the Lord be **a**, 2734
18:32 Oh let not the Lord be **a**, and I will speak 2734
45: 5 be not grieved, nor **a** with yourselves, 2734
Lev 10:16 he was **a** with Eleazar and Ithamar the sons 7107
Dt 1:37 Also the LORD was **a** with me for your 599
4:21 Furthermore the LORD was **a** with me for 599
9: 8 that the LORD was **a** with you to have 599
9:20 the LORD was very **a** with Aaron to have 599
Jdg 18:25 lest **a** fellows run upon thee, and 4751+5315
2Sa 19:42 wherefore then be ye **a** for this matter? 2734
1Ki 8:46 thou be **a** with them, and deliver them to 599
11: 9 the LORD was **a** with Solomon, because 599
2Ki 17:18 Therefore the LORD was very **a** with 599
2Ch 6:36 thou be **a** with them, and deliver them *over* 599
Ezr 9:14 wouldest thou not be **a** with us till *thou* hadst 599
Ne 5: 6 I was very **a** when I heard their cry and 2734
Ps 2:12 lest he be **a**, and ye perish *from* the way, 599
7:11 and God is **a** *with the wicked* every day. 2194
76: 7 may stand in thy sight when once thou art **a**? 639
79: 5 wilt thou be **a**, for ever? shall thy jealousy 599
80: 4 how long wilt thou be **a** against the prayer 6225
85: 5 Wilt thou be **a** with us for ever? wilt thou 599
Pr 14:17 *He that is* soon **a** dealeth foolishly: and 639
21:19 than with a contentious and an **a** woman. 3708
22:24 Make no friendship with an **a** man; and 639
25:23 *doth* an **a** countenance a backbiting tongue. 2194
29:22 An **a** man stirreth up strife, and a furious 639
Ecc 5: 6 wherefore should God be **a** at thy voice, 7107
7: 9 Be not hasty in thy spirit to be **a**: for anger 3707
SS 1: 6 my mother's children were **a** with me; 2787
Isa 12: 1 though thou wast **a** with me, thine anger is 599
Eze 16:42 and I will be quiet, and will be no more **a**. 3707
Da 2:12 For this cause the king was **a** and 1149
Jnh 4: 1 Jonah exceedingly, and he was **very a**. 2734
4: 4 said the LORD, Doest thou well to be **a**? 2734
4: 9 Doest thou well to be **a** for the gourd? 2734
4: 9 he said, I do well to be **a**, *even* unto death. 2734
Mt 5:22 That whosoever is **a** with his brother *3710*
Lk 14:21 of the house being **a** said to his servant, *3710*
15:28 And he was **a**, and would not go in: *3710*
Jn 7:23 are ye **a** at me, because I have made a man *5520*
Eph 4:26 Be ye **a**, and sin not: let not the sun go *3710*
Tit 1: 7 not selfwilled, not **soon a**, not given to *3711*
Rev 11:18 And the nations were **a**, and thy wrath is *3710*

ANGUISH (17)

Ge 42:21 in that we saw the **a** of his soul, when he 6869
Ex 6: 9 they hearkened not unto Moses for **a** of 7115
Dt 2:25 shall tremble, and be **in a** because of thee. 2342
2Sa 1: 9 for **a** is come upon me, because my life *is* 7661
Job 7:11 I will speak in the **a** of my spirit; 6862
15:24 Trouble and **a** shall make him afraid; 4691
Ps 119:143 Trouble and **a** have taken hold on me: 4689
Pr 1:27 when distress and **a** cometh upon you: 6695
Isa 8:22 behold trouble and darkness, dimness of **a**; 6695
30: 6 into the land of trouble and **a**, from whence 6695
Jer 4:31 the **a** as of her that bringeth forth her first 6869
6:24 **a** hath taken hold of us, *and* pain, as of a 6869
49:24 fear hath seized on *her:* **a** and sorrows have 6869
50:43 **a** took hold of him, *and* pangs as of a 6869
Jn 16:21 the child, she remembereth no more the **a**, *2347*
Ro 2: 9 Tribulation and **a**, upon every soul of man *4730*
2Co 2: 4 **a** of heart I wrote unto you with many *4928*

ANIAM (1)

1Ch 7:19 Ahian, and Shechem, and Likhi, and **A**. 593

ANIM (1)

Jos 15:50 And Anab, and Eshtemoh, and **A**, 6044

ANISE (1)

Mt 23:23 for ye pay tithe of mint and **a** and cummin, *432*

ANKLE (1) [ANKLES]

Ac 3: 7 his feet and **a** bones received strength, *4974*

ANKLES (1) [ANKLE]

Eze 47: 3 through the waters; the waters *were* to the **a**. 657

ANNA (1)

Lk 2:36 And there was *one* **A**, a prophetess, *451*

ANNAS (4)

Lk 3: 2 **A** and Caiaphas being the high priests, *452*
Jn 18:13 And led him away to **A** first; for he was *452*
18:24 Now **A** had sent him bound unto Caiaphas *452*
Ac 4: 6 And **A** the high priest, and Caiaphas, and *452*

ANOINT (35) [ANOINTED, ANOINTEDST, ANOINTEST, ANOINTING]

Ex 28:41 shalt **a** them, and consecrate them, and 4886
29: 7 and pour *it* upon his head, and **a** him. 4886
29:36 for it, and thou shalt **a** it, to sanctify it. 4886
30:26 thou shalt **a** the tabernacle of 4886
30:30 thou shalt **a** Aaron and his sons, and 4886
40: 9 **a** the tabernacle, and all that *is* therein, 4886
40:10 thou shalt **a** the altar of the burnt offering, 4886
40:11 thou shalt **a** the laver and his foot, and 4886
40:13 and **a** him, and sanctify him; 4886
40:15 thou shalt **a** them, as thou didst anoint their 4886
40:15 anoint them, as thou didst **a** their father, 4886
Lev 16:32 whom he shall **a**, and whom he shall 4886
Dt 28:40 but thou shalt not **a** *thyself with* the oil; 5480
Jdg 9: 8 The trees went forth on a time to **a** a king 4886
9:15 If in truth ye **a** me king over you, *then* 4886
Ru 3: 3 **a** thee, and put thy raiment upon thee, and 5480
1Sa 9:16 thou shalt **a** him to be captain over my 4886
15: 1 The LORD sent me to **a** thee to be king 4886
16: 3 thou shalt **a** unto me *him* whom I name 4886
16:12 the LORD said, Arise, **a** him: for this *is* 4886
2Sa 14: 2 **a** not *thyself with* oil, but be as a woman 5480
1Ki 1:34 Nathan the prophet **a** him there king over 4886
19:15 **a** Hazael to be king over Syria: 4886
19:16 Jehu the son of Nimshi shalt thou **a** to be 4886
19:16 shalt thou **a** to be prophet in thy room. 4886
Isa 21: 5 drink: arise, ye princes, *and* **a** the shield. 4886
Da 9:24 and prophecy, and to **a** the most Holy. 4886
10: 3 neither did I **a** myself **at all**, till three 5480+5480
Am 6: 6 and **a** themselves *with* the chief ointments: 4886
Mic 6:15 but thou shalt not **a** *thee with* oil; 5480
Mt 6:17 thou fastest, **a** thine head, and wash thy face; *218*
Mk 14: 8 she is come aforehand to **a** my body to *3462*
16: 1 that they might come and **a** him. *218*
Lk 7:46 Mine head with oil thou didst not **a**: but *218*
Rev 3:18 and **a** thine eyes *with* eyesalve, that thou *1472*

ANOINTED (98) [ANOINT]

Ex 29: 2 with oil, and wafers unleavened **a** with oil: 4886
29:29 to be **a** therein, and to be consecrated in 4888
Lev 2: 4 with oil, or unleavened wafers **a** with oil. 4886
4: 3 If the priest that is **a** do sin according to 4899
4: 5 the priest that is **a** shall take of 4899
4:16 the priest that is **a** shall bring of 4899
6:20 unto the LORD in the day when he is **a**; 4886
6:22 the priest of his sons that is **a** in his stead 4899
7:12 unleavened wafers **a** with oil, and 4886
7:36 in the day that he **a** them, *by* a statute for 4886
8:10 **a** the tabernacle and all that *was* therein, 4886
8:11 **a** the altar and all his vessels, both the laver 4886
8:12 Aaron's head, and **a** him, to sanctify him. 4886
Nu 3: 3 the sons of Aaron, the priests which were **a**, 4886
6:15 wafers of unleavened bread **a** with oil, and 4886
7: 1 had **a** it, and sanctified it, and all 4886
7: 1 and had **a** them, and sanctified them; 4886
7:10 of the altar in the day that it was **a**, 4886
7:84 in the day when it was **a**, by the princes of 4886
7:88 dedication of the altar, after *that* it was **a**. 4886
35:25 high priest, which was **a** with the holy oil. 4886
1Sa 2:10 unto his king, and exalt the horn of his **a**. 4899
2:35 and he shall walk before mine **a** for ever. 4899
10: 1 the LORD hath **a** thee to be captain over 4886
12: 3 me before the LORD, and before his **a**: 4899
12: 5 against you, and his **a** *is* witness this day, 4899
15:17 and the LORD **a** thee king over Israel? 4886
16: 6 said, Surely the LORD'S **a** *is* before him. 4899
16:13 and **a** him in the midst of his brethren; 4886
24: 6 the LORD'S **a**, to stretch forth mine hand 4899
24: 6 seeing he *is* the **a** of the LORD. 4899
24:10 against my lord; for he *is* the LORD'S **a**. 4899
26: 9 forth his hand against the LORD'S **a**, 4899
26:11 forth mine hand against the LORD'S **a**: 4899
26:16 have not kept your master, the LORD'S **a**. 4899
26:23 forth mine hand against the LORD'S **a**. 4899
2Sa 1:14 thine hand to destroy the LORD'S **a**? 4899
1:16 saying, I have slain the LORD'S **a**. 4899
1:21 *as though he had* not *been* **a** with oil. 4899
2: 4 there they **a** David king over the house of 4886
2: 7 also the house of Judah have **a** me king 4886
3:39 And I *am this* day weak, though **a** king; and 4886
5: 3 and they **a** David king over Israel. 4886
5:17 when the Philistines heard that they had **a** 4886
12: 7 I **a** thee king over Israel, and I delivered 4886
12:20 and **a** *himself,* and changed his apparel, and 5480
19:10 Absalom, whom we **a** over us, is dead in 4886
19:21 because he cursed the LORD'S **a**? 4899
22:51 sheweth mercy to his **a**, unto David, and 4899
23: 1 the **a** of the God of Jacob, and the sweet 4899
1Ki 1:39 of oil out of the tabernacle, and **a** Solomon. 4886
1:45 Nathan the prophet have **a** him king in 4886
5: 1 for he had heard that they had **a** him king in 4886
2Ki 9: 3 the LORD, I have **a** thee king over Israel. 4886
9: 6 I have **a** thee king over the people of 4886
9:12 the LORD, I have **a** thee king over Israel. 4886
11:12 they made him king, and **a** him; and 4886
23:30 **a** him, and made him king in his father's 4886
1Ch 11: 3 they **a** David king over Israel, according to 4886
14: 8 when the Philistines heard that David was **a** 4886

A

1Ch 16:22 *Saying,* Touch not mine **a**, and do my 4899
29:22 **a** *him* unto the LORD to be the chief 4886
2Ch 6:42 turn not away the face of thine **a**: 4899
22: 7 whom the LORD had **a** to cut off 4886
23:11 Jehoiada and his sons **a** him, and said, 4886
28:15 **a** them, and carried all the feeble of them 5480
Ps 2: 2 the LORD, and against his **a**, *saying,* 4899
18:50 sheweth mercy to his **a**, to David, and to his 4899
20: 6 Now know I that the LORD saveth his **a**; 4899
28: 8 and he *is* the saving strength of his **a**. 4899
45: 7 hath **a** thee *with* the oil of gladness above 4886
84: 9 and look upon the face of thine **a**. 4899
89:20 my servant; with my holy oil have I **a** him: 4886
89:38 thou hast been wroth with thine **a**. 4899
89:51 have reproached the footsteps of thine **a**. 4899
92:10 *of* an unicorn: I shall be **a** with fresh oil. 1101
105:15 *Saying,* Touch not mine **a**, and do my 4899
132:10 sake turn not away the face of thine **a**. 4899
132:17 to bud: I have ordained a lamp for mine **a**. 4899
Isa 45: 1 Thus saith the LORD to his **a**, to Cyrus, 4899
61: 1 the LORD hath **a** me to preach good 4886
La 4:20 the **a** of the LORD, was taken in their pits, 4899
Eze 16: 9 thy blood from thee, and I **a** thee with oil. 5480
28:14 Thou *art* the **a** cherub that covereth; and 4473
Hab 3:13 thy people, *even* for salvation with thine **a**; 4899
Zec 4:14 said he, These *are* the two **a** ones, that stand 3323
Mk 6:13 and **a** with oil many *that were* sick, and *218*
Lk 4:18 he hath **a** me to preach the gospel to *5548*
7:38 his feet, and **a** *them* with the ointment. *218*
7:46 this *woman* hath **a** my feet with ointment. *218*
Jn 9: 6 he **a** the eyes of the blind man with *2025*
9:11 and **a** mine eyes, and said unto me, Go to *2025*
11: 2 (It was *that* Mary which **a** the Lord with *218*
12: 3 and **a** the feet of Jesus, and wiped his feet *218*
Ac 4:27 whom thou hast **a**, both Herod, and *5548*
10:38 How God **a** Jesus of Nazareth with *5548*
2Co 1:21 with you in Christ, and hath **a** us, *is* God; *5548*
Heb 1: 9 hath **a** thee *with* the oil of gladness above *5548*

ANOINTEDST (1) [ANOINT]

Ge 31:13 where thou **a** the pillar, *and* where thou 4886

ANOINTEST (1) [ANOINT]

Ps 23: 5 thou **a** my head with oil; my cup runneth 1878

ANOINTING (28) [ANOINT]

Ex 25: 6 spices for **a** oil, and for sweet incense, 4888
29: 7 shalt thou take the **a** oil, and pour *it* upon 4888
29:21 and of the **a** oil, and sprinkle *it* upon Aaron, 4888
30:25 of the apothecary: it shall be a holy **a** oil. 4888
30:31 This shall be a holy **a** oil unto me 4888
31:11 the **a** oil, and sweet incense for the holy 4888
35: 8 spices for **a** oil, and for the sweet incense, 4888
35:15 the **a** oil, and the sweet incense, and 4888
35:28 and for the **a** oil, and for the sweet incense. 4888
37:29 he made the holy **a** oil, and the pure 4888
39:38 the **a** oil, and the sweet incense, and 4888
40: 9 thou shalt take the **a** oil, and anoint 4888
40:15 for their **a** shall surely be an everlasting 4888
Lev 7:35 This *is the portion* of the **a** of Aaron, and 4888
7:35 of Aaron, and of the **a** of his sons, 4888
8: 2 the **a** oil, and a bullock *for* the sin offering, 4888
8:10 Moses took the **a** oil, and anointed 4888
8:12 he poured of the **a** oil upon Aaron's head, 4888
8:30 Moses took of the **a** oil, and of the blood 4888
10: 7 for the **a** oil of the LORD *is* upon you. 4888
21:10 upon whose head the **a** oil was poured, and 4888
21:12 for the crown of the **a** oil of his God *is* 4888
Nu 4:16 the **a** oil, *and* the oversight of all 4888
18: 8 thee have I given them by reason of the **a**, 4888
Isa 10:27 yoke shall be destroyed because of the **a**. 8081
Jas 5:14 **a** him with oil in the name of the Lord: *218*
1Jn 2:27 But the **a** which ye have received of him *5545*
2:27 but as the same **a** teacheth you of all *things,* *5545*

ANON (2)

Mt 13:20 the word, and **a** with joy receiveth it; *2112*
Mk 1:30 sick of a fever, and **a** they tell him of her. *2112*

ANOTHER (448) [ANOTHER'S]

Ge 4:25 *said she,* hath appointed me **a** seed instead of 312
11: 3 they said one to **a**[S], Go to, let us make 7453
15:10 and laid each piece one against **a**[S]: 7453
26:21 they digged **a** well, and strove for that also: 312
26:22 he removed from thence, and digged **a** well; 312
26:31 betimes in the morning, and sware one to **a**: 251
29:19 to thee, than that I should give her to **a** man: 312
30:24 and said, The LORD shall add to me **a** son. 312
31:49 and thee, when we are absent one from **a**[S]. 7453
37: 9 he dreamed yet **a** dream, and told it his 312
37:19 they said one to **a**[S], Behold, this dreamer 251
42: 1 unto his sons, Why do ye look one upon **a**? NIH
42:21 they said one to **a**[S], We *are* verily guilty 251
42:28 and they were afraid, saying one to **a**[S], 251
43: 7 have ye **a** brother? and we told him NIH
43:33 his youth: and the men marvelled one at **a**[S]. 7453
Ex 10:23 They saw not one **a**[S], neither rose any from 251
16:15 children of Israel saw *it,* they said one to **a**[S], 251
18:16 I judge between one and **a**[S], and I do make 7453
21:10 If he take him **a** *wife;* her food, her raiment, 312
21:18 one smite **a**[S] with a stone, or with *his* fist, 7453
22: 5 in his beast, and shall feed in **a man's** field; 312
22: 9 for any manner of lost *thing,* which **a** NIH
25:20 and their faces *shall look* one to **a**[S]; 251
26: 3 curtains shall be coupled together one to **a**[S]; 269
26: 3 five curtains *shall be* coupled one to **a**[S]. 269
26: 4 make in the uttermost edge of **a** curtain, NIH
26: 5 that the loops may take hold one of **a**[S]. 269
26:17 in one board, set in order one against **a**[S]: 269
26:19 two sockets under **a** board for his two 259
26:21 one board, and two sockets under **a** board. 259
26:25 one board, and two sockets under **a** board. 259
36:10 And he coupled the five curtains one unto **a**: 259
36:10 *the other* five curtains he coupled one unto **a**. 259
Ex 36:11 likewise he made in the uttermost side of **a** NIH
36:12 the second: the loops held one *curtain* to **a**. 259
36:13 coupled the curtains one unto **a** with 259
36:22 had two tenons, equally distant one from **a**: 259
36:24 two sockets under **a** board for his two 259
36:26 one board, and two sockets under **a** board. 259
37: 8 and **a** cherub on the *other* end on that side: 259
37: 9 the mercy seat, with their faces one to **a**[S]; 251
37:19 three bowls made like almonds in **a** branch, 259
Lev 7:10 the sons of Aaron have, one *as much* as **a**[S]. 251
19:11 neither deal falsely, neither lie one to **a**[S]. 5997
20:10 the man that committeth adultery with **a** NIH
25:14 ye shall not oppress one **a**[S]: 251
25:17 Ye shall not therefore oppress one **a**[S]; 5997
25:46 ye shall not rule one over **a**[S] with rigour. 251
26:37 they shall fall one upon **a**[S], as it were before 251
27:20 or if he have sold the field to **a** man, it shall 312
Nu 5:19 uncleanness *with* **a** instead of thy husband, NIH
5:20 if thou hast gone aside *to* **a** instead of thy NIH
5:29 when a wife goeth aside *to* **a** instead of her NIH
8: 8 **a** young bullock shalt thou take for a sin 8145
14: 4 they said one to **a**[S], Let us make a captain, 251
14:24 because he had **a** spirit with him, and 312
23:13 Come, I pray thee, with me unto **a** place, 312
23:27 I pray thee, I will bring thee unto **a** place; 312
36: 9 inheritance remove from *one* tribe to **a** tribe; 312
Dt 4:34 take him a nation from the midst of **a** NIH
20: 5 he die in the battle, and **a** man dedicate it. 312
20: 6 lest he die in the battle, and **a** man eat of it. 312
20: 7 lest he die in the battle, and **a** man take her. 312
21:15 **a** hated, and they have born him children, 259
24: 2 his house, she may go and be **a** man's *wife.* 312
25:11 When men strive together one with **a**[S], 251
28:30 betroth a wife, and **a** man shall lie with her: 312
28:32 thy daughters *shall be* given unto **a** people, 312
29:28 and cast them into **a** land, as *it is* this day. 312
Jdg 2:10 there arose **a** generation after them, 312
6:29 they said one to **a**[S], Who hath done this 7453
9:37 **a** company come along by the plain of 259
10:18 *and* princes of Gilead said one to **a**[S], 7453
16: 7 then shall I be weak, and be as **a** man. 259
16:11 shall I be weak, and be as **a** man. 259
Ru 2: 8 Go not to glean in **a** field, neither go from 312
3:14 she rose up before one could know **a**[S]. And 7453
1Sa 2:25 If one man sin against **a**[S], the judge shall 376
10: 3 **a** carrying three loaves of bread, and 259
10: 3 of bread, and **a** carrying a bottle of wine: 259
10: 6 with them, and shalt be turned into **a** man. 312
10: 9 to go from Samuel, God gave him **a** heart: 312
10:11 the prophets, then the people said one to **a**[S], 7453
13:18 **a** company turned the way to Beth-horon: 259
13:18 **a** company turned *to* the way of the border 259
14:16 and they went on beating down *one* **a**. NIH
17:30 he turned from him towards **a**, and 312
18: 7 the women answered *one* **a** as they played, NIH
20:41 they kissed one **a**[S], and wept one with 7453
20:41 wept one with **a**[S], until David exceeded. 7453
21:11 did they not sing one to **a** of him in dances, NIH
29: 5 of whom they sang one to **a** in dances, NIH
2Sa 11:25 for the sword devoureth one as well as **a**: 2088
18:20 this day, but thou shalt bear tidings **a** day: 312
18:26 the watchman saw **a** man running: and 312
18:26 and said, Behold *a* man running alone. NIH
1Ki 6:27 their wings touched **one a** in 413+3671+3671
7: 8 his house where he dwelt *had* **a** court within 312
11:23 God stirred him up **a** adversary, Rezon NIH
13:10 So he went **a** way, and returned not by 312
14: 5 that she shall **feign** herself **to be a** *woman.* 5234
14: 6 why **feignest** thou thyself **to be a**? 5234
18: 6 Obadiah went **a** way by himself. 259
20:37 he found **a** man, and said, Smite me, I pray 312
21: 6 I will give thee **a** vineyard for it: NIH
22:20 on this manner, and **a** said on that manner. 2088
2Ki 1:11 Again also he sent unto him **a** captain of 312
3:23 surely slain, and they have smitten one **a**[S]: 7453
7: 3 they said one to **a**[S], Why sit we here until 7453
7: 6 they said one to **a**[S], Lo, the king of Israel 251
7: 8 entered into **a** tent, and carried thence *also,* 312
7: 9 they said one to **a**[S], We do not well: this 7453
10:21 house of Baal was full from one end to **a**[S]. 6310
14: 8 Come, let us look one **a** *in* the face. NIH
14:11 Amaziah king of Judah looked one **a** *in* NIH
21:16 he had filled Jerusalem from one end to **a**[S]; 6310
1Ch 2:26 Jerahmeel had also **a** wife, whose name *was* 312
16:20 and from *one* kingdom to **a** people; 312
17: 5 tent to tent, and from *one* tabernacle *to* **a**. NIH
24: 5 were they divided by lot, one *sort* with **a**; 428
26:12 the chief men, *having* wards one against **a**[S], 251
2Ch 18:19 and **a** saying after that manner. 2088
20:23 of Seir, every one helped to destroy **a**[S]. 7453
25:17 Come, let us see one **a** *in* the face. NIH
25:21 they saw one **a** *in* the face, *both* he and NIH
32: 5 **a** wall without, and repaired Millo *in* the city 312
Ezr 4:21 until **a** commandment shall be given from NIH
9:11 have filled it from one end to **a**[S] with 6310
Ne 3:19 **a** piece over against the going up to 8145
3:21 the son of Urijah the son of Koz **a** piece, 8145
3:24 Binnui the son of Henadad **a** piece, 8145
3:27 After them the Tekoites repaired **a** piece, 8145
3:30 and Hanun the sixth son of Zalaph, **a** piece. 8145
4:19 separated upon the wall, one far from **a**[S]. 251
9: 3 **a** fourth *part* they confessed, and NIH
Est 1: 7 (the vessels being diverse **one** from **a**[S],) 3627
1:19 let the king give her royal estate unto **a**[S] 7468
4:14 deliverance arise to the Jews from **a** place; 312
9:19 and *of* sending portions one to **a**[S]. 7453
9:22 of sending portions one to **a**[S], and gifts to 7453
Job 1:16 yet speaking, there came also **a**, and said, 2088
1:17 yet speaking, there came also **a**, and said, 2088
1:18 there came also **a**, and said, Thy sons and 2088
13: 9 or as *one* man mocketh **a**[S], do ye *so* 582
19:27 and mine eyes shall behold, and not **a**; 2114
21:25 **a** dieth in the bitterness of his soul, and 2088
31: 8 *Then* let me sow, and let **a** eat; yea, let my 312
31:10 *Then* let my wife grind unto **a**, and let others 312
Job 41:16 One is so near to **a**, that no air can come 259
41:17 They are joined one to **a**[S], they stick 251
Ps 16: 4 **a** *god:* their drink offerings of blood will I 312
75: 7 he putteth down one, and setteth up **a**. 2088
105:13 When they went from one nation to **a**, 1471
105:13 to another, from *one* kingdom to **a** people; 312
109: 8 Let his days be few; *and* let **a** take his office. 312
145: 4 One generation shall praise thy works to **a**[S], 1755
Pr 25: 9 and discover not a secret *to* **a**: 312
27: 2 Let **a** *man* praise thee, and not thine own 2114
Ecc 1: 4 passeth away, and *a* generation cometh: NIH
4:10 he falleth; for *he hath* not **a** to help him up. 8145
8: 9 one man ruleth over **a** to his own hurt. 120
SS 5: 9 What *is* thy beloved more than *a* beloved, NIH
5: 9 what *is* thy beloved more than *a* beloved, NIH
Isa 3: 5 every one by **a**[S], and every one by his 376
6: 3 one cried unto **a**, and said, Holy, holy, 2088
13: 8 they shall be amazed one at **a**[S]; their faces 7453
28:11 and **a** tongue will he speak to this people. 312
42: 8 my glory will I not give to **a**, neither my 312
44: 5 **a** shall call *himself* by the name of Jacob; 2088
44: 5 **a** shall subscribe *with* his hand unto 2088
48:11 and I will not give my glory unto **a**. 312
57: 8 for thou hast discovered *thyself to* **a** than NIH
65:15 slay thee, and call his servants by **a** name: 312
65:22 They shall not build, and **a** inhabit; 312
65:22 they shall not plant, and **a** eat: 312
66:23 *that* from one new moon to **a**[S], and 2320
66:23 to another, and from one sabbath to **a**[S], 7676
Jer 3: 1 and she go from him, and become **a** man's, 312
13:14 I will dash them one against **a**[S], even 251
18: 4 so he made it again **a** vessel, as seemed 312
18:14 waters that come from **a place** be forsaken? 2114
22:26 into **a** country, where ye were not born; 312
25:26 one with **a**[S], and all the kingdoms of 251
36:28 Take thee again **a** roll, and write in it all 312
36:32 took Jeremiah **a** roll, and gave it to Baruch 312
46:16 made many to fall, yea, one fell upon **a**[S]: 7453
51:31 One post shall run to meet **a**[S], and 7323
51:31 and one messenger to meet **a**[S], 5046
51:46 and after that in *a* year *shall come* a rumour, NIH
Eze 1: 9 Their wings *were* joined one to **a**[S]; they 269
1:11 *wings* of every one *were* joined one to **a**[S], 376
3:13 of the living creatures that touched one **a**[S], 269
4: 8 thou shalt not turn thee from one side to **a**[S], 6654
4:17 be astonied one with **a**[S], and consume away 251
10: 9 one cherub, and **a** wheel by another cherub: 259
10: 9 one cherub, and another wheel by **a** cherub: 259
12: 3 thou shalt remove from thy place to **a** place 312
15: 7 from *one* fire, and **a** fire shall devour them; NIH
17: 7 There was also **a** great eagle with great 259
19: 5 she took **a** of her whelps, *and* made him a 259
22:11 **a**[S] hath lewdly defiled his daughter in law; 376
22:11 **a**[S] in thee hath humbled his sister, 376
24:23 your iniquities, and mourn one towards **a**[S]. 251
33:30 and speak one to **a**, every one to his brother, 259
37:16 take **a** stick, and write upon it, For Joseph, 259
37:17 join them one to **a** into one stick; and 259
40:13 of *one* little chamber to the roof of **a**[S]: 2050.2
40:26 one on this side, and **a** on that side, 259
40:49 one on this side, and **a** on that side. 259
41: 6 *were* three, one over **a**[S], and thirty *in* order; 6763
41:11 the north, and **a** door toward the south: 259
47:14 ye shall inherit it, one as well as **a**[S]: 251
Da 2:39 after thee shall arise **a** kingdom inferior to 317
2:39 **a** third kingdom of brass, which shall bear 317
2:43 they shall not cleave one to **a**, even as iron 1836
5: 6 and his knees smote one against **a**. 1668
5:17 gifts be to thyself, and give thy rewards to **a**; 321
7: 3 came up from the sea, diverse one from **a**. 1668
7: 5 And behold, **a** beast, a second, like to a bear, 317
7: 6 After this I beheld, and lo **a**, like a leopard, 317
7: 8 there came up among them **a** little horn, 317
7:24 **a** shall rise after them; and he shall be 321
8:13 **a** saint said unto that certain *saint* which 259
Hos 3: 3 the harlot, and thou shalt not be for *a* man: NIH
4: 4 Yet let no man strive, nor reprove **a**[S]: 376
Joel 1: 3 and their children **a** generation. 312
2: 8 Neither shall one thrust **a**[S]; they shall walk 251
Am 4: 7 and caused it not to rain upon **a** city: 259
Na 2: 4 they shall justle one against **a** in the broad NIH
Zec 2: 3 and **a** angel went out to meet him, 312
8:21 the inhabitants of one *city* shall go to **a**, 259
11: 9 let the rest eat every one the flesh of **a**[S]. 7468
Mal 3:16 feared the LORD spake often one to **a**[S]: 7453
Mt 2:12 they departed into their own country **a** way. *243*
8: 9 and to **a**, Come, and he cometh; and to my *243*
8:21 And **a** of his disciples said unto him, Lord, *2087*
10:23 they persecute you in this city, flee ye into **a**: *243*
11: 3 he that should come, or do we look for **a**? *2087*
13:24 **A** parable put he forth unto them, saying, *243*
13:31 **A** parable put he forth unto them, saying, *243*
13:33 **A** parable spake he unto them; The kingdom *243*
19: 9 and shall marry **a**, committeth adultery: *243*
21:33 Hear **a** parable: There was a certain *243*
21:35 beat one, and killed **a**, and stoned another. *3739*
21:35 beat one, and killed another, and stoned **a**. *3739*
22: 5 one to his farm, **a** to his merchandise: *3739*
24: 2 shall not be left here one stone upon **a**[S], *3037*
24:10 and shall betray **one a**, and shall hate one *240*
24:10 betray one another, and shall hate **one a**. *240*
25:15 five talents, to **a** two, and to another one; *3739*
25:15 five talents, to another two, and to **a** one; *3739*
25:32 and he shall separate them **one** from **a**, as a *240*
26:71 **a** *maid* saw him, and said unto them that *243*
27:38 one on the right hand, and **a** on the left. *1520*
Mk 4:41 and said **one** to **a**, What *manner of* man is *240*
9:10 questioning *one* with **a** what the rising from NIG
9:50 in yourselves, and have peace **one** with **a**. *240*
10:11 and marry **a**, committeth adultery against *243*
10:12 and be married to **a**, she committeth *243*
12: 4 And again he sent unto them **a** servant; and *243*
12: 5 And again he sent **a**; and him they killed, *243*
13: 2 there shall not be left one stone upon **a**[S], *3037*
14:19 him one by one, *Is* it I? and **a** *said, Is* it I? *243*

Mk 14:58 within three days I will build **a** made without 243
16:12 After that he appeared in **a** form unto two 2087
Lk 2:15 the shepherds said **one to a**, Let us now go 240
6: 6 And it came to pass also on **a** sabbath, 2087
6:11 communed **one** with **a** what they might do to 240
7: 8 and to **a**, Come, and he cometh; and to my 243
7:19 thou he that should come? or look we for **a**? 243
7:20 thou he that should come? or look we for **a**? 243
7:32 and calling **one** to **a**, and saying, We have 240
8:25 saying **one** to **a**, What *manner of man* is 240
9:56 to save *them*. And they went to **a** village. 2087
9:59 And he said unto **a**, Follow me. But he 2087
9:61 And **a** also said, Lord, I will follow thee; 2087
12: 1 insomuch that *they* trode **one** upon **a**, 240
14:19 And **a** said, I have bought five yoke of 2087
14:20 And **a** said, I have married a wife, and 2087
14:31 going to make war against **a** king, 2087
16: 7 Then said he to **a**, And how much owest 2087
16:12 **a** *man's*, who shall give you that which is 245
16:18 and marrieth **a**, committeth adultery: 2087
19:20 And **a** came, saying, Lord, behold, *here is* 2087
19:44 shall not leave in thee one stone upon **a**[S]; 3037
20:11 And again he sent **a** servant: and they beat 2087
21: 6 there shall not be left one stone upon **a**[S], 3037
22:58 And after a little while **a** saw him, and said, 2087
22:59 one hour after **a** confidently affirmed, 243+5100
24:17 *are* these that ye have **one** to **a**, 240
24:32 And they said **one** to **a**, Did not our heart 240
Jn 4:33 Therefore said the disciples **one** to **a**, 240
4:37 *that* saying true, One soweth, and **a** reapeth. 243
5: 7 I am coming, **a** steppeth down before me. 243
5:32 There is **a** that beareth witness of me; and 243
5:43 if **a** shall come in his own name, him ye will 243
5:44 which receive honour **one** of **a**, and seek not 240
13:22 Then the disciples looked **one** on **a**, 240
13:34 I give unto you, That ye love **one a**; 240
13:34 as I have loved you, that ye also love **one a**. 240
13:35 ye are my disciples, if ye have love **one** to **a**. 240
14:16 and he shall give you **a** Comforter, 243
15:12 That ye love **one a**, as I have loved you. 240
15:17 *things* I command you, that ye love **one a**. 240
18:15 Peter followed Jesus, and *so did* **a** disciple: 243
19:37 And again **a** scripture saith, They shall look 2087
21:18 and **a** shall gird thee, and carry *thee* whither 243
Ac 1:20 dwell therein: and his bishoprick let **a** take. 2087
2: 7 and marvelled, saying **one** to **a**, Behold, 240
2:12 and were in doubt, saying one to **a**, 243
7:18 Till **a** king arose, which knew not Joseph. 2087
7:26 ye are brethren; why do ye wrong **one** to **a**? 240
10:28 or come unto **one of a nation**; 246
12:17 And he departed, and went into **a** place. 2087
13:35 Wherefore he saith also in **a** *psalm*, Thou 2087
17: 7 saying that there is **a** king, *one* Jesus. 2087
19:32 Some therefore cried one *thing*, and some **a**: 243
19:38 there are deputies: let them implead **one a**. 240
21: 6 And when we had taken our leave **one** of **a**, 240
21:34 And some cried one *thing*, some **a**, 243
Ro 1:27 burned in their lust **one** towards **a**; 240
2: 1 for wherein thou judgest **a**, 2087
2:15 while accusing or else excusing **one a**;) 240
2:21 Thou therefore which teachest **a**, 2087
7: 3 husband liveth, she be married to **a** man, 2087
7: 3 though she be married to **a** man. 2087
7: 4 that ye should be married to **a**, *even* to him 2087
7:23 But I see **a** law in my members, 2087
9:21 unto honour, and **a** unto dishonour? 3303+3739
12: 5 in Christ, and every one members **one** of **a**. 240
12:10 *Be* kindly affectioned **one** to **a** with 240
12:10 brotherly love; in honour preferring **one a**; 240
12:16 *Be* of the same mind **one** toward **a**. 240
13: 8 Owe no *man* any *thing*, but to love **one a**: 240
13: 8 for he that loveth **a** hath fulfilled the law. 2087
14: 2 one believeth that *he* may eat all *things*: **a**, 3588
14: 4 Who art thou that judgest **a** *man's* servant? 245
14: 5 One man esteemeth one day above **a**[S]: 2250
14: 5 **a** esteemeth every day *alike*. Let every man 3739
14:13 Let us not therefore judge **one a** any more: 240
14:19 and *things* wherewith **one** may edify **a**. 240
15: 5 **one** towards **a** according to Christ Jesus: 240
15: 7 Wherefore receive ye **one a**, as Christ also 240
15:14 all knowledge, able also to admonish **one a**. 240
15:20 lest I should build upon **a** *man's* foundation: 245
16:16 Salute **one a** with a holy kiss. The churches 240
1Co 3: 4 I am of Paul; and **a**, I *am* of Apollos; 2087
3:10 laid the foundation, and **a** buildeth thereon. 243
4: 6 one of you be puffed up for one against **a**. 2087
4: 7 For who maketh thee to differ *from* **a**? and NIG
6: 1 Dare any of you, having a matter against **a**, 2087
6: 7 because ye go to law **one** with **a**. 1438
7: 7 one after this manner, and **a** after that. 3739
10:29 for why is my liberty judged of **a** *man's* 243
11:21 and one is hungry, and **a** is drunken. 3739
11:33 ye come together to eat, tarry **one** for **a**. 240
12: 8 to **a** the word of knowledge by the same 243
12: 9 To **a** faith by the same Spirit; to another 2087
12: 9 to **a** the gifts of healing by the same Spirit; 243
12:10 To **a** the working of miracles; to another 243
12:10 to **a** prophecy; to another discerning of 243
12:10 another prophecy; to **a** discerning of spirits; 243
12:10 of spirits; to **a** *divers* kinds of tongues; 2087
12:10 of tongues; to **a** the interpretation of tongues: 243
12:25 should have the same care **one** for **a**. 240
14:30 If *any thing* be revealed to **a** that sitteth *by*, 243
15:39 **a** flesh of beasts, another of fishes, *and* 243
15:39 of beasts, **a** of fishes, *and* another of birds. 243
15:39 of beasts, another of fishes, *and* **a** of birds. 243
15:40 *is* one, and the *glory* of the terrestrial *is* **a**. 2087
15:41 and **a** glory of the moon, and another glory 243
15:41 glory of the moon, and **a** glory of the stars: 243
15:41 for *one* star differeth from **a** star in glory. NIG
16:20 greet you. Greet ye **one a** with a holy kiss. 240
2Co 10:16 not to boast in **a** *man's* line of *things* made 245
11: 4 For if he that cometh preacheth **a** Jesus, 243
11: 4 or *if* ye receive **a** spirit, which ye have not 2087
11: 4 which ye have not received, or **a** gospel, 2087
2Co 13:12 Greet **one a** with a holy kiss. 240
Gal 1: 6 you into the grace of Christ unto **a** gospel: 2087
1: 7 Which is not **a**; but there be some that 243
5:13 to the flesh, but by love serve **one a**. 240
5:15 But if ye bite and devour **one a**, take heed ye 240
5:15 take heed ye be not consumed **one** of **a**. 240
5:26 provoking **one a**, envying one another. 240
5:26 provoking one another, envying **one a**. 240
6: 4 rejoicing in himself alone, and not in **a**. 2087
Eph 4: 2 with longsuffering, forbearing **one a** in love; 240
4:25 his neighbour: for we are members **one** of **a**. 240
4:32 And be ye kind **one** to **a**, tenderhearted, 240
4:32 to another, tenderhearted, forgiving **one a**, 1438
5:21 Submitting yourselves **one** to **a** in the fear of 240
Col 3: 9 Lie not **one** to **a**, seeing that ye have put off 240
3:13 Forbearing **one a**, and forgiving one another, 240
3:13 one another, and forgiving **one a**, 1438
3:16 and admonishing **one a** in psalms and 1438
1Th 3:12 and abound in love **one** towards **a**, 240
4: 9 yourselves are taught of God to love **one a**. 240
4:18 Wherefore comfort **one a** with these words. 240
5:11 **one a**, even as also ye do. 1520+1520+3588
1Ti 5:21 *one before* **a**, doing nothing by partiality. NIG
Tit 3: 3 and envy, hateful, *and* hating **one a**. 240
Heb 3:13 But exhort **one a** daily, while it is called To 1438
4: 8 would he not afterward have spoken of **a** 243
5: 6 As he saith also in **a** *place*, Thou *art* a priest 2087
7:11 what further need *was there* that **a** priest 2087
7:13 *things* are spoken pertaineth to **a** tribe, 2087
7:15 of Melchisedec there ariseth **a** priest, 2087
10:24 And let us consider **one a** to provoke unto 240
10:25 but exhorting *one* **a**: and so much the more, NIG
Jas 2:25 and had sent *them* out **a** way? 2087
4:11 Speak not evil **one** of **a**, brethren. He that 240
4:12 and to destroy: who art thou that judgest **a**? 2087
5: 9 Grudge not **one** against **a**, brethren, lest ye 240
5:16 Confess *your* faults **one** to **a**, and pray one 240
5:16 and pray **one** for **a**, that ye may be healed. 240
1Pe 1:22 *see that ye* love **one a** with a pure heart 240
3: 8 having **compassion one of a**, love as 4835
4: 9 Use hospitality **one** to **a** without grudging. 240
4:10 *the* gift, *even so* minister the same **one** to **a**, 1438
5: 5 all *of you* be subject **one** to **a**, and be clothed 240
5:14 Greet ye **one a** with a kiss of charity. 240
1Jn 1: 7 we have fellowship **one** with **a**, and 240
3:11 the beginning, that we should love **one a**. 240
3:23 and love **one a**, as he gave us 240
4: 7 Beloved, let us love **one a**: for love is of 240
4:11 so loved us, we ought also to love **one a**. 240
4:12 If we love **one a**, God dwelleth in us, and 240
2Jn 1: 5 had from the beginning, that we love **one a**. 240
Rev 6: 4 And there went out **a** horse *that was* red: and 243
6: 4 the earth, and that they should kill **one a**: 240
7: 2 And I saw **a** angel ascending from the east, 243
8: 3 And **a** angel came and stood at the altar, 243
10: 1 And I saw **a** mighty angel come down from 243
11:10 make merry, and shall send gifts **one** to **a**; 240
12: 3 And there appeared **a** wonder in heaven; and 243
13:11 And I beheld **a** beast coming up out of 243
14: 6 And I saw **a** angel fly in the midst of heaven, 243
14: 8 And there followed **a** angel, saying, 243
14:15 And **a** angel came out of the temple, 243
14:17 And **a** angel came out of the temple which is 243
14:18 And **a** angel came out from the altar, 243
15: 1 And I saw **a** sign in heaven, great and 243
16: 7 And I heard **a** out of the altar say, Even so, 243
18: 1 And after these *things* I saw **a** angel come 243
18: 4 And I heard **a** voice from heaven, saying, 243
20:12 and **a** book was opened, which is *the book* of 243

ANOTHER'S (5) [ANOTHER]

Ge 11: 7 that they may not understand one **a**[S] 7453
Ex 21:35 if one man's ox hurt **a**[S], that he die; 7453+7794
Jn 13:14 your feet; ye also ought to wash **one a** feet. 240
1Co 10:24 *man* seek his own, but every man **a** *wealth*. 2087
Gal 6: 2 Bear ye **one a** burdens, and so fulfil the law 240

ANSWER (131) [ANSWERABLE, ANSWERED, ANSWEREDST, ANSWEREST, ANSWERETH, ANSWERING, ANSWERS]

Ge 30:33 So shall my righteousness **a** for me in time 6030
41:16 God shall **give** Pharaoh **an a** of peace. 6030
45: 3 his brethren could not **a** him; for they were 6030
Dt 20:11 if it **make** thee **a** of peace, and open unto 6030
21: 7 they shall **a** and say, Our hands have not 6030
25: 9 and spit in his face, and shall **a** and say, 6030
27:15 in *a secret place*. And all the people shall **a** 6030
Jos 4: 7 ye shall **a** them, That the waters of Jordan 559
Jdg 5:29 answered *her*, yea, she returned **a** to herself, 561
1Sa 2:16 he would **a** him, *Nay;* but thou shalt give *it* 559
20:10 or what *if* thy father **a** thee roughly? 6030
2Sa 3:11 he could not **a** Abner a word again, because 7725
24:13 see what **a** I shall return *to* him that sent 1697
1Ki 9: 9 they shall **a**, Because they forsook 559
12: 6 How do you advise that *I* may **a** this 1697
12: 7 **a** them, and speak good words to them, 6030
12: 9 What counsel give ye that we may **a** this 1697
18:29 nor any to **a**, nor any that regarded. 6030
2Ki 4:29 **a** him not *again:* and lay my staff upon 6030
18:36 commandment was, saying, **A** him not. 6030
2Ch 10: 6 What counsel give ye *me* to return **a** to this 1697
10: 9 What advice give ye that we may return **a** 1697
10:10 Thus shalt thou **a** the people that spake unto 559
Ezr 4:17 *Then* sent the king an **a** unto Rehum 6600
5: 5 they **returned a** by letter concerning this 8421
5:11 thus they returned us **a**, saying, We are 6600
Ne 5: 8 they their peace, and found nothing *to* **a**. NIH
Est 4:13 Mordecai commanded to **a** Esther, 7725
4:15 Esther bade *them* return Mordecai *this* **a**: NIH
Job 5: 1 Call now, if there be *any* that will **a** thee; 6030
9: 3 he cannot **a** him one of a thousand. 6030
9:14 How much less shall I **a** him, *and* 6030
9:15 *yet* would I not **a**, *but* I would make 6030
9:32 as I *am*, *that* I should **a** him, *and* we should 6030
Job 13:22 call thou, and I will **a**: or let me speak, 6030
13:22 or let me speak, and **a** thou me. 7725
14:15 Thou shalt call, and I will **a** thee: thou wilt 6030
19:16 I called my servant, and he **gave** *me* no **a**; 6030
20: 2 Therefore do my thoughts **cause** me to **a**, 7725
20: 3 spirit of my understanding causeth me to **a**. 6030
23: 5 I would know the words *which* he would **a** 6030
31:14 and when he visiteth, what shall I **a** him? 7725
31:35 my desire *is, that* the Almighty would **a** 6030
32: 1 So these three men ceased to **a** Job, because 6030
32: 3 because they had found no **a**, and *yet* had 4617
32: 5 When Elihu saw that *there was* no **a** in 4617
32:14 neither will I **a** him with your speeches. 7725
32:17 *I said*, I will **a** also my part, I also will shew 6030
32:20 be refreshed: I will open my lips and **a**. 6030
33: 5 If thou canst, **a** me, set *thy words* in order 7725
33:12 I will **a** thee, that God is greater than man. 6030
33:32 If *thou* hast any thing to say, **a** me: speak, 7725
35: 4 I will **a** thee, and thy companions 4405+7725
35:12 none **giveth a**, because of the pride of evil 6030
38: 3 for I will demand of thee, and **a** thou me. 3045
40: 2 *him?* he that reproveth God, let him **a** it. 6030
40: 4 Behold, I am vile; what shall I **a** thee? 7725
40: 5 Once have I spoken; but I will not **a**: yea, 6030
Ps 27: 7 have mercy also upon me, and **a** me. 6030
65: 5 *things* in righteousness wilt thou **a** us, 6030
86: 7 I will call upon thee: for thou wilt **a** me. 6030
91:15 He shall call upon me, and I will **a** him: 6030
102: 2 in the day *when* I call **a** me speedily. 6030
108: 6 save *with* thy right hand, and **a** me. 6030
119:42 So shall I have wherewith to **a** him that 6030
143: 1 in thy faithfulness **a** me, *and* in thy 6030
Pr 1:28 shall they call upon me, but I will not **a**; 6030
15: 1 A soft **a** turneth away wrath: but 4617
15:23 A man hath joy by the **a** of his mouth: and 4617
15:28 The heart of the righteous studieth to **a**: but 6030
16: 1 the **a** of the tongue, *is* from the LORD. 4617
22:21 that *thou* mightest **a** the words *of* truth to 7725
24:26 *man* shall kiss *his* lips that giveth a right **a**. 1697
26: 4 **A** not a fool according to his folly, lest thou 6030
26: 5 **A** a fool according to his folly, lest he be 6030
27:11 I may **a** him that reproacheth me. 1697+7725
29:19 for though he understand he will not **a**. 4617
SS 5: 6 I called him, but he **gave** me no **a**. 6030
Isa 14:32 then **a** the messengers of the nation? 6030
30:19 when *he* shall hear it, he will **a** thee. 6030
36:21 commandment was, saying, **A** him not. 6030
41:28 that, when I asked of them, could **a** a word. 7725
46: 7 *one* shall cry unto him, yet can he not **a**, 6030
50: 2 when I called, *was there* none to **a**? Is my 6030
58: 9 shalt thou call, and the LORD shall **a**; 6030
65:12 because when I called, ye did not **a**; when I 6030
65:24 come to pass, that before they call, I will **a**; 6030
66: 4 because when I called, none did **a**; when I 6030
Jer 5:19 shalt thou **a** them, Like as ye have forsaken 559
7:27 call unto them; but they will not **a** thee. 6030
22: 9 they shall **a**, Because they have forsaken 559
33: 3 I will **a** thee, and shew thee great and 6030
42: 4 *that* whatsoever thing the LORD shall **a** 6030
44:20 all the people which had **given** him *that* **a**, 6030
Eze 14: 4 I the LORD will **a** him that cometh 6030
14: 7 I the LORD will **a** him by myself: 6030
21: 7 that thou shalt **a**, For the tidings; because 559
Da 3:16 we *are* not careful to **a** thee in this matter. 8421
Joel 2:19 the LORD will **a** and say unto his people, 6030
Mic 3: 7 all cover their lips; for *there is* no **a** of God. 4617
Hab 2: 1 and what I shall **a** when I am reproved. 7725
2:11 and the beam out of the timber shall **a** it. 6030
Zec 13: 6 he shall **a**, *Those with* which I was wounded 559
Mt 22:46 And no *man* was able to **a** him a word, 611
25:37 Then shall the righteous **a** him, saying, Lord, 611
25:40 And the King shall **a** and say unto them, 611
25:44 Then shall they also **a** him, saying, Lord, 611
25:45 Then shall he **a** them, saying, Verily I say 611
Mk 11:29 and **a** me, and I will tell you by what 611
11:30 was *it* from heaven, or of men? **a** me. 611
14:40 neither wist they what to **a** him. 611
Lk 11: 7 And he from within shall **a** and say, 611
12:11 ye no thought how or what *thing* ye shall **a**, 626
13:25 and he shall **a** and say unto you, I know you 611
14: 6 And they could not **a** him **again** to these 470
20: 3 I will also ask you one thing; and **a** me: 3004
20:26 and they marvelled at his **a**, and held their 612
21:14 not to meditate before *what ye* shall **a**: 626
22:68 And if I also ask *you*, you will not **a** me, 611
Jn 1:22 that we may give an **a** to them that sent us. 612
19: 9 Whence art thou? But Jesus gave him no **a**. 612
Ac 24:10 I do the more cheerfully **a** for myself: 626
25:16 have licence to **a for** himself concerning 627
26: 2 I shall **a for** myself this day before thee 626
Ro 11: 4 But what saith the **a of God** unto him? 5538
1Co 9: 3 Mine **a** to them that do examine me is this: 627
2Co 5:12 that you may have *somewhat* to **a** them NIG
Col 4: 6 that *you* may know how ye ought to **a** every 611
2Ti 4:16 At my first **a** no *man* stood with me, but 627
1Pe 3:15 *be* ready always to *give* an **a** to every *man* 627
3:21 the **a** of a good conscience toward God,) 1906

ANSWERABLE (1) [ANSWER]

Ex 38:18 in the breadth *was* five cubits, **a** 5980+3807.1

ANSWERED (492) [ANSWER]

Ge 18:27 Abraham **a** and said, Behold now, I have 6030
23: 5 the children of Heth **a** Abraham, saying 6030
23:10 Ephron the Hittite **a** Abraham in 6030
23:14 And Ephron **a** Abraham, saying unto him, 6030
24:50 Laban and Bethuel **a** and said, The thing 6030
27:37 Isaac **a** and said unto Esau, Behold, I have 6030
27:39 Isaac his father **a** and said unto him, 6030
31:14 Rachel and Leah **a** and said unto him, 6030
31:31 Jacob **a** and said to Laban, Because I was 6030
31:36 Jacob **a** and said to Laban, What *is* my 6030
31:43 Laban **a** and said unto Jacob, *These* 6030
34:13 the sons of Jacob **a** Shechem and Hamor 6030
35: 3 who **a** me in the day of my distress, and 6030

Ge 40:18 Joseph **a** and said, This *is* the interpretation 6030
41:16 Joseph **a** Pharaoh, saying, *It is* not in me: 6030
42:22 Reuben **a** them, saying, Spake I not unto 6030
43:28 they **a**, Thy servant our father *is* in good 559
Ex 4: 1 Moses **a** and said, But behold, they will not 6030
15:21 Miriam **a** them, Sing ye to the LORD, 6030
19: 8 all the people **a** together, and said, All that 6030
19:19 Moses spake, and God **a** him by a voice. 6030
24: 3 all the people **a** *with* one voice, and said, 6030
Nu 11:28 **a** and said, My lord Moses, forbid them. 6030
22:18 Balaam **a** and said unto the servants of 6030
23:12 he **a** and said, Must I not take heed to speak 6030
23:26 Balaam **a** and said unto Balak, Told not I 6030
32:31 of Gad and the children of Reuben **a**, 6030
Dt 1:14 ye **a** me, and said, The thing which thou 6030
1:41 ye **a** and said unto me, We have sinned 6030
Jos 1:16 they **a** Joshua, saying, All that thou 6030
2:14 the men **a** her, Our life for yours, if ye utter 559
7:20 Achan **a** Joshua, and said, Indeed I have 6030
9:24 they **a** Joshua, and said, Because it was 6030
15:19 Who **a**, Give me a blessing; for thou hast 559
17:15 Joshua **a** them, If thou *be* a great people, 559
22:21 of Gad and the half tribe of Manasseh **a**, 6030
24:16 the people **a** and said, God forbid that we 6030
Jdg 5:29 Her wise ladies **a** *her*, yea, she returned 6030
7:14 his fellow **a** and said, This *is* nothing else 6030
8: 8 the men of Penuel **a** him as the men of 6030
8: 8 him as the men of Succoth had **a** *him*. 6030
8:18 they **a**, As thou *art*, so *were* they; *each* one 559
8:25 they **a**, We will willingly give *them*. And 559
11:13 the king of the children of Ammon **a** unto 559
15: 6 they **a**, Samson, the son in law of 559
15:10 they **a**, To bind Samson are we come up, 559
18:14 **a** the five men that went to spy out 6030
19:28 none **a**. Then the man took her *up* upon an 6030
20: 4 of the woman that was slain, **a** and said, 6030
Ru 2: 4 And they **a** him, The LORD bless thee. 559
2: 6 the servant that was set over the reapers **a** 6030
2:11 Boaz **a** and said unto her, It hath fully been 6030
3: 9 she **a**, I *am* Ruth thine handmaid: spread 559
1Sa 1:15 Hannah **a** and said, No, my lord, I *am* a 6030
1:17 Eli **a** and said, Go in peace: and the God of 6030
3: 4 LORD called Samuel: and he **a**, Here *am* I. 559
3: 6 he **a**, I called not, my son; lie down again. 559
3:10 Samuel **a**, Speak; for thy servant heareth. 559
3:16 said, Samuel, my son. And he **a**, Here *am* I. 559
4:17 the messenger **a** and said, Israel is fled 6030
4:20 But she **a** not, neither did she regard *it*. 6030
5: 8 they **a**, Let the ark of the God of Israel be 559
6: 4 They **a**, Five golden emerods, and 559
9: 8 the servant **a** Saul again, and said, Behold, 6030
9:12 they **a** them, and said, He is; behold, *he is* 6030
9:19 Samuel **a** Saul, and said, I *am* the seer: 6030
9:21 Saul **a** and said, *Am* not I a Benjamite, 6030
10:12 one of the same place **a** and said, But who 6030
10:22 the LORD **a**, Behold, he hath hid himself 559
11: 2 Nahash the Ammonite **a** them, On this 559
12: 5 ought in my hand. And they **a**, *He is* witness. 559
14:12 And the men of the garrison **a** Jonathan and 6030
14:28 **a** one of the people, and said, Thy father 6030
14:37 hand of Israel? But he **a** him not that day. 6030
14:39 not *a man* among all the people *that* **a** him. 6030
14:44 Saul **a**, God do so and more also: for thou 559
16:18 **a** one of the servants, and said, Behold, 6030
17:27 the people **a** him after this manner, saying, 559
17:30 the people **a** him again after the former 1697
17:58 David **a**, *I am* the son of thy servant Jesse 559
18: 7 the women **a** *one another* as they played, 6030
19:17 Michal **a** Saul, He said unto me, Let me go; 559
20:28 Jonathan **a** Saul, David earnestly asked 6030
20:32 Jonathan **a** Saul his father, and said unto 6030
21: 4 the priest **a** David, and said, *There is* no 6030
21: 5 David **a** the priest, and said unto him, Of a 6030
22: 9 **a** Doeg the Edomite, which *was* set over 6030
22:12 son of Ahitub. And he **a**, Here I *am*, my lord. 559
22:14 Ahimelech **a** the king, and said, And who *is* 6030
23: 4 the LORD **a** him and said, Arise, go down 6030
25:10 Nabal **a** David's servants, and said, Who *is* 6030
26: 6 **a** David and said to Ahimelech the Hittite, 6030
26:14 Abner **a** and said, Who *art* thou *that* criest 6030
26:22 David **a** and said, Behold, the king's spear; 6030
28: 6 the LORD **a** him not, neither by dreams, 6030
28:15 Saul **a**, I am sore distressed; for 559
29: 9 Achish **a** and said to David, I know that 6030
30: 8 he **a** him, Pursue: for thou shalt surely 559
30:22 **a** all the wicked men and *men* of Belial, 6030
2Sa 1: 4 he **a**, That the people are fled from the battle, 559
1: 7 and called unto me. And I **a**, Here *am* I. 559
1: 8 *art* thou? And I **a** him, I *am* an Amalekite. 559
1:13 he **a**, I *am* the son of a stranger, an 559
2:20 and said, *Art* thou Asahel? And he **a**, I *am*. 559
4: 9 David **a** Rechab and Baanah his brother, 6030
9: 6 And he **a**, Behold thy servant. 559
13:12 she **a** him, Nay, my brother, do not force me; 559
13:32 son of Shimeah David's brother, **a** and said, 6030
14: 5 And she **a**, I *am* indeed a widow woman, and 559
14:18 the king **a** and said unto the woman, 6030
14:19 the woman **a** and said, *As* thy soul liveth, 6030
14:32 Absalom **a** Joab, Behold, I sent unto thee, 559
15:21 Ittai **a** the king, and said, *As* the LORD 6030
18: 3 the people **a**, Thou shalt not go forth: for if 559
18:29 Ahimaaz **a**, When Joab sent the king's 559
18:32 Cushi **a**, The enemies of my lord the king, 559
19:21 Abishai the son of Zeruiah **a** and said, Shall 6030
19:26 he **a**, My lord, O king, my servant deceived 559
19:38 the king **a**, Chimham shall go over with me, 559
19:42 all the men of Judah **a** the men of Israel, 6030
19:43 the men of Israel **a** the men of Judah, and 6030
20:17 he **a**, I *am he*. Then she said unto him, 559
20:17 of thine handmaid. And he **a**, I do hear. 559
20:20 Joab **a** and said, Far be it, far be it from me, 6030
21: 1 the LORD **a**, *It is* for Saul, and for *his* 559
21: 5 they **a** the king, The man that consumed us, 559
22:42 *even* unto the LORD, but he **a** them not. 6030
1Ki 1:28 king David **a** and said, Call me Bath-sheba. 6030

1Ki 1:36 Benaiah the son of Jehoiada **a** the king, 6030
1:43 Jonathan **a** and said to Adonijah, Verily our 6030
2:22 king Solomon **a** and said unto his mother, 6030
2:30 Thus said Joab, and thus he **a** me. 6030
3:27 the king **a** and said, Give her the living 6030
11:22 he **a**, Nothing: howbeit let me go in any 559
12:13 the king **a** the people roughly, and 6030
12:16 the people **a** the king, saying, 1697+7725
13: 6 the king **a** and said unto the man of God, 6030
18: 8 he **a** him, I *am*: go, tell thy lord, Behold, 559
18:18 he **a**, I have not troubled Israel; but thou, 559
18:21 And the people **a** him not a word. 6030
18:24 all the people **a** and said, It is well spoken. 6030
18:26 *there was* no voice, nor any that **a**. 6030
20: 4 the king of Israel **a** and said, My lord, 6030
20:11 the king of Israel **a** and said, Tell *him*, Let 6030
20:14 Who shall order the battle? And he **a**, Thou. 559
21: 6 and he **a**, I will not give thee my vineyard. 559
21:20 he **a**, I have found *thee*: because thou hast 559
22:15 he **a** him, Go, and prosper: for the LORD 559
2Ki 1: 8 they **a** him, *He was* a hairy man, and 559
1:10 Elijah **a** and said to the captain of fifty, 6030
1:11 And he **a** and said unto him, O man of God, 6030
1:12 Elijah **a** and said unto them, If I *be* a man 6030
2: 5 he **a**, Yea, I know *it*; hold you your peace. 559
3: 8 he **a**, The way through the wilderness of 559
3:11 one of the king of Israel's servants **a** and 6030
4:13 And she **a**, I dwell among mine own people. 559
4:14 And Gehazi **a**, Verily she hath no child, and 559
4:26 *it* well with the child? And she **a**, *It is* well. 559
6: 2 where we may dwell. And he **a**, Go ye. 559
6: 3 and go with thy servants. And he **a**, I will go. 559
6:16 he **a**, Fear not: for *they* that *be* with us *are* 559
6:22 he **a**, Thou shalt not smite *them*: wouldest 559
6:28 she **a**, This woman said unto me, Give thy 559
7: 2 a lord on whose hand the king leaned **a** 6030
7:13 one of his servants **a** and said, Let *some* 6030
7:19 *that* lord **a** the man of God, and said, 6030
8:12 he **a**, Because I know the evil that thou wilt 559
8:13 Elisha **a**, The LORD hath shewed me *that* 559
8:14 he **a**, He told me *that* thou shouldest surely 559
9:19 Jehu **a**, What hast thou to do with peace? 559
9:22 he **a**, What peace, so long as the whoredoms 559
10:13 And they **a**, We *are* the brethren of Ahaziah; 559
10:15 Jehonadab **a**, It is. If it be, give *me* thine 559
18:36 held their peace, and **a** him not a word: 6030
20:10 Hezekiah **a**, It is a light thing for the shadow 559
20:15 Hezekiah **a**, All *the things* that *are* in mine 559
1Ch 12:17 out to meet them, and **a** and said unto them, 6030
21: 3 Joab **a**, The LORD make his people an 559
21:26 he **a** him from heaven by fire upon the altar 6030
21:28 **a** him in the threshingfloor of Ornan 6030
2Ch 2:11 Huram the king of Tyre **a** in writing, which 559
7:22 it shall be **a**, Because they forsook 559
10:13 the king **a** them roughly; and king 6030
10:14 **a** them after the advice of the young men, 1696
10:16 the people **a** the king, saying, What portion 7725
18: 3 he **a** him, I *am* as thou *art*, and my people as 559
25: 9 the man of God **a**, The LORD is able to 559
29:31 Hezekiah **a** and said, Now ye have 6030
31:10 the chief priest of the house of Zadok **a** him, 559
34:15 Hilkiah **a** and said to Shaphan the scribe, 6030
34:23 she **a** them, Thus saith the LORD God of 559
Ezr 10: 2 of the sons of Elam, **a** and said unto Ezra, 6030
10:12 all the congregation **a** and said *with* a loud 6030
Ne 2:20 **a** I them, and said unto them, 1697+7725
6: 4 and I **a** them after the same manner. 7725
8: 6 all the people **a**, Amen, Amen, with lifting 6030
Est 1:16 Memucan **a** before the king and the princes, 559
5: 4 And Esther **a**, If *it seem* good unto the king, 559
5: 7 **a** Esther, and said, My petition and 6030
6: 7 Haman **a** the king, *For* the man whom 559
7: 3 Esther the queen **a** and said, If I have found 6030
7: 5 the king Ahasuerus **a** and said unto Esther 559
Job 1: 7 Satan **a** the LORD, and said, From going 6030
1: 9 Satan **a** the LORD, and said, Doth Job 6030
2: 2 Satan **a** the LORD, and said, From going 6030
2: 4 Satan **a** the LORD, and said, Skin for 6030
4: 1 Then Eliphaz the Temanite **a** and said, 6030
6: 1 But Job **a** and said, 6030
8: 1 Then **a** Bildad the Shuhite, and said, 6030
9: 1 Then Job **a** and said, 6030
9:16 If I had called, and he had **a** me; *yet* would 6030
11: 1 Then **a** Zophar the Naamathite, and said, 6030
11: 2 Should not the multitude of words be **a**? 6030
12: 1 And Job **a** and said, 6030
15: 1 Then **a** Eliphaz the Temanite, and said, 6030
16: 1 Then Job **a** and said, 6030
18: 1 Then **a** Bildad the Shuhite, and said, 6030
19: 1 Then Job **a** and said, 6030
20: 1 Then **a** Zophar the Naamathite, and said, 6030
21: 1 But Job **a** and said, 6030
22: 1 Then Eliphaz the Temanite **a** and said, 6030
23: 1 Then Job **a** and said, 6030
25: 1 Then **a** Bildad the Shuhite, and said, 6030
26: 1 But Job **a** and said, 6030
32: 6 Elihu the son of Barachel the Buzite **a** and 6030
32:12 you that convinced Job, *or* that **a** his words: 6030
32:15 They were amazed, they **a** no more: 6030
32:16 spake not, but stood still, *and* **a** no more:) 6030
34: 1 Furthermore Elihu **a** and said, 6030
38: 1 the LORD **a** Job out of the whirlwind, 6030
40: 1 Moreover the LORD **a** Job, and said, 6030
40: 3 Then Job **a** the LORD, and said, 6030
40: 6 **a** the LORD unto Job out of 6030
42: 1 Then Job **a** the LORD, and said, 6030
Ps 18:41 *even* unto the LORD, but he **a** them not. 6030
81: 7 I **a** thee in the secret place of thunder: 6030
99: 6 called upon the LORD, and he **a** them. 6030
118: 5 the LORD **a** me, *and set me* in a large 6030
Isa 6:11 he **a**, Until the cities be wasted without 559
21: 9 he **a** and said, Babylon is fallen, is fallen; 6030
36:21 held their peace, and **a** him not a word: 6030
39: 4 Hezekiah **a**, All that *is* in mine house have 559
Jer 7:13 ye heard not; and I called you, but ye **a** not; 6030

Jer 11: 5 Then **a** I, and said, So be it, O LORD. 6030
23:35 to his brother, What hath the LORD **a**? 6030
23:37 the prophet, What hath the LORD **a** thee? 6030
35:17 have called unto them, but they have not **a**. 6030
36:18 Baruch **a** them, He pronounced all these 559
44:15 of Egypt, in Pathros, **a** Jeremiah, saying, 6030
Eze 24:20 I **a** them, The word of the LORD came 559
37: 3 And I **a**, O Lord GOD, thou knowest. 559
Da 2: 5 The king **a** and said to the Chaldeans, 6032
2: 7 They **a** again and said, Let the king tell his 6032
2: 8 The king **a** and said, I know of certainty 6032
2:10 The Chaldeans **a** before the king, and said, 6032
2:14 Daniel **a** with counsel and wisdom to 8421
2:15 He **a** and said to Arioch the king's captain, 6032
2:20 Daniel **a** and said, Blessed be the name of 6032
2:26 The king **a** and said to Daniel, whose name 6032
2:27 Daniel **a** in the presence of the king, and 6032
2:47 The king **a** unto Daniel, and said, Of a truth 6032
3:16 and Abed-nego, **a** and said to the king, 6032
3:24 They **a** and said unto the king, True, O 6032
3:25 He **a** and said, Lo, I see four men loose, 6032
4:19 Belteshazzar **a** and said, My lord, 6032
5:17 Daniel **a** and said before the king, Let thy 6032
6:12 The king **a** and said, The thing *is* true, 6032
6:13 **a** they and said before the king, 6032
Am 7:14 **a** Amos, and said to Amaziah, I *was* no 6030
Mic 6: 5 and what Balaam the son of Beor **a** him; 6030
Hab 2: 2 the LORD **a** me, and said, Write 6030
Hag 2:12 it be holy? And the priests **a** and said, No. 6030
2:13 the priests **a** and said, It shall be unclean. 6030
2:14 **a** Haggai, and said, So *is* this people, and 6030
Zec 1:10 the man that stood among the myrtle trees **a** 6030
1:11 they **a** the angel of the LORD that stood 6030
1:12 the angel of the LORD **a** and said, 6030
1:13 the LORD **a** the angel that talked with me 6030
1:19 he **a** me, These *are* the horns which have 559
3: 4 he **a** and spake unto those that stood before 6030
4: 4 So I **a** and spake to the angel that talked 6030
4: 5 the angel that talked with me **a** and 6030
4: 6 he **a** and spake unto me, saying, This *is* 6030
4:11 **a** I, and said unto him, What *are* these two 6030
4:12 I **a** again, and said unto him, What *be these* 6030
4:13 he **a** me and said, Knowest thou not what 559
5: 2 I **a**, I see a flying roll; the length thereof *is* 559
6: 4 I **a** and said unto the angel that talked with 6030
6: 5 the angel **a** and said unto me, These *are* 6030
Mt 4: 4 But he **a** and said, It is written, Man shall not 611
8: 8 The centurion **a** and said, Lord, I am not 611
11: 4 Jesus **a** and said unto them, Go and 611
11:25 At that time Jesus **a** and said, I thank thee, 611
12:38 certain of the scribes and of the Pharisees **a**, 611
12:39 But he **a** and said to them, An evil and 611
12:48 But he **a** and said unto him that told him, 611
13:11 He **a** and said unto them, Because it is given 611
13:37 He **a** and said unto them, He that soweth 611
14:28 And Peter **a** him and said, Lord, if it be thou, 611
15: 3 But he **a** and said unto them, Why do you 611
15:13 But he **a** and said, Every plant, which my 611
15:15 Then **a** Peter and said unto him, 611
15:23 But he **a** her not a word. And his disciples 611
15:24 But he **a** and said, I am not sent but unto 611
15:26 But he **a** and said, It is not meet to take 611
15:28 Then Jesus **a** and said unto her, O woman, 611
16: 2 He **a** and said unto them, When it is evening, 611
16:16 And Simon Peter **a** and said, Thou art 611
16:17 And Jesus **a** and said unto him, Blessed art 611
17: 4 Then **a** Peter, and said unto Jesus, Lord, it is 611
17:11 And Jesus **a** and said unto them, Elias truly 611
17:17 Then Jesus **a** and said, O faithless and 611
19: 4 And he **a** and said unto them, Have ye not 611
19:27 Then **a** Peter and said unto him, Behold, 611
20:13 But he **a** one of them, and said, Friend, I do 611
20:22 But Jesus **a** and said, Ye know not what ye 611
21:21 Jesus **a** and said unto them, Verily I say unto 611
21:24 And Jesus **a** and said unto them, I also will 611
21:27 And they **a** Jesus, and said, We cannot tell. 611
21:29 He **a** and said, I will not: but afterward he 611
21:30 And he **a** and said, I *go*, sir: and went not. 611
22: 1 And Jesus **a** and spake unto them again by 611
22:29 Jesus **a** and said unto them, Ye do err, 611
24: 4 And Jesus **a** and said unto them, Take heed 611
25: 9 But the wise **a**, saying, *Not so*; lest there be 611
25:12 But he **a** and said, Verily I say unto you, 611
25:26 His lord **a** and said unto him, *Thou* wicked 611
26:23 And he **a** and said, He that dippeth *his* hand 611
26:25 betrayed him, **a** and said, Master, is it I? 611
26:33 Peter **a** and said unto him, Though all *men* 611
26:63 And the high priest **a** and said unto him, 611
26:66 They **a** and said, He is guilty of death. 611
27:12 of the chief priests and elders, he **a** nothing. 611
27:14 And he **a** him to never a word; 611
27:21 The governor **a** and said unto them, 611
27:25 Then **a** all the people, and said, His blood *be* 611
28: 5 And the angel **a** and said unto the women, 611
Mk 3:33 And he **a** them, saying, Who is my mother, 611
5: 9 And he **a**, saying, My name *is* Legion: 611
6:37 He **a** and said unto them, Give ye them to 611
7: 6 He **a** and said unto them, Well hath Esaias 611
7:28 And she **a** and said unto him, Yes, Lord: 611
8: 4 And his disciples **a** him, From whence can a 611
8:28 And they **a**, John the Baptist: but some *say*, 611
9: 5 And Peter **a** and said to Jesus, Master, it is 611
9:12 And he **a** and told them, Elias verily cometh 611
9:17 And one of the multitude **a** and said, Master, 611
9:38 And John **a** him, saying, Master, we saw one 611
10: 3 And he **a** and said unto them, What did 611
10: 5 And Jesus **a** and said unto them, For 611
10:20 And he **a** and said unto him, Master, 611
10:29 And Jesus **a** and said, Verily I say unto you, 611
10:51 And Jesus **a** and said unto him, What wilt 611
11:14 And Jesus **a** and said unto it, No *man* eat 611
11:29 And Jesus **a** and said unto them, I will also 611
11:33 And they **a** and said unto Jesus, We cannot 611
12:28 and perceiving that he had **a** them well, 611
12:29 And Jesus **a** him, The first of all 611

Mk 12:34 And when Jesus saw that he **a** discreetly, *611*
12:35 And Jesus **a** and said, while he taught in *611*
14:20 And he **a** and said unto them, *It is* one of *611*
14:48 And Jesus **a** and said unto them, Are ye *611*
14:61 But he held his peace, and **a** nothing. *611*
15: 3 him of many *things:* but he **a** nothing. *611*
15: 5 But Jesus yet **a** nothing; so that Pilate *611*
15: 9 But Pilate **a** them, saying, Will ye *that* I *611*
15:12 And Pilate **a** and said again unto them, *611*
Lk 1:35 And the angel **a** and said unto her, The Holy *611*
1:60 And his mother **a** and said, Not *so;* but *611*
3:16 John **a**, saying unto *them* all, I indeed *611*
4: 4 And Jesus **a** him, saying, It is written, *611*
4: 8 And Jesus **a** and said unto him, Get thee *611*
7:43 Simon **a** and said, I suppose that *he,* to *611*
8:21 And he **a** and said unto them, My mother *611*
8:50 But when Jesus heard *it,* he **a** him, saying, *611*
9:49 And John **a** and said, Master, we saw one *611*
10:28 And he said unto him, Thou hast **a** right: *611*
10:41 And Jesus **a** and said unto her, Martha, *611*
11:45 Then **a** one of the lawyers, and said unto *611*
13:14 And the ruler of the synagogue **a** with *611*
13:15 The Lord then **a** him, and said, *611*
14: 5 And **a** them, saying, Which of you shall *611*
17:20 of God should come, he **a** them and said, *611*
17:37 And they **a** and said unto him, Where, Lord? *611*
19:40 And he **a** and said unto them, I tell you that, *611*
20: 3 And he **a** and said unto them, I will also ask *611*
20: 7 And they **a**, that *they* could not tell whence *611*
20:24 hath it? They **a** and said, Cesar's. *611*
22:51 And Jesus **a** and said, Suffer ye thus far. *611*
23: 3 And he **a** him and said, Thou sayest *it.* *611*
23: 9 him in many words; but he **a** him nothing. *611*
Jn 1:21 am not. Art thou *that* prophet? And he **a**, No. *611*
1:26 John **a** them, saying, I baptize with water: *611*
1:48 Jesus **a** and said unto him, Before that Philip *611*
1:49 Nathanael **a** and saith unto him, Rabbi, *611*
1:50 Jesus **a** and said unto him, Because I said *611*
2:18 Then **a** the Jews and said unto him, *611*
2:19 Jesus **a** and said unto them, Destroy this *611*
3: 3 Jesus **a** and said unto him, Verily, verily, *611*
3: 5 Jesus **a**, Verily, verily, I say unto thee, *611*
3: 9 Nicodemus **a** and said unto him, How can *611*
3:10 Jesus **a** and said unto him, Art thou **a** master *611*
3:27 John **a** and said, A man can receive nothing, *611*
4:10 Jesus **a** and said unto her, If thou knewest *611*
4:13 Jesus **a** and said unto her, *611*
4:17 The woman **a** and said, I have no husband. *611*
5: 7 The impotent *man* **a** him, Sir, I have no man, *611*
5:11 He **a** them, He that made me whole, *611*
5:17 But Jesus **a** them, My Father worketh *611*
5:19 Then **a** Jesus and said unto them, Verily, *611*
6: 7 Philip **a** him, Two hundred pennyworth of *611*
6:26 Jesus **a** them and said, Verily, verily, I say *611*
6:29 Jesus **a** and said unto them, This is the work *611*
6:43 Jesus therefore **a** and said unto them, *611*
6:68 Then Simon Peter **a** him, Lord, to whom *611*
6:70 Jesus **a** them, Have not I chosen you twelve, *611*
7:16 Jesus **a** them, and said, My doctrine is not *611*
7:20 The people **a** and said, Thou hast **a** devil: *611*
7:21 Jesus **a** and said unto them, I have done one *611*
7:46 The officers **a**, Never man spake like this *611*
7:47 Then **a** them the Pharisees, Are ye also *611*
7:52 They **a** and said unto him, Art thou also of *611*
8:14 Jesus **a** and said unto them, Though I bear *611*
8:19 Jesus **a**, Ye neither know me, nor my Father: *611*
8:33 They **a** him, We be Abraham's seed, and *611*
8:34 Jesus **a** them, Verily, verily, I say unto you, *611*
8:39 They **a** and said unto him, Abraham is our *611*
8:48 Then **a** the Jews, and said unto him, Say we *611*
8:49 Jesus **a**, I have not a devil; but I honour my *611*
8:54 Jesus **a**, If I honour myself, my honour is *611*
9: 3 Jesus **a**, Neither hath this *man* sinned, *611*
9:11 He **a** and said, A man *that is* called Jesus *611*
9:20 His parents **a** them and said, We know that *611*
9:25 He **a** and said, Whether he be a sinner *or* *611*
9:27 He **a** them, I have told you already, and *611*
9:30 The man **a** and said unto them, Why herein *611*
9:34 They **a** and said unto him, Thou wast *611*
9:36 He **a** and said, Who is he, Lord, that I might *611*
10:25 Jesus **a** them, I told you, and ye believe not: *611*
10:32 Jesus **a** them, Many good works have I *611*
10:33 The Jews **a** him, saying, For a good work we *611*
10:34 Jesus **a** them, Is it not written in your law, I *611*
11: 9 Jesus **a**, Are there not twelve hours in *611*
12:23 And Jesus **a** them, saying, The hour is come, *611*
12:30 Jesus **a** and said, This voice came not *611*
12:34 The people **a** him, We have heard out of *611*
13: 7 Jesus **a** and said unto him, What I do thou *611*
13: 8 Jesus **a** him, If I wash thee not, thou hast no *611*
13:26 Jesus **a**, He it is, to whom I shall give a sop, *611*
13:36 Jesus **a** him, Whither I go, thou canst not *611*
13:38 Jesus **a** him, Wilt thou lay down thy life for *611*
14:23 Jesus **a** and said unto him, If a man love me, *611*
16:31 Jesus **a** them, Do ye now believe? *611*
18: 5 They **a** him, Jesus of Nazareth. Jesus saith *611*
18: 8 Jesus **a**, I have told you that I am *he:* if *611*
18:20 Jesus **a** him, I spake openly to the world; *611*
18:23 Jesus **a** him, If I have spoken evil, *611*
18:30 They **a** and said unto him, If he were not a *611*
18:34 Jesus **a** him, Sayest thou this *thing* of *611*
18:35 Pilate **a**, Am I a Jew? Thine own nation and *611*
18:36 Jesus **a**, My kingdom is not of this world: *611*
18:37 Jesus **a**, Thou sayest that I am a king. To this *611*
19: 7 The Jews **a** him, We have a law, and by our *611*
19:11 Jesus **a**, Thou couldest have no power *at all* *611*
19:15 The chief priests **a**, We have no king but *611*
19:22 Pilate **a**, What I have written I have written. *611*
20:28 And Thomas **a** and said unto him, My Lord *611*
21: 5 have ye any meat? They **a** him, No. *611*
Ac 3:12 And when Peter saw *it,* he **a** unto the people, *611*
4:19 But Peter and John **a** and said unto them, *611*
5: 8 And Peter **a** unto her, Tell me whether ye *611*
5:29 Then Peter and the *other* apostles **a** and said, *611*
8:24 Then **a** Simon, and said, Pray ye to the Lord *611*
Ac 8:34 And the eunuch **a** Philip, and said, I pray *611*
8:37 And he **a** and said, I believe that Jesus Christ *611*
9:13 Then Ananias **a**, Lord, I have heard by many *611*
10:46 and magnify God. Then **a** Peter, *611*
11: 9 But *the* voice **a** me again from heaven, *611*
15:13 James **a**, saying, Men *and* brethren, *611*
19:15 And the evil spirit **a** and said, Jesus I know, *611*
21:13 Then Paul **a**, What mean ye to weep and *611*
22: 8 And I **a**, Who art thou, Lord? And he said *611*
22:28 And the chief captain **a**, With a great sum *611*
24:10 governor had beckoned unto him to speak, **a**, *611*
24:25 judgment to come, Felix trembled, and **a**, *611*
25: 4 But Festus **a**, that Paul should be kept at *611*
25: 8 While he **a for himself**, Neither against *626*
25: 9 **a** Paul, and said, Wilt thou go up to *611*
25:12 **a**, Hast thou appealed unto Cesar? *611*
25:16 To whom I **a**, It is not the manner of *611*
26: 1 stretched forth the hand, and **a for** himself: *626*
Rev 7:13 And one of the elders **a**, saying unto me, *611*

ANSWEREDST (2) [ANSWER]
Ps 99: 8 Thou **a** them, O LORD our God: 6030
138: 3 In the day when I cried thou **a** me, *and* 6030

ANSWEREST (6) [ANSWER]
1Sa 26:14 the son of Ner, saying, **A** thou not, Abner? 6030
Job 16: 3 or what emboldeneth thee that thou **a**? 6030
Mt 26:62 and said unto him, **A** thou nothing? *611*
Mk 14:60 and asked Jesus, saying, **A** thou nothing? *611*
15: 4 asked him again, saying, **A** thou nothing? *611*
Jn 18:22 his hand, saying, **A** thou the high priest so? *611*

ANSWERETH (13) [ANSWER]
1Sa 28:15 **a** me no more, neither by prophets, nor by 6030
1Ki 18:24 the God that **a** by fire, let him be God. 6030
Job 12: 4 who calleth upon God, and he **a** him: 6030
Pr 18:13 He that **a a** matter before he heareth *it, it is* 7725
18:23 poor useth intreaties; but the rich **a** roughly. 6030
27:19 As *in* water face **a** to face, so the heart of NIH
Ecc 5:20 because God **a** *him* in the joy of his heart. 6031
10:19 maketh merry: but money **a** all *things.* 6030
Mk 8:29 And Peter **a** and saith unto him, Thou art *611*
9:19 He **a** him, and saith, O faithless generation, *611*
10:24 But Jesus **a** again, and saith unto them, *611*
Lk 3:11 He **a** and saith unto them, He that hath two *611*
Gal 4:25 and **a to** Jerusalem which now is, and is in *4960*

ANSWERING (31) [ANSWER]
Mt 3:15 And Jesus **a** said unto him, Suffer *it to be so* *611*
Mk 11:22 And Jesus **a** saith unto them, Have faith in *611*
11:33 And Jesus **a** saith unto them, Neither do I *611*
12:17 And Jesus **a** said unto them, Render to Cesar *611*
12:24 And Jesus **a** said unto them, Do ye not *611*
13: 2 And Jesus **a** said unto him, Seest thou these *611*
13: 5 And Jesus **a** them began to say, Take heed *611*
15: 2 And he **a** said unto him, Thou sayest *it.* *611*
Lk 1:19 And the angel **a** said unto him, I am Gabriel, *611*
4:12 And Jesus **a** said unto him, It is said, *611*
5: 5 And Simon **a** said unto him, Master, *611*
5:22 he **a** said unto them, What reason ye in your *611*
5:31 And Jesus **a** said unto them, They that are *611*
6: 3 And Jesus **a** them said, Have ye not read so *611*
7:22 Then Jesus **a** said unto them, Go *your way,* *611*
7:40 And Jesus **a** said unto him, Simon, I have *611*
9:19 They **a** said, John the Baptist; but some *say,* *611*
9:20 that I am? Peter **a** said, The Christ of God. *611*
9:41 And Jesus **a** said, O faithless and *611*
10:27 And he **a** said, Thou shalt love the Lord thy *611*
10:30 And Jesus **a** said, A certain man went down *5274*
11:39 And Jesus **a** said unto them, Suppose ye that *611*
13: 8 And he **a** said unto him, Lord, let it alone *611*
14: 3 And Jesus **a** spake unto the lawyers and *611*
15:29 And he **a** said to *his* father, Lo, these many *611*
17:17 And Jesus **a** said, Were there not ten *611*
20:34 And Jesus **a** said unto them, The children of *611*
20:39 Then certain of the scribes **a** said, Master, *611*
23:40 But the other **a** rebuked him, saying, Dost *611*
24:18 **a** said unto him, Art thou only a stranger in *611*
Tit 2: 9 please *them* well in all *things;* not **a again;** *483*

ANSWERS (3) [ANSWER]
Job 21:34 seeing *in* your **a** there remaineth falsehood? 8666
34:36 the end because of *his* **a** for wicked men. 8666
Lk 2:47 were astonished at his understanding and **a**. *612*

ANT (1) [ANTS]
Pr 6: 6 Go to the **a**, thou sluggard; consider her 5244

ANTHOTHIJAH See ANTOTHIJAH

ANTICHRIST (4) [CHRIST]
1Jn 2:18 and as ye have heard that **a** shall come, *500*
2:22 He is **a**, that denieth the Father and the Son. *500*
4: 3 and this is *that spirit of* **a**, whereof you have *500*
2Jn 1: 7 in the flesh. This is a deceiver and an **a**. *500*

ANTICHRISTS (1) [CHRIST]
1Jn 2:18 shall come, even now are there many **a**; *500*

ANTIOCH (19)
Ac 6: 5 and Parmenas, and Nicolas a proselyte of **A**: *491*
11:19 and Cyprus, and **A**, preaching the word to *490*
11:20 Cyrene, which, when they were come to **A**, *490*
11:22 forth Barnabas, that *he* should go as far as **A**. *490*
11:26 he had found him, he brought him unto **A**. *490*
11:26 disciples were called Christians first in **A**. *490*
11:27 days came prophets from Jerusalem unto **A**. *490*
13: 1 Now there were in the church that was at **A** *490*
13:14 they came to **A** in Pisidia, and went into *490*
14:19 And there came thither *certain* Jews from **A** *490*
14:21 *again* to Lystra, and *to* Iconium, and **A**, *490*
14:26 And thence sailed to **A**, from whence they *490*
15:22 men of their own company to **A** with Paul *490*
15:23 the brethren which are of the Gentiles in **A** *490*
Ac 15:30 when they were dismissed, they came to **A**: *490*
15:35 Paul also and Barnabas continued in **A**, *490*
18:22 and saluted the church, he went down to **A**. *490*
Gal 2:11 But when Peter was come to **A**, I withstood *490*
2Ti 3:11 afflictions, which came unto me at **A**, *490*

ANTIPAS (1)
Rev 2:13 even in *those* days wherein **A** *was* my *493*

ANTIPATRIS (1)
Ac 23:31 took Paul, and brought *him* by night to **A**. *494*

ANTIQUITY (1)
Isa 23: 7 *Is* this your joyous *city,* whose **a** *is* of 6927

ANTOTHIJAH (1)
1Ch 8:24 And Hananiah, and Elam, and **A**, 6070

ANTOTHITE (2)
1Ch 11:28 son of Ikkesh the Tekoite, Abi-ezer the **A**, 6069
12: 3 and Berachah, and Jehu the **A**, 6069

ANTS (1) [ANT]
Pr 30:25 The **a** *are* a people not strong, yet they 5244

ANUB (1)
1Ch 4: 8 Coz begat **A**, and Zobebah, and the families 6036

ANVIL (1)
Isa 41: 7 *with* the hammer him that smote the **a**, 6471

ANY (916) [ANYTHING]
Ge 3: 1 Now the serpent was more subtil than **a** 3605
4:15 lest **a** finding him should kill him. 3605
8:12 which returned not again unto him **a more**. 5750
8:21 I will not again curse the ground **a more** 5750
8:21 neither will I again smite **a more** every 5750
9:11 neither shall all flesh be cut off **a more** by 5750
9:11 neither shall there **a more** be a flood to 5750
14:23 that I will not take **a thing** that *is* thine, 3605
17: 5 Neither shall thy name **a more** be called 5750
17:12 or bought with money of **a** stranger, which 3605
18:14 Is **a thing** too hard for the LORD? At 1697
19:12 said unto Lot, Hast thou here **a** besides? 4310
19:22 for I cannot do **a thing** till thou be come 1697
22:12 the lad, neither do thou **a thing** unto him: 3972
24:16 a virgin, neither had **a man** known her: 376
30:31 Jacob said, Thou shalt not give me **a thing**: 3972
31:14 *Is there* yet **a** portion or inheritance for us in NIH
35:10 thy name shall not be called **a more** Jacob, 5750
36:31 before there reigned *a* king over NIH
39: 9 neither hath he kept back **a thing** from me 3972
39:23 to **a thing** *that was* under his hand; 3605+3972
42:16 be proved, whether *there be* **a** truth in you: NIH
43:34 mess was five times so much as **a** of theirs. 3605
47: 6 if thou knowest *a* man of activity amongst NIH
Ex 1:10 to pass, that, when there falleth out **a** war, NIH
8:29 let not Pharaoh deal deceitfully **a more** in 3254
9:29 neither shall there be **a more** hail; 5750
10:15 there remained not **a** green thing in 3605
10:23 neither rose **a** from his place for three days: 376
11: 6 was none like it, nor shall be like it **a more**. 3254
11: 7 against **a** of the children of Israel shall not a 3605
12:39 neither had they prepared for themselves *a* NIH
16:24 not stink, neither was there *a* worm therein. NIH
20: 4 Thou shalt not make unto thee *a* graven NIH
20: 4 **a** likeness *of any thing* that *is* in heaven 3605
20: 4 any likeness *of* **a** *thing* that *is* in heaven NIH
20:10 *in it* thou shalt not do **a** work, thou, nor thy 3605
20:17 his ass, nor **a thing** that *is* thy neighbour's. 3605
21:23 if *a* mischief follow, then thou shalt give NIH
22: 9 for **a manner** of lost *thing,* which *another* 3605
22:10 or an ox, or a sheep, or **a** beast, to keep; 3605
22:20 He that sacrificeth unto *a* god, save unto NIH
22:22 Ye shall not afflict **a** widow, or 3605
22:23 If thou **afflict** them **in a wise**, 6031+6031
22:25 If thou lend money to *a of* my people *that is* NIH
22:31 neither shall ye eat *a* flesh *that is* torn *of* NIH
24:14 if a man have any matters to do, let him 4310
24:14 if any man have *a* matters to do, let him NIH
30:32 neither shall ye make *a other* like it, NIH
30:33 Whosoever compoundeth *a* like it, or NIH
30:33 or whosoever putteth **a** of it upon a stranger, NIH
31:14 for whosoever doeth *a* work therein, that NIH
31:15 whosoever doeth *a* work in the sabbath day, NIH
32:24 Whosoever hath *a* gold, let them break *it* NIH
34: 3 neither let **a man** be seen throughout all 376
34:10 been done in all the earth, nor in **a** nation: 3605
34:24 neither shall **a man** desire thy land, 376
35:24 with whom was found shittim wood for **a** 3605
35:33 to make **a** *manner of* cunning work. 3605
35:35 *even* of them that do **a** work, and of those 3605
36: 6 Let neither man nor woman make **a more** 5750
Lev 1: 2 If *a* man of you bring an offering unto NIH
2: 1 when **a** will offer a meat offering unto 5315
2:11 for ye shall burn no leaven, nor **a** honey, 3605
2:11 *in* **a** offering of the LORD made by fire. NIH
4: 2 **a** of the commandments of the LORD 3605
4: 2 to be done), and shall do against **a** of them: 259
4:13 they have done somewhat against **a** of 3605
4:22 **a** of the commandments of the LORD his 3605
4:27 if **a** one of the common people sin through 259
4:27 while he doeth somewhat against *a of* NIH
5: 2 Or if a soul touch **a** unclean thing, 3605
5:11 neither shall he put *a* frankincense thereon: NIH
5:17 commit **a** *of these things* which are 259+3605
6: 3 in **a** of all *these* that a man doeth, sinning 259
6: 7 it shall be forgiven him for **a** *thing* of all that 259
6:27 of the blood thereof upon *a* garment, NIH
6:30 whereof **a** of the blood is brought into NIH
7: 8 the priest that offereth *a* man's burnt NIH
7:15 he shall not leave *a* of it until the morning. NIH
7:18 if *a* of the flesh of the sacrifice of his peace NIH
7:19 the flesh that toucheth **a** unclean *thing* shall 3605

A

Ref	Context	Strong's
Lev 7:21	Moreover the soul that shall touch **a**	3605
7:21	or **a** unclean beast, or any abominable	NIH
7:21	or **a** abominable unclean *thing,* and eat of	3605
7:24	*with beasts,* may be used in **a** *other* use:	3605
7:26	of fowl or of beast, in **a** of your dwellings.	3605
7:27	Whatsoever soul *it be* that eateth **a** *manner*	3605
11:10	and of **a** living thing which *is* in the waters,	3605
11:32	upon whatsoever **a** of them, when they are	NIH
11:32	whether *it be* **a** vessel of wood, or raiment,	3605
11:32	whatsoever vessel *it be,* wherein **a** work is	NIH
11:33	earthen vessel, whereinto **a** of them falleth,	NIH
11:35	every *thing* whereupon **a** *part* of their	NIH
11:37	if **a** *part* of their carcase fall upon any	NIH
11:37	if *any part* of their carcase fall upon **a**	3605
11:38	if **a** water be put upon the seed, and *any part*	NIH
11:38	**a** *part* of their carcase fall thereon, it *shall*	NIH
11:39	if **a** beast, of which ye may eat, die; he that	4480
11:43	with **a** creeping thing that creepeth,	3605
11:44	neither shall ye defile yourselves with **a**	3605
13:24	Or if there be **a** flesh, in the skin whereof	NIH
13:48	in a skin, or in **a thing** made of skin;	3605
13:49	or in the woof, or in **a** thing of skin;	3605
13:51	in a skin, *or* in **a** work that is made of skin;	3605
13:52	in woollen or in linen, or **a** thing of skin,	3605
13:53	or in the woof, or in **a** thing of skin;	3605
13:57	or in the woof, or in **a** thing of skins;	3605
13:59	*in* the warp, or woof, or **a** thing of skins,	3605
15:2	When **a man** hath a running issue out	376+376
15:6	he that sitteth on **a** thing whereon he sat that	NIH
15:10	whosoever toucheth **a** *thing* that was under	3605
15:10	he that beareth **a** *of* those *things* shall wash	NIH
15:16	if **a man's** seed of copulation go out from	376
15:22	whosoever toucheth **a** thing that she sat	3605
15:23	or on **a** thing whereon she sitteth, when he	NIH
15:24	if **a man** lie with her at all, and her flowers	376
17:10	among you, that eateth **a** *manner of* blood;	3605
17:12	neither shall **a**[S] stranger that sojourneth	1886.1
17:13	which hunteth and catcheth **a** beast or	NIH
18:6	None of you shall approach to **a** that is near	3605
18:21	thou shalt not let **a** of thy seed pass through	NIH
18:23	Neither shalt thou lie with **a** beast to defile	3605
18:23	neither shall **a** woman stand before a beast	NIH
18:24	Defile not you yourselves in **a** of these	3605
18:26	shall not commit **a** of these abominations;	3605
18:26	*neither* **a** of your own nation, nor any	NIH
18:26	nor **a** stranger that sojourneth among you:	NIH
18:29	For whosoever shall commit **a** of these	3605
18:30	that *ye* commit not **a** *one* of *these*	NIH
19:17	thou shalt **in a wise rebuke** thy	3198+3198
19:18	nor **bear a grudge against** the children of	5201
19:26	Ye shall not eat **a** *thing* with the blood:	NIH
19:28	Ye shall not make **a** cuttings in your flesh	NIH
19:28	for the dead, nor print **a** marks upon you:	3793
20:2	that giveth **a** of his seed unto Molech;	NIH
20:4	**a ways hide** their eyes from the man,	5956+5956
20:16	if **a** woman approach unto a beast, and	3605
20:25	by **a** *manner of living thing* that creepeth	3605
21:5	nor **make a cuttings** in their flesh.	8295+8296
21:9	the daughter of **a** priest, if she profane	376
21:11	Neither shall he go in to **a** dead body,	3605
21:17	in their generations that hath **a** blemish,	NIH
21:18	that hath **a** flat nose, or **a** thing superfluous,	NIH
22:4	whoso toucheth **a** *thing that is* unclean *by*	3605
22:5	Or whosoever toucheth **a** creeping thing,	3605
22:6	The soul which hath touched **a** such shall be	NIH
22:11	if the priest buy **a** soul with his money,	NIH
22:23	or a lamb that **hath a thing superfluous** or	8311
22:24	neither shall you make **a** offering *thereof* in	NIH
22:25	offer the bread of your God of **a** of these;	3605
23:22	neither shalt thou gather **a** gleaning of thy	NIH
23:30	whatsoever soul *it be* that doeth **a** work in	3605
24:17	he that killeth **a** man shall surely be put to	3605
25:25	*if* **a** *of* his kin come to redeem it, then	NIH
25:32	may the Levites redeem at **a time.**	5769
25:49	**a** that is nigh of kin unto him of his family	NIH
26:1	neither *shall* ye set up **a** image of stone in	NIH
27:9	all that **a** *man* giveth of such unto	NIH
27:11	if *it be* **a** unclean beast, of which they do	3605
27:19	the field will **in a wise redeem** it,	1350+1350
27:20	it shall not be redeemed **a more.**	5750
Nu 4:15	they shall not touch **a** holy *thing,* lest they	NIH
5:6	woman shall commit **a** sin that men	3605
5:10	whatsoever **a man** giveth the priest, it shall	376
5:12	If **a man's** wife go aside, and commit a	376
6:3	neither shall he drink **a** liquor of grapes,	3605
6:9	And if **a** man die very suddenly by him, and	NIH
9:10	If **a man** of you or of your posterity shall be	376
9:12	it unto the morning, nor break **a** bone of it:	NIH
14:23	neither shall **a** of them that provoked me	3605
15:27	if **a** soul sin through ignorance, then he shall	259
17:13	Whosoever cometh **a thing** near unto	3605
18:5	that there be no wrath **a more** upon	5750
18:20	neither shalt thou have **a** part among them:	NIH
19:11	He that toucheth the dead *body* of **a** man	3605
19:13	Whosoever toucheth the dead *body* of **a**	NIH
20:5	neither *is there* **a** water to drink.	NIH
20:19	without *doing* **a** thing *else,* go through on	NIH
21:5	*there is* no bread, neither *is there* **a** water;	NIH
21:9	to pass, that if **a** serpent had bitten **a** man,	NIH
22:38	have I now **a power at all** to say any	3201+3201
22:38	have I now any power at all to say **a thing**?	3972
23:23	neither *is there* **a** divination against Israel:	NIH
29:7	your souls: ye shall not do **a** work *therein:*	3605
30:5	not **a** of her vows, or of her bonds	3605
30:15	if he shall **a ways make** them **void**	6565+6565
31:19	whosoever hath killed **a** person, and	NIH
31:19	whosoever hath touched **a** slain, purify *both*	NIH
35:11	which killeth **a** person at unawares.	NIH
35:15	that every one that killeth **a** person	NIH
35:22	have cast upon him **a** thing without laying	3605
35:23	Or with **a** stone, wherewith **a** *man* may die,	3605
35:26	if the slayer shall **at a time come**	3318+3318
35:30	Whoso killeth **a** person, the murderer shall	NIH
35:30	one witness shall not testify against **a**	NIH
36:3	*if* they be married to **a** of the sons of	259
Nu 36:8	that possesseth an inheritance in **a** tribe of	NIH
Dt 2:19	of the children of Ammon **a** possession;	NIH
2:37	*nor unto* **a** place of the river Jabbok,	3605
4:16	the similitude of **a** figure, the likeness of	3605
4:17	The likeness of **a** beast that *is* on the earth,	3605
4:17	the likeness of **a** winged fowl that flieth in	3605
4:18	The likeness of **a** *thing* that creepeth on	3605
4:18	the likeness of **a** fish that *is* in the waters	3605
4:23	the likeness of **a** *thing,* which the LORD	3605
4:25	*or* the likeness of **a** *thing,* and shall do evil	3605
4:32	whether there hath been **a** *such thing* as this	NIH
5:8	Thou shalt not make thee **a** graven image,	NIH
5:8	**a** likeness *of any thing* that *is* in heaven	3605
5:8	any likeness *of* **a** *thing* that *is* in heaven	NIH
5:14	*in it* thou shalt not do **a** work, thou, nor thy	3605
5:14	thine ox, nor thine ass, nor **a** of thy cattle,	3605
5:21	or his ass, or **a** *thing* that *is* thy neighbour's.	3605
5:25	of the LORD our God **a more,**	3254+5750
7:7	ye were moe in number than **a** people;	3605
8:9	thou shalt not lack **a** *thing* in it;	3605
12:17	nor **a** of thy vows which thou vowest,	3605
13:11	shall do no more **a** such wickedness as	3509.1
14:1	nor make **a** baldness between your eyes for	NIH
14:3	Thou shalt not eat **a** abominable *thing.*	3605
14:21	Ye shall not eat of **a thing** that dieth of	3605
15:7	**a** of thy gates in thy land which the LORD	259
15:21	if there be **a** blemish therein, *as if it be*	NIH
15:21	*if it be* lame, or blind, *or have* **a** ill blemish,	3605
16:4	neither shall there **a** *thing* of the flesh,	NIH
16:5	sacrifice the passover within **a** of thy gates,	259
16:21	Thou shalt not plant thee a grove *of* **a** trees	3605
16:22	Neither shalt thou set thee up **a** image;	NIH
17:1	unto the LORD thy God **a** bullock,	NIH
17:1	wherein is blemish, *or* **a** evil favouredness:	3605
17:2	within **a** of thy gates which the LORD thy	259
17:3	or moon, or **a** of the host of heaven,	3605
17:15	Thou shalt **in a wise set** *him* king	7760+7760
18:6	if a Levite come from **a** of thy gates out of	259
18:10	There shall not be found among you **a** *one*	NIH
18:16	neither let me see this great fire **a more,**	5750
19:11	if **a man** hate his neighbour, and lie in wait	376
19:15	not rise up against a man for **a** iniquity,	3605
19:15	or for a sin, in any sin that he sinneth:	3605
19:15	or for any sin, in **a** sin that he sinneth:	3605
19:16	If a false witness rise up against **a man** to	376
19:20	shall henceforth commit no more **a**[S] such	1697
21:23	shalt **in a wise bury** him that day;	6912+6912
22:1	**in a case bring** them **again** unto thy	7725+7725
22:6	to be before thee in the way in **a** tree,	3605
22:7	thou shalt **in a wise let** the dam **go,**	7971+7971
22:8	upon thine house, if **a** man fall from thence.	NIH
22:13	If **a man** take a wife, and go in unto her, and	376
23:10	If there be among you **a man,** that is not	376
23:18	*into* the house of the LORD thy God for **a**	3605
23:19	usury of **a** thing that is lent upon usury:	3605
23:24	but thou shalt not put **a** in thy vessel.	NIH
24:5	neither shall he be charged with **a** business:	3605
24:7	If a man be found stealing **a** of his brethren	5315
24:10	When thou dost lend thy brother **a thing,**	3972
24:13	**In a case** thou shalt **deliver** him the pledge **again**	7725+7725
26:14	have I taken away *ought* thereof for **a**	NIH
27:5	thou shalt not lift up **a** iron *tool* upon them.	NIH
27:15	Cursed *be* the man that maketh **a** graven or	NIH
27:21	Cursed *be* he that lieth with **a** *manner of*	3605
28:14	thou shalt not go aside from **a** of the words	3605
28:55	So that *he* will not give to **a** of them of	259
29:23	nor beareth, nor **a** grass groweth therein,	3605
30:4	If **a** of thine be driven out unto the outmost	NIH
31:13	which have not known **a** *thing,* may hear,	NIH
32:28	neither *is there* **a** understanding in them.	NIH
32:39	neither *is there* **a** that can deliver out of my	NIH
Jos 1:5	There shall not **a man** *be able to* stand	376
2:11	neither did there remain **a more** courage in	5750
2:11	there remain any more courage in **a man,**	376
2:19	*shall be* on our head, if **a** hand be upon him.	NIH
5:1	neither was there spirit in them **a more,**	5750
5:12	had the children of Israel manna **a more;**	5750
6:10	nor make **a** noise with your voice,	NIH
6:10	neither shall **a** word proceed out of your	NIH
6:18	**in a wise** keep *yourselves* from	7535
7:12	neither will I be with you **a more,**	3254
8:31	over which no *man* hath lift up **a** iron:	NIH
10:21	none moved his tongue against **a** of	NIH
11:11	utterly destroying *them:* there was not **a** left	3605
11:14	neither left they **a** to breathe.	3605
13:33	unto the tribe of Levi Moses gave not **a**	NIH
20:3	That the slayer that killeth **a** person	NIH
20:9	that whosoever killeth **a** person at unawares	NIH
21:45	There failed not ought of **a** good thing	3605
23:12	Else if ye do **in a wise go back,**	7725+7725
23:13	out **a** *of* these nations from before you;	NIH
Jdg 2:14	that they could not **a longer** stand before	5750
2:21	I also will not henceforth drive out **a** from	376
4:20	when **a** man doth come and inquire of thee,	NIH
4:20	of thee, and say, Is there **a** man here?	NIH
11:25	now *art* thou **a thing better** than	2896+2896
13:4	strong drink, and eat not **a** unclean *thing:*	3605
13:7	neither eat **a** unclean *thing:* for the child	3605
13:14	She may not eat of **a** *thing* that cometh of	3605
13:14	nor eat **a** unclean *thing:* all that I	3605
16:17	become weak, and be like **a** *other* man.	3605
18:7	that might put *them* to shame in **a** thing;	NIH
18:7	and had no business with **a** man.	NIH
18:10	a place where *there is* no want of **a** thing	3605
18:28	and they had no business with **a** man;	NIH
19:19	thy servants: *there is* no want of **a** thing.	3605
20:8	We will not **a** *of us* go to his tent,	376
20:8	neither will we **a** *of us* turn into his house.	376
21:1	There shall not **a** of us give his daughter	376
21:12	that had known no man by lying with **a**	NIH
Ru 1:11	*are there* yet **a** moe sons in my womb,	NIH
2:22	that they meet thee not in **a** other field.	NIH
1Sa 2:2	**neither** *is there* **a** rock like our God.	369+2050.1
2:13	*was, that* when **a** man offered sacrifice,	3605
1Sa 2:16	*if* **a** man said unto him, Let them not fail to	NIH
3:17	if thou hide **a** thing from me of all	NIH
5:5	nor **a** that come *into* Dagon's house,	3605
6:3	**in a wise return** him a trespass	7725+7725
9:2	upward *he was* higher than **a** of the people.	3605
10:23	he was higher than **a** of the people from his	3605
12:3	of whose hand have I received **a** bribe to	NIH
12:4	neither hast thou taken ought of **a man's**	376
13:22	hand of **a** of the people that *were* with Saul	3605
14:24	Cursed *be* the man that eateth **a** food until	NIH
14:24	So none of the people tasted **a** food.	NIH
14:28	Cursed *be* the man that eateth **a** food *this*	NIH
14:52	when Saul saw a strong man, or any valiant	3605
14:52	or **a** valiant man, he took him unto him.	3605
18:25	The king desireth not **a** dowry, but an	NIH
20:12	sounded my father about to morrow **a** time,	NIH
20:26	Nevertheless Saul spake not **a thing** that	3972
20:39	the lad knew not **a thing:** only Jonathan	3972
21:2	Let no man know **a thing** of the business	3972
22:15	let not the king impute **a** thing unto his	NIH
25:15	were not hurt, neither missed we **a thing,**	3972
25:22	morning light **a** *that* pisseth against the wall.	NIH
25:34	morning light **a** *that* pisseth against the wall.	NIH
27:1	to seek me **a more** in any coast of Israel:	5750
27:1	to seek me any more in **a** coast of Israel:	3605
30:2	they slew not **a,** either great or small, but	376
30:12	nor drunk **a** water, three days and	NIH
30:19	nor **a** *thing* that they had taken to them:	3605
2Sa 2:1	Shall I go up into **a** of the cities of Judah?	259
2:28	Israel no more, neither fought they **a more.**	5750
7:6	Whereas I have not dwelt in **a** house since	NIH
7:7	spake I a word with **a** of the tribes of Israel,	259
7:10	children of wickedness afflict them **a more,**	3254
7:22	like thee, neither *is there* **a** God beside thee,	NIH
9:1	Is there yet **a** that is left of the house of	NIH
9:3	*Is there* not yet **a** of the house of Saul,	376
10:19	to help the children of Ammon **a more.**	5750
13:2	thought it hard for him to do **a thing** to her.	3972
14:10	and he shall not touch thee **a more.**	3254+5750
14:11	the revengers of blood to destroy **a more,**	7235
14:14	up *again;* neither doth God respect **a** person:	NIH
14:32	if there be **a** iniquity in me, let him kill me.	NIH
15:2	*that when* **a** man that had a controversy	3605
15:4	that every man which hath **a** suit or	NIH
15:5	that when **a man** came nigh *to him* to do	376
15:11	their simplicity, and they knew not **a** thing.	3605
19:22	shall there **a man** be put to death *this* day in	376
19:28	have I yet to cry **a more** unto the king?	5750
19:29	Why speakest thou **a more** of thy matters?	5750
19:35	can I hear **a more** the voice of singing *men*	5750
19:42	the king's *cost?* or hath he given us **a** gift?	NIH
21:4	neither for us *shalt thou* kill **a man** in Israel.	376
21:5	from remaining in **a** of the coasts of Israel,	3605
1Ki 1:6	his father had not displeased him **at a time**	3117
2:36	**a whither.**	575+575+1886.5+1886.5+2050.1
2:42	**a whither,**	575+575+1886.5+1886.5+2050.1
3:12	neither after thee shall **a** arise like unto thee.	NIH
3:13	that there shall not be **a** among the kings like	376
5:6	for thou knowest that *there is* not among us **a**	376
6:7	axe *nor* **a** tool of iron heard in the house,	3605
8:31	If **a man** trespass against his neighbour, and	376
8:38	and supplication soever be *made* by **a** man,	3605
10:3	there was not **a** thing hid from the king,	NIH
10:20	there was not the like made in **a** kingdom.	3605
11:22	howbeit **let** me **go in a wise.**	7971+7971
15:5	turned not aside from **a** *thing* that he	3605
15:17	that *he* might not suffer **a** to go out or	NIH
15:29	he left not to Jeroboam **a** that breathed,	3605
18:26	But *there was* no voice, nor **a** that answered.	369
18:29	**nor a** to answer, nor any that	369+2050.1
18:29	any to answer, **nor a** that regarded.	369+2050.1
20:33	whether **a** *thing would come* from him,	NIH
20:39	if **by a means** he be **missing,** then	6485+6485
2Ki 2:21	there shall not be from thence **a more** death	5750
4:2	Thine handmaid hath not **a thing** in	3605
4:29	go *thy way:* if thou meet **a man,** salute him	376
4:29	if **a** salute thee, answer him not *again:* and	376
6:33	should I wait for the LORD **a longer**?	5750
10:5	thou shalt bid us; we will not make **a** king:	376
10:14	and forty men; neither left he **a** of them.	376
10:24	*If* **a** of the men whom I have brought into	376
12:4	all the money that cometh into **a man's** heart	376
12:5	**wheresoever a** breach shall be	834+3605+8033
12:13	**a** vessels of gold, or vessels of silver,	3605
14:26	for *there was* **not a** shut up, nor any left,	657
14:26	for *there was* not any shut up, **nor a**	657+2050.1
14:26	nor any left, **nor a** helper for Israel.	369+2050.1
18:5	kings of Judah, nor **a** that were before him.	NIH
18:33	Hath **a** of the gods of the nations delivered at	376
21:8	**a more** out of the land which I gave their	3254
23:25	neither after him arose there **a** like him.	NIH
24:7	the king of Egypt came not again **a more**	5750
1Ch 1:43	**a** king reigned over the children of Israel;	NIH
17:6	spake I a word to **a** of the judges of Israel,	259
17:9	children of wickedness waste them **a more,**	3254
17:20	neither *is there* **a** God besides thee,	NIH
19:19	help the children of Ammon **a more.**	5750
23:26	nor **a** vessels of it for the service thereof.	3605
27:1	their officers that served the king in **a**	3605
28:21	skilful *man,* for **a** *manner of* service:	3605
29:25	had not been on **a** king before him in Israel.	3605
2Ch 1:12	**neither** shall there **a** after thee	3808+2050.1
2:14	also to grave **a** *manner of* graving, and	3605
6:5	neither chose I **a man** to be a ruler over my	376
6:29	what supplication soever shall be *made* of **a**	3605
8:15	the priests and Levites concerning **a** matter,	3605
9:9	**neither** was there **a** such spice as	3808+2050.1
9:19	There was not the like made in **a** kingdom.	3605
9:20	it was *not* **a thing** accounted of in the days	3972
23:19	that none *which was* unclean in **a** thing	3605
32:13	**a ways able** to deliver their lands out	3201+3201
32:15	for no god of **a** nation or kingdom was able	3605
33:8	Neither will I **a more** remove the foot of	3254
34:13	in **a manner of service:**	5656+5656+2050.1
Ezr 1:4	whosoever remaineth in **a** place where he	3605

Ezr 7:24 that *touching* **a** of the priests and Levites, 3606
Ne 2:12 neither told I **a** man what my God had put NIH
2:12 neither *was there* **a** beast with me, save NIH
5:16 work of this wall, neither bought we **a** land: NIH
10:31 or **a** victuals on the sabbath day to sell, 3605
Job 4:20 they perish for ever without **a** regarding *it*. NIH
5: 1 Call now, if there be **a** that will answer thee; NIH
5: 4 **neither** *is there* **a** to deliver *them*. 369+2050.1
6: 6 or is there **a** taste in the white of an egg? NIH
7:10 neither shall his place know him **a more**. 5750
8:12 cut down, it withereth before **a** *other* herb. 3605
9:33 Neither is there **a** daysman betwixt us, NIH
10:22 **without a** order, and *where* 3808+2050.1
15:11 with thee? is there **a** secret thing with thee? NIH
16:17 Not for **a** injustice in mine hands: also my NIH
18:19 his people, nor **a** remaining in his dwellings. NIH
20: 9 neither shall his place **a more** behold him. 5750
21:22 Shall **a** teach God knowledge? seeing he NIH
22: 3 *Is it* **a** pleasure to the Almighty, that thou art NIH
25: 3 Is there **a** number of his armies? and NIH
31: 7 and *if* **a** blot hath cleaved to my hands; NIH
31:19 If I have seen **a** perish for want of clothing, NIH
31:19 of clothing, or **a** poor without covering; NIH
32:21 me not, I pray you, accept **a** man's person, NIH
33:13 for he giveth not account of **a** of his 3605
33:27 *if* **a** say, I have sinned, and perverted *that* NIH
33:32 If *thou* hast **a thing to say**, answer me: 4405
34:27 and would not consider **a** of his ways: 3605
34:31 *chastisement*, I will not offend **a** *more*: NIH
36: 5 despiseth not **a**: *he is* mighty in strength *and* NIH
36:29 Also can **a** understand the spreadings of NIH
37:24 he respecteth not **a** *that are* wise of heart. 3605
Ps 4: 6 many that say, Who will shew us **a** good? NIH
14: 2 to see if there were **a** that did understand, NIH
33:17 neither shall he deliver **a** by his great NIH
34:10 they that seek the LORD shall not want **a** 3605
37: 8 fret not thyself **in a wise** to do evil. 389
38: 3 neither *is there* **a** rest in my bones because NIH
49: 7 can **by a means redeem** *his* brother, 6299+6299
53: 2 to see if there were **a** that did understand, NIH
59: 5 be not merciful to **a** wicked transgressors. 3605
74: 9 *there is* no more **a** prophet: neither *is there* NIH
74: 9 neither *is there* among us **a** that knoweth NIH
81: 9 neither shalt thou worship **a** strange god. NIH
86: 8 neither *are there* **a** *works* like unto thy NIH
91:10 neither shall **a** plague come nigh thy NIH
109:12 neither let there be **a** to favour his fatherless NIH
113:17 neither **a** that go down into silence. 3605
119:133 let not **a** iniquity have dominion over me. 3605
135:17 neither is there **a** breath in their mouths. NIH
139:24 And see if *there be* **a** wicked way in me, and NIH
141: 4 Incline not my heart to **a** evil thing, NIH
146: 2 *praises* unto my God while I have **a** being. NIH
147:20 He hath not dealt so with **a** nation: and 3605
Pr 1:17 vain the net *is* spread in the sight of **a** bird. 3605
6:35 He will not regard **a** ransom; neither will he 3605
14:34 a nation: but sin *is* a reproach to **a** people. NIH
28:17 A man that doeth violence to the blood of **a** NIH
30: 2 Surely I *am* more brutish than **a** man, and NIH
30:30 among beasts, and turneth not away for **a**; 3605
31: 5 pervert the judgment of **a** of the afflicted. 3605
Ecc 1:10 Is there **a** thing whereof it may be said, See, NIH
1:11 **a** remembrance of *things* that are to come NIH
2:10 I withheld not my heart from **a** joy; 3605
3:14 put to it, **nor a thing** taken from it: 369+2050.1
5: 2 let not thine heart be hasty to utter **a** thing NIH
6: 5 nor known **a** *thing*: this hath more rest than NIH
9: 5 the dead know not **a thing**, neither have 3972
9: 5 neither have they **a more** a reward; 5750
9: 6 neither have they **a more** a portion for ever 5750
9: 6 ever in **a** *thing* that is done under the sun. 3605
Isa 1: 5 Why should ye be stricken **a more**? ye will 5750
2: 4 neither shall they learn war **a more**. 5750
2: 7 neither *is there* **a** end of their treasures; NIH
2: 7 neither *is there* **a** end of their chariots: NIH
19:15 Neither shall there be **a** work for Egypt, NIH
26:18 we have not wrought **a** deliverance *in* NIH
27: 3 lest **a** hurt it, I will keep it night and day. NIH
30:20 teachers be removed into a corner **a more**, 5750
33:20 neither shall **a** of the cords thereof be 3605
35: 9 nor **a** ravenous beast shall go up thereon, NIH
36:18 Hath **a** of the gods of the nations delivered 376
44: 8 yea, *there is* no God; I know not **a**. NIH
51:18 neither *is there* **a** that taketh her by the hand NIH
52:14 his visage *was* so marred more than **a** man, NIH
53: 9 neither *was* **a** deceit in his mouth. NIH
54: 4 the reproach of thy widowhood **a more**. 5750
56: 2 and keepeth his hand from doing **a** evil. 3605
59: 4 for justice, **nor a** pleadeth for truth: 369+2050.1
62: 4 neither shall thy land **a more** be termed 5750
Jer 3:16 visit *it*; neither shall *that* be done **a more**. 5750
3:17 neither shall they walk **a more** after 5750
5: 1 if there be **a** that executeth judgment, NIH
9: 4 his neighbour, and trust ye not in **a** brother: 3605
10:20 *is* none to stretch forth my tent **a more**, 5750
14:22 Are there **a** among the vanities of NIH
17:22 neither do ye **a** work, but hallow ye 3605
18:18 and let us not give heed to **a** of his words. 3605
20: 9 of him, nor speak **a more** in his name. 5750
22:11 He shall not return thither **a more**: 5750
22:30 of David, and ruling **a more** in Judah. 5750
23:24 Can **a** hide himself in secret places that I 376
31:12 they shall not sorrow **a more at all**. 3254+5750
31:40 nor thrown down **a more** for ever. 5750
32:27 all flesh: is there **a** thing too hard for me? 3605
33:26 that *I* will not take **a** of his seed *to be* rulers NIH
34:10 should serve themselves of them **a more**, 5750
35: 7 nor have **a**: but all your days ye shall dwell NIH
36:24 nor **a** of his servants that heard all these 3605
37:17 and said, Is there **a** word from the LORD? NIH
38: 5 for the king *is* not *he that* can do **a** thing NIH
42:21 nor **a** *thing* for the which he hath sent me 3605
44:26 of **a** man of Judah in all the land of Egypt, 3605
48: 9 shall be desolate, without **a** to dwell therein. NIH
49:33 abide there, nor **a** son of man dwell in it. NIH
Jer 50:40 **neither** shall **a** son of man dwell 3808+2050.1
51:43 neither doth **a** son of man pass thereby. NIH
51:44 the nations shall not flow *together* **a** more 5750
La 1:12 see if there be **a** sorrow like unto my NIH
3:49 ceaseth not, **without a** intermission, 369+4480
Eze 5: 9 whereunto I will not do **a more** the like, 5750
5:11 mine eye spare, neither will I have **a** pity. 1571
7:11 nor of their multitude, nor of **a** of theirs: 4480
7:13 neither shall **a** strengthen himself in 376
9: 6 come not near **a** man upon whom *is* 3605
12:24 For there shall be no more **a** vain vision nor 3605
12:28 none of my words be prolonged **a more**, 5750
14:11 neither be polluted **a more** with all their 5750
15: 2 What is the vine tree more than **a** tree, *or* 3605
15: 3 Shall wood be taken thereof to do **a** work? NIH
15: 3 will *men* take a pin of it to hang **a** vessel 3605
15: 4 midst of it is burnt. Is it meet for **a** work? NIH
15: 5 how much less shall it be meet yet for **a** NIH
16: 5 eye pitied thee, to do **a** of these unto thee, 259
16:41 and thou also shalt give no hire **a more**. 5750
16:63 never open thy mouth **a more**, because 5750
18: 3 ye shall not have *occasion* **a more** to use 5750
18: 7 hath not oppressed **a**, *but* hath restored *to* 376
18: 8 upon usury, neither hath taken **a** increase, NIH
18:10 *that* doeth the like to **a** one of these *things*, NIH
18:11 that doeth not **a** of those *duties*, but 3605
18:16 Neither hath oppressed **a**, hath not 376
18:23 Have I **a pleasure at all** that 2654+2654
21: 5 out of his sheath: it shall not return **a more**. 5750
23:27 unto them, nor remember Egypt **a more**. 5750
24:13 not be purged from thy filthiness **a more**, 5750
27:36 a terror, and never *shalt* be **a more**. 5704+5769
28:19 and never *shalt* thou *be* **a more**. 5704+5769
28:24 nor **a** grieving thorn of all *that are* round NIH
29:15 neither shall it exalt itself **a more** above 5750
31: 8 nor **a** tree in the garden of God was like 3605
32:13 shall the foot of man trouble them **a more**, 5750
33: 6 and take **a** person from among them, NIH
34:10 the shepherds feed themselves **a more**; 5750
34:29 bear the shame of the heathen **a more**. 5750
36:14 neither bereave thy nations **a more**, 5750
36:15 in thee the shame of the heathen **a more**, 5750
36:15 bear the reproach of the people **a more**, 5750
36:15 shalt thou cause thy nations to fall **a more**, 5750
37:22 into two kingdoms **a more at all**: 5750+5750
37:23 Neither shall they defile themselves **a more** 5750
37:23 nor with **a** of their transgressions: 3605
39: 7 not let *them* pollute my holy name **a more**: 5750
39:10 neither cut down **a** out of the forests; NIH
39:15 when **a** seeth a man's bone, then shall he set NIH
39:28 and have left none of them **a more** there. 5750
39:29 Neither will I hide my face **a more** from 5750
44: 9 of **a** stranger that *is* among the children of 3605
44:13 nor to come near to **a** of my holy *things*, in 3605
44:18 they shall not gird *themselves* with **a** thing NIH
44:21 Neither shall **a** priest drink wine, when they 3605
44:31 The priests shall not eat *of* **a thing** that is 3605
46:16 If the prince give a gift unto **a** of his sons, 376
Da 2:10 *that* asked such things at **a** magician, or 3606
2:30 this secret *is* not revealed to me for **a** NIH
2:30 *any* wisdom that I have more than **a** living, 3606
3:28 that they might not serve nor worship **a** 3606
3:29 which speak **a thing amiss** against the God 7960
6: 4 neither was there **a** error or fault found in 3606
6: 5 We shall not find **a** occasion against this 3606
6: 7 that whosoever shall ask a petition of **a** 3606
6:12 that every man that shall ask *a petition* of **a** 3606
8: 4 neither *was there* **a** that could deliver out of NIH
11:15 neither *shall there be* **a** strength to NIH
11:37 nor the desire of women, nor regard **a** god: 3605
Hos 13:10 where *is* **a** *other* that may save thee in all NIH
14: 3 neither will we say **a more** to the work of 5750
14: 8 *say*, What have I to do **a more** with idols? 5750
Joel 2: 2 the like, neither shall be **a** more after it, 5704
3:17 shall no strangers pass through her **a more**. 5750
Am 6:10 sides of the house, *Is there* yet **a** with thee? NIH
7: 8 I will not again pass by them **a more**: 5750
7:13 prophesy not again **a more** *at* Beth-el: for it 5750
8: 2 I will not again pass by them **a more**. 5750
8: 7 Surely I will never forget **a** of their works. 3605
Ob 1:18 there shall not be **a** remaining of the house NIH
Jnh 3: 7 nor beast, herd nor flock, taste **a thing**: 3972
Mic 4: 3 neither shall they learn war **a more**. 5750
Zep 3:15 of thee: thou shalt not see evil **a more**. 5750
Hag 2:12 or pottage, or wine, or oil, or **a** meat, 3605
2:13 *is* unclean *by* **a** dead body touch **a** of these, 3605
Zec 8:10 no hire for man, **nor a** hire for beast; 369+2050.1
8:10 neither *was there* **a** peace to him that went NIH
9: 8 oppressor shall pass through them **a more**: 5750
13: 3 *that* when **a** shall yet prophesy, then 376
Mal 2:13 that *he* regardeth not the offering **a more**, 5750
Mt 4: 6 **lest at a time** thou dash thy foot against a *3379*
5:25 **lest at a time** the adversary deliver thee to *3379*
5:40 And if **a** man will sue thee at the law, and *3588*
10: 5 into **a** city of the Samaritans enter ye not: NIG
11:27 neither knoweth **a** *man* the Father, save *5100*
12:19 neither shall **a** *man* hear his voice in *5100*
13:15 **lest at a time** they should see with *their* *3379*
13:19 When **a one** heareth the word of *3956*
16:24 **If a** *man* will come after me, let him deny *1536*
18:19 earth as touching **a** thing that they shall ask, *3956*
21: 3 And if **a** *man* say ought unto you, ye shall *5100*
22:16 neither carest thou for **a** *man*: for thou *3762*
22:46 neither durst **a** *man* from that day forth ask *5100*
22:46 that day forth ask him **a moe** *questions*. *3765*
24:17 come down to take **a** *thing* out of his house: *5100*
24:23 Then if **a** *man* shall say unto you, Lo, *5100*
Mk 1:44 See thou say nothing to **a** *man*: but go thy *3367*
4:12 **lest at a time** they should be converted, *3379*
4:22 neither was **a** *thing* kept secret, but that it NIG
4:23 **If a** *man* have ears to hear, let him hear. *1536*
5: 4 in pieces: neither could **a** *man* tame him. *3762*
5:35 why troublest thou the Master **a further**? *2089*
7:16 **If a** *man* have ears to hear, let him hear. *1536*
8:26 go into the town, nor tell *it* to **a** in the town. *5100*
Mk 9: 8 they saw no *man* **a more**, save Jesus only *3765*
9:22 if thou canst do **a** *thing*, have compassion *5100*
9:30 he would not that **a** *man* should know *it*. *5100*
9:35 saith unto them, **If a** *man* desire to be first, *1536*
11: 3 And if **a** *man* say unto you, Why do ye *5100*
11:13 if haply he might find **a** *thing* thereon: *5100*
11:16 And would not suffer that **a** *man* should *5100*
11:16 should carry **a** vessel through the temple. NIG
11:25 forgive, if ye have ought against **a**: *5100*
12:21 took her, and died, neither left he **a** seed: NIG
12:34 And no *man* after that durst ask him **a** NIG
13: 5 to say, Take heed lest **a** *man* deceive you: *5100*
13:15 neither enter *therein*, to take **a** *thing* out of *5100*
13:21 And then if **a** *man* shall say to you, Lo, *5100*
14:31 with thee, I will **not** deny thee **in a wise**. *3364*
14:63 saith, What need we **a further** witnesses? *2089*
15:44 he asked him whether he had been **a while** *3819*
16: 8 **neither** said they **a** *thing* to any *man*; *2532+3762*
16: 8 neither said they any *thing* to **a** *man*; for *3762*
16:18 if they drink **a** deadly *thing*, it shall not hurt *5100*
Lk 3:14 violence to no man, neither accuse **a** falsely; NIG
4:11 **lest at a time** thou dash thy foot against a *3379*
4:40 all they that had **a** sick with divers diseases NIG
8:17 neither **a** *thing* hid, that shall not be known NIG
8:27 neither abode in **a** house, but in the tombs. NIG
8:43 **neither** could be healed of **a**, *3756+3762*
9:23 If **a** *man* will come after me, let him deny *5100*
9:36 told no *man* in those days **a** of *those things* *3762*
10:19 and nothing shall **by a means** hurt you. *3364*
11:11 *If* **a** son shall ask bread of **a** of you that is a *5101*
14: 8 When thou art bidden of **a** *man* to a *5100*
14:26 **If a** *man* come to me, and hate not his *1536*
15:29 **neither** transgressed I **at a time** thy *2532+3763*
19: 8 if I have taken **a** *thing* from any *man* by *5100*
19: 8 if I have taken any *thing* from **a** *man* by *5100*
19:31 And if **a** *man* ask you, Why do ye loose *5100*
20:21 neither acceptest thou the person *of* **a**, but NIG
20:27 which deny that there is **a** resurrection; *3361*
20:28 If **a** *man's* brother die, having a wife, and *5100*
20:36 Neither can they die **a more**: for they are *2089*
20:40 And after that they durst **not** ask him **a** *3762*
21:34 **lest at a time** your hearts be overcharged *3379*
22:16 say unto you, I will not **a more** eat thereof, *3765*
22:35 shoes, lacked ye **a** *thing*? And they said, *5100*
22:71 What need we **a further** witness? *2089*
24:41 he said unto them, Have ye here **a** meat? *5100*
Jn 1: 3 without him was not **a** *thing* made that was *1520*
1:18 No *man* hath seen God **at a time**; the only *4455*
1:46 Can there **a** good *thing* come out of *5100*
2:25 And needed not that **a** should testify of *5100*
4:33 Hath **a** *man* brought him *ought* to eat? *3385*
5:37 Ye have neither heard his voice **at a time**, *4455*
6:46 Not that **a** *man* hath seen the Father, *5100*
6:51 if **a** *man* eat of this bread, he shall live for *5100*
7: 4 For *there is* no *man that* doeth **a** *thing* in *5100*
7:17 If **a** *man* will do his will, he shall know of *5100*
7:37 and cried, saying, If **a** *man* thirst, *5100*
7:48 Have **a** of the rulers or of the Pharisees *3385*
7:51 Doth our law judge **a** man, before it hear *3588*
8:33 were never in bondage to **a** *man*: how *3762*
9:22 that if **a** *man* did confess that he *was* Christ, *5100*
9:31 but if **a** *man* be a worshipper of God, and *5100*
9:32 **a** *man* opened the eyes of one that was born *5100*
10: 9 by me if **a** *man* enter in, he shall be saved, *5100*
10:28 neither shall **a** *man* pluck them out of my *5100*
11: 9 If **a** *man* walk in the day, he stumbleth not, *5100*
11:57 that, if **a** *man* knew where he were, *5100*
12:26 If **a** *man* serve me, let him follow me; and *5100*
12:26 if **a** *man* serve me, him will *my* Father *5100*
12:47 And if **a** *man* hear my words, and *5100*
14:14 If ye shall ask **a** *thing* in my name, I will *5100*
16:30 and needest not that **a** *man* should ask thee: *5100*
18:31 It is not lawful for us to put **a** *man* to death: *3762*
21: 5 saith unto them, Children, have ye **a** meat? *3385*
Ac 4:12 Neither is there salvation in **a** other: *3762*
4:32 neither said **a** *of them* that ought of *1520*
4:34 Neither was there **a** among them that *5100*
9: 2 that if he found **a** of *this* way, whether they *5100*
10:14 for I have never eaten **a** *thing that is* *3956*
10:28 me that *I* should **not** call **a** man common *3367*
10:47 Can **a** *man* forbid water, that these should *5100*
11: 8 **nothing** common or unclean hath
at a time *3763+3956*
13:15 if ye have **a** word of exhortation for NIG
17:25 as though he needed **a** *thing*, seeing he *5100*
19: 2 much as heard whether there be **a** Holy NIG
19:38 have a matter against **a** *man*, the law is *5100*
19:39 But if ye inquire **a** *thing* concerning other *5100*
24:12 with **a** *man*, neither raising up the people, *5100*
24:20 **if** they have found **a** evil doing in me, *1536*
25: 5 this man, **if** there be **a** *wickedness* in him. *1536*
25: 8 have I offended **a** *thing at all*. *5100*
25:11 or have committed **a** *thing* worthy of death, *5100*
25:16 of the Romans to deliver **a** man to die, *5100*
25:17 they were come hither, **without a** delay, *3367*
25:24 crying that he ought not to live **a longer**. *3371*
27:12 **if by a means** they might attain to Phenice, *1513*
27:22 for there shall be no loss of **a** *man's* life NIG
27:34 **not** a hair fall from the head of **a** of you. *3762*
27:42 lest **a** *of them* should swim out, and escape. *5100*
28:21 neither **a** of the brethren that came shewed *5100*
28:21 that came shewed or spake **a** harm of thee. *5100*
Ro 1:10 **if by a means** now at length I might have a *1513*
6: 2 that are dead to sin, live **a longer** therein? *2089*
8: 9 Now **if a** *man* have not the Spirit of Christ, *1536*
8:33 Who shall lay **a** thing to the charge of God's NIG
8:39 Nor height, nor depth, nor **a** other creature, *5100*
9:11 neither having done **a** good or evil, *5100*
11:14 **If by a means** I may provoke to emulation *1513*
13: 8 Owe no *man* **a** *thing*, but to love one *3367*
13: 9 and **if** *there be* **a** other commandment, it is *1536*
14:13 us **not** therefore judge one another **a more**: *3371*
14:14 to him that esteemeth **a** *thing* to be unclean, *5100*
14:21 nor **a** *thing* whereby thy brother stumbleth, NIG
15:18 For I will not dare to speak of **a** of *those* *5100*

A

1Co 1:15 Lest **a** should say that I had baptized in *5100*
1:16 I know not **whether** I baptized **a** other. *1536*
2: 2 For I determined not to know **a** *thing* *5100*
3: 7 neither is he that planteth **a** *thing,* neither *5100*
3:12 Now **if a** *man* build upon this foundation *1536*
3:14 **If a** *man's* work abide which he hath built *1536*
3:15 **If a** *man's* work shall be burnt, he shall *1536*
3:17 **If a** *man* defile the temple of God, *1536*
3:18 **If a** *man* among you seemeth to be wise in *1536*
5:11 **if a** *man that is* called a brother be a *5100*
6: 1 Dare **a** of you, having a matter against *5100*
6:12 I will not be brought under the power of **a**. *5100*
7:12 **If a** brother hath a wife that believeth not, *1536*
7:18 Is **a** *man* called being circumcised? let him *5100*
7:18 Is **a** called in uncircumcision? let him not *5100*
7:36 But **if a** *man* think that *he* behaveth himself *5100*
8: 2 And **if a** *man* think that *he* knoweth any *5100*
8: 2 And if any *man* think that *he* knoweth a *5100*
8: 3 But **if a** *man* love God, the same is known *5100*
8: 9 But take heed **lest by a means** this liberty *3381*
8:10 For **if a** *man* see thee which hast *5100*
9: 7 Who goeth a warfare **a time** at his own *4218*
9:15 than that **a** *man* should make my glorying *5100*
9:27 **lest that by a means**, when I have *3381*
10:19 that the idol is **a** *thing,* or that which is *5100*
10:19 is offered in sacrifice to idols is **a** *thing?* *5100*
10:27 **If a** of them that believe not bid you *to a* *5100*
10:28 But **if a** *man* say unto you, This is offered *5100*
11:16 But **if a** *man* seem to be contentious, *5100*
11:34 And **if a** *man* hunger, let him eat at home; *5100*
14:27 **If a** *man* speak in an *unknown* tongue, *let it* *5100*
14:30 **If a** *thing* be revealed to another that sitteth NIG
14:35 And if they will learn **a** *thing,* let them ask *5100*
14:37 **If a** *man* think himself to be a prophet, or *1536*
14:38 But **if a** *man* be ignorant, let him be *1536*
16:22 **If a** *man* love not the Lord Jesus Christ, *1536*
2Co 1: 4 to comfort them which are in **a** trouble, *3956*
2: 5 But **if a** have caused grief, he hath not *5100*
2:10 To whom ye forgive **a** *thing,* I *forgive* also: *5100*
2:10 for **if** I forgave **a** *thing,* to whom I forgave *1536*
3: 5 ourselves to think **a** *thing* as of ourselves; *5100*
5:17 Therefore **if a** *man be* in Christ, *he is* a new *1536*
6: 3 Giving no offence in **a** *thing,* that *3367*
7:14 For **if** I have boasted **a** *thing* to him of you, *1536*
8:23 Whether **a** *do inquire* of Titus, *he is* my NIG
10: 7 **If a** *man* trust to himself that *he* is Christ's, *1536*
11: 3 But I fear, **lest by a means**, as the serpent *3381*
11:21 Howbeit whereinsoever **a** is bold, (I speak *5100*
12: 6 lest **a** *man* should think of me above *that* *5100*
12:17 Did I make a gain of you by **a** of them *5100*
Gal 1: 8 preach **a other** gospel unto you **than** *that* *3844*
1: 9 **If a** *man* preach any other gospel unto you *1536*
1: 9 **a other** gospel unto you **than** that ye have *3844*
2: 2 **lest by a means** I should run, or had run, *3381*
5: 6 availeth **a** *thing,* nor uncircumcision; *5100*
6:15 availeth **a** *thing,* nor uncircumcision, *5100*
Eph 2: 9 Not of works, lest **a** *man* should boast. *5100*
5: 5 hath **a** inheritance in the kingdom of Christ NIG
5:27 or **a** such *thing;* but that it should be holy *5100*
6: 8 that whatsoever good *thing* **a man** doeth, *1538*
Php 2: 1 **If** *there be* therefore **a** consolation in *1536*
2: 1 consolation in Christ, **if a** comfort of love, *1536*
2: 1 **if a** fellowship of the Spirit, if any bowels *1536*
2: 1 of the Spirit, **if a** bowels and mercies, *1536*
3: 4 **If a** other *man* thinketh that *he hath* *1536*
3:11 **If by a means** I might attain unto *1513*
3:15 and **if** in **a** *thing* ye be otherwise minded, *1536*
4: 8 **if** *there be* **a** virtue, and if *there be* any *1536*
4: 8 *there be* any virtue, and **if** *there be* **a** praise, *1536*
Col 2: 4 lest **a** *man* should beguile you with enticing *5100*
2: 8 Beware lest **a** *man* spoil you through *5100*
2:23 not in **a** honour to the satisfying of *5100*
3:13 if **a** *man* have a quarrel against any: *5100*
3:13 if any *man* have a quarrel against **a**: *5100*
1Th 1: 8 so that we need not to speak **a** *thing.* *5100*
2: 5 For neither **at a time** used we flattering *4218*
2: 9 *we* would not be chargeable unto **a** of you, *5100*
4: 6 and defraud his brother in **a** matter: NIG
5:15 See that none render evil for evil unto **a** *5100*
2Th 2: 3 Let no *man* deceive you by **a** means: *3367*
3: 8 Neither did we eat **a** *man's* bread for *5100*
3: 8 that *we* might not be chargeable to **a** of *5100*
3:10 that **if a** would not work, neither should he *1536*
3:14 And **if a** *man* obey not our word by *this* *5100*
1Ti 1:10 **if** *there be* **a** other *thing that* is contrary to *1536*
5: 4 But **if a** widow have children or nephews, *5100*
5: 8 But **if a** provide not for his own, and *5100*
5:16 **If a** man or woman that believeth have *1536*
6: 3 **If a** *man* teach otherwise, and consent not *1536*
Tit 1: 6 **If a** be blameless, the husband of one wife, *5100*
Heb 1: 5 unto which of the angels said he **at a time,** *4218*
1:13 to which of the angels said he **at a time,** *4218*
2: 1 **lest at a time** we should let *them* slip. *3379*
3:12 lest there be in **a** of you an evil heart of *5100*
3:13 lest **a** of you be hardened through *5100*
4: 1 **a** of you should seem to come short *of it.* *5100*
4:11 lest **a** *man* fall after the same example of *5100*
4:12 and sharper than **a** twoedged sword, *3956*
4:13 Neither is there a creature *that is* not NIG
10:38 but **if a** *man* draw back, my soul shall have NIG
12:15 Looking diligently lest **a** *man* fail of *5100*
12:15 lest **a** root of bitterness springing up trouble *5100*
12:16 Lest there *be* **a** fornicator, or *5100*
12:19 word should not be spoken to them **a more:** *4369*
Jas 1: 5 **If a** of you lack wisdom, let him ask of *5100*
1: 7 that he shall receive **a** *thing* of the Lord. *5100*
1:13 **neither** tempteth he **a** *man:* *1161+3762*
1:23 For **if a** be a hearer of the word, and not a *1536*
1:26 **If a** *man* among you seem to be religious, *1536*
3: 2 **If a** *man* offend not in word, the same *is* a *1536*
5:12 neither by the earth, neither by **a** other oath: *5100*
5:13 Is **a** among you afflicted? let him pray. *5100*
5:13 him pray. Is **a** merry? let him sing psalms. *5100*
5:14 Is **a** sick among you? let him call for *5100*
5:19 if **a** of you do err from the truth, and *5100*
1Pe 3: 1 that, **if a** obey not the word, they also may *1536*
3: 6 and are **not** afraid *with* **a** amazement. *3367*
4:11 **If a** *man* speak, *let him speak* as the oracles *1536*
4:11 **if a** *man* minister, *let him do it* as of *1536*
4:16 Yet if **a** *man suffer* as a Christian, let him NIG
2Pe 1:20 that no prophecy of the scripture is of **a** NIG
3: 9 not willing that **a** should perish, but that all *5100*
1Jn 2: 1 And if **a** *man* sin, we have an advocate with *5100*
2:15 If **a** *man* love the world, the love of *5100*
2:27 and ye need not that **a** *man* teach you: *5100*
4:12 No *man* hath seen God **at a time.** If we *4455*
5:14 that, if we ask **a** *thing* according to his will, *5100*
5:16 If **a** *man* see his brother sin a sin *which is* *5100*
2Jn 1:10 If there come **a** unto you, and bring not this *5100*
Rev 3:20 if **a** *man* hear my voice, and open the door, *5100*
7: 1 on the earth, nor on the sea, nor on **a** tree. *3956*
7:16 shall hunger no more, neither thirst **a more;** *2089*
7:16 shall the sun light on them, nor **a** heat. *3956*
9: 4 neither **a** green *thing,* neither any tree; *3956*
9: 4 neither any green *thing,* neither **a** tree; *3956*
11: 5 And **if a** *man* will hurt them, *1536*
11: 5 and **if a** *man* will hurt them, he must in this *1536*
12: 8 neither was their place found **a more** in *2089*
13: 9 **If a** *man* have an ear, let him hear. *1536*
14: 9 **If a** *man* worship the beast and his image, *1536*
18:11 no *man* buyeth their merchandise **a more:** *3765*
18:22 craft *he be,* shall be found **a more** in thee; *2089*
21: 4 neither shall there be **a more** pain: *2089*
21:27 And there shall in no wise enter into it **a** *3956*
22:18 If **a** *man* shall add unto these *things,* God *5100*
22:19 And if **a** *man* shall take away from *5100*

ANYTHING (1) [ANY]

1Ch 26:28 whosoever had dedicated **a**, *it was* under NIH

APACE (3)

2Sa 18:25 And he **came a**, and drew near. 1980+1980
Ps 68:12 Kings of armies did **flee a**: and 5074+5074
Jer 46: 5 and are **fled a**, and look not back: 4498+5127

APART (24) [PART]

Ex 13:12 That thou shalt **set a** unto the LORD all 5674
Lev 15:19 be blood, she shall be **put a** seven days: 5079
18:19 as long as she is **put a** for her uncleanness. 5079
Ps 4: 3 know that the LORD hath **set a** *him that is* 6395
Eze 22:10 humbled her **that was set a** for pollution. 5079
Zec 12:12 land shall mourn, every family **a;** 905+3807.1
12:12 the family of the house of David **a,** 905+3807.1
12:12 of David apart, and their wives **a;** 905+3807.1
12:12 the family of the house of Nathan **a,** 905+3807.1
12:12 of Nathan apart, and their wives **a;** 905+3807.1
12:13 The family of the house of Levi **a,** 905+3807.1
12:13 of Levi apart, and their wives **a;** 905+3807.1
12:13 the family of Shimei **a,** and 905+3807.1
12:13 of Shimei apart, and their wives **a;** 905+3807.1
12:14 family **a,** and their wives apart. 905+3807.1
12:14 family apart, and their wives **a.** 905+3807.1
Mt 14:13 thence by ship into a desert place **a:** *2398+2596*
14:23 he went up into a mountain **a** to pray: *2398+2596*
17: 1 them up into a high mountain **a,** *2398+2596*
17:19 Then came the disciples to Jesus **a,** *2398+2596*
20:17 the twelve disciples **a** in the way, *2398+2596*
Mk 6:31 Come ye yourselves **a** into a desert *2398+2596*
9: 2 a high mountain **a** by themselves: *2398+2596*
Jas 1:21 Wherefore **lay a** all filthiness and *659*

APELLES (1)

Ro 16:10 Salute **A** approved in Christ. Salute them *559*

APES (2)

1Ki 10:22 and silver, ivory, and **a**, and peacocks. 6971
2Ch 9:21 and silver, ivory, and **a**, and peacocks. 6971

APHARSACHITES (2)

Ezr 5: 6 Shethar-boznai, and his companions the **A**, 671
6: 6 Shethar-boznai, and your companions the **A**, 671

APHARSATHCHITES (1)

Ezr 4: 9 the Dinaites, the **A**, the Tarpelites, 671

APHARSITES (1)

Ezr 4: 9 the Tarpelites, the **A**, the Archevites, 670

APHEK (8)

Jos 12:18 The king of **A**, one; the king of Lasharon, 663
13: 4 unto **A**, to the borders of the Amorites: 663
19:30 Ummah also, and **A**, and Rehob: twenty and 663
1Sa 4: 1 and the Philistines pitched in **A**. 663
29: 1 gathered together all their armies to **A**: 663
1Ki 20:26 and went up to **A**, to fight against Israel. 663
20:30 the rest fled to **A**, into the city; and *there* a 663
2Ki 13:17 for thou shalt smite the Syrians in **A**, 663

APHEKAH (1)

Jos 15:53 And Janum, and Beth-tappuah, and **A**, 664

APHIAH (1)

1Sa 9: 1 son of Bechorath, the son of **A**, a Benjamite, 647

APHIK (1)

Jdg 1:31 nor of Helbah, nor of **A**, nor of Rehob: 663

APHRAH See HOUSE OF APHRAH

APHSES (1)

1Ch 24:15 seventeenth to Hezir, the eighteenth to **A**, 6483

APIECE (8)

Nu 3:47 Thou shalt even take **five** shekels **a** 2568+2568
7:86 *of* incense, *weighing* ten *shekels* **a**, 3709+1886.1
17: 6 every one of their princes gave him a rod **a**, 259
1Ki 7:15 *of* brass, of eighteen cubits high **a**: 259+5982
Eze 10:21 Every one had **four** faces **a**, and every 702+702
Eze 41:24 the doors had two leaves **a**, two turning NIH
Lk 9: 3 neither money; neither have two coats **a**. *303*
Jn 2: 6 the Jews, containing two or three firkins **a**. *303*

APOLLONIA (1)

Ac 17: 1 they had passed through Amphipolis and **A**, *624*

APOLLOS (10)

Ac 18:24 And a certain Jew named **A**, born at *625*
19: 1 it came to pass, that, while **A** was at Corinth, *625*
1Co 1:12 and I of **A**; and I of Cephas; and I of Christ. *625*
3: 4 I am of Paul; and another, I *am* of **A**; *625*
3: 5 and who *is* **A**, but ministers by whom ye *625*
3: 6 I have planted, **A** watered; but God gave *625*
3:22 or **A**, or Cephas, or the world, or life, or *625*
4: 6 to myself and *to* **A** for your sakes; *625*
16:12 As touching *our* brother **A**, I greatly desired *625*
Tit 3:13 the lawyer and **A** on their journey diligently, *625*

APOLLYON (1)

Rev 9:11 but in the Greek *tongue* hath *his* name **A**. *623*

APOSTLE (19) [APOSTLES, APOSTLES', APOSTLESHIP]

Ro 1: 1 a servant of Jesus Christ, called *to be* an **a**, *652*
11:13 inasmuch as I am the **a** of the Gentiles, *652*
1Co 1: 1 called *to be* an **a** of Jesus Christ through *652*
9: 1 Am I not an **a**? am I not free? have I not *652*
9: 2 If I be not an **a** unto others, yet doubtless I *652*
15: 9 that am not meet to be called an **a**, because *652*
2Co 1: 1 an **a** of Jesus Christ by the will of God, and *652*
12:12 Truly the signs of an **a** were wrought among *652*
Gal 1: 1 Paul, an **a**, (not of men, neither by man, but *652*
Eph 1: 1 Paul, an **a** of Jesus Christ by the will of God, *652*
Col 1: 1 an **a** of Jesus Christ by the will of God, and *652*
1Ti 1: 1 an **a** of Jesus Christ by the commandment of *652*
2: 7 and an **a**, (I speak the truth in Christ, *and* *652*
2Ti 1: 1 Paul, an **a** of Jesus Christ by the will of God, *652*
1:11 and an **a**, and a teacher of the Gentiles. *652*
Tit 1: 1 a servant of God, and an **a** of Jesus Christ, *652*
Heb 3: 1 consider the **A** and High Priest of our *652*
1Pe 1: 1 Peter, an **a** of Jesus Christ, to the strangers *652*
2Pe 1: 1 a servant and an **a** of Jesus Christ, *652*

APOSTLES (55) [APOSTLE]

Mt 10: 2 Now the names of the twelve **a** are these; *652*
Mk 6:30 And the **a** gathered themselves together unto *652*
Lk 6:13 he chose twelve, whom also he named **a**; *652*
9:10 And the **a**, when they were returned, *652*
11:49 I will send them prophets and **a**, and *some* of *652*
17: 5 And the **a** said unto the Lord, Increase our *652*
22:14 he sat down, and the twelve **a** with him. *652*
24:10 which told these *things* unto the **a**. *652*
Ac 1: 2 unto the **A** whom he had chosen: *652*
1:26 and he was numbered with the eleven **a**. *652*
2:37 and said unto Peter and *to* the rest of the **a**, *652*
2:43 many wonders and signs were done by the **a**. *652*
4:33 And with great power gave the **a** witness of *652*
4:36 who by the **a** was surnamed Barnabas, *652*
5:12 And by the hands of the **a** were many signs *652*
5:18 And laid their hands on the **a**, and put them *652*
5:29 and the *other* **a** answered and said, *652*
5:34 commanded to put the **a** forth a little space; *652*
5:40 and when they had called the **a**, and *652*
6: 6 Whom they set before the **a**: and when they *652*
8: 1 regions of Judea and Samaria, except the **a**. *652*
8:14 Now when the **a** which were at Jerusalem *652*
9:27 and brought *him* to the **a**, and declared unto *652*
11: 1 And the **a** and brethren that were in Judea *652*
14: 4 part held with the Jews, and part with the **a**. *652*
14:14 *Which* when the **a**, Barnabas and Paul, *652*
15: 2 should go up to Jerusalem unto the **a** and *652*
15: 4 and *of* the **a** and elders, and they declared all *652*
15: 6 And the **a** and elders came together for to *652*
15:22 Then pleased it the **a** and elders, with *652*
15:23 The **a** and elders and brethren *send* greeting *652*
15:33 let go in peace from the brethren unto the **a**. *652*
16: 4 that were ordained of the **a** and elders which *652*
Ro 16: 7 who are of note among the **a**, *652*
1Co 4: 9 For I think that God hath set forth us the **a** *652*
9: 5 as well as other **a**, and *as* the brethren of *652*
12:28 first **a**, secondarily prophets, *652*
12:29 *Are* all **a**? *are* all prophets? *are* all teachers? *652*
15: 7 he was seen of James; then of all the **a**. *652*
15: 9 For I am the least of the **a**, that am not meet *652*
2Co 11: 5 *I* was not a whit behind the very chiefest **a**. *652*
11:13 For such *are* **false a**, deceitful workers, *5570*
11:13 transforming themselves into the **a** of Christ. *652*
12:11 *in* nothing am I behind the very chiefest **a**, *652*
Gal 1:17 Jerusalem to them which were **a** before me; *652*
1:19 But other of the **a** saw I none, save James *652*
Eph 2:20 And are built upon the foundation of the **a** *652*
3: 5 as it is now revealed unto his holy **a** and *652*
4:11 And he gave some, **a**; and some, prophets; *652*
1Th 2: 6 have been burdensome, as *the* **a** of Christ. *652*
2Pe 3: 2 of the commandment of us the **a** of the Lord *652*
Jude 1:17 before of the **a** of our Lord Jesus Christ; *652*
Rev 2: 2 thou hast tried them which say *they* are **a**, *652*
18:20 *thou* heaven, and ye holy **a** and prophets; *652*
21:14 in them the names of the twelve **a** of *652*

APOSTLES' (5) [APOSTLE]

Ac 2:42 And they continued stedfastly in the **a** *652*
4:35 And laid *them down* at the **a** feet: and *652*
4:37 brought the money, and laid *it* at the **a** feet. *652*
5: 2 a certain part, and laid *it* at the **a** feet. *652*
8:18 on of the **a** hands the Holy Ghost was given, *652*

APOSTLESHIP (4) [APOSTLE]

Ac 1:25 That *he* may take part of this ministry and **a**, *651*
Ro 1: 5 By whom we have received grace and **a**, *651*
1Co 9: 2 for the seal of mine **a** are ye in the Lord. *651*
Gal 2: 8 in Peter to the **a** of the circumcision, *651*

APOTHECARIES (1) [APOTHECARY]
Ne 3: 8 repaired Hananiah the son of *one of* the **a**, 7546

APOTHECARIES' (1) [APOTHECARY]
2Ch 16:14 divers kinds *of spices* prepared by the **a** art: 4842

APOTHECARY (4) [APOTHECARIES, APOTHECARIES']
Ex 30:25 ointment compound *after* the art of the **a**: 7543
30:35 a confection *after* the art of the **a**, 7543
37:29 *according to* the work of the **a**. 7543
Ecc 10: 1 Dead flies cause the ointment of the **a** to 7543

APPAIM (2)
1Ch 2:30 the sons of Nadab; Seled, and **A**: but 649
2:31 the sons of **A**; Ishi. And the sons of Ishi; 649

APPAREL (28) [APPARELLED]
Jdg 17:10 by the year, and a suit of **a**, and thy victuals. 899
1Sa 27: 9 and the **a**, and returned, and came to Achish. 899
2Sa 1:24 who put on ornaments of gold upon your **a**. 3830
12:20 anointed *himself*, and changed his **a**, and 8071
14: 2 put on now mourning **a**, and anoint not 899
1Ki 10: 5 their **a**, and his cupbearers, and his ascent 4403
2Ch 9: 4 the attendance of his ministers, and their **a**; 4403
9: 4 his cupbearers also, and their **a**; and 4403
Ezr 3:10 they set the priests in their **a** with trumpets, 3847
Est 5: 1 that Esther put on *her* royal **a**, and stood in NIH
6: 8 Let the royal **a** be brought which the king 3830
6: 9 let *this* **a** and horse be delivered to the hand 3830
6:10 Make haste, *and* take the **a** and the horse, 3830
6:11 took Haman the **a** and the horse, and 3830
8:15 the presence of the king in royal **a** *of* blue 3830
Isa 3:22 The **changeable suits of a**, and 4254
4: 1 eat our own bread, and wear our own **a**: 8071
63: 1 this *that is* glorious in his **a**, travelling in 3830
63: 2 Wherefore *art thou* red in thine **a**, and 3830
Eze 27:24 and broidered work, and in chests of **rich a**, 1264
Zep 1: 8 and all such as are clothed with strange **a**. 4403
Zec 14:14 gold, and silver, and **a**, in great abundance. 899
Ac 1:10 two men stood by them in white **a**; *2066*
12:21 arrayed in royal **a**, sat upon his throne, and *2066*
20:33 have coveted no *man's* silver, or gold, or **a**. *2441*
1Ti 2: 9 that women adorn themselves in modest **a**, *2689*
Jas 2: 2 in goodly **a**, and there come in also a poor *2066*
1Pe 3: 3 of wearing of gold, or of putting on of **a**; *2440*

APPARELLED (2) [APPAREL]
2Sa 13:18 the king's daughters *that were* virgins **a**. 3847
Lk 7:25 they which are gorgeously **a**, and *2441*

APPARENTLY (1)
Nu 12: 8 to mouth, even **a**, and not in dark speeches; 4758

APPEAL (2) [APPEALED]
Ac 25:11 may deliver me unto them. I **a unto** Cesar. *1941*
28:19 *it*, I was constrained to **a unto** Cesar; *1941*

APPEALED (4) [APPEAL]
Ac 25:12 answered, Hast thou **a unto** Cesar? *1941*
25:21 But when Paul had **a** to be reserved unto *1941*
25:25 and *that* he himself hath **a to** Augustus, *1941*
26:32 set at liberty, if he had not **a unto** Cesar. *1941*

APPEAR (54) [APPEARANCE, APPEARANCES, APPEARED, APPEARETH, APPEARING]
Ge 1: 9 unto one place, and let the dry *land* **a**: 7200
30:37 **made** the white **a** which *was* in the rods. 4286
Ex 23:15 and none shall **a** before me empty: 7200
23:17 Three times in the year all thy males shall **a** 7200
34:20 and none shall **a** before me empty. 7200
34:23 men children **a** before the Lord GOD, 7200
34:24 when thou shalt go up to **a** before 7200
Lev 9: 4 for to day the LORD will **a** unto you. 7200
9: 6 the glory of the LORD shall **a** unto you. 7200
13:57 if it **a** still in the garment, either in 7200
16: 2 for I will **a** in the cloud upon the mercy 7200
Dt 16:16 Three times in a year shall all thy males **a** 7200
16:16 they shall not **a** before the LORD empty: 7200
31:11 When all Israel is come to **a** before 7200
Jdg 13:21 the angel of the LORD did no more **a** to 7200
1Sa 1:22 that he may **a** before the LORD, and 7200
2:27 Did I **plainly a** unto the house of thy 1540+1540
2Ch 1: 7 In that night did God **a** unto Solomon, and 7200
Ps 42: 2 when shall I come and **a** before God? 7200
90:16 Let thy work **a** unto thy servants, and 7200
102:16 shall build up Zion, he shall **a** in his glory. 7200
SS 2:12 The flowers **a** on the earth; the time of 7200
4: 1 a flock of goats, that **a** from mount Gilead. 1570
6: 5 thy hair *is* as a flock of goats that **a** from 1570
7:12 *whether* the tender grape **a**, *and* 6605
Isa 1:12 When ye come to **a** before me, who hath 7200
66: 5 he *shall* **a** to your joy, and they shall be 7200
Jer 13:26 skirts upon thy face, that thy shame may **a**. 7200
Eze 21:24 so that in all your doings your sins do **a**; 7200
Mt 6:16 that they may **a** unto men to fast. *5316*
6:18 That thou **a** not unto men to fast, but *5316*
23:27 which indeed **a** beautiful outward, but *5316*
23:28 so ye also outwardly **a** righteous unto men, *5316*
24:30 shall **a** the sign of the Son of man in *5316*
Lk 11:44 for ye are as graves which **a not**, and the men *82*
19:11 the kingdom of God should immediately **a**. *398*
Ac 22:30 the chief priests and all their council to **a**, *2064*
26:16 *of those things* in the which I will **a** unto *3700*
Ro 7:13 But sin, that it might **a** sin, working death *5316*
2Co 5:10 For we must all **a** before the judgment seat *5319*
7:12 you in the sight of God might **a** unto you. *5319*
13: 7 not that we should **a** approved, but that ye *5316*
Col 3: 4 shall **a**, then shall ye also appear with him *5319*
3: 4 then shall ye also **a** with him in glory. *5319*
1Ti 4:15 to them; that thy profiting may **a** to all. *5318*
Heb 9:24 now to **a** in the presence of God for us: *1718*
9:28 unto them that look for him shall he **a** *3700*
Heb 11: 3 seen were not made of *things* which do **a**. *5316*
1Pe 4:18 where shall the ungodly and the sinner **a**? *5316*
5: 4 And when the chief Shepherd shall **a**, *5319*
1Jn 2:28 that, when he shall **a**, we may have *5319*
3: 2 and it doth not yet **a** what we shall be: *5319*
3: 2 but we know that, when he shall **a**, we shall *5319*
Rev 3:18 *that* the shame of thy nakedness do not **a**; *5319*

APPEARANCE (38) [APPEAR]
Nu 9:15 upon the tabernacle as it were the **a** of fire, 4758
9:16 it *by day*, and the **a** of fire by night. 4758
1Sa 16: 7 for man looketh on the **outward a**, but 5869
Eze 1: 5 this *was* their **a**; they had the likeness of a 4758
1:13 their **a** *was* like burning coals of fire, *and* 4758
1:13 coals of fire, *and* like the **a** of lamps: 4758
1:14 and returned as the **a** of a flash of lightning. 4758
1:16 The **a** of the wheels and their work *was* like 4758
1:16 their **a** and their work *was* as it were a 4758
1:26 of a throne, as the **a** of a sapphire stone: 4758
1:26 likeness as the **a** of a man above upon it. 4758
1:27 as the **a** of fire round about within it, 4758
1:27 from the **a** of his loins even upward, 4758
1:27 from the **a** of his loins even downward, 4758
1:27 I saw as it were the **a** of fire, and it had 4758
1:28 As the **a** of the bow that is in the cloud in 4758
1:28 so *was* the **a** of the brightness round about. 4758
1:28 This *was* the **a** of the likeness of the glory 4758
8: 2 I beheld, and lo, a likeness as the **a** of fire: 4758
8: 2 from the **a** of his loins even downward, 4758
8: 2 as the **a** of brightness, as the colour of 4758
10: 1 as the **a** of the likeness of a throne. 4758
10: 9 the **a** of the wheels *was* as the colour of a 4758
40: 3 whose **a** *was* like the appearance of brass, 4758
40: 3 whose appearance *was* like the **a** of brass, 4758
41:21 the **a** *of the one* as the appearance *of* 4758
41:21 the appearance *of the one* as the **a** *of* 4758
42:11 the way before them *was* like the **a** of 4758
43: 3 *it was* according to the **a** of the vision 4758
Da 8:15 there stood before me as the **a** of a man. 4758
10: 6 his face as the **a** of lightning, and his eyes 4758
10:18 and touched me *one* like the **a** of a man, 4758
Joel 2: 4 The **a** of them *is* as the appearance of 4758
2: 4 The appearance of them *is* as the **a** of 4758
Jn 7:24 Judge not according to the **a**, but *3799*
2Co 5:12 *somewhat to answer* them which glory in **a**, *4383*
10: 7 Do ye look on *things* after the **outward a**? *4383*
1Th 5:22 Abstain from all **a** of evil. *1491*

APPEARANCES (2) [APPEAR]
Eze 10:10 *as for* their **a**, they four had one likeness, 4758
10:22 the river of Chebar, their **a** and themselves: 4758

APPEARED (70) [APPEAR]
Ge 12: 7 the LORD **a** unto Abram, and said, 7200
12: 7 an altar unto the LORD, who **a** unto him. 7200
17: 1 the LORD **a** to Abram, and said unto him, 7200
18: 1 the LORD **a** unto him in the plains of 7200
26: 2 the LORD **a** unto him, and said, Go not 7200
26:24 And the LORD **a** unto him the same night, 7200
35: 1 that **a** unto thee when thou fleddest from 7200
35: 7 because there God **a** unto him, when he 1540
35: 9 God **a** unto Jacob again, when he came out 7200
48: 3 God Almighty **a** unto me at Luz in the land 7200
Ex 3: 2 the angel of the LORD **a** unto him in a 7200
3:16 of Isaac, and of Jacob, **a** unto me, saying, 7200
4: 1 will say, The LORD hath not **a** unto thee. 7200
4: 5 and the God of Jacob, hath **a** unto thee. 7200
6: 3 I **a** unto Abraham, unto Isaac, and 7200
14:27 his strength **when** the morning **a**; 6437+3807.1
16:10 the glory of the LORD **a** in the cloud. 7200
Lev 9:23 the glory of the LORD **a** unto all 7200
Nu 14:10 the glory of the LORD **a** in the tabernacle 7200
16:19 the glory of the LORD **a** unto all 7200
16:42 covered it, and the glory of the LORD **a**. 7200
20: 6 and the glory of the LORD **a** unto them. 7200
Dt 31:15 the LORD **a** in the tabernacle in a pillar of 7200
Jdg 6:12 the angel of the LORD **a** unto him, and 7200
13: 3 the angel of the LORD **a** unto the woman, 7200
13:10 unto him, Behold, the man hath **a** unto me, 7200
1Sa 3:21 the LORD **a** again in Shiloh: for 7200
2Sa 22:16 the channels of the sea **a**, the foundations of 7200
1Ki 3: 5 In Gibeon the LORD **a** to Solomon in a 7200
9: 2 That the LORD **a** to Solomon the second 7200
9: 2 as he had **a** unto him at Gibeon. 7200
11: 9 God of Israel, which had **a** unto him twice, 7200
2Ki 2:11 *there* **a** a chariot of fire, and horses of fire, NIH
2Ch 3: 1 where *the LORD* **a** unto David his father, 7200
7:12 the LORD **a** to Solomon by night, and 7200
Ne 4:21 the rising of the morning till the stars **a**. 3318
Jer 31: 3 The LORD hath **a** of old unto me, 7200
Eze 10: 1 **a** over them as it were a sapphire stone, 7200
10: 8 there **a** in the cherubims the form of a 7200
19:11 she **a** in her height with the multitude of her 7200
Da 1:15 at the end of ten days their countenances **a** 7200
8: 1 of king Belshazzar a vision **a** unto me, 7200
8: 1 after that which **a** unto me at the first. 7200
Mt 1:20 *the* angel of the Lord **a** unto him in a *5316*
2: 7 of them diligently what time the star **a**. *5316*
13:26 brought forth fruit, then **a** the tares also. *5316*
17: 3 there **a** unto them Moses and Elias talking *3700*
27:53 went into the holy city, and **a** unto many. *1718*
Mk 9: 4 And there **a** unto them Elias with Moses: *3700*
16: 9 he **a** first to Mary Magdalene, out of whom *5316*
16:12 After that he **a** in another form unto two of *5319*
16:14 Afterward he **a** unto the eleven as they sat *5319*
Lk 1:11 And there **a** unto him an angel of the Lord *3700*
9: 8 And of some, that Elias had **a**; and *5316*
9:31 Who **a** in glory, and spake of his decease *3700*
22:43 And there **a** an angel unto him from *3700*
24:34 Lord is risen indeed, and hath **a** to Simon. *3700*
Ac 2: 3 And there **a** unto them cloven tongues like *3700*
7: 2 The God of glory **a** unto our father *3700*
7:30 there **a** to him in the wilderness of mount *3700*
7:35 a deliverer by the hand of the angel which **a** *3700*
Ac 9:17 that **a** unto thee in the way as thou camest, *3700*
16: 9 And a vision **a** to Paul in the night; *3700*
26:16 for I have **a** unto thee for this *purpose*, to *3700*
27:20 when neither sun nor stars in many days **a**, *2014*
Tit 2:11 that bringeth salvation hath **a** to all men, *2014*
3: 4 and love of God our Saviour toward man **a**, *2014*
Heb 9:26 now once in the end of the world hath he **a** *5319*
Rev 12: 1 And there **a** a great wonder in heaven; *3700*
12: 3 And there **a** another wonder in heaven; and *3700*

APPEARETH (10) [APPEAR]
Lev 13:14 when raw flesh **a** in him, he shall be 7200
13:43 as the leprosy **a** in the skin of the flesh; 4758
Dt 2:30 deliver him into thy hand, as **a** this day. NIH
Ps 84: 7 *every one of them* in Zion **a** before God. 7200
Pr 27:25 The hay **a**, and the tender grass sheweth 1540
Jer 6: 1 for evil **a** out of the north, and 8259
Mal 3: 2 who *shall* stand when he **a**? for he *is* like a 7200
Mt 2:13 *the* angel of the Lord **a** to Joseph in a *5316*
2:19 an angel of the Lord **a** in a dream to Joseph *5316*
Jas 4:14 that **a** for a little *time*, and then *5316*

APPEARING (6) [APPEAR]
1Ti 6:14 until the **a** of our Lord Jesus Christ: *2015*
2Ti 1:10 But is now made manifest by the **a** of our *2015*
4: 1 and the dead at his **a** and his kingdom; *2015*
4: 8 but unto all them also that love his **a**. *2015*
Tit 2:13 and the glorious **a** of the great God and *2015*
1Pe 1: 7 honour and glory at the **a** of Jesus Christ: *602*

APPEASE (1) [APPEASED, APPEASETH]
Ge 32:20 I will **a** him with the present that 3722+6440

APPEASED (2) [APPEASE]
Est 2: 1 when the wrath of king Ahasuerus was **a**, 7918
Ac 19:35 And when the townclerk had **a** the people, *2687*

APPEASETH (1) [APPEASE]
Pr 15:18 but *he that is* slow to anger **a** strife. 8252

APPERTAIN (2) [APPERTAINED, APPERTAINETH]
Nu 16:30 with all that **a** unto them, and they go down NIH
Jer 10: 7 for to thee doth it **a**: forasmuch as among 2969

APPERTAINED (3) [APPERTAIN]
Nu 16:32 all the men that **a** unto Korah, and all *their* NIH
16:33 They, and all that **a** to them, went down NIH
Ne 2: 8 the gates of the palace which **a** to the house, NIH

APPERTAINETH (1) [APPERTAIN]
Lev 6: 5 *and* give it unto him to whom it **a**, in NIH

APPETITE (4)
Job 38:39 for the lion? or fill the **a** of the young lions, 2416
Pr 23: 2 to thy throat, if thou *be* a man **given to a**. 5315
Ecc 6: 7 *is* for his mouth, and yet the **a** is not filled. 5315
Isa 29: 8 and behold, *he is* faint, and his soul hath **a**: 8264

APPHIA (1)
Phm 1: 2 And to *our* beloved **A**, *682*

APPII (1)
Ac 28:15 they came to meet us as far as **A** forum, and *675*

APPIUS See APPII

APPLE (8) [APPLES]
Dt 32:10 he kept him as the **a** of his eye. 380
Ps 17: 8 Keep me as the **a** of the eye, hide me 380+1323
Pr 7: 2 and live; and my law as the **a** of thine eye. 380
SS 2: 3 As the **a tree** among the trees of the wood, 8598
8: 5 I raised thee up under the **a tree**: there thy 8598
La 2:18 no rest; let not the **a** of thine eye cease. 1323
Joel 1:12 the palm tree also, and the **a tree**, 8598
Zec 2: 8 for he that toucheth you toucheth the **a** of his 892

APPLES (3) [APPLE]
Pr 25:11 A word fitly spoken *is like* **a** of gold in 8598
SS 2: 5 Stay me with flagons, comfort me with **a**: 8598
7: 8 of the vine, and the smell of thy nose like **a**; 8598

APPLIED (3) [APPLY]
Ecc 7:25 I **a** mine heart to know, and to search, and 5437
8: 9 **a** my heart unto every work that is done 5414
8:16 When I **a** mine heart to know wisdom, and 5414

APPLY (4) [APPLIED]
Ps 90:12 that we may **a** *our* hearts *unto* wisdom. 935
Pr 2: 2 *and* **a** thine heart to understanding; 5186
22:17 and **a** thine heart unto my knowledge. 7896
23:12 **A** thine heart unto instruction, and thine ears 935

APPOINT (41) [APPOINTED, APPOINTETH, APPOINTMENT]
Ge 30:28 he said, **A** me thy wages, and I will give *it*. 5344
41:34 do *this*, and let him **a** officers over the land, 6485
Ex 21:13 I will **a** thee a place whither he shall flee. 7760
30:16 shalt **a** it for the service of the tabernacle of 5414
Lev 26:16 I will even **a** over you terror, consumption, 6485
Nu 1:50 thou shalt **a** the Levites over the tabernacle 6485
3:10 thou shalt **a** Aaron and his sons, and 6485
4:19 **a** them every one to his service and to his 7760
4:27 ye shall **a** unto them in charge all their 6485
35: 6 which ye shall **a** for the manslayer, that he 5414
35:11 ye shall **a** you cities to be cities of refuge 7136
Jos 20: 2 **A out** for you cities of refuge, 5414
1Sa 8:11 and **a** *them* for himself, for his chariots, and 7760
8:12 he will **a** him captains over thousands, and 7760
2Sa 6:21 to **a** me ruler over the people of 6680
7:10 Moreover I will **a** a place for my people 7760
15:15 *to do* whatsoever my lord the king shall **a**. 977
1Ki 5: 6 servants according to all that thou shalt **a**: 559
5: 9 *in* flotes unto the place that thou shalt **a** me, 7971

A

1Ch 15:16 David spake to the chief of the Levites to a 5975
Ne 7: 3 a watches of the inhabitants of Jerusalem, 5975
Est 2: 3 let the king a officers in all the provinces of 6485
Job 14:13 that thou wouldest a me a set time, and 7896
Isa 26: 1 salvation will *God* a *for* walls and 7896
61: 3 To a unto them that mourn in Zion, to give 7760
Jer 15: 3 I will a over them four kinds, saith 6485
49:19 who *is* a chosen *man, that* I may a over 6485
49:19 who will a me the time? and who *is* that 3259
50:44 who *is* a chosen *man, that* I may a over 6485
50:44 who will a me the time? and who *is* that 3259
51:27 and Ashchenaz; a a captain against her; 6485
Eze 21:19 Also, thou son of man, a thee two ways, 7760
21:20 A a way, that the sword may come to 7760
21:22 to a captains, to open the mouth in 7760
21:22 to a *battering* rams against the gates, to cast 7760
45: 6 ye shall a the possession of the city five 5414
Hos 1:11 a themselves one head, and they shall come 7760
Mt 24:51 and a *him* his portion with the hypocrites: *5087*
Lk 12:46 will a *him* his portion with the unbelievers. *5087*
22:29 And I a unto you a kingdom, as my Father *1303*
Ac 6: 3 whom we may a over this business. *2525*

APPOINTED (126) [APPOINT]

Ge 4:25 *said she,* hath a me another seed instead of 7896
18:14 At the time a I will return unto thee, 4150
24:14 *let the same be* she *that* thou hast a for thy 3198
24:44 the LORD hath a out for my master's son. 3198
Ex 9: 5 the LORD a a set time, saying, 7760
23:15 in the time a of the month Abib; 4150
Nu 9: 2 also keep the passover at his a season. 4150
9: 3 at even, ye shall keep it in his a season: 4150
9: 7 his a season among the children of Israel? 4150
9:13 the offering of the LORD in his a season, 4150
Jos 8:14 he and all his people, at a time a, before 4150
20: 7 they a Kedesh in Galilee in mount 6942
20: 9 These were the cities a for all the children 4152
Jdg 18:11 six hundred men a *with* weapons of war. 2296
18:16 the six hundred men a *with* their weapons 2296
18:17 men that were a *with* weapons of war. 2296
20:38 Now there was an a sign between the men 4150
1Sa 13: 8 according to the set time that Samuel *had* a: NIH
13:11 *that* thou camest not within the days a, and 4150
19:20 Samuel standing *as* a over them, the spirit 5324
20:35 out *into* the field at the time a with David, 4150
21: 2 I have a *my* servants to such and such a 3045
25:30 and shall have a thee ruler over Israel; 6680
29: 4 which thou hast a him, and let him not go 6485
2Sa 17:14 For the LORD had a to defeat the good 6680
20: 5 than the set time which he had a him. 3259
24:15 Israel from the morning even to the time a: 4150
1Ki 1:35 I have a him to be ruler over Israel and 6680
11:18 and a him victuals, and gave him land. 559
12:12 as the king had a, saying, Come to me 1696
20:42 hand a man whom I a to utter destruction, 2764
2Ki 7:17 the king a the lord on whose hand he 6485
8: 6 So the king a unto her a certain officer, 5414
10:24 Jehu a fourscore men without, and said, 7760
11:18 the priest a officers over the house of 7760
18:14 the king of Assyria a unto Hezekiah king of 7760
1Ch 6:48 Their brethren also the Levites *were* a unto 5414
6:49 *were* a for all the work of the *place* most NIH
9:29 *Some* of them also *were* a to oversee 4487
15:17 So the Levites a Heman the son of Joel; 5975
15:19 *were* a to sound with cymbals of brass; NIH
16: 4 he a *certain* of the Levites to minister 5414
2Ch 8:14 he a, according to the order of David his 5975
20:21 he a singers unto the LORD, and 5975
23:18 Also Jehoiada a the offices of the house of 7760
31: 2 Hezekiah a the courses of the priests and 5975
31: 3 *He* a also the king's portion of his substance NIH
33: 8 of the land which I have a for your fathers; 5975
34:22 *they* that the king *had* a, went to Huldah NIH
Ezr 3: 8 a the Levites from twenty years old and 5975
8:20 the princes had a for the service of 5414
10:14 strange wives in our cities come at a times, 2163
Ne 5:14 Moreover from the time that I was a to be 6680
6: 7 thou hast also a prophets to preach of thee 5975
7: 1 and the singers and the Levites were a, 6485
9:17 in their rebellion a a captain to return to 5414
10:34 of our fathers, at times a year by year, 2163
12:31 a two great *companies of them that gave* 5975
12:44 at that time were some a over the chambers 6485
13:30 a the wards of the priests and the Levites, 5975
13:31 at times a, and for the firstfruits. 2163
Est 1: 8 the king had a to all the officers of his 3245
2:15 the keeper of the women, a. 559
4: 5 whom he had a to attend upon her, and 5975
9:27 and according to their *a* time every year; NIH
9:31 times a, according as Mordecai the Jew NIH
Job 7: 1 *Is there* not an a time to man upon earth? 6635
7: 3 and wearisome nights are a to me. 4487
14: 5 thou hast a his bounds that he cannot pass; 6213
14:14 *again?* all the days of my a time will I wait, 6635
20:29 and the heritage a unto him by God. 561
23:14 For he performeth the thing that is a for 2706
30:23 *to* death, and *to* the house a for all living. 4150
Ps 44:11 Thou hast given us like sheep a for meat; NIH
78: 5 a a law in Israel, which he commanded our 7760
79:11 preserve thou those that are a to die; 1121+8546
81: 3 in the time a, on our solemn feast day. 3677
102:20 to loose those that are a to death; 1121+8546
104:19 He a the moon for seasons: the sun 6213
Pr 7:20 with him, *and* will come home at the day a. 3677
8:29 when he a the foundations of the earth: 2710
31: 8 of all such as are a to destruction. 1121+2475
Isa 1:14 and your a feasts my soul hateth: 4150
14:31 and none *shall be* alone in his a times. 4151
28:25 and the a barley and the rye *in* their place? 5567
44: 7 order for me, since I a the ancient people? 7760
Jer 5:24 he reserveth unto us the a weeks of 2708
8: 7 stork in the heaven knoweth her a times; 4150
33:25 *if* I have not a the ordinances of heaven and 7760
46:17 *but* a noise; he hath passed the time a. 4150
47: 7 against the sea shore? there hath he a it. 3259
Eze 4: 6 I have a thee each day for a year. 5414
36: 5 which have a my land into their possession 5414
43:21 he shall burn it in the a place of the house, 4662
Da 1: 5 the king a them a daily provision of 4487
1:10 who hath a your meat and your drink: 4487
8:19 for at the time a the end *shall be.* 4150
10: 1 the thing *was* true, but the time a *was* long: 6635
11:27 for yet the end *shall be* at the time a. 4150
11:29 At the time a he shall return, and 4150
11:35 of the end: because *it is* yet for a time a. 4150
Mic 6: 9 hear ye the rod, and who hath a it. 3259
Hab 2: 3 For the vision *is* yet for an a time, but 4150
Mt 26:19 And the disciples did as Jesus had a them; *4929*
27:10 for the potter's field, as the Lord a me. *4929*
28:16 into a mountain where Jesus had a them. *5021*
Lk 3:13 Exact no more than that which is a you. *1299*
10: 1 After these *things* the Lord a other seventy *322*
22:29 a kingdom, as my Father hath a unto me; *1303*
Ac 1:23 And they a two, Joseph called Barsabas, *2476*
7:44 as he had a, speaking unto Moses, *1299*
17:26 and hath determined the times before a, *4384*
17:31 Because he hath a a day, in the which he *2476*
20:13 for so had he a, minding himself to go *1299*
22:10 thee of all *things* which are a for thee to do. *5021*
28:23 And when they had a him a day, *5021*
1Co 4: 9 us the apostles last, as *it were* a to death: *1935*
Gal 4: 2 and governors until the time a of the father. *4287*
1Th 3: 3 for yourselves know that we are a *2749*
5: 9 For God hath not a us to wrath, but *5087*
2Ti 1:11 Whereunto I am a a preacher, and *5087*
Tit 1: 5 ordain elders in every city, as I had a thee: *1299*
Heb 1: 2 whom he hath a heir of all *things,* by whom *5087*
3: 2 Who was faithful to him that a him, as also *4160*
9:27 And as it is a unto men once to die, but *606*
1Pe 2: 8 whereunto also they were a. *5087*

APPOINTETH (1) [APPOINT]

Da 5:21 and *that* he a over it whomsoever he will. 6966

APPOINTMENT (4) [APPOINT]

Nu 4:27 At the a of Aaron and his sons shall be all 6310
2Sa 13:32 for by the a of Absalom *this* hath been 6310
Ezr 6: 9 according to the a of the priests which *are* 3983
Job 2:11 for they had made an a together to come to 3259

APPREHEND (2) [APPREHENDED]

2Co 11:32 *with a garrison,* desirous to a me: *4084*
Php 3:12 I follow *after,* if that I may a *that* for which *2638*

APPREHENDED (3) [APPREHEND]

Ac 12: 4 And when he had a him, he put *him* in *4084*
Php 3:12 *that* for which also I am a of Christ Jesus. *2638*
3:13 Brethren, I count not myself to have a: but *2638*

APPROACH (19) [APPROACHED, APPROACHETH, APPROACHING]

Lev 18: 6 None of you shall a to any that is near of 7126
18:14 thou shalt not a to his wife: 7126
18:19 Also thou shalt not a unto a woman to 7126
20:16 if a woman a unto any beast, and lie down 7126
21:17 let him not a to offer the bread of his God. 7126
21:18 *he be* that hath a blemish, he shall not a: 7126
Nu 4:19 when they a unto the most holy *things:* 5066
Dt 20: 2 that the priest shall a and speak unto 5066
20: 3 you a *this* day unto battle against your 7131
31:14 Behold, thy days a that *thou* must die: 7126
Jos 8: 5 that *are* with me, will a unto the city: 7126
Job 40:19 he that made him can make his sword to a 5066
Ps 65: 4 causest to a *unto thee, that* he may dwell *in* 7126
Jer 30:21 him to draw near, and he shall a unto me: 5066
30:21 for who *is* this that engaged his heart to a 5066
Eze 42:13 where the priests that a unto the LORD 7138
42:14 shall a to *those things* which *are* for 7126
43:19 which a unto me, to minister unto me, 7138
1Ti 6:16 in the light which no *man* can a unto; *676*

APPROACHED (2) [APPROACH]

2Sa 11:20 Wherefore a ye *so* nigh unto the city when 5066
2Ki 16:12 the king a to the altar, and offered thereon. 7126

APPROACHETH (1) [APPROACH]

Lk 12:33 where no thief a, neither moth corrupteth. *1448*

APPROACHING (2) [APPROACH]

Isa 58: 2 of justice; they take delight in a to God. 7132
Heb 10:25 and so much the more, as ye see the day a. *1448*

APPROVE (3) [APPROVED, APPROVEST, APPROVETH, APPROVING]

Ps 49:13 yet their posterity a their sayings. Selah. 7521
1Co 16: 3 whomsoever you shall a by *your* letters, *1381*
Php 1:10 That ye may a *things* that are excellent; *1381*

APPROVED (8) [APPROVE]

Ac 2:22 a man a of God among you by miracles and *584*
Ro 14:18 Christ *is* acceptable to God, and a of men. *1384*
16:10 Salute Apelles a in Christ. Salute them *1384*
1Co 11:19 that they *which are* a may be made *1384*
2Co 7:11 In all *things* ye have a yourselves to be *4921*
10:18 For not he that commendeth himself is a, *1384*
13: 7 not that we should appear a, but that ye *1384*
2Ti 2:15 Study to shew thyself a unto God, *1384*

APPROVEST (1) [APPROVE]

Ro 2:18 and a the *things* that are more excellent, *1381*

APPROVETH (1) [APPROVE]

La 3:36 subvert a man in his cause, the Lord a not. 7200

APPROVING (1) [APPROVE]

2Co 6: 4 But in all *things* a ourselves as *4921*

APRONS (2)

Ge 3: 7 fig leaves together, and made themselves a. 2290
Ac 19:12 brought unto the sick handkerchiefs or a, *4612*

APT (4)

2Ki 24:16 all *that were* strong *and* a for war, 6213
1Ch 7:40 genealogy of them *that were* a to the war NIH
1Ti 3: 2 given to hospitality, a to teach; *1317*
2Ti 2:24 but be gentle unto all *men,* a to teach, *1317*

AQUEDUCT See CONDUIT

AQUILA (6)

Ac 18: 2 And found a certain Jew named A, born in *207*
18:18 into Syria, and with him Priscilla and A: *207*
18:26 whom when A and Priscilla had heard, *207*
Ro 16: 3 and A my helpers in Christ Jesus: *207*
1Co 16:19 A and Priscilla salute you much in the Lord, *207*
2Ti 4:19 Salute Prisca and A, and the household of *207*

AR (6)

Nu 21:15 that goeth down to the dwelling of A, 6144
21:28 it hath consumed A of Moab, *and* the lords 6144
Dt 2: 9 I have given A unto the children of Lot *for* 6144
2:18 Thou art to pass over *through* A, the coast 6144
2:29 the Moabites which dwell in A, did unto 6144
Isa 15: 1 Because in the night A of Moab is laid 6144

ARA (1)

1Ch 7:38 of Jether; Jephunneh, and Pispah, and A. 690

ARAB (1) [ARABIA, ARABIAN, ARABIANS]

Jos 15:52 A, and Dumah, and Eshean, 694

ARABAH (2) [BETH-ARABAH]

Jos 18:18 passed along toward the side over against A 6160
18:18 Arabah northward, and went down unto A: 6160

ARABIA (8) [ARAB]

1Ki 10:15 *of* all the kings of A, and *of* the governors 6153
2Ch 9:14 all the kings of A and governors of 6152
Isa 21:13 The burden upon A. In the forest in Arabia 6152
21:13 In the forest in A shall ye lodge, O ye 6152
Jer 25:24 all the kings of A, and all the kings of 6152
Eze 27:21 A, and all the princes of Kedar, 6152
Gal 1:17 but I went into A, and returned again unto *688*
4:25 For *this* Agar is mount Sinai in A, and *688*

ARABIAN (4) [ARAB]

Ne 2:19 the Ammonite, and Geshem the A, 6163
6: 1 Geshem the A, and the rest of our enemies, 6163
Isa 13:20 neither shall the A pitch tent there; 6163
Jer 3: 2 sat for them, as the A in the wilderness; 6163

ARABIANS (6) [ARAB]

2Ch 17:11 the A brought him flocks, seven thousand 6163
21:16 and of the A, that *were* near the Ethiopians: 6163
22: 1 for the band *of men* that came with the A to 6163
26: 7 against the A that dwelt in Gur-baal, and 6163
Ne 4: 7 the A, and the Ammonites, and 6163
Ac 2:11 Cretes and A, we do hear them speak in our *690*

ARAD (5)

Nu 21: 1 *when* king A the Canaanite, which dwelt *in* 6166
33:40 king A the Canaanite, which dwelt in 6166
Jos 12:14 king of Hormah, one; the king of A, one; 6166
Jdg 1:16 of Judah, which *lieth* in the south of A; 6166
1Ch 8:15 And Zebadiah, and A, and Ader, 6166

ARAH (4)

1Ch 7:39 the sons of Ulla; A, and Haniel, and Rezia. 733
Ezr 2: 5 The children of A, seven hundred seventy 733
Ne 6:18 the son in law of Shechaniah the son of A; 733
7:10 The children of A, six hundred fifty and two. 733

ARAM (10) [ARAM-NAHARAIM, ARAM-ZOBAH, ARAMITESS, BETH-ARAM, PADAN-ARAM]

Ge 10:22 and Asshur, and Arphaxad, and Lud, and A. 758
10:23 the children of A; Uz, and Hul, and Gether, 758
22:21 Buz his brother, and Kemuel the father of A, 758
Nu 23: 7 the king of Moab hath brought me from A, 758
1Ch 1:17 A, and Uz, and Hul, and Gether, and 758
2:23 he took Geshur, and A, with the towns of 758
7:34 Ahi, and Rohgah, Jehubbah, and A. 758
Mt 1: 3 Phares begat Esrom; and Esrom begat A; *689*
1: 4 And A begat Aminadab; and *689*
Lk 3:33 which was *the son* of A, which was *the son* *689*

ARAM MAACAH See SYRIA-MAACHAH

ARAMAIC See SYRIACK

ARAMEAN See ARAMITESS

ARAMEANS See SYRIANS

ARAMITESS (1) [ARAM]

1Ch 7:14 his concubine the A bare Machir the father 761

ARAM-NAHARAIM (1) [ARAM]

Ps 60: T when he strove with A and 763

ARAM-ZOBAH (1) [ARAM, ZOBAH]

Ps 60: T he strove with Aram-naharaim and with A, 760

ARAN (2)

Ge 36:28 The children of Dishan *are* these; Uz, and A. 765
1Ch 1:42 *and* Jakan. The sons of Dishan; Uz, and A. 765

ARARAT (2)

Ge 8: 4 day of the month, upon the mountains of A. 780
Jer 51:27 call together against her the kingdoms of A, 780

ARAUNAH (9) [ORNAN]
2Sa 24:16 was by the threshingplace of **A** the Jebusite. 728
24:18 in the threshingfloor of **A** the Jebusite. 728
24:20 **A** looked, and saw the king and his servants 728
24:20 **A** went out, and bowed himself before 728
24:21 **A** said, Wherefore is my lord the king come 728
24:22 **A** said unto David, Let my lord the king take 728
24:23 All *these things* did **A**, *as* a king, give unto 728
24:23 **A** said unto the king, The LORD thy God 728
24:24 the king said unto **A**, Nay; but I will surely 728

ARBA (2) [ARBAH, KIRJATH-ARBA]
Jos 14:15 which **A** *was* a great man among NIH
15:13 *even* the city of **A** the father of Anak, 704

ARBAH (2) [ARBA]
Ge 35:27 unto the city of **A**, which *is* Hebron, 704
Jos 21:11 they gave them the city of **A** the father of 704

ARBATHITE (2)
2Sa 23:31 Abialbon the **A**, Azmaveth the Barhumite, 6164
1Ch 11:32 Hurai of the brooks of Gaash, Abiel the **A**, 6164

ARBITE (1)
2Sa 23:35 Hezrai the Carmelite, Paarai the **A**, 701

ARCHANGEL (2) [ANGEL]
1Th 4:16 with the voice of the **a**, and with the trump *743*
Jude 1: 9 Yet Michael the **a**, when contending with *743*

ARCHELAUS (1)
Mt 2:22 But when he heard that **A** did reign in Judea *745*

ARCHER (2) [ARCHERS]
Ge 21:20 in the wilderness, and became an **a**. 7199+7235
Jer 51: 3 Against *him that* bendeth let the **a** bend his 1869

ARCHERS (12) [ARCHER]
Ge 49:23 The **a** have sorely grieved him, and 1167+2671
Jdg 5:11 *They that are delivered* from the noise of **a** 2686
1Sa 31: 3 the **a** hit him; 376+3384+7198+871.1+1886.1
31: 3 hit him; and he was sore wounded of the **a**. 3384
1Ch 8:40 **a**, and had many sons, and 1869+7198
10: 3 the **a** hit him, and 4175+7198+871.1+1886.1
10: 3 hit him, and he was wounded of the **a**. 3384
2Ch 35:23 the **a** shot at king Josiah; and the king said 3384
Job 16:13 His **a** compass me round about, he cleaveth 7228
Isa 21:17 the residue of the number of **a**, the mighty 7198
22: 3 are fled together, they are bound by the **a**: 7198
Jer 50:29 Call together the **a** against Babylon: all ye 7228

ARCHES (15)
Eze 40:16 the gate round about, and likewise to the **a**: 361
40:21 the **a** thereof were after the measure of 361
40:22 and their **a**, and their palm trees, 361
40:22 and the **a** thereof *were* before them. 361
40:24 the **a** thereof according to these measures. 361
40:25 in it and in the **a** thereof round about, 361
40:26 up to it, and the **a** thereof *were* before them: 361
40:29 the posts thereof, and the **a** thereof, 361
40:29 in it and in the **a** thereof round about: 361
40:30 the **a** round about *were* five and 361
40:31 the **a** thereof *were* toward the utter court; 361
40:33 and the posts thereof, and the **a** thereof, 361
40:33 and in the **a** thereof round about: 361
40:34 the **a** thereof *were* toward the outward court; 361
40:36 the **a** thereof, and the windows to it round 361

ARCHEVITES (1)
Ezr 4: 9 the Tarpelites, the Apharsites, the **A**, 756

ARCHI (1)
Jos 16: 2 passeth along unto the borders of **A** *to* 757

ARCHIPPUS (2)
Col 4:17 And say to **A**, Take heed to the ministry *751*
Phm 1: 2 and **A** our fellowsoldier, and to the church *751*

ARCHITE (5)
2Sa 15:32 Hushai the **A** *came* to meet him with his coat 757
16:16 to pass, when Hushai the **A**, David's friend, 757
17: 5 Call now Hushai the **A** also, and let us hear 757
17:14 The counsel of Hushai the **A** *is* better than 757
1Ch 27:33 and Hushai the **A** *was* the king's companion: 757

ARCTURUS (2)
Job 9: 9 Which maketh **A**, Orion, and Pleiades, and 5906
38:32 or canst thou guide **A** with his sons? 5906

ARD (3) [ARDITES]
Ge 46:21 and Rosh, Muppim, and Huppim, and **A**. 714
Nu 26:40 the sons of Bela were **A** and Naaman: 714
26:40 *of* **A**, the family of the Ardites: *and* NIH

ARDITES (1) [ARD]
Nu 26:40 *of Ard,* the family of the **A**: *and* of Naaman, 716

ARDON (1)
1Ch 2:18 sons *are* these; Jesher, and Shobab, and **A**. 715

ARE (2946) [BE] See Index of Articles, Etc.

ARELI (2) [ARELITES]
Ge 46:16 Shuni, and Ezbon, Eri, and Arodi, and **A**. 692
Nu 26:17 the Arodites: of **A**, the family of the Arelites. 692

ARELITES (1) [ARELI]
Nu 26:17 of the Arodites: of Areli, the family of the **A**. 692

AREOPAGITE (1) [AREOPAGUS]
Ac 17:34 among the which *was* Dionysius the **A**, and *698*

AREOPAGUS (1) [AREOPAGITE, MARS' HILL]
Ac 17:19 took him, and brought him unto **A**, saying, *697*

ARETAS (1)
2Co 11:32 In Damascus the governor under **A** the king *702*

ARGOB (5)
Dt 3: 4 threescore cities, all the region of **A**, 709
3:13 all the region of **A**, with all Bashan, which 709
3:14 the country of **A** unto the coasts of Geshuri 709
1Ki 4:13 to him *also pertained* the region of **A**, 709
2Ki 15:25 of the king's house, with **A** and Arieh; 709

ARGUING (1) [ARGUMENTS]
Job 6:25 right words! but what doth your **a** reprove? 3198

ARGUMENTS (1) [ARGUING]
Job 23: 4 cause before him, and fill my mouth *with* **a**. 8433

ARIDAI (1)
Est 9: 9 and Arisai, and **A**, and Vajezatha, 742

ARIDATHA (1)
Est 9: 8 And Poratha, and Adalia, and **A**, 743

ARIEH (1)
2Ki 15:25 of the king's house, with Argob and **A**; 745

ARIEL (6)
Ezr 8:16 for **A**, for Shemaiah, and for Elnathan, and 740
Isa 29: 1 Woe to **A**, to Ariel, the city *where* David 740
29: 1 Woe to Ariel, to **A**, the city *where* David 740
29: 2 Yet I will distress **A**, and there shall be 740
29: 2 and sorrow: and it shall be unto me as **A**. 740
29: 7 of all the nations that fight against **A**, 740

ARIGHT (5) [RIGHT]
Ps 50:23 to him that ordereth *his* conversation **a** will NIH
78: 8 a generation *that* **set** not their heart **a**, and 3559
Pr 15: 2 The tongue of the wise **useth** knowledge **a**: 3190
23:31 in the cup, *when* it moveth itself **a**. 4339+871.1
Jer 8: 6 and heard, *but* they spake not **a**: 3651

ARIMATHEA (4)
Mt 27:57 there came a rich man of **A**, named Joseph, *707*
Mk 15:43 Joseph of **A**, an honourable counseller, *707*
Lk 23:51 of them;) *he was* of **A**, a city of the Jews: *707*
Jn 19:38 And after this Joseph of **A**, being a disciple *707*

ARIOCH (7)
Ge 14: 1 **A** king of Ellasar, Chedorlaomer king of 746
14: 9 king of Shinar, and **A** king of Ellasar; 746
Da 2:14 wisdom to **A** the captain of the king's guard, 746
2:15 and said to **A** the king's captain, 746
2:15 Then **A** made the thing known to Daniel. 746
2:24 Therefore Daniel went in unto **A**, whom 746
2:25 **A** brought in Daniel before the king in haste, 746

ARISAI (1)
Est 9: 9 and **A**, and Aridai, and Vajezatha, 747

ARISE (149) [RISE]
Ge 13:17 **A**, walk through the land in the length of it 6965
19:15 saying, **A**, take thy wife, and thy two 6965
21:18 **A**, lift up the lad, and hold him in thine 6965
27:19 **a**, I pray thee, sit and eat of my venison, 6965
27:31 Let my father **a**, and eat of his son's 6965
27:43 **a**, flee thou to Laban my brother to Haran; 6965
28: 2 **A**, go to Padan-aram, to the house of 6965
31:13 now **a**, get thee out from this land, 6965
35: 1 **A**, go up to Beth-el, and dwell there: 6965
35: 3 let us **a**, and go up to Beth-el; and I will 6965
41:30 there shall **a** after them seven years of 6965
43: 8 Send the lad with me, and we will **a** and go; 6965
43:13 your brother, and **a**, go again unto the man: 6965
Dt 9:12 the LORD said unto me, **A**, get thee down 6965
10:11 the LORD said unto me, **A**, take thy 6965
13: 1 If there **a** among you a prophet, or 6965
17: 8 If there **a** a matter too hard for thee in NIH
17: 8 shalt thou **a**, and get thee up into the place 6965
Jos 1: 2 now therefore **a**, go over this Jordan, thou, 6965
8: 1 people of war with thee, and **a**, go up *to* Ai: 6965
Jdg 5:12 **a**, Barak, and lead thy captivity captive, 6965
7: 9 unto him, **A**, get thee down unto the host; 6965
7:15 returned into the host of Israel, and said, **A**; 6965
18: 9 they said, **A**, that we may go up against 6965
20:40 when the flame began to **a up** out of 5927
1Sa 9: 3 servants with thee, and **a**, go seek the asses. 6965
16:12 the LORD said, **A**, anoint him: for this *is* 6965
23: 4 And the LORD answered him and said, **A**, 6965
2Sa 2:14 Let the young men now **a**, and play before 6965
2:14 play before us. And Joab said, Let them **a**. 6965
3:21 I will **a** and go, and will gather all Israel 6965
11:20 if so be that the king's wrath **a**, and he say 5927
13:15 And Amnon said unto her, **A**, be gone. 6965
15:14 with him at Jerusalem, **A**, and let us flee; 6965
17: 1 I will **a** and pursue after David *this* night: 6965
17:21 **A**, and pass quickly over the water: 6965
19: 7 Now therefore **a**, go forth, and 6965
22:39 and wounded them, that they could not **a**: 6965
1Ki 3:12 neither after thee shall any **a** like unto thee. 6965
14: 2 **A**, I pray thee, and disguise thyself, 6965
14:12 **A** thou therefore, get thee to thine own 6965
17: 9 **A**, get thee to Zarephath, which *belongeth* 6965
19: 5 touched him, and said unto him, **A** *and* eat. 6965
19: 7 and touched him, and said, **A** *and* eat; 6965
21: 7 **a**, *and* eat bread, and let thine heart be 6965
21:15 and was dead, that Jezebel said to Ahab, **A**, 6965
21:18 **A**, go down to meet Ahab king of Israel, 6965
2Ki 1: 3 **A**, go up to meet the messengers of 6965
8: 1 **A**, and go thou and thine household, and 6965
9: 2 **make** him **a up** from among his brethren, 6965
1Ch 22:16 **A** *therefore,* and be doing, and the LORD 6965
22:19 **a** therefore, and build ye the sanctuary of 6965
2Ch 6:41 Now therefore **a**, O LORD God, into thy 6965
Ezr 10: 4 **A**; for *this* matter *belongeth* unto thee: 6965
Ne 2:20 therefore we his servants will **a** and build: 6965
Est 1:18 Thus *shall there* **a** too much contempt and NIH
4:14 deliverance **a** to the Jews from another 5975
Job 7: 4 When shall I **a**, and the night be gone? 6965
25: 3 and upon whom doth not his light **a**? 6965
Ps 3: 7 **A**, O LORD; save me, O my God: 6965
7: 6 **A**, O LORD, in thine anger, lift up thyself 6965
9:19 **A**, O LORD; let not man prevail: let 6965
10:12 **A**, O LORD; O God, lift up thine hand: 6965
12: 5 the needy, now will I **a**, saith the LORD; 6965
17:13 **A**, O LORD, disappoint him, cast him 6965
44:23 O Lord? **a**, cast *us* not off for ever. 6974
44:26 **A** for our help, and redeem us for thy 6965
68: 1 Let God **a**, let his enemies be scattered: 6965
74:22 **A**, O God, plead thine own cause: 6965
78: 6 *who* should **a** and declare *them* to their 6965
82: 8 **A**, O God, judge the earth: for thou shalt 6965
88:10 shall the dead **a** *and* praise thee? Selah. 6965
89: 9 when the waves thereof **a**, thou stillest 5375
102:13 Thou shalt **a**, *and* have mercy upon Zion: 6965
109:28 when they **a**, let them be ashamed; but 6965
132: 8 **A**, O LORD, into thy rest; thou, and 6965
Pr 6: 9 when wilt thou **a** out of thy sleep? 6965
31:28 Her children **a up**, and call her blessed; 6965
SS 2:13 **A**, my love, my fair one, and come away. 6965
Isa 21: 5 drink: **a**, ye princes, *and* anoint the shield. 6965
23:12 **a**, pass over *to* Chittim; there also shalt 6965
26:19 *together with* my dead body shall they **a**. 6965
31: 2 will **a** against the house of the evildoers, 6965
49: 7 to a servant of rulers, Kings shall see and **a**, 6965
52: 2 the dust; **a**, *and* sit down, O Jerusalem: 6965
60: 1 **A**, shine; for thy light is come, and 6965
60: 2 the LORD shall **a** upon thee, and his glory 2224
Jer 1:17 **a**, and speak unto them all that I command 6965
2:27 their trouble they will say, **A**, and save us. 6965
2:28 let them **a**, if they can save thee in the time 6965
6: 4 war against her; **a**, and let us go up at noon. 6965
6: 5 **A**, and let us go by night, and let us destroy 6965
8: 4 the LORD; Shall they fall, and not **a**? 6965
13: 4 **a**, go to Euphrates, and hide it there in a 6965
13: 6 **A**, go to Euphrates, and take the girdle 6965
18: 2 **A**, and go down *to* the potter's house, and 6965
31: 6 **A** ye, and let us go up *to* Zion unto 6965
46:16 **A**, and let us go again to our own people, 6965
49:28 **A** ye, go up to Kedar, and spoil the men of 6965
49:31 **A**, get you up unto the wealthy nation, 6965
La 2:19 **A**, cry out in the night: in the beginning of 6965
Eze 3:22 he said unto me, **A**, go forth into the plain, 6965
Da 2:39 after thee shall **a** another kingdom inferior 6966
7: 5 said thus unto it, **A**, devour much flesh. 6966
7:17 four kings, *which* shall **a** out of the earth. 6966
7:24 of this kingdom *are* ten kings *that* shall **a**: 6966
Hos 10:14 Therefore shall a tumult **a** among thy 6965
Am 7: 2 *by* whom shall Jacob **a**? for he *is* small. 6965
7: 5 *by* whom shall Jacob **a**? for he *is* small. 6965
Ob 1: 1 **A** ye, and let us rise up against her in battle. 6965
Jnh 1: 2 **A**, go to Nineveh, *that* great city, and 6965
1: 6 **a**, call upon thy God, if so be that God will 6965
3: 2 **A**, go unto Nineveh, *that* great city, and 6965
4: 8 it came to pass, when the sun did **a**, 2224
Mic 2:10 **A** ye, and depart; for this *is* not *your* rest: 6965
4:13 **A** and thresh, O daughter of Zion: for I will 6965
6: 1 **A**, contend thou before the mountains, and 6965
7: 8 when I fall, I shall **a**; when I sit in darkness, 6965
Hab 2:19 to the dumb stone, **A**, it shall teach! 5782
Mal 4: 2 righteousness **a** with healing in his wings; 2224
Mt 2:13 **A**, and take the young child and his mother, *1453*
2:20 **A**, and take the young child and his mother, *1453*
9: 5 be forgiven thee; or to say, **A**, and walk? *1453*
9: 6 **A**, take up thy bed, and go unto thine *1453*
17: 7 and said, **A**, and be not afraid. *1453*
24:24 For there shall **a** false Christs, and *1453*
Mk 2: 9 or to say, **A**, and take up thy bed, and walk? *1453*
2:11 **A**, and take up thy bed, and go thy way into *1453*
5:41 Damsel (I say unto thee) **a**. *1453*
Lk 5:24 **A**, and take up thy couch, and go into thine *1453*
7:14 he said, Young man, I say unto thee, **A**. *1453*
8:54 by the hand, and called, saying, Maid, **a**. *1453*
15:18 I will **a** and go to my father, and will say *450*
17:19 And he said unto him, **A**, go *thy way:* thy *450*
24:38 and why do thoughts **a** in your hearts? *305*
Jn 14:31 *even* so I do. **A**, let us go hence. *1453*
Ac 8:26 **A**, and go toward the south unto the way that *450*
9: 6 **A**, and go into the city, and it shall be told *450*
9:11 **A**, and go into the street which is called *450*
9:34 **a**, and make thy bed. And he arose *450*
9:40 and turning *him* to the body said, Tabitha, **a**. *450*
10:20 **A** therefore, and get *thee* down, and go with *450*
11: 7 I heard a voice saying unto me, **A**, Peter; *450*
12: 7 and raised him up, saying, **A up** quickly. *450*
20:30 Also of your own selves shall men **a**, *450*
22:10 said unto me, **A**, and go into Damascus; *450*
22:16 **a**, and be baptized, and wash away thy sins, *450*
Eph 5:14 and **a** from the dead, and Christ shall give *450*
2Pe 1:19 day dawn, and the day star **a** in your hearts: *393*

ARISETH (11) [RISE]
1Ki 18:44 Behold, there **a** a little cloud out of the sea, 5927
Ps 104:22 The sun **a**, they gather themselves together, 2224
112: 4 Unto the upright there **a** light in 2224
Ecc 1: 5 The sun also **a**, and the sun goeth down, 2224
Isa 2:19 when he **a** to shake terribly the earth. 6965
2:21 when he **a** to shake terribly the earth. 6965
Na 3:17 *but* when the sun **a** they flee away, and 2224
Mt 13:21 or persecution **a** because of the word, *1096*
Mk 4:17 or persecution **a** for the word's sake, *1096*
Jn 7:52 and look: for out of Galilee **a** no prophet. *1453*
Heb 7:15 of Melchisedec there **a** another priest, *450*

ARISING (1) [RISE]
Est 7: 7 the king **a** from the banquet of wine in his 6965

A

ARISTARCHUS (5)
Ac 19:29 and having caught Gaius and **A**, men of *708*
20: 4 and of the Thessalonians, **A** and Secundus; *708*
27: 2 *one* **A**, a Macedonian of Thessalonica, *708*
Col 4:10 **A** my fellowprisoner saluteth you, and *708*
Phm 1:24 Marcus, **A**, Demas, Lucas, *708*

ARISTOBULUS' (1)
Ro 16:10 Salute them which are of **A** *household.* *711*

ARK (230)
Ge 6:14 Make thee an **a** of gopher wood; 8392
6:14 rooms shalt thou make *in* the **a**, and 8392
6:15 of the **a** *shall be* three hundred cubits, 8392
6:16 A window shalt thou make to the **a**, and 8392
6:16 the door of the **a** shalt thou set in the side 8392
6:18 thou shalt come into the **a**, thou, and 8392
6:19 of every *sort* shalt thou bring into the **a**, 8392
7: 1 Come thou and all thy house into the **a**; 8392
7: 7 into the **a**, because of the waters of 8392
7: 9 went in two and two unto Noah into the **a**, 8392
7:13 wives of his sons with them, into the **a**; 8392
7:15 they went in unto Noah into the **a**, two and 8392
7:17 bare up the **a**, and it was lift up above 8392
7:18 and the **a** went upon the face of the waters. 8392
7:23 and *they* that *were* with him in the **a**. 8392
8: 1 and all the cattle that *was* with him in the **a**: 8392
8: 4 the **a** rested in the seventh month, on 8392
8: 6 that Noah opened the window of the **a** 8392
8: 9 she returned unto him into the **a**, for 8392
8: 9 and pulled her in unto him into the **a**. 8392
8:10 again he sent forth the dove out of the **a**; 8392
8:13 Noah removed the covering of the **a**, and 8392
8:16 Go forth of the **a**, thou, and thy wife, and 8392
8:19 after their kinds, went forth out of the **a**. 8392
9:10 from all that go out of the **a**, to every beast 8392
9:18 that went forth of the **a**, were Shem, and 8392
Ex 2: 3 she took for him an **a** of bulrushes, and 8392
2: 5 when she saw the **a** among the flags, she 8392
25:10 they shall make an **a** of shittim wood: 727
25:14 the staves into the rings by the sides of the **a**, 727
25:14 the ark, that the **a** may be borne with them. 727
25:15 The staves shall be in the rings of the **a**: 727
25:16 thou shalt put into the **a** the Testimony 727
25:21 shalt put the mercy seat above upon the **a**; 727
25:21 in the **a** thou shalt put the Testimony that I 727
25:22 which *are* upon the **a** of the Testimony, 727
26:33 within the vail the **a** of the Testimony: 727
26:34 thou shalt put the mercy seat upon the **a** of 727
30: 6 the vail that *is* by the **a** of the Testimony, 727
30:26 and the **a** of the Testimony, 727
31: 7 the **a** of the Testimony, and the mercy seat 727
35:12 The **a**, and the staves thereof, *with* the mercy 727
37: 1 Bezaleel made the **a** *of* shittim wood: 727
37: 5 the staves into the rings by the sides of the **a**, 727
37: 5 rings by the sides of the ark, to bear the **a**. 727
39:35 The **a** of the Testimony, and the staves 727
40: 3 thou shalt put therein the **a** of the Testimony, 727
40: 3 the Testimony, and cover the **a** with the vail. 727
40: 5 the incense before the **a** of the Testimony, 727
40:20 he took and put the Testimony into the **a**, 727
40:20 set the staves on the **a**, and put the mercy 727
40:20 and put the mercy seat above upon the **a**: 727
40:21 And he brought the **a** into the tabernacle, and 727
40:21 and covered the **a** of the Testimony; 727
Lev 16: 2 before the mercy seat, which *is* upon the **a**; 727
Nu 3:31 their charge *shall be* the **a**, and the table, 727
4: 5 and cover the **a** of Testimony with it: 727
7:89 seat that *was* upon the **a** of Testimony, 727
10:33 the **a** of the covenant of the LORD went 727
10:35 when the **a** set forward, that Moses said, 727
14:44 nevertheless the **a** of the covenant of the 727
Dt 10: 1 into the mount, and make thee an **a** of wood. 727
10: 2 and thou shalt put them in the **a**. 727
10: 3 I made an **a** of shittim wood, and hewed two 727
10: 5 and put the tables in the **a** which I had made; 727
10: 8 to bear the **a** of the covenant of the LORD, 727
31: 9 which bare the **a** of the covenant of 727
31:25 which bare the **a** of the covenant of 727
31:26 put it in the side of the **a** of the covenant of 727
Jos 3: 3 When ye see the **a** of the covenant of 727
3: 6 Take up the **a** of the covenant, and pass over 727
3: 6 And they took up the **a** of the covenant, and 727
3: 8 the priests that bear the **a** of the covenant, 727
3:11 Behold, the **a** of the covenant, *even* the Lord 727
3:13 of the priests that bear the **a** of the LORD, 727
3:14 the priests bearing the **a** *of* the covenant 727
3:15 as they that bare the **a** were come unto 727
3:15 the feet of the priests that bare the **a** were 727
3:17 the priests that bare the **a** *of* the covenant of 727
4: 5 Pass over before the **a** of the LORD your 727
4: 7 before the **a** of the covenant of the LORD; 727
4: 9 which bare the **a** of the covenant stood: 727
4:10 For the priests which bare the **a** stood in 727
4:11 that the **a** of the LORD passed over, and 727
4:16 Command the priests that bear the **a** of 727
4:18 when the priests that bare the **a** of 727
6: 4 seven priests shall bear before the **a** seven 727
6: 6 Take up the **a** of the covenant, and let seven 727
6: 6 of rams' horns before the **a** of the LORD. 727
6: 7 let him that is armed pass on before the **a** of 727
6: 8 the **a** of the covenant of the LORD 727
6: 9 the rereward came after the **a**, *the priests* 727
6:11 So the **a** of the LORD compassed the city, 727
6:12 and the priests took up the **a** of the LORD. 727
6:13 the **a** of the LORD went on continually, 727
6:13 the rereward came after the **a** of the LORD, 727
7: 6 fell to the earth upon his face before the **a** of 727
8:33 stood on this side the **a** and on that side 727
8:33 which bare the **a** of the covenant of 727
Jdg 20:27 (for the **a** of the covenant of God *was* there 727
1Sa 3: 3 where the **a** of God *was*, and Samuel was 727
4: 3 Let us fetch the **a** of the covenant of 727
4: 4 that they might bring from thence the **a** of 727
1Sa 4: 4 *were* there with the **a** of the covenant of 727
4: 5 when the **a** of the covenant of the LORD 727
4: 6 they understood that the **a** of the LORD 727
4:11 the **a** of God was taken; and the two sons of 727
4:13 for his heart trembled for the **a** of God. 727
4:17 are dead, and the **a** of God is taken. 727
4:18 when he made mention of the **a** of God, 727
4:19 when she heard the tidings that the **a** of God 727
4:21 because the **a** of God was taken, and because 727
4:22 from Israel: for the **a** of God is taken. 727
5: 1 the Philistines took the **a** of God, and 727
5: 2 When the Philistines took the **a** of God, they 727
5: 3 face to the earth before the **a** of the LORD. 727
5: 4 to the ground before the **a** of the LORD; 727
5: 7 The **a** of the God of Israel shall not abide 727
5: 8 What shall we do with the **a** of the God of 727
5: 8 Let the **a** of the God of Israel be carried 727
5: 8 they carried the **a** of the God of Israel about 727
5:10 Therefore they sent the **a** of God *to* Ekron. 727
5:10 came to pass, as the **a** of God came *to* Ekron, 727
5:10 They have brought about the **a** of the God of 727
5:11 Send away the **a** of the God of Israel, and 727
6: 1 the **a** of the LORD was in the country of 727
6: 2 What shall we do to the **a** of the LORD? 727
6: 3 If ye send away the **a** of the God of Israel, 727
6: 8 take the **a** of the LORD, and lay it upon 727
6:11 they laid the **a** of the LORD upon the cart, 727
6:13 and saw the **a**, and rejoiced to see *it*. 727
6:15 the Levites took down the **a** of the LORD, 727
6:18 whereon they set down the **a** of the LORD: 727
6:19 they had looked into the **a** of the LORD, 727
6:21 The Philistines have brought again the **a** of 727
7: 1 fetched up the **a** of the LORD, and 727
7: 1 sanctified Eleazar his son to keep the **a** of 727
7: 2 to pass, while the **a** abode in Kirjath-jearim, 727
14:18 said unto Ahiah, Bring hither the **a** of God. 727
14:18 For the **a** of God was at that time with 727
2Sa 6: 2 to bring up from thence the **a** of God, 727
6: 3 they set the **a** of God upon a new cart, and 727
6: 4 *was* at Gibeah, accompanying the **a** of God: 727
6: 4 the ark of God: and Ahio went before the **a**. 727
6: 6 Uzzah put forth *his hand* to the **a** of God, 727
6: 7 *his* error; and there he died by the **a** of God. 727
6: 9 How shall the **a** of the LORD come to me? 727
6:10 So David would not remove the **a** of 727
6:11 the **a** of the LORD continued *in* the house 727
6:12 unto him, because of the **a** of God. 727
6:12 brought up the **a** of God from the house of 727
6:13 that when they that bare the **a** of the LORD 727
6:15 all the house of Israel brought up the **a** of 727
6:16 as the **a** of the LORD came *into* the city of 727
6:17 they brought in the **a** of the LORD, and 727
7: 2 but the **a** of God dwelleth within curtains. 727
11:11 The **a**, and Israel, and Judah, abide in tents; 727
15:24 bearing the **a** of the covenant of God: 727
15:24 they set down the **a** of God; and 727
15:25 Carry back the **a** of God *into* the city: 727
15:29 Abiathar carried the **a** of God again *to* 727
1Ki 2:26 thou barest the **a** of the Lord GOD before 727
3:15 stood before the **a** of the covenant of 727
6:19 to set there the **a** of the covenant of 727
8: 1 that *they* might bring up the **a** of 727
8: 3 of Israel came, and the priests took up the **a**. 727
8: 4 they brought up the **a** of the LORD, and 727
8: 5 *were* with him before the **a**, sacrificing sheep 727
8: 6 the priests brought in the **a** of the covenant 727
8: 7 forth *their* two wings over the place of the **a**, 727
8: 7 the cherubims covered the **a** and the staves 727
8: 9 *There was* nothing in the **a** save the two 727
8:21 I have set there a place for the **a**, wherein *is* 727
1Ch 6:31 of the LORD, after that the **a** had rest. 727
13: 3 let us bring again the **a** of our God to us: 727
13: 5 to bring the **a** of God from Kirjath-jearim. 727
13: 6 to bring up thence the **a** of God the LORD, 727
13: 7 they carried the **a** of God in a new cart out of 727
13: 9 Uzza put forth his hand to hold the **a**; 727
13:10 smote him, because he put his hand to the **a**: 727
13:12 How shall I bring the **a** of God *home* to me? 727
13:13 So David brought not the **a** *home* to himself 727
13:14 the **a** of God remained with the family of 727
15: 1 prepared a place for the **a** of God, and 727
15: 2 None ought to carry the **a** of God but 727
15: 2 the LORD chosen to carry the **a** of God, 727
15: 3 to bring up the **a** of the LORD unto his 727
15:12 that you may bring up the **a** of the LORD 727
15:14 bring up the **a** of the LORD God of Israel. 727
15:15 the children of the Levites bare the **a** of God 727
15:23 and Elkanah *were* doorkeepers for the **a**. 727
15:24 did blow with the trumpets before the **a** of 727
15:24 and Jehiah *were* doorkeepers for the **a**. 727
15:25 went to bring up the **a** of the covenant of 727
15:26 when God helped the Levites that bare the **a** 727
15:27 all the Levites that bare the **a**, and 727
15:28 Thus all Israel brought up the **a** of 727
15:29 *as* the **a** of the covenant of the LORD came 727
16: 1 So they brought the **a** of God, and set it in 727
16: 4 to minister before the **a** of the LORD, 727
16: 6 before the **a** of the covenant of God. 727
16:37 So he left there before the **a** of the covenant 727
16:37 to minister before the **a** continually, 727
17: 1 the **a** of the covenant of the LORD 727
22:19 to bring the **a** of the covenant of the LORD, 727
28: 2 rest for the **a** of the covenant of the LORD, 727
28:18 covered the **a** of the covenant of the LORD. 727
2Ch 1: 4 the **a** of God had David brought up from 727
5: 2 to bring up the **a** of the covenant of 727
5: 4 of Israel came; and the Levites took up the **a**. 727
5: 5 they brought up the **a**, and the tabernacle of 727
5: 6 that were assembled unto him before the **a**, 727
5: 7 the priests brought in the **a** of the covenant 727
5: 8 forth *their* wings over the place of the **a**, 727
5: 8 the cherubims covered the **a** and the staves 727
5: 9 they drew out the staves *of the* **a**, that NIH
5: 9 were seen from the **a** before the oracle; 727
5:10 *There was* nothing in the **a** save the two 727
2Ch 6:11 in it have I put the **a**, wherein *is* the covenant 727
6:41 resting place, thou, and the **a** of thy strength: 727
8:11 whereunto the **a** of the LORD hath come. 727
35: 3 Put the holy **a** in the house which Solomon 727
Ps 132: 8 into thy rest; thou, and the **a** of thy strength. 727
Jer 3:16 The **a** of the covenant of the LORD: 727
Mt 24:38 until the day that Noe entered into the **a**, *2787*
Lk 17:27 until the day that Noe entered into the **a**, *2787*
Heb 9: 4 the **a** of the covenant overlaid round about *2787*
11: 7 prepared an **a** to the saving of his house; *2787*
1Pe 3:20 while the **a** was a preparing, wherein few, *2787*
Rev 11:19 there was seen in his temple the **a** of his *2787*

ARKITE (2)
Ge 10:17 And the Hivite, and the **A**, and the Sinite, 6208
1Ch 1:15 And the Hivite, and the **A**, and the Sinite, 6208

ARKITES See ARCHI; ARCHITE

ARM (67) [ARMED, ARMHOLES, ARMIES, ARMOUR, ARMOURBEARER, ARMOURY, ARMS, ARMY]
Ex 6: 6 I will redeem you with a stretched out **a**, 2220
15:16 by the greatness of thine **a** they shall be *as* 2220
Nu 31: 3 **A** some of yourselves unto the war, and 2502
Dt 4:34 by a stretched out **a**, and by great terrors, 2220
5:15 a mighty hand and by a stretched out **a**: 2220
7:19 the mighty hand, and the stretched out **a**, 2220
9:29 mighty power and by thy stretched out **a**. 2220
11: 2 his mighty hand, and his stretched out **a**, 2220
26: 8 with an outstretched **a**, and with great 2220
33:20 teareth the **a** with the crown of the head. 2220
1Sa 2:31 that I will cut off thine **a**, and the arm of 2220
2:31 thine arm, and the **a** of thy father's house, 2220
2Sa 1:10 the bracelet that *was* on his **a**, and 2220
1Ki 8:42 thy strong hand, and of thy stretched out **a**;) 2220
2Ki 17:36 with great power and a stretched out **a**, 2220
2Ch 6:32 thy mighty hand, and thy stretched out **a**; 2220
32: 8 With him *is* an **a** of flesh; but with us *is* 2220
Job 26: 2 *how* savest thou the **a** *that hath* no strength? 2220
31:22 *Then* let mine **a** fall from *my* shoulder 3802
31:22 and mine **a** be broken from the bone. 248
35: 9 they cry out by reason of the **a** of 2220
38:15 and the high **a** shall be broken. 2220
40: 9 Hast thou an **a** like God? or, canst thou 2220
Ps 10:15 Break thou the **a** of the wicked and the evil 2220
44: 3 neither did their own **a** save them: 2220
44: 3 thine **a**, and the light of thy countenance, 2220
77:15 Thou hast with *thine* **a** redeemed thy 2220
89:10 scattered thine enemies with thy strong **a**. 2220
89:13 Thou hast a mighty **a**: strong is thy hand, 2220
89:21 mine **a** also shall strengthen him. 2220
98: 1 and his holy **a**, hath gotten him the victory. 2220
136:12 a strong hand, and with a stretched out **a**: 2220
SS 8: 6 upon thine heart, as a seal upon thine **a**: 2220
Isa 9:20 shall eat every man the flesh of his own **a**: 2220
17: 5 the corn, and reapeth the ears *with* his **a**; 2220
30:30 shall shew the lighting down of his **a**, 2220
33: 2 be thou their **a** every morning, 2220
40:10 strong *hand*, and his **a** *shall* rule for him: 2220
40:11 he shall gather the lambs with his **a**, and 2220
48:14 and his **a** *shall be on* the Chaldeans. 2220
51: 5 upon me, and on mine **a** shall they trust. 2220
51: 9 awake, put on strength, O **a** of the LORD; 2220
52:10 The LORD hath made bare his holy **a** in 2220
53: 1 to whom is the **a** of the LORD revealed? 2220
59:16 therefore his **a** brought salvation unto him; 2220
62: 8 his right hand, and by the **a** of his strength, 2220
63: 5 mine own **a** brought salvation unto me; 2220
63:12 the right hand of Moses *with* his glorious **a**, 2220
Jer 17: 5 maketh flesh his **a**, and whose heart 2220
21: 5 an outstretched hand and with a strong **a**, 2220
27: 5 my great power and by my outstretched **a**, 2220
32:17 by thy great power and stretched out **a**, 2220
32:21 with a stretched out **a**, and with great terror; 248
48:25 and his **a** is broken, saith the LORD. 2220
Eze 4: 7 thine **a** *shall be* uncovered, and thou shalt 2220
20:33 with a stretched out **a**, and with fury poured 2220
20:34 with a stretched out **a**, and with fury poured 2220
30:21 I have broken the **a** of Pharaoh king of 2220
31:17 *they that were* his **a**, *that* dwelt under his 2220
Da 11: 6 she shall not retain the power of the **a**; 2220
11: 6 of the arm; neither shall he stand, nor his **a**: 2220
Zec 11:17 the sword *shall be* upon his **a**, and upon his 2220
11:17 his **a** shall be clean dried up, and his right 2220
Lk 1:51 He hath shewed strength with his **a**; he hath *1023*
Jn 12:38 to whom hath the **a** of the Lord been *1023*
Ac 13:17 and with a high **a** brought he them out of it. *1023*
1Pe 4: 1 **a** yourselves likewise with the same mind: *3695*

ARMAGEDDON (1)
Rev 16:16 into a place called in the Hebrew tongue **A**. *717*

ARMED (30) [ARM]
Ge 14:14 he **a** his trained *servants*, born in his own 7324
Nu 31: 5 of *every* tribe, twelve thousand **a** for war. 2502
32:17 we ourselves will **go** ready **a** before 2502
32:20 if ye will **go a** before the LORD to war, 2502
32:21 will go all of you **a** over Jordan before 2502
32:27 every man **a** for war, before the LORD to 2502
32:29 every man **a** to battle, before the LORD, 2502
32:30 if they will not pass over with you **a**, 2502
32:32 We will pass over **a** before the LORD *into* 2502
Dt 3:18 ye shall pass over **a** before your brethren 2502
Jos 1:14 ye shall pass before your brethren **a**, all 2571
4:12 passed over **a** before the children of Israel, 2571
6: 7 let him that is **a** pass on before the ark of 2502
6: 9 the **a** men went before the priests that blew 2502
6:13 the **a** men went before them; but 2502
Jdg 7:11 outside of the **a** *men* that *were* in the host. 2571
1Sa 17: 5 his head, and he *was* **a** with a coat of mail; 3847
17:38 Saul **a** David with his armour, and he put a 3847
17:38 his head; also he **a** him with a coat *of mail*. 3847
1Ch 12: 2 *They were* **a** with bows, and could use both 5401

1Ch 12:23 of the bands that were ready a to the war, 2502
12:24 and eight hundred, ready a to the war. 2502
2Ch 17:17 with him a men with bow and shield two 5401
28:14 So the a men left the captives and the spoil 2502
Job 39:21 He goeth on to meet the a men. 5402
Ps 78: 9 of Ephraim, being a, and carrying bows, 5401
Pr 6:11 that travelleth, and thy want as an a man. 4043
24:34 that travelleth; and thy want as an a man. 4043
Isa 15: 4 the a soldiers of Moab shall cry out; 2502
Lk 11:21 When a strong man a keepeth his palace, 2528

ARMENIA (2)

2Ki 19:37 they escaped into the land of A. 780
Isa 37:38 and they escaped into the land of A: 780

ARMHOLES (2) [ARM, HOLE]

Jer 38:12 rags under thine a under the cords. 679+3027
Eze 13:18 to the women that sew pillows to all a, 679+3027

ARMIES (43) [ARM]

Ex 6:26 from the land of Egypt according to their a. 6635
7: 4 bring forth mine a, and my people 6635
12:17 I brought your a out of the land of Egypt: 6635
12:51 of Israel out of the land of Egypt by their a. 6635
Nu 1: 3 and Aaron shall number them by their a. 6635
2: 3 the camp of Judah pitch throughout their a: 6635
2: 9 and four hundred, throughout their a. 6635
2:10 of the camp of Reuben according to their a: 6635
2:16 four hundred and fifty, throughout their a. 6635
2:18 the camp of Ephraim according to their a: 6635
2:24 and an hundred, throughout their a. 6635
2:25 of Dan shall be on the north side by their a: 6635
10:14 the children of Judah according to their a: 6635
10:18 of Reuben set forward according to their a: 6635
10:22 Ephraim set forward according to their a: 6635
10:28 the children of Israel according to their a, 6635
33: 1 Egypt with their a under the hand of Moses 6635
Dt 20: 9 that they shall make captains of the a to 6635
1Sa 17: 1 gathered together their a to battle, 4264
17: 8 he stood and cried unto the a of Israel, and 4634
17:10 I defy the a of Israel this day; 4634
17:23 out of the a of the Philistines, and 4634
17:26 that he should defy the a of the living God? 4634
17:36 seeing he hath defied the a of the living 4634
17:45 the God of the a of Israel, whom thou hast 4634
23: 3 if we come to Keilah against the a of 4634
28: 1 that the Philistines gathered their a together 4264
29: 1 gathered together all their a to Aphek: 4264
2Ki 25:23 when all the captains of the a, they and 2428
25:26 and great, and the captains of the a, 2428
1Ch 11:26 Also the valiant men of the a were, Asahel 2428
2Ch 16: 4 sent the captains of his a against the cities 2428
Job 25: 3 Is there any number of his a? and 1416
Ps 44: 9 us to shame; and goest not forth with our a. 6635
60:10 O God, which didst not go out with our a? 6635
68:12 Kings of a did flee apace: and she that 6635
SS 6:13 As it were the company of two a. 4264
Isa 34: 2 all nations, and his fury upon all their a: 6635
Mt 22: 7 and he sent forth his a, and destroyed those 4753
Lk 21:20 ye shall see Jerusalem compassed with a, 4760
Heb 11:34 in fight, turned to flight the a of the aliens. 3925
Rev 19:14 And the a which were in heaven followed 4753
19:19 and the kings of the earth, and their a, 4753

ARMONI (1)

2Sa 21: 8 she bare unto Saul, A and Mephibosheth; 764

ARMOUR (24) [ARM]

1Sa 14: 1 said unto the young man that bare his a, 3627
14: 6 said to the young man that bare his a, 3627
17:38 Saul armed David with his a, and he put a 4055
17:39 David girded his sword upon his a, and 4055
17:54 it to Jerusalem; but he put his a in his tent. 3627
31: 9 stripped off his a, and sent into the land of 3627
31:10 they put his a in the house of Ashtaroth: 3627
2Sa 2:21 one of the young men, and take thee his a. 2488
18:15 ten young men that bare Joab's a 3627
1Ki 10:25 and a, and spices, horses, and mules, 5402
22:38 licked up his blood; and they washed his a; 2185
2Ki 3:21 all that were able to put on a, 2290+2296
10: 2 and horses, a fenced city also, and a; 5402
20:13 all the house of his a, and all that was 3627
1Ch 10: 9 his a, and sent into the land of 3627
10:10 they put his a in the house of their gods, 3627
Isa 22: 8 thou didst look in that day to the a of 5402
39: 2 all the house of his a, and all that was 3627
Eze 38: 4 all of them clothed with all sorts of a, even NIH
Lk 11:22 he taketh from him all his a wherein he 3833
Ro 13:12 of darkness, and let us put on the a of light. 3696
2Co 6: 7 by the a of righteousness on the right hand 3696
Eph 6:11 Put on the whole a of God, that ye may be 3833
6:13 Wherefore take unto you the whole a of 3833

ARMOURBEARER (18) [ARM, BEAR]

Jdg 9:54 hastily unto the young man his a, 3627+5375
1Sa 14: 7 his a said unto him, Do all that is in 3627+5375
14:12 answered Jonathan and his a, 3627+5375
14:12 Jonathan said unto his a, Come up 3627+5375
14:13 upon his feet, and his a after him: 3627+5375
14:13 and his a slew after him 3627+5375
14:14 which Jonathan and his a made, was 3627+5375
14:17 and his a were not there. 3627+5375
16:21 him greatly; and he became his a. 3627+5375
31: 4 said Saul unto his a, Draw thy 3627+5375
31: 4 his a would not; for he was sore 3627+5375
31: 5 when his a saw that Saul was dead, 3627+5375
31: 6 three sons, and his a, and all his men, 3627+5375
2Sa 23:37 a to Joab the son of Zeruiah, 3627+5375
1Ch 10: 4 said Saul to his a, Draw thy sword, 3627+5375
10: 4 his a would not; for he was sore 3627+5375
10: 5 when his a saw that Saul was dead, 3627+5375
11:39 the a of Joab the son of Zeruiah, 3627+5375

ARMOURY (3) [ARM]

Ne 3:19 going up to the a at the turning of the wall. 5402
SS 4: 4 is like the tower of David builded for an a, 8530
Jer 50:25 The LORD hath opened his a, and 214

ARMS (29) [ARM]

Ge 49:24 the a of his hands were made strong by 2220
Dt 33:27 and underneath are the everlasting a: 2220
Jdg 15:14 the cords that were upon his a became as 2220
16:12 he brake them from off his a like a thread. 2220
2Sa 22:35 so that a bow of steel is broken by mine a. 2220
2Ki 9:24 smote Jehoram between his a, and 2220
Job 22: 9 the a of the fatherless have been broken. 2220
Ps 18:34 so that a bow of steel is broken by mine a. 2220
37:17 For the a of the wicked shall be broken: but 2220
Pr 31:17 loins with strength, and strengtheneth her a. 2220
Isa 44:12 and worketh it with the strength of his a: 2220
49:22 they shall bring thy sons in their a, and 2684
51: 5 and mine a shall judge the people; 2220
Eze 13:20 I will tear them from your a, and will let 2220
30:22 will break his a, the strong, and that which 2220
30:24 I will strengthen the a of the king of 2220
30:24 I will break Pharaoh's a, and he shall 2220
30:25 I will strengthen the a of the king of 2220
30:25 and the a of Pharaoh shall fall down; 2220
Da 2:32 his breast and his a of silver, his belly and 1872
10: 6 his a and his feet like in colour to polished 2220
11:15 the a of the south shall not withstand, 2220
11:22 with the a of a flood shall they be 2220
11:31 a shall stand on his part, and they shall 2220
Hos 7:15 I have bound and strengthened their a, 2220
11: 3 Ephraim also to go, taking them by their a; 2220
Mk 9:36 And when he had taken him in his a, 1723
10:16 And he took them up in his a, put his 1723
Lk 2:28 Then took he him up in his a, and 43

ARMY (82) [ARM]

Ge 26:26 and Phichol the chief captain of his a. 6635
Ex 14: 9 of Pharaoh, and his horsemen, and his a) 2428
Dt 11: 4 what he did unto the a of Egypt, unto their 2428
Jdg 4: 7 the captain of Jabin's a, with his chariots 6635
8: 6 that we should give bread unto thine a? 6635
9:29 Increase thine a, and come out. 6635
1Sa 4: 2 they slew of the a in the field about four 4634
4:12 there ran a man of Benjamin out of the a, 4634
4:16 I am he that came out of the a, and I fled to 4634
4:16 of the army, and I fled to day out of the a. 4634
17:21 had put the battle in array, a against army. 4634
17:21 had put the battle in array, army against a. 4634
17:22 ran into the a, and came and saluted his 4634
17:48 and ran toward the a to meet the Philistine. 4634
1Ki 20:19 of the city, and the a which followed them. 2428
20:25 number thee an a, like the army that thou 2428
20:25 like the a that thou hast lost, horse for 2428
2Ki 25: 5 the a of the Chaldees pursued after 2428
25: 5 and all his a were scattered from him. 2428
25:10 all the a of the Chaldees, that were with 2428
1Ch 20: 1 to battle, Joab led forth the power of the a, 6635
27:34 and the general of the king's a was Joab. 6635
2Ch 13: 3 Abijah set the battle in array with an a of 2428
14: 8 Asa had an a of men that bare targets and 2428
20:21 as they went out before the a, and to say, 2502
24:24 For the a of the Syrians came with a small 2428
25: 7 O king, let not the a of Israel go with thee; 6635
25: 9 which I have given to the a of Israel? 1416
25:10 the a that was come to him out of Ephraim, 1416
25:13 the soldiers of the a which Amaziah sent 1416
26:13 under their hand was an a, three 2428+6635
Ne 2: 9 Now the king had sent captains of the a and 2428
4: 2 before his brethren and the a of Samaria, 2428
Job 29:25 and sat chief, and dwelt as a king in the a, 1416
SS 6: 4 as Jerusalem, terrible as an a with banners. NIH
6:10 the sun, and terrible as an a with banners? NIH
Isa 36: 2 unto king Hezekiah with a great a. 2426
43:17 the chariot and horse, the a and the power; 2428
Jer 32: 2 the king of Babylon's a besieged 2428
34: 1 all his a, and all the kingdoms of the earth 2428
34: 7 When the king of Babylon's a fought 2428
34:21 into the hand of the king of Babylon's a, 2428
35:11 let us go to Jerusalem for fear of the a of 2428
35:11 and for fear of the a of the Syrians: 2428
37: 5 Pharaoh's a was come forth out of Egypt: 2428
37: 7 Behold, Pharaoh's a, which is come forth 2428
37:10 For though ye had smitten the whole a of 2428
37:11 that when the a of the Chaldeans was 2428
37:11 up from Jerusalem for fear of Pharaoh's a, 2428
38: 3 into the hand of the king of Babylon's a, 2428
39: 1 of Babylon and all his a against Jerusalem, 2428
39: 5 the Chaldeans' a pursued after them, and 2428
46: 2 against the a of Pharaoh-necho king of 2428
46:22 for they shall march with an a, and 2428
52: 4 he and all his a, against Jerusalem, and 2428
52: 8 the a of the Chaldeans pursued after 2428
52: 8 and all his a was scattered from him. 2428
52:14 all the a of the Chaldeans, that were with 2428
Eze 17:17 Neither shall Pharaoh with his mighty a 2428
27:10 and of Lud and of Phut were in thine a, 2428
27:11 The men of Arvad with thine a were upon 2428
29:18 his a to serve a great service against Tyrus: 2428
29:18 yet had he no wages, nor his a, for Tyrus, 2428
29:19 her prey; and it shall be the wages for his a. 2428
32:31 and all his a slain by the sword, 2428
37:10 up upon their feet, an exceeding great a. 2428
38: 4 and all thine a, horses and horsemen, 2428
38:15 a great company, and a mighty a: 2428
Da 3:20 men that were in his a to bind Shadrach, 2429
4:35 he doeth according to his will in the a of 2429
11: 7 which shall come with an a, and shall enter 2428
11:13 come after certain years with a great a 2428
11:25 against the king of the south with a great a; 2428
11:25 up to battle with a very great and mighty a; 2428
11:26 shall destroy him, and his a shall overflow: 2428
Joel 2:11 LORD shall utter his voice before his a: 2428
2:20 will remove far off from you the northern a, NIH
Joel 2:25 my great a which I sent among you. 2428
Zec 9: 8 encamp about mine house because of the a, 4675
Ac 23:27 then came I with an a, and rescued him, 4753
Rev 9:16 And the number of the a of the horsemen 4753
19:19 him that sat on the horse, and against his a. 4753

ARNAN (1)

1Ch 3:21 the sons of A, the sons of Obadiah, 770

ARNON (25)

Nu 21:13 and pitched on the other side of A, 769
21:13 for A is the border of Moab, between Moab 769
21:14 he did in the Red sea, and in the brooks of A, 769
21:24 and possessed his land from A unto Jabbok, 769
21:26 all his land out of his hand, even unto A. 769
21:28 and the lords of the high places of A. 769
22:36 which is in the border of A, which is in 769
Dt 2:24 take your journey, and pass over the river A: 769
2:36 which is by the brink of the river of A, and 769
3: 8 from the river of A unto mount Hermon; 769
3:12 which is by the river A, and half mount 769
3:16 I gave from Gilead even unto the river A, 769
4:48 which is by the bank of the river A, 769
Jos 12: 1 from the river A unto mount Hermon, and 769
12: 2 which is upon the bank of the river of A, and 769
13: 9 that is upon the bank of the river A, and 769
13:16 that is on the bank of the river A, and 769
Jdg 11:13 from A even unto Jabbok, and unto Jordan: 769
11:18 pitched on the other side of A, but came not 769
11:18 of Moab: for A was the border of Moab. 769
11:22 from A even unto Jabbok, and from 769
11:26 all the cities that be along by the coasts of A, 769
2Ki 10:33 from Aroer, which is by the river A, 769
Isa 16: 2 daughters of Moab shall be at the fords of A. 769
Jer 48:20 and cry; tell ye it in A, that Moab is spoiled, 769

AROD (1)

Nu 26:17 Of A, the family of the Arodites: of Areli, 720

ARODI (1) [ARODITES]

Ge 46:16 Shuni, and Ezbon, Eri, and A, and Areli. 722

ARODITES (1) [ARODI]

Nu 26:17 Of Arod, the family of the A: of Areli, 722

AROER (16) [AROERITE]

Nu 32:34 of Gad built Dibon, and Ataroth, and A, 6177
Dt 2:36 From A, which is by the brink of the river 6177
3:12 from A, which is by the river Arnon, and 6177
4:48 From A, which is by the bank of the river 6177
Jos 12: 2 who dwelt in Heshbon, and ruled from A, 6177
13: 9 From A, that is upon the bank of the river 6177
13:16 their coast was from A, that is on the bank 6177
13:25 of Ammon, unto A that is before Rabbah; 6177
Jdg 11:26 in A and her towns, and in all the cities that 6177
11:33 he smote them from A, even till thou come 6177
1Sa 30:28 to them which were in A, and to them 6177
2Sa 24: 5 they passed over Jordan, and pitched in A, 6177
2Ki 10:33 and the Manassites, from A, 6177
1Ch 5: 8 the son of Joel, who dwelt in A, even unto 6177
Isa 17: 2 The cities of A are forsaken: they shall be 6177
Jer 48:19 O inhabitant of A, stand by the way and 6177

AROERITE (1) [AROER]

1Ch 11:44 Shama and Jehiel the sons of Hothan the A, 6200

AROMA See ODOUR; SAVOUR

AROSE (168) [RISE]

Ge 19:15 when the morning a, then the angels 5927
19:33 not when she lay down, nor when she a. 6965
19:35 the younger a, and lay with him; and 6965
19:35 not when she lay down, nor when she a. 6965
24:10 he a, and went to Mesopotamia, unto 6965
24:61 Rebekah a, and her damsels, and they rode 6965
37: 7 and lo, my sheaf a, and also stood upright; 6965
38:19 she a, and went away, and laid by her vail 6965
Ex 1: 8 Now there a up a new king over Egypt, 6965
Dt 34:10 there a not a prophet since in Israel like 6965
Jos 8: 3 So Joshua a, and all the people of war, 6965
8:19 the ambush a quickly out of their place, 6965
18: 8 the men a, and went away: and 6965
24: 9 a and warred against Israel, and sent and 6965
Jdg 2:10 there a another generation after them, 6965
3:20 God unto thee. And he a out of his seat. 6965
4: 9 Deborah a, and went with Barak to Kedesh. 6965
5: 7 they ceased in Israel, until that I Deborah a, 6965
5: 7 I Deborah arose, that I a a mother in Israel. 6965
6:28 when the men of the city a early in 7925
8:21 Gideon a, and slew Zebah and Zalmunna, 6965
10: 1 after Abimelech there a to defend Israel 6965
10: 3 after him a Jair, a Gileadite, and 6965
13:11 Manoah a, and went after his wife, and 6965
16: 3 a at midnight, and took the doors of 6965
19: 3 her husband a, and went after her, to speak 6965
19: 5 when they a early in the morning, that he 7925
19: 8 he a early in the morning on the fifth day 7925
20: 8 all the people a as one man, saying, 6965
20:18 the children of Israel a, and went up to 6965
Ru 1: 6 she a with her daughters in law, that she 6965
1Sa 3: 6 Samuel a and went to Eli, and said, 6965
3: 8 he a and went to Eli, and said, Here am I; 6965
5: 3 when they of Ashdod a early on 7925
5: 4 when they a early on the morrow morning, 7925
9:26 they a early: and it came to pass about 7925
9:26 Saul a, and they went out both of them, 6965
13:15 Samuel a, and gat him up from Gilgal unto 6965
17:35 when he a against me, I caught him by his 6965
17:48 when the Philistine a, and came and 6965
17:52 the men of Israel and of Judah a, and 6965
18:27 Wherefore David a and went, he and 6965
20:25 Jonathan a, and Abner sat by Saul's side, 6965
20:34 So Jonathan a from the table in fierce 6965
20:41 David a out of a place toward the south, 6965

1Sa 20:42 he **a** and departed: and Jonathan went *into* 6965
21:10 David **a**, and fled that day for fear of Saul, 6965
23:13 **a** and departed out of Keilah, and 6965
23:16 Jonathan Saul's son **a**, and went to David 6965
23:24 they **a**, and went to Ziph before Saul: but 6965
24: 4 David **a**, and cut off the skirt of Saul's robe 6965
25: 1 David **a**, and went down to the wilderness 6965
25:41 she **a**, and bowed herself *on her* face to 6965
26: 2 Saul **a**, and went down to the wilderness of 6965
26: 5 David **a**, and came to the place where Saul 6965
27: 2 David **a**, and he passed over with the six 6965
28:23 So he **a** from the earth, and sat upon 6965
28:25 Then they **a up**, and went away that night. 6965
31:12 All the valiant men **a**, and went all night, 6965
2Sa 2:15 there **a** and went over by number twelve of 6965
6: 2 David **a**, and went with all the people that 6965
11: 2 that David **a** from off his bed, and 6965
12:17 the elders of his house **a**, *and went* to him, 6965
12:20 David **a** from the earth, and washed, and 6965
13:29 all the king's sons **a**, and every man gat 6965
13:31 the king **a**, and tare his garments, and 6965
14:23 So Joab **a** and went to Geshur, and 6965
14:31 Joab **a**, and came to Absalom unto *his* 6965
15: 9 Go in peace. So he **a**, and went to Hebron. 6965
17:22 David **a**, and all the people that *were* with 6965
17:23 **a**, and gat him *home* to his house, to his 6965
23:10 He **a**, and smote the Philistines until his 6965
1Ki 1:50 **a**, and went, and caught hold on the horns 6965
2:40 Shimei **a**, and saddled his ass, and went to 6965
8:54 he **a** from before the altar of the LORD, 6965
11:18 they **a** out of Midian, and came *to* Paran: 6965
11:40 Jeroboam **a**, and fled *into* Egypt, 6965
14: 4 **a**, and went *to* Shiloh, and came *to* 6965
14:17 Jeroboam's wife **a**, and departed, and 6965
17:10 So he **a** and went to Zarephath. And when 6965
19: 3 when he saw *that*, he **a**, and went for his 6965
19: 8 he **a**, and did eat and drink, and went in 6965
19:21 he **a**, and went after Elijah, and 6965
2Ki 1:15 he **a**, and went down with him unto 6965
4:30 not leave thee. And he **a**, and followed her. 6965
7: 7 Wherefore they **a** and fled in the twilight, 6965
7:12 the king **a** in the night, and said unto his 6965
8: 2 the woman **a**, and did after the saying of 6965
9: 6 he **a**, and went into the house; and 6965
10:12 he **a** and departed, and came *to* Samaria. 6965
11: 1 she **a** and destroyed all the seed royal. 6965
12:20 his servants **a**, and made a conspiracy, 6965
19:35 when they **a early** in the morning, behold, 7925
23:25 neither after him **a** there *any* like him. 6965
25:26 of the armies, **a**, and came *to* Egypt: 6965
1Ch 10:12 They **a**, all the valiant men, and took away 6965
20: 4 that there **a** war at Gezer with 5975
2Ch 22:10 she **a** and destroyed all the seed royal of 6965
29:12 the Levites **a**, Mahath the son of Amasai, 6965
30:14 they **a** and took away the altars that *were* in 6965
30:27 the priests the Levites **a** and blessed 6965
36:16 until the wrath of the LORD **a** against his 5927
Ezr 9: 5 at the evening sacrifice I **a up** from my 6965
10: 5 **a** Ezra, and made the chief priests, 6965
Ne 2:12 I **a** in the night, I and *some* few men with 6965
Est 8: 4 So Esther **a**, and stood before the king, 6965
Job 1:20 Job **a**, and rent his mantle, and shaved his 6965
19:18 I **a**, and they spake against me. 6965
29: 8 and the aged **a**, *and* stood *up*. 6965
Ps 76: 9 When God **a** to judgment, to save all 6965
Ecc 1: 5 and hasteth to his place where he **a**. 2224
Isa 37:36 when they **a early** in the morning, behold, 7925
Jer 41: 2 **a** Ishmael the son of Nethaniah, and the ten 6965
Eze 3:23 I **a**, and went forth into the plain: and 6965
Da 6:19 the king **a** very early in the morning, and 6966
Jnh 3: 3 So Jonah **a**, and went unto Nineveh, 6965
3: 6 he **a** from his throne, and he laid his robe 6965
Mt 2:14 When he **a**, he took the young child and 1453
2:21 And he **a**, and took the young child and 1453
8:15 and she **a**, and ministered unto them. 1453
8:24 there **a** a great tempest in the sea, 1096
8:26 Then he **a**, and rebuked the winds and 1453
9: 7 And he **a**, and departed to his house. 1453
9: 9 Follow me. And he **a**, and followed him. 450
9:19 And Jesus **a**, and followed him, and *so* 1453
9:25 and took her by the hand, and the maid **a**. 1453
25: 7 Then all those virgins **a**, and trimmed their 1453
26:62 And the high priest **a**, and said unto him, 450
27:52 and many bodies of saints which slept **a**, 1453
Mk 2:12 And immediately he **a**, took up the bed, and 1453
2:14 Follow me. And he **a** and followed him. 450
4:37 And there **a** a great storm of wind, and 1096
4:39 And he **a**, and rebuked the wind, and 1326
5:42 And straightway the damsel **a**, and walked; 450
7:24 And from thence he **a**, and went into 450
9:27 him by the hand, and lifted him up; and he **a**. 450
14:57 And there **a** certain, and bare false witness 450
Lk 1:39 And Mary **a** in those days, and went into 450
4:38 And he **a** out of the synagogue, and 450
4:39 and immediately she **a** and ministered unto 450
6: 8 *forth* in the midst. And he **a** and stood *forth*. 450
6:48 and when the flood **a**, the stream beat 1096
8:55 her spirit came again, and she **a** straightway: 450
9:46 Then there **a** a reasoning among them, 1525
15:14 there **a** a mighty famine in that land; 1096
15:20 And he **a**, and came to his father. But when 450
23: 1 And the whole multitude of them **a**, and 450
24:12 Then **a** Peter, and ran unto the sepulchre; 450
Jn 3:25 Then there **a** a question between *some* of 1096
6:18 And the sea **a** by reason of a great wind 1326
11:29 As soon as she heard *that*, she **a** quickly, 1453
Ac 5: 6 And the young men **a**, wound him up, and 450
6: 1 there **a** a murmuring of the Grecians 1096
6: 9 Then there **a** certain of the synagogue, 450
7:18 Till another king **a**, which knew not Joseph. 450
8:27 And he **a** and went: and behold, a man of 450
9: 8 And Saul **a** from the earth; and when his 1453
9:18 sight forthwith, and **a**, and was baptized, 450
9:34 and make thy bed. And he **a** immediately. 450
9:39 Then Peter **a** and went with them. When he 450

Ac 11:19 **a** about Stephen travelled as far as Phenice, 1096
19:23 And the same time there **a** no small stir 1096
23: 7 there **a** a dissension between the Pharisees 1096
23: 9 And there **a** a great cry: and the scribes *that* 1096
23: 9 the scribes *that were* of the Pharisees' part **a**, 450
23:10 And when there **a** a great dissension, 1096
27:14 But not long after there **a** against it a 906
Rev 9: 2 and there **a** a smoke out of the pit, as 305

ARPAD (4) [ARPHAD]

2Ki 18:34 Where *are* the gods of Hamath, and of **A**? 774
19:13 the king of **A**, and the king of the city of 774
Isa 10: 9 *is* not Hamath as **A**? *is* not Samaria as 774
Jer 49:23 Hamath is confounded, and **A**: for they have 774

ARPHAD (2) [ARPAD]

Isa 36:19 Where *are* the gods of Hamath and **A**? 774
37:13 the king of **A**, and the king of the city of 774

ARPHAXAD (10)

Ge 10:22 and Asshur, and **A**, and Lud, and Aram. 775
10:24 And **A** begat Salah; and Salah begat Eber. 775
11:10 and begat **A** two years after the flood: 775
11:11 Shem lived after he begat **A** five hundred 775
11:12 **A** lived five and thirty years, and 775
11:13 **A** lived after he begat Salah four hundred 775
1Ch 1:17 and **A**, and Lud, and Aram, and Uz, and Hul, 775
1:18 And **A** begat Shelah, and Shelah begat Eber. 775
1:24 Shem, **A**, Shelah, 775
Lk 3:36 which was *the son* of **A**, which was *the son* 742

ARRAY (34) [ARRAYED]

Jdg 20:20 the men of Israel **put** *themselves* **in a** to 6186
20:22 **set** *their* battle again **in a** in the place where 6186
20:22 they **put** *themselves* **in a** the first day. 6186
20:30 **put** *themselves* **in a** against Gibeah, as at 6186
20:33 and **put** *themselves* **in a** at Baal-tamar: 6186
1Sa 4: 2 the Philistines **put** *themselves* **in a** against 6186
17: 2 **set** the battle **in a** against the Philistines. 6186
17: 8 are ye come out to **set** *your* battle **in a**? 6186
17:21 and the Philistines had **put** *the battle* **in a**, 6186
2Sa 10: 8 **put** the battle **in a** *at* the entering in of 6186
10: 9 and **put** *them* **in a** against the Syrians: 6186
10:10 that he might **put** *them* **in a** against 6186
10:17 the Syrians **set** *themselves* **in a** against 6186
1Ki 20:12 Set *yourselves in* **a**. And they set NIH
20:12 they set *themselves in* **a** against the city. NIH
1Ch 19: 9 **put** the battle **in a** *before* the gate of 6186
19:10 and **put** *them* **in a** against the Syrians. 6186
19:11 they **set** *themselves* **in a** against 6186
19:17 and **set** *the battle* **in a** against them. 6186
19:17 So when David had **put** the battle **in a** 6186
2Ch 13: 3 Abijah **set** the battle **in a** with an army of 631
13: 3 Jeroboam also **set** the battle **in a** against 6186
14:10 they **set** the battle **in a** in the valley of 6186
Est 6: 9 that they may **a** the man *withal* whom 3847
Job 6: 4 the terrors of God do **set** *themselves* **in a** 6186
40:10 and **a** thyself with glory and beauty. 3847
Isa 22: 7 the horsemen shall **set** themselves **in a** at 7896
Jer 6:23 **set in a** as men for war against thee, 6186
43:12 he shall **a** himself **with** the land of Egypt, 5844
50: 9 they shall **set** *themselves* **in a** against her; 6186
50:14 **Put** *yourselves* **in a** against Babylon round 6186
50:42 *every one* **put in a**, like a man to the battle, 6186
Joel 2: 5 as a strong people **set in** battle **a**. 6186
1Ti 2: 9 broided hair, or gold, or pearls, or costly **a**; 2441

ARRAYED (11) [ARRAY]

Ge 41:42 **a** him in vestures of fine linen, and put a 3847
2Ch 5:12 and their brethren, *being* **a** in white linen, 3847
28:15 **a** them, and shod them, and gave them to 3847
Est 6:11 **a** Mordecai, and brought him on horseback 3847
Mt 6:29 in all his glory was not **a** like one of these. 4016
Lk 12:27 *that* Solomon in all his glory was not **a** like 4016
23:11 mocked *him*, and **a** him in a gorgeous robe, 4016
Ac 12:21 **a** in royal apparel, sat upon his throne, and 1746
Rev 7:13 What are these which are **a** in white robes? 4016
17: 4 And the woman was **a in** purple and 4016
19: 8 granted that she should be **a** in fine linen, 4016

ARRIVED (2)

Lk 8:26 And they **a** at the country of the Gadarenes, 2668
Ac 20:15 and the next *day* we **a** at Samos, and tarried 3846

ARROGANCY (4)

1Sa 2: 3 let *not* **a** come out of your mouth: 6277
Pr 8:13 **a**, and the evil way, and the froward mouth, 1347
Isa 13:11 I will cause the **a** of the proud to cease, and 1347
Jer 48:29 his **a**, and his pride, and the haughtiness of 1347

ARROW (16) [ARROWS]

1Sa 20:36 as the lad ran, he shot an **a** beyond him. 2678
20:37 when the lad was come to the place of the **a** 2678
20:37 the lad, and said, *Is* not the **a** beyond thee? 2678
2Ki 9:24 the **a** went out at his heart, and he sunk 2678
13:17 The **a** of the LORD'S deliverance, and 2671
13:17 and the **a** of deliverance from Syria: 2671
19:32 nor shoot an **a** there, nor come before it 2671
Job 41:28 The **a** cannot make him flee: 1121+7198
Ps 11: 2 they make ready their **a** upon the string, 2671
64: 7 God shall shoot at them *with* an **a**; 2671
91: 5 by night; *nor* for the **a** *that* flieth by day; 2671
Pr 25:18 *is* a maul, and a sword, and a sharp **a**. 2671
Isa 37:33 nor shoot an **a** there, nor come before it 2671
Jer 9: 8 Their tongue *is as* an **a** shot out; it speaketh 2671
La 3:12 his bow, and set me as a mark for the **a**. 2671
Zec 9:14 and his **a** shall go forth as the lightning: 2671

ARROWS (41) [ARROW]

Nu 24: 8 and pierce *them* through *with* his **a**. 2671
Dt 32:23 upon them; I will spend mine **a** upon them. 2671
32:42 I will make mine **a** drunk with blood, and 2671
1Sa 20:20 I will shoot three **a** on the side *thereof*, as 2671
20:21 I will send a lad, *saying*, Go, find out the **a**. 2671

1Sa 20:21 Behold, the **a** *are* on this side of thee, take 2671
20:22 young man, Behold, the **a** *are* beyond thee; 2671
20:36 Run, find out now the **a** which I shoot. 2671
20:38 Jonathan's lad gathered up the **a**, and 2671
2Sa 22:15 he sent out **a**, and scattered them; lightning, 2671
2Ki 13:15 Elisha said unto him, Take bow and **a**. 2671
13:15 arrows. And he took unto him bow and **a**. 2671
13:18 he said, Take the **a**. And he took *them*. And 2671
1Ch 12: 2 *hurling* stones and *shooting* **a** out of a bow, 2671
2Ch 26:15 to shoot **a** and great stones withal. 2671
Job 6: 4 For the **a** of the Almighty *are* within me, 2671
Ps 7:13 he ordaineth his **a** against the persecutors. 2671
18:14 Yea, he sent out his **a**, and scattered them; 2671
21:12 *when* thou shalt make ready *thine* **a** upon NIH
38: 2 For thine **a** stick fast in me, and thy hand 2671
45: 5 Thine **a** *are* sharp in the heart of the king's 2671
57: 4 whose teeth *are* spears and **a**, and 2671
58: 7 *when* he bendeth *his bow to shoot* his **a**, 2671
64: 3 *and* bend *their bows to shoot* their **a**, 2671
76: 3 There brake he the **a** of the bow, the shield, 7565
77:17 sent out a sound: thine **a** also went abroad. 2687
120: 4 Sharp **a** of the mighty, with coals of 2671
127: 4 As **a** *are* in the hand of a mighty *man*; so 2671
144: 6 shoot out thine **a**, and destroy them. 2671
Pr 26:18 *man* who casteth firebrands, **a**, and death, 2671
Isa 5:28 Whose **a** *are* sharp, and all their bows bent, 2671
7:24 With **a** and with bows shall *men* come 2671
Jer 50: 9 their **a** *shall be* as of a mighty expert *man*; 2671
50:14 that bend the bow, shoot at her, spare no **a**: 2671
51:11 Make bright the **a**: gather the shields: 2671
La 3:13 He hath caused the **a**s of his quiver to enter 1121
Eze 5:16 When I shall send upon them the evil **a** of 2671
21:21 he made *his* **a** bright, he consulted with 2671
39: 3 will cause thine **a** to fall out of thy right 2671
39: 9 the bows and the **a**, and the handstaves, and 2671
Hab 3:11 at the light of thine **a** they went, *and* at 2671

ART (495) [ARTS]

Ge 3: 9 and said unto him, Where **a** thou? NIH
3:14 thou **a** cursed above all cattle, and NIH
3:19 for dust thou **a**, and unto dust shalt thou NIH
4: 6 LORD said unto Cain, Why **a** thou wroth? NIH
4:11 now **a** thou cursed from the earth, NIH
12:11 I know that thou **a** a fair woman to look NIH
12:13 Say, I pray thee, thou **a** my sister: that it NIH
13:14 look from the place where thou **a** NIH
16:11 thou **a** with child, and shalt bear a son, and NIH
17: 8 the land wherein thou **a** a stranger, NIH
20: 3 said to him, Behold, thou **a** *but* a dead man, NIH
23: 6 thou **a** a mighty prince among us: in NIH
24:23 said, Whose daughter **a** thou? tell me, I pray NIH
24:47 and said, Whose daughter **a** thou? NIH
24:60 and said unto her, Thou **a** our sister, NIH
26:16 from us; for thou **a** much mightier than we. NIH
26:29 thou **a** now the blessed of the LORD. NIH
27:18 he said, Here *am* I; who **a** thou, my son? NIH
27:24 he said, **A** thou my very son Esau? And he NIH
27:32 Isaac his father said unto him, Who **a** thou? NIH
28: 4 inherit the land wherein thou **a** a stranger, NIH
29:14 Surely thou **a** my bone and my flesh. NIH
29:15 Because thou **a** my brother, shouldest thou NIH
32:17 and asketh thee, saying, Whose **a** thou? NIH
39: 9 from me but thee, because thou **a** his wife: NIH
41:39 *there is* none so discreet and wise as thou **a**: NIH
44:18 thy servant: for thou **a** even as Pharaoh. NIH
45:19 Now thou **a** commanded, this do ye; NIH
46:30 have seen thy face, because thou **a** yet alive. NIH
47: 8 Pharaoh said unto Jacob, How old **a** thou? NIH
49: 3 Reuben, thou **a** my firstborn, my might, and NIH
49: 8 thou **a** *he* whom thy brethren shall praise: NIH
49: 9 from the prey, my son, thou **a** gone up: NIH
Ex 4:25 said, Surely a bloody husband **a** thou to me. NIH
4:26 A bloody husband *thou* **a**, because of NIH
18:18 thou **a** not able to perform it thyself alone. NIH
30:25 an ointment compound *after* the **a** of 4639
30:35 a confection *after* the **a** of the apothecary, 4639
33: 3 of thee; for thou **a** a stiffnecked people: NIH
34:10 all the people among which thou **a** shall see NIH
Lev 27:12 valuest it, *who* **a** the priest, so shall it be. NIH
Nu 14:14 *for* they have heard that thou LORD **a** NIH
14:14 that thou LORD **a** seen face to face, and NIH
21:29 thou **a** undone, O people of Chemosh: NIH
Dt 2:18 Thou **a** to pass over *through* Ar, the coast of NIH
4:30 When thou **a** in tribulation, and all these NIH
4:38 and mightier than thou **a**, to bring thee in, NIH
7: 6 For thou **a** a holy people unto the LORD NIH
7:19 unto all the people of whom thou **a** afraid. NIH
8:10 When thou hast eaten and **a** full, then NIH
8:12 Lest *when* thou hast eaten and **a** full, and NIH
9: 1 Thou **a** to pass over Jordan *this* day, to go in NIH
9: 6 for thou **a** a stiffnecked people. NIH
14: 2 For thou **a** a holy people unto the LORD NIH
14:21 for thou **a** a holy people unto the LORD. NIH
14:24 for thee, so that thou **a** not able to carry it; NIH
17:14 When thou **a** come unto the land which NIH
18: 9 When thou **a** come into the land which NIH
26: 1 when thou **a** come in unto the land which NIH
27: 3 words of this law, when thou **a** passed over, NIH
27: 9 this day thou **a** become the people of NIH
28:10 all people of the earth shall see that thou **a** NIH
32:15 thou **a** waxed fat, thou art grown thick, NIH
32:15 thou art waxed fat, thou **a** grown thick, NIH
32:15 thou **a** covered *with fatness;* then he forsook NIH
32:18 Of the Rock *that* begat thee thou **a** NIH
33:29 Happy **a** thou, O Israel: who *is* like unto NIH
Jos 5:13 **A** thou for us, or for our adversaries? NIH
13: 1 Thou **a** old *and* stricken in years, and NIH
17:17 Thou **a** a great people, and hast great power: NIH
Jdg 8:18 they answered, As thou **a**, so *were* they; NIH
11: 2 for thou **a** the son of a strange woman. NIH
11:12 that thou **a** come against me to fight in my NIH
11:25 now **a** thou any thing better than Balak NIH
11:35 thou **a** one of them that trouble me: 1961
12: 5 said unto him, **A** thou an Ephraimite? NIH
13: 3 Behold now, thou **a** barren, and bearest not: NIH

Jdg 13:11 A thou the man that spakest unto NIH
Ru 2: 9 and when thou a athirst, go unto the vessels, NIH
2:11 a come unto a people which thou knewest NIH
2:12 under whose wings thou a come to trust. NIH
3: 9 he said, Who a thou? And she answered, NIH
3: 9 thine handmaid; for thou a a near kinsman. NIH
3:11 doth know that thou a a virtuous woman. NIH
3:16 in law, she said, Who a thou, my daughter? NIH
1Sa 8: 5 thou a old, and thy sons walk not in thy NIH
10: 2 When thou a departed from me to day, then NIH
10: 5 when thou a come thither *to* the city, NIH
17:28 for thou a come down that *thou* mightest NIH
17:33 Thou a not able to go against this Philistine NIH
17:33 for thou a *but* a youth, and he a man of war NIH
17:58 to him, Whose son a thou, *thou* young man? NIH
19: 3 beside my father in the field where thou a, NIH
21: 1 Why a thou alone, and no man with thee? NIH
24:17 said to David, Thou a more righteous than I: NIH
26:14 and said, Who a thou *that* criest to the king? NIH
26:15 said to Abner, A not thou a *valiant* man? NIH
28:12 hast thou deceived me? for thou a Saul. NIH
29: 9 I know that thou a good in my sight, NIH
30:13 whence a thou? And he said, I *am* a young NIH
2Sa 1: 8 he said unto me, Who a thou? And I NIH
1:13 young man that told him, Whence a thou? NIH
2:20 behind him, and said, A thou Asahel? NIH
7:22 Wherefore thou a great, O LORD God: NIH
7:24 and thou, LORD, a become their God. NIH
7:28 thou a that God, and thy words be true, and NIH
9: 2 the king said unto him, A thou Ziba? NIH
12: 7 And Nathan said to David, Thou a the man. NIH
13: 4 Why a thou, *being* the king's son, lean from NIH
15: 2 unto him, and said, Of what city a thou? NIH
15:19 for thou a a stranger, and also an exile. NIH
15:27 unto Zadok the priest, A *not* thou a seer? NIH
16: 8 and, behold, thou a *taken* to thy mischief, NIH
16: 8 thy mischief, because thou a a bloody man. NIH
16:21 all Israel shall hear that thou a abhorred of NIH
18: 3 now *thou* a worth ten thousand of us: NIH
19:13 A thou not *of* my bone, and *of* my flesh? NIH
20: 9 to Amasa, A thou in health, my brother? NIH
20:17 unto her, the woman said, A thou Joab? NIH
22:29 For thou a my lamp, O LORD: and NIH
1Ki 1:42 for thou a a valiant man, and bringest good NIH
2: 9 for thou a a wise man, and knowest what NIH
2:26 thine own fields; for thou a worthy of death: NIH
6:12 *Concerning* this house which thou a in NIH
13:14 A thou the man of God that camest from NIH
13:18 I *am* a prophet also as thou a; and an angel NIH
17:18 a thou come unto me to call my sin to NIH
17:24 Now *by* this I know that thou a a man of NIH
18: 7 and said, A thou that my lord Elijah? NIH
18:17 unto him, A thou he that troubleth Israel? NIH
18:36 let it be known *this* day that thou a God in NIH
18:37 that this people may know that thou a NIH
20:36 behold, as soon as thou a departed from me, NIH
22: 4 I *am* as thou a, my people as thy people, my NIH
2Ki 1: 4 from *that* bed on which thou a gone up, NIH
1: 6 from *that* bed on which thou a gone up, NIH
1:16 down off *that* bed on which thou a gone up, NIH
3: 7 I *am* as thou a, my people as thy people, NIH
4: 4 when thou a come in, thou shalt shut NIH
19:15 thou a the God, *even* thou alone, of all NIH
19:19 may know that thou a the LORD God, NIH
1Ch 17:26 thou a God, and hast promised this NIH
29:11 and *thou* a exalted as head above all. NIH
2Ch 14:11 O LORD, thou a our God; let not man NIH
16:14 *of spices* prepared by the apothecaries' a: 4639
18: 3 I *am* as thou a, and my people as thy NIH
20: 6 of our fathers, a not thou God in heaven? NIH
20: 7 A not thou our God, who didst drive out NIH
25:16 A thou made of the king's counsel? NIH
Ezr 7:14 Forasmuch as *thou* a sent of the king, and NIH
9:15 O LORD God of Israel, thou a righteous: NIH
Ne 2: 2 thy countenance sad, seeing thou a not sick? NIH
9: 6 Thou, *even* thou, a LORD alone; thou hast NIH
9: 7 Thou a the LORD the God, who didst NIH
9: 8 performed thy words; for thou a righteous: NIH
9:17 thou a a God ready to pardon, gracious and NIH
9:31 for thou a a gracious and merciful God, NIH
9:33 Howbeit thou a just in all that is brought NIH
Est 4:14 who knoweth whether thou a come to NIH
Job 4: 5 it toucheth thee, and thou a troubled. NIH
15: 7 A thou the first man *that* was born? or NIH
17:14 I have said to corruption, Thou a my father: NIH
17:14 *Thou* a my mother, and my sister. NIH
22: 3 to the Almighty, that thou a righteous? NIH
30:21 Thou a become cruel to me: with thy strong NIH
31:24 said to the fine gold, *Thou* a my confidence; NIH
33:12 Behold, *in* this thou a not just: I will answer NIH
34:18 *Is it fit* to say to a king, *Thou* a wicked? *and* NIH
35: 8 Thy wickedness *may hurt* a man as thou a; NIH
Ps 2: 7 LORD hath said unto me, Thou a my Son; NIH
3: 3 thou, O LORD, a a shield for me; NIH
5: 4 For thou a not a God that hath pleasure in NIH
8: 4 What *is* man, that thou a mindful of him? NIH
10:14 thou a the helper of the fatherless. 1961
16: 2 hast said unto the LORD, Thou a my Lord: NIH
22: 1 *why* a *thou so* far from helping me, *and* NIH
22: 3 thou a holy, O thou that inhabitest NIH
22: 9 But thou a he that took me out of the womb: NIH
22:10 thou a my God from my mother's belly. NIH
23: 4 for thou a with me; thy rod and thy staff NIH
25: 5 for thou a the God of my salvation; on thee NIH
31: 3 For thou a my rock and my fortress; NIH
31: 4 laid privily for me: for thou a my strength. NIH
31:14 in thee, O LORD: I said, Thou a my God. NIH
32: 7 Thou a my hiding place; thou shalt preserve NIH
40:17 thou a my help and my deliverer; make no NIH
42: 5 Why a thou cast down, O my soul? and NIH
42: 5 *why* a thou disquieted in me? hope thou in NIH
42:11 Why a thou cast down, O my soul? and NIH
42:11 why a thou disquieted within me? hope thou NIH
43: 2 For thou a the God of my strength: why NIH
43: 5 Why a thou cast down, O my soul? and NIH
Ps 43: 5 why a thou disquieted within me? hope in NIH
44: 4 Thou a my King, O God: NIH
45: 2 Thou a fairer than the children of men: NIH
63: 1 O God, thou a my God; early will I seek NIH
65: 5 *who* a the confidence of all the ends of NIH
66: 3 unto God, How terrible a *thou in* thy works! NIH
68:35 *thou* a terrible out of thy holy places: NIH
70: 5 thou a my help and my deliverer; NIH
71: 3 for thou a my rock and my fortress. NIH
71: 5 For thou a my hope, O Lord GOD: NIH
71: 5 *thou* a my trust from my youth. NIH
71: 6 thou a he that took me out of my mother's NIH
71: 7 unto many; but thou a my strong refuge. NIH
76: 4 Thou a more glorious *and* excellent than NIH
76: 7 Thou, *even* thou, a to be feared: and NIH
76: 7 stand in thy sight when once thou a angry? NIH
77:14 Thou a the God that doest wonders: NIH
83:18 a the most High over all the earth. NIH
86: 5 Lord, a good, and ready to forgive; NIH
86:10 For thou a great, and doest wondrous NIH
86:10 doest wondrous *things:* thou a God alone. NIH
86:15 a a God full of compassion, and gracious, NIH
89:17 For thou a the glory of their strength: and NIH
89:26 Thou a my Father, my God, and the rock of NIH
90: 2 from everlasting to everlasting, thou a God. NIH
92: 8 LORD, a *most* high for evermore. NIH
93: 2 established of old: thou a from everlasting. NIH
97: 9 LORD, a High above all the earth: NIH
97: 9 the earth: thou a exalted far above all gods. NIH
102:27 thou a the same, and thy years shall have no NIH
104: 1 O LORD my God, thou a very great; NIH
104: 1 thou a clothed with honour and majesty. NIH
110: 4 Thou a a priest for ever after the order of NIH
118:21 hast heard me, and a become my salvation. NIH
118:28 Thou a my God, and I will praise thee: NIH
118:28 *thou* a my God, I will exalt thee. NIH
119:12 Blessed a thou, O LORD: teach me thy NIH
119:57 *Thou* a my portion, O LORD: I have said NIH
119:68 Thou a good, and doest good; teach me thy NIH
119:114 Thou a my hiding place and my shield: NIH
119:137 Righteous a thou, O LORD, and NIH
119:151 Thou a near, O LORD; and all thy NIH
137: 8 of Babylon, who a *to be* destroyed; NIH
139: 3 and a acquainted *with* all my ways. NIH
139: 8 If I ascend up *into* heaven, thou a there: if I NIH
139: 8 I make my bed in hell, behold, thou a *there.* NIH
140: 6 I said unto the LORD, Thou a my God: NIH
142: 5 Thou a my refuge *and* my portion in NIH
143:10 Teach me to do thy will; for thou a my God: NIH
Pr 6: 2 Thou a snared with the words of thy mouth, NIH
6: 2 thou a taken with the words of thy mouth, NIH
6: 3 when thou a come into the hand of thy NIH
7: 4 Say unto wisdom, Thou a my sister; and NIH
24:24 saith unto the wicked, Thou a righteous; NIH
Ecc 10:17 Blessed a thou, O land, when thy king *is* NIH
SS 1:15 Behold, thou a fair, my love; behold, NIH
1:15 thou *art* fair, my love; behold, thou a fair; NIH
1:16 Behold, thou a fair, my beloved, yea, NIH
2:14 O my dove, *that* a in the clefts of the rock, NIH
4: 1 Behold, thou a fair, my love; behold, NIH
4: 1 thou *art* fair, my love; behold, thou a fair; NIH
4: 7 Thou a all fair, my love; *there is* no spot in NIH
6: 4 Thou a beautiful, O my love, as Tirzah, NIH
7: 6 How fair and how pleasant a thou, O love, NIH
Isa 14: 8 of Lebanon, *saying,* Since thou a laid down, NIH
14:10 unto thee, A thou also become weak as we? NIH
14:10 weak as we? a thou become like unto us? NIH
14:12 How a thou fallen from heaven, O Lucifer, NIH
14:12 *how* a thou cut down to the ground, NIH
14:19 thou a cast out of thy grave like an NIH
14:31 O city; thou, whole Palestina, a dissolved: NIH
22: 1 that thou a wholly gone up to NIH
22: 2 Thou *that* a full *of* stirs, a tumultuous city, NIH
25: 1 O LORD, thou a my God; I will exalt thee, NIH
26:15 thou a glorified: thou hadst removed *it* far NIH
37:16 thou a the God, *even* thou alone, of all NIH
37:20 the earth may know that thou a the LORD, NIH
41: 8 thou, Israel, a my servant, Jacob whom I NIH
41: 9 and said unto thee, Thou a my servant; NIH
43: 1 I have called *thee* by thy name; thou a mine. NIH
44:17 and saith, Deliver me; for thou a my god. NIH
44:21 O Jacob and Israel; for thou a my servant: NIH
44:21 I have formed thee; thou a my servant: NIH
45:15 Verily thou a a God that hidest thyself, NIH
47: 8 *thou that* a given to pleasures, that dwellest NIH
47:13 Thou a wearied in the multitude of thy NIH
48: 4 Because I knew that thou a obstinate, and NIH
49: 3 said unto me, Thou a my servant, O Israel, NIH
51: 9 A thou not it that hath cut Rahab, *and* NIH
51:10 A thou not it which hath dried the sea, NIH
51:12 who a thou, that thou shouldest be afraid of NIH
51:16 and say unto Zion, Thou a my people. NIH
57: 8 *thyself to another* than me, and a gone up; NIH
57:10 Thou a wearied in the greatness of thy way; NIH
63: 2 Wherefore a *thou* red in thine apparel, and NIH
63:16 Doubtless thou a our father, NIH
63:16 thou, O LORD, a our father, our redeemer; NIH
64: 5 behold, thou a wroth; for we have sinned: NIH
64: 8 now, O LORD, thou a our father; we *are* NIH
Jer 2:21 a thou turned *into* the degenerate plant of a NIH
2:23 *thou* a a swift dromedary traversing her NIH
2:27 Saying to a stock, Thou a my father; and NIH
3: 4 My father, thou a the guide of my youth? NIH
3:22 unto thee; for thou a the LORD our God. NIH
4:30 when thou a spoiled, what wilt thou do? NIH
10: 6 thou a great, and thy name *is* great in might. NIH
12: 1 Righteous a thou, O LORD, when I plead NIH
12: 2 thou a near in their mouth, and far from NIH
14: 9 a in the midst of us, and we are called by NIH
14:22 a not thou he, O LORD our God? therefore NIH
15: 6 saith the LORD, thou a gone backward: NIH
17:14 and I shall be saved: for thou a my praise. NIH
17:17 unto me: thou a my hope in the day of evil. NIH
20: 7 thou a stronger than I, and hast prevailed: NIH
22: 6 Thou a Gilead unto me, *and* the head of NIH
Jer 31:18 be turned; for thou a the LORD my God. NIH
39:17 the hand of the men of whom thou a afraid. NIH
49:12 a thou he *that* shall altogether go NIH
50:24 thou a also taken, O Babylon, and thou wast NIH
50:24 thou a found, and also caught, because NIH
51:20 Thou a my battle axe *and* weapons of war: NIH
La 5:22 rejected us; thou a very wroth against us. NIH
Eze 3: 5 For thou a not sent to a people of a strange NIH
16: 7 and thou a come to excellent ornaments: 1961
16:34 given unto thee, therefore thou a contrary. 1961
16:45 Thou a thy mother's daughter, that lotheth NIH
16:45 thou a the sister of thy sisters, which lothed NIH
16:54 in that thou a a comfort unto them. NIH
22: 4 Thou a become guilty in thy blood that thou NIH
22: 4 draw near, and a come *even* unto thy years: NIH
22: 5 *which* a infamous *and* much vexed. NIH
22:24 Thou a the land that is not cleansed, NIH
23:30 *and* because thou a polluted with their idols. NIH
26:17 say to thee, How a thou destroyed, *that wast* NIH
27: 3 O thou that a situate at the entry of the sea, NIH
27: 3 *which* a a merchant of the people for many NIH
28: 2 yet thou a a man, and not God, though thou NIH
28: 3 Behold, thou a wiser than Daniel; *there is* NIH
28:14 Thou a the anointed cherub that covereth; NIH
31: 2 Whom a thou like in thy greatness? NIH
31:18 To whom a thou thus like in glory and NIH
32: 2 Thou a like a young lion of the nations, and NIH
32: 2 and thou a as a whale in the seas: NIH
33:32 thou a unto them as a very lovely song *of* NIH
38:13 say unto thee, A thou come to take a spoil? NIH
38:17 A thou he of whom I have spoken in old NIH
40: 4 shew *them* unto thee a thou brought hither: NIH
Da 2:26 A thou able to make known unto me 383
2:37 Thou, O king, a a king of kings: for the God NIH
2:38 over them all. Thou a this head of gold. NIH
4:18 thou a able; for the spirit of the holy gods *is* NIH
4:22 O king, that a grown and become strong: NIH
5:13 and said unto Daniel, A thou that Daniel, NIH
5:13 which a of the children of the captivity of NIH
5:27 Thou a weighed in the balances, and NIH
5:27 in the balances, and a found wanting. NIH
9:23 I am come to shew *thee;* for thou a greatly NIH
Hos 2:23 *were* not my people, Thou a my people; NIH
2:23 and they shall say, *Thou* a my God. NIH
Ob 1: 2 among the heathen: thou a greatly despised. NIH
1: 5 if robbers by night, (how a thou cut off!) NIH
Jnh 1: 8 *is* thy country? and of what people a thou? NIH
4: 2 for I knew that thou a a gracious God, and NIH
Mic 2: 7 O *thou that* a named the house of Jacob, is NIH
Na 1:14 I will make thy grave; for thou a vile. NIH
3: 8 A thou better than populous No, that was NIH
Hab 1:12 A thou not from everlasting, O LORD my NIH
1:13 *Thou* a of purer eyes than to behold evil, NIH
2:16 Thou a filled *with* shame for glory: NIH
Zec 4: 7 Who a thou, O great mountain? NIH
Mt 2: 6 a not the least among the princes of Juda: *1510*
5:25 whiles thou a in the way with him; *1510*
6: 9 Our Father which a in heaven, Hallowed be NIG
8:29 a thou come hither to torment us before NIG
11: 3 A thou he that should come, or do we look *1510*
11:23 Capernaum, which a exalted unto heaven, NIG
14:33 saying, Of a truth thou a the Son of God. *1510*
16:14 Some *say that thou* a John the Baptist: NIG
16:16 Peter answered and said, Thou a the Christ, *1510*
16:17 and said unto him, Blessed a thou, *1510*
16:18 That thou a Peter, and upon this rock I will *1510*
16:23 thou a an offence unto me: for thou *1510*
22:16 we know that thou a true, and teachest *1510*
25:24 Lord, I knew thee that thou a a hard man, *1510*
26:50 unto him, Friend, wherefore a thou come? NIG
26:73 to Peter, Surely thou also a *one* of them; *1510*
27:11 saying, A thou the King of the Jews? *1510*
Mk 1:11 *saying,* Thou a my beloved Son, in whom I *1510*
1:24 a thou come to destroy us? I know thee who NIG
1:24 I know thee who thou a, the Holy One of *1510*
3:11 and cried, saying, Thou a the Son of God. *1510*
8:29 and saith unto him, Thou a the Christ. *1510*
12:14 we know that thou a true, and carest for no *1510*
12:34 Thou a not far from the kingdom of God. *1510*
14:61 and said unto him, A thou the Christ, *1510*
14:70 again to Peter, Surely thou a *one* of them: *1510*
14:70 for thou a a Galilean, and thy speech *1510*
15: 2 asked him, A thou the King of the Jews? *1510*
Lk 1:28 and said, Hail, *thou that* a highly favoured, NIG
1:28 *is* with thee: blessed a thou among women. NIG
1:42 Blessed a thou among women, and NIG
3:22 which said, Thou a my beloved Son; *1510*
4:34 a thou come to destroy us? I know thee who NIG
4:34 I know thee who thou a, the Holy One of *1510*
4:41 and saying, Thou a Christ the Son of God. *1510*
7:19 saying, A thou he that should come? *1510*
7:20 saying, A thou he that should come? *1510*
10:15 Capernaum, which a exalted to heaven, NIG
10:41 thou a careful and troubled about many NIG
11: 2 ye pray, say, Our Father which a in heaven, NIG
12:58 *as thou* a in the way, give diligence that NIG
13:12 Woman, thou a loosed from thy infirmity. NIG
14: 8 When thou a bidden of any *man* to a NIG
14:10 But when thou a bidden, go and sit down in NIG
15:31 thou a ever with me, and all that I have is *1510*
16:25 now he is comforted, and thou a tormented. NIG
19:21 feared thee, because thou a an austere man: *1510*
22:32 and when thou a converted, strengthen thy NIG
22:58 saw him, and said, Thou a also of them. *1510*
22:67 A thou the Christ? tell us. And he said unto *1510*
22:70 said they all, A thou then the Son of God? *1510*
23: 3 saying, A thou the King of the Jews? *1510*
23:40 seeing thou a in the same condemnation? *1510*
24:18 A thou only a stranger in Jerusalem, and NIG
Jn 1:19 from Jerusalem to ask him, Who a thou? *1510*
1:21 A thou Elias? And he saith, I am not. *1510*
1:21 A thou *that* prophet? And he answered, No. *1510*
1:22 Then said they unto him, Who a thou? *1510*
1:42 he said, Thou a Simon the son of Jona: *1510*
1:49 unto him, Rabbi, thou a the Son of God; *1510*

A

Jn 1:49 the Son of God; thou **a** the King of Israel. *1510*
3: 2 we know that thou **a** a teacher come from NIG
3:10 **A** thou a master of Israel, and knowest not *1510*
4:12 **A** thou greater than our father Jacob, *1510*
4:19 Sir, I perceive that thou **a** a prophet. *1510*
5:14 said unto him, Behold, thou **a** made whole: NIG
6:69 and are sure that thou **a** *that* Christ, *1510*
7:52 and said unto him, **A** thou also of Galilee? *1510*
8:25 Then said they unto him, Who **a** thou? *1510*
8:48 Say we not well that thou **a** a Samaritan, *1510*
8:53 **A** thou greater than our father Abraham, *1510*
8:57 Thou **a** not yet fifty years old, and hast thou *2192*
9:28 reviled him, and said, Thou **a** his disciple; *1510*
11:27 I believe that thou **a** the Christ, the Son of *1510*
17:21 as thou, Father, *a* in me, and I in thee, NIG
18:17 **A** not thou also *one* of this man's disciples? *1510*
18:25 **A** not thou also *one* of his disciples? *1510*
18:33 unto him, **A** thou the King of the Jews? *1510*
18:37 said unto him, **A** thou a king then? *1510*
19: 9 and saith unto Jesus, Whence **a** thou? *1510*
19:12 let this *man* go, thou **a** not Cesar's friend: *1510*
21:12 of the disciples durst ask him, Who **a** thou? *1510*
Ac 4:24 and said, Lord, thou **a** God, which hast NIG
8:23 For I perceive that thou **a** in the gall of *1510*
9: 5 And he said, Who **a** thou, Lord? And *1510*
10:33 and thou hast well done that thou **a** come. NIG
12:15 And they said unto her, Thou **a** mad. NIG
13:33 Thou **a** my Son, this day have I begotten *1510*
17:29 or stone, graven by **a** and man's device. *5078*
21:22 for they will hear that thou **a** come. NIG
21:38 **A** not thou *that* Egyptian, which before *1510*
22: 8 And I answered, Who **a** thou, Lord? *1510*
22:27 said unto him, Tell me, **a** thou a Roman? *1510*
26: 1 Thou **a** permitted to speak for thyself. NIG
26:15 And I said, Who **a** thou, Lord? And he said, *1510*
26:24 a loud voice, Paul, thou **a** beside thyself; NIG
Ro 2: 1 Therefore thou **a** inexcusable, O man, *1510*
2: 1 O man, whosoever thou **a** that judgest: NIG
2:17 thou **a** called a Jew, and restest in the law, NIG
2:19 And **a** confident that thou thyself art a guide NIG
2:19 And art confident that thou thyself **a** a *1510*
3: 4 and mightest overcome when thou **a** judged. NIG
9:20 who **a** thou that repliest against God? *1510*
14: 4 Who **a** thou that judgest another *man's* *1510*
1Co 7:21 **A** thou called *being* a servant? care not for NIG
7:27 **A** thou bound unto a wife? seek not to be NIG
7:27 **A** thou loosed from a wife? seek not a wife. NIG
Gal 4: 7 Wherefore thou **a** no more a servant, but *1510*
1Ti 6:12 whereunto thou **a** also called, and NIG
Heb 1: 5 Thou **a** my Son, this day have I begotten *1510*
1:12 but thou **a** the same, and thy years shall not *1510*
2: 6 What is man, that thou **a** mindful of him? NIG
5: 5 but he that said unto him, Thou **a** my Son, *1510*
5: 6 As he saith also in another *place*, Thou ***a*** a NIG
7:17 Thou ***a*** a priest for ever after the order of NIG
7:21 Thou ***a*** a priest for ever after the order of NIG
12: 5 nor faint when thou **a** rebuked of him: NIG
Jas 2:11 thou **a** become a transgressor of the law. NIG
4:11 thou **a** not a doer of the law, but a judge. *1510*
4:12 to destroy: who **a** thou that judgest another? *1510*
Rev 2: 5 therefore from whence thou **a** fallen, NIG
2: 9 tribulation, and poverty, (but thou **a** rich) *1510*
3: 1 hast a name that thou livest, and **a** dead. *1510*
3:15 thy works, that thou **a** neither cold nor hot: *1510*
3:16 So *then* because thou **a** lukewarm, and *1510*
3:17 and knowest not that thou **a** wretched, and *1510*
4:11 Thou **a** worthy, O Lord, to receive glory *1510*
5: 9 Thou **a** worthy to take the book, and *1510*
11:17 which **a**, and wast, and art to come; *1510*
11:17 which art, and wast, and **a** to come; NIG
15: 4 for *thou* only **a** holy: for all nations shall NIG
16: 5 Thou **a** righteous, O Lord, which art, and *1510*
16: 5 O Lord, which **a**, and wast, and shalt be, *1510*

ARTAXERXES (14) [ARTAXERXES']

Ezr 4: 7 in the days of **A** wrote Bishlam, Mithredath, 783
4: 7 of their companions, unto **A** king of Persia; 783
4: 8 against Jerusalem to **A** the king in this sort: 783
4:11 they sent unto him, *even* unto **A** the king: 783
6:14 of Cyrus, and Darius, and **A** king of Persia. 783
7: 1 these things, in the reign of **A** king of Persia, 783
7: 7 in the seventh year of **A** the king. 783
7:11 that the king **A** gave unto Ezra the priest, 783
7:12 **A**, king of kings, unto Ezra the priest, 783
7:21 I, *even* I **A** the king, do make a decree to all 783
8: 1 me from Babylon, in the reign of **A** the king. 783
Ne 2: 1 *in* the twentieth year of **A** the king, *that* wine 783
5:14 unto the two and thirtieth year of **A** the king, 783
13: 6 thirtieth year of **A** king of Babylon came I 783

ARTAXERXES' (1) [ARTAXERXES]

Ezr 4:23 Now when the copy of king **A** letter *was* 783

ARTEMAS (1)

Tit 3:12 When I shall send **A** unto thee, or Tychicus, *734*

ARTEMIS See DIANA

ARTIFICER (2) [ARTIFICERS]

Ge 4:22 an instructor of every **a** in brass and iron: 2794
Isa 3: 3 and the cunning **a**, and the eloquent orator. 2791

ARTIFICERS (2) [ARTIFICER]

1Ch 29: 5 *of* work *to be made* by the hands of **a**. 2796
2Ch 34:11 Even to the **a** and builders gave they *it*, to 2796

ARTILLERY (1)

1Sa 20:40 Jonathan gave his **a** unto his lad, and 3627

ARTS (1) [ART]

Ac 19:19 Many also of them which used **curious a** *4021*

ARUBBOTH See ARUBOTH

ARUBOTH (1)

1Ki 4:10 The son of Hesed, in **A**; to him *pertained* 700

ARUMAH (1)

Jdg 9:41 Abimelech dwelt at **A**: and Zebul thrust out 725

ARVAD (2) [ARVADITE]

Eze 27: 8 of Zidon and **A** were thy mariners: 719
27:11 The men of **A** with thine army *were* upon 719

ARVADITE (2) [ARVAD]

Ge 10:18 the **A**, and the Zemarite, and the Hamathite: 721
1Ch 1:16 the **A**, and the Zemarite, and the Hamathite. 721

ARZA (1)

1Ki 16: 9 drinking *himself* drunk *in* the house of **A** 777

AS (3520) [FORASMUCH, INASMUCH] See Index of Articles, Etc.

ASA (59) [ASA'S]

1Ki 15: 8 of David: and **A** his son reigned in his stead. 609
15: 9 king of Israel reigned **A** over Judah. 609
15:11 **A** did *that* which *was* right in the eyes of 609
15:13 **A** destroyed her idol, and burnt *it* by 609
15:16 there was war between **A** and Baasha king of 609
15:17 *any* to go out or come in to **A** king of Judah. 609
15:18 **A** took all the silver and the gold that were 609
15:18 king **A** sent them to Ben-hadad, the son of 609
15:20 So Ben-hadad hearkened unto king **A**, and 609
15:22 king **A** made a proclamation throughout all 609
15:22 king **A** built with them Geba of Benjamin, 609
15:23 The rest of all the acts of **A**, and all his 609
15:24 **A** slept with his fathers, and was buried with 609
15:25 Israel in the second year of **A** king of Judah, 609
15:28 Even in the third year of **A** king of Judah did 609
15:32 there was war between **A** and Baasha king of 609
15:33 In the third year of **A** king of Judah *began* 609
16: 8 sixth year of **A** king of Judah *began* Elah 609
16:10 and seventh year of **A** king of Judah, 609
16:15 seventh year of **A** king of Judah did Zimri 609
16:23 first year of **A** king of Judah *began* Omri to 609
16:29 eighth year of **A** king of Judah *began* Ahab 609
22:41 Jehoshaphat the son of **A** *began* to reign over 609
22:43 he walked in all the ways of **A** his father; 609
22:46 which remained in the days of his father **A**, 609
1Ch 3:10 Abia his son, **A** his son, Jehoshaphat his son, 609
9:16 Berechiah the son of **A**, the son of Elkanah, 609
2Ch 14: 1 **A** his son reigned in his stead. In his days 609
14: 2 **A** did *that* which *was* good and right in 609
14: 8 And **A** had an army *of men* that bare targets 609
14:10 **A** went out against him, and they set 609
14:11 **A** cried unto the LORD his God, and said, 609
14:12 the LORD smote the Ethiopians before **A**, 609
14:13 **A** and the people that *were* with him pursued 609
15: 2 he went out to meet **A**, and said unto him, 609
15: 2 Hear ye me, **A**, and all Judah and Benjamin; 609
15: 8 when **A** heard these words, and the prophecy 609
15:10 in the fifteenth year of the reign of **A**. 609
15:16 also *concerning* Maachah the mother of **A** 609
15:16 and **A** cut down her idol, and stamped *it*, and 609
15:17 nevertheless the heart of **A** was perfect all 609
15:19 the five and thirtieth year of the reign of **A**. 609
16: 1 thirtieth year of the reign of **A** Baasha king 609
16: 1 none go out or come in to **A** king of Judah. 609
16: 2 **A** brought out silver and gold out of 609
16: 4 And Ben-hadad hearkened unto king **A**, and 609
16: 6 **A** the king took all Judah; and they carried 609
16: 7 at that time Hanani the seer came to **A** king 609
16:10 **A** was wroth with the seer, and put him *in* a 609
16:10 of this *thing*. And **A** oppressed *some* of 609
16:11 behold, the acts of **A**, first and last, lo, 609
16:12 **A** in the thirty and ninth year of his reign 609
16:13 **A** slept with his fathers, and died in the one 609
17: 2 of Ephraim, which **A** his father had taken. 609
20:32 he walked in the way of **A** his father, and 609
21:12 nor in the ways of **A** king of Judah, 609
Jer 41: 9 *was* it which **A** the king had made for fear of 609
Mt 1: 7 and Roboam begat Abia; and Abia begat **A**; *760*
1: 8 And **A** begat Josaphat; and Josaphat begat *760*

ASA'S (1) [ASA]

1Ki 15:14 nevertheless **A** heart was perfect with 609

ASAHEL (18)

2Sa 2:18 of Zeruiah there, Joab, and Abishai, and **A**: 6214
2:18 and **A** *was as* light of foot as a wild roe. 6214
2:19 **A** pursued after Abner; and in going he 6214
2:20 looked behind him, and said, *Art* thou **A**? 6214
2:21 **A** would not turn aside from following of 6214
2:22 Abner said again to **A**, Turn thee aside 6214
2:23 that as many as came to the place where **A** 6214
2:30 of David's servants nineteen men and **A**. 6214
2:32 they took up **A**, and buried him in 6214
3:27 that he died, for the blood of **A** his brother. 6214
3:30 he had slain their brother **A** at Gibeon in 6214
23:24 **A** the brother of Joab *was* one of the thirty; 6214
1Ch 2:16 of Zeruiah; Abishai, and Joab, and **A**, three. 6214
11:26 Also the valiant *men* of the armies *were*, **A** 6214
27: 7 the fourth month *was* **A** the brother of Joab, 6214
2Ch 17: 8 **A**, and Shemiramoth, and Jehonathan, and 6214
31:13 **A**, and Jerimoth, and Jozabad, and Eliel, 6214
Ezr 10:15 Only Jonathan the son of **A** and 6214

ASAHIAH (2)

2Ki 22:12 and **A** a servant of the king's, saying, 6222
22:14 Ahikam, and Achbor, and Shaphan, and **A**, 6222

ASAIAH (6)

1Ch 4:36 **A**, and Adiel, and Jesimiel, and Benaiah, 6222
6:30 Shimea his son, Haggiah his son, **A** his son. 6222
9: 5 the Shilonites; **A** the firstborn, and his sons. 6222
15: 6 **A** the chief, and his brethren two hundred 6222
1Ch 15:11 for Uriel, **A**, and Joel, Shemaiah, and Eliel, 6222
2Ch 34:20 and **A** a servant of the king's, saying, 6222

ASAPH (45) [ASAPH'S]

2Ki 18:18 and Joah the son of **A** the recorder. 623
18:37 and Joah the son of **A** the recorder, 623
1Ch 6:39 his brother **A**, who stood on his right hand, 623
6:39 *even* **A** the son of Berachiah, the son of 623
9:15 of Micah, the son of Zichri, the son of **A**; 623
15:17 and of his brethren, **A** the son of Berechiah; 623
15:19 So the singers, Heman, **A**, and Ethan, 623
16: 5 **A** the chief, and next to him Zechariah, Jeiel, 623
16: 5 but **A** made a sound with cymbals; 623
16: 7 to thank the LORD into the hand of **A** 623
16:37 the ark of the covenant of the LORD **A** 623
25: 1 separated to the service of the sons of **A**, 623
25: 2 Of the sons of **A**; Zaccur, and Joseph, and 623
25: 2 the sons of **A** under the hands of Asaph, 623
25: 2 the sons of Asaph under the hands of **A**, 623
25: 6 according to the king's order *to* **A**, Jeduthun, 623
25: 9 Now the first lot came forth for **A** to Joseph: 623
26: 1 the son of Kore, of the sons of **A**. 623
2Ch 5:12 all of them of **A**, of Heman, of Jeduthun, 623
20:14 son of Mattaniah, a Levite of the sons of **A**, 623
29:13 of the sons of **A**; Zechariah, and Mattaniah: 623
29:30 with the words of David, and of **A** the seer. 623
35:15 the singers the sons of **A** *were* in their place, 623
35:15 **A**, and Heman, and Jeduthun the king's seer; 623
Ezr 2:41 the children of **A**, an hundred twenty and 623
3:10 and the Levites the sons of **A** with cymbals, 623
Ne 2: 8 a letter unto **A** the keeper of the king's 623
7:44 the children of **A**, an hundred forty and 623
11:17 son of Micha, the son of Zabdi, the son of **A**, 623
11:22 Of the sons of **A**, the singers *were* over 623
12:35 of Michaiah, the son of Zaccur, the son of **A**: 623
12:46 and **A** of old *there were* chief of the singers, 623
Ps 50: T A Psalm of **A**. 623
73: T A Psalm of **A**. 623
74: T Maschil of **A**. 623
75: T Al-taschith, A Psalm *or* Song of **A**. 623
76: T on Neginoth, A Psalm *or* Song of **A**. 623
77: T chief Musician, to Jeduthun, A Psalm of **A**. 623
78: T Maschil of **A**. 623
79: T A Psalm of **A**. 623
80: T upon Shoshannim-Eduth, A Psalm of **A**. 623
81: T chief Musician upon Gittith, *A Psalm* of **A**. 623
82: T A Psalm of **A**. 623
83: T A Song *or* Psalm of **A**. 623
Isa 36:22 and Joah, the son of **A**, the recorder, 623

ASAPH'S (1) [ASAPH]

Isa 36: 3 the scribe, and Joah, **A** son, the recorder. 623

ASAREEL (1)

1Ch 4:16 of Jehaleleel; Ziph, and Ziphah, Tiria, and **A**. 840

ASAREL See ASAREEL

ASARELAH (1)

1Ch 25: 2 Zaccur, and Joseph, and Nethaniah, and **A**, 841

ASCEND (13) [ASCENDED, ASCENDETH, ASCENDING, ASCENT]

Jos 6: 5 the people shall **a up** every man straight 5927
Ps 24: 3 Who shall **a** into the hill of the LORD? 5927
135: 7 He **causeth** the vapours **to a** from the ends 5927
139: 8 If I **a up** *into* heaven, thou *art* there: if I 5266
Isa 14:13 hast said in thine heart, I will **a** *into* heaven, 5927
14:14 I will **a** above the heights of the clouds; 5927
Jer 10:13 he **causeth** the vapours **to a** from the ends 5927
51:16 he **causeth** the vapours **to a** from the ends 5927
Eze 38: 9 Thou shalt **a** and come like a storm, 5927
Jn 6:62 if ye shall see the Son of man **a up** where he *305*
20:17 I **a** unto my Father, and your Father; *305*
Ro 10: 6 not in thine heart, Who shall **a** into heaven? *305*
Rev 17: 8 and shall **a** out of the bottomless *pit*, and *305*

ASCENDED (19) [ASCEND]

Ex 19:18 the smoke thereof **a** as the smoke of a 5927
Nu 13:22 they **a** by the south, and came unto Hebron; 5927
Jos 8:20 the smoke of the city **a up** to heaven, and 5927
8:21 that the smoke of the city **a**, then 5927
10: 7 So Joshua **a** from Gilgal, he, and all 5927
15: 3 **a up** on the south side unto Kadesh-barnea, 5927
Jdg 13:20 that the angel of the LORD **a** in the flame 5927
20:40 the flame of the city **a up** to heaven. 5927
Ps 68:18 Thou hast **a** on high, thou hast led captivity 5927
Pr 30: 4 Who hath **a up** *into* heaven, or descended? 5927
Jn 3:13 And no *man* hath **a up** to heaven, but he that *305*
20:17 me not; for I am not yet **a** to my Father: *305*
Ac 2:34 For David is not **a** into the heavens: but *305*
25: 1 after three days he **a** from Cesarea to *305*
Eph 4: 8 Wherefore *he* saith, When he **a up** on high, *305*
4: 9 (Now that he **a**, what is it but that he also *305*
4:10 He that descended is the same also that **a up** *305*
Rev 8: 4 **a up** before God out of the angel's hand. *305*
11:12 And they **a up** to heaven in a cloud; and *305*

ASCENDETH (2) [ASCEND]

Rev 11: 7 the beast that **a** out of the bottomless *pit* *305*
14:11 And the smoke of their torment **a up** for ever *305*

ASCENDING (5) [ASCEND]

Ge 28:12 behold the angels of God **a** and 5927
1Sa 28:13 unto Saul, I saw gods **a** out of the earth. 5927
Lk 19:28 he went before, **a up** to Jerusalem. *305*
Jn 1:51 and the angels of God **a** and *305*
Rev 7: 2 And I saw another angel **a** from the east, *305*

ASCENT (4) [ASCEND]

Nu 34: 4 turn from the south to the **a** of Akrabbim, 4608
2Sa 15:30 David went up by the **a** of *mount* Olivet, 4608
1Ki 10: 5 his **a** *by* which he went up *unto* the house 5930
2Ch 9: 4 his **a** *by* which he went up *into* the house of 5944

ASCRIBE (3) [ASCRIBED]
Dt 32: 3 the LORD: **a** ye greatness unto our God. 3051
Job 36: 3 and will **a** righteousness to my Maker. 5414
Ps 68:34 **A** ye strength unto God: his excellency *is* 5414

ASCRIBED (2) [ASCRIBE]
1Sa 18: 8 They have **a** unto David ten thousands, and 5414
18: 8 and to me they have **a** *but* thousands: 5414

ASENATH (3)
Ge 41:45 he gave him to wife **A** the daughter of 621
41:50 which **A** the daughter of Poti-pherah priest 621
46:20 which **A** the daughter of Poti-pherah priest 621

ASER (2) [ASHER]
Lk 2:36 the daughter of Phanuel, of the tribe of **A**: *768*
Rev 7: 6 Of the tribe of **A** *were* sealed twelve *768*

ASH (1)
Isa 44:14 he planteth an **a**, and the rain doth nourish 766

ASHAMED (122) [SHAME]
Ge 2:25 the man and his wife, and were not **a**. 954
Nu 12:14 in her face, should she not be **a** seven days? 3637
Jdg 3:25 And they tarried till *they* were **a**: and behold, 954
2Sa 10: 5 meet them, because the men were greatly **a**: 3637
19: 3 as people being **a** steal away when they flee 3637
2Ki 2:17 when they urged him till *he* was **a**, he said, 954
8:11 his countenance stedfastly, until *he* was **a**: 954
1Ch 19: 5 for the men were greatly **a**. And the king 3637
2Ch 30:15 the priests and the Levites were **a**, and 3637
Ezr 8:22 For I was **a** to require of the king a band *of* 954
9: 6 I am **a** and blush to lift up my face to thee, 954
Job 6:20 had hoped; they came thither, and were **a**. 2659
11: 3 thou mockest, shall no man **make** *thee* **a**? 3637
19: 3 you are not **a** *that* you make yourselves 954
Ps 6:10 Let all mine enemies be **a** and sore vexed: 954
6:10 let them return *and* be **a** suddenly. 954
25: 2 let me not be **a**, let not mine enemies 954
25: 3 Yea, let none that wait on thee be **a**: let them 954
25: 3 let them be **a** which transgress without 954
25:20 let me not be **a**; for I put my trust in thee. 954
31: 1 do I put my trust; let me never be **a**: 954
31:17 Let me not be **a**, O LORD; for I have called 954
31:17 let the wicked be **a**, *and* let them be silent in 954
34: 5 were lightened: and their faces were not **a**. 2659
35:26 Let them be **a** and brought to confusion 954
37:19 They shall not be **a** in the evil time: and 954
40:14 Let them be **a** and confounded together that 954
69: 6 O Lord GOD of hosts, be **a** for my sake: 954
70: 2 Let them be **a** and confounded that seek after 954
74:21 O let not the oppressed return **a**: let 3637
86:17 that they which hate me may see *it*, and be **a**: 954
109:28 when they arise, let them be **a**; but let thy 954
119: 6 shall I not be **a**, when I have respect unto all 954
119:46 also before kings, and will not be **a**. 954
119:78 Let the proud be **a**; for they dealt perversely 954
119:80 heart be sound in thy statutes; that I be not **a**. 954
119:116 I may live: and let me not be **a** of my hope. 954
127: 5 they shall not be **a**, but they shall speak with 954
Pr 12: 4 she that **maketh a** *is* as rottenness in his 954
Isa 1:29 For they shall be **a** of the oaks which ye 954
20: 5 be afraid and **a** of Ethiopia their expectation, 954
23: 4 Be thou **a**, O Zidon: for the sea hath spoken, 954
24:23 moon shall be confounded, and the sun **a**, 954
26:11 and be **a** for *their* envy at the people; 954
29:22 the house of Jacob, Jacob shall not now be **a**, 954
30: 5 They were all **a** of a people *that* could not 954
33: 9 Lebanon is **a** *and* hewn down: Sharon is 2659
41:11 that were incensed against thee shall be **a** 954
42:17 turned back, they shall be **greatly a**, 954+1322
44: 9 they see not, nor know; that they may be **a**. 954
44:11 Behold, all his fellows shall be **a**: and 954
44:11 they shall fear, *and* they shall be **a** together. 954
45:16 They shall be **a**, and also confounded, all of 954
45:17 ye shall not be **a** nor confounded world 954
45:24 all that are incensed against him shall be **a**. 954
49:23 for they shall not be **a** that wait for me. 954
50: 7 like a flint, and I know that I shall not be **a**. 954
54: 4 Fear not; for thou shalt not be **a**: neither be 954
65:13 my servants shall rejoice, but ye shall be **a**: 954
66: 5 *shall* appear to your joy, and they shall be **a**. 954
Jer 2:26 As the thief is **a** when he is found, so is 1322
2:26 when he is found, so is the house of Israel **a**; 954
2:36 thou also shalt be **a** of Egypt, as thou wast 954
2:36 ashamed of Egypt, as thou wast **a** of Assyria. 954
3: 3 a whore's forehead, thou refusedst to be **a**. 3637
6:15 Were they **a** when they had committed 954
6:15 nay, they were not **at all a**, neither 954+954
8: 9 The wise *men* are **a**, they are dismayed and 954
8:12 Were they **a** when they had committed 954
8:12 nay, they were not **at all a**, neither 954+954
12:13 and they shall be **a** of your revenues because 954
14: 3 they were **a** and confounded, and 954
14: 4 the plowmen were **a**, they covered their 954
15: 9 she hath been **a** and confounded: and 954
17:13 all that forsake thee shall be **a**, and they that 954
20:11 they shall be greatly **a**: for they shall not 954
22:22 surely then shalt thou be **a** and 954
31:19 I was **a**, yea, even confounded, because I did 954
48:13 Moab shall be **a** of Chemosh, as the house of 954
48:13 as the house of Israel was **a** of Beth-el their 954
50:12 she that bare you shall be **a**: 2659
Eze 16:27 which are **a** of thy lewd way. 3637
16:61 be **a**, when thou shalt receive thy sisters, 3637
32:30 with their terror *they are* **a** of their might; 954
36:32 be **a** and confounded for your own ways, 954
43:10 that they may be **a** of their iniquities: 3637
43:11 if they be **a** of all that they have done, 3637
Hos 4:19 they shall be **a** because of their sacrifices. 954
10: 6 and Israel shall be **a** of his own counsel. 954
Joel 1:11 Be ye **a**, O ye husbandmen; howl, O ye 954
2:26 with you: and my people shall never be **a**. 954
2:27 none else: and my people shall never be **a**. 954
Mic 3: 7 shall the seers be **a**, and the diviners 954
Zep 3:11 In that day shalt thou not be **a** for all thy 954
Zec 9: 5 for her expectation shall be **a**; and the king 3001
13: 4 *that* the prophets shall be **a** every one of his 954
Mk 8:38 Whosoever therefore shall be **a** of me and *1870*
8:38 of him also shall the Son of man be **a**, *1870*
Lk 9:26 For whosoever shall be **a** of me and of my *1870*
9:26 of him shall the Son of man be **a**, *1870*
13:17 said these *things*, all his adversaries were **a**: *2617*
16: 3 the stewardship: I cannot dig; to beg I am **a**. *153*
Ro 1:16 For I am not **a** of the gospel of Christ: for it *1870*
5: 5 And hope **maketh** not **a**; because the love *2617*
6:21 then *in those things* whereof ye are now **a**? *1870*
9:33 whosoever believeth on him shall not be **a**. *2617*
10:11 Whosoever believeth on him shall not be **a**. *2617*
2Co 7:14 boasted any *thing* to him of you, I am not **a**; *2617*
9: 4 should be **a** in this *same* confident boasting. *2617*
10: 8 not for your destruction, I should not be **a**: *153*
Php 1:20 that in nothing I shall be **a**, but *that* with all *153*
2Th 3:14 no company with him, that he may be **a**. *1788*
2Ti 1: 8 therefore **a** of the testimony of our Lord, *1870*
1:12 suffer these *things*: nevertheless I am not **a**: *1870*
1:16 refreshed me, and was not **a** of my chain: *1870*
2:15 a workman that **needeth not to be a**, *422*
Tit 2: 8 that he that is of the contrary *part* may be **a**, *1788*
Heb 2:11 for which cause he is not **a** to call them *1870*
11:16 wherefore God is not **a** to be called their *1870*
1Pe 3:16 they may be **a** that falsely accuse your good *2617*
4:16 *man suffer* as a Christian, let him not be **a**; *153*
1Jn 2:28 and not be **a** before him at his coming. *153*

ASHAN (4)
Jos 15:42 Libnah, and Ether, and **A**, 6228
19: 7 Ain, Remmon, and Ether, and **A**; four cities 6228
1Ch 4:32 Ain, Rimmon, and Tochen, and **A**, 6228
6:59 **A** with her suburbs, and Beth-shemesh with 6228

ASHBEA (1)
1Ch 4:21 that wrought fine linen, of the house of **A**, 791

ASHBEL (3) [ASHBELITES]
Ge 46:21 and **A**, Gera, and Naaman, Ehi, and Rosh, 788
Nu 26:38 of **A**, the family of the Ashbelites: 788
1Ch 8: 1 **A** the second, and Aharah the third, 788

ASHBELITES (1) [ASHBEL]
Nu 26:38 of Ashbel, the family of the **A**: of Ahiram, 789

ASHCHENAZ (2)
1Ch 1: 6 of Gomer; **A**, and Riphath, and Togarmah. 813
Jer 51:27 her the kingdoms of Ararat, Minni, and **A**; 813

ASHDOD (21) [ASHDODITES]
Jos 11:22 only in Gaza, in Gath, and in **A**, 795
15:46 all that *lay* near **A**, with their villages: 795
15:47 **A** *with* her towns and her villages, Gaza *with* 795
1Sa 5: 1 and brought it from Eben-ezer unto **A**. 795
5: 3 when **they of A** arose early on the morrow, 796
5: 5 tread on the threshold of Dagon in **A** unto 795
5: 6 of the LORD was heavy upon **them of A**, 796
5: 6 with emerods, *even* **A** and the coasts thereof. 795
5: 7 when the men of **A** saw that *it was* so, they 795
6:17 for **A** one, for Gaza one, for Askelon one, 795
2Ch 26: 6 the wall of **A**, and built cities about Ashdod, 795
26: 6 built cities about **A**, and among 795
Ne 13:23 also saw I Jews *that* had married wives **of A**, 796
13:24 their children spake half **in the speech of A**, 797
Isa 20: 1 In the year that Tartan came unto **A**, 795
20: 1 sent him,) and fought against **A**, and took it; 795
Jer 25:20 and Ekron, and the remnant of **A**: 795
Am 1: 8 And I will cut off the inhabitant from **A**, and 795
3: 9 Publish in the palaces at **A**, and in 795
Zep 2: 4 they shall drive out **A** at the noon day, 795
Zec 9: 6 a bastard shall dwell in **A**, and I will cut off 795

ASHDODITES (1) [ASHDOD]
Ne 4: 7 the Arabians, and the Ammonites, and the **A**, 796

ASHDOTHITES (1)
Jos 13: 3 the Gazathites, and the **A**, the Eshkalonites, 796

ASHDOTH-PISGAH (3)
Dt 3:17 *even* the salt sea, under **A** eastward. 798
Jos 12: 3 and from the south, under **A**: 798
13:20 And Beth-peor, and **A**, and Beth-jeshimoth, 798

ASHER (43) [ASER, ASHERITES]
Ge 30:13 call me blessed: and she called his name **A**. 836
35:26 of Zilpah, Leah's handmaid; Gad, and **A**: 836
46:17 And the sons of **A**; Jimnah, and Ishuah, and 836
49:20 Out of **A** his bread *shall be* fat, and he shall 836
Ex 1: 4 Dan, and Naphtali, Gad, and **A**. 836
Nu 1:13 Of **A**; Pagiel the son of Ocran. 836
1:40 Of the children of **A**, *by* their generations, 836
1:41 *even* of the tribe of **A**, *were* forty and 836
2:27 that encamp by him *shall be* the tribe of **A**: 836
2:27 the captain of the children of **A** *shall be* 836
7:72 prince of the children of **A**, *offered*: 836
10:26 over the host of the tribe of the children of **A** 836
13:13 Of the tribe of **A**, Sethur the son of Michael. 836
26:44 *Of* the children of **A** after their families: 836
26:46 the name of the daughter of **A** *was* Sarah. 836
26:47 These *are* the families of the sons of **A** 836
34:27 the prince of the tribe of the children of **A**, 836
Dt 27:13 and **A**, and Zebulun, Dan, and Naphtali. 836
33:24 of **A** he said, *Let* Asher *be* blessed with 836
33:24 he said, *Let* **A** *be* blessed with children; 836
Jos 17: 7 the coast of Manasseh was from **A** *to* 836
17:10 and they met together in **A** on the north, and 836
17:11 and in **A** Beth-shean and her towns, 836
19:24 the children of **A** according to their families. 836
19:31 the children of **A** according to their families, 836
19:34 reacheth to **A** on the west side, and to Judah 836
21: 6 out of the tribe of **A**, and out of the tribe of 836
Jos 21:30 out of the tribe of **A**, Mishal with her 836
Jdg 1:31 Neither did **A** drive out the inhabitants of 836
5:17 **A** continued on the sea shore, and abode in 836
6:35 he sent messengers unto **A**, and 836
7:23 out of **A**, and out of all Manasseh, and 836
1Ki 4:16 Baanah the son of Hushai *was* in **A** and 836
1Ch 2: 2 Joseph, and Benjamin, Naphtali, Gad, and **A**. 836
6:62 out of the tribe of **A**, and out of the tribe of 836
6:74 out of the tribe of **A**; Mashal with her 836
7:30 The sons of **A**; Imnah, and Isuah, and Ishuai, 836
7:40 All these *were* the children of **A**, heads of 836
12:36 of **A**, such as went forth to battle, expert in 836
2Ch 30:11 Nevertheless divers of **A** and Manasseh and 836
Eze 48: 2 east side unto the west side, a *portion for* **A**. 836
48: 3 by the border of **A**, from the east side even 836
48:34 one gate of Gad, one gate of **A**, one gate of 836

ASHERITES (1) [ASHER]
Jdg 1:32 the **A** dwelt among the Canaanites, 843

ASHES (43)
Ge 18:27 unto the Lord, which *am but* dust and **a**: 665
Ex 9: 8 Take to you handfuls of **a** of the furnace, 6368
9:10 they took **a** of the furnace, and stood before 6368
27: 3 thou shalt make his pans to **receive** his **a**, 1878
Lev 1:16 altar on the east part, by the place of the **a**: 1880
4:12 where the **a** are poured out, and burn him 1880
4:12 where the **a** are poured out shall he be 1880
6:10 take up the **a** which the fire hath consumed 1880
6:11 carry forth the **a** without the camp unto a 1880
Nu 4:13 they shall **take away** the **a** from the altar, 1878
19: 9 a man *that is* clean shall gather up the **a** of 665
19:10 he that gathereth the **a** of the heifer shall 665
19:17 **a** of the burnt *heifer* of purification for sin, 6083
2Sa 13:19 Tamar put **a** on her head, and rent her 665
1Ki 13: 3 the **a** that *are* upon it shall be poured out. 1880
13: 5 and the **a** poured out from the altar, 1880
20:38 and disguised himself with **a** upon his face. 666
20:41 and took the **a** away from his face; 666
2Ki 23: 4 and carried the **a** of them *unto* Beth-el. 6083
Est 4: 1 put on sackcloth with **a**, and went out into 665
4: 3 wailing; *and* many lay in sackcloth and **a**. 665
Job 2: 8 and he sat down among the **a**. 665
13:12 Your remembrances *are* like unto **a**, 665
30:19 the mire, and I am become like dust and **a**. 665
42: 6 I abhor *myself*, and repent in dust and **a**. 665
Ps 102: 9 For I have eaten **a** like bread, and 665
147:16 like wool: he scattereth the hoarfrost like **a**. 665
Isa 44:20 He feedeth on **a**: a deceived heart hath 665
58: 5 and **a** *under him?* wilt thou call this a fast, 665
61: 3 to give unto them beauty for **a**, the oil of joy 665
Jer 6:26 *thee* with sackcloth, and wallow thyself in **a**: 665
25:34 wallow yourselves *in the* **a**, ye principal of NIH
31:40 of the **a**, and all the fields unto the brook of 1880
La 3:16 gravel stones, he hath covered me with **a**. 665
Eze 27:30 they shall wallow themselves in the **a**: 665
28:18 I will bring thee to **a** upon the earth in 665
Da 9: 3 with fasting, and sackcloth, and **a**: 665
Jnh 3: 6 and covered *him* with sackcloth, and sat in **a**. 665
Mal 4: 3 for they shall be **a** under the soles of your 665
Mt 11:21 have repented long ago in sackcloth and **a**. *4700*
Lk 10:13 ago repented, sitting in sackcloth and **a**. *4700*
Heb 9:13 and the **a** of a heifer sprinkling the unclean, *4700*
2Pe 2: 6 **turning** the cities of Sodom and Gomorrha
into a *5077*

ASHHUR See ASHUR

ASHIMA (1)
2Ki 17:30 and the men of Hamath made **A**, 807

ASHKELON (9) [ASKELON, ESHKALONITES]
Jdg 14:19 he went down *to* **A**, and slew thirty men of 831
Jer 25:20 **A**, and Azzah, and Ekron, and the remnant 831
47: 5 **A** is cut off *with* the remnant of their valley: 831
47: 7 the LORD hath given it a charge against **A**, 831
Am 1: 8 and him that holdeth the sceptre from **A**, and 831
Zep 2: 4 Gaza shall be forsaken, and **A** a desolation: 831
2: 7 in the houses of **A** shall they lie down in 831
Zec 9: 5 **A** shall see *it*, and fear; Gaza also *shall see* 831
9: 5 from Gaza, and **A** shall not be inhabited. 831

ASHKENAZ (1)
Ge 10: 3 of Gomer; **A**, and Riphath, and Togarmah. 813

ASHNAH (2)
Jos 15:33 in the valley, Eshtaol, and Zoreah, and **A**, 823
15:43 And Jiphtah, and **A**, and Nezib, 823

ASHPENAZ (1)
Da 1: 3 the king spake unto **A** the master of his 828

ASHRIEL (1)
1Ch 7:14 The sons of Manasseh; **A**, whom she bare: 844

ASHTAROTH (11) [ASHTORETH]
Jos 9:10 and to Og king of Bashan, which *was* at **A**. 6252
12: 4 of the giants, that dwelt at **A** and at Edrei, 6252
13:12 in Bashan, which reigned in **A** and in Edrei, 6252
13:31 half Gilead, and **A**, and Edrei, cities of 6252
Jdg 2:13 the LORD, and served Baal and **A**. 6252
10: 6 **A**, and the gods of Syria, and the gods of 6252
1Sa 7: 3 the strange gods and **A** from among you, 6252
7: 4 of Israel did put away Baalim and **A**, 6252
12:10 and have served Baalim and **A**: 6252
31:10 they put his armour *in* the house of **A**: and 6253
1Ch 6:71 with her suburbs, and **A** with her suburbs: 6252

ASHTERATHITE (1)
1Ch 11:44 Uzzia the **A**, Shama and Jehiel the sons of 6254

ASHTEROTH KARNAIM (1)
Ge 14: 5 and smote the Rephaims in **A**, 6255

ASHTORETH (3) [ASHTAROTH]
1Ki 11: 5 For Solomon went after **A** the goddess of 6253
11:33 have worshipped **A** the goddess of 6253
2Ki 23:13 for **A** the abomination of the Zidonians, 6253

ASHUR (2) [ASHURITES]
1Ch 2:24 Abiah Hezron's wife bare him **A** the father 806
4: 5 **A** the father of Tekoa had two wives, Helah 806

ASHURBANIPAL See ASNAPPER

ASHURI See ASHURITES

ASHURITES (2) [ASHUR]
2Sa 2: 9 over the **A**, and over Jezreel, and 805
Eze 27: 6 the company of the **A** have made thy 839

ASHVATH (1)
1Ch 7:33 sons of Japhlet; Pasach, and Bimhal, and **A**. 6220

ASIA (21)
Ac 2: 9 in Judea, and Cappadocia, in Pontus, and **A**, *773*
6: 9 and of them of Cilicia and of **A**, *773*
16: 6 of the Holy Ghost to preach the word in **A**, *773*
19:10 that all they which dwelt in **A** heard *773*
19:22 but he himself stayed in **A** for a season. *773*
19:26 but almost throughout all **A**, this Paul hath *773*
19:27 whom all **A** and the world worshippeth. *773*
19:31 And certain of the **chief of A**, which were *775*
20: 4 And there accompanied him into **A** Sopater *773*
20: 4 and **of A**, Tychicus and Trophimus. *774*
20:16 because he would not spend the time in **A**: *773*
20:18 from the first day that I came into **A**, *773*
21:27 the Jews which were of **A**, when they saw *773*
24:18 Whereupon certain Jews from **A** found me *773*
27: 2 meaning to sail by the coasts of **A**; *773*
1Co 16:19 The churches of **A** salute you. Aquila and *773*
2Co 1: 8 of our trouble which came to us in **A**, *773*
2Ti 1:15 that all they which are in **A** be turned away *773*
1Pe 1: 1 Galatia, Cappadocia, **A**, and Bithynia, *773*
Rev 1: 4 John to the seven churches which are in **A**: *773*
1:11 *it* unto the seven churches which are in **A**; *773*

ASIDE (72) [SIDE]
Ex 3: 3 I will now **turn a**, and see this great sight, 5493
3: 4 when the LORD saw that he **turned a** to 5493
32: 8 They have **turned a** quickly out of the way 5493
Nu 5:12 If any man's wife **go a**, and commit a 7847
5:19 if thou hast not **gone a** *to* uncleanness *with* 7847
5:20 if thou hast **gone a** *to another* instead of thy 7847
5:29 when a wife **goeth a** *to another* instead of 7847
22:23 the ass **turned a** out of the way, and 5186
Dt 5:32 ye shall not **turn a** *to* the right hand or 5493
9:12 **turned a** out of the way which I 5493
9:16 ye had **turned a** quickly out of the way 5493
11:16 ye **turn a**, and serve other gods, and 5493
11:28 **turn a** out of the way which I command 5493
17:20 that *he* **turn** not **a** from the commandment, 5493
28:14 thou shalt not **go a** from any of the words 5493
31:29 **turn a** from the way which I have 5493
Jos 23: 6 that *ye* **turn** not **a** therefrom *to* the right 5493
Jdg 14: 8 he **turned a** to see the carcase of the lion: 5493
19:12 We will not **turn a** hither into the city of a 5493
19:15 they **turned a** thither, to go in *and* to lodge 5493
Ru 4: 1 *Ho,* such a one, **turn a**, sit down here. 5493
4: 1 down here. And he **turned a**, and sat down. 5493
1Sa 6:12 **turned** not **a** *to* the right hand or *to* the left; 5493
8: 3 **turned a** after lucre, and took bribes, and 5186
12:20 yet **turn** not **a** from following the LORD, 5493
12:21 **turn** ye not **a**: for *then should ye go* after 5493
2Sa 2:21 **Turn** thee **a** to thy right hand or to thy left, 5186
2:21 Asahel would not **turn a** from following of 5493
2:22 to Asahel, **Turn** thee **a** from following me: 5493
2:23 Howbeit he refused to **turn a**: 5493
3:27 Joab **took** him **a** in the gate to speak with 5186
6:10 David **carried** it **a** *into* the house of 5186
18:30 the king said *unto him,* **Turn a**, *and* 5437
18:30 And he **turned a**, and stood still. 5437
1Ki 15: 5 **turned** not **a** from any *thing* that he 5493
20:39 a man **turned a**, and brought a man unto 5493
22:32 they **turned a** to fight against him: and 5493
22:43 he **turned** not **a** from it, doing *that* which 5493
2Ki 4: 4 and thou shalt **set a** *that* which *is* full. 5265
22: 2 **turned** not **a** *to* the right hand or *to* the left. 5493
1Ch 13:13 **carried** it **a** into the house of Obed-edom 5186
Job 6:18 The paths of their way are **turned a**; 3943
Ps 14: 3 They are all **gone a**, they are *all* together 5493
40: 4 not the proud, nor such as **turn a** to lies. 7750
78:57 they were **turned a** like a deceitful bow. 2015
101: 3 I hate the work of them that **turn a**; *it* shall 7750
125: 5 As for such as **turn a** *unto* their crooked 5186
SS 1: 7 for why should I be as one that **turneth a** 5844
6: 1 whither is thy beloved **turned a**? that we 6437
Isa 10: 2 To **turn a** the needy from judgment, and 5186
29:21 and **turn a** the just for a thing of nought. 5186
30:11 ye out of the way, **turn a** out of the path, 5186
44:20 a deceived heart hath **turned** him **a**, that he 5186
Jer 14: 8 as a wayfaring man *that* **turneth a** to tarry 5186
15: 5 or who shall **go a** to ask how thou doest? 5493
La 3:11 He hath **turned a** my ways, and pulled me 5493
3:35 To **turn a** the right of a man before the face 5186
Am 2: 7 the poor, and **turn a** the way of the meek: 5186
5:12 they **turn a** the poor in the gate *from their* 5186
Mal 3: 5 that **turn a** the stranger *from his right,* and 5186
Mt 2:22 he **turned a** into the parts of Galilee: *402*
Mk 7: 8 For **laying a** the commandment of God, *863*
7:33 And he took him **a** from *2398+2596*
Lk 9:10 **went a** privately into a desert place *5298*
Jn 13: 4 riseth from supper, and **laid a** *his* garments; *5087*
Ac 4:15 But when they had commanded them to **go a** *565*
23:19 by the hand, and **went** *with him* **a** privately, *402*
26:31 And when they were **gone a**, they talked *402*
1Ti 1: 6 swerved have **turned a** unto vain jangling; *1624*
5:15 For some are already **turned a** after Satan. *1624*
Heb 12: 1 let us **lay a** every weight, and the sin which *659*
1Pe 2: 1 Wherefore **laying a** all malice, and all guile, *659*

ASIEL (1)
1Ch 4:35 the son of Seraiah, the son of **A**, 6221

ASK (109) [ASKED, ASKEST, ASKETH, ASKING]
Ge 32:29 Wherefore *is* it *that* thou dost **a** after my 7592
34:12 **A** me **never so much** dowry and gift, 3966+7235
Nu 27:21 who shall **a** *counsel* for him after 7592
Dt 4:32 For **a** now of the days that are past, 7592
4:32 *a* from the one side of heaven unto NIH
13:14 and make search, and **a** diligently; 7592
32: 7 **a** thy father, and he will shew thee; 7592
Jos 4: 6 *that* when your children **a** *their fathers* in 7592
4:21 When your children shall **a** their fathers in 7592
15:18 she moved him to **a** of her father a field: 7592
Jdg 1:14 she moved him to **a** of her father a field: 7592
18: 5 unto him, **A** *counsel,* we pray thee, of God, 7592
1Sa 12:19 unto all our sins *this* evil, to **a** us a king. 7592
25: 8 **A** thy young men, and they will shew thee. 7592
28:16 Wherefore then dost thou **a** of me, 7592
2Sa 14:18 I pray thee, the thing that I shall **a** thee. 7592
20:18 They shall **surely a** *counsel* at Abel: 7592+7592
1Ki 2:16 now I **a** one **petition** of thee, 7592+7596
2:20 the king said unto her, **A on**, my mother: 7592
2:22 why dost thou **a** Abishag the Shunammite 7592
2:22 **a** for him the kingdom also; for he *is* mine 7592
3: 5 and God said, **A** what I shall give thee. 7592
14: 5 the wife of Jeroboam cometh to **a** a thing of 1875
2Ki 2: 9 said unto Elisha, **A** what I shall do for thee, 7592
2Ch 1: 7 and said unto him, **A** what I shall give thee. 7592
20: 4 to **a** *help* of the LORD: 1245
Job 12: 7 **a** now the beasts, and they shall teach thee; 7592
Ps 2: 8 **A** of me, and I shall give *thee* the heathen 7592
Isa 7:11 **A** thee a sign of the LORD thy God; ask it 7592
7:11 **a** it either in the depth, or in the height 7592
7:12 Ahaz said, I will not **a**, neither will I tempt 7592
45:11 **A** me of *things* to come concerning my 7592
58: 2 they **a** of me the ordinances of justice; 7592
Jer 6:16 the ways, and see, and **a** for the old paths, 7592
15: 5 or who shall go aside to **a** how thou doest? 7592
18:13 **A** ye now among the heathen, who hath 7592
23:33 the prophet, or a priest, shall **a** thee, saying, 7592
30: 6 **A** ye now, and see whether a man doth 7592
38:14 said unto Jeremiah, I *will* **a** thee a thing; 7592
48:19 **a** him that fleeth, and her that escapeth, *and* 7592
50: 5 They shall **a** the way *to* Zion with their 7592
La 4: 4 the young children **a** bread, *and* no man 7592
Da 6: 7 that whosoever shall **a** a petition of any 1156
6:12 that every man that shall **a** *a petition* of any 1156
Hos 4:12 My people **a** *counsel* at their stocks, and 7592
Hag 2:11 **A** now the priests *concerning* the law, 7592
Zec 10: 1 **A** ye of the LORD rain in the time of 7592
Mt 6: 8 *things* ye have need of, before ye **a** him. *154*
7: 7 **A**, and it shall be given you; seek, and *154*
7: 9 whom if his son **a** bread, will he give him a *154*
7:10 Or if he **a** a fish, will he give him a serpent? *154*
7:11 heaven give good *things* to them that **a** him? *154*
14: 7 an oath to give her whatsoever she would **a**. *154*
18:19 earth as touching any thing that they shall **a**, *154*
20:22 and said, Ye know not what ye **a**. *154*
21:22 And all *things,* whatsoever ye shall **a** in *154*
21:24 said unto them, I also will **a** you one thing, *2065*
22:46 neither durst any *man* from that day forth **a** *1905*
27:20 the multitude that they should **a** Barabbas, *154*
Mk 6:22 **A** of me whatsoever thou wilt, and I will *154*
6:23 Whatsoever thou shalt **a** of me, I will give *it* *154*
6:24 and said unto her mother, What shall I **a**? *154*
9:32 not *that* saying, and were afraid to **a** him. *1905*
10:38 said unto them, Ye know not what ye **a**: *154*
11:29 I will also **a** of you one question, and *1905*
12:34 And no *man* after that durst **a** him *any* *1905*
Lk 6: 9 I will **a** you one *thing;* Is it lawful on *1905*
6:30 that taketh away thy *goods* **a** *them* not **again**. *523*
9:45 and they feared to **a** him of that saying. *2065*
11: 9 I say unto you, **A**, and it shall be given you; *154*
11:11 *If* a son shall **a** bread of any of you that is a *154*
11:11 or if *he* **a** a fish, will he for a fish give him a NIG
11:12 Or if he shall **a** an egg, will he offer him a *154*
11:13 give the Holy Spirit to them that **a** him? *154*
12:48 of him they will **a** the more. *154*
19:31 And if any *man* **a** you, Why do ye loose *2065*
20: 3 said unto them, I will also **a** you one thing; *2065*
20:40 And after that they durst not **a** him any *1905*
22:68 And if I also **a** *you,* you will not answer *2065*
Jn 1:19 and Levites from Jerusalem to **a** him, *2065*
9:21 he is of age; **a** him: he shall speak for *2065*
9:23 said his parents, He is of age; **a** him. *2065*
11:22 even now, whatsoever thou wilt **a** of God, *154*
13:24 that *he* should **a** who it should be of whom *4441*
14:13 And whatsoever ye shall **a** in my name, *154*
14:14 If ye shall **a** any *thing* in my name, I will do *154*
15: 7 ye shall **a** what ye will, and it shall be done *154*
15:16 that whatsoever ye shall **a** of the Father in *154*
16:19 knew that they were desirous to **a** him, *2065*
16:23 And in that day ye shall **a** me nothing. *2065*
16:23 Whatsoever ye shall **a** the Father in my *154*
16:24 **a**, and ye shall receive, that your joy may be *154*
16:26 At that day ye shall **a** in my name: and I say *154*
16:30 and needest not that any *man* should **a** thee: *2065*
18:21 **a** them which heard *me,* what I have said *1905*
21:12 And none of the disciples durst **a** him, *1833*
Ac 3: 2 to **a** alms of them that entered into *154*
10:29 I **a** therefore for what intent ye have sent *4441*
1Co 14:35 And if they will learn any *thing,* let them **a** *1905*
Eph 3:20 do exceeding abundantly above all that we **a** *154*
Jas 1: 5 If any of you lack wisdom, let him **a** of God, *154*
1: 6 But let him **a** in faith, nothing wavering: *154*
4: 2 and war, yet ye have not, because ye **a** not. *154*
4: 3 Ye **a**, and receive not, because ye ask amiss, *154*
4: 3 Ye ask, and receive not, because ye **a** amiss, *154*
1Jn 3:22 And whatsoever we **a**, we receive of him, *154*
5:14 that, if we **a** any *thing* according to his will, *154*
5:15 if we know that he hear us, whatsoever we **a**, *154*
1Jn 5:16 he shall **a**, and he shall give him life for *154*

ASKED (119) [ASK]
Ge 24:47 I **a** her, and said, Whose daughter *art* thou? 7592
26: 7 the men of the place **a** *him* of his wife; and 7592
32:29 Jacob **a** *him,* and said, Tell *me,* I pray thee, 7592
37:15 the man **a** him, saying, What seekest thou? 7592
38:21 he **a** the men of that place, saying, Where *is* 7592
40: 7 he **a** Pharaoh's officers that *were* with him 7592
43: 7 The man **a** us **straitly** of our state, 7592+7592
43:27 he **a** them of *their* welfare, and said, *Is* your 7592
44:19 My lord **a** his servants, saying, Have ye a 7592
Ex 18: 7 they **a** each other of *their* welfare; and 7592
Jos 9:14 **a** not *counsel* at the mouth of the LORD. 7592
19:50 LORD they gave him the city which he **a**, 7592
Jdg 1: 1 that the children of Israel **a** the LORD, 7592
5:25 He **a** water, *and* she gave *him* milk; 7592
6:29 when they inquired and **a**, they said, 1245
13: 6 I **a** him not whence he *was,* neither told he 7592
20:18 of God, and **a** *counsel* of God, and said, 7592
20:23 and **a** *counsel* of the LORD, saying, 7592
1Sa 1:17 *thee* thy petition that thou hast **a** of him. 7592
1:20 *saying,* Because I have **a** him of 7592
1:27 given me my petition which I **a** of him: 7592
8:10 unto the people that **a** of him a king. 7592
14:37 Saul **a** *counsel* of God, Shall I go down 7592
19:22 he **a** and said, Where *are* Samuel and 7592
20: 6 David **earnestly a** *leave* of me that 7592+7592
20:28 David **earnestly a** *leave* of me *to go* 7592+7592
1Ki 3:10 the Lord, that Solomon had **a** this thing. 7592
3:11 Because thou hast **a** this thing, and hast not 7592
3:11 and hast not **a** for thyself long life; 7592
3:11 neither hast **a** riches for thyself, nor hast 7592
3:11 nor hast **a** the life of thine enemies; 7592
3:11 hast **a** for thyself understanding to discern 7592
3:13 also given thee *that* which thou hast not **a**, 7592
10:13 what*soever* she **a**, besides *that* which 7592
2Ki 2:10 he said, Thou hast **a** a hard thing: 7592
8: 6 when the king **a** the woman, she told him. 7592
2Ch 1:11 thou hast not **a** riches, wealth, or honour, 7592
1:11 thine enemies, neither yet hast **a** long life; 7592
1:11 hast **a** wisdom and knowledge for thyself, 7592
9:12 what*soever* she **a**, besides *that* which she 7592
Ezr 5: 9 **a** we those elders, *and* said unto them thus, 7593
5:10 We **a** their names also, to certify thee, 7593
Ne 1: 2 I **a** them concerning the Jews that had 7592
Job 21:29 Have ye not **a** them that go by the way? 7592
Ps 21: 4 He **a** life of thee, *and* thou gavest *it* him, 7592
105:40 *The people* **a**, and he brought quails, and 7592
Isa 30: 2 *into* Egypt, and have not **a** *at* my mouth; 7592
41:28 that, when I **a** of them, could answer a 7592
65: 1 I am sought of *them that* **a** not *for me:* I am 7592
Jer 36:17 they **a** Baruch, saying, Tell us now, 7592
37:17 and the king **a** him secretly in his house, 7592
38:27 all the princes unto Jeremiah, and **a** him: 7592
Da 2:10 *that* **a** such things at any magician, or 7593
7:16 that stood *by,* and **a** him the truth of all this. 1156
Mt 12:10 And they **a** him, saying, Is it lawful to heal *1905*
16:13 he **a** his disciples, saying, Whom do men *2065*
17:10 And his disciples **a** him, saying, Why then *1905*
22:23 say that there is no resurrection, and **a** him, *1905*
22:35 **a** *him a question,* tempting him, and saying, *1905*
22:41 were gathered together, Jesus **a** them, *1905*
27:11 and the governor **a** him, saying, Art thou *1905*
Mk 4:10 they that were about him with the twelve **a** *2065*
5: 9 And he **a** him, What *is* thy name? And he *1905*
6:25 and **a**, saying, I will that thou give me by *154*
7: 5 Then the Pharisees and scribes **a** him, *1905*
7:17 his disciples **a** him concerning the parable. *1905*
8: 5 And he **a** them, How many loaves have ye? *1905*
8:23 hands upon him, he **a** him if he saw ought. *1905*
8:27 and by the way he **a** his disciples, *1905*
9:11 And they **a** him, saying, Why say *1905*
9:16 And he **a** the scribes, What question ye *1905*
9:21 And he **a** his father, How long is it ago *1905*
9:28 his disciples **a** him privately, Why could *1905*
9:33 and being in the house he **a** them, *1905*
10: 2 And the Pharisees came to *him,* and **a** him, *1905*
10:10 And in the house his disciples **a** him again *1905*
10:17 kneeled to him, and **a** him, Good Master, *1905*
12:18 is no resurrection; and they **a** him, saying, *1905*
12:28 **a** him, Which is the first commandment of *1905*
13: 3 and John and Andrew **a** him privately, *1905*
14:60 and **a** Jesus, saying, Answerest thou *1905*
14:61 Again the high priest **a** him, and said unto *1905*
15: 2 And Pilate **a** him, Art thou the King of *1905*
15: 4 And Pilate **a** him again, saying, *1905*
15:44 he **a** him whether he had been any while *1905*
Lk 1:63 And he **a for** a writing table, and wrote, *154*
3:10 And the people **a** him, saying, What shall *1905*
8: 9 And his disciples **a** him, saying, *1905*
8:30 And Jesus **a** him, saying, What is thy *1905*
9:18 and he **a** them, saying, Whom say *1905*
15:26 the servants, and **a** what these *things* meant. *4441*
18:18 And a certain ruler **a** him, saying, *1905*
18:36 the multitude pass by, he **a** what it meant. *4441*
18:40 and when he was come near, he **a** him, *1905*
20:21 And they **a** him, saying, Master, we know *1905*
20:27 there is any resurrection; and they **a** him, *1905*
21: 7 And they **a** him, saying, Master, *1905*
22:64 and **a** him, saying, Prophesy, who is it that *1905*
23: 3 And Pilate **a** him, saying, Art thou the King *1905*
23: 6 he **a** whether the man were a Galilean. *1905*
Jn 1:21 And they **a** him, What then? Art thou *2065*
1:25 And they **a** him, and said unto him, *2065*
4:10 thou wouldest have **a** of him, and he would *154*
5:12 Then **a** they him, What man is that which *2065*
9: 2 And his disciples **a** him, saying, Master, *2065*
9:15 Then again the Pharisees also **a** him how he *2065*
9:19 And they **a** them, saying, Is this your son, *2065*
16:24 Hitherto have ye **a** nothing in my name: ask, *154*
18: 7 Then **a** he them again, Whom seek ye? *1905*
18:19 high priest then **a** Jesus of his disciples, *2065*
Ac 1: 6 come together, they **a** of him, saying, Lord, *1905*
3: 3 John about to go into the temple, **a** an alms. *2065*

Ac 4: 7 they **a**, By what power, or by what name, 4441
5:27 the council: and the high priest **a** them, 1905
10:18 And called, and **a** whether Simon, 4441
23:19 **a** *him,* What is that thou hast to tell me? 4441
23:34 *the letter,* he **a** of what province he was: 1905
25:20 I **a** *him* whether he would go to Jerusalem, 3004
Ro 10:20 manifest unto them that **a** not **after** me. 1905

ASKELON (3) [ASHKELON]
Jdg 1:18 **A** with the coast thereof, and Ekron with 831
1Sa 6:17 for Gaza one, for **A** one, for Gath one, 831
2Sa 1:20 not in Gath, publish *it* not in the streets of **A**; 831

ASKEST (3) [ASK]
Jdg 13:18 Why **a** thou thus after my name, seeing it *is* 7592
Jn 4: 9 *is it that* thou, being a Jew, **a** drink of me, 154
18:21 Why **a** thou me? ask them which heard *me,* 1905

ASKETH (11) [ASK]
Ge 32:17 and **a** thee, saying, Whose *art* thou? 7592
Ex 13:14 it shall be when thy son **a** thee in time to 7592
Dt 6:20 *And* when thy son **a** thee in time to come, 7592
Mic 7: 3 the prince **a**, and the judge *asketh* for a 7592
7: 3 prince asketh, and the judge *a* for a reward; NIH
Mt 5:42 Give to him that **a** thee, and from him that 154
7: 8 For every one that **a** receiveth; and he that 154
Lk 6:30 Give to every man that **a** of thee; and of him 154
11:10 For every one that **a** receiveth; and he that 154
Jn 16: 5 and none of you **a** me, Whither goest thou? 2065
1Pe 3:15 **a** you a reason of the hope that is in you with 154

ASKING (7) [ASK]
1Sa 12:17 in the sight of the LORD, in **a** you a king. 7592
1Ch 10:13 also for **a** *counsel of one that had* a familiar 7592
Ps 78:18 they tempted God in their heart by **a** meat 7592
Lk 2:46 both hearing them, and **a** them *questions.* 1905
Jn 8: 7 So when they continued **a** him, he lift up 2065
1Co 10:25 *that* eat, **a** no **question** for conscience sake: 350
10:27 eat, **a** no **question** for conscience sake. 350

ASLEEP (16) [SLEEP]
Jdg 4:21 for he was **fast a** and weary. So he died. 7290
1Sa 26:12 for they *were* all **a**; because a deep sleep 3463
SS 7: 9 causing the lips of *those that are* **a** to speak. 3463
Jnh 1: 5 of the ship; and he lay, and was **fast a**. 7290
Mt 8:24 was covered with the waves: but he was **a**. 2518
26:40 and findeth them **a**, and saith unto Peter, 2518
26:43 And he came and found them **a** again: 2518
Mk 4:38 in the hinder part of the ship, **a** on a pillow: 2518
14:40 when he returned, he found them **a** again, 2518
Lk 8:23 But as they sailed he **fell a**: and there came 879
Ac 7:60 And when he had said this, he **fell a**. 2837
1Co 15: 6 unto this present, but some are **fallen a**. 2837
15:18 Then they also which are **fallen a** in Christ 2837
1Th 4:13 brethren, concerning them which are **a**, 2837
4:15 Lord shall not prevent them which are **a**. 2837
2Pe 3: 4 for since the fathers **fell a**, all *things* 2837

ASNAH (1)
Ezr 2:50 The children of **A**, the children of Mehunim, 619

ASNAPPAR (1)
Ezr 4:10 whom the great and noble **A** brought over, 620

ASP (1) [ASPS]
Isa 11: 8 child shall play on the hole of the **a**, 6620

ASPATHA (1)
Est 9: 7 And Parshandatha, and Dalphon, and **A**, 630

ASPS (4) [ASP]
Dt 32:33 of dragons, and the cruel venom of **a**. 6620
Job 20:14 is turned, *it is* the gall of **a** within him. 6620
20:16 He shall suck the poison of **a**: the viper's 6620
Ro 3:13 the poison of **a** *is* under their lips: 785

ASRIEL (2) [ASRIELITES]
Nu 26:31 *of* **A**, the family of the Asrielites: and 844
Jos 17: 2 for the children of **A**, and for the children of 844

ASRIELITES (1) [ASRIEL]
Nu 26:31 *of* Asriel, the family of the **A**: and 845

ASS (86) [ASS'S, ASSES]
Ge 22: 3 saddled his **a**, and took two of his young 2543
22: 5 his young men, Abide you here with the **a**; 2543
42:27 his sack to give his **a** provender in the inn, 2543
44:13 laded every man his **a**, and returned to 2543
49:14 Issachar *is* a strong **a** couching down 2543
Ex 4:20 set them upon an **a**, and he returned to 2543
13:13 every firstling of an **a** thou shalt redeem 2543
20:17 nor his maidservant, nor his ox, nor his **a**, 2543
21:33 not cover it, and an ox or an **a** fall therein; 2543
22: 4 hand alive, whether it be ox, or **a**, or sheep; 2543
22: 9 for **a**, for sheep, for raiment, *or* for any 2543
22:10 If a man deliver unto his neighbour an **a**, or 2543
23: 4 thine enemy's ox or his **a** going astray, 2543
23: 5 If thou see the **a** of him that hateth thee 2543
23:12 that thine ox and thine **a** may rest, and 2543
34:20 the firstling of an **a** thou shalt redeem with 2543
Nu 16:15 I have not taken one **a** from them, 2543
22:21 saddled his **a**, and went with the princes of 860
22:22 Now he was riding upon his **a**, and his two 860
22:23 the **a** saw the angel of the LORD standing 860
22:23 the **a** turned aside out of the way, and 860
22:23 Balaam smote the **a**, to turn her *into* the way. 860
22:25 when the **a** saw the angel of the LORD, 860
22:27 when the **a** saw the angel of the LORD, 860
22:27 was kindled, and he smote the **a** with a staff. 860
22:28 And the LORD opened the mouth of the **a**, 860
22:29 Balaam said unto the **a**, Because thou hast 860
22:30 the **a** said unto Balaam, *Am* not I thine ass, 860
22:30 the ass said unto Balaam, *Am* not I thine **a**, 860

Nu 22:32 Wherefore hast thou smitten thine **a** these 860
22:33 the **a** saw me, and turned from me these 860
Dt 5:14 thy maidservant, nor thine ox, nor thine **a**, 2543
5:21 or his **a**, or any *thing* that *is* thy 2543
22: 3 In like manner shalt thou do with his **a**; and 2543
22: 4 Thou shalt not see thy brother's **a** or his ox 2543
22:10 shalt not plow with an ox and an **a** together. 2543
28:31 thine **a** *shall be* violently taken away from 2543
Jos 6:21 and old, and ox, and sheep, and **a**, 2543
15:18 she lighted off *her* **a**; and Caleb said unto 2543
Jdg 1:14 she lighted from off *her* **a**; and Caleb said 2543
6: 4 for Israel, neither sheep, nor ox, nor **a**. 2543
10: 4 had thirty sons that rode on thirty **a colts**, 5895
12:14 that rode on threescore and ten **a colts**: 5895
15:15 he found a new jawbone of an **a**, and 2543
15:16 Samson said, With the jawbone of an **a**, 2543
15:16 with the jaw of an **a** have I slain a thousand 2543
19:28 the man took her *up* upon an **a**, and the man 2543
1Sa 12: 3 or whose **a** have I taken? or whom have I 2543
15: 3 and suckling, ox and sheep, camel and **a**. 2543
16:20 Jesse took an **a** *laden* with bread, and 2543
25:20 it was *so, as* she rode on the **a**, that she 2543
25:23 lighted off the **a**, and fell before David on 2543
25:42 and rose, and rode upon an **a**, 2543
2Sa 17:23 he saddled *his* **a**, and arose, and gat him 2543
19:26 for thy servant said, I will saddle me an **a**, 2543
1Ki 2:40 saddled his **a**, and went to Gath to Achish 2543
13:13 he said unto his sons, Saddle me the **a**. 2543
13:13 So they saddled him the **a**: and he rode 2543
13:23 he had drunk, that he saddled for him the **a**, 2543
13:24 was cast in the way, and the **a** stood by it, 2543
13:27 spake to his sons, saying, Saddle me the **a**. 2543
13:28 the **a** and the lion standing by the carcase: 2543
13:28 had not eaten the carcase, nor torn the **a**. 2543
13:29 and laid it upon the **a**, and brought it back: 2543
2Ki 4:24 she saddled an **a**, and said to her servant, 860
Job 6: 5 Doth the **wild a** bray when he hath grass? 6501
24: 3 They drive away the **a** of the fatherless, 2543
39: 5 Who hath sent out the **wild a** free? or 6501
39: 5 or who hath loosed the bands of the **wild a**? 6171
Pr 26: 3 a bridle for the **a**, and a rod for the fools' 2543
Isa 1: 3 his owner, and the **a** his master's crib: 2543
32:20 forth *thither* the feet of the ox and the **a**. 2543
Jer 2:24 A **wild a** used to the wilderness, 6501
22:19 He shall be buried *with* the burial of an **a**, 2543
Hos 8: 9 up *to* Assyria, a **wild a** alone by himself: 6501
Zec 9: 9 riding upon an **a**, and upon a colt the foal of 2543
9: 9 upon an ass, and upon a colt the foal of an **a**. 860
14:15 of the **a**, and of all the beasts that shall be 2543
Mt 21: 2 and straightway ye shall find an **a** tied, and 3688
21: 5 and sitting upon an **a**, and a colt the foal of 3688
21: 5 upon an ass, and a colt the foal of an **a**. 5268
21: 7 And brought the **a**, and the colt, and put on 3688
Lk 13:15 sabbath loose his ox or *his* **a** from the stall, 3688
14: 5 Which of you shall have an **a** or an ox 3688
Jn 12:14 And Jesus, when he had found a **young a**, 3678
2Pe 2:16 the dumb **a** speaking with man's voice 5268

ASS'S (4) [ASS]
Ge 49:11 the vine, and his **a** colt unto the choice vine; 860
2Ki 6:25 until an **a** head was *sold* for fourscore 2543
Job 11:12 though man be born *like* a **wild a** colt. 6501
Jn 12:15 thy King cometh, sitting on an **a** colt. 3688

ASSAULT (2) [ASSAULTED]
Est 8:11 the people and province that would **a** them, 6696
Ac 14: 5 And when there was an **a** made both of 3730

ASSAULTED (1) [ASSAULT]
Ac 17: 5 and **a** the house of Jason, and sought to 2186

ASSAY (1) [ASSAYED, ASSAYING]
Job 4: 2 *If we* **a** to commune with thee, wilt thou be 5254

ASSAYED (4) [ASSAY]
Dt 4:34 Or hath God **a** to go *and* take him a nation 5254
1Sa 17:39 his sword upon his armour, and he **a** to go; 2974
Ac 9:26 he **a** to join himself to the disciples: 3987
16: 7 come to Mysia, they **a** to go into Bithynia: 3985

ASSAYING (1) [ASSAY]
Heb 11:29 which the Egyptians **a** to do were drowned. 3984

ASSEMBLE (20) [ASSEMBLED, ASSEMBLIES, ASSEMBLING, ASSEMBLY]
Nu 10: 3 all the assembly shall **a** themselves to thee 3259
2Sa 20: 4 **A** me the men of Judah *within* three days, 2199
20: 5 So Amasa went to **a** *the men of* Judah: but 2199
Isa 11:12 shall **a** the outcasts of Israel, and 622
45:20 **A** yourselves and come; draw near 6908
48:14 All ye, **a** yourselves, and hear; 6908
Jer 4: 5 **A** yourselves, and let us go into the defenced 622
8:14 **a** yourselves, and let us enter into 622
12: 9 come ye, **a** all the beasts of the field, 622
21: 4 and I will **a** them into the midst of this city. 622
Eze 11:17 **a** you out of the countries where ye have 622
39:17 beast of the field, **A** yourselves, and come; 6908
Da 11:10 and shall **a** a multitude of great forces: 622
Hos 7:14 they **a** themselves for corn and wine, *and* 1481
Joel 2:16 **a** the elders, gather the children, and 6908
3:11 **A** yourselves, and come, all ye heathen, 5789
Am 3: 9 **A** yourselves upon the mountains of 622
Mic 2:12 I will **surely a**, O Jacob, all of thee; 622+622
4: 6 will I **a** her that halteth, and I will gather her 622
Zep 3: 8 that I may **a** the kingdoms, to pour upon 6908

ASSEMBLED (37) [ASSEMBLE]
Ex 38: 8 which **a** *at* the door of the tabernacle of 6633
Nu 1:18 they **a** all the congregation **together** on 6950
Jos 18: 1 the children of Israel **a together** *at* Shiloh, 6950
Jdg 10:17 the children of Israel **a** themselves **together**, 622
1Sa 2:22 how they lay with the women that **a** *at* 6633
14:20 all the people that *were* with him **a** 2199
1Ki 8: 1 Solomon **a** the elders of Israel, and all 6950

1Ki 8: 2 all the men of Israel **a** themselves unto king 6950
8: 5 of Israel, that were **a** unto him, 3259
12:21 he **a** all the house of Judah, with the tribe of 6950
1Ch 15: 4 David **a** the children of Aaron, and 622
28: 1 David **a** all the princes of Israel, the princes 6950
2Ch 5: 2 Solomon **a** the elders of Israel, and all 6950
5: 3 Wherefore all the men of Israel **a** 6950
5: 6 all the congregation of Israel that were **a** 3259
20:26 on the fourth day they **a** themselves in 6950
30:13 there **a** *at* Jerusalem much people to keep 622
Ezr 9: 4 were **a** unto me every one that trembled at 622
10: 1 there **a** unto him out of Israel a very great 6908
Ne 9: 1 the children of Israel were **a** with fasting, 622
Est 9:18 the Jews that *were* at Shushan **a together** 6950
Ps 48: 4 For lo, the kings were **a**, they passed by 3259
Isa 43: 9 be gathered together, and let the people be **a**: 622
Jer 5: 7 **a** themselves **by troops** *in* the harlots' 1413
Eze 38: 7 all thy company that are **a** unto thee, and 6950
Da 6: 6 princes **a** *together* to the king, 7284
6:11 these men **a**, and found Daniel praying 7284
6:15 these men **a** unto the king, and said unto 7284
Mt 26: 3 Then **a together** the chief priests, and 4863
26:57 where the scribes and the elders were **a**. 4863
28:12 And when they were **a** with the elders, and 4863
Mk 14:53 **with** him were **a** all the chief priests and 4905
Jn 20:19 the disciples were **a** for fear of the Jews, 4863
Ac 1: 4 And, being **a together with** them, 4871
4:31 was shaken where they were **a together**; 4863
11:26 that a whole year they **a** themselves with 4863
15:25 good unto us, being **a** with one accord, 1096

ASSEMBLIES (6) [ASSEMBLE]
Ps 86:14 the **a** of violent *men* have sought after my 5712
Ecc 12:11 and as nails fastened *by* the masters of **a**, 627
Isa 1:13 new moons and sabbaths, the calling of **a**, 4744
4: 5 upon her **a**, a cloud and smoke by day, and 4744
Eze 44:24 keep my laws and my statutes in all mine **a**; 4150
Am 5:21 and I will not smell in your **solemn a**. 6116

ASSEMBLING (2) [ASSEMBLE]
Ex 38: 8 of the lookingglasses of *the women* **a**, 6633
Heb 10:25 Not forsaking the **a** of ourselves **together**, 1997

ASSEMBLY (49) [ASSEMBLE]
Ge 49: 6 unto their **a**, mine honour, be not thou 6951
Ex 12: 6 the whole **a** of the congregation of Israel 6951
16: 3 to kill this whole **a** with hunger. 6951
Lev 4:13 the thing be hid from the eyes of the **a**, and 6951
8: 4 the **a** was gathered together unto the door 5712
23:36 it *is* a **solemn a**; *and* ye shall do no servile 6116
Nu 8: 9 thou shalt gather the whole **a** of 5712
10: 2 mayest use them for the calling of the **a**, 5712
10: 3 all the **a** shall assemble themselves to thee 5712
14: 5 Aaron fell on their faces before all the **a** of 6951
16: 2 two hundred and fifty princes of the **a**, 5712
20: 6 Aaron went from the presence of the **a** unto 6951
20: 8 gather thou the **a** together, thou, and 5712
29:35 On the eighth day ye shall have a **solemn a**; 6116
Dt 5:22 **a** in the mount out of the midst of the fire, 6951
9:10 of the midst of the fire in the day of the **a**. 6951
10: 4 of the midst of the fire in the day of the **a**: 6951
16: 8 on the seventh day *shall be* a **solemn a** to 6116
18:16 thy God in Horeb in the day of the **a**, 6951
Jdg 20: 2 presented themselves in the **a** of the people 6951
21: 8 to the camp from Jabesh-gilead to the **a**. 6951
1Sa 17:47 all this **a** shall know that the LORD saveth 6951
2Ki 10:20 Jehu said, Proclaim a **solemn a** for Baal. 6116
2Ch 7: 9 in the eighth day they made a **solemn a**: 6116
30:23 the whole **a** took counsel to keep other 6951
Ne 5: 7 And I set a great **a** against them. 6952
8:18 on the eighth day *was* a **solemn a**, 6116
Ps 22:16 the **a** of the wicked have inclosed me: 5712
89: 7 God *is* greatly to be feared in the **a** of 5475
107:32 and praise him in the **a** of the elders. 4186
111: 1 in the **a** of the upright, and *in* 5475
Pr 5:14 evil in the midst of the congregation and **a**. 5712
Jer 6:11 and upon the **a** of young men together: 5475
9: 2 *be* all adulterers, an **a** of treacherous *men.* 6116
15:17 I sat not in the **a** of the mockers, 5475
26:17 and spake to all the **a** of the people, saying, 6951
50: 9 cause to come up against Babylon an **a** of 6951
La 1:15 he hath called an **a** against me to crush my 4150
2: 6 he hath destroyed his **places of the a**: 4150
Eze 13: 9 they shall not be in the **a** of my people, 5475
23:24 and wheels, and with an **a** of people, 6951
Joel 1:14 call a **solemn a**, gather the elders *and* 6116
2:15 in Zion, sanctify a fast, call a **solemn a**: 6116
Zep 3:18 *them that are* sorrowful for the **solemn a**, 4150
Ac 19:32 for the **a** was confused; and the more part 1577
19:39 it shall be determined in a lawful **a**. 1577
19:41 he had thus spoken, he dismissed the **a**. 1577
Heb 12:23 To the **general a**, and church of 3831
Jas 2: 2 For if there come unto your **a** a man with a 4864

ASSENT (1) [ASSENTED]
2Ch 18:12 *declare* good to the king **with** one **a**; 6310

ASSENTED (1) [ASSENT]
Ac 24: 9 And the Jews also **a**, saying that these 4934

ASSES (64) [ASS]
Ge 12:16 **he a**, and menservants, and maidservants, 2543
12:16 and maidservants, and **she a**, and camels. 860
24:35 and maidservants, and camels, and **a**. 2543
30:43 and menservants, and camels, and **a**. 2543
32: 5 **a**, flocks, and menservants, and 2543
32:15 and ten bulls, twenty **she a**, and ten foals. 860
34:28 their **a**, and that which *was* in the city, and 2543
36:24 as he fed the **a** of Zibeon his father. 2543
42:26 they laded their **a** with the corn, and 2543
43:18 and take us for bondmen, and our **a**. 2543
43:24 their feet; and he gave their **a** provender. 2543
44: 3 the men were sent away, they and their **a**. 2543
45:23 ten **a** laden with the good things of Egypt, 2543

Ge 45:23 and ten **she a** laden with corn and bread and 860
47:17 and for the cattle of the herds, and for the **a**: 2543
Ex 9: 3 upon the horses, upon the **a**, upon 2543
Nu 31:28 the beeves, and of the **a**, and of the sheep: 2543
31:30 of the beeves, of the **a**, and of the flocks, 2543
31:34 And threescore and one thousand **a**, 2543
31:39 the **a** *were* thirty thousand and 2543
31:45 And thirty thousand **a** and five hundred, 2543
Jos 7:24 his **a**, and his sheep, and his tent, and all 2543
9: 4 took old sacks upon their **a**, and 2543
Jdg 5:10 Speak, ye that ride on white **a**, ye that sit in 860
19: 3 his servant with him, and a couple of **a**: 2543
19:10 *there were* with him two **a** saddled, 2543
19:19 there is both straw and provender for our **a**; 2543
19:21 his house, and gave provender unto the **a**: 2543
1Sa 8:16 and your **a**, and put *them* to his work. 2543
9: 3 the **a** of Kish Saul's father were lost. 860
9: 3 servants with thee, and arise, go seek the **a**. 860
9: 5 lest my father leave *caring* for the **a**, and 860
9:20 as for thine **a** that were lost three days ago, 860
10: 2 The **a** which thou wentest to seek are found: 860
10: 2 lo, thy father hath left the care of the **a**, and 860
10:14 he said, To seek the **a**: and when we saw that 860
10:16 He told us plainly that the **a** were found. 860
22:19 and sucklings, and oxen, and **a**, and sheep, 2543
25:18 hundred cakes *of figs*, and laid *them* on **a**. 2543
27: 9 the **a**, and the camels, and the apparel, and 2543
2Sa 16: 1 with a couple of **a** saddled, and upon them 2543
16: 2 The **a** *be* for the king's household to ride 2543
2Ki 4:22 one of the young men, and one of the **a**, 860
7: 7 left their tents, and their horses, and their **a**, 2543
7:10 and **a** tied, and the tents as they *were*. 2543
1Ch 5:21 *of* **a** two thousand, and *of* men an hundred 2543
12:40 brought bread on **a**, and on camels, and 2543
27:30 over the **a** *was* Jehdeiah the Meronothite: 860
2Ch 28:15 carried all the feeble of them upon **a**, 2543
Ezr 2:67 *their* **a**, six thousand seven hundred and 2543
Ne 7:69 six thousand seven hundred and twenty **a**. 2543
13:15 and bringing in sheaves, and lading **a**; 2543
Job 1: 3 five hundred **she a**, and a very great 860
1:14 and the **a** feeding beside them: 860
24: 5 Behold, *as* **wild a** in the desert, go they 6501
42:12 yoke of oxen, and a thousand **she a**. 860
Ps 104:11 of the field: the **wild a** quench their thirst. 6501
Isa 21: 7 a chariot of **a**, *and* a chariot of camels; 2543
30: 6 their riches upon the shoulders of **young a**, 5895
30:24 the **young a** that ear the ground shall eat 5895
32:14 a joy of **wild a**, a pasture of flocks; 6501
Jer 14: 6 the **wild a** did stand in the high places, 6501
Eze 23:20 whose flesh *is as* the flesh of **a**, and 2543
Da 5:21 and his dwelling *was* with the **wild a**: 6167

ASSHUR (8) [ASSHURIM]

Ge 10:11 Out of that land went forth **A**, and 804
10:22 and **A**, and Arphaxad, and Lud, and Aram. 804
Nu 24:22 until **A** shall carry thee away captive. 804
24:24 and shall afflict **A**, and shall afflict Eber, and 804
1Ch 1:17 **A**, and Arphaxad, and Lud, and Aram, and 804
Eze 27:23 **A**, *and* Chilmad, *were* thy merchants. 804
32:22 **A** *is* there and all her company: his graves 804
Hos 14: 3 **A** shall not save us: we will not ride upon 804

ASSHURIM (1) [ASSHUR]

Ge 25: 3 the sons of Dedan were **A**, and Letushim, 805

ASSHURITES See ASSHURIM

ASSIGNED (3)

Ge 47:22 for the priests had a portion **a** them of 3807.1
Jos 20: 8 they **a** Bezer in the wilderness upon 5414
2Sa 11:16 that he **a** Uriah unto a place where he 5414

ASSIR (5)

Ex 6:24 of Korah; **A**, and Elkanah, and Abiasaph: 617
1Ch 3:17 the sons of Jeconiah; **A**, Salathiel his son, 617
6:22 his son, Korah his son, **A** his son, 617
6:23 his son, and Ebiasaph his son, and **A** his son, 617
6:37 The son of Tahath, the son of **A**, the son of 617

ASSIST (1)

Ro 16: 2 *that* ye **a** her in whatsoever business she *3936*

ASSOCIATE (1)

Isa 8: 9 **A** yourselves, O ye people, and ye shall be 7489

ASSOS (2)

Ac 20:13 we went before to ship, and sailed unto **A**, *789*
20:14 And when he met with us at **A**, we took him *789*

ASSUR (2)

Ezr 4: 2 since the days of Esar-haddon king of **A**, 804
Ps 83: 8 **A** also is joined with them: they have holpen 804

ASSURANCE (7) [ASSURE]

Dt 28:66 and night, and shalt have none **a** of thy life: 539
Isa 32:17 of righteousness quietness and **a** for ever. 983
Ac 17:31 *whereof* he hath given **a** unto all *men*, in *4102*
Col 2: 2 unto all riches of the **full a** of *4136*
1Th 1: 5 and in the Holy Ghost, and in much **a**; *4136*
Heb 6:11 diligence to the **full a** of hope unto the end: *4136*
10:22 Let us draw near with a true heart in **full a** *4136*

ASSURE (1) [ASSURANCE, ASSURED, ASSUREDLY]

1Jn 3:19 the truth, and shall **a** our hearts before him. *3982*

ASSURED (3) [ASSURE]

Lev 27:19 estimation unto it, and it shall be **a** to him. 6965
Jer 14:13 but I will give you **a** peace in this place. 571
2Ti 3:14 which thou hast learned and hast been **a** of, *4104*

ASSUREDLY (9) [ASSURE]

1Sa 28: 1 said unto David, **Know** thou **a**, 3045+3045
1Ki 1:13 **A** Solomon thy son shall reign after me, 3588
1:17 *saying*, **A** Solomon thy son shall reign after 3588
1:30 **A** Solomon thy son shall reign after me, 3588
Jer 32:41 I will plant them in this land **a** with 571+871.1
38:17 If thou wilt **a go forth** unto the king 3318+3318
49:12 to drink of the cup have **a drunken**; 8354+8354
Ac 2:36 Therefore let all the house of Israel know **a**, *806*
16:10 **a gathering** that the Lord had called us for *4822*

ASSWAGE (1) [ASSWAGED]

Job 16: 5 the moving of my lips should **a** *your grief*. 2820

ASSWAGED (2) [ASSWAGE]

Ge 8: 1 to pass over the earth, and the waters **a**; 7918
Job 16: 6 Though I speak, my grief is not **a**: and 2820

ASSYRIA (118) [ASSYRIAN, ASSYRIANS]

Ge 2:14 that *is it* which goeth toward the east of **A**. 804
25:18 *is* before Egypt, as thou goest towards **A**: 804
2Ki 15:19 *And* Pul the king of **A** came against the land: 804
15:20 shekels *of* silver, to give to the king of **A**. 804
15:20 So the king of **A** turned back, and stayed not 804
15:29 of Israel came Tiglath-pileser king of **A**, 804
15:29 of Naphtali, and carried them captive to **A**. 804
16: 7 sent messengers to Tiglath-pileser king of **A**, 804
16: 8 and sent *it for* a present to the king of **A**. 804
16: 9 the king of **A** hearkened unto him: for 804
16: 9 for the king of **A** went up against Damascus, 804
16:10 Damascus to meet Tiglath-pileser king of **A**, 804
16:18 the house of the LORD for the king of **A**. 804
17: 3 him came up Shalmaneser king of **A**; 804
17: 4 the king of **A** found conspiracy in Hoshea: 804
17: 4 brought no present to the king of **A**, as *he* 804
17: 4 therefore the king of **A** shut him up, and 804
17: 5 the king of **A** came up throughout all 804
17: 6 the king of **A** took Samaria, and 804
17: 6 carried Israel away into **A**, and placed them 804
17:23 out of their own land to **A** unto this day. 804
17:24 the king of **A** brought *men* from Babylon, 804
17:26 Wherefore they spake to the king of **A**, 804
17:27 the king of **A** commanded, saying, 804
18: 7 he rebelled against the king of **A**, and 804
18: 9 *that* Shalmaneser king of **A** came up against 804
18:11 the king of **A** did carry away Israel unto 804
18:11 king of Assyria did carry away Israel unto **A**, 804
18:13 **A** come up against all the fenced cities of 804
18:14 Hezekiah king of Judah sent to the king of **A** 804
18:14 the king of **A** appointed unto Hezekiah king 804
18:16 had overlaid, and gave it to the king of **A**. 804
18:17 the king of **A** sent Tartan and Rabsaris and 804
18:19 Thus saith the great king, the king of **A**, 804
18:23 give pledges to my lord the king of **A**, and 804
18:28 the word of the great king, the king of **A**: 804
18:30 be delivered into the hand of the king of **A**. 804
18:31 for thus saith the king of **A**, Make *an* 804
18:33 all his land out of the hand of the king of **A**? 804
19: 4 whom the king of **A** his master hath sent to 804
19: 6 *with* which the servants of the king of **A** 804
19: 8 found the king of **A** warring against Libnah: 804
19:10 be delivered into the hand of the king of **A**. 804
19:11 thou hast heard what the kings of **A** have 804
19:17 the kings of **A** have destroyed the nations 804
19:20 against Sennacherib king of **A** I have heard. 804
19:32 saith the LORD concerning the king of **A**, 804
19:36 So Sennacherib king of **A** departed, and 804
20: 6 and this city out of the hand of the king of **A**; 804
23:29 against the king of **A** to the river Euphrates: 804
1Ch 5: 6 whom Tilgath-pilneser king of **A** carried 804
5:26 Israel stirred up the spirit of Pul king of **A**, 804
5:26 the spirit of Tilgath-pilneser king of **A**, 804
2Ch 28:16 Ahaz send unto the kings of **A** to help him. 804
28:20 Tilgath-pilneser king of **A** came unto him, 804
28:21 the princes, and gave *it* unto the king of **A**: 804
30: 6 escaped out of the hand of the kings of **A**. 804
32: 1 *thereof*, Sennacherib king of **A** came, 804
32: 4 Why should the kings of **A** come, and 804
32: 7 be not afraid nor dismayed for the king of **A**, 804
32: 9 After this did Sennacherib king of **A** send 804
32:10 Thus saith Sennacherib king of **A**, 804
32:11 deliver us out of the hand of the king of **A**? 804
32:21 and captains in the camp of the king of **A**. 804
32:22 from the hand of Sennacherib the king of **A**, 804
33:11 the captains of the host of the king of **A**, 804
Ezr 6:22 turned the heart of the king of **A** unto them, 804
Ne 9:32 since the time of the kings of **A** unto this 804
Isa 7:17 departed from Judah; *even* the king of **A**. 804
7:18 and for the bee that *is* in the land of **A**. 804
7:20 by the king of **A**, the head, and the hair of 804
8: 4 shall be taken away before the king of **A**. 804
8: 7 *even* the king of **A**, and all his glory: 804
10:12 the fruit of the stout heart of the king of **A**, 804
11:11 which shall be left from **A**, and from Egypt, 804
11:16 of his people, which shall be left from **A**; 804
19:23 shall there be a highway out of Egypt to **A**, 804
19:23 the Egyptian into **A**, and the Egyptians shall 804
19:24 Israel be the third with Egypt and with **A**, 804
19:25 **A** the work of my hands, and Israel mine 804
20: 1 (when Sargon the king of **A** sent him,) 804
20: 4 So shall the king of **A** lead away 804
20: 6 for help to be delivered from the king of **A**: 804
27:13 which were ready to perish in the land of **A**, 804
36: 1 *that* Sennacherib king of **A** came up against 804
36: 2 the king of **A** sent Rabshakeh from Lachish 804
36: 4 Thus saith the great king, the king of **A**, 804
36: 8 to my master the king of **A**, and I will give 804
36:13 ye the words of the great king, the king of **A**. 804
36:15 be delivered into the hand of the king of **A**. 804
36:16 for thus saith the king of **A**, Make *an* 804
36:18 his land out of the hand of the king of **A**? 804
37: 4 whom the king of **A** his master hath sent to 804
37: 6 where*with* the servants of the king of **A** have 804
37: 8 found the king of **A** warring against Libnah: 804
37:10 not be given into the hand of the king of **A**. 804
37:11 thou hast heard what the kings of **A** have 804
37:18 the kings of **A** have laid waste all 804
Isa 37:21 prayed to me against Sennacherib king of **A**: 804
37:33 saith the LORD concerning the king of **A**, 804
37:37 So Sennacherib king of **A** departed, and 804
38: 6 and this city out of the hand of the king of **A**: 804
Jer 2:18 or what hast thou to do in the way of **A**, 804
2:36 of Egypt, as thou wast ashamed of **A**. 804
50:17 first the king of **A** hath devoured him; and 804
50:18 his land, as I have punished the king of **A**. 804
Eze 23: 7 *with* all them *that were* the chosen men of **A**, 804
Hos 7:11 they call *to* Egypt, they go *to* **A**. 804
8: 9 For they are gone up *to* **A**, a wild ass alone 804
9: 3 and they shall eat unclean *things* in **A**. 804
10: 6 It shall be also carried unto **A** *for* a present 804
11:11 of Egypt, and as a dove out of the land of **A**: 804
Mic 5: 6 they shall waste the land of **A** with 804
7:12 day *also* he shall come even to thee from **A**, 804
Na 3:18 Thy shepherds slumber, O king of **A**: 804
Zep 2:13 his hand against the north, and destroy **A**; 804
Zec 10:10 the land of Egypt, and gather them out of **A**; 804
10:11 the pride of **A** shall be brought down, and 804

ASSYRIAN (13) [ASSYRIA]

Isa 10: 5 O **A**, the rod of mine anger, and the staff in 804
10:24 that dwellest in Zion, be not afraid of the **A**: 804
14:25 That *I* will break the **A** in my land, and 804
19:23 the **A** shall come into Egypt, and 804
23:13 *till* the **A** founded it for them that dwell in 804
30:31 of the LORD shall the **A** be beaten down, 804
31: 8 shall the **A** fall with the sword, not of a 804
52: 4 and the **A** oppressed them without cause. 804
Eze 31: 3 the **A** *was* a cedar in Lebanon with fair 804
Hos 5:13 went Ephraim to the **A**, and sent to king 804
11: 5 the **A** shall be his king, because they refused 804
Mic 5: 5 when the **A** shall come into our land: 804
5: 6 thus shall he deliver *us* from the **A**, when he 804

ASSYRIANS (10) [ASSYRIA]

2Ki 19:35 smote in the camp of the **A** an hundred 804
Isa 19:23 and the Egyptians shall serve *with* the **A**. 804
37:36 smote in the camp of the **A** an hundred and 804
La 5: 6 *and to* the **A**, to be satisfied *with* bread. 804
Eze 16:28 hast played the whore also with the **A**, 804+1121
23: 5 on her lovers, on the **A** *her* neighbours, 804
23: 9 into the hand of the **A**, upon whom 804+1121
23:12 She doted upon the **A** *her* neighbours, 804+1121
23:23 Shoa, and Koa, all the **A** with them: 804+1121
Hos 12: 1 and they do make a covenant with the **A**, and 804

ASTAROTH (1)

Dt 1: 4 king of Bashan, which dwelt at **A** in Edrei: 6252

ASTONIED (10) [ASTONISHMENT]

Ezr 9: 3 my head and of my beard, and sat down **a**. 8074
9: 4 and I sat **a** until the evening sacrifice. 8074
Job 17: 8 Upright *men* shall be **a** at this, and 8074
18:20 They that come after *him* shall be **a** at his 8074
Isa 52:14 As many were **a** at thee; his visage *was* so 8074
Jer 14: 9 Why shouldest thou be as a man **a**, as a 1724
Eze 4:17 be **a** one with another, and consume away 8074
Da 3:24 Nebuchadnezzar the king was **a**, and 8429
4:19 was **a** for one hour, and his thoughts 8075
5: 9 *was* changed in him, and his lords *were* **a**. 7672

ASTONISHED (34) [ASTONISHMENT]

Lev 26:32 enemies which dwell therein shall be **a** at it. 8074
1Ki 9: 8 every one that passeth by it shall be **a**, and 8074
Job 21: 5 be **a**, and lay *your* hand upon *your* mouth. 8074
26:11 of heaven tremble and are **a** at his reproof. 8539
Jer 2:12 Be **a**, O ye heavens, at this, and be horribly 8074
4: 9 the priests shall be **a**, and the prophets shall 8074
18:16 every one that passeth thereby shall be **a**, 8074
19: 8 every one that passeth thereby shall be **a** 8074
49:17 every one that goeth by it shall be **a**, and 8074
50:13 every one that goeth by Babylon shall be **a**, 8074
Eze 3:15 remained there **a** among them seven days. 8074
26:16 tremble at every moment, and be **a** at thee. 8074
27:35 All the inhabitants of the isles shall be **a** at 8074
28:19 thee among the people shall be **a** at thee: 8074
Da 8:27 I was **a** at the vision, but none understood 8074
Mt 7:28 the people were **a** at his doctrine: *1605*
13:54 insomuch that they were **a**, and said, *1605*
22:33 heard *this*, they were **a** at his doctrine. *1605*
Mk 1:22 And they were **a** at his doctrine: for he *1605*
5:42 And they were **a** with a great astonishment. *1839*
6: 2 and many hearing *him* were **a**, saying, *1605*
7:37 And were beyond measure **a**, saying, *1605*
10:24 And the disciples were **a** at his words. *2284*
10:26 And they were **a** out of measure, *1605*
11:18 because all the people was **a** at his doctrine. *1605*
Lk 2:47 And all that heard him were **a** at his *1839*
4:32 And they were **a** at his doctrine: for his *1605*
5: 9 For he was **a**, *2285+4023*
8:56 And her parents were **a**: but he charged *1839*
24:22 women *also* of our company **made** us **a**, *1839*
Ac 9: 6 And he trembling and **a** said, Lord, *2284*
10:45 of the circumcision which believed were **a**, *1839*
12:16 opened *the door*, and saw him, they were **a**. *1839*
13:12 being **a** at the doctrine of the Lord. *1605*

ASTONISHMENT (21) [ASTONIED, ASTONISHED]

Dt 28:28 and blindness, and **a** of heart: 8541
28:37 thou shalt become an **a**, a proverb, and a 8047
2Ch 7:21 shall be an **a** to every one that passeth by it; 8074
29: 8 to **a**, and to hissing, as ye see with your 8047
Ps 60: 3 thou hast made us to drink the wine *of* **a**. 8653
Jer 8:21 I hurt; I am black; **a** hath taken hold on me. 8047
25: 9 make them an **a**, and a hissing, and 8047
25:11 whole land shall be a desolation, *and* an **a**; 8047
25:18 a desolation, an **a**, a hissing, and a curse; 8047
29:18 and an **a**, and a hissing, and a reproach, 8047
42:18 and an **a**, and a curse, and a reproach; 8047
44:12 an **a**, and a curse, and a reproach. 8047
44:22 an **a**, and a curse, without an inhabitant, 8047
51:37 an **a**, and a hissing, without an inhabitant. 8047

Jer 51:41 how is Babylon become an **a** among 8047
Eze 4:16 shall drink water by measure, and with **a**: 8078
5:15 an **a** unto the nations that *are* round about 4923
12:19 and drink their water with **a**, 8078
23:33 sorrow, *with* the cup of **a** and desolation, 8047
Zec 12: 4 I will smite every horse with **a**, and 8541
Mk 5:42 And they were astonished with a great **a**. *1611*

ASTRAY (22)

Ex 23: 4 meet thine enemy's ox or his ass **going a**, 8582
Dt 22: 1 not see thy brother's ox or his sheep **go a**, 5080
Ps 58: 3 they **go a** as soon as they be born, speaking 8582
119:67 Before I was afflicted I **went a**: but 7683
119:176 I have **gone a** like a lost sheep; seek thy 8582
Pr 5:23 in the greatness of his folly he shall **go a**. 7686
7:25 decline to her ways, **go** not **a** in her paths. 8582
28:10 Whoso **causeth** the righteous **to go a** in an 7686
Isa 53: 6 All we like sheep have **gone a**; we have 8582
Jer 50: 6 their shepherds have **caused** them **to go a**, 8582
Eze 14:11 That the house of Israel may **go** no more **a** 8582
44:10 away far from me, when Israel **went a**, 8582
44:10 which **went a** away from me after their 8582
44:15 the children of Israel **went a** from me, 8582
48:11 which **went** not **a** when the children of 8582
48:11 astray when the children of Israel **went a**, 8582
48:11 of Israel went astray, as the Levites **went a**. 8582
Mt 18:12 and one of them be **gone a**, doth he not *4105*
18:12 and seeketh that which is **gone a**? *4105*
18:13 of the ninety and nine which **went** not **a**. *4105*
1Pe 2:25 For ye were as sheep **going a**; but are now *4105*
2Pe 2:15 forsaken the right way, and are **gone a**, *4105*

ASTROLOGER (1) [ASTROLOGERS, ASTROLOGIANS]

Da 2:10 things at any magician, or **a**, or Chaldean. 826

ASTROLOGERS (7) [ASTROLOGER]

Isa 47:13 Let now the **a**, the stargazers, 1895+8064
Da 1:20 *and* **a** that *were* in all his realm. 825
2: 2 the **a**, and the sorcerers, and the Chaldeans, 825
4: 7 the **a**, the Chaldeans, and the soothsayers: 826
5: 7 The king cried aloud to bring in the **a**, 826
5:11 **a**, Chaldeans, *and* soothsayers; 826
5:15 now the wise *men,* the **a**, have been brought 826

ASTROLOGIANS (1) [ASTROLOGER]

Da 2:27 hath demanded cannot the wise *men,* the **a**, 826

ASUNDER (21)

Lev 1:17 the wings thereof, *but* shall not **divide** *it* **a**: 914
5: 8 head from his neck, but shall not **divide** *it* **a**: 914
Nu 16:31 that the ground **clave a** that *was* under 1234
2Ki 2:11 and horses of fire, and parted them both **a**; 996
Job 16:12 I was at ease, but he hath **broken** me **a**: 6565
16:13 he **cleaveth** my reins **a**, and doth not spare; 6398
Ps 2: 3 Let us **break** their bands **a**, and cast away 5423
129: 4 he hath **cut a** the cords of the wicked. 7112
Jer 50:23 is the hammer of the whole earth **cut a** 1438
Eze 30:16 No shall be **rent a**, and Noph *shall have* 1234
Hab 3: 6 he beheld, and **drove a** the nations; and 5425
Zec 11:10 I took my staff, *even* Beauty, and **cut** it **a**, 1438
11:14 I **cut a** mine other staff, *even* Bands, that I 1438
Mt 19: 6 hath joined together, let not man **put a**. *5563*
24:51 And shall **cut** him **a**, and appoint *him* his *1371*
Mk 5: 4 and the chains had been **plucked a** by him, *1288*
10: 9 hath joined together, let not man **put a**. *5563*
Ac 1:18 he **burst a** in the midst, and all his bowels *2997*
15:39 sharp *between them,* that they **departed a** *673*
Heb 4:12 piercing even to the **dividing a** of soul and *3311*
11:37 they were **sawn a**, were tempted, *4249*

ASUPPIM (2)

1Ch 26:15 and to his sons the house of **A**. 624
26:17 four a day, and toward **A** two *and* two. 624

ASWAN See SYENE

ASYNCRITUS (1)

Ro 16:14 Salute **A**, Phlegon, Hermas, Patrobas, *799*

AT (1571)

Ge 3:24 he placed **a** the east of the garden of Eden 4480
4: 7 if thou doest not well, sin lieth **a** the door. 3807.1
6: 6 on the earth, and it grieved him **a** his heart. 413
8: 6 it came to pass **a** the end of forty days, 4480
9: 5 **a** the hand of every beast will I require it, 4480
9: 5 will I require it, and **a** the hand of man; 4480
9: 5 **a** the hand of every man's brother will I 4480
13: 3 unto the place where his tent had been **a** 871.1
13: 4 which he had made there **a** the first: 871.1
14:17 **a** the valley of Shaveh, which *is* the king's 413
17:21 which Sarah shall bear unto thee **a** this set NIH
18:14 **A** the time appointed I will return unto 3807.1
19: 1 there came two angels to Sodom **a** even; 871.1
19: 6 Lot went out **a** the door unto them, and 1886.5
19:11 they smote the men that *were* **a** the door of NIH
20:13 **a** every place whither we shall come, say of 413
21: 2 **a** the set time of which God had spoken 3807.1
21:22 it came to pass **a** that time, that Abimelech 871.1
21:32 Thus they made a covenant **a** Beer-sheba: 871.1
22:19 and Abraham dwelt **a** Beer-sheba. 871.1
23:10 *even* of all that went in **a** the gate of his NIH
23:18 before all that went in **a** the gate of his city. NIH
24:11 a well of water **a** the time of the evening, 3807.1
24:21 the man wondering **a** her held his peace, 3807.1
24:30 behold, he stood by the camels **a** the well. 5921
24:55 abide with us *a few* days, **a the least** ten; 176
24:57 call the damsel, and inquire **a** her mouth. NIH
24:63 Isaac went out to meditate in the field **a** 3807.1
25:32 Esau said, Behold, I *am* **a the point** to die: 1980
26: 8 of the Philistines looked out **a** a window, 1157
27:41 days of mourning for my father are **a hand**; 7126
28:19 the name of *that* city *was called* Luz **a** 3807.1
31:10 it came to pass **a** the time that the cattle 871.1
Ge 33:10 then receive my present **a** my hand: 4480
33:19 **a** the hand of the children of Hamor, 4480
38: 1 it came to pass **a** that time, that Judah went 871.1
38: 5 and he was **a** Chezib, when she bare him. 871.1
38:11 Remain a widow **a** thy father's house, NIH
41: 1 it came to pass **a** the end of two full years, 4480
43:21 *were still* ill favoured, as **a** the beginning. 871.1
43:16 for *these* men shall dine with me **a** noon. 871.1
43:18 sacks **a** the first time *are* we brought in; 871.1
43:19 they communed with him **a** the door of NIH
43:20 we came indeed down **a** the first time to 871.1
43:25 the present against Joseph came **a** noon: 871.1
43:33 and the men marvelled one **a** another. 413
44:12 *and* began **a** the eldest, and left at 871.1
44:12 began at the eldest, and left **a** the youngest: 871.1
45: 3 for they were troubled **a** his presence. 4480
48: 3 God Almighty appeared unto me **a** Luz in 871.1
49:13 Zebulun shall dwell **a** the haven of 3807.1
49:19 but he shall overcome **a** the last. NIH
49:23 grieved him, and shot **a** *him,* and hated him: NIH
49:27 and **a** night he shall divide the spoil. 3807.1
Ex 2: 5 came down to wash *herself* **a** the river; 5921
4:25 of her son, and cast *it* **a** his feet, and said, 3807.1
5:23 hast thou **delivered** thy people **a all**. 5337+5337
8:32 Pharaoh hardened his heart **a** this time 871.1
9:14 For I will **a** this time send all my plagues 871.1
12: 9 nor **sodden a all** with water, but 1310+1311
12:18 on the fourteenth day of the month **a** even, 871.1
12:18 and twentieth day of the month **a** even. 871.1
12:22 none of you shall go out **a** the door of his 4480
12:29 that **a** midnight the LORD smote all 871.1
12:41 it came to pass **a** the end of the four 4480
16: 6 **A** even, then ye shall know that the LORD NIH
16:12 **A even** ye shall eat flesh, and 996+6153+1886.1
16:13 that **a** even the quails came up, 871.1
18: 5 where he encamped **a** the mount of God: NIH
18:22 let them judge the people **a** all seasons: 871.1
18:26 they judged the people **a** all seasons: 871.1
19:15 against the third day: come not **a** *your* wives. 413
19:17 they stood **a** the nether part of the mount. 871.1
22:23 they **cry a all** unto me, I will surely 6817+6817
22:26 **a all take** thy neighbour's raiment **to pledge**, 2254+2254
28: 7 *thereof* joined **a** the two edges thereof; 413
28:14 two chains *of* pure gold **a** the ends; NIH
28:22 **a** the ends *of* wreathen work *of* pure gold. NIH
29:39 lamb thou shalt offer **a even**: 996+6153+1886.1
29:41 lamb thou shalt offer **a even**, 996+6153+1886.1
29:42 **a** the door of the tabernacle of NIH
30: 8 lighteth the lamps **a even**, 996+6153+1886.1
32: 4 he received *them* **a** their hand, and 4480
33: 8 stood every man **a** his tent door, and NIH
33: 9 stood **a** the door of the tabernacle, and NIH
33:10 all the people saw the cloudy pillar stand **a** NIH
34:22 and the feast of ingathering **a** the year's end. NIH
35:15 the hanging for the door **a** the entering in 3807.1
36:29 coupled together **a** the head thereof, to one 413
38: 8 which assembled **a** the door of NIH
39:15 upon the breastplate chains **a the ends**, 1383
40: 8 and hang up the hanging **a** the court gate. NIH
40:28 he set up the hanging **a** the door of NIH
Lev 1: 3 he shall offer it of his own voluntary will **a** 413
1:15 the blood thereof shall be wrung out **a** 5921
3: 2 kill it **a** the door of the tabernacle of NIH
4: 7 shall pour all the blood of the bullock **a** 413
4: 7 which *is* **a** the door of the tabernacle of NIH
4:18 shall pour out all the blood **a** the bottom of 413
4:18 which *is* **a** the door of the tabernacle of NIH
4:25 shall pour out his blood **a** the bottom of 413
4:30 shall pour out all the blood thereof **a** 413
4:34 shall pour out all the blood thereof **a** 413
5: 9 the rest of the blood shall be wrung out **a** 413
6:20 it in the morning, and half thereof **a** night. 871.1
7:18 be **eaten a all** on the third day, 398+398
8:15 poured the blood **a** the bottom of the altar, 413
8:31 Boil the flesh **a** the door of the tabernacle of NIH
8:33 the days of your consecration be **a an end**: 4390
8:35 Therefore shall ye abide **a** the door of NIH
9: 9 poured out the blood **a** the bottom of 413
13: 5 *if* the plague in his sight be **a a stay**, *and* 5975
13:37 if the scall be in his sight **a a stay**, and 5975
14:11 **a** the door of the tabernacle of NIH
15:24 if any man **lie with** her **a all**, 854+7901+7901
16: 2 that he come not **a** all times into the holy 871.1
16: 7 present them before the LORD **a** the door NIH
16:29 do no work **a** *all, whether it be* one of your NIH
17: 6 **a** the door of the tabernacle of NIH
18: 9 *whether she be* born **a** home, or NIH
19: 5 ye shall offer it **a** your own will. 3807.1
19: 7 if it be **eaten a all** on the third day, it *is* 398+398
19:20 not **a all redeemed**, nor freedom 6299+6299
22:19 *Ye shall offer* **a** your own will a male 3807.1
22:29 unto the LORD, offer *it* **a** your own will. 3807.1
23: 5 In the fourteenth *day* of the first month **a** 996
23:32 in the ninth *day* of the month **a** even, 871.1
25:32 may the Levites redeem **a** any time. NIH
26:32 which dwell therein shall be astonished **a** it. 5921
27:10 if he shall **a all change** beast for 4171+4171
27:13 if he will **a all redeem** it, then 1350+1350
27:16 a homer of barley seed *shall be valued* **a** 871.1
27:31 if a man will **a all redeem** *ought* of 1350+1350
27:33 if he **change** it **a all**, then both it and 4171+4171
Nu 3:39 Aaron numbered **a** the commandment of 5921
4:27 **A** the appointment of Aaron and his sons 5921
6: 6 the LORD he shall come **a** no dead body. 5921
6:18 **a** the door of the tabernacle of NIH
9: 2 keep the passover **a** his appointed season. 871.1
9: 3 In the fourteenth day of this month, **a** even, 996
9: 5 first month **a** even in the wilderness of Sinai: 996
9:11 The fourteenth day of the second month **a** 996
9:15 **a** even there was upon the tabernacle as it 871.1
9:18 **A** the commandment of the LORD 5921
9:18 **a** the commandment of the LORD they 5921
9:23 **A** the commandment of the LORD they 5921
9:23 **a** the commandment of the LORD they 5921
Nu 9:23 **a** the commandment of the LORD by 5921
10: 3 **a** the door of the tabernacle of 413
11: 6 *there is* nothing **a** all, beside *this* manna, NIH
11:20 until it come out **a** your nostrils, and it be 4480
11:35 *unto* Hazeroth; and abode **a** Hazeroth. 871.1
13:30 Let us **go up a once**, and possess it; 5927+5927
16:34 round about them fled **a** the cry of them: 3807.1
19:19 *himself* in water, and shall be clean **a** even. 871.1
20:24 ye rebelled against my word **a** the water 3807.1
21:11 from Oboth, and pitched **a** Ije-abarim, 871.1
21:15 **a** the stream of the brooks that goeth down NIH
21:30 We have shot **a** them; Heshbon is perished NIH
21:33 he, and all his people, to the battle **a** Edrei. NIH
21:34 of the Amorites, which dwelt **a** Heshbon. 871.1
22: 4 *was* king of the Moabites **a** that time. 871.1
22:20 God came unto Balaam **a** night, and NIH
22:38 have I now **any power a all** to say 3201+3201
23:25 Neither **curse** them **a all**, nor bless 5344+5344
23:25 them at all, nor **bless** them **a all**. 1288+1288
24: 1 he went not, as **a other times**, 6471+6471+871.1
27:14 to sanctify me **a** the water before their 871.1
27:21 **a** his word shall they go out, and at his 5921
27:21 **a** his word shall they come in, *both* he, and 5921
28: 4 lamb shalt thou offer **a even**; 996+6153+1886.1
28: 8 lamb shalt thou offer **a even**: 996+6153+1886.1
30: 4 and her father shall hold his peace **a** her: 3807.1
30: 6 if she **had a all** a husband, 1961+1961+3807.1
30: 7 held his peace **a** her in the day that he 3807.1
30:11 heard *it,* and held his peace **a** her, 3807.1
30:14 if her husband altogether hold his peace **a** 3807.1
30:14 he held his peace **a** her in the day that he 3807.1
31:12 unto the camp **a** the plains of Moab, 413
33:14 from Alush, and encamped **a** Rephidim, 871.1
33:16 of Sinai, and pitched **a** Kibroth-hattaavah. 871.1
33:17 and encamped **a** Hazeroth. 871.1
33:19 and pitched **a** Rimmon-parez. 871.1
33:21 from Libnah, and pitched **a** Rissah. 871.1
33:26 from Makheloth, and encamped **a** Tahath. 871.1
33:27 from Tahath, and pitched **a** Tarah. 871.1
33:30 and encamped **a** Moseroth. 871.1
33:32 and encamped **a** Hor-hagidgad. 871.1
33:34 from Jotbathah, and encamped **a** Ebronah. 871.1
33:35 and encamped **a** Ezion-gaber. 871.1
33:38 Aaron the priest went up into mount Hor **a** 5921
34: 5 and the goings out of it shall be **a** the sea. 1886.5
34: 9 the goings out of it shall be **a** Hazar-enan: NIH
34:12 the goings out of it shall be **a** the salt sea: NIH
35:11 which killeth *any* person **a** unawares. 871.1
35:20 or hurl **a** him by laying of wait, that he die; 5921
35:26 if the slayer shall **a any time come** 3318+3318
Dt 1: 4 which dwelt **a** Astaroth in Edrei: 871.1
1: 9 I spake unto you **a** that time, saying, I am 871.1
1:16 I charged your judges **a** that time, saying, 871.1
1:18 I commanded you **a** that time all the things 871.1
2:32 he and all his people, to fight **a** Jahaz. NIH
2:34 we took all his cities **a** that time, and 871.1
3: 1 he and all his people, to battle **a** Edrei. NIH
3: 2 of the Amorites, which dwelt **a** Heshbon. 871.1
3: 4 we took all his cities **a** that time, there was 871.1
3: 8 we took **a** that time out of the hand of 871.1
3:12 *which* we possessed **a** that time, from 871.1
3:18 I commanded you **a** that time, saying, 871.1
3:21 I commanded Joshua **a** that time, saying, 871.1
3:23 I besought the LORD **a** that time, saying, 871.1
4:14 the LORD commanded me **a** that time to 871.1
4:46 who dwelt **a** Heshbon, whom Moses and 871.1
5: 5 between the LORD and you **a** that time, 871.1
6:24 might preserve us alive, as *it is* **a** this day. NIH
7:21 Thou shalt not be affrighted **a** them: 4480+6440
7:22 thou mayest not consume them **a once**, 4118
8:16 to do thee good **a** thy latter end; 871.1
8:19 if thou **do a all forget** the LORD 7911+7911
9:11 it came to pass **a** the end of forty days and 4480
9:18 as **a** the first, forty days and forty nights: NIH
9:19 the LORD hearkened unto me **a** that time 871.1
9:22 **a** Taberah, and at Massah, and 871.1
9:22 and **a** Massah, and at Kibroth-hattaavah, 871.1
9:22 and at Massah, and **a** Kibroth-hattaavah, 871.1
9:25 as I fell down **a** *the first;* because NIH
10: 1 **A** that time the LORD said unto me, 871.1
10: 8 **A** that time the LORD separated the tribe 871.1
10:10 the LORD hearkened unto me **a** that time 871.1
14:28 **A** the end of three years thou shalt bring 4480
15: 1 **A** the end of *every* seven years thou shalt 4480
15: 9 seventh year, the year of release, is **a hand**; 7126
16: 4 which thou sacrificedst the first day **a** 871.1
16: 6 **a** the place which the LORD thy God shall 413
16: 6 thou shalt sacrifice the passover **a** even, 871.1
16: 6 **a** the going down of the sun, *at* the season 3509.1
16: 6 **a** the season that thou camest forth out of NIH
17: 6 **A** the mouth of two witnesses, or 5921
17: 6 **a** the mouth of one witness he shall not be 5921
19:15 **a** the mouth of two witnesses, or at 5921
19:15 or **a** the mouth of three witnesses, shall 5921
21:14 thou shalt not **sell** her **a all** for 4376+4376
23:24 thou mayest eat grapes thy fill **a** thine 3509.1
24: 5 *but* he shall be free **a** home one year, and 3807.1
24:15 **A** his day thou shalt give *him* his hire, 871.1
28:29 thou shalt grope **a** noondays, as the blind 871.1
28:67 **a** even thou shalt say, Would God it were 871.1
31:10 **A** the end of *every* seven years, 4480
32:35 for the day of their calamity *is* **a hand**, and 7138
32:51 of Israel **a** the waters of Meribah-Kadesh, 871.1
33: 3 they sat down **a** thy feet; *every one* shall 3807.1
33: 8 whom thou didst prove **a** Massah, *and* 871.1
33: 8 *with* whom thou didst strive **a** the waters of 5921
Jos 5: 2 **A** that time the LORD said unto Joshua, 871.1
5: 3 circumcised the children of Israel **a** the hill 413
5:10 the month **a** even in the plains of Jericho. 871.1
6:16 it came to pass **a** the seventh time, 871.1
6:26 Joshua adjured *them* **a** that time, saying, 871.1
7: 7 **a all brought** this people **over** 5674+5674
8: 5 as **a** the first, that we will flee before them, 871.1
8: 6 will say, *They* flee before us, as **a** the first: 871.1
8:14 he and all his people, **a** a time appointed, 3807.1

A

Jos 8:29 cast it **a** the entering of the gate of the city, 413
9: 6 they went to Joshua unto the camp **a** Gilgal, NIH
9:10 king of Bashan, which *was* **a** Ashtaroth. 871.1
9:14 asked not *counsel* **a** the mouth of NIH
9:16 it came to pass **a** the end of three days after 4480
10:10 slew them *with* **a** great slaughter **a** Gibeon, 871.1
10:16 and hid themselves in a cave **a** Makkedah. 871.1
10:17 The five kings are found hid in a cave **a** 871.1
10:21 to the camp to Joshua **a** Makkedah in peace: NIH
10:27 it came to pass **a** the time of the going 3807.1
10:42 and their land did Joshua take **a** one time, NIH
11: 5 and pitched together **a** the waters of Merom, 413
11:10 Joshua **a** that time turned back, and 871.1
11:21 **a** that time came Joshua, and cut off 871.1
12: 4 that dwelt **a** Ashtaroth and at Edrei, 871.1
12: 4 that dwelt at Ashtaroth and **a** Edrei, 871.1
15: 4 goings out of that coast were **a** the sea: 1886.5
15: 5 of the sea **a** the uttermost part of Jordan: 4480
15: 7 and the goings out thereof were **a** En-rogel: 413
15: 8 which *is* **a** the end of the valley of 413
15:11 goings out of the border were **a** the sea. 1886.5
15:63 of Judah **a** Jerusalem unto this day. 871.1
16: 3 and the goings out thereof are **a** the sea. 1886.5
16: 7 and came to Jericho, and went out **a** Jordan. NIH
16: 8 and the goings out thereof were **a** the sea. 1886.5
17: 9 and the outgoings of it were **a** the sea: 1886.5
18: 1 of Israel assembled together **a** Shiloh, NIH
18: 9 came *again* to Joshua to the host **a** Shiloh. NIH
18:12 the goings out thereof were **a** 1886.5
18:14 the goings out thereof were **a** Kirjath-baal, 413
18:19 the outgoings of the border were **a** 1886.5
18:19 of the salt sea **a** the south end of Jordan: 1886.5
19:22 the outgoings of their border were **a** Jordan: NIH
19:29 the outgoings thereof are **a** the sea from 1886.5
19:33 and the outgoings thereof were **a** Jordan: NIH
19:51 **a** the door of the tabernacle of NIH
20: 4 stand **a** the entering of the gate of the city, NIH
20: 9 that whosoever killeth *any* person **a** 871.1
21: 2 they spake unto them **a** Shiloh in the land 871.1
21: 3 **a** the commandment of the LORD, these 413
22:11 **a** the passage of the children of Israel. 413
22:12 gathered themselves together **a** Shiloh, NIH
Jdg 3: 2 **a the least** such as before knew nothing 7535
3:29 they slew *of* Moab **a** that time about ten 871.1
4: 4 of Lapidoth, she judged Israel **a** that time. 871.1
4:10 he went up with ten thousand men **a** his 871.1
5:27 **A** her feet he bowed, he fell, he lay down: 996
5:27 **a** her feet he bowed, he fell: where he 996
5:28 The mother of Sisera looked out **a** a 1157
7:25 Zeeb they slew **a** the winepress of Zeeb, 871.1
8:18 of men *were they* whom ye slew **a** Tabor? 871.1
9: 5 he went unto his father's house **a** Ophrah, 1886.5
9:41 Abimelech dwelt **a** Arumah: and 871.1
11:39 it came to pass **a** the end of two months, 4480
12: 2 my people were **a** great strife with NIH
12: 6 and slew him **a** the passages of Jordan: 413
12: 6 there fell **a** that time of the Ephraimites 871.1
12:10 died Ibzan, and was buried **a** Beth-lehem. 871.1
13:23 and a meat offering **a** our hands, 4480
13:23 **a** *this* time have told us *such things* as these. NIH
13:25 to **move** him **a times** in the camp of Dan, 6470
14: 4 for **a** that time the Philistines had 871.1
16: 3 arose **a** midnight, and took the doors of 871.1
16:20 I will go out as **a other times** 6471+6471+871.1
16:28 that I may be **a once** avenged of 259
16:30 So the dead which he slew **a** his death 871.1
18:27 unto a people *that were* **a** quiet and secure: NIH
18:29 howbeit the name of the city *was* Laish **a** 3807.1
19:16 man from his work out of the field **a** even, 871.1
19:22 *and* beat **a** the door, and spake to the master 5921
19:26 fell down **a** the door of the man's house NIH
19:27 the woman his concubine *was* fallen down **a** NIH
20:15 the children of Benjamin were numbered **a** 871.1
20:16 every one could sling stones **a** a hair *breadth*, 413
20:20 in array to fight against them **a** Gibeah. 413
20:30 as **a other times**. 6471+6471+871.1
20:31 **a other times**, in 6471+6471+871.1
20:32 *are* smitten down before us, as **a** the first. 871.1
20:33 and put *themselves* in array **a** Baal-tamar: 871.1
21:14 Benjamin came again **a** that time; and 871.1
21:22 for ye did not give unto them **a** *this* time, 3509.1
21:24 the children of Israel departed thence **a** 871.1
Ru 2:14 **A** mealtime come thou hither, and eat of 3807.1
3: 7 he went to lie down **a** the end of the heap 871.1
3: 8 it came to pass **a** midnight, that the man 871.1
3: 8 and behold, a woman lay **a** his feet. NIH
3:10 in the latter end than **a** the beginning, NIH
3:14 she lay **a** his feet until the morning: and NIH
1Sa 2:22 **a** the door of the tabernacle of NIH
2:29 Wherefore kick ye **a** my sacrifice and 871.1
2:29 ye at my sacrifice and **a** mine offering, 871.1
3: 2 it came to pass **a** that time, when Eli *was* 871.1
3:10 and called as **a other times**, 6471+6471+871.1
3:11 **a** which both the ears of every one that NIH
6:10 the cart, and shut up their calves **a** home: 871.1
9: 8 I have here **a** hand the fourth part of a 871.1
10: 2 in the border of Benjamin **a** Zelzah; 871.1
13:11 gathered themselves together **a** Michmash; NIH
14:18 For the ark of God was **a** that time with 871.1
16: 4 the elders of the town trembled **a** his 3807.1
17: 1 were gathered together **a** Shochoh, NIH
17:15 to feed his father's sheep **a** Beth-lehem. NIH
18:10 his hand, as **a other times**: 3117+3117+871.1
18:19 it came to pass **a** the time when Merab 871.1
19:19 Behold, David *is* **a** Naioth in Ramah. 871.1
19:22 Behold, *they be* **a** Naioth in Ramah. 871.1
20: 5 should not fail to sit with the king **a** meat: 3807.1
20: 5 in the fields unto the third *day* **a** even. 871.1
20: 6 If thy father **a all miss** me, then say, 6485+6485
20:16 *saying*, Let the LORD even require *it* **a** 4480
20:20 side *thereof*, as *though* I shot **a** a mark. 3807.1
20:25 as **a other times**, *even* upon a 6471+6471+871.1
20:33 Saul cast a javelin **a** him to smite him: 5921
20:35 that Jonathan went out *into* the field **a** 3807.1
21: 1 Ahimelech was afraid **a** the meeting of 3807.1
1Sa 21: 4 have kept themselves **a least** from women. 389
22: 8 against me, to lie in wait, as **a** this day? NIH
22:13 rise against me, to lie in wait, as **a** this day? NIH
22:14 goeth **a** thy bidding, and *is* honourable in 413
23:29 and dwelt in strong holds **a** En-gedi. NIH
25: 1 and buried him in his house **a** Ramah. 871.1
25:24 fell **a** his feet, and said, Upon me, my lord, 5921
26: 7 his spear stuck in the ground **a** his bolster: NIH
26: 8 the spear even to the earth **a once**, 259+6471
26:11 take thou now the spear that *is* **a** his bolster, NIH
26:16 and the cruse of water that *was* **a** his bolster. NIH
27: 3 David dwelt with Achish **a** Gath, he and 871.1
28: 7 woman that hath a familiar spirit **a** En-dor. 871.1
30: 8 David inquired **a** the LORD, saying, 871.1
30:21 whom they had made also to abide **a** 871.1
31:13 buried *them* under a tree **a** Jabesh, 871.1
2Sa 2:32 and they came to Hebron **a break of day**. 215
3:30 he had slain their brother Asahel **a** Gibeon 871.1
3:32 up his voice, and wept **a** the grave of Abner; 413
4: 5 of Ish-bosheth, who lay on a bed **a** noon. NIH
6: 4 house of Abinadab which *was* **a** Gibeah, 871.1
8: 3 as he went to recover his border **a** the river 871.1
9: 7 thou shalt eat bread **a** my table continually. 5921
9:10 son shall eat bread alway **a** my table. 5921
9:11 *said the king*, he shall eat **a** my table, 5921
9:13 for he did eat continually **a** the king's table; 5921
10: 5 Tarry **a** Jericho until your beards be 871.1
10: 8 put the battle in array **a** the entering in of NIH
11: 1 **a** the time when kings go forth *to battle*, 3807.1
11: 1 But David tarried *still* **a** Jerusalem. 871.1
11: 9 Uriah slept **a** the door of the king's house NIH
11:13 **a** even he went out to lie on his bed with 871.1
13: 5 that I may see *it*, and eat *it* **a** her hand. 4480
13: 6 in my sight, that I may eat **a** her hand. 4480
14:26 (for it was **a** every year's end that he polled 4480
14:26 he weighed the hair of his head **a** two NIH
15: 8 a vow while I abode **a** Geshur in Syria, 871.1
15:14 servants that *were* with him **a** Jerusalem, 871.1
16: 3 the king, Behold, he abideth **a** Jerusalem: 871.1
16: 6 he cast stones **a** David, and at all NIH
16: 6 and **a** all the servants of king David: NIH
16:13 threw stones **a** him, and cast dust. 5980+3807.1
16:23 *was* as if a man had inquired **a** the oracle 871.1
17: 7 hath given *is* not good **a** this time. 871.1
17: 9 when *some* of them be overthrown **a** 871.1
19: 9 all the people were **a strife** throughout all 1777
19:28 among them that did eat **a** thine own table. NIH
19:32 of sustenance while he lay **a** Mahanaim; 871.1
19:42 have we **eaten a all** of the king's *cost*? 398+398
20: 3 David came to his house **a** Jerusalem; and NIH
20: 8 When they *were* **a** the great stone which *is* 5973
20:18 They shall surely ask *counsel* **a** Abel: 871.1
21:18 again a battle with the Philistines **a** Gob: 871.1
22:16 **a** the rebuking of the LORD, at the blast 871.1
22:16 **a** the blast of the breath of his nostrils. 4480
23: 8 eight hundred, whom he slew **a** one time. 871.1
24: 8 they came *to* Jerusalem **a** the end of nine 4480
24:24 but I will surely buy *it* of thee **a** a price: 871.1
1Ki 1: 6 his father had not displeased him **a** any 4480
2: 7 and let them be of *those* that eat **a** thy table: NIH
2: 8 but he came down to meet me **a** Jordan, and NIH
2:26 I will not **a** this time put thee to death, 871.1
2:39 it came to pass **a** the end of three years, 4480
3:20 she rose **a** midnight, and took my son from 871.1
5:14 were in Lebanon, *and* two months **a** home: 871.1
7:30 **a** the side of every addition. 4480
8: 2 Solomon **a** the feast in the month Ethanim, 871.1
8: 9 of stone, which Moses put there **a** Horeb, 871.1
8:59 his people Israel **a all times**, 3117+3117+871.1
8:61 to keep his commandments, as **a** this day. NIH
8:65 **a** that time Solomon held a feast, and 871.1
9: 2 as he had appeared unto him **a** Gibeon. 871.1
9: 6 *But* if you shall **a all turn** from following 7725
9: 8 **a** this house, *which* is high, every one that NIH
9:10 it came to pass **a** the end of twenty years, 4480
10:22 For the king had **a** sea a navy of Tharshish 871.1
10:26 for chariots, and with the king **a** Jerusalem. 871.1
10:28 received the linen yarn **a** a price. 871.1
11:29 it came to pass **a** that time when Jeroboam 871.1
12:27 in the house of the LORD **a** Jerusalem, 871.1
13:20 it came to pass, as they sat **a** the table, 413
14: 1 **A** that time Abijah the son of Jeroboam 871.1
14: 6 as she came in **a** the door, that he said, 871.1
15:18 of Syria, that dwelt **a** Damascus, saying, 871.1
15:27 Baasha smote him **a** Gibbethon, 871.1
18:19 four hundred, which eat **a** Jezebel's table. NIH
18:27 it came to pass **a** noon, that Elijah mocked 871.1
18:36 it came to pass **a** *the time of* the offering of 871.1
18:36 *that* I have done all these things **a** thy 871.1
18:44 it came to pass **a** the seventh *time*, that he 871.1
19: 6 the coals, and a cruse of water **a** his head. NIH
20: 9 All that thou didst send for to thy servant **a** 871.1
20:16 they went out **a** noon. But Ben-hadad *was* 871.1
20:22 for **a** the return of the year the king of 3807.1
20:26 it came to pass **a** the return of the year, 3807.1
22: 5 **a** the word of the LORD to day. 3509.1
22:20 he may go up and fall **a** Ramoth-gilead? 871.1
22:28 If thou **return a all** in peace, 7725+7725
22:34 a *certain* man drew a bow **a** a venture, 3807.1
22:35 against the Syrians, and died **a** even: 871.1
22:48 for the ships were broken **a** Ezion-geber. 871.1
2Ki 2: 3 the sons of the prophets that *were* **a** Beth-el NIH
2: 5 the sons of the prophets that *were* **a** Jericho 871.1
2:15 which *were* to view **a** Jericho saw him, 871.1
2:18 again to him, (for he tarried **a** Jericho,) 871.1
4:17 bare a son **a** that season that Elisha had 3807.1
4:37 fell **a** his feet, and bowed herself to 5921
5: 9 and stood **a** the door of the house of Elisha. NIH
5:20 in not receiving **a** his hands *that* which he 4480
6:32 shut the door, and hold him fast **a** the door: 871.1
7: 3 there were four leprous men **a** the entering NIH
8: 3 it came to pass **a** the seven years' end, 4480
8:22 Then Libnah revolted **a** the same time. 871.1
8:29 which the Syrians had given him **a** Ramah, 871.1
9: 7 of the LORD, **a** the hand of Jezebel. 4480
2Ki 9:24 the arrow went out **a** his heart, and he sunk 4480
9:27 *And they did so* **a** the going up to Gur, 871.1
9:30 tired her head, and looked out **a** a window. 1157
9:31 as Jehu entered in **a** the gate, she said, *Had* 871.1
10: 8 Lay ye them *in* two heaps **a** the entering in NIH
10:12 *And* as he *was* **a** the shearing house in NIH
10:14 slew them **a** the pit of the shearing house, 413
11: 6 a third *part shall be* **a** the gate of Sur; and 871.1
11: 6 a third *part* **a** the gate behind the guard: 871.1
12: 4 *account*, the money that every man is **set a**, 6187
13:20 the land **a** the coming in of the year. NIH
14:10 glory *of this*, and tarry **a** home: for why 871.1
14:11 one another *in* the face **a** Beth-shemesh, 871.1
14:13 **a** Beth-shemesh, and came *to* Jerusalem, 871.1
14:20 he was buried **a** Jerusalem with his fathers 871.1
16: 6 **A** that time Rezin king of Syria recovered 871.1
16:10 and saw an altar that *was* **a** Damascus: 871.1
17:25 it was **a** the beginning of their dwelling 871.1
18:10 **a** the end of three years they took it: 4480
18:16 **A** that time did Hezekiah cut off *the gold* 871.1
18:33 **delivered a all** his land out of 5337+5337
19:21 of Jerusalem hath shaken her head **a** thee. 310
19:36 went and returned, and dwelt **a** Nineveh. 871.1
20:12 **A** that time Berodach-baladan, the son of 871.1
23: 6 burnt it **a** the brook Kidron, and stampt *it* 871.1
23: 8 which *were* on a man's left hand **a** the gate 871.1
23:11 **a** the entering in of the house of 4480
23:15 Moreover the altar that *was* **a** Beth-el, *and* 871.1
23:29 he slew him **a** Megiddo, when he had seen 871.1
23:33 Pharaoh-nechoh put him in bands **a** Riblah 871.1
24: 3 Surely **a** the commandment of the LORD 5921
24:10 **A** that time the servants of 871.1
25:21 slew them **a** Riblah in the land of Hamath. 871.1
25:25 the Chaldees that were with him **a** Mizpah. 871.1
1Ch 2:55 the families of the scribes which **dwelt a** 3427
4:28 they dwelt **a** Beer-sheba, and Moladah, 871.1
4:29 And **a** Bilhah, and at Ezem, and at Tolad, 871.1
4:29 And at Bilhah, and **a** Ezem, and at Tolad, 871.1
4:29 And at Bilhah, and at Ezem, and **a** Tolad, 871.1
4:30 **a** Bethuel, and at Hormah, and at Ziklag, 871.1
4:30 at Bethuel, and **a** Hormah, and at Ziklag, 871.1
4:30 at Bethuel, and at Hormah, and **a** Ziklag, 871.1
4:31 **a** Beth-marcaboth, and Hazar-susim, and 871.1
4:31 and **a** Beth-birei, and at Shaaraim. 871.1
4:31 and at Beth-birei, and **a** Shaaraim. 871.1
8:29 **a** Gibeon dwelt the father of Gibeon; 871.1
9:34 their generations; these dwelt **a** Jerusalem. 871.1
9:38 they also dwelt with their brethren **a** 871.1
11:11 three hundred slain *by him* **a** one time. 871.1
11:13 He was with David **a** Pas-dammim, and 871.1
11:16 garrison *was* then **a** Beth-lehem. 871.1
11:17 the well of Beth-lehem, that *is* **a** the gate. 871.1
12:22 For **a** *that* time day by day there came to 3807.1
12:32 all their brethren *were* **a** their 5921
13: 3 for we inquired not **a** it in the days of Saul. NIH
14: 3 David took moe wives **a** Jerusalem: and 871.1
15:13 For because ye *did it* not **a** the first, 871.1
15:29 **out a** a window saw king David dancing 1157
16:33 out **a** the presence of the LORD, 4480+3807.1
16:39 in the high place that *was* **a** Gibeon, 871.1
17: 9 waste them any more, as **a** the beginning, 871.1
19: 5 Tarry **a** Jericho until your beards be 871.1
20: 1 **a** the time that kings go out *to battle*, Joab 3807.1
20: 1 David tarried **a** Jerusalem. And Joab smote 871.1
20: 4 that there arose war **a** Gezer with 871.1
20: 4 **a which time** Sibbechai the Hushathite slew 227
20: 6 yet again there was war **a** Gath, where was 871.1
21:19 David went up **a** the saying of Gad, 871.1
21:28 **A** that time when David saw that 871.1
21:29 *were* **a** that season in the high place at 871.1
21:29 *were* at that season in the high place **a** 871.1
23:30 praise the LORD, and likewise **a** even; 3807.1
26:18 **A** Parbar westward, four at the causeway, 3807.1
26:18 four **a** the causeway, *and* two at Parbar. 3807.1
26:18 four at the causeway, *and* two **a** Parbar. 3807.1
26:31 mighty *men* of valour **a** Jazer of Gilead. 871.1
28: 7 and my judgments, as **a** this day. NIH
28:21 all the people *will be* wholly **a** thy 3807.1
2Ch 1: 3 went to the high place that *was* **a** Gibeon; 871.1
1: 4 for he had pitched a tent for it **a** Jerusalem. 871.1
1: 6 which *was* **a** the tabernacle of 3807.1
1:13 high place that *was* **a** Gibeon *to* Jerusalem, 871.1
1:14 and with the king **a** Jerusalem. 871.1
1:15 gold **a** Jerusalem *as plenteous* as stones, 871.1
1:16 received the linen yarn **a** a price. 871.1
3: 1 the LORD **a** Jerusalem in mount Moriah, 871.1
5:10 tables which Moses put *therein* **a** Horeb, 871.1
5:12 stood **a** the east *end* of the altar, and NIH
7: 8 Also **a** the same time Solomon kept 871.1
8: 1 it came to pass **a** the end of twenty years, 4480
8:14 the porters also by their courses **a** every 3807.1
8:17 to Eloth, **a** the sea side in the land of Edom. 5921
9: 1 Solomon with hard questions **a** Jerusalem, 871.1
9:25 and with the king **a** Jerusalem. 871.1
13:18 of Israel were brought under **a** that time, 871.1
14:10 in the valley of Zephathah **a** Mareshah. 3807.1
15:10 So they gathered themselves together **a** NIH
15:15 all Judah rejoiced **a** the oath: for they had 5921
15:16 and burnt *it* **a** the brook Kidron. 871.1
16: 2 of Syria, that dwelt **a** Damascus, saying, 871.1
16: 7 **a** that time Hanani the seer came to Asa 871.1
18: 4 **a** the word of the LORD to day. 3509.1
18: 9 they sat in a void place **a** the entering in of NIH
18:19 he may go up and fall **a** Ramoth-gilead? 871.1
18:33 a *certain* man drew a bow **a** a venture, 3807.1
19: 4 Jehoshaphat dwelt **a** Jerusalem: and 871.1
20:16 ye shall find them **a** the end of the brook, 871.1
22: 5 Hazael king of Syria **a** Ramoth-gilead: 871.1
22: 6 of the wounds which were given him **a** 871.1
22: 6 to see Jehoram the son of Ahab **a** Jezreel, 871.1
23: 5 a third *part shall be* **a** the king's house; 871.1
23: 5 a third *part* **a** the gate of the foundation: 871.1
23:13 the king stood **a** his pillar at the entering in, 5921
23:13 the king stood at his pillar **a** the entering 871.1
23:19 he set the porters **a** the gates of the house of 5921

A

2Ch 24: 8 a the king's commandment they made a NIH
24: 8 set it without a the gate of the house of 871.1
24:11 that a what time the chest was brought 871.1
24:21 stoned him with stones a 871.1
24:23 it came to pass a the end of the year, 3807.1
25:19 abide now a home; why shouldest thou 871.1
25:21 Amaziah king of Judah, a Beth-shemesh, 871.1
25:23 a Beth-shemesh, and brought him to 871.1
26: 9 built towers in Jerusalem a the corner gate, 5921
26: 9 a the valley gate, and at the turning of 5921
26: 9 a the turning of the wall, and 5921
28:16 A that time did king Ahaz send unto 871.1
30: 1 to the house of the LORD a Jerusalem, 871.1
30: 3 For they could not keep it a that time, 871.1
30: 5 the LORD God of Israel a Jerusalem: 871.1
30:13 there assembled a Jerusalem much people NIH
30:21 the children of Israel that were present a 871.1
31:13 a the commandment of Hezekiah the king, 871.1
32: 9 unto all Judah that were a Jerusalem, 871.1
32:33 of Jerusalem did him honour a his death. 871.1
33:14 even to the entering in a the fish gate, and 871.1
35:15 and the porters waited a every gate; 3807.1
35:17 were present kept the passover a that time, 871.1
35:23 the archers shot a king Josiah; and 3807.1
36: 3 the king of Egypt put him down a 871.1
36: 7 and put them in his temple a Babylon. 871.1
Ezr 1: 2 he hath charged me to build him a house a 871.1
2:68 house of the LORD which is a Jerusalem, 871.1
3: 8 unto the house of God a Jerusalem, 3807.1
4:10 are on this side the river, and a such a time. NIH
4:11 on this side the river, and a such a time. 3706
4:17 beyond the river: Peace, and a such a time. 3706
4:24 the house of the God which is a Jerusalem. 871.2
5: 2 began to build the house of God which is a 871.2
5: 3 A the same time came to them Tatnai, 871.2
5:17 which is there a Babylon, whether it be so, 871.2
5:17 to build this house of God a Jerusalem, 871.2
6: 2 there was found a Achmetha, in the palace 871.2
6: 3 concerning the house of God a Jerusalem, 871.2
6: 5 out of the temple which is a Jerusalem, 871.2
6: 5 brought again unto the temple which is a 871.2
6: 9 of the priests which are a Jerusalem, 871.2
6:12 to destroy this house of God which is a 871.2
6:17 offered a the dedication of this house of 3807.2
6:18 the service of God, which is a Jerusalem; 871.2
7:12 perfect peace, and a such a time. 3706
8:17 unto Iddo the chief a the place Casiphia, 871.1
8:17 the Nethinims, a the place Casiphia, 871.1
8:21 I proclaimed a fast there, a the river Ahava, 5921
8:29 chief of the fathers of Israel, a Jerusalem, 871.1
8:34 and all the weight was written a that time. 871.1
9: 4 trembled a the words of the God of Israel, 871.1
9: 5 a the evening sacrifice I arose up from my 871.1
10: 3 of those that tremble a the commandment 871.1
10:14 in our cities come a appointed times, 3807.1
Ne 2:12 had put in my heart to do a Jerusalem: 3807.1
3:19 up to the armoury a the turning of the wall. NIH
4:22 Likewise a the same time said I unto 871.1
5:17 Moreover there were a my table an hundred NIH
6: 1 (though a that time I had not set up 5704
6: 7 prophets to preach of thee a Jerusalem, 871.1
7: 5 of them which came up a the first, 871.1
9:37 a their pleasure, and we are in great 3509.1
10:34 a times appointed year by year, 3807.1
11: 1 the rulers of the people dwelt a Jerusalem: 871.1
11: 2 offered themselves to dwell a Jerusalem. 871.1
11: 4 a Jerusalem dwelt certain of the children 871.1
11: 6 All the sons of Perez that dwelt a 871.1
11:22 The overseer also of the Levites a 871.1
11:24 was a the king's hand in all matters 3807.1
11:25 some of the children of Judah dwelt a 871.1
11:25 a Dibon, and in the villages thereof, and 871.1
11:25 a Jekabzeel, and in the villages thereof, 871.1
11:26 a Jeshua, and at Moladah, and 871.1
11:26 and a Moladah, and at Beth-phelet, 871.1
11:26 and at Moladah, and a Beth-phelet, 871.1
11:27 a Hazar-shual, and at Beer-sheba, and 871.1
11:27 a Beer-sheba, and in the villages thereof, 871.1
11:28 a Ziklag, and at Mekonah, and in 871.1
11:28 a Mekonah, and in the villages thereof, 871.1
11:29 a En-rimmon, and at Zareah, and 871.1
11:29 and a Zareah, and at Jarmuth, 871.1
11:29 and at Zareah, and a Jarmuth, 871.1
11:30 a Lachish, and the fields thereof, at Azekah, NIH
11:30 a Azekah, and in the villages thereof. NIH
11:31 of Benjamin from Geba dwelt a Michmash, NIH
11:32 And a Anathoth, Nob, Ananiah, NIH
12:25 were porters keeping the ward a 871.1
12:27 a the dedication of the wall of Jerusalem 871.1
12:37 a the fountain gate, which was over against 5921
12:37 a the going up of the wall, above the house 871.1
12:44 a that time were some appointed over 871.1
13: 6 in all this time was not I a Jerusalem: 871.1
13:19 some of my servants set I a the gates, 5921
13:31 a times appointed, and for the firstfruits. 871.1
Est 1:12 the queen Vashti refused to come a 871.1
4: 8 that was given a Shushan to destroy them, 871.1
4:14 For if thou altogether holdest thy peace a 871.1
5: 6 the king said unto Esther a the banquet of 871.1
5:13 long as I see Mordecai the Jew sitting a 871.1
6:10 the Jew, that sitteth a the king's gate: 871.1
7: 2 on the second day a the banquet of wine, 871.1
7: 3 let my life be given me a my petition, and 871.1
7: 3 my petition, and my people a my request: 871.1
8: 3 fell down a his feet, and besought 6440+3807.1
8: 9 were the king's scribes called a that time 871.1
8:14 the decree was given a Shushan the palace. 871.1
9:14 the decree was given a Shushan; and they 871.1
9:15 and slew three hundred men a Shushan; 871.1
9:18 the Jews that were a Shushan assembled 871.1
Job 2:10 shall we receive good a the hand of 854+4480
3:13 I should have slept: then had I been a rest, 5117
3:17 and there the weary be a rest. 5117
5:22 A destruction and famine thou shalt 3807.1
5:23 the beasts of the field shall be a peace with 7999

Job 9:23 he will laugh a the trial of the innocent. 3807.1
12: 5 in the thought of him that is a ease. 7600
15:12 thee away? and what do thine eyes wink a, NIH
15:23 the day of darkness is ready a his hand. 871.1
16: 4 against you, and shake mine head a you. 5921
16:12 I was a ease, but he hath broken me 7961
17: 8 Upright men shall be astonied a this, and 5921
18:12 and destruction shall be ready a his side. 3807.1
18:20 come after him shall be astonied a his day, 5921
19:25 that he shall stand a the latter day upon NIH
21:12 and rejoice a the sound of the organ. 3807.1
21:23 full strength, being wholly a ease and quiet. 7946
22:21 now thyself with him, and be a peace: 7999
23:15 Therefore am I troubled a his presence: 4480
26:11 and are astonished a his reproof. 4480
27:23 Men shall clap their hands a him, and 5921
29:21 and waited, and kept silence a my counsel. 3926
31: 9 if I have laid wait a my neighbour's door; 5921
31:29 If I rejoiced a the destruction of him that 871.1
34:20 people shall be troubled a midnight, 2676+3915
37: 1 A this also my heart trembleth, and 3807.1
39:22 He mocketh a fear, and is not affrighted; 3807.1
39:27 Doth the eagle mount up a thy command, 5921
41: 9 shall not one be cast down even a the sight 413
41:26 The sword of him that layeth a him cannot NIH
41:29 he laugheth a the shaking of a spear. 3807.1
Ps 7: 4 evil unto him that was a peace with me; 7999
9: 3 they shall fall and perish a thy presence. 4480
10: 5 as for all his enemies, he puffeth a them. 871.1
11: 2 that they may privily shoot a the upright 3807.1
12: 5 in safety from him that puffeth a him. 3807.1
16: 8 because he is a my right hand, I shall not be 4480
16:11 a thy right hand there are pleasures for 871.1
18:12 A the brightness that was before him his 4480
18:15 of the world were discovered a thy rebuke, 4480
18:15 a the blast of the breath of thy nostrils. 4480
25:13 His soul shall dwell a ease; and his seed 871.1
30: T Song a the dedication of the house of NIH
30: 4 give thanks a the remembrance of his 3807.1
34: 1 I will bless the LORD a all times: 871.1
35: 8 Let destruction come upon him a unawares; NIH
35:26 brought to confusion together that rejoice a NIH
37:13 The Lord shall laugh a him: for he seeth 3807.1
39: 5 verily every man a his best state is 5324
39:12 unto my cry; hold not thy peace a my tears: NIH
42: 7 Deep calleth unto deep a the noise of thy 3807.1
52: 6 shall see, and fear, and shall laugh a him: 5921
55: 6 for then would I fly away, and be a rest. 7931
55:17 Evening, and morning, and a noon, will I NIH
55:20 hands against such as be a peace with him: NIH
59: 6 They return a evening: they make a noise 3807.1
59: 8 thou, O LORD, shalt laugh a them; 3807.1
59:14 a evening let them return; and let them 3807.1
62: 8 Trust in him a all times; ye people, 871.1
64: 4 That they may shoot in secret a the perfect: NIH
64: 4 suddenly do they shoot a him, and fear not. NIH
64: 7 God shall shoot a them with an arrow; NIH
65: 8 the uttermost parts are afraid a thy tokens: 4480
68: 2 let the wicked perish a the presence of God. 4480
68: 8 the heavens also dropped a the presence of 4480
68: 8 even Sinai itself was moved a the presence 4480
68:12 she that tarried a home divided the spoil. NIH
68:29 Because of thy temple a Jerusalem shall 5921
73: 3 For I was envious a the foolish, when I 871.1
74: 6 the carved work thereof a once with axes 3162
76: 6 A thy rebuke, O God of Jacob, both 4480
80:16 they perish a the rebuke of thy 4480
81: 7 I proved thee a the waters of Meribah. 5921
83: 9 to Sisera, as to Jabin, a the brook of Kison: 871.1
83:10 Which perished a En-dor: they became as 871.1
91: 6 nor for the destruction that wasteth a NIH
91: 7 A thousand shall fall a thy side, and 4480
91: 7 thy side, and ten thousand a thy right hand; 4480
97: 5 The hills melted like wax a 4480+3807.1
97: 5 at the presence of the LORD, a 4480+3807.1
97:12 give thanks a the remembrance of his 3807.1
99: 5 our God, and worship a his footstool; 3807.1
99: 9 our God, and worship a his holy hill; 3807.1
104: 7 A thy rebuke they fled; at the voice of thy 4480
104: 7 a the voice of thy thunder they hasted 4480
105:22 To bind his princes a his pleasure; and 871.1
106: 3 and he that doeth righteousness a all times. 871.1
106: 7 provoked him a the sea, even at the Red 5921
106: 7 him at the sea, even a the Red sea. 871.1
106:32 They angered him also a the waters of 5921
107:27 and are a their wit's end. 1104+2451+3605
109: 6 and let Satan stand a his right hand. 5921
109:31 For he shall stand a the right hand of 3807.1
110: 1 unto my Lord, Sit thou a my right hand, 3807.1
110: 5 The Lord a thy right hand shall strike 5921
114: 7 a the presence of the Lord, 4480+3807.1
114: 7 a the presence of the God of Jacob; 4480
118:13 Thou hast thrust sore a me that I might fall: NIH
119:20 that it hath unto thy judgments a all times. 871.1
119:45 I will walk a liberty: for I seek thy 871.1
119:62 A midnight I will rise to give thanks 2676+3915
119:162 I rejoice a thy word, as one that findeth 5921
123: 4 with the scorning of those that are a ease, 7600
132: 6 Lo, we heard of it a Ephratah: we found it 871.1
132: 7 we will worship a his footstool. 3807.1
135:21 out of Zion, which dwelleth a Jerusalem. NIH
141: 7 Our bones are scattered a the grave's 3807.1
Pr 1:23 Turn you a my reproof: behold, I will 3807.1
1:25 ye have set a nought all my counsel, and 6544
1:26 I also will laugh a your calamity; I will 871.1
4:19 they know not a what they stumble. 871.1
5:11 thou mourn a the last, when thy flesh and 871.1
5:19 let her breasts satisfy thee a all times; and 871.1
7: 6 For a the window of my house I looked 871.1
7:12 the streets, and lieth in wait a every corner.) 681
7:19 For the goodman is not a home, he is gone 871.1
7:20 will come home a the day appointed. 3807.1
8: 3 She crieth a the gates, at the entry 3027+3807.1
8: 3 crieth at the gates, a the entry of the city, 3807.1
8: 3 of the city, a the coming in at the doors. NIH

Pr 8: 3 of the city, at the coming in a the doors. NIH
8:34 watching daily a my gates, waiting at 5921
8:34 my gates, waiting a the posts of my doors. NIH
9:14 For she sitteth a the door of her house, 3807.1
14: 9 Fools make a mock a sin: but among 3887
14:19 and the wicked a the gates of the righteous. 5921
16: 7 he maketh even his enemies to be a peace 7999
17: 5 he that is glad a calamities shall not be 3807.1
17:17 A friend loveth a all times, and a brother is 871.1
20:21 An inheritance may be gotten hastily a 871.1
21:13 Whoso stoppeth his ears a the cry of 4480
23:30 They that tarry long a the wine; they that 5921
23:32 A the last it biteth like a serpent, and NIH
24:19 of evil men, neither be thou envious a 871.1
28:18 he that is perverse in his ways shall fall a 871.1
29:21 shall have him become his son a the length. NIH
30:17 The eye that mocketh a his father, and 3807.1
Ecc 5: 6 wherefore should God be angry a thy 5921
5: 8 in a province, marvel not a the matter: 5921
10: 2 A wise man's heart is a his right hand; 3807.1
10: 2 his right hand; but a fool's heart a his left. 3807.1
12: 4 he shall rise up a the voice of the bird, 3807.1
12: 6 or the pitcher be broken a the fountain, or 5921
12: 6 or the wheel broken a the cistern. 413
SS 1: 7 thou makest thy flock to rest a noon: 871.1
1:12 While the king sitteth a his table, 871.1
2: 9 our wall, he looketh forth a the windows, NIH
7:13 a our gates are all manner of pleasant fruits, 5921
8:11 Solomon had a vineyard a Baal-hamon; 871.1
Isa 1:12 who hath required this a your hand, to tread 4480
1:26 I will restore thy judges as a the first, and 871.1
1:26 and thy counsellers as a the beginning: 871.1
6: 4 the posts of the door moved a the voice of 4480
7: 3 a the end of the conduit of the upper pool in 413
7:23 where there were a thousand vines a a 871.1
9: 1 when a the first he lightly afflicted 3509.1
10:26 to the slaughter of Midian a the rock Oreb: 871.1
10:28 a Michmash he hath laid up his carriages: 3807.1
10:29 they have taken up their lodging a Geba; NIH
10:32 As yet shall he remain a Nob that day: 871.1
13: 6 for the day of the LORD is a hand; 7138
13: 8 they shall be amazed one a another; their 413
14: 7 The whole earth is a rest, and is quiet: 5117
14: 8 the fir trees rejoice a thee, and the cedars 3807.1
14: 9 moved for thee to meet thee a thy coming: NIH
16: 2 the daughters of Moab shall be a the fords NIH
16: 4 for the extortioner is a an end, the spoiler 656
17: 7 A that day shall a man look to his Maker, 871.1
17:14 behold a eveningtide trouble; and 3807.1
19: 1 the idols of Egypt shall be moved a his 4480
19:19 a pillar a the border thereof to the LORD. 681
20: 2 A the same time spake the LORD by 871.1
21: 3 I was bowed down a the hearing of it; I 4480
21: 3 of it; I was dismayed a the seeing of it. 4480
22: 7 shall set themselves in array a the gate. 1886.5
23: 5 As a the report concerning Egypt, so NIH
23: 5 shall they be sorely pained a the report of NIH
26:11 and be ashamed for their envy a the people; NIH
27:13 the LORD in the holy mount a Jerusalem. 871.1
28:15 and with hell are we a agreement; 6213
29: 5 yea, it shall be a an instant suddenly. 3807.1
30: 2 into Egypt, and have not asked a my mouth; NIH
30: 4 For his princes were a Zoan, and 871.1
30:13 whose breaking cometh suddenly a an 3807.1
30:17 One thousand shall flee a the rebuke 4480+6440
30:17 a the rebuke of five shall ye flee: 4480+6440
30:19 For the people shall dwell in Zion a 871.1
30:19 he will be very gracious unto thee a 3807.1
32: 9 Rise up, ye women that are a ease, hear my 7600
32:11 Tremble, ye women that are a ease; 7600
33: 3 A the noise of the tumult the people fled; 4480
33: 3 a the lifting up of thyself the nations were 4480
37:22 of Jerusalem hath shaken her head a thee. 310
37:37 went and returned, and dwelt a Nineveh. 871.1
39: 1 A that time Merodach-baladan, the son of 871.1
42:14 I will destroy and devour a once. 3162
47:14 there shall not be a coal to warm a, nor fire NIH
50: 2 Is my hand shortened a all, that it 7114+7114
50: 2 behold, a my rebuke I dry up the sea, 871.1
51:17 which hast drunk a the hand of the LORD 4480
51:20 they lie a the head of all the streets, as a 871.1
52:14 As many were astonied a thee; his visage 5921
52:15 the kings shall shut their mouths a him: 5921
59:10 we stumble a noonday as in the night; 871.1
60: 4 thy daughters shall be nursed a thy side. 5921
60:14 themselves down a the soles of thy feet; 5921
64: 1 that the mountains might flow down a thy 4480
64: 2 that the nations may tremble a thy 4480
64: 3 the mountains flowed down a thy presence. 4480
66: 2 a contrite spirit, and trembleth a my word. 5921
66: 5 of the LORD, ye that tremble a his word; 413
66: 8 or shall a nation be born a once? for 259+6471
Jer 1:15 they shall set every one his throne a NIH
1:17 be not dismayed a their faces, lest I 4480
2:12 O ye heavens, a this, and be horribly afraid, 5921
2:24 that snuffeth up the wind a her pleasure; 871.1
3:17 A that time they shall call Jerusalem 871.1
4: 9 it shall come to pass a that day, saith 871.1
4:11 A that time shall it be said to this people 871.1
4:19 I am pained a my very heart; my heart NIH
4:26 all the cities thereof were broken down a 4480
5:22 will ye not tremble a my presence, 4480
6: 4 against her; arise, and let us go up a noon. 871.1
6:15 nay, they were not a all ashamed, 954+954
6:15 a the time that I visit them they shall be 871.1
7: 2 that enter in a these gates to worship 871.1
7:12 where I set my name a the first, and 871.1
8: 1 A that time, saith the LORD, they shall 871.1
8:12 nay, they were not a all ashamed, 954+954
8:16 the whole land trembled a the sound of 4480
10: 2 and be not dismayed a the signs of heaven; 4480
10: 2 for the heathen are dismayed a them. 4480
10:10 a his wrath the earth shall tremble, and 4480
10:18 I will sling out the inhabitants of the land a 871.1
11:12 they shall not save them a all in 3467+3467

Jer 15: 8 of the young men a spoiler **a** noonday: 871.1
17:11 of his days, and **a** his end shall be a fool. 871.1
17:27 even entering in **a** the gates of Jerusalem 871.1
18: 7 **A** *what* instant I shall speak concerning a NIH
18: 9 **a** *what* instant I shall speak concerning a NIH
20:16 the morning, and the shouting **a** noontide; 871.1
23:23 *Am* I a God **a** hand, saith the LORD, and 4480
23:32 they shall not **profit** this people **a all**, 3276+3276
25:15 Take the wine cup of this fury **a** mine hand, 4480
25:17 took I the cup **a** the LORD'S hand, and 4480
25:28 if they refuse to take the cup **a** thine hand 4480
25:33 the slain of the LORD shall be **a** that day 871.1
26:19 and all Judah **put** him **a all to death**? 4191+4191
27:18 and **a** Jerusalem, go not to Babylon. 871.1
29:10 accomplished **a** Babylon I will visit you, 3807.1
29:25 unto all the people that *are* **a** Jerusalem, 871.1
31: 1 **A** the same time, saith the LORD, will I 871.1
31:12 they shall not sorrow **any more a all**. 3254+5750
32:20 and hast made thee a name, as **a** this day; NIH
33: 7 and will build them, as **a** the first. 871.1
33:11 the captivity of the land as **a** the first, 871.1
33:15 In those days, and **a** that time, will I cause 871.1
34: 8 all the people which *were* **a** Jerusalem, 871.1
34:14 **A** the end of seven years let ye go every 4480
34:16 whom ye had set **a** liberty at their pleasure, NIH
34:16 whom ye had set at liberty **a** their 3807.1
35:11 of the Syrians: so we dwell **a** Jerusalem. 871.1
36:10 in the higher court **a** the entry of the new NIH
36:17 How didst thou write all these words **a** his 4480
36:27 the words which Baruch wrote **a** the mouth 4480
39:10 them vineyards and fields **a** the same time. 871.1
40:10 I *will* dwell **a** Mizpah to serve 871.1
41: 3 *even* with Gedaliah **a** Mizpah, and 871.1
43: 9 which *is* **a** the entry of Pharaoh's house in 871.1
44: 1 which dwell **a** Migdol, and at Tahpanhes, 871.1
44: 1 **a** Tahpanhes, and at Noph, and in 871.1
44: 1 **a** Noph, and in the country of Pathros, 871.1
44: 6 they are wasted *and* desolate, as **a** this day. NIH
44:22 a curse, without an inhabitant, as **a** this day. NIH
44:23 this evil is happened unto you, as **a** this day. NIH
45: 1 words in a book **a** the mouth of Jeremiah, 4480
46:27 be in rest and **a ease**, and none shall make 7599
47: 3 **A** the noise of the stamping of the hoofs of 4480
47: 3 strong *horses*, **a** the rushing of his chariots, 4480
47: 3 *and* **a** the rumbling of his wheels, the fathers NIH
48:11 Moab hath been **a ease** from his youth, and 7599
48:41 the mighty *men's* hearts in Moab **a** that 871.1
49:17 and shall hiss **a** all the plagues thereof. 5921
49:21 The earth is moved **a** the noise of their fall, 4480
49:21 **a** the cry, the noise thereof was heard in NIH
49:22 **a** that day shall the heart of the mighty 871.1
50:11 ye are grown fat as the heifer **a** grass, NIH
50:13 be astonished, and hiss **a** all her plagues. 5921
50:14 bend the bow, shoot **a** her, spare no arrows: 413
50:46 **A** the noise of the taking of Babylon 4480
51:31 of Babylon that his city is taken **a** *one* end, 4480
51:49 **a** Babylon shall fall the slain of all 3807.1
La 1: 7 saw her, *and* did mock **a** her sabbaths. 5921
1:20 sword bereaveth, **a** home *there is* as death. 871.1
2:15 All that pass by clap *their* hands **a** thee; 5921
2:15 wag their head **a** the daughter of Jerusalem, 5921
3:56 hide not thine ear **a** my breathing, at my 3807.1
3:56 not thine ear at my breathing, **a** my cry. 3807.1
Eze 2: 6 their words, nor be dismayed **a** their looks, 4480
3: 9 them not, neither be dismayed **a** their looks, 4480
3:15 I came to them of the captivity **a** Tel-abib, NIH
3:16 it came to pass **a** the end of seven days, 4480
3:17 therefore hear the word **a** my mouth, and 4480
3:18 but his blood will I require **a** thine hand. 4480
3:20 but his blood will I require **a** thine hand. 4480
8: 5 northward **a** the gate of the altar this 3807.1
8:16 **a** the door of the temple of the LORD, NIH
9: 6 *is* the mark; and begin **a** my sanctuary. 4480
9: 6 they began **a** the ancient men which *were* 871.1
10:19 *every one* stood **a** the door of the east gate NIH
11: 1 behold **a** the door of the gate five and 871.1
12: 4 thou shalt go forth **a** even in their sight, 871.1
12:23 The days are **a hand**, and the effect of 7126
14: 3 I be **inquired of a all** by them? 1875+1875
16: 4 *thee;* thou wast not **salted a all**, 4414+4414
16: 4 not salted at all, nor **swaddled a all**. 2853+2853
16:25 Thou hast built thy high place **a** every head 413
16:46 her daughters that dwell **a** thy left hand: 5921
16:46 that dwelleth **a** thy right hand, *is* Sodom 4480
16:57 as **a** the time of *thy* reproach of NIH
18:23 Have I **any pleasure a all** that 2654+2654
20:32 cometh into your mind shall not **be a all**, 1961
21:19 choose *it*, **a** the head of the way to the city. 871.1
21:21 For the king of Babylon stood **a** the parting 413
21:21 **a** the head of the two ways, to use 871.1
21:22 **A** his right hand was the divination for 871.1
22:13 I have smitten mine hand **a** thy dishonest 413
22:13 **a** thy blood which hath been in the midst of 5921
23:42 a voice of a multitude being **a ease** *was* 7961
24:18 **a** even my wife died; and I did in 871.1
26:10 thy walls shall shake **a** the noise of 4480
26:15 Shall not the isles shake **a** the sound of thy 4480
26:16 shall tremble **a** every moment, and 3807.1
26:16 at every moment, and be astonished **a** thee. 5921
26:18 in the sea shall be troubled **a** thy departure. 4480
27: 3 O thou that art situate **a** the entry of the sea, 5921
27:28 The suburbs shall shake **a** the sound of 3807.1
27:35 of the isles shall be astonished **a** thee, 5921
27:36 among the people shall hiss **a** thee; 5921
28:19 the people shall be astonished **a** thee: 5921
29: 7 and **madest** all their loins **to be a a stand**. 5976
29:13 **A** the end of forty years will I gather 4480
30:18 **A** Tehaphnehes also the day shall be 871.1
31:16 I made the nations to shake **a** the sound of 4480
32:10 I will make many people amazed **a** thee, 5921
32:10 they shall tremble **a** every moment, 3807.1
33: 6 his blood will I require **a** the watchman's 4480
33: 7 thou shalt hear the word **a** my mouth, 4480
33: 8 but his blood will I require **a** thine hand. 4480
34:10 I will require my flock **a** their hand, and 4480
Eze 35:15 As thou didst rejoice **a** the inheritance of 3807.1
36: 8 of Israel; for they are **a hand** to come. 7126
36:11 will do better *unto you* than **a** your NIH
37:22 into two kingdoms **any more a all**: 5750+5750
38:10 *that* **a** the same time shall things come into 871.1
38:11 I will go *to* them that are **a rest**, that dwell 8252
38:18 it shall come to pass **a** the same time when 871.1
38:20 shall shake **a** my presence, and 4480
39:20 Thus ye shall be filled **a** my table *with* 5921
40:40 **a** the side without, as one goeth up to 413
40:40 which *was* **a** the porch of the gate, 3807.1
40:44 which *was* **a** the side of the north gate; 413
40:44 one **a** the side of the east gate *having* 413
41:12 **a** the end toward the west *was* seventy NIH
44:11 *having* charge **a** the gates of the house, and 413
44:17 *that* when they enter in **a** the gates of 413
44:25 they shall come **a** no dead person to defile 413
46: 2 he shall worship **a** the threshold of the gate: 5921
46: 3 **a** the door of this gate before the LORD in NIH
46:19 the entry, which *was* **a** the side of the gate, 5921
47: 1 of the house, **a** the south *side* of the altar. 4480
47: 7 **a** the bank of the river *were* very many trees 413
48:28 border of Gad, **a** the south side southward, 413
48:32 **a** the east side four thousand and 413
48:33 **a** the south side four thousand and NIH
48:34 **A** the west side four thousand and NIH
Da 1: 5 that **a** the end thereof they might stand 4480
1:15 **a** the end of ten days their countenances 4480
1:18 Now **a** the end of the days that the king 3807.1
2:10 *that* asked such things **a** any magician, or 3807.2
3: 5 *That* **a what time** ye hear 0.2+1768+5732+871.2
3: 7 Therefore **a** that time, when all the people 871.2
3: 8 Wherefore **a** that time certain Chaldeans 871.2
3:15 Now if ye be ready that **a** what time ye 871.2
4: 4 I Nebuchadnezzar was **a** rest in mine 871.2
4: 8 **a** the last Daniel came in before me, 5705
4:29 **A** the end of twelve months he walked in 3807.2
4:34 **a** the end of the days I Nebuchadnezzar 3807.2
4:36 **A** the same time my reason returned unto 871.2
5: 3 the house of God which *was* **a** Jerusalem; 871.2
6:24 ever they came **a** the bottom of the den. 3807.2
8: 1 after that which appeared unto me **a** 871.1
8: 2 I saw, that I *was* **a** Shushan *in* the palace, 871.1
8:17 **a** the time of the end *shall be* the vision. 3807.1
8:19 for **a** the time appointed the end *shall be*. 3807.1
8:27 I was astonished **a** the vision, but 5921
9: 7 but unto us confusion of faces, as **a** this day; NIH
9:15 and hast gotten thee renown, as **a** this day; NIH
9:21 whom I had seen in the vision **a** 871.1
9:23 **A** the beginning of thy supplications 871.1
10: 3 neither did I **anoint** myself **a all**, till 5480+5480
11:27 and they shall speak lies **a** one table; 5921
11:27 for yet the end *shall be* **a** the time 3807.1
11:29 **A** the time appointed he shall return, and 3807.1
11:40 **a** the time of the end shall the king of 871.1
11:40 end shall the king of the south push **a** him: 5973
11:43 and the Ethiopians *shall be* **a** his steps. 871.1
12: 1 **a** that time shall Michael stand up, 871.1
12: 1 **a** that time thy people shall be delivered, 871.1
12:13 and stand in thy lot **a** the end of the days. 3807.1
Hos 1: 5 it shall come to pass **a** that day, that I will 871.1
2:16 it shall be **a** that day, saith the LORD, 871.1
4:12 My people ask *counsel* **a** their stocks, and 871.1
5: 8 cry aloud **a** Beth-aven, after thee, NIH
9:10 the firstripe in the fig tree **a** her first time: 871.1
11: 7 the most High, none **a all** would exalt *him*. 3162
Joel 1:15 for the day of the LORD *is* **a hand**, and 7138
2: 1 the LORD cometh, for *it is* **nigh a hand**; 7138
2: 9 they shall enter in **a** the windows like a 1157
Am 1:13 they have ript up the women with child **a** NIH
3: 5 and have **taken** nothing **a all**? 3920+3920
3: 9 Publish in the palaces **a** Ashdod, and in 871.1
4: 3 ye shall go out **a** the breaches, every *cow at* NIH
4: 3 every *cow* **a** *that which is* before her; NIH
4: 4 **a** Gilgal multiply transgression; and NIH
6: 1 Woe to them *that are* **a ease** in Zion, and 7600
7:13 But prophesy not again any more **a** Beth-el: NIH
8: 9 that I will cause the sun to go down **a** 871.1
Ob 1: 7 the men that were **a** peace with thee have NIH
Mic 1:10 Declare ye *it* not **a** Gath, weep ye not at 871.1
1:10 ye *it* not at Gath, **weep** ye not **a all**: 1058+1058
3: 4 he will even hide his face from them **a** that 871.1
7:16 and be confounded **a** all their might: 4480
Na 1: 3 will not **a all acquit** *the wicked:* 5352+5352
1: 5 The mountains quake **a** him, and the hills 4480
1: 5 the earth is burnt **a** his presence, yea, 4480
3:10 dashed in pieces **a** the top of all the streets: 871.1
Hab 1:10 they shall scoff **a** the kings, and the princes 871.1
2: 3 but **a** the end it shall speak, and not lie: 3807.1
2: 5 *he is* a proud man, neither **keepeth a home**, 5115
2:19 and *there is* no breath **a** all in the midst of it. NIH
3: 5 and burning coals went forth **a** his feet. 3807.1
3:11 **a** the light of thine arrows they went, *and* 3807.1
3:11 *and* **a** the shining of thy glittering spear. 3807.1
3:16 my lips quivered **a** the voice: 3807.1
Zep 1: 7 Hold thy peace **a** the presence of the Lord 4480
1: 7 for the day of the LORD *is* **a hand**: 7138
1:12 it shall come to pass **a** that time, *that* I will 871.1
2: 4 they shall drive out Ashdod **a** the noon 871.1
3:19 **a** that time I *will* undo all that afflict thee: 871.1
3:20 **A** that time will I bring you *again*, even in 871.1
Zec 1:11 all the earth sitteth still, and is **a rest**. 8252
1:15 displeased with the heathen *that are* **a ease**: 7600
3: 1 Satan standing **a** his right hand to resist 5921
3: 8 for they *are* men **wondered a**: for behold, 4159
7: 5 ye **a all fast** *unto* me, *even to* me? 6684+6684
11:13 a goodly price that I was prised **a** of them. NIH
12: 8 he that is feeble among them **a** that day 871.1
14: 7 *that* **a** evening time it shall be light. 3807.1
14:14 Judah also shall fight **a** Jerusalem; and 871.1
Mal 1:10 neither will I accept an offering **a** your 4480
1:13 a weariness *is it!* and ye have snuffed **a** it, NIH
2: 7 and they should seek the law **a** his mouth: 4480
2: 8 ye have caused many to stumble **a** the law; 871.1
2:13 or receiveth *it with* good will **a** your hand. 4480
Mt 3: 2 for the kingdom of heaven is **a hand**. *1448*
4: 6 **lest a any time** thou dash thy foot against a *3379*
4:17 for the kingdom of heaven is **a hand**. *1448*
5:25 **lest a any time** the adversary deliver thee *3379*
5:34 But I say unto you, Swear not **a all**; *3654*
5:40 And if any man will **sue** thee **a the law**, *2919*
7:13 Enter ye in **a** the strait gate: for wide *is* *1223*
7:28 the people were astonished **a** his doctrine: *1909*
8: 6 my servant lieth **a** home sick of the palsy, *1722*
9: 9 sitting **a** the receipt of custom: *1909*
9:10 as Jesus **sat a meat** in the house, behold, *345*
10: 7 saying, The kingdom of heaven is **a hand**. *1448*
10:35 For I am come to **set** a man **a variance** *1369*
11:22 for Tyre and Sidon **a** the day of judgment, *1722*
11:25 **A** that time Jesus answered and said, *1722*
12: 1 **A** that time Jesus went on the sabbath day *1722*
12:41 they repented **a** the preaching of Jonas; *1519*
13:15 **lest a any time** they should see with *their* *3379*
13:49 So shall it be **a** the end of the world: *1722*
14: 1 **A** that time Herod the tetrarch heard of *1722*
14: 9 and them which **sat with** him **a meat**, *4873*
15:17 that whatsoever entereth in **a** the mouth NIG
15:30 and cast them *down* **a** Jesus' feet; *3844*
18: 1 **A** the same time came the disciples unto *1722*
18:29 And his fellowservant fell down **a** his feet, *1519*
19: 4 that he which made *them* **a** the beginning *575*
22:33 *this*, they were astonished **a** his doctrine. *1909*
23: 6 And love the uppermost rooms **a** feasts, *1722*
24:33 know that it is near, *even* **a** the doors. *1909*
24:41 Two *women shall be* grinding **a** the mill; *1722*
25: 6 And **a midnight** there was a cry *3319+3571*
25:27 **a** my coming I should have received mine NIG
26: 7 and poured *it* on his head, as he **sat a meat**. *345*
26:18 The Master saith, My time is **a hand**; *1451*
26:18 I will keep the passover **a** thy house with *4314*
26:45 the hour is **a hand**, and the Son of man is *1448*
26:46 behold, he is **a hand** that doth betray me. *1448*
26:60 **A the last** came two false witnesses, *5306*
27:15 Now **a** *that* feast the governor was wont to *2596*
Mk 1:15 and the kingdom of God is **a hand**: *1448*
1:22 And they were astonished **a** his doctrine: *1909*
1:32 And **a even**, when the sun did set, *1096+3798*
1:33 And all the city was gathered together **a** *4314*
2:14 he saw Levi the *son* of Alpheus sitting **a** *1909*
2:15 that as *Jesus* **sat a meat** in his house, *2621*
4:12 **lest a any time** they should be converted, *3379*
5:22 and when he saw him, he fell **a** his feet, *4314*
5:23 daughter **lieth a the point of death**: *2079+2192*
6: 3 with us? And they were offended **a** him. *1722*
7:25 heard of him, and came and fell **a** his feet: *4314*
9:12 suffer many *things*, and be **set a nought**. *1847*
10:22 And he was sad **a** *that* saying, and *1909*
10:24 And the disciples were astonished **a** his *1909*
11: 1 and Bethany, **a** the mount of Olives, *4314*
11:18 all the people was astonished **a** his *1909*
12: 2 And **a** the season he sent to the husbandmen NIG
12: 4 and **a** him they cast stones, and NIG
12:17 that are God's. And they marvelled **a** him. *1909*
12:39 and the uppermost rooms **a** feasts: *1722*
13:29 know that it is nigh, *even* **a** the doors. *1909*
13:35 **a even**, or at midnight, or at *3796*
13:35 or **a midnight**, or at the cockcrowing, or *3317*
13:35 or **a** the cockcrowing, or in the morning: NIG
14: 3 house of Simon the leper, as he **sat a meat**, *2621*
14:42 us go; lo, he that betrayeth me is **a hand**. *1448*
14:54 the servants, and warmed himself **a** the fire. *4314*
15: 6 Now **a** *that* feast he released unto them one *2596*
15:34 And **a** the ninth hour Jesus cried with a loud NIG
16: 2 they came unto the sepulchre **a** the rising of NIG
16:14 appeared unto the eleven as they **sat a meat**, *345*
Lk 1:10 were praying without **a** the time of incense. NIG
1:14 gladness; and many shall rejoice **a** his birth. *1909*
1:29 And when she saw *him*, she was troubled **a** *1909*
2:18 And all they that heard *it* wondered **a** those *4012*
2:33 his mother marvelled **a** those *things* which *1909*
2:41 every year **a** the feast of the passover. NIG
2:47 And all that heard him were astonished **a** *1909*
4:11 **lest a any time** thou dash thy foot against a *3379*
4:18 to set **a** liberty *them that are* bruised, *1722*
4:22 wondered **a** the gracious words which *1909*
4:32 And they were astonished **a** his doctrine: *1909*
5: 5 nevertheless **a** thy word I will let down *1909*
5: 8 When Simon Peter saw *it*, he **fell down a** *4363*
5: 9 **a** the draught of the fishes which they had *1909*
5:27 named Levi, sitting **a** the receipt of custom: *1909*
7: 9 heard these *things*, he marvelled **a** him, NIG
7:37 when she knew that *Jesus* **sat a meat** in *345*
7:38 And stood **a** his feet behind *him* weeping, *3844*
7:49 And they that **sat a meat with** *him* began *4873*
8:19 and could not **come a** him for the press. *4940*
8:26 And they arrived **a** the country of *1519*
8:35 sitting **a** the feet of Jesus, clothed, and *3844*
8:41 and he fell down **a** Jesus' feet, and *3844*
9:31 which he should accomplish **a** Jerusalem. *1722*
9:43 And they were all amazed **a** the mighty *1909*
9:43 But while they wondered every one **a** all *1909*
9:61 which are **a** *home* in my house. NIG
10:14 for Tyre and Sidon **a** the judgment, *1722*
10:32 when he was **a** the place, came and *2596*
10:39 which also sat **a** Jesus' feet, and heard his *3844*
11: 5 and shall go unto him **a** midnight, and NIG
11:32 for they repented **a** the preaching of Jonas; *1519*
12:40 for the Son of man cometh **a** an hour when NIG
12:46 for *him*, and **a** an hour when he is not ware, *1722*
13: 1 There were present **a** that season some that *1722*
13:24 Strive to enter in **a** the strait gate: for many, *1223*
13:25 and to knock **a** the door, saying, Lord, Lord, NIG
14:10 presence of them that **sit a meat with** thee. *4873*
14:14 for thou shalt be recompensed **a** *1722*
14:15 **sat a meat with** *him* heard these *things*, he *4873*
14:17 And sent his servant **a** supper time to say to NIG
15:29 **neither** transgressed I **a any time** *2532+3763*
16:20 which was laid **a** his gate, full of sores, *4314*
17:16 And fell down on *his* face **a** his feet, *3844*
19: 5 for to day I must abide **a** thy house. *1722*

Lk 19:23 that a my coming I might have required NIG
19:29 a the mount called *the mount* of Olives, *4314*
19:30 a your entering ye shall find a colt tied, NIG
19:37 *even* now a the descent of the mount of *4314*
19:42 even thou, **a least** in this thy day, *1065+2532*
20:10 And a the season he sent a servant to *1722*
20:26 and they marvelled a his answer, and *1909*
20:37 are raised, even Moses shewed a the bush, *1909*
20:40 they durst not ask him any *question* **a** *all.* NIG
20:46 and the chief rooms a feasts; *1722*
21:30 selves that summer is now **nigh a hand.** *1451*
21:31 ye that the kingdom of God is **nigh a hand.** *1451*
21:34 **lest a any time** your hearts be overcharged *3379*
21:37 and a night he went out, and abode in NIG
22:27 he that **sitteth a meat,** or he that serveth? *345*
22:27 *is* not he that **sitteth a meat?** but I am *345*
22:30 and drink a my table in my kingdom, *1909*
22:40 And when he was a the place, he said unto *1909*
23: 7 who himself also was a Jerusalem at that *1722*
23: 7 who himself also was at Jerusalem a that *1722*
23:11 with his men of war **set** him **a nought,** *1848*
23:12 for before they were a enmity between *1722*
23:17 he must release one unto them a the feast.) *2596*
23:18 And they cried out **all a once,** saying, *3826*
24:12 wondering in himself a that which was NIG
24:22 which were early a the sepulchre; *1909*
24:27 And beginning a Moses and all the prophets, *575*
24:30 as he **sat a meat** with them, he took bread, *2625*
24:47 among all nations, beginning a Jerusalem. *575*
Jn 1:18 No *man* hath seen God **a any time;** *4455*
2:10 Every man **a the beginning** doth set forth *4412*
2:13 And the Jews' passover was **a hand,** and *1451*
2:23 Now when he was in Jerusalem a *1722*
4:21 nor *yet* a Jerusalem, worship the Father. *1722*
4:45 having seen all *the things* that he did a *1722*
4:45 *things* that he did at Jerusalem a the feast: *1722*
4:46 whose son was sick a Capernaum. *1722*
4:47 his son: for he was **a the point of** death. *3195*
4:52 Yesterday a the seventh hour the fever left NIG
4:53 So the father knew that *it was* a the same *1722*
5: 2 Now there is a Jerusalem by the sheep *1722*
5: 4 For an angel went down a a *certain* season *2596*
5:28 Marvel not a this: for the hour is coming, NIG
5:37 Ye have neither heard his voice **a any time,** *4455*
6:21 immediately the ship was a the land *1909*
6:39 but should raise it up *again* a the last day. *1722*
6:40 and I will raise him up *a* the last day. NIG
6:41 The Jews then murmured a him, because *4012*
6:44 and I will raise him up *a* the last day. NIG
6:54 and I will raise him up *a* the last day. NIG
6:61 in himself that his disciples murmured a it, *4012*
7: 2 the Jews' feast of tabernacles was **a hand.** *1451*
7:11 Then the Jews sought him a the feast, and *1722*
7:23 are ye angry a me, because I have made a NIG
8: 7 among you, let him first cast a stone a her. *1909*
8: 9 beginning a the eldest, *even* unto the last: *575*
8:59 Then took they up stones to cast a him: but *1909*
10:22 And it was a Jerusalem *the feast of* *1722*
10:40 into the place where John a **first** baptized; *4412*
11:24 rise again in the resurrection a the last day. *1722*
11:32 and saw him, she fell down a his feet, *1519*
11:49 unto them, Ye know **nothing a all,** *3756+3762*
11:55 And the Jews' passover was **nigh a hand:** *1451*
12: 2 them that **sat a the table with** him. *4873*
12:16 understood not his disciples a the **first:** *4412*
12:20 them that came up to worship a the feast: *1722*
13:28 Now no *man* a the table knew for what NIG
14:20 A that day ye shall know that I *am* in my *1722*
16: 4 And these *things* I said not unto you a *1537*
16:26 A that day ye shall ask in my name: and *1722*
18:16 But Peter stood a the door without. *4314*
18:38 saith unto them, I find in him no fault *a all.* NIG
18:39 that I should release unto you one a *1722*
19:11 Thou couldest have no power *a all* against NIG
19:39 which a the first came to Jesus by night, and NIG
19:42 *day;* for the sepulchre was **nigh a hand.** *1451*
20:11 But Mary stood without a the sepulchre *4314*
20:12 the one a the head, and the other at the feet, *4314*
20:12 the one at the head, and the other a the feet, *4314*
20:19 Then the same day a evening, being the first NIG
21: 1 again to the disciples a the sea of Tiberias; *1909*
21:20 which also leaned on his breast a supper, *1722*
Ac 1: 6 wilt thou a this time restore again *1722*
1:19 And it was known unto all the dwellers a NIG
2: 5 And there were dwelling a Jerusalem Jews, *1722*
2:14 of Judea, and all *ye* that dwell a Jerusalem, NIG
3: 1 John went up together into the temple a *1909*
3: 2 whom they laid daily a the gate of *4314*
3:10 for alms a the Beautiful gate of the temple: *1909*
3:10 amazement a that which had happened unto *1909*
3:12 Ye men of Israel, why marvel ye a this? *1909*
4: 6 were gathered together a Jerusalem. *1519*
4:11 This is the stone which was **set a nought** of *1848*
4:18 commanded them not to speak **a all** nor *2527*
4:35 And laid *them down* a the apostles' feet: *3844*
4:37 the money, and laid *it* a the apostles' feet. *3844*
5: 2 certain part, and laid *it* a the apostles' feet. *3844*
5: 9 have buried thy husband *are* a the door, *1909*
5:10 Then fell she down straightway a his feet, *3844*
5:15 that **a the least** the shadow of Peter passing *2579*
7:13 And a the second time Joseph was made *1722*
7:26 **set** them **a one** *again,* saying, *1515+1519+4900*
7:29 Then fled Moses a this saying, and was a *1722*
7:31 When Moses saw *it,* he wondered a NIG
7:58 the witnesses laid down their clothes a a *3844*
8: 1 And a that time there was a great *1722*
8: 1 against the church which was a Jerusalem; *1722*
8:14 Now when the apostles which were a *1722*
8:35 and began a the same scripture, and *575*
8:40 But Philip was found a Azotus: and *1519*
9:10 And there was a certain disciple a *1722*
9:13 how much evil he hath done to thy saints a *1722*
9:19 with the disciples which were a Damascus. *1722*
9:22 confounded the Jews which dwelt a *1722*
9:27 how he had preached boldly a Damascus in *1722*

Ac 9:28 them coming in and going out a Jerusalem. *1519*
9:32 also to the saints which dwelt a Lydda. NIG
9:35 And all that dwelt a Lydda and Saron saw NIG
9:36 Now there was a Joppa a certain disciple *1722*
10:11 as *it had been* a great sheet knit a the four NIG
10:25 and fell down a *his* feet, and *1909*
10:30 and a the ninth hour I prayed in my house, *3360*
11: 8 **nothing** common or unclean hath
a any time *3763+3956*
11:15 fell on them, as on us a the beginning. *1722*
12:13 And as Peter knocked a the door of the gate, NIG
13: 1 Now there were in the church that was a *1722*
13: 5 And when they were a Salamis, *1722*
13:12 being astonished a the doctrine of the Lord. *1909*
13:27 For they that dwell a Jerusalem, and *1722*
14: 8 And there sat a certain man a Lystra, *1722*
15:14 Simeon hath declared how God a the first NIG
16: 2 of by the brethren that were a Lystra *1722*
16: 4 and elders which were a Jerusalem. *1722*
16:25 And a midnight Paul and Silas prayed, and *2596*
17:13 word of God was preached of Paul a Berea, *1722*
17:16 Now while Paul waited for them a Athens, *1722*
17:30 the times of *this* ignorance God **winked a;** *5237*
18:22 And when he had landed a Cesarea, and *1519*
18:24 born **a Alexandria,** an eloquent man, *and* *221*
19: 1 to pass that, while Apollos was a Corinth, *1722*
19:17 and Greeks also **dwelling a** Ephesus; *2730*
19:26 that not alone a Ephesus, but NIG
19:27 our craft is in danger to be set a nought; *1519*
20: 5 These going before tarried for us a Troas. *1722*
20:14 And when he met with us a Assos, we took *1519*
20:15 and the next *day* we arrived a Samos, and *1519*
20:15 arrived at Samos, and tarried a Trogyllium; *1722*
20:16 to be a Jerusalem the day of Pentecost. *1519*
20:18 after what manner I have been with you a NIG
21: 3 and sailed into Syria, and landed a Tyre: *1519*
21:11 So shall the Jews a Jerusalem bind the man *1722*
21:13 also to die a Jerusalem for the name of *1519*
21:24 with them, and be a charges with them, NIG
22: 3 yet brought up in this city a the feet of *3844*
23:11 so must thou bear witness also a Rome. *1519*
23:23 two hundred, a the third hour of the night; *575*
25: 4 that Paul should be kept a Cesarea, and *1722*
25: 8 have I offended any *thing a all.* NIG
25:10 said Paul, I stand a Cesar's judgment seat, *1909*
25:15 About whom, when I was a Jerusalem, *1519*
25:23 a Festus' commandment Paul was brought NIG
25:24 both a Jerusalem, and *also* here, crying that *1722*
26: 4 which was a the first among mine own *575*
26: 4 first among mine own nation a Jerusalem, *1722*
26:13 **A midday,** O king, I saw in the way *2250+3319*
26:20 and a Jerusalem, and throughout all NIG
26:32 This man might have been **set a liberty,** *630*
27: 3 And the next *day* we touched a Sidon. *1519*
28:12 And landing a Syracuse, we tarried *there* *1519*
Ro 1:10 if by any means now **a length** I might have *4218*
1:15 the gospel to you that are a Rome also. *1722*
3:26 *I say,* a this time his righteousness: *1722*
4:20 He staggered not a the promise of God *1519*
8:34 that is risen *again,* who is even a the right *1722*
9: 9 A this time will I come, and Sara shall have *2596*
9:32 For they stumbled a *that* stumblingstone; NIG
11: 5 a *this* present time also there is a remnant *1722*
13:12 The night is far spent, the day is **a hand:** *1448*
14:10 or why dost thou **set a nought** thy brother? *1848*
15:26 for the poor saints which are a Jerusalem. *1722*
16: 1 which is a servant of the church which is a *1722*
16: S *sent* by Phebe servant of the church a *1722*
1Co 1: 2 Unto the church of God which is a Corinth, *1722*
7:39 she is a liberty to be married to whom she NIG
8:10 knowledge **sit a meat** in the idol's temple, *2621*
9: 7 Who goeth a warfare any time a his own NIG
9:13 they which **wait a** the altar are partakers *4332*
11:34 And if any *man* hunger, let him eat a home; *1722*
14:16 unlearned say Amen a thy giving of thanks, *1909*
14:27 or a the most *by* three, and *that* by course; NIG
14:35 *thing,* let them ask their husbands a home: *1722*
15: 6 of above five hundred brethren a **once;** *2178*
15:23 afterward they that are Christ's a his *1722*
15:29 for the dead, if the dead rise not **a all?** *3654*
15:32 men I have fought with beasts a Ephesus, *1722*
15:52 in the twinkling of an eye, a the last trump: *1722*
16: 8 But I will tarry a Ephesus until Pentecost. *1722*
16:12 *his* will was not **a all** to come at this time; *3843*
16:12 *his* will was not at all to come **a this time;** *3568*
2Co 1: 1 unto the church of God which is a Corinth, *1722*
4:18 While we **look** not a the *things* which are *4648*
4:18 but a the *things* which are not seen: NIG
5: 6 whilst we are **a home** in the body, *1736*
8:14 *that* now a *this* time your abundance *may* *1722*
Gal 4:12 *am* as ye *are:* ye have not injured me **a all.** *3762*
4:13 I preached the gospel unto you a the **first.** *4387*
Eph 1: 1 to the saints which are a Ephesus, and *1722*
1:20 set *him* a his own right hand in *1722*
2:12 That a that time ye were without Christ, *1722*
3:13 Wherefore I desire that *ye* faint not a my *1722*
Php 1: 1 to all the saints in Christ Jesus which are a *1722*
2:10 That a the name of Jesus every knee should *1722*
4: 5 known unto all men. The Lord *is* **a hand.** *1451*
4:10 that now a the **last** your care of me hath *4218*
Col 1: 2 faithful brethren in Christ which are a *1722*
2: 1 and *for* them a Laodicea, and *for* as many *1722*
1Th 2: 2 as ye know, a Philippi, *1722*
2: 5 For neither **a any time** used we flattering *4218*
2:19 our Lord Jesus Christ a his coming? *1722+3588*
3: 1 we thought it good to be left a Athens *1722*
3:13 a the coming of our Lord Jesus Christ with *1722*
5:13 *And* be a peace among yourselves. NIG
2Th 2: 2 from us, as that the day of Christ is **a hand.** *1764*
3:11 working **not a all,** but are busybodies. *3367*
1Ti 1: 3 As I besought thee to abide *still* a Ephesus, *1722*
5: 4 let them learn first to shew piety a home, NIG
2Ti 1:18 *things* he ministered *unto me* a Ephesus, *1722*
2:26 *who are* taken captive by him a his will. *1519*
3:11 afflictions, which came unto me a Antioch, *1722*

2Ti 3:11 unto me at Antioch, a Iconium, at Lystra; *1722*
3:11 unto me at Antioch, at Iconium, a Lystra; *1722*
4: 1 and the dead a his appearing and his *2596*
4: 6 and the time of my departure is **a hand.** *2186*
4: 8 righteous judge, shall give me a that day: *1722*
4:13 The cloke that I left a Troas with Carpus, *1722*
4:16 A my first answer no *man* stood with me, *1722*
4:20 Erastus abode a Corinth: but *1722*
4:20 but Trophimus have I left a Miletum sick. *1722*
Tit 2: 5 *be* discreet, chaste, **keepers a home,** good, *3626*
Heb 1: 1 God, who a **sundry** times and in divers *3588*
1: 5 which of the angels said he **a any time,** *4218*
1:13 to which of the angels said he **a any time,** *4218*
2: 1 **lest a any time** we should let *them* slip. *3379*
2: 3 which a the first began to be spoken by NIG
7:13 of which no *man* **gave attendance a** *4337*
9:17 otherwise it is of **no** strength **a all** whilst *3379*
12: 2 is set down a the right hand of the throne of *1722*
13:23 ye that *our* brother Timothy is **set a liberty;** *630*
Jas 3:11 Doth a fountain send forth a the same place *1537*
1Pe 1: 7 and glory a the appearing of Jesus Christ: *1722*
1:13 unto you a the revelation of Jesus Christ; *1722*
2: 8 *even to them* which stumble a the word, NIG
4: 7 But the end of all *things* is **a hand:** be ye *1448*
4:17 judgment must begin a the house of God: *575*
4:17 and if *it* first *begin* a us, what *shall* the end *575*
5:13 The *church that is* a Babylon, *1722*
1Jn 1: 5 God is light, and in him is no darkness **a** all. NIG
2:28 not be ashamed before him a his coming. *1722*
4:12 No *man* hath seen God **a any time.** If we *4455*
Rev 1: 3 are written therein: for the time is **a hand.** *1451*
1:17 when I saw him, I fell a his feet as dead. *4314*
3:20 Behold, I stand a the door, and knock: *1909*
8: 3 another angel came and stood a the altar, *1909*
18:14 shalt find them **no more a all.** *3361+3756+3765*
18:21 and shall be found **no** more **a all.** *3364*
18:22 shall be heard **no** more **a all** in thee; *3364*
18:22 shall be heard **no** more **a all** in thee; *3364*
18:23 a candle shall shine **no** more **a all** in thee; *3364*
18:23 of the bride shall be heard **no** more **a all** in *3364*
19: 2 hath avenged the blood of his servants a *1537*
19:10 And I fell a his feet to worship him. And he *1715*
21:12 and a the gates twelve angels, and *1909*
21:25 And the gates of it shall **not** be shut **a all** by *3364*
22:10 of this book: for the time is **a hand.** *1451*

ATAD (2)
Ge 50:10 they came to the threshingfloor of **A,** 329
50:11 saw the mourning in the floor of **A,** they 329

ATARAH (1)
1Ch 2:26 had also another wife, whose name *was* **A;** 5851

ATAROTH (5)
Nu 32: 3 **A,** and Dibon, and Jazer, and Nimrah, and 5852
32:34 of Gad built Dibon, and **A,** and Aroer, 5852
Jos 16: 2 along unto the borders of Archi *to* **A,** 5852
16: 7 it went down from Janohah *to* **A,** and 5852
1Ch 2:54 **A,** the house of Joab, and half of 5852

ATAROTH-ADAR (1) [ATAROTH-ADDAR]
Jos 18:13 the border descended *to* **A,** near the hill that 5853

ATAROTH-ADDAR (1) [ATAROTH-ADAR]
Jos 16: 5 of their inheritance on the east side was **A,** 5853

ATE (3) [EAT]
Ps 106:28 and a the sacrifices of the dead. 398
Da 10: 3 I a no pleasant bread, neither came flesh nor 398
Rev 10:10 book out of the angel's hand, and a it **up;** *2719*

ATER (5)
Ezr 2:16 The children of **A** of Hezekiah, ninety and 333
2:42 the children of **A,** the children of Talmon, 333
Ne 7:21 The children of **A** of Hezekiah, ninety and 333
7:45 the children of **A,** the children of Talmon, 333
10:17 **A,** Hizkijah, Azzur, 333

ATHACH (1)
1Sa 30:30 and to *them* which *were* in **A,** 6269

ATHAIAH (1)
Ne 11: 4 **A** the son of Uzziah, the son of Zechariah, 6265

ATHALIAH (17)
2Ki 8:26 his mother's name *was* **A,** the daughter of 6271
11: 1 when **A** the mother of Ahaziah saw that her 6271
11: 2 in the bedchamber from **A,** so that he was 6271
11: 3 six years. And **A** *did* reign over the land. 6271
11:13 when **A** heard the noise of the guard *and* 6271
11:14 **A** rent her clothes, and cried, Treason, 6271
11:20 they slew **A** with the sword *beside* 6271
1Ch 8:26 And Shamsherai, and Shehariah, and **A,** 6271
2Ch 22: 2 His mother's name also *was* **A** the daughter 6271
22:10 when **A** the mother of Ahaziah saw that her 6271
22:11 hid him from **A,** so that she slew him not. 6271
22:12 God six years: and **A** reigned over the land. 6271
23:12 Now when **A** heard the noise of the people 6271
23:13 **A** rent her clothes, and said, Treason, 6271
23:21 after that they had slain **A** with the sword. 6271
24: 7 For the sons of **A,** *that* wicked woman, 6271
Ezr 8: 7 Jeshaiah the son of **A,** and with him 6271

ATHENIANS (1) [ATHENS]
Ac 17:21 (For all the **A** and strangers which were *117*

ATHENS (7) [ATHENIANS]
Ac 17:15 that conducted Paul brought him unto **A:** *116*
17:16 Now while Paul waited for them at **A,** his *116*
17:22 midst of Mars' hill, and said, *Ye* men of **A,** *117*
18: 1 After these *things* Paul departed from **A,** and *116*
1Th 3: 1 we thought it good to be left at **A** alone; *116*
5: S unto the Thessalonians was written from **A.** *116*

A

2Th 3: S to the Thessalonians was written from **A**. *116*

ATHIRST (5) [THIRST]

Jdg 15:18 he was sore **a**, and called on the LORD, 6770
Ru 2: 9 when thou art **a**, go unto the vessels, and 6770
Mt 25:44 or **a**, or a stranger, or naked, or sick, or *1372*
Rev 21: 6 I will give unto him that is **a** of the fountain *1372*
22:17 And let him that is **a** come. And whosoever *1372*

ATHLAI (1)

Ezr 10:28 Jehohanan, Hananiah, Zabbai, *and* **A**. 6270

ATONEMENT (81) [ATONEMENTS]

Ex 29:33 eat those *things* wherewith the **a** was **made**, 3722
29:36 every day a bullock *for* a sin offering for **a**: 3725
29:36 when thou hast **made an a** for it, and 3722
29:37 Seven days thou shalt **make an a** for 3722
30:10 Aaron shall **make an a** upon the horns of it 3722
30:10 once in the year shall he **make a** upon it 3722
30:15 the LORD, to **make an a** for your souls. 3722
30:16 thou shalt take the **a** money of the children 3725
30:16 the LORD, to **make an a** for your souls. 3722
32:30 peradventure I shall **make an a** for your 3722
Lev 1: 4 it shall be accepted for him to **make a** for 3722
4:20 the priest shall **make an a** for them, and 3722
4:26 the priest shall **make an a** for him as 3722
4:31 the priest shall **make an a** for him, and 3722
4:35 the priest shall **make an a** for his sin that 3722
5: 6 the priest shall **make an a** for him 3722
5:10 the priest shall **make an a** for him for his 3722
5:13 the priest shall **make an a** for him as 3722
5:16 the priest shall **make an a** for him with 3722
5:18 the priest shall **make an a** for him 3722
6: 7 the priest shall **make an a** for him before 3722
7: 7 the priest that **maketh a** therewith shall 3722
8:34 commanded to do, to **make an a** for you. 3722
9: 7 **make an a** for thyself, and for the people: 3722
9: 7 of the people, and **make an a** for them; 3722
10:17 to **make a** for them before the LORD? 3722
12: 7 before the LORD, and **make an a** for her; 3722
12: 8 the priest shall **make an a** for her, and 3722
14:18 the priest shall **make an a** for him before 3722
14:19 **make an a** for him that is to be cleansed 3722
14:20 the priest shall **make an a** for him, and 3722
14:21 to **make an a** for him, and one tenth deal of 3722
14:29 to **make an a** for him before the LORD. 3722
14:31 the priest shall **make an a** for him that is to 3722
14:53 open fields, and **make an a** for the house: 3722
15:15 the priest shall **make an a** for him before 3722
15:30 the priest shall **make an a** for her before 3722
16: 6 **make an a** for himself, and for his house. 3722
16:10 to **make an a** with him, *and* to let him go 3722
16:11 shall **make an a** for himself, and for his 3722
16:16 he shall **make an a** for the holy *place*, 3722
16:17 **make an a** in the holy *place*, until he come 3722
16:17 have **made an a** for himself, and for his 3722
16:18 *is* before the LORD, and **make an a** for it; 3722
16:24 **make an a** for himself, and for the people. 3722
16:27 whose blood was brought in to **make a** in 3722
16:30 For on that day shall *the priest* **make an a** 3722
16:32 shall **make** the **a**, and shall put on the linen 3722
16:33 he shall **make an a** for the holy sanctuary, 3722
16:33 he shall **make an a** for the tabernacle of 3722
16:33 he shall **make an a** for the priests, and 3722
16:34 to **make an a** for the children of Israel for 3722
17:11 upon the altar to **make an a** for your souls: 3722
17:11 for it *is* the blood *that* **maketh an a** for 3722
19:22 the priest shall **make an a** for him with 3722
23:27 seventh month *there shall be* a day of **a**: 3725
23:28 for it *is* a day of **a**, to make an atonement 3725
23:28 to **make an a** for you before the LORD 3722
25: 9 in the day of **a** shall ye make the trumpet 3725
Nu 5: 8 beside the ram of the **a**, whereby an 3725
5: 8 whereby an **a** shall be **made** for him. 3722
6:11 a burnt offering, and **make an a** for him, 3722
8:12 the LORD, to **make an a** for the Levites. 3722
8:19 and to **make an a** for the children of Israel: 3722
8:21 Aaron **made an a** for them to cleanse them. 3722
15:25 the priest shall **make an a** for all 3722
15:28 the priest shall **make an a** for the soul that 3722
15:28 before the LORD, to **make an a** for him; 3722
16:46 the congregation, and **make an a** for them: 3722
16:47 on incense, and **made an a** for the people. 3722
25:13 and **made an a** for the children of Israel. 3722
28:22 for a sin offering, to **make an a** for you. 3722
28:30 one kid of the goats, to **make an a** for you. 3722
29: 5 for a sin offering, to **make an a** for you: 3722
29:11 beside the sin offering of **a**, and 3725
31:50 to **make an a** for our souls before 3722
2Sa 21: 3 wherewith shall I **make** the **a**, that ye may 3722
1Ch 6:49 most holy, and to **make an a** for Israel, 3722
2Ch 29:24 upon the altar, to **make an a** for all Israel: 3722
Ne 10:33 for the sin offerings to **make an a** for 3722
Ro 5:11 by whom we have now received the **a**. *2643*

ATONEMENTS (1) [ATONEMENT]

Ex 30:10 year with the blood of the sin offering of **a**: 3725

ATROTH SHOPHAN (1)

Nu 32:35 **A**, and Jaazer, and Jogbehah, 5855

ATTAI (4)

1Ch 2:35 his servant to wife; and she bare him **A**. 6262
2:36 **A** begat Nathan, and Nathan begat Zabad, 6262
12:11 **A** the sixth, Eliel the seventh, 6262
2Ch 11:20 and **A**, and Ziza, and Shelomith. 6262

ATTAIN (6) [ATTAINED]

Ps 139: 6 for me; it is high, I cannot **a unto** it. 3807.1
Pr 1: 5 a man of understanding shall **a** unto wise 7069
Eze 46: 7 lambs according as his hand shall **a unto**, 5381
Hos 8: 5 how long *will it be* ere they **a** to innocency? 3201
Ac 27:12 if by any means they might **a** to Phenice, *2658*
Php 3:11 If by any means I might **a** unto *2658*

ATTAINED (10) [ATTAIN]

Ge 47: 9 have not **a unto** the days of the years of 5381
2Sa 23:19 howbeit he **a** not unto the *first* three. 935
23:23 than the thirty, but he **a** not to the *first* three. 935
1Ch 11:21 howbeit he **a** not to the *first* three. 935
11:25 among the thirty, but **a** not to the *first* three: 935
Ro 9:30 have **a** to righteousness, *2638*
9:31 hath not **a** to the law of righteousness. *5348*
Php 3:12 Not as though I had already **a**, either were *2983*
3:16 Nevertheless, whereto we have *already* **a**, *5348*
1Ti 4: 6 of good doctrine, whereunto thou hast **a**. *3877*

ATTALIA (1)

Ac 14:25 the word in Perga, they went down into **A**: *825*

ATTEND (11) [ATTENDANCE, ATTENDED, ATTENDING, ATTENT, ATTENTIVE, ATTENTIVELY]

Est 4: 5 whom he had appointed to **a upon** her, and 6440
Ps 17: 1 Hear the right, O LORD, **a unto** my cry, 7181
55: 2 **A** unto me, and hear me: I mourn in my 7181
61: 1 Hear my cry, O God; **a** unto my prayer. 7181
86: 6 and **a** to the voice of my supplications. 7181
142: 6 **A** unto my cry; for I am brought very low: 7181
Pr 4: 1 of a father, and **a** to know understanding. 7181
4:20 My son, **a** to my words; incline thine ear 7181
5: 1 **a** unto my wisdom, *and* bow thine ear to 7181
7:24 and **a to** the words of my mouth. 7181
1Co 7:35 that you may **a upon** the Lord without *2145*

ATTENDANCE (4) [ATTEND]

1Ki 10: 5 and the **a** of his ministers, and their apparel, 4612
2Ch 9: 4 and the **a** of his ministers, and their apparel; 4612
1Ti 4:13 Till I come, **give a** to reading, *4337*
Heb 7:13 of which no *man* **gave a at** the altar. *4337*

ATTENDED (3) [ATTEND]

Job 32:12 Yea, I **a** unto you, and behold, *there was* 995
Ps 66:19 *But* verily God hath heard *me;* he hath **a** to 7181
Ac 16:14 that *she* **a unto** the *things* which were *4337*

ATTENDING (1) [ATTEND]

Ro 13: 6 **a continually** upon this very *thing.* *4342*

ATTENT (2) [ATTEND]

2Ch 6:40 *let* thine ears *be* **a** unto the prayer *that is* 7183
7:15 mine ears **a** unto the prayer *that is made* in 7183

ATTENTIVE (5) [ATTEND]

Ne 1: 6 Let thine ear now be **a**, and thine eyes 7183
1:11 let now thine ear be **a** to the prayer of thy 7183
8: 3 the ears of all the people *were* **a** unto NIH
Ps 130: 2 let thine ears be **a** to the voice of my 7183
Lk 19:48 for all the people were **very a** to hear him. *1582*

ATTENTIVELY (1) [ATTEND]

Job 37: 2 **Hear a** the noise of his voice, and 8085

ATTIRE (3) [ATTIRED]

Pr 7:10 there met him a woman *with* the **a** of a 7897
Jer 2:32 forget her ornaments, *or* a bride her **a**? 7196
Eze 23:15 **exceeding in dyed a** upon their 2871+5628

ATTIRED (1) [ATTIRE]

Lev 16: 4 and with the linen mitre shall he be **a**: 6801

AUDIENCE (12)

Ge 23:10 Abraham in the **a** of the children of Heth, 241
23:13 he spake unto Ephron in the **a** of the people 241
23:16 which he had named in the **a** of the sons of 241
Ex 24: 7 the covenant, and read in the **a** of the people: 241
1Sa 25:24 speak in thine **a**, and hear the words of thine 241
1Ch 28: 8 in the **a** of our God, keep and seek for all 241
Ne 13: 1 in the book of Moses in the **a** of the people; 241
Lk 7: 1 ended all his sayings in the **a** of the people, *189*
20:45 Then **in** the **a** of all the people he said unto *191*
Ac 13:16 Men of Israel, and *ye* that fear God, **give a**. *191*
15:12 and **gave a** to Barnabas and Paul, *191*
22:22 And they **gave** him **a** unto this word, and *191*

AUGMENT (1)

Nu 32:14 to **a** yet the fierce anger of the LORD 5595

AUGUSTUS (3) [AUGUSTUS']

Lk 2: 1 *that* there went out a decree from Cesar **A**, *828*
Ac 25:21 to be reserved unto the hearing of **A**, *4575*
25:25 and *that* he himself hath appealed to **A**, *4575*

AUGUSTUS' (1) [AUGUSTUS]

Ac 27: 1 *one* named Julius, a centurion of **A** band. *4575*

AUL (2)

Ex 21: 6 master shall bore his ear through with an **a**; 4836
Dt 15:17 thou shalt take an **a**, and thrust *it* through 4836

AUNT (1)

Lev 18:14 not approach to his wife: she *is* thine **a**. 1733

AUSTERE (2)

Lk 19:21 For I feared thee, because thou art an **a** man: *840*
19:22 Thou knewest that I was an **a** man, taking up *840*

AUTHOR (3)

1Co 14:33 For God is not *the* **a** of confusion, but NIG
Heb 5: 9 he became the **a** of eternal salvation unto all *159*
12: 2 Looking unto Jesus the **a** and finisher of *our* *747*

AUTHORITIES (1) [AUTHORITY]

1Pe 3:22 angels and **a** and powers being made *1849*

AUTHORITY (37) [AUTHORITIES]

Est 9:29 and Mordecai the Jew, wrote with all **a**, 8633
Pr 29: 2 When the righteous are **in a**, the people 7235
Mt 7:29 For he taught them as *one* having **a**, and *1849*
8: 9 For I am a man under **a**, having soldiers *1849*
20:25 they *that are* great **exercise a upon** them. *2715*
21:23 By what **a** doest thou these *things?* and *1849*
21:23 these *things?* and who gave thee this **a**? *1849*
21:24 I in like wise will tell you by what **a** I do *1849*
21:27 Neither tell I you by what **a** I do these *1849*
Mk 1:22 for he taught them as *one* that had **a**, and *1849*
1:27 for with a commandeth he even the unclean *1849*
10:42 and their great ones **exercise a upon** them. *2715*
11:28 By what **a** doest thou these *things?* and *1849*
11:28 who gave thee this **a** to do these *things?* *1849*
11:29 I will tell you by what **a** I do these *things.* *1849*
11:33 Neither do I tell you by what **a** I do these *1849*
13:34 and gave **a** to his servants, and to every *1849*
Lk 4:36 for with **a** and power he commandeth *1849*
7: 8 For I also am a man set under **a**, *1849*
9: 1 and gave them power and **a** over all devils, *1849*
19:17 in a very little, have thou **a** over ten cities. *1849*
20: 2 by what **a** doest thou these *things?* or *1849*
20: 2 or who is he that gave thee this **a**? *1849*
20: 8 Neither tell I you by what **a** I do these *1849*
20:20 him unto the power and **a** of the governor. *1849*
22:25 they that **exercise a upon** them are called *1850*
Jn 5:27 And hath given him **a** to execute judgment *1849*
Ac 8:27 an eunuch **of great a** under Candace queen *1413*
9:14 And here he hath **a** from the chief priests to *1849*
26:10 having received **a** from the chief priests; *1849*
26:12 Whereupon as I went to Damascus with **a** *1849*
1Co 15:24 have put down all rule and all **a** and power. *1849*
2Co 10: 8 I should boast somewhat more of our **a**, *1849*
1Ti 2: 2 For kings, and *for* all that are in **a**; that we *5247*
2:12 nor to **usurp a over** the man, but to be in *831*
Tit 2:15 and exhort, and rebuke with all **a**. *2003*
Rev 13: 2 him his power, and his seat, and great **a**. *1849*

AVA (1)

2Ki 17:24 from **A**, and from Hamath, and 5755

AVAILETH (4)

Est 5:13 Yet all this **a** me nothing, so long as I see 7737
Gal 5: 6 For in Jesus Christ neither circumcision **a** *2480*
6:15 For in Christ Jesus neither circumcision **a** *2480*
Jas 5:16 fervent prayer of a righteous *man* **a** much. *2480*

AVEN (3) [BETH-AVEN]

Eze 30:17 The young men of **A** and of Phi-beseth shall 205
Hos 10: 8 The high places also of **A**, the sin of Israel, 205
Am 1: 5 cut off the inhabitant from the plain of **A**, 206

AVENGE (17) [VENGEANCE]

Lev 19:18 Thou shalt not **a**, nor bear any grudge 5358
26:25 shall **a the quarrel** of *my* covenant: 5358+5359
Nu 31: 2 **A** the children of Israel of 5358+5360
31: 3 and **a** the LORD of Midian. 5360+5414
Dt 32:43 for he will **a** the blood of his servants, and 5358
1Sa 24:12 and thee, and the LORD **a** me of thee: 5358
2Ki 9: 7 that I may **a** the blood of my servants 5358
Est 8:13 that day to **a** themselves on their enemies. 5358
Isa 1:24 and **a** me of mine enemies: 5358
Jer 46:10 that *he* may **a** him of his adversaries: 5358
Hos 1: 4 I will **a** the blood of Jezreel upon the house 6485
Lk 18: 3 unto him, saying, **A** me of mine adversary. *1556*
18: 5 this widow troubleth me, I will **a** her, *1556*
18: 7 And shall not God **a** his own *1557+3588+4160*
18: 8 I tell you that he will **a** them speedily. *1557*
Ro 12:19 **a** not yourselves, but *rather* give place unto *1556*
Rev 6:10 **a** our blood on them that dwell on *1556*

AVENGED (16) [VENGEANCE]

Ge 4:24 If Cain shall be **a** sevenfold, truly Lamech 5358
Jos 10:13 until the people had **a** themselves upon 5358
Jdg 15: 7 yet will I be **a** of you, and after *that* I will 5358
16:28 that I may be at once **a** of 5358+5359
1Sa 14:24 that I may be **a** on mine enemies. 5358
18:25 to be **a** of the king's enemies. 5358
25:31 or that my lord hath **a** himself: 3467
2Sa 4: 8 the LORD hath **a** my lord the king 5360+5414
18:19 how that the LORD hath **a** him of his 8199
18:31 for the LORD hath **a** thee *this* day of all 8199
Jer 5: 9 shall not my soul be **a** on such a nation as 5358
5:29 shall not my soul be **a** on such a nation as 5358
9: 9 shall not my soul be **a** on such a nation as 5358
Ac 7:24 and **a** him that was oppressed, *1557+4160*
Rev 18:20 for God hath **a** you on her. *2917+2919*
19: 2 hath **a** the blood of his servants at her hand. *1556*

AVENGER (9) [VENGEANCE]

Nu 35:12 be unto you cities for refuge from the **a**; 1350
Dt 19: 6 Lest the **a** of the blood pursue the slayer, 1350
19:12 deliver him into the hand of the **a** of blood, 1350
Jos 20: 3 they shall be your refuge from the **a** of 1350
20: 5 if the **a** of blood pursue after him, then 1350
20: 9 not die by the hand of the **a** of blood, 1350
Ps 8: 2 that *thou* mightest still the enemy and the **a**. 5358
44:16 by reason of the enemy and **a**. 5358
1Th 4: 6 because that the Lord *is* the **a** of all such, *1558*

AVENGETH (2) [VENGEANCE]

2Sa 22:48 *It is* God that **a** me, and that bringeth 5360+5414
Ps 18:47 *It is* God that **a** me, and subdueth 5360+5414

AVENGING (3) [VENGEANCE]

Jdg 5: 2 Praise ye the LORD for the **a** of 6544+6546
1Sa 25:26 *from* **a** thyself with thine own hand, now let 3467
25:33 and *from* **a** myself with mine own hand. 3467

AVERSE (1)

Mic 2: 8 that pass by securely *as men* **a** from war. 7725

AVIM (1) [AVIMS]

Jos 18:23 And **A**, and Parah, and Ophrah, 5761

AVIMS (1) [AVIM]
Dt 2:23 the **A** which dwelt in Hazerim, *even* unto 5761

AVITES (2)
Jos 13: 3 the Gittites, and the Ekronites; also the **A**: 5761
2Ki 17:31 the **A** made Nibhaz and Tartak, and 5761

AVITH (2)
Ge 36:35 his stead: and the name of his city *was* **A**. 5762
1Ch 1:46 his stead: and the name of his city *was* **A**. 5762

AVOID (5) [AVOIDED, AVOIDING, AVOUCHED]
Pr 4:15 **A** it, pass not by it, turn from it, and 6544
Ro 16:17 which ye have learned; and **a** them. *1578*
1Co 7: 2 Nevertheless, to **a** fornication, let every *1223*
2Ti 2:23 But foolish and unlearned questions **a**, *3868*
Tit 3: 9 But **a** foolish questions, and genealogies, *4026*

AVOIDED (1) [AVOID]
1Sa 18:11 *it.* And David **a** out of his presence twice. 5437

AVOIDING (2) [AVOID]
2Co 8:20 **A** this, that no *man* should blame us in this *4724*
1Ti 6:20 **a** profane *and* vain babblings, and *1624*

AVOUCHED (2) [AVOID]
Dt 26:17 Thou hast **a** the LORD *this* day to be thy 559
26:18 the LORD hath **a** thee *this* day to be his 559

AVVA See AVA

AVVIM See AVIM

AVVITES See AVIMS; AVITES

AWAIT (1) [WAIT]
Ac 9:24 But their **laying a** was known of Saul. *1917*

AWAKE (42) [WAKE]
Jdg 5:12 **A**, awake, Deborah: awake, awake, utter a 5782
5:12 Awake, **a**, Deborah: awake, awake, utter a 5782
5:12 **a**, awake, utter a song: arise, Barak, and 5782
5:12 awake, **a**, utter a song: arise, Barak, and 5782
Job 8: 6 surely now he would **a** for thee, and 5782
14:12 the heavens *be* no more, they shall not **a**, 6974
Ps 7: 6 **a** for me *to* the judgment *that* thou hast 5782
17:15 be satisfied, when *I* **a**, *with* thy likeness. 6974
35:23 Stir up thyself, and **a** to my judgment, 6974
44:23 **A**, why sleepest thou, O Lord? arise, cast *us* 5782
57: 8 **A up**, my glory; awake, psaltery and harp: 5782
57: 8 Awake up, my glory; **a**, psaltery and harp: 5782
57: 8 and harp: I *myself* will **a** early. 5782
59: 4 without *my* fault: **a** to help me, and behold. 5782
59: 5 the God of Israel, **a** to visit all the heathen: 6974
108: 2 **A**, psaltery and harp: I *myself* will awake 5782
108: 2 and harp: I *myself* will **a** early. 5782
139:18 than the sand: when I **a**, I am still with thee. 6974
Pr 23:35 when shall I **a**? I will seek it yet again. 6974
SS 2: 7 ye stir not up, nor **a** *my* love, till he please. 5782
3: 5 ye stir not up, nor **a** *my* love, till he please. 5782
4:16 **A**, O north wind; and come thou south; 5782
8: 4 stir not up, nor **a** *my* love, until he please. 5782
Isa 26:19 **A** and sing, ye that dwell in dust: for thy 6974
51: 9 **A**, awake, put on strength, O arm of 5782
51: 9 Awake, **a**, put on strength, O arm of 5782
51: 9 **a**, as *in* the ancient days, *in* the generations 5782
51:17 **A**, awake, stand up, O Jerusalem, 5782
51:17 Awake, **a**, stand up, O Jerusalem, 5782
52: 1 **A**, awake; put on thy strength, O Zion; 5782
52: 1 Awake, **a**; put on thy strength, O Zion; 5782
Da 12: 2 that sleep in the dust of the earth shall **a**, 6974
Joel 1: 5 **A**, ye drunkards, and weep; and howl, 6974
Hab 2: 7 **a** that *shall* vex thee, and thou shalt be for 3364
2:19 Woe unto him that saith to the wood, **A**; 6974
Zec 13: 7 **A**, O sword, against my shepherd, and 5782
Mk 4:38 and they **a** him, and say unto him, Master, *1326*
Lk 9:32 and when they were **a**, they saw his glory, *1235*
Jn 11:11 but I go, that I may **a** him **out of sleep**. *1852*
Ro 13:11 that now *it is* high time to **a** out of sleep: *1453*
1Co 15:34 **A** to righteousness, and sin not: for some *1594*
Eph 5:14 **A** thou that sleepest, and arise from *1453*

AWAKED (8) [WAKE]
Ge 28:16 Jacob **a** out of his sleep, and he said, 3364
Jdg 16:14 he **a** out of his sleep, and went away with 3364
1Sa 26:12 and no man saw *it*, nor knew *it*, neither **a**: 6974
1Ki 18:27 *or* peradventure he sleepeth, and must be **a**. 3364
2Ki 4:31 and told him, saying, The child is not **a**. 6974
Ps 3: 5 I laid me down and slept; I **a**; for 6974
78:65 the Lord **a** as one out of sleep, *and* like a 3364
Jer 31:26 Upon this I **a**, and beheld; and my sleep 6974

AWAKEST (2) [WAKE]
Ps 73:20 *so*, O Lord, when *thou* **a**, thou shalt despise 5782
Pr 6:22 and *when* thou **a**, it shall talk *with* thee. 6974

AWAKETH (3) [WAKE]
Ps 73:20 As a dream when *one* **a**; *so*, O Lord, 6974
Isa 29: 8 he eateth; but he **a**, and his soul *is* empty: 6974
29: 8 he **a**, and behold, *he is* faint, and his soul 6974

AWAKING (1) [WAKE]
Ac 16:27 of the prison **a out of** his **sleep**, *1096+1853*

AWARE (3) [WARE]
SS 6:12 Or ever I was **a**, my soul made me *like* 3045
Jer 50:24 also taken, O Babylon, and thou wast not **a**: 3045
Lk 11:44 the men that walk over *them* are not **a** *of* *1492*

AWAY (916) [CASTAWAY]
Ge 12:20 they **sent** him **a**, and his wife, and all that 7971
15:11 upon the carcases, Abram **drove** them **a**. 5380
18: 3 **pass** not **a**, I pray thee, from thy servant: 5674
21:14 her shoulder, and the child, and **sent** her **a**: 7971
21:25 servants had **violently taken a**. 1497
24:54 and he said, **Send** me **a** unto my master. 7971
24:56 send me **a** that I may go to my master. 7971
24:59 they **sent a** Rebekah their sister, and her 7971
25: 6 **sent** them **a** from Isaac his son, while he 7971
26:27 ye hate me, and have **sent** me **a** from you? 7971
26:29 but good, and have **sent** thee **a** in peace: 7971
26:31 Isaac **sent** them **a**, and they departed from 7971
27:35 and hath **taken a** thy blessing. 3947
27:36 he **took a** my birthright; and behold, 3947
27:36 behold, now he hath **taken a** my blessing. 3947
27:44 a few days, until thy brother's fury **turn a**; 7725
27:45 Until thy brother's anger **turn a** from thee, 7725
28: 5 Isaac **sent a** Jacob: and he went to 7971
28: 6 **sent** him **a** to Padan-aram, to take him a 7971
30:15 wouldest thou **take a** my son's mandrakes 3947
30:23 and said, God hath **taken a** my reproach: 622
30:25 that Jacob said unto Laban, **Send** me **a**, 7971
31: 1 Jacob hath **taken a** all that *was* our 3947
31: 9 Thus God hath **taken a** the cattle of your 5337
31:18 he **carried a** all his cattle, and all his goods 5090
31:20 Jacob **stale a unawares** to Laban 1589+3820
31:26 that thou hast **stolen a unawares** to 1589+3824
31:26 **carried a** my daughters, as captives taken 5090
31:27 Wherefore didst thou **flee a** secretly, 1272
31:27 flee away secretly, and **steal a from** me; 1589
31:27 that I might have **sent** thee **a** with mirth, 7971
31:42 surely thou hadst **sent** me **a** now empty. 7971
35: 2 **Put a** the strange gods that *are* among you, 5493
38:19 **went a**, and laid by her vail from her, and 1980
40:15 For **indeed** I was **stolen a** out of 1589+1589
42:36 ye will take Benjamin **a**: all these things are NIH
43:14 that he may **send a** your other brother, and 7971
44: 3 the men were **sent a**, they and their asses. 7971
45:24 So he **sent** his brethren **a**, and 7971
Ex 2: 9 **Take** this child **a**, and nurse it for me, and 1980
2:17 the shepherds came and **drove** them **a**: but 1644
8: 8 that he may **take a** the frogs from me, and 5493
8:28 only you shall not go **very far a**: 7368+7368
10:17 that he may **take a** from me this death only. 5493
10:19 which **took a** the locusts, and cast them 5375
12:15 even the first day ye shall **put a** leaven out 7673
12:28 the children of Israel **went a**, and did as 1980
13:19 ye shall carry up my bones **a** hence with 4480
13:22 He **took** not **a** the pillar of the cloud by 4185
14:11 hast thou **taken** us **a** to die in 3947
15:15 all the inhabitants of Canaan shall **melt a**. 4127
18:18 Thou wilt **surely wear a**, both thou, 5034+5034
19:24 **A**, get thee down, and thou shalt come up, 1980
22:10 it die, or be hurt, or **driven a**, no man 7617
23:25 I will **take** sickness **a** from the midst of 5493
33:23 I will **take a** mine hand, and thou shalt see 5493
Lev 1:16 he shall **pluck a** his crop with his feathers, 5493
3: 4 with the kidneys, it shall he **take a**. 5493
3:10 with the kidneys, it shall he **take a**. 5493
3:15 with the kidneys, it shall he **take a**. 5493
4: 9 with the kidneys, it shall he **take a**, 5493
4:31 he shall **take a** all the fat thereof, as the fat 5493
4:31 as the fat is **taken a** from off the sacrifice 5493
4:35 he shall **take a** all the fat thereof, as the fat 5493
4:35 as the fat of the lamb is **taken a** from 5493
6: 2 or in a **thing taken a by violence**, or 1498
6: 4 that which he **took violently a**, 1497+1500
7: 4 with the kidneys, it shall he **take a**: 5493
14:40 the priest shall command that they **take a** 2502
14:43 after *that* he hath **taken a** the stones, and 2502
16:21 shall **send** *him* **a** by the hand of a fit man 7971
21: 7 neither shall they take a woman **put a** from 1644
25:25 hath sold **a** *some* of his possession, and 4480
26:39 they that are left of you shall **pine a** in their 4743
26:39 of their fathers shall they **pine a** with them. 4743
26:44 I will not **cast** them **a**, neither will I abhor 3988
Nu 4:13 they shall **take a** the **ashes** from the altar, 1878
11: 6 now our soul *is* **dried a**: *there is* nothing at 3002
14:43 because ye are **turned a** from the LORD, 7725
17:10 thou shalt **quite take a** their murmurings 3615
20:21 wherefore Israel turned **a from** him. 4480+5921
21: 7 that he **take a** the serpents from us. 5493
24:22 until Asshur shall **carry** thee **a captive**. 7617
25: 4 the LORD may be **turned a** from Israel. 7725
25:11 hath **turned** my wrath **a** from the children 7725
27: 4 father be **done a** from among his family, 1639
32:15 For if ye **turn a** from after him, he will yet 7725
36: 4 shall their inheritance be **taken a** from 1639
Dt 7: 4 For they will **turn a** thy son from following 5493
7:15 the LORD will **take a** from thee all 5493
13: 5 he hath spoken to **turn** *you* **a** from 5627
13: 5 So shalt thou **put** the evil **a** from the midst 1197
13:10 he hath sought to **thrust** thee **a** from 5080
15:13 thou shalt not **let** him **go a** empty: 7971
15:16 he say unto thee, I will not **go a** from thee; 3318
15:18 when thou **sendest** him **a** free from thee; 7971
17: 7 So thou shalt **put** the evil **a** from among 1197
17:12 and thou shalt **put a** the evil from Israel. 1197
17:17 wives to himself, that his heart **turn** not **a**: 5493
19:13 thou shalt **put a** *the guilt of* innocent blood 1197
19:19 shalt thou **put** the evil **a** from among you. 1197
21: 9 So shalt thou **put a** the *guilt of* innocent 1197
21:21 so shalt thou **put** evil **a** from among you; 1197
22:19 his wife; he may not **put** her **a** all his days. 7971
22:21 so shalt thou **put** evil **a** from among you. 1197
22:22 so shalt thou **put a** evil from Israel. 1197
22:24 so thou shalt **put a** evil from among you. 1197
22:29 he may not **put** her **a** all his days. 7971
23:14 thing in thee, and turn **a from** thee. 310+4480
24: 4 Her former husband, which **sent** her **a**, 7971
24: 7 and thou shalt **put** evil **a** from among you. 1197
26:13 I have **brought a** the hallowed *things* out 1197
26:14 neither have I **taken a** *ought* thereof for 1197
28:26 of the earth, and no man shall **fray** *them* **a**. 2729
28:31 thine ass *shall be* **violently taken a** from 1497
29:18 whose heart **turneth a** *this* day from 6437
30:17 If thine heart **turn a**, so that thou wilt not 6437
30:17 shalt be **drawn a**, and worship other gods, 5080
Jos 2:21 she **sent** them **a**, and they departed: and 7971
5: 9 *This* day have I **rolled a** the reproach of 1556
7:13 until ye **take a** the accursed thing from 5493
8: 3 *men* of valour, and **sent** them **a** by night. 7971
8:16 and were **drawn a** from the city. 5423
18: 8 the men arose, and **went a**: and 1980
22: 6 So Joshua blessed them, and **sent** them **a**: 7971
22: 7 when Joshua **sent** them **a** also unto their 7971
22:16 to **turn a** *this* day from following 7725
22:18 that ye must **turn a** *this* day from following 7725
24:14 **put a** the gods which your fathers served 5493
24:23 Now therefore **put a**, *said he*, the strange 5493
Jdg 3:18 he **sent a** the people that bare the present. 7971
4:15 down off *his* chariot, and **fled a** on his feet. 5127
4:17 Howbeit Sisera **fled a** on his feet to the tent 5127
5:21 The river of Kishon **swept** them **a**, 1640
8:21 **took a** the ornaments that *were* on their 3947
9:21 Jotham **ran a**, and fled, and went to Beer, 5127
10:16 they **put a** the strange gods from among 5493
11:13 Because Israel **took a** my land, when they 3947
11:15 Israel **took** not **a** the land of Moab, 3947
11:38 he **sent** her **a** *for* two months: and she went 7971
15:17 that he **cast a** the jawbone out of his hand, 7993
16: 3 **went a** with them, bar and all, and put *them* 5265
16:14 **went a** with the pin of the beam, and 5265
18:24 Ye have **taken a** my gods which I made, 3947
18:24 I made, and the priest, and ye are **gone a**: 1980
19: 2 **went a** from him unto her father's house to 1980
20:13 them to death, and **put a** evil from Israel. 1197
20:31 *and* were **drawn a** from the city; 5423
1Sa 1:14 thou be drunken? **put a** thy wine from thee. 5493
5:11 **Send a** the ark of the God of Israel, and 7971
6: 3 If ye **send a** the ark of the God of Israel, 7971
6: 8 side thereof; and **send** it **a**, that it may go. 7971
7: 3 *then* **put a** the strange gods and Ashtaroth 5493
7: 4 the children of Israel did **put a** Baalim 5493
9:26 saying, Up, that I may **send** thee **a**. 7971
10:25 Samuel **sent** all the people **a**, every man to 7971
14:16 the multitude **melted a**, and they went on 4127
15:27 as Samuel turned about to **go a**, he laid 1980
17:26 and **taketh a** the reproach from Israel? 5493
19:10 he **slipt a** out of Saul's presence, and 6362
19:17 and **sent a** mine enemy, that he is escaped? 7971
20:13 I will shew it thee, and **send** thee **a**, 7971
20:22 *thy way*: for the LORD hath **sent** thee **a**. 7971
20:29 let me **get a**, I pray thee, and see my 4422
21: 6 hot bread in the day when it was **taken a**. 3947
23: 5 **brought a** their cattle, and smote them *with* 5090
23:26 David made haste to **get a** for fear of Saul; 1980
24:19 will he let him go well **a**? 1870+871.1
25:10 that **break a** every man from his master. 6555
26:12 they **gat** them **a**, and no man saw *it*, nor 1980
27: 9 **took a** the sheep, and the oxen, and 3947
28: 3 Saul had **put a** those that had familiar 5493
28:25 Then they arose up, and **went a** that night. 1980
30: 2 but **carried** *them* **a**, and went on their way. 5090
30:18 all that the Amalekites had **carried a**: 3947
30:22 that they may **lead** *them* **a**, and depart. 5090
2Sa 1:21 the shield of the mighty is **vilely cast a**, 1602
3:21 David **sent** Abner **a**; and he went in peace. 7971
3:22 for he had **sent** him **a**, and he was gone in 7971
3:23 he hath **sent** him **a**, and he is gone in peace. 7971
3:24 why *is* it *that* thou hast **sent** him **a**, and 7971
4: 7 and **gat** them **a** through the plain all night. 1980
4:11 your hand, and **take** you **a** from the earth? 1197
5: 6 Except thou **take a** the blind and the lame, 5493
7:15 my mercy shall not **depart a** from him, as I 5493
7:15 from Saul, whom I **put a** before thee. 4480+5493
10: 4 *even* to their buttocks, and **sent** them **a**. 7971
12:13 The LORD also hath **put a** thy sin; 5674
13:16 this evil in **sending** me **a** *is* greater than 7971
17:18 they **went** both of them **a** quickly, and 1980
18: 3 for if we **flee a**, they will not care for 5127+5127
18: 9 and the mule that *was* under him **went a**. 5674
19: 3 as people being ashamed **steal a** when they 1589
19:41 brethren the men of Judah **stolen** thee **a**, 1589
22:46 Strangers shall **fade a**, and they shall be 5034
23: 6 *shall be* all of them as thorns **thrust a**, 5074
23: 9 and the men of Israel were **gone a**: 5927
24:10 **take a** the iniquity of thy servant; 5674
1Ki 2:31 that thou mayest **take a** the innocent blood, 5493
2:39 that two of the servants of Shimei **ran a** 1272
8:46 that they **carry** them **a captives** unto 7617+7617
8:48 which **led** them **a captive**, and pray unto 7617
8:66 On the eighth day he **sent** the people **a**: and 7971
11: 2 *for* surely they will **turn a** your heart after 5186
11: 3 and his wives **turned a** his heart. 5186
11: 4 *that* his wives **turned a** his heart after other 5186
11:13 Howbeit I will not **rend a** all the kingdom; 7167
14: 8 **rent** the kingdom **a** from the house of 7167
14:10 will **take a** the remnant of the house of 1197
14:10 as *a man* **taketh a** dung, till it be all gone. 1197
14:26 he **took a** the treasures of the house of 3947
14:26 of the king's house; he even **took a** all: 3947
14:26 he **took a** all the shields of gold which 3947
15:12 he **took a** the sodomites out of the land, 5674
15:22 they **took a** the stones of Ramah, and 5375
16: 3 I will **take a** the posterity of Baasha, and 1197
19: 4 *is* enough; now, O LORD, **take a** my life; 3947
19:10 am left; and they seek my life, to **take** it **a**. 3947
19:14 am left; and they seek my life, to **take** it **a**. 3947
20: 6 they shall put *it* in their hand, and **take** *it* **a**. 3947
20:24 do this thing, **Take** the kings **a**, every man 5493
20:34 *said Ahab*, I will **send** thee **a** with *this* 7971
20:34 made a covenant with him, and **sent** him **a**. 7971
20:41 and **took** the ashes **a** from his face; 5493
21: 4 **turned a** his face, and would eat no bread. 5437
21:21 will **take a** thy posterity, and will cut off 1197
22:43 the high places were not **taken a**; 5493
2Ki 2: 3 Knowest thou that the LORD will **take a** 3947
2: 5 Knowest thou that the LORD will **take a** 3947
2: 9 do for thee, before I be **taken a** from thee. 3947
3: 2 for he **put a** the image of Baal that his 5493
4:27 Gehazi came near to **thrust** her **a**. And 1920
5: 2 had **brought a captive** out of the land of 7617

2Ki 5:11 and **went a**, and said, Behold, I thought, 1980
5:12 So he turned and **went a** in a rage. 1980
6:23 he **sent** them **a**, and they went to their 7971
6:32 a murderer hath sent to **take a** mine head? 5493
7:15 which the Syrians had **cast a** in their haste. 7993
12: 3 the high places were not **taken a**: 5493
12:18 of Syria: and he **went a** from Jerusalem. 5927
14: 4 Howbeit the high places were not **taken a**: 5493
17: 6 **carried** Israel **a** into Assyria, and 1540
17:11 whom the LORD **carried a** before them; 1540
17:23 So was Israel **carried a** out of their own 1540
17:28 one of the priests whom they had **carried a** 1540
17:33 nations whom they **carried a** from thence. 1540
18:11 the king of Assyria did **carry a** Israel unto 1540
18:22 and whose altars Hezekiah hath **taken a**, 5493
18:24 wilt thou **turn a** the face of one captain of 7725
18:32 **take** you **a** to a land like your own land, 3947
20:18 shall they take *a*; and they shall be eunuchs NIH
23:11 he **took a** the horses that the kings of Judah 7673
23:19 Josiah **took a**, and did to them according to 5493
23:24 and in Jerusalem, did Josiah **put a**, 1197
23:34 and took Jehoahaz *a*: and he came *to* Egypt, NIH
24:14 he **carried a** all Jerusalem, and all 1540
24:15 he **carried a** Jehoiachin to Babylon, and 1540
25:11 the fugitives that **fell a** to the king of 5307
25:11 the captain of the guard **carry a**. 1540
25:14 wherewith they ministered, took they *a*. NIH
25:15 *in* silver, the captain of the guard took *a*. NIH
25:21 So Judah was **carried a** out of their land. 1540
1Ch 5: 6 king of Assyria **carried a captive**: 1540
5:21 they **took a** their cattle; *of* their camels fifty 7617
5:26 he **carried** them **a**, even the Reubenites, 1540
6:15 when the LORD **carried a** Judah 1540
7:21 they came down to take *a* their cattle. NIH
8: 8 country of Moab, after he had **sent** them **a**; 7971
8:13 who **drove a** the inhabitants of Gath: 1272
9: 1 *who* were **carried a** to Babylon for their 1540
10:12 **took a** the body of Saul, and the bodies of 5375
12:19 the Philistines upon advisement **sent** him **a**, 7971
14:14 **turn a** from them, and come upon them 5437
17:13 I will not **take** my mercy **a** from him, as I 5493
19: 4 hard by *their* buttocks, and **sent** them **a**. 7971
21: 8 **do a** the iniquity of thy servant; 5674
2Ch 6:36 they **carry** them **a captives** unto a 7617+7617
6:42 **turn** not **a** the face of thine anointed: 7725
7:10 month he **sent** the people **a** into their tents, 7971
7:19 if ye **turn a**, and forsake my statutes and 7725
9:12 **went a** to her own land, she and 1980
12: 9 **took a** the treasures of the house of 3947
12: 9 he **carried a** also the shields of gold which 3947
14: 3 For he **took a** the altars of the strange *gods,* 5493
14: 5 Also he **took a** out of all the cities of Judah 5493
14:13 and they **carried a** very much spoil. 5375
14:15 **carried a** sheep and camels in abundance, 7617
15: 8 **put a** the abominable idols out of all 5674
15:17 the high places were not **taken a** out of 5493
16: 6 they **carried a** the stones of Ramah, and 5375
17: 6 moreover he **took a** the high places and 5493
19: 3 in that thou hast **taken a** the groves out of 1197
20:25 his people came to **take a** the spoil of them, 962
20:25 more than they could **carry a**: 4853
20:33 Howbeit the high places were not **taken a**: 5493
21:17 **carried a** all the substance that was found 7617
25:12 did the children of Judah **carry a captive**, 7617
25:27 Now after the time that Amaziah did **turn a** 5493
28: 5 **carried a** a great multitude of them
captives, 7617+7633
28: 8 the children of Israel **carried a captive** of 7617
28: 8 **took** also **a** much spoil from them, and 962
28:17 and smitten Judah, and **carried a** captives. 7617
28:21 For Ahaz **took a a portion** *out* of the house 2505
29: 6 have **turned a** their faces from 5437
29:10 that his fierce wrath may **turn a** from us. 7725
29:19 which king Ahaz in his reign did **cast a** in 2186
30: 8 that the fierceness of his wrath may **turn a** 7725
30: 9 and will not **turn a** *his* face from you, 5493
30:14 **took a** the altars that *were* in Jerusalem, 5493
30:14 all the altars for incense **took** they **a**, and 5493
32:12 Hath not the same Hezekiah **taken a** his 5493
33:15 he **took a** the strange gods, and the idol out 5493
34:33 Josiah **took a** all the abominations out of 5493
35:23 the king said to his servants, **Have** me **a**; 5674
36:20 from the sword **carried** he **a** to Babylon; 1540
Ezr 2: 1 *of* those which had been **carried a**, 1473
2: 1 of Babylon had **carried a** unto Babylon, 1540
5:12 **carried** the people **a** into Babylon. 1541
8:35 children of those that had been **carried a**, 1473
9: 4 of those that had been **carried a**; 1473
10: 3 with our God to **put a** all the wives, 3318
10: 6 of **them** that had been **carried a**. 1473
10: 8 of **those** that had been **carried a**. 1473
10:19 they gave their hands that *they* would **put a** 3318
Ne 7: 6 *of* those that had been **carried a**, 1473
7: 6 the king of Babylon had **carried a**, 1540
Est 2: 6 Who had been **carried a** from Jerusalem 1540
2: 6 **carried a** with Jeconiah king of Judah, 1540
2: 6 the king of Babylon had **carried a**. 1540
4: 4 and to **take a** his sackcloth from him: 5493
8: 3 besought him with tears to **put a** 5674
Job 1:15 Sabeans fell *upon them,* and **took** them **a**; 3947
1:17 have **carried** them **a**, yea, and slain 3947
1:21 the LORD hath taken *a*; blessed be NIH
4:21 not their excellency *which is* in them **go a**? 5265
6:15 *and* as the stream of brooks they **pass a**; 5674
7: 9 *As* the cloud is consumed and **vanisheth a**: 1980
7:21 and **take a** mine iniquity? 5674
8: 4 he have **cast** them **a** for their transgression; 7971
8:20 God will not **cast a** a perfect *man,* neither 3988
9:12 Behold, he **taketh a**, who can hinder him? 2862
9:25 than a post: they **flee a**, they see no good. 1272
9:26 They are **passed a** as the swift ships: as 2498
9:34 Let him **take** his rod **a** from me, and let not 5493
11:14 **put** it **far a**, and let not wickedness dwell 7368
11:16 *and* remember *it* as waters *that* **pass a**: 5674
12:17 He **leadeth** counsellers **a** spoiled, and 1980
Job 12:19 He **leadeth** princes **a** spoiled, and 1980
12:20 He **removeth a** the speech of the trusty, 5493
12:20 and taketh **a** the understanding of the aged. NIH
12:24 He **taketh a** the heart of the chief of 5493
14:10 man dieth, and **wasteth a**: yea, man giveth 2522
14:19 thou **washest a** the things which grow out 7857
14:20 his countenance, and **sendest** him **a**. 7971
15:12 Why doth thine heart **carry** thee **a**? and 3947
15:30 by the breath of his mouth shall he **go a**. 5493
20: 8 He shall **fly a** as a dream, and shall not be 5774
20: 8 he shall be **chased a** as a vision of 5074
20:19 he hath **violently taken a** a house which he 1497
20:28 *his goods shall* **flow a** in the day of his 5064
21:18 and as chaff that the storm **carrieth a**. 1589
22: 9 Thou hast **sent** widows **a** empty, and 7971
22:23 **put a** iniquity **far** from thy tabernacles. 7368
24: 2 they **violently take a** flocks, and 1497
24: 3 They **drive a** the ass of the fatherless, 5090
24:10 and they **take a** the sheaf *from* the hungry; 5375
27: 2 *who* hath **taken a** my judgment; 5493
27: 8 hath gained, when God **taketh a** his soul? 7953
27:20 a tempest **stealeth** him **a** in the night. 1589
27:21 The east wind **carrieth** him **a**, and 5375
28: 4 are dried up, they are **gone a** from men. 5128
30:12 they **push a** my feet, and they raise up 7971
30:15 and my welfare **passeth a** as a cloud. 5674
32:22 *so doing* my Maker would soon **take** me **a**. 5375
33:21 His flesh is **consumed a**, that it cannot be 3615
34: 5 and God hath **taken a** my judgment. 5493
34:20 shall be troubled at midnight, and **pass a**: 5674
34:20 the mighty shall be **taken a** without hand. 5493
36:18 *beware* lest he **take** thee **a** with *his* stroke: 5496
Ps 1: 4 *are* like the chaff which the wind **driveth a**. 5086
2: 3 and **cast a** their cords from us. 7993
18:22 and I did not **put a** his statutes from me. 5493
18:45 The strangers shall **fade a**, and be afraid 5034
27: 9 *far* from me; **put** not thy servant **a** in anger: 5186
28: 3 **Draw** me not **a** with the wicked, and 4900
31:13 against me, they devised to **take a** my life. 3947
34: T who **drove** him **a**, and he departed. 1644
37:20 into smoke shall they consume *a*. NIH
37:36 Yet he **passed a**, and lo, he *was* not: yea, 5674
39:10 Remove thy stroke **a from** me: I am 4480+5921
39:11 thou **makest** his beauty **to consume a** like 4529
48: 5 they were troubled, *and* **hasted a**. 2648
49:17 For when he dieth he shall **carry** nothing **a**: 3947
51:11 **Cast** me not **a** from thy presence; and 7993
52: 5 he shall **take** thee **a**, and pluck thee out of 2846
55: 6 *for then* would I **fly a**, and be at rest. 5774
58: 7 Let them **melt a** as waters *which* run 3988
58: 8 let *every one of them* **pass a**: 1980
58: 9 he shall **take** them **a as with a whirlwind**, 8175
64: 8 all that see them shall **flee a**. 5074
65: 3 thou shalt **purge** them **a**. 3722
66:20 which hath not **turned a** my prayer, 5493
68: 2 As smoke is **driven a**, *so* drive *them* away: 5086
68: 2 As smoke is driven away, *so* **drive** *them* **a**: 5086
69: 4 then I restored *that* which I took not **a**. 1497
78:38 many a time **turned** he his anger **a**, and 7725
78:39 a wind that **passeth a**, and cometh not 1980
79: 9 deliver us, and **purge a** our sins, for thy 3722
85: 3 Thou hast **taken a** all thy wrath: thou hast 622
88: 8 Thou hast **put a** mine acquaintance **far** 7368
90: 5 Thou **carriest** them **a as with a flood**; 2229
90: 9 For all our days are **passed a** in thy wrath: 6437
90:10 sorrow; for it is soon cut off, and we **fly a**. 5774
102:24 **take** me not **a** in the midst of my days: 5927
104: 7 at the voice of thy thunder they **hasted a**. 2648
104:29 thou **takest a** their breath, they die, and 622
106:23 to **turn a** his wrath, lest *he* should destroy 7725
112:10 he shall gnash *with* his teeth, and **melt a**: 4549
119:37 **Turn a** mine eyes from beholding vanity; 5674
119:39 **Turn a** my reproach which I fear: for thy 5674
119:119 Thou **puttest a** all the wicked of the earth 7673
132:10 For thy servant David's sake **turn** not **a** 7725
137: 3 For there they that **carried** us **a captive** 7617
144: 4 his days *are* as a shadow that **passeth a**. 5674
Pr 1:19 *which* **taketh a** the life of the owners 3947
1:32 For the **turning a** of the simple shall slay 4878
4:15 pass not by it, turn from it, and **pass a**. 5674
4:16 their sleep is **taken a**, unless they cause 1497
4:24 **Put a** from thee a froward mouth, and 5493
6:33 and his reproach shall not be **wiped a**. 4229
10: 3 he **casteth a** the substance of the wicked. 1920
14:32 The wicked is **driven a** in his wickedness: 1760
15: 1 A soft answer **turneth a** wrath: but 7725
19:26 *his* father, *and* **chaseth a** *his* mother, 1272
20: 8 judgment scattereth *a* all evil with his eyes. NIH
20:30 The blueness of a wound **cleanseth a** evil: 8562
22:27 why should he **take a** thy bed from under 3947
23: 5 they **fly a** as an eagle *toward* heaven. 5774
24:18 and he **turn a** his wrath from him. 7725
25: 4 **Take a** the dross from the silver, and 1898
25: 5 **Take a** the wicked *from* before the king, 1898
25:10 thee to shame, and thine infamy **turn** not **a**. 7725
25:20 *As* he that **taketh a** a garment in cold 5710
25:23 The north wind **driveth a** rain: so *doth* an 2342
28: 9 He that **turneth a** his ear from hearing 5493
29: 8 into a snare: but wise *men* **turn a** wrath. 7725
30:30 among beasts, and **turneth** not **a** for any; 7725
Ecc 1: 4 *One* generation **passeth a**, and 1980
3: 5 A time to **cast a** stones, and a time to 7993
3: 6 to lose; a time to keep, and a time to **cast a**; 7993
5:15 which he may **carry a** in his hand. 1980
11:10 thy heart, and **put a** evil from thy flesh: 5674
SS 2:10 Rise up, my love, my fair one, and **come a**. 1980
2:13 Arise, my love, my fair one, and **come a**. 1980
2:17 the shadows **flee a**, turn, my beloved, and 5127
4: 6 Until the day break, and the shadows **flee a**, 5127
5: 7 the keepers of the walls **took a** my vail 5375
6: 5 **Turn a** thine eyes from me, for they have 5437
Isa 1: 4 unto anger, they are **gone a** backward. 2114
1:13 of assemblies, **I cannot a with**; 3201+3808
1:16 **put a** the evil of your doings from before 5493
1:25 purely **purge a** thy dross, and take away all 6884
Isa 1:25 away thy dross, and **take a** all thy tin: 5493
3: 1 doth **take a** from Jerusalem and from Judah 5493
3:18 In that day the Lord will **take a** the bravery 5493
4: 1 called by thy name, to **take a** our reproach. 622
4: 4 When the Lord shall have **washed a** 7364
5: 5 I *will* **take a** the hedge thereof, and it shall 5493
5:23 **take a** the righteousness of the righteous 5493
5:24 they have **cast a** the law of the LORD of 3988
5:25 For all this his anger is not **turned a**, but 7725
5:29 shall **carry** *it* **a safe**, and none shall deliver 6403
6: 7 thine iniquity is **taken a**, and thy sin 5493
6:12 the LORD have **removed** men **far a**, and 7368
8: 4 the spoil of Samaria shall be **taken a** before 5375
9:12 For all this his anger is not **turned a**, but 7725
9:17 For all this his anger is not **turned a**, but 7725
9:21 For all this his anger is not **turned a**, but 7725
10: 2 to **take a** the right **from** the poor of my 1497
10: 4 For all this his anger is not **turned a**, but 7725
10:27 *that* his burden shall be **taken a** from off 5493
12: 1 thine anger is **turned a**, and 7725
15: 6 for the hay is **withered a**, the grass faileth, 3001
15: 7 shall they **carry a** to the brook of 5375
16:10 gladness is **taken a**, and joy out of 622
17: 1 Damascus *is* **taken a** from *being* a city, and 5493
18: 5 and **take a** *and* cut down the branches. 5493
19: 6 they shall **turn** the rivers **far a**; 2186
19: 7 shall wither, be **driven a**, and *be* no *more.* 5086
20: 4 So shall the king of Assyria **lead a** 5090
22: 4 Therefore said I, **Look a** from me; I will 8159
22:17 the LORD will **carry** thee **a** with a mighty 2904
24: 4 The earth mourneth *and* **fadeth a**, 5034
24: 4 the world languisheth *and* **fadeth a**, 5034
25: 8 the Lord GOD will **wipe a** tears from off 4229
25: 8 the rebuke of his people shall he **take a** 5493
27: 9 and this *is* all the fruit to **take a** his sin; 5493
28:17 the hail shall **sweep a** the refuge of lies, 3261
29: 5 ones *shall be* as chaff that **passeth a**: 5674
30:22 thou shalt **cast** them **a** as a menstruous 2219
31: 7 For in that day every man shall **cast a** his 3988
35:10 and sorrow and sighing shall **flee a**. 5127
36: 7 and whose altars Hezekiah hath **taken a**, 5493
36: 9 wilt thou **turn a** the face of one captain of 7725
36:17 **take** you **a** to a land like your own land, 3947
39: 7 which thou shalt beget, shall they **take a**; 3947
40:24 the whirlwind shall **take** them **a** as stubble. 5375
41: 9 I have chosen thee, and not **cast** thee **a**. 3988
41:16 the wind shall **carry** them **a**, and 5375
49:19 they that swallowed thee up shall be **far a**. 7368
49:25 the captives of the mighty shall be **taken a**, 3947
50: 1 mother's divorcement, whom I have **put a**? 7971
50: 1 your transgressions *is* your mother **put a**. 7971
50: 5 I was not rebellious, neither **turned a** back. 5472
51: 6 for the heavens shall **vanish a** like smoke, 4414
51:11 joy; *and* sorrow and mourning shall **flee a**. 5127
52: 5 that my people is **taken a** for nought? 3947
57: 1 merciful men *are* **taken a**, none considering 622
57: 1 righteous is **taken a** from the evil *to come.* 622
57:13 the wind shall **carry** them all **a**; 5375
58: 9 Here I *am.* If thou **take a** from the midst of 5493
58:13 If thou **turn a** thy foot from the sabbath, 7725
59:13 **departing a** from our God, 5253
59:14 judgment is **turned a** backward, and 5253
64: 6 like the wind, have **taken** us **a**. 5375
Jer 1: 3 unto the **carrying a** of Jerusalem **captive** in 1540
2:24 *in* her occasion who can **turn** her **a**? 7725
3: 1 If a man **put a** his wife, and she go from 7971
3: 8 Israel committed adultery I had **put** her **a**, 7971
3:19 My father; and shalt not **turn a** from me. 7725
4: 1 if thou wilt **put a** thine abominations out of 5493
4: 4 **take a** the foreskins of your heart, ye men 5493
5:10 **take a** her battlements; for they *are* not 5493
5:25 Your iniquities have **turned a** these *things,* 5186
6: 4 for the day **goeth a**, for the shadows of 6437
6:29 in vain: for the wicked are not **plucked a**. 5423
7:29 *O Jerusalem,* and **cast** *it* **a**, and take up a 7993
7:33 of the earth; and none shall **fray** *them* **a**. 2729
8: 4 not arise? shall he **turn a**, and not return? 7725
8:13 I have given them shall **pass a from** them. 5674
13:17 the LORD'S flock is **carried a captive**. 7617
13:19 Judah shall be **carried a captive** all of it, 1540
13:19 of it, it shall be wholly **carried a captive**. 1540
13:24 **passeth a** by the wind of the wilderness. 5674
15:15 **take** me not **a** in thy longsuffering: 3947
16: 5 for I have **taken a** my peace from this 622
18:20 *and* to **turn a** thy wrath from them. 7725
22:10 *but* weep sore for him that **goeth a**: for he 1980
23: 2 **driven** them **a**, and have not visited them: 5080
24: 1 **carried a captive** Jeconiah the son of 1540
24: 5 them that are **carried a captive** of Judah, 1546
27:20 when he **carried a captive** Jeconiah 1540
28: 3 king of Babylon **took a** from this place, 3947
28: 6 all that is **carried a captive**, from Babylon 1473
29: 1 the elders which were **carried a captives**, 1473
29: 1 **carried a captive** from Jerusalem to 1540
29: 4 unto all that are **carried a captives**, 1473
29: 4 whom I have **caused to be carried a** from 1540
29: 7 have **caused** you **to be carried a captives**, 1540
29:14 I will **turn a** your captivity, and I will 7725
29:14 I **caused** you **to be carried a captive**. 1540
32:40 that I will not **turn a** from them, to do them 7725
33:26 will I **cast a** the seed of Jacob, and 3988
37:13 Thou **fallest a** to the Chaldeans. 5307
37:14 *It is* false; I **fall** not **a** to the Chaldeans. 5307
38:22 in the mire, *and* they are **turned a** back. 5472
39: 9 **carried a captive** *into* Babylon 1540
39: 9 those that **fell a**, that fell to him, with 5307
40: 1 that were **carried a captive** of Jerusalem 1546
40: 1 which were **carried a captive** unto 1540
40: 7 of *them* that were not **carried a captive** to 1540
41:10 Ishmael **carried a captive** all the residue of 7617
41:10 son of Nethaniah **carried** them **a captive**, 7617
41:14 **carried a captive** from Mizpah cast about 7617
43: 3 and **carry** us **a captives** *into* Babylon. 1540
43:12 burn them, and **carry** them **a captives**: 7617
46: 5 I seen them dismayed *and* **turned a** back? 5472

Jer 46: 6 Let not the swift **flee a**, nor the mighty *man* 5127
46:15 Why are thy valiant *men* **swept a**? 5502
46:21 are turned back, *and* are **fled a** together; 5127
48: 9 unto Moab, that it may flee and **get a**: 3318
49:19 suddenly make him run **a from** her: 4480+5921
49:29 their flocks shall they take **a**: they shall take NIH
50: 6 they have **turned** them **a** *on* the mountains: 7725
50:17 the lions have **driven** *him* **a**: 5080
50:44 make them suddenly run **a from** her: 4480+5921
51:50 escaped the sword, go **a**, stand not still: NIH
52:15 **carried a captive** *certain* of the poor of 1540
52:15 those that **fell a**, that fell to the king of 5307
52:18 wherewith they ministered, took they **a**. NIH
52:19 *in* silver, took the captain of the guard **a**. NIH
52:27 Thus Judah was **carried a captive** out of 1540
52:28 whom Nebuchadrezzar **carried a captive**: 1540
52:29 **carried a captive** from Jerusalem eight 1540
52:30 **carried a captive** *of* the Jews seven 1540
La 2: 6 he hath **violently taken a** his tabernacle, 2554
2:14 thine iniquity, to **turn a** thy captivity; 7725
4: 9 for these **pine a**, stricken through for *want* 2100
4:15 touch not, when they **fled a** and wandered: 5132
4:22 will no more **carry** thee **a into captivity**: 1540
Eze 3:14 **took** me **a**, and I went in bitterness, in 3947
4:17 and **consume a** for their iniquity. 4743
11:18 they shall **take a** all the detestable things 5493
14: 6 **turn a** your faces from all your 7725
16: 9 I **throughly washed a** thy blood from thee, 7857
16:50 therefore I **took** them **a** as I saw *good*. 5493
18:24 when the righteous **turneth a** from his 7725
18:26 When a righteous *man* **turneth a** from his 7725
18:27 when the wicked *man* **turneth a** from his 7725
18:28 **turneth a** from all his transgressions that 7725
18:31 **Cast a** from you all your transgressions, 7993
20: 7 **Cast** ye **a** every man the abominations of 7993
20: 8 they did not every man **cast a** 7993
23:25 they shall **take a** thy nose and thine ears; 5493
23:26 of thy clothes, and **take a** thy fair jewels. 3947
23:29 shall take **a** all thy labour, and shall leave NIH
24:16 I **take a** from thee the desire of thine eyes 3947
24:23 ye shall **pine a** for your iniquities, and 4743
26:16 **lay a** their robes, and put off their broidered 5493
30: 4 they shall take **a** her multitude, and NIH
33: 4 if the sword come, and **take** him **a**, 3947
33: 6 among them, he is taken **a** in his iniquity; NIH
33:10 and we **pine a** in them, how should we then 4743
34: 4 ye brought again that which was **driven a**, 5080
34:16 bring again that which was **driven a**, and 5080
36:26 I will **take a** the stony heart out of your 5493
38:13 to **carry a** silver and gold, to take *away* 5375
38:13 and gold, to take **a** cattle and goods, NIH
43: 9 **put a** their whoredom, and the carcases of their kings, **far** 7368
44:10 the Levites that are **gone a far** from me, 7368
44:10 which went astray **a from** me after 4480+5921
44:22 their wives a widow, nor her that is **put a**: 1644
45: 9 **take a** your exactions from my people, 7311
Da 1:16 Thus Melzar **took a** the portion of their 5375
2:35 the wind **carried** them **a**, that no place was 5376
4:14 let the beasts **get a** from under it, and 5111
7:12 they had their dominion **taken a**: 5709
7:14 which shall not **pass a**, and his kingdom 5709
7:26 they shall **take a** his dominion, to consume 5709
8:11 by him the daily *sacrifice* was **taken a**, and 7311
9:16 thy fury be **turned a** from thy city 7725
11:12 *And* when he hath **taken a** the multitude, 5375
11:31 shall **take a** the daily *sacrifice*, and 5493
11:44 to destroy, and **utterly** to **make a** many. 2763
12:11 *that* the daily *sacrifice* shall be **taken a**, 5493
Hos 1: 6 but I will **utterly take** them **a**. 5375+5375
2: 2 **put a** her whoredoms out of her sight, 5493
2: 9 take **a** my corn in the time thereof, and NIH
2:17 For I will **take a** the names of Baalim out 5493
4: 3 the fishes of the sea also shall be **taken a**. 622
4:11 and wine and new wine take **a** the heart. NIH
5:14 I, *even* I, will tear and **go a**; I will take 1980
5:14 I will **take a**, and none shall rescue *him*. 5375
6: 4 and as the early dew *it* **goeth a**. 1980
9:11 their glory shall **fly a** like a bird, from 5774
9:17 My God will **cast** them **a**, because they did 3988
13: 3 and as the early dew that **passeth a**, 1980
13:11 in mine anger, and took *him* **a** in my wrath. NIH
14: 2 **Take a** all iniquity, and receive *us* 5375
14: 4 for mine anger is **turned a** from him. 7725
Joel 1: 7 he hath made it clean bare, and **cast** *it* **a**; 7993
1:12 joy is **withered a** from the sons of men. 3001
Am 1: 3 I will not **turn a** *the punishment* thereof; 7725
1: 6 I will not **turn a** *the punishment* thereof; 7725
1: 6 they **carried a captive** the whole captivity, 1540
1: 9 I will not **turn a** *the punishment* thereof; 7725
1:11 I will not **turn a** *the punishment* thereof; 7725
1:13 I will not **turn a** *the punishment* thereof; 7725
2: 1 I will not **turn a** *the punishment* thereof; 7725
2: 4 I will not **turn a** *the punishment* thereof; 7725
2: 6 I will not **turn a** *the punishment* thereof; 7725
2:16 the mighty shall **flee a** naked in that day, 5127
4: 2 that he will **take** you **a** with hooks, and 5375
4:10 the sword, and have **taken a** your horses; 7628
5:23 **Take** thou **a** from me the noise of thy 5493
6: 3 Ye that **put far a** the evil day, and 5077
7:11 Israel shall **surely** be **led a captive** 1540+1540
7:12 go, **flee** thee **a** into the land of Judah, and 1272
9: 1 he that fleeth of them shall not **flee a**, and 5127
Ob 1:11 the strangers **carried a captive** his forces, 7617
Jnh 3: 9 repent, and **turn a** from his fierce anger, 7725
Mic 1:11 **Pass** ye **a**, thou inhabitant of Saphir, 5674
2: 2 by violence; and houses, and **take** *them* **a**: 5375
2: 4 **turning a** he hath divided our fields. 7725
2: 9 from their children have ye taken **a** my NIH
Na 2: 2 For the LORD hath turned **a** NIH
2: 7 Huzzab shall be **led a captive**, she shall be 1540
2: 8 yet they *shall* **flee a**. Stand, stand, *shall they* 5127
3:10 Yet *was* she carried **a**, she went into 1473
3:16 the cankerworm spoileth, and **flieth a**. 5774
3:17 *but* when the sun ariseth they **flee a**, and 5074

Zep 2: 7 shall visit them, and **turn a** their captivity. 7725
3:11 I will **take a** out of the midst of thee them 5493
3:15 The LORD hath **taken a** thy judgments, 5493
Zec 3: 4 **Take a** the filthy garments from him. 5493
7:11 pulled **a** the shoulder, and stopped their 5637
9: 7 I will **take a** his blood out of his mouth, 5493
10:11 and the sceptre of Egypt shall **depart a**. 5493
14:12 Their flesh *shall* **consume a** while they 4743
14:12 their eyes shall **consume a** in their holes, 4743
14:12 their tongue shall **consume a** in their 4743
Mal 2: 3 and *one* shall **take** you **a** with it. 5375
2: 6 and did **turn** many **a** from iniquity. 7725
2:16 of Israel, saith that he hateth **putting a**: 7971
3: 7 ye are **gone a** from mine ordinances, 5493
Mt 1:11 about the time they were **carried a** to 3350
1:17 from David until the **carrying a** into 3350
1:17 from the **carrying a** into Babylon unto 3350
1:19 was minded to **put** her **a** privily. 630
5:31 been said, Whosoever shall **put a** his wife, 630
5:32 That whosoever shall **put a** his wife, 630
5:40 and take **a** thy coat, let him have *thy* cloke NIG
5:42 that would borrow of thee **turn** not thou **a**. 654
8:31 suffer us to **go a** into the herd of swine. 565
13: 6 because *they* had not root, they **withered a**. 3583
13:12 from him shall be **taken a** even that he hath. 142
13:19 **catcheth a** that which was sown in his heart. 726
13:36 Then Jesus **sent** the multitude **a**, and 863
13:48 the good into vessels, but cast the bad **a**. 1854
14:15 **send** the multitude **a**, that they may go into 630
14:22 other side, while he **sent** the multitudes **a**. 630
14:23 And when he had **sent** the multitudes **a**, 630
15:23 and besought him, saying, **Send** her **a**; 630
15:32 and I will not **send** them **a** fasting, lest they 630
15:39 And he **sent a** the multitude, and took ship, 630
19: 3 Is it lawful for a man to **put a** his wife for 630
19: 7 a writing of divorcement, and to **put** her **a**? 630
19: 8 hearts suffered you to **put a** your wives: 630
19: 9 unto you, Whosoever shall **put a** his wife, 630
19: 9 whoso marrieth her *which is* **put a** doth 630
19:22 man heard *that* saying, he **went a** sorrowful: 565
21:19 And presently the fig tree **withered a**. 3583
21:20 How soon is the fig tree **withered a**! 3583
22:13 Bind him hand and foot, and **take** him **a**, 142
24:35 Heaven and earth shall **pass a**, but 3928
24:35 pass away, but my words shall not **pass a**. 3928
24:39 until the flood came, and **took** *them* all **a**; 142
25:29 from him that hath not shall be **taken a** even 142
25:46 And these shall **go a** into everlasting 565
26:42 He **went a** again the second time, and 565
26:42 if this cup may not **pass a** from me, 3928
26:44 and **went a** again, and prayed the third time, 565
26:57 Jesus **led** *him* **a** to Caiaphas the high priest, 520
27: 2 they **led** *him* **a**, and delivered him to Pontius 520
27:31 on him, and **led** him **a** to crucify *him*. 520
27:64 and steal him **a**, and say unto the people, NIG
28:13 by night, and stole him **a** while we slept. NIG
28:16 Then the eleven disciples went **a** into NIG
Mk 1:43 charged him, and forthwith **sent** him **a**; 1544
2:20 when the bridegroom shall be **taken a** from 522
2:21 else the new piece that filled it up **taketh a** 575
4: 6 and because *it* had no root, it **withered a**. 3583
4:15 **taketh a** the word that was sown in their 142
4:36 And when they had **sent a** the multitude, 863
5:10 he would not **send** them **a** out of the country. 649
6:36 **Send** them **a**, that they may go into 630
6:45 unto Bethsaida, while he **sent a** the people. 630
6:46 And when he had **sent** them **a**, he departed 657
8: 3 And if I **send** them **a** fasting to their own 630
8: 9 about four thousand: and he **sent** them **a**. 630
8:26 And he **sent** him **a** to his house, saying, 649
9:18 and gnasheth with his teeth, and **pineth a**: 3583
10: 2 Is it lawful for a man to **put a** *his* wife? 630
10: 4 write a bill of divorcement, and to **put** *her* **a**. 630
10:11 Whosoever shall **put a** his wife, and 630
10:12 And if a woman shall **put a** her husband, 630
10:22 was sad at *that* saying, and **went a** grieved: 565
10:50 **casting a** his garment, rose, and came to 577
11:21 fig tree which thou cursedst is **withered a**. 3583
12: 3 and beat *him*, and **sent** *him* **a** empty. 649
12: 4 and **sent** *him* **a** shamefully handled. 649
13:31 Heaven and earth shall **pass a**: but 3928
13:31 pass away: but my words shall not **pass a**. 3928
14:36 unto thee; **take a** this cup from me: 3911
14:39 And again he **went a**, and prayed, and 565
14:44 same is he; take him, and **lead** *him* **a** safely. 520
14:53 And they **led** Jesus **a** to the high priest: and 520
15: 1 and **carried** *him* **a**, and delivered *him* to 667
15:16 And the soldiers **led** him **a** into the hall, 520
16: 3 Who shall **roll** us **a** the stone from the door 617
16: 4 they saw that the stone was **rolled a**: 617
Lk 1:25 on *me*, to **take a** my reproach among men. 851
1:53 and the rich he hath **sent** empty **a**. 1821
2:15 as the angels were **gone a** from them into 565
5:35 when the bridegroom shall be **taken a** from 522
6:29 him that **taketh a** thy cloke forbid not *to* 142
6:30 of him that **taketh a** thy *goods* ask *them* not 142
8: 6 it **withered a**, because *it* lacked moisture. 3583
8:12 and **taketh a** the word out of their hearts, 142
8:13 and in time of temptation **fall a**. 868
8:38 be with him: but Jesus **sent** him **a**, saying, 630
9:12 And *when* the day began to **wear a**, then 2827
9:12 and said unto him, **Send** the multitude **a**, 630
9:25 and lose himself, or be **cast a**? 2210
10:42 which shall not be **taken a** from her. 851
11:52 for ye have **taken a** the key of knowledge: 142
13:15 from the stall, and **lead** *him* **a** to watering? 520
16: 3 for my lord **taketh a** from me 851
16:18 Whosoever **putteth a** his wife, and 630
16:18 whosoever marrieth her that is **put a** from 630
17:31 let him not come down to **take** it **a**: 142
19:26 even that he hath shall be **taken a** from him. 142
20:10 beat him, and **sent** *him* **a** empty. 1821
20:11 *him* shamefully, and **sent** *him* **a** empty. 1821
21:24 and shall be **led a captive** into all nations: 163
21:32 This generation shall not **pass a**, till all be 3928

Lk 21:33 Heaven and earth shall **pass a**: but 3928
21:33 pass away: but my words shall not **pass a**. 3928
23:18 **A with** this *man*, and release unto us 142
23:26 And as they **led** him **a**, they laid hold upon 520
24: 2 And they found the stone **rolled a** from 617
Jn 1:29 of God, which **taketh a** the sin of the world. 142
4: 8 (For his disciples were **gone a** unto the city 565
5:13 for Jesus had **conveyed** himself **a**, 1593
6:22 but *that* his disciples were **gone a** alone; 565
6:67 Jesus unto the twelve, Will ye also **go a**? 5217
10:40 And **went a** again beyond Jordan into 565
11:39 Jesus said, **Take** ye **a** the stone. Martha, 142
11:41 Then they **took a** the stone *from the place* 142
11:48 and **take a** both our place and nation. 142
12:11 by reason of him many of the Jews **went a**, 5217
14:28 unto you, I **go a**, and come *again* unto you. 5217
15: 2 in me that beareth not fruit he **taketh a**: 142
16: 7 the truth; It is expedient for you that I **go a**: 565
16: 7 for if I **go** not **a**, the Comforter will not come 565
18:13 And **led** him **a** to Annas first; for he was 520
19:15 **A with** *him*, away with *him*, crucify him. 142
19:15 Away with *him*, **a with** *him*, crucify him. 142
19:16 And they took Jesus, and **led** *him* **a**. 520
19:31 be broken, and *that* they might be **taken a**. 142
19:38 besought Pilate that he might **take a** 142
20: 1 seeth the stone **taken a** from the sepulchre. 142
20: 2 They have **taken a** the Lord out of 142
20:10 Then the disciples **went a** again unto their 565
20:13 Because they have **taken a** my Lord, and 142
20:15 thou hast laid him, and I will **take** him **a**. 142
Ac 3:26 in **turning a** every one of you from *his* 654
5:37 and **drew a** much people after him: 868
7:27 that did his neighbour wrong **thrust** him **a**, 683
7:43 and I will **carry** you **a** beyond Babylon. 3351
8:33 In his humiliation his judgment was **taken a**: 142
8:39 the Spirit of the Lord **caught a** Philip, 726
10:23 on the morrow Peter **went a** with them, 1831
13: 3 laid *their* hands on them, they **sent** *them* **a**. 630
13: 8 seeking to turn **a** the deputy **from** the faith. 575
17:10 And the brethren immediately **sent a** Paul 1599
17:14 immediately the brethren **sent a** Paul to go 1821
19:26 hath persuaded and **turned a** much people, 3179
20: 6 And we **sailed a** from Philippi after 1602
20:30 speaking perverse *things*, to **draw a** 645
21:36 people followed *after*, crying, **A with** him. 142
22:16 arise, and be baptized, and **wash a** thy sins, 628
22:22 said, **A with** such *a fellow* from the earth: 142
24: 7 with great violence **took** *him* **a** out of our 520
27:20 that we should be saved was then **taken a**. 4014
Ro 11: 1 I say then, Hath God **cast a** his people? 683
11: 2 God hath not **cast a** his people which he 683
11:15 For if the **casting a** of them *be* 580
11:26 and shall **turn a** ungodliness from Jacob: 654
11:27 unto them, when I shall **take a** their sins. 851
1Co 5: 2 deed might be **taken a** from among you. 1808
5:13 Therefore **put a** from among yourselves 1808
7:11 and let not the husband **put a** *his* wife. 863
7:12 to dwell with him, let him not **put** her **a**. 863
7:31 *it*: for the fashion of this world **passeth a**. 3855
12: 2 **carried a** unto *these* dumb idols, *even* as ye 520
13: 8 *there be* knowledge, it shall **vanish a**. 2673
13:10 then that which is in part shall be **done a**. 2673
13:11 I became a man, I **put a** childish *things*. 2673
2Co 3: 7 which *glory* was to be **done a**: 2673
3:11 For if that which is **done a** *was* glorious, 2673
3:14 **untaken a** in the reading of the old 343+3361
3:14 which *vail* is **done a** in Christ. 2673
3:16 turn to the Lord, the vail shall be **taken a**. 4014
5:17 old *things* are **past a**; behold, all *things* are 3928
Gal 2:13 was **carried a with** their dissimulation. 4879
Eph 4:25 Wherefore **putting a** lying, speak every man 659
4:31 and evil speaking, be **put a** from you, 142
Col 1:23 *be* not **moved a** from the hope of 3334
2Th 2: 3 *not come*, except there come a **falling a** first, 646
1Ti 1:19 which some having **put a**, concerning faith 683
2Ti 1:15 which are in Asia be **turned a from** me; 654
3: 5 the power thereof: **from** such **turn a**. 665
3: 6 laden with sins, **led a** with divers lusts, 71
4: 4 And they shall **turn a** *their* ears from 654
Heb 6: 6 If they shall **fall a**, to renew *them* again 3895
8:13 and waxeth old *is* ready to **vanish a**. 854
9:26 to **put a** sin by the sacrifice of himself. 115
10: 4 of bulls and of goats should **take a** sins. 851
10: 9 He **taketh a** the first, that he may establish 337
10:11 which can never **take a** sins: 4014
10:35 **Cast** not **a** therefore your confidence, 577
12:25 **turn a from** him that *speaketh* from heaven: 654
Jas 1:10 as the flower of the grass he shall **pass a**. 3928
1:11 also shall the rich *man* **fade a** in his ways. 3133
1:14 when he is **drawn a** of his own lust, and 1828
4:14 for a little *time*, and then **vanisheth a**. 853
1Pe 1: 4 and undefiled, and that **fadeth not a**, 263
1:24 and the flower thereof **falleth a**: 1601
3:21 us (not the **putting a** of the filth of the flesh, 595
5: 4 receive a crown of glory that **fadeth not a**. 262
2Pe 3:10 in the which the heavens shall **pass a** with a 3928
3:17 being **led a with** the error of the wicked, 4879
1Jn 2:17 And the world **passeth a**, and the lust 3855
3: 5 that he was manifested to **take a** our sins; 142
Rev 7:17 God shall **wipe a** all tears from their eyes. 1813
12:15 cause her to be **carried a of the flood**. 4216
16:20 And every island fled **a**, and the mountains NIG
17: 3 So he **carried** me **a** in the spirit into 667
20:11 face the earth and the heaven fled **a**; and NIG
21: 1 and the first earth were **passed a**; 3928
21: 4 And God shall **wipe a** all tears from their 1813
21: 4 for the former *things* are **passed a**. 565
21:10 And he **carried** me **a** in the spirit to a great 667
22:19 And if any *man* shall **take a** from the words 851
22:19 God shall **take a** his part out of the book of 851

AWE (3)

Ps 4: 4 **Stand in a**, and sin not: commune with 7264
33: 8 inhabitants of the world **stand in a** of him. 1481
119:161 but my heart **standeth in a** of thy word. 6342

B

AWOKE (8) [WAKE]
Ge 9:24 Noah **a** from his wine, and knew what his 3364
41: 4 well favoured and fat kine. So Pharaoh **a**. 3364
41: 7 And Pharaoh **a**, and behold, *it was* a dream. 3364
41:21 *still* ill favoured, as at the beginning. So I **a**. 3364
Jdg 16:20 And he **a** out of his sleep, and said, 3364
1Ki 3:15 Solomon **a**; and behold, *it was* a dream. 3364
Mt 8:25 And his disciples came to *him*, and **a** him, *1453*
Lk 8:24 And they came to *him*, and **a** him, saying, *1326*

AXE (11) [AXES]
Dt 19: 5 his hand fetcheth a stroke with the **a** to cut 1631
20:19 trees thereof by forcing an **a** against them: 1631
Jdg 9:48 Abimelech took an **a** in his hand, and 7134
1Sa 13:20 and his coulter, and his **a**, and his mattock. 7134
1Ki 6: 7 that there was neither hammer nor **a** *nor* 1631
2Ki 6: 5 a beam, the **a head** fell into the water: 1270
Isa 10:15 Shall the **a** boast itself against him that 1631
Jer 10: 3 of the hands of the workman, with the **a**. 4621
51:20 Thou *art* my **battle a** *and* weapons of war: 4661
Mt 3:10 And now also the **a** is laid unto the root of *513*
Lk 3: 9 And now also the **a** is laid unto the root of *513*

AXES (7) [AXE]
1Sa 13:21 for the **a**, and to sharpen the goads. 7134
2Sa 12:31 under **a** of iron, and made them pass 4037
1Ch 20: 3 and with harrows of iron, and with **a**. 4050
Ps 74: 5 as he had lifted up **a** upon the thick trees. 7134
74: 6 the carved work thereof at once with **a** 3781
Jer 46:22 come against her with **a**, as hewers of 7134
Eze 26: 9 with his **a** he shall break down thy towers. 2719

AXLETREES (2)
1Ki 7:32 the **a** of the wheels *were* joined to the base: 3027
7:33 their **a**, and their naves, and their felloes, 3027

AZAL (1)
Zec 14: 5 valley of the mountains shall reach unto **A**: 682

AZALIAH (2)
2Ki 22: 3 *that* the king sent Shaphan the son of **A**, 683
2Ch 34: 8 he sent Shaphan the son of **A**, and Maaseiah 683

AZANIAH (1)
Ne 10: 9 both Jeshua the son of **A**, Binnui of the sons 245

AZARAEL (1)
Ne 12:36 Shemaiah, and **A**, Milalai, Gilalai, Maai, 5832

AZAREEL (5)
1Ch 12: 6 Jesiah, and **A**, and Joezer, and Jashobeam, 5832
25:18 The eleventh *to* **A**, *he*, his sons, and 5832
27:22 Of Dan, **A** the son of Jeroham. These *were* 5832
Ezr 10:41 **A**, and Shelemiah, Shemariah, 5832
Ne 11:13 Amashai the son of **A**, the son of Ahasai, 5832

AZAREL See AZARAEL; AZAREEL

AZARIAH (49) [ABED-NEGO, UZZIAH]
1Ki 4: 2 he had; **A** the son of Zadok the priest, 5838
4: 5 **A** the son of Nathan *was* over the officers: 5838
2Ki 14:21 all the people of Judah took **A**, which *was* 5838
15: 1 **A** son of Amaziah king of Judah to reign. 5838
15: 6 the rest of the acts of **A**, and all that he did, 5838
15: 7 So **A** slept with his fathers; and they buried 5838
15: 8 eighth year of **A** king of Judah did 5838
15:17 thirtieth year of **A** king of Judah *began* 5838
15:23 In the fiftieth year of **A** king of Judah 5838
15:27 fiftieth year of **A** king of Judah Pekah 5838
1Ch 2: 8 And the sons of Ethan; **A**. 5838
2:38 And Obed begat Jehu, and Jehu begat **A**, 5838
2:39 **A** begat Helez, and Helez begat Eleasah, 5838
3:12 his son, **A** his son, Jotham his son, 5838
6: 9 Ahimaaz begat **A**, and Azariah begat 5838
6: 9 begat Azariah, and **A** begat Johanan, 5838
6:10 Johanan begat **A**, (he *it is* that executed 5838
6:11 **A** begat Amariah, and Amariah begat 5838
6:13 begat Hilkiah, and Hilkiah begat **A**, 5838
6:14 **A** begat Seraiah, and Seraiah begat 5838
6:36 of Elkanah, the son of Joel, the son of **A**, 5838
9:11 **A** the son of Hilkiah, the son of 5838
2Ch 15: 1 the spirit of God came upon **A** the son of 5838
21: 2 **A**, and Jehiel, and Zechariah, and Azariah, 5838
21: 2 and **A**, and Michael, and Shephatiah: 5838
22: 6 **A** the son of Jehoram king of Judah went 5838
23: 1 **A** the son of Jeroham, and Ishmael the son 5838
23: 1 **A** the son of Obed, and Maaseiah the son of 5838
26:17 **A** the priest went in after him, and with him 5838
26:20 **A** the chief priest, and all the priests, 5838
28:12 **A** the son of Johanan, Berechiah the son of 5838
29:12 the son of Amasai, and Joel the son of **A**, 5838
29:12 the son of Abdi, and **A** the son of Jehalelel: 5838
31:10 **A** the chief priest of the house of Zadok 5838
31:13 and **A** the ruler of the house of God. 5838
Ezr 7: 1 of Seraiah, the son of **A**, the son of Hilkiah, 5838
7: 3 the son of **A**, the son of Meraioth, 5838
Ne 3:23 After him repaired **A** the son of Maaseiah 5838
3:24 from the house of **A** unto the turning *of* 5838
7: 7 **A**, Raamiah, Nahamani, Mordecai, Bilshan, 5838
8: 7 Kelita, **A**, Jozabad, Hanan, Pelaiah, and 5838
10: 2 Seraiah, **A**, Jeremiah, 5838
12:33 And **A**, Ezra, and Meshullam, 5838
Jer 43: 2 spake **A** the son of Hoshaiah, and 5838
Da 1: 6 Daniel, Hananiah, Mishael, and **A**: 5838
1: 7 of Meshach; and to **A**, of Abed-nego. 5838
1:11 set over Daniel, Hananiah, Mishael, and **A**, 5838
1:19 like Daniel, Hananiah, Mishael, and **A**: 5838
2:17 Mishael, and **A**, his companions: 5839

AZAZ (1)
1Ch 5: 8 Bela the son of **A**, the son of Shema, 5811

AZAZIAH (3)
1Ch 15:21 and Obed-edom, and Jeiel, and **A**, 5812
27:20 children of Ephraim, Hoshea the son of **A**: 5812
2Ch 31:13 **A**, and Nahath, and Asahel, and Jerimoth, 5812

AZBUK (1)
Ne 3:16 After him repaired Nehemiah the son of **A**, 5802

AZEKAH (7)
Jos 10:10 and smote them to **A**, and unto Makkedah. 5825
10:11 stones from heaven upon them unto **A**, 5825
15:35 Jarmuth, and Adullam, Socoh, and **A**, 5825
1Sa 17: 1 pitched between Shochoh and **A**, 5825
2Ch 11: 9 And Adoraim, and Lachish, and **A**, 5825
Ne 11:30 *at* **A**, and *in* the villages thereof. 5825
Jer 34: 7 were left, against Lachish, and against **A**: 5825

AZEL (6)
1Ch 8:37 *was* his son, Eleasah his son, **A** his son: 682
8:38 And **A** had six sons, whose names *are* these, 682
8:38 and Hanan. All these *were* the sons of **A**. 682
9:43 Rephaiah his son, Eleasah his son, **A** his son. 682
9:44 And **A** had six sons, whose names *are* these, 682
9:44 and Hanan: these *were* the sons of **A**. 682

AZEM (2)
Jos 15:29 Baalah, and Iim, and **A**, 6107
19: 3 And Hazar-shual, and Balah, and **A**, 6107

AZGAD (4)
Ezr 2:12 The children of **A**, a thousand two hundred 5803
8:12 of the sons of **A**; Johanan the son of 5803
Ne 7:17 The children of **A**, two thousand three 5803
10:15 Bunni, **A**, Bebai, 5803

AZIEL (1)
1Ch 15:20 **A**, and Shemiramoth, and Jehiel, and Unni, 5815

AZIZA (1)
Ezr 10:27 and Jeremoth, and Zabad, and **A**. 5819

AZMAVETH (8) [BETH-AZMAVETH]
2Sa 23:31 Abialbon the Arbathite, **A** the Barhumite, 5820
1Ch 8:36 Jehoadah begat Alemeth, and **A**, and Zimri; 5820
9:42 and Jarah begat Alemeth, and **A**, and Zimri; 5820
11:33 **A** the Baharumite, Eliahba the Shaalbonite, 5820
12: 3 Jeziel, and Pelet, the sons of **A**; and 5820
27:25 over the king's treasures *was* **A** the son of 5820
Ezr 2:24 The children of **A**, forty and two. 5820
Ne 12:29 and out of the fields of Geba and **A**: 5820

AZMON (3)
Nu 34: 4 go on *to* Hazar-addar, and pass on to **A**: 6111
34: 5 the border shall fetch a compass from **A** 6111
Jos 15: 4 *From thence* it passed toward **A**, and 6111

AZNOTH-TABOR (1) [TABOR]
Jos 19:34 *then* the coast turneth westward *to* **A**, and 243

AZOR (2)
Mt 1:13 Abiud begat Eliakim; and Eliakim begat **A**; *107*
1:14 And **A** begat Sadoc; and Sadoc begat *107*

AZOTUS (1)
Ac 8:40 But Philip was found at **A**: and *108*

AZRIEL (3)
1Ch 5:24 **A**, and Jeremiah, and Hodaviah, and 5837
27:19 of Naphtali, Jerimoth the son of **A**: 5837
Jer 36:26 Seraiah the son of **A**, and Shelemiah 5837

AZRIKAM (6)
1Ch 3:23 Elioenai, and Hezekiah, and **A**, three. 5840
8:38 **A**, Bocheru, and Ishmael, and Sheariah, 5840
9:14 the son of **A**, the son of Hashabiah, of 5840
9:44 **A**, Bocheru, and Ishmael, and Sheariah, 5840
2Ch 28: 7 **A** the governor of the house, and Elkanah 5840
Ne 11:15 the son of **A**, the son of Hashabiah, the son 5840

AZUBAH (4)
1Ki 22:42 his mother's name *was* **A** the daughter of 5806
1Ch 2:18 son of Hezron begat *children* of **A** *his* wife, 5806
2:19 when **A** was dead, Caleb took unto him 5806
2Ch 20:31 his mother's name *was* **A** the daughter of 5806

AZUR (2)
Jer 28: 1 *that* Hananiah the son of **A** the prophet, 5809
Eze 11: 1 among whom I saw Jaazaniah the son of **A**, 5809

AZZAH (3)
Dt 2:23 *even* unto **A**, the Caphtorims, which came 5804
1Ki 4:24 from Tiphsah even to **A**, over all the kings 5804
Jer 25:20 **A**, and Ekron, and the remnant of Ashdod: 5804

AZZAN (1)
Nu 34:26 children of Issachar, Paltiel the son of **A**. 5821

AZZUR (1)
Ne 10:17 Ater, Hizkijah, **A**, 5809

B

BAAL (63) [BAAL'S, BAAL-BERITH, BAAL-GAD, BAAL-HAMON, BAAL-HANAN, BAAL-HAZOR, BAAL-HERMON, BAAL-MEON, BAAL-PEOR, BAAL-PERAZIM, BAAL-SHALISHA, BAAL-TAMAR, BAAL-ZEBUB, BAAL-ZEPHON, BAALIM, BAMOTH-BAAL, GUR-BAAL, JERUBBAAL, KIRJATH-BAAL, MERIB-BAAL]
Nu 22:41 brought him up *into* the high places of **B**, 1168
Jdg 2:13 the LORD, and served **B** and Ashtaroth. 1168
6:25 throw down the altar of **B** that thy father 1168
6:28 the altar of **B** was cast down, and the grove 1168
6:30 because he hath cast down the altar of **B**, 1168
6:31 that stood against him, Will ye plead for **B**? 1168
6:32 saying, Let **B** plead against him, because 1168
1Ki 16:31 went and served **B**, and worshipped him. 1168
16:32 he reared up an altar for **B** *in* the house of 1168
16:32 up an altar for Baal *in* the house of **B**, 1168
18:19 the prophets of **B** four hundred and fifty, 1168
18:21 if **B**, *then* follow him. And the people 1168
18:25 Elijah said unto the prophets of **B**, 1168
18:26 called on the name of **B** from morning even 1168
18:26 even until noon, saying, O **B**, hear us. 1168
18:40 said unto them, Take the prophets of **B**; 1168
19:18 all the knees which have not bowed unto **B**, 1168
22:53 For he served **B**, and worshipped him, and 1168
2Ki 3: 2 for he put away the image of **B** that his 1168
10:18 and said unto them, Ahab served **B** a little; 1168
10:19 therefore call unto me all the prophets of **B**, 1168
10:19 for I have a great sacrifice *to do* to **B**; 1168
10:19 that *he* might destroy the worshippers of **B**. 1168
10:20 Proclaim a solemn assembly for **B**. 1168
10:21 all the worshippers of **B** came, so that there 1168
10:21 they came *into* the house of **B**; and 1168
10:21 the house of **B** was full from one end to 1168
10:22 vestments for all the worshippers of **B**. 1168
10:23 *into* the house of **B**, and said unto 1168
10:23 said unto the worshippers of **B**, Search, and 1168
10:23 the LORD, but the worshippers of **B** only. 1168
10:25 and went to the city of the house of **B**. 1168
10:26 forth the images out of the house of **B**, 1168
10:27 they brake down the image of **B**, and 1168
10:27 brake down the house of **B**, and made it a 1168
10:28 Thus Jehu destroyed **B** out of Israel. 1168
11:18 people of the land went *into* the house of **B**, 1168
11:18 slew Mattan the priest of **B** before 1168
17:16 all the host of heaven, and served **B**. 1168
21: 3 he reared up altars for **B**, and made a grove, 1168
23: 4 all the vessels that were made for **B**, 1168
23: 5 them also that burnt incense unto **B**, to 1168
1Ch 4:33 *were* round about the same cities, unto **B**. 1168
5: 5 Micah his son, Reaia his son, **B** his son, 1168
8:30 and Zur, and Kish, and **B**, and Nadab, 1168
9:36 Zur, and Kish, and **B**, and Ner, and Nadab, 1168
2Ch 23:17 all the people went *to* the house of **B**, and 1168
23:17 slew Mattan the priest of **B** before 1168
Jer 2: 8 the prophets prophesied by **B**, and 1168
7: 9 burn incense unto **B**, and walk after other 1168
11:13 *even* altars to burn incense unto **B**. 1168
11:17 me to anger in offering incense unto **B**. 1168
12:16 as they taught my people to swear by **B**; 1168
19: 5 They have built also the high places of **B**, 1168
19: 5 sons with fire *for* burnt offerings unto **B**, 1168
23:13 they prophesied in **B**, and caused my 1168
23:27 their fathers have forgotten my name for **B**. 1168
32:29 roofs they have offered incense unto **B**, 1168
32:35 they built the high places of **B**, which *are* in 1168
Hos 2: 8 and gold, *which* they prepared for **B**. 1168
13: 1 but when he offended in **B**, he died. 1168
Zep 1: 4 I will cut off the remnant of **B** from this 1168
Ro 11: 4 have not bowed the knee to *the image of* **B**. *896*

BAAL'S (1) [BAAL]
1Ki 18:22 **B** prophets *are* four hundred and fifty men. 1168

BAALAH (5)
Jos 15: 9 the border was drawn *to* **B**, which *is* 1173
15:10 the border compassed from **B** westward 1173
15:11 passed along *to* mount **B**, and went out *unto* 1173
15:29 **B**, and Iim, and Azem, 1173
1Ch 13: 6 David went up, and all Israel, to **B**, *that is*, 1173

BAALATH (3) [BAALATH-BEER]
Jos 19:44 And Eltekeh, and Gibbethon, and **B**, 1191
1Ki 9:18 **B**, and Tadmor in the wilderness, in 1191
2Ch 8: 6 **B**, and all the store cities that Solomon had, 1191

BAALATH-BEER (1) [BAALATH, BEER]
Jos 19: 8 that *were* round about these cities to **B**, 1192

BAAL-BERITH (2) [BAAL, BERITH]
Jdg 8:33 after Baalim, and made **B** their god. 1170
9: 4 ten *pieces* of silver out of the house of **B**, 1170

BAALE OF JUDAH (1) [JUDAH]
2Sa 6: 2 that *were* with him from **B**, 1184

BAAL-GAD (3) [BAAL, GAD]
Jos 11:17 even unto **B** in the valley of Lebanon under 1171
12: 7 from **B** in the valley of Lebanon even unto 1171
13: 5 from **B** under mount Hermon unto 1171

BAAL-HAMON (1) [BAAL]
SS 8:11 Solomon had a vineyard at **B**; he let out 1174

BAAL-HANAN (5) [BAAL, HANAN]
Ge 36:38 **B** the son of Achbor reigned in his stead. 1177
36:39 **B** the son of Achbor died, and 1177
1Ch 1:49 **B** the son of Achbor reigned in his stead. 1177
1:50 when **B** was dead, Hadad reigned in his 1177
27:28 *were* in the low plains *was* **B** the Gederite: 1177

BAAL-HAZOR (1) [BAAL, HAZOR]
2Sa 13:23 that Absalom had sheepshearers in **B**, 1178

BAAL-HERMON (2) [BAAL, HERMON]
Jdg 3: 3 from mount **B** unto the entering in of 1179
1Ch 5:23 they increased from Bashan unto **B** and 1179

BAALI (1)
Hos 2:16 call *me* Ishi; and shalt call me no more **B**. 1180

BAALIM (18) [BAAL]
Jdg 2:11 in the sight of the LORD, and served **B**: 1168
3: 7 their God, and served **B** and the groves. 1168
8:33 went a whoring after **B**, and 1168
10: 6 served **B**, and Ashtaroth, and the gods of 1168
10:10 have forsaken our God, and *also* served **B**. 1168
1Sa 7: 4 the children of Israel did put away **B** and 1168
12:10 and have served **B** and Ashtaroth: 1168
1Ki 18:18 of the LORD, and thou hast followed **B**. 1168
2Ch 17: 3 of his father David, and sought not unto **B**; 1168
24: 7 of the LORD did they bestow upon **B**. 1168
28: 2 and made also molten images for **B**. 1168
33: 3 he reared up altars for **B**, and made groves, 1168
34: 4 they brake down the altars of **B** in his 1168
Jer 2:23 I am not polluted, I have not gone after **B**? 1168
9:14 after **B**, which their fathers taught them: 1168
Hos 2:13 I will visit upon her the days of **B**, 1168
2:17 For I will take away the names of **B** out of 1168
11: 2 they sacrificed unto **B**, and burned incense 1168

BAALIS (1)
Jer 40:14 Dost thou certainly know that **B** the king of 1185

BAAL-MEON (3) [BAAL, BETH-BAAL-MEON, BETH-MEON]
Nu 32:38 Nebo, and **B**, (*their* names being changed,) 1186
1Ch 5: 8 who dwelt in Aroer, even unto Nebo and **B**: 1186
Eze 25: 9 Beth-jeshimoth, **B**, and Kiriathaim, 1186

BAAL-PEOR (6) [BAAL, PEOR]
Nu 25: 3 Israel joined himself unto **B**: and the anger 1187
25: 5 every one his men that were joined unto **B**. 1187
Dt 4: 3 seen what the LORD did because of **B**: 1187
4: 3 for all the men that followed **B**, the LORD 1187
Ps 106:28 They joined themselves also unto **B**, and 1187
Hos 9:10 *but* they went to **B**, and 1187

BAAL-PERAZIM (4) [BAAL, PERAZIM]
2Sa 5:20 David came to **B**, and David smote them 1188
5:20 he called the name of that place **B**. 1188
1Ch 14:11 So they came up to **B**; and David smote 1188
14:11 they called the name of that place **B**. 1188

BAALS See BAALIM

BAAL-SHALISHA (1) [BAAL, SHALISHA]
2Ki 4:42 there came a man from **B**, and brought 1190

BAAL-TAMAR (1) [BAAL, TAMAR]
Jdg 20:33 and put *themselves* in array at **B**: 1193

BAAL-ZEBUB (4) [BAAL]
2Ki 1: 2 inquire of **B** the god of Ekron whether I 1176
1: 3 *that* ye go to inquire of **B** the god of Ekron? 1176
1: 6 *that* thou sendest to inquire of **B** the god of 1176
1:16 to inquire of **B** the god of Ekron, 1176

BAAL-ZEPHON (3) [BAAL, ZEPHON]
Ex 14: 2 and the sea, over against **B**: 1189
14: 9 by the sea, beside Pi-hahiroth, before **B**. 1189
Nu 33: 7 again unto Pi-hahiroth, which *is* before **B**: 1189

BAANA (2)
1Ki 4:12 **B** the son of Ahilud; *to him pertained* 1195
Ne 3: 4 unto them repaired Zadok the son of **B**. 1195

BAANAH (10)
2Sa 4: 2 the name of the one *was* **B**, and the name of 1196
4: 5 Rechab and **B**, went, and came about 1196
4: 6 and Rechab and **B** his brother escaped. 1196
4: 9 David answered Rechab and **B** his brother, 1196
23:29 Heleb the son of **B**, a Netophathite, Ittai 1196
1Ki 4:16 **B** the son of Hushai *was* in Asher and 1195
1Ch 11:30 Heled the son of **B** the Netophathite, 1196
Ezr 2: 2 Bilshan, Mizpar, Bigvai, Rehum, **B**. 1196
Ne 7: 7 Bilshan, Mispereth, Bigvai, Nehum, **B**. 1196
10:27 Malluch, Harim, **B**. 1196

BAARA (1)
1Ch 8: 8 them away; Hushim and **B** *were* his wives. 1199

BAASEIAH (1)
1Ch 6:40 The son of Michael, the son of **B**, the son 1202

BAASHA (28)
1Ki 15:16 and **B** king of Israel all their days. 1201
15:17 And **B** king of Israel went up against Judah, 1201
15:19 *and* break thy league with **B** king of Israel, 1201
15:21 when **B** heard *thereof*, that he left off 1201
15:22 timber thereof, where*with* **B** had builded; 1201
15:27 **B** the son of Ahijah, of the house of 1201
15:27 **B** smote him at Gibbethon, 1201
1Ki 15:28 year of Asa king of Judah did **B** slay him, 1201
15:32 and **B** king of Israel all their days. 1201
15:33 **B** the son of Ahijah to reign over all Israel 1201
16: 1 came to Jehu the son of Hanani against **B**, 1201
16: 3 I will take away the posterity of **B**, and 1201
16: 4 Him that dieth of **B** in the city shall 1201
16: 5 Now the rest of the acts of **B**, and what he 1201
16: 6 So **B** slept with his fathers, and was buried 1201
16: 7 came the word of the LORD against **B**, 1201
16: 8 the son of **B** to reign over Israel in Tirzah, 1201
16:11 his throne, *that* he slew all the house of **B**: 1201
16:12 Thus did Zimri destroy all the house of **B**, 1201
16:12 which he spake against **B** by Jehu 1201
16:13 For all the sins of **B**, and the sins of Elah 1201
21:22 like the house of **B** the son of Ahijah, 1201
2Ki 9: 9 and like the house of **B** the son of Ahijah: 1201
2Ch 16: 1 thirtieth year of the reign of Asa **B** king of 1201
16: 3 go, break thy league with **B** king of Israel, 1201
16: 5 when **B** heard *it*, that he left off building of 1201
16: 6 where*with* **B** was a building; 1201
Jer 41: 9 king had made for fear of **B** king of Israel: 1201

BABBLER (2) [BABBLING]
Ecc 10:11 and a **b** is no better. 1167+3956+1886.1
Ac 17:18 And some said, What will this **b** say? *4691*

BABBLING (1) [BABBLER, BABBLINGS]
Pr 23:29 who hath **b**? who hath wounds without 7879

BABBLINGS (2) [BABBLING]
1Ti 6:20 avoiding profane *and* **vain b**, and *2757*
2Ti 2:16 But shun profane *and* **vain b**: for they will *2757*

BABE (6) [BABES]
Ex 2: 6 behold, the **b** wept. And she had 5288
Lk 1:41 of Mary, the **b** leaped in her womb; *1025*
1:44 the **b** leaped in my womb for joy. *1025*
2:12 Ye shall find *the* **b** wrapped in swaddling *1025*
2:16 and Joseph, and the **b** lying in a manger. *1025*
Heb 5:13 in the word of righteousness: for he is a **b**. *3516*

BABEL (2) [BABYLON]
Ge 10:10 the beginning of his kingdom was **B**, and 894
11: 9 Therefore is the name of it called **B**; because 894

BABES (9) [BABE]
Ps 8: 2 Out of the mouth of **b** and sucklings hast 5768
17:14 leave the rest of their *substance* to their **b**. 5768
Isa 3: 4 *be* their princes, and **b** shall rule over them. 8586
Mt 11:25 and prudent, and hast revealed them unto **b**. *3516*
21:16 Out of the mouth of **b** and sucklings thou *3516*
Lk 10:21 and prudent, and hast revealed them unto **b**: *3516*
Ro 2:20 An instructor of the foolish, a teacher of **b**, *3516*
1Co 3: 1 but as unto carnal, *even* as unto **b** in Christ. *3516*
1Pe 2: 2 As newborn **b**, desire the sincere milk of *1025*

BABOONS See PEACOCKS

BABYLON (286) [BABEL, BABYLON'S, BABYLONIANS, BABYLONISH]
2Ki 17:24 the king of Assyria brought *men* from **B**, 894
17:30 And the men of **B** made Succoth-benoth, and 894
20:12 king of **B**, sent letters and a present unto 894
20:14 are come from a far country, *even* from **B**. 894
20:17 store unto this day, shall be carried unto **B**: 894
20:18 be eunuchs in the palace of the king of **B**. 894
24: 1 In his days Nebuchadnezzar king of **B** came 894
24: 7 for the king of **B** had taken from the river of 894
24:10 king of **B** came up *against* Jerusalem, 894
24:11 Nebuchadnezzar king of **B** came against 894
24:12 the king of Judah went out to the king of **B**, 894
24:12 the king of **B** took him in the eighth year of 894
24:15 he carried away Jehoiachin to **B**, and 894
24:15 he *into* captivity from Jerusalem to **B**. 894
24:16 even them the king of **B** brought captive to 894
24:16 the king of Babylon brought captive to **B**. 894
24:17 the king of **B** made Mattaniah his father's 894
24:20 that Zedekiah rebelled against the king of **B**. 894
25: 1 *that* Nebuchadnezzar king of **B** came, he, 894
25: 6 brought him up to the king of **B** to Riblah; 894
25: 7 with fetters of brass, and carried him *to* **B**. 894
25: 8 year of king Nebuchadnezzar king of **B**, 894
25: 8 a servant of the king of **B**, *unto* Jerusalem: 894
25:11 the fugitives that fell away to the king of **B**, 894
25:13 *in pieces*, and carried the brass of them to **B**. 894
25:20 and brought them to the king of **B** to Riblah: 894
25:21 the king of **B** smote them, and slew them at 894
25:22 whom Nebuchadnezzar king of **B** had left, 894
25:23 heard that the king of **B** had made Gedaliah 894
25:24 dwell in the land, and serve the king of **B**; 894
25:27 of the month, *that* Evil-merodach king of **B**, 894
25:28 throne of the kings that *were* with him in **B**; 894
1Ch 9: 1 *who* were carried away to **B** for their 894
2Ch 32:31 *of* the ambassadors of the princes of **B**, 894
33:11 bound him with fetters, and carried him to **B**. 894
36: 6 him came up Nebuchadnezzar king of **B**, 894
36: 6 and bound him in fetters, to carry him to **B**. 894
36: 7 the vessels of the house of the LORD to **B**, 894
36: 7 to Babylon, and put them in his temple at **B**. 894
36:10 Nebuchadnezzar sent, and brought him to **B**, 894
36:18 and of his princes; all *these* he brought *to* **B**. 894
36:20 from the sword carried he away to **B**; 894
Ezr 1:11 that were brought up from **B** unto Jerusalem. 894
2: 1 whom Nebuchadnezzar the king of **B** had 894
2: 1 king of Babylon had carried away unto **B**, 894
5:12 the hand of Nebuchadnezzar the king of **B**, 895
5:12 and carried the people away into **B**. 895
5:13 in the first year of Cyrus the king of **B** 895
5:14 brought them into the temple of **B**, those did 895
5:14 Cyrus the king take out of the temple of **B**, 895
5:17 which *is* there at **B**, whether it be *so*, that a 895
6: 1 where the treasures were laid up in **B**. 895
6: 5 brought unto **B**, be restored, and 895
7: 6 This Ezra went up from **B**; and he *was* a 894
Ezr 7: 9 of the first month began he to go up from **B**, 894
7:16 that thou canst find in all the province of **B**, 895
8: 1 of them that went up with me from **B**, 894
Ne 7: 6 whom Nebuchadnezzar the king of **B** had 894
13: 6 thirtieth year of Artaxerxes king of **B** came I 894
Est 2: 6 whom Nebuchadnezzar the king of **B** had 894
Ps 87: 4 of Rahab and **B** to them that know me: 894
137: 1 By the rivers of **B**, there we sat down, yea, 894
137: 8 O daughter of **B**, who art *to be* destroyed; 894
Isa 13: 1 The burden of **B**, which Isaiah the son of 894
13:19 **B**, the glory of kingdoms, the beauty of 894
14: 4 take up this proverb against the king of **B**, 894
14:22 cut off from **B** the name, and remnant, and 894
21: 9 he answered and said, **B** is fallen, is fallen; 894
39: 1 king of **B**, sent letters and a present to 894
39: 3 from a far country unto me, *even* from **B**. 894
39: 6 in store until this day, shall be carried *to* **B**: 894
39: 7 be eunuchs in the palace of the king of **B**. 894
43:14 For your sake I have sent to **B**, and 894
47: 1 and sit in the dust, O virgin daughter of **B**, 894
48:14 he will do his pleasure on **B**, and his arm 894
48:20 Go ye forth of **B**, flee ye from 894
Jer 20: 4 give all Judah into the hand of the king of **B**, 894
20: 4 he shall carry them captive into **B**, and 894
20: 5 and take them, and carry them to **B**. 894
20: 6 thou shalt come *to* **B**, and there thou shalt 894
21: 2 for Nebuchadrezzar king of **B** maketh war 894
21: 4 wherewith ye fight against the king of **B**, and 894
21: 7 into the hand of Nebuchadrezzar king of **B**, 894
21:10 shall be given into the hand of the king of **B**, 894
22:25 into the hand of Nebuchadrezzar king of **B**, 894
24: 1 after that Nebuchadrezzar king of **B** had 894
24: 1 from Jerusalem, and had brought them *to* **B**. 894
25: 1 the first year of Nebuchadrezzar king of **B**; 894
25: 9 Nebuchadrezzar the king of **B**, my servant, 894
25:11 these nations shall serve the king of **B** 894
25:12 *that* I will punish the king of **B**, and that 894
27: 6 the hand of Nebuchadnezzar the king of **B**, 894
27: 8 the same Nebuchadnezzar the king of **B**, 894
27: 8 their neck under the yoke of the king of **B**, 894
27: 9 saying, Ye shall not serve the king of **B**: 894
27:11 their neck under the yoke of the king of **B**, 894
27:12 your necks under the yoke of the king of **B**, 894
27:13 the nation that will not serve the king of **B**? 894
27:14 saying, Ye shall not serve the king of **B**: 894
27:16 *shall* now shortly be brought again from **B**: 894
27:17 not unto them; serve the king of **B**, and live: 894
27:18 king of Judah, and at Jerusalem, go not to **B**. 894
27:20 Which Nebuchadnezzar king of **B** took not, 894
27:20 king of Judah from Jerusalem to **B**, 894
27:22 They shall be carried to **B**, and there shall 894
28: 2 I have broken the yoke of the king of **B**. 894
28: 3 that Nebuchadnezzar king of **B** took away 894
28: 3 away from this place, and carried them *to* **B**: 894
28: 4 of Judah, that went into **B**, saith the LORD: 894
28: 4 for I will break the yoke of the king of **B**. 894
28: 6 carried away captive, from **B** into this place. 894
28:11 **B** from the neck of all nations within 894
28:14 *they* may serve Nebuchadnezzar king of **B**; 894
29: 1 carried away captive from Jerusalem to **B**; 894
29: 3 whom Zedekiah king of Judah sent unto **B** to 894
29: 3 unto Babylon to Nebuchadnezzar king of **B**, 894
29: 4 to be carried away from Jerusalem unto **B**; 894
29:10 years be accomplished at **B** I will visit you, 894
29:15 The LORD hath raised us up prophets in **B**; 894
29:20 whom I have sent from Jerusalem to **B**: 894
29:21 into the hand of Nebuchadrezzar king of **B**; 894
29:22 by all the captivity of Judah which *are* in **B**, 894
29:22 whom the king of **B** roasted in the fire; 894
29:28 For therefore he sent unto us *in* **B**, saying, 894
32: 3 give this city into the hand of the king of **B**, 894
32: 4 be delivered into the hand of the king of **B**, 894
32: 5 he shall lead Zedekiah *to* **B**, and there shall 894
32:28 into the hand of Nebuchadrezzar king of **B**, 894
32:36 into the hand of the king of **B** by the sword, 894
34: 1 when Nebuchadnezzar king of **B**, and all his 894
34: 2 give this city into the hand of the king of **B**, 894
34: 3 eyes shall behold the eyes of the king of **B**, 894
34: 3 thee mouth to mouth, and thou shalt go *to* **B**. 894
35:11 when Nebuchadrezzar king of **B** came up 894
36:29 The king of **B** shall certainly come 894
37: 1 whom Nebuchadrezzar king of **B** made king 894
37:17 be delivered into the hand of the king of **B**. 894
37:19 The king of **B** shall not come against you, 894
38:23 shalt be taken by the hand of the king of **B**: 894
39: 1 came Nebuchadrezzar king of **B** and all his 894
39: 3 And all the princes of the king of **B** came in, 894
39: 3 the residue of the princes of the king of **B**. 894
39: 5 king of **B** to Riblah in the land of Hamath, 894
39: 6 the king of **B** slew the sons of Zedekiah in 894
39: 6 also the king of **B** slew all the nobles of 894
39: 7 bound him with chains to carry him to **B**. 894
39: 9 **B** the remnant of the people that remained in 894
39:11 Now Nebuchadrezzar king of **B** gave charge 894
40: 1 which were carried away captive unto **B**. 894
40: 4 good unto thee to come with me *into* **B**, 894
40: 4 it seem ill unto thee to come with me *into* **B**, 894
40: 5 whom the king of **B** hath made governor 894
40: 7 heard that the king of **B** had made Gedaliah 894
40: 7 that were not carried away captive to **B**; 894
40: 9 dwell in the land and serve the king of **B**, 894
40:11 heard that the king of **B** had left a remnant of 894
41: 2 whom the king of **B** had made governor over 894
41:18 whom the king of **B** made governor in 894
42:11 Be not afraid of the king of **B**, of whom ye 894
43: 3 to death, and carry us away captives *into* **B**. 894
43:10 and take Nebuchadrezzar the king of **B**, 894
44:30 into the hand of Nebuchadrezzar king of **B**, 894
46: 2 which Nebuchadrezzar king of **B** smote in 894
46:13 how Nebuchadrezzar king of **B** should come 894
46:26 into the hand of Nebuchadrezzar king of **B**, 894
49:28 which Nebuchadrezzar king of **B** shall smite, 894
49:30 for Nebuchadrezzar king of **B** hath taken 894
50: 1 The word that the LORD spake against **B** 894
50: 2 say, **B** is taken, Bel is confounded, 894

Jer 50: 8 Remove out of the midst of B, and go forth 894
50: 9 cause to come up against B an assembly of 894
50:13 every one that goeth by B shall be 894
50:14 Put *yourselves* in array against B round 894
50:16 Cut off the sower from B, and him that 894
50:17 last this Nebuchadrezzar king of B hath 894
50:18 I *will* punish the king of B and his land, 894
50:23 how is B become a desolation among 894
50:24 art also taken, O B, and thou wast not aware: 894
50:28 that flee and escape out of the land of B, 894
50:29 Call together the archers against B: all ye 894
50:34 to the land, and disquiet the inhabitants of B. 894
50:35 upon the inhabitants of B, and upon her 894
50:42 to the battle, against thee, O daughter of B. 894
50:43 The king of B hath heard the report of them, 894
50:45 of the LORD, that he hath taken against B; 894
50:46 At the noise of the taking of B the earth is 894
51: 1 I *will* raise up against B, and against them 894
51: 2 will send unto B fanners, that shall fan her, 894
51: 6 Flee out of the midst of B, and deliver every 894
51: 7 B *hath been* a golden cup in the LORD'S 894
51: 8 B is suddenly fallen and destroyed: howl for 894
51: 9 We would have healed B, but she is not 894
51:11 for his device *is* against B, to destroy it; 894
51:12 Set up the standard upon the walls of B, 894
51:12 which he spake against the inhabitants of B. 894
51:24 I will render unto B and to all the inhabitants 894
51:29 of the LORD shall be performed against B, 894
51:29 to make the land of B a desolation without 894
51:30 The mighty *men* of B have forborn to fight, 894
51:31 to shew the king of B that his city is taken at 894
51:33 The daughter of B *is* like a threshingfloor, 894
51:34 Nebuchadrezzar the king of B hath devoured 894
51:35 done to me and *to* my flesh *be* upon B, 894
51:37 B shall become heaps, a dwelling place for 894
51:41 how is B become an astonishment among 894
51:42 The sea is come up upon B: she is covered 894
51:44 I will punish Bel in B, and I will bring forth 894
51:44 more unto him: yea, the wall of B shall fall. 894
51:47 do judgment upon the graven images of B: 894
51:48 and all that *is* therein, shall sing for B: 894
51:49 As B *hath caused* the slain of Israel to fall, 894
51:49 so at B shall fall the slain of all the earth. 894
51:53 Though B should mount up *to* heaven, and 894
51:54 A sound of a cry *cometh* from B, and 894
51:55 Because the LORD *hath* spoiled B, and 894
51:56 *even* upon B, and her mighty *men* are taken, 894
51:58 The broad walls of B shall be utterly broken, 894
51:59 Judah *into* B in the fourth year of his reign. 894
51:60 a book all the evil that should come upon B, 894
51:60 all these words that are written against B. 894
51:61 When thou comest *to* B, and shalt see, and 894
51:64 Thus shall B sink, and shall not rise from 894
52: 3 that Zedekiah rebelled against the king of B. 894
52: 4 *that* Nebuchadrezzar king of B came, he and 894
52: 9 carried him up unto the king of B to Riblah 894
52:10 the king of B slew the sons of Zedekiah 894
52:11 the king of B bound him in chains, and 894
52:11 carried him to B, and put him in prison till 894
52:12 year of Nebuchadrezzar king of B, 894
52:12 *which* served the king of B, into Jerusalem, 894
52:15 that fell to the king of B, and the rest of 894
52:17 and carried all the brass of them to B. 894
52:26 and brought them to the king of B to Riblah. 894
52:27 the king of B smote them, and put them to 894
52:31 *that* Evil-merodach king of B in the *first* year 894
52:32 throne of the kings that *were* with him in B, 894
52:34 a continual diet given him of the king of B, 894
Eze 12:13 I will bring him to B *to* the land of 894
17:12 the king of B is come *to* Jerusalem, and 894
17:12 princes thereof, and led them with him to B; 894
17:16 *even* with him in the midst of B he shall die. 894
17:20 I will bring him to B, and will plead with 894
19: 9 in chains, and brought him to the king of B: 894
21:19 that the sword of the king of B may come: 894
21:21 For the king of B stood at the parting of 894
24: 2 the king of B set himself against Jerusalem 894
26: 7 bring upon Tyrus Nebuchadrezzar king of B, 894
29:18 Nebuchadrezzar king of B caused his army 894
29:19 of Egypt unto Nebuchadrezzar king of B; 894
30:10 by the hand of Nebuchadrezzar king of B. 894
30:24 I will strengthen the arms of the king of B, 894
30:25 I will strengthen the arms of the king of B, 894
30:25 put my sword into the hand of the king of B, 894
32:11 The sword of the king of B shall come *upon* 894
Da 1: 1 Nebuchadnezzar king of B *unto* Jerusalem, 894
2:12 to destroy all the wise *men* of B. 895
2:14 was gone forth to slay the wise *men* of B: 895
2:18 not perish with the rest of the wise *men* of B. 895
2:24 had ordained to destroy the wise *men* of B: 895
2:24 unto him; Destroy not the wise *men* of B: 895
2:48 him ruler over the whole province of B, 895
2:48 of the governors over all the wise *men* of B. 895
2:49 over the affairs of the province of B: 895
3: 1 up in the plain of Dura, in the province of B. 895
3:12 hast set over the affairs of the province of B, 895
3:30 and Abed-nego, in the province of B. 895
4: 6 to bring in all the wise *men* of B before me, 895
4:29 he walked in the palace of the kingdom of B. 895
4:30 The king spake, and said, *Is* not this great B, 895
5: 7 king spake, and said to the wise *men* of B, 895
7: 1 In the first year of Belshazzar king of B 895
Mic 4:10 in the field, and thou shalt go *even* to B; 894
Zec 2: 7 O Zion, that dwellest *with* the daughter of B. 894
6:10 which are come from B, and come thou 894
Mt 1:11 about the time they were carried away to B: *897*
1:12 And after they were brought to B, *897*
1:17 from David until the carrying away into B *897*
1:17 from the carrying away into B unto Christ *897*
Ac 7:43 and I will carry you away beyond B. *897*
1Pe 5:13 The *church that is* at B, elected together with *897*
Rev 14: 8 saying, B is fallen, is fallen, *that* great city, *897*
16:19 great B came in remembrance before God, *897*
17: 5 name written, MYSTERY, B THE GREAT, *897*
18: 2 saying, B the great is fallen, is fallen, and *897*
Rev 18:10 saying, Alas, alas, *that* great city B, *897*
18:21 Thus with violence shall *that* great city B be *897*

BABYLON'S (8) [BABYLON]

Jer 32: 2 then the king of B army besieged Jerusalem: 894
34: 7 When the king of B army fought against 894
34:21 into the hand of the king of B army, 894
38: 3 be given into the hand of the king of B army, 894
38:17 go forth unto the king of B princes, 894
38:18 if thou wilt not go forth to the king of B 894
38:22 *be* brought forth to the king of B princes, 894
39:13 Rab-mag, and all the king of B princes; 894

BABYLONIA See BABYLONISH; CHALDEA; CHALDEANS

BABYLONIANS (4) [BABYLON]

Ezr 4: 9 the Apharsites, the Archevites, the B, 896
Eze 23:15 *after* the manner of the B of Chaldea, 894+1121
23:17 the B came to her into the bed of love, 894+1121
23:23 The B, and all the Chaldeans, Pekod, 894+1121

BABYLONISH (1) [BABYLON]

Jos 7:21 When I saw among the spoils a goodly B 8152

BACA (1)

Ps 84: 6 *Who* passing through the valley of B make 1056

BACHRITES (1)

Nu 26:35 of Becher, the family of the B: of Tahan, 1076

BACK (155) [BACKBITERS, BACKBITETH, BACKBITING, BACKBITINGS, BACKS, BACKSIDE, BACKSLIDER, BACKSLIDING, BACKSLIDINGS, BACKWARD, CROOKBACKT, HORSEBACK]

Ge 14:16 he brought b all the goods, and 7725
19: 9 they said, Stand b. And they said *again,* 1973
19:26 But his wife looked b from behind him, and NIH
38:29 to pass, as he drew b his hand, that, behold, 7725
39: 9 neither hath he kept b any thing from me 2820
Ex 14:21 the LORD caused the sea to go *b* by a NIH
18: 2 Moses' wife, after he had sent her *b,* NIH
23: 4 shalt surely bring it b to him again. 7725+7725
33:23 mine hand, and thou shalt see my b parts: 268
Lev 3: 9 it shall he take off hard by the b bone; 6096
Nu 9: 7 wherefore are we kept b, that *we* may not 1639
13:26 brought b word unto them, and unto all 7725
22:34 if it displease thee, I will get me b again. 7725
24:11 the LORD hath kept thee b from honour. 4513
Dt 23:13 shalt turn b and cover that which cometh 7725
Jos 8:20 the wilderness turned b upon the pursuers. 2015
8:26 For Joshua drew not his hand b, 7725
11:10 Joshua at that time turned b, and 7725
23:12 Else if ye do in any wise go b, 7725+7725
Jdg 11:35 mouth unto the LORD, and I cannot go b. 7725
18:26 he turned and went b unto his house. 7725
Ru 1:15 thy sister in law is gone b unto her people, 7725
2: 6 It *is* the Moabitish damsel that came b with 7725
1Sa 10: 9 that when he had turned his b to go from 7926
15:11 for he is turned b from following me, and 7725
25:34 which hath kept me b from hurting thee, 4513
2Sa 1:22 the bow of Jonathan turned not b, and 268
12:23 can I bring him b again? I shall go to him, 7725
15:20 I may, return thou, and take b thy brethren: 7725
15:25 Carry b the ark of God *into* the city: 7725
17: 3 I will bring b all the people unto thee: 7725
18:16 after Israel: for Joab held b the people. 2820
19:10 ye not a word of bringing the king b? 7725
19:11 Why are ye the last to bring the king b to 7725
19:12 then are ye the last to bring b the king? 7725
19:37 Let thy servant, I pray thee, turn b again, 7725
19:43 not be first had in bringing b our king? 7725
1Ki 13:18 Bring him b with thee into thine house, 7725
13:19 So he went b with him, and did eat bread in 7725
13:20 came unto the prophet that brought him b: 7725
13:22 camest b, and hast eaten bread and 7725
13:23 for the prophet whom he had brought b. 7725
13:26 when the prophet that brought him b from 7725
13:29 and laid it upon the ass, and brought it b: 7725
14: 9 me to anger, and hast cast me behind thy b: 1458
14:28 brought them b into the guard chamber. 7725
18:37 *that* thou hast turned their heart b again. 5437
19:20 he said unto him, Go b again: for what 7725
19:21 he returned b from him, and took a yoke 7725
22:26 carry him b unto Amon the governor of 7725
22:33 that they turned b from pursuing him. 7725
2Ki 1: 5 when the messengers turned b unto him, 7725
1: 5 said unto them, Why are ye now turned b? 7725
2:13 went b, and stood by the bank of Jordan; 7725
2:24 he turned b, and looked on them, and 310
8:29 king Joram went b to be healed in Jezreel 7725
15:20 So the king of Assyria turned b, and 7725
19:28 I will turn thee b by the way by which 7725
20: 9 forward ten degrees, or go b ten degrees? 7725
1Ch 21:20 Ornan turned b, and saw the angel; and 7725
2Ch 13:14 when Judah looked b, behold, the battle 6437
18:25 carry him b to Amon the governor of 7725
18:32 they turned b *again* from pursuing him. 7725
19: 4 brought them b unto the LORD God of 7725
25:13 soldiers of the army which Amaziah sent b, 7725
34:16 and brought the king word b again, saying, 7725
Ne 2:15 turned b, and entered by the gate of 7725
Job 23:12 Neither have I gone b from 4185
26: 9 He holdeth b the face of *his* throne, *and* 270
33:18 He keepeth b his soul from the pit, and 2820
33:30 To bring b his soul from the pit, to be 7725
34:27 Because they turned b from him, and 5493
39:22 neither turneth he b from the sword. 7725
Ps 9: 3 When mine enemies are turned b, they shall 268
14: 7 when the LORD bringeth b the captivity 7725
19:13 Keep b thy servant also from 2820
21:12 shalt thou make them turn their b, 7926
35: 4 let them be turned b and brought to 268
Ps 44:10 Thou makest us to turn b from the enemy: 268
44:18 Our heart is not turned b, neither have our 268
53: 3 Every one of them is gone b, they are 5472
53: 6 When God bringeth b the captivity of his 7725
56: 9 *unto thee,* then shall mine enemies turn b: 268
70: 3 Let them be turned b for a reward of their 7725
78: 9 carrying bows, turned *b* in the day of battle. NIH
78:41 they turned *b* and tempted God, and NIH
78:57 turned *b,* and dealt unfaithfully like their NIH
80:18 So will not we go *b* from thee: quicken us, NIH
85: 1 thou hast brought b the captivity of Jacob. 7725
114: 3 sea saw *it,* and fled: Jordan was driven b. 268
114: 5 thou Jordan, *that* thou wast driven b? 268
129: 3 The plowers plowed upon my b: they made 1354
129: 5 be confounded and turned b that hate Zion. 268
Pr 10:13 a rod *is* for the b of him that is void of 1460
19:29 for scorners, and stripes for the b of fools. 1460
26: 3 bridle for the ass, and a rod for the fools' b. 1460
Isa 14:27 *is* stretched out, and who shall turn it b? 7725
31: 2 bring evil, and will not call b his words: 5493
37:29 I will turn thee b by the way by which 7725
38:17 for thou hast cast all my sins behind thy b. 1460
42:17 They shall be turned b, they shall be greatly 268
43: 6 Give *up;* and to the south, Keep not b: 3607
50: 5 I was not rebellious, neither turned away b. 268
50: 6 I gave my b to the smiters, and my cheeks 1460
Jer 2:27 for they have turned *their* b unto me, and 6203
4: 8 of the LORD is not turned b from us. 7725
4:28 not repent, neither will I turn b from it. 7725
6: 9 turn b thine hand as a grapegatherer into 7725
8: 5 is this people of Jerusalem slidden b *by* a 7725
11:10 They are turned b to the iniquities of their 7725
18:17 I will shew them the b, and not the face, 6203
21: 4 I *will* turn b the weapons of war that *are* in 5437
32:33 they have turned unto me the b, and not 6203
38:22 sunk in the mire, *and* they are turned away b. 268
40: 5 Now while he was not yet gone b, *he said,* 7725
40: 5 *he said,* Go b also to Gedaliah the son of 7725
42: 4 *it* unto you; I will keep nothing b from you. 4513
46: 5 I seen them dismayed *and* turned away b? 268
46: 5 and are fled apace, and look not b: 6437
46:21 for they also are turned b, *and* are fled 6437
47: 3 the fathers shall not look b to *their* children 6437
48:10 cursed *be* he that keepeth b his sword from 4513
48:39 how hath Moab turned the b with shame! 6203
49: 8 Flee ye, turn b, dwell deep, O inhabitants 6437
La 1:13 a net for my feet, he hath turned me b: 268
2: 3 he hath drawn b his right hand from before 268
Eze 23:35 cast me behind thy b, therefore bear thou 1458
24:14 I will do *it;* I will not go b, neither will I 6544
38: 4 I will turn thee b, and put hooks into thy 7725
38: 8 the land *that is* brought b from the sword, 7725
39: 2 I will turn thee b, and leave but the sixth 7725
44: 1 he brought me b the way of the gate of 7725
Da 7: 6 which had upon the b of it four wings of a 1355
Hos 4:16 For Israel slideth b as a backsliding heifer: 5637
Na 2: 8 stand, *shall they cry;* but none shall look b. 6437
Zep 1: 6 them that are turned b from the LORD; 5472
3:20 when I turn b your captivity before your 7725
Mt 24:18 let him which is in the field return b *3694*
28: 2 came and rolled b the stone from the door, *617*
Mk 13:16 And let him that is in the field not turn b *1994*
Lk 2:45 they turned b again to Jerusalem, *5290*
8:37 went *up* into the ship, and returned *b again.* NIG
9:62 and looking b, is fit for *1519+3588+3694*
17:15 turned b, and with a loud voice glorified *5290*
17:31 let him likewise not return b. *1519+3588+3694*
Jn 6:66 of his disciples went b, *565+1519+3588+3694*
20:14 thus said, she turned herself b, *1519+3588+3694*
Ac 5: 2 And kept b *part* of the price, his wife also *3557*
5: 3 and to keep b *part* of the price of the land? *3557*
7:39 in their hearts turned *b again* into Egypt, NIG
20:20 *And* how I kept b nothing that was *5288*
Ro 11:10 may not see, and bow down their b alway. *3577*
Heb 10:38 but if *any man* draw b, my soul shall have *5288*
10:39 But we are not of *them* who draw b unto *5289*
Jas 5: 4 which is of you kept b by fraud, crieth: *650*

BACKBITERS (1) [BACK, BITE]

Ro 1:30 B, haters of God, despiteful, proud, *2637*

BACKBITETH (1) [BACK, BITE]

Ps 15: 3 *He that* b not with his tongue, nor doeth 7270

BACKBITING (1) [BACK, BITE]

Pr 25:23 so *doth* an angry countenance a b tongue. 5643

BACKBITINGS (1) [BACK, BITE]

2Co 12:20 envyings, wraths, strifes, b, whisperings, *2636*

BACKS (8) [BACK]

Ex 23:27 I will make all thine enemies turn their b 6203
Jos 7: 8 when Israel turneth *their* b before their 6203
7:12 *but* turned *their* b before their enemies, 6203
Jdg 20:42 Therefore they turned *their b* before NIH
2Ch 29: 6 of the LORD, and turned *their* b. 6203
Ne 9:26 cast thy law behind their b, and slew thy 1458
Eze 8:16 *with* their b toward the temple of 268
10:12 their b, and their hands, and their wings, 1354

BACKSIDE (3) [BACK, SIDE]

Ex 3: 1 he led the flock to the b of the desert, and 310
26:12 shall hang over the b of the tabernacle. 268
Rev 5: 1 throne a book written within and on the b, *3693*

BACKSLIDER (1) [BACK, SLIDE]

Pr 14:14 The b in heart shall be filled with his own 5472

BACKSLIDING (12) [BACK, SLIDE]

Jer 3: 6 Hast thou seen *that* which b Israel hath 4878
3: 8 when for all the causes whereby b Israel 4878
3:11 The b Israel hath justified herself more than 4878
3:12 say, Return, thou b Israel, saith 4878
3:14 Turn, O b children, saith the LORD; for I 7726

Jer 3:22 ye **b** children, *and* I will heal your 7726
8: 5 of Jerusalem slidden back *by* a perpetual **b**? 4878
31:22 long wilt thou go about, O thou **b** daughter? 7728
49: 4 thy flowing valley, O **b** daughter? 7728
Hos 4:16 For Israel slideth back as a **b** heifer: 5637
11: 7 my people are bent to **b** from me: 4878
14: 4 I will heal their **b**, I will love them freely: 4878

BACKSLIDINGS (4) [BACK, SLIDE]
Jer 2:19 correct thee, and thy **b** shall reprove thee: 4878
3:22 backsliding children, *and* I will heal your **b**. 4878
5: 6 are many, *and* their **b** are increased. 4878
14: 7 for our **b** are many; we have sinned against 4878

BACKWARD (18) [BACK]
Ge 9:23 went **b**, and covered the nakedness of their 322
9:23 their faces *were* **b**, and they saw not their 322
49:17 the horse heels, so that his rider shall fall **b**. 268
1Sa 4:18 that he fell from off the seat **b** by the side of 322
2Ki 20:10 nay, but let the shadow return **b** ten degrees. 322
20:11 he brought the shadow ten degrees **b**, 322
Job 23: 8 he *is* not *there;* and **b**, but I cannot perceive 268
Ps 40:14 let them be driven **b** and put to shame that 268
70: 2 let them be turned **b**, and put to confusion, 268
Isa 1: 4 of Israel unto anger, they are gone away **b**. 268
28:13 fall **b**, and be broken, and snared, and taken. 268
38: 8 down in the sun dial of Ahaz, ten degrees **b**. 322
44:25 that turneth wise *men* **b**, and maketh their 268
59:14 judgment is turned away **b**, and 268
Jer 7:24 and went **b**, and not forward. 268+3807.1
15: 6 saith the LORD, thou art gone **b**: 268
La 1: 8 yea, she sigheth, and turneth **b**. 268
Jn 18: 6 I am *he,* they went **b**, *1519+3588+3694*

BAD (18) [BADNESS, WORSE, WORST]
Ge 24:50 we cannot speak unto thee **b** or good. 7451
31:24 thou speak not to Jacob either good or **b**. 7451
31:29 thou speak not to Jacob either good or **b**. 7451
Lev 27:10 a good for a **b**, or a bad for a good: 7451
27:10 a good for a bad, or a **b** for a good: 7451
27:12 shall value it, whether it be good or **b**: 7451
27:14 shall estimate it, whether it be good or **b**: 7451
27:33 He shall not search whether it be good or **b**, 7451
Nu 13:19 that they dwell in, whether it *be* good or **b**; 7451
24:13 to do *either* good or **b** of mine own mind; 7451
2Sa 13:22 unto his brother Amnon neither good nor **b**: 7451
14:17 *is* my lord the king to discern good and **b**: 7451
1Ki 3: 9 that *I* may discern between good and **b**: 7451
Ezr 4:12 building the rebellious and the **b** city, and 873
Jer 24: 2 which could not be eaten, they were so **b**. 7455
Mt 13:48 the good into vessels, but cast the **b** away. *4550*
22:10 all as many as they found, both **b** and good: *4190*
2Co 5:10 that he hath done, whether *it be* good or **b**. *2556*

BADE (18) [BID]
Ge 43:17 the man did as Joseph **b**; and the man 559
Ex 16:24 they laid it up till the morning, as Moses **b**: 6680
Nu 14:10 all the congregation **b** stone them with 559
Jos 11: 9 Joshua did unto them as the LORD **b** him: 559
Ru 3: 6 to all that her mother in law **b** her. 6680
1Sa 24:10 *some* **b** *me* kill thee: but *mine eye* spared 559
2Sa 1:18 (Also he **b** *them* teach the children of Judah 559
14:19 he **b** me, and he put all these words in 6680
2Ch 10:12 as the king **b**, saying, Come again to me on 1696
Est 4:15 Esther **b** *them* return Mordecai *this answer:* 559
Mt 16:12 Then understood they how that he **b** *them* *3004*
Lk 14: 9 And he that **b** thee and him come and *2564*
14:10 that when he that **b** thee cometh, he may *2564*
14:12 Then said he also to him that **b** him, *2564*
14:16 man made a great supper, and **b** many: *2564*
Ac 11:12 And the Spirit **b** me go with them, *3004*
18:21 But **b** them **farewell**, saying, I must by all *657*
22:24 **b** that he should be examined by scourging; *3004*

BADEST (1) [BID]
Ge 27:19 I have done according as thou **b** me: 1696

BADGERS' (14)
Ex 25: 5 dyed red, and **b** skins, and shittim wood, 8476
26:14 dyed red, and a covering above of **b** skins. 8476
35: 7 dyed red, and **b** skins, and shittim wood, 8476
35:23 skins of rams, and **b** skins, brought *them.* 8476
36:19 and a covering of **b** skins above *that.* 8476
39:34 the covering of **b** skins, and the vail of 8476
Nu 4: 6 shall put thereon the covering of **b** skins, 8476
4: 8 cover the same with a covering of **b** skins, 8476
4:10 thereof within a covering of **b** skins, 8476
4:11 cover it with a covering of **b** skins, and 8476
4:12 cover them with a covering of **b** skins, and 8476
4:14 they shall spread upon it a covering of **b** 8476
4:25 the covering of the **b skins** that *is* above 8476
Eze 16:10 shod thee *with* **b** *skin,* and I girded thee 8476

BADNESS (1) [BAD]
Ge 41:19 I never saw in all the land of Egypt for **b**: 7455

BAG (11) [BAGS]
Dt 25:13 Thou shalt not have in thy **b** divers weights, 3599
1Sa 17:40 put them in a shepherd's **b** which he had, 3627
17:49 David put his hand in *his* **b**, and 3627
Job 14:17 My transgression *is* sealed up in a **b**, and 6872
Pr 7:20 He hath taken a **b** of money with him, 6872
16:11 all the weights of the **b** *are* his work. 3599
Isa 46: 6 They lavish gold out of the **b**, and 3599
Mic 6:11 and with the **b** of deceitful weights? 3599
Hag 1: 6 earneth wages *to put it* into a **b** with holes. 6872
Jn 12: 6 and had the **b**, and bare what was put *1101*
13:29 *of them* thought, because Judas had the **b**, *1101*

BAGGAGE See STUFF

BAGS (3) [BAG]
2Ki 5:23 and bound two talents of silver in two **b**, 2754
12:10 they put up *in* **b**, and told the money that NIH

Lk 12:33 provide yourselves **b** which wax not old, *905*

BAHARUMITE (1)
1Ch 11:33 Azmaveth the **B**, Eliahba the Shaalbonite, 978

BAHURIM (5)
2Sa 3:16 with her along weeping behind her to **B**. 980
16: 5 when king David came to **B**, behold, 980
17:18 came to a man's house in **B**, which had a 980
19:16 which *was* of **B**, hasted and came down with 980
1Ki 2: 8 Shimei the son of Gera, a Benjamite of **B**, 980

BAJITH (1)
Isa 15: 2 He is gone up *to* **B**, and *to* Dibon, the high 1006

BAKBAKKAR (1)
1Ch 9:15 **B**, Heresh, and Galal, and Mattaniah 1230

BAKBUK (2)
Ezr 2:51 The children of **B**, the children of Hakupha, 1227
Ne 7:53 The children of **B**, the children of Hakupha, 1227

BAKBUKIAH (3)
Ne 11:17 **B** the second among his brethren, and 1229
12: 9 Also **B** and Unni, their brethren, *were* over 1229
12:25 Mattaniah, and **B**, Obadiah, Meshullam, 1229

BAKE (9) [BAKED, BAKEMEATS, BAKEN, BAKER, BAKERS, BAKERS', BAKETH]
Ge 19: 3 did **b** unleavened bread, and they did eat. 644
Ex 16:23 **b** *that* which you will bake *to day,* and 644
16:23 bake *that* which you will **b** *to day,* and 644
Lev 24: 5 take fine flour, and **b** twelve cakes thereof: 644
26:26 ten women shall **b** your bread in one oven, 644
1Sa 28:24 and did **b** unleavened bread thereof: 644
2Sa 13: 8 cakes in his sight, and did **b** the cakes. 1310
Eze 4:12 thou shalt **b** it with dung that cometh out of 5746
46:20 where they shall **b** the meat offering; 644

BAKED (4) [BAKE]
Ex 12:39 they **b** unleavened cakes of the dough which 644
Nu 11: 8 and **b** *it* in pans, and made cakes *of* it: 1310
1Ch 23:29 for *that which is* **b** *in* the pan, and for that NIH
Isa 44:19 also I have **b** bread upon the coals thereof; 644

BAKED GOODS See BAKEMEATS

BAKEMEATS (1) [BAKE, MEAT]
Ge 40:17 of all *manner of* **b** for Pharaoh; 644+3978+4639

BAKEN (9) [BAKE]
Lev 2: 4 oblation of a meat offering **b** in the oven, 3989
2: 5 if thy oblation *be* a meat offering *b* in a pan, NIH
2: 7 if thy oblation *be* a meat offering **b** in NIH
6:17 It shall not be **b** *with* leaven. I have given it 644
6:21 *and when it is* **b**, thou shalt bring it in: 7246
6:21 the **b** pieces of the meat offering shalt thou 8601
7: 9 all the meat offering that is **b** in the oven, 644
23:17 be *of* fine flour; they shall be **b** *with* leaven; 644
1Ki 19: 6 *there was* a cake **b on the coals**, and 7529

BAKER (8) [BAKE]
Ge 40: 1 *his* **b** had offended their lord the king of 644
40: 5 the butler and the **b** of the king of Egypt, 644
40:16 When the chief **b** saw that the interpretation 644
40:20 and of the chief **b** among his servants. 644
40:22 he hanged the chief **b**: as Joseph had 644
41:10 the guard's house, *both* me and the chief **b**: 644
Hos 7: 4 *are* all adulterers, as an oven heated by the **b**, 644
7: 6 their **b** sleepeth all the night; *in* the morning 644

BAKERS (2) [BAKE]
Ge 40: 2 of the butlers, and against the chief of the **b**. 644
1Sa 8:13 and to be cooks, and to be **b**. 644

BAKERS' (1) [BAKE]
Jer 37:21 him daily a piece of bread out of the **b** street, 644

BAKETH (1) [BAKE]
Isa 44:15 yea, he kindleth *it,* and **b** bread; yea, 644

BALAAM (60) [BALAAM'S]
Nu 22: 5 therefore unto **B** the son of Beor to Pethor, 1109
22: 7 they came unto **B**, and spake unto him 1109
22: 8 and the princes of Moab abode with **B**. 1109
22: 9 God came unto **B**, and said, What men *are* 1109
22:10 **B** said unto God, Balak the son of Zippor, 1109
22:12 God said unto **B**, Thou shalt not go with 1109
22:13 **B** rose up in the morning, and said unto 1109
22:14 and said, **B** refuseth to come with us. 1109
22:16 they came to **B**, and said to him, Thus saith 1109
22:18 **B** answered and said unto the servants of 1109
22:20 God came unto **B** at night, and said unto 1109
22:21 **B** rose up in the morning, and saddled his 1109
22:23 **B** smote the ass, to turn her *into* the way. 1109
22:27 of the LORD, she fell down under **B**: 1109
22:28 she said unto **B**, What have I done unto 1109
22:29 **B** said unto the ass, Because thou hast 1109
22:30 And the ass said unto **B**, *Am* not I thine ass, 1109
22:31 Then the LORD opened the eyes of **B**, and 1109
22:34 **B** said unto the angel of the LORD, I have 1109
22:35 the angel of the LORD said unto **B**, 1109
22:35 So **B** went with the princes of Balak. 1109
22:36 when Balak heard that **B** was come, he 1109
22:37 Balak said unto **B**, Did I not earnestly send 1109
22:38 **B** said unto Balak, Lo, I am come unto 1109
22:39 **B** went with Balak, and they came *unto* 1109
22:40 sent to **B**, and to the princes that *were* with 1109
22:41 that Balak took **B**, and brought him up *into* 1109
23: 1 **B** said unto Balak, Build me here seven 1109
23: 2 Balak did as **B** had spoken; and Balak and 1109
23: 2 and **B** offered on *every* altar a bullock and 1109
23: 3 **B** said unto Balak, Stand by thy burnt 1109

Nu 23: 4 God met **B**: and he said unto him, I have 1109
23:11 Balak said unto **B**, What hast thou done 1109
23:16 the LORD met **B**, and put a word in his 1109
23:25 Balak said unto **B**, Neither curse them at 1109
23:26 **B** answered and said unto Balak, Told not I 1109
23:27 Balak said unto **B**, Come, I pray thee, I will 1109
23:28 Balak brought **B** *unto* the top of Peor, 1109
23:29 **B** said unto Balak, Build me here seven 1109
23:30 Balak did as **B** had said, and offered a 1109
24: 1 when **B** saw that it pleased the LORD to 1109
24: 2 **B** lift up his eyes, and he saw Israel abiding 1109
24: 3 **B** the son of Beor hath said, and the man 1109
24:10 Balak's anger was kindled against **B**, and 1109
24:10 Balak said unto **B**, I called thee to curse 1109
24:12 **B** said unto Balak, Spake I not also to thy 1109
24:15 **B** the son of Beor hath said, and the man 1109
24:25 **B** rose up, and went and returned to his 1109
31: 8 **B** also the son of Beor they slew with 1109
31:16 children of Israel, through the counsel of **B**, 1109
Dt 23: 4 they hired against thee **B** the son of Beor of 1109
23: 5 thy God would not hearken unto **B**; 1109
Jos 13:22 **B** also the son of Beor, the soothsayer, 1109
24: 9 and called **B** the son of Beor to curse you: 1109
24:10 I would not hearken unto **B**; therefore 1109
Ne 13: 2 and with water, but hired **B** against them, 1109
Mic 6: 5 and what **B** the son of Beor answered him; 1109
2Pe 2:15 following the way of **B** *the son* of Bosor, *903*
Jude 1:11 ran greedily after the error of **B** for reward, *903*
Rev 2:14 hast there them that hold the doctrine of **B**, *903*

BALAAM'S (3) [BALAAM]
Nu 22:25 the wall, and crusht **B** foot against the wall: 1109
22:27 **B** anger was kindled, and he smote the ass 1109
23: 5 the LORD put a word in **B** mouth, and 1109

BALAC (1) [BALAK]
Rev 2:14 who taught **B** to cast a stumblingblock *904*

BALADAN (2)
2Ki 20:12 the son of **B**, king of Babylon, sent letters 1081
Isa 39: 1 the son of **B**, king of Babylon, sent letters 1081

BALAH (1)
Jos 19: 3 And Hazar-shual, and **B**, and Azem, 1088

BALAK (42) [BALAC, BALAK'S]
Nu 22: 2 **B** the son of Zippor saw all that Israel had 1111
22: 4 **B** the son of Zippor *was* king of 1111
22: 7 and spake unto him the words of **B**. 1111
22:10 **B** the son of Zippor, king of Moab, 1111
22:13 said unto the princes of **B**, Get you into 1111
22:14 they went unto **B**, and said, 1111
22:15 **B** sent yet again princes, more, and 1111
22:16 said to him, Thus saith **B** the son of Zippor, 1111
22:18 and said unto the servants of **B**, 1111
22:18 If **B** would give me his house full *of* silver 1111
22:35 So Balaam went with the princes of **B**. 1111
22:36 when **B** heard that Balaam was come, he 1111
22:37 **B** said unto Balaam, Did I not earnestly 1111
22:38 Balaam said unto **B**, Lo, I am come unto 1111
22:39 Balaam went with **B**, and they came *unto* 1111
22:40 **B** offered oxen and sheep, and sent to 1111
22:41 that **B** took Balaam, and brought him up 1111
23: 1 Balaam said unto **B**, Build me here seven 1111
23: 2 **B** did as Balaam had spoken; and Balak 1111
23: 2 **B** and Balaam offered on *every* altar a 1111
23: 3 Balaam said unto **B**, Stand by thy burnt 1111
23: 5 Return unto **B**, and thus thou shalt speak. 1111
23: 7 **B** the king of Moab hath brought me from 1111
23:11 **B** said unto Balaam, What hast thou done 1111
23:13 **B** said unto him, Come, I pray thee, 1111
23:15 he said unto **B**, Stand here by thy burnt 1111
23:16 and said, Go again unto **B**, and say thus. 1111
23:17 **B** said unto him, What hath the LORD 1111
23:18 his parable, and said, Rise up, **B**, and hear; 1111
23:25 **B** said unto Balaam, Neither curse them at 1111
23:26 Balaam answered and said unto **B**, Told not 1111
23:27 **B** said unto Balaam, Come, I pray thee, 1111
23:28 **B** brought Balaam *unto* the top of Peor, 1111
23:29 Balaam said unto **B**, Build me here seven 1111
23:30 **B** did as Balaam had said, and offered a 1111
24:10 **B** said unto Balaam, I called thee to curse 1111
24:12 Balaam said unto **B**, Spake I not also to thy 1111
24:13 If **B** would give me his house full *of* silver 1111
24:25 to his place: and **B** also went his way. 1111
Jos 24: 9 **B** the son of Zippor, king of Moab, arose 1111
Jdg 11:25 now *art* thou any thing better than **B** the son 1111
Mic 6: 5 remember now what **B** king of Moab 1111

BALAK'S (1) [BALAK]
Nu 24:10 **B** anger was kindled against Balaam, and 1111

BALANCE (8) [BALANCES, BALANCINGS]
Job 31: 6 Let me be weighed in an even **b**, that God 3976
Ps 62: 9 to be laid in the **b**, they *are* altogether 3976
Pr 11: 1 A false **b** *is* abomination to the LORD: 3976
16:11 A just weight and **b** *are* the LORD'S: 3976
20:23 unto the LORD; and a false **b** *is* not good. 3976
Isa 40:12 mountains in scales, and the hills in a **b**? 3976
40:15 and are counted as the small dust of the **b**: 3976
46: 6 weigh silver in the **b**, *and* hire a goldsmith, 7070

BALANCES (10) [BALANCE]
Lev 19:36 Just **b**, just weights, a just ephah, and a just 3976
Job 6: 2 my calamity laid in the **b** together! 3976
Jer 32:10 weighed *him* the money in the **b**. 3976
Eze 5: 1 take thee **b** to weigh, and divide *the hair.* 3976
45:10 Ye shall have just **b**, and a just ephah, and 3976
Da 5:27 Thou art weighed in the **b**, and art found 3977
Hos 12: 7 a merchant, the **b** of deceit *are* in his hand: 3976
Am 8: 5 shekel great, and falsifying the **b** by deceit? 3976
Mic 6:11 Shall I count *them* pure with the wicked **b**, 3976
Rev 6: 5 he that sat on him had a **pair of b** in his *2218*

BALANCINGS (1) [BALANCE]
Job 37:16 Dost thou know the **b** of the clouds, 4657

BALD (16) [BALDNESS]
Lev 11:22 the **b locust** after his kind, and the beetle 5556
13:40 whose hair is fallen off his head, he *is* **b**: 7142
13:41 *his head toward* his face, he *is* **forehead b**: 1371
13:42 if there be in the **b head**, or bald forehead, 7146
13:42 or **b forehead**, a white reddish sore; 1372
13:42 it *is* a leprosy sprung up in his **b head**, or 7146
13:42 up in his bald head, or his **b forehead**. 1372
13:43 of the sore *be* white reddish in his **b head**, 7146
13:43 or in his **b forehead**, as the leprosy 1372
2Ki 2:23 and said unto him, Go up, thou **b head**; 7142
2:23 Go up, thou bald head; go up, thou **b head**. 7142
Jer 16: 6 nor **make** themselves **b** for them: 7139
48:37 For every head *shall be* **b**, and every beard 7144
Eze 27:31 **make** themselves **utterly b** for thee, 7139+7139
29:18 every head *was* **made b**, and 7139
Mic 1:16 **Make** thee **b**, and poll thee for thy delicate 7139

BALDNESS (9) [BALD]
Lev 21: 5 They shall not **make b** upon their 7139+7144
Dt 14: 1 nor make *any* **b** between your eyes for 7144
Isa 3:24 instead of well set hair **b**; and instead of a 7144
15: 2 on all their heads *shall be* **b**, *and* 7144
22:12 and to **b**, and to girding with sackcloth: 7144
Jer 47: 5 **B** is come upon Gaza; Ashkelon is cut off 7144
Eze 7:18 upon all faces, and **b** upon all their heads. 7144
Am 8:10 upon all loins, and **b** upon every head; 7144
Mic 1:16 enlarge thy **b** as the eagle; 7144

BALL (1)
Isa 22:18 and toss thee like a **b** into a large country: 1754

BALM (6)
Ge 37:25 camels bearing spicery and **b** and myrrh, 6875
43:11 a little **b**, and a little honey, spices, and 6875
Jer 8:22 *Is there* no **b** in Gilead; *is there* no 6875
46:11 Go up *into* Gilead, and take **b**, O virgin, 6875
51: 8 take **b** for her pain, if so be she may be 6875
Eze 27:17 and Pannag, and honey, and oil, and **b**. 6875

BAMAH (1)
Eze 20:29 the name thereof is called **B** unto this day. 1117

BAMOTH (2) [BAMOTH-BAAL]
Nu 21:19 *to* Nahaliel: and from Nahaliel *to* **B**: 1120
21:20 from **B** *in* the valley, that *is* in the country 1120

BAMOTH-BAAL (1) [BAMOTH, BAAL]
Jos 13:17 Dibon, and **B**, and Beth-baal-meon, 1120

BAND (20) [BANDED, BANDS, HEADBANDS]
Ex 39:23 *with* a **b** round about the hole, *that* it should 8193
1Sa 10:26 there went with him a **b of men**, 2428
1Ki 11:24 unto him, and became captain over a **b**, 1416
2Ki 13:21 they spied a **b** *of men;* and they cast 1416
1Ch 12:18 and made them captains of the **b**. 1416
12:21 they helped David against the **b** *of* 1416
2Ch 22: 1 for the **b** *of men* that came with 1416
Ezr 8:22 to require of the king a **b** *of soldiers* 2428
Job 38: 9 and thick darkness a **swaddling b** for it, 2854
39:10 Canst thou bind the unicorn *with* his **b** in 5688
Da 4:15 even with a **b** of iron and brass, in the tender 613
4:23 even with a **b** of iron and brass, in the tender 613
Mt 27:27 gathered unto him the whole **b** *of soldiers.* *4686*
Mk 15:16 and they call together the whole **b**. *4686*
Jn 18: 3 having received a **b** *of men,* and *4686*
18:12 Then the **b** and the captain and officers of *4686*
Ac 10: 1 a centurion of the **b** called the Italian *band,* *4686*
10: 1 a centurion of the band called the Italian *b,* NIG
21:31 tidings came unto the chief captain of the **b**, *4686*
27: 1 named Julius, a centurion of Augustus' **b**. *4686*

BANDED (1) [BAND]
Ac 23:12 certain of the Jews **b together**, *4160+4963*

BANDS (46) [BAND]
Ge 32: 7 and herds, and the camels, into two **b**; 4264
32:10 this Jordan; and now I am become two **b**. 4264
Lev 26:13 I have broken the **b** of your yoke, and 4133
Jdg 15:14 and his **b** loosed from off his hands. 612
2Sa 4: 2 son had two men *that were* captains of **b**: 1416
2Ki 6:23 So the **b** of Syria came no more into 1416
13:20 the **b** of the Moabites invaded the land *at* 1416
23:33 Pharaoh-nechoh **put** him **in b** at Riblah in 631
24: 2 the LORD sent against him **b** of 1416
24: 2 **b** of the Syrians, and bands of 1416
24: 2 **b** of the Moabites, and bands of 1416
24: 2 **b** of the children of Ammon, and sent them 1416
1Ch 7: 4 *were* **b** of soldiers for war, six and 1416
12:23 these *are* the numbers of the **b** that were 7218
2Ch 26:11 of fighting *men,* that went out to war by **b**, 1416
Job 1:17 The Chaldeans made out three **b**, and 7218
38:31 of Pleiades, or loose the **b** of Orion? 4189
39: 5 or who hath loosed the **b** of the wild ass? 4147
Ps 2: 3 Let us break their **b** asunder, and cast away 4147
73: 4 For *there are* no **b** in their death: but 2784
107:14 of death, and brake their **b** in sunder. 4147
119:61 The **b** of the wicked have robbed me: *but* 2256
Pr 30:27 no king, yet go they forth all of them **by b**; 2686
Ecc 7:26 heart *is* snares and nets, *and* her hands *as* **b**: 612
Isa 28:22 ye not mockers, lest your **b** be made strong: 4147
52: 2 loose thyself from the **b** of thy neck, 4147
58: 6 to loose the **b** of wickedness, to undo 2784
Jer 2:20 I have broken thy yoke, *and* burst thy **b**; 4147
Eze 3:25 they shall put **b** upon thee, and shall bind 5688
4: 8 I will lay **b** upon thee, and thou shalt not 5688
12:14 that *are* about him to help him, and all his **b**; 102
17:21 all his fugitives with all his **b** shall fall by 102
34:27 when I have broken the **b** of their yoke, and 4133
38: 6 Gomer, and all his **b**; the house of Togarmah 102
Eze 38: 6 *of* the north quarters, and all his **b**: 102
38: 9 and all thy **b**, and many people with thee. 102
38:22 upon his **b**, and upon the many people that 102
39: 4 all thy **b**, and the people that *is* with thee: 102
Hos 11: 4 them with cords of a man, with **b** of love: 5688
Zec 11: 7 I called Beauty, and the other I called **B**; 2254
11:14 I cut asunder mine other staff, *even* **B**, 2254
Lk 8:29 and he brake the **b**, and was driven of *1199*
Ac 16:26 and every one's **b** were loosed. *1199*
22:30 he loosed him from *his* **b**, and *1199*
27:40 and loosed the rudder **b**, and hoised up *2202*
Col 2:19 and **b** having nourishment ministered, *4886*

BANI (15)
2Sa 23:36 the son of Nathan of Zobah, **B** the Gadite, 1137
1Ch 6:46 The son of Amzi, the son of **B**, the son of 1137
9: 4 son of Omri, the son of Imri, the son of **B**, 1137
Ezr 2:10 The children of **B**, six hundred forty and 1137
10:29 of the sons of **B**; Meshullam, Malluch, and 1137
10:34 Of the sons of **B**; Maadai, Amram, and Uel, 1137
10:38 And **B**, and Binnui, Shimei, 1137
Ne 3:17 repaired the Levites, Rehum the son of **B**. 1137
8: 7 **B**, and Sherebiah, Jamin, Akkub, 1137
9: 4 Jeshua, and **B**, Kadmiel, Shebaniah, Bunni, 1137
9: 4 **B**, *and* Chenani, and cried with a loud voice 1137
9: 5 Jeshua and Kadmiel, **B**, Hashabniah, 1137
10:13 Hodijah, **B**, Beninu. 1137
10:14 Parosh, Pahath-moab, Elam, Zatthu, **B**, 1137
11:22 Levites at Jerusalem *was* Uzzi the son of **B**, 1137

BANISHED (2) [BANISHMENT]
2Sa 14:13 the king doth not fetch *home* again his **b**. 5080
14:14 that *his* **b** be not expelled from him. 5080

BANISHMENT (2) [BANISHED]
Ezr 7:26 or to **b**, or to confiscation of goods, or 8332
La 2:14 seen for thee false burdens and **causes of b**. 4065

BANK (14) [BANKS]
Ge 41:17 behold, I stood upon the **b** of the river: 8193
Dt 4:48 which *is* by the **b** of the river Arnon, 8193
Jos 12: 2 which *is* upon the **b** of the river of Arnon, 8193
13: 9 that *is* upon the **b** of the river Arnon, and 8193
13:16 that *is* on the **b** of the river Arnon, and 8193
2Sa 20:15 they cast up a **b** against the city, and 5550
2Ki 2:13 went back, and stood by the **b** of Jordan; 8193
19:32 before it *with* shield, nor cast a **b** against it. 5550
Isa 37:33 it *with* shields, nor cast a **b** against it. 5550
Eze 47: 7 at the **b** of the river *were* very many trees 8193
47:12 by the river upon the **b** thereof, on this side 8193
Da 12: 5 the one on this side of the **b** of the river, 8193
12: 5 the other on that side of the **b** of the river. 8193
Lk 19:23 then gavest not thou my money into the **b**, *5132*

BANKS (5) [BANK]
Jos 3:15 (for Jordan overfloweth all his **b** all 1415
4:18 flowed over all his **b**, as *they did* before. 1415
1Ch 12:15 when it had overflown all his **b**; 1415
Isa 8: 7 over all his channels, and go over all his **b**: 1415
Da 8:16 I heard a man's voice between *the* **b** *of* Ulai, NIH

BANNER (3) [BANNERS]
Ps 60: 4 Thou hast given a **b** to them that fear thee, 5251
SS 2: 4 and his **b** over me *was* love. 1714
Isa 13: 2 Lift ye up a **b** upon the high mountain, 5251

BANNERS (3) [BANNER]
Ps 20: 5 the name of our God we will **set up** *our* **b**: 1713
SS 6: 4 as Jerusalem, terrible as *an army* **with b**. 1713
6:10 as the sun, *and* terrible as *an army* with **b**? 1713

BANQUET (14) [BANQUETING, BANQUETINGS]
Est 5: 4 Haman come *this* day unto the **b** that I have 4960
5: 5 Haman came to the **b** that Esther had 4960
5: 6 the king said unto Esther at the **b** of wine, 4960
5: 8 Haman come to the **b** that I shall prepare 4960
5:12 the king unto the **b** that she had prepared 4960
5:14 go thou in merrily with the king unto the **b**. 4960
6:14 hasted to bring Haman unto the **b** that 4960
7: 1 Haman came to **b** with Esther the queen. 8354
7: 2 Esther on the second day at the **b** of wine, 4960
7: 7 the king arising from the **b** of wine in his 4960
7: 8 garden into the place of the **b** of wine; 4960
Job 41: 6 Shall the companions **make a b** of him? 3739
Da 5:10 and his lords, came into the **b** house: 4961
Am 6: 7 the **b** of them that stretched themselves 4797

BANQUETING (1) [BANQUET]
SS 2: 4 He brought me to the **b** house, and 3196

BANQUETINGS (1) [BANQUET]
1Pe 4: 3 revellings, **b**, and abominable idolatries: *4224*

BAPTISM (22) [BAPTIZE]
Mt 3: 7 the Pharisees and Sadducees come to his **b**, *908*
20:22 to be baptized *with* the **b** that I am baptized *908*
20:23 be baptized *with* the **b** that I am baptized *908*
21:25 The **b** of John, whence was it? from heaven, *908*
Mk 1: 4 preach the **b** of repentance for the remission *908*
10:38 be baptized with the **b** that I am baptized *908*
10:39 *with* the **b** that I am baptized *withal* shall ye *908*
11:30 The **b** of John, was *it* from heaven, or *908*
Lk 3: 3 preaching the **b** of repentance for *908*
7:29 being baptized *with* the **b** of John. *908*
12:50 But I have a **b** to be baptized *with;* and *908*
20: 4 The **b** of John, was it from heaven, or *908*
Ac 1:22 Beginning from the **b** of John, unto *that* *908*
10:37 after the **b** which John preached; *908*
13:24 **b** of repentance to all the people of Israel. *908*
18:25 of the Lord, knowing only the **b** of John. *908*
19: 3 ye baptized? And they said, Unto John's **b**. *908*
19: 4 John verily baptized *with* the **b** of *908*
Ro 6: 4 Therefore we are buried with him by **b** into *908*
Eph 4: 5 One Lord, one faith, one **b**, *908*
Col 2:12 Buried with him in **b**, wherein also you are *908*
1Pe 3:21 The like figure whereunto *even* **b** doth also *908*

BAPTISMS (1) [BAPTIZE]
Heb 6: 2 Of the doctrine of **b**, and of laying on of *909*

BAPTIST (14) [BAPTIZE]
Mt 3: 1 In those days came John the **B**, preaching in *910*
11:11 hath not risen a greater than John the **B**: *910*
11:12 And from the days of John the **B** until now *910*
14: 2 said unto his servants, This is John the **B**; *910*
16:14 they said, Some *say that thou art* John the **B**: *910*
17:13 that he spake unto them of John the **B**. *910*
Mk 6:14 That John the **B** was risen from the dead, *907*
6:24 I ask? And she said, The head of John the **B**. *910*
6:25 and by in a charger the head of John the **B**. *910*
8:28 And they answered, John the **B**: but *910*
Lk 7:20 John **B** hath sent us unto thee, saying, *910*
7:28 is not a greater prophet than John the **B**: *910*
7:33 For John the **B** came neither eating bread nor *910*
9:19 They answering said, John the **B**; but *910*

BAPTIST'S (1) [BAPTIZE]
Mt 14: 8 said, Give me here John **B** head in a charger. *910*

BAPTIZE (9) [BAPTISM, BAPTISMS, BAPTIST, BAPTIST'S, BAPTIZED, BAPTIZEST, BAPTIZETH, BAPTIZING]
Mt 3:11 I indeed **b** you with water unto repentance: *907*
3:11 he shall **b** you with the Holy Ghost, and *907*
Mk 1: 4 John did **b** in the wilderness, and preach *907*
1: 8 but he shall **b** you with the Holy Ghost. *907*
Lk 3:16 unto *them* all, I indeed **b** you with water; *907*
3:16 he shall **b** you with the Holy Ghost and *907*
Jn 1:26 John answered them, saying, I **b** with water: *907*
1:33 but he that sent me to **b** with water, the same *907*
1Co 1:17 For Christ sent me not to **b**, but to preach *907*

BAPTIZED (61) [BAPTIZE]
Mt 3: 6 And were **b** of him in Jordan, *907*
3:13 Galilee to Jordan unto John, to be **b** of him. *907*
3:14 I have need to be **b** of thee, and comest thou *907*
3:16 And Jesus, when he was **b**, went up *907*
20:22 to be **b** *with* the baptism that I am baptized *907*
20:22 to be baptized *with* the baptism that I am **b** *907*
20:23 be **b** *with* the baptism that I am baptized *907*
20:23 be baptized *with* the baptism that I am **b** *907*
Mk 1: 5 and were all **b** of him in the river *of* Jordan, *907*
1: 8 I indeed have **b** you with water: but he shall *907*
1: 9 of Galilee, and was **b** of John in Jordan. *907*
10:38 be **b** *with* the baptism that I am baptized *907*
10:38 be baptized *with* the baptism that I am **b** *907*
10:39 *with* the baptism that I am **b** *withal* shall ye *907*
10:39 that I am baptized *withal* shall ye be **b**: *907*
16:16 He that believeth and is **b** shall be saved; but *907*
Lk 3: 7 the multitude that came forth to be **b** of him, *907*
3:12 Then came also publicans to be **b**, and *907*
3:21 Now when all the people were **b**, it came to *907*
3:21 to pass, *that* Jesus also being **b**, and praying, *907*
7:29 being **b** *with* the baptism of John. *907*
7:30 God against themselves, being not **b** of him. *907*
12:50 But I have a baptism to be **b** *with;* and *907*
Jn 3:22 and there he tarried with them, and **b**. *907*
3:23 water there: and they came, and were **b**. *907*
4: 1 Jesus made and **b** moe disciples than John, *907*
4: 2 (Though Jesus himself **b** not, but *907*
10:40 Jordan into the place where John at first **b**; *907*
Ac 1: 5 For John truly **b** with water; but ye shall be *907*
1: 5 ye shall be **b** with the Holy Ghost not many *907*
2:38 be **b** every one of you in the name of Jesus *907*
2:41 they that gladly received his word were **b**: *907*
8:12 they were **b**, both men and women. *907*
8:13 and when he was **b**, he continued with *907*
8:16 only they were **b** in the name of the Lord *907*
8:36 *here is* water; what doth hinder me to be **b**? *907*
8:38 both Philip and the eunuch; and he **b** him. *907*
9:18 sight forthwith, and arose, and was **b**, *907*
10:47 *man* forbid water, that these should not be **b**, *907*
10:48 And he commanded them to be **b** in *907*
11:16 how that he said, John indeed **b** with water; *907*
11:16 but ye shall be **b** with the Holy Ghost. *907*
16:15 And when she was **b**, and her household, *907*
16:33 and was **b**, he and all his, straightway. *907*
18: 8 Corinthians hearing believed, and were **b**. *907*
19: 3 said unto them, Unto what then were ye **b**? *907*
19: 4 John verily **b** *with* the baptism of *907*
19: 5 When they heard *this,* they were **b** in *907*
22:16 arise, and be **b**, and wash away thy sins, *907*
Ro 6: 3 many of us as were **b** into Jesus Christ were *907*
6: 3 into Jesus Christ were **b** into his death? *907*
1Co 1:13 for you? or were ye **b** in the name of Paul? *907*
1:14 I thank God that I **b** none of you, but Crispus *907*
1:15 Lest any should say that I had **b** in mine own *907*
1:16 And I **b** also the household of Stephanas: *907*
1:16 besides, I know not whether I **b** any other. *907*
10: 2 And were all **b** unto Moses in the cloud and *907*
12:13 For by one Spirit are we all **b** into one body, *907*
15:29 Else what shall they do which are **b** for *907*
15:29 not at all? why are they then **b** for the dead? *907*
Gal 3:27 For as many of you as have been **b** into *907*

BAPTIZEST (1) [BAPTIZE]
Jn 1:25 and said unto him, Why **b** thou then, *907*

BAPTIZETH (2) [BAPTIZE]
Jn 1:33 the same is he which **b** with the Holy Ghost. *907*
3:26 the same **b**, and all *men* come to him. *907*

BAPTIZING (4) [BAPTIZE]
Mt 28:19 **b** them in the name of the Father, and of *907*
Jn 1:28 beyond Jordan, where John was **b**. *907*
1:31 to Israel, therefore am I come **b** with water. *907*
3:23 And John also was **b** in Aenon near to *907*

BAR (7) [BARS]
Ex 26:28 the middle b in the midst of the boards 1280
36:33 he made the middle b to shoot through 1280
Nu 4:10 of badgers' skins, and shall put it upon a b. 4132
4:12 badgers' skins, and shall put them on a b: 4132
Jdg 16: 3 b and all, and put them upon his shoulders, 1280
Ne 7: 3 b them: and appoint watches of 270
Am 1: 5 I will break also the b of Damascus, and 1280

BARABBAS (11)
Mt 27:16 they had then a notable prisoner, called B. 912
27:17 unto you? B, or Jesus which is called Christ? 912
27:20 the multitude that they should ask B, 912
27:21 will ye that I release unto you? They said, B. 912
27:26 Then released he B unto them: 912
Mk 15: 7 And there was one named B, which lay 912
15:11 that he should rather release B unto them. 912
15:15 released B unto them, and delivered Jesus, 912
Lk 23:18 Away with this man, and release unto us B: 912
Jn 18:40 they all again, saying, Not this man, but B. 912
18:40 but Barabbas. Now B was a robber. 912

BARACHEL (2)
Job 32: 2 was kindled the wrath of Elihu the son of B 1292
32: 6 Elihu the son of B the Buzite answered 1292

BARACHIAS (1) [BERECHIAH]
Mt 23:35 Abel unto the blood of Zacharias son of B, 914

BARAK (14)
Jdg 4: 6 called B the son of Abinoam out of 1301
4: 8 B said unto her, If thou wilt go with me, 1301
4: 9 Deborah arose, and went with B to Kedesh. 1301
4:10 B called Zebulun and Naphtali to Kedesh; 1301
4:12 they shewed Sisera that B the son of 1301
4:14 Deborah said unto B, Up; for this is the day 1301
4:14 So B went down from mount Tabor, and 1301
4:15 with the edge of the sword before B; 1301
4:16 B pursued after the chariots, and after 1301
4:22 behold, as B pursued Sisera, Jael came out 1301
5: 1 and B the son of Abinoam on that day, 1301
5:12 arise, B, and lead thy captivity captive, 1301
5:15 with Deborah; even Issachar, and also B: 1301
Heb 11:32 and of B, and of Samson, and of Jephthae; 913

BARAKEL See BARACHEL

BARBARIAN (3) [BARBARIANS, BARBAROUS]
1Co 14:11 I shall be unto him that speaketh a b, and 915
14:11 and he that speaketh shall be a b unto me. 915
Col 3:11 b, Scythian, bond nor free: 915

BARBARIANS (2) [BARBARIAN]
Ac 28: 4 And when the b saw the venomous beast 915
Ro 1:14 I am debtor both to the Greeks, and to the b; 915

BARBAROUS (1) [BARBARIAN]
Ac 28: 2 And the b **people** shewed us no little 915

BARBED (1)
Job 41: 7 Canst thou fill his skin with b **irons**? or 7905

BARBER'S (1)
Eze 5: 1 take thee a b rasor, and cause it to pass 1532

BARBS See PRICKS

BARE (186) [BAREFOOT, BAREST, BEAR]
Ge 4: 1 she conceived, and b Cain, and said, I have 3205
4: 2 she again b his brother Abel. And Abel was 3205
4:17 his wife; and she conceived, and b Enoch: 3205
4:20 Adah b Jabal: he was the father of such as 3205
4:22 Zillah, she also b Tubal-cain, an instructor 3205
4:25 she b a son, and called his name Seth: 3205
6: 4 they b children to them, the same became 3205
7:17 b **up** the ark, and it was lift up above 5375
16: 1 Now Sarai Abram's wife b him no 3205
16:15 Hagar b Abram a son: and Abram called 3205
16:15 his son's name, which Hagar b, Ishmael. 3205
16:16 years old, when Hagar b Ishmael to Abram. 3205
19:37 the firstborn b a son, and called his name 3205
19:38 she also b a son, and called his name 3205
20:17 and his maidservants; and they b children. 3205
21: 2 and b Abraham a son in his old age, 3205
21: 3 unto him, whom Sarah b to him, Isaac. 3205
22:24 she b also Tebah, and Gaham, and 3205
24:24 the son of Milcah, which she b unto Nahor. 3205
24:36 Sarah my master's wife b a son to my 3205
24:47 Nahor's son, whom Milcah b unto him: 3205
25: 2 she b him Zimran, and Jokshan, and 3205
25:12 Sarah's handmaid, b unto Abraham: 3205
25:26 Isaac was threescore years old when she b 3205
29:32 b a son, and she called his name Reuben: 3205
29:33 she conceived again, and b a son; and said, 3205
29:34 she conceived again, and b a son; and said, 3205
29:35 she conceived again, and b a son: and 3205
30: 1 when Rachel saw that she b Jacob no 3205
30: 5 And Bilhah conceived, and b Jacob a son. 3205
30: 7 conceived again, and b Jacob a second son. 3205
30:10 And Zilpah Leah's maid b Jacob a son. 3205
30:12 Zilpah Leah's maid b Jacob a second son. 3205
30:17 she conceived, and b Jacob the fifth son. 3205
30:19 conceived again, and b Jacob the sixth son. 3205
30:21 afterwards she b a daughter, and called her 3205
30:23 she conceived, and b a son; and said, 3205
31: 8 be thy wages; then all the cattle b speckled: 3205
31: 8 be thy hire; then b all the cattle ringstraked. 3205
31:39 I b the **loss** of it; of my hand didst thou 2398
34: 1 daughter of Leah, which she b unto Jacob, 3205
36: 4 Adah b to Esau Eliphaz; and 3205
36: 4 to Esau Eliphaz; and Bashemath b Reuel; 3205
36: 5 Aholibamah b Jeush, and Jaalam, and 3205
36:12 Esau's son; and she b to Eliphaz Amalek: 3205
Ge 36:14 she b to Esau Jeush, and Jaalam, and 3205
38: 3 she conceived, and b a son; and he called 3205
38: 4 she conceived again, and b a son; and 3205
38: 5 she yet again conceived, and b a son; and 3205
38: 5 and he was at Chezib, when she b him. 3205
41:50 of Poti-pherah priest of On b unto him. 3205
44:27 Ye know that my wife b me two sons: 3205
46:15 which she b unto Jacob in Padan-aram, 3205
46:18 these she b unto Jacob, even sixteen souls. 3205
46:20 of Poti-pherah priest of On b unto him. 3205
46:25 his daughter, and she b these unto Jacob: 3205
Ex 2: 2 the woman conceived, and b a son: and 3205
2:22 she b him a son, and he called his name 3205
6:20 to wife; and she b him Aaron and Moses: 3205
6:23 she b him Nadab, and Abihu, Eleazar, and 3205
6:25 of Putiel to wife; and she b him Phinehas: 3205
19: 4 how I b you on eagles' wings, and 5375
Lev 13:45 his head b, and he shall put a covering 6544
13:55 whether it be b **within** or without. 7146
Nu 13:23 and they b it between two upon a staff; 5375
26:59 whom her mother b to Levi in Egypt: 3205
26:59 she b unto Amram Aaron and Moses, and 3205
Dt 1:31 seen how that the LORD thy God b thee, 5375
31: 9 which b the ark of the covenant of 5375
31:25 which b the ark of the covenant of 5375
Jos 3:15 as they that b the ark were come unto 5375
3:15 the feet of the priests that b the ark were 5375
3:17 the priests that b the ark of the covenant of 5375
4: 9 which b the ark of the covenant stood: 5375
4:10 For the priests which b the ark stood in 5375
4:18 when the priests that b the ark of 5375
8:33 which b the ark of the covenant of 5375
Jdg 3:18 he sent away the people that b the present. 5375
8:31 she also b him a son, whose name he called 3205
11: 2 Gilead's wife b him sons; and his wife's 3205
13: 2 and his wife was barren, and b not. 3205
13:24 the woman b a son, and called his name 3205
Ru 4:12 of Pharez, whom Tamar b unto Judah, 3205
4:13 gave her conception, and she b a son. 3205
1Sa 1:20 that she b a son, and called his name 3205
2:21 and b three sons and two daughters. 3205
14: 1 said unto the young man that b his armour, 5375
14: 6 Jonathan said to the young man that b his 5375
17:41 the man that b the shield went before him. 5375
2Sa 6:13 that when they that b the ark of the LORD 5375
11:27 and she became his wife, and b him a son. 3205
12:15 the child that Uriah's wife b unto David, 3205
12:24 she b a son, and he called his name 3205
18:15 ten young men that b Joab's armour 5375
21: 8 whom she b unto Saul, Armoni and 3205
1Ki 1: 6 and his mother b him after Absalom. 3205
5:15 and ten thousand that b burdens, 5375
9:23 which b **rule** over the people that wrought 7287
10: 2 with camels that b spices, and very much 5375
11:20 the sister of Tahpenes b him Genubath his 3205
14:28 that the guard b them, and brought them 5375
2Ki 4:17 b a son at that season that Elisha had said 3205
5:23 his servants; and they b them before him. 5375
1Ch 1:32 she b Zimran, and Jokshan, and Medan, 3205
2: 4 Tamar his daughter in law b him Pharez 3205
2:17 Abigail b Amasa: and the father of Amasa 3205
2:19 took unto him Ephrath, which b him Hur. 3205
2:21 threescore years old; and she b him Segub. 3205
2:24 Abiah Hezron's wife b him Ashur 3205
2:29 and she b him Ahban, and Molid. 3205
2:35 his servant to wife; and she b him Attai. 3205
2:46 b Haran, and Moza, and Gazez: 3205
2:48 Caleb's concubine, b Sheber, and Tirhanah. 3205
2:49 She b also Shaaph the father of 3205
4: 6 Naarah b him Ahuzam, and Hepher, and 3205
4: 9 Because I b him with sorrow. 3205
4:17 she b Miriam, and Shammai, and Ishbah 2029
4:18 his wife Jehudijah b Jered the father of 3205
7:14 sons of Manasseh; Ashriel, whom she b: 3205
7:14 his concubine the Aramitess b Machir 3205
7:16 Maachah the wife of Machir b a son, and 3205
7:18 his sister Hammoleketh b Ishod, and 3205
7:23 b a son, and he called his name Beriah, 3205
12:24 The children of Judah that b shield and 5375
15:15 the children of the Levites b the ark of God 5375
15:26 when God helped the Levites that b the ark 5375
15:27 all the Levites that b the ark, and 5375
2Ch 8:10 and fifty, that b **rule** over the people. 7287
9: 1 camels that b spices, and gold in 5375
11:19 Which b him children; Jeush, and 3205
11:20 which b him Abijah, and Attai, and Ziza, 3205
14: 8 Asa had an army of men that b targets and 5375
14: 8 that b shields and drew bows, two hundred 5375
Ne 4:17 they that b burdens, with those that laded, 5375
5:15 yea, even their servants b **rule** over 7980
Pr 17:25 his father, and bitterness to her that b him. 3205
23:25 be glad, and she that b thee shall rejoice. 3205
SS 6: 9 she is the choice one of her that b her. 3205
8: 5 there she brought thee forth that b thee. 3205
Isa 8: 3 and she conceived, and b a son. 3205
22: 6 Elam b the quiver with chariots of men 5375
32:11 **make** ye b, and gird sackcloth upon your 6209
47: 2 **make** b the leg, uncover the thigh, 2834
51: 2 your father, and unto Sarah that b you: 2342
52:10 The LORD hath **made** b his holy arm in 2834
53:12 he b the sin of many, and made intercession 5375
63: 9 he b them, and carried them all the days of 5190
Jer 13:22 skirts discovered, and thy heels **made** b. 2554
16: 3 concerning their mothers that b them, and 3205
20:14 let not the day wherein my mother b me be 3205
22:26 thy mother that b thee, into another 3205
49:10 I have **made** Esau b, I have uncovered his 2834
50:12 she that b you shall be ashamed: 3205
Eze 12: 7 and I b it upon my shoulder in their sight. 5375
16: 7 is grown, whereas thou wast naked and b. 6181
16:22 when thou wast naked and b, and 6181
16:39 thy fair jewels, and leave thee naked and b. 6181
19:11 rods for the sceptres of them that b **rule**, 4910
23: 4 were mine, and they b sons and daughters. 3205
23:29 and shall leave thee naked and b: 6181
Eze 23:37 caused their sons, whom they b unto me, 3205
Hos 1: 3 which conceived, and b him a son. 3205
1: 6 she conceived again, and b a daughter. 3205
1: 8 she conceived, and b a son. 3205
Joel 1: 7 he hath made it clean b, and cast it away; 2834
Mt 8:17 took our infirmities, and b our sicknesses. 941
Mk 14:56 For many b **false witness** against him, but 5576
14:57 and b **false witness** against him, saying, 5576
Lk 4:22 And all b him **witness**, and wondered at 3140
7:14 and they that b him stood still. And he said, 941
8: 8 and sprang up, and b fruit an hundredfold. 4160
11:27 Blessed is the womb that b thee, and 941
23:29 and the wombs that never b, and the paps 1080
Jn 1:15 John b **witness** of him, and cried, saying, 3140
1:32 And John b **record**, saying, I saw the Spirit 3140
1:34 and b **record** that this is the Son of God. 3140
2: 8 the governor of the feast. And they b it. 5342
5:33 unto John, and he b **witness** unto the truth. 3140
12: 6 had the bag, and b what was put therein. 941
12:17 and raised him from the dead, b **record**. 3140
19:35 And he that saw it b **record**, and his record 3140
Ac 15: 8 which knoweth the hearts, b them **witness**, 3140
1Co 15:37 but b grain, it may chance of wheat, or 1131
1Pe 2:24 Who his own self b our sins in his own body 399
Rev 1: 2 Who b **record** of the word of God, and 3140
22: 2 which b twelve manner of fruits, and 4160

BAREFOOT (4) [BARE, FOOT]
2Sa 15:30 and had his head covered, and he went b: 3182
Isa 20: 2 And he did so, walking naked and b. 3182
20: 3 b three years for a sign and wonder upon 3182
20: 4 young and old, naked and b, 3182

BAREST (3) [BARE]
1Ki 2:26 thou b the ark of the Lord GOD before 5375
Isa 63:19 We are thine: thou never b **rule** over them; 4910
Jn 3:26 to whom thou b **witness**, behold, the same 3140

BARHUMITE (1)
2Sa 23:31 Abialbon the Arbathite, Azmaveth the B, 1273

BARIAH (1)
1Ch 3:22 Igeal, and B, and Neariah, and Shaphat, six. 1282

BAR-JESUS (1)
Ac 13: 6 a false prophet, a Jew, whose name was B: 919

BAR-JONA (1)
Mt 16:17 said unto him, Blessed art thou, Simon B: 920

BARK (1) [BARKED]
Isa 56:10 they are all dumb dogs, they cannot b; 5024

BARKED (1) [BARK]
Joel 1: 7 hath laid my vine waste, and b my fig tree: 7111

BARKOS (2)
Ezr 2:53 The children of B, the children of Sisera, 1302
Ne 7:55 The children of B, the children of Sisera, 1302

BARLEY (37)
Ex 9:31 the flax and the b was smitten: for 8184
9:31 for the b was in the ear, and the flax was 8184
Lev 27:16 a homer of b seed shall be valued at fifty 8184
Nu 5:15 the tenth part of an ephah of b meal; 8184
Dt 8: 8 b, and vines, and fig trees, and 8184
Jdg 7:13 a cake of b bread tumbled into the host of 8184
Ru 1:22 Beth-lehem in the beginning of b harvest. 8184
2:17 and it was about an ephah of b. 8184
2:23 of Boaz to glean unto the end of b harvest 8184
3: 2 he winnoweth b to night in 8184
3:15 he measured six measures of b, and laid it 8184
3:17 These six measures of b gave he me; 8184
2Sa 14:30 field is near mine, and he hath b there; 8184
17:28 and flour, and parched corn, and beans, 8184
21: 9 in the first days, in the beginning of b 8184
1Ki 4:28 B also and straw for the horses and 8184
2Ki 4:42 twenty loaves of b, and full ears of corn in 8184
7: 1 two measures of b for a shekel, in the gate 8184
7:16 two measures of b for a shekel, 8184
7:18 Two measures of b for a shekel, and 8184
1Ch 11:13 where was a parcel of ground full of b; 8184
2Ch 2:10 twenty thousand measures of b, and 8184
2:15 the wheat, and the b, the oil, and the wine, 8184
27: 5 measures of wheat, and ten thousand of b. 8184
Job 31:40 instead of wheat, and cockle instead of b. 8184
Isa 28:25 the appointed b and the rye in their place? 8184
Jer 41: 8 and of b, and of oil, and of honey. 8184
Eze 4: 9 b, and beans, and lentiles, and millet, and 8184
4:12 thou shalt eat it as b cakes, and thou shalt 8184
13:19 me among my people for handfuls of b 8184
45:13 the sixth part of an ephah of a homer of b: 8184
Hos 3: 2 for a homer of b, and a half homer of 8184
3: 2 a homer of barley, and a half homer of b: 8184
Joel 1:11 ye vinedressers, for the wheat and for the b; 8184
Jn 6: 9 which hath five b loaves, and two small 2916
6:13 with the fragments of the five b loaves, 2916
Rev 6: 6 and three measures of b for a penny; 2915

BARN (4) [BARNFLOOR, BARNS]
Job 39:12 home thy seed, and gather it into thy b? 1637
Hag 2:19 Is the seed yet in the b? yea, as yet the vine, 4035
Mt 13:30 burn them: but gather the wheat into my b. 596
Lk 12:24 which neither have storehouse nor b; and 596

BARNABAS (29) [JOSES]
Ac 4:36 who by the apostles was surnamed B, 921
9:27 But B took him, and brought him to 921
11:22 and they sent forth B, that he should go as 921
11:25 Then departed B to Tarsus, for to seek Saul: 921
11:30 sent it to the elders by the hands of B and 921
12:25 And B and Saul returned from Jerusalem, 921
13: 1 as B, and Simeon that was called Niger, and 921

Ac 13: 2 Separate me **B** and Saul for the work *921*
13: 7 who called for **B** and Saul, and desired to *921*
13:43 religious proselytes followed Paul and **B**: *921*
13:46 Then Paul and **B** waxed bold, and said, *921*
13:50 and raised persecution against Paul and **B**, *921*
14:12 And they called **B**, Jupiter; and Paul, *921*
14:14 *Which* when the apostles, **B** and Paul, *921*
14:20 the next day he departed with **B** to Derbe. *921*
15: 2 and **B** had no small dissension and *921*
15: 2 they determined that Paul and **B**, and *921*
15:12 and gave audience to **B** and Paul, *921*
15:22 own company to Antioch with Paul and **B**; *921*
15:25 chosen men unto you with our beloved **B** *921*
15:35 Paul also and **B** continued in Antioch, *921*
15:36 And some days after Paul said unto **B**, Let us *921*
15:37 And **B** determined to take with *them* John, *921*
15:39 and *so* **B** took Mark, and sailed unto Cyprus; *921*
1Co 9: 6 Or I only and **B**, have not we power to *921*
Gal 2: 1 after I went up again to Jerusalem with **B**, *921*
2: 9 to me and **B** the right hands of fellowship; *921*
2:13 insomuch that **B** also was carried away with *921*
Col 4:10 saluteth you, and Marcus, sister's son to **B**, *921*

BARNFLOOR (1) [BARN, FLOOR]
2Ki 6:27 out of the **b**, or out of the winepress? 1637

BARNS (4) [BARN]
Pr 3:10 So shall thy **b** be filled *with* plenty, and 618
Joel 1:17 are laid desolate, the **b** are broken down; 4460
Mt 6:26 neither do they reap, nor gather into **b**; *596*
Lk 12:18 I will pull down my **b**, and build greater; and *596*

BARREL (3) [BARRELS]
1Ki 17:12 a handful of meal in a **b**, and a little oil in a 3537
17:14 The **b** of meal shall not waste, neither shall 3537
17:16 *And* the **b** of meal wasted not, neither did 3537

BARRELS (1) [BARREL]
1Ki 18:33 Fill four **b** *with* water, and pour *it* on 3537

BARREN (23) [BARRENNESS]
Ge 11:30 But Sarai was **b**; she had no child. 6135
25:21 LORD for his wife, because she *was* **b**: 6135
29:31 he opened her womb: but Rachel *was* **b**. 6135
Ex 23:26 cast their young, nor be **b**, in thy land: 6135
Dt 7:14 shall not be male or **female b** among you, 6135
Jdg 13: 2 and his wife *was* **b**, and bare not. 6135
13: 3 Behold now, thou *art* **b**, and bearest not: 6135
1Sa 2: 5 so that the **b** hath born seven; and she that 6135
2Ki 2:19 but the water *is* naught, and the ground **b**. 7921
2:21 be from thence any more death or **b** *land.* 7921
Job 24:21 He evil entreateth the **b** *that* beareth not: 6135
39: 6 and the **b** *land* his dwellings. 4420
Ps 113: 9 He maketh the **b** *woman* to keep house, 6135
Pr 30:16 The grave; and the **b** womb; the earth *that* 6115
SS 4: 2 beareth twins, and none *is* **b** among them. 7909
6: 6 and *there is* not one **b** among them. 7909
Isa 54: 1 Sing, O **b**, thou *that* didst not bear; 6135
Joel 2:20 will drive him into a land **b** and desolate, 6723
Lk 1: 7 because that Elisabeth was **b**, and they both *4723*
1:36 the sixth month with her, who was called **b**. *4723*
23:29 Blessed *are* the **b**, and the wombs that *4723*
Gal 4:27 is written, Rejoice, *thou* **b** that bearest not; *4723*
2Pe 1: 8 they make *you that ye shall* neither *be* **b** nor *692*

BARRENNESS (1) [BARREN]
Ps 107:34 A fruitful land into **b**, for the wickedness of 4420

BARS (38) [BAR]
Ex 26:26 thou shalt make **b** *of* shittim wood; five for 1280
26:27 five **b** for the boards of the other side of 1280
26:27 five **b** for the boards of the side of 1280
26:29 their rings *of* gold *for* places for the **b**: 1280
26:29 and thou shalt overlay the **b** with gold. 1280
35:11 his **b**, his pillars, and his sockets, 1280
36:31 he made **b** of shittim wood; five for 1280
36:32 five **b** for the boards of the other side of 1280
36:32 five **b** for the boards of the tabernacle for 1280
36:34 their rings *of* gold *to be* places for the **b**, 1280
36:34 for the bars, and overlaid the **b** with gold. 1280
39:33 his **b**, and his pillars, and his sockets, 1280
40:18 put in the **b** thereof, and reared up his 1280
Nu 3:36 the **b** thereof, and the pillars thereof, and 1280
4:31 the **b** thereof, and the pillars thereof, and 1280
Dt 3: 5 *were* fenced *with* high walls, gates, and **b**; 1280
1Sa 23: 7 entering into a town that hath gates and **b**. 1280
1Ki 4:13 great cities *with* walls and brasen **b**: 1280
2Ch 8: 5 fenced cities, *with* walls, gates, and **b**; 1280
14: 7 about *them* walls, and towers, gates, and **b**, 1280
Ne 3: 3 the locks thereof, and the **b** thereof. 1280
3: 6 and the locks thereof, and the **b** thereof. 1280
3:13 the **b** thereof, and a thousand cubits on 1280
3:14 the locks thereof, and the **b** thereof. 1280
3:15 the **b** thereof, and the wall of the pool of 1280
Job 17:16 They shall go down *to* the **b** of the pit, 905
38:10 it my decreed *place,* and set **b** and doors, 1280
40:18 pieces of brass; his bones *are* like **b** of iron. 4300
Ps 107:16 of brass, and cut the **b** of iron in sunder. 1280
147:13 For he hath strengthened the **b** of thy gates; 1280
Pr 18:19 *their* contentions *are* like the **b** of a castle. 1280
Isa 45: 2 of brass, and cut in sunder the **b** of iron: 1280
Jer 49:31 which have neither gates nor **b**, 1280
51:30 burnt her dwelling places; her **b** are broken. 1280
La 2: 9 he hath destroyed and broken her **b**: 1280
Eze 38:11 and having neither **b** nor gates, 1280
Jnh 2: 6 the earth *with* her **b** *was* about me for ever: 1280
Na 3:13 thine enemies: the fire shall devour thy **b**. 1280

BARSABAS (2)
Ac 1:23 And they appointed two, Joseph called **B**, *923*
15:22 *namely,* Judas surnamed **B**, and Silas, *923*

BARSABBAS See BARSABAS

BARTHOLOMEW (4)
Mt 10: 3 Philip, and **B**; Thomas, and Matthew *918*
Mk 3:18 and **B**, and Matthew, and Thomas, and *918*
Lk 6:14 his brother, James and John, Philip and **B**, *918*
Ac 1:13 Philip, and Thomas, **B**, and Matthew, *918*

BARTIMEUS (1)
Mk 10:46 of people, blind **B**, the son of Timeus, *924*

BARUCH (26)
Ne 3:20 After him **B** the son of Zabbai earnestly 1263
10: 6 Daniel, Ginnethon, **B**, 1263
11: 5 Maaseiah the son of **B**, the son of 1263
Jer 32:12 I gave the evidence of the purchase unto **B** 1263
32:13 And I charged **B** before them, saying, 1263
32:16 of the purchase unto **B** the son of Neriah, 1263
36: 4 Jeremiah called **B** the son of Neriah: and 1263
36: 4 **B** wrote from the mouth of Jeremiah all 1263
36: 5 Jeremiah commanded **B**, saying, I *am* shut 1263
36: 8 **B** the son of Neriah did according to all that 1263
36:10 read **B** in the book the words of Jeremiah *in* 1263
36:13 when **B** read the book in the ears of 1263
36:14 the son of Cushi, unto **B**, saying, 1263
36:14 So **B** the son of Neriah took the roll in his 1263
36:15 read it in our ears. So **B** read *it* in their ears. 1263
36:16 afraid both one and other, and said unto **B**, 1263
36:17 they asked **B**, saying, Tell us now, 1263
36:18 **B** answered them, He pronounced all these 1263
36:19 Then said the princes unto **B**, Go, hide thee, 1263
36:26 to take **B** the scribe and Jeremiah 1263
36:27 the words which **B** wrote at the mouth of 1263
36:32 gave it to **B** the scribe, the son of Neriah; 1263
43: 3 **B** the son of Neriah setteth thee on against 1263
43: 6 the prophet, and **B** the son of Neriah. 1263
45: 1 the prophet spake unto **B** the son of Neriah, 1263
45: 2 the God of Israel, unto thee, O **B**; 1263

BARZILLAI (12)
2Sa 17:27 and **B** the Gileadite of Rogelim, 1271
19:31 **B** the Gileadite came down from Rogelim, 1271
19:32 Now **B** was a very aged man, 1271
19:33 the king said unto **B**, Come thou over with 1271
19:34 **B** said unto the king, How long have I to 1271
19:39 the king kissed **B**, and blessed him; 1271
21: 8 up for Adriel the son of **B** the Meholathite: 1271
1Ki 2: 7 shew kindness unto the sons of **B** 1271
Ezr 2:61 the children of Koz, the children of **B**; 1271
2:61 which took a wife of the daughters of **B** 1271
Ne 7:63 the children of Koz, the children of **B**, 1271
7:63 which took *one* of the daughters of **B** 1271

BASE (18) [BASER, BASES, BASEST]
2Sa 6:22 than thus, and will be **b** in mine own sight: 8217
1Ki 7:27 four cubits *was* the length of one **b**, and 4350
7:29 upon the ledges *there was* a **b** above: and 3653
7:30 every **b** had four brasen wheels, and 4350
7:31 thereof *was* round *after* the work of the **b**, 3653
7:32 of the wheels *were* joined to the **b**: 4350
7:34 undersetters to the four corners of one **b**: 4350
7:34 the undersetters *were of* the *very* **b** itself. 4350
7:35 in the top of the **b** *was there* a round 4350
7:35 on the top of the **b** the ledges thereof and 4350
Job 30: 8 of fools, yea, children of **b men**: 1097+8034
Isa 3: 5 and the **b** against the honourable. 7034
Eze 17:14 That the kingdom might be **b**, that *it* might 8217
29:14 and they shall be there a **b** kingdom. 8217
Zec 5:11 and set there upon her own **b**. 4350
Mal 2: 9 and **b** before all the people, 8217
1Co 1:28 And **b** *things* of the world, and *things* which *36*
2Co 10: 1 who in presence *am* **b** among you, but *5011*

BASEMATH See BASHEMATH; BASMATH

BASER (1) [BASE]
Ac 17: 5 unto *them* certain lewd fellows of the **b sort**, *60*

BASES (16) [BASE]
1Ki 7:27 he made ten **b** of brass; four cubits *was* 4350
7:28 the work of the **b** *was on* this *manner:* they 4350
7:37 After this *manner* he made the ten **b**: all of 4350
7:38 *and* upon every one of the ten **b** one laver. 4350
7:39 he put five **b** on the right side of the house, 4350
7:43 And the ten **b**, and ten lavers on the bases; 4350
7:43 And the ten bases, and ten lavers on the **b**; 4350
2Ki 16:17 king Ahaz cut off the borders of the **b**, and 4350
25:13 the **b**, and the brasen sea that *was* in 4350
25:16 the **b** which Solomon had made for 4350
2Ch 4:14 He made also **b** and lavers made he upon 4350
4:14 also bases and lavers made he upon the **b**; 4350
Ezr 3: 3 they set the altar upon his **b**; for fear *was* 4350
Jer 27:19 concerning the **b**, and concerning 4350
52:17 the **b**, and the brasen sea that *was* in 4350
52:20 twelve brasen bulls that *were* under the **b**, 4350

BASEST (2) [BASE]
Eze 29:15 It shall be the **b** of the kingdoms; 8217
Da 4:17 he will, and setteth up over it the **b** of men. 8215

BASHAN (59) [BASHAN-HAVOTH-JAIR]
Nu 21:33 they turned and went up *by* the way of **B**: 1316
21:33 Og the king of **B** went out against them, 1316
32:33 the kingdom of Og king of **B**, the land, 1316
Dt 1: 4 dwelt in Heshbon, and Og the king of **B**, 1316
3: 1 we turned, and went up the way to **B**: and 1316
3: 1 Og the king of **B** came out against us, he 1316
3: 3 Og also, the king of **B**, and all his people: 1316
3: 4 region of Argob, the kingdom of Og in **B**. 1316
3:10 all Gilead, and all **B**, unto Salchah and 1316
3:10 and Edrei, cities of the kingdom of Og in **B**. 1316
3:11 For only Og king of **B** remained of 1316
3:13 the rest of Gilead, and all **B**, *being* 1316
3:13 all the region of Argob, with all **B**, which 1316
4:43 and Golan in **B**, of the Manassites. 1316
4:47 the land of Og king of **B**, two kings of 1316
29: 7 the king of Heshbon, and Og the king of **B**, 1316
32:14 and rams of the breed of **B**, and goats, 1316
33:22 Dan *is* a lion's whelp: he shall leap from **B**. 1316
Jos 9:10 to Og king of **B**, which *was* at Ashtaroth. 1316
12: 4 the coast of Og king of **B**, *which was* of 1316
12: 5 mount Hermon, and in Salcah, and in all **B**, 1316
13:11 all mount Hermon, and all **B** unto Salcah; 1316
13:12 All the kingdom of Og in **B**, which reigned 1316
13:30 their coast was from Mahanaim, all **B**, 1316
13:30 all the kingdom of Og king of **B**, and all 1316
13:30 of Jair, which *are* in **B**, threescore cities: 1316
13:31 and Edrei, cities of the kingdom of Og in **B**, 1316
17: 1 man of war, therefore he had Gilead and **B**. 1316
17: 5 beside the land of Gilead and **B**, 1316
20: 8 Golan in **B** out of the tribe of Manasseh. 1316
21: 6 out of the half tribe of Manasseh in **B**, 1316
21:27 *they gave* Golan in **B** with her suburbs, 1316
22: 7 Moses had given *possession* in **B**: 1316
1Ki 4:13 which *is* in **B**, threescore great cities *with* 1316
4:19 king of the Amorites, and of Og king of **B**; 1316
2Ki 10:33 *is* by the river Arnon, even Gilead and **B**. 1316
1Ch 5:11 against them, in the land of **B** unto Salchah: 1316
5:12 the next, and Jaanai, and Shaphat in **B**. 1316
5:16 they dwelt in Gilead in **B**, and in her towns, 1316
5:23 they increased from **B** unto Baal-hermon 1316
6:62 out of the tribe of Manasseh in **B**, 1316
6:71 Golan in **B** with her suburbs, and Ashtaroth 1316
Ne 9:22 of Heshbon, and the land of Og king of **B**. 1316
Ps 22:12 strong *bulls* of **B** have beset me round. 1316
68:15 The hill of God *is as* the hill of **B**; a high 1316
68:15 hill of Bashan; a high hill *as* the hill of **B**. 1316
68:22 The Lord said, I will bring again from **B**, 1316
135:11 Og king of **B**, and all the kingdoms of 1316
136:20 Og the king of **B**: for his mercy *endureth* 1316
Isa 2:13 and lifted up, and upon all the oaks of **B**, 1316
33: 9 and **B** and Carmel shake off *their fruits.* 1316
Jer 22:20 lift up thy voice in **B**, and cry from 1316
50:19 he shall feed on Carmel and **B**, and his soul 1316
Eze 27: 6 *Of* the oaks of **B** have they made thine oars; 1316
39:18 of bullocks, all of them fatlings of **B**. 1316
Am 4: 1 Hear this word, ye kine of **B**, that *are* in 1316
Mic 7:14 let them feed *in* **B** and Gilead, as *in* 1316
Na 1: 4 **B** languisheth, and Carmel, and the flower 1316
Zec 11: 2 howl, O ye oaks of **B**; for the forest of 1316

BASHAN-HAVOTH-JAIR (1) [BASHAN, HAVOTH-JAIR, JAIR]
Dt 3:14 after his own name, **B**, unto this day. 1316+2334

BASHEMATH (6)
Ge 26:34 and **B** the daughter of Elon the Hittite: 1315
36: 3 **B** Ishmael's daughter, sister of Nebajoth. 1315
36: 4 bare to Esau Eliphaz; and **B** bare Reuel; 1315
36:10 Reuel the son of **B** the wife of Esau. 1315
36:13 these were the sons of **B** Esau's wife. 1315
36:17 these *are* the sons of **B** Esau's wife. 1315

BASIC PRINCIPLES See RUDIMENTS

BASIN; BASINS See BASON; BASONS; LAVER

BASKET (23) [BASKETS]
Ge 40:17 in the uppermost **b** *there was* of all *manner* 5536
40:17 the birds did eat them out of the **b** upon my 5536
Ex 29: 3 thou shalt put them into one **b**, and 5536
29: 3 bring them in the **b**, with the bullock and 5536
29:23 one wafer out of the **b** of the unleavened 5536
29:32 of the ram, and the bread that *is* in the **b**, 5536
Lev 8: 2 and two rams, and a **b** of unleavened bread; 5536
8:26 out of the **b** of unleavened bread, that *was* 5536
8:31 there eat it with the bread that *is* in the **b** of 5536
Nu 6:15 a **b** of unleavened bread, cakes *of* fine flour 5536
6:17 with the **b** of unleavened bread: 5536
6:19 one unleavened cake out of the **b**, and 5536
Dt 26: 2 shalt put *it* in a **b**, and shalt go unto 2935
26: 4 the priest shall take the **b** out of thine hand, 2935
28: 5 Blessed *shall be* thy **b** and thy store. 2935
28:17 Cursed *shall be* thy **b** and thy store. 2935
Jdg 6:19 the flesh he put in a **b**, and he put the broth 5536
Jer 24: 2 One **b** *had* very good figs, *even* like the figs 1731
24: 2 the other **b** *had* very naughty figs, 1731
Am 8: 1 unto me: and behold, a **b** of summer fruit. 3619
8: 2 I said, A **b** of summer fruit. Then said 3619
Ac 9:25 and let *him* down by the wall in a **b**. *4711*
2Co 11:33 And through a window in a **b** was I let *4553*

BASKETS (15) [BASKET]
Ge 40:16 behold, *I had* three white **b** on my head: 5536
40:18 The three **b** *are* three days: 5536
2Ki 10: 7 put their heads in **b**, and sent him *them* to 1731
Jer 6: 9 thine hand as a grapegatherer into the **b**. 5552
24: 1 two **b** of figs *were* set before the temple of 1736
Mt 14:20 the fragments that remained twelve **b** full. *2894*
15:37 the broken *meat* that was left seven **b** full. *4711*
16: 9 five thousand, and how many **b** ye took up? *2894*
16:10 and how many **b** ye took up? *4711*
Mk 6:43 And they took up twelve **b** full of *2894*
8: 8 up of the broken *meat* that was left seven **b**. *4711*
8:19 how many **b** full of fragments took ye up? *2894*
8:20 how many **b** full of fragments took ye up? *4711*
Lk 9:17 fragments that remained to them twelve **b**. *2894*
Jn 6:13 filled twelve **b** with the fragments of *2894*

BASMATH (1)
1Ki 4:15 he also took **B** the daughter of Solomon to 1315

BASON (5) [BASONS]
Ex 12:22 dip *it* in the blood that *is* in the **b**, and 5592
12:22 side posts with the blood that *is* in the **b**; 5592
1Ch 28:17 *gold* by weight for **every b**; 3713+3713+2050.1
28:17 weight for **every b** of silver: 3713+3713+2050.1
Jn 13: 5 he poureth water into a **b**, and began to *3537*

B

BASONS (18) [BASON]
Ex 24: 6 Moses took half of the blood, and put *it* in **b**; 101
27: 3 his **b**, and his fleshhooks, and his firepans: 4219
38: 3 the **b**, *and* the fleshhooks, and the firepans: 4219
Nu 4:14 the fleshhooks, and the shovels, and the **b**, 4219
2Sa 17:28 **b**, and earthen vessels, and wheat, and 5592
1Ki 7:40 made the lavers, and the shovels, and the **b**. 4219
7:45 the pots, and the shovels, and the **b**: and 4219
7:50 the **b**, and the spoons, and the censers *of* 4219
2Ki 12:13 snuffers, **b**, trumpets, any vessels of gold, 4219
1Ch 28:17 for the golden **b** *he gave gold* by weight for 3713
2Ch 4: 8 the left. And he made an hundred **b** of gold. 4219
4:11 made the pots, and the shovels, and the **b**. 4219
4:22 the **b**, and the spoons, and the censers, 4219
Ezr 1:10 Thirty **b** of gold, silver basons of a second 3713
1:10 silver **b** of a second sort four hundred and 3713
8:27 Also twenty **b** of gold, of a thousand 3713
Ne 7:70 fifty **b**, five hundred and thirty priests' 4219
Jer 52:19 the **b**, and the firepans, and the bowls, and 5592

BASTARD (2) [BASTARDS]
Dt 23: 2 A **b** shall not enter into the congregation of 4464
Zec 9: 6 a **b** shall dwell in Ashdod, and I will cut off 4464

BASTARDS (1) [BASTARD]
Heb 12: 8 are partakers, then are ye **b**, and not sons. *3541*

BAT (2) [BATS]
Lev 11:19 after her kind, and the lapwing, and the **b**. 5847
Dt 14:18 after her kind, and the lapwing, and the **b**. 5847

BATH (6) [BATHS]
Isa 5:10 ten acres of vineyard shall yield one **b**, and 1324
Eze 45:10 just balances, and a just ephah, and a just **b**. 1324
45:11 and the **b** shall be of one measure, 1324
45:11 that the **b** may contain the tenth part of a 1324
45:14 the ordinance of oil, the **b** *of* oil, 1324
45:14 *ye shall offer* the tenth part of a **b** out of 1324

BATHE (18) [BATHED]
Lev 15: 5 **b** *himself* in water, and be unclean until 7364
15: 6 **b** *himself* in water, and be unclean until 7364
15: 7 **b** *himself* in water, and be unclean until 7364
15: 8 **b** *himself* in water, and be unclean until 7364
15:10 **b** *himself* in water, and be unclean until 7364
15:11 **b** *himself* in water, and be unclean until 7364
15:13 **b** his flesh in running water, and shall be 7364
15:18 they shall *both* **b** *themselves* in water, and 7364
15:21 **b** *himself* in water, and be unclean until 7364
15:22 **b** *himself* in water, and be unclean until 7364
15:27 **b** *himself* in water, and be unclean until 7364
16:26 **b** his flesh in water, and afterward come 7364
16:28 **b** his flesh in water, and afterward he shall 7364
17:15 **b** *himself* in water, and be unclean until 7364
17:16 if he wash *them* not, nor **b** his flesh; then 7364
Nu 19: 7 he shall **b** his flesh in water, and 7364
19: 8 **b** his flesh in water, and shall be unclean 7364
19:19 **b** *himself* in water, and shall be clean at 7364

BATHED (1) [BATHE]
Isa 34: 5 For my sword shall be **b** in heaven: behold, 7301

BATH-RABBIM (1)
SS 7: 4 the *fish*pools in Heshbon, by the gate of **B**: 1337

BATHS (9) [BATH]
1Ki 7:26 of lilies: it contained two thousand **b**. 1324
7:38 one laver contained forty **b**: *and* every laver 1324
2Ch 2:10 twenty thousand **b** of wine, and 1324
2:10 of wine, and twenty thousand **b** of oil. 1324
4: 5 *and* it received and held three thousand **b**. 1324
Ezr 7:22 to an hundred **b** *of* wine, and to an hundred 1325
7:22 to an hundred **b** *of* oil, and salt without 1325
Eze 45:14 out of the cor, *which is* a homer of ten **b**; 1324
45:14 a homer of ten baths; for ten **b** *are* a homer: 1324

BATH-SHEBA (11)
2Sa 11: 3 *one* said, *Is* not this **B**, the daughter of 1339
12:24 David comforted **B** his wife, and went in 1339
1Ki 1:11 Wherefore Nathan spake unto **B** the mother 1339
1:15 **B** went in unto the king into the chamber: 1339
1:16 **B** bowed, and did obeisance unto the king. 1339
1:28 king David answered and said, Call me **B**. 1339
1:31 **B** bowed *with her* face *to* the earth, and 1339
2:13 Adonijah the son of Haggith came to **B** 1339
2:18 **B** said, Well; I will speak for thee unto 1339
2:19 **B** therefore went unto king Solomon, 1339
Ps 51: T came unto him, after he had gone in to **B**. 1339

BATH-SHUA (1)
1Ch 3: 5 four, of **B** the daughter of Ammiel: 1340

BATS (1) [BAT]
Isa 2:20 to worship, to the moles and to the **b**; 5847

BATTERED (1) [BATTERING]
2Sa 20:15 all the people that *were* with Joab **b** 7843

BATTERING (2) [BATTERED]
Eze 4: 2 and set **b** rams against it round about. NIH
21:22 to appoint **b** rams against the gates, to cast a NIH

BATTLE (170) [BATTLEMENT, BATTLEMENTS, BATTLES]
Ge 14: 8 they joined **b** with them in the vale of 4421
Nu 21:33 he, and all his people, to the **b** at Edrei. 4421
31:14 which came from the **b**. 4421+6635
31:21 unto the men of war which went to the **b**, 4421
31:27 who went out to **b**, and between all 6635
31:28 of the men of war which went out to **b**: 6635
32:27 before the LORD to **b**, as my lord saith. 4421
32:29 every man armed to **b**, before the LORD, 4421
Dt 2: 9 neither contend with them *in* **b**: 4421
2:24 to possess *it*, and contend with him *in* **b**. 4421
3: 1 he and all his people, to **b** *at* Edrei. 4421
20: 1 When thou goest out to **b** against thine 4421
20: 2 shall be, when ye are come nigh unto the **b**, 4421
20: 3 you approach *this* day unto **b** against your 4421
20: 5 lest he die in the **b**, and another man 4421
20: 6 lest he die in the **b**, and another man eat of 4421
20: 7 lest he die in the **b**, and another man take 4421
29: 7 came out against us unto **b**, and we smote 4421
Jos 4:13 war passed over before the LORD unto **b**, 4421
8:14 men of the city went out against Israel to **b**, 4421
11:19 of Gibeon: all *other* they took in **b**. 4421
11:20 that *they* should come against Israel *in* **b**, 4421
22:33 did not intend to go up against them in **b**, 6635
Jdg 8:13 Gideon the son of Joash returned from **b** 4421
20:14 to go out to **b** against the children of Israel. 4421
20:18 Which of us shall go up first to the **b** 4421
20:20 the men of Israel went out to **b** against 4421
20:22 set *their* **b** again in array in the place where 4421
20:23 Shall I go *up* again to **b** against the children 4421
20:28 Shall I yet again go out to **b** against 4421
20:34 men out of all Israel, and the **b** was sore: 4421
20:39 And when the men of Israel retired in the **b**, 4421
20:39 are smitten down before us, as *in* the first **b**. 4421
20:42 the **b** overtook them; and them which *came* 4421
1Sa 4: 1 Israel went out against the Philistines to **b**, 4421
4: 2 when they joined **b**, Israel was smitten 4421
7:10 the Philistines drew near to **b** against Israel: 4421
13:22 So it came to pass in the day of **b**, that there 4421
14:20 and they came to the **b**: 4421
14:22 they also followed hard after them in the **b**. 4421
14:23 and the **b** passed over *unto* Beth-aven. 4421
17: 1 gathered together their armies to **b**, 4421
17: 2 set the **b** in array against the Philistines. 4421
17: 8 Why are ye come out to set *your* **b** in 4421
17:13 of Jesse went *and* followed Saul to the **b**: 4421
17:13 that went to the **b** *were* Eliab the firstborn, 4421
17:20 forth to the fight, and shouted for the **b**. 4421
17:21 and the Philistines had put *the* **b** in array, NIH
17:28 art come down that *thou* mightest see the **b**. 4421
17:47 for the **b** *is* the LORD'S, and he will give 4421
26:10 or he shall descend into **b**, and perish. 4421
28: 1 that thou shalt go out with me to **b**, thou 4264
29: 4 and let him not go down with us to **b**, 4421
29: 4 lest in the **b** he be an adversary to us: 4421
29: 9 He shall not go up with us to the **b**. 4421
30:24 as his part *is* that goeth down to the **b**, so 4421
31: 3 the **b** went sore against Saul, and 4421
2Sa 1: 4 That the people are fled from the **b**, and 4421
1:25 are the mighty fallen in the midst of the **b**! 4421
2:17 there was a very sore **b** that day; and 4421
3:30 their brother Asahel at Gibeon in the **b**. 4421
10: 8 put the **b** in array *at* the entering in of 4421
10: 9 When Joab saw that the front of the **b** was 4421
10:13 with him, unto the **b** against the Syrians: 4421
11: 1 at the time when kings go forth *to* **b**, that NIH
11:15 ye Uriah in the forefront of the hottest **b**, 4421
11:25 make thy **b** *more* strong against the city, 4421
17:11 and *that* thou go to **b** in thine own person. 7128
18: 6 and the **b** was in the wood of Ephraim; 4421
18: 8 For the **b** was there scattered over the face 4421
19: 3 ashamed steal away when they flee in **b**. 4421
19:10 whom we anointed over us, is dead in **b**. 4421
21:17 Thou shalt go no more out with us to **b**, 4421
21:18 that there was again a **b** with the Philistines 4421
21:19 there was again a **b** in Gob with 4421
21:20 there was yet a **b** in Gath, where was a man 4421
22:40 For thou hast girded me with strength to **b**: 4421
23: 9 *that* were there gathered together to **b**, 4421
1Ki 8:44 If thy people go out to **b** against their 4421
20:14 he said, Who shall order the **b**? And he 4421
20:29 that in the seventh day the **b** was joined: 4421
20:39 servant went out into the midst of the **b**; 4421
22: 4 Wilt thou go with me to **b** *to* 4421
22: 6 Shall I go against Ramoth-gilead to **b**, or 4421
22:15 shall we go against Ramoth-gilead to **b**, or 4421
22:30 I will disguise myself, and enter into the **b**; 4421
22:30 disguised himself, and went into the **b**. 4421
22:35 the **b** increased that day: and the king was 4421
2Ki 3: 7 wilt thou go with me against Moab to **b**? 4421
3:26 when the king of Moab saw that the **b** was 4421
1Ch 5:20 for they cried to God in the **b**, and he was 4421
7:11 *soldiers, fit* to go out *for* war and **b**. 4421
7:40 *and* to **b** *was* twenty and six thousand men. 4421
10: 3 the **b** went sore against Saul, and 4421
11:13 the Philistines were gathered together to **b**, 4421
12: 8 *and* men of war *fit* for the **b**, that could 4421
12:19 came with the Philistines against Saul to **b**: 4421
12:33 Of Zebulun, such as went forth to **b**, 6635
12:36 such as went forth to **b**, expert in war, 6635
12:37 all *manner of* instruments of war for the **b**, 4421
14:15 *that* then thou shalt go out to **b**: 4421
19: 7 together from their cities, and came to **b**. 4421
19: 9 put the **b** in array *before* the gate of 4421
19:10 Now when Joab saw that the **b** was set 4421
19:14 drew nigh before the Syrians unto the **b**; 4421
19:17 and set *the* **b** in array against them. NIH
19:17 So when David had put the **b** in array 4421
20: 1 at the time that kings go out *to* **b**, Joab led NIH
2Ch 13: 3 Abijah set the **b** in array with an army of 4421
13: 3 Jeroboam also set the **b** in array against 4421
13:14 behold, the **b** *was* before and behind: 4421
14:10 they set the **b** in array in the valley of 4421
18: 5 Shall we go to Ramoth-gilead to **b**, or 4421
18:14 shall we go to Ramoth-gilead to **b**, or 4421
18:29 I will disguise myself, and will go to the **b**; 4421
18:29 disguised himself; and they went to the **b**. 4421
18:34 the **b** increased that day: howbeit the king 4421
20: 1 came against Jehoshaphat to **b**. 4421
20:15 for the **b** *is* not yours, but God's. 4421
20:17 Ye shall not need to fight in this *b*: set NIH
25: 8 if thou *wilt* go, do *it*, be strong for the **b**: 4421
25:13 that *they* should not go with him to **b**, fell 4421
Job 15:24 against him, as a king ready to the **b**. 3593
38:23 of trouble, against the day of **b** and war? 7128
39:25 he smelleth the **b** afar off, the thunder of 4421
41: 8 upon him, remember the **b**, do no more. 4421
Ps 18:39 hast girded me *with* strength unto the **b**: 4421
24: 8 and mighty, the LORD mighty *in* **b**. 4421
55:18 in peace from the **b** *that was* against me: 7128
76: 3 the shield, and the sword, and the **b**. 4421
78: 9 carrying bows, turned *back* in the day of **b**. 7128
89:43 and hast not made him to stand in the **b**. 4421
140: 7 thou hast covered my head in the day of **b**. 5402
Pr 21:31 The horse *is* prepared against the day of **b**: 4421
Ecc 9:11 nor the **b** to the strong, neither yet bread to 4421
Isa 9: 5 For every **b** of the warrior *is* with confused 5430
13: 4 of hosts mustereth the host of the **b**. 4421
22: 2 *are* not slain with the sword, nor dead in **b**. 4421
27: 4 set the briers *and* thorns against me in **b**? 4421
28: 6 for strength to them that turn the **b** to 4421
42:25 the fury of his anger, and the strength of **b**: 4421
Jer 8: 6 his course, as the horse rusheth into the **b**. 4421
18:21 their young men *be* slain by the sword in **b**. 4421
46: 3 the buckler and shield, and draw near to **b**. 4421
49:14 and come against her, and rise up to the **b**. 4421
50:22 A sound of **b** *is* in the land, and of great 4421
50:42 in array, like a man to the **b**, against thee, 4421
51:20 Thou *art* my **b axe** *and* weapons of war: 4661
Eze 7:14 to make all ready; but none goeth to the **b**: 4421
13: 5 to stand in the **b** in the day of the LORD. 4421
Da 11:20 be destroyed, neither in anger, nor in **b**. 4421
11:25 the king of the south shall be stirred up to **b** 4421
Hos 1: 7 nor by sword, nor by **b**, by horses, nor by 4421
2:18 and the sword and the **b** out of the earth, 4421
10: 9 the **b** in Gibeah against the children of 4421
10:14 Shalman spoiled Beth-arbel in the day of **b**: 4421
Joel 2: 5 as a strong people set in **b** array. 4421
Am 1:14 with shouting in the day of **b**, 4421
Ob 1: 1 Arise ye, and let us rise up against her in **b**. 4421
Zec 9:10 and the **b** bow shall be cut off: 4421
10: 3 made them as his goodly horse in the **b**. 4421
10: 4 out of him the nail, out of him the **b** bow, 4421
10: 5 *enemies* in the mire of the streets in the **b**: 4421
14: 2 gather all nations against Jerusalem to **b**; 4421
14: 3 as when he fought in the day of **b**. 7128
1Co 14: 8 who shall prepare himself to the **b**? *4171*
Rev 9: 7 *were* like unto horses prepared unto **b**; *4171*
9: 9 of chariots of many horses running to **b**. *4171*
16:14 to gather them to the **b** of that great day of *4171*
20: 8 and Magog, to gather them together to **b**: *4171*

BATTLEMENT (1) [BATTLE]
Dt 22: 8 then thou shalt make a **b** for thy roof, 4624

BATTLEMENTS (1) [BATTLE]
Jer 5:10 take away her **b**; for they *are* not 5189

BATTLES (6) [BATTLE]
1Sa 8:20 and go out before us, and fight our **b**. 4421
18:17 valiant for me, and fight the LORD'S **b**. 4421
25:28 my lord fighteth the **b** of the LORD, 4421
1Ch 26:27 Out of the spoils won in **b** did they dedicate 4421
2Ch 32: 8 our God to help us, and to fight our **b**. 4421
Isa 30:32 and in **b** of shaking will he fight with it. 4421

BAVAI (1) [BINNUI]
Ne 3:18 their brethren, **B** the son of Henadad, 942

BAY (6)
Jos 15: 2 salt sea, from the **b** that looketh southward: 3956
15: 5 **b** of the sea at the uttermost part of Jordan: 3956
18:19 **b** of the salt sea at the south end of Jordan: 3956
Ps 37:35 and spreading himself like a green **b tree**. 249
Zec 6: 3 in the fourth chariot grisled *and* **b** horses. 554
6: 7 the **b** went forth, and sought to go that *they* 554

BAZLITH (1) [BAZLUTH]
Ne 7:54 The children of **B**, the children of Mehida, 1213

BAZLUTH (1) [BAZLITH]
Ezr 2:52 The children of **B**, the children of Mehida, 1213

BDELLIUM (2)
Ge 2:12 land *is* good: there *is* **b** and the onyx stone. 916
Nu 11: 7 and the colour thereof as the colour of **b**. 916

BE (7012) [AM, ARE, BEEN, BEING, HOWBEIT, IS, WAS, WAST, WERE, WERT, WILL] See Index of Articles, Etc.

BE ESHTARAH See BEESHTERAH

BEACON (1)
Isa 30:17 till ye be left as a **b** upon the top of a 8650

BEALIAH (1)
1Ch 12: 5 **B**, and Shemariah, and Shephatiah 1183

BEALOTH (1)
Jos 15:24 Ziph, and Telem, and **B**, 1175

BEAM (15) [BEAMS]
Jdg 16:14 went away with the pin of the **b**, and 708
1Sa 17: 7 the staff of his spear *was* like a weaver's **b**; 4500
2Sa 21:19 staff of whose spear *was* like a weaver's **b**. 4500
1Ki 7: 6 and the **thick b** *were* before them. 5646
2Ki 6: 2 take thence every man a **b**, and let us make 6982
6: 5 as one was felling a **b**, the axe head fell into 6982
1Ch 11:23 hand *was* a spear like a weaver's **b**; 4500
20: 5 whose spear staff *was* like a weaver's **b**. 4500
Hab 2:11 and the **b** out of the timber shall answer it. 3714
Mt 7: 3 considerest not the **b** that is in thine own *1385*
7: 4 and behold, a **b** *is* in thine own eye? *1385*
7: 5 first cast out the **b** out of thine own eye; *1385*
Lk 6:41 perceivest not the **b** that is in thine own *1385*
6:42 when thou thyself beholdest not the **b** that *1385*
6:42 cast out first the **b** out of thine own eye, *1385*

BEAMS (12) [BEAM]
1Ki 6: 6 that *the* **b** should not be fastened in NIH
6: 9 covered the house with **b** and boards of 1356
6:36 rows of hewed stone, and a row of cedar **b**. 3773
7: 2 cedar pillars, with cedar **b** upon the pillars. 3773
7: 3 *was* covered with cedar above upon the **b**, 6763
7:12 a row of cedar **b**, both for the inner court of 3773
2Ch 3: 7 the **b**, the posts, and the walls thereof, and 6982
Ne 2: 8 that he may give me timber to **make b** for 7136
3: 3 who *also* **laid** the **b** thereof, and set up 7136
3: 6 they **laid** the **b** thereof, and set up the doors 7136
Ps 104: 3 Who **layeth** the **b** of his chambers in 7136
SS 1:17 The **b** of our house *are* cedar, *and* 6982

BEANS (2)
2Sa 17:28 parched *corn,* and **b**, and lentiles, and 6321
Eze 4: 9 **b**, and lentiles, and millet, and fitches, and 6321

BEAR (214) [ARMOURBEARER, BARE, BEARERS, BEAREST, BEARETH, BEARING, BEARS, BIRTH, BIRTHDAY, BIRTHRIGHT, BORN, BORNE, CHILDBEARING, CUPBEARER, CUPBEARERS, FIRSTBORN, HOMEBORN, NEWBORN, STANDARD-BEARER, TALEBEARER]
Ge 4:13 My punishment *is* greater than *I* can **b**. 5375
13: 6 the land was not **able to b** them, that they 5375
16:11 shalt **b** a son, and shalt call his name 3205
17:17 and shall Sarah, that is ninety years old, **b**? 3205
17:19 Sarah thy wife shall **b** thee a son indeed; 3205
17:21 which Sarah shall **b** unto thee at this set 3205
18:13 Shall I of a surety **b** *a child,* which am old? 3205
22:23 these eight Milcah did **b** to Nahor, 3205
30: 3 she shall **b** upon my knees, that I may also 3205
36: 7 they were strangers could not **b** them 5375
43: 9 then let me **b the blame** for ever: 2398
44:32 I shall **b the blame** to my father for ever. 2398
49:15 bowed his shoulder to **b**, and became a 5445
Ex 18:22 and they shall **b** *the burden* with thee. 5375
20:16 Thou shalt not **b** false witness against thy 6030
25:27 be for places of the staves to **b** the table. 5375
27: 7 be upon the two sides of the altar, to **b** it. 5375
28:12 Aaron shall **b** their names before 5375
28:29 Aaron shall **b** the names of the children of 5375
28:30 Aaron shall **b** the judgment of the children 5375
28:38 that Aaron may **b** the iniquity of the holy 5375
28:43 in the holy *place;* that they **b** not iniquity, 5375
30: 4 they shall be for places for the staves to **b** it 5375
37: 5 rings by the sides of the ark, to **b** the ark. 5375
37:14 the places for the staves to **b** the table. 5375
37:15 and overlaid them with gold, to **b** the table. 5375
37:27 to be places for the staves to **b** it withal. 5375
38: 7 rings on the sides of the altar, to **b** it withal; 5375
Lev 5: 1 do not utter *it,* then he shall **b** his iniquity. 5375
5:17 yet is he guilty, and shall **b** his iniquity. 5375
7:18 the soul that eateth of it shall **b** his iniquity. 5375
10:17 *God* hath given it you to **b** the iniquity of 5375
12: 5 if she **b** a maid child, then she shall be 3205
16:22 the goat shall **b** upon him all their iniquities 5375
17:16 bathe his flesh; then he shall **b** his iniquity. 5375
19: 8 Therefore *every one* that eateth it shall **b** 5375
19:18 nor **b any grudge against** the children of 5201
20:17 sister's nakedness; he shall **b** his iniquity. 5375
20:19 his near kin: they shall **b** their iniquity. 5375
20:20 they shall **b** their sin; they shall die 5375
22: 9 lest they **b** sin for it, and die therefore, if 5375
22:16 Or **suffer** them **to b** the iniquity of trespass, 5375
24:15 Whosoever curseth his God shall **b** his sin. 5375
Nu 1:50 they shall **b** the tabernacle, and all 5375
4:15 the sons of Kohath shall come to **b** *it:* but 5375
4:25 they shall **b** the curtains of the tabernacle, 5375
5:31 and this woman shall **b** her iniquity. 5375
7: 9 *that* they should **b** upon *their* shoulders. 5375
9:13 appointed season, that man shall **b** his sin. 5375
11:14 I am not able to **b** all this people alone, 5375
11:17 they shall **b** the burden of the people with 5375
11:17 with thee, that thou **b** *it* not thyself alone. 5375
14:27 How long *shall I* **b** with this evil NIH
14:33 **b** your whoredoms, until your carcases be 5375
14:34 shall ye **b** your iniquities, *even* forty years, 5375
18: 1 thy father's house with thee shall **b** 5375
18: 1 thy sons with thee shall **b** the iniquity of 5375
18:22 of the congregation, lest they **b** sin, and die. 5375
18:23 and they shall **b** their iniquity: 5375
18:32 ye shall **b** no sin by reason of it, when ye 5375
30:15 heard *them;* then he shall **b** her iniquity. 5375
Dt 1: 9 I am not able to **b** you myself alone: 5375
1:12 How can I myself alone **b** your cumbrance, 5375
1:31 as a man doth **b** his son, in all the way that 5375
5:20 Neither shalt thou **b** false witness against 6030
10: 8 to **b** the ark of the covenant of the LORD, 5375
28:57 and towards her children which she shall **b**: 3205
Jos 3: 8 thou shalt command the priests that **b** 5375
3:13 of the priests that **b** the ark of the LORD, 5375
4:16 Command the priests that **b** the ark of 5375
6: 4 seven priests shall **b** before the ark seven 5375
6: 6 let seven priests **b** seven trumpets of rams' 5375
Jdg 13: 3 but thou shalt conceive, and **b** a son. 3205
13: 5 For lo, thou *shalt* conceive, and **b** a son; 3205
13: 7 Behold, thou *shalt* conceive, and **b** a son; 3205
Ru 1:12 also to night, and should also **b** sons; 3205
1Sa 17:34 there came a lion and a **b**, and took a lamb 1677
17:36 Thy servant slew both the lion and the **b**: 1677
17:37 out of the paw of the **b**, he will deliver me 1677
2Sa 17: 8 as a **b** robbed of her whelps in the field: 1677
18:19 Let me now run, and **b** the king **tidings**, 1319
18:20 Thou *shalt* not **b**[S] tidings this day, but 376
18:20 but thou shalt **b tidings** another day: 1319
18:20 this day thou shalt **b** no **tidings**, because 1319
1Ki 3:21 it was not my son, which I did **b**. 3205
21:10 to **b witness against** him, saying, 5749
2Ki 18:14 *that* which thou puttest on me will I **b**. 5375
19:30 take root downward, and **b** fruit upward. 6213
1Ch 5:18 men *able to* **b** buckler and sword, and 5375
2Ch 2: 2 and ten thousand men to **b** burdens, NIH
Est 1:22 that every man should **b rule** in his own 8323
Ps 75: 3 *are* dissolved: I **b up** the pillars of it. Selah. 8505
89:50 *how* I do **b** in my bosom *the reproach of* all 5375
91:12 They shall **b** thee **up** in *their* hands, 5375
Pr 9:12 but *if* thou scornest, thou alone shalt **b** *it.* 5375
12:24 The hand of the diligent shall **b rule**: but 4910
17:12 *Let* a **b** robbed of her whelps meet a man, 1677
18:14 but a wounded spirit who can **b**? 5375
28:15 *As* a roaring lion, and a ranging **b**; *so is* a 1677
30:21 and for four *which* it cannot **b**: 5375
Isa 1:14 a trouble unto me; I am weary to **b** *them.* 5375
7:14 **b** a Son, and shall call his name Immanuel. 3205
11: 7 the cow and the **b** shall feed; their young 1677
37:31 take root downward, and **b** fruit upward. 6213
46: 4 will I carry *you:* I have made, and I will **b**; 5375
46: 7 They **b** him upon the shoulder, they carry 5375
52:11 ye clean, that **b** the vessels of the LORD. 5375
53:11 justify many; for he shall **b** their iniquities. 5445
54: 1 Sing, O barren, thou *that* didst not **b**; 3205
Jer 5:31 and the priests **b rule** by their means; 7287
10:19 I said, Truly this *is* a grief, and I must **b** it. 5375
17:21 **b** no burden on the sabbath day, 5375
17:27 not to **b** a burden, even entering in at 5375
29: 6 that they may **b** sons and daughters; 3205
31:19 because I did **b** the reproach of my youth. 5375
44:22 So that the LORD could no longer **b**, 5375
La 3:10 He *was* unto me *as* a **b** lying in wait, *and* 1677
3:27 *It is* good for a man that he **b** the yoke in 5375
Eze 4: 4 shalt lie upon it thou shalt **b** their iniquity. 5375
4: 5 shalt thou **b** the iniquity of the house of 5375
4: 6 thou shalt **b** the iniquity of the house of 5375
12: 6 In their sight shalt thou **b** *it* upon *thy* 5375
12:12 the prince that *is* among them shall **b** upon 5375
14:10 they shall **b** the punishment of their 5375
16:52 **b** thine own shame for thy sins that thou 5375
16:52 be thou confounded also, and **b** thy shame, 5375
16:54 That thou mayest **b** thine own shame, and 5375
17: 8 that *it* might **b** fruit, that *it* might be a 5375
17:23 and **b** fruit, and be a goodly cedar: 6213
18:19 doth not the son **b** the iniquity of 5375
18:20 The son shall not **b** the iniquity of 5375
18:20 neither shall the father **b** the iniquity of 5375
23:35 therefore **b** thou also thy lewdness and thy 5375
23:49 and ye shall **b** the sins of your idols: 5375
32:30 **b** their shame with them that go down to 5375
34:29 neither **b** the shame of the heathen any 5375
36: 7 that *are* about you, they shall **b** their shame. 5375
36:15 neither shalt thou **b** the reproach of 5375
44:10 their idols; they shall even **b** their iniquity. 5375
44:12 Lord GOD, and they shall **b** their iniquity. 5375
44:13 holy *place:* but they shall **b** their shame, 5375
46:20 that *they* **b** *them* not **out** into the utter 3318
Da 2:39 which shall **b rule** over all the earth. 7981
7: 5 like to a **b**, and it raised up itself on one 1678
Hos 9:16 their root is dried up, they shall **b** no fruit: 6213
13: 8 I will meet them as a **b** *that is* bereaved of 1677
Am 5:19 man did flee from a lion, and a **b** met him; 1677
7:10 the land is not able to **b** all his words. 3557
Mic 6:16 ye shall **b** the reproach of my people. 5375
7: 9 I will **b** the indignation of the LORD, 5375
Zep 1:11 cut down; all they that **b** silver are cut off. 5187
Hag 2:12 If one **b** holy flesh in the skirt of his 5375
Zec 5:10 with me, Whither do these **b** the ephah? 1980
6:13 he shall **b** the glory, and shall sit and 5375
Mt 3:11 than I, whose shoes I am not worthy to **b**: *941*
4: 6 and in *their* hands they shall **b** thee **up**, *142*
19:18 not steal, Thou shalt not **b false witness**, *5576*
27:32 by name: him they compelled to **b** his cross. *142*
Mk 10:19 Do not **b false witness**, Defraud not, *5576*
15:21 of Alexander and Rufus, to **b** his cross. *142*
Lk 1:13 and thy wife Elisabeth shall **b** thee a son, *1080*
4:11 And in *their* hands they shall **b** thee **up**, *142*
11:48 Truly ye **b witness** that ye allow the deeds *3140*
13: 9 And if it **b** fruit, *well:* and if not, *then* *4160*
14:27 And whosoever doth not **b** his cross, and *941*
18: 7 unto him, though he **b long** with them? *3114*
18:20 Do not steal, Do not **b false witness**, *5576*
23:26 laid the cross, that *he* might **b** *it* after Jesus. *5342*
Jn 1: 7 for a witness, to **b witness** of the Light, *3140*
1: 8 but *was sent* to **b witness** of *that* Light. *3140*
2: 8 and **b** unto the governor of the feast. *5342*
3:28 Ye yourselves **b** me **witness**, that I said, I *3140*
5:31 If I **b witness** of myself, my witness is not *3140*
5:36 the same works that I do, **b witness** of me, *3140*
8:14 unto them, Though I **b record** of myself, *3140*
8:18 I am *one* that **b witness** of myself, and *3140*
10:25 in my Father's name, they **b witness** of me. *3140*
15: 4 As the branch cannot **b** fruit of itself, *5342*
15: 8 is my Father glorified, that ye **b** much fruit; *5342*
15:27 And ye also shall **b witness**, because *3140*
16:12 to say unto you, but ye cannot **b** *them* now. *941*
18:23 If I have spoken evil, **b witness** of the evil: *3140*
18:37 that I should **b witness** unto the truth. *3140*
Ac 9:15 to **b** my name before the Gentiles, and kings, *941*
15:10 neither our fathers nor we were able to **b**? *941*
18:14 reason would that I should **b with** you: *430*
22: 5 As also the high priest doth **b** me **witness**, *3140*
23:11 so must thou **b witness** also at Rome. *3140*
27:15 and could not **b up into** the wind, we let *her* *503*
Ro 10: 2 For I **b** them **record** that they have a zeal *3140*
13: 9 not steal, Thou shalt not **b false witness**, *5576*
15: 1 that are strong ought to **b** the infirmities of *941*
1Co 3: 2 for hitherto ye were not able *to* **b** *it,* neither NIG
10:13 way to escape, that ye may be able to **b** *it.* *5297*
15:49 we shall also **b** the image of the heavenly. *5409*
2Co 8: 3 I **b record**, *yea,* and beyond *their* power *3140*
11: 1 Would *to God* you could **b with** me a little *430*
11: 1 a little in *my* folly: and indeed **b with** me. *430*
11: 4 not accepted, ye might well **b with** *him.* *430*
Gal 4:15 for I **b** you **record**, that if *it had been* *3140*
5:10 he that troubleth you shall **b** *his* judgment, *941*
6: 2 **B** ye one another's burdens, and so fulfil *941*
6: 5 For every man shall **b** his own burden. *941*
6:17 for I **b** in my body the marks of the Lord *941*
Col 4:13 For I **b** him **record**, that he hath a great *3140*
1Ti 5:14 *women* marry, **b children**, guide the house, *5041*
Heb 9:28 So Christ was once offered to **b** the sins of *399*
Jas 3:12 the fig tree, my brethren, **b** olive berries? *4160*
1Jn 1: 2 and we have seen *it,* and **b witness**, and *3140*
5: 7 For there are three that **b record** in heaven, *3140*
5: 8 And there are three that **b witness** in earth, *3140*
3Jn 1:12 yea, and we also **b record**; and ye know *3140*
Rev 2: 2 how thou canst not **b** *them which are* evil: *941*
13: 2 and his feet *were* as *the feet* of a **b**, and *715*

BEARD (16) [BEARDS]
Lev 13:29 hath a plague upon the head or the **b**; 2206
13:30 *even* a leprosy upon the head or **b**. 2206
14: 9 off his head and his **b** and his eyebrows, 2206
19:27 neither shalt thou mar the corners of thy **b**. 2206
21: 5 shall they shave off the corner of their **b**, 2206
1Sa 17:35 I caught *him* by his **b**, and smote him, and 2206
21:13 and let his spittle fall down upon his **b**. 2206
2Sa 19:24 nor trimmed his **b**, nor washed his clothes, 8222
20: 9 Joab took Amasa by the **b** with the right 2206
Ezr 9: 3 pluckt off the hair of my head and of my **b**, 2206
Ps 133: 2 that ran down upon the **b**, *even* Aaron's 2206
133: 2 ran down upon the beard, *even* Aaron's **b**: 2206
Isa 7:20 of the feet: and it shall also consume the **b**. 2206
15: 2 *shall be* baldness, *and* every **b** cut off. 2206
Jer 48:37 every head *shall be* bald, and every **b** clipt: 2206
Eze 5: 1 *it* to pass upon thine head and upon thy **b**: 2206

BEARDS (4) [BEARD]
2Sa 10: 4 shaved off the *one* half of their **b**, and 2206
10: 5 Tarry at Jericho until your **b** be grown, and 2206
1Ch 19: 5 Tarry at Jericho until your **b** be grown, and 2206
Jer 41: 5 having their **b** shaven, and their clothes 2206

BEARERS (3) [BEAR]
2Ch 2:18 ten thousand of them *to be* **b of burdens**, 5449
34:13 Also *they were* over the **b of burdens**, and 5449
Ne 4:10 The strength of the **b of burdens** is 5449

BEAREST (5) [BEAR]
Jdg 13: 3 Behold now, thou *art* barren, and **b** not: 3205
Ps 106: 4 with the favour *that thou* **b** unto thy people: NIH
Jn 8:13 said unto him, Thou **b record** of thyself; *3140*
Ro 11:18 thou **b** not the root, but the root thee. *941*
Gal 4:27 it is written, Rejoice, *thou* barren that **b** not; *5088*

BEARETH (26) [BEAR]
Lev 11:25 whosoever **b** *ought* of the carcase of them 5375
11:28 he that **b** the carcase of them shall wash his 5375
11:40 he also that **b** the carcase of it shall wash 5375
15:10 he that **b** *any of* those *things* shall wash his 5375
Nu 11:12 as a nursing father **b** the sucking child, 5375
Dt 25: 6 *that* the firstborn which she **b** shall succeed 3205
29:18 lest there should be among you a root that **b** 6509
29:23 salt, *and* burning, *that* it is not sown, nor **b**, 6779
32:11 taketh them, **b** them on her wings: 5375
Job 16: 8 my leanness rising up in me **b witness** to 6030
24:21 He evil entreateth the barren *that* **b** not: and 3205
Pr 25:18 A man that **b** false witness against his 6030
29: 2 when the wicked **b rule**, the people mourn. 4910
SS 4: 2 whereof every one **b twins**, and none *is* 8382
6: 6 whereof every one **b twins**, and *there is* not 8382
Joel 2:22 for the tree **b** her fruit, the fig tree and 5375
Mt 13:23 and understandeth *it;* which also **b fruit**, *2592*
Jn 5:32 There is another that **b witness** of me; and *3140*
8:18 the Father that sent me **b witness** of me. *3140*
15: 2 Every branch in me that **b** not fruit he *5342*
15: 2 and every *branch* that **b** fruit, he purgeth it, *5342*
Ro 8:16 The Spirit itself **b witness with** our spirit, *4828*
13: 4 be afraid; for he **b** not the sword in vain: *5409*
1Co 13: 7 **B** all *things,* believeth all *things,* hopeth all *4722*
Heb 6: 8 But that which **b** thorns and briers *is* *1627*
1Jn 5: 6 And it is the Spirit that **b witness**, because *3140*

BEARING (22) [BEAR]
Ge 1:29 I have given you every herb **b** seed, 2232
16: 2 the LORD hath restrained me from **b**: 3205
29:35 she called his name Judah; and left **b**. 3205
30: 9 When Leah saw that she had left **b**, she 3205
37:25 from Gilead with their camels **b** spicery 5375
Nu 10:17 of Merari set forward, **b** the tabernacle. 5375
10:21 the Kohathites set forward, **b** the sanctuary: 5375
Jos 3: 3 the priests the Levites **b** it, then ye shall 5375
3:14 the priests **b** the ark *of* the covenant before 5375
6: 8 that the seven priests **b** the seven trumpets 5375
6:13 seven priests **b** seven trumpets of rams' 5375
1Sa 17: 7 *of* iron: and one **b** a shield went before him. 5375
2Sa 15:24 with him, **b** the ark of the covenant of God: 5375
Ps 126: 6 goeth forth and weepeth, **b** precious seed, 5375
Mk 14:13 there shall meet you a man **b** a pitcher of *941*
Lk 22:10 shall a man meet you, **b** a pitcher of water; *941*
Jn 19:17 And he **b** his cross went forth into a place *941*
Ro 2:15 their conscience **also b witness**, and *their* *4828*
9: 1 my conscience **also b** me **witness** in *4828*
2Co 4:10 Always **b about** in the body the dying of *4064*
Heb 2: 4 God **also b** *them* **witness**, both with signs *4901*
13:13 unto him without the camp, **b** his reproach. *5342*

BEARS (2) [BEAR]
2Ki 2:24 there came forth two she **b** out of the wood, 1677
Isa 59:11 We roar all like **b**, and mourn sore like 1677

BEAST (180) [BEAST'S, BEASTS]
Ge 1:24 and **b** of the earth after his kind: 2416
1:25 God made the **b** of the earth after his kind, 2416
1:30 to every **b** of the earth, and to every fowl of 2416
2:19 LORD God formed every **b** of the field, 2416
2:20 fowl of the air, and to every **b** of the field; 2416
3: 1 of the field which the LORD God had 2416
3:14 all cattle, and above every **b** of the field; 2416
6: 7 **b**, and the creeping thing, and the fowls of 929
7: 2 Of every clean **b** thou shalt take to thee by 929
7:14 every **b** after his kind, and all the cattle 2416

Ge 7:21 of **b**, and of every creeping thing that 2416
8:19 Every **b**, every creeping thing, and 2416
8:20 took of every clean **b**, and of every clean 929
9: 2 the dread of you shall be upon every **b** of 2416
9: 5 at the hand of every **b** will I require it, and 2416
9:10 and of every **b** of the earth with you; 2416
9:10 go out of the ark, to every **b** of the earth. 2416
34:23 and every **b** of theirs *be* ours? 929
37:20 will say, *Some* evil **b** hath devoured him: 2416
37:33 son's coat; an evil **b** hath devoured him; 2416
Ex 8:17 and it became lice in man, and in **b**; 929
8:18 so there were lice upon man, and upon **b**. 929
9: 9 and upon **b**, throughout all the land of Egypt. 929
9:10 forth *with* blains upon man, and upon **b**. 929
9:19 and **b** which shall be found in the field, 929
9:22 and upon **b**, and upon every herb of the field, 929
9:25 all that *was* in the field, both man and **b**; 929
11: 7 not a dog move his tongue, against man or **b**: 929
12:12 in the land of Egypt, both man and **b**; 929
13: 2 the children of Israel, *both* of man and of **b**: 929
13:12 every firstling that cometh of a **b** which thou 929
13:15 the firstborn of man, and the firstborn of **b**: 929
19:13 whether *it be* **b** or man, it shall not live: 929
21:34 owner of them; and the dead *b* shall be his. NIH
22: 5 shall put in his **b**, and shall feed in another 1165
22:10 or an ox, or a sheep, or any **b**, to keep; 929
22:19 Whosoever lieth with a **b** shall surely be put 929
23:29 and the **b** of the field multiply against thee. 2416
Lev 5: 2 whether *it be* a carcase of an unclean **b**, or a 2416
7:21 or *any* unclean **b**, or any abominable unclean 929
7:24 And the fat of the **b that dieth of itself**, and 5038
7:25 For whosoever eateth the fat of the **b**, 929
7:26 *whether it be* of fowl or of **b**, in any of your 929
11:26 *The carcases* of every **b** which divideth 929
11:39 if any **b**, of which ye may eat, die; he that 929
11:47 between the **b** that may be eaten and 2416
11:47 be eaten and the **b** that may not be eaten. 2416
17:13 which hunteth and catcheth *any* **b** or 2416
18:23 Neither shalt thou lie with any **b** to defile 929
18:23 neither shall any woman stand before a **b** to 929
20:15 if a man lie with a **b**, he shall surely be put to 929
20:15 be put to death: and ye shall slay the **b**. 929
20:16 if a woman approach unto any **b**, and 929
20:16 thou shalt kill the woman and the **b**: 929
20:25 shall not make your souls abominable by **b**, 929
24:18 he that killeth a **b** shall make it good; 929
24:18 a beast shall make it good; **b** for beast. 5315
24:18 a beast shall make it good; beast for **b**. 5315
24:21 he that killeth a **b**, he shall restore it: and 929
25: 7 thy cattle, and for the **b** that *are* in thy land, 2416
27: 9 if *it be* a **b**, whereof *men* bring an offering 929
27:10 and if he shall at all change **b** for beast, then 929
27:10 and if he shall at all change beast for **b**, then 929
27:11 if *it be* any unclean **b**, of which they do not 929
27:11 then he shall present the **b** before the priest: 929
27:27 if *it be* of an unclean **b**, then he shall redeem 929
27:28 *both* of man and **b**, and of the field of his 929
Nu 3:13 all the firstborn in Israel, both man and **b**: 929
8:17 children of Israel *are* mine, *both* man and **b**: 929
31:26 *both* of man and of **b**, thou, and Eleazar 929
31:47 *both* of man and of **b**, and gave them unto 929
Dt 4:17 The likeness of any **b** that *is* on the earth, 929
14: 6 every **b** that parteth the hoof, and 929
27:21 *be* he that lieth with any *manner of* **b**. 929
Jdg 20:48 as the **b**, and all that came to hand: 929
2Ki 14: 9 there passed by a wild **b** that *was* in 2416
2Ch 25:18 there passed by a wild **b** that *was* in 2416
Ne 2:12 neither *was there any* **b** with me, save 929
2:12 beast with me, save the **b** that I rode upon. 929
2:14 *there was* no place for the **b** that *was* under 929
Job 39:15 or *that* the wild **b** may break them. 2416
Ps 36: 6 O LORD, thou preservest man and **b**. 929
50:10 For every **b** of the forest *is* mine, *and* 2416
73:22 *was* I, and ignorant: I was *as* a **b** before thee. 929
80:13 and the **wild b** of the field doth devour it. 2123
104:11 They give drink to every **b** of the field: 2416
135: 8 the firstborn of Egypt, both of man and **b**. 929
147: 9 He giveth to the **b** his food, *and* to the young 929
Pr 12:10 A righteous *man* regardeth the life of his **b**: 929
Ecc 3:19 that a man hath no preeminence above a **b**: 929
3:21 the spirit of the **b** that goeth downward to 929
Isa 35: 9 nor *any* ravenous **b** shall go up thereon, 2416
43:20 The **b** of the field shall honour me, 2416
46: 1 *they are* a burden to the weary *b*. NIH
63:14 As a **b** goeth down into the valley, the Spirit 929
Jer 7:20 upon **b**, and upon the trees of the field, and 929
9:10 the fowl of the heavens and the **b** are fled; 929
21: 6 the inhabitants of this city, both man and **b**: 929
27: 5 the man and the **b** that *are* upon the ground, 929
31:27 *with* the seed of man, and *with* the seed of **b**. 929
32:43 ye say, *It is* desolate without man or **b**; 929
33:10 *shall be* desolate without man and without **b**, 929
33:10 and without inhabitant, and without **b**, 929
33:12 *is* desolate without man and without **b**, 929
36:29 shall cause to cease from thence man and **b**? 929
50: 3 they shall depart, both man and **b**. 929
51:62 neither man nor **b**, but that it shall be 929
Eze 14:13 upon it, and will cut off man and **b** from it: 929
14:17 the land; so that I cut off man and **b** from it: 929
14:19 it in blood, to cut off from it man and **b**: 929
14:21 and the noisome **b**, and the pestilence, 2416
14:21 the pestilence, to cut off from it man and **b**? 929
25:13 and will cut off man and **b** from it; 929
29: 8 upon thee, and cut off man and **b** out of thee. 929
29:11 through it, nor foot of **b** shall pass through it, 929
34: 8 my flock became meat to every **b** of 2416
34:28 neither shall the **b** of the land devour them; 2416
36:11 I will multiply upon you man and **b**; and 929
39:17 to every **b** of the field, 2416
44:31 of itself, or torn, whether it be fowl or **b**. 929
Da 7: 5 behold, another **b**, a second, like to a bear, 2423
7: 6 the **b** had also four heads; and 2423
7: 7 behold, a fourth **b**, dreadful and terrible, 2423
7:11 I beheld *even* till the **b** *was* slain, and 2423
7:19 I would know the truth of the fourth **b**, 2423
Da 7:23 The fourth **b** shall be the fourth kingdom 2423
Hos 13: 8 them like a lion: the wild **b** shall tear them. 2416
Jnh 3: 7 his nobles, saying, Let neither man nor **b**, 929
3: 8 But let man and **b** be covered with sackcloth, 929
Mic 1:13 of Lachish, bind the chariot to the **swift b**: 7409
Zep 1: 3 I will consume man and **b**; I will consume 929
Zec 8:10 there was no hire for man, nor any hire for **b**; 929
Lk 10:34 and set him on his own **b**, and brought him *2934*
Ac 28: 4 saw the *venomous* **b** hang on his hand, *2342*
28: 5 And he shook off the **b** into the fire, and *2342*
Heb 12:20 And if *so much as* a **b** touch the mountain, *2342*
Rev 4: 7 And the first **b** *was* like a lion, and *2226*
4: 7 and the second **b** like a calf, and the third *2226*
4: 7 and the third **b** had a face as a man, and *2226*
4: 7 and the fourth **b** *was* like a flying eagle. *2226*
6: 3 I heard the second **b** say, Come and see. *2226*
6: 5 I heard the third **b** say, Come and see. *2226*
6: 7 I heard the voice of the fourth **b** say, Come *2226*
11: 7 the **b** that ascendeth out of the bottomless *2342*
13: 1 and saw a **b** rise up out of the sea, *2342*
13: 2 And the **b** which I saw was like unto a *2342*
13: 3 and all the world wondered after the **b**. *2342*
13: 4 the dragon which gave power unto the **b**: *2342*
13: 4 and they worshipped the **b**, saying, Who *is* *2342*
13: 4 the beast, saying, Who *is* like unto the **b**? *2342*
13:11 And I beheld another **b** coming up out of *2342*
13:12 all the power of the first **b** before him, *2342*
13:12 which dwell therein to worship the first **b**, *2342*
13:14 he had power to do in the sight of the **b**; *2342*
13:14 that *they* should make an image to the **b**, *2342*
13:15 power to give life unto the image of the **b**, *2342*
13:15 that the image of the **b** should both speak, *2342*
13:15 the image of the **b** should be killed. *2342*
13:17 or the name of the **b**, or the number of his *2342*
13:18 understanding count the number of the **b**: *2342*
14: 9 If any *man* worship the **b** and his image, *2342*
14:11 who worship the **b** and his image, and *2342*
15: 2 them that had gotten the victory over the **b**, *2342*
16: 2 upon the men which had the mark of the **b**, *2342*
16:10 poured out his vial upon the seat of the **b**; *2342*
16:13 and out of the mouth of the **b**, and out of *2342*
17: 3 saw a woman sit upon a scarlet coloured **b**, *2342*
17: 7 and of the **b** that carrieth her, which hath *2342*
17: 8 The **b** that thou sawest was, and is not; and *2342*
17: 8 when they behold the **b** that was, and is not, *2342*
17:11 And the **b** that was, and is not, even he is *2342*
17:12 receive power as kings one hour with the **b**. *2342*
17:13 give their power and strength unto the **b**. *2342*
17:16 the ten horns which thou sawest upon the **b**, *2342*
17:17 and give their kingdom unto the **b**, *2342*
19:19 And I saw the **b**, and the kings of the earth, *2342*
19:20 And the **b** was taken, and with him *2342*
19:20 them that had received the mark of the **b**, *2342*
20: 4 and which had not worshipped the **b**, *2342*
20:10 where the **b** and the false prophet *are*, and *2342*

BEAST'S (1) [BEAST]

Da 4:16 and let a **b** heart be given unto him; 2423

BEASTS (156) [BEAST]

Ge 7: 2 of **b** that *are* not clean by two, the male and 929
7: 8 Of clean **b**, and of beasts that *are* not clean, 929
7: 8 and of **b** that *are* not clean, and of fowls, and 929
31:39 That which was torn *of b* I brought not unto NIH
36: 6 his cattle, and all his **b**, and all his substance, 929
45:17 lade your **b**, and go, get you unto the land 1165
Ex 11: 5 *is* behind the mill; and all the firstborn of **b**. 929
22:31 ye eat *any* flesh *that is* torn *of* **b** in the field; NIH
23:11 what they leave the **b** of the field shall eat. 2416
Lev 7:24 the fat of that which is torn *with* **b**, may be NIH
11: 2 These *are* the **b** which ye shall eat among 2416
11: 2 eat among all the **b** that *are* on the earth. 929
11: 3 cheweth the cud, among the **b**, 929
11:27 among all *manner of* **b** that go on *all* four, 2416
11:46 This *is* the law of the **b**, and of the fowl, and 929
17:15 that which was torn *with* **b**, *whether it be* NIH
20:25 put difference between clean **b** and unclean, 929
22: 8 is torn *with* **b**, he shall not eat to defile NIH
26: 6 I will rid evil **b** out of the land, neither shall 2416
26:22 I will also send wild **b** among you, which 2416
27:26 Only the firstling of the **b**, which should be 929
Nu 18:15 *whether it be* of men or **b**, shall be thine: 929
18:15 the firstling of unclean **b** shalt thou redeem. 929
20: 8 give the congregation and their **b** drink. 1165
20:11 the congregation drank, and their **b** *also*. 1165
31:11 and all the prey, *both* of men and of **b**. 929
31:30 of all *manner of* **b**, and give them unto 929
35: 3 and for their goods, and for all their **b**. 2416
Dt 7:22 lest the **b** of the field increase upon thee. 2416
14: 4 These *are* the **b** which ye shall eat: the ox, 929
14: 6 *and* cheweth the cud amongst the **b**: 929
28:26 unto the **b** of the earth, and no man shall fray 929
32:24 I will also send the teeth of **b** upon them, 929
1Sa 17:44 the fowls of the air, and to the **b** of the field. 929
17:46 of the air, and to the **wild b** of the earth; 2416
2Sa 21:10 them by day, nor the **b** of the field by night. 2416
1Ki 4:33 he spake also of **b**, and of fowl, and 929
18: 5 and mules alive, that we leese not all the **b**. 929
2Ki 3:17 *both* ye, and your cattle, and your **b**. 929
2Ch 32:28 stalls for all *manner of* **b**, 929+929+2050.1
Ezr 1: 4 and with gold, and with goods, and with **b**, 929
1: 6 and with **b**, and with precious things, 929
Job 5:22 neither shalt thou be afraid of the **b** of 2416
5:23 the **b** of the field shall be at peace with 2416
12: 7 But ask now the **b**, and they shall teach thee; 929
18: 3 Wherefore are we counted as **b**, *and* 929
35:11 Who teacheth us more than the **b** of 929
37: 8 the **b** go into dens, and remain in their 2416
40:20 forth food, where all the **b** of the field play. 2416
Ps 8: 7 and oxen, yea, and the **b** of the field; 929
49:12 abideth not: he is like the **b** *that* perish. 929
49:20 understandeth not, is like the **b** *that* perish. 929
50:11 and the **wild b** of the field *are* mine. 2123
79: 2 the flesh of thy saints unto the **b** of 2416
104:20 wherein all the **b** of the forest do creep 2416
Ps 104:25 both small and great **b**. 2416
148:10 **B**, and all cattle; creeping things, and 2416
Pr 9: 2 She hath killed her **b**; she hath mingled her 2874
30:30 A lion *which is* strongest among **b**, and 929
Ecc 3:18 *they* might see that they themselves are **b**. 929
3:19 which befalleth the sons of men befalleth **b**; 929
Isa 1:11 offerings of rams, and the fat of **fed b**; 4806
13:21 **wild b of the desert** shall lie there; and 6728
13:22 the **wild b of the islands** shall cry in their 338
18: 6 of the mountains, and to the **b** of the earth: 929
18: 6 all the **b** of the earth shall winter upon them. 929
30: 6 The burden of the **b** of the south: into 929
34:14 The **wild b of the desert** shall also meet 6728
34:14 shall also meet with the **wild b of the island**, 338
40:16 nor the **b** thereof sufficient *for* a burnt 2416
46: 1 their idols were upon the **b**, and upon 2416
56: 9 All ye **b** of the field, come to devour, 2416
56: 9 come to devour, *yea*, all ye **b** in the forest. 2416
66:20 and upon mules, and upon **swift b**, 3753
Jer 7:33 of the heaven, and for the **b** of the earth; 929
12: 4 the **b** are consumed, and the birds; because 929
12: 9 come ye, assemble all the **b** of the field, 2416
15: 3 and the **b** of the earth, to devour and destroy. 929
16: 4 fowls of heaven, and for the **b** of the earth. 929
19: 7 of the heaven, and for the **b** of the earth. 929
27: 6 the **b** of the field have I given him also to 2416
28:14 and I have given him the **b** of the field also. 2416
34:20 of the heaven, and to the **b** of the earth. 929
50:39 Therefore the **wild b of the desert** with the 6728
50:39 the **wild b of the islands** shall dwell *there*, 338
Eze 5:17 So will I send upon you famine and evil **b**, 2416
8:10 abominable **b**, and all the idols of the house 929
14:15 If I cause noisome **b** to pass through 2416
14:15 no man may pass through because of the **b**: 2416
29: 5 I have given thee for meat to the **b** of 2416
31: 6 under his branches did all the **b** of the field 2416
31:13 all the **b** of the field shall be upon his 2416
32: 4 I will fill the **b** of the whole earth with thee. 2416
32:13 I will destroy also all the **b** thereof from 929
32:13 any more, nor the hoofs of **b** trouble them. 929
33:27 field will I give to the **b** to be devoured, 2416
34: 5 they became meat to all the **b** of the field, 2416
34:25 will cause the evil **b** to cease out of 2416
38:20 the **b** of the field, and all creeping things 2416
39: 4 and *to* the **b** of the field to be devoured. 2416
Da 2:38 the **b** of the field and the fowls of 2423
4:12 the **b** of the field had shadow under it, and 2423
4:14 let the **b** get away from under it, and 2423
4:15 *let* his portion *be* with the **b** in the grass of 2423
4:21 under which the **b** of the field dwelt, and 2423
4:23 *let* his portion *be* with the **b** of the field, 2423
4:25 thy dwelling shall be with the **b** of the field, 2423
4:32 thy dwelling *shall be* with the **b** of the field: 2423
5:21 his heart was made like the **b**, and 2423
7: 3 four great **b** came up from the sea, 2423
7: 7 it *was* diverse from all the **b** that *were* 2423
7:12 As concerning the rest of the **b**, they had 2423
7:17 These great **b**, which *are* four, *are* four 2423
8: 4 so that no **b** might stand before him, 2416
Hos 2:12 and the **b** of the field shall eat them. 2416
2:18 a covenant for them with the **b** of the field, 2416
4: 3 with the **b** of the field, and with the fowls 2416
Joel 1:18 How do the **b** groan! the herds of cattle are 929
1:20 The **b** of the field cry also unto thee: for 929
2:22 Be not afraid, ye **b** of the field: for 929
Am 5:22 I regard the peace offerings of your **fat b**. 4806
Mic 5: 8 people as a lion among the **b** of the forest, 929
Hab 2:17 the spoil of **b**, *which* made them afraid, 929
Zep 2:14 in the midst of her, all the **b** of the nations: 2416
2:15 a desolation, a place for **b** to lie down in! 2416
Zec 14:15 and of all the **b** that shall be in these tents, 929
Mk 1:13 and was with the **wild b**; and the angels *2342*
Ac 7:42 have ye offered to me **slain b** and *4968*
10:12 Wherein were all *manner of* **fourfooted b** *5074*
10:12 and **wild b**, and creeping things, and *2342*
11: 6 and saw **fourfooted b** of the earth, and *5074*
11: 6 and **wild b**, and creeping things, and fowls *2342*
23:24 And provide *them* **b**, that they may set Paul *2934*
Ro 1:23 and **fourfooted b**, and creeping things. *5074*
1Co 15:32 of men I have **fought with b** at Ephesus, *2341*
15:39 another flesh of **b**, another of fishes, *and* *2934*
Tit 1:12 *are* alway liars, evil **b**, slow bellies. *2342*
Heb 13:11 For the bodies of those **b**, whose blood is *2226*
Jas 3: 7 For every kind of **b**, and of birds, and *2342*
2Pe 2:12 But these, as natural brute **b**, made to be *2226*
Jude 1:10 but what they know naturally, as brute **b**, *2226*
Rev 4: 6 *were* four **b** full of eyes before and behind. *2226*
4: 8 And the four **b** had each of them six wings *2226*
4: 9 And when *those* **b** give glory and honour *2226*
5: 6 in the midst of the throne and of the four **b**, *2226*
5: 8 the four **b** and four *and* twenty elders fell *2226*
5:11 about the throne and the **b** and the elders: *2226*
5:14 And the four **b** said, Amen. And the four *2226*
6: 1 one of the four **b** saying, Come and see. *2226*
6: 6 heard a voice in the midst of the four **b** say, *2226*
6: 8 and with death, and with the **b** of the earth. *2342*
7:11 and *about* the elders and the four **b**, and *2226*
14: 3 and before the four **b**, and the elders: *2226*
15: 7 And one of the four **b** gave unto the seven *2226*
18:13 and **b**, and sheep, and horses, and chariots, *2934*
19: 4 twenty elders and the four **b** fell down and *2226*

BEAT (36) [BEATEN, BEATEST, BEATETH, BEATING]

Ex 30:36 thou shalt **b** *some* of it very small, and 7833
39: 3 they did **b** the gold into thin plates, and 7554
Nu 11: 8 or **b** *it* in a mortar, and baked *it* in pans, and 1743
Dt 25: 3 **b** him above these *with* many stripes, then 5221
Jdg 8:17 he **b down** the tower of Penuel, and 5422
9:45 and **b down** the city, and sowed it *with* salt. 5422
19:22 *and* **b** at the door, and spake to the master 1849
Ru 2:17 until even, and **b out** that she had gleaned: 2251
2Sa 22:43 did I **b** them *as* **small** as the dust of 7833
2Ki 3:25 they **b down** the cities, and *on* every good 2040
13:25 Three times did Joash **b** him, and 5221
23:12 did the king **b down**, and brake *them* down 5422

Ps 18:42 did I **b** them **small** as the dust before 7833
89:23 I will **b down** his foes before his face, and 3807
Pr 23:14 Thou shalt **b** him with the rod, and 5221
Isa 2:4 they shall **b** their swords into plowshares, 3807
3:15 mean ye *that* ye **b** my people **to pieces**, 1792
27:12 *that* the LORD shall **b off** from 2251
41:15 **b** *them* **small**, and shalt make the hills as 1854
Joel 3:10 **B** your plowshares into swords, and 3807
Jnh 4:8 the sun **b** upon the head of Jonah, that he 5221
Mic 4:3 they shall **b** their swords into plowshares, 3807
4:13 thou shalt **b in pieces** many people: and 1854
Mt 7:25 and the winds blew, and **b upon** that house; 4363
7:27 and the winds blew, and **b upon** that house; 4350
21:35 husbandmen took his servants, and **b** one, 1194
Mk 4:37 and the waves **b** into the ship, so that it was 1911
12:3 and **b** *him*, and sent *him* away empty. 1194
Lk 6:48 the stream **b vehemently upon** that house, 4366
6:49 **against** which the stream did **b vehemently**, 4366
12:45 and shall begin to **b** the menservants and 5180
20:10 but the husbandmen **b** him, and sent *him* 1194
20:11 and they **b** him also, and entreated *him* 1194
Ac 16:22 their clothes, and commanded to **b** *them*. 4463
18:17 and **b** *him* before the judgment seat. 5180
22:19 **b** in every synagogue them that believed on 1194

BEATEN (40) [BEAT]

Ex 5:14 had set over them, were **b**, *and* demanded, 5221
5:16 behold, thy servants *are* **b**; but the fault *is* 5221
25:18 *of* **b work** shalt thou make them, in the two 4749
25:31 *of* **b work** shall the candlestick be made: 4749
25:36 all it *shall be* one **b work** *of* pure gold. 4749
27:20 that they bring thee pure oil olive **b** for 3795
29:40 with the fourth part of a hin of **b** oil; 3795
37:7 **b out of one piece** made he them, on 4749
37:17 *of* **b work** made he the candlestick; 4749
37:22 all of it *was* one **b work** *of* pure gold. 4749
Lev 2:14 by the fire, *even* corn **b out** of full ears. 1643
2:16 *part* of the **b corn** thereof, and *part* of 1643
16:12 and his hands full of sweet incense **b small**, 1851
24:2 that they bring unto thee pure oil olive **b** for 3795
Nu 8:4 this work of the candlestick *was of* **b** gold, 4749
8:4 unto the flowers thereof, *was* **b work**: 4749
28:5 mingled with the fourth *part* of a hin of **b** 3795
Dt 25:2 if the wicked *man be* worthy to be **b**, 5221
25:2 to be **b** before his face, according to his 5221
Jos 8:15 all Israel *made as if they* were **b** before 5060
2Sa 2:17 Abner was **b**, and the men of Israel, before 5062
1Ki 10:16 made two hundred targets *of* **b** gold: 7820
10:17 *he made* three hundred shields *of* **b** gold; 7820
2Ch 2:10 twenty thousand measures of **b** wheat, and 4347
9:15 made two hundred targets *of* **b** gold: 7820
9:15 six hundred *shekels* of **b** gold went to one 7820
9:16 three hundred shields *made he of* **b** gold: 7820
34:7 had **b** the graven images into powder, and 3807
Pr 23:35 not sick; they have **b** me, *and* I felt *it* not: 1986
Isa 27:9 altar as chalkstones that are **b in sunder**, 5310
28:27 the fitches are **b out** with a staff, and 2251
30:31 the LORD shall the Assyrian be **b down**, 2865
Jer 46:5 their mighty ones are **b down**, and are fled 3807
Mic 1:7 graven images thereof shall be **b to pieces**, 3807
Mk 13:9 and in the synagogues ye shall be **b**: 1194
Lk 12:47 to his will, shall be **b** with many *stripes*. 1194
12:48 shall be **b** with few *stripes*. For unto 1194
Ac 5:40 **b** *them*, they commanded that *they* should 1194
16:37 They have **b** us openly uncondemned, 1194
2Co 11:25 Thrice was I **b with rods**, once was I 4463

BEATEST (2) [BEAT]

Dt 24:20 When thou **b** thine olive tree, thou shalt not 2251
Pr 23:13 for *if* thou **b** him with the rod, he shall not 5221

BEATETH (1) [BEAT]

1Co 9:26 so fight I, not as one that **b** the air: 1194

BEATING (3) [BEAT]

1Sa 14:16 and they went on **b down** *one another*. 1986
Mk 12:5 him they killed, and many others; **b** some, 1194
Ac 21:32 and the soldiers, they left **b** of Paul. 5180

BEAUTIES (1) [BEAUTY]

Ps 110:3 in the **b** of holiness from the womb of 1926

BEAUTIFUL (23) [BEAUTY]

Ge 29:17 but Rachel was **b** and well favoured. 3303+8389
Dt 21:11 seest among the captives a **b** woman, 3303+8389
1Sa 16:12 *and* withal of a **b** countenance, and 3303
25:3 and of a **b** countenance: 3303
2Sa 11:2 and the woman *was* very **b** to look upon. 2896
Est 2:7 and the maid *was* fair and **b**; 2896+4758
Ps 48:2 **B** for situation, the joy of the whole earth, 3303
Ecc 3:11 He hath made every *thing* **b** in his time: 3303
SS 6:4 Thou *art* **b**, O my love, as Tirzah, 3303
7:1 How **b** are thy feet with shoes, O prince's 3302
Isa 4:2 day shall the branch of the LORD be **b** 6643
52:1 put on thy **b** garments, O Jerusalem, 8597
52:7 How **b** upon the mountains are the feet of 4998
64:11 Our holy and our **b** house, where our 8597
Jer 13:20 the flock *that* was given thee, thy **b** flock? 8597
48:17 is the strong staff broken, *and* the **b** rod! 8597
Eze 16:12 thine ears, and a **b** crown upon thine head. 8597
16:13 thou wast exceeding **b**, and thou didst 3302
23:42 their hands, and **b** crowns upon their heads. 8597
Mt 23:27 which indeed appear **b** outward, but 5611
Ac 3:2 at the gate of the temple which is called **B**, 5611
3:10 sat for alms at the **B** gate of the temple: 5611
Ro 10:15 How **b** *are* the feet of them that preach 5611

BEAUTIFY (3) [BEAUTY]

Ezr 7:27 to **b** the house of the LORD which *is* in 6286
Ps 149:4 he will **b** the meek with salvation. 6286
Isa 60:13 to **b** the place of my sanctuary; 6286

BEAUTY (49) [BEAUTIES, BEAUTIFUL, BEAUTIFY]

Ex 28:2 for Aaron thy brother, for glory and for **b**. 8597
28:40 thou make for them, for glory and for **b**. 8597
2Sa 1:19 The **b** of Israel *is* slain upon thy high 6643
14:25 to be so much praised as Absalom for his **b**: 3303
1Ch 16:29 worship the LORD in the **b** of holiness. 1927
2Ch 3:6 the house with precious stones for **b**: 8597
20:21 that should praise the **b** of holiness, as *they* 1927
Est 1:11 to shew the people and the princes her **b**: 3308
Job 40:10 and array thyself with glory and **b**. 1926
Ps 27:4 to behold the **b** of the LORD, and 5278
29:2 worship the LORD in the **b** of holiness. 1927
39:11 thou makest his **b** to consume away like a 2530
45:11 So shall the king greatly desire thy **b**: for he 3308
49:14 their **b** shall consume *in* the grave from 6699
50:2 Out of Zion, the perfection of **b**, God hath 3308
90:17 let the **b** of the LORD our God be upon 5278
96:6 strength and **b** *are* in his sanctuary. 8597
96:9 O worship the LORD in the **b** of holiness: 1927
Pr 6:25 Lust not after her **b** in thine heart; 3308
20:29 and the **b** of old men *is* the gray head. 1926
31:30 Favour *is* deceitful, and **b** *is* vain: *but* 3308
Isa 3:24 of sackcloth; *and* burning instead of **b**. 3308
13:19 the **b** of the Chaldees' excellency, 8597
28:1 whose glorious **b** *is* a fading flower, 8597
28:4 the glorious **b**, which *is* on the head of 8597
28:5 for a diadem of **b**, unto the residue of his 8597
33:17 Thine eyes shall see the king in his **b**: 3308
44:13 of a man, according to the **b** of a man; 8597
53:2 *there is* no **b** that we should desire him. 4758
61:3 to give unto them **b** for ashes, the oil of joy 6287
La 1:6 from the daughter of Zion all her **b** is 1926
2:1 cast down from heaven *unto* the earth the **b** 8597
2:15 the city that *men* call The perfection of **b**, 3308
Eze 7:20 As for the **b** of his ornament, he set it in 6643
16:14 went forth among the heathen for thy **b**: 3308
16:15 thou didst trust in thine own **b**, and 3308
16:25 hast made thy **b** to be abhorred, and 3308
27:3 O Tyrus, thou hast said, I *am* of perfect **b**. 3308
27:4 the seas, thy builders have perfected thy **b**. 3308
27:11 round about; they have made thy **b** perfect. 3308
28:7 they shall draw their swords against the **b** 3308
28:12 the sum, full *of* wisdom, and perfect in **b**. 3308
28:17 Thine heart was lifted up because of thy **b**, 3308
31:8 garden of God was like unto him in his **b**. 3308
32:19 Whom dost thou pass **in b**? go down, and 5276
Hos 14:6 his **b** shall be as the olive tree, and his 1935
Zec 9:17 *is* his goodness, and how great *is* his **b**! 3308
11:7 the one I called **B**, and the other I called 5278
11:10 I took my staff, *even* **B**, and cut it asunder, 5278

BEBAI (6)

Ezr 2:11 The children of **B**, six hundred twenty and 893
8:11 of the sons of **B**; Zechariah the son of Bebai, 893
8:11 Zechariah the son of **B**, and with him twenty 893
10:28 Of the sons also of **B**; Jehohanan, Hananiah, 893
Ne 7:16 The children of **B**, six hundred twenty and 893
10:15 Bunni, Azgad, **B**, 893

BECAME (106) [BECOME]

Ge 2:7 the breath of life; and man **b** a living soul. 1961
2:10 thence it was parted, and **b** into four heads. 1961
6:4 the same ***b*** mighty *men* which *were* of old, NIH
19:26 from behind him, and she **b** a pillar of salt. 1961
20:12 daughter of my mother; and she **b** my wife. 1961
21:20 dwelt in the wilderness, and **b** an archer. 1961
24:67 and took Rebekah, and she **b** his wife; 1961
26:13 and grew until he **b** very **great**: 1431
44:32 For thy servant **b surety** for the lad unto 6148
47:20 over them: so the land **b** Pharaoh's. 1961
47:26 of the priests only, *which* **b** not Pharaoh's. 1961
49:15 to bear, and **b** a servant unto tribute. 1961
Ex 2:10 unto Pharaoh's daughter, and he **b** her son. 1961
4:3 he cast it on the ground, and it **b** a serpent; 1961
4:4 caught it, and it **b** a rod in his hand: 1961+3807.1
7:10 and before his servants, and it **b** a serpent. 1961
7:12 every man his rod, and they **b** serpents: 1961
8:17 the earth, and it **b** lice in man, and in beast; 1961
8:17 all the dust of the land **b** lice throughout all 1961
9:10 it **b** a boil breaking forth *with* blains upon 1961
9:24 in all the land of Egypt since it **b** a nation. 1961
36:13 with the taches: so it **b** one tabernacle. 1961
Nu 12:10 behold, Miriam ***b*** leprous, *white* as snow: NIH
26:10 and fifty men: and they **b** a sign. 1961+3807.1
Dt 26:5 **b** there a nation, great, mighty, and 1961
Jos 7:5 hearts of the people melted, and **b** as water. 1961
14:14 **b** the inheritance of Caleb the son 1961+3807.1
24:32 it **b** the inheritance of the children 1961+3807.1
Jdg 1:30 among them, and **b** tributaries. 1961+3807.1
1:33 Beth-anath **b** tributaries unto them. 1961+3807.1
1:35 so that they **b** tributaries. 1961+3807.1
8:27 which *thing* **b** a snare unto Gideon, and 1961
15:14 the cords that *were* upon his arms **b** as flax 1961
17:5 one of his sons, who **b** his priest. 1961
17:12 the young man **b** his priest, and was in 1961
Ru 4:16 laid it in her bosom, and **b** nurse unto it. 1961
1Sa 10:12 Therefore it **b** a proverb, *Is* Saul also 1961
16:21 him greatly; and he **b** his armourbearer. 1961
18:29 and Saul **b** David's enemy continually. 1961
22:2 unto him; and he **b** a captain over them: 1961
25:37 heart died within him, and he **b** *as* a stone. 1961
25:42 the messengers of David, and **b** his wife. 1961
2Sa 2:25 **b** one troop, and stood on the top of a hill. 1961
4:4 made haste to flee, that he fell, and **b lame**. 6452
8:2 *so* the Moabites **b** David's servants, and 1961
8:6 the Syrians **b** servants to David, 1961
8:14 and all they of Edom **b** David's servants. 1961
11:27 and she **b** his wife, and bare him a son. 1961
1Ki 11:24 men unto him, and **b** captain over a band, 1961
12:30 this thing **b** a sin: for the people went *to* 1961
13:6 restored him again, and **b** as *it was* before. 1961
13:33 he **b** *one of* the priests of the high places. 1961
13:34 this thing **b** sin unto the house of Jeroboam, 1961
2Ki 17:3 Hoshea **b** his servant, and gave him 1961
17:15 **b** vain, and *went* after the heathen that *were* NIH
24:1 and Jehoiakim **b** his servant three years: 1961
1Ch 18:2 the Moabites **b** David's servants, and 1961
18:6 the Syrians **b** David's servants, and 1961
18:13 and all the Edomites **b** David's servants. 1961
19:19 made peace with David, and **b** his servants: NIH
2Ch 27:6 So Jotham **b mighty**, because he prepared 2388
Ne 9:25 **b fat**, and delighted themselves in thy great 8080
Est 8:17 And many of the people of the land **b Jews**; 3054
Ps 69:11 for my garment; and I **b** a proverb to them. 1961
83:10 at En-dor: they **b** *as* dung for the earth. 1961
109:25 I **b** also a reproach unto them: *when* they 1961
Jer 51:30 their might hath failed; they **b** as women: 1961
Eze 17:6 and **b** a spreading vine of low stature, 1961
17:6 so it **b** a vine, and brought forth branches, 1961
19:3 it **b** a young lion, and it learned to catch 1961
19:6 he **b** a young lion, and learned to catch 1961
23:10 she **b** famous among women; for they had 1961
31:5 his branches **b** long because of NIH
34:5 they **b** meat to all the beasts of the field, 1961
34:8 surely because my flock **b** a prey, and 1961
34:8 my flock **b** meat to every beast of the field, 1961
36:4 which **b** a prey and derision to the residue 1961
Da 2:35 **b** like the chaff of the summer 1934
2:35 the stone that smote the image **b** a great 1934
8:4 but he did according to his will, and **b** great. NIH
10:15 my face toward the ground, and I **b dumb**. 481
Ob 1:12 thy brother in the day that he **b** a stranger; NIH
Mt 28:4 the keepers did shake, and **b** as dead *men*. 1096
Mk 9:3 And his raiment **b** shining, exceeding white 1096
Ac 10:10 And he **b** very hungry, and would have 1096
Ro 1:21 but **b** vain in their imaginations, and NIG
1:22 *themselves* to be wise, they **b** fools, NIG
6:18 from sin, ye **b** the servants of righteousness. NIG
1Co 9:20 And unto the Jews I **b** as a Jew, that I might 1096
9:22 To the weak **b** I as weak, that I might gain 1096
13:11 but when I **b** a man, I put away childish 1096
2Co 8:9 he was rich, *yet* for your sakes he **b** poor, NIG
Php 2:8 and **b** obedient unto death, 1096
1Th 1:6 And ye **b** followers of us, and of the Lord, 1096
2:14 **b** followers of the churches of God which 1096
Heb 2:10 For it **b** him, for whom *are* all *things*, and 4241
5:9 he **b** the author of eternal salvation unto all 1096
7:26 For such a high priest **b** us, *who is* holy, 4241
10:33 whilst ye **b** companions of them that were 1096
11:7 **b** heir of the righteousness which is by 1096
Rev 6:12 and the sun **b** black as sackcloth of hair, 1096
6:12 sackcloth of hair, and the moon **b** as blood; 1096
8:8 and the third *part* of the sea **b** blood; 1096
8:11 third *part* of the waters **b** wormwood; 1096+1519
16:3 and it **b** as the blood of a dead *man*: and 1096
16:4 and fountains of waters; and they **b** blood. 1096

BECAMEST (2) [BECOME]

1Ch 17:22 for ever; and thou, LORD, **b** their God. 1961
Eze 16:8 saith the Lord GOD, and thou **b** mine. 1961

BECAUSE (1209)

Ge 2:3 **b** that in it he had rested from all his work 3588
2:23 **b** she was taken out of Man. 3588
3:10 the garden, and I was afraid, **b** I *was* naked; 3588
3:14 **B** thou hast done this, thou *art* cursed above 3588
3:17 **B** thou hast hearkened unto the voice of thy 3588
3:20 **b** she was the mother of all living. 3588
5:29 **b of** the ground which the LORD hath 4480
7:7 the ark, **b of** the waters of the flood. 4480+6440
11:9 **b** the LORD did there confound 3588
12:13 and my soul shall live **b of** thee. 1558+871.1
12:17 with great plagues **b of** Sarai Abram's wife. 5921
16:11 **b** the LORD hath heard thy affliction. 3588
18:20 **B** the cry of Sodom and Gomorrah is great, 3588
18:20 is great, and **b** their sin is very grievous; 3588
19:13 **b** the cry of them is waxen great before 3588
20:11 Abraham said, **B** I thought, Surely the fear 3588
20:18 **b** of Sarah Abraham's wife. 1697+5921
21:11 in Abraham's sight **b of** his son. 182+5921
21:12 it not be grievous in thy sight **b of** the lad, 5921
21:12 of the lad, and **b of** thy bondwoman; 5921
21:13 will I make a nation, **b** he *is* thy seed. 3588
21:25 **b of** a well of water, 182+5921
21:31 **b** there they sware both of them. 3588
22:16 for **b** thou hast done this thing, 834+3282
22:18 **b** thou hast obeyed my voice. 834+6118
25:21 the LORD for his wife, **b** she *was* barren: 3588
25:28 loved Esau, **b** he did eat of *his* venison: 3588
26:5 **B** that Abraham obeyed my voice, and 6118
26:7 for Rebekah; **b** she *was* fair to look upon. 3588
26:9 said unto him, **B** I said, Lest I die for her. 3588
26:20 of the well Esek; **b** they strove with him. 3588
27:20 **B** the LORD thy God brought *it* to me. 3588
27:23 discerned him not, **b** his hands were hairy, 3588
27:41 **b of** the blessing wherewith his father 5921
27:46 of my life **b of** the daughters of Heth: 4480+6440
28:11 tarried there all night, **b** the sun was set; 3588
29:15 **B** thou *art* my brother, shouldest thou 3588
29:33 **B** the LORD hath heard that I *was* hated, 3588
29:34 unto me, **b** I have born him three sons: 3588
30:18 **b** I have given my maiden to my husband: 834
30:20 dwell with me, **b** I have born him six sons: 3588
31:30 **b** thou sore longedst after thy father's 3588
31:31 and said to Laban, **B** I was afraid: 3588
32:32 **b** he touched the hollow of Jacob's thigh in 3588
33:11 **b** God hath dealt graciously with me, and 3588
33:11 graciously with me, and **b** I have enough. 3588
34:7 **b** he had wrought folly in Israel in lying 3588
34:13 and said, **b** he had defiled Dinah their sister: 834
34:19 **b** he had delight in Jacob's daughter: 3588
34:27 the city, **b** they had defiled their sister. 834
35:7 **b** there God appeared unto him, when he 3588
36:7 could not bear them **b of** their cattle. 4480+6440
37:3 **b** he *was* the son of his old age: 3588
38:15 to be a harlot; **b** she had covered her face. 3588
38:26 **b** that I gave her not to Shelah my son. 3588
39:9 from me but thee, **b** thou *art* his wife: 834+871.1
39:23 **b** the LORD *was* with him, and 834+871.1
41:32 *it is* **b** the thing *is* established by God, and 3588
41:57 **b that** the famine was *so* sore in all lands. 3588
43:18 **b** they were brought into Joseph's house; 3588

Ge 43:18 **B of** the money that was returned in 1697+5921
43:32 **b** the Egyptians might not eat bread with 3588
46:30 I have seen thy face, **b** thou *art* yet alive. 3588
47:20 his field, **b** the famine prevailed over them: 3588
49: 4 **b** thou wentest up to thy father's bed; then 3588
Ex 1:12 **b of** the children of Israel. 4480+6440
1:19 **B** the Hebrew women *are* not as 3588
1:21 it came to pass, **b** the midwives feared God, 3588
2:10 and she said, **B** I drew him out of the water. 3588
4:26 husband *thou art,* **b of** the circumcision. 3807.1
5:21 **b** you have made our savour to be abhorred 834
8:12 Moses cried unto the LORD **b of** the frogs 5921
9:11 stand before Moses **b of** the boils; 4480+6440
12:39 **b** they were thrust out of Egypt, and 3588
13: 8 **b of** that *which* the LORD did unto 5668+871.1
14:11 **B** *there were* no graves in Egypt, 4480
17: 7 **b** of the chiding of the children of Israel, 5921
17: 7 **b** they tempted the LORD, saying, Is 5921
17:16 **B** the LORD hath sworn *that* the LORD 3588
18:15 **B** the people come unto me to inquire of 3588
19:18 **b** the LORD descended upon it in 4480+6440
29:33 shall not eat *thereof,* **b** they *are* holy. 3588
29:34 with fire: it shall not be eaten, **b** it *is* holy. 3588
32:35 **b** they made the calf, which Aaron 834+5921
40:35 **b** the cloud abode thereon, and the glory of 3588
Lev 6: 4 it shall be, **b** he hath sinned, and is guilty, 3588
6: 9 **b of** the burning upon the altar all night 5921
10:13 **b** it *is* thy due, and thy sons' due, 3588
11: 4 **b** he cheweth the cud, but divideth not 3588
11: 5 **b** he cheweth the cud, but divideth not 3588
11: 6 **b** he cheweth the cud, but divideth not 3588
14:48 the house clean, **b** the plague is healed. 3588
15: 2 out of his flesh, **b** *of* his issue he *is* unclean. NIH
16:16 **b of** the uncleanness of the children of 4480
16:16 **b of** their transgressions in all their sins: 4480
19: 8 **b** he hath profaned the hallowed *thing* of 3588
19:20 not be put to death, **b** she was not free. 3588
20: 3 **b** he hath given of his seed unto Molech, to 3588
21:23 nigh unto the altar, **b** he hath a blemish; 3588
22: 7 eat of the holy *things;* **b** it *is* his food. 3588
22:25 **b** their corruption *is* in them, *and* 3588
26:10 bring forth the old **b** of the new. 4480+6440
26:35 **b** it did not rest in your sabbaths, when ye 834
26:43 **b**, even because they despised my 3282
26:43 even **b** they despised my judgments, 3282+871.1
26:43 and **b** their soul abhorred my statutes. NIH
Nu 3:13 **B** all the firstborn *are* mine; *for* on the day 3588
6: 7 **b** the consecration of his God *is* upon his 3588
6:12 shall be lost, **b** his separation was defiled. 3588
7: 9 **b** the service of the sanctuary belonging 3588
9:13 **b** he brought not the offering of 3588
11: 3 **b** the fire of the LORD burnt among them. 3588
11:14 this people alone, **b** *it is* too heavy for me. 3588
11:20 **b** that ye have despised the LORD which 3282
11:34 **b** there they buried the people that lusted. 3588
12: 1 **b of** the Ethiopian woman whom he 182+5921
13:24 **b of** the cluster of grapes which 182+5921
14:16 **B** the LORD was not able to bring this 4480
14:22 **B** all *those* men which have seen my glory, 3588
14:24 **b** he had another spirit with him, and 6118
14:43 ye shall fall by the sword: **b** ye 3588+3651+5921
15:31 **B** he hath despised the word of the LORD, 3588
15:34 **b** it was not declared what should be done 3588
19:13 **b** the water of separation was not sprinkled 3588
19:20 **b** he hath defiled the sanctuary of 3588
20:12 and Aaron, **B** ye believed me not, 3282
20:13 **b** the children of Israel strove with 834
20:24 **b** ye rebelled against my word at 834+5921
21: 4 was much discouraged **b of** the way. 871.1
22: 3 afraid of the people, **b** they *were* many: 3588
22: 3 **b of** the children of Israel. 4480+6440
22:22 God's anger was kindled **b** he went: and 3588
22:29 said unto the ass, **B** thou hast mocked me: 3588
22:32 **b** *thy* way is perverse before me: 3588
25:13 **b** he was zealous for his God, and 834+8478
26:62 **b** there was no inheritance given them 3588
27: 4 from among his family, **b** he hath no son? 3588
30: 5 forgive her, **b** her father disallowed her. 3588
30:14 **b** he held his peace at her in the day that he 3588
32:11 **b** they have not wholly followed me: 3588
32:17 shall dwell in the fenced cities **b of** 4480+6440
32:19 **b** our inheritance is fallen to us on *this* side 3588
35:28 **B** he should have remained in the city of 3588
Dt 1:27 and said, **B** the LORD hated us, 871.1
1:36 **b** he hath wholly followed 834+3282
2: 5 **b** I have given mount Seir unto Esau *for* a 3588
2: 9 **b** I have given Ar unto the children of Lot 3588
2:19 **b** I have given it unto the children of Lot 3588
2:25 and be in anguish **b of** thee. 4480+6440
4: 3 seen what the LORD did **b of** Baal-peor: 871.1
4:37 **b** he loved thy fathers, therefore 3588+8478
7: 7 **b** ye were more in number than any people; 4480
7: 8 **b** the LORD loved you, and because 4480
7: 8 **b** he would keep the oath which he had 4480
8:20 **b** ye would not be obedient unto the voice 6118
9:18 **b of** all your sins which ye sinned, 5921
9:25 as I fell down *at the first;* **b** the LORD had 3588
9:28 **B** the LORD was not able to bring them 4480
9:28 **b** he hated them, he hath brought them out 4480
12:20 eat flesh, **b** thy soul longeth to eat flesh; 3588
13: 5 **b** he hath spoken to turn *you* away from 3588
13:10 **b** he hath sought to thrust thee away from 3588
14: 8 the swine, **b** it divideth the hoof, 3588
14:29 (**b** he hath no part nor inheritance with 3588
15: 2 **b** it is called the LORD'S release. 3588
15:10 **b** that for this thing the LORD thy God 3588
15:16 **b** he loveth thee and thine house, because 3588
15:16 and thine house, **b** he is well with thee; 3588
16:15 **b** the LORD thy God shall bless thee in all 3588
18:12 **b of** these abominations the LORD 1558+871.1
19: 6 **b** the way is long, and slay him; 3588
20: 3 neither be ye terrified **b of** them; 4480+6440
21:14 of her, **b** thou hast humbled her. 834+8478
22:19 **b** he hath brought up an evil name upon a 3588
22:21 **b** she hath wrought folly in Israel, to play 3588

Dt 22:24 the damsel, **b** she cried not, 834+1697+5921
22:24 **b** he hath humbled his 834+1697+5921
22:29 **b** he hath humbled her, he may not put 834+8478
23: 4 **B** they met you not with bread 834+1697+5921
23: 4 **b** they hired against thee Balaam the son of 834
23: 5 **b** the LORD thy God loved thee. 3588
23: 7 **b** thou wast a stranger in his land. 3588
24: 1 **b** he hath found some uncleanness in her: 3588
27:20 **b** he uncovereth his father's skirt. 3588
28:20 **b of** the wickedness of thy doings, 4480+6440
28:45 **b** thou hearkenedst not unto the voice of 3588
28:47 **B** thou servedst not the LORD thy 834+8478
28:55 **b** he hath nothing left him in the siege, and 4480
28:62 **b** thou wouldest not obey the voice of 3588
29:25 **B** they have forsaken the covenant of 834+5921
31:17 **b** our God *is* not amongst us? 3588+5921
31:29 **b** ye will do evil in the sight of the LORD, 3588
32: 3 **B** I will publish the name of the LORD: 3588
32:19 **b** of the provoking of his sons, 4480
32:47 *is* not a vain thing for you; **b** it *is* your life: 3588
32:51 **B** ye trespassed against me among 834+5921
32:51 **b** ye sanctified me not in the midst of 834+5921
33:21 **b** there, *in* a portion of the lawgiver, *was he* 3588
Jos 2: 9 inhabitants of the land faint **b of** you. 4480+6440
2:11 more courage in any man, **b of** you: 4480+6440
2:24 of the country do faint **b of** us. 4480+6440
5: 1 any more, **b of** the children of Israel. 4480+6440
5: 6 **b** they obeyed not the voice of the LORD: 834
5: 7 **b** they had not circumcised them by 3588
6: 1 shut up **b of** the children of Israel: 4480+6440
6:17 **b** she hid the messengers that we sent. 3588
6:25 **b** she hid the messengers, which Joshua 3588
7:12 before their enemies, **b** they were accursed: 3588
7:15 **b** he hath transgressed the covenant of 3588
7:15 and **b** he hath wrought folly in Israel. 3588
9: 9 **b of** the name of the LORD thy God: 3807.1
9:18 **b** the princes of the congregation had sworn 3588
9:20 **b** of the oath which we sware unto them. 5921
9:24 said, **B** it was certainly told thy servants, 3588
9:24 sore afraid of our lives **b of** you, 4480+6440
10: 2 feared greatly, **b** Gibeon *was* a great city, 3588
10: 2 **b** it *was* greater than Ai, and all the men 3588
10:42 **b** the LORD God of Israel fought for 3588
11: 6 said unto Joshua, Be not afraid **b of** them: 6440
14: 9 **b** thou hast wholly followed the LORD 3588
14:14 **b** that he wholly followed the LORD God 3282
17: 1 **b** he was a man of war, therefore he had 3588
17: 6 **B** the daughters of Manasseh had an 3588
20: 5 **b** he smote his neighbour unwittingly, 3588
22:31 **b** ye have not committed this trespass 834
23: 3 hath done unto all these nations **b** 4480+6440
Jdg 1:19 of the valley, **b** they had chariots of iron. 3588
2:18 for it repented the LORD **b** of their 6440
2:20 **B** that this people hath transgressed my 3282
3:12 **b** they had done evil in the sight of 3588+5921
5:23 **b** they came not to the help of the LORD, 3588
6: 2 **b of** the Midianites the children of 4480+6440
6: 6 **b of** the Midianites; 4480+6440
6: 7 unto the LORD **b of** the Midianites, 182+5921
6:22 for **b** I have seen an angel of 3651+5921
6:27 **b** he feared his father's household, 834+3509.1
6:30 **b** he hath cast down the altar of Baal, and 3588
6:30 **b** he hath cut down the grove that *was* by it. 3588
6:31 for himself, **b** *one* hath cast down his altar. 3588
6:32 **b** he hath thrown down his altar. 3588
8:20 for he feared, **b** he *was* yet a youth. 3588
8:24 golden earrings, **b** they *were* Ishmaelites.) 3588
9:18 the men of Shechem, **b** he *is* your brother;) 3588
10:10 both **b** we have forsaken our God, and 3588
11:13 **B** Israel took away my land, when they 3588
12: 4 men of Gilead smote Ephraim, **b** they said, 3588
13:22 We shall surely die, **b** we have seen God. 3588
14:17 that he told her, **b** she lay sore upon him: 3588
15: 6 **b** he had taken his wife, and given her to 3588
18:28 **b** it *was* far from Zidon, and they had no 3588
20:36 **b** they trusted unto the liers in wait which 3588
21:15 **b** that the LORD had made a breach in 3588
21:22 **b** we reserved not to each man his wife in 3588
1Sa 1: 6 **b** the LORD had shut up her womb. 3588
1:20 *saying,* **B** I have asked him of the LORD. 3588
2: 1 mine enemies; **b** I rejoice in thy salvation. 3588
2:25 their father, **b** the LORD would slay them. 3588
3:13 **b** his sons made themselves vile, and 3588
4:21 **b** the ark of God was taken, and because 413
4:21 and **b of** her father in law and her husband. 413
6:19 **b** they had looked into the ark of 3588
6:19 **b** the LORD had smitten *many* of 3588
8:18 shall cry out in that day **b of** 4480+6440+3807.1
9:13 until he come, **b** he doth bless the sacrifice; 3588
9:16 my people, **b** their cry is come unto me. 3588
10: 1 *Is it* not **b** the LORD hath anointed thee to 3588
12:10 **b** we have forsaken the LORD, and 3588
12:22 **b** it hath pleased the LORD to make you 3588
13:11 **B** I saw that the people were scattered from 3588
13:14 **b** thou hast not kept *that* which the LORD 3588
14:29 **b** I tasted a little of this honey. 3588
15:23 **B** thou hast rejected the word of 3282
15:24 **b** I feared the people, and obeyed their 3588
16: 7 height of his stature; **b** I have refused him: 3588
17:32 to Saul, Let no man's heart fail **b of** him; 5921
18: 3 **b** he loved him as his own soul. 871.1
18:12 **b** the LORD was with him, and 3588
18:16 **b** he went out and came in before them. 3588
19: 4 **b** he hath not sinned against thee, and 3588
19: 4 **b** his works *have been* to thee-ward very 3588
20:17 David to swear again, **b** he loved him: 3588
20:18 shalt be missed, **b** thy seat will be empty. 3588
20:34 **b** his father had done him shame. 3588
21: 8 **b** the king's business required haste. 3588
22:17 **b** their hand also *is* with David, and 3588
22:17 **b** they knew when he fled, and did not 3588
24: 5 **b** he had cut off Saul's skirt. 834+5921
25:28 **b** my lord fighteth the battles of 3588
26:12 **b** a deep sleep from the LORD was fallen 3588
26:16 to die, **b** ye have not kept your master, 834

1Sa 26:21 **b** my soul was precious in thine eyes 834+8478
28:18 **B** thou obeyedst not the voice of 834+3509.1
28:20 was sore afraid, **b of** the words of Samuel: 4480
30: 6 **b** the soul of all the people was grieved, 3588
30:13 left me, **b** three days agone I fell sick. 3588
30:16 **b of** all the great spoil that they had taken 871.1
30:22 and said, **B** they went not with us, 834+3282
2Sa 1: 9 upon me, **b** my life *is* yet whole in me. 3588
1:10 **b** I was sure that he could not live after *that* 3588
1:12 of Israel; **b** they were fallen by the sword. 3588
2: 6 you this kindness, **b** ye have done this thing. 834
3:11 Abner a word again, **b** he feared him. 4480
3:30 **b** he had slain their brother Asahel at 834+5921
6: 8 **b** the LORD had made a breach upon 5921
6:12 all that *pertaineth* unto him, **b of** 5668+871.1
8:10 **b** he had fought against Hadadezer, 834+5921
10: 5 **b** the men were greatly ashamed: 3588
12: 6 **b** he did this thing, and because he 834+6118
12: 6 he did this thing, and **b** he had no pity. 834+5921
12:10 **b** thou hast despised me, and 3588+6118
12:14 **b** by this deed thou hast given great 3588
12:25 he called his name Jedidiah, **b of** 5668+871.1
13:22 **b** he had forced his sister 834+1697+5921
14:15 *it is* **b** the people have made me afraid: 3588
14:26 he polled *it:* **b** *the hair* was heavy on him, 3588
16: 8 to thy mischief, **b** thou *art* a bloody man. 3588
16:10 **b** the LORD hath said unto him, 3588
18:20 **b** the king's son is dead. 3588+3651+5921
19:21 **b** he cursed the LORD'S anointed? 3588
19:26 go to the king; **b** thy servant *is* lame. 3588
19:42 of Israel, **B** the king *is* near of kin to us: 3588
21: 1 **b** he slew the Gibeonites. 834+5921
21: 7 **b of** the LORD'S oath that *was* between 5921
22: 8 heaven moved and shook, **b** he was wroth. 3588
22:20 he delivered me, **b** he delighted in me. 3588
23: 6 **b** they cannot be taken with hands: 3588
1Ki 1:50 Adonijah feared **b** of Solomon, and 4480+6440
2: 7 I fled **b of** Absalom thy brother. 4480+6440
2:26 **b** thou barest the ark of the Lord GOD 3588
2:26 **b** thou hast been afflicted in all where*in* my 3588
3: 2 **b** there was no house built unto the name of 3588
3:11 **B** thou hast asked this thing, and 834+3282
3:19 child died in the night; **b** she overlaid it. 834
7:47 **b** they were exceeding many: 4480
8:11 not stand to minister **b of** the cloud: 4480+6440
8:33 **b** they have sinned against thee, and 834
8:35 is no rain, **b** they have sinned against thee; 3588
8:64 **b** the brasen altar that *was* before 3588
9: 9 **B** they forsook the LORD their God, 834+5921
10: 9 **b** the LORD loved Israel for ever, 871.1
11: 9 **b** his heart was turned from the LORD 3588
11:33 **B** that they have forsaken me, and 3282
11:34 **b** he kept my commandments and 834
14:13 **b** in him there is found *some* good thing 3282
14:15 **b** they have made their groves, 834+3282
14:16 he shall give Israel up **b of** the sins 1558+871.1
15: 5 **B** David did *that* which *was* right in the eyes 834
15:13 **b** she had made an idol in a grove; 834
15:30 **B of** the sins of Jeroboam which he sinned, 5921
16: 7 of Jeroboam; and **b** he killed him. 834+5921
17: 7 **b** there had been no rain in the land. 3588
19: 7 *and* eat; **b** the journey *is* too great for thee. 3588
19:14 **b** the children of Israel have forsaken thy 3588
20:28 the LORD, **B** the Syrians have said, 834+3282
20:36 **B** thou hast not obeyed the voice of 834+3282
20:42 **B** thou hast let go out of *thy* hand a man 3282
21: 2 garden of herbs, **b** it *is* near unto my house: 3588
21: 4 **b of** the word which Naboth the Jezreelite 5921
21: 6 **B** I spake unto Naboth the Jezreelite, and 3588
21:20 I have found *thee:* **b** thou hast sold thyself 3282
21:29 **b** he humbleth himself before me, 3282+3588
2Ki 1: 3 *Is it* not **b** *there is* not a God in Israel, 4480
1: 6 *Is it* not **b** *there is* not a God in Israel, 4480
1:16 *is it* not **b** *there is* no God in Israel to 4480
1:17 king of Judah; **b** he had no son. 3588
5: 1 **b** by him the LORD had given deliverance 3588
8:12 **B** I know the evil that thou wilt do unto 3588
8:29 the son of Ahab in Jezreel, **b** he was sick. 3588
9:14 all Israel, **b of** Hazael king of Syria. 4480+6440
10:30 **B** thou hast done well in executing 834+3282
13: 4 **b** the king of Syria oppressed them. 3588
13:23 had respect unto them, **b of** his 4616+3807.1
15:16 **b** they opened not *to him,* therefore 3588
17:26 **b** they know not the manner of 834+3509.1
18:12 **B** they obeyed not the voice of 834+5921
19:28 **B** thy rage against me and thy tumult is 3282
21:11 **B** Manasseh king of Judah hath done 834+3282
21:15 **B** they have done *that* which *was* evil 834+3282
22: 7 into their hand, **b** they dealt faithfully. 3588
22:13 **b** our fathers have not hearkened unto 834+5921
22:17 **B** they have forsaken me, and 834+8478
22:19 **B** thine heart was tender, and thou hast 3282
23:26 **b of** all the provocations that Manasseh had 5921
1Ch 1:19 **b** in his days the earth was divided: 3588
4: 9 saying, **B** I bare *him* with sorrow. 3588
4:41 **b** *there was* pasture there for their flocks. 3588
5: 9 **b** their cattle were multiplied in the land of 3588
5:20 of them; **b** they put their trust in him. 3588
5:22 down many slain, **b** the war *was* of God. 3588
7:21 **b** they came down to take *away* their cattle. 3588
7:23 name Beriah, **b** it went evil with his house. 3588
9:27 **b** the charge *was* upon them, and 3588
12: 1 while he yet kept himself close **b of** 4480+6440
13:10 **b** he put his hand to the ark: 834+5921
13:11 **b** the LORD had made a breach upon 3588
14: 2 up on high, **b of** his people Israel. 5668+871.1
15:13 For **b** ye *did it* not at the first, 4100+3807.1
15:22 instructed about the song, **b** he *was* skilful. 3588
16:33 **b** he cometh to judge the earth. 3588
16:41 the LORD, **b** his mercy *endureth* for ever; 3588
18:10 **b** he had fought against Hadarezer, 834+5921
19: 2 **b** his father shewed kindness to me. 3588
21: 8 have sinned greatly, **b** I have done this thing: 834
21:30 for he was afraid **b of** the sword of 4480+6440
22: 8 **b** thou hast shed much blood upon the earth 3588

B

1Ch 23:28 **B** their office *was* to wait on the sons of 3588
27:23 **b** the LORD had said *he* would increase 3588
27:24 **b** there fell wrath for it against Israel; 2050.1
28: 3 **b** thou *hast been* a man of war, and 3588
29: 3 **b** I have set my affection to the house of 2050.1
29: 9 **b** with perfect heart they offered willingly 3588
2Ch 1:11 **B** this was in thine heart, and 834+3282
2:11 **B** the LORD hath loved his people, 871.1
6:24 the enemy, **b** they have sinned against thee; 3588
6:26 is no rain, **b** they have sinned against thee; 3588
7: 2 **b** the glory of the LORD had filled 3588
7: 6 **b** his mercy *endureth* for ever, when David 3588
7: 7 **b** the brasen altar which Solomon had made 3588
7:22 **B** they forsook the LORD God of 834+5921
8:11 **b** *the places are* holy, whereunto the ark of 3588
9: 8 **b** thy God loved Israel, to establish them 871.1
12: 2 **b** they had transgressed against 3588
12: 5 gathered together to Jerusalem **b of** 4480+6440
12:14 **b** he prepared not his heart to seek 3588
13:18 **b** they relied upon the LORD God of their 3588
14: 6 **b** the LORD had given him rest. 3588
14: 7 **b** we have sought the LORD our God, 3588
15:16 **b** she had made an idol in a grove: 834
16: 7 **B** thou hast relied on the king of Syria, and 871.1
16: 8 yet, **b** thou didst rely on the LORD, 871.1
16:10 **b of** this *thing*. And Asa oppressed *some* of 5921
17: 3 **b** he walked in the first ways of his father 3588
20:37 **B** thou hast joined thyself with Ahaziah, 3509.1
21: 3 gave he to Jehoram; **b** he *was* the firstborn. 3588
21: 7 **b of** the covenant that he had made 4616+3807.1
21:10 **b** he had forsaken the LORD God of his 3588
21:12 **B** thou hast not walked in the ways of 834+8478
22: 6 **b of** the wounds which were given him at 3588
22: 6 the son of Ahab at Jezreel, **b** he was sick. 3588
22: 9 **B**, said they, he *is* the son of Jehoshaphat, 3588
24:16 **b** he had done good in Israel, both towards 3588
24:20 **b** ye have forsaken the LORD, he hath 3588
24:24 **b** they had forsaken the LORD God of 3588
25:16 **b** thou hast done this, and hast not 3588
25:20 **b** they sought after the gods of Edom. 3588
26:20 to go out, **b** the LORD had smitten him. 3588
27: 6 **b** he prepared his ways before the LORD 3588
28: 6 **b** they had forsaken the LORD God of 871.1
28: 9 **b** the LORD God of your fathers was 871.1
28:19 the LORD brought Judah low **b of** 5668+871.1
28:23 **B** the gods of the kings of Syria help them, 3588
30: 3 **b** the priests had not sanctified themselves 3588
34:21 **b** our fathers have not kept the word 834+5921
34:25 **B** they have forsaken me, and 834+8478
34:27 **B** thine heart was tender, and thou didst 3282
35:14 **b** the priests the sons of Aaron *were busied* 3588
36:15 **b** he had compassion on his people, and 3588
Ezr 3: 3 **b of** the people of *those* countries: 4480
3:11 **b** *he is* good, for his mercy *endureth* for 3588
3:11 **b** the foundation of the house of 5921
4:14 Now **b** we have maintenance 1768+3606+6903
8:22 **b** we had spoken unto the king, saying, 3588
9: 4 **b of** the transgression of those that had 5921
9:15 for *we* cannot stand before thee **b of** this. 5921
10: 6 for he mourned **b of** the transgression of 5921
10: 9 trembling **b of** *this* matter, and for the great 5921
Ne 4: 9 them day and night, **b of** them. 4480+6440
5: 3 that we might buy corn, **b of** the dearth. 871.1
5: 9 **b of** the reproach of the heathen our 4480
5:15 but so did not I, **b of** the fear of God. 4480+6440
5:18 **b** the bondage was heavy upon this people. 3588
6:18 **b** he *was* the son in law of Shechaniah 3588
8:12 **b** they had understood the words that were 3588
9:37 whom thou hast set over us **b of** our sins: 871.1
9:38 **b of** all this we make a sure covenant, and 871.1
13: 2 **B** they met not the children of Israel with 3588
13:29 **b** they have defiled the priesthood, and 5921
Est 1:15 **b** she hath not performed 834+5921
8: 7 **b** he laid his hand upon the Jews. 834+5921
9: 3 **b** the fear of Mordecai fell upon them. 3588
9:24 **B** Haman the son of Hammedatha, 3588
Job 3:10 **B** it shut not up the doors of my *mother's* 3588
6:20 They were confounded **b** they had hoped; 3588
8: 9 **b** our days upon earth *are* a shadow:) 3588
11:16 **B** thou shalt forget *thy* misery, *and* 3588
11:18 thou shalt be secure, **b** there is hope; yea, 3588
15:27 **B** he covereth his face with his fatness, and 3588
17:12 the light *is* short, **b** of darkness. 4480+6440
18:15 dwell in his tabernacle, **b** *it is* none of his: 4480
20:19 **B** he hath oppressed *and* hath forsaken 3588
20:19 *b* he hath violently taken away a house NIH
23:17 **B** I was not cut off before the darkness, 3588
29:12 **B** I delivered the poor that cried, and 3588
30:11 **B** he hath loosed my cord, and afflicted me, 3588
31:25 If I rejoiced **b** my wealth *was* great, and 3588
31:25 and **b** mine hand had gotten much; 3588
32: 1 **b** he *was* righteous in his own eyes. 3588
32: 2 **b** he justified himself rather than God. 5921
32: 3 **b** they had found no answer, and 834+5921
32: 4 Job had spoken, **b** they *were* elder than he. 3588
34:27 **B** they turned back from him, and 3651+5921
34:36 the end **b of** *his* answers for wicked men. 5921
35:12 none giveth answer, **b of** the pride of 4480+6440
35:15 **b** *it is* not *so*, he hath visited *in* his anger; 3588
36:18 **B** *there is* wrath, *beware* lest he take thee 3588
38:21 Knowest thou *it*, **b** thou wast then born? or 3588
38:21 born? or **b** the number of thy days *is* great? NIH
39:11 Wilt thou trust him, **b** his strength *is* great? 3588
39:17 **B** God hath deprived her of wisdom, 3588
Ps 5: 8 **b of** mine enemies; 4616+3807.1
5:11 ever shout for joy, **b** thou defendest them: 2050.1
6: 7 Mine eye is consumed **b of** grief; it waxeth 4480
6: 7 it waxeth old **b of** all mine enemies. 871.1
7: 6 up thyself **b of** the rage of mine enemies: 871.1
8: 2 hast thou ordained strength **b of** 4616+3807.1
13: 6 **b** he hath dealt bountifully with me. 3588
14: 6 of the poor, **b** the LORD *is* his refuge. 3588
16: 8 **b** *he is* at my right hand, I shall not be 3588
18: 7 and were shaken, **b** he was wroth. 3588
18:19 he delivered me, **b** he delighted in me. 3588
Ps 27:11 in a plain path, **b of** mine enemies. 4616+3807.1
28: 5 **B** they regard not the works of the LORD, 3588
28: 6 **b** he hath heard the voice of my 3588
31:10 my strength faileth **b of** mine iniquity, and 871.1
33:21 in him, **b** we have trusted in his holy name. 3588
37: 1 Fret not thyself **b of** evildoers, neither be 871.1
37: 7 **b of** him who prospereth *in* his way, 871.1
37: 7 **b of** the man who bringeth wicked devices 871.1
37:40 and save them, **b** they trust in him. 3588
38: 3 *is* no soundness in my flesh **b of** 4480+6440
38: 3 *is there any* rest in my bones **b of** 4480+6440
38: 5 My wounds stink *and* are corrupt **b** 4480+6440
38:20 **b** I follow *the thing that* good *is*. 8478
39: 9 I opened not my mouth; **b** thou didst *it*. 3588
41:11 **b** mine enemy doth not triumph over me. 3588
42: 9 **b of** the oppression of the enemy? 871.1
43: 2 **b of** the oppression of the enemy? 871.1
44: 3 **b** thou hadst a favour unto them. 3588
45: 4 *in* thy majesty ride prosperously **b of** 1697+5921
48:11 daughters of Judah be glad, **b of** 4616+3807.1
52: 9 **b** thou hast done *it*: and I will wait on thy 3588
53: 5 *them* to shame, **b** God hath despised them. 3588
55: 3 **B of** the voice of the enemy, because of 4480
55: 3 of the voice of the enemy, **b of** 4480+6440
55:19 **B** they have no changes, therefore they fear 834
59: 9 *B of* his strength will I wait upon thee: NIH
60: 4 *it* may be displayed **b of** the truth. 4480+6440
60: 8 my shoe: Philistia, triumph thou **b of** me. 5921
63: 3 **B** thy lovingkindness *is* better than life, 3588
63: 7 **B** thou hast been my help, therefore in 3588
68:29 **B of** thy temple at Jerusalem shall kings 4480
69: 7 **B** for thy sake I have borne reproach; 3588
69:18 deliver me **b of** mine enemies. 4616+3807.1
78:22 **B** they believed not in God, and trusted not 3588
86:17 **b** thou, LORD, hast holpen me, and 3588
91: 9 **B** thou hast made the LORD, *which is* my 3588
91:14 **B** he hath set his love upon me, therefore 3588
91:14 set him on high, **b** he hath known my name. 3588
97: 8 daughters of Judah rejoiced, **b of** 4616+3807.1
102:10 **B of** thine indignation and thy wrath: 4480+6440
106:33 **B** they provoked his spirit, so that he spake 3588
107:11 **B** they rebelled against the words of God, 3588
107:17 Fools **b of** their transgression, and because 4480
107:17 **b of** their iniquities, are afflicted. 4480
107:26 their soul is melted **b of** trouble. 871.1
107:30 are they glad **b** they be quiet; so he bringeth 3588
109:16 **B** that he remembered not to shew mercy, 3282
109:21 **b** thy mercy *is* good, deliver thou me. 3588
116: 1 **b** he hath heard my voice *and* 3588
116: 2 **B** he hath inclined his ear unto me, 3588
118: 1 *he is* good: **b** his mercy *endureth* for ever. 3588
119:53 **b of** the wicked that forsake thy law. 4480
119:56 This I had, **b** I kept thy precepts. 3588
119:62 unto thee **b of** thy righteous judgments. 5921
119:74 they see me; **b** I have hoped in thy word. 3588
119:100 than the ancients, **b** I keep thy precepts. 3588
119:136 down mine eyes, **b** they keep not thy law. 5921
119:139 **b** mine enemies have forgotten thy words. 3588
119:158 and was grieved; **b** they kept not thy word. 834
119:164 I praise thee **b of** thy righteous judgments. 5921
122: 9 **B of** the house of the LORD our 4616+3807.1
Pr 1:24 **B** I have called, and ye refused; I have 3282
21: 7 destroy them; **b** they refuse to do judgment. 3588
22:22 Rob not the poor, **b** he *is* poor: 3588
24:13 My son, eat thou honey, **b** *it is* good; and 3588
24:19 **b of** evil *men*, neither be thou envious at 871.1
Ecc 2:17 **b** the work that is wrought under the sun *is* 3588
2:18 **b** I should leave it unto the man that shall 7945
4: 9 **b** they have a good reward for their labour. 834
5:20 **b** God answereth *him* in the joy of his 3588
8: 6 **B** to every purpose there is time and 3588
8:11 **B** sentence *against* an evil work is not 834
8:13 as a shadow; **b** he feareth not before God. 834
8:15 **b** a man hath no better *thing* under the sun, 834
8:17 **b** though a man labour to seek *it* out, 7945+871.1
10:15 **b** he knoweth not how to go to the city. 834
12: 3 the grinders cease **b** they are few, and 3588
12: 5 **b** man goeth to his long home, and 3588
12: 9 moreover, **b** the Preacher was wise, he still 7945
SS 1: 3 **B of** the savour of thy good ointments thy 3807.1
1: 6 **b** I *am* black, because the sun hath looked 7945
1: 6 I *am* black, **b** the sun hath looked upon me: 7945
3: 8 sword upon his thigh **b of** fear in the night. 4480
Isa 2: 6 **b** they be replenished from the east, and 3588
3: 8 **b** their tongue and their doings *are* against 3588
3:16 **B** the daughters of Zion are haughty, 3282+3588
5:13 into captivity, **b** *they have* no knowledge: 4480
5:24 **b** they have cast away the law of 3588
6: 5 **b** I *am* a man of unclean lips, and I dwell in 3588
7: 5 **B** Syria, Ephraim, and the son of 3282+3588
7:24 **b** all the land shall become briers and 3588
8:20 to this word, *it is* **b** *there is* no light in them. 834
10:27 shall be destroyed **b of** the anointing. 4480+6440
14:20 **b** thou hast destroyed thy land, *and* 3588
14:29 **b** the rod of him that smote thee is broken: 3588
15: 1 **B** in the night Ar of Moab is laid waste, *and* 3588
15: 1 **b** in the night Kir of Moab is laid waste, 3588
17: 9 they left **b of** the children of Israel: 4480+6440
17:10 **B** thou hast forgotten the God of thy 3588
19:16 **b of** the shaking of the hand of 4480+6440
19:17 **b of** the counsel of the LORD of 4480+6440
19:20 unto the LORD **b of** the oppressors, 4480+6440
22: 4 **b of** the spoiling of the daughter of my 5921
24: 5 **b** they have transgressed the laws, 3588
26: 3 *is* stayed *on thee*: **b** he trusteth in thee. 3588
28:15 **B** ye have said, We have made a covenant 3588
28:28 **b** he will not ever be threshing it, nor break 3588
30:12 **B** ye despise this word, and trust in 3282
31: 1 and trust in chariots, **b** *they are* many; 3588
31: 1 in horsemen, **b** they are very strong; but 3588
32:14 **B** the palaces shall be forsaken; 3588
37:29 **B** thy rage against me, and thy tumult, 3282
40: 7 **b** the spirit of the LORD bloweth upon it: 3588
43:20 **b** I give waters in the wilderness, *and* 3588
48: 4 **B** I knew that thou *art* obstinate, and 4480
Isa 49: 7 princes also shall worship, **b of** 4616+3807.1
50: 2 **b** *there is* no water, and dieth for thirst. 4480
51:13 **b of** the fury of the oppressor, 4480+6440
53: 9 **b** he had done no violence, neither *was any* 5921
53:12 **b** he hath poured out his soul unto 834+8478
55: 5 not thee shall run unto thee **b of** 4616+3807.1
60: 5 **b** the abundance of the sea shall be 3588
60: 9 Holy One of Israel, **b** he hath glorified thee. 3588
61: 1 **b** the LORD hath anointed me to preach 3282
64: 7 consumed us, **b of** our iniquities. 3027+871.1
65:12 **b** when I called, ye did not answer; when I 3282
65:16 **b** the former troubles are forgotten, and 3588
65:16 and **b** they are hid from mine eyes. 3588
66: 4 **b** when I called, none did answer; when I 3282
Jer 2:35 Yet thou sayest, **B** I am innocent, surely his 3588
2:35 with thee, **b** thou sayest, I have not sinned. 5921
4: 4 **b of** the evil of your doings. 4480+6440
4:17 **b** she hath been rebellious against me, 3588
4:18 **b** *it is* bitter, because it reacheth unto thine 3588
4:18 *it is* bitter, **b** it reacheth unto thine heart. 3588
4:19 my peace, **b** thou hast heard, O my soul, 3588
4:28 **b** I have spoken *it*, I have purposed 3588+5921
4:31 for my soul is wearied **b of** murderers. 3807.1
5: 6 **b** their transgressions are many, *and* 3588
5:14 **B** ye speak this word, behold, I will make 3282
6:19 **b** they have not hearkened unto my words, 3588
6:30 call them, **b** the LORD hath rejected them. 3588
7:13 now, **b** ye have done all these works, saith 3282
8:14 **b** we have sinned against the LORD. 3588
8:19 **b of** them that dwell in a far country: 4480
9:10 **b** they are burnt up, so that none can pass 3588
9:13 **B** they have forsaken my law which I set 5921
9:19 **b** we have forsaken the land, because 3588
9:19 the land, **b** our dwellings have cast *us* out. 3588
10: 5 must needs be borne, **b** they cannot go. 3588
12: 4 **b** they said, He shall not see our last end. 3588
12:11 made desolate, **b** no man layeth *it* to heart. 3588
12:13 **b of** the fierce anger of the LORD. 4480
13:17 **b** the LORD'S flock is carried away 3588
13:25 **b** thou hast forgotten me, and trusted in 834
14: 4 **B** the ground is chapt, for there was 5668+871.1
14: 5 and forsook *it*, **b** there was no grass. 3588
14: 6 their eyes did fail, **b** *there was* no grass. 3588
14:16 **b of** the famine and the sword; 4480+6440
15: 4 into all kingdoms of the earth, **b of** 1558+871.1
15:17 I sat alone **b of** thy hand: 4480+6440
16:11 **B** your fathers have forsaken me, 834+5921
16:18 **b** they have defiled my land, they have 5921
17:13 **b** they have forsaken the LORD, 3588
18:15 **B** my people hath forgotten me, they have 3588
19: 4 **B** they have forsaken me, and 834+3282
19: 8 and hiss **b of** all the plagues thereof. 5921
19:13 **b of** all the houses upon whose roofs they 3807.1
19:15 **b** they have hardened their necks, that *they* 3588
20: 8 **b** the word of the LORD was made a 3588
20:17 **B** he slew me not from the womb; or that my 834
21:12 **b of** the evil of your doings. 4480+6440
22: 9 **B** they have forsaken the covenant of 834+5921
22:15 thou reign, **b** thou closest *thyself* in cedar? 3588
23: 9 within me is broken **b of** the prophets; 3807.1
23: 9 **b of** the LORD, and because of 4480+6440
23: 9 and **b of** the words of his holiness. 4480+6440
23:10 for **b of** swearing the land mourneth; 4480+6440
23:38 **B** you say this word, The burden of 3282
25: 8 **B** ye have not heard my words, 834+3282
25:16 **b of** the sword that I will send among 4480+6440
25:27 **b of** the sword which I will send among 6440
25:37 **b of** the fierce anger of the LORD. 4480+6440
25:38 **b of** the fierceness of the oppressor, 4480+6440
25:38 and **b of** his fierce anger. 4480+6440
26: 3 **b of** the evil of their doings. 4480+6440
28:16 **b** thou hast taught rebellion against 3588
29:15 **B** ye have said, The LORD hath raised us 3588
29:19 **B** they have not hearkened to my 834+8478
29:23 **B** they have committed villany in 834+3282
29:25 **B** thou hast sent letters in thy name 834+3282
29:31 **B** that Shemaiah hath prophesied unto you, 3282
29:32 **b** he hath taught rebellion against 3588
30:14 of thine iniquity; *b* thy sins were increased. NIH
30:15 *b* thy sins were increased, I have done these NIH
30:17 **b** they called thee an Outcast, *saying*, This 3588
31:15 comforted for her children, **b** they *were* not. 3588
31:19 **b** I did bear the reproach of my youth. 3588
32:24 that fight against it, **b of** the sword, 4480+6440
32:32 **B of** all the evil of the children of Israel and 5921
35:16 **B** the sons of Jonadab the son of Rechab 3588
35:17 **b** I have spoken unto them, but they have 3282
35:18 **B** ye have obeyed the commandment 834+3282
39:18 **b** thou hast put thy trust in me, saith 3588
40: 3 **b** ye have sinned against the LORD, and 3588
41: 9 whom he had slain **b of** Gedaliah, 3027+871.1
41:18 **B of** the Chaldeans: for they were 4480+6440
41:18 **b** Ishmael the son of Nethaniah had slain 3588
44: 3 **B** of their wickedness which they 4480+6440
44:22 **b of** the evil of your doings, *and* 4480+6440
44:22 *and* **b of** the abominations which ye 4480+6440
44:23 **B** you have burnt incense, and 834+4480+6440
44:23 **b** ye have sinned against the LORD, and 834
46:15 stood not, **b** the LORD did drive them. 3588
46:21 **b** the day of their calamity was come upon 3588
46:23 **b** they are more than the grasshoppers, and 3588
47: 4 **B of** the day that cometh to spoil all 5921
48: 7 For **b** thou hast trusted in thy works and 3282
48:36 **b** the riches *that* he hath gotten are 3651+5921
48:42 **b** he hath magnified *himself* against 3588
48:45 the shadow of Heshbon **b of** the force: 4480
50: 7 **b** they have sinned against 834+8478
50:11 **B** ye were glad, because ye rejoiced, O ye 3588
50:11 Because ye were glad, **b** ye rejoiced, O ye 3588
50:11 **b** ye are grown fat as the heifer at grass, 3588
50:13 **B of** the wrath of the LORD it shall not be 4480
50:24 **b** thou hast striven against the LORD. 3588
51:11 **b** *it is* the vengeance of the LORD, 3588
51:51 are confounded, **b** we have heard reproach: 3588
51:55 **B** the LORD *hath* spoiled Babylon, and 3588

Jer 51:56 **B** the spoiler is come upon her, *even* upon 3588
La 1: 3 Judah is gone into captivity **b of** affliction, 4480
1: 3 of affliction, and **b of** great servitude: 4480
1: 4 **b** none come to the solemn feasts: 4480
1: 8 **b** they have seen her nakedness: 3588
1:16 **b** the comforter that *should* relieve my soul 3588
1:16 are desolate, **b** the enemy prevailed. 3588
2:11 **b** the children and the sucklings swoon in 871.1
3:22 not consumed, **b** his compassions fail not. 3588
3:28 **b** he hath borne *it* upon him. 3588
3:51 **b of** all the daughters of my city. 4480
5: 9 bread with *the peril of* our lives **b of** 4480+6440
5:10 Our skin was black like an oven **b of** 4480+6440
5:18 **B of** the mountain of Zion, which is 5921
Eze 3:20 **b** thou hast not given him warning, he shall 3588
3:21 not sin, he shall surely live, **b** he is warned; 3588
5: 7 **B** ye multiplied more than the nations that 3282
5: 9 more the like, **b of** all thine abominations. 3282
5:11 **b** thou hast defiled my sanctuary with all 3282
6: 9 **b** I am broken with their whorish heart, 834
7:19 **b** it is the stumblingblock of their iniquity. 3588
12:19 **b of** the violence of all them that dwell 4480
13: 8 **B** ye have spoken vanity, and seen lies, 3282
13:10 **B**, even because they have seduced my 3282
13:10 even **b** they have seduced my 3282+871.1
13:22 **B** *with* lies *ye* have made the heart of 3282
14: 5 **b** they are all estranged from me through 834
14:15 may pass through **b of** the beasts: 4480+6440
15: 8 **b** they have committed a trespass, saith 3282
16:15 playedst the harlot **b of** thy renown, and 5921
16:28 with the Assyrians, **b** thou wast unsatiable; 4480
16:36 **B** thy filthiness was poured out, and 3282
16:43 **B** thou hast not remembered the days 834+3282
16:63 never open thy mouth any more, **b of** 4480+6440
18:18 *As for* his father, **b** he cruelly oppressed, 3588
18:28 **B** he considereth, and turneth away from 2050.1
20:16 **B** they despised my judgments, and walked 3282
20:24 **B** they had not executed my judgments, but 3282
21: 7 shalt answer, For the tidings; **b** it cometh: 3588
21:13 **B** *it is* a trial, and what if *the sword* 3588
21:24 **B** ye have made your iniquity to be 3282
21:24 **b**, *I say*, that ye are come to remembrance, 3282
21:28 to consume **b of** the glittering: 4616+3807.1
22:19 **B** ye are all become dross, 3282
23:30 **b** thou hast gone a whoring after 871.1
23:30 **b** thou art polluted with their idols. 834+5921
23:35 **B** thou hast forgotten me, and cast me 3282
23:45 **b** they *are* adulteresses, and blood *is* in their 3588
24:13 **b** I have purged thee, and thou wast not 3282
25: 3 **B** thou saidst, Aha, against my sanctuary, 3282
25: 6 **B** thou hast clapped *thine* hands, and 3282
25: 8 **B that** Moab and Seir do say, Behold, 3282
25:12 **B that** Edom hath dealt against the house 3282
25:15 **B** the Philistines have dealt by revenge, and 3282
26: 2 **b** that Tyrus hath said against Jerusalem, 3282
28: 2 **B** thine heart *is* lifted up, and thou hast 3282
28: 5 and thine heart is lifted up **b of** thy riches: 871.1
28: 6 **B** thou hast set thine heart as the heart of 3282
28:17 Thine heart was lifted up **b of** thy beauty, 871.1
29: 6 **b** they have been a staff of reed to 3282
29: 9 **b** he hath said, The river *is* mine, and 3282
29:20 **b** they wrought for me, saith the Lord 834
31: 5 became long **b of** the multitude of waters, 4480
31:10 **B** thou hast lifted up thyself in height, 834+3282
33:29 **b of** all their abominations which they have 5921
34: 5 they were scattered, **b** *there is* no shepherd: 4480
34: 8 surely **b** my flock became a prey, and 3282
34: 8 **b** *there was* no shepherd, neither did my 4480
34:21 **B** ye have thrust with side and 3282
35: 5 **B** thou hast had a perpetual hatred, and 3282
35:10 **B** thou hast said, These two nations and 3282
35:15 **b** it was desolate, so will I do unto 834+5921
36: 2 **B** the enemy hath said against you, Aha, 3282
36: 3 **B** *they* have made *you* 3282+3282+871.1
36: 6 **b** ye have borne the shame of the heathen: 3282
36:13 **B** they say unto you, Thou *land* devourest 3282
39:23 **b** they trespassed against me, 834+5921
44: 2 **b** the LORD, the God of Israel, 3588
44: 7 my covenant **b of** all your abominations. 413
44:12 **B** they ministered unto them before 834+3282
47: 9 of fish, **b** these waters shall come thither: 3588
47:12 **b** their waters they issued out of 3588
Da 2: 8 **b** ye see the thing is gone from 1768+3606+6903
3:22 Therefore **b** the king's 1768+4481
3:29 shall be made a dunghill: **b** 1768+3606+6903
4: 9 **b** I know that the spirit of the holy gods *is* 1768
6: 3 **b** an excellent spirit *was* in 1768+3606+6903
6:23 found upon him, **b** he believed in his God. 1768
7:11 I beheld then **b of** the voice of the great 4481
9: 7 **b of** their trespass that they have 871.1
9: 8 to our fathers, **b** we have sinned against thee. 834
9:11 of God, **b** we have sinned against him. 3588
9:16 **b** for our sins, and for the iniquities of our 3588
11:35 of the end: **b** *it is* yet for a time appointed. 3588
Hos 4: 1 **b** *there is* no truth, nor mercy, 3588
4: 6 **b** thou hast rejected knowledge, I will also 3588
4:10 **b** they have left off to take heed to 3588
4:13 and elms, **b** the shadow thereof *is* good: 3588
4:19 they shall be ashamed **b of** their sacrifices. 4480
5: 1 **b** ye have been a snare on Mizpah, and 3588
5:11 **b** he willingly walked after 3588
7:13 **b** they have transgressed against me: 3588
8: 1 **b** they have transgressed my covenant, and 3282
8:11 **B** Ephraim hath made many altars to sin, 3588
9: 6 For lo, they are gone **b of** destruction: 4480
9:17 **b** they did not hearken unto him: 3588
10: 3 have no king, **b** we feared not the LORD; 3588
10: 5 shall fear **b of** the calves of Beth-aven: 3807.1
10: 5 the glory thereof, **b** it is departed from it. 3588
10:13 **b** thou didst trust in thy way, in 3588
10:15 unto you **b of** your great wickedness; 4480+6440
11: 5 shall be his king, **b** they refused to return. 3588
11: 6 and devour *them*, **b of** their own counsels. 4480
Joel 1: 5 all ye drinkers of wine, **b of** the new wine, 5921
1:11 **b** the harvest of the field is perished. 3588

Joel 1:12 **b** joy is withered away from the sons of 3588
1:18 are perplexed, **b** they have no pasture; 3588
2:20 shall come up, **b** he hath done great things. 3588
3: 5 **B** ye have taken my silver and my gold, and 834
3:19 **b** they have shed innocent blood in their 834
Am 1: 3 **b** they have threshed Gilead with threshing 5921
1: 6 **b** they carried away captive the whole 5921
1: 9 **b** they delivered up the whole captivity to 5921
1:11 **b** he did pursue his brother with the sword, 5921
1:13 **b** they have ript up the women with child at 5921
2: 1 **b** he burnt the bones of the king of Edom 5921
2: 4 **b** they have despised the law of 5921
2: 6 **b** they sold the righteous for silver, and 5921
4:12 *and* **b** I will do this unto thee, 3588+6118
Jnh 1:10 of the LORD, **b** he had told them. 3588
Mic 2: 1 practise it, **b** it is in the power of their hand. 3588
2:10 for this *is* not *your* rest: **b** it is 5668+871.1
6:13 in making *thee* desolate **b of** thy sins. 5921
7: 9 **b** I have sinned against him, until he plead 3588
7:13 be desolate **b of** them that dwell therein, 5921
7:17 LORD our God, and shall fear **b of** thee. 4480
7:18 his anger for ever, **b** he delighteth in mercy. 3588
Na 3: 4 **B of** the multitude of the whoredoms of 4480
3:11 also shalt seek strength **b of** the enemy. 4480
Hab 1:16 **b** by them their portion *is* fat, and 3588
2: 3 for it; **b** it will surely come, it will not tarry. 3588
2: 5 Yea also, **b** he transgresseth *by* wine, *he is* 3588
2: 8 **B** thou hast spoiled many nations, all 3588
2: 8 **b of** men's blood, and *for* the violence of 4480
2:17 **b** of men's blood, and *for* the violence of 4480
Zep 1:17 that they shall walk like blind *men*, **b** 3588
2:10 **b** they have reproached and 3588
3:11 more be haughty **b of** my holy mountain. 871.1
Hag 1: 9 **B of** mine house that *is* waste, and ye run 3282
Zec 8:10 that went out or came in **b of** the affliction: 4480
9: 8 encamp about mine house **b of** the army, 4480
9: 8 **b of** him that passeth by, and because 4480
9: 8 that passeth by, and **b of** him that returneth: 4480
10: 2 were troubled, **b** *there was* no shepherd. 3588
10: 5 **b** the LORD *is* with them, and the riders 3588
11: 2 the cedar is fallen; **b** the mighty are spoiled: 834
Mal 2: 2 them already, **b** ye do not lay *it* to heart. 3588
2:14 Wherefore? **B** the LORD hath been 3588+5921
Mt 2:18 and would not be comforted, **b** they are not. *3754*
5:36 **b** thou canst not make one hair white or *3754*
7:14 **B** strait *is* the gate, and narrow *is* the way, *3754*
9:36 with compassion on them, **b** they fainted, *3754*
11:20 works were done, **b** they repented not. *3754*
11:25 **b** thou hast hid these *things* from the wise *3754*
12:41 **b** they repented at the preaching of Jonas; *3754*
13: 5 **b** *they* had no deepness of earth: *1223+3588*
13: 6 and **b** *they* had not root, *1223+3588*
13:11 **B** it is given unto you to know *3754*
13:13 **b** they seeing see not; and hearing they hear *3754*
13:21 or persecution ariseth **b of** the word, *1223*
13:58 mighty works there, **b of** their unbelief. *1223*
14: 5 **b** they counted him as a prophet. *3754*
15:32 **b** they continue with me now three days, *3754*
16: 7 saying, *It is* **b** we have taken no bread. *3754*
16: 8 **b** ye have brought no bread? *3754*
17:20 Jesus said unto them, **B of** your unbelief: *1223*
18: 7 Woe unto the world **b of** offences: for it *575*
18:32 thee all that debt, **b** thou desiredst me: *1893*
19: 8 **b of** the hardness of your hearts suffered *4314*
20: 7 They say unto him, **B** no *man* hath hired us. *3754*
20:15 mine own? Is thine eye evil, **b** I am good? *3754*
20:31 **b** they should hold their peace: *2443*
21:46 **b** they took him for a prophet. *1894*
23:29 **b** ye build the tombs of the prophets, and *3754*
24:12 And **b** iniquity shall abound, the love *1223+3588*
26:31 All ye shall be offended **b** of me this night: *1722*
26:33 Though all *men* shall be offended **b of** thee, *1722*
27: 6 into the treasury, **b** it is the price of blood. *1893*
27:19 many *things* this day in a dream **b of** him. *1223*
Mk 1:34 not the devils to speak, **b** they knew him. *3754*
3: 9 ship should wait on him **b of** the multitude, *1223*
3:30 **B** they said, He hath an unclean spirit. *3754*
4: 5 sprang up, **b** *it* had no depth of earth: *1223+3588*
4: 6 **b** *it* had no root, it withered away. *1223+3588*
4:29 putteth in the sickle, **b** the harvest is come. *3754*
5: 4 **B** that he had been often bound with fetters *1223*
6: 6 And he marvelled **b of** their unbelief. *1223*
6:34 **b** they were as sheep not having a *3754*
7:19 **B** it entereth not into his heart, but into *3754*
8: 2 **b** they have now been with me three days, *3754*
8:16 saying, *It is* **b** we have no bread. *3754*
8:17 Why reason ye, **b** ye have no bread? *3754*
9:38 and we forbad him, **b** he followeth not us. *3754*
9:41 **b** ye belong to Christ, verily I say unto you, *3754*
11:18 **b** all the people was astonished at his *3754*
12:24 therefore err, **b** ye know not the scriptures, NIG
14:27 All ye shall be offended **b of** me this night: *1722*
15:42 **b** it was the preparation, that is, the day *1893*
16:14 **b** they believed not them which had seen *3754*
Lk 1: 7 **b that** Elisabeth was barren, and they both *2530*
1:20 **b** thou believest not my words, *473+3739*
2: 4 (**b** he was of the house and lineage of *1223+3588*
2: 7 **b** there was no room for them in the inn. *1360*
4:18 The Spirit of the Lord *is* upon me, **b** *1752+3739*
5:19 they might bring him in **b of** the multitude, *1223*
8: 6 withered away, **b** *it* lacked moisture. *1223+3588*
8:30 **b** many devils were entered into him. *3754*
9: 7 **b** that it was said of some, *1223+3588*
9:49 we forbad him, **b** he followeth not with us. *3754*
9:53 **b** his face was *as though he* would go to *3754*
10:20 **b** your names are written in heaven. *3754*
11: 8 **b** *he* is his friend, yet because of his *1223+3588*
11: 8 yet **b of** his importunity he will rise and *1223*
11:18 **b** ye say that I cast out devils through *3754*
12:17 **b** I have no room where to bestow my *3754*
13: 2 the Galileans, **b** they suffered such *things?* *3754*
13:14 **b** that Jesus had healed on the sabbath day, *3754*
15:27 **b** he hath received him *safe and* sound. *3754*
16: 8 the unjust steward, **b** he had done wisely: *3754*
17: 9 Doth he thank that servant **b** he did *3754*

Lk 18: 5 Yet **b** this widow troubleth me, I will *1223+3588*
19: 3 not for the press, **b** he was little of stature. *3754*
19:11 **b** he was nigh to Jerusalem, and *1223+3588*
19:11 and *b* they thought that the kingdom of God NIG
19:17 **b** thou hast been faithful in a very little, *3754*
19:21 For I feared thee, **b** thou art an austere man: *3754*
19:31 say unto him, **B** the Lord hath need of him. *3754*
19:44 **b** thou knewest not the time of thy *473+3739*
23: 8 **b** *he* had heard many *things* of him; *1223+3588*
Jn 1:50 and said unto him, **B** I said unto thee, *3754*
2:24 unto them, **b** he knew all *men*, *1223+3588*
3:18 **b** he hath not believed in the name of *3754*
3:19 rather than light, **b** their deeds were evil. *1063*
3:23 to Salim, **b** there was much water there: *3754*
3:29 **b of** the bridegroom's voice: *1223*
4:41 many moe believed **b of** his own word; *1223*
4:42 *Now* we believe, not **b of** thy saying: *1223*
5:16 **b** he had done these *things* on the sabbath *3754*
5:18 **b** he not only had broken the sabbath, but *3754*
5:27 judgment also, **b** he is the Son of man. *3754*
5:30 is just; **b** I seek not mine own will, *3754*
6: 2 **b** they saw his miracles which he did on *3754*
6:26 not **b** ye saw *the* miracles, but because *3754*
6:26 but **b** ye did eat of the loaves, and *3754*
6:41 The Jews then murmured at him, **b** he said, *3754*
7: 1 in Jewry, **b** the Jews sought to kill him. *3754*
7: 7 but me it hateth, **b** I testify of it, that *3754*
7:22 not **b** it is of Moses, but of the fathers; *3754*
7:23 **b** I have made a man every whit whole on *3754*
7:30 hands on him, **b** his hour was not yet come. *3754*
7:39 *given;* **b** that Jesus was not yet glorified.) *3754*
7:43 was a division among the people **b of** him. *1223*
8:22 **b** he saith, Whither I go, ye cannot come. *3754*
8:37 to kill me, **b** my word hath no place in you. *3754*
8:43 *even* **b** ye cannot hear my word. *3754*
8:44 not in the truth, **b** there is no truth in him. *3754*
8:45 And **b** I tell *you* the truth, ye believe me *3754*
8:47 hear *them* not, **b** ye are not of God. *3754*
9:16 of God, **b** he keepeth not the sabbath day. *3754*
9:22 spake his parents, **b** they feared the Jews: *3754*
10:13 **b** he is a hireling, and careth not for *3754*
10:17 **b** I lay down my life, that I might take it *3754*
10:26 **b** ye are not of my sheep, as I said unto *1063*
10:33 and **b** that thou, being a man, *3754*
10:36 **b** I said, I am the Son of God? *3754*
11: 9 **b** he seeth the light of this world. *3754*
11:10 he stumbleth, **b** there is no light in him. *3754*
11:42 **b of** the people which stand by I said *it*, that *1223*
12: 6 but **b** he was a thief, and had the bag, and *3754*
12:11 **B** that **by reason of** him many of the Jews *1223*
12:30 This voice came not **b of** me, but for your *1223*
12:39 could not believe, **b that** Esaias said again, *3754*
12:42 **b of** the Pharisees they did not confess *him*, *1223*
13:29 some *of them* thought, **b** Judas had the bag, *1893*
14:12 these shall he do; **b** I go unto my Father. *3754*
14:17 **b** it seeth him not, neither knoweth him: *3754*
14:19 but ye see me: **b** I live, ye shall live also. *3754*
14:28 If ye loved me, ye would rejoice, **b** I said, *3754*
15:19 but **b** ye are not of the world, but I have *3754*
15:21 **b** they know not him that sent me. *3754*
15:27 **b** ye have been with me from *3754*
16: 3 **b** they have not known the Father, nor me. *3754*
16: 4 you at the beginning, **b** I was with you. *3754*
16: 6 But **b** I have said these *things* unto you, *3754*
16: 9 Of sin, **b** they believe not on me; *3754*
16:10 **b** I go to my Father, and ye see me no *3754*
16:11 **b** the prince of this world is judged. *3754*
16:16 and ye shall see me, **b** I go to the Father. *3754*
16:17 ye shall see me: and, **B** I go to the Father? *3754*
16:21 in travail hath sorrow, **b** her hour is come: *3754*
16:27 **b** ye have loved me, and have believed that *3754*
16:32 *yet* I am not alone, **b** the Father is with me. *3754*
17:14 hated them, **b** they are not of the world, *3754*
19: 7 to die, **b** he made himself the Son of God. *3754*
19:31 Jews therefore, **b** it was the preparation, *1893*
19:42 **b of** the Jews' preparation *day;* for *1223*
20:13 **B** they have taken away my Lord, and *3754*
20:29 Thomas, **b** thou hast seen me, thou hast *3754*
21:17 Peter was grieved **b** he said unto him *3754*
Ac 2: 6 **b that** every man heard them speak in his *3754*
2:24 **b** it was not possible that he should be *2530*
2:27 **B** thou wilt not leave my soul in hell, *3754*
4:21 they might punish them, **b of** the people: *1223*
6: 1 **b** their widows were neglected in the daily *3754*
8:11 **b** that of long time *he* had bewitched them *1223*
8:20 **b** thou hast thought that the gift of God *3754*
10:45 **b** that on the Gentiles also was poured out *3754*
12: 3 And **b** he saw it pleased the Jews, NIG
12:20 **b** their country was nourished by *1223*
12:23 **b** he gave not God the glory: *473+3739*
13:27 and their rulers, **b** they knew him not, NIG
14:12 Mercurius, **b** he was the chief speaker. *1894*
16: 3 **b of** the Jews which were in those quarters: *1223*
17:18 **b** he preached unto them Jesus, and *3754*
17:31 **B** he hath appointed a day, in the which he *1360*
18: 2 (**b that** Claudius had commanded all *1223+3588*
18: 3 And **b** *he* was of the same craft, *1223+3588*
20:16 **b** he would not spend the time in Asia: *3704*
22:29 he was a Roman, and **b** he had bound him. *3754*
22:30 **b** he would have known the certainty NIG
24:11 **B** that thou mayest understand, that there NIG
25:20 And **b** I doubted of such *manner of* NIG
26: 2 **b** I shall answer for myself this day before NIG
26: 3 Especially **b** *I know* thee to be expert in all NIG
27: 4 **b** the winds were contrary. *1223+3588*
27: 9 **b** the fast was now already past, *1223+3588*
27:12 And **b** the haven was not commodious to NIG
28: 2 **b** of the present rain, and because of *1223*
28: 2 of the present rain, and **b of** the cold. *1223*
28:18 **b** there was no cause of death in me. *1223+3588*
28:20 **b that** for the hope of Israel I am bound *1752*
Ro 1:19 **B** that which may be known of God is *1360*
1:21 **B that**, when they knew God, they glorified *1360*
3: 2 **b** that unto them were committed *1063*
4:15 **B** the law worketh wrath: for where no law *1063*

Ro 5: 5 b the love of God is shed abroad in our 3754
6:15 b we are not under the law, but 3754
6:19 of men b of the infirmity of your flesh: 1223
8: 7 B the carnal mind *is* enmity against God: 1360
8:10 Christ *be* in you, the body *is* dead b of sin; 1223
8:10 but the Spirit *is* life b of righteousness. 1223
8:21 B the creature itself also shall be delivered 3754
8:27 b he maketh intercession for the saints 3754
9: 7 Neither, b they are the seed of Abraham, 3754
9:28 b a short work will the Lord make upon 3754
9:32 B *they sought it* not by faith, but as *it were* 3754
11:20 b of unbelief they were broken off, and NIG
14:23 is damned if he eat, b *he eateth* not of faith: 3754
15:15 b of the grace that is given to me of God, 1223
1Co 1:25 B the foolishness of God is wiser than men; 3754
2:14 neither can he know *them,* b they are 3754
3:13 for the day shall declare *it,* b it shall be 3754
6: 7 b ye go to law one with another. 3754
11:10 to have power on *her* head b of the angels. 1223
12:15 If the foot shall say, B I am not the hand, 3754
12:16 B I am not the eye, I am not of the body; 3754
15: 9 b I persecuted the church of God. 1360
15:15 b we have testified of God that he raised up 3754
2Co 2:13 in my spirit, b I found not Titus my brother: NIG
5:14 b we thus judge, that if one died for all, then NIG
7:13 b his spirit was refreshed by you all. 3754
11: 7 b I have preached to you the gospel of God 3754
11:11 b I love you not? God knoweth. 3754
Gal 2: 4 b of false brethren unawares brought in, 1223
2:11 him to the face, b he was *to be* blamed. 3754
3:19 It was added b of transgressions, till 5484
4: 6 And b ye are sons, God hath sent forth 3754
4:16 become your enemy, b I tell you the truth? 5620
Eph 4:18 is in them, b of the blindness of their heart: 1223
5: 6 b of these *things* cometh the wrath of God 1223
5:16 Redeeming the time, b the days are evil. 3754
Php 1: 7 of you all, b I have you in *my* heart; 1223+3588
2:26 b that ye had heard that he had been sick. 1360
2:30 B for the work of Christ he was nigh unto 3754
4:17 Not b I desire a gift: but I desire fruit that 3754
1Th 2: 8 also our own souls, b ye were dear unto us. 1360
2: 9 b *we* would not be chargeable unto 3588+4314
2:13 also thank we God without ceasing, b, 3754
4: 6 b that the Lord *is* the avenger of all such, 1360
2Th 1: 3 b that your faith groweth exceedingly, and 3754
1:10 to be admired in all them that believe (b 3754
2:10 b they received not the love of 473+3739
2:13 b God hath from the beginning chosen you 3754
3: 9 Not b we have not power, but to make 3754
1Ti 1:13 b I did *it* ignorantly in unbelief. 3754
4:10 b we trust in the living God, 3754
5:12 b they have cast off *their* first faith. 3754
6: 2 them not despise *them,* b they are brethren; 3754
6: 2 b they are faithful and beloved, 3754
Phm 1: 7 b the bowels of the saints are refreshed by 3754
Heb 3:19 that they could not enter in b of unbelief. 1223
4: 6 first preached entered not in b of unbelief, 1223
6:13 b he could swear by no greater, he sware 1893
7:23 b *they* were not suffered to continue by NIG
7:24 But this *man,* b he continueth ever, 1223+3588
8: 9 b they continued not in my covenant, and I 3754
10: 2 b that the worshippers once purged 1223+3588
11: 5 was not found, b God had translated him: 1360
11:11 b she judged him faithful who had 1893
11:23 b they saw *he was* a proper child; 1360
Jas 1:10 b as the flower of the grass he shall pass 3754
4: 2 war, yet ye have not, b ye ask not. 1223+3588
4: 3 Ye ask, and receive not, b ye ask amiss, 1360
1Pe 1:16 B it is written, Be ye holy; for I am holy. 1360
2:21 b Christ also suffered for us, leaving us an 3754
5: 8 b your adversary the devil, as a roaring 3754
1Jn 2: 8 b the darkness is past, and the true light 3754
2:11 b that darkness hath blinded his eyes. 3754
2:12 b *your* sins are forgiven you for his name's 3754
2:13 b ye have known him that is from 3754
2:13 b you have overcome the wicked one. 3754
2:13 little children, b ye have known the Father. 3754
2:14 b ye have known him that is from 3754
2:14 b ye are strong, and the word of God 3754
2:21 written unto you b ye know not the truth, 3754
2:21 but b ye know it, and that no lie is of 3754
3: 1 world knoweth us not, b it knew him not. 3754
3: 9 and he cannot sin, b he is born of God. 3754
3:12 B his own works were evil, and his 3754
3:14 death unto life, b we love the brethren. 3754
3:16 love *of God,* b he laid down his life for us: 3754
3:22 b we keep his commandments, and 3754
4: 1 b many false prophets are gone out into 3754
4: 4 b greater is he that is in you, than he that is 3754
4: 9 b that God sent his only begotten Son into 3754
4:13 he in us, b he hath given us of his Spirit. 3754
4:17 boldness in the day of judgment: b as he is, 3754
4:18 b fear hath torment. He that feareth is not 3754
4:19 We love him, b he first loved us. 3754
5: 6 that beareth witness, b the Spirit is truth. 3754
5:10 b he believeth not the record that God gave 3754
3Jn 1: 7 B that for his name's sake they went forth, NIG
Jude 1:16 persons in admiration b of advantage. 5484
Rev 1: 7 all kindreds of the earth shall wail b of him. 1909
2: 4 against thee, b thou hast left thy first love. 3754
2:14 b thou hast there them that hold 3754
2:20 b thou sufferest *that* woman Jezebel, 3754
3:10 B thou hast kept the word of my patience, 3754
3:16 So *then* b thou art lukewarm, and 3754
3:17 B thou sayest, I am rich, and increased with 3754
5: 4 b no *man* was found worthy to open and 3754
8:11 died of the waters, b they were made bitter. 3754
11:10 b these two prophets tormented them that 3754
11:17 b thou hast taken *to thee* thy great power, 3754
12:12 b he knoweth that he hath *but* a short time. NIG
14: 8 b she made all nations drink of the wine of 3754
16: 5 and shalt be, b thou hast judged thus. 3754
16:11 of heaven b of their pains and their sores, 1537
16:21 b of the plague of the hail; 1537

BECHER (5)

Ge 46:21 and B, and Ashbel, Gera, and Naaman, Ehi, 1071
Nu 26:35 of B, the family of the Bachrites: of Tahan, 1071
1Ch 7: 6 Bela, and B, and Jediael, three. 1071
7: 8 the sons of B; Zemira, and Joash, and 1071
7: 8 and Alameth. All these *are* the sons of B. 1071

BECHORATH (1)

1Sa 9: 1 son of Abiel, the son of Zeror, the son of B, 1064

BECKONED (6) [BECKONING]

Lk 1:22 for he b unto them, and 1269
5: 7 And they b unto *their* partners, which were 2656
Jn 13:24 Simon Peter therefore b to him, that *he* 3506
Ac 19:33 And Alexander b with the hand, and 2678
21:40 and b with the hand unto the people. 2678
24:10 after that the governor had b unto him to 3506

BECKONING (2) [BECKONED]

Ac 12:17 b unto them with the hand to hold their 2678
13:16 and b with *his* hand said, Men of Israel, and 2678

BECOME (135) [BECAME, BECAMEST, BECOMETH]

Ge 3:22 Behold, the man is b as one of us, to know 1961
9:15 the waters shall no more b a flood to 1961
18:18 Seeing that Abraham shall surely b a 1961+1961
24:35 my master greatly; and he is b great: NIH
32:10 and now I am b two bands. 1961+3807.1
34:16 and we will b one people. 1961+3807.1
37:20 and we shall see what will b of his dreams. 1961
48:19 I know *it:* he also shall b a people, and 1961
48:19 and his seed shall b a multitude of nations. 1961
Ex 4: 9 the river shall b blood upon the dry *land.* 1961
7: 9 *it* before Pharaoh, *and* it shall b a serpent. 1961
7:19 their pools of water, that they may b blood; 1961
8:16 that it may b lice throughout all the land of 1961
9: 9 it shall b small dust in all the land of Egypt, 1961
15: 2 and song, and he is b my salvation: 1961
15: 6 O LORD, is b glorious in power: 142
23:29 lest the land b desolate, and the beast of 1961
32: 1 land of Egypt, we wot not what is b of him. 1961
32:23 land of Egypt, we wot not what is b of him. 1961
Lev 19:29 and the land b full of wickedness. 4390
Nu 5:24 the curse shall enter into her, and b bitter. NIH
5:27 b bitter, and her belly shall swell, and NIH
Dt 27: 9 this day thou art b the people of 1961
28:37 thou shalt b an astonishment, a proverb, 1961
Jos 9:13 our shoes are b old by reason of the very 1086
Jdg 16:17 I shall b weak, and be like any *other* man. 1961
1Sa 28:16 departed from thee, and is b thine enemy? 1961
2Sa 7:24 for ever; and thou, LORD, art b their God. 1961
1Ki 2:15 is turned about, and is b my brother's: 1961
14: 3 he shall tell thee what shall b of the child. 1961
2Ki 21:14 they shall b a prey and a spoil to all their 1961
22:19 that *they* should b a desolation and a curse, 1961
Est 2:11 how Esther did, and what should b of her. 6213
Job 7: 5 my skin is broken, and b loathsome. 3988
15:28 which are ready to b heaps. 6257
21: 7 b old, yea, are mighty *in* power? 6275
30:19 the mire, and I am b like dust and ashes. 4911
30:21 Thou art b cruel to me: with thy strong 2015
Ps 14: 3 all gone aside, they are *all* together b filthy: NIH
28: 1 I b like them that go down into the pit. 4911
53: 3 is gone back, they are altogether b filthy; NIH
62:10 not in oppression, and b not vain in robbery: NIH
69: 8 I am b a stranger unto my brethren, and 1961
69:22 Let their table b a snare before them: and 1961
69:22 *have been* for *their* welfare, *let it* b a trap. NIH
79: 4 We are b a reproach to our neighbours, 1961
109: 7 him be condemned: and let his prayer b sin. 1961
118:14 and song, and is b my salvation. 1961
118:21 thou hast heard me, and art b my salvation. 1961
118:22 The stone *which* the builders refused is b 1961
119:83 For I am b like a bottle in the smoke; *yet* do 1961
Pr 29:21 child shall have him b *his* son at the length. 1961
Isa 1:21 How is the faithful city b a harlot! *it was* 1961
1:22 Thy silver is b dross, thy wine mixt with 1961
7:24 all the land shall b briers and thorns. 1961
12: 2 and *my* song; he also is b my salvation. 1961
14:10 say unto thee, Art thou also b weak as we? 2470
14:10 weak as we? art thou b like unto us? 4911
19:11 the wise counsellers of Pharaoh is b brutish: NIH
19:13 The princes of Zoan are b fools, the princes NIH
29:11 the vision of all is b unto you as the words 1961
34: 9 and the land thereof shall b burning pitch. 1961
35: 7 the parched ground shall b a pool, and 1961
59: 6 Their webs shall not b garments, 1961
60:22 A little one shall b a thousand, and a small 1961
Jer 2: 5 have walked after vanity, and are b vain? 1891
3: 1 go from him, and b another man's, 1961+3807.1
5:13 the prophets shall b wind, and the word *is* 1961
5:27 they are b great, and waxen rich. NIH
7:11 my name, b a den of robbers in your eyes? 1961
10:21 For the pastors are b brutish, and have not NIH
22: 5 that this house shall b a desolation. 1961
26:18 Jerusalem shall b heaps, and the mountain 1961
49:13 that Bozrah shall b a desolation, a reproach, 1961
50:23 how is Babylon b a desolation among 1961
50:37 midst of her; and they shall b as women: 1961
51:37 Babylon shall b heaps, a dwelling place for 1961
51:41 how is Babylon b an astonishment among 1961
La 1: 1 *how* is she b as a widow! she *that was* great 1961
1: 1 the provinces, *how* is she b tributary! 1961
1: 2 with her, they are b her enemies. 1961
1: 6 her princes are b like harts *that* find no 1961
1:11 O LORD, and consider; for I am b vile. 1961
4: 1 How is the gold b dim! *how* is the most 6004
4: 3 the daughter of my people *is* b cruel, NIH
4: 8 it is withered, it is b like a stick. 1961
Eze 22: 4 Thou art b guilty in thy blood that thou hast NIH
22:18 of man, the house of Israel is to me b dross: 1961
22:19 Because ye are all b dross, 1961
26: 5 and it shall b a spoil to the nations. 1961
36:35 This land that was desolate is b like 1961
36:35 and desolate and ruined cities *are* b fenced, NIH
37:17 and they shall b one in thine hand. 1961
Da 4:22 *is* thou, O king, that art grown and b strong: NIH
9:16 thy people *are* b a reproach to all *that are* NIH
11:23 and shall b strong with a small people. NIH
Hos 12: 8 Ephraim said, Yet I am b rich, I have 6238
13:15 his spring shall b dry, and his fountain shall NIH
13:16 Samaria shall b desolate; for she hath NIH
Jnh 4: 5 till he might see what would b of the city. 1961
Mic 3:12 Jerusalem shall b heaps, and the mountain 1961
Zep 1:13 Therefore their goods shall b a 1961+3807.1
2:15 how is she b a desolation, a place for beasts 1961
Zec 4: 7 before Zerubbabel *thou shalt* b a plain: and NIH
Mt 18: 3 ye be converted, and b as little children, 1096
21:42 the same is b the head of the corner: 1096+1519
Mk 1:17 and I will make you to b fishers of men. 1096
12:10 rejected is b the head of the corner: 1096+1519
Lk 20:17 the same is b the head of the corner? 1096+1519
Jn 1:12 to them gave he power to b the sons of 1096
Ac 4:11 which is b the head of the corner. 1096+1519
7:40 land of Egypt, we wot not what is b of him. 1096
12:18 among the soldiers, what was b of Peter. 1096
Ro 3:12 of the way, they are together b unprofitable; NIG
3:19 and all the world may b guilty before God. 1096
4:18 that he might b the father of many nations; 1096
6:22 and b servants to God, ye have your fruit NIG
7: 4 ye also are b dead to the law by the body of NIG
7:13 that sin by the commandment might b 1096
1Co 3:18 let him b a fool, that he may be wise. 1096
7:18 let him not b uncircumcised. Is any called 1986
8: 9 b a stumblingblock to them that are weak. 1096
13: 1 I am b *as* sounding brass, or a tinkling 1096
15:20 *and* b the firstfruits of them that slept. 1096
2Co 5:17 are passed away; behold, all *things* are b new. 1096
12:11 I am b a fool in glorying; ye have 1096
Gal 4:16 Am I therefore b your enemy, because I tell 1096
5: 4 Christ is b of no effect unto you, 2673
Tit 2: 1 But speak thou *the things* which b sound 4241
Phm 1: 6 That the communication of thy faith may b 1096
Heb 5:12 and are b such as have need of milk, and 1096
Jas 2: 4 and are b judges of evil thoughts? 1096
2:11 thou art b a transgressor of the law. 1096
Rev 11:15 The kingdoms of *this* world are b 1096
18: 2 is fallen, and is b the habitation of devils, 1096

BECOMETH (15) [BECOME]

Ps 93: 5 holiness b thine house, O LORD, for ever. 4998
Pr 10: 4 *He* b poor that dealeth *with* a slack hand: NIH
17: 7 Excellent speech b not a fool: much less do 5000
17:18 b surety in the presence of his 6148+6161
Ecc 4:14 also *he that is* born in his kingdom b poor. NIH
Mt 3:15 for thus it b us to fulfil all righteousness. 4241
13:22 choke the word, and he b unfruitful. 1096
13:32 and b a tree, so that the birds of the air 1096
Mk 4:19 choke the word, and it b unfruitful. 1096
4:32 and b greater than all herbs, and 1096
Ro 16: 2 as b saints, and *that* ye assist her in 516
Eph 5: 3 be once named amongst you, as b saints; 4241
Php 1:27 Only let your conversation be as it b 516
1Ti 2:10 But (which b women professing godliness) 4241
Tit 2: 3 *that they be* in behaviour as b holiness, 2412

BECORATH See BECHORATH

BED (90) [BED'S, BEDCHAMBER, BEDS, BEDSTEAD]

Ge 48: 2 strengthened himself, and sat upon the b. 4296
49: 4 because thou wentest up to thy father's b; 4904
49:33 he gathered up his feet into the b, and 4296
Ex 8: 3 upon thy b, and into the house of thy 4296
21:18 *his* fist, and he die not, but keepeth *his* b: 4904
Lev 15: 4 Every b, whereon he lieth that hath 4904
15: 5 whosoever toucheth his b shall wash his 4904
15:21 whosoever toucheth her b shall wash his 4904
15:23 if it *be* on *her* b, or on *any* thing whereon 4904
15:24 all the b whereon he lieth shall be unclean. 4904
15:26 Every b whereon she lieth all the days of 4904
15:26 shall be unto her as the b of her separation: 4904
1Sa 19:13 laid *it* in the b, and put a pillow of goats' 4296
19:15 saying, Bring him up to me in the b, that I 4296
19:16 behold *there was* an image in the b, 4296
28:23 he arose from the earth, and sat upon the b. 4296
2Sa 4: 5 who lay on a b at noon. 4904+7901
4: 7 he lay on his b in his bedchamber, and 4296
4:11 person in his own house upon his b? 4904
11: 2 that David arose from off his b, and 4904
11:13 at even he went out to lie on his b with 4904
13: 5 Lay *thee* down on thy b, and make thyself 4904
1Ki 1:47 And the king bowed himself upon the b. 4904
17:19 he abode, and laid him upon his own b. 4296
21: 4 he laid him down upon his b, and 4296
2Ki 1: 4 Thou shalt not come down from *that* b on 4296
1: 6 thou shalt not come down from *that* b on 4296
1:16 thou shalt not come down off *that* b on 4296
4:10 let us set for him there a b, and a table, and 4296
4:21 laid him on the b of the man of God, and 4296
4:32 the child was dead, *and* laid upon his b. 4296
1Ch 5: 1 but, forasmuch as he defiled his father's b, 3326
2Ch 16:14 laid him in the b which was filled *with* 4904
24:25 and slew him on his b, and he died: 4296
Est 7: 8 Haman was fallen upon the b whereon 4296
Job 7:13 When I say, My b shall comfort me, 6210
17:13 I have made my b in the darkness. 3326
33:15 upon men, in slumberings upon the b; 4904
33:19 He is chastened also with pain upon his b, 4904
Ps 4: 4 with your own heart upon your b, 4904
6: 6 all the night make I my b to swim; 4296
36: 4 He deviseth mischief upon his b; he setteth 4904
41: 3 The LORD will strengthen him upon the b 6210
41: 3 thou wilt make all his b in his sickness. 4904
63: 6 When I remember thee upon my b, *and* 3326
132: 3 of my house, nor go up into my b; 3326+6210
139: 8 if I make my b in hell, behold, thou *art* 3331
Pr 7:16 I have deckt my b *with* coverings of 6210
7:17 I have perfumed my b *with* myrrh, aloes, 4904
22:27 why should he take away thy b from under 4904

Pr 26:14 his hinges, so doth the slothful upon his b. 4296
SS 1:16 yea, pleasant: also our b is green. 6210
3: 1 By night on my b I sought him whom my 4904
3: 7 Behold his b, which is Solomon's; 4296
5:13 His cheeks are as a b of spices, as sweet 6170
Isa 28:20 For the b is shorter than that a man can 4702
57: 7 and high mountain hast thou set thy b: 4904
57: 8 thou hast enlarged thy b, and made thee a 4904
57: 8 thou lovedst their b where thou sawest it. 4904
Eze 23:17 the Babylonians came to her into the b of 4904
23:41 satest upon a stately b, and a table prepared 4296
32:25 They have set her a b in the midst of 4904
Da 2:28 the visions of thy head upon thy b, 4903
2:29 thoughts came into thy mind upon thy b, 4903
4: 5 the thoughts upon my b and the visions of 4903
4:10 were the visions of mine head in my b; 4903
4:13 I saw in the visions of my head upon my b, 4903
7: 1 a dream and visions of his head upon his b: 4903
Am 3:12 that dwell in Samaria in the corner of a b, 4296
Mt 9: 2 him a man sick of the palsy, lying on a b: 2825
9: 6 take up thy b, and go unto thine house. 2825
Mk 2: 4 they let down the b wherein the sick of 2895
2: 9 to say, Arise, and take up thy b, and walk? 2895
2:11 and take up thy b, and go thy way into 2895
2:12 took up the b, and went forth before them 2895
4:21 to be put under a bushel, or under a b? 2825
7:30 gone out, and her daughter laid upon the b. 2825
Lk 5:18 men brought in a b a man which was taken 2825
8:16 it with a vessel, or putteth it under a b; 2825
11: 7 and my children are with me in b; 2845
17:34 that night there shall be two men in one b; 2825
Jn 5: 8 unto him, Rise, take up thy b, and walk. 2895
5: 9 and took up his b, and walked: 2895
5:10 it is not lawful for thee to carry thy b. 2895
5:11 said unto me, Take up thy b, and walk. 2895
5:12 said unto thee, Take up thy b, and walk? 2895
Ac 9:33 which had kept his b eight years, and was 2895
9:34 arise, and make thy b. And he arose 4766
Heb 13: 4 is honourable in all, and the b undefiled: 2845
Rev 2:22 I will cast her into a b, and them that 2825

BED'S (1) [BED]
Ge 47:31 And Israel bowed himself upon the b head. 4296

BEDAD (2)
Ge 36:35 Husham died, and Hadad the son of B, 911
1Ch 1:46 Husham was dead, Hadad the son of B, 911

BEDAN (2)
1Sa 12:11 B, and Jephthah, and Samuel, and 917
1Ch 7:17 the sons of Ulam; B. These were the sons of 917

BEDCHAMBER (6) [BED, CHAMBER]
Ex 8: 3 into thy b, and upon thy bed, and 2315+4904
2Sa 4: 7 he lay on his bed in his b, and 2315+4904
2Ki 6:12 the words that thou speakest in thy b. 2315+4904
11: 2 in the b from Athaliah, so that he 2315+4296
2Ch 22:11 and put him and his nurse in a b. 2315+4296
Ecc 10:20 and curse not the rich in thy b: 2315+4904

BEDEIAH (1)
Ezr 10:35 Benaiah, B, Chelluh, 912

BEDROOM See BEDCHAMBER

BEDS (10) [BED]
2Sa 17:28 Brought b, and basons, and earthen vessels, 4904
Est 1: 6 the b were of gold and silver, upon a 4296
Ps 149: 5 in glory: let them sing aloud upon their b. 4904
SS 6: 2 to the b of spices, to feed in the gardens, 6170
Isa 57: 2 they shall rest in their b, each one walking 4904
Hos 7:14 their heart, when they howled upon their b: 4904
Am 6: 4 That lie upon b of ivory, and 4296
Mic 2: 1 devise iniquity, and work evil upon their b! 4904
Mk 6:55 began to carry about in b those that were 2895
Ac 5:15 the streets, and laid them on b and couches, 2825

BEDSTEAD (2) [BED]
Dt 3:11 behold, his b was a bedstead of iron; is it 6210
3:11 behold, his bedstead was a b of iron; is it 6210

BEE (1) [BEES]
Isa 7:18 and for the b that is in the land of Assyria. 1682

BEELIADA (1)
1Ch 14: 7 And Elishama, and B, and Eliphalet. 1182

BEELZEBUB (7)
Mt 10:25 they have called the master of the house B, 954
12:24 out devils, but by B the prince of the devils. 954
12:27 And if I by B cast out devils, by whom do 954
Mk 3:22 He hath B, and by the prince of the devils 954
Lk 11:15 He casteth out devils through B the chief of 954
11:18 ye say that I cast out devils through B. 954
11:19 And if I by B cast out devils, by whom do 954

BEEN (331) [BE]
Ge 13: 3 unto the place where his tent had b at 1961
26: 8 to pass, when he had b there a long time, NIH
31: 5 the God of my father hath b with me. 1961
31:38 This twenty years have I b with thee; NIH
31:41 Thus have I b twenty years in thy house; NIH
31:42 and the fear of Isaac, had b with me, 1961
38:26 and said, She hath b more righteous than I; NIH
45: 6 For these two years hath the famine b in NIH
46:32 for their trade hath b to feed cattle; 1961
46:34 Thy servants' trade hath b about cattle from 1961
47: 9 evil have the days of the years of my life b, NIH
Ex 2:22 I have b a stranger in a strange land. 1961
9:18 as hath not b in Egypt since 1961
14:12 For it had b better for us to serve NIH
18: 3 he said, I have b an alien in a strange land: 1961
21:29 it hath b testified to his owner, and he hath NIH
34:10 such as have not b done in all the earth, NIH
Lev 10:19 should it have b accepted in the sight of NIH
13: 7 after that he hath b seen of the priest for his NIH
Nu 19:20 the water of separation hath not b sprinkled NIH
Dt 2: 7 years the LORD thy God hath b with thee; NIH
4:32 whether there hath b any such thing as this 1961
4:32 as this great thing is, or hath b heard like it? NIH
9: 7 ye have b rebellious against the LORD. 1961
9:24 You have b rebellious against the LORD 1961
15:18 for he hath b worth a double hired servant NIH
21: 3 which hath not b wrought with, and NIH
31:27 ye have b rebellious against the LORD; 1961
Jos 7: 7 would to God we had b content, and NIH
9: 4 and made as if they had b ambassadors, NIH
10:27 cast them into the cave wherein they had b NIH
23: 9 no man hath b able to stand before you unto NIH
Jdg 16: 8 seven green withs which had not b dried, NIH
16:17 for I have b a Nazarite unto God from my NIH
Ru 2:11 unto her, It hath fully b shewed me, 5046+5046
1Sa 1:13 therefore Eli thought she had b drunken. NIH
4: 7 for there hath not b such a thing heretofore. 1961
4: 9 unto the Hebrews, as they have b[S] to you: 5647
4:17 there hath b also a great slaughter among 1961
9:24 for unto this time hath it b kept for thee NIH
14:29 how mine eyes have b enlightened, because NIH
14:30 for had there not b now a much greater NIH
14:38 and see wherein this sin hath b this day. 1961
15:21 the chief of the things which should have b NIH
18:19 daughter should have b given to David, NIH
19: 4 his works have b to thee-ward very good: NIH
20:13 be with thee, as he hath b with my father. 1961
21: 5 Of a truth women have b kept from us about NIH
25:28 evil hath not b found in thee all thy days. NIH
25:34 surely there had not b left unto Nabal by NIH
29: 3 which hath b with me these days, or 1961
29: 6 thou hast b upright, and thy going out and NIH
29: 8 so long as I have b with thee unto this day, 1961
2Sa 1:21 as though he had not b anointed with oil. NIH
1:26 very pleasant hast thou b unto me: thy love NIH
12: 8 if that had b too little, I would moreover NIH
13:20 Hath Amnon thy brother b with thee? 1961
13:32 b determined from the day that he forced NIH
14:32 it had b good for me to have been there still: NIH
14:32 it had been good for me to have b there still: NIH
15:34 as I have b thy father's servant hitherto, so NIH
1Ki 1:37 As the LORD hath b with my lord 1961
2:26 thou hast b afflicted in all wherein my NIH
14: 8 yet thou hast not b as my servant David, 1961
16:31 as if it had b a light thing for him to walk in NIH
17: 7 because there had b no rain in the land. 1961
19:10 I have b very jealous for the LORD God of NIH
19:14 I have b very jealous for the LORD God of NIH
2Ki 4:13 thou hast b careful for us with all this care; NIH
20:12 for he had heard that Hezekiah had b sick. NIH
1Ch 17: 8 I have b with thee whithersoever thou hast 1961
28: 3 because thou hast b a man of war, and NIH
29:25 had not b on any king before him in Israel. 1961
2Ch 1:12 the kings have had that have b before thee, NIH
15: 3 Now for a long season Israel hath b without NIH
23: 9 and shields, that had b king David's, NIH
Ezr 2: 1 of those which had b carried away, NIH
4:18 The letter which ye sent unto us hath b NIH
4:19 search hath b made, and it is found that this NIH
4:19 and sedition have b made therein. NIH
4:20 There have b mighty kings also over 1934
5:16 since that time even until now hath it b in NIH
8:35 Also the children of those that had b carried NIH
9: 2 and rulers hath b chief in this trespass. 1961
9: 4 of the transgression of those that had b NIH
9: 7 Since the days of our fathers have we b in a NIH
9: 7 b delivered into the hand of the kings of NIH
9: 8 now for a little space grace hath b shewed 1961
10: 6 of the transgression of them that had b NIH
10: 8 of those that had b carried away. NIH
Ne 2: 1 Now I had not b beforetime sad in his 1961
5:15 the former governors that had b before me NIH
7: 6 of those that had b carried away, NIH
13:10 had not b given them: for the Levites NIH
Est 2: 6 Who had b carried away from Jerusalem NIH
2: 6 b carried away with Jeconiah king of Judah, NIH
2:12 after that she had b twelve months, NIH
4:11 I have not b called to come in unto the king NIH
6: 3 dignity hath b done to Mordecai for this? NIH
7: 4 if we had b sold for bondmen and NIH
Job 3:13 For now should I have lien still and b quiet, NIH
3:13 I should have slept: then had I b at rest, NIH
3:16 Or as a hidden untimely birth I had not b; 1961
10:19 I should have b as though I had not been; I NIH
10:19 have been as though I had not b; 1961+1961
10:19 I should have b carried from the womb to NIH
22: 9 the arms of the fatherless have b broken. NIH
31: 9 If mine heart have b deceived by a woman, NIH
31:27 my heart hath b secretly enticed, or NIH
38:17 Have the gates of death b opened unto thee? NIH
42:11 all they that had b of his acquaintance NIH
Ps 25: 6 for they have b ever of old. NIH
27: 9 thou hast b my help; leave me not, 1961
35:14 I behaved myself as though he had b my NIH
37:25 I have b young, and now am old; yet have I 1961
42: 3 My tears have b my meat day and night, 1961
50: 8 to have b continually before me. NIH
50:18 and hast b partaker with adulterers. NIH
59:16 for thou hast b my defence and refuge in 1961
60: 1 hast scattered us, thou hast b displeased; NIH
61: 3 For thou hast b a shelter for me, and 1961
63: 7 Because thou hast b my help, therefore 1961
69:22 that which should have b for their welfare, NIH
71: 6 By thee have I b holden up from the womb: NIH
73:14 For all the day long have I b plagued, and 1961
85: 1 thou hast b favourable unto thy land: NIH
89:38 thou hast b wroth with thine anointed. NIH
90: 1 thou hast b our dwelling place in all 1961
94:17 Unless the LORD had b my help, my soul NIH
115:12 The LORD hath b mindful of us: he will NIH
119:54 Thy statutes have b my songs in the house 1961
119:71 It is good for me that I have b afflicted; that NIH
Ps 119:92 Unless thy law had b my delights, I should NIH
124: 1 If it had not b the LORD who was on our NIH
124: 2 If it had not b the LORD who was on our NIH
143: 3 in darkness, as those that have b long dead. NIH
Pr 7:26 yea, many strong men have b slain by her. NIH
Ecc 1: 9 The thing that hath b, it is that which shall 1961
1:10 it hath b already of old time, which was 1961
1:16 all they that have b before me in Jerusalem: 1961
2:12 even that which hath b already done. NIH
3:15 That which hath b, is now; and that which 1961
3:15 that which is to be hath already b; and God 1961
4: 3 is he than both they, which hath not yet b, 1961
4:16 even of all that have b before them: 1961
6:10 That which hath b is named already, and 1961
Isa 1: 6 they have not b closed, neither bound up, NIH
1: 9 we should have b as Sodom, and we should 1961
1: 9 and we should have b like unto Gomorrah. NIH
5: 4 What could have b done more to my NIH
17:10 hast not b mindful of the rock of thy NIH
23:16 the city, thou harlot that hast b forgotten; NIH
25: 4 For thou hast b a strength to the poor, 1961
26:17 so have we b in thy sight, O LORD. 1961
26:18 We have b with child, we have been in pain, NIH
26:18 We have been with child, we have b in pain, NIH
30:24 which hath b winnowed with the shovel and NIH
38: 9 when he had b sick, and was recovered of NIH
39: 1 for he had heard that he had b sick, and NIH
40:21 hath it not b told you from the beginning? NIH
42:14 I have b still, and refrained myself: NIH
43: 4 thou hast b honourable, and I have loved NIH
43:22 but thou hast b weary of me, O Israel. NIH
48:18 had thy peace b as a river, and 1961
48:19 Thy seed also had b as the sand, and 1961
48:19 his name should not have b cut off nor NIH
49:21 I was left alone; these, where had they b? NIH
52:15 for that which had not b told them shall they NIH
57:11 of whom hast thou b afraid or feared, NIH
60:15 Whereas thou hast b forsaken and hated, so 1961
66: 2 all those things have b, saith the LORD: 1961
Jer 2:31 Have I b a wilderness unto Israel? a land of 1961
3: 2 and see where thou hast not b lien with. NIH
3: 3 Therefore the showers have b withholden, NIH
3: 3 and there hath b no latter rain; 1961
4:17 because she hath b rebellious against me, NIH
15: 9 she hath b ashamed and confounded: and NIH
20:17 or that my mother might have b my grave, 1961
22:21 This hath b thy manner from thy youth, NIH
28: 8 The prophets that have b before me and 1961
32:31 For this city hath b to me as a provocation 1961
34:14 a Hebrew, which hath b sold unto thee; NIH
42:18 my fury hath b poured forth upon NIH
43: 5 whither they had b driven, to dwell in NIH
44:18 have b consumed by the sword and by NIH
48:11 Moab hath b at ease from his youth, and NIH
48:11 hath not b emptied from vessel to vessel, NIH
50: 6 My people hath b lost sheep: 1961
50:29 for she hath b proud against the LORD, NIH
51: 5 For Israel hath not b forsaken, nor Judah of NIH
51: 7 Babylon hath b a golden cup in NIH
Eze 2: 5 yet shall know that there hath b a prophet 1961
4:14 behold, my soul hath not b polluted: NIH
10:10 as if a wheel had b in the midst of a wheel. 1961
11:17 of the countries where ye have b scattered, NIH
16:31 hast not b as a harlot, in that thou scornest 1961
20:41 the countries wherein ye have b scattered; NIH
20:43 all your doings, wherein ye have b defiled; NIH
22:13 at thy blood which hath b in the midst of 1961
28:13 Thou hast b in Eden the garden of God; 1961
29: 6 they have b a staff of reed to the house of 1961
33:33 shall they know that a prophet hath b 1961
34:12 where they have b scattered in the cloudy NIH
38: 8 of Israel, which have b always waste: 1961
Da 5:15 have b brought in before me, that they NIH
9:12 for under the whole heaven hath not b done NIH
9:12 been done as hath b done upon Jerusalem. NIH
Hos 5: 1 because ye have b a snare on Mizpah, and 1961
5: 2 though I have b a rebuker of them all. NIH
Joel 1: 2 Hath this b in your days, or even in 1961
2: 2 there hath not b ever the like, neither shall 1961
Ob 1:16 and they shall be as though they had not b. 1961
Mic 5: 2 whose goings forth have b from of old, NIH
Zep 3:19 fame in every land where they have b put to NIH
Zec 1: 2 The LORD hath b sore displeased with NIH
Mal 1: 9 this hath b by your means: will he regard 1961
2: 9 kept my ways, but have b partial in the law. 5375
2:14 Because the LORD hath b witness NIH
3:13 Your words have b stout against me, NIH
Mt 1: 6 Solomon of her that had b the wife of Urias; NIG
5:31 It hath b said, Whosoever shall put away his NIG
5:33 ye have heard that it hath b said by them of NIG
5:38 Ye have heard that it hath b said, An eye for NIG
5:43 Ye have heard that it hath b said, Thou shalt NIG
11:21 had b done in Tyre and Sidon they would NIG
11:23 mighty works, which have b done in thee, NIG
11:23 been done in thee, had b done in Sodom, NIG
13:35 I will utter things which have b kept secret NIG
23:30 If we had b in the days of our fathers, 1510
23:30 we would not have b partakers with them 1510
25:21 thou hast b faithful over a few things, I will 1510
25:23 thou hast b faithful over a few things, I will 1510
26: 9 For this ointment might have b sold for NIG
26:24 it had b good for that man if he had not 1510
26:24 been good for that man if he had not b born. NIG
Mk 5: 4 Because that he had b often bound with NIG
5: 4 the chains had b plucked asunder by him, NIG
5:18 he that had b possessed with the devil NIG
6:49 they supposed it had b a spirit, and 1510
8: 2 they have now b with me three days, 4357
14: 5 For it might have b sold for more than three 1410
14: 5 and have b given to the poor. NIG
14:21 good were it for that man if he had never b NIG
15:44 he asked him whether he had b any while NIG
16:10 and told them that had b with him, 1096
16:11 and had b seen of her, believed not. NIG
Lk 1: 4 those things, wherein thou hast b instructed. NIG

Lk 1:70 which have **b** since the world began:) NIG
2:44 supposing him to have **b** in the company, *1510*
4:16 to Nazareth, where he had **b** brought up: *1510*
7:10 found the servant whole that had **b** sick. NIG
8: 2 which had **b** healed of evil spirits and *1510*
10:13 for if the mighty works had **b** done in Tyre NIG
10:13 and Sidon, which have **b** done in you, NIG
16:11 ye have not **b** faithful in the unrighteous *1096*
16:12 And if ye have not **b** faithful in that which *1096*
19:17 because thou hast **b** faithful in a very little, *1096*
24:21 But we trusted that it had **b** he which *1510*
Jn 5: 6 knew that he had **b** now a long time *in that* *2192*
9:18 that he had **b** blind, and received his sight, *1510*
11:21 Lord, if thou hadst **b** here, my brother had *1510*
11:32 saying unto him, Lord, if thou hadst **b** here, *1510*
11:39 he stinketh: for he hath **b** *dead* four days. *1510*
12: 1 where Lazarus was which had **b** dead, NIG
12:38 to whom hath the arm of the Lord **b** NIG
14: 9 Have I **b** so long time with you, and *1510*
15:27 ye have **b** with me from the beginning. *1510*
Ac 1:16 this scripture must needs have **b** fulfilled, NIG
4:13 of them, that they had **b** with Jesus. *1510*
4:16 for that indeed a notable miracle hath **b** NIG
5:26 the people, lest they should have **b** stoned. NIG
6:15 saw his face as it had **b** the face of an angel. NIG
7:52 of whom ye have **b** now the betrayers and *1096*
9:18 there fell from his eyes **as it had b** scales: *5616*
10:11 as *it had* **b** a great sheet knit at the four NIG
11: 5 vessel descend, as *it had* **b** a great sheet, NIG
13: 1 which had **b** brought up with Herod NIG
13:46 of God should first have **b** spoken to you: NIG
14:19 out of the city, supposing he had **b** dead. NIG
14:26 from whence they had **b** recommended to *1510*
15: 7 And when there had **b** much disputing, *1096*
16:27 supposing that the prisoners had **b** fled. NIG
19:21 to Jerusalem, saying, After I have **b** there, *1096*
20:18 after what manner I have **b** with you at all *1096*
23:10 fearing lest Paul should have **b** pulled in NIG
23:27 the Jews, and should have **b** killed of them: NIG
24:10 Forasmuch as I know that thou hast **b** of *1510*
24:19 Who ought to have **b** here before thee, and NIG
24:26 He hoped also that money should have **b** NIG
25:14 And when they had **b** there many days, *1304*
26:32 This man might have **b** set at liberty, NIG
Ro 6: 5 For if we have **b** planted together in *1096*
9:29 we had **b** as Sodoma, and been made like *1096*
9:29 and **b** made like unto Gomorrha. NIG
11:34 of the Lord? or who hath **b** his counseller? *1096*
15:22 For which cause also I have **b** much NIG
15:27 For if the Gentiles have **b** made partakers NIG
16: 2 for she hath **b** a succourer of many, and *1096*
1Co 1:11 For it hath **b** declared unto me of you, NIG
12:13 and have **b** all made to drink into one Spirit. NIG
2Co 11: 6 we *have* **b** throughly made manifest among NIG
11:21 as though we had **b** weak. NIG
11:25 a night and a day I have **b** in the deep; *4160*
12:11 for I ought to have **b** commended of you: NIG
Gal 3: 1 before whose eyes Jesus Christ hath **b** NIG
3:21 for if there had **b** a law given which could NIG
3:21 verily righteousness should have **b** by *1510*
3:27 For as many of you as have **b** baptized into NIG
4:15 I bear you record, that if *it had* **b** possible, NIG
5:13 For, brethren, ye have **b** called unto liberty; NIG
Eph 3: 9 beginning of the world hath **b** hid in God, NIG
4:21 and have **b** taught by him, as the truth is in NIG
Php 2:26 that ye had heard that he had **b** sick. NIG
Col 1:26 *Even* the mystery which hath **b** hid from NIG
2: 7 stablished in the faith, as ye have **b** taught, NIG
4:11 of God, which have **b** a comfort unto me. *1096*
1Th 2: 6 when we might have **b** burdensome, *1510*
2Th 2:15 hold the traditions which ye have **b** taught, NIG
1Ti 5: 9 years old, having **b** the wife of one man, *1096*
2Ti 3:14 thou hast learned and hast **b** assured of, NIG
Tit 1: 9 Holding fast the faithful word as *he* hath **b** NIG
Heb 8: 7 For if that first *covenant* had **b** faultless, *1510*
8: 7 should no place have **b** sought for NIG
11:15 if they had **b** mindful of that *country* from NIG
13: 9 which have not profited them that have **b** NIG
Jas 3: 7 is tamed, and hath **b** tamed of mankind: NIG
5: 5 lived in pleasure on the earth, and **b** wanton; NIG
2Pe 2:21 For it had **b** better for them not to have *1510*
1Jn 2:19 for if they had **b** of us, they would *no doubt* *1510*
Rev 5: 6 stood a Lamb as *it had* **b** slain, having seven NIG
17: 2 the inhabiters of the earth have **b** made NIG

BEER (2) [BAALATH-BEER, BEER-ELIM, BEER-LAHAI-ROI, BEER-SHEBA]

Nu 21:16 from thence *they went* to **B**: that *is* the well 876
Jdg 9:21 and fled, and went to **B**, and dwelt there, 876

BEERA (1)

1Ch 7:37 Shamma, and Shilshah, and Ithran, and **B**. 878

BEERAH (1)

1Ch 5: 6 **B** his son, whom Tilgath-pilneser king of 880

BEER-ELIM (1) [BEER, ELIM]

Isa 15: 8 and the howling thereof *unto* **B**. 879

BEERI (2)

Ge 26:34 to wife Judith the daughter of **B** the Hittite, 882
Hos 1: 1 the son of **B**, in the days of Uzziah, Jotham, 882

BEER-LAHAI-ROI (1) [BEER, LAHAI-ROI, WELL]

Ge 16:14 Wherefore the well was called **B**; behold, 883

BEEROTH (6) [BEEROTHITE, BEEROTHITES]

Dt 10: 6 from **B** of the children of Jaakan *to* Mosera: 881
Jos 9:17 and Chephirah, and **B**, and Kirjath-jearim. 881
18:25 Gibeon, and Ramah, and **B**, 881
2Sa 4: 2 (for **B** also was reckoned to Benjamin: 881
Ezr 2:25 Chephirah, and **B**, seven hundred and forty 881
Ne 7:29 Chephirah, and **B**, seven hundred forty and 881

BEEROTHITE (4) [BEEROTH]

2Sa 4: 2 the sons of Rimmon a **B**, of the children of 886
4: 5 And the sons of Rimmon the **B**, Rechab and 886
4: 9 the sons of Rimmon the **B**, and said unto 886
23:37 Zelek the Ammonite, Naharai the **B**, 886

BEEROTHITES (1) [BEEROTH]

2Sa 4: 3 the **B** fled to Gittaim, and were sojourners 886

BEER-SHEBA (34) [BEER, SHEBA, SHEBAH]

Ge 21:14 and wandered in the wilderness of **B**. 884
21:31 Wherefore he called that place **B**; because 884
21:32 Thus they made a covenant at **B**: then 884
21:33 *Abraham* planted a grove in **B**, and 884
22:19 and they rose up and went together to **B**; 884
22:19 to Beer-sheba; and Abraham dwelt at **B**. 884
26:23 And he went up from thence to **B**. 884
26:33 the name of the city *is* **B** unto this day. 884
28:10 Jacob went out from **B**, and went toward 884
46: 1 came to **B**, and offered sacrifices unto 884
46: 5 Jacob rose up from **B**: and the sons of Israel 884
Jos 15:28 And Hazar-shual, and **B**, and Bizjothjah, 884
19: 2 they had in their inheritance **B**, or Sheba, 884
Jdg 20: 1 from Dan even to **B**, with the land of Gilead, 884
1Sa 3:20 all Israel from Dan even to **B** knew that 884
8: 2 of his second, Abiah: *they were* judges in **B**. 884
2Sa 3:10 and over Judah, from Dan even to **B**. 884
17:11 from Dan even to **B**, as the sand that *is* by 884
24: 2 from Dan even to **B**, and number ye 884
24: 7 went out to the south of Judah, *even to* **B**. 884
24:15 there died of the people from Dan even to **B** 884
1Ki 4:25 and under his fig tree, from Dan even to **B**, 884
19: 3 went for his life, and came *to* **B**, 884
2Ki 12: 1 And his mother's name *was* Zibiah of **B**. 884
23: 8 from Geba to **B**, and brake down the high 884
1Ch 4:28 they dwelt at **B**, and Moladah, and 884
21: 2 Go, number Israel from **B** even to Dan; 884
2Ch 19: 4 he went out again through the people from **B** 884
24: 1 His mother's name also *was* Zibiah of **B**. 884
30: 5 throughout all Israel, from **B** even to Dan, 884
Ne 11:27 and at **B**, and *in* the villages thereof, 884
11:30 they dwelt from **B** unto the valley of 884
Am 5: 5 nor enter *into* Gilgal, and pass not *to* **B**: 884
8:14 O Dan, liveth; and, The manner of **B** liveth; 884

BEES (3) [BEE]

Dt 1:44 as **b** do, and destroyed you in Seir, 1682
Jdg 14: 8 *there was* a swarm of **b** and honey in 1682
Ps 118:12 They compassed me about like **b**; they are 1682

BEESHTERAH (1)

Jos 21:27 and **B** with her suburbs; two cities. 1203

BEETLE (1)

Lev 11:22 the **b** after his kind, and the grasshopper 2728

BEEVES (7)

Lev 22:19 of the **b**, of the sheep, or of the goats. 1241
22:21 or a freewill offering in **b** or sheep, it shall 1241
Nu 31:28 of the **b**, and of the asses, and of the sheep: 1241
31:30 of the **b**, of the asses, and of the flocks, 1241
31:33 And threescore and twelve thousand **b**, 1241
31:38 the **b** *were* thirty and six thousand; of 1241
31:44 And thirty and six thousand **b**, 1241

BEFALL (9) [BEFALLEN, BEFALLETH, BEFELL]

Ge 42: 4 he said, Lest peradventure mischief **b** him. 7122
42:38 if mischief **b** him by the way in the which 7122
44:29 take this also from me, and mischief **b** him, 7136
49: 1 that I may tell you *that* which shall **b** you in 7122
Dt 31:17 and many evils and troubles shall **b** them; 4672
31:29 evil will **b** you in the latter days; because 7122
Ps 91:10 There shall no evil **b** thee, neither shall 413+579
Da 10:14 what shall **b** thy people in the latter days: 7136
Ac 20:22 not knowing the *things* that shall **b** me *4876*

BEFALLEN (7) [BEFALL]

Lev 10:19 the LORD; and such things have **b** me: 7122
Nu 20:14 Thou knowest all the travail that hath **b** us: 4672
Dt 31:21 when many evils and troubles are **b** them, 4672
Jdg 6:13 be with us, why then is all this **b** us? 4672
1Sa 20:26 for he thought, **Something** hath **b** him, 4745
Est 6:13 all his friends every *thing* that had **b** him. 7136
Mt 8:33 **what was b to** the possessed of the devils. *3588*

BEFALLETH (3) [BEFALL]

Ecc 3:19 For that which **b** the sons of men befalleth 4745
3:19 For that which befalleth the sons of men **b** 4745
3:19 befalleth beasts; even one thing **b** them: 4745

BEFELL (5) [BEFALL]

Ge 42:29 and told him all that **b** unto them; 7136
Jos 2:23 of Nun, and told him all *things* that **b** them: 4672
2Sa 19: 7 that **b** thee from thy youth until now. 935+5921
Mk 5:16 And they that saw *it* told them how it **b** to *1096*
Ac 20:19 which **b** me by the lying in wait of *4819*

BEFORE (1799) [BEFOREHAND, BEFORETIME]

Ge 2: 5 every plant of the field **b** it was in the earth, 2962
2: 5 and every herb of the field **b** it grew: 2962
6:11 The earth also was corrupt **b** God, 6440+3807.1
6:13 The end of all flesh is come **b** me; 6440+3807.1
7: 1 for thee have I seen righteous **b** me 6440+3807.1
10: 9 He was a mighty hunter **b** 6440+3807.1
10: 9 the mighty hunter **b** the LORD. 6440+3807.1
11:28 Haran died **b** his father Terah in 5921+6440
12:15 saw her, and commended her **b** Pharaoh: 413
13: 9 *Is* not the whole land **b** thee? 6440+3807.1
13:10 it *was* well watered every where, **b** 6440+3807.1
13:13 and sinners **b** the LORD exceedingly. 3807.1
17: 1 walk **b** me, and be thou perfect. 6440+3807.1
17:18 O that Ishmael might live **b** thee! 6440+3807.1
18: 8 he had dressed, and set *it* **b** them; 6440+3807.1
18:22 Abraham stood yet **b** the LORD. 6440+3807.1
19: 4 **b** they lay down, the men of the city, 2962
19:13 the cry of them is waxen great **b** the face of 854
19:27 place where he stood **b** the LORD: 854+6440
20:15 Behold, my land *is* **b** thee: 6440+3807.1
23: 3 Abraham stood up from **b** his dead, and 6440
23:12 Abraham bowed down himself **b** 6440+3807.1
23:17 which *was* **b** Mamre, the field, and 6440+3807.1
23:18 **b** all that went in at the gate of his city. 871.1
23:19 of the field of Machpelah **b** Mamre: 5921+6440
24: 7 he shall send his angel **b** thee, and 6440+3807.1
24:15 **b** he had done speaking, that behold, 2962
24:33 there was set *meat* **b** him to eat: but 6440+3807.1
24:40 The LORD, **b** whom I walk, 6440+3807.1
24:45 **b** I had done speaking in mine heart, 2962
24:51 Behold, Rebekah *is* **b** thee, 6440+3807.1
25: 9 Zohar the Hittite, which *is* **b** Mamre; 5921+6440
25:18 that *is* **b** Egypt, as thou goest towards 5921+6440
27: 4 that my soul may bless thee **b** I die. 2962+871.1
27: 7 **b** the LORD before my death. 6440+3807.1
27: 7 before the LORD **b** my death. 6440+3807.1
27:10 that he may bless thee **b** his death. 6440+3807.1
27:33 I have eaten of all **b** thou camest, 2962+871.1
29:26 to give the younger **b** the firstborn. 6440+3807.1
30:30 For *it was* little which thou hadst **b** 6440+3807.1
30:33 when it shall come for my hire **b** thy face: 3807.1
30:38 **b** the flocks in the gutters in 5227+3807.1
30:39 the flocks conceived **b** the rods, and 413
30:41 that Jacob laid the rods **b** the eyes of 3807.1
31: 2 behold, it *was* not toward him as **b**. 8032+8543
31: 5 that it *is* not toward me as **b**; 8032+8543
31:32 **b** our brethren discern thou what *is* thine 5048
31:35 my lord that I cannot rise up **b** thee; 4480+6440
31:37 set *it* here **b** my brethren and thy brethren, 5048
32: 3 Jacob sent messengers **b** him to 6440+3807.1
32:16 Pass over **b** me, and put a space 6440+3807.1
32:17 and whose *are* these **b** thee? 6440+3807.1
32:20 with the present that goeth **b** me, 6440+3807.1
32:21 So went the present over **b** him: and 5921+6440
33: 3 he passed over **b** them, and 6440+3807.1
33:12 and let us go, and I will go **b** thee. 5048+3807.1
33:14 I pray thee, pass over **b** his servant: 6440+3807.1
33:14 according as the cattle that goeth **b** 6440+3807.1
33:18 and pitched his tent **b** the city. 854+6440
34:10 the land shall be **b** you; dwell and 6440+3807.1
36:31 that reigned in the land of Edom, **b** 6440+3807.1
37:18 even **b** he came near unto them, 2962+871.1
40: 9 behold, a vine *was* **b** me; 6440+3807.1
41:43 they cried **b** him, Bow the knee: 6440+3807.1
41:46 he stood **b** Pharaoh king of Egypt. 6440+3807.1
41:50 unto Joseph were born two sons **b** 2962+871.1
42: 6 bowed down themselves **b** him *with* their 3807.1
42:24 and bound him **b** their eyes. 3807.1
43: 9 set him **b** thee, then let me bear 6440+3807.1
43:14 God Almighty give you mercy **b** 6440+3807.1
43:15 *to* Egypt, and stood **b** Joseph. 6440+3807.1
43:33 they sat **b** him, the firstborn 6440+3807.1
43:34 *and sent* messes unto them from **b** him: 6440
44:14 and they fell **b** him on the ground. 6440+3807.1
45: 1 Joseph could not refrain himself **b** all 3807.1
45: 5 did send me **b** you to preserve life. 6440+3807.1
45: 7 God sent me **b** you to preserve you 6440+3807.1
45:28 I will go and see him **b** I die. 2962+871.1
46:28 he sent Judah **b** him unto Joseph, 6440+3807.1
47: 6 The land of Egypt *is* **b** thee; in 6440+3807.1
47: 7 his father, and set him **b** Pharaoh: 6440+3807.1
47:10 and went out from **b** Pharaoh. 6440+3807.1
47:19 Wherefore shall we die **b** thine eyes, 3807.1
48: 5 of Egypt **b** I came unto thee into Egypt, 5704
48:15 God, **b** whom my fathers Abraham 6440+3807.1
48:20 and he set Ephraim **b** Manasseh. 6440+3807.1
49: 8 thy father's children shall bow down **b** 3807.1
49:30 *is* **b** Mamre, in the land of Canaan, 5921+6440
50:13 of Ephron the Hittite, **b** Mamre. 5921+6440
50:16 did command **b** he died, saying, 6440+3807.1
50:18 also went and fell down **b** his face; 3807.1
Ex 4: 3 became a serpent; and Moses fled from **b** it. 6440
4:21 do all *those* wonders **b** Pharaoh, 6440+3807.1
6:12 Moses spake **b** the LORD, saying, 6440+3807.1
6:30 Moses said **b** the LORD, Behold, 6440+3807.1
7: 9 cast *it* **b** Pharaoh, *and* it shall 6440+3807.1
7:10 Aaron cast down his rod **b** 6440+3807.1
7:10 **b** his servants, and it became a 6440+3807.1
8:20 the morning, and stand **b** Pharaoh; 6440+3807.1
8:26 of the Egyptians **b** their eyes, 3807.1
9:10 the furnace, and stood **b** Pharaoh; 6440+3807.1
9:11 the magicians could not stand **b** 6440+3807.1
9:13 stand **b** Pharaoh, and say unto him, 6440+3807.1
10: 1 I might shew these my signs **b** him: 7130+871.1
10: 3 thou refuse to humble thyself **b** me? 4480+6440
10:10 look *to it*; for evil *is* **b** you. 5048+6440
10:14 very grievous *were they*; **b** them 6440+3807.1
11:10 did all these wonders **b** Pharaoh: 6440+3807.1
12:34 the people took their dough **b** it was 2962
13:21 the LORD went **b** them by day in 6440+3807.1
13:22 the pillar of fire by night, *from* **b** 6440+3807.1
14: 2 that they turn and encamp **b** 6440+3807.1
14: 2 over against Baal-zephon: **b** 5226+3807.1
14: 9 beside Pi-hahiroth, **b** Baal-zephon. 6440+3807.1
14:19 which went **b** the camp of Israel, 6440+3807.1
14:19 pillar of the cloud went from **b** their **face**, 6440
16: 9 of Israel, Come near **b** the LORD: 6440+3807.1
16:33 lay it up **b** the LORD, to be kept for your 6440
16:34 so Aaron laid it up **b** 6440+3807.1
17: 5 Go on **b** the people, and take with 6440+3807.1
17: 6 I will stand **b** thee there upon 6440+3807.1
18:12 with Moses' father in law **b** God. 6440+3807.1
19: 2 and there Israel camped **b** the mount. 5048
19: 7 laid **b** their faces all these words which 3807.1
20: 3 Thou shalt have no other gods **b** me. 5921+6440
20:20 that his fear may be **b** your faces, that ye 5921
21: 1 which thou shalt set **b** them. 6440+3807.1
22: 9 the cause of both parties shall come **b** 5704
23:15 and none shall appear **b** me empty: 6440
23:17 males shall appear **b** the Lord GOD. 413+6440

Ex 23:20 Behold, I send an Angel **b** thee, 6440+3807.1
23:23 For mine Angel shall go **b** thee, 6440+3807.1
23:27 I will send my fear **b** thee, and 6440+3807.1
23:28 I will send hornets **b** thee, 6440+3807.1
23:28 and the Hittite, from **b** thee. 6440+3807.1
23:29 I will not drive them out from **b** thee in one 6440
23:30 and little I will drive them out from **b** thee, 6440
23:31 and thou shalt drive them out **b** thee. 6440
25:30 the table shewbread **b** me alway. 6440+3807.1
27:21 which *is* **b** the Testimony, Aaron and 5921
27:21 evening to morning **b** the LORD: 6440+3807.1
28:12 Aaron shall bear their names **b** 6440+3807.1
28:25 of the ephod **b** it. 413+4136+6440
28:29 **b** the LORD continually. 6440+3807.1
28:30 when he goeth in **b** the LORD: 6440+3807.1
28:30 his heart **b** the LORD continually. 6440+3807.1
28:35 unto the holy *place* **b** the LORD, 6440+3807.1
28:38 may be accepted **b** the LORD. 6440+3807.1
29:10 **b** the tabernacle of 6440+3807.1
29:11 thou shalt kill the bullock **b** 6440+3807.1
29:23 bread that *is* **b** the LORD: 6440+3807.1
29:24 *for* a wave offering **b** the LORD. 6440+3807.1
29:25 for a sweet savour **b** the LORD: 6440+3807.1
29:26 *for* a wave offering **b** the LORD: 6440+3807.1
29:42 of the congregation **b** the LORD: 6440+3807.1
30: 6 thou shalt put it **b** the vail that *is* by 6440+3807.1
30: 6 *is* by the ark of the Testimony, **b** 6440+3807.1
30: 8 a perpetual incense **b** the LORD 6440+3807.1
30:16 children of Israel **b** the LORD, 6440+3807.1
30:36 put of it **b** the Testimony in 6440+3807.1
32: 1 make us gods, which shall go **b** us; 6440+3807.1
32: 5 Aaron saw *it,* he built an altar **b** it; 6440+3807.1
32:23 Make us gods, which shall go **b** us: 6440+3807.1
32:34 behold, mine Angel shall go **b** 6440+3807.1
33: 2 I will send an angel **b** thee; and 6440+3807.1
33:19 I will make all my goodness pass **b** 5921+6440
33:19 the name of the LORD **b** thee; 6440+3807.1
34: 3 neither let the flocks nor herds feed **b** 413+4136
34: 6 the LORD passed by **b** him, and 5921+6440
34:10 **b** all thy people I will do marvels, such as 5048
34:11 I drive out **b** thee the Amorite, and 4480+6440
34:20 and none shall appear **b** me empty. 6440
34:23 children appear **b** the Lord GOD, 854+6440
34:24 For I will cast out the nations **b** thee, 4480+6440
34:24 when thou shalt go up to appear **b** 854+6440
34:34 when Moses went in **b** the LORD 6440+3807.1
39:18 of the ephod, **b** it. 413+4136+6440
40: 5 incense **b** the ark of the Testimony, 6440+3807.1
40: 6 **b** the door of the tabernacle of 6440+3807.1
40:23 he set the bread in order upon it **b** 6440+3807.1
40:25 he lighted the lamps **b** the LORD; 6440+3807.1
40:26 tent of the congregation **b** the vail: 6440+3807.1
Lev 1: 3 of the congregation **b** the LORD. 6440+3807.1
1: 5 he shall kill the bullock **b** 6440+3807.1
1:11 the altar northward **b** the LORD: 6440+3807.1
3: 1 he shall offer it without blemish **b** 6440+3807.1
3: 7 then shall he offer it **b** the LORD. 6440+3807.1
3: 8 **b** the tabernacle of 6440+3807.1
3:12 then he shall offer it **b** the LORD. 6440+3807.1
3:13 **b** the tabernacle of 6440+3807.1
4: 4 of the congregation **b** the LORD; 6440+3807.1
4: 4 and kill the bullock **b** the LORD. 6440+3807.1
4: 6 sprinkle of the blood seven times **b** 6440+3807.1
4: 6 seven times before the LORD, **b** 854+6440
4: 7 of sweet incense **b** the LORD, 6440+3807.1
4:14 bring him **b** the tabernacle of 6440+3807.1
4:15 head of the bullock **b** the LORD: 6440+3807.1
4:15 shall be killed **b** the LORD. 6440+3807.1
4:17 sprinkle *it* seven times **b** 6440+3807.1
4:17 before the LORD, *even* **b** the vail. 854+6440
4:18 of the altar which *is* **b** the LORD, 6440+3807.1
4:24 the burnt offering **b** the LORD: 6440+3807.1
6: 7 atonement for him **b** the LORD: 6440+3807.1
6:14 the sons of Aaron shall offer it **b** 6440+3807.1
6:14 shall offer it before the LORD, **b** 413+6440
6:25 offering be killed **b** the LORD: 6440+3807.1
7:30 *for* a wave offering **b** the LORD. 6440+3807.1
8:26 that *was* **b** the LORD, he took one 6440+3807.1
8:27 waved them *for* a wave offering **b** 6440+3807.1
8:29 *for* a wave offering **b** the LORD: 6440+3807.1
9: 2 and offer *them* **b** the LORD. 6440+3807.1
9: 4 to sacrifice **b** the LORD; 6440+3807.1
9: 5 **b** the tabernacle of the congregation: 413+6440
9: 5 drew near and stood **b** the LORD. 6440+3807.1
9:21 *for* a wave offering **b** the LORD; 6440+3807.1
9:24 there came a fire out from **b** 6440+3807.1
10: 1 offered strange fire **b** the LORD, 6440+3807.1
10: 2 and they died **b** the LORD. 6440+3807.1
10: 3 **b** all the people I will be glorified. 5921+6440
10: 4 carry your brethren from **b** the sanctuary 6440
10:15 to wave *it for* a wave offering **b** 6440+3807.1
10:17 atonement for them **b** the LORD? 6440+3807.1
10:19 their burnt offering **b** the LORD; 6440+3807.1
12: 7 Who shall offer it **b** the LORD, 6440+3807.1
14:11 those *things,* **b** the LORD, *at* 6440+3807.1
14:12 wave them *for* a wave offering **b** 6440+3807.1
14:16 finger seven times **b** the LORD: 6440+3807.1
14:18 atonement for him **b** the LORD. 6440+3807.1
14:23 tabernacle of the congregation, **b** 6440+3807.1
14:24 *for* a wave offering **b** the LORD: 6440+3807.1
14:27 hand seven times **b** the LORD: 6440+3807.1
14:29 to make an atonement for him **b** 6440+3807.1
14:31 is to be cleansed **b** the LORD. 6440+3807.1
14:36 that they empty the house, **b** 2962+871.1
15:14 come **b** the LORD unto the door 6440+3807.1
15:15 for him **b** the LORD for his issue. 6440+3807.1
15:30 **b** the LORD for the issue of her 6440+3807.1
16: 1 offered **b** the LORD, and died; 6440+3807.1
16: 2 *place* within the vail **b** the mercy seat, 413+6440
16: 7 present them **b** the LORD *at* 6440+3807.1
16:10 shall be presented alive **b** 6440+3807.1
16:12 off the altar **b** the LORD, 4480+6440+3807.1
16:13 upon the fire **b** the LORD, 6440+3807.1
16:14 **b** the mercy seat shall he sprinkle 6440+3807.1
16:15 mercy seat, and **b** the mercy seat: 6440+3807.1

Lev 16:18 unto the altar that *is* **b** the LORD, 6440+3807.1
16:30 from all your sins **b** the LORD. 6440+3807.1
17: 4 **b** the tabernacle of the LORD; 6440+3807.1
18:23 neither shall any woman stand **b** a 6440+3807.1
18:24 are defiled which I cast out **b** you: 4480+6440
18:27 *were* **b** you, and the land is 6440+3807.1
18:28 out the nations that *were* **b** you. 6440+3807.1
18:30 which were committed **b** you, and 6440+3807.1
19:14 nor put a stumblingblock **b** 6440+3807.1
19:22 **b** the LORD for his sin which he 6440+3807.1
19:32 Thou shalt rise up **b** the hoary head, 4480+6440
20:23 of the nation, which I cast out **b** you: 4480+6440
23:11 he shall wave the sheaf **b** 6440+3807.1
23:20 *for* a wave offering **b** the LORD, 6440+3807.1
23:28 to make an atonement for you **b** 6440+3807.1
23:40 ye shall rejoice **b** the LORD your 6440+3807.1
24: 3 morning **b** the LORD continually: 6440+3807.1
24: 4 **b** the LORD continually. 6440+3807.1
24: 6 upon the pure table **b** the LORD. 6440+3807.1
24: 8 in order **b** the LORD continually, 6440+3807.1
26: 7 they shall fall **b** you by the sword. 6440+3807.1
26: 8 shall fall **b** you by the sword. 6440+3807.1
26:17 ye shall be slain **b** your enemies; 6440+3807.1
26:37 were **b** a sword, when none pursueth: 4480+6440
26:37 ye shall have no power to stand **b** 6440+3807.1
27: 8 he shall present himself **b** 6440+3807.1
27:11 shall present the beast **b** the priest: 6440+3807.1
Nu 3: 4 Nadab and Abihu died **b** 6440+3807.1
3: 4 when they offered strange fire **b** 6440+3807.1
3: 6 present them **b** Aaron the priest, 6440+3807.1
3: 7 **b** the tabernacle of 6440+3807.1
3:38 those that encamp **b** the tabernacle 6440+3807.1
3:38 tabernacle toward the east, *even* **b** 6440+3807.1
5:16 her near, and set her **b** the LORD: 6440+3807.1
5:18 the priest shall set the woman **b** 6440+3807.1
5:25 shall wave the offering **b** 6440+3807.1
5:30 shall set the woman **b** the LORD, 6440+3807.1
6:12 the days that were **b** shall be lost, because 7223
6:16 the priest shall bring *them* **b** 6440+3807.1
6:20 *for* a wave offering **b** the LORD: 6440+3807.1
7: 3 they brought their offering **b** 6440+3807.1
7: 3 they brought them **b** the tabernacle. 6440+3807.1
7:10 offered their offering **b** the altar. 6440+3807.1
8: 9 thou shalt bring the Levites **b** 6440+3807.1
8:10 thou shalt bring the Levites **b** 6440+3807.1
8:11 Aaron shall offer the Levites **b** 6440+3807.1
8:13 thou shalt set the Levites **b** Aaron, 6440+3807.1
8:13 **b** his sons, and offer them *for* an 6440+3807.1
8:21 them *as* an offering **b** the LORD; 6440+3807.1
8:22 of the congregation **b** Aaron, 6440+3807.1
8:22 before Aaron, and **b** his sons: 6440+3807.1
9: 6 they came **b** Moses and before 6440+3807.1
9: 6 and **b** Aaron on that day: 6440+3807.1
10: 9 ye shall be remembered **b** 6440+3807.1
10:10 to you for a memorial **b** your God: 6440+3807.1
10:33 **b** them *in* the three days' journey, 6440+3807.1
10:35 let them that hate thee flee **b** thee. 4480+6440
11: 6 at all, beside *this* manna, *b* our eyes. NIH
11:20 have wept **b** him, saying, Why 6440+3807.1
13:22 built seven years **b** Zoan in Egypt.) 6440+3807.1
13:30 Caleb stilled the people **b** Moses, and said, 413
14: 5 Aaron fell on their faces **b** all 6440+3807.1
14:10 the congregation **b** all the children of Israel. 413
14:14 *that* thou goest **b** them, by day time 6440+3807.1
14:37 died by the plague **b** the LORD. 6440+3807.1
14:42 ye be not smitten **b** your enemies. 6440+3807.1
14:43 and the Canaanites *are* there **b** you, 6440+3807.1
15:15 shall the stranger be **b** the LORD. 6440+3807.1
15:25 their sin offering **b** the LORD, 6440+3807.1
15:28 when he sinneth by ignorance **b** 6440+3807.1
16: 2 they rose up **b** Moses, with certain 6440+3807.1
16: 7 put incense in them **b** the LORD 6440+3807.1
16: 9 to stand **b** the congregation to 6440+3807.1
16:16 and all thy company **b** the LORD, 6440+3807.1
16:17 bring ye **b** the LORD every man 6440+3807.1
16:38 for they offered them **b** 6440+3807.1
16:40 near to offer incense **b** the LORD; 6440+3807.1
16:43 Aaron came **b** the tabernacle of 413+6440
17: 4 the congregation **b** the Testimony, 6440+3807.1
17: 7 Moses laid up the rods **b** 6440+3807.1
17: 9 **b** the LORD unto all the children 6440+3807.1
17:10 rod again **b** the Testimony, 6440+3807.1
18: 2 thy sons with thee *shall minister* **b** 6440+3807.1
18:19 it *is* a covenant of salt for ever **b** 6440+3807.1
19: 3 and *one* shall slay her **b** his face: 3807.1
19: 4 sprinkle of her blood directly **b** 6440
20: 3 our brethren died **b** the LORD! 6440+3807.1
20: 8 and speak ye unto the rock **b** their eyes; 3807.1
20: 9 Moses took the rod from **b** 6440+3807.1
20:10 the congregation together **b** the rock, 413+6440
21:11 in the wilderness which *is* **b** Moab, 5921+6440
22:32 because *thy* way is perverse **b** me: 5048+3807.1
25: 4 hang them up **b** the LORD against 3807.1
25: 6 who *were* weeping *b* the door of NIH
26:61 when they offered strange fire **b** 6440+3807.1
27: 2 they stood **b** Moses, and before 6440+3807.1
27: 2 **b** Eleazar the priest, and before 6440+3807.1
27: 2 **b** the princes and all 6440+3807.1
27: 5 Moses brought their cause **b** 6440+3807.1
27:14 to sanctify me at the water **b** their eyes: 3807.1
27:17 Which may go out **b** them, and 6440+3807.1
27:17 which may go in **b** them, and 6440+3807.1
27:19 set him **b** Eleazar the priest, and 6440+3807.1
27:19 and **b** all the congregation; 6440+3807.1
27:21 he shall stand **b** Eleazar the priest, 6440+3807.1
27:21 judgment of Urim **b** the LORD: 6440+3807.1
27:22 set him **b** Eleazar the priest, and 6440+3807.1
27:22 and **b** all the congregation: 6440+3807.1
31:50 for our souls **b** the LORD. 6440+3807.1
31:54 children of Israel **b** the LORD. 6440+3807.1
32: 4 smote **b** the congregation of Israel, 6440+3807.1
32:17 armed **b** the children of Israel, 6440+3807.1
32:20 go armed **b** the LORD to war, 6440+3807.1
32:21 armed over Jordan **b** the LORD, 6440+3807.1
32:21 until he hath driven out his enemies from **b** 6440

Nu 32:22 the land be subdued **b** the LORD: 6440+3807.1
32:22 be guiltless **b** the LORD, and 4480
32:22 guiltless before the LORD, and **b** Israel; 4480
32:22 this land shall be your possession **b** 6440+3807.1
32:27 every man armed for war, **b** 6440+3807.1
32:29 every man armed to battle, **b** 6440+3807.1
32:29 the land shall be subdued **b** you; 6440+3807.1
32:32 We will pass over armed **b** 6440+3807.1
33: 7 which *is* **b** Baal-zephon: 5921+6440
33: 7 and they pitched **b** Migdol. 6440+3807.1
33: 8 they departed from **b** *Pi*-hahiroth, and 6440
33:47 in the mountains of Abarim, **b** 6440+3807.1
33:52 all the inhabitants of the land from **b** you, 6440
33:55 out the inhabitants of the land from **b** you; 6440
35:12 until he stand **b** the congregation in 6440+3807.1
36: 1 **b** Moses, and before the princes, 6440+3807.1
36: 1 before Moses, and **b** the princes, 6440+3807.1
Dt 1: 8 Behold, I have set the land **b** you: 6440+3807.1
1:21 thy God hath set the land **b** thee: 6440+3807.1
1:22 We will send men **b** us, and 6440+3807.1
1:30 LORD your God which goeth **b** 6440+3807.1
1:30 that he did for you in Egypt **b** your eyes; 3807.1
1:33 Who went in the way **b** you, 6440+3807.1
1:38 which standeth **b** thee, he shall go in 6440
1:42 lest ye be smitten **b** your enemies. 6440+3807.1
1:45 ye returned and wept **b** 6440+3807.1
2:12 when they had destroyed them from **b** 6440
2:21 the LORD destroyed them **b** them; 4480+6440
2:22 when he destroyed the Horims from **b** 6440
2:31 to give Sihon and his land **b** thee: 6440+3807.1
2:33 our God delivered him **b** us; 6440+3807.1
3:18 ye shall pass over armed **b** your 6440+3807.1
3:28 for he shall go over **b** this people, 6440+3807.1
4: 8 which I set **b** you *this* day? 6440+3807.1
4:10 **b** the LORD thy God in Horeb, 6440+3807.1
4:32 that are past, which were **b** thee, 6440+3807.1
4:34 God did for you in Egypt **b** your eyes? 3807.1
4:38 To drive out nations from **b** thee greater 6440
4:44 this *is* the law which Moses set **b** 6440+3807.1
5: 7 Thou shalt have none other gods **b** 5921+6440
6:19 To cast out all thine enemies from **b** thee, 6440
6:22 and upon all his household, **b** our eyes: 3807.1
6:25 **b** the LORD our God, 6440+3807.1
7: 1 hath cast out many nations **b** thee, 4480+6440
7: 2 thy God shall deliver them **b** thee; 6440+3807.1
7:22 put out those nations **b** thee by little 4480+6440
7:24 there shall no man *be able to* stand **b** 6440+871.1
8:20 which the LORD destroyeth **b** your face, 4480
9: 2 can stand **b** the children of Anak! 6440+3807.1
9: 3 God *is* he which goeth over **b** thee; 6440+3807.1
9: 3 and he shall bring them down **b** thy face: 3807.1
9: 4 hath cast them out from **b** thee, 6440+3807.1
9: 4 LORD doth drive them out from **b** thee. 6440
9: 5 thy God doth drive them out from **b** thee, 6440
9:17 two hands, and brake them **b** your eyes. 3807.1
9:18 I fell down **b** the LORD, as at 6440+3807.1
9:25 Thus I fell down **b** the LORD 6440+3807.1
10: 8 to stand **b** the LORD to minister 6440+3807.1
10:11 Arise, take thy journey **b** 6440+3807.1
11:23 out all these nations from **b** you, 6440+3807.1
11:25 shall no man *be able to* stand **b** 6440+871.1
11:26 **b** you *this* day a blessing and 6440+3807.1
11:32 which I set **b** you *this* day. 6440+3807.1
12: 7 there ye shall eat **b** the LORD 6440+3807.1
12:12 ye shall rejoice **b** the LORD your 6440+3807.1
12:18 thou must eat them **b** the LORD 6440+3807.1
12:18 thou shalt rejoice **b** the LORD thy 6440+3807.1
12:29 God shall cut off the nations from **b** thee, 6440
12:30 after that they be destroyed from **b** thee; 6440
14:23 thou shalt eat **b** the LORD thy 6440+3807.1
14:26 thou shalt eat there **b** the LORD thy 6440+3807.1
15:20 Thou shalt eat it **b** the LORD thy 6440+3807.1
16:11 thou shalt rejoice **b** the LORD thy 6440+3807.1
16:16 **b** the LORD thy God in the place 854+6440
16:16 shall not appear **b** the LORD empty: 854+6440
17:12 to minister there **b** the LORD thy God, NIH
17:18 *which is* **b** the priests the Levites: 6440+3807.1
18: 7 which stand there **b** the LORD. 6440+3807.1
18:12 thy God doth drive them out from **b** thee. 6440
19:17 *is,* shall stand **b** the LORD, 6440+3807.1
19:17 *is,* shall stand before the LORD, **b** 6440+3807.1
21:16 firstborn **b** the son of the hated, 5921+6440
22: 6 If a bird's nest chance to be **b** thee 6440+3807.1
22:17 they shall spread the cloth **b** 6440+3807.1
23:14 to give up thine enemies **b** thee; 6440+3807.1
24: 4 that *is* abomination **b** the LORD: 6440+3807.1
24:13 unto thee **b** the LORD thy God. 6440+3807.1
25: 2 to be beaten **b** his face, according to his 3807.1
26: 4 set it down **b** the altar of 6440+3807.1
26: 5 and say **b** the LORD thy God, 6440+3807.1
26:10 thou shalt set it **b** the LORD thy 6440+3807.1
26:10 worship **b** the LORD thy God: 6440+3807.1
26:13 thou shalt say **b** the LORD thy 6440+3807.1
27: 7 and rejoice **b** the LORD thy God. 6440+3807.1
28: 7 up against thee *to be* smitten **b** thy face: 3807.1
28: 7 and flee **b** thee seven ways. 6440+3807.1
28:25 thee *to be* smitten **b** thine enemies: 6440+3807.1
28:25 and flee seven ways **b** them: 6440+3807.1
28:31 Thine ox *shall be* slain **b** thine eyes, and 3807.1
28:31 *be* violently taken away from **b** thy face, 3807.1
28:66 thy life shall hang in doubt **b** thee; 4480+5048
29: 2 Ye have seen all that the LORD did **b** 3807.1
29:10 Ye stand *this* day all of you **b** 6440+3807.1
29:15 us *this* day **b** the LORD our God, 6440+3807.1
30: 1 which I have set **b** thee, and 6440+3807.1
30:15 I have set **b** thee *this* day life and 6440+3807.1
30:19 *that* I have set **b** you life and death, 6440+3807.1
31: 3 he will go over **b** thee, *and* he will 6440+3807.1
31: 3 destroy these nations from **b** thee, 6440+3807.1
31: 3 *and* Joshua, he shall go over **b** thee, 6440+3807.1
31: 5 the LORD shall give them up **b** your 3807.1
31: 8 he *it is* that doth go **b** thee; 6440+3807.1
31:11 When all Israel is come to appear **b** 854+6440
31:11 thou shalt read this law **b** all Israel in their 5048
31:21 *even* now, **b** I have brought them 2962+871.1

B

Dt 32:52 Yet thou shalt see the land **b** *thee;* 4480+5048
33: 1 the children of Israel **b** his death. 6440+3807.1
33:10 they shall put incense **b** thee, and 639+871.1
33:27 he shall thrust out the enemy from **b** thee; 6440
Jos 1: 5 stand **b** thee all the days of thy life: 6440+3807.1
1:14 ye shall pass **b** your brethren 6440+3807.1
2: 8 **b** they were laid down, she came up unto 2962
3: 1 and lodged there **b** they passed over. 2962
3: 6 and pass over **b** the people. 6440+3807.1
3: 6 and went **b** the people. 6440+3807.1
3:10 *that* he will without fail drive out from **b** 6440
3:11 passeth over **b** you into Jordan. 6440+3807.1
3:14 ark *of* the covenant **b** the people; 6440+3807.1
4: 5 Pass over **b** the ark of the LORD 6440+3807.1
4: 7 **b** the ark of the covenant of 4480+6440
4:12 over armed **b** the children of Israel, 6440+3807.1
4:13 over **b** the LORD unto battle, 6440+3807.1
4:18 over all his banks, as *they did* **b**. 8032+8543
4:23 dried up the waters of Jordan from **b** you, 6440
4:23 which he dried up from **b** us, until we were 6440
5: 1 of Jordan from **b** the children of Israel, 6440
6: 4 seven priests shall bear **b** the ark 6440+3807.1
6: 5 shall ascend up every man **straight b** him. 5048
6: 6 horns **b** the ark of the LORD. 6440+3807.1
6: 7 let him that is armed pass on **b** 6440+3807.1
6: 8 horns passed on **b** the LORD, 6440+3807.1
6: 9 the armed men went **b** the priests 6440+3807.1
6:13 **b** the ark of the LORD went on 6440+3807.1
6:13 the armed men went **b** them; but 6440+3807.1
6:20 every man **straight b** him, and they took 5048
6:26 saying, Cursed *be* the man **b** 6440+3807.1
7: 4 and they fled **b** the men of Ai. 6440+3807.1
7: 5 for they chased them *from* **b** 6440+3807.1
7: 6 fell to the earth upon his face **b** 6440+3807.1
7: 8 when Israel turneth *their* backs **b** 6440+3807.1
7:12 could not stand **b** their enemies, 6440+3807.1
7:12 *but* turned *their* backs **b** their 6440+3807.1
7:13 thou canst not stand **b** thine 6440+3807.1
7:23 and laid them out **b** the LORD. 6440+3807.1
8: 5 the first, that we will flee **b** them, 6440+3807.1
8: 6 *They* flee **b** us, as at the first: 6440+3807.1
8: 6 therefore we will flee **b** them. 6440+3807.1
8:10 elders of Israel, **b** the people *to* Ai. 6440+3807.1
8:11 came **b** the city, and pitched on the north 5048
8:14 at a time appointed, **b** the plain; 6440+3807.1
8:15 *as if they* were beaten **b** them, 6440+3807.1
8:33 and on that side **b** the priests the Levites, 5048
8:33 LORD had commanded **b**, 7223+871.1+1886.1
8:35 which Joshua read not **b** all 5048
9:24 all the inhabitants of the land from **b** you, 6440
10: 5 encamped **b** Gibeon, and made war against 5921
10: 8 shall not a man of them stand **b** thee. 6440+871.1
10:10 the LORD discomfited them **b** 6440+3807.1
10:11 as they fled from **b** Israel, *and* were in 6440
10:12 Amorites **b** the children of Israel, 6440+3807.1
10:14 there was no day like that **b** it or 6440+3807.1
11: 6 I deliver them up all slain **b** Israel: 6440+3807.1
13: 3 From Sihor, which *is* **b** Egypt, 5921+6440
13: 6 them will I drive out from **b** the children of 6440
13:25 unto Aroer that *is* **b** Rabbah; 5921+6440
14:15 the name of Hebron **b** *was* 6440+3807.1
15: 7 that *is* **b** the going up to Adummim, 5227
15: 8 **b** the valley of Hinnom westward, 5921+6440
15:15 of Debir **b** *was* Kirjath-sepher. 6440+3807.1
17: 4 they came near **b** Eleazar 6440+3807.1
17: 4 **b** Joshua the son of Nun, and 6440+3807.1
17: 4 of Nun, and **b** the princes, saying, 6440+3807.1
17: 7 that *lieth* **b** Shechem; 5921+6440
18: 1 And the land was subdued **b** them. 6440+3807.1
18: 6 that I may cast lots for you here **b** 6440+3807.1
18: 8 that I may here cast lots for you **b** 6440+3807.1
18:10 for them in Shiloh **b** the LORD: 6440+3807.1
18:14 from the hill that *lieth* **b** Beth-horon 5921+6440
18:16 **b** the valley of the son of Hinnom, 5921+6440
19:11 to the river that *is* **b** Jokneam; 5921+6440
19:46 and Rakkon, with the border **b** Japho. 4136
19:51 by lot in Shiloh **b** the LORD, 6440+3807.1
20: 6 until he stand **b** the congregation 6440+3807.1
20: 9 until he stood **b** the congregation. 6440+3807.1
21:44 a man of all their enemies **b** them; 6440+871.1
22:27 **b** him with our burnt offerings, 6440+3807.1
22:29 our God that *is* **b** his tabernacle. 6440+3807.1
23: 5 he shall expel them from **b** you, and 6440
23: 9 For the LORD hath driven out from **b** you 6440
23: 9 no man hath *been able to* stand **b** 6440+871.1
23:13 *any of* these nations from **b** you; 6440+3807.1
24: 1 they presented themselves **b** God. 6440+3807.1
24: 8 and I destroyed them from **b** you. 6440
24:12 I sent the hornet **b** you, 6440+3807.1
24:12 which drave them out from **b** you, 6440
24:18 the LORD drave out from **b** us all 6440
Jdg 1:10 (now the name of Hebron **b** *was* 6440+3807.1
1:11 the name of Debir **b** *was* Kirjath-sepher. 6440
1:23 the name of the city **b** *was* Luz.) 6440+3807.1
2: 3 I will not drive them out from **b** you; 6440
2:14 any longer stand **b** their enemies. 6440+3807.1
2:21 **b** them of the nations which Joshua left 6440
3: 2 such as **b** knew nothing thereof: 6440+3807.1
3:27 from the mount, and he **b** them. 6440+3807.1
4:14 is not the LORD gone out **b** thee? 6440+3807.1
4:15 the edge of the sword **b** Barak; 6440+3807.1
4:23 of Canaan **b** the children of Israel. 6440+3807.1
5: 5 The mountains melted from **b** the LORD, 6440
5: 5 *even* that Sinai from **b** the LORD God of 6440
6: 9 drave them out from **b** you, and gave you 6440
6:18 forth my present, and set *it* **b** thee. 6440+3807.1
7:24 **b** them the waters unto Beth-barah and 3807.1
8:13 returned from battle **b** the sun was up, 4480
8:28 Thus was Midian subdued **b** 6440+3807.1
9:39 Gaal went out **b** the men of 6440+3807.1
9:40 he fled **b** him, and many were 4480+6440
11: 9 the LORD deliver them **b** me, 6440+3807.1
11:11 Jephthah uttered all his words **b** 6440+3807.1
11:23 the Amorites from **b** his people Israel, 6440
11:24 LORD our God shall drive out from **b** us, 6440
Jdg 11:33 subdued **b** the children of Israel. 4480+6440
12: 5 the passages of Jordan **b** the Ephraimites: 3807.1
14:16 Samson's wife wept **b** him, and said, 5921
14:17 she wept **b** him the seven days, while their 5921
14:18 seventh day **b** the sun went down, 2962+871.1
16: 3 to the top of a hill that *is* **b** Hebron. 5921+6440
16:20 I will go out as at other times **b**, and NIH
18: 6 **b** the LORD *is* your way wherein ye go. 5227
18:21 the cattle and the carriage **b** them. 6440+3807.1
20:23 and wept **b** the LORD until even, 6440+3807.1
20:26 sat there **b** the LORD, and 6440+3807.1
20:26 and peace offerings **b** the LORD. 6440+3807.1
20:28 of Aaron, stood **b** it in those days,) 6440+3807.1
20:32 smitten down **b** us, as at the first. 6440+3807.1
20:35 the LORD smote Benjamin **b** 6440+3807.1
20:39 Surely they are smitten down **b** us, 6440+3807.1
20:42 Therefore they turned *their backs* **b** 6440+3807.1
21: 2 abode there till even **b** God, and 6440+3807.1
Ru 3:14 she rose up **b** one could know 2962+871.1
4: 4 Buy *it* **b** the inhabitants, and before 5048
4: 4 and **b** the elders of my people. 5048
1Sa 1:12 continued praying **b** the LORD, 6440+3807.1
1:15 poured out my soul **b** the LORD. 6440+3807.1
1:19 worshipped **b** the LORD, and 6440+3807.1
1:22 that he may appear **b** the LORD, and 854+6440
2:11 unto the LORD **b** Eli the priest. 854+6440
2:15 Also **b** they burnt the fat, the priest's 2962+871.1
2:17 men was very great **b** the LORD: 854+6440
2:18 Samuel ministered **b** the LORD, 854+6440
2:21 And the child Samuel grew **b** the LORD. 5973
2:28 to wear an ephod **b** me? 6440+3807.1
2:30 should walk **b** me for ever: 6440+3807.1
2:35 walk **b** mine anointed for ever. 6440+3807.1
3: 1 ministered unto the LORD **b** Eli. 6440+3807.1
4: 2 Israel was smitten **b** the Philistines: 6440+3807.1
4: 3 smitten us to day **b** the Philistines? 6440+3807.1
4:17 Israel is fled **b** the Philistines, and 6440+3807.1
5: 3 the earth **b** the ark of the LORD. 6440+3807.1
5: 4 ground **b** the ark of the LORD; 6440+3807.1
6:20 Who is able to stand **b** this holy 6440+3807.1
7: 6 poured *it* out **b** the LORD, and 6440+3807.1
7:10 and they were smitten **b** Israel. 6440+3807.1
8:11 and *some* shall run **b** his chariots. 6440+3807.1
8:20 go out **b** us, and fight our battles. 6440+3807.1
9:12 said, He is; behold, *he is* **b** you: 6440+3807.1
9:13 ye shall straightway find him, **b** he 2962+871.1
9:15 in his ear a day **b** Saul came, 6440+3807.1
9:19 go up **b** me *unto* the high place; 6440+3807.1
9:24 *was* upon it, and set *it* **b** Saul. 6440+3807.1
9:24 which is left; set *it* **b** thee, *and* eat: 6440+3807.1
9:27 Bid the servant pass on **b** us, (and 6440+3807.1
10: 5 and a pipe, and a harp, **b** them; 6440+3807.1
10: 8 thou shalt go down **b** me *to* Gilgal; 6440+3807.1
10:19 present yourselves **b** the LORD 6440+3807.1
10:25 and laid *it* up **b** the LORD. 6440+3807.1
11:15 there they made Saul king **b** 6440+3807.1
11:15 *of* peace offerings **b** the LORD; 6440+3807.1
12: 2 now behold, the king walketh **b** 6440+3807.1
12: 2 I have walked **b** you from my 6440+3807.1
12: 3 here I *am*: witness against me **b** 5048
12: 3 me before the LORD, and **b** his anointed: 5048
12: 7 that I may reason with you **b** 6440+3807.1
12:16 which the LORD will do **b** your eyes. 3807.1
14:13 they fell **b** Jonathan; and 6440+3807.1
14:21 the Philistines **b that time**, 865+8032+3509.1
15:30 **b** the elders of my people, and 5048
15:30 elders of my people, and **b** Israel, 5048
15:33 Samuel hewed Agag in pieces **b** 6440+3807.1
16: 6 Surely the LORD's anointed *is* **b** him. 5048
16: 8 and made him pass **b** Samuel. 6440+3807.1
16:10 seven of his sons to pass **b** Samuel. 6440+3807.1
16:16 thy servants *which are* **b** thee, 6440+3807.1
16:21 David came to Saul, and stood **b** 6440+3807.1
16:22 Let David, I pray thee, stand **b** me; 6440+3807.1
17: 7 one bearing a shield went **b** him. 6440+3807.1
17:31 they rehearsed *them* **b** Saul: 6440+3807.1
17:41 that bare the shield *went* **b** him. 6440+3807.1
17:57 brought him **b** Saul with the head 6440+3807.1
18:13 went out and came in **b** the people. 6440+3807.1
18:16 he went out and came in **b** them. 6440+3807.1
19:24 prophesied **b** Samuel in like 6440+3807.1
20: 1 came and said **b** Jonathan, 6440+3807.1
20: 1 what *is* my sin **b** thy father, that he 6440+3807.1
21: 6 that was taken from **b** the LORD, 6440+3807.1
21: 7 that day, detained **b** the LORD; 6440+3807.1
21:13 he changed his behaviour **b** them, 5869+871.1
22: 4 he brought them **b** the king of Moab: 854+6440
23:18 they two made a covenant **b** 6440+3807.1
23:24 they arose, and went to Ziph **b** 6440+3807.1
25:19 said unto her servants, Go on **b** me; 6440+3807.1
25:23 fell **b** David on her face, and 639+3807.1
26: 1 of Hachilah, *which is* **b** Jeshimon? 5921+6440
26: 3 which *is* **b** Jeshimon, by the way. 5921+6440
26:19 cursed *be* they **b** the LORD; 6440+3807.1
26:20 let not my blood fall to the earth **b** 4480+5048
28:22 let me set a morsel of bread **b** thee; 6440+3807.1
28:25 she brought *it* **b** Saul, and before 6440+3807.1
28:25 *it* before Saul, and **b** his servants; 6440+3807.1
30:20 *which* they drave **b** those *other* 6440+3807.1
31: 1 the men of Israel fled from **b** 6440
2Sa 2:14 men now arise, and play **b** us. 6440+3807.1
2:17 of Israel, **b** the servants of David. 6440+3807.1
2:24 that *lieth* **b** Giah *by* the way of 5921+6440
3:28 my kingdom *are* guiltless **b** 4480+5973
3:31 and mourn **b** Abner. 6440+3807.1
3:34 as *a man* falleth **b** wicked men, *so* 6440+3807.1
5: 3 them in Hebron **b** the LORD: 6440+3807.1
5:20 forth upon mine enemies **b** me, 6440+3807.1
5:24 for then shall the LORD go out **b** 6440+3807.1
6: 4 of God: and Ahio went **b** the ark. 6440+3807.1
6: 5 all the house of Israel played **b** 6440+3807.1
6:14 David danced **b** the LORD with 6440+3807.1
6:16 and dancing **b** the LORD; 6440+3807.1
6:17 and peace offerings **b** the LORD. 6440+3807.1
6:21 unto Michal, *It was* **b** the LORD, 6440+3807.1
2Sa 6:21 which chose me **b** thy father, and before all 4480
6:21 me before thy father, and **b** all his house, 4480
6:21 therefore will I play **b** the LORD. 6440+3807.1
7:15 whom I put away **b** thee. 6440+3807.1
7:16 shall be stablished for ever **b** thee: 6440+3807.1
7:18 sat **b** the LORD, and he said, 6440+3807.1
7:23 terrible, for thy land, **b** thy people, 4480+6440
7:26 David be established **b** thee. 6440+3807.1
7:29 *it* may continue for ever **b** thee: 6440+3807.1
10: 6 of Ammon saw that they stank **b** David, 871.1
10: 9 front of the battle was against him **b** 4480+6440
10:13 the Syrians: and they fled **b** him. 4480+6440
10:14 *then* fled they *also* **b** Abishai, and 4480+6440
10:15 saw that they were smitten **b** Israel, 6440+3807.1
10:16 the host of Hadarezer *went* **b** them. 6440+3807.1
10:18 the Syrians fled **b** Israel; and 4480+6440
10:19 saw that they were smitten **b** Israel, 6440+3807.1
11:13 he did eat and drink **b** him; 6440+3807.1
12:11 I will take thy wives **b** thine eyes, and 3807.1
12:12 I will do this thing **b** all Israel, and 5048
12:12 this thing before all Israel, and **b** the sun. 5048
12:20 they set bread **b** him, and he did eat. 3807.1
13: 9 a pan, and poured *them* out **b** him; 6440+3807.1
14:33 his face to the ground **b** the king: 6440+3807.1
15: 1 horses, and fifty men to run **b** him. 6440+3807.1
15:18 him from Gath, passed on **b** the king. 5921+6440
18: 7 were slain **b** the servants of David, 6440+3807.1
18:28 he fell down to the earth upon his face **b** 3807.1
19: 8 all the people came **b** the king: 6440+3807.1
19:13 if thou be not captain of the host **b** 6440+3807.1
19:17 they went over Jordan **b** the king. 6440+3807.1
19:18 Shimei the son of Gera fell down **b** 6440+3807.1
19:28 but dead men **b** my lord the king: 3807.1
20: 8 *is* in Gibeon, Amasa went **b** them. 6440+3807.1
21: 9 them in the hill **b** the LORD: 6440+3807.1
22:13 Through the brightness **b** him were coals of 5048
22:23 For all his judgments *were* **b** me: 5048+3807.1
22:24 I was also upright **b** him, and have kept 3807.1
24:13 wilt thou flee three months **b** thine 6440+3807.1
24:20 bowed himself **b** the king *on* his face 3807.1
1Ki 1: 2 let her stand **b** the king, and let her 6440+3807.1
1: 5 and fifty men to run **b** him. 6440+3807.1
1:23 when he was come in **b** the king, 6440+3807.1
1:23 he bowed himself **b** the king with his face 3807.1
1:25 they eat and drink **b** him, and say, 6440+3807.1
1:28 and stood **b** the king. 6440+3807.1
1:32 And they came **b** the king. 6440+3807.1
2: 4 to walk **b** me in truth with all their 6440+3807.1
2:26 the Lord GOD **b** David my father, 6440+3807.1
2:45 established **b** the LORD for ever. 6440+3807.1
3: 6 according as he walked **b** thee in 6440+3807.1
3:12 so that there was none like thee **b** 6440+3807.1
3:15 stood **b** the ark of the covenant of 6440+3807.1
3:16 unto the king, and stood **b** him. 6440+3807.1
3:22 Thus they spake **b** the king. 6440+3807.1
3:24 they brought a sword **b** the king. 6440+3807.1
6: 3 the porch **b** the temple of the house, 5921+6440
6: 3 ten cubits *was* the breadth thereof **b** 5921+6440
6: 7 was built *of* stone made ready **b** *it was* NIH
6:17 the house, that *is*, the temple **b** it, 6440+3807.1
6:21 by the chains of gold **b** the oracle; 6440+3807.1
7: 6 the porch *was* **b** them: and *the other* 5921+6440
7: 6 and the thick beam *were* **b** them. 5921+6440
7:49 five on the left, **b** the oracle, 6440+3807.1
8: 5 *were* with him **b** the ark, 6440+3807.1
8: 8 out in the holy *place* **b** the oracle, 5921+6440
8:22 Solomon stood **b** the altar of 6440+3807.1
8:23 walk **b** thee with all their heart: 6440+3807.1
8:25 that they walk **b** me as thou hast 6440+3807.1
8:25 me as thou hast walked **b** me. 6440+3807.1
8:28 thy servant prayeth **b** thee to day: 6440+3807.1
8:31 come **b** thine altar in this house: 6440+3807.1
8:33 be smitten down **b** the enemy, 6440+3807.1
8:50 give them compassion **b** them who 6440+3807.1
8:54 from **b** the altar of the LORD, 6440+3807.1
8:59 made supplication **b** the LORD, 6440+3807.1
8:62 offered sacrifice **b** the LORD. 6440+3807.1
8:64 *was* **b** the house of the LORD: 6440+3807.1
8:64 the brasen altar that *was* **b** 6440+3807.1
8:65 Hamath unto the river of Egypt, **b** 6440+3807.1
9: 3 that thou hast made **b** me: 6440+3807.1
9: 4 if thou wilt walk **b** me, as David 6440+3807.1
9: 6 my statutes which I have set **b** you, 6440+3807.1
9:25 the altar that *was* **b** the LORD. 6440+3807.1
10: 8 which stand continually **b** thee, *and* 6440+3807.1
11: 7 in the hill that *is* **b** Jerusalem, and 5921+6440
11:36 a light alway **b** me in Jerusalem, 6440+3807.1
12: 6 that stood **b** Solomon his father while 854+6440
12: 8 with him, *and* which stood **b** him: 6440+3807.1
12:30 for the people went *to worship* **b** 6440+3807.1
13: 6 and became as *it was* **b**. 7223+871.1+1886.1
14: 9 hast done evil above all that were **b** 6440+3807.1
14:24 cast out **b** the children of Israel. 4480+6440
15: 3 which he had done **b** him: 6440+3807.1
16:25 did worse than all that *were* **b** him. 6440+3807.1
16:30 LORD above all that *were* **b** him. 6440+3807.1
16:33 the kings of Israel that were **b** him. 6440+3807.1
17: 1 the LORD God of Israel liveth, **b** 6440+3807.1
17: 3 the brook Cherith, that *is* **b** Jordan. 5921+6440
17: 5 the brook Cherith, that *is* **b** Jordan. 5921+6440
18:15 *As* the LORD of hosts liveth, **b** 6440+3807.1
18:46 **b** Ahab to the entrance of Jezreel. 6440+3807.1
19:11 upon the mount **b** the LORD. 6440+3807.1
19:11 in pieces the rocks **b** the LORD; 6440+3807.1
19:19 *with* twelve yoke *of oxen* **b** him, 6440+3807.1
20:27 the children of Israel pitched **b** them like 5048
21:10 set two men, sons of Belial, **b** him, to bear 5048
21:13 two men, children of Belial, and sat **b** him: 5048
21:26 whom the LORD cast out **b** 4480+6440
21:29 humbleth himself **b** me? 4480+6440+3807.1
21:29 because he humbleth himself **b** me, 4480+6440
22:10 all the prophets prophesied **b** them. 6440+3807.1
22:21 stood **b** the LORD, and said, 6440+3807.1
2Ki 1:13 came and fell on his knees **b** 5048+3807.1
2: 9 Ask what I shall do for thee, **b** I be 2962+871.1

2Ki 2:15 bowed themselves to the ground **b** him. 3807.1
3:14 *As* the LORD of hosts liveth, **b** 6440+3807.1
3:24 so that they fled **b** them: 4480+6440
4:12 he had called her, she stood **b** him. 6440+3807.1
4:31 Gehazi passed on **b** them, and 6440+3807.1
4:38 of the prophets *were* sitting **b** him: 6440+3807.1
4:43 should I set this **b** an hundred men? 6440+3807.1
4:44 So he set *it* **b** them, and they did 6440+3807.1
5:15 and came, and stood **b** him: 6440+3807.1
5:16 the LORD liveth, **b** whom I stand, 6440+3807.1
5:23 and they bare *them* **b** him. 6440+3807.1
5:25 he went in, and stood **b** his master. 413
6:22 set bread and water **b** them, 6440+3807.1
6:32 *the king* sent a man from **b** him: 6440+3807.1
8: 9 came and stood **b** him, and said, 6440+3807.1
10: 4 Behold, two kings stood not **b** him: 6440+3807.1
11:18 the priest of Baal **b** the altars. 6440+3807.1
14:12 Judah was put to the worse **b** 6440+3807.1
15:10 smote him **b** the people, and slew him, and 6905
16: 3 whom the LORD cast out from **b** 6440
16:14 which *was* **b** the LORD, from 6440+3807.1
17: 2 the kings of Israel that were **b** him. 6440+3807.1
17: 8 whom the LORD cast out from **b** 6440
17:11 the LORD carried away **b** them; 4480+6440
18: 5 of Judah, nor *any* that were **b** him. 6440+3807.1
18:22 worship **b** this altar in Jerusalem? 6440+3807.1
19:14 and spread it **b** the LORD. 6440+3807.1
19:15 Hezekiah prayed **b** the LORD, 6440+3807.1
19:26 *as* corn blasted **b** it be grown up. 6440+3807.1
19:32 an arrow there, nor **come b** it *with* shield, 6923
20: 3 how I have walked **b** thee in truth 6440+3807.1
21: 2 whom the LORD cast out **b** 4480+6440
21: 9 destroyed **b** the children of Israel. 4480+6440
21:11 which *were* **b** him, and hath made 6440+3807.1
22:10 And Shaphan read it **b** the king. 6440+3807.1
22:19 hast humbled thyself **b** the LORD, 4480+6440
22:19 rent thy clothes, and wept **b** me; 6440+3807.1
23: 3 made a covenant **b** the LORD, 6440+3807.1
23:13 the high places that *were* **b** 5921+6440
23:25 like unto him was there no king **b** 6440+3807.1
25: 7 they slew the sons of Zedekiah **b** his 3807.1
25:29 he did eat bread continually **b** him 6440+3807.1
1Ch 1:43 **b** *any* king reigned over 6440+3807.1
5:25 whom God destroyed **b** them. 4480+6440
6:32 they ministered **b** the dwelling 6440+3807.1
10: 1 the men of Israel fled from **b** 6440
11: 3 them in Hebron **b** the LORD; 6440+3807.1
11:13 and the people fled from **b** the Philistines. 6440
13: 8 played **b** God with all *their* might, 6440+3807.1
13:10 to the ark: and there he died **b** God. 6440+3807.1
14:15 for God is gone forth **b** thee to 6440+3807.1
15:24 did blow with the trumpets **b** 6440+3807.1
16: 1 and peace offerings **b** God. 6440+3807.1
16: 4 minister **b** the ark of the LORD, 6440+3807.1
16: 6 **b** the ark of the covenant of God. 6440+3807.1
16:29 bring an offering, and come **b** him: 6440+3807.1
16:30 Fear **b** him, all the earth: 4480+6440+3807.1
16:37 So he left there **b** the ark of 6440+3807.1
16:37 to minister **b** the ark continually, 6440+3807.1
16:39 his brethren the priests, **b** 6440+3807.1
17: 8 have cut off all thine enemies from **b** thee, 6440
17:13 I took *it* from *him* that was **b** thee: 6440+3807.1
17:16 king came and sat **b** the LORD, 6440+3807.1
17:21 by driving out nations from **b** thy people, 6440
17:24 thy servant *be* established **b** thee. 6440+3807.1
17:25 found *in his heart* to pray **b** thee. 6440+3807.1
17:27 that *it* may be **b** thee for ever: 6440+3807.1
19: 7 who came and pitched **b** Medeba. 6440+3807.1
19: 9 put the battle in array *b* the gate of the city: NIH
19:10 saw that the battle was set against him **b** 6440
19:14 nigh **b** the Syrians unto the battle; 6440+3807.1
19:14 unto the battle; and they fled **b** him. 4480+6440
19:15 they likewise fled **b** Abishai his 4480+6440
19:16 they were put to the worse **b** Israel, 6440+3807.1
19:16 the host of Hadarezer *went* **b** them. 6440+3807.1
19:18 the Syrians fled **b** Israel; and 4480+6440+3807.1
19:19 they were put to the worse **b** Israel, 6440+3807.1
21:12 or three months to be destroyed **b** thy 4480+6440
21:30 David could not go **b** it to inquire 6440+3807.1
22: 5 prepared abundantly **b** his death. 6440+3807.1
22:18 the land is subdued **b** the LORD, 6440+3807.1
22:18 the LORD, and **b** his people. 6440+3807.1
23:13 to burn incense **b** the LORD, 6440+3807.1
23:31 continually **b** the LORD: 6440+3807.1
24: 2 Nadab and Abihu died **b** their 6440+3807.1
24: 6 wrote them **b** the king, and 6440+3807.1
24: 6 *b* the chief of the fathers of the priests and NIH
28: 4 **b** all the house of my father to be king over 4480
29:10 the LORD **b** all the congregation: 5869+3807.1
29:15 For we *are* strangers **b** thee, and 6440+3807.1
29:22 drink **b** the LORD on that day 6440+3807.1
29:25 been on any king **b** him in Israel. 6440+3807.1
2Ch 1: 5 put **b** the tabernacle of the LORD: 6440+3807.1
1: 6 to the brasen altar **b** the LORD, 6440+3807.1
1:10 go out and come in **b** this people: 6440+3807.1
1:12 have had that *have been* **b** thee, 6440+3807.1
1:13 from **b** the tabernacle of 6440+3807.1
2: 4 *and* to burn **b** him sweet incense, 6440+3807.1
2: 6 save only to burn sacrifice **b** him? 6440+3807.1
3:15 Also he made **b** the house two 6440+3807.1
3:17 he reared up the pillars **b** the temple, 5921+6440
4:20 burn after the manner **b** the oracle, 6440+3807.1
5: 6 were assembled unto him **b** the ark, 6440+3807.1
5: 9 were seen from the ark **b** the oracle; 5921+6440
6:12 he stood **b** the altar of the LORD 6440+3807.1
6:13 kneeled *down* upon his knees **b** all 5048
6:14 walk **b** thee with all their hearts: 6440+3807.1
6:16 my law, as thou hast walked **b** me. 6440+3807.1
6:19 which thy servant prayeth **b** thee: 6440+3807.1
6:22 come **b** thine altar in this house; 6440+3807.1
6:24 be put to the worse **b** the enemy, 6440+3807.1
6:24 supplication **b** thee in this house; 6440+3807.1
6:36 deliver them *over* **b** *their* enemies, 6440+3807.1
7: 4 all the people offered sacrifices **b** 6440+3807.1
7: 6 the priests sounded trumpets **b** them, and 5048

2Ch 7: 7 *was* **b** the house of the LORD: 6440+3807.1
7:17 *as for* thee, if thou wilt walk **b** me, 6440+3807.1
7:19 which I have set **b** you, and 6440+3807.1
8:12 which he had built **b** the porch, 6440+3807.1
8:14 to praise and minister **b** the priests, 5048
9: 7 which stand continually **b** thee, and 6440+3807.1
9:11 there were none such seen **b** in 6440+3807.1
10: 6 **b** Solomon his father while he *yet* 6440+3807.1
10: 8 up with him, that stood **b** him. 6440+3807.1
13:13 so they were **b** Judah, and 6440+3807.1
13:14 behold, the battle *was* **b** and behind: 6440
13:15 and all Israel **b** Abijah and Judah. 6440+3807.1
13:16 the children of Israel fled **b** Judah: 4480+6440
14: 5 and the kingdom was quiet **b** him. 6440+3807.1
14: 7 and bars, *while* the land *is* yet **b** us; 6440+3807.1
14:12 smote the Ethiopians **b** Asa, 6440+3807.1
14:12 before Asa, and **b** Judah; 6440+3807.1
14:13 for they were destroyed **b** 6440+3807.1
14:13 before the LORD, and **b** his host; 6440+3807.1
15: 8 *was* **b** the porch of the LORD. 6440+3807.1
18: 9 all the prophets prophesied **b** them. 6440+3807.1
18:20 stood **b** the LORD, and said, 6440+3807.1
19: 2 upon thee from **b** the LORD. 6440+3807.1
19:11 also the Levites *shall be* officers **b** 6440+3807.1
20: 5 in the house of the LORD, **b** 6440+3807.1
20: 7 this land **b** thy people Israel, 4480+6440+3807.1
20: 9 **b** this house, and in thy presence, 6440+3807.1
20:13 all Judah stood **b** the LORD, 6440+3807.1
20:16 of the brook, **b** the wilderness of Jeruel. 6440
20:18 the inhabitants of Jerusalem fell **b** 6440+3807.1
20:21 as *they* went out **b** the army, and 6440+3807.1
23:17 the priest of Baal **b** the altars. 6440+3807.1
24:14 the rest of the money **b** the king 6440+3807.1
25: 8 God shall make thee fall **b** 6440+3807.1
25:14 bowed down himself **b** them, and 6440+3807.1
25:22 Judah was put to the worse **b** 6440+3807.1
26:19 **b** the priests in the house of 6440+3807.1
27: 6 he prepared his ways **b** the LORD 6440+3807.1
28: 3 had cast out **b** the children of Israel. 4480+6440
28: 9 he went out **b** the host that came to 6440+3807.1
28:14 the spoil **b** the princes and all 6440+3807.1
29:11 hath chosen you to stand **b** him, 6440+3807.1
29:19 they *are* **b** the altar of the LORD. 6440+3807.1
29:23 goats for the sin offering **b** the king 6440+3807.1
30: 9 **b** them that lead them captive, 6440+3807.1
31:20 and truth **b** the LORD his God. 6440+3807.1
32:12 Ye shall worship **b** one altar, and 6440+3807.1
33: 2 whom the LORD had cast out **b** 4480+6440
33: 7 which I have chosen **b** all the tribes of 4480
33: 9 whom the LORD had destroyed **b** 4480+6440
33:12 humbled himself greatly **b** 4480+6440+3807.1
33:19 graven images, **b** he was humbled: 6440+3807.1
33:23 humbled not himself **b** 4480+6440+3807.1
34:18 And Shaphan read it **b** the king. 6440+3807.1
34:24 they have read **b** the king of Judah: 6440+3807.1
34:27 didst humble thyself **b** God, 4480+6440+3807.1
34:27 humbledst thyself **b** me, and 6440+3807.1
34:27 rend thy clothes, and weep **b** me; 6440+3807.1
34:31 made a covenant **b** the LORD, 6440+3807.1
36:12 humbled not himself **b** 4480+6440+3807.1
Ezr 3:12 of this house was laid **b** their eyes, 871.1
4:18 sent unto us *hath been* plainly read **b** me. 6925
4:23 king Artaxerxes' letter *was* read **b** Rehum, 6925
7:19 *those* deliver thou **b** the God of Jerusalem. 6925
7:28 hath extended mercy unto me **b** 6440+3807.1
7:28 and **b** all the king's mighty princes. 3807.1
8:21 might afflict ourselves **b** our God, 6440+3807.1
8:29 keep *them,* until ye weigh *them* **b** 6440+3807.1
9:15 behold, we *are* **b** thee in our 6440+3807.1
9:15 cannot stand **b** thee because of this. 6440+3807.1
10: 1 himself down **b** the house of God, 6440+3807.1
10: 6 Ezra rose up from **b** the house of 6440+3807.1
Ne 1: 4 and prayed **b** the God of heaven, 6440+3807.1
1: 6 which I pray **b** thee now, day and 6440+3807.1
2: 1 the king, *that* wine *was* **b** him: 6440+3807.1
2:13 even **b** the dragon well, and to 413+6440
4: 2 he spake **b** his brethren and 6440+3807.1
4: 5 their sin be blotted out from **b** thee: 6440+3807.1
4: 5 *thee* to anger **b** the builders. 5048+3807.1
5:15 **b** me were chargeable unto 6440+3807.1
6:19 they reported his good deeds **b** 6440+3807.1
8: 1 the street that *was* **b** the water gate; 6440+3807.1
8: 2 Ezra the priest brought the law **b** 6440+3807.1
8: 3 he read therein **b** the street that *was* 6440+3807.1
8: 3 *was* **b** the water gate from 6440+3807.1
8: 3 **b** the men and the women, and those that 5048
9: 8 foundest his heart faithful **b** thee, 6440+3807.1
9:11 thou didst divide the sea **b** them, so 6440+3807.1
9:24 thou subduedst **b** them 6440+3807.1
9:28 had rest, they did evil again **b** thee: 6440+3807.1
9:32 all the trouble seem little **b** thee, 6440+3807.1
9:35 fat land which thou gavest **b** them, 6440+3807.1
12:36 of God, and Ezra the scribe **b** them. 6440+3807.1
13: 4 **b** this, Eliashib the priest, 6440+3807.1
13:19 Jerusalem began to be dark **b** the sabbath, 6440
Est 1: 3 of the provinces, *being* **b** him: 6440+3807.1
1:11 To bring Vashti the queen **b** 6440+3807.1
1:16 Memucan answered **b** the king and 6440+3807.1
1:17 the queen to be brought in **b** him, 6440+3807.1
1:19 That Vashti come no *more* **b** king 6440+3807.1
2:11 Mordecai walked every day **b** 6440+3807.1
2:23 book of the chronicles **b** the king. 6440+3807.1
3: 7 that *is,* the lot, **b** Haman from day 6440+3807.1
4: 2 came even **b** the king's gate: 6440+3807.1
4: 6 which *was* **b** the king's gate. 6440+3807.1
4: 8 request **b** him for her people. 4480+6440+3807.1
6: 1 they were read **b** the king. 6440+3807.1
6: 9 of the city, and proclaim **b** him, 6440+3807.1
6:11 of the city, and proclaimed **b** him, 6440+3807.1
6:13 *be* of the seed of the Jews, **b** 6440+3807.1
6:13 but shalt surely fall **b** him. 6440+3807.1
7: 6 Haman was afraid **b** the king 4480+6440+3807.1
7: 8 Will he force the queen also **b** me in 5973
7: 9 said **b** the king, Behold also, 6440+3807.1
8: 1 Mordecai came **b** the king; 6440+3807.1

Est 8: 3 Esther spake yet again **b** the king, 6440+3807.1
8: 4 Esther arose, and stood **b** the king, 6440+3807.1
8: 5 the thing seem right **b** the king, and 6440+3807.1
9:11 the palace was brought **b** the king. 6440+3807.1
9:25 when *Esther* came **b** the king, 6440+3807.1
Job 1: 6 came to present themselves **b** the LORD, 5921
2: 1 came to present themselves **b** the LORD, 5921
2: 1 them to present himself **b** the LORD. 5921
3:24 For my sighing cometh **b** I eat, and 6440+3807.1
4:15 a spirit passed **b** my face; the hair of my 5921
4:16 an image *was* **b** mine eyes, 5048+3807.1
4:19 which are crushed **b** the moth? 6440+3807.1
8:12 it withereth **b** any *other* herb. 6440+3807.1
8:16 He *is* green **b** the sun, and 6440+3807.1
10:21 **B** I go whence I shall not return, 2962+871.1
13:15 I will maintain mine own ways **b** him. 413+6440
13:16 a hypocrite shall not come **b** him. 6440+3807.1
15: 4 and restrainest prayer **b** God. 6440+3807.1
15: 7 or wast thou made **b** the hills? 6440+3807.1
15:32 It shall be accomplished **b** his time, 3808+871.1
18:20 as **they that went b** were affrighted. 6931
21: 8 and their offspring **b** their eyes. 3807.1
21:18 They are as stubble **b** the wind, and 6440+3807.1
21:33 as *there are* innumerable **b** him. 6440+3807.1
23: 4 I would order *my* cause **b** him, and 6440+3807.1
23:17 Because I was not cut off **b** 4480+6440
26: 6 Hell *is* naked **b** him, and destruction hath 5048
30:11 have also let loose the bridle **b** me. 4480+6440
33: 5 *thy words* in order **b** me, stand up. 6440+3807.1
35:14 not see him, *yet* judgment *is* **b** him; 6440+3807.1
41:10 who then is able to stand **b** me? 6440+3807.1
41:22 sorrow is turned into joy **b** him. 6440+3807.1
42:10 gave Job twice as much as he had **b**. NIH
42:11 *had been of* his acquaintance **b**, 6440+3807.1
Ps 5: 8 make thy way straight **b** my face. 3807.1
16: 8 I have set the LORD always **b** 5048+3807.1
18: 6 cry came **b** him, *even* into his ears. 6440+3807.1
18:12 At the brightness *that was* **b** him his thick 5048
18:22 For all his judgments *were* **b** me, 5048+3807.1
18:23 I was also upright **b** him, and I kept myself 5973
18:42 did I beat them small as the dust **b** 5921+6440
22:25 I will pay my vows **b** them that fear him. 5048
22:27 of the nations shall worship **b** thee. 6440+3807.1
22:29 down to the dust shall bow **b** him: 6440+3807.1
23: 5 Thou preparest a table **b** me in 6440+3807.1
26: 3 For thy lovingkindness *is* **b** mine 5048+3807.1
31:19 them that trust in thee **b** the sons of men! 5048
31:22 in my haste, I am cut off from **b** thine eyes: 5048
34: T when he changed his behaviour **b** 6440+3807.1
35: 5 Let them be as chaff **b** the wind: 6440+3807.1
36: 1 *that there is* no fear of God **b** his eyes. 5048
38: 9 Lord, all my desire *is* **b** thee; and 5048
38:17 to halt, and my sorrow *is* continually **b** me. 5048
39: 1 a bridle, while the wicked *is* **b** me. 5048+3807.1
39: 5 and mine age *is* as nothing **b** thee: 5048
39:13 that I may recover strength, **b** I go 2962+871.1
41:12 and settest me **b** thy face for ever. 3807.1
42: 2 when shall I come and appear **b** God? 6440
44:15 My confusion *is* continually **b** me, and 5048
50: 3 a fire shall devour **b** him, and 6440+3807.1
50: 8 *to have been* continually **b** me. 5048+3807.1
50:21 and set *them* in order **b** thine eyes. 3807.1
51: 3 my transgressions: and my sin *is* ever **b** me. 5048
52: 9 on thy name; for *it is* good **b** thy saints. 5048
54: 3 have not set God **b** them. Selah. 5048+3807.1
56:13 that *I* may walk **b** God in the light 6440+3807.1
57: 6 they have digged a pit **b** me, 6440+3807.1
58: 9 **B** your pots can feel the thorns, 2962+871.1
61: 7 He shall abide **b** God for ever: 6440+3807.1
62: 8 pour out your heart **b** him: 6440+3807.1
68: 1 them also that hate him flee **b** him. 4480+6440
68: 2 as wax melteth **b** the fire, *so* let 4480+6440
68: 3 be glad; let them rejoice **b** God: 6440+3807.1
68: 4 his name JAH, and rejoice **b** him. 6440+3807.1
68: 7 thou wentest forth **b** thy people, 6440+3807.1
68:25 The singers **went b**, the players on 6923
69:19 mine adversaries *are* all **b** thee. 5048
69:22 Let their table become a snare **b** 6440+3807.1
72: 9 in the wilderness shall bow **b** him; 6440+3807.1
72:11 Yea, all kings shall fall down **b** him: 3807.1
73:22 *was* I, and ignorant: I was *as* a beast **b** thee. 5973
78:55 He cast out the heathen also **b** them, 4480+6440
79:11 the sighing of the prisoner come **b** 6440+3807.1
80: 2 **B** Ephraim and Benjamin and 6440+3807.1
80: 9 Thou preparedst *room* **b** it, and 6440+3807.1
83:13 a wheel; as the stubble **b** the wind. 6440+3807.1
84: 7 *every one of them* in Zion appeareth **b** God. 413
85:13 Righteousness shall go **b** him; and 6440+3807.1
86: 9 shall come and worship **b** thee, 6440+3807.1
86:14 and have not set thee **b** them. 5048+3807.1
88: 1 I have cried day *and* night **b** thee: 5048
88: 2 Let my prayer come **b** thee: 6440+3807.1
89:14 mercy and truth shall **go b** thy face. 6923
89:23 I will beat down his foes **b** his face, and 4480
89:36 for ever, and his throne as the sun **b** me. 5048
90: 2 **B** the mountains were brought forth, 2962+871.1
90: 8 Thou hast set our iniquities **b** thee, 5048+3807.1
95: 2 Let us **come b** his presence with 6923
95: 6 us kneel **b** the LORD our Maker. 6440+3807.1
96: 6 Honour and majesty *are* **b** him: 6440+3807.1
96: 9 of holiness: fear **b** him, all the earth. 4480+6440
96:13 **B** the LORD, for he cometh, 6440+3807.1
97: 3 A fire goeth **b** him, and burneth up 6440+3807.1
98: 6 make a joyful noise **b** the LORD, 6440+3807.1
98: 9 **B** the LORD; for he cometh to 6440+3807.1
100: 2 come **b** his presence with singing. 3807.1
101: 3 I will set no wicked thing **b** mine 5048+3807.1
102: T out his complaint **b** the LORD. 6440+3807.1
102:28 seed shall be established **b** thee. 6440+3807.1
105:17 He sent a man **b** them, 6440+3807.1
106:23 had not Moses his chosen stood **b** 6440+3807.1
109:15 Let them be **b** the LORD continually, 5048
116: 9 I will walk **b** the LORD in 6440+3807.1
119:30 of truth: thy judgments have I laid *b* me. NIH
119:46 I will speak of thy testimonies also **b** kings, 5048

B

B

Ps 119:67 **B** I was afflicted I went astray: but 2962
119:168 thy testimonies: for all my ways *are* **b** thee. 5048
119:169 Let my cry come near **b** thee, 6440+3807.1
119:170 Let my supplication come **b** thee: 6440+3807.1
138: 1 **b** the gods will I sing *praise* unto thee. 5048
139: 5 Thou hast beset me behind and **b**, and 6924
141: 2 Let my prayer be set forth **b** thee *as* 6440+3807.1
141: 3 Set a watch, O LORD, **b** my mouth; 3807.1
142: 2 I poured out my complaint **b** him; 6440+3807.1
142: 2 I shewed **b** him my trouble. 6440+3807.1
147:17 who can stand **b** his cold? 6440+3807.1
Pr 4:25 and let thine eyelids look straight **b** thee. 5048
5:21 For the ways of man *are* **b** the eyes of 5227
8:22 beginning of his way, **b** his works of old. 6924
8:25 **B** the mountains were settled, before 2962+871.1
8:25 the mountains were settled, **b** 6440+3807.1
8:30 *his* delight, rejoicing always **b** him; 6440+3807.1
14:19 The evil bow **b** the good; and 6440+3807.1
15:11 Hell and destruction *are* **b** the LORD: 5048
15:33 and **b** honour *is* humility. 6440+3807.1
16:18 Pride *goeth* **b** destruction, and 6440+3807.1
16:18 and a haughty spirit **b** a fall. 6440+3807.1
17:14 **b** *it* be meddled with. 6440+3807.1
17:24 Wisdom *is* **b** him that hath 854+6440
18:12 **B** destruction the heart of man is 6440+3807.1
18:12 and **b** honour *is* humility. 6440+3807.1
18:13 He that answereth a matter **b** he 2962+871.1
18:16 and bringeth him **b** great *men.* 6440+3807.1
22:29 he shall stand **b** kings; he shall not 6440+3807.1
22:29 he shall not stand **b** mean *men.* 6440+3807.1
23: 1 consider diligently what *is* **b** thee: 6440+3807.1
25: 5 Take away the wicked *from* **b** 6440+3807.1
25:26 A righteous *man* falling down **b** 6440+3807.1
26:26 his wickedness shall be shewed **b** 871.1
27: 4 but who is able to stand **b** envy? 6440+3807.1
30: 7 of thee; deny me *them* not **b** I die: 2962+871.1
Ecc 1:10 of old time, which was **b** us. 4480+6440+3807.1
1:16 that have been **b** me in Jerusalem: 6440+3807.1
2: 7 all that were in Jerusalem **b** me: 6440+3807.1
2: 9 increased more than all that were **b** 6440+3807.1
2:26 give to *him that is* good **b** God. 6440+3807.1
3:14 that *men* should fear **b** him. 4480+6440+3807.1
4:16 *even* of all that have been **b** them: 6440+3807.1
5: 2 be hasty to utter *any* thing **b** God: 6440+3807.1
5: 6 neither say thou **b** the angel, that it 6440+3807.1
6: 8 the poor, that knoweth to walk **b** the living? 5048
7:17 why shouldest thou die **b** thy time? 3808+871.1
8:12 fear God, which fear **b** him: 4480+6440+3807.1
8:13 he feareth not **b** God. 4480+6440+3807.1
9: 1 or hatred *by* all *that is* **b** them. 6440+3807.1
SS 8:12 My vineyard, which *is* mine, *is* **b** 6440+3807.1
Isa 1:12 When ye come to appear **b** me, who hath 6440
1:16 put away the evil of your doings from **b** 5048
7:16 For **b** the child shall know to refuse 2962+871.1
8: 4 For **b** the child shall have 2962+871.1
8: 4 taken away **b** the king of Assyria. 6440+3807.1
9: 3 they joy **b** thee according to the joy 6440+3807.1
9:12 The Syrians **b**, and the Philistines 4480+6924
13:16 shall be dashed to pieces **b** their eyes; 3807.1
17:13 chaff of the mountains **b** the wind, 6440+3807.1
17:13 a rolling thing **b** the whirlwind. 6440+3807.1
17:14 behold at eveningtide trouble; *and* **b** 2962+871.1
23:18 for them that dwell **b** the LORD, 6440+3807.1
24:23 in Jerusalem, and **b** his ancients gloriously. 5048
28: 4 *and* as the hasty fruit **b** the summer; 2962+871.1
30: 8 write it **b** them in a table, and note it in a 854
30:11 the Holy One of Israel to cease from **b** us. 6440
36: 7 Ye shall worship **b** this altar? 6440+3807.1
37:14 and spread it **b** the LORD. 6440+3807.1
37:27 *as* corn blasted **b** it be grown up. 6440+3807.1
37:33 an arrow there, nor **come b** it *with* shields, 6923
38: 3 how I have walked **b** thee in truth 6440+3807.1
40:10 *is* with him, and his work **b** him. 6440+3807.1
40:17 All nations **b** him *are* as nothing; and 5048
41: 1 Keep silence **b** me, O islands; and let 413
41: 2 gave the nations **b** him, and 6440+3807.1
42: 9 new *things* do I declare: **b** they 2962+871.1
42:16 I will make darkness light **b** them, 6440+3807.1
43:10 understand that I *am* he: **b** me there 6440+3807.1
43:13 Yea, **b** the day *was* I *am* he; and *there is* 4480
45: 1 to subdue nations **b** him; 6440+3807.1
45: 1 to open **b** him the two leaved gates; 6440+3807.1
45: 2 I will go **b** thee, and make 6440+3807.1
47:14 not *be* a coal to warm at, *nor* fire to sit **b** it. 5048
48: 5 the beginning declared *it* to thee; **b** 2962+871.1
48: 7 even **b** the day when thou heardest 6440+3807.1
48:19 cut off nor destroyed from **b** me. 6440+3807.1
49:16 *my* hands; thy walls *are* continually **b** me. 5048
52:12 for the LORD will go **b** you; and 6440+3807.1
53: 2 For he shall grow up **b** him as a 6440+3807.1
53: 7 as a sheep **b** her shearers is dumb, 6440+3807.1
55:12 the hills shall break forth **b** you 6440+3807.1
57:16 for the spirit should fail **b** 4480+6440+3807.1
58: 8 thy righteousness shall go **b** thee; 6440+3807.1
59:12 For our transgressions are multiplied **b** 5048
61:11 and praise to spring forth **b** all the nations. 5048
62:11 *is* with him, and his work **b** him. 6440+3807.1
63:12 dividing the water **b** them, to make 4480+6440
65: 6 Behold, *it is* written **b** me: I will 6440+3807.1
65:12 did evil **b** mine eyes, and did choose *that* 871.1
65:24 to pass, that **b** they call, I will answer; 2962
66: 4 they did evil **b** mine eyes, and chose *that* in 871.1
66: 7 **B** she travailed, she brought forth; 2962+871.1
66: 7 she brought forth; **b** her pain came, 2962+871.1
66:22 *shall* remain **b** me, saith 6440+3807.1
66:23 shall all flesh come to worship **b** 6440+3807.1
Jer 1: 5 **B** I formed thee in the belly I knew 2962+871.1
1: 5 **b** thou camest forth out of the womb 2962+871.1
1:17 lest I confound thee **b** them. 6440+3807.1
2:22 *yet* thine iniquity *is* marked **b** me, 6440+3807.1
6: 7 spoil is heard in her; **b** me 5921+6440
6:21 I will lay stumblingblocks **b** this people, and 413
7:10 come and stand **b** me in this house, 6440+3807.1
8: 2 they shall spread them **b** the sun, and 3807.1
9:13 my law which I set **b** them, 6440+3807.1
Jer 13:16 glory to the LORD your God, **b** 2962+871.1
13:16 **b** your feet stumble upon the dark 2962+871.1
15: 1 and Samuel stood **b** me, 6440+3807.1
15: 9 to the sword **b** their enemies, 6440+3807.1
15:19 *and* thou shalt stand **b** me: 6440+3807.1
17:16 out of my lips was **right b** thee. 5227+6440
18:17 as *with* an east wind **b** the enemy; 6440+3807.1
18:20 Remember that I stood **b** thee to 6440+3807.1
18:23 but let them be overthrown **b** thee; 6440+3807.1
19: 7 fall by the sword **b** their enemies, 6440+3807.1
21: 8 I set **b** you the way of life, and 6440+3807.1
24: 1 two baskets of figs *were* set **b** 6440+3807.1
26: 4 in my law, which I have set **b** you, 6440+3807.1
28: 8 The prophets that have been **b** me 6440+3807.1
28: 8 **b** thee of old prophesied both 6440+3807.1
29:21 and he shall slay them **b** your eyes; 3807.1
30:20 shall be established **b** me, 6440+3807.1
31:36 If those ordinances depart from **b** 6440+3807.1
31:36 from being a nation **b** me for ever. 6440+3807.1
32:12 the book of the purchase, **b** 5869+3807.1
32:13 I charged Baruch **b** them, saying, 5869+3807.1
32:30 done evil **b** me from their youth: 5869+871.1
32:31 *I* should remove it **from b** my face, 4480+5921
33: 9 an honour **b** all the nations of the earth, 3807.1
33:18 **b** me to offer burnt 4480+6440+3807.1
33:24 should be no more a nation **b** them. 6440+3807.1
34: 5 the former kings which were **b** 6440+3807.1
34:15 ye had made a covenant **b** me in 6440+3807.1
34:18 which they had made **b** me, 6440+3807.1
35: 5 I set **b** the sons of the house of 6440+3807.1
35:19 want a man to stand **b** me for ever. 6440+3807.1
36: 7 their supplication **b** the LORD, 6440+3807.1
36: 9 *that* they proclaimed a fast **b** 6440+3807.1
36:22 *a fire on* the hearth burning **b** him. 6440+3807.1
37:20 I pray thee, be accepted **b** thee, 6440+3807.1
38:10 the prophet out of the dungeon, **b** 2962+871.1
38:26 my supplication **b** the king, 6440+3807.1
39: 6 the sons of Zedekiah in Riblah **b** his eyes: 3807.1
39:16 they shall be *accomplished* in that day **b** 6440
40: 4 behold, all the land *is* **b** thee: 6440+3807.1
42: 2 our supplication be accepted **b** 6440+3807.1
42: 9 to present your supplication **b** him: 6440+3807.1
44:10 I set **b** you and before your fathers. 6440+3807.1
44:10 I set before you and **b** your fathers. 6440+3807.1
47: 1 the prophet against the Philistines, **b** 2962+871.1
49:19 that shepherd that will stand **b** me? 6440+3807.1
49:37 to be dismayed **b** their enemies, 6440+3807.1
49:37 and **b** them that seek their life: 6440+3807.1
50: 8 and be as the he goats **b** the flocks. 6440+3807.1
50:44 that shepherd that will stand **b** me? 6440+3807.1
52:10 slew the sons of Zedekiah **b** his eyes: 3807.1
52:33 he did continually eat bread **b** him 6440+3807.1
La 1: 5 gone *into* captivity **b** the enemy. 6440+3807.1
1: 6 they are gone without strength **b** 6440+3807.1
1:22 Let all their wickedness come **b** 6440+3807.1
2: 3 he hath drawn back his right hand from **b** 6440
2:19 pour out thine heart like water **b** the face of 5227
3:35 To turn aside the right of a man **b** the face 5048
Eze 2:10 he spread it **b** me; and it *was* 6440+3807.1
3:20 I lay a stumblingblock **b** him, 6440+3807.1
4: 1 lay it **b** thee, and pourtray upon it 6440+3807.1
6: 4 I will cast down your slain *men* **b** 6440+3807.1
6: 5 the children of Israel **b** their idols; 6440+3807.1
8: 1 and the elders of Judah sat **b** me, 6440+3807.1
8:11 there stood **b** them seventy men of 6440+3807.1
9: 6 men which *were* **b** the house. 6440+3807.1
14: 1 of Israel unto me, and sat **b** me. 6440+3807.1
14: 3 put the stumblingblock of their iniquity **b** 5227
14: 4 putteth the stumblingblock of his iniquity **b** 5227
14: 7 putteth the stumblingblock of his iniquity **b** 5227
16:18 mine oil and mine incense **b** them. 6440+3807.1
16:19 thou hast even set it **b** them for a 6440+3807.1
16:50 and committed abomination **b** me: 6440+3807.1
16:57 **B** thy wickedness was discovered, 2962+871.1
20: 1 of the LORD, and sat **b** me. 6440+3807.1
20: 9 not be polluted **b** the heathen, 5869+3807.1
20:14 that *it* should not be polluted **b** 5869+3807.1
20:41 be sanctified in you **b** the heathen. 5869+3807.1
21: 6 and with bitterness sigh **b** their eyes. 3807.1
22:30 stand in the gap **b** me for the land, 6440+3807.1
23:24 I will set judgment **b** them, and 6440+3807.1
23:41 and a table prepared **b** it, 6440+3807.1
28: 9 Wilt thou yet say **b** him that 6440+3807.1
28:17 I will lay thee **b** kings, that *they* 6440+3807.1
30:24 he shall groan **b** him *with* 6440+3807.1
32:10 I shall brandish my sword **b** them; 5921+6440
33:31 they sit **b** thee *as* my people, and 6440+3807.1
36:17 their way was **b** me as 6440+3807.1
36:23 when I shall be sanctified in you **b** their 3807.1
37:20 writest shall be in thine hand **b** their eyes. 3807.1
38:16 be sanctified in thee, O Gog, **b** their eyes. 3807.1
40:12 The space also **b** the little 6440+3807.1
40:22 the arches thereof *were* **b** them. 6440+3807.1
40:26 the arches thereof *were* **b** them: 6440+3807.1
40:47 and the altar *that was* **b** the house. 6440+3807.1
41: 4 twenty cubits, **b** the temple: 413+6440
41:12 Now the building that *was* **b** 413+6440
41:22 *is* the table that *is* **b** the LORD. 6440+3807.1
42: 1 which *was* **b** the building toward the north. 5048
42: 2 **B** the length of an hundred cubits *was* 413+6440
42: 4 **b** the chambers *was* a walk of ten 6440+3807.1
42: 8 **b** the temple *were* an hundred cubits. 5921+6440
42:11 the way **b** them *was* like 6440+3807.1
42:12 *even* the way directly **b** the wall 6440+871.1
42:13 which *are* **b** the separate place, 413+6440
43:24 thou shalt offer them **b** 6440+3807.1
44: 3 sit in it to eat bread **b** the LORD; 6440+3807.1
44: 4 the way of the north gate **b** the house: 413+6440
44:11 they shall stand **b** them to minister 6440+3807.1
44:12 ministered unto them **b** their idols, 6440+3807.1
44:15 they shall stand **b** me to offer unto 6440+3807.1
44:22 or a widow that **had** a priest **b**. 1961+4480
45: 7 **b** the oblation of the holy *portion,* and 413+6440
45: 7 and **b** the possession of the city, 413+6440
46: 3 gate **b** the LORD in the sabbaths 6440+3807.1
Eze 46: 9 **b** the LORD in the solemn feasts, 6440+3807.1
Da 1: 5 they might stand **b** the king. 6440+3807.1
1:13 be looked upon **b** thee, 6440+3807.1
1:18 them in **b** Nebuchadnezzar. 6440+3807.1
1:19 therefore stood they **b** the king. 6440+3807.1
2: 2 So they came and stood **b** the king. 6440+3807.1
2: 9 and corrupt words to speak **b** me, 6925
2:10 The Chaldeans answered **b** the king, and 6925
2:11 there is none other that can shew it **b** 6925
2:24 bring me in **b** the king, and I will shew unto 6925
2:25 Arioch brought in Daniel **b** the king in 6925
2:31 *was* excellent, stood **b** thee; 6903+3807.2
2:36 we will tell the interpretation thereof **b** 6925
3: 3 they stood **b** the image that 6903+3807.2
3:13 Then they brought these men **b** the king. 6925
4: 6 bring in all the wise *men* of Babylon **b** me, 6925
4: 7 I told the dream **b** them; but they *did* not 6925
4: 8 at the last Daniel came in **b** me, 6925
4: 8 and **b** him I told the dream, *saying,* 6925
5: 1 and drank wine **b** the thousand. 6903+3807.2
5:13 was Daniel brought in **b** the king. *And* 6925
5:15 have been brought in **b** me, that they should 6925
5:17 Daniel answered and said **b** the king, 6925
5:19 trembled and feared **b** him: 4481+6925
5:23 brought the vessels of his house **b** thee, 6925
6:10 prayed, and gave thanks **b** his God, as he 6925
6:11 and making supplication **b** his God. 6925
6:12 spake **b** the king concerning the king's 6925
6:13 answered they and said **b** the king, 6925
6:18 were instruments of musick brought **b** him: 6925
6:22 forasmuch as **b** him innocency was found 6925
6:22 also **b** thee, O king, have I done no hurt. 6925
6:26 and fear **b** the God of Daniel: 4481+6925
7: 7 diverse from all the beasts that *were* **b** it; 6925
7: 8 **b** whom there were three of the first 4481+6925
7:10 stream issued and came forth from **b** him: 6925
7:10 ten thousand times ten thousand stood **b** 6925
7:13 of days, and they brought him near **b** him. 6925
7:20 came up, and **b** whom three fell; 4481+6925
8: 3 there stood **b** the river a ram which 6440+3807.1
8: 4 so that no beasts might stand **b** 6440+3807.1
8: 6 which I had seen standing **b** 6440+3807.1
8: 7 power in the ram to stand **b** him, 6440+3807.1
8:15 there stood **b** me as the appearance 5048+3807.1
9:10 which he set **b** us by his servants 6440+3807.1
9:13 yet made we not our prayer **b** the LORD 6440
9:18 **b** thee for our righteousnesses, 6440+3807.1
9:20 presenting my supplication **b** 6440+3807.1
10:12 to chasten thyself **b** thy God, 6440+3807.1
10:16 and said unto him that stood **b** me, 5048+3807.1
11:16 and none shall stand **b** him: 6440+3807.1
11:22 they be overflown from **b** him, 6440+3807.1
Hos 7: 2 have beset them about; they are **b** my face. 5048
Joel 1:16 Is not the meat cut off **b** our eyes, *yea,* joy 5048
2: 3 A fire devoureth **b** them; and 6440+3807.1
2: 3 the land *is* as the garden of Eden **b** 6440+3807.1
2: 6 **B** their face *the* people shall be much 4480
2:10 The earth shall quake **b** them; 6440+3807.1
2:11 the LORD shall utter his voice **b** 6440+3807.1
2:31 the moon into blood, **b** the great 6440+3807.1
Am 1: 1 two year **b** the earthquake. 6440+3807.1
2: 9 Yet destroyed I the Amorite **b** them, 4480+6440
4: 3 every *cow at that which is* **b** her; 5048
9: 4 though they go into captivity **b** 6440+3807.1
Jnh 1: 2 their wickedness is come up **b** me. 6440+3807.1
4: 2 Therefore I fled **b** unto Tarshish: for I knew 6923
Mic 1: 4 as wax **b** the fire, *and* as the waters 4480+6440
2:13 The breaker is come up **b** them: 6440+3807.1
2:13 their king shall pass **b** them, and 6440+3807.1
6: 1 contend thou **b** the mountains, and let NIH
6: 4 I sent **b** thee Moses, Aaron, and 6440+3807.1
6: 6 Wherewith shall I **come b** the LORD, *and* 6923
6: 6 *and* bow myself **b** the high God? 3807.1
6: 6 shall I **come b** him with burnt offerings, 6923
Na 1: 6 Who can stand **b** his indignation? 6440+3807.1
2: 1 He that dasheth in pieces is come up **b** thy 5921
Hab 1: 3 for spoiling and violence *are* **b** me: 5048+3807.1
2:20 let all the earth keep silence **b** him. 4480+6440
3: 5 **B** him went the pestilence, and 6440+3807.1
Zep 2: 2 **B** the decree bring forth, *before* 2962+871.1
2: 2 bring forth, *b* the day pass as the chaff, NIH
2: 2 the day pass as the chaff, **b** 2962+3808+871.1
2: 2 the LORD come upon you, **b** 2962+3808+871.1
3:20 when I turn back your captivity **b** your 3807.1
Hag 1:12 the people did fear **b** the LORD. 4480+6440
2:14 and so *is* this nation **b** me, 6440+3807.1
2:15 from **b** a stone was laid upon a stone in 2962
Zec 2:13 Be silent, O all flesh, **b** the LORD: 4480+6440
3: 1 **b** the angel of the LORD, 6440+3807.1
3: 3 and stood **b** the angel. 6440+3807.1
3: 4 spake unto those that stood **b** him, 6440+3807.1
3: 8 and thy fellows that sit **b** thee: 6440+3807.1
3: 9 the stone that I have laid **b** Joshua; 6440+3807.1
4: 7 **b** Zerubbabel *thou shalt* become a 6440+3807.1
6: 5 *which* go forth from standing **b** the Lord of 5921
7: 2 and their men, to pray **b** the LORD, 6440
8:10 For **b** these days there was no hire 6440+3807.1
8:21 Let us go speedily to pray **b** the LORD, 6440
8:22 in Jerusalem, and to pray **b** the LORD. 6440
12: 8 as the angel of the LORD **b** them. 6440+3807.1
14: 4 which *is* **b** Jerusalem on the east, and 5921+6440
14: 5 like as ye fled from **b** the earthquake in 6440
14:20 shall be like the bowls **b** the altar. 6440+3807.1
Mal 2: 5 and was afraid **b** my name. 4480+6440
2: 9 and base **b** all the people, 3807.1
3: 1 and he shall prepare the way **b** me: 6440+3807.1
3:11 vine **cast** her **fruit b the time** in the field, 7921
3:14 that we have walked mournfully **b** 4480+6440
3:16 **b** him for them that feared 6440+3807.1
4: 5 I *will* send you Elijah the prophet **b** 6440+3807.1
Mt 1:18 **b** they came together, she was found *2228+4250*
2: 9 **went b** them, till it came and stood over *4254*
5:12 persecuted they the prophets which were **b** *4253*
5:16 Let your light so shine **b** men, that they *1715*
5:24 Leave there thy gift **b** the altar, and go thy *1715*

Mt 6: 1 Take heed that *ye* do not your alms **b** men, *1715*
6: 2 *thine* alms, do not sound a trumpet **b** thee, *1715*
6: 8 *things* ye have need of, **b** ye ask him. *3588+4253*
7: 6 neither cast ye your pearls **b** swine, *1715*
8:29 art thou come hither to torment us **b** *4253*
10:18 And ye shall be brought **b** governors and *1909*
10:32 therefore shall confess me **b** men, *1715*
10:32 him will I confess also **b** my Father which *1715*
10:33 But whosoever shall deny me **b** men, *1715*
10:33 him will I also deny **b** my Father which is *1715*
11:10 Behold, I send my messenger **b** thy face, *4253*
11:10 which shall prepare thy way **b** thee. *1715*
14: 6 daughter of Herodias danced **b** *1722+3319+3588*
14: 8 being **b instructed** of her mother, said, *4264*
14:22 and to **go b** him unto the other side, *4254*
17: 2 And was transfigured **b** them: and his face *1715*
21: 9 And the multitudes that **went b**, *4254*
21:31 the harlots **go** into the kingdom of God **b** *4254*
24:25 Behold, I have **told** you **b**. *4302*
24:38 For as in the days that were **b** the flood *4253*
25:32 And **b** him shall be gathered all nations: *1715*
26:32 But after I am risen *again,* I will **go b** you *4254*
26:34 unto thee, That this night, **b** *the* cock crow, *4250*
26:70 But he denied **b** *them* all, saying, I know *1715*
26:75 which said unto him, **B** *the* cock crow, *4250*
27:11 And Jesus stood **b** the governor: and *1715*
27:24 and washed *his* hands **b** the multitude, *561*
27:29 and they bowed the knee **b** him, and *1715*
28: 7 and behold, he **goeth b** you into Galilee; *4254*
Mk 1: 2 Behold, I send my messenger **b** thy face, *4253*
1: 2 which shall prepare thy way **b** thee. *1715*
1:35 rising up a great while **b day**, he went out, *1773*
2:12 took up the bed, and went forth **b** *them* all; *1726*
3:11 **fell down b** him, and cried, saying, *4363*
5:33 came and **fell down b** him, and told him all *4363*
6:41 gave *them* to his disciples to **set b** them; *3908*
6:45 to **go** to the other side **b** unto Bethsaida, *4254*
8: 6 and gave to his disciples to **set b** *them;* and *3908*
8: 6 and they did **set** *them* **b** the people. *3908*
8: 7 and commanded to **set** them also **b** *them.* *3908*
9: 2 and he was transfigured **b** them. *1715*
10:32 up to Jerusalem; and Jesus **went b** them: *4254*
11: 9 And they that **went b**, and they that *4254*
13: 9 and ye shall be brought **b** rulers and *1909*
14:28 that I am risen, I will **go b** you into Galilee. *4254*
14:30 in this night, **b** *the* cock crow twice, *2228+4250*
14:72 **B** *the* cock crow twice, thou shalt deny me *4250*
15:42 that is, the **day b the sabbath**, *4315*
16: 7 and Peter that he **goeth b** you into Galilee: *4254*
Lk 1: 6 And they were both righteous **b** God, *1799*
1: 8 *that* while he executed the priest's office **b** *1725*
1:17 And he shall go **b** him in the spirit and *4281*
1:75 In holiness and righteousness **b** him, all *1799*
1:76 for thou shalt go **b** the face of the Lord to *4253*
2:21 named of the angel **b** he was conceived in *4253*
2:26 **b** he had seen the Lord's Christ. *2228+4250*
2:31 Which thou hast prepared **b** the face of all *2596*
5:18 to bring him in, and to lay *him* **b** him. *1799*
5:19 tiling with *his* couch into the midst **b** Jesus. *1715*
5:25 And immediately he rose up **b** them, and *1799*
7:27 Behold, I send my messenger **b** thy face, *4253*
7:27 which shall prepare thy way **b** thee. *1715*
8:28 and **fell down b** him, and with a loud voice *4363*
8:47 came trembling, and **falling down b** him, *4363*
8:47 she declared unto him **b** all the people for *1799*
9:16 gave to the disciples to **set b** the multitude. *3908*
9:52 And sent messengers **b** his face: and *4253*
10: 1 and two **b** his face into every city and *4253*
10: 8 eat such *things* as are **set b** you: *3908*
11: 6 to me, and I have nothing to **set b** him: *3908*
11:38 that he had not first washed **b** dinner. *4253*
12: 6 and not one of them is forgotten **b** God? *1799*
12: 8 Whosoever shall confess me **b** men, *1715*
12: 8 him shall the Son of man also confess **b** *1715*
12: 9 But he that denieth me **b** men shall be *1799*
12: 9 men shall be denied **b** the angels of God. *1799*
14: 2 And behold, there was a certain man **b** him, *1715*
15:18 I have sinned against heaven, and **b** thee, *1799*
16:15 Ye are they which justify yourselves **b** *1799*
18:39 And they which **went b** rebuked him, *4254*
19: 4 And he **ran b**, *4390*
19:27 bring hither, and slay *them* **b** me. *1715*
19:28 he went **b**, ascending up to Jerusalem. *1715*
20:26 not take hold of his words **b** the people: *1726*
21:12 But **b** all these, they shall lay their hands on *4253*
21:12 being brought **b** kings and rulers for my *1909*
21:14 not to **meditate b** *what ye* shall answer: *4304*
21:36 to pass, and to stand **b** the Son of man. *1715*
22:15 eat this passover with you **b** I suffer: *3588+4253*
22:34 **b** that thou shalt thrice deny that *thou* *2228+4250*
22:47 **went b** them, and drew near unto Jesus to *4281*
22:61 **B** *the* cock crow, thou shalt deny me thrice. *4250*
23:12 for **b** they were at enmity between *4391*
23:14 and behold, I, having examined *him* **b** you, *1799*
23:53 wherein **never** man **b** was laid. *3756+3764*
24:19 in deed and word **b** God and all the people: *1726*
24:43 And he took *it,* and did eat **b** them. *1799*
Jn 1:15 cometh after me is **preferred b** me: *1096+1715*
1:15 me is preferred before me: for he was **b** me. *4413*
1:27 who coming after me is preferred **b** me, *1715*
1:30 a man which is **preferred b** me: *1096+1715*
1:30 is preferred before me: for he was **b** me. *4413*
1:48 unto him, **B that** Philip called thee, *3588+4253*
3:28 am not the Christ, but that I am sent **b** him. *1715*
5: 7 I am coming, another steppeth down **b** me. *4253*
6:62 the Son of man ascend up where he was **b**? *4387*
7:51 **b** it hear him, and know what he doeth? *4387*
8:58 I say unto you, **B** Abraham was, I am. *4250*
9: 8 they which **b** had seen him that he was *4387*
10: 4 he goeth **b** them, and the sheep follow him: *1715*
10: 8 All that ever came **b** me are thieves and *4253*
11:55 the country up to Jerusalem **b** the passover, *4253*
12: 1 Then Jesus six days **b** the passover came to *4253*
12:37 he had done so many miracles **b** them, *1715*
13: 1 Now **b** the feast of the passover, *4253*

Jn 13:19 Now I tell you **b** it come, that, *3588+4253*
14:29 And now I have told you **b** it come to pass, *4250*
15:18 ye know that it hated me **b** *it hated* you. *4412*
17: 5 I had with thee **b** the world was. *3588+4253*
17:24 for thou lovedst me **b** the foundation of *4253*
Ac 1:16 mouth of David **spake b** concerning Judas, *4302*
2:20 **b** *that* great and notable day of the Lord *4250*
2:25 I foresaw the Lord always **b** my **face**, *1799*
2:31 He **seeing** *this* **b**, spake of the resurrection *4275*
3:18 But *those things,* which God **b** had **shewed** *4293*
3:20 which **b** was **preached** unto you: *4296*
4:10 *even* by him doth this *man* stand **here b** *1799*
4:28 and thy counsel **determined b** to be done. *4309*
5:23 the keepers standing without **b** the doors: *4253*
5:27 brought them, they set *them* **b** the council: *1722*
5:36 For **b** these days rose up Theudas, *4253*
6: 6 Whom they set **b** the apostles: and *1799*
7: 2 **b** he dwelt in Charran, *2228+4250*
7:40 unto Aaron, Make us gods to **go b** us: *4313*
7:45 whom God drave out **b** the face of our *575*
7:46 Who found favour **b** God, and desired to *1799*
7:52 they have slain them which **shewed b** of *4293*
8:32 and like a lamb dumb **b** his shearer, so *1726*
9:15 to bear my name **b** the Gentiles, and kings, *1799*
10: 4 thine alms are come up for a memorial **b** *1799*
10:17 Simon's house, and **stood b** the gate, *2186*
10:30 a man stood **b** me in bright clothing, *1799*
10:33 therefore are we all here present **b** God, *1799*
10:41 but unto witnesses **chosen b** of God, *4401*
12: 6 and *the* keepers **b** the door kept the prison. *4253*
12:14 ran in, and told how Peter stood **b** the gate. *4253*
13:24 When John had first preached **b** his *4253+4383*
14:13 which was **b** their city, brought oxen and *4253*
16:29 and **fell down b** Paul and Silas, *4363*
16:34 he **set meat b** *them,* and rejoiced, *3908+5132*
17:26 hath determined the times **b appointed**, *4384*
18:17 and beat *him* **b** the judgment seat. *1715*
19: 9 but spake evil of *that* way **b** the multitude, *1799*
19:19 and burned *them* **b** all *men:* and *1799*
20: 5 These **going b** tarried for us at Troas. *4281*
20:13 And we **went b** to ship, and sailed unto *4281*
21:29 (For they had **seen b** with him in the city *4308*
21:38 which **b** these days madest an uproar, and *4253*
22:30 brought Paul down, and set *him* **b** them. *1519*
23: 1 I have lived in all good conscience **b** God NIG
23:30 to say **b** thee what *they had* against him. *1909*
23:33 to the governor, **presented** Paul also **b** him. *3936*
24:19 Who ought to have been here **b** thee, and *1909*
24:20 doing in me, while I stood **b** the council, *1909*
25: 9 and there be judged of these *things* **b** me? *1909*
25:16 **b** that he which is accused have *2228+4250*
25:26 Wherefore I have brought him forth **b** you, *1909*
25:26 and specially **b** thee, O king Agrippa, that, *1909*
26: 2 I shall answer for myself this day **b** thee *1909*
26:26 For the king knoweth of these *things,* **b** *4314*
27:24 Paul; thou must be **brought b** Cesar: *3936*
Ro 2:13 (For not the hearers of the law *are* just **b** *3844*
3: 9 for we have **b proved** both Jews and *4256*
3:18 There is no fear of God **b** their eyes. *561*
3:19 all the world may become **guilty b** God. *5267*
4: 2 he hath whereof to glory; but not **b** God. *4314*
4:17 **b** *him* whom he believed, *even* God, *2713*
9:29 And as Esaias **said b**, Except the Lord of *4302*
14:10 for we shall all **stand b** the judgment seat *3936*
14:22 have *it* to thyself **b** God. Happy *is* he that *1799*
16: 7 the apostles, who also were in Christ **b** me. *4253*
1Co 2: 7 God ordained **b** the world unto our glory: *4253*
4: 5 Therefore judge nothing **b** the time, *4253*
6: 1 go to law **b** the unjust, and not before *1909*
6: 1 law before the unjust, and not **b** the saints? *1909*
6: 6 with brother, and that **b** the unbelievers. *1909*
10:27 whatsoever is **set b** you, eat, asking no *3908*
11:21 For in eating every one **taketh b** *other* his *4301*
2Co 1:15 I was minded to come unto you **b**, *4387*
5:10 For we must all appear **b** the judgment seat *1715*
7: 3 not *this* to condemn *you:* for I have **said b**, *4302*
7:14 even so our boasting, which *I made* **b** Titus, *1909*
8:10 who have **begun b**, not only to do, but *4278*
8:24 and **b** the churches, the proof of your *1519+4383*
9: 5 that they would **go b** unto you, and *4281*
9: 5 whereof *ye* **had notice b**, that the same *4293*
12:19 we speak **b** God in Christ: but *we do* all *2714*
13: 2 I **told** *you* **b**, and foretell *you,* as if I were *4302*
Gal 1: 9 As we **said b**, so say I now again, If any *4302*
1:17 to them which were apostles **b** me; *4253*
1:20 I write unto you, behold, **b** God, I lie not. *1799*
2:12 For **b** that certain came from James, he did *4253*
2:14 I said unto Peter **b** *them* all, If thou, being a *1715*
3: 1 **b** whose eyes Jesus Christ hath been *2596*
3: 8 **preached b the gospel** unto Abraham, *4283*
3:17 that was **confirmed b** of God in Christ, *4300*
3:23 But **b** faith came, we were kept *3588+4253*
5:21 of the which I **tell** you **b**, as I have also told *4302*
Eph 1: 4 According as he hath chosen us in him **b** *4253*
1: 4 be holy and without blame **b** him in love: *2714*
2:10 which God hath **b ordained** that we should *4282*
Php 3:13 forth unto those *things which are* **b**, *1715*
Col 1: 5 whereof ye **heard b** in the word of the truth *4257*
1:17 And he is **b** all *things,* and by him all *things* *4253*
1Th 2: 2 But even after that we had **suffered b**, and *4310*
3: 4 we **told** you **b** that we should suffer *4302*
3: 9 we joy for your sakes **b** our God; *1715*
3:13 your hearts unblameable in holiness **b** God, *1715*
1Ti 1:13 Who was **b** a blasphemer, and a persecutor, *4387*
1:18 according to the prophecies which **went b** *4254*
5: 4 for that is good and acceptable **b** God. *1799*
5:19 an accusation, but **b** two or three witnesses. *1909*
5:20 Them that sin rebuke **b** all, that others also *1799*
5:21 I charge *thee* **b** God, and the Lord Jesus *1799*
5:21 *one* **b** *another,* doing nothing by partiality. NIG
5:24 are open beforehand, **going b** to judgment; *4254*
6:12 hast professed a good profession **b** many *1799*
6:13 quickeneth all *things,* and **b** Christ Jesus, NIG
6:13 who **b** Pontius Pilate witnessed a good *1909*
2Ti 1: 9 which was given us in Christ Jesus **b** *4253*

2Ti 2:14 charging *them* **b** the Lord that *they* strive *1799*
4: 1 I charge *thee* therefore **b** God, and the Lord *1799*
4:21 Do thy diligence to come **b** winter. *4253*
4: S when Paul was **brought b** Nero the second *3936*
Tit 1: 2 cannot lie, promised **b** the world began; *4253*
Heb 6:18 refuge to lay hold upon the hope **set b** *us:* *4295*
7:18 commandment **going b** for the weakness *4254*
10:15 a witness to us: for after that *he* had **said b**, *4302*
11: 5 for **b** his translation he had this testimony, *4253*
12: 1 run with patience the race that is **set b** us, *4295*
12: 2 who for the joy that was **set b** him endured *4295*
Jas 1:27 Pure religion and undefiled **b** God and *3844*
2: 6 and draw you **b** the judgment seats? *1519*
5: 9 the judge standeth **b** the door. *4253*
1Pe 1:20 Who verily was foreordained **b** *4253*
2Pe 2:11 bring not railing accusation against them **b** *3844*
3: 2 which were **spoken b** by the holy prophets, *4302*
3:17 beloved, seeing ye **know** *these things* **b**, *4267*
1Jn 2:28 and not be ashamed **b** him at his coming. *575*
3:19 the truth, and shall assure our hearts **b** him. *1715*
3Jn 1: 6 Which have borne witness of thy charity **b** *1799*
Jude 1: 4 who were **b** of old **ordained** to this *4270*
1:17 **spoken b** of the apostles of our Lord Jesus *4302*
1:24 to present *you* faultless **b the presence** of *2714*
Rev 1: 4 from the seven spirits which are **b** his *1799*
2:14 a stumblingblock **b** the children of Israel, *1799*
3: 2 for I have not found thy works perfect **b** *1799*
3: 5 but I will confess his name **b** my Father, *1799*
3: 5 name before my Father, and **b** his angels. *1799*
3: 8 I have set **b** thee an open door, and no *man* *1799*
3: 9 make them to come and worship **b** thy feet, *1799*
4: 5 And *there were* seven lamps of fire burning **b** *1799*
4: 6 And **b** the throne *there was* a sea of glass *1799*
4: 6 *were* four beasts full of eyes **b** and behind. *1715*
4:10 twenty elders fall down **b** him that sat on *1799*
4:10 and cast their crowns **b** the throne, *1799*
5: 8 *and* twenty elders fell down **b** the Lamb, *1799*
7: 9 stood **b** the throne, and before the Lamb, *1799*
7: 9 stood before the throne, and **b** the Lamb, *1799*
7:11 and fell **b** the throne on their faces, and *1799*
7:15 Therefore are they **b** the throne of God, and *1799*
8: 2 And I saw the seven angels which stood **b** *1799*
8: 3 the golden altar which was **b** the throne. *1799*
8: 4 ascended up **b** God out of the angel's hand. *1799*
9:13 horns of the golden altar which is **b** God, *1799*
10:11 Thou must prophesy again **b** many peoples, *1909*
11: 4 the two candlesticks standing **b** the God of *1799*
11:16 which sat **b** God on their seats, *1799*
12: 4 the dragon stood **b** the woman which was *1799*
12:10 which accused them **b** our God day and *1799*
13:12 all the power of the first beast **b** him, *1799*
14: 3 And they sung as *it were* a new song **b** *1799*
14: 3 and **b** the four beasts, and the elders: *1799*
14: 5 for they are without fault **b** the throne of *1799*
15: 4 all nations shall come and worship **b** thee; *1799*
16:19 great Babylon came in remembrance **b** *1799*
19:20 false prophet that wrought miracles **b** him, *1799*
20:12 the dead, small and great, stand **b** God; *1799*
22: 8 I fell down to worship **b** the feet of *1715*

BEFOREHAND (5) [BEFORE]

Mk 13:11 **take** no **thought b** what ye shall speak, *4305*
2Co 9: 5 and **make up b** your bounty, whereof *ye* *4294*
1Ti 5:24 Some men's sins are **open b**, going before *4271*
5:25 the good works *of some* are **manifest b**; *4271*
1Pe 1:11 when it **testified b** the sufferings of Christ, *4303*

BEFORETIME (11) [BEFORE, TIME]

Dt 2:12 The Horims also dwelt in Seir **b**; 6440+3807.1
Jos 11:10 for Hazor **b** *was* the head of all 6440+3807.1
20: 5 hated him not **b**. 4480+8032+8543
1Sa 9: 9 (**B** in Israel, when a man went to 6440+3807.1
9: 9 for *he that is* now *called* a Prophet was **b** 6440
10:11 knew him **b** saw that behold, 865+4480+8032
2Sa 7:10 afflict them any more, as **b**, 7223+871.1+1886.1
2Ki 13: 5 of Israel dwelt in their tents, as **b**. 8032+8543
Ne 2: 1 Now I had not been ***b*** sad in his presence. NIH
Isa 41:26 **b**, that we may say, *He is* 4480+6440+3807.1
Ac 8: 9 which **b** in the *same* city used sorcery, and *4391*

BEG (3) [BEGGAR, BEGGARLY, BEGGED, BEGGING]

Ps 109:10 children be continually vagabonds, and **b**: 7592
Pr 20: 4 therefore shall he **b** in harvest, and 7592
Lk 16: 3 I cannot dig; to **b** I am ashamed. *1871*

BEGAN (178) [BEGIN]

Ge 4:26 **b** *men* to call upon the name of 2490
6: 1 when men **b** to multiply on the face of 2490
9:20 Noah **b** *to be* a husbandman, and he planted 2490
10: 8 he **b** to be a mighty *one* in the earth. 2490
41:54 the seven years of dearth **b** to come, 2490
44:12 *and* **b** at the eldest, and left at the youngest: 2490
Dt 1: 5 **b** Moses to declare this law, saying, 2974
Jdg 13:25 the spirit of the LORD **b** to move him at 2490
16:19 she **b** to afflict him, and his strength went 2490
16:22 Howbeit the hair of his head **b** to grow 2490
19:25 when the **day b** to spring, they let her go. 7837
20:31 they **b** to smite of the people, *and* kill, as at 2490
20:39 Benjamin **b** to smite *and* kill of the men of 2490
20:40 when the flame **b** to arise up out of the city 2490
1Sa 3: 2 his eyes ***b*** *to wax* dim, *that* he could not 2490
2Sa 2:10 years old when he ***b*** to reign over Israel, NIH
5: 4 David *was* thirty years old when he ***b*** to NIH
1Ki 6: 1 that he ***b*** to build the house of the LORD. NIH
14:21 and one years old when he ***b*** to reign, NIH
15:25 Nadab the son of Jeroboam ***b*** to reign over NIH
15:33 In the third year of Asa king of Judah ***b*** NIH
16: 8 sixth year of Asa king of Judah ***b*** Elah NIH
16:11 it came to pass, when he ***b*** to reign, as soon NIH
16:23 first year of Asa king of Judah ***b*** Omri to NIH
16:29 eighth year of Asa king of Judah ***b*** Ahab NIH
22:41 Jehoshaphat the son of Asa ***b*** to reign over NIH
22:42 and five years old when he ***b*** to reign; NIH
22:51 Ahaziah the son of Ahab ***b*** to reign over NIH

B

2Ki 3: 1 Now Jehoram the son of Ahab **b** to reign NIH
8:16 son of Jehoshaphat king of Judah **b** to reign. NIH
8:17 two years old was he when he **b** to reign; NIH
8:26 twenty years old *was* Ahaziah when he **b** to NIH
9:29 son of Ahab **b** Ahaziah to reign over Judah. NIH
10:32 In those days the LORD **b** to cut Israel 2490
11:21 Seven years old *was* Jehoash when he **b** to NIH
12: 1 In the seventh year of Jehu Jehoash **b** to NIH
13: 1 of Jehu **b** to reign over Israel in Samaria, NIH
13:10 seventh year of Joash king of Judah **b** NIH
14: 2 and five years old when he **b** to reign, NIH
14:23 Joash king of Israel **b** to reign in Samaria, NIH
15: 1 seventh year of Jeroboam king of Israel **b** NIH
15: 2 Sixteen years old was he when he **b** to NIH
15:13 Shallum the son of Jabesh **b** to reign in NIH
15:17 thirtieth year of Azariah king of Judah **b** NIH
15:23 Menahem **b** to reign over Israel in Samaria, NIH
15:27 Remaliah **b** to reign over Israel in Samaria, NIH
15:32 **b** Jotham the son of Uzziah king of Judah to NIH
15:33 twenty years old was he when he **b** to reign, NIH
15:37 In those days the LORD **b** to send against 2490
16: 1 the son of Jotham king of Judah **b** to reign. NIH
16: 2 Twenty years old *was* Ahaz when he **b** to NIH
17: 1 In the twelfth year of Ahaz king of Judah **b** NIH
18: 1 the son of Ahaz king of Judah **b** to reign. NIH
18: 2 five years old was he when he **b** to reign; NIH
21: 1 Manasseh *was* twelve years old when he **b** NIH
21:19 and two years old when he **b** to reign, NIH
22: 1 Josiah *was* eight years old when he **b** to NIH
23:31 and three years old when he **b** to reign; NIH
23:36 and five year old when he **b** to reign; NIH
24: 8 *was* eighteen years old when he **b** to reign, NIH
24:18 and one years old when he **b** to reign, NIH
25:27 of Babylon, in the year that he **b** to reign, NIH
1Ch 1:10 he **b** to be mighty upon the earth. 2490
27:24 Joab the son of Zeruiah **b** to number, but 2490
2Ch 3: 1 Solomon **b** to build the house of 2490
3: 2 he **b** to build in the second *day* of 2490
12:13 and forty years old when he **b** to reign, NIH
13: 1 Jeroboam **b** Abijah to reign over Judah. NIH
20:22 when they **b** to sing and to praise, 2490
20:31 and five years old when he **b** to reign, NIH
21: 5 and two years old when he **b** to reign, NIH
21:20 two *years* old was he when he **b** to reign, NIH
22: 2 two years old *was* Ahaziah when he **b** to NIH
24: 1 Joash *was* seven years old when he **b** to NIH
25: 1 and five years old *when* he **b** to reign, NIH
26: 3 Sixteen years old *was* Uzziah when he **b** to NIH
27: 1 and five years old when he **b** to reign, NIH
27: 8 and twenty years old when he **b** to reign, NIH
28: 1 Ahaz *was* twenty years old when he **b** to NIH
29: 1 Hezekiah **b** to reign *when he was* five and NIH
29:17 Now they **b** on the first *day* of the first 2490
29:27 when the burnt offering **b**, the song of 2490
29:27 the song of the LORD **b** *also* with 2490
31: 7 In the third month they **b** to lay 2490
31:10 Since *the people* **b** to bring the offerings 2490
31:21 in every work that he **b** in the service of 2490
33: 1 Manasseh *was* twelve years old when he **b** NIH
33:21 and twenty years old when he **b** to reign, NIH
34: 1 Josiah *was* eight years old when he **b** to NIH
34: 3 he **b** to seek after the God of David his 2490
34: 3 in the twelfth year he **b** to purge Judah and 2490
36: 2 and three years old when he **b** to reign, NIH
36: 5 and five years old when he **b** to reign, NIH
36: 9 Jehoiachin *was* eight years old when he **b** to NIH
36:11 and twenty years old when he **b** to reign, NIH
Ezr 3: 6 From the first day of the seventh month **b** 2490
3: 8 **b** Zerubbabel the son of Shealtiel, and 2490
5: 2 **b** to build the house of God which *is* at 8271
7: 9 For upon the first *day* of the first month **b** 3246
Ne 4: 7 *and* that the breaches **b** to be stopped, then 2490
13:19 that when the gates of Jerusalem **b** to be NIH
Jer 52: 1 and twenty year old when he **b** to reign, NIH
Eze 9: 6 they **b** at the ancient men which *were* 2490
Jnh 3: 4 Jonah **b** to enter into the city a day's 2490
Mt 4:17 From that time Jesus **b** to preach, and to say, *756*
11: 7 Jesus **b** to say unto the multitudes *756*
11:20 Then **b** he to upbraid the cities wherein most *756*
12: 1 and **b** to pluck the ears of corn, and to eat. *756*
16:21 From that time forth **b** Jesus to shew unto his *756*
16:22 and **b** to rebuke him, saying, Be it far from *756*
26:22 and **b** every one of them to say unto him, *756*
26:37 and **b** to be sorrowful and very heavy. *756*
26:74 Then **b** he to curse and to swear, *saying,* I *756*
28: 1 as it **b** to dawn towards the first *day* of NIG
Mk 1:45 and **b** to publish *it* much, and to blaze abroad *756*
2:23 and his disciples **b**, as they went, to pluck *756*
4: 1 And he **b** again to teach by the sea side: and *756*
5:17 And they **b** to pray him to depart out of their *756*
5:20 **b** to publish in Decapolis how great *things* *756*
6: 2 was come, he **b** to teach in the synagogue: *756*
6: 7 and **b** to send them forth by two and two; *756*
6:34 and he **b** to teach them many *things.* *756*
6:55 **b** to carry about in beds those that were sick, *756*
8:11 came forth, and **b** to question with him, *756*
8:31 And he **b** to teach them, that the Son of man *756*
8:32 And Peter took him, and **b** to rebuke him. *756*
10:28 Then Peter **b** to say unto him, Lo, we have *756*
10:32 **b** to tell them what *things* should happen *756*
10:41 And when the ten heard *it,* they **b** to be much *756*
10:47 he **b** to cry out, and say, Jesus, *thou* Son of *756*
11:15 and **b** to cast out them that sold and *756*
12: 1 And he **b** to speak unto them by parables. *756*
13: 5 And Jesus answering them **b** to say, *756*
14:19 And they **b** to be sorrowful, and to say unto *756*
14:33 and **b** to be sore amazed, and to be very *756*
14:65 And some **b** to spit on him, and to cover his *756*
14:69 and **b** to say to them that stood by, This is *756*
14:71 But he **b** to curse and to swear, *saying,* I *756*
15: 8 And the multitude crying aloud **b** to desire *756*
15:18 And **b** to salute him, Hail, King of the Jews. *756*
Lk 1:70 which have been **since** the world **b**:) *575*
3:23 And Jesus himself **b** *to be* about thirty years *756*
4:21 And he **b** to say unto them, This day is this *756*
Lk 5: 7 filled both the ships, so that they **b** to sink. NIG
5:21 the scribes and the Pharisees **b** to reason, *756*
7:15 And he that was dead sat up, and **b** to speak. *756*
7:24 he **b** to speak unto the people concerning *756*
7:38 and **b** to wash his feet with tears, and *756*
7:49 And they that sat at meat with *him* **b** to say *756*
9:12 And *when* the day **b** to wear away, then *756*
11:29 he **b** to say, This is an evil generation: *756*
11:53 and the Pharisees **b** to urge *him* vehemently, *756*
12: 1 he **b** to say unto his disciples first *of all,* *756*
14:18 And they all with one *consent* **b** to make *756*
14:30 This man **b** to build, and was not able to *756*
15:14 famine in that land; and he **b** to be in want. *756*
15:24 and is found. And they **b** to be merry. *756*
19:37 the whole multitude of the disciples **b** to *756*
19:45 and **b** to cast out them that sold therein, *756*
20: 9 Then **b** he to speak to the people this *756*
22:23 And they **b** to inquire among themselves, *756*
23: 2 And they **b** to accuse him, saying, We found *756*
Jn 4:52 them the hour when he **b to amend.** *2192+2866*
9:32 **Since** the world **b** was it not heard that any *1537*
13: 5 and **b** to wash the disciples' feet, and to wipe *756*
Ac 1: 1 of all that Jesus **b** both to do and teach, *756*
2: 4 and **b** to speak with other tongues, as *756*
3:21 of all his holy prophets **since** the world **b**. *575*
8:35 and **b** at the same scripture, and *756*
10:37 and **b** from Galilee, after the baptism which *756*
11:15 And as I **b** to speak, the Holy Ghost fell on *756*
18:26 And he **b** to speak boldly in the synagogue: *756*
24: 2 And when he was called *forth,* Tertullus **b** to *756*
27:35 and when he had broken *it,* he **b** to eat. *756*
Ro 16:25 was kept secret **since** the **world b**, *166+5550*
2Ti 1: 9 us in Christ Jesus before the **world b**, *166+5550*
Tit 1: 2 promised before the **world b**; *166+5550*
Heb 2: 3 which at the first **b** to be spoken by *2983*

BEGAT (225) [BEGET]

Ge 4:18 Irad **b** Mehujael: and Mehujael begat 3205
4:18 Mehujael **b** Methusael: and 3205
4:18 begat Methusael: and Methusael **b** Lamech. 3205
5: 3 and **b** *a son* in his own likeness, 3205
5: 4 and he **b** sons and daughters: 3205
5: 6 an hundred and five years, and **b** Enos: 3205
5: 7 Seth lived after he **b** Enos eight hundred 3205
5: 7 seven years, and **b** sons and daughters: 3205
5: 9 And Enos lived ninety years, and **b** Cainan: 3205
5:10 Enos lived after he **b** Cainan eight hundred 3205
5:10 and fifteen years, and **b** sons and daughters: 3205
5:12 lived seventy years, and **b** Mahalaleel: 3205
5:13 Cainan lived after he **b** Mahalaleel eight 3205
5:13 forty years, and **b** sons and daughters: 3205
5:15 lived sixty and five years, and **b** Jared: 3205
5:16 Mahalaleel lived after he **b** Jared eight 3205
5:16 thirty years, and **b** sons and daughters: 3205
5:18 and two years, and he **b** Enoch: 3205
5:19 Jared lived after he **b** Enoch eight hundred 3205
5:19 hundred years, and **b** sons and daughters: 3205
5:21 and five years, and **b** Methuselah: 3205
5:22 Enoch walked with God after he **b** 3205
5:22 hundred years, and **b** sons and daughters: 3205
5:25 and seven years, and **b** Lamech: 3205
5:26 Methuselah lived after he **b** Lamech seven 3205
5:26 and two years, and **b** sons and daughters: 3205
5:28 hundred eighty and two years, and **b** a son: 3205
5:30 Lamech lived after he **b** Noah five hundred 3205
5:30 and five years, and **b** sons and daughters: 3205
5:32 and Noah **b** Shem, Ham, and Japheth. 3205
6:10 Noah **b** three sons, Shem, Ham, and 3205
10: 8 Cush **b** Nimrod: he began to be a mighty 3205
10:13 Mizraim **b** Ludim, and Anamim, and 3205
10:15 Canaan **b** Sidon his firstborn, and Heth, 3205
10:24 Arphaxad **b** Salah; and Salah begat Eber. 3205
10:24 Arphaxad begat Salah; and Salah **b** Eber. 3205
10:26 Joktan **b** Almodad, and Sheleph, and 3205
11:10 and **b** Arphaxad two years after the flood: 3205
11:11 Shem lived after he **b** Arphaxad five 3205
11:11 hundred years, and **b** sons and daughters. 3205
11:12 lived five and thirty years, and **b** Salah: 3205
11:13 Arphaxad lived after he **b** Salah four 3205
11:13 three years, and **b** sons and daughters. 3205
11:14 And Salah lived thirty years, and **b** Eber: 3205
11:15 Salah lived after he **b** Eber four hundred 3205
11:15 three years, and **b** sons and daughters. 3205
11:16 lived four and thirty years, and **b** Peleg: 3205
11:17 Eber lived after he **b** Peleg four hundred 3205
11:17 thirty years, and **b** sons and daughters. 3205
11:18 And Peleg lived thirty years, and **b** Reu: 3205
11:19 Peleg lived after he **b** Reu two hundred 3205
11:19 nine years, and **b** sons and daughters. 3205
11:20 lived two and thirty years, and **b** Serug: 3205
11:21 Reu lived after he **b** Serug two hundred 3205
11:21 seven years, and **b** sons and daughters. 3205
11:22 And Serug lived thirty years, and **b** Nahor: 3205
11:23 Serug lived after he **b** Nahor two hundred 3205
11:23 hundred years, and **b** sons and daughters. 3205
11:24 lived nine and twenty years, and **b** Terah: 3205
11:25 Nahor lived after he **b** Terah an hundred 3205
11:25 nineteen years, and **b** sons and daughters. 3205
11:26 and **b** Abram, Nahor, and Haran. 3205
11:27 Terah **b** Abram, Nahor, and Haran; and 3205
11:27 and Haran; and Haran **b** Lot. 3205
22:23 Bethuel **b** Rebekah: these eight Milcah did 3205
25: 3 Jokshan **b** Sheba, and Dedan. And the sons 3205
25:19 of Isaac, Abraham's son: Abraham **b** Isaac: 3205
Lev 25:45 *are* with you, which they **b** in your land: 3205
Nu 26:29 Machir **b** Gilead: of Gilead *come* 3205
26:58 of the Korahites. And Kohath **b** Amram. 3205
Dt 32:18 Of the Rock *that* **b** thee thou art unmindful, 3205
Jdg 11: 1 the son of a harlot: and Gilead **b** Jephthah. 3205
Ru 4:18 generations of Pharez: Pharez **b** Hezron, 3205
4:19 Hezron **b** Ram, and Ram begat 3205
4:19 begat Ram, and Ram **b** Amminadab, 3205
4:20 Amminadab **b** Nahshon, and 3205
4:20 begat Nahshon, and Nahshon **b** Salmon, 3205
4:21 And Salmon **b** Boaz, and Boaz begat Obed, 3205
Ru 4:21 And Salmon begat Boaz, and Boaz **b** Obed, 3205
4:22 And Obed **b** Jesse, and Jesse begat David. 3205
4:22 And Obed begat Jesse, and Jesse **b** David. 3205
1Ch 1:10 Cush **b** Nimrod: he began to be mighty 3205
1:11 Mizraim **b** Ludim, and Anamim, and 3205
1:13 Canaan **b** Zidon his firstborn, and Heth, 3205
1:18 Arphaxad **b** Shelah, and Shelah begat Eber. 3205
1:18 Arphaxad begat Shelah, and Shelah **b** Eber. 3205
1:20 Joktan **b** Almodad, and Sheleph, and 3205
1:34 Abraham **b** Isaac. The sons of Isaac; Esau 3205
2:10 Ram **b** Amminadab; and Amminadab begat 3205
2:10 Amminadab **b** Nahshon, prince of 3205
2:11 Nahshon **b** Salma, and Salma begat Boaz, 3205
2:11 Nahshon begat Salma, and Salma **b** Boaz, 3205
2:12 And Boaz **b** Obed, and Obed begat Jesse, 3205
2:12 And Boaz begat Obed, and Obed **b** Jesse, 3205
2:13 Jesse **b** his firstborn Eliab, and 3205
2:18 Caleb the son of Hezron **b** *children* of 3205
2:20 And Hur **b** Uri, and Uri begat Bezaleel. 3205
2:20 And Hur begat Uri, and Uri **b** Bezaleel. 3205
2:22 Segub **b** Jair, who had three and 3205
2:36 Attai **b** Nathan, and Nathan begat Zabad, 3205
2:36 Attai begat Nathan, and Nathan **b** Zabad, 3205
2:37 Zabad **b** Ephlal, and Ephlal begat Obed, 3205
2:37 Zabad begat Ephlal, and Ephlal **b** Obed, 3205
2:38 And Obed **b** Jehu, and Jehu begat Azariah, 3205
2:38 And Obed begat Jehu, and Jehu **b** Azariah, 3205
2:39 Azariah **b** Helez, and Helez begat Eleasah, 3205
2:39 Azariah begat Helez, and Helez **b** Eleasah, 3205
2:40 Eleasah **b** Sisamai, and Sisamai begat 3205
2:40 begat Sisamai, and Sisamai **b** Shallum, 3205
2:41 Shallum **b** Jekamiah, and Jekamiah begat 3205
2:41 begat Jekamiah, and Jekamiah **b** Elishama. 3205
2:44 Shema **b** Raham, the father of Jorkoam: 3205
2:44 father of Jorkoam: and Rekem **b** Shammai. 3205
2:46 and Moza, and Gazez: and Haran **b** Gazez. 3205
4: 2 And Reaiah the son of Shobal **b** Jahath; and 3205
4: 2 and Jahath **b** Ahumai, and Lahad. 3205
4: 8 Coz **b** Anub, and Zobebah, and the families 3205
4:11 Chelub the brother of Shuah **b** Mehir, 3205
4:12 Eshton **b** Beth-rapha, and Paseah, and 3205
4:14 Meonothai **b** Ophrah: and Seraiah begat 3205
4:14 Seraiah **b** Joab, the father of the valley of 3205
6: 4 Eleazar **b** Phinehas, Phinehas begat 3205
6: 4 begat Phinehas, Phinehas **b** Abishua, 3205
6: 5 Abishua **b** Bukki, and Bukki begat Uzzi, 3205
6: 5 Abishua begat Bukki, and Bukki **b** Uzzi, 3205
6: 6 Uzzi **b** Zerahiah, and Zerahiah begat 3205
6: 6 begat Zerahiah, and Zerahiah **b** Meraioth, 3205
6: 7 Meraioth **b** Amariah, and Amariah begat 3205
6: 7 begat Amariah, and Amariah **b** Ahitub, 3205
6: 8 Ahitub **b** Zadok, and Zadok begat 3205
6: 8 begat Zadok, and Zadok **b** Ahimaaz, 3205
6: 9 Ahimaaz **b** Azariah, and Azariah begat 3205
6: 9 begat Azariah, and Azariah **b** Johanan, 3205
6:10 Johanan **b** Azariah, (he *it is* that executed 3205
6:11 Azariah **b** Amariah, and Amariah begat 3205
6:11 begat Amariah, and Amariah **b** Ahitub, 3205
6:12 Ahitub **b** Zadok, and Zadok begat Shallum, 3205
6:12 Ahitub begat Zadok, and Zadok **b** Shallum, 3205
6:13 Shallum **b** Hilkiah, and Hilkiah begat 3205
6:13 begat Hilkiah, and Hilkiah **b** Azariah, 3205
6:14 Azariah **b** Seraiah, and Seraiah begat 3205
6:14 begat Seraiah, and Seraiah **b** Jehozadak, 3205
7:32 Heber **b** Japhlet, and Shomer, and Hotham, 3205
8: 1 Now Benjamin **b** Bela his firstborn, 3205
8: 7 he removed them, and **b** Uzza, and Ahihud. 3205
8: 8 Shaharaim **b** *children* in the country of 3205
8: 9 he **b** of Hodesh his wife, Jobab, and Zibia, 3205
8:11 And of Hushim he **b** Abitub, and Elpaal. 3205
8:32 Mikloth **b** Shimeah. And these also dwelt 3205
8:33 Ner **b** Kish, and Kish begat Saul, and 3205
8:33 Kish **b** Saul, and Saul begat Jonathan, and 3205
8:33 Saul **b** Jonathan, and Malchishua, and 3205
8:34 *was* Merib-baal; and Merib-baal **b** Micah. 3205
8:36 Ahaz **b** Jehoadah; and Jehoadah begat 3205
8:36 Jehoadah **b** Alemeth, and Azmaveth, and 3205
8:36 and Zimri; and Zimri **b** Moza, 3205
8:37 Moza **b** Binea: Rapha *was* his son, 3205
9:38 Mikloth **b** Shimeam. And they also dwelt 3205
9:39 Ner **b** Kish; and Kish begat Saul; and 3205
9:39 Kish **b** Saul; and Saul begat Jonathan, and 3205
9:39 Saul **b** Jonathan, and Malchishua, and 3205
9:40 *was* Merib-baal: and Merib-baal **b** Micah. 3205
9:42 Ahaz **b** Jarah; and Jarah begat Alemeth, 3205
9:42 Jarah **b** Alemeth, and Azmaveth, and 3205
9:42 and Zimri; and Zimri **b** Moza; 3205
9:43 Moza **b** Binea; and Rephaiah his son, 3205
14: 3 and David **b** moe sons and daughters. 3205
2Ch 11:21 **b** twenty and eight sons, and 3205
13:21 **b** twenty and two sons, and 3205
24: 3 two wives; and he **b** sons and daughters. 3205
Ne 12:10 Jeshua **b** Joiakim, Joiakim also begat 3205
12:10 Joiakim also **b** Eliashib, and Eliashib begat 3205
12:10 also begat Eliashib, and Eliashib **b** Joiada, NIH
12:11 Joiada **b** Jonathan, and Jonathan begat 3205
12:11 begat Jonathan, and Jonathan **b** Jaddua. 3205
Pr 23:22 Hearken unto thy father that **b** thee, and 3205
Jer 16: 3 concerning their fathers that **b** them in this 3205
Da 11: 6 he that **b** her, and he that strengthened her 3205
Zec 13: 3 his mother that **b** him shall say unto him, 3205
13: 3 his mother that **b** him shall thrust him 3205
Mt 1: 2 Abraham **b** Isaac; and Isaac begat Jacob; *1080*
1: 2 and Isaac **b** Jacob; and Jacob begat Judas *1080*
1: 2 and Jacob **b** Judas and his brethren; *1080*
1: 3 And Judas **b** Phares and Zara of Thamar; *1080*
1: 3 and Phares **b** Esrom; and Esrom begat *1080*
1: 3 Phares begat Esrom; and Esrom **b** Aram; *1080*
1: 4 And Aram **b** Aminadab; and *1080*
1: 4 and Aminadab **b** Naasson; and *1080*
1: 4 begat Naasson; and Naasson **b** Salmon; *1080*
1: 5 And Salmon **b** Booz of Rachab; and *1080*
1: 5 and Booz **b** Obed of Ruth; and Obed begat *1080*
1: 5 begat Obed of Ruth; and Obed **b** Jesse; *1080*
1: 6 And Jesse **b** David the king; and David *1080*

Mt 1: 6 David the king b Solomon of *her that had* *1080*
1: 7 And Solomon b Roboam; and *1080*
1: 7 and Roboam b Abia; and Abia begat Asa; *1080*
1: 7 and Roboam begat Abia; and Abia b Asa; *1080*
1: 8 And Asa b Josaphat; and Josaphat begat *1080*
1: 8 and Josaphat b Joram; and Joram begat *1080*
1: 8 Josaphat begat Joram; and Joram b Ozias; *1080*
1: 9 And Ozias b Joatham; and Joatham begat *1080*
1: 9 and Joatham b Achaz; and Achaz begat *1080*
1: 9 begat Achaz; and Achaz b Ezekias; *1080*
1:10 And Ezekias b Manasses; and *1080*
1:10 and Manasses b Amon; and Amon begat *1080*
1:10 Manasses begat Amon; and Amon b Josias; *1080*
1:11 And Josias b Jechonias and his brethren, *1080*
1:12 brought to Babylon, Jechonias b Salathiel; *1080*
1:12 begat Salathiel; and Salathiel b Zorobabel; *1080*
1:13 And Zorobabel b Abiud; and Abiud begat *1080*
1:13 and Abiud b Eliakim; and Eliakim begat *1080*
1:13 Abiud begat Eliakim; and Eliakim b Azor; *1080*
1:14 And Azor b Sadoc; and Sadoc begat *1080*
1:14 and Sadoc b Achim; and Achim begat *1080*
1:14 Sadoc begat Achim; and Achim b Eliud; *1080*
1:15 And Eliud b Eleazar; and Eleazar begat *1080*
1:15 and Eleazar b Matthan; and Matthan begat *1080*
1:15 begat Matthan; and Matthan b Jacob; *1080*
1:16 And Jacob b Joseph the husband of Mary, *1080*
Ac 7: 8 and so *Abraham* b Isaac, and *1080*
7: 8 and Isaac b Jacob; and Jacob *begat* NIG
7: 8 and Jacob *b* the twelve patriarchs. NIG
7:29 in the land of Madian, where he b two sons. *1080*
Jas 1:18 Of his own will b he us with the word of *616*
1Jn 5: 1 every one that loveth him that b loveth him *1080*

BEGET (10) [BEGAT, BEGETTEST, BEGETTETH, BEGOTTEN, FIRSTBEGOTTEN]
Ge 17:20 twelve princes shall he b, and I will make 3205
Dt 4:25 When thou shalt b children, and 3205
28:41 Thou shalt b sons and daughters, but 3205
2Ki 20:18 which thou shalt b, shall they take *away;* 3205
Ecc 6: 3 If a man b an hundred *children,* and 3205
Isa 39: 7 which thou shalt b, shall they take away; 3205
Jer 29: 6 Take ye wives, and b sons and daughters; 3205
Eze 18:10 If he b a son *that is* a robber, a shedder of 3205
18:14 Now lo, *if* he b a son, that seeth all his 3205
47:22 which shall b children among you: 3205

BEGETTEST (2) [BEGET]
Ge 48: 6 which thou b after them, shall be thine, *and* 3205
Isa 45:10 him that saith unto *his* father, What b thou? 3205

BEGETTETH (3) [BEGET]
Pr 17:21 He that b a fool *doeth it* to his sorrow: and 3205
23:24 he that b a wise *child* shall have joy of him. 3205
Ecc 5:14 he b a son, and *there is* nothing in his hand. 3205

BEGGAR (3) [BEG]
1Sa 2: 8 *and* lifteth up the b from the dunghill, to set 34
Lk 16:20 And there was a certain b named Lazarus, *4434*
16:22 And it came to pass that the b died, and *4434*

BEGGARLY (1) [BEG]
Gal 4: 9 turn ye again to the weak and b elements, *4434*

BEGGED (3) [BEG]
Mt 27:58 He went to Pilate, and b the body of Jesus. *154*
Lk 23:52 went unto Pilate, and b the body of Jesus. *154*
Jn 9: 8 said, Is not this he that sat and b? *4319*

BEGGING (3) [BEG]
Ps 37:25 righteous forsaken, nor his seed b bread. 1245
Mk 10:46 son of Timeus, sat by the *high*way side b. *4319*
Lk 18:35 a certain blind man sat by the way side b: *4319*

BEGIN (27) [BEGAN, BEGINNEST, BEGINNING, BEGINNINGS, BEGUN]
Ge 11: 6 all one language; and this they b to do: 2490
Dt 2:24 b to possess *it,* and contend with him in 2490
2:25 This day will I b to put the dread of thee 2490
2:31 b to possess, that *thou* mayest inherit his 2490
16: 9 b to number the seven weeks from *such* 2490
Jos 3: 7 This day will I b to magnify thee in 2490
Jdg 10:18 What man *is he* that will b to fight against 2490
13: 5 he shall b to deliver Israel out of the hand 2490
1Sa 3:12 when I b, I will also make an end. 2490
22:15 Did I then b to inquire of God for him? 2490
2Ki 8:25 the son of Jehoram king of Judah *b* to reign. NIH
Ne 11:17 *was* the principal to b the thanksgiving in 8462
Jer 25:29 I b to bring evil on the city which is called 2490
Eze 9: 6 whom *is* the mark; and b at my sanctuary. 2490
Mt 24:49 And shall b to smite *his* fellowservants, and *756*
Lk 3: 8 and b not to say within yourselves, *756*
12:45 and shall b to beat the menservants and *756*
13:25 and ye b to stand without, and to knock at *756*
13:26 Then shall ye b to say, We have eaten and *756*
14: 9 thou b with shame to take the lowest room. *756*
14:29 is not able to finish *it,* all that behold *it* b to *756*
21:28 And when these *things* b to come to pass, *756*
23:30 Then shall they b to say to the mountains, *756*
2Co 3: 1 Do we b again to commend ourselves? or *756*
1Pe 4:17 For the time *is come* that judgment must b at *756*
4:17 and if *it* first *b* at us, what *shall* the end *be* NIG
Rev 10: 7 when he shall b to sound, the mystery of *3195*

BEGINNEST (1) [BEGIN]
Dt 16: 9 *time as thou* b *to put* the sickle to the corn. 2490

BEGINNING (106) [BEGIN]
Ge 1: 1 In the b God created the heaven and 7225
10:10 the b of his kingdom was Babel, and Erech, 7225
13: 3 the place where his tent had been at the b, 8462
41:21 but they *were still* ill favoured, as at the b. 8462
49: 3 my might, and the b of my strength, 7225
Ex 12: 2 This month *shall be* unto you the b of 7218
Dt 11:12 from the b of the year even unto the end of 7225
21:17 for he *is* the b of his strength; the right of 7225
32:42 from the b of revenges upon the enemy. 7218
Jdg 7:19 came unto the outside of the camp *in* the b 7218
Ru 1:22 they came *to* Beth-lehem in the b of barley 8462
3:10 kindness in the latter end than at the b, 7223
2Sa 21: 9 in the first *days,* in the b of barley harvest. 8462
21:10 from the b of harvest until water dropped 8462
2Ki 17:25 *so* it was at the b of their dwelling there, 8462
1Ch 17: 9 waste them any more, as at the b, 7223
Ezr 4: 6 reign of Ahasuerus, in the b of his reign, 8462
Job 8: 7 Though thy b was small, yet thy latter end 7225
42:12 the latter end of Job more than his b: 7225
Ps 111:10 The fear of the LORD *is* the b of wisdom: 7225
119:160 Thy word *is* true *from* the b: and every one 7218
Pr 1: 7 The fear of the LORD *is* the b of 7225
8:22 The LORD possessed me *in* the b of his 7225
8:23 from the b, or ever the earth was. 7218
9:10 The fear of the LORD *is* the b of wisdom: 8462
17:14 The b of strife *is as* when one letteth out 7225
20:21 inheritance *may be* gotten hastily at the b; 7223
Ecc 3:11 that God maketh from the b to the end. 7218
7: 8 Better *is* the end of a thing than the b 7225
10:13 The b of the words of his mouth *is* 8462
Isa 1:26 at the first, and thy counsellers as at the b: 8462
18: 2 to a people terrible from their b hitherto; 4480
18: 7 from a people terrible from their b hitherto; 4480
40:21 hath it not been told you from the b? 7218
41: 4 done *it,* calling the generations from the b? 7218
41:26 Who hath declared from the b, that we may 7218
46:10 Declaring the end from the b, and 7225
48: 3 have declared the former *things* from the b; 227
48: 5 I have even from the b declared *it* to thee; 227
48: 7 They are created now, and not from the b; 227
48:16 I have not spoken in secret from the b; 7218
64: 4 For since the b of the world *men* 4480+5769
Jer 17:12 A glorious high throne from the b *is* 7223
26: 1 In the b of the reign of Jehoiakim the son 7225
27: 1 In the b of the reign of Jehoiakim the son 7225
28: 1 in the b of the reign of Zedekiah king of 7225
49:34 b of the reign of Zedekiah king of Judah, 7225
La 2:19 in the b of the watches, pour out thine heart 7218
Eze 40: 1 in the b of the year, in the tenth *day* of 7218
Da 9:21 whom I had seen in the vision at the b, 8462
9:23 At the b of thy supplications 8462
Hos 1: 2 The b of the word of the LORD by Hosea. 8462
Am 7: 1 he formed grasshoppers in the b of 8462
Mic 1:13 she *is* the b of the sin to the daughter of 7225
Mt 14:30 and b to sink, he cried, saying, Lord, *756*
19: 4 that he which made *them* at the b made them *746*
19: 8 your wives: but from the b it was not so. *746*
20: 8 them *their* hire, b from the last unto the first. *756*
24: 8 All these *are* the b of sorrows. *746*
24:21 such as was not since the b of the world to *746*
Mk 1: 1 The b of the gospel of Jesus Christ, the Son *746*
10: 6 But from the b of the creation God made *746*
13:19 such as was not from the b of the creation *746*
Lk 1: 2 which from the b were eyewitnesses, and *746*
23: 5 all Jewry, b from Galilee to this place. *756*
24:27 And b at Moses and all the prophets, *756*
24:47 his name among all nations, b at Jerusalem. *756*
Jn 1: 1 In the b was the Word, and the Word was *746*
1: 2 The same was in the b with God. *746*
2:10 Every man at the b doth set forth good *4412*
2:11 This b of miracles did Jesus in Cana of *746*
6:64 For Jesus knew from the b who they were *746*
8: 9 by one, b at the eldest, *even* unto the last: *756*
8:25 the same that I said unto you *from* the b. *746*
8:44 He was a murderer from the b, and *746*
15:27 because ye have been with me from the b. *746*
16: 4 And these *things* I said not unto you at the b, *746*
Ac 1:22 B from the baptism of John, unto *that same* *756*
11: 4 But Peter *rehearsed the matter* from the b, *756*
11:15 Holy Ghost fell on them, as on us at the b. *746*
15:18 are all his works from the b of the world. *575*
26: 5 Which knew me from the b, if they would *509*
Eph 3: 9 which from the b of the world hath been hid *165*
Php 4:15 know also, that in the b of the gospel, *746*
Col 1:18 who is the b, the firstborn from the dead; *746*
2Th 2:13 God hath from the b chosen you to salvation *746*
Heb 1:10 in the b hast laid the foundation of the earth; *746*
3:14 if we hold the b of *our* confidence stedfast *746*
7: 3 having neither b of days, nor end of life; *746*
2Pe 2:20 the latter *end* is worse with them than the b. *4413*
3: 4 all *things* continue as *they were* from the b *746*
1Jn 1: 1 *That* which was from the b, which we have *746*
2: 7 old commandment which ye had from the b. *746*
2: 7 is the word which ye have heard from the b. *746*
2:13 ye have known him that is from the b. *746*
2:14 ye have known him that is from the b. *746*
2:24 in you, which ye have heard from the b. *746*
2:24 If *that* which ye have heard from the b shall *746*
3: 8 of the devil; for the devil sinneth from the b. *746*
3:11 this is the message that ye heard from the b, *746*
2Jn 1: 5 but *that* which we had from the b, that we *746*
1: 6 That, as ye have heard from the b, ye should *746*
Rev 1: 8 am Alpha and Omega, the b and the ending, *746*
3:14 true witness, the b of the creation of God; *746*
21: 6 I am Alpha and Omega, the b and the end. *746*
22:13 the b and the end, the first and the last. *746*

BEGINNINGS (4) [BEGIN]
Nu 10:10 solemn days, and in the b of your months, 7218
28:11 in the b of your months ye shall offer a 7218
Eze 36:11 and will do better *unto you* than at your b: 7221
Mk 13: 8 and troubles: these *are* the b of sorrows. *746*

BEGOTTEN (24) [BEGET]
Ge 5: 4 the days of Adam after he had b Seth were 3205
Lev 18:11 b of thy father, she *is* thy sister, thou shalt 4138
Nu 11:12 have I b them, that thou shouldest say unto 3205
Dt 23: 8 The children that are b of them shall enter 3205
Jdg 8:30 had threescore and ten sons of his body b: 3318
Job 38:28 a father? or who hath b the drops of dew? 3205
Ps 2: 7 Thou *art* my Son; *this* day have I b thee. 3205
Isa 49:21 Who hath b me these, seeing I have lost my 3205
Hos 5: 7 for they have b strange children: now shall 3205
Jn 1:14 the glory as of the only b of the Father,) *3439*
1:18 the only b Son, which is in the bosom of *3439*
3:16 the world, that he gave his only b Son, *3439*
3:18 in the name of the only b Son of God. *3439*
Ac 13:33 Thou art my Son, this day have I b thee. *1080*
1Co 4:15 for in Christ Jesus I have b you through *1080*
Phm 1:10 whom I have b in my bonds: *1080*
Heb 1: 5 Thou art my Son, this day have I b thee? *1080*
5: 5 Thou art my Son, to day have I b thee. *1080*
11:17 the promises offered up *his* only b *son,* *3439*
1Pe 1: 3 b us again unto a lively hope by *313*
1Jn 4: 9 that God sent his only b Son into the world, *3439*
5: 1 that begat loveth him also that is b of him. *1080*
5:18 but he that is b of God keepeth himself, *1080*
Rev 1: 5 *and* the first b of the dead, and the prince *4416*

BEGUILE (2) [BEGUILED, BEGUILING]
Col 2: 4 lest any *man* should b you with enticing *3884*
2:18 Let no *man* b you of your reward in a *2603*

BEGUILED (5) [BEGUILE]
Ge 3:13 The serpent b me, and I did eat. 5377
29:25 for Rachel? wherefore then hast thou b me? 7411
Nu 25:18 wherewith they have b you in the matter of 5230
Jos 9:22 Wherefore have ye b us, saying, 7411
2Co 11: 3 as the serpent b Eve through his subtilty, so *1818*

BEGUILING (1) [BEGUILE]
2Pe 2:14 cannot cease from sin; b unstable souls: *1185*

BEGUN (13) [BEGIN]
Nu 16:46 gone out from the LORD; the plague is b. 2490
16:47 the plague was b among the people: 2490
25: 1 the people b to commit whoredom with 2490
Dt 2:31 I have b to give Sihon and his land before 2490
3:24 thou hast b to shew thy servant thy 2490
Est 6:13 before whom thou hast b to fall, thou shalt 2490
9:23 the Jews undertook to do as they had b, 2490
Mt 18:24 And when he had b to reckon, one was *756*
2Co 8: 6 that as he had b, so he would also finish in *4278*
8:10 who have b before, not only to do, but *4278*
Gal 3: 3 having b in the Spirit, are ye now made *1728*
Php 1: 6 b a good work in you will perform *it* until *1728*
1Ti 5:11 for when they have *b to* wax wanton against NIG

BEHALF (13) [BEHAVE, BEHAVED, BEHAVETH, BEHAVIOUR, BEHEADED]
Ex 27:21 on the b of the children of Israel. 854+4480
2Sa 3:12 Abner sent messengers to David on his b, 8478
2Ch 16: 9 to shew himself strong in the b of *them* 5973
Job 36: 2 thee that *I have* yet to speak on God's b. 3807.1
Da 11:18 a prince for his own b shall cause NIH
Ro 16:19 all *men.* I am glad therefore on your b: *1909*
1Co 1: 4 I thank my God always on your b, for *4012*
2Co 1:11 thanks may be given by many on our b. *5228*
5:12 but give you occasion to glory on our b, *5228*
8:24 of your love, and of our boasting on your b. *5228*
9: 3 boasting of you should be in vain in this b; *3313*
Php 1:29 For unto you it is given in the b of Christ, *5228*
1Pe 4:16 but let him glorify God on this b. *3313*

BEHAVE (6) [BEHALF]
Dt 32:27 adversaries should b themselves strangely, 5234
1Ch 19:13 let us b ourselves valiantly for our people, 2388
Ps 101: 2 I will b myself wisely in a perfect way. 7919
Isa 3: 5 the child shall b himself proudly against 7292
1Co 13: 5 Doth not b itself unseemly, seeketh not her *807*
1Ti 3:15 oughtest to b thyself in the house of God, *390*

BEHAVED (9) [BEHALF]
1Sa 18: 5 Saul sent him, *and* b himself wisely: 7919
18:14 David b himself wisely in all his ways; 7919
18:15 Saul saw that he b himself very wisely, 7919
18:30 *that* David b himself more wisely than all 7919
Ps 35:14 I b myself as though *he had been* my friend 1980
131: 2 Surely I have b and quieted myself, as a 7737
Mic 3: 4 as they have b themselves ill in their 7489
1Th 2:10 unblameably we b ourselves among you *1096*
2Th 3: 7 for we b not ourselves disorderly among *812*

BEHAVETH (1) [BEHALF]
1Co 7:36 *he* b himself uncomely toward his virgin, *807*

BEHAVIOUR (4) [BEHALF]
1Sa 21:13 he changed his b before them, and 2940
Ps 34: T when he changed his b before Abimelech; 2940
1Ti 3: 2 vigilant, sober, of good b, given to *2887*
Tit 2: 3 *that they be* in b as becometh holiness, *2688*

BEHEADED (7) [BEHALF]
Dt 21: 6 hands over the heifer that is b in the valley: 6202
2Sa 4: 7 b him, and took his head, and 5493+7218
Mt 14:10 And he sent, and b John in the prison. *607*
Mk 6:16 heard *thereof,* he said, It is John, whom I b: *607*
6:27 and he went and b him in the prison, *607*
Lk 9: 9 And Herod said, John have I b: but who is *607*
Rev 20: 4 *I saw* the souls of them that were b for *3990*

BEHELD (53) [BEHOLD]
Ge 12:14 the Egyptians b the woman that she *was* 7200
13:10 up his eyes, and b all the plain of Jordan, 7200
19:28 all the land of the plain, and b, and lo, 7200
31: 2 And Jacob b the countenance of Laban, and 7200
48: 8 Israel b Joseph's sons, and said, Who *are* 7200
Nu 21: 9 he b the serpent of brass, he lived. 413+5027
23:21 He hath not b iniquity in Jacob, 5027
Jdg 16:27 women, that b while Samson made sport. 7200
1Sa 26: 5 David b the place where Saul lay, and 7200
1Ch 21:15 the LORD b, and he repented him of 7200
Job 31:26 If I b the sun when it shined, or the moon 7200
Ps 119:158 I b the transgressors, and was grieved; 7200

Ps 142: 4 **b**, but *there was* no man that would know 7200
Pr 7: 7 **b** among the simple ones, I discerned 7200
Ecc 8:17 I **b** all the work of God, that a man cannot 7200
Isa 41:28 For I **b**, and *there was* no man; 7200
Jer 4:23 I **b** the earth, and lo, *it was* without form, 7200
4:24 I **b** the mountains, and lo, they trembled, 7200
4:25 I **b**, and lo, *there was* no man, and all 7200
4:26 I **b**, and lo, the fruitful place *was* a 7200
31:26 Upon this I awaked, and **b**; and my sleep 7200
Eze 1:15 Now as I **b** the living creatures, behold one 7200
8: 2 I **b**, and lo, a likeness as the appearance of 7200
37: 8 when I **b**, lo, the sinews and the flesh came 7200
Da 7: 4 I **b** till the wings thereof were pluckt, and 2370
7: 6 After this I **b**, and lo another, like a 2370
7: 9 I **b** till the thrones were cast *down*, and 2370
7:11 I **b** then because of the voice of the great 2370
7:11 I **b** *even* till the beast *was* slain, and 2370
7:21 I **b**, and the same horn made war with 2370
Hab 3: 6 he **b**, and drove asunder the nations; and 7200
Mt 19:26 But Jesus **b** *them*, and said unto them, *1689*
Mk 9:15 when they **b** him, were greatly amazed, and *1492*
12:41 **b** how the people cast money into *2334*
15:47 Mary *the mother* of Joses **b** where he was *2334*
Lk 10:18 I **b** Satan as lightning fall from heaven. *2334*
19:41 come near, he **b** the city, and wept over it, *1492*
20:17 And he **b** them, and said, What is this then *1689*
22:56 But a certain maid **b** him as he sat by *1492*
23:55 and **b** the sepulchre, and how his body was *2300*
24:12 he **b** the linen clothes laid by themselves, *991*
Jn 1:14 and dwelt among us, (and we **b** his glory, *2300*
1:42 And when Jesus **b** him, he said, Thou art *1689*
Ac 1: 9 he had spoken these *things*, while they **b**, *991*
17:23 For as I passed by, and **b** your devotions, *333*
Rev 5: 6 And I **b**, and lo, in the midst of the throne *1492*
5:11 And I **b**, and I heard the voice of many *1492*
6: 5 And I **b**, and lo a black horse; and he that *1492*
6:12 And I **b** when he had opened the sixth seal, *1492*
7: 9 After this I **b**, and lo, a great multitude, *1492*
8:13 And I **b**, and heard an angel flying through *1492*
11:12 in a cloud; and their enemies **b** them. *2334*
13:11 And I **b** another beast coming up out of *1492*

BEHEMOTH (1)

Job 40:15 Behold now **b**, which I made with thee; 930

BEHIND (74)

Ge 18:10 heard *it in* the tent door, which *was* **b** him. 310
19:17 look not **b** thee, neither stay thou in all 310
19:26 his wife looked back from **b** him, and 310
22:13 behold **b** *him* a ram caught in a thicket by 310
32:18 my lord Esau: and behold, also he *is* **b** us. 310
32:20 Behold, thy servant Jacob *is* **b** us. 310
Ex 10:26 go with us; there shall not a hoof be **left b**; 7604
11: 5 of the maidservant that *is* **b** the mill; 310
14:19 of Israel, removed and went **b** them; 310+4480
14:19 before their face, and stood **b** them: 310+4480
Lev 25:51 If *there be* yet many years ***b***, according unto NIH
Nu 3:23 The families of the Gershonites shall pitch **b** 310
Dt 25:18 *even* all that were feeble **b** thee, when thou 310
Jos 8: 2 lay thee an ambush for the city **b** it. 310+4480
8: 4 wait against the city, *even* **b** the city: 310+4480
8:14 liers in ambush against him **b** the city. 310+4480
8:20 when the men of Ai looked **b** them, they 310
Jdg 18:12 unto this day: behold, *it is* **b** Kirjath-jearim. 310
20:40 the Benjamites looked **b** them, and behold, 310
1Sa 21: 9 it *is here* wrapt in a cloth **b** the ephod: 310
24: 8 when Saul looked **b** him, David stooped 310
30: 9 where those that were **left b** stayed. 3498
30:10 for two hundred abode ***b***, which were so NIH
2Sa 1: 7 And when he looked **b** him, he saw me, and 310
2:20 Abner looked **b** him, and said, *Art* thou 310
2:23 *rib*, that the spear came out **b** him; 310+4480
3:16 her husband went with her along weeping **b** 310
5:23 *but* fetch a compass **b** them, and come upon 310
10: 9 battle was against him before and **b**, 268+4480
13:34 people by the way of the hill side **b** him. 310
1Ki 10:19 and the top of the throne *was* round **b**: 310+4480
14: 9 me to anger, and hast cast me **b** thy back: 310
2Ki 6:32 *is* not the sound of his master's feet **b** him? 310
9:18 turn thee **b** me. And the watchman told, 310+413
9:19 thou to do with peace? turn thee **b** me. 310+413
11: 6 and a third *part* at the gate **b** the guard: 310
1Ch 19:10 the battle was set against him before and **b**, 268
2Ch 13:13 ambushment to come about **b** them: 310+4480
13:13 and the ambushment *was* **b** them. 310+4480
13:14 behold, the battle *was* before and **b**: 268
Ne 4:13 Therefore set I in the lower places **b** 310+4480
4:16 and the rulers *were* **b** all the house of Judah. 310
9:26 cast thy law **b** their backs, and slew thy 310
Ps 50:17 and castest my words **b** thee. 310
139: 5 Thou hast beset me **b** and before, and 268
SS 2: 9 behold, he standeth **b** our wall, he looketh 310
Isa 9:12 Syrians before, and the Philistines **b**; 268+4480
30:21 thine ears shall hear a word **b** thee, 310+4480
38:17 for thou hast cast all my sins **b** thy back. 310
57: 8 **B** the doors also and the posts hast thou set 310
66:17 purify themselves in the gardens **b** one *tree* 310
Eze 3:12 and I heard **b** me a voice of a great rushing, 310
23:35 cast me **b** thy back, therefore bear thou also 310
41:15 the separate place which *was* **b** it, 310+5921
Joel 2: 3 before them; and **b** them a flame burneth: 310
2: 3 and **b** them a desolate wilderness; 310
2:14 and repent, and leave a blessing **b** him; 310
Zec 1: 8 **b** him *were there* red horses, speckled, and 310
Mt 9:20 came **b** *him*, and touched the hem of his *3693*
16:23 and said unto Peter, Get thee **b** me, Satan: *3694*
Mk 5:27 came in the press **b**, and touched his *3693*
8:33 saying, Get thee **b** me, Satan: *3694*
12:19 and leave *his* wife ***b*** *him*, and leave no NIG
Lk 2:43 the child Jesus **tarried b** in Jerusalem; *5278*
4: 8 and said unto him, Get thee **b** me, Satan: *3694*
7:38 And stood at his feet **b** *him* weeping, and *3694*
8:44 Came **b** *him*, and touched the border of his *3693*
1Co 1: 7 So that ye **come b** in no gift; waiting for *5302*
2Co 11: 5 For I suppose *I* was not a whit **b** the very *5302*
12:11 for *in* nothing am I **b** the very chiefest *5302*
Php 3:13 *I do*, forgetting those *things which are* **b**, *3694*
Col 1:24 fill up that which is **b** of the afflictions of *5303*
Rev 1:10 and heard **b** me a great voice, as of a *3694*
4: 6 *were* four beasts full of eyes before and **b**. *3693*

BEHOLD (1326) [BEHELD, BEHOLDEST, BEHOLDETH, BEHOLDING]

Ge 1:29 God said, **B**, I have given you every herb 2009
1:31 that he had made, and **b**, *it was* very good. 2009
3:22 the LORD God said, **B**, the man is 2005
4:14 **B**, thou hast driven me out *this* day from 2005
6:12 upon the earth, and **b**, it was corrupt; 2009
6:13 and **b**, I will destroy them with the earth. 2009
6:17 **b**, I, even I, do bring a flood of waters upon 2009
8:13 looked, and **b**, the face of the ground was 2009
9: 9 **b** I establish my covenant with you and 2009
11: 6 **B**, the people *is* one, and they have all one 2005
12:11 that he said unto Sarai his wife, **B** now, 2009
12:19 now therefore **b** thy wife, take *her*, and 2009
15: 3 Abram said, **B**, to me thou hast given no 2005
15: 4 **b**, the word of the LORD *came* unto him, 2009
15:17 **b** a smoking furnace, and a burning lamp 2009
16: 2 Sarai said unto Abram, **B** now, the LORD 2009
16: 6 said unto Sarai, **B**, thy maid *is* in thy hand; 2009
16:11 **B**, thou *art* with child, and shalt bear a son, 2009
16:14 **b**, *it is* between Kadesh and Bered. 2009
17: 4 *As for* me, **b**, my covenant *is* with thee, and 2009
17:20 **B**, I have blessed him, and will make him 2009
18: 9 Sarah thy wife? And he said, **B**, in the tent. 2009
18:27 Abraham answered and said, **B** now, I have 2009
18:31 he said, **B** now, I have taken upon me to 2009
19: 2 **B** now, my lords, turn in, I pray you, 2009
19: 8 **B** now, I have two daughters which have 2009
19:19 **B** now, thy servant hath found grace in thy 2009
19:20 **B** now, this city *is* near to flee unto, and 2009
19:34 **B**, I lay yesternight with my father: 2005
20: 3 said to him, **B**, thou *art but* a dead man, 2009
20:15 Abimelech said, **B**, my land *is* before thee: 2009
20:16 unto Sarah he said, **B**, I have given thy 2009
20:16 **b**, he *is* to thee a covering of the eyes, 2009
22: 1 Abraham: and he said, **B**, *here* I *am*. 2009
22: 7 he said, **B** the fire and the wood: but 2009
22:13 **b** behind *him* a ram caught in a thicket by 2009
22:20 it was told Abraham, saying, **B**, Milcah, 2009
24:13 **B**, I stand *here* by the well of water; and 2009
24:15 that **b**, Rebekah came out, who was born to 2009
24:30 and **b**, he stood by the camels at the well. 2009
24:43 **B**, I stand by the well of water; and it shall 2009
24:45 I had done speaking in mine heart, **b**, 2009
24:51 **B**, Rebekah *is* before thee, take *her*, and go, 2009
24:63 he lift up his eyes, and saw, and, **b**, 2009
25:24 **b**, *there were* twins in her womb. 2009
25:32 Esau said, **B**, I *am* at the point to die: and 2009
26: 8 saw, and **b**, Isaac *was* sporting with 2009
26: 9 and said, **B**, of a surety she *is* thy wife: 2009
27: 1 My son: and he said unto him, **B**, *here am* I. 2009
27: 2 he said, **B** now, I am old, I know not 2009
27: 6 spake unto Jacob her son, saying, **B**, 2009
27:11 **B**, Esau my brother *is* a hairy man, and 2005
27:36 **b**, now he hath taken away my blessing. 2009
27:37 Isaac answered and said unto Esau, **B**, 2005
27:39 his father answered and said unto him, **B**, 2009
27:42 said unto him, **B**, thy brother Esau, 2009
28:12 **b** a ladder set up on the earth, and the top 2009
28:12 **b** the angels of God ascending and 2009
28:13 **b**, the LORD stood above it, and said, 2009
28:15 **b**, I *am* with thee, and will keep thee in all 2009
29: 2 he looked, and **b** a well in the field, and lo, 2009
29: 6 **b**, Rachel his daughter cometh with 2009
29:25 to pass, that in the morning, **b**, it *was* Leah: 2009
30: 3 she said, **B** my maid Bilhah, go in unto her; 2009
30:34 Laban said, **B**, I would it might be 2005
31: 2 and **b**, it *was* not toward him as before. 2009
31:10 up mine eyes, and saw in a dream, and **b**, 2009
31:51 to Jacob, **B** this heap, and behold *this* pillar, 2009
31:51 to Jacob, Behold this heap, and **b** *this* pillar, 2009
32:18 my lord Esau: and **b**, also he *is* behind us. 2009
32:20 say ye moreover, **B**, thy servant Jacob *is* 2009
33: 1 looked, and **b**, Esau came, and with him 2009
34:21 for the land, **b**, *it is* large enough for them; 2009
37: 7 For, **b**, we *were* binding sheaves in 2009
37: 7 **b**, your sheaves stood round about, and 2009
37: 9 told it his brethren, and said, **B**, I have 2009
37: 9 **b**, the sun and the moon and the eleven 2009
37:15 a *certain* man found him, and **b**, *he was* 2009
37:19 one to another, **B**, this dreamer cometh. 2009
37:25 they lift up their eyes and looked, and **b**, 2009
37:29 **b**, Joseph *was* not in the pit; and he rent his 2009
38:13 **B** thy father in law goeth up to Timnath to 2009
38:23 **b**, I sent this kid, and thou hast not found 2009
38:24 and also, **b**, she *is* with child by whoredom. 2009
38:27 her travail, that, **b**, twins *were* in her womb. 2009
38:29 back his hand, that, **b**, his brother came out: 2009
39: 8 and said unto his master's wife, **B**, 2005
40: 6 looked upon them, and **b**, they *were* sad. 2009
40: 9 said to him, In my dream, **b**, a vine *was* 2009
40:16 unto Joseph, I also *was* in my dream, and **b**, 2009
41: 1 and **b**, he stood by the river. 2009
41: 2 **b**, there came up out of the river seven well 2009
41: 3 **b**, seven other kine came up after them out 2009
41: 5 **b**, seven ears of corn came up upon one 2009
41: 6 **b**, seven thin ears and blasted with the east 2009
41: 7 And Pharaoh awoke, and **b**, *it was* a dream. 2009
41:17 Pharaoh said unto Joseph, In my dream, **b**, 2009
41:18 **b**, there came up out of the river seven 2009
41:19 **b**, seven other kine came up after them, 2009
41:22 I saw in my dream, and **b**, seven ears came 2009
41:23 **b**, seven ears, withered, thin, *and* 2009
41:29 **B**, there come seven years of great plenty 2009
42: 2 he said, **B**, I have heard that there is corn in 2009
42:13 **b**, the youngest *is this* day with our father, 2009
42:22 therefore, **b**, also his blood is required. 2009
42:27 for **b**, it *was* in his sack's mouth. 2009
42:35 that **b**, every man's bundle of money *was* in 2009
Ge 43:21 to the inn, that we opened our sacks, and **b**, 2009
44: 8 **B**, the money, which we found in our 2005
44:16 **b**, we *are* my lord's servants, both we, and 2009
45:12 **b**, your eyes see, and the eyes of my 2009
47: 1 and **b**, they *are* in the land of Goshen. 2009
47:23 **B**, I have bought you *this* day and your land 2005
48: 1 that *one* told Joseph, **B**, thy father *is* sick: 2009
48: 2 *one* told Jacob, and said, **B**, thy son Joseph 2009
48: 4 said unto me, **B**, I will make thee fruitful, 2009
48:21 Israel said unto Joseph, **B**, I die: but 2009
50:18 and they said, **B**, we *be* thy servants. 2009
Ex 1: 9 he said unto his people, **B**, the people of 2009
2: 6 **b**, the babe wept. And she had compassion 2009
2:13 when he went out the second day, **b**, 2009
3: 2 he looked, and **b**, the bush burned with fire, 2009
3: 9 Now therefore, **b**, the cry of the children of 2009
3:13 Moses said unto God, **B**, *when* I come unto 2009
4: 1 Moses answered and said, But **b**, they will 2005
4: 6 when he took it out, **b**, his hand *was* 2009
4: 7 plucked it out of his bosom, and **b**, it was 2009
4:14 also, **b**, he cometh forth to meet thee: and 2009
4:23 **b**, I will slay thy son, *even* thy firstborn. 2009
5: 5 Pharaoh said, **B**, the people of the land now 2005
5:16 **b**, thy servants *are* beaten; but the fault *is* in 2009
6:12 Moses spake before the LORD, saying, **B**, 2005
6:30 **B**, I *am* of uncircumcised lips, and 2005
7:16 and **b**, hitherto thou wouldest not hear. 2009
7:17 **b**, I will smite with the rod that *is* in mine 2009
8: 2 if thou refuse to let *them* go, **b**, I will smite 2009
8:21 Else, if thou wilt not let my people go, **b**, 2009
8:29 Moses said, **B**, I go out from thee, and 2009
9: 3 **B**, the hand of the LORD is upon thy 2009
9: 7 Pharaoh sent, and, **b**, there was not one of 2009
9:18 **B**, to morrow about *this* time I will cause it 2009
10: 4 Else, if thou refuse to let my people go, **b**, 2009
14:10 and **b**, the Egyptians marched after them; 2009
14:17 I, **b**, I will harden the hearts of 2009
16: 4 said the LORD unto Moses, **B**, I will rain 2009
16:10 they looked toward the wilderness, and **b**, 2009
16:14 when the dew that lay was gone up, **b**, 2009
17: 6 **B**, I will stand before thee there upon 2009
23:20 **B**, I send an Angel before thee, to keep thee 2009
24: 8 and said, **B** the blood of the covenant, 2009
24:14 **b**, Aaron and Hur *are* with you: if any man 2009
31: 6 I, **b**, I have given with him Aholiab, the son 2009
32: 9 I have seen this people, and **b**, it *is* a 2009
32:34 **b**, mine Angel shall go before thee: 2009
33:21 the LORD said, **B**, *there is* a place by me, 2009
34:10 he said, **B**, I make a covenant: before all 2009
34:11 **b**, I drive out before thee the Amorite, and 2009
34:30 saw Moses, **b**, the skin of his face shone; 2009
39:43 Moses did look upon all the work, and **b**, 2009
Lev 10:16 goat of the sin offering, and **b**, it was burnt: 2009
10:18 **B**, the blood of it was not brought in within 2005
10:19 Aaron said unto Moses, **B**, *this* day have 2005
13: 5 **b**, *if* the plague in his sight be at a stay, *and* 2009
13: 6 **b**, *if* the plague *be* somewhat dark, and 2009
13: 8 *if* the priest see that **b**, the scab spreadeth in 2009
13:10 the priest shall see *him*: and **b**, *if* the rising 2009
13:13 **b**, *if* the leprosy have covered all his flesh, 2009
13:17 **b**, *if* the plague be turned into white; then 2009
13:20 if, when the priest seeth it, **b**, it *be* in sight 2009
13:21 if the priest look on it, and **b**, *there be* no 2009
13:25 **b**, *if* the hair in the bright spot be turned 2009
13:26 if the priest look on it, and **b**, *there be* no 2009
13:30 **b**, *if* it *be* in sight deeper than the skin; and 2009
13:31 **b**, it *be* not in sight deeper than the skin, 2009
13:32 **b**, *if* the scall spread not, and there be in it 2009
13:34 **b**, *if* the scall be not spread in the skin, 2009
13:36 **b**, *if* the scall be spread in the skin, 2009
13:39 **b**, *if* the bright spots in the skin of their 2009
13:43 **b**, *if* the rising of the sore *be* white reddish 2009
13:53 if the priest shall look, and **b**, the plague be 2009
13:55 **b**, *if* the plague have not changed his 2009
13:56 if the priest look, and **b**, the plague *be* 2009
14: 3 the priest shall look, and **b**, *if* the plague of 2009
14:37 he shall look on the plague, and **b**, *if* 2009
14:39 **b**, *if* the plague be spread in the walls of 2009
14:44 the priest shall come and look, and **b**, *if* 2009
14:48 shall come in, and look *upon it*, and **b**, 2009
25:20 **b**, we shall not sow, nor gather in our 2005
Nu 3:12 I, **b**, I have taken the Levites from among 2009
12: 8 the similitude of the LORD shall he **b**: 5027
12:10 **b**, Miriam *became* leprous, *white* as snow: 2009
12:10 upon Miriam, and **b**, *she was* leprous. 2009
16:42 **b**, the cloud covered it, and the glory of 2009
16:47 **b**, the plague was begun among the people: 2009
17: 8 **b**, the rod of Aaron for the house of Levi 2009
17:12 **B**, we die, we perish, we all perish. 2005
18: 6 I, **b**, I have taken your brethren the Levites 2009
18: 8 the LORD spake unto Aaron, **B**, I also 2009
18:21 **b**, I have given the children of Levi all 2009
20:16 **b**, we *are* in Kadesh, a city in the uttermost 2009
22: 5 to call him, saying, **B**, there is a people 2009
22: 5 **b**, they cover the face of the earth, and 2009
22:11 **B**, *there is* a people come out of Egypt, 2009
22:32 **b**, I went out to withstand thee, because 2009
23: 9 rocks I see him, and from the hills I **b** him: 7789
23:11 and **b**, thou hast blessed *them* altogether. 2009
23:17 when he came to him, **b**, he stood by his 2009
23:20 **B**, I have received *commandment* to bless: 2009
23:24 **B**, the people shall rise up as a great lion, 2005
24:10 I called thee to curse mine enemies, and **b**, 2009
24:14 now **b**, I go unto my people: come 2009
24:17 I shall **b** him, but not nigh: there shall come 7789
25: 6 **b**, one of the children of Israel came and 2009
25:12 Wherefore say, **B**, I give unto him my 2009
31:16 **B**, these caused the children of Israel, 2005
32: 1 the land of Gilead, that **b**, the place *was* a 2009
32:14 **b**, ye are risen up in your fathers' stead, 2009
32:23 if ye will not do so, **b**, ye have sinned 2009
Dt 1: 8 **B**, I have set the land before you: go in and 7200
1:10 your God hath multiplied you, and **b**, 2009
1:21 **B**, the LORD thy God hath set the land 7200
2:24 **b**, I have given into thy hand Sihon 7200

Dt 2:31 B, I have begun to give Sihon and his land 7200
3:11 b, his bedstead *was* a bedstead of iron; *is* it 2009
3:27 eastward, and b *it* with thine eyes: 7200
4: 5 B, I have taught you statutes and 7200
5:24 ye said, B, the LORD our God hath 2005
9:13 saying, I have seen this people, and b, it *is* 2009
9:16 I looked, and b, ye had sinned against 2009
10:14 B, the heaven and the heaven of heavens *is* 2005
11:26 B, I set before you *this* day a blessing and 7200
13:14 b, *if it be* truth, *and* the thing certain, *that* 2009
17: 4 and b, *it is* true, *and* the thing certain, 2009
19:18 b, *if* the witness *be* a false witness, *and* 2009
26:10 now, b, I have brought the firstfruits of 2009
31:14 the LORD said unto Moses, B, thy days 2005
31:16 B, thou shalt sleep with thy fathers; 2009
31:27 b, while I am yet alive with you *this* day, 2005
32:49 b the land of Canaan, which I give unto 7200
Jos 2: 2 it was told the king of Jericho, saying, B, 2009
2:18 B, *when* we come into the land, thou shalt 2009
3:11 B, the ark of the covenant, *even* the Lord of 2009
5:13 that he lift up his eyes and looked, and b, 2009
7:21 b, they *are* hid in the earth in the midst of 2009
7:22 b, *it was* hid in his tent, and the silver under 2009
8: 4 he commanded them, saying, B, ye shall lie 7200
8:20 they saw, and b, the smoke of the city 2009
9:12 but now, b, it is dry, and it is mouldy: 2009
9:13 we filled, *were* new; and b, they be rent: 2009
9:25 now, b, we *are* in thine hand: as it seemeth 2009
14:10 And now b, the LORD hath kept me alive, 2009
22:11 B, the children of Reuben and the children 2009
22:28 that we may say *again,* B the pattern of 7200
23: 4 B, I have divided unto you *by lot* these 7200
23:14 b, *this* day I am going the way of all 2009
24:27 Joshua said unto all the people, B, this 2009
Jdg 1: 2 b, I have delivered the land into his hand. 2009
3:24 when they saw that b, the doors of 2009
3:25 b, he opened not the doors of the parlour; 2009
3:25 they took a key, and opened *them:* and b, 2009
4:22 b, as Barak pursued Sisera, Jael came out 2009
4:22 when he came into her *tent,* b, Sisera lay 2009
6:15 b, my family *is* poor in Manasseh, and I *am* 2009
6:28 b, the altar of Baal was cast down, and 2009
6:37 B, I will put a fleece of wool in the floor; 2009
7:13 when Gideon was come, b, *there was* a 2009
7:13 and said, B, I dreamed a dream, and lo, 2009
7:17 b, when I come to the outside of the camp, 2009
8:15 said, B Zebah and Zalmunna, with whom 2009
9:31 saying, B, Gaal the son of Ebed and 2009
9:31 and b, they fortify the city against thee. 2009
9:33 b, *when* he and the people that *is* with him 2009
9:36 Gaal saw the people, he said to Zebul, B, 2009
9:43 laid wait in the field, and looked, and b, 2009
11:34 came *to* Mizpeh unto his house, and b, 2009
13: 3 said unto her, B now, thou *art* barren, and 2009
13: 7 B, thou *shalt* conceive, and bear a son; 2009
13:10 shewed her husband, and said unto him, B, 2009
14: 5 b, a young lion roared against him. 2009
14: 8 b, *there was* a swarm of bees and honey in 2009
14:16 he said unto her, B, I have not told *it* my 2009
16:10 B, thou hast mocked me, and told me lies: 2009
17: 2 also in mine ears, b, the silver *is* with me; 2009
18: 9 have seen the land, and b, it *is* very good: 2009
18:12 unto this day: b, *it is* behind Kirjath-jearim. 2009
19: 9 the damsel's father, said unto him, B now, 2009
19: 9 b, the day groweth to an end, lodge here, 2009
19:16 b, there came an old man from his work out 2009
19:22 b, the men of the city, certain sons of 2009
19:24 B, *here is* my daughter a maiden, and 2009
19:27 b, the woman his concubine *was* fallen 2009
20: 7 B, ye *are* all children of Israel; give here 2009
20:40 the Benjamites looked behind them, and b, 2009
21: 8 b, there came none to the camp from 2009
21: 9 For the people were numbered, and b, 2009
21:19 they said, B, *there is* a feast of the LORD 2009
21:21 see, and b, if the daughters of Shiloh come 2009
Ru 1:15 she said, B, thy sister in law is gone back 2009
2: 4 b, Boaz came from Beth-lehem, and 2009
3: 2 B, he winnoweth barley to night in 2009
3: 8 and b, a woman lay *at* his feet. 2009
4: 1 b, the kinsman of whom Boaz spake came 2009
1Sa 2:31 B, the days come, that I will cut off thine 2009
3:11 to Samuel, B, I will do a thing in Israel, 2009
5: 3 of Ashdod arose early on the morrow, b, 2009
5: 4 they arose early on the morrow morning, b, 2009
8: 5 B, thou art old, and thy sons walk not in thy 2009
9: 6 he said unto him, B now, *there is* in this 2009
9: 7 b, *if* we go, what shall we bring the man? 2009
9: 8 servant answered Saul again, and said, B, 2009
9:12 and said, He is; b, *he is* before you: 2009
9:14 b, Samuel came out against them, for to go 2009
9:17 B the man whom I spake to thee of: 2009
9:24 *Samuel* said, B that which is left; set *it* 2009
10: 8 b, I will come down unto thee, to offer 2009
10:10 the hill, b, a company of prophets met him; 2009
10:11 all that knew him beforetime saw that b, 2009
10:22 the LORD answered, B, he hath hid 2009
11: 5 b, Saul came after the herd out of the field; 2009
12: 1 Samuel said unto all Israel, B, I have 2009
12: 2 now b, the king walketh before you: and 2009
12: 2 grayheaded; and b, my sons *are* with you: 2009
12: 3 B, here I *am:* witness against me before 2009
12:13 therefore b the king whom ye have chosen, 2009
12:13 and b, the LORD hath set a king over you. 2009
13:10 the burnt offering, b, Samuel came; 2009
14: 7 b, I *am* with thee according to thy heart. 2009
14: 8 said Jonathan, B, we will pass over unto 2009
14:11 the Philistines said, B, the Hebrews come 2009
14:16 b, the multitude melted away, and 2009
14:17 b Jonathan and his armourbearer *were* not 2009
14:20 b, every man's sword was against his 2009
14:26 come into the wood, b the honey dropped; 2009
14:33 they told Saul, saying, B, the people sin 2009
15:12 Saul came to Carmel, and b, 2009
15:22 B, to obey *is* better than sacrifice, *and* 2009
16:11 the youngest, and b, he keepeth the sheep 2009

1Sa 16:15 Saul's servants said unto him, B now, 2009
16:18 answered one of the servants, and said, B, 2009
17:23 as he talked with them, b, there came up 2009
18:17 said to David, B my elder daughter Merab, 2009
18:22 say, B, the king hath delight in thee, and 2009
19:16 come in, b *there was* an image in the bed, 2009
19:19 it was told Saul, saying, B, David *is* at 2009
19:22 *one* said, B, *they be* at Naioth in Ramah. 2009
20: 2 b, my father will do nothing *either* great or 2009
20: 5 B, to morrow *is* the new moon, and 2009
20:12 *or* the third *day,* and b, *if there be* good 2009
20:21 b, I will send a lad, *saying,* Go, find out 2009
20:21 If I expressly say unto the lad, B, 2009
20:22 young man, B, the arrows *are* beyond thee; 2009
20:23 matter which thou and I have spoken of, b, 2009
21: 9 whom thou slewest in the valley of Elah, b, 2009
23: 1 they told David, saying, B, the Philistines 2009
23: 3 unto him, B, we *be* afraid here in Judah: 2009
24: 1 that it was told him, saying, B, David *is* in 2009
24: 4 B the day of which the LORD said unto 2009
24: 4 B, I will deliver thine enemy into thine 2009
24: 9 saying, B, David seeketh thy hurt? 2009
24:10 B, this day thine eyes have seen how that 2009
24:20 now b, I know well that thou shalt surely 2009
25:14 men told Abigail, Nabal's wife, saying, B, 2009
25:19 Go on before me; b, I come after you. 2009
25:20 b, David and his men came down against 2009
25:36 b, he held a feast in his house, like the feast 2009
25:41 herself *on her* face to the earth, and said, B, 2009
26: 7 b, Saul lay sleeping within the trench, and 2009
26:21 b, I have played the fool, and have erred 2009
26:22 David answered and said, B, the king's 2009
26:24 b, as thy life was much set by this day in 2009
28: 7 his servants said to him, B, *there is* a 2009
28: 9 the woman said unto him, B, thou knowest 2009
28:21 he was sore troubled, and said unto him, B, 2009
30: 3 to the city, and b, *it was* burnt with fire; 2009
30:16 b *they were* spread abroad upon all 2009
30:26 B a present for you of the spoil of 2009
2Sa 1: 2 came even to pass on the third day, that b, 2009
1: 6 b, Saul leaned upon his spear; 2009
1:18 b, *it is* written in the book of Jasher.) 2009
3:12 b, my hand *shall be* with thee, to bring 2009
3:22 b, the servants of David and Joab came 2009
3:24 b, Abner came unto thee; why *is* it *that* 2009
4: 8 B the head of Ish-bosheth the son of Saul 2009
4:10 When one told me, saying, B, Saul is dead, 2009
5: 1 spake, saying, B, we *are* thy bone and 2009
9: 4 B, he *is in* the house of Machir, the son of 2009
9: 6 And he answered, B thy servant. 2009
12:11 Thus saith the LORD, B, I will raise up 2009
12:18 for they said, B, while the child was *yet* 2009
13:24 said, B now, thy servant hath 2009
13:34 watch lift up his eyes, and looked, and b, 2009
13:35 said unto the king, B, the king's sons come: 2009
13:36 that b, the king's sons came, and lift up 2009
14: 7 b, the whole family is risen against thine 2009
14:21 unto Joab, B now, I have done this thing: 2009
14:32 B, I sent unto thee, saying, Come hither, 2009
15:15 the king's servants said unto the king, B, 2009
15:26 b, *here am* I, let him do to me as seemeth 2009
15:32 b, Hushai the Archite *came* to meet him 2009
15:36 B, *they have* there with them their two 2009
16: 1 David was a little past the top *of the hill,* b, 2009
16: 3 unto the king, B, he abideth at Jerusalem: 2009
16: 4 said the king to Ziba, B, thine *are* all that 2009
16: 5 when king David came to Bahurim, b, 2009
16: 8 and, b, thou *art taken* to thy mischief, 2009
16:11 and to all his servants, B, my son, 2009
17: 9 B, he is hid now in some pit, or in some 2009
18:10 man saw *it,* and told Joab, and said, B, 2009
18:11 b, thou sawest *him,* and why didst thou not 2009
18:24 and looked, and b a man running alone. 2009
18:26 and said, B *another* man running alone. 2009
18:31 b, Cushi came; and Cushi said, Tidings, 2009
19: 1 b, the king weepeth and mourneth for 2009
19: 8 b, the king doth sit in the gate. 2009
19:20 therefore, b, I am come the first *this* day of 2009
19:37 b thy servant Chimham; let him go over 2009
19:41 b, all the men of Israel came to the king, 2009
20:21 the woman said unto Joab, B, his head *shall* 2009
24:22 b, *here be* oxen for burnt sacrifice, and 7200
1Ki 1:14 B, while thou yet talkest there with 2009
1:18 now b, Adonijah reigneth; and now, 2009
1:23 told the king, saying, B Nathan the prophet. 2009
1:25 b, they eat and drink before him, and say, 2009
1:42 while he yet spake, b, Jonathan the son of 2009
1:51 it was told Solomon, saying, B, 2009
2: 8 b, *thou hast* with thee Shimei the son of 2009
2:29 of the LORD; and b, *he is* by the altar. 2009
2:39 they told Shimei, saying, B, thy servants *be* 2009
3:12 B, I have done according to thy word: lo, 2009
3:15 Solomon awoke; and b, *it was* a dream. 2009
3:21 to give my child suck, b, it was dead: 2009
3:21 b, it was not my son, which I did bear. 2009
5: 5 b, I purpose to build a house unto the name 2009
8:27 b, the heaven and heaven of heavens 2009
10: 7 I came, and mine eyes had seen *it:* and b, 2009
11:22 But what *hast* thou lacked with me, that b, 2009
11:31 thus saith the LORD, the God of Israel, B, 2009
12:28 b thy gods, O Israel, which brought thee up 2009
13: 1 b, there came a man of God out of Judah by 2009
13: 2 B, a child *shall be* born unto the house of 2009
13: 3 B, the altar *shall be* rent, and the ashes that 2009
13:25 b, men passed by, and saw the carcase cast 2009
14: 2 b, there *is* Ahijah the prophet, which told 2009
14: 5 the LORD said unto Ahijah, B, the wife of 2009
14:10 Therefore, b, I will bring evil upon 2009
14:19 b they *are* written in the book of 2009
15:19 b, I have sent unto thee a present of silver 2009
16: 3 B, I will take away the posterity of Baasha, 2009
17: 9 b, I have commanded a widow woman 2009
17:10 when he came to the gate of the city, b, 2009
17:12 b, I *am* gathering two sticks, that I may go 2009
18: 7 Obadiah was in the way, b Elijah met him: 2009

1Ki 18: 8 I *am:* go, tell thy lord, B, Elijah *is here.* 2009
18:11 Go, tell thy lord, B, Elijah *is here.* 2009
18:14 Go, tell thy lord, B, Elijah *is here:* and 2009
18:44 B, there ariseth a little cloud out of the sea, 2009
19: 5 b then, an angel touched him, and 2009+2088
19: 6 he looked, and b, *there was* a cake baken 2009
19: 9 b, the word of the LORD *came* to him, 2009
19:11 b, the LORD passed by, and a great and 2009
19:13 b, *there came* a voice unto him, and said, 2009
20:13 b, there came a prophet unto Ahab king of 2009
20:13 b, I will deliver it into thine hand *this* day; 2009
20:31 his servants said unto him, B now, we have 2009
20:36 b, as soon as thou art departed from me, a 2009
20:39 b, a man turned aside, and brought a man 2009
21:18 b, *he is* in the vineyard of Naboth, 2009
21:21 B, I will bring evil upon thee, and will take 2009
22:13 Micaiah spake unto him, saying, B now, 2009
22:23 Now therefore b, the LORD hath put a 2009
22:25 Micaiah said, B, thou shalt see in that day, 2009
2Ki 1: 9 b, he sat on the top of a hill. And he spake 2009
1:14 B, there came fire down from heaven, and 2009
2:11 *as* they still went on, and talked, that b, 2009
2:16 they said unto him, B now, there be with 2009
2:19 B, I pray thee, the situation of this city *is* 2009
3:20 when the meat offering was offered, that b, 2009
4: 9 she said unto her husband, B now, 2009
4:13 And he said unto him, Say now unto her, B, 2009
4:25 his servant, B, *yonder is* that Shunammite: 2009
4:32 b, the child was dead, *and* laid upon his 2009
5: 6 Now when this letter is come unto thee, b, 2009
5:11 and went away, and said, B, I thought, 2009
5:15 he said, B, now I know that *there is* no God 2009
5:20 servant of Elisha the man of God, said, B, 2009
5:22 My master hath sent me, saying, B, 2009
6: 1 of the prophets said unto Elisha, B now, 2009
6:13 it was told him, saying, B, *he is* in Dothan. 2009
6:15 gone forth, b, a host compassed the city 2009
6:17 b, the mountain was full *of* horses and 2009
6:20 and b, *they were* in the midst of Samaria. 2009
6:25 b, they besieged it, until an ass's head was 2009
6:30 the wall, and the people looked, and b, 2009
6:33 while he yet talked with them, b, 2009
6:33 he said, B, this evil *is* of the LORD; 2009
7: 2 said, B, *if* the LORD would make 2009
7: 2 he said, B, thou shalt see *it* with thine eyes, 2009
7: 5 camp of Syria, b, *there was* no man there. 2009
7:10 b, *there was* no man there, neither voice of 2009
7:13 that remain, which are left in the city, (b, 2009
7:13 b, *I say,* they *are even* as all the multitude 2009
7:19 answered the man of God, and said, Now b, 2009
7:19 he said, B, thou shalt see *it* with thine eyes, 2009
8: 5 that b, the woman, whose son he had 2009
9: 5 when he came, b, the captains of the host 2009
10: 4 said, B, two kings stood not before him: 2009
10: 9 b, I conspired against my master, and 2009
11:14 when she looked, b, the king stood by a 2009
13:21 that b, they spied a band *of men;* and 2009
15:11 the rest of the acts of Zachariah, b, they *are* 2009
15:15 and his conspiracy which he made, b, 2009
15:26 the acts of Pekahiah, and all that he did, b, 2009
15:31 of the acts of Pekah, and all that he did, b, 2009
17:26 b, they slay them, because they know not 2009
18:21 Now b, thou trustest upon the staff of this 2009
19: 7 B, I will send a blast upon him, and he shall 2009
19: 9 B, he is come out to fight against thee: 2009
19:11 B, thou hast heard what the kings of 2009
19:35 the morning, b, they *were* all dead corpses. 2009
20: 5 b, I will heal thee: on the third day thou 2009
20:17 B, the days come, that all that *is* in thine 2009
21:12 B, I *am* bringing *such* evil upon Jerusalem 2009
22:16 Thus saith the LORD, B, I will bring evil 2009
22:20 B therefore, I will gather thee unto thy 2009
1Ch 9: 1 b, they *were* written in the book of 2009
11: 1 B, we *are* thy bone and thy flesh. 2009
11:25 B, he was honourable among the thirty, but 2009
22: 9 B, a son *shall be* born to thee, who shall be 2009
22:14 Now b, in my trouble I have prepared for 2009
28:21 b, the courses of the priests and the Levites, 2009
29:29 the acts of David the king, first and last, b, 2009
2Ch 2: 4 B, I build a house to the name of 2009
2: 8 b, my servants *shall be* with thy servants, 2009
2:10 b, I will give to thy servants, the hewers 2009
6:18 b, heaven and the heaven of heavens 2009
9: 6 I came, and mine eyes had seen *it:* and b, 2009
13:12 b, God *himself is* with us for *our* captain, 2009
13:14 b, the battle *was* before and behind: 2009
16: 3 b, I have sent thee silver and gold; go, 2009
16:11 b, the acts of Asa, first and last, lo, they *are* 2009
18:12 to call Micaiah spake to him, saying, B, 2009
18:22 Now therefore b, the LORD hath put a 2009
18:24 Micaiah said, B, thou shalt see on that day 2009
19:11 b, Amariah the chief priest *is* over you in 2009
20: 2 b, they *be* in Hazazon-tamar, which *is* 2009
20:10 now b, the children of Ammon and Moab 2009
20:11 B, I say, *how* they reward us, to come to 2009
20:16 b, they come up by the cliff of Ziz; and 2009
20:24 they looked unto the multitude, and b, 2009
20:34 b they *are* written in the book of Jehu 2009
21:14 B, *with* a great plague will the LORD 2009
23: 3 he said unto them, B, the king's son shall 2009
23:13 she looked, and b, the king stood at his 2009
24:27 b they *are* written in the story of the book 2009
25:26 rest of the acts of Amaziah, first and last, b, 2009
26:20 and all the priests, looked upon him, and b, 2009
28: 9 B, because the LORD God of your fathers 2009
28:26 his acts and of all his ways, first and last, b, 2009
29:19 have we prepared and sanctified, and b, 2009
32:32 the acts of Hezekiah, and his goodness, b, 2009
33:18 b, they *are written* in the book of the kings 2009
33:19 b, they *are* written among the sayings of 2009
34:24 Thus saith the LORD, B, I will bring evil 2009
34:28 B, I will gather thee to thy fathers, and 2009
35:25 and b, they *are* written in the lamentations. 2009
35:27 his deeds, first and last, b, they *are* written 2009
36: 8 he did, and that which was found in him, b, 2009

Ezr 9:15 **b**, we *are* before thee in our trespasses: 2009
Ne 9:36 **B**, we *are* servants *this* day, and *for* the land 2009
9:36 eat the fruit thereof and the good thereof, **b**, 2009
Est 6: 5 unto him, **B**, Haman standeth in the court. 2009
7: 9 said before the king, **B** also, 2009
8: 7 the queen and to Mordecai the Jew, **B**, 2009
Job 1:12 **B**, all that he hath *is* in thy power; 2009
1:19 **b**, there came a great wind from 2009
2: 6 said unto Satan, **B**, he *is* in thine hand; 2009
4: 3 **B**, thou hast instructed many, and thou hast 2009
4:18 **B**, he put no trust in his servants; and his 2005
5:17 **B**, happy *is* the man whom God correcteth: 2009
8:19 **B**, this *is* the joy of his way, and out of 2005
8:20 **B**, God will not cast away a perfect *man,* 2005
9:12 **B**, he taketh away, who can hinder him? 2005
12:14 **B**, he breaketh down, and it cannot be built 2005
12:15 **B**, he withholdeth the waters, and they dry 2005
13:18 **B** now, I have ordered *my* cause; I know 2009
15:15 **B**, he putteth no trust in his saints; yea, 2005
16:19 **b** my witness *is* in heaven, and my record *is* 2009
19: 7 **B**, I cry out *of* wrong, but I am not heard: 2005
19:27 and mine eyes shall **b**, and not another; 7200
20: 9 neither shall his place any more **b** him. 7789
21:27 **B**, I know your thoughts, and the devices 2005
22:12 **b** the height of the stars, how high they are. 7200
23: 8 **B**, I go forward, but he *is* not *there;* and 2005
23: 9 I cannot **b** *him:* he hideth *himself* on 2372
24: 5 **B**, *as* wild asses in the desert, go they forth 2005
25: 5 **B** *even* to the moon, and it shineth not; yea, 2005
27:12 **B**, all ye yourselves have seen *it;* why then 2005
28:28 **B**, the fear of the Lord, that *is* wisdom; 2005
31:35 **b**, my desire *is, that* the Almighty would 2005
32:11 **B**, I waited for your words; I gave ear to 2005
32:12 Yea, I attended unto you, and **b**, *there was* 2009
32:19 **B**, my belly *is* as wine *which* hath no vent; 2009
33: 2 **B** now I have opened my mouth, my tongue 2009
33: 6 **B**, I *am* according to thy wish in God's 2005
33: 7 **B**, my terror shall not make thee afraid, 2009
33:10 **B**, he findeth occasions against me, 2005
33:12 **B**, *in* this thou art not just: I will answer 2005
34:29 he hideth *his* face, who then can **b** him? 7789
35: 5 **b** the clouds *which* are higher than thou. 7789
36: 5 **B**, God *is* mighty, and despiseth not *any: he* 2005
36:22 **B**, God exalteth by his power: who teacheth 2005
36:24 that thou magnify his work, which men **b**. 7891
36:25 man may see it; man may **b** *it* afar off. 5027
36:26 **B**, God *is* great, and we know *him* not, 2005
36:30 **B**, he spreadeth his light upon it, and 2005
39:29 seeketh the prey, *and* her eyes **b** afar off. 5027
40: 4 **B**, I am vile; what shall I answer thee? 2005
40:11 **b** every one *that is* proud, and abase him. 7200
40:15 **B** now behemoth, which I made with thee; 2009
40:23 **B**, he drinketh up a river, *and* hasteth not: 2005
41: 9 **B**, the hope of him is in vain: shall *not one* 2005
Ps 7:14 **B**, he travaileth with iniquity, and 2009
11: 4 his eyes **b**, his eyelids try, the children of 2372
11: 7 his countenance doth **b** the upright. 2372
17: 2 let thine eyes **b** the things that are equal. 2372
17:15 *for* me, I will **b** thy face in righteousness: 2372
27: 4 to **b** the beauty of the LORD, and 2372
33:18 **B**, the eye of the LORD *is* upon them that 2009
37:37 Mark the perfect *man,* and **b** the upright: 7200
39: 5 **B**, thou hast made my days *as* a 2009
46: 8 Come, **b** the works of the LORD, 2372
51: 5 **B**, I was shapen in iniquity; and in sin did 2005
51: 6 **B**, thou desirest truth in the inward parts: 2005
54: 4 **B**, God *is* mine helper: the Lord *is* with 2009
59: 4 without *my* fault: awake to help me, and **b**. 7200
59: 7 **B**, they belch out with their mouth: 2009
66: 7 his power for ever; his eyes **b** the nations: 6822
73:12 **B**, these *are* the ungodly, who prosper in 2009
73:15 **B**, I should offend *against* the generation of 2009
78:20 **B**, he smote the rock, that the waters 2005
80:14 from heaven, and **b**, and visit this vine; 7200
84: 9 **B**, O God our shield, and look upon 7200
87: 4 **b** Philistia, and Tyre, with Ethiopia; 2009
91: 8 Only with thine eyes shalt thou **b** and 5027
102:19 from heaven did the LORD **b** the earth; 5027
113: 6 Who humbleth *himself* to **b** *the things that* 7200
119:18 that I may **b** wondrous *things* out of thy 5027
119:40 **B**, I have longed after thy precepts: 2009
121: 4 **B**, he that keepeth Israel shall neither 2009
123: 2 **B**, as the eyes of servants *look* unto 2009
128: 4 **B**, that thus shall the man be blessed that 2009
133: 1 **B**, how good and how pleasant *it is* for 2009
134: 1 **B**, bless ye the LORD, all ye servants of 2009
139: 8 if I make my bed in hell, **b**, thou *art there.* 2009
Pr 1:23 **b**, I will pour out my spirit unto you, I will 2009
7:10 **b**, there met him a woman *with* the attire of 2009
11:31 **B**, the righteous shall be recompensed in 2005
23:33 Thine eyes shall **b** strange *women,* and 7200
24:12 If thou sayest, **B**, we knew it not; doth not 2005
Ecc 1:14 and **b**, all *is* vanity and vexation of spirit. 2009
2: 1 enjoy pleasure: and **b**, this also *is* vanity. 2009
2:11 **b**, all *was* vanity and vexation of spirit, and 2009
2:12 I turned myself to **b** wisdom, and madness, 7200
4: 1 **b**, the tears of such as were oppressed, and 2009
5:18 **B** *that* which I have seen: *it is* good and 2009
7:27 **B**, this have I found, saith the Preacher, 7200
11: 7 a pleasant *thing it is* for the eyes to **b** 7200
SS 1:15 **B**, thou *art* fair, my love; behold, thou *art* 2009
1:15 thou *art* fair, my love; **b**, thou *art* fair; 2009
1:16 **B**, thou *art* fair, my beloved, yea, pleasant: 2009
2: 8 **b**, he cometh leaping upon the mountains, 2009
2: 9 **b**, he standeth behind our wall, he looketh 2009
3: 7 **B** his bed, which *is* Solomon's; 2009
3:11 **b** king Solomon with the crown where*with* 7200
4: 1 **B**, thou *art* fair, my love; behold, thou *art* 2009
4: 1 thou *art* fair, my love; **b**, thou *art* fair; 2009
Isa 3: 1 For **b**, the Lord, the LORD of hosts, 2009
5: 7 he looked for judgment, but **b** oppression; 2009
5: 7 for righteousness, but **b** a cry. 2009
5:26 and **b**, they shall come with speed swiftly: 2009
5:30 **b** darkness *and* sorrow, and the light is 2009
7:14 **B**, a Virgin shall conceive, and bear a Son, 2009

Isa 8: 7 Now therefore **b**, the Lord bringeth up 2009
8:18 **B**, I and the children whom the LORD 2009
8:22 **b** trouble and darkness, dimness of anguish; 2009
10:33 **B**, the Lord, the LORD of hosts, shall lop 2009
12: 2 **B**, God *is* my salvation; I will trust, and 2009
13: 9 **B**, the day of the LORD cometh, 2009
13:17 **B**, I will stir up the Medes against them, 2009
17: 1 **B**, Damascus *is* taken away from *being* a 2009
17:14 **b** at eveningtide trouble; *and* before 2009
19: 1 **B**, the LORD rideth upon a swift cloud, 2009
20: 6 say in that day, **B**, such *is* our expectation, 2009
21: 9 **b**, here cometh a chariot of men, *with* a 2009
22:13 **b** joy and gladness, slaying oxen, and 2009
22:17 **B**, the LORD will carry thee away with a 2009
23:13 **B** the land of the Chaldeans; this people 2005
24: 1 **B**, the LORD maketh the earth empty, and 2009
26:10 and will not **b** the majesty of the LORD. 7200
26:21 For **b**, the LORD cometh out of his place 2009
28: 2 **B**, the Lord hath a mighty and 2009
28:16 Therefore thus saith the Lord GOD, **B**, 2009
29: 8 a hungry *man* dreameth, and **b**, he eateth; 2009
29: 8 a thirsty *man* dreameth, and **b**, he drinketh; 2009
29: 8 **b**, *he is* faint, and his soul hath appetite: 2009
29:14 Therefore, **b**, I will proceed to do a 2009
30:27 **B**, the name of the LORD cometh from 2009
32: 1 **B**, a king shall reign in righteousness, and 2005
33: 7 **B**, their valiant ones shall cry without: 2005
33:17 they shall **b** the land that is very far off. 7200
34: 5 **b**, it shall come down upon Idumea, and 2009
35: 4 **b**, your God will come *with* vengeance, 2009
37: 7 **B**, I will send a blast upon him, and he shall 2009
37:11 **B**, thou hast heard what the kings of 2009
37:36 the morning, **b**, they *were* all dead corpses. 2009
38: 5 **b**, I will add unto thy days fifteen years. 2009
38: 8 **B**, I will bring again the shadow of 2009
38:11 I shall **b** man no more with the inhabitants 5027
38:17 **B**, for peace I had great bitterness: but 2009
39: 6 **B**, the days come, that all that *is* in thine 2009
40: 9 say unto the cities of Judah, **B** your God. 2009
40:10 **B**, the Lord GOD will come with strong 2009
40:10 **b**, his reward *is* with him, and his work 2009
40:15 **B**, the nations *are* as a drop of a bucket, and 2005
40:15 **b**, he taketh up the isles as a very little 2005
40:26 **b** who hath created these *things,* that 7200
41:11 **B**, all they that were incensed against thee 2005
41:15 **B**, I will make thee a new sharp threshing 2009
41:23 that we may be dismayed, and **b** *it* together. 7200
41:24 **B**, ye *are* of nothing, and your work of 2005
41:27 The first *shall say* to Zion, **B**, behold them: 2009
41:27 The first *shall say* to Zion, Behold, **b** them: 2009
41:29 **B**, they *are* all vanity; their works *are* 2005
42: 1 **B** my servant, whom I uphold; mine elect, 2005
42: 9 **B**, the former *things* are come to pass, and 2009
43:19 **B**, I will do a new *thing;* now it shall spring 2009
44:11 **B**, all his fellows shall be ashamed: and 2005
47:14 **B**, they shall be as stubble; the fire shall 2009
48: 7 lest thou shouldest say, **B**, I knew them. 2009
48:10 **B**, I have refined thee, but not with silver; 2009
49:12 **B**, these shall come from far: and lo, 2009
49:16 **B**, I have graven thee upon the palms of *my* 2005
49:18 Lift up thine eyes round about, and **b**: 7200
49:21 **B**, I was left alone; these, where *had* they 2005
49:22 Thus saith the Lord GOD, **B**, I will lift up 2009
50: 1 **B**, for your iniquities have you sold 2005
50: 2 **b**, at my rebuke I dry up the sea, I make 2005
50: 9 **B**, the Lord GOD will help me; who *is* he 2005
50:11 **B**, all ye that kindle a fire, that compass 2005
51:22 *that* pleadeth the cause of his people, **B**, 2009
52: 6 day that I *am* he that doth speak: **b**, *it is* I. 2009
52:13 **B**, my servant shall deal prudently, he shall 2009
54:11 tossed with tempest, *and* not comforted, **b**, 2009
54:15 **B**, they shall surely gather together, *but* 2005
54:16 **B**, I have created the smith that bloweth 2009
55: 4 **B**, I have given him *for* a witness to 2005
55: 5 **B**, thou shalt call a nation *that* thou knowest 2005
56: 3 let the eunuch say, **B**, I *am* a dry tree. 2005
58: 3 **B**, in the day of your fast you find pleasure, 2005
58: 4 **B**, ye fast for strife and debate, and to smite 2005
59: 1 **B**, the LORD'S hand is not shortened, 2005
59: 9 we wait for light, but **b** obscurity; 2009
60: 2 For **b**, the darkness shall cover the earth, 2009
62:11 **B**, the LORD hath proclaimed unto 2009
62:11 daughter of Zion, **B**, thy salvation cometh; 2009
62:11 **b**, his reward *is* with him, and his work 2009
63:15 **b** from the habitation of thy holiness and 7200
64: 5 **b**, thou art wroth; for we have sinned: 2005
64: 9 **b**, see, we beseech thee, we *are* all thy 2005
65: 1 I said, **B** me, behold me, unto a nation *that* 2009
65: 1 I said, Behold me, **b** me, unto a nation *that* 2009
65: 6 **B**, *it is* written before me: I will not keep 2009
65:13 **B**, my servants shall eat, but ye shall be 2009
65:13 **b**, my servants shall drink, but ye shall be 2009
65:13 **b**, my servants shall rejoice, but ye shall be 2009
65:14 **B**, my servants shall sing for joy of heart, 2009
65:17 For, **b**, I create new heavens and a new 2009
65:18 for **b**, I create Jerusalem a rejoicing, and 2009
66:12 For thus saith the LORD, **B**, I will extend 2009
66:15 For **b**, the LORD will come with fire, and 2009
Jer 1: 6 said I, Ah, Lord GOD, **b**, I cannot speak: 2009
1: 9 the LORD said unto me, **B**, I have put my 2009
1:18 For **b**, I have made thee *this* day a defenced 2009
2:35 **B**, I *will* plead with thee, because 2009
3: 5 **B**, thou hast spoken and done evil *things* as 2009
3:22 **B**, we come unto thee; for thou *art* 2009
4:13 **B**, he shall come up as clouds, and 2009
4:16 **b**, publish against Jerusalem, *that* watchers 2009
5:14 Because ye speak this word, **b**, I will make 2009
6:10 **b**, their ear *is* uncircumcised, and 2009
6:10 **b**, the word of the LORD is unto them a 2009
6:19 **b**, I will bring evil upon this people, 2009
6:21 Therefore thus saith the LORD, **B**, I will 2009
6:22 Thus saith the LORD, **B**, a people cometh 2009
7: 8 **B**, ye trust in lying words, *that* cannot 2009
7:11 **B**, even I have seen *it,* saith the LORD. 2009
7:20 **B**, mine anger and my fury *shall be* poured 2009

Jer 7:32 Therefore, **b**, the days come, saith 2009
8:15 *and* for a time of health, and **b** trouble. 2009
8:17 For **b**, I will send serpents, cockatrices, 2009
8:19 **B** the voice of the cry of the daughter of my 2009
9: 7 of hosts, **B**, I will melt them, and try them; 2009
9:15 **B**, I *will* feed them, *even* this people, with 2009
9:25 **B**, the days come, saith the LORD, that I 2009
10:18 For thus saith the LORD, **B**, I will sling 2009
10:22 **B**, the noise of the bruit is come, and 2009
11:11 the LORD, **B**, I *will* bring evil upon them, 2009
11:22 the LORD of hosts, **B**, I will punish them: 2009
12:14 **B**, I will pluck them out of their land, and 2009
13: 7 **b**, the girdle was marred, it was profitable 2009
13:13 say unto them, Thus saith the LORD, **B**, 2009
13:20 and **b** them that come from the north: 7200
14:13 **b**, the prophets say unto them, Ye shall not 2009
14:18 the field, then **b** the slain with the sword: 2009
14:18 then **b** them that are sick with famine: 2009
14:19 and for the time of healing, and **b** trouble. 2009
16: 9 **B**, I will cause to cease out of this place in 2009
16:12 for **b**, ye walk every one after 2009
16:14 Therefore **b**, the days come, saith 2009
16:16 **B**, I will send for many fishers, saith 2009
16:21 Therefore **b**, I *will* this once cause them to 2009
17:15 **B**, they say unto me, Where *is* the word of 2009
18: 3 and **b**, he wrought a work on the wheels. 2009
18: 6 **B**, as the clay *is* in the potter's hand, so 2009
18:11 **B**, I frame evil against you, and devise a 2009
19: 3 **B**, I *will* bring evil upon this place, 2009
19: 6 Therefore **b**, the days come, saith 2009
19:15 **B**, I will bring upon this city and upon all 2009
20: 4 For thus saith the LORD, **B**, I will make 2009
20: 4 thine eyes *shall* **b** *it;* and I will give all 7200
21: 4 **B**, I *will* turn back the weapons of war that 2009
21: 8 **B**, I set before you the way of life, and 2009
21:13 **B**, I *am* against thee, O inhabitant of 2009
23: 2 **b**, I will visit upon you the evil of your 2009
23: 5 **B**, the days come, saith the LORD, that I 2009
23: 7 Therefore **b**, the days come, saith 2009
23:15 **B**, I will feed them with wormwood, and 2009
23:19 **B**, a whirlwind of the LORD is gone forth 2009
23:30 Therefore **b**, I *am* against the prophets, 2009
23:31 **B**, I *am* against the prophets, saith 2009
23:32 **B**, I *am* against them that prophesy false 2009
23:39 Therefore **b**, I, even I, will utterly forget 2009
24: 1 The LORD shewed me, and **b**, 2009
25: 9 **B**, I will send and take all the families of 2009
25:32 Thus saith the LORD of hosts, **B**, 2009
26:14 As for me, **b**, I *am* in your hand: do with 2009
27:16 prophets that prophesy unto you, saying, **B**, 2009
28:16 **B**, I will cast thee from off the face of 2009
29:17 **B**, I will send upon them the sword, 2009
29:21 **B**, I will deliver them into the hand of 2009
29:32 **B**, I will punish Shemaiah the Nehelamite, 2009
29:32 neither shall he **b** the good that I will do for 7200
30:18 **B**, I *will* bring again the captivity of 2009
30:23 **B**, the whirlwind of the LORD goeth forth 2009
31: 8 **B**, I *will* bring them from the north country, 2009
31:27 **B**, the days come, saith the LORD, that I 2009
31:31 **B**, the days come, saith the LORD, that I 2009
31:38 **B**, the days come, saith the LORD, 2009
32: 3 and say, Thus saith the LORD, **B**, 2009
32: 4 to mouth, and his eyes shall **b** his eyes: 7200
32: 7 **B**, Hanameel the son of Shallum thine 2009
32:17 **b**, thou hast made the heaven and the earth 2009
32:24 **B** the mounts, they are come *unto* the city 2009
32:24 is come to pass; and **b**, thou seest *it.* 2009
32:27 **B**, I *am* the LORD, the God of all flesh: is 2009
32:28 **B**, I *will* give this city into the hand of 2009
32:37 **B**, I *will* gather them out of all countries, 2009
33: 6 **B**, I *will* bring it health and cure, and I will 2009
33:14 **B**, the days come, saith the LORD, that I 2009
34: 2 **B**, I *will* give this city into the hand of 2009
34: 3 thine eyes shall **b** the eyes of the king of 7200
34:17 **b**, I proclaim a liberty for you, saith 2009
34:22 **B**, I *will* command, saith the LORD, and 2009
35:17 **B**, I will bring upon Judah and upon all 2009
37: 7 **B**, Pharaoh's army, which is come forth to 2009
38: 5 the king said, **B**, he *is* in your hand: 2009
38:22 **b**, all the women that are left in the king of 2009
39:16 **B**, I *will* bring my words upon this city for 2009
40: 4 now **b**, I loose thee *this* day from the chains 2009
40: 4 **b**, all the land *is* before thee: whither it 7200
40:10 As for me, **b**, I *will* dwell at Mizpah to 2009
42: 2 *but* a few of many, as thine eyes do **b** us:) 7200
42: 4 said unto them, I have heard *you;* **b**, 2009
43:10 **B**, I *will* send and take Nebuchadrezzar 2009
44: 2 **b**, this day they *are* a desolation, and 2009
44:11 **B**, I will set my face against you for evil, 2009
44:26 **B**, I have sworn by my great name, 2009
44:27 **B**, I *will* watch over them for evil, and 2009
44:30 **B**, I *will* give Pharaoh-hophra king of 2009
45: 4 **B**, *that* which I have built *will* I break 2009
45: 5 for **b**, I *will* bring evil upon all flesh, 2009
46:25 **B**, I will punish the multitude of No, and 2009
46:27 for **b**, I *will* save thee from afar off, and 2009
47: 2 **B**, waters rise up out of the north, and 2009
48:12 Therefore **b**, the days come, saith 2009
48:40 **B**, he shall fly as an eagle, and shall spread 2009
49: 2 Therefore **b**, the days come, saith 2009
49: 5 **B**, I will bring a fear upon thee, saith 2009
49:12 **B**, they whose judgment *was* not to drink of 2009
49:19 **B**, he shall come up like a lion from 2009
49:22 **B**, he shall come up and fly as the eagle, 2009
49:35 **B**, I *will* break the bow of Elam, the chief 2009
50:12 **b**, the hindermost of the nations *shall be* a 2009
50:18 **B**, I *will* punish the king of Babylon and his 2009
50:31 **B**, I *am* against thee, *O thou* most proud, 2009
50:41 **B**, a people shall come from the north, and 2009
50:44 **B**, he shall come up like a lion from 2009
51: 1 **B**, I *will* raise up against Babylon, and 2009
51:25 **B**, I *am* against thee, O destroying 2009
51:36 **B**, I *will* plead thy cause, and 2009
51:47 Therefore **b**, the days come, that I will do 2009
51:52 Wherefore **b**, the days come, saith 2009

La 1: 9 O LORD, **b** my affliction: for the enemy 7200
1:12 **b**, and see if there be any sorrow like unto 5027
1:18 I pray you, all people, and **b** my sorrow: 7200
1:20 **B**, O LORD; for I *am* in distress: my 7200
2:20 **B**, O LORD, and consider to whom thou 7200
3:50 the LORD look down, and **b** from heaven. 7200
3:63 **B** their sitting down, and their rising up; 5027
5: 1 upon us: consider, and **b** our reproach. 7200
Eze 1: 4 I looked, and **b**, a whirlwind came out of 2009
1:15 **b** one wheel upon the earth by the living 2009
2: 9 when I looked, **b**, a hand *was* sent unto me; 2009
3: 8 **B**, I have made thy face strong against their 2009
3:23 **b**, the glory of the LORD stood there, 2009
3:25 thou, O son of man, **b**, they shall put bands 2009
4: 8 **b**, I will lay bands upon thee, and thou shalt 2009
4:14 said I, Ah Lord GOD, **b**, my soul *hath* not 2009
4:16 Moreover he said unto me, Son of man, **b**, 2009
5: 8 **B**, I, even I, *am* against thee, and 2009
6: 3 **B**, I, *even* I, *will* bring a sword upon you, 2009
7: 5 An evil, an only evil, **b**, is come. 2009
7: 6 is come: it watcheth for thee; **b**, it is come. 2009
7:10 **B** the day, behold, it is come: the morning 2009
7:10 Behold the day, **b**, it is come: the morning 2009
8: 4 **b**, the glory of the God of Israel *was* there, 2009
8: 5 mine eyes the way toward the north, and **b**, 2009
8: 7 and when I looked, **b** a hole in the wall. 2009
8: 8 when I had digged in the wall, **b** a door. 2009
8: 9 **b** the wicked abominations that they do 7200
8:10 **b** every form of creeping things, and 2009
8:14 **b**, there sat women weeping for Tammuz. 2009
8:16 **b**, *at* the door of the temple of the LORD, 2009
9: 2 **b**, six men came from the way of the higher 2009
9:11 **b**, the man clothed with linen, which *had* 2009
10: 1 I looked, and **b**, in the firmament that *was* 2009
10: 9 **b** the four wheels by the cherubims, 2009
11: 1 **b** at the door of the gate five and 2009
12:27 Son of man, **b**, *they of* the house of Israel 2009
13: 8 seen lies, therefore **b**, I *am* against you, 2009
13:20 **B**, I *am* against your pillows, where*with* ye 2009
14:22 Yet **b**, therein shall be left a remnant that 2009
14:22 **b**, they *shall* come forth unto you, and 2009
15: 4 **B**, it is cast into the fire for fuel; the fire 2009
15: 5 **B**, when it was whole, it was meet for no 2009
16: 8 I passed by thee, and looked upon thee, **b**, 2009
16:27 **B** therefore, I have stretched out my hand 2009
16:37 **B** therefore, I will gather all thy lovers, 2009
16:43 hast fretted me in all these *things*; **b** 1887
16:44 **B**, every one that useth proverbs shall use 2009
16:49 **B**, this was the iniquity of thy sister Sodom, 2009
17: 7 **b**, this vine did bend her roots toward him, 2009
17:10 Yea **b**, *being* planted, shall it prosper? shall 2009
17:12 not what these *things mean?* tell *them*, **B**, 2009
18: 4 **B**, all souls *are* mine; as the soul of 2005
20:47 **B**, I *will* kindle a fire in thee, and it shall 2009
21: 3 **B**, I *am* against thee, and will draw forth 2009
21: 7 **b**, it cometh, and shall be brought to pass, 2009
22: 6 **B**, the princes of Israel, every one were in 2009
22:13 **B** therefore, I have smitten mine hand at 2009
22:19 ye are all become dross, **b** therefore, 2009
23:22 **B**, I will raise up thy lovers against thee, 2009
23:28 **B**, I *will* deliver thee into the hand *of them* 2009
24:16 Son of man, **b**, I take away from thee 2009
24:21 **B**, I *will* profane my sanctuary, 2009
25: 4 **B** therefore, I *will* deliver thee to the men 2009
25: 7 **B** therefore, I will stretch out mine hand 2009
25: 8 Because that Moab and Seir do say, **B**, 2009
25: 9 Therefore **b**, I *will* open the side of Moab 2009
25:16 **B**, I *will* stretch out mine hand upon 2009
26: 3 **B**, I *am* against thee, O Tyrus, and 2009
26: 7 **B**, I *will* bring upon Tyrus Nebuchadrezzar 2009
28: 3 **B**, thou *art* wiser than Daniel; *there is* no 2009
28: 7 **B** therefore, I *will* bring strangers upon 2009
28:17 lay thee before kings, that *they* may **b** thee. 7200
28:18 the earth in the sight of all them that **b** thee. 7200
28:22 **B**, I *am* against thee, O Zidon; and I will be 2009
29: 3 **B**, I *am* against thee, Pharaoh king of 2009
29: 8 **B**, I *will* bring a sword upon thee, and 2009
29:10 **B** therefore, I *am* against thee, and 2009
29:19 **B**, I *will* give the land of Egypt unto 2009
30:22 **B**, I *am* against Pharaoh king of Egypt, and 2009
31: 3 **B**, the Assyrian *was* a cedar in Lebanon 2009
34:10 **B**, I *am* against the shepherds; and I will 2009
34:11 **B**, I, *even* I, will both search my sheep, and 2009
34:17 **B**, I judge between cattle and cattle, 2009
34:20 **B**, I, *even* I, will judge between the fat 2009
35: 3 **B**, O mount Seir, I *am* against thee, and 2009
36: 6 **B**, I have spoken in my jealousy and in my 2009
36: 9 For **b**, I *am* for you, and I will turn unto 2009
37: 2 **b**, *there were* very many in the open valley; 2009
37: 5 **B**, I *will* cause breath to enter into you, and 2009
37: 7 **b** a shaking, and the bones came together, 2009
37:11 **b**, they say, Our bones are dried, and 2009
37:12 **B**, O my people, I *will* open your graves, 2009
37:19 **B**, I *will* take the stick of Joseph, which *is* 2009
37:21 **B**, I *will* take the children of Israel from 2009
38: 3 **B**, I *am* against thee, O Gog, the chief 2009
39: 1 **B**, I *am* against thee, O Gog, the chief 2009
39: 8 **B**, it is come, and it is done, saith the Lord 2009
40: 3 brought me thither, and **b**, *there was* a man, 2009
40: 4 **b** with thine eyes, and hear with thine ears, 7200
40: 5 **b** a wall on the outside of the house round 2009
40:24 the south, and **b** a gate toward the south: 2009
43: 2 **b**, the glory of the God of Israel came from 2009
43: 5 **b**, the glory of the LORD filled the house. 2009
43:12 most holy. **B**, this *is* the law of the house. 2009
44: 4 I looked, and **b**, the glory of the LORD 2009
44: 5 **b** with thine eyes, and hear with thine ears 7200
46:19 **b**, there *was* a place on the two sides 2009
46:21 **b**, in every corner of the court *there was* a 2009
47: 1 **b**, waters issued out from under 2009
47: 2 *by* the way that looketh east*ward*; and **b**, 2009
47: 7 Now when I had returned, **b**, at the bank of 2009
Da 2:31 Thou, O king, sawest, and **b** a great image. 431
4:10 I saw, and **b**, a tree in the midst of the earth, 431
4:13 **b**, a watcher and a holy one came down from 431

Da 7: 2 and said, I saw in my vision by night, and **b**, 718
7: 5 **b**, another beast, a second, like to a bear, 718
7: 7 **b**, a fourth beast, dreadful and terrible, and 718
7: 8 I considered the horns, and **b**, there came up 431
7: 8 **b**, in this horn *were* eyes like the eyes of 431
7:13 I saw in the night visions, and **b**, *one* like 718
8: 3 I lifted up mine eyes, and saw, and **b**, 2009
8: 5 as I was considering, **b**, a he goat came 2009
8:15 and sought for the meaning, then **b**, 2009
8:19 he said, **B**, I *will* make thee know what 2009
9:18 **b** our desolations, and the city which is 7200
10: 5 Then I lift up mine eyes, and looked, and **b**, 2009
10:10 **b**, a hand touched me, which set me upon 2009
10:16 **b**, *one* like the similitude of the sons of 2009
11: 2 **B**, there *shall* stand up yet three kings in 2009
12: 5 and **b**, there stood other two, 2009
Hos 2: 6 Therefore **b**, I will hedge up thy way with 2009
2:14 Therefore **b**, I *will* allure her, and bring her 2009
Joel 2:19 will answer and say unto his people, **B**, 2009
3: 1 For **b**, in those days, and in that time, 2009
3: 7 **B**, I *will* raise them out of the place whither 2009
Am 2:13 **B**, I am pressed under you, as a cart is 2009
3: 9 and **b** the great tumults in the midst thereof, 7200
6:11 For **b**, the LORD commandeth, and 2009
6:14 **b**, I *will* raise up against you a nation, 2009
7: 1 **b**, he formed grasshoppers in the beginning 2009
7: 4 **b**, the Lord GOD called to contend by 2009
7: 7 **b**, the Lord stood upon a wall made by a 2009
7: 8 said the Lord, **B**, I *will* set a plumbline in 2009
8: 1 unto me: and **b**, a basket of summer fruit. 2009
8:11 **B**, the days come, saith the Lord GOD, 2009
9: 8 **B**, the eyes of the Lord GOD *are* upon 2009
9:13 **B**, the days come, saith the LORD, 2009
Ob 1: 2 **B**, I have made thee small among 2009
Mic 1: 3 For **b**, the LORD cometh forth out of his 2009
2: 3 **B**, against this family do I devise an evil, 2009
7: 9 to the light, *and* I shall **b** his righteousness. 7200
7:10 mine eyes shall **b** her: now shall she be 7200
Na 1:15 **B** upon the mountains the feet of him that 2009
2:13 **B**, I *am* against thee, saith the LORD of 2009
3: 5 **B**, I *am* against thee, saith the LORD of 2009
3:13 **B**, thy people in the midst of thee *are* 2009
Hab 1: 3 me iniquity, and **cause** *me* **to b** grievance? 5027
1: 5 **B** ye among the heathen, and regard, and 7200
1:13 *Thou art* of purer eyes than to **b** evil, and 7200
2: 4 **B**, his soul *which* is lifted up is not upright 2009
2:13 **B**, *is it* not of the LORD of hosts that 2009
2:19 **B**, it *is* laid over *with* gold and silver, and 2009
Zep 3:19 **B**, at that time I *will* undo all that afflict 2009
Zec 1: 8 **b** a man riding upon a red horse, and 2009
1:11 walked to and fro through the earth, and **b**, 2009
1:18 I up mine eyes, and saw, and **b** four horns. 2009
2: 1 lift up mine eyes again, and looked, and **b**, 2009
2: 3 **b**, the angel that talked with me went forth, 2009
2: 9 For **b**, I *will* shake mine hand upon them, 2009
3: 4 unto him he said, **B**, I have caused thine 7200
3: 8 for **b**, I *will* bring forth my servant 2009
3: 9 For **b** the stone that I have laid before 2009
3: 9 **b**, I *will* engrave the graving thereof, 2009
4: 2 I said, I have looked, and **b**, a candlestick 2009
5: 1 mine eyes, and looked, and **b**, a flying roll. 2009
5: 7 **b**, there *was* lift up a talent of lead: and 2009
5: 9 Then lift I up mine eyes, and looked, and **b**, 2009
6: 1 and lift up mine eyes, and looked, and **b**, 2009
6: 8 he upon me, and spake unto me, saying, **B**, 7200
6:12 **B** the man whose name *is* The BRANCH; 2009
8: 7 **B**, I *will* save my people from the east 2009
9: 4 **B**, the Lord will cast her out, and he will 2009
9: 9 **b**, thy King cometh unto thee: he *is* just, 2009
12: 2 **B**, I *will* make Jerusalem a cup of trembling 2009
14: 1 **B**, the day of the LORD cometh, and 2009
Mal 1:13 Ye said also, **B**, what a weariness *is it!* and 2009
2: 3 **B**, I *will* corrupt your seed, and 2009
3: 1 **B**, I *will* send my messenger, and he shall 2009
3: 1 **b**, he *shall* come, saith the LORD of hosts. 2009
4: 1 For **b**, the day cometh, that *shall* burn as an 2009
4: 5 **B**, I *will* send you Elijah the prophet before 2009
Mt 1:20 But while he thought on these *things*, **b**, *2400*
1:23 **B**, a virgin shall be with child, and *2400*
2: 1 **b**, there came wise men from the east to *2400*
2:13 And when they were departed, **b**, *the* angel *2400*
2:19 But when Herod was dead, **b**, an angel of *2400*
4:11 and **b**, angels came and ministered unto *2400*
6:26 **B** the fowls of the air: for they sow not, *1689*
7: 4 and **b**, a beam *is* in thine own eye? *2400*
8: 2 And **b**, there came a leper and *2400*
8:24 And **b**, there arose a great tempest in *2400*
8:29 And **b**, they cried out, saying, What have *2400*
8:32 and **b**, the whole herd of swine ran *2400*
8:34 And **b**, the whole city came out to meet *2400*
9: 2 And **b**, they brought to him a man sick of *2400*
9: 3 And **b**, certain of the scribes said within *2400*
9:10 **b**, many publicans and sinners came and *2400*
9:18 **b**, there came a *certain* ruler, and *2400*
9:20 (And **b**, a woman, which was diseased with *2400*
9:32 As they went out, **b**, they brought to him a *2400*
10:16 **B**, I send you forth as sheep in the midst of *2400*
11: 8 **b**, they that wear soft *clothing* are in kings' *2400*
11:10 For this is *he*, of whom it is written, **B**, *2400*
11:19 **B** a man gluttonous, and a winebibber, *2400*
12: 2 the Pharisees saw *it*, they said unto him, **B**, *2400*
12:10 And **b**, there was a man which had *his* hand *2400*
12:18 **B** my servant, whom I have chosen; my *2400*
12:41 and **b**, a greater than Jonas *is* here. *2400*
12:42 and **b**, a greater than Solomon *is* here. *2400*
12:46 **b**, *his* mother and his brethren stood *2400*
12:47 **B**, thy mother and thy brethren stand *2400*
12:49 and said, **B** my mother and my brethren. *2400*
13: 3 saying, **B**, a sower went forth to sow; *2400*
15:22 And **b**, a woman of Canaan came out of *2400*
17: 3 And **b**, there appeared unto them Moses *2400*
17: 5 While he yet spake, **b**, a bright cloud *2400*
17: 5 and **b** a voice out of the cloud, which said, *2400*
18:10 That in heaven their angels do always **b** *991*
19:16 And **b**, one came and said unto him, *2400*

Mt 19:27 Then answered Peter and said unto him, **B**, *2400*
20:18 **B**, we go up to Jerusalem; and the Son of *2400*
20:30 And **b**, two blind men sitting by the way *2400*
21: 5 **B**, thy King cometh unto thee, meek, and *2400*
22: 4 are bidden, **B**, I have prepared my dinner: *2400*
23:34 Wherefore **b**, I send unto you prophets, and *2400*
23:38 **B**, your house is left unto you desolate. *2400*
24:25 **B**, I have told you before. *2400*
24:26 shall say unto you, **B**, he is in the desert; *2400*
24:26 **b**, *he is* in the secret chambers; believe *it* *2400*
25: 6 was a cry made, **B**, the bridegroom cometh; *2400*
25:20 **b**, I have gained besides them five talents *2396*
25:22 **b**, I have gained two other talents besides *2396*
26:45 **b**, the hour is at hand, and the Son of man *2400*
26:46 **b**, he is at hand that doth betray me. *2400*
26:51 And **b**, one of them which were with Jesus *2400*
26:65 **b**, now ye have heard his blasphemy. *2396*
27:51 And **b**, the vail of the temple was rent in *2400*
28: 2 And **b**, there was a great earthquake: for *2400*
28: 7 and **b**, he goeth before you into Galilee; *2400*
28: 9 **b**, Jesus met them, saying, *All* hail. *2400*
28:11 Now when they were going, **b**, some of *2400*
Mk 1: 2 As it is written in the prophets, **B**, I send *2400*
2:24 And the Pharisees said unto him, **B**, why do *2396*
3:32 **B**, thy mother and thy brethren without *2400*
3:34 and said, **B** my mother and my brethren. *2396*
4: 3 Hearken; **B**, there went out a sower to sow: *2400*
5:22 And **b**, there cometh one of the rulers of *2400*
10:33 *Saying*, **B**, we go up to Jerusalem; and *2400*
11:21 Master, **b**, the fig tree which thou cursedst *2396*
13:23 ye heed: **b**, I have foretold you all *things*. *2400*
14:41 **b**, the Son of man is betrayed into *2400*
15: 4 **b** how many *things* they witness against *2396*
15:35 when they heard *it*, said, **B**, he calleth Elias. *2400*
16: 6 is not here: **b** the place where they laid him. *2396*
Lk 1:20 And **b**, thou shalt be dumb, and not able to *2400*
1:31 And **b**, thou shalt conceive in *thy* womb, *2400*
1:36 And **b**, thy cousin Elisabeth, she hath also *2400*
1:38 Mary said, **B** the handmaid of the Lord; *2400*
1:48 for **b**, from henceforth all generations shall *2400*
2:10 for **b**, I bring you good tidings of great joy, *2400*
2:25 And **b**, there was a man in Jerusalem, *2400*
2:34 **B**, this *child* is set for the fall and *2400*
2:48 **b**, thy father and I have sought thee *2400*
5:12 in a certain city, **b** a man full of leprosy: *2400*
5:18 And **b**, men brought in a bed a man which *2400*
6:23 ye in that day, and leap *for joy*: for **b**, *2400*
7:12 **b**, there was a dead man carried out, *2400*
7:25 **B**, they which are gorgeously apparelled, *2400*
7:27 This is *he*, of whom it is written, **B**, I send *2400*
7:34 **B** a gluttonous man, and a winebibber, *2400*
7:37 And **b**, a woman in the city, which was a *2400*
8:41 And **b**, there came a man named Jairus, and *2400*
9:30 And **b**, there talked with him two men, *2400*
9:38 And **b**, a man of the company cried out, *2400*
10: 3 **b**, I send you forth as lambs among wolves. *2400*
10:19 **B**, I give unto you power to tread on *2400*
10:25 And **b**, a certain lawyer stood up, and *2400*
11:31 and **b**, a greater than Solomon *is* here. *2400*
11:32 and **b**, a greater than Jonas *is* here. *2400*
11:41 and **b**, all *things* are clean unto you. *2400*
13: 7 said he unto the dresser of his vineyard, **B**, *2400*
13:11 And **b**, there was a woman which had a *2400*
13:30 And **b**, there are last which shall be first, *2400*
13:32 Go ye, and tell that fox, **B**, I cast out devils, *2400*
13:35 **B**, your house is left unto you desolate: and *2400*
14: 2 And **b**, there was a certain man before him, *2400*
14:29 is not able to finish *it*, all that **b** *it* begin to *2334*
17:21 for **b**, the kingdom of God is within you. *2400*
18:31 and said unto them, **B**, we go up to *2400*
19: 2 And **b**, *there was* a man named Zaccheus, *2400*
19: 8 **B**, Lord, the half of my goods I give to *2400*
19:20 saying, Lord, **b**, *here is* thy pound, *2400*
21: 6 *As for* these *things* which ye **b**, the days *2334*
21:29 a parable; **B** the fig tree, and all the trees; *1492*
22:10 And he said unto them, **B**, when ye are *2400*
22:21 But **b**, the hand of him that betrayeth me *is* *2400*
22:31 And the Lord said, Simon, Simon, **b**, Satan *2400*
22:38 And they said, Lord, **b**, here *are* two *2400*
22:47 **b** a multitude, and he that was called Judas, *2400*
23:14 and **b**, I, having examined *him* before you, *2400*
23:29 For **b**, the days are coming, in the which *2400*
23:50 And **b**, *there was* a man named Joseph, *2400*
24: 4 as they were *much* perplexed thereabout, **b**, *2400*
24:13 And **b**, two of them went *that* same day to a *2400*
24:39 **B** my hands and my feet, that it is I myself: *1492*
24:49 And **b**, I send the promise of my Father *2400*
Jn 1:29 and saith, **B** the Lamb of God, which taketh *2396*
1:36 as he walked, he saith, **B** the Lamb of God. *2396*
1:47 and saith of him, **B** an Israelite indeed, *2396*
3:26 **b**, the same baptizeth, and all *men* come to *2396*
4:35 **b**, I say unto you, Lift up your eyes, and *2400*
5:14 and said unto him, **B**, thou art made whole: *2396*
11: 3 saying, Lord, **b**, he whom thou lovest is *2396*
11:36 Then said the Jews, **B**, how he loved him. *2396*
12:15 **b**, thy King cometh, sitting on an ass's colt. *2400*
12:19 **b**, the world is gone after him. *2396*
16:32 **B**, the hour cometh, yea, is now come, *2400*
17:24 that they may **b** my glory, which thou hast *2334*
18:21 said unto them: **b**, they know what I said. *2396*
19: 4 went forth again, and saith unto them, **B**, *2396*
19: 5 And *Pilate* saith unto them, **B** the man. *2396*
19:14 and he saith unto the Jews, **B** your King. *2396*
19:26 saith unto his mother, Woman, **b** thy son. *2400*
19:27 Then saith he to the disciple, **B** thy mother. *2400*
20:27 Reach hither thy finger, and **b** my hands; *2396*
Ac 1:10 stedfastly toward heaven as he went *up*, **b**, *2400*
2: 7 and marvelled, saying one to another, **B**, *2400*
4:29 And now, Lord, **b** their threatenings: *1896*
5: 9 **b**, the feet of them which have buried thy *2400*
5:25 Then came one and told them, saying, **B**, *2400*
5:28 and **b**, ye have filled Jerusalem with your *2400*
7:31 as he drew near to **b** *it*, the voice of *2657*
7:32 Then Moses trembled, and durst not **b**. *2657*
7:56 And said, **B**, I see the heavens opened, *2400*

Ac 8:27 and **b**, a man of Ethiopia, an eunuch of 2400
9:10 Ananias. And he said, **B**, I *am here,* Lord. 2400
9:11 called Saul, of Tarsus: for, **b**, he prayeth, 2400
10:17 **b**, the men which were sent from Cornelius 2400
10:19 said unto him, **B**, three men seek thee: 2400
10:21 and said, **B**, I am he whom ye seek: 2400
10:30 the ninth hour I prayed in my house, and **b**, 2400
11:11 And **b**, immediately there were three men 2400
12:7 And **b**, *the* angel of the Lord came upon 2400
13:11 And now **b**, the hand of the Lord *is* upon 2400
13:25 I am not *he.* But **b**, there cometh *one* after 2400
13:41 **B** *ye* despisers, and wonder, and perish: 1492
16:1 and **b**, a certain disciple was there, 2400
20:22 And now **b**, I go bound in the spirit unto 2400
20:25 And now **b**, I know that ye all, 2400
Ro 2:17 **B**, thou art called a Jew, and restest in 2396
9:33 As it is written, **B**, I lay in Sion a 2400
11:22 **B** therefore the goodness and severity of 2396
1Co 10:18 **B** Israel after the flesh: are not they which 991
15:51 **B**, I shew you a mystery; We shall not all 2400
2Co 3:7 **stedfastly b** the face of Moses for the glory 816
5:17 past away; **b**, all *things* are become new. 2400
6:2 **b**, now *is* the accepted time; behold, now *is* 2400
6:2 **b**, now *is* the day of salvation.) 2400
6:9 as dying, and **b**, we live; as chastened, and 2400
7:11 For **b** this selfsame *thing,* that ye sorrowed 2400
12:14 **B**, the third *time* I am ready to come to you; 2400
Gal 1:20 I write unto you, **b**, before God, I lie not. 2400
5:2 **B**, I Paul say unto you, that if ye be 2396
Heb 2:13 **B**, I, and the children which God hath given 2400
8:8 *he* saith, **B**, the days come, saith the Lord, 2400
Jas 3:3 **B**, we put bits in the horses' mouths, 2400
3:4 **B** also the ships, which though they be so 2400
3:5 **B**, how great a matter a little fire kindleth. 2400
5:4 **B**, the hire of the labourers which have 2400
5:7 **B**, the husbandman waiteth for the precious 2400
5:9 **b**, the judge standeth before the door. 2400
5:11 **B**, we count them happy which endure. 2400
1Pe 2:6 **B**, I lay in Sion a chief corner stone, elect, 2400
2:12 by *your* good works, *which* they shall **b**, 2029
3:2 While they **b** your chaste conversation 2029
1Jn 3:1 **B**, what manner of love the Father hath 1492
Jude 1:14 from Adam, prophesied of these, saying, **B**, 2400
Rev 1:7 **B**, he cometh with clouds; and every eye 2400
1:18 and **b**, I am alive for evermore, Amen; and 2400
2:10 **b**, the devil shall cast *some* of you into 2400
2:22 **B**, I *will* cast her into a bed, and them that 2400
3:8 **b**, I have set before thee an open door, and 2400
3:9 **B**, I *will* make *them* of the synagogue of 2400
3:9 **b**, I will make them to come and 2400
3:11 **B**, I come quickly: hold *that* fast which 2400
3:20 **B**, I stand at the door, and knock: if any 2400
4:1 After this I looked, and **b**, a door *was* 2400
4:2 and **b**, a throne was set in heaven, and 2400
5:5 **b**, the Lion of the tribe of Juda, the root of 2400
6:2 And I saw, and **b** a white horse: and he that 2400
6:8 And I looked, and **b** a pale horse: and 2400
9:12 *and* **b**, there come two woes more hereafter. 2400
11:14 *and* **b**, the third woe cometh quickly. 2400
12:3 and **b** a great red dragon, having seven 2400
14:14 and **b** a white cloud, and upon the cloud 2400
15:5 And after that I looked, and **b**, the temple 2400
16:15 **B**, I come as a thief. Blessed *is* he that 2400
17:8 when they **b** the beast that was, and is not, 991
19:11 I saw heaven opened, and **b** a white horse; 2400
21:3 **B**, the tabernacle of God *is* with men, and 2400
21:5 the throne said, **B**, I make all *things* new. 2400
22:7 **B**, I come quickly: blessed *is* he that 2400
22:12 And **b**, I come quickly; and my reward *is* 2400

BEHOLDEST (4) [BEHOLD]

Ps 10:14 Thou hast seen *it;* for thou **b** mischief and 5027
Mt 7:3 And why **b** thou the mote that is in thy 991
Lk 6:41 And why **b** thou the mote that is in thy 991
6:42 when thou thyself **b** not the beam that is in 991

BEHOLDETH (4) [BEHOLD]

Job 24:18 he **b** not the way of the vineyards. 6437
41:34 He **b** all high *things:* he *is* a king over all 7200
Ps 33:13 from heaven; he **b** all the sons of men. 7200
Jas 1:24 For he **b** himself, and goeth his way, and 2657

BEHOLDING (15) [BEHOLD]

Ps 119:37 Turn away mine eyes from **b** vanity; *and* 7200
Pr 15:3 *are* in every place, **b** the evil and the good. 6822
Ecc 5:11 saving the **b** *of them* with their eyes? 7207
Mt 27:55 And many women were there **b** afar off, 2334
Mk 10:21 Then Jesus **b** him loved him, and said unto 1689
Lk 23:35 And the people stood **b**. And the rulers also 2334
23:48 **b** the *things* which were done, smote their 2334
23:49 from Galilee, stood afar off, **b** these *things.* 3708
Ac 4:14 And **b** the man which was healed standing 991
8:13 **b** *the* miracles and signs *which were* done. 2334
14:9 who **stedfastly b** him, and perceiving that he 816
23:1 **earnestly b** the council, said, Men *and* 816
2Co 3:18 with open face **b as in a glass** the glory of 2734
Col 2:5 joying and **b** your order, and the stedfastness 991
Jas 1:23 he is like unto a man **b** his natural face in a 2657

BEHOVED (2)

Lk 24:46 and thus it **b** Christ to suffer, and to rise 1163
Heb 2:17 Wherefore in all *things* it **b** him to be made 3784

BEING (291) [BE]

Ge 18:12 shall I have pleasure, my lord **b** old also? NIH
19:16 the LORD **b** merciful unto him: NIH
21:4 Abraham circumcised his son Isaac **b** eight NIH
24:27 I *b* in the way, the LORD led me to NIH
34:30 I *b* few in number, they shall gather NIH
35:29 unto his people, *b* old and full of days: NIH
37:2 Joseph, *b* seventeen years old, was feeding NIH
50:26 Joseph died, *b* an hundred and ten years old: NIH
Ex 12:34 their kneadingtroughs **b** bound up in their NIH
13:15 all that openeth the matrix, **b** males; NIH
22:14 or die, the owner thereof *b* not with it, NIH
28:16 Foursquare it shall be *b* doubled; a span NIH
32:18 neither *is it* the voice of *them that* cry for **b** NIH
39:9 and a span the breadth thereof, *b* doubled. NIH
Lev 21:4 *b* a chief man among his people, to profane NIH
24:8 *b taken* from the children of Israel *by* an NIH
Nu 1:44 and the princes of Israel, *b* twelve men: NIH
22:24 a wall *b* on this side, and a wall on that side. NIH
30:3 a bond, *b* in her father's house in her youth; NIH
30:16 *b yet* in her youth *in* her father's house. NIH
31:32 *b* the rest of the prey which the men of war NIH
32:38 and Baal-meon, (*their* names **b** changed,) NIH
Dt 3:13 and all Bashan, *b* the kingdom of Og, NIH
17:8 *b* matters of controversy within thy gates: NIH
22:24 because she cried not, *b* in the city; NIH
32:31 even our enemies themselves *b* judges. NIH
Jos 9:23 there shall none of you be freed from **b** NIH
21:10 *b* of the families of the Kohathites, NIH
24:29 died, *b* an hundred and ten years old. NIH
Jdg 2:8 died, *b* an hundred and ten years old. NIH
9:5 *b* threescore and ten persons, upon one NIH
1Sa 2:18 *b* a child, girded *with* a linen ephod. NIH
15:23 he hath also rejected thee from **b** king. NIH
15:26 the LORD hath rejected thee from **b** king 1961
26:13 hill afar off; a great space *b* between them: NIH
2Sa 8:13 the valley of salt, *b* eighteen thousand *men.* NIH
13:4 Why *art* thou, *b* the king's son, lean from NIH
13:14 but, *b* stronger than she, forced her, and NIH
19:3 as people **b** ashamed steal away when they NIH
21:16 he **b** girded *with* a new *sword,* thought to NIH
1Ki 1:41 Wherefore *is this* noise of the city **b** in an NIH
2:27 So Solomon thrust out Abiathar from **b** 1961
11:17 to go *into* Egypt; Hadad *b yet* a little child. NIH
15:13 even her he removed from **b** queen, because NIH
16:7 his hands, in **b** like the house of Jeroboam; 1961
20:15 all the children of Israel, *b* seven thousand. NIH
2Ki 8:16 of Israel, Jehoshaphat *b* then king of Judah, NIH
10:6 Now the king's sons, *b* seventy persons, NIH
12:11 they gave the money, **b** told, into the hands NIH
1Ch 9:19 their fathers, *b* over the host of the LORD, NIH
24:6 one principal household **b** taken for Eleazar, NIH
2Ch 5:12 and their brethren, **b** arrayed in white linen, NIH
13:3 chosen men, *b* mighty *men* of valour. NIH
15:16 he removed her from **b** queen, because NIH
21:20 eight years, and departed without **b** desired. NIH
26:21 and dwelt *in* a several house, *b* a leper; NIH
Ezr 6:11 and **b** set up, let him be hanged thereon; NIH
10:19 *b* guilty, *they offered* a ram of the flock for NIH
Ne 6:11 *b* as I *am,* would go into the temple to save NIH
Est 1:3 and princes of the provinces, *b* before him: NIH
1:7 (the vessels **b** diverse one from another,) NIH
3:15 **b** hastened by the king's commandment, NIH
8:14 **b** hastened and pressed on by the king's NIH
Job 4:7 I pray thee, who *ever* perished, **b** innocent? NIH
21:23 his full strength, *b* wholly at ease and quiet. NIH
42:17 So Job died, *b* old and full of days. NIH
Ps 49:12 Nevertheless man *b* in honour abideth not: NIH
65:6 fast the mountains; *b* girded with power: NIH
69:4 *b* mine enemies wrongfully, are mighty: NIH
78:9 of Ephraim, **b** armed, *and* carrying bows, NIH
78:38 he, *b* full of compassion, forgave *their* NIH
83:4 and let us cut them off from *b* a nation; NIH
104:33 to my God **while I have** my **b**. 5750+871.1
107:10 of death, *b* bound in affliction and iron; NIH
139:16 did see my **substance, yet b unperfect;** 1564
146:2 unto my God **while I have** *any* **b**. 5750+871.1
Pr 3:26 and shall keep thy foot from **b** taken. NIH
29:1 that **b** often reproved hardeneth *his* neck, NIH
SS 3:8 They all hold swords, *b* expert in war: NIH
3:10 the midst thereof **b** paved *with* love, NIH
Isa 3:26 and she *b* desolate shall sit upon the ground. NIH
17:1 Damascus *is* taken away from **b** a city, and NIH
40:13 or *b* his counseller hath taught him? NIH
65:20 the sinner *b* an hundred years old shall be NIH
Jer 2:25 Withhold thy foot from **b** unshod, and NIH
12:11 *b* desolate it mourneth unto me; NIH
17:16 I have not hastened from *b* a pastor to NIH
31:36 the seed of Israel also shall cease from **b** a 1961
34:9 *b* a Hebrew or a Hebrewess, go free; NIH
40:1 when he had taken him **b** bound in chains NIH
48:2 come, and let us cut it off from *b* a nation. NIH
48:42 Moab shall be destroyed from *b* a people, NIH
Eze 17:10 Yea behold, *b* planted, shall it prosper? NIH
23:42 a voice of a multitude **b** at ease *was* with NIH
47:8 *which* **b** brought forth into the sea, NIH
48:22 *b* in the midst *of that* which is the prince's, NIH
Da 3:27 **b** gathered together, saw these men, NIH
5:31 *b* about threescore and two year old. NIH
6:10 his windows **b** open in his chamber toward NIH
8:22 Now that **b** broken, whereas four stood up NIH
9:21 at the beginning, **b** caused to fly swiftly, NIH
Mt 1:19 **b** a just *man,* and not willing to make her a 1510
1:23 which **b** interpreted is, God with us. NIG
1:24 Then Joseph **b** raised from sleep did as NIG
2:12 And **b** warned of God in a dream that *they* NIG
2:22 **b** warned of God in a dream, NIG
7:11 If ye then, **b** evil, know how to give good 1510
12:34 O generation of vipers, how can ye, **b** evil, 1510
14:8 **b** before instructed of her mother, said, NIG
Mk 3:5 **b** grieved for the hardness of their hearts, NIG
5:41 which is, **b** interpreted, Damsel (I say unto NIG
8:1 In those days the multitude **b** very great, 1510
9:33 and **b** in the house he asked them, 1096
14:3 And **b** in Bethany in the house of Simon 1510
15:22 which is, **b** interpreted, The place of a skull. NIG
15:34 which is, **b** interpreted, My God, my God, NIG
Lk 1:74 that *we* **b** delivered out of the hand of our NIG
2:5 Mary his espoused wife, **b** great with child. 1510
3:1 Pontius Pilate **b** governor of Judea, and NIG
3:1 and Herod **b** tetrarch of Galilee, and NIG
3:2 Annas and Caiaphas **b** the high priests, 1909
3:19 **b** reproved by him for Herodias his brother NIG
3:21 *that* Jesus also **b** baptized, and praying, NIG
3:23 thirty years of age, **b** (as was supposed) 1510
4:1 And Jesus **b** full of the Holy Ghost returned NIG
4:2 **B** forty days tempted of the devil. And in NIG
4:15 in their synagogues, **b** glorified of all. NIG
7:29 **b** baptized *with* the baptism of John. NIG
7:30 against themselves, **b** not baptized of him. NIG
8:25 And they **b** afraid wondered, saying one to NIG
11:13 If ye then, **b** evil, know how to give good 5225
13:16 And ought not this *woman,* **b** a daughter of 1510
14:21 of the house **b** angry said to his servant, NIG
16:23 **b** in torments, and seeth Abraham afar off, 5225
20:36 of God, **b** the children of the resurrection. 1510
21:12 **b** brought before kings and rulers for my NIG
22:3 **b** of the number of the twelve. 1510
22:44 And **b** in an agony he prayed more 1096
Jn 1:38 (which is to say, **b** interpreted, Master,) NIG
1:41 which is, **b** interpreted, the Christ. NIG
4:6 Jesus therefore, **b** wearied with *his* journey, NIG
4:9 *is it that* thou, **b** a Jew, askest drink of me, 1510
5:13 himself away, a multitude **b** in *that* place. 1510
6:71 *that* should betray him, **b** one of the twelve. 1510
7:50 that came to *Jesus* by night, **b** one of them,) 1510
8:9 And they which heard *it,* **b** convicted by NIG
10:33 and because that thou, **b** a man, 1510
11:49 **b** the high priest that *same* year, said unto 1510
11:51 but **b** high priest that year, he prophesied 1510
13:2 And supper **b** ended, the devil having now NIG
14:25 I spoken unto you, **b** *yet* present with you. NIG
18:26 **b** *his* kinsman whose ear Peter cut off, 1510
19:38 **b** a disciple of Jesus, but secretly for fear of 1510
20:19 day at evening, **b** the first *day* of the week, 1510
20:26 *then* came Jesus, the doors **b** shut, NIG
Ac 1:3 **b** seen of them forty days, and speaking of NIG
1:4 And, **b** assembled together with them, NIG
2:23 **b** delivered by the determinate counsel and NIG
2:30 Therefore **b** a prophet, and knowing that 5225
2:33 Therefore **b** by the right hand of God NIG
3:1 at the hour of prayer, **b** the ninth *hour.* NIG
4:2 **B** grieved that they taught the people, and NIG
4:23 And **b** let go, they went to their own NIG
4:36 (which is, **b** interpreted, The son of NIG
5:2 his wife also **b** privy *to it,* and brought a NIG
7:55 But he, **b** full of the Holy Ghost, looked up 5225
13:4 So they, **b** sent forth by the Holy Ghost, NIG
13:12 **b** astonished at the doctrine of the Lord. NIG
14:8 **b** a cripple from his mother's womb, 5225
15:3 And **b** brought on their way by the church, NIG
15:21 **b** read in the synagogues every sabbath day. NIG
15:25 good unto us, **b** assembled with one accord, NIG
15:32 and Silas, **b** prophets also themselves, 1510
15:40 **b** recommended by the brethren unto NIG
16:18 **b** grieved, turned and said to the spirit, NIG
16:20 saying, These men, **b** Jews, do exceedingly 5225
16:21 us to receive, neither to observe, **b** Romans. 1510
16:37 **b** Romans, and have cast *us* into prison; 5225
17:28 in him we live, and move, and **have** our **b**; 1510
18:25 and **b** fervent in the spirit, he spake and NIG
19:40 there **b** no cause whereby we may give an 5225
20:9 named Eutychus, **b** fallen into a deep sleep: NIG
22:11 **b** led by the hand of them that were with NIG
26:11 and **b** exceedingly mad against them, NIG
27:2 a Macedonian of Thessalonica, **b** with us. 1510
27:18 And we **b** exceedingly tossed with a NIG
Ro 1:20 **b** understood by the things that are made, NIG
1:29 **B** filled with all unrighteousness, NIG
2:18 more excellent, **b** instructed out of the law; NIG
3:21 **b** witnessed by the law and the prophets; NIG
3:24 **B** justified freely by his grace through NIG
4:11 the faith which he had *yet* **b** uncircumcised: 1722
4:12 which he had **b** *yet* uncircumcised. NIG
4:19 And **b** not weak in faith, he considered not NIG
4:21 And **b** fully persuaded that, what he had NIG
5:1 Therefore **b** justified by faith, we have NIG
5:9 more then, **b** now justified by his blood, NIG
5:10 much more, **b** reconciled, we shall be saved NIG
6:9 Knowing that Christ **b** raised from the dead NIG
6:18 **B** then made free from sin, ye became NIG
6:22 But now **b** made free from sin, and NIG
7:6 the law, *that* **b** dead wherein we were held; NIG
9:11 (For *the children* **b** not yet born, NIG
10:3 For they **b** ignorant of God's righteousness, NIG
11:17 and thou, **b** a wild olive tree, wert graffed 1510
12:5 So we, **b** many, are one body in Christ, and NIG
15:16 **b** sanctified by the Holy Ghost. NIG
1Co 4:12 **b** reviled, we bless; being persecuted, NIG
4:12 we bless; **b** persecuted, we suffer *it:* NIG
4:13 **B** defamed, we intreat: we are made as NIG
7:18 Is any *man* called **b** circumcised? let him NIG
7:21 Art thou called **b** a servant? care not for it: NIG
7:22 the Lord, **b** a servant, is the Lord's freeman: NIG
7:22 he that is called, *b* free, is Christ's servant. NIG
8:7 and their conscience **b** weak is defiled. 1510
9:21 (**b** not without law to God, but under 1510
10:17 For we **b** many are one bread, *and* NIG
12:12 of *that* one body, **b** many, are one body: 1510
2Co 5:3 be that **b** clothed we shall not be found NIG
5:4 are in *this* tabernacle do groan, **b** burdened: NIG
8:17 but **b** more forward, of his own accord he 5225
9:11 **B** enriched in every *thing* to all NIG
10:1 but **b** absent am bold toward you: NIG
11:9 have kept myself **from b burdensome** to you, 4
12:16 nevertheless, **b** crafty, I caught you with 5225
13:2 **b** absent now I write to them which NIG
13:10 Therefore I write these *things* **b** absent, NIG
13:10 lest **b** present I should use sharpness, NIG
Gal 1:14 **b** more exceedingly zealous of 5225
2:3 neither Titus, who was with me, **b** a Greek, 1510
2:14 unto Peter before *them* all, If thou, **b** a Jew, 5225
3:13 the curse of the law, **b** made a curse for us: NIG
Eph 1:11 **b** predestinated according to the purpose of NIG
1:18 The eyes of your understanding **b** NIG
2:11 that ye **b** in time passed Gentiles in NIG
2:12 **b** aliens from the commonwealth of Israel, NIG
2:20 Jesus Christ himself **b** the chief corner 1510
3:17 that ye, **b** rooted and grounded in love, NIG
4:18 **b** alienated from the life of God through 1510
4:19 Who **b** past feeling have given themselves NIG

Php 1: 6 **B** confident of this very *thing,* that he which NIG
1:11 **B** filled with the fruits of righteousness, NIG
2: 2 same love, **b** of one accord, of one mind. NIG
2: 6 Who, **b** in the form of God, thought it not *5225*
2: 8 And **b** found in fashion as a man, NIG
3:10 **b** made conformable unto his death; NIG
Col 1:10 **b** fruitful in every good work, and NIG
2: 2 **b** knit together in love, and unto all riches NIG
2:13 **b** dead in *your* sins and the uncircumcision *1510*
1Th 2: 8 So **b** affectionately desirous of you, NIG
2:17 **b** taken from you for a short time in NIG
1Ti 2:14 the woman **b** deceived was in NIG
3: 6 lest **b** lifted up with pride he fall into NIG
3:10 the office of a deacon, **b** *found* blameless. *1510*
2Ti 1: 4 desiring to see thee, **b** mindful of thy tears, NIG
3:13 and worse, deceiving, and **b** deceived. NIG
Tit 1:16 but in works they deny *him,* **b** abominable, *1510*
3: 7 That **b** justified by his grace, we should be NIG
3:11 and sinneth, **b** condemned of himself. *1510*
Phm 1: 9 *Yet* for love's sake I rather beseech *thee,* **b** *1510*
Heb 1: 3 Who **b** the brightness of *his* glory, and *1510*
1: 4 **B** made so much better than the angels, NIG
2:18 For in that he himself hath suffered **b** NIG
4: 1 a promise **b** left *us* of entering into his rest, NIG
4: 2 not **b** mixed with faith in them that heard *it.* NIG
5: 9 And **b** made perfect, he became the author NIG
7: 2 first **b** by interpretation King of NIG
7:12 For the priesthood **b** changed, there is made NIG
9:11 But Christ **b** come a high priest of good NIG
11: 4 his gifts: and by it he **b** dead yet speaketh. NIG
11: 7 **b** warned of God of *things* not seen as yet, NIG
11:37 **b** destitute, afflicted, tormented; NIG
13: 3 as **b** yourselves also in the body. *1510*
Jas 1:25 continueth *therein,* he **b** not a forgetful *1096*
2:17 if it hath not works, is dead, **b** alone. NIG
1Pe 1: 7 **b** much more precious than of gold that NIG
1:23 **B** born again, not of corruptible seed, but NIG
2: 8 which stumble at the word, **b** disobedient: NIG
2:24 that we, **b** dead to sins, should live unto NIG
3: 5 **b** in subjection unto their own husbands: NIG
3: 7 and as **b** heirs together of the grace of life; NIG
3:18 **b** put to death in the flesh, but quickened by NIG
3:22 and powers **b** made subject unto him. NIG
5: 3 Neither as **b** lords over *God's* heritage, but NIG
5: 3 but **b** ensamples to the flock. *1096*
2Pe 3: 6 then was, **b** overflowed with water, NIG
3:12 wherein the heavens **b** on fire shall be NIG
3:17 **b** led away with the error of the wicked, NIG
Rev 1:12 And **b** turned, I saw seven golden NIG
12: 2 And she **b** with child cried, travailing in *2192*
14: 4 **b** the firstfruits unto God and to the Lamb. NIG

BEKAH (1)
Ex 38:26 A **b** for every man, *that is,* half a shekel, 1235

BEKER See BACHRITES; BECHER

BEL (3)
Isa 46: 1 **B** boweth down, Nebo stoopeth, their idols 1078
Jer 50: 2 say, Babylon is taken, **B** is confounded, 1078
51:44 I will punish **B** in Babylon, and I will bring 1078

BELA (13) [BELAH, BELAITES]
Ge 14: 2 and the king of **B**, which *is* Zoar. 1106
14: 8 and the king of **B** (the same *is* Zoar); 1106
36:32 **B** the son of Beor reigned in Edom: and 1106
36:33 **B** died, and Jobab the son of Zerah of 1106
Nu 26:38 of **B**, the family of the Belaites: of Ashbel, 1106
26:40 the sons of **B** were Ard and Naaman: 1106
1Ch 1:43 the children of Israel; **B** the son of Beor: 1106
1:44 when **B** was dead, Jobab the son of Zerah 1106
5: 8 **B** the son of Azaz, the son of Shema, 1106
7: 6 **B**, and Becher, and Jediael, three. 1106
7: 7 the sons of **B**; Ezbon, and Uzzi, and Uzziel, 1106
8: 1 Now Benjamin begat **B** his firstborn, 1106
8: 3 the sons of **B** were, Addar, and Gera, and 1106

BELAH (1) [BELA]
Ge 46:21 the sons of Benjamin *were* **B**, and Becher, 1106

BELAITES (1) [BELA]
Nu 26:38 of Bela, the family of the **B**: of Ashbel, 1108

BELCH (1)
Ps 59: 7 Behold, they **b out** with their mouth: 5042

BELIAL (17)
Dt 13:13 *Certain* men, the children of **B**, are gone 1100
Jdg 19:22 the men of the city, certain sons of **B**, 1100
20:13 deliver *us* the men, the children of **B**, 1100
1Sa 1:16 not thine handmaid for a daughter of **B**: 1100
2:12 Now the sons of Eli *were* sons of **B**; 1100
10:27 the children of **B** said, How shall this *man* 1100
25:17 for he *is such* a son of **B**, that *a man* cannot 1100
25:25 I pray thee, regard this man of **B**, 1100
30:22 answered all the wicked men and *men* of **B**, 1100
2Sa 16: 7 thou bloody man, and thou man of **B**: 1100
20: 1 there happened to be there a man of **B**, 1100
23: 6 *the sons of* **B** *shall be* all of them as thorns 1100
1Ki 21:10 set two men, sons of **B**, before him, to bear 1100
21:13 two men, children of **B**, and sat before him: 1100
21:13 the men of **B** witnessed against him, 1100
2Ch 13: 7 the children of **B**, and have strengthened 1100
2Co 6:15 And what concord hath Christ with **B**? or *955*

BELIED (1)
Jer 5:12 They have **b** the LORD, and said, *It is* not 3584

BELIEF (1) [BELIEVE]
2Th 2:13 of the Spirit and **b** of the truth: *4102*

BELIEVE (144) [BELIEF, BELIEVED, BELIEVERS, BELIEVEST, BELIEVETH, BELIEVING, UNBELIEF]
Ex 4: 1 and said, But behold, they will not **b** me, 539
4: 5 That they may **b** that the LORD God of 539
4: 8 it shall come to pass, if they will not **b** thee, 539
4: 8 that they will **b** the voice of the latter sign. 539
4: 9 if they will not **b** also these two signs, 539
19: 9 when I speak with thee, and **b** thee for ever. 539
Nu 14:11 how long will it be ere they **b** me, for all 539
Dt 1:32 Yet in this thing ye did not **b** the LORD 539
2Ki 17:14 that did not **b** in the LORD their God. 539
2Ch 20:20 **B** in the LORD your God, so shall you be 539
20:20 **b** his prophets, so shall ye prosper. 539
32:15 you on this *manner,* neither yet **b** him: 539
Job 9:16 *yet* would I not **b** that he had hearkened unto 539
39:12 Wilt thou **b** him, that he will bring home thy 539
Pr 26:25 When he speaketh fair, **b** him not: for *there* 539
Isa 7: 9 If ye will not **b**, surely ye shall not be 539
43:10 that ye may know and **b** me, and 539
Jer 12: 6 **b** them not, though they speak fair *words* 539
Hab 1: 5 *which* ye will not **b**, though it be told *you.* 539
Mt 9:28 unto them, **B** ye that I am able to do this? *4100*
18: 6 one of these little ones which **b** in me, *4100*
21:25 say unto us, Why did ye not then **b** him? *4100*
21:32 not afterward, that *ye* might **b** him. *4100*
24:23 Lo, here *is* Christ, or there; **b** *it* not. *4100*
24:26 *he is* in the secret chambers; **b** *it* not. *4100*
27:42 down from the cross, and we will **b** him. *4100*
Mk 1:15 God is at hand: repent ye, and **b** the gospel. *4100*
5:36 of the synagogue, Be not afraid, only **b**. *4100*
9:23 Jesus said unto him, If thou canst **b**, *4100*
9:24 cried out, and said with tears, Lord, I **b**; *4100*
9:42 offend one of *these* little ones that **b** in me, *4100*
11:23 shall **b** that *those things* which he saith *4100*
11:24 **b** that ye receive *them,* and ye shall have *4100*
11:31 he will say, Why then did ye not **b** him? *4100*
13:21 here *is* Christ; or lo, *he is* there; **b** *him* not: *4100*
15:32 now from the cross, that we may see and **b**. *4100*
16:17 And these signs shall follow them that **b**; *4100*
Lk 8:12 lest they should **b** and be saved. *4100*
8:13 which for a while **b**, and in time of *4100*
8:50 **b** only, and she shall be made whole. *4100*
22:67 said unto them, If I tell you, ye will not **b**: *4100*
24:25 slow of heart to **b** all that the prophets have *4100*
Jn 1: 7 that all *men* through him might **b**. *4100*
1:12 of God, *even* to them that **b** on his name: *4100*
3:12 I have told you earthly *things,* and ye **b** not, *4100*
3:12 and ye believe not, how shall ye **b**, *4100*
4:21 unto her, Woman, **b** me, the hour cometh, *4100*
4:42 *Now* we **b**, not because of thy saying: *4100*
4:48 ye see signs and wonders, ye will not **b**. *4100*
5:38 for whom he hath sent, him ye **b** not. *4100*
5:44 How can ye **b**, which receive honour one of *4100*
5:47 But if ye **b** not his writings, how shall ye *4100*
5:47 not his writings, how shall ye **b** my words? *4100*
6:29 that ye **b** on *him* whom he hath sent. *4100*
6:30 thou then, that we may see, and **b** thee? *4100*
6:36 That ye also have seen me, and **b** not. *4100*
6:64 But there are some of you that **b** not. *4100*
6:69 And we **b** and are sure that thou art *that* *4100*
7: 5 For neither did his brethren **b** in him. *4100*
7:39 which they that **b** on him should receive: *4100*
8:24 for if ye **b** not that I am *he,* ye shall die in *4100*
8:45 because I tell *you* the truth, ye **b** me not. *4100*
8:46 And if I say the truth, why do ye not **b** me? *4100*
9:18 But the Jews did not **b** concerning him, *4100*
9:35 unto him, Dost thou **b** on the Son of God? *4100*
9:36 Who is he, Lord, that I might **b** on him? *4100*
9:38 And he said, Lord, I **b**. And he worshipped *4100*
10:25 answered them, I told you, and ye **b** not: *4100*
10:26 But ye **b** not, because ye are not of my *4100*
10:37 I do not the works of my Father, **b** me not. *4100*
10:38 But if I do, though ye **b** not me, believe *4100*
10:38 though ye believe not me, **b** the works: *4100*
10:38 that ye may know, and **b**, that the Father *is* *4100*
11:15 that I was not there, to the intent ye may **b**; *4100*
11:27 I **b** that thou art the Christ, the Son of God, *4100*
11:40 I not unto thee, that, if thou wouldest **b**, *4100*
11:42 *it,* that they may **b** that thou hast sent me. *4100*
11:48 let him thus alone, all *men* will **b** on him: *4100*
12:36 While ye have light, **b** in the light, that ye *4100*
12:39 Therefore they could not **b**, because *4100*
12:47 hear my words, and **b** not, I judge him not: *4100*
13:19 it is come to pass, ye may **b** that I am *he.* *4100*
14: 1 ye **b** in God, believe also in me. *4100*
14: 1 ye believe in God, **b** also in me. *4100*
14:11 **B** me that I *am* in the Father, and the Father *4100*
14:11 or else **b** me for the very works' sake. *4100*
14:29 that, when it is come to pass, ye might **b**. *4100*
16: 9 Of sin, because they **b** not on me; *4100*
16:30 by this we **b** that thou camest forth from *4100*
16:31 Jesus answered them, Do ye now **b**? *4100*
17:20 for them also which shall **b** on me through *4100*
17:21 that the world may **b** that thou hast sent me. *4100*
19:35 knoweth that he saith true, that ye might **b**. *4100*
20:25 thrust my hand into his side, I will not **b**. *4100*
20:31 that ye might **b** that Jesus is the Christ, *4100*
Ac 8:37 said, I **b** that Jesus Christ is the Son of God. *4100*
13:39 And by him all that **b** are justified from all *4100*
13:41 a work which you shall in no wise **b**, *4100*
15: 7 should hear the word of the gospel, and **b**. *4100*
15:11 But we **b** that through the grace of the Lord *4100*
16:31 **B** on the Lord Jesus Christ, and thou shalt *4100*
19: 4 that they should **b** on him which should *4100*
21:20 many thousands of Jews there are which **b**, *4100*
21:25 As touching the Gentiles which **b**, we have *4100*
27:25 for I **b** God, that it shall be even as it was *4100*
Ro 3: 3 For what if some did **not b**? shall their *569*
3:22 Christ unto all and upon all them that **b**: *4100*
4:11 he might be the father of all them that **b**, *4100*
4:24 if we **b** on him that raised up Jesus our *4100*
6: 8 we **b** that we shall also live with him: *4100*
10: 9 shalt **b** in thine heart that God hath raised *4100*
10:14 how shall they **b** *in him* of whom they have *4100*
15:31 delivered from them that do **not b** in Judea; *544*
1Co 1:21 of preaching to save them that **b**. *4100*
10:27 If any of them that **b not** bid you *to a feast,* *571*
11:18 be divisions among you; and I partly **b** *it.* *4100*
14:22 not to them that **b**, but to them that believe *4100*
14:22 to them that believe, but to them that **b not**: *571*
14:22 prophesying *serveth* not for them that **b not**, *571*
14:22 that believe not, but for them which **b**. *4100*
2Co 4: 4 hath blinded the minds of them which **b not**, *571*
4:13 I spoken; we also **b**, and therefore speak; *4100*
Gal 3:22 Jesus Christ might be given to them that **b**. *4100*
Eph 1:19 greatness of his power to us-ward who **b**, *4100*
Php 1:29 not only to **b** on him, but also to suffer for *4100*
1Th 1: 7 So that ye were ensamples to all that **b** in *4100*
2:10 we behaved ourselves among you that **b**: *4100*
2:13 effectually worketh also in you that **b**. *4100*
4:14 For if we **b** that Jesus died and rose again, *4100*
2Th 1:10 and to be admired in all them that **b** *4100*
2:11 strong delusion, that they should **b** a lie: *4100*
1Ti 1:16 hereafter **b** on him to life everlasting. *4100*
4: 3 with thanksgiving of them which **b** *4103*
4:10 of all men, specially of those that **b**. *4103*
2Ti 2:13 If we **b not**, *yet* he abideth faithful: *569*
Heb 10:39 but of *them* that **b** to the saving of the soul. *4102*
11: 6 for he that cometh to God must **b** that he is, *4100*
Jas 2:19 doest well: the devils also **b**, and tremble. *4100*
1Pe 1:21 Who by him do **b** in God, that raised him *4100*
2: 7 Unto you therefore which **b** *he is* precious: *4100*
1Jn 3:23 That we should **b** on the name of his Son *4100*
4: 1 **b** not every spirit, but try the spirits *4100*
5:13 These *things* have I written unto you that **b** *4100*
5:13 that ye may **b** on the name of the Son of *4100*

BELIEVED (115) [BELIEVE]
Ge 15: 6 he **b** in the LORD; and he counted it to him 539
45:26 And *Jacob's* heart fainted, for he **b** them not. 539
Ex 4:31 the people **b**: and when they heard that 539
14:31 and **b** the LORD, and his servant Moses. 539
Nu 20:12 and Aaron, Because ye **b** me not, 539
Dt 9:23 and ye **b** him not, nor hearkened to his voice. 539
1Sa 27:12 Achish **b** David, saying, He hath made his 539
1Ki 10: 7 Howbeit I **b** not the words, until I came, and 539
2Ch 9: 6 Howbeit I **b** not their words, until I came, 539
Job 29:24 *If* I laughed on them, they **b** *it* not; and 539
Ps 27:13 *I had fainted,* unless I had **b** to see 539
78:22 Because they **b** not in God, and trusted not 539
78:32 and **b** not for his wondrous works. 539
106:12 Then **b** they his words; they sang his praise. 539
106:24 the pleasant land, they **b** not his word: 539
116:10 I **b**, therefore have I spoken: I was greatly 539
119:66 knowledge: for I have **b** thy commandments. 539
Isa 53: 1 Who hath **b** our report? and to whom is 539
Jer 40:14 But Gedaliah the son of Ahikam **b** them not. 539
La 4:12 would not have **b** that the adversary and 539
Da 6:23 found upon him, because he **b** in his God. 540
Jnh 3: 5 So the people of Nineveh **b** God, and 539
Mt 8:13 and as thou hast **b**, *so* be it done unto thee. *4100*
21:32 the way of righteousness, and ye **b** him not: *4100*
21:32 but the publicans and the harlots **b** him: and *4100*
Mk 16:11 was alive, and had been seen of her, **b not**. *569*
16:13 told *it* unto the residue: neither **b** they them. *4100*
16:14 they **b** not them which had seen him after *4100*
Lk 1: 1 things which are **most surely b** among us, *4135*
1:45 And blessed *is* she that **b**: for there shall be *4100*
20: 5 he will say, Why then **b** ye him not? *4100*
24:11 to them as idle tales, and they **b** them **not**. *569*
24:41 And while they yet **b not** for joy, and *569*
Jn 2:11 forth his glory; and his disciples **b** on him. *4100*
2:22 and they **b** the scripture, and the word *4100*
2:23 in the feast *day,* many **b** in his name, *4100*
3:18 he hath not **b** in the name of the only *4100*
4:39 And many of the Samaritans of that city **b** *4100*
4:41 And many moe **b** because of his own word; *4100*
4:50 And the man **b** the word that Jesus had *4100*
4:53 and himself **b**, and his whole house. *4100*
5:46 For had ye **b** Moses, ye would have *4100*
5:46 ye believed Moses, ye would have **b** me: *4100*
6:64 the beginning who they were that **b** not, *4100*
7:31 And many of the people **b** on him, and said, *4100*
7:48 of the rulers or of the Pharisees **b** on him? *4100*
8:30 As he spake these *words,* many **b** on him. *4100*
8:31 Then said Jesus to those Jews which **b** on *4100*
10:42 And many **b** on him there. *4100*
11:45 seen *the things* which Jesus did, **b** on him. *4100*
12:11 of the Jews went away, and **b** on Jesus. *4100*
12:37 before them, *yet* they **b** not on him: *4100*
12:38 he spake, Lord, who hath **b** our report? *4100*
12:42 among the *chief* rulers also many **b** on him; *4100*
16:27 and have **b** that I came out from God. *4100*
17: 8 and they have **b** that thou didst send me. *4100*
20: 8 first to the sepulchre, and he saw, and **b**. *4100*
20:29 because thou hast seen me, thou hast **b**: *4100*
20:29 *are they* that have not seen, and *yet* have **b**. *4100*
Ac 2:44 And all that **b** were together, *4100*
4: 4 many of them which heard the word **b**; *4100*
4:32 And the multitude of them that **b** were of *4100*
8:12 But when they **b** Philip preaching *4100*
8:13 Then Simon himself **b** also: and when he *4100*
9:26 of him, and **b** not that he was a disciple. *4100*
9:42 all Joppa; and many **b** in the Lord. *4100*
10:45 And they of the circumcision which **b** were *4103*
11:17 unto us, who **b** on the Lord Jesus Christ; *4100*
11:21 and a great number **b**, and turned unto *4100*
13:12 the deputy, when he saw what was done, **b**, *4100*
13:48 as many as were ordained to eternal life **b**. *4100*
14: 1 both of the Jews and *also* of the Greeks **b**. *4100*
14:23 them to the Lord, on whom they **b**. *4100*
15: 5 certain of the sect of the Pharisees which **b**, *4100*
16: 1 certain woman, *which was* a Jewess, and **b**; *4103*
17: 4 And some of them **b**, and consorted with *3982*
17: 5 But the Jews which **b not**, moved with envy, *544*
17:12 Therefore many of them **b**; also of *4100*
17:34 certain men clave unto him, and **b**: *4100*
18: 8 **b** on the Lord with all his house; *4100*
18: 8 and many of the Corinthians hearing **b**, and *4100*
18:27 helped them much which had **b** through *4100*
19: 2 ye received the Holy Ghost since ye **b**? *4100*
19: 9 and **b not**, but spake evil of *that* way before *544*
19:18 And many that **b** came, and confessed, and *4100*

B

Ac 22:19 beat in every synagogue them that **b** on *4100*
27:11 Nevertheless the centurion **b** the master and *3982*
28:24 And some **b** the *things* which were spoken, *3982*
28:24 *things* which were spoken, and some **b not.** *569*
Ro 4: 3 Abraham **b** God, and it was counted unto *4100*
4:17 before *him* whom he **b**, *even* God, *4100*
4:18 Who against hope **b** in hope, that he might *4100*
10:14 they call on *him* in whom they have not **b**? *4100*
10:16 Esaias saith, Lord, who hath **b** our report? *4100*
11:30 For as ye in times past have **not b** God, *544*
11:31 *Even* so have these also now **not b**, *544*
13:11 *is* our salvation nearer than when we **b**. *4100*
1Co 3: 5 *is* Apollos, but ministers by whom ye **b**, *4100*
15: 2 unto you, unless ye have **b** in vain. *4100*
15:11 *it were* I or they, so we preach, and so ye **b**. *4100*
2Co 4:13 is written, I **b**, *and* therefore have I spoken; *4100*
Gal 2:16 even we have **b** in Jesus Christ, *4100*
3: 6 Even as Abraham **b** God, and it was *4100*
Eph 1:13 in whom also after that ye **b**, ye were *4100*
2Th 1:10 (because our testimony among you was **b**) *4100*
2:12 That they all might be damned who **b** not *4100*
1Ti 3:16 **b** on in the world, received up into glory. *4100*
2Ti 1:12 for I know whom I have **b**, and I am *4100*
Tit 3: 8 that they which have **b** in God might be *4100*
Heb 3:18 enter into his rest, but to them that **b not**? *544*
4: 3 For we which have **b** do enter into rest, *4100*
11:31 Rahab perished not with them that **b not**, *544*
Jas 2:23 Abraham **b** God, and it was imputed unto *4100*
1Jn 4:16 and **b** the love that God hath to us. *4100*
Jude 1: 5 afterward destroyed them that **b** not. *4100*

BELIEVERS (2) [BELIEVE]
Ac 5:14 And **b** were the more added to the Lord, *4100*
1Ti 4:12 but be thou an example of the **b**, in word, *4103*

BELIEVEST (8) [BELIEVE]
Lk 1:20 because thou **b** not my words, which shall *4100*
Jn 1:50 I saw thee under the fig tree, **b** thou? *4100*
11:26 believeth in me shall never die. **B** thou this? *4100*
14:10 **B** thou not that I am in the Father, and *4100*
Ac 8:37 If thou **b** with all *thine* heart, *thou* mayest. *4100*
26:27 King Agrippa, **b** thou the prophets? I know *4100*
26:27 thou the prophets? I know that thou **b**. *4100*
Jas 2:19 Thou **b** that there is one God; thou doest *4100*

BELIEVETH (45) [BELIEVE]
Job 15:22 He **b** not that *he* shall return out of darkness, 539
39:24 neither **b** he that *it is* the sound of 539
Pr 14:15 The simple **b** every word: but the prudent 539
Isa 28:16 he that **b** shall not make haste. 539
Mk 9:23 all *things are* possible to him that **b**. *4100*
16:16 He that **b** and is baptized shall be saved; *4100*
16:16 be saved; but he that **b not** shall be damned. *569*
Jn 3:15 That whosoever **b** in him should not perish, *4100*
3:16 that whosoever **b** in him should not perish, *4100*
3:18 He that **b** on him is not condemned: but *4100*
3:18 but he that **b** not is condemned already, *4100*
3:36 He that **b** on the Son hath everlasting life: *4100*
3:36 and he that **b not** the Son shall not see life; *544*
5:24 and **b** on him that sent me, hath everlasting *4100*
6:35 and he that **b** on me shall never thirst. *4100*
6:40 and **b** on him, may have everlasting life: *4100*
6:47 He that **b** on me hath everlasting life. *4100*
7:38 He that **b** on me, as the scripture hath said, *4100*
11:25 he that **b** in me, though he were dead, *4100*
11:26 and **b** in me shall never die. *4100*
12:44 Jesus cried and said, He that **b** on me, *4100*
12:44 **b** not on me, but on him that sent me. *4100*
12:46 that whosoever **b** on me should not abide in *4100*
14:12 verily, I say unto you, He that **b** on me, *4100*
Ac 10:43 that through his name whosoever **b** in him *4100*
Ro 1:16 of God unto salvation to every one that **b**; *4100*
3:26 and the justifier of him which **b** in Jesus. *4102*
4: 5 but **b** on him that justifieth the ungodly, *4100*
9:33 whosoever **b** on him shall not be ashamed. *4100*
10: 4 law for righteousness to every one that **b**. *4100*
10:10 For with the heart *man* **b** unto *4100*
10:11 Whosoever **b** on him shall not be ashamed. *4100*
14: 2 For one **b** that *he* may eat all *things:* *4100*
1Co 7:12 If any brother hath a wife that **b not**, and *571*
7:13 the woman which hath a husband that **b not**, *571*
13: 7 Beareth all *things*, **b** all *things*, hopeth all *4100*
14:24 and there come in one that **b not**, or *571*
2Co 6:15 or what part hath he that **b** with an infidel? *4103*
1Ti 5:16 If any man or **woman that b** have widows, *4103*
1Pe 2: 6 he that **b** on him shall not be confounded. *4100*
1Jn 5: 1 Whosoever **b** that Jesus is the Christ is born *4100*
5: 5 but he that **b** that Jesus is the Son of God? *4100*
5:10 He that **b** on the Son of God hath *4100*
5:10 he that **b** not God hath made him a liar; *4100*
5:10 he **b** not the record that God gave of his *4100*

BELIEVING (8) [BELIEVE]
Mt 21:22 ye shall ask in prayer, **b**, ye shall receive. *4100*
Jn 20:27 *it* into my side: and be not faithless, but **b**. *4103*
20:31 that **b** ye might have life through his name. *4100*
Ac 16:34 and rejoiced, **b** in God with all his house. *4100*
24:14 **b** all *things* which are written in the law *4100*
Ro 15:13 of hope fill you with all joy and peace in **b**, *4100*
1Ti 6: 2 And they that have **b** masters, let them not *4103*
1Pe 1: 8 though now ye see *him* not, yet **b**, *4100*

BELL (4) [BELLS]
Ex 28:34 A golden **b** and a pomegranate, a golden 6472
28:34 a golden **b** and a pomegranate, 6472
39:26 A **b** and a pomegranate, a bell and 6472
39:26 and a pomegranate, a **b** and a pomegranate, 6472

BELLIES (1) [BELLY]
Tit 1:12 Cretians *are* alway liars, evil beasts, slow **b**. *1064*

BELLOW (1) [BELLOWS]
Jer 50:11 fat as the heifer at grass, and **b** as bulls; 6670

BELLOWS (1) [BELLOW]
Jer 6:29 The **b** are burnt, the lead is consumed of 4647

BELLS (4) [BELL]
Ex 28:33 and **b** of gold between them round about: 6472
39:25 they made **b** of pure gold, and put the bells 6472
39:25 put the **b** between the pomegranates upon 6472
Zec 14:20 In that day shall there be upon the **b** of 4698

BELLY (49) [BELLIES]
Ge 3:14 upon thy **b** shalt thou go, and dust shalt 1512
Lev 11:42 Whatsoever goeth upon the **b**, and 1512
Nu 5:21 make thy thigh to rot, and thy **b** to swell; 990
5:22 to make *thy* **b** to swell, and *thy* thigh to rot: 990
5:27 and her **b** shall swell, and her thigh shall rot: 990
25: 8 of Israel, and the woman through her **b**. 6897
Jdg 3:21 from his right thigh, and thrust it into his **b**: 990
3:22 he could not draw the dagger out of his **b**; 990
1Ki 7:20 over against the **b** which *was* by 990
Job 3:11 give up the ghost when I came out of the **b**? 990
15: 2 and fill his **b** *with* the east wind? 990
15:35 forth vanity, and their **b** prepareth deceit. 990
20:15 up again: God shall cast them out of his **b**. 990
20:20 Surely he shall not feel quietness in his **b**, 990
20:23 *When* he is about to fill his **b**, *God* shall cast 990
32:19 Behold, my **b** *is* as wine *which* hath no vent; 990
40:16 and his force *is* in the navel of his **b**. 990
Ps 17:14 whose **b** thou fillest *with* thy hid *treasure:* 990
22:10 thou *art* my God from my mother's **b**. 990
31: 9 consumed with grief, *yea*, my soul and my **b**. 990
44:25 to the dust: our **b** cleaveth unto the earth. 990
Pr 13:25 his soul: but the **b** of the wicked shall want. 990
18: 8 go down *into* the innermost parts of the **b**. 990
18:20 A man's **b** shall be satisfied with the fruit of 990
20:27 searching all the inward parts of the **b**. 990
20:30 so *do* stripes the inward parts of the **b**. 990
26:22 go down *into* the innermost parts of the **b**. 990
SS 5:14 his **b** *is as* bright ivory overlaid *with* 4578
7: 2 thy **b** *is like* a heap of wheat set about with 990
Isa 46: 3 which are borne *by me* from the **b**, which are 990
Jer 1: 5 Before I formed thee in the **b** I knew thee; 990
51:34 he hath filled his **b** with my delicates, 3770
Eze 3: 3 cause thy **b** to eat, and fill thy bowels with 990
Da 2:32 arms of silver, his **b** and his thighs of brass, 4577
Jnh 1:17 Jonah was in the **b** of the fish three days 4578
2: 1 the LORD his God out of the fish's **b**, 4578
2: 2 out of the **b** of hell cried I, *and* thou heardest 990
Hab 3:16 When I heard, my **b** trembled; my lips 990
Mt 12:40 and three nights in the whale's **b**; *2836*
15:17 entereth in at the mouth goeth into the **b**, *2836*
Mk 7:19 it entereth not into his heart, but into the **b**, *2836*
Lk 15:16 And he would fain have filled his **b** with *2836*
Jn 7:38 out of his **b** shall flow rivers of living *2836*
Ro 16:18 not our Lord Jesus Christ, but their own **b**; *2836*
1Co 6:13 Meats for the **b**, and the belly for meats: *2836*
6:13 Meats for the belly, and the **b** for meats: *2836*
Php 3:19 whose God *is their* **b**, and *whose* glory *is* in *2836*
Rev 10: 9 and it shall make thy **b** bitter, but it shall be *2836*
10:10 as soon as I had eaten it, my **b** was bitter. *2836*

BELONG (12) [BELONGED, BELONGEST, BELONGETH, BELONGING]
Ge 40: 8 unto them, *Do* not interpretations ***b*** to God? NIH
Lev 27:24 to whom the possession of the land *did* **b**. NIH
Nu 1:50 and over all *things* that ***b*** to it: NIH
Dt 29:29 The secret *things* ***b*** unto the LORD our NIH
29:29 *those things* which are revealed ***b*** unto us NIH
Ps 47: 9 for the shields of the earth ***b*** unto God: he is NIH
68:20 unto GOD the Lord ***b*** the issues from NIH
Pr 24:23 These *things* also ***b*** to the wise. *It is* not NIH
Da 9: 9 To the Lord our God ***b*** mercies and NIH
Mk 9:41 because ye **b** to Christ, verily I say unto *1510*
Lk 19:42 thy day, the *things* which **b unto** thy peace! *4314*
1Co 7:32 careth for the *things* that **b** to the Lord, NIG

BELONGED (11) [BELONG]
Jos 17: 8 Tappuah on the border of Manasseh ***b*** to NIH
1Sa 21: 7 the chiefest of the herdmen that ***b*** to Saul. NIH
1Ki 1: 8 Rei, and the mighty *men* which ***b*** to David, NIH
16:15 which ***b*** to the Philistines. NIH
2Ki 14:28 and Hamath, *which* ***b*** to Judah, for Israel, NIH
1Ch 2:23 All these ***b*** *to* the sons of Machir the father NIH
13: 6 *that is*, to Kirjath-jearim, which ***b*** to Judah, NIH
2Ch 26:23 the field of the burial which ***b*** to the kings; NIH
Est 1: 9 the royal house which ***b*** to king Ahasuerus. NIH
2: 9 with **such things as b** to her, and seven 4490
Lk 23: 7 And as soon as he knew that he **b** unto *1510*

BELONGEST (1) [BELONG]
1Sa 30:13 And David said unto him, To whom ***b*** thou? NIH

BELONGETH (21) [BELONG]
Nu 8:24 This *is it* that ***b*** unto the Levites: NIH
Dt 32:35 To me ***b*** vengeance, and recompence; NIH
Jdg 19:14 *they were* by Gibeah, which ***b*** to Benjamin. NIH
20: 4 I came into Gibeah that ***b*** to Benjamin, I NIH
1Sa 17: 1 which ***b*** to Judah, and pitched between NIH
30:14 upon *the coast* which ***b*** to Judah, and NIH
1Ki 15:27 at Gibbethon, which ***b*** to the Philistines; NIH
17: 9 which ***b*** to Zidon, and dwell there: NIH
19: 3 which ***b*** to Judah, and left his servant there. NIH
2Ki 14:11 the face at Beth-shemesh, which ***b*** to Judah. NIH
2Ch 25:21 at Beth-shemesh, which ***b*** to Judah. NIH
Ezr 10: 4 Arise; for *this* matter ***b*** unto thee: we also NIH
Ps 3: 8 Salvation ***b*** unto the LORD: thy blessing *is* NIH
62:11 have I heard this; that power ***b*** unto God. NIH
62:12 Also unto thee, O Lord, ***b*** mercy: for thou NIH
94: 1 O LORD God, to whom vengeance ***b***; NIH
94: 1 O God, to whom vengeance ***b***, shew thyself. NIH
Da 9: 7 righteousness ***b*** unto thee, but unto us NIH
9: 8 O Lord, to us ***b*** confusion of face, to our NIH
Heb 5:14 But strong meat **b** to *them that are* of full *1510*
10:30 Vengeance ***b*** unto me, I will recompense, NIG

BELONGING (5) [BELONG]
Nu 7: 9 the service of the sanctuary **b unto** them 5921
Ru 2: 3 her hap was to light on a part of the field ***b*** NIH
1Sa 6:18 cities of the Philistines ***b*** to the five lords, NIH
Pr 26:17 *and* meddleth with strife ***b*** not to him, NIH
Lk 9:10 went aside privately into a desert place **b** to NIG

BELONGINGS See STUFF

BELOVED (111) [LOVE]
Dt 21:15 one **b**, and another hated, and they have born 157
21:15 born him children, *both* the **b** and the hated; 157
21:16 *that* he may not make the son of the **b** 157
33:12 The **b** of the LORD shall dwell in safety 3039
Ne 13:26 who was **b** of his God, and God made him 157
Ps 60: 5 That thy **b** may be delivered; save *with* thy 3039
108: 6 That thy **b** may be delivered: save *with* thy 3039
127: 2 of sorrows: *for* so he giveth his **b** sleep. 3039
Pr 4: 3 tender and only ***b*** in the sight of my mother. NIH
SS 1:14 My **b** *is* unto me *as* a cluster of camphire in 1730
1:16 Behold, thou *art* fair, my **b**, yea, pleasant: 1730
2: 3 of the wood, so *is* my **b** among the sons. 1730
2: 8 The voice of my **b**! behold, he cometh 1730
2: 9 My **b** *is* like a roe or a young hart: behold, 1730
2:10 My **b** spake, and said unto me, Rise up, my 1730
2:16 My **b** *is* mine, and I *am* his: he feedeth 1730
2:17 my **b**, and be thou like a roe or a young hart 1730
4:16 Let my **b** come into his garden, and eat his 1730
5: 1 drink, yea, drink abundantly, O **b**. 1730
5: 2 *it is* the voice of my **b** that knocketh *saying,* 1730
5: 4 My **b** put in his hand by the hole *of* 1730
5: 5 I rose up to open to my **b**; and my hands 1730
5: 6 I opened to my **b**; but my beloved had 1730
5: 6 my **b** had withdrawn himself, *and* 1730
5: 8 if ye find my **b**, that ye tell him, that I *am* 1730
5: 9 What *is* thy **b** more than *another* beloved, 1730
5: 9 What *is* thy beloved more than *another* **b**, 1730
5: 9 what *is* thy **b** more than *another* beloved, 1730
5: 9 what *is* thy beloved more than *another* **b**, 1730
5:10 My **b** *is* white and ruddy, the chiefest 1730
5:16 This *is* my **b**, and this *is* my friend, 1730
6: 1 Whither is thy **b** gone, O thou fairest 1730
6: 1 whither is thy **b** turned aside? that we may 1730
6: 2 My **b** is gone down into his garden, to 1730
6: 3 I *am* my beloved's, and my **b** *is* mine: 1730
7: 9 for my **b**, that goeth *down* sweetly, 1730
7:11 Come, my **b**, let us go forth *into* the field; 1730
7:13 old, *which* I have laid up for thee, O my **b**. 1730
8: 5 from the wilderness, leaning upon her **b**? 1730
8:14 my **b**, and be thou like to a roe or to a 1730
Isa 5: 1 a song of my **b** touching his vineyard. 1730
Jer 11:15 What hath my **b** to do in mine house, 3039
12: 7 I have given the **dearly b** of my soul into 3033
Da 9:23 come to shew *thee;* for thou *art* **greatly b**: 2532
10:11 said unto me, O Daniel, a man **greatly b**, 2532
10:19 said, O man **greatly b**, fear not: peace *be* 2532
Hos 3: 1 Go yet, love a woman **b** of *her* friend, yet an 157
9:16 yet will I slay *even* the **b** *fruit* of their 4261
Mt 3:17 saying, This is my **b** Son, in whom I am well *27*
12:18 my **b**, in whom my soul is well pleased: *27*
17: 5 which said, This is my **b** Son, in whom I am *27*
Mk 1:11 *saying,* Thou art my **b** Son, in whom I am *27*
9: 7 out of the cloud, saying, This is my **b** Son: *27*
Lk 3:22 from heaven, which said, Thou art my **b** Son; *27*
9:35 out of the cloud, saying, This is my **b** Son: *27*
20:13 I will send my **b** son: it may be they will *27*
Ac 15:25 to send chosen men unto you with our **b** *27*
Ro 1: 7 that be in Rome, **b** of God, called *to be* saints: *27*
9:25 my people; and her **b**, which was not beloved. *25*
9:25 my people; and her beloved, which was not **b**. *25*
11:28 the election, *they are* **b** for the fathers' sakes. *27*
12:19 **Dearly b**, avenge not yourselves, but *27*
16: 8 Greet Amplias my **b** in the Lord. *27*
16: 9 Urban our helper in Christ, and Stachys my **b**. *27*
16:12 Salute the **b** Persis, which laboured much in *27*
1Co 4:14 to shame you, but as my **b** sons I warn *you.* *27*
4:17 who is my **b** son, and faithful in the Lord, *27*
10:14 Wherefore, my **dearly b**, flee from idolatry. *27*
15:58 Therefore, my **b** brethren, be ye stedfast, *27*
2Co 7: 1 Having therefore these promises, **dearly b**, *27*
12:19 but *we do* all *things*, **dearly b**, for your *27*
Eph 1: 6 wherein he hath made us accepted in the **b**: *25*
6:21 a **b** brother and faithful minister in the Lord, *27*
Php 2:12 Wherefore, my **b**, as ye have always obeyed, *27*
4: 1 my brethren **dearly b** and longed for, my joy *27*
4: 1 crown, so stand fast in the Lord, *my* **dearly b**. *27*
Col 3:12 holy and **b**, bowels of mercies, kindness, *25*
4: 7 *who is* a **b** brother, and a faithful minister and *27*
4: 9 With Onesimus, a faithful and **b** brother, *27*
4:14 Luke, the **b** physician, and Demas, greet you. *27*
1Th 1: 4 Knowing, brethren **b**, your election of God. *25*
2Th 2:13 brethren **b** of the Lord, because God hath *25*
1Ti 6: 2 *them* service, because they are faithful and **b**, *27*
2Ti 1: 2 To Timothy, *my* **dearly b** son: Grace, mercy, *27*
Phm 1: 1 unto Philemon *our* **dearly b**, and *27*
1: 2 And to *our* **b** Apphia, *27*
1:16 a brother **b**, specially to me, but how much *27*
Heb 6: 9 But, **b**, we are persuaded better *things* of you, *27*
Jas 1:16 Do not err, my **b** brethren. *27*
1:19 Wherefore, my **b** brethren, let every man be *27*
2: 5 Hearken, my **b** brethren, Hath not God chosen *27*
1Pe 2:11 **Dearly b**, I beseech *you* as strangers and *27*
4:12 **B**, think it not strange concerning the fiery *27*
2Pe 1:17 This is my **b** Son, in whom I am well pleased. *27*
3: 1 This second epistle, **b**, I now write unto you; *27*
3: 8 But, **b**, be not ignorant of this one *thing*, that *27*
3:14 Wherefore, **b**, seeing that ye look for such *27*
3:15 even as our **b** brother Paul also according to *27*
3:17 Ye therefore, **b**, seeing ye know *these things* *27*
1Jn 3: 2 **B**, now are we the sons of God, and it doth *27*
3:21 **B**, if our heart condemn us not, *then* have we *27*
4: 1 **B**, believe not every spirit, but try the spirits *27*
4: 7 **B**, let us love one another: for love is of God; *27*
4:11 **B**, if God so loved us, we ought also to love *27*

3Jn 1: 2 **B**, I wish above all *things* that thou mayest 27
1: 5 **B**, thou doest faithfully whatsoever thou doest 27
1:11 **B**, follow not *that which is* evil, but 27
Jude 1: 3 **B**, when I gave all diligence to write unto you 27
1:17 But, **b**, remember ye the words which were 27
1:20 But ye, **b**, building up yourselves on your 27
Rev 20: 9 the camp of the saints about, and the **b** city: 25

BELOVED'S (2) [LOVE]
SS 6: 3 I *am* my **b**, and my beloved *is* 1730+3807.1
7:10 I *am* my **b**, and his desire *is* 1730+3807.1

BELOW See DOWNWARD; NETHER; NETHERMOST

BELSHAZZAR (8)
Da 5: 1 **B** the king made a great feast to a thousand 1113
5: 2 **B**, whiles *he* tasted the wine, 1113
5: 9 *was* king **B** greatly troubled, and 1113
5:22 thou his son, O **B**, hast not humbled thine 1113
5:29 commanded **B**, and they clothed Daniel 1113
5:30 In that night *was* **B** the king of 1113
7: 1 In the first year of **B** king of Babylon 1113
8: 1 In the third year of the reign of king **B** a 1112

BELTESHAZZAR (10) [DANIEL]
Da 1: 7 for he gave unto Daniel *the name of* **B**; and 1095
2:26 and said to Daniel, whose name *was* **B**, 1096
4: 8 whose name *was* **B**, according to the name 1096
4: 9 O **B**, master of the magicians, because 1096
4:18 Now thou, O **B**, declare the interpretation 1096
4:19 Daniel, whose name *was* **B**, was astonied 1096
4:19 The king spake, and said, **B**, let not 1096
4:19 **B** answered and said, My lord, the dream 1096
5:12 the same Daniel, whom the king named **B**: 1096
10: 1 unto Daniel, whose name was called **B**; 1095

BEMOAN (5) [BEMOANED, BEMOANING]
Jer 15: 5 or who shall **b** thee? or who shall go aside 5110
16: 5 neither go to lament nor **b** them: 5110
22:10 Weep ye not for the dead, neither **b** him: 5110
48:17 All ye that are about him, **b** him; and all ye 5110
Na 3: 7 who will **b** her? whence shall I seek 5110

BEMOANED (1) [BEMOAN]
Job 42:11 they **b** him, and comforted him over all 5110

BEMOANING (1) [BEMOAN]
Jer 31:18 I have surely heard Ephraim **b** himself *thus;* 5110

BEN (1)
1Ch 15:18 **B**, and Jaaziel, and Shemiramoth, and 1122

BENAIAH (42)
2Sa 8:18 **B** the son of Jehoiada *was over* both 1141
20:23 **B** the son of Jehoiada *was* over 1141
23:20 **B** the son of Jehoiada, the son of a valiant 1141
23:22 These *things* did **B** the son of Jehoiada, 1141
23:30 **B** the Pirathonite, Hiddai of the brooks of 1141
1Ki 1: 8 **B** the son of Jehoiada, and Nathan 1141
1:10 **B**, and the mighty *men,* and Solomon his 1141
1:26 **B** the son of Jehoiada, and thy servant 1141
1:32 the prophet, and **B** the son of Jehoiada. 1141
1:36 **B** the son of Jehoiada answered the king, 1141
1:38 **B** the son of Jehoiada, and the Cherethites, 1141
1:44 **B** the son of Jehoiada, and the Cherethites, 1141
2:25 king Solomon sent by the hand of **B** the son 1141
2:29 Solomon sent **B** the son of Jehoiada, 1141
2:30 **B** came to the tabernacle of the LORD, 1141
2:30 And **B** brought the king word again, saying, 1141
2:34 So **B** the son of Jehoiada went up, and 1141
2:35 the king put **B** the son of Jehoiada in his 1141
2:46 So the king commanded **B** the son of 1141
4: 4 **B** the son of Jehoiada *was* over the host: 1141
1Ch 4:36 and Asaiah, and Adiel, and Jesimiel, and **B**, 1141
11:22 **B** the son of Jehoiada, the son of a valiant 1141
11:24 These *things* did **B** the son of Jehoiada, and 1141
11:31 the children of Benjamin, **B** the Pirathonite, 1141
15:18 **B**, and Maaseiah, and Mattithiah, and 1141
15:20 and Unni, and Eliab, and Maaseiah, and **B**, 1141
15:24 Amasai, and Zechariah, and **B**, and Eliezer, 1141
16: 5 and Eliab, and **B**, and Obed-edom: 1141
16: 6 **B** also and Jahaziel the priests with 1141
18:17 **B** the son of Jehoiada *was* over 1141
27: 5 the third month *was* **B** the son of Jehoiada, 1141
27: 6 This *is that* **B**, *who was* mighty among 1141
27:14 the eleventh month *was* **B** the Pirathonite, 1141
27:34 after Ahithophel *was* Jehoiada the son of **B**, 1141
2Ch 20:14 the son of **B**, the son of Jeiel, the son of 1141
31:13 Eliel, and Ismachiah, and Mahath, and **B**, 1141
Ezr 10:25 and Eleazar, and Malchijah, and **B**. 1141
10:30 Adna, and Chelal, **B**, Maaseiah, Mattaniah, 1141
10:35 **B**, Bedeiah, Chelluh, 1141
10:43 Zabad, Zebina, Jadau, and Joel, **B**. 1141
Eze 11: 1 Pelatiah the son of **B**, princes of the people. 1141
11:13 that Pelatiah the son of **B** died. 1141

BEN-AMMI (1)
Ge 19:38 she also bare a son, and called his name **B**: 1151

BENCHES (1)
Eze 27: 6 of the Ashurites have made thy **b** *of* ivory, 7175

BEND (8) [BENDETH, BENDING, BENT]
Ps 11: 2 For lo, the wicked **b** *their* bow, they make 1869
64: 3 *and* **b** *their bows to shoot* their arrows, 1869
Jer 9: 3 they **b** their tongues *like* their bow *for* lies: 1869
46: 9 and the Lydians, that handle *and* **b** the bow. 1869
50:14 all ye that **b** the bow, shoot at her, spare no 1869
50:29 all ye that **b** the bow, camp against it round 1869
51: 3 Against *him that* bendeth let the archer **b** 1869
Eze 17: 7 this vine did **b** her roots toward him, and 3719

BEN-DEKER See SON OF DEKAR

BENDETH (2) [BEND]
Ps 58: 7 *when* he **b** *his bow to shoot* his arrows, 1869
Jer 51: 3 Against *him that* **b** let the archer bend his 1869

BENDING (1) [BEND]
Isa 60:14 that afflicted thee shall come **b** unto thee; 7817

BENEATH (28)
Ge 35: 8 was buried **b** Beth-el under an oak: 4480+8478
Ex 20: 4 or that *is* in the earth **b**, or that *is* in 4480+8478
26:24 shall be coupled together **b**, 4295+4480+3807.1
27: 5 the compass of the altar **b**, 4295+4480+3807.1
28:33 ***b*** upon the hem of it thou shalt make NIH
32:19 of his hands, and brake them **b** the mount. 8478
36:29 they were coupled **b**, 4295+4480+3807.1
38: 4 **b** unto the midst of it. 4295+4480+3807.1
Dt 4:18 fish that *is* in the waters **b** the earth: 4480+8478
4:39 heaven above, and upon the earth **b**: 4480+8478
5: 8 or that *is* in the earth **b**, or that *is* in 4480+8478
5: 8 or that *is* in the waters **b** the earth: 4480+8478
28:13 be above only, and thou shalt not be **b**; 4295
33:13 the dew, and for the deep that coucheth **b**, 8478
Jos 2:11 God in heaven above, and in earth **b**. 4480+8478
Jdg 7: 8 of Midian was **b** him in the valley. 4480+8478
1Ki 4:12 which *is* by Zartanah **b** Jezreel, 4480+8478
7:29 **b** the lions and oxen *were certain* 4480+8478
8:23 in heaven above, or on earth **b**, 4480+8478
Job 18:16 His roots shall be dried up **b**, 4480+8478
Pr 15:24 to the wise, that *he* may depart from hell **b**. 4295
Isa 14: 9 Hell from **b** is moved for thee to meet *thee* 8478
51: 6 and look upon the earth **b**: 4480+8478
Jer 31:37 of the earth searched out **b**, 4295+3807.1
Am 2: 9 his fruit from above, and his roots from **b**. 8478
Mk 14:66 And as Peter was **b** in the palace, *2736*
Jn 8:23 And he said unto them, Ye are from **b**; I am *2736*
Ac 2:19 in heaven above, and signs in the earth **b**; *2736*

BENE-BERAK (1)
Jos 19:45 And Jehud, and **B**, and Gath-rimmon, 1139

BENEFACTORS (1)
Lk 22:25 exercise authority upon them are called **b**. *2110*

BENEFICIAL See EXPEDIENT

BENEFIT (5) [BENEFITS]
2Ch 32:25 not again according to the **b** *done* unto him; 1576
Jer 18:10 the good, wherewith I said *I* would **b** them. 3190
2Co 1:15 you before, that you might have a second **b**; *5485*
1Ti 6: 2 are faithful and beloved, partakers of the **b**. *2108*
Phm 1:14 that thy **b** should not be as *it were* of *18*

BENEFITS (3) [BENEFIT]
Ps 68:19 *who* daily loadeth us *with* **b**, *even* the God NIH
103: 2 O my soul, and forget not all his **b**: 1576
116:12 unto the LORD *for* all his **b** towards me? 8408

BENE-JAAKAN (2) [JAAKAN]
Nu 33:31 departed from Moseroth, and pitched in **B**. 1142
33:32 they removed from **B**, and encamped at 1142

BENEVOLENCE (1)
1Co 7: 3 Let the husband render unto the wife due **b**: *2133*

BEN-HADAD (27)
1Ki 15:18 king Asa sent them to **B**, the son of 1130
15:20 So **B** hearkened unto king Asa, and sent 1130
20: 1 **B** the king of Syria gathered all his host 1130
20: 2 the city, and said unto him, Thus saith **B**, 1130
20: 5 said, Thus speaketh **B**, saying, Although I 1130
20: 9 he said unto the messengers of **B**, 1130
20:10 And **B** sent unto him, and said, The gods do 1130
20:12 when ***B*** heard this message, as he *was* NIH
20:16 **B** *was* drinking *himself* drunk in 1130
20:17 **B** sent out, and they told him, saying, 1130
20:20 **B** the king of Syria escaped on a horse with 1130
20:26 that **B** numbered the Syrians, and went up 1130
20:30 **B** fled, and came into the city, into an inner 1130
20:32 said, Thy servant **B** saith, I pray thee, 1130
20:33 catch *it:* and they said, Thy brother **B**. 1130
20:33 **B** came forth to him; and he caused him to 1130
20:34 ***B*** said unto him, The cities, which my NIH
2Ki 6:24 that **B** king of Syria gathered all his host, 1130
8: 7 **B** the king of Syria was sick; and it was 1130
8: 9 Thy son **B** king of Syria hath sent me to 1130
13: 3 into the hand of **B** the son of Hazael, 1130
13:24 and **B** his son reigned in his stead. 1130
13:25 the hand of **B** the son of Hazael the cities, 1130
2Ch 16: 2 king's house, and sent to **B** king of Syria, 1130
16: 4 **B** hearkened unto king Asa, and sent 1130
Jer 49:27 and it shall consume the palaces of **B**. 1130
Am 1: 4 which shall devour the palaces of **B**. 1130

BEN-HAIL (1)
2Ch 17: 7 *even* to **B**, and to Obadiah, and 1134

BEN-HANAN (1)
1Ch 4:20 *were,* Amnon, and Rinnah, **B**, and Tilon. 1135

BEN-HESED See SON OF HESED

BENINU (1)
Ne 10:13 Hodijah, Bani, **B**. 1148

BENJAMIN (162) [BEN-ONI, BENJAMIN'S, BENJAMITE, BENJAMITES]
Ge 35:18 name Ben-oni: but his father called him **B**. 1144
35:24 The sons of Rachel; Joseph, and **B**: 1144
42: 4 **B**, Joseph's brother, Jacob sent not with his 1144
42:36 ye will take **B** *away:* all these things are 1144
43:14 may send away your other brother, and **B**. 1144
43:15 took double money in their hand, and **B**; 1144
43:16 when Joseph saw **B** with them, he said to 1144
43:29 saw his brother **B**, his mother's son, and 1144
45:12 eyes see, and the eyes of my brother **B**, 1144
45:14 and wept upon his neck. 1144
45:22 to **B** he gave three hundred *pieces* of silver, 1144
46:19 sons of Rachel Jacob's wife; Joseph, and **B**. 1144
46:21 the sons of **B** *were* Belah, and Becher, and 1144
49:27 **B** shall ravin *as* a wolf: in the morning he 1144
Ex 1: 3 Issachar, Zebulun, and **B**, 1144
Nu 1:11 Of **B**; Abidan the son of Gideoni. 1144
1:36 Of the children of **B**, *by* their generations, 1144
1:37 *even* of the tribe of **B**, *were* thirty and 1144
2:22 the tribe of **B**: and the captain of the sons of 1144
2:22 the captain of the sons of **B** *shall be* Abidan 1144
7:60 prince of the children of **B**, *offered:* 1144
10:24 of **B** *was* Abidan the son of Gideoni. 1144
13: 9 Of the tribe of **B**, Palti the son of Raphu. 1144
26:38 The sons of **B** after their families: of Bela, 1144
26:41 These *are* the sons of **B** after their families: 1144
34:21 Of the tribe of **B**, Elidad the son of Chislon. 1144
Dt 27:12 and Judah, and Issachar, and Joseph, and **B**: 1144
33:12 *And* of **B** he said, The beloved of 1144
Jos 18:11 the lot of the tribe of the children of **B** 1144
18:20 *was* the inheritance of the children of **B**, 1144
18:21 **B** according to their families were Jericho, 1144
18:28 This *is* the inheritance of the children of **B** 1144
21: 4 and out of the tribe of **B**, thirteen cities. 1144
21:17 out of the tribe of **B**, Gibeon with her 1144
Jdg 1:21 the children of **B** did not drive out 1144
1:21 the Jebusites dwell with the children of **B** 1144
5:14 after thee, **B**, among thy people; out of 1144
10: 9 against **B**, and against the house of 1144
19:14 *were* by Gibeah, which *belongeth* to **B**. 1144
20: 3 (Now the children of **B** heard that 1144
20: 4 I came into Gibeah that *belongeth* to **B**, I 1144
20:10 may do, when they come to Gibeah of **B**, 1144
20:12 of Israel sent men through all the tribe of **B**, 1144
20:13 the children of **B** would not hearken to 1144
20:14 the children of **B** gathered themselves 1144
20:15 the children of **B** were numbered at that 1144
20:17 the men of Israel, beside **B**, were numbered 1144
20:18 first to the battle against the children of **B**? 1144
20:20 men of Israel went out to battle against **B**; 1144
20:21 the children of **B** came forth out of Gibeah, 1144
20:23 battle against the children of **B** my brother? 1144
20:24 against the children of **B** the second day. 1144
20:25 **B** went forth against them out of Gibeah 1144
20:28 battle against the children of **B** my brother, 1144
20:30 against the children of **B** on the third day, 1144
20:31 the children of **B** went out against 1144
20:32 the children of **B** said, They *are* smitten 1144
20:35 the LORD smote **B** before Israel: and 1144
20:36 So the children of **B** saw that they were 1144
20:39 **B** began to smite *and* kill of the men of 1144
20:41 turned *again,* the men of **B** were amazed: 1144
20:44 there fell of **B** eighteen thousand men; all 1144
20:46 So that all which fell that day of **B** were 1144
20:48 Israel turned again upon the children of **B**, 1144
21: 1 any of us give his daughter unto **B** to wife. 1144
21: 6 the children of Israel repented them for **B** 1144
21:13 of **B** that *were* in the rock Rimmon, 1144
21:14 **B** came again at that time; and they gave 1144
21:15 the people repented them for **B**, because 1144
21:16 seeing the women are destroyed out of **B**? 1144
21:17 inheritance for them that be escaped of **B**, 1144
21:18 Cursed *be* he that giveth a wife to **B**. 1144
21:20 they commanded the children of **B**, 1144
21:21 of Shiloh, and go *to* the land of **B**. 1144
21:23 the children of **B** did so, and took *them* 1144
1Sa 4:12 there ran a man of **B** out of the army, and 1144
9: 1 Now there was a man of **B**, whose name 1144
9:16 I will send thee a man out of the land of **B**, 1144
9:21 least of all the families of the tribe of **B**? 1144
10: 2 sepulchre in the border of **B** at Zelzah; 1144
10:20 to come near, the tribe of **B** was taken. 1144
10:21 When he had caused the tribe of **B** to come 1144
13: 2 were with Jonathan in Gibeah of **B**: 1144
13:15 gat him up from Gilgal *unto* Gibeah of **B**. 1144
13:16 present with them, abode in Gibeah of **B**: 1144
14:16 the watchmen of Saul in Gibeah of **B** 1144
2Sa 2: 9 and over **B**, and over all Israel. 1144
2:15 and went over by number twelve of **B**, 1144
2:25 the children of **B** gathered themselves 1144
2:31 the servants of David had smitten of **B**, and 1144
3:19 Abner also spake in the ears of **B**: and 1144
3:19 that seemed *good* to the whole house of **B**. 1144
4: 2 Rimmon a Beerothite, of the children of **B**: 1144
4: 2 (for Beeroth also was reckoned to **B**: 1144
19:17 *there were* a thousand men of **B** with him, 1144
21:14 buried they in the country of **B** in Zelah, 1144
23:29 of Ribai out of Gibeah of the children of **B**, 1144
1Ki 4:18 Shimei the son of Elah, in **B**: 1144
12:21 with the tribe of **B**, an hundred and 1144
12:23 unto all the house of Judah and **B**, and 1144
15:22 king Asa built with them Geba of **B**, and 1144
1Ch 2: 2 Dan, Joseph, and **B**, Naphtali, Gad, and 1144
6:60 out of the tribe of **B**; Geba with her 1144
6:65 out of the tribe of the children of **B**, these 1144
7: 6 *The sons of* **B**; Bela, and Becher, and 1144
7:10 **B**, and Ehud, and Chenaanah, and Zethan, 1144
8: 1 Now **B** begat Bela his firstborn, Ashbel 1144
8:40 and fifty. All these *are* of the sons of **B**. 1144
9: 3 of the children of **B**, and of the children of 1144
9: 7 of the sons of **B**; Sallu the son of 1144
11:31 that pertained to the children of **B**, 1144
12: 2 out of a bow, *even* of Saul's brethren of **B**. 1144
12:16 there came of the children of **B** and 1144
12:29 of the children of **B**, the kindred of Saul, 1144
21: 6 and **B** counted he not among them: 1144
27:21 of **B**, Jaasiel the son of Abner: 1144
2Ch 11: 1 *of* the house of Judah and **B** an hundred and 1144
11: 3 and to all Israel in Judah and **B**, saying, 1144
11:10 and Hebron, which *are* in Judah and in **B**, 1144
11:12 having Judah and **B** on his side. 1144

2Ch 11:23 throughout all the countries of Judah and **B**, 1144
14: 8 out of **B**, that bare shields and drew bows, 1144
15: 2 Hear ye me, Asa, and all Judah and **B**; 1144
15: 8 idols out of all the land of Judah and **B**, 1144
15: 9 he gathered all Judah and **B**, and 1144
17:17 of **B**; Eliada a mighty *man* of valour, and 1144
25: 5 of *their* fathers, throughout all Judah and **B**: 1144
31: 1 and the altars out of all Judah and **B**, 1144
34: 9 remnant of Israel, and of all Judah and **B**; 1144
34:32 **B** to stand *to it*. And the inhabitants of 1144
Ezr 1: 5 up the chief of the fathers of Judah and **B**, 1144
4: 1 **B** heard that the children of the captivity 1144
10: 9 **B** gathered themselves together *unto* 1144
10:32 **B**, Malluch, *and* Shemariah. 1144
Ne 3:23 After him repaired **B** and Hashub over 1144
11: 4 children of Judah, and of the children of **B**. 1144
11: 7 these *are* the sons of **B**; Sallu the son of 1144
11:31 The children also of **B** from Geba *dwelt at* 1144
11:36 Levites *were* divisions *in* Judah, *and* in **B**. 1144
12:34 Judah, and **B**, and Shemaiah, and Jeremiah, 1144
Ps 68:27 There *is* little **B** *with* their ruler, the princes 1144
80: 2 Before Ephraim and **B** and Manasseh stir 1144
Jer 1: 1 that *were* in Anathoth in the land of **B**: 1144
6: 1 O ye children of **B**, gather yourselves to 1144
17:26 from the land of **B**, and from the plain, and 1144
20: 2 the stocks that *were* in the high gate of **B**, 1144
32: 8 in Anathoth, which *is* in the country of **B**: 1144
32:44 and take witnesses in the land of **B**, 1144
33:13 in the land of **B**, and in the places about 1144
37:12 out of Jerusalem to go *into* the land of **B**, 1144
37:13 when he was in the gate of **B**, a captain of 1144
38: 7 the king then sitting in the gate of **B**; 1144
Eze 48:22 the border of Judah and the border of **B**, 1144
48:23 unto the west side, **B** *shall have* a *portion*. 1144
48:24 by the border of **B**, from the east side unto 1144
48:32 of Joseph, one gate of **B**, one gate of Dan. 1144
Hos 5: 8 cry aloud *at* Beth-aven, after thee, O **B**. 1144
Ob 1:19 of Samaria: and **B** *shall possess* Gilead. 1144
Ac 13:21 a man of the tribe of **B**, *by the space of* forty *958*
Ro 11: 1 of the seed of Abraham, *of* the tribe of **B**. *958*
Php 3: 5 of the stock of Israel, of the tribe of **B**, *958*
Rev 7: 8 Of the tribe of **B** *were* sealed twelve *958*

BENJAMIN'S (4) [BENJAMIN]
Ge 43:34 **B** mess was five times so much as any of 1144
44:12 and the cup was found in **B** sack. 1144
45:14 he fell upon his brother **B** neck, and wept; 1144
Zec 14:10 from **B** gate unto the place of the first gate, 1144

BENJAMITE (9) [BENJAMIN]
Jdg 3:15 the son of Gera, a **B**, a man lefthanded: 1145
1Sa 9: 1 the son of Aphiah, a **B**, 376+1121+3227
9:21 Saul answered and said, *Am* not I a **B**, 1145
2Sa 16:11 how much more now *may this* **B** *do it*? let 1145
19:16 a **B**, which *was* of Bahurim, hasted and 1145
20: 1 *was* Sheba, the son of Bichri, a **B**: 376+3227
1Ki 2: 8 Shimei the son of Gera, a **B** of Bahurim, 1145
Est 2: 5 son of Shimei, the son of Kish, a **B**; 376+3227
Ps 7: T concerning the words of Cush the **B**. 1121

BENJAMITES (8) [BENJAMIN]
Jdg 19:16 in Gibeah: but the men of the place *were* **B**. 1145
20:35 the children of Israel destroyed of the **B** 1144
20:36 for the men of Israel gave place to the **B**, 1144
20:40 the **B** looked behind them, and behold, 1144
20:43 *Thus* they inclosed the **B** round about, 1144
1Sa 9: 4 he passed through the land of the **B**, but 3228
22: 7 that stood about him, Hear now, ye **B**; 1145
1Ch 27:12 *was* Abiezer the Anetothite, of the **B**: 1145

BENO (2)
1Ch 24:26 and Mushi: the sons of Jaaziah; **B**. 1121
24:27 **B**, and Shoham, and Zaccur, and Ibri. 1121

BEN-ONI (1) [BENJAMIN]
Ge 35:18 (for she died) that she called his name **B**: 1126

BENT (8) [BEND]
Ps 7:12 he hath **b** his bow, and made it ready. 1869
37:14 and have **b** their bow, to cast down the poor 1869
Isa 5:28 arrows *are* sharp, and all their bows **b**, 1869
21:15 from the **b** bow, and from the grievousness 1869
La 2: 4 He hath **b** his bow like an enemy: *he* stood 1869
3:12 He hath **b** his bow, and set me as a mark 1869
Hos 11: 7 my people are **b** to backsliding from me: 8511
Zec 9:13 When I have **b** Judah for me, filled the bow 1869

BEN-ZOHETH (1)
1Ch 4:20 And the sons of Ishi *were*, Zoheth, and **B**. 1132

BEON (1)
Nu 32: 3 and Elealeh, and Shebam, and Nebo, and **B**, 1194

BEOR (10) [BOSOR]
Ge 36:32 Bela the son of **B** reigned in Edom: and 1160
Nu 22: 5 unto Balaam the son of **B** to Pethor, 1160
24: 3 Balaam the son of **B** hath said, and the man 1160
24:15 Balaam the son of **B** hath said, and the man 1160
31: 8 Balaam also the son of **B** they slew with 1160
Dt 23: 4 they hired against thee Balaam the son of **B** 1160
Jos 13:22 Balaam also the son of **B**, the soothsayer, 1160
24: 9 called Balaam the son of **B** to curse you: 1160
1Ch 1:43 the children of Israel; Bela the son of **B**: 1160
Mic 6: 5 what Balaam the son of **B** answered him; 1160

BERA (1)
Ge 14: 2 *That these* made war with **B** king of 1298

BERACAH See BERACHAH

BERACHAH (3)
1Ch 12: 3 and **B**, and Jehu the Antothite, 1294
2Ch 20:26 assembled themselves in the valley of **B**; 1293
20:26 was called, The valley of **B**, unto *this* day. 1293

BERACHIAH (1)
1Ch 6:39 *even* Asaph the son of **B**, the son of 1296

BERAIAH (1)
1Ch 8:21 Adaiah, and **B**, and Shimrath, the sons of 1256

BEREA (3)
Ac 17:10 sent away Paul and Silas by night unto **B**: *960*
17:13 the word of God was preached of Paul at **B**, *960*
20: 4 accompanied him into Asia Sopater of **B**; *961*

BEREAVE (6) [BEREAVED, BEREAVETH]
Ecc 4: 8 whom do I labour, and **b** my soul of good? 2637
Jer 15: 7 I will **b** *them* **of children**, I will destroy my 7921
Eze 5:17 and evil beasts, and they shall **b** thee; 7921
36:12 shalt no more henceforth **b** them **of men**. 7921
36:14 neither **b** thy nations any more, saith 7921
Hos 9:12 bring up their children, yet will I **b** them, 7921

BEREAVED (6) [BEREAVE]
Ge 42:36 unto them, Me have ye **b of** my **children**: 7921
43:14 If I be **b of** my **children**, I am bereaved. 7921
43:14 If I be bereaved of my children, I am **b**. 7921
Jer 18:21 let their wives be **b of** their **children**, and 7909
Eze 36:13 devourest up men, and hast **b** thy nations; 7921
Hos 13: 8 meet them as a bear *that is* **b of** her **whelps**, 7909

BEREAVETH (1) [BEREAVE]
La 1:20 abroad the sword **b**, at home *there is* as 7921

BERECHIAH (10) [BARACHIAS]
1Ch 3:20 Ohel, and **B**, and Hasadiah, Jushabhesed, 1296
9:16 and **B** the son of Asa, the son of Elkanah, 1296
15:17 of his brethren, Asaph the son of **B**; and 1296
15:23 **B** and Elkanah *were* doorkeepers for 1296
2Ch 28:12 **B** the son of Meshillemoth, and 1296
Ne 3: 4 them repaired Meshullam the son of **B**, 1296
3:30 After him repaired Meshullam the son of **B** 1296
6:18 the daughter of Meshullam the son of **B**. 1296
Zec 1: 1 the son of **B**, the son of Iddo the prophet, 1296
1: 7 the son of **B**, the son of Iddo the prophet, 1296

BERED (2)
Ge 16:14 behold, *it is* between Kadesh and **B**. 1260
1Ch 7:20 **B** his son, and Tahath his son, and 1260

BEREKIAH See BARACHIAS; BERECHIAH

BERI (1)
1Ch 7:36 Harnepher, and Shual, and **B**, and Imrah, 1275

BERIAH (11) [BERIITES]
Ge 46:17 and Ishui, and **B**, and Serah their sister: 1283
46:17 and the sons of **B**; Heber, and Malchiel. 1283
Nu 26:44 of **B**, the family of the Beriites. 1283
26:45 Of the sons of **B**: of Heber, the family of 1283
1Ch 7:23 he called his name **B**, because it went evil 1283
7:30 and Ishuai, and **B**, and Serah their sister. 1283
7:31 the sons of **B**; Heber, and Malchiel, who *is* 1283
8:13 **B** also, and Shema, who *were* heads of 1283
8:16 and Ispah, and Joha, the sons of **B**; 1283
23:10 *were*, Jahath, Zina, and Jeush, and **B**. 1283
23:11 Jeush and **B** had not many sons; therefore 1283

BERIITES (1) [BERIAH]
Nu 26:44 the Jesuites: of Beriah, the family of the **B**. 1284

BERITES (1)
2Sa 20:14 and *to* Beth-maachah, and all the **B**: 1276

BERITH (1) [BAAL-BERITH]
Jdg 9:46 into a hold of the house of the god **B**. 1286

BERNICE (3)
Ac 25:13 and **B** came unto Cesarea to salute Festus. *959*
25:23 and **B**, with great pomp, and were entered *959*
26:30 and **B**, and they that sat with them: *959*

BERODACH-BALADAN (1) [MERODACH-BALADAN]
2Ki 20:12 At that time **B**, the son of Baladan, king of 1255

BEROTHAH (1)
Eze 47:16 Hamath, **B**, Sibraim, which *is* between 1268

BEROTHAI (1) [BEROTHITE]
2Sa 8: 8 from Betah, and from **B**, cities of 1268

BEROTHITE (1) [BEROTHAI]
1Ch 11:39 Zelek the Ammonite, Naharai the **B**, 1307

BERRIES (2)
Isa 17: 6 three **b** in the top of the uppermost bough, 1620
Jas 3:12 Can the fig tree, my brethren, bear **olive b**? *1636*

BERYL (8)
Ex 28:20 the fourth row a **b**, and an onyx, and 8658
39:13 the fourth row, a **b**, an onyx, and a jasper: 8658
SS 5:14 His hands *are as* gold rings set with the **b**: 8658
Eze 1:16 their work *was* like unto the colour of a **b**: 8658
10: 9 the wheels *was* as the colour of a **b** stone. 8658
28:13 the **b**, the onyx, and the jasper, 8658
Da 10: 6 His body also *was* like the **b**, and his face 8658
Rev 21:20 the eighth, **b**; the ninth, a topaz; the tenth, *969*

BESAI (2)
Ezr 2:49 the children of Paseah, the children of **B**, 1153
Ne 7:52 The children of **B**, the children of Meunim, 1153

BESEECH (67) [BESEECHING, BESOUGHT]
Ex 3:18 now let us go, **we b thee**, three days' 4994
33:18 And he said, **I b thee**, shew me thy glory. 4994
Nu 12:11 Alas, my lord, **I b thee**, lay not the sin upon 4994
12:13 Heal her now, O God, **I b thee**. 4994
14:17 now, **I b thee**, let the power of my Lord be 4994
14:19 Pardon, **I b thee**, the iniquity of this people 4994
1Sa 23:11 God of Israel, **I b thee**, tell thy servant. 4994
2Sa 13:24 **I b thee**, and his servants go with thy 4994
16: 4 I **humbly b** thee *that* I may find grace in 7812
24:10 now, **I b thee**, O LORD, take away 4994
2Ki 19:19 O LORD our God, **I b thee**, 4994
20: 3 **I b thee**, O LORD, remember now how I 577
1Ch 21: 8 now, **I b thee**, do away the iniquity of thy 4994
2Ch 6:40 Now, my God, let, **I b thee**, thine eyes be 4994
Ne 1: 5 said, **I b thee**, O LORD God of heaven, 577
1: 8 Remember, **I b thee**, the word that thou 4994
1:11 O Lord, **I b thee**, let now thine ear be 577
Job 10: 9 Remember, **I b thee**, that thou hast made 4994
42: 4 Hear, **I b thee**, and I will speak: I will 4994
Ps 80:14 Return, **we b thee**, O God *of* hosts: 4994
116: 4 O LORD, I **b** thee, deliver my soul. 577
118:25 Save now, **I b thee**, O LORD: 577
118:25 O LORD, **I b thee**, send now prosperity. 577
119:108 Accept, **I b thee**, the freewill offerings of 4994
Isa 38: 3 Remember now, O LORD, **I b thee**, 4994
64: 9 behold, see, **we b thee**, we *are* all thy 4994
Jer 38: 4 **We b thee**, let this man be put to death: 4994
38:20 **I b thee**, the voice of the LORD, which I 4994
42: 2 unto Jeremiah the prophet, Let, **we b thee**, 4994
Da 1:12 Prove thy servants, **I b thee**, ten days; and 4994
9:16 **I b thee**, let thine anger and thy fury be 4994
Am 7: 2 I said, O Lord GOD, forgive, **I b thee**: 4994
7: 5 Then said I, O Lord GOD, cease, **I b thee**: 4994
Jnh 1:14 said, We **b** thee, O LORD, we beseech 577
1:14 We beseech thee, O LORD, **we b thee**, 4994
4: 3 Therefore now, O LORD, take, **I b thee**, 4994
Mal 1: 9 **b** God that he will be gracious unto 2470+6440
Mk 7:32 and they **b** him to put *his* hand upon him. *3870*
Lk 8:28 God most high? I **b** thee, torment me not. *1189*
9:38 saying, Master, I **b** thee, look upon my son: *1189*
Ac 21:39 and, I **b** thee, suffer me to speak unto *1189*
26: 3 wherefore I **b** thee to hear me patiently. *1189*
Ro 12: 1 I **b** you therefore, brethren, by the mercies *3870*
15:30 Now I **b** you, brethren, for the Lord Jesus *3870*
16:17 Now I **b** you, brethren, mark them which *3870*
1Co 1:10 Now I **b** you, brethren, by the name of our *3870*
4:16 Wherefore I **b** you, be ye followers of me. *3870*
16:15 I **b** you, brethren, (ye know the house of *3870*
2Co 2: 8 Wherefore I **b** you that *you* would confirm *3870*
5:20 for Christ, as though God did **b** *you* by us: *3870*
6: 1 *as* workers together *with him*, **b** *you* also *3870*
10: 1 Now I Paul myself **b** you by the meekness *3870*
10: 2 But I **b** *you*, that I may not be bold when I *1189*
Gal 4:12 Brethren, I **b** you, be as I *am*; for I *am* as ye *1189*
Eph 4: 1 **b** you that *ye* walk worthy of the vocation *3870*
Php 4: 2 I **b** Euodias, and beseech Syntyche, *3870*
4: 2 I beseech Euodias, and **b** Syntyche, *3870*
1Th 4: 1 Furthermore then we **b** you, brethren, and *2065*
4:10 but we **b** you, brethren, that *ye* increase *3870*
5:12 And we **b** you, brethren, to know them *2065*
2Th 2: 1 Now we **b** you, brethren, by the coming of *2065*
Phm 1: 9 *Yet* for love's sake I rather **b** *thee*, being *3870*
1:10 I **b** thee for my son Onesimus, whom I *3870*
Heb 13:19 But I **b** *you* the rather to do this, that I may *3870*
13:22 And I **b** you, brethren, suffer the word of *3870*
1Pe 2:11 I **b** *you* as strangers and pilgrims, *3870*
2Jn 1: 5 And now I **b** thee, lady, not as though I *2065*

BESEECHING (3) [BESEECH]
Mt 8: 5 there came unto him a centurion, **b** him, *3870*
Mk 1:40 **b** him, and kneeling down to him, and *3870*
Lk 7: 3 **b** him that he would come and heal his *2065*

BESET (6)
Jdg 19:22 **b** the house **round about**, *and* beat at 5437
20: 5 **b** the house **round about** upon me by 5437
Ps 22:12 strong *bulls* of Bashan have **b** me **round**. 3803
139: 5 Thou hast **b** me behind and before, and 6696
Hos 7: 2 now their own doings have **b** them **about**; 5437
Heb 12: 1 and the sin which doth so **easily b** *us*, and *2139*

BESIDE (95) [BESIDES]
Ge 31:50 if thou shalt take *other* wives **b** my 5921
Ex 12:37 on foot *that were* men, **b** 905+4480+3807.1
14: 9 the sea, **b** Pi-hahiroth, before Baal-zephon. 5921
29:12 pour all the blood **b** the bottom of the altar. 413
Lev 1:16 cast it **b** the altar on the east part, by 681
9:17 burnt *it* upon the altar, **b** 905+4480+3807.1
10:12 by fire, and eat it without leaven **b** the altar: 681
23:38 **B** the sabbaths of the LORD, 905+4480+3807.1
23:38 **b** your gifts, and beside all 905+4480+3807.1
23:38 **b** all your vows, and beside 905+4480+3807.1
23:38 **b** all your freewill offerings, 905+4480+3807.1
Nu 5: 8 *even* to the priest; **b** the ram 905+4480+3807.1
5:20 *some* man hath lain with thee **b** thine 1107+4480
11: 6 at all, **b** *this* manna, *before* our eyes. 1115
16:49 seven hundred, **b** them that 905+4480+3807.1
24: 6 *and* as cedar trees **b** the waters. 5921
28:10 **b** the continual burnt offering, and his drink 5921
28:23 Ye shall offer these **b** 905+4480+3807.1
28:24 it shall be offered **b** the continual burnt 5921
29: 6 **B** the burnt offering of 905+4480+3807.1
29:11 the goats *for* a sin offering; **b** 905+4480+3807.1
29:16 the goats *for* a sin offering; **b** 905+4480+3807.1
29:19 the goats *for* a sin offering; **b** 905+4480+3807.1
29:22 one goat for a sin offering; **b** 905+4480+3807.1
29:25 the goats *for* a sin offering; **b** 905+4480+3807.1
29:28 one goat for a sin offering; **b** 905+4480+3807.1
29:31 one goat for a sin offering; **b** 905+4480+3807.1
29:34 one goat for a sin offering; **b** 905+4480+3807.1
29:38 one goat for a sin offering; **b** 905+4480+3807.1
31: 8 **b** *the rest of* them that were slain; 5921
Dt 3: 5 **b** unwalled towns a great many. 905+3807.1
11:30 over against Gilgal, **b** the plains of Moreh? 681
18: 8 shall have like portions to eat, **b** 905+3807.1
19: 9 add three cities moe for thee, **b** these three: 5921

Dt 29: 1 Israel in the land of Moab, **b** 905+4480+3807.1
Jos 3:16 the city Adam, that *is* **b** Zaretan: 4480+6654
7: 2 which *is* **b** Beth-aven, on the east side of 5973
12: 9 king of Ai, which *is* **b** Beth-el, one; 4480+6654
13: 4 Mearah that *is* **b** the Sidonians, 3807.1
17: 5 **b** the land of Gilead and 905+4480+3807.1
22:19 in building you an altar **b** the altar of 1107+4480
Jdg 6:37 *it be* dry upon all the earth **b**, then shall I NIH
7: 1 up early, and pitched **b** the well of Harod: 5921
8:26 **b** ornaments, and collars, and 905+4480+3807.1
8:26 **b** the chains that *were* about 905+4480+3807.1
11:34 **b** her he had neither son nor daughter. 4480
20:15 **b** the inhabitants of Gibeah, 905+3807.1
20:17 the men of Israel, **b** Benjamin, 905+4480+3807.1
20:36 liers in wait which they had set **b** Gibeah. 413
Ru 2:14 she sat **b** the reapers: and he reached 4480+6654
1Sa 2: 2 for *there is* none **b** thee: neither *is there* any 1115
4: 1 to battle, and pitched **b** Eben-ezer: 5921
19: 3 stand **b** my father in the field 3027+3807.1
2Sa 7:22 like thee, neither *is there any* God **b** thee, 2108
13:23 in Baal-hazor, which *is* **b** Ephraim: 5973
15: 2 and stood **b** the way of the gate: 3027+5921
15:18 all his servants passed on **b** him; and 3027+5921
1Ki 3:20 at midnight, and took my son from **b** me, 681
4:23 an hundred sheep, **b** harts, and 905+4480+3807.1
9:26 which *is* **b** Eloth, on the shore of the Red 854
10:19 of the seat, and two lions stood **b** the stays. 681
11:25 to Israel all the days of Solomon, **b** 854+2050.1
13:31 of God *is* buried; lay my bones **b** his bones: 681
2Ki 11:20 they slew Athaliah with the sword **b** NIH
12: 9 a hole in the lid of it, and set it **b** the altar, 681
21:16 from one end to another; **b** 905+4480+3807.1
1Ch 3: 9 *were* all the sons of David, **b** 905+4480+3807.1
2Ch 20: 1 and with them *other* **b** the Ammonites, 4480
26:19 of the LORD, from **b** the incense altar. 3807.1
31:16 **B** their genealogy of males, 905+4480+3807.1
Ezr 1: 6 **b** all *that* was willingly 905+5921+3807.1
2:65 **B** their servants and 905+4480+3807.1
Ne 5:15 and wine, **b** forty shekels of silver; 310
7:67 **B** their manservants and 905+4480+3807.1
8: 4 and **b** him stood Mattithiah, and Shema, and 681
Job 1:14 and the asses feeding **b** them: 3027+5921
Ps 23: 2 he leadeth me **b** the still waters. 5921
73:25 *there is* none upon earth *that* I desire **b** thee. 5973
SS 1: 8 and feed thy kids **b** the shepherds' tents. 5921
Isa 32:20 Blessed *are* ye that sow **b** all waters, 5921
43:11 and **b** me *there is* no saviour. 1107+4480
45:21 *there is* no God **else b** me; 1107+4480+5750
45:21 just God and a saviour; *there is* none **b** me. 2108
Jer 36:21 the princes which stood **b** the king. 4480+5921
Eze 9: 2 they went in, and stood **b** the brasen altar. 681
10: 6 then he went in, and stood **b** the wheels. 681
10:16 the same wheels also turned not from **b** 681
Hos 13: 4 no god but me: for *there is* no saviour **b** me. 1115
Zep 2:15 in her heart, I *am*, and *there is* none **b** me: 5750
Mt 14:21 five thousand men, **b** women and children. 5565
15:38 four thousand men, **b** women and children. 5565
Mk 3:21 hold on him: for they said, He is **b himself**. 1839
Lk 24:21 and **b** all this, to day is the third day since 4862
Ac 26:24 with a loud voice, Paul, thou art **b thyself**; 3105
2Pe 1: 5 And **b** this, giving all diligence, add to your 2532

BESIDES (45) [BESIDE]

Ge 19:12 men said unto Lot, Hast thou here any **b**? 5750
26: 1 was a famine in the land, **b** 905+4480+3807.1
46:26 which came out of his loins, **b** 905+4480+3807.1
Lev 6:10 the altar, and he shall put them **b** the altar. 681
7:13 **B** the cakes, he shall offer *for* his offering 5921
18:18 her nakedness, **b** the other in her life *time*. 5921
Nu 6:21 LORD for his separation, **b** 905+4480+3807.1
28:15 **b** the continual burnt offering, and his drink 5921
28:31 Ye shall offer *them* **b** 905+4480+3807.1
29:39 LORD in your set feasts, **b** 905+4480+3807.1
Dt 4:35 *there is* none else **b** him. 905+4480+3807.1
Jos 22:29 **b** the altar of the LORD our 905+4480+3807.1
Ru 4: 4 for *there is* none to redeem *it* **b** thee; and 2108
1Ki 5:16 **B** the chief of Solomon's 905+4480+3807.1
10:13 what*soever* she asked, **b** *that* 905+4480+3807.1
10:15 **B** *that he had* of the merchantmen, 905+4480+3807.1
22: 7 *Is there* not here a prophet of the LORD **b**, 5750
1Ch 17:20 like thee, neither *is there any* God **b** thee, 2108
2Ch 9:12 what*soever* she asked, **b** *that* 905+4480+3807.1
9:14 **B** *that which* chapmen 905+4480+3807.1
17:19 These waited on the king, **b** 905+4480+3807.1
18: 6 *Is there* not here a prophet of the LORD **b**, 5750
Ezr 1: 4 **b** the freewill offering for the house of God 5973
Ne 5:17 **b** those that came unto us from among 2050.1
Isa 26:13 *other* lords **b** thee have had dominion over 2108
44: 6 the last; and **b** me *there is* no God. 1107+4480
44: 8 Is there a God **b** me? yea, *there is* no 1107+4480
45: 5 *there is* none else, *there is* no God **b** me: 2108
45: 6 and from the west, that *there is* none **b** me. 1107
47: 8 in thine heart, I *am*, and none else **b** me; 5750
47:10 in thine heart, I *am*, and none else **b** me. 5750
56: 8 **b** those that are gathered unto him. 3807.1
64: 4 neither hath the eye seen, O God, **b** thee, 2108
Jer 36:32 there were added **b** unto them many like 5750
Eze 10:19 the wheels also *were* **b** them, and 5980+3807.1
11:22 their wings, and the wheels **b** them; 5980+3807.1
32:13 the beasts thereof from **b** the great waters; 5921
Da 11: 4 even for others **b** those. 905+4480+3807.1
Mt 25:20 I have gained **b** them five talents moe. 1909
25:22 I have gained two other talents **b** them. 1909
Lk 16:26 And **b** all this, between us and you there is 1909
1Co 1:16 **b**, I know not whether I baptized any other. 3062
2Co 5:13 For whether we be **b ourselves**, *it is* to 1839
11:28 **B** those *things* that are without, that which 5565
Phm 1:19 thou **owest** unto me even thine own self **b**. 4359

BESIEGE (11) [BESIEGED, SIEGE]

Dt 20:12 war against thee, then thou shalt **b** it: 5921+6696
20:19 When thou shalt **b** a city a long time, 6696
28:52 he shall **b** thee in all thy gates, until thy 6887
28:52 he shall **b** thee in all thy gates throughout 6887
1Sa 23: 8 go down *to* Keilah, to **b** David and his men. 6696
1Ki 8:37 if their enemy **b** them in the land of their 6887
2Ki 24:11 against the city, and his servants *did* **b** it. 6696
2Ch 6:28 if their enemies **b** them in the cities of their 6887
Isa 21: 2 **b**, O Media; all the sighing thereof have I 6696
Jer 21: 4 which **b** you without the walls, and I will 6696
21: 9 falleth to the Chaldeans that **b** you, he shall 6696

BESIEGED (23) [BESIEGE]

2Sa 11: 1 the children of Ammon, and **b** Rabbah. 6696
20:15 and **b** him in Abel of Beth-maachah, 6696
1Ki 16:17 and all Israel with him, and they **b** Tirzah. 6696
20: 1 he went up and **b** Samaria, and 6696
2Ki 6:24 all his host, and went up, and **b** Samaria. 6696
6:25 behold, they **b** it, until an ass's head was 6696
16: 5 they **b** Ahaz, but could not overcome *him*. 6696
17: 5 went up *to* Samaria, and **b** it three years. 6696
18: 9 Assyria came up against Samaria, and **b** it. 6696
19:24 have I dried up all the rivers of **b** *places*. 4693
24:10 and the city was **b**. 4692+871.1+1886.1
25: 2 the city was **b** unto 935+4692+871.1+1886.1
1Ch 20: 1 of Ammon, and came and **b** Rabbah. 6696
Ecc 9:14 and **b** it, and built great bulwarks against it: 5437
Isa 1: 8 lodge in a garden of cucumbers, as a **b** city. 5341
37:25 I dried up all the rivers of the **b** *places*. 4693
Jer 32: 2 the king of Babylon's army **b** Jerusalem: 6696
37: 5 when the Chaldeans that **b** Jerusalem heard 6696
39: 1 his army against Jerusalem, and they **b** it. 6696
52: 5 So the city was **b** unto 935+4692+871.1+1886.1
Eze 4: 3 it shall be **b**, and thou shalt 4692+871.1+1886.1
6:12 and is **b** shall die by the famine: 5341
Da 1: 1 king of Babylon *unto* Jerusalem, and **b** it. 6696

BESODEIAH (1)

Ne 3: 6 son of Paseah, and Meshullam the son of **B**; 1152

BESOM (1)

Isa 14:23 I will sweep it with the **b** of destruction, 4292

BESOR (3)

1Sa 30: 9 *were* with him, and came to the brook **B**, 1308
30:10 that they could not go over the brook **B**. 1308
30:21 they had made also to abide at the brook **B**: 1308

BESOUGHT (44) [BESEECH]

Ge 42:21 when he **b** us, and we would not hear; 2603
Ex 32:11 Moses **b** the LORD his God, 853+2470+6440
Dt 3:23 I **b** the LORD at that time, saying, 413+2603
2Sa 12:16 David therefore **b** God for the child; and 1245
1Ki 13: 6 the man of God **b** the LORD, and 2470+6440
2Ki 1:13 **b** him, and said unto him, O man of God, 2603
13: 4 Jehoahaz **b** the LORD, and 2470+6440
2Ch 33:12 he **b** the LORD his God, and 853+2470+6440
Ezr 8:23 So we fasted and **b** our God for this: and 1245
Est 8: 3 **b** him with tears to put away the mischief 2603
Jer 26:19 **b** the LORD, and the LORD 853+2470+6440
Mt 8:31 So the devils **b** him, saying, If thou cast us 3870
8:34 they **b** *him* that he would depart out of their 3870
14:36 And **b** him that they might only touch 3870
15:23 And his disciples came and **b** him, saying, 2065
18:29 and **b** him, saying, Have patience with me, 3870
Mk 5:10 And he **b** him much that he would not send 3870
5:12 And all the devils **b** him, saying, Send us 3870
5:23 And **b** him greatly, saying, My little 3870
6:56 **b** him that they might touch if it were but 3870
7:26 she **b** him that he would cast forth the devil 2065
8:22 man unto him, and **b** him to touch him. 3870
Lk 4:38 with a great fever; and they **b** him for her. 2065
5:12 and **b** him, saying, Lord, if thou wilt, 1189
7: 4 came to Jesus, they **b** him instantly, saying, 3870
8:31 And they **b** him that he would not 3870
8:32 they **b** him that he would suffer them to 3870
8:37 round about **b** him to depart from them; 2065
8:38 departed **b** him that *he* might be with him: 1189
8:41 **b** him that *he* would come into his house: 3870
9:40 And I **b** thy disciples to cast him out; and 1189
11:37 a certain Pharisee **b** him to dine with him: 2065
Jn 4:40 they **b** him that *he* would tarry with them: 2065
4:47 and **b** him that he would come down, and 2065
19:31 **b** Pilate that their legs might be broken, and 2065
19:38 **b** Pilate that he might take away the body 2065
Ac 13:42 the Gentiles **b** that these words might be 3870
16:15 and her household, she **b** *us*, saying, 3870
16:39 And they came and **b** them, and 3870
21:12 that place, **b** him not to go up to Jerusalem. 3870
25: 2 Jews informed him against Paul, and **b** him, 3870
27:33 Paul **b** *them* all to take meat, saying, 3870
2Co 12: 8 For this *thing* I **b** the Lord thrice, that it 3870
1Ti 1: 3 As I **b** thee to abide *still* at Ephesus, when I 3870

BEST (25) [GOOD]

Ge 43:11 take of the **b fruits** in the land in your 2173
47: 6 in the **b** of the land make thy father and 4315
47:11 in the **b** of the land, in the land of Rameses, 4315
Ex 22: 5 of the **b** of his own field, and of the best of 4315
22: 5 of the **b** of his own vineyard, shall he make 4315
Nu 18:12 All the **b** of the oil, and all the best of 2459
18:12 and all the **b** of the wine, and of the wheat, 2459
18:29 of all the **b** thereof, *even* the hallowed *part* 2459
18:30 When ye have heaved the **b** thereof from it, 2459
18:32 when ye have heaved from it the **b** of it: 2459
36: 6 marry to whom they **think b**; 2896+5869+871.1
Dt 23:16 where it **liketh** him **b**: 2896+871.1+1886.1
1Sa 8:14 *even* the **b** *of them*, and give *them* to his 2896
15: 9 the **b** of the sheep, and of the oxen, and 4315
15:15 for the people spared the **b** of the sheep and 4315
2Sa 18: 4 unto them, What seemeth you **b** I will do. 3190
1Ki 10:18 of ivory, and overlaid it with the **b** gold. 6338
2Ki 10: 3 Look even out the **b** and meetest of your 2896
Est 2: 9 her maids unto the **b** *place* of the house of 2896
Ps 39: 5 verily every man **at** his **b state** *is* altogether 5324
SS 7: 9 the roof of thy mouth like the **b** wine, 2896
Eze 31:16 the choice and **b** of Lebanon, all that drink 2896
Mic 7: 4 The **b** of them *is* as a brier: the *most* 2896
Lk 15:22 Bring forth the **b** robe, and put *it* on him; 4413
1Co 12:31 But covet earnestly the **b** gifts: and 2909

BESTEAD (1)

Isa 8:21 shall pass through it, **hardly b** and hungry: 7185

BESTIR (1)

2Sa 5:24 *that* then thou shalt **b** thyself: 2782

BESTOW (9) [BESTOWED]

Ex 32:29 that he may **b** upon you a blessing *this* day. 5414
Dt 14:26 thou shalt **b** *that* money for whatsoever thy 5414
2Ch 24: 7 of the LORD did they **b** upon Baalim. 6213
Ezr 7:20 which thou shalt have occasion to **b**, 5415
7:20 **b** *it* out of the king's treasure house. 5415
Lk 12:17 I have no room where to **b** my fruits? 4863
12:18 and there will I **b** all my fruits and 4863
1Co 12:23 upon these we **b** more abundant honour; 4060
13: 3 And though I **b** all my goods **to feed** 5595

BESTOWED (14) [BESTOW]

1Ki 10:26 whom he **b** in the cities for chariots, and 5148
2Ki 5:24 from their hand, and **b** *them* in the house: 6485
12:15 delivered the money to be **b** on workmen: 5414
1Ch 29:25 **b** upon him *such* royal majesty as had not 5414
2Ch 9:25 whom he **b** in the chariot cities, and 3240
Isa 63: 7 according to all that the LORD hath **b on** 1580
63: 7 which he hath **b on** them according to his 1580
Jn 4:38 you to reap *that* whereon ye **b** no **labour**: 2872
Ro 16: 6 Greet Mary, who **b** much **labour** on us. 2872
1Co 15:10 his grace which was **b** upon me was not in NIG
2Co 1:11 that for the gift **b** upon us by the means of NIG
8: 1 we do you to wit of the grace of God **b** on 1325
Gal 4:11 lest I have **b** upon you **labour** in vain. 2872
1Jn 3: 1 what manner of love the Father hath **b** upon 1325

BETAH (1)

2Sa 8: 8 from **B**, and from Berothai, cities of 984

BETEN (1)

Jos 19:25 and Hali, and **B**, and Achshaph, 991

BETH BIRI See BETH-BIREI

BETH HAKKEREM See BETH-HACCEREM

BETH HARAM See BETH-ARAM

BETH MAACAH See BETH-MAACHAH

BETH OPHRAH See HOUSE OF APHRAH

BETH PELET See BETH-PALET; BETH-PHELET

BETHABARA (1)

Jn 1:28 These *things* were done in **B** beyond Jordan, 962

BETH-ANATH (3) [ANATH]

Jos 19:38 Horem, and **B**, and Beth-shemesh; 1043
Jdg 1:33 of Beth-shemesh, nor the inhabitants of **B**; 1043
1:33 and of **B** became tributaries unto them. 1043

BETH-ANOTH (1)

Jos 15:59 Maarath, and **B**, and Eltekon; six cities with 1042

BETHANY (11)

Mt 21:17 he left them, and went out of the city into **B**; 963
26: 6 Now when Jesus was in **B**, in the house of 963
Mk 11: 1 unto Bethphage and **B**, at the mount of 963
11:11 he went out unto **B** with the twelve. 963
11:12 when they were come from **B**, he was 963
14: 3 And being in **B** in the house of Simon 963
Lk 19:29 when he was come nigh to Bethphage and **B**, 963
24:50 And he led them out as far as to **B**, and 963
Jn 11: 1 *named* Lazarus, of **B**, the town of Mary and 963
11:18 Now **B** was nigh unto Jerusalem, 963
12: 1 six days before the passover came to **B**, 963

BETH-ARABAH (3) [ARABAH]

Jos 15: 6 and passed along by the north of **B**; 1026
15:61 In the wilderness, **B**, Middin, and Secacah, 1026
18:22 And **B**, and Zemaraim, and Beth-el, 1026

BETH-ARAM (1) [ARAM]

Jos 13:27 **B**, and Beth-nimrah, and Succoth, and 1027

BETH-ARBEL (1)

Hos 10:14 as Shalman spoiled **B** in the day of battle: 1009

BETH-AVEN (7) [AVEN]

Jos 7: 2 which *is* beside **B**, on the east side of 1007
18:12 out thereof were at the wilderness of **B**. 1007
1Sa 13: 5 and pitched in Michmash, eastward from **B**. 1007
14:23 that day: and the battle passed over *unto* **B**. 1007
Hos 4:15 neither go ye up *to* **B**, nor swear, 1007
5: 8 cry aloud *at* **B**, after thee, O Benjamin. 1007
10: 5 shall fear because of the calves of **B**: 1007

BETH-AZMAVETH (1) [AZMAVETH]

Ne 7:28 The men of **B**, forty and two. 1041

BETH-BAAL-MEON (1) [BAAL-MEON]

Jos 13:17 the plain; Dibon, and Bamoth-baal, and **B**, 1010

BETH-BARAH (2)

Jdg 7:24 take before them the waters unto **B** and 1012
7:24 and took the waters unto **B** and Jordan. 1012

BETH-BIREI (1)

1Ch 4:31 and at **B**, and at Shaaraim. 1011

BETH-CAR (1)

1Sa 7:11 and smote them, until *they came* under **B**. 1033

BETH-DAGON (2) [DAGON]
Jos 15:41 **B**, and Naamah, and Makkedah; 1016
19:27 turneth *toward* the sunrising *to* **B**, and 1016

BETH-DIBLATHAIM (1)
Jer 48:22 upon Dibon, and upon Nebo, and upon **B**, 1015

BETH-EL (66) [BETHELITE, EL-BETH-EL, GOD, HOUSE]
Ge 12: 8 thence unto a mountain on the east of **B**, 1008
12: 8 *having* **B** on the west, and Hai on the east: 1008
13: 3 on his journeys from the south even to **B**, 1008
13: 3 been at the beginning, between **B** and Hai; 1008
28:19 he called the name of that place **B**: but 1008
31:13 I *am* the God of **B**, where thou anointedst 1008
35: 1 Arise, go up to **B**, and dwell there: 1008
35: 3 let us arise, and go up to **B**; and I will make 1008
35: 6 that *is*, **B**, he and all the people that *were* 1008
35: 8 she was buried beneath **B** under an oak: 1008
35:15 of the place where God spake with him, **B**. 1008
35:16 they journeyed from **B**; and there was but 1008
Jos 7: 2 on the east side of **B**, and spake unto them, 1008
8: 9 abode between **B** and Ai, on the west side 1008
8:12 set them to lie in ambush between **B** and 1008
8:17 there was not a man left in Ai or **B**, 1008
12: 9 one; the king of Ai, which *is* beside **B**, one; 1008
12:16 king of Makkedah, one; the king of **B**, one; 1008
16: 1 goeth up from Jericho throughout mount **B**, 1008
16: 2 goeth out from **B** to Luz, and passeth along 1008
18:13 to the side of Luz, which *is* **B**, southward; 1008
18:22 And Beth-arabah, and Zemaraim, and **B**, 1008
Jdg 1:22 of Joseph, they also went up *against* **B**: 1008
1:23 the house of Joseph sent to descry **B**. 1008
4: 5 between Ramah and **B** in mount Ephraim: 1008
21:19 *in a place* which *is* on the north side of **B**, 1008
21:19 highway that goeth up from **B** to Shechem, 1008
1Sa 7:16 he went from year to year in circuit *to* **B**, 1008
10: 3 meet thee three men going up to God *to* **B**, 1008
13: 2 with Saul in Michmash and in mount **B**, 1008
30:27 To *them* which *were* in **B**, and to *them* 1008
1Ki 12:29 he set the one in **B**, and the other put he in 1008
12:32 he offered upon the altar (so did he in **B**,) 1008
12:32 he placed in **B** the priests of the high places 1008
12:33 in **B** the fifteenth day of the eighth month, 1008
13: 1 Judah by the word of the LORD unto **B**: 1008
13: 4 which had cried against the altar in **B**, 1008
13:10 returned not by the way that he came to **B**. 1008
13:11 Now there dwelt an old prophet in **B**; and 1008
13:11 that the man of God had done *that* day in **B**: 1008
13:32 word of the LORD against the altar in **B**, 1008
2Ki 2: 2 for the LORD hath sent me to **B**. 1008
2: 2 not leave thee. So they went down *to* **B**. 1008
2: 3 the sons of the prophets that *were* at **B** 1008
2:23 he went up from thence *unto* **B**: and as he 1008
10:29 *to wit*, the golden calves that *were in* **B**, and 1008
17:28 away from Samaria came and dwelt in **B**, 1008
23: 4 and carried the ashes of them *unto* **B**. 1008
23:15 Moreover the altar that *was* at **B**, *and* 1008
23:17 that thou hast done against the altar of **B**. 1008
23:19 to all the acts that he had done in **B**. 1008
1Ch 7:28 habitations *were*, **B** and the towns thereof, 1008
2Ch 13:19 **B** with the towns thereof, and Jeshanah 1008
Ezr 2:28 The men of **B** and Ai, two hundred twenty 1008
Ne 7:32 The men of **B** and Ai, an hundred twenty 1008
11:31 and Aija, and **B**, and *in* their villages, 1008
Jer 48:13 as the house of Israel was ashamed of **B** 1008
Hos 10:15 So shall **B** do unto you because of your 1008
12: 4 he found him *in* **B**, and there he spake with 1008
Am 3:14 upon him I will also visit the altars of **B**: 1008
4: 4 Come *to* **B**, and transgress; *at* Gilgal 1008
5: 5 seek not **B**, nor enter *into* Gilgal, and 1008
5: 5 into captivity, and **B** shall come to nought. 1008
5: 6 and *there be* none to quench *it* in **B**. 1008
7:10 Amaziah *the* priest of **B** sent to Jeroboam 1008
7:13 prophesy not again any more *at* **B**: for it *is* 1008

BETHELITE (1) [BETH-EL]
1Ki 16:34 In his days did Hiel the **B** build Jericho: 1017

BETH-EMEK (1)
Jos 19:27 of Jiphthah-el toward the north side *of* **B**, 1025

BETHER (1)
SS 2:17 or a young hart upon the mountains of **B**. 1335

BETHESDA (1)
Jn 5: 2 which is called in the Hebrew tongue **B**, *964*

BETH-EZEL (1) [EZEL]
Mic 1:11 came not forth *in* the mourning of **B**; 1018

BETH-GADER (1)
1Ch 2:51 of Beth-lehem, Hareph the father of **B**. 1013

BETH-GAMUL (1) [GAMUL]
Jer 48:23 and upon **B**, and upon Beth-meon, 1014

BETH-HACCEREM (2)
Ne 3:14 the son of Rechab, the ruler of part of **B**; 1021
Jer 6: 1 in Tekoa, and set up a sign of fire in **B**: 1021

BETH-HARAN (1) [HARAN]
Nu 32:36 Beth-nimrah, and **B**, fenced cities: and 1028

BETH-HOGLA (1) [BETH-HOGLAH]
Jos 15: 6 the border went up *to* **B**, and passed along 1031

BETH-HOGLAH (2) [BETH-HOGLA]
Jos 18:19 the border passed along to the side of **B** 1031
18:21 and **B**, and the valley of Keziz, 1031

BETH-HORON (14)
Jos 10:10 them *along* the way that goeth up to **B**, 1032
10:11 *and* were in the going down to **B**, 1032
16: 3 unto the coast of **B** the nether, and 1032
16: 5 side was Ataroth-addar, unto **B** the upper; 1032
18:13 that *lieth* on the south side of the nether **B**. 1032
18:14 from the hill that *lieth* before **B** southward; 1032
21:22 with her suburbs, and **B** with her suburbs; 1032
1Sa 13:18 another company turned the way to **B**: and 1032
1Ki 9:17 Solomon built Gezer, and **B** the nether, 1032
1Ch 6:68 with her suburbs, and **B** with her suburbs, 1032
7:24 who built **B** the nether, and the upper, and 1032
2Ch 8: 5 Also he built **B** the upper, and Beth-horon 1032
8: 5 **B** the nether, fenced cities, *with* walls, 1032
25:13 from Samaria even unto **B**, and smote three 1032

BETHINK (2) [THINK]
1Ki 8:47 *Yet if* they shall **b** themselves in 413+3820+7725
2Ch 6:37 *Yet if* they **b** themselves in 413+3824+7725

BETH-JESHIMOTH (3) [BETH-JESIMOTH]
Jos 12: 3 *even* the salt sea on the east, the way to **B**; 1020
13:20 and Ashdoth-pisgah, and **B**, 1020
Eze 25: 9 the country, **B**, Baal-meon, and Kiriathaim, 1020

BETH-JESIMOTH (1) [BETH-JESHIMOTH]
Nu 33:49 from **B** *even* unto Abel-shittim in the plains 1020

BETH-LEBAOTH (1)
Jos 19: 6 **B**, and Sharuhen; thirteen cities and 1034

BETHLEHEM, BETH-LEHEM (39) [BETH-LEHEM-JUDAH, BETH-LEHEMITE, BETHLEHEM]
Ge 35:19 buried in the way to Ephrath, which *is* **B**. 1035
48: 7 there in the way of Ephrath; the same *is* **B**. 1035
Jos 19:15 Nahallal, and Shimron, and Idalah, and **B**: 1035
Jdg 12: 8 And after him Ibzan of **B** judged Israel. 1035
12:10 Then died Ibzan, and was buried at **B**. 1035
Ru 1:19 So they two went until they came *to* **B**. 1035
1:19 it came to pass, when they were come *to* **B**, 1035
1:22 they came *to* **B** in the beginning of barley 1035
2: 4 Boaz came from **B**, and said unto 1035
4:11 worthily in Ephratah, and be famous in **B**: 1035
1Sa 16: 4 which the LORD spake, and came *to* **B**. 1035
17:15 from Saul to feed his father's sheep *at* **B**. 1035
20: 6 *leave* of me that *he* might run *to* **B** his city: 1035
20:28 earnestly asked *leave* of me *to go* to **B**: 1035
2Sa 2:32 the sepulchre of his father, which *was in* **B**. 1035
23:14 garrison of the Philistines *was* then *in* **B**. 1035
23:15 give me drink *of* the water of the well of **B**, 1035
23:16 drew water out of the well of **B**, that *was* by 1035
23:24 of the thirty; Elhanan the son of Dodo *of* **B**, 1035
1Ch 2:51 Salma the father of **B**, Hareph the father of 1035
2:54 **B**, and the Netophathites, Ataroth, 1035
4: 4 the firstborn of Ephratah, the father of **B**. 1035
11:16 and the Philistines' garrison *was* then at **B**. 1035
11:17 give me drink *of* the water of the well of **B**, 1035
11:18 drew water out of the well of **B**, that *was* by 1035
11:26 of Joab, Elhanan the son of Dodo of **B**, 1035
2Ch 11: 6 He built even **B**, and Etam, and Tekoa, 1035
Ezr 2:21 The children of **B**, an hundred twenty and 1035
Ne 7:26 The men of **B** and Netophah, an hundred 1035
Jer 41:17 which *is* by **B**, to go to enter *into* Egypt, 1035
Mic 5: 2 thou, **B** Ephratah, *though thou be* little 1035
Mt 2: 1 Now when Jesus was born in **B** of Judea in *965*
2: 5 And they said unto him, In **B** of Judea: *965*
2: 6 And thou **B**, *in* the land of Juda, art not *965*
2: 8 And he sent them to **B**, and said, Go and *965*
2:16 and slew all the children that were in **B**, and *965*
Lk 2: 4 unto the city of David, which is called **B**; *965*
2:15 Let us now go *even* unto **B**, and see this *965*
Jn 7:42 and out of the town of **B**, where David was? *965*

BETH-LEHEMITE (4) [BETH-LEHEM]
1Sa 16: 1 and go, I will send thee to Jesse the **B**: 1022
16:18 Behold, I have seen a son of Jesse the **B**, 1022
17:58 *I am* the son of thy servant Jesse the **B**. 1022
2Sa 21:19 a **B**, slew *the brother of* Goliath the Gittite, 1022

BETH-LEHEM-JUDAH (10) [BETH-LEHEM, JUDAH]
Jdg 17: 7 there was a young man out of **B** of 1035+3063
17: 8 **B** to sojourn where he could find *a* 1035+3063
17: 9 I *am* a Levite of **B**, and I go to 1035+3063
19: 1 took to him a concubine out of **B**. 1035+3063
19: 2 him unto her father's house to **B**, 1035+3063
19:18 We are passing from **B** toward 1035+3063
19:18 I went to **B**, but I am *now* going *to* 1035+3063
Ru 1: 1 a *certain* man of **B** went to sojourn in 1035+3063
1: 2 and Chilion, Ephrathites of **B**. 1035+3063
1Sa 17:12 *was* the son of that Ephrathite of **B**, 1035+3063

BETH-MAACHAH (2) [ABEL-BETH-MAACHAH]
2Sa 20:14 unto Abel, and *to* **B**, and all the Berites: 1038
20:15 they came and besieged him in Abel of **B**, 1038

BETH-MARCABOTH (2)
Jos 19: 5 And Ziklag, and **B**, and Hazar-susah, 1024
1Ch 4:31 at **B**, and Hazar-susim, and at Beth-birei, 1024

BETH-MEON (1) [BAAL-MEON]
Jer 48:23 and upon Beth-gamul, and upon **B**, 1010

BETH-NIMRAH (2) [NIMRAH]
Nu 32:36 **B**, and Beth-haran, fenced cities: and 1039
Jos 13:27 and **B**, and Succoth, and Zaphon, 1039

BETH-PALET (1) [BETH-PHELET]
Jos 15:27 And Hazar-gaddah, and Heshmon, and **B**, 1046

BETH-PAZZEZ (1)
Jos 19:21 and En-gannim, and En-haddah, and **B**; 1048

BETH-PEOR (4) [PEOR]
Dt 3:29 So we abode in the valley over against **B**. 1047
4:46 side Jordan, in the valley over against **B**, 1047
34: 6 valley in the land of Moab, over against **B**: 1047
Jos 13:20 **B**, and Ashdoth-pisgah, and 1047

BETHPHAGE (3)
Mt 21: 1 and were come to **B**, unto the mount of *967*
Mk 11: 1 unto **B** and Bethany, at the mount of Olives, *967*
Lk 19:29 when he was come nigh to **B** and Bethany, *967*

BETH-PHELET (1) [BETH-PALET]
Ne 11:26 And at Jeshua, and at Moladah, and at **B**, 1046

BETH-RAPHA (1) [RAPHA]
1Ch 4:12 Eshton begat **B**, and Paseah, and Tehinnah 1051

BETH-REHOB (2) [REHOB]
Jdg 18:28 and it was in the valley that *lieth* by **B**. 1050
2Sa 10: 6 of Ammon sent and hired the Syrians of **B**, 1050

BETHSAIDA (7)
Mt 11:21 Woe unto thee, Chorazin, woe unto thee, **B**: *966*
Mk 6:45 and to go to the other side before unto **B**, *966*
8:22 And he cometh to **B**; and they bring a blind *966*
Lk 9:10 a desert place belonging to the city called **B**. *966*
10:13 Woe unto thee, Chorazin, woe unto thee, **B**: *966*
Jn 1:44 Now Philip was of **B**, the city of Andrew *966*
12:21 which was of **B** of Galilee, and desired him, *966*

BETH-SHAN (3) [BETH-SHEAN]
1Sa 31:10 and they fastened his body to the wall of **B**. 1052
31:12 the bodies of his sons from the wall of **B**, 1052
2Sa 21:12 which had stolen them from the street of **B**, 1052

BETH-SHEAN (6) [BETH-SHAN]
Jos 17:11 in Issachar and in Asher **B** and her towns, 1052
17:16 *both they* who *are* of **B** and her towns, and 1052
Jdg 1:27 did Manasseh drive out *the inhabitants of* **B** 1052
1Ki 4:12 *pertained* Taanach and Megiddo, and all **B**, 1052
4:12 beneath Jezreel, from **B** to Abel-meholah, 1052
1Ch 7:29 **B** and her towns, Taanach and her towns, 1052

BETH-SHEMESH (21)
Jos 15:10 went down *to* **B**, and passed on *to* Timnah: 1053
19:22 reacheth to Tabor, and Shahazimah, and **B**; 1053
19:38 Migdal-el, Horem, and Beth-anath, and **B**; 1053
21:16 with her suburbs, *and* **B** with her suburbs; 1053
Jdg 1:33 did Naphtali drive out the inhabitants of **B**, 1053
1:33 nevertheless the inhabitants of **B** and 1053
1Sa 6: 9 goeth up *by* the way of his own coast *to* **B**, 1053
6:12 kine took the straight way to the way of **B**, 1053
6:12 went after them unto the border of **B**. 1053
6:13 *they of* **B** *were* reaping *their* wheat harvest 1053
6:15 the men of **B** offered burnt offerings and 1053
6:19 he smote the men of **B**, because they had 1053
6:20 the men of **B** said, Who is able to stand 1053
1Ki 4: 9 in Shaalbim, and **B**, and Elon-beth-hanan: 1053
2Ki 14:11 Judah looked one another *in* the face at **B**, 1053
14:13 at **B**, and came *to* Jerusalem, and 1053
1Ch 6:59 with her suburbs, and **B** with her suburbs: 1053
2Ch 25:21 *both* he and Amaziah king of Judah, at **B**, 1053
25:23 at **B**, and brought him *to* Jerusalem, and 1053
28:18 and had taken **B**, and Ajalon, and Gederoth, 1053
Jer 43:13 He shall break also the images of **B**, that *is* 1053

BETH-SHEMITE (2) [BETH-SHITTAH]
1Sa 6:14 a **B**, and stood there, where *there was* a 1030
6:18 unto this day in the field of Joshua, the **B**. 1030

BETH-SHITTAH (1) [BETH-SHEMITE]
Jdg 7:22 the host fled to **B** in Zererath, *and* to 1029

BETH-TAPPUAH (1) [TAPPUAH]
Jos 15:53 And Janum, and **B**, and Aphekah, 1054

BETHUEL (10)
Ge 22:22 and Hazo, and Pildash, and Jidlaph, and **B**. 1328
22:23 **B** begat Rebekah: these eight Milcah did 1328
24:15 who was born to **B**, son of Milcah, the wife 1328
24:24 I *am* the daughter of **B** the son of Milcah, 1328
24:47 she said, The daughter of **B**, Nahor's son, 1328
24:50 Laban and **B** answered and said, The thing 1328
25:20 the daughter of **B** the Syrian of 1328
28: 2 to the house of **B** thy mother's father; 1328
28: 5 son of **B** the Syrian, the brother of 1328
1Ch 4:30 And at **B**, and at Hormah, and at Ziklag, 1328

BETHUL (1)
Jos 19: 4 And Eltolad, and **B**, and Hormah, 1329

BETH-ZUR (4) [ZUR]
Jos 15:58 Halhul, **B**, and Gedor, 1049
1Ch 2:45 *was* Maon: and Maon *was* the father of **B**. 1049
2Ch 11: 7 And **B**, and Shoco, and Adullam, 1049
Ne 3:16 of Azbuk, the ruler of the half part of **B**, 1049

BETIMES (5) [TIME]
Ge 26:31 they **rose up b** in the morning, and 7925
2Ch 36:15 his messengers, **rising up b**, and sending; 7925
Job 8: 5 If thou wouldest **seek** unto God **b**, and 7836
24: 5 they forth to their work; **rising b** for a prey: 7836
Pr 13:24 but he that loveth him chasteneth him **b**. 7836

BETONIM (1)
Jos 13:26 from Heshbon unto Ramath-mizpeh, and **B**; 993

BETRAY (18) [BETRAYED, BETRAYERS, BETRAYEST, BETRAYETH]
1Ch 12:17 if *ye be come* to **b** me to mine enemies, 7411
Mt 24:10 and shall **b** one another, and shall hate one *3860*
26:16 that time he sought opportunity to **b** him. *3860*

Mt 26:21 I say unto you, that one of you shall **b** me. 3860
26:23 with me in the dish, the same shall **b** me. 3860
26:46 behold, he is at hand that doth **b** me. 3860
Mk 13:12 Now the brother shall **b** the brother to 3860
14:10 unto the chief priests, to **b** him unto them. 3860
14:11 sought how he might conveniently **b** him. 3860
14:18 One of you which eateth with me shall **b** 3860
Lk 22: 4 captains, how he might **b** him unto them. 3860
22: 6 sought opportunity to **b** him unto them in 3860
Jn 6:64 that believed not, and who should **b** him. 3860
6:71 for he *it was that* should **b** him, being one 3860
12: 4 Simon's *son,* which should **b** him, 3860
13: 2 of Judas Iscariot, Simon's *son,* to **b** him; 3860
13:11 For he knew who should **b** him; therefore 3860
13:21 I say unto you, that one of you shall **b** me. 3860

BETRAYED (19) [BETRAY]
Mt 10: 4 and Judas Iscariot, who also **b** him. 3860
17:22 The Son of man shall be **b** into the hands of 3860
20:18 the Son of man shall be **b** unto the chief 3860
26: 2 and the Son of man is **b** to be crucified. 3860
26:24 that man by whom the Son of man is **b**: 3860
26:25 which **b** him, answered and said, Master, is 3860
26:45 the Son of man is **b** into the hands of 3860
26:48 Now he that **b** him gave them a sign, 3860
27: 3 Then Judas, which had **b** him, when he saw 3860
27: 4 I have sinned in that I have **b** *the* innocent 3860
Mk 3:19 And Judas Iscariot, which also **b** him. 3860
14:21 to that man by whom the Son of man is **b**: 3860
14:41 the Son of man is **b** into the hands of 3860
14:44 And he that **b** him had given them a token, 3860
Lk 21:16 And ye shall be **b** both by parents, and 3860
22:22 but woe unto that man by whom he is **b**. 3860
Jn 18: 2 Judas also, which **b** him, knew the place: 3860
18: 5 Judas also, which **b** him, stood with them. 3860
1Co 11:23 *same* night in which he was **b** took bread: 3860

BETRAYERS (1) [BETRAY]
Ac 7:52 of whom ye have been now the **b** and 4273

BETRAYEST (1) [BETRAY]
Lk 22:48 Judas, **b** thou the Son of man with a kiss? 3860

BETRAYETH (3) [BETRAY]
Mk 14:42 let us go; lo, he that **b** me is at hand. 3860
Lk 22:21 the hand of him that **b** me *is* with me on 3860
Jn 21:20 and said, Lord, which is he that **b** thee? 3860

BETROTH (4) [BETROTHED]
Dt 28:30 Thou shalt **b** a wife, and another man shall 781
Hos 2:19 I will **b** thee unto me for ever; yea, I will 781
2:19 I will **b** thee unto me in righteousness, and 781
2:20 I will even **b** thee unto me in faithfulness: 781

BETROTHED (9) [BETROTH]
Ex 21: 8 who hath **b** her to himself, then shall he let 3259
21: 9 if he have **b** her unto his son, he shall deal 3259
22:16 And if a man entice a maid that is not **b**, and 781
Lev 19:20 **b** to a husband, and not at all redeemed, nor 2778
Dt 20: 7 what man *is there* that hath **b** a wife, and 781
22:23 If a damsel *that is* a virgin be **b** unto a 781
22:25 But if a man find a **b** damsel in the field, and 781
22:27 *and* the **b** damsel cried, and *there was* none 781
22:28 which is not **b**, and lay hold on her, and 781

BETTER (117) [GOOD]
Ge 29:19 Laban said, *It is* **b** that I give her to thee, 2896
Ex 14:12 For *it had been* **b** for us to serve 2896
Nu 14: 3 were it not **b** for us to return into Egypt? 2896
Jdg 8: 2 of Ephraim **b** than the vintage of Abi-ezer? 2896
9: 2 Whether *is* **b** for you, either that all 2896
11:25 now *art* thou **any thing b** than Balak 2896+2896
18:19 *is it* **b** for thee to be a priest unto the house 2896
Ru 4:15 which *is* **b** to thee than seven sons, 2896
1Sa 1: 8 *am* not I **b** to thee than ten sons? 2896
15:22 to obey *is* **b** than sacrifice, *and* to hearken 2896
15:28 to a neighbour of thine, *that is* **b** than thou. 2896
27: 1 *there is* nothing **b** for me than that I should 2896
2Sa 17:14 The counsel of Hushai the Archite *is* **b** than 2896
18: 3 now *it is* **b** that thou succour us out of 2896
1Ki 1:47 God **make** the name of Solomon **b** than thy 3190
2:32 two men more righteous and **b** than he, 2896
19: 4 my life; for I *am* not **b** than my fathers. 2896
21: 2 I will give thee for it a **b** vineyard than it; 2896
2Ki 5:12 **b** than all the waters of Israel? 2896
2Ch 21:13 father's house, *which were* **b** than thyself: 2896
Est 1:19 royal estate unto another *that is* **b** than she. 2896
Ps 37:16 A little that a righteous *man hath is* **b** than 2896
63: 3 Because thy lovingkindness *is* **b** than life, 2896
69:31 *This* also shall please the LORD **b than** 4480
84:10 For a day in thy courts *is* **b** than a thousand. 2896
118: 8 *It is* **b** to trust in the LORD than to put 2896
118: 9 *It is* **b** to trust in the LORD than to put 2896
119:72 The law of thy mouth *is* **b** unto me than 2896
Pr 3:14 For the merchandise of it *is* **b** than 2896
8:11 For wisdom *is* **b** than rubies; and all 2896
8:19 My fruit *is* **b** than gold, yea, than fine gold; 2896
12: 9 *is* **b** than he that honoureth himself, and 2896
15:16 **B** *is* little with the fear of the LORD than 2896
15:17 **B** *is* a dinner of herbs where love is, than a 2896
16: 8 **B** *is* a little with righteousness than great 2896
16:16 How much **b** *is it* to get wisdom than gold! 2896
16:19 **B** *it is to be* of an humble spirit with 2896
16:32 *He that is* slow to anger *is* **b** than 2896
17: 1 **B** *is* a dry morsel, and quietness therewith, 2896
19: 1 **B** *is* the poor that walketh in his integrity, 2896
19:22 and a poor *man is* **b** than a liar. 2896
21: 9 *It is* **b** to dwell in a corner of the housetop, 2896
21:19 *It is* **b** to dwell in the wilderness, than with 2896
25: 7 For **b** *it is* that it be said unto thee, 2896
25:24 *It is* **b** to dwell in a corner of the housetop, 2896
27: 5 Open rebuke *is* **b** than secret love. 2896
27:10 *for* **b** *is* a neighbour *that is* near than a 2896
28: 6 **B** *is* the poor that walketh in his 2896
Ecc 2:24 *There is* nothing **b** for a man, *than* that he 2896
3:22 I perceive that *there is* nothing **b**, 2896
4: 3 Yea, **b** *is he* than both they, which hath not 2896
4: 6 **B** *is* a handful *with* quietness, than both 2896
4: 9 Two *are* **b** than one; because they have a 2896
4:13 **B** *is* a poor and a wise child than an old and 2896
5: 5 **B** *is it* that thou shouldest not vow, 2896
6: 3 I say, *that* an untimely birth *is* **b** than he. 2896
6: 9 **B** *is* the sight of the eyes than 2896
6:11 that increase vanity, what *is* man the **b**? 3148
7: 1 A *good* name *is* **b** than precious ointment; 2896
7: 2 *It is* **b** to go to the house of mourning, 2896
7: 3 Sorrow *is* **b** than laughter: for by 2896
7: 3 of the countenance the heart is **made b**. 3190
7: 5 *It is* **b** to hear the rebuke of the wise, 2896
7: 8 **B** *is* the end of a thing than the beginning 2896
7: 8 the patient in spirit *is* **b** than the proud in 2896
7:10 that the former days were **b** than these? 2896
8:15 a man hath no **b** *thing* under the sun, 2896
9: 4 for a living dog *is* **b** than a dead lion. 2896
9:16 said I, Wisdom *is* **b** than strength: 2896
9:18 Wisdom *is* **b** than weapons of war: but 2896
10:11 without enchantment; and a babbler is no **b**. 3504
SS 1: 2 of his mouth: for thy love *is* **b** than wine. 2896
4:10 how much **b** is thy love than wine! and 2895
Isa 56: 5 a name **b** than *of* sons and *of* daughters: 2896
La 4: 9 *They that be* slain with the sword are **b** than 2896
Eze 36:11 will **do b** *unto you* than at your beginnings: 2895
Da 1:20 he found them ten times **b than** all 5921
Hos 2: 7 for then *was it* **b** with me than now. 2896
Am 6: 2 *be they* **b** than these kingdoms? or 2896
Jnh 4: 3 for *it is* **b** for me to die than to live. 2896
4: 8 and said, *It is* **b** for me to die than to live. 2896
Na 3: 8 Art thou **b** than populous No, that was 3190
Mt 6:26 Are ye not much **b than** they? 1308
12:12 How much then is a man **b than** a sheep? 1308
18: 6 it were **b** for him that a millstone were 4851
18: 8 it is **b** for thee to enter into life halt or 2570
18: 9 it is **b** for thee to enter into life with one 2570
Mk 9:42 it is **b** for him that a millstone were hanged 2570
9:43 it is **b** for thee to enter into life maimed, 2570
9:45 it is **b** for thee to enter halt into life, 2570
9:47 it is **b** for thee to enter into the kingdom of 2570
Lk 5:39 desireth new: for he saith, The old is **b**. 5543
12:24 how much more are ye **b than** the fowls? 1308
17: 2 It were **b** for him that a millstone were 3081
Ro 3: 9 are we **b** *than they?* No, in no wise: for we 4284
1Co 7: 9 for it is **b** to marry than to burn. 2909
7:38 he that giveth *her* not in marriage doeth **b**. 2908
8: 8 for neither, if we eat, are we the **b**; neither, 4052
9:15 for *it were* **b** for me to die, than that 2570+3123
11:17 that you come together not for the **b**, but 2909
Php 1:23 and to be with Christ; *which is* far **b**: 2909
2: 3 *let* each esteem other **b than** themselves. 5242
Heb 1: 4 Being made so much **b than** the angels, 2909
6: 9 we are persuaded **b** *things* of you, and 2909
7: 7 all contradiction the less is blessed of the **b**. 2909
7:19 the bringing in of a **b** hope *did;* by 2909
7:22 much was Jesus made a surety of a **b** 2909
8: 6 by how much also he is the mediator of a **b** 2909
8: 6 which was established upon **b** promises. 2909
9:23 the heavenly *things* themselves with **b** 2909
10:34 in yourselves that *ye* have in heaven a **b** 2909
11:16 But now they desire a **b** *country,* that is, 2909
11:35 that they might obtain a **b** resurrection: 2909
11:40 God having provided some **b** *thing* for us, 2909
12:24 that speaketh **b** *things* than *that of* Abel. 2909
1Pe 3:17 For *it is* **b**, if the will of God be so, that *ye* 2909
2Pe 2:21 For it had been **b** for them not to have 2909

BETTERED (1) [GOOD]
Mk 5:26 and was nothing **b**, but rather grew worse, 5623

BETWEEN (232)
Ge 3:15 And I will put enmity **b** thee and the woman, 996
3:15 and the woman, and **b** thy seed and her seed; 996
9:12 the token of the covenant which I make **b** me 996
9:13 it shall be for a token of a covenant **b** me and 996
9:15 which *is* **b** me and you and every living 996
9:16 remember the everlasting covenant **b** God 996
9:17 which I have established **b** me and all flesh 996
10:12 Resen **b** Nineveh and Calah: the same *is* a 996
13: 3 been at the beginning, **b** Beth-el and Hai; 996
13: 7 there was a strife **b** the herdmen of Abram's 996
13: 8 **b** me and thee, and between my herdmen 996
13: 8 and **b** my herdmen and thy herdmen; 996
15:17 a burning lamp that passed **b** those pieces. 996
16: 5 her eyes: the LORD judge **b** me and thee. 996
16:14 behold, *it is* **b** Kadesh and Bered. 996
17: 2 And I will make my covenant **b** me and thee, 996
17: 7 I will establish my covenant **b** me and thee 996
17:10 **b** me and you and thy seed after thee; 996
20: 1 dwelled **b** Kadesh and Shur, and 996
31:44 and let it be for a witness **b** me and thee. 996
31:48 This heap *is* a witness **b** me and thee *this* 996
31:49 he said, The LORD watch **b** me and thee, 996
48:12 Joseph brought them out from **b** his knees, 5973
49:10 nor a lawgiver from **b** his feet, until Shiloh 996
49:14 Issachar *is* a strong ass couching down **b** two 996
Ex 8:23 I will put a division **b** my people and thy 996
9: 4 the LORD shall sever **b** the cattle of Israel 996
11: 7 doth put a difference **b** the Egyptians 996
13: 9 for a memorial **b** thine eyes, that 996
13:16 thine hand, and for frontlets **b** thine eyes: 996
14: 2 **b** Migdol and the sea, over against 996
14:20 And it came **b** the camp of the Egyptians and 996
16: 1 wilderness of Sin, which *is* **b** Elim and Sinai, 996
18:16 I judge **b** one and another, and I do make 996
22:11 *Then* shall an oath of the LORD be **b** them 996
25:22 from **b** the two cherubims which *are* upon 996
26:33 the vail shall divide unto you **b** the holy 996
28:33 bells of gold **b** them round about: 8432+871.1
30:18 thou shalt put it **b** the tabernacle of 996
31:13 for it *is* a sign **b** me and you throughout your 996
31:17 It *is* a sign **b** me and the children of Israel for 996
Ex 39:25 put the bells **b** the pomegranates 8432+871.1
39:25 round about **b** the pomegranates; 8432+871.1
40: 7 thou shalt set the laver **b** the tent of 996
40:30 he set the laver **b** the tent of the congregation 996
Lev 10:10 that *ye* may put difference **b** holy and 996
10:10 and unholy, and **b** unclean and clean; 996
11:47 To make a difference **b** the unclean and 996
11:47 **b** the beast that may be eaten and the beast 996
20:25 put difference **b** clean beasts and unclean, 996
20:25 and unclean, and **b** unclean fowls and clean: 996
26:46 which the LORD made **b** him and 996
Nu 7:89 ark of Testimony, from **b** the two cherubims: 996
11:33 while the flesh *was* yet **b** their teeth, ere it 996
13:23 and they bare it **b** two upon a staff; 871.1
16:48 he stood **b** the dead and the living; and 996
21:13 border of Moab, **b** Moab and the Amorites. 996
26:56 the possession thereof be divided **b** many 996
30:16 **b** a man and his wife, between the father and 996
30:16 and his wife, **b** the father and his daughter, 996
31:27 **b** them that took the war upon them, 996
31:27 out to battle, and **b** all the congregation: 996
35:24 the congregation shall judge **b** the slayer 996
Dt 1: 1 in the plain over against the Red *sea,* **b** 996
1:16 Hear *the causes* **b** your brethren, and 996
1:16 judge righteously **b** every man and his 996
1:39 which *in that* day had no knowledge **b** good NIH
5: 5 (I stood **b** the LORD and you at that time, 996
6: 8 and they shall be as frontlets **b** thine eyes. 996
11:18 that they may be as frontlets **b** your eyes. 996
14: 1 nor make *any* baldness **b** your eyes for 996
17: 8 **b** blood and blood, between plea and plea, 996
17: 8 **b** plea and plea, and between stroke and 996
17: 8 and plea, and **b** stroke and stroke, 996
19:17 **b** whom the controversy *is,* shall stand 3807.1
25: 1 If there be a controversy **b** men, and 996
28:57 young one that cometh out from **b** her feet, 996
33:12 day long, and he shall dwell **b** his shoulders. 996
Jos 3: 4 Yet there shall be a space **b** you and it, 996
8: 9 abode **b** Beth-el and Ai, on the west side of 996
8:11 of Ai: now *there was* a valley **b** them and Ai. 996
8:12 set them to lie in ambush **b** Beth-el and Ai, 996
18:11 the coast of their lot came forth **b** 996
22:25 For the LORD hath made Jordan a border **b** 996
22:27 *that* it *may be* a witness **b** us, and you, and 996
22:28 but it *is* a witness **b** us and you. 996
22:34 *be* a witness **b** us that the LORD *is* God. 996
24: 7 he put darkness **b** you and the Egyptians, 996
Jdg 4: 5 she dwelt under the palm tree of Deborah **b** 996
4:17 for *there was* peace **b** Jabin the king of 996
9:23 God sent an evil spirit **b** Abimelech and 996
11:10 The LORD be witness **b** us, if we do not so 996
11:27 the LORD the Judge be judge *this* day **b** 996
13:25 in the camp of Dan, **b** Zorah and Eshtaol. 996
15: 4 and put a firebrand in the midst **b** two tails. 996
16:25 them sport: and they set him **b** the pillars. 996
16:31 buried him **b** Zorah and Eshtaol in 996
20:38 Now there was an appointed sign **b** 3807.1
1Sa 4: 4 of hosts, which dwelleth *b* the cherubims: NIH
7:12 set *it* **b** Mizpeh and Shen, and called 996
7:14 there was peace **b** Israel and the Amorites. 996
14: 4 **b** the passages, *by* which Jonathan sought to 996
14:42 Cast *lots* **b** me and Jonathan my son. 996
17: 1 pitched **b** Shochoh and Azekah, 996
17: 3 other side: and *there was* a valley **b** them. 996
17: 6 and a target of brass **b** his shoulders. 996
20: 3 *there is* but a step **b** me and death. 996
20:23 the LORD *be* **b** thee and me for ever. 996
20:42 The LORD be **b** me and thee, and 996
20:42 and **b** my seed and thy seed for ever. 996
24:12 The LORD judge **b** me and thee, and 996
24:15 judge **b** me and thee, and see, and plead my 996
26:13 of a hill afar off; a great space *being* **b** them: 996
2Sa 3: 1 Now there was long war **b** the house of Saul 996
3: 6 while there was war **b** the house of Saul and 996
6: 2 of hosts that dwelleth *b* the cherubims. NIH
18: 9 he was taken up **b** the heaven and the earth; 996
18:24 David sat **b** the two gates: and the watchman 996
19:35 *and* can I discern **b** good and evil? can thy 996
21: 7 of the LORD'S oath that *was* **b** them, 996
21: 7 **b** David and Jonathan the son of Saul. 996
1Ki 3: 9 that *I* may discern **b** good and bad: 996
5:12 there was peace **b** Hiram and Solomon; and 996
7:28 and the borders *were* **b** the ledges: 996
7:29 on the borders that *were* **b** the ledges *were* 996
7:46 in the clay ground **b** Succoth and Zarthan. 996
14:30 there was war **b** Rehoboam and Jeroboam all 996
15: 6 there was war **b** Rehoboam and Jeroboam all 996
15: 7 And there was war **b** Abijam and Jeroboam. 996
15:16 there was war **b** Asa and Baasha king of 996
15:19 *There is* a league **b** me and thee, *and* 996
15:19 and thee, *and* **b** my father and thy father: 996
15:32 there was war **b** Asa and Baasha king of 996
18: 6 So they divided the land **b** them to pass 3807.1
18:21 and said, How long halt ye **b** two opinions? 5921
18:42 upon the earth, and put his face **b** his knees, 996
22: 1 they continued three years without war **b** 996
22:34 smote the king of Israel **b** the joints of 996
2Ki 9:24 smote Jehoram **b** his arms, and the arrow 996
11:17 Jehoiada made a covenant **b** the LORD 996
11:17 **b** the king also and the people. 996
16:14 from **b** the altar and the house of 996
19:15 which dwellest *b* the cherubims, thou *art* NIH
25: 4 by night *by* the way of the gate **b** two walls, 996
1Ch 13: 6 that dwelleth *b* the cherubims, whose name NIH
21:16 saw the angel of the LORD stand **b** 996
2Ch 4:17 in the clay ground **b** Succoth and 996
12:15 *there were* wars **b** Rehoboam and NIH
13: 2 And there was war **b** Abijah and Jeroboam. 996
16: 3 *There is* a league **b** me and thee, as *there was* 996
16: 3 thee, as *there was* **b** my father and thy father: 996
18:33 smote the king of Israel **b** the joints of 996
19:10 **b** blood and blood, between law and 996
19:10 and blood, **b** law and commandment, 996
23:16 Jehoiada made a covenant **b** him, and 996
23:16 **b** all the people, and between the king, 996

2Ch 23:16 between all the people, and **b** the king, 996
Ne 3:32 **b** the going up of the corner unto the sheep 996
Job 41:16 near to another, that no air can come **b** them. 996
Ps 80: 1 thou that dwellest *b* the cherubims, NIH
99: 1 he sitteth *b* the cherubims; let the earth be NIH
Pr 18:18 to cease, and parteth **b** the mighty. 996
Isa 22:11 Ye made also a ditch **b** the two walls for 996
37:16 God of Israel, that dwellest *b* the cherubims, NIH
59: 2 But your iniquities have separated **b** you and 996
Jer 7: 5 if you throughly execute judgment **b** a man 996
34:18 calf in twain, and passed **b** the parts thereof, 996
34:19 which passed **b** the parts of the calf; 996
42: 5 LORD be a true and faithful witness **b** us, 871.1
52: 7 night *by* the way of the gate **b** the two walls, 996
La 1: 3 all her persecutors overtook her **b** the straits. 996
Eze 4: 3 set it *for* a wall of iron **b** thee and the city: 996
8: 3 the spirit lift me up **b** the earth and 996
8:16 **b** the porch and the altar, *were* about five 996
10: 2 said, Go in **b** the wheels, *even* under 996
10: 2 fill thine hand *with* coals of fire from **b** 996
10: 6 saying, Take fire from **b** the wheels, 996
10: 6 between the wheels, from **b** the cherubims; 996
10: 7 *one* cherub stretched forth his hand from **b** 996
10: 7 unto the fire that *was* **b** the cherubims, 996
18: 8 hath executed true judgment **b** man and man, 996
20:12 my sabbaths, to be a sign **b** me and them, 996
20:20 they shall be a sign **b** me and you, that *ye* 996
22:26 they have put no difference **b** the holy 996
22:26 neither have they shewed *difference* **b** 996
34:17 Behold, I judge **b** cattle and cattle, 996
34:17 and cattle, **b** the rams and the he goats. 3807.1
34:20 will judge **b** the fat cattle and between 996
34:20 between the fat cattle and **b** the lean cattle. 996
34:22 be a prey; and I will judge **b** cattle and cattle. 996
40: 7 **b** the little chambers *were* five cubits; and 996
41:10 **b** the chambers *was* the wideness of twenty 996
41:18 so that a palm tree *was* **b** a cherub and a 996
42:20 to make a separation **b** the sanctuary and 996
43: 8 by my posts, and the wall **b** me and them, 996
44:23 they shall teach my people *the difference* **b** 996
44:23 and cause them to discern **b** the unclean and 996
47:16 which *is* **b** the border of Damascus and 996
48:22 **b** the border of Judah and the border of 996
Da 7: 5 *it had* three ribs in the mouth of it **b** the teeth 997
8: 5 and the goat *had* a notable horn **b** his eyes. 996
8:16 I heard a man's voice **b** *the banks of* Ulai, 996
8:21 the great horn that *is* **b** his eyes *is* the first 996
11:45 he shall plant the tabernacles of his palace **b** 996
Hos 2: 2 and her adulteries from **b** her breasts; 996
Joel 2:17 weep **b** the porch and the altar, and let them 996
Jnh 4:11 persons that cannot discern **b** their right hand 996
Zec 5: 9 they lift up the ephah **b** the earth and 996
6: 1 there came four chariots out from **b** two 996
6:13 the counsel of peace shall be **b** them both. 996
9: 7 and his abominations from **b** his teeth: 996
11:14 that I might break the brotherhood **b** Judah 996
Mal 2:14 Because the LORD hath been witness **b** 996
3:18 and discern **b** the righteous and the wicked, 996
3:18 **b** him that serveth God and *him* that serveth 996
Mt 18:15 go and tell him his fault **b** thee and *3342*
23:35 whom ye slew **b** the temple and the altar. *3342*
Lk 11:51 which perished **b** the altar and the temple: *3342*
16:26 **b** us and you there is a great gulf fixed: *3342*
23:12 for before they were at enmity **b** *4314*
Jn 3:25 Then there arose a question **b** *some* of *1537*
Ac 12: 6 the same night Peter was sleeping **b** two *3342*
15: 9 And put no difference **b** us and them, *3342*
15:39 sharp *b them,* that they departed asunder NIG
23: 7 there arose a dissension **b** the Pharisees and NIG
26:31 they talked **b** themselves, saying, *4314*
Ro 1:24 to dishonour their own bodies **b** *1722*
10:12 For there is no difference **b** the Jew and *5037*
1Co 6: 5 not one that shall be able to judge **b** *303+3319*
7:34 There is **difference** *also* **b** a wife and a *3307*
Eph 2:14 down the middle wall of partition *b us;* NIG
1Ti 2: 5 and one mediator **b** God and men, NIG

BETWIXT (16)

Ge 17:11 it shall be a token of the covenant **b** me and 996
23:15 shekels of silver; what *is* that **b** me and thee? 996
26:28 we said, Let there be now an oath **b** us, 996
26:28 *even* **b** us and thee, and let us make a 996
30:36 And he set three days' journey **b** himself and 996
31:37 thy brethren, that they may judge **b** us both. 996
31:50 with us; see, God *is* witness **b** me and thee. 996
31:51 *this* pillar, which I have cast **b** me and thee; 996
31:53 of Nahor, the God of their father, judge **b** us. 996
32:16 and put a space **b** drove and drove. 996
Job 9:33 Neither is there *any* daysman **b** us, 996
36:32 it *not to shine* by *the cloud* that **cometh b**. 6293
SS 1:13 unto me; he shall lie all night **b** my breasts. 996
Isa 5: 3 judge, I pray you, **b** me and my vineyard. 996
Jer 39: 4 king's garden, by the gate **b** the two walls: 996
Php 1:23 For I am in a strait **b** two, having a desire to *1537*

BEULAH (1)

Isa 62: 4 shalt be called Hephzi-bah, and thy land **B**: 1166

BEWAIL (6) [BEWAILED, BEWAILETH]

Lev 10: 6 **b** the burning which the LORD hath 1058
Dt 21:13 **b** her father and her mother a full month: 1058
Jdg 11:37 and **b** my virginity, I and my fellows. 1058+5921
Isa 16: 9 Therefore I will **b** with the weeping of 1058
2Co 12:21 *that* I shall **b** many which have sinned *3996*
Rev 18: 9 with her, shall **b** her, and lament for her, *2799*

BEWAILED (3) [BEWAIL]

Jdg 11:38 and **b** her virginity upon the mountains. 1058
Lk 8:52 And all wept, and **b** her: but he said, *2875*
23:27 of women, which also **b** and lamented him. *2875*

BEWAILETH (1) [BEWAIL]

Jer 4:31 *that* **b** herself, *that* spreadeth her hands, 3306

BEWARE (28)

Ge 24: 6 **B** thou that thou bring not my son thither 8104
Ex 23:21 **B** of him, and obey his voice, provoke him 8104
Dt 6:12 *Then* **b** lest thou forget the LORD, 8104
8:11 **B** that thou forget not the LORD thy God, 8104
15: 9 **B** that there be not a thought in thy wicked 8104
Jdg 13: 4 Now therefore **b**, I pray thee, and drink not 8104
13:13 Of all that I said unto the woman let her **b**. 8104
2Sa 18:12 **B** *that* none *touch* the young man Absalom. 8104
2Ki 6: 9 **B** that *thou* pass not such a place; 8104
Job 36:18 *b* lest he take thee away with *his* stroke: NIH
Pr 19:25 Smite a scorner, and the simple will **b**: and 6191
Isa 36:18 *B* lest Hezekiah persuade you, saying, NIH
Mt 7:15 **B** of false prophets, which come to you in *4337*
10:17 But **b** of men: for they will deliver you up *4337*
16: 6 and **b** of the leaven of the Pharisees and *4337*
16:11 that *ye* should **b** of the leaven of *4337*
16:12 he bade *them* not **b** of the leaven of bread, *4337*
Mk 8:15 **b** of the leaven of the Pharisees, and *of* *991*
12:38 **B** of the scribes, which love to go in long *991*
Lk 12: 1 *of all,* **B** ye of the leaven of the Pharisees, *4337*
12:15 Take heed, and **b** of covetousness: *5442*
20:46 **B** of the scribes, which desire to walk in *4337*
Ac 13:40 **B** therefore, lest that come upon you, *991*
Php 3: 2 **B** of dogs, beware of evil workers, beware of *991*
3: 2 Beware of dogs, **b** of evil workers, *991*
3: 2 beware of evil workers, **b** of the concision. *991*
Col 2: 8 **B** lest any *man* spoil you through philosophy *991*
2Pe 3:17 ye know *these things* before, **b** lest ye also, *5442*

BEWITCHED (3)

Ac 8: 9 and **b** the people of Samaria, giving out that *1839*
8:11 that of long time *he* had **b** them with *1839*
Gal 3: 1 O foolish Galatians, who hath **b** you, *940*

BEWRAY (1) [BEWRAYETH]

Isa 16: 3 hide the outcasts; **b** not him that wandereth. 1540

BEWRAYETH (3) [BEWRAY]

Pr 27:16 ointment of his right hand, *which* **b** *itself.* 7121
29:24 own soul: he heareth cursing, and **b** *it* not. 5046
Mt 26:73 *one* of them; for thy speech **b** thee. *1212+4160*

BEYOND (54)

Ge 35:21 spread his tent **b** the tower of Edar. 1973+4480
50:10 which *is* **b** Jordan, and there they 5676+871.1
50:11 which *is* **b** Jordan. 5676+871.1
Lev 15:25 or if it run **b** the time of her separation; 5921
Nu 22:18 I cannot **go b** the word of the LORD my 5674
24:13 I cannot **go b** the commandment of 5674
Dt 3:20 your God hath given them **b** Jordan: 5676+871.1
3:25 see the good land that *is* **b** Jordan, 5676+871.1
30:13 Neither *is* it **b** the sea, that *thou* 4480+5676
Jos 9:10 that *were* **b** Jordan, to Sihon king of 5676+871.1
13: 8 gave them, **b** Jordan eastward, 5676+871.1
18: 7 have received their inheritance **b** Jordan on 5676
Jdg 3:26 **passed b** the quarries, and escaped unto 5674
5:17 Gilead abode **b** Jordan: and why did 5676+871.1
1Sa 20:22 Behold, the arrows *are* **b** thee; 1973+4480
20:36 *And* as the lad ran, he shot an arrow **b** him. 5674
20:37 said, *Is* not the arrow **b** thee? 1973+4480+2050.1
2Sa 10:16 brought out the Syrians that *were* **b** 4480+5676
1Ki 4:12 unto *the place that is* **b** Jokneam: 4480+5676
14:15 shall scatter them **b** the river, 4480+5676
1Ch 19:16 drew forth the Syrians that *were* **b** 4480+5676
2Ch 20: 2 thee from **b** the sea on this side Syria; 5676
Ezr 4:17 in Samaria, and *unto* the rest **b** the river: 5675
4:20 which have ruled over all *countries* **b** 5675
6: 6 *therefore,* Tatnai, governor **b** the river, 5675
6: 6 which *are* **b** the river, be ye far from 5675
6: 8 *even* of the tribute **b** the river, 5675
7:21 to all the treasurers which *are* **b** the river, 5675
7:25 which may judge all the people that *are* **b** 5675
Ne 2: 7 let letters be given me to the governors **b** 5676
2: 9 I came to the governors **b** the river, and 5676
12:38 **from b** the tower of the furnaces 4480+5921
Isa 7:20 *namely,* by them **b** the river, by the king of 5676
9: 1 the sea, **b** Jordan, in Galilee of the nations. 5676
18: 1 which *is* **b** the rivers of Ethiopia: 4480+5676
Jer 22:19 cast forth **b** the gates of Jerusalem. 1973+4480
25:22 of the isles which *are* **b** the sea, 5676+871.1
Am 5:27 you to go into captivity **b** Damascus, 1973+4480
Zep 3:10 From **b** the rivers of Ethiopia my 5676
Mt 4:15 *by* the way of the sea, **b** Jordan, Galilee of *4008*
4:25 and *from* Judea, and *from* **b** Jordan. *4008*
19: 1 and came into the coasts of Judea **b** Jordan; *4008*
Mk 3: 8 and from Idumea, and *from* **b** Jordan; *4008*
6:51 they were sore amazed in themselves **b** *1537*
7:37 And were **b measure** astonished, saying, *5249*
Jn 1:28 These *things* were done in Bethabara **b** *4008*
3:26 Rabbi, *he* that was with thee **b** Jordan, *4008*
10:40 And went away again **b** Jordan into *4008*
Ac 7:43 and I will carry you away **b** Babylon. *1900*
2Co 8: 3 *b their* power *they were* willing of *5228*
10:14 For we **stretch** not ourselves **b** *our* *5239*
10:16 To preach the gospel in the *regions* **b** you, *5238*
Gal 1:13 how that **b measure** I persecuted *2596+5236*
1Th 4: 6 That no *man* **go b** and defraud his brother *5233*

BEZAI (3)

Ezr 2:17 The children of **B**, three hundred twenty 1209
Ne 7:23 The children of **B**, three hundred twenty 1209
10:18 Hodijah, Hashum, **B**, 1209

BEZALEEL (9)

Ex 31: 2 I have called by name **B** the son of Uri, 1212
35:30 the LORD hath called by name **B** the son 1212
36: 1 wrought **B** and Aholiab, and every wise 1212
36: 2 Moses called **B** and Aholiab, and every 1212
37: 1 **B** made the ark *of* shittim wood: two cubits 1212
38:22 **B** the son of Uri, the son of Hur, of the tribe 1212
1Ch 2:20 And Hur begat Uri, and Uri begat **B**. 1212
2Ch 1: 5 that **B** the son of Uri, the son of Hur, 1212
Ezr 10:30 Mattaniah, **B**, and Binnui, and Manasseh. 1212

BEZALEL See BEZALEEL

BEZEK (3)

Jdg 1: 4 they slew *of* them in **B** ten thousand men. 966
1: 5 they found Adoni-bezek in **B**: and 966
1Sa 11: 8 when he numbered them in **B**, the children 966

BEZER (5)

Dt 4:43 *Namely,* **B** in the wilderness, in the plain 1221
Jos 20: 8 they assigned **B** in the wilderness upon 1221
21:36 **B** with her suburbs, and Jahazah with her 1221
1Ch 6:78 **B** in the wilderness with her suburbs, and 1221
7:37 **B**, and Hod, and Shamma, and Shilshah, 1221

BICHRI (8)

2Sa 20: 1 *was* Sheba, the son of **B**, a Benjamite: 1075
20: 2 *and* followed Sheba the son of **B**: 1075
20: 6 Now shall Sheba the son of **B** do us more 1075
20: 7 to pursue after Sheba the son of **B**. 1075
20:10 brother pursued after Sheba the son of **B**. 1075
20:13 to pursue after Sheba the son of **B**. 1075
20:21 Sheba the son of **B** by name, 1075
20:22 they cut off the head of Sheba the son of **B**, 1075

BICRI See BICHRI

BID (17) [BADE, BADEST, BIDDEN, BIDDETH, BIDDING]

Nu 15:38 **b** them that they make them fringes in 559
Jos 6:10 of your mouth, until the day I **b** you shout; 559
1Sa 9:27 **B** the servant pass on before us, (and 559
2Sa 2:26 ere thou **b** the people return from following 559
2Ki 4:24 slack not *thy* riding for me, except I **b** thee. 559
5:13 *if* the prophet had **b** thee *do some* great 1696
10: 5 and will do all that thou shalt **b** us; 559
Jnh 3: 2 preach unto it the preaching that I **b** thee. 1696
Zep 1: 7 prepared a sacrifice, he hath **b** his guests. 6942
Mt 14:28 **b** thou, **b** me come unto thee on the water. *2753*
22: 9 as many as ye shall find, **b** to the marriage. *2564*
23: 3 therefore whatsoever they **b** you observe, *3004*
Lk 9:61 but let me first go **b** them **farewell**, *657*
10:40 **b** her therefore that she help me. *3004*
14:12 lest they also **b** thee **again**, and *479*
1Co 10:27 If any of them that believe not **b** you *to a* *2564*
2Jn 1:10 into *your* house, neither **b** him God speed: *3004*

BIDDEN (14) [BID]

1Sa 9:13 *and* afterwards they eat that be **b**. 7121
9:22 the chiefest place among them that were **b**, 7121
2Sa 16:11 let him curse; for the LORD hath **b** him. 559
Mt 1:24 did as the angel of the Lord had **b** him, *4367*
22: 3 to call them that were **b** to the wedding: *2564*
22: 4 saying, Tell them which are **b**, Behold, *2564*
22: 8 but they which were **b** were not worthy. *2564*
Lk 7:39 Now when the Pharisee which had **b** him *2564*
14: 7 put forth a parable to those which were **b**, *2564*
14: 8 When thou art **b** of any *man* to a wedding, *2564*
14: 8 lest a more honourable *man* than thou be **b** *2564*
14:10 But when thou art **b**, go and sit down in *2564*
14:17 at supper time to say to them that were **b**, *2564*
14:24 That none of those men which were **b** shall *2564*

BIDDETH (1) [BID]

2Jn 1:11 For he that **b** him God speed is partaker of *3004*

BIDDING (1) [BID]

1Sa 22:14 goeth at thy **b**, and *is* honourable in thine 4928

BIDE (1)

Ro 11:23 they also, if they **b** not **still in** unbelief, *1961*

BIDKAR (1)

2Ki 9:25 said *Jehu* to **B** his captain, Take up, *and* 920

BIER (2)

2Sa 3:31 And king David *himself* followed the **b**. 4296
Lk 7:14 And he came and touched the **b**: and *4673*

BIGTHA (1)

Est 1:10 **B**, and Abagtha, Zethar, and Carcas, 903

BIGTHAN (1)

Est 2:21 **B** and Teresh, of those which kept the door, 904

BIGTHANA (1)

Est 6: 2 that Mordecai had told of **B** and Teresh, 904

BIGVAI (6)

Ezr 2: 2 Bilshan, Mizpar, **B**, Rehum, Baanah. 902
2:14 The children of **B**, two thousand fifty and 902
8:14 Of the sons also of **B**; Uthai, and Zabbud, 902
Ne 7: 7 Bilshan, Mispereth, **B**, Nehum, Baanah. 902
7:19 The children of **B**, two thousand threescore 902
10:16 Adonijah, **B**, Adin, 902

BILDAD (5)

Job 2:11 **B** the Shuhite, and Zophar the Naamathite: 1085
8: 1 Then answered **B** the Shuhite, and said, 1085
18: 1 Then answered **B** the Shuhite, and said, 1085
25: 1 Then answered **B** the Shuhite, and said, 1085
42: 9 the Temanite and **B** the Shuhite *and* 1085

BILEAM (1)

1Ch 6:70 with her suburbs, and **B** with her suburbs, 1109

BILGAH (3)

1Ch 24:14 The fifteenth to **B**, the sixteenth to Immer, 1083
Ne 12: 5 Miamin, Maadiah, **B**, 1083
12:18 Of **B**, Shammua; of Shemaiah, Jehonathan; 1083

BILGAI (1)

Ne 10: 8 Maaziah, **B**, Shemaiah: these *were* 1084

BILHAH (11)
Ge 29:29 Laban gave to Rachel his daughter **B** his 1090
30: 3 she said, Behold my maid **B**, go in unto 1090
30: 4 she gave him **B** her handmaid to wife: and 1090
30: 5 And **B** conceived, and bare Jacob a son. 1090
30: 7 **B** Rachel's maid conceived again, and 1090
35:22 and lay with **B** his father's concubine: 1090
35:25 the sons of **B**, Rachel's handmaid; Dan, 1090
37: 2 the lad *was* with the sons of **B**, and with 1090
46:25 These *are* the sons of **B**, which Laban gave 1090
1Ch 4:29 And at **B**, and at Ezem, and at Tolad, 1090
7:13 and Jezer, and Shallum, the sons of **B**. 1090

BILHAN (4)
Ge 36:27 Ezer *are* these; **B**, and Zaavan, and Akan. 1092
1Ch 1:42 The sons of Ezer; **B**, and Zavan, *and* Jakan. 1092
7:10 The sons also of Jediael; **B**: and the sons of 1092
7:10 the sons of **B**; Jeush, and Benjamin, and 1092

BILL (7)
Dt 24: 1 let him write her a **b** of divorcement, and 5612
24: 3 write her a **b** of divorcement, and giveth *it* 5612
Isa 50: 1 Where *is* the **b** of your mother's 5612
Jer 3: 8 put her away, and given her a **b** of divorce; 5612
Mk 10: 4 Moses suffered to write a **b** of divorcement, *975*
Lk 16: 6 Take thy **b**, and sit down quickly, and *1121*
16: 7 unto him, Take thy **b**, and write fourscore. *1121*

BILLOWS (2)
Ps 42: 7 all thy waves and thy **b** are gone over me. 1530
Jnh 2: 3 all thy **b** and thy waves passed over me. 4867

BILSHAN (2)
Ezr 2: 2 **B**, Mizpar, Bigvai, Rehum, Baanah. 1114
Ne 7: 7 Mordecai, **B**, Mispereth, Bigvai, Nehum, 1114

BIMHAL (1)
1Ch 7:33 of Japhlet; Pasach, and **B**, and Ashvath. 1118

BIND (49) [BINDETH, BINDING, BOUND]
Ex 28:28 they shall **b** the breastplate by the rings 7405
39:21 they did **b** the breastplate by his rings unto 7405
Nu 30: 2 or swear an oath to **b** his soul with a bond; 631
30: 3 **b** *herself by* a bond, *being* in her father's 631
Dt 6: 8 thou shalt **b** them for a sign upon thine 7194
11:18 and **b** them for a sign upon your hand, 7194
14:25 **b up** the money in thine hand, and shalt go 6696
Jos 2:18 thou shalt **b** this line of scarlet thread in 7194
Jdg 15:10 To **b** Samson are we come up, 631
15:12 said unto him, We are come down to **b** thee, 631
15:13 we will **b** thee **fast**, and deliver thee 631+631
16: 5 that we may **b** him to afflict him: 631
16: 7 If they **b** me with seven green withs that 631
16:11 If they **b** me **fast** with new ropes that 631+631
Job 31:36 my shoulder, *and* **b** it *as* a crown to me. 6029
38:31 Canst thou **b** the sweet influences of 7194
39:10 Canst thou **b** the unicorn *with* his band in 7194
40:13 dust together; *and* **b** their faces in secret. 2280
41: 5 a bird? or wilt thou **b** him for thy maidens? 7194
Ps 105:22 To **b** his princes at his pleasure; and 631
118:27 **b** the sacrifice with cords, *even* unto 631
149: 8 To **b** their kings with chains, and 631
Pr 3: 3 **b** them about thy neck; write them upon 7194
6:21 **B** them continually upon thine heart, *and* 7194
7: 3 **B** them upon thy fingers, write them upon 7194
Isa 8:16 **B up** the testimony, seal the law among my 6887
49:18 and **b** them *on thee,* as a bride *doth.* 7194
61: 1 he hath sent me to **b up** the broken-hearted, 2280
Jer 51:63 *that* thou shalt **b** a stone to it, and cast it 7194
Eze 3:25 shall **b** thee with them, and thou shalt not go 631
5: 3 a few in number, and **b** them in thy skirts. 6696
24:17 **b** the tire of thine head upon thee, and 2280
30:21 to put a roller to **b** it, to make it strong to 2280
34:16 will **b up** that which was broken, and 2280
Da 3:20 men that *were* in his army to **b** Shadrach, 3729
Hos 6: 1 he hath smitten, and he will **b** us **up**. 2280
10:10 when *they* shall **b** themselves in their two 631
Mic 1:13 of Lachish, **b** the chariot to the swift beast: 7573
Mt 12:29 except he first **b** the strong *man?* and then *1210*
13:30 and **b** them in bundles to burn them: *1210*
16:19 whatsoever thou shalt **b** on earth shall be *1210*
18:18 Whatsoever ye shall **b** on earth shall be *1210*
22:13 **B** him hand and foot, and take him away, *1210*
23: 4 For they **b** heavy burdens and grievous to *1195*
Mk 3:27 except he will first **b** the strong *man;* and *1210*
5: 3 and no *man* could **b** him, no, not with *1210*
Ac 9:14 chief priests to **b** all that call on thy name. *1210*
12: 8 Gird thyself, and **b on** thy sandals. *5265*
21:11 So shall the Jews at Jerusalem **b** the man *1210*

BINDETH (9) [BIND]
Job 5:18 For he maketh sore, and **b up**: 2280
26: 8 He **b up** the waters in his thick clouds; and 6887
28:11 He **b** the floods from overflowing; and 2280
30:18 it **b** me **about** as the collar of my coat. 247
36:13 heap up wrath: they cry not when he **b** them. 631
Ps 129: 7 his hand; nor he that **b sheaves** his bosom. 6014
147: 3 the broken in heart, and **b up** their wounds. 2280
Pr 26: 8 As *he that* **b** a stone in a sling, so *is* he that 6872
Isa 30:26 in the day that the LORD **b up** the breach 2280

BINDING (5) [BIND]
Ge 37: 7 we *were* **b** sheaves in the field, and lo, 481
49:11 **B** his foal unto the vine, and his ass's colt 631
Ex 28:32 it shall have a **b** of woven work round 8193
Nu 30:13 and every **b** oath to afflict the soul, 632
Ac 22: 4 **b** and delivering into prisons both men and *1195*

BINEA (2)
1Ch 8:37 Moza begat **B**: Rapha *was* his son, 1150
9:43 Moza begat **B**; and Rephaiah his son, 1150

BINNUI (7) [BAVAI]
Ezr 8:33 and Noadiah the son of **B**, Levites; 1131
10:30 Mattaniah, Bezaleel, and **B**, and Manasseh. 1131
10:38 And Bani, and **B**, Shimei, 1131
Ne 3:24 After him repaired **B** the son of Henadad 1131
7:15 The children of **B**, six hundred forty and 1131
10: 9 **B** of the sons of Henadad, Kadmiel; 1131
12: 8 Jeshua, **B**, Kadmiel, Sherebiah, Judah, *and* 1131

BIRD (28) [BIRD'S, BIRDS, BIRDS']
Ge 7:14 fowl after his kind, every **b** of every sort. 6833
Lev 14: 6 As for the living **b**, he shall take it, and 6833
14: 6 the living **b** in the blood of the bird *that* 6833
14: 6 the living bird in the blood of the **b** *that* 6833
14: 7 shall let the living **b** loose into the open 6833
14:51 the living **b**, and dip them in the blood of 6833
14:51 dip them in the blood of the slain **b**, 6833
14:52 cleanse the house with the blood of the **b**, 6833
14:52 with the living **b**, and with the cedar wood, 6833
14:53 he shall let go the living **b** out of the city 6833
Job 41: 5 Wilt thou play with him as *with* a **b**? or 6833
Ps 11: 1 to my soul, Flee *as* a **b** *to* your mountain? 6833
124: 7 Our soul is escaped as a **b** out of the snare 6833
Pr 1:17 the net *is* spread in the sight of any **b**. 1167+3671
6: 5 and as a **b** from the hand of the fowler. 6833
7:23 as a **b** hasteth to the snare, and knoweth not 6833
26: 2 As the **b** by wandering, as the swallow by 6833
27: 8 As a **b** that wandereth from her nest, so *is* a 6833
Ecc 10:20 for a **b** of the air shall carry the voice, and 5775
12: 4 he shall rise up at the voice of the **b**, and 6833
Isa 16: 2 *that,* as a wandering **b** cast out of the nest, 5775
46:11 Calling a **ravenous b** from the east, 5861
Jer 12: 9 Mine heritage *is* unto me *as* a speckled **b**, 5861
La 3:52 chased me sore, like a **b**, without cause. 6833
Hos 9:11 their glory shall fly away like a **b**, from 5775
11:11 They shall tremble as a **b** out of Egypt, and 6833
Am 3: 5 Can a **b** fall in a snare upon the earth, 6833
Rev 18: 2 and a cage of every unclean and hateful **b**. *3732*

BIRD'S (1) [BIRD]
Dt 22: 6 If a **b** nest chance to be before thee in 6833

BIRDS (24) [BIRD]
Ge 15:10 against another: but the **b** divided he not. 6833
40:17 the **b** did eat them out of the basket upon 5775
40:19 and the **b** shall eat thy flesh from off thee. 5775
Lev 14: 4 for him that is to be cleansed two **b** alive 6833
14: 5 the priest shall command that one of the **b** 6833
14:49 he shall take to cleanse the house two **b**, 6833
14:50 he shall kill the one of the **b** in an earthen 6833
Dt 14:11 *Of* all clean **b** ye shall eat. 6833
2Sa 21:10 suffered neither the **b** of the air to rest on 5775
Ps 104:17 Where the **b** make their nests: *as for* 6833
Ecc 9:12 and as the **b** that are caught in the snare; 6833
SS 2:12 the time of the singing *of* **b** is come, and NIH
Isa 31: 5 As **b** flying, so will the LORD of hosts 6833
Jer 4:25 and all the **b** of the heavens were fled. 5775
5:27 As a cage *is* full *of* **b**, so *are* their houses 5775
12: 4 the beasts are consumed, and the **b**; 5775
12: 9 the **b** round about *are* against her; 5861
Eze 39: 4 I will give thee unto the ravenous **b** of 6833
Mt 8:20 have holes, and the **b** of the air *have* nests; *4071*
13:32 so that the **b** of the air come and lodge in *4071*
Lk 9:58 have holes, and **b** of the air *have* nests; *4071*
Ro 1:23 and to **b**, and fourfooted beasts, and *4071*
1Co 15:39 another of fishes, *and* another of **b**. *4421*
Jas 3: 7 and of **b**, and of serpents, and of *things* in *4071*

BIRDS' (1) [BIRD]
Da 4:33 eagles' *feathers,* and his nails like **b** *claws.* 6853

BIRSHA (1)
Ge 14: 2 with **B** king of Gomorrah, Shinab king of 1306

BIRTH (15) [BEAR]
Ex 28:10 rest on the other stone, according to their **b**. 8435
2Ki 19: 3 for the children are come to the **b**, and 4866
Job 3:16 Or as a hidden **untimely b** I had not been; 5309
Ps 58: 8 *like* the **untimely b** of a woman, *that* they 5309
Ecc 6: 3 I say, *that* an **untimely b** *is* better than he. 5309
7: 1 the day of death than the day of one's **b**. 3205
Isa 37: 3 for the children are come to the **b**, and 4866
66: 9 Shall I **bring to the b**, and not cause to 7665
Eze 16: 3 Thy **b** and thy nativity *is* of the land of 4351
Hos 9:11 from the **b**, and from the womb, and 3205
Mt 1:18 Now the **b** of Jesus Christ was on this wise: *1083*
Lk 1:14 gladness; and many shall rejoice at his **b**. *1083*
Jn 9: 1 he saw a man *which was* blind from *his* **b**. *1079*
Gal 4:19 of whom I **travail in b** again until Christ be *5605*
Rev 12: 2 **travailing in b**, and pained to be delivered. *5605*

BIRTHDAY (3) [BEAR, DAY]
Ge 40:20 third day, *which was* Pharaoh's **b**, 3117+3205
Mt 14: 6 But when Herod's **b** was kept, the daughter *1077*
Mk 6:21 that Herod on his **b** made a supper to his *1077*

BIRTHRIGHT (10) [BEAR, RIGHT]
Ge 25:31 And Jacob said, Sell me *this* day thy **b**. 1062
25:32 and what profit shall this **b** do to me? 1062
25:33 sware to him: and he sold his **b** unto Jacob. 1062
25:34 and went his way: thus Esau despised *his* **b**. 1062
27:36 he took away my **b**; and behold, now he 1062
43:33 the firstborn according to his **b**, and 1062
1Ch 5: 1 his **b** was given unto the sons of Joseph 1062
5: 1 genealogy is not to be reckoned after the **b**. 1062
5: 2 the chief ruler; but the **b** *was* Joseph's:) 1062
Heb 12:16 who for one morsel of meat sold his **b**. *4415*

BIRZAITH See BIRZAVITH

BIRZAVITH (1)
1Ch 7:31 and Malchiel, who *is* the father of **B**. 1269

BISHLAM (1)
Ezr 4: 7 in the days of Artaxerxes wrote **B**, 1312

BISHOP (6) [BISHOPRICK, BISHOPS]
1Ti 3: 1 If a man desire the **office of a b**, *1984*
3: 2 A **b** then must be blameless, the husband of *1985*
2Ti 4: S ordained the first **b** of the church of *1985*
Tit 1: 7 For a **b** must be blameless, as the steward *1985*
3: S ordained the first **b** of the church of *1985*
1Pe 2:25 unto the Shepherd and **B** of your souls. *1985*

BISHOPRICK (1) [BISHOP]
Ac 1:20 dwell therein: and his **b** let another take. *1984*

BISHOPS (1) [BISHOP]
Php 1: 1 are at Philippi, with the **b** and deacons: *1985*

BIT (3) [BITE, BITS]
Nu 21: 6 among the people, and they **b** the people; 5391
Ps 32: 9 whose mouth must be held in with **b** and 4964
Am 5:19 his hand on the wall, and a serpent **b** him. 5391

BITE (7) [BACKBITERS, BACKBITETH, BACKBITING, BACKBITINGS, BIT, BITETH, BITTEN, HUNGER-BITTEN]
Ecc 10: 8 breaketh a hedge, a serpent shall **b** him. 5391
10:11 Surely the serpent will **b** without 5391
Jer 8:17 and they shall **b** you, saith the LORD. 5391
Am 9: 3 command the serpent, and he shall **b** them: 5391
Mic 3: 5 that **b** with their teeth, and cry, Peace; 5391
Hab 2: 7 Shall they not rise up suddenly that *shall* **b** 5391
Gal 5:15 But if ye **b** and devour one another, *1143*

BITETH (2) [BITE]
Ge 49:17 that **b** the horse heels, so that his rider shall 5391
Pr 23:32 At the last it **b** like a serpent, and 5391

BITHIAH (1)
1Ch 4:18 these *are* the sons of **B** the daughter of 1332

BITHRON (1)
2Sa 2:29 went *through* all **B**, and they came *to* 1338

BITHYNIA (2)
Ac 16: 7 come to Mysia, they assayed to go into **B**: *978*
1Pe 1: 1 Galatia, Cappadocia, Asia, and **B**, *978*

BITS (1) [BIT]
Jas 3: 3 Behold, we put **b** in the horses' mouths, *5469*

BITTEN (2) [BITE]
Nu 21: 8 shall come to pass, that every one that is **b**, 5391
21: 9 to pass, that if a serpent had **b** *any* man, 5391

BITTER (38) [BITTERLY, BITTERNESS]
Ge 27:34 he cried with a great and exceeding **b** cry, 4751
Ex 1:14 they **made** their lives **b** with hard bondage, 4843
12: 8 *and* with **b** *herbs* they shall eat it. 4844
15:23 of the waters of Marah, for they *were* **b**: 4751
Nu 5:18 the priest shall have in his hand the **b** water 4751
5:19 be thou free from this **b** water that causeth 4751
5:23 and he shall blot *them* out with the **b** water: 4751
5:24 he shall cause the woman to drink the **b** 4751
5:24 curse shall enter into her, and become **b**. 4751
5:27 become **b**, and her belly shall swell, and 4751
9:11 eat it with unleavened bread and **b** *herbs.* 4844
Dt 32:24 with burning heat, and with **b** destruction: 4815
32:32 *are* grapes of gall, their clusters *are* **b**: 4846
2Ki 14:26 the affliction of Israel, *that it was* very **b**: 4784
Est 4: 1 the city, and cried *with* a loud and a **b** cry; 4751
Job 3:20 that is in misery, and life unto the **b** in soul; 4751
13:26 For thou writest **b** *things* against me, and 4846
23: 2 Even to day *is* my complaint **b**: my stroke 4805
Ps 64: 3 *bows to shoot* their arrows, *even* **b** words: 4751
Pr 5: 4 her end is **b** as wormwood, sharp as a 4751
27: 7 *to* the hungry soul every **b** *thing is* sweet. 4751
Ecc 7:26 I find more **b** than death the woman, 4751
Isa 5:20 that put **b** for sweet, and sweet for bitter! 4751
5:20 that put bitter for sweet, and sweet for **b**! 4751
24: 9 strong drink shall be **b** to them that drink it. 4843
Jer 2:19 and see that *it is* an evil *thing* and **b**, 4751
4:18 because *it is* **b**, because it reacheth unto 4751
6:26 *as* for an only *son,* most **b** lamentation: 8563
31:15 in Ramah, lamentation, *and* **b** weeping; 8563
Eze 27:31 thee with bitterness of heart *and* **b** wailing. 4751
Am 8:10 an only *son,* and the end thereof as a **b** day. 4751
Hab 1: 6 up the Chaldeans, *that* **b** and hasty nation, 4751
Col 3:19 love *your* wives, and be not **b** against them. *4087*
Jas 3:11 forth at the same place sweet *water* and **b**? *4089*
3:14 But if ye have **b** envying and strife in your *4089*
Rev 8:11 of the waters, because they were **made b**. *4087*
10: 9 and it shall **make** thy belly **b**, but it shall be *4087*
10:10 as soon as I had eaten it, my belly was **b**. *4087*

BITTERLY (9) [BITTER]
Jdg 5:23 curse ye **b** the inhabitants thereof; 779
Ru 1:20 for the Almighty hath **dealt** very **b** with 4843
Isa 22: 4 I will weep **b**, labour not to comfort me, 4843
33: 7 the ambassadors of peace shall weep **b**. 4751
Eze 27:30 shall cry **b**, and shall cast up dust upon 4751
Hos 12:14 Ephraim provoked *him* to anger **most b**: 8563
Zep 1:14 the mighty *man* shall cry there **b**. 4751
Mt 26:75 me thrice. And he went out, and wept **b**. *4090*
Lk 22:62 And Peter went out, and wept **b**. *4090*

BITTERN (3)
Isa 14:23 I will also make it a possession for the **b**, 7090
34:11 the cormorant and the **b** shall possess it; 7090
Zep 2:14 the **b** shall lodge in the upper lintels of it; 7090

BITTERNESS (22) [BITTER]
1Sa 1:10 she *was* in **b** of soul, and prayed unto 4751

1Sa 15:32 Agag said, Surely the b of death is past. 4751
2Sa 2:26 knowest thou not that it will be b in 4751
Job 7:11 I will complain in the b of my soul. 4751
9:18 me to take my breath, but filleth me with b. 4472
10: 1 I will speak in the b of my soul. 4751
21:25 another dieth in the b of his soul, and 4751
Pr 14:10 The heart knoweth his own b; and 4787
17:25 to his father, and b to her that bare him. 4470
Isa 38:15 go softly all my years in the b of my soul. 4751
38:17 Behold, for peace I had great b: 4751+4843
La 1: 4 her virgins are afflicted, and she is in b. 4843
3:15 He hath filled me with b, he hath made me 4844
Eze 3:14 took me away, and I went in b, in the heat 4751
21: 6 thy loins; and with b sigh before their eyes. 4814
27:31 they shall weep for thee with b of heart and 4751
Zec 12:10 for his only son, and shall be in b for him, 4843
12:10 for him, as one that is in b for his firstborn. 4843
Ac 8:23 For I perceive that thou art in the gall of b, 4088
Ro 3:14 Whose mouth is full of cursing and b: 4088
Eph 4:31 Let all b, and wrath, and anger, and 4088
Heb 12:15 lest any root of b springing up trouble you, 4088

BIZIOTHIAH See BIZJOTHJAH

BIZJOTHJAH (1)
Jos 15:28 And Hazar-shual, and Beer-sheba, and B, 964

BIZTHA (1)
Est 1:10 B, Harbona, Bigtha, and Abagtha, Zethar, 968

BLACK (18) [BLACKER, BLACKISH, BLACKNESS]
Lev 13:31 the skin, and that there is no b hair in it; 7838
13:37 and that there is b hair grown up therein; 7838
1Ki 18:45 that the heaven was b with clouds and 6937
Est 1: 6 of red, and blue, and white, and b marble. 5508
Job 30:30 My skin is b upon me, and my bones are 7835
Pr 7: 9 in the evening, in the b and dark night: 380
SS 1: 5 I am b, but comely, O ye daughters of 7838
1: 6 because I am b, because the sun hath 7840
5:11 his locks are bushy, and b as a raven. 7838
Jer 4:28 earth mourn, and the heavens above be b: 6937
8:21 I am b; astonishment hath taken hold on 6937
14: 2 they are b unto the ground; and the cry of 6937
La 5:10 Our skin was b like an oven because of 3648
Zec 6: 2 and in the second chariot b horses; 7838
6: 6 The b horses which are therein go forth 7838
Mt 5:36 thou canst not make one hair white or b. 3189
Rev 6: 5 And I beheld, and lo a b horse; and he that 3189
6:12 and the sun became b as sackcloth of hair, 3189

BLACKER (1) [BLACK]
La 4: 8 Their visage is b than a coal; they are not 2821

BLACKISH (1) [BLACK]
Job 6:16 Which are b by reason of the ice, and 6937

BLACKNESS (6) [BLACK]
Job 3: 5 dwell upon it; let the b of the day terrify it. 3650
Isa 50: 3 I clothe the heavens with b, and I make 6940
Joel 2: 6 be much pained: all faces shall gather b. 6289
Na 2:10 all loins, and the faces of them all gather b. 6289
Heb 12:18 burned with fire, nor unto b, and darkness, 1105
Jude 1:13 to whom is reserved the b of darkness for 2217

BLADE (5)
Jdg 3:22 the haft also went in after the b; and the fat 3851
3:22 the fat closed upon the b, so that he could 3851
Job 31:22 let mine arm fall from my shoulder b, 7929
Mt 13:26 But when the b was sprung up, and 5528
Mk 4:28 first the b, then the ear, after that the full 5528

BLAINS (2)
Ex 9: 9 shall be a boil breaking forth with b upon 76
9:10 it became a boil breaking forth with b upon 76

BLAME (4) [BLAMED, BLAMELESS, UNBLAMEABLE]
Ge 43: 9 then let me bear the b for ever: 2398
44:32 I shall bear the b to my father for ever. 2398
2Co 8:20 that no man should b us in this abundance 3469
Eph 1: 4 be holy and without b before him in love: 299

BLAMED (2) [BLAME]
2Co 6: 3 in any thing, that the ministry be not b: 3469
Gal 2:11 him to the face, because he was to be b. 2607

BLAMELESS (15) [BLAME]
Ge 44:10 shall be my servant; and ye shall be b. 5355
Jos 2:17 We will be b of this thine oath which thou 5355
Jdg 15: 3 Now shall I be more b than the Philistines, 5352
Mt 12: 5 in the temple profane the sabbath, and are b? 338
Lk 1: 6 and ordinances of the Lord b. 273
1Co 1: 8 that ye may be b in the day of our Lord Jesus 410
Php 2:15 That ye may be b and harmless, the sons of 273
3: 6 the righteousness which is in the law, b. 273
1Th 5:23 body be preserved b unto the coming of our 274
1Ti 3: 2 A bishop then must be b, the husband of one 423
3:10 use the office of a deacon, being found b. 410
5: 7 things give in charge, that they may be b. 423
Tit 1: 6 If any be b, the husband of one wife, 410
1: 7 For a bishop must be b, as the steward of 410
2Pe 3:14 found of him in peace, without spot, and b. 298

BLASPHEME (10) [BLASPHEMED, BLASPHEMER, BLASPHEMERS, BLASPHEMEST, BLASPHEMETH, BLASPHEMIES, BLASPHEMING, BLASPHEMOUS, BLASPHEMOUSLY, BLASPHEMY]
2Sa 12:14 given great occasion to the enemies of the LORD to b, 5006+5006
1Ki 21:10 Thou didst b God and the king. 1288
21:13 Naboth did b God and the king. 1288
Ps 74:10 shall the enemy b thy name for ever? 5006
Mk 3:28 blasphemies wherewith soever they shall b: 987
3:29 But he that shall b against the Holy Ghost 987
Ac 26:11 every synagogue, and compelled them to b; 987
1Ti 1:20 unto Satan, that they may learn not to b. 987
Jas 2: 7 Do not they b that worthy name by 987
Rev 13: 6 to b his name, and his tabernacle, and 987

BLASPHEMED (16) [BLASPHEME]
Lev 24:11 the Israelitish woman's son b the name of 5344
2Ki 19: 6 servants of the king of Assyria have b me. 1442
19:22 Whom hast thou reproached and b? and 1442
Ps 74:18 that the foolish people have b thy name. 5006
Isa 37: 6 servants of the king of Assyria have b me. 1442
37:23 Whom hast thou reproached and b? and 1442
52: 5 and my name continually every day is b. 5006
65: 7 the mountains, and b me upon the hills: 2778
Eze 20:27 Yet in this your fathers have b me, in that 1442
Ac 18: 6 and b, he shook his raiment, and said unto 987
Ro 2:24 For the name of God is b among the Gentiles 987
1Ti 6: 1 the name of God and his doctrine be not b. 987
Tit 2: 5 that the word of God be not b. 987
Rev 16: 9 and b the name of God, which hath power 987
16:11 And b the God of heaven because of their 987
16:21 and men b God because of the plague of 987

BLASPHEMER (1) [BLASPHEME]
1Ti 1:13 Who was before a b, and a persecutor, and 989

BLASPHEMERS (2) [BLASPHEME]
Ac 19:37 of churches, nor yet b of your goddess. 987
2Ti 3: 2 covetous, boasters, proud, b, disobedient to 989

BLASPHEMEST (1) [BLASPHEME]
Jn 10:36 and sent into the world, Thou b; 987

BLASPHEMETH (5) [BLASPHEME]
Lev 24:16 he that b the name of the LORD, he shall 5344
24:16 when he b the name of the LORD, shall 5344
Ps 44:16 the voice of him that reproacheth and b; 1442
Mt 9: 3 scribes said within themselves, This man b. 987
Lk 12:10 unto him that b against the Holy Ghost it 987

BLASPHEMIES (6) [BLASPHEME]
Eze 35:12 that I have heard all thy b which thou hast 5007
Mt 15:19 fornications, thefts, false witness, b: 988
Mk 2: 7 Why doth this man thus speak b? who can 988
3:28 b wherewith soever they shall blaspheme: 988
Lk 5:21 saying, Who is this which speaketh b? 988
Rev 13: 5 him a mouth speaking great things and b; 988

BLASPHEMING (1) [BLASPHEME]
Ac 13:45 were spoken by Paul, contradicting and b. 987

BLASPHEMOUS (2) [BLASPHEME]
Ac 6:11 We have heard him speak b words against 989
6:13 This man ceaseth not to speak b words 989

BLASPHEMOUSLY (1) [BLASPHEME]
Lk 22:65 And many other things b spake they against 987

BLASPHEMY (14) [BLASPHEME]
2Ki 19: 3 is a day of trouble, and of rebuke, and b: 5007
Isa 37: 3 is a day of trouble, and of rebuke, and of b: 5007
Mt 12:31 of sin and b shall be forgiven unto men: 988
12:31 the b against the Holy Ghost shall not be 988
26:65 rent his clothes, saying, He hath spoken b; 987
26:65 behold, now ye have heard his b. 988
Mk 7:22 an evil eye, b, pride, foolishness: 988
14:64 Ye have heard the b: what think ye? 988
Jn 10:33 but for b; and because that thou, being a 988
Col 3: 8 wrath, malice, b, filthy communication out 988
Rev 2: 9 I know the b of them which say they are 988
13: 1 and upon his heads the name of b. 988
13: 6 And he opened his mouth in b against God, 988
17: 3 full of names of b, having seven heads and 988

BLAST (8) [BLASTED, BLASTING]
Ex 15: 8 with the b of thy nostrils the waters were 7307
Jos 6: 5 that when they make a long b with 4900
2Sa 22:16 at the b of the breath of his nostrils. 5397
2Ki 19: 7 I will send a b upon him, and he shall hear 7307
Job 4: 9 By the b of God they perish, and by 5397
Ps 18:15 at the b of the breath of thy nostrils. 5397
Isa 25: 4 when the b of the terrible ones is as a storm 7307
37: 7 I will send a b upon him, and he shall hear 7307

BLASTED (5) [BLAST]
Ge 41: 6 b with the east wind sprang up after them. 7710
41:23 withered, thin, and b with the east wind, 7710
41:27 the seven empty ears b with the east wind 7710
2Ki 19:26 and as corn b before it be grown up. 7711
Isa 37:27 and as corn b before it be grown up. 7711

BLASTING (5) [BLAST]
Dt 28:22 the sword, and with b, and with mildew; 7711
1Ki 8:37 b, mildew, locust, or if there be caterpillar; 7711
2Ch 6:28 if there be b, or mildew, locusts, or 7711
Am 4: 9 I have smitten you with b and mildew: 7711
Hag 2:17 I smote you with b and with mildew and 7711

BLASTUS (1)
Ac 12:20 having made B the king's chamberlain their 986

BLAZE (1)
Mk 1:45 it much, and to b abroad the matter, 1310

BLEATING (1) [BLEATINGS]
1Sa 15:14 then this b of the sheep in mine ears, 6963

BLEATINGS (1) [BLEATING]
Jdg 5:16 the sheepfolds, to hear the b of the flocks? 8292

BLEMISH (62) [BLEMISHES]
Ex 12: 5 Your lamb shall be without b, a male of 8549
29: 1 young bullock, and two rams without b, 8549
Lev 1: 3 of the herd, let him offer a male without b: 8549
1:10 he shall bring it a male without b. 8549
3: 1 he shall offer it without b before 8549
3: 6 male or female, he shall offer it without b. 8549
4: 3 a young bullock without b unto 8549
4:23 a kid of the goats, a male without b; 8549
4:28 a kid of the goats, a female without b, 8549
4:32 he shall bring it a female without b. 8549
5:15 LORD a ram without b out of the flocks, 8549
5:18 he shall bring a ram without b out of 8549
6: 6 a ram without b out of the flock, with thy 8549
9: 2 without b, and offer them before 8549
9: 3 first year, without b, for a burnt offering; 8549
14:10 day he shall take two he lambs without b, 8549
14:10 one ewe lamb of the first year without b, 8549
21:17 seed in their generations that hath any b, 3971
21:18 For whatsoever man he be that hath a b, 3971
21:20 or that hath a b in his eye, or be scurvy, or 8400
21:21 No man that hath a b, of the seed of Aaron 3971
21:21 he hath a b; he shall not come nigh to offer 3971
21:23 nigh unto the altar, because he hath a b; 3971
22:19 offer at your own will a male without b, 8549
22:20 But whatsoever hath a b, that shall ye not 3971
22:21 to be accepted; there shall be no b therein. 3971
23:12 without b of the first year for a burnt 8549
23:18 seven lambs without b of the first year, 8549
24:19 if a man cause a b in his neighbour; as he 3971
24:20 as he hath caused a b in a man, so shall it 3971
Nu 6:14 one he lamb of the first year without b for 8549
6:14 one ewe lamb of the first year without b 8549
6:14 and one ram without b for peace offerings, 8549
19: 2 wherein is no b, and upon which never 3971
28:19 first year: they shall be unto you without b: 8549
28:31 (they shall be unto you without b) 8549
29: 2 seven lambs of the first year without b: 8549
29: 8 first year; they shall be unto you without b: 8549
29:13 of the first year; they shall be without b: 8549
29:20 fourteen lambs of the first year without b; 8549
29:23 fourteen lambs of the first year without b; 8549
29:29 fourteen lambs of the first year without b: 8549
29:32 fourteen lambs of the first year without b: 8549
29:36 seven lambs of the first year without b: 8549
Dt 15:21 if there be any b therein, as if it be lame, 3971
15:21 as if it be lame, or blind, or have any ill b, 3971
17: 1 wherein is b, or any evil favouredness: 3971
2Sa 14:25 crown of his head there was no b in him. 3971
Eze 43:22 of the goats without b for a sin offering; 8549
43:23 thou shalt offer a young bullock without b, 8549
43:23 and a ram out of the flock without b. 8549
43:25 and a ram out of the flock, without b. 8549
45:18 thou shalt take a young bullock without b, 8549
45:23 seven rams without b daily the seven days; 8549
46: 4 sabbath day shall be six lambs without b, 8549
46: 4 without blemish, and a ram without b. 8549
46: 6 it shall be a young bullock without b, 8549
46: 6 and a ram: they shall be without b. 8549
46:13 of a lamb of the first year without b: 8549
Da 1: 4 Children in whom was no b, but 3971
Eph 5:27 but that it should be holy and without b. 299
1Pe 1:19 as of a lamb without b and without spot: 299

BLEMISHES (2) [BLEMISH]
Lev 22:25 corruption is in them, and b be in them: 3971
2Pe 2:13 Spots they are and b, sporting themselves 3470

BLENDED See APOTHECARIES'

BLENDED WINE See LIQUOR

BLESS (127) [BLESSED, BLESSEDNESS, BLESSEST, BLESSETH, BLESSING, BLESSINGS]
Ge 12: 2 and I will b thee, and make thy name great; 1288
12: 3 I will b them that bless thee, and curse him 1288
12: 3 I will bless them that b thee, and curse him 1288
17:16 I will b her, and give thee a son also of her: 1288
17:16 I will b her, and she shall be a mother of 1288
22:17 That in blessing I will b thee, and 1288
26: 3 I will be with thee, and will b thee; 1288
26:24 will b thee, and multiply thy seed for my 1288
27: 4 that my soul may b thee before I die. 1288
27: 7 b thee before the LORD before my death. 1288
27:10 that he may b thee before his death. 1288
27:19 eat of my venison, that thy soul may b me. 1288
27:25 my son's venison, that my soul may b thee. 1288
27:31 his son's venison, that thy soul may b me. 1288
27:34 B me, even me also, O my father. 1288
27:38 b me, even me also, O my father. And Esau 1288
28: 3 God Almighty b thee, and make thee 1288
32:26 I will not let thee go, except thou b me. 1288
48: 9 I pray thee, unto me, and I will b them. 1288
48:16 redeemed me from all evil, b the lads; 1288
48:20 saying, In thee shall Israel b, saying, 1288
49:25 who shall b thee with blessings of heaven 1288
Ex 12:32 ye have said, and be gone; and b me also. 1288
20:24 I will come unto thee, and I will b thee. 1288
23:25 and he shall b thy bread, and thy water; 1288
Nu 6:23 On this wise ye shall b the children of 1288
6:24 The LORD b thee, and keep thee: 1288
6:27 the children of Israel; and I will b them. 1288
23:20 I have received commandment to b: 1288
23:25 curse them at all, nor b them at all. 1288+1288
24: 1 saw that it pleased the LORD to b Israel, 1288
Dt 1:11 so many moe as ye are, and b you, 1288
7:13 love thee, and b thee, and multiply thee: 1288
7:13 he will also b the fruit of thy womb, and 1288
8:10 thou shalt b the LORD thy God for 1288
10: 8 and to b in his name, unto this day. 1288
14:29 that the LORD thy God may b thee in all 1288
15: 4 for the LORD shall greatly b thee 1288+1288
15:10 thy God shall b thee in all thy works, 1288
15:18 the LORD thy God shall b thee in all that 1288
16:15 the LORD thy God shall b thee in all thy 1288
21: 5 and to b in the name of the LORD; 1288
23:20 that the LORD thy God may b thee in all 1288
24:13 may sleep in his own raiment, and b thee: 1288

Dt 24:19 that the LORD thy God may **b** thee in all 1288
26:15 **b** thy people Israel, and the land which thou 1288
27:12 shall stand upon mount Gerizzim to **b** 1288
28: 8 he shall **b** thee in the land which 1288
28:12 and to **b** all the work of thine hand: 1288
29:19 that he **b** himself in his heart, saying, I shall 1288
30:16 the LORD thy God shall **b** thee in the land 1288
33:11 **B**, LORD, his substance, and accept 1288
Jos 8:33 that they should **b** the people of Israel. 1288
Jdg 5: 9 among the people. **B** ye the LORD. 1288
Ru 2: 4 they answered him, The LORD **b** thee. 1288
1Sa 9:13 he come, because he doth **b** the sacrifice; 1288
2Sa 6:20 David returned to **b** his household. 1288
7:29 Therefore now let it please thee to **b** 1288
8:10 to **b** him, because he had fought against 1288
21: 3 that ye may **b** the inheritance of 1288
1Ki 1:47 moreover the king's servants came to **b** our 1288
1Ch 4:10 Oh that thou wouldest **b** me **indeed**, 1288+1288
16:43 and David returned to **b** his house. 1288
17:27 let it please thee to **b** the house of thy 1288
23:13 unto him, and to **b** in his name for ever. 1288
29:20 Now **b** the LORD your God. 1288
Ne 9: 5 *and* **b** the LORD your God for ever and 1288
Ps 5:12 For thou, LORD, wilt **b** the righteous; 1288
16: 7 I will **b** the LORD, who hath given me 1288
26:12 in the congregations will I **b** the LORD. 1288
28: 9 Save thy people, and **b** thine inheritance: 1288
29:11 the LORD will **b** his people with peace. 1288
34: 1 I will **b** the LORD at all times: his praise 1288
62: 4 they **b** with their mouth, but they curse 1288
63: 4 Thus will I **b** thee while I live: I will lift up 1288
66: 8 O **b** our God, ye people, and make 1288
67: 1 God be merciful unto us, and **b** us; *and* 1288
67: 6 *and* God, *even* our own God, shall **b** us. 1288
67: 7 God shall **b** us; and all the ends of the earth 1288
68:26 **B** ye God in the congregations, *even* 1288
96: 2 Sing unto the LORD, **b** his name; 1288
100: 4 be thankful unto him, *and* **b** his name. 1288
103: 1 **B** the LORD, O my soul: and all that is 1288
103: 1 and all that is within me, ***b*** his holy name. NIH
103: 2 **B** the LORD, O my soul, and forget not 1288
103:20 **B** the LORD, ye his angels, that excel in 1288
103:21 **B** ye the LORD, all ye his hosts; 1288
103:22 **B** the LORD, all his works in all places of 1288
103:22 of his dominion: **b** the LORD, O my soul. 1288
104: 1 **B** the LORD, O my soul. O LORD my 1288
104:35 **B** thou the LORD, O my soul. Praise ye 1288
109:28 Let them curse, but **b** thou: when they 1288
115:12 he will **b** *us;* he will bless the house of 1288
115:12 he will bless *us;* he will **b** the house of 1288
115:12 of Israel; he will **b** the house of Aaron. 1288
115:13 He will **b** them that fear the LORD, *both* 1288
115:18 we will **b** the LORD from this time forth 1288
128: 5 The LORD shall **b** thee out of Zion: and 1288
129: 8 we **b** you in the name of the LORD. 1288
132:15 I will **abundantly b** her provision: 1288+1288
134: 1 Behold, **b** ye the LORD, all ye servants of 1288
134: 2 hands *in* the sanctuary, and **b** the LORD. 1288
134: 3 made heaven and earth **b** thee out of Zion. 1288
135:19 **B** the LORD, O house of Israel: bless 1288
135:19 of Israel: **b** the LORD, O house of Aaron: 1288
135:20 **B** the LORD, O house of Levi: ye that 1288
135:20 ye that fear the LORD, **b** the LORD. 1288
145: 1 and I will **b** thy name for ever and ever. 1288
145: 2 Every day will I **b** thee; and I will praise 1288
145:10 O LORD; and thy saints shall **b** thee. 1288
145:21 let all flesh **b** his holy name for ever and 1288
Pr 30:11 their father, and doth not **b** their mother. 1288
Isa 19:25 Whom the LORD of hosts shall **b**, saying, 1288
65:16 earth shall **b** himself in the God of truth; 1288
Jer 4: 2 the nations shall **b** themselves in him, and 1288
31:23 The LORD **b** thee, O habitation of justice, 1288
Hag 2:19 brought forth: from this day will I **b** *you.* 1288
Mt 5:44 Love your enemies, **b** them that curse you, *2127*
Lk 6:28 **B** them that curse you, and pray for them *2127*
Ac 3:26 raised up his Son Jesus, sent him to **b** you, *2127*
Ro 12:14 **B** them which persecute you: bless, and *2127*
12:14 which persecute you: **b**, and curse not. *2127*
1Co 4:12 being reviled, we **b**; being persecuted, *2127*
10:16 The cup of blessing which we **b**, is it not *2127*
14:16 Else when thou shalt **b** with the spirit, *2127*
Heb 6:14 Surely blessing I will **b** thee, and *2127*
Jas 3: 9 Therewith **b** we God, even the Father; and *2127*

BLESSED (302) [BLESS]

Ge 1:22 God **b** them, saying, Be fruitful, and 1288
1:28 God **b** them, and God said unto them, 1288
2: 3 God **b** the seventh day, and sanctified it: 1288
5: 2 **b** them, and called their name Adam, in 1288
9: 1 God **b** Noah and his sons, and said unto 1288
9:26 he said, **B** *be* the LORD God of Shem; 1288
12: 3 in thee shall all families of the earth be **b**. 1288
14:19 he **b** him, and said, Blessed *be* Abram of 1288
14:19 said, **B** *be* Abram of the most high God, 1288
14:20 **b** *be* the most high God, which hath 1288
17:20 I have **b** him, and will make him fruitful, 1288
18:18 all the nations of the earth shall be **b** in 1288
22:18 seed shall all the nations of the earth be **b**; 1288
24: 1 the LORD had **b** Abraham in all things. 1288
24:27 **B** *be* the LORD God of my master 1288
24:31 he said, Come in, thou **b** of the LORD; 1288
24:35 the LORD hath **b** my master greatly; and 1288
24:48 **b** the LORD God of my master Abraham, 1288
24:60 they **b** Rebekah, and said unto her, Thou *art* 1288
25:11 of Abraham, that God **b** his son Isaac; 1288
26: 4 seed shall all the nations of the earth be **b**; 1288
26:12 an hundredfold: and the LORD **b** him. 1288
26:29 in peace: thou *art* now the **b** of the LORD. 1288
27:23 as his brother Esau's hands: so he **b** him. 1288
27:27 of his raiment, and **b** him, and said, See, 1288
27:27 smell of a field which the LORD hath **b**: 1288
27:29 curseth thee, and **b** *be* he that blesseth thee. 1288
27:33 of all before thou camest, and have **b** him? 1288
27:33 have blessed him? yea, *and* he shall be **b**. 1288
27:41 of the blessing wherewith his father **b** him: 1288
Ge 28: 1 **b** him, and charged him, and said unto him, 1288
28: 6 When Esau saw that Isaac had **b** Jacob, and 1288
28: 6 that as he **b** him he gave him a charge, 1288
28:14 seed shall all the families of the earth be **b**. 1288
30:13 am I, for the daughters will **call** me **b**: 833
30:27 that the LORD hath **b** me for thy sake. 1288
30:30 the LORD hath **b** thee since my coming: 1288
31:55 his sons and his daughters, and **b** them: 1288
32:29 ask after my name? And he **b** him there. 1288
35: 9 he came out of Padan-aram, and **b** him. 1288
39: 5 that the LORD **b** the Egyptian's house for 1288
47: 7 him before Pharaoh: and Jacob **b** Pharaoh. 1288
47:10 Jacob **b** Pharaoh, and went out from before 1288
48: 3 me at Luz in the land of Canaan, and **b** me, 1288
48:15 he **b** Joseph, and said, God, before whom 1288
48:20 he **b** them that day, saying, In thee shall 1288
49:28 their father spake unto them, and **b** them; 1288
49:28 every one according to his blessing he **b** 1288
Ex 18:10 Jethro said, **B** *be* the LORD, who hath 1288
20:11 wherefore the LORD **b** the sabbath day, 1288
39:43 so had they done it: and Moses **b** them. 1288
Lev 9:22 **b** them, and came down from offering of 1288
9:23 and came out, and **b** the people: 1288
Nu 22: 6 for I wot that *he* whom thou blessest *is* **b**, 1288
22:12 shalt not curse the people: for they *are* **b**. 1288
23:11 behold, thou hast **b** *them* **altogether**. 1288+1288
23:20 and he hath **b**; and I cannot reverse it. 1288
24: 9 **B** *is* he that blesseth thee, and cursed *is* he 1288
24:10 thou hast **altogether b** *them* these 1288+1288
Dt 2: 7 For the LORD thy God hath **b** thee in all 1288
7:14 Thou shalt be **b** above all people: 1288
12: 7 where*in* the LORD thy God hath **b** thee. 1288
14:24 when the LORD thy God hath **b** thee: 1288
15:14 God hath **b** thee thou shalt give unto him. 1288
16:10 as the LORD thy God hath **b** thee: 1288
28: 3 **B** *shalt* thou *be* in the city, and blessed *shalt* 1288
28: 3 in the city, and **b** *shalt* thou *be* in the field. 1288
28: 4 **B** *shall be* the fruit of thy body, and 1288
28: 5 **B** *shall be* thy basket and thy store. 1288
28: 6 **B** *shalt* thou *be* when thou comest in, and 1288
28: 6 and **b** *shalt* thou *be* when thou goest out. 1288
33: 1 wherewith Moses the man of God **b** 1288
33:13 he said, **B** of the LORD *be* his land, 1288
33:20 of Gad he said, **B** *be* he that enlargeth Gad: 1288
33:24 he said, *Let* Asher *be* **b** with children; 1288
Jos 14:13 Joshua **b** him, and gave unto Caleb the son 1288
17:14 forasmuch as the LORD hath **b** me 1288
22: 6 So Joshua **b** them, and sent them away: and 1288
22: 7 away also unto their tents, then he **b** them, 1288
22:33 the children of Israel **b** God, and did not 1288
24:10 therefore he **b** you **still**: 1288+1288
Jdg 5:24 **B** above women shall Jael the wife of 1288
5:24 **b** shall she be above women in the tent. 1288
13:24 and the child grew, and the LORD **b** him. 1288
17: 2 **B** *be thou* of the LORD, my son. 1288
Ru 2:19 **b** be he that did take knowledge of thee. 1288
2:20 her daughter in law, **B** *be* he of the LORD, 1288
3:10 he said, **B** *be* thou of the LORD, 1288
4:14 women said unto Naomi, **B** *be* the LORD, 1288
1Sa 2:20 Eli **b** Elkanah and his wife, and said, 1288
15:13 said unto him, **B** *be* thou of the LORD: 1288
23:21 Saul said, **B** *be* ye of the LORD; for ye 1288
25:32 to Abigail, **B** *be* the LORD God of Israel, 1288
25:33 **b** *be* thy advice, and blessed *be* thou, 1288
25:33 blessed *be* thy advice, and **b** *be* thou, 1288
25:39 Nabal was dead, he said, **B** *be* the LORD, 1288
26:25 said to David, **B** *be* thou, my son David: 1288
2Sa 2: 5 said unto them, **B** *be* ye of the LORD, 1288
6:11 the LORD **b** Obed-edom, and all his 1288
6:12 The LORD hath **b** the house of 1288
6:18 he **b** the people in the name of the LORD 1288
7:29 let the house of thy servant be **b** for ever. 1288
13:25 howbeit he would not go, but **b** him. 1288
18:28 and said, **B** *be* the LORD thy God, 1288
19:39 the king kissed Barzillai, and **b** him; 1288
22:47 **b** *be* my rock; and exalted be the God of 1288
1Ki 1:48 the king, **B** *be* the LORD God of Israel, 1288
2:45 king Solomon *shall be* **b**, and the throne of 1288
5: 7 and said, **B** *be* the LORD *this* day, 1288
8:14 and **b** all the congregation of Israel: 1288
8:15 he said, **B** *be* the LORD God of Israel, 1288
8:55 **b** all the congregation of Israel *with* a loud 1288
8:56 **B** *be* the LORD, that hath given rest unto 1288
8:66 they **b** the king, and went unto their tents 1288
10: 9 **B** be the LORD thy God, which delighted 1288
1Ch 13:14 the LORD **b** the house of Obed-edom, 1288
16: 2 he **b** the people in the name of the LORD. 1288
16:36 **B** *be* the LORD God of Israel for ever and 1288
17:27 O LORD, and *it shall be* **b** for ever. 1288
26: 5 Peulthai the eighth: for God **b** him. 1288
29:10 Wherefore David **b** the LORD before all 1288
29:10 David said, **B** *be* thou, LORD God of 1288
29:20 all the congregation **b** the LORD God of 1288
2Ch 2:12 **B** *be* the LORD God of Israel, that made 1288
6: 3 and **b** the whole congregation of Israel: 1288
6: 4 he said, **B** *be* the LORD God of Israel, 1288
9: 8 **B** be the LORD thy God, which delighted 1288
20:26 of Berachah; for there they **b** the LORD: 1288
30:27 priests the Levites arose and **b** the people: 1288
31: 8 they **b** the LORD, and his people Israel. 1288
31:10 for the LORD hath **b** his people; and 1288
Ezr 7:27 **B** *be* the LORD God of our fathers, 1288
Ne 8: 6 Ezra **b** the LORD, the great God. And all 1288
9: 5 **b** be thy glorious name, which *is* exalted 1288
11: 2 the people **b** all the men, that willingly 1288
Job 1:10 thou hast **b** the work of his hands, and 1288
1:21 the LORD hath taken *away;* **b** be 1288
29:11 When the ear heard *me,* then it **b** me; and 833
31:20 If his loins have not **b** me, and *if* he were 1288
42:12 So the LORD **b** the latter end of Job more 1288
Ps 1: 1 **B** *is* the man that walketh not in the counsel 835
2:12 **b** *are* all they that put their trust in him. 835
18:46 **b** *be* my rock; and let the God of my 1288
21: 6 For thou hast made him most **b** for ever: 1293
28: 6 **B** *be* the LORD, because he hath heard 1288
Ps 31:21 **B** *be* the LORD: for he hath shewed me 1288
32: 1 **B** *is* he whose transgression *is* forgiven, 835
32: 2 **B** *is* the man unto whom the LORD 835
33:12 **B** *is* the nation whose God *is* the LORD; 835
34: 8 *is* good: **b** *is* the man *that* trusteth in him. 835
37:22 For such as be **b** of him shall inherit 1288
37:26 and lendeth; and his seed *is* **b**. 1293
40: 4 **B** *is that* man that maketh the LORD his 835
41: 1 **B** *is* he that considereth the poor: 835
41: 2 him alive; *and* he shall be **b** upon the earth: 833
41:13 **B** *be* the LORD God of Israel from 1288
45: 2 thy lips: therefore God hath **b** thee for ever. 1288
49:18 Though whiles he lived he **b** his soul: and 1288
65: 4 **B** *is the man whom* thou choosest, and 835
66:20 **B** *be* God, which hath not turned away my 1288
68:19 **B** *be* the Lord, *who* daily loadeth us *with* 1288
68:35 and power unto *his* people. **B** *be* God. 1288
72:17 *men* shall be **b** in him: all nations shall call 1288
72:17 blessed in him: all nations shall **call** him **b**. 833
72:18 **B** *be* the LORD God, the God of Israel, 1288
72:19 **b** *be* his glorious name for ever: and let 1288
84: 4 **B** *are* they that dwell in thy house: they will 835
84: 5 **B** *is* the man whose strength *is* in thee; 835
84:12 of hosts, **b** *is* the man that trusteth in thee. 835
89:15 **B** *is* the people that know the joyful sound: 835
89:52 **B** *be* the LORD for evermore. Amen, and 1288
94:12 **B** *is* the man whom thou chastenest, 835
106: 3 **B** *are* they that keep judgment, *and* he that 835
106:48 **B** *be* the LORD God of Israel from 1288
112: 1 **B** *is* the man *that* feareth the LORD, 835
112: 2 the generation of the upright shall be **b**. 1288
113: 2 **B** be the name of the LORD from this 1288
115:15 You *are* **b** of the LORD which made 1288
118:26 **B** *be* he that cometh in the name of 1288
118:26 we have **b** you out of the house of 1288
119: 1 **B** *are* the undefiled in the way, who walk in 835
119: 2 **B** *are* they that keep his testimonies, *and* 835
119:12 **B** *art* thou, O LORD: teach me thy 1288
124: 6 **B** *be* the LORD, who hath not given us *as* 1288
128: 1 **B** *is* every one that feareth the LORD; 835
128: 4 that thus shall the man be **b** that feareth 1288
135:21 **B** *be* the LORD out of Zion, 1288
144: 1 **B** *be* the LORD my strength, 1288
147:13 he hath **b** thy children within thee. 1288
Pr 5:18 Let thy fountain be **b**: and rejoice with 1288
8:32 for **b** *are they that* keep my ways. 835
8:34 **B** *is* the man that heareth me, watching daily 835
10: 7 The memory of the just *is* **b**: but the name 1293
20: 7 in his integrity: his children *are* **b** after him. 835
20:21 but the end thereof shall not be **b**. 1288
22: 9 He that hath a bountiful eye shall be **b**; 1288
31:28 Her children arise up, and **call** her **b**; 833
Ecc 10:17 **B** *art* thou, O land, when thy king *is* the son 835
SS 6: 9 The daughters saw her, and **b** her; *yea,* 833
Isa 19:25 **B** *be* Egypt my people, and Assyria 1288
30:18 of judgment: **b** *are* all they that wait for him. 835
32:20 **B** *are* ye that sow beside all waters, that send 835
51: 2 him alone, and **b** him, and increased him. 1288
56: 2 **B** *is* the man *that* doeth this, and the son of 835
61: 9 they *are* the seed *which* the LORD hath **b**. 1288
65:23 for they *are* the seed of the **b** of 1288
66: 3 he that burneth incense, *as if* he **b** an idol. 1288
Jer 17: 7 **B** *is* the man that trusteth in the LORD, 1288
20:14 the day wherein my mother bare me be **b**. 1288
Eze 3:12 *saying,* **B** *be* the glory of the LORD from 1288
Da 2:19 Then Daniel **b** the God of heaven. 1289
2:20 **B** be the name of God for ever and ever: 1289
3:28 said, **B** *be* the God of Shadrach, Meshach, 1289
4:34 I **b** the most High, and I praised and 1289
12:12 **B** *is* he that waiteth, and cometh to 835
Zec 11: 5 they that sell them say, **B** *be* the LORD; 1288
Mal 3:12 all nations shall **call** you **b**: for ye shall be a 833
Mt 5: 3 **B** *are* the poor in spirit: for theirs is *3107*
5: 4 **B** *are* they that mourn: for they shall be *3107*
5: 5 **B** *are* the meek: for they shall inherit *3107*
5: 6 **B** *are* they which do hunger and thirst after *3107*
5: 7 **B** *are* the merciful: for they shall obtain *3107*
5: 8 **B** *are* the pure in heart: for they shall see *3107*
5: 9 **B** *are* the peacemakers: for they shall be *3107*
5:10 **B** *are* they which are persecuted for *3107*
5:11 **B** are ye, when *men* shall revile you, and *3107*
11: 6 And **b** is *he,* whosoever shall not be *3107*
13:16 But **b** *are* your eyes, for they see: and *3107*
14:19 he **b**, and brake, and gave the loaves to *his* *2127*
16:17 and said unto him, **B** art thou, *3107*
21: 9 **B** *is* he that cometh in the name of *2127*
23:39 **B** is he that cometh in the name of *2127*
24:46 **B** *is* that servant, whom his lord when he *3107*
25:34 on his right hand, Come, ye **b** of my Father, *2127*
26:26 and **b** *it,* and brake *it,* and gave *it* to *2127*
Mk 6:41 and **b**, and brake the loaves, and gave *them* *2127*
8: 7 and he **b**, and commanded to set them also *2127*
10:16 put *his* hands upon them, and **b** them. *2127*
11: 9 **B** *is* he that cometh in the name of *2127*
11:10 **B** *be* the kingdom of our father David, *2127*
14:22 and **b**, and brake *it,* and gave to them, and *2127*
14:61 Art thou the Christ, the Son of the **B**? *2128*
Lk 1:28 *is* with thee: **b** *art* thou among women. *2127*
1:42 **B** *art* thou among women, and blessed *is* *2127*
1:42 and **b** *is* the fruit of thy womb. *2127*
1:45 And **b** *is* she that believed: for there shall *3107*
1:48 henceforth all generations shall **call** me **b**. *3106*
1:68 **B** *be* the Lord God of Israel; for he hath *2128*
2:28 he him *up* in his arms, and **b** God, and said, *2127*
2:34 And Simeon **b** them, and said unto Mary *2127*
6:20 on his disciples, and said, **B** *be ye* poor: *3107*
6:21 **B** *are ye* that hunger now: for ye shall be *3107*
6:21 **B** *are ye* that weep now: for ye shall laugh. *3107*
6:22 **B** are ye, when men shall hate you, and *3107*
7:23 And **b** is *he,* whosoever shall not be *3107*
9:16 he **b** them, and brake, and gave to *2127*
10:23 **B** *are* the eyes which see *the things* that ye *3107*
11:27 **B** *is* the womb that bare thee, and the paps *3107*
11:28 **b** *are* they that hear the word of God, and *3107*
12:37 **B** *are* those servants, whom the lord when *3107*

Lk 12:38 and find *them* so, **b** are those servants. 3107
12:43 **B** *is* that servant, whom his lord when he 3107
13:35 **B** *is he* that cometh in the name of 2127
14:14 And thou shalt be **b**; for they cannot 3107
14:15 **B** *is he* that shall eat bread in the kingdom 3107
19:38 **B** *be* the King that cometh in the name of 2127
23:29 **B** *are* the barren, and the wombs that never 3107
24:30 and **b** *it*, and brake, and gave to them. 2127
24:50 and he lift up his hands, and **b** them. 2127
24:51 And it came to pass, while he **b** them, 2127
Jn 12:13 **B** *is* the King of Israel that cometh in 2127
20:29 **b** *are* they that have not seen, and *yet* have 3107
Ac 3:25 seed shall all the kindreds of the earth be **b**. 1757
20:35 he said, It is more **b** to give than to receive. 3107
Ro 1:25 more than the Creator, who is **b** for ever. 2128
4: 7 *Saying*, **B** *are they* whose iniquities are 3107
4: 8 **B** *is* the man to whom the Lord will not 3107
9: 5 *came*, who is over all, God **b** for ever. 2128
2Co 1: 3 **B** *be* God, even the Father of our Lord 2128
11:31 which is **b** for evermore, knoweth that I lie 2128
Gal 3: 8 *saying*, In thee shall all nations be **b**. 1757
3: 9 they which be of faith are **b** with faithful 2127
Eph 1: 3 **B** *be* the God and Father of our Lord Jesus 2128
1: 3 who hath **b** us with all spiritual blessings in 2127
1Ti 1:11 According to the glorious gospel of the **b** 3107
6:15 *who is* the **b** and only Potentate, the King 3107
Tit 2:13 Looking for *that* **b** hope, and the glorious 3107
Heb 7: 1 from the slaughter of the kings, and **b** him; 2127
7: 6 and **b** him that had the promises. 2127
7: 7 And without all contradiction the less is **b** 2127
11:20 By faith Isaac **b** Jacob and Esau concerning 2127
11:21 he was a dying, **b** both the sons of Joseph; 2127
Jas 1:12 **B** *is* the man that endureth temptation: 3107
1:25 of the work, this *man* shall be **b** in his deed. 3107
1Pe 1: 3 **B** *be* the God and Father of our Lord Jesus 2128
Rev 1: 3 **B** *is* he that readeth, and they that hear 3107
14:13 **B** *are* the dead which die in the Lord from 3107
16:15 **B** *is* he that watcheth, and keepeth his 3107
19: 9 **B** *are* they which are called unto 3107
20: 6 **B** and holy *is* he that hath part in the first 3107
22: 7 **b** *is* he that keepeth the sayings of 3107
22:14 **B** *are* they that do his commandments, that 3107

BLESSEDNESS (3) [BLESS]

Ro 4: 6 Even as David also describeth the **b** of 3108
4: 9 *Cometh* this **b** then upon the circumcision 3108
Gal 4:15 Where is then the **b** you spake of? for I 3108

BLESSEST (3) [BLESS]

Nu 22: 6 for I wot that *he* whom thou **b** *is* blessed, 1288
1Ch 17:27 for thou **b**, O LORD, and *it shall be* 1288
Ps 65:10 with showers: thou **b** the springing thereof. 1288

BLESSETH (8) [BLESS]

Ge 27:29 curseth thee, and blessed *be* he that **b** thee. 1288
Nu 24: 9 Blessed *is* he that **b** thee, and cursed *is* he 1288
Dt 15: 6 For the LORD thy God **b** thee, as he 1288
Ps 10: 3 **b** the covetous, *whom* the LORD 1288
107:38 He **b** them also, so that they are multiplied 1288
Pr 3:33 but he **b** the habitation of the just. 1288
27:14 He that **b** his friend with a loud voice, 1288
Isa 65:16 That he who **b** himself in the earth shall 1288

BLESSING (67) [BLESS]

Ge 12: 2 make thy name great; and thou shalt be a **b**: 1293
22:17 That in **b** I will bless thee, and 1288
27:12 I shall bring a curse upon me, and not a **b**. 1293
27:30 as soon as Isaac had made an end of **b** 1288
27:35 with subtilty, and hath taken away thy **b**. 1293
27:36 and behold, now he hath taken away my **b**. 1293
27:36 he said, Hast thou not reserved a **b** for me? 1293
27:38 his father, Hast thou but one **b**, my father? 1293
27:41 of the **b** wherewith his father blessed him: 1293
28: 4 give thee the **b** of Abraham, to thee, and 1293
33:11 I pray thee, my **b** that is brought to thee; 1293
39: 5 the **b** of the LORD was upon all that he 1293
49:28 every one according to his **b** he blessed 1293
Ex 32:29 that he may bestow upon you a **b** *this* day. 1293
Lev 25:21 I will command my **b** upon you in the sixth 1293
Dt 11:26 I set before you *this* day a **b** and a curse; 1293
11:27 A **b**, if ye obey the commandments of 1293
11:29 that thou shalt put the **b** upon mount 1293
12:15 according to the **b** of the LORD thy God 1293
16:17 according to the **b** of the LORD thy God 1293
23: 5 thy God turned the curse into a **b** unto thee, 1293
28: 8 The LORD shall command the **b** upon 1293
30: 1 the **b** and the curse, which I have set before 1293
30:19 set before you life and death, **b** and cursing: 1293
33: 1 this *is* the **b**, wherewith Moses the man of 1293
33: 7 this *is the* **b** of Judah: and he said, Hear, NIH
33:16 let *the* **b** come upon the head of Joseph, and NIH
33:23 and full *with* the **b** of the LORD: 1293
Jos 15:19 Who answered, Give me a **b**; for thou hast 1293
Jdg 1:15 she said unto him, Give me a **b**: for thou 1293
1Sa 25:27 now this **b** which thine handmaid hath 1293
2Sa 7:29 with thy **b** let the house of thy servant be 1293
2Ki 5:15 I pray thee, take a **b** of thy servant. 1293
Ne 9: 5 which *is* exalted above all **b** and praise. 1293
13: 2 howbeit our God turned the curse into a **b**. 1293
Job 29:13 The **b** of him that was ready to perish came 1293
Ps 3: 8 thy **b** *is* upon thy people. Selah. 1293
24: 5 He shall receive the **b** from the LORD, 1293
109:17 as he delighted not in **b**, so let it be far from 1293
129: 8 by say, The **b** of the LORD *be* upon you: 1293
133: 3 for there the LORD commanded the **b**, 1293
Pr 10:22 The **b** of the LORD, it maketh rich, and 1293
11:11 By the **b** of the upright the city is exalted: 1293
11:26 **b** *shall be* upon the head of him that selleth 1293
24:25 and a good **b** shall come upon them. 1293
Isa 19:24 *even* a **b** in the midst of the land: 1293
44: 3 thy seed, and my **b** upon thine offspring: 1293
65: 8 and *one* saith, Destroy it not; for a **b** *is* in it: 1293
Eze 34:26 and the places round about my hill a **b**; 1293
34:26 in his season; there shall be showers of **b**. 1293
44:30 that he may cause the **b** to rest in thine 1293
Joel 2:14 and repent, and leave a **b** behind him; 1293
Zec 8:13 so will I save you, and ye shall be a **b**: 1293
Mal 3:10 windows of heaven, and pour you out a **b**, 1293
Lk 24:53 in the temple, praising and **b** God. 2127
Ro 15:29 I shall come in the fulness of the **b** of 2129
1Co 10:16 The cup of **b** which we bless, is it not 2129
Gal 3:14 That the **b** of Abraham might come on 2129
Heb 6: 7 whom it is dressed, receiveth **b** from God: 2129
6:14 Surely **b** I will bless thee, and multiplying I 2127
12:17 when he would have inherited the **b**, he was 2129
Jas 3:10 Out of the same mouth proceedeth **b** and 2129
1Pe 3: 9 but contrariwise **b**; knowing that ye are 2127
3: 9 thereunto called, that ye should inherit a **b**. 2129
Rev 5:12 and strength, and honour, and glory, and **b**. 2129
5:13 **B**, and honour, and glory, and power, 2129
7:12 **B**, and glory, and wisdom, and 2129

BLESSINGS (12) [BLESS]

Ge 49:25 who shall bless thee *with* **b** of heaven 1293
49:25 **b** of the deep that lieth under, blessings of 1293
49:25 **b** of the breasts, and of the womb: 1293
49:26 The **b** of thy father have prevailed above 1293
49:26 **b** of my progenitors unto the utmost bound 1293
Dt 28: 2 all these **b** shall come on thee, and 1293
Jos 8:34 all the words of the law, the **b** and cursings, 1293
Ps 21: 3 For thou preventest him *with* the **b** of 1293
Pr 10: 6 **B** *are* upon the head of the just: but 1293
28:20 A faithful man shall abound with **b**: but 1293
Mal 2: 2 a curse upon you, and will curse your **b**: 1293
Eph 1: 3 who hath blessed us with all spiritual **b** in 2129

BLEW (23) [BLOW]

Jos 6: 8 the LORD, and **b** with the trumpets: 8628
6: 9 before the priests that **b** *with* the trumpets, 8628
6:13 on continually, and **b** with the trumpets: 8628
6:16 when the priests **b** with the trumpets, 8628
6:20 So the people shouted when *the priests* **b** 8628
Jdg 3:27 that he **b** a trumpet in the mountain of 8628
6:34 came upon Gideon, and he **b** a trumpet; 8628
7:19 they **b** the trumpets, and brake the pitchers 8628
7:20 the three companies **b** the trumpets, and 8628
7:22 the three hundred **b** the trumpets, and 8628
1Sa 13: 3 the Philistines heard *of it*. And Saul **b** 8628
2Sa 2:28 So Joab **b** a trumpet, and all the people 8628
18:16 Joab **b** the trumpet, and the people returned 8628
20: 1 he **b** a trumpet, and said, We have no part 8628
20:22 he **b** a trumpet, and they retired from 8628
1Ki 1:39 they **b** the trumpet; and all the people said, 8628
2Ki 9:13 and **b** with trumpets, saying, Jehu is king. 8628
11:14 of the land rejoiced, and **b** with trumpets: 8628
Mt 7:25 and the winds **b**, and beat upon that house; 4154
7:27 and the winds **b**, and beat upon that house; 4154
Jn 6:18 sea arose by reason of a great wind that **b**. 4154
Ac 27:13 And when the south wind **b** softly, 5285
28:13 and after one day the south wind **b**, and 1920

BLIND (82) [BLINDED, BLINDETH, BLINDFOLDED, BLINDNESS]

Ex 4:11 the dumb, or deaf, or the seeing, or the **b**? 5787
Lev 19:14 nor put a stumblingblock before the **b**, but 5787
21:18 a **b** man, or a lame, or he that hath a flat 5787
22:22 **B**, or broken, or maimed, or having a wen, 5788
Dt 15:21 *if it be* lame, or **b**, *or have* any ill blemish, 5787
16:19 for a gift doth **b** the eyes of the wise, and 5786
27:18 Cursed *be* he that maketh the **b** to wander 5787
28:29 as the **b** gropeth in darkness, and thou shalt 5787
1Sa 12: 3 *any* bribe to **b** mine eyes therewith? 5956
2Sa 5: 6 Except thou take away the **b** and the lame, 5787
5: 8 the Jebusites, and the lame and the **b**, 5787
5: 8 The **b** and the lame shall not come into 5787
Job 29:15 I was eyes to the **b**, and feet *was* I to 5787
Ps 146: 8 The LORD openeth *the eyes of* the **b**: 5787
Isa 29:18 the eyes of the **b** shall see out of obscurity, 5787
35: 5 the eyes of the **b** shall be opened, and 5787
42: 7 To open the **b** eyes, to bring out 5787
42:16 I will bring the **b** by a way *that* they knew 5787
42:18 ye deaf; and look, ye **b**, that *ye* may see. 5787
42:19 Who *is* **b**, but my servant? or deaf, as my 5787
42:19 who *is* **b** as he that is perfect, and blind as 5787
42:19 is perfect, and **b** as the LORD'S servant? 5787
43: 8 Bring forth the **b** people that have eyes, and 5787
56:10 His watchmen *are* **b**: they are all ignorant, 5787
59:10 We grope for the wall like the **b**, and 5787
Jer 31: 8 *and* with them the **b** and the lame, 5787
La 4:14 They have wandered *as* **b** *men* in 5787
Zep 1:17 that they shall walk like **b** *men*, because 5787
Mal 1: 8 if ye offer the **b** for sacrifice, *is it* not evil? 5787
Mt 9:27 two **b men** followed him, crying, and 5185
9:28 into the house, the **b men** came to him: 5185
11: 5 The **b** receive their sight, and the lame 5185
12:22 one possessed with a devil, **b**, and dumb: 5185
12:22 insomuch that the **b** and dumb both spake 5185
15:14 they be **b** leaders of the blind. And if 5185
15:14 they be blind leaders of the **b**. And if 5185
15:14 And if the **b** lead the blind, both shall fall 5185
15:14 And if the blind lead the **b**, both shall fall 5185
15:30 **b**, dumb, maimed, and many others, and 5185
15:31 the lame to walk, and the **b** to see: 5185
20:30 two **b men** sitting by the way side, 5185
21:14 And *the* **b** and *the* lame came to him in 5185
23:16 Woe unto you, *ye* **b** guides, which say, 5185
23:17 *Ye* fools and **b**: for whether is greater, 5185
23:19 *Ye* fools and **b**: for whether *is* greater, 5185
23:24 *Ye* **b** guides, which strain out a gnat, and 5185
23:26 *Thou* **b** Pharisee, cleanse first that *which is* 5185
Mk 8:22 and they bring a **b man** unto him, and 5185
8:23 And he took the **b man** by the hand, and 5185
10:46 of people, **b** Bartimeus, the son of Timeus, 5185
10:49 And they call the **b man**, saying unto him, 5185
10:51 The **b man** said unto him, Lord, that I 5185
Lk 4:18 and recovering of sight to the **b**, 5185
6:39 unto them, Can the **b** lead the blind? 5185
6:39 unto them, Can the blind lead the **b**? 5185
7:21 and unto many *that were* **b** he gave sight. 5185
7:22 how that the **b** see, the lame walk, 5185
14:13 call the poor, the maimed, the lame, the **b**: 5185
14:21 and the maimed, and the halt, and the **b**. 5185
18:35 a certain **b man** sat by the way side 5185
Jn 5: 3 lay a great multitude of impotent *folk*, of **b**, 5185
9: 1 he saw a man *which was* **b** from *his* birth. 5185
9: 2 or his parents, that he was born **b**? 5185
9: 6 he anointed the eyes of the **b man** with 5185
9: 8 which before had seen him that he was **b**, 5185
9:13 to the Pharisees him that aforetime was **b**. 5185
9:17 They say unto the **b man** again, 5185
9:18 that he had been **b**, and received his sight, 5185
9:19 Is this your son, who ye say was born **b**? 5185
9:20 that this is our son, and that he was born **b**: 5185
9:24 Then again called they the man that was **b**, 5185
9:25 I know, that, whereas I was **b**, now I see. 5185
9:32 opened the eyes of one that was born **b**. 5185
9:39 and that they which see might be made **b**. 5185
9:40 and said unto him, Are we **b** also? 5185
9:41 Jesus said unto them, If ye were **b**, 5185
10:21 a devil. Can a devil open the eyes of the **b**? 5185
11:37 this *man*, which opened the eyes of the **b**, 5185
Ac 13:11 and thou shalt be **b**, not seeing the sun for a 5185
Ro 2:19 that thou thyself art a guide of the **b**, 5185
2Pe 1: 9 But he that lacketh these *things* is **b**, and 5185
Rev 3:17 and miserable, and poor, and **b**, and naked: 5185

BLINDED (5) [BLIND]

Jn 12:40 He hath **b** their eyes, and hardened their 5186
Ro 11: 7 hath obtained *it*, and the rest were **b**, 4456
2Co 3:14 But their minds were **b**: for until this day 4456
4: 4 In whom the god of this world hath **b** 5186
1Jn 2:11 because that darkness hath **b** his eyes. 5186

BLINDETH (1) [BLIND]

Ex 23: 8 for the gift **b** the wise, and perverteth 5786

BLINDFOLDED (1) [BLIND]

Lk 22:64 And when they had **b** him, they stroke him 4028

BLINDNESS (7) [BLIND]

Ge 19:11 that *were at* the door of the house with **b**, 5575
Dt 28:28 and **b**, and astonishment of heart: 5788
2Ki 6:18 said, Smite this people, I pray thee, with **b**. 5575
6:18 he smote them with **b** according to 5575
Zec 12: 4 will smite every horse of the people with **b**. 5788
Ro 11:25 that **b** in part is happened to Israel, until 4457
Eph 4:18 is in them, because of the **b** of their heart: 4457

BLOCKED See FENCED

BLOOD (447) [BLOODGUILTINESS, BLOODTHIRSTY, BLOODY]

Ge 4:10 the voice of thy brother's **b** crieth unto me 1818
4:11 to receive thy brother's **b** from thy hand. 1818
9: 4 *which is* the **b** thereof, shall you not eat. 1818
9: 5 surely your **b** of your lives will I require; 1818
9: 6 Whoso sheddeth man's **b**, by man shall his 1818
9: 6 man's blood, by man shall his **b** be shed: 1818
37:22 Shed no **b**, *but* cast him into this pit that *is* 1818
37:26 *it* if we slay our brother, and conceal his **b**? 1818
37:31 of the goats, and dipped the coat in the **b**; 1818
42:22 therefore, behold, also his **b** is required. 1818
49:11 in wine, and his clothes in the **b** of grapes: 1818
Ex 4: 9 the river shall become **b** upon the dry *land*. 1818
7:17 in the river, and they shall be turned to **b**. 1818
7:19 pools of water, that they may become **b**; 1818
7:19 *that* there may be **b** throughout all the land 1818
7:20 that *were* in the river were turned to **b**. 1818
7:21 there was **b** throughout all the land of 1818
12: 7 they shall take of the **b**, and strike *it* on 1818
12:13 the **b** shall be to you for a token upon 1818
12:13 where you *are*: and when I see the **b**, 1818
12:22 dip *it* in the **b** that *is* in the bason, and 1818
12:22 the two side posts with the **b** that *is* in 1818
12:23 when he seeth the **b** upon the lintel, and 1818
22: 2 he die, *there shall* no **b** *be shed* for him. 1818
22: 3 upon him, *there shall be* **b** *shed* for him; 1818
23:18 Thou shalt not offer the **b** of my sacrifice 1818
24: 6 Moses took half of the **b**, and put *it* in 1818
24: 6 and half of the **b** he sprinkled on the altar. 1818
24: 8 Moses took the **b**, and sprinkled *it* on 1818
24: 8 and said, Behold the **b** of the covenant, 1818
29:12 thou shalt take of the **b** of the bullock, and 1818
29:12 pour all the **b** beside the bottom of the altar. 1818
29:16 thou shalt take his **b**, and sprinkle *it* round 1818
29:20 take of his **b**, and put *it* upon the tip of 1818
29:20 sprinkle the **b** upon the altar round about. 1818
29:21 thou shalt take of the **b** that *is* upon 1818
30:10 the **b** of the sin offering of atonements: 1818
34:25 Thou shalt not offer the **b** of my sacrifice 1818
Lev 1: 5 shall bring the **b**, and sprinkle the blood 1818
1: 5 sprinkle the **b** round about upon the altar 1818
1:11 shall sprinkle his **b** round about upon 1818
1:15 the **b** thereof shall be wrung out at the side 1818
3: 2 Aaron's sons the priests shall sprinkle the **b** 1818
3: 8 Aaron's sons shall sprinkle the **b** thereof 1818
3:13 the sons of Aaron shall sprinkle the **b** 1818
3:17 your dwellings, *that* ye eat neither fat nor **b**. 1818
4: 5 is anointed shall take of the bullock's **b**, 1818
4: 6 the priest shall dip his finger in the **b**, and 1818
4: 6 sprinkle of the **b** seven times before 1818
4: 7 the priest shall put *some* of the **b** upon 1818
4: 7 shall pour all the **b** of the bullock at 1818
4:16 **b** to the tabernacle of the congregation: 1818
4:17 priest shall dip his finger *in some* of the **b**, 1818
4:18 he shall put *some* of the **b** upon the horns 1818
4:18 shall pour out all the **b** at the bottom of 1818
4:25 the priest shall take of the **b** of the sin 1818
4:25 shall pour out his **b** at the bottom of 1818
4:30 the priest shall take of the **b** thereof with 1818
4:30 shall pour out all the **b** thereof at 1818
4:34 the priest shall take of the **b** of the sin 1818

Book	Ref	Context	No.
Lev	4:34	shall pour out all the **b** thereof at	1818
	5: 9	he shall sprinkle of the **b** of the sin offering	1818
	5: 9	the rest of the **b** shall be wrung out at	1818
	6:27	when there is sprinkled of the **b** thereof	1818
	6:30	whereof *any* of the **b** is brought into	1818
	7: 2	the **b** thereof shall he sprinkle round about	1818
	7:14	it shall be the priest's that sprinkleth the **b**	1818
	7:26	Moreover ye shall eat no *manner of* **b**,	1818
	7:27	soul *it be* that eateth any *manner of* **b**,	1818
	7:33	that offereth the **b** of the peace offerings,	1818
	8:15	he slew *it;* and Moses took the **b**, and put *it*	1818
	8:15	poured the **b** at the bottom of the altar, and	1818
	8:19	Moses sprinkled the **b** upon the altar round	1818
	8:23	he slew *it;* and Moses took of the **b** of it,	1818
	8:24	Moses put of the **b** upon the tip of their	1818
	8:24	Moses sprinkled the **b** upon the altar round	1818
	8:30	of the **b** which *was* upon the altar, and	1818
	9: 9	the sons of Aaron brought the **b** unto him:	1818
	9: 9	he dipt his finger in the **b**, and put *it* upon	1818
	9: 9	poured out the **b** at the bottom of the altar:	1818
	9:12	Aaron's sons presented unto him the **b**,	1818
	9:18	Aaron's sons presented unto him the **b**,	1818
	10:18	the **b** of it was not brought in within	1818
	12: 4	continue in the **b** of her purifying three and	1818
	12: 5	she shall continue in the **b** of her purifying	1818
	12: 7	shall be cleansed from the issue of her **b**.	1818
	14: 6	the living bird in the **b** of the bird *that was*	1818
	14:14	the priest shall take *some* of the **b** of	1818
	14:17	upon the **b** of the trespass offering:	1818
	14:25	the priest shall take *some* of the **b** of	1818
	14:28	upon the place of the **b** of the trespass	1818
	14:51	dip them in the **b** of the slain bird, and	1818
	14:52	he shall cleanse the house with the **b** of	1818
	15:19	an issue, *and* her issue in her flesh be **b**,	1818
	15:25	if a woman have an issue of her **b** many	1818
	16:14	he shall take of the **b** of the bullock, and	1818
	16:14	of the **b** with his finger seven times.	1818
	16:15	bring his **b** within the vail, and do with that	1818
	16:15	do with that **b** as he did with the blood of	1818
	16:16	do with that blood as he did with the **b** of	1818
	16:18	shall take of the **b** of the bullock, and of	1818
	16:18	of the **b** of the goat, and put *it* upon	1818
	16:19	he shall sprinkle of the **b** upon it with his	1818
	16:27	whose **b** was brought in to make atonement	1818
	17: 4	**b** shall be imputed unto that man; he hath	1818
	17: 4	he hath shed **b**; and that man shall be cut	1818
	17: 6	the priest shall sprinkle the **b** upon the altar	1818
	17:10	among you, that eateth any *manner of* **b**;	1818
	17:10	set my face against *that* soul that eateth **b**,	1818
	17:11	For the life of the flesh *is* in the **b**: and	1818
	17:11	for it *is* the **b** *that* maketh an atonement for	1818
	17:12	of Israel, No soul of you shall eat **b**,	1818
	17:12	stranger that sojourneth among you eat **b**.	1818
	17:13	he shall even pour out the **b** thereof, and	1818
	17:14	of all flesh; the **b** of it *is* for the life thereof:	1818
	17:14	Ye shall eat the **b** of no *manner of* flesh:	1818
	17:14	for the life of all flesh *is* the **b** thereof:	1818
	19:16	neither shalt thou stand against the **b** of thy	1818
	19:26	Ye shall not eat *any thing* with the **b**:	1818
	20: 9	or his mother; his **b** *shall be* upon him.	1818
	20:11	be put to death; their **b** *shall be* upon them.	1818
	20:12	their **b** *shall be* upon them.	1818
	20:13	be put to death; their **b** *shall be* upon them.	1818
	20:16	be put to death; their **b** *shall be* upon them.	1818
	20:18	she hath uncovered the fountain of her **b**:	1818
	20:27	with stones: their **b** *shall be* upon them.	1818
Nu	18:17	thou shalt sprinkle their **b** upon the altar,	1818
	19: 4	Eleazar the priest shall take of her **b** with	1818
	19: 4	sprinkle of her **b** directly before	1818
	19: 5	her skin, and her flesh, and her **b**, with her	1818
	23:24	eat *of* the prey, and drink the **b** of the slain.	1818
	35:19	The revenger of **b** himself shall slay	1818
	35:21	the revenger of **b** shall slay the murderer,	1818
	35:24	the revenger of **b** according to these	1818
	35:25	slayer out of the hand of the revenger of **b**,	1818
	35:27	the revenger of **b** find him without	1818
	35:27	and the revenger of **b** kill the slayer;	1818
	35:27	kill the slayer; he shall not be guilty of **b**:	1818
	35:33	wherein ye *are:* for **b** it defileth the land:	1818
	35:33	the land cannot be cleansed of the **b** that is	1818
	35:33	but by the **b** of him that shed it.	1818
Dt	12:16	Only ye shall not eat the **b**, ye shall pour it	1818
	12:23	Only be sure that thou eat not the **b**: for	1818
	12:23	for the **b** *is* the life; and thou mayest not eat	1818
	12:27	the flesh and the **b**, upon the altar of	1818
	12:27	the **b** of thy sacrifices shall be poured out	1818
	15:23	Only thou shalt not eat the **b** thereof;	1818
	17: 8	between **b** and blood, between plea and	1818
	17: 8	between blood and **b**, between plea and	1818
	19: 6	Lest the avenger of the **b** pursue the slayer,	1818
	19:10	That innocent **b** be not shed in thy land,	1818
	19:10	*for* an inheritance, and *so* **b** be upon thee.	1818
	19:12	him into the hand of the avenger of **b**,	1818
	19:13	thou shalt put away *the guilt of* innocent **b**	1818
	21: 7	and say, Our hands have not shed this **b**,	1818
	21: 8	lay not innocent **b** unto thy people of	1818
	21: 8	And the **b** shall be forgiven them.	1818
	21: 9	the *guilt of* innocent **b** from among you,	1818
	22: 8	that thou bring not **b** upon thine house,	1818
	32:14	thou didst drink the pure **b** of the grape.	1818
	32:42	I will make mine arrows drunk with **b**, and	1818
	32:42	*and that* with the **b** of the slain and of	1818
	32:43	for he will avenge the **b** of his servants, and	1818
Jos	2:19	his **b** *shall be* upon his head, and we *will be*	1818
	2:19	his **b** *shall be* on our head, if *any* hand be	1818
	20: 3	shall be your refuge from the avenger of **b**.	1818
	20: 5	if the avenger of **b** pursue after him, then	1818
	20: 9	not die by the hand of the avenger of **b**,	1818
Jdg	9:24	their **b** be laid upon Abimelech their	1818
1Sa	14:32	and the people did eat *them* with the **b**.	1818
	14:33	the LORD, in that they eat with the **b**.	1818
	14:34	not against the LORD in eating with the **b**.	1818
	19: 5	then wilt thou sin against innocent **b**,	1818
	25:26	withholden thee from coming to *shed* **b**,	1818
	25:31	either that thou hast shed **b** causeless, or	1818
1Sa	25:33	kept me this day from coming to *shed* **b**,	1818
	26:20	let not my **b** fall to the earth before the face	1818
2Sa	1:16	said unto him, Thy **b** *be* upon thy head;	1818
	1:22	From the **b** of the slain, from the fat of	1818
	3:27	that he died, for the **b** of Asahel his brother.	1818
	3:28	ever from the **b** of Abner the son of Ner:	1818
	4:11	therefore now require his **b** of your hand,	1818
	14:11	the revengers of **b** to destroy any more,	1818
	16: 8	upon thee all the **b** of the house of Saul,	1818
	20:12	Amasa wallowed in **b** in the midst of	1818
	23:17	*is not this* the **b** of the men that went in	1818
1Ki	2: 5	shed the **b** of war in peace, and put	1818
	2: 5	put the **b** of war upon his girdle that *was*	1818
	2: 9	head bring thou down *to* the grave with **b**.	1818
	2:31	that thou mayest take away the innocent **b**,	1818
	2:32	the LORD shall return his **b** upon his own	1818
	2:33	Their **b** shall therefore return upon the head	1818
	2:37	thy **b** shall be upon thine own head.	1818
	18:28	till the **b** gushed out upon them.	1818
	21:19	In the place where dogs licked the **b** of	1818
	21:19	the blood of Naboth shall dogs lick thy **b**,	1818
	22:35	the **b** ran out of the wound into the midst of	1818
	22:38	the dogs licked up his **b**; and they washed	1818
2Ki	3:22	saw the water on the other side *as* red as **b**:	1818
	3:23	they said, This *is* **b**: the kings are surely	1818
	9: 7	that I may avenge the **b** of my servants	1818
	9: 7	the **b** of all the servants of the LORD,	1818
	9:26	Surely I have seen yesterday the **b** of	1818
	9:26	and the **b** of his sons, saith the LORD;	1818
	9:33	*some* of her **b** was sprinkled on the wall,	1818
	16:13	sprinkled the **b** of his peace offerings,	1818
	16:15	sprinkle upon it all the **b** of the burnt	1818
	16:15	burnt offering, and all the **b** of the sacrifice:	1818
	21:16	Moreover Manasseh shed innocent **b** very	1818
	24: 4	also *for* the innocent **b** that he shed: for he	1818
	24: 4	for he filled Jerusalem *with* innocent **b**;	1818
1Ch	11:19	*I* should do this *thing:* shall I drink the **b**	1818
	22: 8	Thou hast shed **b** abundantly, and	1818
	22: 8	thou hast shed much **b** upon the earth in my	1818
	28: 3	*hast been* a man of war, and hast shed **b**.	1818
2Ch	19:10	between **b** and blood, between law and	1818
	19:10	between blood and **b**, between law and	1818
	24:25	for the **b** of the sons of Jehoiada the priest,	1818
	29:22	the priests received the **b**, and sprinkled *it*	1818
	29:22	they sprinkled the **b** upon the altar:	1818
	29:22	and they sprinkled the **b** upon the altar.	1818
	29:24	they made reconciliation with their **b** upon	1818
	30:16	the priests sprinkled the **b**, *which they*	1818
	35:11	the priests sprinkled *the b* from their hands,	NIH
Job	16:18	cover not thou my **b**, and let my cry have	1818
	39:30	Her young ones also suck up **b**: and where	1818
Ps	9:12	When he maketh inquisition for **b**, he	1818
	16: 4	their drink offerings of **b** will I not offer,	1818
	30: 9	What profit *is there* in my **b**, when I go	1818
	50:13	the flesh of bulls, or drink the **b** of goats?	1818
	58:10	he shall wash his feet in the **b** of	1818
	68:23	That thy foot may be dipped in the **b** of	1818
	72:14	and precious shall their **b** be in his sight.	1818
	78:44	had turned their rivers into **b**; and	1818
	79: 3	Their **b** have they shed like water round	1818
	79:10	of the **b** of thy servants which is shed.	1818
	94:21	the righteous, and condemn the innocent **b**.	1818
	105:29	He turned their waters into **b**, and	1818
	106:38	shed innocent **b**, *even* the blood of their	1818
	106:38	*even* the **b** of their sons and of their	1818
	106:38	and the land was polluted with **b**.	1818
Pr	1:11	Come with us, let us lay wait for **b**,	1818
	1:16	feet run to evil, and make haste to shed **b**.	1818
	1:18	they lay wait for their own **b**; they lurk	1818
	6:17	and hands that shed innocent **b**,	1818
	12: 6	words of the wicked *are* to lie in wait *for* **b**:	1818
	28:17	A man that doeth violence to the **b** of *any*	1818
	30:33	the wringing of the nose bringeth forth **b**:	1818
Isa	1:11	I delight not in the **b** of bullocks, or	1818
	1:15	I will not hear: your hands are full *of* **b**.	1818
	4: 4	shall have purged the **b** of Jerusalem from	1818
	9: 5	confused noise, and garments rolled in **b**;	1818
	15: 9	For the waters of Dimon shall be full *of* **b**:	1818
	26:21	the earth also shall disclose her **b**, and	1818
	33:15	that stoppeth his ears from hearing of **b**,	1818
	34: 3	the mountains shall be melted with their **b**.	1818
	34: 6	The sword of the LORD is filled *with* **b**,	1818
	34: 6	*and* with the **b** of lambs and goats,	1818
	34: 7	their land shall be soaked with **b**, and	1818
	49:26	they shall be drunken with their own **b**,	1818
	59: 3	For your hands are defiled with **b**, and	1818
	59: 7	and they make haste to shed innocent **b**:	1818
	63: 3	their **b** shall be sprinkled upon my	5332
	66: 3	an oblation, *as if he offered* swine's **b**;	1818
Jer	2:34	Also in thy skirts is found the **b** of the souls	1818
	7: 6	and shed not innocent **b** in this place,	1818
	18:21	pour out their *b* by the force of the sword;	NIH
	19: 4	have filled this place *with* the **b** of	1818
	22: 3	neither shed innocent **b** in this place.	1818
	22:17	for to shed innocent **b**, and for oppression,	1818
	26:15	ye shall surely bring innocent **b** upon	1818
	46:10	be satiate and made drunk with their **b**:	1818
	48:10	*be* he that keepeth back his sword from **b**.	1818
	51:35	my **b** upon the inhabitants of Chaldea,	1818
La	4:13	that *have* shed the **b** of the just in the midst	1818
	4:14	they have polluted themselves with **b**, so	1818
Eze	3:18	but his **b** will I require at thine hand.	1818
	3:20	but his **b** will I require at thine hand.	1818
	5:17	pestilence and **b** shall pass through thee;	1818
	9: 9	the land is full *of* **b**, and the city full *of*	1818
	14:19	pour out my fury upon it in **b**, to cut off	1818
	16: 6	and saw thee polluted in thine own **b**,	1818
	16: 6	I said unto thee *when thou wast* in thy **b**,	1818
	16: 6	I said unto thee *when thou wast* in thy **b**,	1818
	16: 9	I throughly washed away thy **b** from thee,	1818
	16:22	and bare, *and* wast polluted in thy **b**.	1818
	16:36	by the **b** of thy children, which thou didst	1818
	16:38	that break wedlock and shed **b** are judged;	1818
	16:38	and I will give thee **b** in fury and jealousy.	1818
	18:10	a shedder of **b**, and *that* doeth the like to	1818
Eze	18:13	he shall surely die; his **b** shall be upon him.	1818
	19:10	Thy mother *is* like a vine in thy **b**,	1818
	21:32	thy **b** shall be in the midst of the land;	1818
	22: 3	The city sheddeth **b** in the midst of it,	1818
	22: 4	Thou art become guilty in thy **b** that thou	1818
	22: 6	one were in thee to their power to shed **b**.	1818
	22: 9	In thee are men that carry tales to shed **b**:	1818
	22:12	In thee have they taken gifts to shed **b**;	1818
	22:13	at thy **b** which hath been in the midst of	1818
	22:27	to shed **b**, *and* to destroy souls, to get	1818
	23:37	**b** *is* in their hands, and with their idols have	1818
	23:45	and after the manner of *women* that shed **b**;	1818
	23:45	*are* adulteresses, and **b** *is* in their hands.	1818
	24: 7	For her **b** is in the midst of her; she set it	1818
	24: 8	I have set her **b** upon the top of a rock,	1818
	28:23	into her pestilence, and **b** into her streets;	1818
	32: 6	I will also water with thy **b** the land	1818
	33: 4	his **b** shall be upon his own head.	1818
	33: 5	took not warning; his **b** shall be upon him.	1818
	33: 6	his **b** will I require at the watchman's hand.	1818
	33: 8	but his **b** will I require at thine hand.	1818
	33:25	Ye eat with the **b**, and lift up your eyes	1818
	33:25	up your eyes toward your idols, and shed **b**:	1818
	35: 5	hast shed *the b of* the children of Israel by	NIH
	35: 6	I will prepare thee unto **b**, and blood shall	1818
	35: 6	thee unto blood, and **b** shall pursue thee:	1818
	35: 6	sith thou hast not hated **b**, even blood shall	1818
	35: 6	not hated blood, even **b** shall pursue thee.	1818
	36:18	for the **b** that they had shed upon the land,	1818
	38:22	against him with pestilence and with **b**;	1818
	39:17	of Israel, that ye may eat flesh, and drink **b**.	1818
	39:18	drink the **b** of the princes of the earth,	1818
	39:19	*ye* be full, and drink **b** till *ye* be drunken,	1818
	43:18	and to sprinkle **b** thereon.	1818
	43:20	thou shalt take of the **b** thereof, and put *it*	1818
	44: 7	the fat and the **b**, and they have broken my	1818
	44:15	me to offer unto me the fat and the **b**,	1818
	45:19	the priest shall take of the **b** of the sin	1818
Hos	1: 4	I will avenge the **b** of Jezreel upon	1818
	4: 2	they break out, and **b** toucheth blood.	1818
	4: 2	they break out, and blood toucheth **b**.	1818
	6: 8	that work iniquity, *and is* polluted with **b**.	1818
	12:14	therefore shall he leave his **b** upon him, and	1818
Joel	2:30	the earth, **b**, and fire, and pillars of smoke.	1818
	2:31	the moon into **b**, before the great and	1818
	3:19	they have shed innocent **b** in their land.	1818
	3:21	For I will cleanse their **b** *that* I have not	1818
Jnh	1:14	man's life, and lay not upon us innocent **b**:	1818
Mic	3:10	They build up Zion with **b**, and	1818
	7: 2	they all lie in wait for **b**; they hunt every	1818
Hab	2: 8	because of men's **b**, and *for* the violence of	1818
	2:12	Woe to him that buildeth a town with **b**,	1818
	2:17	because of men's **b**, and *for* the violence of	1818
Zep	1:17	their **b** shall be poured out as dust, and	1818
Zec	9: 7	I will take away his **b** out of his mouth,	1818
	9:11	by the **b** of thy covenant I have sent forth	1818
Mt	9:20	which was **diseased with an issue of b**	*131*
	16:17	for flesh and **b** hath not revealed *it* unto thee,	*129*
	23:30	partakers with them in the **b** of the prophets.	*129*
	23:35	That upon you may come all the righteous **b**	*129*
	23:35	from the **b** of righteous Abel unto the blood	*129*
	23:35	from the blood of righteous Abel unto the **b**	*129*
	26:28	For this is my **b** of the new testament,	*129*
	27: 4	sinned in that I have betrayed *the* innocent **b**.	*129*
	27: 6	into the treasury, because it is the price of **b**.	*129*
	27: 8	was called, The field of **b**, unto this day.	*129*
	27:24	I am innocent of the **b** of this just *person:*	*129*
	27:25	said, His **b** *be* on us, and on our children.	*129*
Mk	5:25	which had an issue of **b** twelve years,	*129*
	5:29	And straightway the fountain of her **b** was	*129*
	14:24	This is my **b** of the new testament,	*129*
Lk	8:43	And a woman having an issue of **b** twelve	*129*
	8:44	and immediately her issue of **b** stanched.	*129*
	11:50	That the **b** of all the prophets, which was	*129*
	11:51	From the **b** of Abel unto the blood of	*129*
	11:51	From the blood of Abel unto the **b** of	*129*
	13: 1	whose **b** Pilate had mingled with their	*129*
	22:20	This cup *is* the new testament in my **b**,	*129*
	22:44	his sweat was as it were great drops of **b**	*129*
Jn	1:13	Which were born, not of **b**, nor of the will of	*129*
	6:53	and drink his **b**, ye have no life in you.	*129*
	6:54	and drinketh my **b**, hath eternal life;	*129*
	6:55	is meat indeed, and my **b** is drink indeed.	*129*
	6:56	and drinketh my **b**, dwelleth in me, and I in	*129*
	19:34	and forthwith came there out **b** and water.	*129*
Ac	1:19	Aceldama, that is to say, The field of **b**.	*129*
	2:19	**b**, and fire, and vapour of smoke:	*129*
	2:20	and the moon into **b**, before *that* great and	*129*
	5:28	and intend to bring this man's **b** upon us.	*129*
	15:20	and *from* things strangled, and *from* **b**.	*129*
	15:29	and from **b**, and from things strangled, and	*129*
	17:26	And hath made of one **b** all nations of men	*129*
	18: 6	unto them, Your **b** *be* upon your own heads;	*129*
	20:26	that I *am* pure from the **b** of all *men.*	*129*
	20:28	which he hath purchased with his own **b**.	*129*
	21:25	and from **b**, and from strangled, and	*129*
	22:20	And when the **b** of thy martyr Stephen was	*129*
Ro	3:15	Their feet *are* swift to shed **b**:	*129*
	3:25	*to be* a propitiation through faith in his **b**,	*129*
	5: 9	more then, being now justified by his **b**,	*129*
1Co	10:16	is it not the communion of the **b** of Christ?	*129*
	11:25	This cup is the new testament in my **b**:	*129*
	11:27	shall be guilty of the body and **b** of the Lord.	*129*
	15:50	and **b** cannot inherit the kingdom of God;	*129*
Gal	1:16	I conferred not with flesh and **b**:	*129*
Eph	1: 7	In whom we have redemption through his **b**,	*129*
	2:13	far off are made nigh by the **b** of Christ.	*129*
	6:12	For we wrestle not against flesh and **b**, but	*129*
Col	1:14	In whom we have redemption through his **b**,	*129*
	1:20	having made peace through the **b** of his	*129*
Heb	2:14	as the children are partakers of flesh and **b**,	*129*
	9: 7	not without **b**, which he offered for himself,	*129*
	9:12	Neither by the **b** of goats and calves,	*129*
	9:12	by his own **b** he entered in once into	*129*
	9:13	For if the **b** of bulls and of goats, and	*129*

B

Heb 9:14 How much more shall the **b** of Christ, *129*
9:18 the first *testament* was dedicated without **b**. *129*
9:19 he took the **b** of calves and of goats, *129*
9:20 This *is* the **b** of the testament which God *129*
9:21 Moreover he sprinkled with **b** both *129*
9:22 all *things* are by the law purged with **b**; *129*
9:22 and without **shedding of b** is no remission. *130*
9:25 the holy *place* every year with **b** of others; *129*
10: 4 For *it is* not possible that the **b** of bulls and *129*
10:19 boldness to enter into the holiest by the **b** of *129*
10:29 and hath counted the **b** of the covenant, *129*
11:28 he kept the passover, and the sprinkling of **b**, *129*
12: 4 Ye have not yet resisted unto **b**, *129*
12:24 and to the **b** of sprinkling, that speaketh *129*
13:11 whose **b** is brought into the sanctuary by *129*
13:12 he might sanctify the people with his own **b**, *129*
13:20 through the **b** of the everlasting covenant, *129*
1Pe 1: 2 and sprinkling of the **b** of Jesus Christ: *129*
1:19 But with the precious **b** of Christ, as of a *129*
1Jn 1: 7 the **b** of Jesus Christ his Son cleanseth us *129*
5: 6 This is he that came by water and **b**, *129*
5: 6 not by water only, but by water and **b**. *129*
5: 8 in earth, the Spirit, and the water, and the **b**: *129*
Rev 1: 5 and washed us from our sins in his own **b**, *129*
5: 9 hast redeemed us to God by thy **b** out of *129*
6:10 avenge our **b** on them that dwell on *129*
6:12 sackcloth of hair, and the moon became as **b**; *129*
7:14 and made them white in the **b** of the Lamb. *129*
8: 7 there followed hail and fire mingled with **b**, *129*
8: 8 and the third *part* of the sea became **b**; *129*
11: 6 have power over waters to turn them to **b**, *129*
12:11 And they overcame him by the **b** of *129*
14:20 and **b** came out of the winepress, *even* unto *129*
16: 3 and it became as the **b** of a dead *man*: and *129*
16: 4 and fountains of waters; and they became **b**. *129*
16: 6 For they have shed the **b** of saints and *129*
16: 6 and thou hast given them **b** to drink; *129*
17: 6 And I saw the woman drunken with the **b** of *129*
17: 6 and with the **b** of the martyrs of Jesus: *129*
18:24 And in her was found the **b** of prophets, and *129*
19: 2 hath avenged the **b** of his servants at her *129*
19:13 And he *was* clothed with a vesture dipt in **b**: *129*

BLOOD GUILT See BLOODGUILTINESS

BLOOD RELATIVES See KINDRED; KINDREDS

BLOODGUILTINESS (1) [BLOOD, GUILT]
Ps 51:14 Deliver me from **b**, O God, thou God of my 1818

BLOODTHIRSTY (1) [BLOOD, THIRST]
Pr 29:10 The **b** hate the upright: but the just 376+1818

BLOODY (16) [BLOOD]
Ex 4:25 and said, Surely a **b** husband *art* thou to me. 1818
4:26 A **b** husband *thou art*, because of 1818
2Sa 16: 7 thou **b** man, and thou man of Belial: 1818
16: 8 to thy mischief, because thou *art* a **b** man. 1818
21: 1 for *his* **b** house, because he slew 1818
Ps 5: 6 the LORD will abhor the **b** and 1818
26: 9 soul with sinners, nor my life with **b** men: 1818
55:23 **b** and deceitful men shall not live out half 1818
59: 2 of iniquity, and save me from **b** men. 1818
139:19 depart from me therefore, ye **b** men. 1818
Eze 7:23 for the land is full *of* **b** crimes, and the city 1818
22: 2 wilt thou judge, wilt thou judge the **b** city? 1818
24: 6 Woe to the **b** city, to the pot whose scum *is* 1818
24: 9 saith the Lord GOD; Woe to the **b** city! 1818
Na 3: 1 Woe to the **b** city! it *is* all full *of* lies *and* 1818
Ac 28: 8 Publius lay sick of a fever and of a **b flixe**: *1420*

BLOOMED (1)
Nu 17: 8 and **b** blossoms, and yielded almonds. 6692

BLOSSOM (6) [BLOSSOMED, BLOSSOMS]
Nu 17: 5 man's rod, whom I shall choose, shall **b**: 6524
Isa 5:24 and their **b** shall go up as dust: 6525
27: 6 Israel shall **b** and bud, and fill the face of 6692
35: 1 the desert shall rejoice, and **b** as the rose. 6524
35: 2 It shall **b abundantly** and 6524+6524
Hab 3:17 Although the fig tree shall not **b**, 6524

BLOSSOMED (1) [BLOSSOM]
Eze 7:10 the rod hath **b**, pride hath budded. 6692

BLOSSOMS (2) [BLOSSOM]
Ge 40:10 as though it budded, *and* her **b** shot forth; 5322
Nu 17: 8 and bloomed **b**, and yielded almonds. 6731

BLOT (13) [BLOTTED, BLOTTETH, BLOTTING]
Ex 32:32 if not, **b** me, I pray thee, out of thy book 4229
32:33 against me, him will I **b out** of my book. 4229
Nu 5:23 he shall **b** *them* **out** with the bitter water: 4229
Dt 9:14 and **b out** their name from under heaven: 4229
25:19 *that* thou shalt **b out** the remembrance of 4229
29:20 the LORD shall **b out** his name from 4229
2Ki 14:27 the LORD said not that *he* would **b out** 4229
Job 31: 7 and *if any* **b** hath cleaved to my hands; 3971
Ps 51: 1 thy tender mercies **b out** my transgressions. 4229
51: 9 from my sins, and **b out** all mine iniquities. 4229
Pr 9: 7 rebuketh a wicked *man getteth* himself a **b**. 3971
Jer 18:23 neither **b out** their sin from thy sight, but 4229
Rev 3: 5 I will not **b out** his name out of the book of *1813*

BLOTTED (6) [BLOT]
Ne 4: 5 let not their sin be **b out** from before thee: 4229
Ps 69:28 Let them be **b out** of the book of the living, 4229
109:13 following let their name be **b out**. 4229
109:14 and let not the sin of his mother be **b out**. 4229
Isa 44:22 I have **b out**, as a thick cloud, 4229
Ac 3:19 be converted, that your sins may be **b out**, *1813*

BLOTTETH (1) [BLOT]
Isa 43:25 *am* he that **b out** thy transgressions for 4229

BLOTTING (1) [BLOT]
Col 2:14 **B out** the handwriting of ordinances that *1813*

BLOW (39) [BLEW, BLOWETH, BLOWING, BLOWN]
Ex 15:10 Thou didst **b** with thy wind, the sea covered 5398
Nu 10: 3 when they shall **b** with them, all 8628
10: 4 if they **b** *but* with one *trumpet*, then 8628
10: 5 When ye **b** an alarm, then the camps that 8628
10: 6 When you **b** an alarm the second time, then 8628
10: 6 they shall **b** an alarm for their journeys. 8628
10: 7 you shall **b**, but you shall not sound an 8628
10: 8 the priests, shall **b** with the trumpets; 8628
10: 9 then ye shall **b an alarm** with the trumpets; 7321
10:10 ye shall **b** with the trumpets over your 8628
31: 6 and the trumpets to **b** in his hand. 8643
Jos 6: 4 and the priests shall **b** with the trumpets. 8628
Jdg 7:18 When I **b** with a trumpet, I and all that *are* 8628
7:18 **b** ye the trumpets also on every side of all 8628
7:20 the trumpets in their right hands to **b** 8628
1Ki 1:34 **b** ye with the trumpet, and say, God save 8628
1Ch 15:24 did **b** with the trumpets before the ark of 2690
Ps 39:10 I am consumed by the **b** of thine hand. 8409
78:26 He **caused** an east wind **to b** in the heaven: 5265
81: 3 **B up** the trumpet in the new moon, in 8628
147:18 he **causeth** his wind **to b**, *and* the waters 5380
SS 4:16 **b** upon my garden, *that* the spices thereof 6315
Isa 40:24 he shall also **b** upon them, and they shall 5398
Jer 4: 5 and say, **B** ye the trumpet in the land: 8628
6: 1 **b** the trumpet in Tekoa, and set up a sign of 8628
14:17 *with* a great breach, *with* a very grievous **b**. 4347
51:27 **b** the trumpet among the nations, 8628
Eze 21:31 I will **b** against thee in the fire of my wrath, 6315
22:20 to **b** the fire upon it, to melt *it*; so will I 5301
22:21 **b** upon you in the fire of my wrath, and 5301
33: 3 he **b** the trumpet, and warn the people; 8628
33: 6 **b** not the trumpet, and the people be not 8628
Hos 5: 8 **B** ye the cornet in Gibeah, *and* the trumpet 8628
Joel 2: 1 **B** ye the trumpet in Zion, and sound an 8628
2:15 **B** the trumpet in Zion, sanctify a fast, call a 8628
Hag 1: 9 when ye brought *it* home, I did **b** upon it. 5301
Zec 9:14 the Lord GOD shall **b** the trumpet, and 8628
Lk 12:55 And when *ye see* the south wind **b**, ye say, *4154*
Rev 7: 1 that the wind should not **b** on the earth, *4154*

BLOWETH (4) [BLOW]
Isa 18: 3 and when *he* **b** a trumpet, hear ye. 8628
40: 7 because the spirit of the LORD **b** upon it: 5380
54:16 I have created the smith that **b** the coals in 5301
Jn 3: 8 The wind **b** where it listeth, and *4154*

BLOWING (4) [BLOW]
Lev 23:24 a memorial of **b of trumpets**, a holy 8643
Nu 29: 1 it is a day of **b** the **trumpets** unto you. 8643
Jos 6: 9 *priests* going on, and **b** with the trumpets. 8628
6:13 *priests* going on, and **b** with the trumpets. 8628

BLOWN (4) [BLOW]
Job 20:26 a fire not **b** shall consume him; it shall go 5301
Isa 27:13 *that* the great trumpet shall be **b**, and 8628
Eze 7:14 They have **b** the trumpet, even to make all 8628
Am 3: 6 Shall a trumpet be **b** in the city, and 8628

BLOWS See STRIPE; STRIPES

BLUE (50) [BLUENESS]
Ex 25: 4 **b**, and purple, and scarlet, and fine linen, 8504
26: 1 twined linen, and **b**, and purple, and scarlet: 8504
26: 4 thou shalt make loops of **b** upon the edge of 8504
26:31 thou shalt make a vail *of* **b**, and purple, 8504
26:36 *of* **b**, and purple, and scarlet, and 8504
27:16 *of* **b**, and purple, and scarlet, and 8504
28: 5 **b**, and purple, and scarlet, and fine linen. 8504
28: 6 *of* **b**, and *of* purple, *of* scarlet, and 8504
28: 8 *of* **b**, and purple, and scarlet, and 8504
28:15 *of* **b**, and *of* purple, and *of* scarlet, and 8504
28:28 unto the rings of the ephod with a lace of **b**, 8504
28:31 shalt make the robe of the ephod all of **b**. 8504
28:33 of it thou shalt make pomegranates of **b**, 8504
28:37 thou shalt put it on a **b** lace, that it may be 8504
35: 6 **b**, and purple, and scarlet, and fine linen, 8504
35:23 with whom was found **b**, and purple, and 8504
35:25 *both* of **b**, and of purple, *and* of scarlet, 8504
35:35 in **b**, and in purple, in scarlet, and in fine 8504
36: 8 twined linen, and **b**, and purple, and scarlet: 8504
36:11 he made loops of **b** on the edge of one 8504
36:35 he made a vail *of* **b**, and purple, and scarlet, 8504
36:37 a hanging for the tabernacle door *of* **b**, 8504
38:18 *of* **b**, and purple, and scarlet, and 8504
38:23 an embroiderer in **b**, and in purple, and 8504
39: 1 of the **b**, and purple, and scarlet, they made 8504
39: 2 **b**, and purple, and scarlet, and fine twined 8504
39: 3 to work *it* in the **b**, and in the purple, and 8504
39: 5 **b**, and purple, and scarlet, and fine twined 8504
39: 8 **b**, and purple, and scarlet, and fine twined 8504
39:21 unto the rings of the ephod with a lace of **b**, 8504
39:22 robe of the ephod *of* woven work, all of **b**. 8504
39:24 the hems of the robe pomegranates of **b**, 8504
39:29 **b**, and purple, and scarlet, *of* needlework; 8504
39:31 they tied unto it a lace of **b**, to fasten *it* on 8504
Nu 4: 6 shall spread over *it* a cloth wholly of **b**, and 8504
4: 7 of shewbread they shall spread a cloth of **b**, 8504
4: 9 they shall take a cloth of **b**, and cover 8504
4:11 golden altar they shall spread a cloth of **b**, 8504
4:12 put *them* in a cloth of **b**, and cover them 8504
15:38 the fringe of the borders a ribband of **b**: 8504
2Ch 2: 7 **b**, and that can skill to grave with 8504
2:14 in **b**, and in fine linen, and in crimson; 8504
3:14 he made the vail *of* **b**, and purple, and 8504
Est 1: 6 **b** *hangings*, fastened with cords of fine 8504
1: 6 of red, and **b**, and white, and black **marble**. 8336
8:15 presence of the king in royal apparel *of* **b** 8504
Jer 10: 9 **b** and purple *is* their clothing: they *are* all 8504
Eze 23: 6 *Which were* clothed with **b**, captains and 8504
27: 7 **b** and purple from the isles of Elishah was 8504
27:24 in **b** clothes, and broidered work, and 8504

BLUENESS (1) [BLUE]
Pr 20:30 The **b** of a wound cleanseth away evil: so 2250

BLUNT (1)
Ecc 10:10 If the iron be **b**, and he do not whet 6949

BLUSH (3)
Ezr 9: 6 and **b** to lift up my face to thee, 3637
Jer 6:15 not at all ashamed, neither could they **b**: 3637
8:12 not at all ashamed, neither could they **b**: 3637

BOANERGES (1)
Mk 3:17 (and he surnamed them **B**, which is, *993*

BOAR (1)
Ps 80:13 The **b** out of the wood doth waste it, and 2386

BOARD (17) [BOARDS]
Ex 26:16 Ten cubits *shall be* the length of a **b**, and 7175
26:16 and a half *shall be* the breadth of one **b**. 7175
26:17 Two tenons *shall there be* in one **b**, set in 7175
26:19 two sockets under one **b** for his two tenons, 7175
26:19 two sockets under another **b** for his two 7175
26:21 two sockets under one **b**, and two sockets 7175
26:21 and two sockets under another **b**. 7175
26:25 two sockets under one **b**, and two sockets 7175
26:25 and two sockets under another **b**. 7175
36:21 The length of a **b** *was* ten cubits, and 7175
36:21 and the breadth of a **b** one cubit and a half. 7175
36:22 One **b** had two tenons, equally distant one 7175
36:24 two sockets under one **b** for his two tenons, 7175
36:24 two sockets under another **b** for his two 7175
36:26 two sockets under one **b**, and two sockets 7175
36:26 and two sockets under another **b**. 7175
36:30 *of* silver, under every **b** two sockets. 7175

BOARDS (41) [BOARD]
Ex 26:15 thou shalt make **b** for the tabernacle *of* 7175
26:17 thus shalt thou make for all the **b** of 7175
26:18 thou shalt make the **b** for the tabernacle, 7175
26:18 twenty **b** on the south side southward. 7175
26:19 forty sockets of silver under the twenty **b**; 7175
26:20 on the north side *there shall be* twenty **b**: 7175
26:22 tabernacle westward thou shalt make six **b**. 7175
26:23 two **b** shalt thou make for the corners of 7175
26:25 they shall be eight **b**, and their sockets *of* 7175
26:26 five for the **b** of the one side of 7175
26:27 five bars for the **b** of the other side of 7175
26:27 five bars for the **b** of the side of 7175
26:28 the middle bar in the midst of the **b** shall 7175
26:29 thou shalt overlay the **b** with gold, and 7175
27: 8 Hollow with **b** shalt thou make it: as it was 3871
35:11 his taches, and his **b**, his bars, his pillars, 7175
36:20 he made **b** for the tabernacle *of* shittim 7175
36:22 thus did he make for all the **b** of 7175
36:23 he made **b** for the tabernacle; twenty boards 7175
36:23 twenty **b** for the south side southward: 7175
36:24 of silver he made under the twenty **b**; 7175
36:25 toward the north corner, he made twenty **b**, 7175
36:27 of the tabernacle westward he made six **b**. 7175
36:28 two **b** made he for the corners of 7175
36:30 there were eight **b**; and their sockets *were* 7175
36:31 five for the **b** of the one side of 7175
36:32 five bars for the **b** of the other side of 7175
36:32 five bars for the **b** of the tabernacle for 7175
36:33 through the **b** from the one end to the other. 7175
36:34 he overlaid the **b** with gold, and made their 7175
38: 7 it withal; he made *the altar* hollow with **b**. 3871
39:33 his **b**, his bars, and his pillars, and 7175
40:18 set up the **b** thereof, and put in the bars 7175
Nu 3:36 charge of the sons of Merari *shall be* the **b** 7175
4:31 the **b** of the tabernacle, and the bars 7175
1Ki 6: 9 the house with beams and **b** of cedar. 7713
6:15 walls of the house within with **b** of cedar, 6763
6:16 both the floor and the walls with **b** of cedar: 6763
SS 8: 9 a door, we will inclose her with **b** of cedar. 3871
Eze 27: 5 They have made all thy *ship* **b** of fir trees 3871
Ac 27:44 some on **b**, and some on broken pieces of *4548*

BOAST (20) [BOASTED, BOASTERS, BOASTEST, BOASTETH, BOASTING, BOASTINGS]
1Ki 20:11 *harness* **b** himself as he that putteth *it* off. 1984
2Ch 25:19 and thine heart lifteth thee up to **b**: 3513
Ps 34: 2 My soul shall **make** her **b** in the LORD: 1984
44: 8 In God we **b** all the day long, and praise thy 1984
49: 6 **b** themselves in the multitude of their 1984
94: 4 *and* all the workers of iniquity **b** themselves? 559
97: 7 graven images, that **b** themselves of idols: 1984
Pr 27: 1 **B** not thyself of to morrow; for thou 1984
Isa 10:15 Shall the axe **b** itself against him that 6286
61: 6 and in their glory shall you **b** yourselves. 3235
Ro 2:17 in the law, and **makest** thy **b** of God, *2744*
2:23 Thou that **makest** thy **b** of the law, *2744*
11:18 **B** not **against** the branches: but if thou *2620*
11:18 but if thou **b**, thou bearest not the root, but *2620*
2Co 9: 2 for which I **b** of you to them of Macedonia, *2744*
10: 8 For though I should **b** somewhat more of *2744*
10:13 But we will not **b** of *things* without *our* *2744*
10:16 not to **b** in another *man's* line of *things* *2744*
11:16 fool receive me, that I may **b** myself a little. *2744*
Eph 2: 9 Not of works, lest any *man* should **b**. *2744*

BOASTED (2) [BOAST]
Eze 35:13 Thus with your mouth ye have **b** against 1431
2Co 7:14 For if I have **b** any *thing* to him of you, *2744*

BOASTERS (2) [BOAST]
Ro 1:30 haters of God, despiteful, proud, **b**, *213*
2Ti 3: 2 covetous, **b**, proud, blasphemers, *213*

BOASTEST (1) [BOAST]
Ps 52: 1 Why **b** thou thyself in mischief, O mighty 1984

BOASTETH (4) [BOAST]
Ps 10: 3 For the wicked **b** of his heart's desire, and 1984
Pr 20:14 but when he is gone his way, then he **b**. 1984
25:14 Whoso **b** himself of a false gift *is like* 1984
Jas 3: 5 is a little member, and **b** great things. *3166*

BOASTING (9) [BOAST]
Ac 5:36 up Theudas, **b** himself to be somebody; *3004*
Ro 3:27 Where *is* **b** then? It is excluded. By what *2746*
2Co 7:14 even so our **b**, which *I made* before Titus, *2746*
8:24 of your love, and of our **b** on your behalf. *2746*
9: 3 lest our **b** of you should be in vain in this *2745*
9: 4 be ashamed in this *same* confident **b**. *2746*
10:15 Not **b** of *things* without *our* measure, *2744*
11:10 no *man* shall stop me of this **b** in *2746*
11:17 as *it were* foolishly, in this confidence of **b**. *2746*

BOASTINGS (1) [BOAST]
Jas 4:16 But now ye rejoice in your **b**: all such *212*

BOAT (6) [BOATS]
2Sa 19:18 there went over a **ferry b** to carry over 5679
Jn 6:22 sea saw that there was none other **b** there, *4142*
6:22 Jesus went not with his disciples into the **b**, *4142*
Ac 27:16 we had much work to come by the **b**: *4627*
27:30 when they had let down the **b** into the sea, *4627*
27:32 Then the soldiers cut off the ropes of the **b**, *4627*

BOATS (1) [BOAT]
Jn 6:23 (Howbeit there came other **b** from Tiberias *4142*

BOAZ (24) [BOOZ]
Ru 2: 1 family of Elimelech; and his name *was* **B**. 1162
2: 3 on a part of the field *belonging* unto **B**, 1162
2: 4 **B** came from Beth-lehem, and said unto 1162
2: 5 said **B** unto his servant that was set over 1162
2: 8 said **B** unto Ruth, Hearest thou not, 1162
2:11 **B** answered and said unto her, It hath fully 1162
2:14 **B** said unto her, At mealtime come thou 1162
2:15 **B** commanded his young men, saying, 1162
2:19 name with whom I wrought to day *is* **B**. 1162
2:23 So she kept fast by the maidens of **B** to 1162
3: 2 now *is* not **B** of our kindred, with whose 1162
3: 7 when **B** had eaten and drunk, and his heart 1162
4: 1 went **B** up *to* the gate, and sat him down 1162
4: 1 the kinsman of whom **B** spake came by; 1162
4: 5 said **B**, What day thou buyest the field of 1162
4: 8 Therefore the kinsman said unto **B**, Buy *it* 1162
4: 9 **B** said unto the elders, and *unto* all 1162
4:13 So **B** took Ruth, and she was his wife: and 1162
4:21 Salmon begat **B**, and Boaz begat Obed, 1162
4:21 Salmon begat Boaz, and **B** begat Obed, 1162
1Ki 7:21 left pillar, and called the name thereof **B**. 1162
1Ch 2:11 Nahshon begat Salma, and Salma begat **B**, 1162
2:12 And **B** begat Obed, and Obed begat Jesse, 1162
2Ch 3:17 and the name of *that on* the left **B**. 1162

BOCHERU (2)
1Ch 8:38 **B**, and Ishmael, and Sheariah, and Obadiah, 1074
9:44 **B**, and Ishmael, and Sheariah, and Obadiah, 1074

BOCHIM (2)
Jdg 2: 1 of the LORD came up from Gilgal to **B**, 1066
2: 5 they called the name of that place **B**: and 1066

BODIES (33) [BODY]
Ge 47:18 sight of my lord, but our **b**, and our lands: 1472
1Sa 31:12 the **b** of his sons from the wall of 1472
1Ch 10:12 the **b** of his sons, and brought them to 1480
2Ch 20:24 they *were* **dead b** fallen to the earth, and 6297
20:25 in abundance both riches with the **dead b**, 6297
Ne 9:37 also they have dominion over our **b**, and 1472
Job 13:12 like unto ashes, your **b** to bodies of clay. 1354
13:12 like unto ashes, your bodies to **b** of clay. 1354
Ps 79: 2 The **dead b** of thy servants have they given 5038
110: 6 he shall fill *the places with* the **dead b**; 1472
Jer 31:40 the whole valley of the **dead b**, and of 6297
33: 5 *it is* to fill them with the **dead b** of men, 6297
34:20 their **dead b** shall be for meat unto 5038
41: 9 Ishmael had cast all the **dead b** of the men, 6297
Eze 1:11 one to another, and two covered their **b**. 1472
1:23 which covered on that *side*, their **b**. 1472
Da 3:27 upon whose **b** the fire had no power, 1655
3:28 the king's word, and yielded their **b**, 1655
Am 8: 3 *there shall be* many **dead b** in every place; 6297
Mt 27:52 and many **b** of saints which slept arose, *4983*
Jn 19:31 that the **b** should not remain upon the cross *4983*
Ro 1:24 to dishonour their own **b** between *4983*
8:11 mortal **b** by his Spirit that dwelleth in you. *4983*
12: 1 that *ye* present your **b** a living sacrifice, *4983*
1Co 6:15 Know ye not that your **b** are the members *4983*
15:40 *There are* also celestial **b**, and *4983*
15:40 *are* also celestial bodies, and **b** terrestrial: *4983*
Eph 5:28 men to love their wives as their own **b**. *4983*
Heb 10:22 and *our* **b** washed with pure water. *4983*
13:11 For the **b** of those beasts, whose blood is *4983*
Rev 11: 8 And their **dead b** *shall lie* in the street of *4430*
11: 9 nations shall see their **dead b** three days *4430*
11: 9 shall not suffer their **dead b** to be put in *4430*

BODILY (4) [BODY]
Lk 3:22 And the Holy Ghost descended in a **b** shape *4984*
2Co 10:10 but *his* **b** presence *is* weak, and *his* speech *4983*
Col 2: 9 dwelleth all the fulness of the Godhead **b**. *4985*
1Ti 4: 8 For **b** exercise profiteth little: *4984*

BODY (174) [BODIES, BODILY, BODY'S, BUSYBODIES, BUSYBODY]
Ex 24:10 as it were the **b** of heaven in *his* clearness. 6106
Lev 21:11 Neither shall he go in to any dead **b**, 5315
Nu 6: 6 the LORD he shall come at no dead **b**. 5315
9: 6 who were defiled by the **dead b** of a man, 5315
9: 7 We *are* defiled by the **dead b** of a man: 5315
9:10 shall be unclean by reason of a **dead b**, 5315
19:11 He that toucheth the dead **b** of any man NIH
19:13 Whosoever toucheth the dead **b** of *any* man NIH
19:16 or a dead **b**, or a bone of a man, or a grave, NIH
Dt 21:23 His **b** shall not remain all night upon 5038
28: 4 Blessed *shall be* the fruit of thy **b**, and 990
28:11 in the fruit of thy **b**, and in the fruit of thy 990
28:18 Cursed *shall be* the fruit of thy **b**, and 990
28:53 thou shalt eat the fruit of thine own **b**, 990
30: 9 in the fruit of thy **b**, and in the fruit of thy 990
Jdg 8:30 and ten sons of his **b** begotten: 3409
1Sa 31:10 they fastened his **b** to the wall of 1472
31:12 took the **b** of Saul and the bodies of his 1472
2Ki 8: 5 king how he had restored a dead **b** to life, NIH
1Ch 10:12 took away the **b** of Saul, and the bodies of 1480
Job 19:17 for the children's *sake* of mine *own* **b**. 990
19:26 *though* after my skin *worms* destroy this **b**, NIH
20:25 It is drawn, and cometh out of the **b**; yea, 1465
Ps 132:11 Of the fruit of thy **b** will I set upon thy 990
Pr 5:11 when thy flesh and thy **b** are consumed, 7607
Isa 10:18 and of his fruitful field, both soul and **b**: 1320
26:19 *together with* my **dead b** shall they arise. 5038
51:23 thou hast laid thy **b** as the ground, and 1460
Jer 26:23 cast his **dead b** into the graves of 5038
36:30 his **dead b** shall be cast out in the day to 5038
La 4: 7 they were more ruddy *in* **b** than rubies, 6106
Eze 10:12 their whole **b**, and their backs, and 1320
Da 4:33 and his **b** was wet with the dew of heaven, 1655
5:21 and his **b** was wet with the dew of heaven; 1655
7:11 his **b** destroyed, and given to the burning 1655
7:15 grieved in my spirit in the midst of *my* **b**, 5085
10: 6 His **b** also *was* like the beryl, and his face 1472
Mic 6: 7 the fruit of my **b** *for* the sin of my soul? 990
Hag 2:13 If *one that is* unclean *by* a **dead b** touch 5315
Mt 5:29 not *that* thy whole **b** should be cast into *4983*
5:30 not *that* thy whole **b** should be cast into *4983*
6:22 The light of the **b** is the eye: if therefore *4983*
6:22 be single, thy whole **b** shall be full of light. *4983*
6:23 thy whole **b** shall be full of darkness. *4983*
6:25 nor yet for your **b**, what ye shall put on. *4983*
6:25 more than meat, and the **b** than raiment? *4983*
10:28 And fear not them which kill the **b**, but *4983*
10:28 is able to destroy both soul and **b** in hell. *4983*
14:12 And his disciples came, and took up the **b**, *4983*
26:12 that she hath poured this ointment on my **b**, *4983*
26:26 and said, Take, eat; this is my **b**. *4983*
27:58 went to Pilate, and begged the **b** of Jesus. *4983*
27:58 Then Pilate commanded the **b** to be *4983*
27:59 And when Joseph had taken the **b**, *4983*
Mk 5:29 she felt in *her* **b** that she was healed of *that* *4983*
14: 8 she is come aforehand to anoint my **b** to *4983*
14:22 to them, and said, Take, eat: this is my **b**. *4983*
14:51 having a linen cloth cast about *his* naked **b**; NIG
15:43 unto Pilate, and craved the **b** of Jesus. *4983*
15:45 *it* of the centurion, he gave the **b** to Joseph. *4983*
Lk 11:34 The light of the **b** is the eye: *4983*
11:34 is single, thy whole **b** also is full of light; *4983*
11:34 *eye* is evil, thy **b** also *is* full of darkness. *4983*
11:36 If thy whole **b** therefore *be* full of light, *4983*
12: 4 Be not afraid of them that kill the **b**, and *4983*
12:22 neither for the **b**, what ye shall put on. *4983*
12:23 than meat, and the **b** *is more* than raiment. *4983*
17:37 Wheresoever the **b** *is*, thither will *4983*
22:19 This is my **b** which is given for you: *4983*
23:52 went unto Pilate, and begged the **b** of Jesus. *4983*
23:55 the sepulchre, and how his **b** was laid. *4983*
24: 3 and found not the **b** of the Lord Jesus. *4983*
24:23 And when they found not his **b**, they came, *4983*
Jn 2:21 But he spake of the temple of his **b**. *4983*
19:38 that he might take away the **b** of Jesus: *4983*
19:38 He came therefore, and took the **b** of Jesus. *4983*
19:40 Then took they the **b** of Jesus, and wound it *4983*
20:12 at the feet, where the **b** of Jesus had lain. *4983*
Ac 9:40 and turning *him* to the **b** said, Tabitha, *4983*
19:12 So that from his **b** were brought unto *5559*
Ro 4:19 he considered not his own **b** now dead, *4983*
6: 6 *him*, that the **b** of sin might be destroyed, *4983*
6:12 Let not sin therefore reign in your mortal **b**, *4983*
7: 4 ye also are become dead to the law by the **b** *4983*
7:24 who shall deliver me from the **b** of this *4983*
8:10 *be* in you, the **b** *is* dead because of sin; *4983*
8:13 the Spirit do mortify the deeds of the **b**, *4983*
8:23 *to wit*, the redemption of our **b**. *4983*
12: 4 For as we have many members in one **b**, *4983*
12: 5 are one **b** in Christ, and every one members *4983*
1Co 5: 3 I verily, as absent in **b**, but present in spirit, *4983*
6:13 Now the **b** *is* not for fornication, but for *4983*
6:13 but for the Lord; and the Lord for the **b**. *4983*
6:16 that he which is joined to a harlot is one **b**? *4983*
6:18 Every sin that a man doeth is without the **b**; *4983*
6:18 fornication sinneth against his own **b**. *4983*
6:19 know ye not that your **b** is the temple of *4983*
6:20 therefore glorify God in your **b**, and in your *4983*
7: 4 The wife hath not power of her own **b**, but *4983*
7: 4 the husband hath not power of his own **b**, *4983*
7:34 that she may be holy both in **b** and in spirit: *4983*
9:27 But I keep under my **b**, and bring *it* into *4983*
10:16 is it not the communion of the **b** of Christ? *4983*
10:17 we being many are one bread, *and* one **b**: *4983*
11:24 this is my **b**, which is broken for you: *4983*
11:27 shall be guilty of the **b** and blood of *4983*
11:29 to himself, not discerning the Lord's **b**. *4983*
12:12 For as the **b** is one, and hath many *4983*
12:12 and all the members of *that* one **b**, *4983*
12:12 of *that* one body, being many, are one **b**: *4983*
12:13 by one Spirit are we all baptized into one **b**, *4983*
12:14 For the **b** is not one member, but many. *4983*
12:15 I am not the hand, I am not of the **b**; *4983*
12:15 not of the body; is it therefore not of the **b**? *4983*
12:16 Because I am not the eye, I am not of the **b**; *4983*
12:16 not of the body; is it therefore not of the **b**? *4983*
12:17 If the whole **b** *were* an eye, where *were* *4983*
1Co 12:18 set the members every one of them in the **b**, *4983*
12:19 were all one member, where *were* the **b**? *4983*
12:20 now *are they* many members, yet *but* one **b**. *4983*
12:22 Nay, much more those members of the **b**, *4983*
12:23 And those *members* of the **b**, which we *4983*
12:24 but God hath tempered the **b** together, *4983*
12:25 That there should be no schism in the **b**; but *4983*
12:27 Now ye are the **b** of Christ, and members in *4983*
13: 3 and though I give my **b** to be burned, *4983*
15:35 raised up? and with what **b** do they come? *4983*
15:37 thou sowest not that **b** that shall be, but *4983*
15:38 But God giveth it a **b** as it hath pleased *4983*
15:38 pleased him, and to every seed his own **b**. *4983*
15:44 It is sown a natural **b**; it is raised a spiritual *4983*
15:44 a natural body; it is raised a spiritual **b**. *4983*
15:44 There is a natural **b**, and there is a spiritual *4983*
15:44 is a natural body, and there is a spiritual **b**. *4983*
2Co 4:10 Always bearing about in the **b** the dying of *4983*
4:10 of Jesus might be made manifest in our **b**. *4983*
5: 6 whilst we are at home in the **b**, *4983*
5: 8 and willing rather to be absent from the **b**, *4983*
5:10 one may receive the *things done* in *his* **b**, *4983*
12: 2 years ago, (whether in the **b**, I cannot tell; *4983*
12: 2 or whether out of the **b**, I cannot tell: *4983*
12: 3 (whether in the **b**, or out of the body, *4983*
12: 3 in the body, or out of the **b**, I cannot tell: *4983*
Gal 6:17 for I bear in my **b** the marks of the Lord *4983*
Eph 1:23 Which is his **b**, the fulness of him that *4983*
2:16 both unto God in one **b** by the cross, *4983*
3: 6 and **of the same b**, and partakers of his *4954*
4: 4 *There is* one **b**, and one Spirit, even as ye *4983*
4:12 for the edifying of the **b** of Christ: *4983*
4:16 From whom the whole **b** fitly joined *4983*
4:16 maketh increase of the **b** unto the edifying *4983*
5:23 the church: and he is the saviour of the **b**. *4983*
5:30 For we are members of his **b**, of his flesh, *4983*
Php 1:20 now also Christ shall be magnified in my **b**, *4983*
3:21 Who shall change our vile **b**, that it may be *4983*
3:21 may be fashioned like unto his glorious **b**, *4983*
Col 1:18 And he is the head of the **b**, the church: *4983*
1:22 In the **b** of his flesh through death, *4983*
2:11 in putting off the **b** of the sins of the flesh, *4983*
2:17 of *things* to come; but the **b** *is* of Christ. *4983*
2:19 from which all the **b** by joints and *4983*
2:23 and humility, and neglecting of the **b**, *4983*
3:15 to the which also ye are called in one **b**; *4983*
1Th 5:23 **b** be preserved blameless unto the coming *4983*
Heb 5:10 but a **b** hast thou prepared me: *4983*
10:10 of the **b** of Jesus Christ once for all. *4983*
13: 3 as being yourselves also in the **b**. *4983*
Jas 2:16 not those *things which are* needful to the **b**; *4983*
2:26 For as the **b** without the spirit is dead, so *4983*
3: 2 *and* able also to bridle the whole **b**. *4983*
3: 3 obey us; and we turn about their whole **b**. *4983*
3: 6 that it defileth the whole **b**, and setteth on *4983*
1Pe 2:24 self bare our sins in his own **b** on the tree, *4983*
Jude 1: 9 the devil he disputed about the **b** of Moses, *4983*

BODY'S (1) [BODY]
Col 1:24 of Christ in my flesh for his **b** sake, *4983*

BOHAN (2)
Jos 15: 6 the border went up *to* the stone of **B** the son 932
18:17 descended *to* the stone of **B** the son of 932

BOIL (16) [BOILED, BOILING, BOILS]
Ex 9: 9 shall be a **b** breaking forth *with* blains upon 7822
9:10 it became a **b** breaking forth *with* blains 7822
9:11 for the **b** was upon the magicians, and 7822
Lev 8:31 **B** the flesh *at* the door of the tabernacle of 1310
13:18 in the skin thereof, was a **b**, and is healed, 7822
13:19 in the place of the **b** there be a white rising, 7822
13:20 it *is* a plague of leprosy broken out of the **b**. 7822
13:23 his place, *and* spread not, it *is* a burning **b**; 7822
2Ki 20: 7 they took and laid *it* on the **b**, and 7822
Job 41:31 He **maketh** the deep **to b** like a pot: 7570
Isa 38:21 lay *it* for a plaister upon the **b**, and he shall 7822
64: 2 the fire **causeth** the waters **to b**, 1158
Eze 24: 5 *and* **make** it **b well**, and let them 7570+7571
46:20 This *is* the place where the priests shall **b** 1310
46:24 These *are* the places of them that **b**, 1310
46:24 where the ministers of the house shall **b** 1310

BOILED (3) [BOIL]
1Ki 19:21 **b** their flesh with the instruments of 1310
2Ki 6:29 So we **b** my son, and did eat him: and I said 1310
Job 30:27 My bowels **b**, and rested not: the days of 7570

BOILING (1) [BOIL]
Eze 46:23 *it was* made *with* **b places** under the rows 4018

BOILS (2) [BOIL]
Ex 9:11 not stand before Moses because of the **b**; 7822
Job 2: 7 smote Job with sore **b** from the sole of his 7822

BOKERU See BOCHERU

BOKIM See BOCHIM

BOLD (11) [BOLDLY, BOLDNESS, EMBOLDENED, EMBOLDENETH]
Pr 28: 1 but the righteous are **b** as a lion. 982
Ac 13:46 Then Paul and Barnabas **waxed b**, and said, *3955*
Ro 10:20 But Esaias is **very b**, and saith, I was found *662*
2Co 10: 1 but being absent am **b** toward you: *2292*
10: 2 But I beseech *you*, that I may not be **b** *2292*
10: 2 wherewith I think to be **b** against some, *5111*
11:21 Howbeit whereinsoever any is **b**, (I speak *5111*
11:21 any is bold, (I speak foolishly,) I am **b** also. *5111*
Php 1:14 are much more **b** to speak the word without *5111*
1Th 2: 2 we were **b** in our God to speak unto you *3955*
Phm 1: 8 though I might be much **b** in Christ to *3954*

B

BOLDLY (13) [BOLD]
Ge 34:25 came upon the city **b**, and slew all the males. 983
Mk 15:43 and went in **b** unto Pilate, and craved *5111*
Jn 7:26 he speaketh **b**, and they say nothing unto *3954*
Ac 9:27 how he had **preached b** at Damascus in *3955*
9:29 And he spake **b** in the name of the Lord *3955*
14: 3 abode they **speaking b** in the Lord, *3955*
18:26 And he began to **speak b** in the synagogue: *3955*
19: 8 and **spake b** for the space of three months, *3955*
Ro 15:15 I have written the **more b** unto you in some *5112*
Eph 6:19 that *I* may open my mouth **b**, *1722+3954*
6:20 that therein I may **speak b**, as I ought to *3955*
Heb 4:16 come **b** unto the throne of grace, *3326+3954*
13: 6 So that we may **b** say, The Lord *is* my *2292*

BOLDNESS (10) [BOLD]
Ecc 8: 1 and the **b** of his face shall be changed. 5797
Ac 4:13 Now when they saw the **b** of Peter and *3954*
4:29 that with all **b** *they* may speak thy word, *3954*
4:31 and they spake the word of God with **b**. *3954*
2Co 7: 4 Great *is* my **b of speech** toward you, *3954*
Eph 3:12 In whom we have **b** and access with *3954*
Php 1:20 but *that* with all **b**, as always, *so* now also *3954*
1Ti 3:13 great **b** in the faith which is in Christ Jesus. *3954*
Heb 10:19 **b** to enter into the holiest by the blood of *3954*
1Jn 4:17 that we may have **b** in the day of judgment: *3954*

BOLLED (1)
Ex 9:31 barley *was* in the ear, and the flax *was* **b**. 1392

BOLSTER (6)
1Sa 19:13 put a pillow of goats' *hair* for his **b**, and 4763
19:16 with a pillow of goats' *hair* for his **b**. 4763
26: 7 and his spear stuck in the ground *at* his **b**: 4763
26:11 take thou now the spear that *is at* his **b**, and 4763
26:12 and the cruse of water from Saul's **b**; 4763
26:16 and the cruse of water that *was at* his **b**. 4763

BOLT (1) [BOLTED]
2Sa 13:17 out from me, and **b** the door after her. 5274

BOLTED (1) [BOLT]
2Sa 13:18 brought her out, and **b** the door after her. 5274

BOLTS See LOCKS

BOND (19) [BONDAGE, BONDMAID, BONDMAIDS, BONDMAN, BONDMEN, BONDS, BONDSERVANT, BONDSERVICE, BONDWOMAN, BONDWOMEN]
Nu 30: 2 or swear an oath to bind his soul with a **b**; 632
30: 3 bind *herself* by a **b**, *being* in her father's 632
30: 4 her **b** wherewith she hath bound her soul, 632
30: 4 every **b** wherewith she hath bound her soul 632
30:10 or bound her soul by a **b** with an oath; 632
30:11 every **b** wherewith she bound her soul shall 632
30:12 or concerning the **b** of her soul, shall not 632
Job 12:18 He looseth the **b** of kings, and girdeth their 4148
Eze 20:37 I will bring you into the **b** of the covenant: 4562
Lk 13:16 be loosed from this **b** on the sabbath day? *1199*
Ac 8:23 gall of bitterness, and *in* the **b** of iniquity. *4886*
1Co 12:13 or Gentiles, whether *we be* **b** or free; *1401*
Gal 3:28 Jew nor Greek, there is neither **b** nor free, *1401*
Eph 4: 3 the unity of the Spirit in the **b** of peace. *4886*
6: 8 of the Lord, whether *he be* **b** or free. *1401*
Col 3:11 barbarian, Scythian, **b** *nor* free: *1401*
3:14 *on* charity, which is the **b** of perfectness. *4886*
Rev 13:16 and great, rich and poor, free and **b**, *1401*
19:18 and the flesh of all *men*, both free and **b**, *1401*

BONDAGE (39) [BOND]
Ex 1:14 they made their lives bitter with hard **b**, 5656
2:23 children of Israel sighed by reason of the **b**, 5656
2:23 cry came up unto God by reason of the **b**. 5656
6: 5 of Israel, whom the Egyptians **keep in b**; 5647
6: 6 I will rid you out of their **b**, and I will 5656
6: 9 Moses for anguish of spirit, and for cruel **b**. 5656
13: 3 came out from Egypt, out of the house of **b**; 5650
13:14 us out from Egypt, from the house of **b**: 5650
20: 2 of the land of Egypt, out of the house of **b**. 5650
Dt 5: 6 of the land of Egypt, from the house of **b**. 5650
6:12 of the land of Egypt, from the house of **b**. 5650
8:14 of the land of Egypt, from the house of **b**; 5650
13: 5 and redeemed you out of the house of **b**, 5650
13:10 of the land of Egypt, from the house of **b**. 5650
26: 6 and afflicted us, and laid upon us hard **b**: 5656
Jos 24:17 from the house of **b**, and which did those 5650
Jdg 6: 8 and brought you forth out of the house of **b**; 5650
Ezr 9: 8 and give us a little reviving in our **b**. 5659
9: 9 yet our God hath not forsaken us in our **b**, 5659
Ne 5: 5 we **bring into b** our sons and our daughters 3533
5: 5 *some* of our daughters are **brought unto b** 3533
5:18 because the **b** was heavy upon this people. 5656
9:17 appointed a captain to return to their **b**: 5659
Isa 14: 3 from the hard **b** wherein thou wast made to 5656
Jn 8:33 were never **in b** to any *man:* how sayest *1398*
Ac 7: 6 and that they should **bring** them **into b**, and *1402*
7: 7 And the nation to whom they shall be **in b** *1398*
Ro 8:15 For ye have not received the spirit of **b** *1397*
8:21 **b** of corruption into the glorious liberty of *1397*
1Co 7:15 or a sister is not **under b** in such *cases:* but *1402*
2Co 11:20 For ye suffer, if a man **bring** you **into b**, *2615*
Gal 2: 4 that they might **bring** us **into b**: *2615*
4: 3 were **in b** under the elements of the world: *1402*
4: 9 whereunto ye desire again to be **in b**? *1398*
4:24 which gendereth to **b**, which is Agar. *1397*
4:25 which now is, and is **in b** with her children. *1398*
5: 1 be not entangled again with the yoke of **b**. *1397*
Heb 2:15 of death were all their lifetime subject to **b**. *1397*
2Pe 2:19 of the same is he **brought in b**. *1402*

BONDMAID (2) [BOND, MAID]
Lev 19:20 lieth carnally with a woman that *is* a **b**, 8198
Gal 4:22 the one by a **b**, the other by a freewoman. *3814*

BONDMAIDS (2) [BOND, MAID]
Lev 25:44 Both thy bondmen, and thy **b**, which thou 519
25:44 of them shall ye buy bondmen and **b**. 519

BONDMAN (7) [BOND, MAN]
Ge 44:33 let thy servant abide instead of the lad a **b** 5650
Dt 15:15 thou shalt remember that thou wast a **b** in 5650
16:12 thou shalt remember that thou wast a **b** in 5650
24:18 thou shalt remember that thou wast a **b** in 5650
24:22 thou shalt remember that thou wast a **b** in 5650
1Ki 9:22 children of Israel did Solomon make no **b**: 5650
Rev 6:15 and the mighty *men*, and every **b**, and *1401*

BONDMEN (16) [BOND, MAN]
Ge 43:18 upon us, and take us for **b**, and our asses. 5650
44: 9 him die, and we also will be my lord's **b**. 5650
Lev 25:42 land of Egypt: they shall not be sold as **b**. 5650
25:44 Both thy **b**, and thy bondmaids, which thou 5650
25:44 of them shall ye buy **b** and bondmaids. 5650
25:46 a possession; they shall be your **b** for ever: 5647
26:13 land of Egypt, that *ye* should not be their **b**; 5650
Dt 6:21 thy son, We were Pharaoh's **b** in Egypt; 5650
7: 8 redeemed you out of the house of **b**, 5650
28:68 ye shall be sold unto your enemies for **b** 5650
Jos 9:23 shall none of you be freed from being **b**, 5650
2Ki 4: 1 come to take unto him my two sons to be **b**. 5650
2Ch 28:10 Jerusalem for **b** and bondwomen unto you: 5650
Ezr 9: 9 For we *were* **b**; yet our God hath not 5650
Est 7: 4 if we had been sold for **b** and bondwomen, 5650
Jer 34:13 of Egypt, out of the house of **b**, saying, 5650

BONDS (26) [BOND]
Nu 30: 5 of her **b** wherewith she hath bound her soul, 632
30: 7 her **b** wherewith she bound her soul shall 632
30:14 her vows, or all her **b**, which *are* upon her: 632
Ps 116:16 of thy handmaid: thou hast loosed my **b**. 4147
Jer 5: 5 altogether broken the yoke, *and* burst the **b**. 4147
27: 2 Make thee **b** and yokes, and put them upon 4147
30: 8 will burst thy **b**, and strangers shall no 4147
Na 1:13 off thee, and will burst thy **b** in sunder. 4147
Ac 20:23 saying that **b** and afflictions abide me. *1199*
23:29 laid to his charge worthy of death or of **b**. *1199*
25:14 There is a certain man left in **b** by Felix: *1198*
26:29 altogether such as I am, except these **b**. *1199*
26:31 man doeth nothing worthy of death or of **b**. *1199*
Eph 6:20 For which I am an ambassador in **b**: *254*
Php 1: 7 inasmuch as both in my **b**, and *in* *1199*
1:13 So that my **b** in Christ are manifest in all *1199*
1:14 in the Lord, waxing confident by my **b**, *1199*
1:16 supposing to add affliction to my **b**: *1199*
Col 4: 3 mystery of Christ, for which I am also **in b**: *1210*
4:18 Remember my **b**. Grace *be* with you. *1199*
2Ti 2: 9 suffer trouble, as an evil doer, *even* unto **b**; *1199*
Phm 1:10 whom I have begotten in my **b**: *1199*
1:13 ministered unto me in the **b** of the gospel: *1199*
Heb 10:34 For ye had compassion *of me* in my **b**, *1199*
11:36 yea, moreover of **b** and imprisonment: *1199*
13: 3 Remember *them that are* **in b**, as bound *1198*

BONDSERVANT (1) [BOND, SERVE]
Lev 25:39 thou shalt not compel him to serve as a **b**: 5650

BONDSERVICE (1) [BOND, SERVE]
1Ki 9:21 upon those did Solomon levy a tribute of **b** 5647

BONDWOMAN (8) [BOND, WOMAN]
Ge 21:10 unto Abraham, Cast out this **b** and her son: 519
21:10 for the son of this **b** shall not be heir with my 519
21:12 because of the lad, and because of thy **b**; 519
21:13 also of the son of the **b** will I make a nation, 519
Gal 4:23 But he who was of the **b** was born after *3814*
4:30 Cast out the **b** and her son: for the son of *3814*
4:30 for the son of the **b** shall not be heir with *3814*
4:31 we are not children of *the* **b**, but of the free. *3814*

BONDWOMEN (3) [BOND, WOMAN]
Dt 28:68 sold unto your enemies for bondmen and **b**, 8198
2Ch 28:10 Jerusalem for bondmen and **b** unto you: 8198
Est 7: 4 if we had been sold for bondmen and **b**, 8198

BONE (20) [BONES, JAWBONE]
Ge 2:23 This *is* now **b** of my bones, and flesh of my 6106
29:14 to him, Surely thou *art* my **b** and my flesh. 6106
Ex 12:46 neither shall ye break a **b** thereof. 6106
Lev 3: 9 it shall he take off hard by the **back b**; 6096
Nu 9:12 it unto the morning, nor break any **b** of it: 6106
19:16 or a dead *body*, or a **b** of a man, or a grave, 6106
19:18 and upon him that touched a **b**, or one slain, 6106
Jdg 9: 2 remember also that I *am* your **b** and 6106
2Sa 5: 1 Behold, we *are* thy **b** and thy flesh. 6106
19:13 *Art* thou not *of* my **b**, and *of* my flesh? 6106
1Ch 11: 1 Behold, we *are* thy **b** and thy flesh. 6106
Job 2: 5 touch his **b** and his flesh, and he will curse 6106
19:20 My **b** cleaveth to my skin and to my flesh, 6106
31:22 and mine arm be broken from the **b**. 7070
Ps 3: 7 smitten all mine enemies *upon* the **cheek b**; 3895
Pr 25:15 and a soft tongue breaketh the **b**. 1634
Eze 37: 7 and the bones came together, **b** to his bone. 6106
37: 7 and the bones came together, bone to his **b**. 6106
39:15 when *any* seeth a man's **b**, then shall he set 6106
Jn 19:36 be fulfilled, A **b** of him shall not be broken. *3747*

BONES (99) [BONE]
Ge 2:23 This *is* now bone of my **b**, and flesh of my 6106
50:25 and ye shall carry up my **b** from hence. 6106
Ex 13:19 Moses took the **b** of Joseph with him: 6106
13:19 ye shall carry up my **b** away hence with 6106
Nu 24: 8 shall break their **b**, and pierce *them* through 6106
Jos 24:32 the **b** of Joseph, which the children of Israel 6106
Jdg 19:29 divided her, *together* with her **b**, 6106
1Sa 31:13 they took their **b**, and buried *them* under a 6106
2Sa 19:12 *are* my brethren, ye *are* my **b** and my flesh: 6106
21:12 David went and took the **b** of Saul and 6106
21:12 the **b** of Jonathan his son from the men of 6106
21:13 he brought up from thence the **b** of Saul 6106
21:13 of Saul and the **b** of Jonathan his son; 6106
21:13 they gathered the **b** of them that were 6106
21:14 the **b** of Saul and Jonathan his son buried 6106
1Ki 13: 2 and men's **b** shall be burnt upon thee. 6106
13:31 God *is* buried; lay my **b** beside his bones: 6106
13:31 God *is* buried; lay my bones beside his **b**: 6106
2Ki 13:21 touched the **b** of Elisha, he revived, and 6106
23:14 and filled their places *with* the **b** of men. 6106
23:16 took the **b** out of the sepulchres, and 6106
23:18 Let him alone; let no man move his **b**. 6106
23:18 So they let his **b** alone, with the bones of 6106
23:18 with the **b** of the prophet that came out of 6106
23:20 burnt men's **b** upon them, and returned *to* 6106
1Ch 10:12 buried their **b** under the oak in Jabesh, and 6106
2Ch 34: 5 he burnt the **b** of the priests upon their 6106
Job 4:14 trembling, which made all my **b** to shake. 6106
10:11 and hast fenced me with **b** and sinews. 6106
20:11 His **b** are full *of the sin of* his youth, 6106
21:24 and his **b** are moistened with marrow. 6106
30:17 My **b** are pierced in me in the night season: 6106
30:30 upon me, and my **b** are burnt with heat. 6106
33:19 and the multitude of his **b** *with* strong *pain:* 6106
33:21 and his **b** *that* were not seen stick out. 6106
40:18 His **b** *are as* strong pieces of brass; 6106
40:18 pieces of brass; his **b** *are* like bars of iron. 1634
Ps 6: 2 O LORD, heal me; for my **b** are vexed. 6106
22:14 out like water, and all my **b** are out of joint: 6106
22:17 I may tell all my **b**: they look *and* 6106
31:10 of mine iniquity, and my **b** are consumed. 6106
32: 3 my **b** waxed old through my roaring all 6106
34:20 He keepeth all his **b**: not one of them is 6106
35:10 All my **b** shall say, LORD, who *is* like 6106
38: 3 neither *is there any* rest in my **b** because 6106
42:10 *As* with a sword in my **b**, mine enemies 6106
51: 8 *that* the **b** *which* thou hast broken may 6106
53: 5 for God hath scattered the **b** of him that 6106
102: 3 like smoke, and my **b** are burnt as a hearth. 6106
102: 5 reason of the voice of my groaning my **b** 6106
109:18 bowels like water, and like oil into his **b**. 6106
141: 7 Our **b** are scattered at the grave's mouth, 6106
Pr 3: 8 be health to thy navel, and marrow to thy **b**. 6106
12: 4 maketh ashamed *is* as rottenness in his **b**. 6106
14:30 the flesh: but envy the rottenness of the **b**. 6106
15:30 *and* a good report maketh the **b** fat. 6106
16:24 sweet to the soul, and health to the **b**. 6106
17:22 a medicine: but a broken spirit drieth the **b**. 1634
Ecc 11: 5 *nor* how the **b** *do grow* in the womb of her 6106
Isa 38:13 *that,* as a lion, so will he break all my **b**: 6106
58:11 thy soul in drought, and make fat thy **b**: 6106
66:14 and your **b** shall flourish like an herb: 6106
Jer 8: 1 they shall bring out the **b** of the kings of 6106
8: 1 the **b** of his princes, and the bones of 6106
8: 1 the **b** of the priests, and the bones of 6106
8: 1 the **b** of the prophets, and the bones of 6106
8: 1 the **b** of the inhabitants of Jerusalem, out of 6106
20: 9 heart as a burning fire shut up in my **b**, 6106
23: 9 because of the prophets; all my **b** shake; 6106
50:17 king of Babylon hath **broken** his **b**. 6105
La 1:13 From above hath he sent fire into my **b**, and 6106
3: 4 hath he made old; he hath broken my **b**. 6106
4: 8 their skin cleaveth to their **b**; it is withered, 6106
Eze 6: 5 I will scatter your **b** round about your 6106
24: 4 and the shoulder; fill *it with* the choice **b**. 6106
24: 5 burn also the **b** under it, *and* make it boil 6106
24: 5 and let them seethe the **b** of it therein. 6106
24:10 and spice it well, and let the **b** be burnt. 6106
32:27 but their iniquities shall be upon their **b**, 6106
37: 1 the midst of the valley which *was* full *of* **b**, 6106
37: 3 said unto me, Son of man, can these **b** live? 6106
37: 4 Prophesy upon these **b**, and say unto them, 6106
37: 4 these bones, and say unto them, O ye dry **b**, 6106
37: 5 Thus saith the Lord GOD unto these **b**; 6106
37: 7 and the **b** came together, bone to his bone. 6106
37:11 these **b** *are* the whole house of Israel: 6106
37:11 Our **b** are dried, and our hope is lost: 6106
Da 6:24 brake all their **b** in pieces or ever they came 1635
Am 2: 1 he burnt the **b** of the king of Edom into 6106
6:10 to bring out the **b** out of the house, and 6106
Mic 3: 2 off them, and their flesh from off their **b**; 6106
3: 3 they break their **b**, and chop *them* in pieces, 6106
Hab 3:16 rottenness entered into my **b**, and 6106
Zep 3: 3 they **gnaw** not the **b** till the morrow. 1633
Mt 23:27 but are within full of dead *men's* **b**, and *3747*
Lk 24:39 for a spirit hath not flesh and **b**, as ye see *3747*
Ac 3: 7 his feet and ankle **b** received strength, NIG
Eph 5:30 of his body, of his flesh, and of his **b**. *3747*
Heb 11:22 and gave commandment concerning his **b**. *3747*

BONNETS (6)
Ex 28:40 **b** shalt thou make for them, for glory and 4021
29: 9 Aaron and his sons, and put the **b** on them: 4021
39:28 goodly **b** *of* fine linen, and linen breeches 4021
Lev 8:13 them *with* girdles, and put **b** upon them; 4021
Isa 3:20 The **b**, and the ornaments of the legs, and 6287
Eze 44:18 They shall have linen **b** upon their heads, 6287

BOOK (188) [BOOKS]
Ge 5: 1 This *is* the **b** of the generations of Adam. 5612
Ex 17:14 Write this *for* a memorial in a **b**, and 5612
24: 7 he took the **b** of the covenant, and read in 5612
32:32 out of thy **b** which thou hast written. 5612
32:33 against me, him will I blot out of my **b**. 5612
Nu 5:23 the priest shall write these curses in a **b**, 5612
21:14 Wherefore it is said in the **b** of the wars of 5612
Dt 17:18 **b** out of *that which is* before the priests 5612
28:58 words of this law that are written in this **b**, 5612
28:61 which *is* not written in the **b** of this law, 5612
29:20 all the curses that are written in this **b** shall 5612
29:21 that are written in this **b** of the law: 5612
29:27 it all the curses that are written in this **b**: 5612
30:10 his statutes which are written in this **b** of 5612
31:24 end of writing the words of this law in a **b**, 5612

Dt 31:26 Take this **b** of the law, and put it in the side 5612
Jos 1: 8 This **b** of the law shall not depart out of thy 5612
8:31 as it is written in the **b** of the law of Moses, 5612
8:34 according to all that is written in the **b** of 5612
10:13 *Is* not this written in the **b** of Jasher? So 5612
18: 9 described it by cities into seven parts in a **b**, 5612
23: 6 to do all that is written in the **b** of the law 5612
24:26 Joshua wrote these words in the **b** of 5612
1Sa 10:25 wrote *it* in a **b**, and laid *it* up before 5612
2Sa 1:18 behold, *it is* written in the **b** of Jasher.) 5612
1Ki 11:41 *are* they not written in the **b** of the acts of 5612
14:19 behold they *are* written in the **b** of 5612
14:29 *are* they not written in the **b** of 5612
15: 7 *are* they not written in the **b** of 5612
15:23 *are* they not written in the **b** of 5612
15:31 *are* they not written in the **b** of 5612
16: 5 *are* they not written in the **b** of 5612
16:14 *are* they not written in the **b** of 5612
16:20 *are* they not written in the **b** of 5612
16:27 *are* they not written in the **b** of 5612
22:39 *are* they not written in the **b** of 5612
22:45 *are* they not written in the **b** of 5612
2Ki 1:18 *are* they not written in the **b** of 5612
8:23 *are* they not written in the **b** of 5612
10:34 *are* they not written in the **b** of 5612
12:19 *are* they not written in the **b** of 5612
13: 8 *are* they not written in the **b** of 5612
13:12 *are* they not written in the **b** of 5612
14: 6 is written in the **b** of the law of Moses, 5612
14:15 *are* they not written in the **b** of 5612
14:18 *are* they not written in the **b** of 5612
14:28 *are* they not written in the **b** of 5612
15: 6 *are* they not written in the **b** of 5612
15:11 they *are* written in the **b** of the chronicles of 5612
15:15 they *are* written in the **b** of the chronicles of 5612
15:21 *are* they not written in the **b** of 5612
15:26 they *are* written in the **b** of the chronicles of 5612
15:31 they *are* written in the **b** of the chronicles of 5612
15:36 *are* they not written in the **b** of 5612
16:19 *are* they not written in the **b** of 5612
20:20 *are* they not written in the **b** of 5612
21:17 *are* they not written in the **b** of 5612
21:25 *are* they not written in the **b** of 5612
22: 8 I have found the **b** of the law in the house 5612
22: 8 Hilkiah gave the **b** to Shaphan, and he read 5612
22:10 Hilkiah the priest hath delivered me a **b**. 5612
22:11 when the king had heard the words of the **b** 5612
22:13 concerning the words of this **b** that is 5612
22:13 not hearkened unto the words of this **b**, 5612
22:16 *even* all the words of the **b** which the king 5612
23: 2 he read in their ears all the words of the **b** 5612
23: 3 of this covenant that were written in this **b**. 5612
23:21 as it is written in the **b** of this covenant. 5612
23:24 **b** that Hilkiah the priest found *in* the house 5612
23:28 *are* they not written in the **b** of 5612
24: 5 *are* they not written in the **b** of 5612
1Ch 9: 1 they *were* written in the **b** of the kings of 5612
29:29 they *are* written in the **b** of Samuel the seer, 1697
29:29 in the **b** of Nathan the prophet, and in 1697
29:29 the prophet, and in the **b** of Gad the seer, 1697
2Ch 9:29 *are* they not written in the **b** of Nathan 1697
12:15 *are* they not written in the **b** of Shemaiah 1697
16:11 they *are* written in the **b** of the kings of 5612
17: 9 *had* the **b** of the law of the LORD with 5612
20:34 behold they *are* written in the **b** of Jehu 1697
20:34 who is mentioned in the **b** of the kings of 5612
24:27 behold they *are* written in the story of the **b** 5612
25: 4 *did* as it is written in the law in the **b** of 5612
25:26 *are* they not written in the **b** of the kings of 5612
27: 7 lo they *are* written in the **b** of the kings of 5612
28:26 they *are* written in the **b** of the kings of 5612
32:32 *and* in the **b** of the kings of Judah and 5612
33:18 they *are written* in the **b** of the kings of 1697
34:14 Hilkiah the priest found a **b** of the law of 5612
34:15 I have found the **b** of the law in the house 5612
34:15 And Hilkiah delivered the **b** to Shaphan. 5612
34:16 Shaphan carried the **b** to the king, and 5612
34:18 Hilkiah the priest hath given me a **b**. 5612
34:21 concerning the words of the **b** that is found: 5612
34:21 to do after all that is written in this **b**. 5612
34:24 *even* all the curses that are written in the **b** 5612
34:30 he read in their ears all the words of the **b** 5612
34:31 of the covenant which are written in this **b**. 5612
35:12 as it is written in the **b** of Moses. 5612
35:27 they *are* written in the **b** of the kings of 5612
36: 8 they *are* written in the **b** of the kings of 5612
Ezr 4:15 That search may be made in the **b** of 5609
4:15 so shalt thou find in the **b** of the records, 5609
6:18 as it is written in the **b** of Moses. 5609
Ne 8: 1 scribe to bring the **b** of the law of Moses, 5612
8: 3 people *were attentive* unto the **b** of the law. 5612
8: 5 Ezra opened the **b** in the sight of all 5612
8: 8 So they read in the **b** in the law of God 5612
8:18 last day, he read in the **b** of the law of God. 5612
9: 3 read in the **b** of the law of the LORD their 5612
12:23 *were* written in the **b** of the chronicles, 5612
13: 1 On that day they read in the **b** of Moses in 5612
Est 2:23 it was written in the **b** of the chronicles 5612
6: 1 he commanded to bring the **b** of records of 5612
9:32 of Purim; and *it was* written in the **b**. 5612
10: 2 *are* they not written in the **b** of 5612
Job 19:23 O that they were printed in a **b**! 5612
31:35 and *that* mine adversary had written a **b**. 5612
Ps 40: 7 in the volume of the **b** *it is* written of me, 5612
56: 8 tears into thy bottle: *are they* not in thy **b**? 5612
69:28 Let them be blotted out of the **b** of 5612
139:16 in thy **b** all *my members* were written, 5612
Isa 29:11 unto you as the words of a **b** that is sealed, 5612
29:12 the **b** is delivered to *him* that is not learned, 5612
29:18 day shall the deaf hear the words of the **b**, 5612
30: 8 it before them in a table, and note it in a **b**, 5612
34:16 Seek ye out of the **b** of the LORD, and 5612
Jer 25:13 *even* all that is written in this **b**, which 5612
30: 2 words that I have spoken unto thee in a **b**. 5612
32:12 that subscribed the **b** of the purchase, 5612
Jer 36: 2 Take thee a roll of a **b**, and write therein all 5612
36: 4 he had spoken unto him, upon a roll of a **b**. 5612
36: 8 reading in the **b** the words of the LORD *in* 5612
36:10 read Baruch in the **b** the words of Jeremiah 5612
36:11 had heard out of the **b** all the words of 5612
36:13 when Baruch read the **b** in the ears of 5612
36:18 and I wrote *them* with ink in the **b**. 5612
36:32 **b** which Jehoiakim king of Judah had burnt 5612
45: 1 when he had written these words in a **b** at 5612
51:60 So Jeremiah wrote in a **b** all the evil that 5612
51:63 thou hast made an end of reading this **b**, 5612
Eze 2: 9 unto me; and lo, a roll of a **b** *was* therein; 5612
Da 12: 1 one that *shall* be found written in the **b**. 5612
12: 4 O Daniel, shut up the words, and seal the **b**, 5612
Na 1: 1 The **b** of the vision of Nahum 5612
Mal 3:16 a **b** of remembrance was written before him 5612
Mt 1: 1 The **b** of the generation of Jesus Christ, *976*
Mk 12:26 have ye not read in the **b** of Moses, how in *976*
Lk 3: 4 As it is written in the **b** of the words of *976*
4:17 And there was delivered unto him the **b** of *975*
4:17 And when he had opened the **b**, he found *975*
4:20 And he closed the **b**, and he gave *it* again to *975*
20:42 And David himself saith in the **b** of Psalms, *976*
Jn 20:30 his disciples, which are not written in this **b**: *975*
Ac 1:20 For it is written in the **b** of Psalms, Let his *976*
7:42 as it is written in the **b** of the prophets, O *ye* *976*
Gal 3:10 are written in the **b** of the law to do them. *975*
Php 4: 3 whose names *are* in the **b** of life. *976*
Heb 9:19 and sprinkled both the **b**, and all the people, *975*
10: 7 I come (in the volume of the **b** it is written of *975*
Rev 1:11 write in a **b**, and send *it* unto the seven *975*
3: 5 I will not blot out his name out of the **b** of *976*
5: 1 him that sat on the throne a **b** written within *975*
5: 2 Who is worthy to open the **b**, and to loose *975*
5: 3 under the earth, was able to open the **b**, *975*
5: 4 was found worthy to open and to read the **b**, *975*
5: 5 hath prevailed to open the **b**, and to loose *975*
5: 7 took the **b** out of the right hand of him that *975*
5: 8 And when he had taken the **b**, the four beasts *975*
5: 9 Thou art worthy to take the **b**, and to open *975*
10: 2 And he had in his hand a **little b** open: and *974*
10: 8 take the **little b** which is open in the hand of *974*
10: 9 and said unto him, Give me the **little b**. *974*
10:10 And I took the **little b** out of the angel's *974*
13: 8 whose names are not written in the **b** of life *976*
17: 8 whose names were not written in the **b** of *975*
20:12 and another **b** was opened, which is *the book* *975*
20:12 book was opened, which is *the* **b** of life: NIG
20:15 in the **b** of life was cast into the lake of fire. *976*
21:27 they which are written in the Lamb's **b** of *975*
22: 7 the sayings of the prophecy of this **b**. *975*
22: 9 of them which keep the sayings of this **b**: *975*
22:10 not the sayings of the prophecy of this **b**: *975*
22:18 heareth the words of the prophecy of this **b**, *975*
22:18 him the plagues that are written in this **b**: *975*
22:19 from the words of the **b** of this prophecy, *976*
22:19 God shall take away his part out of the **b** of *976*
22:19 *from* the *things* which are written in this **b**. *975*

BOOKS (8) [BOOK]

Ecc 12:12 of making many **b** *there is* no end; and 5612
Da 7:10 judgment was set, and the **b** were opened. 5609
9: 2 understood by **b** the number of the years, 5612
Jn 21:25 not contain the **b** that should be written. *975*
Ac 19:19 used curious arts brought their **b** together, *976*
2Ti 4:13 bring *with thee*, and the **b**, *but* especially *975*
Rev 20:12 stand before God; and the **b** were opened: *975*
20:12 of those *things* which were written in the **b**, *975*

BOOTH (2) [BOOTHS]

Job 27:18 a moth, and as a **b** *that* the keeper maketh. 5521
Jnh 4: 5 there made him a **b**, and sat under it in 5521

BOOTHS (9) [BOOTH]

Ge 33:17 him a house, and made **b** for his cattle: 5521
Lev 23:42 Ye shall dwell in **b** seven days; all that are 5521
23:42 all that are Israelites born shall dwell in **b**: 5521
23:43 I made the children of Israel to dwell in **b**, 5521
Ne 8:14 that the children of Israel should dwell in **b** 5521
8:15 of thick trees, to make **b**, as it is written. 5521
8:16 and brought *them*, and made themselves **b**, 5521
8:17 come again out of the captivity made **b**, 5521
8:17 captivity made booths, and sat under the **b**: 5521

BOOTIES (1) [BOOTY]

Hab 2: 7 and thou shalt be for **b** unto them? 4933

BOOTY (3) [BOOTIES]

Nu 31:32 the **b**, *being* the rest of the prey which 4455
Jer 49:32 their camels shall be a **b**, and the multitude 957
Zep 1:13 Therefore their goods shall become a **b**, 4933

BOOZ (3) [BOAZ]

Mt 1: 5 And Salmon begat **B** of Rachab; and *1003*
1: 5 and **B** begat Obed of Ruth; and Obed begat *1003*
Lk 3:32 *the son* of Obed, which was *the son* of **B**, *1003*

BOR ASHAN See CHOR-ASHAN

BORDER (158) [BORDERS]

Ge 10:19 the **b** of the Canaanites was from Sidon, 1366
49:13 of ships; and his **b** *shall be* unto Zidon. 3411
Ex 19:12 *not* up into the mount, or touch the **b** of it: 7097
25:25 thou shalt make unto it a **b** of a 4526
25:25 thou shalt make a golden crown to the **b** 4526
25:27 Over against the **b** shall the rings be for 4526
28:26 two ends of the breastplate in the **b** thereof, 8193
37:12 Also he made thereunto a **b** of a 4526
37:12 made a crown of gold for the **b** thereof 4526
37:14 Over against the **b** were the rings, 4526
39:19 upon the **b** of it, which *was* on the side of 8193
Nu 20:16 in Kadesh, a city in the uttermost of thy **b**: 1366
20:21 to give Israel passage through his **b**: 1366
21:13 for Arnon *is* the **b** of Moab, between Moab 1366
Nu 21:15 of Ar, and lieth upon the **b** of Moab. 1366
21:23 not suffer Israel to pass through his **b**: 1366
21:24 for the **b** of the children of Ammon *was* 1366
22:36 which *is* in the **b** of Arnon, which *is* in 1366
33:44 and pitched in Ije-abarim, in the **b** of Moab. 1366
34: 3 your south **b** shall be the outmost coast of 1366
34: 4 your **b** shall turn from the south to 1366
34: 5 the **b** shall fetch a compass from Azmon 1366
34: 6 *as for* the western **b**, you shall even have 1366
34: 6 you shall even have the great sea for a **b**: 1366
34: 6 sea for a border: this shall be your west **b**. 1366
34: 7 this shall be your north **b**: from the great 1366
34: 8 From mount Hor ye shall point out *your* **b** NIH
34: 8 the goings forth of the **b** shall be to Zedad: 1366
34: 9 the **b** shall go on to Ziphron, and the goings 1366
34: 9 be at Hazar-enan: this shall be your north **b**. 1366
34:10 ye shall point out your east **b** from 1366
34:11 the **b** shall descend, and shall reach unto 1366
34:12 the **b** shall go down to Jordan, and 1366
35:26 *without* the **b** of the city of his refuge, 1366
Dt 3:16 half the valley, and the **b**, even unto 1366
3:16 *which is* the **b** of the children of Ammon; 1366
12:20 the LORD thy God shall enlarge thy **b**, 1366
Jos 4:19 in Gilgal, in the east **b** of Jericho. 7097
12: 2 *which is* the **b** of the children of Ammon; 1366
12: 5 unto the **b** of the Geshurites and 1366
12: 5 the **b** of Sihon king of Heshbon. 1366
13:10 unto the **b** of the children of Ammon; 1366
13:11 the **b** of the Geshurites and Maachathites, 1366
13:23 the **b** of the children of Reuben was Jordan, 1366
13:23 the **b** *thereof*. This *was* the inheritance of 1366
13:26 and from Mahanaim unto the **b** of Debir; 1366
13:27 Sihon king of Heshbon, Jordan and *his* **b**, 1366
15: 1 *even* to the **b** of Edom, the wilderness of 1366
15: 2 their south **b** was from the shore of the salt 1366
15: 5 the east **b** *was* the salt sea, *even* unto 1366
15: 5 *their* **b** in the north quarter *was* from 1366
15: 6 the **b** went up *to* Beth-hogla, and 1366
15: 6 the **b** went up *to* the stone of Bohan the son 1366
15: 7 the **b** went up toward Debir from the valley 1366
15: 7 the **b** passed towards the waters of 1366
15: 8 the **b** went up *by* the valley of the son of 1366
15: 8 the **b** went up to the top of the mountain 1366
15: 9 the **b** was drawn from the top of the hill 1366
15: 9 the **b** was drawn *to* Baalah, which *is* 1366
15:10 the **b** compassed from Baalah westward 1366
15:11 the **b** went out unto the side of Ekron 1366
15:11 the **b** was drawn to Shicron, and 1366
15:11 and the goings out of the **b** were at the sea. 1366
15:12 the west **b** *was* to the great sea, and 1366
15:47 and the great sea, and the **b** *thereof*. 1366
16: 5 the **b** of the children of Ephraim according 1366
16: 5 **b** of their inheritance on the east side was 1366
16: 6 the **b** went out toward the sea *to* 1366
16: 6 the **b** went about eastward *unto* 1366
16: 8 The **b** went *out* from Tappuah westward 1366
17: 7 the **b** went *along* on the right hand unto 1366
17: 8 Tappuah on the **b** of Manasseh *belonged* to 1366
17:10 *it was* Manasseh's, and the sea is his **b**; 1366
18:12 their **b** on the north side was from Jordan; 1366
18:12 the **b** went up to the side of Jericho on 1366
18:13 the **b** went over from thence toward Luz, 1366
18:13 the **b** descended *to* Ataroth-adar, near 1366
18:14 the **b** was drawn *thence*, and compassed 1366
18:15 the **b** went out on the west, and went out to 1366
18:16 the **b** came down to the end of 1366
18:19 the **b** passed along to the side of 1366
18:19 the outgoings of the **b** were at the north bay 1366
18:20 Jordan was the **b** of it on the east side. 1379
19:10 the **b** of their inheritance was unto Sarid: 1366
19:11 their **b** went up toward the sea, and 1366
19:12 the sunrising unto the **b** of Chisloth-tabor, 1366
19:14 the **b** compasseth it on the north side *to* 1366
19:18 their **b** was toward Jezreel, and Chesulloth, 1366
19:22 and the outgoings of their **b** were *at* Jordan: 1366
19:25 their **b** was Helkath, and Hali, and Beten, 1366
19:46 and Rakkon, with the **b** before Japho. 1366
22:25 For the LORD hath made Jordan a **b** 1366
24:30 they buried him in the **b** of his inheritance 1366
Jdg 2: 9 they buried him in the **b** of his inheritance 1366
7:22 *and* to the **b** of Abel-meholah, 8193
11:18 but came not within the **b** of Moab: 1366
11:18 of Moab: for Arnon *was* the **b** of Moab. 1366
1Sa 6:12 after them unto the **b** of Beth-shemesh. 1366
10: 2 sepulchre in the **b** of Benjamin at Zelzah; 1366
13:18 another company turned *to* the way of the **b** 1366
2Sa 8: 3 as he went to recover his **b** at the river 3027
1Ki 4:21 of the Philistines, and unto the **b** of Egypt: 1366
2Ki 3:21 on armour, and upward, and stood in the **b**. 1366
2Ch 9:26 of the Philistines, and to the **b** of Egypt. 1366
Ps 78:54 he brought them to the **b** of his sanctuary, 1366
Pr 15:25 but he will establish the **b** of the widow. 1366
Isa 19:19 and a pillar at the **b** thereof to the LORD. 1366
37:24 I will enter *into* the height of his **b**, *and* 7093
Jer 31:17 children shall come again to their own **b**. 1366
50:26 Come against her from the **utmost b**, 7093
Eze 11:10 I will judge you in the **b** of Israel; and 1366
11:11 *but* I will judge you in the **b** of Israel: 1366
29:10 from the tower of Syene even unto the **b** of 1366
43:13 the **b** thereof by the edge thereof round 1366
43:17 the **b** about it *shall be* half a cubit; and 1366
43:20 of the settle, and upon the **b** round about: 1366
45: 7 from the west **b** unto the east border. 1366
45: 7 from the west border unto the east **b**. 1366
47:13 This *shall be* the **b**, whereby ye shall inherit 1366
47:15 this *shall be* the **b** of the land toward 1366
47:16 which *is* between the **b** of Damascus and 1366
47:16 border of Damascus and the **b** of Hamath; 1366
47:17 the **b** from the sea shall be Hazar-enan, 1366
47:17 the **b** of Damascus, and the north 1366
47:17 the north northward, and the **b** of Hamath. 1366
47:18 *by* Jordan, from the **b** unto the east sea. 1366
47:20 side also *shall be* the great sea from the **b**, 1366
48: 1 Hazar-enan, the **b** of Damascus northward, 1366
48: 2 by the **b** of Dan, from the east side unto 1366

B

Eze 48: 3 by the **b** of Asher, from the east side even 1366
48: 4 by the **b** of Naphtali, from the east side 1366
48: 5 by the **b** of Manasseh, from the east side 1366
48: 6 by the **b** of Ephraim, from the east side 1366
48: 7 by the **b** of Reuben, from the east side unto 1366
48: 8 by the **b** of Judah, from the east side unto 1366
48:12 *a thing* most holy by the **b** of the Levites. 1366
48:13 over against the **b** of the priests, the Levites 1366
48:21 thousand of the oblation toward the east **b**, 1366
48:21 and twenty thousand toward the west **b**, 1366
48:22 between the **b** of Judah and the border of 1366
48:22 the border of Judah and the **b** of Benjamin, 1366
48:24 by the **b** of Benjamin, from the east side 1366
48:25 by the **b** of Simeon, from the east side unto 1366
48:26 by the **b** of Issachar, from the east side unto 1366
48:27 by the **b** of Zebulun, from the east side unto 1366
48:28 by the **b** of Gad, at the south side 1366
48:28 the **b** shall be even from Tamar *unto* 1366
Joel 3: 6 that *ye* might remove them far from their **b**. 1366
Am 1:13 at Gilead, that *they* might enlarge their **b**: 1366
6: 2 or their **b** greater than your border? 1366
6: 2 or their border greater than your **b**? 1366
Ob 1: 7 have brought thee *even* to the **b**: 1366
Zep 2: 8 and magnified *themselves* against their **b**. 1366
Zec 9: 2 Hamath also shall **b** thereby; Tyrus, and 1379
Mal 1: 4 shall call them, The **b** of wickedness, and, 1366
1: 5 The LORD will be magnified from the **b** 1366
Mk 6:56 touch if it were but the **b** of his garment: *2899*
Lk 8:44 and touched the **b** of his garment: *2899*

BORDERS (43) [BORDER]

Ge 23:17 that *were* in all the **b** round about, 1366
47:21 **b** of Egypt even to the *other* end thereof. 1366
Ex 8: 2 behold, I will smite all thy **b** with frogs: 1366
16:35 until they came unto the **b** of the land of 7097
34:24 the nations before thee, and enlarge thy **b**: 1366
Nu 15:38 **b** of their garments throughout their 3671
15:38 that they put upon the fringe of the **b** a 3671
20:17 nor *to* the left, until we have passed thy **b**. 1366
21:22 the king's *high* way, until we be past thy **b**. 1366
35:27 him without the **b** of the city of his refuge, 1366
Jos 11: 2 the valley, and in the **b** of Dor on the west, 5299
13: 2 all the **b** of the Philistines, and all Geshuri, 1552
13: 3 even unto the **b** of Ekron northward, 1366
13: 4 unto Aphek, to the **b** of the Amorites: 1366
16: 2 passeth along unto the **b** of Archi *to* 1366
22:10 when they came unto the **b** of Jordan, 1552
22:11 in the **b** of Jordan, at the passage of 1552
1Ki 7:28 the bases *was on* this *manner:* they had **b**, 4526
7:28 and the **b** *were* between the ledges: 4526
7:29 on the **b** that *were* between the ledges *were* 4526
7:31 the mouth of it *were* gravings with their **b**, 4526
7:32 under the **b** *were* four wheels; and 4526
7:35 and the **b** thereof *were* of the same. 4526
7:36 on the **b** thereof, he graved cherubims, 4526
2Ki 16:17 king Ahaz cut off the **b** of the bases, and 4526
18: 8 *even* unto Gaza, and the **b** thereof, 1366
19:23 I will enter *into* the lodgings of his **b**, *and* 7093
1Ch 5:16 in all the suburbs of Sharon, upon their **b**. 8444
7:29 by the **b** of the children of Manasseh, 3027
Ps 74:17 Thou hast set all the **b** of the earth: 1367
147:14 He maketh peace *in* thy **b**, *and* filleth thee 1366
SS 1:11 We will make thee **b** of gold with studs of 8447
Isa 15: 8 For the cry is gone round about the **b** of 1366
54:12 and all thy **b** of pleasant stones. 1366
60:18 wasting nor destruction within thy **b**; 1366
Jer 15:13 and *that* for all thy sins, even in all thy **b**. 1366
17: 3 high places for sin, throughout all thy **b**. 1366
Eze 27: 4 Thy **b** *are* in the midst of the seas, 1366
45: 1 This *shall be* holy in all the **b** thereof round 1366
Mic 5: 6 and when he treadeth within our **b**. 1366
Mt 4:13 in the **b** of Zabulon and Nephthalim: *3725*
23: 5 and enlarge the **b** of their garments, *2899*
Mk 7:24 and went into the **b** of Tyre and Sidon, and *3181*

BORE (2) [BORED]

Ex 21: 6 his master shall **b** his ear **through** with an 7527
Job 41: 2 or **b** his jaw **through** with a thorn? 5344

BORED (1) [BORE]

2Ki 12: 9 **b** a hole in the lid of it, and set it beside 5344

BORN (154) [BEAR]

Ge 4:18 unto Enoch was **b** Irad: and Irad begat 3205
4:26 to Seth, *to* him also there was **b** a son; and 3205
6: 1 the earth, and daughters were **b** unto them, 3205
10: 1 and unto them were sons **b** after the flood. 3205
10:21 the elder, even to him were *children* **b**. 3205
10:25 unto Eber were **b** two sons: the name of 3205
14:14 he armed his trained *servants*, **b** in his own 3211
15: 3 and lo, **one b** in my house is mine heir. 1121
17:12 he **that is b** in the house, or bought with 3211
17:13 He **that is b** in thy house, and he that is 3211
17:17 Shall *a child* **b** unto him that is an 3205
17:23 all **that were b** in his house, and all that 3211
17:27 **b** in the house, and bought with money of 3211
21: 3 the name of his son that was **b** unto him, 3205
21: 5 when his son Isaac was **b** unto him. 3205
21: 7 for I have **b** *him* a son in his old age. 3205
21: 9 which she had **b** unto Abraham, mocking. 3205
22:20 she hath also **b** children unto thy brother 3205
24:15 who was **b** to Bethuel, son of Milcah, 3205
29:34 unto me, because I have **b** him three sons: 3205
30:20 with me, because I have **b** him six sons: 3205
30:25 it came to pass, when Rachel had **b** Joseph, 3205
31:43 or unto their children which they have **b**? 3205
35:26 which were **b** to him in Padan-aram. 3205
36: 5 which were **b** unto him in the land of 3205
41:50 unto Joseph were **b** two sons before 3205
46:20 unto Joseph in the land of Egypt were **b** 3205
46:22 the sons of Rachel, which were **b** to Jacob: 3205
46:27 which were **b** him in Egypt, *were* two 3205
48: 5 which were **b** unto thee in the land of Egypt 3205
Ex 1:22 Every son that is **b** ye shall cast into 3209
Ex 12:19 whether he be a stranger, or **b** in the land. 249
12:48 and he shall be as one that is **b** in the land: 249
21: 4 and she have **b** him sons or daughters; 3205
Lev 12: 2 have conceived seed, and **b** a man child: 3205
12: 7 This *is* the law for her that hath **b** a male or 3205
18: 9 *whether she be* **b** at home, or born abroad, 4138
18: 9 *whether she be* born at home, or **b** abroad, 4138
19:34 shall be unto you as **one b amongst** you, 249
22:11 shall eat of it, and **he that is b** in his house: 3211
23:42 all that are Israelites **b** shall dwell in booths: 249
24:16 well the stranger, as he **that is b in the land**, 249
Nu 9:14 and for him **that was b** in the land. 249
15:13 All that are **b of the country** shall do these 249
15:29 *both for* him **that is b** amongst the children 249
15:30 *whether he be* **b in the land**, or a stranger, 249
26:60 unto Aaron was **b** Nadab, and Abihu, 3205
Dt 21:15 and they have **b** him children, 3205
Jos 5: 5 all the people *that were* **b** in the wilderness 3209
8:33 the stranger, as he that was **b among** them; 249
Jdg 13: 8 we shall do unto the child that shall be **b**. 3205
18:29 of Dan their father, who was **b** unto Israel: 3205
Ru 4:15 better to thee than seven sons, hath **b** him. 3205
4:17 a name, saying, There is a son **b** to Naomi; 3205
1Sa 2: 5 so that the barren hath **b** seven; and she that 3205
4:20 *unto her,* Fear not; for thou hast **b** a son. 3205
2Sa 3: 2 unto David were sons **b** in Hebron: and 3205
3: 5 These were **b** to David in Hebron. 3205
5:13 were yet sons and daughters **b** to David. 3205
5:14 these *be* the names of those that were **b** 3209
12:14 the child also that is **b** unto thee shall surely 3209
14:27 unto Absalom there were **b** three sons, and 3205
21:20 *in* number; and he also was **b** to the giant. 3205
21:22 These four were **b** to the giant in Gath, and 3205
1Ki 13: 2 a child *shall be* **b** unto the house of David, 3205
1Ch 1:19 unto Eber were **b** two sons: the name of 3205
2: 3 *which* three were **b** unto him of 3205
2: 9 sons also of Hezron, that were **b** unto him; 3205
3: 1 which were **b** unto him in Hebron; 3205
3: 4 *These* six were **b** unto him in Hebron; and 3205
3: 5 these were **b** unto him in Jerusalem; 3205
7:21 whom the men of Gath that were **b** in *that* 3205
20: 8 These were **b** unto the giant in Gath; and 3205
22: 9 Behold, a son *shall be* **b** to thee, who shall 3205
26: 6 Also unto Shemaiah his son were sons **b**, 3205
Ezr 10: 3 such as are **b** of them, according to 3205
Job 1: 2 there were **b** unto him seven sons and 3205
3: 3 Let the day perish wherein I was **b**, and 3205
5: 7 Yet man is **b** unto trouble, as the sparks fly 3205
11:12 though man be **b** *like* a wild ass's colt. 3205
14: 1 Man *that is* **b** of a woman *is* of few days, 3205
15: 7 *Art* thou the first man *that* was **b**? or 3205
15:14 *he which is* **b** of a woman, that he should 3205
25: 4 how can he be clean *that is* **b** of a woman? 3205
38:21 Knowest thou *it*, because thou wast then **b**? 3205
Ps 22:31 righteousness unto a people that *shall be* **b**, 3205
58: 3 they go astray **as soon as** they be **b**, 990+4480
78: 6 *them, even* the children *which* should be **b**; 3205
87: 4 Tyre, with Ethiopia; this *man* was **b** there. 3205
87: 5 be said, This and that man was **b** in her: 3205
87: 6 *up* the people, *that* this *man* was **b** there. 3205
Pr 17:17 at all times, and a brother is **b** for adversity. 3205
Ecc 2: 7 maidens, and had servants **b** in *my* house; 1121
3: 2 A time to be **b**, and a time to die; a time to 3205
4:14 whereas also *he that is* **b** in his kingdom 3205
Isa 9: 6 For unto us a child is **b**, unto us a Son is 3205
66: 8 *or* shall a nation be **b** at once? for as soon 3205
Jer 16: 3 concerning the daughters that are **b** in this 3209
20:14 Cursed *be* the day wherein I was **b**: let not 3205
20:15 saying, A man child is **b** unto thee; 3205
22:26 into another country, where ye were not **b**; 3205
Eze 16: 4 in the day thou wast **b** thy navel was not 3205
16: 5 of thy person, in the day that thou wast **b**. 3205
47:22 they shall be unto you as **b in the country** 249
Hos 2: 3 and set her as *in* the day that she was **b**, and 3205
Mt 1:16 of whom was **b** Jesus, who is called Christ. *1080*
2: 1 Now when Jesus was **b** in Bethlehem of *1080*
2: 2 Where is he that is **b** King of the Jews? *5088*
2: 4 of them where Christ should be **b**. *1080*
11:11 Among *them that are* **b** of women there *1084*
19:12 so **b** from *their* mother's womb: *1080*
26:24 good for that man if he had not been **b**. *1080*
Mk 14:21 were it for that man if he had never been **b**. *1080*
Lk 1:35 also *that* holy thing which shall be **b** of thee *1080*
2:11 For unto you is **b** this day in the city of *5088*
7:28 Among *those that are* **b** of women there is *1084*
Jn 1:13 Which were **b**, not of blood, nor of the will *1080*
3: 3 I say unto thee, Except a man be **b** again, *1080*
3: 4 How can a man be **b** when he is old? *1080*
3: 4 time into his mother's womb, and be **b**? *1080*
3: 5 Except a man be **b** of water and *of* *1080*
3: 6 That which is **b** of the flesh is flesh; and *1080*
3: 6 and that which is **b** of the Spirit is spirit. *1080*
3: 7 that I said unto thee, Ye must be **b** again. *1080*
3: 8 so is every one that is **b** of the Spirit. *1080*
8:41 they to him, We be not **b** of fornication; *1080*
9: 2 or his parents, that he was **b** blind? *1080*
9:19 Is this your son, who ye say was **b** blind? *1080*
9:20 that this is our son, and that he was **b** blind: *1080*
9:32 opened the eyes of one that was **b** blind. *1080*
9:34 Thou wast altogether **b** in sins, and *1080*
16:21 for joy that a man is **b** into the world. *1080*
18:37 To this end was I **b**, and for this cause came *1080*
Ac 2: 8 in our own tongue, wherein we were **b**? *1080*
7:20 In which time Moses was **b**, and *1080*
18: 2 **b** in Pontus, lately come from Italy, *1085*
18:24 **b** at Alexandria, an eloquent man, *and* *1085*
22: 3 *am* a Jew, **b** in Tarsus, *a city* in Cilicia, *1080*
22:28 And Paul said, But I was *free* **b**. *1080*
Ro 9:11 (For *the children* being not yet **b**, *1080*
1Co 15: 8 of me also, as of one **b out of due time**. *1626*
Gal 4:23 But he who was of the bondwoman was **b** *1080*
4:29 he that was **b** after the flesh persecuted him *1080*
4:29 persecuted him that was *b* after the Spirit, NIG
Heb 11:23 By faith Moses, when he was **b**, was hid *1080*
1Pe 1:23 Being **b again**, not of corruptible seed, but *313*
1Jn 2:29 one which doeth righteousness is **b** of him. *1080*
3: 9 Whosoever is **b** of God doth not commit *1080*
3: 9 and he cannot sin, because he is **b** of God. *1080*
4: 7 and every one that loveth is **b** of God, and *1080*
5: 1 that Jesus is the Christ is **b** of God: *1080*
5: 4 For whatsoever is **b** of God overcometh *1080*
5:18 We know that whosoever is **b** of God *1080*
Rev 12: 4 for to devour her child as soon as it was **b**. *5088*

BORN OF A FORBIDDEN MARRIAGE See BASTARD; BASTARDS

BORNE (31) [BEAR]

Ex 25:14 of the ark, that the ark may be **b** with them. 5375
25:28 that the table may be **b** with them. 5375
Jdg 16:29 on which it was **b up**, of the one with his 5564
Job 34:31 I have **b** *chastisement*, I will not offend 5375
Ps 55:12 I could have **b** *it:* neither *was it* he that 5375
69: 7 Because for thy sake I have **b** reproach; 5375
Isa 46: 3 which are **b** *by me* from the belly, 6006
53: 4 Surely he hath **b** our griefs, and carried our 5375
66:12 ye shall be **b** upon *her* sides, and 5375
Jer 10: 5 they **must needs be b**, because 5375+5375
15: 9 She that hath **b** seven languisheth: she hath 3205
15:10 that thou hast **b** me a man of strife and 3205
La 3:28 because he hath **b** *it* upon him. 5190
5: 7 *and are* not; *and* we have **b** their iniquities. 5445
Eze 16:20 whom thou hast **b** unto me, and these hast 3205
16:58 Thou hast **b** thy lewdness and thine 5375
32:24 yet have they **b** their shame with them that 5375
32:25 yet have they **b** their shame with them that 5375
36: 6 ye have **b** the shame of the heathen: 5375
39:26 After that they have **b** their shame, and all 5375
Am 5:26 ye have **b** the tabernacle of your Moloch 5375
Mt 20:12 which have **b** the burden and heat of the day. *941*
23: 4 bind heavy burdens and **grievous to be b**, *1419*
Mk 2: 3 one sick of the palsy, *which was* **b** of four. *142*
Lk 11:46 ye lade men *with* burdens **grievous to be b**, *1419*
Jn 5:37 which hath sent me, hath **b witness** of me. *3140*
20:15 if thou have **b** him *hence*, tell me where thou *941*
Ac 21:35 that he was **b** of the soldiers for the violence *941*
1Co 15:49 And as we have **b** the image of the earthy, *5409*
3Jn 1: 6 Which have **b witness** of thy charity before *3140*
Rev 2: 3 And hast **b**, and hast patience, and for my *941*

BORROW (8) [BORROWED, BORROWER, BORROWETH]

Ex 3:22 every woman shall **b** of her neighbour, and 7592
11: 2 let every man **b** of his neighbour, and 7592
22:14 if a man **b** *ought* of his neighbour, and it be 7592
Dt 15: 6 unto many nations, but thou shalt not **b**; 5670
28:12 unto many nations, and thou shalt not **b**. 3867
2Ki 4: 3 **b** thee vessels abroad of all thy neighbours, 7592
4: 3 *even* empty vessels; **b** not a few. NIH
Mt 5:42 from him that would **b** of thee turn not thou *1155*

BORROWED (3) [BORROW]

Ex 12:35 they **b** of the Egyptians jewels of silver, 7592
2Ki 6: 5 and said, Alas, master, for it *was* **b**. 7592
Ne 5: 4 We have **b** money for the king's tribute, 3867

BORROWER (2) [BORROW]

Pr 22: 7 the poor, and the **b** *is* servant to the lender. 3867
Isa 24: 2 the seller; as *with* the lender, so *with* the **b**; 3867

BORROWETH (1) [BORROW]

Ps 37:21 The wicked **b**, and payeth not again: but 3867

BOSCATH (1)

2Ki 22: 1 *was* Jedidah, the daughter of Adaiah of **B**. 1218

BOSOM (41)

Ge 16: 5 I have given my maid into thy **b**; and 2436
Ex 4: 6 unto him, Put now thine hand into thy **b**. 2436
4: 6 he put his hand into his **b**: and when he 2436
4: 7 he said, Put thine hand into thy **b** again. 2436
4: 7 he put his hand into his **b** again; and 2436
4: 7 plucked it out of his **b**, and behold, it was 2436
Nu 11:12 shouldest say unto me, Carry them in thy **b**, 2436
Dt 13: 6 or the wife of thy **b**, or thy friend, 2436
28:54 toward the wife of his **b**, and towards 2436
28:56 shall be evil towards the husband of her **b**, 2436
Ru 4:16 laid it in her **b**, and became nurse unto it. 2436
2Sa 12: 3 lay in his **b**, and was unto him as a 2436
12: 8 thy master's wives into thy **b**, and 2436
1Ki 1: 2 let her cherish him, and let her lie in thy **b**, 2436
3:20 laid it in her **b**, and laid her dead child in 2436
3:20 her bosom, and laid her dead child in my **b**. 2436
17:19 he took him out of her **b**, and carried him 2436
Job 31:33 as Adam, by hiding mine iniquity in my **b**: 2243
Ps 35:13 and my prayer returned into mine own **b**. 2436
74:11 even thy right hand? pluck *it* out of thy **b**. 2436
79:12 sevenfold into their **b** their reproach, 2436
89:50 *how* I do bear in my **b** *the reproach of* all 2436
129: 7 his hand; nor he that bindeth sheaves his **b**. 2683
Pr 5:20 and embrace the **b** of a stranger? 2436
6:27 Can a man take fire in his **b**, and his clothes 2436
17:23 A wicked *man* taketh a gift out of the **b** to 2436
19:24 A slothful *man* hideth his hand in *his* **b**, and 6747
21:14 and a reward in the **b** strong wrath. 2436
26:15 The slothful hideth his hand in *his* **b**; 6747
Ecc 7: 9 be angry: for anger resteth in the **b** of fools. 2436
Isa 40:11 carry *them* in his **b**, *and* shall gently lead 2436
65: 6 even recompense into their **b**, 2436
65: 7 I measure their former work into their **b**. 2436
Jer 32:18 into the **b** of their children after them: 2436
La 2:12 soul was poured out into their mothers' **b**. 2436
Mic 7: 5 of thy mouth from her that lieth in thy **b**. 2436
Lk 6:38 running over, shall *men* give into your **b**. *2859*
16:22 carried by the angels into Abraham's **b**: *2859*
16:23 Abraham afar off, and Lazarus in his **b**. *2859*
Jn 1:18 which is in the **b** of the Father, he hath *2859*
13:23 Now there was leaning on Jesus' **b** one of *2859*

BOSOR (1) [BEOR]
2Pe 2:15 following the way of Balaam *the son of* **B**, *1007*

BOSSES (1)
Job 15:26 *his* neck, upon the thick **b** of his bucklers: 1354

BOTCH (2)
Dt 28:27 The LORD will smite thee with the **b** of 7822
28:35 with a sore **b** that cannot be healed, 7822

BOTH (361)
Ge 2:25 they were **b** naked, the man and his wife, 8147
3: 7 the eyes of them **b** were opened, and 8147
6: 7 **b** man, and beast, and the creeping thing, 4480
7:21 ***b*** of fowl, and of cattle, and of beast, and NIH
7:23 **b** man, and cattle, and the creeping things, 4480
8:17 ***b*** of fowl, and of cattle, and of every NIH
9:23 laid *it* upon **b** their shoulders, and 8147
19: 4 the house round, **b** old and young, 4480+5704
19:11 with blindness, **b** small and great: 4480+5704
19:36 Thus were **b** the daughters of Lot with 8147
21:27 and **b** of them made a covenant. 8147
21:31 because there they sware **b** of them. 8147
22: 6 a knife; and they went **b** of them together. 8147
22: 8 so they went **b** of them together. 8147
24:25 We have **b** straw and provender enough, 1571
24:44 **B** drink thou, and I will also draw for thy 1571
27:45 why should I be deprived also of you **b** *in* 8147
31:37 that they may judge betwixt us **b**. 8147
36:24 the children of Zibeon; **b** Aiah, and Anah: 2050.1
40: 5 they dreamed a dream **b** of them, each man 8147
41:10 the guard's house, ***b*** me and the chief baker: NIH
42:35 when ***b*** they and their father saw NIH
43: 8 **b** we, and thou, *and* also our little ones. 1571
44: 9 **b** let him die, and we also will be my 2050.1
44:16 **b** we, and *he* also with whom the cup is 1571
46:34 even until now, **b** we, *and* also our fathers: 1571
47: 3 *are* shepherds, **b** we, *and* also our fathers. 1571
47:19 die before thine eyes, **b** we and our land? 1571
48:13 Joseph took them **b**, Ephraim in his right 8147
50: 9 there went up with him **b** chariots and 1571
Ex 5:14 your task in making brick **b** yesterday 1571
7:19 **b** in *vessels of* wood, and in *vessels of* 2050.1
8: 4 the frogs shall come up ***b*** on thee, and NIH
9:25 *was* in the field, **b** man and beast; 4480+5704
12:12 the land of Egypt, **b** man and beast; 4480+5704
12:31 my people, **b** you and the children of Israel; 1571
13: 2 the children of Israel, ***b*** of man and of beast: NIH
13:15 **b** the firstborn of man, and 4480+5704
18:18 **b** thou, and this people that *is* with thee: 1571
22: 9 the cause of **b** parties shall come before 8147
22:11 an oath of the LORD be between them **b**, 8147
26:24 thus shall it be for them **b**; they shall be for 8147
29:44 I will sanctify also **b** Aaron and his sons, NIH
32:15 the tables *were* written on **b** their sides; 8147
35:22 they came, **b** men **and** women, as many as 5921
35:25 ***b*** of blue, and of purple, *and* of scarlet, NIH
35:34 ***b*** he, and Aholiab, the son of Ahisamach, NIH
36:29 thus he did to **b** of them in both the corners. 8147
36:29 thus he did to both of them in **b** the corners. 8147
37:26 ***b*** the top of it, and the sides thereof round NIH
Lev 6:28 it shall be **b** scoured, and rinsed in water. 2050.1
8:11 all his vessels, **b** the laver and his foot, 2050.1
9: 3 a calf and a lamb, **b** of the first year, NIH
15:18 they shall ***b*** bathe *themselves* in water, and NIH
16:21 Aaron shall lay **b** his hands upon the head 8147
17:15 he shall **b** wash his clothes, and 2050.1
20:11 **b** of them shall surely be put to death; their 8147
20:12 **b** of them shall surely be put to death: 8147
20:13 **b** of them have committed an abomination: 8147
20:14 they shall be burnt with fire, **b** he **and** 2050.1
20:18 **b** of them shall be cut off from among their 8147
21:22 his God, ***b*** of the most holy, and of the holy. NIH
22:28 shall not kill it and her young **b** in one day. NIH
25:41 ***b*** he and his children with him, and NIH
25:44 **B** thy bondmen, and thy bondmaids, 2050.1
25:54 of jubile, ***b*** he, and his children with him. NIH
27:28 ***b*** of man and beast, and of the field of his NIH
27:33 **b** it **and** the change thereof shall be holy; 2050.1
Nu 3:13 all the firstborn in Israel, **b** man and beast: 4480
5: 3 **B** male and female shall ye put out, without 4480
7: 1 **b** the altar and all the vessels thereof, and 2050.1
7:13 **b** of them *were* full *of* fine flour mingled 8147
7:19 **b** of them full *of* fine flour mingled with oil 8147
7:25 **b** of them full *of* fine flour mingled with oil 8147
7:31 **b** of them full *of* fine flour mingled with oil 8147
7:37 **b** of them full *of* fine flour mingled with oil 8147
7:43 **b** of them full *of* fine flour mingled with oil 8147
7:49 **b** of them full *of* fine flour mingled with oil 8147
7:55 **b** of them full *of* fine flour mingled with oil 8147
7:61 **b** of them full *of* fine flour mingled with oil 8147
7:67 **b** of them full *of* fine flour mingled with oil 8147
7:73 **b** of them full *of* fine flour mingled with oil 8147
7:79 **b** of them full *of* fine flour mingled with oil 8147
8:17 of Israel *are* mine, ***b*** man and beast: NIH
9:14 **b** for the stranger, and for him that was 2050.1
12: 5 and Miriam: and they **b** came forth. 8147
15:15 One ordinance *shall be* **b** for you *of* NIH
15:29 ***b*** *for* him that is born amongst the children NIH
16:11 For which cause ***b*** thou and all thy company NIH
25: 8 thrust **b** of them through, the man of Israel, 8147
27:21 ***b*** he, and all the children of Israel with him, NIH
31:11 and all the prey, ***b*** of men and of beasts. NIH
31:19 purify ***b*** yourselves and your captives on NIH
31:26 ***b*** of man and of beast, thou, and Eleazar NIH
31:28 ***b*** of the persons, and of the beeves, and NIH
31:47 ***b*** of man and of beast, and gave them unto NIH
35:15 ***b*** for the children of Israel, and for NIH
Dt 19:17 **b** the men, between whom the controversy 8147
21:15 him children, ***b*** the beloved and the hated; NIH
22:22 they shall **b** of them die, *both* the man that 8147
22:22 ***b*** the man that lay with the woman, and NIH
22:24 ye shall bring them **b** out unto the gate of 8147
23:18 for even **b** these *are* abomination unto 8147
Dt 30:19 that ***b*** thou and thy seed may live: NIH
32:25 shall destroy **b** the young man and 1571
Jos 6:21 **b** man and woman, young and old, 4480+5704
8:25 **b** of men and women, *were* twelve 4480+5704
14:11 for war, **b** to go out, and to come in. 2050.1
17:16 ***b*** *they* who *are* of Beth-shean and NIH
Jdg 5:30 of divers colours of needlework on **b** sides, NIH
6: 5 *for* **b** they and their camels were without 2050.1
8:22 **b** thou, and thy son, and thy son's son also: 1571
10:10 **b** because we have forsaken our God, and 2050.1
15: 5 burnt up **b** the shocks, and also the standing 4480
19: 6 and did eat and drink **b** of them together: 8147
19: 8 until afternoon, and they did eat **b** of them. 8147
19:19 Yet there is **b** straw and provender for our 1571
Ru 1: 5 and Chilion died also **b** of them; 8147
1Sa 2:26 was in favour **b** with the LORD, and 1571
2:34 in one day they shall die **b** of them. 8147
3:11 *at* which **b** the ears of every one that 8147
5: 4 **b** the palms of his hands *were* cut off upon 8147
5: 9 **b** small and great, and they had emerods in 4480
6:18 ***b*** of fenced cities, and of country villages, NIH
9:26 they went out **b** of them, he and Samuel, 8147
12:14 shall **b** ye and also the king that reigneth 1571
12:25 ye shall be consumed, **b** ye and your king. 1571
14:11 **b** of them discovered themselves unto 8147
15: 3 slay **b** man and woman, infant and 4480
17:36 Thy servant slew **b** the lion and the bear: 1571
20:11 And they went out **b** of them *into* the field. 8147
20:42 forasmuch as we have sworn **b** of us in 8147
22:19 **b** men and women, children and sucklings, 4480
25: 6 liveth *in prosperity,* Peace *be* **b** *to* thee, 2050.1
25:16 They were a wall unto us **b** by night and 1571
25:43 and they were also **b** of them his wives. 8147
26:25 thou shalt **b** do great things, and also shalt 1571
2Sa 8:18 Benaiah the son of Jehoiada *was over* **b** 2050.1
9:13 king's table; and *was* lame on **b** his feet. 8147
15:25 and shew me **b** it, and his habitation: NIH
16:23 *was* all the counsel of Ahithophel **b** with 1571
17:18 they went **b** of them away quickly, and 8147
1Ki 3:13 thou hast not asked, **b** riches, and honour: 1571
6: 5 ***b*** of the temple and of the oracle: NIH
6:15 **b** the floor of the house, and the walls of 4480
6:16 **b** the floor and the walls with boards of 4480
6:25 **b** the cherubims *were* of one measure and 8147
7:12 **b** for the inner court of the house of 2050.1
7:50 *of* gold, **b** for the doors of the inner house, NIH
2Ki 2:11 horses of fire, and parted them **b** asunder; 8147
3:17 ***b*** ye, and your cattle, and your beasts. NIH
6:15 a host compassed the city **b** with horses 2050.1
17:41 **b** their children, and their children's 1571
21:12 heareth of it, **b** his ears shall tingle. 8147
23: 2 all the people, **b** small and great: 4480+3807.1
23:15 **b** that altar and the high place he brake 1571
25:26 **b** small and great, and the captains of 4480
1Ch 12: 2 could use **b** the right hand and the left in NIH
12:15 ***b*** toward the east, and toward the west. NIH
15:12 sanctify yourselves, ***b*** ye and your brethren, NIH
16: 3 **b** man and woman, to every one a loaf of 4480
23:29 **B** for the shewbread, and for the fine 2050.1
24: 3 **b** Zadok of the sons of Eleazar, and 2050.1
28:15 ***b*** for the candlestick, and *also for* the lamps NIH
29:12 **B** riches and honour *come* of thee, and 2050.1
2Ch 20:25 they found among them in abundance **b** 2050.1
24:16 **b** towards God, and *towards* his house. 2050.1
25:21 ***b*** he and Amaziah king of Judah, NIH
26:10 **b** in the low country, and in the plains: 2050.1
27: 5 **b** the second year, and the third. 2050.1
31:17 **B** *to* the genealogy of the priests by 2050.1
32:26 ***b*** he and the inhabitants of Jerusalem, so NIH
Ezr 3: 5 **b** of the new moons, and of all the set 2050.1
6: 9 **b** young bullocks, and rams, and lambs, 2050.3
Ne 1: 6 **b** I and my father's house have sinned. 2050.1
4:16 the *other* half of them held **b** the spears, 2050.1
8: 2 the law before the congregation **b of** 4480+5704
10: 9 **b** Jeshua the son of Azaniah, Binnui of 2050.1
12:27 **b** with thanksgivings, and with singing, 2050.1
12:28 **b** out of the plain country round about 2050.1
12:45 **b** the singers and the porters kept 2050.1
Est 1: 5 **b** unto great and small, seven days, in 4480
1:20 **b** to great and small. 4480+3807.1
2:23 therefore they were **b** hanged on a tree: 8147
3:13 all Jews, **b** young and old, little children 4480
8:11 ***b*** little ones and women, and *to take* NIH
9:20 of the king Ahasuerus, ***b*** nigh and far, NIH
Job 9:33 *that* might lay his hand upon us **b**. 8147
15:10 With us *are* **b** the grayheaded and 1571
Ps 4: 8 I will **b** lay me down in peace, and sleep: 3162
49: 2 **B** low and high, rich and poor, together. 1571
58: 9 a whirlwind, **b** living, and in *his* wrath. 3644
64: 6 **b** the inward *thought* of every one *of* 2050.1
76: 6 **b** the chariot and horse *are* cast into a 2050.1
104:25 **b** small and great beasts. 2050.1
115:13 that fear the LORD, ***b*** small and great. NIH
135: 8 the firstborn of Egypt, **b** of man and beast. NIH
139:12 and the light *are* **b** alike *to thee.* NIH
148:12 **B** young men, and maidens; old men, and 2050.1
Pr 17:15 even they **b** *are* abomination to 8147
20:10 **b** of them *are* alike abomination to 8147
20:12 the LORD hath made even **b** of them. 8147
24:22 and who knoweth the ruin of them **b**? 8147
26:10 The great *God* that formed all *things* **b** 2050.1
27: 3 but a fool's wrath *is* heavier than them **b**. 8147
29:13 the LORD lighteneth **b** their eyes. 8147
Ecc 4: 3 Yea, better *is he* than **b** *they,* which hath 8147
4: 6 than **b** the **hands** full *with* travail and 2651
8: 5 a wise *man's* heart discerneth ***b*** time and NIH
11: 6 that, or whether they ***b*** *shall be* alike good. 8147
Isa 1:31 they shall **b** burn together, and none shall 8147
7:16 abhorrest shall be forsaken of **b** her kings. 8147
8:14 for a rock of offence to **b** the houses of 8147
10:18 and of his fruitful field, **b** soul and body: 4480
13: 9 cruel **b** *with* wrath and fierce anger, to lay 2050.1
18: 5 he shall **b** cut off the sprigs with pruning 2050.1
31: 3 **b** he that helpeth shall fall, and he that is 2050.1
38:15 he hath **b** spoken unto me, and 2050.1
Isa 44:12 The smith *with* the tongs **b** worketh in 2050.1
Jer 5:24 **b** the former and the latter, in his season: NIH
9:10 **b** the fowl of the heavens and the beast are 4480
14:18 **b** the prophet and the priest go about into a 1571
16: 6 **B** the great and the small shall die in this 2050.1
21: 6 inhabitants of this city, **b** man and beast: 2050.1
23:11 For **b** prophet and priest are profane; yea, 1571
26: 5 **b** rising up early, and sending *them,* but 2050.1
28: 8 before thee of old prophesied **b** against 2050.1
31:13 the dance, **b** young men and old together: 2050.1
32:11 ***b*** that which was sealed *according to* NIH
32:14 **b** which is sealed, and this evidence 2050.1
36:16 they were afraid **b** one **and** other, and 413
44:25 your wives have **b** spoken with your 2050.1
46:12 the mighty, *and* they are fallen **b** together. 8147
50: 3 they shall depart, **b** man and beast. 4480
51:12 for the LORD hath **b** devised and 1571
51:46 a rumour shall **b** come *one* year, and 2050.1
La 3:26 *It is* good *that a man should* **b** hope and 2050.1
Eze 9: 6 **b** maids, and little children, and women: 2050.1
14:22 be brought forth, **b** sons and daughters: NIH
15: 4 the fire devoureth **b** the ends of it, and 8147
21:19 **b twain** shall come forth out of one land: 8147
23:13 she was defiled, *that* they took **b** one way, 8147
23:29 **b** thy lewdness and thy whoredoms. 2050.1
34:11 **b** search my sheep, and seek them out. 2050.1
39: 9 **b** the shields and the bucklers, the bows 2050.1
42:11 all their goings out *were* **b** according to 2050.1
Da 8:13 to give **b** the sanctuary and the host to be 2050.1
11:27 **b** these kings' hearts *shall be* to do 8147
Mic 5: 8 **b** treadeth down, and teareth in pieces, 2050.1
7: 3 That *they* may do evil with **b** hands NIH
Na 3: 3 The horseman lifteth up **b** the bright 2050.1
Zep 2:14 **b** the cormorant and the bittern shall lodge 1571
Zec 6:13 counsel of peace shall be between them **b**. 8147
12: 2 when they shall be in the siege **b** 1571+2050.1
Mt 9:17 wine into new bottles, and **b** are preserved. *297*
10:28 rather fear him which is able to destroy **b** *2532*
12:22 that the blind and dumb **b** spake and saw. *2532*
13:30 Let **b** grow together until the harvest: and *297*
15:14 lead the blind, **b** shall fall into the ditch. *297*
22:10 all as many as they found, **b** bad and good: *5037*
Mk 6:30 told him all *things,* **b** what they had done, *2532*
7:37 he maketh **b** the deaf to hear, and the dumb *2532*
Lk 1: 6 And they were **b** righteous before God, *297*
1: 7 and they **b** were *now* well stricken in years. *297*
2:46 **b** hearing them, and asking them *2532*
5: 7 and filled **b** the ships, so that they began to *297*
5:36 *then* **b** the new maketh a rent, and the piece *2532*
5:38 be put into new bottles; and **b** are preserved. *297*
6:39 the blind? shall they not **b** fall into the ditch? *297*
7:42 nothing to pay, he frankly forgave *them* **b**. *297*
21:16 And ye shall be betrayed **b** by parents, and *2532*
22:33 to go with thee, **b** into prison, and to death. *2532*
Jn 2: 2 And **b** Jesus was called, and his disciples, *2532*
4:36 that **b** he that soweth and he that reapeth *2532*
7:28 Ye **b** know **me**, and ye know whence I am: *2504*
9:37 Thou hast **b** seen him, and it is he that *2532*
11:48 and take away **b** our place and nation. *2532*
11:57 Now **b** the chief priests and the Pharisees *2532*
12:28 *saying,* I have **b** glorified *it,* and *2532*
15:24 but now have they **b** seen and hated both *2532*
15:24 both seen and hated **b** me and my Father. *2532*
20: 4 So they ran **b** together: and the other *1417*
Ac 1: 1 of all that Jesus began **b** to do and teach, *5037*
1: 8 ye shall be witnesses unto me **b** in *5037*
1:13 where abode **b** Peter, and James, and John, *5037*
2:29 that he is **b** dead and buried, and *2532*
2:36 ye have crucified, **b** Lord and Christ. *2532*
4:27 **b** Herod, and Pontius Pilate, with *5037*
5:14 the Lord, multitudes **b** of men and women.) *5037*
8:12 they were baptized, **b** men and women. *5037*
8:38 and they went down **b** into the water, *297*
8:38 into the water, **b** Philip and the eunuch; *5037*
10:39 which he did **b** in the land of the Jews, *5037*
14: 1 that they went ***b*** together into the synagogue NIG
14: 1 that a great multitude **b** of the Jews and *5037*
14: 5 And when there was an assault made **b** of *5037*
19:10 word of the Lord Jesus, **b** Jews and Greeks. *5037*
20:21 Testifying **b** to the Jews, and *also* to *5037*
21:12 And when we heard these *things,* **b** we, and *5037*
22: 4 and delivering into prisons **b** men and *5037*
23: 8 angel nor spirit: but the Pharisees confess **b**. *297*
24:15 of the dead, **b** of the just and unjust. *5037*
25:24 **b** at Jerusalem, and *also* here, crying that he *5037*
26:16 a witness **b** of *these things* which thou hast *5037*
26:22 this day, witnessing **b** to small and great, *5037*
26:29 all that hear me this day, were **b** almost, NIG
28:23 **b** out of the law of Moses, and *out of* *5037*
Ro 1:12 with you by the mutual faith **b** of you *5037*
1:14 I am debtor **b** to the Greeks, and to *5037*
1:14 **b** to the wise, and to the unwise. *5037*
3: 9 for we have before proved **b** Jews and *5037*
11:33 O the depth of the riches **b** of the wisdom *2532*
14: 9 For to this end Christ **b** died, and rose, *2532*
14: 9 that he might be Lord **b** of the dead and *2532*
1Co 1: 2 of Jesus Christ our Lord, **b** theirs and ours: *5037*
1:24 **b** Jews and Greeks, Christ the power of *5037*
4: 5 who **b** will bring to light the hidden *things* *2532*
4:11 Even unto this present hour we **b** hunger, *2532*
6:13 but God shall destroy **b** it and them. *2532*
6:14 And God hath **b** raised up the Lord, and *2532*
7:29 that **b** they that have wives be as though *2532*
7:34 that she may be holy **b** in body and *2532*
2Co 9:10 to the sower **b** minister bread for *your* food, *2532*
Eph 1:10 **b** which are in heaven, and which are on *5037*
2:14 who hath made **b** one, and hath broken *297*
2:16 And *that* he might reconcile **b** unto God in *297*
2:18 For through him we **b** have access by one *297*
Php 1: 7 **inasmuch as b** in my bonds, and *in* *5037*
2:13 For it is God which worketh in you **b** to *2532*
4: 9 Those *things,* which ye have **b** learned, and *2532*
4:12 I know **b** *how* to be abased, and I know *2532*
4:12 in all *things* I am instructed **b** to be full and *2532*
4:12 be hungry, **b** to abound and to suffer need. *2532*

B

1Th 2:15 Who **b** killed the Lord Jesus, and their own *2532*
5:15 **b** among yourselves, and to all *men.* *2532*
2Th 3: 4 that ye **b** do and will do *the things* which *2532*
1Ti 4:10 For therefore we **b** labour and *2532*
4:16 for in doing this thou shalt **b** save thyself, *2532*
Tit 1: 9 that he may be able by sound doctrine **b** to *2532*
Phm 1:16 unto thee, **b** in the flesh, and in the Lord? *2532*
Heb 2: 4 **b** with signs and wonders, and with divers *5037*
2:11 For **b** he that sanctifieth and they who are *5037*
5: 1 that he may offer **b** gifts and sacrifices for *5037*
5:14 their senses exercised to discern **b** good *5037*
6:19 **b** sure and stedfast, and which entereth into *5037*
9: 9 in which were offered **b** gifts and *5037*
9:19 and sprinkled **b** the book, and all *5037*
9:21 Moreover he sprinkled with blood **b** *2532*
10:33 whilst ye were made a gazingstock **b** by *5037*
11:21 was a dying, blessed **b** the sons of Joseph; *1538*
Jas 3:12 so *can* no fountain **b** yield salt water and NIG
2Pe 3: 1 in **b** which I stir up your pure minds by way NIG
3:18 To him *be* glory **b** now and for ever. Amen. *2532*
2Jn 1: 9 of Christ, he hath **b** the Father and the Son. *2532*
Jude 1:25 dominion and power, **b** now and ever. *2532*
Rev 13:15 that the image of the beast should **b** speak, *2532*
13:16 **b** small and great, rich and poor, free and NIG
19: 5 and ye that fear him, **b** small and great. *2532*
19:18 and the flesh of all *men,* **b** free and bond, *5037*
19:18 *men,* both free and bond, **b** small and great. *2532*
19:20 *These* **b** were cast alive into a lake of fire *1417*

BOTTLE (15) [BOTTLES]
Ge 21:14 and a **b** of water, and gave *it* unto Hagar, 2573
21:15 the water was spent in the **b**, and she cast 2573
21:19 filled the **b** *with* water, and gave the lad 2573
Jdg 4:19 she opened a **b** of milk, and gave him 4997
1Sa 1:24 a **b** of wine, and brought him *unto* 5035
10: 3 of bread, and another carrying a **b** of wine: 5035
16:20 a **b** of wine, and a kid, and sent *them* by 4997
2Sa 16: 1 hundred of summer fruits, and a **b** of wine. 5035
Ps 56: 8 put thou my tears into thy **b**: *are they* not in 4997
119:83 For I am become like a **b** in the smoke; 4997
Jer 13:12 of Israel, Every **b** shall be filled *with* wine: 5035
13:12 Do we not certainly know that every **b** shall 5035
19: 1 Go and get a potter's earthen **b**, and *take* of 1228
19:10 shalt thou break the **b** in the sight of 1228
Hab 2:15 that puttest thy **b** to *him,* and makest *him* 2573

BOTTLES (19) [BOTTLE]
Jos 9: 4 and wine **b**, old, and rent, and bound up; 4997
9:13 these **b** of wine, which we filled, *were* new; 4997
1Sa 25:18 two **b** of wine, and five sheep ready 5035
Job 32:19 hath no vent; it is ready to burst like new **b**. 178
38:37 or who can stay the **b** of heaven, 5035
Jer 48:12 shall empty his vessels, and break their **b**. 5035
Hos 7: 5 princes have made *him* sick *with* **b** of wine; 2534
Mt 9:17 Neither do *men* put new wine into old **b**: *779*
9:17 else the **b** break, and the wine runneth out, *779*
9:17 and the wine runneth out, and the **b** perish: *779*
9:17 but they put new wine into new **b**, and *779*
Mk 2:22 And no *man* putteth new wine into old **b**: *779*
2:22 else the new wine doth burst the **b**, and *779*
2:22 the wine is spilled, and the **b** will be marred: *779*
2:22 but new wine must be put into new **b**. *779*
Lk 5:37 And no *man* putteth new wine into old **b**; *779*
5:37 else the new wine will burst the **b**, and *779*
5:37 and be spilled, and the **b** shall perish. *779*
5:38 But new wine must be put into new **b**; and *779*

BOTTOM (20) [BOTTOMLESS, BOTTOMS]
Ex 15: 5 they sank into the **b** as a stone. 4688
29:12 pour all the blood beside the **b** of the altar. 3247
Lev 4: 7 at the **b** of the altar of the burnt offering, 3247
4:18 shall pour out all the blood at the **b** of 3247
4:25 shall pour out his blood at the **b** of the altar 3247
4:30 shall pour out all the blood thereof at the **b** 3247
4:34 shall pour out all the blood thereof at the **b** 3247
5: 9 shall be wrung out at the **b** of the altar: 3247
8:15 poured the blood at the **b** of the altar, and 3247
9: 9 poured out the blood at the **b** of the altar: 3247
Job 36:30 light upon it, and covereth the **b** of the sea. 8328
SS 3:10 the **b** thereof *of* gold, the covering of it *of* 7507
Eze 43:13 even the **b** *shall be* a cubit, and the breadth 2436
43:14 from the **b** *upon* the ground *even* to 2436
43:17 and the **b** thereof *shall be* a cubit about; and 2436
Da 6:24 or ever they came at the **b** of the den. 773
Am 9: 3 though they be hid from my sight in the **b** 7172
Zec 1: 8 among the myrtle trees that *were* in the **b**; 4699
Mt 27:51 was rent in twain from the top to the **b**; *2736*
Mk 15:38 was rent in twain from the top to the **b**. *2736*

BOTTOMLESS (7) [BOTTOM]
Rev 9: 1 and to him was given the key of the **b** pit. *12*
9: 2 And he opened the **b** pit; and there arose a *12*
9:11 *which is* the angel of the **b** *pit,* whose name in *12*
11: 7 the beast that ascendeth out of the **b** *pit* shall *12*
17: 8 and shall ascend out of the **b** *pit,* and go into *12*
20: 1 having the key of the **b** *pit* and a great chain *12*
20: 3 And cast him into the **b** *pit,* and shut him up, *12*

BOTTOMS (1) [BOTTOM]
Jnh 2: 6 I went down to the **b** of the mountains; 7095

BOUGH (7) [BOUGHS]
Ge 49:22 Joseph *is* a **fruitful b**, *even* a fruitful 1121+6509
49:22 *even* a **fruitful b** by a well; 1121+6509
Jdg 9:48 cut down a **b** from the trees, and took it, 7754
9:49 people likewise cut down every man his **b**, 7754
Isa 10:33 LORD of hosts, shall lop the **b** with terror: 6288
17: 6 three berries in the top of the **uppermost b**, 534
17: 9 shall his strong cities be as a forsaken **b**, 2793

BOUGHS (18) [BOUGH]
Lev 23:40 ye shall take you on the first day the **b** of 6529
23:40 the **b** of thick trees, and willows of 6057
Dt 24:20 thou shalt not **go over the b** again: 6286
2Sa 18: 9 the mule went under the **thick b** of a great 7730
Job 14: 9 it will bud, and bring forth **b** like a plant. 7105
Ps 80:10 the **b** thereof *were like* the goodly cedars. 6057
80:11 She sent out her **b** unto the sea, and 7105
SS 7: 8 palm tree, I will take hold of the **b** thereof: 5577
Isa 27:11 When the **b** thereof are withered, they shall 7105
Eze 17:23 and it shall bring forth **b**, and bear fruit, and 6057
31: 3 and his top was among the **thick b**. 5688
31: 5 his **b** were multiplied, and his branches 5634
31: 6 fowls of heaven made their nests in his **b**, 5589
31: 8 the fir trees were not like his **b**, and 5589
31:10 he hath shot up his top among the **thick b**, 5688
31:12 his **b** are broken by all the rivers of 6288
31:14 shoot up their top among the **thick b**, 5688
Da 4:12 the fowls of the heaven dwelt in the **b** 6056

BOUGHT (44) [BUY]
Ge 17:12 or **b** with money of any stranger, which *is* 4736
17:13 he **that is b** with thy money, must needs be 4736
17:23 and all **that were b** with his money, 4736
17:27 and **b** with money of the stranger, 4736
33:19 he **b** a parcel of a field, where he had 7069
39: 1 **b** him of the hand of the Ishmeelites, 7069
47:14 land of Canaan, for the corn which they **b**: 7666
47:20 Joseph **b** all the land of Egypt for Pharaoh; 7069
47:22 Only the land of the priests **b** he not; for 7069
47:23 I have **b** you *this* day and your land for 7069
49:30 which Abraham **b** with the field of Ephron 7069
50:13 which Abraham **b** with the field for a 7069
Ex 12:44 every man's servant that is **b** for money, 4736
Lev 25:28 of him that hath **b** it until the year of jubile: 7069
25:30 to him that **b** it throughout his generations: 7069
25:50 he shall reckon with him that **b** him from 7069
25:51 out of the money that he was **b** for. 4736
27:22 unto the LORD a field which he hath **b**, 4736
27:24 shall return unto him of whom it was **b**, 7069
Dt 32: 6 *is* not he thy father *that* hath **b** thee? hath he 7069
Jos 24:32 in a parcel of ground which Jacob **b** of 7069
Ru 4: 9 that I have **b** all that *was* Elimelech's, and 7069
2Sa 12: 3 which he had **b** and nourished up: 7069
24:24 So David **b** the threshingfloor and the oxen 7069
1Ki 16:24 he **b** the hill Samaria of Shemer for two 7069
Ne 5:16 work of this wall, neither **b** we *any* land: 7069
Isa 43:24 Thou hast **b** me no sweet cane with money, 7069
Jer 32: 9 I **b** the field of Hanameel my uncle's son, 7069
32:43 fields shall be **b** in this land, whereof ye 7069
Hos 3: 2 So I **b** her to me for fifteen *pieces* of silver, 3739
Mt 13:46 went and sold all that he had, and **b** it. *59*
21:12 cast out all them that sold and **b** in the temple, *59*
27: 7 and **b** with them the potter's field, to bury *59*
Mk 11:15 to cast out them that sold and **b** in the temple, *59*
15:46 And he **b** fine linen, and took him down, and *59*
16: 1 and Salome, had **b** *sweet* spices, that they *59*
Lk 14:18 I have **b** a piece of ground, and I must needs *59*
14:19 I have **b** five yoke of oxen, and I go to prove *59*
17:28 they did eat, they drank, they **b**, they sold, *59*
19:45 out them that sold therein, and *them that* **b**; *59*
Ac 7:16 laid in the sepulchre that Abraham **b** for a *5608*
1Co 6:20 For ye are **b** with a price: therefore *59*
7:23 Ye are **b** with a price; be not ye the servants *59*
2Pe 2: 1 even denying the Lord that **b** them, and *59*

BOUND (104) [BIND, BOUNDS]
Ge 22: 9 **b** Isaac his son, and laid him on the altar 6123
38:28 and **b** upon his hand a scarlet thread, 7194
39:20 a place where the king's prisoners *were* **b**: 631
40: 3 the prison, the place where Joseph *was* **b**. 631
40: 5 king of Egypt, which *were* **b** in the prison. 631
42:19 brethren be **b** in the house of your prison: 631
42:24 them Simeon, and **b** him before their eyes. 631
44:30 seeing that his life *is* **b up** in *the lad's* life; 7194
49:26 unto the **utmost b** of the everlasting hills: 8379
Ex 12:34 their kneadingtroughs being **b up** in their 6887
Lev 8: 7 of the ephod, and **b** *it* unto him therewith. 640
Nu 19:15 which hath no covering **b** upon it, 6616
30: 4 and her bond wherewith she hath **b** her soul, 631
30: 4 every bond wherewith she hath **b** her soul 631
30: 5 of her bonds wherewith she hath **b** her soul, 631
30: 6 out of her lips, wherewith she **b** her soul; 631
30: 7 her bonds wherewith she **b** her soul shall 631
30: 8 wherewith she **b** her soul, of none effect: 631
30: 9 wherewith they have **b** their souls, 631
30:10 or **b** her soul by a bond with an oath; 631
30:11 every bond wherewith she **b** her soul shall 631
Jos 2:21 and she **b** the scarlet line in the window. 7194
9: 4 and wine bottles, old, and rent, and **b up**; 6887
Jdg 15:13 they **b** him with two new cords, and 631
16: 6 wherewith thou mightest be **b** to afflict thee. 631
16: 8 had not been dried, and she **b** him with them. 631
16:10 I pray thee, wherewith thou mightest be **b**. 631
16:12 and **b** him therewith, and said unto him,. 631
16:13 tell me wherewith thou mightest be **b**. 631
16:21 to Gaza, and **b** him with fetters of brass; 631
1Sa 25:29 the soul of my lord shall be **b** in the bundle 6887
2Sa 3:34 Thy hands *were* not **b**, nor thy feet put into 631
2Ki 5:23 and **b** two talents of silver in two bags, 6696
17: 4 of Assyria shut him up, and **b** him *in* prison. 631
25: 7 **b** him with fetters of brass, and carried him 631
2Ch 33:11 **b** him with fetters, and carried him to 631
36: 6 **b** him in fetters, to carry him to Babylon. 631
Job 36: 8 if *they be* **b** in fetters, *and* be holden in cords 631
38:20 That thou shouldest take it to the **b** thereof, 1366
Ps 68: 6 he bringeth out those which are **b** with 615
104: 9 Thou hast set a **b** *that* they may not pass 1366
107:10 of death, *being* **b** in affliction and iron; 615
Pr 22:15 Foolishness *is* **b** in the heart of a child; *but* 7194
30: 4 who hath **b** the waters in a garment? 6887
Isa 1: 6 they have not been closed, neither **b up**, 2280
22: 3 are fled together, they are **b** by the archers: 631
22: 3 all that are found in thee are **b** together, 631
61: 1 the opening of the prison to *them that are* **b**; 631
Jer 5:22 which have placed the sand *for* the **b** of 1366
30:13 plead thy cause, that thou mayest be **b up**: 4205
39: 7 **b** him with chains to carry him to Babylon. 631
40: 1 when he had taken him being **b** in chains 631
Jer 52:11 and the king of Babylon **b** him in chains, and 631
La 1:14 The yoke of my transgressions is **b** by his 8244
Eze 27:24 **b** with cords, and made of cedar, 2280
30:21 lo, it shall not be **b up** to be healed, to put a 2280
34: 4 neither have ye **b up** that which was 2280
Da 3:21 these men were **b** in their coats, 3729
3:23 fell down **b** into the midst of the burning 3729
3:24 Did not we cast three men **b** into the midst 3729
Hos 4:19 The wind hath **b** her **up** in her wings, and 6887
5:10 of Judah were like them that remove the **b**: 1366
7:15 Though I have **b** *and* strengthened their 3256
13:12 The iniquity of Ephraim *is* **b up**; his sin *is* 6887
Na 3:10 and all her great *men* were **b** in chains. 7576
Mt 14: 3 and **b** him, and put *him* in prison for *1210*
16:19 shalt bind on earth shall be **b** in heaven: *1210*
18:18 ye shall bind on earth shall be **b** in heaven: *1210*
27: 2 And when they had **b** him, they led *him* *1210*
Mk 5: 4 Because that he had been often **b** with *1210*
6:17 and **b** him in prison for Herodias' sake, *1210*
15: 1 and **b** Jesus, and carried *him* away, and *1210*
15: 7 *which lay* **b** with them that had made *1210*
Lk 8:29 and he was kept **b** with chains and *1196*
10:34 And went to *him,* and **b up** his wounds, *2611*
13:16 whom Satan hath **b**, lo *these* eighteen years, *1210*
Jn 11:44 **b** hand and foot with graveclothes: *1210*
11:44 and his face was **b about** with a napkin. *4019*
18:12 officers of the Jews took Jesus, and **b** him, *1210*
18:24 Now Annas had sent him **b** unto Caiaphas *1210*
Ac 9: 2 he might bring *them* **b** unto Jerusalem. *1210*
9:21 might bring them **b** unto the chief priests? *1210*
12: 6 between two soldiers, **b** with two chains: *1210*
20:22 I go **b** in the spirit unto Jerusalem, *1210*
21:11 and **b** his *own* hands and feet, and said, *1210*
21:13 for I am ready not to be **b** only, but also to *1210*
21:33 commanded *him* to be **b** with two chains; *1210*
22: 5 **b** unto Jerusalem, for to be punished. *1210*
22:25 And as they **b** him with thongs, Paul said *4385*
22:29 was a Roman, and because he had **b** him. *1210*
23:12 and **b** themselves **under a curse**, *332*
23:14 have **b** ourselves **under a great curse**, *331+332*
23:21 which have **b** themselves **with an oath**, *332*
24:27 to shew the Jews a pleasure, left Paul **b**. *1210*
28:20 that for the hope of Israel I am **b with** this *4029*
Ro 7: 2 For the woman which hath a husband is **b** *1210*
1Co 7:27 Art thou **b** unto a wife? seek not to be *1210*
7:39 The wife is **b** by the law as long as her *1210*
2Th 1: 3 We are **b** to thank God always for you, *3784*
2:13 But we are **b** to give thanks alway to God *3784*
2Ti 2: 9 unto bonds; but the word of God is not **b**. *1210*
Heb 13: 3 as **b with** *them; and* them which suffer *4887*
Rev 9:14 Loose the four angels which are **b** in *1210*
20: 2 and Satan, and **b** him a thousand years, *1210*

BOUNDARY STONE See LANDMARK

BOUNDLESS See INFINITE

BOUNDS (8) [BOUND]
Ex 19:12 thou shalt **set b** unto the people round 1379
19:23 **Set b about** the mount, and sanctify it. 1379
23:31 I will set thy **b** from the Red sea even unto 1366
Dt 32: 8 he set the **b** of the people according to 1367
Job 14: 5 thou hast appointed his **b** that he cannot 2706
26:10 He hath compassed the waters with **b**, 2706
Isa 10:13 I have removed the **b** of the people, and 1367
Ac 17:26 and the **b** of their habitation; *3734*

BOUNTIFUL (2) [BOUNTY]
Pr 22: 9 He that hath a **b** eye shall be blessed; for he 2896
Isa 32: 5 called liberal, nor the churl said *to be* **b**. 7771

BOUNTIFULLY (6) [BOUNTY]
Ps 13: 6 because he hath **dealt b** with me. 1580
116: 7 for the LORD hath **dealt b** with thee. 1580
119:17 **Deal b** with thy servant, *that* I may live, 1580
142: 7 me about; for thou shalt **deal b** with me. 1580
2Co 9: 6 he which soweth **b** shall reap also *1909+2129*
9: 6 soweth bountifully shall reap also **b**. *1909+2129*

BOUNTIFULNESS (1) [BOUNTY]
2Co 9:11 Being enriched in every *thing* to all **b**, *572*

BOUNTY (3) [BOUNTIFUL, BOUNTIFULLY, BOUNTIFULNESS]
1Ki 10:13 *that* which Solomon gave her of his royal **b**. 3027
2Co 9: 5 and make up beforehand your **b**, *2129*
9: 5 as *a matter of* **b**, and not as *of* *2129*

BOW (99) [BOWED, BOWETH, BOWING, BOWMEN, BOWS, BOWSHOT, RAINBOW]
Ge 9:13 I do set my **b** in the cloud, and it shall be 7198
9:14 that the **b** shall be seen in the cloud: 7198
9:16 the **b** shall be in the cloud; and I will look 7198
27: 3 thy quiver and thy **b**, and go out to 7198
27:29 serve thee, and nations **b down** to thee: 7812
27:29 and let thy mother's sons **b down** to thee: 7812
37:10 thy brethren indeed come to **b down** 7812
41:43 and they cried before him, **B the knee**: 86
48:22 the Amorite with my sword and with my **b**. 7198
49: 8 thy father's children shall **b down** before 7812
49:24 his **b** abode in strength, and the arms of his 7198
Ex 11: 8 **b down** themselves unto me, saying, 7812
20: 5 Thou shalt not **b down** thyself to them, 7812
23:24 Thou shalt not **b down** to their gods, 7812
Lev 26: 1 of stone in your land, to **b down** unto it: 7812
Dt 5: 9 Thou shalt not **b down** thyself unto them, 7812
Jos 23: 7 serve them, nor **b** yourselves unto them. 7812
24:12 *but* not with thy sword, nor with thy **b**. 7198
Jdg 2:19 to serve them, and to **b down** unto them; 7812
1Sa 18: 4 to his sword, and to his **b**, and to his girdle. 7198
2Sa 1:18 teach the children of Judah the *use of the* **b**: 7198
1:22 the **b** of Jonathan turned not back, and 7198
22:35 so that a **b** of steel is broken *by* mine arms. 7198
1Ki 22:34 a *certain* man drew a **b** at a venture, 7198

2Ki 5:18 and I **b** myself *in* the house of Rimmon: 7812
5:18 when I **b down** myself *in* the house of 7812
6:22 captive with thy sword and with thy **b**? 7198
9:24 Jehu drew a **b** with his full strength, and 7198
13:15 Elisha said unto him, Take **b** and arrows. 7198
13:15 And he took unto him **b** and arrows. 7198
13:16 king of Israel, Put thine hand upon the **b**. 7198
17:35 nor **b** yourselves to them, nor serve them, 7812
19:16 LORD, **b down** thine ear, and hear: open, 5186
1Ch 5:18 and to shoot with **b**, and skilful in war, 7198
12: 2 and *shooting* arrows out of a **b**, 7198
2Ch 17:17 with him armed *men* with **b** and shield two 7198
18:33 a *certain* man drew a **b** at a venture, 7198
Job 20:24 *and* the **b** of steel shall strike him through. 7198
29:20 in me, and my **b** was renewed in my hand. 7198
31:10 and let others **b down** upon her. 3766
39: 3 They **b** themselves, they bring forth their 3766
Ps 7:12 he hath bent his **b**, and made it ready. 7198
11: 2 For lo, the wicked bend *their* **b**, they make 7198
18:34 so that a **b** of steel is broken *by* mine arms. 7198
22:29 all they that go down to the dust shall **b** 3766
31: 2 **B down** thine ear to me; deliver me 5186
37:14 and have bent their **b**, to cast down the poor 7198
44: 6 For I will not trust in my **b**, neither shall 7198
46: 9 he breaketh the **b**, and cutteth the spear in 7198
58: 7 *when* he bendeth *his* **b** *to shoot* his arrows, NIH
72: 9 They that dwell in the wilderness shall **b** 3766
76: 3 There brake he the arrows of the **b**, 7198
78:57 they were turned aside like a deceitful **b**. 7198
86: 1 **B down** thine ear, O LORD, hear me: 5186
95: 6 O come, let us worship and **b down**: let us 3766
144: 5 **B** thy heavens, O LORD, and come down: 5186
Pr 5: 1 *and* **b** thine ear to my understanding: 5186
14:19 The evil **b** before the good; and the wicked 7817
22:17 **B down** thine ear, and hear the words of 5186
Ecc 12: 3 the strong men shall **b** themselves, and 5791
Isa 10: 4 Without me they shall **b down** under 3766
21:15 from the bent **b**, and from the grievousness 7198
41: 2 *to* his sword, *and* as driven stubble *to* his **b**. 7198
45:23 not return, That unto me every knee shall **b**, 3766
46: 2 They stoop, they **b down** together; 3766
49:23 they shall **b down** to thee *with their* face 7812
51:23 to thy soul, **B down**, that we may go over: 7812
58: 5 *is it* to **b down** his head as a bulrush, and 3721
60:14 **b** themselves **down** at the soles of thy feet; 7812
65:12 and ye shall all **b down** to the slaughter: 3766
66:19 Pul, and Lud, that draw the **b**, *to* Tubal, and 7198
Jer 6:23 They shall lay hold on **b** and spear; they *are* 7198
9: 3 they bend their tongues *like* their **b** *for* lies: 7198
46: 9 the Lydians, that handle *and* bend the **b**. 7198
49:35 Behold, I *will* break the **b** of Elam, 7198
50:14 all ye that bend the **b**, shoot at her, spare no 7198
50:29 all ye that bend the **b**, camp against it round 7198
50:42 They shall hold the **b** and the lance: 7198
51: 3 *him that* bendeth let the archer bend his **b**, 7198
La 2: 4 He hath bent his **b** like an enemy: *he* stood 7198
3:12 He hath bent his **b**, and set me as a mark 7198
Eze 1:28 As the appearance of the **b** that is in 7198
39: 3 I will smite thy **b** out of thy left hand, and 7198
Hos 1: 5 that I will break the **b** of Israel in the valley 7198
1: 7 will not save them by **b**, nor by sword, 7198
2:18 I will break the **b** and the sword and 7198
7:16 they are like a deceitful **b**: their princes 7198
Am 2:15 Neither shall he stand that handleth the **b**; 7198
Mic 6: 6 *and* **b** myself before the high God? 3721
Hab 3: 6 were scattered, the perpetual hills did **b**: 7817
3: 9 Thy **b** was made quite naked, *according to* 7198
Zec 9:10 and the battle **b** shall be cut off: 7198
9:13 filled the **b** *with* Ephraim, and raised up thy 7198
10: 4 out of him the nail, out of him the battle **b**, 7198
Ro 11:10 may not see, and **b down** their back alway. *4781*
14:11 every knee shall **b** to me, and every tongue *2578*
Eph 3:14 For this cause I **b** my knees unto the Father *2578*
Php 2:10 at the name of Jesus every knee should **b**, *2578*
Rev 6: 2 and he that sat on him had a **b**; and a crown *5115*

BOWED (78) [BOW]
Ge 18: 2 tent door, and **b** himself toward the ground, 7812
19: 1 he **b** himself with his face toward 7812
23: 7 and **b** himself to the people of the land, 7812
23:12 Abraham **b down** himself before the people 7812
24:26 the man **b down** his **head**, and 6915
24:48 I **b down** my **head**, and worshipped 6915
33: 3 and **b** himself to the ground seven times, 7812
33: 6 and their children, and they **b** themselves. 7812
33: 7 her children came near, and **b** themselves: 7812
33: 7 and Rachel, and they **b** themselves. 7812
42: 6 **b down** themselves before him *with* their 7812
43:26 and **b** themselves to him to the earth. 7812
43:28 they **b down** their **heads**, and 6915
47:31 And Israel **b** himself upon the bed's head. 7812
48:12 and he **b** himself with his face to the earth. 7812
49:15 **b** his shoulder to bear, and became a 5186
Ex 4:31 then they **b** their **heads** and worshipped. 6915
12:27 the people **b the head** and worshipped. 6915
34: 8 **b** his **head** toward the earth, and 6915
Nu 22:31 he **b down** his **head**, and fell flat on his 6915
25: 2 people did eat, and **b down** to their gods. 7812
Jos 23:16 other gods, and **b** yourselves to them; 7812
Jdg 2:12 **b** themselves unto them, and provoked 7812
2:17 other gods, and **b** themselves unto them: 7812
5:27 At her feet he **b**, he fell, he lay down: at her 3766
5:27 at her feet he **b**, he fell: where he bowed, 3766
5:27 where he **b**, there he fell down dead. 3766
7: 6 all the rest of the people **b down** upon their 3766
16:30 he **b** *himself* with *all his* might; and 5186
Ru 2:10 **b** herself to the ground, and said unto him, 7812
1Sa 4:19 were dead, she **b** herself and travailed; 3766
20:41 to the ground, and **b** himself three times: 7812
24: 8 *with his* face to the earth, and **b** himself. 7812
25:23 on her face, and **b** herself *to* the ground, 7812
25:41 **b** herself *on her* face to the earth, and said, 7812
28:14 *with his* face to the ground, and **b** himself. 7812
2Sa 9: 8 he **b** himself, and said, What *is* thy servant, 7812
14:22 and **b** himself, and thanked the king: 7812
2Sa 14:33 **b** himself on his face to the ground before 7812
18:21 And Cushi **b** himself unto Joab, and ran. 7812
19:14 he **b** the heart of all the men of Judah, 5186
22:10 He **b** the heavens also, and came down; and 5186
24:20 **b** himself before the king *on* his face upon 7812
1Ki 1:16 Bath-sheba **b**, and did obeisance unto 6915
1:23 he **b** himself before the king with his face 7812
1:31 Bath-sheba **b** *with her* face *to* the earth, 6915
1:47 And the king **b** himself upon the bed. 7812
1:53 he came and **b** himself to king Solomon: 7812
2:19 **b** himself unto her, and sat down on his 7812
19:18 all the knees which have not **b** unto Baal, 3766
2Ki 2:15 and **b** themselves to the ground before him. 7812
4:37 **b** herself to the ground, and took up her 7812
1Ch 21:21 **b** himself to David *with his* face to 7812
29:20 **b down** their **heads**, and worshipped 6915
2Ch 7: 3 they **b** themselves *with their* faces to 3766
20:18 Jehoshaphat **b** his **head** *with his* face to 6915
25:14 **b down** himself before them, and 7812
29:29 all that were present with him **b** 3766
29:30 and they **b** their **heads** and worshipped. 6915
Ne 8: 6 they **b** their **heads**, and worshipped 6915
Est 3: 2 the king's gate, **b**, and reverenced Haman: 3766
3: 2 But Mordecai **b** not, nor did *him* reverence. 3766
3: 5 And when Haman saw that Mordecai **b** not, 3766
Ps 18: 9 He **b** the heavens also, and came down: and 5186
35:14 I **b down** heavily, as one that mourneth for 7817
38: 6 I am troubled; I am **b down** greatly; I go 7817
44:25 For our soul is **b down** to the dust: 7743
57: 6 a net for my steps; my soul is **b down**: 3721
145:14 and raiseth up all those that be **b down**. 3721
146: 8 the LORD raiseth them that are **b down**: 3721
Isa 2:11 the haughtiness of men shall be **b down**, 7817
2:17 the loftiness of man shall be **b down**, and 7817
21: 3 I was **b down** at the hearing *of it;* I was 5753
Mt 27:29 and they **b the knee** before him, and *1120*
Lk 13:11 and was **b together**, and could in no wise *4794*
24: 5 and **b down** *their* faces to the earth, *2827*
Jn 19:30 and he **b** *his* head, and gave up the ghost. *2827*
Ro 11: 4 who have not **b** the knee to *the image of* *2578*

BOWELS (39)
Ge 15: 4 he that shall come forth out of thine own **b** 4578
25:23 of people shall be separated from thy **b**; 4578
43:30 for his **b** did yern upon his brother: 7356
Nu 5:22 that causeth the curse shall go into thy **b**, 4578
2Sa 7:12 which shall proceed out of thy **b**, and I will 4578
16:11 Behold, my son, which came forth of my **b**, 4578
20:10 fifth *rib*, and shed out his **b** to the ground, 4578
1Ki 3:26 for her **b** yerned upon her son, and she said, 7356
2Ch 21:15 have great sickness by disease of thy **b**, 4578
21:15 until thy **b** fall out by reason of the sickness 4578
21:18 after all this the LORD smote him in his **b** 4578
21:19 his **b** fell out by reason of his sickness: 4578
32:21 they that came forth of his own **b** slew him 4578
Job 20:14 *Yet* his meat in his **b** is turned, *it is* the gall 4578
30:27 My **b** boiled, and rested not: the days of 4578
Ps 22:14 like wax; it is melted in the midst of my **b**. 4578
71: 6 art he that took me out of my mother's **b**: 4578
109:18 so let it come into his **b** like water, and 7130
SS 5: 4 *of the door,* and my **b** were moved for him. 4578
Isa 16:11 Wherefore my **b** shall sound like a harp for 4578
48:19 the offspring of thy **b** like the gravel 4578
49: 1 from the **b** of my mother hath he made 4578
63:15 the sounding of thy **b** and of thy mercies 4578
Jer 4:19 My **b**, my bowels! I am pained *at* my very 4578
4:19 My bowels, my **b**! I am pained *at* my very 4578
31:20 therefore my **b** are troubled for him; I will 4578
La 1:20 my **b** are troubled; mine heart is turned 4578
2:11 eyes do fail with tears, my **b** are troubled, 4578
Eze 3: 3 and fill thy **b** with this roll that I give thee. 4578
7:19 not satisfy their souls, neither fill their **b**: 4578
Ac 1:18 in the midst, and all his **b** gushed out. *4698*
2Co 6:12 in us, but ye are straitened in your own **b**. *4698*
Php 1: 8 how *greatly* I long after you all in the **b** of *4698*
2: 1 of the Spirit, if any **b** and mercies, *4698*
Col 3:12 holy and beloved, **b** of mercies, kindness, *4698*
Phm 1: 7 the **b** of the saints are refreshed by thee, *4698*
1:12 therefore receive him, that is, mine own **b**: *4698*
1:20 thee in the Lord: refresh my **b** in the Lord. *4698*
1Jn 3:17 shutteth up his **b** *of compassion* from him, *4698*

BOWETH (3) [BOW]
Jdg 7: 5 likewise every one that **b down** upon his 3766
Isa 2: 9 the mean man **b down**, and the great man 7817
46: 1 Bel **b down**, Nebo stoopeth, their idols 3766

BOWING (4) [BOW]
Ge 24:52 the LORD, ***b** himself* to the earth. NIH
Ps 17:11 they have set their eyes **b down** to 5186
62: 3 as a **b** wall *shall ye be, and as* a tottering 5186
Mk 15:19 and **b** *their* knees worshipped him. *5087*

BOWL (17) [BOWLS]
Nu 7:13 thirty *shekels*, one silver **b** of seventy 4219
7:19 thirty *shekels*, one silver **b** of seventy 4219
7:25 thirty *shekels*, one silver **b** of seventy 4219
7:31 thirty *shekels*, one silver **b** of seventy 4219
7:37 thirty *shekels*, one silver **b** of seventy 4219
7:43 thirty *shekels*, a silver **b** of seventy shekels, 4219
7:49 thirty *shekels*, one silver **b** of seventy 4219
7:55 thirty *shekels*, one silver **b** of seventy 4219
7:61 thirty *shekels*, one silver **b** of seventy 4219
7:67 thirty *shekels*, one silver **b** of seventy 4219
7:73 thirty *shekels*, one silver **b** of seventy 4219
7:79 thirty *shekels*, one silver **b** of seventy 4219
7:85 and thirty *shekels*, each **b** seventy: 4219
Jdg 6:38 the dew out of the fleece, a **b** full *of* water. 5602
Ecc 12: 6 or the golden **b** be broken, or the pitcher be 1543
Zec 4: 2 with a **b** upon the top of it, and his seven 1531
4: 3 one upon the right *side* of the **b**, and 1543

BOWLS (24) [BOWL]
Ex 25:29 and covers thereof, and **b** thereof, 4518
25:31 his **b**, his knops, and his flowers, 1375
25:33 Three **b** made like unto almonds, *with* a 1375
25:33 three **b** made like almonds in the other 1375
25:34 in the candlestick *shall be* four **b** made like 1375
37:16 and his **b**, and *his* covers to cover withal, 4518
37:17 his **b**, his knops, and his flowers, 1375
37:19 Three **b** made after the fashion of almonds 1375
37:19 three **b** made like almonds in another 1375
37:20 in the candlestick *were* four **b** made like 1375
Nu 4: 7 and the **b**, and covers to cover withal: 4518
7:84 twelve silver **b**, twelve spoons of gold: 4219
1Ki 7:41 the two **b** of the chapiters that *were* on 1543
7:41 to cover the two **b** of the chapiters which 1543
7:42 to cover the two **b** of the chapiters that 1543
7:50 And the **b**, and the snuffers, and the basons, 5592
2Ki 12:13 *for* the house of the LORD **b** of silver, 5592
25:15 the **b**, *and* such *things* as *were of* gold, 4219
1Ch 28:17 *for* the fleshhooks, and the **b**, and the cups: 4219
Jer 52:18 the **b**, and the spoons, and all the vessels of 4219
52:19 the **b**, and the caldrons, and 4219
Am 6: 6 That drink wine in **b**, and 4219
Zec 9:15 they shall be filled like **b**, *and* as 4219
14:20 house shall be like the **b** before the altar. 4219

BOWMEN (1) [BOW, MAN]
Jer 4:29 for the noise of the horsemen and **b**; 7198+7411

BOWS (14) [BOW]
1Sa 2: 4 The **b** of the mighty *men are* broken, and 7198
1Ch 12: 2 *They were* armed with **b**, and could use 7198
2Ch 14: 8 that bare shields and drew **b**, two hundred 7198
26:14 and **b**, and slings to cast stones. 7198
Ne 4:13 with their swords, their spears, and their **b**. 7198
4:16 the shields, and the **b**, and the habergeons; 7198
Ps 37:15 their own heart, and their **b** shall be broken. 7198
64: 3 *and* bend *their* **b** *to shoot* their arrows, NIH
78: 9 of Ephraim, *being* armed, *and* carrying **b**, 7198
Isa 5:28 arrows *are* sharp, and all their **b** bent, 7198
7:24 and with **b** shall *men* come thither; 7198
13:18 *Their* **b** also shall dash the young men to 7198
Jer 51:56 are taken, *every one of* their **b** is broken: 7198
Eze 39: 9 the **b** and the arrows, and the handstaves, 7198

BOWSHOT (1) [BOW, SHOOT]
Ge 21:16 *him* a good way off, as it were a **b**: 2909+7198

BOX (8)
2Ki 9: 1 take this **b** of oil in thine hand, and go *to* 6378
9: 3 take the **b** of oil, and pour *it* on his head, 6378
Isa 41:19 *and* the pine, and the **b tree** together: 8391
60:13 fir tree, the pine tree, and the **b** together, 8391
Mt 26: 7 an **alabaster b** of very precious ointment, *211*
Mk 14: 3 there came a woman having an **alabaster b** *211*
14: 3 and she brake the **b**, and poured *it* on his *211*
Lk 7:37 brought an **alabaster b** of ointment, *211*

BOY (1) [BOYS]
Joel 3: 3 have given a **b** for a harlot, and sold a girl 3206

BOYS (2) [BOY]
Ge 25:27 the **b** grew: and Esau was a cunning hunter, 5288
Zec 8: 5 the streets of the city shall be full *of* **b** and 3206

BOYSTEROUS (1)
Mt 14:30 But when he saw the wind **b**, he was afraid; *2478*

BOZEZ (1)
1Sa 14: 4 the name of the one *was* **B**, and the name of 949

BOZKATH (1)
Jos 15:39 Lachish, and **B**, and Eglon, 1218

BOZRAH (9)
Ge 36:33 Jobab the son of Zerah of **B** reigned in his 1224
1Ch 1:44 Jobab the son of Zerah of **B** reigned in his 1224
Isa 34: 6 for the LORD hath a sacrifice in **B**, and 1224
63: 1 from Edom, with dyed garments from **B**? 1224
Jer 48:24 upon **B**, and upon all the cities of the land 1224
49:13 that **B** shall become a desolation, a 1224
49:22 as the eagle, and spread his wings over **B**: 1224
Am 1:12 which shall devour the palaces of **B**. 1224
Mic 2:12 I will put them together as the sheep of **B**, 1223

BRACELET (1) [BRACELETS]
2Sa 1:10 the **b** that *was* on his arm, and have brought 685

BRACELETS (10) [BRACELET]
Ge 24:22 two **b** for her hands of ten *shekels* weight 6781
24:30 the earring and **b** upon his sister's hands, 6781
24:47 upon her face, and the **b** upon her hands. 6781
38:18 thy **b**, and thy staff that *is* in thine hand. 6616
38:25 *are* these, the signet, and **b**, and staff. 6616
Ex 35:22 *and* brought **b**, and earrings, and rings, and 2397
Nu 31:50 chains, and **b**, rings, earrings, and tablets, 6781
Isa 3:19 The chains, and the **b**, and the mufflers, 8285
Eze 16:11 I put **b** upon thine hands, and a chain on thy 6781
23:42 which put **b** upon their hands, and 6781

BRAIDED See BROIDED; PLAITING

BRAIDS See LOCKS

BRAKE (73) [BREAK]
Ex 9:25 of the field, and **b** every tree of the field. 7665
32: 3 all the people **b off** the golden earrings 6561
32:19 his hands, and **b** them beneath the mount. 7665
Dt 9:17 two hands, and **b** them before your eyes. 7665
Jdg 7:19 and **b** the pitchers that *were* in their hands. 5310
7:20 **b** the pitchers, and held the lamps in their 7665
9:53 Abimelech's head, and **all to b** his skull. 7533
16: 9 he **b** the withs, as a thread of tow is broken 5423
16:12 he **b** them from off his arms like a thread. 5423
1Sa 4:18 of the gate, and his neck **b**, and he died: 7665

2Sa 23:16 the three mighty *men* **b** through the host of 1234
1Ki 19:11 **b in pieces** the rocks before the LORD; 7665
2Ki 10:27 they **b down** the image of Baal, and 5422
10:27 **b down** the house of Baal, and made it a 5422
11:18 went *into* the house of Baal, and **b** it **down**; 5422
11:18 and his images **b** they **in pieces** throughly, 7665
14:13 **b down** the wall of Jerusalem from the gate 6555
18: 4 **b** the images, and cut down the groves, and 7665
18: 4 **b in pieces** the brasen serpent that Moses 3807
23: 7 he **b down** the houses of the sodomites, 5422
23: 8 **b down** the high places of the gates that 5422
23:12 **b** *them* **down** from thence, and cast the dust 7323
23:14 he **b in pieces** the images, and cut down 7665
23:15 that altar and the high place he **b down**, 5422
25:10 **b down** the walls of Jerusalem round 5422
1Ch 11:18 the three **b** through the host of 1234
2Ch 14: 3 **b down** the images, and cut down 7665
21:17 **b into** it, and carried away all the substance 1234
23:17 **b** it **down**, and brake his altars and his 5422
23:17 **b** his altars and his images **in pieces**, and 7665
25:23 **b down** the wall of Jerusalem from the gate 6555
26: 6 **b down** the wall of Gath, and the wall of 6555
31: 1 **b** the images *in pieces*, and cut down 7665
34: 4 they **b down** the altars of Baalim in his 5422
34: 4 he **b** *in pieces*, and made dust *of them*, and 7665
36:19 **b down** the wall of Jerusalem, and burnt all 5422
Job 29:17 I **b** the jaws of the wicked, and pluckt 7665
38: 8 shut up the sea with doors, when it **b forth**, 1518
38:10 **b up** for it my decreed *place*, and set bars 7665
Ps 76: 3 There **b** he the arrows of the bow, 7665
105:16 the land: he **b** the whole staff of bread. 7665
105:33 fig trees; and **b** the trees of their coasts. 7665
106:29 and the plague **b in** upon them. 6555
107:14 of death, and **b** their bands **in sunder**. 5423
Jer 28:10 off the prophet Jeremiah's neck, and **b** it. 7665
31:32 which my covenant they **b**, although I was 6565
39: 8 and **b down** the walls of Jerusalem. 5422
52:14 **b down** all the walls of Jerusalem round 5422
52:17 the Chaldeans **b**, and carried all the brass of 7665
Eze 17:16 oath he despised, and whose covenant he **b**, 6565
Da 2: 1 was troubled, and his sleep **b** from him. 1961
2:34 of iron and clay, and **b** them **in pieces**. 1855
2:45 *that* it **b in pieces** the iron, the brass, 1855
6:24 **b** all their bones **in pieces** or ever they 1855
7: 7 it devoured and **b in pieces**, and 1855
7:19 **b in pieces**, and stamped the residue with 1855
8: 7 and smote the ram, and **b** his two horns: 7665
Mt 14:19 and **b**, and gave the loaves to *his* disciples, *2806*
15:36 and **b** *them*, and gave to his disciples, and *2806*
26:26 and blessed *it*, and **b** *it*, and gave *it* to *2806*
Mk 6:41 and **b** the loaves, and gave *them* to his *2622*
8: 6 and **b**, and gave to his disciples to set *2806*
8:19 When I **b** the five loaves among five *2806*
14: 3 and she **b** the box, and poured *it* on his *4937*
14:22 and **b** *it*, and gave to them, and said, Take, *2806*
Lk 5: 6 a great multitude of fishes: and their net **b**. *1284*
8:29 and he **b** the bands, and was driven of *1284*
9:16 and **b**, and gave to the disciples to set *2622*
22:19 and **b** *it*, and gave unto them, saying, *2806*
24:30 and blessed *it*, and **b**, and gave to them. *2806*
Jn 19:32 and **b** the legs of the first, and of the other *2608*
19:33 he was dead already, they **b** not his legs: *2608*
1Co 11:24 given thanks, he **b** *it*, and said, Take, eat: *2806*

BRAKEST (5) [BREAK]
Ex 34: 1 that were in the first tables, which thou **b**. 7665
Dt 10: 2 that were in the first tables which thou **b**, 7665
Ps 74:13 thou **b** the heads of the dragons in 7665
74:14 Thou **b** the heads of leviathan **in pieces**, 7533
Eze 29: 7 thou **b**, and madest all their loins to be at a 7665

BRAMBLE (4) [BRAMBLES]
Jdg 9:14 said all the trees unto the **b**, Come thou, 329
9:15 the **b** said unto the trees, If in truth ye anoint 329
9:15 let fire come out of the **b**, and devour 329
Lk 6:44 nor of a **b bush** gather they grapes. *942*

BRAMBLES (1) [BRAMBLE]
Isa 34:13 nettles and **b** in the fortresses thereof: 2336

BRANCH (37) [BRANCHES]
Ex 25:33 *with* a knop and a flower in one **b**; 7070
25:33 bowls made like almonds in the other **b**, 7070
37:17 his shaft, and his **b**, his bowls, his knops, 7070
37:19 made after the fashion of almonds in one **b**, 7070
37:19 bowls made like almonds in another **b**, 7070
Nu 13:23 cut down from thence a **b** with one cluster 2156
Job 8:16 and his **b** shooteth forth in his garden, 3127
14: 7 and that the **tender b** thereof will not cease. 3127
15:32 his time, and his **b** shall not be green. 3712
18:16 and above shall his **b** be cut off. 7105
29:19 and the dew lay all night upon my **b**. 7105
Ps 80:15 the **b** *that* thou madest strong for thyself. 1121
Pr 11:28 but the righteous shall flourish as a **b**. 5929
Isa 4: 2 In that day shall the **b** of the LORD be 6780
9:14 off from Israel head and tail, **b** and rush, 3712
11: 1 and a **B** shall grow out of his roots: 5342
14:19 cast out of thy grave like an abominable **b**, 5342
17: 9 and an uppermost **b**, which they left because 534
19:15 which the head or tail, **b** or rush, may do. 3712
25: 5 the **b** of the terrible ones shall be brought 2159
60:21 the **b** of my planting, the work of my 5342
Jer 23: 5 that I will raise unto David a righteous **B**, 6780
33:15 will I cause the **B** of righteousness to grow 6780
Eze 8:17 and lo, they put the **b** to their nose. 2156
15: 2 *than* a **b** which is among the trees of 2156
17: 3 and took the **highest b** of the cedar: 6788
17:22 I will also take of the **highest b** of the high 6788
Da 11: 7 out of a **b** of her roots shall *one* stand up *in* 5342
Zec 3: 8 I *will* bring forth my servant the **B**. 6780
6:12 Behold the man whose name *is* The **B**; 6780
Mal 4: 1 that it shall leave them neither root nor **b**. 6057
Mt 24:32 When his **b** is yet tender, and putteth forth *2798*
Mk 13:28 When her **b** is yet tender, and putteth forth *2798*
Jn 15: 2 Every **b** in me that beareth not fruit he *2814*
15: 2 and every *b* that beareth fruit, he purgeth it, NIG
15: 4 As the **b** cannot bear fruit of itself, except it *2814*
15: 6 he is cast forth as a **b**, and is withered; *2814*

BRANCHES (75) [BRANCH]
Ge 40:10 in the vine *were* three **b**: and it *was* as 8299
40:12 of it: The three **b** *are* three days: 8299
49:22 by a well; *whose* **b** run over the wall. 1323
Ex 25:31 his shaft, and his **b**, his bowls, his knops, 7070
25:32 six **b** shall come out of the sides of it; 7070
25:32 three **b** of the candlestick out of the one 7070
25:32 three **b** of the candlestick out of the other 7070
25:33 in the six **b** that come out of 7070
25:35 *there shall be* a knop under two **b** of 7070
25:35 a knop under two **b** of the same, and a knop 7070
25:35 and a knop under two **b** of the same, 7070
25:35 according to the six **b** that proceed out of 7070
25:36 and their **b** shall be of the same: 7070
37:18 six **b** going out of the sides thereof; 7070
37:18 three **b** of the candlestick out of the one 7070
37:18 three **b** of the candlestick out of the other 7070
37:19 throughout the six **b** going out of 7070
37:21 a knop under two **b** of the same, and a knop 7070
37:21 a knop under two **b** of the same, and a knop 7070
37:21 and a knop under two **b** of the same, 7070
37:21 according to the six **b** going out of it. 7070
37:22 Their knops and their **b** were of the same: 7070
Lev 23:40 **b** of palm trees, and the boughs of thick 3709
Ne 8:15 fetch olive **b**, and pine branches, and 5929
8:15 pine **b**, and myrtle branches, and 6086
8:15 myrtle **b**; and palm branches, and 5929
8:15 palm **b**, and branches of thick trees, 5929
8:15 palm branches, and **b** of thick trees, 5929
Job 15:30 the flame shall dry up his **b**, and by 3127
Ps 80:11 unto the sea, and her **b** unto the river. 3127
104:12 their habitation, *which* sing among the **b**. 6073
Isa 16: 8 her **b** are stretched out, they are gone over 7976
17: 6 *or* five in the outmost fruitful **b** thereof, 5585
18: 5 and take away *and* cut down the **b**. 5189
27:10 he lie down, and consume the **b** thereof. 5585
Jer 11:16 fire upon it, and the **b** of it are broken. 1808
Eze 17: 6 whose **b** turned toward him, and the roots 1808
17: 6 and brought forth **b**, and shot forth sprigs. 905
17: 7 and shot forth her **b** toward him, 1808
17: 8 that *it* might bring forth **b**, and that *it* might 6057
17:23 in the shadow of the **b** thereof shall they 1808
19:10 and **full of b** by reason of many waters. 6058
19:11 her stature was exalted among the **thick b**, 5688
19:11 in her height with the multitude of her **b**. 1808
19:14 fire is gone out of a rod of her **b**, *which* hath 905
31: 3 *was* a cedar in Lebanon with fair **b**, 6057
31: 5 his **b** became long because of the multitude 6288
31: 6 under his **b** did all the beasts of the field 6288
31: 7 fair in his greatness, in the length of his **b**: 1808
31: 8 and the chesnut trees were not like his **b**; 6288
31: 9 made him fair by the multitude of his **b**: 1808
31:12 and in all the valleys his **b** are fallen, 1808
31:13 the beasts of the field shall be upon his **b**: 6288
36: 8 ye shall shoot forth your **b**, and yield your 6057
Da 4:14 Hew down the tree, and cut off his **b**, 6056
4:14 from under it, and the fowls from his **b**: 6056
4:21 upon whose **b** the fowls of the heaven had 6056
Hos 11: 6 shall consume his **b**, and devour *them*, 905
14: 6 His **b** shall spread, and his beauty shall be 3127
Joel 1: 7 cast *it* away; the **b** thereof are made white. 8299
Na 2: 2 emptied them out, and marred their **vine b**. 2156
Zec 4:12 What *be these* two olive **b** which through 7641
Mt 13:32 of the air come and lodge in the **b** thereof. *2798*
21: 8 others cut down **b** from the trees, and *2798*
Mk 4:32 than all herbs, and shooteth out great **b**; *2798*
11: 8 and others cut down **b** off the trees, *4746*
Lk 13:19 the fowls of the air lodged in the **b** of it. *2798*
Jn 12:13 Took **b** of palm trees, and went forth to meet *902*
15: 5 I am the vine, ye *are* the **b**: He that abideth *2814*
Ro 11:16 and if the root *be* holy, so *are* the **b**. *2798*
11:17 And if some of the **b** be broken off, and *2798*
11:18 Boast not against the **b**: but if thou boast, *2798*
11:19 Thou wilt say then, The **b** were broken off, *2798*
11:21 For if God spared not the natural **b**, *2798*
11:24 which be the natural *b*, be graffed into their NIG

BRAND (1) [BRANDS, FIREBRAND, FIREBRANDS]
Zec 3: 2 *is* not this a **b** pluckt out of the fire? 181

BRANDISH (1)
Eze 32:10 when I shall **b** my sword before them; 5774

BRANDS (1) [BRAND]
Jdg 15: 5 when he had set the **b** on fire, he let *them* 3940

BRASEN (29) [BRASS]
Ex 27: 4 upon the net shalt thou make four **b** rings in 5178
35:16 The altar of burnt offering with his **b** grate, 5178
38: 4 he made for the altar a **b** grate of network 5178
38:10 *were* twenty, and their **b** sockets twenty; 5178
38:30 the **b** altar, and the brasen grate for it, and 5178
38:30 the **b** grate for it, and all the vessels of 5178
39:39 The **b** altar, and his grate of brass, his 5178
Lev 6:28 if it be sodden in a **b** pot, it shall be both 5178
Nu 16:39 Eleazar the priest took the **b** censers, 5178
1Ki 4:13 great cities *with* walls and **b** bars: 5178
7:30 every base had four **b** wheels, and plates of 5178
8:64 the **b** altar that *was* before the LORD *was* 5178
14:27 king Rehoboam made in their stead **b** 5178
2Ki 16:14 he brought also the **b** altar, which *was* 5178
16:15 the **b** altar shall be for me to inquire *by*. 5178
16:17 took down the sea from off the **b** oxen that 5178
18: 4 brake in pieces the **b** serpent that Moses 5178
25:13 the **b** sea that *was* in the house of 5178
1Ch 18: 8 wherewith Solomon made the **b** sea, and 5178
2Ch 1: 5 Moreover the **b** altar, that Bezaleel the son 5178
1: 6 Solomon went up thither to the **b** altar 5178
6:13 For Solomon had made a **b** scaffold, of five 5178
7: 7 the **b** altar which Solomon had made was 5178
Jer 1:18 and **b** walls against the whole land, 5178
15:20 I will make thee unto this people a fenced **b** 5178
52:17 the **b** sea that *was* in the house of 5178
52:20 twelve **b** bulls that *were* under the bases, 5178
Eze 9: 2 they went in, and stood beside the **b** altar. 5178
Mk 7: 4 of cups, and pots, **b vessels**, and of tables. *5473*

BRASS (126) [BRASEN]
Ge 4:22 an instructor of every artificer in **b** and 5178
Ex 25: 3 shall take of them; gold, and silver, and **b**, 5178
26:11 thou shalt make fifty taches of **b**, and 5178
26:37 thou shalt cast five sockets of **b** for them. 5178
27: 2 the same: and thou shalt overlay it with **b**. 5178
27: 3 all the vessels thereof thou shalt make *of* **b**. 5178
27: 4 shalt make for it a grate of network *of* **b**; 5178
27: 6 of shittim wood, and overlay them with **b**. 5178
27:10 and their twenty sockets *shall be of* **b**; 5178
27:11 twenty pillars and their twenty sockets *of* **b**; 5178
27:17 *shall be of* silver, and their sockets *of* **b**. 5178
27:18 *of* fine twined linen, and their sockets *of* **b**. 5178
27:19 and all the pins of the court, *shall be of* **b**. 5178
30:18 Thou shalt also make a laver *of* **b**, and 5178
30:18 his foot *also of* **b**, to wash *withal*: and 5178
31: 4 to work in gold, and in silver, and in **b**, 5178
35: 5 of the LORD; gold, and silver, and **b**, 5178
35:24 and **b** brought the LORD'S offering: 5178
35:32 to work in gold, and in silver, and in **b**, 5178
36:18 he made fifty taches of **b** to couple the tent 5178
36:38 with gold: but their five sockets *were of* **b**. 5178
38: 2 were of the same: and he overlaid it with **b**. 5178
38: 3 all the vessels thereof made he *of* **b**. 5178
38: 5 rings for the four ends of the grate of **b**, 5178
38: 6 *of* shittim wood, and overlaid them with **b**. 5178
38: 8 he made the laver *of* **b**, and the foot of it *of* 5178
38: 8 the laver *of* brass, and the foot of it *of* **b**, 5178
38:11 *were* twenty, and their sockets *of* **b** twenty; 5178
38:17 the sockets for the pillars *were of* **b**; 5178
38:19 *were* four, and their sockets *of* **b** four; 5178
38:20 and of the court round about, *were of* **b**. 5178
38:29 the **b** of the offering *was* seventy talents, 5178
39:39 his grate of **b**, his staves, and all his 5178
Lev 26:19 your heaven as iron, and your earth as **b**: 5154
Nu 21: 9 Moses made a serpent of **b**, and put it upon 5178
21: 9 when he beheld the serpent of **b**, he lived. 5178
31:22 the **b**, the iron, the tin, and the lead, 5178
Dt 8: 9 and out of whose hills thou mayest dig **b**. 5178
28:23 thy heaven that *is* over thy head shall be **b**, 5178
33:25 Thy shoes *shall be* iron and **b**; and as thy 5178
Jos 6:19 and gold, and vessels of **b** and iron, 5178
6:24 the gold, and the vessels of **b** and of iron, 5178
22: 8 with **b**, and with iron, and with very much 5178
Jdg 16:21 to Gaza, and bound him with **fetters of b**; 5178
1Sa 17: 5 *he had* a helmet of **b** upon his head, and 5178
17: 5 of the coat *was* five thousand shekels *of* **b**. 5178
17: 6 *he had* greaves of **b** upon his legs, and 5178
17: 6 and a target of **b** between his shoulders. 5178
17:38 and he put a helmet of **b** upon his head; 5178
2Sa 8: 8 king David took exceeding much **b**. 5178
8:10 and vessels of gold, and vessels of **b**: 5178
21:16 three hundred *shekels* of **b** *in* weight, 5178
1Ki 7:14 his father *was* a man of Tyre, a worker in **b**: 5178
7:14 and cunning to work all works in **b**. 5178
7:15 For he cast two pillars *of* **b**, of eighteen 5178
7:16 he made two chapiters *of* molten **b**, to set 5178
7:27 he made ten bases of **b**; four cubits *was* 5178
7:30 had four brasen wheels, and plates of **b**: 5178
7:38 made he ten lavers of **b**: one laver 5178
7:45 the house of the LORD, *were of* bright **b**. 5178
7:47 neither was the weight of the **b** found out. 5178
2Ki 25: 7 bound him with **fetters of b**, and 5178
25:13 the pillars of **b** that *were in* the house of 5178
25:13 and carried the **b** of them to Babylon. 5178
25:14 all the vessels of **b** wherewith they 5178
25:16 the **b** of all these vessels was without 5178
25:17 and the chapiter upon it *was* **b**: 5178
25:17 upon the chapiter round about, all *of* **b**: 5178
1Ch 15:19 *were appointed* to sound with cymbals of **b**; 5178
18: 8 of Hadarezer, brought David very much **b**, 5178
18: 8 and the pillars, and the vessels of **b**. 5178
18:10 *manner of* vessels of gold and silver and **b**. 5178
22: 3 and **b** in abundance without weight; 5178
22:14 of **b** and iron without weight; for it is in 5178
22:16 the gold, the silver, and the **b**, and the iron, 5178
29: 2 the **b** for *things of* brass, the iron for *things* 5178
29: 2 the brass for *things of* **b**, the iron for *things* 5178
29: 7 *of* **b** eighteen thousand talents, and 5178
2Ch 2: 7 in **b**, and in iron, and in purple, and 5178
2:14 in **b**, in iron, in stone, and in timber, 5178
4: 1 Moreover he made an altar of **b**, 5178
4: 9 and overlaid the doors of them with **b**. 5178
4:16 for the house of the LORD *of* bright **b**. 5178
4:18 for the weight of the **b** could not be found 5178
12:10 which king Rehoboam made shields of **b**, 5178
24:12 and **b** to mend the house of the LORD. 5178
Job 6:12 the strength of stones? or *is* my flesh of **b**? 5153
28: 2 the earth, and **b** *is* molten *out of* the stone. 5154
40:18 His bones *are as* strong pieces of **b**; 5154
41:27 iron as straw, *and* **b** as rotten wood. 5154
Ps 107:16 For he hath broken the gates of **b**, and 5178
Isa 45: 2 I will break in pieces the gates of **b**, and 5154
48: 4 thy neck *is* an iron sinew, and thy brow **b**: 5154
60:17 For **b** I will bring gold, and for iron I will 5178
60:17 and for wood **b**, and for stones iron: 5178
Jer 6:28 *they are* **b** and iron; they *are* all corrupters. 5178
52:17 Also the pillars of **b** that *were* in the house 5178
52:17 and carried all the **b** of them to Babylon. 5178
52:18 all the vessels of **b** wherewith they 5178
52:20 the **b** of all these vessels was without 5178
52:22 a chapiter of **b** *was* upon it; and the height 5178
52:22 upon the chapiters round about, all *of* **b**. 5178
Eze 1: 7 sparkled like the colour of burnished **b**. 5178
22:18 all they *are* **b**, and tin, and iron, and lead, 5178
22:20 and **b**, and iron, and lead, and tin, 5178
24:11 that the **b** of it may be hot, and may burn, 5178

Eze 27:13 of men and vessels of **b** in thy market. 5178
40: 3 appearance *was* like the appearance of **b**, 5178
Da 2:32 arms of silver, his belly and his thighs of **b**, 5174
2:35 the clay, the **b**, the silver, and the gold, 5174
2:39 another third kingdom of **b**, which shall 5174
2:45 the **b**, the clay, the silver, and the gold; 5174
4:15 even with a band of iron and **b**, in 5174
4:23 even with a band of iron and **b**, in 5174
5: 4 of **b**, of iron, of wood, and of stone. 5174
5:23 gold, of **b**, iron, wood, and stone, which see 5174
7:19 whose teeth *were of* iron, and his nails *of* **b**; 5174
10: 6 and his feet like in colour to polished **b**, 5178
Mic 4:13 horn iron, and I will make thy hoofs **b**: 5154
Zec 6: 1 and the mountains *were* mountains of **b**. 5178
Mt 10: 9 nor silver, nor **b** in your purses; *5475*
1Co 13: 1 I am become *as* sounding **b**, or a tinkling *5475*
Rev 1:15 And his feet like unto **fine b**, as if they *5474*
2:18 a flame of fire, and his feet *are* like **fine b**; *5474*
9:20 idols of gold, and silver, and **b**, and stone, *5470*
18:12 and of **b**, and iron, and marble, *5475*

BRAVE See VALIANT; VALOUR

BRAVERY (1)
Isa 3:18 In that day the Lord will take away the **b** of 8597

BRAWLER (1) [BRAWLERS, BRAWLING]
1Ti 3: 3 but patient, **not a b**, not covetous; *269*

BRAWLERS (1) [BRAWLER]
Tit 3: 2 To speak evil of no *man*, to be **no b**, *but* *269*

BRAWLING (2) [BRAWLER]
Pr 21: 9 than with a **b** woman in a wide house. 4066
25:24 than with a **b** woman and in a wide house. 4066

BRAY (2) [BRAYED]
Job 6: 5 Doth the wild ass **b** when he hath grass? or 5101
Pr 27:22 Though thou shouldest **b** a fool in a mortar 3806

BRAYED (1) [BRAY]
Job 30: 7 Among the bushes they **b**; under the nettles 5101

BRAZEN See IMPUDENT

BREACH (22) [BREACHES]
Ge 38:29 *this* **b** *be* upon thee: therefore his name was 6556
Lev 24:20 **B** for breach, eye for eye, tooth for tooth: 7667
24:20 Breach for **b**, eye for eye, tooth for tooth: 7667
Nu 14:34 and ye shall know my **b of promise**. 8569
Jdg 21:15 that the LORD had made a **b** in the tribes 6556
2Sa 5:20 enemies before me, as the **b** of waters. 6556
6: 8 LORD had **made a b** upon Uzzah: 6555+6556
2Ki 12: 5 the house, wheresoever any **b** shall be found. 919
1Ch 13:11 LORD had **made a b** upon Uzza: 6555+6556
15:13 the LORD our God **made a b** upon us, 6555
Ne 6: 1 and *that* there was no **b** left therein; 6556
Job 16:14 He breaketh me *with* **b** upon breach, 6556
16:14 He breaketh me *with* breach upon **b**, 6556
Ps 106:23 his chosen stood before him in the **b**, 6556
Pr 15: 4 but perverseness therein *is* a **b** in the spirit. 7667
Isa 7: 6 let us **make a b** therein for us, and set a 1234
30:13 iniquity shall be to you as a **b** ready to fall, 6556
30:26 in the day that the LORD bindeth up the **b** 7667
58:12 thou shalt be called, The repairer of the **b**, 6556
Jer 14:17 of my people is broken *with* a great **b**, 7667
La 2:13 for thy **b** *is* great like the sea: who can heal 7667
Eze 26:10 men enter into a city wherein is **made a b**. 1234

BREACHES (15) [BREACH]
Jdg 5:17 on the sea shore, and abode in his **b**. 4664
1Ki 11:27 repaired the **b** of the city of David his 6556
2Ki 12: 5 let them repair the **b** of the house, 919
12: 6 priests had not repaired the **b** of the house. 919
12: 7 Why repair ye not the **b** of the house? 919
12: 7 but deliver it for the **b** of the house. 919
12: 8 neither to repair the **b** of the house. 919
12:12 hewed stone to repair the **b** of the house of 919
22: 5 of the LORD, to repair the **b** of the house, 919
Ne 4: 7 *and* that the **b** began to be stopped, then 6555
Ps 60: 2 broken it: heal the **b** thereof; for it shaketh. 7667
Isa 22: 9 Ye have seen also the **b** of the city of 1233
Am 4: 3 ye shall go out *at* the **b**, every *cow at that* 6556
6:11 he will smite the great house *with* **b**, and 7447
9:11 that is fallen, and close up the **b** thereof; 6556

BREAD (361) [SHEWBREAD]
Ge 3:19 In the sweat of thy face shalt thou eat **b**, 3899
14:18 Melchizedek king of Salem brought forth **b** 3899
18: 5 I will fetch a morsel of **b**, and comfort ye 3899
19: 3 did bake **unleavened b**, and they did eat. 4682
21:14 took **b**, and a bottle of water, and gave *it* 3899
25:34 Jacob gave Esau **b** and pottage of lentiles; 3899
27:17 she gave the savoury meat and the **b**, 3899
28:20 will give me **b** to eat, and raiment to put on, 3899
31:54 the mount, and called his brethren to eat **b**: 3899
31:54 they did eat **b**, and tarried all night in 3899
37:25 they sat down to eat **b**: and they lift up their 3899
39: 6 ought he had, save the **b** which he did eat. 3899
41:54 but in all the land of Egypt there was **b**. 3899
41:55 the people cried to Pharaoh for **b**: 3899
43:25 for they heard that they should eat **b** there. 3899
43:31 and refrained himself, and said, Set on **b**. 3899
43:32 the Egyptians might not eat **b** with 3899
45:23 ten she asses laden with corn and **b** and 3899
47:12 and all his father's household, *with* **b**, 3899
47:13 *there was* no **b** in all the land; for 3899
47:15 came unto Joseph, and said, Give us **b**: 3899
47:17 Joseph gave them **b** *in exchange* for horses, 3899
47:17 he fed them with **b** for all their cattle for 3899
47:19 buy us and our land for **b**, and we and 3899
49:20 Out of Asher his **b** *shall be* fat, and he shall 3899
Ex 2:20 left the man? call him, that he may eat **b**. 3899
12: 8 roast with fire, and **unleavened b**; 4682
Ex 12:15 Seven days shall ye eat **unleavened b**; 4682
12:15 for whosoever eateth **leavened b** from 2557
12:17 ye shall observe the *feast of* **unleavened b**; 4682
12:18 ye shall eat **unleavened b**, until the one and 4682
12:20 your habitations shall ye eat **unleavened b**. 4682
13: 3 *place:* there shall no **leavened b** be eaten. 2557
13: 6 Seven days thou shalt eat **unleavened b**, 4682
13: 7 **Unleavened b** shall be eaten seven days; 4682
13: 7 there shall no **leavened b** be seen with thee, 2557
16: 3 *and* when we did eat **b** to the full; 3899
16: 4 Behold, I will rain **b** from heaven for you; 3899
16: 8 to eat, and in the morning **b** to the full; 3899
16:12 and in the morning ye shall be filled *with* **b**; 3899
16:15 This *is* the **b** which the LORD hath given 3899
16:22 sixth day they gathered twice as much **b**, 3899
16:29 he giveth you on the sixth day the **b** of two 3899
16:32 that they may see the **b** wherewith I have 3899
18:12 to eat **b** with Moses' father in law before 3899
23:15 Thou shalt keep the feast of **unleavened b**: 4682
23:15 thou shalt eat **unleavened b** seven days, 4682
23:18 the blood of my sacrifice with **leavened b**; 2557
23:25 and he shall bless thy **b**, and thy water; 3899
29: 2 unleavened **b**, and cakes unleavened 3899
29:23 one loaf of **b**, and one cake of oiled bread, 3899
29:23 one cake of oiled **b**, and one wafer out of 3899
29:23 **unleavened b** that *is* before the LORD: 4682
29:32 of the ram, and the **b** that *is* in the basket, 3899
29:34 or of the **b**, remain unto the morning, then 3899
34:18 The feast of **unleavened b** shalt thou keep: 4682
34:18 seven days thou shalt eat **unleavened b**, 4682
34:28 he did neither eat **b**, nor drink water. 3899
40:23 he set the **b** in order upon it before 3899
Lev 6:16 *with* **unleavened b** shall it be eaten in 4682
7:13 he shall offer *for* his offering leavened **b** 3899
8: 2 two rams, and a basket of **unleavened b**; 4682
8:26 out of the basket of **unleavened b**, that *was* 4682
8:26 a cake of oiled **b**, and one wafer, and 3899
8:31 there eat it with the **b** that *is* in the basket of 3899
8:32 and of the **b** shall ye burn with fire. 3899
21: 6 *and* the **b** of their God, they do offer: 3899
21: 8 for he offereth the **b** of thy God: 3899
21:17 let him not approach to offer the **b** of his 3899
21:21 he shall not come nigh to offer the **b** of his 3899
21:22 He shall eat the **b** of his God, *both* of 3899
22:25 ye offer the **b** of your God of any of these; 3899
23: 6 the feast of **unleavened b** unto the LORD: 4682
23: 6 seven days ye must eat **unleavened b**. 4682
23:14 ye shall eat neither **b**, nor parched *corn*, nor 3899
23:18 ye shall offer with the **b** seven lambs 3899
23:20 the priest shall wave them with the **b** of 3899
24: 7 that it may be on the **b** for a memorial, 3899
26: 5 ye shall eat your **b** to the full, and dwell in 3899
26:26 when I have broken the staff of your **b**, 3899
26:26 ten women shall bake your **b** in one oven, 3899
26:26 they shall deliver *you* your **b** again by 3899
Nu 4: 7 and the continual **b** shall be thereon: 3899
6:15 a basket of **unleavened b**, cakes *of* fine 4682
6:15 wafers of **unleavened b** anointed with oil, 4682
6:17 with the basket of **unleavened b**: 4682
9:11 *and* eat it with **unleavened b** and 4682
14: 9 the people of the land; for they *are* **b** for us: 3899
15:19 *that* when ye eat of the **b** of the land, 3899
21: 5 for *there is* no **b**, neither *is there any* water; 3899
21: 5 and our soul loatheth *this* light **b**. 3899
28: 2 *and* my **b** for my sacrifices made by fire, 3899
28:17 seven days shall **unleavened b** be eaten. 4682
Dt 8: 3 thee know that man doth not live by **b** only, 3899
8: 9 A land wherein thou shalt eat **b** without 3899
9: 9 I neither did eat **b** nor drink water: 3899
9:18 I did neither eat **b**, nor drink water, because 3899
16: 3 Thou shalt eat no **leavened b** with it; 2557
16: 3 seven days shalt thou eat **unleavened b** 4682
16: 3 bread therewith, *even* the **b** of affliction; 3899
16: 4 there shall be no **leavened b** seen with thee 7603
16: 8 Six days thou shalt eat **unleavened b**: and 4682
16:16 in the feast of **unleavened b**, and in 4682
23: 4 Because they met you not with **b** and 3899
29: 6 Ye have not eaten **b**, neither have you 3899
Jos 9: 5 all the **b** of their provision was dry *and* 3899
9:12 This our **b** we took hot for our provision 3899
Jdg 7:13 a cake of barley **b** tumbled into the host of 3899
8: 5 loaves of **b** unto the people that follow me; 3899
8: 6 that we should give **b** unto thine army? 3899
8:15 that we should give **b** unto thy men *that are* 3899
13:16 thou detain me, I will not eat of thy **b**: 3899
19: 5 Comfort thine heart *with* a morsel of **b**, and 3899
19:19 there is **b** and wine also for me, and for thy 3899
Ru 1: 6 had visited his people in giving them **b**. 3899
2:14 eat of the **b**, and dip thy morsel in 3899
1Sa 2: 5 *were* full have hired out themselves for **b**; 3899
2:36 him for a piece of silver and a morsel of **b**, 3899
2:36 priests' offices, that *I* may eat a piece of **b**. 3899
9: 7 for the **b** is spent in our vessels, and *there is* 3899
10: 3 another carrying three loaves of **b**, and 3899
10: 4 salute thee, and give thee two *loaves* of **b**; 3899
16:20 Jesse took an ass *laden* with **b**, and a bottle 3899
21: 3 give *me* five *loaves of* **b** in mine hand, or 3899
21: 4 *There is* no common **b** under mine hand, 3899
21: 4 under mine hand, but there is hallowed **b**; 3899
21: 5 and *the* **b** *is in* a manner common, yea, NIH
21: 6 So the priest gave him hallowed *b*: for there NIH
21: 6 hallowed *bread:* for there was no **b** there 3899
21: 6 to put hot **b** in the day when it was taken 3899
22:13 in that thou hast given him **b** and a sword, 3899
25:11 Shall I then take my **b**, and my water, and 3899
28:20 for he had eaten no **b** all the day, nor all 3899
28:22 and let me set a morsel of **b** before thee; 3899
28:24 and did bake **unleavened b** thereof: 4682
30:11 to David, and gave him **b**, and he did eat; 3899
30:12 for he had eaten no **b**, nor drunk *any* water, 3899
2Sa 3:29 that falleth on the sword, or that lacketh **b**. 3899
3:35 and more also, if I taste **b**, or ought else, 3899
6:19 to every one a cake of **b**, and a good piece 3899
9: 7 and thou shalt eat **b** at my table continually. 3899
9:10 Mephibosheth thy master's son shall eat **b** 3899
2Sa 12:17 would not, neither did he eat **b** with them. 3899
12:20 they set **b** before him, and he did eat. 3899
12:21 child was dead, thou didst rise and eat **b**. 3899
16: 1 upon them two hundred *loaves of* **b**, and 3899
16: 2 the **b** and summer fruit for the young men 3899
1Ki 13: 8 neither will I eat **b** nor drink water in this 3899
13: 9 saying, Eat no **b**, nor drink water, 3899
13:15 unto him, Come home with me, and eat **b**. 3899
13:16 neither will I eat **b** nor drink water with 3899
13:17 Thou shalt eat no **b** nor drink water there, 3899
13:18 that he may eat **b** and drink water. 3899
13:19 and did eat **b** in his house, and drank water. 3899
13:22 hast eaten **b** and drunk water in the place, 3899
13:22 say to thee, Eat no **b**, and drink no water; 3899
13:23 after he had eaten **b**, and after he had 3899
17: 6 the ravens brought him **b** and flesh in 3899
17: 6 and **b** and flesh in the evening; 3899
17:11 I pray thee, a morsel of **b** in thine hand. 3899
18: 4 in a cave, and fed them *with* **b** and water.) 3899
18:13 in a cave, and fed them *with* **b** and water? 3899
21: 4 turned away his face, and would eat no **b**. 3899
21: 5 is thy spirit so sad, that thou eatest no **b**? 3899
21: 7 *and* eat **b**, and let thine heart be merry: 3899
22:27 feed him with **b** of affliction and with water 3899
2Ki 4: 8 and she constrained him to eat **b**. 3899
4: 8 he passed by, he turned in thither to eat **b**. 3899
4:42 brought the man of God **b** of the firstfruits, 3899
6:22 set **b** and water before them, that they may 3899
18:32 and wine, a land of **b** and vineyards, 3899
23: 9 they did eat of the **unleavened b** among 4682
25: 3 there was no **b** for the people of the land. 3899
25:29 he did eat **b** continually before him all 3899
1Ch 12:40 brought **b** on asses, and on camels, and 3899
16: 3 to every one a loaf of **b**, and a good piece 3899
2Ch 8:13 *even* in the feast of **unleavened b**, and 4682
18:26 feed him with **b** of affliction and with water 3899
30:13 feast of **unleavened b** in the second month, 4682
30:21 **unleavened b** seven days with great 4682
35:17 the feast of **unleavened b** seven days. 4682
Ezr 6:22 kept the feast of **unleavened b** seven days 4682
10: 6 he did eat no **b**, nor drink water: 3899
Ne 5:14 my brethren have not eaten the **b** of 3899
5:15 had taken of them **b** and wine, beside forty 3899
5:18 yet for *all* this required not I the **b** of 3899
9:15 gavest them **b** from heaven for their 3899
13: 2 they met not the children of Israel with **b** 3899
Job 15:23 He wandereth abroad for **b**, *saying*, Where 3899
22: 7 thou hast withholden **b** from the hungry. 3899
27:14 his offspring shall not be satisfied *with* **b**. 3899
28: 5 *As for* the earth, out of it cometh **b**: and 3899
33:20 So that his life abhorreth **b**, and his soul 3899
42:11 and did eat **b** with him in his house: 3899
Ps 14: 4 who eat up my people *as* they eat **b**, *and* 3899
37:25 righteous forsaken, nor his seed begging **b**. 3899
41: 9 in whom I trusted, which did eat *of* my **b**, 3899
53: 4 who eat up my people *as* they eat **b**: 3899
78:20 the streams overflowed; can he give **b** also? 3899
80: 5 Thou feedest them with the **b** of tears; and 3899
102: 4 like grass; so that I forget to eat my **b**. 3899
102: 9 For I have eaten ashes like **b**, and 3899
104:15 and **b** *which* strengtheneth man's heart. 3899
105:16 the land: he brake the whole staff of **b**. 3899
105:40 and satisfied them *with* the **b** of heaven. 3899
109:10 let them seek *their* **b** also out of their NIH
127: 2 to sit up late, to eat the **b** of sorrows: 3899
132:15 her provision: I will satisfy her poor *with* **b**. 3899
Pr 4:17 For they eat the **b** of wickedness, and 3899
6:26 woman *a man is brought* to a piece of **b**: 3899
9: 5 eat of my **b**, and drink of the wine *which* I 3899
9:17 are sweet, and **b** *eaten* in secret is pleasant. 3899
12: 9 that honoureth himself, and lacketh **b**. 3899
12:11 that tilleth his land shall be satisfied *with* **b**: 3899
20:13 *and* thou shalt be satisfied *with* **b**. 3899
20:17 **B** of deceit *is* sweet to a man; but 3899
22: 9 for he giveth of his **b** to the poor. 3899
23: 6 Eat thou not the **b** of *him that hath* an evil 3899
25:21 thine enemy *be* hungry, give him **b** to eat; 3899
28:19 that tilleth his land shall have plenty *of* **b**: 3899
28:21 for for a piece of **b** *that* man will transgress. 3899
31:27 and eateth not the **b** of idleness. 3899
Ecc 9: 7 Go *thy way*, eat thy **b** with joy, and 3899
9:11 to the strong, neither yet **b** to the wise, 3899
11: 1 Cast thy **b** upon the waters: for thou shalt 3899
Isa 3: 1 the whole stay of **b**, and the whole stay of 3899
3: 7 for in my house *is* neither **b** nor clothing: 3899
4: 1 We will eat our own **b**, and wear our own 3899
21:14 they prevented with their **b** him that fled. 3899
28:28 **B** *corn* is bruised; because he will not ever 3899
30:20 *though* the Lord give you the **b** of 3899
30:23 **b** of the increase of the earth, and it shall be 3899
33:16 **b** *shall be* given him; his waters *shall be* 3899
36:17 and wine, a land of **b** and vineyards. 3899
44:15 yea, he kindleth *it*, and baketh **b**; yea, 3899
44:19 also I have baked **b** upon the coals thereof; 3899
51:14 not die in the pit, nor that his **b** should fail. 3899
55: 2 do ye spend money for *that which is* not **b**? 3899
55:10 give seed to the sower, and **b** to the eater: 3899
58: 7 *Is it* not to deal thy **b** to the hungry, and 3899
Jer 5:17 thy **b**, *which* thy sons and thy daughters 3899
37:21 that *they* should give him daily a piece of **b** 3899
37:21 until all the **b** in the city were spent. 3899
38: 9 he is: for *there is* no more **b** in the city. 3899
41: 1 and there they did eat **b** together in Mizpah. 3899
42:14 sound of the trumpet, nor have hunger of **b**; 3899
52: 6 that there was no **b** for the people of 3899
52:33 he did continually eat **b** before him all 3899
La 1:11 All her people sigh, they seek **b**; they have 3899
4: 4 the young children ask **b**, *and* no man 3899
5: 6 *and* to the Assyrians, to be satisfied *with* **b**. 3899
5: 9 We gat our **b** with *the peril of* our lives 3899
Eze 4: 9 in one vessel, and make thee **b** thereof, 3899
4:13 eat their defiled **b** among the Gentiles, 3899
4:15 and thou shalt prepare thy **b** therewith. 3899
4:16 I will break the staff of **b** in Jerusalem: 3899
4:16 they shall eat **b** by weight, and with care; 3899

Eze 4:17 That they may want **b** and water, and 3899
5:16 upon you, and will break your staff of **b**: 3899
12:18 eat thy **b** with quaking, and drink thy water 3899
12:19 They shall eat their **b** with carefulness, and 3899
13:19 for handfuls of barley and for pieces of **b**, 3899
14:13 will break the staff of the **b** thereof, and 3899
16:49 fulness of **b**, and abundance of idleness was 3899
18: 7 hath given his **b** to the hungry, and 3899
18:16 *but* hath given his **b** to the hungry, and 3899
24:17 cover not *thy* lips, and eat not the **b** of men. 3899
24:22 not cover *your* lips, nor eat the **b** of men. 3899
44: 3 he shall sit in it to eat **b** before the LORD; 3899
44: 7 when ye offer my **b**, the fat and the blood, 3899
45:21 of seven days; **unleavened b** shall be eaten. 4682
Da 10: 3 I ate no pleasant **b**, neither came flesh nor 3899
Hos 2: 5 that give *me* my **b** and my water, my wool 3899
9: 4 their sacrifices *shall be* unto them as the **b** 3899
9: 4 for their **b** for their soul shall not come *into* 3899
Am 4: 6 and want of **b** in all your places: 3899
7:12 and there eat **b**, and prophesy there: 3899
8:11 not a famine of **b**, nor a thirst for water, but 3899
Ob 1: 7 *they that eat* thy **b** have laid a wound under 3899
Hag 2:12 with his skirt do touch **b**, or pottage, or 3899
Mal 1: 7 *Ye* offer polluted **b** upon mine altar; and 3899
Mt 4: 3 command that these stones be made **b**. *740*
4: 4 Man shall not live by **b** alone, but by every *740*
6:11 Give us this day our daily **b**. *740*
7: 9 whom if his son ask **b**, will he give him a *740*
15: 2 they wash not their hands when they eat **b**. *740*
15:26 It is not meet to take the children's **b**, and *740*
15:33 should we have so much **b** in the wilderness, *740*
16: 5 the other side, they had forgotten to take **b**. *740*
16: 7 saying, *It is* because we have taken no **b**. *740*
16: 8 because ye have brought no **b**? *740*
16:11 that I spake *it* not to you concerning **b**, *740*
16:12 he bade *them* not beware of the leaven of **b**, *740*
26:17 *of* **unleavened b** the disciples came to Jesus, *106*
26:26 Jesus took **b**, and blessed *it*, and brake *it*, and *740*
Mk 3:20 so that they could not so much as eat **b**. *740*
6: 8 no scrip, no **b**, no money in *their* purse: *740*
6:36 and *into* the villages, and buy themselves **b**: *740*
6:37 and buy two hundred pennyworth of **b**, *740*
7: 2 saw some of his disciples eat **b** with defiled, *740*
7: 5 the elders, but eat **b** with unwashen hands? *740*
7:27 for it is not meet to take the children's **b**, and *740*
8: 4 these *men* with **b** here in the wilderness? *740*
8:14 Now *the disciples* had forgotten to take **b**, *740*
8:16 saying, *It is* because we have no **b**. *740*
8:17 Why reason ye, because ye have no **b**? *740*
14: 1 *feast of* the passover, and *of* **unleavened b**: *106*
14:12 And the first day of **unleavened b**, *106*
14:22 Jesus took **b**, and blessed, and brake *it*, and *740*
Lk 4: 3 command this stone that it be made **b**. *740*
4: 4 That man shall not live by **b** alone, but *740*
7:33 For John the Baptist came neither eating **b** *740*
9: 3 neither staves, nor scrip, neither **b**, *740*
11: 3 Give us day by day our daily **b**. *740*
11:11 *If* a son shall ask **b** of any of you that is a *740*
14: 1 chief Pharisees to eat **b** on the sabbath day, *740*
14:15 Blessed *is he* that shall eat **b** in the kingdom *740*
15:17 hired *servants* of my father's have **b** enough *740*
22: 1 Now the feast of **unleavened b** drew nigh, *106*
22: 7 Then came the day of **unleavened b**, *106*
22:19 And he took **b**, and gave thanks, and *740*
24:30 he took **b**, and blessed *it*, and brake, and *740*
24:35 how he was known of them in breaking of **b**. *740*
Jn 6: 5 Whence shall we buy **b**, that these may eat? *740*
6: 7 Two hundred pennyworth of **b** is not *740*
6:23 nigh unto the place where they did eat **b**, *740*
6:31 He gave them **b** from heaven to eat. *740*
6:32 Moses gave you not *that* **b** from heaven; *740*
6:32 my Father giveth you the true **b** from *740*
6:33 For the **b** of God is he which cometh down *740*
6:34 unto him, Lord, evermore give us this **b**. *740*
6:35 And Jesus said unto them, I am the **b** of life: *740*
6:41 I am the **b** which came down from heaven. *740*
6:48 I am *that* **b** of life. *740*
6:50 This is the **b** which cometh down from *740*
6:51 I am the living **b** which came down from *740*
6:51 if any *man* eat of this **b**, he shall live for *740*
6:51 and the **b** that I will give is my flesh, which I *740*
6:58 This is *that* **b** which came down from *740*
6:58 he that eateth *of* this **b** shall live for ever. *740*
13:18 He that eateth **b** with me hath lift up his heel *740*
21: 9 of coals there, and fish laid thereon, and **b**. *740*
21:13 and taketh **b**, and giveth them, and *740*
Ac 2:42 and in breaking of **b**, and in prayers. *740*
2:46 and breaking **b** from house to house, did eat *740*
12: 3 (Then were the days of **unleavened b**.) *106*
20: 6 Philippi after the days of **unleavened b**, *106*
20: 7 when the disciples came together to break **b**, *740*
20:11 was come up *again*, and had broken **b**, *740*
27:35 he took **b**, and gave thanks to God in *740*
1Co 5: 8 but with the **unleavened b** of sincerity and *106*
10:16 The **b** which we break, is it not *740*
10:17 For we being many are one **b**, *and* one body: *740*
10:17 for we are all partakers of *that* one **b**. *740*
11:23 *same* night in which he was betrayed took **b**: *740*
11:26 For as often as ye eat this **b**, and drink this *740*
11:27 Wherefore whosoever shall eat this **b**, and *740*
11:28 and so let him eat of *that* **b**, and drink of *that* *740*
2Co 9:10 to the sower both minister **b** for *your* food, *740*
2Th 3: 8 Neither did we eat any *man's* **b** for nought; *740*
3:12 quietness they work, and eat their own **b**. *740*

BREAD OF THE PRESENCE See SHEWBREAD

BREADTH (87) [BROAD, HANDBREADTH]

Ge 6:15 the **b** of it fifty cubits, and the height of it 7341
13:17 the land in the length of it and in the **b** of it; 7341
Ex 25:10 a cubit and a half the **b** thereof, and a cubit 7341
25:17 and a cubit and a half the **b** thereof. 7341
25:23 a cubit the **b** thereof, and a cubit and a half 7341
26: 2 and the **b** of one curtain four cubits: 7341
26: 8 and the **b** of one curtain four cubits: 7341
Ex 26:16 and a half *shall be* the **b** of one board. 7341
27:12 *for* the **b** of the court on the west side *shall* 7341
27:13 the **b** of the court on the east side eastward 7341
27:18 the **b** fifty every where, and the height five 7341
28:16 and a span *shall be* the **b** thereof. 7341
30: 2 the length thereof, and a cubit the **b** thereof; 7341
36: 9 and the **b** of one curtain four cubits: 7341
36:15 and four cubits *was* the **b** of one curtain: 7341
36:21 and the **b** of a board one cubit and a half. 7341
37: 1 a cubit and a half the **b** of it, and a cubit 7341
37: 6 and one cubit and a half the **b** thereof. 7341
37:10 a cubit the **b** thereof, and a cubit and a half 7341
37:25 of it *was* a cubit, and the **b** of it a cubit; 7341
38: 1 and five cubits the **b** thereof; 7341
38:18 and the height in the **b** *was* five cubits, 7341
39: 9 and a span the **b** thereof, *being* doubled. 7341
Dt 2: 5 of their land, no, not so much as a foot **b**; 4096
3:11 four cubits the **b** of it, after the cubit of a 7341
Jdg 20:16 every one could sling stones at a hair *b*, and NIH
1Ki 6: 2 the **b** thereof twenty *cubits*, and the height 7341
6: 3 according to the **b** of the house; 7341
6: 3 ten cubits *was* the **b** thereof before 7341
6:20 twenty cubits in **b**, and twenty cubits in 7341
7: 2 the **b** thereof fifty cubits, and the height 7341
7: 6 fifty cubits, and the **b** thereof thirty cubits: 7341
7:27 four cubits the **b** thereof, and three cubits 7341
2Ch 3: 3 threescore cubits, and the **b** twenty cubits. 7341
3: 4 *of it was* according to the **b** of the house, 7341
3: 8 the length whereof *was* according to the **b** 7341
3: 8 and the **b** thereof twenty cubits: 7341
4: 1 twenty cubits the **b** thereof, and ten cubits 7341
Ezr 6: 3 *and* the **b** thereof threescore cubits; 6613
Job 37:10 and the **b** of the waters is straitened. 7341
38:18 Hast thou perceived the **b** of the earth? 7338
Isa 8: 8 out of his wings shall fill the **b** of thy land, 7341
Eze 40: 5 six cubits *long* by the cubit and a **hand b**: 2948
40: 5 so he measured the **b** of the building, 7341
40:11 he measured the **b** of the entry of the gate, 7341
40:13 the **b** *was* five and twenty cubits, 7341
40:19 he measured the **b** from the forefront of 7341
40:20 the length thereof, and the **b** thereof. 7341
40:21 and the **b** five and twenty cubits. 7341
40:25 and the **b** five and twenty cubits. 7341
40:36 and the **b** five and twenty cubits. 7341
40:48 the **b** of the gate *was* three cubits on this 7341
40:49 *was* twenty cubits, and the **b** eleven cubits; 7341
41: 1 *which was* the **b** of the tabernacle. 7341
41: 2 the **b** of the door *was* ten cubits; and 7341
41: 2 forty cubits: and the **b**, twenty cubits. 7341
41: 3 and the **b** of the door, seven cubits. 7341
41: 4 and the **b**, twenty cubits, before the temple: 7341
41: 5 the **b** of *every* side chamber, four cubits, 7341
41: 7 the **b** of the house *was still* upward, 7341
41:11 the **b** of the place that was left *was* five 7341
41:14 Also the **b** of the face of the house, and 7341
42: 2 the north door, and the **b** *was* fifty cubits. 7341
42: 4 *was* a walk of ten cubits **b** inward, 7341
43:13 The cubit *is* a cubit and a **hand b**; even 2948
43:13 the **b** a cubit, and the border thereof by 7341
43:14 *shall be* two cubits, and the **b** one cubit; 7341
43:14 *shall be* four cubits, and the **b** *one* cubit. 7341
45: 1 and the **b** *shall be* ten thousand. 7341
45: 2 with five hundred *in b*, square round about; NIH
45: 3 twenty thousand, and the **b** of ten thousand: 7341
45: 5 *the* ten thousand of **b**, shall also 7341
48: 8 *of* five and twenty thousand *reeds in* **b**, 7341
48: 9 *in* length, and *of* ten thousand *in* **b**. 7341
48:10 and toward the west ten thousand *in* **b**, 7341
48:10 toward the east ten thousand *in* **b**, and 7341
48:13 thousand *in* length, and ten thousand *in* **b**: 7341
48:13 twenty thousand, and the **b** ten thousand. 7341
48:15 that are left in the **b** over against the five 7341
Da 3: 1 *and* the **b** thereof six cubits: 6613
Hab 1: 6 which *shall* march through the **b** of 4800
Zec 2: 2 to see what *is* the **b** thereof, and what *is* 7341
5: 2 twenty cubits, and the **b** thereof ten cubits. 7341
Eph 3:18 to comprehend with all saints what *is* the **b**, *4114*
Rev 20: 9 And they went up on the **b** of the earth, and *4114*
21:16 and the length is as large as the **b**: *4114*
21:16 The length and the **b** and the height of it are *4114*

BREAK (140) [BRAKE, BRAKEST, BREAKER, BREAKEST, BREAKETH, BREAKING, BREAKINGS, BROKEN, BROKEN-HEARTED, BROKENFOOTED, BROKENHANDED, COVENANT-BREAKERS, TRUCEBREAKERS]

Ge 19: 9 *even* Lot, and came near to **b** the door. 7665
27:40 that thou shalt **b** his yoke from off thy 6561
Ex 12:46 the house; neither shall ye **b** a bone thereof. 7665
13:13 not redeem *it*, then thou shalt **b** his **neck**: 6202
19:21 lest they **b through** unto the LORD to 2040
19:22 lest the LORD **b forth** upon them. 6555
19:24 the people **b through** to come up unto 2040
19:24 the LORD, lest he **b forth** upon them. 6555
22: 6 If fire **b out**, and catch in thorns, so that 3318
23:24 and **quite b down** their images. 7665+7665
32: 2 said unto them, **B off** the golden earrings, 6561
32:24 Whosoever hath *any* gold, let them **b** *it* **off**. 6561
34:13 **b** their images, and cut down their groves: 7665
34:20 redeem *him* not, then shalt thou **b** his **neck**. 6202
Lev 11:33 *is* in it shall be unclean; and ye shall **b** it. 7665
13:12 if a leprosy **b out abroad** in the skin, 6524+6524
14:43 plague come again, and **b out** in the house, 6524
14:45 he shall **b down** the house, the stones of it, 5422
26:15 *but* that ye **b** my covenant: 6565
26:19 I will **b** the pride of your power; and I will 7665
26:44 and to **b** my covenant with them: 6565
Nu 9:12 of it unto the morning, nor **b** any bone of it: 7665
24: 8 shall **b** their bones, and pierce *them* 1633
30: 2 he shall not **b** his word, he shall do 2490
Dt 7: 5 **b down** their images, and cut down their 7665
12: 3 **b** their pillars, and burn their groves with 7665
31:16 **b** my covenant which I have made with 6565
31:20 and provoke me, and **b** my covenant. 6565
Jdg 2: 1 I said, I will never **b** my covenant with you. 6565
8: 9 again in peace, I will **b down** this tower. 5422
1Sa 25:10 that **b away** every man from his master. 6555
2Sa 2:32 and they came to Hebron **at b of day**. 215
1Ki 15:19 **b** thy league with Baasha king of Israel, 6565
2Ki 3:26 to **b through** *even* unto the king of Edom: 1234
25:13 did the Chaldees **b** *in pieces*, and 7665
2Ch 16: 3 go, **b** thy league with Baasha king of Israel, 6565
Ezr 9:14 Should we again **b** thy commandments, and 6565
Ne 4: 3 he shall even **b down** their stone wall. 6555
Job 13:25 Wilt thou **b** a leaf driven to and fro? and 6206
19: 2 my soul, and **b** me **in pieces** with words? 1792
34:24 He shall **b in pieces** mighty *men* without 7489
39:15 or *that* the wild beast may **b** them. 1758
Ps 2: 3 Let us **b** their bands **asunder**, and 5423
2: 9 Thou shalt **b** them with a rod of iron; 7489
10:15 **B** thou the arm of the wicked and the evil 7665
58: 6 **B** their teeth, O God, in their mouth: 2040
58: 6 **b out** the great teeth of the young lions, 5422
72: 4 and shall **b in pieces** the oppressor. 1792
74: 6 now they **b down** the carved work thereof 1986
89:31 If they **b** my statutes, and keep not my 2490
89:34 My covenant will I not **b**, nor alter 2490
94: 5 They **b in pieces** thy people, O LORD, 1792
141: 5 an excellent oil, *which* shall not **b** my head: 5106
Ecc 3: 3 a time to **b down**, and a time to build *up*; 6555
SS 2:17 Until the day **b**, and the shadows flee away, 6315
4: 6 Until the day **b**, and the shadows flee away, 6315
Isa 5: 5 *and* **b down** the wall thereof, and it shall be 6555
14: 7 *and* is quiet: they **b forth** *into* singing. 6476
14:25 That *I* will **b** the Assyrian in my land, and 7665
28:24 he open and **b the clods** of his ground? 7702
28:28 nor **b** *it with* the wheel of his cart, 2000
30:14 he shall **b** it as the breaking of the potters' 7665
35: 6 for in the wilderness shall waters **b out**, and 1234
38:13 *that*, as a lion, so will he **b** all my bones: 7665
42: 3 A bruised reed shall he not **b**, and 7665
44:23 **b forth** *into* singing, ye mountains, 6476
45: 2 I will **b in pieces** the gates of brass, and 7665
49:13 and **b forth** *into* singing, O mountains: 6476
52: 9 **B forth** into joy, sing together, ye waste 6476
54: 1 **b forth** *into* singing, and cry aloud, 6476
54: 3 For thou shalt **b forth** *on* the right hand and 6555
55:12 the hills shall **b forth** before you *into* 6476
58: 6 go free, and *that* ye **b** every yoke? 5423
58: 8 shall thy light **b forth** as the morning, and 1234
Jer 1:14 Out of the north an evil shall **b forth** upon 6605
4: 3 **B up** your fallow ground, and sow not 5214
14:21 remember, **b** not thy covenant with us. 6565
15:12 Shall iron **b** the northern iron and the steel? 7489
19:10 shalt thou **b** the bottle in the sight of 7665
19:11 Even so will I **b** this people and this city, as 7665
28: 4 for I will **b** the yoke of the king of Babylon. 7665
28:11 will I **b** the yoke of Nebuchadnezzar king 7665
30: 8 *that* I will **b** his yoke from off thy neck, and 7665
31:28 to **b down**, and to throw down, and 5422
33:20 If you can **b** my covenant of the day, and 6565
43:13 He shall **b** also the images of 7665
45: 4 *that* which I have built *will* I **b down**, and 2040
48:12 shall empty his vessels, and **b** their bottles. 5310
49:35 Behold, I *will* **b** the bow of Elam, the chief 7665
51:20 for with thee will I **b in pieces** the nations, 5310
51:21 with thee will I **b in pieces** the horse and 5310
51:21 with thee will I **b in pieces** the chariot and 5310
51:22 With thee also will I **b in pieces** man and 5310
51:22 with thee will I **b in pieces** old and young; 5310
51:22 with thee will I **b in pieces** the young man 5310
51:23 I will also **b in pieces** with thee 5310
51:23 with thee will I **b in pieces** the husbandman 5310
51:23 with thee will I **b in pieces** captains and 5310
Eze 4:16 I will **b** the staff of bread in Jerusalem: 7665
5:16 upon you, and will **b** your staff of bread: 7665
13:14 So will I **b down** the wall that ye have 2040
14:13 will **b** the staff of the bread thereof, and 7665
16:38 as *women* that **b wedlock** and shed blood 5003
16:39 and shall **b down** thy high places: 5422
17:15 such *things*? or shall he **b** the covenant, 6565
23:34 thou shalt **b** the sheards thereof, and 1633
26: 4 the walls of Tyrus, and **b down** her towers: 2040
26: 9 with his axes he shall **b down** thy towers. 5422
26:12 they shall **b down** thy walls, and 2040
29: 7 thou didst **b**, and rent all their shoulder: 7533
30:18 when I shall **b** there the yokes of Egypt: 7665
30:22 will **b** his arms, the strong, and that which 7665
30:24 I will **b** Pharaoh's arms, and he shall groan 7665
Da 2:40 all these, shall it **b in pieces** and bruise. 1855
2:44 *but* it shall **b in pieces** and consume all 1855
4:27 **b off** thy sins by righteousness, and 6562
7:23 and shall tread it down, and **b** it **in pieces**. 1855
Hos 1: 5 that I will **b** the bow of Israel in the valley 7665
2:18 I will **b** the bow and the sword and 7665
4: 2 they **b out**, and blood toucheth blood. 6555
10: 2 he shall **b down** their altars, he shall spoil 6202
10:11 shall plow, *and* Jacob shall **b** his **clods**. 7702
10:12 reap in mercy; **b up** your fallow ground: 5214
Joel 2: 7 his ways, and they shall not **b** their ranks: 5670
Am 1: 5 I will **b** also the bar of Damascus, and 7665
5: 6 lest he **b out** like fire *in* the house of 6743
Mic 3: 3 they **b** their bones, and chop *them* in 6476
Na 1:13 For now will I **b** his yoke from off thee, 7665
Zec 11:10 that *I* might **b** my covenant which I had 6565
11:14 that I might **b** the brotherhood between 6565
Mt 5:19 shall **b** one of these least commandments, *3089*
6:19 and where thieves **b through** and steal: *1358*
6:20 where thieves do not **b through** nor steal: *1358*
9:17 else the bottles **b**, and the wine runneth out, *4486*
12:20 A bruised reed shall he not **b**, and *2608*
Ac 20: 7 when the disciples came together to **b** *2806*
20:11 *even* till **b of day**, so he departed. *827*
21:13 mean ye to weep and to **b** mine heart? *4919*
1Co 10:16 The bread which we **b**, is it not *2806*
Gal 4:27 **b forth** and cry, thou that travailest not: *4486*

BREAKER (2) [BREAK]

Mic 2:13 The **b** is come up before them: they have 6555

Ro 2:25 but if thou be a **b** of the law, *3848*

BREAKEST (1) [BREAK]
Ps 48: 7 Thou **b** the ships of Tarshish with an east 7665

BREAKETH (17) [BREAK]
Ge 32:26 he said, Let me go, for the day **b**. And he 5927
Job 9:17 For he **b** me with a tempest, and 7779
12:14 he **b down**, and it cannot be built *again:* he 2040
16:14 He **b** me *with* breach upon breach, 6555
28: 4 The flood **b out** from the inhabitant; *even* 6555
Ps 29: 5 The voice of the LORD **b** the cedars; yea, 7665
29: 5 yea, the LORD **b** the cedars of Lebanon. 7665
46: 9 he **b** the bow, and cutteth the spear in 7665
119:20 My soul **b** for the longing *that it hath* unto 1638
Pr 25:15 and a soft tongue **b** the bone. 7665
Ecc 10: 8 whoso **b** a hedge, a serpent shall bite him. 6555
Isa 59: 5 that which is crushed **b out** *into* a viper. 1234
Jer 19:11 this city, as *one* **b** a potter's vessel, 7665
23:29 like a hammer *that* **b** the rock **in pieces**? 6327
La 4: 4 ask bread, *and* no man **b** *it* unto them. 6566
Da 2:40 forasmuch as iron **b in pieces** and 1855
2:40 all *things:* and as iron that **b** all these, 7490

BREAKING (18) [BREAK]
Ge 32:24 there wrestled a man with him until the **b** of 5927
Ex 9: 9 shall be a boil **b forth** *with* blains upon 6524
9:10 it became a boil **b forth** *with* blains upon 6524
22: 2 If a thief be found **b up**, and be smitten that 4290
1Ch 14:11 by mine hand like the **b forth** of waters: 6556
Job 30:14 They came *upon me* as a wide **b in** *of* 6556
Ps 144:14 *that there be* no **b in**, nor going out; 6556
Isa 22: 5 **b down** the walls, and of crying to 6979
30:13 whose **b** cometh suddenly at an instant. 7667
30:14 he shall break it as the **b** of the potters' 7667
Eze 16:59 which hast despised the oath in **b** 6565
17:18 Seeing he despised the oath by **b** 6565
21: 6 thou son of man, with the **b** of *thy* loins; 7670
Hos 13:13 long in *the place of* the **b forth** of children. 4866
Lk 24:35 how he was known of them in **b** of bread. *2800*
Ac 2:42 and in **b** of bread, and in prayers. *2800*
2:46 and **b** bread from house to house, did eat *2806*
Ro 2:23 through **b** the law dishonourest thou God? *3847*

BREAKINGS (1) [BREAK]
Job 41:25 by reason of **b** they purify themselves. 7667

BREAST (18) [BREASTPLATE, BREASTPLATES, BREASTS]
Ex 29:26 thou shalt take the **b** of the ram of Aaron's 2373
29:27 thou shalt sanctify the **b** of the wave 2373
Lev 7:30 by fire, the fat with the **b**, it shall he bring, 2373
7:30 that the **b** may be waved *for* a wave 2373
7:31 but the **b** shall be Aaron's and his sons'. 2373
7:34 For the wave **b** and the heave shoulder 2373
8:29 Moses took the **b**, and waved it *for* a wave 2373
10:14 the wave **b** and heave shoulder shall ye eat 2373
10:15 the wave **b** shall they bring with 2373
Nu 6:20 with the wave **b** and heave shoulder: 2373
18:18 as the wave **b** and as the right shoulder are 2373
Job 24: 9 They pluck the fatherless from the **b**, and 7699
Isa 60:16 the Gentiles, and shalt suck the **b** of kings: 7699
La 4: 3 Even the sea monsters draw out the **b**, 7699
Da 2:32 his **b** and his arms of silver, his belly and 2306
Lk 18:13 unto heaven, but smote upon his **b**, saying, *4738*
Jn 13:25 He then lying on Jesus' **b** saith unto him, *4738*
21:20 which also leaned on his **b** at supper, and *4738*

BREASTPLATE (28) [BREAST, PLATE]
Ex 25: 7 stones to be set in the ephod, and in the **b**. 2833
28: 4 a **b**, and an ephod, and a robe, and 2833
28:15 thou shalt make the **b** of judgment *with* 2833
28:22 thou shalt make upon the **b** chains at 2833
28:23 thou shalt make upon the **b** two rings of 2833
28:23 put the two rings on the two ends of the **b**. 2833
28:24 two rings *which are* on the ends of the **b**. 2833
28:26 the two ends of the **b** in the border thereof, 2833
28:28 they shall bind the **b** by the rings thereof 2833
28:28 that the **b** be not loosed from the ephod. 2833
28:29 Israel in the **b** of judgment upon his heart, 2833
28:30 thou shalt put in the **b** of judgment 2833
29: 5 the **b**, and gird him with the curious girdle 2833
35: 9 stones to be set for the ephod, and for the **b**. 2833
35:27 to be set, for the ephod, and for the **b**; 2833
39: 8 he made the **b** *of* cunning work, like 2833
39: 9 It was foursquare; they made the **b** double: 2833
39:15 they made upon the **b** chains at the ends, 2833
39:16 put the two rings in the two ends of the **b**. 2833
39:17 gold in the two rings on the ends of the **b**. 2833
39:19 put *them* on the two ends of the **b**, upon 2833
39:21 they did bind the **b** by his rings unto 2833
39:21 that the **b** might not be loosed from 2833
Lev 8: 8 he put the **b** upon him: also he put in 2833
8: 8 also he put in the **b** the Urim and 2833
Isa 59:17 For he put on righteousness as a **b**, and 8302
Eph 6:14 and having on the **b** of righteousness; *2382*
1Th 5: 8 be sober, putting on the **b** of faith and love; *2382*

BREASTPLATES (3) [BREAST, PLATE]
Rev 9: 9 And they had **b**, as *it were* breastplates of *2382*
9: 9 they had breastplates, as *it were* **b** of iron; *2382*
9:17 having **b** of fire, and of jacinth, and *2382*

BREASTS (27) [BREAST]
Ge 49:25 blessings of the **b**, and of the womb: 7699
Lev 9:20 they put the fat upon the **b**, and he burnt 2373
9:21 the **b** and the right shoulder Aaron waved 2373
Job 3:12 or why the **b** that I should suck? 7699
21:24 His **b** are full *of* milk, and his bones are 5845
Ps 22: 9 me hope *when I was* upon my mother's **b**. 7699
Pr 5:19 let her **b** satisfy thee at all times; and 1717
SS 1:13 unto me; he shall lie all night betwixt my **b**. 7699
4: 5 Thy two **b** *are* like two young roes *that are* 7699
7: 3 Thy two **b** *are* like two young roes *that are* 7699
SS 7: 7 a palm tree, and thy **b** to clusters *of grapes*. 7699
7: 8 now also thy **b** shall be as clusters of 7699
8: 1 that sucked the **b** of my mother! 7699
8: 8 We have a little sister, and she hath no **b**: 7699
8:10 I *am* a wall, and my **b** like towers: then 7699
Isa 28: 9 from the milk, *and* drawn from the **b**. 7699
66:11 be satisfied with the **b** of her consolations; 7699
Eze 16: 7 *thy* **b** are fashioned, and thine hair is 7699
23: 3 there were their **b** pressed, and there they 7699
23: 8 they bruised the **b** of her virginity, and 1717
23:34 sheards thereof, and pluck off thine own **b**: 7699
Hos 2: 2 and her adulteries from between her **b**; 7699
9:14 give them a miscarrying womb and dry **b**. 7699
Joel 2:16 the children, and those that suck the **b**: 7699
Na 2: 7 the voice of doves, tabring upon their **b**. 3824
Lk 23:48 were done, smote their **b**, and returned. *4738*
Rev 15: 6 having their **b** girded with golden girdles. *4738*

BREATH (42) [BREATHE]
Ge 2: 7 and breathed into his nostrils the **b** of life; 5397
6:17 to destroy all flesh, wherein *is* the **b** of life, 7307
7:15 and two of all flesh, wherein *is* the **b** of life. 7307
7:22 All in whose nostrils *was* the **b** of 5397+7307
2Sa 22:16 at the blast of the **b** of his nostrils. 7307
1Ki 17:17 so sore, that there was no **b** left in him. 5397
Job 4: 9 by the **b** of his nostrils are they consumed. 7307
9:18 He will not suffer me to take my **b**, but 7307
12:10 living *thing,* and the **b** of all mankind. 7307
15:30 and by the **b** of his mouth shall he go away. 7307
17: 1 My **b** is corrupt, my days are extinct, 7307
19:17 My **b** is strange to my wife, though I 7307
27: 3 All the while my **b** *is* in me, and the spirit 5397
33: 4 the **b** of the Almighty hath given me life. 5397
34:14 he gather unto himself his spirit and his **b**; 5397
37:10 By the **b** of God frost is given: and 5397
41:21 His **b** kindleth coals, and a flame goeth out 5315
Ps 18:15 at the blast of the **b** of thy nostrils. 7307
33: 6 all the host of them by the **b** of his mouth. 7307
104:29 thou takest away their **b**, they die, and 7307
135:17 neither is there *any* **b** in their mouths. 7307
146: 4 His **b** goeth forth, he returneth to his earth; 7307
150: 6 Let every *thing that hath* **b** praise 5397
Ecc 3:19 yea, they have all one **b**; so that a man hath 7307
Isa 2:22 ye from man, whose **b** *is* in his nostrils: 5397
11: 4 with the **b** of his lips shall he slay 7307
30:28 his **b**, as an overflowing stream, shall reach 7307
30:33 the **b** of the LORD, like a stream of 5397
33:11 your **b**, *as* fire, shall devour you. 7307
42: 5 he that giveth **b** unto the people upon it, 5397
Jer 10:14 *is* falsehood, and *there is* no **b** in them. 7307
51:17 *is* falsehood, and *there is* no **b** in them. 7307
La 4:20 The **b** of our nostrils, the anointed of 7307
Eze 37: 5 I *will* cause **b** to enter into you, and ye shall 7307
37: 6 and put **b** in you, and ye shall live; 7307
37: 8 them above: but *there was* no **b** in them. 7307
37: 9 O **b**, and breathe upon these slain, that they 7307
37:10 the **b** came into them, and they lived, and 7307
Da 5:23 the God in whose hand thy **b** *is,* and 5396
10:17 strength in me, neither is there **b** left in me. 5397
Hab 2:19 and *there is* no **b** at all in the midst of it. 7307
Ac 17:25 he giveth to all life, and **b**, and all *things;* *4157*

BREATHE (4) [BREATH, BREATHED, BREATHETH, BREATHING]
Jos 11:11 *them:* there was not any left to **b**: 5397
11:14 destroyed them, neither left they any to **b**. 5397
Ps 27:12 up against me, and such as **b out** cruelty. 3307
Eze 37: 9 O breath, and **b** upon these slain, that they 5301

BREATHED (4) [BREATHE]
Ge 2: 7 and **b** into his nostrils the breath of life; 5301
Jos 10:40 but utterly destroyed all that **b**, 5397
1Ki 15:29 he left not to Jeroboam any that **b**, until *he* 5397
Jn 20:22 he **b on** *them,* and saith unto them, *1720*

BREATHETH (1) [BREATHE]
Dt 20:16 thou shalt save alive nothing that **b**: 5397

BREATHING (2) [BREATHE]
La 3:56 hide not thine ear at my **b**, at my cry. 7309
Ac 9: 1 yet **b out** threatenings and slaughter against *1709*

BRED (1) [BREED]
Ex 16:20 the morning, and it **b** worms, and stank: 7311

BREECHES (5)
Ex 28:42 thou shalt make them linen **b** to cover *their* 4370
39:28 fine linen, and linen **b** *of* fine twined linen, 4370
Lev 6:10 *his* linen **b** shall he put upon his flesh, and 4370
16: 4 and he shall have the linen **b** upon his flesh, 4370
Eze 44:18 and shall have linen **b** upon their loins; 4370

BREED (2) [BRED, BREEDING]
Ge 8:17 that they may **b abundantly** in the earth, 8317
Dt 32:14 and rams of the **b** of Bashan, and goats, 1121

BREEDING (1) [BREED]
Zep 2: 9 *even* the **b** of nettles, and saltpits, and 4476

BRETHREN (563) [BROTHER]
Ge 9:22 of his father, and told his two **b** without. 251
9:25 a servant of servants shall he be unto his **b**. 251
13: 8 my herdmen and thy herdmen; for we *be* **b**. 251
16:12 he shall dwell in the presence of all his **b**. 251
19: 7 And said, I pray you, **b**, do not *so* wickedly. 251
24:27 led me to the house of my master's **b**. 251
25:18 *and* he died in the presence of all his **b**. 251
27:29 be lord over thy **b**, and let thy mother's sons 251
27:37 all his **b** have I given to him for servants; 251
29: 4 Jacob said unto them, My **b**, whence *be* ye? 251
31:23 he took his **b** with him, and pursued after 251
31:25 Laban with his **b** pitched in the mount of 251
31:32 before our **b** discern thou what *is* thine with 251
31:37 set *it* here before my **b** and thy brethren, 251
Ge 31:37 set *it* here before my brethren and thy **b**, 251
31:46 Jacob said unto his **b**, Gather stones; and 251
31:54 the mount, and called his **b** to eat bread: 251
34:11 Shechem said unto her father and unto her **b**, 251
34:25 Simeon and Levi, Dinah's **b**, took each man 251
37: 2 years old, was feeding the flock with his **b**; 251
37: 4 when his **b** saw that their father loved him 251
37: 4 their father loved him more than all his **b**, 251
37: 5 dreamed a dream, and he told *it* his **b**: 251
37: 8 his **b** said to him, Shalt thou indeed reign 251
37: 9 told it his **b**, and said, Behold, I have 251
37:10 And he told *it* to his father, and to his **b**: and 251
37:10 thy **b** indeed come to bow down ourselves to 251
37:11 his **b** envied him; but his father observed 251
37:12 his **b** went to feed their father's flock in 251
37:13 Do not thy **b** feed *the flock* in Shechem? 251
37:14 see whether it be well with thy **b**, and well 251
37:16 he said, I seek my **b**: tell me, I pray thee, 251
37:17 Joseph went after his **b**, and found them in 251
37:23 to pass, when Joseph was come unto his **b**, 251
37:26 Judah said unto his **b**, What profit *is it* if we 251
37:27 *and* our flesh. And his **b** were content. 251
37:30 he returned unto his **b**, and said, The child *is* 251
38: 1 that Judah went down from his **b**, and 251
38:11 as his **b** *did.* And Tamar went and dwelt *in* 251
42: 3 Joseph's ten **b** went down to buy corn in 251
42: 4 Joseph's brother, Jacob sent not with his **b**; 251
42: 6 Joseph's **b** came, and bowed down 251
42: 7 Joseph saw his **b**, and he knew them, but 251
42: 8 Joseph knew his **b**, but they knew not him. 251
42:13 they said, Thy servants *are* twelve **b**, 251
42:19 If ye *be* true *men,* let one of your **b** be bound 251
42:28 he said unto his **b**, My money is restored; 251
42:32 We *be* twelve **b**, sons of our father; one *is* 251
42:33 true *men;* leave one of your **b** *here* with me, 251
44:14 and his **b** came to Joseph's house; 251
44:33 to my lord; and let the lad go up with his **b**. 251
45: 1 Joseph made himself known unto his **b**. 251
45: 3 Joseph said unto his **b**, I *am* Joseph; doth my 251
45: 3 his **b** could not answer him; for they were 251
45: 4 Joseph said unto his **b**, Come near to me, 251
45:15 Moreover he kissed all his **b**, and wept upon 251
45:15 and after that his **b** talked with him. 251
45:16 saying, Joseph's **b** are come: 251
45:17 said unto Joseph, Say unto thy **b**, This do ye; 251
45:24 So he sent his **b** away, and they departed: 251
46:31 Joseph said unto his **b**, and unto his father's 251
46:31 say unto him, My **b**, and my father's house, 251
47: 1 My father and my **b**, and their flocks, and 251
47: 2 he took some of his **b**, *even* five men, and 251
47: 3 Pharaoh said unto his **b**, What *is* your 251
47: 5 Thy father and thy **b** are come unto thee: 251
47: 6 of the land make thy father and **b** to dwell; 251
47:11 Joseph placed his father and his **b**, and 251
47:12 his **b**, and all his father's household, 251
48: 6 shall be called after the name of their **b** in 251
48:22 I have given to thee one portion above thy **b**, 251
49: 5 Simeon and Levi *are* **b**; instruments of 251
49: 8 Judah, thou *art he* whom thy **b** shall praise: 251
49:26 the head of him *that was* separate from his **b**. 251
50: 8 of Joseph, and his **b**, and his father's house: 251
50:14 he, and his **b**, and all that went up with him 251
50:15 when Joseph's **b** saw that their father was 251
50:17 thee now, the trespass of thy **b**, and their sin; 251
50:18 his **b** also went and fell down before his 251
50:24 Joseph said unto his **b**, I die: and God will 251
Ex 1: 6 and all his **b**, and all that generation. 251
2:11 that he went out unto his **b**, and looked on 251
2:11 an Egyptian smiting a Hebrew, *one* of his **b**. 251
4:18 return unto my **b** which *are* in Egypt, and 251
Lev 10: 4 carry your **b** from before the sanctuary out 251
10: 6 let your **b**, the whole house of Israel, 251
21:10 *he that is* the high priest among his **b**, 251
25:46 over your **b** the children of Israel, ye shall 251
25:48 one of his **b** may redeem him: 251
Nu 8:26 shall minister with their **b** in the tabernacle 251
16:10 and all thy **b** the sons of Levi with thee: 251
18: 2 thy **b** also *of* the tribe of Levi, the tribe of 251
18: 6 I have taken your **b** the Levites from among 251
20: 3 Would God that we had died when our **b** 251
25: 6 brought unto his **b** a Midianitish *woman* in 251
27: 4 a possession among the **b** of our father. 251
27: 7 of an inheritance among their father's **b**; 251
27: 9 then ye shall give his inheritance unto his **b**. 251
27:10 if he have no **b**, then ye shall give his 251
27:10 shall give his inheritance unto his father's **b**. 251
27:11 if his father have no **b**, then ye shall give his 251
32: 6 Shall your **b** go to war, and shall ye sit here? 251
Dt 1:16 Hear *the causes* between your **b**, and 251
1:28 our **b** have discouraged our heart, saying, 251
2: 4 Ye are to pass through the coast of your **b** 251
2: 8 when we passed by from our **b** the children 251
3:18 ye shall pass over armed before your **b** 251
3:20 the LORD have given rest unto your **b**, 251
10: 9 Levi hath no part nor inheritance with his **b**; 251
15: 7 **b** within any of thy gates in thy land which 251
17:15 *one* from among thy **b** shalt thou set king 251
17:20 That his heart be not lifted up above his **b**, 251
18: 2 shall they have no inheritance among their **b**: 251
18: 7 as all his **b** the Levites *do,* which stand there 251
18:15 the midst of thee, of thy **b**, like unto me; 251
18:18 raise them up a Prophet from among their **b**, 251
24: 7 If a man be found stealing any of his **b** of 251
24:14 *whether he be* of thy **b**, or of thy strangers 251
25: 5 If **b** dwell together, and one of them die, and 251
33: 9 neither did he acknowledge his **b**, nor knew 251
33:16 head of him *that was* separated from his **b**. 251
33:24 let him be acceptable to his **b**, and let him 251
Jos 1:14 ye shall pass before your **b** armed, all 251
1:15 Until the LORD have given your **b** rest, 251
2:13 my **b**, and my sisters, and all that they have, 251
2:18 and thy **b**, and all thy father's household, 251
6:23 her mother, and her **b**, and all that she had; 251
14: 8 Nevertheless my **b** that went up with me 251
17: 4 to give us an inheritance among our **b**. 251

B

Jos 17: 4 an inheritance among the **b** of their father. 251
22: 3 Ye have not left your **b** these many days 251
22: 4 your God hath given rest unto your **b**, 251
22: 7 among their **b** on *this* side Jordan westward. 251
22: 8 divide the spoil of your enemies with your **b**. 251
Jdg 8:19 he said, They *were* my **b**, *even* the sons of 251
9: 1 went to Shechem unto his mother's **b**, 251
9: 3 his mother's **b** spake of him in the ears of all 251
9: 5 slew his **b** the sons of Jerubbaal, 251
9:24 which aided him in the killing of his **b**. 251
9:26 Gaal the son of Ebed came with his **b**, and 251
9:31 son of Ebed and his **b** be come to Shechem; 251
9:41 Zebul thrust out Gaal and his **b**, that *they* 251
9:56 did unto his father, in slaying his seventy **b**: 251
11: 3 Jephthah fled from his **b**, and dwelt in 251
14: 3 a woman among the daughters of thy **b**, 251
16:31 his **b** and all the house of his father came 251
18: 8 they came unto their **b** *to* Zorah and Eshtaol: 251
18: 8 and their **b** said unto them, What *say* ye? 251
18:14 said unto their **b**, Do ye know that there is in 251
19:23 said unto them, Nay, my **b**, *nay,* I pray you, 251
20:13 to the voice of their **b** the children of Israel: 251
21:22 or their **b** come unto us to complain, 251
Ru 4:10 of the dead be not cut off from among his **b**, 251
1Sa 16:13 and anointed him in the midst of his **b**: 251
17:17 Take now for thy **b** an ephah of this parched 251
17:17 ten loaves, and run *to* the camp to thy **b**; 251
17:18 look how thy **b** fare, and take their pledge. 251
17:22 *into* the army, and came and saluted his **b**. 251
20:29 let me get away, I pray thee, and see my **b**. 251
22: 1 when his **b** and all his father's house heard 251
30:23 said David, Ye shall not do so, my **b**, 251
2Sa 2:26 bid the people return from following their **b**? 251
3: 8 to his **b**, and to his friends, and have not 251
15:20 I may, return thou, and take back thy **b**: 251
19:12 Ye *are* my **b**, ye *are* my bones and my flesh: 251
19:41 Why have our **b** the men of Judah stolen 251
1Ki 1: 9 called all his **b** the king's sons, and all 251
12:24 nor fight against your **b** the children of 251
2Ki 9: 2 make him arise up from among his **b**, and 251
10:13 Jehu met with the **b** of Ahaziah king of 251
10:13 they answered, We *are* the **b** of Ahaziah; 251
23: 9 eat of the unleavened bread among their **b**. 251
1Ch 4: 9 And Jabez was more honourable than his **b**: 251
4:27 his **b** had not many children, neither did all 251
5: 2 For Judah prevailed above his **b**, and of him 251
5: 7 his **b** by their families, when the genealogy 251
5:13 their **b** of the house of their fathers *were,* 251
6:44 their **b** the sons of Merari *stood* on the left 251
6:48 Their **b** also the Levites *were* appointed unto 251
7: 5 their **b** among all the families of Issachar 251
7:22 many days, and his **b** came to comfort him. 251
8:32 these also dwelt with their **b** in Jerusalem, 251
9: 6 Jeuel, and their **b**, six hundred and ninety. 251
9: 9 their **b**, according to their generations, 251
9:13 their **b**, heads of the house of their fathers, 251
9:17 and Talmon, and Ahiman, and their **b**: 251
9:19 son of Ebiasaph, the son of Korah, and his **b**, 251
9:25 their **b**, *which were* in their villages, *were* to 251
9:32 *other* of their **b**, of the sons of 251
9:38 they also dwelt with their **b** at Jerusalem, 251
9:38 brethren at Jerusalem, over against their **b**. 251
12: 2 out of a bow, *even* of Saul's **b** of Benjamin. 251
12:32 and all their **b** *were* at their commandment. 251
12:39 drinking: for their **b** had prepared for them. 251
13: 2 let us send abroad unto our **b** every where, 251
15: 5 the chief, and his **b** an hundred and twenty: 251
15: 6 the chief, and his **b** two hundred and twenty: 251
15: 7 the chief, and his **b** an hundred and thirty: 251
15: 8 Shemaiah the chief, and his **b** two hundred: 251
15: 9 Eliel the chief, and his **b** fourscore: 251
15:10 the chief, and his **b** an hundred and twelve. 251
15:12 sanctify yourselves, *both* ye and your **b**, 251
15:16 **b** *to be* the singers with instruments of 251
15:17 of his **b**, Asaph the son of Berechiah; and 251
15:17 of the sons of Merari their **b**, Ethan the son 251
15:18 And with them their **b** of the second degree, 251
16: 7 LORD into the hand of Asaph and his **b**. 251
16:37 the covenant of the LORD Asaph and his **b**, 251
16:38 And Obed-edom with their **b**, threescore and 251
16:39 Zadok the priest, and his **b** the priests, before 251
23:22 and their **b** the sons of Kish took them. 251
23:32 and the charge of the sons of Aaron their **b**, 251
24:31 These likewise cast lots over against their **b** 251
24:31 fathers over against their younger **b**. 251
25: 7 with their **b** *that were* instructed in the songs 251
25: 9 who with his **b** and sons *were* twelve: 251
25:10 *he,* his sons, and his **b**, *were* twelve: 251
25:11 to Izri, *he,* his sons, and his **b**, *were* twelve: 251
25:12 *he,* his sons, and his **b**, *were* twelve: 251
25:13 *he,* his sons, and his **b**, *were* twelve: 251
25:14 *he,* his sons, and his **b**, *were* twelve: 251
25:15 *he,* his sons, and his **b**, *were* twelve: 251
25:16 *he,* his sons, and his **b**, *were* twelve: 251
25:17 *he,* his sons, and his **b**, *were* twelve: 251
25:18 *he,* his sons, and his **b**, *were* twelve: 251
25:19 *he,* his sons, and his **b**, *were* twelve: 251
25:20 *he,* his sons, and his **b**, *were* twelve: 251
25:21 *he,* his sons, and his **b**, *were* twelve: 251
25:22 *he,* his sons, and his **b**, *were* twelve: 251
25:23 *he,* his sons, and his **b**, *were* twelve: 251
25:24 *he,* his sons, and his **b**, *were* twelve: 251
25:25 *he,* his sons, and his **b**, *were* twelve: 251
25:26 *he,* his sons, and his **b**, *were* twelve: 251
25:27 *he,* his sons, and his **b**, *were* twelve: 251
25:28 *he,* his sons, and his **b**, *were* twelve: 251
25:29 *he,* his sons, and his **b**, *were* twelve: 251
25:30 *he,* his sons, and his **b**, *were* twelve: 251
25:31 *he,* his sons, and his **b**, *were* twelve. 251
26: 7 whose **b** *were* strong men, Elihu, and 251
26: 8 they and their sons and their **b**, able men for 251
26: 9 Meshelemiah had sons and **b**, strong men, 251
26:11 all the sons and **b** of Hosah *were* thirteen. 251
26:25 And his **b** by Eliezer; Rehabiah his son, and 251
26:26 his **b** *were* over all the treasures of 251
1Ch 26:28 under the hand of Shelomith, and of his **b**. 251
26:30 Hashabiah and his **b**, men of valour, 251
26:32 his **b**, men of valour, *were* two thousand 251
27:18 Of Judah, Elihu, *one* of the **b** of David: 251
28: 2 and said, Hear me, my **b**, and my people: 251
2Ch 5:12 of Jeduthun, with their sons and their **b**, 251
11: 4 Ye shall not go up, nor fight against your **b**: 251
11:22 Maachah the chief, to be ruler among his **b**: 251
19:10 to you of your **b** that dwell in their cities, 251
19:10 *so* wrath come upon you, and upon your **b**: 251
21: 2 he had **b** the sons of Jehoshaphat, Azariah, 251
21: 4 slew all his **b** with the sword, and *divers* also 251
21:13 also hast slain thy **b** of thy father's house, 251
22: 8 the sons of the **b** of Ahaziah, that ministered 251
28: 8 captive of their **b** two hundred thousand, 251
28:11 which ye have taken captive of your **b**: 251
28:15 *to* Jericho, the city of palm trees, to their **b**: 251
29:15 they gathered their **b**, and 251
29:34 wherefore their **b** the Levites did help them, 251
30: 7 be not ye like your fathers, and like your **b**, 251
30: 9 your **b** and your children *shall find* 251
31:15 *their* set office, to give to their **b** by courses, 251
35: 5 families of the fathers of your **b** the people, 251
35: 6 and sanctify yourselves, and prepare your **b**, 251
35: 9 his **b**, and Hashabiah and Jeiel and Jozabad, 251
35:15 for their **b** the Levites prepared for them. 251
Ezr 3: 2 his **b** the priests, and Zerubbabel the son of 251
3: 2 his **b**, and builded the altar of the God of 251
3: 8 the remnant of their **b** the priests and 251
3: 9 stood Jeshua *with* his sons and his **b**, 251
3: 9 *with* their sons and their **b** the Levites. 251
6:20 for their **b** the priests, and for themselves. 251
7:18 and to thy **b**, to do with the rest of the silver 252
8:17 and *to* his **b** the Nethinims, at the place 251
8:18 Sherebiah, with his sons and his **b**, eighteen; 251
8:19 sons of Merari, his **b** and their sons, twenty; 251
8:24 Hashabiah, and ten of their **b** with them, 251
10:18 sons of Jeshua the son of Jozadak, and his **b**; 251
Ne 1: 2 one of my **b**, came, he and *certain* men of 251
3: 1 Eliashib the high priest rose up with his **b** 251
3:18 After him repaired their **b**, Bavai the son of 251
4: 2 he spake before his **b** and the army of 251
4:14 *is* great and terrible, and fight for your **b**, 251
4:23 So neither I, nor my **b**, nor my servants, 251
5: 1 and of their wives against their **b** the Jews. 251
5: 5 Yet now our flesh *is* as the flesh of our **b**, 251
5: 8 We after our ability have redeemed our **b** 251
5: 8 the heathen; and will you even sell your **b**? 251
5:10 I likewise, *and* my **b**, and my servants, 251
5:14 my **b** have not eaten the bread of 251
10:10 their **b**, Shebaniah, Hodijah, Kelita, Pelaiah, 251
10:29 They clave to their **b**, their nobles, and 251
11:12 their **b** that did the work of the house *were* 251
11:13 his **b**, chief of the fathers, two hundred forty 251
11:14 their **b**, mighty *men* of valour, an hundred 251
11:17 and Bakbukiah the second among his **b**, and 251
11:19 Talmon, and their **b** that kept the gates, 251
12: 7 and of their **b** in the days of Jeshua. 251
12: 8 *was* over the thanksgiving, he and his **b**. 251
12: 9 Also Bakbukiah and Unni, their **b**, *were* over 251
12:24 with their **b** over against them, to praise *and* 251
12:36 his **b**, Shemaiah, and Azarael, Milalai, 251
13:13 their office *was* to distribute unto their **b**. 251
Est 10: 3 and accepted of the multitude of his **b**, 251
Job 6:15 My **b** have dealt deceitfully as a brook, *and* 251
19:13 He hath put my **b** far from me, and 251
42:11 came there unto him all his **b**, and all his 251
42:15 father gave them inheritance among their **b**. 251
Ps 22:22 I will declare thy name unto my **b**: in 251
69: 8 I am become a stranger unto my **b**, and 251
122: 8 For my **b** and companions' sakes, I will now 251
133: 1 how pleasant *it is* for **b** to dwell together in 251
Pr 6:19 and he that soweth discord among **b**. 251
17: 2 have part of the inheritance among the **b**. 251
19: 7 All the **b** of the poor do hate him: how much 251
Isa 66: 5 Your **b** that hated you, that cast you out for 251
66:20 they shall bring all your **b** *for* an offering 251
Jer 7:15 as I have cast out all your **b**, *even* the whole 251
12: 6 For even thy **b**, and the house of thy father, 251
29:16 *of* your **b** that are not gone forth with you 251
35: 3 his **b**, and all his sons, and the whole house 251
41: 8 he forbare, and slew them not among their **b**. 251
49:10 and his **b**, and his neighbours, and he *is* not. 251
Eze 11:15 Son of man, thy **b**, *even* thy brethren, 251
11:15 Son of man, thy brethren, *even* thy **b**, 251
Hos 2: 1 Say ye unto your **b**, Ammi; and to your 251
13:15 Though he be fruitful among *his* **b**, an east 251
Mic 5: 3 the remnant of his **b** shall return unto 251
Mt 1: 2 begat Jacob; and Jacob begat Judas and his **b**; *80*
1:11 And Josias begat Jechonias and his **b**, *80*
4:18 saw two **b**, Simon called Peter, and *80*
4:21 he saw other two **b**, James the *son* of *80*
5:47 And if ye salute your **b** only, what do ye more *80*
12:46 behold, *his* mother and his **b** stood without, *80*
12:47 Behold, thy mother and thy **b** stand without, *80*
12:48 Who is my mother? and who are my **b**? *80*
12:49 and said, Behold my mother and my **b**. *80*
13:55 called Mary? and his **b**, James, and Joses, *80*
19:29 or **b**, or sisters, or father, or mother, or wife, *80*
20:24 moved with indignation against the two **b**. *80*
22:25 Now there were with us seven **b**: and the first, *80*
23: 8 is your Master, *even* Christ; and all ye are **b**. *80*
25:40 done *it* unto one of the least of these my **b**, *80*
28:10 go tell my **b** that they go into Galilee, and *80*
Mk 3:31 There came then *his* **b** and his mother, and, *80*
3:32 thy mother and thy **b** without seek for thee. *80*
3:33 saying, Who is my mother, or my **b**? *80*
3:34 and said, Behold my mother and my **b**. *80*
10:29 or **b**, or sisters, or father, or mother, or wife, *80*
10:30 and **b**, and sisters, and mothers, and children, *80*
12:20 Now there were seven **b**: and the first took a *80*
Lk 8:19 Then came to him *his* mother and his **b**, and *80*
8:20 Thy mother and thy **b** stand without, *80*
8:21 my **b** are these which hear the word of God, *80*
14:12 or a supper, call not thy friends, nor thy **b**, *80*
Lk 14:26 and wife, and children, and **b**, and sisters, yea, *80*
16:28 For I have five **b**; that he may testify unto *80*
18:29 or parents, or **b**, or wife, or children, for *80*
20:29 There were therefore seven **b**: and the first *80*
21:16 by parents, and **b**, and kinsfolks, and friends; *80*
22:32 when thou art converted, strengthen thy **b**. *80*
Jn 2:12 and his mother, and his **b**, and his disciples: *80*
7: 3 His **b** therefore said unto him, Depart hence, *80*
7: 5 For neither did his **b** believe in him. *80*
7:10 But when his **b** were gone up, then went he *80*
20:17 but go to my **b**, and say unto them, I ascend *80*
21:23 Then went this saying abroad among the **b**, *80*
Ac 1:14 and Mary the mother of Jesus, and with his **b**. *80*
1:16 Men *and* **b**, this scripture must needs have *80*
2:29 Men *and* **b**, let *me* freely speak unto you of *80*
2:37 of the apostles, Men *and* **b**, what shall we do? *80*
3:17 And now, **b**, I wot that through ignorance ye *80*
3:22 Lord your God raise up unto you of your **b**, *80*
6: 3 Wherefore, **b**, look ye out among you seven *80*
7: 2 And he said, Men, **b**, and fathers, hearken; *80*
7:13 second time Joseph was made known to his **b**; *80*
7:23 it came into his heart to visit his **b** *80*
7:25 For he supposed his **b** would have understood *80*
7:26 set them at one *again,* saying, Sirs, ye are **b**; *80*
7:37 Lord your God raise up unto you of your **b**, *80*
9:30 Which when the **b** knew, they brought him *80*
10:23 and certain **b** from Joppa accompanied him. *80*
11: 1 **b** that were in Judea heard that the Gentiles *80*
11:12 Moreover these six **b** accompanied me, and *80*
11:29 determined to send relief unto the **b** which *80*
12:17 shew these *things* unto James, and to the **b**. *80*
13:15 saying, *Ye* men *and* **b**, if ye have *any* word of *80*
13:26 Men *and* **b**, children of the stock of Abraham, *80*
13:38 Be it known unto you therefore, men *and* **b**, *80*
14: 2 made their minds evil affected against the **b**. *80*
15: 1 which came down from Judea taught the **b**, *80*
15: 3 and they caused great joy unto all the **b**. *80*
15: 7 Peter rose up, and said unto them, Men *and* **b**, *80*
15:13 James answered, saying, Men *and* **b**, *80*
15:22 and Silas, chief *men* among the **b**: *80*
15:23 **b** *send* greeting unto the brethren which are of *80*
15:23 brethren *send* greeting unto the **b** which are of *80*
15:32 exhorted the **b** with many words, and *80*
15:33 they were let go in peace from the **b** unto *80*
15:36 visit our **b** in every city where we have *80*
15:40 being recommended by the **b** unto the grace *80*
16: 2 Which was well reported of by the **b** that were *80*
16:40 and when they had seen the **b**, they comforted *80*
17: 6 and certain **b** unto the rulers of the city, *80*
17:10 And the **b** immediately sent away Paul and *80*
17:14 immediately the **b** sent away Paul to go as *it* *80*
18:18 and then took his leave of the **b**, and *80*
18:27 the **b** wrote, exhorting the disciples to receive *80*
20:32 And now, **b**, I commend you to God, and *80*
21: 7 and saluted the **b**, and abode with them one *80*
21:17 come to Jerusalem, the **b** received us gladly. *80*
22: 1 Men, **b**, and fathers, hear ye my defence *80*
22: 5 from whom also I received letters unto the **b**, *80*
23: 1 beholding the council, said, Men *and* **b**, *80*
23: 5 Then said Paul, I wist not, **b**, that he was *80*
23: 6 Men *and* **b**, I am a Pharisee, the son of a *80*
28:14 Where we found **b**, and were desired to tarry *80*
28:15 And from thence, when the **b** heard of us, *80*
28:17 come together, he said unto them, Men *and* **b**, *80*
28:21 neither any of the **b** that came shewed or *80*
Ro 1:13 Now I would not have you ignorant, **b**, *80*
7: 1 Know ye not, **b**, (for I speak to them that *80*
7: 4 Wherefore, my **b**, ye also are become dead to *80*
8:12 Therefore, **b**, we are debtors, not to the flesh, *80*
8:29 he might be the firstborn amongst many **b**. *80*
9: 3 myself were accursed from Christ for my **b**, *80*
10: 1 **B**, my heart's desire and prayer to God for *80*
11:25 For I would not, **b**, that ye should be ignorant *80*
12: 1 you therefore, **b**, by the mercies of God, *80*
15:14 my **b**, that ye also are full of goodness, *80*
15:15 Nevertheless, **b**, I have written the more *80*
15:30 Now I beseech you, **b**, for the Lord Jesus *80*
16:14 Hermes, and the **b** which are with them. *80*
16:17 Now I beseech you, **b**, mark them which *80*
1Co 1:10 Now I beseech you, **b**, by the name of our *80*
1:11 my **b**, by them which are of the *house* of *80*
1:26 For ye see your calling, **b**, how that not many *80*
2: 1 And I, **b**, when I came to you, came not with *80*
3: 1 And I, **b**, could not speak unto you as unto *80*
4: 6 And these *things,* **b**, I have in a figure *80*
6: 5 one that shall be able to judge between his **b**? *80*
6: 8 ye do wrong, and defraud, and that *your* **b**. *80*
7:24 **B**, let every man, wherein he is called, *80*
7:29 But this I say, **b**, the time *is* short: *80*
8:12 But when ye sin so against the **b**, and *80*
9: 5 and *as* the **b** of the Lord, and Cephas? *80*
10: 1 Moreover, **b**, I would not that ye should be *80*
11: 2 Now I praise you, **b**, that you remember me in *80*
11:33 Wherefore, my **b**, when ye come together to *80*
12: 1 Now concerning spiritual *gifts,* **b**, I would not *80*
14: 6 Now, **b**, if I come unto you speaking with *80*
14:20 **B**, be not children in understanding: *80*
14:26 How is it then, **b**? when ye come together, *80*
14:39 Wherefore, **b**, covet to prophesy, and *80*
15: 1 Moreover, **b**, I declare unto you the gospel *80*
15: 6 he was seen of above five hundred **b** at once; *80*
15:50 **b**, that flesh and blood cannot inherit *80*
15:58 Therefore, my beloved **b**, be ye stedfast, *80*
16:11 come unto me: for I look for him with the **b**. *80*
16:12 desired him to come unto you with the **b**: *80*
16:15 I beseech you, **b**, (ye know the house of *80*
16:20 All the **b** greet you. Greet ye one another with *80*
2Co 1: 8 For we would not, **b**, have you ignorant of our *80*
8: 1 Moreover, **b**, we do you to wit of the grace of *80*
8:23 our **b** *be inquired of, they are* the messengers *80*
9: 3 Yet have I sent the **b**, lest our boasting of you *80*
9: 5 I thought it necessary to exhort the **b**, *80*
11: 9 the **b** which came from Macedonia supplied: *80*
11:26 *in* perils in the sea, *in* perils among **false b**; *5569*
13:11 Finally, **b**, farewell. Be perfect, be of good *80*

Gal 1: 2 And all the **b** which are with me, unto *80*
1:11 But I certify you, **b**, that the gospel which was *80*
2: 4 because of **false b** unawares brought in, *5569*
3:15 **B**, I speak after the manner of men; Though *it* *80*
4:12 **B**, I beseech you, be as I *am*; for I *am* as ye *80*
4:28 Now we, **b**, as Isaac was, are the children of *80*
4:31 So then, **b**, we are not children of *80*
5:11 And I, **b**, if I yet preach circumcision, why do *80*
5:13 For, **b**, ye have been called unto liberty; *80*
6: 1 **B**, if a man be overtaken in a fault, ye which *80*
6:18 **B**, the grace of our Lord Jesus Christ *be* with *80*
Eph 6:10 Finally, my **b**, be strong in the Lord, and *80*
6:23 Peace *be* to the **b**, and love with faith, *80*
Php 1:12 But I would ye should understand, **b**, that *80*
1:14 And many of the **b** in the Lord, *80*
3: 1 Finally, my **b**, rejoice in the Lord. To write *80*
3:13 **B**, I count not myself to have apprehended: *80*
3:17 **B**, be followers together of me, and *80*
4: 1 my **b** dearly beloved and longed for, my joy *80*
4: 8 Finally, **b**, whatsoever *things* are true, *80*
4:21 The **b** which are with me greet you. *80*
Col 1: 2 and faithful **b** in Christ which are at Colosse: *80*
4:15 Salute the **b** which are in Laodicea, and *80*
1Th 1: 4 Knowing, **b** beloved, your election of God. *80*
2: 1 For yourselves, **b**, know our entrance in unto *80*
2: 9 For ye remember, **b**, our labour and travail: *80*
2:14 For ye, **b**, became followers of the churches *80*
2:17 But we, **b**, being taken from you for a short *80*
3: 7 Therefore, **b**, we were comforted over you in *80*
4: 1 **b**, and exhort *you* by the Lord Jesus, *80*
4:10 And indeed ye do it towards all the **b** which *80*
4:10 but we beseech you, **b**, that *ye* increase more *80*
4:13 **b**, concerning them which are asleep, that ye *80*
5: 1 But of the times and the seasons, **b**, ye have *80*
5: 4 But ye, **b**, are not in darkness, that *that* day *80*
5:12 And we beseech you, **b**, to know them which *80*
5:14 Now we exhort you, **b**, warn *them that are* *80*
5:25 **B**, pray for us. *80*
5:26 Greet all the **b** with a holy kiss. *80*
5:27 that *this* epistle be read unto all the holy **b**. *80*
2Th 1: 3 **b**, as it is meet, because that your faith *80*
2: 1 Now we beseech you, **b**, by the coming of our *80*
2:13 **b** beloved of the Lord, because God hath from *80*
2:15 **b**, stand fast, and hold the traditions which ye *80*
3: 1 Finally, **b**, pray for us, that the word of *80*
3: 6 Now we command you, **b**, in the name of our *80*
3:13 But ye, **b**, be not weary in well doing. *80*
1Ti 4: 6 If thou put the **b** in remembrance of these *80*
5: 1 *him* as a father; *and* the younger *men* as **b**; *80*
6: 2 let them not despise *them*, because they are **b**; *80*
2Ti 4:21 Pudens, and Linus, and Claudia, and all the **b**. *80*
Heb 2:11 which cause he is not ashamed to call them **b**, *80*
2:12 Saying, I will declare thy name unto my **b**, *80*
2:17 it behoved him to be made like unto *his* **b**, *80*
3: 1 Wherefore, holy **b**, partakers of the heavenly *80*
3:12 Take heed, **b**, lest there be in any of you an *80*
7: 5 that is, of their **b**, though they come out of *80*
10:19 Having therefore, **b**, boldness to enter into *80*
13:22 And I beseech you, **b**, suffer the word of *80*
Jas 1: 2 My **b**, count *it* all joy when ye fall into divers *80*
1:16 Do not err, my beloved **b**. *80*
1:19 Wherefore, my beloved **b**, let every man be *80*
2: 1 My **b**, have not the faith of our Lord Jesus *80*
2: 5 Hearken, my beloved **b**, Hath not God chosen *80*
2:14 What *doth it* profit, my **b**, though a man say *80*
3: 1 My **b**, be not many masters, knowing that we *80*
3:10 cursing. My **b**, these *things* ought not so to be. *80*
3:12 Can the fig tree, my **b**, bear olive berries? *80*
4:11 Speak not evil one of another, **b**. He that *80*
5: 7 Be patient therefore, **b**, unto the coming of *80*
5: 9 one against another, **b**, lest ye be condemned: *80*
5:10 Take, my **b**, the prophets, who have spoken in *80*
5:12 But above all *things*, my **b**, swear not, *80*
5:19 **B**, if any of you do err from the truth, and *80*
1Pe 1:22 the Spirit unto unfeigned **love of** the **b**, *5360*
3: 8 **love as b**, *be* pitiful, *be* courteous: *5361*
5: 9 accomplished in your **b** that are in the world. *81*
2Pe 1:10 Wherefore the rather, **b**, give diligence to *80*
1Jn 2: 7 **B**, I write no new commandment unto you, *80*
3:13 Marvel not, my **b**, if the world hate you. *80*
3:14 from death unto life, because we love the **b**. *80*
3:16 and we ought to lay down *our* lives for the **b**. *80*
3Jn 1: 3 when *the* **b** came and testified of the truth *that* *80*
1: 5 faithfully whatsoever thou doest to the **b**, *80*
1:10 neither doth he himself receive the **b**, and *80*
Rev 6:11 until their fellowservants also and their **b**, *80*
12:10 for the accuser of our **b** is cast down, *80*
19:10 and of thy **b** that have the testimony of Jesus: *80*
22: 9 and of thy **b** the prophets, and of them which *80*

BRETHREN'S (1) [BROTHER]

Dt 20: 8 lest his **b** heart faint as well as his heart. 251

BRIBE (2) [BRIBERY, BRIBES]

1Sa 12: 3 of whose hand have I received *any* **b** to 3724
Am 5:12 they take a **b**, and they turn aside the poor 3724

BRIBERY (1) [BRIBE]

Job 15:34 and fire shall consume the tabernacles of **b**. 7810

BRIBES (3) [BRIBE]

1Sa 8: 3 and took **b**, and perverted judgment. 7810
Ps 26:10 *is* mischief, and their right hand is full *of* **b**. 7810
Isa 33:15 that shaketh his hands from holding of **b**, 7810

BRICK (7) [BRICKKILN, BRICKS]

Ge 11: 3 **make b**, and burn *them* thoroughly. 3835+3843
11: 3 they had **b** for stone, and slime had they for 3843
Ex 1:14 in **b**, and in all manner of service in 3843
5: 7 give the people straw to **make b**, 3835+3843
5:14 your task in **making b** both yesterday 3835
5:16 thy servants, and they say to us, Make **b**: 3843
Isa 65: 3 and burneth incense upon **altars of b**; 3843

BRICKKILN (3) [BRICK]

2Sa 12:31 of iron, and made them pass through the **b**: 4404
Jer 43: 9 and hide them in the clay in the **b**, 4404
Na 3:14 and tread the morter, make strong the **b**. 4404

BRICKS (4) [BRICK]

Ex 5: 8 the tale of the **b**, which they did make 3843
5:18 given you, yet shall ye deliver the tale of **b**. 3843
5:19 Ye shall not minish *ought* from your **b** of 3843
Isa 9:10 The **b** are fallen down, but we will build 3843

BRIDE (14) [BRIDECHAMBER, BRIDEGROOM, BRIDEGROOM'S]

Isa 49:18 and bind them *on thee*, as a **b** *doth*. 3618
61:10 and as a **b** adorneth *herself* with her jewels. 3618
62: 5 *as* the bridegroom rejoiceth over the **b**, *so* 3618
Jer 2:32 forget her ornaments, *or* a **b** her attire? 3618
7:34 of the bridegroom, and the voice of the **b**: 3618
16: 9 of the bridegroom, and the voice of the **b**. 3618
25:10 the voice of the **b**, the sound of 3618
33:11 of the bridegroom, and the voice of the **b**, 3618
Joel 2:16 of his chamber, and the **b** out of her closet. 3618
Jn 3:29 He that hath the **b** is the bridegroom: but *3565*
Rev 18:23 of the **b** shall be heard no more at all in *3565*
21: 2 prepared as a **b** adorned for her husband. *3565*
21: 9 saying, *Come* hither, I will shew thee the **b**, *3565*
22:17 And the Spirit and the **b** say, Come. And let *3565*

BRIDECHAMBER (3) [BRIDE]

Mt 9:15 Can the children of the **b** mourn, *3567*
Mk 2:19 unto them, Can the children of the **b** fast, *3567*
Lk 5:34 Can ye make the children of the **b** fast, *3567*

BRIDEGROOM (23) [BRIDE]

Ps 19: 5 Which *is* as a **b** coming out of his chamber, 2860
Isa 61:10 as a **b** decketh *himself* with ornaments, and 2860
62: 5 *as* the **b** rejoiceth over the bride, *so* 2860
Jer 7:34 the voice of the **b**, and the voice of 2860
16: 9 the voice of the **b**, and the voice of 2860
25:10 the voice of the **b**, and the voice of 2860
33:11 the voice of the **b**, and the voice of 2860
Joel 2:16 let the **b** go forth of his chamber, and 2860
Mt 9:15 as long as the **b** is with them? *3566*
9:15 when the **b** shall be taken from them, and *3566*
25: 1 their lamps, and went forth to meet the **b**. *3566*
25: 5 While the **b** tarried, they all slumbered and *3566*
25: 6 was a cry made, Behold, the **b** cometh; *3566*
25:10 And while they went to buy, the **b** came; *3566*
Mk 2:19 while the **b** is with them? *3566*
2:19 as long as they have the **b** with them, *3566*
2:20 when the **b** shall be taken away from them, *3566*
Lk 5:34 while the **b** is with them? *3566*
5:35 when the **b** shall be taken away from them, *3566*
Jn 2: 9 the governor of the feast called the **b**, *3566*
3:29 He that hath the bride is the **b**: but *3566*
3:29 but the friend of the **b**, which standeth and *3566*
Rev 18:23 and the voice of the **b** and of the bride shall *3566*

BRIDEGROOM'S (1) [BRIDE]

Jn 3:29 rejoiceth greatly because of the **b** voice: *3566*

BRIDE-PRICE See DOWRY

BRIDLE (9) [BRIDLES, BRIDLETH]

2Ki 19:28 my **b** in thy lips, and I will turn thee back 4964
Job 30:11 they have also let loose the **b** before me. 7448
41:13 *or* who can come *to him* with his double **b**? 7448
Ps 32: 9 mouth must be held in with bit and **b**, 7448
39: 1 I will keep my mouth with a **b**, while 4269
Pr 26: 3 a **b** for the ass, and a rod for the fools' 4964
Isa 30:28 *there shall be* a **b** in the jaws of the people, 7448
37:29 my **b** in thy lips, and I will turn thee back 4964
Jas 3: 2 *and* able also to **b** the whole body. *5468*

BRIDLES (1) [BRIDLE]

Rev 14:20 *even* unto the horse **b**, by the space of a *5469*

BRIDLETH (1) [BRIDLE]

Jas 1:26 and **b** not his tongue, but deceiveth his own *5468*

BRIEFLY (2)

Ro 13: 9 it is **b comprehended** in this saying, *346*
1Pe 5:12 I have written **b**, exhorting, and *1223+3641*

BRIER (3) [BRIERS]

Isa 55:13 instead of the **b** shall come up the myrtle 5636
Eze 28:24 there shall be no more a pricking **b** unto 5544
Mic 7: 4 The best of them *is* as a **b**: the *most* upright 2312

BRIERS (12) [BRIER]

Jdg 8: 7 the thorns of the wilderness and with **b**. 1303
8:16 thorns of the wilderness and **b**, and 1303
Isa 5: 6 but there shall come up **b** and thorns: 8068
7:23 it shall *even* be for **b** and thorns. 8068
7:24 all the land shall become **b** and thorns. 8068
7:25 there shall not come thither the fear of **b** 8068
9:18 it shall devour the **b** and thorns, and 8068
10:17 and devour his thorns and his **b** in one day; 8068
27: 4 who would set the **b** *and* thorns against me 8068
32:13 of my people shall come up thorns *and* **b**; 8068
Eze 2: 6 though **b** and thorns *be* with thee, and 5621
Heb 6: 8 that which beareth thorns and **b** *is* rejected, *5146*

BRIGANDINE (1) [BRIGANDINES]

Jer 51: 3 against *him that* lifteth himself up in his **b**: 5630

BRIGANDINES (1) [BRIGANDINE]

Jer 46: 4 furbish the spears, *and* put on the **b**. 5630

BRIGHT (29) [BRIGHTNESS]

Lev 13: 2 or **b spot**, and it be in the skin of his flesh 934
13: 4 If the **b spot** *be* white in the skin of his flesh, 934
13:19 or a **b spot**, white, *and* somewhat reddish, 934
13:23 if the **b spot** stay in his place, *and* 934
13:24 quick *flesh* that burneth have a white **b spot**, 934
13:25 *if* the hair in the **b spot** be turned white, and 934
13:26 *there be* no white hair in the **b spot**, and it *be* 934
13:28 if the **b spot** stay in his place, *and* spread not 934
13:38 have in the skin of their flesh **b spots**, 934
13:38 their flesh bright spots, *even* white **b spots**; 934
13:39 *if* the **b spots** in the skin of their flesh *be* 934
14:56 for a rising, and for a scab, and for a **b spot**: 934
1Ki 7:45 the house of the LORD, *were of* **b** brass. 4803
2Ch 4:16 for the house of the LORD *of* **b** brass. 4838
Job 37:11 the thick cloud: he scattereth his **b** cloud: 216
37:21 now *men* see not the **b** light which *is* in 925
SS 5:14 his belly *is as* **b** ivory overlaid *with* 6247
Jer 51:11 **Make b** the arrows: gather the shields: 1305
Eze 1:13 the fire was **b**, and out of the fire went forth 5051
21:15 ah, *it is* made **b**, *it is* wrapt up for 1300
21:21 he **made** *his* arrows **b**, he consulted with 7043
27:19 **b** iron, cassia, and calamus, were in thy 6219
32: 8 All the **b** lights of heaven will I make dark 3974
Na 3: 3 The horseman lifteth up both the **b** sword 3851
Zec 10: 1 *so* the LORD *shall* make **b clouds**, and 2385
Mt 17: 5 behold, a **b** cloud overshadowed them: *5460*
Lk 11:36 as when the **b shining** of a candle doth give *796*
Ac 10:30 a man stood before me in **b** clothing, *2986*
Rev 22:16 of David, *and* the **b** and morning star. *2986*

BRIGHTNESS (22) [BRIGHT]

2Sa 22:13 Through the **b** before him were coals of fire 5051
Job 31:26 when it shined, or the moon walking *in* **b**; 3368
Ps 18:12 At the **b** *that was* before him his thick 5051
Isa 59: 9 for **b**, *but* we walk in darkness. 5054
60: 3 to thy light, and kings to the **b** of thy rising. 5051
60:19 neither for **b** shall the moon give light unto 5051
62: 1 the righteousness thereof go forth as **b**, 5051
Eze 1: 4 a **b** *was* about it, and out of the midst 5051
1:27 of fire, and it had **b** round about. 5051
1:28 so *was* the appearance of the **b** round about. 5051
8: 2 as the appearance of **b**, as the colour of 2096
10: 4 the court was full of the **b** of the LORD'S 5051
28: 7 of thy wisdom, and they shall defile thy **b**. 3314
28:17 corrupted thy wisdom by reason of thy **b**: 3314
Da 2:31 This great image, whose **b** *was* excellent, 2122
4:36 mine honour and **b** returned unto me; 2122
12: 3 they that be wise shall shine as the **b** of 2096
Am 5:20 not light? even very dark, and no **b** in it? 5051
Hab 3: 4 *his* **b** was as the light; he had horns *coming* 5051
Ac 26:13 above the **b** of the sun, shining round about *2987*
2Th 2: 8 and shall destroy with the **b** of his coming: *2015*
Heb 1: 3 Who being the **b** of *his* glory, and *541*

BRIM (10) [BRIMSTONE]

Jos 3:15 the ark were dipped in the **b** of the water, 7097
1Ki 7:23 ten cubits from the one **b** to the other: 8193
7:24 under the **b** of it round about *there were* 8193
7:26 the **b** thereof was wrought like the brim of 8193
7:26 the brim thereof was wrought like the **b** of 8193
2Ch 4: 2 a molten sea of ten cubits from **b** to brim, 8193
4: 2 a molten sea of ten cubits from brim to **b**, 8193
4: 5 the **b** of it like the work of the brim of a 8193
4: 5 the brim of it like the work of the **b** of a 8193
Jn 2: 7 with water. And they filled them up to **the b**. *507*

BRIMSTONE (15) [BRIM, STONE]

Ge 19:24 upon Gomorrah **b** and fire from 1614
Dt 29:23 *And that* the whole land thereof *is* **b**, and 1614
Job 18:15 **b** shall be scattered upon his habitation. 1614
Ps 11: 6 fire and **b**, and a horrible tempest: 1614
Isa 30:33 like a stream of **b**, doth kindle it. 1614
34: 9 the dust thereof into **b**, and the land thereof 1614
Eze 38:22 and great hailstones, fire, and **b**. 1614
Lk 17:29 of Sodom it rained fire and **b** from heaven, *2303*
Rev 9:17 breastplates of fire, and of jacinth, and **b**: *2306*
9:17 their mouths issued fire and smoke and **b**. *2303*
9:18 by the fire, and by the smoke, and by the **b**, *2303*
14:10 and **b** in the presence of the holy angels, *2303*
19:20 cast alive into a lake of fire burning with **b**. *2303*
20:10 them was cast into the lake of fire and **b**, *2303*
21: 8 in the lake which burneth with fire and **b**: *2303*

BRING (727) [BRINGERS, BRINGEST, BRINGETH, BRINGING, BROUGHT, BROUGHTEST]

Ge 1:11 God said, Let the earth **b forth** grass, 1876
1:20 Let the waters **b forth abundantly** 8317+8318
1:24 Let the earth **b forth** the living creature 3318
3:16 in sorrow thou shalt **b forth** children; and 3205
3:18 and thistles shall it **b forth** to thee; 6779
6:17 even I, do **b** a flood of waters upon the earth, 935
6:19 two of every *sort* shalt thou **b** into the ark, 935
8:17 **B forth** with thee every living thing that *is* 3318
9: 7 **b forth abundantly** in the earth, and 8317
9:14 when I **b a cloud** over the earth, 6049+6051
18:16 went with them to **b** them **on** the **way**. 7971
18:19 that the LORD may **b** upon Abraham that 935
19: 5 **b** them **out** unto us, that we may know 3318
19: 8 **b** them **out** unto you, and do ye to them as 3318
19:12 hast in the city, **b** *them* **out** of *this* place: 3318
24: 5 **must I needs b** thy son **again** unto 7725+7725
24: 6 thou that thou **b** not my son thither **again**. 7725
24: 8 my oath: only **b** not my son thither **again**. 7725
27: 4 such as I love, and **b** *it* to me, that I may eat; 935
27: 5 to the field to hunt for venison, *and* to **b** *it*. 935
27: 7 **B** me venison, and make me savoury meat, 935
27:10 thou shalt **b** *it* to thy father, that he may eat, 935
27:12 I shall **b** a curse upon me, and not a blessing. 935
27:25 **B** *it* **near** to me, and I will eat of my son's 5066
28:15 and will **b** thee **again** into this land; 7725
37:14 well with the flocks; and **b** me word **again**. 7725
38:24 **B** her **forth**, and let her be burnt. 3318
40:14 unto Pharaoh, and **b** me **out** of this house: 3318
41:32 by God, and God will shortly **b** it **to pass**. 6213
42:20 **b** your youngest brother unto me; so 935
42:34 **b** your youngest brother unto me: then 935
42:37 Slay my two sons, if I **b** him not to thee: 935

Ge 42:37 my hand, and I will **b** him to thee **again**. 7725
42:38 shall ye **b down** my gray hairs with sorrow 3381
43: 7 that he would say, **B** your brother **down**? 3381
43: 9 if I **b** him not unto thee, and set him before 935
43:16 **B** *these* men home, and slay, and 935
44:21 unto thy servants, **B** him **down** unto me, 3381
44:29 ye shall **b down** my gray hairs with sorrow 3381
44:31 thy servants shall **b down** the gray hairs of 3381
44:32 If I **b** him not unto thee, then I shall bear 935
45:13 ye shall haste and **b down** my father hither. 3381
45:19 your wives, and **b** your father, and come. 5375
46: 4 I will also **surely b** thee **up** *again:* 5927+5927
48: 9 **B** them, I pray thee, unto me, and I will 3947
48:21 **b** you **again** unto the land of your fathers. 7725
50:20 it unto good, to **b to pass**, as *it is* this day, 6213
50:24 **b** you out of this land unto the land which 5927
Ex 3: 8 to **b** them **up** out of that land unto a good 5927
3:10 that thou mayest **b forth** my people 3318
3:11 that I should **b forth** the children of Israel 3318
3:17 I will **b** you **up** out of the affliction of 5927
6: 6 I will **b** you **out** from under the burdens of 3318
6: 8 I will **b** you **in** unto the land, *concerning* 935
6:13 to **b** the children of Israel out of the land of 3318
6:26 **B out** the children of Israel from the land of 3318
6:27 to **b out** the children of Israel from Egypt: 3318
7: 4 **b forth** mine armies, *and* my people 3318
7: 5 **b out** the children of Israel from among 3318
8: 3 the river shall **b forth** frogs **abundantly**, 8317
8:18 so with their enchantments to **b forth** lice, 3318
10: 4 to morrow will I **b** the locusts into thy coast: 935
11: 1 Yet will I **b** one plague *more* upon Pharaoh, 935
12:51 **b** the children of Israel **out** of the land of 3318
13: 5 it shall be when the LORD shall **b** thee into 935
13:11 it shall be when the LORD shall **b** thee into 935
15:17 Thou shalt **b** them **in**, and plant them in 935
16: 5 day they shall prepare *that* which they **b in**; 935
18:19 that thou mayest **b** the causes unto God: 935
18:22 *that* every great matter they shall **b** unto 935
21: 6 his master shall **b** him unto the judges; 5066
21: 6 he shall also **b** him to the door, or unto 5066
22:13 *then* let him **b** it *for* witness, *and* he shall not 935
23: 4 shalt **surely b** it **back** to him **again**. 7725+7725
23:19 **b** *into* the house of the LORD thy God. 935
23:20 to **b** thee into the place which I have 935
23:23 **b** thee **in** unto the Amorites, and the Hittites, 935
25: 2 of Israel, that they **b** me an offering: 3947
26:33 that thou mayest **b in** thither within the vail 935
27:20 that they **b** thee pure oil olive beaten for 3947
29: 3 **b** them in the basket, with the bullock and 7126
29: 4 his sons thou shalt **b** unto the door of 7126
29: 8 thou shalt **b** his sons, and put coats upon 7126
32: 2 and of your daughters, and **b** *them* unto me. 935
32:12 say, For mischief did he **b** them **out**, to slay 3318
33:12 See, thou sayest unto me, **B up** this people: 5927
34:26 **b** *unto* the house of the LORD thy God. 935
35: 5 let him **b** it, an offering of the LORD; 935
35:29 whose heart made them willing to **b** for all 935
36: 5 The people **b** much more than enough for 935
40: 4 thou shalt **b in** the table, and set in order 935
40: 4 thou shalt **b in** the candlestick, and light 935
40:12 thou shalt **b** Aaron and his sons unto 7126
40:14 thou shalt **b** his sons, and clothe them with 7126
Lev 1: 2 If *any* man of you **b** an offering unto 7126
1: 2 ye shall **b** your offering of the cattle, 7126
1: 5 shall **b** the blood, and sprinkle the blood 7126
1:10 he shall **b** it a male without blemish. 7126
1:13 the priest shall **b** *it* all, and burn *it* upon 7126
1:14 he shall **b** his offering of turtledoves, or 7126
1:15 the priest shall **b** it unto the altar, and 7126
2: 2 And he shall **b** it to Aaron's sons the priests: 935
2: 4 if thou **b** an oblation of a meat offering 7126
2: 8 thou shalt **b** the meat offering that is made of 935
2: 8 unto the priest, he shall **b** it unto the altar. 5066
2:11 which ye shall **b** unto the LORD, 7126
4: 3 let him **b** for his sin, which he hath sinned, 7126
4: 4 he shall **b** the bullock unto the door of 935
4: 5 **b** it to the tabernacle of the congregation: 935
4:14 **b** him before the tabernacle of 935
4:16 the priest that is anointed shall **b** of 935
4:23 he shall **b** his offering, a kid of the goats, 935
4:28 he shall **b** his offering, a kid of the goats, 935
4:32 if he **b** a lamb for a sin offering, he shall 935
4:32 he shall **b** it a female without blemish. 935
5: 6 he shall **b** his trespass offering unto 935
5: 7 if he be not able to **b** a lamb, then he shall 5060
5: 7 he shall **b** for his trespass, which he hath 935
5: 8 he shall **b** them unto the priest, who shall 935
5:11 if he be not **able to b** two 3027+5381
5:11 he that sinned shall **b** for his offering 935
5:12 shall he **b** it to the priest, and the priest shall 935
5:15 he shall **b** for his trespass unto the LORD a 935
5:18 he shall **b** a ram without blemish out of 935
6: 6 he shall **b** his trespass offering unto 935
6:21 *and when it is* baken, thou shalt **b** it **in**: 935
7:29 **b** his oblation unto the LORD of 935
7:30 His own hands shall **b** the offerings of 935
7:30 by fire, the fat with the breast, it shall he **b**, 935
10:15 the wave breast shall they **b** with 935
12: 6 she shall **b** a lamb of the first year for a burnt 935
12: 8 if she be not **able to b** a lamb, 1767+3027+4672
12: 8 she shall **b** two turtles, or two young 3947
14:23 he shall **b** them on the eighth day for his 935
15:29 young pigeons, and **b** them unto the priest, 935
16: 9 Aaron shall **b** the goat upon which 7126
16:11 Aaron shall **b** the bullock of the sin 7126
16:12 beaten small, and **b** *it* within the vail: 935
16:15 **b** his blood within the vail, and do with that 935
16:20 and the altar, he shall **b** the live goat: 7126
17: 5 To the end that the children of Israel may **b** 935
17: 5 even that they may **b** them unto the LORD, 935
18: 3 of Canaan, whither I **b** you, shall ye not do: 935
19:21 he shall **b** his trespass offering unto 935
20:22 the land, whither I **b** you to dwell therein, 935
23:10 ye shall **b** a sheaf of the firstfruits of your 935
23:17 Ye shall **b** out of your habitations two wave 935
Lev 24: 2 that they **b** unto thee pure oil olive beaten 3947
24:14 **B forth** him that hath cursed without 3318
24:23 that they should **b forth** him that had 3318
25:21 it shall **b forth** fruit for three years. 6213
26:10 **b forth** the old because of the new. 3318
26:21 I will **b** seven *times* moe plagues upon you 3254
26:25 I will **b** a sword upon you, that shall avenge 935
26:31 **b** your sanctuaries **unto desolation**, and 8074
26:32 I will **b** the land **into desolation**: and 8074
27: 9 whereof *men* **b** an offering unto 7126
Nu 3: 6 **B** the tribe of Levi **near**, and present them 7126
5: 9 which they **b** unto the priest, shall be his. 7126
5:15 shall the man **b** his wife unto the priest, 935
5:15 he shall **b** her offering for her, the tenth *part* 935
5:16 the priest shall **b** her **near**, and set her 7126
6:10 And on the eighth day he shall **b** two turtles, 935
6:12 shall **b** a lamb of the first year for a trespass 935
6:16 the priest shall **b** *them* before the LORD, 7126
8: 9 thou shalt **b** the Levites before 7126
8:10 thou shalt **b** the Levites before the LORD: 7126
11:16 **b** them unto the tabernacle of 3947
13:20 good courage, and **b** of the fruit of the land. 3947
14: 8 he will **b** us into this land, and give it us; 935
14:16 Because the LORD was not able to **b** this 935
14:24 him will I **b** into the land whereinto he went; 935
14:31 them will I **b in**, and they shall know 935
14:37 Even *those* men that did **b up** the evil 3318
15: 4 **b** a meat offering of a tenth deal *of* flour 7126
15: 9 shall he **b** with a bullock a meat offering of 7126
15:10 thou shalt **b** for a drink offering half a hin 7126
15:18 When ye come into the land whither I **b** you, 935
15:25 they shall **b** their offering, a sacrifice made 935
15:27 he shall **b** a she goat of the first year for a 7126
16: 9 to **b** you **near** to himself to do the service 7126
16:17 **b** ye before the LORD every man his 7126
17:10 **B** Aaron's rod **again** before the Testimony, 7725
18: 2 the tribe of thy father, **b** thou with thee, 7126
18:13 which they shall **b** unto the LORD, shall be 935
18:15 which they **b** unto the LORD, *whether it* 7126
19: 2 that they **b** thee a red heifer without spot, 3947
19: 3 that he may **b** her **forth** without the camp, 3318
20: 5 out of Egypt, to **b** us in unto this evil place? 935
20: 8 thou shalt **b forth** to them water out of 3318
20:12 ye shall not **b** this congregation into the land 935
20:25 his son, and **b** them **up** *unto* mount Hor: 5927
22: 8 *this* night, and I will **b** you word **again**, 7725
23:27 I pray thee, I will **b** thee unto another place; 3947
27:17 lead them out, and which may **b** them **in**; 935
28:26 when ye **b** a new meat offering unto 7126
32: 5 for a possession, *and* **b** us not **over** Jordan. 5674
Dt 1:17 for you, **b** *it* unto me, and I will hear it. 7126
1:22 **b** us word **again** by what way we must go 7725
4:38 and mightier than thou *art*, to **b** thee **in**, 935
6:23 us out from thence, that he might **b** us **in**, 935
7: 1 When the LORD thy God shall **b** thee into 935
7:26 Neither shalt thou **b** an abomination into 935
9: 3 and he shall **b** them **down** before thy face: 3665
9:28 Because the LORD was not able to **b** them 935
12: 6 thither ye shall **b** your burnt offerings, and 935
12:11 thither shall ye **b** all that I command you; 935
14:28 At the end of three years thou shalt **b forth** 3318
17: 5 shalt thou **b forth** that man or that woman, 3318
21: 4 the elders of that city shall **b down** 3381
21:12 thou shalt **b** her home to thine house; and 935
21:19 **b** him **out** unto the elders of his city, and 3318
22: 1 thou shalt **in any case b** them **again** 7725+7725
22: 2 thou shalt **b** it unto thine own house, and 622
22: 8 that thou **b** not blood upon thine house, 7760
22:14 **b up** an evil name upon her, and say, I took 3318
22:15 **b forth** *the tokens of* the damsel's virginity 3318
22:21 they shall **b out** the damsel to the door of 3318
22:24 ye shall **b** them both **out** unto the gate of 3318
23:18 Thou shalt not **b** the hire of a whore, or 935
24:11 the man to whom thou dost lend shall **b out** 3318
26: 2 which thou shalt **b** of thy land that 935
28:36 The LORD shall **b** thee, and thy king 1980
28:49 The LORD shall **b** a nation against thee 5375
28:60 Moreover he will **b** upon thee all 7725
28:61 them will the LORD **b** upon thee, 5927
28:63 to destroy you, and to **b** you **to nought**; 8045
28:68 the LORD shall **b** thee *into* Egypt **again** 7725
29:27 to **b** upon it all the curses that are written in 935
30: 5 the LORD thy God will **b** thee into the land 935
30:12 **b** it unto us, that we may hear it, and do it? 3947
30:13 **b** it unto us, that we may hear it, and do it? 3947
31:23 for thou shalt **b** the children of Israel into 935
33: 7 voice of Judah, and **b** him unto his people: 935
Jos 2: 3 **B forth** the men that are come to thee, 3318
2:18 thou shalt **b** thy father, and thy mother, and 622
6:22 **b out** thence the woman, and all that she 3318
10:22 **b out** those five kings unto me out of 3318
18: 6 and **b** *the description* hither to me, 935
23:15 shall the LORD **b** upon you all evil things, 935
Jdg 6:13 Did not the LORD **b** us **up** from Egypt? 5927
6:18 **b forth** my present, and set *it* before thee. 3318
6:30 unto Joash, **B out** thy son, that he may die: 3318
7: 4 **b** them **down** unto the water, and I will try 3381
11: 9 If ye **b** me *home* **again** to fight against 7725
19: 3 speak friendly unto her, *and* to **b** her **again**, 7725
19:22 **B forth** the man that came into thine house, 3318
19:24 them I will **b out** now, and humble ye 3318
Ru 3:15 **B** the vail that *thou hast* upon thee, and 3051
1Sa 1:22 *then* I will **b** him, that he may appear before 935
4: 4 that they might **b** from thence the ark of 5375
6: 7 and **b** their calves home from them: 7725
9: 7 *if* we go, what shall we **b** the man? 935
9: 7 *there is* not a present to **b** to the man of God: 935
9:23 **B** the portion which I gave thee, of which I 5414
11:12 **b** the men, that we may put them to death. 5414
13: 9 **B hither** a burnt offering to me, and peace 5066
14:18 said unto Ahiah, **B hither** the ark of God. 5066
14:34 **B** me **hither** every man his ox, and 5066
15:32 **B** you **hither** to me Agag the king of 5066
16:17 a man that can play well, and **b** *him* to me. 935
19:15 saying, **B** him **up** to me in the bed, that I 5927
1Sa 20: 8 for why shouldest thou **b** me to thy father? 935
23: 9 to Abiathar the priest, **B hither** the ephod. 5066
27:11 to **b** *tidings to* Gath, saying, Lest they should 935
28: 8 **b** me *him* **up**, whom I shall name unto thee. 5927
28:11 the woman, Whom shall I **b up** unto thee? 5927
28:11 unto thee? And he said, **B** me **up** Samuel. 5927
28:15 Why hast thou disquieted me, to **b** me **up**? 5927
30: 7 I pray thee, **b** me **hither** the ephod. 5066
30:15 Canst thou **b** me **down** to this company? 3381
30:15 and I will **b** thee **down** to this company. 3381
2Sa 2: 3 his men that *were* with him did David **b up**, 5927
3:12 *be* with thee, to **b about** all Israel unto thee. 5437
3:13 except thou first **b** Michal Saul's daughter, 935
6: 2 to **b up** from thence the ark of God, 5927
9:10 thou shalt **b in** *the fruits*, that thy master's 935
12:23 can I **b** him **back** again? I shall go to him, 7725
13:10 **B** the meat *into* the chamber, that I may eat 935
13:10 **b** him to me, and he shall not touch thee any 935
14:21 **b** the young man Absalom **again**. 7725
15: 8 **b** me **again indeed** *to* Jerusalem, 7725+7725
15:14 **b** evil upon us, and smite the city with 5080
15:25 he will **b** me **again**, and shew me *both* it, 7725
17: 3 I will **b back** all the people unto thee: 7725
17:13 shall all Israel **b** ropes to that city, and 5375
17:14 to the intent that the LORD might **b** evil 935
19:11 Why are ye the last to **b** the king **back** to 7725
19:12 then are ye the last to **b back** the king? 7725
22:28 *that* thou mayest **b** *them* **down**. 8213
1Ki 1:33 mine own mule, and **b** him **down** to Gihon: 3381
2: 9 his hoar head **b** thou **down** *to* the grave 3381
3:24 the king said, **B** me a sword. And they 3947
5: 9 My servants shall **b** *them* **down** from 3381
8: 1 that *they* might **b up** the ark of 5927
8: 4 those did the priests and the Levites **b up**. 5927
8:32 the wicked, to **b** his way upon his head; 5414
8:34 **b** them **again** unto the land which thou 7725
10:29 did they **b** *them* **out** by their means. 3318
12:21 to **b** the kingdom **again** to Rehoboam 7725
13:18 **B** him **back** with thee into thine house, 7725
14:10 I will **b** evil upon the house of Jeroboam, 935
17:11 said, **B** me, I pray thee, a morsel of bread in 3947
17:13 **b** *it* unto me, and after make for thee and 3318
20:33 he said, Go ye, **b** him. Then Ben-hadad 3947
21:21 I will **b** evil upon thee, and will take away 935
21:29 before me, I will not **b** the evil in his days: 935
21:29 in his son's days will I **b** the evil upon his 935
2Ki 2:20 **B** me a new cruse, and put salt therein. 3947
3:15 now **b** me a minstrel. And it came to pass, 3947
4: 6 she said unto her son, **B** me yet a vessel. 5066
4:41 he said, Then **b** meal. And he cast *it* into 3947
6:19 and I will **b** you to the man whom ye seek. 1980
10:22 **B forth** vestments for all the worshippers 3318
12: 4 heart to **b** *into* the house of the LORD, 935
19: 3 and *there is* not strength to **b forth**. 3205
22:16 I will **b** evil upon this place, and upon 935
22:20 all the evil which I will **b** upon this place. 935
23: 4 to **b forth** out of the temple of the LORD 3318
1Ch 9:28 that they should **b** them **in** and out by tale. 935
13: 3 And let us **b again** the ark of our God to us: 5437
13: 5 to **b** the ark of God from Kirjath-jearim. 935
13: 6 to **b up** thence the ark of God the LORD, 5927
13:12 How shall I **b** the ark of God *home* to me? 935
15: 3 to **b up** the ark of the LORD unto his 5927
15:12 that ye may **b up** the ark of the LORD 5927
15:14 the Levites sanctified themselves to **b up** 5927
15:25 went to **b up** the ark of the covenant of 5927
16:29 **b** an offering, and come before him: 5375
21: 2 **b** the number of them to me, that I may 935
21:12 advise thyself what word I shall **b again** to 7725
22:19 to **b** the ark of the covenant of the LORD, 935
2Ch 2:16 we will **b** it to thee *in* flotes by sea *to* Joppa; 935
5: 2 to **b up** the ark of the covenant of 5927
5: 5 these did the priests *and* the Levites **b up**. 5927
6:25 **b** them **again** unto the land which thou 7725
11: 1 that *he* might **b** the kingdom **again** to 7725
24: 6 required of the Levites to **b in** out of Judah 935
24: 9 to **b in** to the LORD the collection that 935
24:19 to them, to **b** them **again** unto the LORD; 7725
28:13 Ye shall not **b in** the captives hither: 935
29:31 come near and **b** sacrifices and 935
31:10 Since *the people* began to **b** the offerings 935
34:24 I will **b** evil upon this place, and upon 935
34:28 see all the evil that I will **b** upon this place, 935
Ezr 1: 8 those did Cyrus king of Persia **b forth** 3318
1:11 All *these* did Sheshbazzar **b up** with *them* 5927
3: 7 to **b** cedar trees from Lebanon to the sea of 935
8:17 that *they* should **b** unto us ministers for 935
8:30 to **b** *them* to Jerusalem unto the house of our 935
Ne 1: 9 will **b** them unto the place that I have chosen 935
5: 5 we **b into bondage** our sons and our 3533
8: 1 they spake unto Ezra the scribe to **b** the book 935
9:29 that *thou* mightest **b** them **again** unto thy 7725
10:31 *if* the people of the land **b** ware or 935
10:34 to **b** *it* into the house of our God, 935
10:35 to **b** the firstfruits of our ground, and 935
10:36 of our flocks, to **b** to the house of our God, 935
10:37 *that* we should **b** the firstfruits of our dough, 935
10:38 the Levites shall **b up** the tithe of the tithes 5927
10:39 the children of Levi shall **b** the offering of 935
11: 1 to **b** one of ten to dwell in Jerusalem 935
12:27 to **b** them to Jerusalem, to keep 935
13:18 *did not* our God **b** all this evil upon us, and 935
13:18 yet ye **b more** wrath upon Israel by 3254
Est 1:11 To **b** Vashti the queen before the king with 935
3: 9 to **b** *it* into the king's treasuries. 935
6: 1 he commanded to **b** the book of records of 935
6: 9 **b** him on horseback through the street of 7392
6:14 hasted to **b** Haman unto the banquet that 935
Job 6:22 Did I say, **B** unto me? or, Give a reward for 3051
10: 9 and wilt thou **b** me into dust **again**? 7725
14: 4 Who can **b** a clean *thing* out of an unclean? 5414
14: 9 it will bud, and **b forth** boughs like a plant. 6213
15:35 **b forth** vanity, and their belly prepareth 3205
18:14 and it shall **b** him to the king of terrors. 6805
30:23 For I know *that* thou wilt **b** me *to* death, 7725

Job 33:30 To **b back** his soul from the pit, to be 7725
38:32 Canst thou **b forth** Mazzaroth in his 3318
39: 1 when the wild goats of the rock **b forth**? 3205
39: 2 knowest thou the time when they **b forth**? 3205
39: 3 they **b forth** their young ones, 6398
39:12 that he will **b home** thy seed, and gather *it* 7725
40:12 on every one *that is* proud, *and* **b** him **low**; 3665
40:20 Surely the mountains **b** him **forth** food, 5375
Ps 18:27 but wilt **b down** high looks. 8213
25:17 O **b** thou me **out** of my distresses. 3318
37: 5 trust also in him; and he shall **b** *it* **to pass**. 6213
37: 6 he shall **b forth** thy righteousness as 3318
38: T A Psalm of David, to **b to remembrance**. 2142
43: 3 let them **b** me unto thy holy hill, and to thy 935
55:23 shalt **b** them **down** into the pit of 3381
59:11 and **b** them **down**, O Lord our shield. 3381
60: 9 Who will **b** me *into* the strong city? 2986
68:22 The Lord said, I will **b again** from Bashan, 7725
68:22 I will **b** *my people* **again** from the depths of 7725
68:29 Jerusalem shall kings **b** presents unto thee. 2986
70: T *A Psalm of* David, to **b to remembrance**. 2142
71:20 shalt **b** me **up** again from the depths of 5927
72: 3 The mountains shall **b** peace to the people, 5375
72:10 of Tarshish and *of* the isles shall **b** presents: 7725
76:11 let all that be round about him **b** presents 2986
81: 2 Take a psalm, and **b** hither the timbrel, 5414
92:14 They shall still **b forth fruit** in old age; 5107
94:23 he shall **b** upon them their own iniquity, 7725
96: 8 **b** an offering, and come into his courts. 5375
104:14 that *he* may **b forth** food out of the earth; 3318
108:10 Who will **b** me *into* the strong city? 2986
142: 7 **B** my soul **out** of prison, that *I* may praise 3318
143:11 for thy righteousness' sake **b** my soul **out** 3318
144:13 *that* our sheep may **b forth thousands** and 503
Pr 4: 8 she shall **b** thee **to honour**, when thou dost 3513
19:24 will not so much as **b** it to his mouth **again**. 7725
26:15 it grieveth him to **b** it **again** to his mouth. 7725
27: 1 thou knowest not what a day may **b forth**. 3205
29: 8 Scornful men **b** a city **into a snare**: but 6315
29:23 A man's pride shall **b** him **low**: but 8213
Ecc 3:22 for who shall **b** him to see what shall be after 935
11: 9 that for all these *things* God will **b** thee into 935
12:14 For God shall **b** every work into judgment, 935
SS 8: 2 *and* **b** thee into my mother's house, 935
8:11 every one for the fruit thereof was to **b** a 935
Isa 1:13 **B** no more vain oblations; incense *is* an 935
5: 2 he looked that *it* should **b forth** grapes, and 6213
5: 4 when I looked that *it* should **b forth** grapes, 6213
7:17 The LORD shall **b** upon thee, and upon thy 935
14: 2 shall take them, and **b** them to their place: 935
15: 9 for I will **b** more upon Dimon, lions upon 7896
23: 4 I travail not, nor **b forth children**, 3205
23: 4 I nourish up young men, *nor* **b up** virgins. 7311
23: 9 to **b into contempt** all the honourable of 7043
25: 5 Thou shalt **b down** the noise of strangers, 3665
25:11 he shall **b down** their pride together with 8213
25:12 the high fort of thy walls shall he **b down**, 7817
25:12 lay low, *and* **b** to the ground, *even* to 5060
28:21 and **b to pass** his act, his strange act. 5647
31: 2 will **b** evil, and will not call back his words: 935
33:11 conceive chaff, ye shall **b forth** stubble: 3205
37: 3 and *there is* not strength to **b forth**. 3205
38: 8 I will **b again** the shadow of the degrees, 7725
41:21 **b forth** your strong *reasons*, saith the King 5066
41:22 Let them **b** *them* **forth**, and shew us what 5066
42: 1 he shall **b forth** judgment to the Gentiles. 3318
42: 3 he shall **b forth** judgment unto truth. 3318
42: 7 to **b out** the prisoners from the prison, *and* 3318
42:16 I will **b** the blind by a way *that* they knew 1980
43: 5 I will **b** thy seed from the east, and 935
43: 6 **b** my sons from far, and my daughters from 935
43: 8 **B forth** the blind people that have eyes, 3318
43: 9 shew us former *things*? let them **b forth** 5414
45: 8 let them **b forth** salvation, and 6509
45:21 Tell ye, and **b** *them* **near**; yea, let them take 5066
46: 8 **b** *it* **again** to mind, O ye transgressors. 7725
46:11 yea, I have spoken *it*, I will also **b** it **to pass**; 935
46:13 I **b near** my righteousness; it shall not be 7126
49: 5 to **b** Jacob **again** to him, Though Israel be 7725
49:22 they shall **b** thy sons in *their* arms, and 935
52: 8 when the LORD shall **b again** Zion. 7725
55:10 the earth, and **maketh** it **b forth** and bud, 3205
56: 7 Even them will I **b** to my holy mountain, and 935
58: 7 that thou **b** the poor that are cast out *to thy* 935
59: 4 conceive mischief, and **b forth** iniquity. 3205
60: 6 they shall **b** gold and incense; and 5375
60: 9 to **b** thy sons from far, their silver and 935
60:11 that *men* may **b** unto thee the forces of 935
60:17 For brass I will **b** gold, and for iron I will 935
60:17 for iron I will **b** silver, and for wood brass, 935
63: 6 I will **b down** their strength to the earth. 3381
65: 9 I will **b forth** a seed out of Jacob, and 3318
65:23 not labour in vain, nor **b forth** for trouble; 3205
66: 4 and will **b** their fears upon them; 935
66: 8 the earth be **made to b forth** in one day? 2342
66: 9 Shall I **b to the birth**, and not cause to 7665
66: 9 bring to the birth, and not **cause to b forth**? 3205
66: 9 shall I **cause to b forth**, and shut 3205
66:20 they shall **b** all your brethren *for* an offering 935
66:20 as the children of Israel **b** an offering in a 935
Jer 3:14 two of a family, and I will **b** you *to* Zion: 935
4: 6 for I will **b** evil from the north, and a great 935
5:15 Lo, I will **b** a nation upon you from far, 935
6:19 behold, I will **b** evil upon this people, 935
8: 1 they shall **b out** the bones of the kings of 3318
10:24 in thine anger, lest thou **b** me **to nothing**. 4591
11: 8 I will **b** upon them all the words of this 935
11:11 the LORD, Behold, I *will* **b** evil upon them, 935
11:23 for I will **b** evil upon the men of Anathoth, 935
12: 2 they grow, yea, they **b forth** fruit: thou *art* 6213
12:15 will **b** them **again**, every man to his 7725
15:19 will I **b** thee **again**, *and* thou shalt stand 7725
16:15 I will **b** them **again** into their land that I 7725
17:18 **b** upon them the day of evil, and 935
17:21 nor **b** *it* in by the gates of Jerusalem; 935
Jer 17:24 to **b in** no burden through the gates of this 935
18:22 when thou shalt **b** a troop suddenly upon 935
19: 3 Behold, I *will* **b** evil upon this place, 935
19:15 I will **b** upon this city and upon all her towns 935
23: 3 and will **b** them **again** to their folds; 7725
23:12 for I will **b** evil upon them, *even* the year of 935
23:40 I will **b** an everlasting reproach upon you, 5414
24: 6 and I will **b** them **again** to this land: 7725
25: 9 will **b** them against this land, and against 935
25:13 I will **b** upon that land all my words which I 935
25:29 I begin to **b evil** on the city which is called 7489
26:15 ye shall surely **b** innocent blood upon 5414
27:11 the nations that **b** their neck under the yoke 935
27:12 **B** your necks under the yoke of the king of 935
27:22 will I **b** them **up**, and restore them to this 5927
28: 3 Within two full years *will* I **b again** into 7725
28: 4 I *will* **b again** to this place Jeconiah the son 7725
28: 6 to **b again** the vessels of the LORD'S 7725
29:14 I will **b** you **again** into the place whence I 7725
30: 3 that I will **b again** the captivity of my 7725
30:18 I *will* **b again** the captivity of Jacob's tents, 7725
31: 8 I *will* **b** them from the north country, and 935
31:23 when I shall **b again** their captivity; 7725
31:32 to **b** them **out** of the land of Egypt; 3318
32:37 and I will **b** them **again** unto this place, and 7725
32:42 will I **b** upon them all the good that I have 935
33: 6 I will **b** it health and cure, and I will cure 5927
33:11 of them that shall **b** the sacrifice of praise 935
35: 2 and **b** them *into* the house of the LORD, 935
35:17 I will **b** upon Judah and upon all 935
36:31 I will **b** upon them, and upon the inhabitants 935
38:23 So they *shall* **b out** all thy wives and thy 3318
39:16 I *will* **b** my words upon this city for evil, and 935
41: 5 to **b** *them to* the house of the LORD. 935
42:17 escape from the evil that I *will* **b** upon them. 935
45: 5 for behold, I *will* **b** evil upon all flesh, 935
48:44 for I will **b** upon it, *even* upon Moab, 935
48:47 Yet will I **b again** the captivity of Moab in 7725
49: 5 Behold, I will **b** a fear upon thee, saith 935
49: 6 afterward I will **b again** the captivity of 7725
49: 8 for I will **b** the calamity of Esau upon him, 935
49:16 I will **b** thee **down** from thence, saith 3381
49:32 I will **b** their calamity from all sides thereof, 935
49:36 upon Elam will I **b** the four winds from 935
49:37 I will **b** evil upon them, *even* my fierce 935
49:39 *that* I will **b again** the captivity of Elam, 7725
50:19 I will **b** Israel **again** to his habitation, and 7725
51:40 I will **b** them **down** like lambs to 3381
51:44 I will **b forth** out of his mouth that which 3318
51:64 shall not rise from the evil that I *will* **b** upon 935
La 1:21 *it:* thou wilt **b** the day *that* thou hast called, 935
Eze 5:17 and I will **b** the sword upon thee. 935
6: 3 *will* **b** a sword upon you, and I will destroy 935
7:24 Wherefore I will **b** the worst of the heathen, 935
11: 7 but *I* will **b** you **forth** out of the midst of it. 3318
11: 8 I will **b** a sword upon you, saith the Lord 935
11: 9 I will **b** you **out** of the midst thereof, and 3318
12: 4 shalt thou **b forth** thy stuff by day in their 3318
12:13 I will **b** him to Babylon *to* the land of 935
13:14 and **b** it **down** to the ground, 5060
14:17 Or *if* I **b** a sword upon that land, and say, 935
16:40 They shall also **b up** a company against 5927
16:53 When I shall **b again** their captivity, 7725
16:53 *will I* **b** *again* the captivity of thy captives in NIH
17: 8 that *it* might **b forth** branches, and that *it* 6213
17:20 I will **b** him to Babylon, and will plead with 935
17:23 it shall **b forth** boughs, and bear fruit, and 5375
20: 6 to **b** them **forth** of the land of Egypt into a 3318
20:15 that *I* would not **b** them into the land which I 935
20:34 I will **b** you **out** from the people, and 3318
20:35 I will **b** you into the wilderness of 935
20:37 I will **b** you into the bond of the covenant: 935
20:38 I will **b** them **forth** out of the country 3318
20:41 when I **b** you **out** from the people, and 3318
20:42 when I shall **b** you into the land of Israel, 935
21:29 to **b** thee upon the necks of *them that are* 5414
23:22 and I will **b** them against thee on every side; 935
23:46 *I will* **b up** a company upon them, and 5927
24: 6 **b** it **out** piece by piece; let no lot fall upon 3318
26: 7 I *will* **b** upon Tyrus Nebuchadrezzar king of 935
26:19 when *I* shall **b up** the deep upon thee, 5927
26:20 When I shall **b** thee **down** with them that 3381
28: 7 I *will* **b** strangers upon thee, 935
28: 8 They shall **b** thee **down** to the pit, and 3381
28:18 will I **b forth** a fire from the midst of thee, 3318
28:18 I will **b** thee to ashes upon the earth in 5414
29: 4 I will **b** thee **up** out of the midst of thy 5927
29: 8 I *will* **b** a sword upon thee, and cut off man 935
29:14 I will **b again** the captivity of Egypt, and 7725
31: 6 the beasts of the field **b forth** their **young**, 3205
32: 3 and they shall **b** thee **up** in my net. 5927
32: 9 when I shall **b** thy destruction among 935
33: 2 unto them, When I **b** the sword upon a land, 935
34:13 I will **b** them **out** from the people, and 3318
34:13 will **b** them to their own land, and feed them 935
34:16 **b again** that which was driven away, and 7725
36:11 beast; and they shall increase and **b fruit**: 6509
36:24 and will **b** you into your own land. 935
37: 6 will **b up** flesh upon you, and cover you 5927
37:12 and **b** you into the land of Israel. 935
37:21 every side, and **b** them into their own land: 935
38: 4 I will **b** thee **forth**, and all thine army, 3318
38:16 latter days, and I will **b** thee against my land, 935
38:17 that *I* would **b** thee against them? 935
39: 2 and will **b** thee upon the mountains of Israel: 935
39:25 Now will I **b again** the captivity of Jacob, 7725
47:12 it shall **b forth new fruit** according to his 1069
Da 1: 3 that *he* should **b** *certain* of the children of 935
1:18 that the king had said *he* should **b** them **in**, 935
2:24 **b** me **in** before the king, and I will shew 5954
3:13 *his* rage and fury commanded to **b** Shadrach, 858
4: 6 Therefore made I a decree to **b in** all 5954
5: 2 commanded to **b** the golden and 858
5: 7 The king cried aloud to **b in** the astrologers, 5954
9:24 to **b in** everlasting righteousness, and to seal 935
Hos 2:14 **b** her *into* the wilderness, and 1980
7:12 I will **b** them **down** as the fowls of 3381
9:12 Though they **b up** their children, yet will I 1431
9:13 Ephraim *shall* **b forth** his children to 3318
9:16 yea, though they **b forth**, yet will I slay 3205
Joel 3: 1 when I shall **b again** the captivity of Judah 7725
3: 2 will **b** them **down** into the valley of 3381
3:11 and he shall **b down** thy strength from thee, 3381
Am 4: 1 say to their masters, **B**, and let us drink. 935
4: 4 **b** your sacrifices *every* morning, *and* 935
6:10 to **b out** the bones out of the house, and 3318
8:10 I will **b up** sackcloth upon all loins, and 5927
9: 2 up *to* heaven, thence will I **b** them **down**: 3381
9:14 I will **b again** the captivity of my people of 7725
Ob 1: 3 Who shall **b** me **down** *to* the ground? 3381
1: 4 thence will I **b** thee **down**, saith 3381
Jnh 1:13 Nevertheless the men rowed hard to **b** *it* to 7725
Mic 1:15 Yet will I **b** an heir unto thee, O inhabitant 935
4:10 Be in pain, and **labour to b forth**, 1518
7: 9 he will **b** me **forth** to the light, *and* I shall 3318
Zep 1:17 I will **b distress** upon men, that they shall 6887
2: 2 Before the decree **b forth**, *before* the day 3205
3: 5 every morning doth he **b** his judgment to 5414
3:10 of my dispersed, shall **b** mine offering. 2986
3:20 At that time will I **b** you *again*, even in 935
Hag 1: 6 Ye have sown much, and **b in** little; *ye* eat, 935
1: 8 and **b** wood, and build the house; 935
Zec 3: 8 I *will* **b forth** my servant the BRANCH. 935
4: 7 he shall **b forth** the headstone *thereof with* 3318
5: 4 I will **b** it **forth**, saith the LORD of hosts, 3318
8: 8 I will **b** them, and they shall dwell in 935
10: 6 and I will **b** them *again* **to place** them; 3427
10:10 I will **b** them **again** also out of the land of 7725
10:10 and I will **b** them into the land of Gilead and 935
13: 9 I will **b** the third *part* through the fire, and 935
Mal 3:10 **B** ye all the tithes into the storehouse, that 935
Mt 1:21 And she shall **b forth** a son, and thou shalt *5088*
1:23 and shall **b forth** a son, and they shall call *5088*
2: 8 when ye have found *him*, **b** me **word again**, *518*
2:13 and be thou there until I **b** thee **word**: *3004*
3: 8 **B forth** therefore fruits meet for *4160*
5:23 Therefore if thou **b** thy gift to the altar, and *4374*
7:18 A good tree cannot **b forth** evil fruit, *4160*
7:18 neither *can* a corrupt tree **b forth** good *4160*
14:18 He said, **B** them hither to me. *5342*
17:17 long shall I suffer you? **b** him hither to me. *5342*
21: 2 with her: loose *them*, and **b** *them* unto me. *71*
28: 8 and did run to **b** his disciples **word**. *518*
Mk 4:20 the word, and receive *it*, and **b forth fruit**, *2592*
7:32 And they **b** unto him one *that was* deaf, and *5342*
8:22 and they **b** a blind man unto him, and *5342*
9:19 long shall I suffer you? **b** him unto me. *5342*
11: 2 never man sat; loose him, and **b** *him*. *71*
12:15 ye me? **b** me a penny, that I may see *it*. *5342*
15:22 And they **b** him unto the place Golgotha, *5342*
Lk 1:31 and **b forth** a son, and shalt call his name *5088*
2:10 I **b** you **good tidings** of great joy, *2097*
3: 8 **B forth** therefore fruits worthy of *4160*
5:18 and they sought *means* to **b** him **in**, and *1533*
5:19 not find by what *way* they might **b** him **in** *1533*
6:43 neither doth a corrupt tree **b forth** good *4160*
8:14 of *this* life, and **b** no fruit **to perfection**. *5052*
8:15 keep *it*, and **b forth fruit** with patience. *2592*
9:41 with you, and suffer you? **B** thy son hither. *4317*
12:11 And when they **b** you unto the synagogues, *4374*
14:21 and **b in** hither the poor, and the maimed, *1521*
15:22 **B forth** the best robe, and put *it* on him; *1627*
15:23 And **b hither** the fatted calf, and kill *it*; and *5342*
19:27 over them, **b** hither, and slay *them* before me. *71*
19:30 never man sat: loose him, and **b** *him hither*. *71*
Jn 10:16 them also I must **b**, and they shall hear my *71*
14:26 and **b** all *things* **to** your **remembrance**, *5279*
15: 2 he purgeth it, that it may **b forth** more fruit. *5342*
15:16 that you should go and **b forth** fruit, and *5342*
18:29 What accusation **b** you against this man? *5342*
19: 4 saith unto them, Behold, I **b** him forth to you, *71*
21:10 **B** of the fish which ye have now caught. *5342*
Ac 5:28 and intend to **b** this man's blood upon us. *1863*
7: 6 and that they should **b** them **into bondage**, *1402*
9: 2 he might **b** *them* bound unto Jerusalem. *71*
9:21 came hither for that *intent*, that he might **b** *71*
12: 4 intending after Easter to **b** him **forth** to *321*
17: 5 and sought to **b** them **out** to the people. *71*
22: 5 to Damascus, to **b** them which were there, *71*
23:10 among them, and to **b** *him* into the castle. *71*
23:15 that he **b** him **down** unto you to morrow, *2609*
23:17 **B** this young man unto the chief captain: *520*
23:18 and prayed *me* to **b** this young man unto thee, *71*
23:20 **b down** Paul to morrow into the council, *2609*
23:24 and **b** *him* **safe** unto Felix the governor. *1295*
24:17 Now after many years I came to **b** alms to *4160*
Ro 7: 4 that we should **b forth fruit** unto God. *2592*
7: 5 did work in our members to **b forth fruit** *2592*
10: 6 (that is, to **b** Christ **down** *from above*:) *2609*
10: 7 (that is, to **b up** Christ **again** from the dead.) *321*
10:15 and **b glad tidings** of good *things*! *2097*
1Co 1:19 will **b to nothing** the understanding of *114*
1:28 are not, to **b to nought** *things* that are: *2673*
4: 5 who both will **b to light** the hidden *things* *5461*
4:17 who shall **b** you **into remembrance** of my *363*
9:27 under my body, and **b** *it* **into subjection**: *1396*
16: 3 them will I send to **b** your liberality unto *667*
16: 6 that ye may **b** me **on** my **journey** *4311*
2Co 11:20 For ye suffer, if a man **b** you **into bondage**, *2615*
Gal 2: 4 that they might **b** us **into bondage**: *2615*
3:24 was our schoolmaster *to* **b** *us* unto Christ, NIG
Eph 6: 4 but **b** them **up** in the nurture and *1625*
1Th 4:14 them also which sleep in Jesus will God **b** *71*
2Ti 4:11 Take Mark, and **b** *him* with thee: for he is *71*
4:13 **b** *with thee*, and the books, *but* *5342*
Tit 3:13 **B** Zenas the lawyer and Apollos
on their **journey** *4311*
1Pe 3:18 for the unjust, that he might **b** us to God, *4317*
2Pe 2: 1 who **privily** shall **b in** damnable heresies, *3919*
2: 1 and **b upon** themselves swift destruction. *1863*

2Pe 2:11 **b** not railing accusation against them before *5342*
2Jn 1:10 come any unto you, and **b** not this doctrine, *5342*
3Jn 1: 6 whom if thou **b forward on** their **journey** *4311*
Jude 1: 9 durst not **b against** *him* a railing *2018*
Rev 21:24 the kings of the earth do **b** their glory and *5342*
21:26 And they shall **b** the glory and honour of *5342*

BRINGERS (1) [BRING]

2Ki 10: 5 the **b up** *of the children,* sent to Jehu, saying, 539

BRINGEST (5) [BRING]

1Ki 1:42 thou *art* a valiant man, and **b** good **tidings**. 1319
Job 14: 3 a one, and **b** me into judgment with thee? 935
Isa 40: 9 O Zion, that **b good tidings**, get thee up 1319
40: 9 O Jerusalem, that **b good tidings**, lift up 1319
Ac 17:20 For thou **b** certain strange *things* to our *1533*

BRINGETH (79) [BRING]

Ex 6: 7 which **b** you **out** from under the burdens of 3318
Lev 11:45 For I *am* the LORD that **b** you **up** out of 5927
17: 4 **b** it not unto the door of the tabernacle of 935
17: 9 **b** it not unto the door of the tabernacle of 935
Dt 8: 7 For the LORD thy God **b** thee into a good 935
14:22 thy seed, that the field **b forth** year by year. 3318
1Sa 2: 6 he **b down** *to* the grave, and bringeth up. 3381
2: 6 he bringeth down *to* the grave, and **b up**. 5927
2: 7 and maketh rich: he **b low**, and lifteth up. 8213
2Sa 18:26 And the king said, He also **b tidings**. 1319
22:48 and that **b down** the people under me, 3381
22:49 that **b** me **forth** from mine enemies: 3318
Job 12: 6 into whose hand God **b** *abundantly.* 935
12:22 and **b out** to light the shadow of death. 3318
19:29 for wrath *b* the punishments of the sword, NIH
28:11 and the thing that is hid **b** he **forth** *to* light. 3318
Ps 1: 3 of water, that **b forth** his fruit in his season; 5414
14: 7 when the LORD **b back** the captivity of 7725
33:10 **b** the counsel of the heathen **to nought**: 6331
37: 7 of the man who **b** wicked devices **to pass**. 6213
53: 6 When God **b back** the captivity of his 7725
68: 6 he **b out** those which are bound with 3318
107:28 and he **b** them **out** of their distresses. 3318
107:30 so he **b** them unto their desired haven. 5148
135: 7 the rain; he **b** the wind **out** of his treasuries. 3318
Pr 10:31 The mouth of the just **b forth** wisdom: but 5107
16:30 moving his lips he **b** evil **to pass**. 3615
18:16 room for him, and **b** him before great *men.* 5148
19:26 a son that causeth shame, and **b reproach**. 2659
20:26 the wicked, and **b** the wheel over them. 7725
21:27 *when* he **b** it with a wicked mind? 935
29:15 child left *to himself* **b** his mother **to shame**. 954
29:21 He that **delicately b up** his servant from a 6445
29:25 The fear of man **b** a snare: but 5414
30:33 Surely the churning of milk **b forth** butter, 3318
30:33 and the wringing of the nose **b forth** blood: 3318
30:33 so the forcing of wrath **b forth** strife. 3318
31:14 merchant's ships; she **b** her food from afar. 935
Ecc 2: 6 to water therewith the wood that **b forth** 6779
Isa 8: 7 the Lord **b up** upon them the waters of 5927
26: 5 For he **b down** them that dwell on high; 7817
26: 5 *even* to the ground; he **b** it *even* to the dust. 5060
40:23 That **b** the princes to nothing; he maketh 5414
40:26 *things,* that **b out** their host by number: 3318
41:27 give to Jerusalem one that **b good tidings**. 1319
43:17 Which **b forth** the chariot and horse, 3318
52: 7 are the feet of him that **b good tidings**, 1319
52: 7 that **b good tidings** of good, that publisheth 1319
54:16 and that **b forth** an instrument for his work; 3318
61:11 For as the earth **b forth** her bud, and as 3318
Jer 4:31 as of her that **b forth** her **first child**, 1069
10:13 and **b forth** the wind out of his treasures. 3318
51:16 and **b forth** the wind out of his treasures. 3318
Eze 29:16 which **b** *their* iniquity **to remembrance**, 2142
Hos 10: 1 empty vine, he **b forth** fruit unto himself: 7737
Na 1:15 the feet of him that **b good tidings**, 1319
Hag 1:11 upon *that* which the ground **b forth**, and 3318
Mt 3:10 every tree which **b** not **forth** good fruit is *4160*
7:17 *Even* so every good tree **b forth** good fruit; *4160*
7:17 but a corrupt tree **b forth** evil fruit. *4160*
7:19 Every tree that **b** not **forth** good fruit is *4160*
12:35 treasure of the heart **b forth** good *things:* *1544*
12:35 an evil man out of the evil treasure **b forth** *1544*
13:23 and **b forth**, some an hundred*fold,* some *4160*
13:52 which **b forth** out of his treasure *things* *1544*
17: 1 and **b** them **up** into a high mountain apart, *399*
Mk 4:28 For the earth **b forth fruit** of herself; *2592*
Lk 3: 9 which **b** not **forth** good fruit is hewn down, *4160*
6:43 For a good tree **b** not **forth** corrupt fruit; *4160*
6:45 of his heart **b forth** that which is good; *4393*
6:45 of his heart **b forth** that which is evil: *4393*
Jn 12:24 but if it die, it **b forth** much fruit. *5342*
15: 5 and I in him, the same **b forth** much fruit: *5342*
Col 1: 6 and **b forth fruit**, as *it doth* also in you, *2592*
Tit 2:11 For the grace of God that **b** salvation hath NIG
Heb 1: 6 when he **b in** the firstbegotten into *1521*
6: 7 **b forth** herbs meet for them by whom it is *5088*
Jas 1:15 when lust hath conceived, it **b forth** sin: *5088*
1:15 and sin, when it is finished, **b forth** death. *616*

BRINGING (24) [BRING]

Ex 12:42 for **b** them **out** from the land of Egypt: 3318
36: 6 So the people were restrained from **b**. 935
Nu 5:15 of memorial, **b** iniquity **to remembrance**. 2142
14:36 by **b up** a slander upon the land, 3318
2Sa 19:10 speak ye not a word of **b** the king **back**? 7725
19:43 should not be first had in **b back** our king? 7725
1Ki 10:22 **b** gold, and silver, ivory, and apes, and 5375
2Ki 21:12 I *am* **b** *such* evil upon Jerusalem and Judah, 935
2Ch 9:21 once came the ships of Tarshish **b** gold, 5375
Ne 13:15 and **b in** sheaves, and lading asses; 935
Ps 126: 6 with rejoicing, **b** his sheaves *with him.* 5375
Jer 17:26 **b** burnt offerings, and sacrifices, and 935
17:26 and incense, and **b** *sacrifices of* praise, 935
Eze 20: 9 in **b** them **forth** out of the land of Egypt. 3318
Da 9:12 that judged us, by **b** upon us a great evil: 935

Mt 21:43 given to a nation **b forth** the fruits thereof. *4160*
Mk 2: 3 **b** one sick of the palsy, *which was* borne of *5342*
Lk 24: 1 **b** the spices which they had prepared, and *5342*
Ac 5:16 **b** sick *folks,* and *them which were* vexed *5342*
Ro 7:23 **b** me **into captivity** to the law of sin which *163*
2Co 10: 5 **b into captivity** every thought to *163*
Heb 2:10 by whom *are* all *things,* in **b** many sons unto *71*
7:19 the **b in** of a better hope *did;* by the which *1898*
2Pe 2: 5 **b in** the flood upon the world of *1863*

BRINK (6)

Ge 41: 3 stood by the *other* kine upon the **b** of 8193
Ex 2: 3 she laid *it* in the flags by the river's **b**. 8193
7:15 thou shalt stand by the river's **b** against he 8193
Dt 2:36 which *is* by the **b** of the river of Arnon, and 8193
Jos 3: 8 When ye are come to the **b** of the water of 7097
Eze 47: 6 caused me to return to the **b** of the river. 8193

BROAD (36) [BREADTH, BROADER]

Ex 27: 1 five cubits long, and five cubits **b**; 7341
Nu 16:38 let them make them **b** plates *for* a covering 7555
16:39 they were **made b** *plates for* a covering of 7554
1Ki 6: 6 The nethermost chamber *was* five cubits **b**, 7341
6: 6 the middle *was* six cubits **b**, and the third 7341
6: 6 and the third *was* seven cubits **b**: 7341
2Ch 6:13 and five cubits **b**, and three cubits high, and 7341
Ne 3: 8 they fortified Jerusalem unto the **b** wall. 7342
12:38 tower of the furnaces even unto the **b** wall; 7342
Job 36:16 thee out of the strait *into* a **b place**, 7338
Ps 119:96 *but* thy commandment *is* exceeding **b**. 7342
SS 3: 2 the city in the streets and in the **b ways**, 7339
Isa 33:21 *will be* unto us a place of **b** rivers 3027+7342
Jer 5: 1 and know, and seek in the **b places** thereof, 7339
51:58 The **b** walls of Babylon shall be utterly 7342
Eze 40: 6 of the gate, *which was* one reed **b**; 7341
40: 6 *of the gate, which was* one reed **b**. 7341
40: 7 *was* one reed long, and one reed **b**; 7341
40:29 cubits long, and five and twenty cubits **b**. 7341
40:30 and twenty cubits long, and five cubits **b**. 7341
40:33 cubits long, and five and twenty cubits **b**. 7341
40:42 and a cubit and a half **b**, and one cubit high: 7341
40:43 a **hand b**, fastened round about: 2948
40:47 and an hundred cubits **b**, foursquare; 7341
41: 1 six cubits **b** on the one side, and six cubits 7341
41: 1 one side, and six cubits **b** on the other side, 7341
41:12 end toward the west *was* seventy cubits **b**; 7341
42:11 the north, as long as they, *and* as **b** as they: 7341
42:20 hundred *reeds* long, and five hundred **b**, 7341
43:16 twelve **b**, square in the four squares thereof. 7341
43:17 and fourteen **b** in the four squares thereof; 7341
45: 6 the possession of the city five thousand **b**, 7341
46:22 joined *of* forty *cubits* long and thirty **b**: 7341
Na 2: 4 justle one against another in the **b ways**: 7339
Mt 7:13 for wide *is* the gate, and **b** *is* the way, *2149*
23: 5 they **make b** their phylacteries, and *4115*

BROADER (1) [BROAD]

Job 11: 9 *is* longer than the earth, and **b** than the sea. 7342

BROIDED (1) [BROIDERED]

1Ti 2: 9 and sobriety; not with **b hair**, *4117*

BROIDERED (8) [BROIDED]

Ex 28: 4 a robe, and a **b** coat, a mitre, and a girdle: 8665
Eze 16:10 I clothed thee also with **b work**, and 7553
16:13 *was of* fine linen, and silk, and **b work**; 7553
16:18 tookest thy **b** garments, and 7553
26:16 their robes, and put off their **b** garments: 7553
27: 7 Fine linen with **b work** from Egypt was 7553
27:16 **b work**, and fine linen, and coral, and 7553
27:24 and **b work**, and in chests of rich apparel, 7553

BROILED (1)

Lk 24:42 And they gave him a piece of a **b** fish, and *3702*

BROKEN (186) [BREAK]

Ge 7:11 all the fountains of the great deep **b up**, 1234
17:14 off from his people; he hath **b** my covenant. 6565
38:29 she said, How hast thou **b forth**? 6555
Lev 6:28 vessel wherein it is sodden shall be **b**: 7665
11:35 or ranges for pots, they shall be **b down**: 5422
13:20 it *is* a plague of leprosy **b out** of the boil. 6524
13:25 it *is* a leprosy **b out** of the burning: 6524
15:12 toucheth which hath the issue, shall be **b**: 7665
21:20 be scurvy, or scabbed, or hath his stones **b**; 4790
22:22 or **b**, or maimed, or having a wen, or 7665
22:24 which is bruised, or crushed, or **b**, or cut; 5423
26:13 I have **b** the bands of your yoke, and 7665
26:26 *And* when I have **b** the staff of your bread, 7665
Nu 15:31 hath **b** his commandment, that soul shall 6565
Jdg 5:22 were the horsehoofs **b** by the means of 1986
16: 9 as a thread of tow is **b** when it toucheth 5423
1Sa 2: 4 The bows of the mighty *men are* **b**, and 2844
2:10 of the LORD shall be **b to pieces**; 2865
2Sa 5:20 The LORD hath **b forth** upon mine 6555
22:35 so that a bow of steel is **b** *by* mine arms. 5181
1Ki 18:30 the altar of the LORD that was **b down**. 2040
22:48 for the ships were **b** at Ezion-geber. 7665
2Ki 11: 6 watch of the house, that it be **not b down**. 4535
25: 4 the city was **b up**, and all the men of war 1234
1Ch 14:11 God hath **b in upon** mine enemies by mine 6555
2Ch 20:37 the LORD hath **b** thy works. 6555
20:37 the ships were **b**, that they were not able to 7665
24: 7 wicked woman, had **b up** the house of God; 6555
25:12 of the rock, that they all were **b in pieces**. 1234
32: 5 built up all the wall that was **b**, and raised *it* 6555
33: 3 which Hezekiah his father had **b down**, 5422
34: 7 when he had **b down** the altars and 5422
Ne 1: 3 the wall of Jerusalem also *is* **b down**, and 6555
2:13 which were **b down**, and the gates thereof 6555
Job 4:10 and the teeth of the young lions, are **b**. 5421
7: 5 my skin is **b**, and become loathsome. 7280
16:12 I was at ease, but he hath **b** me **asunder**: 6565
17:11 My days are past, my purposes are **b off**, 5423

Job 22: 9 and the arms of the fatherless have been **b**. 1792
24:20 and wickedness shall be **b** as a tree. 7665
31:22 and mine arm be **b** from the bone. 7665
38:15 is withholden, and the high arm shall be **b**. 7665
Ps 3: 7 thou hast **b** the teeth of the ungodly. 7665
18:34 so that a bow of steel is **b** *by* mine arms. 5181
31:12 as a dead man out of mind: I am like a **b** vessel. 6
34:18 *is* nigh unto them that are of a **b** heart; 7665
34:20 keepeth all his bones: not one of them is **b**. 7665
37:15 their own heart, and their bows shall be **b**. 7665
37:17 For the arms of the wicked shall be **b**: but 7665
38: 8 I am feeble and sore **b**: I have roared by 1794
44:19 Though thou hast **sore b** us in the place of 1794
51: 8 *that* the bones *which* thou hast **b** may 1794
51:17 The sacrifices of God *are* a **b** spirit: 7665
51:17 a **b** and a contrite heart, O God, thou wilt 7665
55:20 at peace with him: he hath **b** his covenant. 2490
60: 2 made the earth to tremble; thou hast **b** it: 6480
69:20 Reproach hath **b** my heart; and I am full of 7665
80:12 Why hast thou *then* **b down** her hedges, so 6555
89:10 Thou hast **b** Rahab **in pieces**, as one that is 1792
89:40 Thou hast **b down** all his hedges; thou hast 6555
107:16 For he hath **b** the gates of brass, and cut 7665
109:16 that *he* might even slay the **b** in heart. 3512
124: 7 the snare is **b**, and we are escaped. 7665
147: 3 He healeth the **b** in heart, and bindeth up 7665
Pr 3:20 By his knowledge the depths are **b up**, and 1234
6:15 suddenly shall he be **b** without remedy. 7665
15:13 but by sorrow of the heart the spirit *is* **b**. 5218
17:22 a medicine: but a **b** spirit drieth the bones. 5218
24:31 and the stone wall thereof was **b down**. 2040
25:19 *man* in time of trouble *is like* a **b** tooth, 7465
25:28 his own spirit *is like* a city *that is* **b down**, 6555
Ecc 4:12 and a threefold cord is not quickly **b**. 5423
12: 6 or the golden bowl be **b**, or the pitcher be 7533
12: 6 or the pitcher be **b** at the fountain, or 7665
12: 6 the fountain, or the wheel **b** at the cistern. 7533
Isa 5:27 nor the latchet of their shoes be **b**: 5423
7: 8 and five years shall Ephraim be **b**, 2865
8: 9 O ye people, and ye shall be **b in pieces**; 2865
8: 9 gird yourselves, and ye shall be **b in pieces**; 2865
8: 9 gird yourselves, and ye shall be **b in pieces**. 2865
8:15 fall, and be **b**, and be snared, and be taken. 7665
9: 4 For thou hast **b** the yoke of his burden, and 2865
14: 5 The LORD hath **b** the staff of the wicked, 7665
14:29 because the rod of him that smote thee is **b**: 7665
16: 8 the lords of the heathen have **b down** 1986
19:10 they shall be **b** *in* the purposes thereof, 1792
21: 9 all the graven images of her gods he hath **b** 7665
22:10 the houses have ye **b down** to fortify 5422
24: 5 the ordinance, **b** the everlasting covenant. 6565
24:10 The city of confusion is **b down**: 7665
24:19 The earth is **utterly b down**, 7489+7489
27:11 thereof are withered, they shall be **b off**: 7665
28:13 and be **b**, and snared, and taken. 7665
30:14 of the potters' vessel that is **b in pieces**; 3807
33: 8 he hath **b** the covenant, he hath despised 6565
33:20 neither shall any of the cords thereof be **b**. 5423
36: 6 Lo, thou trustest in the staff of this **b** reed, 7533
Jer 2:13 **b** cisterns, that can hold no water. 7665
2:16 Tahapanes have **b** the crown of thy head. 7462
2:20 For of old time I have **b** thy yoke, *and* 7665
4:26 all the cities thereof were **b down** at 5422
5: 5 these have altogether **b** the yoke, *and* 7665
10:20 is spoiled, and all my cords are **b**: 5423
11:10 the house of Judah have **b** my covenant 6565
11:16 fire upon it, and the branches of it are **b**. 7489
14:17 for the virgin daughter of my people is **b** 7665
22:28 *Is* this man Coniah a despised **b** idol? *is he* 5310
23: 9 Mine heart within me is **b** because of 7665
28: 2 I have **b** the yoke of the king of Babylon. 7665
28:12 **b** the yoke from off the neck of the prophet 7665
28:13 Thou hast **b** the yokes of wood; but 7665
33:21 *Then* may also my covenant be **b** with 6565
37:11 **b up** from Jerusalem for fear of Pharaoh's 5927
39: 2 ninth *day* of the month, the city was **b up**. 1234
48:17 How is the strong staff **b**, *and* the beautiful 7665
48:20 Moab is confounded; for it is **b down**: howl 2865
48:25 cut off, and his arm is **b**, saith the LORD. 7665
48:38 for I have **b** Moab like a vessel wherein *is* 7665
48:39 They shall howl, *saying,* How is it **b down**! 2865
50: 2 is confounded, Merodach is **b in pieces**; 2865
50: 2 are confounded, her images are **b in pieces**. 2865
50:17 king of Babylon hath **b** his **bones**. 6105
50:23 of the whole earth cut asunder and **b**! 7665
51:30 burnt her dwelling places; her bars are **b**. 7665
51:56 *men* are taken, *every one of* their bows is **b**: 2865
51:58 walls of Babylon shall be **utterly b**, 6209+6209
52: 7 the city was **b up**, and all the men of war 1234
La 2: 9 he hath destroyed and **b** her bars: 7665
3: 4 skin hath he made old; he hath **b** my bones. 7665
3:16 He hath also **b** my teeth with gravel stones, 1638
Eze 6: 4 be desolate, and your images shall be **b**: 7665
6: 6 your idols may be **b** and cease, and 7665
6: 9 because I am **b** with their whorish heart, 7665
17:19 and my covenant that he hath **b**, 6331
19:12 her strong rods were **b** and withered; 6561
26: 2 she is **b** *that was* the gates of the people: 7665
27:26 the east wind hath **b** thee in the midst of 7665
27:34 *In* the time when *thou shalt be* **b** by the seas 7665
30: 4 and her foundations shall be **b down**. 2040
30:21 I have **b** the arm of Pharaoh king of Egypt; 7665
30:22 his arms, the strong, and that which was **b**; 7665
31:12 his boughs are **b** by all the rivers of 7665
32:28 thou shalt be **b** in the midst of 7665
34: 4 neither have ye bound up that which was **b**, 7665
34:16 will bind up that which was **b**, and 7665
34:27 when I have **b** the bands of their yoke, and 7665
44: 7 they have **b** my covenant because of all 6565
Da 2:35 **b to pieces** together, and became like 1855
2:42 shall be partly strong, and partly **b**. 8406
8: 8 when he was strong, the great horn was **b**; 7665
8:22 Now that being **b**, whereas four stood up 7665
8:25 of princes; but he shall be **b** without hand. 7665
11: 4 his kingdom shall be **b**, and shall be 7665

Da 11:22 overflown from before him, and shall be **b**; 7665
Hos 5:11 Ephraim *is* oppressed *and* **b** in judgment, 7533
8: 6 but the calf of Samaria shall be **b in pieces**. 7616
Joel 1:17 are laid desolate, the barns are **b down**; 2040
Jnh 1: 4 in the sea, so that the ship was like to be **b**. 7665
Mic 2:13 they have **b up**, and have passed through 6555
Zec 11:11 it was **b** in that day: and so the poor of 6565
11:16 nor heal that that is **b**, nor feed that that 7665
Mt 15:37 they took up of the **b** *meat* that was left *2801*
21:44 shall fall on this stone shall be **b**: *4917*
24:43 not have suffered his house to be **b up**. *1358*
Mk 2: 4 and when they had **b** *it* **up**, they let down *1846*
5: 4 asunder by him, and the fetters **b in pieces**: *4937*
8: 8 they took up of the **b** *meat* that was left *2801*
Lk 12:39 have suffered his house to be **b through**. *1358*
20:18 shall fall upon that stone shall be **b**; *4917*
Jn 5:18 because he not only had **b** the sabbath, but *3089*
7:23 that the law of Moses should not be **b**; *3089*
10:35 of God came, and the scripture cannot be **b**; *3089*
19:31 besought Pilate that their legs might be **b**, *2608*
19:36 be fulfilled, A bone of him shall not be **b**. *4937*
21:11 there were so many, *yet* was not the net **b**. *4977*
Ac 13:43 Now when the congregation was **b up**, *3089*
20:11 was come up *again*, and had **b** bread, *2806*
27:35 and when he had **b** *it*, he began to eat. *2806*
27:41 the hinder part was **b** with the violence of *3089*
27:44 and some on **b**[S] **pieces** of the ship. *5100*
Ro 11:17 And if some of the branches be **b off**, and *1575*
11:19 wilt say then, The branches were **b off**, *1575*
11:20 because of unbelief they were **b off**, and *1575*
1Co 11:24 this is my body, which is **b** for you: this do *2806*
Eph 2:14 hath **b down** the middle wall of partition *3089*
Rev 2:27 of a potter *shall* they be **b to shivers**: *4937*

BROKENFOOTED (1) [BREAK, FOOT]

Lev 21:19 Or a man that is **b**, or brokenhanded, 7272+7667

BROKENHANDED (1) [BREAK, HAND]

Lev 21:19 Or a man that is brokenfooted, or **b**, 3027+7667

BROKEN-HEARTED (2) [BREAK, HEART]

Isa 61: 1 he hath sent me to bind up the **b**, to 3820+7665
Lk 4:18 he hath sent me to heal the **b**, to preach *4937*

BRONZE See BRASEN; BRASS; STEEL

BROOD (1)

Lk 13:34 as a hen *doth gather* her **b** under *her* wings, *3555*

BROOK (39) [BROOKS]

Ge 32:23 sent them over the **b**, and sent over that he 5158
Lev 23:40 boughs of thick trees, and willows of the **b**; 5158
Nu 13:23 they came unto the **b** of Eshcol, and 5158
13:24 The place was called the **b** Eshcol, because 5158
Dt 2:13 *said I*, and get you over the **b** Zered. 5158
2:13 And we went over the **b** Zered. 5158
2:14 until we were come over the **b** Zered, 5158
9:21 I cast the dust thereof into the **b** that 5158
1Sa 17:40 chose him five smooth stones out of the **b**, 5158
30: 9 *were* with him, and came to the **b** Besor, 5158
30:10 faint that they could not go over the **b** 5158
30:21 whom they had made also to abide at the **b** 5158
2Sa 15:23 the king also *himself* passed over the **b** 5158
17:20 They be gone over the **b** of water. 4323
1Ki 2:37 goest out, and passest over the **b** Kidron, 5158
15:13 her idol, and burnt *it* by the **b** Kidron. 5158
17: 3 and hide thyself by the **b** Cherith, 5158
17: 4 it shall be, *that* thou shalt drink of the **b**; 5158
17: 5 for he went and dwelt by the **b** Cherith, 5158
17: 6 flesh in the evening; and he drank of the **b**. 5158
17: 7 that the **b** dried up, because there had been 5158
18:40 Elijah brought them down to the **b** Kishon, 5158
2Ki 23: 6 unto the **b** Kidron, and burnt it at the brook 5158
23: 6 burnt it at the **b** Kidron, and stampt *it* small 5158
23:12 and cast the dust of them into the **b** Kidron. 5158
2Ch 15:16 and stamped *it*, and burnt *it* at the **b** Kidron. 5158
20:16 ye shall find them at the end of the **b**, 5158
29:16 *it*, to carry *it* out abroad into the **b** Kidron. 5158
30:14 they away, and cast *them* into the **b** Kidron. 5158
32: 4 the **b** that ran through the midst of the land, 5158
Ne 2:15 went I up in the night by the **b**, and viewed 5158
Job 6:15 My brethren have dealt deceitfully as a **b**, 5158
40:22 the willows of the **b** compass him about. 5158
Ps 83: 9 as *to* Sisera, as *to* Jabin, at the **b** of Kison: 5158
110: 7 He shall drink of the **b** in the way: therefore 5158
Pr 18: 4 the wellspring of wisdom *as* a flowing **b**. 5158
Isa 15: 7 shall they carry away to the **b** of 5158
Jer 31:40 and all the fields unto the **b** of Kidron, 5158
Jn 18: 1 forth with his disciples over the **b** Cedron, *5493*

BROOKS (15) [BROOK]

Nu 21:14 did in the Red sea, and *in* the **b** of Arnon, 5158
21:15 *at* the stream of the **b** that goeth down to 5158
Dt 8: 7 a land of **b** of water, of fountains and 5158
2Sa 23:30 the Pirathonite, Hiddai of the **b** of Gaash, 5158
1Ki 18: 5 unto all fountains of water, and unto all **b**: 5158
1Ch 11:32 Hurai of the **b** of Gaash, Abiel 5158
Job 6:15 *and* as the stream of **b** they pass away; 5158
20:17 the floods, the **b** of honey and butter. 5158
22:24 and *the gold of* Ophir as the stones of the **b**. 5158
Ps 42: 1 As the hart panteth after the water **b**, so 650
Isa 19: 6 *and* the **b** of defence shall be emptied and 2975
19: 7 The paper reeds by the **b**, by the mouth of 2975
19: 7 by the mouth of the **b**, and every thing 2975
19: 7 and every thing sown by the **b**, shall wither, 2975
19: 8 all they that cast angle into the **b** shall 2975

BROOM See BESOM

BROTH (3)

Jdg 6:19 he put the **b** in a pot, and brought *it* out 4839
6:20 lay *them* upon this rock, and pour out the **b**. 4839
Isa 65: 4 **b** of abominable *things is in* their vessels; 4839

BROTHER (367) [BRETHREN, BRETHREN'S, BROTHER'S, BROTHERHOOD, BROTHERLY, BROTHERS']

Ge 4: 2 she again bare his **b** Abel. And Abel was a 251
4: 8 Cain talked with Abel his **b**: and it came to 251
4: 8 that Cain rose up against Abel his **b**, and 251
4: 9 said unto Cain, Where *is* Abel thy **b**? 251
9: 5 at the hand of every man's **b** will I require 251
10:21 the **b** of Japheth the elder, even to him were 251
14:13 **b** of Eshcol, and brother of Aner: 251
14:13 brother of Eshcol, and **b** of Aner: 251
14:14 when Abram heard that his **b** was taken 251
14:16 also brought again his **b** Lot, and his goods, 251
20: 5 she, even she herself said, He *is* my **b**: in 251
20:13 we shall come, say of me, He *is* my **b**. 251
20:16 I have given thy **b** a thousand *pieces* of 251
22:20 she hath also born children unto thy **b** 251
22:21 Buz his **b**, and Kemuel the father of Aram, 251
22:23 Milcah did bear to Nahor, Abraham's **b**. 251
24:15 of Milcah, the wife of Nahor, Abraham's **b**, 251
24:29 Rebekah had a **b**, and his name *was* Laban: 251
24:53 he gave also to her **b** and to her mother 251
24:55 her **b** and her mother said, Let the damsel 251
25:26 after that came his **b** out, and his hand took 251
27: 6 I heard thy father speak unto Esau thy **b**, 251
27:11 Esau my **b** *is* a hairy man, and I *am* a smooth 251
27:23 his hands were hairy, as his **b** Esau's hands: 251
27:30 that Esau his **b** came in from his hunting. 251
27:35 Thy **b** came with subtilty, and hath taken 251
27:40 sword shalt thou live, and shalt serve thy **b**; 251
27:41 are at hand; then will I slay my **b** Jacob. 251
27:42 said unto him, Behold, thy **b** Esau, 251
27:43 and arise, flee thou to Laban my **b** to Haran; 251
28: 2 of the daughters of Laban thy mother's **b**. 251
28: 5 the **b** of Rebekah, Jacob's and 251
29:10 the daughter of Laban his mother's **b**, 251
29:10 the sheep of Laban his mother's **b**, 251
29:10 watered the flock of Laban his mother's **b**. 251
29:12 Jacob told Rachel that he *was* her father's **b**, 251
29:15 Because thou *art* my **b**, shouldest thou 251
32: 3 him to Esau his **b** unto the land of Seir, 251
32: 6 We came to thy **b** Esau, and also he cometh 251
32:11 I pray thee, from the hand of my **b**, 251
32:13 came to his hand a present for Esau his **b**; 251
32:17 When Esau my **b** meeteth thee, and 251
33: 3 seven times, until he came near to his **b**. 251
33: 9 Esau said, I have enough, my **b**; keep that 251
35: 1 thou fleddest from the face of Esau thy **b**. 251
35: 7 when he fled from the face of his **b**. 251
36: 6 went into the country from the face of his **b** 251
37:26 What profit *is it* if we slay our **b**, and 251
37:27 be upon him; for he *is* our **b** *and* our flesh. 251
38: 8 and marry her, and raise up seed to thy **b**. 251
38: 9 lest that he should give seed to his **b**. 251
38:29 back his hand, that, behold, his **b** came out: 251
38:30 afterward came out his **b**, that had the scarlet 251
42: 4 Benjamin, Joseph's **b**, Jacob sent not with 251
42:15 except your youngest **b** come hither. 251
42:16 let him fetch your **b**, and ye shall be kept in 251
42:20 bring your youngest **b** unto me; so shall your 251
42:21 We *are* verily guilty concerning our **b**, 251
42:34 bring your youngest **b** unto me: then shall I 251
42:34 ye *are* true *men*: *so* will I deliver you your **b**, 251
42:38 for his **b** is dead, and he is left alone: 251
43: 3 not see my face, except your **b** *be* with you. 251
43: 4 If thou wilt send our **b** with us, we will go 251
43: 5 not see my face, except your **b** *be* with you. 251
43: 6 as to tell the man whether ye had yet a **b**? 251
43: 7 have ye *another* **b**? and we told him 251
43: 7 know that he would say, Bring your **b** down? 251
43:13 Take also your **b**, and arise, go again unto 251
43:14 that he may send away your other **b**, and 251
43:29 saw his **b** Benjamin, his mother's son, and 251
43:29 and said, *Is* this your younger **b**, 251
43:30 for his bowels did yern upon his **b**: 251
43:30 saying, Have ye a father, or a **b**? 251
44:20 his **b** is dead, and he alone is left of his 251
44:23 Except your youngest **b** come down with 251
44:26 if our youngest **b** be with us, then will we go 251
44:26 except our youngest **b** *be* with us. 251
45: 4 he said, I *am* Joseph your **b**, whom ye sold 251
45:12 eyes see, and the eyes of my **b** Benjamin, 251
45:14 And he fell upon his **b** Benjamin's neck, and 251
48:19 truly his younger **b** shall be greater than he, 251
Ex 4:14 and he said, Is not Aaron the Levite thy **b**? 251
7: 1 and Aaron thy **b** shall be thy prophet. 251
7: 2 Aaron thy **b** shall speak unto Pharaoh, 251
28: 1 take thou unto thee Aaron thy **b**, and his 251
28: 2 shalt make holy garments for Aaron thy **b**, 251
28: 4 shall make holy garments for Aaron thy **b**, 251
28:41 thou shalt put them upon Aaron thy **b**, and 251
32:27 slay every man his **b**, and every man his 251
32:29 every man upon his son, and upon his **b**; 251
Lev 16: 2 said unto Moses, Speak unto Aaron thy **b**, 251
18:14 not uncover the nakedness of thy father's **b**, 251
19:17 Thou shalt not hate thy **b** in thine heart: 251
21: 2 his son, and for his daughter, and for his **b**, 251
25:25 If thy **b** be waxen poor, and hath sold away 251
25:25 then shall he redeem that which his **b** sold. 251
25:35 if thy **b** be waxen poor, and fallen in decay 251
25:36 fear thy God; that thy **b** may live with thee. 251
25:39 if thy **b** *that dwelleth* by thee be waxen poor, 251
25:47 thy **b** *that dwelleth* by him wax poor, and 251
Nu 6: 7 for his **b**, or for his sister, when they die: 251
20: 8 Aaron thy **b**, and speak ye unto the rock 251
20:14 Thus saith thy **b** Israel, Thou knowest all 251
27:13 thy people, as Aaron thy **b** was gathered. 251
36: 2 of Zelophehad our **b** unto his daughters. 251
Dt 1:16 righteously between every man and his **b**, 251
13: 6 If thy **b**, the son of thy mother, or thy son, or 251
15: 2 not exact *it* of his neighbour, or of his **b**; 251
15: 3 *that* which is thine with thy **b** thine hand 251
15: 7 nor shut thine hand from thy poor **b**: 251
15: 9 and thine eye be evil against thy poor **b**, and 251
Dt 15:11 Thou shalt open thine hand wide unto thy **b**, 251
15:12 *And* if thy **b**, a Hebrew man, or a Hebrew 251
17:15 set a stranger over thee, which *is* not thy **b**. 251
19:18 *and* hath testified falsely against his **b**; 251
19:19 as he had thought to have done unto his **b**: 251
22: 1 in any case bring them again unto thy **b**. 251
22: 2 if thy **b** *be* not nigh unto thee, or *if* thou 251
22: 2 it shall be with thee until thy **b** seek after it, 251
23: 7 shalt not abhor an Edomite; for he *is* thy **b**: 251
23:19 Thou shalt not lend upon usury to thy **b**; 251
23:20 unto thy **b** thou shalt not lend upon usury: 251
24:10 When thou dost lend thy **b** any thing, 7453
25: 3 then thy **b** should seem vile unto thee. 251
25: 5 her **husband's b** shall go in unto her, and 2993
25: 5 **perform the duty of a husband's b** unto 2992
25: 6 succeed in the name of his **b** which is dead, 251
25: 7 My **husband's b** refuseth to raise up unto 2993
25: 7 to raise up unto his **b** a name in Israel, 251
25: 7 not **perform the duty of** my **husband's b**. 2992
28:54 his eye shall be evil toward his **b**, and 251
32:50 as Aaron thy **b** died in mount Hor, and 251
Jos 15:17 the son of Kenaz, the **b** of Caleb, took it: 251
Jdg 1: 3 Judah said unto Simeon his **b**, Come up with 251
1:13 the son of Kenaz, Caleb's younger **b**, took it: 251
1:17 Judah went with Simeon his **b**, and they slew 251
3: 9 the son of Kenaz, Caleb's younger **b**. 251
9: 3 follow Abimelech; for they said, He *is* our **b**. 251
9:18 the men of Shechem, because he *is* your **b**;) 251
9:21 and dwelt there, for fear of Abimelech his **b**. 251
9:24 their blood be laid upon Abimelech their **b**, 251
20:23 against the children of Benjamin my **b**? 251
20:28 against the children of Benjamin my **b**, 251
21: 6 of Israel repented them for Benjamin their **b**, 251
Ru 4: 3 parcel of land, which *was* our **b** Elimelech's: 251
1Sa 14: 3 Ahiah, the son of Ahitub, Ichabod's **b**, 251
17:28 Eliab his eldest **b** heard when he spake unto 251
20:29 my **b**, he hath commanded me *to be there*: 251
26: 6 the son of Zeruiah, **b** to Joab, saying, 251
2Sa 1:26 I am distressed for thee, my **b** Jonathan: 251
2:22 then should I hold up my face to Joab thy **b**? 251
2:27 had gone up every one from following his **b**. 251
3:27 that he died, for the blood of Asahel his **b**. 251
3:30 So Joab and Abishai his **b** slew Abner, 251
3:30 he had slain their **b** Asahel at Gibeon in 251
4: 6 and Rechab and Baanah his **b** escaped. 251
4: 9 David answered Rechab and Baanah his **b**, 251
10:10 he delivered into the hand of Abishai his **b**, 251
13: 3 *was* Jonadab, the son of Shimeah David's **b**: 251
13: 4 I love Tamar, my **b** Absalom's sister. 251
13: 7 Go now *to* thy **b** Amnon's house, and 251
13: 8 So Tamar went *to* her **b** Amnon's house; and 251
13:10 *them* into the chamber to Amnon her **b**. 251
13:12 answered him, Nay, my **b**, do not force me; 251
13:20 Absalom her **b** said unto her, Hath Amnon 251
13:20 unto her, Hath Amnon thy **b** been with thee? 251
13:20 he *is* thy **b**; regard not this thing. So Tamar 251
13:20 So Tamar remained desolate *in* her **b** 251
13:22 Absalom spake unto his **b** Amnon neither NIH
13:26 I pray thee, let my **b** Amnon go with us. 251
13:32 the son of Shimeah David's **b**, answered and 251
14: 7 they said, Deliver him that smote his **b**, 251
14: 7 kill him, for the life of his **b** whom he slew; 251
18: 2 Joab's **b**, and a third part under the hand of 251
20: 9 said to Amasa, *Art* thou in health, my **b**? 251
20:10 Abishai his **b** pursued after Sheba the son of 251
21:19 slew *the* **b** *of* Goliath the Gittite, NIH
21:21 Jonathan the son of Shimea the **b** of David 251
23:18 Abishai, the **b** of Joab, the son of Zeruiah, 251
23:24 Asahel the **b** of Joab *was* one of the thirty; 251
1Ki 1:10 and the mighty *men*, and Solomon his **b**, 251
2: 7 to me when I fled because of Absalom thy **b**. 251
2:21 be given to Adonijah thy **b** to wife. 251
2:22 for he *is* mine elder **b**; even for him, and 251
9:13 *are* these which thou hast given me, my **b**? 251
13:30 they mourned over him, *saying*, Alas, my **b**. 251
20:32 And he said, *Is* he yet alive? he *is* my **b**. 251
20:33 catch *it*: and they said, Thy **b** Ben-hadad. 251
2Ki 24:17 Mattaniah his **father's b** king in his stead, 1730
1Ch 2:32 the sons of Jada the **b** of Shammai; Jether, 251
2:42 Now the sons of Caleb the **b** of Jerahmeel 251
4:11 Chelub the **b** of Shuah begat Mehir, 251
6:39 his **b** Asaph, who stood on his right hand, 251
7:16 the name of his **b** *was* Sheresh; and his sons 251
7:35 the son of his **b** Helem; Zophah, and Imna, 251
8:39 the sons of Eshek his **b** *were*, Ulam his 251
11:20 Abishai the **b** of Joab, he was chief of 251
11:26 of the armies *were*, Asahel the **b** of Joab, 251
11:38 Joel the **b** of Nathan, Mibhar the son of 251
11:45 the son of Shimri, and Joha his **b**, the Tizite, 251
19:11 he delivered unto the hand of Abishai his **b**, 251
19:15 they likewise fled before Abishai his **b**, and 251
20: 5 Elhanan the son of Jair slew Lahmi the **b** of 251
20: 7 Jonathan the son of Shimea David's **b** slew 251
24:25 The **b** of Michah *was* Isshiah: of the sons of 251
26:22 Zetham, and Joel his **b**, *which were* over 251
27: 7 the fourth month *was* Asahel the **b** of Joab, 251
2Ch 31:12 *was* ruler, and Shimei his **b** *was* the next. 251
31:13 the hand of Cononiah and Shimei his **b**, 251
36: 4 the king of Egypt made Eliakim his **b** king 251
36: 4 Necho took Jehoahaz his **b**, and carried him 251
36:10 made Zedekiah his **b** king over Judah and 251
Ne 5: 7 You exact usury, every one of his **b**. 251
7: 2 That I gave my **b** Hanani, and Hananiah 251
Job 22: 6 For thou hast taken a pledge from thy **b** for 251
30:29 I am a **b** to dragons, and a companion to 251
Ps 35:14 as though *he had been* my friend *or* **b**: 251
49: 7 *of them* can by any means redeem *his* **b**, 251
50:20 Thou sittest *and* speakest against thy **b**; 251
Pr 17:17 at all times, and a **b** is born for adversity. 251
18: 9 He also that is slothful in his work *is* **b** to 251
18:19 A **b** offended *is harder to be won* than a 251
18:24 there is a friend *that* sticketh closer than a **b**. 251
27:10 *for* better *is* a neighbour *that is* near than a **b** 251
Ecc 4: 8 a second; yea, he hath neither child nor **b**: 251
SS 8: 1 O that thou *wert* as my **b**, that sucked 251

Isa 3: 6 When a man shall take hold of his **b** *of* 251
9:19 the fuel of the fire: no man shall spare his **b**. 251
19: 2 they shall fight every one against his **b**, and 251
41: 6 *every one* said to his **b**, Be of good courage. 251
Jer 9: 4 of his neighbour, and trust ye not in any **b**: 251
9: 4 for every **b** will utterly supplant, and 251
22:18 shall not lament for him, *saying*, Ah my **b**! 251
23:35 every one to his **b**, What hath the LORD 251
31:34 every man his **b**, saying, Know the LORD: 251
34: 9 serve himself of them, *to wit*, of a Jew his **b**. 251
34:14 years let ye go every man his **b** a Hebrew, 251
34:17 every one to his **b**, and every man to his 251
Eze 18:18 spoiled *his* **b** by violence, and did *that* which 251
33:30 every one to his **b**, saying, Come, I pray you, 251
38:21 every man's sword shall be against his **b**. 251
44:25 for **b**, or for sister that hath had no husband, 251
Hos 12: 3 He took his **b** by the heel in the womb, and 251
Am 1:11 because he did pursue his **b** with the sword, 251
Ob 1:10 For *thy* violence against thy **b** Jacob shame 251
1:12 of thy **b** in the day that he became a stranger; 251
Mic 7: 2 they hunt every man his **b** *with* a net. 251
Hag 2:22 come down, every one by the sword of his **b**. 251
Zec 7: 9 and compassions every man to his **b**: 251
7:10 let none of you imagine evil against his **b** in 251
Mal 1: 2 *was* not Esau Jacob's **b**? saith the LORD: 251
2:10 deal treacherously every man against his **b**, 251
Mt 4:18 Simon called Peter, and Andrew his **b**, *80*
4:21 James the *son* of Zebedee, and John his **b**, *80*
5:22 That whosoever is angry with his **b** without a *80*
5:22 and whosoever shall say to his **b**, Raca, *80*
5:23 there rememberest that thy **b** hath ought *80*
5:24 first be reconciled to thy **b**, and then come *80*
7: 4 Or how wilt thou say to thy **b**, Let me pull out *80*
10: 2 who is called Peter, and Andrew his **b**; *80*
10: 2 the *son* of Zebedee, and John his **b**; *80*
10:21 And the **b** shall deliver up the brother to *80*
10:21 And the brother shall deliver up the **b** to *80*
12:50 the same is my **b**, and sister, and mother. *80*
14: 3 prison for Herodias' sake, his **b** Philip's wife. *80*
17: 1 and John his **b**, and bringeth them up into a *80*
18:15 Moreover if thy **b** shall trespass against thee, *80*
18:15 if he shall hear thee, thou hast gained thy **b**. *80*
18:21 how oft shall my **b** sin against me, and I *80*
18:35 forgive not every one his **b** their trespasses. *80*
22:24 his **b** shall marry his wife, and raise up seed *80*
22:24 marry his wife, and raise up seed unto his **b**. *80*
22:25 and, having no issue, left his wife unto his **b**: *80*
Mk 1:16 and Andrew his **b** casting a net into the sea: *80*
1:19 James the *son* of Zebedee, and John his **b**, *80*
3:17 the *son* of Zebedee, and John the **b** of James; *80*
3:35 the same is my **b**, and my sister, and mother. *80*
5:37 and James, and John the **b** of James. *80*
6: 3 the **b** of James, and Joses, and of Juda, and *80*
6:17 prison for Herodias' sake, his **b** Philip's wife: *80*
12:19 If a man's **b** die, and leave *his* wife *behind* *80*
12:19 that his **b** should take his wife, and raise up *80*
12:19 take his wife, and raise up seed unto his **b**. *80*
13:12 Now the **b** shall betray the brother to death, *80*
13:12 Now the brother shall betray the **b** to death, *80*
Lk 3: 1 and his **b** Philip tetrarch of Iturea and of *80*
3:19 being reproved by him for Herodias his **b** *80*
6:14 and Andrew his **b**, James and John, Philip and *80*
6:16 *And* Judas *the* **b** of James, and NIG
6:42 Either how canst thou say to thy **b**, Brother, *80*
6:42 Either how canst thou say to thy brother, **B**, *80*
12:13 Master, speak to my **b**, that *he* divide *80*
15:27 And he said unto him, Thy **b** is come; *80*
15:32 for this thy **b** was dead, and is alive again; and *80*
17: 3 If thy **b** trespass against thee, rebuke him; and *80*
20:28 If any *man's* **b** die, having a wife, and he die *80*
20:28 that his **b** should take *his* wife, and raise up *80*
20:28 take *his* wife, and raise up seed unto his **b**. *80*
Jn 1:40 followed him, was Andrew, Simon Peter's **b**. *80*
1:41 He first findeth his own **b** Simon, and *80*
6: 8 Andrew, Simon Peter's **b**, saith unto him, *80*
11: 2 feet with her hair, whose **b** Lazarus was sick.) *80*
11:19 Mary, to comfort them concerning their **b**. *80*
11:21 if thou hadst been here, my **b** had not died. *80*
11:23 Jesus saith unto her, Thy **b** shall rise again. *80*
11:32 if thou hadst been here, my **b** had not died. *80*
Ac 1:13 Simon Zelotes, and Judas *the* **b** of James. NIG
9:17 on him said, **B** Saul, the Lord, *even* Jesus, *80*
12: 2 And he killed James the **b** of John with *80*
21:20 the Lord, and said unto him, Thou seest, **b**, *80*
22:13 unto me, and stood, and said unto me, **B** Saul, *80*
Ro 14:10 But why dost thou judge thy **b**? or why dost *80*
14:10 or why dost thou set at nought thy **b**? for we *80*
14:15 But if thy **b** be grieved with *thy* meat, *80*
14:21 nor *any thing* whereby thy **b** stumbleth, or *80*
16:23 of the city saluteth you, and Quartus a **b**. *80*
1Co 1: 1 through the will of God, and Sosthenes *our* **b**, *80*
5:11 if any *man that is* called a **b** be a fornicator, or *80*
6: 6 But **b** goeth to law with brother, and *80*
6: 6 But brother goeth to law with **b**, and *80*
7:12 If any **b** hath a wife that believeth not, and *80*
7:15 A **b** or a sister is not under bondage in such *80*
8:11 And through thy knowledge shall the weak **b** *80*
8:13 Wherefore, if meat make my **b** to offend, *80*
8:13 world standeth, lest I make my **b** to offend. *80*
16:12 As touching *our* **b** Apollos, I greatly desired *80*
2Co 1: 1 and Timothy *our* **b**, unto the church of God *80*
2:13 in my spirit, because I found not Titus my **b**: *80*
8:18 And we have sent with him the **b**, *80*
8:22 And we have sent with them our **b**, whom we *80*
12:18 I desired Titus, and with *him* I sent a **b**. *80*
Gal 1:19 apostles saw I none, save James the Lord's **b**. *80*
Eph 6:21 a beloved **b** and faithful minister in the Lord, *80*
Php 2:25 my **b**, and companion in labour, and *80*
Col 1: 1 by the will of God, and Timotheus *our* **b**, *80*
4: 7 *who is* a beloved **b**, and a faithful minister *80*
4: 9 With Onesimus, a faithful and beloved **b**, *80*
1Th 3: 2 our **b**, and minister of God, and *80*
4: 6 go beyond and defraud his **b** in *any* matter: *80*
2Th 3: 6 that ye withdraw yourselves from every **b** that *80*
3:15 not as an enemy, but admonish *him* as a **b**. *80*
Phm 1: 1 a prisoner of Jesus Christ, and Timothy *our* **b**, *80*
1: 7 bowels of the saints are refreshed by thee, **b**. *80*
1:16 a **b** beloved, specially to me, but how much *80*
1:20 Yea, **b**, let me have joy of thee in the Lord: *80*
Heb 8:11 and every man his **b**, saying, Know the Lord: *80*
13:23 Know ye that *our* **b** Timothy is set at liberty; *80*
Jas 1: 9 Let the **b** of low degree rejoice in that he is *80*
2:15 If a **b** or sister be naked, and destitute of daily *80*
4:11 He that speaketh evil of *his* **b**, and judgeth his *80*
4:11 and judgeth his **b**, speaketh evil of the law, *80*
1Pe 5:12 By Silvanus, a faithful **b** unto you, as I *80*
2Pe 3:15 even as our beloved **b** Paul also according to *80*
1Jn 2: 9 and hateth his **b**, is in darkness *even* until *80*
2:10 He that loveth his **b** abideth in the light, and *80*
2:11 But he that hateth his **b** is in darkness, and *80*
3:10 is not of God, neither he that loveth not his **b**. *80*
3:12 *who* was of *that* wicked one, and slew his **b**. *80*
3:14 He that loveth not *his* **b** abideth in death. *80*
3:15 Whosoever hateth his **b** is a murderer: and *80*
3:17 and seeth his **b** hath need, and shutteth up his *80*
4:20 I love God, and hateth his **b**, he is a liar: *80*
4:20 for he that loveth not his **b** whom he hath *80*
4:21 That he who loveth God love his **b** also. *80*
5:16 If any *man* see his **b** sin a sin *which is* not *80*
Jude 1: 1 the servant of Jesus Christ, and **b** of James, *80*
Rev 1: 9 who also am your **b**, and companion in *80*

BROTHER'S (35) [BROTHER]

Ge 4: 9 And he said, I know not: *Am* I my **b** keeper? 251
4:10 the voice of thy **b** blood crieth unto me from 251
4:11 mouth to receive thy **b** blood from thy hand. 251
4:21 his **b** name *was* Jubal: he was the father of 251
10:25 earth divided; and his **b** name *was* Joktan. 251
12: 5 Lot his **b** son, and all their substance that 251
14:12 they took Lot, Abram's **b** son, who dwelt in 251
24:48 to take my master's **b** daughter unto his son. 251
27:44 him a few days, until thy **b** fury turn away; 251
27:45 Until thy **b** anger turn away from thee, and 251
38: 8 Go in unto thy **b** wife, and marry her, and 251
38: 9 to pass, when he went in unto his **b** wife, 251
Lev 18:16 not uncover the nakedness of thy **b** wife: 251
18:16 of thy brother's wife: it *is* thy **b** nakedness. 251
20:21 if a man shall take his **b** wife, it *is* an 251
20:21 he hath uncovered his **b** nakedness; 251
Dt 22: 1 Thou shalt not see thy **b** ox or his sheep go 251
22: 3 with all lost *thing* of thy **b**, which he hath 251
22: 4 Thou shalt not see thy **b** ass or his ox fall 251
25: 7 if the man like not to take his **b wife**, then 2994
25: 7 let his **b wife** go up to the gate unto 2994
25: 9 shall his **b wife** come unto him in 2994
25: 9 *that* man that will not build up his **b** house. 251
1Ki 2:15 turned about, and is become my **b**: 251+3807.1
1Ch 1:19 was divided: and his **b** name *was* Joktan. 251
Job 1:13 and drinking wine in their eldest **b** house: 251
1:18 and drinking wine in their eldest **b** house: 251
Pr 27:10 neither go *into* thy **b** house in the day of thy 251
Mt 7: 3 beholdest thou the mote that is in thy **b** eye, *80*
7: 5 clearly to cast out the mote out of thy **b** eye. *80*
Mk 6:18 It is not lawful for thee to have thy **b** wife. *80*
Lk 6:41 beholdest thou the mote that is in thy **b** eye, *80*
6:42 to pull out the mote that is in thy **b** eye. *80*
Ro 14:13 or an occasion to fall in *his* **b** way. *80*
1Jn 3:12 his own works were evil, and his **b** righteous. *80*

BROTHERHOOD (2) [BROTHER]

Zec 11:14 that I might break the **b** between Judah and 264
1Pe 2:17 Honour all *men*. Love the **b**. Fear God. *81*

BROTHERLY (6) [BROTHER]

Am 1: 9 and remembered not the **b** covenant: 251
Ro 12:10 affectioned one to another with **b love**; *5360*
1Th 4: 9 But as touching **b love** ye need not that *I* *5360*
Heb 13: 1 Let **b love** continue. *5360*
2Pe 1: 7 And to godliness **b kindness**; and *5360*
1: 7 and to **b kindness** charity. *5360*

BROTHERS See BRETHREN

BROTHERS' (1) [BROTHER]

Nu 36:11 were married unto their **father's b** sons: 1730

BROUGHT (864) [BRING]

Ge 1:12 the earth **b forth** grass, *and* herb yielding 3318
1:21 which the waters **b forth abundantly**, 8317
2:19 **b** *them* unto Adam to see what he would call 935
2:22 made he a woman, and **b** her unto the man. 935
4: 3 that Cain **b** of the fruit of the ground an 935
4: 4 he also **b** of the firstlings of his flock and 935
14:16 he **b back** all the goods, and also brought 7725
14:16 also **b again** his brother Lot, and his goods, 7725
14:18 Melchizedek king of Salem **b forth** bread 3318
15: 5 he **b** him **forth** abroad, and said, Look now 3318
15: 7 I *am* the LORD that **b** thee **out** of Ur of 3318
19:16 they **b** him **forth**, and set him without 3318
19:17 when they had **b** them **forth** abroad, that he 3318
20: 9 that thou hast **b** on me and on my kingdom a 935
24:53 the servant **b forth** jewels of silver, and 3318
24:67 And Isaac **b** her into his mother Sarah's tent, 935
26:10 thou shouldest have **b** guiltiness upon us. 935
27:14 and fetched, and **b** *them* to his mother: 935
27:20 Because the LORD thy God **b** *it* to me. 7136
27:25 he **b** *it* **near** to him, and he did eat: and 5066
27:25 he did eat: and he **b** him wine, and he drank. 935
27:31 **b** *it* unto his father, and said unto his father, 935
27:33 **b** *it* me, and I have eaten of all before thou 935
29:13 and kissed him, and **b** him to his house. 935
29:23 he took Leah his daughter, and **b** her to him; 935
30:14 the field, and **b** them unto his mother Leah. 935
30:39 **b forth** cattle ringstraked, speckled, and 3205
31:39 That which was torn *of beasts* I **b** not unto 935
33:11 I pray thee, my blessing that is **b** to thee; 935
37: 2 and Joseph **b** unto his father their evil report. 935
37:28 of silver: and they **b** Joseph into Egypt. 935
37:32 of many colours, and they **b** *it* to their father; 935
Ge 38:25 When she *was* **b forth**, she sent to her 3318
39: 1 Joseph was **b down** to Egypt; and Potiphar, 3381
39: 1 which had **b** him **down** thither. 3381
39:14 he hath **b in** a Hebrew unto us to mock us; 935
39:17 Hebrew servant, which thou hast **b** unto us, 935
40:10 the clusters thereof **b forth ripe** grapes: 1310
41:14 and they **b** him **hastily** out of the dungeon: 7323
41:47 years the earth **b forth** by handfuls. 6213
43: 2 up the corn which they had **b** out of Egypt, 935
43:12 the money that was **b again** in the mouth of 7725
43:17 and the man **b** the men into Joseph's house. 935
43:18 because they were **b into** Joseph's house; 935
43:18 in our sacks at the first time *are* we **b in**; 935
43:21 and we have **b** it **again** in our hand. 7725
43:22 other money have we **b down** in our hands 3381
43:23 And he **b** Simeon **out** unto them. 3318
43:24 And the man **b** the men into Joseph's house, 935
43:26 they **b** him the present which *was* in their 935
44: 8 we **b again** unto thee out of the land of 7725
46: 7 and all his seed **b** he with him into Egypt. 935
46:32 and they have **b** their flocks, and their herds, 935
47: 7 Joseph **b in** Jacob his father, and set him 935
47:14 Joseph **b** the money into Pharaoh's house. 935
47:17 they **b** their cattle unto Joseph: and 935
48:10 he **b** them **near** unto him; and he kissed 5066
48:12 Joseph **b** them **out** from between his knees, 3318
48:13 right hand, and **b** *them* **near** unto him. 5066
50:23 Manasseh were **b up** upon Joseph's knees. 3205
Ex 2:10 and she **b** him unto Pharaoh's daughter, and 935
3:12 When thou hast **b forth** the people out of 3318
8: 7 and **b up** frogs upon the land of Egypt. 5927
8:12 of the frogs which he had **b** against 7760
9:19 shall not be **b** home, the hail shall come 622
10: 8 and Aaron were **b again** unto Pharaoh: 7725
10:13 the LORD **b** an east wind upon the land 5090
10:13 it was morning, the east wind **b** the locusts. 5375
12:17 I **b** your armies **out** of the land of Egypt: 3318
12:39 the dough which they **b forth** out of Egypt, 3318
13: 3 **b** you **out** from this *place*: there shall no 3318
13: 9 hand hath the LORD **b** thee **out** of Egypt. 3318
13:14 By strength of hand the LORD **b** us **out** 3318
13:16 hand the LORD **b** us **forth** out of Egypt. 3318
15:19 the LORD **b again** the waters of the sea 7725
15:22 So Moses **b** Israel from the Red sea, and 5265
15:26 which I have **b** upon the Egyptians: 7760
16: 3 for ye have **b** us **forth** into this wilderness, 3318
16: 6 hath **b** you **out** from the land of Egypt: 3318
16:32 when I **b** you **forth** from the land of Egypt. 3318
17: 3 Wherefore *is* this *that* thou hast **b** us **up** out 5927
18: 1 that the LORD had **b** Israel **out** of Egypt; 3318
18:26 the hard causes they **b** unto Moses, but every 935
19: 4 on eagles' wings, and **b** you unto myself. 935
19:17 Moses **b forth** the people out of the camp 3318
20: 2 which have **b** thee **out** of the land of Egypt, 3318
22: 8 the master of the house shall be **b** unto 7126
29:10 thou shalt **cause** a bullock **to be b** before 7126
29:46 that **b** them **forth** out of the land of Egypt, 3318
32: 1 the man that **b** us **up** out of the land of 5927
32: 3 *were* in their ears, and **b** *them* unto Aaron. 935
32: 4 which **b** thee **up** out of the land of Egypt. 5927
32: 6 burnt offerings, and **b** peace offerings; 5066
32: 8 which have **b** thee **up** out of the land of 5927
32:11 which thou hast **b forth** out of the land of 3318
32:21 that thou hast **b** *so* great a sin upon them? 935
32:23 the man that **b** us **up** out of the land of 5927
33: 1 the people which thou hast **b up** out of 5927
35:21 they **b** the LORD'S offering to the work of 935
35:22 *and* **b** bracelets, and earrings, and rings, and 935
35:23 skins of rams, and badgers' skins, **b** *them*. 935
35:24 of silver and brass **b** the LORD'S offering: 935
35:24 wood for any work of the service, **b** *it*. 935
35:25 and **b** that which they had spun, *both* of blue, 935
35:27 the rulers **b** onyx stones, and stones to be set, 935
35:29 The children of Israel **b** a willing offering 935
36: 3 which the children of Israel had **b** for 935
36: 3 to make it *withal*. And they **b** yet unto him 935
39:33 they **b** the tabernacle unto Moses, the tent, 935
40:21 he **b** the ark into the tabernacle, and set up 935
Lev 6:30 whereof *any* of the blood is **b** into 935
8: 6 Moses **b** Aaron and his sons, and 7126
8:13 Moses **b** Aaron's sons, and put coats upon 7126
8:14 he **b** the bullock *for* the sin offering: and 5066
8:18 he **b** the ram for the burnt offering: and 7126
8:22 he **b** the other ram, the ram of consecration: 7126
8:24 he **b** Aaron's sons, and Moses put of 7126
9: 5 they **b** *that* which Moses commanded 3947
9: 9 the sons of Aaron **b** the blood unto him: 7126
9:15 he **b** the people's offering, and took 7126
9:16 he **b** the burnt offering, and offered it 7126
9:17 he **b** the meat offering, and took a handful 7126
10:18 the blood of it was not **b in** within the holy 935
13: 2 he shall be **b** unto Aaron the priest, or 935
13: 9 in a man, then he shall be **b** unto the priest; 935
14: 2 his cleansing: He shall be **b** unto the priest: 935
16:27 whose blood was **b in** to make atonement in 935
19:36 which **b** you **out** of the land of Egypt. 3318
22:27 is **b forth**, then it shall be seven days under 3205
22:33 That **b** you **out** of the land of Egypt, to be 3318
23:14 until the selfsame day that ye have **b** an 935
23:15 from the day that ye **b** the sheaf of the wave 935
23:43 when I **b** them **out** of the land of Egypt: 3318
24:11 they **b** him unto Moses: (and his mother's 935
25:38 which **b** you **forth** out of the land of Egypt, 3318
25:42 which I **b forth** out of the land of Egypt: 3318
25:55 they *are* my servants whom I **b forth out** of 3318
26:13 which **b** you **forth** out of the land of Egypt, 3318
26:41 have **b** them into the land of their enemies; 935
26:45 whom I **b forth** out of the land of Egypt in 3318
Nu 6:13 he shall be **b** unto the door of the tabernacle 935
7: 3 And they **b** their offering before the LORD, 935
7: 3 and they **b** them before the tabernacle. 7126
9:13 he **b** not the offering of the LORD in his 7126
11:31 **b** quails from the sea, and let *them* fall by 1468
12:15 journeyed not till Miriam was **b in** *again*. 622
13:23 *they* **b** of the pomegranates, and of the figs. NIH

Nu 13:26 **b back** word unto them, and unto all 7725
13:32 they **b up** an evil report of the land which 3318
14: 3 wherefore *hath* the LORD **b** us unto this 935
15:33 they that found him gathering sticks **b** him 7126
15:36 all the congregation **b** him without 3318
15:41 which **b** you **out** of the land of Egypt, to be 3318
16:10 he hath **b** thee **near** *to him,* and all thy 7126
16:13 *Is it* a small thing that thou hast **b** us **up** out 5927
16:14 Moreover thou hast not **b** us into a land that 935
17: 8 **b forth** buds, and bloomed blossoms, and 3318
17: 9 Moses **b out** all the rods from before 3318
20: 4 why have ye **b up** the congregation of 935
20:16 an angel, and hath **b** us **forth** out of Egypt: 3318
21: 5 Wherefore have ye **b** us **up** out of Egypt to 5927
22:41 and **b** him **up** *into* the high places of Baal, 5927
23: 7 Balak the king of Moab hath **b** me from 5148
23:14 he **b** him *into* the field of Zophim, to 3947
23:22 God **b** them **out** of Egypt; he hath as it 3318
23:28 Balak **b** Balaam *unto* the top of Peor, 3947
24: 8 God **b** him **forth** out of Egypt; he hath as it 3318
25: 6 **b** unto his brethren a Midianitish *woman* in 7126
27: 5 Moses **b** their cause before the LORD. 7126
31:12 they **b** the captives, and the prey, and 935
31:50 therefore **b** an oblation for the LORD, 7126
31:54 **b** it into the tabernacle of the congregation, 935
32:17 until we have **b** them unto their place: 935
Dt 1:25 **b** *it* **down** unto us, and brought us word 3381
1:25 unto us, and **b** us word **again**, and said, 7725
1:27 he hath **b** us **forth** out of the land of Egypt, 3318
4:20 **b** you **forth** out of the iron furnace, 3318
4:37 **b** thee **out** in his sight with his mighty 3318
5: 6 which **b** thee **out** of the land of Egypt, 3318
5:15 *that* the LORD thy God **b** thee **out** thence 3318
6:10 when the LORD thy God shall have **b** thee 935
6:12 which **b** thee **forth** out of the land of 3318
6:21 the LORD **b** us **out** of Egypt with a 3318
6:23 he **b** us **out** from thence, that he might 3318
7: 8 hath the LORD **b** you **out** with a mighty 3318
7:19 where*by* the LORD thy God **b** thee **out**: 3318
8:14 which **b** thee **forth** out of the land of 3318
8:15 who **b** thee **forth** water out of the rock of 3318
9: 4 LORD hath **b** me **in** to possess this land: 935
9:12 for thy people which thou hast **b forth** out 3318
9:26 which thou hast **b forth** out of Egypt with a 3318
9:28 he hath **b** them **out** to slay them in 3318
11:29 when the LORD thy God hath **b** thee **in** 935
13: 5 which **b** you **out** of the land of Egypt, and 3318
13:10 which **b** thee **out** of the land of Egypt, 3318
16: 1 thy God **b** thee **forth** out of Egypt by night. 3318
20: 1 which **b** thee **up** out of the land of Egypt. 5927
22:19 he hath **b up** an evil name upon a virgin of 3318
26: 8 the LORD **b** us **forth** out of Egypt with a 3318
26: 9 he hath **b** us into this place, and hath given 935
26:10 behold, I have **b** the firstfruits of the land, 935
26:13 I have **b away** the hallowed *things* out of 1197
29:25 he **b** them **forth** out of the land of Egypt: 3318
31:20 *For* when I shall have **b** them into the land 935
31:21 before I have **b** them into the land which I 935
33:14 for the precious fruits **b** forth by the sun, NIH
Jos 2: 6 she had **b** them **up** to the roof of the house, 5927
6:23 **b out** Rahab, and her father, and 3318
6:23 they **b out** all her kindred, and left them 3318
7: 7 thou **at all b** this people **over** Jordan, 5674+5674
7:14 ye shall be **b** according to your tribes: 7126
7:16 in the morning, and **b** Israel by their tribes; 7126
7:17 he **b** the family of Judah; and he took 7126
7:17 he **b** the family of the Zarhites man by 7126
7:18 he **b** his household man by man; and 7126
7:23 **b** them unto Joshua, and unto all the children 935
7:24 and they **b** them *unto* the valley of Achor. 5927
8:23 of Ai they took alive, and **b** him to Joshua. 7126
10:23 **b forth** those five kings unto him out of 3318
10:24 when they **b out** those kings unto Joshua, 3318
14: 7 I **b** him word **again** as *it was* in mine heart. 7725
22:32 children of Israel, and **b** them word **again**. 7725
24: 5 amongst them: and afterward I **b** you **out**. 3318
24: 6 I **b** your fathers **out** of Egypt: and 3318
24: 7 and **b** the sea upon them, and covered them; 935
24: 8 I **b** you into the land of the Amorites, 935
24:17 he *it is* that **b** us **up** and our fathers out of 5927
24:32 which the children of Israel **b up** out of 5927
Jdg 1: 7 they **b** him *to* Jerusalem, and there he died. 935
2: 1 have **b** you unto the land which I sware unto 935
2:12 which **b** them **out** of the land of Egypt, and 3318
3:17 he **b** the present unto Eglon king of Moab: 7126
5:25 she **b forth** butter in a lordly dish. 7126
6: 8 I **b** you **up** from Egypt, and brought you 5927
6: 8 **b** you **forth** out of the house of bondage; 3318
6:19 **b** *it* **out** unto him under the oak, and 3318
7: 5 So he **b down** the people unto the water: 3381
7:25 **b** the heads of Oreb and Zeeb to Gideon on 935
11:35 thou hast **b** me **very low**, and 3766+3766
14:11 that they **b** thirty companions to be with 3947
15:13 new cords, and **b** him **up** from the rock. 5927
16: 8 the lords of the Philistines **b up** to her 5927
16:18 up unto her, and **b** money in their hand. 5927
16:21 **b** him **down** to Gaza, and bound him with 3381
16:31 **b** *him* **up**, and buried him between Zorah 5927
18: 3 and said unto him, Who **b** thee hither? 935
19: 3 she **b** him *into* her father's house: and 935
19:21 So he **b** him into his house, and 935
19:25 his concubine, and **b** *her* forth unto them; 3318
21:12 they **b** them unto the camp *to* Shiloh, 935
Ru 1:21 the LORD hath **b** me *home* **again** empty: 7725
2:18 she **b forth**, and gave to her that she had 3318
1Sa 1:24 **b** him *unto* the house of the LORD *in* 935
1:25 they slew a bullock, and **b** the child to Eli. 935
2:14 all that the fleshhook **b up** the priest took 5927
2:19 little coat, and **b** *it* to him from year to year, 5927
5: 1 and **b** it from Eben-ezer unto Ashdod. 935
5: 2 they **b** it *into* the house of Dagon, and set it 935
5:10 They have **b about** the ark of the God of 5437
6:21 The Philistines have **b again** the ark of 7725
7: 1 **b** it into the house of Abinadab in the hill, 935
8: 8 **b** them **up** out of Egypt even unto this day, 5927

1Sa 9:22 **b** them into the parlour, and made them sit in 935
10:18 I **b up** Israel out of Egypt, and 5927
10:27 they despised him, and **b** him no presents. 935
12: 6 that **b** your fathers **up** out of the land of 5927
12: 8 which **b forth** your fathers out of Egypt, 3318
14:34 all the people **b** every man his ox with him 5066
15:15 They have **b** them from the Amalekites: 935
15:20 have **b** Agag the king of Amalek, and 935
16:12 he sent, and **b** him **in**. Now he *was* ruddy, 935
17:54 head of the Philistine, and **b** it *to* Jerusalem; 935
17:57 **b** him before Saul with the head of 935
18:27 David **b** their foreskins, and they gave them 935
19: 7 Jonathan **b** David to Saul, and he was in his 935
20: 8 for thou hast **b** thy servant into a covenant of 935
21: 8 for I have neither **b** my sword nor my 3947
21:14 *is* mad: wherefore *then* have ye **b** him to me? 935
21:15 that ye have **b** this *fellow* to play the mad 935
22: 4 he **b** them before the king of Moab: and 5148
23: 5 **b away** their cattle, and smote them *with* a 5090
25:27 which thine handmaid hath **b** unto my lord, 935
25:35 of her hand *that* which she had **b** him, 935
28:25 she **b** *it* before Saul, and before his 5066
30: 7 Abiathar **b thither** the ephod to David. 5066
30:11 **b** him to David, and gave him bread, and 3947
30:16 when he had **b** him **down**, behold *they* 3381
2Sa 1:10 and have **b** them hither unto my lord. 935
2: 8 son of Saul, and **b** him **over** *to* Mahanaim; 5674
3:22 a troop, and **b in** a great spoil with them: 935
3:26 which **b** him **again** from the well of Sirah: 7725
4: 8 they **b** the head of Ish-bosheth unto David *to* 935
4:10 is dead, thinking to have **b good tidings**, 1319
6: 3 **b** it out of the house of Abinadab that *was* 5375
6: 4 they **b** it out of the house of Abinadab 5375
6:12 **b up** the ark of God from the house of 5927
6:15 all the house of Israel **b up** the ark of 5927
6:17 they **b in** the ark of the LORD, and set it in 935
7: 6 I **b up** the children of Israel out of Egypt, 5927
7:18 *is* my house, that thou hast **b** me hitherto? 935
8: 2 became David's servants, and **b** gifts. 5375
8: 6 became servants to David, and **b** gifts. 5375
8: 7 of Hadadezer, and **b** them *to* Jerusalem. 935
8:10 *Joram* **b** with him vessels of silver, and 1961
10:16 **b out** the Syrians that *were* beyond 3318
12:30 he **b forth** the spoil of the city in great 3318
12:31 he **b forth** the people that *were* therein, 3318
13:10 **b** *them* into the chamber to Amnon her 935
13:11 when she had **b** *them* unto him to eat, he 5066
13:18 his servant **b** her **out**, and bolted the door 3318
14:23 to Geshur, and **b** Absalom *to* Jerusalem. 935
17:28 **B** beds, and basons, and earthen vessels, 5066
19:41 **b** the king, and his household, and all David's
men with him, **over** 5674
21: 8 whom she **b up** for Adriel the son of 3205
21:13 he **b up** from thence the bones of Saul and 5927
22:20 He **b** me **forth** also into a large place: he 3318
23:16 by the gate, and took *it,* and **b** *it* to David: 935
1Ki 1: 3 a Shunammite, and **b** her to the king. 935
1:38 king David's mule, and **b** him to Gihon. 1980
1:53 and they **b** him **down** from the altar. 3381
2:30 Benaiah **b** the king word **again**, saying, 7725
2:40 Shimei went, and **b** his servants from Gath. 935
3: 1 and **b** her into the city of David, 935
3:24 a sword. And they **b** a sword before the king. 935
4:21 they **b** presents, and served Solomon all 5066
4:28 dromedaries **b** they unto the place where 935
5:17 they **b** great stones, costly stones, *and* 5265
6: 7 *of* stone made ready *before it was* **b** *thither:* 4551
7:51 Solomon **b in** the *things* which David his 935
8: 4 they **b up** the ark of the LORD, and 5927
8: 6 the priests **b in** the ark of the covenant of 935
8:16 Since the day that I **b forth** my people 3318
8:21 when he **b** them **out** of the land of Egypt. 3318
9: 9 who **b forth** their fathers out of the land of 3318
9: 9 hath the LORD **b** upon them all this evil. 935
9:28 and twenty talents, and **b** *it* to king Solomon. 935
10:11 navy also of Hiram, that **b** gold from Ophir, 5375
10:11 **b in** from Ophir great plenty of almug trees, 935
10:25 they **b** every man his present, vessels of 935
10:28 Solomon had horses **b out** of Egypt, and 4161
12:28 which **b** thee **up** out of the land of Egypt. 5927
13:20 came unto the prophet that **b** him **back**: 7725
13:23 *wit,* for the prophet whom he had **b back**. 7725
13:26 when the prophet that **b** him **back** from 7725
13:29 and laid it upon the ass, and **b** it **back**: 7725
14:28 and **b** them **back** into the guard chamber. 7725
15:15 he **b in** *the things* which his father had 935
17: 6 the ravens **b** him bread and flesh in 935
17:20 hast thou also **b evil** upon the widow with 7489
17:23 **b** him **down** out of the chamber into 3381
18:40 Elijah **b** them **down** to the brook Kishon, 3381
20: 9 and **b** him word **again**. 7725
20:39 **b** a man unto me, and said, Keep this man: 935
22:37 So the king died, and was **b** *to* Samaria; and 935
2Ki 2:20 and put salt therein. And they **b** *it* to him. 3947
4: 5 upon her sons, who **b** *the vessels* to her; 5066
4:20 **b** him to his mother, he sat on her knees till 935
4:42 and **b** the man of God bread of the firstfruits, 935
5: 2 had **b away captive** out of the land of 7617
5: 6 he **b** the letter to the king of Israel, saying, 935
5:20 in not receiving at his hands *that* which he **b**: 935
10: 1 to them that **b up** Ahab's *children,* saying, 539
10: 6 the great *men* of the city, which **b** them **up**. 1431
10: 8 They have **b** the heads of the king's sons. 935
10:22 of Baal. And he **b** them **forth** vestments. 3318
10:24 *If* any of the men whom I *have* **b** into your 935
10:26 they **b forth** the images **out of** the house of 3318
11: 4 **b** them to him *into* the house of the LORD, 935
11:12 he **b forth** the king's son, and put 3318
11:19 they **b down** the king from the house of 3381
12: 4 *things* that is **b** *into* the house of the LORD, 935
12: 9 that was **b** *into* the house of the LORD. 935
12:13 of the money that was **b** *into* the house of 935
12:16 sin money was not **b** *into* the house of 935
14:20 they **b** him on horses: and he was buried at 5375
16:14 he **b** also the brasen altar, which *was* before 7126

2Ki 17: 4 **b** no present to the king of Assyria, as *he* 5927
17: 7 which had **b** them **up** out of the land of 5927
17:24 the king of Assyria **b** *men* from Babylon, 935
17:27 Carry thither one of the priests whom ye **b** 1540
17:36 who **b** you **up** out of the land of Egypt with 5927
19:25 now have I **b** it **to pass**, that thou shouldest 935
20:11 he **b** the shadow ten degrees backward, 7725
20:20 and a conduit, and **b** water into the city, 935
22: 4 that he may sum the silver which is **b** *into* 935
22: 9 and **b** the king word **again**, and said, 7725
22:20 this place. And they **b** the king word **again**. 7725
23: 6 he **b out** the grove from the house of 3318
23: 8 he **b** all the priests out of the cities of Judah, 935
23:30 **b** him *to* Jerusalem, and buried him in his 935
24:16 even them the king of Babylon **b** captive to 935
25: 6 **b** him **up** to the king of Babylon to Riblah; 5927
25:20 **b** them to the king of Babylon to Riblah: 1980
1Ch 5:26 **b** them unto Halah, and Habor, and Hara, 935
10:12 **b** them to Jabesh, and buried their bones 935
11:18 by the gate, and took *it,* and **b** *it* to David: 935
11:19 for with *the jeopardy of* their lives they **b** it. 935
12:40 **b** bread on asses, and on camels, and 935
13:13 So David **b** not the ark *home* to himself to 5493
14:17 the LORD **b** the fear of him upon all 5414
15:28 Thus all Israel **b up** the ark of the covenant 5927
16: 1 So they **b** the ark of God, and set it in 935
17: 5 the day that I **b up** Israel unto this day; 5927
17:16 *is* mine house, that thou hast **b** me hitherto? 935
18: 2 became David's servants, and **b** gifts. 5375
18: 6 became David's servants, and **b** gifts. 5375
18: 7 of Hadarezer, and **b** them *to* Jerusalem. 935
18: 8 of Hadarezer, **b** David very much brass, 3947
18:11 the gold that he **b** from all *these* nations; 5375
20: 2 he **b** also exceeding much spoil *out* **of** 3318
20: 3 he **b out** the people that *were* in it, and 3318
22: 4 they of Tyre **b** much cedar wood to David. 935
2Ch 1: 4 the ark of God had David **b up** from 5927
1:16 Solomon had horses **b out** of Egypt, and 4161
1:17 **b forth** out of Egypt a chariot for six 3318
1:17 **b** they **out** *horses* for all the kings of 3318
5: 1 Solomon **b in** *all the things* that David his 935
5: 5 they **b up** the ark, and the tabernacle of 5927
5: 7 the priests **b in** the ark of the covenant of 935
6: 5 Since the day that I **b forth** my people out 3318
7:22 which **b** them **forth** out of the land of 3318
7:22 hath he **b** all this evil upon them. 935
8:11 Solomon **b up** the daughter of Pharaoh out 5927
8:18 talents of gold, and **b** *them* to king Solomon. 935
9:10 which **b** gold from Ophir, brought algum 935
9:10 **b** algum trees and precious stones. 935
9:12 besides *that* which she had **b** unto the king. 935
9:14 *that which* chapmen and merchants **b**. 935
9:14 governors of the country **b** gold and silver to 935
9:24 they **b** every man his present, vessels of 935
9:28 they **b** unto Solomon horses **out** of Egypt, 3318
10: 8 the young men that were **b up** with him, 1431
10:10 the young men that were **b up** with him 1431
12:11 and **b** them **again** into the guard chamber. 7725
13:18 Thus the children of Israel were **b under** at 3665
15:11 of the spoil *which* they had **b**, seven hundred 935
15:18 he **b** *into* the house of God *the things* that his 935
16: 2 Asa **b out** silver and gold out of 3318
17: 5 all Judah **b** to Jehoshaphat presents; and 5414
17:11 Also *some* of the Philistines **b** Jehoshaphat 935
17:11 the Arabians **b** him flocks, seven thousand 935
19: 4 **b** them **back** unto the LORD God of their 7725
22: 9 he *was* hid in Samaria,) and **b** him to Jehu: 935
23:11 they **b out** the king's son, and put upon him 3318
23:14 Jehoiada the priest **b out** the captains of 3318
23:20 **b down** the king from the house of 3381
24:10 and **b in**, and cast into the chest, 935
24:11 that at *what* time the chest was **b** unto 935
24:14 when they had finished *it,* they **b** the rest of 935
25:12 **b** them unto the top of the rock, and 935
25:14 that he **b** the gods of the children of Seir, and 935
25:23 **b** him *to* Jerusalem, and brake down the wall 935
25:28 they **b** him upon horses, and buried him 5375
28: 5 of them captives, and **b** *them to* Damascus. 935
28: 8 spoil from them, and **b** the spoil to Samaria. 935
28:15 and **b** them *to* Jericho, the city of palm trees, 935
28:19 For the LORD **b** Judah **low** because 3665
28:27 they **b** him not into the sepulchres of 935
29: 4 he **b in** the priests and the Levites, and 935
29:16 **b out** all the uncleanness that they found in 3318
29:21 And they **b** seven bullocks, and seven rams, 935
29:23 they **b forth** the he goats for the sin 5066
29:31 the congregation **b in** sacrifices and 935
29:32 which the congregation **b**, was threescore 935
30:15 **b in** the burnt offerings *into* the house of 935
31: 5 the children of Israel **b in abundance** 7235
31: 5 the tithe of all *things* **b** they in abundantly. 935
31: 6 they also **b in** the tithe of oxen and sheep, 935
31:12 **b in** the offerings and the tithes and 935
32:23 many **b** gifts unto the LORD to Jerusalem, 935
32:30 **b** it **straight** down to the west *side* of 3474
33:11 Wherefore the LORD **b** upon them 935
33:13 **b** him **again** *to* Jerusalem into his kingdom. 7725
34: 9 they delivered the money that was **b** *into* 935
34:14 when they **b** out the money that was 3318
34:14 when they brought out the money that was **b** 935
34:16 **b** the king word **back** again, saying, 7725
34:28 of the same. So they **b** the king word **again**. 7725
35:24 they **b** him *to* Jerusalem, and he died, and 1980
36:10 Nebuchadnezzar sent, and **b** him to Babylon, 935
36:17 Therefore he **b** upon them the king of 5927
36:18 and of his princes; all *these* he **b** *to* Babylon. 935
Ezr 1: 7 Also Cyrus the king **b forth** the vessels of 3318
1: 7 which Nebuchadnezzar had **b forth** out of 3318
1:11 were **b up** from Babylon unto Jerusalem. 5927
4: 2 king of Assur, which **b** us **up** hither. 5927
4:10 the great and noble Asnappar **b over**, 1541
5:14 **b** them into the temple of Babylon, 2987
6: 5 **b** unto Babylon, be restored, and 2987
6: 5 **b** *again* unto the temple which *is* at 1946
8:18 by the good hand of our God upon us they **b** 935

Ne 4:15 God had **b** their counsel **to nought**, that we 6565
5: 5 *some* of our daughters are **b unto bondage** 3533
8: 2 Ezra the priest **b** the law before 935
8:16 and **b** *them*, and made themselves booths, 935
9:18 This *is* thy God that **b** thee **up** out of Egypt, 5927
9:33 Howbeit thou *art* just in all that is **b** upon us; 935
12:31 I **b up** the princes of Judah upon the wall, 5927
13: 9 thither **b** I **again** the vessels of the house of 7725
13:12 **b** all Judah the tithe of the corn and the new 935
13:15 which they **b** *into* Jerusalem on the sabbath 935
13:16 which **b** fish, and all *manner of* ware, and 935
13:19 *that* there should no burden be **b in** on 935
Est 1:17 Vashti the queen to be **b in** before him, 935
2: 7 he **b up** Hadassah, that *is*, Esther, his uncle's 539
2: 8 that Esther was **b** *also* unto the king's 3947
2:20 like as when she was **b up** with him. 545
6: 8 Let the royal apparel be **b** which the king 935
6:11 **b** him **on horseback** through the street of 7392
9:11 in Shushan the palace was **b** before the king. 935
Job 4:12 Now a thing was **secretly b** to me, and 1589
10:18 then hast thou **b** me **forth** out of the womb? 3318
14:21 they are **b low**, but he perceiveth *it* not of 6819
21:30 they shall be **b forth** to the day of wrath. 2986
21:32 Yet shall he be **b** to the grave, and 2986
24:24 for a little while, but are gone and **b low**, 4355
31:18 (For from my youth he was **b up** *with* me, 1431
42:11 all the evil that the LORD had **b** upon him: 935
Ps 7:14 conceived mischief, and **b forth** falsehood. 3205
18:19 He **b** me **forth** also into a large place; 3318
20: 8 They are **b down** and fallen: but we are 3766
22:15 and thou hast **b** me into the dust of death. 8239
30: 3 thou hast **b up** my soul from the grave: 5927
35: 4 and **b to confusion** that devise my hurt. 2659
35:26 **b to confusion** together that rejoice at mine 2659
40: 2 He **b** me **up** also out of a horrible pit, out of 5927
45:14 She shall be **b** unto the king in raiment of 2986
45:14 that follow her *shall be* **b** unto thee. 935
45:15 With gladness and rejoicing shall they be **b**: 2986
71:24 for they are **b unto shame**, that seek my 2659
73:19 How are they **b** into desolation, as *in* a NIH
78:16 He **b** streams also **out** of the rock, and 3318
78:26 and by his power he **b in** the south wind. 5090
78:54 he **b** them to the border of his sanctuary, 935
78:71 young he **b** him to feed Jacob his people, 935
79: 8 speedily prevent us: for we are **b** very **low**. 1809
80: 8 Thou hast **b** a vine **out** of Egypt: thou hast 5265
81:10 which **b** thee out of the land of Egypt: 5927
85: 1 thou hast **b back** the captivity of Jacob. 7725
89:40 thou hast **b** his strong holds to ruin. 7760
90: 2 Before the mountains were **b forth**, or 3205
105:30 Their land **b forth** frogs **in abundance**, 8317
105:37 He **b** them **forth** also with silver and gold: 3318
105:40 he **b** quails, and satisfied them *with* 935
105:43 he **b forth** his people with joy, *and* 3318
106:42 they were **b into subjection** under their 3665
106:43 and were **b low** for their iniquity. 4355
107:12 Therefore he **b down** their heart with 3665
107:14 He **b** them **out** of darkness and the shadow 3318
107:39 are minished and **b low** through oppression, 7817
116: 6 the simple: I was **b low**, and he helped me. 1809
136:11 **b out** Israel from among them: for his 3318
142: 6 Attend unto my cry; for I am **b** very **low**: 1809
Pr 6:26 woman *a man is* **b** to a piece of bread: NIH
8:24 When *there were* no depths, I was **b forth**; 2342
8:25 were settled, before the hills was I **b forth**: 2342
8:30 *as* **one b up** *with him*: and I was daily *his* 525
Ecc 12: 4 all the daughters of musick shall be **b low**; 7817
SS 1: 4 the king hath **b** me *into* his chambers: 935
2: 4 He **b** me to the banqueting house, and 935
3: 4 until I had **b** him into my mother's house, 935
8: 5 there thy mother **b** thee **forth**: there she 2254
8: 5 there she **b** *thee* **forth** *that* bare thee. 2254
Isa 1: 2 I have nourished and **b up** children, and 7311
2:12 one that is lifted up; and he shall be **b low**: 8213
5: 2 forth grapes, and it **b forth** wild grapes. 6213
5: 4 bring forth grapes, **b** it **forth** wild grapes? 6213
5:15 the mean man shall be **b down**, and 7817
14:11 Thy pomp is **b down** *to* the grave, *and* 3381
14:15 Yet thou shalt be **b down** to hell, to 3381
15: 1 Ar of Moab is laid waste, *and* **b to silence**; 1820
15: 1 Kir of Moab is laid waste, *and* **b to silence**; 1820
18: 7 In that time shall the present be **b** unto 2986
21:14 The inhabitants of the land of Tema **b** 857+7125
23:13 up the palaces thereof; *and* he **b** it to ruin. 7760
25: 5 branch of the terrible ones shall be **b low**. 6030
26:18 in pain, we have as it were **b forth** wind; 3205
29: 4 thou shalt be **b down**, *and* shalt speak out 8213
29:20 For the terrible one is **b** to nought, and 656
37:26 now have I **b** it **to pass**, that thou shouldest 935
43:14 have **b down** all their nobles, and 3381
43:23 Thou hast not **b** me the small cattle of thy 935
45:10 or to the woman, What hast thou **b forth**? 2342
48:15 I have **b** him, and he shall make his way 935
49:21 who hath **b up** these? Behold, I was left 1431
51:18 among all the sons *whom* she hath **b forth**; 3205
51:18 the hand of all the sons *that* she hath **b up**. 1431
53: 7 he is **b** as a lamb to the slaughter, and as a 2986
59:16 therefore his arm **b salvation** unto him; and 3467
60:11 the Gentiles, and *that* their kings *may be* **b**. 5090
62: 9 they that have **b** it **together** shall drink it in 6908
63: 5 mine own arm **b salvation** unto me; 3467
63:11 *saying*, Where *is* he that **b** them **up** out of 5927
66: 7 Before she travailed, she **b forth**; before 3205
66: 8 as Zion travailed, she **b forth** her children. 3205
Jer 2: 6 Where *is* the LORD that **b** us **up** out of 5927
2: 7 I **b** you into a plentiful country, to eat 935
2:27 and to a stone, Thou hast **b** me **forth**: 3205
7:22 day that I **b** them **out** of the land of Egypt, 3318
10: 9 Silver spread into plates is **b** from Tarshish, 935
11: 4 that I **b** them **forth** out of the land of Egypt, 3318
11: 7 that I **b** them **up** out of the land of Egypt, 5927
11:19 a lamb *or* an ox *that* is **b** to the slaughter; 2986
15: 8 I have **b** upon them against the mother of 935
16:14 that **b up** the children of Israel out of 5927
16:15 that **b up** the children of Israel from 5927
Jer 20: 3 that Pashur **b forth** Jeremiah out of 3318
20:15 Cursed *be* the man who **b tidings** to my 1319
23: 7 which **b up** the children of Israel out of 5927
23: 8 which **b up** and which led the seed of 5927
24: 1 from Jerusalem, and had **b** them *to* Babylon. 935
26:23 and **b** him unto Jehoiakim the king; 935
27:16 *shall* now shortly be **b again** from Babylon: 7725
32:21 hast **b forth** thy people Israel out of 3318
32:42 Like as I have **b** all this great evil upon this 935
34:11 **b** them **into subjection** for servants and 3533
34:13 that I **b** them **forth** out of the land of Egypt, 3318
34:16 to return, and **b** them **into subjection**, to be 3533
35: 4 And I **b** them *into* the house of the LORD, 935
37:14 took Jeremiah, and **b** him to the princes. 935
38:22 *be* **b forth** to the king of Babylon's princes, 3318
39: 5 they **b** him **up** to Nebuchadnezzar king of 5927
40: 3 Now the LORD hath **b** *it*, and 935
41:16 whom he had **b again** from Gibeon: 7725
44: 2 Ye have seen all the evil that I have **b** upon 935
50:25 hath **b forth** the weapons of his 3318
51:10 The LORD hath **b forth** our 3318
52:26 **b** them to the king of Babylon to Riblah. 1980
52:31 of Judah, and **b** him **forth** out of prison; 3318
La 2: 2 he hath **b** *them* **down** to the ground: 5060
2:22 and **b up** hath mine enemy consumed. 7235
3: 2 and **b** *me into* darkness, but not *into* light. 1980
4: 5 they that were **b up** in scarlet embrace 539
Eze 8: 3 and **b** me in the visions of God to Jerusalem, 935
8: 7 he **b** me to the door of the court; and when I 935
8:14 he **b** me to the door of the gate of 935
8:16 he **b** me into the inner court of the LORD'S 935
11: 1 **b** me unto the east gate of the LORD'S 935
11:24 **b** me in vision by the Spirit of God into 935
12: 7 I **b forth** my stuff by day, as stuff for 3318
12: 7 I **b** *it* **forth** in the twilight, *and* I bare *it* 3318
14:22 shall be left a remnant that shall be **b forth**, 3318
14:22 the evil that I have **b** upon Jerusalem, 935
14:22 *even* concerning all that I have **b** upon it. 935
17: 6 and **b forth** branches, and shot forth sprigs. 6213
17:24 I the LORD have **b down** the high tree, 8213
19: 3 she **b up** one of her whelps: it became a 5927
19: 4 they **b** him with chains unto the land of 935
19: 9 in chains, and **b** him to the king of Babylon: 935
19: 9 they **b** him into holds, that his voice should 935
20:10 of Egypt, and **b** them into the wilderness. 935
20:14 the heathen, in whose sight I **b** them **out**. 3318
20:22 the heathen, in whose sight I **b** them **forth**. 3318
20:28 *For* when I had **b** them into the land, *for* 935
21: 7 behold, it cometh, and shall be **b to pass**, 1961
23: 8 Neither left she her whoredoms ***b*** from NIH
23:27 thy whoredom ***b*** from the land of Egypt: NIH
23:42 with the men of the common sort *were* **b** 935
27: 6 *of* ivory, ***b*** out of the isles of Chittim. NIH
27:15 they **b** thee *for* a present horns of ivory and 7725
27:26 Thy rowers have **b** thee into great waters: 935
29: 5 thou shalt not be **b together**, nor gathered: 622
30:11 of the nations, *shall be* **b** to destroy the land: 935
31:18 yet shalt thou be **b down** with the trees of 3381
34: 4 neither have ye **b again** that which was 7725
37:13 and **b** you **up** out of your graves, 5927
38: 8 into the land *that is* **b back** from the sword, 7725
38: 8 it is **b forth** out of the nations, and 3318
39:27 When I have **b** them **again** from the people, 7725
40: 1 the LORD was upon me, and **b** me thither. 935
40: 2 In the visions of God **b** he me into the land 935
40: 3 he **b** me thither, and behold, *there was* a 935
40: 4 might shew *them* unto thee art thou **b** hither: 935
40:17 Then **b** he me into the outward court, and lo, 935
40:24 After that he **b** me toward the south, and 1980
40:28 he **b** me to the inner court by the south gate: 935
40:32 he **b** me into the inner court toward the east: 935
40:35 he **b** me to the north gate, and measured *it* 935
40:48 he **b** me to the porch of the house, and 935
40:49 *he* ***b*** *me* by the steps whereby they went up NIH
41: 1 Afterward he **b** me to the temple, and 935
42: 1 he **b** me **forth** into the utter court, the way 3318
42: 1 he **b** me into the chamber that *was* over 935
42:15 he **b** me **forth** toward the gate whose 3318
43: 1 Afterward he **b** me to the gate, *even* 1980
43: 5 took me up, and **b** me into the inner court; 935
44: 1 he **b** me **back** the way of the gate of 7725
44: 4 **b** he me the way of the north gate before 935
44: 7 In that ye have **b** *into my sanctuary* 935
46:19 After, he **b** me through the entry, which *was* 935
46:21 Then he **b** me **forth** into the utter court, and 3318
47: 1 Afterward he **b** me **again** unto the door of 7725
47: 2 **b** he me **out** *of* the way of the gate 3318
47: 3 and he **b** me through the waters; 5674
47: 4 a thousand, and **b** me through the waters; 5674
47: 4 measured a thousand, and **b** me **through**; 5674
47: 6 hast thou seen *this?* Then he **b** me, and 1980
47: 8 *which* being **b forth** into the sea, the waters 3318
Da 1: 2 he **b** the vessels *into* the treasure house of his 935
1: 9 Now God had **b** Daniel into favour and 5414
1:18 the prince of the eunuchs **b** them **in** before 935
2:25 Arioch **b in** Daniel before the king in haste, 5954
3:13 Then they **b** these men before the king. 858
5: 3 they **b** the golden vessels that were taken out 858
5:13 was Daniel **b in** before the king. *And* 5954
5:13 whom the king my father **b out** of Jewry? 858
5:15 have been **b in** before me, that they should 5954
5:23 they have **b** the vessels of his house before 858
6:16 they **b** Daniel, and cast *him* into the den of 858
6:17 a stone was **b**, and laid upon the mouth of 858
6:18 neither were instruments of musick **b** 5954
6:24 they **b** those men which had accused Daniel, 858
7:13 of days, and they **b** him **near** before him. 7127
9:14 watched upon the evil, and **b** it upon us: 935
9:15 that hast **b** thy people **forth** out of the land 3318
11: 6 they that **b** her, and he that begat her, and 935
Hos 12:13 by a prophet the LORD **b** Israel out of 5927
Am 2:10 Also I **b** you **up** from the land of Egypt, 5927
3: 1 against the whole family which I **b up** from 5927
9: 7 Have not I **b up** Israel out of the land of 5927
Ob 1: 7 All the men of thy confederacy have **b** thee 7971
Jnh 2: 6 yet hast thou **b up** my life from corruption, 5927
Mic 5: 3 time *that* she which travaileth hath **b forth**: 3205
6: 4 For I **b** thee **up** out of the land of Egypt, 5927
Na 2: 7 she shall be **b up**, and her maids *shall* lead 5927
Hag 1: 9 and when ye **b** *it* home, I did blow upon it. 935
2:19 and the olive tree, hath not **b forth**: 5375
Zec 10:11 the pride of Assyria shall be **b down**, and 3381
Mal 1:13 ye **b** *that which was* torn, and the lame, and 935
1:13 the lame, and the sick; thus ye **b** an offering: 935
Mt 1:12 And after they were **b** to Babylon, *3350*
1:25 And knew her not till she had **b forth** her *5088*
4:24 they **b** unto him all sick people that were *4374*
8:16 they **b** unto him many *that were* possessed *4374*
9: 2 they **b** to him a man sick of the palsy, *4374*
9:32 they **b to** him a dumb man possessed with a *4374*
10:18 And ye shall be **b** before governors and kings *71*
11:23 unto heaven, shalt be **b down** to hell: *2601*
12:22 Then was **b** unto him one possessed with a *4374*
12:25 divided against itself is **b to desolation**; *2049*
13: 8 fell into good ground, and **b forth** fruit, *1325*
13:26 and **b forth** fruit, then appeared the tares *4160*
14:11 And his head was **b** in a charger, and *5342*
14:11 to the damsel: and she **b** *it* to her mother. *5342*
14:35 and **b unto** him all that were diseased; *4374*
16: 8 because ye have **b** no bread? *2983*
17:16 And I **b** him to thy disciples, and *4374*
18:24 had begun to reckon, one was **b** unto him, *4374*
19:13 Then were there **b unto** him little children, *4374*
21: 7 And **b** the ass, and the colt, and put on them *71*
22:19 And they **b** unto him a penny. *4374*
25:20 five talents came and **b** other five talents, *4374*
27: 3 **b again** the thirty pieces of silver to the chief *654*
Mk 1:32 they **b** unto him all that were diseased, and *5342*
4: 8 and **b forth**, some thirty, and some sixty, *5342*
4:21 Is a candle **b** to be put under a bushel, or *2064*
4:29 But when the fruit is **b forth**, *3860*
6:27 and commanded his head to be **b**: *5342*
6:28 And **b** his head in a charger, and gave it to *5342*
9:17 Master, I have **b** unto thee my son, *5342*
9:20 And they **b** him unto him: and when he saw *5342*
10:13 And they **b** young children to him, that he *4374*
10:13 *his* disciples rebuked those that **b** *them*. *4374*
11: 7 And they **b** the colt to Jesus, and cast their *71*
12:16 And they **b** *it*. And he saith unto them, *5342*
13: 9 and ye shall be **b** before rulers and kings *2476*
Lk 1:57 should be delivered; and she **b forth** a son. *1080*
2: 7 And she **b forth** her firstborn son, and *5088*
2:22 they **b** him to Jerusalem, to present *him* to *321*
2:27 and when the parents **b in** the child Jesus, *1521*
3: 5 and every mountain and hill shall be **b low**; *5013*
4: 9 And he **b** him to Jerusalem, and set him on a *71*
4:16 came to Nazareth, where he had been **b up**: *5142*
4:40 sick with divers diseases **b** them unto him; *71*
5:11 And when they had **b** *their* ships to land, *2609*
5:18 men **b** in a bed a man which was taken with *5342*
7:37 **b** an alabaster box of ointment, *2865*
10:34 and **b** him to an inn, and took care of him. *71*
11:17 divided against itself is **b to desolation**; *2049*
12:16 of a certain rich man **b forth plentifully**: *2164*
18:15 And they **b** unto him also infants, that he *4374*
18:40 and commanded him to be **b** unto him: *71*
19:35 And they **b** him to Jesus: and they cast their *71*
21:12 being **b** before kings and rulers for my name's *71*
22:54 **b** him **into** the high priest's house. *1521*
23:14 unto them, Ye have **b** this man unto me, *4374*
Jn 1:42 And he **b** him to Jesus. And when Jesus *71*
4:33 Hath any *man* **b** him *ought* to eat? *5342*
7:45 they said unto them, Why have ye not **b** him? *71*
8: 3 Pharisees **b** unto him a woman taken in *71*
9:13 They **b** to the Pharisees him that aforetime *71*
18:16 unto her that kept the door, and **b in** Peter. *1521*
19:13 he **b** Jesus forth, and sat down in *71*
19:39 and **b** a mixture of myrrh and aloes, *5342*
Ac 4:34 **b** the prices of the *things* that were sold, *5342*
4:37 sold *it*, and **b** the money, and laid *it* at *5342*
5: 2 also being privy *to it*, and **b** a certain part, *5342*
5:15 Insomuch that *they* **b forth** the sick into *1627*
5:19 prison doors, and **b** them **forth**, and said, *1806*
5:21 and sent to the prison to have them **b**. *71*
5:26 the officers, and **b** them without violence: *71*
5:27 And when they had **b** them, they set *them* *71*
5:36 were scattered, and **b** to nought. *1096*
6:12 and caught him, and **b** *him* to the council, *71*
7:36 He **b** them **out**, after that he had shewed *1806*
7:40 which **b** us **out** of the land of Egypt, *1806*
7:45 Which also our fathers that came after **b in** *1521*
9: 8 the hand, and **b** *him* **into** Damascus. *1521*
9:27 and **b** *him* to the apostles, and declared unto *71*
9:30 they **b** him **down** to Cesarea, and sent him *2609*
9:39 they **b** him into the upper chamber: *321*
11:26 he had found him, he **b** him unto Antioch. *71*
12: 6 And when Herod would have **b** him **forth**, *4254*
12:17 how the Lord had **b** him **out** of the prison. *1806*
13: 1 which had been **b up with** Herod *4939*
13:17 and with a high arm **b** he them **out** of it. *1806*
14:13 **b** oxen and garlands unto the gates, and *5342*
15: 3 And being **b on** their **way** by the church, *4311*
16:16 which **b** her masters much gain by *3930*
16:20 And **b** them **to** the magistrates, saying, *4317*
16:30 And **b** them out, and said, Sirs, what must I *4254*
16:34 And when he had **b** them into his house, *321*
16:39 and **b** *them* **out**, and desired *them* to depart *1806*
17:15 And they that conducted Paul **b** him unto *71*
17:19 took him, and **b** him unto Areopagus, saying, *71*
18:12 against Paul, and **b** him to the judgment seat, *71*
19:12 So that from his body were **b** unto the sick *2018*
19:19 used curious arts **b** their books **together**, *4851*
19:24 **b** no small gain unto the craftsmen; *3930*
19:37 For ye have **b** *hither* these men, *which are* *71*
20:12 And they **b** the young man alive, and were not *71*
21: 5 *our way;* and *they* all **b** us **on** our way, *4311*
21:16 and **b** *with them* one Mnason of Cyprus, *71*
21:28 and further **b** Greeks also **into** *1521*
21:29 that Paul had **b into** the temple.) *1521*
22: 3 yet **b up** in this city at the feet of Gamaliel, *397*

Ac 22:24 The chief captain commanded him to be **b** *71*
22:30 and **b** Paul **down**, and set *him* before them. *2609*
23:18 and **b** *him* to the chief captain, and said, *71*
23:28 I **b** him **forth** into their council: *2609*
23:31 took Paul, and **b** *him* by night to Antipatris. *71*
25: 6 the judgment seat, commanded Paul to be **b**. *71*
25:17 and commanded the man to be **b** *forth*. *71*
25:18 **b** none accusation of *such things* as I *2018*
25:23 at Festus' commandment Paul was **b** *forth*. *71*
25:26 Wherefore I have **b** him **forth** before you, *4254*
27:24 Paul; thou must be **b before** Cesar: *3936*
Ro 15:24 and to be **b on** my **way** thitherward by you, *4311*
1Co 6:12 but I will not be **b under** the **power** of any. *1850*
15:54 shall be **b to pass** the saying that is written, *1096*
2Co 1:16 of you to be **b on** *my* **way** toward Judea. *4311*
Gal 2: 4 because of false brethren **unawares b in**, *3920*
1Th 3: 6 and **b** us **good tidings** of your faith and *2097*
1Ti 5:10 if she have **b up children**, if she have *5044*
6: 7 For we **b** nothing into *this* world, *and it is* *1533*
2Ti 1:10 hath **b** life and immortality **to light** through *5461*
4: S when Paul was **b before** Nero the second *3936*
Heb 13:11 whose blood is **b** into the sanctuary by *1533*
13:20 that **b again** from the dead our Lord Jesus, *321*
Jas 5:18 gave rain, and the earth **b forth** her fruit. *985*
1Pe 1:13 hope to the end for the grace that is *to be* **b** *5342*
2Pe 2:19 of the same is he **b in bondage**. *1402*
Rev 12: 5 And she **b forth** a man child, who was to *5088*
12:13 he persecuted the woman which **b forth** *5088*

BROUGHTEST (13) [BRING]
Ex 32: 7 which thou **b** out of the land of Egypt, 5927
Nu 14:13 the Egyptians shall hear *it*, (for thou **b up** 5927
Dt 9:28 Lest the land whence thou **b** us **out** say, 3318
9:29 which thou **b out** by thy mighty power and 3318
2Sa 5: 2 thou wast he that leddest out and **b** in Israel: 935
1Ki 8:51 which thou **b forth** out of Egypt, 3318
8:53 when thou **b** our fathers **out** of Egypt, 3318
1Ch 11: 2 thou *wast* he that leddest out and **b in** Israel: 935
Ne 9: 7 **b** him **forth** out of Ur of the Chaldees, and 3318
9:15 **b forth** water for them out of the rock for 3318
9:23 **b** them into the land, *concerning* which thou 935
Ps 66:11 Thou **b** us into the net; thou laidst affliction 935
66:12 but thou **b** us **out** into a wealthy *place*. 3318

BROW (2) [EYEBROWS]
Isa 48: 4 thy neck *is* an iron sinew, and thy **b** brass: 4696
Lk 4:29 led him unto the **b** of the hill whereon their *3790*

BROWN (4)
Ge 30:32 all the **b** cattle among the sheep, and 2345
30:33 the goats, and **b** amongst the sheep, 2345
30:35 all the **b** amongst the sheep, and gave *them* 2345
30:40 and all the **b** in the flock of Laban; 2345

BRUISE See STRIPE; STRIPES

BRUISE (8) [BRUISED, BRUISES, BRUISING, BRUIT]
Ge 3:15 it shall **b** thy head, and thou shalt bruise his 7779
3:15 bruise thy head, and thou shalt **b** his heel. 7779
Isa 28:28 of his cart, nor **b** it *with* his horsemen. 1854
53:10 Yet it pleased the LORD to **b** him; he hath 1792
Jer 30:12 Thy **b** *is* incurable, *and* thy wound *is* 7667
Da 2:40 all these, shall it break in pieces and **b**. 7490
Na 3:19 *There is* no healing of thy **b**; thy wound *is* 7667
Ro 16:20 And the God of peace shall **b** Satan under *4937*

BRUISED (9) [BRUISE]
Lev 22:24 not offer unto the LORD that which is **b**, 4600
2Ki 18:21 thou trustest upon the staff of this **b** reed, 7533
Isa 28:28 Bread *corn* is **b**; because he will not ever be 1854
42: 3 A **b** reed shall he not break, and 7533
53: 5 *he was* **b** for our iniquities: 1792
Eze 23: 3 and there they **b** the teats of their virginity. 6213
23: 8 they **b** the breasts of her virginity, and 6213
Mt 12:20 A **b** reed shall he not break, and *4937*
Lk 4:18 to the blind, to set at liberty *them that are* **b**, *2352*

BRUISES (1) [BRUISE]
Isa 1: 6 *but* wounds, and **b**, and putrifying sores: 2250

BRUISING (2) [BRUISE]
Eze 23:21 in **b** thy teats by the Egyptians for the paps 6213
Lk 9:39 and **b** him hardly departeth from him. *4937*

BRUIT (2) [BRUISE]
Jer 10:22 the noise of the **b** is come, and a great 8052
Na 3:19 all that hear the **b** of thee shall clap 8088

BRUTE (2) [BRUTISH]
2Pe 2:12 But these, as natural **b** beasts, made to be *249*
Jude 1:10 but what they know naturally, as **b** beasts, *249*

BRUTISH (11) [BRUTE]
Ps 49:10 likewise the fool and the **b person** perish, 1198
92: 6 A **b** man knoweth not; neither doth a fool 1198
94: 8 Understand, ye **b** among the people: and 1197
Pr 12: 1 but he that hateth reproof *is* **b**. 1198
30: 2 Surely I *am* more **b** than *any* man, and 1198
Isa 19:11 wise counsellers of Pharaoh is become **b**: 1197
Jer 10: 8 they are altogether **b** and foolish: the stock 1197
10:14 Every man is **b** in *his* knowledge: 1197
10:21 For the pastors are become **b**, and have not 1197
51:17 Every man is **b** by *his* knowledge; 1197
Eze 21:31 deliver thee into the hand of **b** men, *and* 1197

BUBASTIS See PHI-BESETH

BUCKET (1) [BUCKETS]
Isa 40:15 the nations *are* as a drop of a **b**, and 1805

BUCKETS (1) [BUCKET]
Nu 24: 7 He shall pour the water out of his **b**, and 1805

BUCKLER (11) [BUCKLERS]
2Sa 22:31 he *is* a **b** to all them that trust in him. 4043
1Ch 5:18 men *able to* bear **b** and sword, and to shoot 4043
12: 8 the battle, that could handle shield and **b**, 7420
Ps 18: 2 my **b**, and the horn of my salvation, *and* 4043
18:30 he *is* a **b** to all those that trust in him. 4043
35: 2 Take hold of shield and **b**, and stand up for 6793
91: 4 his truth *shall be thy* shield and **b**. 5507
Pr 2: 7 *he is* a **b** to them that walk uprightly. 4043
Jer 46: 3 Order ye the **b** and shield, and draw near to 4043
Eze 23:24 *which* shall set against thee **b** and shield 6793
26: 8 against thee, and lift up the **b** against thee. 6793

BUCKLERS (5) [BUCKLER]
2Ch 23: 9 **b**, and shields, that *had been* king David's, 4043
Job 15:26 on *his* neck, upon the thick bosses of his **b**: 4043
SS 4: 4 whereon there hang a thousand **b**, 4043
Eze 38: 4 *of armour, even* a great company *with* **b** 6793
39: 9 both the shields and the **b**, the bows and 6793

BUD (11) [BUDDED, BUDS]
Job 14: 9 *Yet* through the scent of water it will **b**, and 6524
38:27 to cause the **b** of the tender herb to spring 4161
Ps 132:17 There will I **make** the horn of David to **b**: 6779
SS 7:12 *and* the pomegranates **b forth**: 5340
Isa 18: 5 when the **b** is perfect, and the sour grape is 6525
27: 6 Israel shall blossom and **b**, and fill the face 6524
55:10 the earth, and maketh it bring forth and **b**, 6779
61:11 For as the earth bringeth forth her **b**, and 6780
Eze 16: 7 I have caused thee to multiply as the **b** of 6780
29:21 **cause** the horn of the house of Israel
to b forth, 6779
Hos 8: 7 the **b** shall yield no meal: if so be it yield, 6780

BUDDED (5) [BUD]
Ge 40:10 it *was* as though it **b**, *and* her blossoms shot 6524
Nu 17: 8 rod of Aaron for the house of Levi was **b**, 6524
SS 6:11 vine flourished, *and* the pomegranates **b**. 5340
Eze 7:10 the rod hath blossomed, pride hath **b**. 6524
Heb 9: 4 and Aaron's rod that **b**, and the tables of *985*

BUDS (1) [BUD]
Nu 17: 8 brought forth **b**, and bloomed blossoms, 6525

BUFFET (2) [BUFFETED]
Mk 14:65 and to **b** him, and to say unto him, *2852*
2Co 12: 7 the messenger of Satan to **b** me, lest I *2852*

BUFFETED (3) [BUFFET]
Mt 26:67 Then did they spit in his face, and **b** him; *2852*
1Co 4:11 and are **b**, and have no certain dwelling *2852*
1Pe 2:20 glory *is it*, if, when ye be **b** for your faults, *2852*

BUILD (162) [BUILDED, BUILDEDST, BUILDER, BUILDERS, BUILDEST, BUILDETH, BUILDING, BUILDINGS, BUILT, MASTERBUILDER]
Ge 11: 4 Go to, let us **b** us a city and a tower, 1129
11: 8 all the earth: and they left off to **b** the city. 1129
Ex 20:25 of stone, thou shalt not **b** it *of* hewn stone: 1129
Nu 23: 1 **B** me here seven altars, and prepare me 1129
23:29 **B** me here seven altars, and prepare me 1129
32:16 We will **b** sheepfolds here for our cattle, 1129
32:24 **B** ye cities for your little ones, and folds for 1129
Dt 20:20 thou shalt **b** bulwarks against the city that 1129
25: 9 man that will not **b up** his brother's house. 1129
27: 5 there shalt thou **b** an altar unto the LORD 1129
27: 6 Thou shalt **b** the altar of the LORD thy 1129
28:30 thou shalt **b** a house, and thou shalt not 1129
Jos 22:26 Let us now prepare to **b** us an altar, 1129
22:29 to **b** an altar for burnt offerings, for meat 1129
Jdg 6:26 **b** an altar unto the LORD thy God upon 1129
Ru 4:11 which two did **b** the house of Israel: 1129
1Sa 2:35 I will **b** him a sure house; and he shall walk 1129
2Sa 7: 5 Shalt thou **b** me a house for me to dwell in? 1129
7: 7 Why **b** ye not me a house of cedar? 1129
7:13 He shall **b** a house for my name, and I will 1129
7:27 to thy servant, saying, I will **b** thee a house: 1129
24:21 of thee, to **b** an altar unto the LORD, 1129
1Ki 2:36 **B** thee a house in Jerusalem, and 1129
5: 3 **b** a house unto the name of the LORD his 1129
5: 5 I purpose to **b** a house unto the name of 1129
5: 5 thy room, he shall **b** a house unto my name. 1129
5:18 prepared timber and stones to **b** the house. 1129
6: 1 that he *began* to **b** the house of the LORD. 1129
8:16 out of all the tribes of Israel to **b** a house, 1129
8:17 it was in the heart of David my father to **b** a 1129
8:18 Whereas it was in thine heart to **b** a house 1129
8:19 Nevertheless thou shalt not **b** the house; but 1129
8:19 he shall **b** the house unto my name. 1129
9:15 for to **b** the house of the LORD, and his 1129
9:19 that which Solomon desired to **b** in 1129
9:24 had built for her: then did he **b** Millo. 1129
11: 7 did Solomon **b** a high place for Chemosh, 1129
11:38 **b** thee a sure house, as I built for David, 1129
16:34 In his days did Hiel the Bethelite **b** Jericho: 1129
1Ch 14: 1 and carpenters, to **b** him a house. 1129
17: 4 Thou shalt not **b** me a house to dwell in: 1129
17:10 thee that the LORD will **b** thee a house. 1129
17:12 He shall **b** me a house, and I will stablish 1129
17:25 hast told thy servant that *thou* wilt **b** him a 1129
21:22 that I may **b** an altar therein unto 1129
22: 2 he set masons to hew wrought stones to **b** 1129
22: 6 charged him to **b** a house for the LORD 1129
22: 7 it was in my mind to **b** a house unto 1129
22: 8 thou shalt not **b** a house unto my name, 1129
22:10 He shall **b** a house for my name; and 1129
22:11 and **b** the house of the LORD thy God, 1129
22:19 and **b** ye the sanctuary of the LORD God, 1129
28: 2 *As for me*, I *had* in mine heart to **b** a house 1129
28: 3 Thou shalt not **b** a house for my name, 1129
28: 6 he shall **b** my house and my courts: 1129
28:10 for the LORD hath chosen thee to **b** a 1129
29:16 all this store that we have prepared to **b** 1129
1Ch 29:19 to do all *these things*, and to **b** the palace, 1129
2Ch 2: 1 Solomon determined to **b** a house for 1129
2: 3 didst send him cedars to **b** him a house to 1129
2: 4 I **b** a house to the name of the LORD my 1129
2: 5 the house which I **b** *is* great: for great *is* our 1129
2: 6 who is able to **b** him a house, seeing 1129
2: 6 who *am* I then, that I should **b** him a house, 1129
2: 9 for the house which I am about to **b** *shall* 1129
2:12 that might **b** a house for the LORD, and 1129
3: 1 Solomon began to **b** the house of 1129
3: 2 he began to **b** in the second *day* of 1129
6: 5 **b** a house *in*, that my name might be there; 1129
6: 7 **b** a house for the name of the LORD God 1129
6: 8 Forasmuch as it was in thine heart to **b** a 1129
6: 9 Notwithstanding thou shalt not **b** the house; 1129
6: 9 thy loins, he shall **b** the house for my name. 1129
8: 6 all that Solomon desired to **b** in Jerusalem, 1129
14: 7 Let us **b** these cities, and make about *them* 1129
35: 3 the son of David king of Israel did **b**; 1129
36:23 he hath charged me to **b** him a house in 1129
Ezr 1: 2 he hath charged me to **b** him a house at 1129
1: 3 **b** the house of the LORD God of Israel, 1129
1: 5 to go up to **b** the house of the LORD 1129
4: 2 and said unto them, Let us **b** with you: 1129
4: 3 You have nothing to do with us to **b** a 1129
4: 3 we ourselves together will **b** unto 1129
5: 2 began to **b** the house of God which *is* at 1124
5: 3 Who hath commanded you to **b** this house, 1124
5: 9 Who commanded you to **b** this house, and 1124
5:11 **b** the house that was builded these many 1124
5:13 made a decree to **b** this house of God. 1124
5:17 king to **b** this house of God at Jerusalem, 1124
6: 7 the elders of the Jews **b** this house of God 1124
Ne 2: 5 of my fathers' sepulchres, that I may **b** it. 1129
2:17 come, and let us **b** *up* the wall of Jerusalem, 1129
2:18 they said, Let us rise up and **b**. So they 1129
2:20 therefore we his servants will arise and **b**: 1129
3: 3 the fish gate did the sons of Hassenaah **b**, 1129
4: 3 he said, Even *that* which they **b**, if a fox go 1129
4:10 so that we are not able to **b** the wall. 1129
Ps 28: 5 he shall destroy them, and not **b** them **up**. 1129
51:18 unto Zion: **b** thou the walls of Jerusalem. 1129
69:35 save Zion, and will **b** the cities of Judah: 1129
89: 4 and **b up** thy throne to all generations. 1129
102:16 When the LORD shall **b up** Zion, he shall 1129
127: 1 Except the LORD **b** the house, 1129
127: 1 the house, they labour in vain that **b** it: 1129
147: 2 The LORD doth **b up** Jerusalem: 1129
Pr 24:27 in the field; and afterwards **b** thine house. 1129
Ecc 3: 3 a time to break down, and a time to **b** *up*; 1129
SS 8: 9 we will **b** upon her a palace of silver: 1129
Isa 9:10 but we will **b** *with* hewn stones: 1129
45:13 he shall **b** my city, and he shall let go my 1129
58:12 *they that shall be* of thee shall **b** the old 1129
60:10 the sons of strangers shall **b up** thy walls, 1129
61: 4 they shall **b** the old wastes, they shall raise 1129
65:21 they shall **b** houses, and inhabit *them*; and 1129
65:22 They shall not **b**, and another inhabit; 1129
66: 1 where *is* the house that ye **b** unto me? 1129
Jer 1:10 and to throw down, to **b**, and to plant. 1129
18: 9 concerning a kingdom, to **b** and to plant *it*; 1129
22:14 I will **b** me a wide house and 1129
24: 6 I will **b** them, and not pull *them* down; and 1129
29: 5 **B** ye houses, and dwell *in them*; and 1129
29:28 **b** ye houses, and dwell *in them*; and 1129
31: 4 Again I will **b** thee, and thou shalt be built, 1129
31:28 to **b**, and to plant, saith the LORD. 1129
33: 7 to return, and will **b** them, as at the first. 1129
35: 7 Neither shall ye **b** house, nor sow seed, 1129
35: 9 Nor to **b** houses for us to dwell in: 1129
42:10 will I **b** you, and not pull *you* down, and 1129
Eze 4: 2 **b** a fort against it, and cast a mount against 1129
11: 3 Which say, *It is* not near; *let us* **b** houses: 1129
21:22 the gates, to cast a mount, *and* to **b** a fort. 1129
28:26 shall **b** houses, and plant vineyards; 1129
36:36 know that I the LORD **b** the ruined *places*, 1129
Da 9:25 to **b** Jerusalem unto the Messiah the Prince 1129
Am 9:11 and I will **b** it as *in* the days of old: 1129
9:14 they shall **b** the waste cities, and 1129
Mic 3:10 They **b up** Zion with blood, and 1129
Zep 1:13 they shall also **b** houses, but not inhabit 1129
Hag 1: 8 and bring wood, and **b** the house; 1129
Zec 5:11 To **b** it a house in the land of Shinar: 1129
6:12 and he shall **b** the temple of the LORD: 1129
6:13 Even he shall **b** the temple of the LORD; 1129
6:15 and **b** in the temple of the LORD, 1129
9: 3 Tyrus did **b** herself a strong hold, and 1129
Mal 1: 4 we will return and **b** the desolate places; 1129
1: 4 They shall **b**, but I will throw down; 1129
Mt 16:18 and upon this rock I will **b** my church; *3618*
23:29 because ye **b** the tombs of the prophets, and *3618*
26:61 the temple of God, and to **b** it in three days. *3618*
Mk 14:58 within three days I will **b** another made *3618*
Lk 11:47 for ye **b** the sepulchres of the prophets, and *3618*
11:48 killed them, and ye **b** their sepulchres. *3618*
12:18 I will pull down my barns, and **b** greater; *3618*
14:28 For which of you, intending to **b** a tower, *3618*
14:30 This man began to **b**, and was not able to *3618*
Ac 7:49 what house will ye **b** me? saith the Lord: or *3618*
15:16 and will **b again** the tabernacle of David, *456*
15:16 and I will **b again** the ruins thereof, and *456*
20:32 which is able to **b** *you* up, and to give you *2026*
Ro 15:20 lest I should **b** upon another *man's* *3618*
1Co 3:12 Now if any *man* **b** upon this foundation *2026*
Gal 2:18 For if I **b** again the *things* which I *3618*

BUILDED (49) [BUILD]
Ge 4:17 he **b** a city, and called the name of the city, 1129
8:20 Noah **b** an altar unto the LORD; and 1129
10:11 **b** Nineveh, and the city Rehoboth, and 1129
11: 5 and the tower, which the children of men **b**. 1129
12: 7 there **b** he an altar unto the LORD, 1129
12: 8 there he **b** an altar unto the LORD, and 1129
26:25 he **b** an altar there, and called upon 1129
Ex 24: 4 **b** an altar under the hill, and twelve pillars, 1129

Nu 32:38 other names unto the cities which they **b**. 1129
Jos 22:16 in that ye have **b** you an altar, that ye might 1129
1Ki 8:27 how much less this house that I have **b**? 1129
8:43 which I have **b**, is called by thy name. 1129
15:22 timber thereof, where*with* Baasha had **b**; 1129
2Ki 23:13 which Solomon the king of Israel had **b** for 1129
1Ch 22: 5 the house *that is* to be **b** for the LORD 1129
Ezr 3: 2 and **b** the altar of the God of Israel, 1129
4: 1 **b** the temple unto the LORD God of 1129
4:13 if this city be **b**, and the walls set up *again,* 1124
4:16 if this city be **b** *again,* and the walls thereof 1124
4:21 *that* this city be not **b**, until *another* 1124
5: 8 which *is* **b** *with* great stones, and timber *is* 1124
5:11 build the house that was **b** these many 1124
5:11 which a great king of Israel **b** and set up. 1124
5:15 and let the house of God be **b** in his place. 1124
6: 3 Let the house be **b**, the place where they 1124
6:14 the elders of the Jews **b**, and they prospered 1124
6:14 they **b**, and finished *it,* according to 1124
Ne 3: 2 next unto him **b** the men of Jericho. 1129
3: 2 And next to them **b** Zaccur the son of Imri. 1129
4: 1 that when Sanballat heard that we **b** 1129
4:17 They which **b** on the wall, and they that 1129
4:18 had his sword girded by his side, and *so* **b**. 1129
6: 1 heard that I had **b** the wall, and *that* there 1129
7: 4 few therein, and the houses *were* not **b**, 1129
12:29 for the singers had **b** them villages round 1129
Job 20:19 taken away a house which he **b** not; 1129
Ps 122: 3 Jerusalem *is* **b** as a city that is compact 1129
Pr 9: 1 Wisdom hath **b** her house, she hath hewn 1129
24: 3 Through wisdom is a house **b**; and 1129
Ecc 2: 4 I **b** me houses; I planted me vineyards: 1129
SS 4: 4 Thy neck *is* like the tower of David **b** for 1129
Jer 30:18 the city shall be **b** upon her own heap, and 1129
La 3: 5 He hath **b** against me, and compassed *me* 1129
Eze 36:10 be inhabited, and the wastes shall be **b**: 1129
36:33 in the cities, and the wastes shall be **b**. 1129
Lk 17:28 they sold, they planted, they **b**; *3618*
Eph 2:22 In whom you also are **b together** for a *4925*
Heb 3: 3 inasmuch as he who hath **b** the house hath *2680*
3: 4 For every house is **b** by some *man;* but *2680*

BUILDEDST (1) [BUILD]

Dt 6:10 and goodly cities, which thou **b** not, 1129

BUILDER (1) [BUILD]

Heb 11:10 whose **b** and maker *is* God. *5079*

BUILDERS (15) [BUILD]

1Ki 5:18 Solomon's **b** and Hiram's builders did hew 1129
5:18 Hiram's **b** did hew *them,* and 1129
2Ki 12:11 they laid it out to the carpenters and **b**, 1129
22: 6 **b**, and masons, and to buy timber and 1129
2Ch 34:11 and **b** gave they *it,* to buy hewn stone, 1129
Ezr 3:10 when the **b** laid the foundation of 1129
Ne 4: 5 have provoked *thee* to anger before the **b**. 1129
4:18 For the **b**, every one had his sword girded 1129
Ps 118:22 The stone *which* the **b** refused is become 1129
Eze 27: 4 the seas, thy **b** have perfected thy beauty. 1129
Mt 21:42 The stone which the **b** rejected, *3618*
Mk 12:10 The stone which the **b** rejected is become *3618*
Lk 20:17 is written, The stone which the **b** rejected, *3618*
Ac 4:11 the stone which was set at nought of you **b**, *3618*
1Pe 2: 7 the stone which the **b** disallowed, *3618*

BUILDEST (5) [BUILD]

Dt 22: 8 When thou **b** a new house, then thou shalt 1129
Ne 6: 6 for which cause thou **b** the wall, that thou 1129
Eze 16:31 In that thou **b** thine eminent place in 1129
Mt 27:40 and **b** *it* in three days, save thyself. *3618*
Mk 15:29 the temple, and **b** *it* in three days, *3618*

BUILDETH (9) [BUILD]

Jos 6:26 that riseth up and **b** this city Jericho: 1129
Job 27:18 He **b** his house as a moth, and as a booth 1129
Pr 14: 1 Every wise woman **b** her house: but 1129
Jer 22:13 Woe unto him that **b** his house by 1129
Hos 8:14 hath forgotten his Maker, and **b** temples; 1129
Am 9: 6 *It is* he that **b** his stories in the heaven, and 1129
Hab 2:12 Woe to him that **b** a town with blood, and 1129
1Co 3:10 laid the foundation, and another **b thereon**. *2026*
3:10 every man take heed how he **b thereupon**. *2026*

BUILDING (37) [BUILD]

Jos 22:19 in **b** you an altar beside the altar of 1129
1Ki 3: 1 until he had made an end of **b** his own 1129
6: 7 the house, when it was **in b**, was built *of* 1129
6: 7 iron heard in the house, while it was **in b**. 1129
6:12 *Concerning* this house which thou art in **b**, 1129
6:38 fashion of it. So was he seven years in **b** it. 1129
7: 1 Solomon was **b** his own house thirteen 1129
9: 1 when Solomon had finished the **b** of 1129
15:21 Baasha heard *thereof,* that he left off **b** 1129
1Ch 28: 2 of our God, and had made ready for the **b**: 1129
2Ch 3: 3 instructed for the **b** of the house of God. 1129
16: 5 when Baasha heard *it,* that he left off **b** of 1129
16: 6 timber thereof, where*with* Baasha was a **b**; 1129
Ezr 4: 4 people of Judah, and troubled them in **b**, 1129
4:12 **b** the rebellious and the bad city, and 1124
5: 4 are the names of the men that make this **b**? 1147
5:16 that time even until now *hath it been* in **b**, 1124
6: 8 these Jews for the **b** of this house of God: 1124
Ecc 10:18 By much slothfulness the **b** decayeth; and 4746
Eze 17:17 by casting up mounts, and **b** forts, to cut off 1129
40: 5 so he measured the breadth of the **b**, 1146
41:12 Now the **b** that *was* before the separate 1146
41:12 the wall of the **b** *was* five cubits thick 1146
41:13 the separate place, and the **b**, with the walls 1140
41:15 he measured the length of the **b** over 1146
42: 1 which *was* before the **b** toward the north. 1146
42: 5 and than the middlemost of the **b**. 1146
42: 6 *the* **b** was straitened more than the lowest NIH
42:10 the separate place, and over against the **b**. 1146
46:23 *there was* a row *of* **b** round about in them, NIH

Jn 2:20 Forty and six years was this temple in **b**, *3618*
1Co 3: 9 ye are God's husbandry, *ye are* God's **b**. *3619*
2Co 5: 1 we have a **b** of God, a house not made with *3619*
Eph 2:21 In whom all the **b** fitly framed together *3619*
Heb 9:11 with hands, that is to say, not of this **b**, *2937*
Jude 1:20 **b up** yourselves on your most holy faith, *2026*
Rev 21:18 And the **b** of the wall of it was *of* jasper: *1739*

BUILDINGS (3) [BUILD]

Mt 24: 1 to *him* for to shew him the **b** of the temple. *3619*
Mk 13: 1 manner of stones and what **b** *are here.* *3619*
13: 2 said unto him, Seest thou these great **b**? *3619*

BUILT (171) [BUILD]

Ge 13:18 and **b** there an altar unto the LORD. 1129
22: 9 Abraham **b** an altar there, and laid 1129
33:17 **b** him a house, and made booths for his 1129
35: 7 he **b** there an altar, and called the place 1129
Ex 1:11 they **b** for Pharaoh treasure cities, Pithom 1129
17:15 Moses **b** an altar, and called the name of it 1129
32: 5 when Aaron saw *it,* he **b** an altar before it; 1129
Nu 13:22 *were.* (Now Hebron was **b** seven years 1129
21:27 let the city of Sihon be **b** and prepared: 1129
23:14 **b** seven altars, and offered a bullock and 1129
32:34 the children of Gad **b** Dibon, and Ataroth, 1129
32:37 the children of Reuben **b** Heshbon, and 1129
Dt 8:12 hast **b** goodly houses, and dwelt *therein;* 1129
13:16 be a heap for ever; it shall not be **b** again. 1129
20: 5 What man *is there* that hath **b** a new house, 1129
Jos 8:30 Joshua **b** an altar unto the LORD God of 1129
19:50 and he **b** the city, and dwelt therein. 1129
22:10 the half tribe of Manasseh **b** there an altar 1129
22:11 the half tribe of Manasseh have **b** an altar 1129
22:23 That we have **b** us an altar to turn from 1129
24:13 cities which ye **b** not, and ye dwell in them; 1129
Jdg 1:26 **b** a city, and called the name thereof Luz: 1129
6:24 Gideon **b** an altar there unto the LORD, 1129
6:28 was offered upon the altar that was **b**. 1129
18:28 And they **b** a city, and dwelt therein, 1129
21: 4 **b** there an altar, and offered burnt offerings 1129
1Sa 7:17 and there he **b** an altar unto the LORD. 1129
14:35 Saul **b** an altar unto the LORD: the same 1129
14:35 the same was the first altar that he **b** unto 1129
2Sa 5: 9 David **b** round about from Millo and 1129
5:11 masons: and they **b** David a house. 1129
24:25 David **b** there an altar unto the LORD, 1129
1Ki 3: 2 there was no house **b** unto the name of 1129
6: 2 the house which king Solomon **b** for 1129
6: 5 against the wall of the house he **b** chambers 1129
6: 7 was **b** *of* stone made ready *before it was* 1129
6: 9 So he **b** the house, and finished it; and 1129
6:10 *then* he **b** chambers against all the house, 1129
6:14 So Solomon **b** the house, and finished it. 1129
6:15 he **b** the walls of the house within with 1129
6:16 he **b** twenty cubits on the sides of 1129
6:16 he even **b** *them* for it within, *even* for 1129
6:36 he **b** the inner court *with* three rows of 1129
7: 2 He **b** also the house of the forest of 1129
8:13 I have **surely b** thee a house to dwell 1129+1129
8:20 have **b** a house for the name of the LORD 1129
8:44 *toward* the house that I have **b** for thy 1129
8:48 and the house which I have **b** for thy name: 1129
9: 3 hallowed this house, which thou hast **b**, 1129
9:10 when Solomon had **b** the two houses, 1129
9:17 Solomon **b** Gezer, and Beth-horon 1129
9:24 her house which *Solomon* had **b** for her: 1129
9:25 peace offerings upon the altar which he **b** 1129
10: 4 and the house that he had **b**, 1129
11:27 Solomon **b** Millo, *and* repaired the breaches 1129
11:38 as I **b** for David, and will give Israel unto 1129
12:25 Jeroboam **b** Shechem in mount Ephraim, 1129
12:25 went out from thence, and **b** Penuel. 1129
14:23 For they also **b** them high places, and 1129
15:17 **b** Ramah, that *he* might not suffer *any* to go 1129
15:22 king Asa **b** with them Geba of Benjamin, 1129
15:23 all that he did, and the cities which he **b**, 1129
16:24 **b** *on* the hill, and called the name of 1129
16:24 and called the name of the city which he **b**, 1129
16:32 house of Baal, which he had **b** in Samaria. 1129
18:32 *with* the stones he **b** an altar in the name of 1129
22:39 which he made, and all the cities that he **b**, 1129
2Ki 14:22 He **b** Elath, and restored it to Judah, 1129
15:35 He **b** the higher gate of the house of 1129
16:11 Urijah the priest **b** an altar according to all 1129
16:18 the covert for the sabbath that they had **b** in 1129
17: 9 they **b** them high places in all their cities, 1129
21: 3 For he **b** *up* again the high places which 1129
21: 4 And he **b** altars in the house of the LORD, 1129
21: 5 he **b** altars for all the host of heaven in 1129
25: 1 and they **b** forts against it round about. 1129
1Ch 6:10 in the temple that Solomon **b** in Jerusalem:) 1129
6:32 until Solomon had **b** the house of 1129
7:24 who **b** Beth-horon the nether, and 1129
8:12 and Shamed, who **b** Ono, and Lod, 1129
11: 8 he **b** the city round about, even from Millo 1129
17: 6 Why have ye not **b** me a house of cedars? 1129
21:26 David **b** there an altar unto the LORD, 1129
22:19 into the house that is *to be* **b** to the name of 1129
2Ch 6: 2 I have **b** a house of habitation for thee, and 1129
6:10 have **b** the house for the name of 1129
6:18 how much less this house which I have **b**? 1129
6:33 may know that this house which I have **b** is 1129
6:34 the house which I have **b** for thy name; 1129
6:38 toward the house which I have **b** for thy 1129
8: 1 wherein Solomon had **b** the house of 1129
8: 2 Solomon **b** them, and caused the children 1129
8: 4 he **b** Tadmor in the wilderness, and all 1129
8: 4 all the store cities, which he **b** in Hamath. 1129
8: 5 Also he **b** Beth-horon the upper, and 1129
8:11 David unto the house that he had **b** for her: 1129
8:12 which he had **b** before the porch, 1129
9: 3 of Solomon, and the house that he had **b**, 1129
11: 5 and **b** cities for defence in Judah. 1129
11: 6 He **b** even Beth-lehem, and Etam, and 1129
14: 6 he **b** fenced cities in Judah: for the land had 1129

2Ch 14: 7 rest on every side. So they **b** and prospered. 1129
16: 1 **b** Ramah, to the intent that *he* might let 1129
16: 6 and he **b** therewith Geba and Mizpah. 1129
17:12 he **b** in Judah castles, and cities of store. 1129
20: 8 have **b** thee a sanctuary therein for thy 1129
26: 2 He **b** Eloth, and restored it to Judah, 1129
26: 6 **b** cities about Ashdod, and among 1129
26: 9 Moreover Uzziah **b** towers in Jerusalem at 1129
26:10 Also he **b** towers in the desert, and 1129
27: 3 He **b** the high gate of the house of 1129
27: 3 and on the wall of Ophel he **b** much. 1129
27: 4 Moreover he **b** cities in the mountains of 1129
27: 4 and in the forests he **b** castles and towers. 1129
32: 5 **b up** all the wall that was broken, and 1129
33: 3 For he **b** again the high places which 1129
33: 4 Also he **b** altars in the house of 1129
33: 5 he **b** altars for all the host of heaven in 1129
33:14 Now after this he **b** a wall without the city 1129
33:15 all the altars that he had **b** in the mount of 1129
33:19 the places wherein he **b** high places, and 1129
Ne 3: 1 the priests, and they **b** the sheep gate; 1129
3:13 they **b** it, and set up the doors thereof, 1129
3:14 he **b** it, and set up the doors thereof, 1129
3:15 he **b** it, and covered it, and set up the doors 1129
4: 6 So **b** we the wall; and all the wall was 1129
7: 1 when the wall was **b**, and I had set up 1129
Job 3:14 which **b** desolate places for themselves; 1129
12:14 it cannot be **b** *again:* he shutteth up a man, 1129
22:23 thou shalt be **b** *up,* thou shalt put away 1129
Ps 78:69 he **b** his sanctuary like high *palaces,* like 1129
89: 2 I have said, Mercy shall be **b up** for ever: 1129
Ecc 9:14 besieged it, and **b** great bulwarks against it: 1129
Isa 5: 2 **b** a tower in the midst of it, and also made a 1129
25: 2 strangers to be no city; it shall never be **b**. 1129
44:26 Ye shall be **b**, and I will raise up 1129
44:28 even saying to Jerusalem, Thou shalt be **b**; 1129
Jer 7:31 they have **b** the high places of Tophet, 1129
12:16 shall they be **b** in the midst of my people. 1129
19: 5 They have **b** also the high places of Baal, 1129
31: 4 and thou shalt be **b**, O virgin of Israel: 1129
31:38 that the city shall be **b** to the LORD from 1129
32:31 of my fury from the day that they **b** it even 1129
32:35 they **b** the high places of Baal, which *are* in 1129
45: 4 *that* which I have **b** *will* I break down, and 1129
52: 4 and **b** forts against it round about. 1129
Eze 13:10 one **b up** a wall, and lo, others daubed it 1129
16:24 *That* thou hast also **b** unto thee an eminent 1129
16:25 Thou hast **b** thy high place at every head of 1129
26:14 spread nets upon; thou shalt be **b** no more: 1129
Da 4:30 that I have **b** for the house of the kingdom 1124
9:25 the street shall be **b** again, and the wall, 1129
Am 5:11 ye have **b** houses of hewn stone, but 1129
Mic 7:11 *In* the day that thy walls are *to be* **b**, *in* that 1129
Hag 1: 2 time that the LORD'S house should be **b**. 1129
Zec 1:16 my house shall be **b** in it, saith the LORD 1129
8: 9 hosts was laid, that the temple might be **b**. 1129
Mt 7:24 a wise man, which **b** his house upon a rock: *3618*
7:26 which **b** his house upon the sand: *3618*
21:33 and **b** a tower, and let it out to husbandmen, *3618*
Mk 12: 1 and **b** a tower, and let it out to husbandmen, *3618*
Lk 4:29 brow of the hill whereon their city was **b**, *3618*
6:48 He is like a man which **b** a house, and *3618*
6:49 is like a man that without a foundation **b** a *3618*
7: 5 our nation, and he hath **b** us a synagogue. *3618*
Ac 7:47 But Solomon **b** him a house. *3618*
1Co 3:14 work abide which he hath **b thereupon**, *2026*
Eph 2:20 And are **b** upon the foundation of *2026*
Col 2: 7 Rooted and **b up** in him, and stablished in *2026*
Heb 3: 4 some *man;* but he that **b** all *things is* God. *2680*
1Pe 2: 5 as lively stones, are **b** *up* a spiritual house, *3618*

BUKKI (5)

Nu 34:22 of the children of Dan, **B** the son of Jogli. 1231
1Ch 6: 5 Abishua begat **B**, and Bukki begat Uzzi, 1231
6: 5 Abishua begat Bukki, and **B** begat Uzzi, 1231
6:51 **B** his son, Uzzi his son, Zerahiah his son, 1231
Ezr 7: 4 of Zerahiah, the son of Uzzi, the son of **B**, 1231

BUKKIAH (2)

1Ch 25: 4 **B**, Mattaniah, Uzziel, Shebuel, and 1232
25:13 The sixth *to* **B**, *he,* his sons, and 1232

BUL (1)

1Ki 6:38 in the eleventh year, in the month **B**, 945

BULL (2) [BULLOCK, BULLOCK'S, BULLOCKS, BULLS]

Job 21:10 Their **b** gendereth, and faileth not; 7794
Isa 51:20 head of all the streets, as a **wild b** *in* a net: 8377

BULLOCK (104) [BULL]

Ex 29: 1 Take one young **b**, and two rams 1241+6499
29: 3 in the basket, with the **b** and the two rams. 6499
29:10 thou shalt cause a **b** to be brought before 6499
29:10 shall put their hands upon the head of the **b**. 6499
29:11 thou shalt kill the **b** before the LORD, 6499
29:12 thou shalt take of the blood of the **b**, and 6499
29:14 the flesh of the **b**, and his skin, and his 6499
29:36 thou shalt offer every day a **b** *for* a sin 6499
Lev 1: 5 he shall kill the **b** before the LORD: 1121+1241
4: 3 a young **b** without blemish unto 1241+6499
4: 4 he shall bring the **b** unto the door of 6499
4: 4 and kill the **b** before the LORD. 6499
4: 7 shall pour all the blood of the **b** at 6499
4: 8 he shall take off from it all the fat of the **b** 6499
4:10 As it was taken off from the **b** of 7794
4:11 the skin of the **b**, and all his flesh, with his 6499
4:12 Even the whole **b** shall he carry forth 6499
4:14 shall offer a young **b** for the sin, 1241+6499
4:15 upon the head of the **b** before the LORD: 6499
4:15 and the **b** shall be killed before the LORD. 6499
4:20 he shall do with the **b** as he did with 6499
4:20 as he did with the **b** for a sin offering, 6499
4:21 he shall carry forth the **b** without the camp, 6499

Lev 4:21 and burn him as he burned the first **b**: 6499
8: 2 a **b** *for* the sin offering, and two rams, and 6499
8:14 he brought the **b** *for* the sin offering: and 6499
8:14 upon the head of the **b** *for* the sin offering. 6499
8:17 the **b**, and his hide, his flesh, and his dung, 6499
9: 4 Also a **b** and a ram for peace offerings, 7794
9:18 He slew also the **b** and the ram *for* a 7794
9:19 the fat of the **b** and of the ram, the rump, 7794
16: 3 with a young **b** for a sin offering, 1241+6499
16: 6 Aaron shall offer *his* **b** of the sin offering, 6499
16:11 Aaron shall bring the **b** of the sin offering, 6499
16:11 shall kill the **b** of the sin offering which *is* 6499
16:14 he shall take of the blood of the **b**, and 6499
16:15 that blood as he did with the blood of the **b**, 6499
16:18 shall take of the blood of the **b**, and of 6499
16:27 the **b** for the sin offering, and the goat for 6499
22:23 Either a **b** or a lamb that hath any thing 7794
22:27 When a **b**, or a sheep, or a goat, is brought 7794
23:18 and one young **b**, and two rams: 1241+6499
Nu 7:15 One young **b**, one ram, one lamb of 1241+6499
7:21 One young **b**, one ram, one lamb of 1241+6499
7:27 One young **b**, one ram, one lamb of 1241+6499
7:33 One young **b**, one ram, one lamb of 1241+6499
7:39 One young **b**, one ram, one lamb of 1241+6499
7:45 One young **b**, one ram, one lamb of 1241+6499
7:51 One young **b**, one ram, one lamb of 1241+6499
7:57 One young **b**, one ram, one lamb of 1241+6499
7:63 One young **b**, one ram, one lamb of 1241+6499
7:69 One young **b**, one ram, one lamb of 1241+6499
7:75 One young **b**, one ram, one lamb of 1241+6499
7:81 One young **b**, one ram, one lamb of 1241+6499
8: 8 let them take a young **b** with his 1241+6499
8: 8 another young **b** shalt thou take for a 1241+6499
15: 8 when thou preparest a **b** *for* a burnt 1121+1241
15: 9 shall he bring with a **b** a meat 1121+1241
15:11 Thus shall it be done for one **b**, or for one 7794
15:24 one young **b** for a burnt offering, 1241+6499
23: 2 and Balaam offered on *every* altar a **b** and 6499
23: 4 I have offered upon *every* altar a **b** and 6499
23:14 and offered a **b** and a ram on *every* altar. 6499
23:30 and offered a **b** and a ram on *every* altar. 6499
28:12 meat offering, mingled with oil, for one **b**; 6499
28:14 shall be half a hin of wine unto a **b**, 6499
28:20 three tenth deals shall ye offer for a **b**, and 6499
28:28 three tenth deals unto one **b**, two tenth 6499
29: 2 one young **b**, one ram, *and* 1241+6499
29: 3 three tenth deals for a **b**, *and* two tenth 6499
29: 8 one young **b**, one ram, *and* 1241+6499
29: 9 three tenth deals to a **b**, *and* two tenth deals 6499
29:14 three tenth deals unto every **b** of 6499
29:36 one **b**, one ram, seven lambs of the first 6499
29:37 and their drink offerings for the **b**, 6499
Dt 15:19 shalt do no work with the firstling of thy **b**, 7794
17: 1 sacrifice unto the LORD thy God *any* **b**, 7794
33:17 His glory *is like* the firstling of his **b**, and 7794
Jdg 6:25 said unto him, Take thy father's young **b**, 7794
6:25 even the second **b** of seven years old, and 6499
6:26 take the second **b**, and offer a burnt 6499
6:28 the second **b** was offered upon the altar that 6499
1Sa 1:25 they slew a **b**, and brought the child to Eli. 6499
1Ki 18:23 let them choose one **b** for themselves, and 6499
18:23 no fire *under*: and I will dress the other **b**, 6499
18:25 Choose you one **b** for yourselves, and 6499
18:26 they took the **b** which was given them, and 6499
18:33 cut the **b** in pieces, and laid *him* on 6499
2Ch 13: 9 to consecrate himself with a young **b** 1241+6499
Ps 50: 9 I will take no **b** out of thy house, *nor* he 6499
69:31 than an ox *or* **b** that hath horns *and* hoofs. 6499
Isa 65:25 and the lion shall eat straw like the **b**: 1241
Jer 31:18 as a **b** unaccustomed *to the yoke*; turn thou 5695
Eze 43:19 a young **b** for a sin offering. 1241+6499
43:21 Thou shalt take the **b** also of the sin 6499
43:22 the altar, as they did cleanse *it* with the **b**. 6499
43:23 offer a young **b** without blemish, 1241+6499
43:25 they shall also prepare a young **b**, 1241+6499
45:18 thou shalt take a young **b** without 1241+6499
45:22 for all the people of the land a **b** *for* a sin 6499
45:24 prepare a meat offering *of* an ephah for a **b**, 6499
46: 6 *shall be* a young **b** without blemish, 1241+6499
46: 7 an ephah for a **b**, and an ephah for a ram, 6499
46:11 the meat offering shall be an ephah to a **b**, 6499

BULLOCK'S (3) [BULL]

Lev 4: 4 shall lay his hand upon the **b** head, and 6499
4: 5 the priest that is anointed shall take of the **b** 6499
4:16 **b** blood to the tabernacle of 6499

BULLOCKS (45) [BULL]

Nu 7:87 oxen for the burnt offering *were* twelve **b**, 6499
7:88 the peace offerings *were* twenty and four **b**, 6499
8:12 lay their hands upon the heads of the **b**: 6499
23:29 prepare me here seven **b** and seven rams. 6499
28:11 two young **b**, and one ram, 1241+6499
28:19 two young **b**, and one ram, and 1241+6499
28:27 two young **b**, one ram, seven lambs 1241+6499
29:13 thirteen young **b**, two rams, *and* 1241+6499
29:14 deals unto every bullock of the thirteen **b**, 6499
29:17 day *ye shall offer* twelve young **b**, 1241+6499
29:18 and their drink offerings for the **b**, 6499
29:20 on the third day eleven **b**, two rams, 6499
29:21 and their drink offerings for the **b**, 6499
29:23 on the fourth day ten **b**, two rams, *and* 6499
29:24 and their drink offerings for the **b**, 6499
29:26 on the fifth day nine **b**, two rams, *and* 6499
29:27 and their drink offerings for the **b**, 6499
29:29 And on the sixth day eight **b**, two rams, *and* 6499
29:30 and their drink offerings for the **b**, 6499
29:32 on the seventh day seven **b**, two rams, *and* 6499
29:33 and their drink offerings for the **b**, 6499
1Sa 1:24 with three **b**, and one ephah of flour, and 6499
1Ki 18:23 Let them therefore give us two **b**; and 6499
1Ch 15:26 that they offered seven **b** and seven rams. 6499
29:21 *even* a thousand **b**, a thousand rams, *and* 6499
2Ch 29:21 they brought seven **b**, and seven rams, and 6499
29:22 So they killed the **b**, and the priests 1241
2Ch 29:32 was threescore and ten **b**, an hundred rams, 1241
30:24 did give to the congregation a thousand **b** 6499
30:24 gave to the congregation a thousand **b** 6499
35: 7 of thirty thousand, and three thousand **b**: 1241
Ezr 6: 9 both young **b**, and rams, and lambs, 8450
6:17 of this house of God an hundred **b**, 8450
7:17 mayest buy speedily with this money **b**, 8450
8:35 twelve **b** for all Israel, ninety and six rams, 6499
Job 42: 8 Therefore take unto you now seven **b** and 6499
Ps 51:19 then shall they offer **b** upon thine altar. 6499
66:15 incense of rams; I will offer **b** with goats. 1241
Isa 1:11 I delight not in the blood of **b**, or of lambs, 6499
34: 7 down with them, and the **b** with the bulls; 6499
Jer 46:21 men *are* in the midst of her like fatted **b**; 5695
50:27 Slay all her **b**; let them go down to 6499
Eze 39:18 of rams, of lambs, and of goats, of **b**, all of 6499
45:23 seven **b** and seven rams without blemish 6499
Hos 12:11 they sacrifice **b** in Gilgal; yea, their altars 7794

BULLS (10) [BULL]

Ge 32:15 forty kine, and ten **b**, twenty she asses, and 6499
Ps 22:12 Many **b** have compassed me: strong *bulls* 6499
22:12 strong *b* of Bashan have beset me round. NIH
50:13 Will I eat the flesh of **b**, or drink the blood of 47
68:30 the multitude of the **b**, with the calves of 47
Isa 34: 7 down with them, and the bullocks with the **b**; 47
Jer 50:11 fat as the heifer at grass, and bellow as **b**; 47
52:20 twelve brasen **b** that *were* under the bases, 1241
Heb 9:13 For if the blood of **b** and of goats, and *5022*
10: 4 For *it is* not possible that the blood of **b** and *5022*

BULRUSH (1) [BULRUSHES, RUSH]

Isa 58: 5 *is it* to bow down his head as a **b**, and 100

BULRUSHES (2) [BULRUSH, RUSH]

Ex 2: 3 she took for him an ark of **b**, and daubed it 1573
Isa 18: 2 even in vessels of **b** upon the waters, 1573

BULWARKS (5)

Dt 20:20 thou shalt build **b** against the city that 4692
2Ch 26:15 *men*, to be on the towers and upon the **b**, 6438
Ps 48:13 Mark ye well her **b**, consider her palaces; 2430
Ecc 9:14 and besieged it, and built great **b** against it: 4685
Isa 26: 1 salvation will *God* appoint *for* walls and **b**. 2426

BUNAH (1)

1Ch 2:25 and **B**, and Oren, and Ozem, *and* Ahijah. 946

BUNCH (1) [BUNCHES]

Ex 12:22 ye shall take a **b** of hyssop, and dip *it* in 92

BUNCHES (3) [BUNCH]

2Sa 16: 1 an hundred **b of raisins**, and an hundred of 6778
1Ch 12:40 cakes *of figs*, and **b of raisins**, and wine, 6778
Isa 30: 6 their treasures upon the **b** of camels, to a 1707

BUNDLE (4) [BUNDLES]

Ge 42:35 every man's **b** of money *was* in his sack: 6872
1Sa 25:29 the soul of my lord shall be bound in the **b** 6872
SS 1:13 A **b** of myrrh *is* my well-beloved unto me; 6872
Ac 28: 3 And when Paul had gathered a **b** of sticks, *4128*

BUNDLES (2) [BUNDLE]

Ge 42:35 and their father saw the **b** of money, 6872
Mt 13:30 the tares, and bind them in **b** to burn them: *1197*

BUNNI (3)

Ne 9: 4 **B**, Sherebiah, Bani, *and* Chenani, and 1138
10:15 **B**, Azgad, Bebai, 1138
11:15 the son of Hashabiah, the son of **B**; 1138

BURDEN (69) [BURDENED, BURDENS, BURDENSOME]

Ex 18:22 and they shall bear *the* **b** with thee. NIH
23: 5 of him that hateth thee lying under his **b**, 4853
Nu 4:15 These *things are* the **b** of the sons of 4853
4:19 them every one to his service and to his **b**: 4853
4:31 this *is* the charge of their **b**, according to all 4853
4:32 the instruments of the charge of their **b**. 4853
4:47 the service of the **b** in the tabernacle of 4853
4:49 to his service, and according to his **b**: 4853
11:11 that *thou* layest the **b** of all this people upon 4853
11:17 they shall bear the **b** of the people with 4853
Dt 1:12 and your **b**, and your strife? 4853
2Sa 15:33 on with me, then thou shalt be a **b** unto me: 4853
19:35 should thy servant be yet a **b** unto my lord 4853
2Ki 5:17 be given to thy servant two mules' **b** of 4853
8: 9 forty camels' **b**, and came and stood before 4853
9:25 his father, the LORD laid this **b** upon him; 4853
2Ch 35: 3 *it shall* not *be* a **b** upon your shoulders: 4853
Ne 13:19 *that* there should no **b** be brought in on 4853
Job 7:20 against thee, so that I am a **b** to myself? 4853
Ps 38: 4 as a heavy **b** they are too heavy for me. 4853
55:22 Cast thy **b** upon the LORD, and he shall 3053
81: 6 I removed his shoulder from the **b**: 5447
Ecc 12: 5 the grasshopper shall be a **b**, and desire 5445
Isa 9: 4 For thou hast broken the yoke of his **b**, and 5448
10:27 *that* his **b** shall be taken away from off thy 5448
13: 1 The **b** of Babylon, which Isaiah the son of 4853
14:25 and his **b** depart from off their shoulders. 5448
14:28 In the year that king Ahaz died was this **b**. 4853
15: 1 The **b** of Moab. Because in the night Ar of 4853
17: 1 The **b** of Damascus. Behold, Damascus *is* 4853
19: 1 The **b** of Egypt. Behold, the LORD rideth 4853
21: 1 The **b** of the desert of the sea. 4853
21:11 The **b** of Dumah. He calleth to me out of 4853
21:13 The **b** upon Arabia. In the forest in Arabia 4853
22: 1 The **b** of the valley of vision. What aileth 4853
22:25 and the **b** that *was* upon it shall be cut off: 4853
23: 1 The **b** of Tyre. Howl, ye ships of Tarshish; 4853
30: 6 The **b** of the beasts of the south: into 4853
30:27 *with* his anger, and the **b** *thereof is* heavy: 4858
46: 1 *they are* a **b** to the weary *beast*. 4853
Isa 46: 2 they could not deliver the **b**, but 4853
Jer 17:21 bear no **b** on the sabbath day, 4853
17:22 Neither carry forth a **b** out of your houses 4853
17:24 to bring in no **b** through the gates of this 4853
17:27 not to bear a **b**, even entering in at the gates 4853
23:33 saying, What *is* the **b** of the LORD? 4853
23:33 thou shalt then say unto them, What **b**? 4853
23:34 that shall say, The **b** of the LORD, 4853
23:36 the **b** of the LORD shall ye mention no 4853
23:36 for every man's word shall be his **b**; for ye 4853
23:38 sith ye say, The **b** of the LORD; therefore 4853
23:38 The **b** of the LORD, and I have sent unto 4853
23:38 Ye shall not say, The **b** of the LORD; 4853
Eze 12:10 This **b** *concerneth* the prince in Jerusalem, 4853
Hos 8:10 they shall sorrow a little for the **b** of 4853
Na 1: 1 The **b** of Nineveh. The book of the vision 4853
Hab 1: 1 The **b** which Habakkuk the prophet did see. 4853
Zep 3:18 of thee, *to whom* the reproach of it *was* a **b**. 4864
Zec 9: 1 The **b** of the word of the LORD in 4853
12: 1 The **b** of the word of the LORD for Israel, 4853
12: 3 all that **b** themselves with it shall be cut in 6006
Mal 1: 1 The **b** of the word of the LORD to Israel 4853
Mt 11:30 For my yoke *is* easy, and my **b** is light. *5413*
20:12 which have borne the **b** and heat of the day. *922*
Ac 15:28 to lay upon you no greater **b** than these *922*
21: 3 for there the ship was to unlade *her* **b**. *1117*
2Co 12:16 But be it so, I did not **b** you: nevertheless, *2599*
Gal 6: 5 For every man shall bear his own **b**. *5413*
Rev 2:24 they speak; I will put upon you none other **b**. *922*

BURDENED (2) [BURDEN]

2Co 5: 4 that are in *this* tabernacle do groan, being **b**: *916*
8:13 not that other *men* be eased, and you **b**: *2347*

BURDENS (25) [BURDEN]

Ge 49:14 a strong ass couching down between **two b**: 4942
Ex 1:11 taskmasters to afflict them with their **b**. 5450
2:11 unto his brethren, and looked on their **b**: 5450
5: 4 from their works? get you unto your **b**. 5450
5: 5 and you make them rest from their **b**. 5450
6: 6 I will bring you out from under the **b** of 5450
6: 7 which bringeth you out from under the **b** of 5450
Nu 4:24 of the Gershonites, to serve, and for **b**: 4853
4:27 in all their **b**, and in all their service: 4853
4:27 appoint unto them in charge all their **b**. 4853
1Ki 5:15 and ten thousand that bare **b**, 5449
2Ch 2: 2 and ten thousand men to bear **b**, 5449
2:18 ten thousand of them *to be* **bearers of b**, 5449
24:27 the greatness of the **b** *laid* upon him, and 4853
34:13 Also *they were* over the **bearers of b**, and 5449
Ne 4:10 The strength of the **bearers of b** is 5449
4:17 and they that bare **b**, *with* those that laded, 5447
13:15 grapes, and figs, and all *manner of* **b**, 4853
Isa 58: 6 to undo the heavy **b**, and to let the oppressed 92
La 2:14 have seen for thee false **b** and causes of 4864
Am 5:11 the poor, and ye take from him **b** of wheat: 4864
Mt 23: 4 For they bind heavy **b** and grievous to be *5413*
Lk 11:46 for ye lade men *with* **b** grievous to be *5413*
11:46 ye yourselves touch not the **b** with one of *5413*
Gal 6: 2 Bear ye one another's **b**, and so fulfil the law *922*

BURDENSOME (5) [BURDEN]

Zec 12: 3 in that day will I make Jerusalem a **b** stone 4614
2Co 11: 9 in all *things* I have kept myself **from being b** *4*
12:13 except *it be* that I myself was not **b** to you? *2655*
12:14 to come to you; and I will not be **b** to you: *2655*
1Th 2: 6 when we might have been **b**, *922+1722*

BURIAL (6) [BURY]

2Ch 26:23 field of the **b** which *belonged* to the kings; 6900
Ecc 6: 3 with good, and also *that* he have no **b**; 6900
Isa 14:20 Thou shalt not be joined with them in **b**, 6900
Jer 22:19 He shall be buried *with* the **b** of an ass, 6900
Mt 26:12 ointment on my body, she did *it* for my **b**. *1779*
Ac 8: 2 And devout men carried Stephen *to his* **b**, NIG

BURIED (106) [BURY]

Ge 15:15 in peace; thou shalt be **b** in a good old age. 6912
23:19 Abraham **b** Sarah his wife in the cave of 6912
25: 9 Ishmael **b** him in the cave of Machpelah, 6912
25:10 there was Abraham **b**, and Sarah his wife. 6912
35: 8 she was **b** beneath Beth-el under an oak: 6912
35:19 and was **b** in the way to Ephrath, 6912
35:29 and his sons Esau and Jacob **b** him. 6912
48: 7 I **b** her there in the way of Ephrath; 6912
49:31 There they **b** Abraham and Sarah his wife; 6912
49:31 there they **b** Isaac and Rebekah his wife; 6912
49:31 and Rebekah his wife; and there I **b** Leah. 6912
50:13 **b** him in the cave of the field of 6912
50:14 to bury his father, after he had **b** his father. 6912
Nu 11:34 because there they **b** the people that lusted. 6912
20: 1 and Miriam died there, and was **b** there. 6912
33: 4 For the Egyptians **b** all *their* firstborn, 6912
Dt 10: 6 there Aaron died, and there he was **b**; 6912
34: 6 he **b** him in a valley in the land of Moab, 6912
Jos 24:30 they **b** him in the border of his inheritance 6912
24:32 up out of Egypt, **b** they in Shechem, 6912
24:33 they **b** him in a hill that pertained to 6912
Jdg 2: 9 they **b** him in the border of his inheritance 6912
8:32 was **b** in the sepulchre of Joash his father, 6912
10: 2 three years, and died, and was **b** in Shamir. 6912
10: 5 And Jair died, and was **b** in Camon. 6912
12: 7 and was **b** in *one of* the cities of Gilead. 6912
12:10 Then died Ibzan, and was **b** at Beth-lehem. 6912
12:12 was **b** in Aijalon in the country of Zebulun. 6912
12:15 was **b** in Pirathon in the land of Ephraim, 6912
16:31 **b** him between Zorah and Eshtaol in 6912
Ru 1:17 thou diest, will I die, and there will I be **b**: 6912
1Sa 25: 1 and **b** him in his house at Ramah. 6912
28: 3 and **b** him in Ramah, even in his own city. 6912
31:13 **b** *them* under a tree at Jabesh, and 6912
2Sa 2: 4 men of Jabesh-gilead *were they* that **b** Saul. 6912
2: 5 your lord, *even* unto Saul, and have **b** him. 6912
2:32 and **b** him in the sepulchre of his father, 6912

2Sa 3:32 they **b** Abner in Hebron: and the king lift 6912
4:12 **b** *it* in the sepulchre of Abner in Hebron. 6912
17:23 and was **b** in the sepulchre of his father. 6912
19:37 *and be* **b** by the grave of my father and NIH
21:14 Jonathan his son **b** they in the country of 6912
1Ki 2:10 his fathers, and was **b** in the city of David. 6912
2:34 he was **b** in his own house in 6912
11:43 and was **b** in the city of David his father: 6912
13:31 it came to pass, after he had **b** him, that he 6912
13:31 the sepulchre wherein the man of God *is* **b**; 6912
14:18 they **b** him; and all Israel mourned for him, 6912
14:31 was **b** with his fathers in the city of David. 6912
15: 8 and they **b** him in the city of David: 6912
15:24 was **b** with his fathers in the city of David 6912
16: 6 slept with his fathers, and was **b** in Tirzah: 6912
16:28 with his fathers, and was **b** in Samaria: 6912
22:37 *to* Samaria; and they **b** the king in Samaria. 6912
22:50 was **b** with his fathers in the city of David 6912
2Ki 8:24 was **b** with his fathers in the city of David: 6912
9:28 **b** him in his sepulchre with his fathers in 6912
10:35 they **b** him in Samaria. And Jehoahaz his 6912
12:21 they **b** him with his fathers in the city of 6912
13: 9 with his fathers; and they **b** him in Samaria: 6912
13:13 Joash was **b** in Samaria with the kings of 6912
13:20 Elisha died, and they **b** him. And the bands 6912
14:16 was **b** in Samaria with the kings of Israel; 6912
14:20 he was **b** at Jerusalem with his fathers in 6912
15: 7 they **b** him with his fathers in the city of 6912
15:38 was **b** with his fathers in the city of David 6912
16:20 was **b** with his fathers in the city of David: 6912
21:18 was **b** in the garden of his own house, 6912
21:26 he was **b** in his sepulchre in the garden of 6912
23:30 and **b** him in his own sepulchre. 6912
1Ch 10:12 **b** their bones under the oak in Jabesh, and 6912
2Ch 9:31 and he was **b** in the city of David his father: 6912
12:16 his fathers, and was **b** in the city of David: 6912
14: 1 and they **b** him in the city of David: 6912
16:14 they **b** him in his own sepulchres, which he 6912
21: 1 was **b** with his fathers in the city of David. 6912
21:20 Howbeit they **b** him in the city of David, 6912
22: 9 when they had slain him, they **b** him: 6912
24:16 they **b** him in the city of David among 6912
24:25 they **b** him in the city of David, but 6912
24:25 they **b** him not in the sepulchres of 6912
25:28 **b** him with his fathers in the city of Judah. 6912
26:23 they **b** him with his fathers in the field of 6912
27: 9 and they **b** him in the city of David: 6912
28:27 they **b** him in the city, *even* in Jerusalem: 6912
32:33 they **b** him in the chiefest of the sepulchres 6912
33:20 and they **b** him *in* his own house: 6912
35:24 was **b** in *one of the* sepulchres of his 6912
Job 27:15 Those that remain of him shall be **b** in 6912
Ecc 8:10 so I saw the wicked **b**, who had come and 6912
Jer 8: 2 they shall not be gathered, nor be **b**; 6912
16: 4 neither shall they be **b**; *but* they shall be as 6912
16: 6 they shall not be **b**, neither shall *men* 6912
20: 6 shalt be **b** there, thou, and all thy friends, 6912
22:19 He shall be **b** *with* the burial of an ass, 6912
25:33 not be lamented, neither gathered, nor **b**; 6912
Eze 39:15 till the buriers have **b** it in the valley of 6912
Mt 14:12 the body, and **b** it, and went and told Jesus. *2290*
Lk 16:22 the rich *man* also died, and was **b**; *2290*
Ac 2:29 that he is both dead and **b**, and *2290*
5: 6 him up, and carried *him* out, and **b** *him.* *2290*
5: 9 the feet of them which have **b** thy husband *2290*
5:10 carrying *her* forth, **b** *her* by her husband. *2290*
Ro 6: 4 Therefore we are **b with** him by baptism *4916*
1Co 15: 4 And that he was **b**, and that he rose *again* *2290*
Col 2:12 **B with** him in baptism, wherein also you *4916*

BURIERS (1) [BURY]

Eze 39:15 till the **b** have buried it in the valley of 6912

BURN (138) [BURNED, BURNETH, BURNING, BURNINGS, BURNT]

Ge 11: 3 **b** *them* **thoroughly.** 8313+8316+3807.1
44:18 let not thine anger **b** against thy servant: 2734
Ex 12:10 of it until the morning ye shall **b** with fire. 8313
27:20 for the light, to **cause** the lamp **to b** always. 5927
29:13 *is* upon them, and **b** *them* upon the altar. 6999
29:14 shalt thou **b** with fire without the camp: 8313
29:18 thou shalt **b** the whole ram upon the altar: 6999
29:25 **b** *them* upon the altar for a burnt offering, 6999
29:34 then thou shalt **b** the remainder with fire: 8313
30: 1 thou shalt make an altar to **b** incense upon: 4729
30: 7 Aaron shall **b** thereon sweet incense every 6999
30: 7 the lamps, he shall **b incense** upon it. 6999
30: 8 lamps at even, he shall **b incense** upon it, 6999
30:20 to **b** offering made by fire unto 6999
Lev 1: 9 the priest shall **b** all on the altar, *to be* a 6999
1:13 shall bring *it* all, and **b** *it* upon the altar: 6999
1:15 and wring off his head, and **b** *it* on the altar; 6999
1:17 the priest shall **b** it upon the altar, upon 6999
2: 2 the priest shall **b** the memorial of it upon 6999
2: 9 and shall **b** *it* upon the altar: 6999
2:11 for ye shall **b** no leaven, nor any honey, 6999
2:16 the priest shall **b** the memorial of it, *part* of 6999
3: 5 Aaron's sons shall **b** it on the altar upon 6999
3:11 the priest shall **b** it upon the altar: *it is* 6999
3:16 the priest shall **b** them upon the altar: *it is* 6999
4:10 the priest shall **b** them upon the altar of 6999
4:12 and **b** him on the wood with fire: 8313
4:19 all his fat from him, and **b** *it* upon the altar. 6999
4:21 and **b** him as he burned the first bullock: 8313
4:26 he shall **b** all his fat upon the altar, as 6999
4:31 the priest shall **b** *it* upon the altar for a 6999
4:35 the priest shall **b** them upon the altar, 6999
5:12 a memorial thereof, and **b** *it* on the altar, 6999
6:12 the priest shall **b** wood on it every morning, 1197
6:12 he shall **b** thereon the fat of the peace 6999
6:15 shall **b** *it upon* the altar *for* a sweet savour, 6999
7: 5 the priest shall **b** them upon the altar *for* an 6999
7:31 the priest shall **b** the fat upon the altar: but 6999
8:32 and of the bread shall ye **b** with fire. 8313

Lev 13:52 He shall therefore **b** *that* garment, 8313
13:55 it *is* unclean; thou shalt **b** it in the fire; it *is* 8313
13:57 it *is* a spreading *plague:* thou shalt **b** that 8313
16:25 the fat of the sin offering shall he **b** upon 6999
16:27 they shall **b** in the fire their skins, and their 8313
17: 6 **b** the fat for a sweet savour unto 6999
24: 2 to **cause** the lamps **to b** continually. 5927
Nu 5:26 **b** *it* upon the altar, and afterward shall 6999
18:17 shalt **b** their fat *for* an offering made by 6999
19: 5 *one* shall **b** the heifer in his sight; her skin, 8313
19: 5 and her blood, with her dung, shall he **b**: 8313
Dt 5:23 (for the mountain did **b** with fire,) 1197
7: 5 and **b** their graven images with fire. 8313
7:25 The graven images of their gods shall ye **b** 8313
12: 3 their pillars, and **b** their groves with fire; 8313
13:16 shalt **b** with fire the city, and all the spoil 8313
32:22 shall **b** unto the lowest hell, and 3344
Jos 11: 6 their horses, and **b** their chariots with fire. 8313
11:13 save Hazor only; *that* did Joshua **b**. 8313
Jdg 9:52 went hard unto the door of the tower to **b** it 8313
12: 1 we will **b** thine house upon thee with fire. 8313
14:15 lest we **b** thee and thy father's house with 8313
1Sa 2:16 Let them **not fail to b** the fat 6999+6999
2:28 to offer upon mine altar, to **b** incense, 6999
1Ki 13: 1 Jeroboam stood by the altar to **b incense**. 6999
13: 2 of the high places that **b incense** upon thee, 6999
2Ki 16:15 Upon the great altar **b** the morning burnt 6999
18: 4 the children of Israel did **b incense** to it: 6999
23: 5 **b incense** in the high places in the cities of 6999
1Ch 23:13 for ever, to **b incense** before the LORD, 6999
2Ch 2: 4 *and* to **b** before him sweet incense, and 6999
2: 6 save only to **b sacrifice** before him? 6999
4:20 that they should **b** after the manner before 1197
13:11 And they **b** unto the LORD every morning 6999
13:11 with the lamps thereof, to **b** every evening: 1197
26:16 to **b incense** upon the altar of incense. 6999
26:18 to **b incense** unto the LORD, but to 6999
26:18 of Aaron, that are consecrated to **b incense**: 6999
26:19 and *had* a censer in his hand to **b incense**: 6999
28:25 high places to **b incense** unto other gods, 6999
29:11 should minister unto him, and **b incense**. 6999
32:12 before one altar, and **b incense** upon it? 6999
Ne 10:34 to **b** upon the altar of the LORD our God, 1197
Ps 79: 5 for ever? shall thy jealousy **b** like fire? 1197
89:46 for ever? shall thy wrath **b** like fire? 1197
Isa 1:31 they shall both **b** together, and none shall 1197
10:17 it shall **b** and devour his thorns and 1197
27: 4 go through them, I would **b** them together. 6702
40:16 Lebanon *is* not sufficient to **b**, nor 1197
44:15 shall it be for a man to **b**: for he will take 1197
47:14 shall be as stubble; the fire shall **b** them; 8313
Jer 4: 4 **b** that none can quench *it*, because of 1197
7: 9 **b incense** unto Baal, and walk after other 6999
7:20 and it shall **b**, and shall not be quenched. 1197
7:31 to **b** their sons and their daughters in 8313
11:13 *even* altars to **b incense** unto Baal. 6999
15:14 in mine anger, *which* shall **b** upon you. 3344
17: 4 a fire in mine anger, *which* shall **b** for ever. 3344
19: 5 to **b** their sons with fire *for* burnt offerings 8313
21:10 king of Babylon, and he shall **b** it with fire. 8313
21:12 **b** that none can quench *it*, because of 1197
32:29 fire on this city, and **b** it with the houses, 8313
34: 2 king of Babylon, and he shall **b** it with fire: 8313
34: 5 before thee, so shall they **b** *odours* for thee; 8313
34:22 against it, and take it, and **b** it with fire: 8313
36:25 to the king that *he* would not **b** the roll: 8313
37: 8 this city, and take it, and **b** it with fire. 8313
37:10 man in his tent, and **b** this city with fire. 8313
38:18 they shall **b** it with fire, and thou shalt not 8313
43:12 he shall **b** them, and carry them away 8313
43:13 gods of the Egyptians shall he **b** with fire. 8313
44: 3 in that *they* went to **b incense**, *and* to serve 6999
44: 5 to **b** no **incense** unto other gods. 6999
44:17 to **b incense** unto the queen of heaven, and 6999
44:18 since we left off to **b incense** to the queen 6999
44:25 to **b incense** to the queen of heaven, and 6999
Eze 5: 2 Thou shalt **b** with fire a third *part* in 1197
5: 4 the midst of the fire, and **b** them in the fire; 8313
16:41 they shall **b** thine houses with fire, and 8313
23:47 and **b up** their houses with fire. 8313
24: 5 **b** also the bones under it, *and* make it boil 1752
24:11 may **b**, and *that* the filthiness of it may be 2787
39: 9 shall set on fire and **b** the weapons, 5400
39: 9 and they shall **b** them with fire seven years: 1197
39:10 for they shall **b** the weapons with fire: 1197
43:21 he shall **b** it in the appointed place of 8313
Hos 4:13 **b incense** upon the hills, under oaks and 6999
Na 2:13 I will **b** her chariots in the smoke, and 1197
Hab 1:16 their net, and **b incense** unto their drag; 6999
Mal 4: 1 the day cometh, that *shall* **b** as an oven; 1197
4: 1 the day that cometh shall **b** them **up**, saith 3857
Mt 3:12 will **b up** the chaff with unquenchable fire. *2618*
13:30 and bind them in bundles to **b** them: *2618*
Lk 1: 9 his lot was to **b incense** when he went into *2370*
3:17 the chaff he will **b** with fire unquenchable. *2618*
24:32 to another, Did not our heart **b** within us, *2545*
1Co 7: 9 for it is better to marry than to **b**. *4448*
2Co 11:29 am not weak? who is offended, and I **b** not? *4448*
Rev 17:16 and shall eat her flesh, and **b** her with fire. *2618*

BURNED (22) [BURN]

Ex 3: 2 the bush **b** with fire, and the bush was not 1197
Lev 4:21 and burn him as he **b** the first bullock: 8313
8:16 and their fat, and Moses **b** *it* upon the altar. 6999
Dt 9:15 from the mount, and the mount **b** with fire: 1197
Jos 7:25 him *with* stones, and **b** them with fire, 8313
11:13 Israel **b** none of them, save Hazor only; 8313
2Ch 25:14 before them, and **b incense** unto them. 6999
34:25 and have **b incense** unto other gods, 6999
Est 1:12 the king very wroth, and his anger **b** in him. 1197
Ps 39: 3 within me, while I was musing the fire **b**: 1197
Isa 24: 6 therefore the inhabitants of the earth are **b**, 2787
42:25 and it **b** him, yet he laid *it* not to heart. 1197
La 2: 3 he **b** against Jacob like a flaming fire, 1197
Eze 15: 5 when the fire hath devoured it, and it is **b**? 2787

Hos 11: 2 and **b incense** to graven images. 6999
Jn 15: 6 and cast *them* into the fire, and they are **b**. *2545*
Ac 19:19 and **b** *them* before all *men:* and *2618*
Ro 1:27 **b** in their lust one towards another; *1572*
1Co 13: 3 and though I give my body to be **b**, *2545*
Heb 6: 8 *is* nigh unto cursing; whose end *is* to be **b**. *2740*
12:18 and that **b** with fire, nor unto blackness, *2545*
Rev 1:15 unto fine brass, as if they **b** in a furnace; *4448*

BURNETH (18) [BURN]

Lev 13:24 the quick *flesh* that **b** have a white bright 4348
16:28 he that **b** them shall wash his clothes, and 8313
Nu 19: 8 he that **b** her shall wash his clothes in 8313
Ps 46: 9 spear in sunder; he **b** the chariot in the fire. 8313
83:14 As the fire **b** a wood, and as the flame 1197
97: 3 and **b up** his enemies round about. 3857
Isa 9:18 For wickedness **b** as the fire: it shall devour 1197
44:16 He **b** part thereof in the fire; with part 8313
62: 1 and the salvation thereof as a lamp *that* **b**. 1197
64: 2 As *when* the melting fire **b**, the fire causeth 6919
65: 3 and **b incense** upon altars of brick; 6999
65: 5 smoke in my nose, a fire that **b** all the day. 3344
66: 3 he that **b** incense, *as if* he blessed an idol. 2142
Jer 48:35 and him that **b incense** to his gods. 6999
Hos 7: 6 *in* the morning it **b** as a flaming fire. 1197
Joel 2: 3 before them; and behind them a flame **b**: 3857
Am 6:10 uncle shall take him up, and he that **b** him, 5635
Rev 21: 8 shall have their part in the lake which **b** *2545*

BURNING (60) [BURN]

Ge 15:17 a **b** lamp that passed between those pieces. 784
Ex 21:25 **B** for burning, wound for wound, stripe for 3555
21:25 Burning for **b**, wound for wound, stripe for 3555
Lev 6: 9 of the **b** upon the altar all night unto 4169
6: 9 and the fire of the altar shall be **b** in it. 3344
6:12 the fire upon the altar shall be **b** in it; 3344
6:13 The fire shall ever be **b** upon the altar; 3344
10: 6 bewail the **b** which the LORD hath 8316
13:23 in his place, *and* spread not, it *is* a **b** boil; 6867
13:24 in the skin whereof *there is* a hot **b**, and 4348
13:25 the skin; it *is* a leprosy broken out of the **b**: 4348
13:28 it *is* a rising of the **b**, and the priest shall 4348
13:28 for it *is* an inflammation of the **b**. 4348
16:12 he shall take a censer full of **b coals** of fire 1513
26:16 consumption, and the **b ague**, that shall 6920
Nu 16:37 that he take up the censers out of the **b**, and 8316
19: 6 cast *it* into the midst of the **b** of the heifer. 8316
Dt 28:22 and with an **extreme b**, and with the sword, 2746
29:23 salt, *and* **b**, *that* it is not sown, nor beareth, 8316
32:24 devoured with **b heat**, and with bitter 7565
2Ch 16:14 they **made** a very great **b** for him. 8313+8316
21:19 his people made no **b** for him, like 8316
21:19 no burning for him, like the **b** of his fathers. 8316
Job 41:19 Out of his mouth go **b lamps**, *and* sparks of 3940
Ps 140:10 Let **b coals** fall upon them: let them be cast 1513
Pr 16:27 up evil: and in his lips *there is* as a **b** fire. 6867
26:21 *As* coals *are* to **b coals**, and wood to fire; so 1513
26:23 **B** lips and a wicked heart *are like* a 1814
Isa 3:24 of sackcloth; *and* **b** instead of beauty. 3587
4: 4 spirit of judgment, and by the spirit of **b**. 1197
9: 5 but *this* shall be with **b** *and* fuel of fire. 8316
10:16 under his glory he shall kindle a **b** like 3350
10:16 he shall kindle a burning like the **b** of a fire. 3350
30:27 **b** *with* his anger, and the burden *thereof is* 1197
34: 9 and the land thereof shall become **b** pitch. 1197
Jer 20: 9 *his word* was in mine heart as a **b** fire shut 1197
36:22 *there was a fire on* the hearth **b** before him. 1197
44: 8 **b incense** unto other gods in the land of 6999
Eze 1:13 their appearance *was* like **b** coals of fire, 1197
Da 3: 6 be cast into the midst of a **b** fiery furnace. 3345
3:11 *that* he should be cast into the midst of a **b** 3345
3:15 hour into the midst of a **b** fiery furnace; 3345
3:17 able to deliver us from the **b** fiery furnace, 3345
3:20 *and* to cast *them* into the **b** fiery furnace. 3345
3:21 were cast into the midst of the **b** fiery 3345
3:23 fell down bound into the midst of the **b** 3345
3:26 near to the mouth of the **b** fiery furnace, 3345
7: 9 the fiery flame, *and* his wheels *as* **b** fire. 1815
7:11 body destroyed, and given to the **b** flame. 3346
Am 4:11 ye were as a firebrand pluckt out of the **b**: 8316
Hab 3: 5 and **b coals** went forth at his feet. 7565
Lk 12:35 loins be girded about, and *your* lights **b**; *2545*
Jn 5:35 He was a **b** and a shining light: and ye were *2545*
Jas 1:11 the sun is no sooner risen with a **b heat**, *2742*
Rev 4: 5 *there were* seven lamps of fire **b** before *2545*
8: 8 as *it were* a great mountain **b** with fire was *2545*
8:10 **b** as *it were* a lamp, and it fell upon *2545*
18: 9 when they shall see the smoke of her **b**, *4451*
18:18 cried when they saw the smoke of her **b**, *4451*
19:20 alive into a lake of fire **b** with brimstone. *2545*

BURNINGS (3) [BURN]

Isa 33:12 the people shall be *as* the **b** of lime: 4955
33:14 amongst us shall dwell *with* everlasting **b**? 4168
Jer 34: 5 with the **b** of thy fathers, the former kings 4955

BURNISHED (1)

Eze 1: 7 and they sparkled like the colour of **b** brass. 7044

BURNT (442) [BURN]

Ge 8:20 and offered **b offerings** on the altar. 5930
22: 2 offer him there for a **b offering** upon one of 5930
22: 3 clave the wood for the **b offering**, and 5930
22: 6 Abraham took the wood of the **b offering**, 5930
22: 7 but where *is* the lamb for a **b offering**? 5930
22: 8 provide himself a lamb for a **b offering**: 5930
22:13 offered him up for a **b offering** in the stead 5930
38:24 Bring her forth, and let her be **b**. 8313
Ex 3: 3 see this great sight, why the bush is not **b**. 1197
10:25 give us also sacrifices and **b offerings**, 5930
18:12 took a **b offering** and sacrifices for God: 5930
20:24 shalt sacrifice thereon thy **b offerings**, and 5930
24: 5 which offered **b offerings**, and 5930
29:18 it *is* a **b offering** unto the LORD: it *is* a 5930

Ex 29:25 burn *them* upon the altar for a **b offering**, 5930
29:42 *This shall be* a continual **b offering** 5930
30: 9 nor **b sacrifice**, nor meat offering; 5930
30:28 the altar of **b offering** with all his vessels, 5930
31: 9 the altar of **b offering** with all his furniture, 5930
32: 6 offered **b offerings**, and brought peace 5930
32:20 and **b** *it* in the fire, and ground *it* to powder, 8313
35:16 The altar of **b offering** with his brasen 5930
38: 1 he made the altar of **b offering** *of* shittim 5930
40: 6 thou shalt set the altar of the **b offering** 5930
40:10 thou shalt anoint the altar of the **b offering**, 5930
40:27 he **b** sweet incense thereon; as the LORD 6999
40:29 he put the altar of **b offering** *by* the door of 5930
40:29 offered upon it the **b offering** and the meat 5930
Lev 1: 3 If his offering *be* a **b sacrifice** of the herd, 5930
1: 4 his hand upon the head of the **b offering**; 5930
1: 6 he shall flay the **b offering**, and cut it into 5930
1: 9 *to be* a **b sacrifice**, an offering made by 5930
1:10 the sheep, or of the goats, for a **b sacrifice**; 5930
1:13 it *is* a **b sacrifice**, an offering made by fire, 5930
1:14 if the **b sacrifice** for his offering to 5930
1:17 it *is* a **b sacrifice**, an offering made by fire, 5930
2:12 they shall not be **b** on the altar for a sweet 5927
3: 5 burn it on the altar upon the **b sacrifice**, 5930
4: 7 at the bottom of the altar of the **b offering**, 5930
4:10 burn them upon the altar of the **b offering**. 5930
4:12 the ashes are poured out shall he be **b**. 8313
4:18 at the bottom of the altar of the **b offering**, 5930
4:24 they kill the **b offering** before the LORD: 5930
4:25 *it* upon the horns of the altar of **b offering**, 5930
4:25 at the bottom of the altar of **b offering**. 5930
4:29 sin offering in the place of the **b offering**. 5930
4:30 *it* upon the horns of the altar of **b offering**, 5930
4:33 in the place where they kill the **b offering**. 5930
4:34 *it* upon the horns of the altar of **b offering**, 5930
5: 7 sin offering, and the other for a **b offering**. 5930
5:10 he shall offer the second *for* a **b offering**, 5930
6: 9 This *is* the law of the **b offering**: 5930
6: 9 It *is* the **b offering**, because of the burning 5930
6:10 consumed with the **b offering** on the altar, 5930
6:12 lay the **b offering** in order upon it; 5930
6:22 ever unto the LORD; it shall be wholly **b**. 6999
6:23 shall be wholly ***b***: it shall not be eaten. NIH
6:25 In the place where the **b offering** is killed 5930
6:30 shall be eaten: it shall be **b** in the fire. 8313
7: 2 In the place where they kill the **b offering** 5930
7: 8 priest that offereth *any* man's **b offering**, 5930
7: 8 of the **b offering** which he hath offered. 5930
7:17 on the third day shall be **b** with fire. 8313
7:19 shall not be eaten; it shall be **b** with fire: 8313
7:37 This *is* the law of the **b offering**, of 5930
8:17 his dung, he **b** with fire without the camp; 8313
8:18 he brought the ram for the **b offering**: and 5930
8:20 Moses **b** the head, and the pieces, and 6999
8:21 and Moses **b** the whole ram upon the altar: 6999
8:21 it *was* a **b sacrifice** for a sweet savour, *and* 5930
8:28 **b** *them* on the altar upon the burnt offering: 6999
8:28 burnt *them* on the altar upon the **b offering**: 5930
9: 2 a ram for a **b offering**, without blemish, 5930
9: 3 without blemish, for a **b offering**; 5930
9: 7 thy **b offering**, and make an atonement for 5930
9:10 liver of the sin offering, he **b** upon the altar; 6999
9:11 the hide he **b** with fire without the camp. 8313
9:12 he slew the **b offering**; and Aaron's sons 5930
9:13 they presented the **b offering** unto him, 5930
9:13 and the head: and he **b** *them* upon the altar. 6999
9:14 **b** *them* upon the burnt offering on the altar. 6999
9:14 burnt *them* upon the **b offering** on the altar. 5930
9:16 he brought the **b offering**, and offered it 5930
9:17 a handful thereof, and **b** *it* upon the altar, 6999
9:17 beside the **b sacrifice** of the morning. 5930
9:20 the breasts, and he **b** the fat upon the altar: 6999
9:22 and the **b offering**, and peace offerings. 5930
9:24 consumed upon the altar the **b offering** and 5930
10:16 of the sin offering, and behold, it was **b**: 8313
10:19 and their **b offering** before the LORD; 5930
12: 6 a lamb of the first year for a **b offering**, 5930
12: 8 the one for the **b offering**, and the other for 5930
13:52 *is* a fretting leprosy; it shall be **b** in the fire. 8313
14:13 kill the sin offering and the **b offering**, 5930
14:19 and afterward he shall kill the **b offering**: 5930
14:20 the priest shall offer the **b offering** and 5930
14:22 a sin offering, and the other a **b offering**. 5930
14:31 the other *for* a **b offering**, with the meat 5930
15:15 sin offering, and the other *for* a **b offering**; 5930
15:30 sin offering, and the other *for* a **b offering**; 5930
16: 3 a sin offering, and a ram for a **b offering**. 5930
16: 5 a sin offering, and one ram for a **b offering**. 5930
16:24 offer his **b offering**, and the burnt offering 5930
16:24 the **b offering** of the people, and make an 5930
17: 8 that offereth a **b offering** or sacrifice, 5930
19: 6 until the third day, it shall be **b** in the fire. 8313
20:14 they shall be **b** with fire, both he and they; 8313
21: 9 her father: she shall be **b** with fire. 8313
22:18 will offer unto the LORD for a **b offering**; 5930
23:12 first year for a **b offering** unto the LORD. 5930
23:18 they shall be *for* a **b offering** unto 5930
23:37 a **b offering**, and a meat offering, 5930
Nu 6:11 the other for a **b offering**, and make an 5930
6:14 first year without blemish for a **b offering**, 5930
6:16 offer his sin offering, and his **b offering**: 5930
7:15 one lamb of the first year, for a **b offering**: 5930
7:21 one lamb of the first year, for a **b offering**: 5930
7:27 one lamb of the first year, for a **b offering**: 5930
7:33 one lamb of the first year, for a **b offering**: 5930
7:39 one lamb of the first year, for a **b offering**: 5930
7:45 one lamb of the first year, for a **b offering**: 5930
7:51 one lamb of the first year, for a **b offering**: 5930
7:57 one lamb of the first year, for a **b offering**: 5930
7:63 one lamb of the first year, for a **b offering**: 5930
7:69 one lamb of the first year, for a **b offering**: 5930
7:75 one lamb of the first year, for a **b offering**: 5930
7:81 one lamb of the first year, for a **b offering**: 5930
7:87 All the oxen for the **b offering** *were* twelve 5930
8:12 the other *for* a **b offering**, unto the LORD, 5930

Nu 10:10 with the trumpets over your **b offerings**, 5930
11: 1 the fire of the LORD **b** among them, and 1197
11: 3 the fire of the LORD **b** among them. 1197
15: 3 a **b offering**, or a sacrifice in performing a 5930
15: 5 shalt thou prepare with the **b offering** 5930
15: 8 thou preparest a bullock *for* a **b offering**, 5930
15:24 offer one young bullock for a **b offering**, 5930
16:39 wherewith they that were **b** had offered; 8313
19:17 ashes of the **b** *heifer* of purification for sin, 8316
23: 3 Stand by thy **b offering**, and I will go: 5930
23: 6 lo, *he* stood by his **b sacrifice**, he, and 5930
23:15 unto Balak, Stand here by thy **b offering**, 5930
23:17 he stood by his **b offering**, and the princes 5930
28: 3 spot day by day, *for* a continual **b offering**. 5930
28: 6 *It is* a continual **b offering**, which was 5930
28:10 *This is* the **b offering** of every sabbath, 5930
28:10 beside the continual **b offering**, and 5930
28:11 shall offer a **b offering** unto the LORD; 5930
28:13 *for* a **b offering** *of* a sweet savour, 5930
28:14 this *is* the **b offering** of every month 5930
28:15 besides the continual **b offering**, and 5930
28:19 by fire *for* a **b offering** unto the LORD; 5930
28:23 Ye shall offer these beside the **b offering** in 5930
28:23 which *is* for a continual **b offering**. 5930
28:24 be offered beside the continual **b offering**, 5930
28:27 ye shall offer the **b offering** for a sweet 5930
28:31 offer *them* besides the continual **b offering**, 5930
29: 2 ye shall offer a **b offering** for a sweet 5930
29: 6 Beside the **b offering** of the month, and 5930
29: 6 the daily **b offering**, and his meat offering, 5930
29: 8 ye shall offer a **b offering** unto the LORD 5930
29:11 the continual **b offering**, and the meat 5930
29:13 ye shall offer a **b offering**, a sacrifice made 5930
29:16 beside the continual **b offering**, his meat 5930
29:19 beside the continual **b offering**, and 5930
29:22 beside the continual **b offering**, and 5930
29:25 beside the continual **b offering**, his meat 5930
29:28 beside the continual **b offering**, and 5930
29:31 beside the continual **b offering**, his meat 5930
29:34 beside the continual **b offering**, his meat 5930
29:36 ye shall offer a **b offering**, a sacrifice made 5930
29:38 beside the continual **b offering**, and 5930
29:39 for your **b offerings**, and for your meat 5930
31:10 they **b** all their cities wherein they dwelt, 8313
Dt 4:11 the mountain **b** with fire unto the midst of 1197
9:21 **b** it with fire, and stamped it, *and* ground *it* 8313
12: 6 thither ye shall bring your **b offerings**, and 5930
12:11 your **b offerings**, and your sacrifices, 5930
12:13 **b offerings** in every place that thou seest: 5930
12:14 there thou shalt offer thy **b offerings**, and 5930
12:27 thou shalt offer thy **b offerings**, the flesh 5930
12:31 their daughters they have **b** in the fire to 8313
27: 6 thou shalt offer **b offerings** thereon unto 5930
32:24 *They shall be* **b** with hunger, and 4198
33:10 and whole ***b sacrifice*** upon thine altar. NIH
Jos 6:24 they **b** the city with fire, and all that *was* 8313
7:15 with the accursed thing shall be **b** with fire, 8313
8:28 Joshua **b** Ai, and made it a heap for ever, 8313
8:31 they offered thereon **b offerings** unto 5930
11: 9 their horses, and **b** their chariots with fire. 8313
11:11 left to breathe: and he **b** Hazor with fire. 8313
22:23 or if to offer thereon **b offering** or 5930
22:26 not for **b offering**, nor for sacrifice: 5930
22:27 LORD before him with our **b offerings**, 5930
22:28 not for **b offerings**, nor for sacrifices; 5930
22:29 to build an altar for **b offerings**, for meat 5930
Jdg 6:26 offer a **b sacrifice** with the wood of 5930
11:31 and I will offer it up *for* a **b offering**. 5930
13:16 if thou wilt offer a **b offering**, thou must 5930
13:23 he would not have received a **b offering** 5930
15: 5 **b up** both the shocks, and also the standing 1197
15: 6 came up, and **b** her and her father with fire. 8313
15:14 arms became as flax that was **b** with fire, 1197
18:27 edge of the sword, and **b** the city with fire. 8313
20:26 offered **b offerings** and peace offerings 5930
21: 4 offered **b offerings** and peace offerings. 5930
1Sa 2:15 Also before they **b** the fat, the priest's 6999
6:14 offered the kine a **b offering** unto 5930
6:15 men of Beth-shemesh offered **b offerings** 5930
7: 9 offered it *for* a **b offering** wholly unto 5930
7:10 as Samuel was offering up the **b offering**, 5930
10: 8 to offer **b offerings**, *and* to sacrifice 5930
13: 9 Bring hither a **b offering** to me, and peace 5930
13: 9 And he offered the **b offering**. 5930
13:10 had made an end of offering the **b offering**, 5930
13:12 myself therefore, and offered a **b offering**. 5930
15:22 the LORD *as great* delight in **b offerings** 5930
30: 1 and smitten Ziklag, and **b** it with fire; 8313
30: 3 to the city, and behold, *it was* **b** with fire; 8313
30:14 south of Caleb; and we **b** Ziklag with fire. 8313
31:12 and came to Jabesh, and **b** them there. 8313
2Sa 5:21 and David and his men **b** them. 5375
6:17 David offered **b offerings** and 5930
6:18 had made an end of offering **b offerings** 5930
23: 7 they shall be **utterly b** with fire in 8313+8313
24:22 *here be* oxen for **b sacrifice**, and threshing 5930
24:24 neither will I offer **b offerings** unto 5930
24:25 offered **b offerings** and peace offerings. 5930
1Ki 3: 3 he sacrificed and **b incense** in high places. 6999
3: 4 a thousand **b offerings** did Solomon offer 5930
3:15 offered up **b offerings**, and offered peace 5930
8:64 for there he offered **b offerings**, and meat 5930
8:64 *was* too little to receive the **b offerings**, 5930
9:16 **b** it with fire, and slain the Canaanites that 8313
9:25 in a year did Solomon offer **b offerings** 5930
9:25 he **b incense** upon the altar that *was* before 6999
11: 8 which **b incense** and sacrificed unto their 6999
12:33 he offered upon the altar, and **b incense**. 6999
13: 2 and men's bones shall be **b** upon thee. 8313
15:13 her idol, and **b** *it* by the brook Kidron. 8313
16:18 **b** the king's house over him with fire, and 8313
18:33 pour *it* on the **b sacrifice**, and on the wood. 5930
18:38 consumed the **b sacrifice**, and the wood, 5930
22:43 and **b incense** yet in the high places. 6999
2Ki 1:14 **b up** the two captains of the former fifties 398

2Ki 3:27 offered him *for* a **b offering** upon the wall. 5930
5:17 **b offering** nor sacrifice unto other gods, 5930
10:24 went in to offer sacrifices and **b offerings**, 5930
10:25 had made an end of offering the **b offering**, 5930
10:26 out of the house of Baal, and **b** them. 8313
12: 3 and **b incense** in the high places. 6999
14: 4 and **b incense** on the high places. 6999
15: 4 and **b incense** still on the high places. 6999
15:35 and **b incense** still in the high places. 6999
16: 4 and **b incense** in the high places, 6999
16:13 he **b** his burnt offering and his meat 6999
16:13 he burnt his **b offering** and his meat 5930
16:15 the great altar burn the morning **b offering**, 5930
16:15 the king's **b sacrifice**, and his meat 5930
16:15 with the **b offering** of all the people of 5930
16:15 upon it all the blood of the **b offering**, 5930
17:11 there they **b incense** in all the high places, 6999
17:31 the Sepharvites **b** their children in fire to 8313
22:17 and have **b incense** unto other gods, 6999
23: 4 he **b** them without Jerusalem in the fields 8313
23: 5 them also that **b incense** unto Baal, to 6999
23: 6 **b** it at the brook Kidron, and stamp *it* small 8313
23: 8 places where the priests had **b incense**, 6999
23:11 and **b** the chariots of the sun with fire. 8313
23:15 **b** the high place, *and* stamped *it* small to 8313
23:15 stamped *it* small to powder, and **b** the grove. 8313
23:16 and **b** *them* upon the altar, and polluted it, 8313
23:20 **b** men's bones upon them, and returned *to* 8313
25: 9 he **b** the house of the LORD, and 8313
25: 9 and every great *man's* house **b** he with fire. 8313
1Ch 6:49 offered upon the altar of the **b offering**, 5930
14:12 a commandment, and they were **b** with fire. 8313
16: 1 they offered **b sacrifices** and 5930
16: 2 made an end of offering the **b offerings** 5930
16:40 To offer **b offerings** unto the LORD upon 5930
16:40 altar of the **b offering** continually morning 5930
21:23 lo, I give *thee* the oxen *also* for **b offerings**, 5930
21:24 nor offer **b offerings** without cost. 5930
21:26 offered **b offerings** and peace offerings, 5930
21:26 heaven by fire upon the altar of **b offering**. 5930
21:29 and the altar of the **b offering**, 5930
22: 1 this *is* the altar of the **b offering** for Israel. 5930
23:31 to offer all **b sacrifices** unto the LORD in 5930
29:21 offered **b offerings** unto the LORD, 5930
2Ch 1: 6 and offered a thousand **b offerings** upon it. 5930
2: 4 *for* the **b offerings** morning and evening, 5930
4: 6 for the **b offering** they washed in them; 5930
7: 1 consumed the **b offering** and the sacrifices; 5930
7: 7 for there he offered **b offerings**, and the fat 5930
7: 7 was not able to receive the **b offerings**, 5930
8:12 Solomon offered **b offerings** unto 5930
13:11 every evening **b sacrifices** and 5930
15:16 stamped *it*, and **b** *it* at the brook Kidron. 8313
23:18 to offer the **b offerings** of the LORD, as it 5930
24:14 they offered **b offerings** in the house of 5930
28: 3 Moreover he **b incense** in the valley of 6999
28: 3 **b** his children in the fire after 1197
28: 4 and **b incense** in the high places, 6999
29: 7 have not **b incense** nor offered burnt 6999+7004
29: 7 **b offerings** in the holy *place* unto the God 5930
29:18 the altar of **b offering**, with all the vessels 5930
29:24 for the king commanded *that* the **b offering** 5930
29:27 to offer the **b offering** upon the altar. 5930
29:27 when the **b offering** began, the song of 5930
29:28 all *this continued* until the **b offering** was 5930
29:31 as many as were of a free heart **b offerings**. 5930
29:32 the number of the **b offerings**, which 5930
29:32 all these *were* for a **b offering** to 5930
29:34 that they could not flay all the **b offerings**: 5930
29:35 also the **b offerings** *were* in abundance, 5930
29:35 the drink offerings for *every* **b offering**. 5930
30:15 brought in the **b offerings** *into* the house of 5930
31: 2 the priests and Levites for **b offerings** and 5930
31: 3 portion of his substance for the **b offerings**, 5930
31: 3 for the morning and evening **b offerings**, 5930
31: 3 the **b offerings** for the sabbaths, and for 5930
34: 5 he **b** the bones of the priests upon their 8313
35:12 they removed the **b offerings**, that they 5930
35:14 *were busied* in offering of **b offerings** 5930
35:16 to offer **b offerings** upon the altar of 5930
36:19 they **b** the house of God, and brake down 8313
36:19 **b** all the palaces thereof with fire, and 8313
Ezr 3: 2 to offer **b offerings** thereon, 5930
3: 3 they offered **b offerings** thereon unto 5930
3: 3 *even* **b offerings** morning and evening. 5930
3: 4 *offered* the daily **b offerings** by number, 5930
3: 5 afterward *offered* the continual **b offering**, 5930
3: 6 they to offer **b offerings** unto the LORD. 5930
6: 9 for the **b offerings** of the God of heaven, 5928
8:35 offered **b offerings** unto the God of Israel, 5930
8:35 all *this was* a **b offering** unto the LORD. 5930
Ne 1: 3 and the gates thereof are **b** with fire. 3341
2:17 and the gates thereof are **b** with fire: 3341
4: 2 out of the heaps of the rubbish which are **b**? 8313
10:33 for the continual **b offering**, of 5930
Job 1: 5 offered **b offerings** *according to* 5930
1:16 hath **b up** the sheep, and the servants, and 1197
30:30 upon me, and my bones are **b** with heat. 2787
42: 8 and offer up for yourselves a **b offering**; 5930
Ps 20: 3 all thy offerings, and accept thy **b sacrifice**. 5930
40: 6 **b offering** and sin offering hast thou not 5930
50: 8 thee for thy sacrifices or thy **b offerings**, 5930
51:16 I give *it*: thou delightest not in **b offering**. 5930
51:19 with **b offering** and whole *burnt offering*: 5930
51:19 burnt offering and whole ***b offering***: then NIH
66:13 I will go *into* thy house with **b offerings**: 5930
66:15 I will offer unto thee **b sacrifices** of 5930
74: 8 they have **b up** all the synagogues of God 8313
80:16 *It is* **b** with fire, *it is* cut down: they perish 8313
102: 3 like smoke, and my bones are **b** as a hearth. 2787
106:18 their company; the flame **b up** the wicked. 3857
Pr 6:27 fire in his bosom, and his clothes not be **b**? 8313
6:28 go upon hot coals, and his feet not be **b**? 3554
Isa 1: 7 *is* desolate, your cities *are* **b** *with* fire: 8313
1:11 I am full *of* the **b offerings** of rams, and 5930

Isa 33:12 *as* thorns cut up shall they be **b** in the fire. 3341
40:16 beasts thereof sufficient *for* a **b offering**. 5930
43: 2 through the fire, thou shalt not be **b**; 3554
43:23 me the small cattle of thy **b offerings**; 5930
44:19 to say, I have **b** part of it in the fire; 8313
56: 7 their **b offerings** and their sacrifices *shall* 5930
61: 8 I hate robbery for **b offering**; 5930
64:11 our fathers praised thee, is **b up** with fire: 8316
65: 7 which have **b incense** upon the mountains, 6999
Jer 1:16 have **b incense** unto other gods, and 6999
2:15 his cities are **b** without inhabitant. 3341
6:20 your **b offerings** *are* not acceptable, 5930
6:29 The bellows are **b**, the lead is consumed of 2787
7:21 Put your **b offerings** unto your sacrifices, 5930
7:22 concerning **b offerings** or sacrifices: 5930
9:10 because they are **b up**, so that none can 3341
9:12 *and* is **b up** like a wilderness, 3341
14:12 when they offer **b offering** and an oblation, 5930
17:26 bringing **b offerings**, and sacrifices, and 5930
18:15 they have **b incense** to vanity, and 6999
19: 4 and have **b incense** in it unto other gods, 6999
19: 5 to burn their sons with fire *for* **b offerings** 5930
19:13 have **b incense** unto all the host of heaven, 6999
33:18 want a man before me to offer **b offerings**, 5930
36:27 after that the king had **b** the roll, and 8313
36:28 which Jehoiakim the king of Judah hath **b**. 8313
36:29 Thou hast **b** this roll, saying, Why hast thou 8313
36:32 Jehoiakim king of Judah had **b** in the fire: 8313
38:17 and this city shall not be **b** with fire; 8313
38:23 thou shalt **cause** this city **to be b** with fire. 8313
39: 8 the Chaldeans **b** the king's house, and 8313
44:15 their wives had **b incense** unto other gods, 6999
44:19 when we **b incense** to the queen of heaven, 6999
44:21 The incense that ye **b** in the cities of Judah, 6999
44:23 Because you have **b incense**, and because 6999
49: 2 and her daughters shall be **b** with fire: 3341
51:25 the rocks, and will make thee a **b** mountain. 8316
51:30 they have **b** her dwelling places; her bars 3341
51:32 the reeds they have **b** with fire, and the men 8313
51:58 her high gates shall be **b** with fire; 3341
52:13 **b** the house of the LORD, and the king's 8313
52:13 all the houses of the great *men*, **b** he with 8313
Eze 15: 4 both the ends of it, and the midst of it is **b**. 2787
20:47 the south to the north shall be **b** therein. 6866
24:10 and spice it well, and let the bones be **b**. 2787
40:38 where they washed the **b offering**. 5930
40:39 to slay thereon the **b offering** and the sin 5930
40:42 *were* of hewn stone for the **b offering**, 5930
40:42 wherewith they slew the **b offering** 5930
43:18 to offer **b offerings** thereon, and to sprinkle 5930
43:24 they shall offer them up *for* a **b offering** 5930
43:27 the priests shall make your **b offerings** 5930
44:11 they shall slay the **b offering** and 5930
45:15 for a **b offering**, and for peace offerings, 5930
45:17 be the prince's part *to give* **b offerings**, 5930
45:17 and the **b offering**, and the peace offerings, 5930
45:23 he shall prepare a **b offering** to the LORD, 5930
45:25 according to the **b offering**, and 5930
46: 2 the priests shall prepare his **b offering** and 5930
46: 4 the **b offering** that the prince shall offer 5930
46:12 prince shall prepare a voluntary **b offering** 5930
46:12 he shall prepare his **b offering** and his 5930
46:13 Thou shalt daily prepare a **b offering** unto 5930
46:15 every morning *for* a continual **b offering**. 5930
Hos 2:13 where*in* she **b incense** to them, and 6999
6: 6 knowledge of God more than **b offerings**. 5930
Joel 1:19 the flame hath **b** all the trees of the field. 3857
Am 2: 1 he **b** the bones of the king of Edom into 8313
5:22 Though ye offer me **b offerings** and 5930
Mic 1: 7 all the hires thereof shall be **b** with the fire, 8313
6: 6 shall I come before him with **b offerings**, 5930
Na 1: 5 the earth is **b** at his presence, yea, 5375
Mt 13:40 the tares are gathered and **b** in the fire; *2618*
22: 7 those murderers, and **b up** their city. *1714*
Mk 12:33 is more than all **whole b offerings** and *3646*
1Co 3:15 If any *man's* work shall be **b**, he shall *2618*
Heb 10: 6 In **b offerings** and *sacrifices* for sin thou *3646*
10: 8 Sacrifice and offering and **b offerings** and *3646*
13:11 high priest for sin, are **b** without the camp. *2618*
2Pe 3:10 the works that are therein shall be **b up**. *2618*
Rev 8: 7 and the third *part* of trees was **b up**, and all *2618*
8: 7 was burnt up, and all green grass was **b up**. *2618*
18: 8 famine; and she shall be **utterly b** with fire: *2618*

BURST (9) [BURSTING]

Job 32:19 no vent; it is **ready to b** like new bottles. 1234
Pr 3:10 and thy presses shall **b out** with new wine. 6555
Jer 2:20 I have broken thy yoke, *and* **b** thy bands; 5423
5: 5 broken the yoke, *and* **b** the bonds. 5423
30: 8 will **b** thy bonds, and strangers shall no 5423
Na 1:13 off thee, and will **b** thy bonds **in sunder**. 5423
Mk 2:22 else the new wine doth **b** the bottles, and *4486*
Lk 5:37 else the new wine will **b** the bottles, and *4486*
Ac 1:18 he **b asunder** in the midst, and all his *2997*

BURSTING (1) [BURST]

Isa 30:14 that there shall not be found in the **b** of it a 4386

BURY (39) [BURIAL, BURIED, BURIERS, BURYING, BURYINGPLACE]

Ge 23: 4 that I may **b** my dead out of my sight. 6912
23: 6 in the choice of our sepulchres **b** thy dead; 6912
23: 6 but that thou mayest **b** thy dead. 6912
23: 8 If it be your mind that I should **b** my dead 6912
23:11 sons of my people give I it thee: **b** thy dead. 6912
23:13 take *it* of me, and I will **b** my dead there. 6912
23:15 betwixt me and thee? **b** therefore thy dead. 6912
47:29 with me; **b** me not, I pray thee, in Egypt: 6912
47:30 of Egypt, and **b** me in their buryingplace. 6912
49:29 **b** me with my fathers in the cave that *is* in 6912
50: 5 the land of Canaan, there shalt thou **b** me. 6912
50: 5 and **b** my father, and I will come again. 6912
50: 6 Pharaoh said, Go up, and **b** thy father, 6912
50: 7 Joseph went up to **b** his father: and 6912
50:14 all that went up with him to **b** his father, 6912
Dt 21:23 shalt **in any wise b** him that day; 6912+6912
1Ki 2:31 he hath said, and fall upon him, and **b** him; 6912
11:15 of the host was gone up to **b** the slain, 6912
13:29 came to the city, to mourn and to **b** him. 6912
13:31 **b** me in the sepulchre wherein the man of 6912
14:13 all Israel shall mourn for him, and **b** him: 6912
2Ki 9:10 *there shall be* none to **b** *her*. And he opened 6912
9:34 Go, see now this cursed *woman*, and **b** her: 6912
9:35 they went to **b** her: but they found no more 6912
Ps 79: 3 and *there was* none to **b** *them*. 6912
Jer 7:32 for they shall **b** in Tophet, till there be no 6912
14:16 they *shall* have none to **b** them, them, 6912
19:11 they shall **b** *them* in Tophet, till *there be* no 6912
19:11 *them* in Tophet, till *there be* no place to **b**. 6912
Eze 39:11 there shall they **b** Gog and all his 6912
39:13 all the people of the land shall **b** *them;* and 6912
39:14 passing through the land to **b** with 6912
Hos 9: 6 gather them up, Memphis shall **b** them: 6912
Mt 8:21 Lord, suffer me first to go and **b** my father. *2290*
8:22 Follow me; and let the dead **b** their dead. *2290*
27: 7 them the potter's field, to **b** strangers in. *5027*
Lk 9:59 Lord, suffer me first to go and **b** my father. *2290*
9:60 said unto him, Let the dead **b** their dead: *2290*
Jn 19:40 as the manner of the Jews is to **b**. *1779*

BURYING (4) [BURY]

2Ki 13:21 to pass, as they were **b** a man, that behold, 6912
Eze 39:12 seven months shall the house of Israel be **b** 6912
Mk 14: 8 come aforehand to anoint my body to the **b**. *1780*
Jn 12: 7 against the day of my **b** hath she kept this. *1780*

BURYINGPLACE (7) [BURY, PLACE]

Ge 23: 4 give me a possession of a **b** with you, that I 6913
23: 9 it me for a possession of a **b** amongst you. 6913
23:20 for a possession of a **b** by the sons of Heth. 6913
47:30 me out of Egypt, and bury me in their **b**. 6900
49:30 Ephron the Hittite for a possession of a **b**. 6913
50:13 a possession of a **b** of Ephron the Hittite, 6913
Jdg 16:31 and Eshtaol in the **b** of Manoah his father. 6913

BUSH (11) [BUSHES, BUSHY]

Ex 3: 2 in a flame of fire out of the midst of a **b**: 5572
3: 2 the **b** burned with fire, and the bush was 5572
3: 2 with fire, and the **b** was not consumed. 5572
3: 3 see this great sight, why the **b** is not burnt. 5572
3: 4 called unto him out of the midst of the **b**, 5572
Dt 33:16 *for* the good will of him that dwelt in the **b**: 5572
Mk 12:26 how in the **b** God spake unto him, saying, *942*
Lk 6:44 nor of a **bramble b** gather they grapes. *942*
20:37 dead are raised, even Moses shewed at the **b**, *942*
Ac 7:30 an angel of the Lord in a flame of fire in a **b**. *942*
7:35 of the angel which appeared to him in the **b**. *942*

BUSHEL (3)

Mt 5:15 and put it under a **b**, but on a candlestick; *3426*
Mk 4:21 Is a candle brought to be put under a **b**, or *3426*
Lk 11:33 neither under a **b**, but on a candlestick, *3426*

BUSHES (3) [BUSH]

Job 30: 4 Who cut up mallows by the **b**, and 7880
30: 7 Among the **b** they brayed; under the nettles 7880
Isa 7:19 and upon all thorns, and upon all **b**. 5097

BUSHY (1) [BUSH]

SS 5:11 his locks *are* **b**, *and* black as a raven. 8534

BUSIED (1) [BUSY]

2Ch 35:14 the priests the sons of Aaron *were* **b** in NIH

BUSINESS (29) [BUSY]

Ge 39:11 that *Joseph* went into the house to do his **b**; 4399
Dt 24: 5 neither shall he be charged with any **b**: 1697
Jos 2:14 Our life for yours, if ye utter not this our **b**. 1697
2:20 if thou utter this our **b**, then we will be quit 1697
Jdg 18: 7 the Zidonians, and had no **b** with *any* man. 1697
18:28 and they had no **b** with *any* man; 1697
1Sa 20:19 didst hide thyself when the **b** was *in hand*, 4639
21: 2 The king hath commanded me a **b**, and 1697
21: 2 Let no man know any thing of the **b** 1697
21: 8 because the king's **b** required haste. 1697
1Ch 26:29 his sons *were* for the outward **b** over Israel, 4399
26:30 Jordan westward in all the **b** of the LORD, 4399
2Ch 13:10 of Aaron, and the Levites *wait* upon *their* **b**: 4399
17:13 he had much **b** in the cities of Judah: and 4399
32:31 Howbeit in *the* **b** *of* the ambassadors of NIH
Ne 11:16 had the oversight of the outward **b** of 4399
11:22 the singers *were* over the **b** of the house of 4399
13:30 and the Levites, every one in his **b**; 4399
Est 3: 9 of those that have the charge of the **b**, 4399
Ps 107:23 to the sea in ships, that do **b** in great waters; 4399
Pr 22:29 Seest thou a man diligent in his **b**? he shall 4399
Ecc 5: 3 a dream cometh through the multitude of **b**; 6045
8:16 and to see the **b** that is done upon the earth: 6045
Da 8:27 afterward I rose up, and did the king's **b**; 4399
Lk 2:49 ye not that I must be about my Father's **b**? NIG
Ac 6: 3 wisdom, whom we may appoint over this **b**. *5532*
Ro 12:11 Not slothful in **b**; fervent in spirit; *4710*
16: 2 *that* ye assist her in whatsoever **b** she hath *4229*
1Th 4:11 and to do your own **b**, and to work with NIG

BUSY (1) [BUSIED, BUSINESS, BUSYBODIES, BUSYBODY]

1Ki 20:40 as thy servant was **b** here and there, he was 6213

BUSYBODIES (2) [BUSY, BODY]

2Th 3:11 working not at all, but are **b**. *4020*
1Ti 5:13 and not only idle, but tattlers also and **b**, *4021*

BUSYBODY (1) [BUSY, BODY]

1Pe 4:15 or as a **b in other men's matters**. *244*

BUT (3994) See Index of Articles, Etc.

BUTLER (8) [BUTLERS, BUTLERSHIP]

Ge 40: 1 *that* the **b** of the king of Egypt and *his* 8248
40: 5 the **b** and the baker of the king of Egypt, 8248
40: 9 the chief **b** told his dream to Joseph, and 8248
40:13 the former manner when thou wast his **b**. 8248
40:20 he lifted up the head of the chief **b** and of 8248
40:21 he restored the chief **b** unto his butlership 8248
40:23 Yet did not the chief **b** remember Joseph, 8248
41: 9 spake the chief **b** unto Pharaoh, saying, 8248

BUTLERS (1) [BUTLER]

Ge 40: 2 against the chief of the **b**, and against 8248

BUTLERSHIP (1) [BUTLER]

Ge 40:21 he restored the chief butler unto his **b** 4945

BUTTER (11)

Ge 18: 8 he took **b**, and milk, and the calf which he 2529
Dt 32:14 **B** of kine, and milk of sheep, with fat of 2529
Jdg 5:25 she brought forth **b** in a lordly dish. 2529
2Sa 17:29 **b**, and sheep, and cheese of kine, for David, 2529
Job 20:17 the floods, the brooks of honey and **b**. 2529
29: 6 When *I* washed my steps with **b**, and 2529
Ps 55:21 *words of* his mouth were smoother than **b**, 4260
Pr 30:33 the churning of milk bringeth forth **b**, 2529
Isa 7:15 **B** and honey shall he eat, that he may know 2529
7:22 of milk *that they* shall give he shall eat **b**: 2529
7:22 for **b** and honey shall every one eat that is 2529

BUTTOCKS (3)

2Sa 10: 4 *even* to their **b**, and sent them away. 8357
1Ch 19: 4 their garments in the midst hard by *their* **b**, 4667
Isa 20: 4 and barefoot, even with *their* **b** uncovered, 8357

BUY (56) [BOUGHT, BUYER, BUYEST, BUYETH]

Ge 41:57 came into Egypt to Joseph for to **b** *corn;* 7666
42: 2 you down thither, and **b** for us from thence; 7666
42: 3 Joseph's ten brethren went down to **b** corn 7666
42: 5 the sons of Israel came to **b** *corn* among 7666
42: 7 From the land of Canaan to **b** food. 7666
42:10 but to **b** food are thy servants come. 7666
43: 2 said unto them, Go again, **b** us a little food. 7666
43: 4 with us, we will go down and **b** thee food: 7666
43:20 we came indeed down at the first time to **b** 7666
43:22 we brought down in our hands to **b** food: 7666
44:25 father said, Go again, *and* **b** us a little food. 7666
47:19 **b** us and our land for bread, and we and 7069
Ex 21: 2 If thou **b** a Hebrew servant, six years he 7069
Lev 22:11 if the priest **b** *any* soul with his 7069+7075
25:15 the jubile thou shalt **b** of thy neighbour, 7069
25:44 of them shall ye **b** bondmen and 7069
25:45 of them shall ye **b**, and of their families that 7069
Dt 2: 6 Ye shall **b** meat of them for money, that ye 7666
2: 6 ye shall also **b** water of them for money, 3739
28:68 and bondwomen, and no man shall **b** *you*. 7069
Ru 4: 4 **B** *it* before the inhabitants, and before 7069
4: 5 thou must **b** *it* also of Ruth the Moabitess, 7069
4: 8 the kinsman said unto Boaz, **B** *it* for thee. 7069
2Sa 24:21 David said, To **b** the threshingfloor of thee, 7069
24:24 I will **surely b** *it* of thee at a price: 7069+7069
2Ki 12:12 to **b** timber and hewed stone to repair 7069
22: 6 to **b** timber and hewn stone to repair 7069
1Ch 21:24 I will **verily b** *it* for the full price: 7069+7069
2Ch 34:11 and builders gave they *it*, to **b** hewn stone, 7069
Ezr 7:17 That thou mayest **b** speedily with this 7066
Ne 5: 3 houses, that we might **b** corn, because 3947
10:31 *that* we would not **b** *it* of them on 3947
Pr 23:23 **B** the truth, and sell *it* not; *also* wisdom, 7069
Isa 55: 1 come ye, **b**, and eat; yea, come, buy wine 7666
55: 1 **b** wine and milk without money and 7666
Jer 32: 7 **B** thee my field that *is* in Anathoth: 7069
32: 7 for the right of redemption *is* thine to **b** *it*. 7069
32: 8 said unto me, **B** my field, I pray thee, that *is* 7069
32: 8 and the redemption *is* thine; **b** *it* for thyself. 7069
32:25 **B** thee the field for money, and 7069
32:44 *Men* shall **b** fields for money, and 7069
Am 8: 6 That *we* may **b** the poor for silver, and 7069
Mt 14:15 into the villages, and **b** themselves victuals. *59*
25: 9 rather to them that sell, and **b** for yourselves. *59*
25:10 And while they went to **b**, the bridegroom *59*
Mk 6:36 and *into* the villages, and **b** themselves bread: *59*
6:37 and **b** two hundred pennyworth of bread, *59*
Lk 9:13 we should go and **b** meat for all this people. *59*
22:36 no sword, let him sell his garment, and **b** one. *59*
Jn 4: 8 were gone away unto the city to **b** meat.) *59*
6: 5 Whence shall we **b** bread, that these may eat? *59*
13:29 **B** *those things* that we have need of against *59*
1Co 7:30 and they that **b**, as though they possessed not; *59*
Jas 4:13 there a year, and **b and sell**, and get gain: *1710*
Rev 3:18 I counsel thee to **b** of me gold tried in the fire, *59*
13:17 And that no *man* might **b** or sell, save he that *59*

BUYER (3) [BUY]

Pr 20:14 *It is* naught, *it is* naught, saith the **b**: but 7069
Isa 24: 2 as *with* the **b**, so *with* the seller; 7069
Eze 7:12 let not the **b** rejoice, nor the seller mourn: 7069

BUYEST (2) [BUY]

Lev 25:14 or **b** *ought* of thy neighbour's hand, ye shall 7069
Ru 4: 5 What day thou **b** the field of the hand of 7069

BUYETH (3) [BUY]

Pr 31:16 She considereth a field, and **b** it: with 3947
Mt 13:44 and selleth all that he hath, and **b** that field. *59*
Rev 18:11 for no *man* **b** their merchandise any more: *59*

BUZ (3)

Ge 22:21 **B** his brother, and Kemuel the father of 938
1Ch 5:14 of Jeshishai, the son of Jahdo, the son of **B**; 938
Jer 25:23 and **B**, and all *that are* in the utmost corners, 938

BUZI (1)
Eze 1: 3 the son of **B**, in the land of the Chaldeans by 941

BUZITE (2)
Job 32: 2 the wrath of Elihu the son of Barachel the **B**, 940
32: 6 Elihu the son of Barachel the **B** answered 940

BY (2633) [HEREBY, THEREBY, WHEREBY] See Index of Articles, Etc.

BYWAYS (1) [WAY]
Jdg 5: 6 and the travellers walked *through* **b**. 734+6128

BYWORD (6) [WORD]
Dt 28:37 an astonishment, a proverb, and a **b**, 8148
1Ki 9: 7 be a proverb and a **b** among all people: 8148
2Ch 7:20 to be a proverb and a **b** among all nations. 8148
Job 17: 6 He hath made me also a **b** of the people; 4914
30: 9 And now am I their song, yea, I am their **b**. 4405
Ps 44:14 Thou makest us a **b** among the heathen, 4912

C

CABBON (1)
Jos 15:40 And **C**, and Lahmam, and Kithlish, 3522

CABINS (1)
Jer 37:16 into the **c**, and Jeremiah had remained there 2588

CABUL (2)
Jos 19:27 Neiel, and goeth out to **C** on the left hand, 3521
1Ki 9:13 he called them the land of **C** unto this day. 3521

CAESAR; CAESAR'S See CESAR; CESAR'S

CAESAREA See CESAREA

CAGE (2)
Jer 5:27 As a **c** *is* full *of* birds, so *are* their houses 3619
Rev 18: 2 and a **c** of every unclean and hateful bird. *5438*

CAIAPHAS (9)
Mt 26: 3 palace of the high priest, who was called **C**, *2533*
26:57 on Jesus led *him* away to **C** the high priest, *2533*
Lk 3: 2 Annas and **C** being the high priests, *2533*
Jn 11:49 And one of them, *named* **C**, being the high *2533*
18:13 for he was father in law to **C**, which was *2533*
18:14 Now **C** was he, which gave counsel to *2533*
18:24 Now Annas had sent him bound unto **C** *2533*
18:28 Then led they Jesus from **C** unto the hall of *2533*
Ac 4: 6 and **C**, and John, and Alexander, and *2533*

CAIN (20)
Ge 4: 1 she conceived, and bare **C**, and said, I have 7014
4: 2 of sheep, but **C** was a tiller of the ground. 7014
4: 3 that **C** brought of the fruit of the ground an 7014
4: 5 unto **C** and to his offering he had not 7014
4: 5 **C** was very wroth, and his countenance fell. 7014
4: 6 the LORD said unto **C**, Why art thou 7014
4: 8 **C** talked with Abel his brother: and it came 7014
4: 8 that **C** rose up against Abel his brother, and 7014
4: 9 the LORD said unto **C**, Where *is* Abel thy 7014
4:13 **C** said unto the LORD, My punishment *is* 7014
4:15 unto him, Therefore whosoever slayeth **C**, 7014
4:15 the LORD set a mark upon **C**, lest any 7014
4:16 **C** went out from the presence of 7014
4:17 **C** knew his wife; and she conceived, and 7014
4:24 If **C** shall be avenged sevenfold, 7014
4:25 seed instead of Abel, whom **C** slew. 7014
Jos 15:57 **C**, Gibeah, and Timnah; ten cities with 7014
Heb 11: 4 unto God a more excellent sacrifice than **C**, *2535*
1Jn 3:12 Not as **C**, *who* was of *that* wicked one, and *2535*
Jude 1:11 for they have gone in the way of **C**, and *2535*

CAINAN (7)
Ge 5: 9 And Enos lived ninety years, and begat **C**: 7018
5:10 Enos lived after he begat **C** eight hundred 7018
5:12 **C** lived seventy years, and 7018
5:13 **C** lived after he begat Mahalaleel eight 7018
5:14 all the days of **C** were nine hundred 7018
Lk 3:36 Which was *the son* of **C**, which was *the son* *2536*
3:37 *son* of Maleleel, which was *the son* of **C**, *2536*

CAKE (13) [CAKES]
Ex 29:23 one **c** of oiled bread, and one wafer out of 2471
Lev 8:26 he took one unleavened **c**, and a cake of 2471
8:26 a **c** of oiled bread, and one wafer, and 2471
24: 5 two tenth deals shall be *in* one **c**. 2471
Nu 6:19 one unleavened **c** out of the basket, and 2471
15:20 Ye shall offer up a **c** *of* the first of your 2471
Jdg 7:13 a **c** of barley bread tumbled into the host of 6742
1Sa 30:12 they gave him a piece of a **c** *of figs*, and 1690
2Sa 6:19 to every one a **c** of bread, and a good piece 2471
1Ki 17:12 I have not a **c**, but a handful of meal in a 4580
17:13 make me thereof a little **c** first, and bring *it* 5692
19: 6 *there was* a **c** baken on the coals, and 5692
Hos 7: 8 the people; Ephraim is a **c** not turned. 5692

CAKES (25) [CAKE]
Ge 18: 6 knead *it*, and make **c** upon the hearth. 5692
Ex 12:39 they baked unleavened **c** of the dough 5692
29: 2 **c** unleavened tempered with oil, and 2471
Lev 2: 4 *it shall be* unleavened **c** of fine flour 2471
7:12 unleavened **c** mingled with oil, 2471
7:12 and **c** mingled with oil, of fine flour, fried. 2471
7:13 Besides the **c**, he shall offer *for* his offering 2471
24: 5 take fine flour, and bake twelve **c** thereof: 2471
Nu 6:15 **c** *of* fine flour mingled with oil, and 2471
11: 8 and baked *it* in pans, and made **c** *of* it: 5692
Jos 5:11 unleavened **c**, and parched *corn* in NIH
Jdg 6:19 and unleavened **c** *of* an ephah of flour: NIH
6:20 Take the flesh and the unleavened **c**, and NIH
6:21 touched the flesh and the unleavened **c**; and NIH
6:21 the unleavened **c**. Then the angel of NIH
1Sa 25:18 two hundred **c** *of figs*, and laid *them* on 1690
2Sa 13: 6 **make** *me* a couple of **c** in my sight, 3823+3834
13: 8 kneaded *it*, and **made c** in his sight, and 3823
13: 8 made cakes in his sight, and did bake the **c**. 3834
13:10 Tamar took the **c** which she had made, and 3834
1Ch 12:40 **c** *of figs*, and bunches of raisins, and wine, 1690
23:29 for the unleavened **c**, and for *that which is* 7550
Jer 7:18 to make **c** to the queen of heaven, and 3561
44:19 did we make her **c** to worship her, and 3561
Eze 4:12 thou shalt eat it *as* barley **c**, and thou shalt 5692

CALAH (2)
Ge 10:11 and the city Rehoboth, and **C**, 3625
10:12 Resen between Nineveh and **C**: the same *is* 3625

CALAMITIES (3) [CALAMITY]
Ps 57: 1 I make my refuge, until *these* **c** be overpast. 1942
141: 5 for yet my prayer also *shall be* in their **c**. 7451
Pr 17: 5 he that is glad at **c** shall not be unpunished. 343

CALAMITY (19) [CALAMITIES]
Dt 32:35 for the day of their **c** *is* at hand, and 343
2Sa 22:19 They prevented me in the day of my **c**: but 343
Job 6: 2 my **c** laid in the balances together! 1942
30:13 They mar my path, they set forward my **c**, 1942
Ps 18:18 They prevented me in the day of my **c**: but 343
Pr 1:26 I also will laugh at your **c**; I will mock when 343
6:15 Therefore shall his **c** come suddenly; 343
19:13 A foolish son *is* the **c** of his father: and 1942
24:22 For their **c** shall rise suddenly; and 343
27:10 *into* thy brother's house in the day of thy **c**: 343
Jer 18:17 and not the face, in the day of their **c**. 343
46:21 the day of their **c** was come upon them, 343
48:16 The **c** of Moab *is* near to come, and 343
49: 8 for I will bring the **c** of Esau upon him, 343
49:32 and I will bring their **c** from all sides thereof, 343
Eze 35: 5 the force of the sword in the time of their **c**, 343
Ob 1:13 the gate of my people in the day of their **c**: 343
1:13 on their affliction in the day of their **c**, 343
1:13 on their substance in the day of their **c**; 343

CALAMUS (3)
Ex 30:23 and of sweet **c** two hundred and 7070
SS 4:14 **c** and cinnamon, with all trees of 7070
Eze 27:19 bright iron, cassia, and **c**, were in thy 7070

CALCOL (1) [CHALCOL]
1Ch 2: 6 and Ethan, and Heman, and **C**, and Dara: 3633

CALDRON (6) [CALDRONS]
1Sa 2:14 *it* into the pan, or kettle, or **c**, or pot; 7037
Job 41:20 goeth smoke, as *out of* a seething pot or **c**. 100
Eze 11: 3 this *city is* the **c**, and we *be* the flesh. 5518
11: 7 they *are* the flesh, and this *city is* the **c**: 5518
11:11 This *city* shall not be your **c**, neither shall 5518
Mic 3: 3 as for the pot, and as flesh within the **c**. 7037

CALDRONS (3) [CALDRON]
2Ch 35:13 in **c**, and in pans, and divided *them* speedily 1731
Jer 52:18 The **c** also, and the shovels, and 5518
52:19 the **c**, and the candlesticks, and the spoons, 5518

CALEB (32) [CALEB'S, CALEB-EPHRATAH]
Nu 13: 6 the tribe of Judah, **C** the son of Jephunneh. 3612
13:30 **C** stilled the people before Moses, and said, 3612
14: 6 son of Nun, and **C** the son of Jephunneh, 3612
14:24 my servant **C**, because he had another spirit 3612
14:30 save **C** the son of Jephunneh, and 3612
14:38 son of Nun, and **C** the son of Jephunneh, 3612
26:65 save **C** the son of Jephunneh, and 3612
32:12 Save **C** the son of Jephunneh the Kenezite, 3612
34:19 the tribe of Judah, **C** the son of Jephunneh. 3612
Dt 1:36 Save **C** the son of Jephunneh, he shall see 3612
Jos 14: 6 **C** the son of Jephunneh the Kenezite said 3612
14:13 gave unto **C** the son of Jephunneh Hebron 3612
14:14 became the inheritance of **C** the son of 3612
15:13 unto **C** the son of Jephunneh he gave a part 3612
15:14 And **C** drove thence the three sons of Anak, 3612
15:16 **C** said, He that smiteth Kirjath-sepher, and 3612
15:17 the son of Kenaz, the brother of **C**, took it: 3612
15:18 and **C** said unto her, What wouldest thou? 3612
21:12 gave they to **C** the son of Jephunneh for his 3612
Jdg 1:12 **C** said, He that smiteth Kirjath-sepher, and 3612
1:14 and **C** said unto her, What wilt thou? 3612
1:15 **C** gave her the upper springs and the nether 3612
1:20 they gave Hebron unto **C**, as Moses said: 3612
1Sa 25: 3 his doings; and he *was* **of the house of C**. 3614
30:14 to Judah, and upon the south of **C**; 3612
1Ch 2:18 **C** the son of Hezron begat *children* of 3612
2:19 **C** took unto him Ephrath, which bare him 3612
2:42 Now the sons of **C** the brother of Jerahmeel 3612
2:49 and the daughter of **C** *was* Achsah. 3612
2:50 These were the sons of **C** the son of Hur, 3612
4:15 the sons of **C** the son of Jephunneh; Iru, 3612
6:56 they gave to **C** the son of Jephunneh. 3612

CALEB'S (4) [CALEB]
Jdg 1:13 son of Kenaz, **C** younger brother, took it: 3612
3: 9 the son of Kenaz, **C** younger brother. 3612
1Ch 2:46 **C** concubine, bare Haran, and Moza, and 3612
2:48 Maachah, **C** concubine, bare Sheber, and 3612

CALEB-EPHRATAH (1) [CALEB, EPHRATAH]
1Ch 2:24 after that Hezron was dead in **C**, then 3613

CALF (29) [CALF'S, CALVE, CALVED, CALVES, CALVETH]
Ge 18: 7 fetcht a **c** tender and good, and 1121+1241
18: 8 the **c** which he had dressed, and set *it* 1121+1241
Ex 32: 4 after he had made it a molten **c**: 5695
32: 8 they have made them a molten **c**, and 5695
32:19 that he saw the **c**, and the dancing: 5695
32:20 he took the **c** which they had made, and 5695
32:24 it into the fire, and there came out this **c**. 5695
32:35 because they made the **c**, which Aaron 5695
Lev 9: 2 Take thee a young **c** for a sin 1241+5695
9: 3 a **c** and a lamb, both of the first year, 5695
9: 8 the altar, and slew the **c** of the sin offering, 5695
Dt 9:16 your God, *and* had made you a molten **c**: 5695
9:21 the **c** which ye had made, and burnt it with 5695
1Sa 28:24 the woman had a fat **c** in the house; and 5695
Ne 9:18 when they had made them a molten **c**, and 5695
Job 21:10 their cow calveth, and **casteth** not **her c**. 7921
Ps 29: 6 He maketh them also to skip like a **c**; 5695
106:19 They made a **c** in Horeb, and 5695
Isa 11: 6 the **c** and the young lion and the fatling 5695
27:10 there shall the **c** feed, and there shall he lie 5695
Jer 34:18 when they cut the **c** in twain, and 5695
34:19 which passed between the parts of the **c**; 5695
Hos 8: 5 Thy **c**, O Samaria, hath cast *thee* off; 5695
8: 6 the **c** of Samaria shall be broken in pieces. 5695
Lk 15:23 And bring hither the fatted **c**, and kill *it*; *3448*
15:27 and thy father hath killed the fatted **c**, *3448*
15:30 thou hast killed for him the fatted **c**. *3448*
Ac 7:41 And they **made a c** in those days, and *3447*
Rev 4: 7 and the second beast like a **c**, and the third *3448*

CALF'S (1) [CALF]
Eze 1: 7 the sole of their feet *was* like the sole of a **c** 5695

CALKERS (2)
Eze 27: 9 wise *men* thereof were in thee thy **c**: 919+2388
27:27 thy **c**, and the occupiers of thy 919+2388

CALL (196) [CALLED, CALLEDST, CALLEST, CALLETH, CALLING]
Ge 2:19 unto Adam to see what he would **c** them: 7121
4:26 began *men* to **c** upon the name of 7121
16:11 bear a son, and shalt **c** his name Ishmael; 7121
17:15 thou shalt not **c** her name Sarai, but 7121
17:19 son indeed; and thou shalt **c** his name Isaac: 7121
24:57 We will **c** the damsel, and inquire at her 7121
30:13 am I, for the daughters will **c** me **blessed**: 833
46:33 when Pharaoh shall **c** you, and shall say, 7121
Ex 2: 7 **c** to thee a nurse of the Hebrew women, 7121
2:20 left the man? **c** him, that he may eat bread. 7121
34:15 and *one* **c** thee, and thou eat of his sacrifice; 7121
Nu 16:12 Moses sent to **c** Dathan and Abiram, 7121
22: 5 to **c** him, saying, Behold, there is a people 7121
22:20 If the men come to **c** thee, rise up, *and* 7121
22:37 Did I not earnestly send unto thee to **c** thee? 7121
Dt 2:11 but the Moabites **c** them Emims. 7121
2:20 and the Ammonites **c** them Zamzummims; 7121
3: 9 (*Which* Hermon the Sidonians **c** Sirion; and 7121
3: 9 call Sirion; and the Amorites **c** it Shenir;) 7121
4: 7 *is* in all *things that* we **c** upon him *for*? 7121
4:26 I **c** heaven and earth **to witness** against you 5749
25: 8 the elders of his city shall **c** him, and 7121
30: 1 thou shalt **c** *them* to mind among all 7725
30:19 I **c** heaven and earth **to record** *this* day 5749
31:14 **c** Joshua, and present yourselves in 7121
31:28 **c** heaven and earth **to record** against them. 5749
33:19 They shall **c** the people *unto* the mountain; 7121
Jdg 12: 1 and didst not **c** us to go with thee? 7121
16:25 that they said, **C** for Samson, that he may 7121
21:13 and to **c** peaceably unto them. 7121
Ru 1:20 unto them, **C** me not Naomi, call me Mara: 7121
1:20 unto them, Call me not Naomi, **c** me Mara: 7121
1:21 why *then* **c** ye me Naomi, seeing 7121
1Sa 3: 6 and said, Here *am* I; for thou didst **c** me. 7121
3: 8 and said, Here *am* I; for thou didst **c** me. 7121
3: 9 it shall be, if he **c** thee, that thou shalt say, 7121
12:17 I will **c** unto the LORD, and he shall send 7121
16: 3 **c** Jesse to the sacrifice, and I will shew thee 7121
22:11 the king sent to **c** Ahimelech the priest, 7121
2Sa 17: 5 **C** now Hushai the Archite also, and let us 7121
22: 4 I will **c on** the LORD, who is *worthy* to be 7121
1Ki 1:28 and said, **C** me Bath-sheba. 7121
1:32 **C** me Zadok the priest, and Nathan 7121
8:52 to hearken unto them in all that they **c for** 7121
17:18 unto me to **c** my sin **to remembrance**, 2142
18:24 **c** ye on the name of your gods, and I will 7121
18:24 and I will **c** on the name of the LORD: 7121
18:25 **c** on the name of your gods, but put no fire 7121
22:13 the messenger that was gone to **c** Micaiah 7121
2Ki 4:12 to Gehazi his servant, **C** this Shunammite. 7121
4:15 he said, **C** her. And when he had called her, 7121
4:36 and said, **C** this Shunammite. 7121
5:11 **c** on the name of the LORD his God, and 7121
10:19 **c** unto me all the prophets of Baal, 7121
1Ch 16: 8 thanks unto the LORD, **c** upon his name, 7121
2Ch 18:12 the messenger that went to **c** Micaiah spake 7121
Job 5: 1 **C** now, if there be *any* that will answer 7121
13:22 **c** thou, and I will answer: or let me speak, 7121
14:15 Thou shalt **c**, and I will answer thee: 7121
27:10 the Almighty? will he always **c upon** God? 7121
Ps 4: 1 Hear me when I **c**, O God of my 7121
4: 3 the LORD will hear when I **c** unto him. 7121
14: 4 they eat bread, *and* **c** not **upon** the LORD. 7121
18: 3 I will **c upon** the LORD, who is *worthy* to 7121
20: 9 LORD: let the king hear us when we **c**. 7121
49:11 they **c** *their* lands after their own names. 7121
50: 4 He shall **c** to the heavens from above, and 7121
50:15 **c upon** me in the day of trouble: I will 7121
55:16 *As for* me, I will **c** upon God; and 7121
72:17 in him: all nations shall **c** him **blessed**. 833

Ps 77: 6 I **c to remembrance** my song in the night: 2142
80:18 quicken us, and we will **c** upon thy name. 7121
86: 5 in mercy unto all them that **c upon** thee. 7121
86: 7 In the day of my trouble I will **c upon** thee: 7121
91:15 He shall **c upon** me, and I will answer him: 7121
99: 6 Samuel among them that **c upon** his name; 7121
102: 2 in the day *when* I **c** answer me speedily. 7121
105: 1 thanks unto the LORD; **c** upon his name: 7121
116: 2 will I **c upon** *him* as long as I live. 7121
116:13 and **c** upon the name of the LORD. 7121
116:17 and will **c** upon the name of the LORD. 7121
145:18 *is* nigh unto all them that **c upon** him, 7121
145:18 upon him, to all that **c upon** him in truth. 7121
Pr 1:28 shall they **c upon** me, but I will not answer; 7121
7: 4 and **c** understanding *thy* kinswoman: 7121
8: 4 Unto you, O men, I **c**; and my voice *is* to 7121
9:15 To **c** passengers who go right *on* their 7121
31:28 Her children arise up, and **c** her **blessed**; 833
Isa 5:20 Woe unto them that **c** evil good, and good 559
7:14 bear a Son, and shall **c** his name Immanuel. 7121
8: 3 to me, **C** his name Maher-shalal-hash-baz. 7121
12: 4 Praise the LORD, **c** upon his name, 7121
22:12 in that day did the Lord GOD of hosts **c** to 7121
22:20 that I will **c** my servant Eliakim the son of 7121
31: 2 bring evil, and will not **c back** his words: 5493
34:12 They shall **c** the nobles thereof *to* 7121
41:25 from the rising of the sun shall he **c** upon 7121
44: 5 another shall **c** *himself* by the name of 7121
44: 7 shall **c**, and shall declare it, and set it in 7121
45: 3 the LORD, which **c** *thee* by thy name, 7121
48: 2 For they **c** themselves of the holy city, and 7121
48:13 *when* I **c** unto them, they stand *up* together. 7121
55: 5 thou shalt **c** a nation *that* thou knowest not, 7121
55: 6 be found, **c** ye **upon** him while he is near: 7121
58: 5 and ashes *under him?* wilt thou **c** this a fast, 7121
58: 9 shalt thou **c**, and the LORD shall answer; 7121
58:13 **c** the sabbath a delight, the holy of 7121
60:14 they shall **c** thee, The city of the LORD, 7121
60:18 thou shalt **c** thy walls Salvation, and 7121
61: 6 *men* shall **c** you the Ministers of our God: 559
62:12 they shall **c** them, The holy people, 7121
65:15 and **c** his servants by another name: 7121
65:24 to pass, that before they **c**, I will answer; 7121
Jer 1:15 I will **c** all the families of the kingdoms of 7121
3:17 At that time they shall **c** Jerusalem 7121
3:19 I said, Thou shalt **c** me, My father; and 7121
6:30 Reprobate silver shall *men* **c** them, because 7121
7:27 thou shalt also **c** unto them; but they will 7121
9:17 **c** for the mourning *women*, that they may 7121
10:25 upon the families that **c** not on thy name: 7121
25:29 for I *will* **c** for a sword upon all 7121
29:12 shall ye **c upon** me, and ye shall go and 7121
33: 3 **C** unto me, and I will answer thee, and 7121
50:29 **C together** the archers against Babylon: 8085
51:27 **c together** against her the kingdoms of 8085
La 2:15 *saying, Is* this the city that *men* **c** The 559
Eze 21:23 he will **c to remembrance** the iniquity, 2142
36:29 I will **c** for the corn, and will increase it, 7121
38:21 I will **c** *for* a sword against him throughout 7121
39:11 they shall **c** *it* The valley of Hamon-gog. 7121
Da 2: 2 the king commanded to **c** the magicians, 7121
Hos 1: 4 LORD said unto him, **C** his name Jezreel; 7121
1: 6 said unto him, **C** her name Lo-ruhamah: 7121
1: 9 said *God,* **C** his name Lo-ammi: for ye *are* 7121
2:16 saith the LORD, *that* thou shalt **c** *me* Ishi; 7121
2:16 call *me* Ishi; and shalt **c** me no more Baali. 7121
7:11 they **c** to Egypt, they go *to* Assyria. 7121
Joel 1:14 **c** a solemn assembly, gather the elders *and* 7121
2:15 sanctify a fast, **c** a solemn assembly: 7121
2:32 *that* whosoever shall **c** on the name of 7121
2:32 in the remnant whom the LORD *shall* **c**. 7121
Am 5:16 they shall **c** the husbandman to mourning, 7121
Jnh 1: 6 **c** upon thy God, if so be that God will think 7121
Zep 3: 9 that they may all **c** upon the name of 7121
Zec 3:10 shall ye **c** every man his neighbour, under 7121
13: 9 they shall **c** on my name, and I will hear 7121
Mal 1: 4 they shall **c** them, The border of 7121
3:12 all nations shall **c** you **blessed**: for ye shall 833
3:15 now we **c** the proud **happy**; yea, they that 833
Mt 1:21 a son, and thou shalt **c** his name JESUS: *2564*
1:23 a son, and they shall **c** his name Emmanuel, *2564*
9:13 for I am not come to **c** *the* righteous, but *2564*
10:25 how much more *shall they* **c** them of his NIG
20: 8 **C** the labourers, and give them *their* hire, *2564*
22: 3 And sent forth his servants to **c** them that *2564*
22:43 How then doth David in spirit **c** him Lord, *2564*
22:45 If David then **c** him Lord, how is he his *2564*
23: 9 And **c** no *man* your father upon the earth: *2564*
Mk 2:17 I came not to **c** *the* righteous, but sinners to *2564*
10:49 And they **c** the blind man, saying unto him, *5455*
15:12 *that* I shall do *unto him* whom ye **c** *3004*
15:16 and they **c together** the whole band. *4779*
Lk 1:13 thee a son, and thou shalt **c** his name John. *2564*
1:31 forth a son, and shalt **c** his name JESUS. *2564*
1:48 all generations shall **c** me **blessed**. *3106*
5:32 I came not to **c** *the* righteous, but sinners to *2564*
6:46 And why **c** ye me, Lord, Lord, and do not *2564*
14:12 a dinner or a supper, **c** not thy friends, *5455*
14:13 **c** the poor, the maimed, the lame, the blind: *2564*
Jn 4:16 Go, **c** thy husband, and come hither. *5455*
13:13 Ye **c** me Master and Lord: and ye say well; *5455*
15:15 Henceforth I **c** you not servants; for *3004*
Ac 2:21 *that* whosoever shall **c on** the name of *1941*
2:39 *even* as many as the Lord our God shall **c**. *4341*
9:14 chief priests to bind all that **c on** thy name. *1941*
10: 5 and **c for** *one* Simon, whose surname is *3343*
10:15 hath cleansed, *that* **c** not thou **common**. *2840*
10:28 God hath shewed me that *I* should not **c** any *3004*
10:32 therefore to Joppa, and **c hither** Simon, *3333*
11: 9 hath cleansed, *that* **c** not thou **common**. *2840*
11:13 Send men to Joppa, and **c for** Simon, *3343*
19:13 took upon them to **c** over them which had *3687*
24:14 that after the way which they **c** heresy, so *3004*
24:25 have a convenient season, I will **c for** thee. *3333*
Ro 9:25 saith also in Osee, I will **c** *them* my people, *2564*
Ro 10:12 over all *is* rich unto all that **c upon** him. *1941*
10:13 For whosoever shall **c upon** the name of *1941*
10:14 shall they **c on** *him* in whom they have not *1941*
1Co 1: 2 with all that in every place **c upon** *1941*
2Co 1:23 Moreover I **c** God **for** a record upon my *1941*
2Ti 1: 5 When I **c** to remembrance the unfeigned *2983*
2:22 with them that **c on** the Lord out of a pure *1941*
Heb 2:11 for which cause he is not ashamed to **c** *2564*
10:32 But **c to remembrance** the former days, *363*
Jas 5:14 let him **c for** the elders of the church; and *4341*
1Pe 1:17 And if ye **c on** the Father, who without *1941*

CALLED (623) [CALL]

Ge 1: 5 God **c** the light Day, and the darkness he 7121
1: 5 the light Day, and the darkness he **c** Night. 7121
1: 8 God **c** the firmament Heaven. And 7121
1:10 God **c** the dry *land* Earth; and the gathering 7121
1:10 the gathering together of the waters **c** he 7121
2:19 whatsoever Adam **c** every living creature, 7121
2:23 she shall be **c** Woman, because she was 7121
3: 9 the LORD God **c** unto Adam, and 7121
3:20 Adam **c** his wife's name Eve; because 7121
4:17 builded a city, and **c** the name of the city, 7121
4:25 she bare a son, and **c** his name Seth: 7121
4:26 he **c** his name Enos; then began *men* to call 7121
5: 2 blessed them, and **c** their name Adam, 7121
5: 3 after his image; and **c** his name Seth: 7121
5:29 he **c** his name Noah, saying, This *same* 7121
11: 9 Therefore is the name of it **c** Babel; 7121
12: 8 and **c** upon the name of the LORD. 7121
12:18 Pharaoh **c** Abram, and said, What *is* this 7121
13: 4 there Abram **c** on the name of the LORD. 7121
16:13 she **c** the name of the LORD that spake 7121
16:14 Wherefore the well was **c** Beer-lahai-roi; 7121
16:15 Abram **c** his son's name, which Hagar bare, 7121
17: 5 Neither shall thy name any more be **c** 7121
19: 5 they **c** unto Lot, and said unto him, 7121
19:22 Therefore the name of the city was **c** Zoar. 7121
19:37 firstborn bare a son, and **c** his name Moab: 7121
19:38 also bare a son, and **c** his name Ben-ammi: 7121
20: 8 **c** all his servants, and told all these things 7121
20: 9 Abimelech **c** Abraham, and said unto him, 7121
21: 3 Abraham **c** the name of his son that was 7121
21:12 her voice; for in Isaac shall thy seed be **c**. 7121
21:17 the angel of God **c** to Hagar out of heaven, 7121
21:31 Wherefore he **c** that place Beer-sheba; 7121
21:33 **c** there on the name of the LORD, 7121
22:11 the angel of the LORD **c** unto him out of 7121
22:14 Abraham **c** the name of that place 7121
22:15 the angel of the LORD **c** unto Abraham 7121
24:58 they **c** Rebekah, and said unto her, Wilt 7121
25:25 a hairy garment; and they **c** his name Esau. 7121
25:26 on Esau's heel; and his name was **c** Jacob: 7121
25:30 I *am* faint: therefore was his name **c** Edom. 7121
26: 9 Abimelech **c** Isaac, and said, Behold, of a 7121
26:18 he **c** their names after the names by which 7121
26:18 the names by which his father had **c** them. 7121
26:20 he **c** the name of the well Esek; because 7121
26:21 for that also: and he **c** the name of it Sitnah. 7121
26:22 he **c** the name of it Rehoboth; and he said, 7121
26:25 **c** upon the name of the LORD, and 7121
26:33 he **c** it Shebah: therefore the name of 7121
27: 1 he **c** Esau his eldest son, and said unto him, 7121
27:42 she sent and **c** Jacob her younger son, and 7121
28: 1 Isaac **c** Jacob, and blessed him, and 7121
28:19 he **c** the name of that place Beth-el: but 7121
28:19 the name of *that* city *was* **c** Luz at the first. NIH
29:32 and bare a son, and she **c** his name Reuben: 7121
29:33 this *son* also: and she **c** his name Simeon. 7121
29:34 three sons: therefore was his name **c** Levi. 7121
29:35 therefore she **c** his name Judah; and 7121
30: 6 me a son: therefore **c** she his name Dan. 7121
30: 8 and she **c** his name Naphtali. 7121
30:11 A troop cometh: and she **c** his name Gad. 7121
30:13 call me blessed: and she **c** his name Asher. 7121
30:18 my husband: and she **c** his name Issachar. 7121
30:20 him six sons: and she **c** his name Zebulun. 7121
30:21 she bare a daughter, and **c** her name Dinah. 7121
30:24 she **c** his name Joseph; and said, 7121
31: 4 Jacob sent and **c** Rachel and Leah to 7121
31:47 Laban **c** it Jegar-sahadutha: but 7121
31:47 it Jegar-sahadutha: but Jacob **c** it Galeed. 7121
31:48 Therefore was the name of it **c** Galeed; 7121
31:54 the mount, and **c** his brethren to eat bread: 7121
32: 2 and he **c** the name of that place Mahanaim. 7121
32:28 Thy name shall be **c** no more Jacob, but 559
32:30 Jacob **c** the name of the place Peniel: for I 7121
33:17 the name of the place is **c** Succoth. 7121
33:20 there an altar, and **c** it El-Elohe-Israel. 7121
35: 7 there an altar, and **c** the place El-beth-el: 7121
35: 8 and the name of it was **c** Allon-bachuth. 7121
35:10 thy name shall not be **c** any more Jacob, but 7121
35:10 shall be thy name: and he **c** his name Israel. 7121
35:15 Jacob **c** the name of the place where God 7121
35:18 (for she died) that she **c** his name Ben-oni: 7121
35:18 but his father **c** him Benjamin. 7121
38: 3 and bare a son; and he **c** his name Er. 7121
38: 4 and bare a son; and she **c** his name Onan. 7121
38: 5 and bare a son; and **c** his name Shelah: 7121
38:29 therefore his name was **c** Pharez. 7121
38:30 upon his hand: and his name was **c** Zarah. 7121
39:14 That she **c** unto the men of her house, and 7121
41: 8 and **c for** all the magicians of Egypt, 7121
41:14 Pharaoh sent and **c** Joseph, and 7121
41:45 Pharaoh **c** Joseph's name 7121
41:51 Joseph **c** the name of the firstborn 7121
41:52 the name of the second **c** he Ephraim: 7121
47:29 he **c** his son Joseph, and said unto him, 7121
48: 6 shall be **c** after the name of their brethren in 7121
49: 1 Jacob **c** unto his sons, and said, 7121
50:11 wherefore the name of it was **c** 7121
Ex 1:18 the king of Egypt **c for** the midwives, and 7121
2: 8 the maid went and **c** the child's mother. 7121
2:10 she **c** his name Moses: and she said, 7121
2:22 *him* a son, and he **c** his name Gershom: 7121
Ex 3: 4 God **c** unto him out of the midst of 7121
7:11 Pharaoh also **c** the wise men and 7121
8: 8 Pharaoh **c for** Moses and Aaron, and said, 7121
8:25 Pharaoh **c** for Moses and for Aaron, and 7121
9:27 **c** for Moses and Aaron, and said unto them, 7121
10:16 Pharaoh **c** for Moses and Aaron in haste; 7121
10:24 Pharaoh **c** unto Moses, and said, Go ye, 7121
12:21 Moses **c** for all the elders of Israel, and 7121
12:31 he **c** for Moses and Aaron by night, and 7121
15:23 the name of it was **c** Marah. 7121
16:31 the house of Israel **c** the name thereof 7121
17: 7 he **c** the name of the place Massah, and 7121
17:15 an altar, and **c** the name of it Jehovah-nissi: 7121
19: 3 the LORD **c** unto him out of the mountain, 7121
19: 7 and **c** for the elders of the people, 7121
19:20 the LORD **c** Moses *up* to the top of 7121
24:16 the seventh day he **c** unto Moses out of 7121
31: 2 I have **c** by name Bezaleel the son of Uri, 7121
33: 7 **c** it the Tabernacle of the Congregation. 7121
34:31 Moses **c** unto them; and Aaron and all 7121
35:30 the LORD hath **c** by name Bezaleel 7121
36: 2 Moses **c** Bezaleel and Aholiab, and every 7121
Lev 1: 1 the LORD **c** unto Moses, and spake unto 7121
9: 1 *that* Moses **c** Aaron and his sons, and 7121
10: 4 Moses **c** Mishael and Elzaphan, the sons of 7121
Nu 11: 3 he **c** the name of the place Taberah: 7121
11:34 he **c** the name of that place 7121
12: 5 of the tabernacle, and **c** Aaron and Miriam: 7121
13:16 Moses **c** Oshea the son of Nun, Jehoshua. 7121
13:24 The place was **c** the brook Eshcol, because 7121
21: 3 and he **c** the name of the place Hormah. 7121
24:10 I **c** thee to curse mine enemies, and behold, 7121
25: 2 they **c** the people unto the sacrifices of their 7121
32:41 towns thereof, and **c** them Havoth-jair. 7121
32:42 and **c** it Nobah, after his own name. 7121
Dt 3:13 all Bashan, which was **c** the land of giants. 7121
3:14 **c** them after his own name, 7121
5: 1 Moses **c** all Israel, and said unto them, 7121
15: 2 because it is **c** the LORD'S release. 7121
25:10 his name shall be **c** in Israel, The house of 7121
28:10 that thou art **c** by the name of the LORD; 7121
29: 2 Moses **c** unto all Israel, and said unto them, 7121
31: 7 Moses **c** unto Joshua, and said unto him in 7121
Jos 4: 4 Joshua **c** the twelve men, whom he had 7121
5: 9 Wherefore the name of the place is **c** Gilgal 7121
6: 6 Joshua the son of Nun **c** the priests, and 7121
7:26 Wherefore the name of that place was **c**, 7121
8:16 all the people that *were* in Ai were **c** 2199
9:22 Joshua **c** for them, and he spake unto them, 7121
10:24 that Joshua **c** for all the men of Israel, and 7121
19:47 and dwelt therein, and **c** Leshem, Dan, 7121
22: 1 Joshua **c** the Reubenites, and the Gadites, 7121
22:34 the children of Gad **c** the altar *Ed:* for it 7121
23: 2 Joshua **c** for all Israel, *and* for their elders, 7121
24: 1 **c** for the elders of Israel, and for their 7121
24: 9 and **c** Balaam the son of Beor to curse you: 7121
Jdg 1:17 and the name of the city was **c** Hormah. 7121
1:26 built a city, and **c** the name thereof Luz: 7121
2: 5 they **c** the name of that place Bochim: and 7121
4: 6 **c** Barak the son of Abinoam out of 7121
4:10 Barak **c** Zebulun and Naphtali to Kedesh; 2199
6:24 unto the LORD, and **c** it Jehovah-shalom: 7121
6:32 Therefore on that day he **c** him Jerubbaal, 7121
8:31 him a son, whose name he **c** Abimelech. 7760
9:54 he **c** hastily unto the young man his 7121
10: 4 which are **c** Havoth-jair unto this day, 7121
12: 2 when I **c** you, ye delivered me not out of 2199
13:24 woman bare a son, and **c** his name Samson: 7121
14:15 have ye **c** us to take that we have? *is it* not 7121
15:17 of his hand, and **c** that place Ramath-lehi. 7121
15:18 sore athirst, and **c** on the LORD, and said, 7121
15:19 wherefore he **c** the name thereof 7121
16:18 and **c** for the lords of the Philistines, 7121
16:19 she **c** for a man, and she caused *him* to 7121
16:25 they **c** for Samson out of the prison house; 7121
16:28 Samson **c** unto the LORD, and said, 7121
18:12 wherefore they **c** that place Mahaneh-dan 7121
18:29 they **c** the name of the city Dan, after 7121
Ru 4:17 born to Naomi; and they **c** his name Obed: 7121
1Sa 1:20 that she bare a son, and **c** his name Samuel, 7121
3: 4 That the LORD **c** Samuel: and 7121
3: 5 he said, I **c** not; lie down again. And he 7121
3: 6 the LORD **c** yet again, Samuel. 7121
3: 6 he answered, I **c** not, my son; lie down 7121
3: 8 the LORD **c** Samuel again the third time. 7121
3: 8 Eli perceived that the LORD had **c** 7121
3:10 stood, and **c** as at other times, Samuel, 7121
3:16 Eli **c** Samuel, and said, Samuel, my son. 7121
6: 2 the Philistines **c** for the priests and 7121
7:12 and Shen, and **c** the name of it Eben-ezer, 7121
9: 9 for *he that is* now **c** a Prophet was NIH
9: 9 *called* a Prophet was beforetime **c** a Seer.) 7121
9:26 that Samuel **c** Saul to the top of the house, 7121
10:17 Samuel **c** the people **together** unto 6817
12:18 So Samuel **c** unto the LORD; and 7121
13: 4 the people were **c together** after Saul *to* 6817
16: 5 and his sons, and **c** them to the sacrifice. 7121
16: 8 Jesse **c** Abinadab, and made him pass 7121
19: 7 Jonathan **c** David, and Jonathan shewed 7121
23: 8 Saul **c** all the people **together** to war, to go 8085
23:28 they **c** that place Sela-hammahlekoth. 7121
28:15 therefore I have **c** thee, that *thou* mayest 7121
29: 6 Achish **c** David, and said unto him, Surely, 7121
2Sa 1: 7 behind him, he saw me, and **c** unto me. 7121
1:15 David **c** one of the young men, and said, 7121
2:16 wherefore that place was **c** 7121
2:26 Abner **c** to Joab, and said, Shall the sword 7121
5: 9 dwelt in the fort, and **c** it the city of David. 7121
5:20 Therefore he **c** the name of that place 7121
6: 2 whose name is **c** *by* the name of 7121
6: 8 he **c** *the name* of the place Perez-uzzah to 7121
9: 2 when they had **c** him unto David, the king 7121
9: 9 the king **c** to Ziba, Saul's servant, and 7121
11:13 when David had **c** him, he did eat and 7121
12:24 she bare a son, and he **c** his name Solomon: 7121

2Sa 12:25 he c his name Jedidiah, because of 7121
12:28 I take the city, and it be c after my name. 7121
13:17 he c his servant that ministered unto him, 7121
14:33 when he had c for Absalom, he came to 7121
15: 2 Absalom c unto him, and said, Of what city 7121
15:11 hundred men out of Jerusalem, *that were* c; 7121
18:18 he c the pillar after his own name: and it is 7121
18:18 and it is c unto this day, Absalom's place. 7121
18:26 the watchman c unto the porter, and said, 7121
18:28 Ahimaaz c, and said unto the king, All is 7121
21: 2 the king c the Gibeonites, and said unto 7121
22: 7 In my distress I c upon the LORD, and 7121
1Ki 1: 9 c all his brethren the king's sons, and all 7121
1:10 and Solomon his brother, he c not. 7121
1:19 hath c all the sons of the king, and Abiathar 7121
1:19 but Solomon thy servant hath he not c. 7121
1:25 hath c all the king's sons, and the captains 7121
1:26 and thy servant Solomon, hath he not c. 7121
2:36 the king sent and c for Shimei, and 7121
2:42 the king sent and c for Shimei, and 7121
7:21 right pillar, and c the name thereof Jachin: 7121
7:21 the left pillar, and c the name thereof Boaz. 7121
8:43 which I have builded, is c by thy name. 7121
9:13 he c them the land of Cabul unto this day. 7121
12: 3 That they sent and c him. And Jeroboam 7121
12:20 they sent and c him unto the congregation, 7121
16:24 and c the name of the city which he built, 7121
17:10 he c to her, and said, Fetch me, I pray thee, 7121
17:11 as she was going to fetch *it*, he c to her, 7121
18: 3 Ahab c Obadiah, which *was* the governor 7121
18:26 c on the name of Baal from morning even 7121
20: 7 the king of Israel c all the elders of 7121
22: 9 the king of Israel c an officer, and said, 7121
2Ki 3:10 that the LORD hath c these three kings 7121
3:13 for the LORD hath c these three kings 7121
4:12 when he had c her, she stood before him. 7121
4:15 when he had c her, she stood in the door. 7121
4:22 she c unto her husband, and said, Send me, 7121
4:36 he c Gehazi, and said, Call this 7121
4:36 So he c her. And when she was come in 7121
6:11 he c his servants, and said unto them, Will 7121
7:10 they came and c unto the porter of the city: 7121
7:11 he c the porters; and they told *it to* 7121
8: 1 for the LORD hath c for a famine; and 7121
9: 1 Elisha the prophet c one of the children of 7121
12: 7 Then king Jehoash c for Jehoiada the priest, 7121
14: 7 and c the name of it Joktheel unto this day. 7121
18: 4 burn incense to it: and he c it Nehushtan. 7121
18:18 when they had c to the king, there came out 7121
1Ch 4: 9 his mother c his name Jabez, saying, 7121
4:10 Jabez c on the God of Israel, saying, 7121
6:65 these cities, which are c by *their* names. 7121
7:16 bare a son, and she c his name Peresh; 7121
7:23 he c his name Beriah, because it went evil 7121
11: 7 therefore they c it the city of David. 7121
13: 6 the cherubims, whose name is c *on it*. 7121
13:11 wherefore that place is c Perez-uzza to this 7121
14:11 they c the name of that place Baal-perazim. 7121
15:11 David c for Zadok and Abiathar the priests, 7121
21:26 peace offerings, and c upon the LORD; 7121
22: 6 he c for Solomon his son, and charged him 7121
2Ch 3:17 c the name of *that on* the right hand Jachin, 7121
6:33 house which I have built is c by thy name. 7121
7:14 If my people, which are c by my name, 7121
10: 3 they sent and c him. So Jeroboam and 7121
18: 8 the king of Israel c for one *of his* officers, 7121
20:26 therefore the name of the same place was c, 7121
24: 6 the king c for Jehoiada the chief, and 7121
Ezr 2:61 the Gileadite, and was c after their name: 7121
Ne 5:12 I c the priests, and took an oath of them, 7121
7:63 *to* wife, and was c after their name. 7121
Est 2:14 in her, and *that* she were c by name. 7121
3:12 were the king's scribes c on the thirteenth 7121
4: 5 c Esther for Hatach, *one* of the king's 7121
4:11 who is not c, *there is* one law of his to put 7121
4:11 I have not been c to come in unto the king 7121
5:10 he sent and c for his friends, and Zeresh his 935
8: 9 were the king's scribes c at that time in 7121
9:26 Wherefore they c these days Purim after 7121
Job 1: 4 sent and c for their three sisters to eat and 7121
9:16 If I had c, and he had answered me; 7121
19:16 I c my servant, and he gave *me* no answer; 7121
42:14 And he c the name of the first, Jemima; and 7121
Ps 17: 6 I have c upon thee, for thou wilt hear me, 7121
18: 6 In my distress I c upon the LORD, and 7121
31:17 O LORD; for I have c upon thee: 7121
50: 1 c the earth from the rising of the sun unto 7121
53: 4 they eat bread: they have not c upon God. 7121
79: 6 upon the kingdoms that have not c upon thy 7121
88: 9 LORD, I have c daily upon thee, I have 7121
99: 6 they c upon the LORD, and he answered 7121
105:16 Moreover, he c *for* a famine upon the land: 7121
116: 4 c I upon the name of the LORD; 7121
118: 5 I c upon the LORD in distress: 7121
Pr 1:24 Because I have c, and ye refused; I have 7121
16:21 The wise in heart shall be c prudent: and 7121
24: 8 He that deviseth to do evil shall be c a 7121
SS 5: 6 I c him, but he gave me no answer. 7121
Isa 1:26 afterward thou shalt be c, The city of 7121
4: 1 only let us be c by thy name, to take away 7121
4: 3 that remaineth in Jerusalem, shall be c holy, 559
9: 6 his name shall be c Wonderful, Counsellor, 7121
13: 3 I have also c my mighty ones for mine 7121
19:18 one shall be c, The city of destruction. 559
31: 4 when a multitude of shepherds is c forth 7121
32: 5 The vile person shall be no more c liberal, 7121
35: 8 and it shall be c The way of holiness; 7121
41: 2 c him to his foot, gave the nations before 7121
41: 9 c thee from the chief men thereof, and 7121
42: 6 I the LORD have c thee in righteousness, 7121
43: 1 redeemed thee, I have c *thee* by thy name; 7121
43: 7 *Even* every one that is c by my name: for I 7121
43:22 thou hast not c upon me, O Jacob; but 7121
45: 4 mine elect, I have even c thee by thy name: 7121
47: 1 for thou shalt no more be c tender and 7121
Isa 47: 5 for thou shalt no more be c, The lady of 7121
48: 1 which are c by the name of Israel, and 7121
48: 8 wast c a transgressor from the womb. 7121
48:12 Hearken unto me, O Jacob, and Israel my c; 7121
48:15 I, *even* I, have spoken; yea, I have c him: 7121
49: 1 The LORD hath c me from the womb; 7121
50: 2 when I c, *was there* none to answer? Is my 7121
51: 2 for I c him alone, and blessed him, and 7121
54: 5 The God of the whole earth shall he be c. 7121
54: 6 for the LORD hath c thee as a woman 7121
56: 7 for mine house shall be c a house of prayer 7121
58:12 thou shalt be c, The repairer of the breach, 7121
61: 3 that they might be c trees of righteousness, 7121
62: 2 thou shalt be c by a new name, which 7121
62: 4 thou shalt be c Hephzi-bah, and thy land 7121
62:12 thou shalt be c, Sought out, A city not 7121
63:19 over them; they were not c by thy name. 7121
65: 1 unto a nation *that* was not c by my name. 7121
65:12 because when I c, ye did not answer; 7121
66: 4 because when I c, none did answer; when I 7121
Jer 7:10 this house, which is c by my name, and say, 7121
7:11 Is this house, which is c by my name, 7121
7:13 heard not; and I c you, but ye answered not; 7121
7:14 which is c by my name, wherein ye trust, 7121
7:30 in the house which is c by my name, 7121
7:32 that it shall no more be c Tophet, 559
11:16 The LORD c thy name, A green olive 7121
12: 6 yea, they have c a multitude after thee: 7121
14: 9 the midst of us, and we are c by thy name; 7121
15:16 for I am c by thy name, O LORD God of 7121
19: 6 that this place shall no more be c Tophet, 7121
20: 3 The LORD hath not c thy name Pashur, 7121
23: 6 this *is* his name whereby he shall be c, 7121
25:29 I begin to bring evil on the city which is c 7121
30:17 because they c thee an Outcast, 7121
32:34 which is c by my name, to defile it. 7121
33:16 this *is the name* wherewith she shall be c, 7121
34:15 me in the house which is c by my name. 7121
35:17 I have c unto them, but they have not 7121
36: 4 Jeremiah c Baruch the son of Neriah: and 7121
42: 8 c he Johanan the son of Kareah, and all 7121
La 1:15 he hath c an assembly against me to crush 7121
1:19 I c for my lovers, *but* they deceived me: 7121
1:21 *it:* thou wilt bring the day *that* thou hast c, 7121
2:22 Thou hast c as *in* a solemn day my terrors 7121
3:55 I c upon thy name, O LORD, out of 7121
3:57 Thou drewest near in the day *that* I c upon 7121
Eze 9: 3 he c to the man clothed *with* linen, 7121
20:29 the name thereof is c Bamah unto this day. 7121
Da 5:12 now let Daniel be c, and he will shew 7123
8:16 which c, and said, Gabriel, make this *man* 7121
9:18 and the city which is c by thy name: 7121
9:19 thy city and thy people are c by thy name. 7121
10: 1 whose name was c Belteshazzar; 7121
Hos 11: 1 I loved him, and c my son out of Egypt. 7121
11: 2 *As* they c them, so they went from them: 7121
11: 7 though they c them to the most High, 7121
Am 7: 4 the Lord GOD c to contend by fire, and 7121
9:12 of all the heathen, which are c by my name, 7121
Hag 1:11 I c *for* a drought upon the land, and 7121
Zec 8: 3 Jerusalem shall be c a city of truth; and 7121
11: 7 the one I c Beauty, and the other I called 7121
11: 7 I called Beauty, and the other I c Bands; 7121
Mt 1:16 of whom was born Jesus, who is c Christ. 3004
1:25 firstborn son: and *he* c his name JESUS. 2564
2: 7 when he had privily c the wise men, 2564
2:15 saying, Out of Egypt have I c my son. 2564
2:23 he came and dwelt in a city c Nazareth: 3004
2:23 by the prophets, He shall be c a Nazarene. 2564
4:18 Simon c Peter, and Andrew his brother, 3004
4:21 mending their nets; and he c them. 2564
5: 9 for they shall be c the children of God. 2564
5:19 he shall be c the least in the kingdom of 2564
5:19 teach *them,* the same shall be c great in 2564
10: 1 And when he had c unto *him* his twelve 4341
10: 2 who is c Peter, and Andrew his brother; 3004
10:25 If they have c the master of the house 2564
13:55 is not his mother c Mary? and his brethren, 3004
15:10 And he c the multitude, and said unto them, 4341
15:32 Then Jesus c his disciples unto *him,* and 4341
18: 2 And Jesus c a little child unto *him,* and 4341
18:32 Then his lord, after that he had c him, 4341
20:16 the first last: for many be c, but few chosen. 2822
20:25 But Jesus c them unto *him,* and said, 4341
20:32 And Jesus stood still, and c them, and said, 5455
21:13 My house shall be c the house of prayer; 2564
22:14 For many are c, but few *are* chosen. 2822
23: 7 and to be c of men, Rabbi, Rabbi. 2564
23: 8 But be not ye c Rabbi: for one is your 2564
23:10 Neither be ye c masters: for one is your 2564
25:14 *who* c his own servants, and delivered unto 2564
26: 3 of the high priest, who was c Caiaphas, 3004
26:14 Then one of the twelve, c Judas Iscariot, 3004
26:36 with them unto a place c Gethsemane, 3004
27: 8 Wherefore that field was c, The field of 2564
27:16 then a notable prisoner, c Barabbas. 3004
27:17 Barabbas, or Jesus which is c Christ? 3004
27:22 shall I do then with Jesus which is c Christ? 3004
27:33 And when they were come unto a place c 3004
Mk 1:20 And straightway he c them: and they left 2564
3:23 And he c them unto *him,* and said unto 4341
7:14 And when he had c all the people unto 4341
8: 1 Jesus c his disciples unto *him,* and 4341
8:34 And when he had c the people unto *him* 4341
9:35 and c the twelve, and saith unto them, 5455
10:42 But Jesus c them to *him,* and saith unto 4341
10:49 stood still, and commanded him to be c. 5455
11:17 My house shall be c of all nations the house 2564
12:43 And he c unto *him* his disciples, and 4341
14:72 And Peter c to mind the word that Jesus said 363
15:16 led him away into the hall, c Pretorium; 3739
Lk 1:32 and shall be c the Son of the Highest: 2564
1:35 be born of thee shall be c the Son of God. 2564
1:36 the sixth month with her, who was c barren. 2564
1:59 and they c him Zacharias, after the name of 2564
Lk 1:60 and said, Not *so;* but he shall be c John. 2564
1:61 There is none of thy kindred that is c by 2564
1:62 to his father, how he would have him c. 2564
1:76 child, shalt be c the prophet of the Highest: 2564
2: 4 the city of David, which is c Bethlehem; 2564
2:21 his name was c JESUS, which was *so* 2564
2:23 the womb shall be c holy to the Lord;) 2564
6:13 it was day, he c unto *him* his disciples: 4377
6:15 the *son* of Alpheus, and Simon c Zelotes, 2564
7:11 *day* after, *that* he went into a city c Nain; 2564
8: 2 and infirmities, Mary c Magdalene, 2564
8:54 her by the hand, and c, saying, Maid, arise. 5455
9: 1 Then he c his twelve disciples together, 4779
9:10 place belonging to the city c Bethsaida. 2564
10:39 And she had a sister c Mary, which also sat 2564
13:12 he c *her* to *him,* and said unto her, Woman, 4377
15:19 And am no more worthy to be c thy son: 2564
15:21 and am no more worthy to be c thy son. 2564
15:26 And he c one of the servants, and 4341
16: 2 And he c him, and said unto him, How *is* it 5455
16: 5 So he c every one of his lord's debtors unto 4341
18:16 But Jesus c them unto *him,* and said, 4341
19:13 And he c his ten servants, and 2564
19:15 he commanded these servants to be c unto 5455
19:29 at the mount c *the mount* of Olives, 2564
21:37 abode in the mount that is c *the mount* of 2564
22: 1 bread drew nigh, which is c the Passover. 3004
22:25 they that exercise authority upon them are c 2564
22:47 and he that was c Judas, one of the twelve, 3004
23:13 when he had c together the chief priests 4779
23:33 which is c Calvary, there they crucified 2564
24:13 went *that* same day to a village c Emmaus, 3686
Jn 1:42 thou shalt be c Cephas, which is by 2564
1:48 said unto him, Before that Philip c thee, 5455
2: 2 And both Jesus was c, and his disciples, 2564
2: 9 the governor of the feast c the bridegroom, 5455
4: 5 he to a city of Samaria, which is c Sychar, 3004
4:25 that Messias cometh, which is c Christ: 3004
5: 2 which is c in the Hebrew tongue Bethesda, 1951
9:11 A man *that is* c Jesus made clay, and 3004
9:18 until they c the parents of him that had 5455
9:24 Then again c they the man that was blind, 5455
10:35 If he c them gods, unto whom the word of 3004
11:16 Then said Thomas, which is c Didymus, 3004
11:28 and c Mary her sister secretly, saying, 5455
11:54 into a city c Ephraim, and there continued 3004
12:17 that was with him when he c Lazarus out of 5455
15:15 but I have c you friends; for all *things* that I 3004
18:33 and c Jesus, and said unto him, Art thou 5455
19:13 seat in a place *that is* c the Pavement, 3004
19:17 forth into a place c *the place* of a skull, 3004
19:17 a skull, which is c in the Hebrew Golgotha: 3004
20:24 But Thomas, one of the twelve, c Didymus, 3004
21: 2 and Thomas c Didymus, and Nathanael of 3004
Ac 1:12 unto Jerusalem from the mount c Olivet, 2564
1:19 insomuch as that field is c in their proper 2564
1:23 they appointed two, Joseph c Barsabas, 2564
3: 2 the gate of the temple which is c Beautiful, 3004
3:11 unto them in the porch that is c Solomon's, 2564
4:18 And they c them, and commanded them not 2564
5:21 and c the council together, and all 4779
5:40 and when they had c the apostles, and 4341
6: 2 c the multitude of the disciples unto *them,* 4341
6: 9 which is c *the synagogue* of the Libertines, 3004
7:14 and c his father Jacob to *him,* and all his 3333
8: 9 But there was a certain man, c Simon, 3686
9:11 and go into the street which is c Straight, 2564
9:11 inquire in the house of Judas for *one* c Saul, 3686
9:21 not this he that destroyed them which c on 1941
9:36 which by interpretation is c Dorcas: 3004
9:41 and when he had c the saints and widows, 5455
10: 1 There was a certain man in Cesarea c 3686
10: 1 a centurion of the band c the Italian *band,* 2564
10: 7 he c two of his household servants, and 5455
10:18 And c, and asked whether Simon, 5455
10:23 Then c he them in, and lodged *them.* And 1528
10:24 and had c together his kinsmen and near 4779
11:26 the disciples were c Christians first in 5537
13: 1 and Simeon that was c Niger, and Lucius of 2564
13: 2 Saul for the work whereunto I have c them. 4341
13: 7 who c for Barnabas and Saul, and 4341
13: 9 Then Saul, (who also *is* c Paul,) filled with NIG
14:12 And they c Barnabas, Jupiter; and Paul, 2564
15:17 upon whom my name is c, saith the Lord, 1941
16:10 assuredly gathering that the Lord had c us 4341
16:29 Then he c for a light, and sprang in, and 154
19:25 Whom he c together with the workmen of 4867
19:40 For we are in danger to be c in question for 1458
20: 1 Paul c unto *him* the disciples, and 4341
20:17 to Ephesus, and c the elders of the church. 3333
23: 6 resurrection of the dead I am c in question. 2919
23:17 Then Paul c one of the centurions unto 4341
23:18 Paul the prisoner c me unto *him,* and 4341
23:23 And he c unto *him* two centurions, saying, 4341
24: 2 And when he was c *forth,* Tertullus began 2564
24:21 dead I am c in question by you this day. 2919
27: 8 came unto a place *which is* c The fair 2564
27:14 it a tempestuous wind, c Euroclydon. 2564
27:16 under a certain island *which is* c Clauda, 2564
28: 1 then they knew that the island was c Melita. 2564
28:17 days Paul c the chief of the Jews together: 4779
28:20 For this cause therefore have I c for you, 3870
Ro 1: 1 a servant of Jesus Christ, c *to be* an apostle, 2822
1: 6 Among whom are ye also *the* c of Jesus 2822
1: 7 be in Rome, beloved of God, c *to be* saints: 2822
2:17 thou art c a Jew, and restest in the law, and 2028
7: 3 to another man, she shall be c an adulteress: 5537
8:28 to them who are *the* c according to *his* 2822
8:30 whom he did predestinate, them he also c: 2564
8:30 and whom he c, them he also justified: and 2564
9: 7 but, In Isaac shall thy seed be c. 2564
9:24 Even us, whom he hath c, not of the Jews 2564
9:26 there shall they be c the children of 2564
1Co 1: 1 c *to be* an apostle of Jesus Christ through 2822
1: 2 are sanctified in Christ Jesus, c *to be* saints, 2822

C

1Co 1: 9 by whom ye were **c** unto the fellowship of *2564*
1:24 But unto them which are **c**, both Jews and *2822*
1:26 not many mighty, not many noble, *are* **c**: NIG
5:11 if any *man that is* **c** a brother be a *3687*
7:15 in such *cases:* but God hath **c** us to peace. *2564*
7:17 as the Lord hath **c** every one, so let him *2564*
7:18 Is any *man* **c** being circumcised? let him *2564*
7:18 Is any **c** in uncircumcision? let him not be *2564*
7:20 abide in the same calling wherein he was **c**. *2564*
7:21 Art thou **c** *being* a servant? care not for it: *2564*
7:22 For he that is **c** in the Lord, *being* a servant, *2564*
7:22 likewise also he that is **c**, *being* free, *2564*
7:24 Brethren, let every man, wherein he is **c**, *2564*
8: 5 For though there be that are **c** gods, *3004*
15: 9 that am not meet to be **c** an apostle, because *2564*
Gal 1: 6 soon removed from him that **c** you into *2564*
1:15 my mother's womb, and **c** *me* by his grace, *2564*
5:13 For, brethren, ye have been **c** unto liberty; *2564*
Eph 2:11 who are **c** Uncircumcision by that which is *3004*
2:11 **c** the Circumcision in the flesh made by *3004*
4: 1 worthy of the vocation wherewith ye are **c**, *2564*
4: 4 even as ye are **c** in one hope of your *2564*
Col 3:15 to the which also ye are **c** in one body; *2564*
4:11 And Jesus, which is **c** Justus, who are of *3004*
1Th 2:12 who hath **c** you unto his kingdom and *2564*
4: 7 For God hath not **c** us unto uncleanness, but *2564*
2Th 2: 4 and exalteth himself above all that is **c** God, *3004*
2:14 Whereunto he **c** you by our gospel, to *2564*
1Ti 6:12 whereunto thou art also **c**, and *2564*
6:20 and oppositions of science **falsely** so **c**: *5581*
2Ti 1: 9 hath saved us, and **c** *us* with a holy calling, *2564*
Heb 3:13 one another daily, while it is **c** To day; *2564*
5: 4 but he that is **c** of God, as *was* Aaron. *2564*
5:10 **C** of God a high priest after the order of *4316*
7:11 and not be **c** after the order of Aaron? *3004*
9: 2 the shewbread; which is **c** the sanctuary. *3004*
9: 3 the tabernacle which is **c** the holiest of all; *3004*
9:15 they which are **c** might receive the promise *2564*
11: 8 when he was **c** to go out into a place which *2564*
11:16 wherefore God is not ashamed to be **c** their *1941*
11:18 was said, That in Isaac shall thy seed be **c**: *2564*
11:24 refused to be **c** the son of Pharaoh's *3004*
Jas 2: 7 *that* worthy name by the which ye are **c**? *1941*
2:23 and he was **c** the Friend of God. *2564*
1Pe 1:15 But as he which hath **c** you is holy, so be ye *2564*
2: 9 **c** you out of darkness into his marvellous *2564*
2:21 For *even* hereunto were ye **c**: because *2564*
3: 9 knowing that ye are thereunto **c**, that ye *2564*
5:10 who hath **c** us into his eternal glory by *2564*
2Pe 1: 3 through the knowledge of him that hath **c** *2564*
1Jn 3: 1 that we should be **c** the sons of God: *2564*
Jude 1: 1 and preserved *in* Jesus Christ, *and* **c**: *2822*
Rev 1: 9 was in the isle that is **c** Patmos, for *2564*
8:11 And the name of the star is **c** Wormwood: *3004*
11: 8 which spiritually is **c** Sodom and Egypt, *2564*
12: 9 **c** the devil, and Satan, which deceiveth *2564*
16:16 place **c** in the Hebrew tongue Armageddon. *2564*
17:14 and they that are with him *are* **c**, and *2822*
19: 9 Blessed *are* they which are **c** unto *2564*
19:11 and he that sat upon him *was* **c** Faithful and *2564*
19:13 and his name is **c** The Word of God. *2564*

CALLEDST (4) [CALL]

Jdg 8: 1 hast thou served us thus, that *thou* **c** us not, 7121
1Sa 3: 5 and said, Here *am* I; for thou **c** me. 7121
Ps 81: 7 Thou **c** in trouble, and I delivered thee; 7121
Eze 23:21 Thus thou **c to remembrance** the lewdness 6485

CALLEST (3) [CALL]

Mt 19:17 he said unto him, Why **c** thou me good? *3004*
Mk 10:18 Jesus said unto him, Why **c** thou me good? *3004*
Lk 18:19 Jesus said unto him, Why **c** thou me good? *3004*

CALLETH (31) [CALL]

1Ki 8:43 do according to all that the stranger **c** to 7121
2Ch 6:33 do according to all that the stranger **c** to 7121
Job 12: 4 who **c** upon God, and he answereth him: 7121
Ps 42: 7 Deep **c** unto deep at the noise of thy 7121
147: 4 of the stars; he **c** them all by *their* names. 7121
Pr 18: 6 and his mouth **c** for strokes. 7121
Isa 21:11 He **c** to me out of Seir, Watchman, what of 7121
40:26 he **c** them all by names by the greatness of 7121
59: 4 None **c** for justice, nor any pleadeth for 7121
64: 7 *there is* none that **c** upon thy name, 7121
Hos 7: 7 *there is* none among them that **c** unto me. 7121
Am 5: 8 that **c** for the waters of the sea, and 7121
9: 6 he that **c** for the waters of the sea, and 7121
Mt 27:47 they heard *that,* said, This *man* **c** for Elias. *5455*
Mk 3:13 and **c unto** *him* whom he would: *4341*
6: 7 And he **c unto** *him* the twelve, and *4341*
10:49 Be of good comfort, rise; he **c** thee. *5455*
12:37 David therefore himself **c** him Lord; and *3004*
15:35 when they heard *it,* said, Behold, he **c** Elias. *5455*
Lk 15: 6 he **c together** *his* friends and neighbours, *4779*
15: 9 **c** *her* friends and *her* neighbours **together**, *4779*
20:37 when he **c** the Lord the God of Abraham, *3004*
20:44 David therefore **c** him Lord, how is he then *2564*
Jn 10: 3 and he **c** his own sheep by name, and *2564*
11:28 saying, The Master is come, and **c for** thee. *5455*
Ro 4:17 **c** those *things* which be not as though they *2564*
9:11 not of works, but of him that **c**;) *2564*
1Co 12: 3 that no *man* speaking by the Spirit of God **c** *3004*
Gal 5: 8 *This* persuasion *cometh* not of him that **c** *2564*
1Th 5:24 Faithful *is* he that **c** you, who also will do *2564*
Rev 2:20 which **c** herself a prophetess, to teach and *3004*

CALLING (24) [CALL]

Nu 10: 2 that thou mayest use them for the **c** of 4744
Isa 1:13 and sabbaths, the **c** of assemblies, 7121
41: 4 done *it,* **c** the generations from 7121
46:11 **C** a ravenous bird from the east, the man 7121
Eze 23:19 in **c to remembrance** the days of her 2142
Mt 11:16 in the markets, and **c unto** their fellows, *4377*
Mk 3:31 and, standing without, sent unto him, **c** him. *5455*
Mk 11:21 And Peter **c to remembrance** saith unto *363*
15:44 and **c unto** *him* the centurion, he asked him *4341*
Lk 7:19 And John **c unto** *him* two of his disciples *4341*
7:32 and **c** one **to** another, and saying, We have *4377*
Ac 7:59 **c upon** *God,* and saying, Lord Jesus, *1941*
22:16 away thy sins, **c on** the name of the Lord. *1941*
Ro 11:29 and **c** of God *are* without repentance. *2821*
1Co 1:26 For ye see your **c**, brethren, how that not *2821*
7:20 Let every man abide in the same **c** wherein *2821*
Eph 1:18 that ye may know what is the hope of his **c**, *2821*
4: 4 even as ye are called in one hope of your **c**; *2821*
Php 3:14 prize of the high **c** of God in Christ Jesus. *2821*
2Th 1:11 our God would count you worthy of *this* **c**, *2821*
2Ti 1: 9 hath saved us, and called *us* with a holy **c**, *2821*
Heb 3: 1 holy brethren, partakers of the heavenly **c**, *2821*
1Pe 3: 6 *Even* as Sara obeyed Abraham, **c** him lord: *2564*
2Pe 1:10 give diligence to make your **c** and *2821*

CALLOUS See FAT; FATNESS

CALLOUSED See GROSS

CALM (6)

Ps 107:29 He maketh the storm a **c**, so that the waves 1827
Jnh 1:11 do unto thee, that the sea may be **c** unto us? 8367
1:12 into the sea; so shall the sea be **c** unto you: 8367
Mt 8:26 and the sea; and there was a great **c**. *1055*
Mk 4:39 the wind ceased, and there was a great **c**. *1055*
Lk 8:24 and they ceased, and there was a **c**. *1055*

CALNEH (2)

Ge 10:10 Erech, and Accad, and **C**, in the land of 3641
Am 6: 2 Pass ye *unto* **C**, and see; and from thence 3641

CALNO (1)

Isa 10: 9 *Is* not **C** as Carchemish? *is* not Hamath as 3641

CALVARY (1) [GOLGOTHA]

Lk 23:33 which is called **C**, there they crucified him, *2898*

CALVE (2) [CALF]

Job 39: 1 *or* canst thou mark when the hinds do **c**? 2342
Ps 29: 9 voice of the LORD **maketh** the hinds **to c**, 2342

CALVED (1) [CALF]

Jer 14: 5 the hind also **c** in the field, and forsook *it,* 3205

CALVES (18) [CALF]

1Sa 6: 7 the cart, and bring their **c** home from them: 1121
6:10 to the cart, and shut up their **c** at home: 1121
14:32 and **c**, and slew *them* on the ground: 1121+1241
1Ki 12:28 made two **c** of gold, and said unto them, 5695
12:32 sacrificing unto the **c** that he had made: 5695
2Ki 10:29 *to wit,* the golden **c** that *were* in Beth-el, 5695
17:16 *even* two **c**, and made a grove, and 5695
2Ch 11:15 and for the **c** which he had made. 5695
13: 8 and *there are* with you golden **c**, 5695
Ps 68:30 of the bulls, with the **c** of the people, 5695
Hos 10: 5 shall fear because of the **c** of Beth-aven: 5697
13: 2 Let the men that sacrifice kiss the **c**. 5695
14: 2 so will we render the **c** of our lips. 6499
Am 6: 4 and the **c** out of the midst of the stall; 5695
Mic 6: 6 with burnt offerings, with **c** of a year old? 5695
Mal 4: 2 shall go forth, and grow up as **c** of the stall. 5695
Heb 9:12 Neither by the blood of goats and **c**, *3448*
9:19 he took the blood of **c** and of goats, *3448*

CALVETH (1) [CALF]

Job 21:10 their cow **c**, and casteth not her calf. 6403

CAME (2096) [COME]

Ge 4: 3 in process of time it **c to pass**, that Cain 1961
4: 8 it **c to pass**, when they were in the field, 1961
6: 1 it **c to pass**, when men began to multiply 1961
6: 4 when the sons of God **c in** unto 935
7:10 it **c to pass** after seven days, that the waters 1961
8: 6 it **c to pass** at the end of forty days, 1961
8:11 And the dove **c in** to him in the evening; and 935
8:13 it **c to pass** in the six hundredth and 1961
10:14 and Casluhim, (out of whom **c** Philistim) 3318
11: 2 it **c to pass**, as they journeyed from 1961
11: 5 the LORD **c down** to see the city and 3381
11:31 and they **c** unto Haran, and dwelt there. 935
12: 5 and into the land of Canaan they **c**. 935
12:11 it **c to pass**, when he was come near to 1961
12:14 it **c to pass**, that, when Abram was come 1961
13:18 **c** and dwelt in the plain of Mamre, which *is* 935
14: 1 it **c to pass** in the days of Amraphel king of 1961
14: 5 in the fourteenth year **c** Chedorlaomer, and 935
14: 7 **c** to En-mishpat, which *is* Kadesh, and 935
14:13 there **c** one that had escaped, and told Abram 935
15: 1 of the LORD **c** unto Abram in a vision, 1961
15: 4 the word of the LORD **c** unto him, saying, NIH
15:11 when the fowls **c down** upon the carcases, 3381
15:17 it **c to pass**, that, when the sun went down, 1961
19: 1 there **c** two angels to Sodom at even; and 935
19: 5 Where *are* the men which **c in** to thee this 935
19: 8 **c** they under the shadow of my roof. 935
19: 9 they said *again, This* one *fellow* **c in** to 935
19: 9 *even* Lot, and **c near** to break the door. 5066
19:17 it **c to pass**, when they had brought them 1961
19:29 it **c to pass**, when God destroyed the cities 1961
19:34 it **c to pass** on the morrow, that 1961
20: 3 But God **c** to Abimelech in a dream by night, 935
20:13 it **c to pass**, when God caused me to 1961
21:22 it **c to pass** at that time, that Abimelech 1961
22: 1 it **c to pass** after these things, that God did 1961
22: 9 they **c** to the place which God had told him 935
22:20 it **c to pass** after these things, that it was 1961
23: 2 Abraham **c** to mourn for Sarah, and to weep 935
24:15 it **c to pass**, before he had done speaking, 1961
24:15 that behold, Rebekah **c out**, who was born 3318
24:16 to the well, and filled her pitcher, and **c up**. 5927
24:22 it **c to pass**, as the camels had done 1961
Ge 24:30 it **c to pass**, when he saw the earring and 1961
24:30 that he **c** unto the man; and behold, he stood 935
24:32 the man **c** into the house: and he ungirded 935
24:42 I **c** this day unto the well, and said, 935
24:45 Rebekah **c forth** with her pitcher on her 3318
24:52 it **c to pass**, that, when Abraham's servant 1961
24:62 Isaac **c** from the way of the well Lahai-roi; 935
25:11 it **c to pass** after the death of Abraham, 1961
25:25 the first **c out** red, all over like a hairy 3318
25:26 after that **c** his brother **out**, and his hand 3318
25:29 and Esau **c** from the field, and he *was* faint: 935
26: 8 it **c to pass**, when he had been there a long 1961
26:32 it **c to pass** the same day, that Isaac's 1961
26:32 that Isaac's servants **c**, and told him 935
27: 1 it **c to pass**, that when Isaac was old, and 1961
27:18 he **c** unto his father, and said, My father: 935
27:27 he **c near**, and kissed him: and he smelled 5066
27:30 it **c to pass**, as soon as Isaac had made an 1961
27:30 that Esau his brother **c** in from his hunting. 935
27:35 Thy brother **c** with subtilty, and hath taken 935
29: 1 **c** into the land of the people of the east. 1980
29: 9 with them, Rachel **c** with her father's sheep: 935
29:10 it **c to pass**, when Jacob saw Rachel 1961
29:13 it **c to pass**, when Laban heard the tidings 1961
29:23 it **c to pass** in the evening, that he took 1961
29:25 it **c to pass**, that in the morning, behold, 1961
30:16 Jacob **c** out of the field in the evening, and 935
30:25 it **c to pass**, when Rachel had born Joseph, 1961
30:30 For *it was* little which thou hadst before I **c**, NIH
30:38 watering troughs when the flocks **c** to drink, 935
30:38 that they should conceive when they **c** to 935
30:41 it **c to pass**, whensoever the stronger cattle 1961
31:10 it **c to pass** at the time that the cattle 1961
31:24 God **c** to Laban the Syrian in a dream by 935
32: 6 We **c** to thy brother Esau, and also he 935
32:13 took of that which **c** to his hand a present for 935
33: 1 Esau **c**, and with him four hundred men. 935
33: 3 seven times, until he **c near** to his brother. 5066
33: 6 the handmaidens **c near**, they and 5066
33: 7 Leah also with her children **c near**, and 5066
33: 7 after **c** Joseph **near** and Rachel, and 5066
33:18 Jacob **c** to Shalem, a city of Shechem, 935
33:18 of Canaan, when he **c** from Padan-aram; 935
34: 7 the sons of Jacob **c** out of the field when 935
34:20 Shechem his son **c** unto the gate of their city, 935
34:25 it **c to pass** on the third day, when they 1961
34:25 **c** upon the city boldly, and slew all 935
34:27 The sons of Jacob **c** upon the slain, and 935
35: 6 So Jacob **c** to Luz, which *is* in the land of 935
35: 9 when he **c** out of Padan-aram, and 935
35:17 it **c to pass**, when she was in hard labour, 1961
35:18 it **c to pass**, as her soul was in departing 1961
35:22 it **c to pass**, when Israel dwelt in that land, 1961
35:27 Jacob **c** unto Isaac his father unto Mamre, 935
36:16 these *are* the dukes *that* **c** of Eliphaz in NIH
36:17 these *are* the dukes *that* **c** of Reuel in NIH
36:18 these *were* the dukes *that* **c** of Aholibamah NIH
36:29 These *are* the dukes *that* **c** of the Horites; NIH
36:30 these *are* the dukes *that* **c** of Hori, NIH
36:40 these *are* the names of the dukes *that* **c** of NIH
37:14 of the vale of Hebron, and he **c** to Shechem. 935
37:18 afar off, even before he **c near** unto them, 7126
37:23 it **c to pass**, when Joseph was come unto 1961
37:25 a company of Ishmeelites **c** from Gilead with 935
38: 1 it **c to pass** at that time, that Judah went 1961
38: 9 it **c to pass**, when he went in unto his 1961
38:18 and **c in** unto her, and she conceived by him. 935
38:24 it **c to pass** about three months after, that it 1961
38:27 it **c to pass** in the time of her travail, that, 1961
38:28 it **c to pass**, when she travailed, that *the one* 1961
38:28 a scarlet thread, saying, This **c out** first. 3318
38:29 it **c to pass**, as he drew back his hand, that, 1961
38:29 his hand, that, behold, his brother **c out**: 3318
38:30 afterward **c out** his brother, that had 3318
39: 5 it **c to pass** from the time *that* he had made 1961
39: 7 it **c to pass** after these things, that his 1961
39:10 it **c to pass**, as she spake to Joseph day by 1961
39:11 it **c to pass** about this time, that *Joseph* 1961
39:13 it **c to pass**, when she saw that he had left 1961
39:14 he **c in** unto me to lie with me, and I cried 935
39:15 it **c to pass**, when he heard that I lifted up 1961
39:16 up his garment by her, until his lord **c** home. 935
39:17 brought unto us, **c in** unto me to mock me: 935
39:18 it **c to pass**, as I lift up my voice and cried, 1961
39:19 it **c to pass**, when his master heard 1961
40: 1 it **c to pass** after these things, *that* the butler 1961
40: 6 Joseph **c in** unto them in the morning, and 935
40:20 it **c to pass** the third day, *which was* 1961
41: 1 it **c to pass** at the end of two full years, 1961
41: 2 there **c up** out of the river seven well 5927
41: 3 seven other kine **c up** after them out of 5927
41: 5 seven ears of corn **c up** upon one stalk, 5927
41: 8 it **c to pass** in the morning that his spirit 1961
41:13 it **c to pass**, as he interpreted to us, so 1961
41:14 changed his raiment, and **c in** unto Pharaoh. 935
41:18 there **c up** out of the river seven kine, 5927
41:19 seven other kine **c up** after them, poor and 5927
41:22 seven ears **c up** in one stalk, full and good: 5927
41:27 ill favoured kine that **c up** after them *are* 5927
41:50 born two sons before the years of famine **c**, 935
41:57 all countries **c** into Egypt to Joseph for to 935
42: 5 the sons of Israel **c** to buy *corn* among those 935
42: 5 Israel came to buy *corn* among those that **c**: 935
42: 6 Joseph's brethren **c**, and bowed down 935
42:29 they **c** unto Jacob their father unto the land 935
42:35 it **c to pass** as they emptied their sacks, 1961
43: 2 it **c to pass**, when they had eaten up 1961
43:19 they **c near** to the steward of Joseph's 5066
43:20 we **c indeed down** at the first time to 3381+3381
43:21 it **c to pass**, when we came to the inn, 1961
43:21 it came to pass, when we **c** to the inn, 935
43:25 they made ready the present against Joseph **c** 935
43:26 when Joseph **c** home, they brought him 935
44:14 and his brethren **c** to Joseph's house; 935
44:18 Judah **c near** unto him, and said, O my 5066

Ge 44:24 it **c to pass** when we came up unto thy 1961
44:24 it came to pass when we **c up** unto thy 5927
45: 4 they **c near**. And he said, I *am* Joseph your 5066
45:25 **c** *into* the land of Canaan unto Jacob their 935
46: 1 **c** to Beer-sheba, and offered sacrifices unto 935
46: 6 **c** into Egypt, Jacob, and all his seed with 935
46: 8 which **c** into Egypt, Jacob and his sons: 935
46:26 All the souls that **c** with Jacob into Egypt, 935
46:26 which **c out** of his loins, besides Jacob's 3318
46:27 which **c** into Egypt, *were* threescore and ten. 935
46:28 and they **c** into the land of Goshen. 935
47: 1 Joseph **c** and told Pharaoh, and said, 935
47:15 all the Egyptians **c** unto Joseph, and said, 935
47:18 they **c unto** him the second year, and 935
48: 1 it **c to pass** after these things, that *one* told 1961
48: 5 of Egypt before I **c** unto thee into Egypt, 935
48: 7 as for me, when I **c** from Padan, Rachel died 935
50:10 they **c** to the threshingfloor of Atad, which *is* 935
Ex 1: 1 of the children of Israel, which **c** into Egypt; 935
1: 1 every man and his household **c** with Jacob. 935
1: 5 all the souls that **c** *out of* the loins of Jacob 3318
1:21 it **c to pass**, because the midwives feared 1961
2: 5 the daughter of Pharaoh **c down** to wash 3381
2:11 it **c to pass** in those days, when Moses was 1961
2:16 they **c** and drew water, and filled the troughs 935
2:17 the shepherds **c** and drove them away: but 935
2:18 when they **c** to Reuel their father, he said, 935
2:23 it **c to pass** in process of time, that the king 1961
2:23 their cry **c up** unto God by reason of 5927
3: 1 **c** to the mountain of God, *even* to Horeb. 935
4:24 it **c to pass** by the way in the inn, that 1961
5:15 the officers of the children of Israel **c** and 935
5:20 in the way, as they **c forth** from Pharaoh: 3318
5:23 For since I **c** to Pharaoh to speak in thy 935
6:28 it **c to pass** on the day *when* the LORD 1961
8: 6 the frogs **c up**, and covered the land of 5927
8:24 there **c** a grievous swarm *of flies* into 935
10: 3 Moses and Aaron **c in** unto Pharaoh, and 935
12:29 it **c to pass**, that at midnight the LORD 1961
12:41 it **c to pass** at the end of the four hundred 1961
12:41 even the selfsame day it **c to pass**, 1961
12:51 it **c to pass** the selfsame day, *that* 1961
13: 3 this day, *in* which ye **c out** from Egypt, 3318
13: 4 *This* day **c** ye **out** in the month Abib. 3318
13: 8 did unto me when I **c forth** out of Egypt. 3318
13:15 it **c to pass**, when Pharaoh would hardly let 1961
13:17 it **c to pass**, when Pharaoh had let 1961
14:20 And it **c** between the camp of the Egyptians 935
14:20 that the one **c** not **near** the other all 7126
14:24 it **c to pass**, that in the morning watch 1961
14:28 all the host of Pharaoh that **c** into the sea 935
15:23 when they **c** to Marah, they could not drink 935
15:27 they **c** to Elim, where *were* twelve wells of 935
16: 1 of Israel **c** unto the wilderness of Sin, 935
16:10 it **c to pass**, as Aaron spake unto the whole 1961
16:13 it **c to pass**, that at even the quails came up, 1961
16:13 that at even the quails **c up**, and 5927
16:22 it **c to pass**, *that* on the sixth day they 1961
16:22 all the rulers of the congregation **c** and 935
16:27 it **c to pass**, *that* there went out *some* of 1961
16:35 forty years, until they **c** to a land inhabited; 935
16:35 until they **c** unto the borders of the land of 935
17: 8 **c** Amalek, and fought with Israel in 935
17:11 it **c to pass**, when Moses held up his hand, 1961
18: 5 **c** with his sons and his wife unto Moses into 935
18: 7 of *their* welfare; and they **c** into the tent. 935
18:12 Aaron **c**, and all the elders of Israel, to eat 935
18:13 it **c to pass** on the morrow, that Moses sat 1961
19: 1 the same day **c** they *into* the wilderness of 935
19: 7 Moses **c** and called for the elders of 935
19:16 it **c to pass** on the third day in the morning, 1961
19:20 And the LORD **c down** upon mount Sinai, 3381
21: 3 If he **c in** by himself, he shall go out by 935
22:15 *it* good: if it *be* a hired *thing*, it **c** for his hire. 935
24: 3 Moses **c** and told the people all the words of 935
32:19 it **c to pass**, as soon as he came nigh unto the 1961
32:19 as soon as he **c nigh** unto the camp, that he 7126
32:24 cast it into the fire, and there **c out** this calf. 3318
32:30 it **c to pass** on the morrow, that Moses said 1961
33: 7 it **c to pass**, *that* every one which sought 1961
33: 8 it **c to pass**, when Moses went out unto 1961
33: 9 it **c to pass**, as Moses entered into 1961
34:29 it **c to pass**, when Moses came down from 1961
34:29 when Moses **c down** from mount Sinai 3381
34:29 when he **c down** from the mount, 3381
34:32 afterward all the children of Israel **c nigh**: 5066
34:34 he took the vail off, until he **c out**. 3318
34:34 he **c out**, and spake unto the children of 3318
35:21 they **c**, every one whose heart stirred him up, 935
35:22 they **c**, both men and women, as many as 935
36: 4 **c** every man from his work which they 935
40:17 it **c to pass** in the first month in the second 1961
40:32 when they **c near** unto the altar, 7126
Lev 9: 1 it **c to pass** on the eighth day, *that* Moses 1961
9:22 **c down** from offering of the sin offering, 3381
9:23 and **c out**, and blessed the people: 3318
9:24 there **c** a fire **out** from before the LORD, 3318
Nu 4:47 every one that **c** to do the service of 935
7: 1 it **c to pass** on the day that Moses had fully 1961
9: 6 they **c** before Moses and before Aaron on 7126
10:11 it **c to pass** on the twentieth *day* of 1961
10:21 *other* did set up the tabernacle against they **c**. 935
10:35 it **c to pass**, when the ark set forward, 1961
11:20 saying, Why **c** we **forth** out of Egypt? 3318
11:25 the LORD **c down** in a cloud, and 3381
11:25 it **c to pass**, that when the spirit rested upon 1961
12: 4 of the congregation. And they three **c out**. 3318
12: 5 the LORD **c down** in the pillar of 3381
12: 5 and Miriam: and they both **c forth**. 3318
13:22 ascended by the south, and **c** unto Hebron; 935
13:23 they **c** unto the brook of Eshcol, and 935
13:26 they went and **c** to Moses, and to Aaron, 935
13:27 We **c** unto the land whither thou sentest us, 935
14:45 the Amalekites **c down**, and the Canaanites 3381
16:27 Dathan and Abiram **c out**, and stood *in* 3318
Nu 16:31 it **c to pass**, as he had made an end of 1961
16:35 there **c out** a fire from the LORD, and 3318
16:42 it **c to pass**, when the congregation was 1961
16:43 Aaron **c** before the tabernacle of 935
17: 8 it **c to pass**, that on the morrow Moses 1961
19: 2 no blemish, *and* upon which never **c** yoke: 5927
20: 1 **c** the children of Israel, *even* the whole 935
20:11 the water **c out** abundantly, and 3318
20:20 Edom **c out** against him with much people, 3318
20:22 from Kadesh, and **c** *unto* mount Hor. 935
20:28 Moses and Eleazar **c down** from the mount. 3381
21: 1 heard *tell* that Israel **c** *by* the way of 935
21: 7 Therefore the people **c** to Moses, and said, 935
21: 9 put it upon a pole, and it **c to pass**, that if a 1961
21:23 and he **c** *to* Jahaz, and fought against Israel. 935
22: 7 they **c** unto Balaam, and spake unto him 935
22: 9 God **c** unto Balaam, and said, What men *are* 935
22:16 they **c** to Balaam, and said to him, Thus saith 935
22:20 God **c** unto Balaam at night, and said unto 935
22:39 with Balak, and they **c** *unto* Kirjath-huzoth. 935
22:41 it **c to pass** on the morrow, that Balak took 1961
23:17 when he **c** to him, behold, he stood by his 935
24: 2 and the spirit of God **c** upon him. 1961
25: 6 one of the children of Israel **c** and 935
26: 1 it **c to pass** after the plague, that 1961
27: 1 **c** the daughters of Zelophehad, the son of 7126
31:14 over hundreds, which **c** from the battle. 935
31:48 captains of hundreds, **c near** unto Moses: 7126
32: 2 the children of Reuben **c** and spake unto 935
32:11 Surely none of the men that **c up** out of 5927
32:16 they **c near** unto him, and said, We will 5066
33: 9 they removed from Marah, and **c** unto Elim: 935
36: 1 **c near**, and spake before Moses, and before 7126
Dt 1: 3 it **c to pass** in the fortieth year, in 1961
1:19 commanded us; and we **c** to Kadesh-barnea. 935
1:22 ye **c near** unto me every one of you, and 7126
1:24 **c** unto the valley of Eshcol, and searched it 935
1:31 way that ye went, until ye **c** into this place. 935
1:44 **c out** against you, and chased you, as bees 3318
2:14 the space in which we **c** from 1980
2:16 So it **c to pass**, when all the men of war 1961
2:23 which **c forth** out of Caphtor, 3318
2:32 Sihon **c out** against us, he and all his 3318
3: 1 and Og the king of Bashan **c out** against us, 3318
4:11 ye **c near** and stood under the mountain; 7126
4:45 of Israel, after they **c forth** out of Egypt, 3318
5:23 it **c to pass**, when ye heard the voice out of 1961
5:23 that ye **c near** unto me, *even* all the heads 7126
9: 7 until ye **c** unto this place, ye have been 935
9:11 And it **c to pass** at the end of forty days and 1961
9:15 So I turned and **c down** from the mount, 3381
10: 5 turned myself and **c down** from the mount, 3381
11: 5 in the wilderness, until ye **c** into this place; 935
11:10 as the land of Egypt, from whence ye **c out**, 3318
22:14 say, I took this woman, and when I **c** to her, 7126
23: 4 in the way, when ye **c forth** out of Egypt; 3318
29: 7 when ye **c** unto this place, Sihon the king of 935
29: 7 **c out** against us unto battle, and we smote 3318
29:16 how we **c** through the nations which ye 5674
31:24 it **c to pass**, when Moses had made an end 1961
32:17 they knew not, *to* new *gods that* **c** newly **up**, 935
32:44 Moses **c** and spake all the words of this song 935
33: 2 The LORD **c** from Sinai, and rose up from 935
33: 2 and he **c** with ten thousands of saints: 857
33:21 he **c** *with* the heads of the people, 857
Jos 1: 1 the servant of the LORD it **c to pass**, 1961
2: 1 **c** *into* a harlot's house, named Rahab, and 935
2: 2 there **c** men in hither to night of the children 935
2: 4 There **c** men unto me, but I wist not whence 935
2: 5 it **c to pass** *about the time* of shutting of 1961
2: 8 she **c up** unto them upon the roof; 5927
2:10 Red sea for you, when you **c out** of Egypt; 3318
2:22 **c** unto the mountain, and abode there three 935
2:23 **c** to Joshua the son of Nun, and told him all 935
3: 1 **c** to Jordan, he and all the children of Israel, 935
3: 2 it **c to pass** after three days, that 1961
3:14 it **c to pass**, when the people removed from 1961
3:16 That the waters which **c down** from above 3381
3:16 those that **c down** toward the sea of 3381
4: 1 it **c to pass**, when all the people were clean 1961
4:11 it **c to pass**, when all the people were clean 1961
4:18 it **c to pass**, when the priests that bare 1961
4:19 the people **c up** out of Jordan on the tenth 5927
4:22 Israel **c over** this Jordan on dry *land*. 5674
5: 1 it **c to pass**, when all the kings of 1961
5: 4 All the people that **c out** of Egypt, 3318
5: 4 by the way, after they **c out** of Egypt. 3318
5: 5 Now all the people that **c out** were 3318
5: 5 by the way as they **c forth** out of Egypt, 3318
5: 6 which **c out** of Egypt, were consumed, 3318
5: 8 it **c to pass**, when they had done 1961
5:13 it **c to pass**, when Joshua was by Jericho, 1961
6: 1 of Israel: none went out, and none **c in**. 935
6: 8 it **c to pass**, when Joshua had spoken unto 1961
6: 9 the rereward **c** after the ark, *the priests* 1980
6:11 they **c** *into* the camp, and lodged in 935
6:13 the rereward **c** after the ark of the LORD, 1980
6:15 it **c to pass** on the seventh day, that they 1961
6:16 it **c to pass** at the seventh time, when 1961
6:20 it **c to pass**, when the people heard 1961
8:11 **c** before the city, and pitched on the north 935
8:14 it **c to pass**, when the king of Ai saw *it*, that 1961
8:24 it **c to pass**, when Israel had made an end 1961
9: 1 it **c to pass**, when all the kings which *were* 1961
9:12 on the day we **c forth** to go unto you; 3318
9:16 it **c to pass** at the end of three days after 1961
9:17 and **c** unto their cities on the third day. 935
10: 1 Now it **c to pass**, when Adoni-zedek king 1961
10: 9 Joshua therefore **c** unto them suddenly, *and* 935
10:11 it **c to pass**, as they fled from before Israel, 1961
10:20 it **c to pass**, when Joshua and the children 1961
10:24 it **c to pass**, when they brought out those 1961
10:24 they **c near**, and put their feet upon 7126
10:27 it **c to pass** at the time of the going down of 1961
10:33 Horam king of Gezer **c up** to help Lachish; 5927
Jos 11: 1 it **c to pass**, when Jabin king of Hazor had 1961
11: 5 they **c** and pitched together at the waters of 935
11: 7 So Joshua **c**, and all the people of war with 935
11:21 at that time **c** Joshua, and cut off 935
14: 6 the children of Judah **c** unto Joshua in 5066
15:18 it **c to pass**, as she came *unto him*, that she 1961
15:18 as she **c** *unto him*, that she moved him to ask 935
16: 7 and **c** to Jericho, and went out *at* Jordan. 6293
17: 4 they **c near** before Eleazar the priest, and 7126
17:13 Yet it **c to pass**, when the children of Israel 1961
18: 9 and **c** *again* to Joshua to the host *at* Shiloh. 935
18:11 Benjamin **c up** according to their families: 5927
18:11 the coast of their lot **c forth** between 3318
18:16 the border **c down** to the end of 3381
19: 1 the second lot **c forth** to Simeon, *even* for 3318
19:10 the third lot **c up** for the children of 5927
19:17 *And* the fourth lot **c out** to Issachar, for 3318
19:24 the fifth lot **c out** for the tribe of 3318
19:32 The sixth lot **c out** to the children of 3318
19:40 *And* the seventh lot **c out** for the tribe of 3318
21: 1 **c near** the heads of the fathers of 5066
21: 4 the lot **c out** for the families of 3318
21:45 unto the house of Israel; all **c to pass**. 935
22:10 And when they **c** unto the borders of Jordan, 935
22:15 And they **c** unto the children of Reuben, and 935
23: 1 it **c to pass** a long time after that 1961
24: 6 you **c** unto the sea; and the Egyptians 935
24:11 ye went over Jordan, and **c** unto Jericho: 935
24:29 it **c to pass** after these things, that Joshua 1961
Jdg 1: 1 Now after the death of Joshua it **c to pass**, 1961
1:14 it **c to pass**, when she came *to him*, that she 1961
1:14 when she **c** *to him*, that she moved him to 935
1:28 it **c to pass**, when Israel was strong, 1961
2: 1 an angel of the LORD **c up** from Gilgal to 5927
2: 4 it **c to pass**, when the angel of the LORD 1961
2:19 it **c to pass**, when the judge was dead, 1961
3:10 the spirit of the LORD **c** upon him, and 1961
3:20 Ehud **c** unto him; and he was sitting in a 935
3:22 dagger out of his belly; and the dirt **c out**. 3318
3:24 When he was gone out, his servants **c**; and 935
3:27 it **c to pass**, when he was come, that he 1961
4: 5 the children of Israel **c up** to her for 5927
4:22 Jael **c out** to meet him, and said unto him, 3318
4:22 when he **c** into her *tent*, behold, Sisera lay 935
5:14 out of Machir **c down** governors, and out of 3381
5:19 The kings **c** *and* fought, then fought 935
5:23 they **c** not to the help of the LORD, 935
6: 3 that the Midianites **c up**, and 5927
6: 3 of the east, even they **c up** against them; 5927
6: 5 For they **c up** with their cattle and 5927
6: 5 and they **c** as grasshoppers for multitude; 935
6: 7 it **c to pass**, when the children of Israel 1961
6:11 there **c** an angel of the LORD, and 935
6:25 it **c to pass** the same night, that the LORD 1961
6:34 the spirit of the LORD **c upon** Gideon, 3847
6:35 unto Naphtali; and they **c up** to meet them. 5927
7: 9 it **c to pass** the same night, that the LORD 1961
7:13 and **c** unto a tent, and smote it that it fell, and 935
7:19 **c** unto the outside of the camp *in* 935
8: 4 Gideon **c** to Jordan, *and* passed over, he, 935
8:15 And he **c** unto the men of Succoth, and said, 935
8:33 it **c to pass**, as soon as Gideon was dead, 1961
9:25 they robbed all that **c along** *that* way by 5674
9:26 Gaal the son of Ebed **c** with his brethren, 935
9:42 it **c to pass** on the morrow, that the people 1961
9:52 Abimelech **c** unto the tower, and 935
9:57 upon them **c** the curse of Jotham the son of 935
11: 4 it **c to pass** in process of time, that 1961
11:13 when they **c up** out of Egypt, from Arnon 5927
11:16 when Israel **c up** from Egypt, and 5927
11:16 unto the Red sea, and **c** to Kadesh; 935
11:18 **c** by the east side of the land of Moab, and 935
11:18 but **c** not within the border of Moab: 935
11:29 the spirit of the LORD **c** upon Jephthah, 1961
11:34 Jephthah **c** *to* Mizpeh unto his house, and 935
11:34 his daughter **c out** to meet him with 3318
11:35 it **c to pass**, when he saw her, that he rent 1961
11:39 it **c to pass** at the end of two months, 1961
13: 6 the woman **c** and told her husband, saying, 935
13: 6 A man of God **c** unto me, and 935
13: 9 the angel of God **c** again unto the woman as 935
13:10 unto me, that **c** unto me the *other* day. 935
13:11 and **c** to the man, and said unto him, 935
13:20 For it **c to pass**, when the flame went up 1961
14: 2 he **c up**, and told his father and his mother, 5927
14: 5 and **c** to the vineyards of Timnath: 935
14: 6 the spirit of the LORD **c mightily** upon 6743
14: 9 **c** to his father and mother, and he gave 1980
14:11 it **c to pass**, when they saw him, that they 1961
14:14 Out of the eater **c forth** meat, and out of 3318
14:14 and out of the strong **c forth** sweetness. 3318
14:15 it **c to pass** on the seventh day, that they 1961
14:17 it **c to pass** on the seventh day, that he told 1961
14:19 the spirit of the LORD **c** upon him, and 6743
15: 1 it **c to pass** within a while after, in the time 1961
15: 6 the Philistines **c up**, and burnt her and her 5927
15:14 *And* when he **c** unto Lehi, the Philistines 935
15:14 the spirit of the LORD **c mightily** upon 6743
15:17 it **c to pass**, when he had made an end of 1961
15:19 *was* in the jaw, and there **c** water thereout; 3318
15:19 his spirit **c again**, and he revived: 7725
16: 4 it **c to pass** afterward, that he loved a 1961
16: 5 the lords of the Philistines **c up** unto her, 5927
16:16 it **c to pass**, when she pressed him daily 1961
16:18 the lords of the Philistines **c up** unto her, 5927
16:25 it **c to pass**, when their hearts were merry, 1961
16:31 and all the house of his father **c down**, 3381
17: 8 he **c** *to* mount Ephraim to the house of 935
18: 2 who when they **c** *to* mount Ephraim, to 935
18: 7 **c** to Laish, and saw the people that *were* 935
18: 8 they **c** unto their brethren *to* Zorah and 935
18:13 and **c** unto the house of Micah. 935
18:15 **c** to the house of the young man the Levite, 935
18:17 *and* **c in** thither, *and* took the graven image, 935
18:27 the priest which he had, and **c** unto Laish, 935

Jdg 19: 1 it **c to pass** in those days, when *there was* 1961
19: 5 it **c to pass** on the fourth day, when they 1961
19:10 and departed, and **c** over against Jebus, 935
19:16 there **c** an old man from his work out of 935
19:22 Bring forth the man that **c** into thine house, 935
19:26 **c** the woman in the dawning of the day, 935
19:30 **c up** out of the land of Egypt unto this day: 5927
20: 4 I **c** into Gibeah that *belongeth* to Benjamin, I 935
20:21 the children of Benjamin **c forth** out of 3318
20:24 the children of Israel **c near** against 7126
20:26 **c** *unto* the house of God, and wept, and 935
20:33 the liers in wait of Israel **c forth** out of their 1518
20:34 there **c** against Gibeah ten thousand chosen 935
20:42 them which **c** out of the cities they NIH
20:48 as the beast, and all that **c to hand**: 4672
20:48 they set on fire all the cities that they **c to**. 4672
21: 2 the people **c** *to* the house of God, and 935
21: 4 it **c to pass** on the morrow, that the people 1961
21: 5 **c** not **up** with the congregation unto 5927
21: 5 *him* that **c** not **up** to the LORD *to* Mizpeh, 5927
21: 8 that **c** not **up** *to* Mizpeh to the LORD? 5927
21: 8 there **c** none to the camp from Jabesh-gilead 935
21:14 Benjamin **c again** at that time; and 7725
Ru 1: 1 Now it **c to pass** in the days when 1961
1: 2 they **c** *into* the country of Moab, and 935
1:19 So they two went until they **c** *to* Beth-lehem. 935
1:19 it **c to pass**, when they were come *to* 1961
1:22 they **c** *to* Beth-lehem in the beginning of 935
2: 3 **c**, and gleaned in the field after the reapers: 935
2: 4 Boaz **c** from Beth-lehem, and said unto 935
2: 6 It *is* the Moabitish damsel that **c back** with 7725
2: 7 so she **c**, and hath continued even from 935
3: 7 the end of the heap *of corn*: and she **c** softly, 935
3: 8 it **c to pass** at midnight, that the man was 1961
3:14 Let it not be known that a woman **c** *into* 935
3:16 when she **c** to her mother in law, she said, 935
4: 1 the kinsman of whom Boaz spake **c by**; 5674
1Sa 1:12 it **c to pass**, as she continued praying 1961
1:19 and returned, and **c** to their house to Ramah: 935
1:20 Wherefore it **c to pass**, when the time was 1961
2:13 the priest's servant **c**, while the flesh was in 935
2:14 in Shiloh unto all the Israelites that **c** thither. 935
2:15 the priest's servant **c**, and said to the man 935
2:19 when she **c up** with her husband to offer 5927
2:27 there **c** a man of God unto Eli, and said unto 935
3: 2 it **c to pass** at that time, when Eli *was* laid 1961
3:10 the LORD **c**, and stood, and called as at 935
4: 1 the word of Samuel **c** to all Israel. 1961
4: 5 the covenant of the LORD **c** into the camp, 935
4:12 **c** *to* Shiloh the same day with his clothes 935
4:13 when he **c**, lo, Eli sat upon a seat *by* 935
4:13 when the man **c** into the city, and told *it*, all 935
4:14 And the man **c in** hastily, and told Eli. 935
4:16 I *am* he that **c** out of the army, and I fled to 935
4:18 it **c to pass**, when he made mention of 1961
4:19 and travailed; for her pains **c** upon her. 2015
5:10 it **c to pass**, as the ark of God came *to* 1961
5:10 it came to pass, as the ark of God **c** *to* Ekron, 935
6:14 the cart **c** into the field of Joshua, 935
7: 1 the men of Kirjath-jearim **c**, and fetched up 935
7: 2 it **c to pass**, while the ark abode in 1961
7:11 and smote them, until *they* **c** under Beth-car. NIH
7:13 and they **c** no more into the coast of Israel: 935
8: 1 it **c to pass**, when Samuel was old, that he 1961
8: 4 and **c** to Samuel unto Ramah, 935
9:12 make haste now, for he **c** to day to the city; 935
9:14 behold, Samuel **c out** against them, for to 3318
9:15 told Samuel in his ear a day before Saul **c**, 935
9:26 it **c to pass** about the spring of the day, 1961
10: 9 and all those signs **c to pass** that day. 935
10:10 when they **c** thither to the hill, behold, 935
10:10 the spirit of God **c** upon him, and 6743
10:11 it **c to pass**, when all that knew him 1961
10:13 end of prophesying, he **c** *to* the high place. 935
10:14 that *they were* no where, we **c** to Samuel. 935
11: 1 Nahash the Ammonite **c up**, and 5927
11: 4 **c** the messengers *to* Gibeah of Saul, and 935
11: 5 Saul **c** after the herd out of the field; 935
11: 6 the spirit of God **c** upon Saul when he 6743
11: 7 and they **c out** with one consent. 3318
11: 9 they said unto the messengers that **c**, 935
11: 9 the messengers **c** and shewed *it* to the men of 935
11:11 they **c** into the midst of the host in 935
11:11 it **c to pass**, that they which remained were 1961
12:12 of the children of Ammon **c** against you, 935
13: 5 they **c up**, and pitched in Michmash, 5927
13: 8 *had appointed*: but Samuel **c** not *to* Gilgal; 935
13:10 it **c to pass**, that as soon as he had made an 1961
13:10 the burnt offering, behold, Samuel **c**; 935
13:17 the spoilers **c out** of the camp of 3318
13:22 So it **c to pass** in the day of battle, 1961
14: 1 Now it **c to pass** upon a day, that Jonathan 1961
14:19 it **c to pass**, while Saul talked unto 1961
14:20 and they **c** to the battle: 935
14:25 all *they of* the land **c** to a wood; and 935
15: 2 him in the way, when he **c up** from Egypt. 5927
15: 5 Saul **c** to a city of Amalek, and laid wait in 935
15: 6 of Israel, when they **c up** out of Egypt. 5927
15:10 **c** the word of the LORD unto Samuel, 1961
15:12 Saul **c** to Carmel, and behold, 935
15:13 Samuel **c** to Saul: and Saul said unto him, 935
15:32 Agag **c** unto him delicately. And Agag said, 1980
15:35 Samuel **c** no **more** to see Saul until the day 3254
16: 4 the LORD spake, and **c** *to* Beth-lehem. 935
16: 6 it **c to pass**, when they were come, that he 1961
16:13 the spirit of the LORD **c** upon David from 6743
16:21 David **c** to Saul, and stood before him: and 935
16:23 it **c to pass**, when the *evil* spirit from God 1961
17:20 he **c** to the trench, as the host was going 935
17:22 *into* the army, and **c** and saluted his brethren. 935
17:23 behold, there **c up** the champion, 5927
17:34 there **c** a lion and a bear, and took a lamb out 935
17:41 the Philistine **c on** and drew near 1980+1980
17:48 it **c to pass**, when the Philistine arose, and 1961
17:48 **c** and drew nigh to meet David, that David 1980

1Sa 18: 1 it **c to pass**, when he made an end of 1961
18: 6 it **c to pass** as they came, when David was 1961
18: 6 it came to pass as they **c**, when David was 935
18: 6 that the women **c out** of all cities of Israel, 3318
18:10 it **c to pass** on the morrow, that the evil 1961
18:10 that the evil spirit from God **c** upon Saul, 6743
18:13 and he went out and **c in** before the people. 935
18:16 because he went out and **c in** before them. 935
18:19 it **c to pass** at the time when Merab Saul's 1961
18:30 it **c to pass**, after they went forth, 1961
19:18 **c** to Samuel to Ramah, and told him all that 935
19:22 and **c** to a great well that *is* in Sechu: 935
19:23 prophesied, until he **c** to Naioth in Ramah. 935
20: 1 **c** and said before Jonathan, What have I 935
20:27 it **c to pass** on the morrow, *which was* 1961
20:35 it **c to pass** in the morning, that Jonathan 1961
20:38 gathered up the arrows, and **c** to his master. 935
21: 1 **c** David to Nob to Ahimelech the priest: 935
21: 5 since I **c out**, and the vessels of the young 3318
22: 5 and **c** *into* the forest of Hareth. 935
22:11 in Nob: and they **c** all of them to the king. 935
23: 6 it **c to pass**, when Abiathar the son of 1961
23: 6 *that* he **c down** *with* an ephod in his hand. 3381
23:19 **c up** the Ziphites to Saul to Gibeah, saying, 5927
23:25 wherefore he **c down** *into* a rock, and 3381
23:27 there **c** a messenger unto Saul, saying, 935
24: 1 it **c to pass**, when Saul was returned from 1961
24: 3 he **c** to the sheepcotes by the way, where 935
24: 5 it **c to pass** afterward, that David's heart 1961
24:16 it **c to pass**, when David had made an end 1961
25: 9 when David's young men **c**, they spake to 935
25:12 and **c** and told him all those sayings. 935
25:20 that she **c down** by the covert of the hill, 3381
25:20 David and his men **c down** against her; 3381
25:36 Abigail **c** to Nabal; and behold, he held a 935
25:37 it **c to pass** in the morning, when the wine 1961
25:38 it **c to pass** about ten days *after*, that 1961
26: 1 the Ziphites **c** unto Saul to Gibeah, saying, 935
26: 3 he saw that Saul **c** after him into 935
26: 5 and **c** to the place where Saul had pitched: 935
26: 7 and Abishai **c** to the people by night: 935
26:15 for there **c** one of the people **in** to destroy 935
27: 9 the apparel, and returned, and **c** to Achish. 935
28: 1 it **c to pass** in those days, that 1961
28: 4 and **c** and pitched in Shunem: 935
28: 8 with him, and they **c** to the woman by night: 935
28:21 the woman **c** unto Saul, and saw that he was 935
30: 1 it **c to pass**, when David and his men were 1961
30: 3 So David and his men **c** to the city, and 935
30: 9 that *were* with him, and **c** to the brook Besor, 935
30:12 he had eaten, his spirit **c again** to him: 7725
30:21 David **c** to the two hundred men, which were 935
30:21 when David **c near** to the people, he 5066
30:23 delivered the company that **c** against us into 935
30:26 when David **c** to Ziklag, he sent of the spoil 935
31: 7 fled; and the Philistines **c** and dwelt in them. 935
31: 8 it **c to pass** on the morrow, when 1961
31: 8 when the Philistines **c** to strip the slain, 935
31:12 and **c** to Jabesh, and burnt them there. 935
2Sa 1: 1 Now it **c to pass** after the death of Saul, 1961
1: 2 It **c** even **to pass** on the third day, that 1961
1: 2 a man **c** out of the camp from Saul with his 935
1: 2 *so* it was, when he **c** to David, that he fell to 935
2: 1 it **c to pass** after this, that David inquired of 1961
2: 4 the men of Judah **c**, and there they anointed 935
2:23 fifth *rib*, that the spear **c out** behind him; 3318
2:23 it **c to pass**, that as many as came to 1961
2:23 that as many as **c** to the place where Asahel 935
2:29 *through* all Bithron, and they **c** *to* Mahanaim. 935
2:32 and they **c** to Hebron at break of day. NIH
3: 6 it **c to pass**, while there was war between 1961
3:20 So Abner **c** to David *to* Hebron, and 935
3:22 of David and Joab **c** from *pursuing* a troop, 935
3:23 Abner the son of Ner **c** to the king, and 935
3:24 Joab **c** to the king, and said, What hast thou 935
3:24 behold, Abner **c** unto thee; why *is* it *that* 935
3:25 that he **c** to deceive thee, and to know thy 935
3:35 when all the people **c** to cause David to eat 935
4: 4 was five years old when the tidings **c** of Saul 935
4: 4 it **c to pass**, as she made haste to flee, 1961
4: 5 **c** about the heat of the day to the house of 935
4: 6 they **c** thither into the midst of the house, 935
4: 7 For when they **c** *into* the house, he lay on his 935
5: 1 **c** all the tribes of Israel to David unto 935
5: 3 So all the elders of Israel **c** to the king to 935
5:17 all the Philistines **c up** to seek David; 5927
5:18 The Philistines also **c** and spread themselves 935
5:20 David **c** to Baal-perazim, and David smote 935
5:22 the Philistines **c up** yet again, and 5927
6: 6 And when they **c** to Nachon's threshingfloor, 935
6:16 as the ark of the LORD **c** *into* the city of 935
6:20 Michal the daughter of Saul **c out** to meet 3318
7: 1 it **c to pass**, when the king sat in his house, 1961
7: 4 it **c to pass** that night, that the word of 1961
7: 4 that the word of the LORD **c** unto Nathan, 1961
8: 1 after this it **c to pass**, that David smote 1961
8: 5 when the Syrians of Damascus **c** to succour 935
10: 1 it **c to pass** after this, that the king of 1961
10: 2 David's servants **c** *into* the land of 935
10: 8 the children of Ammon **c out**, and put 3318
10:14 the children of Ammon, and **c** *to* Jerusalem. 935
10:16 they **c** *to* Helam; and Shobach the captain of 935
10:17 and passed over Jordan, and **c** to Helam. 935
11: 1 it **c to pass**, after the year was expired, 1961
11: 2 it **c to pass** in an eveningtide, that David 1961
11: 4 and she **c in** unto him, and he lay with her; 935
11:14 it **c to pass** in the morning, that David 1961
11:16 it **c to pass**, when Joab observed the city, 1961
11:22 **c** and shewed David all that Joab had sent 935
11:23 **c out** unto us *into* the field, and we were 3318
12: 1 he **c** unto him, and said unto him, 935
12: 4 there **c** a traveller unto the rich man, and 935
12:18 it **c to pass** on the seventh day, that 1961
12:20 **c** *into* the house of the LORD, and 935
12:20 he **c** to his own house; and when he required, 935

2Sa 13: 1 it **c to pass** after this, that Absalom the son 1961
13:23 it **c to pass** after two full years, 1961
13:24 Absalom **c** to the king, and said, 935
13:30 it **c to pass**, while they *were* in the way, 1961
13:30 in the way, that tidings **c** to David, saying, 935
13:34 there **c** much people by the way of the hill 1980
13:36 it **c to pass**, as soon as he had made an end 1961
13:36 the king's sons **c**, and lift up their voice and 935
14:31 **c** to Absalom unto *his* house, and said unto 935
14:33 So Joab **c** to the king, and told him: and 935
14:33 he **c** to the king, and bowed himself on his 935
15: 1 it **c to pass** after this, that Absalom 1961
15: 2 *that when* any man that had a controversy **c** 935
15: 5 that when any man **c nigh** *to him* to do him 7126
15: 6 to all Israel that **c** to the king for judgment: 935
15: 7 it **c to pass** after forty years, that Absalom 1961
15:13 there **c** a messenger to David, saying, 935
15:18 six hundred men which **c** after him from 935
15:32 it **c to pass**, that *when* David was come to 1961
15:32 Hushai the Archite *c* to meet him with his NIH
15:37 So Hushai David's friend **c** *into* the city, and 935
15:37 *into* the city, and Absalom **c** *into* Jerusalem. 935
16: 5 And when king David **c** to Bahurim, behold, 935
16: 5 thence **c out** a man of the family of 3318
16: 5 he **c forth**, and cursed still as he came. 3318
16: 5 he came forth, and cursed still as he **c**. 3318
16:11 my son, which **c forth** of my bowels, 3318
16:14 **c** weary, and refreshed themselves there. 935
16:15 **c** *to* Jerusalem, and Ahithophel with him. 935
16:16 it **c to pass**, when Hushai the Archite, 1961
17:18 **c** to a man's house in Bahurim, which had a 935
17:20 when Absalom's servants **c** to the woman to 935
17:21 it **c to pass**, after they were departed, 1961
17:21 that they **c up** out of the well, and went and 5927
17:24 David **c** to Mahanaim. And Absalom passed 935
17:27 it **c to pass**, when David was come to 1961
18: 4 all the people **c out** by hundreds and 3318
18:25 And he **c apace**, and drew near. 1980+1980
18:31 behold, Cushi **c**; and Cushi said, Tidings, 935
19: 5 Joab **c** *into* the house to the king, and said, 935
19: 8 all the people **c** before the king: for Israel 935
19:15 So the king returned, and **c** to Jordan. 935
19:15 Judah **c** to Gilgal, to go to meet the king, 935
19:16 **c** down with the men of Judah to meet king NIH
19:24 Mephibosheth the son of Saul **c down** to 3381
19:24 departed until the day he **c** *again* in peace. 935
19:25 it **c to pass**, when he was come *to* 1961
19:31 Barzillai the Gileadite **c down** from 3381
19:41 all the men of Israel **c** to the king, and 935
20: 3 David **c** to his house *at* Jerusalem; and 935
20:12 when he saw that every one that **c** by him 935
20:15 they **c** and besieged him in Abel of 935
21:18 it **c to pass** after this, that there was again a 1961
22:10 He bowed the heavens also, and **c down**; 3381
23:13 **c** to David in the harvest time unto the cave 935
24: 6 they **c** to Gilead, and to the land of 935
24: 6 and they **c** to Dan-jaan, and about to Zidon, 935
24: 7 **c** *to* the strong hold of Tyre, and *to* all 935
24: 8 they **c** *to* Jerusalem at the end of nine months 935
24:11 the word of the LORD **c** unto the prophet 1961
24:13 So Gad **c** to David, and told him, and 935
24:18 Gad **c** that day to David, and said unto him, 935
1Ki 1:22 with the king, Nathan the prophet also **c in**. 935
1:28 she **c** into the king's presence, and 935
1:32 son of Jehoiada. And they **c** before the king. 935
1:40 all the people **c up** after him, and 5927
1:42 Jonathan the son of Abiathar the priest **c**: 935
1:47 moreover the king's servants **c** to bless our 935
1:53 he **c** and bowed himself to king Solomon: 935
2: 7 for so they **c** to me when I fled because of 7126
2: 8 he **c down** to meet me *at* Jordan, and 3381
2:13 Adonijah the son of Haggith **c** to Bath-sheba 935
2:28 tidings **c** to Joab: for Joab had turned after 935
2:30 Benaiah **c** to the tabernacle of the LORD, 935
2:39 it **c to pass** at the end of three years, 1961
3:15 he **c** *to* Jerusalem, and stood before the ark 935
3:16 **c** there two women, *that were* harlots, 935
3:18 it **c to pass** the third day after that I was 1961
4:27 for all that **c** unto king Solomon's table, 7131
4:34 there **c** of all people to hear the wisdom of 935
5: 7 it **c to pass**, when Hiram heard the words 1961
6: 1 it **c to pass** in the four hundred and 1961
6:11 the word of the LORD **c** to Solomon, 1961
7:14 he **c** to king Solomon, and wrought all his 935
8: 3 all the elders of Israel **c**, and the priests took 935
8: 9 when they **c out** of the land of Egypt. 3318
8:10 it **c to pass**, when the priests were come out 1961
9: 1 it **c to pass**, when Solomon had finished 1961
9:10 it **c to pass** at the end of twenty years, 1961
9:12 Hiram **c out** from Tyre to see the cities 3318
9:24 Pharaoh's daughter **c up** out of the city of 5927
9:28 they **c** to Ophir, and fet from thence gold, 935
10: 1 she **c** to prove him with hard questions. 935
10: 2 she **c** to Jerusalem with a very great train, 935
10: 7 until I **c**, and mine eyes had seen *it*: and 935
10:10 there **c** no more such abundance of spices as 935
10:12 there **c** no such almug trees, nor were seen 935
10:14 Now the weight of gold that **c** to Solomon in 935
10:22 once in three years **c** the navy of Tharshish, 935
10:29 a chariot **c up** and went out of Egypt for six 5927
11: 4 For it **c to pass**, when Solomon was old, 1961
11:15 For it **c to pass**, when David was in Edom, 1961
11:18 they arose out of Midian, and **c** *to* Paran: 935
11:18 they **c** *to* Egypt, unto Pharaoh king of Egypt; 935
11:29 it **c to pass** at that time when Jeroboam 1961
12: 2 it **c to pass**, when Jeroboam the son of 1961
12: 3 and all the congregation of Israel **c**, 935
12:12 all the people **c** to Rehoboam the third day, 935
12:20 it **c to pass**, when all Israel heard that 1961
12:22 the word of God **c** unto Shemaiah the man 1961
13: 1 there **c** a man of God out of Judah by 935
13: 4 it **c to pass**, when king Jeroboam heard 1961
13:10 returned not by the way that he **c** to Beth-el. 935
13:11 his son **c** and told him all the works that 935
13:12 the man of God went, which **c** from Judah. 935

1Ki 13:20 it **c to pass**, as they sat at the table, that 1961
13:20 that the word of the LORD **c** unto 1961
13:21 he cried unto the man of God that **c** from 935
13:23 it **c to pass**, after he had eaten bread, and 1961
13:25 they **c** and told *it* in the city where the old 935
13:29 the old prophet **c** to the city, to mourn and 935
13:31 it **c to pass**, after he had buried him, that he 1961
14: 4 went *to* Shiloh, and **c** *to* the house of Ahijah. 935
14: 6 as she **c in** at the door, that he said, Come in, 935
14:17 wife arose, and departed, and **c** to Tirzah: 935
14:17 *and* when she **c** to the threshold of the door, 935
14:25 it **c to pass** in the fifth year of king 1961
14:25 *that* Shishak king of Egypt **c up** against 5927
15:21 it **c to pass**, when Baasha heard *thereof,* 1961
15:29 it **c to pass**, when he reigned, *that* he smote 1961
16: 1 the word of the LORD **c** to Jehu the son of 1961
16: 7 **c** the word of the LORD against Baasha, 1961
16:11 it **c to pass**, when he *began* to reign, 1961
16:18 it **c to pass**, when Zimri saw that the city 1961
16:31 it **c to pass**, as if it had been a light thing 1961
17: 2 the word of the LORD **c** unto him, saying, 1961
17: 7 it **c to pass** after a while, that the brook 1961
17: 8 the word of the LORD **c** unto him, saying, 1961
17:10 when he **c** to the gate of the city, behold, 935
17:17 it **c to pass** after these things, *that* the son 1961
17:22 the soul of the child **c** into him **again**, and 7725
18: 1 it **c to pass** *after* many days, that the word 1961
18: 1 that the word of the LORD **c** to Elijah in 1961
18:17 it **c to pass**, when Ahab saw Elijah, 1961
18:21 Elijah **c** unto all the people, and said, How 5066
18:27 it **c to pass** at noon, that Elijah mocked 1961
18:29 it **c to pass**, when midday was past, and 1961
18:30 all the people **c near** unto him. And he 5066
18:31 unto whom the word of the LORD **c**, 1961
18:36 it **c to pass** at *the time of* the offering of 1961
18:36 that Elijah the prophet **c near**, and said, 5066
18:44 it **c to pass** at the seventh *time,* that he said, 1961
18:45 it **c to pass** in the mean while, that 1961
19: 3 went for his life, and **c** *to* Beer-sheba, 935
19: 4 and **c** and sat down under a juniper tree: 935
19: 7 the angel of the LORD **c again** the second 7725
19: 9 he **c** thither unto a cave, and lodged there; 935
19: 9 the word of the LORD **c** to him, and NIH
19:13 *there* **c** a voice unto him, and said, NIH
20: 5 the messengers **c again**, and said, 7725
20:12 it **c to pass**, when *Ben-hadad* heard this 1961
20:13 there **c** a prophet unto Ahab king of Israel, 5066
20:19 princes of the provinces **c out** of the city, 3318
20:22 the prophet **c** to the king of Israel, and 5066
20:26 it **c to pass** at the return of the year, 1961
20:28 there **c** a man of God, and spake unto 5066
20:30 Ben-hadad fled, and **c** into the city, into an 935
20:32 and **c** to the king of Israel, and said, 935
20:33 Ben-hadad **c forth** to him; and he caused 3318
20:43 and displeased, and **c** to Samaria. 935
21: 1 it **c to pass** after these things, *that* Naboth 1961
21: 4 Ahab **c** into his house heavy and displeased 935
21: 5 Jezebel his wife **c** to him, and said unto him, 935
21:13 there **c in** two men, children of Belial, and 935
21:15 it **c to pass**, when Jezebel heard that 1961
21:16 it **c to pass**, when Ahab heard that Naboth 1961
21:17 the word of the LORD **c** to Elijah 1961
21:27 it **c to pass**, when Ahab heard those words, 1961
21:28 the word of the LORD **c** to Elijah 1961
22: 2 it **c to pass** on the third year, that 1961
22: 2 that Jehoshaphat the king of Judah **c down** 3381
22:15 So he **c** to the king. And the king said unto 935
22:21 there **c forth** a spirit, and stood before 3318
22:32 it **c to pass**, when the captains of 1961
22:33 it **c to pass**, when the captains of 1961
2Ki 1: 6 There **c** a man **up** to meet us, and said unto 5927
1: 7 What manner of man *was he* which **c up** to 5927
1:10 there **c down** fire from heaven, and 3381
1:12 the fire of God **c down** from heaven, and 3381
1:13 and **c** and fell on his knees before Elijah, and 935
1:14 there **c** fire **down** from heaven, and 3381
2: 1 it **c to pass**, when the LORD would take 1961
2: 3 that *were at* Beth-el **c forth** to Elisha, 3318
2: 4 I will not leave thee. So they **c** *to* Jericho. 935
2: 5 prophets that *were* at Jericho **c** to Elisha, 5066
2: 9 it **c to pass**, when they were gone over, 1961
2:11 it **c to pass**, *as* they still went on, 1961
2:15 they **c** to meet him, and bowed themselves to 935
2:18 when they **c again** to him, (for he tarried at 7725
2:23 there **c forth** little children out of the city, 3318
2:24 there **c forth** two she bears out of 3318
3: 5 it **c to pass**, when Ahab was dead, that 1961
3:15 it **c to pass**, when the minstrel played, 1961
3:15 that the hand of the LORD **c** upon him. 1961
3:20 it **c to pass** in the morning, when the meat 1961
3:20 there **c** water by the way of Edom, and 935
3:24 when they **c** to the camp of Israel, 935
4: 6 it **c to pass**, when the vessels were full, 1961
4: 7 she **c** and told the man of God. And he said, 935
4:11 that he **c** thither, and he turned into 935
4:25 and **c** unto the man of God to mount Carmel. 935
4:25 it **c to pass**, when the man of God saw her 1961
4:27 when she **c** to the man of God to the hill, 935
4:27 Gehazi **c near** to thrust her away. And 5066
4:38 Elisha **c again** to Gilgal: and *there was* a 7725
4:39 and **c** and shred *them* into the pot of pottage: 935
4:40 it **c to pass**, as they were eating of 1961
4:42 there **c** a man from Baal-shalisha, and 935
5: 7 it **c to pass**, when the king of Israel had 1961
5: 9 So Naaman **c** with his horses and with his 935
5:13 his servants **c near**, and spake unto him, 5066
5:14 his flesh **c again** like unto the flesh of a 7725
5:15 his company, and **c**, and stood before him: 935
5:24 when he **c** to the tower, he took *them* from 935
6: 4 when they **c** to Jordan, they cut down wood. 935
6:14 they **c** by night, and compassed the city 935
6:18 when they **c down** to him, Elisha prayed 3381
6:20 it **c to pass**, when they were come *into* 1961
6:23 So the bands of Syria **c** no more into the land 935
6:24 it **c to pass** after this, that Ben-hadad king 1961
2Ki 6:30 it **c to pass**, when the king heard the words 1961
6:32 ere the messenger **c** to him, he said to 935
6:33 the messenger **c down** unto him: 3381
7: 8 when these lepers **c** to the uttermost part of 935
7: 8 went and hid *it;* and **c again**, and 7725
7:10 So they **c** and called unto the porter of 935
7:10 We **c** to the camp of the Syrians, and behold, 935
7:17 who spake when the king **c down** to him. 3381
7:18 it **c to pass** as the man of God had spoken 1961
8: 3 it **c to pass** at the seven years' end, that 1961
8: 5 it **c to pass**, *as* he was telling the king how 1961
8: 7 Elisha **c** *to* Damascus; and Ben-hadad 935
8: 9 and **c** and stood before him, and said, 935
8:14 he departed from Elisha, and **c** to his master; 935
8:15 it **c to pass** on the morrow, that he took a 1961
9: 5 when he **c**, behold, the captains of the host 935
9:11 Jehu **c forth** to the servants of his lord: 3318
9:11 wherefore **c** this mad *fellow* to thee? And he 935
9:17 he spied the company of Jehu as he **c**, and 935
9:18 The messenger **c** to them, but he cometh not 935
9:19 which **c** to them, and said, Thus saith 935
9:20 He **c** even unto them, and cometh not again: 935
9:22 it **c to pass**, when Joram saw Jehu, that he 1961
9:36 Wherefore they **c again**, and told him. 7725
10: 7 it **c to pass**, when the letter came to them, 1961
10: 7 it came to pass, when the letter **c** to them, 935
10: 8 there **c** a messenger, and told him, saying, 935
10: 9 it **c to pass** in the morning, that he went 1961
10:12 he arose and departed, and **c** *to* Samaria. 1980
10:17 when he **c** *to* Samaria, he slew all that 935
10:21 all the worshippers of Baal **c**, so that there 935
10:21 so that there was not a man left that **c** not. 935
10:21 they **c** *into* the house of Baal; and the house 935
10:25 it **c to pass**, as soon as he had made an end 1961
11: 9 on the sabbath, and **c** to Jehoiada the priest. 935
11:13 she **c** to the people *into* the temple of 935
11:16 which the horses **c** *into* the king's house: 3996
11:19 **c** *by* the way of the gate of the guard *to* 935
12:10 the king's scribe and the high priest **c up**, 5927
13:14 Joash the king of Israel **c down** unto him, 3381
13:21 it **c to pass**, as they were burying a man, 1961
14: 5 it **c to pass**, as soon as the kingdom was 1961
14:13 **c** *to* Jerusalem, and brake down the wall of 935
15:12 the fourth *generation.* And so it **c to pass.** 1961
15:14 **c** *to* Samaria, and smote Shallum the son of 935
15:19 *And* Pul the king of Assyria **c** against 935
15:29 In the days of Pekah king of Israel **c** 935
16: 5 Pekah son of Remaliah king of Israel **c up** 5927
16: 6 the Syrians **c** *to* Elath, and dwelt there unto 935
16:11 Urijah the priest made *it* against king Ahaz **c** 935
17: 3 Against him **c up** Shalmaneser king of 5927
17: 5 the king of Assyria **c up** throughout all 5927
17:28 whom they had carried away from Samaria **c** 935
18: 1 Now it **c to pass** in the third year of Hoshea 1961
18: 9 it **c to pass** in the fourth year of king 1961
18: 9 *that* Shalmaneser king of Assyria **c up** 5927
18:17 they went up and **c** *to* Jerusalem. And when 935
18:17 they **c** and stood by the conduit of the upper 935
18:18 there **c out** to them Eliakim the son of 3318
18:37 **c** Eliakim the son of Hilkiah, which *was* over 935
19: 1 it **c to pass**, when king Hezekiah heard *it,* 1961
19: 5 So the servants of king Hezekiah **c** to Isaiah. 935
19:33 By the way that he **c**, *by the same* shall he 935
19:35 it **c to pass** that night, that the angel of 1961
19:37 it **c to pass**, as he was worshipping *in* 1961
20: 1 the prophet Isaiah the son of Amoz **c** to him, 935
20: 4 it **c to pass**, afore Isaiah was gone out *into* 1961
20: 4 that the word of the LORD **c** to him, 1961
20:14 **c** Isaiah the prophet unto king Hezekiah, 935
20:14 from whence **c** they unto thee? 935
21:15 since the day their fathers **c forth** out of 3318
22: 3 it **c to pass** in the eighteenth year of king 1961
22: 9 Shaphan the scribe **c** to the king, and 935
22:11 it **c to pass**, when the king had heard 1961
23: 9 **c** not **up** to the altar of the LORD in 5927
23:17 which **c** from Judah, and proclaimed these 935
23:18 with the bones of the prophet that **c** out of 935
23:34 and took Jehoahaz *away:* and he **c** *to* Egypt, 935
24: 1 Nebuchadnezzar king of Babylon **c up**, 5927
24: 3 of the LORD **c** *this* upon Judah, 1961
24: 7 the king of Egypt **c** not again any more **out** 3318
24:10 king of Babylon **c up** *against* Jerusalem, 5927
24:11 Nebuchadnezzar king of Babylon **c** against 935
24:20 of the LORD it **c to pass** in Jerusalem 1961
25: 1 it **c to pass** in the ninth year of his reign, 1961
25: 1 *that* Nebuchadnezzar king of Babylon **c**, he, 935
25: 8 **c** Nebuzar-adan, captain of the guard, 935
25:23 there **c** to Gedaliah *to* Mizpah, even Ishmael 935
25:25 it **c to pass** in the seventh month, 1961
25:25 **c**, and ten men with him, and 935
25:26 captains of the armies, arose, and **c** *to* Egypt: 935
25:27 it **c to pass** in the seven and thirtieth year 1961
1Ch 1:12 and Casluhim, (of whom **c** the Philistines,) 3318
2:53 of them **c** the Zareathites, and 3318
2:55 These *are* the Kenites that **c** of Hemath, 935
4:41 these written by name **c** in the days of 935
5: 2 his brethren, and of him **c** the chief ruler; NIH
7:21 they **c down** to take *away* their cattle. 3381
7:22 and his brethren **c** to comfort him. 935
10: 7 fled: and the Philistines **c** and dwelt in them. 935
10: 8 it **c to pass** on the morrow, when 1961
10: 8 when the Philistines **c** to strip the slain, 935
11: 3 Therefore **c** all the elders of Israel to the king 935
12: 1 Now these *are they* that **c** to David to Ziklag, 935
12:16 And there **c** of the children of Benjamin and 935
12:18 the spirit **c upon** Amasai, *who was* chief of 3847
12:19 when he **c** with the Philistines against Saul 935
12:22 For at *that* time day by day there **c** to David 935
12:23 *and* **c** to David to Hebron, to turn 935
12:38 keep rank, **c** with a perfect heart to Hebron, 935
13: 9 when they **c** unto the threshingfloor of 935
14: 9 the Philistines **c** and spread themselves in 935
14:11 So they **c up** to Baal-perazim; and 5927
15:26 it **c to pass**, when God helped the Levites 1961
15:29 it **c to pass**, *as* the ark of the covenant of 1961
1Ch 15:29 *as* the ark of the covenant of the LORD **c** to 935
17: 1 Now it **c to pass**, as David sat in his house, 1961
17: 3 it **c to pass** the same night, that the word of 1961
17: 3 that the word of God **c** to Nathan, saying, 1961
17:16 David the king **c** and sat before the LORD, 935
18: 1 Now after this it **c to pass**, that David 1961
18: 5 when the Syrians of Damascus **c** to help 935
19: 1 Now it **c to pass** after this, that Nahash 1961
19: 2 So the servants of David **c** into the land of 935
19: 7 who **c** and pitched before Medeba. 935
19: 7 together from their cities, and **c** to battle. 935
19: 9 the children of Ammon **c out**, and put 3318
19:15 into the city. Then Joab **c** *to* Jerusalem. 935
19:17 **c** upon them, and set *the battle* in array 935
20: 1 it **c to pass**, that after the year was expired, 1961
20: 1 of Ammon, and **c** and besieged Rabbah. 935
20: 4 it **c to pass** after this, that there arose war at 1961
21: 4 throughout all Israel, and **c** *to* Jerusalem. 935
21:11 So Gad **c** to David, and said unto him, 935
21:21 And as David **c** to Ornan, Ornan looked and 935
22: 8 the word of the LORD **c** to me, saying, 1961
24: 7 Now the first lot **c forth** to Jehoiarib, 3318
24:28 Of Mahli **c** Eleazar, who had no sons. NIH
25: 9 Now the first lot **c forth** for Asaph to 3318
26:14 they cast lots; and his lot **c out** northward. 3318
26:16 and Hosah *the lot* **c** *forth* westward, NIH
27: 1 which **c in** and went out month by month 935
2Ch 1:13 Solomon **c** *from his journey* to the high 935
5: 4 all the elders of Israel **c**; and the Levites took 935
5:10 of Israel, when they **c out** of Egypt. 3318
5:11 it **c to pass**, when the priests were come out 1961
5:13 It **c** even **to pass**, as the trumpeters and 1961
7: 1 the fire **c down** from heaven, and 3381
7: 3 children of Israel saw how the fire **c down**, 3381
7:11 all that **c** into Solomon's heart to make in 935
8: 1 it **c to pass** at the end of twenty years, 1961
9: 1 she **c** to prove Solomon with hard questions 935
9: 6 until I **c**, and mine eyes had seen *it:* and 935
9:13 Now the weight of gold that **c** to Solomon in 935
9:21 every three years once **c** the ships of 935
10: 2 it **c to pass**, when Jeroboam the son of 1961
10: 3 So Jeroboam and all Israel **c** and spake to 935
10:12 all the people **c** to Rehoboam on the third 935
11: 2 the word of the LORD **c** to Shemaiah 1961
11:14 and **c** to Judah and Jerusalem: 1980
11:16 the LORD God of Israel **c** *to* Jerusalem, 935
12: 1 it **c to pass**, when Rehoboam had 1961
12: 2 it **c to pass**, *that* in the fifth year of king 1961
12: 2 king of Egypt **c up** against Jerusalem, 5927
12: 3 the people *were* without number that **c** with 935
12: 4 *pertained* to Judah, and **c** to Jerusalem. 935
12: 5 Then **c** Shemaiah the prophet to Rehoboam, 935
12: 7 the word of the LORD **c** to Shemaiah, 1961
12: 9 So Shishak king of Egypt **c up** against 5927
12:11 the guard **c** and fet them, and brought them 935
13:15 it **c to pass**, that God smote Jeroboam and 1961
14: 9 there **c out** against them Zerah 3318
14: 9 three hundred chariots; and **c** unto Mareshah. 935
14:14 for the fear of the LORD **c** upon them: 1961
15: 1 the spirit of God **c** upon Azariah the son of 1961
15: 5 nor to him that **c in**, but great vexations *were* 935
16: 1 Baasha king of Israel **c up** against Judah, 5927
16: 5 it **c to pass**, when Baasha heard *it,* that he 1961
16: 7 at that time Hanani the seer **c** to Asa king of 935
18:20 there **c out** a spirit, and stood before 3318
18:23 Zedekiah the son of Chenaanah **c near**, 5066
18:31 it **c to pass**, when the captains of 1961
18:32 For it **c to pass**, that when the captains of 1961
20: 1 It **c to pass** after this also, *that* the children 1961
20: 1 **c** against Jehoshaphat to battle. 935
20: 2 there **c** *some* that told Jehoshaphat, saying, 935
20: 4 even out of all the cities of Judah they **c** to 935
20:10 when they **c** out of the land of Egypt, but 935
20:14 **c** the spirit of the LORD in the midst of 1961
20:24 when Judah **c** toward the watch tower in 935
20:25 his people **c** to take away the spoil of them, 935
20:28 they **c** *to* Jerusalem with psalteries and harps 935
21:12 there **c** a writing to him from Elijah 935
21:17 they **c up** into Judah, and brake into it, and 5927
21:19 it **c to pass**, that in process of time, after 1961
22: 1 for the band *of men* that **c** with the Arabians 935
22: 8 it **c to pass**, that when Jehu was executing 1961
23: 2 the fathers of Israel, and they **c** to Jerusalem. 935
23:12 she **c** to the people *into* the house of 935
23:20 they **c** through the high gate *into* the king's 935
24: 4 it **c to pass** after this, *that* Joash was 1961
24:11 Now it **c to pass**, that at *what* time the chest 1961
24:11 and the high priest's officer **c** and 935
24:17 Now after the death of Jehoiada **c** the princes 935
24:18 wrath **c** upon Judah and Jerusalem for this 1961
24:20 the spirit of God **c upon** Zechariah the son 3847
24:23 it **c to pass** at the end of the year, *that* 1961
24:23 *that* the host of Syria **c up** against him: 5927
24:23 they **c** to Judah and Jerusalem, and 935
24:24 For the army of the Syrians **c** with a small 935
25: 3 Now it **c to pass**, when the kingdom was 1961
25: 7 there **c** a man of God to him, saying, O king, 935
25:14 Now it **c to pass**, after that Amaziah was 1961
25:16 it **c to pass**, as he talked with him, that 1961
25:20 for it **c** of God, that *he* might deliver them NIH
28: 9 he went out before the host that **c** to 935
28:12 stood up against them that **c** from the war, 935
28:20 Tilgath-pilneser king of Assyria **c** unto him, 935
29:15 and sanctified themselves, and **c**, 935
29:17 on the eighth day of the month **c** they to 935
30:11 humbled themselves, and **c** to Jerusalem. 935
30:25 all the congregation that **c** out of Israel, and 935
30:25 the strangers that **c** out of the land of Israel, 935
30:27 their prayer **c** *up* to his holy dwelling place, 935
31: 5 as soon as the commandment **c abroad**, 6555
31: 8 and the princes **c** and saw the heaps, 935
32: 1 *thereof,* Sennacherib king of Assyria **c**, 935
32:21 they that **c forth** of his own bowels slew 3329
32:26 that the wrath of the LORD **c** not upon 935
34: 9 when they **c** to Hilkiah the high priest, 935

C

2Ch 34:19 it **c to pass**, when the king had heard 1961
35:20 Necho king of Egypt **c up** to fight against 5927
35:22 and **c** to fight in the valley of Megiddo. 935
36: 6 Against him **c up** Nebuchadnezzar king of 5927
Ezr 2: 1 **c again** unto Jerusalem and Judah, 7725
2: 2 Which **c** with Zerubbabel: Jeshua, 935
2:68 when they **c** to the house of the LORD 935
4: 2 they **c** to Zerubbabel, and to the chief of 5066
4:12 that the Jews which **c up** from thee to us 5559
5: 3 At the same time **c** to them Tatnai, 858
5: 5 them to cease, till the matter **c** to Darius: 1946
5:16 **c** the same Sheshbazzar, *and* laid 858
7: 8 he **c** *to* Jerusalem in the fifth month, 935
7: 9 on the first *day* of the fifth month **c** he to 935
8:32 we **c** *to* Jerusalem, and abode there three 935
9: 1 the princes **c** to me, saying, The people of 5066
10: 6 *when* he **c** thither, he did eat no bread, 1980
Ne 1: 1 it **c to pass** in the month Chisleu, *in* 1961
1: 2 my brethren, **c**, he and *certain* men of Judah; 935
1: 4 it **c to pass**, when I heard these words, 1961
2: 1 it **c to pass** in the month Nisan, *in* 1961
2: 9 I **c** to the governors beyond the river, and 935
2:11 So I **c** to Jerusalem, and was there three 935
4: 1 it **c to pass**, that when Sanballat heard that 1961
4: 7 it **c to pass**, *that* when Sanballat, and 1961
4:12 it **c to pass**, that when the Jews which 1961
4:12 that when the Jews which dwelt by them **c**, 935
4:15 it **c to pass**, when our enemies heard that it 1961
4:16 it **c to pass** from that time forth, *that* 1961
5:17 besides those that **c** unto us from among 935
6: 1 Now it **c to pass**, when Sanballat, and 1961
6:10 Afterward I **c** *unto* the house of Shemaiah 935
6:16 it **c to pass**, that when all our enemies 1961
6:17 and *the letters* of Tobiah **c** unto them. 935
7: 1 Now it **c to pass**, when the wall was built, 1961
7: 5 genealogy of them which **c up** at the first, 5927
7: 6 **c again** to Jerusalem and to Judah, 7725
7: 7 Who **c** with Zerubbabel, Jeshua, Nehemiah, 935
7:73 when the seventh month **c**, the children of 5060
13: 3 Now it **c to pass**, when they had heard 1961
13: 6 king of Babylon **c** I unto the king, 935
13: 7 I **c** to Jerusalem, and understood of the evil 935
13:19 it **c to pass**, that when the gates of 1961
13:21 From that time forth **c** they no *more* on 935
Est 1: 1 Now it **c to pass** in the days of Ahasuerus, 1961
1:17 to be brought in before him, but she **c** not. 935
2: 8 So it **c to pass**, when the king's 1961
2:13 thus **c** *every* maiden unto the king; 935
2:14 she **c in** unto the king no more, except 935
3: 4 Now it **c to pass**, when they spake daily 1961
4: 2 **c** even before the king's gate: for none might 935
4: 3 the king's commandment and his decree **c**, 5060
4: 4 and her chamberlains **c** and told *it* her. 935
4: 9 Hatach **c** and told Esther the words of 935
5: 1 Now it **c to pass** on the third day, 1961
5: 5 Haman **c** to the banquet that Esther had 935
5:10 when he **c** home, he sent and called for his 935
6: 6 So Haman **c in**. And the king said unto him, 935
6:12 Mordecai **c again** to the king's gate. 7725
6:14 **c** the king's chamberlains, and hasted to 5060
7: 1 Haman **c** to banquet with Esther the queen. 935
8: 1 Mordecai **c** before the king; for Esther had 935
8:17 the king's commandment and his decree **c**, 5060
9:25 when *Esther* **c** before the king, 935
Job 1: 6 Now there was a day when the sons of God **c** 935
1: 6 the LORD, and Satan **c** also among them. 935
1:14 And there **c** a messenger unto Job, and said, 935
1:16 yet speaking, there **c** also another, and said, 935
1:17 yet speaking, there **c** also another, and said, 935
1:18 there **c** also another, and said, Thy sons and 935
1:19 there **c** a great wind from the wilderness, and 935
1:21 Naked **c** I **out** of my mother's womb, and 3318
2: 1 **c** to present themselves before the LORD, 935
2: 1 Satan **c** also among them to present himself 935
2:11 they **c** every one from his own place; 935
3:11 give up the ghost when I **c out** of the belly? 3318
3:26 had I rest, neither was I quiet; yet trouble **c**. 935
4:14 Fear **c upon** me, and trembling, 7122
6:20 had hoped; they **c** thither, and were ashamed. 935
26: 4 and whose spirit **c** from thee? 3318
29:13 of him that was ready to perish **c** upon me: 935
30:14 They **c** *upon me* as a wide breaking in *of* 857
30:26 evil **c** *unto me:* and when I waited for light, 935
30:26 and when I waited for light, there **c** darkness. 935
38:29 Out of whose womb **c** the ice? and 3318
42:11 **c** there unto him all his brethren, and all his 935
Ps 18: 6 and my cry **c** before him, *even* into his ears. 935
18: 9 He bowed the heavens also, and **c down**: 3381
27: 2 and my foes, **c** upon me to eat up my flesh, 7126
51: T when Nathan the prophet **c** unto him, 935
52: T when Doeg the Edomite **c** and told Saul, and 935
54: T when the Ziphims **c** and said to Saul, 935
78:21 and anger also **c up** against Israel; 5927
78:31 The wrath of God **c** upon them, and 5927
88:17 They **c round about** me daily like water; 5437
105:19 Until the time that his word **c**: the word of 935
105:23 Israel also **c** *into* Egypt; and Jacob sojourned 935
105:31 there **c** divers sorts *of flies, and* lice in all 935
105:34 the locusts **c**, and caterpillars, and 935
Pr 7:15 Therefore **c** I **forth** to meet thee, 3318
Ecc 5:15 As he **c forth** of his mother's womb, 3318
5:15 naked shall he return to go as he **c**, and 935
5:16 *that* in all points as he **c**, so shall he go: 935
9:14 there **c** a great king against it, and 935
SS 4: 2 even shorn, which **c up** from the washing; 5927
Isa 7: 1 it **c to pass** in the days of Ahaz the son of 1961
11:16 day that he **c up** out of the land of Egypt. 5927
20: 1 In the year that Tartan **c** unto Ashdod, 935
30: 4 at Zoan, and his ambassadors **c** to Hanes. 5060
36: 1 Now it **c to pass** in the fourteenth year of 1961
36: 1 *that* Sennacherib king of Assyria **c up** 5927
36: 3 **c forth** unto him Eliakim, Hilkiah's son, 3318
36:22 **c** Eliakim, the son of Hilkiah, that *was* over 935
37: 1 it **c to pass**, when king Hezekiah heard *it,* 1961
37: 5 So the servants of king Hezekiah **c** to Isaiah. 935
Isa 37:34 By the way that he **c**, *by the same* shall he 935
37:38 it **c to pass**, as he was worshipping *in* 1961
38: 1 Isaiah the prophet the son of Amoz **c** unto 935
38: 4 **c** the word of the LORD to Isaiah, saying, 1961
39: 3 **c** Isaiah the prophet unto king Hezekiah, 935
39: 3 from whence **c** they unto thee? 935
41: 5 of the earth were afraid, drew near, and **c**. 857
48: 3 I did *them* suddenly, and they **c to pass**. 935
48: 5 *it* to thee; before it **c to pass** I shewed *it* thee: 935
50: 2 Wherefore, when I **c**, *was there* no man? 935
66: 7 before her pain **c**, she was delivered of a 935
Jer 1: 2 To whom the word of the LORD **c** in 1961
1: 3 It **c** also in the days of Jehoiakim the son of 1961
1: 4 the word of the LORD **c** unto me, saying, 1961
1:11 the word of the LORD **c** unto me, saying, 1961
1:13 the word of the LORD **c** unto me 1961
2: 1 Moreover the word of the LORD **c** to me, 1961
3: 9 it **c to pass** through the lightness of her 1961
7: 1 The word that **c** to Jeremiah from 1961
7:25 Since the day that your fathers **c forth** out 3318
7:31 *them* not, neither **c** it into my heart. 5927
8:15 no good **c**; *and* for a time of health, and NIH
11: 1 The word that **c** to Jeremiah from 1961
13: 3 the word of the LORD **c** unto me 1961
13: 6 it **c to pass** after many days, that 1961
13: 8 the word of the LORD **c** unto me, saying, 1961
14: 1 The word of the LORD that **c** to Jeremiah 1961
14: 3 they **c** to the pits, *and* found no water; 935
16: 1 The word of the LORD **c** also unto me, 1961
17:16 **that which c out of** my lips was right 4161
18: 1 The word which **c** to Jeremiah from 1961
18: 5 the word of the LORD **c** to me, saying, 1961
19: 5 nor spake *it,* neither **c** *it* into my mind: 5927
19:14 **c** Jeremiah from Tophet, whither the LORD 935
20: 3 it **c to pass** on the morrow, that Pashur 1961
20:18 Wherefore **c** I **forth** out of the womb to see 3318
21: 1 The word which **c** unto Jeremiah from 1961
24: 4 Again the word of the LORD **c** unto me, 1961
25: 1 The word that **c** to Jeremiah concerning all 1961
26: 1 king of Judah **c** this word from the LORD, 1961
26: 8 Now it **c to pass**, when Jeremiah had made 1961
26:10 they **c up** from the king's house *unto* 5927
27: 1 **c** this word unto Jeremiah from 1961
28: 1 it **c to pass** the same year, in the beginning 1961
28:12 the word of the LORD **c** unto Jeremiah 1961
29:30 **c** the word of the LORD unto Jeremiah, 1961
30: 1 The word that **c** to Jeremiah from 1961
32: 1 The word that **c** to Jeremiah from 1961
32: 6 The word of the LORD **c** unto me, saying, 1961
32: 8 So Hanameel mine uncle's son **c** to me in 935
32:23 they **c in**, and possessed it; but they obeyed 935
32:26 **c** the word of the LORD unto Jeremiah, 1961
32:35 them not, neither **c** it into my mind, 5927
33: 1 Moreover the word of the LORD **c** unto 1961
33:19 the word of the LORD **c** unto Jeremiah, 1961
33:23 Moreover the word of the LORD **c** to 1961
34: 1 The word which **c** unto Jeremiah from 1961
34: 8 *This is* the word that **c** unto Jeremiah from 1961
34:12 Therefore the word of the LORD **c** to 1961
35: 1 The word which **c** unto Jeremiah from 1961
35:11 it **c to pass**, when Nebuchadrezzar king of 1961
35:11 king of Babylon **c up** into the land, 5927
35:12 **c** the word of the LORD unto Jeremiah, 1961
36: 1 it **c to pass** in the fourth year of Jehoiakim 1961
36: 1 *that* this word **c** unto Jeremiah from 1961
36: 9 it **c to pass** in the fifth year of Jehoiakim 1961
36: 9 *to* all the people that **c** from the cities of 935
36:14 took the roll in his hand, and **c** unto them. 935
36:16 Now it **c to pass** when they had heard all 1961
36:23 it **c to pass**, *that* when Jehudi had read 1961
36:27 the word of the LORD **c** to Jeremiah, 1961
37: 4 Now Jeremiah **c in** and went out among 935
37: 6 **c** the word of the LORD unto the prophet 1961
37:11 it **c to pass**, *that* when the army of 1961
38:27 **c** all the princes unto Jeremiah, and 935
39: 1 **c** Nebuchadrezzar king of Babylon and 935
39: 3 all the princes of the king of Babylon **c in**, 935
39: 4 it **c to pass**, *that* when Zedekiah the king of 1961
39:15 Now the word of the LORD **c** unto 1961
40: 1 The word which **c** to Jeremiah from 1961
40: 8 they **c** to Gedaliah to Mizpah, even Ishmael 935
40:12 **c** *to* the land of Judah, to Gedaliah, unto 935
40:13 *were* in the fields, **c** to Gedaliah to Mizpah, 935
41: 1 Now it **c to pass** in the seventh month, 1961
41: 1 **c** unto Gedaliah the son of Ahikam to 935
41: 4 it **c to pass** the second day after *he* had 1961
41: 5 That there **c** certain from Shechem, 935
41: 6 it **c to pass**, as he met them, he said unto 1961
41: 7 *so,* when they **c** into the midst of the city, 935
41:13 Now it **c to pass**, *that* when all the people 1961
42: 1 the least even unto the greatest, **c** near, 5066
42: 7 it **c to pass** after ten days, that the word of 1961
42: 7 that the word of the LORD **c** unto 1961
43: 1 it **c to pass**, *that* when Jeremiah had made 1961
43: 7 So they **c** *into* the land of Egypt: for they 935
43: 7 the LORD: thus **c** they *even* to Tahpanhes. 935
43: 8 **c** the word of the LORD unto Jeremiah in 1961
44: 1 The word that **c** to Jeremiah *concerning* all 1961
44:21 remember them, and **c** it *not* into his mind? 5927
46: 1 The word of the LORD which **c** to 1961
47: 1 The word of the LORD that **c** to Jeremiah 1961
49:34 The word of the LORD that **c** to Jeremiah 1961
52: 3 of the LORD it **c to pass** in Jerusalem 1961
52: 4 it **c to pass** in the ninth year of his reign, 1961
52: 4 *that* Nebuchadrezzar king of Babylon **c**, he 935
52:12 **c** Nebuzar-adan, captain of the guard, 935
52:31 it **c to pass** in the seven and thirtieth year 1961
La 1: 9 last end; therefore she **c down** wonderfully: 3381
Eze 1: 1 Now it **c to pass** in the thirtieth year, in 1961
1: 3 The word of the LORD **c expressly** 1961+1961
1: 4 behold, a whirlwind **c** out of the north, 935
1: 5 Also out of the midst thereof **c** the likeness NIH
3:15 Then I **c** to them of the captivity *at* Tel-abib, 935
3:16 it **c to pass** at the end of seven days, 1961
3:16 that the word of the LORD **c** unto me, 1961
Eze 4:14 neither **c** there abominable flesh into my 935
6: 1 the word of the LORD **c** unto me, saying, 1961
7: 1 Moreover the word of the LORD **c** unto 1961
8: 1 it **c to pass** in the sixth year, in the sixth 1961
9: 2 six men **c** from the way of the higher gate, 935
9: 8 it **c to pass**, while they were slaying them, 1961
10: 6 it **c to pass**, *that* when he had commanded 1961
11:13 it **c to pass**, when I prophesied, 1961
11:14 Again the word of the LORD **c** unto me, 1961
12: 1 The word of the LORD also **c** unto me, 1961
12: 8 in the morning **c** the word of the LORD 1961
12:17 Moreover the word of the LORD **c** to me, 1961
12:21 the word of the LORD **c** unto me, saying, 1961
12:26 Again the word of the LORD **c** to me, 1961
13: 1 the word of the LORD **c** unto me, saying, 1961
14: 1 **c** certain of the elders of Israel unto me, 935
14: 2 the word of the LORD **c** unto me, saying, 1961
14:12 The word of the LORD **c** again to me, 1961
15: 1 the word of the LORD **c** unto me, saying, 1961
16: 1 Again the word of the LORD **c** unto me, 1961
16:23 it **c to pass** after all thy wickedness, (woe, 1961
17: 1 the word of the LORD **c** unto me, saying, 1961
17: 3 **c** unto Lebanon, and took the highest branch 935
17:11 Moreover the word of the LORD **c** unto 1961
18: 1 the word of the LORD **c** unto me again, 1961
20: 1 it **c to pass** in the seventh year, in the fifth 1961
20: 1 *that* certain of the elders of Israel **c** to inquire 935
20: 2 **c** the word of the LORD unto me, saying, 1961
20:45 Moreover the word of the LORD **c** unto 1961
21: 1 the word of the LORD **c** unto me, saying, 1961
21: 8 Again the word of the LORD **c** unto me, 1961
21:18 The word of the LORD **c** unto me again, 1961
22: 1 Moreover the word of the LORD **c** unto 1961
22:17 the word of the LORD **c** unto me, saying, 1961
22:23 the word of the LORD **c** unto me, saying, 1961
23: 1 The word of the LORD **c** again unto me, 1961
23:17 the Babylonians **c** to her into the bed of love, 935
23:39 they **c** the same day into my sanctuary to 935
23:40 whom a messenger *was* sent; and lo, they **c**: 935
24: 1 the word of the LORD **c** unto me, saying, 1961
24:15 Also the word of the LORD **c** unto me, 1961
24:20 The word of the LORD **c** unto me, saying, 1961
25: 1 The word of the LORD **c** again unto me, 1961
26: 1 it **c to pass** in the eleventh year, in the first 1961
26: 1 *that* the word of the LORD **c** unto me, 1961
27: 1 The word of the LORD **c** again unto me, 1961
28: 1 The word of the LORD **c** again unto me, 1961
28:11 Moreover the word of the LORD **c** unto 1961
28:20 Again the word of the LORD **c** unto me, 1961
29: 1 the word of the LORD **c** unto me, saying, 1961
29:17 it **c to pass** in the seven and twentieth year, 1961
29:17 the word of the LORD **c** unto me, saying, 1961
30: 1 The word of the LORD **c** again unto me, 1961
30:20 it **c to pass** in the eleventh year, in the first 1961
30:20 *that* the word of the LORD **c** unto me, 1961
31: 1 it **c to pass** in the eleventh year, in the third 1961
31: 1 *that* the word of the LORD **c** unto me, 1961
32: 1 it **c to pass** in the twelfth year, in 1961
32: 1 *that* the word of the LORD **c** unto me, 1961
32:17 It **c to pass** also in the twelfth year, in 1961
32:17 *that* the word of the LORD **c** unto me, 1961
33: 1 Again the word of the LORD **c** unto me, 1961
33:21 it **c to pass** in the twelfth year of our 1961
33:21 *that* one that had escaped out of Jerusalem **c** 935
33:22 in the evening, afore he that was escaped **c**; 935
33:22 my mouth, until *he* **c** to me in the morning; 935
33:23 the word of the LORD **c** unto me, saying, 1961
34: 1 the word of the LORD **c** unto me, saying, 1961
35: 1 Moreover the word of the LORD **c** unto 1961
36:16 Moreover the word of the LORD **c** unto 1961
37: 7 and the bones **c together**, bone to his bone. 7126
37: 8 the sinews and the flesh **c up** upon them, 5927
37:10 the breath **c** into them, and they lived, and 935
37:15 The word of the LORD **c** again unto me, 1961
38: 1 the word of the LORD **c** unto me, saying, 1961
40: 6 **c** he unto the gate which looketh toward 935
43: 2 the glory of the God of Israel **c** from the way 935
43: 3 vision that I saw when I **c** to destroy the city: 935
43: 4 the glory of the LORD **c** into the house by 935
46: 9 *by* the way of the gate whereby he **c in**, 935
47: 1 the waters **c down** from under from 3381
Da 1: 1 **c** Nebuchadnezzar king of Babylon *unto* 935
2: 2 So they **c** and stood before the king. 935
2:29 thy thoughts **c** *into thy mind* upon thy bed, 5559
3: 8 at that time certain Chaldeans **c near**, 7127
3:26 Nebuchadnezzar **c near** to the mouth of 7127
3:26 Abed-nego, **c forth** of the midst of the fire. 5312
4: 7 **c in** the magicians, the astrologers, 5954
4: 8 at the last Daniel **c in** before me, 5954
4:13 and a holy one **c down** from heaven; 5182
4:28 All this **c** upon the king Nebuchadnezzar. 4291
5: 5 In the same hour **c forth** fingers of a man's 5312
5: 8 **c in** all the king's wise *men:* but they could 5954
5:10 and his lords, **c** into the banquet house: 5954
6:12 they **c near**, and spake before the king 7127
6:20 when he **c** to the den, he cried with a 7127
6:24 or ever they **c** at the bottom of the den. 4291
7: 3 four great beasts **c up** from the sea, 5559
7: 8 there **c up** among them another little horn, 5559
7:10 stream issued and **c forth** from before him: 5312
7:13 *one* like the Son of man **c** with the clouds of 858
7:13 **c** to the Ancient of days, and they brought 4291
7:16 I **c near** unto one of them that stood *by,* 7127
7:20 *of* the other which **c up**, and before whom 5559
7:22 Until the Ancient of days **c**, and 858
7:22 the time **c** that the saints possessed 4291
8: 2 it **c to pass**, when I saw, that I *was* at 1961
8: 3 than the other, and the higher **c up** last. 5927
8: 5 a he goat **c** from the west on the face of 935
8: 6 he **c** to the ram that had two horns, which I 935
8: 8 for it **c up** four notable ones toward 5927
8: 9 And out of one of them **c forth** a little horn, 3318
8:15 it **c to pass**, when I, *even* I Daniel, had seen 1961
8:17 So he **c** near where I stood: and when he 935
8:17 when he **c**, I was afraid, and fell upon my 935

Book	Ref	Context	No.
Da	9: 2	where*of* the word of the LORD **c** to	1961
	9:23	supplications the commandment **c forth**,	3318
	10: 3	neither **c** flesh nor wine in my mouth,	935
	10:13	one of the chief princes, **c** to help me;	935
	10:18	there **c again** and touched me *one* like	3254
Hos	1: 1	The word of the LORD that **c** unto Hosea,	1961
	2:15	as *in* the day when she **c up** out of the land	5927
Joel	1: 1	The word of the LORD that **c** to Joel	1961
Am	6: 1	the nations, to whom the house of Israel **c**!	935
	7: 2	it **c to pass**, *that* when they had made an	1961
Ob	1: 5	If thieves **c** to thee, if robbers by night,	935
	1: 5	if the grape-gatherers **c** to thee, would they	935
Jnh	1: 1	Now the word of the LORD **c** unto Jonah	1961
	1: 6	So the shipmaster **c** to him, and said unto	7126
	2: 7	my prayer **c in** unto thee, into thine holy	935
	3: 1	the word of the LORD **c** unto Jonah	1961
	3: 6	For word **c** unto the king of Nineveh, and	5060
	4: 8	it **c to pass**, when the sun did arise,	1961
	4:10	which **c up** in a night, and perished in a	1961
Mic	1: 1	The word of the LORD that **c** to Micah	1961
	1:11	the inhabitant of Zaanan **c** not **forth** *in*	3318
	1:12	evil **c down** from the LORD unto the gate	3381
Hab	3: 3	God **c** from Teman, and the Holy One from	935
	3:14	they **c out as a whirlwind** to scatter me:	5590
Zep	1: 1	The word of the LORD which **c** unto	1961
Hag	1: 1	**c** the word of the LORD by Haggai	1961
	1: 3	**c** the word of the LORD by Haggai	1961
	1: 9	*Ye* looked for much, and lo, *it* **c** to little;	NIH
	1:14	they **c** and did work in the house of	935
	2: 1	**c** the word of the LORD by the prophet	1961
	2: 5	with you when ye **c out** of Egypt,	3318
	2:10	**c** the word of the LORD by Haggai	1961
	2:16	when *one* **c** to a heap of twenty *measures*,	935
	2:16	when *one* **c** to the pressfat for to draw out	935
	2:20	again the word of the LORD **c** unto	1961
Zec	1: 1	**c** the word of the LORD unto Zechariah,	1961
	1: 7	**c** the word of the LORD unto Zechariah,	1961
	4: 1	the angel that talked with me **c again**, and	7725
	4: 8	Moreover the word of the LORD **c** unto	1961
	5: 9	there **c out** two women, and the wind *was*	3318
	6: 1	there **c** four chariots **out** from between two	3318
	6: 9	the word of the LORD **c** unto me, saying,	1961
	7: 1	it **c to pass** in the fourth year of king	1961
	7: 1	*that* the word of the LORD **c** unto	1961
	7: 4	**c** the word of the LORD of hosts unto me,	1961
	7: 8	the word of the LORD **c** unto Zechariah,	1961
	7:12	**c** a great wrath from the LORD of hosts.	1961
	8: 1	Again the word of the LORD of hosts **c** *to*	1961
	8:10	went out or **c in** because of the affliction:	935
	8:18	the word of the LORD of hosts **c** unto me,	1961
	10: 4	Out of him **c forth** the corner, out of him	3318
	14:16	**c** against Jerusalem shall even go up from	935
Mt	1:18	before they **c together**, she was found with	4905
	2: 1	there **c** wise men from the east to	3854
	2: 9	till it **c** and stood over where the young	2064
	2:21	his mother, and **c** into the land of Israel.	2064
	2:23	And he **c** and dwelt in a city called	2064
	3: 1	In those days **c** John the Baptist,	3854
	4: 3	And when the tempter **c to** him, he said,	4334
	4:11	behold, angels **c** and ministered unto him.	4334
	4:13	he **c** and dwelt in Capernaum,	2064
	5: 1	when he was set, his disciples **c** unto him:	4334
	7:25	and the floods **c**, and the winds blew, and	2064
	7:27	and the floods **c**, and the winds blew, and	2064
	7:28	And it **c to pass**, when Jesus had ended	1096
	8: 2	there **c** a leper and worshipped him, saying,	2064
	8: 5	there **c** unto him a centurion,	4334
	8:19	And a certain scribe **c**, and said unto him,	4334
	8:25	And his disciples **c to** *him*, and awoke him,	4334
	8:34	the whole city **c out** to meet Jesus:	1831
	9: 1	and passed over, and **c** into his own city.	2064
	9:10	And it **c to pass**, as Jesus sat at meat in	1096
	9:10	many publicans and sinners **c** and sat down	2064
	9:14	Then **c to** him the disciples of John, saying,	4334
	9:18	there **c** a *certain* ruler, and worshipped him,	2064
	9:20	**c** behind *him*, and touched the hem of his	4334
	9:23	And when Jesus **c** into the ruler's house,	2064
	9:28	into the house, the blind men **c to** him:	4334
	10:34	on earth: I **c** not to send peace, but a sword	2064
	11: 1	And it **c to pass**, when Jesus had made an	1096
	11:18	For John **c** neither eating nor drinking, and	2064
	11:19	The Son of man **c** eating and drinking, and	2064
	12:42	for she **c** from the uttermost parts of	2064
	12:44	return into my house from whence I **c out**;	1831
	13: 4	and the fowls **c** and devoured them up:	2064
	13:10	And the disciples **c**, and said unto him,	4334
	13:25	his enemy **c** and sowed tares among	2064
	13:27	So the servants of the householder **c** and	4334
	13:36	and his disciples **c unto** him, saying,	4334
	13:53	And it **c to pass**, *that* when Jesus had	1096
	14:12	And his disciples **c**, and took up the body,	4334
	14:15	his disciples **c to** him, saying, *This* is a	4334
	14:33	Then they that were in the ship **c** and	2064
	14:34	they **c** into the land of Gennesaret.	2064
	15: 1	Then **c** to Jesus scribes and Pharisees,	4334
	15:12	Then **c** his disciples, and said unto him,	4334
	15:22	a woman of Canaan **c** out of the same	1831
	15:23	And his disciples **c** and besought him,	4334
	15:25	Then **c** she and worshipped him, saying,	2064
	15:29	and **c** nigh unto the sea of Galilee;	2064
	15:30	And great multitudes **c** unto him,	4334
	15:39	took ship, and **c** into the coasts of Magdala.	2064
	16: 1	The Pharisees also with the Sadducees **c**,	4334
	16:13	When Jesus **c** into the coasts of Cesarea	2064
	17: 7	And Jesus **c** and touched them, and said,	4334
	17: 9	And as they **c down** from the mountain,	2597
	17:14	there **c** to him a *certain* man, kneeling down	4334
	17:19	Then **c** the disciples to Jesus apart,	4334
	17:24	they that received tribute money **c to** Peter,	4334
	18: 1	At the same time **c** the disciples unto Jesus,	4334
	18:21	Then **c** Peter to him, and said, Lord,	4334
	18:31	and **c** and told unto their lord all that was	2064
	19: 1	And it **c to pass**, *that* when Jesus had	1096
	19: 1	**c** into the coasts of Judea beyond Jordan;	2064
	19: 3	The Pharisees also **c unto** him,	4334
Mt	19:16	And behold, one **c** and said unto him,	4334
	20: 9	And when they **c** that *were hired* about	2064
	20:10	But when the first **c**, they supposed that	2064
	20:20	Then **c to** him the mother of Zebedee's	4334
	20:28	Even as the Son of man **c** not to be	2064
	21:14	and *the* lame **c to** him in the temple;	4334
	21:19	he **c** to it, and found nothing thereon,	2064
	21:23	the elders of the people **c unto** him as he	4334
	21:28	and he **c to** the first, and said, Son, go work	4334
	21:30	And he **c to** the second,	4334
	21:32	For John **c** unto you in the way of	2064
	22:11	And when the king **c in** to see the guests,	1525
	22:23	The same day **c to** him *the* Sadducees,	4334
	24: 1	his disciples **c to** *him* for to shew him	4334
	24: 3	the disciples **c unto** him privately, saying,	4334
	24:39	And knew not until the flood **c**, and	2064
	25:10	while they went to buy, the bridegroom **c**;	2064
	25:11	Afterward **c** also the other virgins, saying,	2064
	25:20	*so* he that had received five talents **c** and	4334
	25:22	He also that had received two talents **c** and	4334
	25:24	he which had received the one talent **c**	4334
	25:36	I was in prison, and ye **c** unto me.	2064
	25:39	we thee sick, or in prison, and **c** unto thee?	2064
	26: 1	And it **c to pass**, when Jesus had finished	1096
	26: 7	There **c unto** him a woman having an	4334
	26:17	unleavened bread the disciples **c to** Jesus,	4334
	26:43	And he **c** and found them asleep again:	2064
	26:47	**c**, and with him a great multitude with	2064
	26:49	And forthwith he **c to** Jesus, and said, Hail,	4334
	26:50	Then **c** they, and laid hands on Jesus, and	4334
	26:60	yea, though many false witnesses **c**,	4334
	26:60	they none. At the last **c** two false witnesses,	4334
	26:69	and a damsel **c unto** him, saying, Thou also	4334
	26:73	And after a while **c unto** *him* they that	4334
	27:32	And as they **c out**, they found a man of	1831
	27:53	And **c out** of the graves after his	1831
	27:57	there **c** a rich man of Arimathea,	2064
	27:62	and Pharisees **c together** unto Pilate,	4863
	28: 1	**c** Mary Magdalene and the other Mary to	2064
	28: 2	and **c** and rolled back the stone from	4334
	28: 9	And they **c** and held him by the feet, and	4334
	28:11	some of the watch **c** into the city, and	2064
	28:13	His disciples **c** by night, and stole him	2064
	28:18	And Jesus **c** and spake unto them, saying,	4334
Mk	1: 9	And it **c to pass** in those days, *that* Jesus	1096
	1: 9	*that* Jesus **c** from Nazareth of Galilee, and	2064
	1:11	And there **c** a voice from heaven,	1096
	1:14	John was put in prison, Jesus **c** into Galilee,	2064
	1:26	cried with a loud voice, he **c out** of him.	1831
	1:31	And he **c** and took her by the hand, and	4334
	1:38	preach there also: for therefore **c** I **forth**.	1831
	1:40	And there **c** a leper to him, beseeching him,	2064
	1:45	and they **c** to him from every quarter.	2064
	2:15	And it **c to pass**, that as *Jesus* sat at meat in	1096
	2:17	I **c** not to call *the* righteous, but sinners to	2064
	2:23	And it **c to pass**, that he went through	1096
	3: 8	heard what great *things* he did, **c** unto him.	2064
	3:13	*him* whom he would: and they **c** unto him.	565
	3:22	And the scribes which **c down** from	2597
	3:31	There **c** then *his* brethren and his mother,	2064
	4: 4	And it **c to pass**, as *he* sowed, some fell by	1096
	4: 4	and the fowls of the air **c** and devoured it	2064
	5: 1	And they **c** over unto the other side of	2064
	5:27	**c** in the press behind, and touched his	2064
	5:33	**c** and fell down before him, and told him	2064
	5:35	there **c** from the ruler of the synagogue's	2064
	6: 1	from thence, and **c** into his own country;	2064
	6:22	the daughter of the said Herodias **c in**,	1525
	6:25	And she **c in** straightway with haste unto	1525
	6:29	And when his disciples heard *of it*, they **c**	2064
	6:33	outwent them, and **c together** unto him.	4905
	6:34	And Jesus, when he **c out**, saw much	1831
	6:35	his disciples **c** unto him, and said, *This* is a	4334
	6:53	they **c** into the land of Genesaret, and	2064
	7: 1	Then **c together** unto him the Pharisees,	4863
	7: 1	of the scribes, which **c** from Jerusalem.	2064
	7:25	heard of him, and **c** and fell at his feet:	2064
	7:31	and Sidon, he **c** unto the sea of Galilee,	2064
	8: 3	by the way: for divers of them **c** from far.	2240
	8:10	and **c** into the parts of Dalmanutha.	2064
	8:11	And the Pharisees **c forth**, and began to	1831
	9: 7	and a voice **c** out of the cloud, saying,	2064
	9: 9	And as they **c down** from the mountain,	2597
	9:14	And when he **c** to *his* disciples, he saw a	2064
	9:21	How long is it ago since this **c** unto him?	1096
	9:25	saw that the people **c running together**,	1998
	9:26	and **c out** of *him*: and he was as one dead;	1831
	9:33	And he **c** to Capernaum: and being in	2064
	10: 2	And the Pharisees **c** to *him*, and asked him,	4334
	10:17	there **c** one **running**, and kneeled to him,	4370
	10:45	For even the Son of man **c** not to be	2064
	10:46	And they **c** to Jericho: and as he went out	2064
	10:50	away his garment, rose, and **c** to Jesus.	2064
	11: 1	And when they **c nigh** to Jerusalem,	1448
	11:13	he **c**, if haply he might find any *thing*	2064
	11:13	and when he **c** to it, he found nothing but	2064
	12:28	And one of the scribes **c**, and having heard	4334
	12:42	And there **c** a certain poor widow, and	2064
	14: 3	there **c** a woman having an alabaster box of	2064
	14:16	and **c** into the city, and found as he had said	2064
	14:32	And they **c** to a place which was named	2064
	15:41	many other *women* which **c up with** him	4872
	15:43	**c**, and went in boldly unto Pilate, and	2064
	16: 2	they **c** unto the sepulchre at the rising of	2064
Lk	1: 8	And it **c** to **pass**, *that* while he executed	1096
	1:22	And when he **c out**, he could not speak	1831
	1:23	And it **c to pass** *that*, as soon as the days of	1096
	1:28	And the angel **c in** unto her, and said, Hail,	1525
	1:41	And it **c to pass** *that*, when Elisabeth heard	1096
	1:57	Now Elisabeth's **full** time **c** that she should	4130
	1:59	And it **c to pass**, *that* on the eighth day they	1096
	1:59	*that* on the eighth day they **c** to circumcise	2064
	1:65	And fear **c** on all that dwelt round about	1096
	2: 1	And it **c to pass** in those days, *that* there	1096
	2: 9	*the* angel of the Lord **c upon** them, and	2186
Lk	2:15	And it **c to pass**, as the angels were gone	1096
	2:16	And they **c** with haste, and found Mary,	2064
	2:27	And he **c** by the Spirit into the temple: and	2064
	2:46	And it **c to pass**, *that* after three days they	1096
	2:51	and **c** to Nazareth, and was subject unto	2064
	3: 2	the word of God **c** unto John the son of	1096
	3: 3	And he **c** into all the country about Jordan,	2064
	3: 7	Then said he to the multitude that **c forth** to	1607
	3:12	Then **c** also publicans to be baptized, and	2064
	3:21	it **c to pass**, *that* Jesus also being baptized,	1096
	3:22	and a voice **c** from heaven, which said,	1096
	4:16	And he **c** to Nazareth, where he had been	2064
	4:31	And **c down** to Capernaum, a city of	2718
	4:35	he **c out** of him, and hurt him not.	1831
	4:41	And devils also **c out** of many, crying out,	1831
	4:42	and **c** unto him, and stayed him,	2064
	5: 1	And it **c to pass** that, as the people pressed	1096
	5: 7	And they **c**, and filled both the ships, so	2064
	5:12	And it **c to pass**, when he was in a certain	1096
	5:15	and great multitudes **c together** to hear,	4905
	5:17	And it **c to pass** on a certain day, as he was	1096
	5:32	I **c** not to call *the* righteous, but sinners to	2064
	6: 1	And it **c to pass** on the second sabbath after	1096
	6: 6	And it **c to pass** also on another sabbath,	1096
	6:12	And it **c to pass** in those days, *that* he went	1096
	6:17	And he **c down** with them, and stood in	2597
	6:17	which **c** to hear him, and to be healed of	2064
	7: 4	And when they **c** to Jesus, they besought	3854
	7:11	And it **c to pass** the *day* after, *that* he went	1096
	7:12	Now when he **c nigh** to the gate of the city,	1448
	7:14	And he **c** and touched the bier: and	4334
	7:16	And there **c** a fear on all:	2983
	7:33	For John the Baptist **c** neither eating bread	2064
	7:45	this *woman* since the time I **c in** hath not	1525
	8: 1	And it **c to pass** afterward, that he went	1096
	8:19	Then **c** to him *his* mother and his brethren,	3854
	8:22	Now it **c to pass** on a certain day, that he	1096
	8:23	there **c down** a storm of wind on the lake;	2597
	8:24	And they **c** to *him*, and awoke him, saying,	4334
	8:35	and **c** to Jesus, and found the man, out of	2064
	8:40	And it **c to pass** that, when Jesus was	1096
	8:41	there **c** a man named Jairus, and he was a	2064
	8:44	**C** behind *him*, and touched the border of	4334
	8:47	she **c** trembling, and falling down before	2064
	8:51	And when he **c into** the house,	1525
	8:55	And her spirit **c again**, and she arose	1994
	9:12	then **c** the twelve, and said unto him,	4334
	9:18	And it **c to pass**, as he was alone praying,	1096
	9:28	And it **c to pass** about an eight days after	1096
	9:33	And it **c to pass**, as they departed from	1096
	9:34	there **c** a cloud, and overshadowed them:	1096
	9:35	And there **c** a voice out of the cloud,	1096
	9:37	And it **c to pass**, *that* on the next day,	1096
	9:51	And it **c to pass**, when the time was come	1096
	9:57	And it **c to pass** *that*, as they went in	1096
	10:31	And by chance there **c down** a certain	2597
	10:32	**c** and looked *on him*, and passed by on	2064
	10:33	as he journeyed, **c** where he was:	2064
	10:38	Now it **c to pass**, as they went, that he	1096
	10:40	much serving, and **c** to *him*, and said, Lord,	2186
	11: 1	And it **c to pass** *that*, as he was praying in a	1096
	11:14	And it **c to pass**, when the devil was gone	1096
	11:24	I will return unto my house whence I **c out**.	1831
	11:27	And it **c to pass**, as he spake these *things*, a	1096
	11:31	for she **c** from the utmost parts of the earth	2064
	13: 6	and he **c** and sought fruit thereon,	2064
	13:31	The same day there **c** certain *of*	4334
	14: 1	And it **c to pass**, as he went into the house	1096
	14:21	So that servant **c**, and shewed his lord these	3854
	15:17	And when he **c** to himself, he said, How	2064
	15:20	And he arose, and **c** to his father. But when	2064
	15:25	and as he **c** and drew nigh to the house,	2064
	15:28	therefore **c** his father **out** and intreated him.	1831
	16:21	moreover the dogs **c** and licked his sores.	2064
	16:22	And it **c to pass** that the beggar died, and	1096
	17:11	And it **c to pass**, as he went to Jerusalem,	1096
	17:14	And it **c to pass** *that*, as they went,	1096
	17:27	and the flood **c**, and destroyed *them* all.	2064
	18: 3	and she **c** unto him, saying, Avenge me of	2064
	18:35	And it **c to pass**, *that* as he was come nigh	1096
	19: 5	And when Jesus **c** to the place, he looked	2064
	19: 6	and **c down**, and received him joyfully.	2597
	19:15	And it **c to pass**, that when he was	1096
	19:16	Then **c** the first, saying, Lord, thy pound	3854
	19:18	And the second **c**, saying, Lord, thy pound	2064
	19:20	And another **c**, saying, Lord, behold, *here is*	2064
	19:29	And it **c to pass**, when he was come nigh to	1096
	20: 1	And it **c to pass**, *that* on one of those days,	1096
	20: 1	and the scribes **c upon** *him* with the elders,	2186
	20:27	Then **c** to *him* certain of the Sadducees,	4334
	21:38	And all the people **c early in the morning**	3719
	22: 7	Then **c** the day of unleavened bread,	2064
	22:39	And he **c out**, and went, as he was wont, to	1831
	22:66	the chief priests and the scribes **c together**,	4863
	23:48	And all the people that **c together** to that	4836
	23:55	which **c with** him from Galilee,	4905
	24: 1	in the morning, they **c** unto the sepulchre,	2064
	24: 4	And it **c to pass**, as they were *much*	1096
	24:15	And it **c to pass**, that while they communed	1096
	24:23	they found not his body, they **c**, saying,	2064
	24:30	And it **c to pass**, as he sat at meat with	1096
	24:51	And it **c to pass**, while he blessed them,	1096
Jn	1: 7	The same **c** for a witness, to bear witness of	2064
	1:11	He **c** unto his own, and his own received	2064
	1:17	*but* grace and truth **c** by Jesus Christ.	1096
	1:39	They **c** and saw where he dwelt, and	2064
	3: 2	The same **c** to Jesus by night, and said unto	2064
	3:13	but he that **c down** from heaven, *even*	2597
	3:22	After these *things* **c** Jesus and his disciples	2064
	3:23	water there: and they **c**, and were baptized.	3854
	3:26	And they **c** unto John, and said unto him,	2064
	4:27	And upon this **c** his disciples, and	2064
	4:30	they went out of the city, and **c** unto him.	2064
	4:46	So Jesus **c** again into Cana of Galilee,	2064
	6:23	(Howbeit there **c** other boats from Tiberias	2064

Jn 6:24 and c to Capernaum, seeking for Jesus. 2064
6:38 For I c down from heaven, not to do mine 2597
6:41 I am the bread which c down from heaven. 2597
6:42 then that he saith, I c down from heaven? 2597
6:51 I am the living bread which c down from 2597
6:58 This is that bread which c down from 2597
7:45 Then c the officers to the chief priests and 2064
7:50 (he that c to Jesus by night, being one of 2064
8: 2 And early in the morning he c again into 3854
8: 2 the temple, and all the people c unto him; 2064
8:14 for I know whence I c, and whither I go; 2064
8:42 for I proceeded forth and c from God; 2240
8:42 and came from God; neither c I of myself, 2064
9: 7 way therefore, and washed, and c seeing. 2064
10: 8 All that ever c before me are thieves and 2064
10:24 Then c the Jews round about him, and 2944
10:35 unto whom the word of God c, and 1096
11:17 Then when Jesus c, he found that he had 2064
11:19 And many of the Jews c to Martha and 2064
11:29 that, she arose quickly, and c unto him. 2064
11:33 the Jews also weeping which c with her, 4905
11:44 And he that was dead c forth, bound hand 1831
11:45 Then many of the Jews which c to Mary, 2064
12: 1 Then Jesus six days before the passover c 2064
12: 9 and they c not for Jesus' sake only, 2064
12:20 them that c up to worship at the feast: 305
12:21 The same c therefore to Philip, which was 4334
12:27 but for this cause c I unto this hour. 2064
12:28 Then c there a voice from heaven, saying, I 2064
12:30 This voice c not because of me, but 1096
12:47 for I c not to judge the world, but to save 2064
16:27 and have believed that I c out from God. 1831
16:28 I c forth from the Father, and am come into 1831
17: 8 have known surely that I c out from thee, 1831
18:37 I born, and for this cause c I into the world, 2064
19: 5 Then c Jesus forth, wearing the crown of 1831
19:32 Then c the soldiers, and brake the legs of 2064
19:33 But when they c to Jesus, and saw that he 2064
19:34 and forthwith c there out blood and water. 1831
19:38 He c therefore, and took the body of Jesus. 2064
19:39 And there c also Nicodemus, which at 2064
19:39 which at the first c to Jesus by night, and 2064
20: 3 that other disciple, and c to the sepulchre. 2064
20: 4 outrun Peter, and c first to the sepulchre. 2064
20: 8 which c first to the sepulchre, and he saw, 2064
20:18 Mary Magdalene c and told the disciples 2064
20:19 c Jesus and stood in the midst, and 2064
20:24 was not with them when Jesus c. 2064
20:26 then c Jesus, the doors being shut, 2064
21: 8 And the other disciples c in a little ship; 2064
Ac 2: 2 And suddenly there c a sound from heaven 1096
2: 6 the multitude c together, and 4905
2:43 And fear c upon every soul: and 1096
4: 1 and the Sadducees, c upon them, 2186
4: 5 And it c to pass on the morrow, that their 1096
5: 5 great fear c on all them that heard these 1096
5: 7 his wife, not knowing what was done, c in. 1525
5:10 and the young men c in, and found her 1525
5:11 And great fear c upon all the church, and 1096
5:16 There c also a multitude out of the cities 4905
5:21 But the high priest c, and they that were 3854
5:22 But when the officers c, and found them 3854
5:25 Then c one and told them, saying, Behold, 3854
6:12 and c upon him, and caught him, and 2186
7: 4 Then c he out of the land of the Chaldeans, 1831
7:11 Now there c a dearth over all the land of 2064
7:23 it c into his heart to visit his brethren 305
7:31 behold it, the voice of the Lord c unto him, 1096
7:45 Which also our fathers that c after brought 1237
8: 7 c out of many that were possessed with 1831
8:36 on their way, they c unto a certain water: 2064
8:40 in all the cities, till he c to Cesarea. 2064
9: 3 And as he journeyed, he c near Damascus: 1448
9:21 c hither for that intent, that he might bring 2064
9:32 And it c to pass, as Peter passed throughout 1096
9:32 c down also to the saints which dwelt at 2718
9:37 And it c to pass in those days, that she was 1096
9:43 And it c to pass, that he tarried many days 1096
10:13 And there c a voice to him, Rise, Peter; kill, 1096
10:29 Therefore c I unto you without gainsaying, 2064
10:45 as many as c with Peter, because that on 4905
11: 5 heaven by four corners; and it c even to me: 2064
11:22 Then tidings of these things c unto the ears 191
11:23 when he c, and had seen the grace of God, 3854
11:26 And it c to pass, that a whole year they 1096
11:27 And in these days c prophets from 2718
11:28 which c to pass in the days of Claudius 1096
12: 7 the angel of the Lord c upon him, and 2186
12:10 they c unto the iron gate that leadeth unto 2064
12:12 And when he had considered the thing, he c 2064
12:13 a damsel c to hearken, named Rhoda. 4334
12:20 but they c with one accord to him, and, 3918
13:13 from Paphos, they c to Perga in Pamphylia: 2064
13:14 they c to Antioch in Pisidia, and went into 3854
13:31 c up with him from Galilee to Jerusalem, 4872
13:44 c almost the whole city together to hear 4863
13:51 their feet against them, and c unto Iconium. 2064
14: 1 And it c to pass in Iconium, that they went 1096
14:19 And there c thither certain Jews from 1904
14:20 he rose up, and c into the city: 1525
14:24 throughout Pisidia, they c to Pamphylia. 2064
15: 1 And certain men which c down from Judea 2718
15: 6 elders c together for to consider of this 4863
15:30 they were dismissed, they c to Antioch: 2064
16: 1 Then c he to Derbe and Lystra: and behold, 2658
16: 8 And they passing by Mysia c down to 2597
16:11 we c with a straight course to 2113
16:16 And it c to pass, as we went to prayer, 1096
16:18 out of her. And he c out the same hour. 1831
16:29 and c trembling, and fell down before Paul 1096
16:39 And they c and besought them, and 2064
17: 1 and Apollonia, they c to Thessalonica, 2064
17:13 they c thither also, and stirred up 2064
18: 1 departed from Athens, and c to Corinth; 2064
18: 2 to depart from Rome:) and c unto them. 4334
Ac 18:19 And he c to Ephesus, and left them there: 2658
18:24 and mighty in the scriptures, c to Ephesus. 2658
19: 1 And it c to pass, that, while Apollos was at 1096
19: 1 through the upper coasts c to Ephesus: 2064
19: 6 upon them, the Holy Ghost c on them; 2064
19:18 And many that believed c, and confessed, 2064
20: 2 them much exhortation, he c into Greece, 2064
20: 6 and c unto them to Troas in five days; 2064
20: 7 when the disciples c together to break 4863
20:14 we took him in, and c to Mitylene. 2064
20:15 and c the next day over against Chios; 2658
20:15 and the next day we c to Miletus. 2064
20:18 from the first day that I c into Asia, 1910
21: 1 And it c to pass, that after we were gotten 1096
21: 1 we c with a straight course unto Cos, and 2064
21: 7 we c to Ptolemais, and saluted the brethren, 2658
21: 8 company departed, and c unto Cesarea: 2064
21:10 there c down from Judea a certain prophet, 2718
21:31 tidings c unto the chief captain of the band, 305
21:33 Then the chief captain c near, and 1448
21:35 And when he c upon the stairs, so it was, 1096
22: 6 And it c to pass that, as I made my journey, 1096
22:11 them that were with me, I c into Damascus. 2064
22:13 C unto me, and stood, and said unto me, 2064
22:17 And it c to pass that, when I was come 1096
22:27 Then the chief captain c, and said unto him, 4334
23:14 And they c to the chief priests and elders, 4334
23:27 then c I with an army, and rescued him, 2186
23:33 when they c to Cesarea, and 1525
24: 7 But the chief captain Lysias c upon us, and 3928
24:17 Now after many years I c to bring alms to 3854
24:24 when Felix c with his wife Drusilla, 3854
24:27 Porcius Festus c into Felix' room: 1240+2983
25: 7 the Jews which c down from Jerusalem 2597
25:13 Bernice c unto Cesarea to salute Festus. 2658
27: 5 sea of Cilicia and Pamphylia, we c to Myra, 2718
27: 8 c unto a place which is called The fair 2064
27:44 And so it c to pass, that they escaped all 1096
28: 3 there c a viper out of the heat, and 1831
28: 8 And it c to pass, that the father of Publius 1096
28: 9 diseases in the island, c, and were healed: 4334
28:13 we fet a compass, and c to Rhegium: 2658
28:13 and we c the next day to Puteoli: 2064
28:15 they c to meet us as far as Appii forum, and 1831
28:16 And when we c to Rome, the centurion 2064
28:17 And it c to pass, that after three days Paul 1096
28:21 neither any of the brethren that c shewed or 3854
28:23 a day, there c many to him into his lodging; 2240
28:30 and received all that c in unto him, 1531
Ro 5:18 judgment c upon all men to condemnation; NIG
5:18 by the righteousness of one the free gift c NIG
7: 9 but when the commandment c, sin revived, 2064
9: 5 of whom as concerning the flesh Christ c, NIG
1Co 2: 1 And I, brethren, when I c to you, came not 2064
2: 1 c not with excellency of speech or 2064
14:36 c the word of God out from you? or came it 1831
14:36 of God out from you? or c it unto you only? 2658
15:21 For since by man c death, by man came also NIG
15:21 by man c also the resurrection of the dead. NIG
2Co 1: 8 have you ignorant of our trouble which c to 1096
1:23 that to spare you I c not as yet unto Corinth. 2064
2: 3 I wrote this same unto you, lest, when I c, 2064
2:12 when I c to Troas to preach Christ's gospel, 2064
11: 9 brethren which c from Macedonia supplied: 2064
Gal 1:21 Afterwards I c into the regions of Syria and 2064
2: 4 who c in privily to spy out our liberty 3922
2:12 For before that certain c from James, he did 2064
3:23 But before faith c, we were kept under 2064
Eph 2:17 And c and preached peace to you which 2064
1Th 1: 5 For our gospel c not unto you in word only, 1096
3: 4 even as it c to pass, and ye know. 1096
3: 6 But now when Timotheus c from you unto 2064
1Ti 1:15 that Christ Jesus c into the world to save 2064
2Ti 3:11 afflictions, which c unto me at Antioch, 1096
Heb 3:16 howbeit not all that c out of Egypt by 1831
11:15 of that country from whence they c out, 1831
2Pe 1:17 when there c such a voice to him from 5342
1:18 And this voice which c from heaven we 5342
1:21 For the prophecy c not in old time by 5342
1Jn 5: 6 This is he that c by water and blood, 2064
3Jn 1: 3 when the brethren c and testified of 2064
Rev 5: 7 And he c and took the book out of the right 2064
7:13 arrayed in white robes? and whence c they? 2064
7:14 These are they which c out of great 2064
8: 3 And another angel c and stood at the altar, 2064
8: 4 which c with the prayers of the saints, NIG
9: 3 And there c out of the smoke locusts upon 1831
14:15 And another angel c out of the temple, 1831
14:17 And another angel c out of the temple 1831
14:18 And another angel c out from the altar, 1831
14:20 and blood c out of the winepress, even unto 1831
15: 6 And the seven angels c out of the temple, 1831
16:17 there c a great voice out of the temple of 1831
16:19 great Babylon c in remembrance before 3415
17: 1 And there c one of the seven angels which 2064
19: 5 And a voice c out of the throne, saying, 1831
20: 9 and fire c down from God out of heaven, 2597
21: 9 And there c unto me one of the seven 2064

CAMEL (9) [CAMEL'S, CAMELS, CAMELS']

Ge 24:64 when she saw Isaac, she lighted off the c. 1581
Lev 11: 4 as the c, because he cheweth the cud, but 1581
Dt 14: 7 as the c, and the hare, and the coney: 1581
1Sa 15: 3 and suckling, ox and sheep, c and ass. 1581
Zec 14:15 of the c, of the ass, and of all the beasts 1581
Mt 19:24 It is easier for a c to go through the eye of a 2574
23:24 which strain out a gnat, and swallow a c. 2574
Mk 10:25 It is easier for a c to go through the eye of a 2574
Lk 18:25 For it is easier for a c to go through a 2574

CAMEL'S (3) [CAMEL]

Ge 31:34 put them in the c furniture, and sat upon 1581
Mt 3: 4 And the same John had his raiment of c 2574
Mk 1: 6 And John was clothed with c hair, and 2574

CAMELS (47) [CAMEL]

Ge 12:16 and maidservants, and she asses, and c. 1581
24:10 the servant took ten c of the camels of his 1581
24:10 the servant took ten camels of the c of his 1581
24:11 he made his c to kneel down without 1581
24:14 Drink, and I will give thy c drink also: 1581
24:19 she said, I will draw water for thy c also, 1581
24:20 well to draw water, and drew for all his c. 1581
24:22 it came to pass, as the c had done drinking, 1581
24:30 and behold, he stood by the c at the well. 1581
24:31 prepared the house, and room for the c. 1581
24:32 he ungirded his c, and gave straw and 1581
24:32 and gave straw and provender for the c, and 1581
24:35 and maidservants, and c, and asses. 1581
24:44 drink thou, and I will also draw for thy c: 1581
24:46 said, Drink, and I will give thy c drink also: 1581
24:46 so I drank, and she made the c drink also. 1581
24:61 they rode upon the c, and followed 1581
24:63 and saw, and, behold, the c were coming. 1581
30:43 and menservants, and c, and asses. 1581
31:17 and set his sons and his wives upon c; 1581
32: 7 the flocks, and herds, and the c, into two 1581
32:15 Thirty milch c with their colts, forty kine, 1581
37:25 from Gilead with their c bearing spicery 1581
Ex 9: 3 upon the c, upon the oxen, and upon 1581
Jdg 6: 5 both they and their c were without number: 1581
7:12 their c were without number, as the sand by 1581
1Sa 27: 9 the c, and the apparel, and returned, and 1581
30:17 young men, which rode upon c, and fled. 1581
1Ki 10: 2 with c that bare spices, and very much 1581
1Ch 5:21 of their c fifty thousand, and of sheep two 1581
12:40 on c, and on mules, and on oxen, and meat, 1581
27:30 Over the c also was Obil the Ishmaelite: 1581
2Ch 9: 1 c that bare spices, and gold in abundance, 1581
14:15 and carried away sheep and c in abundance, 1581
Ezr 2:67 Their c, four hundred thirty and five; 1581
Ne 7:69 Their c, four hundred thirty and five: 1581
Est 8:10 riders on mules, c, and young dromedaries: 327
8:14 posts that rode upon mules and c went out, 327
Job 1: 3 three thousand c, and five hundred yoke of 1581
1:17 fell upon the c, and have carried them 1581
42:12 six thousand c, and a thousand yoke of 1581
Isa 21: 7 a chariot of asses, and a chariot of c; 1581
30: 6 their treasures upon the bunches of c, to a 1581
60: 6 The multitude of c shall cover thee, 1581
Jer 49:29 and all their vessels, and their c; 1581
49:32 their c shall be a booty, and the multitude 1581
Eze 25: 5 I will make Rabbah a stable for c, and 1581

CAMELS' (3) [CAMEL]

Jdg 8:21 the ornaments that were on their c necks. 1581
8:26 beside the chains that were about their c 1581
2Ki 8: 9 forty c burden, and came and stood before 1581

CAMEST (28) [COME]

Ge 16: 8 he said, Hagar, Sarai's maid, whence c thou? 935
24: 5 again unto the land from whence thou c? 3318
27:33 I have eaten of all before thou c, and 935
Ex 23:15 for in it thou c out from Egypt: 3318
34:18 for in the month Abib thou c out from 3318
Nu 22:37 wherefore c thou not unto me? am I not 1980
Dt 2:37 land of the children of Ammon thou c not, 7126
16: 3 for thou c forth out of the land of Egypt in 3318
16: 3 c forth out of the land of Egypt all the days 3318
16: 6 at the season that thou c forth out of Egypt. 3318
1Sa 13:11 that thou c not within the days appointed, 935
17:28 and he said, Why c thou down hither? 3381
2Sa 11:10 unto Uriah, C thou not from thy journey? 935
15:20 Whereas thou c but yesterday, should I this 935
1Ki 13: 9 nor turn again by the same way that thou c. 1980
13:14 Art thou the man of God that c from Judah? 935
13:17 nor turn again to go by the way that thou c. 1980
13:22 c back, and hast eaten bread and 7725
2Ki 19:28 turn thee back by the way by which thou c. 935
Ne 9:13 Thou c down also upon mount Sinai, and 3381
Isa 37:29 turn thee back by the way by which thou c. 935
64: 3 thou c down, the mountains flowed down 3381
Jer 1: 5 before thou c forth out of the womb I 3318
Eze 32: 2 thou c forth with thy rivers, and 1518
Mt 22:12 how c thou in hither not having a wedding 1525
Jn 6:25 said unto him, Rabbi, when c thou hither? 1096
16:30 by this we believe that thou c forth from 1831
Ac 9:17 appeared unto thee in the way as thou c, 2064

CAMON (1)

Jdg 10: 5 And Jair died, and was buried in C. 7056

CAMP (136) [CAMPED, CAMPS, ENCAMP, ENCAMPED, ENCAMPETH, ENCAMPING]

Ex 14:19 which went before the c of Israel, removed 4264
14:20 it came between the c of the Egyptians and 4264
14:20 camp of the Egyptians and the c of Israel; 4264
16:13 even the quails came up, and covered the c: 4264
19:16 that all the people that was in the c 4264
19:17 Moses brought forth the people out of the c 4264
29:14 shalt thou burn with fire without the c: 4264
32:17 There is a noise of war in the c. 4264
32:19 as soon as he came nigh unto the c, that he 4264
32:26 Moses stood in the gate of the c, and said, 4264
32:27 and out from gate to gate throughout the c, 4264
33: 7 pitched it without the c, afar off from 4264
33: 7 afar off from the c, and called it 4264
33: 7 the Congregation, which was without the c. 4264
33:11 he turned again into the c: but his servant 4264
36: 6 caused it to be proclaimed throughout the c, 4264
Lev 4:12 carry forth without the c unto a clean place, 4264
4:21 shall carry forth the bullock without the c, 4264
6:11 carry forth the ashes without the c unto a 4264
8:17 his dung, he burnt with fire without the c; 4264
9:11 the hide he burnt with fire without the c. 4264
10: 4 from before the sanctuary out of the c. 4264
10: 5 and carried them in their coats out of the c; 4264
13:46 without the c shall his habitation be. 4264
14: 3 the priest shall go forth out of the c; and 4264

Lev 14: 8 after that he shall come into the c, and 4264
16:26 in water, and afterward come into the c. 4264
16:27 place, shall one carry forth without the c; 4264
16:28 and afterward he shall come into the c. 4264
17: 3 in the c, or that killeth it out of the camp, 4264
17: 3 in the camp, or that killeth it out of the c, 4264
24:10 and a man of Israel strove together in the c; 4264
24:14 forth him that hath cursed without the c; 4264
24:23 bring forth him that had cursed out of the c, 4264
Nu 1:52 every man by his own c, and every man by 4264
2: 3 c of Judah pitch throughout their armies: 4264
2: 9 All that were numbered in the c of Judah 4264
2:10 the c of Reuben according to their armies: 4264
2:16 All that were numbered in the c of Reuben 4264
2:17 c of the Levites in the midst of the camp: 4264
2:17 camp of the Levites in the midst of the c: 4264
2:18 the c of Ephraim according to their armies: 4264
2:24 All that were numbered of the c of Ephraim 4264
2:25 The standard of the c of Dan shall be on 4264
2:31 All they that were numbered in the c of 4264
4: 5 when the c setteth forward, Aaron shall 4264
4:15 of the sanctuary, as the c is to set forward; 4264
5: 2 that they put out of the c every leper, and 4264
5: 3 ye put out, without the c shall ye put them; 4264
5: 4 did so, and put them out without the c: 4264
10:14 In the first place went the standard of the c 4264
10:18 the standard of the c of Reuben set forward 4264
10:22 the standard of the c of the children of 4264
10:25 the standard of the c of the children of Dan 4264
10:34 them by day, when they went out of the c. 4264
11: 1 that were in the uttermost parts of the c. 4264
11: 9 when the dew fell upon the c in the night, 4264
11:26 there remained two of the men in the c, 4264
11:26 and they prophesied in the c. 4264
11:27 Eldad and Medad do prophesy in the c. 4264
11:30 Moses gat him into the c, he and the elders 4264
11:31 from the sea, and let them fall by the c, 4264
11:31 round about the c, and as it were two cubits 4264
11:32 all abroad for themselves round about the c. 4264
12:14 let her be shut out from the c seven days, 4264
12:15 Miriam was shut out from the c seven days: 4264
14:44 and Moses, departed not out of the c. 4264
15:35 shall stone him with stones without the c. 4264
15:36 the congregation brought him without the c, 4264
19: 3 that he may bring her forth without the c, 4264
19: 7 afterward he shall come into the c, and 4264
19: 9 lay them up without the c in a clean place, 4264
31:12 unto the c at the plains of Moab, which are 4264
31:13 went forth to meet them without the c. 4264
31:19 do ye abide without the c seven days: 4264
31:24 and afterward ye shall come into the c. 4264
Dt 23:10 shall he go abroad out of the c, he shall not 4264
23:10 of the camp, he shall not come within the c: 4264
23:11 is down, he shall come into the c again. 4264
23:12 Thou shalt have a place also without the c, 4264
23:14 thy God walketh in the midst of thy c, 4264
23:14 before thee; therefore shall thy c be holy: 4264
29:11 your wives, and thy stranger that is in thy c, 4264
Jos 5: 8 that they abode in their places in the c, 4264
6:11 they came into the c, and lodged in 4264
6:11 came into the camp, and lodged in the c. 4264
6:14 the city once, and returned into the c: 4264
6:18 make the c of Israel a curse, and trouble it. 4264
6:23 and left them without the c of Israel. 4264
9: 6 they went to Joshua unto the c at Gilgal, 4264
10: 6 the men of Gibeon sent unto Joshua to the c 4264
10:15 and all Israel with him, unto the c to Gilgal. 4264
10:21 all the people returned to the c to Joshua at 4264
10:43 and all Israel with him, unto the c to Gilgal. 4264
Jdg 7:17 behold, when I come to the outside of the c, 4264
7:18 the trumpets also on every side of all the c, 4264
7:19 came unto the outside of the c in 4264
7:21 every man in his place round about the c: 4264
13:25 began to move him at times in the c of Dan, 4264
21: 8 there came none to the c from 4264
21:12 they brought them unto the c to Shiloh, 4264
1Sa 4: 3 when the people were come into the c, 4264
4: 5 covenant of the LORD came into the c, 4264
4: 6 of this great shout in the c of the Hebrews? 4264
4: 6 the ark of the LORD was come into the c. 4264
4: 7 for they said, God is come into the c. 4264
13:17 the spoilers came out of the c of 4264
14:21 which went up with them into the c from 4264
17: 4 there went out a champion out of the c of 4264
17:17 ten loaves, and run to the c to thy brethren; 4264
26: 6 will go down with me to Saul to the c? 4264
2Sa 1: 2 a man came out of the c from Saul with his 4264
1: 3 Out of the c of Israel am I escaped. 4264
1Ki 16:16 the host, king over Israel that day in the c. 4264
2Ki 3:24 when they came to the c of Israel, 4264
6: 8 In such and such a place shall be my c. 8466
7: 5 the twilight, to go unto the c of the Syrians: 4264
7: 5 come to the uttermost part of the c of Syria, 4264
7: 7 even the c as it was, and fled for their life. 4264
7: 8 lepers came to the uttermost part of the c, 4264
7:10 We came to the c of the Syrians, and 4264
7:12 are they gone out of the c to hide 4264
19:35 smote in the c of the Assyrians an hundred 4264
2Ch 22: 1 Arabians to the c had slain all the eldest. 4264
32:21 and captains in the c of the king of Assyria. 4264
Ps 78:28 he let it fall in the midst of their c, 4264
106:16 They envied Moses also in the c, and 4264
Isa 29: 3 I will c against thee round about, and 2583
37:36 smote in the c of the Assyrians an hundred 4264
Jer 50:29 that bend the bow, c against it round about; 2583
Eze 4: 2 set the c also against it, and set battering 4264
Joel 2:11 for his c is very great: for he is strong that 4264
Na 3:17 which c in the hedges in the cold day, but 2583
Heb 13:11 high priest for sin, are burnt without the c. 3925
13:13 go forth therefore unto him without the c, 3925
Rev 20: 9 and compassed the c of the saints about, 3925

CAMPED (1) [CAMP]
Ex 19: 2 and there Israel c before the mount. 2583

CAMPFIRES See SHEEPFOLD

CAMPHIRE (2)
SS 1:14 My beloved is unto me as a cluster of c in 3724
4:13 with pleasant fruits; c, with spikenard, 3724

CAMPS (7) [CAMP]
Nu 2:32 all those that were numbered of the c 4264
5: 3 that they defile not their c, in the midst 4264
10: 2 and for the journeying of the c. 4264
10: 5 the c that lie on the east parts shall go 4264
10: 6 the c that lie on the south side shall take 4264
10:25 which was the rereward of all the c 4264
Am 4:10 I have made the stink of your c to come up 4264

CAN (235) [CANNOT, CANST]
Ge 4:13 My punishment is greater than I c bear. NIH
13:16 that if a man c number the dust of the earth, 3201
31:43 what c I do this day unto these my NIH
39: 9 how then c I do this great wickedness, and NIH
41:15 a dream, and there is none that c interpret it: NIH
41:38 C we find such a one as this is, a man in NIH
44: 1 as much as they c carry, and put every 3201
44:15 wot ye not that such a man as I c certainly NIH
Ex 4:14 I know that he c speak well. And also, NIH
5:11 get you straw where you c find it: yet not NIH
Lev 14:30 the young pigeons, such as he c **get**; 3027+5381
Nu 23:10 Who c count the dust of Jacob, and NIH
Dt 1:12 How c I myself alone bear your cumbrance, NIH
3:24 that c do according to thy works, and NIH
7:17 are moe than I; how c I dispossess them? 3201
9: 2 of whom thou hast heard say, Who c stand NIH
31: 2 this day; I c no more go out and come in: 3201
32:39 neither is there any that c deliver out of my NIH
Jdg 14:12 if you c certainly declare it me within NIH
1Sa 9: 6 peradventure he c shew us our way that we NIH
16: 2 Samuel said, How c I go? if Saul hear it, he NIH
16:17 Provide me now a man that c play well, and NIH
18: 8 and what c he have more but the kingdom? NIH
26: 9 for who c stretch forth his hand against NIH
28: 2 Surely thou shalt know what thy servant c NIH
2Sa 7:20 what c David say more unto thee? for thou, NIH
12:22 Who c tell whether GOD will be gracious NIH
12:23 c I bring him back again? I shall go to him, 3201
14:19 none c turn to the right hand or to the left 786
15:36 send unto me every thing that ye c hear. NIH
19:35 and c I discern between good and evil? can NIH
19:35 c thy servant taste what I eat or what I NIH
19:35 c I hear any more the voice of singing men NIH
1Ki 5: 6 c **skill** to hew timber like unto 3045
1Ch 17:18 What c David speak **more** to thee for 3254+5750
2Ch 1:10 for who c judge this thy people, that is so NIH
2: 7 that c skill to grave with the cunning men NIH
2: 8 for I know that thy servants c skill to cut NIH
Est 8: 6 For how c I endure to see the evil that shall NIH
8: 6 how c I endure to see the destruction of my NIH
Job 3:22 are glad, when they c find the grave? NIH
4: 2 but who c withhold himself from speaking? 3201
6: 6 C that which is unsavoury be eaten without NIH
8:11 C the rush grow up without mire? can NIH
8:11 c the flag grow without water? NIH
9:12 Behold, he taketh away, who c hinder him? NIH
10: 7 there is none that c deliver out of thine NIH
11:10 or gather together, then who c hinder him? NIH
12:14 up a man, and there c be no opening. NIH
14: 4 Who c bring a clean thing out of an NIH
15: 3 with speeches wherewith he c do no good? NIH
22: 2 C a man be profitable unto God, as he that NIH
22:13 c he judge through the dark cloud? NIH
22:17 and what c the Almighty do for them? NIH
23:13 he is in one mind, and who c turn him? and NIH
25: 4 How then c man be justified with God? or NIH
25: 4 how c he be clean that is born of a woman? NIH
26:14 the thunder of his power who c understand? NIH
34:29 giveth quietness, who then c make trouble? NIH
34:29 he hideth his face, who then c behold him? NIH
36:23 or who c say, Thou hast wrought iniquity? NIH
36:26 neither c the number of his years be NIH
36:29 Also c any understand the spreadings of NIH
38:37 Who c number the clouds in wisdom? or NIH
38:37 or who c stay the bottles of heaven, NIH
40:14 thee that thine own right hand c save thee. NIH
40:19 he that made him c make his sword to NIH
40:23 he trusteth that he c draw up Jordan into his NIH
41:13 Who c discover the face of his garment? or NIH
41:13 who c come to him with his double bridle? NIH
41:14 Who c open the doors of his face? his teeth NIH
41:16 to another, that no air c come between them. NIH
42: 2 that no thought c be withholden from thee. NIH
Ps 11: 3 be destroyed, what c the righteous do? NIH
19:12 Who c understand his errors? cleanse thou NIH
22:29 and none c keep alive his own soul. NIH
40: 5 speak of them, they are moe than c be NIH
49: 7 None of them c by any means redeem his NIH
56: 4 I will not fear what flesh c do unto me. NIH
56:11 I will not be afraid what man c do unto me. NIH
58: 9 Before your pots c feel the thorns, he shall NIH
78:19 C God furnish a table in the wilderness? 3201
78:20 streams overflowed; c he give bread also? 3201
78:20 c he provide flesh for his people? NIH
89: 6 For who in the heaven c be compared unto NIH
89: 6 who among the sons of the mighty c be NIH
106: 2 Who c utter the mighty acts of the LORD? NIH
106: 2 who c shew forth all his praise? NIH
118: 6 I will not fear: what c man do unto me? NIH
147:17 like morsels: who c stand before his cold? NIH
Pr 6:27 C a man take fire in his bosom, and NIH
6:28 C one go upon hot coals, and his feet not be NIH
18:14 but a wounded spirit who c bear? NIH
20: 6 but a faithful man who c find? NIH
20: 9 Who c say, I have made my heart clean, NIH
20:24 how c a man then understand his own way? NIH
26:16 than seven men that c render a reason. NIH
31:10 Who c find a virtuous woman? for her price NIH
Ecc 2:12 for what c the man do that cometh after NIH
2:25 For who c eat, or who else can hasten NIH
2:25 or who else c hasten hereunto, more than I? NIH
3:11 that no man c find out the work that God NIH
3:14 nothing c be put to it, nor any thing taken NIH
4:11 have heat: but **how** c one be warm alone? 349
6:12 for who c tell a man what shall be after him NIH
7:13 for who c make that straight, which he hath 3201
7:24 and exceeding deep, who c find it out? NIH
8: 7 shall be: for who c tell him when it shall be? NIH
10:14 and what shall be after him, who c tell him? NIH
SS 8: 7 quench love, neither c the floods drown it: NIH
Isa 28:20 For the bed is shorter than that a man c NIH
28:20 the covering narrower than that he c wrap NIH
38:18 praise thee, death c not celebrate thee: NIH
43: 9 who among them c declare this, and NIH
43:13 there is none that c deliver out of my hand: NIH
46: 7 one shall cry unto him, yet c he not answer, NIH
49:15 C a woman forget her sucking child, NIH
56:11 they are greedy dogs which c never have NIH
Jer 2:13 broken cisterns, that c hold no water. NIH
2:24 in her occasion who c turn her away? NIH
2:28 if they c save thee in the time of thy trouble: NIH
2:32 C a maid forget her ornaments, or a bride NIH
4: 4 burn that none c quench it, because of NIH
5: 1 the broad places thereof, if ye c find a man, NIH
5:22 toss themselves, yet c they not prevail; NIH
5:22 though they roar, yet c they not pass over it? NIH
9:10 that none c pass through them; neither can NIH
9:10 that none can pass through them; neither c NIH
13:23 C the Ethiopian change his skin, or NIH
14:22 vanities of the Gentiles that c cause rain? NIH
14:22 or c the heavens give showers? art not thou NIH
17: 9 and desperately wicked: who c know it? NIH
21:12 burn that none c quench it, because of NIH
23:24 C any hide himself in secret places that I NIH
31:37 If heaven above c be measured, and NIH
33:20 If you c break my covenant of the day, and NIH
38: 5 for the king is not he that c **do** any thing 3201
47: 7 How c it be quiet, seeing the LORD hath NIH
La 2:13 breach is great like the sea: who c heal thee? NIH
Eze 22:14 C thine heart endure, or can thine hands be NIH
22:14 heart endure, or c thine hands be strong, NIH
28: 3 there is no secret that they c hide from thee: NIH
33:32 and c play well on an instrument: NIH
37: 3 unto me, Son of man, c these bones live? NIH
Da 2: 9 I shall know that ye c shew me NIH
2:10 There is not a man upon the earth that c 3202
2:11 there is none other that c shew it before NIH
3:29 there is no other God that c deliver after 3202
4:35 none c stay his hand, or say unto him, NIH
10:17 For how c the servant of this my lord talk 3201
Joel 2:11 and very terrible; and who c abide it? NIH
Am 3: 3 C two walk together, except they be NIH
3: 5 C a bird fall in a snare upon the earth, NIH
3: 8 GOD hath spoken, who c but prophesy? NIH
Jnh 3: 9 Who c tell if God will turn and repent, and NIH
Mic 3:11 among us? none evil c come upon us. NIH
5: 8 and teareth in pieces, and none c deliver. NIH
Na 1: 6 Who c stand before his indignation? and NIH
1: 6 who c abide in the fierceness of his anger? NIH
Mt 6:24 No man c serve two masters: for either he 1410
6:27 Which of you by taking thought c add one 1410
7:18 neither c a corrupt tree bring forth good NIG
9:15 C the children of the bridechamber mourn, 1410
12:29 Or else how c one enter into a strong man's 1410
12:34 generation of vipers, how c ye, being evil, 1410
16: 3 ye c discern the face of the sky; 1097
16: 3 but c ye not discern the signs of the times? 1410
19:25 saying, Who then c be saved? 1410
23:33 **how** c ye escape the damnation of hell? 4459
27:65 go your way, make it as sure as you c. 1492
Mk 2: 7 who c forgive sins but God only? 1410
2:19 C the children of the bridechamber fast, 1410
3:23 in parables, How c Satan cast out Satan? 1410
3:27 No man c enter into a strong man's house, 1410
7:15 a man, that entering into him c defile him: 1410
8: 4 From whence c a man satisfy these men 1410
9: 3 so as no fuller on earth c white them. 1410
9:29 This kind c come forth by nothing, but by 1410
9:39 in my name, that c lightly speak evil of me. 1410
10:26 among themselves, Who then c be saved? 1410
10:38 c ye drink of the cup that I drink of? and 1410
10:39 And they said unto him, We c. And Jesus 1410
Lk 5:21 Who c forgive sins, but God alone? 1410
5:34 C ye make the children of 1410
6:39 unto them, C the blind lead the blind? 1410
12: 4 and after that have no more that they c do. NIG
12:25 And which of you with taking thought c 1410
12:56 ye c discern the face of the sky and of 1492
16:13 No servant c serve two masters: for either 1410
16:26 neither c they pass to us, that would come NIG
18:26 that heard it said, Who then c be saved? 1410
20:36 Neither c they die any more: for they are 1410
Jn 1:46 C there any good thing come out of 1410
3: 2 for no man c do these miracles that thou 1410
3: 4 How c a man be born when he is old? 1410
3: 4 c he enter the second time into his mother's 1410
3: 9 and said unto him, How c these things be? 1410
3:27 and said, A man c receive nothing, 1410
5:19 The Son c do nothing of himself, but 1410
5:30 I c of mine own self do nothing: as I hear, 1410
5:44 How c ye believe, which receive honour 1410
6:44 No man c come to me, except the Father 1410
6:52 How c this man give us his flesh to eat? 1410
6:60 This is a hard saying; who c hear it? 1410
6:65 I unto you, that no man c come unto me, 1410
9: 4 the night cometh, when no man c work. 1410
9:16 How c a man that is a sinner do such 1410
10:21 C a devil open the eyes of the blind? 1410
14: 5 thou goest; and how c we know the way? 1410
15: 4 no more c ye, except ye abide in me. 3779
15: 5 much fruit: for without me ye c do nothing. 1410
Ac 8:31 And he said, How c I, except some man 1410
10:47 C any man forbid water, that these should 1410

C

Ac 24:13 Neither c they prove *the things* whereof 1410
Ro 8: 7 to the law of God, neither indeed c be. 1410
8:31 If God *be* for us, who c *be* against us? NIG
1Co 2:14 neither c he know *them,* because they are 1410
3:11 For other foundation c no *man* lay than that 1410
12: 3 *that* no *man* c say that Jesus is the Lord, 1410
2Co 13: 8 For we c **do** nothing against the truth, but 1410
Php 4:13 I c **do** all *things* through Christ which 2480
1Th 3: 9 For what thanks c we render to God again 1410
1Ti 6: 7 *and it is* certain we c carry nothing out. 1410
6:16 in the light **which no** *man* **c approach unto**; 676
6:16 whom no man hath seen, nor c see: 1410
Heb 5: 2 Who c have compassion on the ignorant, 1410
10: 1 c never with those sacrifices which they 1410
10:11 which c never take away sins: 1410
Jas 2:14 and have not works? c faith save him? 1410
3: 8 But the tongue c no man tame; *it is* an 1410
3:12 C the fig tree, my brethren, bear olive 1410
3:12 so c no fountain *both* yield salt water and NIG
1Jn 4:20 how c he love God whom he hath not seen? 1410
Rev 3: 8 thee an open door, and no *man* c shut it: 1410
9:20 which neither c see, nor hear, nor walk: 1410

CANA (4)

Jn 2: 1 And the third day there was a marriage in C 2580
2:11 This beginning of miracles did Jesus in C 2580
4:46 So Jesus came again into C of Galilee, 2580
21: 2 and Nathanael of C in Galilee, and the *sons* 2580

CANAAN (93) [CANAANITE, CANAANITES, CANAANITESS, CANAANITISH]

Ge 9:18 and Japheth: and Ham *is* the father of C. 3667
9:22 Ham, the father of C, saw the nakedness of 3667
9:25 he said, Cursed *be* C; a servant of servants 3667
9:26 God of Shem; and C shall be his servant. 3667
9:27 tents of Shem; and C shall be his servant. 3667
10: 6 Cush, and Mizraim, and Phut, and C. 3667
10:15 And C begat Sidon his firstborn, and Heth, 3667
11:31 of the Chaldees, to go into the land of C; 3667
12: 5 they went forth to go into the land of C; 3667
12: 5 and into the land of C they came. 3667
13:12 Abram dwelled in the land of C, and 3667
16: 3 Abram had dwelt ten years in the land of C, 3667
17: 8 all the land of C, for an everlasting 3667
23: 2 the same *is* Hebron in the land of C: 3667
23:19 the same *is* Hebron in the land of C. 3667
28: 1 shalt not take a wife of the daughters of C. 3667
28: 6 shalt not take a wife of the daughters of C; 3667
28: 8 Esau seeing that the daughters of C pleased 3667
31:18 for to go to Isaac his father in the land of C. 3667
33:18 city of Shechem, which *is* in the land of C, 3667
35: 6 which *is* in the land of C, that *is,* Beth-el, 3667
36: 2 Esau took his wives of the daughters of C; 3667
36: 5 which were born unto him in the land of C. 3667
36: 6 which he had got in the land of C; 3667
37: 1 his father was a stranger, in the land of C. 3667
42: 5 for the famine was in the land of C. 3667
42: 7 they said, From the land of C to buy food. 3667
42:13 the sons of one man in the land of C; 3667
42:29 unto Jacob their father unto the land of C, 3667
42:32 *is this* day with our father in the land of C. 3667
44: 8 again unto thee out of the land of C: 3667
45:17 and go, get you unto the land of C; 3667
45:25 came *into* the land of C unto Jacob their 3667
46: 6 which they had gotten in the land of C, and 3667
46:12 Er and Onan died in the land of C. And 3667
46:31 which *were* in the land of C, are come unto 3667
47: 1 they have, are come out of the land of C; 3667
47: 4 for the famine *is* sore in the land of C: 3667
47:13 *all* the land of C fainted by reason of 3667
47:14 in the land of C, for the corn which they 3667
47:15 in the land of C, all the Egyptians came 3667
48: 3 appeared unto me at Luz in the land of C, 3667
48: 7 Rachel died by me in the land of C in 3667
49:30 which *is* before Mamre, in the land of C, 3667
50: 5 I have digged for me in the land of C, 3667
50:13 For his sons carried him into the land of C, 3667
Ex 6: 4 to give them the land of C, the land of their 3667
15:15 all the inhabitants of C shall melt away. 3667
16:35 came unto the borders of the land of C. 3667
Lev 14:34 When ye be come into the land of C, 3667
18: 3 after the doings of the land of C, whither I 3667
25:38 to give you the land of C, *and* to be your 3667
Nu 13: 2 that they may search the land of C, 3667
13:17 Moses sent them to spy out the land of C, 3667
26:19 and Er and Onan died in the land of C. 3667
32:30 possessions among you in the land of C. 3667
32:32 before the LORD *into* the land of C, 3667
33:40 which dwelt in the south in the land of C, 3667
33:51 are passed over Jordan into the land of C; 3667
34: 2 When ye come into the land of C; 3667
34: 2 *even* the land of C with the coasts thereof:) 3667
34:29 unto the children of Israel in the land of C. 3667
35:10 ye be come over Jordan into the land of C; 3667
35:14 three cities shall ye give in the land of C, 3667
Dt 32:49 behold the land of C, which I give unto 3667
Jos 5:12 they did eat of the fruit of the land of C that 3667
14: 1 children of Israel inherited in the land of C, 3667
21: 2 spake unto them at Shiloh in the land of C, 3667
22: 9 which *is* in the land of C, to go unto 3667
22:10 that *are* in the land of C, the children of 3667
22:11 built an altar over against the land of C, 3667
22:32 unto the land of C, to the children of Israel, 3667
24: 3 led him throughout all the land of C, and 3667
Jdg 3: 1 *Israel* as had not known all the wars of C; 3667
4: 2 sold them into the hand of Jabin king of C, 3667
4:23 the king of C before the children of Israel. 3667
4:24 prevailed against Jabin the king of C, 3667
4:24 until they had destroyed Jabin king of C. 3667
5:19 fought the kings of C in Taanach by 3667
21:12 camp *to* Shiloh, which *is* in the land of C. 3667
1Ch 1: 8 of Ham; Cush, and Mizraim, Put, and C. 3667
1:13 And C begat Zidon his firstborn, and Heth, 3667
16:18 Saying, Unto thee will I give the land of C, 3667
Ps 105:11 Saying, Unto thee will I give the land of C, 3667
106:38 whom they sacrificed unto the idols of C: 3667
135:11 king of Bashan, and all the kingdoms of C: 3667
Isa 19:18 the land of Egypt speak the language of C, 3667
Eze 16: 3 and thy nativity *is* of the land of C; 3669
16:29 fornication in the land of C unto Chaldea; 3667
Zep 2: 5 O C, the land of the Philistines, I will even 3667
Mt 15:22 a woman **of** C came out of the same coasts, 5478
Ac 7:11 a dearth over all the land of Egypt and C, 5477
13:19 destroyed seven nations in the land of C, 5477

CANAANITE (14) [CANAAN]

Ge 12: 6 of Moreh. And the C *was* then in the land. 3669
13: 7 the C and the Perizzite dwelled then in 3669
38: 2 Judah saw there a daughter of a certain C, 3669
Ex 23:28 the C, and the Hittite, from before thee. 3669
33: 2 I will drive out the C, the Amorite, and 3669
34:11 and the C, and the Hittite, and the Perizzite, 3669
Nu 21: 1 *when* king Arad the C, which dwelt *in* 3669
33:40 king Arad the C, which dwelt in the south 3669
Jos 9: 1 the Hittite, and the Amorite, the C, 3669
11: 3 *And to* the C on the east and on the west, 3669
13: 3 *which* is counted to the C: 3669
Zec 14:21 in that day there shall be no more the C in 3669
Mt 10: 4 Simon the C, and Judas Iscariot, who also 2581
Mk 3:18 and Thaddeus, and Simon the C, 2581

CANAANITES (55) [CANAAN]

Ge 10:18 afterward were the families of the C spread 3669
10:19 the border of the C was from Sidon, as thou 3669
15:21 the C, and the Girgashites, and 3669
24: 3 wife unto my son of the daughters of the C, 3669
24:37 a wife to my son of the daughters of the C, 3669
34:30 the land, amongst the C and the Perizzites: 3669
50:11 when the inhabitants of the land, the C, 3669
Ex 3: 8 unto the place of the C, and the Hittites, 3669
3:17 affliction of Egypt unto the land of the C, 3669
13: 5 shall bring thee into the land of the C, 3669
13:11 shall bring thee into the land of the C, 3669
23:23 and the C, the Hivites, and the Jebusites: 3669
Nu 13:29 the C dwell by the sea, and by the coast of 3669
14:25 and the C dwelt in the valley.) 3669
14:43 and the C *are* there before you, 3669
14:45 the C which dwelt in that hill, and 3669
21: 3 the voice of Israel, and delivered up the C; 3669
Dt 1: 7 *to* the land of the C, and *unto* Lebanon, 3669
7: 1 the C, and the Perizzites, and the Hivites, 3669
11:30 the sun goeth down, in the land of the C, 3669
20:17 the C, and the Perizzites, the Hivites, and 3669
Jos 3:10 fail drive out from before you the C, 3669
5: 1 all the kings of the C, which *were* by 3669
7: 9 For the C and all the inhabitants of the land 3669
12: 8 the Amorites, and the C, the Perizzites, 3669
13: 4 all the land of the C, and Mearah that *is* 3669
16:10 they drave not out the C that dwelt in 3669
16:10 the C dwell among the Ephraimites unto 3669
17:12 but the C would dwell in that land. 3669
17:13 waxen strong, that they put the C to tribute; 3669
17:16 all the C that dwell in the land of the valley 3669
17:18 for thou shalt drive out the C, though they 3669
24:11 the C, and the Hittites, and the Girgashites, 3669
Jdg 1: 1 Who shall go up for us against the C first, 3669
1: 3 my lot, that we may fight against the C; 3669
1: 4 the LORD delivered the C and 3669
1: 5 and they slew the C and the Perizzites. 3669
1: 9 of Judah went down to fight against the C, 3669
1:10 Judah went against the C that dwelt in 3669
1:17 they slew the C that inhabited Zephath, and 3669
1:27 but the C would dwell in that land. 3669
1:28 that they put the C to tribute, and did not 3669
1:29 Neither did Ephraim drive out the C that 3669
1:29 but the C dwelt in Gezer among them. 3669
1:30 the C dwelt among them, and 3669
1:32 the Asherites dwelt among the C, 3669
1:33 he dwelt among the C, the inhabitants of 3669
3: 3 all the C, and the Sidonians, and 3669
3: 5 the children of Israel dwelt among the C, 3669
2Sa 24: 7 *to* all the cities of the Hivites, and of the C: 3669
1Ki 9:16 slain the C that dwelt in the city, and 3669
Ezr 9: 1 *even* of the C, the Hittites, the Perizzites, 3669
Ne 9: 8 with him to give the land of the C, 3669
9:24 the C, and gavest them into their hands, 3669
Ob 1:20 of Israel *shall possess* that of the C, 3669

CANAANITESS (1) [CANAAN]

1Ch 2: 3 unto him of the daughter of Shua the C. 3669

CANAANITISH (2) [CANAAN]

Ge 46:10 Zohar, and Shaul the son of a C woman. 3669
Ex 6:15 Zohar, and Shaul the son of a C **woman**: 3669

CANDACE (1)

Ac 8:27 an eunuch of great authority under C queen 2582

CANDLE (16) [CANDLES, CANDLESTICK, CANDLESTICKS]

Job 18: 6 and his c shall be put out with him. 5216
21:17 How oft is the c of the wicked put out! and 5216
29: 3 When his c shined upon my head, *and* 5216
Ps 18:28 For thou wilt light my c: the LORD my 5216
Pr 20:27 The spirit of man *is* the c of the LORD, 5216
24:20 *man;* the c of the wicked shall be put out. 5216
31:18 *is* good: her c goeth not out by night. 5216
Jer 25:10 of the millstones, and the light of the c. 5216
Mt 5:15 Neither do men light a c, and put it under a 3088
Mk 4:21 Is a c brought to be put under a bushel, or 3088
Lk 8:16 No *man,* when he hath lighted a c, 3088
11:33 No *man,* when he hath lighted a c, putteth *it* 3088
11:36 as when the bright shining of a c doth give 3088
15: 8 doth not light a c, and sweep the house, 3088
Rev 18:23 And the light of a c shall shine no more at 3088
22: 5 and they need no c, neither light of the sun; 3088

CANDLES (1) [CANDLE]

Zep 1:12 *that* I will search Jerusalem with c, and 5216

CANDLESTICK (41) [CANDLE, STICK]

Ex 25:31 thou shalt make a c of pure gold: *of* beaten 4501
25:31 *of* beaten work shall the c be made: 4501
25:32 three branches of the c out of the one side, 4501
25:32 three branches of the c out of the other side: 4501
25:33 in the six branches that come out of the c. 4501
25:34 in the c *shall be* four bowls made like unto 4501
25:35 the six branches that proceed out of the c. 4501
26:35 the c over against the table on the side of 4501
30:27 the c and his vessels, and the altar of 4501
31: 8 the pure c with all his furniture, and 4501
35:14 The c also for the light, and his furniture, 4501
37:17 he made the c *of* pure gold: *of* beaten work 4501
37:17 *of* beaten work made he the c; his shaft, 4501
37:18 three branches of the c out of the one side 4501
37:18 three branches of the c out of the other side 4501
37:19 the six branches going out of the c. 4501
37:20 in the c *were* four bowls made like 4501
39:37 The pure c, *with* the lamps thereof, 4501
40: 4 thou shalt bring in the c, and light 4501
40:24 he put the c in the tent of the congregation, 4501
Lev 24: 4 He shall order the lamps upon the pure c 4501
Nu 3:31 the c, and the altars, and the vessels of 4501
4: 9 cover the c of the light, and his lamps, and 4501
8: 2 lamps shall give light over against the c. 4501
8: 3 lighted the lamps thereof over against the c, 4501
8: 4 this work of the c *was of* beaten gold, 4501
8: 4 had shewed Moses, so he made the c. 4501
2Ki 4:10 a bed, and a table, and a stool, and a c: 4501
1Ch 28:15 by weight for **every** c, 4501+4501+2050.1
28:15 *both* for the c, and *also for* the lamps 4501
28:15 to the use of **every** c. 4501+4501+2050.1
2Ch 13:11 the c of gold with the lamps thereof, 4501
Da 5: 5 wrote over against the c upon the plaister of 5043
Zec 4: 2 I have looked, and behold, a c all of gold, 4501
4:11 two olive trees upon the right *side* of the c 4501
Mt 5:15 and put it under a bushel, but on a c; 3087
Mk 4:21 or under a bed? *and* not to be set on a c? 3087
Lk 8:16 but setteth *it* on a c, that they which enter in 3087
11:33 neither under a bushel, but on a c, 3087
Heb 9: 2 wherein *was* the c, and the table, and 3087
Rev 2: 5 and will remove thy c out of his place, 3087

CANDLESTICKS (12) [CANDLE, STICK]

1Ki 7:49 the c *of* pure gold, five on the right side, 4501
1Ch 28:15 Even the weight for the c of gold, and 4501
28:15 for the c of silver by weight, *both* for 4501
2Ch 4: 7 he made ten c of gold according to their 4501
4:20 Moreover the c with their lamps, that they 4501
Jer 52:19 and the c, and the spoons, and the cups; 4501
Rev 1:12 And being turned, I saw seven golden c; 3087
1:13 And in the midst of the seven c one like 3087
1:20 in my right hand, and the seven golden c. 3087
1:20 the seven c which thou sawest are the seven 3087
2: 1 walketh in the midst of the seven golden c; 3087
11: 4 the two c standing before the God of 3087

CANE (2)

Isa 43:24 Thou hast bought me no **sweet** c with 7070
Jer 6:20 and the sweet c from a far country? 7070

CANKER (1) [CANKERED]

2Ti 2:17 And their word will eat as *doth* a c: 1044

CANKERED (1) [CANKER]

Jas 5: 3 Your gold and silver is c; and the rust of 2728

CANKERWORM (6) [WORM]

Joel 1: 4 that which the locust hath left hath the c 3218
1: 4 that which the c hath left hath 3218
2:25 the c, and the caterpillar, and 3218
Na 3:15 cut thee off, it shall eat thee up like the c: 3218
3:15 make thyself many as the c, make thyself 3218
3:16 of heaven: the c spoileth, and flieth away. 3218

CANNEH (1)

Eze 27:23 Haran, and C, and Eden, the merchants of 3656

CANNOT (184) [CAN]

Ge 19:19 I c escape to the mountain, lest *some* 3201+3808
19:22 for I c do any thing till thou be come 3201+3808
24:50 we c speak unto thee bad or good. 3201+3808
29: 8 they said, We c, until all the flocks 3201+3808
31:35 Let it not displease my lord that I c 3201+3808
32:12 the sea, which c be numbered for multitude. 3808
34:14 said unto them, We c do this thing, 3201+3808
38:22 he returned to Judah, and said, I c find her; 3808
43:22 we c tell who put our money in our sacks. 3808
44:22 my lord, The lad c leave his father: 3201+3808
44:26 we said, We c go down: if our 3201+3808
Ex 10: 5 the earth, that *one* c be able to see the earth: 3808
19:23 people c come up to mount Sinai: 3201+3808
Lev 14:21 c get *so much;* then he shall take one lamb 369
Nu 22:18 I c go beyond the word of 3201+3808
23:20 and he hath blessed; and I c reverse it. 3808
24:13 I c go beyond the commandment of 3201+3808
35:33 the land c be cleansed of the blood that is 3808
Dt 28:35 with a sore botch that c be healed, 3201+3808
Jos 24:19 the people, Ye c serve the LORD: 3201+3808
Jdg 11:35 unto the LORD, and I c go back. 3201+3808
14:13 if ye c declare *it* me, then shall ye 3201+3808
Ru 4: 6 I c redeem *it* for myself, 3201+3808
4: 6 my right to thyself; for I c redeem *it.* 3201+3808
1Sa 12:21 *should ye go* after vain *things,* which c 3808
17:39 said unto Saul, I c go with these; 3201+3808
17:55 *As* thy soul liveth, O king, I c tell. 518
25:17 a son of Belial, that *a man* c speak to him. 4480
2Sa 5: 6 in hither: thinking, David c come in hither. 3808
14:14 which c be gathered up *again;* neither doth 3808
23: 6 because they c be taken with hands: 3808

1Ki 3: 8 that **c** be numbered nor counted for 3808
8:27 and heaven of heavens **c** contain thee; 3808
18:12 I come and tell Ahab, and he **c** find thee, 3808
2Ch 2: 6 and heaven of heavens **c** contain him? 3808
6:18 and the heaven of heavens **c** contain thee; 3808
24:20 of the LORD, that ye **c** prosper? 3808
Ezr 9:15 for *we* **c** stand before thee because of this. 369
Ne 6: 3 a great work, so that I **c** come down: 3201+3808
Job 5:12 that their hands **c** perform *their* enterprise. 3808
6:30 **c** my taste discern perverse things? 518+3808
9: 3 he **c** answer him one of a thousand. 3808
12:14 it **c** be built *again:* he shutteth up a man, 3808
14: 5 thou hast appointed his bounds that he **c** 3808
17:10 for I **c** find *one* wise *man* among you. 3808
19: 8 He hath fenced up my way that I **c** pass, 3808
23: 8 and backward, but I **c** perceive him: 3808
23: 9 I **c** behold *him:* he hideth *himself* on 3808
23: 9 *himself* on the right hand, that I **c** see *him:* 3808
28:15 It **c** be gotten for gold, neither shall silver 3808
28:16 It **c** be valued with the gold of Ophir, 3808
28:17 The gold and the crystal **c** equal it: and 3808
31:31 that we had of his flesh! we **c** be satisfied. 3808
33:21 flesh is consumed away, that it **c** be seen; 4480
36:18 then a great ransom **c** deliver thee. 408
37: 5 *things* doeth he, which we **c** comprehend. 3808
37:19 *for* we **c** order *our speech* by reason of 3808
37:23 *Touching* the Almighty, we **c** find him out: 3808
41:17 they stick together, that they **c** be sundered. 3808
41:23 are firm in themselves; they **c** be moved. 1077
41:26 The sword of him that layeth at him **c** hold: 1097
41:28 The arrow **c** make him flee: slingstones are 3808
Ps 40: 5 they **c** be reckoned up in order unto thee: *if* I 369
77: 4 I am *so* troubled that I **c** speak. 3808
88: 8 *I am* shut up, and I **c** come forth. 3808
93: 1 world also is stablished, *that* it **c** be moved. 1077
125: 1 *which* **c** be removed, *but* abideth for ever. 3808
139: 6 for me; it is high, I **c** attain unto it. 3201+3808
Pr 30:21 and for four *which* it **c** bear: 3201+3808
Ecc 1: 8 man **c** utter *it:* the eye is not satisfied 3201+3808
1:15 *That which is* crooked **c** be made 3201+3808
1:15 that which is wanting **c** be numbered. 3201+3808
8:17 that a man **c** find out the work that is 3201+3808
10:14 a man **c** tell what shall be; and what shall 3808
SS 8: 7 Many waters **c** quench love, neither can 3808
Isa 1:13 calling of assemblies, I **c away with;** 3201+3808
29:11 and he saith, I **c**; for it *is* sealed: 3201+3808
38:18 For the grave **c** praise thee, death can *not* 3808
38:18 they that go down into the pit **c** hope for 3808
44:18 for he hath shut their eyes, that *they* **c** see; 4480
44:18 *and* their hearts, that *they* **c** understand. 4480
44:20 that he **c** deliver his soul, nor say, *Is there* 3808
45:20 and pray unto a god *that* **c** save. 3808
50: 2 my hand shortened at all, that *it* **c** redeem? 4480
56:10 they *are* all dumb dogs, they **c** bark; 3201+3808
56:11 and they *are* shepherds *that* **c** understand: 3808
57:20 when it **c** rest, whose waters cast up 3201+3808
59: 1 hand is not shortened, **that** *it* **c** save; 4480
59: 1 neither his ear heavy, **that** *it* **c** hear: 4480
59:14 in the street, and equity **c** enter. 3201+3808
Jer 1: 6 Ah, Lord GOD, behold, I **c** speak: 3045+3808
4:19 I **c** hold my peace, because thou hast heard, 3808
5:22 sea *by* a perpetual decree, that it **c** pass it: 3808
6:10 and they **c** hearken: 3201+3808
7: 8 ye trust in lying words, *that* **c** profit. 1115
10: 5 must needs be borne, because they **c** go. 3808
10: 5 for they **c** do evil, neither also *is it* in them 3808
14: 9 as a mighty *man that* **c** save? 3201+3808
18: 6 **c** I do with you as this potter? 3201+3808
19:11 that **c** be made whole again: 3201+3808
24: 3 very evil, that **c** be eaten, they are so evil. 3808
24: 8 evil figs, which **c** be eaten, they are so evil; 3808
29:17 vile figs, that **c** be eaten, they are so evil. 3808
33:22 As the host of heaven **c** be numbered, 3808
36: 5 I **c** go *into* the house of the LORD: 3201+3808
46:23 saith the LORD, though it **c** be searched; 3808
49:23 *is* sorrow on the sea; it **c** be quiet. 3201+3808
La 3: 7 He hath hedged me about, that I **c** get out: 3808
4:18 hunt our steps, that *we* **c** go in our streets: 4480
Da 2:27 The secret which the king hath demanded **c** 3809
Hos 1:10 which **c** be measured nor numbered; 3808
Jnh 4:11 that **c** discern between their right hand 3808
Hab 2: 5 **c** be satisfied, but gathereth unto him all 3808
Mt 5:14 A city that is set on a hill **c** be hid. *1410+3756*
6:24 Ye **c** serve God and mammon. *1410+3756*
7:18 A good tree **c** bring forth evil fruit, *1410+3756*
19:11 unto them, All *men* **c** receive this saying, *3756*
21:27 they answered Jesus, and said, We **c** tell. *3756*
26:53 Thinkest thou that I **c** now pray to *1410+3756*
27:42 He saved others; himself he **c** save. *1410+3756*
Mk 2:19 bridegroom with them, they **c** fast. *1410+3756*
3:24 against itself, that kingdom **c** stand. *1410+3756*
3:25 against itself, that house **c** stand. *1410+3756*
3:26 he **c** stand, but hath an end. *1410+3756*
7:18 entereth into the man, *it* **c** defile him; *1410+3756*
11:33 and said unto Jesus, We **c** tell. *3756*
15:31 He saved others; himself he **c** save. *1410+3756*
Lk 11: 7 me in bed; I **c** rise and give thee? *1410+3756*
13:33 for it **c** be that a prophet perish out of *1735+3756*
14:14 for they **c** recompense thee: *2192+3756*
14:20 a wife, and therefore I **c** come. *1410+3756*
14:26 own life also, he **c** be my disciple. *1410+3756*
14:27 and come after me, **c** be my disciple. *1410+3756*
14:33 all that he hath, he **c** be my disciple. *1410+3756*
16: 3 I **c** dig; to beg I am ashamed. *2480+3756*
16:13 Ye **c** serve God and mammon. *1410+3756*
16:26 would pass from hence to you **c**; *1410+3361*
Jn 3: 3 he **c** see the kingdom of God. *1410+3756*
3: 5 he **c** enter into the kingdom of God. *1410+3756*
7: 7 The world **c** hate you; but me it *1410+3756*
7:34 and where I am, *thither* ye **c** come. *1410+3756*
7:36 and where I am, *thither* ye **c** come? *1410+3756*
8:14 but ye **c** tell whence I come, and whither I *3756*
8:21 in your sins: whither I go, ye **c** come. *1410+3756*
8:22 he saith, Whither I go, ye **c** come. *1410+3756*
8:43 *even* because ye **c** hear my word. *1410+3756*

Jn 10:35 and the scripture **c** be broken; *1410+3756*
13:33 the Jews, Whither I go, ye **c** come; *1410+3756*
13:37 Lord, why **c** I follow thee now? *1410+3756*
14:17 whom the world **c** receive, because *1410+3756*
15: 4 As the branch **c** bear fruit of itself, *1410+3756*
16:12 unto you, but ye **c** bear them now. *1410+3756*
16:18 A little while? we **c** tell what he saith. *3756*
Ac 4:16 in Jerusalem; and we **c** deny *it.* *1410+3756*
4:20 For we **c** but speak *the things* which *1410+3756*
5:39 But if it be of God, ye **c** overthrow it; *1410+3756*
15: 1 the manner of Moses, ye **c** be saved. *1410+3756*
19:36 then that these *things* **c be spoken against,** *368*
27:31 these abide in the ship, ye **c** be saved. *1410+3756*
Ro 8: 8 that are in the flesh **c** please God. *1410+3756*
8:26 for us with groanings which **c be uttered.** *215*
1Co 7: 9 But if they **c** contain, let them marry: for it *3756*
10:21 Ye **c** drink the cup of the Lord, and *1410+3756*
10:21 ye **c** be partakers of the Lord's table, *1410+3756*
12:21 And the eye **c** say unto the hand, *1410+3756*
15:50 blood **c** inherit the kingdom of God; *1410+3756*
2Co 12: 2 years ago, (whether in the body, I **c** tell; *3756*
12: 2 or whether out of the body, I **c** tell: *3756*
12: 3 in the body, or out of the body, I **c** tell: *3756*
Gal 3:17 hundred and thirty years after, **c** disannul, *3756*
5:17 so that ye **c** do the *things* that ye would. *3361*
1Ti 5:25 and they that are otherwise **c** be hid. *1410+3756*
2Ti 2:13 abideth faithful: he **c** deny himself. *1410+3756*
Tit 1: 2 In hope of eternal life, which God, that **c lie,** *893*
2: 8 Sound speech that **c be condemned**; that he *176*
Heb 4:15 we have not a high priest which **c** *1410+3361*
9: 5 which *we* **c** now speak particularly. *1510+3756*
12:27 that those *things* which **c** be shaken may *3361*
12:28 we receiving a kingdom which **c be moved,** *761*
Jas 1:13 for God **c be tempted** with evil, *551+1510*
4: 2 ye kill, and desire *to have,* and **c** *1410+3756*
2Pe 1: 9 and **c see far off,** and hath forgotten that *he* *3467*
2:14 full of adultery and that **c cease from** sin; *180*
1Jn 3: 9 he **c** sin, because he is born of God. *1410+3756*

CANNOT SPEAK See DUMB

CANST (51) [CAN]

Ge 41:15 *that* thou **c** understand a dream to interpret NIH
Ex 33:20 he said, Thou **c** not see my face: for there 3201
Dt 28:27 with the itch, where*of* thou **c** not be healed. 3201
Jos 7:13 thou **c** not stand before thine enemies, 3201
Jdg 16:15 said unto him, How **c** thou say, I love thee, NIH
1Sa 30:15 **C** thou bring me down to this company? NIH
2Ki 8: 1 and sojourn wheresoever thou **c** sojourn: NIH
Ezr 7:16 gold that thou **c** find in all the province of NIH
Job 11: 7 **C** thou *by* searching find out God? NIH
11: 7 **c** thou find out the Almighty unto NIH
11: 8 *It is* as high as heaven; what **c** thou do? NIH
11: 8 deeper than hell; what **c** thou know? NIH
22:11 Or darkness, *that* thou **c** not see; and NIH
33: 5 If thou **c**, answer me, set *thy words* in order 3201
38:31 **C** thou bind the sweet influences of NIH
38:32 **C** thou bring forth Mazzaroth in his season? NIH
38:32 or **c** thou guide Arcturus with his sons? NIH
38:33 **c** thou set the dominion thereof in the earth? NIH
38:34 **C** thou lift up thy voice to the clouds, NIH
38:35 **C** thou send lightnings, that they may go, NIH
39: 1 *or* **c** thou mark when the hinds do calve? NIH
39: 2 **C** thou number the months *that* they fulfil? NIH
39:10 **C** thou bind the unicorn *with* his band in NIH
39:20 **C** thou make him afraid as a grasshopper? NIH
40: 9 or, **c** thou thunder with a voice like him? 3807.1
41: 1 **C** thou draw out leviathan with a hook? or NIH
41: 2 **C** thou put a hook into his nose? or bore his NIH
41: 7 **C** thou fill his skin with barbed irons? or NIH
42: 2 I know that thou **c do** every *thing,* and 3201
Pr 3:15 all the things thou **c** desire are not to be NIH
5: 6 are moveable, *that* thou **c** not know *them.* NIH
30: 4 and what *is* his son's name, if thou **c** tell? NIH
Isa 33:19 a people of a deeper speech than *thou* **c** NIH
33:19 *that thou* **c** not understand. NIH
Jer 2:23 How **c** thou say, I am not polluted, I have NIH
12: 5 then how **c** thou contend with horses? NIH
Eze 3: 6 whose words thou **c** not understand. NIH
Da 5:16 that thou **c** make interpretations, 3202
5:16 now if thou **c** read the writing, and 3202
Hab 1:13 to behold evil, and **c** not look on iniquity: 3201
Mt 5:36 thou **c** not make one hair white or black. *1410*
8: 2 Lord, if thou wilt, thou **c** make me clean. *1410*
Mk 1:40 If thou wilt, thou **c** make me clean. *1410*
9:22 if thou **c** do any *thing,* have compassion on *1410*
9:23 Jesus said unto him, If thou **c** believe, *1410*
Lk 5:12 Lord, if thou wilt, thou **c** make me clean. *1410*
6:42 Either how **c** thou say to thy brother, *1410*
Jn 3: 8 but **c** not tell whence it cometh, and *NIG*
13:36 Whither I go, thou **c** not follow me now; *1410*
Ac 21:37 unto thee? Who said, **C** thou **speak** Greek? *1097*
Rev 2: 2 how thou **c** not bear *them which are* evil: *1410*

CAPABLE See VALOUR

CAPERNAUM (16)

Mt 4:13 leaving Nazareth, he came and dwelt in **C**, *2584*
8: 5 And when Jesus was entered into **C**, *2584*
11:23 And thou, **C**, which art exalted unto *2584*
17:24 And when they were come to **C**, they that *2584*
Mk 1:21 And they went into **C**; and straightway on *2584*
2: 1 And again he entered into **C** after *some* *2584*
9:33 And he came to **C**: and being in the house *2584*
Lk 4:23 whatsoever we have heard done in **C**, *2584*
4:31 And came down to **C**, a city of Galilee, and *2584*
7: 1 audience of the people, he entered into **C**. *2584*
10:15 And thou, **C**, which art exalted to heaven, *2584*
Jn 2:12 After this he went down to **C**, he, and *2584*
4:46 certain nobleman, whose son was sick at **C**. *2584*
6:17 a ship, and went over the sea towards **C**. *2584*
6:24 and came to **C**, seeking for Jesus. *2584*
6:59 said he in the synagogue, as he taught in **C**. *2584*

CAPHTHORIM (1) [CAPHTOR]

1Ch 1:12 (of whom came the Philistines,) and **C**. 3732

CAPHTOR (3) [CAPHTHORIM, CAPHTORIM, CAPHTORIMS]

Dt 2:23 which came forth out of **C**, destroyed them, 3731
Jer 47: 4 the remnant of the country of **C**. 3731
Am 9: 7 the Philistines from **C**, and the Syrians 3731

CAPHTORIM (1) [CAPHTOR]

Ge 10:14 (out of whom came Philistim) and **C**. 3732

CAPHTORIMS (1) [CAPHTOR]

Dt 2:23 *even* unto Azzah, the **C**, which came forth 3732

CAPITAL; CAPITALS See CHAPITER; CHAPITERS

CAPPADOCIA (2)

Ac 2: 9 and in Judea, and **C**, in Pontus, and Asia, *2587*
1Pe 1: 1 Galatia, **C**, Asia, and Bithynia, *2587*

CAPTAIN (139) [CAPTAINS]

Ge 21:22 Phichol the **chief c** of his host spake unto 8269
21:32 Phichol the **chief c** of his host, and 8269
26:26 and Phichol the **chief c** of his army. 8269
37:36 an officer of Pharaoh's, *and* **c** of the guard. 8269
39: 1 of Pharaoh, **c** of the guard, an Egyptian, 8269
40: 3 he put them in ward *in* the house of the **c** of 8269
40: 4 the **c** of the guard charged Joseph with 8269
41:10 put me in ward *in* the **c** of the guard's 8269
41:12 a Hebrew, servant to the **c** of the guard; 8269
Nu 2: 3 Nahshon the son of Amminadab *shall be* **c** 5387
2: 5 Nethaneel the son of Zuar *shall be* **c** of 5387
2: 7 Eliab the son of Helon *shall be* **c** of 5387
2:10 the **c** of the children of Reuben *shall be* 5387
2:12 the **c** of the children of Simeon *shall be* 5387
2:14 the **c** of the sons of Gad *shall be* Eliasaph 5387
2:18 the **c** of the sons of Ephraim *shall be* 5387
2:20 the **c** of the children of Manasseh *shall be* 5387
2:22 the **c** of the sons of Benjamin *shall be* 5387
2:25 the **c** of the children of Dan *shall be* 5387
2:27 the **c** of the children of Asher *shall be* 5387
2:29 the **c** of the children of Naphtali *shall be* 5387
14: 4 Let us make a **c**, and let us return into 7218
Jos 5:14 *as* **c** of the host of the LORD am I now 8269
5:15 the **c** of the LORD'S host said unto 8269
Jdg 4: 2 the **c** of whose host *was* Sisera, which 8269
4: 7 the **c** of Jabin's army, with his chariots and 8269
11: 6 said unto Jephthah, Come, and be our **c**, 7101
11:11 the people made him head and **c** over them: 7101
1Sa 9:16 thou shalt anoint him to be **c** over my 5057
10: 1 the LORD hath anointed thee to be **c** over 5057
12: 9 **c** of the host of Hazor, and into the hand of 8269
13:14 the LORD hath commanded him to be **c** 5057
14:50 the name of the **c** of his host *was* Abner, 8269
17:18 carry these ten cheeses unto the **c** of *their* 8269
17:55 said unto Abner, the **c** of the host, Abner, 8269
18:13 and made him his **c** over a thousand; 8269
22: 2 unto him; and he became a **c** over them: 8269
26: 5 and Abner the son of Ner, the **c** of his host: 8269
2Sa 2: 8 Abner the son of Ner, **c** of Saul's host, 8269
5: 2 and thou shalt be a **c** over Israel. 5057
5: 8 *he shall be chief and* **c**. Wherefore they said, NIH
10:16 Shobach the **c** of the host of Hadarezer 8269
10:18 smote Shobach the **c** of their host, who died 8269
17:25 Absalom made Amasa **c**[S] **of** the host 5921
19:13 if thou be not **c** of the host before me 8269
23:19 therefore he was their **c**: howbeit he 8269
24: 2 For the king said to Joab the **c** of the host, 8269
1Ki 1:19 the priest, and Joab the **c** of the host: 8269
2:32 **c** of the host of Israel, and Amasa the son 8269
2:32 the son of Jether, **c** of the host of Judah. 8269
11:15 Joab the **c** of the host was gone up to bury 8269
11:21 that Joab the **c** of the host was dead, 8269
11:24 men unto him, and became **c** over a band, 8269
16: 9 **c** of half *his* chariots, conspired against 8269
16:16 all Israel made Omri, the **c** of the host, 8269
2Ki 1: 9 the king sent unto him a **c** of fifty with his 8269
1:10 Elijah answered and said to the **c** of fifty, 8269
1:11 Again also he sent unto him another **c** of 8269
1:13 he sent again a **c** of the third fifty with his 8269
1:13 the third **c** of fifty went up, and came and 8269
4:13 for to the king, or to the **c** of the host? 8269
5: 1 **c** of the host of the king of Syria, 8269
9: 5 and he said, I have an errand to thee, O **c**. 8269
9: 5 which of all us? And he said, To thee, O **c**. 8269
9:25 said *Jehu* to Bidkar his **c**, Take up, *and* 7991
15:25 a **c** of his, conspired against him, and 7991
18:24 wilt thou turn away the face of one **c** of 6346
20: 5 and tell Hezekiah the **c** of my people, 5057
25: 8 came Nebuzar-adan, **c** of the guard, 7227
25:10 that *were with* the **c** of the guard, 7227
25:11 did Nebuzar-adan the **c** of the guard carry 7227
25:12 the **c** of the guard left of the poor of 7227
25:15 *in* silver, the **c** of the guard took *away.* 7227
25:18 the **c** of the guard took Seraiah the chief 7227
25:20 Nebuzar-adan **c** of the guard took these, 7227
1Ch 11: 6 the Jebusites first shall be chief and **c**. 8269
11:21 honourable than the two; for he was their **c**: 8269
11:42 a **c** of the Reubenites, and thirty with him, 7218
19:16 Shophach the **c** of the host of Hadarezer 8269
19:18 killed Shophach the **c** of the host. 8269
27: 5 The third **c** of the host for the third month 8269
27: 7 The fourth **c** for the fourth month *was* NIH
27: 8 The fifth **c** for the fifth month *was* 8269
27: 9 The sixth **c** for the sixth month *was* Ira NIH
27:10 The seventh **c** for the seventh month *was* NIH
27:11 The eighth **c** for the eighth month *was* NIH
27:12 The ninth **c** for the ninth month *was* Abiezer NIH
27:13 The tenth **c** for the tenth month *was* NIH
27:14 The eleventh **c** for the eleventh month *was* NIH
27:15 The twelfth **c** for the twelfth month *was* NIH

2Ch 13:12 God *himself is* with us for *our* **c**, and 7218
17:15 next to him *was* Jehohanan the **c**, and 8269
Ne 9:17 in their rebellion appointed a **c** to return to 7218
Isa 3: 3 The **c** of fifty, and the honourable *man*, and 8269
36: 9 wilt thou turn away the face of one **c** of 6346
Jer 37:13 a **c** of the ward *was* there, whose name *was* 1167
39: 9 Nebuzar-adan the **c** of the guard carried 7227
39:10 Nebuzar-adan the **c** of the guard left of 7227
39:11 to Nebuzar-adan the **c** of the guard, 7227
39:13 So Nebuzar-adan the **c** of the guard sent, 7227
40: 1 after that Nebuzar-adan the **c** of the guard 7227
40: 2 the **c** of the guard took Jeremiah, and 7227
40: 5 So the **c** of the guard gave him victuals and 7227
41:10 whom Nebuzar-adan the **c** of the guard had 7227
43: 6 every person that Nebuzar-adan the **c** of 7227
51:27 and Ashchenaz; appoint a **c** against her; 2951
52:12 came Nebuzar-adan, **c** of the guard, 7227
52:14 that *were* with the **c** of the guard, 7227
52:15 Nebuzar-adan the **c** of the guard carried 7227
52:16 Nebuzar-adan the **c** of the guard left *certain* 7227
52:19 *in* silver, took the **c** of the guard *away*. 7227
52:24 the **c** of the guard took Seraiah the chief 7227
52:26 So Nebuzar-adan the **c** of the guard took 7227
52:30 **c** of the guard carried away captive *of* 7227
Da 2:14 wisdom to Arioch the **c** of the king's guard, 7229
2:15 and said to Arioch the king's **c**, 7990
Jn 18:12 Then the band and the **c** and officers of *5506*
Ac 4: 1 and the **c** of the temple, and the Sadducees, *4755*
5:24 the *high* priest and the **c** of the temple and *4755*
5:26 Then went the **c** with the officers, and *4755*
21:31 tidings came unto the **chief c** of the band, *5506*
21:32 and when they saw the **chief c** and *5506*
21:33 Then the **chief c** came near, and took him, *5506*
21:37 he said unto the **chief c**, May I speak unto *5506*
22:24 The **chief c** commanded him to be brought *5506*
22:26 heard *that*, he went and told the **chief c**, *5506*
22:27 Then the **chief c** came, and said unto him, *5506*
22:28 And the **chief c** answered, With a great sum *5506*
22:29 and the **chief c** also was afraid, after he *5506*
23:10 there arose a great dissension, the **chief c**, *5506*
23:15 ye with the council signify to the **chief c** *5506*
23:17 said, Bring this young man unto the **chief c**: *5506*
23:18 and brought *him* to the **chief c**, and said, *5506*
23:19 Then the **chief c** took him by the hand, and *5506*
23:22 So the **chief c** then let the young man *5506*
24: 7 But the **chief c** Lysias came *upon us*, and *5506*
24:22 When Lysias the **chief c** shall come down, *5506*
28:16 the prisoners to the **c of the guard**: *4759*
Heb 2:10 to make the **c** of their salvation perfect *747*

CAPTAINS (119) [CAPTAIN]

Ex 14: 7 of Egypt, and **c** over every one of them. 7991
15: 4 his chosen **c** also are drowned in the Red 7991
Nu 31:14 *with* the **c** over thousands, and 8269
31:14 **c** over hundreds, which came from 8269
31:48 the **c** of thousands, and captains of 8269
31:48 and **c** of hundreds, came near unto Moses: 8269
31:52 of the **c** of thousands, and of the captains of 8269
31:52 of thousands, and of the **c** of hundreds, 8269
31:54 Eleazar the priest took the gold of the **c** of 8269
Dt 1:15 **c** over thousands, and captains over 8269
1:15 **c** over hundreds, and captains over fifties, 8269
1:15 **c** over fifties, and captains over tens, and 8269
1:15 **c** over tens, and officers among your tribes. 8269
20: 9 that they shall make **c** of the armies to lead 8269
29:10 your **c** of your tribes, your elders, and 7218
Jos 10:24 said unto the **c** of the men of war which 7101
1Sa 8:12 he will appoint him **c** over thousands, and 8269
8:12 captains over thousands, and **c** over fifties; 8269
22: 7 *and* make you all **c** of thousands, and 8269
22: 7 captains of hundreds, and **c** of hundreds; 8269
2Sa 4: 2 Saul's son had two men *that were* **c** of 8269
18: 1 set **c** of thousands and captains of hundreds 8269
18: 1 of thousands and **c** of hundreds over them. 8269
18: 5 gave all the **c** charge concerning Absalom. 8269
23: 8 that sat in the seat, chief among the **c**; 7991
24: 4 against Joab, and against the **c** of the host. 8269
24: 4 the **c** of the host went out from the presence 8269
1Ki 1:25 the **c** of the host, and Abiathar the priest; 8269
2: 5 what he did to the two **c** of the hosts of 8269
9:22 his **c**, and rulers of his chariots, and 7991
15:20 sent the **c** of the hosts which he had against 8269
20:24 out of his place, and put **c** in their rooms: 6346
22:31 and two **c** that had rule over *his* chariots, 8269
22:32 when the **c** of the chariots saw Jehoshaphat, 8269
22:33 when the **c** of the chariots perceived that it 8269
2Ki 1:14 burnt up the two **c** of the former fifties with 8269
8:21 him about, and the **c** of the chariots: 8269
9: 5 behold, the **c** of the host *were* sitting; 8269
10:25 that Jehu said to the guard and to the **c**, 7991
10:25 the guard and the **c** cast *them* out, and 7991
11: 4 with the **c** and the guard, and brought them 3746
11: 9 the **c** over the hundreds did according to all 8269
11:10 to the **c** over hundreds did the priest give 8269
11:15 Jehoiada the priest commanded the **c** of 8269
11:19 the **c**, and the guard, and all the people of 3746
25:23 when all the **c** of the armies, they and 8269
25:26 and great, and the **c** of the armies, 8269
1Ch 4:42 having for their **c** Pelatiah, and Neariah, 7218
11:11 a Hachmonite, the chief of the **c**: 7991
11:15 Now three of the thirty **c** went down to 7218
12:14 *were* of the sons of Gad, **c** of the host: 7218
12:18 *who was* chief of the **c**, *and he said*, Thine 7970
12:18 and made them **c** of the band. 7218
12:20 **c** of the thousands that *were* of Manasseh. 7218
12:21 *men* of valour, and were **c** in the host. 8269
12:28 and *of* his father's house twenty and two **c**. 8269
12:34 of Naphtali a thousand **c**, and with them 8269
13: 1 David consulted with the **c** of thousands 8269
15:25 elders of Israel, and the **c** over thousands, 8269
25: 1 the **c** of the host separated to the service of 8269
26:26 the **c** over thousands and hundreds, and 8269
26:26 and hundreds, and the **c** of the host, 8269
27: 1 and **c** of thousands and hundreds, 8269
27: 3 of all the **c** of the host for the first month. 8269
1Ch 28: 1 the **c** of the companies that ministered to 8269
28: 1 the **c** over the thousands, and captains over 8269
28: 1 **c** over the hundreds, and the stewards over 8269
29: 6 and the **c** of thousands and of hundreds, 8269
2Ch 1: 2 to the **c** of thousands and of hundreds, and 8269
8: 9 chief of his **c**, and captains of his chariots 7991
8: 9 and **c** of his chariots and horsemen. 8269
11:11 put **c** in them, and store of victual, and 5057
16: 4 sent the **c** of his armies against the cities of 8269
17:14 Of Judah, the **c** of thousands; Adnah 8269
18:30 the **c** of the chariots that *were* with him, 8269
18:31 when the **c** of the chariots saw Jehoshaphat, 8269
18:32 that when the **c** of the chariots perceived 8269
21: 9 compassed him in, and the **c** of the chariots. 8269
23: 1 took the **c** of hundreds, Azariah the son of 8269
23: 9 priest delivered to the **c** of hundreds spears, 8269
23:14 Jehoiada the priest brought out the **c** of 8269
23:20 he took the **c** of hundreds, and the nobles, 8269
25: 5 made them **c** over thousands, and captains 8269
25: 5 over thousands, and **c** over hundreds, 8269
26:11 the hand of Hananiah, *one* of the king's **c**. 8269
32: 6 he set **c** of war over the people, and 8269
32:21 and **c** in the camp of the king of Assyria. 8269
33:11 the **c** of the host of the king of Assyria, 8269
33:14 put **c** of war in all the fenced cities of 8269
Ne 2: 9 Now the king had sent **c** of the army and 8269
Job 39:25 the thunder of the **c**, and the shouting. 8269
Jer 13:21 for thou hast taught them *to be* **c**, *and* 441
40: 7 *Now* when all the **c** of the forces which 8269
40:13 all the **c** of the forces that *were* in the fields, 8269
41:11 all the **c** of the forces that *were* with him, 8269
41:13 all the **c** of the forces that *were* with him, 8269
41:16 all the **c** of the forces that *were* with him, 8269
42: 1 all the **c** of the forces, and Johanan the son 8269
42: 8 all the **c** of the forces which *were* with him, 8269
43: 4 all the **c** of the forces, and all the people, 8269
43: 5 all the **c** of the forces, took all the remnant 8269
51:23 with thee will I break in pieces **c** and rulers. 6346
51:28 the **c** thereof, and all the rulers thereof, and 6346
51:57 her wise *men*, her **c**, and her rulers, and 6346
Eze 21:22 to appoint **c**, to open the mouth in 3733
23: 6 *Which were* clothed with blue, **c** and rulers, 6346
23:12 **c** and rulers clothed most gorgeously, 6346
23:23 **c** and rulers, great lords and renowned, 6346
Da 3: 2 and the **c**, the judges, the treasurers, 6347
3: 3 the governors and **c**, the judges, 6347
3:27 **c**, and the king's counsellers, 6347
6: 7 and the princes, the counsellers and the **c**, 6347
Na 3:17 and thy **c** as the great grasshoppers, 2951
Mk 6:21 **high c**, and chief *estates* of Galilee; *5506*
Lk 22: 4 and communed with the chief priests and **c**, *4755*
22:52 and **c** of the temple, and the elders, *4755*
Ac 25:23 with the **chief c**, and principal men of *5506*
Rev 6:15 and the rich *men*, and the **chief c**, and *5506*
19:18 and the flesh of **c**, and the flesh of mighty *5506*

CAPTIVE (59) [CAPTIVES, CAPTIVITY]

Ge 14:14 Abram heard that his brother was **taken c**, 7617
34:29 their wives **took** they **c**, and spoiled even 7617
Ex 12:29 firstborn of the **c** that *was* in the dungeon; 7628
Nu 24:22 until Asshur shall **carry** thee **away c**. 7617
Dt 21:10 and thou hast **taken** them **c**, 7617+7628
Jdg 5:12 arise, Barak, and **lead** thy captivity **c**, 7617
1Ki 8:48 which **led** them **away c**, and pray unto thee 7617
8:50 before them who **carried** them **c**, 7617
2Ki 5: 2 had **brought away c** out of the land of 7617
6:22 whom thou hast **taken c** with thy sword 7617
15:29 of Naphtali, and **carried** them **c** to Assyria. 1540
16: 9 **carried** *the people of* it **c** to Kir, and slew 1540
24:16 even them the king of Babylon brought **c** to 1473
1Ch 5: 6 king of Assyria **carried away c**: 1540
2Ch 6:37 in the land whither they are **carried c**, 7617
25:12 did the children of Judah **carry away c**, 7617
28: 8 the children of Israel **carried away c** of 7617
28:11 which ye have **taken c** of your brethren: 7617
30: 9 compassion before them that **lead** them **c**, 7617
Ps 68:18 ascended on high, thou hast **led** captivity **c**: 7617
137: 3 For there they that **carried** us **away c** 7617
Isa 49:21 *am* desolate, a **c**, and removing to and fro? 1540
49:24 from the mighty, or the lawful **c** delivered? 7628
51:14 The **c exile** hasteneth that *he* may be 6808
52: 2 bands of thy neck, O **c** daughter of Zion. 7628
Jer 1: 3 unto the **carrying away** of Jerusalem **c** in 1540
13:17 the LORD'S flock is **carried away c**. 7617
13:19 Judah shall be **carried away c** all of it, 1540
13:19 all of it, it shall be wholly **carried away c**. 1540
20: 4 he shall **carry** them **c** into Babylon, and 1540
22:12 in the place whither they have **led** him **c**, 1540
24: 1 **carried away c** Jeconiah the son of 1540
24: 5 them that are **carried away c** of Judah, 1546
27:20 when he **carried away c** Jeconiah the son 1540
28: 6 all that is **carried away c**, from Babylon 1473
29: 1 **carried away c** from Jerusalem to 1540
29:14 I **caused** you **to be carried away c**. 1540
39: 9 **carried away c** *into* Babylon the remnant 1540
40: 1 all that were **carried away c** of Jerusalem 1546
40: 1 which were **carried away c** unto Babylon. 1540
40: 7 of *them* that were not **carried away c** to 1540
41:10 Ishmael **carried away c** all the residue of 7617
41:10 the son of Nethaniah **carried** them **away c**, 7617
41:14 **carried away c** from Mizpah cast about 7617
52:15 **carried away c** *certain* of the poor of 1540
52:27 Thus Judah was **carried away c** out of his 1540
52:28 whom Nebuchadrezzar **carried away c**: 1540
52:29 **carried away c** from Jerusalem eight 1540
52:30 **carried away c** *of* the Jews seven hundred 1540
Am 1: 6 they **carried away c** the whole captivity, 1540
6: 7 Therefore now shall they **go c** with the first 1540
6: 7 shall they go captive with the first that **go c**, 1540
7:11 Israel shall **surely** be **led away c** out 1540+1540
Ob 1:11 in the day that the strangers **carried away c** 7617
Na 2: 7 Huzzab shall be **led away c**, she shall be 1540
Lk 21:24 and shall be **led away c** into all nations: *163*
Eph 4: 8 he **led** captivity **c**, and gave gifts unto men. *162*
2Ti 2:26 *who are* **taken c** by him at his will. *2221*
2Ti 3: 6 and **lead c** silly women laden with sins, *162*

CAPTIVES (43) [CAPTIVE]

Ge 31:26 my daughters, as **c** taken with the sword? 7617
Nu 31: 9 of Israel **took** *all* the women of Midian **c**, 7617
31:12 they brought the **c**, and the prey, and 7628
31:19 *both* yourselves and your **c** on the third day, 7628
Dt 21:11 seest among the **c** a beautiful woman, and 7633
32:42 *that* with the blood of the slain and of the **c**, 7633
1Sa 30: 2 had **taken** the women **c**, that *were* therein: 7617
30: 3 and their daughters, were **taken c**. 7617
30: 5 David's two wives were **taken c**, 7617
1Ki 8:46 that they **carry** them **away c** unto 7617+7617
8:47 in the land whither they were **carried c**, 7617
8:47 in the land of them *that* **carried** them **c**, 7617
2Ki 24:14 *even* ten thousand **c**, and all the craftsmen 1540
2Ch 6:36 they **carry** them **away c** unto a land 7617+7617
6:38 whither they have **carried** them **c**, and 7617
28: 5 **carried away** a great multitude of
them **c**, 7617+7633
28:11 hear me therefore, and deliver the **c** again, 7633
28:13 Ye shall not bring in the **c** hither: 7633
28:14 So the armed men left the **c** and the spoil 7633
28:15 took the **c**, and with the spoil clothed all 7633
28:17 and smitten Judah, and carried away **c**. 7628
Ps 106:46 to be pitied of all those that **carried** them **c**. 7617
Isa 14: 2 and they shall **take** them **c**, whose captives they 7617
14: 2 take them captives, whose **c** they were; 7617
20: 4 the Ethiopians **c**, young and old, naked and 1546
45:13 build my city, and he shall let go my **c**, 1546
49:25 Even the **c** of the mighty shall be taken 7628
61: 1 to proclaim liberty to the **c**, and the opening 7617
Jer 28: 4 with all the **c** of Judah, that went into 1546
29: 1 of the elders which were **carried away c**, 1473
29: 4 of Israel, unto all that are **carried away c**, 1473
29: 7 I have **caused** you **to be carried away c**, 1540
43: 3 and **carry** us **away c** *into* Babylon. 1540
43:12 shall burn them, and **carry** them **away c**: 7617
48:46 for thy sons are taken **c**, and thy daughters 7628
48:46 are taken captives, and thy daughters **c**. 7633
50:33 all that **took** them **c** held them fast; 7617
Eze 1: 1 as I *was* among the **c** by the river of 1473
6: 9 the nations whither they shall be **carried c**, 7617
16:53 *will I bring again* the captivity of thy **c** in 7622
Da 2:25 I have found a man of the **c** of Judah, 1123+1547
11: 8 shall also carry **c** *into* Egypt their gods, 7628
Lk 4:18 to preach deliverance to the **c**, and *164*

CAPTIVITY (127) [CAPTIVE]

Nu 21:29 his daughters into **c** unto Sihon king of 7622
Dt 21:13 she shall put the raiment of her **c** from off 7628
28:41 not enjoy them; for they shall go into **c**. 7628
30: 3 then the LORD thy God will turn thy **c**, 7622
Jdg 5:12 arise, Barak, and lead thy **c** captive, 7628
18:30 of Dan until the day of the **c** of the land. 1540
2Ki 24:15 *those* carried he *into* **c** from Jerusalem to 1473
25:27 thirtieth year of the **c** of Jehoiachin king of 1546
1Ch 5:22 And they dwelt in their steads until the **c**. 1473
6:15 Jehozadak went *into* **c**, when the LORD NIH
2Ch 6:37 and pray unto thee in the land of their **c**, 7628
6:38 and with all their soul in the land of their **c**, 7628
29: 9 and our wives *are* in **c** for this. 7628
Ezr 1:11 **c** that were brought up from Babylon unto 1473
2: 1 of the province that went up out of the **c**, 7628
3: 8 all they that were come out of the **c** *unto* 7628
4: 1 Benjamin heard that the children of the **c** 1473
6:16 and the rest of the children of the **c**, 1547
6:19 the children of the **c** kept the passover upon 1473
6:20 the passover for all the children of the **c**, 1473
6:21 which were come again out of **c**, and 1473
8:35 which were come out of the **c**, offered burnt 7628
9: 7 to **c**, and to a spoil, and to confusion of 7628
10: 7 and Jerusalem unto all the children of the **c**, 1473
10:16 the children of the **c** did so. And Ezra 1473
Ne 1: 2 which were left of the **c**, and 7628
1: 3 The remnant that are left of the **c** there in 7628
4: 4 and give them for a prey in the land of **c**: 7633
7: 6 that went up out of the **c**, *of* those that had 7628
8:17 were come again out of the **c** made booths, 7628
Est 2: 6 **c** which had been carried away with 1473
Job 42:10 the LORD turned the **c** of Job, when he 7622
Ps 14: 7 when the LORD bringeth back the **c** of his 7622
53: 6 When God bringeth back the **c** of his 7622
68:18 ascended on high, thou hast led **c** captive: 7628
78:61 delivered his strength into **c**, and his glory 7628
85: 1 thou hast brought back the **c** of Jacob. 7622
126: 1 When the LORD turned again the **c** of 7870
126: 4 Turn again our **c**, O LORD, as the streams 7622
Isa 5:13 Therefore my people are **gone into c**, 1540
22:17 will carry thee away with a mighty **c**, 2925
46: 2 the burden, but themselves are gone into **c**. 7628
Jer 15: 2 and such as *are* for the **c**, to the captivity. 7628
15: 2 and such as *are* for the captivity, to the **c**. 7628
20: 6 all that dwell in thine house shall go into **c**: 7628
22:22 thy pastors, and thy lovers shall go into **c**: 7628
29:14 I will turn away your **c**, and I will gather 7622
29:16 that are not gone forth with you into **c**; 1473
29:20 the word of the LORD, all *ye of* the **c**, 1473
29:22 by all the **c** of Judah which *are* in Babylon, 1546
29:28 unto us *in* Babylon, saying, This **c** *is* long: NIH
29:31 Send to all them of the **c**, saying, Thus saith 1473
30: 3 that I will bring again the **c** of my people 7622
30:10 and thy seed from the land of their **c**; 7628
30:16 every one of them, shall go into **c**; 7628
30:18 I *will* bring again the **c** of Jacob's tents, and 7622
31:23 when I shall bring again their **c**; 7622
32:44 for I will cause their **c** to return, saith 7622
33: 7 I will cause the **c** of Judah and the captivity 7622
33: 7 of Judah and the **c** of Israel to return, 7622
33:11 For I will cause to return the **c** of the land 7622
33:26 for I will cause their **c** to return, and 7622
43:11 such *as are* for **c** to captivity; and such *as* 7628
43:11 such *as are* for captivity to **c**; and such *as* 7628
46:19 in Egypt, furnish thyself to **go into c**: 1473
46:27 and thy seed from the land of their **c**; 7628

Jer 48: 7 Chemosh shall go forth into **c** *with* his 1473
48:11 vessel to vessel, neither hath he gone into **c**: 1473
48:47 Yet will I bring again the **c** of Moab in 7622
49: 3 for their king shall go into **c**, *and* his priests 1473
49: 6 afterward I will bring again the **c** of 7622
49:39 *that* I will bring again the **c** of Elam, 7622
52:31 thirtieth year of the **c** of Jehoiachin king of 1546
La 1: 3 Judah is **gone into c** because of affliction, 1540
1: 5 her children are gone *into* **c** before 7628
1:18 and my young men are gone into **c**. 7628
2:14 thine iniquity, to turn away thy **c**; 7622
4:22 he will no more **carry** thee **away into c**: 1540
Eze 1: 2 *was* the fifth year of king Jehoiachin's **c**, 1546
3:11 go, get thee to them of the **c**, unto 1473
3:15 I came to them of the **c** *at* Tel-abib, 1473
11:24 of God into Chaldea, to them of the **c**. 1473
11:25 I spake unto them of the **c** all the things that 1473
12: 4 in their sight, as they that go forth into **c**. 1473
12: 7 as stuff for **c**, and in the even I digged 1473
12:11 unto them: they shall remove *and* go into **c**. 7628
16:53 When I shall bring again their **c**, 7622
16:53 the **c** of Sodom and her daughters, and 7622
16:53 the **c** of Samaria and her daughters, then 7622
16:53 *will I bring again* the **c** of thy captives in 7622
25: 3 the house of Judah, when they went into **c**; 1473
29:14 I will bring again the **c** of Egypt, and 7622
30:17 the sword: and these *cities* shall go into **c**. 7628
30:18 cover her, and her daughters shall go into **c**. 7628
33:21 it came to pass in the twelfth year of our **c**, 1546
39:23 of Israel **went into c** for their iniquity: 1540
39:25 Now will I bring again the **c** of Jacob, and 7622
39:28 which **caused** them **to be led into c** among 1540
40: 1 In the five and twentieth year of our **c**, 1546
Da 5:13 which *art* of the children of the **c** of Judah, 1547
6:13 which *is* of the children of the **c** of Judah, 1547
11:33 by flame, by **c**, and by spoil, *many* days. 7628
Hos 6:11 when I returned the **c** of my people. 7622
Joel 3: 1 when I shall bring again the **c** of Judah and 7622
Am 1: 5 the people of Syria shall **go into c** unto Kir, 1540
1: 6 they carried away captive the whole **c**, 1546
1: 9 they delivered up the whole **c** to Edom, 1546
1:15 their king shall go into **c**, he and his princes 1473
5: 5 for Gilgal shall **surely go into c**, 1540+1540
5:27 Therefore will I **cause** you **to go into c** 1540
7:17 Israel shall **surely go into c** forth of 1540+1540
9: 4 though they go into **c** before their enemies, 7628
9:14 I will bring again the **c** of my people of 7622
Ob 1:20 the **c** of this host of the children of Israel 1546
1:20 the **c** of Jerusalem, which *is* in Sepharad, 1546
Mic 1:16 for they are **gone into c** from thee. 1540
Na 3:10 Yet *was* she carried away, she went into **c**: 7628
Hab 1: 9 and they shall gather the **c** as the sand. 7628
Zep 2: 7 God shall visit them, and turn away their **c**. 7622
3:20 when I turn back your **c** before your eyes, 7622
Zec 6:10 Take of *them of* the **c**, *even* of Heldai, of 1473
14: 2 and half of the city shall go forth into **c**, and 1473
Ro 7:23 **bringing** me **into c** to the law of sin which is *163*
2Co 10: 5 **bringing into c** every thought to *163*
Eph 4: 8 he led **c** captive, and gave gifts unto men. *161*
Rev 13:10 He that leadeth into **c** *shall* go into captivity: *161*
13:10 He that leadeth into captivity *shall* go into **c**: *161*

CAPTURE See FETCH; FETCHED

CARAWAY See FITCHES

CARBUNCLE (3) [CARBUNCLES]
Ex 28:17 *first* row *shall be* a sardius, a topaz, and a **c**: 1304
39:10 *the first* row *was* a sardius, a topaz, and a **c**: 1304
Eze 28:13 the emerald, and the **c**, and gold: 1304

CARBUNCLES (1) [CARBUNCLE]
Isa 54:12 thy gates of **c**, and all thy borders of 68+688

CARCAS (1)
Est 1:10 Bigtha, and Abagtha, Zethar, and **C**, 3752

CARCASE (34) [CARCASES]
Lev 5: 2 whether *it be* a **c** of an unclean beast, or a 5038
5: 2 or a **c** of unclean cattle, or the carcase of 5038
5: 2 or the **c** of unclean creeping things, and *if* it 5038
11: 8 ye not eat, and their **c** shall ye not touch; 5038
11:24 whosoever toucheth the **c** of them shall be 5038
11:25 whosoever beareth *ought* of the **c** of them 5038
11:27 whoso toucheth their **c** shall be unclean 5038
11:28 he that beareth the **c** of them shall wash his 5038
11:35 every *thing* whereupon *any part* of their **c** 5038
11:36 that which toucheth their **c** shall be 5038
11:37 if *any part* of their **c** fall upon any sowing 5038
11:38 *any part* of their **c** fall thereon, it *shall be* 5038
11:39 he that toucheth the **c** thereof shall be 5038
11:40 he that eateth of the **c** of it shall wash his 5038
11:40 he also that beareth the **c** of it shall wash 5038
Dt 14: 8 eat of their flesh, nor touch their **dead c**. 5038
28:26 thy **c** shall be meat unto all fowls of the air, 5038
Jos 8:29 they should take his **c** down from the tree, 5038
Jdg 14: 8 and he turned aside to see the **c** of the lion: 4658
14: 8 of bees and honey in the **c** of the lion. 1472
14: 9 had taken the honey out of the **c** of the lion. 1472
1Ki 13:22 thy **c** shall not come unto the sepulchre of 5038
13:24 his **c** was cast in the way, and the ass stood 5038
13:24 ass stood by it, the lion also stood by the **c**. 5038
13:25 saw the **c** cast in the way, and the lion 5038
13:25 in the way, and the lion standing by the **c**: 5038
13:28 he went and found his **c** cast in the way, 5038
13:28 and the ass and the lion standing by the **c**: 5038
13:28 the lion had not eaten the **c**, nor torn 5038
13:29 the prophet took up the **c** of the man of 5038
13:30 he laid his **c** in his own grave; and 5038
2Ki 9:37 the **c** of Jezebel shall be as dung upon 5038
Isa 14:19 stones of the pit; as a **c** trodden under feet. 6297
Mt 24:28 For wheresoever the **c** is, there will *4430*

CARCASES (22) [CARCASE]
Ge 15:11 And when the fowls came down upon the **c**, 6297
Lev 11:11 but you shall have their **c** in abomination. 5038
11:26 *The* **c** of every beast which divideth NIH
26:30 cast your **c** upon the carcases of your idols, 6297
26:30 cast your carcases upon the **c** of your idols, 6297
Nu 14:29 Your **c** shall fall in this wilderness; and 6297
14:32 *as for* you, your **c**, they shall fall in this 6297
14:33 until your **c** be wasted in the wilderness. 6297
1Sa 17:46 I will give the **c** of the host of 6297
Isa 5:25 their **c** were torn in the midst of the streets. 5038
34: 3 their stink shall come up *out of* their **c**, and 6297
66:24 look upon the **c** of the men that have 6297
Jer 7:33 the **c** of this people shall be meat for 5038
9:22 Even the **c** of men shall fall as dung upon 5038
16: 4 their **c** shall be meat for the fowls of 5038
16:18 they have filled mine inheritance with the **c** 5038
19: 7 their **c** will I give to be meat for the fowls 5038
Eze 6: 5 I will lay the **dead c** of the children of 6297
43: 7 nor by the **c** of their kings *in* their high 6297
43: 9 the **c** of their kings, far from me, and I will 6297
Na 3: 3 multitude of slain, and a great number of **c**; 6297
Heb 3:17 had sinned, whose **c** fell in the wilderness? *2966*

CARCASS; CARCASSES See CARCASE; CARCASES

CARCHEMISH (3)
2Ch 35:20 came up to fight against **C** by Euphrates: 3751
Isa 10: 9 *Is* not Calno as **C**? *is* not Hamath as Arpad? 3751
Jer 46: 2 which was by the river Euphrates in **C**, 3751

CARE (20) [CARED, CAREFUL, CAREFULLY, CAREFULNESS, CARELESS, CARELESSLY, CARES, CAREST, CARETH, CARING]
1Sa 10: 2 lo, thy father hath left the **c** of the asses, 1697
2Sa 18: 3 for if we flee away, they will not **c** 3820+7760
18: 3 if half of us die, will they **c** for us: 3820+7760
2Ki 4:13 thou hast been careful for us with all this **c**; 2731
Jer 49:31 that dwelleth **without c**, saith the LORD, 983
Eze 4:16 they shall eat bread by weight, and with **c**; 1674
Mt 13:22 and the **c** of this world, and *3308*
Lk 10:34 brought him to an inn, and **took c of** him. *1959*
10:35 the host, and said unto him, **Take c of** him; *1959*
10:40 dost thou not **c** that my sister hath left me *3199*
1Co 7:21 Art thou called *being* a servant? **c** not **for** it: *3199*
9: 9 out the corn. Doth God **take c for** oxen? *3199*
12:25 *that* the members should **have** the same **c** *3309*
2Co 7:12 that our **c** for you in the sight of God might *4710*
8:16 which put the same **earnest c** into the heart *4710*
11:28 upon me daily, the **c** of all the churches. *3308*
Php 2:20 who will naturally **c for** your state. *3309*
4:10 that now at the last your **c** of me hath *5426*
1Ti 3: 5 how shall he **take c of** the church of God?) *1959*
1Pe 5: 7 Casting all your **c** upon him; for he careth *3308*

CAREAH (1)
2Ki 25:23 Johanan the son of **C**, and Seraiah the son 7143

CARED (3) [CARE]
Ps 142: 4 refuge failed me; no man **c** for my soul. 1875
Jn 12: 6 This he said, not that he **c** for the poor; but *3199*
Ac 18:17 And Gallio **c for** none of those *things*. *3199*

CAREFUL (7) [CARE]
2Ki 4:13 thou hast been **c** for us with all this care; 2729
Jer 17: 8 shall not be **c** in the year of drought, 1672
Da 3:16 we *are* not **c** to answer thee in this matter. 2818
Lk 10:41 thou art **c** and troubled about many *things*: *3309*
Php 4: 6 Be **c** for nothing; but in every *thing* by *3309*
4:10 wherein ye were also **c**, but ye lacked *5426*
Tit 3: 8 in God might be **c** to maintain good works. *5431*

CAREFULLY (4) [CARE]
Dt 15: 5 Only if thou **c hearken** unto 8085+8085
Mic 1:12 For the inhabitant of Maroth **waited c** for 2342
Php 2:28 I sent him therefore the **more c**, that, *4708*
Heb 12:17 though he **sought** it **c** with tears. *1567*

CAREFULNESS (4) [CARE]
Eze 12:18 drink thy water with trembling and with **c**; 1674
12:19 They shall eat their bread with **c**, and 1674
1Co 7:32 But I would have you **without c**. He *that is* *275*
2Co 7:11 what **c** it wrought in you, yea, *4710*

CARELESS (5) [CARE]
Jdg 18: 7 people that *were* therein, how they dwelt **c**, 983
Isa 32: 9 ye **c** daughters, give ear unto my speech. 982
32:10 ye **c** *women*: for the vintage shall fail, 982
32:11 that are at ease; be troubled, ye **c** ones: 982
Eze 30: 9 me in ships to make the **c** Ethiopians afraid, 983

CARELESSLY (3) [CARE]
Isa 47: 8 that dwellest **c**, that sayest in thine 983+3807.1
Eze 39: 6 among them that dwell **c** in the isles: 983+3807.1
Zep 2:15 *is* the rejoicing city that dwelt **c**, 983+3807.1

CARES (3) [CARE]
Mk 4:19 And the **c** of this world, and *3308*
Lk 8:14 and are choked with **c** and riches and *3308*
21:34 and **c** of *this* life, and *so* that day come *3308*

CARESSING See SPORTING

CAREST (3) [CARE]
Mt 22:16 neither **c** thou for any *man*: for thou *3199*
Mk 4:38 Master, **c** thou not that we perish? *3199*
12:14 **c** for no *man*: for thou regardest not *3199*

CARETH (7) [CARE]
Dt 11:12 A land which the LORD thy God **c for**: 1875
Jn 10:13 he is a hireling, and **c** not for the sheep. *3199*
1Co 7:32 He *that is* unmarried **c for** the *things* that *3309*
7:33 But he that is married **c for** the *things that* *3309*
7:34 The unmarried *woman* **c for** the *things* of *3309*
7:34 she that is married **c for** the *things* of *3309*
1Pe 5: 7 all your care upon him; for he **c** for you. *3199*

CARING (1) [CARE]
1Sa 9: 5 lest my father leave **c** for the asses, and NIH

CARMEL (26) [CARMELITE, CARMELITESS]
Jos 12:22 one; the king of Jokneam of **C**, one; 3760
15:55 Maon, **C**, and Ziph, and Juttah, 3760
19:26 reacheth to **C** westward, and 3760
1Sa 15:12 Saul came to **C**, and behold, 3760
25: 2 in Maon, whose possessions *were* in **C**; 3760
25: 2 and he was shearing his sheep in **C**. 3760
25: 5 Get you up to **C**, and go to Nabal, and 3760
25: 7 unto them, all the while they were in **C**. 3760
25:40 of David were come to Abigail to **C**, 3760
1Ki 18:19 *and* gather to me all Israel unto mount **C**, 3760
18:20 the prophets together unto mount **C**. 3760
18:42 Elijah went up to the top of **C**; and he cast 3760
2Ki 2:25 he went from thence to mount **C**, and 3760
4:25 and came unto the man of God to mount **C**. 3760
19:23 of his borders, *and into* the forest of his **C**. 3760
2Ch 26:10 vinedressers in the mountains, and in **C**: 3760
SS 7: 5 Thine head upon thee *is* like **C**, and the hair 3760
Isa 33: 9 and Bashan and **C** shake off *their fruits*. 3760
35: 2 the excellency of **C** and Sharon, they shall 3760
37:24 height of his border, *and* the forest of his **C**. 3760
Jer 46:18 and as **C** by the sea, *so* shall he come. 3760
50:19 he shall feed on **C** and Bashan, and his soul 3760
Am 1: 2 shall mourn, and the top of **C** shall wither. 3760
9: 3 they hide themselves in the top of **C**, 3760
Mic 7:14 solitarily *in* the wood, in the midst of **C**: 3760
Na 1: 4 **C**, and the flower of Lebanon languisheth. 3760

CARMELITE (5) [CARMEL]
1Sa 30: 5 and Abigail the wife of Nabal the **C**. 3761
2Sa 2: 2 and Abigail Nabal's wife the **C**. 3761
3: 3 of Abigail the wife of Nabal the **C**; 3761
23:35 Hezrai the **C**, Paarai the Arbite, 3761
1Ch 11:37 Hezro the **C**, Naarai the son of Ezbai, 3761

CARMELITESS (2) [CARMEL]
1Sa 27: 3 and Abigail the **C**, Nabal's wife. 3761
1Ch 3: 1 the second Daniel, of Abigail the **C**: 3761

CARMI (8) [CARMITES]
Ge 46: 9 Hanoch, and Phallu, and Hezron, and **C**. 3756
Ex 6:14 Hanoch, and Pallu, Hezron, and **C**: 3756
Nu 26: 6 of **C**, the family of the Carmites. 3756
Jos 7: 1 for Achan, the son of **C**, the son of Zabdi, 3756
7:18 Achan, the son of **C**, the son of Zabdi, 3756
1Ch 2: 7 the sons of **C**; Achar, the troubler of Israel, 3756
4: 1 Hezron, and **C**, and Hur, and Shobal. 3756
5: 3 *were*, Hanoch, and Pallu, Hezron, and **C**. 3756

CARMITE See CARMITES

CARMITES (1) [CARMI]
Nu 26: 6 of Carmi, the family of the **C**. 3757

CARNAL (11) [CARNALLY]
Ro 7:14 law is spiritual: but I am **c**, sold under sin. *4559*
8: 7 Because the **c** mind *is* enmity against God: *4561*
15:27 is also to minister unto them in **c** *things*. *4559*
1Co 3: 1 but as unto **c**, *even* as unto babes in Christ. *4559*
3: 3 For ye are yet **c**: for whereas *there is* among *4559*
3: 3 divisions, are ye not **c**, and walk as men? *4559*
3: 4 and another, I *am* of Apollos; are ye not **c**? *4559*
9:11 a great *thing* if we shall reap your **c** *things*? *4559*
2Co 10: 4 (For the weapons of our warfare *are* not **c**, *4559*
Heb 7:16 not after the law of a **c** commandment, but *4559*
9:10 and divers washings, and **c** ordinances, *4561*

CARNALLY (4) [CARNAL]
Lev 18:20 **lie c** with thy 2233+5414+7903+3807.1
19:20 **lieth c with** a woman that 854+2233+7901+7902
Nu 5:13 **a man** lie with her **c**, and it be 376+2233+7902
Ro 8: 6 For to be **c** minded *is* death; *4561*

CARNELIAN See SARDINE

CARPENTER (3) [CARPENTER'S, CARPENTERS]
Isa 41: 7 So the **c** encouraged the goldsmith, *and* 2796
44:13 The **c** stretcheth out *his* rule; 2796+6086
Mk 6: 3 Is not this the **c**, the son of Mary, *5045*

CARPENTER'S (1) [CARPENTER]
Mt 13:55 Is not this the **c** son? is not his mother *5045*

CARPENTERS (9) [CARPENTER]
2Sa 5:11 and cedar trees, and **c**, and masons: 2796+6086
2Ki 12:11 they laid it out to the **c** and builders, 2796+6086
22: 6 Unto **c**, and builders, and masons, and 2796
1Ch 14: 1 timber of cedars, with masons and **c**, 2796+6086
2Ch 24:12 and **c** to repair the house of the LORD, 2796
Ezr 3: 7 money also unto the masons, and to the **c**; 2796
Jer 24: 1 with the **c** and smiths, from Jerusalem, and 2796
29: 2 and Jerusalem, and the **c**, and the smiths, 2796
Zec 1:20 And the LORD shewed me four **c**. 2796

CARPUS (1)
2Ti 4:13 The cloke that I left at Troas with **C**, *2591*

CARRIAGE (3) [CARRIAGES]
Jdg 18:21 and the cattle and the **c** before them. 3520
1Sa 17:22 David left his **c** in the hand of the keeper of 3627
17:22 carriage in the hand of the keeper of the **c**, 3627

CARRIAGES (3) [CARRIAGE]
Isa 10:28 at Michmash he hath laid up his **c**: 3627

Isa 46: 1 your c *were* heavy loaden; *they are* a 5385
Ac 21:15 And after those days we took up our c, and *643*

CARRIED (145) [CARRY]
Ge 31:18 he c away all his cattle, and all his goods 5090
31:26 c away my daughters, as captives taken 5090
46: 5 the sons of Israel c Jacob their father, and 5375
50:13 For his sons c him into the land of Canaan, 5375
Lev 10: 5 and c them in their coats out of the camp; 5375
Jos 4: 8 c them over with them unto the place 5674
Jdg 16: 3 c them up to the top of a hill that *is* before 5927
1Sa 5: 8 Let the ark of the God of Israel be c about 5437
5: 8 they c the ark of the God of Israel about 5437
5: 9 it was *so,* that after they had c it about, 5437
30: 2 but c *them* away, and went on their way. 5090
30:18 all that the Amalekites had c away: 3947
2Sa 6:10 David c it aside *into* the house of 5186
15:29 Abiathar c the ark of God again *to* 7725
1Ki 8:47 in the land whither they were c captives, 7617
8:47 in the land of them *that* c them captives, 7617
8:50 before them who c them captive, 7617
17:19 c him up into a loft, where he abode, and 5927
21:13 they c him forth out of the city, and 3318
2Ki 7: 8 c thence silver, and gold, and raiment, and 5375
7: 8 and c thence *also,* and went and hid *it.* 5375
9:28 his servants c him *in a chariot* to Jerusalem, 7392
15:29 of Naphtali, and c them captive to Assyria. 1540
16: 9 c *the people of* it captive to Kir, and slew 1540
17: 6 c Israel away into Assyria, and placed them 1540
17:11 whom the LORD c away before them; 1540
17:23 So was Israel c away out of their own land 1540
17:28 one of the priests whom they had c away 1540
17:33 the nations whom they c away from thence. 1540
20:17 store unto this day, shall be c unto Babylon: 5375
23: 4 and c the ashes of them *unto* Beth-el. 5375
23:30 his servants c him *in a chariot* dead from 7392
24:13 he c out thence all the treasures of 3318
24:14 he c away all Jerusalem, and all 1540
24:15 he c away Jehoiachin to Babylon, and 1540
24:15 *those* c he *into* captivity from Jerusalem to 1980
25: 7 with fetters of brass, and c him *to* Babylon. 935
25:13 and c the brass of them to Babylon. 5375
25:21 So Judah was c away out of their land. 1540
1Ch 5: 6 king of Assyria c away captive: 1540
5:26 he c them away, even the Reubenites, and 1540
6:15 *captivity,* when the LORD c away Judah 1540
9: 1 *who* were c away to Babylon for their 1540
13: 7 they c the ark of God in a new cart out of 7392
13:13 c it aside into the house of Obed-edom 5186
2Ch 6:37 in the land whither they are c captive, 7617
6:38 whither they have c them captives, and 7617
12: 9 he c away also the shields of gold which 3947
14:13 his host; and they c away very much spoil. 5375
14:15 c away sheep and camels in abundance, 7617
16: 6 they c away the stones of Ramah, and 5375
21:17 c away all the substance that was found in 7617
24:11 and took it, and c it to his place again. 7725
28: 5 c away a great multitude of them
captives, 7617+7633
28: 8 the children of Israel c away captive of 7617
28:15 c all the feeble of them upon asses, 5095
28:17 and smitten Judah, and c away captives. 7617
33:11 him with fetters, and c him to Babylon. 1980
34:16 Shaphan c the book to the king, and 935
36: 4 Jehoahaz his brother, and c him to Egypt. 935
36: 7 Nebuchadnezzar also c of the vessels of 935
36:20 from the sword c he away to Babylon; 1540
Ezr 2: 1 *of* those which had been c away, 1473
2: 1 king of Babylon had c away unto Babylon, 1540
5:12 and c the people away into Babylon. 1541
8:35 the children of those that had been c away, 1473
9: 4 of those that had been c away; 1473
10: 6 of them that had been c away. 1473
10: 8 of those that had been c away. 1473
Ne 7: 6 *of* those that had been c away, 1473
7: 6 the king of Babylon had c away, 1540
Est 2: 6 Who had been c away from Jerusalem with 1540
2: 6 been c away with Jeconiah king of Judah, 1540
2: 6 the king of Babylon had c away. 1540
Job 1:17 have c them away, yea, and slain 3947
5:13 the counsel of the froward is c headlong. 4116
10:19 I should have been c from the womb to 2986
Ps 46: 2 though the mountains be c into the midst of 4131
106:46 be pitied of all those that c them captives. 7617
137: 3 For there they that c us away captive 7617
Isa 39: 6 store until this day, shall be c *to* Babylon: 5375
46: 3 from the belly, which are c from the womb: 5375
49:22 thy daughters shall be c upon *their* 5375
53: 4 he hath borne our griefs, and c our sorrows: 5445
63: 9 bare them, and c them all the days of old. 5375
Jer 13:17 the LORD'S flock is c away captive. 7617
13:19 Judah shall be c away captive all of it, 1540
13:19 all of it, it shall be wholly c away captive. 1540
24: 1 c away captive Jeconiah the son of 1540
24: 5 them that are c away captive of Judah, 1546
27:20 when he c away captive Jeconiah the son 1540
27:22 They shall be c to Babylon, and there shall 935
28: 3 from this place, and c them *to* Babylon: 935
28: 6 all that is c away captive, from Babylon 1473
29: 1 of the elders which were c away captives, 1473
29: 1 c away captive from Jerusalem to 1540
29: 4 of Israel, unto all that are c away captives, 1473
29: 4 whom I have caused to be c away from 1540
29: 7 I have caused you to be c away captives, 1540
29:14 whence I caused you to be c away captive. 1540
39: 9 c away captive *into* Babylon the remnant 1540
40: 1 all that were c away captive of Jerusalem 1546
40: 1 which were c away captive unto Babylon. 1540
40: 7 of *them* that were not c away captive to 1540
41:10 Ishmael c away captive all the residue of 7617
41:10 the son of Nethaniah c them away captive, 7617
41:14 c away captive from Mizpah cast about 7617
52: 9 c him up unto the king of Babylon to 5927
52:11 c him to Babylon, and put him in prison till 935
52:15 c away captive *certain* of the poor of 1540
Jer 52:17 and c all the brass of them to Babylon. 5375
52:27 Thus Judah was c away captive out of his 1540
52:28 whom Nebuchadrezzar c away captive: 1540
52:29 c away captive from Jerusalem eight 1540
52:30 c away captive *of* the Jews seven hundred 1540
Eze 6: 9 nations whither they shall be c captives, 7617
17: 4 young twigs, and c it into a land of traffick; 935
37: 1 c me out in the spirit of the LORD, and 3318
Da 1: 2 which he c *into* the land of Shinar *to* 935
2:35 the wind c them away, that no place was 5376
Hos 10: 6 It shall be also c unto Assyria *for* a present 2986
12: 1 with the Assyrians, and oil is c into Egypt. 2986
Joel 3: 5 have c into your temples my goodly pleasant 935
Am 1: 6 they c away captive the whole captivity, 1540
Ob 1:11 in the day that the strangers c away captive 7617
Na 3:10 Yet *was* she c away, she went into 3807.1
Mt 1:11 about the time they were c away to *3350*
Mk 15: 1 and c *him* away, and delivered *him* to Pilate. *667*
Lk 7:12 behold, there was a dead man c out, *1580*
16:22 was c by the angels into Abraham's bosom: *667*
24:51 was parted from them, and c up into heaven. *399*
Ac 3: 2 man lame from his mother's womb was c, *941*
5: 6 him up, and c *him* out, and buried *him.* *1627*
7:16 And were c over into Sychem, and laid in *3346*
8: 2 And devout men c Stephen *to his burial,* *4792*
21:34 he commanded him to be c into the castle. *71*
1Co 12: 2 c away unto *these* dumb idols, *even* as ye *520*
Gal 2:13 also was c away with their dissimulation. *4879*
Eph 4:14 and c about with every wind of doctrine, *4064*
Heb 13: 9 Be not c about with divers and *4064*
2Pe 2:17 clouds that are c with a tempest; *1643*
Jude 1:12 *they are* without water, c about of winds; *4064*
Rev 12:15 might cause her to be c away of the flood. *4216*
17: 3 So he c me away in the spirit into *667*
21:10 And he c me away in the spirit to a great and *667*

CARRIEST (1) [CARRY]
Ps 90: 5 Thou c them away as with a flood; 2229

CARRIETH (3) [CARRY]
Job 21:18 and as chaff that the storm c away. 1589
27:21 The east wind c him away, and 5375
Rev 17: 7 and of the beast that c her, which hath *941*

CARRY (90) [CARRIED, CARRIEST, CARRIETH, CARRYING]
Ge 37:25 and myrrh, going to c *it* down to Egypt. 3381
42:19 go ye, c corn *for* the famine of your houses: 935
43:11 and c down the man a present, a little balm, 3381
43:12 of your sacks, c *it* again in your hand; 7725
44: 1 as much as they can c, and put every man's 5375
45:27 the wagons which Joseph had sent to c him, 5375
46: 5 in the wagons which Pharaoh had sent to c 5375
47:30 thou shalt c me out of Egypt, and bury me 5375
50:25 and ye shall c up my bones from hence. 5927
Ex 12:46 thou shalt not c forth *ought* of the flesh 3318
13:19 ye shall c up my bones away hence with 5927
14:11 thus with us, to c us forth out of Egypt? 3318
33:15 If thy presence go not *with me,* c us not up 5927
Lev 4:12 Even the whole bullock shall he c forth 3318
4:21 he shall c forth the bullock without 3318
6:11 c forth the ashes without the camp unto a 3318
10: 4 c your brethren from before the sanctuary 5375
14:45 he shall c *them* forth out of the city into an 3318
16:27 *place,* shall *one* c forth without the camp; 3318
Nu 11:12 say unto me, C them in thy bosom, 5375
24:22 until Asshur shall c thee away captive. 7617
Dt 14:24 for thee, so that thou art not able to c it; 5375
28:38 Thou shalt c much seed out *into* the field, 3318
Jos 4: 3 ye shall c them over with you, and 5674
1Sa 17:18 c these ten cheeses unto the captain of *their* 935
20:40 and said unto him, Go, c *them to* the city. 935
2Sa 15:25 C back the ark of God *into* the city: 7725
19:18 there went over a ferry boat to c over 5674
1Ki 8:46 that they c them away captives unto 7617+7617
18:12 that the spirit of the LORD shall c thee 5375
21:10 *then* c him out, and stone him, that he may 3318
22:26 c him back unto Amon the governor of 7725
22:34 Turn thine hand, and c me out of the host; 3318
2Ki 4:19 And he said to a lad, C him to his mother. 5375
9: 2 his brethren, and c him *to* an inner chamber: 935
17:27 C thither one of the priests whom ye 1980
18:11 the king of Assyria did c away Israel unto 1540
25:11 the captain of the guard c away. 1540
1Ch 10: 9 to c tidings unto their idols, and to 1319
15: 2 None ought to c the ark of God but 5375
15: 2 for them hath the LORD chosen to c 5375
23:26 *they* shall no *more* c the tabernacle, nor any 5375
2Ch 2:16 and thou shalt c it up *to* Jerusalem. 5927
6:36 they c them away captives unto a 7617+7617
18:25 c him back to Amon the governor of 7725
18:33 that thou mayest c me out of the host; 3318
20:25 more than they could c away: 4853
25:12 did the children of Judah c away captive, 7617
29: 5 c forth the filthiness out of the holy *place.* 3318
29:16 the Levites took *it,* to c *it* out abroad into 3318
36: 6 bound him in fetters, to c him to Babylon. 1980
Ezr 5:15 c them into the temple that *is* in Jerusalem, 5182
7:15 And to c the silver and gold, which the king 2987
Job 15:12 Why doth thine heart c thee away? and 3947
Ps 49:17 For when he dieth he shall c nothing away: 3947
Ecc 5:15 which he may c away in his hand. 1980
10:20 for a bird of the air shall c the voice, and 1980
Isa 5:29 shall c *it* away safe, and none shall deliver 6403
15: 7 shall they c away to the brook of 5375
22:17 the LORD will c thee away with a mighty 2904
23: 7 her own feet shall c her afar off to sojourn. 2986
30: 6 they will c their riches upon the shoulders 5375
40:11 c *them* in his bosom, *and* shall gently lead 5375
41:16 the wind shall c them away, and the 5375
46: 4 *even* to hoar hairs will I c *you:* I have 5445
46: 4 even I will c, and will deliver *you.* 5445
46: 7 they c him, and set him in his place, and 5445
57:13 the wind shall c them all away; vanity shall 5375
Jer 17:22 Neither c forth a burden out of your 3318
20: 4 he shall c them captive into Babylon, and 1540
20: 5 and take them, and c them to Babylon. 935
39: 7 bound him with chains to c him to Babylon. 935
39:14 son of Shaphan, that *he* should c him home: 3318
43: 3 and c us away captives *into* Babylon. 1540
43:12 shall burn them, and c them away captives: 7617
La 4:22 he will no more c thee away into captivity: 1540
Eze 12: 5 the wall in their sight, and c out thereby. 3318
12: 6 *thy* shoulders, *and* c *it* forth in the twilight: 3318
12:12 they shall dig through the wall to c out 3318
22: 9 In thee are men that c tales to shed blood: 7400
38:13 to c away silver and gold, to take *away* 5375
Da 11: 8 shall also c captives *into* Egypt their gods, 935
Mk 6:55 began to c about in beds those that were *4064*
11:16 should c *any* vessel through the temple. *1308*
Lk 10: 4 C neither purse, nor scrip, nor shoes: and *941*
Jn 5:10 it is not lawful for thee to c *thy* bed. *142*
21:18 and c *thee* whither thou wouldest not. *5342*
Ac 5: 9 *are* at the door, and shall c thee out. *1627*
7:43 and I will c you away beyond Babylon. *3351*
1Ti 6: 7 *and it is* certain we can c nothing out. *1627*

CARRYING (8) [CARRY]
1Sa 10: 3 one c three kids, and another carrying three 5375
10: 3 another c three loaves of bread, and 5375
10: 3 of bread, and another c a bottle of wine: 5375
Ps 78: 9 of Ephraim, *being* armed, *and* c bows, 7411
Jer 1: 3 unto the c away of Jerusalem captive in 1540
Mt 1:17 from David until the c away into Babylon *3350*
1:17 from the c away into Babylon unto Christ *3350*
Ac 5:10 and found her dead, and, c *her* forth, *1627*

CARSHENA (1)
Est 1:14 the next unto him *was* C, Shethar, 3771

CART (15)
1Sa 6: 7 Now therefore make a new c, and take two 5699
6: 7 tie the kine to the c, and bring their calves 5699
6: 8 ark of the LORD, and lay it upon the c; 5699
6:10 tied them to the c, and shut up their calves 5699
6:11 they laid the ark of the LORD upon the c, 5699
6:14 the c came into the field of Joshua, 5699
6:14 they clave the wood of the c, and offered 5699
2Sa 6: 3 they set the ark of God upon a new c, and 5699
6: 3 the sons of Abinadab, drave the new c. 5699
1Ch 13: 7 they carried the ark of God in a new c out 5699
13: 7 and Uzza and Ahio drave the c. 5699
Isa 5:18 of vanity, and sin as it were with a c rope: 5699
28:27 is a c wheel turned about upon the cummin; 5699
28:28 nor break *it with* the wheel of his c, 5699
Am 2:13 as a c is pressed *that is* full *of* sheaves. 5699

CARVED (13) [CARVING]
Jdg 18:18 fetched the c image, the ephod, and 6459
1Ki 6:18 the cedar of the house within *was* c with 4734
6:29 he c all the walls of the house round about 7049
6:29 about *with* c figures of cherubims 4734+6603
6:32 he c upon them carvings of cherubims and 7049
6:35 he c *thereon* cherubims and palm trees and 7049
6:35 *them* with gold fitted upon the c work. 2707
2Ch 33: 7 he set a c image, the idol which he had 6459
33:22 for Amon sacrificed unto all the c images 6456
34: 3 and the c images, and the molten images. 6456
34: 4 and the c images, and the molten images, 6456
Ps 74: 6 now they break down the c work thereof at 6603
Pr 7:16 *with* c *works, with* fine linen of Egypt. 2405

CARVING (2) [CARVED, CARVINGS]
Ex 31: 5 of stones, to set *them,* and in c of timber, 2799
35:33 of stones, to set *them,* and in c of wood, 2799

CARVINGS (1) [CARVING]
1Ki 6:32 he carved upon them c of cherubims and 4734

CASE (8) [CASES]
Ex 5:19 see *that* they *were* in evil c, after it was said, NIH
Dt 19: 4 this *is* the c of the slayer, which shall flee 1697
22: 1 thou shalt in any c bring them again 7725+7725
24:13 In any c thou shalt deliver him the
pledge again 7725+7725
Ps 144:15 Happy *is that* people, that is in such a c: 3602
Mt 5:20 ye shall in no c enter into the kingdom of *3364*
19:10 If the c of the man be so with *his* wife, it is *156*
Jn 5: 6 now a long time *in that* c, he saith unto him, NIG

CASEMENT (1)
Pr 7: 6 window of my house I looked through my c, 822

CASES (1) [CASE]
1Co 7:15 or a sister is not under bondage in such c: NIG

CASIPHIA (2)
Ezr 8:17 unto Iddo the chief at the place C, 3703
8:17 his brethren the Nethinims, at the place C, 3703

CASLUHIM (2)
Ge 10:14 Pathrusim, and C, (out of whom came 3695
1Ch 1:12 Pathrusim, and C, (of whom came 3695

CASLUHITES See CASLUHIM

CASSIA (3)
Ex 30:24 of c five hundred *shekels,* after the shekel 6916
Ps 45: 8 and aloes, *and* c, out of the ivory palaces, 7102
Eze 27:19 bright iron, c, and calamus, were in thy 6916

CAST (501) [CASTAWAY, CASTEDST, CASTEST, CASTETH, CASTING, OUTCAST, OUTCASTS]
Ge 21:10 C out this bondwoman and her son: 1644
21:15 and she c the child under one of the shrubs. 7993
31:38 and thy she goats have not c their young, 7921
31:51 which I have c betwixt me and thee; 3384

Book	Ref	Context	No.
Ge	37:20	and **c** him into some pit, and we will say,	7993
	37:22	**c** him into this pit that *is* in the wilderness,	7993
	37:24	they took him, and **c** him into a pit: and	7993
	39:7	that his master's wife **c** her eyes upon	5375
Ex	1:22	Every son that is born ye shall **c** into	7993
	4:3	he said, **C** it on the ground. And he cast it	7993
	4:3	he **c** it on the ground, and it became a	7993
	4:25	of her son, and **c** *it* at his feet, and said,	5060
	7:9	**c** *it* before Pharaoh, *and* it shall become a	7993
	7:10	Aaron **c** **down** his rod before Pharaoh, and	7993
	7:12	For they **c** **down** every man his rod, and	7993
	10:19	the locusts, and **c** them into the Red sea;	8628
	15:4	and his host hath he **c** into the sea:	3384
	15:25	*which* when he had **c** into the waters,	7993
	22:31	*beasts* in the field; ye shall **c** it to the dogs.	7993
	23:26	There shall nothing **c** their **young**, nor be	7921
	25:12	thou shalt **c** four rings of gold for it, and	3332
	26:37	thou shalt **c** five sockets of brass for them.	3332
	32:19	he **c** the tables out of his hands, and	7993
	32:24	I **c** it into the fire, and there came out this	7993
	34:24	For I will **c** **out** the nations before thee, and	3423
	36:36	and he **c** for them four sockets of silver.	3332
	37:3	he **c** for it four rings of gold, *to be set* by	3332
	37:13	he **c** for it four rings of gold, and put	3332
	38:5	he **c** four rings for the four ends of the grate	3332
	38:27	of the hundred talents of silver were **c**	3332
Lev	1:16	**c** it beside the altar on the east part, by	7993
	14:40	they shall **c** them into an unclean place	7993
	16:8	Aaron shall **c** lots upon the two goats;	5414
	18:24	are defiled which I **c** **out** before you:	7971
	20:23	of the nation, which I **c** **out** before you:	7971
	26:30	**c** your carcases upon the carcases of your	5414
	26:44	I will not **c** them **away**, neither will I abhor	3988
Nu	19:6	**c** *it* into the midst of the burning of	7993
	35:22	have **c** upon him any thing without laying	7993
	35:23	**c** *it* upon him, that he die, and *was* not his	5307
Dt	6:19	To **c** **out** all thine enemies from before	1920
	7:1	hath **c** **out** many nations before thee,	5394
	9:4	thy God hath **c** them **out** from before thee,	1920
	9:17	**c** them out of my two hands, and	7993
	9:21	I **c** the dust thereof into the brook that	7993
	28:40	*with* the oil; for thine olive shall **c** *his fruit*.	5394
	29:28	**c** them into another land, as *it is* this day.	7993
Jos	8:29	**c** it at the entering of the gate of the city,	7993
	10:11	that the LORD **c** **down** great stones from	7993
	10:27	**c** them into the cave wherein they had been	7993
	13:12	for these did Moses smite, and **c** them **out**.	3423
	18:6	that I may **c** lots for you here before	3384
	18:8	that I may here **c** lots for you before	7993
	18:10	Joshua **c** lots for them in Shiloh before	7993
Jdg	6:28	the altar of Baal was **c** **down**, and the grove	5422
	6:30	because he hath **c** **down** the altar of Baal,	5422
	6:31	because *one* hath **c** **down** his altar.	5422
	8:25	did **c** therein every man the earrings of his	7993
	9:53	a certain woman **c** a piece of a millstone	7993
	15:17	that he **c** **away** the jawbone out of his hand,	7993
1Sa	14:42	**C** *lots* between me and Jonathan my son.	5307
	18:11	Saul **c** the javelin; for he said, I will smite	2904
	20:33	Saul **c** a javelin at him to smite him:	2904
2Sa	1:21	the shield of the mighty is **vilely** **c** **away**,	1602
	11:21	did not a woman **c** a piece of a millstone	7993
	16:6	he **c** stones at David, and at all the servants	5619
	16:13	and threw stones at him, and **c** dust.	6080
	18:17	**c** him into a great pit in the wood, and	7993
	20:12	*into* the field, and **c** a cloth upon him,	7993
	20:15	they **c** **up** a bank against the city, and	8210
	20:22	the son of Bichri, and **c** *it* **out** to Joab.	7993
1Ki	7:15	For he **c** two pillars *of* brass, of eighteen	6696
	7:24	the knops *were* **c** *in* two rows, when it was	3332
	7:24	knops *were* cast *in* two rows, when it was **c**.	3333
	7:46	In the plain of Jordan did the king **c** them,	3332
	9:7	for my name, will I **c** **out** of my sight;	7971
	13:24	his carcase was **c** in the way, and the ass	7993
	13:25	saw the carcase **c** in the way, and the lion	7993
	13:28	he went and found his carcase **c** in the way,	7993
	14:9	to anger, and hast **c** me behind thy back:	7993
	14:24	LORD **c** **out** before the children of Israel.	3423
	18:42	he **c** **himself** **down** upon the earth, and	1457
	19:19	passed by him, and **c** his mantle upon him.	7993
	21:26	whom the LORD **c** **out** before the children	3423
2Ki	2:16	**c** him upon some mountain, or into some	7993
	2:21	**c** the salt **in** there, and said, Thus saith	7993
	3:25	*on* every good piece of land **c** every man	7993
	4:41	he **c** *it* into the pot; and he said, Pour out	7993
	6:6	he cut down a stick, and **c** *it* **in** thither;	7993
	7:15	which the Syrians had **c** **away** in their	7993
	9:25	**c** him in the portion of the field of Naboth	7993
	9:26	**c** him into the plat *of ground*, according to	7993
	10:25	the guard and the captains **c** *them* **out**, and	7993
	13:21	they **c** the man into the sepulchre of Elisha:	7993
	13:23	neither **c** he them from his presence as yet.	7993
	16:3	whom the LORD **c** **out** from before	3423
	17:8	whom the LORD **c** **out** from before	3423
	17:20	until *he* had **c** them out of his sight.	7993
	19:18	have **c** their gods into the fire: for they *were*	5414
	19:32	before it *with* shield, nor **c** a bank against it.	8210
	21:2	whom the LORD **c** **out** before the children	3423
	23:6	**c** the powder thereof upon the graves of	7993
	23:12	**c** the dust of them into the brook Kidron.	7993
	23:27	will **c** **off** this city Jerusalem which I have	3988
	24:20	until he had **c** them **out** from his presence,	7993
1Ch	24:31	These likewise **c** lots over against their	5307
	25:8	they **c** lots, ward against *ward*, as well	5307
	26:13	they **c** lots, as well the small as the great,	5307
	26:14	his son, a wise counseller, they **c** lots;	5307
	28:9	forsake him, he will **c** thee **off** for ever.	2186
2Ch	4:3	Two rows *of* oxen *were* **c**, when it was cast.	3332
	4:3	Two rows *of* oxen *were* cast, when it was **c**.	4166
	4:17	In the plain of Jordan did the king **c** them,	3332
	7:20	will I **c** **out** of my sight, and will make it to	7993
	11:14	his sons had **c** them **off** from executing	2186
	13:9	Have ye not **c** **out** the priests of	5080
	20:11	to come to **c** us **out** of thy possession,	1644
	24:10	and brought in, and **c** into the chest,	7993
	25:8	for God hath power to help, and to **c** **down**.	3782
2Ch	25:12	**c** them **down** from the top of the rock,	7993
	26:14	and bows, and slings to **c** stones.	NIH
	28:3	had **c** **out** before the children of Israel.	3423
	29:19	which king Ahaz in his reign did **c** **away** in	2186
	30:14	and **c** *them* into the brook Kidron.	7993
	33:2	whom the LORD had **c** **out** before	3423
	33:15	in Jerusalem, and **c** *them* out of the city.	7993
Ne	1:9	though there were of you **c** **out** unto	5080
	6:16	they were much **c** **down** in their own eyes:	5307
	9:26	**c** thy law behind their backs, and slew thy	7993
	10:34	we **c** the lots *among* the priests, the Levites,	5307
	11:1	the rest of the people also **c** lots, to bring	5307
	13:8	I **c** **forth** all the household stuff of Tobiah	7993
Est	3:7	they **c** Pur, that *is*, the lot, before Haman	5307
	9:24	had **c** Pur, that *is*, the lot, to consume them,	5307
Job	8:4	he have **c** them **away** for their	7971
	8:20	God will not **c** **away** a perfect *man*, neither	3988
	15:33	and shall **c** **off** his flower as the olive.	7993
	18:7	and his own counsel shall **c** him **down**.	7993
	18:8	For he is **c** into a net by his own feet, and	7971
	20:15	up again: God shall **c** them **out** of his belly.	3423
	20:23	*God* shall **c** the fury of his wrath upon him,	7971
	22:29	When *men* are **c** **down**, then thou shalt say,	8213
	27:22	For *God* shall **c** upon him, and not spare:	7993
	29:24	light of my countenance they **c** not **down**.	5307
	30:19	He hath **c** me into the mire, and I am	3384
	39:3	their young ones, they **c** **out** their sorrows.	7971
	40:11	**C** **abroad** the rage of thy wrath: and	6327
	41:9	shall *not one* be **c** **down** even at the sight of	2904
Ps	2:3	and **c** **away** their cords from us.	7993
	5:10	**c** them **out** in the multitude of their	5080
	17:13	O LORD, disappoint him, **c** him **down**:	3766
	18:42	I did **c** them **out** as the dirt in the streets.	7324
	22:10	I was **c** upon thee from the womb: thou *art*	7993
	22:18	among them, and **c** lots upon my vesture.	5307
	36:12	they are **c** **down**, and shall not be able to	1760
	37:14	to **c** **down** the poor and needy, *and* to slay	5307
	37:24	he fall, he shall not be **utterly** **c** **down**:	2904
	42:5	Why art thou **c** **down**, O my soul? and	7817
	42:6	O my God, my soul is **c** **down** within me:	7817
	42:11	Why art thou **c** **down**, O my soul? and	7817
	43:2	why dost thou **c** me **off**? why go I	2186
	43:5	Why art thou **c** **down**, O my soul? and	7817
	44:2	didst afflict the people, and **c** them **out**.	7971
	44:9	thou hast **c** **off**, and put us to shame; and	2186
	44:23	O Lord? arise, **c** *us* not **off** for ever.	2186
	51:11	**C** me not **away** from thy presence; and	7993
	55:3	for they **c** iniquity upon me, and in wrath	4131
	55:22	**C** thy burden upon the LORD, and	7993
	56:7	in *thine* anger **c** **down** the people, O God.	3381
	60:1	O God, thou hast **c** us **off**, thou hast	2186
	60:8	over Edom will I **c** **out** my shoe:	7993
	60:10	*Wilt* not thou, O God, *which* hadst **c** us **off**?	2186
	62:4	They only consult to **c** *him* **down** from his	5080
	71:9	**C** me not **off** in the time of old age;	7993
	74:1	O God, why hast thou **c** *us* **off** for ever?	2186
	74:7	They have **c** fire into thy sanctuary,	7971
	76:6	and horse *are* **c** **into a dead sleep**.	7290
	77:7	Will the Lord **c** **off** for ever? and will he be	2186
	78:49	He **c** upon them the fierceness of his anger,	7971
	78:55	He **c** **out** the heathen also before them, and	1644
	80:8	thou hast **c** **out** the heathen, and planted it.	1644
	89:38	thou hast **c** **off** and abhorred, thou hast been	2186
	89:44	and **c** his throne **down** to the ground.	4048
	94:14	For the LORD will not **c** **off** his people,	5203
	102:10	for thou hast lifted me up, and **c** me **down**.	7993
	108:9	over Edom will I **c** **out** my shoe;	7993
	108:11	*Wilt* not *thou*, O God, *who* hast **c** us **off**?	2186
	140:10	let them be **c** into the fire; into deep pits,	5307
	144:6	**C** **forth** **lightning**, and scatter them:	1299+1300
Pr	1:14	**C** **in** thy lot among us; let us all have one	5307
	7:26	For she hath **c** **down** many wounded: yea,	5307
	16:33	The lot is **c** into the lap; but the whole	2904
	22:10	**C** **out** the scorner, and contention shall go	1644
Ecc	3:5	A time to **c** **away** stones, and a time to	7993
	3:6	a time to keep, and a time to **c** **away**;	7993
	11:1	**C** thy bread upon the waters: for thou shalt	7971
Isa	2:20	In that day a man shall **c** his idols of silver,	7993
	5:24	they have **c** **away** the law of the LORD of	3988
	6:13	when they **c** *their leaves: so* the holy seed	7995
	14:19	thou art **c** out of thy grave like an	7993
	16:2	*that*, as a wandering bird **c** **out** of the nest,	7971
	19:8	all they that **c** angle into the brooks shall	7993
	25:7	the face of the covering **c** over all people,	3874
	26:19	of herbs, and the earth shall **c** **out** the dead.	5307
	28:2	shall **c** **down** to the earth with the hand.	3240
	28:25	doth he not **c** **abroad** the fitches, and	6327
	28:25	**c** in the principal wheat and the appointed	7760
	30:22	thou shalt **c** them **away** as a menstruous	2219
	31:7	For in that day every man shall **c** **away** his	3988
	34:3	Their slain also shall be **c** **out**, and	7993
	34:17	he hath **c** the lot for them, and his hand hath	5307
	37:19	have **c** their gods into the fire: for they *were*	5414
	37:33	it *with* shields, nor **c** a bank against it.	8210
	38:17	for thou hast **c** all my sins behind thy back.	7993
	41:9	I have chosen thee, and not **c** thee **away**.	3988
	57:14	shall say, **C** ye **up**, cast ye up, prepare	5549
	57:14	shall say, Cast ye up, **c** ye **up**, prepare	5549
	57:20	whose waters **c** **up** mire and dirt.	1644
	58:7	that thou bring the poor that are **c** **out** *to thy*	4788
	62:10	**c** **up**, cast up the highway; gather out	5549
	62:10	cast up, **c** **up** the highway; gather out	5549
	66:5	that **c** you **out** for my name's sake, said,	5077
Jer	6:6	and **c** a mount against Jerusalem:	8210
	6:15	time *that* I visit them they shall be **c** **down**,	3782
	7:15	I will **c** you **out** of my sight, as I have cast	7993
	7:15	as I have **c** **out** all your brethren, *even*	7993
	7:29	*O Jerusalem*, and **c** *it* **away**, and take up a	7993
	8:12	of their visitation they shall be **c** **down**,	3782
	9:19	because our dwellings have **c** *us* **out**.	7993
	14:16	shall be **c** **out** in the streets of Jerusalem	7993
	15:1	**c** *them* **out** of my sight, and let them go	7971
	16:13	Therefore will I **c** you out of this land into a	2904
	18:15	to walk *in* paths, *in* a way not **c** **up**;	5549
	22:7	thy choice cedars, and **c** *them* into the fire.	5307
Jer	22:19	and **c** **forth** beyond the gates of Jerusalem.	7993
	22:26	I will **c** thee **out**, and thy mother that bare	2904
	22:28	wherefore are they **c** **out**, he and his seed,	2904
	22:28	and are **c** into a land which they know not?	7993
	23:39	your fathers, *and* **c** *you* out of my presence:	NIH
	26:23	**c** his dead body into the graves of	7993
	28:16	I will **c** thee from off the face of the earth:	7971
	31:37	I will also **c** **off** all the seed of Israel for all	3988
	33:24	hath chosen, he hath even **c** them **off**?	3988
	33:26	will I **c** **away** the seed of Jacob, and	3988
	36:23	**c** *it* into the fire that *was* on the hearth,	7993
	36:30	his dead body shall be **c** **out** in the day to	7993
	38:6	**c** him into the dungeon of Malchiah the son	7993
	38:9	whom they have **c** into the dungeon;	7993
	38:11	took thence old **c** **clouts** and old rotten rags,	5499
	38:12	Put now *these* old **c** **clouts** and rotten rags	5499
	41:7	*and* **c** *them* into the midst of the pit, he, and	NIH
	41:9	Now the pit wherein Ishmael had **c** all	7993
	41:14	carried away captive from Mizpah **c** **about**	5437
	50:26	**c** her **up** as heaps, and destroy her utterly:	5549
	51:34	belly with my delicates, he hath **c** me **out**.	1740
	51:63	to it, and **c** it into the midst of Euphrates:	7993
	52:3	till he had **c** them **out** from his presence,	7993
La	2:1	**c** **down** from heaven *unto* the earth	7993
	2:7	The Lord hath **c** **off** his altar, he hath	2186
	2:10	they have **c** **up** dust upon their heads;	5927
	3:31	For the Lord will not **c** **off** for ever:	2186
	3:53	life in the dungeon, and **c** a stone upon me.	3034
Eze	4:2	a fort against it, and **c** a mount against it;	8210
	5:4	**c** them into the midst of the fire, and	7993
	6:4	I will **c** **down** your slain *men* before your	5307
	7:19	They shall **c** their silver in the streets, and	7993
	11:16	Although I have **c** them **far off** among	7368
	15:4	Behold, it is **c** into the fire for fuel; the fire	5414
	16:5	thou wast **c** **out** in the open field, to	7993
	18:31	**C** **away** from you all your transgressions,	7993
	19:12	she was **c** **down** to the ground, and the east	7993
	20:7	**C** ye **away** every man the abominations of	7993
	20:8	they did not every man **c** **away**	7993
	21:22	the gates, to **c** a mount, *and* to build a fort.	8210
	23:35	**c** me behind thy back, therefore bear thou	7993
	26:8	**c** a mount against thee, and lift up	8210
	27:30	and shall **c** **up** dust upon their heads,	5927
	28:16	I will **c** thee **as profane** out of the mountain	2490
	28:17	I will **c** thee to the ground, I will lay thee	7993
	31:16	when I **c** him **down** to hell with them that	3381
	32:4	I will **c** thee **forth** upon the open field, and	2904
	32:18	**c** them **down**, *even* her, and the daughters	3381
	36:5	with despiteful minds, to **c** it **out** for a prey.	4054
	43:24	the priests shall **c** salt upon them, and	7993
Da	3:6	worshippeth shall the same hour be **c** into	7412
	3:11	*that* he should be **c** into the midst of a	7412
	3:15	ye shall be **c** the same hour into the midst	7412
	3:20	to **c** *them* into the burning fiery furnace.	7412
	3:21	were **c** into the midst of the burning fiery	7412
	3:24	Did not we **c** three men bound into	7412
	6:7	O king, he shall be **c** into the den of lions.	7412
	6:12	O king, shall be **c** into the den of lions?	7412
	6:16	and **c** *him* into the den of lions.	7412
	6:24	they **c** *them* into the den of lions, them,	7412
	7:9	I beheld till the thrones were **c** *down*, and	7412
	8:7	he **c** him **down** to the ground, and	7993
	8:10	it **c** **down** *some* of the host and of the stars	5307
	8:11	and the place of his sanctuary was **c** **down**.	7993
	8:12	and it **c** **down** the truth to the ground;	7993
	11:12	and he shall **c** **down** *many* ten thousands:	5307
	11:15	**c** **up** a mount, and take the most fenced	8210
Hos	8:3	Israel hath **c** **off** *the thing that is* good:	2186
	8:5	Thy calf, O Samaria, hath **c** *thee* **off**;	2186
	9:17	My God will **c** them **away**, because	3988
	14:5	the lily, and **c** **forth** his roots as Lebanon.	5221
Joel	1:7	he hath made it clean bare, and **c** *it* **away**;	7993
	3:3	they have **c** lots for my people; and	3032
Am	1:11	did **c** **off** all pity, and his anger did tear	7843
	4:3	ye shall **c** *them* into the palace, saith	7993
	8:3	they shall **c** *them* **forth** with silence.	7993
	8:8	it shall be **c** **out** and drowned, as *by*	1644
Ob	1:11	**c** lots upon Jerusalem, even thou *wast* as	3032
Jnh	1:5	**c** **forth** the wares that *were* in the ship	2904
	1:7	one to his fellow, Come, and let us **c** lots,	5307
	1:7	So they **c** lots, and the lot fell upon Jonah.	5307
	1:12	Take me up, and **c** me **forth** into the sea;	2904
	1:15	took up Jonah, and **c** him **forth** into the sea:	2904
	2:3	For thou hadst **c** me *into* the deep, in	7993
	2:4	I said, I am **c** **out** of thy sight; yet I will	1644
Mic	2:5	Therefore thou shalt have none that shall **c**	7993
	2:9	The women of my people have ye **c** **out**	1644
	4:7	and her that was **c** **far off** a strong nation:	1972
	7:19	thou wilt **c** all their sins into the depths of	7993
Na	3:6	I will **c** abominable filth upon thee, and	7993
	3:10	they **c** lots for her honourable *men*, and	3032
Zep	3:15	thy judgments, he hath **c** **out** thine enemy:	6437
Zec	1:21	to **c** **out** the horns of the Gentiles,	3034
	5:8	he **c** it into the midst of the ephah; and	7993
	5:8	he **c** the weight of lead upon the mouth	7993
	9:4	the Lord will **c** her **out**, and he will smite	3423
	10:6	shall be as though I had not **c** them **off**:	2186
	11:13	LORD said unto me, **C** it unto the potter:	7993
	11:13	**c** them to the potter *in* the house of	7993
Mal	3:11	**c** her **fruit before the time** in the field,	7921
Mt	3:10	good fruit is hewn down, and **c** into the fire.	*906*
	4:6	If thou be the Son of God, **c** thyself down:	*906*
	4:12	had heard that John was **c** **into prison**,	*3860*
	5:13	but to be **c** **out**, and to be trodden under foot	*906*
	5:25	thee to the officer, and thou be **c** into prison.	*906*
	5:29	offend thee, pluck it out, and **c** *it* from thee:	*906*
	5:29	not *that* thy whole body should be **c** into	*906*
	5:30	offend thee, cut it off, and **c** *it* from thee:	*906*
	5:30	not *that* thy whole body should be **c** into	*906*
	6:30	to day is, and to morrow is **c** into the oven,	*906*
	7:5	first **c** **out** the beam out of thine own eye;	*1544*
	7:5	shalt thou see clearly to **c** **out** the mote out	*1544*
	7:6	neither **c** ye your pearls before swine,	*906*
	7:19	good fruit is hewn down, and **c** into the fire.	*906*
	7:22	and in thy name have **c** **out** devils?	*1544*

Mt 8:12 kingdom shall be **c out** into outer darkness: *1544*
8:16 and he **c out** the spirits with *his* word, and *1544*
8:31 besought him, saying, If thou **c** us **out**, *1544*
9:33 And when the devil was **c out**, the dumb *1544*
10: 1 to **c** them **out**, and to heal all *manner of* *1544*
10: 8 the lepers, raise the dead, **c out** devils: *1544*
12:24 This *fellow* doth not **c out** devils, but by *1544*
12:26 And if Satan **c out** Satan, he is divided *1544*
12:27 And if I by Beelzebub **c out** devils, *1544*
12:27 by whom do your children **c** *them* **out**? *1544*
12:28 But if I **c out** devils by the Spirit of God, *1544*
13:42 And shall **c** them into a furnace of fire: *906*
13:47 *that was* **c** into the sea, and gathered of every *906*
13:48 the good into vessels, but **c** the bad away. *906*
13:50 And shall **c** them into the furnace of fire: *906*
15:17 into the belly, and is **c out** into the draught? *1544*
15:26 take the children's bread, and to **c** *it* to dogs. *906*
15:30 and **c** them *down* at Jesus' feet; *4496*
17:19 and said, Why could not we **c** him **out**? *1544*
17:27 and **c** a hook, and take up the fish that first *906*
18: 8 cut them off, and **c** *them* from thee: *906*
18: 8 or two feet to be **c** into everlasting fire. *906*
18: 9 offend thee, pluck it out, and **c** *it* from thee: *906*
18: 9 rather than having two eyes to be **c** into hell *906*
18:30 but went and **c** him into prison, till he should *906*
21:12 and **c out** all them that sold and bought in *1544*
21:21 Be thou removed, and be thou **c** into the sea; *906*
21:39 and **c** *him* **out** of the vineyard, and *1544*
22:13 him away, and **c** *him* into outer darkness; *1544*
25:30 And **c** ye the unprofitable servant into outer *1544*
27: 5 And he **c down** the pieces of silver in *4496*
27:35 and upon my vesture did they **c** lots. *906*
27:44 crucified with him, **c** the same **in** his **teeth**. *3679*
Mk 1:34 of divers diseases, and **c out** many devils; *1544*
1:39 throughout all Galilee, and **c out** devils. *1544*
3:15 to heal sicknesses, and to **c out** devils: *1544*
3:23 in parables, How can Satan **c out** Satan? *1544*
4:26 as if a man should **c** seed into the ground, *906*
6:13 And they **c out** many devils, and *1544*
7:26 she besought him that he would **c forth** *1544*
7:27 children's bread, and to **c** *it* unto the dogs. *906*
9:18 to thy disciples that they should **c** him **out**; *1544*
9:22 And ofttimes it hath **c** him into the fire, and *906*
9:28 Why could not we **c** him **out**? *1544*
9:42 about his neck, and he were **c** into the sea. *906*
9:45 than having two feet to be **c** into hell, *906*
9:47 than having two eyes to be **c** into hell fire: *906*
11: 7 colt to Jesus, and **c** their garments **on** him; *1911*
11:15 and began to **c out** them that sold and *1544*
11:23 Be thou removed, and be thou **c** into the sea; *906*
12: 4 and at him they **c stones**, and wounded *him* *3036*
12: 8 killed *him*, and **c** *him* **out** of the vineyard. *1544*
12:41 beheld how the people **c** money into *906*
12:41 and many *that were* rich **c** in much. *906*
12:43 That this poor widow hath **c** more in, *906*
12:43 than all they which have **c** into the treasury: *906*
12:44 For all *they* did **c** in of their abundance; *906*
12:44 but she of her want did **c** in all that she had, *906*
14:51 having a linen cloth **c** about *his* naked *4016*
16: 9 out of whom he had **c** seven devils. *1544*
16:17 In my name shall they **c out** devils; *1544*
Lk 1:29 **c in** her **mind** what manner of salutation *1260*
3: 9 good fruit is hewn down, and **c** into the fire. *906*
4: 9 the Son of God, **c** thyself down from hence: *906*
4:29 that *they* might **c** him **down headlong**. *2630*
6:22 reproach *you*, and **c out** your name as evil, *1544*
6:42 **c out** first the beam out of thine own eye, *1544*
9:25 and lose himself, or be **c away**? *2210*
9:40 And I besought thy disciples to **c** him **out**; *1544*
11:18 ye say that I **c out** devils through *1544*
11:19 And if I by Beelzebub **c out** devils, *1544*
11:19 by whom do your sons **c** *them* **out**? *1544*
11:20 But if I with the finger of God **c out** devils, *1544*
12: 5 which after *he* hath killed hath power to **c** *1685*
12:28 in the field, and to morrow is **c** into the oven; *906*
12:58 the officer, and the officer **c** thee into prison. *906*
13:19 which a man took, and **c** into his garden; *906*
13:32 I **c out** devils, and I do cures to day and *1544*
14:35 nor yet for the dunghill; *but men* **c** it out. *906*
17: 2 and he **c** into the sea, than that he should *4496*
19:35 and they **c** their garments **upon** the colt, *1977*
19:43 that thine enemies shall **c** a trench **about** *4016*
19:45 and began to **c out** them that sold therein, *1544*
20:12 and they wounded him also, and **c** *him* **out**. *1544*
20:15 So they **c** him **out** of the vineyard, and *1544*
21: 3 that this poor widow hath **c in** more than *906*
21: 4 For all these have of their abundance **c** in *906*
21: 4 she of her penury hath **c** in all the living that *906*
22:41 withdrawn from them about a stone's **c**, *1000*
23:19 the city, and *for* murder, was **c** into prison.) *906*
23:25 for sedition and murder was **c** into prison, *906*
23:34 And they parted his raiment, and **c** lots. *906*
Jn 3:24 For John was not yet **c** into prison. *906*
6:37 that cometh to me I will in no wise **c out**. *1544*
8: 7 sin among you, let him first **c** a stone at her. *906*
8:59 Then took they up stones to **c** at him: but *906*
9:34 dost thou teach us? And they **c** him **out**. *1544*
9:35 Jesus heard that they had **c** him **out**; *1544*
12:31 now shall the prince of this world be **c out**. *1544*
15: 6 he is **c** forth as a branch, and is withered; *906*
15: 6 and **c** *them* into the fire, and they are burned. *906*
19:24 Let us not rent it, but **c lots** for it, whose it *2975*
19:24 and for my vesture they did **c** lots. *906*
21: 6 **C** the net on the right side of the ship, and *906*
21: 6 They **c** therefore, and now they were not *906*
21: 7 was naked,) and did **c** himself into the sea. *906*
Ac 7:19 that *they* **c out** their young children, *1570+4160*
7:21 And when he was **c out**, *1620*
7:58 And **c** *him* **out** of the city, and stoned *him:* *1544*
12: 8 **C** thy garment **about** thee, and follow me. *4016*
16:23 they **c** *them* into prison, charging the jailor to *906*
16:37 being Romans, and have **c** *us* into prison; *906*
22:23 and **c** *off their* clothes, and threw dust into *4495*
27:19 And the third *day* we **c** *out* with our own *4496*
27:26 Howbeit we must be **c** upon a certain *1601*
Ac 27:29 they **c** four anchors out of the stern, and *4496*
27:30 under colour as though they would have **c** *1614*
27:38 the ship, and **c out** the wheat into the sea. *1544*
27:43 swim should **c** *themselves* first into *the sea,* *641*
Ro 11: 1 I say then, Hath God **c away** his people? *683*
11: 2 God hath not **c away** his people which he *683*
13:12 let us therefore **c off** the works of darkness, *659*
1Co 7:35 not that I may **c** a snare upon you, but *1911*
2Co 4: 9 not forsaken; **c down**, but not destroyed; *2598*
7: 6 that comforteth *those that are* **c down**, *5011*
Gal 4:30 **C out** the bondwoman and her son: for *1544*
1Ti 5:12 because they have **c off** *their* first faith. *114*
Heb 10:35 **C** not **away** therefore your confidence, *577*
2Pe 2: 4 but **c** *them* **down to hell**, and *5020*
Rev 2:10 the devil shall **c** *some* of you into prison, *906*
2:14 who taught Balac to **c** a stumblingblock *906*
2:22 I *will* **c** her into a bed, and them that commit *906*
4:10 and **c** their crowns before the throne, *906*
8: 5 it with fire of the altar, and **c** *it* into the earth: *906*
8: 7 with blood, and they were **c** upon the earth: *906*
8: 8 burning with fire was **c** into the sea: *906*
12: 4 stars of heaven, and did **c** them to the earth: *906*
12: 9 And the great dragon was **c** *out, that* old *906*
12: 9 he was **c** *out* into the earth, and his angels *906*
12: 9 and his angels were **c** *out* with him. *906*
12:10 for the accuser of our brethren is **c down**, *2598*
12:13 And when the dragon saw that he was **c** unto *906*
12:15 And the serpent **c** out of his mouth water as *906*
12:16 swallowed up the flood which the dragon **c** *906*
14:19 **c** *it* into the great winepress of the wrath of *906*
18:19 And they **c** dust on their heads, and cried, *906*
18:21 great millstone, and **c** *it* into the sea, saying, *906*
19:20 *These* both were **c** alive into a lake of fire *906*
20: 3 And **c** him into the bottomless *pit,* and *906*
20:10 And the devil that deceived them was **c** into *906*
20:14 and hell were **c** into the lake of fire. *906*
20:15 in the book of life was **c** into the lake of fire. *906*

CASTAWAY (1) [AWAY, CAST]
1Co 9:27 preached to others, I myself should be a **c**. *96*

CASTEDST (1) [CAST]
Ps 73:18 *places:* thou **c** them **down** into destruction. 5307

CASTEST (3) [CAST]
Job 15: 4 thou **c off** fear, and restrainest prayer 6565
Ps 50:17 and **c** my words behind thee. 7993
88:14 LORD, why **c** thou **off** my soul? 2186

CASTETH (16) [CAST]
Job 21:10 their cow calveth, and **c** not **her calf**. 7921
Ps 147: 6 he **c** the wicked **down** to the ground. 8213
147:17 He **c forth** his ice like morsels: who can 7993
Pr 10: 3 but he **c away** the substance of the wicked. 1920
19:15 Slothfulness **c into** a deep sleep; and 5307
21:22 **c down** the strength of the confidence 3381
26:18 As a mad *man* who **c** firebrands, arrows, 3384
Isa 40:19 it over with gold, and **c** silver chains. 6884
Jer 6: 7 As a fountain **c out** her waters, so 6979
6: 7 her waters, so she **c out** her wickedness: 6979
Mt 9:34 He **c out** the devils through the prince of *1544*
Mk 3:22 by the prince of the devils **c** he **out** devils. *1544*
Lk 11:15 He **c out** devils through Beelzebub *1544*
1Jn 4:18 is no fear in love; but perfect love **c** out fear: *906*
3Jn 1:10 that would, and **c** *them* out of the church. *1544*
Rev 6:13 *even* as a fig tree **c** her untimely figs, when *906*

CASTING (21) [CAST]
2Sa 8: 2 with a line, **c** them **down** to the ground; 7901
1Ki 7:37 all of them had one **c**, one measure, *and* 4165
Ezr 10: 1 **c** himself **down** before the house of God, 5307
Job 6:21 ye see *my* **c down**, and are afraid. 2866
Ps 74: 7 they have defiled *by* **c** *down* the dwelling NIH
89:39 thou hast profaned his crown *by* **c** *it* to NIH
Eze 17:17 by **c up** mounts, and building forts, to cut 8210
Mic 6:14 thy **c down** *shall be* in the midst of thee; 3445
Mt 4:18 and Andrew his brother, **c** a net into the sea: *906*
27:35 and parted his garments, **c** lots: *906*
Mk 1:16 and Andrew his brother **c** a net into the sea: *906*
9:38 we saw one **c out** devils in thy name, and *1544*
10:50 **c away** his garment, rose, and came to Jesus. *577*
15:24 they parted his garments, **c** lots upon them, *906*
Lk 9:49 we saw one **c out** devils in thy name; *1544*
11:14 And he was **c out** a devil, and it was dumb. *1544*
21: 1 saw the rich *men* **c** their gifts into *906*
21: 2 And he saw also a certain poor widow **c** in *906*
Ro 11:15 For if the **c away** of them *be* the reconciling *580*
2Co 10: 5 **C down** imaginations, and every high thing *2507*
1Pe 5: 7 **C** all your care upon him; for he careth for *1977*

CASTLE (9) [CASTLES]
1Ch 11: 5 Nevertheless David took the **c** of Zion, 4686
11: 7 David dwelt in the **c**; therefore they called 4679
Pr 18:19 and *their* contentions *are* like the bars of a **c**. 759
Ac 21:34 he commanded him to be carried into the **c**. *3925*
21:37 And as Paul was to be led into the **c**, *3925*
22:24 commanded him to be brought into the **c**, *3925*
23:10 among them, and to bring *him* into the **c**. *3925*
23:16 he went and entered into the **c**, and *3925*
23:32 to go with him, and returned to the **c**: *3925*

CASTLES (6) [CASTLE]
Ge 25:16 their names, by their towns, and by their **c**; 2918
Nu 31:10 they dwelt, and all their **goodly c**, with fire. 2918
1Ch 6:54 places throughout their **c** in their coasts, 2918
27:25 the cities, and in the villages, and in the **c**, 4026
2Ch 17:12 he built in Judah **c**, and cities of store. 1003
27: 4 and in the forests he built **c** and towers. 1003

CASTOR (1)
Ac 28:11 in the isle, *whose* sign *was* **C and Pollux**. *1359*

CATCH (15) [CATCHETH, CAUGHT]
Ex 22: 6 **c** in thorns, so that the stacks of corn, or 4672
Jdg 21:21 **c** you every man his wife of the daughters 2414
1Ki 20:33 did hastily **c** *it:* and they said, Thy brother 2480
2Ki 7:12 we shall **c** them alive, and get into the city. 8610
Ps 10: 9 he lieth in wait to **c** the poor: he doth catch 2414
10: 9 he doth **c** the poor, when he draweth him 2414
35: 8 and let his net that he hath hid **c** himself: 3920
109:11 Let the extortioner **c** all that he hath; and 5367
Jer 5:26 setteth snares; they set a trap, they **c** men. 3920
Eze 19: 3 a young lion, and it learned to **c** the prey; 2963
19: 6 learned to **c** the prey, *and* devoured men. 2963
Hab 1:15 they **c** them in their net, and gather them in 1641
Mk 12:13 and of the Herodians, to **c** him in *his* words. *64*
Lk 5:10 Fear not; from henceforth thou shalt **c** men. *2221*
11:54 seeking to **c** something out of his mouth, *2340*

CATCHETH (3) [CATCH]
Lev 17:13 which hunteth and **c** *any* beast or fowl that 6718
Mt 13:19 **c away** that which was sown in his heart. *726*
Jn 10:12 and the wolf **c** them, and scattereth *726*

CATERPILLAR (5) [CATERPILLARS]
1Ki 8:37 blasting, mildew, locust, *or* if there be **c**; 2625
Ps 78:46 He gave also their increase unto the **c**, and 2625
Isa 33: 4 shall be gathered *like* the gathering of the **c**: 2625
Joel 1: 4 the cankerworm hath left hath the **c** eaten. 2625
2:25 and the **c**, and the palmerworm, 2625

CATERPILLARS (4) [CATERPILLAR]
2Ch 6:28 there be blasting, or mildew, locusts, or **c**; 2625
Ps 105:34 and **c**, and that without number, 3218
Jer 51:14 Surely I will fill thee *with* men, as *with* **c**; 3218
51:27 cause the horses to come up as the rough **c**. 3218

CATTLE (153)
Ge 1:24 **c**, and creeping thing, and beast of the earth 929
1:25 **c** after their kind, and every thing that 929
1:26 over the **c**, and over all the earth, and 929
2:20 Adam gave names to all **c**, and to the fowl of 929
3:14 thou *art* cursed above all **c**, and above every 929
4:20 as dwell in tents, and *of such as have* **c**. 4735
6:20 after their kind, and of **c** after their kind, 929
7:14 all the **c** after their kind, and every creeping 929
7:21 of **c**, and of beast, and of every creeping 929
7:23 **c**, and the creeping things, and the fowl of 929
8: 1 and all the **c** that *was* with him in the ark: 929
8:17 of **c**, and of every creeping thing that 929
9:10 of the **c**, and of every beast of the earth with 929
13: 2 Abram *was* very rich in **c**, in silver, and 4735
13: 7 a strife between the herdmen of Abram's **c** 4735
13: 7 Abram's cattle and the herdmen of Lot's **c**: 4735
29: 7 neither *is it* time that the **c** should be 4735
30:29 served thee, and how thy **c** was with me. 4735
30:32 from thence all the speckled and spotted **c**, 7716
30:32 all the brown **c** among the sheep, and 7716
30:39 brought forth **c** ringstraked, speckled, and 6629
30:40 put them not unto Laban's **c**. 6629
30:41 whensoever the stronger **c** did conceive, 6629
30:41 rods before the eyes of the **c** in the gutters, 6629
30:42 when the **c** were feeble, he put *them* not in: 6629
30:43 had much **c**, and maidservants, and 6629
31: 8 be thy wages; then all the **c** bare speckled: 6629
31: 8 be thy hire; then bare all the **c** ringstraked. 6629
31: 9 Thus God hath taken away the **c** of your 4735
31:10 it came to pass at the time that the **c** 6629
31:10 the rams which leaped upon the **c** *were* 6629
31:12 all the rams which leap upon the **c** *are* 6629
31:18 he carried away all his **c**, and all his goods 4735
31:18 which he had gotten, the **c** of his getting, 4735
31:41 thy two daughters, and six years for thy **c**: 6629
31:43 *these* **c** *are* my cattle, and all that thou seest 6629
31:43 *these* cattle *are* my **c**, and all that thou seest 6629
33:14 according as the **c** that goeth before me and 4399
33:17 him a house, and made booths for his **c**: 4735
34: 5 now his sons were with his **c** in the field: 4735
34:23 *Shall* not their **c** and their substance and 4735
36: 6 his **c**, and all his beasts, and all his 4735
36: 7 could not bear them because of their **c**. 4735
46: 6 they took their **c**, and their goods, 4735
46:32 for their **trade** hath been **to feed c**; 376+4735
46:34 Thy servants' **trade** hath been **about c** 376+4735
47: 6 then make them rulers over my **c**. 4735
47:16 Joseph said, Give your **c**; and I will give 4735
47:16 I will give you for your **c**, if money fail. 4735
47:17 they brought their **c** unto Joseph: and 4735
47:17 and for the **c** of the herds, and for the asses: 4735
47:17 he fed them with bread for all their **c** for 4735
47:18 is spent; my lord also had our herds of **c**; 929
Ex 9: 3 the hand of the LORD is upon thy **c** which 4735
9: 4 the LORD shall sever between the **c** of 4735
9: 4 the cattle of Israel and the **c** of Egypt: 4735
9: 6 on the morrow, and all the **c** of Egypt died: 4735
9: 6 of the **c** of the children of Israel died not 4735
9: 7 there was not one of the **c** of the Israelites 4735
9:19 *and* gather thy **c**, and all that thou hast in 4735
9:20 his servants and his **c** flee into the houses: 4735
9:21 left his servants and his **c** in the field. 4735
10:26 Our **c** also shall go with us; there shall not a 4735
12:29 in the dungeon; and all the firstborn of **c**. 929
12:38 and flocks, and herds, *even* very much **c**. 4735
17: 3 and our children and our **c** with thirst? 4735
20:10 nor thy maidservant, nor thy **c**, 929
34:19 every firstling amongst thy **c**, *whether* ox 4735
Lev 1: 2 ye shall bring your offering of the **c**, *even* of 929
5: 2 or a carcase of unclean **c**, or the carcase of 929
19:19 Thou shalt not let thy **c** gender with a diverse 929
25: 7 for thy **c**, and for the beast that *are* in thy 929
26:22 destroy your **c**, and make you few in 929
Nu 3:41 the **c** of the Levites instead of all 929
3:41 among the **c** of the children of Israel. 929
3:45 the **c** of the Levites instead of their cattle; 929
3:45 the cattle of the Levites instead of their **c**; 929
20: 4 that we and our **c** should die there? 1165
20:19 if I and my **c** drink *of* thy water, then I will 4735
31: 9 took the spoil of all their **c**, and all their 929

Nu 32: 1 of Gad had a very great multitude of c: 4735
32: 1 that behold, the place *was* a place for c; 4735
32: 4 *is* a land for c, and thy servants have cattle: 4735
32: 4 *is* a land for cattle, and thy servants have c: 4735
32:16 We will build sheepfolds here for our c, 4735
32:26 our wives, our flocks, and all our c, 929
35: 3 the suburbs of them shall be for their c, and 929
Dt 2:35 Only the c we took for a prey unto ourselves, 929
3: 7 all the c, and the spoil of the cities, we took 929
3:19 your wives, and your little ones, and your c, 4735
3:19 (*for* I know that ye have much c,) 4735
5:14 nor thine ox, nor thine ass, nor any of thy c, 929
7:14 female barren among you, or among your c. 929
11:15 I will send grass in thy fields for thy c, 929
13:15 and all that *is* therein, and the c thereof, 929
20:14 and the c, and all that is in the city, 929
28: 4 the fruit of thy ground, and the fruit of thy c, 929
28:11 in the fruit of thy c, and in the fruit of thy 929
28:51 he shall eat the fruit of thy c, and the fruit of 929
30: 9 in the fruit of thy c, and in the fruit of thy 929
Jos 1:14 Your wives, your little ones, and your c, 4735
8: 2 only the spoil thereof, and the c thereof, 929
8:27 Only the c and the spoil of that city Israel 929
11:14 all the spoil of these cities, and the c, 929
14: 4 to dwell *in,* with their suburbs for their c 4735
21: 2 dwell in, with the suburbs thereof for our c. 929
22: 8 with very much c, with silver, and 4735
Jdg 6: 5 For they came up with their c and 4735
18:21 put the little ones and the c and the carriage 4735
1Sa 23: 5 brought away their c, and smote them with 4735
30:20 *which* they drave before those *other* c, and 4735
1Ki 1: 9 oxen and fat c by the stone of Zoheleth, 4806
1:19 and fat c and sheep in abundance, 4806
1:25 hath slain oxen and fat c and sheep in 4806
2Ki 3: 9 the host, and for the c that followed them. 929
3:17 *both* ye, and your c, and your beasts. 4735
1Ch 5: 9 their c were multiplied in the land of 4735
5:21 they took away their c; *of* their camels fifty 4735
7:21 they came down to take *away* their c. 4735
2Ch 14:15 They smote also the tents of c, and 4735
26:10 for he had much c, both in the low country, 4735
35: 8 six hundred *small* c, and three hundred NIH
35: 9 for passover *offerings* five thousand *small* c, NIH
Ne 9:37 over our c, at their pleasure, and we *are* in 929
10:36 of our c, as it is written in the law, and 929
Job 36:33 the c also concerning the vapour. 4735
Ps 50:10 *is* mine, *and* the c upon a thousand hills. 929
78:48 He gave up their c also to the hail, and 1165
104:14 He causeth the grass to grow for the c, and 929
107:38 and suffereth not their c to decrease. 929
148:10 Beasts, and all c; creeping things, and 929
Ecc 2: 7 I had great possessions of great and small c 1241
Isa 7:25 of oxen, and for the treading of lesser c. 7716
30:23 in that day shall thy c feed *in* large 4735
43:23 Thou hast not brought me the small c of 7716
46: 1 idols were upon the beasts, and upon the c: 929
Jer 9:10 neither can *men* hear the voice of the c; 4735
49:32 a booty, and the multitude of their c a spoil: 4735
Eze 34:17 Behold, I judge between c and cattle, 7716
34:17 Behold, I judge between cattle and c, 7716
34:20 will judge between the fat c and 7716
34:20 the fat cattle and between the lean c. 7716
34:22 and I will judge between c and cattle. 7716
34:22 and I will judge between cattle and c. 7716
38:12 which have gotten c and goods, that dwell 4735
38:13 and gold, to take *away* c and goods, 4735
Joel 1:18 the herds of c are perplexed, because 1241
Jnh 4:11 and their left hand; and *also* much c? 929
Hag 1:11 upon c, and upon all the labour of the hands. 929
Zec 2: 4 walls for the multitude of men and c therein: 929
13: 5 for man taught me *to keep* c from my youth. NIH
Lk 17: 7 having a servant plowing or feeding c, *4165*
Jn 4:12 thereof himself, and his children, and his c? *2353*

CAUDA See CLAUDA

CAUGHT (37) [CATCH]

Ge 22:13 behold behind *him* a ram c in a thicket by his 270
39:12 she c him by his garment, saying, Lie with 8610
Ex 4: 4 and c it, and it became a rod in his hand: 2388
Nu 31:32 rest of the prey which the men of war had c, 962
Jdg 1: 6 c him, and cut off his thumbs and his great 270
8:14 c a young man of the men of Succoth, and 3920
15: 4 Samson went and c three hundred foxes, 3920
21:23 of them that danced, whom they c: 1497
1Sa 17:35 I c *him* by his beard, and smote him, and 2388
2Sa 2:16 they c every one his fellow by the head, 2388
18: 9 his head c hold of the oak, and he was 2388
1Ki 1:50 went, and c hold on the horns of the altar. 2388
1:51 he hath c hold on the horns of the altar, 270
2:28 and c hold on the horns of the altar. 2388
11:30 Ahijah c the new garment that *was* on him, 8610
2Ki 4:27 of God to the hill, she c him by the feet: 2388
2Ch 22: 9 and they c him, (for he *was* hid in Samaria,) 3920
Pr 7:13 So she c him, and kissed him, and with an 2388
Ecc 9:12 and as the birds that are c in the snare; 270
Jer 50:24 also c, because thou hast striven against 8610
Mt 14:31 and c him, and said unto him, O thou of *1949*
21:39 And they c him, and cast *him* out of *2983*
Mk 12: 3 And they c him, and beat *him,* and sent *him* *2983*
Lk 8:29 For oftentimes it had c him: and he was *4884*
Jn 21: 3 and that night they c nothing. *4084*
21:10 Bring of the fish which ye have now c. *4084*
Ac 6:12 and came upon *him,* and c him, and *4884*
8:39 the Spirit of the Lord c away Philip, that *726*
16:19 they c Paul and Silas, and drew *them* into *1949*
19:29 and having c Gaius and Aristarchus, men of *4884*
26:21 For these causes the Jews c me in *4815*
27:15 And when the ship was c, and could not *4884*
2Co 12: 2 such a one c up to the third heaven. *726*
12: 4 How that he was c up into paradise, and *726*
12:16 being crafty, I c you with guile. *2983*
1Th 4:17 remain shall be c up together with them in *726*
Rev 12: 5 and her child was c up unto God, and *to* his *726*

CAUL (12) [CAULS]

Ex 29:13 the c *that is* above the liver, and the two 3508
29:22 the c *above* the liver, and the two kidneys, 3508
Lev 3: 4 the c above the liver, with the kidneys, 3508
3:10 the c above the liver, with the kidneys, 3508
3:15 the c above the liver, with the kidneys, 3508
4: 9 the c above the liver, with the kidneys, 3508
7: 4 the c *that is* above the liver, with 3508
8:16 the c *above* the liver, and the two kidneys, 3508
8:25 the c *above* the liver, and the two kidneys, 3508
9:10 and the c above the liver of the sin offering, 3508
9:19 and the kidneys, and the c *above* the liver: 3508
Hos 13: 8 will rent the c of their heart, and there will I 5458

CAULS (1) [CAUL]

Isa 3:18 ornaments *about their feet,* and *their* c, 7636

CAUSE (328) [CAUSED, CAUSELESS, CAUSES, CAUSEST, CAUSETH, CAUSEWAY, CAUSING]

Ge 7: 4 I will c it to rain upon the earth forty days 4305
45: 1 he cried, C every man to go out from me. 3318
Ex 8: 5 c frogs to come up upon the land of Egypt. 5927
9:16 in very deed for this c have I raised 5668+871.1
9:18 to morrow about *this* time I will c it to rain 4305
21:19 shall c *him* to be thoroughly healed. 7495+7495
22: 5 man shall c a field or vineyard to be eaten, 1197
22: 9 the c of both parties shall come before 1697
23: 2 neither shalt thou speak in a c to decline 7379
23: 3 shalt thou countenance a poor *man* in his c. 7379
23: 6 not wrest the judgment of thy poor in his c. 7379
27:20 for the light, to c the lamp to burn always. 5927
29:10 thou shalt c a bullock to be brought before 7126
Lev 14:41 he shall c the house to be scraped within 7106
19:29 thy daughter, to c her to be a whore; 2181
24: 2 to c the lamps to burn continually. 5927
24:19 if a man c a blemish in his neighbour; as he 5414
25: 9 c the trumpet of the jubile to sound on 5674
26:16 consume the eyes, and c sorrow of heart: 1727
Nu 5:24 he shall c the woman to drink the bitter 8248
5:26 afterward shall c the woman to drink 8248
16: 5 and will c *him* to come near unto him: 7126
16: 5 chosen will he c to come near unto him. 7126
16:11 For which c *both* thou and all thy 3651+3807.1
27: 5 Moses brought their c before the LORD. 4941
27: 7 c the inheritance of their father to pass unto 5674
27: 8 ye shall c his inheritance to pass unto his 5674
28: 7 c the strong wine to be poured unto 5258
35:30 testify against *any* person *to* c *him* to die. NIH
Dt 1:17 the c that is too hard for you, bring *it* unto 1697
1:38 for he shall c Israel to inherit it. 5157
3:28 he shall c them to inherit the land which 5157
12:11 shall choose to c his name to dwell there; 7931
17:16 nor c the people to return to Egypt, to 7725
24: 4 thou shalt not c the land to sin, which 2398
25: 2 that the judge shall c him to lie down, and 5307
28: 7 The LORD shall c thine enemies that rise 5414
28:25 The LORD shall c thee *to be* smitten 5414
31: 7 and thou shalt c them to inherit it. 5157
Jos 5: 4 this *is* the c why Joshua did circumcise: 1697
20: 4 shall declare his c in the ears of the elders 1697
23: 7 nor c to swear *by them,* neither serve them, 7650
1Sa 17:29 What have I now done? *Is there* not a c? 1697
19: 5 innocent blood, to slay David without a c? 2600
24:15 plead my c, and deliver me out of thine 7379
25:39 that hath pleaded the c of my reproach from 7379
28: 9 thou a snare for my life, to c me to die? 4191
2Sa 3:35 when all the people came to c David to eat 1262
13:13 I, whither shall I c my shame to go? 1980
13:16 she said unto him, *There is* no c: this evil in 182
15: 4 hath *any* suit or c might come unto me, 4941
1Ki 1:33 c Solomon my son to ride upon mine own 7392
5: 9 will c them to be discharged there, and 5310
8:31 an oath be laid upon him to c him to swear, 422
8:45 and their supplication, and maintain their c. 4941
8:49 thy dwelling place, and maintain their c, 4941
8:59 that *he* maintain the c of his servant, and 4941
8:59 the c of his people Israel at all times, as 4941
11:27 this *was* the c that he lift up *his* hand 1697
12:15 for the c was from the LORD, that *he* 5438
2Ki 19: 7 I will c him to fall by the sword in his own 5307
1Ch 21: 3 why will he be a c of trespass to Israel? 819
2Ch 6:35 and their supplication, and maintain their c. 4941
6:39 maintain their c, and forgive thy people 4941
10:15 for the c was of God, that the LORD 5252
19:10 what c soever shall come to you of your 7379
32:20 for this c Hezekiah the king, and the prophet NIH
Ezr 4:15 for which *c* was this city destroyed. NIH
4:21 now commandment to c these men to cease, 989
5: 5 that they could not c them to cease, till 989
Ne 4:11 and slay them, and c the work to cease. 7673
6: 6 for which c thou buildest the wall, 3651+5921
13:26 even him did outlandish women c to sin. 2398
Est 3:13 to destroy, to kill, and to c to perish, all Jews, 6
5: 5 the king said, C Haman to make haste, 4116
8:11 their life, to destroy, to slay, and to c to perish, 6
Job 2: 3 me against him, to destroy him without c. 2600
5: 8 and unto God would I commit my c: 1700
6:24 c me to understand wherein I have erred. 995
9:17 and multiplieth my wounds without c. 2600
13:18 Behold now, I have ordered *my* c; I know 4941
20: 2 Therefore do my thoughts c me to answer, 7725
23: 4 I would order *my* c before him, and fill my 4941
24: 7 They c the naked to lodge without clothing, 3885
24:10 They c *him* to go naked without clothing, 1980
29:16 and the c *which* I knew not I searched out. 7379
31:13 If I did despise the c of my manservant or 4941
34:11 c every man to find according to *his* ways. 4672
34:28 So that *they* c the cry of the poor to come 935
38:26 To c it to rain on the earth, *where* no man 4305
38:27 c the bud of the tender herb to spring forth? 6779
Ps 7: 4 I have delivered him that without c is mine 7387
9: 4 thou hast maintained my right and my c; 1779
10:17 their heart, thou wilt c thine ear to hear: 7181
25: 3 be ashamed which transgress without c. 7387
35: 1 Plead *my* c, O LORD, with them that NIH
35: 7 For without c have they hid for me their 2600
35: 7 *which* without c they have digged for my 2600
35:19 wink *with* the eye that hate me without a c. 2600
35:23 *even* unto my c, my God and my Lord. 7379
35:27 and be glad, that favour my righteous c: 6664
43: 1 and plead my c against an ungodly nation: 7379
67: 1 *and* c his face to shine upon us; Selah. 215
69: 4 They that hate me without a c are moe than 2600
71: 2 in thy righteousness, and c me to escape: 6403
74:22 Arise, O God, plead thine own c: 7379
76: 8 Thou didst c judgment to be heard from 8085
80: 3 us again, O God, and c thy face to shine; 215
80: 7 O God *of* hosts, and c thy face to shine; 215
80: 9 didst c it to take deep root, and 8327+8328
80:19 O LORD God *of* hosts, c thy face to shine; 215
85: 4 and c thine anger towards us to cease. 6565
109: 3 and fought against me without a c. 2600
119:78 they dealt perversely with me without a c: 8267
119:154 Plead my c, and deliver me: quicken me 7379
119:161 Princes have persecuted me without a c: 2600
140:12 I know that the LORD will maintain the c 1779
143: 8 C me to hear thy lovingkindness in 8085
143: 8 c me to know the way wherein I should 3045
Pr 1:11 us lurk privily for the innocent without c: 2600
3:30 Strive not with a man without c, if he have 2600
4:16 is taken away, unless they c *some* to fall. 3782
8:21 That *I* may c those that love me to inherit 5157
18:17 *He that is* first in his own c *seemeth* just; 7379
22:23 For the LORD will plead their c, and 7379
23:11 *is* mighty; he shall plead their c with thee. 7379
23:29 who hath wounds without c? who hath 2600
24:28 a witness against thy neighbour without c; 2600
25: 9 Debate thy c with thy neighbour *himself;* 7379
29: 7 The righteous considereth the c of the poor: 1779
31: 8 Open thy mouth for the dumb in the c of all 1779
31: 9 and plead the c of the poor and needy. 1777
Ecc 2:20 c my heart to despair of all the labour 2976
5: 6 Suffer not thy mouth to c thy flesh to sin; 2398
7:10 What is *the* c that the former days were NIH
10: 1 c the ointment of the apothecary
to send forth 5042
SS 8: 2 I would c thee to drink of spiced wine, 8248
8:13 hearken to thy voice: c me to hear *it.* 8085
Isa 1:23 neither doth the c of the widow come unto 7379
3:12 they which lead thee c *thee* to err, and 8582
9:16 For the leaders of this people c *them* to err; 8582
10:30 c *it* to be heard unto Laish, O poor 7181
13:10 and the moon shall not c her light to shine. 5050
13:11 I will c the arrogancy of the proud to cease, 7673
27: 6 c them that come of Jacob to take root: 8327
28:12 rest *wherewith* ye may c the weary to rest; 5117
30:11 c the Holy One of Israel to cease from 7673
30:30 shall c his glorious voice to be heard, 8085
32: 6 and he will c the drink of the thirsty to fail. 2637
37: 7 I will c him to fall by the sword in his own 5307
41:21 Produce your c, saith the LORD; 7379
42: 2 nor c his voice to be heard in the street. 8085
49: 8 to c to inherit the desolate heritages; 5157
51:22 thy God *that* pleadeth the c of his people, 7378
52: 4 Assyrian oppressed them without c. 657+871.1
58:14 I will c thee to ride upon the high places of 7392
61:11 c righteousness and praise to spring forth 6779
66: 9 bring to the birth, and not c to bring forth? 3205
66: 9 shall I c to bring forth, and shut 3205
Jer 3:12 I will not c mine anger to fall upon you: 5307
5:28 they judge not the c, the cause of 1779
5:28 the c of the fatherless, yet they prosper; 1779
7: 3 and I will c you to dwell in this place. 7931
7: 7 will I c you to dwell in this place, in 7931
7:34 will I c to cease from the cities of Judah, 7673
11:20 for unto thee have I revealed my c. 7379
13:16 before he c darkness, and before your feet 2821
14:22 the vanities of the Gentiles that can c rain? 1652
15: 4 I will c them to be removed into all 5414
15:11 verily I will c the enemy to entreat thee 6293
16: 9 I will c to cease out of this place in your 7673
16:21 I *will* this once c them to know, 3045
16:21 I will c them to know mine hand and my 3045
17: 4 I will c thee to serve thine enemies in 5647
18: 2 and there I will c thee to hear my words. 8085
19: 7 I will c them to fall by the sword before 5307
19: 9 I will c them to eat the flesh of their sons 398
20:12 on them: for unto thee have I opened my c. 7379
22:16 He judged the c of the poor and needy; then 1779
23:27 Which think to c my people to forget my 7911
23:32 c my people to err by their lies, and 8582
25:15 c all the nations, to whom I send thee,
to drink 8248
29: 8 to your dreams which ye c to be dreamed. 2492
30: 3 I will c them to return to the land that I 7725
30:13 *There is* none to plead thy c, that thou 1779
30:21 I will c him to draw near, and he shall 7126
31: 2 *even* Israel when *I* went to c him to rest. 7280
31: 9 I will c them to walk by the rivers of 1980
32:35 c their sons and their daughters
to pass through 5674
32:35 do this abomination, to c Judah to sin. 2398
32:37 and I will c them to dwell safely: 3427
32:44 for I will c their captivity to return, 7725
33: 7 c the captivity of Judah and the captivity of
Israel to return, 7725
33:11 For I will c to return the captivity of 7725
33:15 c the Branch of righteousness to grow up 6779
33:26 for I will c their captivity to return, 7725
34:22 and c them to return to this city; 7725
36:29 shall c to cease from thence man and 7673
37:20 that thou c me not to return *to* the house of 7725
38:23 thou shalt c this city to be burnt with fire. 8313
38:26 that *he* would not c me to return *to* 7725
42:12 and c you to return to your own land. 7725
48:12 that shall c him to wander, and shall empty 6808
48:35 Moreover I will c to cease in Moab, 7673
49: 2 that I will c an alarm of war to be heard in 8085
49:37 For I will c Elam to be dismayed before 2865

Jer 50: 9 **c to come up** against Babylon an assembly 5927
50:34 he shall throughly plead their **c**, that he may 7379
51:27 **c** the horses **to come up** as the rough 5927
51:36 I *will* plead thy **c**, and take vengeance for 7379
La 3:32 though he **c grief**, yet will he have 3013
3:36 To subvert a man in his **c**, the Lord 7379
3:52 chased me sore, like a bird, **without c**. 2600
3:59 thou hast seen my wrong: judge thou my **c**. 4941
Eze 3: 3 **c** thy belly **to eat**, and fill thy bowels with 398
5: 1 **c** *it* **to pass** upon thine head and upon thy 5674
5:13 I will **c** my fury **to rest** upon them, and 5117
9: 1 **C** them that have charge over the city
to draw near, 7126
14:15 If I **c** noisome beasts **to pass** through 5674
14:23 done **without c** all that I have done in it, 2600
16: 2 **c** Jerusalem **to know** her abominations, 3045
16:21 delivered them to **c** them **to pass through** 5674
16:41 I will **c** thee **to cease** from playing 7673
20: 4 wilt thou judge *them?* **c** them **to know** 3045
20:37 I will **c** you **to pass** under the rod, and 5674
21:17 hands together, and I will **c** my fury **to rest**: 5117
21:30 Shall I **c** *it* **to return** into his sheath? I will 7725
23:48 Thus will I **c** lewdness **to cease** out of 7673
24: 8 That *it* might **c** fury **to come up** to take 5927
24:26 to **c** *thee* **to hear** *it* with *thine* ears? 2045
25: 7 and I will **c** thee **to perish** out of the countries: 6
26: 3 will **c** many nations **to come up** against 5927
26:13 I will **c** the noise of thy songs **to cease**; 7673
26:17 which **c** their terror *to be* on all that haunt 5414
27:30 shall **c** their voice **to be heard** against thee, 8085
29: 4 I will **c** the fish of thy rivers **to stick** unto 1692
29:14 will **c** them **to return** *into* the land of 7725
29:21 **c** the horn of the house of Israel **to bud forth**, 6779
30:13 I will **c** *their* images **to cease** out of Noph; 7673
30:22 I will **c** the sword **to fall** out of his hand. 5307
32: 4 will **c** all the fowls of the heaven **to remain** 7931
32:12 of the mighty will I **c** thy multitude **to fall**, 5307
32:14 **c** their rivers **to run** like oil, saith the Lord 1980
34:10 and **c** them **to cease** from feeding the flock; 7673
34:15 my flock, and I will **c** them **to lie down**, 7257
34:25 will **c** the evil beasts **to cease** out of 7673
34:26 I will **c** the shower **to come down** in his 3381
36:12 Yea, I will **c** men **to walk** upon you, 1980
36:15 Neither will I **c** *men* **to hear** in thee 8085
36:15 neither shalt thou **c** thy nations **to fall** any 3782
36:27 **c** you to walk in my statutes, and ye shall 6213
36:33 I will also **c** *you* **to dwell in** the cities, and 3427
37: 5 I *will* **c** breath **to enter** into you, and ye shall 935
37:12 **c** you **to come up** out of your graves, and 5927
39: 2 will **c** thee **to come up** from the north parts, 5927
39: 3 will **c** thine arrows **to fall** out of thy right 5307
44:23 **c** them **to discern** between the unclean and 3045
44:30 that he may **c** the blessing **to rest** in thine 5117
Da 2:12 **For this c** the king was angry 1836+3606+6903
8:25 also he shall **c** craft **to prosper** in his hand; 6743
9:17 **c** thy face **to shine** upon thy sanctuary that is 215
9:27 **c** the sacrifice and the oblation **to cease**, 7673
11:18 **c** the reproach offered by him **to cease**; 7673
11:18 reproach he shall **c** *it* **to turn** upon him. 7725
11:39 he shall **c** them **to rule over** many, and 4910
Hos 1: 4 will **c to cease** the kingdom of the house of 7673
2:11 I will also **c** all her mirth **to cease**, her feast 7673
Joel 2:23 he will **c to come down** for you the rain, 3381
3:11 thither **c** thy mighty ones **to come down**, 5181
Am 5:27 Therefore will I **c** you **to go into captivity** 1540
6: 3 and **c** the seat of violence **to come near**; 5066
8: 9 that I will **c** the sun **to go down** at noon, and 935
Jnh 1: 7 that we may know **for whose c** this 7945+871.1
1: 8 **for** whose **c** this evil *is* upon us; 834+871.1
Mic 7: 9 until he plead my **c**, and execute judgment 7379
Hab 1: 3 me iniquity, and **c** *me* **to behold** grievance? 5027
Zec 8:12 **c** the remnant of this people **to possess** all 5157
13: 2 **c** the prophets and the unclean spirit **to pass** 5674
Mt 5:22 **without a c** shall be in danger of *1500*
5:32 saving for the **c** of fornication, causeth her *3056*
10:21 *their* parents, and **c** them to be put to death. NIG
19: 3 for a man to put away his wife for every **c**? *156*
19: 5 **For this c** shall a man leave father *1752+3778*
Mk 10: 7 **For this c** shall a man leave his *1752+3778*
13:12 and shall **c** them to be put to death. NIG
Lk 8:47 the people for what **c** she had touched him, *156*
21:16 *some* of you shall they **c** to be put to death. NIG
23:22 I have found no **c** of death in him: I will *158*
Jn 12:18 **For this c** the people also met him, *1223+3778*
12:27 but **for this c** came I unto this hour. *1223+3778*
15:25 in their law, They hated me **without a c**. *1432*
18:37 and **for this c** came I into the world, *1519+3778*
Ac 10:21 what *is* the **c** wherefore ye are come? *156*
13:28 And though they found no **c** of death *in him,* *156*
19:40 there being no **c** whereby we may give an *158*
23:28 And when I would have known the **c** *156*
25:14 Festus declared Paul's **c** unto the king, *2596*
28:18 because there was no **c** of death in me. *156*
28:20 For this **c** therefore have I called for you, *156*
Ro 1:26 **For this c** God gave them up unto *1223+3778*
13: 6 For **for this c** pay you tribute also: *1223+3778*
15: 9 **For this c** I will confess to thee *1223+3778*
15:22 **For which c** also I have been much *1352*
16:17 mark them which **c** divisions and offences *4160*
1Co 4:17 **For this c** have I sent unto you *1223+3778*
11:10 **For this c** ought the woman to have *1223+3778*
11:30 **For this c** many *are* weak and *1223+3778*
2Co 4:16 **For which c** we faint not; but though our *1352*
5:13 or whether we be sober, *it is* for your **c**. NIG
7:12 *I did it* not **for** his **c** that had done *1752*
7:12 nor **for** his **c** that suffered wrong, but *1752*
Eph 3: 1 **For** this **c** I Paul, the prisoner of Jesus *5484*
3:14 **For this c** I bow my knees unto the Father *5484*
5:31 **For this c** shall a man leave his father and *473*
Php 2:18 *For* the same **c** also do ye joy, and NIG
Col 1: 9 **For this c** we also, since the day we *1223+3778*
4:16 **c** that it be read also in the church of *4160*
1Th 2:13 **For this c** also thank we God *1223+3778*
3: 5 **For this c**, when I could no longer *1223+3778*
2Th 2:11 And **for this c** God shall send them *1223+3778*
1Ti 1:16 Howbeit **for this c** I obtained mercy, *1223+3778*
2Ti 1:12 For the which **c** I also suffer these *things*: *156*
Tit 1: 5 **For** this **c** left I thee in Crete, that thou *5484*
Heb 2:11 for which **c** he is not ashamed to call them *156*
9:15 And **for this c** he is the mediator of *1223+3778*
1Pe 4: 6 For **for this c** was the gospel *1519+3778*
Rev 12:15 that he might **c** her to be carried away of *4160*
13:15 **c** that as many as would not worship *4160*

CAUSED (94) [CAUSE]
Ge 2: 5 for the LORD God had not **c** it **to rain** 4305
2:21 the LORD God **c** a deep sleep **to fall** upon 5307
20:13 when God **c** me **to wander** from my 8582
41:52 For God hath **c** me **to be fruitful** in 6509
Ex 14:21 the LORD **c** the sea **to go** *back* by a strong 1980
36: 6 they **c** it **to be proclaimed** 5674+6963
Lev 24:20 as he hath **c** a blemish in a man, so shall it 5414
Nu 31:16 Behold, these **c** the children of Israel, 1961
Dt 34: 4 I have **c** thee **to see** *it* with thine eyes, but 7200
Jdg 16:19 she **c** *him* **to shave off** the seven locks of 1548
1Sa 10:20 had **c** all the tribes of Israel **to come near**, 7126
10:21 **c** the tribe of Benjamin **to come near** by 7126
20:17 Jonathan **c** David to swear **again**, because 3254
2Sa 7:11 have **c** thee **to rest** from all thine enemies. 5117
1Ki 1:38 **c** Solomon **to ride** upon king David's mule, 7392
1:44 they have **c** him **to ride** upon the king's 7392
2:19 and **c** a seat **to be set** for the king's mother; 7760
20:33 and he **c** him **to come up** into the chariot. 5927
2Ki 17:17 **c** their sons and their daughters **to pass** 5674
2Ch 8: 2 and **c** the children of Israel **to dwell** there. 3427
13:13 Jeroboam **c** an ambushment to come **about** 5437
21:11 **c** the inhabitants of Jerusalem **to commit**
fornication, 2181
33: 6 he **c** his children **to pass** through the fire in 5674
34:32 **c** all that were present in Jerusalem and
Benjamin **to stand** 5975
Ezr 6:12 the God that hath **c** his name **to dwell** there 7932
Ne 8: 7 **c** the people **to understand** the law: 995
8: 8 and **c** *them* **to understand** the reading. 995
Est 5:14 and he **c** the gallows **to be made**. 6213
Job 29:13 and I **c** the widow's heart **to sing for joy**. 7442
31:16 or have **c** the eyes of the widow **to fail**; 3615
31:39 have **c** the owners thereof **to lose** their life: 5301
37:15 and **c** the light of his cloud **to shine**? 3313
38:12 *and* **c** the dayspring **to know** his place; 3045
Ps 66:12 Thou hast **c** men **to ride** over our heads; 7392
78:13 the sea, and **c** them **to pass through**; 5674
78:16 and **c** waters **to run down** like rivers. 3381
78:26 He **c** an east wind **to blow** in the heaven: 5265
119:49 upon which thou hast **c** me **to hope**. 3176
Pr 7:21 her much fair speech she **c** him **to yield**, 5186
Isa 19:14 they have **c** Egypt **to err** in every work 8582
43:23 I have not **c** thee **to serve** with an offering, 5647
48:21 he **c** the waters **to flow** out of the rock for 5140
63:14 the Spirit of the LORD **c** him **to rest**: 5117
Jer 12:14 which I have **c** my people Israel **to inherit**; 5157
13:11 have I **c to cleave** unto me the whole house 1692
15: 8 I have **c** *him* **to fall** upon it suddenly, and 5307
18:15 they have **c** them **to stumble** in their ways 3782
23:13 in Baal, and **c** my people Israel **to err**. 8582
23:22 had **c** my people **to hear** my words, then 8085
29: 4 whom I have **c to be carried away** from 1540
29: 7 I have **c** you **to be carried away captives**, 1540
29:14 I **c** you **to be carried away captive**. 1540
29:31 I sent him not, and he **c** you **to trust** in a lie: 982
32:23 thou hast **c** all this evil **to come upon** them: 7122
34:11 **c** the servants and the handmaids, whom they
had let go free, **to return**, 7725
34:16 **c** every man his servant, . . . **to return**, 7725
48: 4 her little ones have **c** a cry **to be heard**. 8085
48:33 I have **c** wine **to fail** from the wine presses: 7673
50: 6 their shepherds have **c** them **to go astray**, 8582
51:49 As Babylon *hath* **c** the slain of Israel to fall, NIH
La 2: 6 **c** the solemn feasts and sabbaths
to be forgotten 7911
2:17 he hath **c** *thine* enemy **to rejoice** over thee, 8055
3:13 He hath **c** the arrows of his quiver **to enter** 935
Eze 3: 2 my mouth, and he **c** me **to eat** that roll. 398
16: 7 I have **c** thee to multiply as the bud of 5414
20:10 Wherefore I **c** them **to go forth** out of 3318
20:26 in that they **c to pass through** *the fire* all 5674
22: 4 thou hast **c** thy days **to draw near**, and 7126
23:37 **c** their sons, whom they bare unto me,
to pass for them **through** 5674
24:13 till I have **c** my fury **to rest** upon thee. 5117
29:18 **c** his army **to serve** a great service against 5647
31:15 he went down to the grave I **c a mourning**: 56
31:15 I **c** Lebanon **to mourn** for him, and all 6937
32:23 which **c** terror in the land of the living. 5414
32:24 which **c** their terror in the land of the living; 5414
32:25 though their terror was **c** in the land of 5414
32:26 though they **c** their terror in the land of 5414
32:32 For I have **c** my terror in the land of 5414
37: 2 And **c** me **to pass** by them round about: and 5674
39:28 which **c** them **to be led into captivity** 1540
44:12 **c** the house of Israel **to fall** into iniquity; 4383
46:21 **c** me **to pass** by the four corners of 5674
47: 6 and **c** me **to return** to the brink of the river. 7725
Da 9:21 at the beginning, being **c to fly** swiftly, 3286
Hos 4:12 the spirit of whoredoms hath **c** *them* **to err**, 8582
Am 2: 4 and their lies **c** them **to err**, 8582
4: 7 I **c** it **to rain** upon one city, and caused it 4305
4: 7 and **c** it not **to rain** upon another city: 4305
Jnh 3: 7 he **c** *it* **to be proclaimed** and 2199
Zec 3: 4 I have **c** thine iniquity **to pass** from thee, 5674
Mal 2: 8 ye have **c** many **to stumble** at the law; 3782
Jn 11:37 have **c** that even this *man* should not have *4160*
Ac 15: 3 and they **c** great joy unto all the brethren. *4160*
2Co 2: 5 But if any have **c grief**, he hath not grieved *3076*

CAUSELESS (2) [CAUSE]
1Sa 25:31 either that thou hast shed blood **c**, or 2600
Pr 26: 2 by flying, so the curse **c** shall not come. 2600

CAUSES (7) [CAUSE]
Ex 18:19 that thou mayest bring the **c** unto God: 1697
18:26 the hard **c** they brought unto Moses, but 1697
Dt 1:16 Hear *the* **c** between your brethren, and NIH
Jer 3: 8 when for all the **c** whereby backsliding Israel 182
La 2:14 thee false burdens and **c of banishment**. 4065
3:58 O Lord, thou hast pleaded the **c** of my soul; 7379
Ac 26:21 **For** these **c** the Jews caught me in *1752*

CAUSEST (2) [CAUSE]
Job 30:22 thou **c** me **to ride** *upon it*, and 7392
Ps 65: 4 **c to approach** *unto thee, that* he may dwell 7126

CAUSETH (32) [CAUSE]
Nu 5:18 in his hand the bitter water that **c** the **curse**: 779
5:19 free from this bitter water that **c the curse**: 779
5:22 this water that **c the curse** shall go into thy 779
5:24 to drink the bitter water that **c the curse**: 779
5:24 the water that **c the curse** shall enter into 779
5:27 that the water that **c the curse** shall enter 779
Job 12:24 **c** them **to wander** in a wilderness *where* 8582
20: 3 the spirit of my understanding **c** me to NIH
37:13 He **c** it **to come**, whether for correction, or 4672
Ps 104:14 He **c** the grass **to grow** for the cattle, and 6779
107:40 **c** them **to wander** in the wilderness, 8582
135: 7 He **c** the vapours **to ascend** from the ends 5927
147:18 he **c** his wind **to blow**, *and* the waters flow. 5380
Pr 10: 5 sleepeth in harvest *is* a son that **c shame**. 954
10:10 He that winketh *with* the eye **c** sorrow: but 5414
14:35 but his wrath is *against* him that **c shame**. 954
17: 2 shall have rule over a son that **c shame**, 954
18:18 The lot **c** contentions **to cease**, and 7673
19:26 *is* a son that **c shame**, and bringeth reproach. 954
19:27 to hear the instruction *that* **c** to err from NIH
28:10 Whoso **c** the righteous **to go astray** in an 7686
Isa 61:11 **c** the things that are sown in it
to spring forth; 6779
64: 2 fire burneth, the fire **c** the waters **to boil**, 1158
Jer 10:13 he **c** the vapours **to ascend** from the ends of 5927
51:16 he **c** the vapours **to ascend** from the ends of 5927
Eze 26: 3 as the sea **c** his waves **to come up**. 5927
44:18 *themselves* with any thing that **c** sweat. 871.1
Mt 5:32 of fornication, **c** her to commit adultery: *4160*
2Co 2:14 which always **c** us **to triumph** in Christ, *2358*
9:11 which **c** through us thanksgiving to God. *2716*
Rev 13:12 and **c** the earth and them which dwell *4160*
13:16 And he **c** all, *both* small and great, rich and *4160*

CAUSEWAY (2) [CAUSE]
1Ch 26:16 by the **c** of the going up, ward against ward. 4546
26:18 four at the **c**, *and* two at Parbar. 4546

CAUSING (4) [CAUSE]
SS 7: 9 **c** the lips of *those that are* asleep **to speak**. 1680
Isa 30:28 in the jaws of the people, **c** *them* **to err**. 8582
Jer 29:10 in **c** you **to return** to this place. 7725
33:12 of shepherds **c** *their* flocks **to lie down**. 7257

CAVE (33) [CAVE'S, CAVES]
Ge 19:30 he dwelt in a **c**, he and his two daughters. 4631
23: 9 That he may give me the **c** of Machpelah, 4631
23:11 and the **c** that *is* therein, I give it thee; 4631
23:17 the **c** which *was* therein, and all the trees 4631
23:19 Abraham buried Sarah his wife in the **c** of 4631
23:20 the field, and the **c** that *is* therein, were 4631
25: 9 Ishmael buried him in the **c** of Machpelah, 4631
49:29 bury me with my fathers in the **c** that *is* in 4631
49:30 In the **c** that *is* in the field of Machpelah, 4631
49:32 of the **c** that *is* therein *was* from 4631
50:13 buried him in the **c** of the field of 4631
Jos 10:16 and hid themselves in a **c** at Makkedah. 4631
10:17 The five kings are found hid in a **c** at 4631
10:18 Roll great stones upon the mouth of the **c**, 4631
10:22 Open the mouth of the **c**, and bring out 4631
10:22 out those five kings unto me out of the **c**. 4631
10:23 forth those five kings unto him out of the **c**, 4631
10:27 cast them into the **c** wherein they had been 4631
1Sa 22: 1 and escaped to the **c** Adullam: 4631
24: 3 the sheepcotes by the way, where *was* a **c**; 4631
24: 3 and his men remained in the sides of the **c**. 4631
24: 7 Saul rose up out of the **c**, and went on *his* 4631
24: 8 went out of the **c**, and cried after Saul, 4631
24:10 thee to day into mine hand in the **c**: 4631
2Sa 23:13 in the harvest time unto the **c** of Adullam: 4631
1Ki 18: 4 hid them *by* fifty in a **c**, and fed them *with* 4631
18:13 of the LORD'S prophets by fifty in a **c**, 4631
19: 9 he came thither unto a **c**, and lodged there; 4631
19:13 and stood *in* the entering in of the **c**. 4631
1Ch 11:15 to the rock to David, into the **c** of Adullam; 4631
Ps 57: T of David, when he fled from Saul in the **c**. 4631
142: T of David; A Prayer when he was in the **c**. 4631
Jn 11:38 It was a **c**, and a stone lay upon it. *4693*

CAVE'S (1) [CAVE]
Jos 10:27 laid great stones in the **c** mouth, 4631

CAVES (6) [CAVE]
Jdg 6: 2 in the mountains, and **c**, and strong holds. 4631
1Sa 13: 6 the people did hide themselves in **c**, and 4631
Job 30: 6 *in* **c** of the earth, and *in* the rocks. 2356
Isa 2:19 into the **c** of the earth, for fear of 4247
Eze 33:27 and in the **c** shall die of the pestilence. 4631
Heb 11:38 and *in* dens and **c** of the earth. *3692*

CEASE (70) [CEASED, CEASETH, CEASING]
Ge 8:22 and winter, and day and night shall not **c**. 7673
Ex 9:29 *and* the thunder shall **c**, neither shall there 2308
Nu 8:25 from the age of fifty years they shall **c** 7725
11:25 upon them, they prophesied, and did not **c**. 3254
17: 5 I will **make to c** from me the murmurings 7918
Dt 15:11 For the poor shall never **c** out of the land: 2308
32:26 **make** the remembrance of them to **c** from 7673
Jos 22:25 shall your children **make** our children **c** 7673

Jdg 15: 7 I be avenged of you, and after *that* I will **c**. 2308
20:28 of Benjamin my brother, or shall I **c**? 2308
1Sa 7: 8 **C** not to cry unto the LORD our God for 2790
2Ch 16: 5 off building of Ramah, and let his work **c**. 7673
Ezr 4:21 now commandment to **cause** these men **to c**, 989
4:23 and **made** them **to c** by force and power. 989
5: 5 that they could not **cause** them **to c**, till 989
Ne 4:11 and slay them, and **cause** the work **to c**. 7673
6: 3 why should the work **c**, whilst I leave it, 7673
Job 3:17 There the wicked **c** *from* troubling; and 2308
10:20 **c** then, and let me alone, that I may take 2308
14: 7 that the tender branch thereof will not **c**. 2308
Ps 37: 8 **C** from anger, and forsake wrath: fret not 7503
46: 9 He **maketh** wars **to c** unto the end of 7673
85: 4 and **cause** thine anger towards us **to c**. 6565
89:44 Thou hast **made** his glory **to c**, and cast his 7673
Pr 18:18 The lot **causeth** contentions **to c**, and 7673
19:27 **C**, my son, to hear the instruction *that* 2308
20: 3 *It is* an honour for a man to **c** from strife: 7674
22:10 go out; yea, strife and reproach shall **c**. 7673
23: 4 not to be rich: **c** from thine own wisdom. 2308
Ecc 12: 3 and the grinders **c** because they are few, and 988
Isa 1:16 doings from before mine eyes; **c** to do evil; 2308
2:22 **C** ye from man, whose breath *is* in his 2308
10:25 the indignation shall **c**, and mine anger in 3615
13:11 will **cause** the arrogancy of the proud **to c**, 7673
16:10 I have **made** *their vintage* shouting **to c**. 7673
17: 3 The fortress also shall **c** from Ephraim, and 7673
21: 2 all the sighing thereof have I **made to c**. 7673
30:11 **cause** the Holy One of Israel **to c** from 7673
33: 1 when thou shalt **c** to spoil, thou shalt be 8552
Jer 7:34 will I **cause to c** from the cities of Judah, 7673
14:17 *with* tears night and day, and let them not **c**: 1820
16: 9 I will **cause to c** out of this place in your 7673
17: 8 neither shall **c** from yielding fruit. 4185
31:36 the seed of Israel also shall **c** from being a 7673
36:29 shall **cause to c** from thence man and 7673
48:35 Moreover I will **cause to c** in Moab, 7673
La 2:18 no rest; let not the apple of thine eye **c**. 1826
Eze 6: 6 your idols may be broken and **c**, and 7673
7:24 will also **make** the pomp of the strong **to c**; 7673
12:23 I will **make** this proverb **to c**, and 7673
16:41 I will **cause** thee **to c** from playing 7673
23:27 Thus will I **make** thy lewdness **to c** from 7673
23:48 Thus will I **cause** lewdness **to c** out of 7673
26:13 I will **cause** the noise of thy songs **to c**; 7673
30:10 **make** the multitude of Egypt **to c** by 7673
30:13 I will **cause** *their* images **to c** out of Noph; 7673
30:18 the pomp of her strength shall **c** in her: 7673
33:28 the pomp of her strength shall **c**; 7673
34:10 and **cause** them **to c** from feeding the flock; 7673
34:25 will **cause** the evil beasts **to c** out of 7673
Da 9:27 **cause** the sacrifice and the oblation **to c**, 7673
11:18 **cause** the reproach offered by him **to c**; 7673
Hos 1: 4 will **cause to c** the kingdom of the house of 7673
2:11 I will also **cause** all her mirth **to c**, her feast 7673
Am 7: 5 said I, O Lord GOD, **c**, I beseech thee: 2308
Ac 13:10 wilt thou not **c** to pervert the right ways of *3973*
1Co 13: 8 whether *there be* tongues, they shall **c**; *3973*
Eph 1:16 **C** not to give thanks for you, *3973*
Col 1: 9 since the day we heard *it*, do not **c** to pray *3973*
2Pe 2:14 full of adultery and that **cannot c from** sin; *180*

CEASED (33) [CEASE]
Ge 18:11 it **c** to be with Sarah after the manner of 2308
Ex 9:33 the thunders and hail **c**, and the rain was 2308
9:34 and the hail and the thunders were **c**, 2308
Jos 5:12 the manna **c** on the morrow after they had 7673
Jdg 2:19 they **c** not from their own doings, nor from 5307
5: 7 *The inhabitants of* the villages **c**, 2308
5: 7 they **c** in Israel, until that I Deborah arose, 2308
1Sa 2: 5 for bread; and *they that were* hungry **c**: 2308
25: 9 those words in the name of David, and **c**. 5117
Ezr 4:24 **c** the work of the house of the God which *is* 989
4:24 So it **c** unto the second year of the reign of 989
Job 32: 1 So these three men **c** to answer Job, 7673
Ps 35:15 I knew *it* not; they did tear *me*, and **c** not: 1826
77: 2 my sore ran in the night, and **c** not: my soul 6313
Isa 14: 4 and say, How hath the oppressor **c**! 7673
14: 4 the oppressor ceased! the golden city **c**! 7673
La 5:14 The elders have **c** from the gate, the young 7673
5:15 The joy of our heart is **c**; our dance is 7673
Jnh 1:15 into the sea: and the sea **c** from her raging. 5975
Mt 14:32 they were come into the ship, the wind **c**. *2869*
Mk 4:39 And the wind **c**, and there was a great calm. *2869*
6:51 up unto them into the ship; and the wind **c**: *2869*
Lk 7:45 time I came in hath not **c** to kiss my feet. *1257*
8:24 the water: and they **c**, and there was a calm. *3973*
11: 1 when he **c**, one of his disciples said unto *3973*
Ac 5:42 they **c** not to teach and preach Jesus Christ. *3973*
20: 1 And after the uproar was **c**, Paul called unto *3973*
20:31 that *by the space of* three years I **c** not to *3973*
21:14 we **c**, saying, The will of the Lord be done. *2270*
Gal 5:11 then is the offence of the cross **c**. *2673*
Heb 4:10 he also hath **c** from his own works, as God *2664*
10: 2 then would they not have **c** to be offered? *3973*
1Pe 4: 1 for he that hath suffered in the flesh hath **c** *3973*

CEASETH (10) [CEASE]
Ps 12: 1 Help, LORD; for the godly *man* **c**; for 1584
49: 8 of their soul is precious, and it **c** for ever:) 2308
Pr 26:20 so where *there is* no talebearer, the strife **c**. 8367
Isa 16: 4 the extortioner is at an end, the spoiler **c**, 3615
24: 8 The mirth of tabrets **c**, the noise of them 7673
24: 8 that rejoice endeth, the joy of the harp **c**. 7673
33: 8 highways lie waste, the wayfaring man **c**: 7673
La 3:49 Mine eye trickleth down, and **c** not, without 1820
Hos 7: 4 *who* **c** from raising after *he* hath kneaded 7673
Ac 6:13 This man **c** not to speak blasphemous *3973*

CEASING (7) [CEASE]
1Sa 12:23 sin against the LORD in **c** to pray for you: 2308
Ac 12: 5 prayer was made **without c** of the church *1618*
Ro 1: 9 that **without c** I make mention of you, *89*
1Th 1: 3 Remembering **without c** your work of faith, *89*
2:13 For this cause also thank we God **without c**, *89*
5:17 Pray **without c**. *89*
2Ti 1: 3 that **without c** I have remembrance of thee in *88*

CEDAR (51) [CEDARS]
Lev 14: 4 clean, and **c** wood, and scarlet, and hyssop: 730
14: 6 the **c** wood, and the scarlet, and the hyssop, 730
14:49 and **c** wood, and scarlet, and hyssop: 730
14:51 he shall take the **c** wood, and the hyssop, 730
14:52 with the **c** wood, and with the hyssop, and 730
Nu 19: 6 the priest shall take **c** wood, and hyssop, 730
24: 6 *and* as **c trees** beside the waters. 730
2Sa 5:11 and **c** trees, and carpenters, and masons: 730
7: 2 I dwell in a house of **c**, but the ark of God 730
7: 7 Why build ye not me a house of **c**? 730
1Ki 4:33 from the **c tree** that *is* in Lebanon even unto 730
5: 6 command thou that they hew me **c trees** out 730
5: 8 will do all thy desire concerning timber of **c**, 730
5:10 So Hiram gave Solomon **c** trees and fir trees 730
6: 9 the house with beams and boards of **c**. 730
6:10 they rested on the house with timber of **c**. 730
6:15 walls of the house within with boards of **c**, 730
6:16 both the floor and the walls with boards of **c**: 730
6:18 the **c** of the house within *was* carved with 730
6:18 all *was* **c**; there was no stone seen. 730
6:20 and *so* covered the altar *which was of* **c**. 730
6:36 rows of hewed stone, and a row of **c** beams. 730
7: 2 thirty cubits, upon four rows of **c** pillars, 730
7: 2 cedar pillars, with **c** beams upon the pillars. 730
7: 3 *it was* covered with **c** above upon the beams, 730
7: 7 *it was* covered with **c** from one side of 730
7:12 a row of **c** beams, both for the inner court of 730
9:11 of Tyre had furnished Solomon with **c** trees 730
2Ki 14: 9 The thistle that *was* in Lebanon sent to the **c** 730
19:23 will cut down the tall **c trees** thereof, *and* 730
1Ch 22: 4 Also **c** trees in abundance: for the Zidonians 730
22: 4 they of Tyre brought much **c** wood to David. 730
2Ch 1:15 **c trees** made he as the sycomore trees that 730
2: 8 Send me also **c** trees, fir trees, and 730
9:27 **c trees** made he as the sycomore trees that 730
25:18 The thistle that *was* in Lebanon sent to the **c** 730
Ezr 3: 7 to bring **c** trees from Lebanon to the sea of 730
Job 40:17 He moveth his tail like a **c**: the sinews of his 730
Ps 92:12 palm tree: he shall grow like a **c** in Lebanon. 730
SS 1:17 The beams of our house *are* **c**, *and* 730
8: 9 a door, we will inclose her with boards of **c**. 730
Isa 41:19 I will plant in the wilderness the **c**, 730
Jer 22:14 *it is* cieled with **c**, and painted with 730
22:15 thou reign, because thou closest *thyself* in **c**? 730
Eze 17: 3 and took the highest branch of the **c**: 730
17:22 also take of the highest branch of the high **c**, 730
17:23 and bear fruit, and be a goodly **c**: 730
27:24 bound with cords, and **made of c**, 729
31: 3 the Assyrian *was* a **c** in Lebanon with fair 730
Zep 2:14 for he shall uncover the **c work**. 731
Zec 11: 2 Howl, fir tree; for the **c** is fallen; because 730

CEDARS (24) [CEDAR]
Jdg 9:15 of the bramble, and devour the **c** of Lebanon. 730
1Ki 7:11 after the measures of hewed stones, and **c**. 730
10:27 **c** made he *to be* as the sycomore trees that 730
1Ch 14: 1 and timber of **c**, with masons and carpenters, 730
17: 1 I dwell in a house of **c**, but the ark of 730
17: 6 Why have ye not built me a house of **c**? 730
2Ch 2: 3 didst send him **c** to build him a house to 730
Ps 29: 5 The voice of the LORD breaketh the **c**; yea, 730
29: 5 yea, the LORD breaketh the **c** of Lebanon. 730
80:10 the boughs thereof *were like* the goodly **c**. 730
104:16 The trees of the LORD are full *of sap;* the **c** 730
148: 9 all hills; fruitful trees, and all **c**: 730
SS 5:15 *is* as Lebanon, excellent as the **c**. 730
Isa 2:13 And upon all the **c** of Lebanon, *that are* high 730
9:10 cut down, but we will change *them into* **c**. 730
14: 8 trees rejoice at thee, *and* the **c** of Lebanon, 730
37:24 I will cut down the tall **c** thereof, *and* 730
44:14 *He* heweth him down **c**, and taketh 730
Jer 22: 7 they shall cut down thy choice **c**, and 730
22:23 of Lebanon, that makest thy nest in the **c**, 730
Eze 27: 5 they have taken **c** from Lebanon to make 730
31: 8 The **c** in the garden of God could not hide 730
Am 2: 9 whose height *was* like the height of the **c**, 730
Zec 11: 1 O Lebanon, that the fire may devour thy **c**. 730

CEDRON (1)
Jn 18: 1 forth with his disciples over the brook **C**, *2748*

CELEBRATE (3)
Lev 23:32 unto even, shall ye **c** your **sabbath**. 7673+7676
23:41 ye shall **c** it in the seventh month. 2287
Isa 38:18 cannot praise thee, death can *not* **c** thee: 1984

CELESTIAL (2)
1Co 15:40 *There are* also **c** bodies, and *2032*
15:40 but the glory of the **c** *is* one, and the *glory* *2032*

CELLARS (2)
1Ch 27:27 for the wine **c** *was* Zabdi the Shiphmite: 214
27:28 the Gederite: and over the **c** of oil *was* Joash: 214

CENCHREA (3)
Ac 18:18 having shorn *his* head in **C**: for he had a *2747*
Ro 16: 1 is a servant of the church which is at **C**: *2747*
16: S *sent* by Phebe servant of the church at **C**. *2747*

CENSER (12) [CENSERS]
Lev 10: 1 took either of them his **c**, and put fire 4289
16:12 he shall take a **c** full of burning coals of fire 4289
Nu 16:17 take every man his **c**, and put incense in 4289
16:17 ye before the LORD every man his **c**, 4289
16:17 thou also, and Aaron, each *of you* his **c**. 4289
16:18 they took every man his **c**, and put fire in 4289
16:46 Take a **c**, and put fire therein from off 4289
2Ch 26:19 and *had* a **c** in his hand to burn incense: 4730
Eze 8:11 with every man his **c** in his hand; 4730
Heb 9: 4 Which had the golden **c**, and the ark of *2369*
Rev 8: 3 and stood at the altar, having a golden **c**; *3031*
8: 5 And the angel took the **c**, and filled it with *3031*

CENSERS (8) [CENSER]
Nu 4:14 *even* the **c**, the fleshhooks, and the shovels, 4289
16: 6 Take you **c**, Korah, and all his company; 4289
16:17 man his censer, two hundred and fifty **c**; 4289
16:37 that he take up the **c** out of the burning, and 4289
16:38 The **c** of these sinners against their own 4289
16:39 Eleazar the priest took the brasen **c**, 4289
1Ki 7:50 and the spoons, and the **c** *of* pure gold; 4289
2Ch 4:22 the basons, and the spoons, and the **c**, 4289

CENSUS See NUMBER; SUM; TAXING

CENTURION (20) [CENTURION'S, CENTURIONS]
Mt 8: 5 there came unto him a **c**, beseeching him, *1543*
8: 8 The **c** answered and said, Lord, I am not *1543*
8:13 And Jesus said unto the **c**, Go thy way; and *1543*
27:54 Now when the **c**, and they that were with *1543*
Mk 15:39 And when the **c**, which stood over against *2760*
15:44 and calling unto *him* the **c**, he asked him *2760*
15:45 And when he knew *it* of the **c**, he gave *2760*
Lk 7: 6 the **c** sent friends to him, saying unto him, *1543*
23:47 Now when the **c** saw what was done, *1543*
Ac 10: 1 a **c** of the band called the Italian *band*, *1543*
10:22 Cornelius the **c**, a just man, and one that *1543*
22:25 Paul said unto the **c** that stood *by*, Is it *1543*
22:26 When the **c** heard *that*, he went and told *1543*
24:23 And he commanded a **c** to keep Paul, *1543*
27: 1 *one* named Julius, a **c** of Augustus' band. *1543*
27: 6 And there the **c** found a ship of Alexandria *1543*
27:11 Nevertheless the **c** believed the master and *1543*
27:31 Paul said to the **c** and to the soldiers, *1543*
27:43 But the **c**, willing to save Paul, kept them *1543*
28:16 the **c** delivered the prisoners to the captain *1543*

CENTURION'S (1) [CENTURION]
Lk 7: 2 And a certain **c** servant, who was dear unto *1543*

CENTURIONS (3) [CENTURION]
Ac 21:32 Who immediately took soldiers and **c**, and *1543*
23:17 Then Paul called one of the **c** unto *him*, and *1543*
23:23 And he called unto *him* two **c**, saying, *1543*

CEPHAS (6) [PETER]
Jn 1:42 thou shalt be called **C**, which is by *2786*
1Co 1:12 I of Apollos; and I of **C**; and I of Christ. *2786*
3:22 or **C**, or the world, or life, or death, or *2786*
9: 5 and *as* the brethren of the Lord, and **C**? *2786*
15: 5 And that he was seen of **C**, then of *2786*
Gal 2: 9 And when James, **C**, and John, *2786*

CEREMONIES (1)
Nu 9: 3 according to all the **c** thereof, shall ye keep 4941

CERTAIN (196) [CERTAINLY, CERTAINTY, UNCERTAIN]
Ge 28:11 he lighted upon a **c** place, and tarried there NIH
37:15 a **c** man found him, and behold, *he was* NIH
38: 1 turned in to a **c** Adullamite, whose name *was* 376
38: 2 Judah saw there a daughter of a **c** Canaanite, 376
Ex 16: 4 shall go out and gather a **c rate** every day, 1697
Nu 9: 6 there were **c** men, who were defiled by NIH
16: 2 with **c** of the children of Israel, two hundred 376
Dt 13:13 *C* men, the children of Belial, are gone out NIH
13:14 behold, *if it be* truth, *and* the thing **c**, *that* 3559
17: 4 and behold, *it is* true, *and* the thing **c**, 3559
25: 2 according to his fault, by a **c** number. NIH
Jdg 9:53 a **c** woman cast a piece of a millstone upon 259
13: 2 there was a **c** man of Zorah, of the family of 259
19: 1 that there was a **c** Levite sojourning on 376
19:22 behold, the men of the city, **c** sons of Belial, 376
Ru 1: 1 a **c** man of Beth-lehem-judah went to NIH
1Sa 1: 1 Now there was a **c** man of 259
21: 7 Now a **c** man of the servants of Saul *was* NIH
2Sa 18:10 And a **c** man saw *it*, and told Joab, and said, 259
1Ki 2:37 thou shalt **know for c** that thou shalt 3045+3045
2:42 unto thee, saying, **Know for a c**, 3045+3045
7:29 oxen *were* **c** additions made of thin work. NIH
11:17 **c** Edomites of his father's servants with him, 376
20:35 a **c** man of the sons of the prophets said unto 259
22:34 a **c** man drew a bow at a venture, and NIH
2Ki 4: 1 Now there cried a **c** woman of the wives of 259
8: 6 So the king appointed unto her a **c** officer, 259
1Ch 9:28 **c** of them had the charge of the ministering NIH
16: 4 he appointed **c** of the Levites to minister NIH
19: 5 there went **c**, and told David how the men NIH
2Ch 8:13 Even after a **c rate** every day, offering 1697
18: 2 after **c** years he went down to Ahab to NIH
18:33 a **c** man drew a bow at a venture, and NIH
28:12 **c** of the heads of the children of Ephraim, 376
Ezr 10:16 Ezra the priest, *with* **c** chief of the fathers, 376
Ne 1: 2 my brethren, came, he and **c** men of Judah; NIH
1: 4 mourned **c** days, and fasted, and NIH
11: 4 at Jerusalem dwelt **c** of the children of NIH
11:23 that a **c portion** *should be* for the singers, 548
12:35 **c** of the priests' sons with trumpets; NIH
13: 6 and after **c** days obtained I *leave* of the king: NIH
13:25 smote **c** of them, and pluckt off their hair, 376
Est 2: 5 *Now* in Shushan the palace there was a **c** 376
3: 8 There is a **c** people scattered abroad and 259
Jer 26:15 **know** ye **for c**, that if ye put me to 3045+3045
26:17 Then rose up **c** of the elders of the land, and 376
26:22 of Achbor, and **c** men with him into Egypt. NIH
41: 5 That there came **c** from Shechem, 376
52:15 away captive **c** of the poor of the people, NIH
52:16 Nebuzar-adan the captain of the guard left **c** NIH
Eze 14: 1 Then came **c** of the elders of Israel unto me, 376
20: 1 *that* **c** of the elders of Israel came to inquire 376
Da 1: 3 that he should bring **c** of the children of NIH
2:45 the dream *is* **c**, and the interpretation 3330

Da 3: 8 Wherefore at that time c Chaldeans came 1400
3:12 There are c Jews whom thou hast set over 1400
8:13 another saint said unto that c *saint* which 6422
8:27 I Daniel fainted, and was sick c days; NIH
10: 5 looked, and behold, a c man clothed *in* linen, 259
11:13 shall certainly come after c years with a 6256
Mt 8:19 And a c scribe came, and said unto him, *1520*
9: 3 c of the scribes said within themselves, *5100*
9:18 there came a c ruler, and worshipped him, NIG
12:38 Then c of the scribes and of the Pharisees *5100*
17:14 there came to him a c man, kneeling down NIG
18:23 the kingdom of heaven likened unto a c king, *444*
20:20 and desiring a c *thing* of him. *5100*
21:28 A c man had two sons; and he came to NIG
21:33 There was a c householder, which planted a *5100*
22: 2 The kingdom of heaven is like unto a c king, *444*
Mk 2: 6 But there were c of the scribes sitting there, *5100*
5:25 And a c woman, which had an issue of *5100*
5:35 ruler of the synagogue's *house* c which said, NIG
7: 1 and c of the scribes, which came from *5100*
7:25 For a c woman, whose young daughter had NIG
11: 5 And c of them that stood there said unto *5100*
12: 1 A c man planted a vineyard, and set a hedge NIG
12:13 And they send unto him c of the Pharisees *5100*
12:42 And there came a c poor widow, and *1520*
14:51 And there followed him a c young man, *5100*
14:57 And there arose c, and bare false witness *5100*
Lk 1: 5 king of Judea, a c priest named Zacharias, *5100*
5:12 it came to pass, when he was in a c city, *1520*
5:17 And it came to pass on a c day, as he was *1520*
6: 2 And c of the Pharisees said unto them, *5100*
7: 2 And a c centurion's servant, who was dear *5100*
7:41 There was a c creditor which had two *5100*
8: 2 And c women, which had been healed of *5100*
8:20 And it was told him *by* c which said, NIG
8:22 Now it came to pass on a c day, that he *1520*
8:27 there met him out of the city a c man, *5100*
9:57 a c *man* said unto him, Lord, I will follow *5100*
10:25 a c lawyer stood up, and tempted him, *5100*
10:30 A c man went down from Jerusalem to *5100*
10:31 And by chance there came down a c priest *5100*
10:33 But a c Samaritan, as he journeyed, *5100*
10:38 they went, that he entered into a c village: *5100*
10:38 a c woman named Martha received him *5100*
11: 1 to pass *that,* as he was praying in a c place, *5100*
11:27 as he spake these *things,* a c woman of *5100*
11:37 a c Pharisee besought him to dine with him: *5100*
12:16 The ground of a c rich man brought forth *5100*
13: 6 A c *man* had a fig tree planted in his *5100*
13:31 The same day there came c *of* *5100*
14: 2 And behold, there was a c man before him, *5100*
14:16 A c man made a great supper, and *5100*
15:11 And he said, A c man had two sons: *5100*
16: 1 There was a c rich man, which had a *5100*
16:19 There was a c rich man, which was clothed *5100*
16:20 And there was a c beggar named Lazarus, *5100*
17:12 And as he entered into a c village, *5100*
18: 9 And he spake this parable unto c which *5100*
18:18 And a c ruler asked him, saying, *5100*
18:35 a c blind man sat by the way side begging: *5100*
19:12 A c nobleman went into a far country to *5100*
20: 9 A c man planted a vineyard, and let it forth *5100*
20:27 Then came to *him* c of the Sadducees, *5100*
20:39 Then c of the scribes answering said, *5100*
21: 2 And he saw also a c poor widow casting in *5100*
22:56 But a c maid beheld him as he sat by *5100*
23:19 (Who for a c sedition made in the city, and *5100*
24: 1 they had prepared, and c *others* with them. *5100*
24:22 c women *also* of our company made us *5100*
24:24 And c of them which were with us went to *5100*
Jn 4:46 And there was a c nobleman, whose son *5100*
5: 4 For an angel went down at a c season into NIG
5: 5 And a c man was there, which had an *5100*
11: 1 Now a c *man* was sick, *named* Lazarus, *5100*
12:20 And there were c Greeks among them that *5100*
Ac 3: 2 And a c man lame from his mother's womb *5100*
5: 1 But a c man named Ananias, with Sapphira *5100*
5: 2 also being privy *to it,* and brought a c part, *5100*
6: 9 Then there arose c of the synagogue, *5100*
8: 9 But there was a c man, called Simon, *5100*
8:36 on *their* way, they came unto a c water: *5100*
9:10 And there was a c disciple at Damascus, *5100*
9:19 Then was Saul c days with the disciples *5100*
9:33 And there he found a c man named Aeneas, *5100*
9:36 Now there was at Joppa a c disciple named *5100*
10: 1 There was a c man in Cesarea called *5100*
10:11 and a c vessel descending unto him, *5100*
10:23 c brethren from Joppa accompanied him. *5100*
10:48 Then prayed they him to tarry c days. *5100*
11: 5 a trance I saw a vision, A c vessel descend, *5100*
12: 1 forth *his* hands to vex c of the church. *5100*
13: 1 the church that was at Antioch c prophets *5100*
13: 6 they found a c sorcerer, a false prophet, *5100*
14: 8 And there sat a c man at Lystra, impotent in *5100*
14:19 And there came thither c Jews from Antioch NIG
15: 1 And c *men* which came down from Judea *5100*
15: 2 and Barnabas, and c other of them, *5100*
15: 5 But there rose up c of the sect of *5100*
15:24 that c which went out from us have *5100*
16: 1 and behold, a c disciple was there, *5100*
16: 1 named Timotheus, the son of a c woman, *5100*
16:12 and we were in that city abiding c days. *5100*
16:14 And a c woman named Lydia, a seller of *5100*
16:16 a c damsel possessed with a spirit of *5100*
17: 5 took unto *them* c lewd fellows of the baser *5100*
17: 6 and c brethren unto the rulers of the city, *5100*
17:18 Then c philosophers of the Epicureans, and *5100*
17:20 For thou bringest c strange *things* to our *5100*
17:28 as c also of your own poets have said, *5100*
17:34 Howbeit c men clave unto him, and *5100*
18: 2 And found a c Jew named Aquila, born in *5100*
18: 7 and entered into a c *man's* house, *5100*
18:24 And a c Jew named Apollos, born at *5100*
19: 1 came to Ephesus: and finding c disciples, *5100*
19:13 Then c of the vagabond Jews, exorcists, *5100*
Ac 19:24 For a c *man* named Demetrius, *5100*
19:31 And c of the chief of Asia, which were his *5100*
20: 9 And there sat in a window a c young man *5100*
21:10 there came down from Judea a c prophet, *5100*
21:16 There went with us also c of the disciples of NIG
23:12 it was day, c of the Jews banded together, *5100*
23:17 for he hath a c *thing* to tell him. *5100*
24: 1 and *with* a c orator *named* Tertullus, *5100*
24:18 Whereupon c Jews from Asia found me *5100*
24:24 And after c days, when Felix came with his *5100*
25:13 And after c days king Agrippa and *5100*
25:14 There is a c man left in bonds by Felix: *5100*
25:19 But had c questions against him of their *5100*
25:26 Of whom I have no c *thing* to write unto *my* *804*
27: 1 c other prisoners unto *one* named Julius, *5100*
27:16 And running under a c island *which is* *5100*
27:26 Howbeit we must be cast upon a c island. *5100*
27:39 but they discovered a c creek with a shore, *5100*
Ro 15:26 Achaia to make a c contribution for *5100*
1Co 4:11 are buffeted, and **have no c dwelling place**; *790*
Gal 2:12 For before that c came from James, he did *5100*
1Ti 6: 7 *and it is* c we can carry nothing out. *1212*
Heb 2: 6 But one in **a c place** testified, saying, *4225*
4: 4 For *he* spake in **a c place** of the seventh *4225*
4: 7 Again he limiteth a c day, saying in David, *5100*
10:27 But a c fearful looking for of judgment and *5100*
Jude 1: 4 For there are c men crept in unawares, *5100*

CERTAINLY (31) [CERTAIN]

Ge 18:10 I will c **return** unto thee according 7725+7725
26:28 **saw** c that the LORD was with 7200+7200
43: 7 could we c **know** that he would say, 3045+3045
44:15 that such a man as I can c **divine**? 5172+5172
50:15 will c **requite** us all the evil which 7725+7725
Ex 3:12 he said, C I will be with thee; and this *shall* 3588
22: 4 If the theft be c **found** in his hand 4672+4672
Lev 5:19 hath c **trespassed** against the LORD. 816+816
24:16 the congregation shall c **stone** him: 7275+7275
Jos 9:24 Because it was c **told** thy servants, 5046+5046
Jdg 14:12 if you can c **declare** it me *within* 5046+5046
1Sa 20: 3 Thy father c **knoweth** that I have 3045+3045
20: 9 for if I **knew** c that evil were 3045+3045
23:10 thy servant hath c **heard** that Saul 8085+8085
25:28 for the LORD will c **make** my lord 6213+6213
1Ki 1:30 in my stead; even so will I c do this day. 3651
2Ki 8:10 unto him, Thou mayest c **recover**: 2421+2421
2Ch 18:27 If thou c **return** in peace, *then* 7725+7725
Pr 23: 5 for *riches* c **make** themselves wings; 6213+6213
Jer 8: 8 c in vain made he *it;* the pen of the scribes *is* 403
13:12 Do we not c **know** that every bottle 3045+3045
25:28 LORD of hosts; Ye shall c **drink**. 8354+8354
36:29 The king of Babylon shall c **come** 935+935
40:14 Dost thou c **know** that Baalis 3045+3045
42:19 **know** c that I have admonished you 3045+3045
42:22 **know** c that ye shall die by 3045+3045
44:17 we will c **do** whatsoever thing goeth 6213+6213
La 2:16 c this *is* the day that we looked for; we have 389
Da 11:10 *one* shall c **come**, and overflow, and 935+935
11:13 shall c **come** after certain years with a 935+935
Lk 23:47 saying, C this was a righteous man. *3689*

CERTAINTY (7) [CERTAIN]

Jos 23:13 **Know for a c** that the LORD your 3045+3045
1Sa 23:23 come ye again to me with the c, and I will 3559
Pr 22:21 That *I* might make thee know the c of 7189
Da 2: 8 I know of c that ye would gain the time, 3330
Lk 1: 4 That thou mightest know the c of *those* *803*
Ac 21:34 when he could not know the c for the tumult, *804*
22:30 he would have known the c wherefore he *804*

CERTIFIED (2) [CERTIFY]

Ezr 4:14 therefore have we sent and c the king; 3046
Est 2:22 Esther c the king *thereof* in Mordecai's 559

CERTIFY (5) [CERTIFIED]

2Sa 15:28 until there come word from you to c me. 5046
Ezr 4:16 We c the king that, if this city be builded 3046
5:10 We asked their names also, to c thee, 3046
7:24 Also *we* c you, that *touching* any of 3046
Gal 1:11 But I c you, brethren, that the gospel which *1107*

CESAR (21) [CESAR'S]

Mt 22:17 Is it lawful to give tribute unto C, or not? *2541*
22:21 unto C the *things* which are Cesar's; *2541*
Mk 12:14 Is it lawful to give tribute to C, or not? *2541*
12:17 Render to C the *things* that are Cesar's, and *2541*
Lk 2: 1 *that* there went out a decree from C *2541*
3: 1 the fifteenth year of the reign of Tiberius C, *2541*
20:22 Is it lawful for us to give tribute unto C, or *2541*
20:25 unto C the *things* which be Cesar's, *2541*
23: 2 and forbidding to give tribute to C, saying *2541*
Jn 19:12 maketh himself a king speaketh against C. *2541*
19:15 priests answered, We have no king but C. *2541*
Ac 11:28 came to pass in the days of Claudius C. *2541*
17: 7 these all do contrary to the decrees of C, *2541*
25: 8 against the temple, nor *yet* against C, *2541*
25:11 may deliver me unto them. I appeal unto C. *2541*
25:12 answered, Hast thou appealed unto C? *2541*
25:12 appealed unto Cesar? unto C shalt thou go. *2541*
25:21 him to be kept till I might send him to C. *2541*
26:32 set at liberty, if he had not appealed unto C. *2541*
27:24 Paul; thou must be brought before C: *2541*
28:19 *it,* I was constrained to appeal unto C; *2541*

CESAR'S (9) [CESAR]

Mt 22:21 They say unto him, C. Then saith he unto *2541*
22:21 unto Cesar the *things* which are C; *2541*
Mk 12:16 And they said unto him, C. *2541*
12:17 Render to Cesar the *things* that are C, and *2541*
Lk 20:24 hath it? They answered and said, C. *2541*
20:25 therefore unto Cesar the *things* which be C, *2541*
Jn 19:12 thou let this *man* go, thou art not C friend: *2541*
Ac 25:10 Then said Paul, I stand at C judgment seat, *2541*
Php 4:22 chiefly they that are of C household. *2541*

CESAREA (17)

Mt 16:13 When Jesus came into the coasts of C *2542*
Mk 8:27 his disciples, into the towns of C Philippi: *2542*
Ac 8:40 preached in all the cities, till he came to C. *2542*
9:30 they brought him down to C, and sent him *2542*
10: 1 There was a certain man in C called *2542*
10:24 And the morrow *after* they entered into C. *2542*
11:11 house where I was, sent from C unto me. *2542*
12:19 And he went down from Judea to C, and *2542*
18:22 And when he had landed at C, and gone up, *2542*
21: 8 company departed, and came unto C: *2542*
21:16 with us also *certain* of the disciples of C, *2542*
23:23 ready two hundred soldiers to go to C, *2542*
23:33 when they came to C, and delivered *2542*
25: 1 after three days he ascended from C to *2542*
25: 4 that Paul should be kept at C, and that he *2542*
25: 6 more than ten days, he went down unto C; *2542*
25:13 and Bernice came unto C to salute Festus. *2542*

CHAFED (1)

2Sa 17: 8 mighty *men,* and they *be* c in their minds, 4751

CHAFF (14)

Job 21:18 and as c that the storm carrieth away. 4671
Ps 1: 4 *are* like the c which the wind driveth away. 4671
35: 5 Let them be as c before the wind: and 4671
Isa 5:24 the flame consumeth the c, *so* their root 2842
17:13 shall be chased as the c of the mountains 4671
29: 5 ones *shall be* as c that passeth away: 4671
33:11 Ye shall conceive c, ye shall bring forth 2842
41:15 *them* small, and shalt make the hills as c. 4671
Jer 23:28 What *is* the c to the wheat? saith 8401
Da 2:35 became like the c of the summer 5784
Hos 13: 3 as the c *that* is driven with a whirlwind out 4671
Zep 2: 2 bring forth, *before* the day pass as the c, 4671
Mt 3:12 will burn up the c with unquenchable fire. *892*
Lk 3:17 the c he will burn with fire unquenchable. *892*

CHAIN (13) [CHAINS]

Ge 41:42 fine linen, and put a gold c about his neck; 7242
1Ki 7:17 of checker work, *and* wreaths of c work, 8333
Ps 73: 6 pride **compasseth** them **about as a c**; 6059
SS 4: 9 one of thine eyes, with one c of thy neck. 6060
La 3: 7 I cannot get out: he hath made my c heavy. 5178
Eze 7:23 Make a c: for the land is full *of* bloody 7569
16:11 upon thine hands, and a c on thy neck. 7242
Da 5: 7 *have* a c of gold about his neck, and 2002
5:16 *have* a c of gold about thy neck, and 2002
5:29 *put* a c of gold about his neck, and made a 2002
Ac 28:20 for the hope of Israel I am bound with this c. *254*
2Ti 1:16 refreshed me, and was not ashamed of my c: *254*
Rev 20: 1 the bottomless *pit* and a great c in his hand. *254*

CHAINS (37) [CHAIN]

Ex 28:14 two c *of* pure gold at the ends; *of* wreathen 8333
28:14 and fasten the wreathen c to the ouches. 8333
28:22 thou shalt make upon the breastplate c at 8331
28:24 thou shalt put the two wreathen c *of* gold in NIH
28:25 *the other* two ends of the two wreathen c NIH
39:15 they made upon the breastplate c at 8333
39:17 they put the two wreathen c *of* gold in NIH
39:18 the two ends of the two wreathen c they NIH
Nu 31:50 c, and bracelets, rings, earrings, and tablets, 685
Jdg 8:26 beside the c that *were* about their camels' 6060
1Ki 6:21 he made a partition by the c of gold before 7572
2Ch 3: 5 fine gold, and set thereon palm trees and c. 8333
3:16 he made c, *as* in the oracle, and put *them* on 8333
3:16 and put *them* on the c. 8333
Ps 68: 6 bringeth out those which are bound with c: 3574
149: 8 To bind their kings with c, and their nobles 2131
Pr 1: 9 grace unto thy head, and c about thy neck. 6060
SS 1:10 rows *of jewels,* thy neck with c *of gold.* 2737
Isa 3:19 The c, and the bracelets, and the mufflers, 5188
40:19 it over with gold, and casteth silver c. 7577
45:14 in c they shall come over, and they shall 2131
Jer 39: 7 bound him with c to carry him to Babylon. 5178
40: 1 when he had taken him being bound in c 246
40: 4 I loose thee *this* day from the c which *were* 246
52:11 the king of Babylon bound him in c, and 5178
Eze 19: 4 they brought him with c unto the land of 2397
19: 9 they put him in ward in c, and brought him 2397
Na 3:10 and all her great *men* were bound in c. 2131
Mk 5: 3 and no *man* could bind him, no, not with c: *254*
5: 4 he had been often bound with fetters and c, *254*
5: 4 and the c had been plucked asunder by him, *254*
Lk 8:29 and he was kept bound with c and in fetters; *254*
Ac 12: 6 between two soldiers, bound with two c: *254*
12: 7 up quickly. And his c fell off from *his* hands. *254*
21:33 commanded *him* to be bound with two c; *254*
2Pe 2: 4 and delivered *them* into c of darkness, *4577*
Jude 1: 6 he hath reserved in everlasting c under *1199*

CHALCEDONY (1)

Rev 21:19 the second, sapphire; the third, a c; *5472*

CHALCOL (1) [CALCOL]

1Ki 4:31 Heman, and C, and Darda, the sons of 3633

CHALDEA (7) [CHALDEAN, CHALDEANS, CHALDEANS', CHALDEES, CHALDEES']

Jer 50:10 C shall be a spoil: all that spoil her shall be 3778
51:24 to all the inhabitants of C all their evil that 3778
51:35 my blood upon the inhabitants of C, 3778
Eze 11:24 me in vision by the Spirit of God into C, 3778
16:29 fornication in the land of Canaan unto C; 3778
23:15 *after* the manner of the Babylonians of C, 3778
23:16 and sent messengers unto them into C. 3778

CHALDEAN (2) [CHALDEA]

Ezr 5:12 the C, who destroyed this house, 3679
Da 2:10 things at any magician, or astrologer, or C. 3779

CHALDEANS (66) [CHALDEA]
Job 1:17 The **C** made out three bands, and fell upon 3778
Isa 23:13 Behold the land of the **C**; this people was 3778
43:14 and the **C**, whose cry *is* in the ships. 3778
47: 1 *there is* no throne, O daughter of the **C**: 3778
47: 5 get thee into darkness, O daughter of the **C**: 3778
48:14 on Babylon, and his arm *shall be on* the **C**. 3778
48:20 Go ye forth of Babylon, flee ye from the **C**, 3778
Jer 21: 4 against the **C**, which besiege you without 3778
21: 9 falleth to the **C** that besiege you, he shall 3778
22:25 of Babylon, and into the hand of the **C**. 3778
24: 5 place *into* the land of the **C** for *their* good. 3778
25:12 the land of the **C**, and will make it 3778
32: 4 shall not escape out of the hand of the **C**, 3778
32: 5 though ye fight with the **C**, ye shall not 3778
32:24 the city is given into the hand of the **C**, 3778
32:25 for the city is given into the hand of the **C**. 3778
32:28 I *will* give this city into the hand of the **C**, 3778
32:29 the **C**, that fight against this city, 3778
32:43 or beast; it is given into the hand of the **C**. 3778
33: 5 They come to fight with the **C**, but *it is* to 3778
35:11 *to* Jerusalem for fear of the army of the **C**, 3778
37: 5 when the **C** that besieged Jerusalem heard 3778
37: 8 the **C** shall come again, and fight against 3778
37: 9 The **C** shall surely depart from us: 3778
37:10 whole army of the **C** that fight against you, 3778
37:11 *that* when the army of the **C** was broken up 3778
37:13 saying, Thou fallest away to the **C**. 3778
37:14 *It is* false; I fall not away to the **C**. 3778
38: 2 he that goeth forth to the **C** shall live; 3778
38:18 this city be given into the hand of the **C**, 3778
38:19 afraid of the Jews that are fallen to the **C**, 3778
38:23 out all thy wives and thy children to the **C**: 3778
39: 8 the **C** burnt the king's house, and 3778
40: 9 their men, saying, Fear not to serve the **C**: 3778
40:10 I *will* dwell at Mizpah to serve the **C**, 3778
41: 3 the **C** that were found there, *and* the men of 3778
41:18 Because of the **C**: for they were afraid of 3778
43: 3 for to deliver us into the hand of the **C**, 3778
50: 1 against the land of the **C** by Jeremiah 3778
50: 8 go forth out of the land of the **C**, and be as 3778
50:25 Lord GOD of hosts in the land of the **C**. 3778
50:35 A sword *is* upon the **C**, saith the LORD, 3778
50:45 he hath purposed against the land of the **C**: 3778
51: 4 Thus the slain shall fall in the land of the **C**, 3778
51:54 great destruction from the land of the **C**: 3778
52: 7 (now the **C** *were* by the city round about:) 3778
52: 8 the army of the **C** pursued after the king, 3778
52:14 all the army of the **C**, that *were* with 3778
52:17 the **C** brake, and carried all the brass of 3778
Eze 1: 3 in the land of the **C** by the river Chebar; 3778
12:13 bring him to Babylon *to* the land of the **C**; 3778
23:14 the images of the **C** pourtrayed with 3778
23:23 all the **C**, Pekod, and Shoa, and Koa, 3778
Da 1: 4 teach the learning and the tongue of the **C**. 3778
2: 2 and the sorcerers, and the **C**, 3778
2: 4 spake the **C** to the king in Syriack, O king, 3778
2: 5 The king answered and said to the **C**, 3779
2:10 The **C** answered before the king, and said, 3779
3: 8 Wherefore at that time certain **C** came near, 3779
4: 7 the astrologers, the **C**, and the soothsayers: 3779
5: 7 the astrologers, the **C**, and the soothsayers. 3779
5:11 astrologers, **C**, *and* soothsayers; 3779
5:30 *was* Belshazzar the king of the **C** slain. 3778
9: 1 was made king over the realm of the **C**; 3778
Hab 1: 6 For lo, I raise up the **C**, *that* bitter and hasty 3778
Ac 7: 4 Then came he out of the land of the **C**, and *5466*

CHALDEANS' (1) [CHALDEA]
Jer 39: 5 the **C** army pursued after them, and 3778

CHALDEES (13) [CHALDEA]
Ge 11:28 in the land of his nativity, in Ur of the **C**. 3778
11:31 went forth with them from Ur of the **C**, 3778
15: 7 that brought thee out of Ur of the **C**, 3778
2Ki 24: 2 LORD sent against him bands of the **C**, 3778
25: 4 (now the **C** *were* against the city round 3778
25: 5 the army of the **C** pursued after the king, 3778
25:10 all the army of the **C**, that *were with* 3778
25:13 did the **C** break *in pieces*, and carried 3778
25:24 Fear not to be the servants of the **C**: 3778
25:25 and the **C** that were with him at Mizpah. 3778
25:26 *to* Egypt: for they were afraid of the **C**. 3778
2Ch 36:17 he brought upon them the king of the **C**, 3778
Ne 9: 7 broughtest him forth out of Ur of the **C**, 3778

CHALDEES' (1) [CHALDEA]
Isa 13:19 the beauty of the **C** excellency, 3778

CHALKSTONES (1) [STONE]
Isa 27: 9 the altar as **c** that are beaten in sunder, 68+1615

CHALLENGETH (1)
Ex 22: 9 for any manner of lost *thing*, which *another* **c** 559

CHAMBER (52) [BEDCHAMBER, CHAMBERING, CHAMBERLAIN, CHAMBERLAINS, CHAMBERS, GUESTCHAMBER]
Ge 43:30 and he entered into *his* **c**, and wept there. 2315
Jdg 3:24 Surely he covereth his feet in *his* summer **c**. 2315
15: 1 he said, I will go in to my wife into the **c**. 2315
16: 9 men lying in wait, abiding with her in the **c**. 2315
16:12 *there were* liers in wait abiding in the **c**. 2315
2Sa 13:10 Bring the meat *into* the **c**, that I may eat of 2315
13:10 brought *them* into the **c** to Amnon her 2315
18:33 went up to the **c** over the gate, and wept: 5944
1Ki 1:15 Bath-sheba went in unto the king into the **c**: 2315
6: 6 The nethermost **c** *was* five cubits broad, 3326
6: 8 The door for the middle **c** *was* in the right 6763
6: 8 up with winding stairs into the middle **c**, NIH
14:28 and brought them back into the guard **c**. 8372
17:23 brought him down out of the **c** into 5944
20:30 **into the** city, into an **inner c** 2315+2315+871.1
1Ki 22:25 into an **inner c** to hide thyself. 2315+2315+871.1
2Ki 1: 2 a lattice in his **upper c** that *was* in Samaria, 5944
4:10 Let us make a little **c**, I pray thee, on 5944
4:11 he turned into the **c**, and lay there. 5944
9: 2 and carry him *to* an **inner c**: 2315+2315+871.1
23:11 by the **c** of Nathan-melech the chamberlain, 3957
23:12 *were* on the top of the **upper c** of Ahaz, 5944
2Ch 12:11 and brought them again into the guard **c**. 8372
18:24 into an **inner c** to hide thyself. 2315+2315+871.1
Ezr 10: 6 went into the **c** of Johanan the son of 3957
Ne 3:30 the son of Berechiah over against his **c**. 5393
13: 4 having the oversight of the **c** of the house 3957
13: 5 he had prepared for him a great **c**, where 3957
13: 7 in preparing him a **c** in the courts of 5393
13: 8 the household stuff of Tobiah out of the **c**. 3957
Ps 19: 5 *is* as a bridegroom coming out of his **c**, 2646
SS 3: 4 and into the **c** of her that conceived me. 2315
Jer 35: 4 into the **c** of the sons of Hanan, the son of 3957
35: 4 of God, which *was* by the **c** of the princes, 3957
35: 4 which *was* above the **c** of Maaseiah the son 3957
36:10 in the **c** of Gemariah the son of Shaphan 3957
36:12 *into* the king's house, into the scribe's **c**: 3957
36:20 they laid up the roll in the **c** of Elishama 3957
36:21 he took it out of Elishama the scribe's **c**. 3957
Eze 40: 7 *every* **little c** *was* one reed long, and 8372
40:13 the gate from the roof of *one* **little c** to 8372
40:45 he said unto me, This **c**, whose prospect *is* 3957
40:46 the **c** whose prospect *is* toward the north *is* 3957
41: 5 the breadth of *every* **side c**, four cubits, 6763
41: 7 increased *from* the lowest **c** to the highest NIH
41: 9 which *was* for the **side c** without, *was* five 6763
42: 1 he brought me into the **c** that *was* over 3957
Da 6:10 his windows being open in his **c** toward 5952
Joel 2:16 let the bridegroom go forth of his **c**, and 2315
Ac 9:37 had washed, they laid *her* in an **upper c**. *5253*
9:39 they brought him into the **upper c**: *5253*
20: 8 And there were many lights in the **upper c**, *5253*

CHAMBERING (1) [CHAMBER]
Ro 13:13 not in **c** and wantonness, not in strife and *2845*

CHAMBERLAIN (6) [CHAMBER]
2Ki 23:11 by the chamber of Nathan-melech the **c**, 5631
Est 2: 3 unto the custody of Hege the king's **c**, 5631
2:14 the king's **c**, which kept the concubines: 5631
2:15 but what Hegai the king's **c**, 5631
Ac 12:20 the king's **c** their friend, *1909+2846+3588*
Ro 16:23 Erastus the **c** of the city saluteth you, and *3623*

CHAMBERLAINS (9) [CHAMBER]
Est 1:10 the seven **c** that served in the presence of 5631
1:12 come at the king's commandment by *his* **c**: 5631
1:15 of the king Ahasuerus by the **c**? 5631
2:21 two of the king's **c**, Bigthan and Teresh, 5631
4: 4 and her **c** came and told *it* her. 5631
4: 5 Esther for Hatach, *one* of the king's **c**, 5631
6: 2 and Teresh, two of the king's **c**, 5631
6:14 came the king's **c**, and hasted to bring 5631
7: 9 Harbonah, one of the **c**, said before 5631

CHAMBERS (66) [CHAMBER]
1Ki 6: 5 against the wall of the house he built **c** 3326
6: 5 of the oracle: and he made **c** round about: 6763
6:10 *then* he built **c** against all the house, 3326
1Ch 9:26 were over the **c** and treasuries of the house 3957
9:33 *who remaining* in the **c** *were* free: 3957
23:28 in the **c**, and in the purifying of all holy 3957
28:11 of the **upper c** thereof, and of the inner 5944
28:12 of all the **c** round about, of the treasuries of 3957
2Ch 3: 9 And he overlaid the **upper c** with gold. 5944
31:11 Hezekiah commanded to prepare **c** in 3957
Ezr 8:29 *in* the **c** of the house of the LORD. 3957
Ne 10:37 the priests, to the **c** of the house of our God; 3957
10:38 our God, to the **c**, into the treasure house. 3957
10:39 of the new wine, and the oil, unto the **c**, 3957
12:44 at that time were some appointed over the **c** 5393
13: 9 I commanded, and they cleansed the **c**: 3957
Job 9: 9 Orion, and Pleiades, and the **c** of the south. 2315
Ps 104: 3 Who layeth the beams of his **c** in 5944
104:13 He watereth the hills from his **c**: the earth is 5944
105:30 frogs in abundance, in the **c** of their kings. 2315
Pr 7:27 way to hell, going down to the **c** of death. 2315
24: 4 by knowledge shall the **c** be filled *with* all 2315
SS 1: 4 the king hath brought me *into* his **c**: we will 2315
Isa 26:20 enter thou into thy **c**, and shut thy doors 2315
Jer 22:13 by unrighteousness, and his **c** by wrong; 5944
22:14 I will build me a wide house and large **c**, 5944
35: 2 into one of the **c**, and give them wine to 3957
Eze 8:12 every man in the **c** of his imagery? 2315
21:14 *are* slain, which **entereth into** their **privy c**. 2314
40: 7 between the **little c** *were* five cubits; and 8372
40:10 the **little c** of the gate eastward *were* three 8372
40:12 The space also before the **little c** *was* one 8372
40:12 the **little c** *were* six cubits on this side, and 8372
40:16 *there were* narrow windows to the **little c**, 8372
40:17 lo, *there were* **c**, and a pavement made for 3957
40:17 thirty **c** *were* upon the pavement. 3957
40:21 the **little c** thereof *were* three on this side 8372
40:29 the **little c** thereof, and the posts thereof, 8372
40:33 the **little c** thereof, and the posts thereof, 8372
40:36 The **little c** thereof, the posts thereof, and 8372
40:38 the **c** and the entries thereof *were* by 3957
40:44 without the inner gate *were* the **c** of 3957
41: 6 the **side c** *were* three, one over another, 6763
41: 6 *was* of the house for the **side c** round about, 6763
41: 7 a winding about still upward to the **side c**: 6763
41: 8 the foundations of the **side c** *were* a full 6763
41: 9 *was* the place of the **side c** that *were* within. 6763
41:10 between the **c** *was* the wideness of twenty 3957
41:11 the doors of the **side c** *were* toward 6763
41:26 *upon* the **side c** of the house, and thick 6763
42: 4 before the **c** *was* a walk of ten cubits 3957
42: 5 Now the upper **c** *were* shorter: for 3957
42: 7 the wall that *was* without over against the **c**, 3957
Eze 42: 7 the utter court on the forepart of the **c**, 3957
42: 8 For the length of the **c** that *were* in the utter 3957
42: 9 from under these **c** *was* the entry on the east 3957
42:10 The **c** *were* in the thickness of the wall of 3957
42:11 of the **c** which *were* toward the north, 3957
42:12 according to the doors of the **c** that *were* 3957
42:13 The north **c** *and* the south chambers, 3957
42:13 The north chambers *and* the south **c**, 3957
42:13 before the separate place, they *be* holy **c**, 3957
44:19 lay them in the holy **c**, and they shall put on 3957
45: 5 for a possession *for* twenty **c**. 3957
46:19 into the holy **c** of the priests, which looked 3957
Mt 24:26 behold, *he is* in the **secret c**; believe *it* not. *5009*

CHAMELEON (1)
Lev 11:30 the **c**, and the lizard, and the snail, and 3581

CHAMOIS (1)
Dt 14: 5 and the pygarg, and the wild ox, and the **c**. 2169

CHAMPAIGN (1)
Dt 11:30 which dwell in the **c** over against Gilgal, 6160

CHAMPION (3)
1Sa 17: 4 there went out a **c** out of 376+1143+1886.1
17:23 behold, there came up the **c**, 376+1143+1886.1
17:51 when the Philistines saw their **c** was dead, 1368

CHANCE (6) [CHANCETH]
Dt 22: 6 If a bird's nest **c to be** before thee in 7122
1Sa 6: 9 smote us; it *was* a **c** *that* happened to us. 4745
2Sa 1: 6 As I **happened by c** upon mount Gilboa, 7122
Ecc 9:11 but time and **c** happeneth to them all. 6294
Lk 10:31 And by **c** there came down a certain priest *4795*
1Co 15:37 **it may c** of wheat, or of some other *1487+5177*

CHANCELLOR (3)
Ezr 4: 8 Rehum the **c** and Shimshai the scribe 1169+2942
4: 9 *wrote* Rehum the **c**, and Shimshai 1169+2942
4:17 king an answer unto Rehum the **c**, 1169+2942

CHANCETH (1) [CHANCE]
Dt 23:10 reason of *uncleanness* that **c** him by night, 7137

CHANGE (26) [CHANGEABLE, CHANGED, CHANGERS, CHANGERS', CHANGES, CHANGEST, CHANGETH, CHANGING, UNCHANGEABLE]
Ge 35: 2 and be clean, and **c** your garments: 2498
Lev 27:10 nor **c** it, a good for a bad, or a bad for a 4171
27:10 if he shall **at all c** beast for beast, 4171+4171
27:33 it be good or bad, neither shall he **c** it: 4171
27:33 if he **c** it **at all**, then both it and 4171+4171
27:33 both it and the **c** thereof shall be holy; 8545
Jdg 14:12 you thirty sheets and thirty **c** of garments: 2487
14:13 me thirty sheets and thirty **c** of garments. 2487
14:19 gave **c** *of garments* unto them which 2487
Job 14:14 appointed time will I wait, till my **c** come. 2487
17:12 They **c** the night into day: the light *is* short, 7760
Ps 102:26 as a vesture shalt thou **c** them, and 2498
Pr 24:21 meddle not with them that are **given to c**: 8138
Isa 9:10 cut down, but we will **c** *them into* cedars. 2498
Jer 2:36 gaddest thou about *so* much to **c** thy way? 8138
13:23 Can the Ethiopian **c** his skin, or the leopard 2015
Da 7:25 most High, and think to **c** times and laws: 8133
Hos 4: 7 *therefore* will I **c** their glory into shame. 4171
Hab 1:11 shall *his* mind **c**, and he shall pass over, 2498
Zec 3: 4 and *I will* clothe thee with **c of raiment**. 4254
Mal 3: 6 For I *am* the LORD, I **c** not; therefore 8138
Ac 6:14 shall **c** the customs which Moses delivered *236*
Ro 1:26 for even their women did **c** the natural use *3337*
Gal 4:20 be present with you now, and to **c** my voice; *236*
Php 3:21 Who shall **c** our vile body, that it may be *3345*
Heb 7:12 there is made of necessity a **c** also of *3331*

CHANGEABLE (1) [CHANGE]
Isa 3:22 The **c suits of apparel**, and the mantles, 4254

CHANGED (43) [CHANGE]
Ge 31: 7 deceived me, and **c** my wages ten times; 2498
31:41 and thou hast **c** my wages ten times. 2498
41:14 he shaved *himself*, and **c** his raiment, and 2498
Lev 13:16 be **c** unto white, he shall come unto 2015
13:55 *if* the plague have not **c** his colour, and 2015
Nu 32:38 and Baal-meon, (*their* names being **c**,) 5437
1Sa 21:13 he **c** his behaviour before them, and 8138
2Sa 12:20 and anointed *himself*, and **c** his apparel, and 2498
2Ki 24:17 in his stead, and **c** his name *to* Zedekiah. 5437
25:29 **c** his prison garments: and he did eat bread 8132
Job 30:18 great force *of my disease* is my garment **c**: 2664
Ps 34: T when he **c** his behaviour before Abimelech; 8138
102:26 shalt thou change them, and they shall be **c**: 2498
106:20 Thus they **c** their glory into the similitude 4171
Ecc 8: 1 and the boldness of his face shall be **c**. 8132
Isa 24: 5 have transgressed the laws, **c** the ordinance, 2498
Jer 2:11 Hath a nation **c** *their* gods, which *are* yet no 3235
2:11 my people have **c** their glory for *that which* 4171
48:11 taste remained in him, and his sent is not **c**. 4171
52:33 **c** his prison garments: and he did 8138
La 4: 1 *how* is the most fine gold **c**! the stones of 8132
Eze 5: 6 she hath **c** my judgments into wickedness 4784
Da 2: 9 words to speak before me, till the time be **c**: 8133
3:19 the form of his visage was **c** against 8133
3:27 head singed, neither were their coats **c**, 8133
3:28 have **c** the king's word, and yielded their 8133
4:16 Let his heart be **c** from man's, and let a 8133
5: 6 the king's countenance was **c**, and 8133
5: 9 his countenance *was* **c** in him, and his lords 8133
5:10 trouble thee, nor let thy countenance be **c**. 8133
6: 8 and sign the writing, that *it* be not **c**, 8133
6:15 which the king establisheth may be **c**. 8133
6:17 that the purpose might not be **c** concerning 8133
7:28 troubled me, and my countenance **c** in me: 8133

Mic 2: 4 he hath c the portion of my people: 4171
Ac 28: 6 they c their minds, and said that he was a 3328
Ro 1:23 And c the glory of the uncorruptible God 236
1:25 Who c the truth of God into a lie, and 3337
1Co 15:51 We shall not all sleep, but we shall all be c, 236
15:52 be raised incorruptible, and we shall be c. 236
2Co 3:18 are c into the same image from glory to 3339
Heb 1:12 shalt thou fold them up, and they shall be c: 236
7:12 For the priesthood being c, there is made of 3346

C

CHANGERS (1) [CHANGE]
Jn 2:14 and doves, and the c of money sitting: 2773

CHANGERS' (1) [CHANGE]
Jn 2:15 and poured out the c money, and 2855

CHANGES (7) [CHANGE]
Ge 45:22 To all of them he gave each man c of 2487
45:22 pieces of silver, and five c of raiment. 2487
2Ki 5: 5 pieces of gold, and ten c of raiment. 2487
5:22 a talent of silver, and two c of garments. 2487
5:23 with two c of garments, and laid them upon 2487
Job 10:17 upon me; c and war are against me. 2487
Ps 55:19 Because they have no c, therefore they fear 2487

CHANGEST (1) [CHANGE]
Job 14:20 thou c his countenance, and sendest him 8138

CHANGETH (2) [CHANGE]
Ps 15: 4 He that sweareth to his own hurt, and c not. 4171
Da 2:21 he c the times and the seasons: he removeth 8133

CHANGING (1) [CHANGE]
Ru 4: 7 concerning redeeming and concerning c, 8545

CHANNEL (1) [CHANNELS]
Isa 27:12 that the LORD shall beat off from the c of 7641

CHANNELS (3) [CHANNEL]
2Sa 22:16 the c of the sea appeared, the foundations of 650
Ps 18:15 the c of waters were seen, and 650
Isa 8: 7 he shall come up over all his c, and go over 650

CHANT (1)
Am 6: 5 That c to the sound of the viol, and 6527

CHAPEL (1)
Am 7:13 for it is the king's c, and it is the king's 4720

CHAPITER (13) [CHAPITERS]
1Ki 7:16 the height of the one c was five cubits, and 3805
7:16 the height of the other c was five cubits: 3805
7:17 seven for the one c, and seven for the other 3805
7:17 the one chapiter, and seven for the other c. 3805
7:18 and so did he for the other c. 3805
7:20 in rows round about upon the other c. 3805
7:31 the mouth of it within the c and above was 3805
2Ki 25:17 eighteen cubits, and the c upon it was brass: 3805
25:17 the height of the c three cubits; and 3805
25:17 pomegranates upon the c round about, all 3805
2Ch 3:15 the c that was on the top of each of them 6858
Jer 52:22 a c of brass was upon it; and the height of 3805
52:22 the height of one c was five cubits, 3805

CHAPITERS (16) [CHAPITER]
Ex 36:38 he overlaid their c and their fillets with 7218
38:17 the overlaying of their c of silver; and all 7218
38:19 the overlaying of their c and their fillets of 7218
38:28 and overlaid their c, and filleted them. 7218
1Ki 7:16 he made two c of molten brass, to set upon 3805
7:17 for the c which were upon the top of 3805
7:18 to cover the c that were upon the top, with 3805
7:19 (And the c that were upon the top of 3805
7:20 the c upon the two pillars had 3805
7:41 the two bowls of the c that were on the top 3805
7:41 to cover the two bowls of the c which were 3805
7:42 to cover the two bowls of the c that were 3805
2Ch 4:12 the c which were on the top of the two 3805
4:12 the c which were on the top of the pillars; 3805
4:13 to cover the two pommels of the c which 3805
Jer 52:22 and pomegranates upon the c round about, 3805

CHAPMEN (1) [MAN]
2Ch 9:14 Besides that which c and merchants 376+1886.1

CHAPT (1)
Jer 14: 4 Because the ground is c, for there was no 2865

CHARASHIM (1)
1Ch 4:14 begat Joab, the father of the valley of C; 2798

CHARGE (102) [CHARGEABLE, CHARGED, CHARGEDST, CHARGES, CHARGEST, CHARGING, OVERCHARGE]
Ge 26: 5 kept my c, my commandments, my statutes, 4931
28: 6 that as he blessed him he gave him a c, 6680
Ex 6:13 gave them a c unto the children of Israel, 6680
19:21 said unto Moses, Go down, c the people, 5749
Lev 8:35 keep the c of the LORD, that ye die not: 4931
Nu 1:53 the Levites shall keep the c of 4931
3: 7 they shall keep his c, and the charge of 4931
3: 7 the c of the whole congregation before 4931
3: 8 the c of the children of Israel, to do 4931
3:25 the c of the sons of Gershon in 4931
3:28 six hundred, keeping the c of the sanctuary. 4931
3:31 their c shall be the ark, and the table, and 4931
3:32 have the oversight of them that keep the c 4931
3:36 c of the sons of Merari shall be the boards 4931
3:38 keeping the c of the sanctuary for 4931
3:38 sanctuary for the c of the children of Israel; 4931
4:27 ye shall appoint unto them in c all their 4931
4:28 their c shall be under the hand of Ithamar 4931
4:31 this is the c of their burden, according to all 4931
Nu 4:32 the instruments of the c of their burden. 4931
5:19 the priest shall c her by an oath, and 7650
5:21 c the woman with an oath of 7621+7650+871.1
8:26 to keep the c, and shall do no service. 4931
8:26 thou do unto the Levites touching their c. 4931
9:19 the children of Israel kept the c of 4931
9:23 they kept the c of the LORD, at 4931
18: 3 they shall keep thy c, and the charge of all 4931
18: 3 thy charge, and the c of all the tabernacle: 4931
18: 4 keep the c of the tabernacle of 4931
18: 5 ye shall keep the c of the sanctuary, and 4931
18: 5 of the sanctuary, and the c of the altar: 4931
18: 8 I also have given thee the c of mine heave 4931
27:19 and give him a c in their sight. 6680
27:23 laid his hands upon him, and gave him a c, 6680
31:30 which keep the c of the tabernacle of 4931
31:47 which kept the c of the tabernacle of 4931
31:49 of the men of war which are under our c, 3027
Dt 3:28 c Joshua, and encourage him, and 6680
11: 1 keep his c, and his statutes, and 4931
21: 8 blood unto thy people of Israel's c. 7130
31:14 the congregation, that I may give him a c. 6680
31:23 he gave Joshua the son of Nun a c, 6680
Jos 22: 3 have kept the c of the commandment of 4931
2Sa 14: 8 and I will give c concerning thee. 6680
18: 5 gave all the captains c concerning 6680
1Ki 2: 3 keep the c of the LORD thy God, to walk 4931
4:28 officers were, every man according to his c. 4941
11:28 he made him ruler over all the c of 5447
2Ki 7:17 hand he leaned to have the c of the gate: 5921
1Ch 9:27 because the c was upon them, and 4931
9:28 certain of them had the c of the ministering 5921
22:12 and give thee c concerning Israel, 6680
23:32 that they should keep the c of 4931
23:32 the c of the holy place, and the charge of 4931
23:32 the c of the sons of Aaron their brethren, 4931
2Ch 13:11 for we keep the c of the LORD our God; 4931
30:17 the Levites had the c of the killing of 5921
Ne 7: 2 gave my brother Hanani, and Hananiah
the ruler of the palace, c 6680
10:32 to c ourselves yearly with the third part of a 5414
Est 3: 9 of those that have the c of the business, 6213
4: 8 to c her that she should go in unto the king, 6680
Job 34:13 Who hath given him a c over the earth? 6485
Ps 35:11 they laid to my c things that I knew not. 7592
91:11 For he shall give his angels c over thee, 6680
SS 2: 7 I c you, O ye daughters of Jerusalem, 7650
3: 5 I c you, O ye daughters of Jerusalem, 7650
5: 8 I c you, O daughters of Jerusalem, if ye 7650
5: 9 another beloved, that thou dost so c us? 7650
8: 4 I c you, O daughters of Jerusalem, that ye 7650
Isa 10: 6 the people of my wrath will I give him a c, 6680
Jer 39:11 gave c concerning Jeremiah to 6680
47: 7 seeing the LORD hath given it a c against 6680
52:25 which had the c of the men of war; 6496
Eze 9: 1 Cause them that have c over the city to 6486
40:45 the keepers of the c of the house. 4931
40:46 the priests, the keepers of the c of the altar: 4931
44: 8 ye have not kept the c of mine holy things: 4931
44: 8 ye have set keepers of my c in my 4931
44:11 having c at the gates of the house, and 6486
44:14 I will make them keepers of the c of 4931
44:15 that kept the c of my sanctuary when 4931
44:16 minister unto me, and they shall keep my c. 4931
48:11 which have kept my c, which went not 4931
Zec 3: 7 if thou wilt keep my c, then thou shalt also 4931
Mt 4: 6 He shall give his angels c concerning thee: 1781
Mk 9:25 Thou dumb and deaf spirit, I c thee, 2004
Lk 4:10 He shall give his angels c over thee, to keep 1781
Ac 7:60 loud voice, Lord, lay not this sin to their c. 2476
8:27 who had the c of all her treasure, and had 1909
16:24 Who, having received such a c, thrust them 3852
23:29 to have nothing laid to his c worthy of 1462
Ro 8:33 Who shall lay any thing to the c of God's 1458
1Co 9:18 I may make the gospel of Christ without c, 77
1Th 5:27 I c you by the Lord that this epistle be read 3726
1Ti 1: 3 that thou mightest c some that they teach 3853
1:18 This c I commit unto thee, son Timothy, 3852
5: 7 And these things give in c, that they may 3853
5:21 I c thee before God, and the Lord Jesus 1263
6:13 I give thee c in the sight of God, 3853
6:17 C them that are rich in this world, that they 3853
2Ti 4: 1 I c thee therefore before God, and the Lord 1263
4:16 I pray God that it may not be laid to their c. 3049

CHARGEABLE (5) [CHARGE]
2Sa 13:25 let us not all now go, lest we be c unto thee. 3513
Ne 5:15 had been before me were c unto the people, 3513
2Co 11: 9 I was c to no man: for that which was 2655
1Th 2: 9 because we would not be c unto any of you, 1912
2Th 3: 8 day, that we might not be c to any of you: 1912

CHARGED (51) [CHARGE]
Ge 26:11 Abimelech c all his people, saying, He that 6680
28: 1 blessed him, and c him, and said unto him, 6680
40: 4 the captain of the guard c Joseph with 6485
49:29 he c them, and said unto them, I am to be 6680
Ex 1:22 Pharaoh c all his people, saying, Every son 6680
Dt 1:16 I c your judges at that time, saying, 6680
24: 5 shall he be c with any business: 5674+5921
27:11 Moses c the people the same day, saying, 6680
Jos 18: 8 Joshua c them that went to describe 6680
22: 5 which Moses the servant of the LORD c 6680
Ru 2: 9 have I not c the young men that they shall 6680
1Sa 14:27 when his father c the people with the oath: 7650
14:28 straitly c the people with an oath, 7650+7650
2Sa 11:19 c the messenger, saying, When thou hast 6680
18:12 for in our hearing the king c thee and 6680
1Ki 2: 1 and he c Solomon his son, saying, 6680
2:43 the commandment that I have c thee with? 6680
13: 9 so was it c me by the word of the LORD, 6680
2Ki 17:15 concerning whom the LORD had c them, 6680
17:35 c them, saying, Ye shall not fear other 6680
1Ch 22: 6 c him to build a house for the LORD God 6680
22:13 judgments which the LORD c Moses with 6680
2Ch 19: 9 he c them, saying, Thus shall ye do in 6680
36:23 he hath c me to build him a house in 6485
Ezr 1: 2 he hath c me to build him a house at 6485
Ne 13:19 c that they should not be opened till after 559
Est 2:10 for Mordecai had c her that she should not 6680
2:20 nor her people; as Mordecai had c her: 6680
Job 1:22 all this Job sinned not, nor c God foolishly. 5414
4:18 his servants; and his angels he c with folly: 7760
Jer 32:13 And I c Baruch before them, saying, 6680
35: 8 of Rechab our father in all that he hath c us, 6680
Mt 9:30 and Jesus straitly c them, saying, See that 1690
12:16 And c them that they should not make him 2008
16:20 Then c he his disciples that they should tell 1291
17: 9 from the mountain, Jesus c them, saying, 1781
Mk 1:43 And he straitly c him, and forthwith sent 1690
3:12 And he straitly c them that they should not 2008
5:43 And he c them straitly that no man should 1291
7:36 And he c them that they should tell no man: 1291
7:36 should tell no man: but the more he c them, 1291
8:15 And he c them, saying, Take heed, 1291
8:30 And he c them that they should tell no man 2008
9: 9 he c them that they should tell no man what 1291
10:48 And many c him that he should hold his 2008
Lk 5:14 And he c him to tell no man: but go, and 3853
8:56 he c them that they should tell no man what 3853
9:21 And he straitly c them, and 2008
Ac 23:22 c him, See thou tell no man that thou hast 3853
1Th 2:11 and comforted and c every one of you, 3143
1Ti 5:16 relieve them, and let not the church be c; 916

CHARGEDST (1) [CHARGE]
Ex 19:23 for thou c us, saying, Set bounds about 5749

CHARGER (17) [CHARGERS]
Nu 7:13 his offering was one silver c, the weight 7086
7:19 He offered for his offering one silver c, 7086
7:25 His offering was one silver c, the weight 7086
7:31 His offering was one silver c of the weight 7086
7:37 His offering was one silver c, the weight 7086
7:43 His offering was one silver c of the weight 7086
7:49 His offering was one silver c, the weight 7086
7:55 His offering was one silver c of the weight 7086
7:61 His offering was one silver c, the weight 7086
7:67 His offering was one silver c, the weight 7086
7:73 His offering was one silver c, the weight 7086
7:79 His offering was one silver c, the weight 7086
7:85 Each c of silver weighing an hundred and 7086
Mt 14: 8 Give me here John Baptist's head in a c. 4094
14:11 And his head was brought in a c, and 4094
Mk 6:25 and by in a c the head of John the Baptist. 4094
6:28 And brought his head in a c, and gave it to 4094

CHARGERS (3) [CHARGER]
Nu 7:84 twelve c of silver, twelve silver bowls, 7086
Ezr 1: 9 thirty c of gold, a thousand chargers of 105
1: 9 a thousand c of silver, nine and 105

CHARGES (6) [CHARGE]
2Ch 8:14 the Levites to their c, to praise and minister 4931
31:16 his daily portion for their service in their c 4931
31:17 and upward, in their c by their courses; 4931
35: 2 he set the priests in their c, and 4931
Ac 21:24 thyself with them, and be at c with them, 1159
1Co 9: 7 goeth a warfare any time at his own c? 3800

CHARGEST (1) [CHARGE]
2Sa 3: 8 that thou c me to day with a fault 6485

CHARGING (2) [CHARGE]
Ac 16:23 into prison, c the jailor to keep them safely: 3853
2Ti 2:14 c them before the Lord that they strive not 1263

CHARIOT (64) [CHARIOTS]
Ge 41:43 he made him to ride in the second c which 4818
46:29 Joseph made ready his c, and went up to 4818
Ex 14: 6 he made ready his c, and took his people 7393
14:25 took off their c wheels, that they drave 4818
Jdg 4:15 so that Sisera lighted down off his c, and 4818
5:28 the lattice, Why is his c so long in coming? 7393
2Sa 8: 4 David houghed all the c horses, but 7393
1Ki 7:33 the wheels was like the work of a c wheel: 4818
10:29 a c came up and went out of Egypt for six 4818
12:18 made speed to get him up to his c, 4818
18:44 Prepare thy c, and get thee down, NIH
20:25 hast lost, horse for horse, and c for chariot: 7393
20:25 hast lost, horse for horse, and chariot for c: 7393
20:33 and he caused him to come up into the c. 4818
22:34 wherefore he said unto the driver of his c, 7395
22:35 the king was stayed up in his c against 4818
22:35 ran out of the wound into the midst of the c. 7393
22:38 one washed the c in the pool of Samaria; 7393
2Ki 2:11 there appeared a c of fire, and horses of 7393
2:12 the c of Israel, and the horsemen thereof. 7393
5: 9 came with his horses and with his c, 7393
5:21 he lighted down from the c to meet him, 4818
5:26 man turned again from his c to meet thee? 4818
7:14 They took therefore two c horses; and 7393
9:16 So Jehu rode in a c, and went to Jezreel; NIH
9:21 his c was made ready. And Joram king of 7393
9:21 each in his c, and they went out against 7393
9:24 out at his heart, and he sunk down in his c. 7393
9:27 after him, and said, Smite him also in the c. 4818
9:28 his servants carried him in a c to Jerusalem, NIH
10:15 and he took him up to him into the c. 4818
10:16 So they made him ride in his c. 7393
13:14 the c of Israel, and the horsemen thereof. 7393
23:30 his servants carried him in a c dead from NIH
1Ch 18: 4 David also houghed all the c horses, but 7393
28:18 gold for the pattern of the c of 4818
2Ch 1:14 which he placed in the c cities, and with 7393
1:17 brought forth out of Egypt a c for six 4818
8: 6 all the c cities, and the cities of 7393
9:25 whom he bestowed in the c cities, and 7393
10:18 made speed to get him up to his c, 4818

2Ch 18:33 therefore he said to his c man, Turn thine 7395
18:34 in his c against the Syrians until the even: 4818
35:24 therefore took him out of that c, 4818
35:24 and put him in the second c that he had; 7393
Ps 46: 9 spear in sunder; he burneth the c in the fire. 5699
76: 6 both the c and horse are cast into a dead 7393
104: 3 who maketh the clouds his c: who walketh 7398
SS 3: 9 King Solomon made himself a c of the wood 668
Isa 21: 7 he saw a c with a couple of horsemen, 7393
21: 7 a c of asses, and a chariot of camels; 7393
21: 7 a chariot of asses, and a c of camels; 7393
21: 9 behold, here cometh a c of men, with a 7393
43:17 Which bringeth forth the c and horse, 7393
Jer 51:21 with thee will I break in pieces the c and 7393
Mic 1:13 of Lachish, bind the c to the swift beast: 4818
Zec 6: 2 In the first c were red horses; and in 4818
6: 2 and in the second c black horses; 4818
6: 3 in the third c white horses; and in the fourth 4818
6: 3 and in the fourth c grisled and bay horses. 4818
9:10 I will cut off the c from Ephraim, and 7393
Ac 8:28 and sitting in his c read Esaias the prophet. 716
8:29 Go near, and join thyself to this c. 716
8:38 And he commanded the c to stand still: and 716

CHARIOTS (113) [CHARIOT]
Ge 50: 9 there went up with him both c and 7393
Ex 14: 7 he took six hundred chosen c, and all 7393
14: 7 all the c of Egypt, and captains over every 7393
14: 9 after them (all the horses and c of Pharaoh, 7393
14:17 upon his c, and upon his horsemen. 7393
14:18 upon his c, and upon his horsemen. 7393
14:23 Pharaoh's horses, his c, and his horsemen. 7393
14:26 upon their c, and upon their horsemen. 7393
14:28 covered the c, and the horsemen, and all 7393
15: 4 Pharaoh's c and his host hath he cast into 4818
15:19 For the horse of Pharaoh went in with his c 7393
Dt 11: 4 of Egypt, unto their horses, and to their c; 7393
20: 1 and c, and a people more than thou, 7393
Jos 11: 4 in multitude, with horses and c very many. 7393
11: 6 their horses, and burn their c with fire. 4818
11: 9 their horses, and burnt their c with fire. 4818
17:16 in the land of the valley have c of iron, 7393
17:18 though they have iron c, and though they be 7393
24: 6 Egyptians pursued after your fathers with c 7393
Jdg 1:19 of the valley, because they had c of iron. 7393
4: 3 for he had nine hundred c of iron; and 7393
4: 7 Jabin's army, with his c and his multitude; 7393
4:13 Sisera gathered together all his c, even nine 7393
4:13 even nine hundred c of iron, and all 7393
4:15 and all his c, and all his host, 7393
4:16 Barak pursued after the c, and after 7393
5:28 in coming? why tarry the wheels of his c? 4818
1Sa 8:11 for his c, and to be his horsemen; 4818
8:11 and some shall run before his c. 4818
8:12 of war, and instruments of his c. 7393
13: 5 thirty thousand c, and six thousand 7393
2Sa 1: 6 the c and horsemen followed hard after 7393
8: 4 And David took from him a thousand c, and NIH
8: 4 but reserved of them for an hundred c. 7393
10:18 David slew the men of seven hundred c of 7393
15: 1 that Absalom prepared him c and horses, 4818
1Ki 1: 5 he prepared him c and horsemen, and 7393
4:26 had forty thousand stalls of horses for his c, 4817
9:19 cities for his c, and cities for his horsemen, 7393
9:22 and rulers of his c, and his horsemen. 7393
10:26 Solomon gathered together c and 7393
10:26 he had a thousand and four hundred c, and 7393
10:26 whom he bestowed in the cities for c, and 7393
16: 9 captain of half his c, conspired against him, 7393
20: 1 and two kings with him, and horses, and c: 7393
20:21 smote the horses and c, and slew 7393
22:31 and two captains that had rule over his c, 7393
22:32 when the captains of the c saw 7393
22:33 when the captains of the c perceived that it 7393
2Ki 6:14 he thither horses, and c, and a great host: 7393
6:15 compassed the city both with horses and c. 7393
6:17 of horses and c of fire round about Elisha. 7393
7: 6 the host of the Syrians to hear a noise of c, 7393
8:21 went over to Zair, and all the c with him: 7393
8:21 him about, and the captains of the c: 7393
10: 2 there are with you c and horses, a fenced 7393
13: 7 and ten c, and ten thousand footmen; 7393
18:24 put thy trust on Egypt for c and 7393
19:23 With the multitude of my c I am come up 7393
23:11 and burnt the c of the sun with fire. 4818
1Ch 18: 4 David took from him a thousand c, and 7393
18: 4 but reserved of them an hundred c. 7393
19: 6 a thousand talents of silver to hire them c 7393
19: 7 So they hired thirty and two thousand c, 7393
19:18 seven thousand men which fought in c, 7393
2Ch 1:14 Solomon gathered c and horsemen: and 7393
1:14 he had a thousand and four hundred c, and 7393
8: 9 and captains of his c and horsemen. 7393
9:25 had four thousand stalls for horses and c, 4818
12: 3 With twelve hundred c, and threescore 7393
14: 9 a thousand thousand, and three hundred c; 4818
16: 8 with very many c and horsemen? 7393
18:30 the captains of the c that were with him, 7393
18:31 when the captains of the c saw 7393
18:32 that when the captains of the c perceived 7393
21: 9 with his princes, and all his c with him: 7393
21: 9 him in, and the captains of the c. 7393
Ps 20: 7 Some trust in c, and some in horses: but 7393
68:17 The c of God are twenty thousand, 7393
SS 1: 9 to a company of horses in Pharaoh's c. 7393
6:12 my soul made me like the c of 4818
Isa 2: 7 neither is there any end of their c: 4818
22: 6 Elam bare the quiver with c of men and 7393
22: 7 that thy choicest valleys shall be full of c, 7393
22:18 there the c of thy glory shall be the shame 4818
31: 1 and trust in c, because they are many; 7393
36: 9 put thy trust on Egypt for c and 7393
37:24 By the multitude of my c am I come up to 7393
66:15 with his c like a whirlwind, to render his 4818
66:20 in c, and in litters, and upon mules, and 7393

Jer 4:13 as clouds, and his c shall be as a whirlwind: 4818
17:25 riding in c and on horses, they, and 7393
22: 4 riding in c and on horses, he, and 7393
46: 9 rage, ye c; and let the mighty men come 7393
47: 3 of his strong horses, at the rushing of his c, 7393
50:37 upon their c, and upon all the mingled 7393
Eze 23:24 they shall come against thee with c, 2021
26: 7 with c, and with horsemen, and companies, 7393
26:10 of the wheels, and of the c, when he shall 7393
27:20 was thy merchant in precious clothes for c. 7396
39:20 be filled at my table with horses and c, 7393
Da 11:40 with c, and with horsemen, and with many 7393
Joel 2: 5 Like the noise of c on the tops of mountains 4818
Mic 5:10 the midst of thee, and I will destroy thy c: 4818
Na 2: 3 the c shall be with flaming torches in 7393
2: 4 The c shall rage in the streets, they shall 7393
2:13 I will burn her c in the smoke, and 7393
3: 2 the pransing horses, and of the jumping c. 4818
Hab 3: 8 upon thine horses and thy c of salvation? 4818
Hag 2:22 I will overthrow the c, and those that ride in 4818
Zec 6: 1 there came four c out from between two 4818
Rev 9: 9 sound of c of many horses running to battle. 716
18:13 horses, and c, and slaves, and souls of men. 4480

CHARITABLY (1) [CHARITY]
Ro 14:15 with thy meat, now walkest thou not c. 26+2596

CHARITY (28) [CHARITABLY]
1Co 8: 1 Knowledge puffeth up, but c edifieth. 26
13: 1 tongues of men and of angels, and have not c, 26
13: 2 and have no c, I am nothing. 26
13: 3 and have not c, it profiteth me nothing. 26
13: 4 C suffereth long, and is kind; charity envieth 26
13: 4 suffereth long, and is kind; c envieth not; 26
13: 4 c vaunteth not itself, is not puffed up, 26
13: 8 C never faileth: 26
13:13 And now abideth faith, hope, c, these three; 26
13:13 these three; but the greatest of these is c. 26
14: 1 Follow after c, and desire spiritual gifts, but 26
16:14 Let all your things be done with c. 26
Col 3:14 And above all these things put on c, which is 26
1Th 3: 6 brought us good tidings of your faith and c, 26
2Th 1: 3 the c of every one of you all towards each 26
1Ti 1: 5 Now the end of the commandment is c out of 26
2:15 in faith and c and holiness with sobriety. 26
4:12 in c, in spirit, in faith, in purity. 26
2Ti 2:22 but follow righteousness, faith, c, peace, 26
3:10 purpose, faith, longsuffering, c, patience, 26
Tit 2: 2 temperate, sound in faith, in c, in patience. 26
1Pe 4: 8 And above all things have fervent c among 26
4: 8 for c shall cover the multitude of sins. 26
5:14 Greet ye one another with a kiss of c. 26
2Pe 1: 7 and to brotherly kindness c. 26
3Jn 1: 6 Which have borne witness of thy c before 26
Jude 1:12 These are spots in your feasts of c when they 26
Rev 2:19 I know thy works, and c, and service, 26

CHARMED (1) [CHARMER, CHARMERS, CHARMING]
Jer 8:17 which will not be c, and they shall bite you, 3908

CHARMER (1) [CHARMED]
Dt 18:11 Or a c, or a consulter with familiar 2266+2267

CHARMERS (2) [CHARMED]
Ps 58: 5 Which will not hearken to the voice of c, 3907
Isa 19: 3 to the c, and to them that have familiar 328

CHARMING (1) [CHARMED]
Ps 58: 5 voice of charmers, c never so wisely. 2266+2267

CHARRAN (2) [HARAN]
Ac 7: 2 was in Mesopotamia, before he dwelt in C, 5488
7: 4 the land of the Chaldeans, and dwelt in C: 5488

CHASE (6) [CHASED, CHASETH, CHASING]
Lev 26: 7 ye shall c your enemies, and they shall fall 7291
26: 8 five of you shall c an hundred, and 7291
26:36 the sound of a shaken leaf shall c them; and 7291
Dt 32:30 How should one c a thousand, and two put 7291
Jos 23:10 One man of you shall c a thousand: for 7291
Ps 35: 5 and let the angel of the LORD c them. 1760

CHASED (13) [CHASE]
Dt 1:44 c you, as bees do, and destroyed you in 7291
Jos 7: 5 for they c them from before the gate even 7291
8:24 in the wilderness wherein they c them, and 7291
10:10 c them along the way that goeth up to 7291
11: 8 c them unto great Zidon, and 7291
Jdg 9:40 Abimelech c him, and he fled before him, 7291
20:43 and c them, and trode them down with ease 7291
Ne 13:28 the Horonite: therefore I c him from me. 1272
Job 18:18 light into darkness, and c out of the world. 5074
20: 8 he shall be c away as a vision of the night. 5074
Isa 13:14 it shall be as the c roe, and as a sheep that 5080
17:13 shall be c as the chaff of the mountains 7291
La 3:52 Mine enemies c me sore, like a bird, 6679+6679

CHASETH (1) [CHASE]
Pr 19:26 wasteth his father, and c away his mother, 1272

CHASING (1) [CHASE]
1Sa 17:53 the children of Israel returned from c after 1814

CHASTE (3)
2Co 11: 2 that I may present you as a c virgin to Christ. 53
Tit 2: 5 To be discreet, c, keepers at home, good, 53
1Pe 3: 2 While they behold your c conversation 53

CHASTEN (6) [CHASTENED, CHASTENEST, CHASTENETH, CHASTENING]
2Sa 7:14 I will c him with the rod of men, and 3198
Ps 6: 1 neither c me in thy hot displeasure. 3256

Ps 38: 1 neither c me in thy hot displeasure. 3256
Pr 19:18 C thy son while there is hope, and let not 3256
Da 10:12 to c thyself before thy God, thy words were 6031
Rev 3:19 As many as I love, I rebuke and c: 3811

CHASTENED (8) [CHASTEN]
Dt 21:18 his mother, and that, when they have c him, 3256
Job 33:19 He is c also with pain upon his bed, and 3198
Ps 69:10 When I wept, and c my soul with fasting, NIH
73:14 have I been plagued, and c every morning. 8433
118:18 The LORD hath c me sore: but 3256+3256
1Co 11:32 when we are judged, we are c of the Lord, 3811
2Co 6: 9 and behold, we live; as c, and not killed; 3811
Heb 12:10 For they verily for a few days c us after 3811

CHASTENEST (1) [CHASTEN]
Ps 94:12 Blessed is the man whom thou c, 3256

CHASTENETH (5) [CHASTEN]
Dt 8: 5 as a man c his son, so the LORD thy God 3256
8: 5 his son, so the LORD thy God c thee. 3256
Pr 13:24 but he that loveth him c him betimes. 4148
Heb 12: 6 For whom the Lord loveth he c, and 3811
12: 7 for what son is he whom the father c not? 3811

CHASTENING (6) [CHASTEN]
Job 5:17 despise not thou the c of the Almighty: 4148
Pr 3:11 My son, despise not the c of the LORD; 4148
Isa 26:16 they poured out a prayer when thy c was 4148
Heb 12: 5 My son, despise not thou the c of the Lord, 3809
12: 7 If ye endure c, God dealeth with you as 3809
12:11 Now no c for the present seemeth to be 3809

CHASTISE (10) [CHASTISED, CHASTISEMENT, CHASTISETH]
Lev 26:28 even I, will c you seven times for your sins. 3256
Dt 22:18 of that city shall take that man and c him; 3256
1Ki 12:11 with whips, but I will c you with scorpions. 3256
12:14 with whips, but I will c you with scorpions. 3256
2Ch 10:11 with whips, but I will c you with scorpions. NIH
10:14 with whips, but I will c you with scorpions. NIH
Hos 7:12 I will c them, as their congregation hath 3256
10:10 It is in my desire that I should c them; and 3256
Lk 23:16 I will therefore c him, and release him. 3811
23:22 I will therefore c him, and let him go. 3811

CHASTISED (6) [CHASTISE]
1Ki 12:11 my father hath c you with whips, but I will 3256
12:14 my father also c you with whips, but I will 3256
2Ch 10:11 my father c you with whips, but I will 3256
10:14 my father c you with whips, but I will 3256
Jer 31:18 bemoaning himself thus; Thou hast c me, 3256
31:18 I was c, as a bullock unaccustomed to 3256

CHASTISEMENT (5) [CHASTISE]
Dt 11: 2 which have not seen the c of the LORD 4148
Job 34:31 I have borne c, I will not offend any more: NIH
Isa 53: 5 the c of our peace was upon him; and 4148
Jer 30:14 with the c of a cruel one, for the multitude 4148
Heb 12: 8 But if ye be without c, whereof all are 3809

CHASTISETH (1) [CHASTISE]
Ps 94:10 He that c the heathen, shall not he correct? 3256

CHATTER (1)
Isa 38:14 Like a crane or a swallow, so did I c: I did 6850

CHEBAR (8)
Eze 1: 1 I was among the captives by the river of C, 3529
1: 3 in the land of the Chaldeans by the river C; 3529
3:15 that dwelt by the river of C, and I sat where 3529
3:23 as the glory which I saw by the river of C: 3529
10:15 living creature that I saw by the river of C. 3529
10:20 under the God of Israel by the river of C; 3529
10:22 same faces which I saw by the river of C, 3529
43: 3 like the vision that I saw by the river C; 3529

CHECK (1)
Job 20: 3 I have heard the c of my reproach, and 4148

CHECKER (1)
1Ki 7:17 And nets of c work, and wreaths of chain 7639

CHEDORLAOMER (5)
Ge 14: 1 C king of Elam, and Tidal king of nations; 3540
14: 4 Twelve years they served C, and in 3540
14: 5 in the fourteenth year came C, and 3540
14: 9 With C the king of Elam, and with Tidal 3540
14:17 him after his return from the slaughter of C, 3540

CHEEK (8) [CHEEK-TEETH, CHEEKS]
1Ki 22:24 and smote Micaiah on the c, and said, 3895
2Ch 18:23 and smote Micaiah upon the c, and said, 3895
Job 16:10 they have smitten me upon the c 3895
Ps 3: 7 smitten all mine enemies upon the c bone; 3895
La 3:30 He giveth his c to him that smiteth him: 3895
Mic 5: 1 the judge of Israel with a rod upon the c. 3895
Mt 5:39 whosoever shall smite thee on thy right c, 4600
Lk 6:29 And unto him that smiteth thee on the one c 4600

CHEEKS (5) [CHEEK]
Dt 18: 3 the shoulder, and the two c, and the maw. 3895
SS 1:10 Thy c are comely with rows of jewels, thy 3895
5:13 His c are as a bed of spices, as sweet 3895
Isa 50: 6 and my c to them that plucked off the hair: 3895
La 1: 2 sore in the night, and her tears are on her c: 3895

CHEEK-TEETH (1) [CHEEK, TOOTH]
Joel 1: 6 of a lion, and he hath the c of a great lion. 4973

CHEER (10) [CHEERETH, CHEERFUL, CHEERFULLY, CHEERFULNESS]
Dt 24: 5 shall c up his wife which he hath taken. 8055

Ecc 11: 9 let thy heart c thee in the days of thy youth, 2895
Mt 9: 2 Son, be of good c; thy sins be forgiven 2293
14:27 spake unto them, saying, Be of good c; 2293
Mk 6:50 and saith unto them, Be of good c: 2293
Jn 16:33 but be of good c; I have overcome 2293
Ac 23:11 stood by him, and said, Be of good c, Paul: 2293
27:22 And now I exhort you to be of good c: 2114
27:25 Wherefore, sirs, be of good c: for I believe 2114
27:36 Then were they all of good c, and they also 2115

CHEERETH (1) [CHEER]
Jdg 9:13 which c God and man, and go to be 8055

CHEERFUL (4) [CHEER]
Pr 15:13 A merry heart maketh a c countenance: but 3190
Zec 8:19 of Judah joy and gladness, and c feasts; 2896
9:17 corn shall make the young men c, and 5107
2Co 9: 7 or of necessity: for God loveth a c giver. 2431

CHEERFULLY (1) [CHEER]
Ac 24:10 I do the more c answer for myself: 2115

CHEERFULNESS (1) [CHEER]
Ro 12: 8 he that sheweth mercy, with c. 2432

CHEESE (2) [CHEESES]
2Sa 17:29 butter, and sheep, and c of kine, for David, 8194
Job 10:10 me out as milk, and cruddled me like c? 1385

CHEESES (1) [CHEESE]
1Sa 17:18 carry these ten c unto the captain of 2461+2757

CHELAL (1)
Ezr 10:30 Adna, and C, Benaiah, Maaseiah, 3636

CHELLUH (1)
Ezr 10:35 Benaiah, Bedeiah, C, 3622

CHELUB (2)
1Ch 4:11 C the brother of Shuah begat Mehir, 3620
27:26 tillage of the ground *was* Ezri the son of C: 3620

CHELUBAI (1)
1Ch 2: 9 born unto him; Jerahmeel, and Ram, and C. 3621

CHEMARIMS (1)
Zep 1: 4 *and* the name of the C with the priests; 3649

CHEMOSH (8)
Nu 21:29 thou art undone, O people of C: he hath 3645
Jdg 11:24 Wilt not thou possess that which C thy god 3645
1Ki 11: 7 did Solomon build a high place for C, 3645
11:33 C the god of the Moabites, and Milcom 3645
2Ki 23:13 for C the abomination of the Moabites, and 3645
Jer 48: 7 C shall go forth into captivity *with* his 3645
48:13 Moab shall be ashamed of C, as the house 3645
48:46 the people of C perisheth: for thy sons are 3645

CHENAANAH (5)
1Ki 22:11 Zedekiah the son of C made him horns of 3668
22:24 Zedekiah the son of C went near, and 3668
1Ch 7:10 C, and Zethan, and Tharshish, and 3668
2Ch 18:10 Zedekiah the son of C had made him horns 3668
18:23 Zedekiah the son of C came near, and 3668

CHENANI (1)
Ne 9: 4 *and* C, and cried with a loud voice unto 3662

CHENANIAH (3)
1Ch 15:22 C, chief of the Levites, *was* for song: 3663
15:27 C the master of the song *with* the singers: 3663
26:29 C and his sons *were* for the outward 3663

CHEPHAR-HAAMMONAI (1)
Jos 18:24 C, and Ophni, and Gaba; twelve cities with 3726

CHEPHIRAH (4)
Jos 9:17 and C, and Beeroth, and Kirjath-jearim. 3716
18:26 And Mizpeh, and C, and Mozah, 3716
Ezr 2:25 C, and Beeroth, seven hundred and forty 3716
Ne 7:29 C, and Beeroth, seven hundred forty and 3716

CHERAN (2)
Ge 36:26 Hemdan, and Eshban, and Ithran, and C. 3763
1Ch 1:41 Amram, and Eshban, and Ithran, and C. 3763

CHERETHIMS (1) [CHERETHITES]
Eze 25:16 I will cut off the C, and destroy 3774

CHERETHITES (9) [CHERETHIMS]
1Sa 30:14 made an invasion *upon* the south of the C, 3774
2Sa 8:18 the son of Jehoiada *was over* both the C 3774
15:18 all the C, and all the Pelethites, and all 3774
20: 7 the C, and the Pelethites, and all the mighty 3774
20:23 Benaiah the son of Jehoiada *was* over the C 3774
1Ki 1:38 the C, and the Pelethites, went down, and 3774
1:44 the C, and the Pelethites, and they have 3774
1Ch 18:17 Benaiah the son of Jehoiada *was* over the C 3774
Zep 2: 5 of the sea coast, the nation of the C! 3774

CHERISH (1) [CHERISHED, CHERISHETH]
1Ki 1: 2 let her c him, and let her lie in thy 1961+5532

CHERISHED (1) [CHERISH]
1Ki 1: 4 c the king, and ministered to him: 1961+5532

CHERISHETH (2) [CHERISH]
Eph 5:29 but nourisheth and c it, even as the Lord 2282
1Th 2: 7 among you, *even* as a nurse c her children: 2282

CHERITH (2)
1Ki 17: 3 and hide thyself by the brook C, 3747
1Ki 17: 5 for he went and dwelt by the brook C, 3747

CHERUB (30) [CHERUBIMS, CHERUBIMS']
Ex 25:19 make one c on the one end, and the other 3742
25:19 one end, and the other c on the other end: 3742
37: 8 One c on the end on this side, and 3742
37: 8 and another c on the *other* end on that side: 3742
2Sa 22:11 he rode upon a c, and did fly: and he was 3742
1Ki 6:24 five cubits *was* the one wing of the c, and 3742
6:24 and five cubits the other wing of the c: 3742
6:25 the other c *was* ten cubits: both 3742
6:26 The height of the one c *was* ten cubits, and 3742
6:26 *was* ten cubits, and so *was it* of the other c. 3742
6:27 the wing of the other c touched the other 3742
2Ch 3:11 *one* wing of the one c *was* five cubits, NIH
3:11 reaching to the wing of the other c. 3742
3:12 *one* wing of the other c *was* five cubits, 3742
3:12 *also,* joining to the wing of the other c. 3742
Ezr 2:59 Tel-harsa, C, Addan, *and* Immer: 3743
Ne 7:61 Tel-haresha, C, Addon, and Immer: 3743
Ps 18:10 he rode upon a c, and did fly: yea, he did 3742
Eze 9: 3 the God of Israel was gone up from the c, 3742
10: 2 *even* under the c, and fill thine hand *with* 3742
10: 4 glory of the LORD went up from the c, 3742
10: 7 *one* c stretched forth his hand from between 3742
10: 9 one wheel by one c, and another wheel by 3742
10: 9 and another wheel by another c: 3742
10:14 the first face *was* the face of a c, and 3742
28:14 Thou *art* the anointed c that covereth; and 3742
28:16 I will destroy thee, O covering c, from 3742
41:18 so that a palm tree *was* between a c and a 3742
41:18 a palm tree *was* between a cherub and a c; 3742
41:18 and a cherub; and *every* c had two faces; 3742

CHERUBIMS (64) [CHERUB]
Ge 3:24 placed at the east of the garden of Eden C, 3742
Ex 25:18 thou shalt make two c *of* gold, *of* beaten 3742
25:19 *even* of the mercy seat shall ye make the c 3742
25:20 the c shall stretch forth *their* wings on high, 3742
25:20 the mercy seat shall the faces of the c be. 3742
25:22 from between the two c which *are* upon 3742
26: 1 *with* c *of* cunning work shalt thou make 3742
26:31 *of* cunning work: *with* c shall it be made: 3742
36: 8 *with* c *of* cunning work made he them. 3742
36:35 *with* c made he it *of* cunning work. 3742
37: 7 he made two c *of* gold, beaten out of one 3742
37: 8 out of the mercy seat made he the c on 3742
37: 9 the c spread out *their* wings on high, 3742
37: 9 the mercy seatward were the faces of the c. 3742
Nu 7:89 ark of Testimony, from between the two c: 3742
1Sa 4: 4 of hosts, which dwelleth *between* the c: 3742
2Sa 6: 2 of hosts that dwelleth *between* the c. 3742
1Ki 6:23 within the oracle he made two c *of* olive 3742
6:25 both the c *were* of one measure and 3742
6:27 And he set the c within the inner house: and 3742
6:27 they stretched forth the wings of the c, so 3742
6:28 And he overlaid the c with gold. 3742
6:29 house round about *with* carved figures of c 3742
6:32 he carved upon them carvings of c and 3742
6:32 spread gold upon the c, and upon the palm 3742
6:35 And he carved *thereon* c and palm trees and 3742
7:29 between the ledges *were* lions, oxen, and c: 3742
7:36 he graved c, lions, and palm trees, 3742
8: 6 holy *place,* even under the wings of the c. 3742
8: 7 For the c spread forth *their* two wings over 3742
8: 7 the c covered the ark and the staves thereof 3742
2Ki 19:15 which dwellest *between* the c, thou *art* 3742
1Ch 13: 6 that dwelleth *between* the c, whose name is 3742
28:18 gold for the pattern of the chariot of the c, 3742
2Ch 3: 7 with gold; and graved c on the walls. 3742
3:10 in the most holy house he made two c of 3742
3:11 the wings of the c *were* twenty cubits long: 3742
3:13 The wings of these c spread themselves 3742
3:14 and fine linen, and wrought c thereon. 3742
5: 7 holy *place,* even under the wings of the c: 3742
5: 8 For the c spread forth *their* wings over 3742
5: 8 the c covered the ark and the staves thereof 3742
Ps 80: 1 thou that dwellest *between* the c, 3742
99: 1 he sitteth *between* the c; let the earth be 3742
Isa 37:16 God of Israel, that dwellest *between* the c, 3742
Eze 10: 1 c there appeared over them as it were a 3742
10: 2 hand *with* coals of fire from between the c, 3742
10: 3 Now the c stood on the right side of 3742
10: 6 between the wheels, from between the c; 3742
10: 7 c unto the fire that *was* between 3742
10: 7 unto the fire that *was* between the c, 3742
10: 8 there appeared in the c the form of a man's 3742
10: 9 I looked, behold the four wheels by the c, 3742
10:15 the c were lifted up. This *is* the living 3742
10:16 when the c went, the wheels went by them: 3742
10:16 when the c lift up their wings to mount up 3742
10:18 of the house, and stood over the c. 3742
10:19 the c lift up their wings, and mounted up 3742
10:20 of Chebar; and I knew that they *were the* c. 3742
11:22 did the c lift up their wings, and the wheels 3742
41:18 *it was* made *with* c and palm trees, so that a 3742
41:20 the ground unto above the door *were* c 3742
41:25 the doors of the temple, c and palm trees, 3742
Heb 9: 5 And over it the c of glory shadowing 5502

CHERUBIMS' (1) [CHERUB]
Eze 10: 5 the sound of the c wings was heard *even* to 3742

CHESALON (1)
Jos 15:10 which *is* C, on the north side, and 3693

CHESED (1)
Ge 22:22 C, and Hazo, and Pildash, and Jidlaph, and 3777

CHESIL (1)
Jos 15:30 And Eltolad, and C, and Hormah, 3686

CHESNUT (2)
Ge 30:37 of green poplar, and of the hazel and c tree; 6196
Eze 31: 8 and the c trees were not like his branches; 6196

CHEST (6) [CHESTS]
2Ki 12: 9 Jehoiada the priest took a c, and bored a hole 727
12:10 saw that *there was* much money in the c, 727
2Ch 24: 8 at the king's commandment they made a c, 727
24:10 and brought in, and cast into the c, 727
24:11 that at *what* time the c was brought unto 727
24:11 high priest's officer came and emptied the c, 727

CHESTS (1) [CHEST]
Eze 27:24 broidered work, and in c of rich apparel, 1595

CHESULLOTH (1)
Jos 19:18 was toward Jezreel, and C, and Shunem, 3694

CHEW (3) [CHEWED, CHEWETH]
Lev 11: 4 these shall ye not eat of them that c the cud, 5927
Dt 14: 7 these ye shall not eat of them that c the cud, 5927
14: 7 for they c the cud, but divide not the hoof; 5927

CHEWED (1) [CHEW]
Nu 11:33 *was* yet between their teeth, ere it was c, 3772

CHEWETH (8) [CHEW]
Lev 11: 3 *is* clovenfooted, *and* c cud, among 5927
11: 4 because he c the cud, but divideth not 5927
11: 5 because he c the cud, but divideth not 5927
11: 6 because he c the cud, but divideth not 5927
11: 7 and *be* clovenfooted, yet he c not the cud; 1641
11:26 *is* not clovenfooted, nor c the cud, 5927
Dt 14: 6 *and* c the cud amongst the beasts: 5927
14: 8 it divideth the hoof, yet c not the cud, NIH

CHEZIB (1)
Ge 38: 5 and he was at C, when she bare him. 3580

CHICKENS (1)
Mt 23:37 even as a hen gathereth her c under *her* 3556

CHICKS See BROOD; CHICKENS

CHIDE (4) [CHIDING]
Ex 17: 2 Wherefore the people did c with Moses, 7378
17: 2 Moses said unto them, Why c you with me? 7378
Jdg 8: 1 And they did c with him sharply. 7378
Ps 103: 9 He will not always c: neither will he keep 7378

CHIDING (1) [CHIDE]
Ex 17: 7 because of the c of the children of Israel, 7379

CHIDON (1)
1Ch 13: 9 they came unto the threshingfloor of C, 3592

CHIEF (338) [CHIEFEST, CHIEFLY]
Ge 21:22 Phichol the c captain of his host spake 8269
21:32 Phichol the c captain of his host, and 8269
26:26 and Phichol the c captain of his army. 8269
40: 2 against the c of the butlers, and against 8269
40: 2 the butlers, and against the c of the bakers. 8269
40: 9 the c butler told his dream to Joseph, and 8269
40:16 When the c baker saw that 8269
40:20 he lifted up the head of the c butler and of 8269
40:20 and of the c baker among his servants. 8269
40:21 he restored the c butler unto his butlership 8269
40:22 he hanged the c baker: as Joseph had 8269
40:23 Yet did not the c butler remember Joseph, 8269
41: 9 spake the c butler unto Pharaoh, saying, 8269
41:10 the guard's house, *both* me and the c baker: 8269
Lev 21: 4 *being* a c man among his people, 1167
Nu 3:24 the c of the house of the father of 5387
3:30 the c of the house of the father of 5387
3:32 *shall be* c over the chief of the Levites, 5387
3:32 *shall be* chief over the c of the Levites, 5387
3:35 the c of the house of the father of 5387
4:34 the c of the congregation numbered 5387
4:46 and Aaron and the c of Israel numbered, 5387
25:14 a prince of a c house among the Simeonites. 1
25:15 head over a people, *and* of a c house in Midian. 1
31:26 and the c fathers of the congregation: 7218
32:28 the c fathers of the tribes of the children of 7218
36: 1 the c fathers of the families of the children 7218
36: 1 the c fathers of the children of Israel: 7218
Dt 1:15 So I took the c of your tribes, wise men, 7218
33:15 for the c things of the ancient mountains, 7218
Jos 22:14 of each c house a prince throughout all 5387
Jdg 20: 2 the c of all the people, *even* of all the tribes 6438
1Sa 14:38 Draw ye near hither, all the c of the people: 6438
15:21 the c of the things which should have been 7225
2Sa 5: 8 *he shall be* c *and captain.* Wherefore they NIH
8:18 and David's sons were c rulers. 3548
20:26 Ira also the Jairite was a c ruler about 3548
23: 8 that sat in the seat, c among the captains; 7218
23:13 three of the thirty c went down, and 7218
23:18 the son of Zeruiah, *was* c among three. 7218
1Ki 5:16 Besides the c of Solomon's officers which 8269
8: 1 the c of the fathers of the children of Israel, 5387
9:23 These *were* the c of the officers that *were* 8269
14:27 committed *them* unto the hands of the c of 8269
2Ki 25:18 the captain of the guard took Seraiah the c 7218
1Ch 5: 2 his brethren, and of him *came* the c ruler; 5057
5: 7 *were* the c, Jeiel, and Zechariah, 7218
5:12 Joel the c, and Shapham the next, and 7218
5:15 son of Guni, c of the house of their fathers. 7218
7: 3 and Joel, Ishiah, five: all of them c *men.* 7218
7:40 *and* mighty *men* of valour, c of the princes. 7218
8:28 c *men.* These dwelt in Jerusalem. 7218
9: 9 All these men *were* c of the fathers in 7218
9:17 and their brethren: Shallum *was* the c; 7218
9:26 For these Levites, the four c porters, 1368
9:33 the singers, c of the fathers of the Levites, 7218
9:34 These c fathers of the Levites *were* chief 7218
9:34 These chief fathers of the Levites *were* c 7218

1Ch 11: 6 smiteth the Jebusites first shall be c 7218
11: 6 the son of Zeruiah went first up, and was c. 7218
11:10 These also are the c of the mighty men 7218
11:11 a Hachmonite, the c of the captains: 7218
11:20 the brother of Joab, he was c of the three: 7218
12: 3 The c was Ahiezer, then Joash, the sons of 7218
12:18 who was c of the captains, and he said, 7218
15: 5 Uriel the c, and his brethren an hundred and 8269
15: 6 Asaiah the c, and his brethren two hundred 8269
15: 7 Joel the c, and his brethren an hundred and 8269
15: 8 Shemaiah the c, and his brethren two 8269
15: 9 Eliel the c, and his brethren fourscore: 8269
15:10 Amminadab the c, and his brethren an 8269
15:12 Ye are the c of the fathers of the Levites: 7218
15:16 David spake to the c of the Levites to 8269
15:22 c of the Levites, was for song: 8269
16: 5 Asaph the c, and next to him Zechariah, 7218
18:17 the sons of David were c about the king. 7223
23: 8 the c was Jehiel, and Zetham, and Joel, 7218
23: 9 These were the c of the fathers of Laadan. 7218
23:11 Jahath was the c, and Zizah the second: 7218
23:16 Of the sons of Gershom, Shebuel was the c. 7218
23:17 the sons of Eliezer were, Rehabiah the c. 7218
23:18 Of the sons of Izhar; Shelomith the c. 7218
23:24 even the c of the fathers, as they were 7218
24: 4 there were moe c men found of the sons of 7218
24: 4 sixteen c men of the house of their fathers, 7218
24: 6 before the c of the fathers of the priests and 7218
24:31 the c of the fathers of the priests and 7218
26:10 Simri the c, (for though he was not 7218
26:10 yet his father made him the c;) 7218
26:12 even among the c men, having wards one 7218
26:21 c fathers, even of Laadan the Gershonite, 7218
26:26 the c fathers, the captains over thousands 7218
26:31 Among the Hebronites was Jerijah the c, 7218
26:32 two thousand and seven hundred c fathers, 7218
27: 1 to wit, the c fathers and captains of 7218
27: 3 Of the children of Perez was the c of all 7218
27: 5 was Benaiah the son of Jehoiada, a c priest: 7218
29: 6 the c of the fathers and princes of the tribes 8269
29:22 him unto the LORD to be the c governor, 5057
2Ch 1: 2 governor in all Israel, the c of the fathers. 7218
5: 2 the c of the fathers of the children of Israel, 5387
8: 9 c of his captains, and captains of his 8269
8:10 these were the c of king Solomon's 8269
11:22 made Abijah the son of Maachah the c, 7218
12:10 committed them to the hands of the c of 8269
17:14 Adnah the c, and with him mighty men of 8269
19: 8 and of the c of the fathers of Israel, 7218
19:11 Amariah the c priest is over you in all 7218
23: 2 the c of the fathers of Israel, and they came 7218
24: 6 the king called for Jehoiada the c, and 7218
26:12 The whole number of the c of the fathers of 7218
26:20 And Azariah the c priest, and all the priests, 7218
31:10 Azariah the c priest of the house of Zadok 7218
35: 9 and Jeiel and Jozabad, c of the Levites, 8269
36:14 Moreover all the c of the priests, and 8269
Ezr 1: 5 rose up the c of the fathers of Judah and 7218
2:68 some of the c of the fathers, when they 7218
3:12 the priests and Levites and c of the fathers, 7218
4: 2 to the c of the fathers, and said unto them, 7218
4: 3 and the rest of the c of the fathers of Israel, 7218
5:10 names of the men that were the c of them. 7217
7: 5 of Eleazar, the son of Aaron the c priest: 7218
7:28 I gathered together out of Israel c men to go 7218
8: 1 These are now the c of their fathers, and 7218
8:16 c men; also for Joiarib, and for Elnathan, 7218
8:17 unto Iddo the c at the place Casiphia, 7218
8:24 I separated twelve of the c of the priests, 8269
8:29 keep them, until ye weigh them before the c 8269
8:29 the Levites, and c of the fathers of Israel, 8269
9: 2 and rulers hath been c in this trespass. 7223
10: 5 made the c priests, the Levites, and 8269
10:16 Ezra the priest, with certain c of the fathers, 7218
Ne 7:70 some of the c of the fathers gave unto 7218
7:71 some of the c of the fathers gave to 7218
8:13 the c of the fathers of all the people, 7218
10:14 The c of the people; Parosh, Pahath-moab, 7218
11: 3 Now these are the c of the province that 7218
11:13 his brethren, c of the fathers, two hundred 7218
11:16 and Jozabad, of the c of the Levites, 7218
12: 7 These were the c of the priests and of their 7218
12:12 of Joiakim were priests, the c of the fathers: 7218
12:22 and Jaddua, were recorded c of the fathers: 7218
12:23 The sons of Levi, the c of the fathers, 7218
12:24 the c of the Levites: Hashabiah, Sherebiah, 7218
12:46 Asaph of old there were c of the singers, 7218
Job 12:24 He taketh away the heart of the c of 7218
29:25 and sat c, and dwelt as a king in the army, 7218
40:19 He is the c of the ways of God: he that 7225
Ps 4: T To the c Musician on Neginoth, A Psalm 5329
5: T To the c Musician upon Nehiloth, A Psalm 5329
6: T To the c Musician on Neginoth upon 5329
8: T To the c Musician upon Gittith, A Psalm of 5329
9: T To the c Musician upon Muth-labben, A 5329
11: T To the c Musician, A Psalm of David. 5329
12: T To the c Musician upon Sheminith, 5329
13: T To the c Musician, A Psalm of David. 5329
14: T To the c Musician, A Psalm of David. 5329
18: T To the c Musician, A Psalm of David, 5329
19: T To the c Musician, A Psalm of David. 5329
20: T To the c Musician, A Psalm of David. 5329
21: T To the c Musician, A Psalm of David. 5329
22: T To the c Musician upon Aijeleth Shahar, 5329
31: T To the c Musician, A Psalm of David. 5329
36: T To the c Musician, A Psalm of David 5329
39: T To the c Musician, even to Jeduthun, 5329
40: T To the c Musician, A Psalm of David. 5329
41: T To the c Musician, A Psalm of David. 5329
42: T To the c Musician, Maschil, for the sons of 5329
44: T To the c Musician for the sons of Korah, 5329
45: T To the c Musician upon Shoshannim, 5329
46: T To the c Musician for the sons of Korah, 5329
47: T To the c Musician, A Psalm for the sons of 5329
49: T To the c Musician, A Psalm for the sons of 5329

Ps 51: T To the c Musician, A Psalm of David, 5329
52: T To the c Musician, Maschil, A Psalm of 5329
53: T To the c Musician upon Mahalath, 5329
54: T To the c Musician on Neginoth, Maschil, 5329
55: T To the c Musician on Neginoth, Maschil, 5329
56: T To the c Musician upon 5329
57: T To the c Musician, Al-taschith, 5329
58: T To the c Musician, Al-taschith, 5329
59: T To the c Musician, Al-taschith, 5329
60: T To the c Musician upon Shushan-eduth, 5329
61: T To the c Musician upon Neginah, A Psalm 5329
62: T To the c Musician, to Jeduthun, A Psalm 5329
64: T To the c Musician, A Psalm of David. 5329
65: T To the c Musician, A Psalm and Song of 5329
66: T To the c Musician, A Song or Psalm. 5329
67: T To the c Musician on Neginoth, A Psalm 5329
68: T To the c Musician, A Psalm or Song of 5329
69: T To the c Musician upon Shoshannim, 5329
70: T To the c Musician, A Psalm of David, 5329
75: T To the c Musician, Al-taschith, A Psalm or 5329
76: T To the c Musician on Neginoth, A Psalm 5329
77: T To the c Musician, to Jeduthun, A Psalm 5329
78:51 the c of their strength in the tabernacles of 7225
80: T To the c Musician upon 5329
81: T To the c Musician upon Gittith, A Psalm of 5329
84: T To the c Musician upon Gittith, A Psalm 5329
85: T To the c Musician, A Psalm for the sons of 5329
88: T To the c Musician upon Mahalath 5329
105:36 in their land, the c of all their strength. 7225
109: T To the c Musician, A Psalm of David. 5329
137: 6 if I prefer not Jerusalem above my c joy. 7218
139: T To the c Musician, A Psalm of David. 5329
140: T To the c Musician, A Psalm of David. 5329
Pr 1:21 She crieth in the c place of concourse, 7218
16:28 and a whisperer separateth c friends. 441
SS 4:14 myrrh and aloes, with all the c spices: 7218
Isa 14: 9 for thee, even all the c ones of the earth; 6260
41: 9 called thee from the c men thereof, and 678
Jer 13:21 them to be captains, and as c over thee: 7218
20: 1 who was also c governor in the house of 5057
31: 7 and shout among the c of the nations: 7218
49:35 break the bow of Elam, the c of their might. 7225
52:24 the captain of the guard took Seraiah the c 7218
La 1: 5 Her adversaries are the c, her enemies 7218
Eze 27:22 they occupied in thy fairs with c of all 7218
38: 2 the c prince of Meshech and Tubal, and 7218
38: 3 O Gog, the c prince of Meshech and Tubal: 7218
39: 1 O Gog, the c prince of Meshech and Tubal: 7218
Da 2:48 c of the governors over all the wise men of 7229
10:13 lo, Michael, one of the c princes, came to 7223
11:41 Moab, and the c of the children of Ammon. 7225
Am 6: 1 which are named c of the nations, 7225
6: 6 and anoint themselves with the c ointments: 7225
Hab 3:19 To the c singer on my stringed instruments. 5329
Mt 2: 4 And when he had gathered all the c priests 749
16:21 things of the elders and c priests and scribes, 749
20:18 of man shall be betrayed unto the c priests 749
20:27 And whosoever will be c among you, 4413
21:15 And when the c priests and scribes saw 749
21:23 the c priests and the elders of the people 749
21:45 And when the c priests and Pharisees had 749
23: 6 at feasts, and the c seats in the synagogues, 4410
26: 3 Then assembled together the c priests, and 749
26:14 called Judas Iscariot, went unto the c priests, 749
26:47 from the c priests and elders of the people. 749
26:59 Now the c priests, and elders, and all 749
27: 1 all the c priests and elders of the people took 749
27: 3 the thirty pieces of silver to the c priests 749
27: 6 And the c priests took the silver pieces, and 749
27:12 And when he was accused of the c priests 749
27:20 But the c priests and elders persuaded 749
27:41 Likewise also the c priests mocking him, 749
27:62 the c priests and Pharisees came together 749
28:11 shewed unto the c priests all the things that 749
Mk 6:21 high captains, and c estates of Galilee; 4413
8:31 the elders, and of the c priests, and scribes, 749
10:33 of man shall be delivered unto the c priests, 749
11:18 And the scribes and c priests heard it, and 749
11:27 there come to him the c priests, and 749
12:39 And the c seats in the synagogues, and 4410
14: 1 and the c priests and the scribes sought how 749
14:10 one of the twelve, went unto the c priests, 749
14:43 from the c priests and the scribes and 749
14:53 with him were assembled all the c priests 749
14:55 And the c priests and all the council sought 749
15: 1 And straightway in the morning the c priests 749
15: 3 And the c priests accused him of many 749
15:10 For he knew that the c priests had delivered 749
15:11 But the c priests moved the people, that he 749
15:31 Likewise also the c priests mocking said 749
Lk 9:22 of the elders and c priests and scribes, 749
11:15 devils through Beelzebub the c of the devils. 758
14: 1 as he went into the house of one of the c 758
14: 7 he marked how they chose out the c rooms; 4411
19: 2 which was the c among the publicans, and 754
19:47 But the c priests and the scribes and 749
19:47 the c of the people sought to destroy him, 4413
20: 1 the c priests and the scribes came upon him 749
20:19 And the c priests and the scribes the same 749
20:46 the synagogues, and the c rooms at feasts; 4411
22: 2 And the c priests and scribes sought how 749
22: 4 and communed with the c priests and 749
22:26 and he that is c, as he that doth serve. 2233
22:52 Then Jesus said unto the c priests, and 749
22:66 the elders of the people and the c priests and 749
23: 4 Then said Pilate to the c priests and to 749
23:10 And the c priests and scribes stood and 749
23:13 when he had called together the c priests 749
23:23 of them and of the c priests prevailed. 749
24:20 And how the c priests and our rulers 749
Jn 7:32 and the c priests sent officers to take him. 749
7:45 Then came the officers to the c priests and 749
11:47 Then gathered the c priests and 749
11:57 Now both the c priests and the Pharisees NIG
12:10 But the c priests consulted that they might 749

Jn 12:42 Nevertheless among the c rulers also many NIG
18: 3 and officers from the c priests and 749
18:35 the c priests have delivered thee unto me: 749
19: 6 When the c priests therefore and officers 749
19:15 The c priests answered, We have no king 749
19:21 Then said the c priests of the Jews to Pilate, 749
Ac 4:23 and reported all that the c priests and elders 749
5:24 and the c priests heard these things, 749
9:14 here he hath authority from the c priests 749
9:21 might bring them bound unto the c priests? 749
13:50 and the c men of the city, and 4413
14:12 Mercurius, because he was the c speaker. 2233
15:22 and Silas, c men among the brethren: 2233
16:12 which is the c city of that part of 4413
17: 4 and of the c women not a few. 4413
18: 8 And Crispus, the c ruler of the synagogue, NIG
18:17 the c ruler of the synagogue, and beat him NIG
19:14 a Jew, and c of the priests, which did so. 749
19:31 And certain of the c of Asia, which were his 775
21:31 tidings came unto the c captain of 5506
21:32 and when they saw the c captain and 5506
21:33 Then the c captain came near, and 5506
21:37 he said unto the c captain, May I speak 5506
22:24 The c captain commanded him to be 5506
22:26 heard that, he went and told the c captain, 5506
22:27 Then the c captain came, and said unto 5506
22:28 And the c captain answered, With a great 5506
22:29 and the c captain also was afraid, after he 5506
22:30 and commanded the c priests and all their 749
23:10 arose a great dissension, the c captain, 5506
23:14 And they came to the c priests and elders, 749
23:15 ye with the council signify to the c captain 5506
23:17 Bring this young man unto the c captain: 5506
23:18 and brought him to the c captain, and said, 5506
23:19 Then the c captain took him by the hand, 5506
23:22 So the c captain then let the young man 5506
24: 7 But the c captain Lysias came upon us, and 5506
24:22 When Lysias the c captain shall come 5506
25: 2 the c of the Jews informed him against 4413
25:15 the c priests and the elders of the Jews 749
25:23 with the c captains, and principal men of 5506
26:10 having received authority from the c priests; 749
26:12 and commission from the c priests, 749
28: 7 were possessions of the c man of the island, 4413
28:17 that after three days Paul called the c of 4413
Eph 2:20 Jesus Christ himself being the c corner 204
1Ti 1:15 the world to save sinners; of whom I am c. 4413
1Pe 2: 6 Behold, I lay in Sion a c corner stone, elect, 204
5: 4 And when the c Shepherd shall appear, 750
Rev 6:15 and the rich men, and the c captains, and 5506

CHIEFEST (9) [CHIEF]

1Sa 2:29 to make yourselves fat with the c of all 7225
9:22 made them sit in the c place among them 7218
21: 7 the c of the herdmen that belonged to Saul. 47
2Ch 32:33 they buried him in the c of the sepulchres 4608
SS 5:10 and ruddy, the c among ten thousand. 1713
Mk 10:44 And whosoever of you will be the c, 4413
2Co 11: 5 I was not a whit behind the very c apostles. 3029
12:11 for in nothing am I behind the very c 3029
1Ti 6: S which is the c city of Phrygia Pacatiana. 3390

CHIEFLY (3) [CHIEF]

Ro 3: 2 c, because that unto them were committed 4412
Php 4:22 c they that are of Cesar's household. 3122
2Pe 2:10 But c them that walk after the flesh in 3122

CHILD (201) [CHILD'S, CHILDBEARING, CHILDHOOD, CHILDISH, CHILDLESS, CHILDREN, CHILDREN'S]

Ge 11:30 But Sarai was barren; she had no c. 2056
16:11 thou art with c, and shalt bear a son, and 2030
17:10 Every man c among you shall be NIH
17:12 every man c in your generations, he that is NIH
17:14 the uncircumcised man c whose flesh of his NIH
17:17 Shall a c be born unto him that is an NIH
18:13 Shall I of a surety bear a c, which am old? NIH
19:36 Thus were both the daughters of Lot with c 2029
21: 8 the c grew, and was weaned: and 3206
21:14 her shoulder, and the c, and sent her away: 3206
21:15 and she cast the c under one of the shrubs. 3206
21:16 she said, Let me not see the death of the c. 3206
37:30 unto his brethren, and said, The c is not; 3206
38:24 also, behold, she is with c by whoredom. 2030
38:25 By the man, whose these are, am I with c: 2030
42:22 unto you, saying, Do not sin against the c; 3206
44:20 old man, and a c of his old age, a little one; 3206
Ex 2: 2 when she saw him that he was a goodly c, NIH
2: 3 and with pitch, and put the c therein; 3206
2: 6 when she had opened it, she saw the c: and 3206
2: 7 that she may nurse the c for thee? 3206
2: 9 Take this c away, and nurse it for me, and 3206
2: 9 And the woman took the c, and nursed it. 3206
2:10 the c grew, and she brought him unto 3206
21:22 hurt a woman with c, so that her fruit 2030
22:22 shall not afflict any widow, or fatherless c. 3490
Lev 12: 2 have conceived seed, and born a man c: 2145
12: 5 if she bear a maid c, then she shall be 5347
22:13 have no c, and is returned unto her father's 2233
Nu 11:12 as a nursing father beareth the sucking c, 3243
Dt 25: 5 and one of them die, and have no c, 1121
Jdg 11:34 she was his only c; beside her he had 3173
13: 5 for the c shall be a Nazarite unto God from 5288
13: 7 neither eat any unclean thing: for the c shall 5288
13: 8 teach us what we shall do unto the c that 5288
13:12 How shall we order the c, and how shall we 5288
13:24 the c grew, and the LORD blessed him. 5288
Ru 4:16 Naomi took the c, and laid it in her bosom, 3206
1Sa 1:11 wilt give unto thine handmaid a man c, then 2233
1:22 I will not go up until the c be weaned, and 5288
1:24 the LORD in Shiloh: and the c was young. 5288
1:25 slew a bullock, and brought the c to Eli. 5288
1:27 For this c I prayed; and the LORD hath 5288
2:11 the c did minister unto the LORD before 5288

1Sa 2:18 being a c, girded with a linen ephod. 5288
2:21 And the c Samuel grew before the LORD. 5288
2:26 the c Samuel grew on, and was in favour 5288
3: 1 the c Samuel ministered unto the LORD 5288
3: 8 perceived that the LORD had called the c. 5288
4:19 Phinehas' wife, was with c, near to be 2030
4:21 she named the c Ichabod, saying, The glory 5288
2Sa 6:23 of Saul had no c unto the day of her death. 2056
11: 5 sent and told David, and said, I am with c. 2030
12:14 the c also that is born unto thee shall surely 1121
12:15 the LORD strake the c that Uriah's wife 3206
12:16 David therefore besought God for the c; 5288
12:18 to pass on the seventh day, that the c died. 3206
12:18 feared to tell him that the c was dead: 3206
12:18 they said, Behold, while the c was yet alive, 3206
12:18 if we tell him that the c is dead? 3206
12:19 David perceived that the c was dead: 3206
12:19 David said unto his servants, Is the c dead? 3206
12:21 thou didst fast and weep for the c, while it 3206
12:21 when the c was dead, thou didst rise and 3206
12:22 While the c was yet alive, I fasted and 3206
12:22 will be gracious to me, that the c may live? 3206
1Ki 3: 7 I am but a little c: I know not how to go out 5288
3:17 I was delivered of a c with her in 3205
3:19 this woman's c died in the night; because 1121
3:20 and laid her dead c in my bosom. 1121
3:21 when I rose in the morning to give my c 1121
3:25 Divide the living c in two, and give half to 3206
3:26 spake the woman whose the living c was 1121
3:26 give her the living c, and in no wise slay it. 3205
3:27 Give her the living c, and in no wise slay it: 3205
11:17 to go into Egypt; Hadad being yet a little c. 5288
13: 2 a c shall be born unto the house of David, 1121
14: 3 shall tell thee what shall become of the c. 5288
14:12 thy feet enter into the city, the c shall die. 3206
14:17 to the threshold of the door, the c died; 5288
17:21 he stretched himself upon the c three times, 3206
17:22 the soul of the c came into him again, and 3206
17:23 Elijah took the c, and brought him down 3206
2Ki 4:14 Verily she hath no c, and her husband is 1121
4:18 when the c was grown, it fell on a day, 3206
4:26 is it well with the c? And she answered, 3206
4:29 and lay my staff upon the face of the c. 5288
4:30 the mother of the c said, As the LORD 5288
4:31 and laid the staff upon the face of the c; 5288
4:31 and told him, saying, The c is not awaked. 5288
4:32 the c was dead, and laid upon his bed. 5288
4:34 lay upon the c, and put his mouth upon his 3206
4:34 he stretched himself upon the c[S]; and 2050.2
4:34 and the flesh of the c waxed warm. 3206
4:35 the c neesed seven times, and the child 5288
4:35 seven times, and the c opened his eyes. 5288
5:14 came again like unto the flesh of a little c, 5288
8:12 and rip up their women with c. 2030
15:16 all the women therein that were with c he 2030
Job 3: 3 it was said, There is a man c conceived. 1397
Ps 131: 2 as a c that is weaned of his mother: 1580
131: 2 his mother: my soul is even as a weaned c. 1580
Pr 20:11 Even a c is known by his doings, 5288
22: 6 Train up a c in the way he should go: and 5288
22:15 Foolishness is bound in the heart of a c; but 5288
23:13 Withhold not correction from the c: for if 5288
23:24 he that begetteth a wise c shall have joy of NIH
29:15 a c left to himself bringeth his mother to 5288
29:21 c shall have him become his son at 5290
Ecc 4: 8 a second; yea, he hath neither c nor brother: 1121
4:13 and a wise c than an old and foolish king, 3206
4:15 with the second c that shall stand up in his 3206
10:16 when thy king is a c, and thy princes eat in 5288
11: 5 do grow in the womb of her that is with c: 4392
Isa 3: 5 the c shall behave himself proudly against 5288
7:16 For before the c shall know to refuse 5288
8: 4 For before the c shall have knowledge to 5288
9: 6 For unto us a c is born, unto us a Son is 3206
10:19 forest shall be few, that a c may write them. 5288
11: 6 and a little c shall lead them. 5288
11: 8 the sucking c shall play on the hole of 3243
11: 8 the weaned c shall put his hand on 1580
26:17 Like as a woman with c, that draweth near 2030
26:18 We have been with c, we have been in 2029
49:15 Can a woman forget her sucking c, that she 5764
54: 1 thou that didst not travail with c: 2342
65:20 for the c shall die an hundred years old; but 5288
66: 7 pain came, she was delivered of a man c. 2145
Jer 1: 6 behold, I cannot speak: for I am a c. 5288
1: 7 the LORD said unto me, Say not, I am a c: 5288
4:31 as of her that bringeth forth her first c, 1069
20:15 saying, A man c is born unto thee; 1121
30: 6 and see whether a man doth travail with c? 3205
31: 8 the woman with c and her that travaileth 2030
31: 8 and her that travaileth with c together: 3205
31:20 is he a pleasant c? for since I spake against 3206
44: 7 from you man and woman, c and suckling, 5768
La 4: 4 The tongue of the sucking c cleaveth to 3243
Hos 11: 1 When Israel was a c, then I loved him, and 5288
13:16 and their women with c shall be ript up. 2030
Am 1:13 they have ript up the women with c at 2030
Mt 1:18 with c of the Holy Ghost. 1064+1722+2192
1:23 a virgin shall be with c, and 1064+1722+2192
2: 8 Go and search diligently for the young c; 3813
2: 9 and stood over where the young c was. 3813
2:11 they saw the young c with Mary his 3813
2:13 and take the young c and his mother, and 3813
2:13 for Herod will seek the young c to destroy 3813
2:14 he took the young c and his mother by 3813
2:20 and take the young c and his mother, and 3813
2:21 and took the young c and his mother, and 3813
10:21 up the brother to death, and the father the c: 5043
17:18 and the c was cured from that very hour. 3816
18: 2 And Jesus called a little c unto him, and 3813
18: 4 shall humble himself as this little c, 3813
18: 5 And whoso shall receive one such little c in 3813
23:15 ye make him twofold more the c of hell 5207
24:19 woe unto them that are with c, 1064+1722+2192
Mk 9:21 this came unto him? And he said, Of a c. 3812
Mk 9:24 And straightway the father of the c cried 3813
9:36 And he took a c, and set him in the midst of 3813
10:15 receive the kingdom of God as a little c, 3813
13:17 But woe to them that are with c, and 1064
Lk 1: 7 And they had no c, because that Elisabeth 5043
1:59 eighth day they came to circumcise the c; 3813
1:66 saying, What manner of c shall this be! 3813
1:76 And thou, c, shalt be called the prophet of 3813
1:80 And the c grew, and waxed strong in spirit, 3813
2: 5 his espoused wife, being great with c. 1471
2:17 which was told them concerning this c. 3813
2:21 accomplished for the circumcising of the c, 3813
2:27 when the parents brought in the c Jesus, 3813
2:34 this c is set for the fall and rising again of NIG
2:40 And the c grew, and waxed strong in spirit, 3813
2:43 the c Jesus tarried behind in Jerusalem; 3816
9:38 look upon my son: for he is mine only c. 3439
9:42 and healed the c, and delivered him again 3816
9:47 of their heart, took a c, and set him by him, 3813
9:48 Whosoever shall receive this c in my name 3813
18:17 as a little c shall in no wise enter therein. 3813
21:23 woe unto them that are with c, 1064+1722+2192
Jn 4:49 unto him, Sir, come down ere my c die. 3813
16:21 but as soon as she is delivered of the c, 3813
Ac 4:27 For of a truth against thy holy c Jesus, 3816
4:30 be done by the name of thy holy c Jesus. 3816
7: 5 his seed after him, when as yet he had no c. 5043
13:10 and all mischief, thou c of the devil, 5207
1Co 13:11 When I was a c, I spake as a child, 3516
13:11 When I was a child, I spake as a c, 3516
13:11 I spake as a child, I understood as a c, 3516
13:11 I understood as a child, I thought as a c: 3516
Gal 4: 1 I say, That the heir, as long as he is a c, 3516
1Th 5: 3 travail upon a woman with c; 1064+1722+2192
2Ti 3:15 And that from a c thou hast known the holy 1025
Heb 11:11 was delivered of a c when she was past 5088
11:23 because they saw he was a proper c; 3813
Rev 12: 2 And she being with c cried, travailing in 1064
12: 4 for to devour her c as soon as it was born. 5043
12: 5 And she brought forth a man c, who was to 5207
12: 5 and her c was caught up unto God, and 5043
12:13 the woman which brought forth the man c. NIG

CHILD'S (4) [CHILD]

Ex 2: 8 And the maid went and called the c mother. 3206
1Ki 17:21 let this c soul come into him again. 3206
Job 33:25 His flesh shall be fresher than a c: he shall 5290
Mt 2:20 for they are dead which sought the young c 3813

CHILDBEARING (1) [BEAR, CHILD]

1Ti 2:15 Notwithstanding she shall be saved in c, 5042

CHILDHOOD (2) [CHILD]

1Sa 12: 2 I have walked before you from my c unto 5271
Ecc 11:10 from thy flesh: for c and youth are vanity. 3208

CHILDISH (1) [CHILD]

1Co 13:11 when I became a man, I put away c things. 3516

CHILDLESS (7) [CHILD]

Ge 15: 2 seeing I go c, and the steward of my house 6185
Lev 20:20 they shall bear their sin; they shall die c. 6185
20:21 his brother's nakedness; they shall be c. 6185
1Sa 15:33 As thy sword hath made women c, so 7921
15:33 so shall thy mother be c among women. 7921
Jer 22:30 saith the LORD, Write ye this man c, 6185
Lk 20:30 the second took her to wife, and he died c. 815

CHILDREN (1803) [CHILD]

Ge 3:16 in sorrow thou shalt bring forth c; and 1121
6: 4 they bare c to them, the same became NIH
10:21 Shem also, the father of all the c of Eber, 1121
10:21 Japheth the elder, even to him were c born. NIH
10:22 The c of Shem; Elam, and Asshur, and 1121
10:23 the c of Aram; Uz, and Hul, and Gether, 1121
11: 5 and the tower, which the c of men builded. 1121
16: 1 Now Sarai Abram's wife bare him no c: and NIH
16: 2 it may be that I may obtain c by her. 1129
18:19 that he will command his c and his 1121
19:38 the same is the father of the c of Ammon 1121
20:17 and his maidservants; and they bare c. NIH
21: 7 that Sarah should have given c suck? 1121
22:20 she hath also born c unto thy brother 1121
23: 5 the c of Heth answered Abraham, saying 1121
23: 7 people of the land, even to the c of Heth. 1121
23:10 Ephron dwelt amongst the c of Heth: and 1121
23:10 Abraham in the audience of the c of Heth, 1121
23:18 possession in the presence of the c of Heth, 1121
25: 4 Eldaah. All these were the c of Keturah. 1121
25:22 the c struggled together within her; and 1121
30: 1 when Rachel saw that she bare Jacob no c, NIH
30: 1 said unto Jacob, Give me c, or else I die. 1121
30: 3 my knees, that I may also have c by her. 1129
30:26 Give me my wives and my c, for whom I 3206
31:43 these c are my children, and these 1121+3807.1
31:43 these children are my c, and these cattle are 1121
31:43 or unto their c which they have born? 1121
32:11 and smite me, and the mother with the c. 1121
32:32 Therefore the c of Israel eat not of 1121
33: 1 he divided the c unto Leah, and 3206
33: 2 he put the handmaids and their c foremost, 3206
33: 2 Leah and her c after, and Rachel and 3206
33: 5 up his eyes, and saw the women and the c; 3206
33: 5 The c which God hath graciously given thy 3206
33: 6 they and their c, and they bowed 3206
33: 7 Leah also with her c came near, and 3206
33:13 My lord knoweth that the c are tender, and 3206
33:14 before me and the c be able to endure, 3206
33:19 at the hand of the c of Hamor, 1121
36:21 the c of Seir in the land of Edom. 1121
36:22 the c of Lotan were Hori and Hemam; and 1121
36:23 the c of Shobal were these; Alvan, and 1121
36:24 these are the c of Zibeon; both Aiah, and 1121
36:25 the c of Anah were these; Dishon, and 1121
Ge 36:26 these are the c of Dishon; Hemdan, and 1121
36:27 The c of Ezer are these; Bilhan, and 1121
36:28 The c of Dishan are these; Uz, and Aran. 1121
36:31 before there reigned any king over the c of 1121
37: 3 Israel loved Joseph more than all his c, 1121
42:36 unto them, Me have ye bereaved of my c: 7921
43:14 If I be bereaved of my c, I am bereaved. 7921
45:10 thy c, and thy children's children, and 1121
45:10 thy children's c, and thy flocks, and 1121
45:21 the c of Israel did so: and Joseph gave them 1121
46: 8 these are the names of the c of Israel, 1121
49: 8 thy father's c shall bow down before thee. 1121
49:32 of the cave that is therein was from the c of 1121
50:23 Joseph saw Ephraim's c of the third 1121
50:23 c also of Machir the son of Manasseh were 1121
50:25 Joseph took an oath of the c of Israel, 1121
Ex 1: 1 Now these are the names of the c of Israel, 1121
1: 7 the c of Israel were fruitful, and 1121
1: 9 the people of the c of Israel are moe and 1121
1:12 were grieved because of the c of Israel. 1121
1:13 the Egyptians made the c of Israel to serve 1121
1:17 but saved the men c alive. 3206
1:18 this thing, and have saved the men c alive? 3206
2: 6 and said, This is one of the Hebrews' c. 3206
2:23 the c of Israel sighed by reason of 1121
2:25 God looked upon the c of Israel, and 1121
3: 9 the cry of the c of Israel is come unto me: 1121
3:10 my people the c of Israel out of Egypt. 1121
3:11 that I should bring forth the c of Israel out 1121
3:13 when I come unto the c of Israel, and 1121
3:14 Thus shalt thou say unto the c of Israel, 1121
3:15 Thus shalt thou say unto the c of Israel, 1121
4:29 gathered together all the elders of the c of 1121
4:31 that the LORD had visited the c of Israel, 1121
5:14 the officers of the c of Israel, 1121
5:15 the officers of the c of Israel came and 1121
5:19 the officers of the c of Israel did see that 1121
6: 5 I have also heard the groaning of the c of 1121
6: 6 Wherefore say unto the c of Israel, I am 1121
6: 9 Moses spake so unto the c of Israel: but 1121
6:11 that he let the c of Israel go out of his land. 1121
6:12 the c of Israel have not hearkened unto me; 1121
6:13 gave them a charge unto the c of Israel, and 1121
6:13 to bring the c of Israel out of the land of 1121
6:26 Bring out the c of Israel from the land of 1121
6:27 to bring out the c of Israel from Egypt: 1121
7: 2 that he send the c of Israel out of his land. 1121
7: 4 mine armies, and my people the c of Israel, 1121
7: 5 bring out the c of Israel from among them. 1121
9: 6 of the cattle of the c of Israel died not one. 1121
9:26 where the c of Israel were, was there no 1121
9:35 neither would he let the c of Israel go; 1121
10:20 so that he would not let the c of Israel go. 1121
10:23 all the c of Israel had light in their 1121
11: 7 against any of the c of Israel shall not a dog 1121
11:10 that he would not let the c of Israel go out 1121
12:26 to pass, when your c shall say unto you, 1121
12:27 who passed over the houses of the c of 1121
12:28 the c of Israel went away, and did as 1121
12:31 my people, both you and the c of Israel; 1121
12:35 the c of Israel did according to the word of 1121
12:37 the c of Israel journeyed from Rameses to 1121
12:37 thousand on foot that were men, beside c. 2945
12:40 Now the sojourning of the c of Israel, 1121
12:42 of all the c of Israel in their generations. 1121
12:50 Thus did all the c of Israel; as the LORD 1121
12:51 that the LORD did bring the c of Israel out 1121
13: 2 whatsoever openeth the womb among the c 1121
13:13 all the firstborn of man amongst thy c shalt 1121
13:15 but all the firstborn of my c I redeem. 1121
13:18 the c of Israel went up harnessed out of 1121
13:19 for he had straitly sworn the c of Israel, 1121
14: 2 Speak unto the c of Israel, that they turn 1121
14: 3 For Pharaoh will say of the c of Israel, 1121
14: 8 and he pursued after the c of Israel: 1121
14: 8 the c of Israel went out with a high hand. 1121
14:10 the c of Israel lift up their eyes, and behold, 1121
14:10 the c of Israel cried out unto the LORD. 1121
14:15 speak unto the c of Israel, that they go 1121
14:16 the c of Israel shall go on dry ground 1121
14:22 the c of Israel went into the midst of the sea 1121
14:29 the c of Israel walked upon dry land in 1121
15: 1 the c of Israel this song unto the LORD, 1121
15:19 the c of Israel went on dry land in the midst 1121
16: 1 all the congregation of the c of Israel came 1121
16: 2 the whole congregation of the c of Israel 1121
16: 3 the c of Israel said unto them, Would to 1121
16: 6 and Aaron said unto all the c of Israel, 1121
16: 9 Say unto all the congregation of the c of 1121
16:10 the whole congregation of the c of Israel, 1121
16:12 I have heard the murmurings of the c of 1121
16:15 when the c of Israel saw it, they said one to 1121
16:17 the c of Israel did so, and gathered, 1121
16:35 the c of Israel did eat manna forty years, 1121
17: 1 all the congregation of the c of Israel 1121
17: 3 to kill us and our c and our cattle with 1121
17: 7 because of the chiding of the c of Israel, 1121
19: 1 when the c of Israel were gone forth out of 1121
19: 3 the house of Jacob, and tell the c of Israel; 1121
19: 6 which thou shalt speak unto the c of Israel. 1121
20: 5 of the fathers upon the c unto the third 1121
20:22 Thus thou shalt say unto the c of Israel, 1121
21: 4 the wife and her c shall be her master's, 3206
21: 5 I love my master, my wife, and my c; 1121
22:24 shall be widows, and your c fatherless. 1121
24: 5 he sent young men of the c of Israel, 1121
24:11 upon the nobles of the c of Israel he laid 1121
24:17 of the mount in the eyes of the c of Israel. 1121
25: 2 Speak unto the c of Israel, that they bring 1121
25:22 thee in commandment unto the c of Israel. 1121
27:20 thou shalt command the c of Israel, 1121
27:21 generations on the behalf of the c of Israel. 1121
28: 1 sons with him, from among the c of Israel, 1121
28: 9 grave on them the names of the c of Israel: 1121
28:11 stones with the names of the c of Israel: 1121

Ex 28:12 *for* stones of memorial unto the **c** of Israel: 1121
28:21 the stones shall be with the names of the **c** 1121
28:29 Aaron shall bear the names of the **c** of 1121
28:30 Aaron shall bear the judgment of the **c** of 1121
28:38 **c** of Israel shall hallow in all their holy 1121
29:28 his sons' by a statute for ever from the **c** of 1121
29:28 it shall be a heave offering from the **c** of 1121
29:43 there I will meet with the **c** of Israel, and 1121
29:45 I will dwell amongst the **c** of Israel, and 1121
30:12 When thou takest the sum of the **c** of Israel 1121
30:16 take the atonement money of the **c** of Israel, 1121
30:16 that it may be a memorial unto the **c** of 1121
30:31 thou shalt speak unto the **c** of Israel, saying, 1121
31:13 Speak thou also unto the **c** of Israel, saying, 1121
31:16 Wherefore the **c** of Israel shall keep 1121
31:17 between me and the **c** of Israel for ever: 1121
32:20 and made the **c** of Israel drink *of it.* 1121
32:28 the **c** of Levi did according to the word of 1121
33: 5 Say unto the **c** of Israel, Ye *are* a 1121
33: 6 the **c** of Israel stript themselves of their 1121
34: 7 the iniquity of the fathers upon the **c**, 1121
34: 7 upon the children's **c**, unto the third and 1121
34:23 Thrice in the year shall all your **men c** 2138
34:30 and all the **c** of Israel saw Moses, 1121
34:32 afterward all the **c** of Israel came nigh: and 1121
34:34 spake unto the **c** of Israel *that* which he was 1121
34:35 the **c** of Israel saw the face of Moses, 1121
35: 1 the congregation of the **c** of Israel together, 1121
35: 4 unto all the congregation of the **c** of Israel, 1121
35:20 all the congregation of the **c** of Israel 1121
35:29 The **c** of Israel brought a willing offering 1121
35:30 Moses said unto the **c** of Israel, See, 1121
36: 3 which the **c** of Israel had brought for 1121
39: 6 with the names of the **c** of Israel. 1121
39: 7 *be* stones for a memorial to the **c** of Israel; 1121
39:14 according to the names of the **c** of Israel, 1121
39:32 the **c** of Israel did according to all that 1121
39:42 so the **c** of Israel made all the work. 1121
40:36 the **c** of Israel went onward in all their 1121
Lev 1: 2 Speak unto the **c** of Israel, and say unto 1121
4: 2 Speak unto the **c** of Israel, saying, If a soul 1121
6:18 All the males among the **c** of Aaron shall 1121
7:23 Speak unto the **c** of Israel, saying, Ye shall 1121
7:29 Speak unto the **c** of Israel, saying, He that 1121
7:34 the heave shoulder have I taken of the **c** of 1121
7:34 statute for ever from among the **c** of Israel. 1121
7:36 to be given them of the **c** of Israel, 1121
7:38 in the day that he commanded the **c** of 1121
9: 3 unto the **c** of Israel thou shalt speak, saying, 1121
10:11 that *ye* may teach the **c** of Israel all 1121
10:14 of peace offerings of the **c** of Israel. 1121
11: 2 Speak unto the **c** of Israel, saying, 1121
12: 2 Speak unto the **c** of Israel, saying, If a 1121
15: 2 Speak unto the **c** of Israel, and say unto 1121
15:31 Thus shall ye separate the **c** of Israel from 1121
16: 5 he shall take of the congregation of the **c** of 1121
16:16 of the uncleanness of the **c** of Israel, 1121
16:19 hallow it from the uncleanness of the **c** of 1121
16:21 confess over him all the iniquities of the **c** 1121
16:34 to make an atonement for the **c** of Israel for 1121
17: 2 unto all the **c** of Israel, and say unto them; 1121
17: 5 To the end that the **c** of Israel may bring 1121
17:12 Therefore I said unto the **c** of Israel, No 1121
17:13 whatsoever man *there be* of the **c** of Israel, 1121
17:14 therefore I said unto the **c** of Israel, 1121
18: 2 Speak unto the **c** of Israel, and say unto 1121
19: 2 Speak unto all the congregation of the **c** of 1121
19:18 nor bear any grudge against the **c** of thy 1121
20: 2 Again, thou shalt say to the **c** of Israel, 1121
20: 2 Whosoever *he be* of the **c** of Israel, or 1121
21:24 and to his sons, and unto all the **c** of Israel. 1121
22: 2 from the holy *things* of the **c** of Israel, 1121
22: 3 that goeth unto the holy *things* which the **c** 1121
22:15 profane the holy *things* of the **c** of Israel, 1121
22:18 unto all the **c** of Israel, and say unto them, 1121
22:32 I will be hallowed among the **c** of Israel: 1121
23: 2 Speak unto the **c** of Israel, and say unto 1121
23:10 Speak unto the **c** of Israel, and say unto 1121
23:24 Speak unto the **c** of Israel, saying, In 1121
23:34 Speak unto the **c** of Israel, saying, The 1121
23:43 I made the **c** of Israel to dwell in booths, 1121
23:44 Moses declared unto the **c** of Israel 1121
24: 2 Command the **c** of Israel, that they bring 1121
24: 8 *being taken* from the **c** of Israel *by* an 1121
24:10 went out among the **c** of Israel: 1121
24:15 thou shalt speak unto the **c** of Israel, saying, 1121
24:23 Moses spake to the **c** of Israel, that they 1121
24:23 the **c** of Israel did as the LORD 1121
25: 2 Speak unto the **c** of Israel, and say unto 1121
25:33 *are* their possession among the **c** of Israel. 1121
25:41 *both* he and his **c** with him, and shall return 1121
25:45 Moreover of the **c** of the strangers that do 1121
25:46 them as an inheritance for your **c** after you, 1121
25:46 over your brethren the **c** of Israel, ye shall 1121
25:54 year of jubile, *both* he, and his **c** with him. 1121
25:55 For unto me the **c** of Israel *are* servants; 1121
26:22 which shall **rob** you **of** your **c**, and 7921
26:46 the **c** of Israel in mount Sinai by the hand 1121
27: 2 Speak unto the **c** of Israel, and say unto 1121
27:34 Moses for the **c** of Israel in mount Sinai. 1121
Nu 1: 2 of all the congregation of the **c** of Israel, 1121
1:10 Of the **c** of Joseph: of Ephraim; 1121
1:20 the **c** of Reuben, Israel's eldest son, *by* their 1121
1:22 Of the **c** of Simeon, *by* their generations, 1121
1:24 Of the **c** of Gad, *by* their generations, 1121
1:26 Of the **c** of Judah, *by* their generations, 1121
1:28 Of the **c** of Issachar, *by* their generations, 1121
1:30 Of the **c** of Zebulun, *by* their generations, 1121
1:32 Of the **c** of Joseph, *namely,* of the children 1121
1:32 *namely,* of the **c** of Ephraim, *by* their 1121
1:34 Of the **c** of Manasseh, *by* their generations, 1121
1:36 Of the **c** of Benjamin, *by* their generations, 1121
1:38 Of the **c** of Dan, *by* their generations, 1121
1:40 Of the **c** of Asher, *by* their generations, 1121
1:42 *Of* the **c** of Naphtali, *throughout* their 1121

Nu 1:45 those that were numbered of the **c** of Israel, 1121
1:49 neither take the sum of them among the **c** 1121
1:52 the **c** of Israel shall pitch their tents, 1121
1:53 upon the congregation of the **c** of Israel: 1121
1:54 the **c** of Israel did according to all that 1121
2: 2 Every man of the **c** of Israel shall pitch by 1121
2: 3 *shall be* captain of the **c** of Judah. 1121
2: 5 of Zuar *shall be* captain of the **c** of Issachar. 1121
2: 7 Helon *shall be* captain of the **c** of Zebulun. 1121
2:10 the captain of the **c** of Reuben *shall be* 1121
2:12 the captain of the **c** of Simeon *shall be* 1121
2:20 the captain of the **c** of Manasseh *shall be* 1121
2:25 the captain of the **c** of Dan *shall be* Ahiezer 1121
2:27 the captain of the **c** of Asher *shall be* Pagiel 1121
2:29 the captain of the **c** of Naphtali *shall be* 1121
2:32 the **c** of Israel by the house of their fathers: 1121
2:33 the Levites were not numbered among the **c** 1121
2:34 the **c** of Israel did according to all that 1121
3: 4 the wilderness of Sinai, and they had no **c**: 1121
3: 8 the charge of the **c** of Israel, to do 1121
3: 9 they *are* wholly given unto him out of the **c** 1121
3:12 I have taken the Levites from among the **c** 1121
3:12 openeth the matrix among the **c** of Israel: 1121
3:15 Number the **c** of Levi after the house of 1121
3:38 sanctuary for the charge of the **c** of Israel; 1121
3:40 males of the **c** of Israel from a month old 1121
3:41 instead of all the firstborn among the **c** of 1121
3:41 firstlings among the cattle of the **c** of Israel. 1121
3:42 all the firstborn among the **c** of Israel. 1121
3:45 of all the firstborn among the **c** of Israel, 1121
3:46 thirteen of the firstborn of the **c** of Israel, 1121
3:50 Of the firstborn of the **c** of Israel took he 1121
5: 2 Command the **c** of Israel, that they put out 1121
5: 4 the **c** of Israel did so, and put them out 1121
5: 4 spake unto Moses, so did the **c** of Israel. 1121
5: 6 Speak unto the **c** of Israel, When a man or 1121
5: 9 every offering of all the holy *things* of the **c** 1121
5:12 Speak unto the **c** of Israel, and say unto 1121
6: 2 Speak unto the **c** of Israel, and say unto 1121
6:23 On this wise ye shall bless the **c** of Israel, 1121
6:27 they shall put my name upon the **c** of Israel; 1121
7:24 prince of the **c** of Zebulun, *did offer:* 1121
7:30 prince of the **c** of Reuben, *did offer:* 1121
7:36 prince of the **c** of Simeon, *did offer:* 1121
7:42 of Deuel, prince of the **c** of Gad, *offered:* 1121
7:48 prince of the **c** of Ephraim, *offered:* 1121
7:54 of Pedahzur, prince of the **c** of Manasseh: 1121
7:60 prince of the **c** of Benjamin, *offered:* 1121
7:66 prince of the **c** of Dan, *offered:* 1121
7:72 of Ocran, prince of the **c** of Asher, *offered:* 1121
7:78 prince of the **c** of Naphtali, *offered:* 1121
8: 6 Take the Levites from among the **c** of 1121
8: 9 whole assembly of the **c** of Israel together: 1121
8:10 the **c** of Israel shall put their hands upon 1121
8:11 LORD *for* an offering of the **c** of Israel, 1121
8:14 the Levites from among the **c** of Israel: 1121
8:16 given unto me from among the **c** of Israel; 1121
8:16 *even instead of* the firstborn of all the **c** of 1121
8:17 For all the firstborn of the **c** of Israel *are* 1121
8:18 for all the firstborn of the **c** of Israel. 1121
8:19 and to his sons from among the **c** of Israel, 1121
8:19 to do the service of the **c** of Israel in 1121
8:19 to make an atonement for the **c** of Israel: 1121
8:19 that there be no plague among the **c** of 1121
8:19 when the **c** of Israel come nigh unto 1121
8:20 and all the congregation of the **c** of Israel, 1121
8:20 the Levites, so did the **c** of Israel unto them. 1121
9: 2 Let the **c** of Israel also keep the passover at 1121
9: 4 Moses spake unto the **c** of Israel, that they 1121
9: 5 commanded Moses, so did the **c** of Israel. 1121
9: 7 his appointed season among the **c** of Israel? 1121
9:10 Speak unto the **c** of Israel, saying, If any 1121
9:17 then after that the **c** of Israel journeyed: 1121
9:17 there the **c** of Israel pitched their tents. 1121
9:18 At the commandment of the LORD the **c** 1121
9:19 the **c** of Israel kept the charge of 1121
9:22 the **c** of Israel abode in their tents, and 1121
10:12 the **c** of Israel took their journeys out of 1121
10:14 of the **c** of Judah according to their armies: 1121
10:15 over the host of the tribe of the **c** of 1121
10:16 over the host of the tribe of the **c** of 1121
10:19 over the host of the tribe of the **c** of Simeon 1121
10:20 over the host of the tribe of the **c** of Gad 1121
10:22 the standard of the camp of the **c** of 1121
10:23 over the host of the tribe of the **c** of 1121
10:24 over the host of the tribe of the **c** of 1121
10:25 the standard of the camp of the **c** of Dan set 1121
10:26 over the host of the tribe of the **c** of Asher 1121
10:27 over the host of the tribe of the **c** of 1121
10:28 Thus *were* the journeyings of the **c** of Israel 1121
11: 4 the **c** of Israel also wept again, and said, 1121
13: 2 which I give unto the **c** of Israel: 1121
13: 3 all those men *were* heads of the **c** of Israel. 1121
13:22 Sheshai, and Talmai, the **c** of Anak, 3211
13:24 of the cluster of grapes which the **c** of Israel 1121
13:26 to all the congregation of the **c** of Israel, 1121
13:28 and moreover we saw the **c** of Anak there. 3211
13:32 they had searched unto the **c** of Israel, 1121
14: 2 all the **c** of Israel murmured against Moses 1121
14: 3 *that* our wives and our **c** should be a prey? 2945
14: 5 of the congregation of the **c** of Israel. 1121
14: 7 they spake unto all the company of the **c** of 1121
14:10 the congregation before all the **c** of Israel. 1121
14:18 of the fathers upon the **c** unto the third 1121
14:27 I have heard the murmurings of the **c** of 1121
14:33 your **c** shall wander in the wilderness forty 1121
14:39 Moses told these sayings unto all the **c** of 1121
15: 2 Speak unto the **c** of Israel, and say unto 1121
15:18 Speak unto the **c** of Israel, and say unto 1121
15:25 for all the congregation of the **c** of Israel, 1121
15:26 all the congregation of the **c** of Israel, 1121
15:29 *both for* him that is born amongst the **c** of 1121
15:32 while the **c** of Israel were in the wilderness, 1121
15:38 Speak unto the **c** of Israel, and bid them 1121
16: 2 with certain of the **c** of Israel, two hundred 1121

Nu 16:27 and their sons, and their **little c**. 2945
16:38 and they shall be a sign unto the **c** of Israel. 1121
16:40 *To be* a memorial unto the **c** of Israel, that 1121
16:41 on the morrow all the congregation of the **c** 1121
17: 2 Speak unto the **c** of Israel, and take of 1121
17: 5 from me the murmurings of the **c** of Israel, 1121
17: 6 Moses spake unto the **c** of Israel, and 1121
17: 9 before the LORD unto all the **c** of Israel: 1121
17:12 the **c** of Israel spake unto Moses, saying, 1121
18: 5 that there be no wrath any more upon the **c** 1121
18: 6 the Levites from among the **c** of Israel: 1121
18: 8 of all the hallowed *things* of the **c** of Israel; 1121
18:11 with all the wave offerings of the **c** of 1121
18:19 which the **c** of Israel offer unto the LORD, 1121
18:20 and thine inheritance among the **c** of Israel. 1121
18:21 I have given the **c** of Levi all the tenth in 1121
18:22 Neither must the **c** of Israel henceforth 1121
18:23 that among the **c** of Israel they have no 1121
18:24 the tithes of the **c** of Israel, which they offer 1121
18:24 Among the **c** of Israel they shall have no 1121
18:26 When ye take of the **c** of Israel the tithes 1121
18:28 which ye receive of the **c** of Israel; 1121
18:32 ye pollute the holy *things* of the **c** of Israel, 1121
19: 2 saying, Speak unto the **c** of Israel, that they 1121
19: 9 it shall be kept for the congregation of the **c** 1121
19:10 it shall be unto the **c** of Israel, and unto 1121
20: 1 came the **c** of Israel, *even* the whole 1121
20:12 to sanctify me in the eyes of the **c** of Israel, 1121
20:13 the **c** of Israel strove with the LORD, 1121
20:19 the **c** of Israel said unto him, We will go by 1121
20:22 the **c** of Israel, *even* the whole 1121
20:24 which I have given unto the **c** of Israel, 1121
21:10 the **c** of Israel set forward, and pitched in 1121
21:24 unto Jabbok, *even* unto the **c** of Ammon: 1121
21:24 for the border of the **c** of Ammon *was* 1121
22: 1 the **c** of Israel set forward, and pitched in 1121
22: 3 was distressed because of the **c** of Israel. 1121
22: 5 which *is* by the river *of* the land of the **c** of 1121
24:17 of Moab, and destroy all the **c** of Sheth. 1121
25: 6 one of the **c** of Israel came and 1121
25: 6 in the sight of all the congregation of the **c** 1121
25: 8 So the plague was stayed from the **c** of 1121
25:11 hath turned my wrath away from the **c** of 1121
25:11 that I consumed not the **c** of Israel in my 1121
25:13 and made an atonement for the **c** of Israel. 1121
26: 2 of all the congregation of the **c** of Israel, 1121
26: 4 commanded Moses and the **c** of Israel, 1121
26: 5 the **c** of Reuben; Hanoch, *of whom cometh* 1121
26:11 Notwithstanding the **c** of Korah died not. 1121
26:15 The **c** of Gad after their families: 1121
26:18 These *are* the families of the **c** of Gad 1121
26:44 *Of* the **c** of Asher after their families: 1121
26:51 These *were* the numbered of the **c** of Israel, 1121
26:62 for they were not numbered among the **c** of 1121
26:62 given them among the **c** of Israel. 1121
26:63 who numbered the **c** of Israel in the plains 1121
26:64 when they numbered the **c** of Israel in 1121
27: 8 thou shalt speak unto the **c** of Israel, saying, 1121
27:11 it shall be unto the **c** of Israel a statute of 1121
27:12 see the land which I have given unto the **c** 1121
27:20 that all the congregation of the **c** of Israel 1121
27:21 *both* he, and all the **c** of Israel with him, 1121
28: 2 Command the **c** of Israel, and say unto 1121
29:40 Moses told the **c** of Israel according to all 1121
30: 1 of the tribes concerning the **c** of Israel, 1121
31: 2 Avenge the **c** of Israel of the Midianites: 1121
31: 9 the **c** of Israel took *all* the women of 1121
31:12 and unto the congregation of the **c** of Israel, 1121
31:16 Behold, these caused the **c** of Israel, 1121
31:18 all the **women c**, that have not known a 2945
31:30 of the **c** of Israel's half, thou shalt take one 1121
31:42 of the **c** of Israel's half, which Moses 1121
31:47 Even of the **c** of Israel's half, Moses took 1121
31:54 *for* a memorial for the **c** of Israel before 1121
32: 1 Now the **c** of Reuben and the children of 1121
32: 1 the **c** of Gad had a very great multitude of 1121
32: 2 The **c** of Gad and the children of Reuben 1121
32: 2 the **c** of Reuben came and spake unto 1121
32: 6 Moses said unto the **c** of Gad and to 1121
32: 6 the children of Gad and to the **c** of Reuben, 1121
32: 7 wherefore discourage ye the heart of the **c** 1121
32: 9 they discouraged the heart of the **c** of Israel, 1121
32:17 will go ready armed before the **c** of Israel, 1121
32:18 until the **c** of Israel have inherited every 1121
32:25 the **c** of Gad and the children of Reuben 1121
32:25 and the **c** of Reuben spake unto Moses, 1121
32:28 the chief fathers of the tribes of the **c** of 1121
32:29 If the **c** of Gad and the children of Reuben 1121
32:29 the **c** of Reuben will pass with you over 1121
32:31 the **c** of Gad and the children of Reuben 1121
32:31 of Gad and the **c** of Reuben answered, 1121
32:33 *even* to the **c** of Gad, and to the children of 1121
32:33 to the **c** of Reuben, and unto half the tribe 1121
32:34 the **c** of Gad built Dibon, and Ataroth, and 1121
32:37 the **c** of Reuben built Heshbon, and 1121
32:39 the **c** of Machir the son of Manasseh went 1121
33: 1 These *are* the journeys of the **c** of Israel, 1121
33: 3 on the morrow after the passover the **c** of 1121
33: 5 the **c** of Israel removed from Rameses, and 1121
33:38 in the fortieth year after the **c** of Israel were 1121
33:40 heard of the coming of the **c** of Israel. 1121
33:51 Speak unto the **c** of Israel, and say unto 1121
34: 2 Command the **c** of Israel, and say unto 1121
34:13 Moses commanded the **c** of Israel, saying, 1121
34:14 For the tribe of the **c** of Reuben according 1121
34:14 the tribe of the **c** of Gad according to 1121
34:20 of the tribe of the **c** of Simeon, Shemuel 1121
34:22 the prince of the tribe of the **c** of Dan, 1121
34:23 The prince of the **c** of Joseph, for the tribe 1121
34:23 for the tribe of the **c** of Manasseh, 1121
34:24 the prince of the tribe of the **c** of Ephraim, 1121
34:25 the prince of the tribe of the **c** of Zebulun, 1121
34:26 the prince of the tribe of the **c** of Issachar, 1121
34:27 the prince of the tribe of the **c** of Asher, 1121
34:28 the prince of the tribe of the **c** of Naphtali, 1121

Nu 34:29 unto the c of Israel in the land of Canaan. 1121
35: 2 Command the c of Israel, that they give 1121
35: 8 *shall be* of the possession of the c of Israel: 1121
35:10 Speak unto the c of Israel, and say unto 1121
35:15 *both* for the c of Israel, and for the stranger, 1121
35:34 for I the LORD dwell among the c of 1121
36: 1 the chief fathers of the families of the c of 1121
36: 1 the chief fathers of the c of Israel: 1121
36: 2 for an inheritance by lot to the c of Israel: 1121
36: 3 sons of the *other* tribes of the c of Israel, 1121
36: 4 when the jubile of the c of Israel shall be, 1121
36: 5 Moses commanded the c of Israel 1121
36: 7 So shall not the inheritance of the c of 1121
36: 7 for every one of the c of Israel shall keep 1121
36: 8 an inheritance in any tribe of the c of Israel, 1121
36: 8 that the c of Israel may enjoy every man 1121
36: 9 every one of the tribes of the c of Israel 1121
36:13 c of Israel in the plains of Moab by Jordan 1121
Dt 1: 3 *that* Moses spake unto the c of Israel, 1121
1:36 to his c, because he hath wholly followed 1121
1:39 which ye said should be a prey, and your c, 1121
2: 4 the coast of your brethren the c of Esau, 1121
2: 8 when we passed by from our brethren the c 1121
2: 9 I have given Ar unto the c of Lot *for* a 1121
2:12 the c of Esau succeeded them, when they 1121
2:19 *when* thou comest nigh over against the c 1121
2:19 for I will not give thee of the land of the c 1121
2:19 I have given it unto the c of Lot *for* a 1121
2:22 As he did to the c of Esau, which dwelt in 1121
2:29 (As the c of Esau which dwell in Seir, and 1121
2:37 Only unto the land of the c of Ammon thou 1121
3: 6 the men, women, and c, of every city. 2945
3:11 *is* it not in Rabbath of the c of Ammon? 1121
3:16 *which is* the border of the c of Ammon; 1121
3:18 armed before your brethren the c of Israel, 1121
4:10 the earth, and *that* they may teach their c. 1121
4:25 When thou shalt beget c, and 1121
4:25 children's c, and ye shall have remained 1121
4:40 with thy c after thee, and that thou mayest 1121
4:44 this *is* the law which Moses set before the c 1121
4:45 which Moses spake unto the c of Israel, 1121
4:46 whom Moses and the c of Israel smote, 1121
5: 9 the iniquity of the fathers upon the c 1121
5:29 well with them, and with their c for ever! 1121
6: 7 thou shalt teach them diligently unto thy c, 1121
9: 2 people great and tall, the c of the Anakims, 1121
9: 2 *say,* Who can stand before the c of Anak! 1121
10: 6 the c of Israel took their journey from 1121
10: 6 from Beeroth of the c of Jaakan *to* Mosera: 1121
11: 2 for *I speak* not with your c which have not 1121
11:19 ye shall teach them your c, speaking of 1121
11:21 may be multiplied, and the days of your c, 1121
12:25 go well with thee, and with thy c after thee, 1121
12:28 with thee, and with thy c after thee for ever, 1121
13:13 *Certain* men, the c of Belial, are gone out 1121
14: 1 Ye *are* the c of the LORD your God: 1121
17:20 he, and his c, in the midst of Israel. 1121
21:15 another hated, and they have born him c, 1121
23: 8 The c that are begotten of them shall enter 1121
24: 7 any of his brethren of the c of Israel, 1121
24:16 fathers shall not be put to death for the c, 1121
24:16 neither shall the c be put to death for 1121
28:54 towards the remnant of his c which he shall 1121
28:55 of the flesh of his c whom he shall eat: 1121
28:57 and towards her c which she shall bear: 1121
29: 1 with the c of Israel in the land of Moab, 1121
29:22 So that the generation to come of your c 1121
29:29 *belong* unto us and to our c for ever, 1121
30: 2 thou and thy c, with all thine heart, and 1121
31:12 c, and thy stranger that *is* within thy gates, 2945
31:13 *that* their c, which have not known *any* 1121
31:19 song for you, and teach it the c of Israel: 1121
31:19 be a witness for me against the c of Israel. 1121
31:22 the same day, and taught it the c of Israel. 1121
31:23 for thou shalt bring the c of Israel into 1121
32: 5 their spot *is* not *the spot* of his c: 1121
32: 8 according to the number of the c of Israel. 1121
32:20 froward generation, c in whom *is* no faith. 1121
32:46 which ye shall command your c to observe 1121
32:49 which I give unto the c of Israel for a 1121
32:51 c of Israel at the waters of 1121
32:51 ye sanctified me not in the midst of the c of 1121
32:52 unto the land which I give the c of Israel. 1121
33: 1 God blessed the c of Israel before his death. 1121
33: 9 his brethren, nor knew his own c: 1121
33:24 Asher he said, *Let* Asher *be* blessed with c; 1121
34: 8 the c of Israel wept for Moses in the plains 1121
34: 9 the c of Israel hearkened unto him, and 1121
Jos 1: 2 I do give to them, *even* to the c of Israel. 1121
2: 2 there came men in hither to night of the c 1121
3: 1 he and all the c of Israel, and lodged there 1121
3: 9 Joshua said unto the c of Israel, 1121
4: 4 whom he had prepared of the c of Israel, 1121
4: 5 the number of the tribes of the c of Israel: 1121
4: 6 *that* when your c ask *their fathers* in time to 1121
4: 7 for a memorial unto the c of Israel for ever. 1121
4: 8 the c of Israel did so as Joshua commanded, 1121
4: 8 the number of the tribes of the c of Israel, 1121
4:12 the c of Reuben, and the children of Gad, 1121
4:12 the c of Gad, and half the tribe of 1121
4:12 passed over armed before the c of Israel, 1121
4:21 he spake unto the c of Israel, saying, 1121
4:21 When your c shall ask their fathers in time 1121
4:22 ye shall let your c know, saying, 1121
5: 1 waters of Jordan from before the c of Israel, 1121
5: 1 them any more, because of the c of Israel. 1121
5: 2 circumcise again the c of Israel the second 1121
5: 3 circumcised the c of Israel at the hill of 1121
5: 6 For the c of Israel walked forty years in 1121
5: 7 their c, *whom* he raised up in their stead, 1121
5:10 the c of Israel encamped in Gilgal, and 1121
5:12 neither had the c of Israel manna any more; 1121
6: 1 straitly shut up because of the c of Israel: 1121
7: 1 the c of Israel committed a trespass in 1121
7: 1 LORD was kindled against the c of Israel. 1121
Jos 7:12 Therefore the c of Israel could not stand 1121
7:23 unto all the c of Israel, and laid them out 1121
8:31 of the LORD commanded the c of Israel, 1121
8:32 which he wrote in the presence of the c of 1121
9:17 the c of Israel journeyed, and came unto 1121
9:18 And the c of Israel smote them not, because 1121
9:26 delivered them out of the hand of the c of 1121
10: 4 peace with Joshua and with the c of Israel. 1121
10:11 whom the c of Israel slew with the sword. 1121
10:12 up the Amorites before the c of Israel, 1121
10:20 the c of Israel had made an end of slaying 1121
10:21 none moved his tongue against any of the c 1121
11:14 the c of Israel took for a prey unto 1121
11:19 a city that made peace with the c of Israel, 1121
11:22 Anakims left in the land of the c of Israel: 1121
12: 1 which the c of Israel smote, and 1121
12: 2 *which is* the border of the c of Ammon; 1121
12: 6 of the LORD and the c of Israel smite: 1121
12: 7 the c of Israel smote on *this* side Jordan on 1121
13: 6 them will I drive out from before the c of 1121
13:10 unto the border of the c of Ammon; 1121
13:13 (Nevertheless the c of Israel expelled not 1121
13:15 Moses gave unto the tribe of the c of 1121
13:22 did the c of Israel slay with the sword 1121
13:23 the border of the c of Reuben was Jordan, 1121
13:23 of the c of Reuben after their families, 1121
13:24 *even* unto the c of Gad according to their 1121
13:25 and half the land of the c of Ammon, 1121
13:28 This *is* the inheritance of the c of Gad after 1121
13:29 tribe of the c of Manasseh by their families. 1121
13:31 *were pertaining* unto the c of Machir 1121
13:31 *even* to the one half of the c of Machir by 1121
14: 1 these *are the countries* which the c of Israel 1121
14: 1 the heads of the fathers of the tribes of the c 1121
14: 4 For the c of Joseph were two tribes, 1121
14: 5 so the c of Israel did, and they divided 1121
14: 6 the c of Judah came unto Joshua in Gilgal: 1121
14:10 while *the c of* Israel wandered in NIH
15: 1 was the lot of the tribe of the c of Judah by 1121
15:12 the coast *thereof.* This *is* the coast of the c 1121
15:13 he gave a part among the c of Judah, 1121
15:14 and Ahiman, and Talmai, the c of Anak. 3211
15:20 This *is* the inheritance of the tribe of the c 1121
15:21 the uttermost cities of the tribe of the c of 1121
15:63 the c of Judah could not drive them out: 1121
15:63 the Jebusites dwell with the c of Judah at 1121
16: 1 the lot of the c of Joseph fell from Jordan 1121
16: 4 So the c of Joseph, Manasseh and Ephraim, 1121
16: 5 the border of the c of Ephraim according to 1121
16: 8 This *is* the inheritance of the tribe of the c 1121
16: 9 the separate cities for the c of Ephraim 1121
16: 9 the inheritance of the c of Manasseh, 1121
17: 2 There was also *a lot* for the rest of the c of 1121
17: 2 for the c of Abiezer, and for the children of 1121
17: 2 for the c of Helek, and for the children of 1121
17: 2 for the c of Asriel, and for the children of 1121
17: 2 for the c of Shechem, and for the children 1121
17: 2 for the c of Hepher, and for the children of 1121
17: 2 of Hepher, and for the c of Shemida: 1121
17: 2 these *were* the male c of Manasseh the son 1121
17: 8 of Manasseh *belonged* to the c of Ephraim; 1121
17:12 Yet the c of Manasseh could not drive out 1121
17:13 when the c of Israel were waxen strong, 1121
17:14 the c of Joseph spake unto Joshua, saying, 1121
17:16 the c of Joseph said, The hill is not enough 1121
18: 1 the whole congregation of the c of Israel 1121
18: 2 there remained among the c of Israel seven 1121
18: 3 Joshua said unto the c of Israel, How long 1121
18:10 there Joshua divided the land unto the c of 1121
18:11 the lot of the tribe of the c of Benjamin 1121
18:11 their lot came forth between the c of Judah 1121
18:11 the children of Judah and the c of Joseph. 1121
18:14 *is* Kirjath-jearim, a city of the c of Judah: 1121
18:20 This *was* the inheritance of the c of 1121
18:21 Now the cities of the tribe of the c of 1121
18:28 This *is* the inheritance of the c of Benjamin 1121
19: 1 *even* for the tribe of the c of Simeon 1121
19: 1 within the inheritance of the c of Judah. 1121
19: 8 This *is* the inheritance of the tribe of the c 1121
19: 9 Out of the portion of the c of Judah *was* 1121
19: 9 *was* the inheritance of the c of Simeon: 1121
19: 9 for the part of the c of Judah was too much 1121
19: 9 the c of Simeon had their inheritance within 1121
19:10 the third lot came up for the c of Zebulun 1121
19:16 This *is* the inheritance of the c of Zebulun 1121
19:17 for the c of Issachar according to their 1121
19:23 This *is* the inheritance of the tribe of the c 1121
19:24 the fifth lot came out for the tribe of the c 1121
19:31 This *is* the inheritance of the tribe of the c 1121
19:32 The sixth lot came out to the c of Naphtali, 1121
19:32 *even* for the c of Naphtali according to their 1121
19:39 This *is* the inheritance of the tribe of the c 1121
19:40 of the c of Dan according to their families. 1121
19:47 the coast of the c of Dan went out *too little* 1121
19:47 the c of Dan went up to fight against 1121
19:48 This *is* the inheritance of the tribe of the c 1121
19:49 the c of Israel gave an inheritance to Joshua 1121
19:51 the heads of the fathers of the tribes of the c 1121
20: 2 Speak to the c of Israel, saying, 1121
20: 9 These were the cities appointed for all the c 1121
21: 1 of the fathers of the tribes of the c of Israel; 1121
21: 3 the c of Israel gave unto the Levites out of 1121
21: 4 the c of Aaron the priest, *which were* of 1121
21: 5 the rest of the c of Kohath had by lot out of 1121
21: 6 the c of Gershon *had* by lot out of 1121
21: 7 The c of Merari by their families *had* out of 1121
21: 8 the c of Israel gave by lot unto the Levites 1121
21: 9 they gave out of the tribe of the c of Judah, 1121
21: 9 out of the tribe of the c of Simeon, these 1121
21:10 Which the c of Aaron, *being* of the families 1121
21:10 *who were* of the c of Levi, had: 1121
21:13 Thus they gave to the c of Aaron the priest 1121
21:19 All the cities of the c of Aaron, the priests, 1121
21:20 the families of the c of Kohath, the Levites 1121
21:20 the Levites which remained of the c of 1121
Jos 21:26 families of the c of Kohath that remained. 1121
21:27 unto the c of Gershon, of the families of 1121
21:34 unto the families of the c of Merari, the rest 1121
21:40 So all the cities for the c of Merari by their 1121
21:41 the possession of the c of Israel *were* forty 1121
22: 9 the c of Reuben and the children of Gad 1121
22: 9 children of Reuben and the c of Gad and 1121
22: 9 departed from the c of Israel out of Shiloh, 1121
22:10 the c of Reuben and the children of Gad 1121
22:10 children of Reuben and the c of Gad and 1121
22:11 the c of Israel heard say, Behold, 1121
22:11 the c of Reuben and the children of Gad 1121
22:11 children of Reuben and the c of Gad and 1121
22:11 of Jordan, at the passage of the c of Israel. 1121
22:12 when the c of Israel heard *of it,* the whole 1121
22:12 c of Israel gathered themselves together *at* 1121
22:13 the c of Israel sent unto the children of 1121
22:13 the children of Israel sent unto the c of 1121
22:13 to the c of Gad, and to the half tribe of 1121
22:15 they came unto the c of Reuben, and to 1121
22:15 to the c of Gad, and to the half tribe of 1121
22:21 the c of Reuben and the children of Gad 1121
22:21 children of Reuben and the c of Gad and 1121
22:24 In time to come your c might speak unto 1121
22:24 come your children might speak unto our c, 1121
22:25 ye c of Reuben and children of Gad; 1121
22:25 ye children of Reuben and c of Gad; 1121
22:25 shall your c make our children cease from 1121
22:25 shall your children make our c cease from 1121
22:27 that your c may not say to our children in 1121
22:27 that your children may not say to our c in 1121
22:30 heard the words that the c of Reuben and 1121
22:30 the c of Gad and the children of Manasseh 1121
22:30 of Gad and the c of Manasseh spake, 1121
22:31 the priest said unto the c of Reuben, 1121
22:31 to the c of Gad, and to the children of 1121
22:31 children of Gad, and to the c of Manasseh, 1121
22:31 now ye have delivered the c of Israel out of 1121
22:32 returned from the c of Reuben, and 1121
22:32 from the c of Gad, out of the land of 1121
22:32 to the c of Israel, and brought them word 1121
22:33 the thing pleased the c of Israel; and 1121
22:33 the c of Israel blessed God, and did not 1121
22:33 to destroy the land wherein the c of Reuben 1121
22:34 the c of Reuben and the children of Gad 1121
22:34 the c of Gad called the altar *Ed:* for it *shall* 1121
24: 4 Jacob and his c went down *into* Egypt. 1121
24:32 which the c of Israel brought up out of 1121
24:32 it became the inheritance of the c of Joseph. 1121
Jdg 1: 1 that the c of Israel asked the LORD, 1121
1: 8 Now the c of Judah had fought against 1121
1: 9 afterward the c of Judah went down to fight 1121
1:16 the c of the Kenite, Moses' father in law, 1121
1:16 the c of Judah *into* the wilderness of Judah, 1121
1:21 the c of Benjamin did not drive out 1121
1:21 the Jebusites dwell with the c of Benjamin 1121
1:34 the Amorites forced the c of Dan into 1121
2: 4 spake these words unto all the c of Israel, 1121
2: 6 the c of Israel went every man unto his 1121
2:11 the c of Israel did evil in the sight of 1121
3: 2 Only that the generations of the c of Israel 1121
3: 5 the c of Israel dwelt among the Canaanites, 1121
3: 7 the c of Israel did evil in the sight of 1121
3: 8 the c of Israel served Chushan-rishathaim 1121
3: 9 when the c of Israel cried unto the LORD, 1121
3: 9 the LORD raised up a deliverer to the c of 1121
3:12 the c of Israel did evil again in the sight of 1121
3:13 he gathered unto him the c of Ammon and 1121
3:14 So the c of Israel served Eglon the king of 1121
3:15 when the c of Israel cried unto the LORD, 1121
3:15 by him the c of Israel sent a present unto 1121
3:27 the c of Israel went down with him from 1121
4: 1 the c of Israel again did evil in the sight of 1121
4: 3 the c of Israel cried unto the LORD: for he 1121
4: 3 twenty years he mightily oppressed the c of 1121
4: 5 the c of Israel came up to her for judgment. 1121
4: 6 take with thee ten thousand men of the c of 1121
4: 6 of Naphtali and of the c of Zebulun? 1121
4:11 *which was* of the c of Hobab the father in 1121
4:23 the king of Canaan before the c of Israel. 1121
4:24 the hand of the c of Israel prospered, 1121
6: 1 the c of Israel did evil in the sight of 1121
6: 2 of the Midianites the c of Israel made them 1121
6: 3 and the Amalekites, and the c of the east, 1121
6: 6 and the c of Israel cried unto the LORD. 1121
6: 7 when the c of Israel cried unto the LORD 1121
6: 8 That the LORD sent a prophet unto the c 1121
6:33 the c of the east were gathered together, 1121
7:12 all the c of the east lay along in the valley 1121
8:10 were left of all the hosts of the c of the east: 1121
8:18 *each* one resembled the c of a king. 1121
8:28 Thus was Midian subdued before the c of 1121
8:33 that the c of Israel turned again, and went a 1121
8:34 the c of Israel remembered not the LORD 1121
10: 6 the c of Israel did evil again in the sight of 1121
10: 6 the gods of the c of Ammon, and the gods 1121
10: 7 and into the hands of the c of Ammon. 1121
10: 8 they vexed and oppressed the c of Israel: 1121
10: 8 all the c of Israel that *were* on the *other* side 1121
10: 9 Moreover the c of Ammon passed over 1121
10:10 the c of Israel cried unto the LORD, 1121
10:11 the LORD said unto the c of Israel, *Did* 1121
10:11 from the c of Ammon, and from 1121
10:15 the c of Israel said unto the LORD, 1121
10:17 the c of Ammon were gathered together, 1121
10:17 the c of Israel assembled themselves 1121
10:18 will begin to fight against the c of Ammon? 1121
11: 4 that the c of Ammon made war against 1121
11: 5 that when the c of Ammon made war 1121
11: 6 that we may fight with the c of Ammon. 1121
11: 8 fight against the c of Ammon, and be our 1121
11: 9 again to fight against the c of Ammon, 1121
11:12 unto the king of the c of Ammon, 1121
11:13 the king of the c of Ammon answered unto 1121
11:14 again unto the king of the c of Ammon: 1121

Jdg 11:15 of Moab, nor the land of the **c** of Ammon: 1121
11:27 be judge *this* day between the **c** of Israel 1121
11:27 the children of Israel and the **c** of Ammon. 1121
11:28 Howbeit the king of the **c** of Ammon 1121
11:29 he passed over *unto* the **c** of Ammon. 1121
11:30 If thou shalt without fail deliver the **c** of 1121
11:31 when I return in peace from the **c** of 1121
11:32 So Jephthah passed over unto the **c** of 1121
11:33 Thus the **c** of Ammon were subdued before 1121
11:33 were subdued before the **c** of Israel. 1121
11:36 of thine enemies, *even* of the **c** of Ammon. 1121
12: 1 thou over to fight against the **c** of Ammon, 1121
12: 2 my people were at great strife with the **c** of 1121
12: 3 passed over against the **c** of Ammon, and 1121
13: 1 the **c** of Israel did evil again in the sight of 1121
14:16 thou hast put forth a riddle unto the **c** of my 1121
14:17 she told the riddle to the **c** of her people. 1121
18: 2 the **c** of Dan sent of their family five men 1121
18:16 which *were* of the **c** of Dan, stood *by* 1121
18:22 and overtook the **c** of Dan. 1121
18:23 they cried unto the **c** of Dan. And they 1121
18:25 the **c** of Dan said unto him, Let not thy 1121
18:26 the **c** of Dan went their way: and 1121
18:30 the **c** of Dan set up the graven image: and 1121
19:12 of a stranger, that *is* not of the **c** of Israel; 1121
19:30 **c** of Israel came up out of the land of Egypt 1121
20: 1 all the **c** of Israel went out, and 1121
20: 3 (Now the **c** of Benjamin heard that 1121
20: 3 the **c** of Israel were gone up *to* Mizpeh.) 1121
20: 3 said the **c** of Israel, Tell *us,* how was this 1121
20: 7 Behold, ye *are* all **c** of Israel; give here 1121
20:13 deliver *us* the men, the **c** of Belial, 1121
20:13 the **c** of Benjamin would not hearken to 1121
20:13 to the voice of their brethren the **c** of Israel: 1121
20:14 the **c** of Benjamin gathered themselves 1121
20:14 to go out to battle against the **c** of Israel. 1121
20:15 the **c** of Benjamin were numbered at that 1121
20:18 the **c** of Israel arose, and went up *to* 1121
20:18 first to the battle against the **c** of Benjamin? 1121
20:19 the **c** of Israel rose up in the morning, and 1121
20:21 the **c** of Benjamin came forth out of 1121
20:23 (And the **c** of Israel went up and 1121
20:23 Shall I go *up* again to battle against the **c** of 1121
20:24 the **c** of Israel came near against 1121
20:24 children of Israel came near against the **c** 1121
20:25 destroyed *down* to the ground of the **c** of 1121
20:26 all the **c** of Israel, and all the people, 1121
20:27 the **c** of Israel inquired of the LORD, 1121
20:28 against the **c** of Benjamin my brother, 1121
20:30 the **c** of Israel went up against the children 1121
20:30 the children of Israel went up against the **c** 1121
20:31 the **c** of Benjamin went out against 1121
20:32 the **c** of Benjamin said, They *are* smitten 1121
20:32 the **c** of Israel said, Let us flee, and 1121
20:35 the **c** of Israel destroyed of the Benjamites 1121
20:36 So the **c** of Benjamin saw that they were 1121
20:48 the men of Israel turned again upon the **c** of 1121
21: 5 the **c** of Israel said, Who *is there* among all 1121
21: 6 the **c** of Israel repented them for Benjamin 1121
21:10 of the sword, with the women and the **c**. 2945
21:13 **c** of Benjamin that *were* in the rock 1121
21:18 for the **c** of Israel have sworn, saying, 1121
21:20 Therefore they commanded the **c** of 1121
21:23 the **c** of Benjamin did so, and took *them* 1121
21:24 the **c** of Israel departed thence at that time, 1121
1Sa 1: 2 Peninnah had **c**, but Hannah had no 3206
1: 2 had children, but Hannah had no **c**. 3206
2: 5 and she that hath many **c** is waxed feeble. 1121
2:28 offerings made by fire of the **c** of Israel? 1121
7: 4 the **c** of Israel did put away Baalim and 1121
7: 6 Samuel judged the **c** of Israel in Mizpeh. 1121
7: 7 when the Philistines heard that the **c** of 1121
7: 7 when the **c** of Israel heard *it,* they were 1121
7: 8 the **c** of Israel said to Samuel, Cease not to 1121
9: 2 *there was* not among the **c** of Israel a 1121
10:18 said unto the **c** of Israel, Thus saith 1121
10:27 the **c** of Belial said, How shall this *man* 1121
11: 8 the **c** of Israel were three hundred thousand, 1121
12:12 when ye saw that Nahash the king of the **c** 1121
14:18 of God was at that time with the **c** of Israel. 1121
14:47 against the **c** of Ammon, and against Edom, 1121
15: 6 for ye shewed kindness to all the **c** of 1121
16:11 Samuel said unto Jesse, Are here all *thy* **c**? 5288
17:53 the **c** of Israel returned from chasing after 1121
22:19 **c** and sucklings, and oxen, and asses, and 5768
26:19 if *they be* the **c** of men, cursed *be* they 1121
30:22 save *to* every man his wife and his **c**, 1121
2Sa 1:18 (Also he bade *them* teach the **c** of Judah 1121
2:25 the **c** of Benjamin gathered themselves 1121
4: 2 a Beerothite, of the **c** of Benjamin: 1121
7: 6 I brought up the **c** of Israel out of Egypt, 1121
7: 7 **c** of Israel spake I a word with any of 1121
7:10 neither shall the **c** of wickedness afflict 1121
7:14 and with the stripes of the **c** of men: 1121
8:12 of the **c** of Ammon, and of the Philistines, 1121
10: 1 that the king of the **c** of Ammon died, and 1121
10: 2 David's servants came *into* the land of the **c** 1121
10: 3 the princes of the **c** of Ammon said unto 1121
10: 6 when the **c** of Ammon saw that they stank 1121
10: 6 the **c** of Ammon sent and hired the Syrians 1121
10: 8 the **c** of Ammon came out, and put 1121
10:10 put *them* in array against the **c** of Ammon. 1121
10:11 if the **c** of Ammon be too strong for thee, 1121
10:14 when the **c** of Ammon saw that the Syrians 1121
10:14 So Joab returned from the **c** of Ammon, 1121
10:19 So the Syrians feared to help the **c** of 1121
11: 1 they destroyed the **c** of Ammon, and 1121
12: 3 grew up together with him, and with his **c**; 1121
12: 9 hast slain him with the sword of the **c** of 1121
12:26 Joab fought against Rabbah of the **c** of 1121
12:31 thus did he unto all the cities of the **c** of 1121
17:27 of Nahash of Rabbah of the **c** of Ammon, 1121
21: 2 (now the Gibeonites *were* not of the **c** of 1121
21: 2 and the **c** of Israel had sworn unto them: 1121
21: 2 Saul sought to slay them in his zeal to the **c** 1121

2Sa 23:29 Ittai the son of Ribai out of Gibeah of the **c** 1121
1Ki 2: 4 saying, If thy **c** take heed to their way, 1121
4:30 the wisdom of all the **c** of the east country, 1121
6: 1 eightieth year after the **c** of Israel were 1121
6:13 I will dwell among the **c** of Israel, and 1121
8: 1 the chief of the fathers of the **c** of Israel, 1121
8: 9 made *a covenant* with the **c** of Israel, 1121
8:25 so that thy **c** take heed to their way, 1121
8:39 knowest the hearts of all the **c** of men;) 1121
8:63 all the **c** of Israel dedicated the house of 1121
9: 6 you or your **c**, and will not keep my 1121
9:20 which *were* not of the **c** of Israel, 1121
9:21 Their **c** that were left after them in the land, 1121
9:21 whom the **c** of Israel also were not able 1121
9:22 of the **c** of Israel did Solomon make no 1121
11: 2 which the LORD said unto the **c** of Israel, 1121
11: 7 the abomination of the **c** of Ammon. 1121
11:33 Milcom the god of the **c** of Ammon, and 1121
12:17 *as for* the **c** of Israel which dwelt in 1121
12:24 nor fight against your brethren the **c** of 1121
12:33 and ordained a feast unto the **c** of Israel: 1121
14:24 the LORD cast out before the **c** of Israel. 1121
18:20 So Ahab sent unto all the **c** of Israel, and 1121
19:10 for the **c** of Israel have forsaken thy 1121
19:14 the **c** of Israel have forsaken thy covenant, 1121
20: 3 thy wives also and thy **c**, *even* 1121
20: 5 and thy gold, and thy wives, and thy **c**; 1121
20: 7 for my **c**, and for my silver, and for my 1121
20:15 *even* all the **c** of Israel, *being* seven 1121
20:27 the **c** of Israel were numbered, and were all 1121
20:27 the **c** of Israel pitched before them like two 1121
20:29 the **c** of Israel slew *of* the Syrians an 1121
21:13 in two men, **c** of Belial, and sat before him: 1121
21:26 whom the LORD cast out before the **c** of 1121
2Ki 2:23 there came forth little **c** out of the city, and 5288
2:24 the wood, and tare forty and two **c** of them. 3206
4: 7 thy debt, and live thou and thy **c** of the rest. 1121
8:12 evil that thou wilt do unto the **c** of Israel: 1121
8:12 wilt dash their **c**, and rip up their women 5768
8:19 to give to him alway a light, *and* to his **c**. 1121
9: 1 Elisha the prophet called one of the **c** of 1121
10: 1 to them that brought up Ahab's *c,* saying, NIH
10: 5 the bringers up *of the c,* sent to Jehu, NIH
10:13 we go down to salute the **c** of the king and 1121
10:13 children of the king and the **c** of the queen. 1121
10:30 thy **c** of the fourth *generation* shall sit on 1121
13: 5 the **c** of Israel dwelt in their tents, 1121
14: 6 the **c** of the murderers he slew not: 1121
14: 6 fathers shall not be put to death for the **c**, 1121
14: 6 nor the **c** be put to death for the fathers; 1121
16: 3 LORD cast out from before the **c** of Israel. 1121
17: 7 that the **c** of Israel had sinned against 1121
17: 8 LORD cast out from before the **c** of Israel, 1121
17: 9 the **c** of Israel did secretly *those* things that 1121
17:22 For the **c** of Israel walked in all the sins of 1121
17:24 cities of Samaria instead of the **c** of Israel: 1121
17:31 the Sepharvites burnt their **c** in fire to 1121
17:34 the LORD commanded the **c** of Jacob, 1121
17:41 both their **c**, and their children's children: 1121
17:41 both their children, and their children's **c**: 1121
18: 4 for unto those days the **c** of Israel did burn 1121
19: 3 for the **c** are come to the birth, and *there is* 1121
19:12 and the **c** of Eden which *were* in Thelasar? 1121
21: 2 whom the LORD cast out before the **c** of 1121
21: 9 LORD destroyed before the **c** of Israel. 1121
23: 6 upon the graves of the **c** of the people. 1121
23:10 which *is* in the valley of the **c** of Hinnom, 1121
23:13 for Milcom the abomination of the **c** of 1121
24: 2 bands of the **c** of Ammon, and sent them 1121
1Ch 1:43 before *any* king reigned over the **c** of Israel; 1121
2:10 begat Nahshon, prince of the **c** of Judah; 1121
2:18 Caleb the son of Hezron begat **c** of Azubah NIH
2:30 and Appaim: but Seled died without **c**. 1121
2:31 Sheshan. And the **c** of Sheshan; Ahlai. 1121
2:32 and Jonathan: and Jether died without **c**. 1121
4:27 his brethren had not many **c**, neither did all 1121
4:27 their family multiply, like to the **c** of Judah. 1121
5:11 the **c** of Gad dwelt over against them, in 1121
5:14 These *are* the **c** of Abihail the son of Huri, 1121
5:23 the **c** of the half tribe of Manasseh dwelt in 1121
6: 3 the **c** of Amram; Aaron, and Moses, and 1121
6:33 these *are* they that waited with their **c**. 1121
6:64 the **c** of Israel gave to the Levites *these* 1121
6:65 they gave by lot out of the tribe of the **c** of 1121
6:65 out of the tribe of the **c** of Simeon, and 1121
6:65 out of the tribe of the **c** of Benjamin, these 1121
6:77 Unto the rest of the **c** of Merari *were given* 1121
7:12 and Huppim, the **c** of Ir, *and* Hushim, 1121
7:29 by the borders of the **c** of Manasseh, 1121
7:29 In these dwelt the **c** of Joseph the son of 1121
7:33 and Ashvath. These *are* the **c** of Japhlet. 1121
7:40 All these *were* the **c** of Asher, heads of 1121
8: 8 Shaharaim begat **c** in the country of Moab, NIH
9: 3 in Jerusalem dwelt of the **c** of Judah, and 1121
9: 3 of the **c** of Benjamin, and of the children of 1121
9: 3 and of the **c** of Ephraim, and Manasseh; 1121
9: 4 of Bani, of the **c** of Pharez the son of Judah. 1121
9:18 they *were* porters in the companies of the **c** 1121
9:23 their **c** had the oversight of the gates of 1121
11:31 that pertained to the **c** of Benjamin, 1121
12:16 there came of the **c** of Benjamin and 1121
12:24 The **c** of Judah that bare shield and 1121
12:25 Of the **c** of Simeon, mighty *men* of valour 1121
12:26 Of the **c** of Levi four thousand and 1121
12:29 of the **c** of Benjamin, the kindred of Saul, 1121
12:30 of the **c** of Ephraim twenty thousand and 1121
12:32 of the **c** of Issachar, *which were men* that 1121
14: 4 Now these *are* the names of *his* **c** which he 3205
15: 4 David assembled the **c** of Aaron, and 1121
15:15 the **c** of the Levites bare the ark of God 1121
16:13 his servant, ye **c** of Jacob, his chosen *ones.* 1121
17: 9 neither shall the **c** of wickedness waste 1121
18:11 from the **c** of Ammon, and from 1121
19: 1 that Nahash the king of the **c** of Ammon 1121
19: 2 into the land of the **c** of Ammon to Hanun, 1121

1Ch 19: 3 the princes of the **c** of Ammon said to 1121
19: 6 when the **c** of Ammon saw that they had 1121
19: 6 the **c** of Ammon sent a thousand talents of 1121
19: 7 the **c** of Ammon gathered themselves 1121
19: 9 the **c** of Ammon came out, and put 1121
19:11 they set *themselves* in array against the **c** of 1121
19:12 if the **c** of Ammon be too strong for thee, 1121
19:15 when the **c** of Ammon saw that the Syrians 1121
19:19 neither would the Syrians help the **c** of 1121
20: 1 wasted the country of the **c** of Ammon, and 1121
20: 3 dealt David with all the cities of the **c** of 1121
20: 4 slew Sippai, *that was* of the **c** of the giant: 3211
24: 2 died before their father, and had no **c**: 1121
26:10 Also Hosah, of the **c** of Merari, had sons; 1121
27: 1 Now the **c** of Israel after their number, 1121
27: 3 Of the **c** of Perez *was* the chief of all 1121
27:10 Helez the Pelonite, of the **c** of Ephraim: 1121
27:14 the Pirathonite, of the **c** of Ephraim: 1121
27:20 Of the **c** of Ephraim, Hoshea the son of 1121
28: 8 leave *it* for an inheritance for your **c** after 1121
2Ch 5: 2 the chief of the fathers of the **c** of Israel, 1121
5:10 made *a covenant* with the **c** of Israel, 1121
6:11 that he made with the **c** of Israel. 1121
6:16 that thy **c** take heed to their way to walk in 1121
6:30 (for thou only knowest the hearts of the **c** of 1121
7: 3 when all the **c** of Israel saw how the fire 1121
8: 2 and caused the **c** of Israel to dwell there. 1121
8: 8 *But* of their **c**, who were left after them in 1121
8: 8 whom the **c** of Israel consumed not, 1121
8: 9 of the **c** of Israel did Solomon make no 1121
10:17 *as for* the **c** of Israel that dwelt in the cities 1121
10:18 the **c** of Israel stoned him with stones, 1121
11:19 Which bare him **c**; Jeush, and Shamariah, 1121
11:23 dispersed of all his **c** throughout all 1121
13: 7 the **c** of Belial, and have strengthened 1121
13:12 O **c** of Israel, fight ye not against 1121
13:16 the **c** of Israel fled before Judah: and 1121
13:18 Thus the **c** of Israel were brought under at 1121
13:18 the **c** of Judah prevailed, because 1121
20: 1 *that* the **c** of Moab, and the children of 1121
20: 1 the **c** of Ammon, and with them *other* 1121
20:10 the **c** of Ammon and Moab and mount Seir, 1121
20:13 their little ones, their wives, and their **c**. 1121
20:19 of the **c** of the Kohathites, and of 1121
20:19 the Kohathites, and of the **c** of the Korhites, 1121
20:22 the LORD set ambushments against the **c** 1121
20:23 For the **c** of Ammon and Moab stood up 1121
21:14 and thy **c**, and thy wives, and all thy goods: 1121
25: 4 he slew not their **c**, but *did* as it is written in 1121
25: 4 saying, The fathers shall not die for the **c**, 1121
25: 4 neither shall the **c** die for the fathers, but 1121
25: 7 *to wit, with* all the **c** of Ephraim. 1121
25:11 and smote *of* the **c** of Seir ten thousand. 1121
25:12 *other* ten thousand *left* alive did the **c** of 1121
25:14 that he brought the gods of the **c** of Seir, 1121
27: 5 the **c** of Ammon gave him the same year an 1121
27: 5 So much did the **c** of Ammon pay unto 1121
28: 3 burnt his **c** in the fire after the abominations 1121
28: 3 LORD had cast out before the **c** of Israel. 1121
28: 8 the **c** of Israel carried away captive of their 1121
28:10 now ye purpose to keep under the **c** of 1121
28:12 certain of the heads of the **c** of Ephraim, 1121
30: 6 of the king, saying, Ye **c** of Israel, 1121
30: 9 your **c** *shall find* compassion before them 1121
30:21 the **c** of Israel that were present at 1121
31: 1 *them all.* Then all the **c** of Israel returned, 1121
31: 5 the **c** of Israel brought in abundance 1121
31: 6 *concerning* the **c** of Israel and Judah, 1121
33: 2 whom the LORD had cast out before the **c** 1121
33: 6 he caused his **c** to pass through the fire in 1121
33: 9 had destroyed before the **c** of Israel. 1121
34:33 countries that *pertained* to the **c** of Israel, 1121
35:17 the **c** of Israel that were present kept 1121
Ezr 2: 1 Now these *are* the **c** of the province that 1121
2: 3 The **c** of Parosh, two thousand an hundred 1121
2: 4 The **c** of Shephatiah, three hundred seventy 1121
2: 5 The **c** of Arah, seven hundred seventy and 1121
2: 6 The **c** of Pahath-moab, of the children of 1121
2: 6 of the **c** of Jeshua *and* Joab, two thousand 1121
2: 7 The **c** of Elam, a thousand two hundred 1121
2: 8 The **c** of Zattu, nine hundred forty and five. 1121
2: 9 The **c** of Zaccai, seven hundred and 1121
2:10 The **c** of Bani, six hundred forty and two. 1121
2:11 The **c** of Bebai, six hundred twenty and 1121
2:12 The **c** of Azgad, a thousand two hundred 1121
2:13 The **c** of Adonikam, six hundred sixty and 1121
2:14 The **c** of Bigvai, two thousand fifty and six. 1121
2:15 The **c** of Adin, four hundred fifty and four. 1121
2:16 The **c** of Ater of Hezekiah, ninety and 1121
2:17 The **c** of Bezai, three hundred twenty and 1121
2:18 The **c** of Jorah, an hundred and twelve. 1121
2:19 The **c** of Hashum, two hundred twenty and 1121
2:20 The **c** of Gibbar, ninety and five. 1121
2:21 The **c** of Beth-lehem, an hundred twenty 1121
2:24 The **c** of Azmaveth, forty and two. 1121
2:25 The **c** of Kirjath-arim, Chephirah, and 1121
2:26 The **c** of Ramah and Gaba, six hundred 1121
2:29 The **c** of Nebo, fifty and two. 1121
2:30 The **c** of Magbish, an hundred fifty and six. 1121
2:31 The **c** of the other Elam, a thousand two 1121
2:32 The **c** of Harim, three hundred and twenty. 1121
2:33 The **c** of Lod, Hadid, and Ono, 1121
2:34 The **c** of Jericho, three hundred forty and 1121
2:35 The **c** of Senaah, three thousand and 1121
2:36 the **c** of Jedaiah, of the house of Jeshua, 1121
2:37 The **c** of Immer, a thousand fifty and two. 1121
2:38 The **c** of Pashur, a thousand two hundred 1121
2:39 The **c** of Harim, a thousand and seventeen. 1121
2:40 the **c** of Jeshua and Kadmiel, of 1121
2:40 of the **c** of Hodaviah, seventy and four. 1121
2:41 The **c** of Asaph, an hundred twenty and 1121
2:42 The **c** of the porters: the children of 1121
2:42 the **c** of Shallum, the children of Ater, 1121
2:42 the **c** of Ater, the children of Talmon, 1121
2:42 the children of Ater, the **c** of Talmon, 1121

C

Ezr 2:42 the **c** of Akkub, the children of Hatita, 1121
2:42 the children of Akkub, the **c** of Hatita, 1121
2:42 the children of Hatita, the **c** of Shobai, 1121
2:43 the **c** of Ziha, the children of Hasupha, 1121
2:43 the children of Ziha, the **c** of Hasupha, 1121
2:43 the children of Hasupha, the **c** of Tabbaoth, 1121
2:44 The **c** of Keros, the children of Siaha, 1121
2:44 the **c** of Siaha, the children of Padon, 1121
2:44 the children of Siaha, the **c** of Padon, 1121
2:45 The **c** of Lebanah, the children of Hagabah, 1121
2:45 the **c** of Hagabah, the children of Akkub, 1121
2:45 the children of Hagabah, the **c** of Akkub, 1121
2:46 The **c** of Hagab, the children of Shalmai, 1121
2:46 the **c** of Shalmai, the children of Hanan, 1121
2:46 the children of Shalmai, the **c** of Hanan, 1121
2:47 The **c** of Giddel, the children of Gahar, 1121
2:47 the **c** of Gahar, the children of Reaiah, 1121
2:47 the children of Gahar, the **c** of Reaiah, 1121
2:48 The **c** of Rezin, the children of Nekoda, 1121
2:48 The children of Rezin, the **c** of Nekoda, 1121
2:48 the children of Nekoda, the **c** of Gazzam, 1121
2:49 The **c** of Uzza, the children of Paseah, 1121
2:49 the **c** of Paseah, the children of Besai, 1121
2:49 the children of Paseah, the **c** of Besai, 1121
2:50 The **c** of Asnah, the children of Mehunim, 1121
2:50 The children of Asnah, the **c** of Mehunim, 1121
2:50 children of Mehunim, the **c** of Nephusim, 1121
2:51 The **c** of Bakbuk, the children of Hakupha, 1121
2:51 the **c** of Hakupha, the children of Harhur, 1121
2:51 the children of Hakupha, the **c** of Harhur, 1121
2:52 The **c** of Bazluth, the children of Mehida, 1121
2:52 the **c** of Mehida, the children of Harsha, 1121
2:52 the children of Mehida, the **c** of Harsha, 1121
2:53 The **c** of Barkos, the children of Sisera, 1121
2:53 The children of Barkos, the **c** of Sisera, 1121
2:53 the children of Sisera, the **c** of Thamah, 1121
2:54 The **c** of Neziah, the children of Hatipha. 1121
2:54 The children of Neziah, the **c** of Hatipha. 1121
2:55 The **c** of Solomon's servants: the children 1121
2:55 the **c** of Sotai, the children of Sophereth, 1121
2:55 the children of Sotai, the **c** of Sophereth, 1121
2:55 the children of Sophereth, the **c** of Peruda, 1121
2:56 The **c** of Jaalah, the children of Darkon, 1121
2:56 the **c** of Darkon, the children of Giddel, 1121
2:56 the children of Darkon, the **c** of Giddel, 1121
2:57 The **c** of Shephatiah, the children of Hattil, 1121
2:57 The children of Shephatiah, the **c** of Hattil, 1121
2:57 the **c** of Pochereth of Zebaim, the children 1121
2:57 of Pochereth of Zebaim, the **c** of Ami. 1121
2:58 and the **c** of Solomon's servants, 1121
2:60 The **c** of Delaiah, the children of Tobiah, 1121
2:60 the **c** of Tobiah, the children of Nekoda, 1121
2:60 the **c** of Nekoda, six hundred fifty and two. 1121
2:61 of the **c** of the priests: the children of 1121
2:61 the **c** of Habaiah, the children of Koz, 1121
2:61 the children of Habaiah, the **c** of Koz, 1121
2:61 the children of Koz, the **c** of Barzillai; 1121
3: 1 and the **c** of Israel *were* in the cities, 1121
4: 1 Benjamin heard that the **c** of the captivity 1121
6:16 the **c** of Israel, the priests, and the Levites, 1123
6:16 and the rest of the **c** of the captivity, 1123
6:19 the **c** of the captivity kept the passover 1121
6:20 killed the passover for all the **c** of 1121
6:21 the **c** of Israel, which were come again out 1121
7: 7 there went up *some* of the **c** of Israel, and 1121
8:35 *Also* the **c** of those that had been carried 1121
9:12 leave *it* for an inheritance to your **c** for 1121
10: 1 congregation *of* men and women and **c**: 3206
10: 7 Jerusalem unto all the **c** of the captivity, 1121
10:16 the **c** of the captivity did so. And Ezra 1121
10:44 of them had wives by *whom* they had **c**. 1121
Ne 1: 6 for the **c** of Israel thy servants, and 1121
1: 6 confess the sins of the **c** of Israel, which we 1121
2:10 a man to seek the welfare of the **c** of Israel. 1121
5: 5 of our brethren, our **c** as their children: 1121
5: 5 of our brethren, our children as their **c**: 1121
7: 6 These *are* the **c** of the province, that went 1121
7: 8 The **c** of Parosh, two thousand an hundred 1121
7: 9 The **c** of Shephatiah, three hundred seventy 1121
7:10 The **c** of Arah, six hundred fifty and two. 1121
7:11 The **c** of Pahath-moab, of the children of 1121
7:11 of the **c** of Jeshua and Joab, two thousand 1121
7:12 The **c** of Elam, a thousand two hundred 1121
7:13 The **c** of Zattu, eight hundred forty and 1121
7:14 The **c** of Zaccai, seven hundred and 1121
7:15 The **c** of Binnui, six hundred forty and 1121
7:16 The **c** of Bebai, six hundred twenty and 1121
7:17 The **c** of Azgad, two thousand three 1121
7:18 The **c** of Adonikam, six hundred threescore 1121
7:19 The **c** of Bigvai, two thousand threescore 1121
7:20 The **c** of Adin, six hundred fifty and five. 1121
7:21 The **c** of Ater of Hezekiah, ninety and 1121
7:22 The **c** of Hashum, three hundred twenty 1121
7:23 The **c** of Bezai, three hundred twenty and 1121
7:24 The **c** of Hariph, an hundred *and* twelve. 1121
7:25 The **c** of Gibeon, ninety and five. 1121
7:34 The **c** of the other Elam, a thousand two 1121
7:35 The **c** of Harim, three hundred and twenty. 1121
7:36 The **c** of Jericho, three hundred forty and 1121
7:37 The **c** of Lod, Hadid, and Ono, 1121
7:38 The **c** of Senaah, three thousand nine 1121
7:39 the **c** of Jedaiah, of the house of Jeshua, 1121
7:40 The **c** of Immer, a thousand fifty and two. 1121
7:41 The **c** of Pashur, a thousand two hundred 1121
7:42 The **c** of Harim, a thousand *and* seventeen. 1121
7:43 the **c** of Jeshua, of Kadmiel, *and* of 1121
7:43 *and* of the **c** of Hodevah, seventy and four. 1121
7:44 the **c** of Asaph, an hundred forty and eight. 1121
7:45 the **c** of Shallum, the children of Ater, 1121
7:45 the **c** of Ater, the children of Talmon, 1121
7:45 the children of Ater, the **c** of Talmon, 1121
7:45 the **c** of Akkub, the children of Hatita, 1121
7:45 the children of Akkub, the **c** of Hatita, 1121
7:45 the **c** of Shobai, an hundred thirty and 1121
7:46 the **c** of Ziha, the children of Hashupha, 1121

Ne 7:46 the children of Ziha, the **c** of Hashupha, 1121
7:46 children of Hashupha, the **c** of Tabbaoth, 1121
7:47 The **c** of Keros, the children of Sia, 1121
7:47 the **c** of Sia, the children of Padon, 1121
7:47 the children of Sia, the **c** of Padon, 1121
7:48 The **c** of Lebana, the children of Hagaba, 1121
7:48 The children of Lebana, the **c** of Hagaba, 1121
7:48 the children of Hagaba, the **c** of Shalmai, 1121
7:49 The **c** of Hanan, the children of Giddel, 1121
7:49 the **c** of Giddel, the children of Gahar, 1121
7:49 the children of Giddel, the **c** of Gahar, 1121
7:50 The **c** of Reaiah, the children of Rezin, 1121
7:50 the **c** of Rezin, the children of Nekoda, 1121
7:50 the children of Rezin, the **c** of Nekoda, 1121
7:51 The **c** of Gazzam, the children of Uzza, 1121
7:51 the **c** of Uzza, the children of Phaseah, 1121
7:51 the children of Uzza, the **c** of Phaseah, 1121
7:52 The **c** of Besai, the children of Meunim, 1121
7:52 The children of Besai, the **c** of Meunim, 1121
7:52 children of Meunim, the **c** of Nephishesim, 1121
7:53 The **c** of Bakbuk, the children of Hakupha, 1121
7:53 the **c** of Hakupha, the children of Harhur, 1121
7:53 the children of Hakupha, the **c** of Harhur, 1121
7:54 The **c** of Bazlith, the children of Mehida, 1121
7:54 the **c** of Mehida, the children of Harsha, 1121
7:54 the children of Mehida, the **c** of Harsha, 1121
7:55 The **c** of Barkos, the children of Sisera, 1121
7:55 the **c** of Sisera, the children of Tamah, 1121
7:55 the children of Sisera, the **c** of Tamah, 1121
7:56 The **c** of Neziah, the children of Hatipha. 1121
7:56 The children of Neziah, the **c** of Hatipha. 1121
7:57 The **c** of Solomon's servants: the children 1121
7:57 the **c** of Sotai, the children of Sophereth, 1121
7:57 the children of Sotai, the **c** of Sophereth, 1121
7:57 the children of Sophereth, the **c** of Perida, 1121
7:58 The **c** of Jaala, the children of Darkon, 1121
7:58 The children of Jaala, the **c** of Darkon, 1121
7:58 the children of Darkon, the **c** of Giddel, 1121
7:59 The **c** of Shephatiah, the children of Hattil, 1121
7:59 The children of Shephatiah, the **c** of Hattil, 1121
7:59 of Hattil, the **c** of Pochereth Zebaim, 1121
7:59 of Pochereth Zebaim, the **c** of Amon. 1121
7:60 and the **c** of Solomon's servants, 1121
7:62 The **c** of Delaiah, the children of Tobiah, 1121
7:62 the **c** of Tobiah, the children of Nekoda, 1121
7:62 the **c** of Nekoda, six hundred forty and two. 1121
7:63 the **c** of Habaiah, the children of Koz, 1121
7:63 the children of Habaiah, the **c** of Koz, 1121
7:63 the children of Koz, the **c** of Barzillai, 1121
7:73 the **c** of Israel *were* in their cities. 1121
8:14 that the **c** of Israel should dwell in booths in 1121
8:17 that day had not the **c** of Israel done so. 1121
9: 1 fourth day of this month the **c** of Israel 1121
9:23 Their **c** also multipliedst thou as the stars of 1121
9:24 So the **c** went in and possessed the land, 1121
10:39 For the **c** of Israel and the children of Levi 1121
10:39 the **c** of Levi shall bring the offering of 1121
11: 3 and the **c** of Solomon's servants. 1121
11: 4 at Jerusalem dwelt *certain* of the **c** of Judah, 1121
11: 4 of Judah, and of the **c** of Benjamin. 1121
11: 4 Of the **c** of Judah; Athaiah the son of 1121
11: 4 the son of Mahalaleel, of the **c** of Perez; 1121
11:24 of the **c** of Zerah the son of Judah, 1121
11:25 *some* of the **c** of Judah dwelt at 1121
11:31 The **c** also of Benjamin from Geba *dwelt at* 1121
12:43 the wives also and the **c** rejoiced: so 3206
12:47 the Levites sanctified *them* unto the **c** of 1121
13: 2 Because they met not the **c** of Israel with 1121
13:16 and sold on the sabbath unto the **c** of Judah, 1121
13:24 their **c** spake half in the speech of Ashdod, 1121
Est 3:13 both young and old, **little c** and women, 2945
5:11 the multitude of his **c**, and all *the things* 1121
Job 5: 4 His **c** are far from safety, and they are 1121
8: 4 If thy **c** have sinned against him, and 1121
17: 5 *his* friends, even the eyes of his **c** shall fail. 1121
19:18 Yea, **young c** despised me; I arose, and 5759
20:10 His **c** shall *seek to* please the poor, and 1121
21:11 little ones like a flock, and their **c** dance. 3206
21:19 God layeth up his iniquity for his **c**: 1121
24: 5 *yieldeth* food for them *and* for *their* **c**. 5288
27:14 If his **c** be multiplied, *it is* for the sword: 1121
29: 5 yet with me, *when* my **c** *were* about me; 5288
30: 8 *They were* **c** of fools, yea, children of base 1121
30: 8 *were* children of fools, yea, **c** of base men: 1121
41:34 *things:* he *is* a king over all the **c** of pride. 1121
Ps 11: 4 eyes behold, his eyelids try, the **c** of men. 1121
12: 1 for the faithful fail from among the **c** of 1121
14: 2 down from heaven upon the **c** of men, 1121
17:14 *with* thy hid *treasure:* they are full *of* **c**, 1121
21:10 and their seed from among the **c** of men. 1121
34:11 Come, ye **c**, hearken unto me: I will teach 1121
36: 7 the **c** of men put their trust under 1121
45: 2 Thou art fairer than the **c** of men: grace is 1121
45:16 Instead of thy fathers shall be thy **c**, 1121
53: 2 God looked down from heaven upon the **c** 1121
66: 5 *he is* terrible *in his* doing toward the **c** of 1121
69: 8 and an alien unto my mother's **c**. 1121
72: 4 he shall save the **c** of the needy, and 1121
73:15 offend *against* the generation of thy **c**. 1121
78: 4 We will not hide *them* from their **c**, 1121
78: 5 *they* should make them known to their **c**: 1121
78: 6 *them, even* the **c** *which* should be born; 1121
78: 6 should arise and declare *them* to their **c**: 1121
78: 9 The **c** of Ephraim, *being* armed, *and* 1121
82: 6 and all of you *are* **c** of the most High. 1121
83: 8 they have holpen the **c** of Lot. Selah. 1121
89:30 If his **c** forsake my law, and walk not in my 1121
90: 3 and sayest, Return, ye **c** of men. 1121
90:16 thy servants, and thy glory unto their **c**. 1121
102:28 The **c** of thy servants shall continue, and 1121
103: 7 unto Moses, his acts unto the **c** of Israel. 1121
103:13 Like as a father pitieth *his* **c**, *so* the LORD 1121
103:17 and his righteousness unto children's **c**; 1121
105: 6 his servant, ye **c** of Jacob, his chosen. 1121
107: 8 *for* his wonderful works to the **c** of men! 1121

Ps 107:15 *for* his wonderful works to the **c** of men! 1121
107:21 *for* his wonderful works to the **c** of men! 1121
107:31 *for* his wonderful works to the **c** of men! 1121
109: 9 Let his **c** be fatherless, and his wife a 1121
109:10 Let his **c** be continually vagabonds, 1121
109:12 let there be any to favour his **fatherless c**. 3490
113: 9 to keep house, *to be* a joyful mother of **c**. 1121
115:14 you more and more, you and your **c**. 1121
115:16 but the earth hath he given to the **c** of men. 1121
127: 3 Lo, **c** *are* an heritage of the LORD: *and* 1121
127: 4 of a mighty *man;* so *are* **c** of the youth. 1121
128: 3 thy **c** like olive plants round about thy 1121
128: 6 thou shalt see thy children's **c**, *and* 1121
132:12 If thy **c** will keep my covenant and 1121
132:12 their **c** also shall sit upon thy throne for 1121
137: 7 the **c** of Edom *in* the day of Jerusalem; 1121
144: 7 of great waters, from the hand of strange **c**; 1121
144:11 and deliver me from the hand of strange **c**, 1121
147:13 thy gates; he hath blessed thy **c** within thee. 1121
148:12 young men, and maidens; old men, and **c**: 5288
148:14 *even* of the **c** of Israel, a people near unto 1121
149: 2 let the **c** of Zion be joyful in their King. 1121
Pr 4: 1 Hear, ye **c**, the instruction of a father, and 1121
5: 7 O ye **c**, and depart not from the words of 1121
7:24 O ye **c**, and attend to the words of my 1121
8:32 Now therefore hearken unto me, O ye **c**: 1121
13:22 leaveth an inheritance to *his* children's **c**: 1121
14:26 and his **c** shall have a place of refuge. 1121
15:11 much more then the hearts of the **c** of men? 1121
17: 6 Children's **c** *are* the crown of old men; and 1121
17: 6 and the glory of **c** *are* their fathers. 1121
20: 7 in his integrity: his **c** *are* blessed after him. 1121
31:28 Her **c** arise up, and call her blessed; 1121
Ecc 6: 3 If a man beget an hundred **c**, and live many NIH
SS 1: 6 my mother's **c** were angry with me; 1121
Isa 1: 2 I have nourished and brought up **c**, and 1121
1: 4 a seed of evildoers, **c** that are corrupters: 1121
2: 6 they please themselves in the **c** of strangers. 3206
3: 4 I will give **c** *to be* their princes, and 5288
3:12 **c** *are* their oppressors, and women rule over 5953
8:18 the **c** whom the LORD hath given me *are* 3206
11:14 and the **c** of Ammon shall obey them. 1121
13:16 Their **c** also shall be dashed to pieces 5768
13:18 of the womb; their eye shall not spare **c**. 1121
14:21 Prepare slaughter for his **c** for the iniquity 1121
17: 3 they shall be as the glory of the **c** of Israel, 1121
17: 9 which they left because of the **c** of Israel: 1121
21:17 the mighty *men* of the **c** of Kedar, shall be 1121
23: 4 saying, I travail not, nor **bring forth c**, 3205
27:12 be gathered one by one, O ye **c** of Israel. 1121
29:23 when he seeth his **c**, the work of mine 3206
30: 1 Woe to the rebellious **c**, saith the LORD, 1121
30: 9 That this *is* a rebellious people, lying **c**, 1121
30: 9 **c** *that* will not hear the law of the LORD: 1121
31: 6 Turn ye unto *him from* whom the **c** of 1121
37: 3 for the **c** are come to the birth, and *there is* 1121
37:12 and the **c** of Eden which *were* in Telassar? 1121
38:19 the father to the **c** shall make known thy 1121
47: 8 a widow, neither shall I know the **loss of c**: 7908
47: 9 in one day, the **loss of c**, and widowhood: 7908
49:17 Thy **c** shall make haste; thy destroyers and 1121
49:20 The **c** which thou shalt have, after thou hast 1121
49:21 seeing I have **lost** my **c**, and *am* desolate, 7921
49:25 contendeth with thee, and I will save thy **c**. 1121
54: 1 for more *are* the **c** of the desolate than 1121
54: 1 the desolate than the **c** of the married wife, 1121
54:13 And all thy **c** *shall be* taught of the LORD; 1121
54:13 and great *shall be* the peace of thy **c**. 1121
57: 4 *are* ye not **c** of transgression, a seed of 3206
57: 5 slaying the **c** in the valleys under the clifts 3206
63: 8 they *are* my people, **c** *that* will not lie: 1121
66: 8 as Zion travailed, she brought forth her **c**. 1121
66:20 as the **c** of Israel bring an offering in a 1121
Jer 2: 9 and with your children's **c** will I plead. 1121
2:16 Also the **c** of Noph and Tahapanes have 1121
2:30 In vain have I smitten your **c**; they received 1121
3:14 Turn, O backsliding **c**, saith the LORD; 1121
3:19 How shall I put thee among the **c**, and 1121
3:21 *and* supplications of the **c** of Israel: 1121
3:22 ye backsliding **c**, *and* I will heal your 1121
4:22 they *are* sottish **c**, and they have none 1121
5: 7 thy **c** have forsaken me, and sworn by *them* 1121
6: 1 O ye **c** of Benjamin, gather yourselves to 1121
6:11 I *will* pour *it* out upon the **c** abroad, and 5768
7:18 The **c** gather wood, and the fathers kindle 1121
7:30 For the **c** of Judah have done evil in my 1121
9:21 to cut off the **c** from without, *and* the young 5768
9:26 the **c** of Ammon, and Moab, and all *that are* 1121
10:20 my **c** are gone forth *of* me, and they *are* not: 1121
15: 7 I will **bereave** *them* **of c**, I will destroy my 7921
16:14 that brought up the **c** of Israel out of 1121
16:15 that brought up the **c** of Israel from the land 1121
17: 2 Whilst their **c** remember their altars and 1121
17:19 and stand in the gate of the **c** of the people, 1121
18:21 Therefore deliver up their **c** to the famine, 1121
18:21 let their wives be **bereaved of** their **c**, and 7909
23: 7 which brought up the **c** of Israel out of 1121
25:21 Edom, and Moab, and the **c** of Ammon, 1121
30:20 Their **c** also shall be as aforetime, and 1121
31:15 Rahel weeping for her **c** refused to be 1121
31:15 children refused to be comforted for her **c**, 1121
31:17 that *thy* **c** shall come again to their own 1121
32:18 fathers into the bosom of their **c** after them: 1121
32:30 For the **c** of Israel and the children of Judah 1121
32:30 the **c** of Judah have only done evil before 1121
32:30 for the **c** of Israel have only provoked me to 1121
32:32 Because of all the evil of the **c** of Israel and 1121
32:32 the children of Israel and of the **c** of Judah, 1121
32:39 the good of them, and of their **c** after them: 1121
38:23 all thy wives and thy **c** to the Chaldeans: 1121
40: 7 women, and **c**, and of the poor of the land, 2945
41:16 and the women, and the **c**, and the eunuchs, 2945
43: 6 **c**, and the king's daughters, and every 2945
47: 3 the fathers shall not look back to *their* **c** for 1121
49: 6 again the captivity of the **c** of Ammon, 1121

Jer 49:11 Leave thy **fatherless c**, I will preserve *them* 3490
50: 4 the c of Israel shall come, they and 1121
50: 4 they and the c of Judah together, going and 1121
50:33 The c of Israel and the children of Judah 1121
50:33 and the c of Judah *were* oppressed together: 1121
La 1: 5 her c are gone *into* captivity before 5768
1:16 my c are desolate, because the enemy 1121
2:11 because the c and the sucklings swoon in 5768
2:19 toward him for the life of thy **young c**, 5768
2:20 women eat their fruit, *and* c of a span long? 5768
3:33 not afflict willingly nor grieve the c of men. 1121
4: 4 the **young c** ask bread, *and* no man 5768
4:10 the pitiful women have sodden their own c: 3206
5:13 men to grind, and the c fell under the wood. 5288
Eze 2: 3 Son of man, I send thee to the c of Israel, 1121
2: 4 For *they are* impudent c and stiff hearted. 1121
3:11 unto the c of thy people, and speak unto 1121
4:13 Even thus shall the c of Israel eat their 1121
6: 5 I will lay the dead carcases of the c of 1121
9: 6 both maids, and **little c**, and women: 2945
16:21 That thou hast slain my c, and 1121
16:36 by the blood of thy c, which thou didst give 1121
16:45 that lotheth their husband and her c; 1121
16:45 which lothed their husbands and their c: 1121
20:18 I said unto their c in the wilderness, 1121
20:21 Notwithstanding the c rebelled against me: 1121
23:39 For when they had slain their c to their 1121
31:14 of the earth, in the midst of the c of men, 1121
33: 2 speak to the c of thy people, and say unto 1121
33:12 son of man, say unto the c of thy people, 1121
33:17 Yet the c of thy people say, The way of 1121
33:30 the c of thy people still are talking against 1121
35: 5 hast shed *the blood of* the c of Israel by 1121
37:16 and for the c of Israel his companions: 1121
37:18 when the c of thy people shall speak unto 1121
37:21 I *will* take the c of Israel from among 1121
37:25 their c, and their children's children for 1121
37:25 and their children's c for ever: 1121
43: 7 where I will dwell in the midst of the c of 1121
44: 9 of any stranger that *is* among the c of 1121
44:15 when the c of Israel went astray from me, 1121
47:22 which shall beget c among you: 1121
47:22 born in the country among the c of Israel; 1121
48:11 which went not astray when the c of Israel 1121
Da 1: 3 that *he* should bring *certain* of the c of 1121
1: 4 **C** in whom *was* no blemish, but 3206
1: 6 Now among these were of the c of Judah, 1121
1:10 liking than the c which *are* of your sort? 3206
1:13 the countenance of the c that eat *of* 3206
1:15 fatter in flesh than all the c which did eat 3206
1:17 As for these four c, God gave them 3206
2:38 wheresoever the c of men dwell, the beasts 1123
5:13 which *art* of the c of the captivity of Judah, 1123
6:13 which *is* of the c of the captivity of Judah, 1123
6:24 den of lions, them, their c, and their wives; 1123
11:41 Moab, and the chief of the c of Ammon. 1121
12: 1 the great prince which standeth for the c of 1121
Hos 1: 2 a wife of whoredoms and c of whoredoms: 3206
1:10 Yet the number of the c of Israel shall be as 1121
1:11 shall the c of Judah and the children of 1121
1:11 and the c of Israel be gathered together, 1121
2: 4 I will not have mercy upon her c; for they 1121
2: 4 for they *be the* c of whoredoms. 1121
3: 1 love of the LORD toward the c of Israel, 1121
3: 4 For the c of Israel shall abide many days 1121
3: 5 Afterward shall the c of Israel return, and 1121
4: 1 the word of the LORD, ye c of Israel: 1121
4: 6 the law of thy God, I will also forget thy c. 1121
5: 7 for they have begotten strange c: now shall 1121
9:12 Though they bring up their c, yet will I 1121
9:13 Ephraim *shall* bring forth his c to 1121
10: 9 the battle in Gibeah against the c of iniquity 1121
10:14 mother was dashed in pieces upon *her* c. 1121
11:10 then the c shall tremble from the west. 1121
13:13 long in *the place of* the breaking forth of c. 1121
Joel 1: 3 Tell ye your c of it, and *let* your children 1121
1: 3 *let* your c *tell* their children, and 1121
1: 3 *let* your children *tell* their c, and 1121
1: 3 and their c another generation. 1121
2:16 gather the c, and those that suck the breasts: 5768
2:23 ye c of Zion, and rejoice in the LORD 1121
3: 6 The c also of Judah and the children of 1121
3: 6 the c of Jerusalem have ye sold unto 1121
3: 8 your daughters into the hand of the c of 1121
3:16 and the strength of the c of Israel. 1121
3:19 for the violence against the c of Judah, 1121
Am 1:13 For three transgressions of the c of 1121
2:11 *Is it* not even thus, O ye c of Israel? 1121
3: 1 hath spoken against you, O c of Israel, 1121
3:12 shall the c of Israel be taken out that dwell 1121
4: 5 for this liketh you, O ye c of Israel, 1121
9: 7 *Are* ye not as c of the Ethiopians unto me, 1121
9: 7 of the Ethiopians unto me, O c of Israel? 1121
Ob 1:12 c of Judah in the day of their destruction; 1121
1:20 the captivity of this host of the c of Israel 1121
Mic 1:16 thee bald, and poll thee for thy delicate c; 1121
2: 9 from their c have ye taken *away* my glory 5768
5: 3 his brethren shall return unto the c of Israel. 1121
Na 3:10 her **young c** also were dashed in pieces at 5768
Zep 1: 8 the king's c, and all such as are clothed 1121
2: 8 and the revilings of the c of Ammon, 1121
2: 9 the c of Ammon as Gomorrah, *even* 1121
Zec 10: 7 yea, their c shall see *it*, and be glad; 1121
10: 9 they shall live with their c, and turn again. 1121
Mal 4: 6 shall turn the heart of the fathers to the c, 1121
4: 6 the heart of the c to their fathers, lest I 1121
Mt 2:16 and slew all the c that were in Bethlehem, *3816*
2:18 Rachel weeping for her c, and would not be *5043*
3: 9 that God is able of these stones to raise up c *5043*
5: 9 for they shall be called the c of God. *5207*
5:45 That ye may be the c of your Father which *5207*
7:11 know how to give good gifts unto your c, *5043*
8:12 But the c of the kingdom shall be cast out *5207*
9:15 Can the c of the bridechamber mourn, *5207*
10:21 and the c shall rise up against *their* parents, *5043*
11:16 It is like unto c sitting in the markets, and *3808*
11:19 sinners. But wisdom is justified of her c. *5043*
12:27 by whom do your c cast *them* out? *5207*
13:38 the good seed are the c of the kingdom; but *5207*
13:38 but the tares are the c of the wicked one; *5207*
14:21 five thousand men, beside women and c. *3813*
15:38 four thousand men, beside women and c. *3813*
17:25 or tribute? of their own c, or of strangers? *5207*
17:26 Jesus saith unto him, Then are the c free. *5207*
18: 3 ye be converted, and become as **little c**, *3813*
18:25 and c, and all that he had, and payment to *5043*
19:13 Then were there brought unto him **little c**, *3813*
19:14 Suffer **little c**, and forbid them not, *3813*
19:29 or father, or mother, or wife, or c, or lands, *5043*
20:20 the mother of Zebedee's c with her sons, *5207*
21:15 and the c crying in the temple, and saying, *3816*
22:24 Moses said, If a man die, having no c, *5043*
23:31 that ye are the c of them which killed *5207*
23:37 how often would I have gathered thy c *5043*
27: 9 whom they of the c of Israel did value; *5207*
27:25 and said, His blood *be* on us, and on our c. *5043*
27:56 and Joses, and the mother of Zebedee's c. *5207*
Mk 2:19 Can the c of the bridechamber fast, *5207*
7:27 Jesus said unto her, Let the c first be filled: *5043*
9:37 Whosoever shall receive one of such c in *3813*
10:13 And they brought **young c** to him, that he *3813*
10:14 Suffer the **little c** to come unto me, and *3813*
10:24 answereth again, and saith unto them, C, *5043*
10:29 or father, or mother, or wife, or c, or lands, *5043*
10:30 and sisters, and mothers, and c, and lands, *5043*
12:19 leave *his* wife *behind him*, and leave no c, *5043*
13:12 and c shall rise up against *their* parents, and *5043*
Lk 1:16 And many of the c of Israel shall he turn to *5207*
1:17 to turn the hearts of the fathers to the c, and *5043*
3: 8 of these stones to raise up c unto Abraham. *5043*
5:34 Can ye make the c of the bridechamber *5207*
6:35 and ye shall be the c of the Highest: *5207*
7:32 They are like unto c sitting in *3813*
7:35 But wisdom is justified of all her c. *5043*
11: 7 is now shut, and my c are with me in bed; *3813*
11:13 know how to give good gifts unto your c: *5043*
13:34 how often would I have gathered thy c *5043*
14:26 and c, and brethren, and sisters, yea, *5043*
16: 8 for the c of this world are in their *5207*
16: 8 in their generation wiser than the c of light. *5207*
18:16 Suffer **little c** to come unto me, and *3813*
18:29 or parents, or brethren, or wife, or c, for *5043*
19:44 with the ground, and thy c within thee: *5043*
20:28 having a wife, and he die **without c**, *815*
20:29 and the first took a wife, and died **without c**. *815*
20:31 the seven also: and they left no c, and died. *5043*
20:34 The c of this world marry, and are given in *5207*
20:36 and are the c of God, being the children of *5207*
20:36 of God, being the c of the resurrection. *5207*
23:28 but weep for yourselves, and for your c. *5043*
Jn 4:12 thereof himself, and his c, and his cattle? *5207*
8:39 saith unto them, If ye were Abraham's c, *5043*
11:52 the c of God that were scattered abroad. *5043*
12:36 in the light, that ye may be the c of light. *5207*
13:33 **Little c**, yet a little while I am with you. *5040*
21: 5 saith unto them, **C**, have ye any meat? *3813*
Ac 2:39 and to your c, and to all that are afar off, *5043*
3:25 Ye are the c of the prophets, and of *5207*
5:21 and all the senate of the c of Israel, and *5207*
7:19 so that *they* cast out their **young c**, *1025*
7:23 his heart to visit his brethren the c of Israel. *5207*
7:37 *that* Moses, which said unto the c of Israel, *5207*
9:15 the Gentiles, and kings, and the c of Israel: *5207*
10:36 The word which *God* sent unto the c of *5207*
13:26 c of the stock of Abraham, and *5207*
13:33 God hath fulfilled the same unto us their c, *5043*
21: 5 with wives and c, till *we were* out of *5043*
21:21 that they *ought* not to circumcise *their* c, *5043*
Ro 8:16 with our spirit, that we are the c of God: *5043*
8:17 And if c, then heirs; heirs of God, and *5043*
8:21 into the glorious liberty of the c of God. *5043*
9: 7 are the seed of Abraham, *are they* all c: *5043*
9: 8 That is, *They which are* the c of the flesh, *5043*
9: 8 of the flesh, these *are* not the c of God: *5043*
9: 8 the c of the promise are counted for *5043*
9:11 (For *the* c being not yet born, neither having NIG
9:26 there shall they be called the c of the living *5207*
9:27 Though the number of the c of Israel be as *5207*
1Co 7:14 else were your c unclean; but now are they *5043*
14:20 Brethren, be not c in understanding: *3813*
14:20 howbeit in malice be ye c, *3515*
2Co 3: 7 that the c of Israel could not stedfastly *5207*
3:13 that the c of Israel could not stedfastly look *5207*
6:13 in the same, (I speak as unto *my* c,) *5043*
12:14 for the c ought not to lay up for the parents, *5043*
12:14 up for the parents, but the parents for the c. *5043*
Gal 3: 7 are of faith, the same are the c of Abraham. *5207*
3:26 For ye are all the c of God by faith in Christ *5207*
4: 3 Even so we, when we were c, were in *3516*
4:19 My **little c**, of whom I travail in birth again *5040*
4:25 which now is, and is in bondage with her c. *5043*
4:27 for the desolate hath many moe c than she *5043*
4:28 as Isaac was, are the c of promise. *5043*
4:31 we are not c of *the* bondwoman, but of *5043*
Eph 1: 5 **adoption of c** by Jesus Christ to himself, *5206*
2: 2 the spirit that now worketh in the c of *5207*
2: 3 and were by nature the c of wrath, even as *5043*
4:14 That we *henceforth* be no more c, tossed to *3516*
5: 1 Be ye therefore followers of God, as dear c; *5043*
5: 6 wrath of God upon the c of disobedience. *5207*
5: 8 *are ye* light in the Lord: walk as c of light: *5043*
6: 1 **C**, obey your parents in the Lord: for this is *5043*
6: 4 ye fathers, provoke not your c to wrath: *5043*
Col 3: 6 of God cometh on the c of disobedience: *5207*
3:20 **C**, obey *your* parents in all *things*: for this *5043*
3:21 provoke not your c *to anger*, lest they be *5043*
1Th 2: 7 *even* as a nurse cherisheth her c: *5043*
2:11 every one of you, as a father *doth* his c, *5043*
5: 5 Ye are all the c of light, and the children of *5207*
5: 5 the children of light, and the c of the day: *5207*
1Ti 3: 4 having *his* c in subjection with all gravity; *5043*
3:12 ruling *their* c and their own houses well. *5043*
5: 4 But if any widow have c or nephews, *5043*
5:10 if she have **brought up c**, if she have *5044*
5:14 *women* marry, **bear c**, guide the house, *5041*
Tit 1: 6 having faithful c not accused of riot or *5043*
2: 4 to love their husbands, to **love** their c, *5388*
Heb 2:13 I, and the c which God hath given me. *3813*
2:14 then as the c are partakers of flesh and *3813*
11:22 made mention of the departing of the c of *5207*
12: 5 which speaketh unto you as unto c, *5207*
1Pe 1:14 As obedient c, not fashioning yourselves *5043*
2Pe 2:14 exercised with covetous practices; cursed c: *5043*
1Jn 2: 1 My **little c**, these *things* write I unto you, *5040*
2:12 **little c**, because *your* sins are forgiven you *5040*
2:13 **little c**, because ye have known the Father. *3813*
2:18 **Little c**, it is the last time: and as ye have *3813*
2:28 And now, **little c**, abide in him; that, *5040*
3: 7 **Little c**, let no *man* deceive you: he that *5040*
3:10 In this the c of God are manifest, and the *5043*
3:10 of God are manifest, and the c of the devil: *5043*
3:18 My **little c**, let us not love in word, *5040*
4: 4 of God, **little c**, and have overcome them: *5040*
5: 2 By this we know that we love the c of God, *5043*
5:21 **Little c**, keep yourselves from idols. Amen. *5040*
2Jn 1: 1 The elder unto the elect lady and her c, *5043*
1: 4 I rejoiced greatly that I found of thy c *5043*
1:13 The c of thy elect sister greet thee. Amen. *5043*
3Jn 1: 4 I have no greater joy than to hear that my c *5043*
Rev 2:14 cast a stumblingblock before the c of Israel, *5207*
2:23 And I will kill her c with death; and all *5043*
7: 4 four thousand of all the tribes of the c of *5207*
21:12 *names* of the twelve tribes of the c of Israel: *5207*

CHILDREN'S (19) [CHILD]

Ge 31:16 from our father, that *is* ours, and our c: 1121
45:10 thy c children, and thy flocks, and 1121
Ex 9: 4 there shall nothing die of all *that is* the c of 1121
34: 7 upon the c children, unto the third and 1121
Dt 4:25 c children, and ye shall have remained long 1121
Jos 14: 9 thy c for ever, because thou hast wholly 1121
2Ki 17:41 both their children, and their c children: 1121
Job 19:17 though I intreated for the c *sake* of mine 1121
Ps 103:17 and his righteousness unto c children; 1121
128: 6 thou shalt see thy c children, *and* 1121+3807.1
Pr 13:22 A good *man* leaveth an inheritance to *his* c 1121
17: 6 C children *are* the crown of old men; and 1121
Jer 2: 9 and with your c children will I plead. 1121
31:29 sour grape, and the c teeth are set on edge. 1121
Eze 18: 2 sour grapes, and the c teeth are set on edge? 1121
37:25 their children, and their c children for ever: 1121
Mt 15:26 It is not meet to take the c bread, and *5043*
Mk 7:27 for it is not meet to take the c bread, and *5043*
7:28 yet the dogs under the table eat of the c *3813*

CHILEAB (1)

2Sa 3: 3 his second, C, of Abigail the wife of Nabal 3609

CHILION (2) [CHILION'S]

Ru 1: 2 the name of his two sons Mahlon and C, 3630
1: 5 Mahlon and C died also both of them; and 3630

CHILION'S (1) [CHILION]

Ru 4: 9 all that *was* C and Mahlon's, of the hand of 3630

CHILMAD (1)

Eze 27:23 Asshur, *and* C, *were* thy merchants. 3638

CHIMHAM (4)

2Sa 19:37 behold thy servant C; let him go over with 3643
19:38 C shall go over with me, and I will do to 3643
19:40 went on to Gilgal, and C went on with him: 3643
Jer 41:17 and dwelt in the habitation of C, 3643

CHIMNEY (1)

Hos 13: 3 of the floor, and as the smoke out of the c. 699

CHINNERETH (3) [CINNEROTH]

Nu 34:11 shall reach unto the side of the sea of C 3672
Dt 3:17 the coast *thereof*, from C even unto the sea 3672
Jos 19:35 Zer, and Hammath, Rakkath, and C, 3672

CHIOS (1)

Ac 20:15 and came the next *day* over against C; *5508*

CHISEL See HEW

CHISELS See PLANES

CHISLEU (2)

Ne 1: 1 it came to pass in the month C, *in* 3691
Zec 7: 1 fourth *day* of the ninth month, *even* in C; 3691

CHISLON (1)

Nu 34:21 the tribe of Benjamin, Elidad the son of C. 3692

CHISLOTH-TABOR (1) [TABOR]

Jos 19:12 *toward* the sunrising unto the border of C, 3696

CHITTIM (6)

Nu 24:24 ships *shall come* from the coast of C, and 3794
Isa 23: 1 from the land of C it is revealed to them. 3794
23:12 arise, pass over *to* C; there also shalt thou 3794
Jer 2:10 For pass over the isles of C, and see; and 3794
Eze 27: 6 *of* ivory, *brought* out of the isles of C. 3794
Da 11:30 For *the* ships of C shall come against him: 3794

CHIUN (1)

Am 5:26 of your Moloch and C your images, 3594

CHLOE (1)

1Co 1:11 by them which are of the *house* of C, *5514*

CHODE (2)
Ge 31:36 Jacob was wroth, and **c** with Laban: and 7378
Nu 20: 3 the people **c** with Moses, and spake, saying, 7378

CHOICE (21) [CHOOSE]
Ge 23: 6 in the **c** of our sepulchres bury thy dead; 4005
49:11 the vine, and his ass's colt unto the **c vine**; 8322
Dt 12:11 all your **c** vows which ye vow unto 4005
1Sa 9: 2 *was* Saul, a **c** *young man*, and a goodly: 970
2Sa 10: 9 he chose of all the **c** *men* of Israel, and 977
2Ki 3:19 every **c** city, and shall fell every good tree, 4004
19:23 trees thereof, *and* the **c** fir trees thereof: 4004
1Ch 7:40 **c** *and* mighty *men* of valour, chief of 1305
19:10 he chose out of all the **c** of Israel, and 977
2Ch 25: 5 found them three hundred thousand **c** *men*, 977
Ne 5:18 *for me* daily *was* one ox *and* six **c** sheep; 1305
Pr 8:10 not silver; and knowledge rather than **c** gold. 977
8:19 than fine gold; and my revenue than **c** silver. 977
10:20 The tongue of the just *is as* **c** silver: the heart 977
SS 6: 9 she *is* the **c** one of her that bare her. 1249
Isa 37:24 cedars thereof, *and* the **c** fir trees thereof: 4005
Jer 22: 7 they shall cut down thy **c** cedars, and 4005
Eze 24: 4 and the shoulder; fill *it with* the **c** bones. 4005
24: 5 Take the **c** of the flock, and burn also 4005
31:16 the **c** and best of Lebanon, all that drink 4005
Ac 15: 7 a good while ago God **made c** among us, *1586*

CHOICEST (2) [CHOOSE]
Isa 5: 2 planted it *with* the **c vine**, and built a tower 8321
22: 7 *that* thy **c** valleys shall be full *of* chariots, 4005

CHOKE (2) [CHOKED]
Mt 13:22 **c** the word, and he becometh unfruitful. *4846*
Mk 4:19 **c** the word, and it becometh unfruitful. *4846*

CHOKED (6) [CHOKE]
Mt 13: 7 and the thorns sprung up, and **c** them: *638*
Mk 4: 7 grew up, and **c** it, and it yielded no fruit. *4846*
5:13 about two thousand,) and were **c** in the sea. *4155*
Lk 8: 7 and the thorns sprang up with *it*, and **c** it. *638*
8:14 and are **c** with cares and riches and *4846*
8:33 down a steep place into the lake, and were **c**. *638*

CHOLER (2)
Da 8: 7 he was **moved with c** against him, and 4843
11:11 king of the south shall be **moved with c**, 4843

CHOOSE (59) [CHOICE, CHOICEST, CHOOSEST, CHOOSETH, CHOOSING, CHOSE, CHOSEN]
Ex 17: 9 **C** us **out** men, and go out, fight with 977
Nu 16: 7 be *that* the man whom the LORD doth **c**, 977
17: 5 man's rod, whom I shall **c**, shall blossom: 977
Dt 7: 7 nor **c** you, because ye were moe in number 977
12: 5 **c** out of all your tribes to put his name there, 977
12:11 God shall **c** to cause his name to dwell there; 977
12:14 in the place which the LORD shall **c** in one 977
12:18 the place which the LORD thy God shall **c**, 977
12:26 go unto the place which the LORD shall **c**: 977
14:23 in the place which he shall **c** to place his 977
14:24 which the LORD thy God shall **c** to set his 977
14:25 the place which the LORD thy God shall **c**: 977
15:20 year in the place which the LORD shall **c**, 977
16: 2 in the place which the LORD shall **c** to 977
16: 6 the place which the LORD thy God shall **c** 977
16: 7 the place which the LORD thy God shall **c**: 977
16:15 God in the place which the LORD shall **c**: 977
16:16 thy God in the place which he shall **c**; 977
17: 8 the place which the LORD thy God shall **c**; 977
17:10 which the LORD shall **c** shall shew thee; 977
17:15 whom the LORD thy God shall **c**: 977
18: 6 unto the place which the LORD shall **c**; 977
23:16 in *that* place which he shall **c** in one of thy 977
26: 2 thy God shall **c** to place his name there. 977
30:19 therefore **c** life, that *both* thou and thy seed 977
31:11 thy God in the place which he shall **c**, 977
Jos 9:27 unto this day, in the place which he should **c**. 977
24:15 **c** you *this* day whom you will serve; 977
1Sa 2:28 did I **c** him out of all the tribes of Israel to be 977
17: 8 **c** you a man for you, and let him come 1262
2Sa 16:18 **c**, his will I be, and with him will I abide. 977
17: 1 Let me now **c out** twelve thousand men, and 977
21: 6 in Gibeah of Saul, whom the LORD did **c**. 972
24:12 I offer thee three *things*; **c** thee one of them, 977
1Ki 14:21 the city which the LORD did **c** out of all 977
18:23 let them **c** one bullock for themselves, and 977
18:25 **C** you one bullock for yourselves, and 977
1Ch 21:10 I offer thee three *things*: **c** thee one of them, 977
21:11 unto him, Thus saith the LORD, **C** thee 6901
Ne 9: 7 who didst **c** Abram, and broughtest him forth 977
Job 9:14 *and* **c out** my words *to reason* with him? 977
34: 4 Let us **c** to us judgment: let us know among 977
34:33 whether thou refuse, or whether thou **c**; 977
Ps 25:12 him shall he teach in the way *that* he shall **c**. 977
47: 4 He shall **c** our inheritance for us, 977
Pr 1:29 and did not **c** the fear of the LORD: 977
3:31 not the oppressor, and **c** none of his ways. 977
Isa 7:15 may know to refuse the evil, and **c** the good. 977
7:16 shall know to refuse the evil, and **c** the good, 977
14: 1 will yet **c** Israel, and set them in their own 977
49: 7 the Holy One of Israel, and he shall **c** thee. 977
56: 4 **c** *the things* that please me, and take hold of 977
65:12 and did **c** *that* wherein I delighted not. 977
66: 4 I also will **c** their delusions, and will bring 977
Eze 21:19 **c** thou a place, choose *it*, at the head of 1254
21:19 **c** *it*, at the head of the way to the city. 1254
Zec 1:17 yet comfort Zion, and shall yet **c** Jerusalem. 977
2:12 in the holy land, and shall **c** Jerusalem again. 977
Php 1:22 of my labour: yet what I shall **c** I wot not. *138*

CHOOSEST (2) [CHOOSE]
Job 15: 5 and thou **c** the tongue of the crafty. 977
Ps 65: 4 Blessed *is the man whom* thou **c**, and 977

CHOOSETH (3) [CHOOSE]
Job 7:15 So that my soul **c** strangling, *and* 977
Isa 40:20 impoverished that he hath no oblation **c** a 977
41:24 of nought: an abomination *is he that* **c** you. 977

CHOOSING (1) [CHOOSE]
Heb 11:25 **C** rather to suffer affliction with the people *138*

CHOP (1)
Mic 3: 3 **c** *them* **in pieces**, as for the pot, and as flesh 6566

CHOR-ASHAN (1)
1Sa 30:30 to *them* which *were* in **C**, and to *them* 3565

CHORAZIN (2)
Mt 11:21 unto thee, **C**, woe unto thee, Bethsaida: *5523*
Lk 10:13 unto thee, **C**, woe unto thee, Bethsaida: *5523*

CHOSE (29) [CHOOSE]
Ge 6: 2 they took them wives of all which they **c**. 977
13:11 Lot **c** him all the plain of Jordan; and 977
Ex 18:25 Moses **c** able men out of all Israel, and 977
Dt 4:37 therefore he **c** their seed after them, and 977
10:15 he **c** their seed after them, *even* you above 977
Jos 8: 3 Joshua **c out** thirty thousand mighty *men* of 977
Jdg 5: 8 They **c** new gods; then *was* war in the gates: 977
1Sa 13: 2 Saul **c** him three thousand *men* of Israel; 977
17:40 **c** him five smooth stones out of the brook, 977
2Sa 6:21 which **c** me before thy father, and before all 977
10: 9 he **c** of all the choice *men* of Israel, and 977
1Ki 8:16 I **c** no city out of all the tribes of Israel to 977
8:16 but I **c** David to be over my people Israel. 977
11:34 whom I **c**, because he kept my 977
1Ch 19:10 he **c** out of all the choice of Israel, and 977
28: 4 Howbeit the LORD God of Israel **c** me 977
2Ch 6: 5 **c** no city among all the tribes of Israel to 977
6: 5 neither **c** I any man to be a ruler over my 977
Job 29:25 I **c out** their way, and sat chief, and dwelt as 977
Ps 78:67 of Joseph, and **c** not the tribe of Ephraim: 977
78:68 **c** the tribe of Judah, the mount Zion which 977
78:70 He **c** David also his servant, and took him 977
Isa 66: 4 and **c** *that* in which I delighted not. 977
Eze 20: 5 In the day when I **c** Israel, and lifted up mine 977
Lk 6:13 and of them he **c** twelve, whom also he *1586*
14: 7 when he marked how they **c out** the chief *1586*
Ac 6: 5 and they **c** Stephen, a man full of faith and *1586*
13:17 The God of this people of Israel **c** our *1586*
15:40 And Paul **c** Silas, and departed, *1951*

CHOSEN (123) [CHOOSE]
Ex 14: 7 he took six hundred **c** chariots, and all 977
15: 4 his **c** captains also are drowned in the Red 4005
Nu 16: 5 even *him* whom he hath **c** will he cause to 977
Dt 7: 6 the LORD thy God hath **c** thee to be a 977
12:21 **c** to put his name there be too far from thee, 977
14: 2 the LORD hath **c** thee to be a peculiar 977
16:11 thy God hath **c** to place his name there. 977
18: 5 For the LORD thy God hath **c** him out of 977
21: 5 for them the LORD thy God hath **c** to 977
Jos 24:22 yourselves that ye have **c** you the LORD, 977
Jdg 10:14 Go and cry unto the gods which ye have **c**; 977
20:15 *which* were numbered seven hundred **c** men. 977
20:16 *there were* seven hundred **c** men lefthanded; 977
20:34 there came against Gibeah ten thousand **c** 977
1Sa 8:18 of your king which ye shall have **c** you; 977
10:24 See ye him whom the LORD hath **c**, 977
12:13 therefore behold the king whom ye have **c**, 977
16: 8 And he said, Neither hath the LORD **c** this. 977
16: 9 And he said, Neither hath the LORD **c** this. 977
16:10 unto Jesse, The LORD hath not **c** these. 977
20:30 **c** the son of Jesse to thine own confusion, 977
24: 2 Saul took three thousand **c** men out of all 977
26: 2 having three thousand **c** men of Israel with 977
2Sa 6: 1 David gathered together all the **c** *men* of 977
1Ki 3: 8 in the midst of thy people which thou hast **c**, 977
8:44 LORD toward the city which thou hast **c**, 977
8:48 the city which thou hast **c**, and the house 977
11:13 and for Jerusalem's sake, which I have **c**. 977
11:32 the city which I have **c** out of all the tribes of 977
11:36 the city which I have **c** me to put my name 977
12:21 fourscore thousand **c** *men*, which were 977
2Ki 21: 7 which I have **c** out of all tribes of Israel, 977
23:27 cast off this city Jerusalem which I have **c**, 977
1Ch 9:22 All these which were **c** to be porters in 1305
15: 2 for them hath the LORD **c** to carry the ark 977
16:13 his servant, ye children of Jacob, his **c** *ones*. 972
16:41 and Jeduthun, and the rest that were **c**, 1305
28: 4 for he hath **c** Judah to be the ruler; and of 977
28: 5 he hath **c** Solomon my son to sit upon 977
28: 6 for I have **c** him to be my son, and I will be 977
28:10 for the LORD hath **c** thee to build a house 977
29: 1 whom alone God hath **c**, *is yet* young and 977
2Ch 6: 6 I have **c** Jerusalem, that my name might be 977
6: 6 have **c** David to be over my people Israel. 977
6:34 unto thee toward this city which thou hast **c**, 977
6:38 *toward* the city which thou hast **c**, and 977
7:12 have **c** this place to myself for a house of 977
7:16 For now have I **c** and sanctified this house, 977
11: 1 fourscore thousand **c** *men*, which were 977
12:13 the city which the LORD had **c** out of all 977
13: 3 of war, *even* four hundred thousand **c** men: 977
13: 3 him with eight hundred thousand **c** men, 977
13:17 slain of Israel five hundred thousand **c** men. 977
29:11 for the LORD hath **c** you to stand before 977
33: 7 which I have **c** before all the tribes of Israel, 977
Ne 1: 9 will bring them unto the place that I have **c** 977
Job 36:21 for this hast thou **c** rather than affliction. 977
Ps 33:12 the people *whom* he hath **c** for his own 977
78:31 of them, and smote down the **c** *men* of Israel. 970
89: 3 I have made a covenant with my **c**, I have 972
89:19 I have exalted *one* **c** out of the people. 977
105: 6 his servant, ye children of Jacob, his **c**. 972
105:26 his servant; *and* Aaron whom he had **c**. 977
105:43 his people with joy, *and* his **c** with gladness: 972
Ps 106: 5 That *I* may see the good of thy **c**, that *I* may 972
106:23 had not Moses his **c** stood before him in 972
119:30 I have **c** the way of truth: thy judgments 977
119:173 hand help me; for I have **c** thy precepts. 977
132:13 For the LORD hath **c** Zion; he hath desired 977
135: 4 For the LORD hath **c** Jacob unto himself, 977
Pr 16:16 to get understanding rather to be **c** than 977
22: 1 A *good* name *is* rather to be **c** than great 977
Isa 1:29 confounded for the gardens that ye have **c**. 977
41: 8 Israel, *art* my servant, Jacob whom I have **c**, 977
41: 9 I have **c** thee, and not cast thee away. 977
43:10 the LORD, and my servant whom I have **c**: 977
43:20 the desert, to give drink to my people, my **c**. 972
44: 1 Jacob my servant; and Israel, whom I have **c**: 977
44: 2 and *thou*, Jeshurun, whom I have **c**. 977
48:10 I have **c** thee in the furnace of affliction. 977
58: 5 Is it such a fast that I have **c**? a day for a man 977
58: 6 *Is* not this the fast that I have **c**? to loose 977
65:15 shall leave your name for a curse unto my **c**: 972
66: 3 they have **c** their own ways, and their soul 977
Jer 8: 3 death shall be **c** rather than life by all 977
33:24 The two families which the LORD hath **c**, 977
48:15 his **c** young men are gone down to 4005
49:19 who *is* a **c** *man*, *that* I may appoint over her? 977
50:44 who *is* a **c** *man*, *that* I may appoint over her? 977
Eze 23: 7 *with* all them *that were* the **c** men of 4005
Da 11:15 shall not withstand, neither his **c** people, 4005
Hag 2:23 for I have **c** thee, saith the LORD of hosts. 977
Zec 3: 2 even the LORD that hath **c** Jerusalem 977
Mt 12:18 Behold my servant, whom I have **c**; my *140*
20:16 the first last: for many be called, but few **c**. *1588*
22:14 For many are called, but few *are* **c**. *1588*
Mk 13:20 but for the elect's sake, whom he hath **c**, *1586*
Lk 10:42 and Mary hath **c** *that* good part, which shall *1586*
23:35 save himself, if he be Christ, the **c** of God. *1588*
Jn 6:70 Have not I **c** you twelve, and one of you is *1586*
13:18 I know whom I have **c**: but that *1586*
15:16 Ye have not **c** me, but I have chosen you, *1586*
15:16 but I have **c** you, and ordained you, *1586*
15:19 but I have **c** you out of the world, therefore *1586*
Ac 1: 2 unto the Apostles whom he had **c**: *1586*
1:24 shew whether of these two thou hast **c**, *1586*
9:15 Go *thy way*: for he is a **c** vessel unto me, *1589*
10:41 but unto witnesses **c before** of God, *even* to *4401*
15:22 to send **c** men of their own company to *1586*
15:25 to send **c** men unto you with our beloved *1586*
22:14 he said, The God of our fathers hath **c** thee, *4400*
Ro 16:13 Salute Rufus **c** in the Lord, and his mother *1588*
1Co 1:27 But God hath **c** the foolish *things* of *1586*
1:27 God hath **c** the weak *things* of the world to *1586*
1:28 hath God **c**, *yea*, and *things* which are not, *1586*
2Co 8:19 who was also **c** of the churches to travel *5500*
Eph 1: 4 According as he hath **c** us in him before *1586*
2Th 2:13 God hath from the beginning **c** you to *138*
2Ti 2: 4 please him who hath **c** *him* **to be a soldier**. *4758*
Jas 2: 5 Hath not God **c** the poor of this world rich *1586*
1Pe 2: 4 indeed of men, but **c** of God, *and* precious, *1588*
2: 9 But ye *are* a **c** generation, a royal *1588*
Rev 17:14 are with him *are* called, and **c**, and faithful. *1588*

CHOZEBA (1)
1Ch 4:22 and the men of **C**, and Joash, and Saraph, 3578

CHRIST (555) [ANTICHRIST, ANTICHRISTS, CHRIST'S, CHRISTIAN, CHRISTIANS, CHRISTS]
Mt 1: 1 The book of the generation of Jesus **C**, *5547*
1:16 of whom was born Jesus, who is called **C**. *5547*
1:17 Babylon unto **C** *are* fourteen generations. *5547*
1:18 Now the birth of Jesus **C** was on this wise: *5547*
2: 4 he demanded of them where **C** should be *5547*
11: 2 had heard in the prison the works of **C**, *5547*
16:16 Peter answered and said, Thou art the **C**, *5547*
16:20 should tell no *man* that he was Jesus the **C**. *5547*
22:42 Saying, What think ye of **C**? whose son is *5547*
23: 8 for one is your Master, *even* **C**; *5547*
23:10 for one is your Master, *even* **C**. *5547*
24: 5 shall come in my name, saying, I am **C**; *5547*
24:23 shall say unto you, Lo, here *is* **C**, or there; *5547*
26:63 that thou tell us whether thou be the **C**, *5547*
26:68 Saying, Prophesy unto us, *thou* **C**, Who is *5547*
27:17 Barabbas, or Jesus which is called **C**? *5547*
27:22 I do then with Jesus which is called **C**? *5547*
Mk 1: 1 The beginning of the gospel of Jesus **C**, *5547*
8:29 and saith unto him, Thou art the **C**. *5547*
9:41 because ye belong to **C**, verily I say unto *5547*
12:35 How say the scribes that **C** is the Son of *5547*
13: 6 saying, I am **C**; and shall deceive many. NIG
13:21 if any *man* shall say to you, Lo, here *is* **C**; *5547*
14:61 and said unto him, Art thou the **C**, the Son *5547*
15:32 Let **C** the King of Israel descend now from *5547*
Lk 2:11 of David a Saviour, which is **C** the Lord. *5547*
2:26 see death, before he had seen the Lord's **C**. *5547*
3:15 of John, whether he were the **C**, or not; *5547*
4:41 and saying, Thou art **C** the Son of God. *5547*
4:41 not to speak: for they knew that he was **C**. *5547*
9:20 I am? Peter answering said, The **C** of God. *5547*
20:41 How say they that **C** is David's son? *5547*
21: 8 saying, I am **C**; and the time draweth near: NIG
22:67 Art thou the **C**? tell us. And he said unto *5547*
23: 2 saying that he himself is **C** a King. *5547*
23:35 save himself, if he be **C**, the chosen of God. *5547*
23:39 saying, If thou be **C**, save thyself and us. *5547*
24:26 Ought not **C** to have suffered these *things*, *5547*
24:46 and thus it behoved **C** to suffer, and to rise *5547*
Jn 1:17 *but* grace and truth came by Jesus **C**. *5547*
1:20 denied not; but confessed, I am not the **C**. *5547*
1:25 if thou be not *that* **C**, nor Elias, neither *that* *5547*
1:41 which is, being interpreted, the **C**. *5547*
3:28 I am not the **C**, but that I am sent before *5547*
4:25 that Messias cometh, which is called **C**: *5547*
4:29 all *things* that ever I did: is not this the **C**? *5547*
4:42 and know that this is indeed the **C**, *5547*
6:69 we believe and are sure that thou art *that* **C**, *5547*
7:26 rulers know indeed that this is the very **C**? *5547*

Jn	7:27	but when **C** cometh, no *man* knoweth	*5547*
	7:31	believed on him, and said, When **C** cometh,	*5547*
	7:41	Others said, This is the **C**. But some said,	*5547*
	7:41	some said, Shall **C** come out of Galilee?	*5547*
	7:42	That **C** cometh of the seed of David, and	*5547*
	9:22	that if any *man* did confess that he *was* **C**,	*5547*
	10:24	to doubt? If thou be the **C**, tell us plainly.	*5547*
	11:27	I believe that thou art the **C**, the Son of	*5547*
	12:34	We have heard out of the law that **C**	*5547*
	17: 3	and Jesus **C**, whom thou hast sent.	*5547*
	20:31	that ye might believe that Jesus is the **C**,	*5547*
Ac	2:30	*he* would raise up **C** to sit on his throne;	*5547*
	2:31	*this* before, spake of the resurrection of **C**,	*5547*
	2:36	whom ye have crucified, both Lord and **C**.	*5547*
	2:38	name of Jesus **C** for the remission of sins,	*5547*
	3: 6	In the name of Jesus **C** of Nazareth rise up	*5547*
	3:18	that **C** should suffer, he hath so fulfilled.	*5547*
	3:20	And he shall send Jesus **C**, which before	*5547*
	4:10	that by the name of Jesus **C** of Nazareth,	*5547*
	4:26	against the Lord, and against his **C**.	*5547*
	5:42	ceased not to teach and preach Jesus **C**.	*5547*
	8: 5	city of Samaria, and preached **C** unto them.	*5547*
	8:12	and the name of Jesus **C**, they were	*5547*
	8:37	I believe that Jesus **C** is the Son of God.	*5547*
	9:20	And straightway he preached **C** in	*5547*
	9:22	at Damascus, proving that this is *very* **C**.	*5547*
	9:34	Aeneas, Jesus **C** maketh thee whole:	*5547*
	10:36	of Israel, preaching peace by Jesus **C**:	*5547*
	11:17	unto us, who believed on the Lord Jesus **C**;	*5547*
	15:11	of the Lord Jesus **C** *we* shall be saved,	*5547*
	15:26	lives for the name of our Lord Jesus **C**.	*5547*
	16:18	I command thee in the name of Jesus **C** to	*5547*
	16:31	Believe on the Lord Jesus **C**, and thou shalt	*5547*
	17: 3	that **C** must needs have suffered, and	*5547*
	17: 3	this Jesus, whom I preach unto you, is **C**.	*5547*
	18: 5	and testified to the Jews *that* Jesus *was* **C**.	*5547*
	18:28	shewing by the scriptures that Jesus was **C**.	*5547*
	19: 4	should come after him, that is, on **C** Jesus.	*5547*
	20:21	and faith toward our Lord Jesus **C**.	*5547*
	24:24	and heard him concerning the faith in **C**.	*5547*
	26:23	That **C** should suffer, *and* that he *should be*	*5547*
	28:31	*things* which concern the Lord Jesus **C**,	*5547*
Ro	1: 1	Paul, a servant of Jesus **C**, called *to be* an	*5547*
	1: 3	Concerning his Son Jesus **C** our Lord,	*5547*
	1: 6	whom are ye also *the* called of Jesus **C**:	*5547*
	1: 7	from God our Father, and the Lord Jesus **C**.	*5547*
	1: 8	I thank my God through Jesus **C** for you	*5547*
	1:16	For I am not ashamed of the gospel of **C**:	*5547*
	2:16	of men by Jesus **C** according to my gospel.	*5547*
	3:22	of God *which is* by faith of Jesus **C** unto all	*5547*
	3:24	through the redemption that is in **C** Jesus:	*5547*
	5: 1	peace with God through our Lord Jesus **C**:	*5547*
	5: 6	in due time **C** died for the ungodly.	*5547*
	5: 8	while we were yet sinners, **C** died for us.	*5547*
	5:11	also joy in God through our Lord Jesus **C**,	*5547*
	5:15	by grace, which is by one man, Jesus **C**,	*5547*
	5:17	shall reign in life by one, Jesus **C**.	*5547*
	5:21	unto eternal life by Jesus **C** our Lord.	*5547*
	6: 3	many of us as were baptized into Jesus **C**	*5547*
	6: 4	that like as **C** was raised up from the dead	*5547*
	6: 8	Now if we be dead with **C**, we believe that	*5547*
	6: 9	Knowing that **C** being raised from the dead	*5547*
	6:11	alive unto God through Jesus **C** our Lord.	*5547*
	6:23	*is* eternal life through Jesus **C** our Lord.	*5547*
	7: 4	become dead to the law by the body of **C**;	*5547*
	7:25	I thank God through Jesus **C** our Lord. So	*5547*
	8: 1	*are* in **C** Jesus who walk not after the flesh,	*5547*
	8: 2	For the law of the Spirit of life in **C** Jesus	*5547*
	8: 9	Now if any *man* have not the Spirit of **C**,	*5547*
	8:10	And if **C** *be* in you, the body *is* dead	*5547*
	8:11	he that raised up **C** from the dead shall also	*5547*
	8:17	heirs of God, and joint-heirs with **C**; if so	*5547*
	8:34	*It is* **C** that died, yea rather, that is risen	*5547*
	8:35	Who shall separate us from the love of **C**?	*5547*
	8:39	love of God, which is in **C** Jesus our Lord.	*5547*
	9: 1	I say the truth in **C**, I lie not, my conscience	*5547*
	9: 3	were accursed from **C** for my brethren,	*5547*
	9: 5	of whom as concerning the flesh **C** *came,*	*5547*
	10: 4	For **C** *is* the end of the law for	*5547*
	10: 6	(that is, to bring **C** down *from above:*)	*5547*
	10: 7	(that is, to bring up **C** again from the dead.)	*5547*
	12: 5	are one body in **C**, and every one members	*5547*
	13:14	But put ye on the Lord Jesus **C**, and	*5547*
	14: 9	For to this end **C** both died, and rose,	*5547*
	14:10	all stand before the judgment seat of **C**.	*5547*
	14:15	not him with thy meat, for whom **C** died.	*5547*
	14:18	For he that in these *things* serveth **C** *is*	*5547*
	15: 3	For even **C** pleased not himself; but, as it is	*5547*
	15: 5	one towards another according to **C** Jesus:	*5547*
	15: 6	even the Father of our Lord Jesus **C**.	*5547*
	15: 7	as **C** also received us, to the glory of God.	*5547*
	15: 8	Now I say that Jesus **C** was a minister of	*5547*
	15:16	That I should be the minister of Jesus **C** to	*5547*
	15:17	whereof *I* may glory through Jesus **C** *in*	*5547*
	15:18	*things* which **C** hath not wrought by me,	*5547*
	15:19	I have fully preached the gospel of **C**.	*5547*
	15:20	preach the gospel, not where **C** was named,	*5547*
	15:29	fulness of the blessing of the gospel of **C**.	*5547*
	16: 3	and Aquila my helpers in **C** Jesus:	*5547*
	16: 5	who is the firstfruits of Achaia unto **C**.	*5547*
	16: 7	the apostles, who also were in **C** before me.	*5547*
	16: 9	Salute Urban our helper in **C**, and	*5547*
	16:10	Salute Apelles approved in **C**. Salute them	*5547*
	16:16	a holy kiss. The churches of **C** salute you.	*5547*
	16:18	*that are* such serve not our Lord Jesus **C**,	*5547*
	16:20	The grace of our Lord Jesus **C** *be* with you.	*5547*
	16:24	The grace of our Lord Jesus **C** *be* with you	*5547*
	16:25	and the preaching of Jesus **C**, according to	*5547*
	16:27	*be* glory through Jesus **C** for ever.	*5547*
1Co	1: 1	called *to be* an apostle of Jesus **C** through	*5547*
	1: 2	to them that are sanctified in **C** Jesus,	*5547*
	1: 2	call upon the name of Jesus **C** our Lord,	*5547*
	1: 3	God our Father, and *from* the Lord Jesus **C**.	*5547*
	1: 4	of God which is given you by Jesus **C**;	*5547*
	1: 6	Even as the testimony of **C** was confirmed	*5547*
1Co	1: 7	for the coming of our Lord Jesus **C**:	*5547*
	1: 8	blameless in the day of our Lord Jesus **C**.	*5547*
	1: 9	the fellowship of his Son Jesus **C** our Lord.	*5547*
	1:10	brethren, by the name of our Lord Jesus **C**,	*5547*
	1:12	I of Apollos; and I of Cephas; and I of **C**.	*5547*
	1:13	Is **C** divided? was Paul crucified for you?	*5547*
	1:17	For **C** sent me not to baptize, but to preach	*5547*
	1:17	lest the cross of **C** should be made of none	*5547*
	1:23	But we preach **C** crucified, unto the Jews a	*5547*
	1:24	**C** the power of God, and the wisdom of	*5547*
	1:30	But of him are ye in **C** Jesus, who of God is	*5547*
	2: 2	save Jesus **C**, and him crucified.	*5547*
	2:16	instruct him? But we have the mind of **C**.	*5547*
	3: 1	but as unto carnal, *even* as unto babes in **C**.	*5547*
	3:11	*man* lay than that is laid, which is Jesus **C**.	*5547*
	3:23	And ye *are* Christ's; and **C** *is* God's.	*5547*
	4: 1	as of the ministers of **C**, and stewards of	*5547*
	4:10	for Christ's sake, but ye *are* wise in **C**;	*5547*
	4:15	you have ten thousand instructors in **C**,	*5547*
	4:15	for in **C** Jesus I have begotten you through	*5547*
	4:17	remembrance of my ways which be in **C**,	*5547*
	5: 4	In the name of our Lord Jesus **C**, when ye	*5547*
	5: 4	with the power of our Lord Jesus **C**,	*5547*
	5: 7	For even **C** our passover is sacrificed for	*5547*
	6:15	not that your bodies are the members of **C**?	*5547*
	6:15	shall I then take the members of **C**, and	*5547*
	8: 6	and one Lord Jesus **C**, by whom *are* all	*5547*
	8:11	the weak brother perish, for whom **C** died?	*5547*
	8:12	their weak conscience, ye sin against **C**.	*5547*
	9: 1	have I not seen Jesus **C** our Lord? are not	*5547*
	9:12	lest we should hinder the gospel of **C**.	*5547*
	9:18	I may make the gospel of **C** without charge,	*5547*
	9:21	law to God, but under the law to **C**,)	*5547*
	10: 4	that followed *them:* and *that* Rock was **C**.	*5547*
	10: 9	Neither let us tempt **C**, as some of them	*5547*
	10:16	is it not the communion of the blood of **C**?	*5547*
	10:16	is it not the communion of the body of **C**?	*5547*
	11: 1	ye followers of me, even as I also *am* of **C**.	*5547*
	11: 3	you know, that the head of every man is **C**;	*5547*
	11: 3	*is* the man; and the head of **C** *is* God.	*5547*
	12:12	being many, are one body: so also *is* **C**.	*5547*
	12:27	Now ye are the body of **C**, and members in	*5547*
	15: 3	how that **C** died for our sins according to	*5547*
	15:12	Now if **C** be preached that he rose from	*5547*
	15:13	resurrection of the dead, then is **C** not risen:	*5547*
	15:14	And if **C** be not risen, then *is* our preaching	*5547*
	15:15	have testified of God that he raised up **C**:	*5547*
	15:16	if the dead rise not, then is not **C** raised:	*5547*
	15:17	And if **C** be not raised, your faith *is* vain;	*5547*
	15:18	Then they also which are fallen asleep in **C**	*5547*
	15:19	If in this life only we have hope in **C**,	*5547*
	15:20	But now is **C** risen from the dead, *and*	*5547*
	15:22	all die, even so in **C** shall all be made alive.	*5547*
	15:23	**C** the firstfruits; afterward they that are	*5547*
	15:31	rejoicing which I have in **C** Jesus our Lord,	*5547*
	15:57	us the victory through our Lord Jesus **C**.	*5547*
	16:22	If any *man* love not the Lord Jesus **C**,	*5547*
	16:23	The grace of *our* Lord Jesus **C** *be* with you.	*5547*
	16:24	My love *be* with you all in **C** Jesus. Amen.	*5547*
2Co	1: 1	an apostle of Jesus **C** by the will of God,	*5547*
	1: 2	God our Father, and *from* the Lord Jesus **C**.	*5547*
	1: 3	even the Father of our Lord Jesus **C**,	*5547*
	1: 5	For as the sufferings of **C** abound in us, so	*5547*
	1: 5	so our consolation also aboundeth by **C**.	*5547*
	1:19	For the Son of God, Jesus **C**, who was	*5547*
	1:21	Now he which stablisheth us with you in **C**,	*5547*
	2:10	your sakes *forgave I it* in the person of **C**;	*5547*
	2:14	which always causeth us to triumph in **C**,	*5547*
	2:15	For we are unto God a sweet savour of **C**,	*5547*
	2:17	of God, in the sight of God speak we in **C**.	*5547*
	3: 3	to be the epistle of **C** ministered by us,	*5547*
	3: 4	And such trust have we through **C** to	*5547*
	3:14	which *vail* is done away in **C**.	*5547*
	4: 4	lest the light of the glorious gospel of **C**,	*5547*
	4: 5	preach not ourselves, but **C** Jesus the Lord;	*5547*
	4: 6	of the glory of God in the face of Jesus **C**.	*5547*
	5:10	all appear before the judgment seat of **C**;	*5547*
	5:14	For the love of **C** constraineth us; because	*5547*
	5:16	though we have known **C** after the flesh,	*5547*
	5:17	Therefore if any *man be* in **C**, *he is* a new	*5547*
	5:18	hath reconciled us to himself by Jesus **C**,	*5547*
	5:19	that God was in **C** reconciling the world	*5547*
	5:20	*Now* then we are ambassadors for **C**,	*5547*
	6:15	And what concord hath **C** with Belial? or	*5547*
	8: 9	For ye know the grace of our Lord Jesus **C**,	*5547*
	8:23	of the churches, *and* the glory of **C**.	*5547*
	9:13	professed subjection unto the gospel of **C**,	*5547*
	10: 1	you by the meekness and gentleness of **C**,	*5547*
	10: 5	every thought to the obedience of **C**;	*5547*
	10:14	as to you also in *preaching* the gospel of **C**:	*5547*
	11: 2	*I* may present *you as* a chaste virgin to **C**.	*5547*
	11: 3	corrupted from the simplicity that is in **C**.	*5547*
	11:10	*As* the truth of **C** is in me, no *man* shall	*5547*
	11:13	themselves into the apostles of **C**.	*5547*
	11:23	Are they ministers of **C**? (I speak as a fool)	*5547*
	11:31	The God and Father of our Lord Jesus **C**,	*5547*
	12: 2	I knew a man in **C** above fourteen years	*5547*
	12: 9	that the power of **C** may rest upon me.	*5547*
	12:19	we speak before God in **C**: but *we do* all	*5547*
	13: 3	Since ye seek a proof of **C** speaking in me,	*5547*
	13: 5	how that Jesus **C** is in you, except ye be	*5547*
	13:14	The grace of the Lord Jesus **C**, and the love	*5547*
Gal	1: 1	but by Jesus **C**, and God the Father,	*5547*
	1: 3	God the Father, and *from* our Lord Jesus **C**,	*5547*
	1: 6	into the grace of **C** unto another gospel:	*5547*
	1: 7	and would pervert the gospel of **C**.	*5547*
	1:10	I should not be the servant of **C**.	*5547*
	1:12	I taught *it,* but by the revelation of Jesus **C**.	*5547*
	1:22	the churches of Judea which were in **C**:	*5547*
	2: 4	out our liberty which we have in **C** Jesus,	*5547*
	2:16	but by the faith of Jesus **C**, even we have	*5547*
	2:16	even we have believed in Jesus **C**,	*5547*
	2:16	that we might be justified by the faith of **C**,	*5547*
	2:17	But if, while we seek to be justified by **C**,	*5547*
	2:17	*is* therefore **C** the minister of sin?	*5547*
Gal	2:20	I am crucified with **C**: nevertheless I live;	*5547*
	2:20	I live; yet not I, but **C** liveth in me:	*5547*
	2:21	*come* by the law, then **C** is dead in vain.	*5547*
	3: 1	before whose eyes Jesus **C** hath been	*5547*
	3:13	**C** hath redeemed us from the curse of	*5547*
	3:14	come on the Gentiles through Jesus **C**;	*5547*
	3:16	but as of one, And to thy seed, which is **C**.	*5547*
	3:17	that was confirmed before of God in **C**,	*5547*
	3:22	that the promise by faith of Jesus **C** might	*5547*
	3:24	was our schoolmaster *to bring us* unto **C**,	*5547*
	3:26	all the children of God by faith in **C** Jesus.	*5547*
	3:27	been baptized into **C** have put on Christ.	*5547*
	3:27	been baptized into Christ have put on **C**.	*5547*
	3:28	nor female: for ye are all one in **C** Jesus.	*5547*
	4: 7	and if a son, then an heir of God through **C**.	*5547*
	4:14	me as an angel of God, *even* as **C** Jesus.	*5547*
	4:19	of whom I travail in birth again until **C** be	*5547*
	5: 1	in the liberty wherewith **C** hath made us	*5547*
	5: 2	be circumcised, **C** shall profit you nothing.	*5547*
	5: 4	**C** is become of no effect unto you,	*5547*
	5: 6	For in Jesus **C** neither circumcision	*5547*
	6: 2	and so fulfil the law of **C**.	*5547*
	6:12	suffer persecution for the cross of **C**.	*5547*
	6:14	save in the cross of our Lord Jesus **C**,	*5547*
	6:15	For in **C** Jesus neither circumcision	*5547*
	6:18	the grace of our Lord Jesus **C** *be* with your	*5547*
Eph	1: 1	an apostle of Jesus **C** by the will of God,	*5547*
	1: 1	at Ephesus, and to the faithful in **C** Jesus:	*5547*
	1: 2	God our Father, and *from* the Lord Jesus **C**.	*5547*
	1: 3	*be* the God and Father of our Lord Jesus **C**,	*5547*
	1: 3	spiritual blessings in heavenly *places* in **C**:	*5547*
	1: 5	adoption of children by Jesus **C** to himself,	*5547*
	1:10	might gather together in one all *things* in **C**,	*5547*
	1:12	praise of his glory, who first trusted in **C**:	*5547*
	1:17	That the God of our Lord Jesus **C**,	*5547*
	1:20	Which he wrought in **C**, when he raised	*5547*
	2: 5	hath quickened *us* together with **C**, (by	*5547*
	2: 6	sit together in heavenly *places* in **C** Jesus:	*5547*
	2: 7	in *his* kindness towards us through **C** Jesus.	*5547*
	2:10	created in **C** Jesus unto good works,	*5547*
	2:12	That at that time ye were without **C**,	*5547*
	2:13	But now in **C** Jesus ye who sometimes	*5547*
	2:13	far off are made nigh by the blood of **C**.	*5547*
	2:20	Jesus **C** himself being the chief corner	*5547*
	3: 1	the prisoner of Jesus **C** for you Gentiles,	*5547*
	3: 4	my knowledge in the mystery of **C**)	*5547*
	3: 6	partakers of his promise in **C** by the gospel:	*5547*
	3: 8	the Gentiles the unsearchable riches of **C**;	*5547*
	3: 9	in God, who created all *things* by Jesus **C**:	*5547*
	3:11	which he purposed in **C** Jesus our Lord:	*5547*
	3:14	knees unto the Father of our Lord Jesus **C**,	*5547*
	3:17	That **C** may dwell in your hearts by faith;	*5547*
	3:19	And to know the love of **C**, which passeth	*5547*
	3:21	Unto him *be* glory in the church by **C** Jesus	*5547*
	4: 7	according to the measure of the gift of **C**.	*5547*
	4:12	for the edifying of the body of **C**:	*5547*
	4:13	measure of the stature of the fulness of **C**:	*5547*
	4:15	*in* all *things,* which is the head, *even* **C**:	*5547*
	4:20	But ye have not so learned **C**;	*5547*
	5: 2	as **C** also hath loved us, and hath given	*5547*
	5: 5	hath *any* inheritance in the kingdom of **C**	*5547*
	5:14	from the dead, and **C** shall give thee light.	*5547*
	5:20	the Father in the name of our Lord Jesus **C**;	*5547*
	5:23	even as **C** *is* the head of the church:	*5547*
	5:24	Therefore as the church is subject unto **C**,	*5547*
	5:25	even as **C** also loved the church, and	*5547*
	5:32	but I speak concerning **C** and the church.	*5547*
	6: 5	in singleness of your heart, as unto **C**;	*5547*
	6: 6	but as the servants of **C**, doing the will of	*5547*
	6:23	from God the Father and the Lord Jesus **C**.	*5547*
	6:24	that love our Lord Jesus **C** in sincerity.	*5547*
Php	1: 1	and Timotheus, the servants of Jesus **C**,	*5547*
	1: 1	to all the saints in **C** Jesus which are at	*5547*
	1: 2	God our Father, and *from* the Lord Jesus **C**.	*5547*
	1: 6	you will perform *it* until the day of Jesus **C**:	*5547*
	1: 8	long after you all in the bowels of Jesus **C**.	*5547*
	1:10	and without offence till the day of **C**;	*5547*
	1:11	which are by Jesus **C** unto the glory and	*5547*
	1:13	So that my bonds in **C** are manifest in all	*5547*
	1:15	Some indeed preach **C** even of envy and	*5547*
	1:16	The one preach **C** of contention,	*5547*
	1:18	in pretence, or in truth, **C** is preached;	*5547*
	1:19	and the supply of the Spirit of Jesus **C**,	*5547*
	1:20	now also **C** shall be magnified in my body,	*5547*
	1:21	For to me to live *is* **C**, and to die *is* gain.	*5547*
	1:23	having a desire to depart, and to be with **C**;	*5547*
	1:26	Jesus **C** for me by my coming to you again.	*5547*
	1:27	be as it becometh the gospel of **C**:	*5547*
	1:29	For unto you it is given in the behalf of **C**,	*5547*
	2: 1	If *there be* therefore any consolation in **C**,	*5547*
	2: 5	mind be in you, which *was* also in **C** Jesus:	*5547*
	2:11	tongue should confess that Jesus **C** *is* Lord,	*5547*
	2:16	that I may rejoice in the day of **C**, that I	*5547*
	2:30	Because for the work of **C** he was nigh	*5547*
	3: 3	and rejoice in **C** Jesus, and have no	*5547*
	3: 7	were gain to me, those I counted loss for **C**.	*5547*
	3: 8	of the knowledge of **C** Jesus my Lord:	*5547*
	3: 8	do count *them but* dung, that I may win **C**,	*5547*
	3: 9	but that which is through the faith of **C**,	*5547*
	3:12	which also I am apprehended of **C** Jesus.	*5547*
	3:14	prize of the high calling of God in **C** Jesus.	*5547*
	3:18	*that they are* the enemies of the cross of **C**:	*5547*
	3:20	we look for the Saviour, the Lord Jesus **C**:	*5547*
	4: 7	your hearts and minds through **C** Jesus.	*5547*
	4:13	I can do all *things* through **C** which	*5547*
	4:19	according to his riches in glory by **C** Jesus.	*5547*
	4:21	Salute every saint in **C** Jesus. The brethren	*5547*
	4:23	The grace of our Lord Jesus **C** *be* with you	*5547*
Col	1: 1	an apostle of Jesus **C** by the will of God,	*5547*
	1: 2	faithful brethren in **C** which are at Colosse:	*5547*
	1: 2	from God our Father and the Lord Jesus **C**.	*5547*
	1: 3	to God and the Father of our Lord Jesus **C**,	*5547*
	1: 4	Since we heard of your faith in **C** Jesus,	*5547*
	1: 7	who is for you a faithful minister of **C**;	*5547*
	1:24	of **C** in my flesh for his body's sake,	*5547*

Col 1:27 which is C in you, the hope of glory: 5547
1:28 that we may present every man perfect in C 5547
2: 2 of God and of the Father, and of C; 5547
2: 5 and the stedfastness of your faith in C. 5547
2: 6 therefore received C Jesus the Lord, 5547
2: 8 the rudiments of the world, and not after C. 5547
2:11 sins of the flesh, by the circumcision of C: 5547
2:17 of *things* to come; but the body *is* of C. 5547
2:20 Wherefore if ye be dead with C from 5547
3: 1 If ye then be risen with C, seek those *things* 5547
3: 1 where C sitteth on the right hand of God. 5547
3: 3 and your life is hid with C in God. 5547
3: 4 When C, *who is* our life, shall appear, then 5547
3:11 bond *nor* free: but C *is* all, and in all. 5547
3:13 even as C forgave you, so also *do* ye. 5547
3:16 Let the word of C dwell in you richly in all 5547
3:24 of the inheritance: for ye serve the Lord C. 5547
4: 3 to speak the mystery of C, for which I am 5547
4:12 is *one* of you, a servant of C, saluteth you, 5547
1Th 1: 1 in God the Father and *in* the Lord Jesus C: 5547
1: 1 from God our Father, and the Lord Jesus C. 5547
1: 3 and patience of hope in our Lord Jesus C, 5547
2: 6 been burdensome, as *the* apostles of C. 5547
2:14 of God which in Judea are in C Jesus: 5547
2:19 of our Lord Jesus C at his coming? 5547
3: 2 and our fellowlabourer in the gospel of C, 5547
3:11 and our Father, and our Lord Jesus C, 5547
3:13 at the coming of our Lord Jesus C with all 5547
4:16 of God: and the dead in C shall rise first: 5547
5: 9 but to obtain salvation by our Lord Jesus C, 5547
5:18 for this *is* the will of God in C Jesus 5547
5:23 unto the coming of our Lord Jesus C. 5547
5:28 The grace of our Lord Jesus C *be* with you. 5547
2Th 1: 1 in God our Father and the Lord Jesus C: 5547
1: 2 from God our Father and the Lord Jesus C. 5547
1: 8 obey not the gospel of our Lord Jesus C: 5547
1:12 That the name of our Lord Jesus C may be 5547
1:12 the grace of our God and the Lord Jesus C. 5547
2: 1 by the coming of our Lord Jesus C, and 5547
2: 2 as from us, as that the day of C is at hand. 5547
2:14 obtaining of the glory of our Lord Jesus C. 5547
2:16 Now our Lord Jesus C himself, and God, 5547
3: 5 of God, and into the patient waiting for C. 5547
3: 6 brethren, in the name of our Lord Jesus C, 5547
3:12 and exhort by our Lord Jesus C, 5547
3:18 The grace of our Lord Jesus C *be* with you 5547
1Ti 1: 1 an apostle of Jesus C by the commandment 5547
1: 1 and Lord Jesus C, *which is* our hope; 5547
1: 2 from God our Father and Jesus C our Lord. 5547
1:12 And I thank C Jesus our Lord, who hath 5547
1:14 with faith and love which is in C Jesus. 5547
1:15 that C Jesus came into the world to save 5547
1:16 that in me first Jesus C might shew forth all 5547
2: 5 between God and men, *the* man C Jesus; 5547
2: 7 (I speak the truth in C, *and* lie not;) 5547
3:13 great boldness in the faith which is in C 5547
4: 6 thou shalt be a good minister of Jesus C, 5547
5:11 they have *begun to* wax wanton against C, 5547
5:21 and the Lord Jesus C, and the elect angels, 5547
6: 3 *even* the *words* of our Lord Jesus C, and 5547
6:13 quickeneth all *things*, and *before* C Jesus, 5547
6:14 until the appearing of our Lord Jesus C: 5547
2Ti 1: 1 an apostle of Jesus C by the will of God, 5547
1: 1 to the promise of life which is in C Jesus, 5547
1: 2 from God the Father and C Jesus our Lord. 5547
1: 9 which was given us in C Jesus before 5547
1:10 by the appearing of our Saviour Jesus C, 5547
1:13 of me, in faith and love which is in C Jesus. 5547
2: 1 be strong in the grace that is in C Jesus. 5547
2: 3 as a good soldier of Jesus C. 5547
2: 8 Remember that Jesus C of the seed of 5547
2:10 which is in C Jesus with eternal glory. 5547
2:19 Let every one that nameth the name of C 5547
3:12 all that will live godly in C Jesus shall 5547
3:15 salvation through faith which is in C Jesus. 5547
4: 1 therefore before God, and the Lord Jesus C, 5547
4:22 The Lord Jesus C *be* with thy spirit. Grace 5547
Tit 1: 1 a servant of God, and an apostle of Jesus C, 5547
1: 4 and the Lord Jesus C our Saviour. 5547
2:13 of the great God and our Saviour Jesus C; 5547
3: 6 us abundantly through Jesus C our Saviour; 5547
Phm 1: 1 a prisoner of Jesus C, and Timothy *our* 5547
1: 3 from God our Father and the Lord Jesus C. 5547
1: 6 good *thing* which is in you in C Jesus. 5547
1: 8 though I might be much bold in C to enjoin 5547
1: 9 and now also a prisoner of Jesus C. 5547
1:23 my fellowprisoner in C Jesus; 5547
1:25 The grace of our Lord Jesus C *be* with your 5547
Heb 3: 1 and High Priest of our profession, C Jesus; 5547
3: 6 But C as a Son over his own house; 5547
3:14 For we are made partakers of C, if we hold 5547
5: 5 So also C glorified not himself to be made 5547
6: 1 leaving the principles of the doctrine of C, 5547
9:11 But C being come a high priest of good 5547
9:14 How much more shall the blood of C, 5547
9:24 For C is not entered into the holy *places* 5547
9:28 So C was once offered to bear the sins of 5547
10:10 offering of the body of Jesus C once for all. 5547
11:26 Esteeming the reproach of C greater riches 5547
13: 8 Jesus C the same yesterday, and to day, and 5547
13:21 well pleasing in his sight, through Jesus C; 5547
Jas 1: 1 a servant of God and of the Lord Jesus C, 5547
2: 1 have not the faith of our Lord Jesus C, 5547
1Pe 1: 1 Peter, an apostle of Jesus C, to 5547
1: 2 and sprinkling of the blood of Jesus C: 5547
1: 3 *be* the God and Father of our Lord Jesus C, 5547
1: 3 the resurrection of Jesus C from the dead, 5547
1: 7 and glory at the appearing of Jesus C: 5547
1:11 what manner of time the Spirit of C which 5547
1:11 it testified beforehand the sufferings of C, 5547
1:13 unto you at the revelation of Jesus C; 5547
1:19 But with the precious blood of C, as of a 5547
2: 5 acceptable to God by Jesus C. 5547
2:21 because C also suffered for us, leaving us 5547
3:16 falsely accuse your good conversation in C. 5547

1Pe 3:18 For C also hath once suffered for sins, 5547
3:21 by the resurrection of Jesus C: 5547
4: 1 then as C hath suffered for us in the flesh, 5547
4:11 all *things* may be glorified through Jesus C, 5547
4:14 If ye be reproached for the name of C, 5547
5: 1 and a witness of the sufferings of C, and 5547
5:10 called us into his eternal glory by C Jesus, 5547
5:14 Peace *be* with you all that are in C Jesus. 5547
2Pe 1: 1 a servant and an apostle of Jesus C, 5547
1: 1 of God and our Saviour Jesus C: 5547
1: 8 in the knowledge of our Lord Jesus C. 5547
1:11 kingdom of our Lord and Saviour Jesus C. 5547
1:14 even as our Lord Jesus C hath shewed me. 5547
1:16 the power and coming of our Lord Jesus C, 5547
2:20 of the Lord and Saviour Jesus C, 5547
3:18 of our Lord and Saviour Jesus C. 5547
1Jn 1: 3 with the Father, and with his Son Jesus C. 5547
1: 7 the blood of Jesus C his Son cleanseth us 5547
2: 1 with the Father, Jesus C *the* righteous: 5547
2:22 but he that denieth that Jesus is the C? 5547
3:23 believe on the name of his Son Jesus C, 5547
4: 2 Every spirit that confesseth that Jesus C is 5547
4: 3 Jesus C is come in the flesh is not of God: 5547
5: 1 Whosoever believeth that Jesus is the C is 5547
5: 6 came by water and blood, *even* Jesus C; 5547
5:20 in him *that is* true, *even* in his Son Jesus C. 5547
2Jn 1: 3 God the Father, and from the Lord Jesus C, 5547
1: 7 who confess not that Jesus C is come in 5547
1: 9 and abideth not in the doctrine of C, 5547
1: 9 He that abideth in the doctrine of C, 5547
Jude 1: 1 the servant of Jesus C, and brother of 5547
1: 1 and preserved *in* Jesus C, *and* called: 5547
1: 4 the only Lord God, and our Lord Jesus C. 5547
1:17 before of the apostles of our Lord Jesus C; 5547
1:21 looking for the mercy of our Lord Jesus C 5547
Rev 1: 1 The Revelation of Jesus C, which God 5547
1: 2 and of the testimony of Jesus C, and of all 5547
1: 5 And from Jesus C, *who is* the faithful 5547
1: 9 in the kingdom and patience of Jesus C, 5547
1: 9 of God, and for the testimony of Jesus C. 5547
11:15 *the kingdoms* of our Lord, and of his C; 5547
12:10 of our God, and the power of his C: 5547
12:17 of God, and have the testimony of Jesus C. 5547
20: 4 and reigned with C a thousand years. 5547
20: 6 but they shall be priests of God and of C, 5547
22:21 The grace of our Lord Jesus C *be* with you 5547

CHRIST'S (16) [CHRIST]

Ro 15:30 for the Lord Jesus C sake, and for the love 5547
1Co 3:23 And ye *are* C; and Christ *is* God's. 5547
4:10 We *are* fools for C sake, but ye *are* wise in 5547
7:22 he that is called, *being* free, is C servant. 5547
15:23 afterward they that are C at his coming. 5547
2Co 2:12 when I came to Troas to *preach* C gospel, 5547
5:20 we pray *you* in C stead, be ye reconciled to 5547
10: 7 If any *man* trust to himself that *he* is C, 5547
10: 7 that, as he *is* C, even so *are* we Christ's. 5547
10: 7 that, as he *is* Christ's, even so *are* we C. 5547
12:10 in persecutions, in distresses for C sake: 5547
Gal 3:29 And if ye *be* C, then are ye Abraham's 5547
5:24 And they that are C have crucified the flesh 5547
Eph 4:32 even as God for C sake hath forgiven you. 5547
Php 2:21 their own, not the *things which are* Jesus C. 5547
1Pe 4:13 inasmuch as ye are partakers of C 5547

CHRISTIAN (2) [CHRIST]

Ac 26:28 Almost thou persuadest me to be a C. 5546
1Pe 4:16 Yet if *any man suffer* as a C, let him not be 5546

CHRISTIANS (1) [CHRIST]

Ac 11:26 the disciples were called C first in Antioch. 5546

CHRISTS (2) [CHRIST]

Mt 24:24 For there shall arise **false** C, and 5580
Mk 13:22 For **false** C and false prophets shall rise, 5580

CHRONICLES (38)

1Ki 14:19 book of the c of the kings of Israel. 1697+3117
14:29 book of the c of the kings of Judah? 1697+3117
15: 7 book of the c of the kings of Judah? 1697+3117
15:23 book of the c of the kings of Judah? 1697+3117
15:31 book of the c of the kings of Israel? 1697+3117
16: 5 book of the c of the kings of Israel? 1697+3117
16:14 book of the c of the kings of Israel? 1697+3117
16:20 book of the c of the kings of Israel? 1697+3117
16:27 book of the c of the kings of Israel? 1697+3117
22:39 book of the c of the kings of Israel? 1697+3117
22:45 book of the c of the kings of Judah? 1697+3117
2Ki 1:18 book of the c of the kings of Israel? 1697+3117
8:23 book of the c of the kings of Judah? 1697+3117
10:34 book of the c of the kings of Israel? 1697+3117
12:19 book of the c of the kings of Judah? 1697+3117
13: 8 book of the c of the kings of Israel? 1697+3117
13:12 book of the c of the kings of Israel? 1697+3117
14:15 book of the c of the kings of Israel? 1697+3117
14:18 book of the c of the kings of Judah? 1697+3117
14:28 book of the c of the kings of Israel? 1697+3117
15: 6 book of the c of the kings of Judah? 1697+3117
15:11 they *are* written in the book of the c 1697+3117
15:15 they *are* written in the book of the c 1697+3117
15:21 book of the c of the kings of Israel? 1697+3117
15:26 they *are* written in the book of the c 1697+3117
15:31 they *are* written in the book of the c 1697+3117
15:36 book of the c of the kings of Judah? 1697+3117
16:19 book of the c of the kings of Judah? 1697+3117
20:20 book of the c of the kings of Judah? 1697+3117
21:17 book of the c of the kings of Judah? 1697+3117
21:25 book of the c of the kings of Judah? 1697+3117
23:28 book of the c of the kings of Judah? 1697+3117
24: 5 book of the c of the kings of Judah? 1697+3117
1Ch 27:24 of the c of king David. 1697+3117+1886.1
Ne 12:23 written in the book of the c, 1697+3117+1886.1
Est 2:23 of the c before the king. 1697+3117+1886.1
6: 1 the book of records of the c; 1697+3117+1886.1

Est 10: 2 the c of the kings of Media 1697+3117+1886.1

CHRYSOLITE (1)

Rev 21:20 sardonyx; the sixth, sardius; the seventh, c; 5555

CHRYSOPRASE See CHRYSOPRASUS

CHRYSOPRASUS (1)

Rev 21:20 beryl; the ninth, a topaz; the tenth, a c; 5556

CHUB (1)

Eze 30: 5 C, and the men of the land that is in league, 3552

CHUN (1)

1Ch 18: 8 and from C, cities of Hadarezer, 3560

CHURCH (80) [CHURCHES]

Mt 16:18 and upon this rock I will build my c; 1577
18:17 shall neglect to hear them, tell *it* unto the c: 1577
18:17 but if he neglect to hear the c, let him be 1577
Ac 2:47 And the Lord added to the c daily such as 1577
5:11 And great fear came upon all the c, and 1577
7:38 that was in the c in the wilderness with 1577
8: 1 against the c which was at Jerusalem; 1577
8: 3 As for Saul, he made havock of the c, 1577
11:22 the ears of the c which was in Jerusalem: 1577
11:26 year they assembled themselves with the c, 1577
12: 1 forth *his* hands to vex certain of the c. 1577
12: 5 prayer was made without ceasing of the c 1577
13: 1 Now there were in the c that was at Antioch 1577
14:23 had ordained them elders **in every** c, 1577+2596
14:27 and had gathered the c together, 1577
15: 3 And being brought on their way by the c, 1577
15: 4 they were received of the c, and *of* 1577
15:22 it the apostles and elders, with the whole c, 1577
18:22 and gone up, and saluted the c, he went 1577
20:17 to Ephesus, and called the elders of the c. 1577
20:28 to feed the c of God, which he hath 1577
Ro 16: 1 which is a servant of the c which is at 1577
16: 5 Likewise *greet* the c that is in their house. 1577
16:23 mine host, and of the whole c, saluteth you. 1577
16: S *sent* by Phebe servant of the c at Cenchrea. 1577
1Co 1: 2 Unto the c of God which is at Corinth, 1577
4:17 in Christ, as I teach every where in every c. 1577
6: 4 to judge who are least esteemed in the c. 1577
10:32 nor to the Gentiles, nor to the c of God: 1577
11:18 first of all, when ye come together in the c, 1577
11:22 and to drink *in?* or despise ye the c of God, 1577
12:28 And God hath set some in the c, 1577
14: 4 but he that prophesieth edifieth *the* c. 1577
14: 5 that the c may receive edifying. 1577
14:12 that ye may excel to the edifying of the c. 1577
14:19 Yet in the c I had rather speak five words 1577
14:23 the whole c be come together into one 1577
14:28 no interpreter, let him keep silence in the c; 1577
14:35 it is a shame for women to speak in the c. 1577
15: 9 because I persecuted the c of God. 1577
16:19 in the Lord, with the c that is in their house. 1577
2Co 1: 1 unto the c of God which is at Corinth, 1577
Gal 1:13 how that beyond measure I persecuted the c 1577
Eph 1:22 him *to be* the head over all *things* to the c, 1577
3:10 by the c the manifold wisdom of God, 1577
3:21 Unto him *be* glory in the c by Christ Jesus 1577
5:23 the wife, even as Christ *is* the head of the c: 1577
5:24 Therefore as the c is subject unto Christ, so 1577
5:25 even as Christ also loved the c, and 1577
5:27 he might present it to himself a glorious c, 1577
5:29 and cherisheth it, even as the Lord the c: 1577
5:32 but I speak concerning Christ and the c. 1577
Php 3: 6 Concerning zeal, persecuting the c; 1577
4:15 no c communicated with me as concerning 1577
Col 1:18 And he is the head of the body, the c: 1577
1:24 flesh for his body's sake, which is the c: 1577
4:15 Nymphas, and the c which is in his house. 1577
4:16 cause that it be read also in the c of 1577
1Th 1: 1 unto the c of the Thessalonians *which is* in 1577
2Th 1: 1 unto the c of the Thessalonians in God our 1577
1Ti 3: 5 how shall he take care of the c of God?) 1577
3:15 which is the c of the living God, the pillar 1577
5:16 relieve them, and let not the c be charged; 1577
2Ti 4: S ordained the first bishop of the c of 1577
Tit 3: S ordained the first bishop of the c of 1577
Phm 1: 2 our fellowsoldier, and to the c in thy house: 1577
Heb 2:12 in the midst of the c will I sing praise unto 1577
12:23 the general assembly, and c of the firstborn, 1577
Jas 5:14 let him call for the elders of the c; and 1577
1Pe 5:13 The *c that is* at Babylon, elected together NIG
3Jn 1: 6 borne witness of thy charity before the c: 1577
1: 9 I wrote unto the c: but Diotrephes, 1577
1:10 that would, and casteth *them* out of the c. 1577
Rev 2: 1 Unto the angel of the c of Ephesus write; 1577
2: 8 And unto the angel of the c in Smyrna 1577
2:12 And to the angel of the c in Pergamos 1577
2:18 And unto the angel of the c in Thyatira 1577
3: 1 And unto the angel of the c in Sardis write; 1577
3: 7 And to the angel of the c in Philadelphia 1577
3:14 And unto the angel of the c of 1577

CHURCHES (37) [CHURCH]

Ac 9:31 Then had the c rest throughout all Judea 1577
15:41 through Syria and Cilicia, confirming the c. 1577
16: 5 And so were the c established in the faith, 1577
19:37 *which are* neither **robbers of** c, nor yet 2417
Ro 16: 4 but also all the c of the Gentiles. 1577
16:16 with a holy kiss. The c of Christ salute you. 1577
1Co 7:17 so let him walk. And so ordain I in all c. 1577
11:16 have no such custom, neither the c of God. 1577
14:33 but of peace, as in all c of the saints. 1577
14:34 Let your women keep silence in the c: for it 1577
16: 1 as I have given order to the c of Galatia, 1577
16:19 The c of Asia salute you. Aquila and 1577
2Co 8: 1 of God bestowed on the c of Macedonia; 1577
8:18 praise *is* in the gospel throughout all the c; 1577
8:19 who was also chosen of the c to travel with 1577

2Co 8:23 *of, they are* the messengers of the c, *1577*
8:24 and before the c, the proof of your love, *1577*
11: 8 I robbed other c, taking wages *of them,* to *1577*
11:28 cometh upon me daily, the care of all the c. *1577*
12:13 is it wherein ye were inferior to other c, *1577*
Gal 1: 2 which are with me, unto the c of Galatia: *1577*
1:22 And was unknown by face unto the c of *1577*
1Th 2:14 became followers of the c of God which in *1577*
2Th 1: 4 So that we ourselves glory in you in the c *1577*
Rev 1: 4 John to the seven c which are in Asia: *1577*
1:11 send *it* unto the seven c which are in Asia; *1577*
1:20 seven stars are the angels of the seven c: *1577*
1:20 which thou sawest are the seven c. *1577*
2: 7 let him hear what the Spirit saith unto the c; *1577*
2:11 let him hear what the Spirit saith unto the c; *1577*
2:17 let him hear what the Spirit saith unto the c; *1577*
2:23 all the c shall know that I am he which *1577*
2:29 let him hear what the Spirit saith unto the c. *1577*
3: 6 let him hear what the Spirit saith unto the c. *1577*
3:13 let him hear what the Spirit saith unto the c. *1577*
3:22 let him hear what the Spirit saith unto the c. *1577*
22:16 to testify unto you these *things* in the c. *1577*

CHURL (2) [CHURLISH]
Isa 32: 5 called liberal, nor the c said *to be* bountiful. 3596
32: 7 The instruments also of the c *are* evil: 3596

CHURLISH (1) [CHURL]
1Sa 25: 3 the man *was* c and evil *in* his doings; and 7186

CHURNING (1)
Pr 30:33 Surely the c of milk bringeth forth butter, 4330

CHUSHAN-RISHATHAIM (4)
Jdg 3: 8 he sold them into the hand of C king of 3573
3: 8 the children of Israel served C eight years. 3573
3:10 the LORD delivered C king of 3573
3:10 his hand; and his hand prevailed against C. 3573

CHUZA (1)
Lk 8: 3 And Joanna the wife of C Herod's steward, *5529*

CIELED (4) [CIELING]
2Ch 3: 5 the greater house he c with fir tree, 2645
Jer 22:14 *it is* c with cedar, and painted with 5603
Eze 41:16 c with wood round about, and *from* 7824
Hag 1: 4 to dwell in your c houses, and this house *lie* 5603

CIELING (1) [CIELED]
1Ki 6:15 floor of the house, and the walls of the c: 5604

CILICIA (8)
Ac 6: 9 and of them of C and of Asia, *2791*
15:23 of the Gentiles in Antioch and Syria and C: *2791*
15:41 And he went through Syria and C, *2791*
21:39 *a city* in C, a citizen of no mean city: *2791*
22: 3 *am* a Jew, born in Tarsus, *a city* in C, *2791*
23:34 and when he understood that *he was* of C; *2791*
27: 5 And when we had sailed over the sea of C *2791*
Gal 1:21 I came into the regions of Syria and C; *2791*

CINNAMON (4)
Ex 30:23 and of sweet c half so much, 7076
Pr 7:17 perfumed my bed *with* myrrh, aloes, and c. 7076
SS 4:14 calamus and c, with all trees of 7076
Rev 18:13 And c, and odours, and ointments, and *2792*

CINNERETH (1) [CINNEROTH]
Jos 13:27 *even* unto the edge of the sea of C on 3672

CINNEROTH (3) [CINNERETH, CHINNERETH]
Jos 11: 2 of the plains south of C, and in the valley, 3672
12: 3 *from* the plain to the sea of C on the east, 3672
1Ki 15:20 and Abel-beth-maachah, and all C, 3672

CIRCLE (1)
Isa 40:22 *It is* he that sitteth upon the c of the earth, 2329

CIRCUIT (3) [CIRCUITS]
1Sa 7:16 he went from year to year in c *to* Beth-el, 5437
Job 22:14 and he walketh *in* the c of heaven. 2329
Ps 19: 6 of the heaven, and his c unto the ends of it: 8622

CIRCUITS (1) [CIRCUIT]
Ecc 1: 6 the wind returneth *again* according to his c. 5439

CIRCUMCISE (10) [CIRCUMCISED, CIRCUMCISING, CIRCUMCISION, UNCIRCUMCISED]
Ge 17:11 ye shall c the flesh of your foreskin; and 5243
Dt 10:16 C therefore the foreskin of your heart, and 4135
30: 6 the LORD thy God will c thine heart, and 4135
Jos 5: 2 c again the children of Israel the second 4135
5: 4 this *is* the cause why Joshua did c: All 4135
Jer 4: 4 C yourselves to the LORD, and take away 4135
Lk 1:59 *that* on the eighth day they came to c *4059*
Jn 7:22 and ye on the sabbath day c a man. *4059*
Ac 15: 5 That it was needful to c them, and *4059*
21:21 saying that they *ought* not to c *their* *4059*

CIRCUMCISED (39) [CIRCUMCISE]
Ge 17:10 Every man *child* among you shall be c. 4135
17:12 he that is eight days old shall be c among 4135
17:13 with thy money, **must needs be** c: 4135+4135
17:14 *child* whose flesh of his foreskin is not c, 4135
17:23 c the flesh of their foreskin in the selfsame 4135
17:24 when he was c *in* the flesh of his foreskin. 4135
17:25 when he was c in the flesh of his foreskin. 4135
17:26 In the selfsame day was Abraham c, and 4135
17:27 money of the stranger, were c with him. 4135
21: 4 Abraham c his son Isaac being eight days 4135
34:15 be as we *be,* that every male of you be c; 4135
34:17 if ye will not hearken unto us, to be c; then 4135
Ge 34:22 be one people, if every male among us be c, 4135
34:22 among us be circumcised, as they *are* c. 4135
34:24 every male was c, all that went out of 4135
Ex 12:44 when thou hast c him, then shall he eat 4135
12:48 let all his males be c, and then let him come 4135
Lev 12: 3 day the flesh of his foreskin shall be c. 4135
Jos 5: 3 c the children of Israel at the hill of 4135
5: 5 Now all the people that came out were c: 4135
5: 5 forth out of Egypt, *them* they had not c. 4135
5: 7 he raised up in their stead, them Joshua c: 4135
5: 7 because they had not c them by the way. 4135
Jer 9:25 that I will punish all *them which are* c with 4135
Ac 7: 8 begat Isaac, and c him the eighth day; *4059*
15: 1 *said,* Except ye be c after the manner of *4059*
15:24 saying, *Ye must* be c, and keep the law: *4059*
16: 3 and took and c him because of the Jews *4059*
Ro 4:11 all them that believe, though they be **not** c; *203*
1Co 7:18 Is any *man* called being c? let him not *4059*
7:18 called in uncircumcision? let him not be c. *4059*
Gal 2: 3 being a Greek, was compelled to be c: *4059*
5: 2 Behold, I Paul say unto you, that if ye be c, *4059*
5: 3 For I testify again to every man that is c, *4059*
6:12 in the flesh, they constrain you to be c; *4059*
6:13 For neither they themselves who are c keep *4059*
6:13 but desire to have you c, that they may *4059*
Php 3: 5 C the eighth day, of the stock of Israel, *4061*
Col 2:11 In whom also ye are c with *4059*

CIRCUMCISING (2) [CIRCUMCISE]
Jos 5: 8 when they had done c all the people, 4135
Lk 2:21 were accomplished for the c of the child, *4059*

CIRCUMCISION (36) [CIRCUMCISE]
Ex 4:26 bloody husband *thou art,* because of the c. 4139
Jn 7:22 Moses therefore gave unto you c, not *4061*
7:23 If a man on the sabbath day receive c, *4061*
Ac 7: 8 And he gave him the covenant of c: and so *4061*
10:45 And they of the c which believed were *4061*
11: 2 they that were of the c contended with him, *4061*
Ro 2:25 For c verily profiteth, if thou keep the law: *4061*
2:25 of the law, thy c is made uncircumcision. *4061*
2:26 not his uncircumcision be counted for c? *4061*
2:27 by the letter and c dost transgress the law? *4061*
2:28 neither *is that* c, which is outward in *4061*
2:29 and c *is that* of the heart, in the spirit, *and* *4061*
3: 1 hath the Jew? or what profit *is there* of c? *4061*
3:30 which shall justify the c by faith, and *4061*
4: 9 this blessedness then upon the c *only,* or *4061*
4:10 when he was in c, or in uncircumcision? *4061*
4:10 Not in c, but in uncircumcision. *4061*
4:11 And he received the sign of c, a seal of *4061*
4:12 And the father of c to them who are not of *4061*
4:12 to them who are not of the c only, *4061*
15: 8 was a minister of the c for the truth of God, *4061*
1Co 7:19 C is nothing, and uncircumcision is *4061*
Gal 2: 7 as *the gospel* of the c *was* unto Peter; *4061*
2: 8 in Peter to the apostleship of the c, *4061*
2: 9 *go* unto the heathen, and they unto the c. *4061*
2:12 fearing them which were of the c. *4061*
5: 6 For in Jesus Christ neither c availeth any *4061*
5:11 And I, brethren, if I yet preach c, why do I *4061*
6:15 For in Christ Jesus neither c availeth any *4061*
Eph 2:11 is called the C in the flesh made by hands; *4061*
Php 3: 3 For we are the c, which worship God in *4061*
Col 2:11 In whom also ye are circumcised with the c *4061*
2:11 of the sins of the flesh, by the c of Christ: *4061*
3:11 c nor uncircumcision, barbarian, Scythian, *4061*
4:11 which is called Justus, who are of the c. *4061*
Tit 1:10 and deceivers, specially they of the c: *4061*

CIRCUMSPECT (1) [CIRCUMSPECTLY]
Ex 23:13 in all *things* that I have said unto you be c: 8104

CIRCUMSPECTLY (1) [CIRCUMSPECT]
Eph 5:15 See then that ye walk c, not as fools, but *199*

CIRCUMSTANCES See DEGREE; DEGREES

CIS (1)
Ac 13:21 and God gave unto them Saul the son of C, *2797*

CISTERN (4) [CISTERNS]
2Ki 18:31 and drink ye every one the waters of his c: 953
Pr 5:15 Drink waters out of thine own c, and 953
Ecc 12: 6 at the fountain, or the wheel broken at the c. 953
Isa 36:16 drink ye every one the waters of his own c; 953

CISTERNS (2) [CISTERN]
Jer 2:13 hewed them out c, broken cisterns, that can 953
2:13 broken c, that can hold no water. 953

CITIES (448) [CITY]
Ge 13:12 Lot dwelled in the c of the plain, and 5892
19:25 he overthrew those c, and all the plain, and 5892
19:25 all the inhabitants of the c, and that which 5892
19:29 when God destroyed the c of the plain, 5892
19:29 when he overthrew the c in the which Lot 5892
35: 5 the terror of God was upon the c that *were* 5892
41:35 of Pharaoh, and let them keep food in the c. 5892
41:48 land of Egypt, and laid up the food in the c: 5892
47:21 he removed them to c from *one* end of 5892
Ex 1:11 they built for Pharaoh treasure c, Pithom 5892
Lev 25:32 Notwithstanding the c of the Levites, *and* 5892
25:32 *and* the houses of the c of their possession, 5892
25:33 for the houses of the c of the Levites *are* 5892
25:34 the field of the suburbs of their c may not 5892
26:25 ye are gathered together within your c, 5892
26:31 I will make your c waste, and bring your 5892
26:33 land shall be desolate, and your c waste. 5892
Nu 13:19 what c *they be* that they dwell in, whether 5892
13:28 and the c *are* walled, *and* very great: 5892
21: 2 my hand, then I will utterly destroy their c. 5892
21: 3 and they utterly destroyed them and their c: 5892
21:25 Israel took all these c: and Israel dwelt in 5892
Nu 21:25 Israel dwelt in all the c of the Amorites, 5892
31:10 they burnt all their c wherein they dwelt, 5892
32:16 here for our cattle, and c for our little ones: 5892
32:17 our little ones shall dwell in the fenced c 5892
32:24 Build ye c for your little ones, and folds for 5892
32:26 our cattle, shall be there in the c of Gilead: 5892
32:33 the land, with the c thereof in the coasts, 5892
32:33 *even* the c of the country round about. 5892
32:36 and Beth-haran, fenced c: 5892
32:38 gave other names unto the c which they 5892
35: 2 of their possession c to dwell in; 5892
35: 2 Levites suburbs for the c round about them. 5892
35: 3 the c shall they have to dwell in; and 5892
35: 4 the suburbs of the c, which ye shall give 5892
35: 5 this shall be to them the suburbs of the c. 5892
35: 6 *among* the c which ye shall give unto 5892
35: 6 the Levites *there shall be* six c for refuge, 5892
35: 6 to them ye shall add forty and two c. 5892
35: 7 *So* all the c which ye shall give to 5892
35: 7 to the Levites *shall be* forty and eight c: 5892
35: 8 the c which ye shall give *shall be* of 5892
35: 8 every one shall give of his c unto 5892
35:11 ye shall appoint you c to be cities of refuge 5892
35:11 ye shall appoint you cities to be c of refuge 5892
35:12 they shall be unto you c for refuge from 5892
35:13 *of these* c which ye shall give six cities 5892
35:13 *of these* cities which ye shall give six c 5892
35:14 Ye shall give three c on *this* side Jordan, 5892
35:14 three c shall ye give in the land of Canaan, 5892
35:14 land of Canaan, *which* shall be c of refuge. 5892
35:15 These six c shall be a refuge, *both* for 5892
Dt 1:22 must go up, and into what c we shall come. 5892
1:28 the c *are* great and walled up to heaven; and 5892
2:34 we took all his c at that time, and 5892
2:35 and the spoil of the c which we took. 5892
2:37 nor *unto* the c in the mountains, 5892
3: 4 we took all his c at that time, there was not 5892
3: 4 threescore c, all the region of Argob, 5892
3: 5 All these c *were* fenced *with* high walls, 5892
3: 7 all the cattle, and the spoil of the c, we took 5892
3:10 All the c of the plain, and all Gilead, and 5892
3:10 Edrei, c of the kingdom of Og in Bashan. 5892
3:12 half mount Gilead, and the c thereof, gave I 5892
3:19 shall abide in your c which I have given 5892
4:41 Moses severed three c on *this* side Jordan 5892
4:42 that fleeing unto one of these c he might 5892
6:10 to Jacob, to give thee great and goodly c, 5892
9: 1 c great and fenced up to heaven, 5892
13:12 If thou shalt hear *say* in one of thy c, 5892
19: 1 and dwellest in their c, and in their houses; 5892
19: 2 Thou shalt separate three c for thee in 5892
19: 5 he shall flee unto one of those c, and live: 5892
19: 7 Thou shalt separate three c for thee. 5892
19: 9 shalt thou add three c moe for thee, 5892
19:11 that he die, and fleeth into one of these c: 5892
20:15 Thus shalt thou do unto all the c *which are* 5892
20:15 which *are* not of the c of these nations. 5892
20:16 of the c of these people, which the LORD 5892
21: 2 they shall measure unto the c which *are* 5892
Jos 9:17 and came unto their c on the third day. 5892
9:17 Now their c *were* Gibeon, and Chephirah, 5892
10: 2 as one of the royal c, and because it *was* 5892
10:19 suffer them not to enter into their c: 5892
10:20 remained of them entered into fenced c. 5892
10:37 all the c thereof, and all the souls that *were* 5892
10:39 and the king thereof, and all the c thereof; 5892
11:12 all the c of those kings, and all the kings of 5892
11:13 *as for* the c that stood still in their strength, 5892
11:14 all the spoil of these c, and the cattle, 5892
11:21 Joshua destroyed them utterly with their c. 5892
13:10 all the c of Sihon king of the Amorites, 5892
13:17 Heshbon, and all her c that *are* in the plain; 5892
13:21 all the c of the plain, and all the kingdom of 5892
13:23 their families, the c and villages thereof. 5892
13:25 all the c of Gilead, and half the land of 5892
13:28 after their families, the c, and their villages. 5892
13:30 of Jair, which *are* in Bashan, threescore c: 5892
13:31 Edrei, c of the kingdom of Og in Bashan, 5892
14: 4 save c to dwell *in,* with their suburbs for 5892
14:12 and *that* the c *were* great *and* fenced: 5892
15: 9 and went out to the c of mount Ephron; 5892
15:21 the uttermost c of the tribe of the children 5892
15:32 all the c *are* twenty and nine, with their 5892
15:36 Gederothaim; fourteen c with their villages. 5892
15:41 Makkedah; sixteen c with their villages. 5892
15:44 and Mareshah; nine c with their villages. 5892
15:51 and Giloh; eleven c with their villages. 5892
15:54 and Zior; nine c with their villages. 5892
15:57 and Timnah; ten c with their villages. 5892
15:59 and Eltekon; six c with their villages. 5892
15:60 and Rabbah; two c with their villages. 5892
15:62 and En-gedi; six c with their villages. 5892
16: 9 the separate c for the children of Ephraim 5892
16: 9 of Manasseh, all the c with their villages. 5892
17: 9 these c of Ephraim *are* among the cities of 5892
17: 9 these cities of Ephraim *are* among the c of 5892
17:12 not drive out *the inhabitants of* those c; 5892
18: 9 described it by c into seven parts in a book, 5892
18:21 Now the c of the tribe of the children of 5892
18:24 and Gaba; twelve c with their villages. 5892
18:28 *and* Kirjath; fourteen c with their villages. 5892
19: 6 and Sharuhen; thirteen c and their villages: 5892
19: 7 Ether, and Ashan; four c and their villages: 5892
19: 8 *were* round about these c to Baalath-beer, 5892
19:15 Beth-lehem: twelve c with their villages. 5892
19:16 to their families, these c with their villages. 5892
19:22 *at* Jordan: sixteen c with their villages. 5892
19:23 to their families, the c and their villages. 5892
19:30 twenty and two c with their villages. 5892
19:31 to their families, these c with their villages. 5892
19:35 the fenced c *are* Ziddim, Zer, and 5892
19:38 nineteen c with their villages. 5892
19:39 to their families, the c and their villages. 5892
19:48 to their families, these c with their villages. 5892
20: 2 Appoint out for you c of refuge, 5892

C

Jos 20: 4 when he that doth flee unto one of those **c** 5892
20: 9 These were the **c** appointed for all 5892
21: 2 the hand of Moses to give us **c** to dwell in, 5892
21: 3 of the LORD, these **c** and their suburbs. 5892
21: 4 and out of the tribe of Benjamin, thirteen **c**. 5892
21: 5 and out of the half tribe of Manasseh, ten **c**. 5892
21: 6 tribe of Manasseh in Bashan, thirteen **c**. 5892
21: 7 and out of the tribe of Zebulun, twelve **c**. 5892
21: 8 unto the Levites these **c** with their suburbs, 5892
21: 9 these **c** which are *here* mentioned by name, 5892
21:16 her suburbs; nine **c** out of those two tribes. 5892
21:18 and Almon with her suburbs; four **c**. 5892
21:19 All the **c** of the children of Aaron, 5892
21:19 *were* thirteen **c** with their suburbs. 5892
21:20 even they had the **c** of their lot out of 5892
21:22 and Beth-horon with her suburbs; four **c**. 5892
21:24 Gath-rimmon with her suburbs; four **c**. 5892
21:25 and Gath-rimmon with her suburbs; two **c**. 5892
21:26 All the **c** *were* ten with their suburbs for 5892
21:27 and Beeshterah with her suburbs; two **c**. 5892
21:29 En-gannim with her suburbs; four **c**. 5892
21:31 and Rehob with her suburbs; four **c**. 5892
21:32 and Kartan with her suburbs; three **c**. 5892
21:33 All the **c** of the Gershonites according to 5892
21:33 families *were* thirteen **c** with their suburbs. 5892
21:35 Nahalal with her suburbs; four **c**. 5892
21:37 and Mephaath with her suburbs; four **c**. 5892
21:39 Jazer with her suburbs; four **c** in all. 5892
21:40 So all the **c** for the children of Merari by 5892
21:40 of the Levites, were *by* their lot twelve **c**. 5892
21:41 All the **c** of the Levites within 5892
21:41 *were* forty and eight **c** with their suburbs. 5892
21:42 These **c** were **every one** with their 5892+5892
21:42 round about them: thus *were* all these **c**. 5892
24:13 **c** which ye built not, and ye dwell in them; 5892
Jdg 10: 4 they had thirty **c**, which are called 5892
11:26 in all the **c** that *be* along by the coasts of 5892
11:33 *even* twenty **c**, and unto the plain of 5892
12: 7 and was buried in *one of* the **c** of Gilead. 5892
20:14 together out of the **c** unto Gibeah, 5892
20:15 numbered at that time out of the **c** twenty 5892
20:42 them which *came* out of the **c** they 5892
20:48 also they set on fire all the **c** that they came 5892
21:23 and repaired the **c**, and dwelt in them. 5892
1Sa 6:18 *according to* the number of all the **c** of 5892
6:18 *both* of fenced **c**, and of country villages, 5892
7:14 the **c** which the Philistines had taken from 5892
18: 6 that the women came out of all **c** of Israel, 5892
30:29 to *them* which *were* in the **c** of 5892
30:29 to *them* which *were* in the **c** of the Kenites, 5892
31: 7 were dead, they forsook the **c**, and fled; 5892
2Sa 2: 1 Shall I go up into any of the **c** of Judah? 5892
2: 3 and they dwelt in the **c** of Hebron. 5892
8: 8 and from Berothai, **c** of Hadadezer, 5892
10:12 for our people, and for the **c** of our God: 5892
12:31 thus did he unto all the **c** of the children of 5892
20: 6 lest he get him fenced **c**, and escape us. 5892
24: 7 *to* all the **c** of the Hivites, and of 5892
1Ki 4:13 threescore great **c** *with* walls and 5892
8:37 enemy besiege them in the land of their **c**; 8179
9:11 king Solomon gave Hiram twenty **c** in 5892
9:12 Hiram came out from Tyre to see the **c** 5892
9:13 What **c** *are* these which thou hast given me, 5892
9:19 all the **c** of store that Solomon had, 5892
9:19 **c** for his chariots, and cities for his 5892
9:19 **c** for his horsemen, and that which 5892
10:26 whom he bestowed in the **c** for chariots, 5892
12:17 of Israel which dwelt in the **c** of Judah, 5892
13:32 high places which *are* in the **c** of Samaria, 5892
15:20 hosts which he had against the **c** of Israel, 5892
15:23 and all that he did, and the **c** which he built, 5892
20:34 *Ben-hadad* said unto him, The **c**, which my 5892
22:39 which he made, and all the **c** that he built, 5892
2Ki 3:25 they beat down the **c**, and *on* every good 5892
13:25 hand of Ben-hadad the son of Hazael the **c**, 5892
13:25 beat him, and recovered the **c** of Israel. 5892
17: 6 river of Gozan, and in the **c** of the Medes. 5892
17: 9 they built them high places in all their **c**, 5892
17:24 placed *them* in the **c** of Samaria instead of 5892
17:24 and dwelt in the **c** thereof. 5892
17:26 and placed in the **c** of Samaria, 5892
17:29 every nation in their **c** wherein they dwelt. 5892
18:11 river of Gozan, and in the **c** of the Medes: 5892
18:13 come up against all the fenced **c** of Judah, 5892
19:25 that thou shouldest be to lay waste fenced **c** 5892
23: 5 incense in the high places in the **c** of Judah, 5892
23: 8 he brought all the priests out of the **c** of 5892
23:19 high places that *were* in the **c** of Samaria, 5892
1Ch 2:22 and twenty **c** in the land of Gilead. 5892
2:23 and the towns thereof, *even* threescore **c**. 5892
4:31 These *were* their **c** unto the reign of David. 5892
4:32 Rimmon, and Tochen, and Ashan, five **c**: 5892
4:33 villages that *were* round about the same **c**, 5892
6:57 to the sons of Aaron they gave the **c** of 5892
6:60 All their **c** throughout their families *were* 5892
6:60 throughout their families *were* thirteen **c**. 5892
6:61 *were* **c** *given* out of the half tribe, NIH
6:61 *of* the half *tribe* of Manasseh, by lot, ten **c**. 5892
6:62 the tribe of Manasseh in Bashan, thirteen **c**. 5892
6:63 and out of the tribe of Zebulun, twelve **c**. 5892
6:64 to the Levites *these* **c** with their suburbs. 5892
6:65 these **c**, which are called by *their* names. 5892
6:66 **c** of their coasts out of the tribe of Ephraim. 5892
6:67 they gave unto them, *of* the **c** of refuge, 5892
9: 2 possessions in their **c** *were*, the Israelites, 5892
10: 7 then they forsook their **c**, and fled: 5892
13: 2 Levites *which are* in their **c** *and* suburbs, 5892
18: 8 and from Chun, **c** of Hadarezer, 5892
19: 7 gathered themselves together from their **c**, 5892
19:13 for our people, and for the **c** of our God: 5892
20: 3 dealt David with all the **c** of the children of 5892
27:25 in the **c**, and in the villages, and in 5892
2Ch 1:14 which he placed in the chariot **c**, and 5892
6:28 if their enemies besiege them in the **c** of 8179
8: 2 That the **c** which Huram had restored to 5892
2Ch 8: 4 all the store **c**, which he built in Hamath. 5892
8: 5 fenced **c**, *with* walls, gates, and bars; 5892
8: 6 all the store **c** that Solomon had, and all 5892
8: 6 all the chariot **c**, and the cities of 5892
8: 6 the **c** of the horsemen, and all that Solomon 5892
9:25 whom he bestowed in the chariot **c**, and 5892
10:17 of Israel that dwelt in the **c** of Judah, 5892
11: 5 and built **c** for defence in Judah. 5892
11:10 *are* in Judah and in Benjamin, fenced **c**. 5892
12: 4 he took the fenced **c** which *pertained* to 5892
13:19 took **c** from him, Beth-el with the towns 5892
14: 5 Also he took away out of all the **c** of Judah 5892
14: 6 he built fenced **c** in Judah: for the land had 5892
14: 7 Let us build these **c**, and make about *them* 5892
14:14 they smote all the **c** round about Gerar; 5892
14:14 they spoiled all the **c**; for there was 5892
15: 8 out of the **c** which he had taken from mount 5892
16: 4 sent the captains of his armies against the **c** 5892
16: 4 and all the store **c** of Naphtali. 5892
17: 2 he placed forces in all the fenced **c** of 5892
17: 2 in the **c** of Ephraim, which Asa his father 5892
17: 7 and to Michaiah, to teach in the **c** of Judah. 5892
17: 9 went about throughout all the **c** of Judah, 5892
17:12 he built in Judah castles, and **c** of store. 5892
17:13 he had much business in the **c** of Judah: 5892
17:19 put in the fenced **c** throughout all Judah. 5892
19: 5 land throughout all the fenced **c** of Judah, 5892
19:10 to you of your brethren that dwell in their **c**, 5892
20: 4 even out of all the **c** of Judah they came to 5892
21: 3 of precious things, with fenced **c** in Judah: 5892
23: 2 gathered the Levites out of all the **c** of 5892
24: 5 Go out unto the **c** of Judah, and gather of 5892
25:13 fell upon the **c** of Judah, from Samaria even 5892
26: 6 built **c** about Ashdod, and among 5892
27: 4 Moreover he built **c** in the mountains of 5892
28:18 The Philistines also had invaded the **c** of 5892
31: 1 all Israel that were present went out to the **c** 5892
31: 1 man to his possession, into their own **c**. 5892
31: 6 and Judah, that dwelt in the **c** of Judah, 5892
31:15 and Shecaniah, in the **c** of the priests, 5892
31:19 *were* in the fields of the suburbs of their **c**, 5892
32: 1 encamped against the fenced **c**, and 5892
32:29 Moreover he provided him **c**, and 5892
33:14 put captains of war in all the fenced **c** of 5892
34: 6 *so did he* in the **c** of Manasseh, and 5892
Ezr 2:70 dwelt in their **c**, and all Israel in their cities. 5892
2:70 dwelt in their cities, and all Israel in their **c**. 5892
3: 1 and the children of Israel *were* in the **c**, 5892
4:10 set in the **c** of Samaria, and the rest *that are* 7149
10:14 wives in our **c** come at appointed times, 5892
Ne 7:73 and all Israel, dwelt in their **c**; 5892
7:73 the children of Israel *were* in their **c**. 5892
8:15 should publish and proclaim in all their **c**, 5892
9:25 they took strong **c**, and a fat land, and 5892
10:37 have the tithes in all the **c** of our tillage. 5892
11: 1 holy city, and nine parts *to dwell* in *other* **c**. 5892
11: 3 in the **c** of Judah dwelt every one in his 5892
11: 3 dwelt every one in his possession in their **c**, 5892
11:20 *and* the Levites, *were* in all the **c** of Judah, 5892
12:44 to gather into them out of the fields of the **c** 5892
Est 9: 2 **c** throughout all the provinces of the king 5892
Job 15:28 he dwelleth in desolate **c**, *and* in houses 5892
Ps 9: 6 thou hast destroyed **c**; their memorial is 5892
69:35 save Zion, and will build the **c** of Judah: 5892
Isa 1: 7 *is* desolate, your **c** *are* burnt *with* fire: 5892
6:11 Until the **c** be wasted without inhabitant, 5892
14:17 a wilderness, and destroyed the **c** thereof; 5892
14:21 nor fill the face of the world *with* **c**. 5892
17: 2 The **c** of Aroer *are* forsaken: they shall be 5892
17: 9 In that day shall his strong **c** be as a 5892
19:18 In that day shall five **c** in the land of Egypt 5892
33: 8 he hath despised the **c**, he regardeth no 5892
36: 1 up against all the defenced **c** of Judah, 5892
37:26 to lay waste defenced **c** *into* ruinous heaps. 5892
40: 9 say unto the **c** of Judah, Behold your God. 5892
42:11 the **c** thereof lift up *their voice*, the villages 5892
44:26 to the **c** of Judah, Ye shall be built, and 5892
54: 3 and make the desolate **c** to be inhabited. 5892
61: 4 they shall repair the waste **c**, 5892
64:10 Thy holy **c** are a wilderness, Zion is a 5892
Jer 1:15 round about, and against all the **c** of Judah. 5892
2:15 his **c** are burnt without inhabitant. 5892
2:28 for *according* to the number of thy **c** are thy 5892
4: 5 and let us go into the defenced **c**. 5892
4: 7 *and* thy **c** shall be laid waste, without an 5892
4:16 give out their voice against the **c** of Judah. 5892
4:26 all the **c** thereof were broken down at 5892
5: 6 a leopard shall watch over their **c**: 5892
5:17 they shall impoverish thy fenced **c**, 5892
7:17 Seest thou not what they do in the **c** of 5892
7:34 will I cause to cease from the **c** of Judah, 5892
8:14 let us enter into the defenced **c**, and let us 5892
9:11 I will make the **c** of Judah desolate, 5892
10:22 to make the **c** of Judah desolate, *and* a den 5892
11: 6 Proclaim all these words in the **c** of Judah, 5892
11:12 shall the **c** of Judah and inhabitants of 5892
11:13 For *according to* the number of thy **c** were 5892
13:19 The **c** of the south shall be shut up, and 5892
17:26 they shall come from the **c** of Judah, and 5892
20:16 let that man be as the **c** which the LORD 5892
22: 6 a wilderness *and* **c** *which* are not inhabited. 5892
25:18 the **c** of Judah, and the kings thereof, *and* 5892
26: 2 and speak unto all the **c** of Judah, 5892
31:21 O virgin of Israel, turn again to these thy **c**, 5892
31:23 in the land of Judah and in the **c** thereof, 5892
31:24 *in* all the **c** thereof together, husbandmen, 5892
32:44 in the **c** of Judah, and in the cities of 5892
32:44 in the **c** of the mountains, and in the cities 5892
32:44 in the **c** of the valley, and in the cities of 5892
32:44 of the valley, and in the **c** of the south: 5892
33:10 *even* in the **c** of Judah, and in the streets of 5892
33:12 and without beast, and in all the **c** thereof, 5892
33:13 In the **c** of the mountains, in the cities of 5892
33:13 in the **c** of the vale, and in the cities of 5892
33:13 in the **c** of the south, and in the land of 5892
Jer 33:13 about Jerusalem, and in the **c** of Judah, 5892
34: 1 and against all the **c** thereof, saying, 5892
34: 7 against all the **c** of Judah that were left, 5892
34: 7 for these defenced **c** remained of the cities 5892
34: 7 for these defenced cities remained of the **c** 5892
34:22 I will make the **c** of Judah a desolation 5892
36: 6 ears of all Judah that come out of their **c**. 5892
36: 9 *to* all the people that came from the **c** of 5892
40: 5 hath made governor over the **c** of Judah, 5892
40:10 and dwell in your **c** that ye have taken. 5892
44: 2 and upon all the **c** of Judah; 5892
44: 6 was kindled in the **c** of Judah and in 5892
44:17 in the **c** of Judah, and in the streets of 5892
44:21 The incense that ye burnt in the **c** of Judah, 5892
48: 9 for the **c** thereof shall be desolate, without 5892
48:15 gone up *out of* her **c**, and his chosen young 5892
48:24 upon all the **c** of the land of Moab, far or 5892
48:28 leave the **c**, and dwell in the rock, and 5892
49: 1 inherit Gad, and his people dwell in his **c**? 5892
49:13 all the **c** thereof shall be perpetual wastes. 5892
49:18 and Gomorrah and the neighbour **c** thereof, NIH
50:32 I will kindle a fire in his **c**, and it shall 5892
50:40 and Gomorrah and the neighbour **c** thereof, NIH
51:43 Her **c** are a desolation, a dry land, and 5892
La 5:11 in Zion, *and* the maids in the **c** of Judah. 5892
Eze 6: 6 In all your dwelling places the **c** shall be 5892
12:20 the **c** that are inhabited shall be laid waste, 5892
19: 7 desolate palaces, and he laid waste their **c**; 5892
25: 9 I *will* open the side of Moab from the **c**, 5892
25: 9 from his **c** *which are* on his frontiers, 5892
26:19 like the **c** that are not inhabited; 5892
29:12 her **c** among the cities *that are* laid waste 5892
29:12 her cities among the **c** *that are* laid waste 5892
30: 7 her **c** shall be in the midst of the cities *that* 5892
30: 7 her cities shall be in the midst of the **c** *that* 5892
30:17 and these **c** shall go into captivity. NIH
35: 4 I will lay thy **c** waste, and thou shalt be 5892
35: 9 and thy **c** shall not return: 5892
36: 4 to the **c** that are forsaken, which became a 5892
36:10 the **c** shall be inhabited, and the wastes 5892
36:33 I will also cause *you* to dwell in the **c**, and 5892
36:35 and ruined **c** *are become* fenced, 5892
36:38 shall the waste **c** be filled *with* flocks of 5892
39: 9 they that dwell in the **c** of Israel shall go 5892
Da 11:15 up a mount, and take the most fenced **c**: 5892
Hos 8:14 and Judah hath multiplied fenced **c**: 5892
8:14 I will send a fire upon his **c**, and it shall 5892
11: 6 the sword shall abide on his **c**, and 5892
13:10 *is any other* that may save thee in all thy **c**? 5892
Am 4: 6 given you cleanness of teeth in all your **c**, 5892
4: 8 So two *or* three **c** wandered unto one city, 5892
9:14 they shall build the waste **c**, and 5892
Ob 1:20 shall possess the **c** of the south. 5892
Mic 5:11 I will cut off the **c** of thy land, and 5892
5:14 of the midst of thee: so will I destroy thy **c**. 5892
7:12 *from* the fortified **c**, and from the fortress 5892
Zep 1:16 the trumpet and alarm against the fenced **c**, 5892
3: 6 their **c** are destroyed, so that there is no 5892
Zec 1:12 mercy on Jerusalem and on the **c** of Judah, 5892
1:17 My **c** through prosperity shall yet be spread 5892
7: 7 and the **c** thereof round about her, 5892
8:20 and the inhabitants of many **c**: 5892
Mt 9:35 And Jesus went about all the **c** and villages, *4172*
10:23 Ye shall not have gone over the **c** of Israel, *4172*
11: 1 thence to teach and to preach in their **c**. *4172*
11:20 Then began he to upbraid the **c** wherein *4172*
14:13 they followed him on foot out of the **c**. *4172*
Mk 6:33 and ran afoot thither out of all **c**, and *4172*
6:56 he entered, into villages, or **c**, or country, *4172*
Lk 4:43 preach the kingdom of God to other **c** also: *4172*
13:22 And he went through the **c** and villages, *4172*
19:17 a very little, have thou authority over ten **c**. *4172*
19:19 likewise to him, Be thou also over five **c**. *4172*
Ac 5:16 There came also a multitude *out* of the **c** *4172*
8:40 passing through he preached in all the **c**, *4172*
14: 6 **c** of Lycaonia, and *unto* the region that lieth *4172*
16: 4 And as they went through the **c**, *4172*
26:11 I persecuted *them* even unto strange **c**. *4172*
2Pe 2: 6 And turning the **c** of Sodom and *4172*
Jude 1: 7 and Gomorrha, and the **c** about them, *4172*
Rev 16:19 three parts, and the **c** of the nations fell: *4172*

CITIZEN (2) [CITIZENS, FELLOWCITIZENS]

Lk 15:15 and joined himself to a **c** of that country; *4177*
Ac 21:39 *a city* in Cilicia, a **c** of no mean city: *4177*

CITIZENS (1) [CITIZEN]

Lk 19:14 But his **c** hated him, and sent a message *4177*

CITIZENSHIP See COMMONWEALTH

CITRON See THYINE

CITY (870) [CITIES]

Ge 4:17 he builded a **c**, and called the name of 5892
4:17 builded a city, and called the name of the **c**, 5892
10:11 and the **c** Rehoboth, and Calah, 5892
10:12 and Calah: the same *is* a great **c**. 5892
11: 4 Go to, let us build us a **c** and a tower, 5892
11: 5 the LORD came down to see the **c** and 5892
11: 8 all the earth: and they left off to build the **c**. 5892
18:24 there be fifty righteous within the **c**: 5892
18:26 I find in Sodom fifty righteous within the **c**, 5892
18:28 wilt thou destroy all the **c** for *lack of* five? 5892
19: 4 the men of the **c**, *even* the men of Sodom, 5892
19:12 and whatsoever thou hast in the **c**, 5892
19:14 for the LORD will destroy this **c**. 5892
19:15 thou be consumed in the iniquity of the **c**. 5892
19:16 him forth, and set him without the **c**. 5892
19:20 this **c** *is* near to flee unto, and it *is* a little 5892
19:21 that I will not overthrow *this* **c**, for 5892
19:22 Therefore the name of the **c** was called 5892
23:10 *even* of all that went in *at* the gate of his **c**, 5892
23:18 before all that went in *at* the gate of his **c**, 5892
24:10 went to Mesopotamia, unto the **c** of Nahor. 5892

Ge 24:11 **c** by a well of water at the time of 5892
24:13 the daughters of the men of the **c** come out 5892
26:33 the name of the **c** *is* Beer-sheba unto this 5892
28:19 the name of *that* **c** *was called* Luz at 5892
33:18 Jacob came to Shalem, a **c** of Shechem, 5892
33:18 and pitched his tent before the **c**. 5892
34:20 his son came unto the gate of their **c**, 5892
34:20 communed with the men of their **c**, saying, 5892
34:24 all that went out of the gate of his **c**; 5892
34:24 all that went out of the gate of his **c**. 5892
34:25 came upon the **c** boldly, and slew all 5892
34:27 spoiled the **c**, because they had defiled their 5892
34:28 that which *was* in the **c**, and that which *was* 5892
35:27 unto the **c** of Arbah, which *is* Hebron, 7151
36:32 and the name of his **c** *was* Dinhabah. 5892
36:35 his stead: and the name of his **c** *was* Avith. 5892
36:39 the name of his **c** *was* Pau; and his wife's 5892
41:48 the field, which *was* round about every **c**, 5892
44: 4 *And* when they were gone out of the **c**, *and* 5892
44:13 every man his ass, and returned to the **c**. 5892
Ex 9:29 As soon as I am gone out of the **c**, 5892
9:33 And Moses went out of the **c** from Pharaoh, 5892
Lev 14:40 them into an unclean place without the **c**: 5892
14:41 off without the **c** into an unclean place: 5892
14:45 he shall carry *them* forth out of the **c** into 5892
14:53 he shall let go the living bird out of the **c** 5892
25:29 if a man sell a dwelling house in a walled **c**, 5892
25:30 the house that *is* in the walled **c** shall be 5892
25:33 that was sold, and the **c** of his possession, 5892
Nu 20:16 a **c** in the uttermost of thy border: 5892
21:26 For Heshbon *was* the **c** of Sihon the king of 5892
21:27 let the **c** of Sihon be built and prepared: 5892
21:28 of Heshbon, a flame from the **c** of Sihon: 7151
22:36 he went out to meet him unto a **c** of Moab, 5892
24:19 shall destroy him that remaineth of the **c**. 5892
35: 4 *shall reach* from the wall of the **c** and 5892
35: 5 ye shall measure from without the **c** *on* 5892
35: 5 and the **c** *shall be* in the midst: 5892
35:25 the congregation shall restore him to the **c** 5892
35:26 *without* the border of the **c** of his refuge, 5892
35:27 without the borders of the **c** of his refuge, 5892
35:28 Because he should have remained in the **c** 5892
35:32 for him that is fled to the **c** of his refuge, 5892
Dt 2:34 the women, and the little ones, of every **c**, 5892
2:36 *from* the **c** that *is* by the river, even unto 5892
2:36 there was not one **c** too strong for us: 7151
3: 4 there was not a **c** which we took not from 7151
3: 6 the men, women, and children, of every **c**. 5892
13:13 have withdrawn the inhabitants of their **c**, 5892
13:15 of that **c** with the edge of the sword, 5892
13:16 shalt burn with fire the **c**, and all the spoil 5892
19:12 the elders of his **c** shall send and fetch him 5892
20:10 When thou comest nigh unto a **c** to fight 5892
20:14 and the cattle, and all that is in the **c**, 5892
20:19 When thou shalt besiege a **c** a long time, 5892
20:20 thou shalt build bulwarks against the **c** that 5892
21: 3 *that* the **c** *which is* next unto the slain *man*, 5892
21: 3 even the elders of that **c** shall take a heifer, 5892
21: 4 the elders of that **c** shall bring down 5892
21: 6 all the elders of that **c**, *that are* next unto 5892
21:19 bring him out unto the elders of his **c**, and 5892
21:20 they shall say unto the elders of his **c**, 5892
21:21 all the men of his **c** shall stone him with 5892
22:15 virginity unto the elders of the **c** in the gate: 5892
22:17 spread the cloth before the elders of the **c**. 5892
22:18 the elders of that **c** shall take *that* man and 5892
22:21 the men of her **c** shall stone her with stones 5892
22:23 a man find her in the **c**, and lie with her; 5892
22:24 bring them both out unto the gate of that **c**, 5892
22:24 because she cried not, *being* in the **c**; 5892
25: 8 the elders of his **c** shall call him, and 5892
28: 3 Blessed *shalt* thou *be* in the **c**, and 5892
28:16 Cursed *shalt* thou *be* in the **c**, and 5892
34: 3 of Jericho, the **c** of palm trees, unto Zoar. 5892
Jos 3:16 from the **c** Adam, that *is* beside Zaretan: 5892
6: 3 ye shall compass the **c**, all *ye* men of war, 5892
6: 3 men of war, *and* go round about the **c** once. 5892
6: 4 the seventh day ye shall compass the **c** 5892
6: 5 the wall of the **c** shall fall down flat, 5892
6: 7 compass the **c**, and let him that is armed 5892
6:11 So the ark of the LORD compassed the **c**, 5892
6:14 the second day they compassed the **c** once, 5892
6:15 compassed the **c** after the same manner 5892
6:15 only on that day they compassed the **c** 5892
6:16 Shout; for the LORD hath given you the **c**. 5892
6:17 the **c** shall be accursed, *even* it, and all that 5892
6:20 so that the people went up into the **c**, 5892
6:20 straight before him, and they took the **c**. 5892
6:21 they utterly destroyed all that *was* in the **c**, 5892
6:24 they burnt the **c** with fire, and all that *was* 5892
6:26 that riseth up and buildeth this **c** Jericho: 5892
8: 1 and his people, and his **c**, and his land: 5892
8: 2 lay thee an ambush for the **c** behind it. 5892
8: 4 Behold, ye shall lie in wait against the **c**, 5892
8: 4 in wait against the city, *even* behind the **c**: 5892
8: 4 go not very far from the **c**, but be ye all 5892
8: 5 that *are* with me, will approach unto the **c**: 5892
8: 6 till we have drawn them from the **c**; 5892
8: 7 up from the ambush, and seize upon the **c**: 5892
8: 8 it shall be, when ye have taken the **c**, 5892
8: 8 taken the city, *that* ye shall set the **c** on fire: 5892
8:11 came before the **c**, and pitched on the north 5892
8:12 and Ai, on the west side of the **c**. 5892
8:13 all the host that *was* on the north of the **c**, 5892
8:13 and their liers in wait on the west of the **c**, 5892
8:14 the men of the **c** went out against Israel to 5892
8:14 liers in ambush against him behind the **c**. 5892
8:16 and were drawn away from the **c**. 5892
8:17 they left the **c** open, and pursued after 5892
8:18 spear that *he had* in his hand toward the **c**. 5892
8:19 they entered *into* the **c**, and took it, and 5892
8:19 and took it, and hasted and set the **c** on fire. 5892
8:20 the smoke of the **c** ascended up to heaven, 5892
8:21 Israel saw that the ambush had taken the **c**, 5892
8:21 that the smoke of the **c** ascended, then 5892

Jos 8:22 the other issued out of the **c** against them; 5892
8:27 the spoil of that **c** Israel took for a prey 5892
8:29 cast it at the entering of the gate of the **c**, 5892
10: 2 because Gibeon *was* a great **c**, 5892
11:19 There was not a **c** that made peace with 5892
13: 9 the **c** that *is* in the midst of the river, and 5892
13:16 the **c** that *is* in the midst of the river, and 5892
15:13 *even* the **c** of Arba the father of Anak, 7151
15:13 Arba the father of Anak, which **c** *is* Hebron. NIH
15:62 and the **c** of salt, and En-gedi; 5892
18:14 a **c** of the children of Judah: 5892
19:29 turneth *to* Ramah, and to the strong **c** Tyre; 5892
19:50 they gave him the **c** which he asked, 5892
19:50 and he built the **c**, and dwelt therein. 5892
20: 4 stand *at* the entering of the gate of the **c**, 5892
20: 4 his cause in the ears of the elders of that **c**, 5892
20: 4 they shall take him into the **c** unto them, 5892
20: 6 he shall dwell in that **c**, until he stand 5892
20: 6 come unto his own **c**, and unto his own 5892
20: 6 own house, unto the **c** from whence he fled. 5892
21:11 they gave them the **c** of Arbah the father of 7151
21:11 which **c** *is* Hebron, in the hill *country* of NIH
21:12 the fields of the **c**, and the villages thereof, 5892
21:13 *to be* a **c** of refuge for the slayer; 5892
21:21 *to be* a **c** of refuge for the slayer; 5892
21:27 *to be* a **c** of refuge for the slayer; 5892
21:32 *to be* a **c** of refuge for the slayer; 5892
21:38 *to be* a **c** of refuge for the slayer; 5892
Jdg 1: 8 the edge of the sword, and set the **c** on fire. 5892
1:16 went up out of the **c** of palm trees with 5892
1:17 and the name of the **c** was called Hormah. 5892
1:23 (Now the name of the **c** before *was* Luz.) 5892
1:24 the spies saw a man come forth out of the **c**, 5892
1:24 the entrance into the **c**, and we will shew 5892
1:25 he shewed them the entrance into the **c**, 5892
1:25 they smote the **c** with the edge of 5892
1:26 built a **c**, and called the name thereof Luz: 5892
3:13 and possessed the **c** of palm trees. 5892
6:27 the men of the **c**, that *he* could not do *it* by 5892
6:28 when the men of the **c** arose early in 5892
6:30 the men of the **c** said unto Joash, Bring out 5892
8:16 he took the elders of the **c**, and thorns of 5892
8:17 tower of Penuel, and slew the men of the **c**. 5892
8:27 and put it in his **c**, *even* in Ophrah: 5892
9:30 when Zebul the ruler of the **c** heard 5892
9:31 and behold, they fortify the **c** against thee. 5892
9:33 thou shalt rise early, and set upon the **c**: 5892
9:35 stood *in* the entering of the gate of the **c**: 5892
9:43 the people *were* come forth out of the **c**; 5892
9:44 stood *in* the entering of the gate of the **c**: 5892
9:45 Abimelech fought against the **c** all that day; 5892
9:45 he took the **c**, and slew the people that *was* 5892
9:45 beat down the **c**, and sowed it *with* salt. 5892
9:51 there was a strong tower within the **c**, and 5892
9:51 all they of the **c**, and shut *it* to them, and 5892
14:18 the men of the **c** said unto him on 5892
16: 2 wait for him all night in the gate of the **c**, 5892
16: 3 took the doors of the gate of the **c**, and 5892
17: 8 the man departed out of the **c** from 5892
18:27 edge of the sword, and burnt the **c** with fire. 5892
18:28 And they built a **c**, and dwelt therein. 5892
18:29 they called the name of the **c** Dan, after 5892
18:29 howbeit the name of the **c** *was* Laish at 5892
19:11 and let us turn in into this **c** of the Jebusites, 5892
19:12 We will not turn aside hither into the **c** of a 5892
19:15 he sat him down in a street of the **c**: 5892
19:17 saw a wayfaring man in the street of the **c**: 5892
19:22 behold, the men of the **c**, certain sons of 5892
20:11 men of Israel were gathered against the **c**, 5892
20:31 *and* were drawn away from the **c**; 5892
20:32 draw them from the **c** unto the highways. 5892
20:37 smote all the **c** with the edge of the sword. 5892
20:38 great flame with smoke rise up out of the **c**. 5892
20:40 arise up out of the **c** *with* a pillar of smoke, 5892
20:40 the flame of the **c** ascended up to heaven. 5892
20:48 as well the men of *every* **c**, as the beast, and 5892
Ru 1:19 that all the **c** was moved about them, and 5892
2:18 she took *it* up, and went *into* the **c**: and 5892
3:11 for all the **c** of my people doth know that 8179
3:15 and laid *it* on her: and he went *into* the **c**. 5892
4: 2 he took ten men of the elders of the **c**, and 5892
1Sa 1: 3 this man went up out of his **c** yearly to 5892
4:13 when the man came into the **c**, and told *it*, 5892
4:13 into the city, and told *it*, all the **c** cried out. 5892
5: 9 the hand of the LORD was against the **c** 5892
5: 9 he smote the men of the **c**, both small and 5892
5:11 a deadly destruction throughout all the **c**; 5892
5:12 and the cry of the **c** went up *to* heaven. 5892
8:22 men of Israel, Go ye every man unto his **c**. 5892
9: 6 *there is* in this **c** a man of God, and *he is* an 5892
9:10 So they went unto the **c** where the man of 5892
9:11 *And* as they went up the hill to the **c**, they 5892
9:12 haste now, for he came to day to the **c**; 5892
9:13 As soon as ye be come *into* the **c**, ye shall 5892
9:14 they went up *into* the **c**: *and* when they 5892
9:14 *and* when they were come into the **c**, 5892
9:25 come down from the high place *into* the **c**, 5892
9:27 they were going down to the end of the **c**, 5892
10: 5 to pass, when thou art come thither *to* the **c**, 5892
15: 5 Saul came to a **c** of Amalek, and laid wait 5892
20: 6 me that *he* might run *to* Beth-lehem his **c**: 5892
20:29 for our family hath a sacrifice in the **c**; and 5892
20:40 and said unto him, Go, carry *them to* the **c**. 5892
20:42 and departed: and Jonathan went *into* the **c**. 5892
22:19 Nob, the **c** of the priests, smote he with 5892
23:10 to Keilah, to destroy the **c** for my sake. 5892
27: 5 thy servant dwell in the royal **c** with thee? 5892
28: 3 buried him in Ramah, even in his own **c**. 5892
30: 3 So David and his men came to the **c**, and 5892
2Sa 5: 7 hold of Zion: the same *is* the **c** of David. 5892
5: 9 in the fort, and called it the **c** of David. 5892
6:10 the LORD unto him into the **c** of David: 5892
6:12 *into* the **c** of David with gladness. 5892
6:16 as the ark of the LORD came *into* the **c** of 5892
10: 3 to search the **c**, and to spy it out, and 5892

2Sa 10:14 *also* before Abishai, and entered *into* the **c**. 5892
11:16 it came to pass, when Joab observed the **c**, 5892
11:17 the men of the **c** went out, and fought with 5892
11:20 *so* nigh unto the **c** when *ye* did fight? 5892
11:25 make thy battle *more* strong against the **c**, 5892
12: 1 unto him, There were two men in one **c**; 5892
12:26 children of Ammon, and took the royal **c**. 5892
12:27 and have taken the **c** of waters. 5892
12:28 and encamp against the **c**, and take it: 5892
12:28 lest I take the **c**, and it be called after my 5892
12:30 he brought forth the spoil of the **c** in great 5892
15: 2 unto him, and said, Of what **c** *art* thou? 5892
15:12 from his **c**, *even* from Giloh, 5892
15:14 and smite the **c** with the edge of the sword. 5892
15:24 all the people had done passing out of the **c**. 5892
15:25 Carry back the ark of God *into* the **c**: 5892
15:27 return *into* the **c** in peace, and your two 5892
15:34 if thou return *to* the **c**, and say unto 5892
15:37 So Hushai David's friend came *into* the **c**, 5892
17:13 if he be gotten into a **c**, then shall all Israel 5892
17:13 shall all Israel bring ropes to that **c**, and 5892
17:17 they might not be seen to come into the **c**: 5892
17:23 to his **c**, and put his household in order, 5892
18: 3 *it is* better that thou succour us out of the **c**. 5892
19: 3 gat them by stealth that day *into* the **c**, 5892
19:37 that I may die in mine own **c**, *and be buried* 5892
20:15 they cast up a bank against the **c**, and 5892
20:16 cried a wise woman out of the **c**, Hear, 5892
20:19 thou seekest to destroy a **c** and a mother in 5892
20:21 him only, and I will depart from the **c**. 5892
20:22 they retired from the **c**, every man to his 5892
24: 5 *on* the right side of the **c** that *lieth* in 5892
1Ki 1:41 Wherefore *is this* noise of the **c** being in an 7151
1:45 thence rejoicing, so that the **c** rang again. 7151
2:10 and was buried in the **c** of David. 5892
3: 1 and brought her into the **c** of David, 5892
8: 1 of the LORD out of the **c** of David, 5892
8:16 I chose no **c** out of all the tribes of Israel to 5892
8:44 shall pray unto the LORD toward the **c** 5892
8:48 the **c** which thou hast chosen, and the house 5892
9:16 slain the Canaanites that dwelt in the **c**, and 5892
9:24 Pharaoh's daughter came up out of the **c** of 5892
11:27 repaired the breaches of the **c** of David his 5892
11:32 the **c** which I have chosen out of all 5892
11:36 the **c** which I have chosen me to put my 5892
11:43 and was buried in the **c** of David his father: 5892
13:25 told *it* in the **c** where the old prophet dwelt. 5892
13:29 the old prophet came to the **c**, to mourn and 5892
14:11 Him that dieth of Jeroboam in the **c** shall 5892
14:12 *and* when thy feet enter into the **c**, the child 5892
14:21 the **c** which the LORD did choose out of 5892
14:31 was buried with his fathers in the **c** of 5892
15: 8 and they buried him in the **c** of David: 5892
15:24 was buried with his fathers in the **c** of 5892
16: 4 Him that dieth of Baasha in the **c** shall 5892
16:18 when Zimri saw that the **c** was taken, 5892
16:24 and called the name of the **c** which he built, 5892
17:10 when he came to the gate of the **c**, behold, 5892
20: 2 to Ahab king of Israel into the **c**, 5892
20:12 they set *themselves in array* against the **c**. 5892
20:19 princes of the provinces came out of the **c**, 5892
20:30 the rest fled to Aphek, into the **c**; and 5892
20:30 Ben-hadad fled, and came into the **c**, 5892
21: 8 and to the nobles that *were* in his **c**, 5892
21:11 the men of his **c**, *even* the elders and 5892
21:11 nobles who *were* the inhabitants in his **c**, 5892
21:13 they carried him forth out of the **c**, and 5892
21:24 Him that dieth of Ahab in the **c** the dogs 5892
22:26 him back unto Amon the governor of the **c**, 5892
22:36 Every man to his **c**, and every man to his 5892
22:50 was buried with his fathers in the **c** of 5892
2Ki 2:19 the men of the **c** said unto Elisha, Behold, 5892
2:19 pray thee, the situation of *this* **c** *is* pleasant, 5892
2:23 there came forth little children out of the **c**, 5892
3:19 ye shall smite every fenced **c**, and 5892
3:19 every choice **c**, and shall fell every good 5892
6:14 came by night, and compassed the **c** about. 5892
6:15 a host compassed the **c** both with horses 5892
6:19 This *is* not the way, neither *is* this the **c**: 5892
7: 4 We will enter *into* the **c**, then the famine *is* 5892
7: 4 the famine *is* in the **c**, and we shall die 5892
7:10 and called unto the porter of the **c**: 5892
7:12 saying, When they come out of the **c**, we 5892
7:12 shall catch them alive, and get into the **c**. 5892
7:13 which are left in **the c**[S], (behold, 1886.3
8:24 was buried with his fathers in the **c** of 5892
9:15 let none go forth *nor* escape out of the **c** to 5892
9:28 sepulchre with his fathers in the **c** of David. 5892
10: 2 and horses, a fenced **c** also, and armour; 5892
10: 5 *he* that *was* over the **c**, the elders also, and 5892
10: 6 *were* with the great *men* of the **c**, 5892
10:25 and went to the **c** of the house of Baal. 5892
11:20 of the land rejoiced, and the **c** was in quiet: 5892
12:21 they buried him with his fathers in the **c** of 5892
14:20 with his fathers in the **c** of David. 5892
15: 7 they buried him with his fathers in the **c** of 5892
15:38 was buried with his fathers in the **c** of 5892
16:20 was buried with his fathers in the **c** of 5892
17: 9 the tower of the watchmen to the fenced **c**. 5892
18: 8 the tower of the watchmen to the fenced **c**. 5892
18:30 this **c** shall not be delivered into the hand of 5892
19:13 the king of the **c** of Sepharvaim, *of* Hena, 5892
19:32 He shall not come into this **c**, nor shoot an 5892
19:33 shall not come into this **c**, saith 5892
19:34 For I will defend this **c**, to save it, for mine 5892
20: 6 this **c** out of the hand of the king of 5892
20: 6 I will defend this **c** for mine own sake, and 5892
20:20 and a conduit, and brought water into the **c**, 5892
23: 8 of the gate of Joshua the governor of the **c**, 5892
23: 8 on a man's left hand at the gate of the **c**. 5892
23:17 the men of the **c** told him, *It is* 5892
23:27 will cast off this **c** Jerusalem which I have 5892
24:10 *against* Jerusalem, and the **c** was besieged. 5892
24:11 king of Babylon came against the **c**, 5892
25: 2 the **c** was besieged unto the eleventh year 5892

C

2Ki 25: 3 *fourth* month the famine prevailed in the **c**, 5892
25: 4 the **c** was broken up, and all the men of war 5892
25: 4 (now the Chaldees *were* against the **c** round 5892
25:11 the rest of the people that were left in the **c**, 5892
25:19 out of the **c** he took an officer that was set 5892
25:19 which were found in the **c**, and 5892
25:19 people of the land that were found in the **c**: 5892
1Ch 1:43 and the name of his **c** *was* Dinhabah. 5892
1:46 his stead: and the name of his **c** *was* Avith. 5892
1:50 the name of his **c** *was* Pai; and his wife's 5892
6:56 the fields of the **c**, and the villages thereof, 5892
6:57 *the* **c** of refuge, and Libnah with her NIH
11: 5 the castle of Zion, which *is* the **c** of David. 5892
11: 7 they called it the **c** of David. 5892
11: 8 he built the **c** round about, even from Millo 5892
11: 8 and Joab repaired the rest of the **c**. 5892
13:13 the ark *home* to himself to the **c** of David, 5892
15: 1 *David* made him houses in the **c** of David, 5892
15:29 of the LORD came to the **c** of David, 5892
19: 9 the battle in array *before* the gate of the **c**: 5892
19:15 Abishai his brother, and entered into the **c**. 5892
20: 2 also exceeding much spoil *out* of the **c**. 5892
2Ch 5: 2 of the LORD out of the **c** of David, 5892
6: 5 **c** among all the tribes of Israel to build a 5892
6:34 they pray unto thee toward this **c** which 5892
6:38 *toward* the **c** which thou hast chosen, and 5892
8:11 **c** of David unto the house that he had built 5892
9:31 he was buried in the **c** of David his father: 5892
11:12 in every **several c** *he put* 5892+5892+2050.1
11:23 and Benjamin, unto every fenced **c**: 5892
12:13 the **c** which the LORD had chosen out of 5892
12:16 and was buried in the **c** of David: 5892
14: 1 and they buried him in the **c** of David: 5892
15: 6 was destroyed of nation, and **c** of city: 5892
15: 6 was destroyed of nation, and city of **c**: 5892
16:14 which he had made for himself in the **c** of 5892
18:25 him back to Amon the governor of the **c**, 5892
19: 5 all the fenced cities of Judah, **c** by city, 5892
19: 5 all the fenced cities of Judah, city by **c**, 5892
21: 1 was buried with his fathers in the **c** of 5892
21:20 Howbeit they buried him in the **c** of David, 5892
23:21 the **c** was quiet, after that they had slain 5892
24:16 they buried him in the **c** of David among 5892
24:25 they buried him in the **c** of David, but 5892
25:28 buried him with his fathers in the **c** of 5892
27: 9 and they buried him in the **c** of David: 5892
28:15 the **c** of palm trees, to their brethren: 5892
28:25 in every **several c** of Judah 5892+5892+2050.1
28:27 they buried him in the **c**, *even* in Jerusalem: 5892
29:20 gathered the rulers of the **c**, and went up *to* 5892
30:10 So the posts passed from **c** to city through 5892
30:10 So the posts passed from city to **c** through 5892
31:19 in every **several c**, the men 5892+5892+2050.1
32: 3 of the fountains which *were* without the **c**: 5892
32: 5 repaired Millo *in* the **c** of David, and 5892
32: 6 to him in the street of the gate of the **c**, 5892
32:18 to trouble them; that they might take the **c**. 5892
32:30 down to the west *side* of the **c** of David. 5892
33:14 Now after this he built a wall without the **c** 5892
33:15 in Jerusalem, and cast *them* out of the **c**. 5892
34: 8 Maaseiah the governor of the **c**, and Joah 5892
Ezr 2: 1 and Judah, every one unto his **c**; 5892
4:12 building the rebellious and the bad **c**, and 7149
4:13 if this **c** be builded, and the walls set up 7149
4:15 and know that this **c** *is* a rebellious city, and 7149
4:15 and know that this city *is* a rebellious **c**, and 7149
4:15 for which *cause* was this **c** destroyed. 7149
4:16 if this **c** be builded *again*, and the walls 7149
4:19 it is found that this **c** of old time *hath* made 7149
4:21 *that* this **c** be not builded, until *another* 7149
10:14 them the elders of **every c**, 5892+5892+2050.1
Ne 2: 3 when the **c**, the place of my fathers' 5892
2: 5 unto the **c** of my fathers' sepulchres, that I 5892
2: 8 for the wall of the **c**, and for the house that 5892
3:15 unto the stairs that go down from the **c** of 5892
7: 4 Now the **c** *was* large and great: but 5892
7: 6 and to Judah, every one unto his **c**; 5892
11: 1 one of ten to dwell in Jerusalem the holy **c**, 5892
11: 9 the son of Senuah *was* second over the **c**. 5892
11:18 All the Levites in the holy **c** *were* two 5892
12:37 they went up by the stairs of the **c** of David, 5892
13:18 bring all this evil upon us, and upon this **c**? 5892
Est 3:15 to drink; but the **c** Shushan was perplexed. 5892
4: 1 went out into the midst of the **c**, and 5892
4: 6 forth to Mordecai unto the street of the **c**, 5892
6: 9 on horseback through the street of the **c**, 5892
6:11 on horseback through the street of the **c**, 5892
8:11 **every c** to gather 3605+5892+5892+2050.1
8:15 and the **c** of Shushan rejoiced and was glad. 5892
8:17 in **every c**, 3605+5892+5892+2050.1
9:28 every province, and **every c**; 5892+5892+2050.1
Job 24:12 Men groan from out of the **c**, and the soul 5892
29: 7 When I went out *to* the gate through the **c**, 7176
39: 7 He scorneth the multitude of the **c**, 7151
Ps 31:21 me his marvellous kindness in a strong **c**. 5892
46: 4 the streams whereof shall make glad the **c** 5892
48: 1 greatly to be praised in the **c** of our God, 5892
48: 2 sides of the north, the **c** of the great King. 7151
48: 8 have we seen in the **c** of the LORD of 5892
48: 8 of the LORD of hosts, in the **c** of our God: 5892
55: 9 for I have seen violence and strife in the **c**. 5892
59: 6 noise like a dog, and go round about the **c**. 5892
59:14 noise like a dog, and go round about the **c**. 5892
60: 9 Who will bring me *into* the strong **c**? 5892
72:16 *they* of the **c** shall flourish like grass of 5892
87: 3 *things* are spoken of thee, O **c** of God. 5892
101: 8 all wicked doers from the **c** of the LORD. 5892
107: 4 a solitary way; they found no **c** to dwell in. 5892
107: 7 that *they* might go to a **c** of habitation. 5892
107:36 that they may prepare a **c** for habitation; 5892
108:10 Who will bring me *into* the strong **c**? 5892
122: 3 Jerusalem *is* builded as a **c** that is compact 5892
127: 1 except the LORD keep the **c**, 5892
Pr 1:21 in the **c** she uttereth her words, *saying*, 5892
8: 3 She crieth at the gates, at the entry of the **c**, 7176
Pr 9: 3 she crieth upon the highest places of the **c**, 7176
9:14 on a seat in the high places of the **c**, 7176
10:15 The rich *man's* wealth *is* his strong **c**: 7151
11:10 well with the righteous, the **c** rejoiceth: 7151
11:11 By the blessing of the upright the **c** is 7176
16:32 that ruleth his spirit than he that taketh a **c**. 5892
18:11 The rich *man's* wealth *is* his strong **c**, and 7151
18:19 *is harder to be won* than a strong **c**: 7151
21:22 A wise *man* scaleth the **c** of the mighty, and 5892
25:28 own spirit *is like* a **c** *that is* broken down, 5892
29: 8 Scornful men bring a **c** into a snare: but 7151
Ecc 7:19 than ten mighty *men* which are in the **c**. 5892
8:10 they were forgotten in the **c** where they had 5892
9:14 *There was* a little **c**, and few men within it; 5892
9:15 and he by his wisdom delivered the **c**; 5892
10:15 because he knoweth not how to go to the **c**. 5892
SS 3: 2 go about the **c** in the streets and in 5892
3: 3 The watchmen that go about the **c** found 5892
5: 7 The watchmen that went about the **c** found 5892
Isa 1: 8 in a garden of cucumbers, as a besieged **c**. 5892
1:21 How is the faithful **c** become a harlot! 7151
1:26 The **c** of righteousness, the faithful city. 5892
1:26 The city of righteousness, the faithful **c**. 7151
14: 4 the oppressor ceased! the **golden c** ceased! 4062
14:31 cry, O **c**; thou, whole Palestina, 5892
17: 1 Damascus *is* taken away from *being* a **c**, 5892
19: 2 **c** against city, *and* kingdom against 5892
19: 2 city against **c**, *and* kingdom against 5892
19:18 one shall be called, The **c** of destruction. 5892
22: 2 full *of* stirs, a tumultuous **c**, a joyous city: 5892
22: 2 full *of* stirs, a tumultuous city, a joyous **c**: 7151
22: 9 Ye have seen also the breaches of the **c** of 5892
23: 7 *Is* this your joyous **c**, whose antiquity *is* of NIH
23: 8 the crowning **c**, whose merchants *are* NIH
23:11 **c**, to destroy the strong holds thereof. NIH
23:16 Take a harp, go about the **c**, thou harlot that 5892
24:10 The **c** of confusion is broken down: 7151
24:12 In the **c** is left desolation, and the gate is 5892
25: 2 For thou hast made of a **c** a heap; *of* a 5892
25: 2 of a city a heap; *of* a defenced **c** a ruin: 7151
25: 2 a palace of strangers to be no **c**; it shall 5892
25: 3 the **c** of the terrible nations shall fear thee. 7151
26: 1 We have a strong **c**; salvation will *God* 5892
26: 5 the lofty **c**, he layeth it low; he layeth it 7151
27:10 Yet the defenced **c** *shall be* desolate, *and* 5892
29: 1 to Ariel, to Ariel, the **c** *where* David dwelt! 7151
32:13 upon all the houses of joy *in* the joyous **c**: 7151
32:14 the multitude of the **c** shall be left; the forts 5892
32:19 and the **c** shall be low in a low place. 5892
33:20 Look upon Zion, the **c** of our solemnities: 7151
36:15 this **c** shall not be delivered into the hand of 5892
37:13 the king of the **c** of Sepharvaim, Hena, and 5892
37:33 He shall not come into this **c**, nor shoot an 5892
37:34 shall not come into this **c**, saith 5892
37:35 For I will defend this **c** to save it for mine 5892
38: 6 this **c** out of the hand of the king of 5892
38: 6 king of Assyria: and I will defend this **c**. 5892
45:13 he shall build my **c**, and he shall let go my 5892
48: 2 For they call themselves of the holy **c**, and 5892
52: 1 O Jerusalem, the holy **c**: 5892
60:14 they shall call thee, The **c** of the LORD, 5892
62:12 be called, Sought out, A **c** not forsaken. 5892
66: 6 A voice of noise from the **c**, a voice from 5892
Jer 1:18 I have made thee *this* day a defenced **c**, and 5892
3:14 I will take you one of a **c**, and two of a 5892
4:29 The whole **c** shall flee for the noise of the 5892
4:29 every **c** *shall be* forsaken, and not a man 5892
6: 6 this is the **c** to be visited; she *is* wholly 5892
8:16 is in it; the **c**, and those that dwell therein. 5892
14:18 if I enter *into* the **c**, then behold them that 5892
15: 8 upon it suddenly, and terrors *upon* the **c**. 5892
17:24 the gates of this **c** on the sabbath day, 5892
17:25 shall there enter into the gates of this **c** 5892
17:25 and this **c** shall remain for ever. 5892
19: 8 I will make this **c** desolate, and a hissing; 5892
19:11 Even so will I break this people and this **c**, 5892
19:12 and *even* make this **c** as Tophet: 5892
19:15 I will bring upon this **c** and upon all her 5892
20: 5 I will deliver all the strength of this **c**, 5892
21: 4 will assemble them into the midst of this **c**. 5892
21: 6 I will smite the inhabitants of this **c**, both 5892
21: 7 such as are left in this **c** from the pestilence, 5892
21: 9 He that abideth in this **c** shall die by 5892
21:10 For I have set my face against this **c** for 5892
22: 8 many nations shall pass by this **c**, and 5892
22: 8 the LORD done thus unto this great **c**? 5892
23:39 the **c** that I gave you and your fathers, *and* 5892
25:29 I begin to bring evil on the **c** which is 5892
26: 6 will make this **c** a curse to all the nations of 5892
26: 9 this **c** shall be desolate without an 5892
26:11 for he hath prophesied against this **c**, as ye 5892
26:12 against this **c** all the words that ye have 5892
26:15 upon this **c**, and upon the inhabitants 5892
26:20 who prophesied against this **c** and 5892
27:17 live: wherefore should this **c** be laid waste? 5892
27:19 residue of the vessels that remain in this **c**, 5892
29: 7 seek the peace of the **c** whither I have 5892
29:16 of all the people that dwelleth in this **c**, 5892
30:18 the **c** shall be builded upon her own heap, 5892
31:38 that the **c** shall be built to the LORD from 5892
32: 3 I *will* give this **c** into the hand of the king 5892
32:24 they are come *unto* the **c** to take it; 5892
32:24 the **c** is given into the hand of 5892
32:25 for the **c** is given into the hand of 5892
32:28 I *will* give this **c** into the hand of 5892
32:29 that fight against this **c**, shall come and 5892
32:29 shall come and set fire on this **c**, and burn it 5892
32:31 For this **c** hath been to me *as* a provocation 5892
32:36 of Israel, concerning this **c**, whereof ye say, 5892
33: 4 concerning the houses of this **c**, 5892
33: 5 wickedness I have hid my face from this **c**. 5892
34: 2 I *will* give this **c** into the hand of the king 5892
34:22 and cause them to return to this **c**; 5892
37: 8 fight against this **c**, and take it, and burn it 5892
37:10 man in his tent, and burn this **c** with fire. 5892
Jer 37:21 until all the bread in the **c** were spent. 5892
38: 2 He that remaineth in this **c** shall die by 5892
38: 3 This **c** shall surely be given into the hand of 5892
38: 4 of the men of war that remain in this **c**, 5892
38: 9 he is: for *there is* no more bread in the **c**. 5892
38:17 and this **c** shall not be burnt with fire; 5892
38:18 shall this **c** be given into the hand of 5892
38:23 thou shalt cause this **c** to be burnt with fire. 5892
39: 2 *day* of the month, the **c** was broken up. 5892
39: 4 and went forth out of the **c** by night, 5892
39: 9 of the people that remained in the **c**, 5892
39:16 I *will* bring my words upon this **c** for evil, 5892
41: 7 *so*, when they came into the midst of the **c**, 5892
46: 8 I will destroy the **c** and the inhabitants 5892
47: 2 the **c**, and them that dwell therein: 5892
48: 8 the spoiler shall come upon every **c**, and 5892
48: 8 upon every city, and no **c** shall escape: 5892
49:25 How is the **c** of praise not left, the city of 5892
49:25 the city of praise not left, the **c** of my joy! 7151
51:31 to shew the king of Babylon that his **c** is 5892
52: 5 So the **c** was besieged unto the eleventh 5892
52: 6 the famine was sore in the **c**, so that there 5892
52: 7 the **c** was broken up, and all the men of war 5892
52: 7 went forth out of the **c** by night *by* the way 5892
52: 7 (now the Chaldeans *were* by the **c** round 5892
52:15 residue of the people that remained in the **c**, 5892
52:25 He took also out of the **c** an eunuch, 5892
52:25 king's person, which were found in the **c**; 5892
52:25 that were found in the midst of the **c**. 5892
La 1: 1 How doth the **c** sit solitary, *that was* full of 5892
1:19 and mine elders gave up the ghost in the **c**, 5892
2:11 the sucklings swoon in the streets of the **c**. 7151
2:12 as the wounded in the streets of the **c**, 5892
2:15 *saying*, *Is* this the **c** that *men* call The 5892
3:51 because of all the daughters of my **c**. 5892
Eze 4: 1 and pourtray upon it *the* **c**, *even* Jerusalem: 5892
4: 3 it *for* a wall of iron between thee and the **c**: 5892
5: 2 with fire a third *part* in the midst of the **c**, 5892
7:15 he that *is* in the **c**, famine and 5892
7:23 bloody crimes, and the **c** is full *of* violence. 5892
9: 1 Cause them that have charge over the **c** to 5892
9: 4 Go through the midst of the **c** through 5892
9: 5 Go ye after him through the **c**, and smite: 5892
9: 7 And they went forth, and slew in the **c**. 5892
9: 9 full *of* blood, and the **c** full *of* perverseness: 5892
10: 2 the cherubims, and scatter *them* over the **c**. 5892
11: 2 and give wicked counsel in this **c**: 5892
11: 3 this **c** *is* the caldron, and we *be* the flesh. NIH
11: 6 Ye have multiplied your slain in this **c**, 5892
11: 7 they *are* the flesh, and this **c** *is* the caldron: NIH
11:11 This **c** shall not be your caldron, NIH
11:23 LORD went up from the midst of the **c**, 5892
11:23 mountain which *is* on the east side of the **c**. 5892
17: 4 of traffick; he set it in a **c** of merchants. 5892
21:19 choose *it*, at the head of the way to the **c**. 5892
22: 2 thou judge, wilt thou judge the bloody **c**? 5892
22: 3 The **c** sheddeth blood in the midst of it, 5892
24: 6 Woe to the bloody **c**, to the pot whose scum 5892
24: 9 saith the Lord GOD; Woe to the bloody **c**! 5892
26:10 as men enter into a **c** wherein is made a 5892
26:17 the renowned **c**, which wast strong in 5892
26:19 When I shall make thee a desolate **c**, 5892
27:32 over thee, *saying*, What **c** *is* like Tyrus, NIH
33:21 came unto me, saying, The **c** is smitten. 5892
39:16 also the name of the **c** *shall be* Hamonah. 5892
40: 1 in the fourteenth year after that the **c** was 5892
40: 2 by which *was* as the frame of a **c** on 5892
43: 3 that I saw when I came to destroy the **c**: 5892
45: 6 ye shall appoint the possession of the **c** five 5892
45: 7 holy *portion*, and of the possession of the **c**, 5892
45: 7 and before the possession of the **c**, 5892
48:15 *shall be* a profane *place* for the **c**, 5892
48:15 and the **c** shall be in the midst thereof. 5892
48:17 the suburbs of the **c** shall be toward 5892
48:18 shall be for food unto them that serve the **c**. 5892
48:19 they that serve the **c** shall serve it out of all 5892
48:20 with the possession of the **c**. 5892
48:21 of the possession of the **c**, over against 5892
48:22 *and* from the possession of the **c**, 5892
48:30 these *are* the goings out of the **c** on 5892
48:31 the gates of the **c** *shall be* after the names of 5892
48:35 the name of the **c** from *that* day *shall be*, 5892
Da 9:16 thy fury be turned away from thy **c** 5892
9:18 and the **c** which is called by thy name: 5892
9:19 for thy **c** and thy people are called by thy 5892
9:24 upon thy people and upon thy holy **c**, 5892
9:26 prince that *shall* come shall destroy the **c** 5892
Hos 6: 8 Gilead *is* a **c** of them that work iniquity, 7151
11: 9 midst of thee: and I will not enter into the **c**. 5892
Joel 2: 9 They shall run to and fro in the **c**; they shall 5892
Am 3: 6 Shall a trumpet be blown in the **c**, and 5892
3: 6 shall there be evil in a **c**, and the LORD 5892
4: 7 I caused it to rain upon one **c**, and caused it 5892
4: 7 and caused it not to rain upon another **c**: 5892
4: 8 So two *or* three cities wandered unto one **c**, 5892
5: 3 The **c** that went out *by* a thousand shall 5892
6: 8 will I deliver up the **c** with all that is 5892
7:17 Thy wife shall be a harlot in the **c**, and 5892
Jnh 1: 2 to Nineveh, *that* great **c**, and cry against it; 5892
3: 2 *that* great **c**, and preach unto it 5892
3: 3 Now Nineveh was an exceeding great **c** of 5892
3: 4 Jonah began to enter into the **c** a day's 5892
4: 5 So Jonah went out of the **c**, and sat on 5892
4: 5 sat on the east side of the **c**, and there made 5892
4: 5 he might see what would become of the **c**. 5892
4:11 should not I spare Nineveh, *that* great **c**, 5892
Mic 4:10 for now shalt thou go forth out of the **c**, and 7151
6: 9 The LORD'S voice crieth unto the **c**, and 5892
Na 3: 1 Woe to the bloody **c**! it *is* all full *of* lies *and* 5892
Hab 2: 8 *of* the **c**, and *of* all that dwell therein. 7151
2:12 with blood, and stablisheth a **c** by iniquity! 7151
2:17 *of* the **c**, and *of* all that dwell therein. 7151
Zep 2:15 This *is* the rejoicing **c** that dwelt carelessly, 5892
3: 1 is filthy and polluted, to the oppressing **c**! 5892
Zec 8: 3 Jerusalem shall be called a **c** of truth; and 5892

Zec 8: 5 the streets of the c shall be full *of* boys and 5892
8:21 the inhabitants of one c shall go to another, NIH
14: 2 the c shall be taken, and the houses rifled, 5892
14: 2 half of the c shall go forth into captivity, 5892
14: 2 of the people shall not be cut off from the c. 5892
Mt 2:23 he came and dwelt in a c called Nazareth: *4172*
4: 5 the devil taketh him *up* into the holy c, *4172*
5:14 A c that is set on a hill cannot be hid. *4172*
5:35 for it is the c of the great King. *4172*
8:33 and went their ways into the c, and *4172*
8:34 the whole c came out to meet Jesus: *4172*
9: 1 and passed over, and came into his own c. *4172*
10: 5 into *any* c of the Samaritans enter ye not: *4172*
10:11 And into whatsoever c or town ye shall *4172*
10:14 when ye depart out of that house or c, *4172*
10:15 in the day of judgment, than for that c. *4172*
10:23 But when they persecute you in this c, *4172*
12:25 and every c or house divided against itself *4172*
21:10 all the c was moved, saying, Who is this? *4172*
21:17 and went out of the c into Bethany; *4172*
21:18 in the morning as he returned into the c, *4172*
22: 7 those murderers, and burnt up their c. *4172*
23:34 and persecute *them* from c to city: *4172*
23:34 and persecute *them* from city to c: *4172*
26:18 Go into the c to such a man, and say unto *4172*
27:53 and went into the holy c, and appeared unto *4172*
28:11 some of the watch came into the c, and *4172*
Mk 1:33 And all the c was gathered together at *4172*
1:45 *Jesus* could no more openly enter into the c, *4172*
5:14 and told *it* in the c, and in the country. *4172*
6:11 in the day of judgment, than for that c. *4172*
11:19 when even was come, he went out of the c. *4172*
14:13 Go ye into the c, and there shall meet you a *4172*
14:16 and came into the c, and found as he had *4172*
Lk 1:26 was sent from God unto a c of Galilee, *4172*
1:39 the hill country with haste, into a c of Juda; *4172*
2: 3 went to be taxed, every one into his own c. *4172*
2: 4 out of the c of Nazareth, into Judea, *4172*
2: 4 into Judea, unto the c of David, *4172*
2:11 For unto you is born this day in the c of *4172*
2:39 into Galilee, to their own c Nazareth. *4172*
4:26 save unto Sarepta, *a* c of Sidon, unto a NIG
4:29 and thrust him out of the c, and led him *4172*
4:29 brow of the hill whereon their c was built, *4172*
4:31 a c of Galilee, and taught them on *4172*
5:12 it came to pass, when he was in a certain c, *4172*
7:11 *day* after, *that* he went into a c called Nain; *4172*
7:12 when he came nigh to the gate of the c, *4172*
7:12 and much people of the c was with her. *4172*
7:37 And behold, a woman in the c, which was a *4172*
8: 1 that he went throughout every c and *4172*
8: 4 and were come to him out of every c, *4172*
8:27 there met him out of the c a certain man, *4172*
8:34 and went and told *it* in the c and in *4172*
8:39 published throughout the whole c how *4172*
9: 5 not receive you, when ye go out of that c, *4172*
9:10 place belonging to the c called Bethsaida. *4172*
10: 1 and two before his face into every c and *4172*
10: 8 And into whatsoever c ye enter, and *4172*
10:10 But into whatsoever c ye enter, and *4172*
10:11 Even the *very* dust of your c, *4172*
10:12 in that day for Sodom, than for that c. *4172*
14:21 quickly into the streets and lanes of the c, *4172*
18: 2 Saying, There was in a c a judge, *4172*
18: 3 And there was a widow in that c; and *4172*
19:41 he beheld the c, and wept over it, *4172*
22:10 Behold, when ye are entered into the c, *4172*
23:19 (Who for a certain sedition made in the c, *4172*
23:51 *he was* of Arimathea, a c of the Jews: *4172*
24:49 but tarry ye in the c of Jerusalem, until ye *4172*
Jn 1:44 of Bethsaida, the c of Andrew and Peter. *4172*
4: 5 Then cometh he to a c of Samaria, which is *4172*
4: 8 were gone away unto the c to buy meat.) *4172*
4:28 and went her way into the c, and saith to *4172*
4:30 Then they went out of the c, and came unto *4172*
4:39 And many of the Samaritans of that c *4172*
11:54 into a c called Ephraim, and there *4172*
19:20 Jesus was crucified was nigh to the c: *4172*
Ac 7:58 And cast *him* out of the c, and stoned *him:* *4172*
8: 5 Then Philip went down to the c of Samaria, *4172*
8: 8 And there was great joy in that c. *4172*
8: 9 which beforetime in the *same* c used *4172*
9: 6 and go into the c, and it shall be told thee *4172*
10: 9 on their journey, and drew nigh unto the c, *4172*
11: 5 I was in the c of Joppa praying: and in a *4172*
12:10 unto the iron gate that leadeth unto the c; *4172*
13:44 whole c together to hear the word of God. *4172*
13:50 and the chief *men* of the c, and *4172*
14: 4 But the multitude of the c was divided: and *4172*
14:13 which was before their c, brought oxen and *4172*
14:19 having stoned Paul, drew *him* out of the c, *4172*
14:20 about him, he rose up, and came into the c: *4172*
14:21 they had preached the gospel to that c, *4172*
15:21 For Moses of old time hath in every c them *4172*
15:36 visit our brethren in every c where we have *4172*
16:12 which is the chief c of *that* part of *4172*
16:12 and we were in that c abiding certain days. *4172*
16:13 And on the sabbath we went out of the c by *4172*
16:14 a seller of purple, of the c of Thyatira, *4172*
16:20 being Jews, do exceedingly trouble our c, *4172*
16:39 and desired *them* to depart out of the c. *4172*
17: 5 and set all the c on an uproar, and assaulted *4172*
17: 6 certain brethren unto the **rulers of the** c, *4173*
17: 8 troubled the people and the **rulers of the** c, *4173*
17:16 when he saw the c wholly given to idolatry. *4172*
18:10 hurt thee: for I have much people in this c. *4172*
19:29 And the whole c was filled with confusion: *4172*
19:35 c of the Ephesians is a worshipper of *4172*
20:23 that the Holy Ghost witnesseth in every c, *4172*
21: 5 and children, till *we were* out of the c: *4172*
21:29 (For they had seen before with him in the c *4172*
21:30 And all the c was moved, and the people *4172*
21:39 *a* c in Cilicia, a citizen of no mean city: NIG
21:39 *a city* in Cilicia, a citizen of no mean c: *4172*
22: 3 *am* a Jew, born in Tarsus, *a* c in Cilicia, NIG
Ac 22: 3 yet brought up in this c at the feet of *4172*
24:12 neither in the synagogues, nor in the c: *4172*
25:23 chief captains, and principal men of the c, *4172*
27: 5 Pamphylia, we came to Myra, *a* c of Lycia. NIG
27: 8 nigh whereunto was the c *of* Lasea. *4172*
Ro 16:23 Erastus the chamberlain of the c saluteth *4172*
2Co 11:26 *in* perils by the heathen, *in* perils in the c, *4172*
11:32 c of the Damascenes *with a garrison,* *4172*
13: S *a* c of Macedonia, by Titus and Lucas. NIG
1Ti 6: S which is the **chiefest** c of Phrygia *3390*
Tit 1: 5 and ordain elders in every c, as I had *4172*
Heb 11:10 For he looked for a c which hath *4172*
11:16 for he hath prepared for them a c. *4172*
12:22 and unto the c of the living God, *4172*
13:14 For here have we no continuing c, but *4172*
Jas 4:13 or to morrow we will go into such a c, *4172*
Rev 3:12 and the name of the c of my God, *which is* *4172*
11: 2 the holy c shall they tread under foot forty *4172*
11: 8 bodies *shall lie* in the street of the great c, *4172*
11:13 and the tenth *part* of the c fell, and in *4172*
14: 8 Babylon is fallen, is fallen, *that* great c, *4172*
14:20 the winepress was trodden without the c, *4172*
16:19 And the great c was *divided* into three *4172*
17:18 woman which thou sawest is *that* great c, *4172*
18:10 saying, Alas, alas, *that* great c Babylon, *4172*
18:10 alas, *that* great city Babylon, **that** mighty c! *4172*
18:16 And saying, Alas, alas, *that* great c, *4172*
18:18 saying, What c *is* like unto *this* great city? NIG
18:18 saying, What *city is* like unto *this* great c? *4172*
18:19 and wailing, saying, Alas, alas, *that* great c, *4172*
18:21 Thus with violence shall *that* great c *4172*
20: 9 camp of the saints about, and the beloved c: *4172*
21: 2 And I John saw the holy c, new Jerusalem, *4172*
21:10 high mountain, and shewed me *that* great c, *4172*
21:14 And the wall of the c had twelve *4172*
21:15 me had a golden reed to measure the c, *4172*
21:16 And the c lieth foursquare, and the length is *4172*
21:16 and he measured the c with the reed, *4172*
21:18 and the c *was* pure gold, like unto clear *4172*
21:19 And the foundations of the wall of the c *4172*
21:21 and the street of the c *was* pure gold, as *it* *4172*
21:23 And the c had no need of the sun, neither of *4172*
22:14 may enter in through the gates into the c. *4172*
22:19 and out of the holy c, and *from* the *things* *4172*

CITY CLERK See TOWNCLERK

CLAD (2)

1Ki 11:29 he had c himself with a new garment; and 3680
Isa 59:17 *for* clothing, and was c **with** zeal as a cloke. 5844

CLAMOROUS (1) [CLAMOUR]

Pr 9:13 A foolish woman *is* c: *she is* simple, and 1993

CLAMOUR (1) [CLAMOROUS]

Eph 4:31 wrath, and anger, and c, and evil speaking, *2906*

CLAN See KINDRED; KINDREDS

CLANGING See TINKLING

CLAP (6) [CLAPPED, CLAPPETH, CLAPT]

Job 27:23 *Men* shall c their hands at him, and 5606
Ps 47: 1 O c *your* hands, all ye people; shout unto 8628
98: 8 Let the floods c *their* hands: let the hills be 4222
Isa 55:12 all the trees of the field shall c *their* hands. 4222
La 2:15 All that pass by c *their* hands at thee; 5606
Na 3:19 all that hear the bruit of thee shall c 8628

CLAPPED (1) [CLAP]

Eze 25: 6 Because thou hast c *thine* hands, and 4222

CLAPPETH (1) [CLAP]

Job 34:37 he c *his hands* amongst us, and 5606

CLAPT (1) [CLAP]

2Ki 11:12 they c their hands, and said, God save 5221

CLASP See TACHES

CLAUDA (1)

Ac 27:16 under a certain island *which is* called C, *2802*

CLAUDIA (1)

2Ti 4:21 and Linus, and C, and all the brethren. *2803*

CLAUDIUS (3)

Ac 11:28 which came to pass in the days of C Cesar. *2804*
18: 2 that C had commanded all Jews to depart *2804*
23:26 C Lysias unto the most excellent governor *2804*

CLAVE (14) [CLEAVE]

Ge 22: 3 c the wood for the burnt offering, and 1234
34: 3 his soul c unto Dinah the daughter of Jacob, 1692
Nu 16:31 that the ground c **asunder** that *was* under 1234
Jdg 15:19 God c a hollow place that *was* in the jaw, 1234
Ru 1:14 her mother in law; but Ruth c unto her. 1692
1Sa 6:14 they c the wood of the cart, and offered 1234
2Sa 20: 2 the men of Judah c unto their king, 1692
23:10 was weary, and his hand c unto the sword: 1692
1Ki 11: 2 their gods: Solomon c unto these in love. 1692
2Ki 18: 6 For he c to the LORD, *and* departed not 1692
Ne 10:29 They c to their brethren, their nobles, and 2388
Ps 78:15 He c the rocks in the wilderness, and 1234
Isa 48:21 he c the rock also, and the waters gushed 1234
Ac 17:34 Howbeit certain men c unto him, and *2853*

CLAWS (3)

Dt 14: 6 cleaveth the cleft *into* two c, *and* 6541
Da 4:33 eagles' *feathers,* and his nails like birds' c. NIH
Zec 11:16 flesh of the fat, and tear their c in pieces. 6541

CLAY (33)

1Ki 7:46 in the c ground between Succoth and 4568
2Ch 4:17 in the c ground between Succoth and 5645
Job 4:19 much less *in* them that dwell in houses of c, 2563
10: 9 that thou hast made me as the c; 2563
13:12 like unto ashes, your bodies to bodies of c. 2563
27:16 as the dust, and prepare raiment as the c; 2563
33: 6 God's stead: I also am formed out of the c. 2563
38:14 It is turned as c *to* the seal; and they stand 2563
Ps 40: 2 out of the miry c, and set my feet upon a 2916
Isa 29:16 down shall be esteemed as the potter's c: 2563
41:25 as *upon* morter, and as the potter treadeth c. 2916
45: 9 Shall the c say to him that fashioneth it, 2563
64: 8 we *are* the c, and thou our potter; and we all 2563
Jer 18: 4 the vessel that he made of c was marred in 2563
18: 6 as the c *is* in the potter's hand, so *are* ye in 2563
43: 9 and hide them in the c in the brickkiln, 4423
Da 2:33 of iron, his feet part of iron and part of c. 2635
2:34 image upon his feet *that were* of iron and c, 2635
2:35 the c, the brass, the silver, and the gold, 2635
2:41 and toes, part of potter's c, and part of iron, 2635
2:41 as thou sawest the iron mixed with miry c. 2635
2:42 part of c, *so* the kingdom shall be partly 2635
2:43 whereas thou sawest iron mixt with miry c, 2635
2:43 to another, even as iron is not mixed with c. 2635
2:45 the brass, the c, the silver, and the gold; 2635
Na 3:14 go into c, and tread the morter, make strong 2916
Hab 2: 6 and to him that ladeth himself with **thick** c! 5671
Jn 9: 6 and made c of the spittle, and he anointed *4081*
9: 6 the eyes of the blind man with the c, *4081*
9:11 A man *that is* called Jesus made c, and *4081*
9:14 the sabbath day when Jesus made the c, *4081*
9:15 He put c upon mine eyes, and I washed, *4081*
Ro 9:21 Hath not the potter power over the c, of *4081*

CLEAN (133) [CLEANNESS, CLEANSE, CLEANSED, CLEANSETH, CLEANSING, UNCLEAN]

Ge 7: 2 Of every c beast thou shalt take to thee by 2889
7: 2 and of beasts that *are* not c by two, the male 2889
7: 8 Of c beasts, and of beasts that *are* not clean, 2889
7: 8 of beasts that *are* not c, and of fowls, and 2889
8:20 took of every c beast, and of every clean 2889
8:20 of every c fowl, and offered burnt offerings 2889
35: 2 and be c, and change your garments: 2891
Lev 4:12 carry forth without the camp unto a c place, 2889
6:11 the ashes without the camp unto a c place. 2889
7:19 *for* the flesh, all that be c shall eat thereof. 2889
10:10 and unholy, and between unclean and c; 2889
10:14 and heave shoulder shall ye eat in a c place; 2889
11:36 *wherein there is* plenty of water, shall be c: 2889
11:37 seed which is to be sown, it *shall be* c. 2889
11:47 a difference between the unclean and the c, 2889
12: 8 an atonement for her, and she shall be c. 2891
13: 6 the skin, the priest shall **pronounce** him c: 2891
13: 6 and he shall wash his clothes, and be c. 2891
13:13 he shall **pronounce** *him* c *that hath* 2891
13:13 the plague: it is all turned white: he *is* c. 2889
13:17 the priest shall **pronounce** *him* c *that hath* 2891
13:17 *him* clean *that hath* the plague: he *is* c. 2889
13:23 and the priest shall **pronounce** him c. 2891
13:28 and the priest shall **pronounce** him c: 2891
13:34 then the priest shall **pronounce** him c: 2891
13:34 and he shall wash his clothes, and be c. 2891
13:37 up therein; the scall is healed, he *is* c: 2889
13:37 and the priest shall **pronounce** him c. 2891
13:39 spot *that* groweth in the skin: he *is* c. 2889
13:40 is fallen off his head, he *is* bald: *yet is* he c. 2889
13:41 his face, he *is* forehead bald: *yet is* he c. 2889
13:58 be washed the second time, and shall be c. 2891
13:59 to **pronounce** it c, or to pronounce it 2891
14: 4 that is to be cleansed two birds alive *and* c, 2889
14: 7 shall **pronounce** him c, and shall let 2891
14: 8 wash *himself* in water, that he may be c: 2891
14: 9 wash his flesh in water, and he shall be c. 2891
14:11 the priest that **maketh** *him* c shall present 2891
14:11 shall present the man that is to be **made** c, 2891
14:20 an atonement for him, and he shall be c. 2891
14:48 the priest shall **pronounce** the house c, 2891
14:53 atonement for the house: and it shall be c. 2891
14:57 teach when *it is* unclean, and when *it is* c: 2889
15: 8 that hath the issue spit upon him that is c; 2889
15:13 his flesh in running water, and shall be c. 2891
15:28 seven days, and after *that* she shall be c. 2891
16:30 *that* ye may be c from all your sins before 2891
17:15 unclean until the even: then shall he be c. 2891
20:25 put difference between c beasts 2889
20:25 and between unclean fowls and c: 2889
22: 4 not eat of the holy *things,* until he be c. 2891
22: 7 he shall be c, and shall afterward eat of 2891
23:22 thou shalt not **make** c **riddance** of 3615
Nu 5:28 if the woman be not defiled, but *be* c; then 2889
8: 7 their clothes, and *so* **make** themselves c. 2891
9:13 the man that *is* c, and is not in a journey, 2889
18:11 every one *that is* c in thy house shall eat of 2889
18:13 every one *that is* c in thine house shall eat 2889
19: 9 a man *that is* c shall gather up the ashes of 2889
19: 9 lay *them* up without the camp in a c place, 2889
19:12 and on the seventh day he shall be c: 2891
19:12 then the seventh day he shall not be c. 2891
19:18 a c person shall take hyssop, and dip *it* in 2889
19:19 the c *person* shall sprinkle upon the unclean 2889
19:19 *himself* in water, and shall be c at even. 2891
31:23 *it* go through the fire, and it shall be c: 2891
31:24 ye shall be c, and afterward ye shall come 2891
Dt 12:15 the unclean and the c may eat thereof, as of 2889
12:22 and the c shall eat of them alike. 2889
14:11 *Of* all c birds ye shall eat. 2889
14:20 *But* of all c fowls ye may eat. 2889
15:22 and the c *person shall eat it* alike, 2889
23:10 that is not c by reason of *uncleanness* that 2889
Jos 3:17 all the people were passed c over Jordan. 8552
4: 1 when all the people were c passed over 8552
4:11 when all the people were c passed over, 8552
1Sa 20:26 Something hath befallen him, he *is* not c; 2889
20:26 he *is* not clean; surely *he is* not c. 2889
2Ki 5:10 come again to thee, and thou shalt be c. 2891
5:12 may I not wash in them, and be c? So he 2891

2Ki 5:13 when he saith to thee, Wash, and be c? 2891
5:14 unto the flesh of a little child, and he was c. 2891
2Ch 30:17 the passovers for every one *that was* not c, 2889
Job 9:30 **make** my hands **never so** c; 1253+2141+871.1
11: 4 doctrine *is* pure, and I am c in thine eyes. 1249
14: 4 Who can bring a c *thing* out of an unclean? 2889
15:14 What *is* man, that he should be c? and 2135
15:15 yea, the heavens are not c in his sight. 2141
17: 9 he that hath c hands shall be stronger and 2889
25: 4 how can he be c *that is* born of a woman? 2135
33: 9 I am c without transgression, I *am* 2134
Ps 19: 9 The fear of the LORD *is* c, enduring for 2889
24: 4 He that hath c hands, and a pure heart; 5355
51: 7 Purge me with hyssop, and I shall be c: 2891
51:10 Create in me a c heart, O God; and renew a 2889
73: 1 to Israel, *even* to such as are of a c heart. 1249
77: 8 Is his mercy c **gone** for ever? doth *his* 656
Pr 14: 4 Where no oxen *are*, the crib *is* c: but 1249
16: 2 All the ways of a man *are* c in his own 2134
20: 9 Who can say, I have **made** my heart c, I am 2135
Ecc 9: 2 to the good and to the c, and to the unclean; 2889
Isa 1:16 Wash ye, **make** you c; put away the evil of 2135
24:19 the earth is c **dissolved**, the earth is 6565+6565
28: 8 *and* filthiness, *so that there is* no place c. NIH
30:24 that ear the ground shall eat c provender, 2548
52:11 be ye c, that bear the vessels of 1305
66:20 in a c vessel *into* the house of the LORD. 2889
Jer 13:27 wilt thou not be **made** c? when *shall it* 2891
Eze 22:26 *difference* between the unclean and the c, 2889
36:25 will I sprinkle c water upon you, and 2889
36:25 clean water upon you, and ye shall be c: 2891
44:23 to discern between the unclean and the c. 2889
Joel 1: 7 he hath **made** it c bare, and cast *it* away; 2834
Zec 11:17 his arm shall be c **dried up**, and 3001+3001
Mt 8: 2 Lord, if thou wilt, thou canst **make** me c. *2511*
8: 3 and touched him, saying, I will; be thou c. *2511*
23:25 for ye **make** c the outside of the cup and *2511*
23:26 that the outside of them may be c also. *2513*
27:59 the body, he wrapped it in a c linen cloth, *2513*
Mk 1:40 If thou wilt, thou canst **make** me c. *2511*
1:41 and saith unto him, I will; be thou c. *2511*
Lk 5:12 Lord, if thou wilt, thou canst **make** me c. *2511*
5:13 be thou c. And immediately the leprosy *2511*
11:39 Now do ye Pharisees **make** c the outside of *2511*
11:41 and behold, all *things* are c unto you. *2513*
Jn 13:10 save to wash *his* feet, but is c every whit: *2513*
13:10 clean every whit: and ye are c, but not all. *2513*
13:11 therefore said he, Ye are not all c. *2513*
15: 3 Now ye are c through the word which I *2513*
Ac 18: 6 blood *be* upon your own heads; I *am* c: *2513*
2Pe 2:18 those that were c escaped from them who *3689*
Rev 19: 8 should be arrayed in fine linen, c and white: *2513*
19:14 clothed in fine linen, white and c. *2513*

CLEANNESS (5) [CLEAN]

2Sa 22:21 according to the c of my hands hath he 1252
22:25 according to my c in his eye sight. 1252
Ps 18:20 according to the c of my hands hath he 1252
18:24 according to the c of my hands in his 1252
Am 4: 6 I also have given you c of teeth in all your 5356

CLEANSE (33) [CLEAN]

Ex 29:36 thou shalt c the altar, when thou hast made 2398
Lev 14:49 he shall take to c the house two birds, and 2398
14:52 he shall c the house with the blood of 2398
16:19 c it, and hallow it from the uncleanness of 2891
16:30 to c you, *that* ye may be clean from all your 2891
Nu 8: 6 among the children of Israel, and c them. 2891
8: 7 thus shalt thou do unto them, to c them: 2891
8:15 thou shalt c them, and offer them *for* an 2891
8:21 Aaron made an atonement for them to c 2891
2Ch 29:15 the LORD, to c the house of the LORD. 2891
29:16 to c *it*, and brought out all the uncleanness 2891
Ne 13:22 I commanded the Levites that they should c 2891
Ps 19:12 *his* errors? c thou me from secret *faults*. 5352
51: 2 from mine iniquity, and c me from my sin. 2891
119: 9 Wherewithal shall a young man c his way? 2135
Jer 4:11 daughter of my people, not to fan, nor to c, 1305
33: 8 I will c them from all their iniquity, 2891
Eze 36:25 and from all your idols, will I c you. 2891
37:23 wherein they have sinned, and will c them: 2891
39:12 burying of them, that *they* may c the land. 2891
39:14 remain upon the face of the earth, to c it: 2891
39:16 *be* Hamonah. Thus shall they c the land. 2891
43:20 round about: thus shalt thou c and purge it. 2398
43:22 they shall c the altar, as they did cleanse *it* 2398
43:22 the altar, as they did c *it* with the bullock. 2398
45:18 without blemish, and c the sanctuary: 2398
Joel 3:21 For I will c their blood *that* I have not 5352
Mt 10: 8 Heal the sick, c the lepers, raise the dead, *2511*
23:26 c first that *which is* within the cup and *2511*
2Co 7: 1 let us c ourselves from all filthiness of *2511*
Eph 5:26 c *it* with the washing of water by the word, *2511*
Jas 4: 8 C *your* hands, *ye* sinners; and purify *your* *2511*
1Jn 1: 9 and to c us from all unrighteousness. *2511*

CLEANSED (39) [CLEAN]

Lev 11:32 be unclean until the even; so it shall be c. 2891
12: 7 she shall be c from the issue of her blood. 2891
14: 4 take for him that is to be c two birds alive 2891
14: 7 he shall sprinkle upon him that is to be c 2891
14: 8 he that is to be c shall wash his clothes, 2891
14:14 the tip of the right ear of him that is to be c, 2891
14:17 the tip of the right ear of him that is to be c, 2891
14:18 pour upon the head of him that is to be c: 2891
14:19 make an atonement for him that is to be c 2891
14:25 the tip of the right ear of him that is to be c, 2891
14:28 the tip of the right ear of him that is to be c, 2891
14:29 put upon the head of him that is to be c, 2891
14:31 for him that is to be c before the LORD. 2891
15:13 when he that hath an issue is c of his issue; 2891
15:28 if she be c of her issue, then she shall 2891
Nu 35:33 the land cannot be c of the blood that is 3722
Jos 22:17 from which we are not c until this day, 2891
2Ch 29:18 We have c all the house of the LORD, and 2891
30:18 and Zebulun, had not c themselves, 2891
30:19 though *he be* not c according to NIH
34: 5 their altars, and c Judah and Jerusalem. 2891
Ne 13: 9 I commanded, and they c the chambers: 2891
13:30 Thus c I them from all strangers, and 2891
Job 35: 3 profit shall I have, *if I be* c from my sin? NIH
Ps 73:13 Verily I have c my heart *in* vain, and 2135
Eze 22:24 say unto her, Thou *art* the land that is not c, 2891
36:33 In the day that I shall have c you from all 2891
44:26 after he is c, they shall reckon unto him 2893
Da 8:14 hundred days; then shall the sanctuary be c. 6663
Joel 3:21 I will cleanse their blood *that* I have not c: 5352
Mt 8: 3 And immediately his leprosy was c. *2511*
11: 5 the lepers are c, and the deaf hear, *2511*
Mk 1:42 leprosy departed from him, and he was c. *2511*
Lk 4:27 and none of them was c, saving Naaman *2511*
7:22 lame walk, the lepers are c, the deaf hear, *2511*
17:14 to pass *that*, as they went, they were c. *2511*
17:17 Jesus answering said, Were there not ten c? *2511*
Ac 10:15 What God hath c, *that* call not thou *2511*
11: 9 What God hath c, *that* call not thou *2511*

CLEANSETH (3) [CLEAN]

Job 37:21 but the wind passeth, and c them. 2891
Pr 20:30 The blueness of a wound c **away** evil: so 8562
1Jn 1: 7 the blood of Jesus Christ his Son c us from *2511*

CLEANSING (10) [CLEAN]

Lev 13: 7 he hath been seen of the priest for his c, 2893
13:35 the scall spread much in the skin after his c; 2893
14: 2 be the law of the leper in the day of his c: 2893
14:23 on the eighth day for his c unto the priest, 2893
14:32 able to get *that which pertaineth* to his c. 2893
15:13 number to himself seven days for his c, 2893
Nu 6: 9 he shall shave his head in the day of his c, 2893
Eze 43:23 When thou hast made an end of c *it*, thou 2398
Mk 1:44 offer for thy c *those things* which Moses *2512*
Lk 5:14 thyself to the priest, and offer for thy c, *2512*

CLEAR (15) [CLEARER, CLEARING, CLEARLY, CLEARNESS]

Ge 24: 8 then thou shalt be c from this my oath: 5352
24:41 shalt thou be c from *this* my oath, 5352
24:41 if they give not thee *one*, thou shalt be c 5355
44:16 or how shall we c ourselves? God hath 6663
Ex 34: 7 *that* will by no means c *the guilty;* 5352+5352
2Sa 23: 4 out of the earth by c **shining** after rain. 5051
Ps 51: 4 thou speakest, *and* be c when thou judgest. 2135
SS 6:10 c as the sun, *and* terrible as *an army* with 1249
Isa 18: 4 I will consider in my dwelling place like a c 6703
Am 8: 9 and I will darken the earth in the c day: 216
Zec 14: 6 *that* the light shall not be c, *nor* dark: 3368
2Co 7:11 approved yourselves to be c in *this* matter. *53*
Rev 21:11 *even* like a jasper stone, c **as crystal**; *2929*
21:18 the city *was* pure gold, like unto c glass. *2513*
22: 1 c as crystal, proceeding out of the throne of *2986*

CLEARER (1) [CLEAR]

Job 11:17 *thine* age shall be c than the noonday; 6965

CLEARING (2) [CLEAR]

Nu 14:18 by no means c *the guilty*, visiting 5352+5352
2Co 7:11 yea, *what* c of yourselves, yea, *627*

CLEARLY (5) [CLEAR]

Job 33: 3 and my lips shall utter knowledge c. 1305
Mt 7: 5 shalt thou **see** c to cast out the mote out of *1227*
Mk 8:25 and he was restored, and saw every *man* c. *5081*
Lk 6:42 shalt thou **see** c to pull out the mote that is *1227*
Ro 1:20 from the creation of the world are c **seen**, *2529*

CLEARNESS (1) [CLEAR]

Ex 24:10 and as it were the body of heaven in *his* c. 2892

CLEAVE (30) [CLAVE, CLEAVED, CLEAVETH, CLOVEN, CLOVENFOOTED]

Ge 2:24 and his mother, and shall c unto his wife: 1692
Lev 1:17 And he shall c it with the wings thereof, *but* 8156
Dt 4: 4 ye that did c unto the LORD your God *are* 1695
10:20 to him shalt thou c, and swear by his name. 1692
11:22 to walk in all his ways, and to c unto him; 1692
13: 4 and you shall serve him, and c unto him. 1692
13:17 there shall c nought of the cursed thing to 1692
28:21 The LORD shall **make** the pestilence c 1692
28:60 wast afraid of; and they shall c unto thee. 1692
30:20 his voice, and that thou mayest c unto him: 1692
Jos 22: 5 to c unto him, and to serve him with all 1692
23: 8 c unto the LORD your God, as ye have 1692
23:12 c unto the remnant of these nations, 1692
2Ki 5:27 therefore of Naaman shall c unto thee, 1692
Job 38:38 and the clods c **fast together**? 1692
Ps 74:15 Thou didst c the fountain and the flood: 1234
101: 3 of them that turn aside; *it* shall not c to me. 1692
102: 5 of my groaning my bones c **to** my skin. 1692
137: 6 let my tongue c to the roof of my mouth; 1692
Isa 14: 1 and they shall c to the house of Jacob. 5596
Jer 13:11 have I **caused to** c unto me the whole 1692
Eze 3:26 I will **make** thy tongue c to the roof of thy 1692
Da 2:43 they shall not c one to another, even as iron 1693
11:34 but many shall c to them with flatteries. 3867
Hab 3: 9 Selah. Thou didst c the earth *with* rivers. 1234
Zec 14: 4 the mount of Olives shall c in the midst 1234
Mt 19: 5 and mother, and shall c **to** his wife: *4347*
Mk 10: 7 his father and mother, and c to his wife; *4347*
Ac 11:23 of heart *they* would c **unto** the Lord. *4357*
Ro 12: 9 *that which is* evil; c to *that which is* good. *2853*

CLEAVED (3) [CLEAVE]

2Ki 3: 3 Nevertheless he c unto the sins of Jeroboam 1692
Job 29:10 their tongue c to the roof of their mouth. 1692
31: 7 and *if any* blot hath c to my hands; 1692

CLEAVETH (13) [CLEAVE]

Dt 14: 6 c the cleft *into* two claws, *and* cheweth 8156
Job 16:13 he c my reins **asunder**, and doth not spare; 6398
19:20 My bone c to my skin and to my flesh, and 1692
Ps 22:15 my tongue c *to* my jaws; and thou hast 1692
41: 8 An evil disease, *say they*, c **fast** unto him: 3332
44:25 down to the dust: our belly c unto the earth. 1692
119:25 My soul c unto the dust: quicken thou me 1692
141: 7 one cutteth and c *wood* upon the earth. 1234
Ecc 10: 9 he that c wood shall be endangered thereby. 1234
Jer 13:11 For as the girdle c to the loins of a man, so 1692
La 4: 4 The tongue of the sucking child c to 1692
4: 8 their skin c to their bones; it is withered, 6821
Lk 10:11 which c **on** us, we do wipe off against you: *2853*

CLEFT (2) [CLEFTS]

Dt 14: 6 cleaveth the c *into* two claws, *and* 8157
Mic 1: 4 the valleys shall be c, as wax before 1234

CLEFTS (4) [CLEFT]

SS 2:14 O my dove, *that art* in the c of the rock, 2288
Jer 49:16 O thou that dwellest in the c of the rock, 2288
Am 6:11 *with* breaches, and the little house *with* c. 1233
Ob 1: 3 thou that dwellest in the c of the rock, 2288

CLEMENCY (1)

Ac 24: 4 thou wouldest hear us of thy c a few words. *1932*

CLEMENT (1)

Php 4: 3 with C also, and *with* other my *2815*

CLEOPAS (1)

Lk 24:18 And the one *of them*, whose name *was* C, *2810*

CLEOPHAS (1)

Jn 19:25 Mary the *wife* of C, and Mary Magdalene. *2832*

CLIFF (1) [CLIFT, CLIFTS]

2Ch 20:16 behold, they come up by the c of Ziz; and 4608

CLIFT (1) [CLIFF]

Ex 33:22 that I will put thee in a c of the rock, and 5366

CLIFTS (3) [CLIFF]

Job 30: 6 To dwell in the c of the valleys, *in* caves of 6178
Isa 2:21 To go into the c of the rocks, and into 5366
57: 5 in the valleys under the c of the rocks? 5585

CLIMB (4) [CLIMBED, CLIMBETH]

Jer 4:29 go into thickets, and c **up** upon the rocks: 5927
Joel 2: 7 *men*; they shall c the wall like men of war; 5927
2: 9 the wall, they shall c **up** upon the houses; 5927
Am 9: 2 though they c **up** *to* heaven, thence will I 5927

CLIMBED (2) [CLIMB]

1Sa 14:13 Jonathan c **up** upon his hands and upon his 5927
Lk 19: 4 and c **up** into a sycomore tree to see him: *305*

CLIMBETH (1) [CLIMB]

Jn 10: 1 but c **up** some other way, the same is a thief *305*

CLING See CLEAVE; CLEAVED; CLEAVETH

CLIP OFF See MAR

CLIPT (1)

Jer 48:37 every head *shall be* bald, and every beard c: 1639

CLOAK See CLOKE; GARMENT; RAIMENT; VESTURE

CLODS (6)

Job 7: 5 flesh is clothed with worms and c of dust; 1487
21:33 The c of the valley shall be sweet unto him, 7263
38:38 and the c cleave fast together? 7263
Isa 28:24 he open and **break the** c of his ground? 7702
Hos 10:11 shall plow, *and* Jacob shall **break** his c. 7702
Joel 1:17 The seed is rotten under their c, the garners 4053

CLOKE (7)

Isa 59:17 *for* clothing, and was clad with zeal as a c. 4598
Mt 5:40 take *away* thy coat, let him have *thy* c also. *2440*
Lk 6:29 him that taketh away thy c forbid not *to* *2440*
Jn 15:22 but now they have no c for their sin. *4392*
1Th 2: 5 as ye know, nor a c of covetousness; *4392*
2Ti 4:13 The c that I left at Troas with Carpus, *5341*
1Pe 2:16 not using *your* liberty for a c of *1942*

CLOPAS See CLEOPHAS

CLOSE (11) [CLOSED, CLOSER, CLOSEST]

Nu 5:13 be **kept** c, and she be defiled, and *there be* 5641
2Sa 22:46 they shall be afraid out of their c **places**. 4526
1Ch 12: 1 while he yet **kept** himself c because of Saul 6113
Job 28:21 and **kept** c from the fowls of the air. 5641
41:15 *his* pride, shut up *together as with* a c seal. 6862
Ps 18:45 and be afraid out of their c **places**. 4526
Jer 42:16 shall **follow** c after you there *in* Egypt; 1692
Da 8: 7 I saw him **come** c unto the ram, and he was 5060
Am 9:11 that is fallen, and c **up** the breaches thereof; 1443
Lk 9:36 And they **kept** *it* c, and told no *man* in *4601*
Ac 27:13 loosing *thence*, they sailed c **by** Crete. *788*

CLOSED (11) [CLOSE]

Ge 2:21 his ribs, and c **up** the flesh instead thereof; 5462
20:18 For the LORD had **fast** c **up** all 6113+6113
Nu 16:33 into the pit, and the earth c upon them: 3680
Jdg 3:22 the fat c upon the blade, so that he could 5462
Isa 1: 6 they have not been c, neither bound up, 2115
29:10 spirit of deep sleep, and hath c your eyes: 6105
Da 12: 9 for the words *are* c **up** and sealed till 5640
Jnh 2: 5 the depth c me **round about**, the weeds 5437

Mt 13:15 dull of hearing, and their eyes they have c; 2576
Lk 4:20 And he c the book, and he gave it again to 4428
Ac 28:27 dull of hearing, and their eyes have they c; 2576

CLOSER (1) [CLOSE]
Pr 18:24 there is a friend that sticketh c than a 1695

CLOSEST (1) [CLOSE]
Jer 22:15 thou reign, because thou c thyself in cedar? 8474

CLOSET (2) [CLOSETS]
Joel 2:16 of his chamber, and the bride out of her c. 2646
Mt 6: 6 enter into thy c, and when thou hast shut 5009

CLOSETS (1) [CLOSET]
Lk 12: 3 that which ye have spoken in the ear in c 5009

CLOTH (18) [CLOTHE, SACKCLOTH, SACKCLOTHES]
Nu 4: 6 shall spread over it a c wholly of blue, and 899
4: 7 of shewbread they shall spread a c of blue, 899
4: 8 they shall spread upon them a c of scarlet, 899
4: 9 they shall take a c of blue, and cover 899
4:11 upon the golden altar they shall spread a c of 899
4:12 put them in a c of blue, and cover them with 899
4:13 from the altar, and spread a purple c thereon: 899
Dt 22:17 they shall spread the c before the elders of 8071
1Sa 19:13 hair for his bolster, and covered it with a c. 899
21: 9 it is here wrapt in a c behind the ephod: 8071
2Sa 20:12 into the field, and cast a c upon him, 899
2Ki 8:15 that he took a thick c, and dipt it in water, 4346
Isa 30:22 shalt cast them away as a menstruous c; 1739
Mt 9:16 No man putteth a piece of new c unto an 4470
27:59 the body, he wrapped it in a clean linen c, 4616
Mk 2:21 No man also seweth a piece of new c on an 4470
14:51 having a linen c cast about his naked body; 4616
14:52 And he left the linen c, and fled from them 4616

CLOTHE (16) [CLOTH, CLOTHED, CLOTHES, CLOTHEST, CLOTHING, GRAVECLOTHES, UNCLOTHED]
Ex 40:14 shalt bring his sons, and c them with coats: 3847
Est 4: 4 she sent raiment to c Mordecai, and to take 3847
Ps 132:16 I will also c her priests with salvation: and 3847
132:18 His enemies will I c with shame: but 3847
Pr 23:21 and drowsiness shall c a man with rags. 3847
Isa 22:21 I will c him with thy robe, and 3847
49:18 thou shalt surely c thee with them all, 3847
50: 3 I c the heavens with blackness, and I make 3847
Eze 26:16 they shall c themselves with trembling; 3847
34: 3 Ye eat the fat, and ye c you with the wool, 3847
Hag 1: 6 ye c you, but there is none warm; and he 3847
Zec 3: 4 and I will c thee with change of raiment. 3847
Mt 6:30 Wherefore, if God so c the grass of the field, 294
6:30 shall he not much more c you, O ye of little NIG
Lk 12:28 If then God so c the grass, which is to day in 294
12:28 how much more will he c you, O ye of little NIG

CLOTHED (73) [CLOTHE]
Ge 3:21 God make coats of skins, and c them. 3847
Lev 8: 7 c him with the robe, and put the ephod 3847
2Sa 1:24 weep over Saul, who c you in scarlet, 3847
1Ch 15:27 David was c with a robe of fine linen, and 3736
21:16 the elders of Israel, who were c in 3680
2Ch 6:41 be c with salvation, and let thy saints 3847
18: 9 c in their robes, and they sat in a void place 3847
28:15 with the spoil c all that were naked among 3847
Est 4: 2 for none might enter into the king's gate c 3830
Job 7: 5 My flesh is c with worms and clods of 3847
8:22 They that hate thee shall be c with shame; 3847
10:11 Thou hast c me with skin and flesh, and 3847
29:14 I put on righteousness, and it c me: 3847
39:19 hast thou c his neck with thunder? 3847
Ps 35:26 let them be c with shame and 3847
65:13 The pastures are c with flocks; the valleys 3847
93: 1 The LORD reigneth, he is c with majesty; 3847
93: 1 the LORD is c with strength, 3847
104: 1 thou art c with honour and majesty. 3847
109:18 As he c himself with cursing like as with 3847
109:29 Let mine adversaries be c with shame, and 3847
132: 9 Let thy priests be c with righteousness; and 3847
Pr 31:21 for all her household are c with scarlet. 3847
Isa 61:10 for he hath c me with the garments of 3847
Eze 7:27 the prince shall be c with desolation, and 3847
9: 2 one man among them was c with linen, 3847
9: 3 he called to the man c with linen, 3847
9:11 behold, the man c with linen, which had 3847
10: 2 he spake unto the man c with linen, and 3847
10: 6 he had commanded the man c with linen, 3847
10: 7 put it into the hands of him that was c with 3847
16:10 I c thee also with broidered work, and 3847
23: 6 Which were c with blue, captains and 3847
23:12 captains and rulers c most gorgeously, 3847
38: 4 all of them c with all sorts of armour, even 3847
44:17 they shall be c with linen garments; 3847
Da 5: 7 shall be c with scarlet, and have a chain of 3848
5:16 thou shalt be c with scarlet, and have a 3848
5:29 they c Daniel with scarlet, and put a chain 3848
10: 5 and behold, a certain man c in linen, 3847
12: 6 one said to the man c in linen, which was 3847
12: 7 I heard the man c in linen, which was upon 3847
Zep 1: 8 and all such as are c with strange apparel. 3847
Zec 3: 3 Now Joshua was c with filthy garments, 3847
3: 5 upon his head, and c him with garments. 3847
Mt 6:31 we drink? or, Wherewithal shall we be c? 4016
11: 8 A man c in soft raiment? behold, they that 294
25:36 Naked, and ye c me: I was sick, and 4016
25:38 and took thee in? or naked, and c thee? 4016
25:43 naked, and ye c me not: sick, and in prison, 4016
Mk 1: 6 And John was c with camel's hair, and 1746
5:15 sitting, and c, and in his right mind: 2439
15:17 And they c him with purple, and platted a 1746
16: 5 on the right side, c in a long white garment; 4016
Lk 7:25 A man c in soft raiment? Behold, they which 294
Lk 8:35 at the feet of Jesus, c, and in his right mind: 2439
16:19 which was c in purple and fine linen, and 1737
2Co 5: 2 earnestly desiring to be c upon with our 1902
5: 3 be that being c we shall not be found 1746
5: 4 that we would be unclothed, but c upon, 1902
1Pe 5: 5 one to another, and be c with humility: 1463
Rev 1:13 c with a garment down to the foot, and 1746
3: 5 the same shall be c in white raiment; 4016
3:18 that thou mayest be c, and that the shame of 4016
4: 4 twenty elders sitting, c in white raiment; 4016
7: 9 c with white robes, and palms in their 4016
10: 1 come down from heaven, c with a cloud: 4016
11: 3 and threescore days, c in sackcloth. 4016
12: 1 a woman c with the sun, and the moon 4016
15: 6 c in pure and white linen, and having their 1746
18:16 that was c in fine linen, and purple, and 4016
19:13 And he was c with a vesture dipt in blood: 4016
19:14 c in fine linen, white and clean. 1746

CLOTHES (105) [CLOTHE]
Ge 37:29 Joseph was not in the pit; and he rent his c. 899
37:34 Jacob rent his c, and put sackcloth upon his 8071
44:13 they rent their c, and laded every man his 8071
49:11 in wine, and his c in the blood of grapes: 5497
Ex 12:34 bound up in their c upon their shoulders. 8071
19:10 and to morrow, and let them wash their c, 8071
19:14 the people; and they washed their c. 8071
31:10 the c of service, and the holy garments for 899
35:19 The c of service, to do service in the holy 899
39: 1 and scarlet, they made c of service, 899
39:41 The c of service to do service in the holy 899
Lev 10: 6 Uncover not your heads, neither rend your c; 899
11:25 of the carcase of them shall wash his c, 899
11:28 beareth the carcase of them shall wash his c, 899
11:40 eateth of the carcase of it shall wash his c, 899
11:40 that beareth the carcase of it shall wash his c, 899
13: 6 a scab: and he shall wash his c, and be clean. 899
13:34 and he shall wash his c, and be clean. 899
13:45 the leper in whom the plague is, his c shall 899
14: 8 he that is to be cleansed shall wash his c, 899
14: 9 he shall wash his c, also he shall wash his 899
14:47 he that lieth in the house shall wash his c; 899
14:47 he that eateth in the house shall wash his c. 899
15: 5 whosoever toucheth his bed shall wash his c, 899
15: 6 he sat that hath the issue shall wash his c, 899
15: 7 of him that hath the issue shall wash his c, 899
15: 8 he shall wash his c, and bathe himself in 899
15:10 beareth any of those things shall wash his c, 899
15:11 he shall wash his c, and bathe himself in 899
15:13 wash his c, and bathe his flesh in running 899
15:21 whosoever toucheth her bed shall wash his c, 899
15:22 any thing that she sat upon shall wash his c, 899
15:27 shall wash his c, and bathe himself in water, 899
16:26 the goat for the scapegoat shall wash his c, 899
16:28 he that burneth them shall wash his c, and 899
16:32 shall put on the linen c, even the holy 899
17:15 he shall both wash his c, and bathe himself 899
21:10 shall not uncover his head, nor rend his c; 899
Nu 8: 7 let them wash their c, and so 899
8:21 were purified, and they washed their c; 899
14: 6 of them that searched the land, rent their c: 899
19: 7 the priest shall wash his c, and he shall bathe 899
19: 8 he that burneth her shall wash his c in water, 899
19:10 the ashes of the heifer shall wash his c, 899
19:19 day he shall purify himself, and wash his c, 899
19:21 the water of separation shall wash his c; 899
31:24 ye shall wash your c on the seventh day, 899
Dt 29: 5 your c are not waxen old upon you, and 8008
Jos 7: 6 Joshua rent his c, and fell to the earth upon 8071
Jdg 11:35 that he rent his c, and said, Alas, 899
1Sa 4:12 came to Shiloh the same day with his c 4055
19:24 he stript off his c also, and prophesied before 899
2Sa 1: 2 out of the camp from Saul with his c rent, 899
1:11 David took hold on his c, and rent them; 899
3:31 Rent your c, and gird you with sackcloth, 899
13:31 all his servants stood by with their c rent. 899
19:24 nor trimmed his beard, nor washed his c, 899
1Ki 1: 1 they covered him with c, but he gat no heat. 899
21:27 that he rent his c, and put sackcloth upon his 899
2Ki 2:12 he took hold of his own c, and rent them in 899
5: 7 that he rent his c, and said, Am I God, to kill 899
5: 8 heard that the king of Israel had rent his c, 899
5: 8 saying, Wherefore hast thou rent thy c? 899
6:30 the words of the woman, that he rent his c; 899
11:14 Athaliah rent her c, and cried, Treason, 899
18:37 to Hezekiah with their c rent, and told him 899
19: 1 king Hezekiah heard it, that he rent his c, 899
22:11 of the book of the law, that he rent his c. 899
22:19 and hast rent thy c, and wept before me; 899
2Ch 23:13 Then Athaliah rent her c, and said, Treason, 899
34:19 heard the words of the law, that he rent his c. 899
34:27 and didst rend thy c, and weep before me; 899
Ne 4:23 which followed me, none of us put off our c, 899
9:21 their c waxed not old, and their feet swelled 8008
Est 4: 1 Mordecai rent his c, and put on sackcloth 899
Job 9:31 the ditch, and mine own c shall abhor me. 8008
Pr 6:27 fire in his bosom, and his c not be burnt? 899
Isa 36:22 to Hezekiah with their c rent, and told him 899
37: 1 king Hezekiah heard it, that he rent his c, 899
Jer 41: 5 their c rent, and having cut themselves, 899
Eze 16:39 they shall strip thee also of thy c, and 899
23:26 They shall also strip thee out of thy c, and 899
27:20 Dedan was thy merchant in precious c for 899
27:24 in blue c, and broidered work, and in chests 1545
Am 2: 8 they lay themselves down upon c laid to 899
Mt 21: 7 and the colt, and put on them their c, 2440
24:18 is in the field return back to take his c. 2440
26:65 Then the high priest rent his c, saying, 2440
Mk 5:28 For she said, If I may touch but his c, 2440
5:30 in the press, and said, Who touched my c? 2440
14:63 Then the high priest rent his c, and saith, 5509
15:20 and put his own c on him, and led him out 2440
Lk 2: 7 and wrapped him in swaddling c, and 4683
2:12 find the babe wrapped in swaddling c, 4683
8:27 and ware no c, neither abode in any house, 2440
Lk 19:36 as he went, they spread their c in the way. 2440
24:12 he beheld the linen c laid by themselves, 3608
Jn 19:40 and wound it in linen c with the spices, 3608
20: 5 and looking in, saw the linen c lying; 3608
20: 6 into the sepulchre, and seeth the linen c lie, 3608
20: 7 not lying with the linen c, but 3608
Ac 7:58 the witnesses laid down their c at a young 2440
14:14 heard of, they rent their c, and ran in among 2440
16:22 and the magistrates rent off their c, and 2440
22:23 and cast off their c, and threw dust into 2440

CLOTHEST (1) [CLOTHE]
Jer 4:30 Though thou c thyself with crimson, 3847

CLOTHING (19) [CLOTHE]
Job 22: 6 for nought, and stripped the naked of their c. 899
24: 7 They cause the naked to lodge without c, 3830
24:10 They cause him to go naked without c, and 3830
31:19 If I have seen any perish for want of c, or 3830
Ps 35:13 when they were sick, my c was sackcloth: 3830
45:13 glorious within: her c is of wrought gold. 3830
Pr 27:26 The lambs are for thy c, and the goats are 3830
31:22 of tapestry; her c is silk and purple. 3830
31:25 Strength and honour are her c; and she shall 3830
Isa 3: 6 saying, Thou hast c, be thou our ruler, and 8071
3: 7 for in my house is neither bread nor c: 8071
23:18 to eat sufficiently, and for durable c. 4374
59:17 put on the garments of vengeance
for c, 3847+8516
Jer 10: 9 blue and purple is their c: they are all 3830
Mt 7:15 which come to you in sheep's c, but 1742
11: 8 they that wear soft c are in kings' houses. NIG
Mk 12:38 which love to go in long c, and 4749
Ac 10:30 behold, a man stood before me in bright c, 2066
Jas 2: 3 have respect to him that weareth the gay c, 2066

CLOUD (107) [CLOUDS, CLOUDY]
Ge 9:13 I do set my bow in the c, and it shall be for 6051
9:14 when I bring a c over the earth, 6049+6051
9:14 that the bow shall be seen in the c: 6051
9:16 the bow shall be in the c; and I will look 6051
Ex 13:21 went before them by day in a pillar of a c, 6051
13:22 He took not away the pillar of the c by day, 6051
14:19 the pillar of the c went from before their 6051
14:20 it was a c and darkness to them, but it gave 6051
14:24 through the pillar of fire and of the c, 6051
16:10 the glory of the LORD appeared in the c. 6051
19: 9 Lo, I come unto thee in a thick c, 6051
19:16 a thick c upon the mount, and the voice of 6051
24:15 into the mount, and a c covered the mount. 6051
24:16 mount Sinai, and the c covered it six days: 6051
24:16 called unto Moses out of the midst of the c. 6051
24:18 Moses went into the midst of the c, and 6051
34: 5 the LORD descended in the c, and 6051
40:34 a c covered the tent of the congregation, 6051
40:35 because the c abode thereon, and the glory 6051
40:36 when the c was taken up from over 6051
40:37 if the c were not taken up, then 6051
40:38 For the c of the LORD was upon 6051
Lev 16: 2 for I will appear in the c upon the mercy 6051
16:13 that the c of the incense may cover 6051
Nu 9:15 the c covered the tabernacle, namely, 6051
9:16 the c covered it by day, and the appearance 6051
9:17 when the c was taken up from 6051
9:17 in the place where the c abode, there 6051
9:18 as long as the c abode upon the tabernacle 6051
9:19 when the c tarried long upon the tabernacle 6051
9:20 when the c was a few days upon 6051
9:21 when the c abode from even unto 6051
9:21 that the c was taken up in the morning, then 6051
9:21 by day or by night that the c was taken up, 6051
9:22 that the c tarried upon the tabernacle, 6051
10:11 that the c was taken up from off 6051
10:12 and the c rested in the wilderness of Paran. 6051
10:34 the c of the LORD was upon them by day, 6051
11:25 the LORD came down in a c, and 6051
12: 5 LORD came down in the pillar of the c, 6051
12:10 the c departed from off the tabernacle; and 6051
14:14 that thy c standeth over them, and that thou 6051
14:14 by day time in a pillar of a c, and in a pillar 6051
16:42 the c covered it, and the glory of 6051
Dt 1:33 what way ye should go, and in a c by day. 6051
5:22 of the c, and of the thick darkness, with a 6051
31:15 appeared in the tabernacle in a pillar of a c: 6051
31:15 the pillar of the c stood over the door of 6051
1Ki 8:10 that the c filled the house of the LORD, 6051
8:11 not stand to minister because of the c: 6051
18:44 there ariseth a little c out of the sea, 5645
2Ch 5:13 that then the house was filled with a c, 6051
5:14 not stand to minister by reason of the c: 6051
Ne 9:19 the pillar of the c departed not from them 6051
Job 3: 5 of death stain it; let a c dwell upon it; 6053
7: 9 As the c is consumed and vanisheth away: 6051
22:13 can he judge through the dark c? NIH
26: 8 and the c is not rent under them. 6051
26: 9 of his throne, and spreadeth his c upon it. 6051
30:15 and my welfare passeth away as a c. 5645
36:32 commandeth it not to shine by the c that NIH
37:11 Also by watering he wearieth the thick c: 5645
37:11 the thick cloud: he scattereth his bright c: 6051
37:15 and caused the light of his c to shine? 6051
38: 9 When I made the c the garment thereof, and 6051
Ps 78:14 In the daytime also he led them with a c, 6051
105:39 He spread a c for a covering; and fire to 6051
Pr 16:15 and his favour is as a c of the latter rain. 5645
Isa 4: 5 a c and smoke by day, and the shining of a 6051
18: 4 and like a c of dew in the heat of harvest. 5645
19: 1 the LORD rideth upon a swift c, and 5645
25: 5 even the heat with the shadow of a c: 5645
44:22 I have blotted out, as a thick c, 5645
44:22 thy transgressions, and, as a c, thy sins: 6051
60: 8 Who are these that fly as a c, and as 5645
La 2: 1 covered the daughter of Zion with a c 5743
3:44 Thou hast covered thyself with a c, that our 6051

Eze 1: 4 a great **c**, and a fire infolding itself, and 6051
1:28 the appearance of the bow that is in the **c** 6051
8:11 his hand; and a thick **c** of incense went up. 6051
10: 3 went in; and the **c** filled the inner court. 6051
10: 4 the house was filled with the **c**, and 6051
30:18 a **c** shall cover her, and her daughters shall 6051
32: 7 I will cover the sun with a **c**, and the moon 6051
38: 9 thou shalt be like a **c** to cover the land, 6051
38:16 people of Israel, as a **c** to cover the land; 6051
Hos 6: 4 for your goodness *is* as a morning **c**, and 6051
13: 3 Therefore they shall be as the morning **c**, 6051
Mt 17: 5 behold, a bright **c** overshadowed them: *3507*
17: 5 and behold a voice out of the **c**, which said, *3507*
Mk 9: 7 And there was a **c** that overshadowed them: *3507*
9: 7 and a voice came out of the **c**, saying, *3507*
Lk 9:34 there came a **c**, and overshadowed them: *3507*
9:34 and they feared as they entered into the **c**. *3507*
9:35 And there came a voice out of the **c**, saying, *3507*
12:54 When ye see a **c** rise out of the west, *3507*
21:27 shall they see the Son of man coming in a **c** *3507*
Ac 1: 9 and a **c** received him out of their sight. *3507*
1Co 10: 1 how that all our fathers were under the **c**, *3507*
10: 2 And were all baptized unto Moses in the **c** *3507*
Heb 12: 1 about with so great a **c** of witnesses, *3509*
Rev 10: 1 come down from heaven, clothed with a **c**: *3507*
11:12 And they ascended up to heaven in a **c**; and *3507*
14:14 and behold a white **c**, and upon the cloud *3507*
14:14 upon the **c** one sat like unto the Son of man, *3507*
14:15 with a loud voice to him that sat on the **c**, *3507*
14:16 And he that sat on the **c** thrust in his sickle *3507*

CLOUDS (49) [CLOUD]

Dt 4:11 *with* darkness, **c**, and thick darkness. 6051
Jdg 5: 4 heavens dropped, the **c** also dropped water. 5645
2Sa 22:12 dark waters, *and* **thick c** of the skies. 5645
23: 4 the sun riseth, *even* a morning without **c**; 5645
1Ki 18:45 that the heaven was black *with* **c** and wind, 5645
Job 20: 6 the heavens, and his head reach unto the **c**; 5645
22:14 **Thick c** *are* a covering to him, that he seeth 5645
26: 8 He bindeth up the waters in his **thick c**; and 5645
35: 5 behold the **c** *which* are higher than thou. 7834
36:28 Which the **c** do drop *and* distil upon man 7834
36:29 can *any* understand the spreadings of the **c**, 5645
36:32 With **c** he covereth the light; and 3709
37:16 Dost thou know the balancings of the **c**, 5645
37:21 see not the bright light which *is* in the **c**: 7834
38:34 Canst thou lift up thy voice to the **c**, 5645
38:37 Who can number the **c** in wisdom? or 7834
Ps 18:11 *were* dark waters *and* **thick c** of the skies. 5645
18:12 *that was* before him his **thick c** passed, 5645
36: 5 *and* thy faithfulness *reacheth* unto the **c**. 7834
57:10 unto the heavens, and thy truth unto the **c**. 7834
68:34 *is* over Israel, and his strength *is* in the **c**. 7834
77:17 The **c** poured out water: the skies sent out a 5645
78:23 Though he had commanded the **c** from 7834
97: 2 **C** and darkness *are* round about him: 6051
104: 3 who maketh the **c** his chariot: who walketh 5645
108: 4 and thy truth *reacheth* unto the **c**. 7834
147: 8 Who covereth the heaven with **c**, 5645
Pr 3:20 broken up, and the **c** drop down the dew. 7834
8:28 When he established the **c** above: when *he* 7834
25:14 boasteth himself of a false gift *is like* **c** 5387
Ecc 11: 3 If the **c** be full *of* rain, they empty 5645
11: 4 and he that regardeth the **c** shall not reap. 5645
12: 2 not darkened, nor the **c** return after the rain: 5645
Isa 5: 6 I will also command the **c** that they rain no 5645
14:14 I will ascend above the heights of the **c**; 5645
Jer 4:13 he shall come up as **c**, and his chariots *shall* 6051
Da 7:13 *one* like the Son of man came with the **c** of 6050
Joel 2: 2 a day of **c** and of thick darkness, 6051
Na 1: 3 the storm, and the **c** *are* the dust of his feet. 6051
Zep 1:15 gloominess, a day of **c** and thick darkness, 6051
Zec 10: 1 *so* the LORD *shall* make **bright c**, and 2385
Mt 24:30 man coming in the **c** of heaven with power *3507*
26:64 of power, and coming in the **c** of heaven. *3507*
Mk 13:26 of man coming in *the* **c** with great power *3507*
14:62 of power, and coming in the **c** of heaven. *3507*
1Th 4:17 be caught up together with them in the **c**, *3507*
2Pe 2:17 **c** that are carried with a tempest; *3507*
Jude 1:12 **c** *they are* without water, carried about of *3507*
Rev 1: 7 Behold, he cometh with **c**; and every eye *3507*

CLOUDY (6) [CLOUD]

Ex 33: 9 the **c** pillar descended, and stood *at* the door 6051
33:10 all the people saw the **c** pillar stand *at* 6051
Ne 9:12 thou leddest them in the day by a **c** pillar; 6051
Ps 99: 7 He spake unto them in the **c** pillar: 6051
Eze 30: 3 even the day of the LORD *is* near, a **c** day; 6051
34:12 where they have been scattered in the **c** 6051

CLOUTED (1) [CLOUTS]

Jos 9: 5 old shoes and **c** upon their feet, and 2921

CLOUTS (2) [CLOUTED]

Jer 38:11 took thence old **cast c** and old rotten rags, 5499
38:12 Put now *these* old **cast c** and rotten rags 5499

CLOVEN (2) [CLEAVE]

Dt 14: 7 the cud, or of them that divide the **c** hoof; 8156
Ac 2: 3 And there appeared unto them **c** tongues *1266*

CLOVENFOOTED (3) [CLEAVE, FOOT]

Lev 11: 3 *is* **c**, *and* cheweth cud, 6541+8156+8157
11: 7 he divide the hoof, and *be* **c**, 6541+8156+8157
11:26 *is* not **c**, nor cheweth the cud, 8156+8157

CLUB See DARTS

CLUBS See STAVES

CLUNG See CLAVE; CLEAVE; CLEAVED; CLEAVETH

CLUSTER (5) [CLUSTERS]

Nu 13:23 cut down from thence a branch with one **c** of 811
13:24 of the **c of grapes** which the children of 811
SS 1:14 My beloved *is* unto me *as* a **c** of camphire in 811
Isa 65: 8 As the new wine is found in the **c**, and 811
Mic 7: 1 *there is* no **c** to eat: my soul desired 811

CLUSTERS (7) [CLUSTER]

Ge 40:10 *and* the **c** thereof brought forth ripe grapes: 811
Dt 32:32 grapes *are* grapes of gall, their **c** *are* bitter: 811
1Sa 25:18 parched *corn*, and an hundred **c of raisins**, 6778
30:12 of a cake *of figs*, and two **c of raisins**: 6778
SS 7: 7 a palm tree, and thy breasts to **c** *of grapes*. 811
7: 8 now also thy breasts shall be as **c** of the vine, 811
Rev 14:18 and gather the **c** of the vine of the earth; *1009*

CNIDUS (1)

Ac 27: 7 and scarce were come over against **C**, *2834*

COAL (4) [COALS]

2Sa 14: 7 and *so* they shall quench my **c** which is left, 1513
Isa 6: 6 unto me, having a **live c** in his hand, 7531
47:14 *there shall* not *be* a **c** to warm at, *nor* fire to 1513
La 4: 8 Their visage is blacker than a **c**; they are 7815

COALS (26) [COAL]

Lev 16:12 he shall take a censer full of **burning c** of 1513
2Sa 22: 9 his mouth devoured: **c** were kindled by it. 1513
22:13 Through the brightness before him were **c** 1513
1Ki 19: 6 *there was* a cake **baken on the c**, and 7529
Job 41:21 His breath kindleth **c**, and a flame goeth out 1513
Ps 18: 8 his mouth devoured: **c** were kindled by it. 1513
18:12 clouds passed, hail-*stones* and **c** of fire. 1513
18:13 gave his voice; hail-*stones* and **c** of fire. 1513
120: 4 arrows of the mighty, with **c** of juniper. 1513
140:10 Let **burning c** fall upon them: let them be 1513
Pr 6:28 Can one go upon **hot c**, and his feet not be 1513
25:22 For thou shalt heap **c of fire** upon his head, 1513
26:21 *As* **c** *are* to burning coals, and wood to fire; 6352
26:21 *As* coals *are* to **burning c**, and wood to 1513
SS 8: 6 the **c** thereof *are* coals of fire, *which hath* a 7565
8: 6 the coals thereof *are* **c** of fire, *which hath* a 7565
Isa 44:12 smith *with* the tongs both worketh in the **c**, 6352
44:19 also I have baked bread upon the **c** thereof; 1513
54:16 I have created the smith that bloweth the **c** 6352
Eze 1:13 their appearance *was* like burning **c** of fire, 1513
10: 2 fill thine hand *with* **c** of fire from between 1513
24:11 set it empty upon the **c** thereof, that 1513
Hab 3: 5 and **burning c** went forth at his feet. 7565
Jn 18:18 stood *there*, who had made a **fire of c**; *439*
21: 9 they saw a **fire of c** there, and fish laid *439*
Ro 12:20 doing thou shalt heap **c** of fire on his head. *440*

COARSE JOKING See JESTING

COAST (62) [COASTS]

Ex 10: 4 morrow will I bring the locusts into thy **c**: 1366
Nu 13:29 dwell by the sea, and by the **c** of Jordan. 3027
20:23 by the **c** of the land of Edom, saying, 1366
22:36 border of Arnon, which *is* in the utmost **c**. 1366
24:24 And ships *shall come* from the **c** of Chittim, 3027
34: 3 wilderness of Zin along by the **c** of Edom, 3027
34: 3 **outmost c** of the salt sea eastward: 4480+7097
34:11 the **c** shall go down from Shepham *to* 1366
Dt 2: 4 Ye are to pass through the **c** of your 1366
2:18 over *through* Ar, the **c** of Moab, *this* day: 1366
3:17 the **c** *thereof*, from Chinnereth even unto 1366
11:24 even unto the uttermost sea shall your **c** be. 1366
16: 4 bread seen with thee in all thy **c** seven days; 1366
19: 8 if the LORD thy God enlarge thy **c**, as he 1366
Jos 1: 4 the going down of the sun, shall be your **c**. 1366
12: 4 the **c** of Og king of Bashan, *which was* of 1366
12:23 The king of Dor in the **c** of Dor, one; 5299
13:16 their **c** was from Aroer, that *is* on the bank 1366
13:25 their **c** was Jazer, and all the cities of 1366
13:30 their **c** was from Mahanaim, all Bashan, 1366
15: 1 *was* the uttermost part of the south **c**. NIH
15: 4 and the goings out of that **c** were at the sea: 1366
15: 4 were at the sea: this shall be your south **c**. 1366
15:12 the **c** *thereof*. This *is* the coast of 1366
15:12 the coast *thereof*. This *is* the **c** of 1366
15:21 the **c** of Edom southward were Kabzeel, 1366
16: 3 goeth down westward to the **c** of Japhleti, 1366
16: 3 unto the **c** of Beth-horon the nether, and 1366
17: 7 the **c** of Manasseh was from Asher *to* 1366
17: 9 the **c** descended *unto* the river Kanah, 1366
17: 9 the **c** of Manasseh also *was* on the north 1366
18: 5 Judah shall abide in their **c** on the south, 1366
18:11 the **c** of their lot came forth between 1366
18:19 south end of Jordan: this *was* the south **c**. 1366
19:22 the **c** reacheth to Tabor, and Shahazimah, 1366
19:29 *then* the **c** turneth *to* Ramah, and to 1366
19:29 the **c** turneth *to* Hosah; and the outgoings 1366
19:29 thereof are at the sea from the **c** to Achzib: 2256
19:33 their **c** was from Heleph, from Allon to 1366
19:34 the **c** turneth westward *to* Aznoth-tabor, 1366
19:41 the **c** of their inheritance was Zorah, and 1366
19:47 the **c** of the children of Dan went out *too* 1366
Jdg 1:18 Also Judah took Gaza with the **c** thereof, 1366
1:18 Askelon with the **c** thereof, and Ekron with 1366
1:18 coast thereof, and Ekron with the **c** thereof. 1366
1:36 the **c** of the Amorites *was* from the going 1366
11:20 trusted not Israel to pass through his **c**: 1366
1Sa 6: 9 if it goeth up *by* the way of his own **c** *to* 1366
7:13 and they came no more into the **c** of Israel: 1366
27: 1 to seek me any more in any **c** of Israel: 1366
30:14 upon *the* **c** which *belongeth* to Judah, and NIH
2Ki 14:25 He restored the **c** of Israel from the entering 1366
1Ch 4:10 enlarge my **c**, and that thine hand might be 1366
Eze 25:16 and destroy the remnant of the sea **c**. 2348
47:16 which *is* by the **c** of Hauran. 1366
48: 1 From the north end to the **c** of the way of 3027
48: 1 Damascus northward, to the **c** of Hamath; 3027
Zep 2: 5 Woe unto the inhabitants of the sea **c**, 2256
2: 6 the sea **c** shall be dwellings *and* cottages for 2256
2: 7 the **c** shall be for the remnant of the house 2256
Mt 4:13 in Capernaum, which is **upon the sea c**, *3864*
Lk 6:17 and *from* the **sea c** of Tyre and Sidon, *3882*

COASTS (51) [COAST]

Ex 10:14 of Egypt, and rested in all the **c** of Egypt: 1366
10:19 there remained not one locust in all the **c** of 1366
Nu 21:13 that cometh out of the **c** of the Amorites: 1366
32:33 the land, with the cities thereof in the **c**, 1367
34: 2 *even* the land of Canaan with the **c** thereof:) 1367
34:12 this shall be your land with the **c** thereof 1367
Dt 3:14 the country of Argob unto the **c** of Geshuri 1366
19: 3 thee a way, and divide the **c** of thy land, 1366
28:40 shalt have olive trees throughout all thy **c**, 1366
Jos 9: 1 in all the **c** of the great sea over against 2348
18: 5 the house of Joseph shall abide in their **c** on 1366
18:20 by the **c** thereof round about, according to 1367
19:49 dividing the land for inheritance by their **c**, 1367
Jdg 11:22 they possessed all the **c** of the Amorites, 1366
11:26 in all the cities that *be* along by the **c** of 3027
18: 2 sent of their family five men from their **c**, 7098
19:29 and sent her into all the **c** of Israel. 1366
1Sa 5: 6 *even* Ashdod and the **c** thereof. 1366
7:14 the **c** thereof did Israel deliver out of 1366
11: 3 that we may send messengers unto all the **c** 1366
11: 7 sent *them* throughout all the **c** of Israel by 1366
2Sa 21: 5 from remaining in any of the **c** of Israel, 1366
1Ki 1: 3 a fair damsel throughout all the **c** of Israel, 1366
2Ki 10:32 Hazael smote them in all the **c** of Israel; 1366
15:16 *were* therein, and the **c** thereof from Tirzah: 1366
1Ch 6:54 places throughout their castles in their **c**, 1366
6:66 cities of their **c** out of the tribe of Ephraim. 1366
21:12 destroying throughout all the **c** of Israel. 1366
2Ch 11:13 all Israel resorted to him out of all their **c**. 1366
Ps 105:31 divers sorts *of flies*, *and* lice in all their **c**. 1366
105:33 their fig trees; and brake the trees of their **c**. 1366
Jer 25:32 shall be raised up from the **c** of the earth. 3411
31: 8 and gather them from the **c** of the earth, *and* 3411
50:41 many kings shall be raised up from the **c** of 3411
Eze 33: 2 the people of the land take a man of their **c**, 7097
Joel 3: 4 and Zidon, and all the **c** of Palestine? 1552
Mt 2:16 and in all the **c** thereof, from two years old *3725*
8:34 *him* that he would depart out of their **c**. *3725*
15:21 and departed into the **c** of Tyre and Sidon. *3313*
15:22 woman of Canaan came out of the same **c**, *3725*
15:39 took ship, and came into the **c** of Magdala. *3725*
16:13 When Jesus came into the **c** of Cesarea *3313*
19: 1 came into the **c** of Judea beyond Jordan; *3725*
Mk 5:17 began to pray him to depart out of their **c**. *3725*
7:31 departing from the **c** of Tyre and Sidon, *3725*
7:31 through the midst of the **c** of Decapolis. *3725*
10: 1 cometh into the **c** of Judea by the farther *3725*
Ac 13:50 Barnabas, and expelled them out of their **c**. *3725*
19: 1 Paul having passed through the upper **c** *3313*
26:20 and throughout all the **c** of Judea, and *then* *5561*
27: 2 meaning to sail by the **c** of Asia; *5117*

COAT (25) [COATS]

Ge 37: 3 and he made him a **c** of many colours. 3801
37:23 that they stript Joseph out of his **c**, 3801
37:23 *his* **c** of many colours that *was* on him; 3801
37:31 they took Joseph's **c**, and killed a kid of 3801
37:31 of the goats, and dipped the **c** in the blood; 3801
37:32 they sent the **c** of many colours, and 3801
37:32 know now whether it *be* thy son's **c** or no. 3801
37:33 he knew it, and said, *It is* my son's **c**; 3801
Ex 28: 4 a robe, and a broidered **c**, a mitre, and 3801
28:39 thou shalt embroider the **c** of fine linen, 3801
29: 5 put upon Aaron the **c**, and the robe of 3801
Lev 8: 7 he put upon him the **c**, and girded him with 3801
16: 4 He shall put on the holy linen **c**, and 3801
1Sa 2:19 Moreover his mother made him a little **c**, 4598
17: 5 and he *was* armed with a **c** of mail; 8302
17: 5 the weight of the **c** *was* five thousand 8302
17:38 also he armed him with a **c** *of mail*. 8302
2Sa 15:32 Archite *came* to meet him with his **c** rent, 3801
Job 30:18 it bindeth me about as the collar of my **c**. 3801
SS 5: 3 I have put off my **c**; how shall I put it on? 3801
Mt 5:40 and take *away* thy **c**, let him have *thy* cloke *5509*
Lk 6:29 away thy cloke forbid not *to take thy* **c** also. *5509*
Jn 19:23 to every soldier a part; and *also his* **c**: *5509*
19:23 now the **c** was without seam, woven from *5509*
21: 7 he girt *his* **fisher's c** unto him, (for he was *1903*

COAT OF ARMOR See HABERGEONS

COATS (14) [COAT]

Ge 3:21 to his wife did the LORD God make **c** of 3801
Ex 28:40 for Aaron's sons thou shalt make **c**, and 3801
29: 8 shalt bring his sons, and put **c** upon them. 3801
39:27 they made **c** *of* fine linen *of* woven work 3801
40:14 shalt bring his sons, and clothe them with **c**: 3801
Lev 8:13 put **c** upon them, and girded them *with* 3801
10: 5 and carried them in their **c** out of the camp; 3801
Da 3:21 these men were bound in their **c**, 5622
3:27 head singed, neither were their **c** changed, 5622
Mt 10:10 neither two **c**, neither shoes, nor yet staves: *5509*
Mk 6: 9 *be* shod with sandals; and not put on two **c**. *5509*
Lk 3:11 and saith unto them, He that hath two **c**, *5509*
9: 3 neither money; neither have two **c** apiece. *5509*
Ac 9:39 and shewing the **c** and garments which *5509*

COBRA See ASP; ASPS

COCK (12) [COCKCROWING]

Mt 26:34 unto thee, That this night, before *the* **c** crow, *220*
26:74 not the man. And immediately *the* **c** crew. *220*
26:75 which said unto him, Before *the* **c** crow, *220*
Mk 14:30 *even* in this night, before *the* **c** crow twice, *220*
14:68 he went out into the porch; and *the* **c** crew. *220*
14:72 And the second time *the* **c** crew. And Peter *220*
14:72 Before *the* **c** crow twice, thou shalt deny me *220*
Lk 22:34 tell thee, Peter, *the* **c** shall not crow this day, *220*

Lk 22:60 while he yet spake, the c crew. 220
22:61 Before the c crow, thou shalt deny me thrice. 220
Jn 13:38 verily, I say unto thee, The c shall not crow, 220
18:27 denied again: and immediately the c crew. 220

COCKATRICE (1) [COCKATRICE', COCKATRICES]
Isa 14:29 of the serpent's root shall come forth a c, 6848

COCKATRICE' (2) [COCKATRICE]
Isa 11: 8 the weaned child shall put his hand on the c 6848
59: 5 They hatch c eggs, and weave the spider's 6848

COCKATRICES (1) [COCKATRICE]
Jer 8:17 I will send serpents, c, among you, 6848

COCKCROWING (1) [COCK, CROW]
Mk 13:35 or at midnight, or at the c, or in the morning: 219

COCKLE (1)
Job 31:40 instead of wheat, and c instead of barley. 890

COFFER (3)
1Sa 6: 8 a trespass offering, in a c by the side thereof; 712
6:11 the c with the mice of gold and the images of 712
6:15 the c that was with it, wherein the jewels of 712

COFFIN (1)
Ge 50:26 and he was put in a c in Egypt. 727

COGITATIONS (1)
Da 7:28 my c much troubled me, and 7476

COINS See PENCE

COLD (18)
Ge 8:22 c and heat, and summer and winter, and 7120
Job 24: 7 that they have no covering in the c. 7135
37: 9 the whirlwind: and c out of the north. 7135
Ps 147:17 like morsels: who can stand before his c? 7135
Pr 20: 4 sluggard will not plow by reason of the c; 2779
25:13 As the c of snow in the time of harvest, so 6793
25:20 As he that taketh away a garment in c 7135
25:25 As c waters to a thirsty soul, so is good 7119
Jer 18:14 shall the c flowing waters that come from 7119
Na 3:17 which camp in the hedges in the c day, but 7135
Mt 10:42 of c water only in the name of a disciple, 5593
24:12 shall abound, the love of many shall wax c. 5594
Jn 18:18 who had made a fire of coals; for it was c: 5592
Ac 28: 2 of the present rain, and because of the c. 5592
2Co 11:27 thirst, in fastings often, in c and nakedness. 5592
Rev 3:15 thy works, that thou art neither c nor hot: 5593
3:15 cold nor hot: I would thou wert c or hot. 5593
3:16 thou art lukewarm, and neither c nor hot, 5593

COL-HOZEH (2)
Ne 3:15 the fountain repaired Shallun the son of C, 3626
11: 5 the son of C, the son of Hazaiah, the son of 3626

COLLAR (1) [COLLARS]
Job 30:18 it bindeth me about as the c of my coat. 6310

COLLARS (1) [COLLAR]
Jdg 8:26 c, and purple raiment that was on the kings 5188

COLLECTION (3)
2Ch 24: 6 in out of Judah and out of Jerusalem the c, 4864
24: 9 to bring in to the LORD the c that Moses 4864
1Co 16: 1 Now concerning the c for the saints, as I 3048

COLLEGE (2)
2Ki 22:14 (now she dwelt in Jerusalem in the c;) and 4932
2Ch 34:22 (now she dwelt in Jerusalem in the c:) and 4932

COLLOPS (1)
Job 15:27 and maketh c of fat on his flanks. 6371

COLONY (1)
Ac 16:12 city of that part of Macedonia, and a c: 2862

COLORFUL See DIVERS; DIVERSE

COLOSSE (1) [COLOSSIANS]
Col 1: 2 faithful brethren in Christ which are at C: 2857

COLOSSIANS (1) [COLOSSE]
Col 4: S Written from Rome to the C by Tychicus 2858

COLOUR (14) [COLOURED, COLOURS]
Lev 13:55 if the plague have not changed his c, and 5869
Nu 11: 7 and the c thereof as the colour of bdellium. 5869
11: 7 and the colour thereof as the c of bdellium. 5869
Pr 23:31 when it giveth his c in the cup, when it 5869
Eze 1: 4 out of the midst thereof as the c of amber, 5869
1: 7 they sparkled like the c of burnished brass. 5869
1:16 their work was like unto the c of a beryl: 5869
1:22 creature was as the c of the terrible crystal, 5869
1:27 I saw as the c of amber, as the appearance 5869
8: 2 appearance of brightness, as the c of amber. 5869
10: 9 the appearance of the wheels was as the c 5869
Da 10: 6 and his feet like in c to polished brass, 5869
Ac 27:30 under c as though they would have cast 4392
Rev 17: 4 woman was arrayed in purple and scarlet c, 2847

COLOURED (1) [COLOUR]
Rev 17: 3 I saw a woman sit upon a scarlet c beast, 2847

COLOURS (12) [COLOUR]
Ge 37: 3 old age: and he made him a coat of many c. 6446
37:23 his coat of many c that was on him; 6446
37:32 they sent the coat of many c, and 6446
Jdg 5:30 to Sisera a prey of divers c, a prey of divers 6648
5:30 a prey of divers c of needlework, 6648
5:30 of divers c of needlework on both sides, 6648
2Sa 13:18 she had a garment of divers c upon her: 6446
13:19 rent her garment of divers c that was on 6446
1Ch 29: 2 of divers c, and all manner of precious 7553
Isa 54:11 I will lay thy stones with fair c, and lay thy 6320
Eze 16:16 deckedst thy high places with divers c, and 2921
17: 3 full of feathers, which had divers c, 7553

COLT (15) [COLTS]
Ge 49:11 and his ass's c unto the choice vine; 1121
Job 11:12 though man be born like a wild ass's c. 5895
Zec 9: 9 upon an ass, and upon a c the foal of an ass. 5895
Mt 21: 2 ye shall find an ass tied, and a c with her: 4454
21: 5 upon an ass, and a c the foal of an ass. 4454
21: 7 and the c, and put on them their clothes, 4454
Mk 11: 2 ye shall find a c tied, whereon never man 4454
11: 4 found the c tied by the door without in a 4454
11: 5 said unto them, What do ye, loosing the c? 4454
11: 7 And they brought the c to Jesus, and 4454
Lk 19:30 at your entering ye shall find a c tied, 4454
19:33 And as they were loosing the c, the owners 4454
19:33 thereof said unto them, Why loose ye the c? 4454
19:35 and they cast their garments upon the c, and 4454
Jn 12:15 thy King cometh, sitting on an ass's c. 4454

COLTS (3) [COLT]
Ge 32:15 Thirty milch camels with their c, forty kine, 1121
Jdg 10: 4 he had thirty sons that rode on thirty ass c, 5895
12:14 that rode on threescore and ten ass c: 5895

COME (1972) [CAME, CAMEST, COMERS, COMEST, COMETH, COMING, COMINGS]
Ge 4:14 it shall c to pass, that every one that findeth 1961
6:13 The end of all flesh is c before me; 935
6:18 thou shalt c into the ark, thou, and thy sons, 935
6:20 two of every sort shall c unto thee, to keep 935
7: 1 C thou and all thy house into the ark; 935
9:14 it shall c to pass, when I bring a cloud over 1961
12:11 when he was c near to enter into Egypt, 7126
12:12 Therefore it shall c to pass, when 1961
12:14 to pass, that, when Abram was c into Egypt, 935
15: 4 he that shall c forth out of thine own 3318
15:14 afterward shall they c out with great 3318
15:16 fourth generation they shall c hither again: 7725
17: 6 of thee, and kings shall c out of thee. 3318
18: 5 for therefore are you c to your servant. 5674
18:21 to the cry of it, which is c unto me; 935
19:22 for I cannot do any thing till thou be c 935
19:31 there is not a man in the earth to c in unto us 935
19:32 C, let us make our father drink wine, and 1980
20: 4 Abimelech had not c near her: and he said, 7126
20:13 at every place whither we shall c, say of me, 935
22: 5 go yonder and worship, and c again to you. 7725
24:13 the daughters of the men of the city c out to 3318
24:14 let it c to pass, that the damsel to whom I 1961
24:31 he said, C in, thou blessed of the LORD; 935
24:43 it shall c to pass, that when the virgin 1961
26:27 Wherefore c ye to me, seeing ye hate me, 935
27:21 C near, I pray thee, that I may feel thee, 5066
27:26 C near now, and kiss me, my son. 5066
27:40 it shall c to pass when thou shalt have 1961
28:21 So that I c again to my father's house in 7725
30:16 meet him, and said, Thou must c in unto me; 935
30:33 righteousness answer for me in time to c, 4279
30:33 when it shall c for my hire before thy face: 935
31:44 Now therefore c thou, let us make a 1980
32: 8 If Esau c to the one company, and smite it, 935
32:11 lest he will c and smite me, and the mother 935
33:14 to endure, until I c unto my lord unto Seir. 935
34: 5 and Jacob held his peace until they were c. 935
35:11 of thee, and kings shall c out of thy loins; 3318
35:16 there was but a little way to c to Ephrath: 935
37:10 thy brethren indeed c to bow down 935+935
37:13 c, and I will send thee unto them. And he 1980
37:20 C now therefore, and let us slay him, and 1980
37:23 when Joseph was c unto his brethren, 935
37:27 C, and let us sell him to the Ishmeelites, 1980
38:16 Go to, I pray thee, let me c in unto thee; 935
38:16 thou give me, that thou mayest c in unto me? 935
41:29 there c seven years of great plenty 935
41:35 gather all the food of those good years that c, 935
41:54 the seven years of dearth began to c, 935
42: 7 and he said unto them, Whence c ye? 935
42: 9 to see the nakedness of the land you are c. 935
42:10 my lord, but to buy food are thy servants c. 935
42:12 to see the nakedness of the land you are c. 935
42:15 except your youngest brother c hither. 935
42:21 not hear; therefore is this distress c upon us. 935
44:23 Except your youngest brother c down with 3381
44:30 therefore when I c to thy servant my father, 935
44:31 It shall c to pass, when he seeth that the lad 1961
44:34 I see the evil that shall c on my father. 4672
45: 4 unto his brethren, C near to me, I pray you. 5066
45: 9 of all Egypt: c down unto me, tarry not: 3381
45:11 and all that thou hast, c to poverty. 3423
45:16 saying, Joseph's brethren are c: 935
45:18 and your households, and c unto me: 935
45:19 for your wives, and bring your father, and c. 935
46:31 were in the land of Canaan, are c unto me; 935
46:33 it shall c to pass, when Pharaoh shall call 1961
47: 1 they have, are c out of the land of Canaan; 935
47: 4 For to sojourn in the land are we c; 935
47: 5 Thy father and thy brethren are c unto thee: 935
47:24 it shall c to pass in the increase, that you 1961
48: 7 there was but a little way to c unto Ephrath: 935
49: 6 O my soul, c not thou into their secret; 935
49:10 from between his feet, until Shiloh c; 935
50: 5 and bury my father, and I will c again. 7725
Ex 1:10 C on, let us deal wisely with them; 3051
1:10 lest they multiply, and it c to pass, that, 1961
1:19 are delivered ere the midwives c in unto 935
2:18 How is it that you are c so soon to day? 935
3: 8 I am c down to deliver them out of 3381
3: 9 the cry of the children of Israel is c unto me: 935
3:10 C now therefore, and I will send thee unto 1980
3:13 when I c unto the children of Israel, and 935
3:18 thou shalt c, thou and the elders of Israel, 935
3:21 it shall c to pass, that, when ye go, ye shall 1961
4: 8 it shall c to pass, if they will not believe 1961
4: 9 it shall c to pass, if they will not believe 1961
7:15 shalt stand by the river's brink against he c; 7125
8: 3 which shall go up and c into thine house, and 935
8: 4 the frogs shall c up both on thee, and 5927
8: 5 cause frogs to c up upon the land of Egypt. 5927
9:19 the hail shall c down upon them, and 3381
10:12 that they may c up upon the land of Egypt, 5927
10:26 must serve the LORD, until we c thither. 935
11: 8 all these thy servants shall c down unto me, 3381
12:23 will not suffer the destroyer to c in unto 935
12:25 it shall c to pass, when ye be come to 1961
12:25 when ye be c to the land which the LORD 935
12:26 it shall c to pass, when your children shall 1961
12:48 and then let him c near and keep it; 7126
13:14 be when thy son asketh thee in time to c, 4279
14:26 that the waters may c again upon 7725
16: 5 it shall c to pass, that on the sixth day they 1961
16: 9 of Israel, C near before the LORD: 7126
17: 6 the rock, and there shall c water out of it, 3318
18: 6 I thy father in law Jethro am c unto thee, and 935
18: 8 all the travail that had c upon them by 4672
18:15 Because the people c unto me to inquire of 935
18:16 When they have a matter, they c unto me; 935
19: 2 were c to the desert of Sinai, and had pitched 935
19: 9 Lo, I c unto thee in a thick cloud, 935
19:11 for the third day the LORD will c down in 3381
19:13 they shall c up to the mount. 5927
19:15 against the third day: c not at your wives. 5066
19:22 which c near to the LORD, 5066
19:23 The people cannot c up to mount Sinai: 5927
19:24 thou shalt c up, thou, and Aaron with thee: 5927
19:24 the people break through to c up unto 5927
20:20 for God is c to prove you, and that his fear 935
20:24 in all places where I record my name I will c 935
21:14 if a man c presumptuously upon his 2102
22: 9 the cause of both parties shall c before 935
22:27 it shall c to pass, when he crieth unto me, 1961
23:27 destroy all the people to whom thou shalt c, 935
24: 1 C up unto the LORD, thou, and Aaron, 5927
24: 2 Moses alone shall c near the LORD: but 5066
24: 2 they shall not c nigh; neither shall 5066
24:12 C up to me into the mount, and be there: 5927
24:14 ye here for us, until we c again unto you: 7725
24:14 have any matters to do, let him c unto them. 5066
25:32 six branches shall c out of the sides of it; 3318
25:33 in the six branches that c out of 3318
28:43 when they c in unto the tabernacle of 935
28:43 when they c near unto the altar to minister 5066
30:20 or when they c near to the altar to minister, 5066
32: 1 Moses delayed to c down out of the mount, 3381
32:26 let him c unto me. And all the sons of Levi NIH
33: 5 I will c up into the midst of thee in a 5927
33:22 it shall c to pass, while my glory passeth 1961
34: 2 c up in the morning unto mount Sinai, and 5927
34: 3 no man shall c up with thee, neither let any 5927
34:30 and they were afraid to c nigh him. 5066
35:10 every wise hearted among you shall c, and 935
36: 2 stirred him up to c unto the work to do it: 7126
Lev 4:23 he hath sinned, c to his knowledge, 3045
4:28 c to his knowledge, then he shall bring his 3045
10: 3 I will be sanctified in them that c nigh me, 7138
10: 4 of Aaron, and said unto them, C near, 7126
10: 6 and lest wrath c upon all the people: NIH
12: 4 she shall touch no hallowed thing, nor c into 935
13:16 unto white, he shall c unto the priest; 935
14: 8 after that he shall c into the camp, and 935
14:34 When ye be c into the land of Canaan, 935
14:35 he that owneth the house shall c and tell 935
14:39 the priest shall c again the seventh day, 7725
14:43 if the plague c again, and break out in 7725
14:44 Then the priest shall c and look, and behold, 935
14:48 if the priest shall c in, and look upon it, 935+935
15:14 c before the LORD unto the door of 935
16: 2 that he c not at all times into the holy place 935
16: 3 Thus shall Aaron c into the holy place: with 935
16:17 atonement in the holy place, until he c out, 3318
16:23 Aaron shall c into the tabernacle of 935
16:24 c forth, and offer his burnt offering, and 3318
16:26 in water, and afterward c into the camp. 935
16:28 and afterward he shall c into the camp. 935
19:19 mingled of linen and woollen c upon thee. 5927
19:23 when ye shall c into the land, and shall have 935
21:21 shall c nigh to offer the offerings of 5066
21:21 he shall not c nigh to offer the bread of his 5066
21:23 nor c nigh unto the altar, because he hath a 5066
23:10 When ye be c into the land which I give unto 935
25: 2 When ye c into the land which I give you, 935
25:22 until her fruits c in ye shall eat of the old 935
25:25 if any of his kin c to redeem it, then shall he 935
Nu 1: 1 in the second year after they were c out of 3318
4: 5 Aaron shall c, and his sons, and they shall 935
4:15 the sons of Kohath shall c to bear it: but 935
5:14 the spirit of jealousy c upon him, and he be 5674
5:14 or if the spirit of jealousy c upon him, and 5674
5:27 it shall c to pass, that, if she be defiled, 1961
6: 5 there shall no rasor c upon his head: 5674
6: 6 unto the LORD he shall c at no dead body. 935
8:19 when the children of Israel c nigh unto 5066
9: 1 after they were c out of the land of Egypt, 3318
10:29 c thou with us, and we will do thee good: 1980
11:17 I will c down and talk with thee there: and 3381
11:20 until it c out at your nostrils, and it be 3318
11:23 whether my word shall c to pass unto thee 7136
12: 4 C out ye three unto the tabernacle of 3318
13:21 of Zin unto Rehob, as men c to Hamath. 935
13:33 the sons of Anak, which c of the giants: NIH
14:30 Doubtless ye shall not c into the land, 935
15: 2 When ye be c into the land of your 935
15:18 When ye c into the land whither I bring you, 935
16: 5 and will cause him to c near unto him: 7126
16: 5 chosen will he cause to c near unto him. 7126

Nu 16:12 of Eliab: which said, We will not **c up**: 5927
16:14 the eyes of these men? we will not **c up**. 5927
16:40 **c near** to offer incense before the LORD; 7126
17: 5 it shall **c to pass**, *that* the man's rod, 1961
18: 3 only they shall not **c nigh** the vessels of 7126
18: 4 and a stranger shall not **c nigh** unto you. 7126
18:22 **c nigh** the tabernacle of the congregation, 7126
19: 7 afterward he shall **c** into the camp, and 935
19:14 all that **c** into the tent, and all that *is* in 935
20: 5 wherefore have ye **made us to c up** out of 5927
20:18 lest I **c out** against thee with the sword. 3318
21: 8 it shall **c to pass**, that every one that is 1961
21:27 **C** *into* Heshbon, let the city of Sihon be built 935
22: 5 Behold, there is a people **c out** from Egypt: 3318
22: 6 **C** now therefore, I pray thee, curse me this 1980
22:11 Behold, *there is* a people **c out** of Egypt, 3318
22:11 **c** now, curse me them; peradventure I shall 1980
22:14 and said, Balaam refuseth to **c** with us. 1980
22:17 **c** therefore, I pray thee, curse me this 1980
22:20 If the men **c** to call thee, rise up, *and* go with 935
22:36 when Balak heard that Balaam was **c**, he 935
22:38 said unto Balak, Lo, I am **c** unto thee: 935
23: 3 peradventure the LORD will **c** to meet 7136
23: 7 *saying*, **C**, curse me Jacob, and come, 1980
23: 7 curse me Jacob, and **c**, defy Israel. 1980
23:13 Balak said unto him, **C**, I pray thee, 1980
23:27 Balak said unto Balaam, **C**, I pray thee, 1980
24:14 **c** *therefore, and* I will advertise thee what 1980
24:17 there shall **c** a Star out of Jacob, and 1869
24:19 Out of Jacob shall **c** *he* that shall have NIH
24:24 ships *shall* **c** from the coast of Chittim, and NIH
26:29 of Gilead **c** the family of the Gileadites. NIH
27:21 at his word they shall **c in**, *both* he, and 935
31:24 and afterward ye shall **c** into the camp. 935
33:38 of Israel were **c out** of the land of Egypt, 3318
33:55 **c to** pass, *that those* which ye let **remain** 3498
33:56 Moreover it shall **c to pass**, *that* I shall do 1961
34: 2 When ye **c** into the land of Canaan; 935
35:10 When ye be **c over** Jordan into the land of 5674
35:26 if the slayer shall **at any time c** 3318+3318
35:32 that he should **c again** to dwell in the land, 7725
Dt 1:20 Ye are **c** unto the mountain of the Amorites, 935
1:22 must go up, and into what cities we shall **c**. 935
2:14 until we were **c over** the brook Zered, 5674
4:30 all these things are **c upon** thee, *even* in 4672
4:46 after they were **c forth** out of Egypt: 3318
6:20 *And* when thy son asketh thee **in time to c**, 4279
7:12 Wherefore it shall **c to pass**, if ye hearken 1961
10: 1 **c up** unto me into the mount, and 5927
11:13 it shall **c to pass**, if you shall hearken 1961
11:29 it shall **c to pass**, when the LORD thy 1961
12: 5 shall ye seek, and thither thou shalt **c**: 935
12: 9 For ye are not as yet **c** to the rest and to 935
13: 2 the sign or the wonder **c to pass**, whereof he 935
14:29 shall **c**, and shall eat and be satisfied; 935
15:19 All the firstling males that **c** of thy herd and 3205
17: 9 And thou shalt **c** unto the priests the Levites, 935
17:14 When thou art **c** unto the land which 935
18: 6 if a Levite **c** from any of thy gates out of all 935
18: 6 **c** with all the desire of his mind unto 935
18: 9 When thou art **c** into the land which 935
18:19 it shall **c to pass**, *that* whosoever will not 1961
18:22 if the thing follow not, nor **c to pass**, that *is* 935
20: 2 shall be, when ye are **c nigh** unto the battle, 7126
21: 2 thy elders and thy judges shall **c forth**, 3318
21: 5 the priests the sons of Levi shall **c near**; 5066
23:10 of the camp, he shall not **c** within the camp: 935
23:11 sun is down, he shall **c** into the camp *again*. 935
24: 1 it **c to pass** that she find no favour in his 1961
24: 9 after that ye were **c forth** out of Egypt. 3318
25: 1 they **c** unto judgment, that *the judges* may 5066
25: 9 shall his brother's wife **c** unto him in 5066
25:17 when ye were **c forth** out of Egypt; 3318
26: 1 when thou art **c in** unto the land which 935
26: 3 that I am **c** unto the country which 935
27:12 the people, when ye are **c over** Jordan; 5674
28: 1 it shall **c to pass**, if thou shalt hearken 1961
28: 2 all these blessings shall **c** on thee, and 935
28: 7 they shall **c out** against thee one way, and 3318
28:15 it shall **c to pass**, if thou wilt not hearken 1961
28:15 that all these curses shall **c** upon thee, and 935
28:24 from heaven shall it **c down** upon thee, 3381
28:43 very high; and thou shalt **c down** very low. 3381
28:45 Moreover all these curses shall **c** upon thee, 935
28:52 until thy high and fenced walls **c down**, 3381
28:63 it shall **c to pass**, *that* as the LORD 1961
29:19 it **c to pass**, when he heareth the words of 1961
29:22 So that the generation **to c** of your children 314
29:22 the stranger that shall **c** from a far land, 935
30: 1 it shall **c to pass**, when all these things are 1961
30: 1 when all these things are **c** upon thee, 935
31: 2 old *this* day; I can no more go out and **c in**: 935
31:11 When all Israel is **c** to appear before 935
31:17 Are not these evils **c upon** us, because our 4672
31:21 And it shall **c to pass**, when many evils and 1961
32:35 the **things that shall c** upon them make 6264
33:16 let *the blessing* **c** upon the head of Joseph, 935
Jos 2: 3 Bring forth the men that are **c** to thee, 935
2: 3 for they be **c** to search out all the country. 935
2:18 Behold, *when* we **c** into the land, thou shalt 935
3: 4 **c** not **near** unto it, that ye may know 7126
3: 8 When ye are **c** to the brink of the water of 935
3: 9 **C** hither, and hear the words of the LORD 5066
3:13 it shall **c to pass**, as soon as the soles of 1961
3:13 *from* the waters that **c down** from above; 3381
3:15 as they that bare the ark were **c** unto Jordan, 935
4: 6 your children ask *their fathers* **in time to c**, 4279
4:16 the Testimony, that they **c up** out of Jordan. 5927
4:17 the priests, saying, **C** ye **up** out of Jordan. 5927
4:18 were **c up** out of the midst of Jordan, 5927
4:21 children shall ask their fathers **in time to c**, 4279
5:14 of the host of the LORD am I now **c**. 935
6: 5 it shall **c to pass**, *that* when *they* make a 1961
6:19 they shall **c** *into* the treasury of the LORD. 935
7:14 shall **c** according to the families *thereof*; 7126

Jos 7:14 LORD shall take shall **c** by households; 7126
7:14 the LORD shall take shall **c** man by man. 7126
8: 5 it shall **c to pass**, when they come out 1961
8: 5 when they **c out** against us, as at the first, 3318
8: 6 (For they will **c out** after us) till we have 3318
9: 6 men of Israel, We be **c** from a far country: 935
9: 8 Who *are* ye? and from whence **c** ye? 935
9: 9 From a very far country thy servants are **c** 935
10: 4 **C up** unto me, and help me, that we may 5927
10: 6 **c up** to us quickly, and save us, and 5927
10:24 **C near**, put your feet upon the necks of 7126
11:20 that *they* should **c against** Israel *in* battle, 7125
14:11 for war, both to go out, and to **c in**. 935
18: 4 of them; and they shall **c** *again* to me. 935
18: 8 the land, and describe it, and **c again** to me, 7725
20: 6 **c** unto his own city, and unto his own house, 935
22:24 **In time to c** your children might speak 4279
22:27 may not say to our children **in time to c**, 4279
22:28 say to us or to our generations **in time to c**, 4279
23: 7 That *ye* **c** not among these nations, these that 935
23:14 all are **c to pass** unto you, *and* not one thing 935
23:15 Therefore it shall **c to pass**, *that* as all good 1961
23:15 *that* as all good things are **c** upon you, 935
Jdg 1: 3 his brother, **C up** with me into my lot, 5927
1:24 the spies saw a man **c forth** out of the city, 3318
1:34 for they would not suffer them to **c down** to 3381
3:27 it came to pass, when he was **c**, that he blew 935
4:20 when any man doth **c** and inquire of thee, 935
4:22 **C**, and I will shew thee the man whom thou 1980
6: 4 till thou **c** *unto* Gaza, and left no sustenance 935
6:18 until I **c** unto thee, and bring forth my 935
6:18 And he said, I will tarry until thou **c again**. 7725
7:13 when Gideon was **c**, behold, *there was* a man 935
7:17 behold, when I **c** to the outside of the camp, 935
7:24 **C down** against the Midianites, and 3381
8: 9 saying, When I **c again** in peace, I will 7725
9:10 to the fig tree, **C** thou, *and* reign over us. 1980
9:12 unto the vine, **C** thou, *and* reign over us. 1980
9:14 the bramble, **C** thou, *and* reign over us. 1980
9:15 *then* **c** *and* put your trust in my shadow: 935
9:15 let fire **c out** of the bramble, and devour 3318
9:20 let fire **c out** from Abimelech, and 3318
9:20 and let fire **c out** from the men of Shechem, 3318
9:24 and ten sons of Jerubbaal might **c**, 935
9:29 Increase thine army, and **c out**. 3318
9:31 of Ebed and his brethren be **c** to Shechem; 935
9:33 the people that *is* with him **c out** against 3318
9:36 there **c** people **down** from the top of 3381
9:37 See there **c** people **down** by the middle of 3381
9:37 another company **c** along by the plain of 935
9:43 the people *were* **c forth** out of the city; 3318
11: 6 said unto Jephthah, **C**, and be our captain, 1980
11: 7 why are ye **c** unto me now when ye are in 935
11:12 that thou art **c** against me to fight in my 935
11:33 even till thou **c** *to* Minnith, *even* twenty 935
12: 3 are ye **c up** unto me this day, 5927
13: 5 bear a son; and no rasor shall **c** on his head: 5927
13: 8 let the man of God which thou didst send **c** 935
13:12 Manoah said, Now let thy words **c to pass**. 935
13:17 that when thy sayings **c to pass** we may do 935
15:10 of Judah said, Why are ye **c up** against us? 5927
15:10 To bind Samson are we **c up**, 5927
15:12 said unto him, We are **c down** to bind thee, 3381
16: 2 *told* the Gazites, saying, Samson is **c** hither. 935
16:17 There hath not **c** a rasor upon mine head; 5927
16:18 saying, **C up** *this* once, for he hath shewed 5927
18:10 ye shall **c** unto a people secure, and to a 935
19:11 **C**, I pray thee, and let us turn in into this 1980
19:13 **C**, and let us draw near to one of *these* 1980
19:23 seeing that this man is **c** into mine house, 935
19:29 when he was **c** into his house, he took a 935
20:10 may do, when they **c** to Gibeah of Benjamin, 935
20:41 for they saw that evil was **c** upon them. 5060
21: 3 of Israel, why is this **c to pass** in Israel, 1961
21:21 if the daughters of Shiloh **c out** to dance in 3318
21:21 **c** ye **out** of the vineyards, and catch you 3318
21:22 or their brethren **c** unto us to complain, 935
Ru 1:19 to pass, when they were **c** *to* Beth-lehem, 935
2:11 art **c** unto a people which thou knewest not 1980
2:12 under whose wings thou art **c** to trust. 935
2:14 At mealtime **c** thou hither, and eat of 5066
4: 3 that is **c again** out of the country of Moab, 7725
4:11 The LORD make the woman that is **c** into 935
1Sa 1:11 and there shall no rasor **c** upon his head. 5927
1:20 when the time was **c about** after 8622+3807.1
2: 3 let *not* arrogancy **c out** of your mouth: 3318
2:31 Behold, the days **c**, that I will cut off thine 935
2:34 that shall **c** upon thy two sons, on Hophni 935
2:36 it shall **c to pass**, *that* every one that is left 1961
2:36 every one that is left in thine house shall **c** 935
4: 3 when the people were **c** into the camp, 935
4: 6 the ark of the LORD was **c** into the camp. 935
4: 7 for they said, God is **c** into the camp. 935
5: 5 of Dagon, nor any that **c** *into* Dagon's house, 935
6: 7 on which there hath **c** no yoke, and tie 5927
6:21 **c** ye **down**, *and* fetch it up to you. 3381
9: 5 *And* when they were **c** to the land of Zuph, 935
9: 5 that *was* with him, **C**, and let us return; 1980
9: 9 thus he spake, **C**, and let us go to the seer: 1980
9:10 Saul to his servant, Well said; **c**, let us go. 1980
9:13 As soon as ye be **c** *into* the city, ye shall 935
9:13 for the people will not eat until he **c**, because 935
9:14 *and* when they were **c** into the city, behold, 935
9:16 my people, because their cry is **c** unto me. 935
9:25 when they were **c down** from the high 3381
10: 3 thou shalt **c** to the plain of Tabor, and 935
10: 5 After that thou shalt **c** to the hill of God, 935
10: 5 it shall **c to pass**, when thou art come 1961
10: 5 to pass, when thou art **c** thither *to* the city, 935
10: 6 the spirit of the LORD will **c** upon thee, 6743
10: 7 let it be, when these signs are **c** unto thee, 935
10: 8 behold, I will **c down** unto thee, to offer 3381
10: 8 till I **c** to thee, and shew thee what thou shalt 935
10:11 What *is* this *that* is **c** unto the son of Kish? 1961
10:20 had **caused** all the tribes of Israel **to c near**, 7126

1Sa 10:21 **caused** the tribe of Benjamin **to c near** by 7126
10:22 if the man should yet **c** thither. 935
11: 3 *be* no man to save us, we will **c out** to thee. 3318
11:10 To morrow we will **c out** unto you, and 3318
11:14 **C**, and let us go *to* Gilgal, and renew 1980
12: 8 When Jacob was **c** *into* Egypt, and 935
13:12 The Philistines will **c down** now upon me 3381
14: 1 **C**, and let us go over to the Philistines' 1980
14: 6 **C**, and let us go over unto the garrison of 1980
14: 9 say thus unto us, Tarry until we **c** to you; 5060
14:10 if they say thus, **C up** unto us; then we will 5927
14:11 the Hebrews **c forth** out of the holes where 3318
14:12 **C up** to us, and we will shew you a thing. 5927
14:12 said unto his armourbearer, **C up** after me: 5927
14:26 when the people were **c** into the wood, 935
16: 2 say, I am **c** to sacrifice to the LORD. 935
16: 5 I am **c** to sacrifice unto the LORD: 935
16: 5 and **c** with me to the sacrifice. 935
16: 6 it came to pass, when they were **c**, that he 935
16:11 for we will not sit down till he **c** hither. 935
16:16 it shall **c to pass**, when the evil spirit from 1961
17: 8 Why are ye **c out** to set *your* battle in 3318
17: 8 a man for you, and let him **c down** to me. 3381
17:25 Have ye seen this man that is **c up**? 5927
17:25 surely to defy Israel is he **c up**: and it shall 5927
17:28 for thou art **c down** that *thou* mightest see 3381
17:44 **C** to me, and I will give thy flesh unto 1980
17:45 I **c** to thee in the name of the LORD of 935
17:52 until thou **c** *to* the valley, and to the gates of 935
19:16 when the messengers were **c in**, behold *there* 935
20: 9 determined by my father to **c** upon thee, 935
20:11 **C**, and let us go out *into* the field. 1980
20:19 **c** to the place where thou didst hide thyself 935
20:21 on this side of thee, take them; then **c** thou: 935
20:24 when the new moon was **c**, the king sat him 1961
20:37 when the lad was **c** to the place of the arrow 935
21:15 shall this *fellow* **c** into my house? 935
22: 3 I pray thee, **c forth**, *and be* with you, 3318
23: 3 if we **c** *to* Keilah against the armies of 1980
23: 7 it was told Saul that David was **c** *to* Keilah. 935
23:10 heard that Saul seeketh to **c** to Keilah, 935
23:11 Will Saul **c down**, as thy servant hath 3381
23:11 And the LORD said, He will **c down**. 3381
23:15 David saw that Saul was **c out** to seek his 3318
23:20 **c down** according to all the desire of thy 3381
23:20 to all the desire of thy soul to **c down**; 3381
23:23 **c** ye **again** to me with the certainty, and 7725
23:23 it shall **c to pass**, if he be in the land, that I 1961
23:27 unto Saul, saying, Haste thee, and **c**; 1980
24:14 After whom is the king of Israel **c out**? 3318
25: 8 for we **c** in a good day: give, I pray thee, 935
25:19 Go on before me; behold, I **c** after you. 935
25:30 it shall **c to pass**, when the LORD shall 1961
25:34 except thou hadst hasted and **c** to meet me, 935
25:40 when the servants of David were **c** to 935
26: 4 and understood that Saul was **c** in very deed. 935
26:10 or his day shall **c** to die; or he shall descend 935
26:20 for the king of Israel is **c out** to seek a flea, 3318
26:22 let one of the young men **c over** and 5674
29:10 thy master's servants that are **c** with thee: 935
30: 1 his men were **c** *to* Ziklag on the third day, 935
31: 4 lest these uncircumcised **c** and thrust me 935
2Sa 1: 9 for anguish is **c upon** me, because my life *is* 270
2:24 the sun went down when they were **c** to 935
3:23 and all the host that *was* with him were **c**, 935
3:26 when Joab was **c out** from David, he sent 3318
5: 6 and the lame, thou shalt not **c in** hither: 935
5: 6 in hither: thinking, David cannot **c in** hither. 935
5: 8 and the lame shall not **c** into the house. 935
5:13 of Jerusalem, after he was **c** from Hebron: 935
5:23 **c** upon them over against the mulberry trees. 935
5:25 smote the Philistines from Geba until thou **c** 935
6: 9 How shall the ark of the LORD **c** to me? 935
7:19 house for a **great while to c**. 4480+7350
9: 6 the son of Saul, was **c** unto David, he fell on 935
10:11 strong for thee, then I will **c** and help thee. 1980
11: 7 when Uriah was **c** unto him, David 935
12: 4 to dress for the wayfaring man that was **c** 935
12: 4 and dressed it for the man that was **c** to him. 935
13: 5 let my sister Tamar **c**, and give me meat, and 935
13: 6 when the king was **c** to see him, Amnon said 935
13: 6 let Tamar my sister **c**, and make *me* a couple 935
13:11 and said unto her, **C** lie with me, my sister. 935
13:35 said unto the king, Behold, the king's sons **c**: 935
14: 3 **c** to the king, and speak on this manner unto 935
14:15 that I am **c** to speak of this thing unto my 935
14:29 him to the king; but he would not **c** to him: 935
14:29 sent again the second time, he would not **c**. 935
14:32 Behold, I sent unto thee, saying, **C** hither, 935
14:32 to say, Wherefore am I **c** from Geshur? 935
15: 4 hath *any* suit or cause might **c** unto me, 935
15:28 until there **c** word from you to certify me. 935
15:32 that *when* David was **c** to the top *of* 935
16: 7 **C out**, come out, thou bloody man, and 3318
16: 7 Come out, **c out**, thou bloody man, and 3318
16:16 David's friend, was **c** unto Absalom, 935
17: 2 And I will **c** upon him while he *is* weary and 935
17: 6 when Hushai was **c** to Absalom, 935
17: 9 it will **c to pass**, when *some* of them be 1961
17:12 So shall we **c** upon him in some place where 935
17:17 for they might not be seen to **c** into the city: 935
17:27 to pass, when David was **c** to Mahanaim, 935
19:11 seeing the speech of all Israel is **c** to 935
19:18 before the king, as he was **c over** Jordan; 5674
19:20 I am **c** the first *this* day of all the house of 935
19:25 when he was **c** *to* Jerusalem to meet 935
19:30 forasmuch as my lord the king is **c** *again* in 935
19:33 **C** thou **over** with me, and I will feed thee 5674
19:39 when the king was **c over**, the king kissed 5674
20:16 say, I pray you, unto Joab, **C near** hither, 7126
20:17 when he was **c near** unto her, the woman 7126
24:13 Shall seven years of famine **c** unto thee in 935
24:21 Wherefore is my lord the king **c** to his 935
1Ki 1:12 Now therefore **c**, let me, I pray thee, 1980
1:14 I also will **c in** after thee, and confirm thy 935

1Ki 1:21 Otherwise it shall **c to pass**, when my lord 1961
1:23 when he was **c in** before the king, he bowed 935
1:35 ye shall **c up** after him, that he may come 5927
1:35 that he may **c** and sit upon my throne; 935
1:42 Adonijah said *unto him*, **C in**; for thou *art* a 935
1:45 they are **c up** from thence rejoicing, so 5927
2:30 said unto him, Thus saith the king, **C forth**. 3318
2:41 from Jerusalem *to* Gath, and was **c again**. 7725
3: 7 little child: I know not *how* to go out or **c in**. 935
6: 1 of Israel were **c out** of the land of Egypt, 3318
8:10 when the priests were **c out** of the holy 3318
8:19 thy son that shall **c forth** out of thy loins, 3318
8:31 the oath **c** before thine altar in this house: 935
8:42 when he shall **c** and pray towards this house; 935
10: 2 when she was **c** to Solomon, she communed 935
11: 2 in to them, neither shall they **c in** unto you: 935
12: 1 for all Israel were **c** *to* Shechem to make him 935
12: 5 yet *for* three days, then **c again** to me. 7725
12:12 saying, **C** to me **again** the third day. 7725
12:20 all Israel heard that Jeroboam was **c again**, 7725
12:21 when Rehoboam was **c** *to* Jerusalem, he 935
13: 7 **C** home with me, and refresh *thyself*, and 935
13:15 unto him, **C** home with me, and eat bread. 1980
13:22 thy carcase shall not **c** unto the sepulchre of 935
13:32 of Samaria, shall **surely c to pass**. 1961+1961
14: 6 that he said, **C in**, thou wife of Jeroboam; 935
14:13 for he only of Jeroboam shall **c** to the grave, 935
15:17 *any* to go out or **c in** to Asa king of Judah. 935
15:19 **c** *and* break thy league with Baasha king of 1980
17:18 art thou **c** unto me to call my sin to 935
17:21 let this child's soul **c** into him **again**. 7725
18:12 it shall **c to pass**, *as soon as* I am gone from 1961
18:12 *so* when I **c** and tell Ahab, and he cannot 935
18:30 said unto all the people, **C near** unto me. 5066
19:17 it shall **c to pass**, *that* him that escapeth 1961
20:17 There are men **c out** of Samaria. 3318
20:18 he said, Whether they be **c out** for peace, 3318
20:18 or whether they be **c out** for war, take them 3318
20:22 the king of Syria will **c up** against thee. 5927
20:33 whether *any thing would* **c** from him, NIH
20:33 and he **caused** him to **c up** into the chariot. 5927
22:27 with water of affliction, until I **c** in peace. 935
2Ki 1: 4 Thou shalt not **c down** from *that* bed on 3381
1: 6 thou shalt not **c down** from *that* bed on 3381
1: 9 man of God, the king hath said, **C down**. 3381
1:10 let fire **c down** from heaven, and 3381
1:11 thus hath the king said, **C down** quickly. 3381
1:12 let fire **c down** from heaven, and 3381
1:16 thou shalt not **c down** off *that* bed on which 3381
3:21 the kings were **c up** to fight against them, 5927
4: 1 the creditor is **c** to take unto him my two 935
4: 4 when thou art **c in**, thou shalt shut the door 935
4:22 I may run to the man of God, and **c again**. 7725
4:32 when Elisha was **c** into the house, behold, 935
4:36 when she was **c in** unto him, he said, 935
5: 6 saying, Now when this letter is **c** unto thee, 935
5: 8 let him **c** now to me, and he shall know that 935
5:10 thy flesh shall **c again** to thee, and 7725
5:11 He will **surely c out** to me, and 3318+3318
5:22 even now there be **c** to me from mount 935
6: 9 a place; for thither the Syrians are **c down**. 5185
6:20 when they were **c** *into* Samaria, that Elisha 935
7: 4 Now therefore **c**, and let us fall unto 1980
7: 5 when they were **c** to the uttermost part of 935
7: 6 and the kings of the Egyptians, to **c** upon us. 935
7: 9 *some* mischief will **c upon** us: 4672
7: 9 now therefore **c**, that we may go and 1980
7:12 saying, When they **c out** of the city, we 3318
8: 1 and it shall also **c** upon the land seven years. 935
8: 7 told him, saying, The man of God is **c** hither. 935
9:16 Ahaziah king of Judah was **c down** to see 3381
9:30 when Jehu was **c** to Jezreel, Jezebel heard *of* 935
9:34 And when he was **c in**, he did eat and drink, 935
10: 6 **c** to me to Jezreel by to morrow *this* time. 935
10:16 **C** with me, and see my zeal for 1980
10:25 Go in, *and* slay them; let none **c forth**. 3318
11: 9 his men that were to **c in** on the sabbath, 935
14: 8 son of Jehu, king of Israel, saying, **C**, 1980
16: 7 **c up**, and save me out of the hand of 5927
16:12 when the king was **c** from Damascus, 935
18:13 **c up** against all the fenced cities of Judah, 5927
18:17 when they were **c up**, they came and 5927
18:25 Am I now **c up** without the LORD against 5927
18:31 **c out** to me, and *then* eat ye every man of 3318
18:32 Until I **c** and take you away to a land like 935
19: 3 for the children are **c** to the birth, and *there is* 935
19: 9 Behold, he is **c out** to fight against thee: 3318
19:23 I am **c up** *to* the height of the mountains, 5927
19:28 and thy tumult is **c up** into mine ears, 5927
19:32 He shall not **c** into this city, nor shoot an 935
19:32 an arrow there, nor **c before** it *with* shield, 6923
19:33 shall not **c** into this city, saith the LORD. 935
20:14 They are **c** from a far country, 935
20:17 Behold, the days **c**, that all that *is* in thine 935
1Ch 9:25 *were* to **c** after seven days from time to time 935
10: 4 lest these uncircumcised **c** and abuse me. 935
11: 5 Jebus said to David, Thou shalt not **c** hither. 935
12:17 If ye be **c** peaceably unto me to help me, 935
12:17 but if *ye be* **c** to betray me to mine enemies, NIH
12:31 by name, to **c** and make David king. 935
14:14 **c** upon them over against the mulberry trees. 935
16:29 bring an offering, and **c** before him: 935
17:11 it shall **c to pass**, when thy days be expired 1961
17:17 house for a **great while to c**, 4480+7350
19: 3 are not his servants **c** unto thee for to search, 935
19: 9 the kings that were **c** *were* by themselves in 935
24:19 service to **c** into the house of the LORD, 935
29:12 Both riches and honour **c** of thee, and NIH
29:14 willingly after this *sort?* for all *things* **c** of NIH
2Ch 1:10 that I may go out and **c in** before this people: 935
5:11 when the priests were **c out** of the holy 3318
6: 9 thy son which shall **c forth** out of thy loins, 3318
6:22 the oath **c** before thine altar in this house; 935
6:32 is **c** from a far country for thy great name's 935
6:32 out arm; if they **c** and pray in this house; 935

2Ch 8:11 whereunto the ark of the LORD hath **c**. 935
9: 1 when she was **c** to Solomon, she communed 935
10: 1 for *to* Shechem were all Israel **c** to make him 935
10: 5 **C again** unto me after three days. 7725
10:12 saying, **C again** to me on the third day. 7725
11: 1 when Rehoboam was **c** *to* Jerusalem, he 935
13:13 Jeroboam caused an ambushment to **c** about 935
16: 1 let none go out or **c in** to Asa king of Judah. 935
18:14 when he was **c** to the king, the king said unto 935
19:10 what cause soever shall **c** to you of your 935
19:10 *so* wrath **c** upon you, and upon your 1961
20:11 to **c** to cast us out of thy possession, 935
20:16 behold, they **c up** by the cliff of Ziz; and 5927
20:22 and mount Seir, which were **c** against Judah; 935
22: 7 for when he was **c**, he went out with 935
23: 6 But let none **c** *into* the house of the LORD, 935
23: 8 took every man his men that were to **c in** on 935
23:15 when she was **c** to the entering of the horse 935
25:10 the army that was **c** to him out of Ephraim, 935
25:14 after that Amaziah was **c** from the slaughter 935
25:17 the son of Jehu, king of Israel, saying, **C**, 1980
28:17 For again the Edomites had **c** and 935
29:31 **c near** and bring sacrifices and 5066
30: 1 that *they* should **c** to the house of 935
30: 5 that *they* should **c** to keep the passover unto 935
30: 9 so that *they shall* **c again** into this land: 7725
32: 2 when Hezekiah saw that Sennacherib was **c**, 935
32: 4 Why should the kings of Assyria **c**, and 935
32:21 when he was **c** *into* the house of his god, 935
35:21 *I* **c** not against thee *this* day, but against NIH
Ezr 3: 1 when the seventh month was **c**, and 5060
3: 8 all they that were **c** out of the captivity *unto* 935
4:12 up from thee to us are **c** unto Jerusalem, 858
6:21 which were **c again** out of captivity, and 7725
8:35 which were **c** out of the captivity, 935
9:13 after all that is **c** upon us for our evil deeds, 935
10: 8 *that* whosoever would not **c** within three 935
10:14 wives in our cities **c** at appointed times, 935
Ne 2: 7 that they may convey me over till I **c** into 935
2:10 **c** a man to seek the welfare of the children of 935
2:17 **c**, and let us build *up* the wall of Jerusalem, 1980
4: 8 conspired all of them together to **c** *and* 935
4:11 till we **c** in the midst among them, and 935
6: 2 and Geshem sent unto me, saying, **C**, 1980
6: 3 a great work, so that I cannot **c down**: 3381
6: 3 whilst I leave it, and **c down** to you? 3381
6: 7 **C** now therefore, and let us take counsel 1980
6:10 for they will **c** to slay thee; yea, in the night 935
6:10 yea, in the night will they **c** to slay thee. 935
8:17 **c again** out of the captivity made booths, 7725
9:32 that hath **c upon** us, on our kings, on our 4672
13: 1 the Moabite should not **c** into 935
13:22 *that* they should **c** *and* keep the gates, 935
Est 1:12 the queen Vashti refused to **c** at the king's 935
1:17 For *this* deed of the queen shall **c abroad** 3318
1:19 That Vashti **c** no *more* before king 935
2:12 Now when every maid's turn was **c** to go in 5060
2:15 was **c** to go in unto the king, she required 5060
4:11 shall **c** unto the king into the inner court, 935
4:11 I have not been called to **c in** unto the king 935
4:14 who knoweth whether thou art **c** to 5060
5: 4 Haman **c** *this* day unto the banquet that I 935
5: 8 Haman **c** to the banquet that I shall prepare 935
5:12 Esther the queen did let no *man* **c in** with 935
6: 4 Now Haman was **c** into the outward court of 935
6: 5 in the court. And the king said, Let him **c in**. 935
8: 6 to see the evil that shall **c unto** my people? 4672
9:26 this *matter*, and which had **c** unto them, 5060
Job 2:11 heard of all this evil that was **c** upon him, 935
2:11 appointment together to **c** to mourn with him 935
3: 6 let it not **c** into the number of the months. 935
3: 7 be solitary, let no joyful voice **c** therein. 935
3:25 thing which I greatly feared is **c upon** me, 857
3:25 and *that* which I was afraid of is **c** unto me. 935
4: 5 now it is **c** upon thee, and thou faintest; 935
5:26 Thou shalt **c** to *thy* grave in a full age, like as 935
7: 9 he that goeth down *to* the grave shall **c up** 5927
8:22 place of the wicked shall **c to nought**. 369
9:32 *and* we should **c** together in judgment. 935
13:13 I may speak, and let **c** on me what *will*. 5674
13:16 for a hypocrite shall not **c** before him. 935
14:14 appointed time will I wait, till my change **c**. 935
14:21 His sons **c to honour**, and he knoweth *it* 3513
15:21 in prosperity the destroyer shall **c** *upon* him. 935
16:22 When a few years are **c**, then I shall go 857
17:10 But *as for* you all, do you return, and **c** now: 935
18:20 They that **c after** *him* shall be astonied at 314
19:12 His troops **c** together, and raise up their way 935
20:22 every hand of the wicked shall **c** *upon* him. 935
22:21 be at peace: thereby good shall **c** *unto* thee. 935
23: 3 find him! *that* I might **c** *even* to his seat! 935
23:10 he hath tried me, I shall **c forth** as gold. 3318
26:10 until the day and night **c to an end**. 8503
34:28 So that *they* **cause** the cry of the poor **to c** 935
37:13 He **causeth** it to **c**, whether for correction, 4672
38:11 Hitherto shalt thou **c**, but no further: 935
41:13 *or* who can **c** *to him* with his double bridle? 935
41:16 to another, that no air can **c** between them. 935
Ps 5: 7 I will **c** *into* thy house in the multitude of thy 935
7: 9 the wickedness of the wicked **c to an end**; 1584
7:16 his violent dealing shall **c down** upon his 3381
9: 6 destructions are **c** to a perpetual **end**: 8552
14: 7 O that the salvation of Israel *were* **c** out of NIH
17: 2 Let my sentence **c forth** from thy presence; 3318
22:31 They shall **c**, and shall declare his 935
24: 7 and the King of glory shall **c in**. 935
24: 9 and the King of glory shall **c in**. 935
32: 6 great waters they shall not **c nigh** unto him. 5060
32: 9 and bridle, lest *they* **c near** unto thee. 7126
34:11 **C**, ye children, hearken unto me: I will 1980
35: 8 Let destruction **c upon** him at unawares; and 935
36:11 Let not the foot of pride **c** against me, and 935
40: 7 said I, Lo, I **c**: in the volume of the book *it is* 935
41: 6 if he **c** to see *me*, he speaketh vanity: 935
42: 2 when shall I **c** and appear before God? 935

Ps 44:17 All this is **c upon** us; yet have we not 935
46: 8 **C**, behold the works of the LORD, 1980
50: 3 Our God shall **c**, and shall not keep silence: 935
52: T David is **c** to the house of Ahimelech. 935
53: 6 O that the salvation of Israel *were* **c** out of NIH
55: 5 Fearfulness and trembling are **c** upon me, 935
65: 2 hearest prayer, unto thee shall all flesh **c**. 935
66: 5 **C** and see the works of God: *he is* terrible 1980
66:16 **C** *and* hear, all ye that fear God, and I will 1980
68:31 Princes shall **c** out of Egypt; Ethiopia shall 857
69: 1 O God; for the waters are **c in** unto *my* soul. 935
69: 2 I am **c** into deep waters, where the floods 935
69:27 and let them not **c** into thy righteousness. 935
71:18 *and* thy power to every one *that* is to **c**. 935
72: 6 He shall **c down** like rain upon the mown 3381
78: 4 shewing to the generation to **c** the praises of 314
78: 6 That the generation to **c** might know *them*, 314
79: 1 the heathen are **c** into thine inheritance; 935
79:11 Let the sighing of the prisoner **c** before thee; 935
80: 2 stir up thy strength, and **c** and save us. 1980
83: 4 **C**, and let us cut them off from *being* a 1980
86: 9 All nations whom thou hast made shall **c** and 935
88: 2 Let my prayer **c** before thee: incline thine ear 935
88: 8 *I am* shut up, and I cannot **c forth**. 3318
91: 7 thy right hand; *but* it shall not **c nigh** thee. 5066
91:10 *neither* shall *any* plague **c nigh** thy 7126
95: 1 O **c**, let us sing unto the LORD: let us 1980
95: 2 Let us **c before** his presence with 6923
95: 6 O **c**, let us worship and bow down: let us 935
96: 8 bring an offering, and **c** into his courts. 935
100: 2 **c** before his presence with singing. 935
101: 2 O when wilt thou **c** unto me? I will walk 935
102: 1 O LORD, and let my cry **c** unto thee. 935
102:13 the time to favour her, yea, the set time, is **c**. 935
102:18 This shall be written for the generation to **c**: 314
109:17 As he loved cursing, so let it **c** *unto* him: as 935
109:18 so let it **c** into his bowels like water, and 935
119:41 Let thy mercies **c** also *unto* me, O LORD, 935
119:77 Let thy tender mercies **c** *unto* me, that I may 935
119:169 Let my cry **c near** before thee, O LORD: 7126
119:170 Let my supplication **c** before thee: 935
126: 6 shall **doubtless c again** with rejoicing, 935+935
132: 3 Surely I will not **c** into the tabernacle of my 935
144: 5 Bow thy heavens, O LORD, and **c down**: 3381
Pr 1:11 If they say, **C** with us, let us lay wait for 1980
3:28 Go, and **c again**, and to morrow I will give; 7725
5: 8 and **c** not **nigh** the door of her house: 7126
6: 3 when thou art **c** into the hand of thy friend; 935
6:11 So shall thy poverty **c** as one that travelleth, 935
6:15 Therefore shall his calamity **c** suddenly; 935
7:18 **C**, let us take our fill of love until 1980
7:20 *and* will **c** home at the day appointed. 935
9: 5 **C**, eat of my bread, and drink of the wine 1980
10:24 The fear of the wicked, it shall **c** *upon* him: 935
11:27 he that seeketh mischief, it shall **c** *unto* him. 935
12:13 *his* lips: but the just shall **c out** of trouble. 3318
20:13 Love not sleep, lest thou **c to poverty**; 3423
22:16 that giveth to the rich, *shall* surely **c** to want. NIH
23:21 and the glutton shall **c to poverty**: 3423
24:25 and a good blessing shall **c** upon them. 935
24:34 So shall thy poverty **c** *as* one that travelleth; 935
25: 4 there shall **c forth** a vessel for the finer. 3318
25: 7 *it is* that it be said unto thee, **C up** hither; 5927
26: 2 by flying, so the curse causeless shall not **c**. 935
28:22 considereth not that poverty shall **c** *upon* 935
31:25 and she shall rejoice in time **to c**. 314
Ecc 1: 7 unto the place from whence the rivers **c**, 1980
1:11 that are to **c** with *those* that shall come after. 314
1:11 are to come with *those* that shall **c** after. 1961
1:16 Lo, I am **c to great estate**, and have gotten 1431
2:16 seeing *that* which now *is*, *in* the days to **c** 935
4:16 they also that **c after** shall not rejoice in him. 314
7:18 for he that feareth God shall **c forth** of 3318
8:10 who had **c** and gone from the place of 935
9: 2 All *things* **c** alike to all: *there is* one event to NIH
12: 1 while the evil days **c** not, nor the years draw 935
SS 2:10 Rise up, my love, my fair one, and **c away**. 1980
2:12 the time of the singing *of birds* is **c**, and 5060
2:13 Arise, my love, my fair one, and **c away**. 1980
4: 8 **C** with me from Lebanon, *my* spouse, 935
4:16 Awake, O north wind; and **c** thou south; 935
4:16 Let my beloved **c** into his garden, and eat his 935
5: 1 I am **c** into my garden, my sister, *my* spouse: 935
7:11 **C**, my beloved, let us go forth *into* 1980
Isa 1:12 When ye **c** to appear before me, who hath 935
1:18 **C** now, and let us reason together, saith 1980
1:23 neither doth the cause of the widow **c** unto 935
2: 2 it shall **c to pass** in the last days, *that* 1961
2: 3 **C** ye, and let us go up to the mountain of 1980
2: 5 **c** ye, and let us walk in the light of 1980
3:24 it shall **c to pass**, *that* instead of sweet 1961
4: 3 it shall **c to pass**, *that* he that is left in Zion, 1961
5: 6 but there shall **c up** briers and thorns: 5927
5:19 of the Holy One of Israel draw nigh and **c**, 935
5:26 and behold, they shall **c** with speed swiftly: 935
7: 7 It shall not stand, neither shall it **c to pass**. 1961
7:17 thy father's house, days that have not **c**, 935
7:18 it shall **c to pass** in that day, *that* 1961
7:19 they shall **c**, and shall rest all of them in 935
7:21 it shall **c to pass** in that day, *that* a man 1961
7:22 it shall **c to pass**, for the abundance of milk 1961
7:23 it shall **c to pass** in that day, *that* every 1961
7:24 and with bows shall *men* **c** thither; 935
7:25 there shall not **c** thither the fear of briers and 935
8: 7 he shall **c up** over all his channels, and 5927
8:10 counsel together, and it shall **c to nought**; 6565
8:21 it shall **c to pass**, that when they shall be 1961
10: 3 and in the desolation *which* shall **c** from far? 935
10:12 Wherefore it shall **c to pass**, *that* when 1961
10:20 it shall **c to pass** in that day, *that* 1961
10:27 it shall **c to pass** in that day, *that* his burden 1961
10:28 He is **c** to Aiath, he is passed to Migron; 935
11: 1 there shall **c forth** a rod out of the stem of 3318
11:11 it shall **c to pass** in that day, *that* the Lord 1961
13: 5 They **c** from a far country, from the end of 935

Isa 13: 6 it shall **c** as a destruction from the Almighty. 935
13:22 her time *is* near to **c**, and her days shall not 935
14: 3 it shall **c to pass** in the day that the LORD 1961
14: 8 art laid down, no feller is **c up** against us. 5927
14:24 as I have thought, so shall it **c to pass**; 1961
14:29 for out of the serpent's root shall **c forth** a 3318
14:31 for there shall **c** from the north a smoke, and 935
16: 8 they are **c** *even* unto Jazer, they wandered 5060
16:12 it shall **c to pass**, when it is seen that Moab 1961
16:12 that he shall **c** to his sanctuary to pray; 935
17: 4 in that day it shall **c to pass**, *that* the glory 1961
19: 1 upon a swift cloud, and shall **c** *into* Egypt: 935
19:23 the Assyrian shall **c** into Egypt, and 935
21:12 if ye will inquire, inquire ye: return, **c**. 857
22: 7 it shall **c to pass**, *that* thy choicest valleys 1961
22:20 it shall **c to pass** in that day, that I will call 1961
23:15 it shall **c to pass** in that day, that Tyre shall 1961
23:17 it shall **c to pass** after the end of seventy 1961
24:10 house is shut up, that no *man may* **c in**. 935
24:18 it shall **c to pass**, *that* he who fleeth from 1961
24:21 it shall **c to pass** in that day, *that* 1961
26:20 **C**, my people, enter thou into thy 1980
27: 6 He shall cause them that **c** of Jacob to take 935
27:11 the women **c**, *and* set them on fire: for it *is* a 935
27:12 it shall **c to pass** in that day, *that* 1961
27:13 it shall **c to pass** in that day, *that* the great 1961
27:13 they shall **c** which were ready to perish in 935
28:15 shall pass through, it shall not **c** *unto* us: 935
29:24 in spirit shall **c to understanding**, 998+3045
30: 6 from whence **c** the young and old lion, NIH
30: 8 that it may be for the time **to c** for ever and 314
30:29 as when one goeth with a pipe to **c** into 935
31: 4 shall the LORD of hosts **c down** to fight 3381
32:10 vintage shall fail, the gathering shall not **c**. 935
32:13 Upon the land of my people shall **c up** 5927
34: 1 **C near**, ye nations, to hear; and hearken, 7126
34: 1 the world, and all things **that c forth** of it. 6631
34: 3 their stink shall **c up** *out of* their carcases, 5927
34: 5 it shall **c down** upon Idumea, and upon 3381
34: 7 the unicorns shall **c down** with them, and 3381
34:13 And thorns shall **c up** *in* her palaces, nettles 5927
35: 4 behold, your God will **c** *with* vengeance, 935
35: 4 *with* a recompence; he will **c** and save you. 935
35:10 **c** *to* Zion with songs and everlasting joy 935
36:10 am I now **c up** without the LORD against 5927
36:16 with me *by* a present, and **c out** to me: 3318
36:17 Until I **c** and take you away to a land like 935
37: 3 for the children are **c** to the birth, and *there is* 935
37: 9 He is **c forth** to make war with thee. 3318
37:24 By the multitude of my chariots am I **c up** 5927
37:29 is **c up** into mine ears, therefore will I put 5927
37:33 He shall not **c** into this city, nor shoot an 935
37:33 an arrow there, nor **c before** it *with* shields, 6923
37:34 shall not **c** into this city, saith the LORD. 935
39: 3 They are **c** from a far country unto me, 935
39: 6 Behold, the days **c**, that all that *is* in thine 935
40:10 the Lord GOD will **c** with strong *hand,* and 935
41: 1 let them **c near**; then let them speak: let us 5066
41: 1 let us **c near** together to judgment. 7126
41:22 end of them; or declare us *things* for to **c**. 935
41:23 Shew the *things* that are **to c** hereafter, 857
41:25 raised up *one* from the north, and he shall **c**: 857
41:25 he shall **c** *upon* princes as *upon* morter, and 935
42: 9 the former *things* are **c to pass**, and 935
42:23 *who* will hearken and hear for the **time to c**? 268
44: 7 and shall **c**, let them shew unto them. 935
45:11 Ask me of *things* **to c** concerning my sons, 857
45:14 shall **c over** unto thee, and they shall be 5674
45:14 they shall **c** after thee, in chains they shall 1980
45:14 in chains they shall **c over**, and they shall 5674
45:20 Assemble yourselves and **c**; draw near 935
45:24 *even* to him shall *men* **c**; and all that are 935
47: 1 **C down**, and sit in the dust, O virgin 3381
47: 9 these two *things* shall **c** to thee *in* a moment 935
47: 9 they shall **c** upon thee in their perfection for 935
47:11 Therefore shall evil **c** upon thee; thou shalt 935
47:11 desolation shall **c** upon thee suddenly, 935
47:13 save thee from *these things* that shall **c** upon 935
48: 1 and are **c forth** out of the waters of Judah, 3318
48:16 **C** ye **near** unto me, hear ye this; I have not 7126
49:12 Behold, these shall **c** from far: and lo, 935
49:18 gather themselves together, *and* **c** to thee. 935
50: 8 *is* mine adversary? let him **c near** to me. 5066
51:11 shall return, and **c** with singing *unto* Zion; 935
51:19 These two *things* are **c unto** thee; who shall 7122
52: 1 for henceforth there shall no more **c** into thee 935
54:14 and from terror; for it shall not **c near** thee. 7126
55: 1 **c** ye to the waters, and he that hath no 1980
55: 1 **c** ye, buy, and eat; yea, come, buy wine and 1980
55: 1 yea, **c**, buy wine and milk without money 1980
55: 3 Incline your ear, and **c** unto me: hear, and 1980
55:13 Instead of the thorn shall **c up** the fir tree, 5927
55:13 instead of the brier shall **c up** the myrtle 5927
56: 1 for my salvation *is* near to **c**, and 935
56: 9 All ye beasts of the field, **c** to devour, 857
56:12 **C** ye, *say they,* I will fetch wine, and we will 857
57: 1 righteous is taken away from the evil *to* **c**. NIH
59:19 When the enemy shall **c in** like a flood, 935
59:20 the redeemer shall **c** to Zion, and unto them 935
60: 1 for thy light is **c**, and the glory of 935
60: 3 the Gentiles shall **c** to thy light, and 1980
60: 4 gather themselves together, they **c** to thee: 935
60: 4 thy sons shall **c** from far, and thy daughters 935
60: 5 the forces of the Gentiles shall **c** unto thee. 935
60: 6 and Ephah; all they from Sheba shall **c**: 935
60: 7 they shall **c up** with acceptance on mine 5927
60:13 The glory of Lebanon shall **c** unto thee, 935
60:14 that afflicted thee shall **c** bending unto thee; 1980
63: 4 and the year of my redeemed is **c**. 935
64: 1 the heavens, that thou wouldest **c down**, 3381
65: 5 Stand by thyself, **c** not **near** to me; 5066
65:17 shall not be remembered, nor **c** into mind. 5927
65:24 it shall **c to pass**, that before they call, I 1961
66:15 the LORD will **c** with fire, and with his 935
66:18 it shall **c**, that *I* will gather all nations and 935

Isa 66:18 tongues; and they shall **c**, and see my glory. 935
66:23 it shall **c to pass**, *that* from one new moon 1961
66:23 shall all flesh **c** to worship before me, 935
Jer 1:15 they shall **c**, and they shall set every one his 935
2: 3 evil shall **c** upon them, saith the LORD. 935
2:31 We are lords; we will **c** no more unto thee? 935
3:16 it shall **c to pass**, when ye be multiplied 1961
3:16 neither shall it **c** to mind: neither shall they 5927
3:18 they shall **c** together out of the land of 935
3:22 Behold, we **c** unto thee; for thou *art* 857
4: 4 lest my fury **c forth** like fire, and burn that 3318
4: 7 The lion is **c up** from his thicket, and 5927
4: 9 it shall **c to pass** at that day, saith 1961
4:12 *Even* a full wind from those *places* shall **c** 935
4:13 he shall **c up** as clouds, and his chariots 5927
4:16 *that* watchers **c** from a far country, and 935
5:12 said, *It is* not he; neither shall evil **c** upon us; 935
5:19 it shall **c to pass**, when ye shall say, 1961
6: 3 The shepherds with their flocks shall **c** unto 935
6:26 for the spoiler shall suddenly **c** upon us. 935
7:10 **c** and stand before me in this house, which is 935
7:32 Therefore, behold, the days **c**, saith 935
8:16 for they are **c**, and have devoured the land, 935
9:17 for the mourning *women,* that they may **c**; 935
9:17 send for cunning *women,* that they may **c**: 935
9:21 For death is **c up** into our windows, *and* 5927
9:25 Behold, the days **c**, saith the LORD, that I 935
10:22 the noise of the bruit is **c**, and a great 935
12: 9 **c** ye, assemble all the beasts of the field, 1980
12: 9 all the beasts of the field, **c** to devour. 857
12:12 The spoilers are **c** upon all high places 935
12:15 it shall **c to pass**, after that I have plucked 1961
12:16 it shall **c to pass**, if they will diligently 1961
13:18 for your principalities shall **c down**, 3381
13:20 and behold them that **c** from the north: 935
13:22 Wherefore **c** these *things* **upon** me? 7122
15: 2 it shall **c to pass**, if they say unto thee, 1961
16:10 it shall **c to pass**, when thou shalt shew this 1961
16:14 the days **c**, saith the LORD, 935
16:19 the Gentiles shall **c** unto thee from the ends 935
17:15 *is* the word of the LORD? let it **c** now. 935
17:19 whereby the kings of Judah **c in**, and by 935
17:24 it shall **c to pass**, if ye diligently hearken 1961
17:26 they shall **c** from the cities of Judah, and 935
18:14 shall the cold flowing waters that **c** from NIH
18:18 **C**, and let us devise devices against 1980
18:18 **C**, and let us smite him with the tongue, 1980
19: 6 the days **c**, saith the LORD, 935
20: 6 thou shalt **c** *to* Babylon, and there thou shalt 935
21:13 which say, Who shall **c down** against us? 5181
22:23 how gracious shalt thou be when pangs **c** 935
23: 5 Behold, the days **c**, saith the LORD, that I 935
23: 7 the days **c**, saith the LORD, 935
23:17 of his own heart, No evil shall **c** upon you. 935
25: 3 the word of the LORD hath **c** unto me, 1961
25:12 it shall **c to pass**, when seventy years are 1961
25:31 A noise shall **c** *even* to the ends of the earth; 935
26: 2 which **c** to worship *in* the LORD'S house, 935
27: 3 by the hand of the messengers which **c** *to* 935
27: 7 son's son, until the very time of his land **c**: 935
27: 8 it shall **c to pass**, *that* the nation and 1961
28: 9 when the word of the prophet shall **c to pass**, 935
30: 3 For lo, the days **c**, saith the LORD, that I 935
30: 8 For it shall **c to pass** in that day, saith 1961
31: 9 They shall **c** with weeping, and 935
31:12 Therefore they shall **c** and sing in the height 935
31:16 they shall **c again** from the land of 7725
31:17 that *thy* children shall **c again** to their own 7725
31:27 Behold, the days **c**, saith the LORD, that I 935
31:28 it shall **c to pass**, *that* like as I have 1961
31:31 Behold, the days **c**, saith the LORD, that I 935
31:38 Behold, the days **c**, saith the LORD, 935
32: 7 son of Shallum thine uncle *shall* **c** unto thee, 935
32:23 thou hast **caused** all this evil **to c upon** 7122
32:24 the mounts, they are **c** *unto* the city to take it; 935
32:24 what thou hast spoken is **c to pass**; and 1961
32:29 shall **c** and set fire on this city, and burn it 935
33: 5 They **c** to fight with the Chaldeans, but *it is* 935
33:14 Behold, the days **c**, saith the LORD, that I 935
35:11 **C**, and let us go *to* Jerusalem for fear of 935
36: 6 the ears of all Judah that **c** out of their cities. 935
36:14 hast read in the ears of the people, and **c**. 1980
36:29 The king of Babylon shall **certainly c** 935+935
37: 5 Pharaoh's army was **c forth** out of Egypt: 3318
37: 7 which is **c forth** to help you, 3318
37: 8 the Chaldeans shall **c again**, and 7725
37:19 The king of Babylon shall not **c** against you, 935
38:25 and they **c** unto thee, and say unto thee, 935
40: 3 his voice, therefore this thing is **c** upon you. 1961
40: 4 If it seem good unto thee to **c** with me *into* 935
40: 4 unto thee to come with me *into* Babylon, **c**; 935
40: 4 if it seem ill unto thee to **c** with me *into* 935
40:10 to serve the Chaldeans, which will **c** unto us: 935
41: 6 unto them, **C** to Gedaliah the son of Ahikam. 935
42: 4 it shall **c to pass**, *that* whatsoever thing 1961
42:16 it shall **c to pass**, *that* the sword, which ye 1961
46: 9 **C up**, ye horses; and rage, ye chariots; and 5927
46: 9 ye chariots; and let the mighty *men* **c forth**; 3318
46:13 Nebuchadrezzar king of Babylon should **c** 935
46:18 and as Carmel by the sea, *so* shall he **c**. 935
46:21 the day of their calamity was **c** upon them, 935
46:22 **c** against her with axes, as hewers of wood. 935
47: 5 Baldness is **c** upon Gaza; Ashkelon is cut off 935
48: 2 **c**, and let us cut it off from *being* a nation. 1980
48: 8 the spoiler shall **c** upon every city, and 935
48:12 the days **c**, saith the LORD, 935
48:16 The calamity of Moab *is* near to **c**, and 935
48:18 **c down** from *thy* glory, and sit in thirst; 3381
48:18 for the spoiler of Moab shall **c** upon thee, 5927
48:21 judgment is **c** upon the plain country; 935
48:45 a fire shall **c forth** out of Heshbon, and 3318
49: 2 the days **c**, saith the LORD, 935
49: 4 her treasures, *saying,* Who shall **c** unto me? 935
49: 9 If grapegatherers **c** to thee, would they not 935
49:14 and **c** against her, and rise up to the battle. 935

Jer 49:19 he shall **c up** like a lion from the swelling 5927
49:22 he shall **c up** and fly as the eagle, and 5927
49:36 whither the outcasts of Elam shall not **c**. 935
49:39 it shall **c to pass** in the latter days, *that* I 1961
50: 4 the children of Israel shall **c**, they and 935
50: 5 *saying,* **C**, and let us join ourselves to 935
50: 9 **cause to c up** against Babylon an assembly 5927
50:26 **C** against her from the utmost border, 935
50:27 for their day is **c**, the time of their visitation. 935
50:31 for thy day is **c**, the time *that* I will visit thee. 935
50:41 a people shall **c** from the north, and a great 935
50:44 he shall **c up** like a lion from the swelling 5927
51:10 **c**, and let us declare in Zion the work of 935
51:13 thine end is **c**, *and* the measure of thy 935
51:27 **cause** the horses **to c up** as the rough 5927
51:33 and the time of her harvest shall **c**. 935
51:42 The sea is **c up** upon Babylon: she is 5927
51:46 a rumour shall both **c** *one* year, and after that 935
51:46 after that in *another* year *shall* **c** a rumour, NIH
51:47 Therefore behold, the days **c**, that I will do 935
51:48 for the spoilers shall **c** unto her from 935
51:50 afar off, and let Jerusalem **c** into your mind. 5927
51:51 for strangers are **c** into the sanctuaries of 935
51:52 the days **c**, saith the LORD, 935
51:53 *yet* from me shall spoilers **c** unto her, 935
51:56 Because the spoiler is **c** upon her, *even* upon 935
51:60 book all the evil that should **c** upon Babylon, 935
La 1: 4 because none **c** to the solemn feasts: 935
1:14 they are wreathed, *and* **c up** upon my neck: 5927
1:22 Let all their wickedness **c** before thee; and 935
3:47 Fear and a snare is **c** upon us, desolation 1961
4:18 our days are fulfilled; for our end is **c**. 935
5: 1 Remember, O LORD, what is **c** upon us: 1961
Eze 5: 4 *for* thereof shall a fire **c forth** into all 3318
7: 2 the end is **c** upon the four corners of 935
7: 3 Now *is* the end **c** upon thee, and I will send NIH
7: 5 An evil, an only evil, behold, is **c**. 935
7: 6 An end is **c**, the end is come: it watcheth for 935
7: 6 An end is come, the end is **c**: it watcheth for 935
7: 6 is come: it watcheth for thee; behold, it is **c**. 935
7: 7 The morning is **c** unto thee, O thou that 935
7: 7 the time is **c**, the day of trouble *is* near, and 935
7:10 Behold the day, behold, it is **c**: the morning 935
7:12 The time is **c**, the day draweth near: let not 935
7:26 Mischief shall **c** upon mischief, and 935
9: 6 **c** not **near** any man upon whom *is* 5066
11: 5 for I know the **things that c into** your 4609
11:16 sanctuary in the countries where they shall **c**. 935
11:18 they shall **c** thither, and they shall take away 935
12:16 among the heathen whither they **c**; 935
12:25 the word that I shall speak shall **c to pass**; 6213
12:27 vision that he seeth *is* for many days *to* **c**, NIH
13:18 will ye save the souls alive *that* **c** unto you? NIH
14:22 they *shall* **c forth** unto you, and ye shall see 3318
16: 7 and thou art **c** to excellent ornaments: 935
16:16 *the like things shall* not **c**, neither shall it be 935
16:33 that *they* may **c** unto thee on every side for 935
17:12 the king of Babylon is **c** *to* Jerusalem, and 935
18: 6 neither hath **c near** to a menstruous 7126
20: 3 the Lord GOD; Are ye **c** to inquire of me? 935
21:19 that the sword of the king of Babylon may **c**: 935
21:19 both twain shall **c forth** out of one land: 3318
21:20 that the sword may **c** to Rabbath of 935
21:24 *I say,* that ye are **c to remembrance**, 2142
21:25 wicked prince of Israel, whose day is **c**, 935
21:27 it shall be no *more,* until he **c** whose right it 935
21:29 whose day is **c**, when *their* iniquity *shall* 935
22: 3 that her time may **c**, and maketh idols 935
22: 4 to draw near, and art **c** *even* unto thy years: 935
23:24 they shall **c** against thee *with* chariots, 935
23:40 that ye have sent for men to **c** from far, 935
24: 8 That *it* might **cause** fury **to c up** to take 5927
24:14 the LORD have spoken *it:* it shall **c to pass**, 935
24:26 *That* he that escapeth in that day shall **c** unto 935
26: 3 will **cause** many nations **to c up** against 5927
26: 3 as the sea **causeth** his waves **to c up**. 5927
26:16 all the princes of the sea shall **c down** from 3381
27:29 of the sea, shall **c down** from their ships, 3381
30: 4 the sword shall **c** upon Egypt, and great pain 935
30: 6 and the pride of her power shall **c down**: 3381
30: 9 great pain shall **c** upon them, as *in* the day 1961
32:11 The sword of the king of Babylon shall **c** 935
33: 3 *If* when he seeth the sword **c** upon the land, 935
33: 4 if the sword **c**, and take him away, his blood 935
33: 6 if the watchman see the sword **c**, and 935
33: 6 if the sword **c**, and take *any* person from 935
33:30 saying, **C**, I pray you, and hear what *is* 935
33:31 they **c** unto thee as the people cometh, and 935
33:33 And when this cometh to pass, (lo, it will **c**) 935
34:26 I will **cause** the shower **to c down** in his 3381
36: 8 my people of Israel; for they are at hand to **c**. 935
37: 9 **C** from the four winds, O breath, and 935
37:12 **cause** you **to c up** out of your graves, and 5927
38: 8 in the latter years thou shalt **c** into the land 935
38: 9 Thou shalt ascend and **c** like a storm, 935
38:10 It shall also **c to pass**, *that* at the same time 1961
38:10 *that* at the same time shall things **c** into thy 5927
38:13 say unto thee, Art thou **c** to take a spoil? 935
38:15 thou shalt **c** from thy place out of the north 935
38:16 thou shalt **c up** against my people of Israel, 5927
38:18 it shall **c to pass** at the same time when 1961
38:18 when Gog shall **c** against the land of Israel, 935
38:18 *that* my fury shall **c up** in my face. 5927
39: 2 will **cause** thee **to c up** from the north 5927
39: 8 Behold, it is **c**, and it is done, saith the Lord 935
39:11 it shall **c to pass** in that day, *that* I will give 1961
39:17 of the field, Assemble yourselves, and **c**; 935
40:46 which **c near** to the LORD to minister 7131
44:13 they shall not **c near** unto me, to do 5066
44:13 nor to **c near** to any of my holy *things,* in 5066
44:15 they shall **c near** to me to minister unto me, 7126
44:16 they shall **c near** to my table, to minister 7126
44:17 it shall **c to pass**, *that* when they enter in at 1961
44:17 no wool shall **c** upon them, whiles they 5927
44:25 they shall **c** at no dead person to defile 935

Eze 45: 4 which shall **c near** to minister unto 7131
46: 9 when the people of the land shall **c** before 935
47: 9 it shall **c to pass**, *that* every thing that 1961
47: 9 whithersoever the rivers shall **c**, shall live: 935
47: 9 of fish, because these waters shall **c** thither: 935
47:10 it shall **c to pass**, *that* the fishers shall stand 1961
47:20 the border, till *a man* **c** over against Hamath. 935
47:22 it shall **c to pass**, *that* ye shall divide it *by* 1961
47:23 it shall **c to pass**, *that* in what tribe 1961
Da 2:29 thy bed, what should **c to pass** hereafter: 1934
2:29 maketh known to thee what shall **c to pass.** 1934
2:45 to the king what shall **c to pass** hereafter: 1934
3: 2 to **c** to the dedication of the image which 858
3:26 **c forth**, and come *hither.* Then Shadrach, 5312
3:26 **c** *hither.* Then Shadrach, Meshach, and 858
4:24 which is **c** upon my lord the king: 4291
8: 7 I saw him **c close** unto the ram, and he was 5060
8:23 when the transgressors are **c to the full,** 8552
9:13 the law of Moses, all this evil is **c** upon us: 935
9:22 I am now **c forth** to give thee skill and 3318
9:23 I am **c** to shew *thee;* for thou *art* greatly 935
9:26 the people of the prince that *shall* **c** shall 935
10:12 words were heard, and I am **c** for thy words. 935
10:14 Now I am **c** to make thee understand what 935
10:20 Knowest thou wherefore I **c** unto thee? 935
10:20 gone forth, lo, the prince of Grecia shall **c.** 935
11: 6 for the king's daughter of the south shall **c** to 935
11: 7 which shall **c** with an army, and shall enter 935
11: 9 So the king of the south shall **c** into *his* 935
11:10 *one* shall **certainly c**, and overflow, 935+935
11:11 shall **c forth** and fight with him, *even* with 3318
11:13 shall **certainly c** after certain years 935+935
11:15 So the king of the north shall **c**, and cast up a 935
11:21 he shall **c** in peaceably, and obtain 935
11:23 for he shall **c up**, and shall become strong 5927
11:29 he shall return, and **c** toward the south; 935
11:30 For *the* ships of Chittim shall **c** against him: 935
11:40 north shall **c** against him **like a whirlwind,** 8175
11:45 yet he shall **c** to his end, and none shall help 935
Hos 1: 5 it shall **c to pass** at that day, that I will 1961
1:10 it shall **c to pass**, *that* in the place where it 1961
1:11 and they shall **c up** out of the land: 5927
2:21 it shall **c to pass** in that day, I will hear, 1961
4:15 **c** not ye *unto* Gilgal, neither go ye up *to* 935
6: 1 **C** and let us return unto the LORD: for he 1980
6: 3 he shall **c** unto us as the rain, as the latter 935
8: 1 *He shall* **c** as an eagle against the house of NIH
9: 4 for their bread for their soul shall not **c** *into* 935
9: 7 The days of visitation are **c**, the days of 935
9: 7 are come, the days of recompence are **c;** 935
10: 8 and the thistle shall **c up** on their altars; 5927
10:12 till he **c** and rain righteousness upon you. 935
13:13 The sorrows of a travailing *woman* shall **c** 935
13:15 among *his* brethren, an east wind shall **c,** 935
13:15 the wind of the LORD *shall* **c up** from 5927
Joel 1: 6 For a nation is **c up** upon my land, strong, 5927
1:13 **c**, lie all night in sackcloth, ye ministers of 935
1:15 as a destruction from the Almighty shall it **c.** 935
2:20 his stink shall **c up**, and his ill savour shall 5927
2:20 his ill savour shall **c up**, because he hath 5927
2:23 he will **cause to c down** for you the rain, 3381
2:28 it shall **c to pass** afterward, that I will pour 1961
2:31 and the terrible day of the LORD **c.** 935
2:32 it shall **c to pass**, *that* whosoever shall call 1961
3: 9 the men of war draw near; let them **c up:** 5927
3:11 **c**, all ye heathen, and gather yourselves 935
3:11 thither **cause** thy mighty ones **to c down,** 5181
3:12 and **c up** to the valley of Jehoshaphat: 5927
3:13 **c**, get you down; for the press is full, the fats 935
3:18 it shall **c to pass** in that day, *that* 1961
3:18 a fountain shall **c forth** of the house of 3318
Am 4: 2 that lo, the days shall **c** upon you, that he 935
4: 4 **C** *to* Beth-el, and transgress; *at* Gilgal 935
4:10 **made** the stink of your camps **to c up** unto 5927
5: 5 and Beth-el shall **c** to nought. 1961
5: 9 that the spoiled shall **c** against the fortress. 935
6: 3 and **cause** the seat of violence **to c near;** 5066
6: 9 it shall **c to pass**, if there remain ten men in 1961
8: 2 The end is **c** upon my people *of* Israel; 935
8: 9 it shall **c to pass** in that day, saith the Lord 1961
8:11 Behold, the days **c**, saith the Lord GOD, 935
9:13 Behold, the days **c**, saith the LORD, 935
Ob 1:21 saviours shall **c up** on mount Zion to judge 5927
Jnh 1: 2 for their wickedness is **c up** before me. 5927
1: 7 one to his fellow, **C**, and let us cast lots, 1980
4: 6 a gourd, and **made** *it* **to c up** over Jonah, 5927
Mic 1: 3 will **c down** and tread upon the high places 3381
1: 9 wound *is* incurable; for it is **c** unto Judah; 935
1: 9 he is **c** unto the gate of my people, *even* to 5060
1:15 he shall **c** unto Adullam the glory of Israel. 935
2:13 The breaker is **c up** before them: they have 5927
3:11 LORD among us? none evil can **c** upon us. 935
4: 1 in the last days it shall **c to pass**, *that* 1961
4: 2 many nations shall **c**, and say, Come, and 1980
4: 2 **C**, and let us go up to the mountain of 1980
4: 8 unto thee shall it **c**, even the first dominion; 857
4: 8 the kingdom shall **c** to the daughter of 935
5: 2 *yet* out of thee shall he **c forth** unto me *that* 3318
5: 5 when the Assyrian shall **c** into our land: 935
5:10 it shall **c to pass** in that day, saith 1961
6: 6 Wherewith shall I **c before** the LORD, 6923
6: 6 shall I **c before** him with burnt offerings, 6923
7:12 *In* that day *also* he shall **c** even to thee from 935
Na 1:11 There is *one* **c out** of thee, that imagineth 3318
2: 1 He that dasheth in pieces is **c up** before thy 5927
3: 7 it shall **c to pass**, *that* all they that look 1961
Hab 1: 8 and their horsemen shall **c** from far; 935
1: 9 They shall **c** all for violence: their faces shall 935
2: 3 it will **surely c**, it will not tarry. 935+935
Zep 1: 8 it shall **c to pass** in the day of 1961
1:10 it shall **c to pass** in that day, saith 1961
1:12 it shall **c to pass** at that time, *that* I will 1961
2: 2 before the fierce anger of the LORD **c** upon 935
2: 2 before the day of the LORD'S anger **c** upon 935
Hag 1: 2 This people say, The time is not **c**, 935
Hag 2: 7 and the desire of all nations shall **c:** 935
2:22 the horses and their riders shall **c down,** 3381
Zec 1:21 said I, What **c** these to do? And he spake, 935
1:21 these are **c** to fray them, to cast out the horns 935
2: 6 **c** *forth,* and flee from the land of the north, NIH
2:10 I **c**, and I will dwell in the midst of thee, 935
6:10 which are **c** from Babylon, and come thou 935
6:10 **c** thou the same day, and go *into* the house of 935
6:15 *they that are* far off shall **c** and build in 935
6:15 *this* shall **c to pass**, if ye will diligently 1961
7:13 Therefore it is **c to pass**, *that* as he cried, 1961
8:13 it shall **c to pass**, *that* as ye were a curse 1961
8:20 *It shall* yet **c** *to pass,* that there shall come NIH
8:20 *It shall* yet *come to pass,* that there shall **c** 935
8:22 strong nations shall **c** to seek the LORD of 935
8:23 In those days *it shall* **c** *to pass,* that ten men NIH
11: 2 for the forest of the vintage is **c down.** 3381
12: 9 it shall **c to pass** in that day, *that* I will seek 1961
12: 9 all the nations that **c** against Jerusalem. 935
13: 2 it shall **c to pass** in that day, saith 1961
13: 3 it shall **c to pass**, *that* when any shall yet 1961
13: 4 it shall **c to pass** in that day, *that* 1961
13: 8 it shall **c to pass**, *that* in all the land, 1961
14: 5 the LORD my God shall **c**, *and* all 935
14: 6 it shall **c to pass** in that day, *that* the light 1961
14: 7 it shall **c to pass**, *that* at evening time it 1961
14:13 it shall **c to pass** in that day, *that* a great 1961
14:16 it shall **c to pass**, *that* every one that is left 1961
14:17 *that* whoso will not **c up** of *all* the families 5927
14:18 if the family of Egypt go not up, and **c** not, 935
14:18 **c** not **up** to keep the feast of tabernacles. 5927
14:19 the punishment of all nations that **c** not **up** 5927
14:21 all they that sacrifice shall **c** and take of 935
Mal 3: 1 ye seek, shall suddenly **c** to his temple, 935
3: 1 behold, he *shall* **c**, saith the LORD of hosts. 935
3: 5 I will **c near** to you to judgment; and I will 7126
4: 6 lest I **c** and smite the earth *with* a curse. 935
Mt 2: 2 star in the east, and are **c** to worship him. *2064*
2: 6 for **out** of thee shall **c** a Governor, that shall *1831*
2: 8 that I may **c** and worship him also. *2064*
2:11 And when they were **c** into the house, *2064*
3: 7 and Sadducees **c** to his baptism, *2064*
3: 7 warned you to flee from the wrath to **c?** *3195*
5:17 Think not that I am **c** to destroy the law, or *2064*
5:17 I am not **c** to destroy, but to fulfil. *2064*
5:24 to thy brother, and then **c** and offer thy gift. *2064*
5:26 Thou shalt by no means **c out** thence, *1831*
6:10 Thy kingdom **c**. Thy will be done in earth, *2064*
7:15 which **c** to you in sheep's clothing, but *2064*
8: 1 When he was **c down** from the mountain, *2597*
8: 7 Jesus saith unto him, I will **c** and heal him. *2064*
8: 8 I am not worthy that thou shouldest **c under** *1525*
8: 9 and to another, **C**, and he cometh; and *2064*
8:11 That many shall **c** from the east and west, *2240*
8:14 And when Jesus was **c** into Peter's house, *2064*
8:16 When the even was **c**, they brought unto *1096*
8:28 And when he was **c** to the other side into *2064*
8:29 art thou **c** hither to torment us before *2064*
8:32 And when they were **c out**, they went into *1831*
9:13 for I am not **c** to call *the* righteous, but *2064*
9:15 but the days will **c**, when the bridegroom *2064*
9:18 but **c** and lay thy hand upon her, and *2064*
9:28 And when he was **c** into the house, *2064*
10:12 And when ye **c into** a house salute it. *1525*
10:13 house be worthy, let your peace **c** upon it: *2064*
10:23 the cities of Israel, till the Son of man be **c.** *2064*
10:34 Think not that I am **c** to send peace on *2064*
10:35 For I am **c** to set a man at variance against *2064*
11: 3 Art thou he that should **c**, or do we look for *2064*
11:14 *it,* this is Elias, which was **for to c.** *2064+3195*
11:28 **C** unto me, all *ye* that labour and are heavy *1205*
12:28 then the kingdom of God is **c** unto you. *5348*
12:32 in this world, neither in the *world* to **c.** *3195*
12:44 and when he is **c**, he findeth *it* empty, *2064*
13:32 so that the birds of the air **c** and lodge in *2064*
13:49 the angels shall **c forth**, and sever *1831*
13:54 And when he was **c** into his own country, *2064*
14:23 and when the evening was **c**, he was there *1096*
14:28 it be thou, bid me **c** unto thee on the water. *2064*
14:29 And he said, **C**. And when Peter was come *2064*
14:29 And when Peter was **c down** out of *2597*
14:32 And when they were **c** into the ship, *1684*
15:18 out of the mouth **c forth** from the heart; *1831*
16: 5 And when his disciples were **c** to the other *2064*
16:24 If any *man* will **c** after me, let him deny *2064*
16:27 For the Son of man shall **c** in the glory of *2064*
17:10 then say the scribes that Elias must first **c?** *2064*
17:11 Elias truly shall first **c**, and restore all *2064*
17:12 That Elias is **c** already, and they knew him *2064*
17:14 And when they were **c** to the multitude, *2064*
17:24 And when they were **c** to Capernaum, *2064*
17:25 And when he was **c into** the house, *1525*
18: 7 for it must needs be that offences **c;** but *2064*
18:11 For the Son of man is **c** to save that which *2064*
19:14 and forbid them not, to **c** unto me: *2064*
19:21 treasure in heaven: and **c** *and* follow me. *1204*
20: 8 So when even was **c**, the lord of *1096*
21: 1 and were **c** to Bethphage, unto the mount of *2064*
21:10 And when he was **c into** Jerusalem, *1525*
21:23 And when he was **c** into the temple, *2064*
21:38 **c**, let us kill him, and let us seize on his *1205*
22: 3 to the wedding: and they would not **c.** *2064*
22: 4 all *things are* ready: **c** unto the marriage. *1205*
23:35 That upon you may **c** all the righteous *2064*
23:36 All these *things* shall **c** upon this *2240*
24: 5 For many shall **c** in my name, saying, I am *2064*
24: 6 for all *these things* must **c to pass**, but *1096*
24:14 unto all nations; and then shall the end **c.** *2240*
24:17 **c down** to take any *thing* out of his house: *2597*
24:42 ye know not what hour your Lord doth **c.** *2064*
24:43 had known in what watch the thief would **c,** *2064*
24:50 The lord of that servant shall **c** in a day *2240*
25:31 When the Son of man shall **c** in his glory, *2064*
25:34 his right hand, **C**, ye blessed of my Father, *1205*
26:20 Now when the even was **c**, he sat down *1096*
Mt 26:50 said unto him, Friend, wherefore art thou **c?** *3918*
26:55 Are ye **c out** as against a thief with swords *1831*
27: 1 When the morning was **c**, all the chief *1096*
27:33 And when they were **c** unto a place called *2064*
27:40 be the Son of God, **c down** from the cross. *2597*
27:42 let him now **c down** from the cross, and *2597*
27:49 let us see whether Elias will **c** to save him. *2064*
27:57 When the even was **c**, there came a rich *1096*
27:64 lest his disciples **c** by night, and steal him *2064*
28: 6 **C**, see the place where the Lord lay. *1205*
28:14 And if this **c to** the governor's **ears,** *191+1909*
Mk 1:17 **C** ye after me, and I will make you to *1205*
1:24 art thou **c** to destroy us? I know thee who *2064*
1:25 saying, Hold thy peace, and **c out** of him. *1831*
1:29 when they were **c out** of the synagogue, *1831*
2: 3 And they **c** unto him, bringing one sick of *2064*
2: 4 And when they could not **c nigh** unto him *4331*
2:18 and they **c** and say unto him, Why do *2064*
2:20 But the days will **c**, when the bridegroom *2064*
4:22 kept secret, but that it should **c** abroad. *2064*
4:29 in the sickle, because the harvest is **c.** *3936*
4:35 And the same day, when the even was **c,** *1096*
5: 2 And when he was **c out** of the ship, *1831*
5: 8 **C out** of the man, *thou* unclean spirit. *1831*
5:15 And they **c** to Jesus, and see him that was *2064*
5:18 And when he was **c** into the ship, he that *1684*
5:23 *I pray thee,* **c** and lay *thy* hands on her, *2064*
5:39 And when he was **c in**, he saith unto them, *1525*
6: 2 And when the sabbath day was **c**, he began *1096*
6:21 And when a convenient day was **c,** *1096*
6:31 **C** ye yourselves apart into a desert place, *1205*
6:47 And when even was **c**, the ship was in *1096*
6:54 And when they were **c out** of the ship, *1831*
7: 4 And *when they* **c** from the market, NIG
7:15 but the *things* which **c out** of him, those are *1607*
7:23 All these evil *things* **c** from within, and *1607*
7:30 And when she was **c** to her house, she found *565*
8:34 said unto them, Whosoever will **c** after me, *2064*
9: 1 till they have seen the kingdom of God **c** *2064*
9:11 Why say the scribes that Elias must first **c?** *2064*
9:13 That Elias is indeed **c**, and they have done *2064*
9:25 **c out** of him, and enter no more into him. *1831*
9:28 And when he was **c into** *the* house, *1525*
9:29 This kind can **c forth** by nothing, but by *1831*
10:14 Suffer the little children to **c** unto me, and *2064*
10:21 and **c**, take up the cross, and follow me. *1204*
10:30 and in the world to **c** eternal life. *2064*
10:35 of Zebedee, **c unto** him, saying, Master, *4365*
11:11 all *things,* and now the eventide was **c,** *1510*
11:12 when they were **c** from Bethany, he was *1831*
11:15 And they **c** to Jerusalem: and Jesus went *2064*
11:19 And when even was **c**, he went out of *1096*
11:23 *those things* which he saith shall **c to pass;** *1096*
11:27 And they **c** again to Jerusalem: and as he *2064*
11:27 there **c** to him the chief priests, and *2064*
12: 7 **c**, let us kill him, and the inheritance shall *1205*
12: 9 he will **c** and destroy the husbandmen, and *2064*
12:14 And when they were **c**, they say unto him, *2064*
12:18 Then **c** unto him *the* Sadducees, which say *2064*
13: 6 For many shall **c** in my name, saying, I am *2064*
13:29 when ye shall see these *things* **c to pass,** *1096*
14: 8 she is **c aforehand** to anoint my body to *4301*
14:41 it is enough, the hour is **c;** behold, the Son *2064*
14:45 And as soon as he was **c**, he goeth *2064*
14:48 and said unto them, Are ye **c out,** *1831*
15:30 Save thyself, and **c down** from the cross. *2597*
15:33 And when the sixth hour was **c**, there was *1096*
15:36 let us see whether Elias will **c** to take him *2064*
15:42 And now when the even was **c**, because *1096*
16: 1 that they might **c** and anoint him. *2064*
Lk 1:35 The Holy Ghost shall **c upon** thee, *1904*
1:43 that the mother of my Lord should **c** to me? *2064*
2:15 and see this thing which is **c to pass**, *1096*
3: 7 warned you to flee from the wrath to **c?** *3195*
4:34 art thou **c** to destroy us? I know thee who *2064*
4:35 saying, Hold thy peace, and **c out** of him. *1831*
4:36 the unclean spirits, and they **c out.** *1831*
5: 7 that *they* should **c** and help them. *2064*
5:17 doctors of the law sitting *by,* which were **c** *2064*
5:35 But the days will **c**, when the bridegroom *2064*
7: 3 beseeching him that he would **c** and *2064*
7: 7 thought I myself worthy to **c** unto thee: *2064*
7: 8 and to another, **C**, and he cometh; and *2064*
7:19 to Jesus, saying, Art thou he that should **c?** *2064*
7:20 When the men were **c** unto him, they said, *3854*
7:20 saying, Art thou he that should **c?** *2064*
7:34 The Son of man is **c** eating and drinking; *2064*
8: 4 and were **c** to him **out of** every city, *1975*
8:17 that shall not be known and **c** abroad. *2064*
8:19 and could not **c at** him for the press. *4940*
8:29 the unclean spirit to **c out** of the man. *1831*
8:41 besought him that *he* would **c into** *1525*
9:23 If any *man* will **c** after me, let him deny *2064*
9:26 when he shall **c** in his own glory, and *in his* *2064*
9:37 when they were **c down** from the hill, *2718*
9:51 when the time was **c** that he should be *4845*
9:54 wilt thou *that* we command fire to **c down** *2597*
9:56 For the Son of man is not **c** to destroy *2064*
10: 1 and place, whither he himself would **c.** *2064*
10: 9 The kingdom of God is **c nigh** unto you. *1448*
10:11 that the kingdom of God is **c nigh** unto *1448*
10:35 when I **c again**, I will repay thee. *1880*
11: 2 Thy kingdom **c**. Thy will be done, as in *2064*
11: 6 For a friend of mine in *his* journey is **c** to *3854*
11:20 no doubt the kingdom of God is **c** upon *5348*
11:22 But when a stronger than he shall **c upon** *1904*
11:33 that they which **c in** may see the light. *1531*
12:37 to meat, and will **c forth** and serve them. *3928*
12:38 And if he shall **c** in the second watch, or *2064*
12:38 or **c** in the third watch, and find *them* so, *2064*
12:39 had known what hour the thief would **c,** *2064*
12:46 The lord of that servant will **c** in a day *2240*
12:49 I am **c** to send fire on the earth; and *2064*
12:51 Suppose ye that I am **c** to give peace on *3854*
13: 7 *these* three years I **c** seeking fruit on this fig *2064*

Lk 13:14 in them therefore **c** and be healed, and 2064
13:29 And they shall **c** from the east, and 2240
13:35 see me, until *the time* **c** when ye shall say, 2240
14: 9 he that bade thee and him **c** and say to thee, 2064
14:17 time to say to them that were bidden, **C**; 2064
14:20 married a wife, and therefore I cannot **c**. 2064
14:23 and hedges, and compel *them* to **c in**, 1525
14:26 If any *man* **c** to me, and hate not his father, 2064
14:27 and **c** after me, cannot be my disciple. 2064
15:27 And he said unto him, Thy brother is **c**; 2240
15:30 But as soon as this thy son was **c**, 2064
16:26 they pass to us, that *would* **c** from thence. NIG
16:28 lest they also **c** into this place of torment. 2064
17: 1 It is impossible but that offences will **c**: 2064
17: 1 but woe *unto him*, through whom they **c**. 2064
17: 7 when he is **c** from the field, Go and 1525
17:20 when the kingdom of God should **c**, 2064
17:22 he said unto the disciples, The days will **c**, 2064
17:31 let him not **c down** to take it away: 2597
18:16 Suffer little children to **c** unto me, and 2064
18:22 have treasure in heaven: and **c**, follow me. 1204
18:30 and in the world to **c** life everlasting. 2064
18:35 to pass, *that* as he was **c nigh** unto Jericho, 1448
18:40 and when he was **c near**, he asked him, 1448
19: 5 Zaccheus, make haste, and **c down**; 2597
19: 9 This day is salvation **c** to this house, 1096
19:10 For the Son of man is **c** to seek and to save 2064
19:13 and said unto them, Occupy till I **c**. 2064
19:29 when he was **c nigh** to Bethphage and 1448
19:37 And when he was **c nigh**, *even* now at 1448
19:41 And when he was **c near**, he beheld 1448
19:43 For the days shall **c** upon thee, that thine 2240
20:14 **c**, let us kill him, that the inheritance may 1205
20:16 He shall **c** and destroy these husbandmen, 2064
21: 6 *things* which ye behold, the days will **c**, 2064
21: 7 *there be* when these *things* shall **c to pass**? 1096
21: 8 for many shall **c** in my name, saying, I am 2064
21: 9 for these *things* must first **c to pass**; but 1096
21:28 And when these *things* begin to **c to pass**, 1096
21:31 when ye see these *things* **c to pass**, 1096
21:34 *so that* day **c upon** you unawares. 2186
21:35 For as a snare shall it **c on** all them 1904
21:36 escape all these *things* that shall **c to pass**, 1096
22:14 And when the hour was **c**, he sat down, and 1096
22:18 the vine, until the kingdom of God shall **c**. 2064
22:45 up from prayer, and was **c** to his disciples, 2064
22:52 and the elders, which were **c** to him, Be ye 3854
22:52 Be ye **c out**, as against a thief, with swords 1831
23:33 And when they were **c** to the place, which is 565
24:12 in himself at that which was **c to pass**. 1096
24:18 which are **c to pass** there in these days? 1096
Jn 1:31 therefore am I **c** baptizing with water. 2064
1:39 He saith unto them, **C** and see. They came 2064
1:46 Can there any good *thing* **c** out of 1510
1:46 Philip saith unto him, **C** and see. 2064
2: 4 I to do with thee? mine hour is not yet **c**. 2240
3: 2 we know that thou art a teacher **c** from 2064
3:19 that light is **c** into the world, and men loved 2064
3:26 the same baptizeth, and all *men* **c** to him. 2064
4:15 that I thirst not, neither **c** hither to draw. 2064
4:16 unto her, Go, call thy husband, and **c** hither. 2064
4:25 when he is **c**, he will tell us all *things*. 2064
4:29 **C**, see a man, which told me all *things* that 1205
4:40 So when the Samaritans were **c** unto him, 2064
4:45 Then when he was **c** into Galilee, 2064
4:47 When he heard that Jesus was **c** out of 2240
4:47 and besought him that he would **c down**, 2597
4:49 unto him, Sir, **c down** ere my child die. 2597
4:54 when he was **c** out of Judea into Galilee. 2064
5:14 sin no more, lest a worse *thing* **c** unto thee. 1096
5:24 and shall not **c** into condemnation; 2064
5:29 And shall **c forth**; they that have done 1607
5:40 And ye will not **c** to me, that ye might have 2064
5:43 I am **c** in my Father's name, and ye receive 2064
5:43 if another shall **c** in his own name, him ye 2064
6: 5 and saw a great company **c** unto him, 2064
6:14 This is of a truth *that* prophet that should **c** 2064
6:15 therefore perceived that they would **c** and 2064
6:16 And when even was *now* **c**, his disciples 1096
6:17 was now dark, and Jesus was not **c** to them. 2064
6:37 All that the Father giveth me shall **c** to me; 2240
6:44 No *man* can **c** to me, except the Father 2064
6:65 said I unto you, that no *man* can **c** unto me, 2064
7: 6 Jesus said unto them, My time is not yet **c**: 3918
7: 8 unto this feast; for my time is not yet **full c**. 4137
7:28 and I am not **c** of myself, but he that sent 2064
7:30 on him, because his hour was not yet **c**. 2064
7:34 *me:* and where I am, *thither* ye cannot **c**. 2064
7:36 *me:* and where I am, *thither* ye cannot **c**? 2064
7:37 *man* thirst, let him **c** unto me, and drink. 2064
7:41 some said, Shall Christ **c** out of Galilee? 2064
8:14 but ye cannot tell whence I **c**, and whither I 2064
8:20 hands on him; for his hour was not yet **c**. 2064
8:21 die in your sins: whither I go, ye cannot **c**. 2064
8:22 because he saith, Whither I go, ye cannot **c**. 2064
9:39 For judgment I am **c** into this world, 2064
10:10 I am **c** that they might have life, and 2064
11:27 Son of God, which should **c** into the world. 2064
11:28 The Master is **c**, and calleth for thee. 3918
11:30 Now Jesus was not yet **c** into the town, but 2064
11:32 Then when Mary was **c** where Jesus was, 2064
11:34 They say unto him, Lord, **c** and see. 2064
11:43 he cried with a loud voice, Lazarus, **c** forth. 1204
11:48 and the Romans shall **c** and take away both 2064
11:56 think ye, that he will not **c** to the feast? 2064
12:12 On the next day much people that were **c** to 2064
12:23 Jesus answered them, saying, The hour is **c**, 2064
12:35 ye have the light, lest darkness **c upon** you: 2638
12:46 I am **c** a light into the world, 2064
13: 1 when Jesus knew that his hour was **c** that 2064
13: 3 and that he was **c** from God, and went to 1831
13:19 Now I tell you before it **c**, that, when it is 1096
13:19 that, when it is **c to pass**, ye may believe 1096
13:33 unto the Jews, Whither I go, ye cannot **c**; 2064
14: 3 I will **c** again, and receive you unto myself; 2064
Jn 14:18 not leave you comfortless: I will **c** to you. 2064
14:23 and we will **c** unto him, and make *our* 2064
14:28 unto you, I go away, and **c** *again* unto you. 2064
14:29 now I have told you before it **c to pass**, 1096
14:29 that, when it is **c to pass**, ye might believe. 1096
15:22 If I had not **c** and spoken unto them, 2064
15:26 But when the Comforter is **c**, whom I will 2064
16: 4 have I told you, that when the time shall **c**, 2064
16: 7 the Comforter will not **c** unto you; 2064
16: 8 And when he is **c**, he will reprove the world 2064
16:13 Howbeit when he, the Spirit of truth, is **c**, 2064
16:13 he speak: and he will shew you *things* to **c**. 2064
16:21 travail hath sorrow, because her hour is **c**: 2064
16:28 from the Father, and am **c** into the world: 2064
16:32 Behold, the hour cometh, yea, is now **c**, 2064
17: 1 to heaven, and said, Father, the hour is **c**; 2064
17:11 but these are in the world, and I **c** to thee. 2064
17:13 And now **c** I to thee; and these *things* I 2064
18: 4 knowing all *things* that should **c** upon him, 2064
21: 4 But when the morning was now **c**, 1096
21: 9 As soon then as they were **c** to land, 576
21:12 Jesus saith unto them, **C** *and* dine. 1205
21:22 If I will that he tarry till I **c**, what *is that* to 2064
21:23 but, If I will that he tarry till I **c**, what *is* 2064
Ac 1: 6 When they therefore were **c together**, 4905
1: 8 that the Holy Ghost is **c upon** you: 1904
1:11 **c** *in* like manner as ye have seen him go 2064
1:13 And when they were **c in**, they went up into 1525
2: 1 And when the day of Pentecost was **fully c**, 4845
2:17 And it shall **c to pass** in the last days, 1510
2:20 *that* great and notable day of the Lord **c**: 2064
2:21 And it shall **c to pass**, *that* whosoever shall 1510
3:19 when *the* times of refreshing shall **c** from 2064
3:23 And it shall **c to pass**, *that* every soul, 1510
5:38 or this work be of men, it will **c to nought**: 2647
7: 3 and **c** into the land which I shall shew thee. 1204
7: 7 and after that shall they **c forth**, and 1831
7:34 and am **c down** to deliver them. 2597
7:34 And now **c**, I will send thee into Egypt. 1204
8:15 Who, when they were **c down**, prayed for 2597
8:24 which ye have spoken **c upon** me. 1904
8:27 and had **c** to Jerusalem for to worship, 2064
8:31 And he desired Philip that *he* would **c up** 305
8:39 And when they were **c up** out of the water, 305
9:26 And when Saul was **c** to Jerusalem, 3854
9:38 desiring *him* that *he* would not delay to **c** to 1330
9:39 When he was **c**, they brought him into 3854
10: 4 thine alms are **c up** for a memorial before 305
10:21 what *is* the cause wherefore ye are **c**? 3918
10:27 and found many *that were* **c together**. 4905
10:28 or **c unto** one of another nation; 4334
10:33 and thou hast well done that thou art **c**. 3854
11: 2 And when Peter was **c up** to Jerusalem, 305
11:11 immediately there were three men already **c** 2186
11:20 which, when they were **c to** Antioch, 1525
12:11 And when Peter was **c** to himself, he said, 1096
13:40 Beware therefore, lest that **c** upon you, 1904
14:11 The gods are **c down** to us in the likeness 2597
14:27 And when they were **c**, and had gathered 3854
15: 4 And when they were **c** to Jerusalem, 3854
16: 7 After they were **c** to Mysia, they assayed to 2064
16: 9 **C over** into Macedonia, and help us. 1224
16:15 **c into** my house, and abide *there*. 1525
16:18 in the name of Jesus Christ to **c out** of her. 1831
16:37 but let them **c** themselves and fetch us out. 2064
17: 6 the world upside down are **c** hither also; 3918
17:15 Timotheus for to **c** to him with all speed, 2064
18: 2 born in Pontus, lately **c** from Italy, with his 2064
18: 5 And Timotheus were **c** from Macedonia, 2718
18:27 who, when he was **c**, helped them much 3854
19: 4 believe on him which should **c** after him, 2064
19:32 knew not wherefore they were **c together**. 4905
20:11 When he therefore was **c up** *again*, and 305
20:18 And when they were **c** to him, he said unto 3854
21:11 And when he was **c** unto us, he took Paul's 2064
21:17 And when we were **c** to Jerusalem, 1096
21:22 the multitude must needs **c together**: 4905
21:22 for they will hear that thou art **c**. 2064
22: 6 and was **c nigh** unto Damascus about noon, 1448
22:17 pass that, when I was **c again** to Jerusalem, 5290
23:15 and we, or ever he **c near**, are ready to kill 1448
23:35 said he, when thine accusers are also **c**. 3854
24: 8 Commanding his accusers to **c** unto thee: 2064
24:22 Lysias the chief captain shall **c down**, 2597
24:23 his acquaintance to minister or **c unto** him. 4334
24:25 temperance, and judgment **to c**, Felix 3195
25: 1 Now when Festus was **c into** the province, 1910
25: 7 And when he was **c**, the Jews which came 3854
25:17 Therefore, when they were **c** hither, 4905
25:23 when Agrippa was **c**, and Bernice, 2064
26: 7 serving *God* day and night, hope to **c**. 2658
26:22 the prophets and Moses did say should **c**: 1096
27: 7 and scarce were **c** over against Cnidus, 1096
27:16 we had much work to **c by** the boat: 1096+4031
27:27 But when the fourteenth night was **c**, as we 1096
28: 6 and saw no harm **c** to him, they changed 1096
28:17 and when they were **c together**, he said 4905
Ro 1:10 journey by the will of God to **c** unto you. 2064
1:13 that oftentimes I purposed to **c** unto you, 2064
3: 8 we say,) Let us do evil, that good may **c**? 2064
3:23 and **c short** of the glory of God; 5302
5:14 who is the figure of *him* that was **to c**. 3195
8:38 nor *things* present, nor *things* to **c**, 3195
9: 9 At this time will I **c**, and Sara shall have a 2064
9:26 And it shall **c to pass**, *that* in the place 1510
11:11 *rather* through their fall salvation *is* **c** unto NIG
11:25 until the fulness of the Gentiles be **c in**. 1525
11:26 There shall **c** out of Sion the Deliverer, and 2240
15:23 having a great desire these many years to **c** 2064
15:24 take my journey into Spain, I will **c** to you: 2064
15:28 to them this fruit, I will **c** by you into Spain. 565
15:29 And I am sure that, when I **c** unto you, 2064
15:29 I shall **c** in the fulness of the blessing of 2064
15:32 That I may **c** unto you with joy by the will 2064
16:19 For your obedience is **c abroad** unto all 864
1Co 1: 7 So that ye **c behind** in no gift; waiting for 5302
2: 6 the princes of this world, that **c to nought**: 2673
3:22 or death, or *things* present, or *things* **to c**; 3195
4: 5 nothing before the time, until the Lord **c**, 2064
4:18 puffed up, as though I would not **c** to you. 2064
4:19 But I will **c** to you shortly, if the Lord will, 2064
4:21 shall I **c** unto you with a rod, or in love, and 2064
7: 5 to fasting and prayer, and **c** together again, 4905
10:11 upon whom the ends of the world are **c**. 2658
11:17 that you **c together** not for the better, but 4905
11:18 of all, when ye **c together** in the church, 4905
11:20 When ye **c together** therefore into one 4905
11:26 ye do shew the Lord's death till he **c**. 2064
11:33 my brethren, when ye **c together** to eat, 4905
11:34 that ye **c** not **together** unto condemnation. 4905
11:34 And the rest will I set in order when I **c**. 2064
13:10 But when *that which is* perfect is **c**, then 2064
14: 6 if I **c** unto you speaking with tongues, 2064
14:23 the whole church be **c together** into one 4905
14:23 and there **c in** *those that are* unlearned, or 1525
14:24 and there **c in** one that believeth not, or 1525
14:26 when ye **c together**, every one of you hath 4905
15:35 raised up? and with what body do they **c**? 2064
16: 2 that there be no gatherings when I **c**. 2064
16: 3 And when I **c**, whomsoever you shall 3854
16: 5 Now I will **c** unto you, when I shall pass 2064
16:10 Now if Timotheus **c**, see that he may be 2064
16:11 him forth in peace, that he may **c** unto me: 2064
16:12 I greatly desired him to **c** unto you with 2064
16:12 but *his* will was not at all to **c** at this time; 2064
16:12 he will **c** when he shall have convenient 2064
2Co 1:15 And in this confidence I was minded to **c** 2064
1:16 and to **c** again out of Macedonia unto you, 2064
2: 1 that *I* would not **c** again to you in 2064
6:17 Wherefore **c out** from among them, and 1831
7: 5 For, when we were **c** into Macedonia, 2064
9: 4 Lest haply if they of Macedonia **c** with me, 2064
10:14 for we are **c** as far as to you also in 5348
12: 1 I will **c** to visions and revelations of 2064
12:14 the third *time* I am ready to **c** to you; 2064
12:20 For I fear, lest, when I **c**, I shall not find 2064
12:21 *And* lest, when I **c** again, my God will 2064
13: 2 and to all other, that, if I **c** again, I will not 2064
Gal 2:11 But when Peter was **c** to Antioch, 2064
2:12 But when they were **c**, he withdrew and 2064
2:21 for if righteousness **c** by the law, then NIG
3:14 That the blessing of Abraham might **c** on 1096
3:19 till the seed should **c** to whom the promise 2064
3:25 But after that faith is **c**, we are no longer 2064
4: 4 But when the fulness of the time was **c**, 2064
Eph 1:21 in this world, but also in that which is **to c**: 3195
2: 7 That in the ages to **c** he might shew 1904
4:13 Till we all **c** in the unity of the faith, and 2658
Php 1:27 that whether I **c** and see you, or *else* be 2064
2:24 the Lord that I also myself shall **c** shortly. 2064
Col 1: 6 Which is **c** unto you, as *it is* in all 3918
2:17 Which are a shadow of *things* **to c**; but 3195
4:10 if he **c** unto you, receive him;) 2064
1Th 1:10 which delivered us from the wrath to **c**. 2064
2:16 for the wrath is **c** upon them to 5348
2:18 Wherefore we would have **c** unto you, 2064
2Th 1:10 When he shall **c** to be glorified in his saints, 2064
2: 3 for *that day shall not* **c**, except there come a NIG
2: 3 for *that day shall not come*, except there **c** a 2064
1Ti 2: 4 and to **c** unto the knowledge of the truth. 2064
3:14 I unto thee, hoping to **c** unto thee shortly: 2064
4: 8 life that now is, and of that which is **to c**. 3195
4:13 Till I **c**, give attendance to reading, 2064
6:19 a good foundation against the **time to c**, 3195
2Ti 3: 1 that in the last days perilous times shall **c**. 1764
3: 7 never able to **c** to the knowledge of 2064
4: 3 For the time will **c** when they will not 1510
4: 9 Do thy diligence to **c** shortly unto me: 2064
4:21 Do thy diligence to **c** before winter. 2064
Tit 3:12 be diligent to **c** unto me to Nicopolis: 2064
Heb 2: 5 hath he not put in subjection the world **to c**, 3195
4: 1 any of you should seem to **c short** *of it*. 5302
4:16 therefore **c** boldly unto the throne of grace, 4334
6: 5 of God, and the powers of the world **to c**, 3195
7: 5 though they **c out** of the loins of Abraham: 1831
7:25 to the uttermost that **c unto** God by him, 4334
8: 8 *he* saith, Behold, the days **c**, saith the Lord, 2064
9:11 But Christ being **c** a high priest of good 3854
9:11 come a high priest of good *things* **to c**, 3195
10: 1 law having a shadow of good *things* **to c**, 3195
10: 7 I **c** (in the volume of the book it is written 2240
10: 9 Then said he, Lo, I **c** to do thy will, O God. 2240
10:37 *and* he that shall **c** will come, and will not 2064
10:37 *and* he that shall come will **c**, and will not 2240
11:20 and Esau concerning *things* **to c**. 3195
11:24 By faith Moses, when he was **c to years**, 3173
12:18 For ye are not **c** unto the mount that might 4334
12:22 But ye are **c unto** mount Sion, and unto 4334
13:14 no continuing city, but we seek one **to c**. 3195
13:23 with whom, if he **c** shortly, I will see you. 2064
Jas 2: 2 For if there **c unto** your assembly a 1525
2: 2 there **c in** also a poor *man* in vile raiment; 1525
4: 1 From whence **c** wars and fightings among NIG
4: 1 **c** *they* not hence, *even* of your lusts that war NIG
5: 1 howl for your miseries that shall **c upon** 1904
1Pe 1:10 who prophesied of the grace *that should* **c** NIG
4:17 For the time *is* **c** that judgment must begin NIG
2Pe 3: 3 that there shall **c** in the last days scoffers, 2064
3: 9 but that all should **c** to repentance. 5562
3:10 But the day of the Lord will **c** as a thief in 2240
1Jn 2:18 and as ye have heard that antichrist shall **c**, 2064
4: 2 that Jesus Christ is **c** in the flesh is of God: 2064
4: 3 Jesus Christ is **c** in the flesh is not of God: 2064
4: 3 whereof you have heard that it should **c**; 2064
5:20 And we know that the Son of God is **c**, and 2240
2Jn 1: 7 who confess not that Jesus Christ is **c** in 2064
1:10 If there **c** any unto you, and bring not this 2064
1:12 but I trust to **c** unto you, and speak face to 2064
3Jn 1:10 Wherefore, if I **c**, I will remember his deeds 2064
Rev 1: 1 *things* which must shortly **c to pass**; 1096

Rev 1: 4 which is, and which was, and which is to **c**; *2064*
1: 8 which is, and which was, and which is to **c**, *2064*
2: 5 or else I *will* **c** unto thee quickly, and *2064*
2:16 or else I *will* **c** unto thee quickly, and *2064*
2:25 *that* which ye have *already* hold fast till I **c**. *2240*
3: 3 I will **c** on thee as a thief, and thou shalt not *2240*
3: 3 thou shalt not know what hour I will **c** upon *2240*
3: 9 I will make them to **c** and worship before *2240*
3:10 which shall **c** upon all the world, to try *2064*
3:11 Behold, I **c** quickly: hold *that* fast which *2064*
3:20 I will **c in** to him, and will sup with him, *1525*
4: 1 **C up** hither, and I will shew thee *things* *305*
4: 8 which was, and is, and is to **c**. *2064*
6: 1 one of the four beasts saying, **C** and see. *2064*
6: 3 I heard the second beast say, **C** and see. *2064*
6: 5 I heard the third beast say, **C** and see. *2064*
6: 7 the voice of the fourth beast say, **C** and see. *2064*
6:17 For the great day of his wrath is **c**; and *2064*
9:12 behold, there **c** two woes more hereafter. *2064*
10: 1 And I saw another mighty angel **c down** *2597*
11:12 from heaven saying unto them, **C up** hither. *305*
11:17 which art, and wast, and art to **c**; *2064*
11:18 and thy wrath is **c**, and the time of the dead, *2064*
12:10 Now is **c** salvation, and strength, and *1096*
12:12 for the devil is **c down** unto you, *2597*
13:13 that he maketh fire **c down** from heaven on *2597*
14: 7 to him; for the hour of his judgment is **c**: *2064*
14:15 for the time is **c** for thee to reap; for *2064*
15: 4 for all nations shall **c** and worship before *2240*
16:13 And I saw three unclean spirits like frogs **c** NIG
16:15 Behold, I **c** as a thief. Blessed *is* he that *2064*
17: 1 talked with me, saying unto me, **C** hither; NIG
17:10 and one is, *and* the other is not yet **c**; *2064*
18: 1 I saw another angel **c down** from heaven, *2597*
18: 4 saying, **C out** of her, my people, that ye be *1831*
18: 8 Therefore shall her plagues **c** in one day, *2240*
18:10 for in one hour is thy judgment **c**. *2064*
18:17 in one hour so great riches is **c to nought**. *2049*
19: 7 for the marriage of the Lamb is **c**, and *2064*
19:17 **C** and gather yourselves together unto *1205*
20: 1 And I saw an angel **c down** from heaven, *2597*
21: 9 and talked with me, saying, **C** hither, I will NIG
22: 7 Behold, I **c** quickly: blessed *is* he that *2064*
22:12 And behold, I **c** quickly; and my reward *is* *2064*
22:17 And the Spirit and the bride say, **C**. And let *2064*
22:17 And let him that heareth say, **C**. And let *2064*
22:17 And let him that is athirst **c**. *2064*
22:20 these *things* saith, Surely I **c** quickly. *2064*
22:20 Amen. Even so, **c**, Lord Jesus. *2064*

COME O LORD See MARAN-ATHA

COMELINESS (5) [COMELY, UNCOMELY]

Isa 53: 2 he hath no form nor **c**; and when we shall 1926
Eze 16:14 for it *was* perfect through my **c**, which I 1926
27:10 and helmet in thee; they set forth thy **c**. 1926
Da 10: 8 for my **c** was turned in me into corruption, 1935
1Co 12:23 our uncomely *parts* have more abundant **c**. *2157*

COMELY (16) [COMELINESS]

1Sa 16:18 a **c** person, and the LORD *is* with him. 8389
Job 41:12 nor *his* power, nor his **c** proportion. 2433
Ps 33: 1 ye righteous: *for* praise is **c** for the upright. 5000
147: 1 our God; for *it is* pleasant; *and* praise is **c**. 5000
Pr 30:29 which go well, yea, four are **c** in going: 3190
Ecc 5:18 *it is* good and **c** *for one* to eat and to drink, 3303
SS 1: 5 I *am* black, but **c**, O ye daughters of 5000
1:10 Thy cheeks are **c** with rows *of jewels*, thy 4998
2:14 *is* thy voice, and thy countenance *is* **c**. 5000
4: 3 like a thread of scarlet, and thy speech *is* **c**: 5000
6: 4 O my love, as Tirzah, **c** as Jerusalem, 5000
Isa 4: 2 **c** for them that are escaped of 8597+3807.1
Jer 6: 2 I have likened the daughter of Zion *to* a **c** 5116
1Co 7:35 but for *that which is* **c**, and that you may *2158*
11:13 is it **c** that a woman pray unto God *4241*
12:24 For our **c** *parts* have no need: *2158*

COMERS (1) [COME]

Heb 10: 1 continually make the **c** *thereunto* perfect. *4334*

COMEST (29) [COME]

Ge 10:19 from Sidon, as thou **c** to Gerar, unto Gaza; 935
13:10 like the land of Egypt, as thou **c** unto Zoar. 935
24:41 *this* my oath, when thou **c** to my kindred; 935
Dt 2:19 *when* thou **c nigh** over against the children 7126
20:10 When thou **c nigh** unto a city to fight 7126
23:24 When thou **c** into thy neighbour's vineyard, 935
23:25 When thou **c** into the standing corn of thy 935
28: 6 Blessed *shalt* thou *be* when thou **c in**, and 935
28:19 Cursed *shalt* thou *be* when thou **c in**, and 935
Jdg 17: 9 Micah said unto him, Whence **c** thou? 935
18:23 that thou **c with** such a **company**? 2199
19:17 Whither goest thou? and whence **c** thou? 935
1Sa 15: 7 from Havilah *until* thou **c** *to* Shur, 935
16: 4 at his coming, and said, **C** thou peaceably? 935
17:43 *Am* I a dog, that thou **c** to me with staves? 935
17:45 Thou **c** to me with a sword, and with a spear, 935
2Sa 1: 3 David said unto him, From whence **c** thou? 935
3:13 Saul's daughter, when thou **c** to see my face. 935
1Ki 2:13 she said, **C** thou peaceably? And he said, 935
19:15 when thou **c**, anoint Hazael to be king over 935
2Ki 5:25 said unto him, Whence **c** *thou*, Gehazi? NIH
9: 2 when thou **c** thither, look out there Jehu 935
Job 1: 7 the LORD said unto Satan, Whence **c** thou? 935
2: 2 said unto Satan, From whence **c** thou? 935
Jer 51:61 When thou **c** *to* Babylon, and shalt see, and 935
Jnh 1: 8 and whence **c** thou? what *is* thy country? and 935
Mt 3:14 to be baptized of thee, and **c** thou to me? *2064*
Lk 23:42 remember me when thou **c** into thy *2064*
2Ti 4:13 when thou **c**, bring *with thee*, and *2064*

COMETH (282) [COME]

Ge 24:43 *that when* the virgin **c forth** to draw *water*, 3318
29: 6 Rachel his daughter **c** with the sheep. 935
30:11 Leah said, A troop **c**: and she called his 935
32: 6 also he **c** to meet thee, and four hundred 1980
37:19 said one to another, Behold, this dreamer **c**. 935
48: 2 and said, Behold, thy son Joseph **c** unto thee: 935
Ex 4:14 also, behold, he **c forth** to meet thee: and 3318
8:20 lo, he **c forth** to the water; and say unto 3318
13:12 every firstling that **c** of a beast which thou 7698
28:35 and when he **c out**, that he die not. 3318
29:30 when he **c** into the tabernacle of 935
Lev 11:34 *that* on which *such* water **c** shall be unclean: 935
Nu 1:51 the stranger that **c nigh** shall be put to 7131
3:10 the stranger that **c nigh** shall be put to 7131
3:38 the stranger that **c nigh** shall be put to 7131
5:30 Or when the spirit of jealousy **c** upon him, 5674
12:12 when he **c out** of his mother's womb. 3318
17:13 Whosoever **c** any thing **near** unto 7131+7131
18: 7 the stranger that **c nigh** shall be put to 7131
21:13 which *is* in the wilderness that **c out** of 3318
26: 5 *of whom* **c** the family of the Hanochites: NIH
Dt 18: 8 beside **that which c of the sale** of his 4465
23:11 it shall be, when evening **c on**, he shall 6437
23:13 and cover that which **c from** thee: 6627
28:57 towards her young one that **c out** from 3318
Jdg 11:31 that whatsoever **c forth** of the doors of my 3318
13:14 She may not eat of any *thing* that **c** of 3318
1Sa 4: 3 that when it **c** among us, it may save us out 935
9: 6 all that he saith **c surely to pass**: 935+935
11: 7 Whosoever **c** not **forth** after Saul and 3318
20:27 Wherefore **c** not the son of Jesse to meat, 935
20:29 Therefore he **c** not unto the king's table. 935
25: 8 whatsoever **c** to thine hand unto thy 4672
28:14 she said, An old man **c up**; and he *is* 5927
2Sa 13: 5 when thy father **c** to see thee, say unto him, 935
18:27 He *is* a good man, and **c** with good tidings. 935
1Ki 8:41 **c** out of a far country for thy name's sake; 935
14: 5 the wife of Jeroboam **c** to ask a thing of thee 935
14: 5 for it shall be, when she **c in**, that she shall 935
2Ki 4:10 it shall be, when he **c** to us, *that* he shall turn 935
6:32 look, when the messenger **c**, shut the door, 935
9:18 came to them, but he **c** not **again**. 7725
9:20 He came even unto them, and **c** not **again**: 7725
10: 2 Now as soon as this letter **c** to you, 935
11: 8 he that **c** within the ranges, let him be slain: 935
11: 8 with the king as he goeth out and as he **c in**. 935
12: 4 all the money that **c** into any man's heart to 5927
12: 9 on the right side as one **c** *into* the house of 935
1Ch 16:33 the LORD, because he **c** to judge the earth. 935
29:16 a house for thine holy name **c** of thine hand, NIH
2Ch 13: 9 that whosoever **c** to consecrate himself with 935
20: 2 There **c** a great multitude against thee from 935
20: 9 If, *when* evil **c** upon us, *as* the sword, 935
20:12 against this great company that **c** against us; 935
23: 7 whosoever *else* **c** into the house, he shall be 935
23: 7 be you with the king when he **c in**, and 935
Job 3:21 Which long for death, but it **c** not; and NIH
3:24 For my sighing **c** before I eat, and 935
5: 6 Although affliction **c** not **forth** of the dust, 3318
5:21 shalt thou be afraid of destruction when it **c**. 935
5:26 like as a shock of corn **c in** in his season. 5927
14: 2 He **c forth** like a flower, and is cut down: 3318
14:18 surely the mountain falling **c to nought**, 5034
20:25 It is drawn, and **c out** of the body; yea, 3318
20:25 yea, the glistering sword **c out** of his gall: 1980
21:17 *how oft* **c** their destruction upon them! 935
27: 9 Will God hear his cry when trouble **c** upon 935
28: 5 *As for* the earth, out of it **c** bread: and 3318
28:20 Whence then **c** wisdom? and where *is* 935
36:32 it *not to shine* by *the cloud* that **c betwixt**. 6293
37: 9 Out of the south **c** the whirlwind: and 935
37:22 Fair weather **c** out of the north: with God *is* 857
Ps 30: 5 endure for a night, but joy **c** in the morning. NIH
62: 1 waiteth upon God: from him **c** my salvation. NIH
75: 6 For promotion **c** neither from the east, NIH
78:39 a wind that passeth away, and **c** not **again**. 7725
96:13 Before the LORD, for he **c**, for he cometh 935
96:13 for he cometh, for he **c** to judge the earth: 935
98: 9 the LORD; for he **c** to judge the earth: 935
118:26 Blessed *be* he that **c** in the name of 935
121: 1 eyes unto the hills, from whence **c** my help. 935
121: 2 My help **c** from the LORD, which made NIH
Pr 1:26 your calamity; I will mock when your fear **c**; 935
1:27 When your fear **c** as desolation, and 935
1:27 and your destruction **c** as a whirlwind; 857
1:27 when distress and anguish **c** upon you: 935
2: 6 out of his mouth **c** knowledge and NIH
3:25 of the desolation of the wicked, when it **c**. 935
11: 2 *When* pride **c**, then cometh shame: but 935
11: 2 *When* pride cometh, then **c** shame: but 935
11: 8 out of trouble, and the wicked **c** in his stead. 935
13: 5 wicked *man* is loathsome, and **c to shame**. 2659
13:10 Only by pride **c** contention: but with 5414
13:12 but *when* the desire **c**, *it is* a tree of life. 935
18: 3 When the wicked **c**, *then* cometh also 935
18: 3 *then* **c** also contempt, and with ignominy 935
18:17 but his neighbour **c** and searcheth him. 935
29:26 *every* man's judgment **c** from the LORD. NIH
Ecc 1: 4 passeth away, and *another* generation **c**: 935
2:12 for what *can* the man *do* that **c** after 935
4:14 For out of prison he **c** to reign; 3318
5: 3 For a dream **c** through the multitude of 935
6: 4 For he **c in** with vanity, and departeth in 935
11: 8 for they shall be many. All that **c** *is* vanity. 935
SS 2: 8 behold, he **c** leaping upon the mountains, 935
3: 6 Who *is* this that **c** out of the wilderness like 5927
8: 5 Who *is* this that **c up** from the wilderness, 5927
Isa 13: 9 Behold, the day of the LORD **c**, cruel both 935
21: 1 *so* it **c** from the desert, from a terrible land. 935
21: 9 behold, here **c** a chariot of men, *with* a 935
21:12 The morning **c**, and also the night: 857
24:18 he that **c up** out of the midst of the pit shall 5927
26:21 the LORD **c out** of his place to punish 3318
28:29 This also **c forth** from the LORD of hosts, 3318
30:13 whose breaking **c** suddenly at an instant. 935
30:27 Behold, the name of the LORD **c** from far, 935
42: 5 forth the earth, and **that which c out** of it; 6631
Isa 55:10 For as the rain **c down**, and the snow from 3381
62:11 daughter of Zion, Behold, thy salvation **c**; 935
63: 1 Who *is* this *that* **c** from Edom, with dyed 935
Jer 6:20 To what purpose **c** there to me incense from 935
6:22 a people **c** from the north country, and 935
17: 6 in the desert, and shall not see when good **c**; 935
17: 8 shall not see when heat **c**, but her leaf shall 935
18:14 Lebanon *which* **c** from the rock of the field? NIH
43:11 when he **c**, he shall smite the land of Egypt, 935
46: 7 Who *is* this *that* **c up** as a flood, 5927
46:20 *is like* a very fair heifer, *but* destruction **c**; 935
46:20 *but* destruction cometh; it **c** out of the north. 935
47: 4 Because of the day that **c** to spoil all 935
50: 3 For out of the north there **c up** a nation 5927
51:54 A sound of a cry **c** from Babylon, and NIH
La 3:37 Who *is* he *that* saith, and it **c to pass**, 1961
Eze 4:12 thou shalt bake it with dung that **c out** of 6627
7:25 Destruction **c**; and they shall seek peace, and 935
14: 4 iniquity before his face, and **c** to the prophet; 935
14: 4 I the LORD will answer him that **c** 935
14: 7 **c** to a prophet to inquire of him concerning 935
20:32 that which **c** into your mind shall not be at 5927
21: 7 shalt answer, For the tidings; because it **c**: 935
21: 7 behold, it **c**, and shall be brought to pass, 935
24:24 when this **c**, ye shall know that I *am* the Lord 935
30: 9 as *in* the day of Egypt: for lo, it **c**. 935
33:30 hear what *is* the word that **c forth** from 3318
33:31 they come unto thee as the people **c**, and 3996
33:33 when this **c to pass**, (lo, it will come) then 935
47: 9 and every *thing* shall live whither the river **c**. 935
Da 11:16 he that **c** against him shall do according to 935
12:12 **c** to the thousand three hundred *and* five 5060
Hos 7: 1 the thief **c in**, *and* the troop *of robbers* 935
Joel 2: 1 for the day of the LORD **c**, for *it is* nigh at 935
Mic 1: 3 the LORD **c forth** out of his place, and 3318
5: 6 when he **c** into our land, and when he 935
7: 4 the day of thy watchmen *and* thy visitation **c**; 935
Hab 3:16 when *he* **c up** unto the people, he will 5927
Zec 9: 9 behold, thy King **c** unto thee: he *is* just, and 935
14: 1 the day of the LORD **c**, and thy spoil shall 935
Mal 4: 1 For behold, the day **c**, that *shall* burn as an 935
4: 1 the day that **c** shall burn them up, saith 935
Mt 3:11 but he that **c** after me is mightier than I, *2064*
3:13 Then **c** Jesus from Galilee to Jordan unto *3854*
5:37 for whatsoever is more than these **c** of evil. *1510*
8: 9 and to another, Come, and he **c**; and to my *2064*
13:19 then **c** the wicked one, and catcheth away *2064*
15:11 but that which **c out** of the mouth, *1607*
17:27 a hook, and take up the fish that first **c up**; *305*
18: 7 woe to that man by whom the offence **c**. *2064*
21: 5 thy King **c** unto thee, meek, and *2064*
21: 9 Blessed *is* he that **c** in the name of *2064*
21:40 When the lord therefore of the vineyard **c**, *2064*
23:39 Blessed is he that **c** in the name of the Lord. *2064*
24:27 For as the lightning **c out** of the east, and *1831*
24:44 an hour as you think not the Son of man **c**. *2064*
24:46 whom his lord when he **c** shall find so *2064*
25: 6 was a cry made, Behold, the bridegroom **c**; *2064*
25:13 day nor the hour wherein the Son of man **c**. *2064*
25:19 a long time the lord of those servants **c**, *2064*
26:36 Then **c** Jesus with them unto a place called *2064*
26:40 And he **c** unto the disciples, and *2064*
26:45 Then **c** he to his disciples, and saith unto *2064*
Mk 1: 7 There **c** one mightier than I after me, *2064*
3:20 And *the* multitude **c together** again, so *4905*
4:15 Satan **c** immediately, and taketh away *2064*
5:22 there **c** one of the rulers of the synagogue, *2064*
5:38 And he **c** to the house of the ruler of *2064*
6:48 about the fourth watch of the night he **c** *2064*
7:20 And he said, That which **c out** of the man, *1607*
8:22 And he **c** to Bethsaida; and they bring a *2064*
8:38 when he **c** in the glory of his Father with *2064*
9:12 Elias verily **c** first, and restoreth all *things*; *2064*
10: 1 **c** into the coasts of Judea by the farther side *2064*
11: 9 Blessed *is* he that **c** in the name of *2064*
11:10 that **c** in the name of the Lord: *2064*
13:35 know not when the master of the house **c**, *2064*
14:17 And in the evening he **c** with the twelve. *2064*
14:37 And he **c**, and findeth them sleeping, and *2064*
14:41 And he **c** the third time, and saith unto *2064*
14:43 **c** Judas, one of the twelve, and with him a *3854*
14:66 there **c** one of the maids of the high priest: *2064*
Lk 3:16 but one mightier than I **c**, the latchet of *2064*
6:47 Whosoever **c** to me, and heareth my *2064*
7: 8 and to another, Come, and he **c**; and to my *2064*
8:12 then **c** the devil, and taketh away the word *2064*
8:49 there **c** one from the ruler of *2064*
11:25 And when he **c**, he findeth *it* swept and *2064*
12:36 that when *he* **c** and knocketh, they may *2064*
12:37 whom the lord when he **c** shall find *2064*
12:40 for the Son of man **c** at an hour when ye *2064*
12:43 whom his lord when he **c** shall find so *2064*
12:54 straightway ye say, There **c** a shower; *2064*
12:55 ye say, There will be heat; and it **c to pass**. *1096*
13:35 Blessed *is* he that **c** in the name of the Lord. *2064*
14:10 that when he that bade thee **c**, he may say *2064*
14:31 that **c** against him with twenty thousand? *2064*
15: 6 And when he **c** home, he calleth together *2064*
17:20 The kingdom of God **c** not with *2064*
18: 8 Nevertheless when the Son of man **c**, shall *2064*
19:38 Blessed *be* the King that **c** in the name of *2064*
Jn 1: 9 which lighteth every man *that* **c** into *2064*
1:15 He that **c** after me is preferred before me: *2064*
1:30 After me **c** a man which is preferred before *2064*
3: 8 but canst not tell whence it **c**, and whither it *2064*
3:20 neither **c** to the light, lest his deeds should *2064*
3:21 But he that doeth truth **c** to the light, *2064*
3:31 He that **c** from above is above all: he that is *2064*
3:31 he that **c** from heaven is above all. *2064*
4: 5 Then **c** he to a city of Samaria, which is *2064*
4: 7 There **c** a woman of Samaria to draw water: *2064*
4:21 unto her, Woman, believe me, the hour **c**, *2064*
4:23 But the hour **c**, and now is, when the true *2064*
4:25 I know that Messias **c**, which is called *2064*
4:35 are yet four months, and *then* **c** harvest? *2064*

Jn 5:44 seek not the honour that c from God only? NIG
6:33 For the bread of God is he which c down 2597
6:35 he that c to me shall never hunger; and 2064
6:37 him that c to me I will in no wise cast out. 2064
6:45 and hath learned of the Father, c unto me. 2064
6:50 This is the bread which c down from 2597
7:27 but when Christ c, no man knoweth whence 2064
7:31 believed on him, and said, When Christ c, 2064
7:42 That Christ c of the seed of David, and 2064
9: 4 is day: the night c, when no man can work. 2064
10:10 The thief c not, but for to steal, and to kill, 2064
11:38 again groaning in himself c to the grave. 2064
12:13 Blessed is the King of Israel that c in 2064
12:15 behold, thy King c, sitting on an ass's colt. 2064
12:22 Philip c and telleth Andrew: and 2064
13: 6 Then c he to Simon Peter: and Peter saith 2064
14: 6 no man c unto the Father, but by me. 2064
14:30 for the prince of this world c, and 2064
15:25 But this c to pass, that the word might be NIG
16: 2 yea, the time c, that whosoever killeth you 2064
16:25 but the time c, when I shall no more speak 2064
16:32 Behold, the hour c, yea, is now come, 2064
18: 3 c thither with lanterns and torches and 2064
20: 1 The first day of the week c Mary 2064
20: 2 and c to Simon Peter, and to the other 2064
20: 6 Then c Simon Peter following him, and 2064
21:13 Jesus then c, and taketh bread, and 2064
Ac 10:32 who, when he c, shall speak unto thee. 3854
13:25 am not he. But behold, there c one after me, 2064
18:21 I must by all means keep this feast that c in 2064
Ro 4: 9 C this blessedness then upon NIG
10:17 So then faith c by hearing, NIG
1Co 15:24 Then c the end, when he shall have NIG
2Co 11: 4 For if he that c preacheth another Jesus, 2064
11:28 that which c upon me daily, the care of all 1999
Gal 5: 8 This persuasion c not of him that calleth NIG
Eph 5: 6 of these things c the wrath of God upon 2064
Col 3: 6 For which things' sake the wrath of God c 2064
1Th 5: 2 day of the Lord so c as a thief in the night. 2064
5: 3 then sudden destruction c upon them, 2186
1Ti 6: 4 whereof c envy, strife, railings, 1096
Heb 6: 7 which drinketh in the rain that c oft upon it, 2064
10: 5 Wherefore when he c into the world, 1525
11: 6 for he that c to God must believe that he is, 4334
Jas 1:17 and c down from the Father of lights, 2597
Jude 1:14 the Lord c with ten thousands of his saints, 2064
Rev 1: 7 Behold, he c with clouds; and every eye 2064
3:12 which c down out of heaven from my God: 2597
11:14 is past; and behold, the third woe c quickly. 2064
17:10 and when he c, he must continue a short 2064

COMFORT (66) [COMFORTABLE, COMFORTABLY, COMFORTED, COMFORTEDST, COMFORTER, COMFORTERS, COMFORTETH, COMFORTLESS, COMFORTS]

Ge 5:29 This same shall c us concerning our work 5162
18: 5 a morsel of bread, and c ye your hearts; 5582
27:42 as touching thee, doth c himself, 5162
37:35 and all his daughters rose up to c him; 5162
Jdg 19: 5 C thine heart with a morsel of bread, and 5582
19: 8 father said, C thine heart, I pray thee. 5582
2Sa 10: 2 David sent to c him by the hand of his 5162
1Ch 7:22 many days, and his brethren came to c him. 5162
19: 2 David sent messengers to c him concerning 5162
19: 2 the children of Ammon to Hanun, to c him. 5162
Job 2:11 to come to mourn with him and to c him. 5162
6:10 should I yet have c; yea, I would harden 5165
7:13 When I say, My bed shall c me, my couch 5162
9:27 I will leave off my heaviness, and c myself: 1082
10:20 and let me alone, that I may take c a little, 1082
21:34 How then c ye me in vain, seeing in your 5162
Ps 23: 4 art with me; thy rod and thy staff they c me. 5162
71:21 my greatness, and c me on every side. 5162
119:50 This is my c in my affliction: for thy word 5165
119:76 thy merciful kindness be for my c, 5162
119:82 for thy word, saying, When wilt thou c me? 5162
SS 2: 5 Stay me with flagons, c me with apples: 7502
Isa 22: 4 labour not to c me, because of the spoiling 5162
40: 1 C ye, comfort ye my people, saith your 5162
40: 1 Comfort ye, c ye my people, saith your 5162
51: 3 For the LORD shall c Zion: he will 5162
51: 3 he will c all her waste places; and he will 5162
51:19 and the sword: by whom shall I c thee? 5162
57: 6 meat offering. Should I receive c in these? 5162
61: 2 vengeance of our God; to c all that mourn; 5162
66:13 his mother comforteth, so will I c you; 5162
Jer 8:18 When I would c myself against sorrow, 4010
16: 7 them in mourning, to c them for the dead; 5162
31:13 will c them, and make them rejoice from 5162
La 1: 2 among all her lovers she hath none to c her: 5162
1:17 forth her hands, and there is none to c her: 5162
1:21 heard that I sigh; there is none to c me: 5162
2:13 what shall I equal to thee, that I may c thee, 5162
Eze 14:23 they shall c you, when ye see their ways 5162
16:54 hast done, in that thou art a c unto them. 5162
Zec 1:17 the LORD shall yet c Zion, and shall yet 5162
10: 2 and have told false dreams; they c in vain: 5162
Mt 9:22 saw her, he said, Daughter, be of good c; 2293
Mk 10:49 saying unto him, Be of good c, rise; 2293
Lk 8:48 he said unto her, Daughter, be of good c: 2293
Jn 11:19 Mary, to c them concerning their brother. 3888
Ac 9:31 and in the c of the Holy Ghost, 3874
Ro 15: 4 and c of the scriptures might have hope. 3874
1Co 14: 3 men to edification, and exhortation, and c. 3889
2Co 1: 3 the Father of mercies, and the God of all c; 3874
1: 4 that we may be able to c them which are in 3870
1: 4 by the c wherewith we ourselves are 3874
2: 7 c him, lest perhaps such a one should be 3870
7: 4 I am filled with c, I am exceeding joyful in 3874
7:13 Therefore we were comforted in your c: 3874
13:11 Be perfect, be of good c, be of one mind, 3870
Eph 6:22 our affairs, and that he might c your hearts. 3870
Php 2: 1 any consolation in Christ, if any c of love, 3890
2:19 that I also may be of good c, when I know 2174
Col 4: 8 might know your estate, and c your hearts; 3870
4:11 of God, which have been a c unto me. 3931
1Th 3: 2 and to c you concerning your faith: 3870
4:18 Wherefore c one another with these words. 3870
5:11 Wherefore c yourselves together, and 3870
5:14 c the feebleminded, support the weak, 3888
2Th 2:17 C your hearts, and stablish you in every 3870

COMFORTABLE (2) [COMFORT]

2Sa 14:17 word of my lord the king shall now be c: 4496
Zec 1:13 with me with good words and c words. 5150

COMFORTABLY (5) [COMFORT]

2Sa 19: 7 and speak c unto thy servants: 3820+5921
2Ch 30:22 Hezekiah spake c unto all the Levites 3820+5921
32: 6 the city, and spake c to them, saying, 3824+5921
Isa 40: 2 Speak ye c to Jerusalem, and 3820+5921
Hos 2:14 the wilderness, and speak c unto her. 3820+5921

COMFORTED (36) [COMFORT]

Ge 24:67 and Isaac was c after his mother's death. 5162
37:35 he refused to be c; and he said, For I will 5162
38:12 Judah was c, and went up unto his 5162
50:21 he c them, and spake kindly unto them. 5162
Ru 2:13 for that thou hast c me, and for that thou 5162
2Sa 12:24 David c Bath-sheba his wife, and went in 5162
13:39 for he was c concerning Amnon, seeing he 5162
Job 42:11 c him over all the evil that the LORD had 5162
Ps 77: 2 and ceased not: my soul refused to be c. 5162
86:17 thou, LORD, hast holpen me, and c me. 5162
119:52 of old, O LORD; and have c myself. 5162
Isa 49:13 for the LORD hath c his people, and 5162
52: 9 for the LORD hath c his people, he hath 5162
54:11 tossed with tempest, and not c, behold, 5162
66:13 and ye shall be c in Jerusalem. 5162
Jer 31:15 children refused to be c for her children, 5162
Eze 5:13 my fury to rest upon them, and I will be c: 5162
14:22 ye shall be c concerning the evil that I have 5162
31:16 shall be c in the nether parts of the earth. 5162
32:31 shall be c over all his multitude, 5162
Mt 2:18 and would not be c, because they are not. 3870
5: 4 are they that mourn: for they shall be c. 3870
Lk 16:25 Lazarus evil things: but now he is c, 3870
Jn 11:31 and c her, when they saw Mary, that she 3888
Ac 16:40 the brethren, they c them, and departed. 3870
20:12 the young man alive, and were not a little c. 3870
Ro 1:12 that I may be c together with you by 4837
1Co 14:31 by one, that all may learn, and all may be c. 3870
2Co 1: 4 wherewith we ourselves are c of God. 3870
1: 6 or whether we be c, it is for your 3870
7: 6 are cast down, c us by the coming of Titus; 3870
7: 7 by the consolation wherewith he was c in 3870
7:13 Therefore we were c in your comfort: yea, 3870
Col 2: 2 That their hearts might be c, being knit 3870
1Th 2:11 and c and charged every one of you, 3888
3: 7 we were c over you in all our affliction and 3870

COMFORTEDST (1) [COMFORT]

Isa 12: 1 thine anger is turned away, and thou c me. 5162

COMFORTER (8) [COMFORT]

Ecc 4: 1 such as were oppressed, and they had no c; 5162
4: 1 there was power; but they had no c. 5162
La 1: 9 she had no c. O LORD, behold my 5162
1:16 the c that should relieve my soul is far from 5162
Jn 14:16 the Father, and he shall give you another C, 3875
14:26 But the C, which is the Holy Ghost, 3875
15:26 But when the C is come, whom I will send 3875
16: 7 go not away, the C will not come unto you; 3875

COMFORTERS (5) [COMFORT]

2Sa 10: 3 thy father, that he hath sent c unto thee? 5162
1Ch 19: 3 thy father, that he hath sent c unto thee? 5162
Job 16: 2 I have heard many such things: miserable c 5162
Ps 69:20 there was none; and for c, but I found none. 5162
Na 3: 7 whence shall I seek c for thee? 5162

COMFORTETH (5) [COMFORT]

Job 29:25 in the army, as one that c the mourners. 5162
Isa 51:12 I, even I, am he that c you: who art thou, 5162
66:13 As one whom his mother c, so will I 5162
2Co 1: 4 Who c us in all our tribulation, that we may 3870
7: 6 that c those that are cast down, 3870

COMFORTLESS (1) [COMFORT]

Jn 14:18 I will not leave you c: I will come to you. 3737

COMFORTS (2) [COMFORT]

Ps 94:19 thoughts within me thy c delight my soul. 8575
Isa 57:18 and restore c unto him and to his mourners. 5150

COMING (100) [COME]

Ge 24:63 and saw, and behold, the camels were c. 935
30:30 the LORD hath blessed thee since my c: 7272
Nu 22:16 I pray thee, hinder thee from c unto me: 1980
33:40 heard of the c of the children of Israel. 935
Jdg 5:28 the lattice, Why is his chariot so long in c? 935
1Sa 10: 5 c down from the high place with a psaltery, 3381
16: 4 the elders of the town trembled at his c, 7125
22: 9 said, I saw the son of Jesse c to Nob, 935
25:26 hath withholden thee from c to shed blood, 935
25:33 which hast kept me this day from c to shed 935
29: 6 thy c in with me in the host is good in my 935
29: 6 since the day of thy c unto me unto this day: 935
2Sa 3:25 to know thy going out and thy c in, and 4126
24:20 the king and his servants c on toward him: 5674
2Ki 10:15 Jehonadab the son of Rechab c to meet him: NIH
13:20 invaded the land at the c in of the year. 935
19:27 and thy c in, and thy rage against me. 935
2Ch 22: 7 the destruction of Ahaziah was of God by c 935
Ezr 3: 8 Now in the second year of their c unto 935
Ps 19: 5 Which is as a bridegroom c out of his 3318
37:13 laugh at him: for he seeth that his day is c. 935
121: 8 going out and thy c in from this time forth, 935
Pr 8: 3 the entry of the city, at the c in at the doors. 3996
Isa 14: 9 is moved for thee to meet thee at thy c: 935
32:19 When it shall hail, c down on the forest; 3381
37:28 and thy c in, and thy rage against me. 935
44: 7 the things that are c, and shall come, let them 857
Jer 8: 7 and the swallow observe the time of their c; 935
Da 4:23 and a holy one c down from heaven, 5182
Mic 7:15 According to the days of thy c out of 3318
Hab 3: 4 as the light; he had horns c out of his hand: NIH
Mal 3: 2 who may abide the day of his c? and 935
4: 5 Elijah the prophet before the c of the great 935
Mt 8:28 c out of the tombs, exceeding fierce, so 1831
16:28 till they see the Son of man c in his 2064
24: 3 and what shall be the sign of thy c, and 3952
24:27 so shall also the c of the Son of man be. 3952
24:30 they shall see the Son of man c in 2064
24:37 so shall also the c of the Son of man be. 3952
24:39 so shall also the c of the Son of man be. 3952
24:48 say in his heart, My lord delayeth his c; 2064
25:27 at my c I should have received mine own 2064
26:64 of power, and c in the clouds of heaven. 2064
Mk 1:10 And straightway c up out of the water, 305
6:31 for there were many c and going, and they 2064
13:26 shall they see the Son of man c in 2064
13:36 Lest c suddenly he find you sleeping. 2064
14:62 of power, and c in the clouds of heaven. 2064
15:21 who passed by, c out of the country, 2064
Lk 2:38 And she c in that instant gave thanks 2186
9:42 And as he was yet a c, the devil threw him 4334
12:45 say in his heart, My lord delayeth his c; 2064
18: 5 lest by her continual c she weary me. 2064
19:23 that at my c I might have required mine 2064
21:26 after those things which are c on the earth: 1904
21:27 shall they see the Son of man c in a cloud 2064
23:26 c out of the country, and on him they laid 2064
23:29 For behold, the days are c, in the which 2064
23:36 c to him, and offering him vinegar, 4334
Jn 1:27 it is, who c after me is preferred before me, 2064
1:29 The next day John seeth Jesus c unto him, 2064
1:47 Jesus saw Nathanael c to him, and saith of 2064
5: 7 but while I am c, another steppeth down 2064
5:25 I say unto you, The hour is c, and now is, 2064
5:28 for the hour is c, in the which all that are in 2064
10:12 seeth the wolf c, and leaveth the sheep, and 2064
11:20 as soon as she heard that Jesus was c, went 2064
12:12 when they heard that Jesus was c to 2064
Ac 7:52 shewed before of the c of the Just One; 1660
9:12 seen in a vision a man named Ananias c in, 1525
9:28 And he was with them c in and going out at 1531
10: 3 an angel of God c in to him, and 1525
10:25 And as Peter was c in, Cornelius met him, 1525
13:24 When John had first preached before his c 1529
17:10 who c thither went into the synagogue of 3854
27:33 And while the day was c on, Paul besought 3195
Ro 15:22 I have been much hindered from c to you. 2064
1Co 1: 7 waiting for the c of our Lord Jesus Christ: 602
15:23 afterward they that are Christ's at his c. 3952
16:17 I am glad of the c of Stephanas and 3952
2Co 7: 6 cast down, comforted us by the c of Titus; 3952
7: 7 And not by his c only, but by 3952
13: 1 This is the third time I am c to you. In 2064
Php 1:26 Jesus Christ for me by my c to you again. 3952
1Th 2:19 presence of our Lord Jesus Christ at his c? 3952
3:13 at the c of our Lord Jesus Christ with all his 3952
4:15 remain unto the c of the Lord shall not 3952
5:23 body be preserved blameless unto the c of 3952
2Th 2: 1 by the c of our Lord Jesus Christ, and 3952
2: 8 shall destroy with the brightness of his c: 3952
2: 9 Even him, whose c is after the working of 3952
Jas 5: 7 brethren, unto the c of the Lord. 3952
5: 8 for the c of the Lord draweth nigh. 3952
1Pe 2: 4 To whom c, as unto a living stone, 4334
2Pe 1:16 the power and c of our Lord Jesus Christ, 3952
3: 4 And saying, Where is the promise of his c? 3952
3:12 and hasting unto the c of the day of God, 3952
1Jn 2:28 and not be ashamed before him at his c. 3952
Rev 13:11 And I beheld another beast c up out of 305
21: 2 c down from God out of heaven, 2597

COMINGS (1) [COME]

Eze 43:11 the c in thereof, and all the forms thereof, 4126

COMMAND (104) [COMMANDED, COMMANDEDST, COMMANDER, COMMANDEST, COMMANDETH, COMMANDING, COMMANDMENT, COMMANDMENTS]

Ge 18:19 that he will c his children and his 6680
27: 8 obey my voice according to that which I c 6680
50:16 Thy father did c before he died, saying, 6680
Ex 7: 2 Thou shalt speak all that I c thee: and 6680
8:27 to the LORD our God, as he shall c us. 559
18:23 God c thee so, then thou shalt be able to 6680
27:20 thou shalt c the children of Israel, that they 6680
34:11 Observe thou that which I c thee this day: 6680
Lev 6: 9 C Aaron and his sons, saying, This is 6680
13:54 the priest shall c that they wash the thing 6680
14: 4 shall the priest c to take for him that is to be 6680
14: 5 the priest shall c that one of the birds be 6680
14:36 the priest shall c that they empty the house, 6680
14:40 the priest shall c that they take away 6680
24: 2 C the children of Israel, that they bring 6680
25:21 I will c my blessing upon you in the sixth 6680
Nu 5: 2 C the children of Israel, that they put out of 6680
9: 8 I will hear what the LORD will c 6680
28: 2 C the children of Israel, and say unto them, 6680
34: 2 C the children of Israel, and say unto them, 6680
35: 2 C the children of Israel, that they give unto 6680
36: 6 This is the thing which the LORD doth c 6680
Dt 2: 4 c thou the people, saying, Ye are to pass 6680
4: 2 Ye shall not add unto the word which I c 6680
4: 2 of the LORD your God which I c you. 6680
4:40 his commandments, which I c thee this day, 6680
6: 2 which I c thee, thou, and thy son, and 6680

Dt 6: 6 these words, which I **c** thee *this* day, 6680
7:11 which I **c** thee *this* day, to do them. 6680
8: 1 All the commandments which I **c** thee *this* 6680
8:11 and his statutes, which I **c** thee *this* day: 6680
10:13 which I **c** thee *this* day for thy good? 6680
11: 8 the commandments which I **c** you *this* day, 6680
11:13 my commandments which I **c** you *this* day, 6680
11:22 all these commandments which I **c** you, 6680
11:27 LORD your God, which I **c** you *this* day: 6680
11:28 turn aside out of the way which I **c** you *this* 6680
12:11 thither shall ye bring all that I **c** you; 6680
12:14 and there thou shalt do all that I **c** thee. 6680
12:28 and hear all these words which I **c** thee, 6680
12:32 What thing soever I **c** you, observe to do it: 6680
13:18 to keep all his commandments which I **c** 6680
15: 5 commandments which I **c** thee *this* day. 6680
15:11 therefore I **c** thee, saying, Thou shalt open 6680
15:15 therefore I **c** thee this thing to day. 6680
18:18 he shall speak unto them all that I shall **c** 6680
19: 7 Wherefore I **c** thee, saying, Thou shalt 6680
19: 9 which I **c** thee *this* day, to love the LORD 6680
24:18 therefore I **c** thee to do this thing. 6680
24:22 of Egypt: therefore I **c** thee to do this thing. 6680
27: 1 Keep all the commandments which I **c** you 6680
27: 4 which I **c** you *this* day, in mount Ebal, and 6680
27:10 and his statutes, which I **c** thee *this* day. 6680
28: 1 to do all his commandments which I **c** thee 6680
28: 8 The LORD shall **c** the blessing upon thee 6680
28:13 which I **c** thee *this* day, to observe and 6680
28:14 any of the words which I **c** thee *this* day, 6680
28:15 and his statutes which I **c** thee *this* day; 6680
30: 2 shalt obey his voice according to all that I **c** 6680
30: 8 do all his commandments which I **c** thee 6680
30:11 For this commandment which I **c** thee *this* 6680
30:16 In that I **c** thee *this* day to love the LORD 6680
32:46 which ye shall **c** your children to observe to 6680
Jos 1:11 **c** the people, saying, Prepare you victuals; 6680
3: 8 thou shalt **c** the priests that bear the ark of 6680
4: 3 **c** you them, saying, Take you hence out of 6680
4:16 **C** the priests that bear the ark of 6680
11:15 so did Moses **c** Joshua, and so did Joshua; 6680
1Sa 16:16 Let our lord now **c** thy servants *which are* 559
1Ki 5: 6 **c** thou that they hew me cedar trees out of 6680
11:38 if thou wilt hearken unto all that I **c** thee, 6680
2Ch 7:13 or if I **c** the locusts to devour the land, or 6680
Job 39:27 Doth the eagle mount up at thy **c**, and make 6310
Ps 42: 8 *Yet* the LORD will **c** his lovingkindness 6680
44: 4 my King, O God: **c** deliverances for Jacob. 6680
Isa 5: 6 I will also **c** the clouds that they rain no 6680
45:11 concerning the work of my hands **c** ye me. 6680
Jer 1: 7 and whatsoever I **c** thee thou shalt speak. 6680
1:17 arise, and speak unto them all that I **c** thee: 6680
11: 4 do them, according to all which I **c** you: 6680
26: 2 all the words that I **c** thee to speak unto 6680
27: 4 **c** them to say unto their masters, Thus saith 6680
34:22 Behold, I *will* **c**, saith the LORD, and 6680
La 1:10 whom thou didst **c** *that* they should not 6680
Am 9: 3 thence will I **c** the serpent, and he shall bite 6680
9: 4 thence will I **c** the sword, and it shall slay 6680
9: 9 I will **c**, and I will sift the house of Israel 6680
Mt 4: 3 of God, **c** that these stones be made bread. *3004*
19: 7 then **c** to give a writing of divorcement, *1781*
27:64 **C** therefore that the sepulchre be made sure *2753*
Mk 10: 3 and said unto them, What did Moses **c** you? *1781*
Lk 4: 3 of God, **c** this stone that it be made bread. *3004*
8:31 And they besought him that he would not **c** *2004*
9:54 wilt thou *that* we **c** fire to come down from *3004*
Jn 15:14 are my friends, if ye do whatsoever I **c** you. *1781*
15:17 These *things* I **c** you, that ye love one *1781*
Ac 5:28 Did not we **straitly c** you that *you* *3852+3853*
15: 5 and to **c** *them* to keep the law of Moses. *3853*
16:18 I **c** thee in the name of Jesus Christ to come *3853*
1Co 7:10 And unto the married I **c**, *yet* not I, but *3853*
2Th 3: 4 and will do the *things* which we **c** you. *3853*
3: 6 Now we **c** you, brethren, in the name of our *3853*
3:12 Now *them that are* such we **c** and exhort by *3853*
1Ti 4:11 These *things* **c** and teach. *3853*

COMMANDED (443) [COMMAND]

Ge 2:16 the LORD God **c** the man, saying, 6680
3:11 whereof I **c** thee that thou shouldest not 6680
3:17 eaten of the tree, of which I **c** thee, saying, 6680
6:22 according to all that God **c** him, so did he. 6680
7: 5 according unto all that the LORD **c** him. 6680
7: 9 and the female, as God had **c** Noah. 6680
7:16 and female of all flesh, as God had **c** him: 6680
12:20 Pharaoh **c** *his* men concerning him: and 6680
21: 4 being eight days old, as God had **c** him. 6680
32: 4 he **c** them, saying, Thus shall ye speak unto 6680
32:17 he **c** the foremost, saying, When Esau my 6680
32:19 so **c** he the second, and the third, and all 6680
42:25 Joseph **c** to fill their sacks *with* corn, and 6680
44: 1 he **c** the steward of his house, saying, 6680
45:19 Now thou art **c**, this do ye; take you 6680
47:11 in the land of Rameses, as Pharaoh had **c**. 6680
50: 2 Joseph **c** his servants the physicians to 6680
50:12 his sons did unto him according as he **c** 6680
Ex 1:17 and did not as the king of Egypt **c** them, but 1696
4:28 and all the signs which he had **c** him. 6680
5: 6 Pharaoh **c** the same day the taskmasters of 6680
7: 6 and Aaron did as the LORD **c** them, 6680
7:10 and they did so as the LORD had **c**: 6680
7:20 and Aaron did so, as the LORD **c**; 6680
12:28 did as the LORD had **c** Moses and Aaron, 6680
12:50 as the LORD **c** Moses and Aaron, so 6680
16:16 This *is* the thing which the LORD hath **c**, 6680
16:34 As the LORD **c** Moses, so Aaron laid it up 6680
19: 7 all these words which the LORD **c** him. 6680
23:15 as I **c** thee, in the time appointed of 6680
29:35 according to all *things* which I have **c** thee: 6680
31: 6 that they may make all that I have **c** thee; 6680
31:11 to all that I have **c** thee shall they do. 6680
32: 8 quickly out of the way which I **c** them: 6680
34: 4 as the LORD had **c** him, and took in his 6680
34:18 as I **c** thee, in the time of the month Abib: 6680
Ex 34:34 the children of Israel *that* which he was **c**. 6680
35: 1 *are* the words which the LORD hath **c**, 6680
35: 4 This *is* the thing which the LORD **c**, 6680
35:10 and make all that the LORD hath **c**; 6680
35:29 which the LORD had **c** to be made by 6680
36: 1 according to all that the LORD had **c**. 6680
36: 5 of the work, which the LORD **c** to make. 6680
38:22 made all that the LORD **c** Moses. 6680
39: 1 for Aaron; as the LORD **c** Moses. 6680
39: 5 fine twined linen; as the LORD **c** Moses. 6680
39: 7 children of Israel; as the LORD **c** Moses. 6680
39:21 from the ephod; as the LORD **c** Moses. 6680
39:26 robe to minister *in;* as the LORD **c** Moses. 6680
39:29 *of* needlework; as the LORD **c** Moses. 6680
39:31 upon the mitre; as the LORD **c** Moses. 6680
39:32 according to all that the LORD **c** Moses, 6680
39:42 According to all that the LORD **c** Moses, 6680
39:43 they had done it as the LORD had **c**, *even* 6680
40:16 according to all that the LORD **c** him, so 6680
40:19 tent above upon it; as the LORD **c** Moses. 6680
40:21 of the Testimony; as the LORD **c** Moses. 6680
40:23 the LORD; as the LORD had **c** Moses. 6680
40:25 the LORD; as the LORD **c** Moses. 6680
40:27 incense thereon; as the LORD **c** Moses. 6680
40:29 the meat offering; as the LORD **c** Moses. 6680
40:32 they washed; as the LORD **c** Moses. 6680
Lev 7:36 Which the LORD **c** to be given them of 6680
7:38 Which the LORD **c** Moses in mount Sinai, 6680
7:38 in the day that he **c** the children of Israel to 6680
8: 4 Moses did as the LORD **c** him; and 6680
8: 5 This *is* the thing which the LORD **c** to be 6680
8: 9 the holy crown; as the LORD **c** Moses. 6680
8:13 upon them; as the LORD **c** Moses. 6680
8:17 without the camp; as the LORD **c** Moses. 6680
8:21 unto the LORD; as the LORD **c** Moses. 6680
8:29 it was Moses' part; as the LORD **c** Moses. 6680
8:31 as I **c**, saying, Aaron and his sons shall eat 6680
8:34 done this day, *so* the LORD hath **c** to do, 6680
8:35 the LORD, that ye die not: for so I am **c**. 6680
8:36 his sons did all things which the LORD **c** 6680
9: 5 they brought *that* which Moses **c** before 6680
9: 6 This *is* the thing which the LORD **c** *that* 6680
9: 7 an atonement for them; as the LORD **c**. 6680
9:10 upon the altar; as the LORD **c** Moses. 6680
9:21 offering before the LORD; as Moses **c**. 6680
10: 1 before the LORD, which he **c** them not. 6680
10:13 of the LORD made by fire: for so I am **c**. 6680
10:15 by a statute for ever; as the LORD hath **c**. 6680
10:18 have eaten it in the holy *place,* as I **c**. 6680
16:34 a year. And he did as the LORD **c** Moses. 6680
17: 2 This *is* the thing which the LORD hath **c**, 6680
24:23 the children of Israel did as the LORD **c** 6680
27:34 which the LORD **c** Moses for the children 6680
Nu 1:19 As the LORD **c** Moses, so he numbered 6680
1:54 according to all that the LORD **c** Moses, 6680
2:33 children of Israel; as the LORD **c** Moses. 6680
2:34 according to all that the LORD **c** Moses. 6680
3:16 to the word of the LORD, as he was **c**. 6680
3:42 Moses numbered, as the LORD **c** him, 6680
3:51 of the LORD, as the LORD **c** Moses. 6680
4:49 numbered of him, as the LORD **c** Moses. 6680
8: 3 the candlestick, as the LORD **c** Moses. 6680
8:20 LORD **c** Moses concerning the Levites, 6680
8:22 as the LORD had **c** Moses concerning 6680
9: 5 according to all that the LORD **c** Moses, 6680
15:23 *Even* all that the LORD hath **c** you by 6680
15:23 from the day that the LORD **c** *Moses,* and 6680
15:36 and he died; as the LORD **c** Moses. 6680
16:47 Aaron took as Moses **c**, and ran into 1696
17:11 Moses did *so:* as the LORD **c** him, so 6680
19: 2 of the law which the LORD hath **c**, 6680
20: 9 rod from before the LORD, as he **c** him. 6680
20:27 Moses did as the LORD **c**: and they went 6680
26: 4 as the LORD **c** Moses and the children of 6680
27:11 of judgment, as the LORD **c** Moses. 6680
27:22 Moses did as the LORD **c** him: and 6680
27:23 as the LORD **c** by the hand of Moses. 1696
29:40 according to all that the LORD **c** Moses. 6680
30: 1 This *is* the thing which the LORD hath **c**. 6680
30:16 which the LORD **c** Moses, between a man 6680
31: 7 the Midianites, as the LORD **c** Moses; 6680
31:21 of the law which the LORD **c** Moses; 6680
31:31 Eleazar the priest did as the LORD **c** 6680
31:41 Eleazar the priest, as the LORD **c** Moses. 6680
31:47 of the LORD; as the LORD **c** Moses. 6680
32:28 So concerning them Moses **c** Eleazar 6680
34:13 Moses **c** the children of Israel, saying, 6680
34:13 which the LORD **c** to give unto the nine 6680
34:29 These *are they* whom the LORD **c** to 6680
36: 2 The LORD **c** my lord to give the land for 6680
36: 2 my lord was **c** by the LORD to give 6680
36: 5 Moses **c** the children of Israel according to 6680
36:10 Even as the LORD **c** Moses, so did 6680
36:13 which the LORD **c** by the hand of Moses 6680
Dt 1:18 I **c** you at that time all the things which ye 6680
1:19 the Amorites, as the LORD our God **c** us; 6680
1:41 according to all that the LORD our God **c** 6680
3:18 I **c** you at that time, saying, The LORD 6680
3:21 I **c** Joshua at that time, saying, Thine eyes 6680
4: 5 even as the LORD my God **c** me, 6680
4:13 which he **c** you to perform, *even* ten 6680
4:14 the LORD **c** me at that time to teach you 6680
5:12 as the LORD thy God hath **c** thee. 6680
5:15 the LORD thy God **c** thee to keep 6680
5:16 as the LORD thy God hath **c** thee; 6680
5:32 as the LORD your God hath **c** you: 6680
5:33 which the LORD your God hath **c** you, 6680
6: 1 which the LORD your God **c** to teach you, 6680
6:17 and his statutes, which he hath **c** thee. 6680
6:20 which the LORD our God hath **c** you? 6680
6:24 the LORD **c** us to do all these statutes, 6680
6:25 the LORD our God, as he hath **c** us. 6680
9:12 turned aside out of the way which I **c** them; 6680
9:16 of the way which the LORD had **c** you. 6680
10: 5 and there they be, as the LORD **c** me. 6680
Dt 12:21 as I have **c** thee, and thou shalt eat in thy 6680
13: 5 the LORD thy God **c** thee to walk in. 6680
17: 3 of the host of heaven, which I have not **c**; 6680
18:20 which I have not **c** him to speak, or 6680
20:17 as the LORD thy God hath **c** thee: 6680
24: 8 as I **c** them, *so* ye shall observe to do. 6680
26:13 thy commandments which thou hast **c** me: 6680
26:14 have done according to all that thou hast **c** 6680
26:16 This day the LORD thy God hath **c** thee to 6680
27: 1 Moses with the elders of Israel **c** 6680
28:45 and his statutes which he **c** thee: 6680
29: 1 which the LORD **c** Moses to make with 6680
31: 5 all the commandments which I have **c** you. 6680
31:10 Moses **c** them, saying, At the end of *every* 6680
31:25 That Moses **c** the Levites, which bare 6680
31:29 turn aside from the way which I have **c** 6680
33: 4 Moses **c** us a law, *even* the inheritance of 6680
34: 9 unto him, and did as the LORD **c** Moses. 6680
Jos 1: 7 all the law, which Moses my servant **c** thee: 6680
1: 9 Have not I **c** thee? Be strong and of a good 6680
1:10 Joshua **c** the officers of the people, saying, 6680
1:13 Moses the servant of the LORD **c** you, 6680
3: 3 they **c** the people, saying, When ye see 6680
4: 8 the children of Israel did so as Joshua **c**, 6680
4:10 LORD **c** Joshua to speak unto the people, 6680
4:10 according to all that Moses **c** Joshua: 6680
4:17 Joshua therefore **c** the priests, saying, 6680
6:10 Joshua had **c** the people, saying, Ye shall 6680
7:11 transgressed my covenant which I **c** them: 6680
8: 4 he **c** them, saying, Behold, ye shall lie in 6680
8: 8 the LORD shall ye do. See, I have **c** you. 6680
8:27 the word of the LORD which he **c** Joshua. 6680
8:29 Joshua **c** that they should take his carcase 6680
8:31 As Moses the servant of the LORD **c** 6680
8:33 as Moses the servant of the LORD had **c** 6680
8:35 There was not a word of all that Moses **c**, 6680
9:24 how that the LORD thy God **c** his servant 6680
10:27 *that* Joshua **c**, and they took them down off 6680
10:40 as the LORD God of Israel **c**. 6680
11:12 as Moses the servant of the LORD **c**. 6680
11:15 As the LORD **c** Moses his servant, so 6680
11:15 undone of all that the LORD **c** Moses. 6680
11:20 destroy them, as the LORD **c** Moses. 6680
13: 6 for an inheritance, as I have **c** thee. 6680
14: 2 as the LORD **c** by the hand of Moses, 6680
14: 5 As the LORD **c** Moses, so the children of 6680
17: 4 The LORD **c** Moses to give us an 6680
21: 2 The LORD **c** by the hand of Moses to give 6680
21: 8 as the LORD **c** by the hand of Moses. 6680
22: 2 Moses the servant of the LORD **c** you, 6680
22: 2 have obeyed my voice in all that I **c** you: 6680
23:16 which he **c** you, and have gone and 6680
Jdg 2:20 my covenant which I **c** their fathers, 6680
3: 4 which he **c** their fathers by the hand of 6680
4: 6 Hath not the LORD God of Israel **c**, 6680
13:14 nor eat any unclean *thing:* all that I **c** her let 6680
21:10 **c** them, saying, Go and smite 6680
21:20 Therefore they **c** the children of Benjamin, 6680
Ru 2:15 up to glean, Boaz **c** his young men, saying, 6680
1Sa 2:29 which I have **c** *in my* habitation; 6680
13:13 of the LORD thy God, which he **c** thee: 6680
13:14 the LORD hath **c** him to be captain over 6680
13:14 thou hast not kept *that* which the LORD **c** 6680
17:20 and took, and went, as Jesse had **c** him; 6680
18:22 Saul **c** his servants, *saying,* Commune with 6680
20:29 he hath **c** me *to be there:* and now, 6680
21: 2 The king hath **c** me a business, and 6680
21: 2 I send thee, and what I have **c** thee: 6680
2Sa 4:12 David **c** *his* young men, and they slew 6680
5:25 David did so, as the LORD had **c** him; 6680
7: 7 whom I **c** to feed my people Israel, saying, 6680
7:11 *as* since the time that I **c** judges *to be* over 6680
9:11 all that my lord the king hath **c** his servant, 6680
13:28 Now Absalom had **c** his servants, saying, 6680
13:28 have not I **c** you? be courageous, and 6680
13:29 did unto Amnon as Absalom had **c**. 6680
18: 5 the king **c** Joab and Abishai and Ittai, 6680
21:14 they performed all that the king **c**. 6680
24:19 saying of Gad, went up as the LORD **c**. 6680
1Ki 2:46 So the king **c** Benaiah the son of Jehoiada; 6680
5:17 the king **c**, and they brought great stones, 6680
8:58 and his judgments, which he **c** our fathers. 6680
9: 4 to do according to all that I have **c** thee, *and* 6680
11:10 had **c** him concerning this thing, that *he* 6680
11:10 but he kept not *that* which the LORD **c**. 6680
11:11 and my statutes, which I have **c** thee, 6680
13:21 which the LORD thy God **c** thee, 6680
15: 5 turned not aside from any *thing* that he **c** 6680
17: 4 and I have **c** the ravens to feed thee there. 6680
17: 9 I have **c** a widow woman there to sustain 6680
22:31 the king of Syria **c** his thirty and 6680
2Ki 11: 5 he **c** them, saying, This *is* the thing that ye 6680
11: 9 to all *things* that Jehoiada the priest **c**: 6680
11:15 Jehoiada the priest **c** the captains of 6680
14: 6 where*in* the LORD **c**, saying, The fathers 6680
16:15 king Ahaz **c** Urijah the priest, saying, 6680
16:16 the priest, according to all that king Ahaz **c**. 6680
17:13 according to all the law which I **c** your 6680
17:27 the king of Assyria **c**, saying, Carry thither 6680
17:34 commandment which the LORD **c** 6680
18: 6 which the LORD **c** Moses. 6680
18:12 all that Moses the servant of the LORD **c**, 6680
21: 8 to do according to all that I have **c** them, 6680
21: 8 all the law that my servant Moses **c** them. 6680
22:12 the king **c** Hilkiah the priest, and Ahikam 6680
23: 4 the king **c** Hilkiah the high priest, and 6680
23:21 the king **c** all the people, saying, Keep 6680
1Ch 6:49 to all that Moses the servant of God had **c**. 6680
14:16 David therefore did as God **c** him: and 6680
15:15 as Moses **c** according to the word of 6680
16:15 the word *which* he **c** to a thousand 6680
16:40 in the law of the LORD, which he **c** Israel; 6680
17: 6 whom I **c** to feed my people, saying, 6680
17:10 since the time that I **c** judges *to be* over my 6680
21:17 *Is it* not I *that* **c** the people to be numbered? 559

1Ch 21:18 the angel of the LORD **c** Gad to say to 559
21:27 the LORD **c** the angel; and he put up his 559
22: 2 David **c** to gather together the strangers that 559
22:17 David also **c** all the princes of Israel to help 6680
23:31 according to the **order c** unto them, 4941
24:19 as the LORD God of Israel had **c** him. 6680
2Ch 7:17 do according to all that I have **c** thee, and 6680
8:14 for so had David the man of God **c**. 4687
14: 4 **c** Judah to seek the LORD God of their 559
18:30 Now the king of Syria had **c** the captains of 6680
23: 8 to all *things* that Jehoiada the priest had **c**, 6680
25: 4 where the LORD **c**, saying, The fathers 6680
29:21 he **c** the priests the sons of Aaron to offer 559
29:24 for the king **c** *that* the burnt offering and 559
29:27 Hezekiah **c** to offer the burnt offering upon 559
29:30 the princes **c** the Levites to *sing* praise unto 559
31: 4 Moreover he **c** the people that dwelt in 559
31:11 Hezekiah **c** to prepare chambers in the house 559
32:12 and **c** Judah and Jerusalem, saying, 559
33: 8 will take heed to do all that I have **c** them, 6680
33:16 **c** Judah to serve the LORD God of Israel. 559
34:20 the king **c** Hilkiah, and Ahikam the son of 6680
35:21 for God **c** me to make haste: forbear thee 559
Ezr 4: 3 as king Cyrus the king of Persia hath **c** us. 6680
4:19 I **c**, and search hath been made, and 2942+7761
5: 3 Who hath **c** you to build this house, 2942+7761
5: 9 Who **c** you to build this house, and 2942+7761
7:23 Whatsoever *is* **c** by the God of heaven, let it 2941
9:11 Which thou hast **c** by thy servants 6680
Ne 8: 1 which the LORD had **c** to Israel. 6680
8:14 the law which the LORD had **c** by Moses, 6680
13: 5 which was **c** *to be given* to the Levites, and 4687
13: 9 I **c**, and they cleansed the chambers: and 559
13:19 I **c** that the gates should be shut, and 559
13:22 I **c** the Levites that they should cleanse 559
Est 1:10 he **c** Mehuman, Biztha, Harbona, Bigtha, 559
1:17 The king Ahasuerus **c** Vashti the queen to be 559
3: 2 for the king had so **c** concerning him. 6680
3:12 Haman had **c** unto the king's lieutenants, 6680
4:13 Mordecai **c** to answer Esther, Think not with 559
4:17 did according to all that Esther had **c** him. 6680
6: 1 he **c** to bring the book of records of 559
8: 9 to all that Mordecai **c** unto the Jews, 6680
9:14 the king **c** it so to be done: and the decree 559
9:25 he **c** by letters *that* his wicked device, 559
Job 38:12 Hast thou **c** the morning since thy days; *and* 6680
42: 9 and did according as the LORD **c** them: 1696
Ps 7: 6 for me *to* the judgment *that* thou hast **c**. 6680
33: 9 and it was *done;* he **c**, and it stood fast. 6680
68:28 Thy God hath **c** thy strength: strengthen, 6680
78: 5 a law in Israel, which he **c** our fathers, 6680
78:23 Though he had **c** the clouds from above, 6680
105: 8 the word *which* he **c** to a thousand 6680
106:34 *concerning* whom the LORD **c** them: 559
111: 9 he hath **c** his covenant for ever: holy and 6680
119: 4 Thou hast **c** *us* to keep thy precepts 6680
119:138 Thy testimonies *that* thou hast **c** *are* 6680
133: 3 for there the LORD **c** the blessing, 6680
148: 5 for he **c**, and they were created. 6680
Isa 13: 3 I have **c** my sanctified ones, I have also 6680
34:16 for my mouth it hath **c**, and his spirit it hath 6680
45:12 out the heavens, and all their host have I **c**. 6680
48: 5 and my molten image, hath **c** them. 6680
Jer 7:22 nor **c** them in the day that I brought them 6680
7:23 this thing **c** I them, saying, Obey my voice, 6680
7:23 walk ye in all the ways that I have **c** you, 6680
7:31 Which I **c** *them* not, neither came it into my 6680
11: 4 Which I **c** your fathers in the day that I 6680
11: 8 of this covenant, which I **c** *them* to do; 6680
13: 5 hid it by Euphrates, as the LORD **c** me. 6680
13: 6 from thence, which I **c** thee to hide there. 6680
14:14 I sent them not, neither have I **c** them, 6680
17:22 ye the sabbath day, as I **c** your fathers. 6680
19: 5 which I **c** not, nor spake *it,* neither came *it* 6680
23:32 yet I sent them not, nor **c** them: 6680
26: 8 had **c** *him* to speak unto all the people, 6680
29:23 in my name, which I have not **c** them; 6680
32:35 which I **c** them not, neither came it into my 6680
35: 6 for Jonadab the son of Rechab our father **c** 6680
35:10 to all that Jonadab our father **c** us. 6680
35:14 that he **c** his sons not to drink wine, 6680
35:16 of their father, which he **c** them; 6680
35:18 done according unto all that he hath **c** you: 6680
36: 5 Jeremiah **c** Baruch, saying, I *am* shut up; 6680
36: 8 to all that Jeremiah the prophet **c** him, 6680
36:26 the king **c** Jerahmeel the son of 6680
37:21 Zedekiah the king **c** that they should 6680
38:10 the king **c** Ebed-melech the Ethiopian, 6680
38:27 to all these words that the king had **c**. 6680
50:21 and do according to all that I have **c** thee. 6680
51:59 The word which Jeremiah the prophet **c** 6680
La 1:17 the LORD hath **c** concerning Jacob, 6680
2:17 he hath fulfilled his word that he had **c** in 6680
Eze 9:11 I have done as thou hast **c** me. 6680
10: 6 *that* when he had **c** the man clothed with 6680
12: 7 I did so as I was **c**: I brought forth my stuff 6680
24:18 and I did in the morning as I was **c**. 6680
37: 7 So I prophesied as I was **c**: and as I 6680
37:10 So I prophesied as he **c** me, and the breath 6680
Da 2: 2 the king **c** to call the magicians, and 559
2:12 **c** to destroy all the wise *men* of Babylon. 560
2:46 **c** that *they* should offer an oblation and 560
3: 4 To you it is **c**, O people, nations, 560
3:13 in *his* rage and fury **c** to bring Shadrach, 560
3:19 **c** that *they* should heat the furnace one seven 560
3:20 he **c** the most mighty men that *were* in his 560
4:26 whereas they **c** to leave the stump of the tree 560
5: 2 **c** to bring the golden and silver vessels 560
5:29 **c** Belshazzar, and they clothed Daniel with 560
6:16 the king **c**, and they brought Daniel, and 560
6:23 **c** that *they* should take Daniel up out of 560
6:24 the king **c**, and they brought those men 560
Am 2:12 **c** the prophets, saying, Prophesy not. 6680
Zec 1: 6 which I **c** my servants the prophets, 6680
Mal 4: 4 which I **c** unto him in Horeb for all Israel, 6680

Mt 8: 4 offer the gift that Moses **c** for a testimony *4367*
10: 5 twelve Jesus sent forth, and **c** them, saying, *3853*
14: 9 with him at meat, he **c** *it* to be given *her.* *2753*
14:19 And he **c** the multitude to sit down on *2753*
15: 4 For God **c**, saying, Honour thy father and *1781*
15:35 And he **c** the multitude to sit down on *2753*
18:25 his lord **c** him to be sold, and his wife, and *2753*
21: 6 the disciples went, and did as Jesus **c** them, *4367*
27:58 Then Pilate **c** the body to be delivered. *2753*
28:20 observe all *things* whatsoever I have **c** you: *1781*
Mk 1:44 thy cleansing *those things* which Moses **c**, *4367*
5:43 **c** that *something* should be given her to eat. *3004*
6: 8 And **c** them that they should take nothing *3853*
6:27 and **c** his head to be brought: *2004*
6:39 And he **c** them to make all sit down by *2004*
8: 6 And he **c** the people to sit down on *3853*
8: 7 and **c** to set them also before *them.* *3004*
10:49 Jesus stood still, and **c** him to be called. *3004*
11: 6 they said unto them even as Jesus had **c**: *1781*
13:34 man his work, and **c** the porter to watch. *1781*
Lk 5:14 for thy cleansing, according as Moses **c**, *4367*
8:29 (For he had **c** the unclean spirit to come out *3853*
8:55 and he **c** to give her meat. *1299*
9:21 and **c** *them* to tell no *man* that *thing;* *3853*
14:22 it is done as thou hast **c**, and yet there is *2004*
17: 9 because he did the *things* that were **c** him? *1299*
17:10 have done all those *things* which are **c** you, *1299*
18:40 and **c** him to be brought unto him: *2753*
19:15 he **c** these servants to be called unto him, *3004*
Jn 8: 5 Now Moses in the law **c** us, that such *1781*
Ac 1: 4 **c** them that *they* should not depart from *3853*
4:15 But when they had **c** them to go aside out *2753*
4:18 **c** them not to speak at all nor teach in *3853*
5:34 and **c** to put the apostles forth a little space; *2753*
5:40 beaten *them,* they **c** that *they* should not *3853*
8:38 And he **c** the chariot to stand still: and *2753*
10:33 to hear all *things* that are **c** thee of God. *4367*
10:42 And he **c** us to preach unto the people, and *3853*
10:48 And he **c** them to be baptized in the name *4367*
12:19 and **c** that *they* should be put to death. *2753*
13:47 For so hath the Lord **c** us, *saying,* I have set *1781*
16:22 rent off their clothes, and **c** to beat *them.* *2753*
18: 2 that Claudius had **c** all Jews to depart from *1299*
21:33 and **c** *him* to be bound with two chains; *2753*
21:34 he **c** him to be carried into the castle. *2753*
22:24 The chief captain **c** him to be brought into *2753*
22:30 and **c** the chief priests and all their council *2753*
23: 2 And the high priest Ananias **c** them that *2004*
23:10 **c** the soldiers to go down, and to take him *2753*
23:31 as it was **c** them, took Paul, and *1299*
23:35 And he **c** him to be kept in Herod's *2753*
24:23 And he **c** a centurion to keep Paul, *1299*
25: 6 in the judgment seat, **c** Paul to be brought. *2753*
25:17 and **c** the man to be brought *forth.* *2753*
25:21 I **c** him to be kept till I might send him to *2753*
27:43 **c** that they which could swim should cast *2753*
1Co 14:34 but *they are* **c** to be under obedience, as also NIG
2Co 4: 6 who **c** the light to shine out of darkness, *3004*
1Th 4:11 to work with your own hands, as we **c** you; *3853*
2Th 3:10 this we **c** you, that if any would not work, *3853*
Heb 12:20 they could not endure that which was **c**, *1291*
Rev 9: 4 And it was **c** them that they should not hurt *3004*

COMMANDEDST (4) [COMMAND]

Ne 1: 7 which thou **c** thy servant Moses. 6680
1: 8 the word that thou **c** thy servant Moses, 6680
9:14 **c** them precepts, statutes, and laws, by 6680
Jer 32:23 they have done nothing of all that thou **c** 6680

COMMANDER (1) [COMMAND]

Isa 55: 4 to the people, a leader and **c** to the people. 6680

COMMANDEST (3) [COMMAND]

Jos 1:16 All that thou **c** us we will do, and 6680
1:18 unto thy words in all that thou **c** him, 6680
Ac 23: 3 and **c** me to be smitten contrary to the law? *2753*

COMMANDETH (13) [COMMAND]

Ex 16:32 This *is* the thing which the LORD **c**, 6680
Nu 32:25 Thy servants will do as my lord **c**. 6680
Job 9: 7 Which **c** the sun, and it riseth not; and 559
36:10 and **c** that they return from iniquity. 559
36:32 **c** it *not to shine* by *the cloud* that cometh 6680
37:12 that they may do whatsoever he **c** them 6680
Ps 107:25 For he **c**, and raiseth the stormy wind, 559
La 3:37 it cometh to pass, *when* the Lord **c** *it* not? 6680
Am 6:11 the LORD **c**, and he will smite the great 6680
Mk 1:27 for with authority **c** he even the unclean *2004*
Lk 4:36 and power he **c** the unclean spirits, *2004*
8:25 for he **c** even the winds and water, and *2004*
Ac 17:30 but now **c** all men every where to repent: *3853*

COMMANDING (4) [COMMAND]

Ge 49:33 when Jacob had made an end of **c** his sons, 6680
Mt 11: 1 when Jesus had made an end of **c** his *1299*
Ac 24: 8 **C** his accusers to come unto thee: *2753*
1Ti 4: 3 to marry, *and* **c** to abstain from meats, NIG

COMMANDMENT (177) [COMMAND]

Ge 45:21 according to the **c** of Pharaoh, and 6310
Ex 17: 1 according to the **c** of the LORD, and 6310
25:22 of all *things* which I will **give** thee **in c** unto 6680
34:32 he **gave** them **in c** all that the LORD had 6680
36: 6 Moses **gave c**, and they caused it to be 6680
38:21 was counted, according to the **c** of Moses, 6310
Nu 3:39 Aaron numbered at the **c** of the LORD, 6310
4:37 Aaron did number according to the **c** of 6310
4:41 Aaron did number according to the **c** of 6310
4:49 According to the **c** of the LORD they 6310
9:18 At the **c** of the LORD the children of 6310
9:18 and at the **c** of the LORD they pitched: 6310
9:20 according to the **c** of the LORD they 6310
9:20 according to the **c** of the LORD they 6310
9:23 At the **c** of the LORD they rested in 6310

Nu 9:23 and at the **c** of the LORD they journeyed: 6310
9:23 at the **c** of the LORD by the hand of 6310
10:13 the **c** of the LORD by the hand of Moses. 6310
13: 3 Moses by the **c** of the LORD sent them 6310
14:41 Wherefore now do ye transgress the **c** of 6310
15:31 hath broken his **c**, that soul shall utterly be 4687
23:20 Behold, I have received **c** to bless: and NIH
24:13 I cannot go beyond the **c** of the LORD, 6310
27:14 For ye rebelled against my **c** in the desert of 6310
33: 2 to their journeys by the **c** of the LORD: 6310
33:38 up into mount Hor at the **c** of the LORD, 6310
Dt 1: 3 the LORD had **given** him **in c** unto them; 6680
1:26 rebelled against the **c** of the LORD your 6310
1:43 rebelled against the **c** of the LORD, and 6310
9:23 you rebelled against the **c** of the LORD 6310
17:20 that *he* turn not aside from the **c**, *to* 4687
30:11 For this **c** which I command thee *this* day, 4687
Jos 1:18 *he be* that doth rebel against thy **c**, 6310
8: 8 according to the **c** of the LORD shall ye 1697
15:13 according to the **c** of the LORD to Joshua, 6310
17: 4 Therefore according to the **c** of the LORD 6310
21: 3 at the **c** of the LORD, these cities and 6310
22: 3 have kept the charge of the **c** of the LORD 4687
22: 5 take diligent heed to do the **c** and the law, 4687
1Sa 12:14 not rebel against the **c** of the LORD, then 6310
12:15 rebel against the **c** of the LORD, then 6310
13:13 thou hast not kept the **c** of the LORD thy 4687
15:13 I have performed the **c** of the LORD. 1697
15:24 for I have transgressed the **c** of the LORD, 6310
2Sa 12: 9 Wherefore hast thou despised the **c** of 1697
1Ki 2:43 and the **c** that I have charged thee with? 4687
13:21 hast not kept the **c** which the LORD thy 4687
2Ki 17:34 **c** which the LORD commanded 4687
17:37 and the ordinances, and the law, and the **c**, 4687
18:36 for the king's **c** was, saying, Answer him 4687
23:35 the money according to the **c** of Pharaoh: 6310
24: 3 Surely at the **c** of the LORD came *this* 6310
1Ch 12:32 and all their brethren *were* at their **c**. 6310
14:12 David **gave a c**, and they were burnt with 559
28:21 and all the people *will be* wholly at thy **c**. 1697
2Ch 8:13 offering according to the **c** of Moses, on 4687
8:15 they departed not *from* the **c** of the king 4687
14: 4 of their fathers, and to do the law and the **c**. 4687
19:10 and blood, between law and **c**, 4687
24: 6 *according to the* **c** of Moses the servant of NIH
24: 8 at the king's **c** they made a chest, and set it 559
24:21 stoned him *with* stones at the **c** of the king 4687
29:15 and came, according to the **c** of the king, 4687
29:25 according to the **c** of David, and of Gad 4687
29:25 *so was* the **c** of the LORD by his prophets. 4687
30: 6 Judah, and according to the **c** of the king, 4687
30:12 give them one heart to do the **c** of the king 4687
31: 5 as soon as the **c** came abroad, the children 1697
31:13 at the **c** of Hezekiah the king, and 4662
35:10 in their courses, according to the king's **c**. 4687
35:15 according to the **c** of David, and Asaph, 4687
35:16 according to the **c** of king Josiah. 4687
Ezr 4:21 Give ye now **c** to cause these men to cease, 2942
4:21 until *another* **c** shall be given from me. 2941
6:14 finished *it,* according to the **c** of the God of 2941
6:14 according to the **c** of Cyrus, and Darius, 2942
8:17 I **sent** them **with c** unto Iddo the chief at 6680
10: 3 of those that tremble at the **c** of our God; 4687
Ne 11:23 For *it was* the king's **c** concerning them, 4687
12:24 according to the **c** of David the man of 4687
12:45 according to the **c** of David, *and* 4687
Est 1:12 come at the king's **c** by *his* chamberlains: 1697
1:15 she hath not performed the **c** of the king 3982
1:19 let there go a royal **c** from him, and let it be 1697
2: 8 when the king's **c** and his decree was heard, 1697
2:20 for Esther did the **c** of Mordecai, like as 3982
3: 3 Why transgressest thou the king's **c**? 4687
3:14 The copy of the writing for a **c** to be given 1881
3:15 being hastened by the king's **c**, and 1697
4: 3 whithersoever the king's **c** and his decree 1697
4: 5 **gave** him **a c** to Mordecai, to know what it 6680
4:10 and **gave** him **c** unto Mordecai: 6680
8:13 The copy of the writing for a **c** to be given 1881
8:14 and pressed on by the king's **c**, 1697
8:17 whithersoever the king's **c** and his decree 1697
9: 1 when the king's **c** and his decree drew near 1697
Job 23:12 Neither have I gone back from the **c** of his 4687
Ps 19: 8 the **c** of the LORD *is* pure, 4687
71: 3 thou hast **given c** to save me; for thou *art* 6680
119:96 all perfection: *but* thy **c** *is* exceeding broad. 4687
147:15 He sendeth forth his **c** *upon* earth: his word 565
Pr 6:20 keep thy father's **c**, and forsake not the law 4687
6:23 For the **c** *is* a lamp; and the law *is* light; and 4687
8:29 that the waters should not pass his **c**; 6310
13:13 he that feareth the **c** shall be rewarded. 4687
19:16 He that keepeth the **c** keepeth his own soul; 4687
Ecc 8: 2 I *counsel thee* to keep the king's **c**, and 6310
8: 5 Whoso keepeth the **c** shall feel no evil 4687
Isa 23:11 the LORD hath **given a c** against 6680
36:21 for the king's **c** was, saying, Answer him 4687
Jer 35:14 they drink none, but obey their father's **c**: 4687
35:16 have performed the **c** of their father, 4687
35:18 Because ye have obeyed the **c** of Jonadab 4687
La 1:18 for I have rebelled against his **c**: 6310
Da 3:22 Therefore because the king's **c** *was* urgent, 4406
9:23 At the beginning of thy supplications the **c** 1697
9:25 *that* from the going forth of the **c** to restore 1697
Hos 5:11 because he willingly walked after the **c**. 6673
Na 1:14 the LORD hath **given a c** concerning thee, 6680
Mal 2: 1 And now, O ye priests, this **c** *is* for you. 4687
2: 4 ye shall know that I have sent this **c** unto 4687
Mt 8:18 he **gave c** to depart unto the other side. *2753*
15: 3 Why do you also transgress the **c** of God by *1785*
15: 6 *he shall be free.* Thus have ye made the **c** of *1785*
22:36 Master, which *is* the great **c** in the law? *1785*
22:38 This is the first and great **c**. *1785*
Mk 7: 8 For laying aside the **c** of God, ye hold *1785*
7: 9 unto them, Full well ye reject the **c** of God, *1785*
12:28 asked him, Which is the first **c** of all? *1785*
12:30 and with all thy strength: this *is* the first **c**. *1785*

Mk 12:31 There is none other **c** greater than these. *1785*
Lk 15:29 neither transgressed I at any time thy **c**: *1785*
23:56 rested the sabbath day according to the **c**. *1785*
Jn 10:18 This **c** have I received of my Father. *1785*
11:57 and the Pharisees had given a **c**, *1785*
12:49 he gave me a **c**, what I should say, and *1785*
12:50 And I know that his **c** is life everlasting: *1785*
13:34 A new **c** I give unto you, That ye love one *1785*
14:31 and as the Father **gave** me **c**, *even* so I do. *1781*
15:12 This is my **c**, That ye love one another, as I *1785*
Ac 15:24 keep the law: to whom we **gave** no *such* **c**: *1291*
17:15 and receiving a **c** unto Silas and Timotheus *1785*
23:30 **gave** **c** to *his* accusers also to say before *3853*
25:23 at Festus' **c** Paul was brought *forth*. *2753*
Ro 7: 8 But sin, taking occasion by the **c**, *1785*
7: 9 but when the **c** came, sin revived, and *1785*
7:10 And the **c**, which was *ordained* to life, *1785*
7:11 For sin, taking occasion by the **c**, *1785*
7:12 *is* holy, and the **c** holy, and just, and good. *1785*
7:13 that sin by the **c** might become exceeding *1785*
13: 9 and if *there be* any other **c**, it is briefly *1785*
16:26 according to the **c** of the everlasting God, *2003*
1Co 7: 6 I speak this by permission, *and* not of **c**. *2003*
7:25 Now concerning virgins I have no **c** of *2003*
2Co 8: 8 I speak not by **c**, but by occasion of *2003*
Eph 6: 2 (which is the first **c** with promise;) *1785*
1Ti 1: 1 an apostle of Jesus Christ by the **c** of God *2003*
1: 5 Now the end of the **c** is charity out of a *3852*
6:14 That thou keep *this* **c** without spot, *1785*
Tit 1: 3 me according to the **c** of God our Saviour; *2003*
Heb 7: 5 **c** to take tithes of the people according to *1785*
7:16 not after the law of a carnal **c**, but after *1785*
7:18 For there is verily a disannulling of the **c** *1785*
11:22 of Israel; and **gave** **c** concerning his bones. *1781*
11:23 and they were not afraid of the king's **c**. *1297*
2Pe 2:21 to turn from the holy **c** delivered unto them. *1785*
3: 2 of the **c** of us the apostles of the Lord and *1785*
1Jn 2: 7 I write no new **c** unto you, but an old *1785*
2: 7 an old **c** which ye had from the beginning. *1785*
2: 7 The old **c** is the word which ye have heard *1785*
2: 8 Again, a new **c** I write unto you, *1785*
3:23 And this is his **c**, That we should believe on *1785*
3:23 and love one another, as he gave us **c**. *1785*
4:21 And this **c** have we from him, That he who *1785*
2Jn 1: 4 as we have received a **c** from the Father. *1785*
1: 5 not as though I wrote a new **c** unto thee, but *1785*
1: 6 This is the **c**, That, as ye have heard from *1785*

COMMANDMENTS (171) [COMMAND]

Ge 26: 5 my charge, my **c**, my statutes, and my laws. 4687
Ex 15:26 wilt give ear to his **c**, and keep all his 4687
16:28 How long refuse ye to keep my **c** and 4687
20: 6 of them that love me, and keep my **c**. 4687
24:12 and a law, and **c** which I have written; 4687
34:28 tables the words of the covenant, the ten **c**. 1697
Lev 4: 2 **c** of the LORD *(concerning things* which 4687
4:13 **c** of the LORD *concerning things* which 4687
4:22 **c** of the LORD his God *concerning things* 4687
4:27 **c** of the LORD *concerning things* which 4687
5:17 to be done by the **c** of the LORD; 4687
22:31 Therefore shall ye keep my **c**, and do them: 4687
26: 3 in my statutes, and keep my **c**, and do them; 4687
26:14 unto me, and will not do all these **c**; 4687
26:15 so that *ye* will not do all my **c**, *but* that ye 4687
27:34 These *are* the **c**, which the LORD 4687
Nu 15:22 ye have erred, and not observed all these **c**, 4687
15:39 remember all the **c** of the LORD, and 4687
15:40 do all my **c**, and be holy unto your God. 4687
36:13 These *are* the **c** and the judgments, 4687
Dt 4: 2 that *ye* may keep the **c** of the LORD your 4687
4:13 he commanded you to perform, *even* ten **c**; 1697
4:40 shalt keep therefore his statutes, and his **c**, 4687
5:10 of them that love me and keep my **c**. 4687
5:29 would fear me, and keep all my **c** always, 4687
5:31 I will speak unto thee all the **c**, and 4687
6: 1 Now these *are* the **c**, the statutes, and 4687
6: 2 to keep all his statutes and his **c**, which I 4687
6:17 You shall diligently keep the **c** of 4687
6:25 if we observe to do all these **c** before 4687
7: 9 and keep his **c** to a thousand generations; 4687
7:11 Thou shalt therefore keep the **c**, and 4687
8: 1 All the **c** which I command thee *this* day 4687
8: 2 whether thou wouldest keep his **c**, or no. 4687
8: 6 Therefore thou shalt keep the **c** of 4687
8:11 in not keeping his **c**, and his judgments, and 4687
10: 4 according to the first writing, the ten **c**, 1697
10:13 To keep the **c** of the LORD, and his 4687
11: 1 and his judgments, and his **c** alway. 4687
11: 8 Therefore shall ye keep all the **c** which I 4687
11:13 if you shall hearken diligently unto my **c** 4687
11:22 For if ye shall diligently keep all these **c** 4687
11:27 if ye obey the **c** of the LORD your God, 4687
11:28 if ye will not obey the **c** of the LORD 4687
13: 4 keep his **c**, and obey his voice, and 4687
13:18 to keep all his **c** which I command thee *this* 4687
15: 5 to observe to do all these **c** which I 4687
19: 9 If thou shalt keep all these **c** to do them, 4687
26:13 according to all thy **c** which thou hast 4687
26:13 I have not transgressed thy **c**, neither have 4687
26:17 his **c**, and his judgments, and to hearken 4687
26:18 and that *thou* shouldest keep all his **c**; 4687
27: 1 Keep all the **c** which I command you *this* 4687
27:10 do his **c** and his statutes, which I command 4687
28: 1 to do all his **c** which I command thee *this* 4687
28: 9 if thou shalt keep the **c** of the LORD thy 4687
28:13 if that thou hearken unto the **c** of 4687
28:15 to observe to do all his **c** and his statutes 4687
28:45 to keep his **c** and his statutes which he 4687
30: 8 do all his **c** which I command thee *this* day. 4687
30:10 to keep his **c** and his statutes which are 4687
30:16 to keep his **c** and his statutes and 4687
31: 5 all the **c** which I have commanded you. 4687
Jos 22: 5 to keep his **c**, and to cleave unto him, and 4687
Jdg 2:17 walked in, obeying the **c** of the LORD; 4687
3: 4 would hearken unto the **c** of the LORD, 4687

1Sa 15:11 and hath not performed my **c**. 1697
1Ki 2: 3 *and* his **c**, and his judgments, and 4687
3:14 to keep my statutes and my **c**, as thy father 4687
6:12 and keep all my **c** to walk in them; 4687
8:58 to keep his **c**, and his statutes, and 4687
8:61 his statutes, and to keep his **c**, as at this day. 4687
9: 6 will not keep my **c** *and* my statutes which I 4687
11:34 he kept my **c** and my statutes: 4687
11:38 to keep my statutes and my **c**, as David my 4687
14: 8 who kept my **c**, and who followed me with 4687
18:18 in that ye have forsaken the **c** of 4687
2Ki 17:13 evil ways, and keep my **c** *and* my statutes, 4687
17:16 they left all the **c** of the LORD their God, 4687
17:19 Also Judah kept not the **c** of the LORD 4687
18: 6 not from following him, but kept his **c**, 4687
23: 3 to keep his **c** and his testimonies and his 4687
1Ch 28: 7 if he be constant to do my **c** and 4687
28: 8 seek for all the **c** of the LORD your God: 4687
29:19 to keep thy **c**, thy testimonies, and 4687
2Ch 7:19 and forsake my statutes and my **c**, 4687
17: 4 walked in his **c**, and not after the doings of 4687
24:20 Why transgress ye the **c** of the LORD, 4687
31:21 in the law, and in the **c**, to seek his God, 4687
34:31 to keep his **c**, and his testimonies, and 4687
Ezr 7:11 *even* a scribe of the words of the **c** of 4687
9:10 say after this? for we have forsaken thy **c**, 4687
9:14 Should we again break thy **c**, and join in 4687
Ne 1: 5 for them that love him and observe his **c**: 4687
1: 7 have not kept the **c**, nor the statutes, nor 4687
1: 9 turn unto me, and keep my **c**, and do them; 4687
9:13 and true laws, good statutes and **c**: 4687
9:16 their necks, and hearkened not to thy **c**, 4687
9:29 hearkened not unto thy **c**, but 4687
9:34 nor hearkened unto thy **c** and thy 4687
10:29 and do all the **c** of the LORD our Lord, 4687
Ps 78: 7 not forget the works of God, but keep his **c**: 4687
89:31 they break my statutes, and keep not my **c**; 4687
103:18 to those that remember his **c** to do them. 6490
103:20 that excel in strength, that do his **c**, 1697
111: 7 *are* verity and judgment; all his **c** *are* sure. 6490
111:10 that do *his* **c**: his praise endureth for ever. NIH
112: 1 the LORD, *that* delighteth greatly in his **c**. 4687
119: 6 when I have respect unto all thy **c**. 4687
119:10 O let me not wander from thy **c**. 4687
119:19 in the earth: hide not thy **c** from me. 4687
119:21 *that are* cursed, which do err from thy **c**. 4687
119:32 I will run the way of thy **c**, when thou shalt 4687
119:35 Make me to go in the path of thy **c**; 4687
119:47 I will delight myself in thy **c**, which I have 4687
119:48 My hands also will I lift up unto thy **c**, 4687
119:60 I made haste, and delayed not to keep thy **c**. 4687
119:66 and knowledge: for I have believed thy **c**. 4687
119:73 me understanding, that I may learn thy **c**. 4687
119:86 All thy **c** *are* faithful: they persecute me 4687
119:98 Thou *through* thy **c** hast made me wiser 4687
119:115 for I will keep the **c** of my God. 4687
119:127 Therefore I love thy **c** above gold; yea, 4687
119:131 and panted: for I longed for thy **c**. 4687
119:143 taken hold on me: *yet* thy **c** *are* my delights. 4687
119:151 *art* near, O LORD; and all thy **c** *are* truth. 4687
119:166 hoped for thy salvation, and done thy **c**. 4687
119:172 of thy word: for all thy **c** *are* righteousness. 4687
119:176 seek thy servant; for I do not forget thy **c**. 4687
Pr 2: 1 receive my words, and hide my **c** with thee; 4687
3: 1 not my law; but let thine heart keep my **c**: 4687
4: 4 heart retain my words: keep my **c**, and live. 4687
7: 1 keep my words, and lay up my **c** with thee. 4687
7: 2 Keep my **c**, and live; and my law as 4687
10: 8 The wise in heart will receive **c**: but 4687
Ecc 12:13 Fear God, and keep his **c**: for this *is* 4687
Isa 48:18 O that thou hadst hearkened to my **c**! then 4687
Da 9: 4 that love him, and to them that keep his **c**; 4687
Am 2: 4 have not kept his **c**, and their lies caused 2706
Mt 5:19 therefore shall break one of these least **c**, *1785*
15: 9 teaching for doctrines the **c** of men. *1778*
19:17 but if thou wilt enter into life, keep the **c**. *1785*
22:40 On these two **c** hang all the law and *1785*
Mk 7: 7 teaching for doctrines the **c** of men. *1778*
10:19 Thou knowest the **c**, Do not commit *1785*
12:29 The first of all the **c** *is*, Hear, O Israel; *1785*
Lk 1: 6 walking in all the **c** and ordinances of *1785*
18:20 Thou knowest the **c**, Do not commit *1785*
Jn 14:15 If ye love me, keep my **c**. *1785*
14:21 He that hath my **c**, and keepeth them, he it *1785*
15:10 If ye keep my **c**, ye shall abide in my love; *1785*
15:10 even as I have kept my Father's **c**, and *1785*
Ac 1: 2 **given** **c** unto the Apostles whom he had *1781*
1Co 7:19 is nothing, but the keeping of the **c** of God. *1785*
14:37 that I write unto you are the **c** of the Lord. *1785*
Eph 2:15 *even* the law of **c** *contained* in ordinances; *1785*
Col 2:22 after the **c** and doctrines of men? *1778*
4:10 (touching whom ye received **c**: *1785*
1Th 4: 2 For ye know what **c** we gave you by *3852*
Tit 1:14 and **c** of men, that turn from the truth. *1785*
1Jn 2: 3 know that we know him, if we keep his **c**. *1785*
2: 4 and keepeth not his **c**, is a liar, and the truth *1785*
3:22 because we keep his **c**, and do those *things* *1785*
3:24 And he that keepeth his **c** dwelleth in him, *1785*
5: 2 of God, when we love God, and keep his **c**. *1785*
5: 3 this is the love of God, that we keep his **c**: *1785*
5: 3 and his **c** are not grievous. *1785*
2Jn 1: 6 And this is love, that we walk after his **c**. *1785*
Rev 12:17 which keep the **c** of God, and have *1785*
14:12 here *are* they that keep the **c** of God, and *1785*
22:14 Blessed *are* they that do his **c**, that they *1785*

COMMEND (7) [COMMENDATION, COMMENDED, COMMENDETH, COMMENDING]

Lk 23:46 he said, Father, into thy hands I **c** my spirit: *3908*
Ac 20:32 I **c** you to God, and to the word of his *3908*
Ro 3: 5 But if our unrighteousness **c** *4921*
16: 1 I **c** unto you Phebe our sister, which is a *4921*
2Co 3: 1 Do we begin again to **c** ourselves? or need *4921*
5:12 For we **c** not ourselves again unto you, but *4921*
10:12 compare ourselves with some that **c** *4921*

COMMENDABLE See THANKWORTHY

COMMENDATION (2) [COMMEND]

2Co 3: 1 as some *others*, epistles of **c** to you, or *4956*
3: 1 to you, or *letters* of **c** from you? *4956*

COMMENDED (6) [COMMEND]

Ge 12:15 Pharaoh saw her, and **c** her before Pharaoh: 1984
Pr 12: 8 A man shall be **c** according to his wisdom: 1984
Ecc 8:15 I **c** mirth, because a man hath no better 7623
Lk 16: 8 And the lord **c** the unjust steward, because *1867*
Ac 14:23 they **c** them to the Lord, on whom they *3908*
2Co 12:11 for I ought to have been **c** of you: for *in* *4921*

COMMENDETH (4) [COMMEND]

Ro 5: 8 But God **c** his love toward us, in that, *4921*
1Co 8: 8 But meat **c** us not to God: for neither, if we *3936*
2Co 10:18 For not he that **c** himself is approved, but *4921*
10:18 himself is approved, but whom the Lord **c**. *4921*

COMMENDING (1) [COMMEND]

2Co 4: 2 by manifestation of the truth **c** ourselves to *4921*

COMMISSION (1) [COMMISSIONS]

Ac 26:12 with authority and **c** from the chief priests, *2011*

COMMISSIONS (1) [COMMISSION]

Ezr 8:36 they delivered the king's **c** unto the king's 1881

COMMIT (75) [COMMITTED, COMMITTEST, COMMITTETH, COMMITTING]

Ex 20:14 Thou shalt not **c adultery**. 5003
Lev 5:15 If a soul **c a trespass**, and 4603+4604
5:17 **c** any *of these things* which are forbidden to 6213
6: 2 **c a trespass** against the LORD, and 4603+4604
18:26 and shall not **c** any of these abominations; 6213
18:29 For whosoever shall **c** any of these 6213
18:29 even the souls that **c** *them* shall be cut off 6213
18:30 that *ye* **c** not *any one* of *these* abominable 6213
20: 5 to **c** whoredom with Molech, from among NIH
Nu 5: 6 or woman shall **c** any sin that men commit, 6213
5: 6 or woman shall commit any sin that men **c**, NIH
5:12 and **c a trespass** against him, 4603+4604
25: 1 the people begun to **c whoredom** with 2181
31:16 to **c** trespass against the LORD in 4560
Dt 5:18 Neither shalt thou **c adultery**. 5003
19:20 shall henceforth **c** no more any such evil 6213
Jos 22:20 **c a trespass** in the accursed thing, 4603+4604
2Sa 7:14 If he **c iniquity**, I will chasten him with 5753
2Ch 21:11 **caused** the inhabitants of Jerusalem
to c fornication, 2181
Job 5: 8 and unto God would I **c** my cause: 7760
34:10 the Almighty, *that he should* **c** iniquity. NIH
Ps 31: 5 Into thine hand I **c** my spirit: thou hast 6485
37: 5 **C** thy way unto the LORD; trust also in 1556
Pr 16: 3 **C** thy works unto the LORD, and 1556
16:12 *It is* an abomination to kings to **c** 6213
Isa 22:21 and I will **c** thy government into his hand: 5414
23:17 shall **c fornication** with all the kingdoms of 2181
Jer 7: 9 **c adultery**, and swear falsely, and 5003
9: 5 *and* weary themselves to **c iniquity**. 5753
23:14 *they* **c adultery**, and walk in lies: 5003
37:21 **c** Jeremiah into the court of the prison, 6485
44: 7 Wherefore **c** ye *this* great evil against your 6213
Eze 3:20 **c** iniquity, and I lay a stumblingblock 6213
8:17 **c** the abominations which they commit 6213
8:17 the abominations which they **c** here? 6213
16:17 of men, and didst **c whoredom** with them, 2181
16:34 none followeth thee to **c whoredoms**: 2181
16:43 thou shalt not **c** *this* lewdness above all 6213
20:30 **c** ye **whoredom** after their abominations? 2181
22: 9 in the midst of thee they **c** lewdness. 6213
23:43 Will they now **c whoredoms** with 2181+8457
33:13 to his own righteousness, and **c** iniquity, 6213
Hos 4:10 they shall **c whoredom**, and shall not 2181
4:13 your daughters shall **c whoredom**, 2181
4:13 and your spouses shall **c adultery**. 5003
4:14 your daughters when they **c whoredom**, 2181
4:14 nor your spouses when they **c adultery**: 5003
6: 9 *in* the way by consent: for they **c** lewdness. 6213
7: 1 for they **c** falsehood; and the thief cometh 6466
Mt 5:27 of old time, Thou shalt not **c adultery**: *3431*
5:32 of fornication, causeth her to **c adultery**: *3429*
19: 9 her *which is* put away doth **c adultery**. *3429*
19:18 Thou shalt not **c adultery**, Thou shalt not *3431*
Mk 10:19 Do not **c adultery**, Do not kill, Do not *3431*
Lk 12:48 and did **c** *things* worthy of stripes, *4160*
16:11 who will **c** to your **trust** the true *riches?* *4100*
18:20 Do not **c adultery**, Do not kill, Do not *3431*
Jn 2:24 But Jesus did not **c** himself unto them, *4100*
Ro 1:32 that they which **c** such *things* are worthy of *4238*
2: 2 to truth against them which **c** such *things*. *4238*
2:22 that sayest a *man* should not **c adultery**, *3431*
2:22 not commit adultery, dost thou **c adultery**? *3431*
2:22 that abhorrest idols, dost thou **c sacrilege**? *2416*
13: 9 For *this*, Thou shalt not **c adultery**, *3431*
1Co 10: 8 Neither let us **c fornication**, as some of *4203*
1Ti 1:18 This charge I **c** unto thee, son Timothy, *3908*
2Ti 2: 2 the same **c** thou to faithful men, who shall *3908*
Jas 2: 9 ye **c** sin, and are convinced of the law as *2038*
2:11 Do not **c adultery**, said also, Do not kill. *3431*
2:11 Now if thou **c** no **adultery**, yet *if* thou kill, *3431*
1Pe 4:19 **c the keeping** of their souls *to him* in well *3908*
1Jn 3: 9 Whosoever is born of God doth not **c** sin; *4160*
Rev 2:14 sacrificed unto idols, and to **c fornication**. *4203*
2:20 and to seduce my servants to **c fornication**, *4203*
2:22 them that **c adultery** with her into great *3431*

COMMITTED (92) [COMMIT]

Ge 39: 8 and he hath **c** all that he hath to my hand; 5414
39:22 the keeper of the prison **c** to Joseph's hand 5414

Lev 4:35 an atonement for his sin that he hath **c**, 2398
5: 7 which he hath **c**, two turtledoves, or 2398
18:30 which were **c** before you, and that ye defile 6213
20:13 both of them have **c** an abomination: 6213
20:23 for they **c** all these *things,* and therefore 6213
Nu 15:24 if *ought* be **c** by ignorance without 6213
Dt 17: 5 which have **c** that wicked thing, 6213
21:22 if a man have **c a sin** worthy of death, and 2399
Jos 7: 1 the children of Israel **c a trespass** in 4603+4604
22:16 What trespass *is* this that ye have **c** against 4603
22:31 ye have not **c** this **trespass** against 4603+4604
Jdg 20: 6 for they have **c** lewdness and folly in Israel. 6213
1Ki 8:47 done perversely, we have **c wickedness**; 7561
14:22 to jealousy with their sins which they had **c**, 2398
14:27 **c** *them* unto the hands of the chief of 6485
1Ch 10:13 **transgression** which he **c** against 4603+4604
2Ch 12:10 **c** *them* to the hands of the chief of 6485
34:16 saying, All that was **c** to thy servants, 5414
Ps 106: 6 we have **c iniquity**, we have done 5753
Jer 2:13 For my people have **c** two evils; they have 6213
3: 8 Israel **c adultery** I had put her away, 5003
3: 9 and **c adultery** with stones and with stocks. 5003
5: 7 they then **c adultery**, and 5003
5:30 and horrible thing is **c** in the land; 1961
6:15 Were they ashamed when they had **c** 6213
8:12 Were they ashamed when they had **c** 6213
16:10 what *is* our **sin** that we have **c** against 2398+2403
29:23 Because they have **c** villany in Israel, and 6213
29:23 have **c adultery** with their neighbours' 5003
39:14 **c** him unto Gedaliah the son of Ahikam 5414
40: 7 had **c** unto him men, and women, and 6485
41:10 guard had **c** to Gedaliah the son of Ahikam: 6485
44: 3 which they have **c** to provoke me to anger, 6213
44: 9 which they have **c** in the land of Judah, and 6213
44:22 of the abominations which ye have **c**; 6213
Eze 6: 9 which they have **c** in all their abominations. 6213
15: 8 because they have **c a trespass**, saith 4603+4604
16:26 Thou hast also **c fornication** with 2181
16:50 and **c** abomination before me: 6213
16:51 Neither hath Samaria **c** half of thy sins; but 2398
16:52 **sins** that thou hast **c** more abominable than 2403
18:12 up his eyes to the idols, hath **c** abomination, 6213
18:21 will turn from all his sins that he hath **c**, 6213
18:22 All his transgressions that he hath **c**, 6213
18:27 away from his wickedness that he hath **c**, 6213
18:28 from all his transgressions that he hath **c**, 6213
20:27 they have **c a trespass** against me. 4603+4604
20:43 own sight for all your evils that ye have **c**. 6213
22:11 one hath **c** abomination with his 6213
23: 3 they **c whoredoms** in Egypt; 2181
23: 3 in Egypt; they **c whoredoms** in their youth: 2181
23: 7 Thus she **c** her whoredoms with them, 5414
23:37 That they have **c adultery**, and blood *is* in 5003
23:37 with their idols have they **c adultery**, and 5003
33:13 for his iniquity that he hath **c**, he shall die 6213
33:16 None of his sins that he hath **c** shall be 2398
33:29 of all their abominations which they have **c**. 6213
43: 8 by their abominations that they have **c**: 6213
44:13 and their abominations which they have **c**. 6213
Da 9: 5 have **c iniquity**, and have done wickedly, 5753
Hos 1: 2 for the land hath **c great whoredom**, 2181+2181
4:18 they have **c whoredom continually**: 2181+2181
Mal 2:11 an abomination is **c** in Israel and 6213
Mt 5:28 **c adultery** with her already in his heart. *3431*
Mk 15: 7 *him,* who had **c** murder in the insurrection. *4160*
Lk 12:48 and to whom *men* have **c** much, of him *3908*
Jn 5:22 but hath **c** all judgment unto the Son: *1325*
Ac 8: 3 haling men and women **c** *them* to prison. *3860*
25:11 or have **c** any *thing* worthy of death, *4238*
25:25 But when I found that he had **c** nothing *4238*
27:40 they **c** *themselves* unto the sea, and *1439*
28:17 though I have **c** nothing against the people, *4160*
Ro 3: 2 that unto them were **c** the oracles of God. *4100*
1Co 9:17 a dispensation *of the gospel* is **c unto** me. *4100*
10: 8 as some of them **c**, and fell in one day three *4203*
2Co 5:19 hath **c** unto us the word of reconciliation. *5087*
11: 7 Have I **c** an offence in abasing myself that *4160*
12:21 and lasciviousness which they have **c**. *4238*
Gal 2: 7 of the uncircumcision was **c** unto me, *4100*
1Ti 1:11 the blessed God, which was **c to** my **trust**. *4100*
6:20 keep that which is **c to** *thy* **trust**, *3872*
2Ti 1:12 which I have **c unto** *him* against that day. *3866*
1:14 *That* good thing which was **c unto** *thee* *3872*
Tit 1: 3 which is **c** unto me according to *4100*
Jas 5:15 and if he have **c** sins, they shall be forgiven *4160*
1Pe 2:23 **c** *himself* to him that judgeth righteously: *3860*
Jude 1:15 ungodly deeds which they have **ungodly c**, *764*
Rev 17: 2 the kings of the earth have **c fornication**, *4203*
18: 3 the kings of the earth have **c fornication** *4203*
18: 9 who have **c fornication** and *4203*

COMMITTEST (1) [COMMIT]

Hos 5: 3 thou **c whoredom**, *and* Israel is defiled. 2181

COMMITTETH (19) [COMMIT]

Lev 20:10 the man that **c adultery** with *another* man's 5003
20:10 *even he* that **c adultery** with his 5003
Ps 10:14 the poor **c** *himself* unto thee; thou art 5800
Pr 6:32 *But* whoso **c adultery** with a woman 5003
Eze 8: 6 that the house of Israel **c** here, 6213
16:32 *But as* a wife that **c adultery**, *which* taketh 5003
18:24 **c** iniquity, *and* doeth according to all 6213
18:26 and **c** iniquity, and dieth in them; 6213
33:18 and **c** iniquity, he shall even die thereby. 6213
Mt 5:32 shall marry her that is divorced **c adultery**. *3429*
19: 9 and shall marry another, **c adultery**: *3429*
Mk 10:11 and marry another, **c adultery** against her. *3429*
10:12 and be married to another, she **c adultery**. *3429*
Lk 16:18 his wife, and marrieth another, **c adultery**: *3431*
16:18 is put away from *her* husband **c adultery**. *3431*
Jn 8:34 Whosoever **c** sin is the servant of sin. *4160*
1Co 6:18 he that **c fornication** sinneth against his *4203*
1Jn 3: 4 Whosoever **c** sin transgresseth also the law: *4160*
3: 8 He that **c** sin is of the devil; for the devil *4160*

COMMITTING (2) [COMMIT]

Eze 33:15 in the statutes of life, without **c** iniquity; 6213
Hos 4: 2 and killing, and stealing, and **c adultery**, 5003

COMMODIOUS (1)

Ac 27:12 because the haven was not **c** to winter in, *428*

COMMON (21) [COMMONLY]

Lev 4:27 if any one of the **c** people sin through 776
Nu 16:29 If these *men* die the **c** death of all men, or 3509.1
1Sa 21: 4 *There is* no **c** bread under mine hand, but 2455
21: 5 and *the bread is in* a manner **c**, yea, 2455
Ecc 6: 1 seen under the sun, and it *is* **c** among men: 7227
Jer 26:23 cast his dead body into the graves of the **c** 1121
31: 5 shall plant, and shall **eat** *them* **as c things**. 2490
Eze 23:42 with the men of the **c** sort *were* brought 7230
Mt 27:27 of the governor took Jesus into the **c hall**, *4232*
Mk 12:37 his son? And the **c** people heard him gladly. *4183*
Ac 2:44 were together, and had all *things* **c**; *2839*
4:32 was his own; but they had all *things* **c**. *2839*
5:18 the apostles, and put them in the **c** prison. *1219*
10:14 for I have never eaten any *thing that is* **c** or *2839*
10:15 God hath cleansed, *that* **call** not thou **c**. *2840*
10:28 shewed me that *I* should not call any man **c** *2839*
11: 8 for nothing **c** or unclean hath at any time *2839*
11: 9 God hath cleansed, *that* **call** not thou **c**. *2840*
1Co 10:13 taken you but such as is **c to man**: *442*
Tit 1: 4 To Titus, *mine* own son after the **c** faith: *2839*
Jude 1: 3 to write unto you of the **c** salvation, *2839*

COMMONLY (2) [COMMON]

Mt 28:15 this saying is **c reported** among the Jews *1310*
1Co 5: 1 It is reported **c** *that there is* fornication *3654*

COMMONWEALTH (1)

Eph 2:12 being aliens from the **c** of Israel, and *4174*

COMMOTION (1) [COMMOTIONS]

Jer 10:22 and a great **c** out of the north country, 7494

COMMOTIONS (1) [COMMOTION]

Lk 21: 9 But when ye shall hear of wars and **c**, be not *181*

COMMUNE (8) [COMMUNED, COMMUNING, COMMUNION]

Ge 34: 6 went out unto Jacob to **c** with him. 1696
Ex 25:22 I will **c** with thee from above the mercy 1696
1Sa 18:22 *saying,* **C** with David secretly, and say, 1696
19: 3 thou *art,* and I will **c** with my father of thee; 1696
Job 4: 2 *If we* assay to **c** with thee, wilt thou be 1697
Ps 4: 4 **c** with your own heart upon your bed, and 559
64: 5 they **c** of laying snares privily; they say, 5608
77: 6 I **c** with mine own heart: and my spirit 7878

COMMUNED (18) [COMMUNE]

Ge 23: 8 he **c** with them, saying, If it be your mind 1696
34: 8 Hamor **c** with them, saying, The soul of my 1696
34:20 and **c** with the men of their city, saying, 1696
42:24 returned to them *again,* and **c** with them, 1696
43:19 they **c** with him *at* the door of the house, 1696
Jdg 9: 1 **c** with them, and with all the family of 1696
1Sa 9:25 *Samuel* **c** with Saul upon the top of 1696
25:39 David sent and **c** with Abigail, to take her 1696
1Ki 10: 2 she **c** with him of all that was in her heart. 1696
2Ki 22:14 in the college;) and they **c** with her. 1696
2Ch 9: 1 she **c** with him of all that was in her heart. 1696
Ecc 1:16 I **c** with mine own heart, saying, Lo, I am 1696
Da 1:19 the king **c** with them; and among them all 1696
Zec 1:14 So the angel that **c** with me said unto me, 1696
Lk 6:11 **c** one with another what they might do to *1255*
22: 4 and **c with** the chief priests and captains, *4814*
24:15 that while they **c** *together* and reasoned, *3656*
Ac 24:26 he sent for him the oftener, and **c** with him. *3656*

COMMUNICATE (4) [COMMUNICATED, COMMUNICATION, COMMUNICATIONS]

Gal 6: 6 Let him that is taught in the word **c** unto *2841*
Php 4:14 well done, that ye did **c with** my affliction. *4790*
1Ti 6:18 ready to distribute, **willing to c**; *2843*
Heb 13:16 But to do good and to **c** forget not: for with *2842*

COMMUNICATED (2) [COMMUNICATE]

Gal 2: 2 **c** unto them *that* gospel which I preach *394*
Php 4:15 no church **c with** me as concerning giving *2841*

COMMUNICATION (6) [COMMUNICATE]

2Sa 3:17 Abner had **c** with the elders of Israel, 1697
2Ki 9:11 unto them, Ye know the man, and his **c**. 7879
Mt 5:37 But let your **c** be, Yea, yea; Nay, nay: *3056*
Eph 4:29 Let no corrupt **c** proceed out of your mouth, *3056*
Col 3: 8 blasphemy, **filthy c** out of your mouth. *148*
Phm 1: 6 That the **c** of thy faith may become *2842*

COMMUNICATIONS (2) [COMMUNICATE]

Lk 24:17 What *manner of* **c** *are* these that ye have *3056*
1Co 15:33 not deceived: evil **c** corrupt good manners. *3657*

COMMUNING (2) [COMMUNE]

Ge 18:33 as soon as he had left **c** with Abraham: 1696
Ex 31:18 when he had made an end of **c** with him 1696

COMMUNION (4) [COMMUNE]

1Co 10:16 is it not the **c** of the blood of Christ? *2842*
10:16 is it not the **c** of the body of Christ? *2842*
2Co 6:14 and what **c** hath light with darkness? *2842*
13:14 and the **c** of the Holy Ghost, *be* with you *2842*

COMPACT (1) [COMPACTED]

Ps 122: 3 Jerusalem *is* builded as a city that is **c** 2266

COMPACTED (1) [COMPACT]

Eph 4:16 and **c** by that which every joint supplieth, *4822*

COMPANIED (1) [COMPANY]

Ac 1:21 Wherefore of these men which have **c with** *4905*

COMPANIES (17) [COMPANY]

Jdg 7:16 divided the three hundred men *into* three **c**, 7218
7:20 the three **c** blew the trumpets, and brake 7218
9:34 they laid wait against Shechem *in* four **c**. 7218
9:43 divided them into three **c**, and laid wait in 7218
9:44 the two *other* **c** ran upon all *the people* that 7218
1Sa 11:11 that Saul put the people *in* three **c**; 7218
13:17 out of the camp of the Philistines *in* three **c**: 7218
2Ki 5: 2 the Syrians had gone out *by* **c**, and 1416
1Ch 9:18 they *were* porters in the **c** of the children of 4264
28: 1 the **c** that ministered to the king **by course**, 4256
Ne 12:31 appointed two great **c** *of them that gave* NIH
12:40 So stood the two **c** *of them that gave* thanks NIH
Job 6:19 the **c** of Sheba waited for them. 1979
Isa 21:13 ye lodge, O ye **travelling c** of Dedanim. 736
57:13 When thou criest, let thy **c** deliver thee; but 6899
Eze 26: 7 with horsemen, and **c**, and much people. 6951
Mk 6:39 sit down **by c** upon the green grass. *4849+4849*

COMPANION (13) [COMPANIONS, COMPANIONS']

Ex 32:27 every man his **c**, and every man his 7453
Jdg 14:20 Samson's wife was *given* to his **c**, whom he 4828
15: 2 hated her; therefore I gave her to thy **c**: 4828
15: 6 had taken his wife, and given her to his **c**. 4828
1Ch 27:33 and Hushai the Archite *was* the king's **c**: 7453
Job 30:29 I am a brother to dragons, and a **c** to owls. 7453
Ps 119:63 I *am* a **c** of all *them* that fear thee, and 2270
Pr 13:20 be wise: but a **c** of fools shall be destroyed. 7462
28: 7 he that is a **c** of riotous *men* shameth his 7462
28:24 the same *is* the **c** of a destroyer. 2270
Mal 2:14 yet *is* she thy **c**, and the wife of thy 2278
Php 2:25 and **c in labour**, and fellowsoldier, but *4904*
Rev 1: 9 and **c** in tribulation, and in the kingdom and *4791*

COMPANIONS (21) [COMPANION]

Jdg 11:38 she went with her **c**, and bewailed her 7464
14:11 that they brought thirty **c** to be with him. 4828
Ezr 4: 7 Mithredath, Tabeel, and the rest of their **c**, 3674
4: 9 Shimshai the scribe, and the rest of their **c**; 3675
4:17 *to* the rest of their **c** that dwell in Samaria, 3675
4:23 Shimshai the scribe, and their **c**, they went 3675
5: 3 and their **c**, and said thus unto them, 3675
5: 6 and his **c** the Apharsachites, 3675
6: 6 and your **c** the Apharsachites, 3675
6:13 side the river, Shethar-boznai, and their **c**, 3675
Job 35: 4 I will answer thee, and thy **c** with thee. 7453
41: 6 Shall the **c** make a banquet of him? 2271
Ps 45:14 the virgins her **c** that follow her *shall be* 7464
SS 1: 7 that turneth aside by the flocks of thy **c**? 2270
8:13 in the gardens, the **c** hearken to thy voice: 2270
Isa 1:23 Thy princes *are* rebellious, and **c** of thieves: 2270
Eze 37:16 and for the children of Israel his **c**: 2270
37:16 and *for* all the house of Israel his **c**: 2270
Da 2:17 to Hananiah, Mishael, and Azariah, his **c**: 2269
Ac 19:29 men of Macedonia, Paul's **c in travel**, *4898*
Heb 10:33 whilst ye became **c** of them that were so *2844*

COMPANIONS' (1) [COMPANION]

Ps 122: 8 For my brethren and **c** sakes, I will now 7453

COMPANY (86) [COMPANIED, COMPANIED]

Ge 32: 8 If Esau come to the one **c**, and smite it, then 4264
32: 8 then the *other* **c** which is left shall escape. 4264
32:21 and himself lodged that night in the **c**. 4264
35:11 a nation and a **c** of nations shall be of thee, 6951
37:25 a **c** of Ishmeelites came from Gilead with 736
50: 9 and horsemen: and it was a very great **c**. 4264
Nu 14: 7 they spake unto all the **c** of the children of 5712
16: 5 And he spake unto Korah and unto all his **c**, 5712
16: 6 Take you censers, Korah, and all his **c**; 5712
16:11 all thy **c** *are* gathered together against 5712
16:16 Be thou and all thy **c** before the LORD, 5712
16:40 that he be not as Korah, and as his **c**: 5712
22: 4 Now shall *this* **c** lick up all *that are* round 6951
26: 9 and against Aaron in the **c** of Korah, 5712
26:10 when that **c** died, what time the fire 5712
27: 3 he was not in the **c** of them that gathered 5712
27: 3 against the LORD in the **c** of Korah; 5712
Jdg 9:37 another **c** come along by the plain of 7218
9:44 the **c** that *was* with him, rushed forward, 7218
18:23 aileth thee, that thou **comest with** such a **c**? 2199
1Sa 10: 5 that thou shalt meet a **c** of prophets coming 2256
10:10 to the hill, behold, a **c** of prophets met him; 2256
13:17 one **c** turned unto the way that leadeth to 7218
13:18 another **c** turned the way to Beth-horon: 7218
13:18 another **c** turned *to* the way of the border 7218
19:20 when they saw the **c** of the prophets 3862
30:15 to him, Canst thou bring me down to this **c**? 1416
30:15 and I will bring thee down to this **c**. 1416
30:23 delivered the **c** that came against us into 1416
2Ki 5:15 he and all his **c**, and came, and stood before 4264
9:17 he spied the **c** of Jehu as he came, and said, 8229
9:17 of Jehu as he came, and said, I see a **c**. 8229
2Ch 9: 1 with a very great **c**, and camels that bare 2428
20:12 for we have no might against this great **c** 1995
24:24 of the Syrians came with a small **c** of men, NIH
Ne 12:38 the other **c** *of them that gave* thanks went NIH
Job 16: 7 thou hast made desolate all my **c**. 5712
34: 8 Which goeth in **c** with the workers of 2274
Ps 55:14 *and* walked unto the house of God in **c**. 7285
68:11 great *was* the **c** of those that published *it.* 6635
68:30 Rebuke the **c** of spearmen, the multitude of 2416
106:17 up Dathan, and covered the **c** of Abiram. 5712
106:18 a fire was kindled in their **c**; the flame burnt 5712
Pr 29: 3 he that **keepeth c with** harlots spendeth *his* 7462
SS 1: 9 to a **c of horses** in Pharaoh's chariots. 5484
6:13 As it were the **c** of two armies. 4246
Jer 31: 8 child together: a great **c** shall return thither. 6951
Eze 16:40 They shall also bring up a **c** against thee, 6951
17:17 and great **c** make for him in the war, 6951

Eze 23:46 *I will* bring up a **c** upon them, and *will* give 6951
23:47 the **c** shall stone them with stones, and 6951
27: 6 the **c** of the Ashurites have made thy 1323
27:27 in all thy **c** which *is* in the midst of thee, 6951
27:34 and all thy **c** in the midst of thee shall fall. 6951
32: 3 spread out my net over thee with a **c** of 6951
32:22 Asshur *is* there and all her **c**: his graves *are* 6951
32:23 the pit, and her **c** is round about her grave: 6951
38: 4 *of armour, even* a great **c** *with* bucklers 6951
38: 7 all thy **c** that are assembled unto thee, and 6951
38:13 hast thou gathered thy **c** to take a prey? to 6951
38:15 upon horses, a great **c**, and a mighty army: 6951
Hos 6: 9 the **c** of priests murder *in* the way by 2267
Lk 2:44 supposing him to have been in the **c**, *4923*
5:29 and there was a great **c** of publicans and *3793*
6:17 and the **c** of his disciples, and a great *3793*
6:22 when they shall separate you *from their* **c**, NIG
9:14 Make them sit down by fifties in a **c**. *2828*
9:38 a man of the **c** cried out, saying, Master, *3793*
11:27 a certain woman of the **c** lift up her voice, *3793*
12:13 And one of the **c** said unto him, Master, *3793*
23:27 And there followed him a great **c** of people, *4128*
24:22 certain women *also* **of** our **c** made us *1537*
Jn 6: 5 *his* eyes, and saw a great **c** come unto him, *3793*
Ac 4:23 they went to their own **c**, and reported all NIG
6: 7 a great **c** of the priests were obedient to *3793*
10:28 *thing* for a man *that is* a Jew to **keep c**, *2853*
13:13 and his **c** loosed from Paphos, *3588+4012*
15:22 to send chosen men of **their own c** to *846*
17: 5 and **gathered a c**, and set all the city on an *3792*
21: 8 And the next day we that were **of** Paul's **c** *4012*
Ro 15:24 if first I be somewhat filled with your **c**. NIG
1Co 5: 9 I wrote unto you in an epistle not to **c with** *4874*
5:11 now I have written unto you not to **keep c**, *4874*
2Th 3:14 note that *man*, and **have** no **c with** him, *4874*
Heb 12:22 and to an **innumerable c** of angels, *3461*
Rev 18:17 every shipmaster, and all the **c** in ships, *3658*

COMPARABLE (1) [COMPARE]
La 4: 2 The precious sons of Zion, **c** to fine gold, 5537

COMPARE (4) [COMPARABLE, COMPARED, COMPARING, COMPARISON]
Isa 40:18 or what likeness will ye **c** unto him? 6186
46: 5 make *me* equal, and **c** me, that we may be 4911
Mk 4:30 or with what comparison shall we **c** it? *3846*
2Co 10:12 **c** ourselves **with** some that commend *4793*

COMPARED (5) [COMPARE]
Ps 89: 6 For who in the heaven can be **c** unto 6186
Pr 3:15 thou canst desire are not to be **c** unto her. 7737
8:11 that may be desired are not to be **c** to it. 7737
SS 1: 9 I have **c** thee, O my love, to a company of 1819
Ro 8:18 **c with** the glory which shall be revealed in *4314*

COMPARING (2) [COMPARE]
1Co 2:13 **c** spiritual *things* with spiritual. *4793*
2Co 10:12 and **c** themselves **amongst** themselves, *4793*

COMPARISON (4) [COMPARE]
Jdg 8: 2 What have I done now **in c of** you? 3509.1
8: 3 what was I able to do **in c of** you? 3509.1
Hag 2: 3 *is it* not in your eyes **in c of** it as nothing? 3644
Mk 4:30 or with what **c** shall we compare it? *3850*

COMPASS (39) [COMPASSED, COMPASSEST, COMPASSETH, COMPASSING]
Ex 27: 5 thou shalt put it under the **c** of the altar 3749
38: 4 the **c** thereof beneath unto the midst of it. 3749
Nu 21: 4 way of the Red sea, to **c** the land of Edom: 5437
34: 5 the border shall **fetch a c** from Azmon unto 5437
Jos 6: 3 ye shall **c** the city, all *ye* men of war, 5437
6: 4 the seventh day ye shall **c** the city seven 5437
6: 7 **c** the city, and let him that is armed pass on 5437
15: 3 up to Adar, and **fetched a c** to Karkaa: 5437
2Sa 5:23 *but* **fetch a c** behind them, and come upon 5437
1Ki 7:15 of twelve cubits did **c** either of them **about**. 5437
7:23 of thirty cubits did **c** it **round about**. 5437+5439
7:35 in the top of the base *was there* a round **c** of 5439
2Ki 3: 9 they **fetcht a c** of seven days' journey: and 5437
11: 8 ye shall **c** the king round about, every man 5362
2Ch 4: 2 round **in c**, and five cubits the height 5439
4: 2 a line of thirty cubits did **c** it round about. 5437
4: 3 of oxen, which did **c** it round about: 5437
23: 7 the Levites shall **c** the king round about, 5362
Job 16:13 His archers **c** me **round about**, he cleaveth 5437
40:22 the willows of the brook **c** him **about**. 5437
Ps 5:12 *with* favour wilt thou **c** him as *with* a 5849
7: 7 congregation of the people **c** thee **about**: 5437
17: 9 *from* my deadly enemies, *who* **c** me **about**. 5362
26: 6 so will I **c** thine altar, O LORD: 5437
32: 7 thou shalt **c** me **about** *with* songs of 5437
32:10 in the LORD, mercy shall **c** him **about**. 5437
49: 5 the iniquity of my heels shall **c** me **about**? 5437
140: 9 *As for* the head of those that **c** me **about**, 4524
142: 7 the righteous shall **c** me **about**; for thou 3803
Pr 8:27 when he set a **c** upon the face of the depth: 2329
Isa 44:13 he marketh it out with the **c**, and maketh it 4230
50:11 a fire, that **c** *yourselves* **about** with sparks: 247
Jer 31:22 *thing* in the earth, A woman shall **c** a man. 5437
31:39 the hill Gareb, and shall **c about** to Goath. 5437
52:21 a fillet of twelve cubits did **c** it; and 5437
Hab 1: 4 for the wicked doth **c about** the righteous; 3803
Mt 23:15 for ye **c** sea and land to make one *4013*
Lk 19:43 and **c** thee **round**, and keep thee in on *4033*
Ac 28:13 And from thence we **fet a c**, *4022*

COMPASSED (44) [COMPASS]
Ge 19: 4 **c** the house **round**, both old and young, 5437
Dt 2: 1 unto me: and we **c** mount Seir many days. 5437
2: 3 Ye have **c** this mountain long enough: 5437
Jos 6:11 So the ark of the LORD **c** the city, 5437
6:14 the second day they **c** the city once, 5437
6:15 **c** the city after the same manner seven 5437
Jos 6:15 only on that day they **c** the city seven times. 5437
15:10 the border **c** from Baalah westward unto 5437
18:14 and **c** the corner of the sea southward, 5437
Jdg 11:18 **c** the land of Edom, and the land of Moab, 5437
16: 2 they **c** *him* **in**, and laid wait for him all 5437
1Sa 23:26 his men **c** David and his men **round about** 5849
2Sa 18:15 young men that bare Joab's armour **c about** 5437
22: 5 When the waves of death **c** me, the floods of 661
22: 6 The sorrows of hell **c** me **about**; the snares 5437
2Ki 6:14 they came by night, and **c** the city **about**. 5362
6:15 a host **c** the city both with horses and 5437
8:21 smote the Edomites which **c** him **about**, 5437
2Ch 18:31 Therefore they **c** about him to fight: but 5437
21: 9 smote the Edomites which **c** him **in**, and 5437
33:14 **c** about Ophel, and raised it up a very great 5437
Job 19: 6 overthrown me, and hath **c** me with his net. 5362
26:10 He hath **c** the waters **with** 2328+5921+6440
Ps 17:11 They have now **c** us *in* our steps: they have 5437
18: 4 The sorrows of death **c** me, and the floods of 661
18: 5 The sorrows of hell **c** me **about**: the snares 5437
22:12 Many bulls have **c** me: strong *bulls* of 5437
22:16 For dogs have **c** me: the assembly of 5437
40:12 For innumerable evils have **c** me **about**: 661
88:17 daily like water; they **c** me **about** together. 5362
109: 3 They **c** me **about** also *with* words of 5437
116: 3 The sorrows of death **c** me, and the pains of 661
118:10 All nations **c** me **about**: but in the name of 5437
118:11 They **c** me **about**; yea, they compassed me 5437
118:11 me about; yea, they **c** me **about**: 5437
118:12 They **c** me **about** like bees; they are 5437
La 3: 5 against me, and **c** *me* with gall and travail. 5362
Jnh 2: 3 of the seas; and the floods **c** me **about**: 5437
2: 5 The waters **c** me **about**, *even* to the soul: 661
Lk 21:20 And when ye shall see Jerusalem **c** with *2944*
Heb 5: 2 for that he himself also is **c with** infirmity. *4029*
11:30 after they were **c about** seven days. *2944*
12: 1 Wherefore seeing we also are **c about** with *4029*
Rev 20: 9 and **c** the camp of the saints **about**, and *2944*

COMPASSEST (1) [COMPASS]
Ps 139: 3 Thou **c** my path and my lying down, and 2219

COMPASSETH (5) [COMPASS]
Ge 2:11 that *is it* which **c** the whole land of Havilah, 5437
2:13 the same *is it* that **c** the whole land of 5437
Jos 19:14 the border **c** it on the north side *to* 5437
Ps 73: 6 Therefore pride **c** them **about as a chain**; 6059
Hos 11:12 Ephraim **c** me **about** with lies, and 5437

COMPASSING (3) [COMPASS]
1Ki 7:24 it **round about** *there were* knops **c** it, 5437+5439
7:24 ten in a cubit, **c** the sea round about: 5362
2Ch 4: 3 ten in a cubit, **c** the sea round about. 5362

COMPASSION (41) [COMPASSIONS]
Ex 2: 6 she **had c** on him, and said, This *is one* of 2550
Dt 13:17 and **have c** upon thee, and multiply thee, 7355
30: 3 **have c** upon thee, and will return and 7355
1Sa 23:21 *be* ye of the LORD; for ye **have c** on me. 2550
1Ki 8:50 give them **c** before them who carried them 7356
8:50 that they may **have c** on them: 7355
2Ki 13:23 **had c** on them, and had respect unto them, 7355
2Ch 30: 9 your children *shall find* **c** before them that 7356
36:15 because he **had c** on his people, and on his 2550
36:17 **had** no **c** upon young man or maiden, 2550
Ps 78:38 he, *being* **full of c**, forgave *their* iniquity, 7349
86:15 O Lord, *art* a God **full of c**, and gracious, 7349
111: 4 the LORD *is* gracious and **full of c**. 7349
112: 4 *he is* gracious, and **full of c**, and righteous. 7349
145: 8 The LORD *is* gracious, and **full of c**; 7349
Isa 49:15 that *she* should not **have c** on the son of her 7355
Jer 12:15 **have c** on them, and will bring them again, 7355
La 3:32 yet will he **have c** according to 7355
Eze 16: 5 any of these unto thee, to **have c** upon thee; 2550
Mic 7:19 He will turn again, he will **have c** upon us; 7355
Mt 9:36 he was **moved with c** on them, because *4697*
14:14 and was **moved with c** toward them, and *4697*
15:32 and said, I **have c** on the multitude, *4697*
18:27 the lord of that servant was **moved with c**, *4697*
18:33 Shouldest not thou also have **had c** on thy *1653*
20:34 So Jesus **had c** *on them*, and touched their *4697*
Mk 1:41 And Jesus, **moved with c**, put forth *his* *4697*
5:19 hath done for thee, and hath **had c** on thee. *1653*
6:34 and was **moved with c** toward them, *4697*
8: 2 I **have c** on the multitude, because *4697*
9:22 but if thou canst do any *thing*, **have c** on us, *4697*
Lk 7:13 he **had c** on her, and said unto her, *4697*
10:33 and when he saw him, he **had c** *on him*, *4697*
15:20 and **had c**, and ran, and fell on his neck, *4697*
Ro 9:15 I will **have c** on whom I will have *3627*
9:15 have compassion on whom I will **have c**. *3627*
Heb 5: 2 Who can **have c** on the ignorant, and *3356*
10:34 For ye **had c** *of me* in my bonds, *4834*
1Pe 3: 8 having **c one of another**, love as brethren, *4835*
1Jn 3:17 and shutteth up his bowels *of* **c** from him, NIG
Jude 1:22 And of some **have c**, making a difference: *1653*

COMPASSIONATE See TENDERHEARTED

COMPASSIONS (2) [COMPASSION]
La 3:22 are not consumed, because his **c** fail not. 7356
Zec 7: 9 shew mercy and **c** every man to his brother: 7356

COMPEL (5) [COMPELLED, COMPELLEST]
Lev 25:39 thou shalt not **c** him **to serve** as a 5647+5656
Est 1: 8 *was* according to the law; none did **c**: 597
Mt 5:41 And whosoever shall **c** thee **to go** a mile, *29*
Mk 15:21 And they **c** one Simon a Cyrenian, *29*
Lk 14:23 and hedges, and **c** *them* to come in, *315*

COMPELLED (6) [COMPEL]
1Sa 28:23 together with the woman, **c** him; 6555
2Ch 21:11 to commit fornication, and **c** Judah *thereto*. 5080
Mt 27:32 Simon by name: him they **c** to bear his cross. *29*
Ac 26:11 every synagogue, and **c** *them* to blaspheme; *315*
2Co 12:11 am become a fool in glorying; ye have **c** me: *315*
Gal 2: 3 being a Greek, was **c** to be circumcised: *315*

COMPELLEST (1) [COMPEL]
Gal 2:14 why **c** thou the Gentiles to live as do *315*

COMPLAIN (4) [COMPLAINED, COMPLAINERS, COMPLAINING, COMPLAINT, COMPLAINTS]
Jdg 21:22 or their brethren come unto us to **c**, 7378
Job 7:11 I will **c** in the bitterness of my soul. 7878
31:38 or that the furrows likewise thereof **c**; 1058
La 3:39 Wherefore doth a living man **c**, a man for 596

COMPLAINED (2) [COMPLAIN]
Nu 11: 1 *when* the people **c**, it displeased the LORD: 596
Ps 77: 3 I **c**, and my spirit was overwhelmed. Selah. 7878

COMPLAINERS (1) [COMPLAIN]
Jude 1:16 These are murmurers, **c**, walking after their *3202*

COMPLAINING (1) [COMPLAIN]
Ps 144:14 going out; that *there be* no **c** in our streets. 6682

COMPLAINT (9) [COMPLAIN]
1Sa 1:16 for out of the abundance of my **c** and 7879
Job 7:13 comfort me, my couch shall ease my **c**; 7879
9:27 If I say, I will forget my **c**, I will leave off 7879
10: 1 of my life; I will leave my **c** upon myself; 7879
21: 4 *As for* me, *is* my **c** to man? and if *it were* 7879
23: 2 Even to day *is* my **c** bitter: my stroke is 7879
Ps 55: 2 I mourn in my **c**, and make a noise; 7879
102: T and poureth out his **c** before the LORD. 7879
142: 2 I poured out my **c** before him; I shewed 7879

COMPLAINTS (1) [COMPLAIN]
Ac 25: 7 and laid many and grievous **c** against Paul, *157*

COMPLETE (3)
Lev 23:15 wave offering; seven sabbaths shall be **c**: 8549
Col 2:10 And ye are **c** in him, which is the head of *4137*
4:12 stand perfect and **c** in all the will of God. *4137*

COMPLETELY See UTTERMOST

COMPOSITION (2)
Ex 30:32 ye make *any other* like it, after the **c** of it: 4971
30:37 to yourselves according to the **c** thereof: 4971

COMPOUND (1) [COMPOUNDETH]
Ex 30:25 an ointment **c** *after* the art of 4842

COMPOUNDETH (1) [COMPOUND]
Ex 30:33 Whosoever **c** *any* like it, or 7543

COMPREHEND (2) [COMPREHENDED]
Job 37: 5 great *things* doeth he, which we cannot **c**. 3045
Eph 3:18 May be able to **c** with all saints what *is* *2638*

COMPREHENDED (3) [COMPREHEND]
Isa 40:12 and **c** the dust of the earth in a measure, and 3557
Jn 1: 5 in darkness; and the darkness **c** it not. *2638*
Ro 13: 9 it is **briefly c** in this saying, namely, *346*

CONANIAH (1)
2Ch 35: 9 **C** also, and Shemaiah and Nethaneel, 3562

CONCEAL (6) [CONCEALED, CONCEALETH]
Ge 37:26 *is it* if we slay our brother, and **c** his blood? 3680
Dt 13: 8 shalt thou spare, neither shalt thou **c** him: 3680
Job 27:11 *that* which *is* with the Almighty will I not **c**. 3582
41:12 I will not **c** his parts, nor *his* power, nor his 2790
Pr 25: 2 *It is* the glory of God to **c** a thing: but 5641
Jer 50: 2 and set up a standard; publish, *and* **c** not: 3582

CONCEALED (2) [CONCEAL]
Job 6:10 for I have not **c** the words of the Holy One. 3582
Ps 40:10 I have not **c** thy lovingkindness and 3582

CONCEALETH (2) [CONCEAL]
Pr 11:13 he that is of a faithful spirit **c** the matter. 3680
12:23 A prudent man **c** knowledge: but the heart 3680

CONCEIT (5) [CONCEITS]
Pr 18:11 strong city, and as a high wall in his own **c**. 4906
26: 5 to his folly, lest he be wise in his own **c**. 5869
26:12 Seest thou a man wise in his own **c**? 5869
26:16 The sluggard *is* wiser in his own **c** than 5869
28:11 The rich man *is* wise in his own **c**; but 5869

CONCEITED See HIGH-MINDED

CONCEITS (2) [CONCEIT]
Ro 11:25 lest ye should be wise in your own **c**; NIG
12:16 of low estate. Be not wise in your own **c**. NIG

CONCEIVE (14) [CONCEIVED, CONCEIVING, CONCEPTION]
Ge 30:38 that they should **c** when they came to drink. 3179
30:41 whensoever the stronger cattle did **c**, 3179
30:41 that they might **c** among the rods. 3179
Nu 5:28 she shall be free, and shall **c seed**. 2232+2233
Jdg 13: 3 bearest not: but thou shalt **c**, and bear a son. 2029
13: 5 For lo, thou *shalt* **c**, and bear a son; and 2030
13: 7 Behold, thou *shalt* **c**, and bear a son; 2030
Job 15:35 They **c** mischief, and bring forth vanity, 2029
Ps 51: 5 in iniquity; and in sin did my mother **c** me. 3179
Isa 7:14 a Virgin shall **c**, and bear a Son, and 2030
33:11 Ye shall **c** chaff, ye shall bring forth 2029
59: 4 *they* **c** mischief, and bring forth iniquity. 2029
Lk 1:31 thou shalt **c** in *thy* womb, and bring forth a *4815*
Heb 11:11 Sara herself received strength to **c** seed, *2602*

C

CONCEIVED (46) [CONCEIVE]

Ge 4: 1 she c, and bare Cain, and said, I have 2029
4:17 knew his wife; and she c, and bare Enoch: 2029
16: 4 he went in unto Hagar, and she c: and 2029
16: 4 when she saw that she had c, her mistress 2029
16: 5 when she saw that she had c, I was 2029
21: 2 For Sarah c, and bare Abraham a son in his 2029
25:21 intreated of him, and Rebekah his wife c. 2029
29:32 Leah c, and bare a son, and she called his 2029
29:33 she c again, and bare a son; and said, 2029
29:34 she c again, and bare a son; and said, 2029
29:35 she c again, and bare a son: and she said, 2029
30: 5 And Bilhah c, and bare Jacob a son. 2029
30: 7 Bilhah Rachel's maid c again, and 2029
30:17 and she c, and bare Jacob the fifth son. 2029
30:19 Leah c again, and bare Jacob the sixth son. 2029
30:23 she c, and bare a son; and said, God hath 2029
30:39 the flocks c before the rods, and 3179
31:10 it came to pass at the time that the cattle c, 3179
38: 3 she c, and bare a son; and he called his 2029
38: 4 she c again, and bare a son; and she called 2029
38: 5 she yet again c, and bare a son; and NIH
38:18 and came in unto her, and she c by him. 2029
Ex 2: 2 the woman c, and bare a son: and when she 2029
Lev 12: 2 If a woman have c **seed**, and born a man 2232
Nu 11:12 Have I c all this people? have I begotten 2029
1Sa 1:20 time was come about after Hannah had c, 2029
2:21 so that she c, and bare three sons and 2029
2Sa 11: 5 the woman c, and sent and told David, and 2029
2Ki 4:17 the woman c, and bare a son at that season 2029
1Ch 7:23 she c, and bare a son, and he called his 2029
Job 3: 3 *in which it was* said, There is a man child c. 2029
Ps 7:14 hath c mischief, and brought forth 2029
SS 3: 4 and into the chamber of her that c me. 2029
Isa 8: 3 the prophetess; and she c, and bare a son. 2029
Jer 49:30 and hath c a purpose against you. 2803
Hos 1: 3 of Diblaim; which c, and bare him a son. 2029
1: 6 she c again, and bare a daughter. And *God* 2029
1: 8 weaned Lo-ruhamah, she c, and bare a son. 2029
2: 5 she that c them hath done shamefully: 2029
Mt 1:20 for that which is c in her is of the Holy 1080
Lk 1:24 And after those days his wife Elisabeth c, 4815
1:36 she hath also c a son in her old age: 4815
2:21 named of the angel before he was c in 4815
Ac 5: 4 why hast thou c this thing in thine heart? 5087
Ro 9:10 but when Rebecca also had c by one, 2845
Jas 1:15 Then when lust hath c, it bringeth forth sin: 4815

CONCEIVING (1) [CONCEIVE]

Isa 59:13 c and uttering from the heart words of 2029

CONCEPTION (3) [CONCEIVE]

Ge 3:16 I will greatly multiply thy sorrow and thy c; 2032
Ru 4:13 the LORD gave her c, and she bare a son. 2032
Hos 9:11 and from the womb, and from the c. 2032

CONCERN (2) [CONCERNETH, CONCERNING]

Ac 28:31 teaching those *things* which c the Lord 4012
2Co 11:30 I will glory of the *things* which c mine NIG

CONCERNETH (2) [CONCERN]

Ps 138: 8 The LORD will perfect that which c me: 1157
Eze 12:10 This burden c the prince in Jerusalem, and NIH

CONCERNING (242) [CONCERN]

Ge 5:29 This *same* shall comfort us c our work and 4480
12:20 Pharaoh commanded *his* men c him: and 5921
19:21 See, I have accepted thee c this thing, 3807.1
24: 9 his master, and sware to him c that matter. 5921
26:32 him c the well which they had digged, 182+5921
42:21 We *are* verily guilty c our brother, 5921
Ex 6: 8 c the which I did swear to give it to NIH
24: 8 which the LORD hath made with you c all 5921
Lev 4: 2 (c *things* which ought not to be done), NIH
4:13 LORD c *things* which should not be done, NIH
4:22 his God c *things* which should not be done, NIH
4:26 make an atonement for him **as** c his sin, 4480
4:27 c *things* which ought not to be done, NIH
5: 6 shall make an atonement for him c his sin. 4480
5:18 for him c his ignorance wherein he erred 5921
6: 3 and lieth c it, and sweareth falsely; 871.1
6:18 c the offerings of the LORD made by fire: 4480
23: 2 say unto them, C the feasts of the LORD, NIH
27:32 c the tithe of the herd, or of the flock, NIH
Nu 8:20 LORD commanded Moses c the Levites, 3807.1
8:22 as the LORD had commanded Moses c 5921
9: 8 what the LORD will command c you. 3807.1
10:29 for the LORD hath spoken good c Israel. 5921
14:30 c which I sware to make you dwell therein, NIH
30: 1 heads of the tribes c the children of Israel, 3807.1
30:12 whatsoever proceeded out of her lips c 3807.1
30:12 or c the bond of her soul, shall not stand: 3807.1
32:28 So c them Moses commanded Eleazar 3807.1
36: 6 command c the daughters of Zelophehad, 3807.1
Jos 14: 6 said unto Moses the man of God c me 182+5921
23:14 which the LORD your God spake c you; 5921
Jdg 15: 3 Samson said c them, Now shall I be more 3807.1
21: 5 For *they* had made a great oath c *him* that 3807.1
Ru 4: 7 in former time in Israel c redeeming 5921
4: 7 concerning redeeming and c changing, 5921
1Sa 3:12 all *things* which I have spoken c his house: 413
25:30 to all the good that he hath spoken c thee, 5921
2Sa 3: 8 that thou chargest me to day with a fault c NIH
7:25 the word that thou hast spoken c thy 5921
7:25 c his house, establish *it* for ever, and do as 5921
11:18 and told David all the **things** c the war; 1697
13:39 for he was comforted c Amnon, seeing he 5921
14: 8 thine house, and I will give charge c thee. 5921
18: 5 all the captains charge c Absalom. 1697+5921
1Ki 2: 4 continue his word which he spake c me, 5921
2:27 which he spake c the house of Eli in Shiloh. 5921
5: 8 I will do all thy desire c timber of cedar, 871.1
5: 8 timber of cedar, and c timber of fir. 871.1
6:12 C this house which thou art in building, NIH
1Ki 8:41 Moreover c a stranger, that *is* not of thy 413
10: 1 of Solomon c the name of the LORD, 3807.1
11: 2 Of the nations c which the LORD said NIH
11:10 had commanded him c this thing, that *he* 5921
22: 8 for he doth not prophesy good c me, but 5921
22:18 thee that he would prophesy no good c me, 5921
22:23 and the LORD hath spoken evil c thee. 5921
2Ki 10:10 which the LORD spake c the house of 5921
17:15 c whom the LORD had charged them, NIH
19:21 word that the LORD hath spoken c him; 5921
19:32 Therefore thus saith the LORD c the king 413
22:13 c the words of this book that is found: 5921
22:13 unto all that which is written c us. 5921
1Ch 11:10 according to the word of the LORD c 5921
17:23 let the thing that thou hast spoken c thy 5921
17:23 and c his house be established for ever, 5921
19: 2 David sent messengers to comfort him c his 5921
22:12 and give thee charge c Israel, 5921
22:13 the LORD charged Moses with c Israel: 5921
23:14 Now c Moses the man of God, his sons NIH
24:21 C Rehabiah: of the sons of Rehabiah, 3807.1
24:29 C Kish: the son of Kish *was* Jerahmeel. 3807.1
26: 1 C the divisions of the porters: Of 3807.1
26:21 *As* c the sons of Laadan; the sons of NIH
2Ch 6:32 Moreover c the stranger, which *is* not of thy 413
8:15 unto the priests and Levites c any matter, 3807.1
8:15 concerning any matter, or c the treasures. 3807.1
12:15 and of Iddo the seer c genealogies? 3807.1
15:16 also c Maachah the mother of Asa the king, NIH
24:27 Now c his sons, and the greatness of NIH
31: 6 c the children of Israel and Judah, that dwelt NIH
31: 9 with the priests and the Levites c the heaps. 5921
34:21 c the words of the book that is found: 5921
34:26 Thus saith the LORD God of Israel c NIH
Ezr 5: 5 they returned answer by letter c this 5922
5:17 let the king send his pleasure to us c this 5922
6: 3 a decree c the house of God at Jerusalem, NIH
7:14 to inquire c Judah and Jerusalem, 5922
10: 2 yet now there is hope in Israel c this *thing*. 5921
Ne 1: 2 I asked them c the Jews that had escaped, 5921
1: 2 were left of the captivity, and c Jerusalem. 5921
9:23 c which thou hadst promised to their NIH
11:23 For *it was* the king's commandment c 5921
11:24 *was* at the king's hand in all matters c 3807.1
13:14 c this, and wipe not out my good deeds that 5921
13:22 c this also, and spare me according to NIH
Est 3: 2 for the king had so commanded c him. 3807.1
9:26 *of that* which they had seen c this *matter*, 5921
Job 36:33 The noise thereof sheweth c it, the cattle 5921
36:33 concerning it, the cattle also c the vapour. 5921
Ps 7: T c the words of Cush the Benjamite. 5921
17: 4 C the works of men, by the word of thy 3807.1
73: 8 and speak wickedly c oppression: NIH
90:13 and let it repent thee c thy servants. 5921
106:34 c whom the LORD commanded them: NIH
119:128 Therefore I esteem all *thy* precepts c all NIH
119:152 C thy testimonies, I have known of old that 4480
135:14 and he will repent himself c his servants. 5921
Ecc 1:13 search out by wisdom c all *things* that are 5921
3:18 I said in my heart c the estate of the sons of 5921
7:10 for thou dost not inquire wisely c this. 5921
Isa 1: 1 which he saw c Judah and Jerusalem in 5921
2: 1 that Isaiah the son of Amoz saw c Judah 5921
8: 1 write in it with a man's pen c 3807.1
16:13 LORD hath spoken c Moab since that time. 413
23: 5 As *at* the report c Egypt, so shall they be 3807.1
29:22 redeemed Abraham, c the house of Jacob, 413
30: 7 therefore have I cried c this, 3807.1
37: 9 he heard say c Tirhakah king of Ethiopia, 5921
37:22 word which the LORD hath spoken c him; 5921
37:33 Therefore thus saith the LORD c the king 413
45:11 Ask me of *things* to come c my sons, and 5921
45:11 c the work of my hands command ye me. 5921
Jer 7:22 c burnt offerings or sacrifices: 1697+5921
14: 1 that came to Jeremiah c the dearth. 1697+5921
14:15 Therefore thus saith the LORD c 5921
16: 3 For thus saith the LORD c the sons and 5921
16: 3 c the daughters that are born in this place, 5921
16: 3 c their mothers that bare them, and 5921
16: 3 c their fathers that begat them in this land; 5921
18: 7 *At what* instant I shall speak c a nation and 5921
18: 7 speak concerning a nation and c a kingdom, 5921
18: 9 *at what* instant I shall speak c a nation, and 5921
18: 9 and c a kingdom, to build and to plant *it*; 5921
22:18 Therefore thus saith the LORD c Jehoiakim 413
23:15 Therefore thus saith the LORD of hosts c 5921
25: 1 The word that came to Jeremiah c all 5921
27:19 For thus saith the LORD of hosts c 413
27:19 c the sea, and concerning the bases, and 5921
27:19 c the bases, and concerning the residue of 5921
27:19 c the residue of the vessels that remain in 5921
27:21 c the vessels that remain *in* the house of 5921
29:31 Thus saith the LORD c Shemaiah 413
30: 4 these *are* the words that the LORD spake c 413
30: 4 spake concerning Israel and c Judah. 413
32:36 the God of Israel, c this city, whereof ye say, 413
33: 4 c the houses of this city, and concerning 5921
33: 4 and c the houses of the kings of Judah, 5921
39:11 c Jeremiah to Nebuzar-adan the captain of 5921
42:19 The LORD hath said c you, O ye remnant 5921
44: 1 The word that came to Jeremiah c all 413
49: 1 C the Ammonites, thus saith the LORD; 3807.1
49: 7 C Edom, thus saith the LORD of hosts; 3807.1
49:23 C Damascus. Hamath is confounded, and 3807.1
49:28 C Kedar, and concerning the kingdoms of 3807.1
49:28 and c the kingdoms of Hazor, 3807.1
52:21 c the pillars, the height of one pillar *was* NIH
La 1:17 the LORD hath commanded c Jacob, 3807.1
Eze 13:16 of Israel which prophesy c Jerusalem, 413
14: 7 to a prophet to inquire of him c me; 871.1
14:22 ye shall be comforted c the evil that I have 5921
14:22 *even* c all that I have brought upon it. NIH
18: 2 that ye use this proverb c the land of Israel, 5921
21:28 Thus saith the Lord GOD c the Ammonites, 413
21:28 the Ammonites, and c their reproach; 413
Eze 36: 6 Prophesy therefore c the land of Israel, and 5921
44: 5 c all the ordinances of the house of 3807.1
45:14 C the ordinance of oil, the bath *of* oil, 2050.1
47:14 c the which I lifted up mine hand to give it NIH
Da 2:18 mercies of the God of heaven c this secret; 5922
5:29 his neck, and made a proclamation c him, 5922
6: 4 against Daniel c the kingdom; 4481+6655
6: 5 except we find *it* against him c the law of 871.2
6:12 spake before the king c the king's decree; 5922
6:17 that the purpose might not be changed c 871.2
7:12 **As** c the rest of the beasts, they had their 2050.3
8:13 How long *shall be* the vision c the daily NIH
Am 1: 1 which he saw c Israel in the days of Uzziah 5921
Ob 1: 1 Thus saith the Lord GOD c Edom; 3807.1
Mic 1: 1 which he saw c Samaria and Jerusalem. 5921
3: 5 Thus saith the LORD c the prophets that 5921
Na 1:14 the LORD hath given a commandment c 5921
Hag 2:11 Ask now the priests c the law, saying, NIH
Mt 4: 6 He shall give his angels charge c thee: 4012
11: 7 Jesus began to say unto the multitudes c 4012
16:11 that I spake *it* not to you c bread, 4012
Mk 5:16 with the devil, and *also* c the swine. 4012
7:17 his disciples asked him c the parable. 4012
Lk 2:17 the saying which was told them c this child. 4012
7:24 he began to speak unto the people c John, 4012
18:31 all *things* that are written by the prophets c NIG
22:37 for the *things* c me have an end. 4012
24:19 C Jesus of Nazareth, which was a prophet 4012
24:27 in all the scriptures the *things* c himself. 4012
24:44 *in* the prophets, and *in* the psalms, c me. 4012
Jn 7:12 much murmuring among the people c him: 4012
7:32 the people murmured such *things* c him; 4012
9:18 But the Jews did not believe c him, that he 4012
11:19 and Mary, to comfort them c their brother. 4012
Ac 1:16 the mouth of David spake before c Judas, 4012
2:25 For David speaketh c him, I foresaw 1519
8:12 preaching the *things* c the kingdom of God, 4012
13:34 And as c that he raised him up from NIG
19: 8 persuading the *things* c the kingdom of 4012
19:39 But if ye inquire any *thing* c other *matters*, 4012
21:24 *things*, whereof they were informed c thee, 4012
22:18 for they will not receive thy testimony c 4012
23:15 inquire something more perfectly c him: 4012
24:24 and heard him c the faith in Christ. 4012
25:16 have licence to answer for himself c 4012
28:21 We neither received letters out of Judea c 4012
28:22 for **as** c this sect, we know that every where 4012
28:23 persuading them c Jesus, both out of 4012
Ro 1: 3 C his Son Jesus Christ our Lord, which was 4012
9: 5 of whom **as** c the flesh Christ *came*, who is 2596
9:27 Esaias also crieth c Israel, Though 5228
11:28 As c the gospel, *they are* enemies for your 2596
16:19 unto *that which is* good, and simple c evil. 1519
1Co 5: 3 c him that hath so done this *deed*, NIG
7: 1 Now c *the things* whereof ye wrote unto 4012
7:25 Now c virgins I have no commandment of 4012
8: 4 **As** c therefore the eating of those things 4012
12: 1 Now c spiritual *gifts*, brethren, I would not 4012
16: 1 Now c the collection for the saints, as I 4012
2Co 8:23 *he is* my partner and fellowhelper c you: 1519
11:21 I speak **as** c reproach, as though we had 2596
Eph 4:22 That ye put off c the former conversation 2596
5:32 but I speak c Christ and the church. 1519
Php 3: 6 C zeal, persecuting the church; 2596
4:15 communicated with me **as** c giving 1519+3056
1Th 3: 2 and to comfort you c your faith: 4012
4:13 brethren, c them which are asleep, that ye 4012
5:18 for this *is* the will of God in Christ Jesus c 1519
1Ti 1:19 put away, c faith have made shipwrack: 4012
6:21 Which some professing have erred c 4012
2Ti 2:18 Who c the truth have erred, saying that 4012
3: 8 men of corrupt minds, reprobate c the faith. 4012
Heb 7:14 of which tribe Moses spake nothing c 4012
11:20 blessed Jacob and Esau c *things* to come. 4012
11:22 and gave commandment c his bones. 4012
1Pe 4:12 think it not strange c the fiery trial which is NIG
2Pe 3: 9 The Lord is not slack c *his* promise, as some NIG
1Jn 2:26 These *things* have I written unto you c 4012

CONCISION (1)

Php 3: 2 beware of evil workers, beware of the c. 2699

CONCLUDE (1) [CONCLUDED, CONCLUSION]

Ro 3:28 Therefore we c that a man is justified by 3049

CONCLUDED (3) [CONCLUDE]

Ac 21:25 c that they observe no such *thing*, save only 2919
Ro 11:32 For God hath c *them* all in unbelief, that he 4788
Gal 3:22 But the scripture hath c all under sin, 4788

CONCLUSION (1) [CONCLUDE]

Ecc 12:13 Let us hear the c of the whole matter: 5490

CONCORD (1)

2Co 6:15 And what c hath Christ with Belial? or 4857

CONCOURSE (2)

Pr 1:21 She crieth in the chief place of c, in 1993
Ac 19:40 whereby we may give an account of this c. 4963

CONCUBINE (22) [CONCUBINES]

Ge 22:24 his c, whose name *was* Reumah, she bare 6370
35:22 and lay with Bilhah his father's c: 6370
36:12 Timna was c to Eliphaz Esau's son; and 6370
Jdg 8:31 his c that *was* in Shechem, she also bare 6370
19: 1 who took to him a c out of 6370
19: 2 his c played the whore against him, and 6370
19: 9 he, and his c, and his servant, his father in 6370
19:10 two asses saddled, his c also *was* with him. 6370
19:24 *here is* my daughter a maiden, and his c; 6370
19:25 so the man took his c, and brought *her* forth 6370
19:27 the woman his c *was* fallen down *at* 6370
19:29 and laid hold on his c, and divided her, 6370
20: 4 to Benjamin, I and my c, to lodge. 6370

Jdg 20: 5 and my c have they forced, that she is dead. 6370
20: 6 I took my c, and cut her in pieces, and 6370
2Sa 3: 7 Saul had a c, whose name *was* Rizpah, 6370
3: 7 hast thou gone in unto my father's c? 6370
21:11 daughter of Aiah, the c of Saul, had done. 6370
1Ch 1:32 Now the sons of Keturah, Abraham's c: 6370
2:46 Caleb's c, bare Haran, and Moza, and 6370
2:48 Maachah, Caleb's c, bare Sheber, and 6370
7:14 his c the Aramitess bare Machir the father 6370

CONCUBINES (17) [CONCUBINE]
Ge 25: 6 unto the sons of the c, which Abraham had, 6370
2Sa 5:13 David took *him* mo c and wives out of 6370
15:16 *which were* c, to keep the house. 6370
16:21 unto Absalom, Go in unto thy father's c, 6370
16:22 Absalom went in unto his father's c in 6370
19: 5 lives of thy wives, and the lives of thy c, 6370
20: 3 the king took the ten women *his* c, 6370
1Ki 11: 3 princesses, and three hundred c: 6370
1Ch 3: 9 beside the sons of the c, and Tamar their 6370
2Ch 11:21 of Absalom above all his wives and his c: 6370
11:21 he took eighteen wives, and threescore c; 6370
Est 2:14 the king's chamberlain, which kept the c: 6370
SS 6: 8 fourscore c, and virgins without number. 6370
6: 9 *yea,* the queens and the c, and they praised 6370
Da 5: 2 and his princes, his wives, and his c, 3904
5: 3 and his princes, his wives, and his c, 3904
5:23 thou, and thy lords, thy wives, and thy c, 3904

CONCUPISCENCE (3)
Ro 7: 8 wrought in me all *manner of* c. 1939
Col 3: 5 evil c, and covetousness, which is idolatry: 1939
1Th 4: 5 Not in the lust of c, even as the Gentiles 1939

CONDEMN (24) [CONDEMNATION, CONDEMNED, CONDEMNEST, CONDEMNETH, CONDEMNING, UNCONDEMNED]
Ex 22: 9 *and* whom the judges shall c, he shall pay 7561
Dt 25: 1 justify the righteous, and c the wicked. 7561
Job 9:20 justify myself, mine own mouth shall c me: 7561
10: 2 I will say unto God, Do not c me; shew me 7561
34:17 and wilt thou c him that is most just? 7561
40: 8 wilt thou c me, that thou mayest be 7561
Ps 37:33 in his hand, nor c him when he is judged. 7561
94:21 of the righteous, and c the innocent blood. 7561
109:31 to save *him* from those that c his soul. 8199
Pr 12: 2 but a man of wicked devices will he c. 7561
Isa 50: 9 will help me; who *is* he *that* shall c me? 7561
54:17 rise against thee in judgment thou shalt c. 7561
Mt 12:41 with this generation, and shall c it: 2632
12:42 with this generation, and shall c it: 2632
20:18 *the* scribes, and they shall c him to death, 2632
Mk 10:33 and they shall c him to death, and 2632
Lk 6:37 c not, and ye shall not be condemned: 2613
11:31 the men of this generation, and c them: 2632
11:32 with this generation, and shall c it: 2632
Jn 3:17 For God sent not his Son into the world to c 2919
8:11 Jesus said unto her, Neither do I c thee: 2632
2Co 7: 3 I speak not *this* to c *you:* for I have said 2633
1Jn 3:20 For if *our* heart c us, God is greater than 2607
3:21 if our heart c us not, *then* have we 2607

CONDEMNATION (12) [CONDEMN]
Lk 23:40 fear God, seeing thou art in the same c? 2917
Jn 3:19 And this is the c, that light is come into 2920
5:24 everlasting life, and shall not come into c; 2920
Ro 5:16 for the judgment *was* by one to c, but 2631
5:18 of one *judgment came* upon all men to c; 2631
8: 1 now no c to them *which are* in Christ Jesus 2631
1Co 11:34 at home; that ye come not together unto c. 2917
2Co 3: 9 For if the ministration of c *be* glory, 2633
1Ti 3: 6 up with pride he fall into the c of the devil. 2917
Jas 3: 1 knowing that we shall receive the greater c. 2917
5:12 and *your* nay, nay; lest ye fall into c. 2920
Jude 1: 4 who were before of old ordained to this c, 2917

CONDEMNED (21) [CONDEMN]
2Ch 36: 3 c the land in an hundred talents of silver 6064
Job 32: 3 had found no answer, and *yet* had c Job. 7561
Ps 109: 7 When he shall be judged, let him be c: and 7563
Am 2: 8 they drink the wine of the c *in* the house of 6064
Mt 12: 7 ye would not have c the guiltless. 2613
12:37 and by thy words thou shalt be c. 2613
27: 3 when he saw that he was c, 2632
Mk 14:64 And they all c him to be guilty of death. 2632
Lk 6:37 condemn not, and ye shall not be c: forgive, 2613
24:20 our rulers delivered him to be c to death, 2917
Jn 3:18 He that believeth on him is not c: but 2919
3:18 but he that believeth not is c already, 2919
8:10 those thine accusers? hath no *man* c thee? 2632
Ro 8: 3 sinful flesh, and for sin, c sin in the flesh: 2632
1Co 11:32 that we should not be c with the world. 2632
Tit 2: 8 Sound speech that **cannot be** c; that he that 176
3:11 is subverted, and sinneth, being c **of himself**. 843
Heb 11: 7 by the which he c the world, and 2632
Jas 5: 6 Ye have c *and* killed the just; *and* he doth 2613
5: 9 one against another, brethren, lest ye be c: 2632
2Pe 2: 6 Gomorrha into ashes c *them* with an 2632

CONDEMNEST (1) [CONDEMN]
Ro 2: 1 thou judgest another, thou c thyself; 2632

CONDEMNETH (4) [CONDEMN]
Job 15: 6 Thine own mouth c thee, and not I; yea, 7561
Pr 17:15 justifieth the wicked, and he that c the just, 7561
Ro 8:34 Who *is* he that c? *It is* Christ that died, 2632
14:22 Happy *is* he that c not himself in *that thing* 2919

CONDEMNING (2) [CONDEMN]
1Ki 8:32 do, and judge thy servants, c the wicked, 7561
Ac 13:27 they have fulfilled *them* in c *him.* 2919

CONDESCEND (1)
Ro 12:16 not high *things,* but c **to** *men* of low estate. 4879

CONDITION (1) [CONDITIONS]
1Sa 11: 2 On this c will I make *a covenant* with you, NIH

CONDITIONS (1) [CONDITION]
Lk 14:32 an ambassage, and desireth c of peace. 3588

CONDUCT (3) [CONDUCTED]
2Sa 19:15 to meet the king, to c the king **over** Jordan. 5674
19:31 Jordan with the king, to c him *over* Jordan. 7971
1Co 16:11 but c him **forth** in peace, that he may come 4311

CONDUCTED (2) [CONDUCT]
2Sa 19:40 all the people of Judah c the king, and 5674
Ac 17:15 And they that c Paul brought him unto 2525

CONDUIT (4)
2Ki 18:17 and stood by the c of the upper pool, 8585
20:20 and a c, and brought water into the city, 8585
Isa 7: 3 at the end of the c of the upper pool in 8585
36: 2 he stood by the c of the upper pool in 8585

CONEY (1) [CONIES, CONY]
Dt 14: 7 *as* the camel, and the hare, and the c: 8227

CONFECTION (1) [CONFECTIONARIES]
Ex 30:35 a c *after* the art of the apothecary, 7545

CONFECTIONARIES (1) [CONFECTION]
1Sa 8:13 he will take your daughters to be c, and 7548

CONFEDERACY (3) [CONFEDERATE]
Isa 8:12 Say ye not, A c, to all *them to* whom this 7195
8:12 all *them to* whom this people shall say, A c; 7195
Ob 1: 7 All the men of thy c have brought thee *even* 1285

CONFEDERATE (3) [CONFEDERACY]
Ge 14:13 and these *were* c with Abram. 1167+1285
Ps 83: 5 *with one* consent: they are c against thee: 1285
Isa 7: 2 of David, saying, Syria is c with Ephraim. 5117

CONFERENCE (1) [CONFERRED]
Gal 2: 6 *to be somewhat* **in c added** nothing to me: 4323

CONFERRED (4) [CONFERENCE]
1Ki 1: 7 he c with Joab the son of Zeruiah, 1697+1961
Ac 4:15 of the council, they c among themselves, 4820
25:12 when he had c with the council, answered, 4814
Gal 1:16 immediately I c not with flesh and blood: 4323

CONFESS (28) [CONFESSED, CONFESSETH, CONFESSING, CONFESSION]
Lev 5: 5 he shall c that he hath sinned in that *thing:* 3034
16:21 c over him all the iniquities of the children 3034
26:40 If they shall c their iniquity, and 3034
Nu 5: 7 they shall c their sin which they have done: 3034
1Ki 8:33 c thy name, and pray, and 3034
8:35 c thy name, and turn from their sin, 3034
2Ch 6:24 shall return and c thy name, and pray and 3034
6:26 c thy name, *and* turn from their sin, 3034
Ne 1: 6 c the sins of the children of Israel, 3034
Job 40:14 will I also c unto thee that thine own right 3034
Ps 32: 5 I will c my transgressions unto the LORD; 3034
Mt 10:32 therefore shall c me before men, 3670
10:32 him will I c also before my Father which is 3670
Lk 12: 8 Whosoever shall c me before men, 3670
12: 8 him shall the Son of man also c before 3670
Jn 9:22 that if any *man* did c that he *was* Christ, 3670
12:42 of the Pharisees they did not c *him,* lest 3670
Ac 23: 8 angel nor spirit: but the Pharisees c both. 3670
24:14 But this I c unto thee, that after the way 3670
Ro 10: 9 That if thou shalt c with thy mouth the Lord 3670
14:11 to me, and every tongue shall c to God. 1843
15: 9 For this cause I will c to thee among 1843
Php 2:11 And *that* every tongue should c that Jesus 1843
Jas 5:16 C *your* faults one to another, and pray one 1843
1Jn 1: 9 If we c our sins, he is faithful and just to 3670
4:15 Whosoever shall c that Jesus is the Son of 3670
2Jn 1: 7 who c not that Jesus Christ is come in 3670
Rev 3: 5 but I will c his name before my Father, and 1843

CONFESSED (7) [CONFESS]
Ezr 10: 1 when he had c, weeping and 3034
Ne 9: 2 stood and c their sins, and the iniquities of 3034
9: 3 *another* fourth *part* they c, and 3034
Jn 1:20 And he c, and denied not; but confessed, I 3670
1:20 and denied not; but c, I am not the Christ. 3670
Ac 19:18 and c, and shewed their deeds. 1843
Heb 11:13 and c that they were strangers and 3670

CONFESSETH (3) [CONFESS]
Pr 28:13 whoso c and forsaketh *them* shall have 3034
1Jn 4: 2 Every spirit that c that Jesus Christ is come 3670
4: 3 And every spirit that c not that Jesus Christ 3670

CONFESSING (3) [CONFESS]
Da 9:20 c my sin and the sin of my people Israel, 3034
Mt 3: 6 were baptized of him in Jordan, c their sins. 1843
Mk 1: 5 of him in the river *of* Jordan, c their sins. 1843

CONFESSION (6) [CONFESS]
Jos 7:19 God of Israel, and make c unto him; 8426
2Ch 30:22 **making** c to the LORD God of their 3034
Ezr 10:11 make c unto the LORD God of your 8426
Da 9: 4 **made** my c, and said, O Lord, the great and 3034
Ro 10:10 with the mouth c is **made** unto salvation. 3670
1Ti 6:13 before Pontius Pilate witnessed a good c; 3671

CONFIDENCE (38) [CONFIDENT]
Jdg 9:26 and the men of Shechem **put** their c in him. 982
2Ki 18:19 What c *is* this where*in* thou trustest? 986
Job 4: 6 *Is* not *this* thy fear, thy c, thy hope; and 3690
18:14 His c shall be rooted out of his tabernacle, 4009
31:24 or have said to the fine gold, *Thou art* my c; 4009
Ps 65: 5 *who art* the c of all the ends of the earth, 4009
118: 8 to trust in the LORD than to **put** c in man. 982
118: 9 trust in the LORD than to **put** c in princes. 982
Pr 3:26 For the LORD shall be thy c, and 3689
14:26 In the fear of the LORD *is* strong c: and 4009
21:22 casteth down the strength of the c thereof. 4009
25:19 C in an unfaithful *man* in time of trouble *is* 4009
Isa 30:15 in quietness and in c shall be your strength: 985
36: 4 What c *is* this where*in* thou trustest? 986
Jer 48:13 of Israel was ashamed of Beth-el their c. 4009
Eze 28:26 yea, they shall dwell with c, when I have 983
29:16 it shall be no more the c of the house of 4009
Mic 7: 5 ye not in a friend, **put** ye not c in a guide: 982
Ac 28:31 with all c, no man forbidding him. 3954
2Co 1:15 And in this c I was minded to come unto 4006
2: 3 having c in you all, that my joy is *the joy* of 3982
7:16 therefore that I **have** c in you in all *things.* 2292
8:22 upon the great c which *I have* in you. 4006
10: 2 not be bold when I am present with *that* c, 4006
11:17 as *it were* foolishly, in this c of boasting. 5287
Gal 5:10 I have c in you through the Lord, that you 3982
Eph 3:12 and access with c by the faith of him. 4006
Php 1:25 And **having** this c, I know that I shall abide 3982
3: 3 in Christ Jesus, and **have** no c in the flesh. 3982
3: 4 Though I *might* also have c in the flesh. 4006
2Th 3: 4 And we have c in the Lord touching you, 3982
Phm 1:21 **Having** c in thy obedience I wrote unto 3982
Heb 3: 6 if we hold fast the c and the rejoicing of 3954
3:14 if we hold the beginning of *our* c stedfast 5287
10:35 Cast not away therefore your c, which hath 3954
1Jn 2:28 we may have c, and not be ashamed before 3954
3:21 us not, *then* have we c towards God. 3954
5:14 And this is the c that we have in him, that, 3954

CONFIDENCES (1) [CONFIDENCE, CONFIDENCES, CONFIDENT]
Jer 2:37 for the LORD hath rejected thy c, and 4009

CONFIDENT (8) [CONFIDENTLY]
Ps 27: 3 should rise against me, in this *will* I *be* c. 982
Pr 14:16 from evil: but the fool rageth, and *is* c. 982
Ro 2:19 And art c that thou thyself art a guide of 3982
2Co 5: 6 Therefore *we are* always c, knowing that, 2292
5: 8 We are c, I say, and willing rather to be 2292
9: 4 should be ashamed in this *same* c boasting. 5287
Php 1: 6 Being c of this very *thing,* that he which 3982
1:14 in the Lord, **waxing** c by my bonds, 3982

CONFIDENTLY (1) [CONFIDENT]
Lk 22:59 space of one hour after another c **affirmed**, 1340

CONFIRM (13) [CONFIRMATION, CONFIRMED, CONFIRMETH, CONFIRMING]
Ru 4: 7 concerning changing, for to c all things; 6965
1Ki 1:14 will come in after thee, and c thy words. 4390
2Ki 15:19 that his hand might be with him to c 2388
Est 9:29 to c this second letter of Purim. 6965
9:31 To c these days of Purim in their times 6965
Ps 68: 9 whereby thou didst c thine inheritance, 3559
Isa 35: 3 ye the weak hands, and c the feeble knees. 553
Eze 13: 6 *others* to hope that *they* would c the word. 6965
Da 9:27 he shall c the covenant with many *for* one 1396
11: 1 *even* I, stood to c and to strengthen him. 2388
Ro 15: 8 to c the promises made unto the fathers: 950
1Co 1: 8 Who shall also c you unto the end, *that ye* 950
2Co 2: 8 Wherefore I beseech you that *you* would c 2964

CONFIRMATION (2) [CONFIRM]
Php 1: 7 and *in* the defence and c of the gospel, 951
Heb 6:16 an oath for c *is* to them an end of all strife. 951

CONFIRMED (13) [CONFIRM]
2Sa 7:24 For thou hast c to thyself thy people Israel 3559
2Ki 14: 5 as soon as the kingdom was c in his hand, 2388
1Ch 14: 2 David perceived that the LORD had c him 3559
16:17 hath c the same to Jacob for a law, *and* 5975
Est 9:32 the decree of Esther c these matters of 6965
Ps 105:10 c the same unto Jacob for a law, *and* 5975
Da 9:12 he hath c his words, which he spake against 6965
Ac 15:32 the brethren with many words, and c *them.* 1991
1Co 1: 6 Even as the testimony of Christ was c in 950
Gal 3:15 *it be* but a man's covenant, *yet if it be* c, 2964
3:17 that was c **before** of God in Christ, the law, 4300
Heb 2: 3 and was c unto us by them that heard *him;* 950
6:17 immutability of his counsel, c *it* by an oath: 3315

CONFIRMETH (3) [CONFIRM]
Nu 30:14 he c them, because he held his peace at her 6965
Dt 27:26 Cursed *be* he that c not *all* the words of this 6965
Isa 44:26 That c the word of his servant, and 6965

CONFIRMING (3) [CONFIRM]
Mk 16:20 and c the word with signs following. 950
Ac 14:22 C the souls of the disciples, *and* 1991
15:41 through Syria and Cilicia, c the churches. 1991

CONFISCATION (1)
Ezr 7:26 or to c of goods, or to imprisonment. 6065

CONFLICT (2)
Php 1:30 Having the same c which ye saw in me, and 73
Col 2: 1 For I would that ye knew what great c I have 73

CONFORMABLE (1) [CONFORMED]
Php 3:10 his sufferings, being **made** c unto his death; 4833

CONFORMED (2) [CONFORMABLE]
Ro 8:29 he also did predestinate *to be* c **to** the image 4832
12: 2 And be not c **to** this world: but be ye 4964

C

CONFOUND (5) [CONFOUNDED]
Ge 11: 7 let us go down, and there c their language, 1101
11: 9 the LORD did there c the language of all 1101
Jer 1:17 at their faces, lest I c thee before them. 2865
1Co 1:27 foolish *things* of the world to c the wise; *2617*
1:27 the world to c the *things which are* mighty; *2617*

CONFOUNDED (50) [CONFOUND]
2Ki 19:26 of small power, they were dismayed and c; 954
Job 6:20 They were c because they had hoped; 954
Ps 22: 5 they trusted in thee, and were not c. 954
35: 4 Let them be c and put to shame that seek 954
40:14 c together that seek after my soul to destroy 2659
69: 6 let not those that seek thee be c for my 3637
70: 2 be ashamed and c that seek after my soul: 2659
71:13 Let them be c *and* consumed that are 954
71:24 for they are c, for they are brought unto 954
83:17 Let them be c and troubled for ever; yea, 954
97: 7 C be all they that serve graven images, 954
129: 5 Let them all be c and turned back that hate 954
Isa 1:29 ye shall be c for the gardens that ye have 2659
19: 9 and they that weave networks, shall be c. 954
24:23 the moon shall be c, and the sun ashamed, 2659
37:27 of small power, they were dismayed and c: 954
41:11 against thee shall be ashamed and c: 3637
45:16 shall be ashamed, and also c, all of them: 3637
45:17 ye shall not be ashamed nor c world 3637
50: 7 will help me; therefore shall I not be c: 3637
54: 4 neither be thou c; for thou shalt not be put 3637
Jer 9:19 we are greatly c, because we have forsaken 954
10:14 every founder is c by the graven image: 954
14: 3 they were ashamed and c, and covered their 3637
15: 9 she hath been ashamed and c: and 2659
17:18 Let them be c that persecute me, but let not 954
17:18 that persecute me, but let not me be c: 954
22:22 be ashamed and c for all thy wickedness. 3637
31:19 yea, even c, because I did bear the reproach 3637
46:24 The daughter of Egypt shall be c; she shall 954
48: 1 Kiriathaim is c *and* taken: Misgab is 954
48: 1 *and* taken: Misgab is c and dismayed. 954
48:20 Moab is c; for it is broken down: howl and 954
49:23 Hamath is c, and Arpad: for they have heard 954
50: 2 say, Babylon is taken, Bel is c, Merodach is 954
50: 2 her idols are c, her images are broken in 954
50:12 Your mother shall be sore c; she that bare 954
51:17 every founder is c by the graven image: 954
51:47 her whole land shall be c, and all her slain 954
51:51 We are c, because we have heard reproach: 954
Eze 16:52 yea, be thou c also, and bear thy shame, 954
16:54 mayest be c in all that thou hast done, 3637
16:63 be c, and never open thy mouth any more, 954
36:32 be ashamed and c for your own ways, 3637
Mic 3: 7 the seers be ashamed, and the diviners c: 2659
7:16 nations shall see and be c at all their might: 954
Zec 10: 5 and the riders on horses shall be c. 3001
Ac 2: 6 and were c, because that every man heard *4797*
9:22 and c the Jews which dwelt at Damascus, *4797*
1Pe 2: 6 and he that believeth on him shall not be c. *2617*

CONFUSED (2) [CONFUSION]
Isa 9: 5 every battle of the warrior *is* with c **noise**, 7494
Ac 19:32 for the assembly was c; and the more part *4797*

CONFUSION (26) [CONFUSED]
Lev 18:23 before a beast to lie down thereto: it *is* c. 8397
20:12 they have wrought c; their blood *shall be* 8397
1Sa 20:30 hast chosen the son of Jesse to thine own c, 1322
20:30 and unto the c of thy mother's nakedness? 1322
Ezr 9: 7 to captivity, and to a spoil, and to c of face, 1322
Job 10:15 *I am* full of c; therefore see thou mine 7036
Ps 35: 4 and **brought to** c that devise my hurt. 2659
35:26 **brought to** c together that rejoice at mine 2659
44:15 My c *is* continually before me, and 3639
70: 2 and **put to** c, that desire my hurt. 3637
71: 1 do I put my trust: let me never be **put to** c. 954
109:29 let them cover *themselves with* their own c, 1322
Isa 24:10 The city of c is broken down: every house 8414
30: 3 and the trust in the shadow of Egypt *your* c. 3639
34:11 and he shall stretch out upon it the line of c, 8414
41:29 their molten images *are* wind and c. 8414
45:16 they shall go to c together *that are* makers 3639
61: 7 and *for* c they shall rejoice in their portion: 3639
Jer 3:25 down in our shame, and our c covereth us: 3639
7:19 *do they* not *provoke* themselves to the c of 1322
20:11 *their* everlasting c shall never be forgotten. 3639
Da 9: 7 but unto us c of faces, as *at* this day; 1322
9: 8 O Lord, to us *belongeth* c of face, to our 1322
Ac 19:29 And the whole city was filled with c: and *4799*
1Co 14:33 For God is not *the author* of c, but of peace, *181*
Jas 3:16 and strife *is*, there *is* c and every evil work. *181*

CONGEALED (1)
Ex 15: 8 the depths were c in the heart of the sea. 7087

CONGRATULATE (1)
1Ch 18:10 to c him, because he had fought against 1288

CONGREGATION (364) [CONGREGATIONS]
Ex 12: 3 Speak ye unto all the c of Israel, saying, 5712
12: 6 the whole assembly of the c of Israel shall 5712
12:19 even that soul shall be cut off from the c of 5712
12:47 All the c of Israel shall keep it. 5712
16: 1 all the c of the children of Israel came unto 5712
16: 2 the whole c of the children of Israel 5712
16: 9 Say unto all the c of the children of Israel, 5712
16:10 as Aaron spake unto the whole c of 5712
16:22 all the rulers of the c came and told Moses. 5712
17: 1 all the c of the children of Israel journeyed 5712
27:21 In the tabernacle of the c without the vail, 4150
28:43 they come in unto the tabernacle of the c, 4150
29: 4 unto the door of the tabernacle of the c, 4150
29:10 to be brought before the tabernacle of the c: 4150
29:11 *by* the door of the tabernacle of the c. 4150
29:30 of the c to minister in the holy *place*. 4150
Ex 29:32 *by* the door of the tabernacle of the c. 4150
29:42 the tabernacle of the c before the LORD: 4150
29:44 I will sanctify the tabernacle of the c, and 4150
30:16 it for the service of the tabernacle of the c; 4150
30:18 shalt put it between the tabernacle of the c 4150
30:20 When they go into the tabernacle of the c, 4150
30:26 thou shalt anoint the tabernacle of the c 4150
30:36 the Testimony in the tabernacle of the c, 4150
31: 7 The tabernacle of the c, and the ark of 4150
33: 7 and called it the Tabernacle of the C. 4150
33: 7 went out unto the Tabernacle of the C, 4150
34:31 all the rulers of the c returned unto him: 5712
35: 1 Moses gathered all the c of the children of 5712
35: 4 Moses spake unto all the c of the children 5712
35:20 all the c of the children of Israel departed 5712
35:21 to the work of the tabernacle of the c, 4150
38: 8 *at* the door of the tabernacle of the c. 4150
38:25 numbered of the c *was* an hundred talents, 5712
38:30 to the door of the tabernacle of the c, 4150
39:32 the tabernacle of the tent of the c finished: 4150
39:40 of the tabernacle, for the tent of the c, 4150
40: 2 set up the tabernacle of the tent of the c. 4150
40: 6 door of the tabernacle of the tent of the c. 4150
40: 7 shalt set the laver between the tent of the c 4150
40:12 unto the door of the tabernacle of the c, 4150
40:22 he put the table in the tent of the c, 4150
40:24 he put the candlestick in the tent of the c, 4150
40:26 he put the golden altar in the tent of the c 4150
40:29 door of the tabernacle of the tent of the c, 4150
40:30 he set the laver between the tent of the c 4150
40:32 When they went into the tent of the c, and 4150
40:34 a cloud covered the tent of the c, and 4150
40:35 was not able to enter into the tent of the c, 4150
Lev 1: 1 unto him out of the tabernacle of the c, 4150
1: 3 the tabernacle of the c before the LORD. 4150
1: 5 *is by* the door of the tabernacle of the c. 4150
3: 2 kill it *at* the door of the tabernacle of the c: 4150
3: 8 and kill it before the tabernacle of the c: 4150
3:13 and kill it before the tabernacle of the c: 4150
4: 4 the tabernacle of the c before the LORD; 4150
4: 5 and bring it to the tabernacle of the c: 4150
4: 7 which *is* in the tabernacle of the c; 4150
4: 7 *is at* the door of the tabernacle of the c. 4150
4:13 if the whole c of Israel sin through 5712
4:14 the c shall offer a young bullock for the sin, 6951
4:14 bring him before the tabernacle of the c. 4150
4:15 the elders of the c shall lay their hands 5712
4:16 bullock's blood to the tabernacle of the c: 4150
4:18 that *is* in the tabernacle of the c, and shall 4150
4:18 *is at* the door of the tabernacle of the c. 4150
4:21 first bullock: it *is* a sin offering for the c. 6951
6:16 in the court of the tabernacle of the c they 4150
6:26 in the court of the tabernacle of the c. 4150
6:30 c to reconcile *withal* in the holy *place*, shall 4150
8: 3 gather thou all the c together unto the door 5712
8: 3 unto the door of the tabernacle of the c. 4150
8: 4 unto the door of the tabernacle of the c. 4150
8: 5 Moses said unto the c, This *is* the thing 5712
8:31 flesh *at* the door of the tabernacle of the c: 4150
8:33 of the tabernacle of the c *in* seven days, 4150
8:35 *at* the door of the tabernacle of the c day 4150
9: 5 commanded before the tabernacle of the c: 4150
9: 5 all the c drew near and stood before 5712
9:23 and Aaron went into the tabernacle of the c, 4150
10: 7 out from the door of the tabernacle of the c, 4150
10: 9 when ye go into the tabernacle of the c, 4150
10:17 given it you to bear the iniquity of the c, 5712
12: 6 unto the door of the tabernacle of the c, 4150
14:11 *at* the door of the tabernacle of the c: 4150
14:23 unto the door of the tabernacle of the c, 4150
15:14 unto the door of the tabernacle of the c, 4150
15:29 to the door of the tabernacle of the c. 4150
16: 5 he shall take of the c of the children of 5712
16: 7 *at* the door of the tabernacle of the c. 4150
16:16 so shall he do for the tabernacle of the c, 4150
16:17 c when he goeth in to make an atonement 4150
16:17 for his household, and for all the c of Israel. 6951
16:20 the holy *place*, and the tabernacle of the c, 4150
16:23 shall come into the tabernacle of the c, 4150
16:33 an atonement for the tabernacle of the c, 4150
16:33 the priests, and for all the people of the c. 6951
17: 4 not unto the door of the tabernacle of the c, 4150
17: 5 unto the door of the tabernacle of the c, 4150
17: 6 *at* the door of the tabernacle of the c, 4150
17: 9 not unto the door of the tabernacle of the c, 4150
19: 2 Speak unto all the c of the children of 5712
19:21 unto the door of the tabernacle of the c, 4150
24: 3 of the Testimony, in the tabernacle of the c, 4150
24:14 upon his head, and let all the c stone him. 5712
24:16 all the c shall certainly stone him: 5712
Nu 1: 1 in the tabernacle of the c, on the first *day* of 4150
1: 2 Take ye the sum of all the c of the children 5712
1:16 These *were* the renowned of the c, 5712
1:18 they assembled all the c together on 5712
1:53 that there be no wrath upon the c of 5712
2: 2 far off about the tabernacle of the c shall 4150
2:17 the tabernacle of the c shall set forward 4150
3: 7 the charge of the whole c before 5712
3: 7 congregation before the tabernacle of the c, 4150
3: 8 the instruments of the tabernacle of the c, 4150
3:25 tabernacle of the c *shall be* the tabernacle, 4150
3:25 for the door of the tabernacle of the c, 4150
3:38 *even* before the tabernacle of the c 4150
4: 3 to do the work in the tabernacle of the c. 4150
4: 4 sons of Kohath in the tabernacle of the c, 4150
4:15 sons of Kohath in the tabernacle of the c. 4150
4:23 to do the work in the tabernacle of the c. 4150
4:25 the tabernacle of the c, his covering, and 4150
4:25 for the door of the tabernacle of the c, 4150
4:28 sons of Gershon in the tabernacle of the c: 4150
4:30 to do the work of the tabernacle of the c. 4150
4:31 to all their service in the tabernacle of the c; 4150
4:33 all their service, in the tabernacle of the c, 4150
4:34 the chief of the c numbered the sons of 5712
4:35 for the work in the tabernacle of the c: 4150
Nu 4:37 *might* do service in the tabernacle of the c, 4150
4:39 for the work in the tabernacle of the c, 4150
4:41 *might* do service in the tabernacle of the c, 4150
4:43 for the work in the tabernacle of the c, 4150
4:47 of the burden in the tabernacle of the c, 4150
6:10 to the door of the tabernacle of the c: 4150
6:13 unto the door of the tabernacle of the c: 4150
6:18 *at* the door of the tabernacle of the c, 4150
7: 5 to do the service of the tabernacle of the c; 4150
7:89 the tabernacle of the c to speak with him, 4150
8: 9 the Levites before the tabernacle of the c: 4150
8:15 to do the service of the tabernacle of the c: 4150
8:19 children of Israel in the tabernacle of the c, 4150
8:20 and all the c of the children of Israel, 5712
8:22 in the tabernacle of the c before Aaron, 4150
8:24 upon the service of the tabernacle of the c: 4150
8:26 their brethren in the tabernacle of the c, 4150
10: 3 thee at the door of the tabernacle of the c. 4150
10: 7 when the c is to be gathered together, you 6951
11:16 bring them unto the tabernacle of the c, 4150
12: 4 out ye three unto the tabernacle of the c. 4150
13:26 and to all the c of the children of Israel, 5712
13:26 unto all the c, and shewed them the fruit of 5712
14: 1 all the c lifted up their voice, and cried; 5712
14: 2 the whole c said unto them, Would God 5712
14: 5 assembly of the c of the children of Israel. 5712
14:10 all the c bade stone them with stones. 5712
14:10 of the c before all the children of Israel. 4150
14:27 How long *shall I bear* with this evil c, 5712
14:35 I will surely do it unto all this evil c, 5712
14:36 and made all the c to murmur against him, 5712
15:15 ordinance *shall be both* for you *of* the c, 6951
15:24 ignorance without the knowledge of the c, 5712
15:24 that all the c shall offer one young bullock 5712
15:25 for all the c of the children of Israel, 5712
15:26 it shall be forgiven all the c of the children 5712
15:33 unto Moses and Aaron, and unto all the c. 5712
15:35 all the c shall stone him with stones without 5712
15:36 all the c brought him without the camp, 5712
16: 2 famous in the c, men of renown: 4150
16: 3 seeing all the c *are* holy, every one of them, 5712
16: 3 lift you up yourselves above the c of 6951
16: 9 hath separated you from the c of Israel, 5712
16: 9 to stand before the c to minister unto them? 5712
16:18 stood *in* the door of the tabernacle of the c 4150
16:19 Korah gathered all the c against them unto 5712
16:19 unto the door of the tabernacle of the c: 4150
16:19 of the LORD appeared unto all the c. 5712
16:21 Separate yourselves from among this c, that 5712
16:22 and wilt thou be wroth with all the c? 5712
16:24 Speak unto the c, saying, Get you up from 5712
16:26 he spake unto the c, saying, Depart, I pray 5712
16:33 and they perished from among the c. 6951
16:41 on the morrow all the c of the children of 5712
16:42 when the c was gathered against Moses and 5712
16:42 they looked toward the tabernacle of the c: 4150
16:43 Aaron came before the tabernacle of the c. 4150
16:45 Get you up from among this c, that I may 5712
16:46 go quickly unto the c, and make an 5712
16:47 and ran into the midst of the c; 6951
16:50 unto the door of the tabernacle of the c: 4150
17: 4 tabernacle of the c before the Testimony, 4150
18: 4 keep the charge of the tabernacle of the c, 4150
18: 6 to do the service of the tabernacle of the c. 4150
18:21 *even* the service of the tabernacle of the c. 4150
18:22 come nigh the tabernacle of the c, 4150
18:23 do the service of the tabernacle of the c, 4150
18:31 for your service in the tabernacle of the c. 4150
19: 4 before the tabernacle of the c seven times: 4150
19: 9 it shall be kept for the c of the children of 5712
19:20 that soul shall be cut off from among the c, 6951
20: 1 the children of Israel, *even* the whole c, 5712
20: 2 there was no water for the c: and 5712
20: 4 why have ye brought up the c of 6951
20: 6 unto the door of the tabernacle of the c, 4150
20: 8 so thou shalt give the c and their beasts 5712
20:10 Aaron gathered the c together before 6951
20:11 and the c drank, and their beasts *also*. 5712
20:12 ye shall not bring this c into the land which 6951
20:22 *even* the whole c, journeyed from Kadesh, 5712
20:27 up into mount Hor in the sight of all the c. 5712
20:29 when all the c saw that Aaron was dead, 5712
25: 6 in the sight of all the c of the children of 5712
25: 6 *before* the door of the tabernacle of the c. 4150
25: 7 saw *it*, he rose up from amongst the c, and 5712
26: 2 Take the sum of all the c of the children of 5712
26: 9 and Abiram, *which were* famous in the c, 5712
27: 2 and before the princes and all the c, 5712
27: 2 *by* the door of the tabernacle of the c, 4150
27:14 in the strife of the c, to sanctify me at 5712
27:16 the spirits of all flesh, set a man over the c, 5712
27:17 that the c of the LORD be not as sheep 5712
27:19 Eleazar the priest, and before all the c; 5712
27:20 that all the c of the children of Israel may 5712
27:21 children of Israel with him, even all the c. 5712
27:22 Eleazar the priest, and before all the c: 5712
31:12 and unto the c of the children of Israel, 5712
31:13 the priest, and all the princes of the c, 5712
31:16 there was a plague among the c of 5712
31:26 the priest, and the chief fathers of the c: 5712
31:27 went out to battle, and between all the c: 5712
31:43 (Now the half that pertained unto the c was 5712
31:54 and brought it into the tabernacle of the c, 4150
32: 2 and unto the princes of the c, saying, 5712
32: 4 the LORD smote before the c of Israel, 5712
35:12 until he stand before the c in judgment. 5712
35:24 the c shall judge between the slayer and 5712
35:25 the c shall deliver the slayer out of the hand 5712
35:25 the c shall restore him to the city of his 5712
Dt 23: 1 shall not enter into the c of the LORD. 6951
23: 2 A bastard shall not enter into the c of 6951
23: 2 shall he not enter into the c of the LORD. 6951
23: 3 Moabite shall not enter into the c of 6951
23: 3 not enter into the c of the LORD for ever: 6951
23: 8 c of the LORD *in* their third generation. 6951

Dt 31:14 yourselves in the tabernacle of the c, 4150
31:14 themselves in the tabernacle of the c. 4150
31:30 Moses spake in the ears of all the c of Israel 6951
33: 4 *even* the inheritance of the c of Jacob. 6952
Jos 8:35 which Joshua read not before all the c of 6951
9:15 and the princes of the c sware unto them. 5712
9:18 the princes of the c had sworn unto them by 5712
9:18 And all the c murmured against the princes. 5712
9:19 all the princes said unto all the c, We have 5712
9:21 and drawers of water unto all the c; 5712
9:27 of wood and drawers of water for the c, 5712
18: 1 the whole c of the children of Israel 5712
18: 1 and set up the tabernacle of the c there. 4150
19:51 *at* the door of the tabernacle of the c. 4150
20: 6 until he stand before the c for judgment, 5712
20: 9 of blood, until he stood before the c. 5712
22:12 c of the children of Israel gathered 5712
22:16 Thus saith the whole c of the LORD, 5712
22:17 although there was a plague in the c of 5712
22:18 he will be wroth with the whole c of Israel. 5712
22:20 and wrath fell on all the c of Israel? 5712
22:30 the princes of the c and heads of 5712
Jdg 20: 1 the c was gathered together as one man, 5712
21: 5 came not up with the c unto the LORD? 6951
21:10 the c sent thither twelve thousand men of 5712
21:13 the whole c sent *some* to speak to 5712
21:16 the elders of the c said, How shall we do 5712
1Sa 2:22 *at* the door of the tabernacle of the c. 4150
1Ki 8: 4 the tabernacle of the c, and all the holy 4150
8: 5 king Solomon, and all the c of Israel, 5712
8:14 face about, and blessed all the c of Israel: 6951
8:14 of Israel: (and all the c of Israel stood;) 6951
8:22 in the presence of all the c of Israel, 6951
8:55 blessed all the c of Israel *with* a loud voice, 6951
8:65 a feast, and all Israel with him, a great c, 6951
12: 3 Jeroboam and all the c of Israel came, and 6951
12:20 that they sent and called him unto the c, 5712
1Ch 6:32 of the tabernacle of the c with singing, 4150
9:21 porter of the door of the tabernacle of the c. 4150
13: 2 David said unto all the c of Israel, If *it seem* 6951
13: 4 all the c said that *they* would do so: for 6951
23:32 keep the charge of the tabernacle of the c, 4150
28: 8 in the sight of all Israel the c of 6951
29: 1 David the king said unto all the c, 6951
29:10 David blessed the LORD before all the c: 6951
29:20 David said to all the c, Now bless 6951
29:20 all the c blessed the LORD God of their 6951
2Ch 1: 3 So Solomon, and all the c with him, went to 6951
1: 3 for there was the tabernacle of the c of 4150
1: 5 and Solomon and the c sought *unto* it. 6951
1: 6 which *was* at the tabernacle of the c, and 4150
1:13 from before the tabernacle of the c, and 4150
5: 5 the tabernacle of the c, and all the holy 4150
5: 6 all the c of Israel that were assembled unto 5712
6: 3 his face, and blessed the whole c of Israel: 6951
6: 3 of Israel: and all the c of Israel stood. 6951
6:12 in the presence of all the c of Israel, 6951
6:13 upon his knees before all the c of Israel, 6951
7: 8 all Israel with him, a very great c, from 6951
20: 5 Jehoshaphat stood in the c of Judah and 6951
20:14 spirit of the LORD in the midst of the c; 6951
23: 3 all the c made a covenant with the king in 6951
24: 6 of the c of Israel, for the tabernacle of 6951
28:14 the spoil before the princes and all the c. 6951
29:23 the sin offering before the king and the c; 6951
29:28 all the c worshipped, and the singers sang, 6951
29:31 the c brought in sacrifices and 6951
29:32 which the c brought, was threescore and 6951
30: 2 and his princes, and all the c in Jerusalem, 6951
30: 4 the thing pleased the king and all the c. 6951
30:13 bread in the second month, a very great c. 6951
30:17 For *there were* many in the c that were not 6951
30:24 Judah did give to the c a thousand bullocks 6951
30:24 the princes gave to the c a thousand 6951
30:25 all the c of Judah, with the priests and 6951
30:25 all the c that came out of Israel, and 6951
31:18 and their daughters, through all the c: 6951
Ezr 2:64 The whole c together *was* forty and 6951
10: 1 unto him out of Israel a very great c *of* men 6951
10: 8 himself separated from the c of those that 6951
10:12 all the c answered and said *with* a loud 6951
10:14 Let now our rulers of all the c stand, and 6951
Ne 5:13 all the c said, Amen, and praised 6951
7:66 The whole c together *was* forty and 6951
8: 2 Ezra the priest brought the law before the c 6951
8:17 all the c of them that were come again out 6951
13: 1 the Moabite should not come into the c of 6951
Job 15:34 For the c of hypocrites *shall be* desolate, 5712
30:28 the sun: I stood up, *and* I cried in the c. 6951
Ps 1: 5 nor sinners in the c of the righteous. 5712
7: 7 So shall the c of the people compass thee 5712
22:22 in the midst of the c will I praise thee. 6951
22:25 My praise *shall be* of thee in the great c: 6951
26: 5 I have hated the c of evildoers; and will not 6951
35:18 I will give thee thanks in the great c: I will 6951
40: 9 have preached righteousness in the great c: 6951
40:10 and thy truth from the great c. 6951
58: 1 Do ye indeed speak righteousness, O c? 482
68:10 Thy c hath dwelt therein: thou, O God, 2416
74: 2 Remember thy c, *which* thou hast 5712
74:19 forget not the c of thy poor for ever. 2416
75: 2 When I shall receive the c I will judge 4150
82: 1 God standeth in the c of the mighty; 5712
89: 5 thy faithfulness also in the c of the saints. 6951
107:32 Let them exalt him also in the c of 6951
111: 1 in the assembly of the upright, and *in* the c. 5712
149: 1 a new song, *and* his praise in the c of saints. 6951
Pr 5:14 I was almost in all evil in the midst of the c 6951
21:16 shall remain in the c of the dead. 6951
26:26 shall be shewed before the *whole* c. 6951
Isa 14:13 I will sit also upon the mount of the c, 4150
Jer 6:18 Therefore hear, ye nations, and know, O c, 5712
30:20 their c shall be established before me, and 5712
La 1:10 *that* they should not enter into thy c. 6951
Hos 7:12 I will chastise them, as their c hath heard. 5712
Joel 2:16 Gather the people, sanctify the c, 6951
Mic 2: 5 cast a cord by lot in the c of the LORD. 6951
Ac 13:43 Now when the c was broken up, many of *4864*

CONGREGATIONS (3) [CONGREGATION]

Ps 26:12 even place: in the c will I bless the LORD. 4721
68:26 Bless ye God in the c, *even* the Lord, 4721
74: 4 Thine enemies roar in the midst of thy c; 4150

CONIAH (3) [JEHOIACHIN]

Jer 22:24 though C the son of Jehoiakim king of 3659
22:28 *Is* this man C a despised broken idol? *is he* 3659
37: 1 reigned instead of C the son of Jehoiakim, 3659

CONIES (2) [CONEY]

Ps 104:18 for the wild goats; *and* the rocks for the c. 8227
Pr 30:26 The c *are but* a feeble folk, yet make they 8227

CONONIAH (2)

2Ch 31:12 over which C the Levite *was* ruler, and 3562
31:13 *were* overseers under the hand of C and 3562

CONQUER (1) [CONQUERING, CONQUERORS]

Rev 6: 2 and he went forth conquering, and to c. *3528*

CONQUERING (1) [CONQUER]

Rev 6: 2 and he went forth c, and to conquer. *3528*

CONQUERORS (1) [CONQUER]

Ro 8:37 in all these *things* we are **more than c** *5245*

CONSCIENCE (31) [CONSCIENCES]

Jn 8: 9 heard *it,* being convicted by *their own* c, *4893*
Ac 23: 1 I have lived in all good c before God until *4893*
24:16 to have always a c void of offence toward *4893*
Ro 2:15 their c also bearing witness, and *their* *4893*
9: 1 my c also bearing me witness in the Holy *4893*
13: 5 not only for wrath, but also for c sake. *4893*
1Co 8: 7 for some with c of the idol unto this hour, *4893*
8: 7 an idol; and their c being weak is defiled. *4893*
8:10 shall not the c of him which is weak be *4893*
8:12 the brethren, and wound their weak c, *4893*
10:25 *that* eat, asking no question for c sake: *4893*
10:27 eat, asking no question for c sake. *4893*
10:28 and *for* c *sake:* for the earth *is* the Lord's, *4893*
10:29 C, I say, not thine own, but of the other's: *4893*
10:29 is my liberty judged of another *man's* c? *4893*
2Co 1:12 the testimony of our c, that in simplicity *4893*
4: 2 to every man's c in the sight of God. *4893*
1Ti 1: 5 and *of* a good c, and *of* faith unfeigned: *4893*
1:19 Holding faith, and a good c; which some *4893*
3: 9 Holding the mystery of the faith in a pure c. *4893*
4: 2 having their c seared with a hot iron; *4893*
2Ti 1: 3 I serve from *my* forefathers with pure c, *4893*
Tit 1:15 but even their mind and c is defiled. *4893*
Heb 9: 9 the service perfect, as pertaining to the c; *4893*
9:14 purge your c from dead works to serve *4893*
10: 2 purged should have had no more c of sins. *4893*
10:22 having *our* hearts sprinkled from an evil c, *4893*
13:18 for we trust we have a good c, in all *things* *4893*
1Pe 2:19 if a man for c toward God endure grief, *4893*
3:16 Having a good c; that, whereas they speak *4893*
3:21 but the answer of a good c toward God,) *4893*

CONSCIENCES (1) [CONSCIENCE]

2Co 5:11 and I trust also are made manifest in your c. *4893*

CONSECRATE (14) [CONSECRATED, CONSECRATION, CONSECRATIONS]

Ex 28: 3 that they may make Aaron's garments to c 6942
28:41 and c them, and sanctify them, 853+3027+4390
29: 9 and thou shalt c Aaron and his sons. 3027+4390
29:33 to c *and* to sanctify them: 853+3027+4390
29:35 seven days shalt thou c them. 3027+4390
30:30 anoint Aaron and his sons, and c them, 6942
32:29 C yourselves to day to the LORD, 3027+4390
Lev 8:33 for seven days shall he c you. 853+3027+4390
16:32 whom he shall c to minister in 853+3027+4390
Nu 6:12 he shall c unto the LORD the days of his 5144
1Ch 29: 5 is willing to c his service *this* day unto 4390
2Ch 13: 9 that whosoever cometh to c himself 3027+4390
Eze 43:26 purify it; and they shall c themselves. 3027+4390
Mic 4:13 and I will c their gain unto the LORD, and 2763

CONSECRATED (14) [CONSECRATE]

Ex 29:29 and to be c in them. 853+3027+4390
Lev 21:10 that is c to put on the garments, 853+3027+4390
Nu 3: 3 he c to minister in the priest's office. 3027+4390
Jos 6:19 of brass and iron, *are* c unto the LORD: 6944
Jdg 17: 5 teraphim, and c one of his sons, 853+3027+4390
17:12 Micah c the Levite; and 853+3027+4390
1Ki 13:33 he c him, and he became *one of* 853+3027+4390
2Ch 26:18 sons of Aaron, that are c to burn incense: 6942
29:31 Now ye have c yourselves unto 3027+4390
29:33 the c *things were* six hundred oxen and 6944
31: 6 the tithe of holy *things* which were c unto 6942
Ezr 3: 5 all the set feasts of the LORD that were c, 6942
Heb 7:28 *maketh* the Son, who is c for evermore. *5048*
10:20 and living way, which he hath c for us, *1457*

CONSECRATION (8) [CONSECRATE]

Ex 29:22 and the right shoulder; for it *is* a ram of c: 4394
29:27 and which is heaved up, of the ram of the c, 4394
29:31 thou shalt take the ram of the c, and 4394
Lev 8:22 he brought the other ram, the ram of c: and 4394
8:29 *for* of the ram of c it was Moses' part; 4394
8:33 until the days of your c be at an end: 4394
Nu 6: 7 because the c of his God *is* upon his head. 5145
6: 9 and he hath defiled the head of his c; 5145

CONSECRATIONS (5) [CONSECRATE]

Ex 29:26 take the breast of the ram of Aaron's c, 4394
29:34 if *ought* of the flesh of the c, or of 4394
Lev 7:37 of the c, and of the sacrifice of the peace 4394
8:28 they *were* c for a sweet savour: it *is* an 4394
8:31 it with the bread that *is* in the basket of c, 4394

CONSENT (15) [CONSENTED, CONSENTEDST, CONSENTING]

Ge 34:15 in this will we c unto you: If ye will be as we 225
34:22 Only herein will the men c unto us for to 225
34:23 only let us c unto them, and they will dwell 225
Dt 13: 8 Thou shalt not c unto him, nor hearken unto 14
Jdg 11:17 he would not c: and Israel abode in Kadesh. 14
1Sa 11: 7 on the people, and they came out with one c. 376
1Ki 20: 8 said unto him, Hearken not *unto him,* nor c. 14
Ps 83: 5 they have consulted together *with one* c: 3820
Pr 1:10 My son, if sinners entice thee, c thou not. 14
Hos 6: 9 company of priests murder *in* the way by c: 7926
Zep 3: 9 of the LORD, to serve him *with* one c. 7926
Lk 14:18 And they all with one c began to make NIG
Ro 7:16 I would not, I c unto the law that *it is* good. *4852*
1Co 7: 5 one the other, except *it be* with c for a time, *4859*
1Ti 6: 3 and c not **to** wholesome words, *4334*

CONSENTED (4) [CONSENT]

2Ki 12: 8 the priests c to receive no *more* money of 225
Da 1:14 So he c to them in this matter, and 8085
Lk 23:51 (The same had not c to the counsel and *4784*
Ac 18:20 to tarry longer time with them, he c not; *1962*

CONSENTEDST (1) [CONSENT]

Ps 50:18 thou c with him, and hast been partaker 7521

CONSENTING (2) [CONSENT]

Ac 8: 1 And Saul was c unto his death. And at that *4909*
22:20 and c unto his death, and kept the raiment *4909*

CONSIDER (67) [CONSIDERED, CONSIDEREST, CONSIDERETH, CONSIDERING]

Ex 33:13 and c that this nation *is* thy people. 7200
Lev 13:13 the priest shall c: and behold, *if* the leprosy 7200
Dt 4:39 therefore *this* day, and c *it* in thine heart, 7725
8: 5 Thou shalt also c in thine heart, that, as a 3045
32: 7 days of old, c the years of many generations: 995
32:29 *that* they would c their latter end! 995
Jdg 18:14 now therefore c what ye have to do. 3045
19:30 c of it, take advice, and speak *your* 7760+3807.1
1Sa 12:24 for c how great things he hath done for you. 7200
25:17 therefore know and c what thou wilt do; 7200
2Ki 5: 7 wherefore c, I pray you, and see how he 3045
Job 11:11 seeth wickedness also; will he not then c *it?* 995
23:15 at his presence: when I c, I am afraid of him. 995
34:27 from him, and would not c any of his ways: 7919
37:14 and c the wondrous works of God. 995
Ps 5: 1 to my words, O LORD, c my meditation. 995
8: 3 When I c thy heavens, the work of thy 7200
9:13 c my trouble *which I suffer* of them that 7200
13: 3 C *and* hear me, O LORD my God: 5027
25:19 C mine enemies; for they are many; and 7200
37:10 thou shalt **diligently** c his place, and it *shall* 995
45:10 O daughter, and c, and incline thine ear; 7200
48:13 Mark ye well her bulwarks, c her palaces; 6448
50:22 Now c this, ye that forget God, lest I tear 995
64: 9 of God; for they shall **wisely** c of his doing. 7919
119:95 to destroy me: *but* I will c thy testimonies. 995
119:153 C mine affliction, and deliver me: for I do 7200
119:159 C how I love thy precepts: quicken me, 7200
Pr 6: 6 thou sluggard; c her ways, and be wise: 7200
23: 1 a ruler, c **diligently** what *is* before thee: 995+995
24:12 doth not he that pondereth the heart c *it?* and 995
Ecc 5: 1 of fools: for they c not that *they* do evil. 3045
7:13 C the work of God: for who can make *that* 7200
7:14 be joyful, but in the day of adversity c: 7200
Isa 1: 3 Israel doth not know, my people doth not c. 995
5:12 neither c the operation of his hands. 7200
14:16 shall narrowly look upon thee, *and* c thee, 995
18: 4 I will c in my dwelling place like a clear 5027
41:20 and know, and c, and understand together, 7760
41:22 what they *be,* that we may c *them,* 3820+7760
43:18 the former *things,* neither c the *things* of old. 995
52:15 *that* which they had not heard shall they c. 995
Jer 2:10 c diligently, and see if there be such a *thing.* 995
9:17 C ye, and call for the mourning *women,* that 995
23:20 in the latter days ye shall c it **perfectly**. 995+998
30:24 of his heart: in the latter days ye shall c it. 995
La 1:11 see, O LORD, and c; for I am become 5027
2:20 and c to whom thou hast done this. 5027
5: 1 come upon us: c, and behold our reproach. 5027
Eze 12: 3 it may be they will c, though they *be* a 7200
Da 9:23 understand the matter, and c the vision. 995
Hos 7: 2 they c not in their hearts *that* I remember all 559
Hag 1: 5 the LORD of hosts; C your ways. 3824+7760
1: 7 the LORD of hosts; C your ways. 3824+7760
2:15 c from this day and upward, 3824+7760
2:18 C now from this day and upward, 3824+7760
2:18 the LORD'S temple was laid, c *it.* 3824+7760
Mt 6:28 C the lilies of the field, how they grow; *2648*
Lk 12:24 C the ravens: for they neither sow nor reap; *2657*
12:27 C the lilies how they grow: they toil not, *2657*
Jn 11:50 Nor c that it is expedient for us, that one *1260*
Ac 15: 6 elders came together for to c of this matter. *1492*
2Ti 2: 7 C what I say; and the Lord give thee *3539*
Heb 3: 1 c the Apostle and High Priest of our *2657*
7: 4 Now c how great this *man was,* unto whom *2334*
10:24 And let us c one another to provoke unto *2657*
12: 3 For c him that endured such contradiction of *357*

CONSIDERED (16) [CONSIDER]

1Ki 3:21 when I had c it in the morning, behold, 413+995
5: 8 I have c *the things* which thou sentest to me 8085
Job 1: 8 Hast thou c my servant Job, 3820+7760
2: 3 Hast thou c my servant Job, 3820+7760
Ps 31: 7 for thou hast c my trouble; thou hast known 7200
77: 5 I have c the days of old, the years of 2803
Pr 24:32 I saw, *and* c *it* well: I looked upon *it,* 3820+7896
Ecc 4: 1 c all the oppressions that *are* done under 7200

C

Ecc 4: 4 Again, I c all travail, and every right work, 7200
4:15 I c all the living which walk under the sun, 7200
9: 1 For all this I c in my heart even to declare 5414
Da 7: 8 I c the horns, and behold, there came up 7920
Mk 6:52 For they c not *the miracle* of the loaves: *4920*
Ac 11: 6 I c, and saw fourfooted beasts of the earth, *2657*
12:12 And when he had c *the thing,* he came to *4894*
Ro 4:19 in faith, he c not his own body now dead, *2657*

CONSIDEREST (2) [CONSIDER]
Jer 33:24 C thou not what this people have spoken, 7200
Mt 7: 3 but c not the beam that is in thine own eye? *2657*

CONSIDERETH (9) [CONSIDER]
Ps 33:15 their hearts alike; he c all their works. 995
41: 1 Blessed *is* he that c the poor: the LORD 7919
Pr 21:12 The righteous *man* **wisely** c the house of 7919
28:22 and c not that poverty shall come *upon* him. 3045
29: 7 The righteous c the cause of the poor: *but* 3045
31:16 She c a field, and buyeth it: with the fruit of 2161
Isa 44:19 none c in his heart, neither *is there* 7725
Eze 18:14 hath done, and c, and doeth not such like, 7200
18:28 Because he c, and turneth away from all his 7200

CONSIDERING (4) [CONSIDER]
Isa 57: 1 none c that the righteous is taken away from 995
Da 8: 5 as I was c, behold, a he goat came from 995
Gal 6: 1 c thyself, lest thou also be tempted. *4648*
Heb 13: 7 faith follow, c the end of *their* conversation. *333*

CONSIST (1) [CONSISTETH]
Col 1:17 is before all *things,* and by him all *things* c. *4921*

CONSISTETH (1) [CONSIST]
Lk 12:15 for a man's life c not in the abundance of *1510*

CONSOLATION (15) [CONSOLATIONS]
Jer 16: 7 neither shall *men* give them the cup of c to 8575
Lk 2:25 and devout, waiting for the c of Israel: *3874*
6:24 that are rich: for ye have received your c. *3874*
Ac 4:36 (which is, being interpreted, The son of c,) *3874*
15:31 when they had read, they rejoiced for the c. *3874*
Ro 15: 5 c grant you to be likeminded one towards *3874*
2Co 1: 5 in us, so our c also aboundeth by Christ. *3874*
1: 6 be afflicted, *it is* for your c and salvation, *3874*
1: 6 be comforted, *it is* for your c and salvation. *3874*
1: 7 the sufferings, so *shall ye be* also of the c. *3874*
7: 7 by the c wherewith he was comforted in *3874*
Php 2: 1 If *there be* therefore any c in Christ, if any *3874*
2Th 2:16 and hath given *us* everlasting c and *3874*
Phm 1: 7 For we have great joy and c in thy love, *3874*
Heb 6:18 for God to lie, we might have a strong c, *3874*

CONSOLATIONS (3) [CONSOLATION]
Job 15:11 *Are* the c of God small with thee? is there 8575
21: 2 diligently my speech, and let this be your c. 8575
Isa 66:11 and be satisfied with the breasts of her c; 8575

CONSORTED (1)
Ac 17: 4 them believed, and c **with** Paul and Silas; *4345*

CONSPIRACY (10) [CONSPIRATORS, CONSPIRED]
2Sa 15:12 the c was strong; for the people increased 7195
2Ki 12:20 **made a** c, and slew Joash *in* 7194+7195
14:19 Now they **made a** c against him in 7194+7195
15:15 and his c which he **made,** behold, 7194+7195
15:30 Hoshea the son of Elah **made a** c 7194+7195
17: 4 the king of Assyria found c in Hoshea: 7195
2Ch 25:27 **made a** c against him in Jerusalem; 7194+7195
Jer 11: 9 A c is found among the men of Judah, and 7195
Eze 22:25 *There is* a c of her prophets in the midst 7195
Ac 23:13 more *than* forty which had made this c. *4945*

CONSPIRATORS (1) [CONSPIRACY]
2Sa 15:31 Ahithophel *is* among the c with Absalom. 7194

CONSPIRED (19) [CONSPIRACY]
Ge 37:18 unto them, they c **against** him to slay him. 5230
1Sa 22: 8 That all of you have c against me, and 7194
22:13 Why have ye c against me, thou and 7194
1Ki 15:27 of the house of Issachar, c against him; 7194
16: 9 c against him, as he *was* in Tirzah, 7194
16:16 Zimri hath c, and hath also slain the king: 7194
2Ki 9:14 the son of Nimshi c against Joram. 7194
10: 9 I c against my master, and slew him: 7194
15:10 Shallum the son of Jabesh c against him, 7194
15:25 c against him, and smote him in Samaria, 7194
21:23 the servants of Amon c against him, and 7194
21:24 all them that had c against king Amon; 7194
2Ch 24:21 they c against him, and stoned him *with* 7194
24:25 his own servants c against him for 7194
24:26 these *are* they that c against him; Zabad 7194
33:24 his servants c against him, and slew him in 7194
33:25 all them that had c against king Amon; 7194
Ne 4: 8 c all of them together to come *and* to fight 7194
Am 7:10 Amos hath c against thee in the midst of 7194

CONSTANT (1) [CONSTANTLY]
1Ch 28: 7 if he be c to do my commandments and 2388

CONSTANTLY (3) [CONSTANT]
Pr 21:28 the man that heareth, speaketh c. 5331+3807.1
Ac 12:15 But she c **affirmed** that it was *even* so. *1340*
Tit 3: 8 and these *things* I will that thou **affirm** c, *1226*

CONSTELLATIONS (1)
Isa 13:10 and the c thereof shall not give their light: 3685

CONSTRAIN (1) [CONSTRAINED, CONSTRAINETH, CONSTRAINT]
Gal 6:12 in the flesh, they c you to be circumcised; *315*

CONSTRAINED (6) [CONSTRAIN]
2Ki 4: 8 a great woman; and she c him to eat bread. 2388
Mt 14:22 And straightway Jesus c his disciples to get *315*
Mk 6:45 And straightway he c his disciples to get into *315*
Lk 24:29 But they c him, saying, Abide with us: *3849*
Ac 16:15 my house, and abide *there.* And she c us. *3849*
28:19 But when the Jews spake against *it,* I was c *315*

CONSTRAINETH (2) [CONSTRAIN]
Job 32:18 am full *of* matter, the spirit within me c me. 6693
2Co 5:14 For the love of Christ c us; because we thus *4912*

CONSTRAINT (1) [CONSTRAIN]
1Pe 5: 2 taking the oversight *thereof,* not **by** c, but *317*

CONSULT (1) [CONSULTATION, CONSULTED, CONSULTER, CONSULTETH]
Ps 62: 4 They only c to cast *him* down from his 3289

CONSULTATION (1) [CONSULT]
Mk 15: 1 the chief priests held a c with the elders *4824*

CONSULTED (13) [CONSULT]
1Ki 12: 6 king Rehoboam c **with** the old men, 3289
12: 8 c with the young men that were grown up 3289
1Ch 13: 1 David c with the captains of thousands and 3289
2Ch 20:21 when he had c with the people, he 3289
Ne 5: 7 I c with myself, and I rebuked the nobles, 4427
Ps 83: 3 thy people, and c against thy hidden ones. 3289
83: 5 For they have c together *with one* consent: 3289
Eze 21:21 he c with images, he looked in the liver. 7592
Da 6: 7 have c **together** to establish a royal statute, 3272
Mic 6: 5 remember now what Balak king of Moab c, 3289
Hab 2:10 Thou hast c shame to thy house by cutting 3289
Mt 26: 4 And c that they might take Jesus by *4823*
Jn 12:10 But the chief priests c that they might put *1011*

CONSULTER (1) [CONSULT]
Dt 18:11 or a c with familiar spirits, or a wizard, or 7592

CONSULTETH (1) [CONSULT]
Lk 14:31 c whether he be able with ten thousand to *1011*

CONSULTS THE DEAD See NECROMANCER

CONSUME (56) [CONSUMED, CONSUMETH, CONSUMING, CONSUMPTION]
Ge 41:30 of Egypt; and the famine shall c the land; 3615
Ex 32:10 hot against them, and that I may c them: 3615
32:12 and to c them from the face of the earth? 3615
33: 3 stiffnecked people: lest I c thee in the way. 3615
33: 5 the midst of thee in a moment, and c thee: 3615
Lev 26:16 that shall c the eyes, and cause sorrow of 3615
Nu 16:21 that I may c them in a moment. 3615
16:45 that I may c them as in a moment. 3615
Dt 5:25 for this great fire will c us: if we hear 398
7:16 thou shalt c all the people which the LORD 398
7:22 thou mayest not c them at once, lest 3615
28:38 *but* little in; for the locust shall c it. 2628
28:42 and fruit of thy land shall the locust c. 3423
32:22 shall c the earth with her increase, and set on 398
Jos 24:20 he will turn and do you hurt, and c you, 3615
1Sa 2:33 *shall be* to c thine eyes, and to grieve thine 3615
2Ki 1:10 down from heaven, and c thee and thy fifty. 398
1:12 down from heaven, and c thee and thy fifty. 398
Ne 9:31 mercies' sake thou didst not **utterly** c them, 3617
Est 9:24 *is,* the lot, to c them, and to destroy them; 2000
Job 15:34 and fire shall c the tabernacles of bribery. 398
20:26 a fire not blown shall c him; it shall go ill 398
24:19 Drought and heat c the snow waters: *so* 1497
Ps 37:20 they shall c; into smoke shall they 3615
37:20 into smoke shall they c *away.* 3615
39:11 thou **makest** his beauty **to** c **away** like a 4529
49:14 their beauty shall c *in* the grave from their 1086
59:13 C *them* in wrath, consume *them,* that they 3615
59:13 c *them,* that they *may* not *be:* and let them 3615
78:33 Therefore their days did he c in vanity, and 3615
Isa 7:20 hair of the feet: and it shall also c the beard. 5595
10:18 shall c the glory of his forest, and of his 3615
27:10 he lie down, and c the branches thereof. 3615
Jer 8:13 I will **surely** c them, saith 622+5486
14:12 I will c them by the sword, and by 3615
49:27 and it shall c the palaces of Ben-hadad. 398
Eze 4:17 with another, and c **away** for their iniquity. 4743
13:13 and great hailstones in *my* fury to c *it.* 3617
20:13 upon them in the wilderness, to c them. 3615
21:28 *it is* furbished, to c because of the glittering: 398
22:15 and will c thy filthiness out of thee. 8552
24:10 c the flesh, and spice it well, and let 8552
35:12 They are laid desolate, they are given us to c. 402
Da 2:44 break in pieces and c all these kingdoms, 5487
7:26 to c and to destroy *it* unto the end. 8046
Hos 11: 6 shall c his branches, and devour *them,* 3615
Zep 1: 2 I will utterly c all *things* from off the land, 5486
1: 3 I will c man and beast; I will consume 5486
1: 3 I will c the fowls of the heaven, and 5486
Zec 5: 4 shall c it with the timber thereof and 3615
14:12 Their flesh *shall* c **away** while they stand 4743
14:12 their eyes shall c **away** in their holes, and 4743
14:12 their tongue shall c **away** in their mouth. 4743
Lk 9:54 from heaven, and c them, even as Elias did? *355*
2Th 2: 8 whom the Lord shall c with the spirit of his *355*
Jas 4: 3 ask amiss, that ye may c *it* upon your lusts. *1159*

CONSUMED (96) [CONSUME]
Ge 19:15 lest thou be c in the iniquity of the city. 5595
19:17 escape to the mountain, lest thou be c. 5595
31:40 the drought c me, and the frost by night; 398
Ex 3: 2 burned with fire, and the bush was not c. 398
15: 7 forth thy wrath, *which* c them as stubble. 398
22: 6 be c *therewith;* he that kindled the fire shall 398
Lev 6:10 take up the ashes which the fire hath c with 398
9:24 c upon the altar the burnt offering and 398
Nu 11: 1 c *them that were* in the uttermost parts of 398
12:12 of whom the flesh is half c when he cometh 398
14:35 in this wilderness they shall be c, and 8552
16:26 of theirs, lest ye be c in all their sins. 5595
16:35 c the two hundred and fifty men that offered 398
17:13 LORD shall die: shall we be c with dying? 8552
21:28 it hath c Ar of Moab, *and* the lords of 398
25:11 that I c not the children of Israel in my 3615
32:13 done evil in the sight of the LORD, was c. 8552
Dt 2:15 from among the host, until they were c. 8552
2:16 when all the men of war were c and 8552
28:21 until he have c thee from off the land, 3615
Jos 5: 6 were c, because they obeyed not the voice 8552
8:24 until they were c, that all the Israelites 8552
10:20 till they were c, that the rest *which* 8552
Jdg 6:21 c the flesh and the unleavened *cakes.* Then 398
1Sa 12:25 ye shall be c, both ye and your king. 5595
15:18 and fight against them until they be c. 3615
2Sa 21: 5 The man that c us, and that devised against 3615
22:38 and turned not again until I had c them. 3615
22:39 I have c them, and wounded them, that they 3615
1Ki 18:38 c the burnt sacrifice, and the wood, and 398
22:11 push the Syrians, until *thou* have c them. 3615
2Ki 1:10 fire from heaven, and c him and his fifty. 398
1:12 down from heaven, and c him and his fifty. 398
7:13 all the multitude of the Israelites that are c:) 8552
13:17 Syrians in Aphek, till *thou* have c *them.* 3615
13:19 hadst thou smitten Syria till *thou* hadst c *it:* 3615
2Ch 7: 1 and c the burnt offering and the sacrifices; 398
8: 8 the land, whom the children of Israel c not, 3615
18:10 these thou shalt push Syria until they be c. 3615
Ezr 9:14 not be angry with us till *thou* hadst c *us,* 3615
Ne 2: 3 and the gates thereof are c with fire? 398
2:13 and the gates thereof were c with fire. 398
Job 1:16 up the sheep, and the servants, and c them; 398
4: 9 and by the breath of his nostrils are they c. 3615
6:17 when it is hot, they are c out of their place. 1846
7: 9 *As* the cloud is c and vanisheth away: so 3615
19:27 *though* my reins be c within me. 3615
33:21 His flesh is c **away,** that it cannot be seen; 3615
Ps 6: 7 Mine eye is c because of grief; it waxeth 6244
18:37 neither did I turn again till they were c. 3615
31: 9 mine eye is c with grief, *yea,* my soul and 6244
31:10 of mine iniquity, and my bones are c. 6244
39:10 from me: I am c by the blow of thine hand. 3615
71:13 *and* c that are adversaries to my soul; 3615
73:19 *in* a moment! they are utterly c with terrors. 5486
78:63 The fire c their young men; and 398
90: 7 For we are c by thine anger, and by thy 3615
102: 3 For my days are c like smoke, and 3615
104:35 Let the sinners be c out of the earth, and 8552
119:87 They had almost c me upon earth; but 3615
119:139 My zeal hath c me, because mine enemies 6789
Pr 5:11 the last, when thy flesh and thy body are c, 3615
Isa 1:28 and they that forsake the LORD shall be c. 3615
16: 4 the oppressors are c out of the land. 8552
29:20 the scorner is c, and all that watch for 3615
64: 7 and hast c us, because of our iniquities. 4127
66:17 and the mouse, shall be c together, 5486
Jer 5: 3 thou hast c them, *but* they have refused to 3615
6:29 bellows are burnt, the lead is c of the fire; 8552
9:16 send a sword after them, till I have c them. 3615
10:25 c him, and have made his habitation 3615
12: 4 the beasts are c, and the birds; because 5595
14:15 and famine shall those prophets be c. 8552
16: 4 they shall be c by the sword, and 3615
20:18 that my days should be c with shame? 3615
24:10 till they be c from off the land that I gave 8552
27: 8 until I have c them by his hand. 8552
36:23 until all the roll was c in the fire that *was* 8552
44:12 they shall all be c, *and* fall in the land of 8552
44:12 they shall *even* be c by the sword, *and* 8552
44:18 have been c by the sword and by 8552
44:27 in the land of Egypt shall be c by the sword 8552
49:37 the sword after them, till I have c them: 3615
La 2:22 and brought up hath mine enemy c. 3615
3:22 *of* the LORD'S mercies that we are not c, 8552
Eze 5:12 with famine shall they be c in the midst of 3615
13:14 and ye shall be c in the midst thereof: 3615
19:12 were broken and withered; the fire c them. 398
22:31 I have c them with the fire of my wrath: 3615
24:11 molten in it, *that* the scum of it may be c. 8552
34:29 they shall be no more c with hunger in 622
43: 8 wherefore I have c them in mine anger. 3615
47:12 not fade, neither shall the fruit thereof be c: 8552
Da 11:16 glorious land, which by his hand shall be c. 3617
Mal 3: 6 therefore ye sons of Jacob are not c. 3615
Gal 5:15 take heed ye be not c one of another. *355*

CONSUMETH (4) [CONSUME]
Job 13:28 he, as a rotten thing, c, as a garment that is 1086
22:20 cut down, but the remnant of them the fire c. 398
31:12 For it *is* a fire *that* c to destruction, and 398
Isa 5:24 the flame c the chaff, *so* their root shall be 7503

CONSUMING (3) [CONSUME]
Dt 4:24 For the LORD thy God *is* a c fire, *even* a 398
9: 3 *as* a c fire he shall destroy them, and he shall 398
Heb 12:29 For our God *is* a c fire. *2654*

CONSUMMATION (1)
Da 9:27 even until the c, and that determined shall 3617

CONSUMPTION (5) [CONSUME]
Lev 26:16 c, and the burning ague, that shall consume 7829
Dt 28:22 The LORD shall smite thee with a c, and 7829
Isa 10:22 the c decreed shall overflow *with* 3631
10:23 For the Lord GOD of hosts shall make a c, 3617
28:22 heard from the Lord GOD of hosts a c, 3617

CONTAIN (7) [CONTAINED, CONTAINETH, CONTAINING]
1Ki 8:27 and heaven of heavens cannot c thee; 3557
18:32 as great as would c two measures of seed. 1004

2Ch 2: 6 and heaven of heavens cannot c him? 3557
6:18 and the heaven of heavens cannot c thee; 3557
Eze 45:11 that the bath may c the tenth part of a 5375
Jn 21:25 not c the books that should be written. *5562*
1Co 7: 9 But if they cannot c, let them marry: for it *1467*

CONTAINED (5) [CONTAIN]
1Ki 7:26 flowers of lilies: it c two thousand baths. 3557
7:38 one laver c forty baths: *and* every laver was 3557
Ro 2:14 do by nature the *things* c in the law, these, NIG
Eph 2:15 *even* the law of commandments c in NIG
1Pe 2: 6 Wherefore also it is c in the scripture, *4023*

CONTAINETH (1) [CONTAIN]
Eze 23:32 to scorn and had in derision; *it* c much. 3557

CONTAINING (1) [CONTAIN]
Jn 2: 6 of the Jews, c two or three firkins apiece. *5562*

CONTEMN (2) [CONTEMNED, CONTEMNETH]
Ps 10:13 Wherefore doth the wicked c God? he hath 5006
Eze 21:13 and what if *the sword* c even the rod? 3988

CONTEMNED (4) [CONTEMN]
Ps 15: 4 In whose eyes a vile *person* is c; but he 959
107:11 of God, and c the counsel of the most High: 5006
SS 8: 7 house for love, it would **utterly** be c. 936+936
Isa 16:14 a hireling, and the glory of Moab shall be c, 7034

CONTEMNETH (1) [CONTEMN]
Eze 21:10 it c the rod of my son, *as* every tree. 3988

CONTEMPT (10) [CONTEMPTIBLE, CONTEMPTUOUSLY]
Est 1:18 Thus *shall there arise* too much c and wrath. 963
Job 12:21 He poureth c upon princes, and 937
31:34 or did the c of families terrify me, that I kept 937
Ps 107:40 He poureth c upon princes, and causeth them 937
119:22 Remove from me reproach and c; for I have 937
123: 3 for we are exceedingly filled *with* c. 937
123: 4 that are at ease, *and with* the c of the proud. 937
Pr 18: 3 *then* cometh also c, and with ignominy 937
Isa 23: 9 to **bring into** c all the honourable of 7043
Da 12: 2 and some to shame *and* everlasting c. 1860

CONTEMPTIBLE (4) [CONTEMPT]
Mal 1: 7 In that ye say, The table of the LORD *is* c. 959
1:12 the fruit thereof, *even* his meat, *is* c. 959
2: 9 Therefore have I also made you c and 959
2Co 10:10 bodily presence *is* weak, and *his* speech c. *1848*

CONTEMPTUOUSLY (1) [CONTEMPT]
Ps 31:18 things proudly and c against the righteous. 937

CONTEND (14) [CONTENDED, CONTENDEST, CONTENDETH, CONTENDING]
Dt 2: 9 the Moabites, neither c with them *in* battle: 1624
2:24 begin to possess *it,* and c with him *in* battle. 1624
Job 9: 3 If he will c with him, he cannot answer him 7378
13: 8 ye accept his person? will ye c for God? 7378
Pr 28: 4 but such as keep the law c with them. 1624
Ecc 6:10 neither may he c with him that *is* mightier 1777
Isa 49:25 for I will c **with** him that contendeth with 7378
50: 8 near that justifieth me; who will c with me? 7378
57:16 For I will not c for ever, neither will I be 7378
Jer 12: 5 then how canst thou c with horses? 8474
18:19 hearken to the voice of them that c **with** 3401
Am 7: 4 the Lord GOD called to c by fire, and 7378
Mic 6: 1 c thou before the mountains, and let 7378
Jude 1: 3 exhort *you* that *ye* should **earnestly** c **for** *1864*

CONTENDED (6) [CONTEND]
Ne 13:11 c I with the rulers, and said, Why is 7378
13:17 I c with the nobles of Judah, and said unto 7378
13:25 I c with them, and cursed them, and 7378
Job 31:13 of my maidservant, when they c with me; 7379
Isa 41:12 not find them, *even* them that c **with** thee: 4695
Ac 11: 2 they that were of the circumcision c with *1252*

CONTENDEST (1) [CONTEND]
Job 10: 2 shew me wherefore thou c with me. 7378

CONTENDETH (3) [CONTEND]
Job 40: 2 Shall he that c with the Almighty instruct 7378
Pr 29: 9 If a wise man c with a foolish man, 8199
Isa 49:25 for I will contend with him that c **with** thee, 3401

CONTENDING (1) [CONTEND]
Jude 1: 9 when c with the devil he disputed about *1252*

CONTENT (16) [CONTENTMENT]
Ge 37:27 *and* our flesh. And his brethren were c. 8085
Ex 2:21 Moses was c to dwell with the man: and 2974
Lev 10:20 Moses heard *that,* he was c. 3190+5869+871.1
Jos 7: 7 would to God we had been c, and dwelt on 2974
Jdg 17:11 the Levite was c to dwell with the man; 2974
19: 6 Be c, I pray thee, and tarry all night, and 2974
2Ki 5:23 Naaman said, Be c, take two talents. 2974
6: 3 Be c, I pray thee, and go with thy servants. 2974
Job 6:28 Now therefore be c, look upon me; for *it is* 2974
Pr 6:35 neither will he **rest** c, though thou givest 14
Mk 15:15 And *so* Pilate, willing to c *2425+4160*
Lk 3:14 *any* falsely; and be c with your wages. *714*
Php 4:11 in whatsoever *state* I am, *therewith* to be c. *842*
1Ti 6: 8 and raiment let us be therewith c. *714*
Heb 13: 5 *and be* c with such *things* as ye have: *714*
3Jn 1:10 and not c therewith, neither doth he himself *714*

CONTENTION (9) [CONTENTIONS, CONTENTIOUS]
Pr 13:10 Only by pride cometh c: but with the well 4683
17:14 therefore leave off c, before *it* be meddled 7379
18: 6 A fool's lips enter into c, and his mouth 7379
22:10 Cast out the scorner, and c shall go out; 4066
Jer 15:10 of strife and a man of c to the whole earth! 4066
Hab 1: 3 and there are *that* raise up strife and c. 4066
Ac 15:39 And the c was so **sharp** *between them,* that *3948*
Php 1:16 The one preach Christ of c, not sincerely, *2052*
1Th 2: 2 unto you the gospel of God with much c. *73*

CONTENTIONS (6) [CONTENTION]
Pr 18:18 The lot causeth c to cease, and 4066
18:19 and *their* c *are* like the bars of a castle. 4066
19:13 the c of a wife *are* a continual dropping. 4066
23:29 who hath c? who hath babbling? who hath 4066
1Co 1:11 *house* of Chloe, that there are c among you. *2054*
Tit 3: 9 and c, and strivings about the law; *2054*

CONTENTIOUS (5) [CONTENTION]
Pr 21:19 than with a c and an angry woman. 4066
26:21 wood to fire; so *is* a c man to kindle strife. 4066
27:15 a very rainy day and a c woman are alike. 4066
Ro 2: 8 But unto them that are c, *2052*
1Co 11:16 But if any *man* seem to be c, we have no *5380*

CONTENTMENT (1) [CONTENT]
1Ti 6: 6 But godliness with c is great gain. *841*

CONTINUAL (33) [CONTINUE]
Ex 29:42 *This shall be* a c burnt offering throughout 8548
Nu 4: 7 and the c bread shall be thereon: 8548
28: 3 spot day by day, *for* a c burnt offering. 8548
28: 6 *It is* a c burnt offering, which was ordained 8548
28:10 beside the c burnt offering, and his drink 8548
28:15 besides the c burnt offering, and his drink 8548
28:23 which *is* for a c burnt offering. 8548
28:24 it shall be offered beside the c burnt 8548
28:31 Ye shall offer *them* besides the c burnt 8548
29:11 the c burnt offering, and the meat offering 8548
29:16 beside the c burnt offering, his meat 8548
29:19 beside the c burnt offering, and the meat 8548
29:22 beside the c burnt offering, and his meat 8548
29:25 beside the c burnt offering, his meat 8548
29:28 beside the c burnt offering, and his meat 8548
29:31 beside the c burnt offering, his meat 8548
29:34 beside the c burnt offering, his meat 8548
29:38 beside the c burnt offering, and his meat 8548
2Ki 25:30 his allowance was a c allowance given him 8548
2Ch 2: 4 *for* the c shewbread, and *for* the burnt 8548
Ezr 3: 5 afterward *offered* the c burnt offering, 8548
Ne 10:33 *for* the c meat offering, and for 8548
10:33 for the c burnt offering, of the sabbaths, 8548
Pr 15:15 but *he that is* of a merry heart *hath* a c feast. 8548
19:13 the contentions of a wife *are* a c dropping. 2956
27:15 A c **dropping** in a very rainy day 1812+2956
Isa 14: 6 the people in wrath *with* a c stroke, 1115+5627
Jer 48: 5 up of Luhith c **weeping** shall go up; 1065+1065
52:34 there was a c diet given him of the king of 8548
Eze 39:14 they shall sever out men of c **employment,** 8548
46:15 every morning *for* a c burnt offering. 8548
Lk 18: 5 lest **by** her c coming she weary me. *1519+5056*
Ro 9: 2 great heaviness and c sorrow in my heart. *88*

CONTINUALLY (81) [CONTINUE]
Ge 6: 5 of his heart *was* only evil c. 3117+3605+1886.1
8: 3 returned from off the earth c: 1980+7725+2050.1
8: 5 the waters decreased c until the tenth 1980
Ex 28:29 *place,* for a memorial before the LORD c. 8548
28:30 Israel upon his heart before the LORD c. 8548
29:38 two lambs of the first year day by day c. 8548
Lev 24: 2 for the light, to cause the lamps to burn c. 8548
24: 3 unto the morning before the LORD c: 8548
24: 4 the pure candlestick before the LORD c. 8548
24: 8 he shall set it in order before the LORD c, 8548
Jos 6:13 the ark of the LORD **went on** c, 1980+1980
1Sa 18:29 became David's enemy c. 3117+3605+1886.1
2Sa 9: 7 and thou shalt eat bread at my table c. 8548
9:13 for he did eat c at the king's table; and *was* 8548
15:12 for the people increased c with Absalom. 1980
19:13 me c in the room of Joab. 3117+3605+1886.1
1Ki 10: 8 which stand c before thee, *and* that hear thy 8548
2Ki 4: 9 a holy man of God, which passeth by us c. 8548
25:29 he did eat bread c before him all the days of 8548
1Ch 16: 6 Jahaziel the priests with trumpets c before 8548
16:11 and his strength, seek his face c. 8548
16:37 his brethren, to minister before the ark c, 8548
16:40 the altar of the burnt offering c morning 8548
23:31 unto them, c before the LORD: 8548
2Ch 9: 7 which stand c before thee, and hear thy 8548
12:15 and Jeroboam c. 3117+3605+1886.1
24:14 of the LORD c all the days of Jehoiada. 8548
Job 1: 5 their hearts. Thus did Job c. 3117+3605+1886.1
Ps 34: 1 all times: his praise *shall* c *be* in my mouth. 8548
35:27 yea, let them say c, Let the LORD be 8548
38:17 to halt, and my sorrow *is* c before me. 8548
40:11 and thy truth c preserve me. 8548
40:16 let such as love thy salvation say c, 8548
42: 3 while *they* c say unto me, 3117+3605+1886.1
44:15 My confusion *is* c before 3117+3605+1886.1
50: 8 burnt offerings, *to have been* c before me. 8548
52: 1 goodness of God *endureth* c. 3117+3605+1886.1
58: 7 Let them melt away as waters *which* **run** c: 1980
69:23 see not; and make their loins c to shake. 8548
70: 4 let such as love thy salvation say c, 8548
71: 3 strong habitation, whereunto *I* may c resort: 8548
71: 6 my praise *shall be* c of thee. 8548
71:14 I will hope c, and will yet praise thee more 8548
72:15 prayer also shall be made for him c; *and* 8548
73:23 Nevertheless I *am* c with thee: thou hast 8548
74:23 those that rise up against thee increaseth c. 8548
109:10 Let his children be c **vagabonds,** 5128+5128
109:15 Let them be before the LORD c, that he 8548
109:19 and for a girdle where*with* he is girded c. 8548
119:44 So shall I keep thy law c for ever and ever. 8548
119:109 My soul *is* c in my hand: yet do I not forget 8548
119:117 and I will have respect unto thy statutes c. 8548
140: 2 c are they gathered together *for* war. 3117+3605
Pr 6:14 he deviseth mischief c; 3605+6256+871.1
6:21 Bind them c upon thine heart, *and* tie them 8548
Ecc 1: 6 it **whirleth about** c, and 1980+5437+5437
Isa 21: 8 I stand c upon the watchtower in 8548
49:16 of *my* hands; thy walls *are* c before me. 8548
51:13 hast feared c every day because of the fury 8548
52: 5 and my name c every day *is* blasphemed. 8548
58:11 the LORD shall guide thee c, and 8548
60:11 Therefore thy gates shall be open c; 8548
65: 3 A people that provoketh me to anger c to 8548
Jer 6: 7 in her; before me c *is* grief and wounds. 8548
33:18 and to do sacrifice c. 3117+3605+1886.1
52:33 he did c eat bread before him all the days of 8548
Eze 46:14 a meat offering c *by* a perpetual ordinance 8548
Da 6:16 Thy God whom thou servest c, 0.2+8411+871.2
6:20 thy God, whom thou servest c, 0.2+8411+871.2
Hos 4:18 they have **committed whoredom** c: 2181+2181
12: 6 and judgment, and wait on thy God c. 8548
Ob 1:16 *so* shall all the heathen drink c, yea, 8548
Na 3:19 whom hath not thy wickedness passed c? 8548
Hab 1:17 and not spare c to slay the nations? 8548
Lk 24:53 And were c in the temple, praising and *1275*
Ac 6: 4 But we will **give** ourselves c **to** prayer, and *4342*
10: 7 soldier of them that **waited on** him c; *4342*
Ro 13: 6 **attending** c upon this very *thing.* *4342*
Heb 7: 3 Son of God; abideth a priest c. *1336+1519+3588*
10: 1 c make the comers *thereunto* *1336+1519+3588*
13:15 offer the sacrifice of praise to God c, *1223+3956*

CONTINUANCE (5) [CONTINUE]
Dt 28:59 of **long** c, and sore sicknesses, and of long 539
28:59 and sore sicknesses, and of **long** c. 539
Ps 139:16 *which* in c were fashioned, when *as yet* 3117
Isa 64: 5 in those is c, and we shall be saved. 5769
Ro 2: 7 To them who by **patient** c in well doing *5281*

CONTINUE (38) [CONTINUAL, CONTINUALLY, CONTINUANCE, CONTINUED, CONTINUETH, CONTINUING]
Ex 21:21 Notwithstanding, if he c a day or two, 5975
Lev 12: 4 c in the blood of her purifying three and 3427
12: 5 she shall c in the blood of her purifying 3427
1Sa 12:14 also the king that reigneth over you c 1961
13:14 now thy kingdom shall not c: the LORD 6965
2Sa 7:29 that *it* may c for ever before thee: 1961
1Ki 2: 4 That the LORD may c his word which he 6965
Job 15:29 not be rich, neither shall his substance c, 6965
17: 2 *doth not* mine eye c in their provocation? 3885
Ps 36:10 O c thy lovingkindness unto them that 4900
49:11 *thought is, that* their houses *shall* c for ever, NIH
102:28 The children of thy servants shall c, and 7931
119:91 They c *this* day according to thine 5975
Isa 5:11 that c until night, *till* wine inflame them! 309
Jer 32:14 earthen vessel, that they may c many days. 5975
Da 11: 8 he shall c *more* years than the king of 5975
Mt 15:32 because they c with me now three days, and *4357*
Jn 8:31 If ye c in my word, *then* are ye my disciples *3306*
15: 9 so have I loved you: c ye in my love. *3306*
Ac 13:43 persuaded them to c in the grace of God. *1961*
14:22 *and* exhorting *them* to c **in** the faith, and *1696*
26:22 obtained help of God, I c unto this day, *2476*
Ro 6: 1 Shall we c **in** sin, that grace may abound? *1961*
11:22 goodness, if thou c **in** *his* goodness: *1961*
Gal 2: 5 that the truth of the gospel might c with *1265*
Php 1:25 and c **with** you all for your furtherance and *4839*
Col 1:23 If ye c **in** the faith grounded and settled, *1961*
4: 2 C **in** prayer, and watch in the same with *4342*
1Ti 2:15 if they c in faith and charity and *3306*
4:16 and unto the doctrine; c **in** them: *1961*
2Ti 3:14 But c thou in *the things* which thou hast *3306*
Heb 7:23 *they* were not suffered to c by reason of *3887*
13: 1 Let brotherly love c. *3306*
Jas 4:13 and c there a year, and buy and sell, and *4160*
2Pe 3: 4 all *things* c as *they were* from the beginning *1265*
1Jn 2:24 ye also shall c in the Son, and in the Father. *3306*
Rev 13: 5 power was given unto him to c forty *and* *4160*
17:10 when he cometh, he must c a short *space.* *3306*

CONTINUED (29) [CONTINUE]
Ge 40: 4 served them: and they c a season in ward. 1961
Jdg 5:17 Asher c on the sea shore, and abode in his 3427
Ru 1: 2 came *into* the country of Moab, and c there. 1961
2: 7 hath c even from the morning until now, 5975
1Sa 1:12 as she c praying before the LORD, 7235
2Sa 6:11 the ark of the LORD c in the house of 3427
1Ki 22: 1 they c three years without war between 3427
2Ch 29:28 all *this* c until the burnt offering was NIH
Ne 5:16 Yea also I c in the work of this wall, 2388
Job 27: 1 Moreover Job c his parable, and said, 3254+5375
29: 1 Moreover Job c his parable, and said, 3254+5375
Ps 72:17 his name shall be c as long as the sun: and 5125
Da 1:21 Daniel c *even* unto the first year of king 1961
Lk 6:12 to pray, and c all night in prayer to God. *1510*
22:28 Ye are they which have c with me in my *1265*
Jn 2:12 and they c there not many days. *3306*
8: 7 So when they c asking him, he lift up *1961*
11:54 and there c with his disciples. *1304*
Ac 1:14 These all c with one accord in prayer and *4342*
2:42 And they c **stedfastly** in the apostles' *4342*
8:13 he c with Philip, and wondered, *4342*
12:16 But Peter c knocking: and when they had *1961*
15:35 Paul also and Barnabas c in Antioch, *1304*
18:11 And he c *there* a year and six months, *2523*
19:10 And this c by the space of two years; so *1096*
20: 7 and c *his* speech until midnight. *3905*
27:33 day that ye have tarried and c fasting, *1300*
Heb 8: 9 because they c not in my covenant, and I *1696*
1Jn 2:19 of us, they would *no doubt* have c with us: *3306*

CONTINUETH (5) [CONTINUE]
Job 14: 2 he fleeth also as a shadow, and c not. 5975
Gal 3:10 Cursed *is* every one that c not in all *things* *1696*
1Ti 5: 5 and c in supplications and prayers night and *4357*
Heb 7:24 But this *man,* because he c ever, hath an *3306*

Jas 1:25 c therein, he being not a forgetful hearer, 3887

CONTINUING (4) [CONTINUE]
Jer 30:23 goeth forth with fury, a c whirlwind: 1641
Ac 2:46 c daily with one accord in the temple, and 4342
Ro 12:12 patient in tribulation; c instant in prayer; 4342
Heb 13:14 For here have we no c city, but we seek one 3306

CONTRADICTING (1) [CONTRADICTION]
Ac 13:45 were spoken by Paul, c and blaspheming. 483

CONTRADICTION (2) [CONTRADICTING]
Heb 7: 7 And without all c the less is blessed of 485
12: 3 For consider him that endured such c of 485

CONTRARIWISE (3) [CONTRARY]
2Co 2: 7 So that c ye ought rather to forgive him, 5121
Gal 2: 7 But c, when they saw that the gospel of 5121
1Pe 3: 9 but c blessing; knowing that ye are 5121

CONTRARY (24) [CONTRARIWISE]
Lev 26:21 if ye walk c unto me, and will not hearken 7147
26:23 by these things, but will walk c unto me; 7147
26:24 will I also walk c unto you, and will punish 7147
26:27 this hearken unto me, but walk c unto me; 7147
26:28 I will walk c unto you also in fury; and 7147
26:40 and that also they have walked c unto me; 7147
26:41 And that I also have walked c unto them, 7147
Est 9: 1 (though it was turned to the c, that the Jews NIH
Eze 16:34 the c is in thee from other women in thy 2016
16:34 is given unto thee, therefore thou art c. 2016
Mt 14:24 tossed with waves: for the wind was c. 1727
Mk 6:48 in rowing; for the wind was c unto them: 1727
Ac 17: 7 and these all do c to the decrees of Cesar, 561
18:13 men to worship God c to the law. 3844
23: 3 commandest me to be smitten c to the law? 3891
26: 9 that I ought to do many things c to 1727
27: 4 under Cyprus, because the winds were c. 1727
Ro 11:24 wert graffed c to nature into a good olive 3844
16:17 offences c to the doctrine which ye have 3844
Gal 5:17 and these are c the one to the other: so 480
Col 2:14 which was c to us, and took it out of 5227
1Th 2:15 they please not God, and are c to all men: 1727
1Ti 1:10 if there be any other thing that is c to sound 480
Tit 2: 8 that he that is of the c part may be ashamed, 1727

CONTRIBUTION (1)
Ro 15:26 Achaia to make a certain c for the poor 2842

CONTRITE (5)
Ps 34:18 and saveth such as be of a c spirit. 1793
51:17 a broken and a c heart, O God, thou wilt 1794
Isa 57:15 holy place, with him also that is of a c and 1793
57:15 and to revive the heart of the c ones. 1792
66: 2 even to him that is poor and of a c spirit, 5223

CONTROVERSIES (1) [CONTROVERSY]
2Ch 19: 8 for the judgment of the LORD, and for c, 7379

CONTROVERSY (13) [CONTROVERSIES]
Dt 17: 8 stroke, being matters of c within thy gates: 7379
19:17 between whom the c is, shall stand before 7379
21: 5 by their word shall every c and 7379
25: 1 If there be a c between men, and they come 7379
2Sa 15: 2 that when any man that had a c came to 7379
Isa 34: 8 the year of recompences for the c of Zion. 7379
Jer 25:31 for the LORD hath a c with the nations, 7379
Eze 44:24 in c they shall stand in judgment; and 7379
Hos 4: 1 for the LORD hath a c with 7379
12: 2 The LORD hath also a c with Judah, and 7379
Mic 6: 2 the LORD'S c, and ye strong foundations 7379
6: 2 for the LORD hath a c with his people, 7379
1Ti 3:16 And without c great is the mystery of 3672

CONVENIENT (9) [CONVENIENTLY]
Pr 30: 8 nor riches; feed me with food c for me: 2706
Jer 40: 4 and c for thee to go, 413+3477+1886.1
40: 5 go wheresoever it seemeth c unto thee to 3477
Mk 6:21 And when a c day was come, that Herod on 2121
Ac 24:25 when I have a c season, I will call for thee. 2540
Ro 1:28 to do those things which are not c; 2520
1Co 16:12 he will come when he shall have c time. 2119
Eph 5: 4 foolish talking, nor jesting, which are not c: 433
Phm 1: 8 bold in Christ to enjoin thee that which is c, 433

CONVENIENTLY (1) [CONVENIENT]
Mk 14:11 And he sought how he might c betray him. 2122

CONVERSANT (2)
Jos 8:35 and the strangers that were c among them. 1980
1Sa 25:15 as long as we were c with them, when we 1980

CONVERSATION (20)
Ps 37:14 needy, and to slay such as be of upright c. 1870
50:23 to him that ordereth his c aright will I shew 1870
2Co 1:12 we have had our c in the world, and 390
Gal 1:13 For ye have heard of my c in time past in 391
Eph 2: 3 Among whom also we all had our c in times 390
4:22 That ye put off concerning the former c 391
Php 1:27 Only let your c be as it becometh the gospel 4176
3:20 For our c is in heaven; from whence also 4175
1Ti 4:12 in word, in c, in charity, in spirit, in faith, 391
Heb 13: 5 Let your c be without covetousness; and 5158
13: 7 faith follow, considering the end of their c. 391
Jas 3:13 let him shew out of a good c his works with 391
1Pe 1:15 you is holy, so be ye holy in all manner of c; 391
1:18 from your vain c received by tradition from 391
2:12 Having your c honest among the Gentiles: 391
3: 1 the word be won by the c of the wives; 391
3: 2 While they behold your chaste c coupled 391
3:16 that falsely accuse your good c in Christ. 391
2Pe 2: 7 vexed with the filthy c of the wicked: 391
3:11 of persons ought ye to be in all holy c 391

CONVERSION (1) [CONVERT]
Ac 15: 3 Samaria, declaring the c of the Gentiles: 1995

CONVERT (2) [CONVERSION, CONVERTED, CONVERTETH, CONVERTING, CONVERTS]
Isa 6:10 with their heart, and c, and be healed. 7725
Jas 5:19 of you do err from the truth, and one c him; 1994

CONVERTED (9) [CONVERT]
Ps 51:13 thy ways; and sinners shall be c unto thee. 7725
Isa 60: 5 the abundance of the sea shall be c unto 2015
Mt 13:15 and should be c, and I should heal them. 1994
18: 3 Except ye be c, and become as little 4762
Mk 4:12 lest at any time they should be c, and 1994
Lk 22:32 and when thou art c, strengthen thy 1994
Jn 12:40 and be c, and I should heal them. 1994
Ac 3:19 Repent ye therefore, and be c, that your 1994
28:27 and should be c, and I should heal them. 1994

CONVERTETH (1) [CONVERT]
Jas 5:20 that he which c the sinner from the error of 1994

CONVERTING (1) [CONVERT]
Ps 19: 7 law of the LORD is perfect, c the soul: 7725

CONVERTS (1) [CONVERT]
Isa 1:27 and her c with righteousness. 7725

CONVEY (2) [CONVEYED]
1Ki 5: 9 I will c them by sea in flotes unto the place 7760
Ne 2: 7 that they may c me over till I come into 5674

CONVEYED (1) [CONVEY]
Jn 5:13 for Jesus had c himself away, a multitude 1593

CONVICT See REPROOF; REPROVE

CONVICTED (1)
Jn 8: 9 And they which heard it, being c by their 1651

CONVINCE (2) [CONVINCED, CONVINCETH]
Tit 1: 9 both to exhort and to c the gainsayers. 1651
Jude 1:15 to c all that are ungodly among them of all 1827

CONVINCED (4) [CONVINCE]
Job 32:12 there was none of you that c Job, or 3198
Ac 18:28 For he mightily c the Jews, and 1246
1Co 14:24 or one unlearned, he is c of all, he is judged 1651
Jas 2: 9 and are c of the law as transgressors. 1651

CONVINCETH (1) [CONVINCE]
Jn 8:46 Which of you c me of sin? And if I say 1651

CONVINCING See INFALLIBLE

CONVOCATION (16) [CONVOCATIONS]
Ex 12:16 in the first day there shall be a holy c, and 4744
12:16 in the seventh day there shall be a holy c to 4744
Lev 23: 3 seventh day is the sabbath of rest, a holy c; 4744
23: 7 In the first day ye shall have a holy c: 4744
23: 8 in the seventh day is a holy c: ye shall do 4744
23:21 that it may be a holy c unto you: 4744
23:24 memorial of blowing of trumpets, a holy c. 4744
23:27 it shall be a holy c unto you; and ye shall 4744
23:35 On the first day shall be a holy c: ye shall 4744
23:36 on the eighth day shall be a holy c unto 4744
Nu 28:18 In the first day shall be a holy c; ye shall 4744
28:25 on the seventh day ye shall have a holy c; 4744
28:26 your weeks be out, ye shall have a holy c; 4744
29: 1 day of the month, ye shall have a holy c; 4744
29: 7 tenth day of this seventh month a holy c; 4744
29:12 of the seventh month ye shall have a holy c; 4744

CONVOCATIONS (3) [CONVOCATION]
Lev 23: 2 which ye shall proclaim to be holy c, 4744
23: 4 are the feasts of the LORD, even holy c, 4744
23:37 which ye shall proclaim to be holy c, 4744

CONVULSION See TARE

CONY (1) [CONEY]
Lev 11: 5 the c, because he cheweth the cud, but 8227

COOK (2) [COOKS]
1Sa 9:23 Samuel said unto the c, Bring the portion 2876
9:24 the c took up the shoulder, and that which 2876

COOKED See SOD; SODDEN

COOKING See SOD; SODDEN

COOKS (1) [COOK]
1Sa 8:13 and to be c, and to be bakers. 2879

COOL (2)
Ge 3: 8 walking in the garden in the c of the day: 7307
Lk 16:24 tip of his finger in water, and c my tongue; 2711

COPIED (1) [COPY]
Pr 25: 1 the men of Hezekiah king of Judah c out. 6275

COPING (1)
1Ki 7: 9 even from the foundation unto the c, and so 2947

COPPER (1) [COPPERSMITH]
Ezr 8:27 and two vessels of fine c, precious as gold. 5178

COPPERSMITH (1) [COPPER, SMITH]
2Ti 4:14 Alexander the c did me much evil: the Lord 5471

COPULATION (3)
Lev 15:16 if any man's seed of c go out from him, 7902
15:17 and every skin, whereon is the seed of c, 7902
15:18 with whom man shall lie with seed of c, 7902

COPY (9) [COPIED]
Dt 17:18 that he shall write him a c of this law in a 4932
Jos 8:32 he wrote there upon the stones a c of 4932
Ezr 4:11 This is the c of the letter that they sent unto 6573
4:23 Now when the c of king Artaxerxes' letter 6573
5: 6 The c of the letter that Tatnai, governor on 6573
7:11 Now this is the c of the letter that the king 6572
Est 3:14 The c of the writing for a commandment to 6572
4: 8 Also he gave him the c of the writing of 6572
8:13 The c of the writing for a commandment to 6572

COR (1)
Eze 45:14 offer the tenth part of a bath out of the c, 3734

CORAL (2)
Job 28:18 No mention shall be made of c, or 7215
Eze 27:16 and fine linen, and c, and agate. 7215

CORBAN (1)
Mk 7:11 shall say to his father or mother, It is C, 2878

CORD (6) [CORDS]
Jos 2:15 she let them down by a c through 2256
Job 30:11 Because he hath loosed my c, and 3499
41: 1 his tongue with a c which thou lettest 2256
Ecc 4:12 and a threefold c is not quickly broken. 2339
12: 6 Or ever the silver c be loosed, or the golden 2256
Mic 2: 5 c by lot in the congregation of the LORD. 2256

CORDS (26) [CORD]
Ex 35:18 and the pins of the court, and their c, 4340
39:40 his c, and his pins, and all the vessels of 4340
Nu 3:26 and the c of it for all the service thereof. 4340
3:37 their sockets, and their pins, and their c. 4340
4:26 their c, and all the instruments of their 4340
4:32 their sockets, and their pins, and their c, 4340
Jdg 15:13 they bound him with two new c, and 5688
15:14 the c that were upon his arms became as 5688
Est 1: 6 blue hangings, fastened with c of fine linen 2256
Job 36: 8 in fetters, and be holden in c of affliction; 2256
Ps 2: 3 and cast away their c from us. 5688
118:27 bind the sacrifice with c, even unto 5688
129: 4 he hath cut asunder the c of the wicked. 5688
140: 5 The proud have hid a snare for me, and c; 2256
Pr 5:22 he shall be holden with the c of his sins. 2256
Isa 5:18 Woe unto them that draw iniquity with c of 2256
33:20 neither shall any of the c thereof be broken. 2256
54: 2 lengthen thy c, and strengthen thy stakes; 4340
Jer 10:20 is spoiled, and all my c are broken: 4340
38: 6 they let down Jeremiah with c. And in 2256
38:11 let them down by c into the dungeon to 2256
38:12 rags under thine armholes under the c. 2256
38:13 So they drew up Jeremiah with c, and 2256
Eze 27:24 bound with c, and made of cedar, 2256
Hos 11: 4 I drew them with c of a man, with bands of 2256
Jn 2:15 when he had made a scourge of small c, 4979

CORE (1)
Jude 1:11 and perished in the gainsaying of C. 2879

CORIANDER (2)
Ex 16:31 it was like c seed, white; and the taste of it 1407
Nu 11: 7 the manna was as c seed, and the colour 1407

CORINTH (6) [CORINTHIANS, CORINTHUS]
Ac 18: 1 Paul departed from Athens, and came to C; 2882
19: 1 came to pass that, while Apollos was at C, 2882
1Co 1: 2 Unto the church of God which is at C, 2882
2Co 1: 1 unto the church of God which is at C, 2882
1:23 that to spare you I came not as yet unto C. 2882
2Ti 4:20 Erastus abode at C: but Trophimus have I 2882

CORINTHIANS (4) [CORINTH]
Ac 18: 8 and many of the C hearing believed, and 2881
1Co 16: S The first epistle to the C was written from 2881
2Co 6:11 O ye C, our mouth is open unto you, 2881
13: S The second epistle to the C was written 2881

CORINTHUS (1) [CORINTH]
Ro 16: S Written to the Romans from C, and sent by 2882

CORMORANT (4)
Lev 11:17 the little owl, and the c, and the great owl, 7994
Dt 14:17 the pelican, and the gier eagle, and the c, 7994
Isa 34:11 the c and the bittern shall possess it; 6893
Zep 2:14 both the c and the bittern shall lodge in 6893

CORN (102) [CORNFLOOR]
Ge 27:28 of the earth, and plenty of c and wine: 1715
27:37 and with c and wine have I sustained him: 1715
41: 5 seven ears of c came up upon one stalk, 7641
41:35 lay up c under the hand of Pharaoh, and 1250
41:49 Joseph gathered c as the sand of the sea, 1250
41:57 came into Egypt to Joseph for to buy c; NIH
42: 1 Now when Jacob saw that there was c in 7668
42: 2 I have heard that there is c in Egypt: 7668
42: 3 Joseph's ten brethren went down to buy c 1250
42: 5 the sons of Israel came to buy c among NIH
42:19 carry c for the famine of your houses: 7668
42:25 commanded to fill their sacks with c, 1250
42:26 they laded their asses with the c, and 7668
43: 2 when they had eaten up the c which they 7668
44: 2 mouth of the youngest, and his c money. 7668
45:23 ten she asses laden with c and bread and 1250
47:14 of Canaan, for the c which they bought: 7668
Ex 22: 6 so that the stacks of c, or the standing corn, 1430
22: 6 of corn, or the standing c, or the field, 7054
Lev 2:14 firstfruits green ears of c dried by the fire, 24
2:14 by the fire, even c beaten out of full ears. 3759
2:16 part of the beaten c thereof, and part of 1643

Lev 23:14 neither bread, nor parched c, nor green ears, NIH
Nu 18:27 as though it were the c of 1715
Dt 7:13 thy land, thy c, and thy wine, and thine oil, 1715
11:14 that thou mayest gather in thy c, and 1715
12:17 not eat within thy gates the tithe of thy c, 1715
14:23 the tithe of thy c, of thy wine, and of thine 1715
16: 9 *as thou* beginnest *to put* the sickle to the c. 7054
16:13 after that thou hast gathered in thy c and 1637
18: 4 The firstfruit *also* of thy c, of thy wine, and 1715
23:25 When thou comest into the **standing** c of 7054
23:25 a sickle unto thy neighbour's **standing** c. 7054
25: 4 muzzle the ox when he treadeth out *the* c. NIH
28:51 which *also* shall not leave thee *either* c, 1715
33:28 fountain of Jacob *shall be* upon a land of c 1715
Jos 5:11 they did eat of the **old** c of the land on 5669
5:11 and parched c in the selfsame day. NIH
5:12 after they had eaten of the **old** c of the land; 5669
Jdg 15: 5 he let *them* go into the **standing** c of 7054
15: 5 also the **standing** c, with the vineyards *and* 7054
Ru 2: 2 glean **ears of** c after *him* in whose sight I 7641
2:14 he reached her parched c, and she did eat, NIH
3: 7 went to lie down at the end of the heap *of* c: NIH
1Sa 17:17 for thy brethren an ephah of this parched c, NIH
25:18 five measures of parched c, and an hundred NIH
2Sa 17:19 and spread **ground** c thereon; 7383
17:28 parched c, and beans, and lentiles, and NIH
2Ki 4:42 and **full ears of** c in the husk thereof. 3759
18:32 a land of c and wine, a land of bread and 1715
19:26 and *as* c blasted before it be grown up. NIH
2Ch 31: 5 brought in abundance the firstfruits of c, 1715
32:28 Storehouses also for the increase of c, and 1715
Ne 5: 2 we take up c *for them,* that we may eat, 1715
5: 3 houses, that we might buy c, because of 1715
5:10 *might* exact of them money and c: 1715
5:11 *of* the c, the wine, and the oil, that ye exact 1715
10:39 of Levi shall bring the offering of the c, 1715
13: 5 the vessels, and the tithes of the c, the new 1715
13:12 brought all Judah the tithe of the c and 1715
Job 5:26 like as a **shock of** c cometh in in his season. 1430
24: 6 They reap *every one* his c in the field: and 1098
24:24 and cut off as the tops of the **ears of** c. 7641
39: 4 are in good liking, they grow up with c; 1250
Ps 4: 7 more than *in* the time *that* their c and 1715
65: 9 thou preparest them c, when thou hast so 1715
65:13 the valleys also are covered over with c; 1250
72:16 There shall be a handful of c in the earth 1250
78:24 and had given them *of* the c of heaven. 1715
Pr 11:26 He that withholdeth c, the people shall 1250
Isa 17: 5 be as when the harvestman gathereth the c, 7054
21:10 O my threshing, and the c of my floor: 1121
28:28 Bread c is bruised; because he will not ever NIH
36:17 a land of c and wine, a land of bread and 1715
37:27 and *as* c blasted before it be grown up. NIH
62: 8 Surely I will no more give thy c *to be* meat 1715
La 2:12 say to their mothers, Where *is* c and wine? 1715
Eze 36:29 I will call for the c, and will increase it, and 1715
Hos 2: 8 For she did not know that I gave her c, and 1715
2: 9 and take *away* my c in the time thereof, and 1715
2:22 And the earth shall hear the c, and the wine, 1715
7:14 they assemble themselves for c and wine, 1715
10:11 *and* loveth to tread out *the* c; but I passed NIH
14: 7 they shall revive *as* the c, and grow as 1715
Joel 1:10 for the c is wasted, the new wine is dried 1715
1:17 are broken down; for the c is withered. 1715
2:19 I *will* send you c, and wine, and oil, and 1715
Am 8: 5 the new moon be gone, that we may sell c? 7668
9: 9 like as c is sifted in a sieve, yet shall not NIH
Hag 1:11 and upon the c, and upon the new wine, and 1715
Zec 9:17 c shall make the young men cheerful, and 1715
Mt 12: 1 went on the sabbath day through the c; *4702*
12: 1 and began to pluck the **ears of** c, and to eat. *4719*
Mk 2:23 that he went through the c **fields** on *4702*
2:23 as they went, to pluck the **ears of** c. *4719*
4:28 then the ear, after that the full c in the ear. *4621*
Lk 6: 1 the first, that he went through the c **fields**; *4702*
6: 1 and his disciples plucked the **ears of** c, and *4719*
Jn 12:24 Except a c of wheat fall into the ground and *2848*
Ac 7:12 But when Jacob heard that there was c in *4621*
1Co 9: 9 the mouth of the ox that **treadeth out the** c. *248*
1Ti 5:18 not muzzle the ox that **treadeth out the** c. *248*

CORNELIUS (10)

Ac 10: 1 was a certain man in Cesarea called C, *2883*
10: 3 coming in to him, and saying unto him, C. *2883*
10: 7 And when the angel which spake unto C *2883*
10:17 the men which were sent from C had made *2883*
10:21 the men which were sent unto him from C; *2883*
10:22 C the centurion, a just man, and one that *2883*
10:24 And C waited for them, and had called *2883*
10:25 C met him, and fell down at *his* feet, and *2883*
10:30 And C said, Four days ago I was fasting *2883*
10:31 And said, C, thy prayer is heard, and *2883*

CORNER (37)

Ex 36:25 *which is* toward the north c, he made 6285
Lev 21: 5 neither shall they shave off the c of their 6285
Jos 18:14 and compassed the c of the sea southward, 6285
2Ki 11:11 from the right c of the temple to the left 3802
11:11 of the temple to the left c of the temple, 3802
14:13 from the gate of Ephraim unto the c gate, 6438
2Ch 25:23 from the gate of Ephraim to the c gate, 6437
26: 9 built towers in Jerusalem at the c gate, 6438
28:24 he made him altars in every c of Jerusalem. 6438
Ne 3:24 the turning *of the wall,* even unto the c. 6438
3:31 gate Miphkad, and to the going up of the c. 6438
3:32 between the going up of the c unto 6438
Job 38: 6 or who laid the c stone thereof; 6438
Ps 118:22 refused is become the head *stone* of the c. 6438
144:12 *that* our daughters *may be* as c **stones,** 2106
Pr 7: 8 Passing through the street near her c; and 6434
7:12 in the streets, and lieth in wait at every c.) 6438
21: 9 *It is* better to dwell in a c of the housetop, 6438
25:24 *It is* better to dwell in a c of the housetop, 6438
Isa 28:16 a precious c *stone,* a sure foundation: 6438
30:20 thy teachers be **removed into a** c any more, 3670
Jer 31:38 tower of Hananeel unto the gate of the c. 6438
31:40 unto the c of the horse gate towards 6438
48:45 shall devour the c of Moab, and the crown 6285
51:26 they shall not take of thee a stone for a c, 6438
Eze 46:21 **every** c of the court *there was* a 4740+4740
Am 3:12 out that dwell in Samaria in the c of a bed, 6285
Zec 10: 4 Out of him came forth the c, out of him 6438
14:10 unto the c gate, and *from* the tower of 6434
Mt 21:42 the same is become the head of the c: *1137*
Mk 12:10 rejected is become the head of the c: *1137*
Lk 20:17 the same is become the head of the c? *1137*
Ac 4:11 which is become the head of the c. *1137*
26:26 for this *thing* was not done in a c. *1137*
Eph 2:20 Jesus Christ himself being the **chief** c *stone;* *204*
1Pe 2: 6 Behold, I lay in Sion a **chief** c stone, elect, *204*
2: 7 the same is made the head of the c, *1137*

CORNER DEFENSES See BULWARKS

CORNERS (39)

Ex 25:12 for it, and put *them* in the four c thereof; 6471
25:26 put the rings in the four c that *are* on 6285
26:23 two boards shalt thou make for the c of 4742
26:24 for them both; they shall be for the two c. 4740
27: 2 the horns of it upon the four c thereof: 6438
27: 4 four brasen rings in the four c thereof. 7098
30: 4 by the two c thereof, upon the two sides of 6763
36:28 two boards made he for the c of 4742
36:29 thus he did to both of them in both the c. 4740
37: 3 rings of gold, *to be set* by the four c of it; 6471
37:13 put the rings upon the four c that *were* in 6285
37:27 by the two c of it, upon the two sides 6763
38: 2 he made the horns thereof on the four c of 6438
Lev 19: 9 thou shalt not wholly reap the c of thy field, 6285
19:27 Ye shall not round the c of your heads, 6285
19:27 neither shalt thou mar the c of thy beard. 6285
23:22 thou shalt not make clean riddance of the c 6285
Nu 24:17 shall smite the c of Moab, and destroy all 6285
Dt 32:26 I said, I would **scatter** them **into** c, I would 6284
1Ki 7:30 the four c thereof had undersetters: under 6471
7:34 *there were* four undersetters to the four c of 6438
Ne 9:22 and nations, and didst divide them into c: 6285
Job 1:19 smote the four c of the house, and it fell 6438
Isa 11:12 of Judah from the four c of the earth. 3671
Jer 9:26 and Moab, and all *that are* in the utmost c, 6285
25:23 and Buz, and all *that are* in the utmost c, 6285
49:32 into all winds them *that are* in the utmost c; 6285
Eze 7: 2 the end is come upon the four c of the land. 3671
41:22 the c thereof, and the length thereof, and 4740
43:20 on the four c of the settle, and upon 6438
45:19 and upon the four c of the settle of the altar, 6438
46:21 caused me to pass by the four c of 4740
46:22 In the four c of the court *there were* courts 4740
46:22 these four c *were* of one measure. 7106
Zec 9:15 filled like bowls, *and* as the c of the altar. 2106
Mt 6: 5 the synagogues and in the c of the streets, *1137*
Ac 10:11 as *it had been* a great sheet knit at the four c, *746*
11: 5 great sheet, let down from heaven by four c; *746*
Rev 7: 1 angels standing on the four c of the earth, *1137*

CORNET (7)

1Ch 15:28 with sound of the c, and with trumpets, and 7782
Ps 98: 6 sound of c make a joyful noise before 7782
Da 3: 5 at what time ye hear the sound of the c, 7162
3: 7 all the people heard the sound of the c, 7162
3:10 man that shall hear the sound of the c, 7162
3:15 that at what time ye hear the sound of the c, 7162
Hos 5: 8 Blow ye the c in Gibeah, *and* the trumpet in 7782

CORNETS (2)

2Sa 6: 5 and on timbrels, and on c, and on cymbals. 4517
2Ch 15:14 and with trumpets, and with c. 7782

CORNFLOOR (1) [CORN, FLOOR]

Hos 9: 1 hast loved a reward upon every c. 1637+1715

CORPSE (1) [CORPSES]

Mk 6:29 heard *of it,* they came and took up his c, *4430*

CORPSES (4) [CORPSE]

2Ki 19:35 the morning, behold, they *were* all dead c. 6297
Isa 37:36 the morning, behold, they *were* all dead c. 6297
Na 3: 3 of carcases; and *there is* none end of *their* c; 1472
3: 3 of *their* corpses; they stumble upon their c: 1472

CORRECT (7) [CORRECTED, CORRECTETH, CORRECTION]

Ps 39:11 When thou with rebukes dost c man for 3256
94:10 that chastiseth the heathen, shall not he c? 3198
Pr 29:17 C thy son, and he shall give thee rest; yea, 3256
Jer 2:19 Thine own wickedness shall c thee, and 3256
10:24 O LORD, c me, but with judgment; not in 3256
30:11 I will c thee in measure, and will not leave 3256
46:28 a full end of thee, but c thee in measure; 3256

CORRECTED (2) [CORRECT]

Pr 29:19 A servant will not be c by words: 3256
Heb 12: 9 have had fathers of our flesh which c *us,* *3810*

CORRECTETH (2) [CORRECT]

Job 5:17 Behold, happy *is* the man whom God c: 3198
Pr 3:12 For whom the LORD loveth he c; even as 3198

CORRECTION (12) [CORRECT]

Job 37:13 whether for c, or for his land, or for mercy. 7626
Pr 3:11 of the LORD; neither be weary of his c: 8433
7:22 or as a fool to the c of the stocks; 4148
15:10 C *is* grievous unto him that forsaketh 4148
22:15 *but* the rod of c shall drive it far from him. 4148
23:13 Withhold not c from the child: for *if* thou 4148
Jer 2:30 I smitten your children; they received no c: 4148
5: 3 *but* they have refused to receive c: 4148
7:28 of the LORD their God, nor receiveth c: 4148
Hab 1:12 thou hast established them for c. 3198
Zep 3: 2 obeyed not the voice; she received not c; 4148
2Ti 3:16 *is* profitable for doctrine, for reproof, for c, *1882*

CORRUPT (33) [CORRUPTED, CORRUPTERS, CORRUPTETH, CORRUPTIBLE, CORRUPTING, CORRUPTION, CORRUPTLY, UNCORRUPTIBLE]

Ge 6:11 The earth also was c before God, and 7843
6:12 looked upon the earth, and behold, it was c; 7843
Dt 4:16 Lest ye c *yourselves,* and make you a 7843
4:25 shall c *yourselves,* and make a graven 7843
31:29 death ye will **utterly** c *yourselves,* 7843+7843
Job 17: 1 My breath is c, my days are extinct, 2254
Ps 14: 1 They are c, they have done abominable 7843
38: 5 My wounds stink *and* are c because of my 4743
53: 1 C are they, and have done abominable 7843
73: 8 They are c, and speak wickedly *concerning* 4167
Pr 25:26 *is as* a troubled fountain, and a c spring. 7843
Eze 20:44 nor according to your c doings, O ye house 7843
23:11 was more c in her inordinate love than she, 7843
Da 2: 9 and c words to speak before me, 7844
11:32 against the covenant shall he c by flatteries: 2610
Mal 1:14 sacrificeth unto the Lord a c *thing:* for I *am* 7843
2: 3 I *will* c your seed, and spread dung upon 1605
Mt 6:19 where moth and rust doth c, and *853*
6:20 where neither moth nor rust doth c, and *853*
7:17 but a c tree bringeth forth evil fruit. *4550*
7:18 neither *can* a c tree bring forth good fruit. *4550*
12:33 or else make the tree c, and his fruit *4550*
12:33 else make the tree corrupt, and his fruit c: *4550*
Lk 6:43 For a good tree bringeth not forth c fruit; *4550*
6:43 neither doth a c tree bring forth good fruit. *4550*
1Co 15:33 evil communications c good manners. *5351*
2Co 2:17 are not as many, which c the word of God: *2585*
Eph 4:22 which is c according to the deceitful lusts; *5351*
4:29 Let no c communication proceed out of *4550*
1Ti 6: 5 Perverse disputings of men of c minds, and *1311*
2Ti 3: 8 men of c minds, reprobate concerning *2704*
Jude 1:10 in those *things* they c themselves. *5351*
Rev 19: 2 which did c the earth with her fornication, *5351*

CORRUPTED (14) [CORRUPT]

Ge 6:12 for all flesh had c his way upon the earth. 7843
Ex 8:24 the land was c by reason of the swarm *of* 7843
32: 7 of the land of Egypt, have c *themselves:* 7843
Dt 9:12 c *themselves;* they are quickly turned aside 7843
32: 5 They have c themselves, their spot *is* not 7843
Jdg 2:19 and c *themselves* more than their fathers, 7843
Eze 16:47 thou wast c more than they in all thy ways. 7843
28:17 thou hast c thy wisdom by reason of thy 7843
Hos 9: 9 They have deeply c *themselves,* as *in* 7843
Zep 3: 7 but they rose early, *and* c all their doings. 7843
Mal 2: 8 ye have c the covenant of Levi, saith 7843
2Co 7: 2 we have wronged no *man,* we have c no *5351*
11: 3 your minds should be c from the simplicity *5351*
Jas 5: 2 Your riches are c, and your garments are *4595*

CORRUPTERS (2) [CORRUPT]

Isa 1: 4 a seed of evildoers, children that are c: 7843
Jer 6:28 *they are* brass and iron; they *are* all c. 7843

CORRUPTETH (1) [CORRUPT]

Lk 12:33 where no thief approacheth, neither moth c. *1311*

CORRUPTIBLE (7) [CORRUPT]

Ro 1:23 God into an image made like to c man, *5349*
1Co 9:25 *things.* Now they *do it* to obtain a c crown; *5349*
15:53 For this c must put on incorruption, and *5349*
15:54 So when this c shall have put on *5349*
1Pe 1:18 were not redeemed with c *things, as* silver *5349*
1:23 not of c seed, but *of* incorruptible, *5349*
3: 4 in *that which is* **not** c, *even the ornament* of *862*

CORRUPTING (1) [CORRUPT]

Da 11:17 give him the daughter of women, c her: 7843

CORRUPTION (21) [CORRUPT]

Lev 22:25 because their c *is* in them, *and* blemishes *be* 4893
2Ki 23:13 *were* on the right hand of the mount of c, 4889
Job 17:14 I have said to c, Thou *art* my father: to 7845
Ps 16:10 wilt thou suffer thine Holy One to see c. 7845
49: 9 he should still live for ever, *and* not see c. 7845
Isa 38:17 to my soul *delivered it* from the pit of c: 1097
Da 10: 8 for my comeliness was turned in me into c, 4889
Jnh 2: 6 yet hast thou brought up my life from c, 7845
Ac 2:27 wilt thou suffer thine Holy One to see c. *1312*
2:31 not left in hell, neither his flesh did see c. *1312*
13:34 *now* no more to return to c, he said on this *1312*
13:35 shalt not suffer thine Holy One to see c. *1312*
13:36 and was laid unto his fathers, and saw c: *1312*
13:37 But he, whom God raised *again,* saw no c. *1312*
Ro 8:21 c into the glorious liberty of the children of *5356*
1Co 15:42 It is sown in c; it is raised in incorruption: *5356*
15:50 of God; neither doth c inherit incorruption. *5356*
Gal 6: 8 soweth to his flesh shall of the flesh reap c; *5356*
2Pe 1: 4 having escaped the c that is in the world *5356*
2:12 and shall utterly perish in their own c; *5356*
2:19 they themselves are the servants of c: *5356*

CORRUPTLY (2) [CORRUPT]

2Ch 27: 2 of the LORD. And the people did yet c. 7843
Ne 1: 7 We have **dealt very** c against thee, 2254+2254

COS (1)

Ac 21: 1 we came with a straight course unto C, and *2972*

COSAM (1)

Lk 3:28 *the son* of Addi, which was *the son* of C, *2973*

COST (4) [COSTLINESS, COSTLY]

2Sa 19:42 have we eaten at all of the king's c? or NIH
24:24 my God of that which doth c me **nothing.** 2600
1Ch 21:24 nor offer burnt offerings **without** c. 2600
Lk 14:28 sitteth not down first, and counteth the c, *1160*

C

COSTLINESS (1) [COST]
Rev 18:19 that had ships in the sea by reason of her **c**: *5094*

COSTLY (6) [COST]
1Ki 5:17 great stones, **c** stones, *and* hewed stones, 3368
7: 9 All these *were of* **c** stones, according to 3368
7:10 the foundation *was of* **c** stones, *even* great 3368
7:11 above *were* **c** stones, after the measures of 3368
Jn 12: 3 **very c**, and anointed the feet of Jesus, and *4186*
1Ti 2: 9 broided hair, or gold, or pearls, or **c** array; *4185*

COTES (1)
2Ch 32:28 for all *manner of* beasts, and **c** for flocks. 220

COTTAGE (2) [COTTAGES]
Isa 1: 8 the daughter of Zion is left as a **c** in a 5521
24:20 a drunkard, and shall be removed like a **c**; 4412

COTTAGES (1) [COTTAGE]
Zep 2: 6 shall be dwellings *and* **c** for shepherds, 3741

COUCH (7) [COUCHED, COUCHES, COUCHETH, COUCHING]
Ge 49: 4 then defiledst thou *it:* he went up to my **c**. 3326
Job 7:13 comfort me, my **c** shall ease my complaint; 4904
38:40 When they **c** in *their* dens, *and* abide in 7817
Ps 6: 6 bed to swim; I water my **c** with my tears. 6210
Am 3:12 the corner of a bed, and in Damascus *in* a **c**. 6210
Lk 5:19 let him down through the tiling with *his* **c** *2826*
5:24 and take up thy **c**, and go into thine house. *2826*

COUCHED (2) [COUCH]
Ge 49: 9 he **c** as a lion, and as an old lion; 7257
Nu 24: 9 He **c**, he lay down as a lion, and as a great 3766

COUCHES (2) [COUCH]
Am 6: 4 stretch themselves upon their **c**, and eat 6210
Ac 5:15 the streets, and laid *them* on beds and **c**, *2895*

COUCHETH (1) [COUCH]
Dt 33:13 for the dew, and for the deep that **c** beneath, 7257

COUCHING (2) [COUCH]
Ge 49:14 Issachar *is* a strong ass **c down** between 7257
Eze 25: 5 and the Ammonites a **c place** for flocks: 4769

COULD (166) [COULDEST]
Ge 13: 6 was great, so that they **c** not dwell together. 3201
27: 1 and his eyes were dim, so that he **c** not see, NIH
36: 7 the land wherein they were strangers **c** not 3201
37: 4 and **c** not speak peaceably unto him. 3201
41: 8 *there was* none that **c** interpret them unto NIH
41:21 it **c** not be known that they had eaten them; NIH
41:24 but *there was* none that **c** declare *it* to me. NIH
43: 7 **c** we certainly know that he would say, NIH
45: 1 Joseph **c** not refrain himself before all them 3201
45: 3 his brethren **c** not answer him; for they 3201
48:10 were dim for age, *so that* he **c** not see. 3201
Ex 2: 3 when she **c** not longer hide him, she took 3201
7:21 the Egyptians **c** not drink of the water of 3201
7:24 for they **c** not drink of the water of 3201
8:18 to bring forth lice, but they **c** not: 3201
9:11 the magicians **c** not stand before Moses 3201
12:39 were thrust out of Egypt, and **c** not tarry, 3201
15:23 they **c** not drink of the waters of Marah, 3201
Nu 9: 6 that they **c** not keep the passover on that 3201
Jos 7:12 Therefore the children of Israel **c** not stand 3201
15:63 the children of Judah **c** not drive them out: 3201
17:12 Yet the children of Manasseh **c** not drive 3201
Jdg 1:19 **c** not drive out the inhabitants of the valley, NIH
2:14 that they **c** not any longer stand before their 3201
3:22 that he **c** not draw the dagger out of his NIH
6:27 men of the city, **that** *he* **c not do** *it* by day, 4480
12: 6 for he **c** not **frame** to pronounce *it* right. 3559
14:14 they **c** not *in* three days expound the riddle. 3201
17: 8 to sojourn where he **c** find *a place:* NIH
20:16 every one **c** sling stones at a hair *breadth,* NIH
Ru 3:14 she rose up before one **c** know another. And NIH
1Sa 3: 2 eyes began *to wax* dim, *that* he **c** not see; 3201
4:15 and his eyes were dim, that he **c** not see. 3201
10:21 when they sought him, he **c** not be found. NIH
23:13 and went whithersoever they **c** go. NIH
30:10 faint that they **c** not go over the brook NIH
30:21 so faint that they **c** not follow David, NIH
2Sa 1:10 I was sure that he **c** not live after *that* he was NIH
3:11 he **c** not answer Abner a word again, 3201
17:20 **c** not find *them,* they returned *to* Jerusalem. NIH
22:39 and wounded them, that they **c** not arise: NIH
1Ki 5: 3 Thou knowest how that David my father **c** 3201
8: 5 that **c** not be told nor numbered for NIH
8:11 So that the priests **c** not stand to minister 3201
13: 4 so that he **c** not pull it in again to him. 3201
14: 4 Ahijah **c** not see; for his eyes were set by 3201
2Ki 3:26 *even* unto the king of Edom: but they **c** not. 3201
4:40 in the pot. And they **c** not eat *thereof.* 3201
16: 5 besieged Ahaz, but **c** not overcome *him.* 3201
1Ch 12: 2 **c** use both the right hand and the left in NIH
12: 8 the battle, that **c** handle shield and buckler, NIH
12:33 of war, fifty thousand, which **c** keep rank: NIH
12:38 All these men of war, that **c** keep rank, NIH
21:30 David **c** not go before it to inquire of God: 3201
2Ch 4:18 for the weight of the brass **c** not be found NIH
5: 6 which **c** not be told nor numbered for NIH
5:14 So that the priests **c** not stand to minister by 3201
7: 2 the priests **c** not enter into the house of 3201
13: 7 tender hearted, and **c** not withstand them. NIH
14:13 that they **c** not recover themselves; NIH
20:25 more than they **c** carry away: NIH
25: 5 forth *to* war, that **c** handle spear and shield. NIH
25:15 which **c** not deliver their own people out of NIH
29:34 that they **c** not flay all the burnt offerings: 3201
30: 3 For they **c** not keep it at that time, because 3201
32:14 that **c** deliver his people out of mine hand, 3201
2Ch 34:12 all that **c** skill of instruments of musick. NIH
Ezr 2:59 they **c** not shew their fathers' house, and 3201
3:13 So that the people **c** not discern the noise of NIH
5: 5 that they **c** not cause them to cease, till NIH
Ne 7:61 they **c** not shew their fathers' house, 3201
8: 2 and all that **c** hear with understanding, NIH
8: 3 and the women, and those that **c** understand; NIH
13:24 **c** not speak in the Jews' language, but 5234
Est 6: 1 On that night **c not** the king sleep, and 5074
7: 4 although the enemy **c** not countervail NIH
9: 2 no man **c** withstand them; for the fear of NIH
Job 4:16 but I **c** not discern the form thereof: NIH
16: 4 I also **c** speak as ye *do:* if your soul were in NIH
16: 4 I **c** heap up words against you, and NIH
31:23 by reason of his highness I **c** not **endure**. 3201
Ps 37:36 yea, I sought him, but he **c** not be found. NIH
55:12 I **c** have borne *it:* neither *was it* he that hated NIH
73: 7 they have more than heart **c** wish. NIH
78:44 and their floods, *that* they **c** not drink. NIH
SS 5: 6 I sought him, but I **c** not find him; I called NIH
Isa 5: 4 What **c** have been done more to my NIH
7: 1 to war against it, but **c** not prevail against it. 3201
30: 5 They were all ashamed of a people *that* **c** NIH
33:23 they **c** not well strengthen their mast, NIH
33:23 their mast, they **c** not spread the sail: NIH
41:28 when I asked of them, **c** answer a word. NIH
46: 2 they **c** not deliver the burden, but 3201
Jer 6:15 not at all ashamed, neither **c** they blush: 3045
8:12 not at all ashamed, neither **c** they blush: 3045
15: 1 *yet* my mind **c** not *be* toward this people: NIH
20: 9 was weary with forbearing, and I **c** not stay. 3201
24: 2 which **c** not be eaten, they were so bad. NIH
44:22 So that the LORD **c** no longer bear, 3201
La 4:14 so that *men* **c** not touch their garments. 3201
4:17 watched for a nation *that* **c** not save *us.* NIH
Eze 31: 8 The cedars in the garden of God **c** not hide NIH
47: 5 *and it was* a river that I **c** not pass over: 3201
47: 5 to swim in, a river that **c** not be passed over. NIH
Da 5: 8 wise *men:* but they **c** not read the writing, 3546
5:15 they **c** not shew the interpretation of 3546
6: 4 they **c** find none occasion nor fault; 3202
8: 4 neither *was there any* that **c** deliver out of NIH
8: 7 there was none that **c** deliver the ram out of NIH
Hos 5:13 yet **c** he not heal you nor cure you of your 3201
Jnh 1:13 hard to bring *it* to the land; but they **c** not: 3201
Mt 17:16 to thy disciples, and they **c** not cure him. *1410*
17:19 and said, Why **c** not we cast him out? *1410*
26:40 What, **c** ye not watch with me one hour? *2480*
27:24 When Pilate saw that he **c** prevail nothing, NIG
Mk 1:45 insomuch that *Jesus* **c** no more openly enter *1410*
2: 4 And when they **c** not come nigh unto him *1410*
3:20 so that they **c** not so much as eat bread. *1410*
5: 3 and no *man* **c** bind him, no, not with *1410*
5: 4 in pieces: neither **c** any *man* tame him. *2480*
6: 5 And he **c** there do no mighty work, *1410*
6:19 and would have killed him; but she **c** not: *1410*
7:24 have no *man* know *it:* but he **c** not be hid. *1410*
9:18 they should cast him out; and they **c** not. *2480*
9:28 him privately, Why **c** not we cast him out? *1410*
14: 8 She hath done what she **c**: she is come NIG
Lk 1:22 he came out, he **c** not speak unto them: *1410*
5:19 And when they **c** not find by what *way* they NIG
6:48 upon that house, and **c** not shake it: *2480*
8:19 and **c** not come at him for the press. *1410*
8:43 upon physicians, neither **c** be healed of any, *2480*
9:40 disciples to cast him out; and they **c** not. *1410*
13:11 and **c** in no wise lift up *herself.* *1410*
14: 6 And they **c** not answer him again to these *2480*
19: 3 and **c** not for the press, because he was *1410*
19:48 And **c** not find what they might do: for all NIG
20: 7 that *they* **c** not tell whence *it was.* NIG
20:26 And they **c** not take hold of his words *2480*
Jn 9:33 this *man* were not of God, he **c** do nothing. *1410*
11:37 **C** not this *man,* which opened the eyes of *1410*
12:39 Therefore they **c** not believe, because *1410*
21:25 I suppose that even the world itself **c** not NIG
Ac 4:14 with them, they **c** say nothing against *it.* *2192*
11:17 what was I, that I **c** withstand God? *1415*
13:39 ye **c** not be justified by the law of Moses. *1410*
21:34 when he **c** not know the certainty for *1410*
22:11 And when I **c** not see for the glory of that NIG
25: 7 against Paul, which they **c** not prove. *2480*
27:15 and **c** not bear up into the wind, we let *her* *1410*
27:43 commanded that they which **c** swim should *1410*
Ro 8: 3 For what the law **c not do**, in that it was *102*
9: 3 For I **c** wish that myself were accursed from NIG
1Co 3: 1 **c** not speak unto you as unto spiritual, but *1410*
13: 2 so that *I* **c** remove mountains, and have no NIG
2Co 3: 7 that the children of Israel **c** not stedfastly *1410*
3:13 that the children of Israel **c** not stedfastly NIG
11: 1 Would *to God* you **c** bear with me a little in NIG
Gal 3:21 for if there had been a law given which **c** *1410*
1Th 3: 1 Wherefore when we **c** no longer forbear, NIG
3: 5 For this cause, when I **c** no longer forbear, NIG
Heb 3:19 So we see that they **c** not enter in because *1410*
6:13 because he **c** swear by no greater, he sware NIG
9: 9 that **c** not make him that did the service *1410*
12:20 (For they **c** not endure that which was NIG
Rev 7: 9 which no *man* **c** number, of all nations, and *1410*
14: 3 and no *man* **c** learn *that* song but *1410*

COULD NOT TALK See DUMB

COULDEST (5) [COULD]
Jer 3: 5 hast spoken and done evil *things* as thou **c**. 3201
Eze 16:28 harlot with them, and yet **c** not be satisfied. NIH
Da 2:47 of secrets, seeing thou **c** reveal this secret. 3202
Mk 14:37 sleepest thou? **c** not thou watch one hour? *2480*
Jn 19:11 Thou **c** have no power *at all* against me, NIG

COULTER (1) [COULTERS]
1Sa 13:20 and his **c**, and his axe, and his mattock. 855

COULTERS (1) [COULTER]
1Sa 13:21 for the **c**, and for the forks, and for the axes, 855

COUNCIL (23) [COUNCILS]
Ps 68:27 the princes of Judah *and* their **c**, the princes 7277
Mt 5:22 Raca, shall be in danger of the **c**: *4892*
12:14 went out, and held a **c** against him, *4824*
26:59 the chief priests, and elders, and all the **c**, *4892*
Mk 14:55 all the **c** sought for witness against Jesus to *4892*
15: 1 with the elders and scribes and the whole **c**, *4892*
Lk 22:66 and led him into their **c**, saying, *4892*
Jn 11:47 the chief priests and the Pharisees a **c**, *4892*
Ac 4:15 commanded them to go aside out of the **c**, *4892*
5:21 and called the **c** together, and all the senate *4892*
5:27 brought them, they set *them* before the **c**: *4892*
5:34 Then stood there up one in the **c**, *4892*
5:41 they departed from the presence of the **c**, *4892*
6:12 and caught him, and brought *him* to the **c**, *4892*
6:15 And all that sat in the **c**, looking stedfastly *4892*
22:30 the chief priests and all their **c** to appear, *4892*
23: 1 earnestly beholding the **c**, said, Men *and* *4892*
23: 6 he cried out in the **c**, Men *and* brethren, *4892*
23:15 ye with the **c** signify to the chief captain *4892*
23:20 bring down Paul to morrow into the **c**, *4892*
23:28 I brought him forth into their **c**: *4892*
24:20 evil doing in me, while I stood before the **c**, *4892*
25:12 when he had conferred with the **c**, *4824*

COUNCILS (2) [COUNCIL]
Mt 10:17 for they will deliver you up to the **c**, and *4892*
Mk 13: 9 for they shall deliver you up to **c**; and in *4892*

COUNSEL (143) [COUNSELLED, COUNSELLER, COUNSELLERS, COUNSELS]
Ex 18:19 I will **give** thee **c**, and God shall be with 3289
Nu 27:21 who shall ask **c** for him after the judgment NIH
31:16 children of Israel, through the **c** of Balaam, 1697
Dt 32:28 For they *are* a nation void of **c**, neither *is* 6098
Jos 9:14 and asked not **c** at the mouth of the LORD. NIH
Jdg 18: 5 said unto him, Ask **c**, we pray thee, of God, NIH
20: 7 of Israel; give here your advice and **c**. 6098
20:18 house of God, and asked **c** of God, and said, NIH
20:23 and asked **c** of the LORD, saying, NIH
1Sa 14:37 Saul asked **c** of God, Shall I go down after NIH
2Sa 15:31 turn the **c** of Ahithophel into foolishness. 6098
15:34 mayest thou for me defeat the **c** of 6098
16:20 Give **c** among you what we shall do. 6098
16:23 the **c** of Ahithophel, which he counselled in 6098
16:23 *was* all the **c** of Ahithophel both with David 6098
17: 7 The **c** that Ahithophel hath **given** *is* 3289+6098
17:11 Therefore I **c** *that* all Israel be generally 3289
17:14 The **c** of Hushai the Archite *is* better than 6098
17:14 Archite *is* better than the **c** of Ahithophel. 6098
17:14 to defeat the good **c** of Ahithophel, 6098
17:15 thus did Ahithophel **c** Absalom and 3289
17:23 when Ahithophel saw that his **c** was not 6098
20:18 They shall surely ask **c** at Abel: NIH
1Ki 1:12 come, let me, I pray thee, **give** thee **c**, 3289+6098
12: 8 **c** of the old men, which they had **given** 3289+6098
12: 9 What **c give** ye that we may answer this 3289
12:13 the old men's **c** that they **gave** him; 3289+6098
12:14 spake to them after the **c** of the young men, 6098
12:28 Whereupon the king **took c**, and made two 3289
2Ki 6: 8 **took c** with his servants, saying, In such 3289
18:20 *I have* **c** and strength for the war. 6098
1Ch 10:13 also for asking **c** of *one that had* a familiar NIH
2Ch 10: 6 king Rehoboam **took c with** the old men 3289
10: 6 What **c give** ye *me* to return answer to this 3289
10: 8 the **c** which the old men **gave** him, 3289+6098
10: 8 **took c with** the young men that were 3289
10:13 king Rehoboam forsook the **c** of the old 6098
22: 5 He walked also after their **c**, and went with 6098
25:16 unto him, Art thou made of the king's **c**? 3289
25:16 and hast not hearkened unto my **c**. 6098
30: 2 For the king had **taken c**, and his princes, 3289
30:23 the whole assembly **took c** to keep other 3289
32: 3 He **took c** with his princes and his mighty 3289
Ezr 10: 3 according to the **c** of my lord, and of those 6098
10: 8 according to the **c** of the princes and 6098
Ne 4:15 God had brought their **c** to nought, that we 6098
6: 7 now therefore, and let us **take c** together. 3289
Job 5:13 the **c** of the froward is carried headlong. 6098
10: 3 and shine upon the **c** of the wicked? 6098
12:13 and strength, he hath **c** and understanding. 6098
18: 7 and his own **c** shall cast him down. 6098
21:16 the **c** of the wicked is far from me. 6098
22:18 but the **c** of the wicked is far from me. 6098
29:21 and waited, and kept silence at my **c**. 6098
38: 2 Who *is* this that darkeneth **c** by words 6098
42: 3 Who *is* he that hideth **c** without 6098
Ps 1: 1 Blessed *is* the man that walketh not in the **c** 6098
2: 2 the rulers **take c** together, against 3245
13: 2 How long shall I take **c** in my soul, 6098
14: 6 You have shamed the **c** of the poor, 6098
16: 7 bless the LORD, who hath **given** me **c**: 3289
20: 4 to thine own heart, and fulfil all thy **c**. 6098
31:13 while they **took c** together against me, 3245
33:10 The LORD bringeth the **c** of the heathen 6098
33:11 The **c** of the LORD standeth for ever, 6098
55:14 We took sweet **c** together, *and* walked unto 5475
64: 2 Hide me from the **secret c** of the wicked; 5475
71:10 they that lay wait for my soul **take c** 3289
73:24 Thou shalt guide me with thy **c**, and 6098
83: 3 They have taken crafty **c** against thy 5475
106:13 forgat his works; they waited not for his **c**: 6098
106:43 they provoked *him* with their **c**, and 6098
107:11 and contemned the **c** of the most High: 6098
Pr 1:25 ye have set at nought all my **c**, and 6098
1:30 They would none of my **c**: they despised all 6098
8:14 **C** *is* mine, and sound wisdom: I *am* 6098
11:14 Where no **c** *is,* the people fall: but in 8458
12:15 but he that hearkeneth unto **c** *is* wise. 6098
15:22 Without **c** purposes *are* disappointed: but 5475
19:20 Hear **c**, and receive instruction, that thou 6098

Pr 19:21 nevertheless the c of the LORD, that shall 6098
20: 5 C in the heart of man is like deep water; 6098
20:18 Every purpose is established by c: and 6098
21:30 is no wisdom nor understanding nor c 6098
24: 6 For by wise c thou shalt make thy war: and 8458
27: 9 the sweetness of a man's friend by hearty c. 6098
Ecc 8: 2 I c thee to keep the king's commandment, NIH
Isa 5:19 let the c of the Holy One of Israel draw 6098
7: 5 have taken evil c against thee, saying, 3289
8:10 Take c together, and it shall come to 5779+6098
11: 2 understanding, the spirit of c and might, 6098
16: 3 Take c, execute judgment; make thy 6098
19: 3 and I will destroy the c thereof: 6098
19:11 the c of the wise counsellers of Pharaoh is 6098
19:17 because of the c of the LORD of hosts, 6098
23: 8 Who hath taken this c against Tyre, 3289
28:29 which is wonderful in c, and excellent in 6098
29:15 seek deep to hide their c from the LORD, 6098
30: 1 saith the LORD, that take c, but not of me; 6098
36: 5 vain words) I have c and strength for war: 6098
40:14 With whom took he c, and who instructed 3289
44:26 and performeth the c of his messengers; 6098
45:21 them near; yea, let them take c together: 3289
46:10 My c shall stand, and I will do all my 6098
46:11 the man that executeth my c from a far 6098
Jer 18:18 nor c from the wise, nor the word from 6098
18:23 thou knowest all their c against me to slay 6098
19: 7 I will make void the c of Judah and 6098
23:18 For who hath stood in the c of the LORD, 5475
23:22 if they had stood in my c, and had caused 5475
32:19 Great in c, and mighty in work: for thine 6098
38:15 if I give thee c, wilt thou not hearken unto 3289
49: 7 is c perished from the prudent? is their 6098
49:20 Therefore hear the c of the LORD, that he 6098
49:30 of Babylon hath taken c against you, 3289+6098
50:45 Therefore hear ye the c of the LORD, 6098
Eze 7:26 from the priest, and c from the ancients. 6098
11: 2 and give wicked c in this city: 3289+6098
Da 2:14 Daniel answered with c and wisdom to 5843
4:27 let my c be acceptable unto thee, and 4431
Hos 4:12 My people ask c at their stocks, and NIH
10: 6 and Israel shall be ashamed of his own c. 6098
Mic 4:12 the LORD, neither understand they his c: 6098
Zec 6:13 the c of peace shall be between them both. 6098
Mt 22:15 took c how they might entangle him in his 4824
27: 1 elders of the people took c against Jesus to 4824
27: 7 And they took c, and bought with them 4824
28:12 and had taken c, they gave large money 4824
Mk 3: 6 straightway took c with the Herodians 4824
Lk 7:30 lawyers rejected the c of God against 1012
23:51 (The same had not consented to the c and 1012
Jn 11:53 took c together for to put him to death. 4823
18:14 Caiaphas was he, which gave c to the Jews, 4823
Ac 2:23 being delivered by the determinate c and 1012
4:28 and thy c determined before to be done. 1012
5:33 cut to the heart, and took c to slay them. 1011
5:38 for if this c or this work be of men, it will 1012
9:23 were fulfilled, the Jews took c to kill him: 4823
20:27 to declare unto you all the c of God. 1012
27:42 And the soldiers' c was to kill 1012
Eph 1:11 all things after the c of his own will: 1012
Heb 6:17 heirs of promise the immutability of his c, 1012
Rev 3:18 I c thee to buy of me gold tried in the fire, 4823

COUNSELLED (4) [COUNSEL]

2Sa 16:23 of Ahithophel, which he c in those days, 3289
17:15 elders of Israel; and thus and thus have I c. 3289
17:21 for thus hath Ahithophel c against you. 3289
Job 26: 3 How hast thou c him that hath no wisdom? 3289

COUNSELLER (14) [COUNSEL]

2Sa 15:12 David's c, from his city, even from Giloh, 3289
1Ch 26:14 Zechariah his son, a wise c, they cast lots; 3289
27:32 Also Jonathan David's uncle was a c, 3289
27:33 Ahithophel was the king's c: and 3289
2Ch 22: 3 for his mother was his c to do wickedly. 3289
Isa 3: 3 the honourable man, and the c, and 3289
9: 6 C, The mighty God, The everlasting Father, 3289
40:13 or being his c hath taught him? 376+6098
41:28 amongst them, and there was no c, that, 3289
Mic 4: 9 is thy c perished? for pangs have taken thee 3289
Na 1:11 evil against the LORD, a wicked c. 3289
Mk 15:43 Joseph of Arimathea, an honourable c, 1010
Lk 23:50 there was a man named Joseph, a c; 1010
Ro 11:34 mind of the Lord? or who hath been his c? 4825

COUNSELLERS (21) [COUNSEL]

2Ch 22: 4 for they were his c after the death of his 3289
Ezr 4: 5 hired c against them, to frustrate their 3289
7:14 of his seven c, to inquire concerning Judah 3272
7:15 his c have freely offered unto the God of 3272
7:28 his c, and before all the king's mighty 3289
8:25 his c, and his lords, and all Israel there 3289
Job 3:14 With kings and c of the earth, which built 3289
12:17 He leadeth c away spoiled, and maketh 3289
Ps 119:24 also are my delight and my c. 376+6098
Pr 11:14 but in the multitude of c there is safety. 3289
12:20 imagine evil: but to the c of peace is joy. 3289
15:22 in the multitude of c they are established. 3289
24: 6 and in multitude of c there is safety. 3289
Isa 1:26 as at the first, and thy c as at the beginning: 3289
19:11 the counsel of the wise c of Pharaoh is 3289
Da 3: 2 the c, the sheriffs, and all the rulers of 1884
3: 3 the c, the sheriffs, and all the rulers of 1884
3:24 up in haste, and spake, and said unto his c, 1907
3:27 governors, and captains, and the king's c, 1907
4:36 and my c and my lords sought unto me; and 1907
6: 7 and the princes, the c and the captains, 1907

COUNSELS (12) [COUNSEL]

Job 37:12 it is turned round about by his c: that they 8458
Ps 5:10 O God; let them fall by their own c; 4156
81:12 heart's lust: and they walked in their own c. 4156
Pr 1: 5 of understanding shall attain unto wise c: 8458
Pr 12: 5 are right: but the c of the wicked are deceit. 8458
22:20 not I written to thee excellent things in c 4156
Isa 25: 1 thy c of old are faithfulness and truth. 6098
47:13 Thou art wearied in the multitude of thy c. 6098
Jer 7:24 walked in the c and in the imagination of 4156
Hos 11: 6 and devour them, because of their own c. 4156
Mic 6:16 the house of Ahab, and ye walk in their c; 4156
1Co 4: 5 and will make manifest the c of the hearts: 1012

COUNT (26) [COUNTED, COUNTETH, COUNTING]

Ex 12: 4 his eating shall make your c for the lamb. 3699
Lev 19:23 c the fruit thereof as uncircumcised: 6188+6190
23:15 ye shall c unto you from the morrow after 5608
25:27 let him c the years of the sale thereof, and 2803
25:52 he shall c with him, and according unto his 2803
Nu 23:10 Who can c the dust of Jacob, and 4487
1Sa 1:16 C not thine handmaid for a daughter of 5414
Job 19:15 and my maidens, c me for a stranger: 2803
31: 4 not he see my ways, and c all my steps? 5608
Ps 87: 6 The LORD shall c, when he writeth up 5608
139:18 If I should c them, they are moe in number 5608
139:22 I c them mine enemies. 1961+3807.1
Mic 6:11 Shall I c them pure with the wicked 2135
Ac 20:24 neither c I my life dear unto myself, so 2192
Php 3: 8 and I c all things but loss for 2233
3: 8 loss of all things, and do c them but dung, 2233
3:13 I c not myself to have apprehended: 3049
2Th 1:11 that our God would c you worthy of this 515
3:15 Yet c him not as an enemy, but 2233
1Ti 6: 1 c their own masters worthy of all honour, 2233
Phm 1:17 If thou c me therefore a partner, 2192
Jas 1: 2 c it all joy when ye fall into divers 2233
5:11 Behold, we c them happy which endure. 3106
2Pe 2:13 as they that c it pleasure to riot in the day 2233
3: 9 his promise, as some men c slackness; 2233
Rev 13:18 Let him that hath understanding c 5585

COUNTED (40) [COUNT]

Ge 15: 6 and he c it to him for righteousness. 2803
30:33 the sheep, that shall be c stolen with me. NIH
31:15 Are we not c of him strangers? for he hath 2803
Ex 38:21 of the tabernacle of Testimony, as it was c, 6485
Lev 25:31 them shall be c as the fields of the country: 2803
Nu 18:30 it shall be c unto the Levites as the increase 2803
Jos 13: 3 which is c to the Canaanite: 2803
1Ki 1:21 and my son Solomon shall be c offenders NIH
3: 8 that cannot be numbered nor c for 5608
1Ch 21: 6 and Benjamin c he not among them: 6485
23:24 as they were c by number of names by their 6485
Ne 13:13 for they were c faithful, and their office 2803
Job 18: 3 Wherefore are we c as beasts, and 2803
41:29 Darts are c as stubble: he laugheth at 2803
Ps 44:22 we are c as sheep for the slaughter. 2803
88: 4 I am c with them that go down into the pit: 2803
106:31 that was c unto him for righteousness unto 2803
Pr 17:28 a fool, when he holdeth his peace, is c wise: 2803
27:14 in the morning, it shall be c a curse to him. 2803
Isa 5:28 their horses' hoofs shall be c like flint, and 2803
32:15 and the fruitful field be c for a forest. 2803
33:18 the receiver? where is he that c the towers? 5608
40:15 and are c as the small dust of the balance: 2803
40:17 they are c to him less than nothing, and 2803
Hos 8:12 my law, but they were c as a strange thing. 2803
Mt 14: 5 because they c him as a prophet. 2192
Mk 11:32 for all men c John, that he was a prophet 2192
Ac 5:41 rejoicing that they were c worthy to suffer 2661
19:19 all men: and they c the price of them, 4860
Ro 2:26 shall not his uncircumcision be c for 3049
4: 3 and it was c unto him for righteousness. 3049
4: 5 the ungodly, his faith is c for righteousness. 3049
9: 8 the children of the promise are c for 3049
Php 3: 7 were gain to me, those I c loss for Christ. 2233
2Th 1: 5 that ye may be c worthy of the kingdom of 2661
1Ti 1:12 hath enabled me, for that he c me faithful, 2233
5:17 Let the elders that rule well be c worthy of 515
Heb 3: 3 For this man was c worthy of more glory 515
7: 6 But he whose descent is not c from them 1075
10:29 and hath c the blood of the covenant, 2233

COUNTENANCE (53) [COUNTENANCES]

Ge 4: 5 And Cain was very wroth, and his c fell. 6440
4: 6 art thou wroth? and why is thy c fallen? 6440
31: 2 Jacob beheld the c of Laban, and behold, 6440
31: 5 said unto them, I see your father's c, that it 6440
Ex 23: 3 Neither shalt thou c a poor man in his 1921
Nu 6:26 The LORD lift up his c upon thee, and 6440
Dt 28:50 A nation of fierce c, which shall not regard 6440
Jdg 13: 6 his c was like the countenance of an angel 4758
13: 6 his countenance was like the c of an angel 4758
1Sa 1:18 and did eat, and her c was no more sad. 6440
16: 7 Look not on his c, or on the height of his 4758
16:12 and withal of a beautiful c, and goodly to 5869
17:42 but a youth, and ruddy, and of a fair c. 4758
25: 3 of good understanding, and of a beautiful c: 8389
2Sa 14:27 was Tamar: she was a woman of a fair c. 4758
2Ki 8:11 he settled his c stedfastly, until he was 6440
Ne 2: 2 Why is thy c sad, seeing thou art not sick? 6440
2: 3 why should not my c be sad, when the city, 6440
Job 14:20 thou changest his c, and sendest him away. 6440
29:24 and the light of my c they cast not down. 6440
Ps 4: 6 lift thou up the light of thy c upon us. 6440
10: 4 The wicked, through the pride of his c, 639
11: 7 his c doth behold the upright. 6440
21: 6 hast made him exceeding glad with thy c. 6440
42: 5 I shall yet praise him for the help of his c. 6440
42:11 who is the health of my c, and my God. 6440
43: 5 who is the health of my c, and my God. 6440
44: 3 the light of thy c, because thou hadst a 6440
80:16 they perish at the rebuke of thy c. 6440
89:15 shall walk, O LORD, in the light of thy c. 6440
90: 8 our secret sins in the light of thy c. 6440
Pr 15:13 A merry heart maketh a cheerful c: but 6440
16:15 In the light of the king's c is life; and 6440
Pr 25:23 so doth an angry c a backbiting tongue. 6440
27:17 so a man sharpeneth the c of his friend. 6440
Ecc 7: 3 for by the sadness of the c the heart is made 6440
SS 2:14 let me see thy c, let me hear thy voice; 4758
2:14 for sweet is thy voice, and thy c is comely. 4758
5:15 his c is as Lebanon, excellent as the cedars. 4758
Isa 3: 9 The shew of their c doth witness against 6440
Eze 27:35 sore afraid, they shall be troubled in their c. 6440
Da 1:13 the c of the children that eat of the portion 4758
5: 6 the king's c was changed, and his thoughts 2122
5: 9 his c was changed in him, and his lords 2122
5:10 trouble thee, nor let thy c be changed. 2122
7:28 troubled me, and my c changed in me: 2122
8:23 a king of fierce c, and understanding dark 6440
Mt 6:16 ye fast, be not as the hypocrites, of a sad c: 4659
28: 3 His c was like lightning, and his raiment 2397
Lk 9:29 the fashion of his c was altered, and 4383
Ac 2:28 thou shalt make me full of joy with thy c. 4383
2Co 3: 7 the face of Moses for the glory of his c; 4383
Rev 1:16 his c was as the sun shineth in his strength. 3799

COUNTENANCES (2) [COUNTENANCE]

Da 1:13 let our c be looked upon before thee, and 4758
1:15 at the end of ten days their c appeared fairer 4758

COUNTERVAIL (1)

Est 7: 4 although the enemy could not c the king's 7737

COUNTETH (3) [COUNT]

Job 19:11 he c me unto him as one of his enemies. 2803
33:10 against me, he c me for his enemy, 2803
Lk 14:28 sitteth not down first, and c the cost, 5585

COUNTING (1) [COUNT]

Ecc 7:27 I found, saith the Preacher, c one by one, NIH

COUNTRIES (55) [COUNTRY]

Ge 10:20 their tongues, in their c, and in their nations. 776
26: 3 I will give all these c, and I will perform 776
26: 4 and will give unto thy seed all these c; 776
41:57 all c came into Egypt to Joseph for to buy 776
Jos 13:32 These are the c which Moses did distribute NIH
14: 1 these are the c which the children of Israel NIH
17:11 of Megiddo and her towns, even three c. 5316
2Ki 18:35 Who are they among all the gods of the c, 776
1Ch 22: 5 of fame and of glory throughout all c: 776
29:30 and over all the kingdoms of the c. 776
2Ch 11:23 all his children throughout all the c of Judah 776
12: 8 and the service of the kingdoms of the c. 776
15: 5 were upon all the inhabitants of the c. 776
20:29 of God was on all the kingdoms of those c, 776
34:33 the c that pertained to the children of Israel, 776
Ezr 3: 3 upon them because of the people of those c: 776
4:20 which have ruled over all c beyond NIH
Ps 110: 6 he shall wound the heads over many c. 776
Isa 8: 9 broken in pieces; and give ear, all ye of far c: 776
37:18 have laid waste all the nations, and their c, 776
Jer 23: 3 flock out of all c whither I have driven them, 776
23: 8 and from all c whither I had driven them; 776
28: 8 thee of old prophesied both against many c, 776
32:37 Behold, I will gather them out of all c, 776
40:11 in Edom, and that were in all the c, 776
Eze 5: 5 of the nations and c that are round about her. 776
5: 6 my statutes more than the c that are round 776
6: 8 when ye shall be scattered through the c. 776
11:16 although I have scattered them among the c, 776
11:16 sanctuary in the c where they shall come. 776
11:17 assemble you out of the c where ye have 776
12:15 the nations, and disperse them in the c. 776
20:23 and disperse them through the c; 776
20:32 as the families of the c, to serve wood and 776
20:34 will gather you out of the c wherein ye are 776
20:41 gather you out of the c wherein ye have been 776
22: 4 unto the heathen, and a mocking to all c. 776
22:15 disperse thee in the c, and will consume thy 776
25: 7 and I will cause thee to perish out of the c: 776
29:12 in the midst of the c that are desolate, 776
29:12 and will disperse them through the c. 776
30: 7 they shall be desolate in the midst of the c 776
30:23 and will disperse them through the c. 776
30:26 the nations, and disperse them among the c; 776
32: 9 into the c which thou hast not known. 776
34:13 gather them from the c, and will bring them 776
35:10 two nations and these two c shall be mine, 776
36:19 and they were dispersed through the c: 776
36:24 gather you out of all c, and will bring you 776
Da 9: 7 through all the c whither thou hast driven 776
11:40 he shall enter into the c, and shall overflow 776
11:41 and many c shall be overthrown: NIH
11:42 shall stretch forth his hand also upon the c: 776
Zec 10: 9 they shall remember me in far c; and 4801
Lk 21:21 let not them that are in the c enter thereinto. 5561

COUNTRY (179) [COUNTRIES, COUNTRYMEN]

Ge 12: 1 Get thee out of thy c, and from thy kindred, 776
14: 7 smote all the c of the Amalekites, and 7704
19:28 the smoke of the c went up as the smoke of a 776
20: 1 journeyed from thence toward the south c, 776
24: 4 thou shalt go unto my c, and to my kindred, 776
24:62 well Lahai-roi; for he dwelt in the south c. 776
25: 6 while he yet lived, eastward, unto the east c. 776
29:26 Laban said, It must not be so done in our c, 4725
30:25 I may go unto mine own place, and to my c. 776
32: 3 unto the land of Seir, the c of Edom. 7704
32: 9 Return unto thy c, and to thy kindred, and 776
34: 2 prince of the c, saw her, he took her, and 776
36: 6 went into the c from the face of his brother 776
42:30 roughly to us, and took us for spies of the c. 776
42:33 And the man, the lord of the c, said unto us, 776
47:27 in the land of Egypt, in the c of Goshen; 776
Lev 16:29 work at all, whether it be one of your own c, 249
17:15 beasts, whether it be one of your own c, 249
24:22 for the stranger, as for one of your own c: 249
25:31 them shall be counted as the fields of the c: 776

C

C

Nu 15:13 All that are born of the c shall do these 249
20:17 Let us pass, I pray thee, through thy c: 776
21:20 that is in the c of Moab, to the top of 7704
32: 4 Even the c which the LORD smote before 776
32:33 even the cities of the c round about. 776
Dt 3:14 Jair the son of Manasseh took all the c of 2256
4:43 in the plain c, of the Reubenites; 776
26: 3 that I am come unto the c which the LORD 776
Jos 2: 2 of the children of Israel to search out the c. 776
2: 3 for they be come to search out all the c. 776
2:24 for even all the inhabitants of the c do faint 776
6:22 unto the two men that had spied out the c, 776
6:27 and his fame was noised throughout all the c. 776
7: 2 unto them, saying, Go up and view the c. 776
9: 6 the men of Israel, We be come from a far c: 776
9: 9 From a very far c thy servants are come 776
9:11 and all the inhabitants of our c spake to us, 776
10:40 So Joshua smote all the c of the hills, and 776
10:41 and all the c of Goshen, even unto Gibeon. 776
11:16 all the south c, and all the land of Goshen, NIH
12: 7 these are the kings of the c which Joshua 776
12: 8 in the south c; the Hittites, the Amorites, NIH
13: 6 All the inhabitants of the hill c from 2022
13:21 were dukes of Sihon, dwelling in the c. 776
17:15 then get thee up to the wood c, and NIH
19:51 So they made an end of dividing the c. 776
21:11 which city is Hebron, in the hill c of Judah, NIH
22: 9 to go unto the c of Gilead, to the land of 776
Jdg 8:28 the c was in quietness forty years in the days 776
11:21 of the Amorites, the inhabitants of that c. 776
12:12 was buried in Aijalon in the c of Zebulun. 776
16:24 the destroyer of our c, which slew many of 776
18:14 five men that went to spy out the c of Laish, 776
20: 6 sent her throughout all the c of 7704
Ru 1: 1 went to sojourn in the c of Moab, 7704
1: 2 they came into the c of Moab, and 7704
1: 6 that she might return from the c of Moab: 7704
1: 6 for she had heard in the c of Moab how that 7704
1:22 which returned out of the c of Moab: 7704
2: 6 back with Naomi out of the c of Moab: 7704
4: 3 that is come again out of the c of Moab, 7704
1Sa 6: 1 the ark of the LORD was in the c of 7704
6:18 both of fenced cities, and of c villages, 6521
14:21 them into the camp from the c round about, NIH
27: 5 them give me a place in some town in the c, 7704
27: 7 the time that David dwelt in the c of 7704
27:11 while he dwelleth in the c of the Philistines. 7704
2Sa 15:23 all the c wept with a loud voice, and all 776
18: 8 was there scattered over the face of all the c: 776
21:14 Jonathan his son buried they in the c of 776
1Ki 4:19 Geber the son of Uri was in the c of Gilead, 776
4:19 in the c of Sihon king of the Amorites, and 776
4:30 the wisdom of all the children of the east c, 6924
8:41 cometh out of a far c for thy name's sake; 776
10:13 So she turned and went to her own c, she and 776
10:15 of Arabia, and of the governors of the c. 776
11:21 Let me depart, that I may go to mine own c. 776
11:22 thou seekest to go to thine own c? 776
20:27 flocks of kids; but the Syrians filled the c. 776
22:36 man to his city, and every man to his own c. 776
2Ki 3:20 of Edom, and the c was filled with water. 776
3:24 smiting the Moabites, even in their c[S]. 1886.3
18:35 that have delivered their c out of mine hand, 776
20:14 Hezekiah said, They are come from a far c, 776
1Ch 8: 8 Shaharaim begat children in the c of Moab, 7704
20: 1 and wasted the c of the children of Ammon, 776
2Ch 6:32 is come from a far c for thy great name's 776
9:14 governors of the c brought gold and silver to 776
26:10 both in the low c, and in the plains: 8219
28:18 also had invaded the cities of the low c, 8219
30:10 from city to city through the c of Ephraim 776
Ne 12:28 both out of the plain c round about 3603
Pr 25:25 a thirsty soul, so is good news from a far c. 776
Isa 1: 7 Your c is desolate, your cities are burnt with 776
13: 5 They come from a far c, from the end of 776
22:18 and toss thee like a ball into a large c: 776
39: 3 They are come from a far c unto me, 776
46:11 man that executeth my counsel from a far c: 776
Jer 2: 7 I brought you into a plentiful c, to eat 776
4:16 that watchers come from a far c, and 776
6:20 from Sheba, and the sweet cane from a far c? 776
6:22 a people cometh from the north c, and 776
8:19 because of them that dwell in a far c: 776
10:22 and a great commotion out of the north c, 776
22:10 he shall return no more, nor see his native c. 776
22:26 into another c, where ye were not born; 776
23: 8 seed of the house of Israel out of the north c, 776
31: 8 I will bring them from the north c, and 776
32: 8 in Anathoth, which is in the c of Benjamin: 776
44: 1 and at Noph, and in the c of Pathros, saying, 776
46:10 in the north c by the river Euphrates. 776
47: 4 the remnant of the c of Caphtor. 339
48:21 judgment is come upon the plain c; 776
50: 9 assembly of great nations from the north c: 776
51: 9 and let us go every one into his own c: 776
Eze 20:38 I will bring them forth out of the c where 776
20:42 into the c for the which I lifted up mine hand 776
25: 9 the glory of the c, Beth-jeshimoth, 776
32:15 the c shall be destitute of that whereof it was 776
34:13 and in all the inhabited places of the c. 776
47: 8 These waters issue out toward the east c, 1552
47:22 they shall be unto you as born in the c 249
Hos 12:12 Jacob fled into the c of Syria, and 7704
Jnh 1: 8 what is thy c? and of what people art thou? 776
4: 2 not this my saying, when I was yet in my c? 127
Zec 6: 6 which are therein go forth into the north c; 776
6: 6 and the grisled go forth toward the south c. 776
6: 8 these that go toward the north c have quieted 776
6: 8 country have quieted my spirit in the north c. 776
8: 7 I will save my people from the east c, and 776
8: 7 from the east country, and from the west c; 776
Mt 2:12 they departed into their own c another way. 5561
8:28 the other side into the c of the Gergesenes, 5561
9:31 spread abroad his fame in all that c. 1093
13:54 And when he was come into his own c, 3968
Mt 13:57 save in his own c, and in his own house. 3968
14:35 they sent out into all that c round about, 4066
21:33 it out to husbandmen, and went into a far c: 589
25:14 of heaven is as a man travelling into a far c, 589
Mk 5: 1 side of the sea, into the c of the Gadarenes. 5561
5:10 he would not send them away out of the c. 5561
5:14 swine fled, and told it in the city, and in the c. 68
6: 1 out from thence, and came into his own c; 3968
6: 4 but in his own c, and among his own kin, 3968
6:36 that they may go into the c round about, and 68
6:56 he entered, into villages, or cities, or c, 68
12: 1 it out to husbandmen, and went into a far c. 589
15:21 who passed by, coming out of the c, the father 68
16:12 of them, as they walked, and went into the c. 68
Lk 1:39 and went into the hill c with haste, into a 3714
1:65 abroad throughout all the hill c of Judea. 3714
2: 8 in the same c shepherds abiding in the field, 63
3: 3 And he came into all the c about Jordan, 4066
4:23 done in Capernaum, do also here in thy c. 3968
4:24 No prophet is accepted in his own c. 3968
4:37 out into every place of the c round about. 4066
8:26 And they arrived at the c of the Gadarenes, 5561
8:34 and went and told it in the city and in the c. 68
8:37 c of the Gadarenes round about besought 4066
9:12 they may go into the towns and c round about, 68
15:13 and took his journey into a far c, and 5561
15:15 and joined himself to a citizen of that c; 5561
19:12 A certain nobleman went into a far c to 5561
20: 9 and went into a far c for a long time. 589
23:26 coming out of the c, and on him they laid 68
Jn 4:44 that a prophet hath no honour in his own c. 3968
11:54 went thence unto a c near to the wilderness, 5561
11:55 many went out of the c up to Jerusalem 5561
Ac 4:36 a Levite, and of the c of Cyprus, 1085
7: 3 Get thee out of thy c, and from thy kindred, 1093
12:20 their c was nourished by the king's 5561
12:20 their country was nourished by the king's c. NIG
13: 7 Which was with the deputy of the c, Sergius NIG
18:23 and went over all the c of Galatia and 5561
27:27 deemed that they drew near to some c; 5561
Heb 11: 9 as in a strange c, dwelling in tabernacles NIG
11:14 things declare plainly that they seek a c. 3968
11:15 if they had been mindful of that c from NIG
11:16 But now they desire a better c, that is, NIG

COUNTRYMEN (2) [COUNTRY, MAN]

2Co 11:26 in perils of robbers, in perils by my own c, 1085
1Th 2:14 have suffered like things of your own c, 4853

COUPLE (10) [COUPLED, COUPLETH, COUPLING, COUPLINGS]

Ex 26: 6 and c the curtains together with the taches: 2266
26: 9 thou shalt c five curtains by themselves, 2266
26:11 and c the tent together, that it may be one. 2266
36:18 fifty taches of brass to c the tent together, 2266
39: 4 made shoulderpieces for it, to c it together: 2266
Jdg 19: 3 his servant with him, and a c of asses: 6776
2Sa 13: 6 make me a c of cakes in my sight, that I 8147
16: 1 with a c of asses saddled, and upon them 6776
Isa 21: 7 he saw a chariot with a c of horsemen, 6776
21: 9 a chariot of men, with a c of horsemen. 6776

COUPLED (12) [COUPLE]

Ex 26: 3 The five curtains shall be c together one to 2266
26: 3 other five curtains shall be c one to another. 2266
26:24 they shall be c together beneath, and 8382
26:24 they shall be c together above 3162+8535
36:10 And he c the five curtains one unto another: 2266
36:10 the other five curtains he c one unto 2266
36:13 c the curtains one unto another with 2266
36:16 he c five curtains by themselves, and six 2266
36:29 they were c beneath, and coupled together 8382
36:29 c together at the head thereof, to one 1961+8535
39: 4 by the two edges was it c together. 2266
1Pe 3: 2 behold your chaste conversation c with fear. NIG

COUPLETH (2) [COUPLE]

Ex 26:10 the edge of the curtain which c the second. 2279
36:17 the edge of the curtain which c the second. 2279

COUPLING (10) [COUPLE]

Ex 26: 4 the one curtain from the selvedge in the c; 2279
26: 4 of another curtain, in the c of the second. 4225
26: 5 of the curtain that is in the c of the second; 4225
26:10 of the one curtain that is outmost in the c, 2279
28:27 over against the other c thereof, 4225
36:11 of one curtain from the selvedge in the c: 4225
36:11 of another curtain, in the c of the second. 4225
36:12 curtain which was in the c of the second: 4225
36:17 the uttermost edge of the curtain in the c, 4225
39:20 of it, over against the other c thereof, 4225

COUPLINGS (1) [COUPLE]

2Ch 34:11 timber for c, and to floor the houses which 4226

COURAGE (20) [COURAGEOUS, COURAGEOUSLY]

Nu 13:20 be ye of good c, and bring of the fruit of 2388
Dt 31: 6 Be strong and of a good c, fear not, nor be 553
31: 7 sight of all Israel, Be strong and of a good c: 553
31:23 and said, Be strong and of a good c: 553
Jos 1: 6 Be strong and of a good c: for unto this 553
1: 9 Be strong and of a good c; be not afraid, 553
1:18 put to death: only be strong and of a good c. 553
2:11 neither did there remain any more c in any 7307
10:25 nor be dismayed, be strong and of good c: 553
2Sa 10:12 Be of good c, and let us play the men for 2388
1Ch 19:13 Be of good c, and let us behave ourselves 2388
22:13 be strong, and of good c; dread not, nor be 553
28:20 Be strong and of good c, and do it: fear not, 553
2Ch 15: 8 he took c, and put away the abominable 2388
Ezr 10: 4 will be with thee: be of good c, and do it. 2388
Ps 27:14 be of good c, and he shall strengthen thine 2388
31:24 Be of good c, and he shall strengthen your 2388
Isa 41: 6 every one said to his brother, Be of good c. 2388
Da 11:25 his c against the king of the south with a 3824
Ac 28:15 Paul saw, he thanked God, and took c. 2294

COURAGEOUS (5) [COURAGE]

Jos 1: 7 Only be thou strong and very c, that thou 553
23: 6 Be ye therefore very c to keep and to do all 2388
2Sa 13:28 not I commanded you? be c, and be valiant. 2388
2Ch 32: 7 Be strong and c, be not afraid nor dismayed 553
Am 2:16 he that is c among the mighty shall 533+3820

COURAGEOUSLY (1) [COURAGE]

2Ch 19:11 Deal c, and the LORD shall be with 2388

COURSE (35) [COURSES]

1Ch 27: 1 of every c were twenty and four thousand. 4256
27: 2 Over the first c for the first month was 4256
27: 2 and in his c were twenty and four thousand. 4256
27: 4 over the c of the second month was Dodai 4256
27: 4 and of his c was Mikloth also the ruler: 4256
27: 4 in his c likewise were twenty and 4256
27: 5 and in his c were twenty and four thousand. 4256
27: 6 and in his c was Ammizabad his son. 4256
27: 7 and in his c were twenty and four thousand. 4256
27: 8 and in his c were twenty and four thousand. 4256
27: 9 and in his c were twenty and four thousand. 4256
27:10 and in his c were twenty and four thousand. 4256
27:11 and in his c were twenty and four thousand. 4256
27:12 and in his c were twenty and four thousand. 4256
27:13 and in his c were twenty and four thousand. 4256
27:14 and in his c were twenty and four thousand. 4256
27:15 and in his c were twenty and four thousand. 4256
28: 1 companies that ministered to the king by c, 4256
2Ch 5:11 were sanctified, and did not then wait by c: 4256
Ezr 3:11 And they sung together by c in praising and NIH
Ps 82: 5 all the foundations of the earth are out of c. 4131
Jer 8: 6 every one turned to his c, as the horse 4794
23:10 their c is evil, and their force is not right. 4794
Lk 1: 5 priest named Zacharias, of the c of Abia: 2183
1: 8 office before God in the order of his c, 2183
Ac 13:25 And as John fulfilled his c, he said, 1408
16:11 we came with a straight c to Samothracia, 2113
20:24 so that I might finish my c with joy, and 1408
21: 1 we came with a straight c unto Cos, and 2113
21: 7 And when we had finished our c from Tyre, 4144
1Co 14:27 or at the most by three, and that by c; 303+3313
Eph 2: 2 ye walked according to the c of this world, 165
2Th 3: 1 that the word of the Lord may have free c, 5143
2Ti 4: 7 I have finished my c, I have kept the faith: 1408
Jas 3: 6 and setteth on fire the c of nature; 5164

COURSES (18) [COURSE]

Jdg 5:20 the stars in their c fought against Sisera. 4546
1Ki 5:14 to Lebanon, ten thousand a month by c: 2487
1Ch 23: 6 David divided them into c among the sons 4256
27: 1 that served the king in any matter of the c, 4256
28:13 Also for the c of the priests and the Levites, 4256
28:21 the c of the priests and the Levites, 4256
2Ch 8:14 the c of the priests to their service, and 4256
8:14 the porters also by their c at every gate: for 4256
23: 8 for Jehoiada the priest dismissed not the c. 4256
31: 2 And Hezekiah appointed the c of the priests 4256
31: 2 of the priests and the Levites after their c, 4256
31:15 set office, to give to their brethren by c, 4256
31:16 service in their charges according to their c; 4256
31:17 and upward, in their charges by their c; 4256
35: 4 after your c, according to the writing of 4256
35:10 in their place, and the Levites in their c, 4256
Ezr 6:18 the Levites in their c, for the service of 4255
Isa 44: 4 among the grass, as willows by the water c. 2988

COURT (122) [COURTS]

Ex 27: 9 thou shalt make the c of the tabernacle: 2691
27: 9 c of fine twined linen of an hundred cubits 2691
27:12 for the breadth of the c on the west side 2691
27:13 the breadth of the c on the east side 2691
27:16 for the gate of the c shall be a hanging of 2691
27:17 All the pillars round about the c shall be 2691
27:18 The length of the c shall be an hundred 2691
27:19 and all the pins of the c, shall be of brass. 2691
35:17 The hangings of the c, his pillars, and 2691
35:17 and the hanging for the door of the c, 2691
35:18 and the pins of the c, and their cords, 2691
38: 9 he made the c: on the south side southward 2691
38: 9 hangings of the c were of fine twined linen, 2691
38:15 for the other side of the c gate, on this hand 2691
38:16 All the hangings of the c round about were 2691
38:17 all the pillars of the c were filleted with 2691
38:18 the hanging for the gate of the c was 2691
38:18 answerable to the hangings of the c. 2691
38:20 and of the c round about, were of brass. 2691
38:31 the sockets of the c round about, and 2691
38:31 the sockets of the c gate, and all the pins of 2691
38:31 and all the pins of the c round about. 2691
39:40 The hangings of the c, his pillars, and his 2691
39:40 the hanging for the c gate, his cords, and 2691
40: 8 thou shalt set up the c round about, and 2691
40: 8 and hang up the hanging at the c gate. 2691
40:33 he reared up the c round about 2691
40:33 and set up the hanging of the c gate. 2691
Lev 6:16 in the c of the tabernacle of 2691
6:26 in the c of the tabernacle of 2691
Nu 3:26 the hangings of the c, and the curtain for 2691
3:26 the curtain for the door of the c, which is by 2691
3:37 the pillars of the c round about, and 2691
4:26 the hangings of the c, and the hanging for 2691
4:26 hanging for the door of the gate of the c, 2691
4:32 the pillars of the c round about, and 2691
2Sa 17:18 in Bahurim, which had a well in his c; 2691
1Ki 6:36 he built the inner c with three rows of 2691
7: 8 his house where he dwelt had another c 2691
7: 9 and so on the outside toward the great c. 2691
7:12 the great c round about was with three rows 2691
7:12 both for the inner c of the house of 2691

1Ki 8:64 **c** that *was* before the house of the LORD: 2691
2Ki 20: 4 afore Isaiah was gone out *into* the middle **c**, 2691
2Ch 4: 9 Furthermore he made the **c** of the priests, 2691
4: 9 the great **c**, and doors for the court, and 5835
4: 9 doors for the **c**, and overlaid the doors of 5835
6:13 and had set it in the midst of the **c**: 5835
7: 7 **c** that *was* before the house of the LORD: 2691
20: 5 the house of the LORD, before the new **c**, 2691
24:21 king in the **c** of the house of the LORD. 2691
29:16 into the **c** of the house of the LORD. 2691
Ne 3:25 high house, that *was* by the **c** of the prison. 2691
Est 1: 5 in the **c** of the garden of the king's palace; 2691
2:11 Mordecai walked every day before the **c** of 2691
4:11 shall come unto the king into the inner **c**, 2691
5: 1 and stood in the inner **c** of the king's house, 2691
5: 2 king saw Esther the queen standing in the **c**, 2691
6: 4 the king said, Who *is* in the **c**? Now Haman 2691
6: 4 Now Haman was come into the outward **c** 2691
6: 5 unto him, Behold, Haman standeth in the **c**. 2691
Isa 34:13 be a habitation of dragons, *and* a **c** for owls. 2681
Jer 19:14 he stood in the **c** of the LORD'S house; 2691
26: 2 Stand in the **c** of the LORD'S house, and 2691
32: 2 Jeremiah the prophet was shut up in the **c** 2691
32: 8 **c** of the prison according to the word of 2691
32:12 before all the Jews that sat in the **c** of 2691
33: 1 while he was yet shut up in the **c** of 2691
36:10 in the higher **c** *at* the entry of the new gate 2691
36:20 they went in to the king into the **c**, but 2691
37:21 commit Jeremiah into the **c** of the prison, 2691
37:21 Thus Jeremiah remained in the **c** of 2691
38: 6 that *was* in the **c** of the prison: 2691
38:13 Jeremiah remained in the **c** of the prison. 2691
38:28 So Jeremiah abode in the **c** of the prison 2691
39:14 took Jeremiah out of the **c** of the prison, 2691
39:15 while he was shut up in the **c** of the prison, 2691
Eze 8: 7 And he brought me to the door of the **c**; and 2691
8:16 he brought me into the inner **c** of 2691
10: 3 went in; and the cloud filled the inner **c**. 2691
10: 4 the **c** was full of the brightness of 2691
10: 5 wings was heard *even* to the utter **c**, 2691
40:14 even unto the post of the **c** round about 2691
40:17 Then brought he me into the outward **c**, and 2691
40:17 a pavement made for the **c** round about: 2691
40:19 unto the forefront of the inner **c** without, 2691
40:20 the gate of the outward **c** that looked 2691
40:23 the gate of the inner **c** *was* over against 2691
40:27 *there was* a gate in the inner **c** toward 2691
40:28 he brought me to the inner **c** by the south 2691
40:31 the arches thereof *were* toward the utter **c**; 2691
40:32 he brought me into the inner **c** toward 2691
40:34 arches thereof *were* toward the outward **c**; 2691
40:37 the posts thereof *were* toward the utter **c**; 2691
40:44 the chambers of the singers in the inner **c**, 2691
40:47 So he measured the **c**, an hundred cubits 2691
41:15 the inner temple, and the porches of the **c**; 2691
42: 1 he brought me forth into the utter **c**, 2691
42: 3 twenty *cubits* which *were* for the inner **c**, 2691
42: 3 the pavement which *was* for the utter **c**, 2691
42: 7 towards the utter **c** on the forepart of 2691
42: 8 that *were* in the utter **c** *was* fifty cubits: 2691
42: 9 as one goeth into them from the utter **c**. 2691
42:10 of the wall of the **c** toward the east, 2691
42:14 not go out of the holy *place* into the utter **c**, 2691
43: 5 me up, and brought me into the inner **c**; 2691
44:17 they enter in at the gates of the inner **c**, 2691
44:17 they minister in the gates of the inner **c**, 2691
44:19 when they go forth into the utter **c**, 2691
44:19 *even* into the utter **c** to the people, 2691
44:21 when they enter into the inner **c**. 2691
44:27 unto the inner **c**, to minister in 2691
45:19 upon the posts of the gate of the inner **c**. 2691
46: 1 The gate of the inner **c** that looketh *toward* 2691
46:20 that *they* bear *them* not out into the utter **c**, 2691
46:21 he brought me forth into the utter **c**, 2691
46:21 me to pass by the four corners of the **c**; 2691
46:21 in every corner of the **c** *there was* a court. 2691
46:21 in every corner of the court *there was* a **c**. 2691
46:22 In the four corners of the **c** *there were* 2691
Am 7:13 it *is* the king's chapel, and it *is* the king's **c**. 1004
Rev 11: 2 But the **c** which is without the temple leave 833

COURTEOUS (1) [COURTEOUSLY]
1Pe 3: 8 of another, love as brethren, *be* pitiful, *be* **c**: 5391

COURTEOUSLY (2) [COURTEOUS]
Ac 27: 3 And Julius **c** entreated Paul, and gave *him* 5364
28: 7 received us, and lodged *us* three days **c**. 5390

COURTS (25) [COURT]
2Ki 21: 5 in the two **c** of the house of the LORD. 2691
23:12 in the two **c** of the house of the LORD, 2691
1Ch 23:28 in the **c**, and in the chambers, and in 2691
28: 6 thy son, he shall build my house and my **c**: 2691
28:12 of the **c** of the house of the LORD, and 2691
2Ch 23: 5 all the people *shall be* in the **c** of the house 2691
33: 5 in the two **c** of the house of the LORD. 2691
Ne 8:16 in their **c**, and in the courts of the house of 2691
8:16 in the **c** of the house of God, and in 2691
13: 7 in preparing him a chamber in the **c** of 2691
Ps 65: 4 *unto thee, that* he may dwell *in* thy **c**: 2691
84: 2 yea, even fainteth for the **c** of the LORD: 2691
84:10 For a day in thy **c** *is* better than a thousand. 2691
92:13 LORD shall flourish in the **c** of our God. 2691
96: 8 bring an offering, and come into his **c**. 2691
100: 4 *and* into his **c** with praise: 2691
116:19 In the **c** of the LORD'S house, in 2691
135: 2 in the **c** of the house of our God, 2691
Isa 1:12 required this at your hand, to tread my **c**? 2691
62: 9 shall drink it in the **c** of my holiness. 2691
Eze 9: 7 the house, and fill the **c** *with* the slain: 2691
42: 6 but had not pillars as the pillars of the **c**: 2691
46:22 In the four corners of the court *there were* **c** 2691
Zec 3: 7 shalt also keep my **c**, and I will give thee 2691
Lk 7:25 and live delicately, are in **kings' c**. 933

COUSIN (1) [COUSINS]
Lk 1:36 And behold, thy **c** Elisabeth, she hath also 4773

COUSINS (1) [COUSIN]
Lk 1:58 her **c** heard how the Lord had shewed great 4773

COVENANT (292) [COVENANT-BREAKERS, COVENANTED, COVENANTS]
Ge 6:18 with thee will I establish my **c**; and 1285
9: 9 behold I establish my **c** with you and 1285
9:11 I will establish my **c** with you; neither shall 1285
9:12 This *is* the token of the **c** which I make 1285
9:13 it shall be for a token of a **c** between me 1285
9:15 I will remember my **c**, which *is* between me 1285
9:16 that I may remember the everlasting **c** 1285
9:17 said unto Noah, This *is* the token of the **c**, 1285
15:18 In the same day the LORD made a **c** with 1285
17: 2 I will make my **c** between me and thee, 1285
17: 4 my **c** *is* with thee, and thou shalt be a father 1285
17: 7 I will establish my **c** between me and thee 1285
17: 7 in their generations for an everlasting **c**, 1285
17: 9 Thou shalt keep my **c** therefore, thou, and 1285
17:10 This *is* my **c**, which ye shall keep, 1285
17:11 it shall be a token of the **c** betwixt me and 1285
17:13 my **c** shall be in your flesh for an 1285
17:13 shall be in your flesh for an everlasting **c**. 1285
17:14 off from his people; he hath broken my **c**. 1285
17:19 I will establish my **c** with him for an 1285
17:19 my covenant with him for an everlasting **c**, 1285
17:21 my **c** will I establish with Isaac, 1285
21:27 and both of them made a **c**. 1285
21:32 Thus they made a **c** at Beer-sheba: then 1285
26:28 and thee, and let us make a **c** with thee; 1285
31:44 come thou, let us make a **c**, I and thou; 1285
Ex 2:24 God remembered his **c** with Abraham, 1285
6: 4 I have also established my **c** with them, 1285
6: 5 in bondage; and I have remembered my **c**. 1285
19: 5 keep my **c**, then ye shall be a peculiar 1285
23:32 Thou shalt make no **c** with them, nor with 1285
24: 7 he took the book of the **c**, and read in 1285
24: 8 and said, Behold the blood of the **c**, 1285
31:16 their generations, *for* a perpetual **c**. 1285
34:10 he said, Behold, I make a **c**: before all thy 1285
34:12 lest thou make a **c** with the inhabitants of 1285
34:15 Lest thou make a **c** with the inhabitants of 1285
34:27 of these words I have made a **c** with thee 1285
34:28 he wrote upon the tables the words of the **c**, 1285
Lev 2:13 neither shalt thou suffer the salt of the **c** of 1285
24: 8 the children of Israel *by* an everlasting **c**. 1285
26: 9 multiply you, and establish my **c** with you. 1285
26:15 my commandments, *but* that ye break my **c**: 1285
26:25 that shall avenge the quarrel of *my* **c**: 1285
26:42 will I remember my **c** with Jacob, and 1285
26:42 also my **c** with Isaac, and also my covenant 1285
26:42 also my **c** with Abraham will I remember; 1285
26:44 them utterly, and to break my **c** with them: 1285
26:45 I will for their sakes remember the **c** of 1285
Nu 10:33 the ark of the **c** of the LORD went before 1285
14:44 nevertheless the ark of the **c** of the LORD, 1285
18:19 it *is* a **c** of salt for ever before the LORD 1285
25:12 Behold, I give unto him my **c** of peace: 1285
25:13 *even* the **c** of an everlasting priesthood; 1285
Dt 4:13 he declared unto you his **c**, which he 1285
4:23 lest ye forget the **c** of the LORD your 1285
4:31 nor forget the **c** of thy fathers which he 1285
5: 2 The LORD our God made a **c** with us in 1285
5: 3 The LORD made not this **c** with our 1285
7: 2 thou shalt make no **c** with them, nor shew 1285
7: 9 which keepeth **c** and mercy with them that 1285
7:12 LORD thy God shall keep unto thee the **c** 1285
8:18 that he may establish his **c** which he sware 1285
9: 9 *even* the tables of the **c** which the LORD 1285
9:11 two tables of stone, *even* the tables of the **c**. 1285
9:15 the two tables of the **c** *were* in my two 1285
10: 8 to bear the ark of the **c** of the LORD, 1285
17: 2 the LORD thy God, in transgressing his **c**, 1285
29: 1 These *are* the words of the **c**, which 1285
29: 1 beside the **c** which he made with them in 1285
29: 9 Keep therefore the words of this **c**, and 1285
29:12 That thou shouldest enter into **c** with 1285
29:14 Neither with you only do I make this **c** 1285
29:21 according to all the curses of the **c** that are 1285
29:25 Because they have forsaken the **c** of 1285
31: 9 which bare the ark of the **c** of the LORD, 1285
31:16 break my **c** which I have made with them. 1285
31:20 and provoke me, and break my **c**. 1285
31:25 which bare the ark of the **c** of the LORD, 1285
31:26 put it in the side of the ark of the **c** of 1285
33: 9 have observed thy word, and kept thy **c**. 1285
Jos 3: 3 When ye see the ark of the **c** of the LORD 1285
3: 6 Take up the ark of the **c**, and pass over 1285
3: 6 they took up the ark of the **c**, and 1285
3: 8 the priests that bear the ark of the **c**, 1285
3:11 Behold, the ark of the **c**, *even* the Lord of 1285
3:14 the priests bearing the ark *of* the **c** before 1285
3:17 the priests that bare the ark *of* the **c** of 1285
4: 7 off before the ark of the **c** of the LORD; 1285
4: 9 priests which bare the ark of the **c** stood: 1285
4:18 when the priests that bare the ark of the **c** of 1285
6: 6 Take up the ark of the **c**, and let seven 1285
6: 8 the ark of the **c** of the LORD followed 1285
7:11 they have also transgressed my **c** which I 1285
7:15 he hath transgressed the **c** of the LORD, 1285
8:33 which bare the ark of the **c** of the LORD, 1285
23:16 When ye have transgressed the **c** of 1285
24:25 So Joshua made a **c** with the people that 1285
Jdg 2: 1 I said, I will never break my **c** with you. 1285
2:20 my **c** which I commanded their fathers, 1285
20:27 (for the ark of the **c** of God *was* there in 1285
1Sa 4: 3 Let us fetch the ark of the **c** of the LORD 1285
4: 4 the ark of the **c** of the LORD of hosts, 1285
4: 4 *were* there with the ark of the **c** of God. 1285
4: 5 when the ark of the **c** of the LORD came 1285
11: 1 Make a **c** with us, and we will serve thee. 1285
1Sa 11: 2 On this *condition* will I make *a* **c** with you, NIH
18: 3 Jonathan and David made a **c**, because 1285
20: 8 for thou hast brought thy servant into a **c** of 1285
20:16 So Jonathan made *a* **c** with the house of NIH
23:18 they two made a **c** before the LORD: and 1285
2Sa 15:24 with him, bearing the ark of the **c** of God: 1285
23: 5 yet he hath made with me an everlasting **c**, 1285
1Ki 3:15 stood before the ark of the **c** of the LORD, 1285
6:19 to set there the ark of the **c** of the LORD. 1285
8: 1 that *they* might bring up the ark of the **c** of 1285
8: 6 the priests brought in the ark of the **c** of 1285
8: 9 when the LORD made *a* **c** with NIH
8:21 wherein *is* the **c** of the LORD, which he 1285
8:23 who keepest **c** and mercy with thy servants 1285
11:11 thou hast not kept my **c** and my statutes, 1285
19:10 the children of Israel have forsaken thy **c**, 1285
19:14 the children of Israel have forsaken thy **c**, 1285
20:34 *Ahab*, I will send thee away with *this* **c**. 1285
20:34 So he made a **c** with him, and sent him 1285
2Ki 11: 4 made a **c** with them, and took an oath of 1285
11:17 Jehoiada made a **c** between the LORD 1285
13:23 because of his **c** with Abraham, Isaac, and 1285
17:15 his **c** that he made with their fathers, and 1285
17:35 With whom the LORD had made a **c**, and 1285
17:38 the **c** that I have made with you ye shall not 1285
18:12 transgressed his **c**, *and* all that Moses 1285
23: 2 **c** which was found in the house of 1285
23: 3 made a **c** before the LORD, to walk after 1285
23: 3 to perform the words of this **c** that were 1285
23: 3 this book. And all the people stood to the **c**. 1285
23:21 as it is written in the book of this **c**. 1285
1Ch 11: 3 David made a **c** with them in Hebron 1285
15:25 went to bring up the ark of the **c** of 1285
15:26 that bare the ark of the **c** of the LORD, 1285
15:28 Thus all Israel brought up the ark of the **c** 1285
15:29 *as* the ark of the **c** of the LORD came to 1285
16: 6 continually before the ark of the **c** of God. 1285
16:15 Be ye mindful always of his **c**; the word 1285
16:16 *Even of the* **c** which he made with NIH
16:17 for a law, *and* to Israel *for* an everlasting **c**, 1285
16:37 So he left there before the ark of the **c** of 1285
17: 1 the ark of the **c** of the LORD *remaineth* 1285
22:19 to bring the ark of the **c** of the LORD, and 1285
28: 2 of rest for the ark of the **c** of the LORD, 1285
28:18 and covered the ark of the **c** of the LORD. 1285
2Ch 5: 2 to bring up the ark of the **c** of the LORD 1285
5: 7 the priests brought in the ark of the **c** of 1285
5:10 when the LORD made *a* **c** with NIH
6:11 put the ark, wherein *is* the **c** of the LORD, 1285
6:14 which keepest **c**, and *shewest* mercy unto 1285
13: 5 *even* to him and to his sons *by* a **c** of salt? 1285
15:12 they entered into a **c** to seek the LORD 1285
21: 7 of the **c** that he had made with David, 1285
23: 1 the son of Zichri, into **c** with him. 1285
23: 3 all the congregation made a **c** with the king 1285
23:16 Jehoiada made a **c** between him, and 1285
29:10 Now *it is* in mine heart to make a **c** with 1285
34:30 **c** that was found *in* the house of 1285
34:31 made a **c** before the LORD, to walk after 1285
34:31 to perform the words of the **c** which are 1285
34:32 of Jerusalem did according to the **c** of God, 1285
Ezr 10: 3 let us make a **c** with our God to put away 1285
Ne 1: 5 that keepeth **c** and mercy for them that love 1285
9: 8 madest a **c** with him to give the land of 1285
9:32 the terrible God, who keepest **c** and mercy, 1285
9:38 because of all this we **make a** sure **c**, and 3772
13:29 the **c** of the priesthood, and of the Levites. 1285
Job 31: 1 I made a **c** with mine eyes; why then 1285
41: 4 Will he make a **c** with thee? wilt thou take 1285
Ps 25:10 truth unto such as keep his **c** and 1285
25:14 that fear him; and he will shew them his **c**. 1285
44:17 neither have we dealt falsely in thy **c**. 1285
50: 5 those that have made a **c** with me by 1285
50:16 *that* thou shouldest take my **c** in thy mouth? 1285
55:20 be at peace with him: he hath broken his **c**. 1285
74:20 Have respect unto the **c**: for the dark places 1285
78:10 They kept not the **c** of God, and refused to 1285
78:37 neither were they stedfast in his **c**. 1285
89: 3 I have made a **c** with my chosen, I have 1285
89:28 and my **c** *shall* stand fast with him. 1285
89:34 My **c** will I not break, nor alter the thing 1285
89:39 Thou hast made void the **c** of thy servant: 1285
103:18 To such as keep his **c**, and to those that 1285
105: 8 He hath remembered his **c** for ever, 1285
105: 9 Which **c** he made with Abraham, and NIH
105:10 for a law, *and* to Israel *for* an everlasting **c**: 1285
106:45 he remembered for them his **c**, and 1285
111: 5 fear him: he will ever be mindful of his **c**. 1285
111: 9 he hath commanded his **c** for ever: holy and 1285
132:12 If thy children will keep my **c** and 1285
Pr 2:17 her youth, and forgetteth the **c** of her God. 1285
Isa 24: 5 the ordinance, broken the everlasting **c**. 1285
28:15 We have made a **c** with death, and with hell 1285
28:18 your **c** with death shall be disannulled, and 1285
33: 8 he hath broken the **c**, he hath despised 1285
42: 6 and give thee for a **c** of the people, 1285
49: 8 and give thee for a **c** of the people, 1285
54:10 neither shall the **c** of my peace be removed, 1285
55: 3 I will make an everlasting **c** with you, 1285
56: 4 that please me, and take hold of my **c**; 1285
56: 6 from polluting it, and taketh hold of my **c**; 1285
57: 8 thy bed, and made thee *a* **c** with them; NIH
59:21 As for me, this *is* my **c** with them, saith 1285
61: 8 and I will make an everlasting **c** with them. 1285
Jer 3:16 no more, The ark of the **c** of the LORD: 1285
11: 2 Hear ye the words of this **c**, and speak unto 1285
11: 3 man that obeyeth not the words of this **c**, 1285
11: 6 Hear ye the words of this **c**, and do them. 1285
11: 8 will bring upon them all the words of this **c**, 1285
11:10 the house of Judah have broken my **c** which 1285
14:21 remember, break not thy **c** with us. 1285
22: 9 Because they have forsaken the **c** of 1285
31:31 that I will make a new **c** with the house of 1285
31:32 Not according to the **c** that I made with 1285
31:32 which my **c** they brake, although I was a 1285

Jer 31:33 this *shall be* the **c** that I will make with 1285
32:40 And I will make an everlasting **c** with them, 1285
33:20 If you can break my **c** of the day, and my 1285
33:20 my **c** of the night, and that there should not 1285
33:21 *Then* may also my **c** be broken with David 1285
33:25 If my **c** *be* not with day and night, *and if* I 1285
34: 8 after that the king Zedekiah had made a **c** 1285
34:10 all the people, which had entered into the **c**, 1285
34:13 I made a **c** with your fathers in the day that 1285
34:15 ye had made a **c** before me in the house 1285
34:18 give the men that have transgressed my **c**, 1285
34:18 of the **c** which they had made before me, 1285
50: 5 *in* a perpetual **c** *that* shall not be forgotten. 1285
Eze 16: 8 unto thee, and entered into a **c** with thee, 1285
16:59 hast despised the oath in breaking the **c**. 1285
16:60 Nevertheless I will remember my **c** with 1285
16:60 I will establish unto thee an everlasting **c**. 1285
16:61 unto thee for daughters, but not by thy **c**. 1285
16:62 I will establish my **c** with thee; and 1285
17:13 made a **c** with him, and hath taken an oath 1285
17:14 *but* that by keeping of his **c** it might stand. 1285
17:15 doeth such *things*? or shall he break the **c**, 1285
17:16 oath he despised, and whose **c** he brake, 1285
17:18 he despised the oath by breaking the **c**, 1285
17:19 and my **c** that he hath broken, 1285
20:37 and I will bring you into the bond of the **c**: 1285
34:25 I will make with them a **c** of peace, and 1285
37:26 Moreover I will make a **c** of peace with 1285
37:26 it shall be an everlasting **c** with them: 1285
44: 7 they have broken my **c** because of all your 1285
Da 9: 4 keeping the **c** and mercy to them that love 1285
9:27 he shall confirm the **c** with many *for* one 1285
11:22 be broken; yea also, the prince of the **c**. 1285
11:28 his heart *shall be* against the holy **c**; and 1285
11:30 and have indignation against the holy **c**: 1285
11:30 with them that forsake the holy **c**. 1285
11:32 such as do wickedly against the **c** shall he 1285
Hos 2:18 in that day will I make a **c** for them with 1285
6: 7 they like men have transgressed the **c**: 1285
8: 1 because they have transgressed my **c**, and 1285
10: 4 swearing falsely in making a **c**: 1285
12: 1 they do make a **c** with the Assyrians, and 1285
Am 1: 9 and remembered not the brotherly **c**: 1285
Zec 9:11 by the blood of thy **c** I have sent forth thy 1285
11:10 that *I* might break my **c** which I had made 1285
Mal 2: 4 that my **c** might be with Levi, saith 1285
2: 5 My **c** was with him of life and peace; and 1285
2: 8 ye have corrupted the **c** of Levi, saith 1285
2:10 by profaning the **c** of our fathers? 1285
2:14 *is* she thy companion, and the wife of thy **c**. 1285
3: 1 even the messenger of the **c**, whom ye 1285
Lk 1:72 to our fathers, and to remember his holy **c**; *1242*
Ac 3:25 of the **c** which God made with our fathers, *1242*
7: 8 And he gave him the **c** of circumcision: and *1242*
Ro 11:27 For this *is* my **c** unto them, when I shall *1242*
Gal 3:15 Though *it be* but a man's **c**, *yet if it be* *1242*
3:17 And this I say, *that* the **c**, that was *1242*
Heb 8: 6 much also he is the mediator of a better **c**, *1242*
8: 7 For if that first *c* had been faultless, *then* NIG
8: 8 when I will make a new **c** with the house of *1242*
8: 9 Not according to the **c** that I made with *1242*
8: 9 because they continued not in my **c**, and I *1242*
8:10 For this *is* the **c** that I will make with *1242*
8:13 A new *c*, he hath made the first old. NIG
9: 1 Then verily the first *c* had also ordinances NIG
9: 4 the ark of the **c** overlaid round about with *1242*
9: 4 rod that budded, and the tables of the **c**; *1242*
10:16 This *is* the **c** that I will make with them *1242*
10:29 and hath counted the blood of the **c**, *1242*
12:24 And to Jesus the mediator of the new **c**, and *1242*
13:20 through the blood of the everlasting **c**, *1242*

COVENANT-BREAKERS (1) [BREAK, COVENANT]

Ro 1:31 Without understanding, **c**, without natural *802*

COVENANTED (4) [COVENANT]

2Ch 7:18 according as I have **c** with David thy father, 3772
Hag 2: 5 *According to* the word that I **c** with you 3772
Mt 26:15 And they **c** with him for thirty pieces of *2476*
Lk 22: 5 they were glad, and **c** to give him money. *4934*

COVENANTS (3) [COVENANT]

Ro 9: 4 and the **c**, and the giving of the law, and *1242*
Gal 4:24 for these are the two **c**; the one from *1242*
Eph 2:12 and strangers from the **c** of promise, *1242*

COVER (72) [COVERED, COVEREDST, COVEREST, COVERETH, COVERING, COVERINGS, COVERS, UNCOVER]

Ex 10: 5 they shall **c** the face of the earth, that *one* 3680
21:33 and not **c** it, and an ox or an ass fall therein; 3680
25:29 and bowls thereof, to **c** withal: 5258
26:13 on this side and on that side, to **c** it. 3680
28:42 thou shalt make them linen breeches to **c** 3680
33:22 will **c** thee with my hand while I pass by: 5526
37:16 and his bowls, and *his* covers to **c** withal, 5258
40: 3 the Testimony, and **c** the ark with the vail. 5526
Lev 13:12 the leprosy **c** all the skin of *him that hath* 3680
16:13 that the cloud of the incense may **c** 3680
17:13 out the blood thereof, and **c** it with dust. 3680
Nu 4: 5 and **c** the ark of Testimony with it: 3680
4: 7 and the bowls, and covers to **c withal**: 5262
4: 8 **c** the same with a covering of badgers' 3680
4: 9 **c** the candlestick of the light, and his lamps, 3680
4:11 **c** it with a covering of badgers' skins, and 3680
4:12 **c** them with a covering of badgers' skins, 3680
22: 5 they **c** the face of the earth, and they abide 3680
Dt 23:13 and **c** that which cometh from thee: 3680
33:12 *the* LORD shall **c** him all the day long, 2653
1Sa 24: 3 *was* a cave; and Saul went in to **c** his feet: 5526
1Ki 7:18 to **c** the chapiters that *were* upon the top, 3680
7:41 to **c** the two bowls of the chapiters which 3680
7:42 to **c** the two bowls of the chapiters that 3680
2Ch 4:12 the two wreaths to **c** the two pommels of 3680
2Ch 4:13 to **c** the two pommels of the chapiters 3680
Ne 4: 5 **c** not their iniquity, and let not their sin be 3680
Job 16:18 **c** not thou my blood, and let my cry have 3680
21:26 in the dust, and the worms shall **c** them. 3680
22:11 not see; and abundance of waters **c** thee. 3680
38:34 that abundance of waters may **c** thee? 3680
40:22 The shady trees **c** him *with* their shadow; 5526
Ps 91: 4 He shall **c** thee with his feathers, and 5526
104: 9 *that* they turn not again to **c** the earth. 3680
109:29 let them **c** *themselves with* their own 5844
139:11 If I say, Surely the darkness shall **c** me; 7779
140: 9 let the mischief of their own lips **c** them. 3680
Isa 11: 9 of the LORD, as the waters **c** the sea. 3680
14:11 is spread under thee, and the worms **c** thee. 4374
22:17 and will **surely** **c** thee. 5844+5844
26:21 her blood, and shall no more **c** her slain. 3680
30: 1 that **c** *with* a covering, but not of my Spirit, 5258
58: 7 when thou seest the naked, that thou **c** him; 3680
59: 6 neither shall they **c** themselves with their 3680
60: 2 the darkness shall **c** the earth, and 3680
60: 6 The multitude of camels shall **c** thee, 3680
Jer 46: 8 he saith, I will go up, *and* will **c** the earth; 3680
Eze 7:18 with sackcloth, and horror shall **c** them; 3680
12: 6 thou shalt **c** thy face, that thou see not 3680
12:12 he shall **c** his face, that he see not 3680
24: 7 it not upon the ground, to **c** it with dust; 3680
24:17 **c** not *thy* lips, and eat not the bread of men. 5844
24:22 ye shall not **c** *your* lips, nor eat the bread of 5844
26:10 of his horses their dust shall **c** thee: 3680
26:19 upon thee, and great waters shall **c** thee; 3680
30:18 a cloud shall **c** her, and her daughters shall 3680
32: 7 I will **c** the heaven, and make the stars 3680
32: 7 I will **c** the sun with a cloud, and the moon 3680
37: 6 **c** you **with** skin, and put breath in you, and 7159
38: 9 thou shalt be like a cloud to **c** the land, 3680
38:16 people of Israel, as a cloud to **c** the land; 3680
Hos 2: 9 and my flax *given* to **c** her nakedness. 3680
10: 8 they shall say to the mountains, **C** us; and 3680
Ob 1:10 thy brother Jacob shame shall **c** thee, 3680
Mic 3: 7 yea, they shall all **c** their lips; for *there is* no 5844
7:10 and shame shall **c** her which said unto me, 3680
Hab 2:14 of the LORD, as the waters **c** the sea. 3680
2:17 For the violence of Lebanon shall **c** thee, 3680
Mk 14:65 and to **c** his face, and to buffet him, and *4028*
Lk 23:30 Fall on us; and to the hills, **C** us. *2572*
1Co 11: 7 For a man indeed ought not to **c** *his* head, *2619*
1Pe 4: 8 for charity shall **c** the multitude of sins. *2572*

COVERED (105) [COVER]

Ge 7:19 that *were* under the whole heaven, were **c**. 3680
7:20 waters prevail; and the mountains were **c**. 3680
9:23 and **c** the nakedness of their father; 3680
24:65 therefore she took a vail, and **c** herself. 3680
38:14 **c** her with a vail, and wrapped herself, and 3680
38:15 to be a harlot; because she had **c** her face. 3680
Ex 8: 6 the frogs came up, and **c** the land of Egypt. 3680
10:15 For they **c** the face of the whole earth, so 3680
14:28 **c** the chariots, and the horsemen, and all 3680
15: 5 The depths have **c** them: they sank into 3680
15:10 didst blow with thy wind, the sea **c** them: 3680
16:13 at even the quails came up, and **c** the camp: 3680
24:15 up into the mount, and a cloud **c** the mount. 3680
24:16 mount Sinai, and the cloud **c** it six days: 3680
37: 9 *and* **c** with their wings over the mercy seat, 5526
40:21 and **c** the ark of the Testimony; 5526
40:34 a cloud **c** the tent of the congregation, and 3680
Lev 13:13 behold, *if* the leprosy have **c** all his flesh, 3680
Nu 4:20 not go in to see when the holy *things* are **c**, 1104
7: 3 six **c** wagons, and twelve oxen; 6632
9:15 the cloud **c** the tabernacle, *namely*, the tent 3680
9:16 the cloud **c** it *by day*, and the appearance of 3680
16:42 the cloud **c** it, and the glory of the LORD 3680
Dt 32:15 thou art **c** *with fatness*; then he forsook God 3780
Jos 24: 7 and brought the sea upon them, and **c** them; 3680
Jdg 4:18 her into the tent, she **c** him with a mantle. 3680
4:19 of milk, and gave him drink, and **c** him. 3680
1Sa 19:13 *hair for* his bolster, and **c** *it* with a cloth. 3680
28:14 man cometh up; and he *is* **c with** a mantle. 5844
2Sa 15:30 and had his head **c**, and he went barefoot: 2645
15:30 all the people that *was* with him **c** every 2645
19: 4 the king **c** his face, and the king cried *with* 3813
1Ki 1: 1 they **c** him with clothes, but he gat no heat. 3680
6: 9 **c** the house with beams and boards of 5603
6:15 *and* he **c** *them* on the inside with wood, and 6823
6:15 **c** the floor of the house with planks of fir. 6823
6:20 and *so* **c** the altar *which was of* cedar. 6823
6:35 **c** *them* with gold fitted upon the carved 6823
7: 3 *it was* **c** with cedar above upon the beams, 5603
7: 7 *it was* **c** with cedar from one side of 5603
8: 7 the cherubims **c** the ark and the staves 5526
2Ki 19: 1 **c** himself with sackcloth, and went *into* 3680
19: 2 the elders of the priests, **c** with sackcloth, 3680
1Ch 28:18 **c** the ark of the covenant of the LORD. 5526
2Ch 5: 8 the cherubims **c** the ark and the staves 3680
Ne 3:15 and **c** it, and set up the doors thereof, 2926
Est 6:12 his house mourning, and having his head **c**. 2645
7: 8 of the king's mouth, they **c** Haman's face. 2645
Job 23:17 *neither* hath he **c** the darkness from my 3680
31:33 If I **c** my transgressions as Adam, by hiding 3680
Ps 32: 1 transgression *is* forgiven, whose sin *is* **c**. 3680
44:15 and the shame of my face hath **c** me, 3680
44:19 and **c** us with the shadow of death. 3680
65:13 the valleys also are **c over** with corn; 5848
68:13 *yet shall ye be as* the wings of a dove **c** 2645
69: 7 borne reproach; shame hath **c** my face. 3680
71:13 let them be **c** *with* reproach and 5844
80:10 The hills were **c** *with* the shadow of it, and 3680
85: 2 of thy people, thou hast **c** all their sin. 3680
89:45 thou hast **c** him **with** shame. Selah. 5844
106:11 the waters **c** their enemies: there was not 3680
106:17 up Dathan, and **c** the company of Abiram. 3680
139:13 thou hast **c** me in my mother's womb. 5526
140: 7 thou hast **c** my head in the day of battle. 5526
Pr 24:31 *and* nettles had **c** the face thereof, and 3680
26:23 a wicked heart *are like* a potsherd **c** with 6823
Pr 26:26 *Whose* hatred is **c** by deceit, his wickedness 3680
Ecc 6: 4 and his name shall be **c** with darkness. 3680
Isa 6: 2 with twain he **c** his face, and with twain he 3680
6: 2 with twain he **c** his feet, and with twain he 3680
29:10 and your rulers, the seers hath he **c**. 3680
37: 1 **c** himself with sackcloth, and went *into* 3680
37: 2 the elders of the priests **c** with sackcloth, 3680
51:16 have **c** thee in the shadow of mine hand, 3680
61:10 he hath **c** me **with** the robe of 3271
Jer 14: 3 and confounded, and **c** their heads. 2645
14: 4 plowmen were ashamed, they **c** their heads. 2645
51:42 she is **c** with the multitude of the waves 3680
51:51 shame hath **c** our faces: for strangers are 3680
La 2: 1 **c** the daughter of Zion **with a cloud** in his 5743
3:16 with gravel stones, he hath **c** me with ashes. 3728
3:43 Thou hast **c** with anger, and persecuted us: 5526
3:44 Thou hast **c** thyself with a cloud, that *our* 5526
Eze 1:11 one to another, and two **c** their bodies. 3680
1:23 which **c** on this *side*, and every one had 3680
1:23 had two, which **c** on that *side*, their bodies. 3680
16: 8 my skirt over thee, and **c** thy nakedness: 3680
16:10 about with fine linen, and I **c** thee *with* silk. 3680
18: 7 and hath **c** the naked with a garment; 3680
18:16 and hath **c** the naked with a garment, 3680
24: 8 the top of a rock, that *it* should not be **c**. 3680
27: 7 the isles of Elishah was that which **c** thee. 4374
31:15 I **c** the deep for him, and I restrained 3680
37: 8 up upon them, and the skin **c** them above: 7159
41:16 to the windows, and the windows *were* **c**; 3680
Jnh 3: 6 and **c** *him* with sackcloth, and sat in ashes. 3680
3: 8 let man and beast be **c** with sackcloth, and 3680
Hab 3: 3 His glory **c** the heavens, and the earth was 3680
Mt 8:24 insomuch that the ship was **c** with *2572*
10:26 for there is nothing **c**, that shall not be *2572*
Lk 12: 2 For there is nothing **c**, that shall not be *4780*
Ro 4: 7 are forgiven, and whose sins are **c**. *1943*
1Co 11: 4 or prophesying, having *his* head **c**, *2596*
11: 6 For if the woman be not **c**, let her also be *2619*
11: 6 woman to be shorn or shaven, let her be **c**. *2619*

COVEREDST (2) [COVER]

Ps 104: 6 Thou **c** it *with* the deep as *with* a garment: 3680
Eze 16:18 tookest thy broidered garments, and **c** them: 3680

COVEREST (2) [COVER]

Dt 22:12 of thy vesture, wherewith thou **c** *thyself*. 3680
Ps 104: 2 Who **c** *thyself with* light as *with* a garment: 5844

COVERETH (27) [COVER]

Ex 29:13 thou shalt take all the fat that **c** the inwards, 3680
29:22 the fat that **c** the inwards, and the caul 3680
Lev 3: 3 the fat that **c** the inwards, and all the fat that 3680
3: 9 the fat that **c** the inwards, and all the fat that 3680
3:14 the fat that **c** the inwards, and all the fat that 3680
4: 8 the fat that **c** the inwards, and all the fat that 3680
7: 3 the rump, and the fat that **c** the inwards, 3680
9:19 that which **c** *the inwards*, and the kidneys, 4374
Nu 22:11 out of Egypt, which **c** the face of the earth: 3680
Jdg 3:24 Surely he **c** his feet in *his* summer chamber. 5526
Job 9:24 he **c** the faces of the judges thereof; if not, 3680
15:27 Because he **c** his face with his fatness, and 3680
36:30 light upon it, and **c** the bottom of the sea. 3680
36:32 With clouds he **c** the light; and 3680
Ps 73: 6 as a chain; violence **c** them *as* a garment. 5848
109:19 Let it be unto him as the garment *which* **c** 5844
147: 8 Who **c** the heaven with clouds, 3680
Pr 10: 6 but violence **c** the mouth of the wicked. 3680
10:11 but violence **c** the mouth of the wicked. 3680
10:12 Hatred stirreth up strifes: but love **c** all sins. 3680
12:16 but a prudent *man* **c** shame. 3680
17: 9 He that **c** a transgression seeketh love; but 3680
28:13 He that **c** his sins shall not prosper: but 3680
Jer 3:25 down in our shame, and our confusion **c** us: 3680
Eze 28:14 Thou *art* the anointed cherub that **c**; and 5526
Mal 2:16 for *one* **c** violence with his garment, 3680
Lk 8:16 **c** it with a vessel, or putteth *it* under a bed; *2572*

COVERING (48) [COVER]

Ge 8:13 Noah removed the **c** of the ark, and looked, 4372
20:16 behold, he *is* to thee a **c** of the eyes, unto all 3682
Ex 22:27 For that *is* his **c** only, it *is* his raiment for 3682
25:20 **c** the mercy seat with their wings, and 5526
26: 7 *of* goats' *hair* to be a **c** upon the tabernacle: 168
26:14 thou shalt make a **c** for the tent *of* rams' 4372
26:14 dyed red, and a **c** above of badgers' skins. 4372
35:11 his tent, and his **c**, his taches, and 4372
35:12 *with* the mercy seat, and the vail of the **c**, 4539
36:19 he made a **c** for the tent *of* rams' skins dyed 4372
36:19 and a **c** of badgers' skins above *that*. 4372
39:34 the **c** of rams' skins dyed red, and 4372
39:34 the **c** of badgers' skins, and the vail of 4372
39:34 of badgers' skins, and the vail of the **c**, 4539
40:19 and put the **c** of the tent above upon it; 4372
40:21 set up the vail of the **c**, and covered the ark 4539
Lev 13:45 he shall **put a c** upon *his* upper lip, and 5844
Nu 3:25 the **c** thereof, and the hanging for the door 4372
4: 5 they shall take down the **c** vail, and 4539
4: 6 shall put thereon the **c** of badgers' skins, 3681
4: 8 cover the same with a **c** of badgers' skins, 4372
4:10 all the vessels thereof within a **c** of 4372
4:11 cover it with a **c** of badgers' skins, and 4372
4:12 cover them with a **c** of badgers' skins, and 4372
4:14 they shall spread upon it a **c** of badgers' 3681
4:15 his sons have made an end of **c** 3680
4:25 his **c**, and the covering of the badgers' skins 4372
4:25 the **c** of the badgers' skins that *is* above 4372
16:38 let them make them broad plates *for* a **c** of 6826
16:39 they were made broad *plates for* a **c** of 6826
19:15 which hath no **c** bound upon it, *is* unclean. 6781
2Sa 17:19 and spread a **c** over the well's mouth, 4539
Job 22:14 Thick clouds *are* a **c** to him, that he seeth 5643
24: 7 that *they have* no **c** in the cold. 3682
26: 6 before him, and destruction hath no **c**. 3682
31:19 for want of clothing, or *any* poor without **c**; 3682

Ps 105:39 He spread a cloud for a **c**; and fire to give 4539
SS 3:10 bottom thereof *of* gold, the **c** of it *of* purple, 4817
Isa 22: 8 he discovered the **c** of Judah, and thou didst 4539
25: 7 the face of the **c** cast over all people, 3875
28:20 the **c** narrower than that *he* can wrap 4541
30: 1 that cover *with* a **c**, but not of my Spirit, 4541
30:22 Ye shall defile also the **c** of thy graven 6826
50: 3 and I make sackcloth their **c**. 3682
Eze 28:13 every precious stone *was* thy **c**, the sardius, 4540
28:16 I will destroy thee, O **c** cherub, from 5526
Mal 2:13 **c** the altar of the LORD *with* tears, *with* 3680
1Co 11:15 to her: for *her* hair is given her for a **c**. *4018*

COVERINGS (2) [COVER]

Pr 7:16 I have deckt my bed *with* **c of tapestry**, 4765
31:22 She maketh herself **c of tapestry**; 4765

COVERS (3) [COVER]

Ex 25:29 and **c** thereof, and bowls thereof, 7184
37:16 and his bowls, and *his* **c** to cover withal, 7184
Nu 4: 7 and the bowls, and **c** to cover withal: 7184

COVERT (9)

1Sa 25:20 that she came down by the **c** of the hill, and 5643
2Ki 16:18 the **c** for the sabbath that they had built in 4329
Job 38:40 *their* dens, *and* abide in the **c** to lie in wait? 5521
40:21 shady trees, in the **c** of the reed, and fens. 5643
Ps 61: 4 I will trust in the **c** of thy wings. Selah. 5643
Isa 4: 6 and for a **c** from storm and from rain. 4563
16: 4 be thou a **c** to them from the face of 5643
32: 2 from the wind, and a **c** from the tempest; 5643
Jer 25:38 He hath forsaken his **c**, as the lion: for their 5520

COVET (8) [COVETED, COVETETH, COVETOUS, COVETOUSNESS]

Ex 20:17 Thou shalt not **c** thy neighbour's house, 2530
20:17 thou shalt not **c** thy neighbour's wife, 2530
Dt 5:21 neither shalt thou **c** thy neighbour's house, 183
Mic 2: 2 they **c** fields, and take *them* by violence; 2530
Ro 7: 7 except the law had said, Thou shalt not **c**. *1937*
13: 9 not bear false witness, Thou shalt not **c**; *1937*
1Co 12:31 But **c earnestly** the best gifts: and yet shew *2206*
14:39 **c** to prophesy, and forbid not to speak with *2206*

COVETED (3) [COVET]

Jos 7:21 then I **c** them, and took them; 2530
Ac 20:33 I have **c** no *man's* silver, or gold, or *1937*
1Ti 6:10 which while some **c after**, they have erred *3713*

COVETETH (2) [COVET]

Pr 21:26 He **c greedily** all the day long: but 183+8378
Hab 2: 9 Woe to him that **c** an evil covetousness to 1214

COVETOUS (9) [COVET]

Ps 10: 3 blesseth the **c**, *whom* the LORD 1214
Lk 16:14 who were **c**, heard all these *things:* and *5366*
1Co 5:10 or with the **c**, or extortioners, or *4123*
5:11 or **c**, or an idolater, or a railer, or *4123*
6:10 Nor thieves, nor **c**, nor drunkards, *4123*
Eph 5: 5 nor unclean *person*, nor **c man** who is an *4123*
1Ti 3: 3 filthy lucre; but patient, not a brawler, **not c**; *866*
2Ti 3: 2 **c**, boasters, proud, blasphemers, *5366*
2Pe 2:14 heart they have exercised with **c practices**; *4124*

COVETOUSNESS (19) [COVET]

Ex 18:21 such as fear God, men of truth, hating **c**; 1215
Ps 119:36 my heart unto thy testimonies, and not to **c**. 1215
Pr 28:16 *but* he that hateth **c** shall prolong *his* days. 1215
Isa 57:17 For the iniquity of his **c** was I wroth, and 1215
Jer 6:13 of them every one *is* **given to c**; 1214+1215
8:10 least even unto the greatest is given to **c**, 1215
22:17 and thine heart *are* not but for thy **c**, 1215
51:13 thine end is come, *and* the measure of thy **c**. 1215
Eze 33:31 *but* their heart goeth after their **c**. 1215
Hab 2: 9 Woe to him that coveteth an evil **c** to his 1215
Mk 7:22 Thefts, **c**, wickedness, deceit, *4124*
Lk 12:15 unto them, Take heed, and beware of **c**: *4124*
Ro 1:29 fornication, wickedness, **c**, maliciousness; *4124*
2Co 9: 5 as *a matter of* bounty, and not as *of* **c**. *4124*
Eph 5: 3 But fornication, and all uncleanness, or **c**, *4124*
Col 3: 5 and **c**, which is idolatry: *4124*
1Th 2: 5 as ye know, nor a cloke of **c**; *4124*
Heb 13: 5 *Let your* conversation *be* **without c**; *and* *866*
2Pe 2: 3 And through **c** shall they with feigned *4124*

COW (6) [COW'S]

Lev 22:28 *whether it be* **c** or ewe, ye shall not kill it 7794
Nu 18:17 the firstling of a **c**, or the firstling of a 7794
Job 21:10 their **c** calveth, and casteth not her calf. 6510
Isa 7:21 *that* a man shall nourish a **young c**, 1241+5697
11: 7 the **c** and the bear shall feed; their young 6510
Am 4: 3 every **c** *at that which is* before her; NIH

COW'S (1) [COW]

Eze 4:15 I have given thee **c** dung for man's dung, 1241

COWS THAT HAVE CALVED See MILCH

COZ (1)

1Ch 4: 8 **C** begat Anub, and Zobebah, and 6976

COZBI (2)

Nu 25:15 Midianitish woman that was slain *was* **C**, 3579
25:18 in the matter of **C**, the daughter of a prince 3579

COZEBA See CHOZEBA

CRACKLING (1)

Ecc 7: 6 For as the **c** of thorns under a pot, so *is* 6963

CRACKNELS (1)

1Ki 14: 3 and **c**, and a cruse of honey, and go to him: 5350

CRAFT (6) [CRAFTINESS, CRAFTSMAN, CRAFTSMEN, CRAFTY, WITCHCRAFT, WITCHCRAFTS]

Da 8:25 through his policy also he shall cause **c** to 4820
Mk 14: 1 sought how they might take him by **c**, *1388*
Ac 18: 3 And because *he* was of the **same c**, *3673*
19:25 ye know that by this **c** we have our wealth. *2039*
19:27 So *that* not only this our **c** is in danger to be *3313*
Rev 18:22 of whatsoever **c** *he be*, shall be found any *5078*

CRAFTINESS (5) [CRAFT]

Job 5:13 He taketh the wise in their own **c**: and 6193
Lk 20:23 But he perceived their **c**, and said unto *3834*
1Co 3:19 He taketh the wise in their own **c**. *3834*
2Co 4: 2 not walking in **c**, nor handling the word of *3834*
Eph 4:14 by the sleight of men, and **cunning c**, *3834*

CRAFTSMAN (2) [CRAFT, MAN]

Dt 27:15 the work of the hands of the **c**, and 2796
Rev 18:22 and no **c**, of whatsoever craft *he be*, shall be *5079*

CRAFTSMEN (7) [CRAFT, MAN]

2Ki 24:14 thousand captives, and all the **c** and smiths: 2796
24:16 **c** and smiths a thousand, all *that were* 2796
1Ch 4:14 of the valley of Charashim; for they were **c**. 2796
Ne 11:35 Lod, and Ono, the valley of **c**. 2791
Hos 13: 2 all of it the work of the **c**: 2796
Ac 19:24 for Diana, brought no small gain unto the **c**; *5079*
19:38 if Demetrius, and the **c** which are with him, *5079*

CRAFTY (4) [CRAFT]

Job 5:12 He disappointeth the devices of the **c**, so 6175
15: 5 and thou choosest the tongue of the **c**. 6175
Ps 83: 3 They have **taken c** counsel against thy 6191
2Co 12:16 nevertheless, being **c**, I caught you with *3835*

CRAG (1)

Job 39:28 upon the **c** of the rock, and the strong place. 8127

CRANE (2)

Isa 38:14 Like a **c** *or* a swallow, so did I chatter: I did 5483
Jer 8: 7 the turtle and the **c** and the swallow observe 5483

CRASHING (1)

Zep 1:10 the second, and a great **c** from the hills. 7667

CRAVED (1) [CRAVETH]

Mk 15:43 boldly unto Pilate, and **c** the body of Jesus. *154*

CRAVETH (1) [CRAVED]

Pr 16:26 for himself; for his mouth **c** it of him. 404

CREATE (8) [CREATED, CREATETH, CREATION, CREATOR, CREATURE, CREATURES]

Ps 51:10 **C** in me a clean heart, O God; and renew a 1254
Isa 4: 5 the LORD will **c** upon every dwelling 1254
45: 7 I form the light, and **c** darkness: I make 1254
45: 7 I make peace, and **c** evil: I the LORD do 1254
57:19 I **c** the fruit of the lips; Peace, peace to *him* 1254
65:17 behold, I **c** new heavens and a new earth: 1254
65:18 and rejoice for ever *in that* which I **c**: 1254
65:18 I **c** Jerusalem a rejoicing, and her people a 1254

CREATED (45) [CREATE]

Ge 1: 1 In the beginning God **c** the heaven and 1254
1:21 God **c** great whales, and every living 1254
1:27 So God **c** man in his own image, in 1254
1:27 own image, in the image of God **c** he him; 1254
1:27 created he him; male and female **c** he them. 1254
2: 3 had rested from all his work which God **c** 1254
2: 4 and of the earth when they were **c**, 1254
5: 1 In the day that God **c** man, in the likeness 1254
5: 2 Male and female **c** he them; and 1254
5: 2 name Adam, in the day when they were **c**. 1254
6: 7 I will destroy man whom I have **c** from 1254
Dt 4:32 since the day that God **c** man upon 1254
Ps 89:12 The north and the south thou hast **c** them: 1254
102:18 the people which *shall be* **c** shall praise 1254
104:30 Thou sendest forth thy spirit, they are **c**: 1254
148: 5 for he commanded, and they were **c**. 1254
Isa 40:26 behold who hath **c** these *things*, that 1254
41:20 and the Holy One of Israel hath **c** it. 1254
42: 5 he that **c** the heavens, and stretched them 1254
43: 1 now thus saith the LORD that **c** thee, 1254
43: 7 for I have **c** him for my glory, I have 1254
45: 8 spring up together; I the LORD have **c** it. 1254
45:12 I have made the earth, and **c** man upon it: I, 1254
45:18 For thus saith the LORD that **c** 1254
45:18 he hath established it, he **c** it not in vain, 1254
48: 7 They are **c** now, and not from 1254
54:16 I have **c** the smith that bloweth the coals in 1254
54:16 and I have **c** the waster to destroy. 1254
Jer 31:22 for the LORD hath **c** a new *thing* in 1254
Eze 21:30 judge thee in the place where thou wast **c**, 1254
28:13 prepared in thee in the day that thou wast **c**. 1254
28:15 in thy ways from the day that thou wast **c**, 1254
Mal 2:10 hath not one God **c** us? why do we deal 1254
Mk 13:19 of the creation which God **c** unto this time, *2936*
1Co 11: 9 Neither was the man **c** for the woman; but *2936*
Eph 2:10 **c** in Christ Jesus unto good works, *2936*
3: 9 in God, who **c** all *things* by Jesus Christ: *2936*
4:24 which after God is **c** in righteousness and *2936*
Col 1:16 For by him were all *things* **c**, that are in *2936*
1:16 all *things* were **c** by him, and for him: *2936*
3:10 after the image of him that **c** him: *2936*
1Ti 4: 3 which God hath **c** to be received with *2936*
Rev 4:11 for thou hast **c** all *things*, and for thy *2936*
4:11 and for thy pleasure they are and were **c**. *2936*
10: 6 who **c** heaven, and the *things* that therein *2936*

CREATETH (1) [CREATE]

Am 4:13 **c** the wind, and declareth unto man what *is* 1254

CREATION (6) [CREATE]

Mk 10: 6 But from the beginning of the **c** God made *2937*
13:19 such as was not from the beginning of the **c** *2937*
Ro 1:20 For the invisible *things* of him from the **c** of *2937*
8:22 For we know that the whole **c** groaneth and *2937*
2Pe 3: 4 as *they were* from the beginning of the **c**. *2937*
Rev 3:14 true witness, the beginning of the **c** of God; *2937*

CREATOR (5) [CREATE]

Ecc 12: 1 Remember now thy **C** in the days of thy 1254
Isa 40:28 the **C** of the ends of the earth, fainteth not, 1254
43:15 your Holy One, the **c** of Israel, your King. 1254
Ro 1:25 and served the creature more than the **C**, *2936*
1Pe 4:19 *to him* in well doing, as unto a faithful **C**. *2939*

CREATURE (29) [CREATE]

Ge 1:20 abundantly the **moving c** that hath life, 5315
1:21 and every living **c** that moveth, 5315
1:24 Let the earth bring forth the living **c** after 5315
2:19 and whatsoever Adam called every living **c**, 5315
9:10 with every living **c** that *is* with you, of 5315
9:12 and you and every living **c** that *is* with you, 5315
9:15 and you and every living **c** of all flesh; 5315
9:16 every living **c** of all flesh that *is* upon 5315
Lev 11:46 of every living **c** that moveth in the waters, 5315
11:46 and of every **c** that creepeth upon the earth: 5315
Eze 1:20 for the spirit of the **living c** *was* in 2416
1:21 for the spirit of the **living c** *was* in 2416
1:22 **living c** *was* as the colour of the terrible 2416
10:15 This *is* the **living c** that I saw by the river of 2416
10:17 for the spirit of the **living c** *was* in them. 2416
10:20 This *is* the **living c** that I saw under 2416
Mk 16:15 the world, and preach the gospel to every **c**. *2937*
Ro 1:25 and served the **c** more than the Creator, *2937*
8:19 For the earnest expectation of the **c** waiteth *2937*
8:20 For the **c** was made subject to vanity, *2937*
8:21 Because the **c** itself also shall be delivered *2937*
8:39 Nor height, nor depth, nor any other **c**, *2937*
2Co 5:17 if any *man be* in Christ, *he is* a new **c**: *2937*
Gal 6:15 any *thing*, nor uncircumcision, but a new **c**. *2937*
Col 1:15 the invisible God, the firstborn of every **c**: *2937*
1:23 which was preached to every **c** which is *2937*
1Ti 4: 4 For every **c** of God *is* good, and nothing to *2938*
Heb 4:13 Neither is there any **c** *that is* not manifest in *2937*
Rev 5:13 And every **c** which is in heaven, and on *2938*

CREATURES (12) [CREATE]

Isa 13:21 their houses shall be full *of* **doleful c**; and 255
Eze 1: 5 thereof *came* the likeness of four **living c**. 2416
1:13 As for the likeness of the **living c**, 2416
1:13 it went up and down among the **living c**; 2416
1:14 the **living c** ran and returned as 2416
1:15 Now as I beheld the **living c**, behold one 2416
1:15 one wheel upon the earth by the **living c**, 2416
1:19 when the **living c** went, the wheels went by 2416
1:19 when the **living c** were lift up from 2416
3:13 of the **living c** that touched one another, 2416
Jas 1:18 we should be a kind of firstfruits of his **c**. *2938*
Rev 8: 9 And the third *part* of the **c** which were in *2938*

CREDIT; CREDITED; CREDITS See IMPUTE; IMPUTED; IMPUTETH; IMPUTING

CREDITOR (3) [CREDITORS]

Dt 15: 2 Every **c** that lendeth *ought* 1167+3027+4874
2Ki 4: 1 the **c** is come to take unto him my two sons 5383
Lk 7:41 There was a certain **c** which had two *1157*

CREDITORS (1) [CREDITOR]

Isa 50: 1 which of my **c** *is it* to whom I have sold 5383

CREEK (1)

Ac 27:39 but they discovered a certain **c** with a shore, *2859*

CREEP (7) [CREEPETH, CREEPING, CREPT]

Lev 11:20 All fowls that **c**, going upon *all* four, 8318
11:29 the creeping things that **c** upon the earth; 8317
11:31 These *are* unclean to you among all that **c**: 8318
11:42 all creeping things that **c** upon the earth, 8317
Ps 104:20 wherein all the beasts of the forest do **c** 7430
Eze 38:20 all creeping things that **c** upon the earth, 7430
2Ti 3: 6 For of this sort are they which **c** into *1744*

CREEPETH (14) [CREEP]

Ge 1:25 every **thing that c** upon the earth after his 7431
1:26 over every creeping thing that **c** upon 7430
1:30 to every *thing* that **c** upon the earth, 7430
7: 8 and of every *thing* that **c** upon the earth, 7430
7:14 every creeping thing that **c** upon the earth 7430
7:21 of every creeping thing that **c** upon 8317
8:17 of every creeping thing that **c** upon 7430
8:19 *and* whatsoever **c** upon the earth, 7430
Lev 11:41 every creeping thing that **c** upon the earth 8317
11:43 abominable with any creeping thing that **c**, 8317
11:44 *of* creeping thing that **c** upon the earth. 7430
11:46 and of every creature that **c** upon the earth: 8317
20:25 by any *manner of living thing* that **c** *on* 7430
Dt 4:18 The likeness of any *thing* that **c** on 7430

CREEPING (29) [CREEP]

Ge 1:24 **c thing**, and beast of the earth after his 7431
1:26 over every **c thing** that creepeth upon 7431
6: 7 and the **c thing**, and the fowls of the air; 7431
6:20 of every **c thing** of the earth after his kind, 7431
7:14 every **c thing** that creepeth upon the earth 7431
7:21 of every **c thing** that creepeth upon 8318
7:23 the **c things**, and the fowl of the heaven; 7431
8:17 of every **c thing** that creepeth upon 7431
8:19 every **c thing**, and every fowl, *and* 7431
Lev 5: 2 or the carcase of unclean **c things**, and *if* it 8318
11:21 flying **c thing** that goeth upon *all* four, 8318
11:23 all *other* flying **c things**, which have four 8318
11:29 the **c things** that creep upon the earth; 8318

Lev 11:41 every c thing that creepeth upon the earth 8318
11:42 all c things that creep upon the earth, 8318
11:43 abominable with any c thing that creepeth, 8318
11:44 of c thing that creepeth upon the earth. 8318
22: 5 Or whosoever toucheth any c thing, 8318
Dt 14:19 every c thing that flieth is unclean unto 8318
1Ki 4:33 and of fowl, and of c things, and of fishes. 7431
Ps 104:25 wherein are things c innumerable, 7431
148:10 all cattle; c things, and flying fowl: 7431
Eze 8:10 behold every form of c things, and 7431
38:20 all c things that creep upon the earth, and 7431
Hos 2:18 and with the c things of the ground: 7431
Hab 1:14 as the c things, that have no ruler over 7431
Ac 10:12 and c things, and fowls of the air. 2062
11: 6 and c things, and fowls of the air. 2062
Ro 1:23 and fourfooted beasts, and c things. 2062

CREPT (1) [CREEP]
Jude 1: 4 For there are certain men c in unawares, 3921

CRESCENS (1)
2Ti 4:10 C to Galatia, Titus unto Dalmatia. 2913

CRETANS See CRETES; CRETIANS

CRETE (5) [CRETES, CRETIANS]
Ac 27: 7 we sailed under C, over against Salmone; 2914
27:12 which is a haven of C, and lieth toward 2914
27:13 loosing thence, they sailed close by C. 2914
27:21 and not have loosed from C, and to have 2914
Tit 1: 5 For this cause left I thee in C, that thou 2914

CRETES (1) [CRETE]
Ac 2:11 C and Arabians, we do hear them speak in 2912

CRETIANS (2) [CRETE]
Tit 1:12 said, The C are alway liars, evil beasts, 2912
3: S the first bishop of the church of the C, 2912

CREW (5) [CROW]
Mt 26:74 not the man. And immediately the cock c. 5455
Mk 14:68 he went out into the porch; and the cock c. 5455
14:72 And the second time the cock c. And Peter 5455
Lk 22:60 while he yet spake, the cock c. 5455
Jn 18:27 denied again: and immediately the cock c. 5455

CRIB (3)
Job 39: 9 be willing to serve thee, or abide by thy c? 18
Pr 14: 4 Where no oxen are, the c is clean: but 18
Isa 1: 3 knoweth his owner, and the ass his master's c: 18

CRICKET See BEETLE

CRIED (199) [CRY]
Ge 27:34 he c with a great and exceeding bitter cry, 6817
39:14 to lie with me, and I c with a loud voice: 7121
39:15 he heard that I lifted up my voice and c, 7121
39:18 it came to pass, as I lift up my voice and c, 7121
41:43 and they c before him, Bow the knee: 7121
41:55 the people c to Pharaoh for bread: 6817
45: 1 he c, Cause every man to go out from me. 7121
Ex 2:23 they c, and their cry came up unto God by 2199
5:15 children of Israel came and c unto Pharaoh, 6817
8:12 Moses c unto the LORD because of 6817
14:10 the children of Israel c out unto 6817
15:25 he c unto the LORD; and the LORD 6817
17: 4 Moses c unto the LORD, saying, 6817
Nu 11: 2 the people c unto Moses; and when Moses 6817
12:13 Moses c unto the LORD, saying, Heal her 6817
14: 1 congregation lifted up their voice, and c; 5414
20:16 when we c unto the LORD, he heard our 6817
Dt 22:24 the damsel, because she c not, being in 6817
22:27 and the betrothed damsel c, and there was 6817
26: 7 when we c unto the LORD God of our 6817
Jos 24: 7 when they c unto the LORD, he put 6817
Jdg 3: 9 when the children of Israel c unto 2199
3:15 when the children of Israel c unto 2199
4: 3 the children of Israel c unto the LORD: 6817
5:28 c through the lattice, Why is his chariot so 2980
6: 6 the children of Israel c unto the LORD. 2199
6: 7 when the children of Israel c unto 2199
7:20 their right hands to blow withal: and they c, 7121
7:21 and all the host ran, and c, and fled. 7321
9: 7 lift up his voice, and c, and said unto them, 7121
10:10 the children of Israel c unto the LORD, 2199
10:12 ye c to me, and I delivered you out of their 6817
18:23 they c unto the children of Dan. And they 7121
1Sa 4:13 into the city, and told it, all the city c out. 2199
5:10 to Ekron, that the Ekronites c out, saying, 2199
7: 9 Samuel c unto the LORD for Israel; and 2199
12: 8 your fathers c unto the LORD, then 2199
12:10 they c unto the LORD, and said, We have 2199
15:11 and he c unto the LORD all night. 2199
17: 8 he stood and c unto the armies of Israel, 7121
20:37 Jonathan c after the lad, and said, Is not 7121
20:38 Jonathan c after the lad, Make speed, haste, 7121
24: 8 and c after Saul, saying, My lord the king. 7121
26:14 David c to the people, and to Abner the son 7121
28:12 saw Samuel, she c with a loud voice: 2199
2Sa 18:25 the watchman c, and told the king. And 7121
19: 4 the king c with a loud voice, O my son 2199
20:16 c a wise woman out of the city, Hear, hear; 7121
22: 7 called upon the LORD, and c to my God: 7121
1Ki 13: 2 he c against the altar in the word of 7121
13: 4 which had c against the altar in Beth-el, 7121
13:21 he c unto the man of God that came from 7121
13:32 For the saying which he c by the word of 7121
17:20 he c unto the LORD, and said, O LORD my 7121
17:21 c unto the LORD, and said, O LORD my 7121
18:28 they c loud, and cut themselves after their 7121
20:39 as the king passed by, he c unto the king: 6817
22:32 to fight against him: and Jehoshaphat c out. 2199
2Ki 2:12 Elisha saw it, and he c, My father, 6817
4: 1 Now there c a certain woman of the wives 6817
4:40 that they c out, and said, O thou man of 6817
6: 5 he c, and said, Alas, master, for it was 6817
6:26 there c a woman unto him, saying, Help, 6817
8: 5 c to the king for her house and for her land. 6817
11:14 rent her clothes, and c, Treason, Treason. 7121
18:28 c with a loud voice in the Jews' language, 7121
20:11 Isaiah the prophet c unto the LORD: and 7121
1Ch 5:20 for they c to God in the battle, and he was 2199
2Ch 13:14 they c unto the LORD, and the priests 6817
14:11 Asa c unto the LORD his God, and said, 7121
18:31 Jehoshaphat c out, and the LORD helped 2199
32:18 they c with a loud voice in the Jews' speech 7121
32:20 the son of Amoz, prayed and c to heaven. 2199
Ne 9: 4 c with a loud voice unto the LORD their 2199
9:27 time of their trouble, when they c unto thee, 6817
9:28 yet when they returned, and c unto thee, 2199
Est 4: 1 the city, and c with a loud and a bitter cry; 2199
Job 29:12 Because I delivered the poor that c, and 7768
30: 5 (they c after them as after a thief;) 7321
30:28 I stood up, and I c in the congregation. 7768
Ps 3: 4 I c unto the LORD with my voice, and 7121
18: 6 upon the LORD, and c unto my God: 7768
18:41 They c, but there was none to save them: 7768
22: 5 They c unto thee, and were delivered: 2199
22:24 but when he c unto him, he heard. 7768
30: 2 I c unto thee, and thou hast healed me. 7768
30: 8 I c to thee, O LORD; and unto 7121
31:22 of my supplications when I c unto thee. 7768
34: 6 This poor man c, and the LORD heard 7121
66:17 I c unto him with my mouth, and he was 7121
77: 1 I c unto God with my voice, even unto God 6817
88: 1 I have c day and night before thee: 6817
88:13 unto thee have I c, O LORD; and in 7768
107: 6 they c unto the LORD in their trouble, 6817
107:13 they c unto the LORD in their trouble, 2199
119:145 I c with my whole heart; hear me, 7121
119:146 I c unto thee; save me, and I shall keep thy 7121
119:147 the dawning of the morning, and c: 7768
120: 1 In my distress I c unto the LORD, and 7121
130: 1 Out of the depths have I c unto thee, 7121
138: 3 In the day when I c thou answeredst me, 7121
142: 1 I c unto the LORD with my voice; 2199
142: 5 I c unto thee, O LORD: I said, Thou art 2199
Isa 6: 3 one c unto another, and said, Holy, holy, 7121
6: 4 the door moved at the voice of him that c, 7121
21: 8 he c, A lion: My lord, I stand continually 7121
30: 7 therefore have I c concerning this, 7121
36:13 c with a loud voice in the Jews' language, 7121
Jer 4:20 Destruction upon destruction is c; for 7121
20: 8 I spake, I c out, I cried violence and spoil; 2199
20: 8 I spake, I cried out, I c violence and spoil; 7121
La 2:18 Their heart c unto the Lord, O wall of 6817
4:15 They c unto them, Depart ye; it is unclean; 7121
Eze 9: 1 He c also in mine ears with a loud voice, 7121
9: 8 my face, and c, and said, Ah Lord GOD, 2199
10:13 it was c unto them in my hearing, O wheel. 7121
11:13 c with a loud voice, and said, Ah Lord 2199
Da 3: 4 a herald c aloud, To you it is commanded, 7123
4:14 He c aloud, and said thus, Hew down 7123
5: 7 The king c aloud to bring in the astrologers, 7123
6:20 he c with a lamentable voice unto Daniel: 2200
Hos 7:14 they have not c unto me with their heart, 2199
Jnh 1: 5 c every man unto his god, and cast forth 2199
1:14 Wherefore they c unto the LORD, and 7121
2: 2 I c by reason of mine affliction unto 7121
2: 2 out of the belly of hell c I, and 7768
3: 4 he c, and said, Yet forty days, and 7121
Zec 1: 4 unto whom the former prophets have c, 7121
6: 8 c he upon me, and spake unto me, saying, 2199
7: 7 the LORD hath c by the former prophets, 7121
7:13 that as he c, and they would not hear; 7121
7:13 so they c, and I would not hear, saith 7121
Mt 8:29 And behold, they c out, saying, What have 2896
14:26 It is a spirit; and they c out for fear. 2896
14:30 to sink, he c, saying, Lord, save me. 2896
15:22 and c unto him, saying, Have mercy on me, 2905
20:30 c out, saying, Have mercy on us, O Lord, 2896
20:31 but they c the more, saying, Have mercy on 2896
21: 9 and that followed, c, saying, Hosanna to 2896
27:23 But they c out the more, saying, Let him be 2896
27:46 And about the ninth hour Jesus c with a loud 310
27:50 when he had c again with a loud voice, 2896
Mk 1:23 a man with an unclean spirit; and he c out, 349
1:26 and c with a loud voice, he came out of 2896
3:11 fell down before him, and c, saying, 2896
5: 7 And c with a loud voice, and said, 2896
6:49 they supposed it had been a spirit, and c out: 349
9:24 straightway the father of the child c out, 2896
9:26 And the spirit c, and rent him sore, and 2896
10:48 but he c the more a great deal, Thou Son of 2896
11: 9 and they that followed, c, saying, Hosanna; 2896
15:13 And they c out again, Crucify him. 2896
15:14 And they c out the more exceedingly, 2896
15:34 And at the ninth hour Jesus c with a loud 994
15:37 And Jesus c with a loud voice, and gave up 863
15:39 saw that he so c out, and gave up the ghost, 2896
Lk 4:33 unclean devil, and c out with a loud voice, 349
8: 8 And when he said these things, he c, 5455
8:28 he c out, and fell down before him, and 349
9:38 a man of the company c out, saying, Master, 310
16:24 And he c and said, Father Abraham, 5455
18:38 And he c, saying, Jesus, thou Son of David, 994
18:39 but he c so much the more, Thou Son of 2896
23:18 And they c out all at once, saying, 349
23:21 But they c, saying, Crucify him, crucify 2019
23:46 And when Jesus had c with a loud voice, 5455
Jn 1:15 John bare witness of him, and c, saying, 2896
7:28 Then c Jesus in the temple as he taught, 2896
7:37 Jesus stood and c, saying, If any man thirst, 2896
11:43 he c with a loud voice, Lazarus, come forth. 2905
12:13 went forth to meet him, and c, Hosanna: 2896
12:44 Jesus c and said, He that believeth on me, 2896
18:40 Then c they all again, saying, Not this man, 2905
19: 6 and officers saw him, they c out, saying, 2905
19:12 but the Jews c out, saying, If thou let this 2896
19:15 But they c out, Away with him, away with 2905
Ac 7:57 Then they c out with a loud voice, and 2896
7:60 and c with a loud voice, Lord, 2896
16:17 The same followed Paul and us, and c, 2896
16:28 But Paul c with a loud voice, saying, 5455
19:28 and c out, saying, Great is Diana of 2896
19:32 Some therefore c one thing, and 2896
19:34 voice about the space of two hours c out, 2896
21:34 And some c one thing, some another, 994
22:23 And as they c out, and cast off their 2905
22:24 he might know wherefore they c so against 2019
23: 6 he c out in the council, Men and brethren, 2896
24:21 one voice, that I c standing among them, 2896
Rev 6:10 And they c with a loud voice, saying, 2896
7: 2 he c with a loud voice to the four angels, 2896
7:10 And c with a loud voice, saying, Salvation 2896
10: 3 And c with a loud voice, as when a lion 2896
10: 3 and when he had c, seven thunders uttered 2896
12: 2 And she being with child c, travailing in 2896
14:18 c with a loud cry to him that had the sharp 5455
18: 2 And he c mightily with a strong voice, 2896
18:18 And c when they saw the smoke of her 2896
18:19 and c, weeping and wailing, saying, Alas, 2896
19:17 and he c with a loud voice, saying to all 2896

CRIES (1) [CRY]
Jas 5: 4 the c of them which have reaped are entered 995

CRIEST (5) [CRY]
Ex 14:15 unto Moses, Wherefore c thou unto me? 6817
1Sa 26:14 and said, Who art thou that c to the king? 7121
Pr 2: 3 if thou c after knowledge, and liftest up thy 7121
Isa 57:13 When thou c, let thy companies deliver 2199
Jer 30:15 Why c thou for thine affliction? thy sorrow 2199

CRIETH (17) [CRY]
Ge 4:10 the voice of thy brother's blood c unto me 6817
Ex 22:27 to pass, when he c unto me, that I will hear; 6817
Job 24:12 the city, and the soul of the wounded c out: 7768
Ps 72:12 For he shall deliver the needy when he c; 7768
84: 2 and my flesh c out for the living God. 7442
Pr 1:20 Wisdom c without; she uttereth her voice in 7442
1:21 She c in the chief place of concourse, in 7121
8: 3 She c at the gates, at the entry of the city, 7442
9: 3 she c upon the highest places of the city, 7121
Isa 26:17 is in pain, and c out in her pangs; 2199
40: 3 The voice of him that c in the wilderness, 7121
Jer 12: 8 the forest; it c out against me: 5414+6963+871.1
Mic 6: 9 The LORD'S voice c unto the city, and 7121
Mt 15:23 saying, Send her away; for she c after us. 2896
Lk 9:39 a spirit taketh him, and he suddenly c out; 2896
Ro 9:27 Esaias also c concerning Israel, Though 2896
Jas 5: 4 which is of you kept back by fraud, c: 2896

CRIME (2) [CRIMES]
Job 31:11 For this is a heinous c; yea, it is an iniquity 2154
Ac 25:16 himself concerning the c laid against him. 1462

CRIMES (2) [CRIME]
Eze 7:23 for the land is full of bloody c, and the city 4941
Ac 25:27 not withal to signify the c laid against him. 156

CRIMINAL; CRIMINALS See MALEFACTOR; MALEFACTORS

CRIMSON (5)
2Ch 2: 7 c, and blue, and that can skill to grave with 3758
2:14 in blue, and in fine linen, and in c; 3758
3:14 c, and fine linen, and wrought cherubims 3758
Isa 1:18 though they be red like c, they shall be as 8438
Jer 4:30 Though thou clothest thyself with c, 8144

CRIPPLE (1)
Ac 14: 8 his feet, being a c from his mother's womb, 5560

CRISPING (1)
Isa 3:22 and the wimples, and the c pins, 2754

CRISPUS (2)
Ac 18: 8 And C, the chief ruler of the synagogue, 2921
1Co 1:14 I baptized none of you, but C and Gaius; 2921

CROOKBACKT (1) [BACK, CROOKED]
Lev 21:20 Or c, or a dwarf, or that hath a blemish in 1384

CROOKED (14) [CROOKBACKT]
Dt 32: 5 they are a perverse and c generation. 6618
Job 26:13 his hand hath formed the c serpent. 1281
Ps 125: 5 As for such as turn aside unto their c ways, 6128
Pr 2:15 Whose ways are c, and they froward in 6141
Ecc 1:15 That which is c cannot be made straight: 5791
7:13 make that straight, which he hath made c? 5791
Isa 27: 1 even leviathan that c serpent; 6129
40: 4 the c shall be made straight, and the rough 6121
42:16 light before them, and c things straight. 4625
45: 2 before thee, and make the c places straight: 1921
59: 8 they have made them c paths: whosoever 6140
La 3: 9 with hewn stone, he hath made my paths c. 5753
Lk 3: 5 and the c shall be made straight, and 4646
Php 2:15 in the midst of a c and perverse nation, 4646

CROP (2) [CROPT]
Lev 1:16 he shall pluck away his c with his feathers, 4760
Eze 17:22 will set it; I will c off from the top of his 6998

CROPT (1) [CROP]
Eze 17: 4 He c off the top of his young twigs, and 6998

CROSS (28) [CROSSWAY]
Mt 10:38 And he that taketh not his c, and 4716
16:24 and take up his c, and follow me. 4716
27:32 by name: him they compelled to bear his c. 4716
27:40 be the Son of God, come down from the c. 4716

Mt 27:42 let him now come down from the **c**, and 4716
Mk 8:34 and take up his **c**, and follow me. 4716
10:21 and come, take up the **c**, and follow me. 4716
15:21 of Alexander and Rufus, to bear his **c**. 4716
15:30 Save thyself, and come down from the **c**. 4716
15:32 the King of Israel descend now from the **c**, 4716
Lk 9:23 him deny himself, and take up his **c** daily, 4716
14:27 And whosoever doth not bear his **c**, and 4716
23:26 of the country, and on him they laid the **c**, 4716
Jn 19:17 And he bearing his **c** went forth into a place 4716
19:19 And Pilate wrote a title, and put *it* on the **c**. 4716
19:25 Now there stood by the **c** of Jesus his 4716
19:31 not remain upon the **c** on the sabbath day, 4716
1Co 1:17 lest the **c** of Christ should be made of none 4716
1:18 For the preaching of the **c** is to them that 4716
Gal 5:11 then is the offence of the **c** ceased. 4716
6:12 suffer persecution for the **c** of Christ. 4716
6:14 save in the **c** of our Lord Jesus Christ, 4716
Eph 2:16 both unto God in one body by the **c**, 4716
Php 2: 8 unto death, even the death of the **c**. 4716
3:18 *that they are* the enemies of the **c** of Christ: 4716
Col 1:20 made peace through the blood of his **c**, 4716
2:14 took it out of the way, nailing it to his **c**; 4716
Heb 12: 2 joy that was set before him endured the **c**, 4716

CROSSWAY (1) [CROSS]
Ob 1:14 Neither shouldest thou have stood in the **c**, 6563

CROUCH (1) [CROUCHETH]
1Sa 2:36 **c** to him for a piece of silver and a morsel 7812

CROUCHETH (1) [CROUCH]
Ps 10:10 He **c**, *and* humbleth himself, that the poor 1794

CROW (7) [COCKCROWING, CREW]
Mt 26:34 That this night, before *the* cock **c**, 5455
26:75 which said unto him, Before *the* cock **c**, 5455
Mk 14:30 *even* in this night, before *the* cock **c** twice, 5455
14:72 Before *the* cock **c** twice, thou shalt deny me 5455
Lk 22:34 Peter, *the* cock shall not **c** this day, 5455
22:61 Before *the* cock **c**, thou shalt deny me 5455
Jn 13:38 verily, I say unto thee, *The* cock shall not **c**, 5455

CROWING See COCKCROWING

CROWN (66) [CROWNED, CROWNEDST, CROWNEST, CROWNETH, CROWNING, CROWNS]
Ge 49:26 on the **c of the head** of him *that was* 6936
Ex 25:11 shalt make upon it a **c** *of* gold round about. 2213
25:24 and make thereto a **c** *of* gold round about. 2213
25:25 thou shalt make a golden **c** to the border 2213
29: 6 his head, and put the holy **c** upon the mitre. 5145
30: 3 thou shalt make unto it a **c** *of* gold round 2213
30: 4 rings shalt thou make to it under the **c** of it, 2213
37: 2 and made a **c** *of* gold to it round about. 2213
37:11 made thereunto a **c** *of* gold round about. 2213
37:12 made a **c** of gold for the border thereof 2213
37:26 also he made unto it a **c** *of* gold round 2213
37:27 he made two rings of gold for it under the **c** 2213
39:30 they made the plate of the holy **c** *of* pure 5145
Lev 8: 9 did he put the golden plate, the holy **c**; 5145
21:12 for the **c** of the anointing oil of his God *is* 5145
Dt 33:20 and teareth the arm with the **c of the head**. 6936
2Sa 1:10 and I took the **c** that *was* upon his head, and 5145
12:30 he took their king's **c** from off his head, 5850
14:25 **c** of his **head** there was no blemish in him. 6936
2Ki 11:12 put the **c** upon him, and *gave him* 5145
1Ch 20: 2 David took the **c** of their king from off his 5850
2Ch 23:11 put upon him the **c**, and *gave him* 5145
Est 1:11 the queen before the king with the **c** royal, 3804
2:17 so that he set the royal **c** upon her head, and 3804
6: 8 the **c** royal which is set upon his head: 3804
8:15 *with* a great **c** of gold, and *with* a garment 5850
Job 2: 7 boils from the sole of his foot unto his **c**. 6936
19: 9 of my glory, and taken the **c** *from* my head. 5850
31:36 upon my shoulder, *and* bind it *as* a **c** to me. 5850
Ps 21: 3 thou settest a **c** of pure gold on his head. 5850
89:39 thou hast profaned his **c** *by casting it* to 5145
132:18 but upon himself shall his **c** flourish. 5145
Pr 4: 9 a **c** of glory shall she deliver *to* thee. 5850
12: 4 A virtuous woman *is* a **c** to her husband: 5850
14:24 The **c** of the wise *is* their riches: *but* 5850
16:31 The hoary head *is* a **c** of glory, *if* it be 5850
17: 6 Children's children *are* the **c** of old men; 5850
27:24 and doth the **c** *endure* to every generation? 5145
SS 3:11 behold king Solomon with the **c** where*with* 5850
Isa 3:17 the **c of the head** of the daughters of Zion, 6936
28: 1 Woe to the **c** of pride, to the drunkards of 5850
28: 3 The **c** of pride, the drunkards of Ephraim, 5850
28: 5 the LORD of hosts be for a **c** of glory, 5850
62: 3 Thou shalt also be a **c** of glory in the hand 5850
Jer 2:16 Tahapanes have broken the **c of** thy **head**. 6936
13:18 shall come down, *even* the **c** of your glory. 5850
48:45 the **c of the head** of the tumultuous ones. 6936
La 5:16 The **c** is fallen *from* our head: woe unto us, 5850
Eze 16:12 and a beautiful **c** upon thine head. 5850
21:26 Remove the diadem, and take off the **c**: 5850
Zec 9:16 for *they shall be as* the stones of a **c**, 5145
Mt 27:29 And when they had platted a **c** of thorns, 4735
Mk 15:17 and platted a **c** of thorns, and put *it* about 4735
Jn 19: 2 And the soldiers platted a **c** of thorns, and 4735
19: 5 wearing the **c** of thorns, and the purple 4735
1Co 9:25 Now they *do it* to obtain a corruptible **c**; 4735
Php 4: 1 my joy and **c**, so stand fast in the Lord, 4735
1Th 2:19 what *is* our hope, or joy, or **c** of rejoicing? 4735
2Ti 4: 8 Henceforth there is laid up for me a **c** of 4735
Jas 1:12 he is tried, he shall receive the **c** of life, 4735
1Pe 5: 4 ye shall receive a **c** of glory that fadeth not 4735
Rev 2:10 unto death, and I will give thee a **c** of life. 4735
3:11 which thou hast, that no *man* take thy **c**. 4735
6: 2 had a bow; and a **c** was given unto him: 4735
12: 1 and upon her head a **c** of twelve stars: 4735
14:14 having on his head a golden **c**, and in his 4735

CROWNED (6) [CROWN]
Ps 8: 5 and hast **c** him *with* glory and honour. 5849
Pr 14:18 but the prudent are **c** *with* knowledge. 3803
SS 3:11 mother **c** him in the day of his espousals, 5849
Na 3:17 Thy **c** *are* as the locusts, and thy captains as 4502
2Ti 2: 5 *yet* is he not **c**, except he strive lawfully. 4737
Heb 2: 9 suffering of death, **c** with glory and honour; 4737

CROWNEDST (1) [CROWN]
Heb 2: 7 thou **c** him with glory and honour, and 4737

CROWNEST (1) [CROWN]
Ps 65:11 Thou **c** the year with thy goodness; and 5849

CROWNETH (1) [CROWN]
Ps 103: 4 who **c** thee *with* lovingkindness and 5849

CROWNING (1) [CROWN]
Isa 23: 8 the **c** *city,* whose merchants *are* princes, 5849

CROWNS (9) [CROWN]
Eze 23:42 and beautiful **c** upon their heads. 5850
Zec 6:11 make **c**, and set *them* upon the head of 5850
6:14 the **c** shall be to Helem, and to Tobijah, 5850
Rev 4: 4 and they had on their heads **c** of gold. 4735
4:10 and ever, and cast their **c** before the throne, 4735
9: 7 on their heads *were* as *it were* **c** like gold, 4735
12: 3 and ten horns, and seven **c** upon his heads. 1238
13: 1 and upon his horns ten **c**, and upon his 1238
19:12 flame of fire, and on his head *were* many **c**; 1238

CRUCIBLE See FINING POT

CRUCIFIED (37) [CRUCIFY]
Mt 26: 2 and the Son of man is betrayed to be **c**. 4717
27:22 *They* all say unto him, Let him be **c**. 4717
27:23 cried out the more, saying, Let him be **c**. 4717
27:26 scourged Jesus, he delivered *him* to be **c**. 4717
27:35 And they **c** him, and parted his garments, 4717
27:38 Then were there two thieves **c** with him, 4717
27:44 The thieves also, which were **c with** 4957
28: 5 for I know that ye seek Jesus, which was **c**. 4717
Mk 15:15 when he had scourged *him*, to be **c**. 4717
15:24 And when they had **c** him, they parted his 4717
15:25 And it was the third hour, and they **c** him. 4717
15:32 that were **c with** him reviled him. 4957
16: 6 Ye seek Jesus of Nazareth, which was **c**: 4717
Lk 23:23 loud voices, requiring that he might be **c**. 4717
23:33 there they **c** him, and the malefactors, 4717
24: 7 and be **c**, and the third day rise again. 4717
24:20 to be condemned to death, and have **c** him. 4717
Jn 19:16 he him therefore unto them to be **c**. 4717
19:18 Where they **c** him, and two other with him, 4717
19:20 for the place where Jesus was **c** was nigh to 4717
19:23 Then the soldiers, when they had **c** Jesus, 4717
19:32 and of the other which was **c with** him. 4957
19:41 Now in the place where he was **c** there was 4717
Ac 2:23 and by wicked hands have **c** and slain: 4362
2:36 whom ye have **c**, both Lord and Christ. 4717
4:10 whom ye **c**, whom God raised from 4717
Ro 6: 6 that our old man is **c with** *him*, that 4957
1Co 1:13 was Paul **c** for you? or were ye baptized in 4717
1:23 But we preach Christ **c**, unto the Jews a 4717
2: 2 among you, save Jesus Christ, and him **c**. 4717
2: 8 *it*, they would not have **c** the Lord of glory. 4717
2Co 13: 4 For though he was **c** through weakness, 4717
Gal 2:20 I am **c with** Christ: nevertheless I live; 4957
3: 1 hath been evidently set forth, **c** among you? 4717
5:24 And they that are Christ's have **c** the flesh 4717
6:14 by whom the world is **c** unto me, and I unto 4717
Rev 11: 8 and Egypt, where also our Lord was **c**. 4717

CRUCIFY (16) [CRUCIFIED]
Mt 20:19 and to **c** *him:* and the third day he shall rise 4717
23:34 and *some* of them ye shall kill and **c**; and 4717
27:31 on him, and led him away to **c** *him.* 4717
Mk 15:13 And they cried out again, **C** him. 4717
15:14 cried out the more exceedingly, **C** him. 4717
15:20 clothes on him, and led him out to **c** him. 4717
15:27 And with him they **c** two thieves; the one 4717
Lk 23:21 But they cried, saying, **C** *him*, crucify him. 4717
23:21 But they cried, saying, Crucify *him*, **c** him. 4717
Jn 19: 6 **C** *him*, crucify *him*. Pilate saith unto them, 4717
19: 6 Crucify *him*, **c** *him*. Pilate saith unto them, 4717
19: 6 and **c** *him:* for I find no fault in him. 4717
19:10 knowest thou not that I have power to **c** 4717
19:15 Away with *him*, away with *him*, **c** him. 4717
19:15 Pilate saith unto them, Shall I **c** your King? 4717
Heb 6: 6 they **c** to themselves the Son of God **afresh**, 388

CRUDDLED (1)
Job 10:10 me out as milk, and **c** me like cheese? 7087

CRUEL (19) [CRUELLY, CRUELTY]
Ge 49: 7 *it was* fierce; and their wrath, for it was **c**: 7185
Ex 6: 9 for anguish of spirit, and for **c** bondage. 7186
Dt 32:33 poison of dragons, and the **c** venom of asps. 393
Job 30:21 Thou art become **c** to me: with thy strong 393
Ps 25:19 and they hate me *with* **c hatred**. 2555+8135
71: 4 of the hand of the unrighteous and **c** *man*. 2556
Pr 5: 9 honour unto others, and thy years unto the **c**: 394
11:17 but *he that is* **c** troubleth his own flesh. 394
12:10 but the tender mercies of the wicked *are* **c**. 394
17:11 a **c** messenger shall be sent against him. 394
27: 4 Wrath *is* **c**, and anger *is* outrageous; but 395
SS 8: 6 strong as death; jealousy *is* **c** as the grave: 7186
Isa 13: 9 **c** both *with* wrath and fierce anger, to lay 394
19: 4 will I give over into the hand of a **c** lord; 7186
Jer 6:23 and spear; they *are* **c**, and have no mercy; 394
30:14 *with* the chastisement of a **c one**, for 394
50:42 they *are* **c**, and will not shew mercy: 394
La 4: 3 the daughter of my people *is become* **c**, 393
Heb 11:36 And others had trial of **c** mockings and NIG

CRUELLY (1) [CRUEL]
Eze 18:18 his father, because he **c oppressed**, 6231+6233

CRUELTY (5) [CRUEL]
Ge 49: 5 instruments of **c** *are in* their habitations. 2555
Jdg 9:24 That the **c** *done* to the threescore and 2555
Ps 27:12 up against me, and such as breathe out **c**. 2555
74:20 of the earth are full *of* the habitations of **c**. 2555
Eze 34: 4 with force and with **c** have ye ruled them. 6531

CRUMBLES See NOUGHT

CRUMBS (3)
Mt 15:27 yet the dogs eat of the **c** which fall from 5589
Mk 7:28 dogs under the table eat of the children's **c**. 5589
Lk 16:21 And desiring to be fed with the **c** which fell 5589

CRUSE (9)
1Sa 26:11 and the **c** of water, and let us go. 6835
26:12 and the **c** of water from Saul's bolster; 6835
26:16 and the **c** of water that *was at* his bolster. 6835
1Ki 14: 3 cracknels, and a **c** of honey, and go to him: 1228
17:12 of meal in a barrel, and a little oil in a **c**: 6835
17:14 not waste, neither shall the **c** of oil fail, 6835
17:16 wasted not, neither did the **c** of oil fail, 6835
19: 6 on the coals, and a **c** of water *at* his head. 6835
2Ki 2:20 Bring me a new **c**, and put salt therein. 6746

CRUSH (4) [CRUSHED, CRUSHT]
Job 39:15 forgetteth that the foot may **c** them, or 2115
La 1:15 he hath called an assembly against me to **c** 7665
3:34 To **c** under his feet all the prisoners of 1792
Am 4: 1 which oppress the poor, which **c** the needy, 7533

CRUSHED (6) [CRUSH]
Lev 22:24 which is bruised, or **c**, or broken, or cut; 3807
Dt 28:33 thou shalt be only oppressed and **c** alway: 7533
Job 4:19 *is* in the dust, which are **c** before the moth? 1792
5: 4 far from safety, and they are **c** in the gate, 1792
Isa 59: 5 that which is **c** breaketh out *into* a viper. 2116
Jer 51:34 he hath **c** me, he hath made me an empty 2000

CRUSHT (1) [CRUSH]
Nu 22:25 and **c** Balaam's foot against the wall: 3905

CRY (181) [CRIED, CRIES, CRIEST, CRIETH, CRYING]
Ge 18:20 Because the **c** of Sodom and Gomorrah is 2201
18:21 done altogether according to the **c** of it, 6818
19:13 the **c** of them is waxen great before the face 6818
27:34 he cried with a great and exceeding bitter **c**, 6818
Ex 2:23 their **c** came up unto God by reason of 7775
3: 7 have heard their **c** by reason of their 6818
3: 9 the **c** of the children of Israel is come unto 6818
5: 8 therefore they **c**, saying, Let us go *and* 6817
11: 6 there shall be a great **c** throughout all 6818
12:30 and there was a great **c** in Egypt; 6818
22:23 they **c at all** unto me, I will surely 6817+6817
22:23 cry at all unto me, I will surely hear their **c**; 6818
32:18 neither *is it* the voice of *them that* **c** for 6030
Lev 13:45 *his* upper lip, and shall **c**, Unclean, unclean. 7121
Nu 16:34 round about them fled at the **c** of them: 6963
Dt 15: 9 he **c** unto the LORD against thee, and it be 7121
24:15 lest he **c** against thee unto the LORD, and 7121
Jdg 10:14 and **c** unto the gods which ye have chosen; 2199
1Sa 5:12 and the **c** of the city went up *to* heaven. 7775
7: 8 Cease not to **c** unto the LORD our God for 2199
8:18 ye shall **c out** in that day because of your 2199
9:16 because their **c** is come unto me. 6818
2Sa 19:28 have I yet to **c** any more unto the king? 2199
22: 7 his temple, and my **c** *did enter* into his ears. 7775
1Ki 8:28 to hearken unto the **c** and to the prayer, 7440
18:27 that Elijah mocked them, and said, **C** aloud: 7121
2Ki 8: 3 she went forth to **c** unto the king for her 6817
2Ch 6:19 to hearken unto the **c** and the prayer which 7440
13:12 sounding trumpets to **c alarm** against you. 7321
20: 9 **c** unto thee in our affliction, then thou wilt 2199
Ne 5: 1 there was a great **c** of the people and 6818
5: 6 I was very angry when I heard their **c** and 2201
9: 9 and heardest their **c** by the Red sea; 2201
Est 4: 1 and cried *with* a loud and a bitter **c**; 2201
9:31 the matters of the fastings and their **c**. 2201
Job 16:18 thou my blood, and let my **c** have no place. 2201
19: 7 I **c out** *of* wrong, but I am not heard: 6817
19: 7 I **c aloud**, but *there is* no judgment. 7768
27: 9 Will God hear his **c** when trouble cometh 6818
30:20 I **c** unto thee, and thou dost not hear me: 7768
30:24 the grave, though *they* **c** in his destruction. 7769
31:38 If my land **c** against me, or that the furrows 2199
34:28 So that *they* cause the **c** of the poor to come 6818
34:28 and he heareth the **c** of the afflicted. 6818
35: 9 oppressions they **make** *the oppressed* **to c**: 2199
35: 9 they **c out** by reason of the arm of 7768
35:12 There they **c**, but none giveth answer, 6817
36:13 up wrath: they **c** not when he bindeth them. 7768
38:41 when his young ones **c** unto God, 7768
Ps 5: 2 Hearken unto the voice of my **c**, my King, 7773
9:12 he forgetteth not the **c** of the humble. 6818
17: 1 the right, O LORD, attend unto my **c**, 7440
18: 6 my **c** came before him, *even* into his ears. 7775
22: 2 I **c** in the daytime, but thou hearest not; 7121
27: 7 Hear, O LORD, *when* I **c** *with* my voice: 7121
28: 1 Unto thee will I **c**, O LORD, my rock; 7121
28: 2 of my supplications, when I **c** unto thee, 7768
34:15 and his ears *are open* unto their **c**. 7775
34:17 *The righteous* **c**, and the LORD heareth, 6817
39:12 O LORD, and give ear unto my **c**; 7775
40: 1 and he inclined unto me, and heard my **c**. 7775
55:17 and at noon, will I pray, and **c aloud**: 1993
56: 9 When I **c** *unto thee*, then shall mine 7121
57: 2 I will **c** unto God most High; unto God that 7121
61: 1 Hear my **c**, O God; attend unto my prayer. 7440
61: 2 From the end of the earth will I **c** unto thee, 7121

Ps 86: 3 unto me, O Lord: for I **c** unto thee daily. 7121
88: 2 before thee; incline thine ear unto my **c**; 7440
89:26 He shall **c unto** me, Thou *art* my Father, 7121
102: 1 O LORD, and let my **c** come unto thee. 7775
106:44 their affliction, when he heard their **c**: 7440
107:19 they **c** unto the LORD in their trouble, 2199
107:28 they **c** unto the LORD in their trouble, 6817
119:169 Let my **c** come near before thee, 7440
141: 1 LORD, I **c unto** thee: make haste unto 7121
141: 1 give ear unto my voice, when I **c** unto thee. 7121
142: 6 Attend unto my **c**; for I am brought very 7440
145:19 he also will hear their **c**, and will save 7775
147: 9 his food, *and* to the young ravens which **c**. 7121
Pr 8: 1 Doth not wisdom **c**? and understanding put 7121
21:13 Whoso stoppeth his ears at the **c** of 2201
21:13 he also shall **c** himself, but shall not be 7121
Ecc 9:17 more than the **c** of him that ruleth among 2201
Isa 5: 7 for righteousness, but behold a **c**. 6818
8: 4 before the child shall have knowledge to **c**, 7121
12: 6 **C out** and shout, thou inhabitant of Zion: 6670
13:22 the wild beasts of the islands shall **c** in their 6030
14:31 **c**, O city; thou, whole Palestina, 2199
15: 4 Heshbon shall **c**, and Elealeh: their voice 2199
15: 4 the armed soldiers of Moab shall **c out**; 7321
15: 5 My heart shall **c out** for Moab; his fugitives 2199
15: 5 they shall raise up a **c** of destruction. 2201
15: 8 For the **c** is gone round about the borders of 2201
19:20 for they shall **c** unto the LORD because of 6817
24:14 they shall **c aloud** from the sea. 6670
29: 9 and wonder; **c** ye **out**, and cry: 8173
29: 9 and wonder; cry ye out, and **c**: 8173
30:19 gracious unto thee at the voice of thy **c**; 2199
33: 7 Behold, their valiant ones shall **c** without: 6817
34:14 and the satyr shall **c** to his fellow; 7121
40: 2 **c** unto her, that her warfare is 7121
40: 6 The voice said, **C**. And he said, What shall 7121
40: 6 he said, What shall I **c**? All flesh *is* grass, 7121
42: 2 He shall not **c**, nor lift up, nor cause his 6817
42:13 he shall **c**, yea, roar; he shall prevail against 7321
42:14 *now* will I **c** like a travailing woman; I will 6463
43:14 and the Chaldeans, whose **c** *is* in the ships. 7440
46: 7 yea, *one* shall **c** unto him, yet can he not 6817
54: 1 break forth *into* singing, and **c aloud**, 6670
58: 1 **C** aloud, spare not, lift up thy voice like a 7121
58: 9 thou shalt **c**, and he shall say, Here I *am*. If 7768
65:14 ye shall **c** for sorrow of heart, and 6817
Jer 2: 2 Go and **c** in the ears of Jerusalem, saying, 7121
3: 4 Wilt thou not from this time **c** unto me, 7121
4: 5 **c**, gather together, and say, 7121
7:16 neither lift up **c** nor prayer for them, 7440
8:19 Behold the voice of the **c** of the daughter of 7775
11:11 though they shall **c** unto me, I will not 2199
11:12 **c** unto the gods unto whom they offer 2199
11:14 neither lift up a **c** or prayer for them: 7440
11:14 time that they **c** unto me for their trouble. 7121
14: 2 and the **c** of Jerusalem is gone up. 6682
14:12 When they fast, I will not hear their **c**; and 7440
18:22 Let a **c** be heard from their houses, 2201
20:16 let him hear the **c** in the morning, and 2201
22:20 Go up *to* Lebanon, and **c**; and lift up thy 6817
22:20 voice in Bashan, and **c** from the passages: 6817
25:34 Howl, ye shepherds, and **c**; and 2199
25:36 A voice of the **c** of the shepherds, and 6818
31: 6 watchmen upon the mount Ephraim shall **c**, 7121
46:12 *of* thy shame, and thy **c** hath filled the land: 6682
46:17 They did **c** there, Pharaoh king of Egypt *is* 7121
47: 2 the men shall **c**, and all the inhabitants of 2199
48: 4 her little ones have caused a **c** to be heard. 2201
48: 5 the enemies have heard a **c** of destruction. 6818
48:20 howl and **c**; tell ye *it* in Arnon, that Moab is 2199
48:31 for Moab, and I will **c out** for all Moab; 2199
48:34 From the **c** of Heshbon *even* unto Elealeh, 2201
49: 3 **c**, ye daughters of Rabbah, gird ye with 6817
49:21 *at* the **c**, the noise thereof was heard in 6818
49:29 they shall **c** unto them, Fear *is* on every 7121
50:46 and the **c** is heard among the nations. 2201
51:54 A sound of a **c** *cometh* from Babylon, and 2201
La 2:19 Arise, **c out** in the night: in the beginning 7442
3: 8 Also when I **c** and shout, he shutteth out 2199
3:56 hide not thine ear at my breathing, at my **c**. 7775
Eze 8:18 though they **c** in mine ears *with* a loud 7121
9: 4 that **c** for all the abominations that be done 602
21:12 **C** and howl, son of man: for it shall be 2199
24:17 Forbear to **c**, make no mourning *for* 602
26:15 at the sound of thy fall, when the wounded **c**, 602
27:28 shake at the sound of the **c** of thy pilots. 2201
27:30 shall **c** bitterly, and shall cast up dust upon 2199
Hos 5: 8 **c aloud** *at* Beth-aven, after thee, 7321
8: 2 Israel shall **c** unto me, My God, we know 2199
Joel 1:14 LORD your God, and **c** unto the LORD, 2199
1:19 O LORD, to thee will I **c**: for the fire hath 7121
1:20 The beasts of the field **c** also unto thee: 6165
Am 3: 4 will a young lion **c** out of his den, 5414+6963
Jnh 1: 2 to Nineveh, *that* great city, and **c** against it; 7121
3: 8 with sackcloth, and **c** mightily unto God: 7121
Mic 3: 4 shall they **c** unto the LORD, but he will 2199
3: 5 that bite with their teeth, and **c**, Peace; 7121
4: 9 Now why dost thou **c out aloud**? *is* 7321+7452
Na 2: 8 stand, *shall they* **c**; but none shall look back. NIH
Hab 1: 2 how long shall I **c**, and thou wilt not hear? 7768
1: 2 *even* **c out** unto thee *of* violence, and 2199
2:11 For the stone shall **c out** of the wall, and 2199
Zep 1:10 *that there shall be* the noise of a **c** from 6818
1:14 the mighty *man* shall **c** there bitterly. 6873
Zec 1:14 **C** thou, saying, Thus saith the LORD of 7121
1:17 **C** yet, saying, Thus saith the LORD of 7121
Mt 12:19 He shall not strive, nor **c**; neither shall any *2905*
25: 6 And at midnight there was a **c** made, *2906*
Mk 10:47 he began to **c out**, and say, Jesus, *thou* Son *2896*
Lk 18: 7 which **c** day and night unto him, though he *994*
19:40 the stones would immediately **c out**. *2896*
Ac 23: 9 And there arose a great **c**: and the scribes *2906*
Ro 8:15 of adoption, whereby we **c**, Abba, Father. *2896*
Gal 4:27 break forth and **c**, thou that travailest not: *994*
Rev 14:18 cried with a loud **c** to him that had *2906*

CRYING (31) [CRY]

1Sa 4:14 when Eli heard the noise of the **c**, he said, 6818
2Sa 13:19 laid her hand on her head, and went on **c**. 2199
Job 39: 7 neither regardeth he the **c** of the driver. 8663
Ps 69: 3 I am weary of my **c**: my throat is dried: 7121
Pr 19:18 is hope, and let not thy soul spare for his **c**. 4191
30:15 hath two daughters, **c**, Give, give. NIH
Isa 22: 5 down the walls, and of **c** to the mountains. 7771
24:11 *There is* a **c** for wine in the streets; all joy is 6682
65:19 be no more heard in her, nor the voice of **c**. 2201
Jer 48: 3 A voice of **c** *shall be* from Horonaim, 6818
Zec 4: 7 *with* shoutings, **c**, Grace, grace unto it. NIH
Mal 2:13 *with* tears, *with* weeping, and *with* **c out**, 603
Mt 3: 3 saying, The voice of one **c** in the wilderness, *994*
9:27 **c**, and saying, *Thou* Son of David, *2896*
21:15 and the children **c** in the temple, and *2896*
Mk 1: 3 The voice of one **c** in the wilderness, *994*
5: 5 **c**, and cutting himself with stones. *2896*
15: 8 And the multitude **c aloud** began to desire *310*
Lk 3: 4 saying, The voice of one **c** in the wilderness, *994*
4:41 And devils also came out of many, **c out**, *2896*
Jn 1:23 I *am* the voice of one **c** in the wilderness, *994*
Ac 8: 7 For unclean spirits, **c** with loud voice, *994*
14:14 and ran in among the people, **c out**, *2896*
17: 6 certain brethren unto the rulers of the city, **c**, *994*
21:28 **C out**, Men of Israel, help: This is the man, *2896*
21:36 multitude of the people followed *after*, **c**, *2896*
25:24 **c** that he ought not to live any longer. *1916*
Gal 4: 6 of his Son into your hearts, **c**, Abba, Father. *2896*
Heb 5: 7 and supplications with strong **c** and *2906*
Rev 14:15 **c** with a loud voice to him that sat on *2896*
21: 4 be no more death, neither sorrow, nor **c**, *2906*

CRYSTAL (5)

Job 28:17 The gold and the **c** cannot equal it: and 2137
Eze 1:22 creature *was* as the colour of the terrible **c**, 7140
Rev 4: 6 throne *there was* a sea of glass like unto **c**: *2930*
21:11 *even* like a jasper stone, **clear as c**; *2929*
22: 1 clear as **c**, proceeding out of the throne of *2930*

CUB; CUBS See WHELP; WHELPS

CUBIT (45) [CUBITS]

Ge 6:16 the ark, and in a **c** shalt thou finish it above; 520
Ex 25:10 a **c** and a half the breadth thereof, and a cubit 520
25:10 and a **c** and a half the height thereof. 520
25:17 and a **c** and a half the breadth thereof. 520
25:23 a **c** the breadth thereof, and a cubit and a half 520
25:23 and a **c** and a half the height thereof. 520
26:13 a **c** on the one side, and a cubit on the other 520
26:13 a **c** on the other side of that which remaineth 520
26:16 a **c** and a half *shall be* the breadth of one 520
30: 2 A **c** *shall be* the length thereof, and a cubit 520
30: 2 length thereof, and a **c** the breadth thereof; 520
36:21 and the breadth of a board one **c** and a half. 520
37: 1 a **c** and a half the breadth of it, and a cubit 520
37: 1 of it, and a **c** and a half the height of it: 520
37: 6 and one **c** and a half the breadth thereof. 520
37:10 a **c** the breadth thereof, and a cubit and a half 520
37:10 and a **c** and a half the height thereof: 520
37:25 the length of it *was* a **c**, and the breadth of it 520
37:25 of it *was* a cubit, and the breadth of it a **c**; 520
Dt 3:11 cubits the breadth of it, after the **c** of a man. 520
Jdg 3:16 dagger which had two edges, of a **c** length; 1574
1Ki 7:24 ten in a **c**, compassing the sea round about: 520
7:31 of it within the chapiter and above *was* a **c**: 520
7:31 *after* the work of the base, a **c** and a half: 520
7:32 the height of a wheel *was* a **c** and half a 520
7:32 height of a wheel *was* a cubit and half a **c**. 520
7:35 *was there* a round compass of half a **c** high: 520
2Ch 4: 3 ten in a **c**, compassing the sea round about. 520
Eze 40: 5 a measuring reed of six cubits *long* by the **c** 520
40:12 the little chambers *was* one **c** *on this side*, 520
40:12 and the space *was* one **c** on that side: 520
40:42 of a **c** and a half long, and a cubit and a half 520
40:42 and a **c** and a half broad, and one cubit high: 520
40:42 and a cubit and a half broad, and one **c** high: 520
42: 4 of ten cubits breadth inward, a way of one **c**; 520
43:13 The **c** *is* a cubit and a hand breadth; even 520
43:13 The cubit *is* a **c** and a hand breadth; even 520
43:13 even the bottom *shall be* a **c**, and the breadth 520
43:13 the breadth a **c**, and the border thereof by 520
43:14 *shall be* two cubits, and the breadth one **c**. 520
43:14 *shall be* four cubits, and the breadth *one* **c**. 520
43:17 and the border about it *shall be* half a **c**; and 520
43:17 the bottom thereof *shall be* a **c** about; and 520
Mt 6:27 thought can add one **c** unto his stature? *4083*
Lk 12:25 taking thought can add to his stature one **c**? *4083*

CUBITS (213) [CUBIT]

Ge 6:15 length of the ark *shall be* three hundred **c**, 520
6:15 the breadth of it fifty **c**, and the height of it 520
6:15 of it fifty cubits, and the height of it thirty **c**. 520
7:20 Fifteen **c** upward did the waters prevail; and 520
Ex 25:10 **two c** and a half *shall be* the length thereof, 520
25:17 **two c** and a half *shall be* the length thereof, 520
25:23 **two c** *shall be* the length thereof, and a cubit 520
26: 2 of one curtain *shall be* eight and twenty **c**, 520
26: 2 and the breadth of one curtain four **c**: 520
26: 8 The length of one curtain *shall be* thirty **c**, 520
26: 8 and the breadth of one curtain four **c**: 520
26:16 Ten **c** *shall be* the length of a board, and 520
27: 1 five **c** long, and five cubits broad; 520
27: 1 five cubits long, and five **c** broad; 520
27: 1 and the height thereof *shall be* three **c**. 520
27: 9 linen of an hundred **c** long for one side: 520
27:11 *shall be* hangings of an hundred **c** long, NIH
27:12 on the west side *shall be* hangings of fifty **c**: 520
27:13 on the east side eastward *shall be* fifty **c**. 520
27:14 of *one* side *of the gate shall be* fifteen **c**: 520
27:15 fifteen **c**: their pillars three, and NIH
27:16 of the court *shall be* a hanging of twenty **c**, 520
27:18 length of the court *shall be* an hundred **c**, 520
27:18 the height five **c** *of* fine twined linen, and 520
Ex 30: 2 **two c** *shall be* the height thereof: the horns 520
36: 9 length of one curtain *was* twenty and eight **c**, 520
36: 9 and the breadth of one curtain four **c**: 520
36:15 The length of one curtain *was* thirty **c**, and 520
36:15 and four **c** *was* the breadth of one curtain: 520
36:21 The length of a board *was* ten **c**, and 520
37: 1 **two c** and a half *was* the length of it, and 520
37: 6 **two c** and a half *was* the length thereof, and 520
37:10 **two c** *was* the length thereof, and a cubit 520
37:25 and **two c** *was* the height of it; 520
38: 1 five **c** *was* the length thereof, and five cubits 520
38: 1 and five **c** the breadth thereof; 520
38: 1 and three **c** the height thereof. 520
38: 9 *were of* fine twined linen, an hundred **c**: 520
38:11 north side *the hangings were* an hundred **c**, 520
38:12 for the west side *were* hangings of fifty **c**, 520
38:13 And for the east side eastward *were* fifty **c**. 520
38:14 of the *one* side *of the gate were* fifteen **c**; 520
38:15 and that hand, *were* hangings of fifteen **c**; 520
38:18 twenty **c** *was* the length, and the height in 520
38:18 and the height in the breadth *was* five **c**, 520
Nu 11:31 as it were **two c** *high* upon the face of 520
35: 4 and outward a thousand **c** round about. 520
35: 5 the city *on* the east side two thousand **c**, 520
35: 5 *on* the south side two thousand **c**, and *on* 520
35: 5 *on* the west side two thousand **c**, and *on* 520
35: 5 and *on* the north side two thousand **c**; 520
Dt 3:11 nine **c** *was* the length thereof, and four cubits 520
3:11 four **c** the breadth of it, after the cubit of a 520
Jos 3: 4 and it, about two thousand **c** by measure: 520
1Sa 17: 4 of Gath, whose height *was* six **c** and a span. 520
1Ki 6: 2 the length thereof *was* threescore **c**, and 520
6: 2 the breadth thereof twenty **c**, and the height NIH
6: 2 twenty *cubits*, and the height thereof thirty **c**. 520
6: 3 twenty **c** *was* the length thereof, according to 520
6: 3 ten **c** *was* the breadth thereof before 520
6: 6 The nethermost chamber *was* five **c** broad, 520
6: 6 the middle *was* six **c** broad, and the third *was* 520
6: 6 and the third *was* seven **c** broad: 520
6:10 chambers against all the house, five **c** high: 520
6:16 he built twenty **c** on the sides of the house, 520
6:17 *is*, the temple before it, was forty **c** *long*. 520
6:20 the oracle in the forepart *was* twenty **c** in 520
6:20 twenty **c** in breadth, and twenty cubits in 520
6:20 and twenty **c** in the height thereof: 520
6:23 two cherubims *of* olive tree, each ten **c** high. 520
6:24 five **c** *was* the one wing of the cherub, and 520
6:24 and five **c** the other wing of the cherub: 520
6:24 the uttermost part of the other *were* ten **c**. 520
6:25 the other cherub *was* ten **c**: both 520
6:26 The height of the one cherub *was* ten **c**, and 520
7: 2 the length thereof *was* an hundred **c**, and 520
7: 2 the breadth thereof fifty **c**, and the height 520
7: 2 fifty cubits, and the height thereof thirty **c**, 520
7: 6 the length thereof *was* fifty **c**, and 520
7: 6 fifty cubits, and the breadth thereof thirty **c**: 520
7:10 stones of ten **c**, and stones of eight cubits. 520
7:10 stones of ten cubits, and stones of eight **c**. 520
7:15 pillars *of* brass, of eighteen **c** high apiece: 520
7:15 a line of twelve **c** did compass either of them 520
7:16 the height of the one chapiter *was* five **c**, and 520
7:16 the height of the other chapiter *was* five **c**: 520
7:19 *were of* lily work in the porch, four **c**). 520
7:23 ten **c** from the one brim to the other: 520
7:23 round all about, and his height *was* five **c**: 520
7:23 a line of thirty **c** did compass it round about. 520
7:27 four **c** *was* the length of one base, and 520
7:27 four **c** the breadth thereof, and three cubits 520
7:27 breadth thereof, and three **c** the height of it. 520
7:38 *and* every laver was four **c**: *and* upon every 520
2Ki 14:13 unto the corner gate, four hundred **c**. 520
25:17 The height of the one pillar *was* eighteen **c**, 520
25:17 the height of the chapiter three **c**; and 520
1Ch 11:23 five **c** *high*; and in the Egyptian's hand *was* a 520
2Ch 3: 3 The length *by* **c** after the first measure *was* 520
3: 3 after the first measure *was* threescore **c**, 520
3: 3 threescore cubits, and the breadth twenty **c**. 520
3: 4 twenty **c**, and the height *was* an hundred and 520
3: 8 twenty **c**, and the breadth thereof twenty 520
3: 8 and the breadth thereof twenty **c**: 520
3:11 the wings of the cherubims *were* twenty **c** 520
3:11 *one* wing of the one *cherub was* five **c**, 520
3:11 the other wing *was likewise* five **c**, 520
3:12 And *one* wing of the other cherub *was* five **c**, 520
3:12 the other wing *was* five **c** *also*, joining to 520
3:13 cherubims spread themselves forth twenty **c**: 520
3:15 house two pillars of thirty and five **c** high, 520
3:15 *was* on the top *of each* of them *was* five **c**. 520
4: 1 twenty **c** the length thereof, and 520
4: 1 twenty **c** the breadth thereof, and ten cubits 520
4: 1 breadth thereof, and ten **c** the height thereof. 520
4: 2 Also he made a molten sea of ten **c** from 520
4: 2 in compass, and five **c** the height thereof; 520
4: 2 a line of thirty **c** did compass it round about. 520
6:13 of five **c** long, and five cubits broad, 520
6:13 five **c** broad, and three cubits high, and 520
6:13 three **c** high, and had set it in the midst of 520
25:23 Ephraim to the corner gate, four hundred **c**. 520
Ezr 6: 3 the height thereof threescore **c**, *and* 521
6: 3 *and* the breadth thereof threescore **c**; 521
Ne 3:13 a thousand **c** on the wall unto the dung gate. 520
Est 5:14 Let a gallows be made of fifty **c** high, and to 520
7: 9 Behold also, the gallows fifty **c** high, 520
Jer 52:21 the height of one pillar *was* eighteen **c**; 520
52:21 a fillet of twelve **c** did compass it; and 520
52:22 the height of one chapiter *was* five **c**, 520
Eze 40: 5 in the man's hand a measuring reed of six **c** 520
40: 7 and between the little chambers *were* five **c**; 520
40: 9 measured he the porch of the gate, eight **c**; 520
40: 9 the posts thereof, two **c**; and the porch of 520
40:11 the breadth of the entry of the gate, ten **c**; 520
40:11 *and* the length of the gate, thirteen **c**. 520
40:12 the little chambers *were* six **c** on this side, 520
40:12 six cubits on this side, and six **c** on that side. 520
40:13 the breadth *was* five and twenty **c**, 520

Eze 40:14 He made also posts *of* threescore c, 520
40:15 of the porch of the inner gate *were* fifty c. 520
40:19 an hundred c east*ward* and north*ward*. 520
40:21 the length thereof *was* fifty c, and 520
40:21 and the breadth five and twenty c. 520
40:23 he measured from gate to gate an hundred c. 520
40:25 the length *was* fifty c, and the breadth five 520
40:25 and the breadth five and twenty c. 520
40:27 gate to gate toward the south an hundred c. 520
40:29 *it was* fifty c long, and five and 520
40:29 cubits long, and five and twenty c broad. 520
40:30 round about *were* five and twenty c long, 520
40:30 and twenty cubits long, and five c broad. 520
40:33 *it was* fifty c long, and five and 520
40:33 cubits long, and five and twenty c broad. 520
40:36 the length *was* fifty c, and the breadth five 520
40:36 and the breadth five and twenty c. 520
40:47 an hundred c long, and an hundred cubits 520
40:47 and an hundred c broad, foursquare; 520
40:48 five c on this side, and five cubits on that 520
40:48 cubits on this side, and five c on that side: 520
40:48 the breadth of the gate *was* three c on this 520
40:48 cubits on this side, and three c on that side. 520
40:49 The length of the porch *was* twenty c, and 520
40:49 *was* twenty cubits, and the breadth eleven c; 520
41: 1 six c broad on the one side, and six cubits 520
41: 1 one side, and six c broad on the other side, 520
41: 2 the breadth of the door *was* ten c; and 520
41: 2 the sides of the door *were* five c on the one 520
41: 2 on the one side, and five c on the other side: 520
41: 2 he measured the length thereof, forty c: and 520
41: 2 forty cubits: and the breadth, twenty c. 520
41: 3 measured the post of the door, two c; 520
41: 3 the door, six c; and the breadth of the door, 520
41: 3 and the breadth of the door, seven c. 520
41: 4 So he measured the length thereof, twenty c; 520
41: 4 and the breadth, twenty c, before the temple: 520
41: 5 he measured the wall of the house, six c; 520
41: 5 the breadth of *every* side chamber, four c, 520
41: 8 side chambers *were* a full reed of six great c. 520
41: 9 for the side chamber without, *was* five c: 520
41:10 c round about the house on every side. 520
41:11 place that was left *was* five c round about. 520
41:12 end toward the west *was* seventy c broad; 520
41:12 the wall of the building *was* five c thick 520
41:12 round about, and the length thereof ninety c. 520
41:13 he measured the house, an hundred c long; 520
41:13 with the walls thereof, an hundred c long; 520
41:14 separate place toward the east, an hundred c. 520
41:15 one side and on the other side, an hundred c, 520
41:22 The altar *of* wood *was* three c high, and 520
41:22 cubits high, and the length thereof two c; 520
42: 2 Before the length of an hundred c *was* 520
42: 2 the north door, and the breadth *was* fifty c. 520
42: 3 Over against the twenty c which *were* for NIH
42: 4 before the chambers *was* a walk of ten c 520
42: 7 the chambers, the length thereof *was* fifty c. 520
42: 8 that *were* in the utter court *was* fifty c: 520
42: 8 and lo, before the temple *were* an hundred c. 520
43:13 these *are* the measures of the altar after the c: 520
43:14 *even* to the lower settle *shall be* two c, 520
43:14 *even* to the greater settle *shall be* four c, 520
43:15 So the altar *shall be* four c; and from 520
43:16 the altar *shall be* twelve c long, twelve NIH
43:17 the settle *shall be* fourteen c long and NIH
45: 2 fifty c round about *for* the suburbs thereof. 520
46:22 *there were* courts joined *of* forty c long NIH
47: 3 forth east*ward*, he measured a thousand c, 520
Da 3: 1 whose height *was* threescore c, *and* 521
3: 1 *and* the breadth thereof six c: 521
Zec 5: 2 the length thereof *is* twenty c, and 520
5: 2 twenty cubits, and the breadth thereof ten c. 520
Jn 21: 8 from land, but as it were two hundred c,) *4083*
Rev 21:17 an hundred *and* forty *and* four c, *4083*

CUCKOW (2)
Lev 11:16 and the c, and the hawk after his kind, 7828
Dt 14:15 and the c, and the hawk after his kind, 7828

CUCUMBERS (2)
Nu 11: 5 the c, and the melons, and the leeks, and 7180
Isa 1: 8 as a lodge in a **garden of c**, as a besieged 4750

CUD (11)
Lev 11: 3 *is* clovenfooted, *and* cheweth c, among 1625
11: 4 shall ye not eat of them that chew the c, 1625
11: 4 because he cheweth the c, but divideth not 1625
11: 5 because he cheweth the c, but divideth not 1625
11: 6 because he cheweth the c, but divideth not 1625
11: 7 *be* clovenfooted, yet he cheweth not the c; 1625
11:26 *is* not clovenfooted, nor cheweth the c, 1625
Dt 14: 6 *and* cheweth the c amongst the beasts: 1625
14: 7 ye shall not eat of them that chew the c, 1625
14: 7 for they chew the c, but divide not the hoof; 1625
14: 8 it divideth the hoof, yet *cheweth* not the c, 1625

CULTIVATED See TILLED; TILLER; TILLEST; TILLETH

CUMBERED (1) [CUMBRANCE]
Lk 10:40 But Martha was c about much serving, and *4049*

CUMBERETH (1) [CUMBRANCE]
Lk 13: 7 find none: cut it down; why c it the ground? *2673*

CUMBRANCE (1) [CUMBERETH, CUMBERED]
Dt 1:12 How can I myself alone bear your c, and 2960

CUMI (1)
Mk 5:41 the hand, and said unto her, TALITHA C; *2891*

CUMMIN (4)
Isa 28:25 scatter the c, and cast in the principal wheat 3646
28:27 is a cart wheel turned about upon the c; 3646
28:27 beaten out with a staff, and the c with a rod. 3646
Mt 23:23 for ye pay tithe of mint and anise and c, and *2951*

CUN See CHUN

CUNNING (33) [CUNNINGLY]
Ge 25:27 Esau was a c hunter, a man of the field; and 3045
Ex 26: 1 *with* cherubims *of* c work shalt thou make 2803
26:31 scarlet, and fine twined linen *of* c work: 2803
28: 6 and fine twined linen, *with* c work. 2803
28:15 the breastplate of judgment *with* c work; 2803
31: 4 To devise c **works**, to work in gold, and 4284
35:33 of wood, to make any *manner of* c work. 4284
35:35 of the c **workman**, and of the embroiderer, 2803
35:35 and of **those that devise c work**. 2803+4284
36: 8 *with* cherubims *of* c work made he them. 2803
36:35 *with* cherubims made he it *of* c work. 2803
38:23 a c **workman**, and an embroiderer in blue, 2803
39: 3 and in the fine linen, *with* c work. 2803
39: 8 he made the breastplate *of* c work, like 2803
1Sa 16:16 seek out a man, *who is* a c player on a harp: 3045
16:18 *that is* c in playing, and a mighty valiant 3045
1Ki 7:14 and c to work all works in brass. 1847
1Ch 22:15 all *manner of* c *men* for every *manner of* 2450
25: 7 *even* all that were c, was two hundred 995
2Ch 2: 7 me now therefore a man c to work in gold, 2450
2: 7 that can skill to grave with the c *men* that 2450
2:13 now I have sent a c man, endued with 2450
2:14 with thy c *men*, and with the cunning *men* 2450
2:14 with the c *men* of my lord David thy father. 2450
26:15 invented by c *men*, to be on the towers and 2803
Ps 137: 5 O Jerusalem, let my right hand forget *her* c. NIH
SS 7: 1 the work of the hands of a c **workman**. 542
Isa 3: 3 and the c artificer, and the eloquent orator. 2450
40:20 he seeketh unto him a c workman to 2450
Jer 9:17 and send for c *women*, that they may come: 2450
10: 9 they *are* all the work of c *men*. 2450
Da 1: 4 c in knowledge, and understanding science, 3045
Eph 4:14 by the sleight of men, and c **craftiness**, *3834*

CUNNINGLY (1) [CUNNING]
2Pe 1:16 For we have not followed c **devised** fables, *4679*

CUP (68) [CUPBEARER, CUPBEARERS, CUPS]
Ge 40:11 Pharaoh's c *was* in my hand: and I took 3563
40:11 pressed them into Pharaoh's c, and I gave 3563
40:11 and I gave the c into Pharaoh's hand. 3563
40:13 thou shalt deliver Pharaoh's c into his hand, 3563
40:21 and he gave the c into Pharaoh's hand: 3563
44: 2 put my c, the silver cup, in the sack's 1375
44: 2 put my cup, the silver c, in the sack's 1375
44:12 and the c was found in Benjamin's sack. 1375
44:16 and *he* also with whom the c is found. 1375
44:17 *but* the man in whose hand the c is found, 1375
2Sa 12: 3 drank of his own c, and lay in his bosom, 3563
1Ki 7:26 thereof was wrought like the brim of a c, 3563
2Ch 4: 5 brim of it like the work of the brim of a c, 3563
Ps 11: 6 *this shall be* the portion of their c. 3563
16: 5 portion of mine inheritance and of my c: 3563
23: 5 my head with oil; my c runneth over. 3563
73:10 and waters of a full c are wrung out to them. NIH
75: 8 For in the hand of the LORD *there is* a c, 3563
116:13 I will take the c of salvation, and call upon 3563
Pr 23:31 when it giveth his colour in the c, *when* it 3563
Isa 51:17 at the hand of the LORD the c of his fury; 3563
51:17 thou hast drunken the dregs of the c of 3563
51:22 I have taken out of thine hand the c of 3563
51:22 *even* the dregs of the c of my fury; 3563
Jer 16: 7 neither shall *men* give them the c of 3563
25:15 Take the wine c of this fury at mine hand, 3563
25:17 took I the c at the LORD'S hand, and 3563
25:28 if they refuse to take the c at thine hand to 3563
49:12 to drink of the c have assuredly drunken; 3563
51: 7 Babylon *hath been* a golden c in 3563
La 4:21 the c also shall pass through unto thee: 3563
Eze 23:31 therefore will I give her c into thine hand. 3563
23:32 Thou shalt drink *of* thy sister's c deep and 3563
23:33 *with* the c of astonishment and desolation, 3563
23:33 desolation, *with* the c of thy sister Samaria. 3563
Hab 2:16 the c of the LORD'S right hand shall be 3563
Zec 12: 2 I *will* make Jerusalem a c of trembling unto 5592
Mt 10:42 c of cold *water* only in the name of a *4221*
20:22 Are ye able to drink *of* the c that I shall *4221*
20:23 Ye shall drink indeed *of* my c, and *4221*
23:25 for ye make clean the outside of the c and *4221*
23:26 cleanse first that *which is* within the c and *4221*
26:27 And he took the c, and gave thanks, and *4221*
26:39 if it be possible, let this c pass from me: *4221*
26:42 if this c may not pass away from me, *4221*
Mk 9:41 For whosoever shall give you a c of water *4221*
10:38 can ye drink *of* the c that I drink *of?* and be *4221*
10:39 Ye shall indeed drink *of* the c that I drink *4221*
14:23 And he took the c, and when he had given *4221*
14:36 unto thee; take away this c from me: *4221*
Lk 11:39 Pharisees make clean the outside of the c *4221*
22:17 And he took *the* c, and gave thanks, and *4221*
22:20 Likewise also the c after supper, saying, *4221*
22:20 This c *is* the new testament in my blood, *4221*
22:42 if thou be willing, remove this c from me: *4221*
Jn 18:11 the c which my Father hath given me, *4221*
1Co 10:16 The c of blessing which we bless, is it not *4221*
10:21 Ye cannot drink the c of the Lord, and *4221*
10:21 the cup of the Lord, and the c of devils: *4221*
11:25 After the same manner also *he took* the c, *4221*
11:25 This c is the new testament in my blood: *4221*
11:26 often as ye eat this bread, and drink this c, *4221*
11:27 and drink *this* c of the Lord unworthily, *4221*
11:28 him eat of *that* bread, and drink of *that* c. *4221*
Rev 14:10 mixture into the c of his indignation; *4221*
16:19 to give unto her the c of the wine of *4221*
17: 4 having a golden c in her hand full of *4221*
18: 6 in the c which she hath filled fill to her *4221*

CUPBEARER (1) [BEAR, CUP]
Ne 1:11 sight of this man. For I was the king's c. 8248

CUPBEARERS (2) [BEAR, CUP]
1Ki 10: 5 his c, and his ascent *by* which he went up 8248
2Ch 9: 4 his c also, and their apparel; and his ascent 8248

CUPS (6) [CUP]
1Ch 28:17 the fleshhooks, and the bowls, and the c: 7184
Isa 22:24 of small quantity, from the vessels of c, 101
Jer 35: 5 and c, and I said unto them, Drink ye wine. 3563
52:19 the candlesticks, and the spoons, and the c; 4518
Mk 7: 4 *as* the washing of c, and pots, *4221*
7: 8 of men, *as* the washing of pots and c: *4221*

CURE (5) [CURED, CURES]
Jer 33: 6 I *will* bring it health and c, and I will cure 4832
33: 6 I will c them, and will reveal unto them 7495
Hos 5:13 yet could he not heal you nor c you of your 1455
Mt 17:16 to thy disciples, and they could not c him. *2323*
Lk 9: 1 authority over all devils, and to c diseases. *2323*

CURED (4) [CURE]
Jer 46:11 many medicines; *for* thou shalt not be c. 8585
Mt 17:18 and the child was c from that *very* hour. *2323*
Lk 7:21 And in that same hour he c many of *their* *2323*
Jn 5:10 therefore said unto him that was c, *2323*

CURES (1) [CURE]
Lk 13:32 and I do c to day and to morrow, and *2392*

CURIOUS (10) [CURIOUSLY]
Ex 28: 8 the c **girdle** of the ephod, which *is* upon it, 2805
28:27 above the c **girdle** of the ephod. 2805
28:28 that *it* may be above the c **girdle** of 2805
29: 5 and gird him with the c **girdle** of the ephod: 2805
35:32 to devise c **works**, to work in gold, and 4284
39: 5 the c **girdle** of his ephod, that *was* upon it, 2805
39:20 above the c **girdle** of the ephod. 2805
39:21 that *it* might be above the c **girdle** of 2805
Lev 8: 7 he girded him with the c **girdle** of 2805
Ac 19:19 Many also of them which used c **arts** *4021*

CURIOUSLY (1) [CURIOUS]
Ps 139:15 c **wrought** in the lowest parts of the earth. 7551

CURRENT (1)
Ge 23:16 of silver, c *money* with the merchant. 5674

CURRY FAVOR See INTREAT; INTREATED; INTREATIES; INTREATY

CURSE (101) [ACCURSED, CURSED, CURSEDST, CURSES, CURSEST, CURSETH, CURSING, CURSINGS]
Ge 8:21 I will not again c the ground any more for 7043
12: 3 that bless thee, and c him that curseth thee: 779
27:12 I shall bring a c upon me, and not a 7045
27:13 said unto him, Upon me *be* thy c, my son: 7045
Ex 22:28 revile the gods, nor c the ruler of thy people. 779
Lev 19:14 Thou shalt not c the deaf, nor put a 7043
Nu 5:18 his hand the bitter water that **causeth** the c: 779
5:19 free from this bitter water that **causeth the** c: 779
5:21 The LORD make thee a c and an oath 423
5:22 this water that **causeth the** c shall go into 779
5:24 to drink the bitter water that **causeth the** c: 779
5:24 the water that **causeth the** c shall enter into 779
5:27 that the water that **causeth the** c shall enter 779
5:27 the woman shall be a c among her people. 423
22: 6 now therefore, I pray thee, c me this people; 779
22:11 come now, c me them; peradventure I shall 6895
22:12 go with them; thou shalt not c the people: 779
22:17 I pray thee, c me this people. 6895
23: 7 c me Jacob, and come, defy Israel. 779
23: 8 How shall I c, whom God hath not cursed? 5344
23:11 I took thee to c mine enemies, and behold, 6895
23:13 see them all: and c me them from thence. 6895
23:25 c them **at all**, nor bless them at all. 5344+5344
23:27 that thou mayest c me them from thence. 6895
24:10 I called thee to c mine enemies, and behold, 6895
Dt 11:26 I set before you *this* day a blessing and a c; 7045
11:28 a c, if ye will not obey the commandments 7045
11:29 mount Gerizim, and the c upon mount Ebal. 7045
23: 4 Beor of Pethor of Mesopotamia, to c thee. 7043
23: 5 the LORD thy God turned the c into a 7045
27:13 these shall stand upon mount Ebal to c; 7045
29:19 to pass, when he heareth the words of this c, 423
30: 1 the blessing and the c, which I have set 7045
Jos 6:18 make the camp of Israel a c, and trouble it. 2764
24: 9 and called Balaam the son of Beor to c you: 7043
Jdg 5:23 C ye Meroz, said the angel of the LORD, 779
5:23 c ye bitterly the inhabitants thereof; 779
9:57 upon them came the c of Jotham the son of 7045
2Sa 16: 9 Why should this dead dog c my lord 7043
16:10 so let him c, because the LORD hath said 7043
16:10 the LORD hath said unto him, C David. 7043
16:11 *do it?* let him alone, and let him c; 7043
1Ki 2: 8 which cursed me *with* a grievous c in 7045
2Ki 22:19 *they* should become a desolation and a c, 7045
Ne 10:29 and entered into a c, and into an oath, 423
13: 2 against them, that *he* should c them: 7043
13: 2 howbeit our God turned the c into a 7045
Job 1:11 that he hath, and he will c thee to thy face. 1288
2: 5 and his flesh, and he will c thee to thy face. 1288
2: 9 still retain thine integrity? c God, and die. 1288
3: 8 Let them c it that curse the day, who are 5344
3: 8 Let them curse it that c the day, who are 779
31:30 my mouth to sin by wishing a c to his soul.) 423
Ps 62: 4 bless with their mouth, but they c inwardly. 7043
109:28 Let them c, but bless thou: when they arise, 7043
Pr 3:33 The c of the LORD *is* in the house of 3994
11:26 withholdeth corn, the people shall c him: 5344
24:24 him shall the people c, nations shall abhor 5344

Pr 26: 2 by flying, so the **c** causeless shall not come. 7045
27:14 the morning, it shall be counted a **c** to him. 7045
28:27 he that hideth his eyes shall have many a **c**. 3994
30:10 lest he **c** thee, and thou be found guilty. 7043
Ecc 7:21 lest thou hear thy servant **c** thee: 7043
10:20 **C** not the king, no not in thy thought; and 7043
10:20 and **c** not the rich in thy bedchamber: 7043
Isa 8:21 **c** their king and their God, and 7043
24: 6 Therefore hath the **c** devoured the earth, and 423
34: 5 and upon the people of my **c**, to judgment. 2764
43:28 have given Jacob to the **c**, and Israel to 2764
65:15 ye shall leave your name for a **c** unto my 7621
Jer 15:10 on usury; *yet* every one of them doth **c** me. 7043
24: 9 a reproach and a proverb, a taunt and a **c**, 7045
25:18 an astonishment, a hissing, and a **c**; 7045
26: 6 will make this city a **c** to all the nations of 7045
29:18 to be a **c**, and an astonishment, and a hissing, 423
29:22 of them shall be taken up a **c** by all 7045
42:18 an astonishment, and a **c**, and a reproach; 7045
44: 8 that *ye* might be a **c** and a reproach among 7045
44:12 an astonishment, and a **c**, and a reproach. 7045
44:22 an astonishment, and a **c**, without an 7045
49:13 a desolation, a reproach, a waste, and a **c**; 7045
La 3:65 Give them sorrow of heart, thy **c** unto them. 8381
Da 9:11 therefore the **c** is poured upon us, and 423
Zec 5: 3 This *is* the **c** that goeth forth over the face of 423
8:13 *that* as ye were a **c** among the heathen, 7045
Mal 2: 2 I will even send a **c** upon you, and 3994
2: 2 a curse upon you, and will **c** your blessings: 779
3: 9 Ye *are* cursed with a **c**: for ye *have* robbed 3994
4: 6 lest I come and smite the earth *with* a **c**. 2764
Mt 5:44 Love your enemies, bless them that **c** you, *2672*
26:74 Then began he to **c** and to swear, *saying*, I *2653*
Mk 14:71 But he began to **c** and to swear, *saying*, I *332*
Lk 6:28 Bless them that **c** you, and pray for them *2672*
Ac 23:12 and **bound** themselves **under a c**, *332*
23:14 have **bound** ourselves **under a great c**, *331+332*
Ro 12:14 them which persecute you: bless, and **c** not. *2672*
Gal 3:10 are of the works of the law are under the **c**: *2671*
3:13 Christ hath redeemed us from the **c** of *2671*
3:13 the curse of the law, being made a **c** for us: *2671*
Jas 3: 9 and therewith **c** we men, which are made *2672*
Rev 22: 3 And there shall be no more **c**: but *2652*

CURSED (72) [CURSE]

Ge 3:14 thou *art* **c** above all cattle, and above every 779
3:17 **c** *is* the ground for thy sake; in sorrow shalt 779
4:11 now *art* thou **c** from the earth, which hath 779
5:29 of the ground which the LORD hath **c**. 779
9:25 he said, **C** *be* Canaan; a servant of servants 779
27:29 **c** *be* every one that curseth thee, and 779
49: 7 **C** *be* their anger, for *it was* fierce; and 779
Lev 20: 9 he hath **c** his father or his mother; his blood 7043
24:11 blasphemed the name *of the LORD*, and **c**. 7043
24:14 Bring forth him that hath **c** without 7043
24:23 that they should bring forth him that had **c** 7043
Nu 22: 6 *is* blessed, and *he* whom thou cursest is **c**. 779
23: 8 How shall I curse, whom God hath not **c**? 6895
24: 9 blesseth thee, and **c** *is* he that curseth thee. 779
Dt 7:26 thine house, lest thou be a **c thing** like it: 2764
7:26 shalt utterly abhor it; for it *is* a **c thing**. 2764
13:17 there shall cleave nought of the **c thing** to 2764
27:15 **C** *be* the man that maketh *any* graven or 779
27:16 **C** *be* he that setteth light by his father or 779
27:17 **C** *be* he that removeth his neighbour's 779
27:18 **C** *be* he that maketh the blind to wander out 779
27:19 **C** *be* he that perverteth the judgment of 779
27:20 **C** *be* he that lieth with his father's wife; 779
27:21 **C** *be* he that lieth with any *manner of* beast. 779
27:22 **C** *be* he that lieth with his sister, 779
27:23 **C** *be* he that lieth with his mother in law. 779
27:24 **C** *be* he that smiteth his neighbour secretly. 779
27:25 **C** *be* he that taketh reward to slay an 779
27:26 **C** *be* he that confirmeth not *all* the words of 779
28:16 **C** *shalt* thou *be* in the city, and cursed *shalt* 779
28:16 *be* in the city, and **c** *shalt* thou *be* in the field. 779
28:17 **C** *shall be* thy basket and thy store. 779
28:18 **C** *shall be* the fruit of thy body, and the fruit 779
28:19 **C** *shalt* thou *be* when thou comest in, and 779
28:19 and **c** *shalt* thou *be* when thou goest out. 779
Jos 6:26 saying, **C** *be* the man before the LORD, 779
9:23 Now therefore ye *are* **c**, and there shall none 779
Jdg 9:27 and did eat and drink, and **c** Abimelech. 7043
21:18 **C** *be* he that giveth a wife to Benjamin. 779
1Sa 14:24 **C** *be* the man that eateth *any* food until 779
14:28 **C** *be* the man that eateth *any* food *this* day. 779
17:43 And the Philistine **c** David by his gods. 7043
26:19 of men, **c** *be* they before the LORD; 779
2Sa 16: 5 he came forth, and **c** still as he came. 7043
16: 7 And thus said Shimei when he **c**, Come out, 7043
16:13 **c** as he went, and threw stones at him, and 7043
19:21 because he **c** the LORD'S anointed? 7043
1Ki 2: 8 which **c** me *with* a grievous curse in the day 7043
2Ki 2:24 and **c** them in the name of the LORD. 7043
9:34 Go, see now this **c** *woman*, and bury her: 779
Ne 13:25 **c** them, and smote certain of them, and 7043
Job 1: 5 sons have sinned, and **c** God in their hearts. 1288
3: 1 this opened Job his mouth, and **c** his day. 7043
5: 3 taking root: but suddenly I **c** his habitation. 5344
24:18 as the waters; their portion is **c** in the earth: 7043
Ps 37:22 and they that be **c** of him shall be cut off. 7043
119:21 Thou hast rebuked the proud *that are* **c**, 779
Ecc 7:22 that thou thyself likewise hast **c** others. 7043
Jer 11: 3 **C** *be* the man that obeyeth not the words of 779
17: 5 **C** *be* the man that trusteth in man, and 779
20:14 **C** *be* the day wherein I was born: let not 779
20:15 **C** *be* the man who brought tidings to my 779
48:10 **C** *be* he that doeth the work of the LORD 779
48:10 **c** *be* he that keepeth back his sword from 779
Mal 1:14 **c** *be* the deceiver, which hath in his flock a 779
2: 2 yea, I have **c** them already, because ye do 779
3: 9 Ye *are* **c** with a curse: for ye *have* robbed 779
Mt 25:41 Depart from me, ye **c**, into everlasting fire, *2672*
Jn 7:49 this people who knoweth not the law are **c**. *1944*
Gal 3:10 **C** *is* every one that continueth not in all *1944*
3:13 **C** *is* every one that hangeth on a tree: *1944*
2Pe 2:14 with covetous practices; **c** children: *2671*

CURSEDST (2) [CURSE]

Jdg 17: 2 about which thou **c**, and spakest of also in 422
Mk 11:21 the fig tree which thou **c** is withered away. *2672*

CURSES (8) [CURSE]

Nu 5:23 the priest shall write these **c** in a book, and 423
Dt 28:15 that all these **c** shall come upon thee, and 7045
28:45 Moreover all these **c** shall come upon thee, 7045
29:20 all the **c** that are written in this book shall lie 423
29:21 according to all the **c** of the covenant that are 423
29:27 to bring upon it all the **c** that are written in 7045
30: 7 the LORD thy God will put all these **c** upon 423
2Ch 34:24 *even* all the **c** that are written in the book 423

CURSEST (1) [CURSE]

Nu 22: 6 *is* blessed, and *he* whom thou **c** is cursed. 779

CURSETH (10) [CURSE]

Ge 12: 3 that bless thee, and curse him that **c** thee: 7043
27:29 cursed *be* every one that **c** thee, and 779
Ex 21:17 he that **c** his father, or his mother, 7043
Lev 20: 9 For every one that **c** his father or his mother 7043
24:15 Whosoever **c** his God shall bear his sin. 7043
Nu 24: 9 blesseth thee, and cursed *is* he that **c** thee. 779
Pr 20:20 Whoso **c** his father or his mother, his lamp 7043
30:11 *There is* a generation *that* **c** their father, and 7043
Mt 15: 4 and, He that **c** father or mother, let him die *2551*
Mk 7:10 and, Whoso **c** father or mother, let him die *2551*

CURSING (12) [CURSE]

Nu 5:21 shall charge the woman with an oath of **c**, 423
Dt 28:20 The LORD shall send upon thee **c**, 3994
30:19 before you life and death, blessing and **c**: 7045
2Sa 16:12 will requite me good for his **c** this day. 7045
Ps 10: 7 His mouth is full *of* **c** and deceit and fraud: 423
59:12 and for **c** and lying *which* they speak. 423
109:17 As he loved **c**, so let it come *unto* him: as 7045
109:18 As he clothed himself with **c** like as with 7045
Pr 29:24 own soul: he heareth **c**, and bewrayeth *it* not. 423
Ro 3:14 Whose mouth is full of **c** and bitterness: *685*
Heb 6: 8 and briers *is* rejected, and *is* nigh unto **c**; *2671*
Jas 3:10 the same mouth proceedeth blessing and **c**. *2671*

CURSINGS (1) [CURSE]

Jos 8:34 the words of the law, the blessings and **c**, 7045

CURTAIN (26) [CURTAINS]

Ex 26: 2 The length of one **c** *shall be* eight and 3407
26: 2 and the breadth of one **c** four cubits: 3407
26: 4 the one **c** from the selvedge in the coupling; 3407
26: 4 make in the uttermost edge of *another* **c**, 3407
26: 5 Fifty loops shalt thou make in the one **c**, 3407
26: 5 the **c** that *is* in the coupling of the second; 3407
26: 8 The length of one **c** *shall be* thirty cubits, 3407
26: 8 and the breadth of one **c** four cubits: 3407
26: 9 shalt double the sixth **c** in the forefront of 3407
26:10 of the one **c** *that is* outmost in the coupling, 3407
26:10 fifty loops in the edge of the **c** which 3407
26:12 the half **c** that remaineth, shall hang over 3407
36: 9 The length of one **c** *was* twenty and 3407
36: 9 and the breadth of one **c** four cubits: 3407
36:11 he made loops of blue on the edge of one **c** 3407
36:11 he made in the uttermost side of *another* **c**, 3407
36:12 Fifty loops made he in one **c**, and 3407
36:12 fifty loops made he in the edge of the **c** 3407
36:12 the second: the loops held one **c** to another. NIH
36:15 The length of one **c** *was* thirty cubits, and 3407
36:15 and four cubits *was* the breadth of one **c**: 3407
36:17 the uttermost edge of the **c** in the coupling, 3407
36:17 fifty loops made he upon the edge of the **c** 3407
Nu 3:26 the **c** for the door of the court, which *is* by 4539
Ps 104: 2 who stretchest out the heavens like a **c**: 3407
Isa 40:22 that stretcheth out the heavens as a **c**, and 1852

CURTAINS (31) [CURTAIN]

Ex 26: 1 tabernacle *with* ten **c** *of* fine twined linen, 3407
26: 2 every one of the **c** shall have one measure. 3407
26: 3 The five **c** shall be coupled together one to 3407
26: 3 *other* five **c** *shall be* coupled one to another. 3407
26: 6 and couple the **c** together with the taches: 3407
26: 7 thou shalt make **c** *of* goats' *hair* to be a 3407
26: 7 the tabernacle: eleven **c** shalt thou make. 3407
26: 8 the eleven **c** *shall be all* of one measure. 3407
26: 9 And thou shalt couple five **c** by themselves, 3407
26: 9 six **c** by themselves, and shalt double 3407
26:12 the remnant that remaineth of the **c** of 3407
26:13 remaineth in the length of the **c** of the tent, 3407
36: 8 tabernacle made ten **c** *of* fine twined linen, 3407
36: 9 four cubits: the **c** *were* all of one size. 3407
36:10 And he coupled the five **c** one unto another: 3407
36:10 *the other* five **c** he coupled one unto 3407
36:13 coupled the **c** one unto another with 3407
36:14 he made **c** *of* goats' *hair* for the tent over 3407
36:14 over the tabernacle: eleven **c** he made them. 3407
36:15 one curtain: the eleven **c** *were* of one size. 3407
36:16 he coupled five **c** by themselves, and six 3407
36:16 by themselves, and six **c** by themselves. 3407
Nu 4:25 they shall bear the **c** of the tabernacle, and 3407
2Sa 7: 2 but the ark of God dwelleth within **c**. 3407
1Ch 17: 1 covenant of the LORD *remaineth* under **c**. 3407
SS 1: 5 as the tents of Kedar, as the **c** of Solomon. 3407
Isa 54: 2 let them stretch forth the **c** of thine 3407
Jer 4:20 my tents spoiled, *and* my **c** in a moment. 3407
10:20 forth my tent any more, and to set up my **c**. 3407
49:29 *away*: they shall take to themselves their **c**, 3407
Hab 3: 7 *and* the **c** of the land of Midian did tremble. 3407

CUSH (8)

Ge 10: 6 **C**, and Mizraim, and Phut, and Canaan. 3568
10: 7 the sons of **C**; Seba, and Havilah, and 3568
10: 8 **C** begat Nimrod: he began to be a mighty 3568
1Ch 1: 8 of Ham; **C**, and Mizraim, Put, and Canaan. 3568
1: 9 the sons of **C**; Seba, and Havilah, and 3568
1:10 **C** begat Nimrod: he began to be mighty 3568
Ps 7: T concerning the words of **C** the Benjamite. 3568
Isa 11:11 from **C**, and from Elam, and from Shinar, 3568

CUSHAN (1)

Hab 3: 7 I saw the tents of **C** in affliction: *and* 3572

CUSHAN-RISHATHAIM See CHUSHAN-RISHATHAIM

CUSHI (10)

2Sa 18:21 said Joab to **C**, Go tell the king what thou 3569
18:21 And **C** bowed himself unto Joab, and ran. 3569
18:22 let me, I pray thee, also run after **C**. 3569
18:23 ran *by* the way of the plain, and overran **C**. 3569
18:31 behold, **C** came; and Cushi said, Tidings, 3569
18:31 and **C** said, Tidings, my lord the king: 3569
18:32 the king said unto **C**, *Is* the young man 3569
18:32 **C** answered, The enemies of my lord 3569
Jer 36:14 the son of **C**, unto Baruch, saying, 3569
Zep 1: 1 which came unto Zephaniah the son of **C**, 3569

CUSTODY (5)

Nu 3:36 under the **c** and charge of the sons of 6486
Est 2: 3 unto the **c** of Hege the king's chamberlain, 3027
2: 8 to the **c** of Hegai, that Esther was brought 3027
2: 8 to the **c** of Hegai, keeper of the women. 3027
2:14 to the **c** of Shaashgaz, the king's 3027

CUSTOM (20) [ACCUSTOMED, CUSTOMS]

Ge 31:35 before thee; for the **c** of women *is* upon me. 1870
Jdg 11:39 she knew no man. And it was a **c** in Israel, 2706
1Sa 2:13 the priests' **c** with the people *was, that* 4941
Ezr 3: 4 **according to the c**, as the duty of every 3509.1
4:13 **c**, and *so* thou shalt endamage the revenue 1983
4:20 and toll, tribute, and **c**, *was* paid unto them. 1983
7:24 to impose toll, tribute, or **c**, upon them. 1983
Jer 32:11 was sealed *according to* the law and **c**, 2706
Mt 9: 9 named Matthew, sitting at the **receipt of c**: *5058*
17:25 of whom do the kings of the earth take **c** or *5056*
Mk 2:14 *son* of Alpheus sitting at the **receipt of c**, *5058*
Lk 1: 9 According to the **c** of the priest's office, *1485*
2:27 to do for him after the **c** of the law, *1480*
2:42 they went up to Jerusalem after the **c** of *1485*
4:16 and, as his **c** was, he went into *1486*
5:27 named Levi, sitting at the **receipt of c**: *5058*
Jn 18:39 But ye have a **c**, that I should release unto *4914*
Ro 13: 7 tribute to whom tribute *is due*; **c** to whom *5056*
13: 7 to whom tribute *is due*; custom to whom **c**; *5056*
1Co 11:16 we have no such **c**, neither the churches of *4914*

CUSTOMS (7) [CUSTOM]

Lev 18:30 commit not *any one* of *these* abominable **c**, 2708
Jer 10: 3 For the **c** of the people *are* vain: for *one* 2708
Ac 6:14 shall change the **c** which Moses delivered *1485*
16:21 And teach **c**, which are not lawful for us to *1485*
21:21 *their* children, neither to walk after the **c**. *1485*
26: 3 *I know* thee to be expert in all **c** and *1485*
28:17 against the people, or **c** of our fathers, *1485*

CUT (320) [CUTTEST, CUTTETH, CUTTING, CUTTINGS]

Ge 9:11 neither shall all flesh be **c off** any more by 3772
17:14 that soul shall be **c off** from his people; 3772
Ex 4:25 **c off** the foreskin of her son, and cast *it* at 3772
9:15 and thou shalt be **c off** from the earth. 3582
12:15 that soul shall be **c off** from Israel. 3772
12:19 even that soul shall be **c off** from 3772
23:23 and the Jebusites: and I will **c** them **off**. 3582
29:17 thou shalt **c** the ram in pieces, and wash 5408
30:33 shall even be **c off** from his people. 3772
30:38 shall even be **c off** from his people. 3772
31:14 that soul shall be **c off** from amongst his 3772
34:13 their images, and **c down** their groves: 3772
39: 3 **c** *it into* wires, to work *it* in the blue, and 7112
Lev 1: 6 the burnt offering, and **c** it into his pieces. 5408
1:12 he shall **c** it into his pieces, with his head 5408
7:20 even that soul shall be **c off** from his 3772
7:21 even that soul shall be **c off** from his 3772
7:25 even the soul that eateth *it* shall be **c off** 3772
7:27 even that soul shall be **c off** from his 3772
8:20 he **c** the ram into pieces; and Moses burnt 5408
17: 4 that man shall be **c off** from among his 3772
17: 9 even that man shall be **c off** from among 3772
17:10 and will **c** him **off** from among his people. 3772
17:14 whosoever eateth it shall be **c off**. 3772
18:29 shall be **c off** from among their people. 3772
19: 8 that soul shall be **c off** from among his 3772
20: 3 and will **c** him **off** from among his people; 3772
20: 5 will **c** him **off**, and all that go a whoring 3772
20: 6 and will **c** him **off** from among his people. 3772
20:17 they shall be **c off** in the sight of their 3772
20:18 both of them shall be **c off** from among 3772
22: 3 that soul shall be **c off** from my presence: 3772
22:24 is bruised, or crushed, or broken, or **c**; 3772
23:29 he shall be **c off** from among his people. 3772
26:30 **c down** your images, and cast your 3772
Nu 4:18 **C** ye not **off** the tribe of the families of 3772
9:13 even the same soul shall be **c off** from 3772
13:23 **c down** from thence a branch with one 3772
13:24 the children of Israel **c down** from thence. 3772
15:30 that soul shall be **c off** from among his 3772
15:31 that soul shall **utterly** be **c off**; 3772+3772
19:13 and that soul shall be **c off** from Israel: 3772
19:20 that soul shall be **c off** from among 3772
Dt 7: 5 **c down** their groves, and burn their graven 1438
12:29 When the LORD thy God shall **c off** 3772
14: 1 ye shall not **c** yourselves, nor make *any* 1413
19: 1 When the LORD thy God hath **c off** 3772
19: 5 a stroke with the axe to **c down** the tree, 3772
20:19 thou shalt not **c** them **down** (for the tree of 3772
20:20 thou shalt destroy and **c** them **down**; 3772

Dt 23: 1 the stones, or hath *his* privy member **c off**, 3772
25:12 thou shalt **c off** her hand, thine eye shall 7112
Jos 3:13 *that* the waters of Jordan shall be **c off** *from* 3772
3:16 *even* the salt sea, failed, *and* were **c off**: 3772
4: 7 That the waters of Jordan were **c off** before 3772
4: 7 the waters of Jordan were **c off**: 3772
7: 9 and **c off** our name from the earth: 3772
11:21 **c off** the Anakims from the mountains, 3772
17:15 **c down** for thyself there in the land of 1254
17:18 for it *is* a wood, and thou shalt **c** it **down**: 1254
23: 4 with all the nations that I have **c off**, 3772
Jdg 1: 6 and **c off** his thumbs and his great toes. 7112
1: 7 their thumbs and their great toes **c off**, 7112
6:25 and **c down** the grove that *is* by it: 3772
6:26 of the grove which thou shalt **c down**. 3772
6:28 the grove was **c down** that *was* by it, and 3772
6:30 he hath **c down** the grove that *was* by it. 3772
9:48 **c down** a bough from the trees, and took it, 3772
9:49 all the people likewise **c down** every man 3772
20: 6 **c** her **in pieces**, and sent her throughout all 5408
21: 6 There is one tribe **c off** from Israel *this* day. 1438
Ru 4:10 that the name of the dead be not **c off** from 3772
1Sa 2:31 that I will **c off** thine arm, and the arm of 1438
2:33 *whom* I shall not **c off** from mine altar, 3772
5: 4 both the palms of his hands *were* **c off** upon 3772
17:51 and slew him, and **c off** his head therewith. 3772
20:15 *also* thou shalt not **c off** thy kindness from 3772
20:15 not when the LORD hath **c off** 3772
24: 4 and **c off** the skirt of Saul's robe privily. 3772
24: 5 because he had **c off** Saul's skirt. 3772
24:11 for in that I **c off** the skirt of thy robe, and 3772
24:21 that thou wilt not **c off** my seed after me, 3772
28: 9 how he hath **c off** those that have familiar 3772
31: 9 they **c off** his head, and stripped off his 3772
2Sa 4:12 **c off** their hands and their feet, and 7112
7: 9 have **c off** all thine enemies out of thy 3772
10: 4 **c off** their garments in the middle, *even* to 3772
20:22 they **c off** the head of Sheba the son of 3772
1Ki 9: 7 will I **c off** Israel out of the land which I 3772
11:16 until he had **c off** every male in Edom:) 3772
13:34 even to **c** *it* **off**, and to destroy *it* from off 3582
14:10 will **c off** from Jeroboam *him that* pisseth 3772
14:14 who shall **c off** the house of Jeroboam that 3772
18: 4 when Jezebel **c off** the prophets of 3772
18:23 **c** it **in pieces**, and lay *it* on wood, and 5408
18:28 **c** themselves after their manner with knives 1413
18:33 **c** the bullock **in pieces**, and laid *him* on 5408
21:21 will **c off** from Ahab *him that* pisseth 3772
2Ki 6: 4 they came to Jordan, they **c down** wood. 1504
6: 6 he **c down** a stick, and cast *it* in thither; 7094
9: 8 I will **c off** from Ahab *him that* pisseth 3772
10:32 days the LORD began to **c** Israel **short**: 7096
16:17 king Ahaz **c off** the borders of the bases, 7112
18: 4 **c down** the groves, and brake in pieces 3772
18:16 At that time did Hezekiah **c off** *the gold* 7112
19:23 will **c down** the tall cedar trees thereof, *and* 3772
23:14 **c down** the groves, and filled their places 3772
24:13 **c in pieces** all the vessels of gold which 7112
1Ch 17: 8 have **c off** all thine enemies from before 3772
19: 4 **c off** their garments in the midst hard by 3772
20: 3 **c** *them* with saws, and with harrows of iron, 7787
2Ch 2: 8 for I know that thy servants can skill to **c** 3772
2:10 to thy servants, the hewers that **c** timber, 3772
2:16 we will **c** wood out of Lebanon, as much as 3772
14: 3 down the images, and **c down** the groves: 1438
15:16 Asa **c down** her idol, and stamped *it*, and 3772
22: 7 whom the LORD had anointed to **c off** 3772
26:21 for he was **c off** from the house of 1504
28:24 **c in pieces** the vessels of the house of God, 7112
31: 1 images *in pieces*, and **c down** the groves, 1438
32:21 which **c off** all the mighty *men* of valour, 3582
34: 4 that *were* on high above them, he **c down**; 1438
34: 7 **c down** all the idols throughout all the land 1438
Job 4: 7 or where were the righteous **c off**? 3582
6: 9 he would let loose his hand, and **c** me **off**! 1214
8:12 it *is* yet in his greenness, *and* not **c down**, 6998
8:14 Whose hope shall be **c off**, and whose trust 6990
11:10 If he **c off**, and shut up, or gather together, 2498
14: 2 cometh forth like a flower, and is **c down**: 5243
14: 7 if it be **c down**, that it will sprout again, 3772
18:16 above shall his branch be **c off**. 5243
21:21 number of his months is **c off in the midst**? 2686
22:16 Which were **c down** out of time, 7059
22:20 Whereas our substance is not **c down**, but 3582
23:17 Because I was not **c off** before 6789
24:24 and **c off** as the tops of the ears of corn. 5243
30: 4 Who **c up** mallows by the bushes, and 6998
36:20 when people are **c off** in their place. 5927
Ps 12: 3 The LORD shall **c off** all flattering lips, 3772
31:22 my haste, I am **c off** from before thine eyes: 1629
34:16 to **c off** the remembrance of them from 3772
37: 2 For they shall soon be **c down** like 5243
37: 9 For evildoers shall be **c off**: but those that 3772
37:22 they that be cursed of him shall be **c off**. 3772
37:28 but the seed of the wicked shall be **c off**. 3772
37:34 when the wicked are **c off**, thou shalt see 3772
37:38 the end of the wicked shall be **c off**. 3772
54: 5 unto mine enemies: **c** them **off** in thy truth. 6789
58: 7 *shoot* his arrows, let them be as **c in pieces**. 4135
75:10 All the horns of the wicked also will I **c off**; 1438
76:12 He shall **c off** the spirit of princes: *he is* 1219
80:16 *It is* burnt with fire, *it is* **c down**: 3683
83: 4 and let us **c** them **off** from *being* a nation; 3582
88: 5 no more: and they are **c off** from thy hand. 1504
88:16 goeth over me; thy terrors have **c** me **off**. 6789
90: 6 in the evening it is **c down**, and withereth. 4135
90:10 for it is soon **c off**, and we fly away. 1468
94:23 shall **c** them **off** in their own wickedness; 6789
94:23 *yea*, the LORD our God shall **c** them **off**. 6789
101: 5 slandereth his neighbour, him will I **c off**: 6789
101: 8 that *I* may **c off** all wicked doers from 3772
107:16 of brass, and **c** the bars of iron **in sunder**. 1438
109:13 Let his posterity be **c off**; *and* in 3772
109:15 that he may **c off** the memory of them from 3772
129: 4 he hath **c asunder** the cords of the wicked. 7112
Ps 143:12 of thy mercy **c off** mine enemies, and 6789
Pr 2:22 the wicked shall be **c off** from the earth, 3772
10:31 but the froward tongue shall be **c out**. 3772
23:18 and thine expectation shall not be **c off**. 3772
24:14 and thy expectation shall not be **c off**. 3772
Isa 9:10 the sycomores are **c down**, but we will 1438
9:14 Therefore the LORD will **c off** from Israel 3772
10: 7 heart to destroy and **c off** nations not a few. 3772
10:34 he shall **c down** the thickets of the forest 5362
11:13 and the adversaries of Judah shall be **c off**: 3772
14:12 *how* art thou **c down** to the ground, 1438
14:22 **c off** from Babylon the name, and remnant, 3772
15: 2 *shall be* baldness, *and* every beard **c off**. 1438
18: 5 he shall both **c off** the sprigs with pruning 3772
18: 5 and take away *and* **c down** the branches. 8456
22:25 place be removed, and be **c down**, and fall; 1438
22:25 the burden that *was* upon it shall be **c off**: 3772
29:20 and all that watch for iniquity are **c off**: 3772
33:12 *as* thorns **c up** shall they be burnt in 3683
37:24 I will **c down** the tall cedars thereof, *and* 3772
38:12 I have **c off** like a weaver my life: he will 7088
38:12 he will **c** me **off** with pining sickness: 1214
45: 2 of brass, and **c in sunder** the bars of iron: 1438
48: 9 will I refrain for thee, that *I* **c** thee not **off**. 3772
48:19 his name should not have been **c off** nor 3772
51: 9 *Art* thou not it that hath **c** Rahab, *and* 2672
53: 8 for he was **c off** out of the land of 1504
55:13 an everlasting sign *that* shall not be **c off**. 3772
56: 5 an everlasting name, that shall not be **c off**. 3772
66: 3 a lamb, *as if* he **c off** a dog's **neck**; 6202
Jer 7:28 is perished, and is **c off** from their mouth. 3772
7:29 **C off** thine hair, *O Jerusalem*, and cast *it* 1494
9:21 to **c off** the children from without, *and* 3772
11:19 let us **c** him **off** from the land of the living, 3772
16: 6 *men* lament for them, nor **c** themselves, 1413
22: 7 they shall **c down** thy choice cedars, and 3772
25:37 the peaceable habitations are **c down** 1826
34:18 when they **c** the calf in twain, and 3772
36:23 he **c** it with the penknife, and cast *it* into 7167
41: 5 having **c** themselves, with offerings and 1413
44: 7 to **c off** from you man and woman, child 3772
44: 8 that ye might **c** yourselves **off**, and that *ye* 3772
44:11 against you for evil, and to **c off** all Judah. 3772
46:23 They shall **c down** her forest, saith 3772
47: 4 *and* to **c off** from Tyrus and Zidon every 3772
47: 5 Ashkelon is **c off** *with* the remnant of their 1820
47: 5 their valley: how long wilt thou **c** thyself? 1413
48: 2 and let us **c** it **off** from *being* a nation. 3772
48: 2 Also thou shalt be **c down**, O Madmen; 1826
48:25 The horn of Moab is **c off**, and his arm is 1438
49:26 all the men of war shall be **c off** in that day, 1826
50:16 **C off** the sower from Babylon, and him that 3772
50:23 is the hammer of the whole earth **c asunder** 1438
50:30 all her men of war shall be **c off** in that day, 1826
51: 6 be not **c off** in her iniquity; for this *is* 1826
51:62 to **c** it **off**, that none shall remain in it, 3772
La 2: 3 He hath **c off** in *his* fierce anger all the horn 1438
3:53 They have **c off** my life in the dungeon, and 6789
3:54 over mine head; *then* I said, I am **c off**. 1504
Eze 6: 6 your images may be **c down**, and 1438
14: 8 I will **c** him **off** from the midst of my 3772
14:13 and will **c off** man and beast from it: 3772
14:17 so that I **c off** man and beast from it: 3772
14:19 it in blood, to **c off** from it man and beast: 3772
14:21 to **c off** from it man and beast? 3772
16: 4 the day thou wast born thy navel was not **c**, 3772
17: 9 and **c off** the fruit thereof, that it wither? 7082
17:17 and building forts, to **c off** many persons: 3772
21: 3 will **c off** from thee the righteous and 3772
21: 4 that I will **c off** from thee the righteous and 3772
25: 7 I will **c** thee **off** from the people, and I will 3772
25:13 and will **c off** man and beast from it; 3772
25:16 I will **c off** the Cherethims, and destroy 3772
29: 8 and **c off** man and beast out of thee. 3772
30:15 and I will **c off** the multitude of No. 3772
31:12 have **c** him **off**, and have left him: 3772
35: 7 **c off** from it him that passeth out and 3772
37:11 our hope is lost: we are **c off** for our parts. 1504
39:10 neither **c down** *any* out of the forests; 2404
Da 2: 5 ye shall be **c** in pieces, and your houses 5648
2:34 Thou sawest till that a stone was **c out** 1505
2:45 was **c out** of the mountain without hands, 1505
3:29 shall be **c** in pieces, and their houses shall 5648
4:14 Hew down the tree, and **c off** his branches, 7113
9:26 and two weeks shall Messiah be **c off**, 3772
Hos 8: 4 made them idols, that they may be **c off**. 3772
10: 7 her king is **c off** as the foam upon 1820
10:15 the king of Israel **utterly** be **c off**. 1820+1820
Joel 1: 5 new wine, for it is **c off** from your mouth. 3772
1: 9 the drink offering is **c off** from the house of 3772
1:16 Is not the meat **c off** before our eyes, 3772
Am 1: 5 **c off** the inhabitant from the plain of Aven, 3772
1: 8 I will **c off** the inhabitant from Ashdod, 3772
2: 3 I will **c off** the judge from the midst 3772
3:14 the horns of the altar shall be **c off**, and 1438
9: 1 **c** them in the head, all of them; and I will 1214
Ob 1: 5 if robbers by night, (how art thou **c off**!) 1820
1: 9 mount of Esau may be **c off** by slaughter. 3772
1:10 cover thee, and thou shalt be **c off** for ever. 3772
1:14 to **c off** those of his that did escape; 3772
Mic 5: 9 and all thine enemies shall be **c off**. 3772
5:10 that I will **c off** thy horses out of the midst 3772
5:11 I will **c off** the cities of thy land, and 3772
5:12 I will **c off** witchcrafts out of thine hand; 3772
5:13 Thy graven images also will I **c off**, and 3772
Na 1:12 yet thus shall they be **c down**, 1494
1:14 out of the house of thy gods will I **c off** 3772
1:15 more pass through thee; he is utterly **c off**. 3772
2:13 I will **c off** thy prey from the earth, and 3772
3:15 the sword shall **c** thee **off**, it shall eat thee 3772
Hab 3:17 the flock shall be **c off** from the fold, and 1504
Zep 1: 3 I will **c off** man from off the land, saith 3772
1: 4 I will **c off** the remnant of Baal from this 3772
1:11 for all the merchant people are **c down**; 1820
1:11 cut down; all they that bear silver are **c off**. 3772
Zep 3: 6 I have **c off** *the* nations: their towers are 3772
3: 7 so their dwelling should not be **c off**, 3772
Zec 5: 3 for every one that stealeth shall be **c off** *as* 5352
5: 3 every one that sweareth shall be **c off** *as* on 5352
9: 6 and I will **c off** the pride of the Philistines. 3772
9:10 I will **c off** the chariot from Ephraim, and 3772
9:10 and the battle bow shall be **c off**: 3772
11: 8 Three shepherds also I **c off** in one month; 3582
11: 9 that that is to be **c off**, let it be cut off; and 3582
11: 9 that that is to be cut off, let it be **c off**; and 3582
11:10 my staff, *even* Beauty, and **c** it **asunder**, 1438
11:14 I **c asunder** mine other staff, *even* Bands, 1438
11:16 *which* shall not visit those that be **c off**, 3582
12: 3 with it shall be **c in pieces**, 8295+8295
13: 2 *that* I will **c off** the names of the idols out 3772
13: 8 two parts therein shall be **c off** *and* die; 3772
14: 2 the residue of the people shall not be **c off** 3772
Mal 2:12 The LORD will **c off** the man that doth 3772
Mt 5:30 offend thee, **c** it **off**, and cast *it* from thee: *1581*
18: 8 **c** them **off**, and cast *them* from thee: *1581*
21: 8 others **c down** branches from the trees, and *2875*
24:51 And shall **c** him **asunder**, and appoint *him* *1371*
Mk 9:43 And if thy hand offend thee, **c** it **off**: it is *609*
9:45 And if thy foot offend thee, **c** it **off**: it is *609*
11: 8 and others **c down** branches off the trees, *2875*
14:47 a servant of the high priest, and **c off** his ear. *851*
Lk 12:46 and will **c** him **in sunder**, and will appoint *1371*
13: 7 **c** it **down**; why cumbereth it the ground? *1581*
13: 9 if not, *then* after that thou shalt **c** it **down**. *1581*
22:50 of the high priest, and **c off** his right ear. *851*
Jn 18:10 high priest's servant, and **c off** his right ear. *609*
18:26 being *his* kinsman whose ear Peter **c off**, *609*
Ac 5:33 When they heard *that*, they were **c** *to* *1282*
7:54 When they heard these *things*, they were **c** *1282*
27:32 Then the soldiers **c off** the ropes of the boat, *609*
Ro 9:28 the work, and **c** *it* **short** in righteousness: *4932*
11:22 otherwise thou also shalt be **c off**. *1581*
11:24 For if thou wert **c out** of the olive tree *1581*
2Co 11:12 that I may **c off** occasion **from** them which *1581*
Gal 5:12 I would they were even **c off** which trouble *609*

CUTH (1) [CUTHAH]

2Ki 17:30 the men of **C** made Nergal, and the men of 3575

CUTHAH (1) [CUTH]

2Ki 17:24 from **C**, and from Ava, and from Hamath, 3575

CUTTEST (1) [CUT]

Dt 24:19 When thou **c down** thine **harvest** in 7105+7114

CUTTETH (6) [CUT]

Job 28:10 He **c out** rivers among the rocks; and 1234
Ps 46: 9 the bow, and **c** the spear **in sunder**; 7112
141: 7 as when one **c** and cleaveth *wood* upon 6398
Pr 26: 6 message by the hand of a fool **c off** the feet, 7096
Jer 10: 3 for *one* **c** a tree out of the forest, the work 3772
22:14 large chambers, and **c** him **out** windows; 7167

CUTTING (5) [CUT]

Ex 31: 5 in **c** of stones, to set *them*, and in carving of 2799
35:33 in the **c** of stones, to set *them*, and 2799
Isa 38:10 I said, in the **c off** of my days, I shall go to 1824
Hab 2:10 shame to thy house by **c off** many people, 7096
Mk 5: 5 crying, and **c** himself with stones. *2629*

CUTTINGS (3) [CUT]

Lev 19:28 Ye shall not make any **c** in your flesh for 8296
21: 5 nor **make any c** in their flesh. 8295+8296
Jer 48:37 upon all the hands *shall be* **c**, and upon 1417

CUZ See CHUZA

CYMBAL (1) [CYMBALS]

1Co 13: 1 become *as* sounding brass, or a tinkling **c**. *2950*

CYMBALS (16) [CYMBAL]

2Sa 6: 5 and on timbrels, and on cornets, and on **c**. 6767
1Ch 13: 8 and with **c**, and with trumpets. 4700
15:16 psalteries and harps and **c**, sounding, 4700
15:19 *were appointed* to sound with **c** of brass; 4700
15:28 the cornet, and with trumpets, and with **c**, 4700
16: 5 with harps; but Asaph made a sound with **c**; 4700
16:42 and **c** for those that should make a sound, 4700
25: 1 with harps, with psalteries, and with **c**: 4700
25: 6 with **c**, psalteries, and harps, for the service 4700
2Ch 5:12 having **c** and psalteries and harps, 4700
5:13 and **c** and instruments of musick, 4700
29:25 Levites *in* the house of the LORD with **c**, 4700
Ezr 3:10 the Levites the sons of Asaph with **c**, 4700
Ne 12:27 *with* **c**, psalteries, and with harps. 4700
Ps 150: 5 Praise him upon the loud **c**: praise him 6767
150: 5 praise him upon the high sounding **c**. 6767

CYPRESS (1)

Isa 44:14 down cedars, and taketh the **c** and the oak, 8645

CYPRUS (8)

Ac 4:36 a Levite, *and* of the country of **C**, *2953*
11:19 and **C**, and Antioch, preaching the word to *2954*
11:20 And some of them were men of **C** and *2953*
13: 4 and from thence they sailed to **C**. *2954*
15:39 *so* Barnabas took Mark, and sailed unto **C**; *2954*
21: 3 Now when we had discovered **C**, we left it *2954*
21:16 and brought *with them* one Mnason of **C**, *2953*
27: 4 we sailed under **C**, because the winds were *2954*

CYRENE (4) [CYRENIAN, CYRENIANS]

Mt 27:32 they found a man of **C**, Simon by name: *2956*
Ac 2:10 and in the parts of Libya about **C**, and *2957*
11:20 some of them were men of Cyprus and **C**, *2956*
13: 1 called Niger, and Lucius **of C**, and Manaen, *2956*

D

CYRENIAN (2) [CYRENE]
Mk 15:21 And they compel one Simon a **C**, 2956
Lk 23:26 a **C**, coming out of the country, and on him 2956

CYRENIANS (1) [CYRENE]
Ac 6: 9 and **C**, and Alexandrians, and of them of 2956

CYRENIUS (1)
Lk 2: 2 (*And* this taxing was first made when **C** 2958

CYRUS (23)
2Ch 36:22 Now in the first year of **C** king of Persia, 3566
36:22 the LORD stirred up the spirit of **C** king 3566
36:23 Thus saith **C** king of Persia, All 3566
Ezr 1: 1 Now in the first year of **C** king of Persia, 3566
1: 1 the LORD stirred up the spirit of **C** king 3566
1: 2 Thus saith **C** king of Persia, The LORD 3566
1: 7 Also **C** the king brought forth the vessels of 3566
1: 8 Even those did **C** king of Persia bring forth 3566
3: 7 according to the grant that they had of **C** 3566
4: 3 as king **C** the king of Persia hath 3566
4: 5 all the days of **C** king of Persia, 3566
5:13 in the first year of **C** the king of Babylon 3567
5:13 **C** made a decree to build this house of 3567
5:14 those did **C** the king take out of the temple 3567
5:17 that a decree *was* made of **C** the king to 3567
6: 3 In the first year of **C** the king *the same* 3567
6: 3 **C** the king made a decree *concerning* 3567
6:14 according to the commandment of **C**, and 3567
Isa 44:28 That saith of **C**, *He is* my shepherd, and 3566
45: 1 to **C**, whose right hand I have holden, to 3566
Da 1:21 *even* unto the first year of king **C**. 3566
6:28 of Darius, and in the reign of **C** the Persian. 3567
10: 1 In the third year of **C** king of Persia a thing 3566

D

DABAREH (1)
Jos 21:28 with her suburbs, **D** with her suburbs, 1705

DABBASHETH (1)
Jos 19:11 reached to **D**, and reached to the river that 1708

DABBESHETH See DABBASHETH

DABERATH (2)
Jos 19:12 *then* goeth out to **D**, and goeth up *to* Japhia, 1705
1Ch 6:72 with her suburbs, **D** with her suburbs, 1705

DAGGER (3)
Jdg 3:16 Ehud made him a **d** which had two edges, 2719
3:21 took the **d** from his right thigh, and thrust it 2719
3:22 that he could not draw the **d** out of his 2719

DAGON (12) [BETH-DAGON, DAGON'S]
Jdg 16:23 to offer a great sacrifice unto **D** their god, 1712
1Sa 5: 2 they brought it *into* the house of **D**, and 1712
5: 2 it *into* the house of Dagon, and set it by **D**. 1712
5: 3 **D** *was* fallen upon his face to the earth 1712
5: 3 they took **D**, and set him in his place again. 1712
5: 4 **D** *was* fallen upon his face to the ground 1712
5: 4 the head of **D** and both the palms of his 1712
5: 4 only *the stump of* **D** was left to him. 1712
5: 5 Therefore neither the priests of **D**, nor any 1712
5: 5 tread on the threshold of **D** in Ashdod unto 1712
5: 7 hand is sore upon us, and upon **D** our god. 1712
1Ch 10:10 and fastened his head *in* the temple of **D**. 1712

DAGON'S (1) [DAGON]
1Sa 5: 5 of Dagon, nor any that come *into* **D** house, 1712

DAILY (63) [DAY]
Ex 5:13 Fulfil your works, *your* **d** 3117+3117+871.1
5:19 your bricks of *your* **d** task. 3117+3117+871.1
16: 5 be twice as much as they gather **d**. 3117+3117
Nu 4:16 the **d** meat offering, and the anointing oil, 8548
28:24 manner ye shall offer **d**, 3117+1886.1+3807.1
29: 6 the **d** burnt offering, and his meat offering, 8548
Jdg 16:16 when she pressed him **d** with 3117+3605+1886.1
2Ki 25:30 a **d** rate for every day, all the days of his 3117
2Ch 31:16 *his* **d** portion for their service 3117+3117+871.1
Ezr 3: 4 **d** burnt offerings by number, 3117+3117+871.1
Ne 5:18 prepared *for me* **d** *was* one ox 259+3117+3807.1
Est 3: 4 when they spake **d** unto him, 3117+3117+2050.1
Ps 13: 2 in my soul, *having* sorrow in my heart **d**? 3119
42:10 while they say **d** unto me, 3117+3605+1886.1
56: 1 he fighting **d** oppresseth me. 3117+3605+1886.1
56: 2 Mine enemies would **d** 3117+3605+1886.1
61: 8 that I may **d** perform my vows. 3117+3117
68:19 *who* **d** loadeth us *with benefits, even* 3117+3117
72:15 *and* **d** shall he be praised. 3117+3605+1886.1
74:22 *man* reproacheth thee **d**. 3117+3605+1886.1
86: 3 for I cry unto thee **d**. 3117+3605+1886.1
88: 9 LORD, I have called **d** upon 3117+3605+871.1
88:17 came round about me **d** 3117+3605+1886.1
Pr 8:30 up *with him:* and I was **d** *his* delight, 3117+3117
8:34 watching **d** at my gates, waiting at 3117+3117
Isa 58: 2 Yet they seek me **d**, and delight to 3117+3117
Jer 7:25 **d** rising up early and sending *them:* 3117
20: 7 **d**, every one mocketh me. 3117+3605+1886.1
20: 8 unto me, and a derision, **d**. 3117+3605+1886.1
37:21 **d** a piece of bread out of 3117+1886.1+3807.1
Eze 30:16 and Noph *shall have* distresses **d**. 3119
45:23 blemish **d** the seven days; 3117+1886.1+3807.1
45:23 goats **d** *for* a sin offering. 3117+1886.1+3807.1
46:13 Thou shalt **d** prepare a 3117+1886.1+3807.1
Da 1: 5 the king appointed them a **d** 3117+3117+871.1
8:11 by him the **d** *sacrifice* was taken away, and 8548
8:12 a host was given *him* against the **d** *sacrifice* 8548
8:13 *be* the vision *concerning* the **d** *sacrifice,* 8548
11:31 shall take away the **d** *sacrifice,* and 8548
12:11 from the time *that* the **d** *sacrifice* shall be 8548
Hos 12: 1 he **d** increaseth lies and 3117+3605+1886.1
Mt 6:11 Give us this day our **d** bread. 1967
26:55 I sat **d** with you teaching in 2250+2596
Mk 14:49 I was **d** with you in the temple 2250+2596
Lk 9:23 and take up his cross **d**, 2250+2596
11: 3 Give us day by day our **d** bread. 1967
19:47 And he taught **d** in the temple. 2250+2596
22:53 When I was **d** with you in 2250+2596
Ac 2:46 continuing **d** with one accord in 2250+2596
2:47 And the Lord added to the church **d** 2250+2596
3: 2 whom they laid **d** at the gate of 2250+2596
5:42 And **d** in the temple, and in every 2250+3956
6: 1 their widows were neglected in the **d** 2522
16: 5 the faith, and increased in number **d**. 2250+2596
17:11 and searched the scriptures **d**, 2250+2596
17:17 in the market **d** with them that 2250+2596+3956
19: 9 **d** in the school of one Tyrannus. 2250+2596
1Co 15:31 in Christ Jesus our Lord, I die **d**. 2250+2596
2Co 11:28 that which cometh upon me **d**, 2250+2596
Heb 3:13 But exhort one another **d**, 1538+2250+2596
7:27 Who needeth not **d**, as *those* high 2250+2596
10:11 And every priest standeth **d** 2250+2596
Jas 2:15 or sister be naked, and destitute of **d** food, 2184

DAINTIES (3) [DAINTY]
Ge 49:20 *shall be* fat, and he shall yield royal **d**. 4574
Ps 141: 4 work iniquity: and let me not eat of their **d**. 4516
Pr 23: 3 Be not desirous of his **d**: for they *are* 4303

DAINTY (3) [DAINTIES]
Job 33:20 life abhorreth bread, and his soul **d** meat. 8378
Pr 23: 6 an evil eye, neither desire thou his **d meats**: 4303
Rev 18:14 and all *things which were* **d** and goodly are 3045

DALAIAH (1)
1Ch 3:24 and Johanan, and **D**, and Anani, seven. 1806

DALE (2)
Ge 14:17 the valley of Shaveh, which *is* the king's **d**. 6010
2Sa 18:18 himself a pillar, which *is* in the king's **d**: 6010

DALMANUTHA (1)
Mk 8:10 his disciples, and came into the parts of **D**. 1148

DALMATIA (1)
2Ti 4:10 Crescens to Galatia, Titus unto **D**. 1149

DALPHON (1)
Est 9: 7 And Parshandatha, and **D**, and Aspatha, 1813

DAM (5)
Ex 22:30 seven days it shall be with his **d**; on 517
Lev 22:27 then it shall be seven days under the **d**; 517
Dt 22: 6 the **d** sitting upon the young, or upon 517
22: 6 thou shalt not take the **d** with the young: 517
22: 7 *But* thou shalt in any wise let the **d** go, 517

DAMAGE (6) [ENDAMAGE]
Ezr 4:22 why should **d** grow to the hurt of the kings? 2257
Est 7: 4 enemy could not countervail the king's **d**. 5143
Pr 26: 6 of a fool cutteth off the feet, *and* drinketh **d**. 2555
Da 6: 2 unto them, and the king should have no **d**. 5142
Ac 27:10 *this* voyage will be with hurt and much **d**, 2209
2Co 7: 9 that ye might **receive d** by us in nothing. 2210

DAMARIS (1)
Ac 17:34 and a woman named **D**, and others with 1152

DAMASCENES (1) [DAMASCUS]
2Co 11:32 **D** *with a garrison,* desirous to apprehend 1153

DAMASCUS (60) [DAMASCENES, SYRIA-DAMASCUS]
Ge 14:15 unto Hobah, which *is* on the left hand of **D**. 1834
15: 2 steward of my house *is* this Eliezer of **D**? 1834
2Sa 8: 5 when the Syrians of **D** came to succour 1834
8: 6 David put garrisons in Syria of **D**: and 1834
1Ki 11:24 slew them *of Zobah:* and they went *to* **D**, 1834
11:24 and dwelt therein, and reigned in **D**. 1834
15:18 king of Syria, that dwelt at **D**, saying, 1834
19:15 return on thy way to the wilderness of **D**: 1834
20:34 thou shalt make streets for thee in **D**, as my 1834
2Ki 5:12 *Are* not Abana and Pharpar, rivers of **D**, 1834
8: 7 Elisha came *to* **D**; and Ben-hadad the king 1834
8: 9 even *of* every good thing of **D**, 1834
14:28 and how he recovered **D**, and Hamath, 1834
16: 9 for the king of Assyria went up against **D**, 1834
16:10 king Ahaz went *to* **D** to meet 1834
16:10 of Assyria, and saw an altar that *was* at **D**: 1834
16:11 to all that king Ahaz had sent from **D**: 1834
16:11 made *it* against king Ahaz came from **D**. 1834
16:12 when the king was come from **D**, the king 1834
1Ch 18: 5 when the Syrians of **D** came to help 1834
2Ch 16: 2 king of Syria, that dwelt at **D**, saying, 1834
24:23 all the spoil of them unto the king of **D**. 1834
28: 5 of them captives, and brought *them to* **D**. 1834
28:23 For he sacrificed unto the gods of **D**, 1834
SS 7: 4 tower of Lebanon which looketh toward **D**. 1834
Isa 7: 8 For the head of Syria *is* **D**, and the head of 1834
7: 8 *is* Damascus, and the head of **D** *is* Rezin; 1834
8: 4 the riches of **D** and the spoil of Samaria 1834
10: 9 not Hamath as Arpad? *is* not Samaria as **D**? 1834
17: 1 The burden of **D**. Behold, Damascus *is* 1834
Isa 17: 1 **D** *is* taken away from *being* a city, and 1834
17: 3 the kingdom from **D**, and the remnant of 1834
Jer 49:23 Concerning **D**. Hamath is confounded, and 1834
49:24 **D** is waxed feeble, *and* turneth herself to 1834
49:27 I will kindle a fire in the wall of **D**, and 1834
Eze 27:18 **D** *was* thy merchant in the multitude of 1834
47:16 which *is* between the border of **D** and 1834
47:17 the border of **D**, and the north northward, 1834
47:18 from **D**, and from Gilead, and from the land 1834
48: 1 Hazar-enan, the border of **D** northward, to 1834
Am 1: 3 For three transgressions of **D**, and for four, 1834
1: 5 I will break also the bar of **D**, and cut off 1834
3:12 in the corner of a bed, and in **D** *in* a couch. 1833
5:27 I cause you to go into captivity beyond **D**, 1834
Zec 9: 1 of Hadrach, and **D** *shall be* the rest thereof: 1834
Ac 9: 2 And desired of him letters to **D** to 1154
9: 3 And as *he* journeyed, he came near **D**: and 1154
9: 8 him by the hand, and brought *him* into **D**. 1154
9:10 And there was a certain disciple at **D**, 1154
9:19 days with the disciples which were at **D**. 1154
9:22 and confounded the Jews which dwelt at **D**, 1154
9:27 how he had preached boldly at **D** in 1154
22: 5 and went to **D**, to bring them which were 1154
22: 6 and was come nigh unto **D** about noon, 1154
22:10 Lord said unto me, Arise, and go into **D**; 1154
22:11 of them that were with me, I came into **D**. 1154
26:12 Whereupon as I went to **D** with authority 1154
26:20 But shewed first unto them of **D**, 1154
2Co 11:32 In **D** the governor under Aretas the king 1154
Gal 1:17 into Arabia, and returned again unto **D**. 1154

DAMNABLE (1) [DAMNATION]
2Pe 2: 1 who privily shall bring in **d** heresies, 684

DAMNATION (11) [DAMNABLE, DAMNED]
Mt 23:14 therefore ye shall receive the greater **d**. 2917
23:33 of vipers, how can ye escape the **d** of hell? 2920
Mk 3:29 but is in danger of eternal **d**. 2920
12:40 long prayers: these shall receive greater **d**. 2917
Lk 20:47 the same shall receive greater **d**. 2917
Jn 5:29 have done evil, unto the resurrection of **d**. 2920
Ro 3: 8 that good may come? whose **d** is just. 2917
13: 2 that resist shall receive to themselves **d**. 2917
1Co 11:29 eateth and drinketh **d** to himself, 2917
1Ti 5:12 Having **d**, because they have cast off *their* 2917
2Pe 2: 3 lingereth not, and their **d** slumbereth not. 684

DAMNED (3) [DAMNATION]
Mk 16:16 but he that believeth not shall be **d**. 2632
Ro 14:23 And he that doubteth is **d** if he eat, because 2632
2Th 2:12 That they all might be **d** who believed not 2919

DAMSEL (40) [DAMSEL'S, DAMSELS]
Ge 24:14 *that* the **d** to whom I shall say, Let down 5291
24:16 the **d** *was* very fair to look upon, a virgin, 5291
24:28 the **d** ran, and told *them of* her mother's 5291
24:55 Let the **d** abide with us *a few* days, at 5291
24:57 We will call the **d**, and inquire at her 5291
34: 3 he loved the **d**, and spake kindly unto 5291
34: 3 the damsel, and spake kindly unto the **d**. 5291
34: 4 saying, Get me this **d** to wife. 3207
34:12 say unto me: but give me the **d** to wife. 5291
Dt 22:15 shall the father of the **d**, and her mother, 5291
22:19 give *them* unto the father of the **d**, because 5291
22:20 *tokens of* virginity be not found for the **d**: 5291
22:21 they shall bring out the **d** to the door of her 5291
22:23 If a **d** *that is* a virgin be betrothed unto a 5291
22:24 the **d**, because she cried not, *being* in 5291
22:25 if a man find a betrothed **d** in the field, and 5291
22:26 unto the **d** thou shalt do nothing; *there is* in 5291
22:26 *there is* in the **d** no sin *worthy* of death: 5291
22:27 *and* the betrothed **d** cried, and *there was* 5291
22:28 If a man find a **d** *that is* a virgin, which is 5291
Jdg 5:30 divided the prey; to every man a **d** *or* two; 7356
19: 3 when the father of the **d** saw him, 5291
Ru 2: 5 was set over the reapers, Whose **d** *is* this? 5291
2: 6 It *is* the Moabitish **d** that came back with 5291
1Ki 1: 3 So they sought for a fair **d** throughout all 5291
1: 4 the **d** *was* very fair, and cherished the king, 5291
Mt 14:11 brought in a charger, and given to the **d**: 2877
26:69 and a **d** came unto him, saying, Thou also 3814
Mk 5:39 and weep? the **d** is not dead, but sleepeth. 3813
5:40 he taketh the father and the mother of the **d**, 3813
5:40 and entereth in where the **d** was lying. 3813
5:41 And he took the **d** by the hand, and 3813
5:41 being interpreted, **D** (I say unto thee) 2877
5:42 And straightway the **d** arose, and walked; 2877
6:22 that sat with *him,* the king said unto the **d**, 2877
6:28 his head in a charger, and gave it to the **d**: 2877
6:28 the damsel: and the **d** gave it to her mother. 2877
Jn 18:17 Then saith the **d** that kept the door unto 3814
Ac 12:13 a **d** came to hearken, named Rhoda. 3814
16:16 a certain **d** possessed with a spirit of 3814

DAMSEL'S (8) [DAMSEL]
Dt 22:15 bring forth *the tokens of* the **d** virginity 5291
22:16 the **d** father shall say unto the elders, I gave 5291
22:29 give unto the **d** father fifty *shekels* of silver, 5291
Jdg 19: 4 his father in law, the **d** father, retained him; 5291
19: 5 the **d** father said unto his son in law, 5291
19: 6 for the **d** father had said unto the man, 5291
19: 8 the **d** father said, Comfort thine heart, 5291
19: 9 the **d** father, said unto him, Behold now, 5291

DAMSELS (3) [DAMSEL]
Ge 24:61 her **d**, and they rode upon the camels, and 5291
1Sa 25:42 with five of hers that went after her; 5291
Ps 68:25 among *them were* the **d** playing with 5959

DAN (72) [DAN-JAAN, DANITES, LESHEM, MAHANEH-DAN]
Ge 14:14 and eighteen, and pursued *them* unto **D**. 1835
30: 6 me a son: therefore called she his name **D**. 1835
35:25 Rachel's handmaid; **D**, and Naphtali: 1835

Ge 46:23 And the sons of **D**; Hushim. 1835
49:16 **D** shall judge his people, as one of 1835
49:17 **D** shall be a serpent by the way, an adder in 1835
Ex 1: 4 **D**, and Naphtali, Gad, and Asher. 1835
31: 6 the son of Ahisamach, of the tribe of **D**: 1835
35:34 the son of Ahisamach, of the tribe of **D**. 1835
38:23 of the tribe of **D**, an engraver, and 1835
Lev 24:11 the daughter of Dibri, of the tribe of **D**:) 1835
Nu 1:12 Of **D**; Ahiezer the son of Ammishaddai. 1835
1:38 Of the children of **D**, *by* their generations, 1835
1:39 *even* of the tribe of **D**, *were* threescore and 1835
2:25 The standard of the camp of **D** *shall be* on 1835
2:25 the captain of the children of **D** *shall be* 1835
2:31 in the camp of **D** *were* an hundred thousand 1835
7:66 prince of the children of **D**, *offered:* 1835
10:25 the camp of the children of **D** set forward, 1835
13:12 Of the tribe of **D**, Ammiel the son of 1835
26:42 These *are* the sons of **D** after their families: 1835
26:42 These *are* the families of **D** after their 1835
34:22 the prince of the tribe of the children of **D**, 1835
Dt 27:13 and Asher, and Zebulun, **D**, and Naphtali. 1835
33:22 of **D** he said, Dan *is* a lion's whelp: he shall 1835
33:22 of Dan he said, **D** *is* a lion's whelp: he shall 1835
34: 1 shewed him all the land of Gilead, unto **D**, 1835
Jos 19:40 children of **D** according to their families. 1835
19:47 the coast of the children of **D** went out *too* 1835
19:47 the children of **D** went up to fight against 1835
19:47 and dwelt therein, and called Leshem, **D**, 1835
19:47 Dan, after the name of **D** their father. 1835
19:48 children of **D** according to their families, 1835
21: 5 out of the tribe of **D**, and out of the half 1835
21:23 out of the tribe of **D**, Eltekeh with her 1835
Jdg 1:34 the Amorites forced the children of **D** into 1835
5:17 why did **D** remain *in* ships? 1835
13:25 to move him at times in the camp of **D**, 1835
18: 2 the children of **D** sent of their family five 1835
18:16 which *were* of the children of **D**, stood *by* 1835
18:22 and overtook the children of **D**. 1835
18:23 they cried unto the children of **D**. And they 1835
18:25 the children of **D** said unto him, Let not thy 1835
18:26 the children of **D** went their way: and 1835
18:29 they called the name of the city **D**, after 1835
18:29 after the name of **D** their father, who was 1835
18:30 the children of **D** set up the graven image: 1835
18:30 his sons were priests to the tribe of **D** until 1839
20: 1 from **D** even to Beer-sheba, with the land 1835
1Sa 3:20 all Israel from **D** even to Beer-sheba knew 1835
2Sa 3:10 over Judah, from **D** even to Beer-sheba. 1835
17:11 from **D** even to Beer-sheba, as the sand that 1835
24: 2 from **D** even to Beer-sheba, and number ye 1835
24:15 there died of the people from **D** even to 1835
1Ki 4:25 his fig tree, from **D** even to Beer-sheba, 1835
12:29 one in Beth-el, and the other put he in **D**. 1835
12:30 *to worship* before the one, *even* unto **D**. 1835
15:20 **D**, and Abel-beth-maachah, and all 1835
2Ki 10:29 that *were in* Beth-el, and that *were* in **D**. 1835
1Ch 2: 2 **D**, Joseph, and Benjamin, Naphtali, Gad, 1835
21: 2 number Israel from Beer-sheba even to **D**; 1835
27:22 Of **D**, Azareel the son of Jeroham. 1835
2Ch 2:14 The son of a woman of the daughters of **D**, 1835
16: 4 **D**, and Abel-maim, and all the store cities 1835
30: 5 all Israel, from Beer-sheba even to **D**, 1835
Jer 4:15 For a voice declareth from **D**, and 1835
8:16 snorting of his horses was heard from **D**: 1835
Eze 27:19 **D** also and Javan going to and fro occupied 1835
48: 1 are his sides east *and* west; a *portion for* **D**. 1835
48: 2 by the border of **D**, from the east side unto 1835
48:32 one gate of Benjamin, one gate of **D**. 1835
Am 8:14 of Samaria, and say, Thy god, O **D**, liveth; 1835

DANCE (8) [DANCED, DANCES, DANCING]

Jdg 21:21 if the daughters of Shiloh come out to **d** in 2342
Job 21:11 little ones like a flock, and their children **d**. 7540
Ps 149: 3 Let them praise his name in the **d**: let them 4234
150: 4 Praise him with the timbrel and **d**: 4234
Ecc 3: 4 to laugh; a time to mourn, and a time to **d**; 7540
Isa 13:21 shall dwell there, and satyrs shall **d** there. 7540
Jer 31:13 shall the virgin rejoice in the **d**, both young 4234
La 5:15 is ceased; our **d** is turned into mourning. 4234

DANCED (6) [DANCE]

Jdg 21:23 of them that **d**, whom they caught: 2342
2Sa 6:14 David **d** before the LORD with all *his* 3769
Mt 11:17 have piped unto you, and ye have not **d**; *3738*
14: 6 the daughter of Herodias **d** before them, *3738*
Mk 6:22 and **d**, and pleased Herod and them that sat *3738*
Lk 7:32 have piped unto you, and ye have not **d**; *3738*

DANCES (6) [DANCE]

Ex 15:20 went out after her with timbrels and with **d**. 4246
Jdg 11:34 out to meet him with timbrels and with **d**: 4246
21:21 daughters of Shiloh come out to dance in **d**, 4246
1Sa 21:11 they not sing one to another of him in **d**, 4246
29: 5 of whom they sang one to another in **d**, 4246
Jer 31: 4 shalt go forth in the **d** of them that make 4234

DANCING (7) [DANCE]

Ex 32:19 the camp, that he saw the calf, and the **d**: 4246
1Sa 18: 6 singing and **d**, to meet king Saul, 4246
30:16 **d**, because of all the great spoil that they 2287
2Sa 6:16 David leaping and **d** before the LORD; 3769
1Ch 15:29 looking out at a window saw king David **d** 7540
Ps 30:11 hast turned for me my mourning into **d**: 4234
Lk 15:25 nigh to the house, he heard musick and **d**. *5525*

DANDLED (1)

Isa 66:12 upon *her* sides, and be **d** upon *her* knees. 8173

DANGER (7) [DANGEROUS]

Mt 5:21 whosoever shall kill shall be **in d** of *1777*
5:22 a cause shall be **in d** of the judgment: *1777*
5:22 Raca, shall be **in d** of the council: *1777*
5:22 *Thou* fool, shall be **in d** of hell fire. *1777*
Mk 3:29 but is in **d** of eternal damnation. *1777*
Ac 19:27 So *that* not only this our craft is **in d** to be *2793*
19:40 For we are **in d** to be called in question for *2793*

DANGEROUS (1) [DANGER]

Ac 27: 9 and when sailing was now **d**, because *2000*

DANIEL (83) [BELTESHAZZAR]

1Ch 3: 1 the second **D**, of Abigail the Carmelitess: 1840
Ezr 8: 2 of the sons of Ithamar; **D**: of the sons of 1840
Ne 10: 6 **D**, Ginnethon, Baruch, 1840
Eze 14:14 Noah, **D**, and Job, were in it, they should 1840
14:20 **D**, and Job, *were* in it, *as* I live, 1840
28: 3 Behold, thou *art* wiser than **D**; *there is* no 1840
Da 1: 6 **D**, Hananiah, Mishael, and Azariah: 1840
1: 7 for he gave unto **D** *the name of* 1840
1: 8 **D** purposed in his heart that he would not 1840
1: 9 Now God had brought **D** into favour and 1840
1:10 the prince of the eunuchs said unto **D**, I fear 1840
1:11 said **D** to Melzar, whom the prince of 1840
1:11 the prince of the eunuchs had set over **D**, 1840
1:17 **D** had understanding in all visions and 1840
1:19 among them all was found none like **D**, 1840
1:21 **D** continued *even* unto the first year of king 1840
2:13 they sought **D** and his fellows to be slain. 1841
2:14 **D** answered with counsel and wisdom to 1841
2:15 Then Arioch made the thing known to **D**. 1841
2:16 **D** went in, and desired of the king that he 1841
2:17 **D** went to his house, and made the thing 1841
2:18 that **D** and his fellows should not perish 1841
2:19 *was* the secret revealed unto **D** in a night 1841
2:19 Then **D** blessed the God of heaven. 1841
2:20 **D** answered and said, Blessed be the name 1841
2:24 Therefore **D** went in unto Arioch, 1841
2:25 Arioch brought in **D** before the king in 1841
2:26 The king answered and said to **D**, 1841
2:27 **D** answered in the presence of the king, and 1841
2:46 worshipped **D**, and commanded that *they* 1841
2:47 The king answered unto **D**, and said, Of a 1841
2:48 the king made **D** a great man, and gave him 1841
2:49 **D** requested of the king, and he set 1841
2:49 but **D** *sat* in the gate of the king. 1841
4: 8 at the last **D** came in before me, 1841
4:19 **D**, whose name *was* Belteshazzar, 1841
5:12 of doubts, were found in the same **D**, 1841
5:12 now let **D** be called, and he will shew 1841
5:13 was **D** brought in before the king. *And* 1841
5:13 *And* the king spake and said unto **D**, 1841
5:13 and said unto Daniel, *Art* thou that **D**, 1841
5:17 **D** answered and said before the king, 1841
5:29 they clothed **D** with scarlet, and *put* a chain 1841
6: 2 three presidents; of whom **D** *was* first: 1841
6: 3 this **D** was preferred above the presidents 1841
6: 4 princes sought to find occasion against **D** 1841
6: 5 shall not find any occasion against this **D**, 1841
6:10 Now when **D** knew that the writing *was* 1841
6:11 found **D** praying and making supplication 1841
6:13 and said before the king, *That* **D**, 1841
6:14 and set *his* heart on **D** to deliver him: 1841
6:16 they brought **D**, and cast *him* into the den 1841
6:16 *Now* the king spake and said unto **D**, 1841
6:17 might not be changed concerning **D**. 1841
6:20 he cried with a lamentable voice unto **D**: 1841
6:20 *and* the king spake and said to **D**, O Daniel, 1841
6:20 *and* the king spake and said to Daniel, O **D**, 1841
6:21 said **D** unto the king, O king, live for ever. 1841
6:23 commanded that *they* should take **D** up out 1841
6:23 So **D** was taken up out of the den, and 1841
6:24 brought those men which had accused **D**, 1841
6:26 *men* tremble and fear before the God of **D**: 1841
6:27 who hath delivered **D** from the power of 1841
6:28 So this **D** prospered in the reign of Darius, 1841
7: 1 Belshazzar king of Babylon **D** had a dream 1841
7: 2 **D** spake and said, I saw in my vision by 1841
7:15 I **D** was grieved in my spirit in the midst of 1841
7:28 *As for* me **D**, my cogitations much troubled 1841
8: 1 *even unto* me **D**, after that which appeared 1840
8:15 when I, *even* I **D**, had seen the vision, and 1840
8:27 I **D** fainted, and was sick *certain* days; 1840
9: 2 In the first year of his reign I **D** understood 1840
9:22 and talked with me, and said, O **D**, 1840
10: 1 king of Persia a thing was revealed unto **D**, 1840
10: 2 In those days I **D** was mourning three full 1840
10: 7 I **D** alone saw the vision: for the men that 1840
10:11 he said unto me, O **D**, a man greatly 1840
10:12 said he unto me, Fear not, **D**: for from 1840
12: 4 thou, O **D**, shut up the words, and seal 1840
12: 5 I **D** looked, and, behold, there stood other 1840
12: 9 he said, Go thy way, **D**: for the words *are* 1840
Mt 24:15 spoken of by **D** the prophet, stand in *1158*
Mk 13:14 spoken of by **D** the prophet, standing where *1158*

DANITES (4) [DAN]

Jdg 13: 2 of the family of the **D**, whose name *was* 1839
18: 1 in those days the tribe of the **D** sought them 1839
18:11 went from thence of the family of the **D**, 1839
1Ch 12:35 of the **D** expert in war twenty and 1839

DAN-JAAN (1) [DAN]

2Sa 24: 6 and they came to **D**, and about to Zidon, 1842

DANNAH (1)

Jos 15:49 And **D**, and Kirjath-sannah, which *is* Debir, 1837

DAPPLED See GRISLED

DARA (1)

1Ch 2: 6 and Ethan, and Heman, and Calcol, and **D**: 1873

DARDA (1)

1Ki 4:31 Heman, and Chalcol, and **D**, the sons of 1862

DARE (5) [DURST]

Job 41:10 None *is so* fierce that **d stir him up**: who 5782
Ro 5: 7 for a good *man* some would even **d** to die. *5111*
Ro 15:18 For I will not **d** to speak of any of *those* *5111*
1Co 6: 1 **D** any of you, having a matter against *5111*
2Co 10:12 For we **d** not make *ourselves* of *5111*

DARE; DARED See DURST

DARICS See DRAMS

DARING See DURST

DARIUS (25)

Ezr 4: 5 even until the reign of **D** king of Persia. 1867
4:24 year of the reign of **D** king of Persia. 1868
5: 5 them to cease, till the matter came to **D**: 1868
5: 6 on *this* side the river, sent unto **D** the king: 1868
5: 7 written thus: Unto **D** the king, all peace. 1868
6: 1 **D** the king made a decree, and search was 1868
6:12 I **D** have made a decree; let it be done with 1868
6:13 according to that which **D** the king had 1868
6:14 and **D**, and Artaxerxes king of Persia. 1868
6:15 *in* the sixth year of the reign of **D** the king. 1868
Ne 12:22 the priests, to the reign of **D** the Persian. 1867
Da 5:31 **D** the Median took the kingdom, 1868
6: 1 It pleased **D** to set over the kingdom an 1868
6: 6 said thus unto him, King **D**, live for ever. 1868
6: 9 Wherefore king **D** signed the writing and 1868
6:25 king **D** wrote unto all people, nations, 1868
6:28 So this Daniel prospered in the reign of **D**, 1868
9: 1 In the first year of **D** the son of Ahasuerus, 1867
11: 1 Also I in the first year of **D** the Mede, 1867
Hag 1: 1 In the second year of **D** the king, in 1867
1:15 in the second year of **D** the king. 1867
2:10 of the ninth *month*, in the second year of **D**, 1867
Zec 1: 1 the eighth month, in the second year of **D**, 1867
1: 7 *is* the month Sebat, in the second year of **D**, 1867
7: 1 it came to pass in the fourth year of king **D**, 1867

DARK (43)

Ge 15:17 that, when the sun went down, and it was **d**, 5939
Lev 13: 6 *if* the plague *be* **somewhat d**, and 3544
13:21 lower than the skin, but *be* **somewhat d**; 3544
13:26 than the *other* skin, but *be* **somewhat d**; 3544
13:28 not in the skin, but it *be* **somewhat d**; 3544
13:56 the plague *be* **somewhat d** after 3544
Nu 12: 8 even apparently, and not in **d speeches**; 2420
Jos 2: 5 when it was **d**, that the men went out: 2822
2Sa 22:12 **d** waters, *and* thick clouds of the skies. 2841
Ne 13:19 Jerusalem began to be **d** before the sabbath, 6751
Job 3: 9 Let the stars of the twilight thereof be **d**; 2821
12:25 They grope *in* the **d** without light, and 2822
18: 6 The light shall be **d** in his tabernacle, and 2821
22:13 can he judge through the **d** *cloud?* 6205
24:16 In the **d** *they* dig *through* houses, 2822
Ps 18:11 his pavilion round about him *were* **d** waters 2824
35: 6 Let their way be **d** and slippery: and let 2822
49: 4 I will open my **d saying** upon the harp. 2420
74:20 for the **d places** of the earth are full *of* 4285
78: 2 in a parable: I will utter **d sayings** of old: 2420
88:12 Shall thy wonders be known in the **d**? and 2822
105:28 He sent darkness, and **made** it **d**; and 2821
Pr 1: 6 the words of the wise, and their **d sayings**. 2420
7: 9 in the evening, in the black and **d** night: 653
Isa 29:15 their works are in the **d**, and they say, 4285
45:19 spoken in secret, in a **d** place of the earth: 2822
Jer 13:16 before your feet stumble upon the **d** 5399
La 3: 6 He hath set me in **d places**, as they that be 4285
Eze 8:12 ancients of the house of Israel do in the **d**, 2822
32: 7 the heaven, and **make** the stars thereof **d**; 6937
32: 8 the bright lights of heaven will I **make d** 6937
34:12 been scattered in the cloudy and **d** day. 6205
Da 8:23 understanding **d sentences**, shall stand up. 2420
Joel 2:10 the sun and the moon shall be **d**, and 6937
Am 5: 8 and **maketh** the day **d** *with* night: 2821
5:20 even **very d**, and no brightness in it? 651
Mic 3: 6 it shall be **d** unto you, that *ye* shall not 2821
3: 6 and the day shall be **d** over them. 6937
Zec 14: 6 *that* the light shall not be clear, *nor* **d**: 7087
Lk 11:36 therefore *be* full of light, having no part **d**, *4652*
Jn 6:17 And it was now **d**, and Jesus was not come *4653*
20: 1 when it was yet **d**, unto the sepulchre, and *4653*
2Pe 1:19 as unto a light that shineth in a **d** place, *850*

DARKEN (1) [DARKENED, DARKENETH, DARKISH, DARKLY, DARKNESS]

Am 8: 9 and I will **d** the earth in the clear day: 2821

DARKENED (19) [DARKEN]

Ex 10:15 of the whole earth, so that the land was **d**; 2821
Ps 69:23 Let their eyes be **d**, that *they* see not; and 2821
Ecc 12: 2 the light, or the moon, or the stars, be not **d**, 2821
12: 3 those that look out of the windows be **d**, 2821
Isa 5:30 and the light is **d** in the heavens thereof. 2821
9:19 wrath of the LORD of hosts is the land **d**, 6272
13:10 the sun shall be **d** in his going forth, and 2821
24:11 all joy is **d**, the mirth of the land is gone. 6150
Eze 30:18 At Tehaphnehes also the day shall be **d**, 2821
Joel 3:15 The sun and the moon shall be **d**, and 6937
Zec 11:17 his right eye shall be **utterly d**. 3543+3543
Mt 24:29 tribulation of those days shall the sun be **d**, *4654*
Mk 13:24 the sun shall be **d**, and the moon shall not *4654*
Lk 23:45 And the sun was **d**, and the vail of *4654*
Ro 1:21 and their foolish heart was **d**. *4654*
11:10 Let their eyes be **d**, that *they* may not see, *4654*
Eph 4:18 Having the understanding **d**, *4654*
Rev 8:12 so as the third *part* of them was **d** and *4654*
9: 2 the air were **d** by reason of the smoke of *4654*

DARKENETH (1) [DARKEN]

Job 38: 2 Who *is* this that **d** counsel by words 2821

DARKISH (1) [DARKEN]

Lev 13:39 spots in the skin of their flesh *be* **d** white; 3544

D

D

DARKLY (1) [DARKEN]

1Co 13:12 For now we see through a glass, **d**; *135+1722*

DARKNESS (162) [DARKEN]

Ge 1: 2 void; and **d** *was* upon the face of the deep. 2822
1: 4 and God divided the light from the **d**. 2822
1: 5 the light Day, and the **d** he called Night. 2822
1:18 the night, and to divide the light from the **d**: 2822
15:12 and, lo, a horror of great **d** fell upon him. 2825
Ex 10:21 that there may be **d** over the land of Egypt, 2822
10:21 land of Egypt, even **d** *which* may be felt. 2822
10:22 there was a thick **d** in all the land of Egypt 2822
14:20 it was a cloud and **d** *to them,* but it gave 2822
20:21 Moses drew near unto the **thick d** where 6205
Dt 4:11 *with* **d**, clouds, and thick darkness. 2822
4:11 *with* darkness, clouds, and **thick d**. 6205
5:22 of the cloud, and of the **thick d**, *with* a 6205
5:23 ye heard the voice out of the midst of the **d**, 2822
28:29 as the blind gropeth in **d**, and thou shalt not 653
Jos 24: 7 he put **d** between you and the Egyptians, 3990
1Sa 2: 9 and the wicked shall be silent in **d**; 2822
2Sa 22:10 and came down; and **d** *was* under his feet. 6205
22:12 he made **d** pavilions round about him, 2822
22:29 and the LORD will lighten my **d**. 2822
1Ki 8:12 said that *he* would dwell in the **thick d**. 6205
2Ch 6: 1 said that *he* would dwell in the **thick d**. 6205
Job 3: 4 Let that day be **d**; let not God regard it 2822
3: 5 Let **d** and the shadow of death stain it; let a 2822
3: 6 *As for* that night, let **d** seize upon it; let it not 652
5:14 They meet with **d** in the daytime, and 2822
10:21 *even* to the land of **d** and the shadow of 2822
10:22 A land of **d**, as darkness itself; *and of* 5890
10:22 A land of darkness, as **d** itself; *and of* 652
10:22 any order, and *where* the light is as **d**. 652
12:22 He discovereth deep *things* out of **d**, and 2822
15:22 believeth not that *he* shall return out of **d**, 2822
15:23 that the day of **d** is ready at his hand. 2822
15:30 He shall not depart out of **d**; the flame shall 2822
17:12 into day: the light *is* short, because of **d**. 2822
17:13 mine house: I have made my bed in the **d**. 2822
18:18 He shall be driven from light into **d**, and 2822
19: 8 cannot pass, and he hath set **d** in my paths. 2822
20:26 All **d** *shall be* hid in his secret places: a fire 2822
22:11 Or **d**, *that* thou canst not see; and 2822
23:17 Because I was not cut off before the **d**, 2822
23:17 *neither* hath he covered the **d** from my face. 652
28: 3 He setteth an end to **d**, and searcheth out all 2822
28: 3 the stones of **d**, and the shadow of death. 652
29: 3 *and when* by his light I walked *through* **d**; 2822
30:26 and when I waited for light, there came **d**. 652
34:22 *There is* no **d**, nor shadow of death, 2822
37:19 we cannot order *our speech* by reason of **d**. 2822
38: 9 and **thick d** a swaddling band for it, 6205
38:19 and *as for* **d**, where *is* the place thereof, 2822
Ps 18: 9 and came down: and **d** *was* under his feet. 6205
18:11 He made **d** his secret place; his pavilion 2822
18:28 the LORD my God will enlighten my **d**. 2822
82: 5 will they understand; they walk on in **d**: 2825
88: 6 laid me in the lowest pit, in **d**, in the deeps. 4285
88:18 far from me, *and* mine acquaintance *into* **d**. 4285
91: 6 *Nor* for the pestilence *that* walketh in **d**; 652
97: 2 Clouds and **d** *are* round about him: 6205
104:20 Thou makest **d**, and it is night: wherein all 2822
105:28 He sent **d**, and made it dark; and 2822
107:10 Such as sit in **d** and in the shadow of death, 2822
107:14 He brought them out of **d** and the shadow 2822
112: 4 Unto the upright there ariseth light in the **d**: 2822
139:11 If I say, Surely the **d** shall cover me; 2822
139:12 Yea, the **d** hideth not from thee; but 2822
139:12 the **d** and the light *are* both alike *to thee.* 2825
143: 3 he hath made me to dwell in **d**, as those that 4285
Pr 2:13 of uprightness, to walk in the ways of **d**; 2822
4:19 The way of the wicked *is* as **d**: they know 653
20:20 his lamp shall be put out in obscure **d**. 2822
Ecc 2:13 excelleth folly, as far as light excelleth **d**. 2822
2:14 *are* in his head; but the fool walketh in **d**: 2822
5:17 All his days also he eateth in **d**, and *he hath* 2822
6: 4 departeth in **d**, and his name shall be 2822
6: 4 and his name shall be covered with **d**. 2822
11: 8 yet let him remember the days of **d**; 2822
Isa 5:20 that put **d** for light, and light for darkness; 2822
5:20 that put darkness for light, and light for **d**; 2822
5:30 behold **d** *and* sorrow, and the light is 2822
8:22 behold trouble and **d**, dimness of anguish; 2825
8:22 of anguish; and *they shall be* driven *to* **d**. 653
9: 2 The people that walked in **d** have seen a 2822
29:18 shall see out of obscurity, and out of **d**. 2822
42: 7 them that sit in **d** out of the prison house. 2822
42:16 I will make **d** light before them, and 4285
45: 3 I will give thee the treasures of **d**, and 2822
45: 7 I form the light, and create **d**: I make peace, 2822
47: 5 Sit thou silent, and get thee into **d**, 2822
49: 9 to *them* that *are* in **d**, Shew yourselves. 2822
50:10 that walketh *in* **d**, and hath no light? 2825
58:10 in obscurity, and thy **d** *be* as the noonday: 653
59: 9 for brightness, *but* we walk in **d**. 653
60: 2 the **d** shall cover the earth, and 2822
60: 2 cover the earth, and **gross d** the people: 6205
Jer 2:31 a land of **d**? wherefore say my people, 3991
13:16 before he **cause d**, and before your feet 2821
13:16 the shadow of death, *and* make *it* **gross d**. 6205
23:12 shall be unto them as slippery *ways* in the **d**: 653
La 3: 2 and brought *me into* **d**, but not *into* light. 2822
Eze 32: 8 set **d** upon thy land, saith the Lord GOD. 2822
Da 2:22 secret *things:* he knoweth what *is* in the **d**, 2816
Joel 2: 2 A day of **d** and of gloominess, a day of 2822
2: 2 a day of clouds and of thick **d**, 6205
2:31 The sun shall be turned into **d**, and 2822
Am 4:13 that maketh the morning **d**, and 5890
5:18 the day of the LORD *is* **d**, and not light. 2822
5:20 *Shall* not the day of the LORD *be* **d**, and 2822
Mic 7: 8 when I sit in **d**, the LORD *shall be* a light 2822
Na 1: 8 and **d** shall pursue his enemies. 2822
Zep 1:15 and desolation, a day of **d** and gloominess, 2822
Zep 1:15 gloominess, a day of clouds and **thick d**, 6205
Mt 4:16 The people which sat in **d** saw great light; *4655*
6:23 be evil, thy whole body shall be **full of d**. *4652*
6:23 If therefore the light that is in thee be **d**, *4655*
6:23 is in thee be darkness, how great *is* that **d**? *4655*
8:12 the kingdom shall be cast out into outer **d**: *4655*
10:27 What I tell you in **d**, *that* speak ye in light: *4653*
22:13 take him away, and cast *him* into outer **d**; *4655*
25:30 ye the unprofitable servant into outer **d**: *4655*
27:45 Now from the sixth hour there was **d** over *4655*
Mk 15:33 there was **d** over the whole land until *4655*
Lk 1:79 To give light to them that sit in **d** and *in* *4655*
11:34 *thine eye* is evil, thy body also *is* **full of d**. *4652*
11:35 that the light which is in thee be not **d**. *4655*
12: 3 Therefore whatsoever ye have spoken in **d** *4653*
22:53 but this is your hour, and the power of **d**. *4655*
23:44 there was a **d** over all the earth until *4655*
Jn 1: 5 And the light shineth in **d**; and the darkness *4653*
1: 5 in darkness; and the **d** comprehended it not. *4653*
3:19 and men loved **d** rather than light, because *4655*
8:12 he that followeth me shall not walk in **d**, *4653*
12:35 ye have the light, lest **d** come upon you: *4653*
12:35 for he that walketh in **d** knoweth not *4653*
12:46 believeth on me should not abide in **d**. *4653*
Ac 2:20 The sun shall be turned into **d**, and *4655*
13:11 there fell on him a mist and a **d**; *4655*
26:18 *and* to turn *them* from **d** to light, and *4655*
Ro 2:19 of the blind, a light of them which are in **d**, *4655*
13:12 let us therefore cast off the works of **d**, and *4655*
1Co 4: 5 will bring to light the hidden *things* of **d**, *4655*
2Co 4: 6 who commanded the light to shine out of **d**, *4655*
6:14 and what communion hath light with **d**? *4655*
Eph 5: 8 For ye were sometimes **d**, but now *are ye* *4655*
5:11 fellowship with the unfruitful works of **d**, *4655*
6:12 against the rulers of the **d** of this world, *4655*
Col 1:13 Who hath delivered us from the power of **d**, *4655*
1Th 5: 4 But ye, brethren, are not in **d**, that *that* day *4655*
5: 5 of the day: we are not of the night, nor of **d**. *4655*
Heb 12:18 burned with fire, nor unto blackness, and **d**, *4655*
1Pe 2: 9 you out of **d** into his marvellous light: *4655*
2Pe 2: 4 to hell, and delivered *them* into chains of **d**, *2217*
2:17 to whom the mist of **d** is reserved for ever. *4655*
1Jn 1: 5 that God is light, and in him is no **d** at all. *4653*
1: 6 and walk in **d**, we lie, and do not the truth: *4655*
2: 8 because the **d** is past, and the true light now *4653*
2: 9 hateth his brother, is in **d** *even* until now. *4653*
2:11 But he that hateth his brother is in **d**, and *4653*
2:11 and walketh in **d**, and knoweth not whither *4653*
2:11 because that **d** hath blinded his eyes. *4653*
Jude 1: 6 under **d** unto the judgment of the great day. *2217*
1:13 to whom is reserved the blackness of **d** for *4655*
Rev 16:10 and his kingdom was **full of d**; and *4656*

DARKON (2)

Ezr 2:56 the children of **D**, the children of Giddel, 1874
Ne 7:58 The children of Jaala, the children of **D**, 1874

DARLING (2)

Ps 22:20 the sword; my **d** from the power of the dog. 3173
35:17 their destructions, my **d** from the lions. 3173

DART (3) [DARTS]

Job 41:26 the spear, the **d**, nor the habergeon. 4551
Pr 7:23 Till a **d** strike through his liver; as a bird 2671
Heb 12:20 shall be stoned, or thrust through with a **d**: *1002*

DARTS (4) [DART]

2Sa 18:14 he took three **d** in his hand, and thrust them 7626
2Ch 32: 5 and made **d** and shields in abundance. 7973
Job 41:29 **D** are counted as stubble: he laugheth at 8455
Eph 6:16 able to quench all the fiery **d** of the wicked. *956*

DASH (7) [DASHED, DASHETH]

2Ki 8:12 wilt **d** their children, and rip up their 7376
Ps 2: 9 thou shalt **d** them **in pieces** like a potter's 5310
91:12 lest thou **d** thy foot against a stone. 5062
Isa 13:18 bows also shall **d** the young men **to pieces**; 7376
Jer 13:14 I will **d** them one against another, even 5310
Mt 4: 6 lest at any time thou **d** thy foot against a *4350*
Lk 4:11 lest at any time thou **d** thy foot against a *4350*

DASHED (5) [DASH]

Ex 15: 6 O LORD, hath **d in pieces** the enemy. 7492
Isa 13:16 Their children also shall be **d to pieces** 7376
Hos 10:14 the mother was **d in pieces** upon *her* 7376
13:16 their infants shall be **d in pieces**, and 7376
Na 3:10 her young children also were **d in pieces** at 7376

DASHETH (2) [DASH]

Ps 137: 9 and **d** thy little ones against the stones. 5310
Na 2: 1 He that **d in pieces** is come up before thy 6327

DATHAN (10)

Nu 16: 1 the son of Levi, and **D** and Abiram, 1885
16:12 Moses sent to call **D** and Abiram, the sons 1885
16:24 the tabernacle of Korah, **D**, and Abiram. 1885
16:25 rose up and went unto **D** and Abiram; 1885
16:27 of Korah, **D**, and Abiram, on every side: 1885
16:27 **D** and Abiram came out, and stood *in* 1885
26: 9 sons of Eliab; Nemuel, and **D**, and Abiram. 1885
26: 9 This *is that* **D** and Abiram, *which were* 1885
Dt 11: 6 what he did unto **D** and Abiram, the sons of 1885
Ps 106:17 The earth opened and swallowed up **D**, and 1885

DAUB (1) [DAUBED, DAUBING]

Eze 13:11 Say unto them which **d** *it with* untempered 2902

DAUBED (7) [DAUB]

Ex 2: 3 **d** it with slime and with pitch, and put 2560
Eze 13:10 and lo, others **d** it *with* untempered *morter:* 2902
13:12 Where *is* the daubing where*with* ye have **d** 2902
13:14 that ye have **d** *with* untempered *morter,* 2902
13:15 upon them that have **d** it *with* untempered 2902
13:15 The wall *is* no *more,* neither they that **d** it; 2902
Eze 22:28 her prophets have **d** them *with* untempered 2902

DAUBING (1) [DAUB]

Eze 13:12 Where *is* the **d** where*with* ye have daubed 2915

DAUGHTER (324) [DAUGHTER'S, DAUGHTERS]

Ge 11:29 Milcah, the **d** of Haran, the father of 1323
11:31 Sarai his **d in law**, his son Abram's wife; 3618
20:12 she *is* the **d** of my father, but not 1323
20:12 of my father, but not the **d** of my mother; 1323
24:23 said, Whose **d** *art* thou? tell me, I pray thee: 1323
24:24 I *am* the **d** of Bethuel the son of Milcah, 1323
24:47 I asked her, and said, Whose **d** *art* thou? 1323
24:47 she said, The **d** of Bethuel, Nahor's son, 1323
24:48 take my master's brother's **d** unto his son. 1323
25:20 the **d** of Bethuel the Syrian of Padan-aram, 1323
26:34 to wife Judith the **d** of Beeri the Hittite, 1323
26:34 and Bashemath the **d** of Elon the Hittite: 1323
28: 9 Mahalath the **d** of Ishmael Abraham's son, 1323
29: 6 Rachel his **d** cometh with the sheep. 1323
29:10 when Jacob saw Rachel the **d** of Laban his 1323
29:18 thee seven years for Rachel thy younger **d**. 1323
29:23 that he took Leah his **d**, and brought her to 1323
29:24 Laban gave unto his **d** Leah Zilpah his 1323
29:28 and he gave him Rachel his **d** to wife *also.* 1323
29:29 Laban gave to Rachel his **d** Bilhah his 1323
30:21 afterwards she bare a **d**, and called her 1323
34: 1 Dinah the **d** of Leah, which she bare unto 1323
34: 3 his soul clave unto Dinah the **d** of Jacob, 1323
34: 5 heard that he had defiled Dinah his **d**: 1323
34: 7 folly in Israel in lying with Jacob's **d**; 1323
34: 8 of my son Shechem longeth for your **d**: 1323
34:17 will we take our **d**, and we will be gone. 1323
34:19 because he had delight in Jacob's **d**: 1323
36: 2 Adah the **d** of Elon the Hittite, and 1323
36: 2 Aholibamah the **d** of Anah the daughter of 1323
36: 2 Aholibamah the daughter of Anah the **d** of 1323
36: 3 Bashemath Ishmael's **d**, sister of Nebajoth. 1323
36:14 the **d** of Anah, daughter of Zibeon, 1323
36:14 of Anah, **d** of Zibeon, Esau's wife: 1323
36:18 *that came* of Aholibamah the **d** of Anah, 1323
36:25 Dishon, and Aholibamah the **d** of Anah. 1323
36:39 the **d** of Matred, the daughter of Mezahab. 1323
36:39 the daughter of Matred, the **d** of Mezahab. 1323
38: 2 Judah saw there a **d** of a certain Canaanite, 1323
38:11 said Judah to Tamar his **d in law**, Remain a 3618
38:12 in process of time the **d** of Shuah Judah's 1323
38:16 (for he knew not that she *was* his **d in law**:) 3618
38:24 Tamar thy **d in law** hath played the harlot; 3618
41:45 he gave him to wife Asenath the **d** of 1323
41:50 which Asenath the **d** of Poti-pherah priest 1323
46:15 Jacob in Padan-aram, with his **d** Dinah: 1323
46:18 whom Laban gave to Leah his **d**, and 1323
46:20 which Asenath the **d** of Poti-pherah priest 1323
46:25 which Laban gave unto Rachel his **d**, and 1323
Ex 1:16 kill him: but if it *be* a **d**, then she shall live. 1323
1:22 the river, and every **d** ye shall save alive. 1323
2: 1 house of Levi, and took *to wife* a **d** of Levi. 1323
2: 5 the **d** of Pharaoh came down to wash 1323
2: 7 said his sister to Pharaoh's **d**, Shall I go 1323
2: 8 Pharaoh's **d** said to her, Go. And the maid 1323
2: 9 Pharaoh's **d** said unto her, Take this child 1323
2:10 she brought him unto Pharaoh's **d**, and 1323
2:21 and he gave Moses Zipporah his **d**. 1323
6:23 **d** of Amminadab, sister of Naashon, 1323
20:10 thou, nor thy son, nor thy **d**, 1323
21: 7 if a man sell his **d** to be a maidservant, 1323
21:31 he have gored a son, or have gored a **d**, 1323
Lev 12: 6 purifying are fulfilled, for a son, or for a **d**, 1323
18: 9 the **d** of thy father, or daughter of thy 1323
18: 9 daughter of thy father, or **d** of thy mother, 1323
18:10 The nakedness of thy son's **d**, or of thy 1323
18:10 thy son's daughter, or of thy daughter's **d**, 1323
18:11 The nakedness of thy father's wife's **d**, 1323
18:15 not uncover the nakedness of thy **d in law**: 3618
18:17 the nakedness of a woman and her **d**, 1323
18:17 neither shalt thou take her son's **d**, or 1323
18:17 or her daughter's **d**, to uncover her 1323
19:29 Do not prostitute thy **d**, to cause her to be a 1323
20:12 if a man lie with his **d in law**, both of them 3618
20:17 his father's **d**, or his mother's daughter, and 1323
20:17 or his mother's **d**, and see her nakedness, 1323
21: 2 his son, and for his **d**, and for his brother, 1323
21: 9 the **d** of any priest, if she profane herself by 1323
22:12 If the priest's **d** also be *married* unto a 1323
22:13 if the priest's **d** be a widow, or divorced, 1323
24:11 the **d** of Dibri, of the tribe of Dan:) 1323
Nu 25:15 that was slain *was* Cozbi, the **d** of Zur; 1323
25:18 the **d** of a prince of Midian, their sister, 1323
26:46 And the name of the **d** of Asher *was* Sarah. 1323
26:59 the **d** of Levi, whom *her mother* bare to 1323
27: 8 cause his inheritance to pass unto his **d**. 1323
27: 9 if he have no **d**, then ye shall give his 1323
30:16 and his wife, between the father and his **d**, 1323
36: 8 every **d**, that possesseth an inheritance in 1323
Dt 5:14 thou, nor thy son, nor thy **d**, nor thy 1323
7: 3 thy **d** thou shalt not give unto his son, 1323
7: 3 nor his **d** shalt thou take unto thy son. 1323
12:18 thy **d**, and thy manservant, and 1323
13: 6 or thy **d**, or the wife of thy bosom, or 1323
16:11 thy **d**, and thy manservant, and 1323
16:14 thy **d**, and thy manservant, and 1323
18:10 his son or his **d** to pass through the fire, 1323
22:16 I gave my **d** unto this man to wife, and 1323
22:17 *her,* saying, I found not thy **d** a maid; 1323
27:22 the **d** of his father, or the daughter of his 1323
27:22 of his father, or the **d** of his mother. 1323
28:56 and towards her son, and towards her **d**, 1323
Jos 15:16 to him will I give Achsah my **d** to wife. 1323
15:17 and he gave him Achsah his **d** to wife. 1323
Jdg 1:12 to him will I give Achsah my **d** to wife. 1323
1:13 and he gave him Achsah his **d** to wife. 1323
11:34 his **d** came out to meet him with timbrels 1323
11:34 beside her he had neither son nor **d**. 1323
11:35 he rent his clothes, and said, Alas, my **d**, 1323

Jdg 11:40 **d** of Jephthah the Gileadite four days in a 1323
19:24 *here is* my **d** a maiden, and his concubine; 1323
21: 1 There shall not any of us give his **d** unto 1323
Ru 1:22 Ruth the Moabitess, her **d in law**, with her, 3618
2: 2 And she said unto her, Go, my **d**. 1323
2: 8 Boaz unto Ruth, Hearest thou not, my **d**? 1323
2:20 Naomi said unto her **d in law**, Blessed *be* 3618
2:22 Naomi said unto Ruth her **d in law**, *It is* 3618
2:22 *It is* good, my **d**, that thou go out with his 1323
3: 1 My **d**, shall I not seek rest for thee, that it 1323
3:10 Blessed *be* thou of the LORD, my **d**: 1323
3:11 now, my **d**, fear not; I will do to thee all 1323
3:16 in law, she said, Who *art* thou, my **d**? 1323
3:18 said she, Sit still, my **d**, until thou know 1323
4:15 for thy **d in law**, which loveth thee, 3618
1Sa 1:16 Count not thine handmaid for a **d** of Belial: 1323
4:19 his **d in law**, Phinehas' wife, was with 3618
14:50 wife *was* Ahinoam, the **d** of Ahimaaz: 1323
17:25 will give him his **d**, and make his father's 1323
18:17 said to David, Behold my elder **d** Merab, 1323
18:19 Saul's **d** should have been given to David, 1323
18:20 Michal Saul's **d** loved David: and they told 1323
18:27 And Saul gave him Michal his **d** to wife. 1323
18:28 and *that* Michal Saul's **d** loved him. 1323
25:44 Saul had given Michal his **d**, David's wife, 1323
2Sa 3: 3 Absalom the son of Maacah the **d** of 1323
3: 7 whose name *was* Rizpah, the **d** of Aiah: 1323
3:13 except thou first bring Michal Saul's **d**, 1323
6:16 Michal Saul's **d** looked through a window, 1323
6:20 Michal the **d** of Saul came out to meet 1323
6:23 Therefore Michal the **d** of Saul had no 1323
11: 3 *Is* not this Bath-sheba, the **d** of Eliam, 1323
12: 3 lay in his bosom, and was unto him as a **d**. 1323
14:27 and one **d**, whose name *was* Tamar: 1323
17:25 that went in to Abigail the **d** of Nahash, 1323
21: 8 the king took the two sons of Rizpah the **d** 1323
21: 8 the five sons of Michal the **d** of Saul, 1323
21:10 Rizpah the **d** of Aiah took sackcloth, and 1323
21:11 it was told David what Rizpah the **d** of 1323
1Ki 3: 1 took Pharaoh's **d**, and brought her into 1323
4:11 which had Taphath the **d** of Solomon to 1323
4:15 he also took Basmath the **d** of Solomon to 1323
7: 8 made also a house for Pharaoh's **d**, 1323
9:16 given it *for* a present unto his **d**, 1323
9:24 Pharaoh's **d** came up out of the city of 1323
11: 1 together with the **d** of Pharaoh, *women of* 1323
15: 2 name *was* Maachah, the **d** of Abishalom. 1323
15:10 name *was* Maachah, the **d** of Abishalom. 1323
16:31 that he took *to* wife Jezebel the **d** of 1323
22:42 his mother's name *was* Azubah the **d** of 1323
2Ki 8:18 for the **d** of Ahab was his wife: and he did 1323
8:26 *was* Athaliah, the **d** of Omri king of Israel. 1323
9:34 and bury her: for she *is* a king's **d**. 1323
11: 2 Jehosheba, the **d** of king Joram, sister of 1323
14: 9 Give thy **d** to my son to wife: 1323
15:33 name *was* Jerusha, the **d** of Zadok. 1323
18: 2 name also *was* Abi, the **d** of Zachariah. 1323
19:21 The virgin the **d** of Zion hath despised thee, 1323
19:21 the **d** of Jerusalem hath shaken her head at 1323
21:19 the **d** of Haruz of Jotbah. 1323
22: 1 *was* Jedidah, the **d** of Adaiah of Boscath. 1323
23:10 or his **d** to pass through the fire to Molech. 1323
23:31 *was* Hamutal, the **d** of Jeremiah of Libnah. 1323
23:36 *was* Zebudah, the **d** of Pedaiah of Rumah. 1323
24: 8 the **d** of Elnathan of Jerusalem. 1323
24:18 *was* Hamutal, the **d** of Jeremiah of Libnah. 1323
1Ch 1:50 the **d** of Matred, the daughter of Mezahab. 1323
1:50 the daughter of Matred, the **d** of Mezahab. 1323
2: 3 *which* three were born unto him of the **d** of 1323
2: 4 Tamar his **d in law** bare him Pharez and 3618
2:21 afterward Hezron went in to the **d** of 1323
2:35 Sheshan gave his **d** to Jarha his servant to 1323
2:49 of Gibea: and the **d** of Caleb *was* Achsah. 1323
3: 2 Absalom the son of Maachah the **d** of 1323
3: 5 four, of Bath-shua the **d** of Ammiel: 1323
4:18 these *are* the sons of Bithiah the **d** of 1323
7:24 (And his **d** *was* Sherah, who built 1323
15:29 that Michal the **d** of Saul looking out at a 1323
2Ch 8:11 Solomon brought up the **d** of Pharaoh out 1323
11:18 Rehoboam took him Mahalath the **d** of 1323
11:18 Abihail the **d** of Eliab the son of Jesse; 1323
11:20 after her he took Maachah the **d** of 1323
11:21 Rehoboam loved Maachah the **d** of 1323
13: 2 His mother's name also *was* Michaiah the **d** 1323
20:31 his mother's name *was* Azubah the **d** of 1323
21: 6 for he had the **d** of Ahab to wife: and 1323
22: 2 His mother's name also *was* Athaliah the **d** 1323
22:11 Jehoshabeath, the **d** of the king, took Joash 1323
22:11 So Jehoshabeath, the **d** of king Jehoram, 1323
25:18 Give thy **d** to my son to wife: 1323
27: 1 name also *was* Jerushah, the **d** of Zadok. 1323
29: 1 name *was* Abijah, the **d** of Zechariah. 1323
Ne 6:18 his son Johanan had taken the **d** of 1323
Est 2: 7 up Hadassah, that *is*, Esther, his uncle's **d**: 1323
2: 7 and mother were dead, took for his own **d**. 1323
2:15 the **d** of Abihail the uncle of Mordecai, 1323
2:15 who had taken *her* for his **d**, was come to 1323
9:29 the **d** of Abihail, and Mordecai the Jew, 1323
Ps 9:14 all thy praise in the gates of the **d** of Zion: 1323
45:10 O **d**, and consider, and incline thine ear; 1323
45:12 the **d** of Tyre *shall be there* with a gift; 1323
45:13 The king's **d** *is* all glorious within: 1323
137: 8 O **d** of Babylon, who art *to be* destroyed; 1323
SS 7: 1 are thy feet with shoes, O prince's **d**! 1323
Isa 1: 8 the **d** of Zion is left as a cottage in a 1323
10:30 Lift up thy voice, O **d** of Gallim: cause *it* to 1323
10:32 his hand *against* the mount of the **d** of Zion, 1323
16: 1 unto the mount of the **d** of Zion. 1323
22: 4 of the spoiling of the **d** of my people. 1323
23:10 thy land as a river, O **d** of Tarshish: 1323
23:12 O thou oppressed virgin, **d** of Zidon: 1323
37:22 The virgin, the **d** of Zion, hath despised 1323
37:22 the **d** of Jerusalem hath shaken her head at 1323
47: 1 and sit in the dust, O virgin **d** of Babylon, 1323
47: 1 *there is* no throne, O **d** of the Chaldeans; 1323

Isa 47: 5 thee into darkness, O **d** of the Chaldeans: 1323
52: 2 the bands of thy neck, O captive **d** of Zion. 1323
62:11 Say ye to the **d** of Zion, Behold, 1323
Jer 4:11 the wilderness toward the **d** of my people, 1323
4:31 the voice of the **d** of Zion, *that* bewaileth 1323
6: 2 I have likened the **d** of Zion *to* a comely 1323
6:14 They have healed also the hurt of *the* **d** *of* NIH
6:23 as men for war against thee, O **d** of Zion. 1323
6:26 O **d** of my people, gird *thee* with sackcloth, 1323
8:11 For they have healed the hurt of the **d** of 1323
8:19 Behold the voice of the cry of the **d** of my 1323
8:21 For the hurt of the **d** of my people am I 1323
8:22 is not the health of the **d** of my people 1323
9: 1 night for the slain of the **d** of my people! 1323
9: 7 for how shall I do for the **d** of my people? 1323
14:17 for the virgin **d** of my people is broken *with* 1323
31:22 wilt thou go about, O thou backsliding **d**? 1323
46:11 and take balm, O virgin, the **d** of Egypt: 1323
46:19 O thou **d** dwelling in Egypt, furnish thyself 1323
46:24 The **d** of Egypt shall be confounded; 1323
48:18 Thou **d** that dost inhabit Dibon, come down 1323
49: 4 thy flowing valley, O backsliding **d**? 1323
50:42 to the battle, against thee, O **d** of Babylon. 1323
51:33 The **d** of Babylon *is* like a threshingfloor, 1323
52: 1 his mother's name *was* Hamutal the **d** of 1323
La 1: 6 from the **d** of Zion all her beauty is 1323
1:15 the **d** of Judah, *as in* a winepress. 1323
2: 1 How hath the Lord covered the **d** of Zion 1323
2: 2 wrath the strong holds of the **d** of Judah; 1323
2: 4 the eye, in the tabernacle of the **d** of Zion: 1323
2: 5 hath increased in the **d** of Judah mourning 1323
2: 8 to destroy the wall of the **d** of Zion: 1323
2:10 The elders of the **d** of Zion sit upon 1323
2:11 for the destruction of the **d** of my people; 1323
2:13 shall I liken to thee, O **d** of Jerusalem? 1323
2:13 I may comfort thee, O virgin **d** of Zion? 1323
2:15 and wag their head at the **d** of Jerusalem, 1323
2:18 unto the Lord, O wall of the **d** of Zion, 1323
3:48 for the destruction of the **d** of my people. 1323
4: 3 the **d** of my people *is* become cruel, like 1323
4: 6 For the punishment of the iniquity of the **d** 1323
4:10 in the destruction of the **d** of my people. 1323
4:21 Rejoice and be glad, O **d** of Edom, 1323
4:22 thine iniquity is accomplished, O **d** of Zion; 1323
4:22 he will visit thine iniquity, O **d** of Edom; 1323
Eze 14:20 they shall deliver neither son nor **d**; 1323
16:44 saying, As *is* the mother, *so is* her **d**. 1323
16:45 Thou *art* thy mother's **d**, that lotheth her 1323
22:11 another hath lewdly defiled his **d in law**; 3618
22:11 thee hath humbled his sister, his father's **d**. 1323
44:25 or for mother, or for son, or for **d**, 1323
Da 11: 6 for the king's **d** of the south shall come to 1323
11:17 he shall give him the **d** of women, 1323
Hos 1: 3 he went and took Gomer the **d** of Diblaim; 1323
1: 6 she conceived again, and bare a **d**. 1323
Mic 1:13 she *is* the beginning of the sin to the **d** of 1323
4: 8 the flock, the strong hold of the **d** of Zion, 1323
4: 8 the kingdom shall come to the **d** of 1323
4:10 and labour to bring forth, O **d** of Zion, 1323
4:13 Arise and thresh, O **d** of Zion: for I will 1323
5: 1 Now gather thyself in troops, O **d** of troops: 1323
7: 6 the **d** riseth up against her mother, 1323
7: 6 the **d in law** against her mother in law; 3618
Zep 3:10 *even* the **d** of my dispersed, shall bring 1323
3:14 Sing, O **d** of Zion; shout, O Israel; be glad 1323
3:14 rejoice with all the heart, O **d** of Jerusalem. 1323
Zec 2: 7 that dwellest *with* the **d** of Babylon. 1323
2:10 Sing and rejoice, O **d** of Zion: for lo, 1323
9: 9 Rejoice greatly, O **d** of Zion; shout, 1323
9: 9 daughter of Zion; shout, O **d** of Jerusalem: 1323
Mal 2:11 and hath married the **d** of a strange god. 1323
Mt 9:18 saying, My **d** is even now dead: *2364*
9:22 and when he saw her, he said, **D**, be of *2364*
10:35 and the **d** against her mother, and *2364*
10:35 and the **d in law** against her mother in law. *3565*
10:37 or **d** more than me is not worthy of me. *2364*
14: 6 the **d** of Herodias danced before them, and *2364*
15:22 my **d** is grievously vexed with a devil. *2364*
15:28 And her **d** was made whole from that *very* *2364*
21: 5 Tell ye the **d** of Sion, Behold, thy King *2364*
Mk 5:23 My **little d** lieth at the point of death: *2365*
5:34 And he said unto her, **D**, thy faith hath *2364*
5:35 *house certain* which said, Thy **d** is dead: *2364*
6:22 And when the **d** of the said Herodias came *2364*
7:25 whose **young d** had an unclean spirit, *2365*
7:26 he would cast forth the devil out of her **d**. *2364*
7:29 go thy way; the devil is gone out of thy **d**. *2364*
7:30 devil gone out, and *her* **d** laid upon the bed. *2364*
Lk 2:36 a prophetess, the **d** of Phanuel, of the tribe *2364*
8:42 For he had one only **d**, about twelve years *2364*
8:48 he said unto her, **D**, be of good comfort: *2364*
8:49 *house*, saying to him, Thy **d** is dead; *2364*
12:53 the mother against the **d**, and the daughter *2364*
12:53 the daughter, and the **d** against the mother; *2364*
12:53 the mother in law against her **d in law**, and *3565*
12:53 and the **d in law** against her mother in law. *3565*
13:16 And ought not this *woman*, being a **d** of *2364*
Jn 12:15 Fear not, **d** of Sion: behold, thy King *2364*
Ac 7:21 Pharaoh's **d** took him up, and *2364*
Heb 11:24 refused to be called the son of Pharaoh's **d**; *2364*

DAUGHTER'S (3) [DAUGHTER]

Lev 18:10 of thy son's daughter, or of thy **d** daughter, 1323
18:17 or her **d** daughter, to uncover her 1323
Dt 22:17 *yet* these *are the tokens of* my **d** virginity. 1323

DAUGHTERS (254) [DAUGHTER]

Ge 5: 4 hundred years: and he begat sons and **d**: 1323
5: 7 seven years, and begat sons and **d**: 1323
5:10 fifteen years, and begat sons and **d**: 1323
5:13 forty years, and begat sons and **d**: 1323
5:16 thirty years, and begat sons and **d**: 1323
5:19 eight hundred years, and begat sons and **d**: 1323
5:22 three hundred years, and begat sons and **d**: 1323
5:26 and two years, and begat sons and **d**: 1323
5:30 and five years, and begat sons and **d**: 1323
6: 1 of the earth, and **d** were born unto them, 1323
6: 2 That the sons of God saw the **d** of men that 1323
6: 4 when the sons of God came in unto the **d** of 1323
11:11 five hundred years, and begat sons and **d**. 1323
11:13 three years, and begat sons and **d**. 1323
11:15 three years, and begat sons and **d**. 1323
11:17 thirty years, and begat sons and **d**. 1323
11:19 nine years, and begat sons and **d**. 1323
11:21 seven years, and begat sons and **d**. 1323
11:23 two hundred years, and begat sons and **d**. 1323
11:25 nineteen years, and begat sons and **d**. 1323
19: 8 I have two **d** which have not known man; 1323
19:12 thy **d**, and whatsoever thou hast in the city, 1323
19:14 which married his **d**, and said, Up, get ye 1323
19:15 saying, Arise, take thy wife, and thy two **d**, 1323
19:16 of his wife, and upon the hand of his two **d**; 1323
19:30 in the mountain, and his two **d** with him; 1323
19:30 and he dwelt in a cave, he and his two **d**. 1323
19:36 Thus were both the **d** of Lot with child by 1323
24: 3 unto my son of the **d** of the Canaanites, 1323
24:13 the **d** of the men of the city come out to 1323
24:37 a wife to my son of the **d** of the Canaanites, 1323
27:46 weary of my life because of the **d** of Heth: 1323
27:46 if Jacob take a wife of the **d** of Heth, 1323
27:46 such as these *which are* of the **d** of the land, 1323
28: 1 Thou shalt not take a wife of the **d** of 1323
28: 2 take thee a wife from thence of the **d** of 1323
28: 6 Thou shalt not take a wife of the **d** of 1323
28: 8 Esau seeing that the **d** of Canaan pleased 1323
29:16 Laban had two **d**: the name of the elder *was* 1323
30:13 Happy am I, for the **d** will call me blessed: 1323
31:26 carried away my **d**, as captives taken with 1323
31:28 not suffered me to kiss my sons and my **d**? 1323
31:31 thou wouldest take by force thy **d** from me. 1323
31:41 I served thee fourteen years for thy two **d**, 1323
31:43 *These* **d** *are* my daughters, and *these* 1323
31:43 *These* daughters *are* my **d**, and *these* 1323
31:43 what can I do *this* day unto these my **d**, or 1323
31:50 If thou shalt afflict my **d**, or if thou shalt 1323
31:50 if thou shalt take *other* wives beside my **d**, 1323
31:55 kissed his sons and his **d**, and blessed them: 1323
34: 1 went out to see the **d** of the land. 1323
34: 9 *and* give your **d** unto us, and take our 1323
34: 9 daughters unto us, and take our **d** unto you. 1323
34:16 will we give our **d** unto you, and we will 1323
34:16 we will take your **d** to us, and we will dwell 1323
34:21 let us take their **d** to us for wives, and let us 1323
34:21 to us for wives, and let us give them our **d**. 1323
36: 2 Esau took his wives of the **d** of Canaan; 1323
36: 6 his **d**, and all the persons of his house, and 1323
37:35 and all his **d** rose up to comfort him; 1323
46: 7 his **d**, and his sons' daughters, and all his 1323
46: 7 his sons' **d**, and all his seed brought he with 1323
46:15 of his sons and his **d** *were* thirty and three. 1323
Ex 2:16 Now the priest of Midian had seven **d**: and 1323
2:20 he said unto his **d**, And where *is* he? why *is* 1323
3:22 put *them* upon your sons, and upon your **d**; 1323
6:25 Eleazar Aaron's son took him *one* of the **d** 1323
10: 9 with our old, with our sons and with our **d**, 1323
21: 4 a wife, and she have born him sons or **d**; 1323
21: 9 he shall deal with her after the manner of **d**. 1323
32: 2 and of your **d**, and bring *them* unto me. 1323
34:16 thou take of their **d** unto thy sons, and 1323
34:16 their **d** go a whoring after their gods, and 1323
Lev 10:14 thou, and thy sons, and thy **d** with thee: 1323
26:29 and the flesh of your **d** shall ye eat. 1323
Nu 18:11 to thy sons and to thy **d** with thee, by a 1323
18:19 and thy sons and thy **d** with thee, 1323
21:29 his **d** into captivity unto Sihon king of 1323
25: 1 to commit whoredom with the **d** of Moab. 1323
26:33 the son of Hepher had no sons, but **d**: 1323
26:33 the names of the **d** of Zelophehad *were* 1323
27: 1 came the **d** of Zelophehad, the son of 1323
27: 1 these *are* the names of his **d**; Mahlah, 1323
27: 7 The **d** of Zelophehad speak right: thou shalt 1323
36: 2 of Zelophehad our brother unto his **d**. 1323
36: 6 command concerning the **d** of Zelophehad, 1323
36:10 so did the **d** of Zelophehad: 1323
36:11 Milcah, and Noah, the **d** of Zelophehad, 1323
Dt 12:12 your **d**, and your menservants, and 1323
12:31 their **d** they have burnt in the fire to their 1323
23:17 There shall be no whore of the **d** of Israel, 1323
28:32 thy **d** *shall be* given unto another people, 1323
28:41 Thou shalt beget sons and **d**, but thou shalt 1323
28:53 the flesh of thy sons and of thy **d**, which 1323
32:19 of the provoking of his sons, and of his **d**. 1323
Jos 7:24 his **d**, and his oxen, and his asses, and his 1323
17: 3 the son of Manasseh, had no sons, but **d**: 1323
17: 3 these *are* the names of his **d**, Mahlah, and 1323
17: 6 Because the **d** of Manasseh had an 1323
Jdg 3: 6 they took their **d** to be their wives, and 1323
3: 6 gave their **d** to their sons, and served their 1323
11:40 *That* the **d** of Israel went yearly to lament 1323
12: 9 thirty **d**, *whom* he sent abroad, and took in 1323
12: 9 took in thirty **d** from abroad for his sons. 1323
14: 1 saw a woman in Timnath of the **d** of 1323
14: 2 I have seen a woman in Timnath of the **d** of 1323
14: 3 *Is there* never a woman among the **d** of thy 1323
21: 7 *we* will not give them of our **d** to wives? 1323
21:18 we may not give them wives of our **d**: 1323
21:21 if the **d** of Shiloh come out to dance in 1323
21:21 catch you every man his wife of the **d** of 1323
Ru 1: 6 she arose with her **d in law**, that she might 3618
1: 7 she was, and her two **d in law** with her; 3618
1: 8 Naomi said unto her two **d in law**, Go, 3618
1:11 Naomi said, Turn again, my **d**: why will 1323
1:12 Turn again, my **d**, go *your way*; for I am 1323
1:13 nay, my **d**; for it grieveth me much for your 1323
1Sa 1: 4 and to all her sons and her **d**, portions: 1323
2:21 and bare three sons and two **d**. 1323
8:13 he will take your **d** to be confectionaries, 1323
14:49 the names of his two **d** *were these*; 1323
30: 3 their wives, and their sons, and their **d**, 1323
30: 6 every man for his sons and for his **d**: 1323

D

1Sa 30:19 nor great, neither sons nor **d**, neither spoil, 1323
2Sa 1:20 lest the **d** of the Philistines rejoice, lest 1323
1:20 lest the **d** of the uncircumcised triumph. 1323
1:24 Ye **d** of Israel, weep over Saul, 1323
5:13 there were yet sons and **d** born to David. 1323
13:18 for with such robes were the king's **d** *that* 1323
19: 5 the lives of thy sons and of thy **d**, and 1323
2Ki 17:17 and their **d** to pass through the fire, 1323
1Ch 2:34 Now Sheshan had no sons, but **d**. 1323
4:27 Shimei had sixteen sons and six **d**; but his 1323
7:15 *was* Zelophehad: and Zelophehad had **d**. 1323
14: 3 and David begat moe sons and **d**. 1323
23:22 Eleazar died, and had no sons, but **d**: and 1323
25: 5 gave to Heman fourteen sons and three **d**. 1323
2Ch 2:14 The son of a woman of the **d** of Dan, and 1323
11:21 and eight sons, and threescore **d**.) 1323
13:21 begat twenty and two sons, and sixteen **d**. 1323
24: 3 him two wives; and he begat sons and **d**. 1323
28: 8 **d**, and took also away much spoil from 1323
29: 9 our sons and our **d** and our wives *are* in 1323
31:18 their wives, and their sons, and their **d**, 1323
Ezr 2:61 which took a wife of the **d** of Barzillai 1323
9: 2 For they have taken of their **d** for 1323
9:12 therefore give not your **d** unto their sons, 1323
9:12 neither take their **d** unto your sons, nor seek 1323
Ne 3:12 of the half part of Jerusalem, he and his **d**. 1323
4:14 your sons, and your **d**, your wives, and 1323
5: 2 We, our sons, and our **d**, *are* many: 1323
5: 5 bondage our sons and our **d** to be servants, 1323
5: 5 *some* of our **d** are brought unto bondage 1323
7:63 which took *one* of the **d** of Barzillai 1323
10:28 their wives, their sons, and their **d**, 1323
10:30 that we would not give our **d** unto 1323
10:30 of the land, nor take their **d** for our sons: 1323
13:25 *saying*, Ye shall not give your **d** unto their 1323
13:25 nor take their **d** unto your sons, or 1323
Job 1: 2 were born unto him seven sons and three **d**. 1323
1:13 when his sons and his **d** *were* eating and 1323
1:18 Thy sons and thy **d** *were* eating and 1323
42:13 He had also seven sons and three **d**. 1323
42:15 no women found *so* fair as the **d** of Job: 1323
Ps 45: 9 Kings' **d** *were* among thy honourable 1323
48:11 let the **d** of Judah be glad, because of thy 1323
97: 8 the **d** of Judah rejoiced, because of thy 1323
106:37 sacrificed their sons and their **d** unto devils, 1323
106:38 *even* the blood of their sons and of their **d**, 1323
144:12 *that* our **d** *may be* as corner stones, 1323
Pr 30:15 The horseleach hath two **d**, *crying*, Give, 1323
31:29 Many **d** have done virtuously, but 1323
Ecc 12: 4 all the **d** of musick shall be brought low; 1323
SS 1: 5 *am* black, but comely, O ye **d** of Jerusalem, 1323
2: 2 among thorns, so *is* my love among the **d**. 1323
2: 7 O ye **d** of Jerusalem, by the roes, and 1323
3: 5 O ye **d** of Jerusalem, by the roes, and 1323
3:10 paved *with* love, for the **d** of Jerusalem. 1323
3:11 O ye **d** of Zion, and behold king Solomon 1323
5: 8 I charge you, O **d** of Jerusalem, if ye find 1323
5:16 and this *is* my friend, O **d** of Jerusalem. 1323
6: 9 The **d** saw her, and blessed her; *yea*, 1323
8: 4 I charge you, O **d** of Jerusalem, that ye stir 1323
Isa 3:16 Because the **d** of Zion are haughty, and 1323
3:17 scab the crown of the head of the **d** of Zion, 1323
4: 4 washed away the filth of the **d** of Zion, 1323
16: 2 the **d** of Moab shall be *at* the fords of 1323
32: 9 ye careless **d**, give ear unto my speech. 1323
43: 6 and my **d** from the ends of the earth; 1323
49:22 thy **d** shall be carried upon *their* shoulders. 1323
56: 5 and a name better than *of* sons and *of* **d**: 1323
60: 4 and thy **d** shall be nursed at *thy* side. 1323
Jer 3:24 and their herds, their sons and their **d**. 1323
5:17 *which* thy sons and thy **d** should eat: 1323
7:31 to burn their sons and their **d** in the fire; 1323
9:20 teach your **d** wailing, and every one her 1323
11:22 their sons and their **d** shall die by famine: 1323
14:16 their wives, nor their sons, nor their **d**: 1323
16: 2 neither shalt thou have sons nor **d** in this 1323
16: 3 concerning the **d** that are born in this place, 1323
19: 9 flesh of their sons and the flesh of their **d**, 1323
29: 6 Take ye wives, and beget sons and **d**; 1323
29: 6 give your **d** to husbands, that they may bear 1323
29: 6 to husbands, that they may bear sons and **d**; 1323
32:35 their **d** to pass through *the fire* unto 1323
35: 8 we, our wives, our sons, nor our **d**; 1323
41:10 *even* the king's **d**, and all the people that 1323
43: 6 the king's **d**, and every person that 1323
48:46 sons are taken captives, and thy **d** captives. 1323
49: 2 and her **d** shall be burnt with fire: 1323
49: 3 cry, ye **d** of Rabbah, gird ye with sackcloth; 1323
La 3:51 mine heart because of all the **d** of my city. 1323
Eze 13:17 set thy face against the **d** of thy people, 1323
14:16 they shall deliver neither sons nor **d**; 1323
14:18 they shall deliver neither sons nor **d**, but 1323
14:22 that shall be brought forth, *both* sons and **d**: 1323
16:20 thou hast taken thy sons and thy **d**, 1323
16:27 the **d** of the Philistines, which are ashamed 1323
16:46 she and her **d** that dwell at thy left hand: 1323
16:46 at thy right hand, *is* Sodom and her **d**. 1323
16:48 she nor her **d**, as thou hast done, thou and 1323
16:48 as thou hast done, thou and thy **d**. 1323
16:49 of idleness was in her and in her **d**, 1323
16:53 the captivity of Sodom and her **d**, and 1323
16:53 and the captivity of Samaria and her **d**, then 1323
16:55 When thy sisters, Sodom and her **d**, 1323
16:55 and her **d** shall return to their former estate, 1323
16:55 and thy **d** shall return to your former estate. 1323
16:57 as *at* the time of *thy* reproach of the **d** of 1323
16:57 *are* round about her, the **d** of the Philistines, 1323
16:61 I will give them unto thee for **d**, but not by 1323
23: 2 were two women, the **d** of one mother: 1323
23: 4 they were mine, and they bare sons and **d**. 1323
23:10 they took her sons and her **d**, and slew her 1323
23:25 they shall take thy sons and thy **d**; and 1323
23:47 they shall slay their sons and their **d**, and 1323
24:21 your **d** whom ye have left shall fall by 1323
24:25 they set their minds, their sons and their **d**, 1323

Eze 26: 6 her **d** which *are* in the field shall be slain by 1323
26: 8 He shall slay with the sword thy **d** in 1323
30:18 cover her, and her **d** shall go into captivity. 1323
32:16 the **d** of the nations shall lament her: 1323
32:18 *even* her, and the **d** of the famous nations, 1323
Hos 4:13 therefore your **d** shall commit whoredom, 1323
4:14 I will not punish your **d** when they commit 1323
Joel 2:28 your sons and your **d** shall prophesy, 1323
3: 8 your **d** into the hand of the children of 1323
Am 7:17 thy sons and thy **d** shall fall by the sword, 1323
Lk 1: 5 and his wife *was* of the **d** of Aaron, and *2364*
23:28 said, **D** of Jerusalem, weep not for me, but *2364*
Ac 2:17 and your sons and your **d** shall prophesy, *2364*
21: 9 And the same *man* had four **d**, virgins, *2364*
2Co 6:18 and ye shall be my sons and **d**, saith *2364*
1Pe 3: 6 whose **d** ye are, as long as ye do well, and *5043*

DAVID (1085) [DAVID'S]

Ru 4:17 he *is* the father of Jesse, the father of **D**. 1732
4:22 And Obed begat Jesse, and Jesse begat **D**. 1732
1Sa 16:13 the spirit of the LORD came upon **D** from 1732
16:19 said, Send me **D** thy son, which *is* with 1732
16:20 and sent *them* by **D** his son unto Saul. 1732
16:21 **D** came to Saul, and stood before him: and 1732
16:22 Let **D**, I pray thee, stand before me; 1732
16:23 that **D** took a harp, and played with his 1732
17:12 Now **D** *was* the son of that Ephrathite of 1732
17:14 **D** *was* the youngest: and the three eldest 1732
17:15 **D** went and returned from Saul to feed his 1732
17:17 Jesse said unto **D** his son, Take now for thy 1732
17:20 **D** rose up early in the morning, and left 1732
17:22 **D** left his carriage in the hand of the keeper 1732
17:23 to the same words: and **D** heard *them*. 1732
17:26 **D** spake to the men that stood by him, 1732
17:28 Eliab's anger was kindled against **D**, and 1732
17:29 **D** said, What have I now done? *Is there* not 1732
17:31 when the words were heard which **D** spake, 1732
17:32 **D** said to Saul, Let no man's heart fail 1732
17:33 Saul said to **D**, Thou art not able to go 1732
17:34 **D** said unto Saul, Thy servant kept his 1732
17:37 **D** said moreover, The LORD that 1732
17:37 Saul said unto **D**, Go, and the LORD be 1732
17:38 Saul armed **D** with his armour, and he put a 1732
17:39 **D** girded his sword upon his armour, and 1732
17:39 for he had not proved *it*. And **D** said unto 1732
17:39 for I have not proved *them*. And **D** put 1732
17:41 Philistine came on and drew near unto **D**; 1732
17:42 looked about, and saw **D**, he disdained him: 1732
17:43 the Philistine said unto **D**, *Am* I a dog, 1732
17:43 And the Philistine cursed **D** by his gods. 1732
17:44 the Philistine said to **D**, Come to me, and 1732
17:45 said **D** to the Philistine, Thou comest to me 1732
17:48 came and drew nigh to meet **D**, that David 1732
17:48 that **D** hasted, and ran *toward* the army to 1732
17:49 **D** put his hand in *his* bag, and took thence a 1732
17:50 So **D** prevailed over the Philistine with a 1732
17:50 but *there was* no sword in the hand of **D**. 1732
17:51 Therefore **D** ran, and stood upon 1732
17:54 **D** took the head of the Philistine, and 1732
17:55 when Saul saw **D** go forth against 1732
17:57 as **D** returned from the slaughter of 1732
17:58 **D** answered, *I am* the son of thy servant 1732
18: 1 of Jonathan was knit with the soul of **D**, 1732
18: 3 Jonathan and **D** made a covenant, because 1732
18: 4 gave it to **D**, and his garments, even to his 1732
18: 5 **D** went out whithersoever Saul sent him, 1732
18: 6 when **D** was returned from the slaughter of 1732
18: 7 his thousands, and **D** his ten thousands. 1732
18: 8 They have ascribed unto **D** ten thousands, 1732
18: 9 Saul eyed **D** from that day and forward. 1732
18:10 **D** played with his hand, as at other times: 1732
18:11 I will smite **D** even to the wall *with it*. And 1732
18:11 And **D** avoided out of his presence twice. 1732
18:12 Saul was afraid of **D**, because the LORD 1732
18:14 **D** behaved himself wisely in all his ways; 1732
18:16 all Israel and Judah loved **D**, because 1732
18:17 Saul said to **D**, Behold my elder daughter 1732
18:18 **D** said unto Saul, Who *am* I? and what *is* 1732
18:19 daughter should have been given to **D**, 1732
18:20 Michal Saul's daughter loved **D**: and 1732
18:21 Wherefore Saul said to **D**, Thou shalt *this* 1732
18:22 *saying*, Commune with **D** secretly, and say, 1732
18:23 servants spake those words in the ears of **D**. 1732
18:23 **D** said, Seemeth it to you a light *thing* to be 1732
18:24 told him, saying, On this manner spake **D**. 1732
18:25 Saul said, Thus shall ye say to **D**, The king 1732
18:25 Saul thought to make **D** fall by the hand of 1732
18:26 when his servants told **D** these words, 1732
18:26 it pleased **D** well to be the king's son in 1732
18:27 Wherefore **D** arose and went, he and 1732
18:27 **D** brought their foreskins, and they gave 1732
18:28 and knew that the LORD *was* with **D**, 1732
18:29 Saul was yet the more afraid of **D**; and 1732
18:30 *that* **D** behaved himself more wisely than 1732
19: 1 to all his servants, that they should kill **D**. 1732
19: 2 Jonathan Saul's son delighted much in **D**: 1732
19: 2 Jonathan told **D**, saying, Saul my father 1732
19: 4 Jonathan spake good of **D** unto Saul his 1732
19: 4 the king sin against his servant, against **D**; 1732
19: 5 innocent blood, to slay **D** without a cause? 1732
19: 7 Jonathan called **D**, and Jonathan shewed 1732
19: 7 Jonathan brought **D** to Saul, and he was in 1732
19: 8 **D** went out, and fought with the Philistines, 1732
19: 9 in his hand: and **D** played with *his* hand. 1732
19:10 Saul sought to smite **D** even to the wall 1732
19:10 and **D** fled, and escaped that night. 1732
19:12 So Michal let **D** down through a window: 1732
19:14 when Saul sent messengers to take **D**, she 1732
19:15 Saul sent the messengers *again* to see **D**, 1732
19:18 So **D** fled, and escaped, and came to 1732
19:19 Behold, **D** *is* at Naioth in Ramah. 1732
19:20 Saul sent messengers to take **D**: and 1732
19:22 and said, Where *are* Samuel and **D**? 1732
20: 1 **D** fled from Naioth in Ramah, and came 1732
20: 3 **D** sware moreover, and said, Thy father 1732

1Sa 20: 4 said Jonathan unto **D**, Whatsoever thy soul 1732
20: 5 **D** said unto Jonathan, Behold, to morrow *is* 1732
20: 6 **D** earnestly asked *leave* of me that *he* might 1732
20:10 said **D** to Jonathan, Who shall tell me? 1732
20:11 Jonathan said unto **D**, Come, and let us go 1732
20:12 Jonathan said unto **D**, O LORD God of 1732
20:12 *if there be* good toward **D**, and I then 1732
20:15 of **D** every one from the face of the earth. 1732
20:16 made *a covenant* with the house of **D**, 1732
20:17 Jonathan caused **D** to swear again, because 1732
20:18 Jonathan said to *D*, To morrow *is* the new NIH
20:24 So **D** hid himself in the field: and when 1732
20:28 **D** earnestly asked *leave* of me *to go* to 1732
20:33 it was determined of his father to slay **D**. 1732
20:34 for he was grieved for **D**, because his father 1732
20:35 *into* the field at the time appointed with **D**, 1732
20:39 only Jonathan and **D** knew the matter. 1732
20:41 **D** arose out of *a place* toward the south, 1732
20:41 wept one with another, until **D** exceeded. 1732
20:42 Jonathan said to **D**, Go in peace, 1732
21: 1 came **D** to Nob to Ahimelech the priest: 1732
21: 1 Ahimelech was afraid at the meeting of **D**, 1732
21: 2 **D** said unto Ahimelech the priest, The king 1732
21: 4 the priest answered **D**, and said, *There is* no 1732
21: 5 **D** answered the priest, and said unto him, 1732
21: 8 **D** said unto Ahimelech, And is there not 1732
21: 9 **D** said, *There is* none like that; give it me. 1732
21:10 **D** arose, and fled that day for fear of Saul, 1732
21:11 unto him, *Is* not this **D** the king of the land? 1732
21:11 his thousands, and **D** his ten thousands? 1732
21:12 **D** laid up these words in his heart, and 1732
22: 1 **D** therefore departed thence, and escaped to 1732
22: 3 **D** went thence *to* Mizpeh of Moab: and 1732
22: 4 they dwelt with him all the while that **D** 1732
22: 5 the prophet Gad said unto **D**, Abide not in 1732
22: 5 **D** departed, and came *into* the forest of 1732
22: 6 When Saul heard that **D** was discovered, 1732
22:14 *so* faithful among all thy servants as **D**, 1732
22:17 because their hand also *is* with **D**, and 1732
22:20 named Abiathar, escaped, and fled after **D**. 1732
22:21 Abiathar shewed **D** that Saul had slain 1732
22:22 **D** said unto Abiathar, I knew *it* that day, 1732
23: 1 they told **D**, saying, Behold, the Philistines 1732
23: 2 Therefore **D** inquired of the LORD, 1732
23: 2 the LORD said unto **D**, Go, and smite 1732
23: 4 **D** inquired of the LORD yet again. 1732
23: 5 So **D** and his men went *to* Keilah, and 1732
23: 5 So **D** saved the inhabitants of Keilah. 1732
23: 6 the son of Ahimelech fled to **D** *to* Keilah, 1732
23: 7 it was told Saul that **D** was come *to* Keilah. 1732
23: 8 down *to* Keilah, to besiege **D** and his men. 1732
23: 9 **D** knew that Saul secretly practised 1732
23:10 said **D**, O LORD God of Israel, 1732
23:12 said **D**, Will the men of Keilah deliver me 1732
23:13 **D** and his men, *which were* about six 1732
23:13 it was told Saul that **D** was escaped from 1732
23:14 **D** abode in the wilderness in strong holds, 1732
23:15 **D** saw that Saul was come out to seek his 1732
23:15 **D** *was* in the wilderness of Ziph in a wood. 1732
23:16 went to **D** *into* the wood, and 1732
23:18 **D** abode in the wood, and Jonathan went to 1732
23:19 Doth not **D** hide himself with us in strong 1732
23:24 **D** and his men *were* in the wilderness of 1732
23:25 his men went to seek *him*. And they told **D**: 1732
23:25 when Saul heard *that*, he pursued after **D** *in* 1732
23:26 **D** and his men on that side of the mountain: 1732
23:26 **D** made haste to get away for fear of Saul; 1732
23:26 for Saul and his men compassed **D** and his 1732
23:28 Saul returned from pursuing after **D**, 1732
23:29 **D** went up from thence, and dwelt in strong 1732
24: 1 Behold, **D** *is* in the wilderness of En-gedi. 1732
24: 2 went to seek **D** and his men upon the rocks 1732
24: 3 **D** and his men remained in the sides of 1732
24: 4 the men of **D** said unto him, Behold the day 1732
24: 4 **D** arose, and cut off the skirt of Saul's robe 1732
24: 7 So **D** stayed his servants with *these* words, 1732
24: 8 **D** also rose afterward, and went out of 1732
24: 8 **D** stooped *with his* face to the earth, and 1732
24: 9 **D** said to Saul, Wherefore hearest thou 1732
24: 9 saying, Behold, **D** seeketh thy hurt? 1732
24:16 when **D** had made an end of speaking these 1732
24:16 that Saul said, *Is* this thy voice, my son **D**? 1732
24:17 he said to **D**, Thou *art* more righteous than 1732
24:22 **D** sware unto Saul. And Saul went home; 1732
24:22 **D** and his men gat them up unto the hold. 1732
25: 1 **D** arose, and went down to the wilderness 1732
25: 4 **D** heard in the wilderness that Nabal did 1732
25: 5 **D** sent out ten young men, and David said 1732
25: 5 **D** said unto the young men, Get you up to 1732
25: 8 hand unto thy servants, and to thy son **D**. 1732
25: 9 to all those words in the name of **D**, 1732
25:10 David's servants, and said, Who *is* **D**? 1732
25:13 **D** said unto his men, Gird you on every 1732
25:13 his sword; and **D** also girded on his sword: 1732
25:13 there went up after **D** about four hundred 1732
25:14 **D** sent messengers out of the wilderness to 1732
25:20 **D** and his men came down against her; 1732
25:21 Now **D** had said, Surely in vain have I kept 1732
25:22 more also do God unto the enemies of **D**, 1732
25:23 when Abigail saw **D**, she hasted, and 1732
25:23 fell before **D** on her face, and 1732
25:32 **D** said to Abigail, Blessed *be* the LORD 1732
25:35 So **D** received of her hand *that* which she 1732
25:39 when **D** heard that Nabal was dead, he said, 1732
25:39 **D** sent and communed with Abigail, to take 1732
25:40 when the servants of **D** were come to 1732
25:40 spake unto her, saying, **D** sent us unto thee, 1732
25:42 she went after the messengers of **D**, and 1732
25:43 **D** also took Ahinoam of Jezreel; and 1732
26: 1 Doth not **D** hide himself in the hill of 1732
26: 2 to seek **D** in the wilderness of Ziph. 1732
26: 3 **D** abode in the wilderness, and he saw that 1732
26: 4 **D** therefore sent out spies, and 1732
26: 5 **D** arose, and came to the place where Saul 1732
26: 5 **D** beheld the place where Saul lay, and 1732

1Sa 26: 6 answered **D** and said to Ahimelech 1732
26: 7 So **D** and Abishai came to the people by 1732
26: 8 said Abishai to **D**, God hath delivered thine 1732
26: 9 **D** said to Abishai, Destroy him not: 1732
26:10 **D** said furthermore, *As* the LORD liveth, 1732
26:12 So **D** took the spear and the cruse of water 1732
26:13 **D** went over *to* the *other* side, and stood on 1732
26:14 **D** cried to the people, and to Abner the son 1732
26:15 **D** said to Abner, *Art* not thou a *valiant* 1732
26:17 and said, *Is* this thy voice, my son **D**? 1732
26:17 **D** said, *It is* my voice, my lord, O king. 1732
26:21 return, my son **D**: for I will no more do thee 1732
26:22 **D** answered and said, Behold, the king's 1732
26:25 Saul said to **D**, Blessed *be* thou, my son 1732
26:25 said to David, Blessed *be* thou, my son **D**: 1732
26:25 So **D** went on his way, and Saul returned to 1732
27: 1 **D** said in his heart, I shall now perish one 1732
27: 2 **D** arose, and he passed over with the six 1732
27: 3 **D** dwelt with Achish at Gath, he and 1732
27: 3 *even* **D** with his two wives, Ahinoam 1732
27: 4 it was told Saul that **D** was fled *to* Gath: 1732
27: 5 **D** said unto Achish, If I have now found 1732
27: 7 the time that **D** dwelt in the country of 1732
27: 8 **D** and his men went up, and invaded 1732
27: 9 **D** smote the land, and left neither man nor 1732
27:10 **D** said, Against the south of Judah, and 1732
27:11 **D** saved neither man nor woman alive, 1732
27:11 So did **D**, and so *will be* his manner all 1732
27:12 Achish believed **D**, saying, He hath made 1732
28: 1 Achish said unto **D**, Know thou assuredly, 1732
28: 2 **D** said to Achish, Surely thou shalt know 1732
28: 2 Achish said to **D**, Therefore will I make 1732
28:17 and given it to thy neighbour, *even* to **D**: 1732
29: 2 **D** and his men passed on in the rereward 1732
29: 3 *Is* not this **D**, the servant of Saul the king of 1732
29: 5 *Is* not this **D**, of whom they sang one to 1732
29: 5 his thousands, and **D** his ten thousands? 1732
29: 6 Achish called **D**, and said unto him, Surely, 1732
29: 8 **D** said unto Achish, But what have I done? 1732
29: 9 Achish answered and said to **D**, I know that 1732
29:11 So **D** and his men rose up early to depart in 1732
30: 1 when **D** and his men were come *to* Ziklag 1732
30: 3 So **D** and his men came to the city, and 1732
30: 4 **D** and the people that *were* with him lift up 1732
30: 6 **D** was greatly distressed; for the people 1732
30: 6 **D** encouraged himself in the LORD his 1732
30: 7 **D** said to Abiathar the priest, 1732
30: 7 Abiathar brought thither the ephod to **D**. 1732
30: 8 **D** inquired at the LORD, saying, Shall I 1732
30: 9 So **D** went, he and the six hundred men that 1732
30:10 **D** pursued, he and four hundred men: 1732
30:11 brought him to **D**, and gave him bread, and 1732
30:13 **D** said unto him, To whom *belongest* thou? 1732
30:15 **D** said to him, Canst thou bring me down to 1732
30:17 **D** smote them from the twilight even unto 1732
30:18 **D** recovered all that the Amalekites had 1732
30:18 carried away: and **D** rescued his two wives. 1732
30:19 they had taken to them: **D** recovered all. 1732
30:20 **D** took all the flocks and the herds, 1732
30:21 **D** came to the two hundred men, 1732
30:21 so faint that they could not follow **D**, 1732
30:21 they went forth to meet **D**, and to meet 1732
30:21 when **D** came near to the people, he saluted 1732
30:22 of those that went with **D**, and said, 1732
30:23 said **D**, Ye shall not do so, my brethren, 1732
30:26 when **D** came to Ziklag, he sent of the spoil 1732
30:31 to all the places where **D** himself and 1732
2Sa 1: 1 when **D** was returned from the slaughter of 1732
1: 1 and **D** had abode two days in Ziklag; 1732
1: 2 *so* it was, when he came to **D**, that he fell to 1732
1: 3 **D** said unto him, From whence comest 1732
1: 4 **D** said unto him, How went the matter? 1732
1: 5 **D** said unto the young man that told him, 1732
1:11 **D** took hold on his clothes, and rent them; 1732
1:13 **D** said unto the young man that told him, 1732
1:14 **D** said unto him, How wast thou not afraid 1732
1:15 **D** called one of the young men, and said, 1732
1:16 **D** said unto him, Thy blood *be* upon thy 1732
1:17 **D** lamented with this lamentation over Saul 1732
2: 1 that **D** inquired of the LORD, saying, 1732
2: 1 **D** said, Whither shall I go up? And he said, 1732
2: 2 So **D** went up thither, and his two wives 1732
2: 3 his men that *were* with him did **D** bring up, 1732
2: 4 there they anointed **D** king over the house 1732
2: 4 they told **D**, saying, *That* the men of 1732
2: 5 **D** sent messengers unto the men of 1732
2:10 But the house of Judah followed **D**. 1732
2:11 the time that **D** was king in Hebron over 1732
2:13 the servants of **D**, went out, and 1732
2:15 of Saul, and twelve of the servants of **D**. 1732
2:17 the men of Israel, before the servants of **D**. 1732
2:31 the servants of **D** had smitten of Benjamin, 1732
3: 1 the house of Saul and the house of **D**: 1732
3: 1 **D** waxed stronger and stronger, and 1732
3: 2 unto **D** were sons born in Hebron: and 1732
3: 5 These were born to **D** in Hebron. 1732
3: 6 the house of Saul and the house of **D**, 1732
3: 8 have not delivered thee into the hand of **D**, 1732
3: 9 as the LORD hath sworn to **D**, even so 1732
3:10 to set up the throne of **D** over Israel and 1732
3:12 Abner sent messengers to **D** on his behalf, 1732
3:14 **D** sent messengers to Ish-bosheth Saul's 1732
3:17 Ye sought for **D** in times past to be king 1732
3:18 do *it*: for the LORD hath spoken of **D**, 1732
3:18 By the hand of my servant **D** I will save my 1732
3:19 Abner went also to speak in the ears of **D** in 1732
3:20 So Abner came to **D** *to* Hebron, and 1732
3:20 **D** made Abner and the men that *were* with 1732
3:21 Abner said unto **D**, I will arise and go, and 1732
3:21 **D** sent Abner away; and he went in peace. 1732
3:22 the servants of **D** and Joab came from 1732
3:22 Abner *was* not with **D** in Hebron; for he 1732
3:26 when Joab was come out from **D**, he sent 1732
3:26 from the well of Sirah: but **D** knew *it* not. 1732
3:28 afterward when **D** heard *it*, he said, I and 1732
2Sa 3:31 **D** said to Joab, and to all the people that 1732
3:31 And king **D** *himself* followed the bier. 1732
3:35 when all the people came to cause **D** to eat 1732
3:35 **D** sware, saying, So do God to me, and 1732
4: 8 the head of Ish-bosheth unto **D** *to* Hebron, 1732
4: 9 **D** answered Rechab and Baanah his 1732
4:12 **D** commanded *his* young men, and 1732
5: 1 came all the tribes of Israel to **D** unto 1732
5: 3 king **D** made a league with them in Hebron 1732
5: 3 and they anointed **D** king over Israel. 1732
5: 4 **D** *was* thirty years old when he *began* to 1732
5: 6 which spake unto **D**, saying, Except thou 1732
5: 6 thinking, **D** cannot come in hither. 1732
5: 7 Nevertheless **D** took the strong hold of 1732
5: 7 hold of Zion: the same *is* the city of **D**. 1732
5: 8 **D** said on that day, Whosoever getteth up to 1732
5: 9 So **D** dwelt in the fort, and called it the city 1732
5: 9 dwelt in the fort, and called it the city of **D**. 1732
5: 9 **D** built round about from Millo and inward. 1732
5:10 **D** went on, and grew great, and the LORD 1732
5:11 Hiram king of Tyre sent messengers to **D**, 1732
5:11 masons: and they built **D** a house. 1732
5:12 **D** perceived that the LORD had 1732
5:13 **D** took *him* mo concubines and wives out 1732
5:13 were yet sons and daughters born to **D**. 1732
5:17 that they had anointed **D** king over Israel, 1732
5:17 all the Philistines came up to seek **D**; 1732
5:17 **D** heard *of it*, and went down to the hold. 1732
5:19 **D** inquired of the LORD, saying, Shall I 1732
5:19 the LORD said unto **D**, Go up: for I will 1732
5:20 **D** came to Baal-perazim, and David smote 1732
5:20 and **D** smote them there, and said, 1732
5:21 and **D** and his men burnt them. 1732
5:23 when **D** inquired of the LORD, he said, 1732
5:25 **D** did so, as the LORD had commanded 1732
6: 1 **D** gathered together all the chosen *men* of 1732
6: 2 **D** arose, and went with all the people that 1732
6: 5 **D** and all the house of Israel played before 1732
6: 8 **D** was displeased, because the LORD had 1732
6: 9 **D** was afraid of the LORD that day, 1732
6:10 So **D** would not remove the ark of 1732
6:10 of the LORD unto him into the city of **D**: 1732
6:10 **D** carried it aside *into* the house of 1732
6:12 it was told king **D**, saying, The LORD 1732
6:12 So **D** went and brought up the ark of God 1732
6:12 *into* the city of **D** with gladness. 1732
6:14 **D** danced before the LORD with all *his* 1732
6:14 and **D** *was* girded *with* a linen ephod. 1732
6:15 So **D** and all the house of Israel brought up 1732
6:16 ark of the LORD came *into* the city of **D**, 1732
6:16 saw king **D** leaping and dancing before 1732
6:17 in the midst of the tabernacle that **D** had 1732
6:17 **D** offered burnt offerings and 1732
6:18 as soon as **D** had made an end of offering 1732
6:20 **D** returned to bless his household. 1732
6:20 the daughter of Saul came out to meet **D**, 1732
6:21 **D** said unto Michal, *It was* before 1732
7: 5 Go and tell my servant **D**, Thus saith 1732
7: 8 so shalt thou say unto my servant **D**, 1732
7:17 all this vision, so did Nathan speak unto **D**. 1732
7:18 went king **D** in, and sat before the LORD, 1732
7:20 what can **D** say more unto thee? for thou, 1732
7:26 let the house of thy servant **D** be 1732
8: 1 that **D** smote the Philistines, and 1732
8: 1 **D** took Metheg-ammah out of the hand of 1732
8: 3 **D** smote also Hadadezer, the son of Rehob, 1732
8: 4 **D** took from him a thousand *chariots*, and 1732
8: 4 **D** houghed all the chariot *horses*, but 1732
8: 5 **D** slew of the Syrians two and 1732
8: 6 Then **D** put garrisons in Syria of Damascus: 1732
8: 6 the Syrians became servants to **D**, 1732
8: 6 the LORD preserved **D** whithersoever he 1732
8: 7 **D** took the shields of gold that were on 1732
8: 8 king **D** took exceeding much brass. 1732
8: 9 When Toi king of Hamath heard that **D** had 1732
8:10 Toi sent Joram his son unto king **D**, 1732
8:11 Which also king **D** did dedicate unto 1732
8:13 **D** gat *him* a name when he returned from 1732
8:14 the LORD preserved **D** whithersoever he 1732
8:15 **D** reigned over all Israel; and David 1732
8:15 **D** executed judgment and justice unto all 1732
9: 1 **D** said, Is there yet *any* that is left of 1732
9: 2 when they had called him unto **D**, the king 1732
9: 5 king **D** sent, and fet him out of the house of 1732
9: 6 the son of Saul, was come unto **D**, he fell 1732
9: 6 **D** said, Mephibosheth. And he answered, 1732
9: 7 **D** said unto him, Fear not: for I will surely 1732
10: 2 said **D**, I will shew kindness unto Hanun 1732
10: 2 **D** sent to comfort him by the hand of his 1732
10: 3 Thinkest thou that **D** doth honour thy 1732
10: 3 hath not **D** *rather* sent his servants unto 1732
10: 5 When they told *it* unto **D**, he sent to meet 1732
10: 6 of Ammon saw that they stank before **D**, 1732
10: 7 when **D** heard *of it*, he sent Joab, and all 1732
10:17 when it was told **D**, he gathered all Israel 1732
10:17 Syrians set *themselves* in array against **D**, 1732
10:18 **D** slew *the men of* seven hundred chariots 1732
11: 1 kings go forth *to battle*, that **D** sent Joab, 1732
11: 1 But **D** tarried *still* at Jerusalem. 1732
11: 2 that **D** arose from off his bed, and 1732
11: 3 **D** sent and inquired after the woman. 1732
11: 4 **D** sent messengers, and took her; and 1732
11: 5 sent and told **D**, and said, I *am* with child. 1732
11: 6 **D** sent to Joab, *saying*, Send me Uriah 1732
11: 6 Uriah the Hittite. And Joab sent Uriah to **D**. 1732
11: 7 **D** demanded *of him* how Joab did, and how 1732
11: 8 **D** said to Uriah, Go down to thy house, 1732
11:10 when they had told **D**, saying, Uriah went 1732
11:10 **D** said unto Uriah, Camest thou not from 1732
11:11 Uriah said unto **D**, The ark, and Israel, and 1732
11:12 **D** said to Uriah, Tarry here to day also, 1732
11:13 when **D** had called him, he did eat and 1732
11:14 that **D** wrote a letter to Joab, and sent *it* by 1732
11:17 fell *some* of the people of the servants of **D**, 1732
11:18 told **D** all the things concerning the war; 1732
2Sa 11:22 shewed **D** all that Joab had sent him for. 1732
11:23 the messenger said unto **D**, Surely the men 1732
11:25 **D** said unto the messenger, Thus shalt thou 1732
11:27 **D** sent and fetched her to his house, and 1732
11:27 the thing that **D** had done displeased 1732
12: 1 the LORD sent Nathan unto **D**. And he 1732
12: 7 Nathan said to **D**, Thou *art* the man. 1732
12:13 **D** said unto Nathan, I have sinned against 1732
12:13 Nathan said unto **D**, The LORD also hath 1732
12:15 the child that Uriah's wife bare unto **D**, 1732
12:16 **D** therefore besought God for the child; and 1732
12:16 **D** fasted, and went in, and lay all night 1732
12:18 the servants of **D** feared to tell him that 1732
12:19 when **D** saw that his servants whispered, 1732
12:19 **D** perceived that the child was dead: 1732
12:19 therefore **D** said unto his servants, Is 1732
12:20 **D** arose from the earth, and washed, and 1732
12:24 **D** comforted Bath-sheba his wife, and 1732
12:27 Joab sent messengers to **D**, and said, I have 1732
12:29 And **D** gathered all the people together, and 1732
12:31 So **D** and all the people returned *unto* 1732
13: 1 that Absalom the son of **D** had a fair sister, 1732
13: 1 and Amnon the son of **D** loved her. 1732
13: 7 **D** sent home to Tamar, saying, Go now *to* 1732
13:21 when king **D** heard of all these things, he 1732
13:30 in the way, that tidings came to **D**, saying, 1732
13:37 And *D* mourned for his son every day. NIH
13:39 *the soul of* king **D** longed to go forth unto 1732
15:13 there came a messenger to **D**, saying, 1732
15:14 **D** said unto all his servants that *were* with 1732
15:22 **D** said to Ittai, Go and pass over. And Ittai 1732
15:30 **D** went up by the ascent of *mount* Olivet, 1732
15:31 *one* told **D**, saying, Ahithophel *is* among 1732
15:31 **D** said, O LORD, I pray thee, turn 1732
15:32 that *when* **D** was come to the top *of* 1732
15:33 Unto whom **D** said, If thou passest on with 1732
16: 1 when **D** was a little past the top *of the hill*, 1732
16: 5 when king **D** came to Bahurim, behold, 1732
16: 6 he cast stones at **D**, and at all the servants 1732
16: 6 at David, and at all the servants of king **D**: 1732
16:10 the LORD hath said unto him, Curse **D**. 1732
16:11 **D** said to Abishai, and to all his servants, 1732
16:13 as **D** and his men went by the way, Shimei 1732
16:23 all the counsel of Ahithophel both with **D** 1732
17: 1 I will arise and pursue after **D** *this* night: 1732
17:16 therefore send quickly, and tell **D**, saying, 1732
17:17 told them; and they went and told king **D**. 1732
17:21 went and told king **D**, and said unto David, 1732
17:21 said unto **D**, Arise, and pass quickly over 1732
17:22 **D** arose, and all the people that *were* with 1732
17:24 **D** came to Mahanaim. And Absalom 1732
17:27 to pass, when **D** was come to Mahanaim, 1732
17:29 for **D**, and for the people that *were* with 1732
18: 1 **D** numbered the people that *were* with him, 1732
18: 2 **D** sent forth a third part of the people under 1732
18: 7 Israel were slain before the servants of **D**, 1732
18: 9 Absalom met the servants of **D**. 1732
18:24 **D** sat between the two gates: and 1732
19:11 king **D** sent to Zadok and to Abiathar 1732
19:16 with the men of Judah to meet king **D**. 1732
19:22 **D** said, What have I to do with you, ye sons 1732
19:43 and we have also more *right* in **D** than ye: 1732
20: 1 a trumpet, and said, We have no part in **D**, 1732
20: 2 every man of Israel went up from after **D**, 1732
20: 3 **D** came to his house *at* Jerusalem; and 1732
20: 6 **D** said to Abishai, Now shall Sheba the son 1732
20:11 and he that *is* for **D**, *let him go* after Joab. 1732
20:21 his hand against the king, *even* against **D**: 1732
20:26 also the Jairite was a chief ruler about **D**. 1732
21: 1 there was a famine in the days of **D** three 1732
21: 1 after year; and **D** inquired of the LORD. 1732
21: 3 Wherefore **D** said unto the Gibeonites, 1732
21: 7 between **D** and Jonathan the son of Saul. 1732
21:11 it was told **D** what Rizpah the daughter of 1732
21:12 **D** went and took the bones of Saul and 1732
21:15 **D** went down, and his servants with him, 1732
21:15 against the Philistines: and **D** waxed faint. 1732
21:16 *with* a new *sword*, thought to have slain **D**. 1732
21:17 the men of **D** sware unto him, saying, 1732
21:21 the son of Shimea the brother of **D** 1732
21:22 fell by the hand of **D**, and by the hand of 1732
22: 1 **D** spake unto the LORD the words of this 1732
22:51 unto **D**, and to his seed for evermore. 1732
23: 1 Now these *be* the last words of **D**. 1732
23: 1 **D** the son of Jesse said, and the man *who* 1732
23: 8 the names of the mighty *men* whom **D** had: 1732
23: 9 *one* of the three mighty *men* with **D**, 1732
23:13 came to **D** in the harvest time unto the cave 1732
23:14 **D** *was* then in a hold, and the garrison of 1732
23:15 **D** longed, and said, Oh that one would give 1732
23:16 by the gate, and took *it*, and brought *it* to **D**: 1732
23:23 *first* three. And **D** set him over his guard. 1732
24: 1 he moved **D** against them to say, Go, 1732
24:10 **D** said unto the LORD, I have sinned 1732
24:11 For when **D** was up in the morning, 1732
24:12 Go and say unto **D**, Thus saith the LORD, 1732
24:13 So Gad came to **D**, and told him, and 1732
24:14 **D** said unto Gad, I am in a great strait: 1732
24:17 **D** spake unto the LORD when he saw 1732
24:18 Gad came that day to **D**, and said unto him, 1732
24:19 **D**, according to the saying of Gad, went up 1732
24:21 **D** said, To buy the threshingfloor of thee, 1732
24:22 Araunah said unto **D**, Let my lord the king 1732
24:24 So **D** bought the threshingfloor and 1732
24:25 **D** built there an altar unto the LORD, and 1732
1Ki 1: 1 Now king **D** was old *and* stricken in years; 1732
1: 8 and the mighty *men* which *belonged* to **D**, 1732
1:11 doth reign, and **D** our lord knoweth *it* not? 1732
1:13 Go and get thee in unto king **D**, and 1732
1:28 king **D** answered and said, Call me 1732
1:31 and said, Let my lord king **D** live for ever. 1732
1:32 king **D** said, Call me Zadok the priest, and 1732
1:37 greater than the throne of my lord king **D**. 1732
1:43 Verily our lord king **D** hath made Solomon 1732
1:47 servants came to bless our lord king **D**, 1732

D

1Ki 2: 1 Now the days of **D** drew nigh that *he* 1732
2:10 So **D** slept with his fathers, and was buried 1732
2:10 his fathers, and was buried in the city of **D**. 1732
2:11 the days that **D** reigned over Israel *were* 1732
2:12 sat Solomon upon the throne of **D** his 1732
2:24 set me on the throne of **D** my father, and 1732
2:26 ark of the Lord GOD before **D** my father, 1732
2:32 my father **D** not knowing *thereof, to wit,* 1732
2:33 upon **D**, and upon his seed, and upon his 1732
2:44 is privy to, that thou didst to **D** my father: 1732
2:45 the throne of **D** shall be established before 1732
3: 1 and brought her into the city of **D**, 1732
3: 3 walking in the statutes of **D** his father: 1732
3: 6 Thou hast shewed unto thy servant **D** my 1732
3: 7 thy servant king instead of **D** my father: 1732
3:14 as thy father **D** did walk, then I will 1732
5: 1 his father: for Hiram was ever a lover of **D**. 1732
5: 3 Thou knowest how that **D** my father could 1732
5: 5 as the LORD spake unto **D** my father, 1732
5: 7 which hath given unto **D** a wise son over 1732
6:12 with thee, which I spake unto **D** thy father: 1732
7:51 Solomon brought in the *things* which **D** his 1732
8: 1 of the LORD out of the city of **D**, 1732
8:15 which spake with his mouth unto **D** my 1732
8:16 but I chose **D** to be over my people Israel. 1732
8:17 it was in the heart of **D** my father to build a 1732
8:18 the LORD said unto **D** my father, 1732
8:20 I am risen up in the room of **D** my father, 1732
8:24 Who hast kept with thy servant **D** my father 1732
8:25 keep with thy servant **D** my father that thou 1732
8:26 which thou spakest unto thy servant **D** my 1732
8:66 that the LORD had done for **D** his servant, 1732
9: 4 as **D** thy father walked, in integrity of heart, 1732
9: 5 as I promised to **D** thy father, saying, 1732
9:24 **D** unto her house which *Solomon* had built 1732
11: 4 his God, as *was* the heart of **D** his father. 1732
11: 6 fully after the LORD, as *did* **D** his father. 1732
11:12 days I will not do it for **D** thy father's sake: 1732
11:13 will give one tribe to thy son for **D** my 1732
11:15 when **D** was in Edom, and Joab the captain 1732
11:21 when Hadad heard in Egypt that **D** slept 1732
11:24 when **D** slew them *of Zobah:* and they went 1732
11:27 repaired the breaches of the city of **D** his 1732
11:33 and my judgments, as *did* **D** his father. 1732
11:34 the days of his life for **D** my servant's sake, 1732
11:36 that **D** my servant may have a light alway 1732
11:38 my commandments, as **D** my servant did; 1732
11:38 as I built for **D**, and will give Israel unto 1732
11:39 I will for this afflict the seed of **D**, but 1732
11:43 and was buried in the city of **D** his father: 1732
12:16 saying, What portion have we in **D**? 1732
12:16 now see to thine own house, **D**. So Israel 1732
12:19 So Israel rebelled against the house of **D** 1732
12:20 was none that followed the house of **D**, 1732
12:26 shall the kingdom return to the house of **D**: 1732
13: 2 a child *shall be* born unto the house of **D**, 1732
14: 8 the kingdom away from the house of **D**, 1732
14: 8 *yet* thou hast not been as my servant **D**, 1732
14:31 was buried with his fathers in the city of **D**. 1732
15: 3 his God, as the heart of **D** his father. 1732
15: 5 Because **D** did *that* which *was* right in 1732
15: 8 and they buried him in the city of **D**: 1732
15:11 the eyes of the LORD, as *did* **D** his father. 1732
15:24 was buried with his fathers in the city of **D** 1732
22:50 was buried with his fathers in the city of **D** 1732
2Ki 8:19 not destroy Judah for **D** his servant's sake, 1732
8:24 was buried with his fathers in the city of **D**: 1732
9:28 sepulchre with his fathers in the city of **D**. 1732
12:21 buried him with his fathers in the city of **D**: 1732
14: 3 of the LORD, yet not like **D** his father: 1732
14:20 Jerusalem with his fathers in the city of **D**. 1732
15: 7 buried him with his fathers in the city of **D**: 1732
15:38 was buried with his fathers in the city of **D** 1732
16: 2 of the LORD his God, like **D** his father. 1732
16:20 was buried with his fathers in the city of **D**: 1732
17:21 For he rent Israel from the house of **D**; and 1732
18: 3 according to all that **D** his father did. 1732
20: 5 saith the LORD, the God of **D** thy father, 1732
21: 7 of which the LORD said to **D**, and 1732
22: 2 walked in all the way of **D** his father, and 1732
1Ch 2:15 Ozem the sixth, **D** the seventh: 1732
3: 1 Now these were the sons of **D**, which were 1732
3: 9 *These were* all the sons of **D**, beside 1732
4:31 These *were* their cities unto the reign of **D**. 1732
6:31 these *are they* whom **D** set over the service 1732
7: 2 whose number *was* in the days of **D** two 1732
9:22 whom **D** and Samuel the seer did ordain in 1732
10:14 turned the kingdom unto **D** the son of Jesse. 1732
11: 1 all Israel gathered themselves to **D** unto 1732
11: 3 **D** made a covenant with them in Hebron 1732
11: 3 they anointed **D** king over Israel, 1732
11: 4 **D** and all Israel went *to* Jerusalem, which *is* 1732
11: 5 the inhabitants of Jebus said to **D**, 1732
11: 5 Nevertheless **D** took the castle of Zion, 1732
11: 5 the castle of Zion, which *is* the city of **D**. 1732
11: 6 **D** said, Whosoever smiteth the Jebusites 1732
11: 7 **D** dwelt in the castle; therefore they called 1732
11: 7 therefore they called it the city of **D**. 1732
11: 9 So **D** waxed greater and greater: for 1732
11:10 the chief of the mighty *men* whom **D** had, 1732
11:11 number of the mighty *men* whom **D** had; 1732
11:13 He was with **D** at Pas-dammim, and 1732
11:15 thirty captains went down to the rock to **D**, 1732
11:16 **D** *was* then in the hold, and the Philistines' 1732
11:17 **D** longed, and said, Oh that one would give 1732
11:18 by the gate, and took *it*, and brought *it* to **D**: 1732
11:18 **D** would not drink *of* it, but poured it out to 1732
11:25 *first* three: and **D** set him over his guard. 1732
12: 1 Now these *are* they that came to **D** to 1732
12: 8 **D** into the hold to the wilderness men of 1732
12:16 of Benjamin and Judah to the hold unto **D**. 1732
12:17 **D** went out to meet them, and answered 1732
12:18 *and he said,* Thine *are we,* **D**, and on thy 1732
12:18 **D** received them, and made them captains 1732
12:19 there fell *some* of Manasseh to **D**, when he 1732

1Ch 12:21 they helped **D** against the band *of* 1732
12:22 For at *that* time day by day there came to **D** 1732
12:23 *and* came to **D** to Hebron, to turn 1732
12:31 by name, to come and make **D** king. 1732
12:38 to Hebron, to make **D** king over all Israel: 1732
12:38 of Israel *were of* one heart to make **D** king. 1732
12:39 there they were with **D** three days, eating 1732
13: 1 **D** consulted with the captains of thousands 1732
13: 2 **D** said unto all the congregation of Israel, 1732
13: 5 So **D** gathered all Israel together, 1732
13: 6 **D** went up, and all Israel, to Baalah, *that is,* 1732
13: 8 **D** and all Israel played before God with all 1732
13:11 **D** was displeased, because the LORD had 1732
13:12 **D** was afraid of God that day, saying, 1732
13:13 So **D** brought not the ark *home* to himself 1732
13:13 not the ark *home* to himself to the city of **D**, 1732
14: 1 Hiram king of Tyre sent messengers to **D**, 1732
14: 2 **D** perceived that the LORD had 1732
14: 3 **D** took moe wives at Jerusalem: and 1732
14: 3 and **D** begat moe sons and daughters. 1732
14: 8 when the Philistines heard that **D** was 1732
14: 8 all the Philistines went up to seek **D**. 1732
14: 8 **D** heard *of it,* and went out against them. 1732
14:10 **D** inquired of God, saying, Shall I go up 1732
14:11 to Baal-perazim; and **D** smote them there. 1732
14:11 **D** said, God hath broken in upon mine 1732
14:12 **D** gave a commandment, and they were 1732
14:14 Therefore **D** inquired again of God; and 1732
14:16 **D** therefore did as God commanded him: 1732
14:17 the fame of **D** went out into all lands; and 1732
15: 1 *D* made him houses in the city of David, NIH
15: 1 *David* made him houses in the city of **D**, 1732
15: 2 **D** said, None ought to carry the ark of God 1732
15: 3 **D** gathered all Israel together to Jerusalem, 1732
15: 4 **D** assembled the children of Aaron, and 1732
15:11 **D** called for Zadok and Abiathar 1732
15:16 **D** spake to the chief of the Levites to 1732
15:25 So **D**, and the elders of Israel, and 1732
15:27 **D** *was* clothed with a robe of fine linen, 1732
15:27 **D** also *had* upon him an ephod of linen. 1732
15:29 of the LORD came to the city of **D**, 1732
15:29 out at a window saw king **D** dancing 1732
16: 1 set it in the midst of the tent that **D** had 1732
16: 2 when **D** had made an end of offering 1732
16: 7 on that day **D** delivered first *this psalm* to 1732
16:43 and **D** returned to bless his house. 1732
17: 1 Now it came to pass, as **D** sat in his house, 1732
17: 1 that **D** said to Nathan the prophet, Lo, 1732
17: 2 Nathan said unto **D**, Do all that *is* in thine 1732
17: 4 Go and tell **D** my servant, Thus saith 1732
17: 7 thus shalt thou say unto my servant **D**, 1732
17:15 all this vision, so did Nathan speak unto **D**. 1732
17:16 **D** the king came and sat before 1732
17:18 What can **D** *speak* more to thee for 1732
17:24 *let* the house of **D** thy servant *be* 1732
18: 1 that **D** smote the Philistines, and 1732
18: 3 **D** smote Hadarezer king of Zobah unto 1732
18: 4 **D** took from him a thousand chariots, and 1732
18: 4 **D** also houghed all the chariot *horses,* but 1732
18: 5 **D** slew of the Syrians two and 1732
18: 6 **D** put *garrisons* in Syria-damascus; 1732
18: 6 Thus the LORD preserved **D** 1732
18: 7 **D** took the shields of gold that were on 1732
18: 8 of Hadarezer, brought **D** very much brass, 1732
18: 9 **D** had smitten all the host of Hadarezer 1732
18:10 He sent Hadoram his son to king **D**, 1732
18:11 Them also king **D** dedicated unto 1732
18:13 Thus the LORD preserved **D** 1732
18:14 So **D** reigned over all Israel, and executed 1732
18:17 the sons of **D** *were* chief about the king. 1732
19: 2 **D** said, I will shew kindness unto Hanun 1732
19: 2 **D** sent messengers to comfort him 1732
19: 2 So the servants of **D** came into the land of 1732
19: 3 Thinkest thou that **D** doth honour thy 1732
19: 5 and told **D** how the men were served. 1732
19: 6 that they had made themselves odious to **D**, 1732
19: 8 when **D** heard *of it,* he sent Joab, and all 1732
19:17 it was told **D**; and he gathered all Israel, 1732
19:17 So when **D** had put the battle in array 1732
19:18 **D** slew of the Syrians seven thousand *men* 1732
19:19 they made peace with **D**, and became his 1732
20: 1 **D** tarried at Jerusalem. And Joab smote 1732
20: 2 **D** took the crown of their king from off his 1732
20: 3 dealt **D** with all the cities of the children of 1732
20: 3 **D** and all the people returned *to* Jerusalem. 1732
20: 8 they fell by the hand of **D**, and by the hand 1732
21: 1 and provoked **D** to number Israel. 1732
21: 2 **D** said to Joab and to the rulers of 1732
21: 5 sum of the number of the people unto **D**. 1732
21: 8 **D** said unto God, I have sinned greatly, 1732
21:10 Go and tell **D**, saying, Thus saith 1732
21:11 So Gad came to **D**, and said unto him, 1732
21:13 **D** said unto Gad, I am in a great strait: 1732
21:16 **D** lift up his eyes, and saw the angel of 1732
21:16 **D** and the elders *of Israel, who were* 1732
21:17 **D** said unto God, *Is it* not I *that* 1732
21:18 the LORD commanded Gad to say to **D**, 1732
21:18 that **D** should go up, and set up an altar 1732
21:19 **D** went up at the saying of Gad, which he 1732
21:21 And as **D** came to Ornan, Ornan looked and 1732
21:21 Ornan looked and saw **D**, and went out of 1732
21:21 bowed himself to **D** *with his* face to 1732
21:22 **D** said to Ornan, Grant me the place of *this* 1732
21:23 And Ornan said unto **D**, Take *it* to thee, and 1732
21:24 king **D** said to Ornan, Nay; but I will verily 1732
21:25 So **D** gave to Ornan for the place six 1732
21:26 **D** built there an altar unto the LORD, and 1732
21:28 At that time when **D** saw that the LORD 1732
21:30 **D** could not go before it to inquire of God: 1732
22: 1 **D** said, This *is* the house of the LORD 1732
22: 2 **D** commanded to gather together 1732
22: 3 **D** prepared iron in abundance for the nails 1732
22: 4 of Tyre brought much cedar wood to **D**. 1732
22: 5 **D** said, Solomon my son *is* young and 1732
22: 5 So **D** prepared abundantly before his death. 1732

1Ch 22: 7 **D** said to Solomon, My son, *as for* me, 1732
22:17 **D** also commanded all the princes of Israel 1732
23: 1 So when **D** was old and full *of* days, 1732
23: 5 which I made, *said* **D**, to praise *therewith.* NIH
23: 6 **D** divided them *into* courses among 1732
23:25 For **D** said, The LORD God of Israel hath 1732
23:27 For by the last words of **D** the Levites 1732
24: 3 **D** distributed them, both Zadok of the sons 1732
24:31 of Aaron in the presence of **D** the king, 1732
25: 1 Moreover **D** and the captains of the host 1732
26:26 of the dedicate *things,* which **D** the king, 1732
26:31 In the fortieth year of the reign of **D** they 1732
26:32 whom king **D** made rulers over 1732
27:18 Of Judah, Elihu, *one* of the brethren of **D**: 1732
27:23 **D** took not the number of them from twenty 1732
27:24 in the account of the chronicles of king **D**. 1732
28: 1 **D** assembled all the princes of Israel, 1732
28: 2 Then **D** the king stood up upon his feet, and 1732
28:11 **D** gave to Solomon his son the pattern of 1732
28:19 All *this, said* **D**, the LORD made me NIH
28:20 **D** said to Solomon his son, Be strong and 1732
29: 1 Furthermore **D** the king said unto all 1732
29: 9 and **D** the king also rejoiced *with* great joy. 1732
29:10 Wherefore **D** blessed the LORD before all 1732
29:10 **D** said, Blessed *be* thou, LORD God of 1732
29:20 **D** said to all the congregation, Now bless 1732
29:22 they made Solomon the son of **D** king 1732
29:23 the LORD as king instead of **D** his father, 1732
29:24 and all the sons likewise of king **D**, 1732
29:26 Thus **D** the son of Jesse reigned over all 1732
29:29 Now the acts of **D** the king, first and last, 1732
2Ch 1: 1 Solomon the son of **D** was strengthened in 1732
1: 4 the ark of God had **D** brought up from 1732
1: 4 to *the place which* **D** had prepared for it: 1732
1: 8 Thou hast shewed great mercy unto **D** my 1732
1: 9 let thy promise unto **D** my father be 1732
2: 3 As thou didst deal with **D** my father, and 1732
2: 7 whom **D** my father did provide. 1732
2:12 who hath given to **D** the king a wise son, 1732
2:14 with the cunning *men* of my lord **D** thy 1732
2:17 after the numbering where*with* **D** his father 1732
3: 1 where *the LORD* appeared unto **D** his 1732
3: 1 in the place that **D** had prepared in 1732
5: 1 Solomon brought in *all the things* that **D** his 1732
5: 2 of the LORD out of the city of **D**, 1732
6: 4 he spake with his mouth to my father **D**, 1732
6: 6 have chosen **D** to be over my people Israel. 1732
6: 7 Now it was in the heart of **D** my father to 1732
6: 8 the LORD said to **D** my father, 1732
6:10 for I am risen up in the room of **D** my 1732
6:15 Thou which hast kept with thy servant **D** 1732
6:16 keep with thy servant **D** my father *that* 1732
6:17 which thou hast spoken unto thy servant **D**. 1732
6:42 remember the mercies of **D** thy servant. 1732
7: 6 which **D** the king had made to praise 1732
7: 6 for ever, when **D** praised by their ministry; 1732
7:10 that the LORD had shewed unto **D**, 1732
7:17 as **D** thy father walked, and do according to 1732
7:18 according as I have covenanted with **D** thy 1732
8:11 **D** unto the house that he had built for her: 1732
8:11 My wife shall not dwell in the house of **D** 1732
8:14 according to the order of **D** his father, 1732
8:14 so had **D** the man of God commanded. 1732
9:31 he was buried in the city of **D** his father: 1732
10:16 saying, What portion have we in **D**? 1732
10:16 *and* now, **D**, see to thine own house. So all 1732
10:19 Israel rebelled against the house of **D** unto 1732
11:17 for three years they walked in the way of **D** 1732
11:18 daughter of Jerimoth the son of **D** *to* wife, 1732
12:16 his fathers, and was buried in the city of **D**: 1732
13: 5 gave the kingdom over Israel to **D** for ever, 1732
13: 6 the servant of Solomon the son of **D**, 1732
13: 8 of the LORD in the hand of the sons of **D**; 1732
14: 1 and they buried him in the city of **D**: 1732
16:14 he had made for himself in the city of **D**, 1732
17: 3 he walked in the first ways of his father **D**, 1732
21: 1 was buried with his fathers in the city of **D**. 1732
21: 7 LORD would not destroy the house of **D**, 1732
21: 7 of the covenant that he had made with **D**, 1732
21:12 Thus saith the LORD God of **D** thy father, 1732
21:20 Howbeit they buried him in the city of **D**, 1732
23: 3 as the LORD hath said of the sons of **D**. 1732
23:18 whom **D** had distributed in the house of 1732
23:18 and with singing, as it was ordained by **D**. 1732
24:16 they buried him in the city of **D** among 1732
24:25 they buried him in the city of **D**, but 1732
27: 9 and they buried him in the city of **D**: 1732
28: 1 the sight of the LORD, like **D** his father: 1732
29: 2 according to all that **D** his father had done. 1732
29:25 according to the commandment of **D**, and 1732
29:26 the Levites stood with the instruments of **D**, 1732
29:27 with the instruments ordained by **D** king of 1732
29:30 unto the LORD with the words of **D**, 1732
30:26 for since the time of Solomon the son of **D** 1732
32: 5 repaired Millo *in* the city of **D**, and 1732
32:30 down to the west *side* of the city of **D**. 1732
32:33 chiefest of the sepulchres of the sons of **D**: 1732
33: 7 of which God had said to **D** and 1732
33:14 this he built a wall without the city of **D**, 1732
34: 2 walked in the ways of **D** his father, and 1732
34: 3 he began to seek after the God of **D** his 1732
35: 3 the son of **D** king of Israel did build; 1732
35: 4 according to the writing of **D** king of Israel, 1732
35:15 according to the commandment of **D**, and 1732
Ezr 3:10 after the ordinance of **D** king of Israel. 1732
8: 2 Daniel: of the sons of **D**; Hattush. 1732
8:20 whom **D** and the princes had appointed for 1732
Ne 3:15 the stairs that go down from the city of **D**. 1732
3:16 *the place* over against the sepulchres of **D**, 1732
12:24 according to the commandment of **D** 1732
12:36 with the musical instruments of **D** the man 1732
12:37 they went up by the stairs of the city of **D**, 1732
12:37 going up of the wall, above the house of **D**, 1732
12:45 according to the commandment of **D**, *and* 1732
12:46 For in the days of **D** and Asaph of old *there* 1732

Ps 3: T A Psalm of **D**, when he fled from Absalom 1732
4: T chief Musician on Neginoth, A Psalm of **D**. 1732
5: T Musician upon Nehiloth, A Psalm of **D**. 1732
6: T Neginoth upon Sheminith, A Psalm of **D**. 1732
7: T Shiggaion of **D**, which he sang unto 1732
8: T chief Musician upon Gittith, A Psalm of **D**. 1732
9: T upon Muth-labben, A Psalm of **D**. 1732
11: T To the chief Musician, *A Psalm* of **D**. 1732
12: T Musician upon Sheminith, A Psalm of **D**. 1732
13: T To the chief Musician, A Psalm of **D**. 1732
14: T To the chief Musician, *A Psalm* of **D**. 1732
15: T A Psalm of **D**. 1732
16: T Michtam of **D**. 1732
17: T A Prayer of **D**. 1732
18: T To the chief Musician, *A Psalm* of **D**, 1732
18:50 to **D**, and to his seed for evermore. 1732
19: T To the chief Musician, A Psalm of **D**. 1732
20: T To the chief Musician, A Psalm of **D**. 1732
21: T To the chief Musician, A Psalm of **D**. 1732
22: T upon Aijeleth Shahar, A Psalm of **D**. 1732
23: T A Psalm of **D**. 1732
24: T A Psalm of **D**. 1732
25: T *A Psalm* of **D**. 1732
26: T *A Psalm* of **D**. 1732
27: T *A Psalm* of **D**. 1732
28: T *A Psalm* of **D**. 1732
29: T A Psalm of **D**. 1732
30: T Song *at* the dedication of the house of **D**. 1732
31: T To the chief Musician, A Psalm of **D**. 1732
32: T *A Psalm* of **D**, Maschil. 1732
34: T *A Psalm* of **D**, when he changed his 1732
35: T *A Psalm* of **D**. 1732
36: T *A Psalm* of **D** the servant of the LORD. 1732
37: T *A Psalm* of **D**. 1732
38: T A Psalm of **D**, to bring to remembrance. 1732
39: T *even* to Jeduthun, A Psalm of **D**. 1732
40: T To the chief Musician, A Psalm of **D**. 1732
41: T To the chief Musician, A Psalm of **D**. 1732
51: T To the chief Musician, A Psalm of **D**, 1732
52: T the chief Musician, Maschil, *A Psalm* of **D**, 1732
52: T **D** is come to the house of Ahimelech. 1732
53: T upon Mahalath, Maschil, *A Psalm* of **D**. 1732
54: T Maschil, *A Psalm* of **D**, when the Ziphims 1732
54: T to Saul, Doth not **D** hide himself with us? 1732
55: T on Neginoth, Maschil, *A Psalm* of **D**. 1732
56: T Michtam of **D**, when the Philistines took 1732
57: T chief Musician, Al-taschith, Michtam of **D**, 1732
58: T chief Musician, Al-taschith, Michtam of **D**. 1732
59: T chief Musician, Al-taschith, Michtam of **D**; 1732
60: T Michtam of **D**, to teach; 1732
61: T Musician upon Neginah, *A Psalm* of **D**. 1732
62: T chief Musician, to Jeduthun, A Psalm of **D**. 1732
63: T A Psalm of **D**, when he was in 1732
64: T To the chief Musician, A Psalm of **D**. 1732
65: T chief Musician, A Psalm *and* Song of **D**. 1732
68: T the chief Musician, A Psalm *or* Song of **D**. 1732
69: T Musician upon Shoshannim, *A Psalm* of **D**. 1732
70: T To the chief Musician, *A Psalm* of **D**, 1732
72:20 The prayers of **D** the son of Jesse are 1732
78:70 He chose **D** also his servant, and took him 1732
86: T A Prayer of **D**. 1732
89: 3 I have sworn unto **D** my servant, 1732
89:20 I have found **D** my servant; with my holy 1732
89:35 by my holiness that I will not lie unto **D**. 1732
89:49 *which* thou swarest unto **D** in thy truth? 1732
101: T A Psalm of **D**. 1732
103: T *A Psalm* of **D**. 1732
108: T A Song *or* Psalm of **D**. 1732
109: T To the chief Musician, A Psalm of **D**. 1732
110: T A Psalm of **D**. 1732
122: T A Song of degrees of **D**. 1732
122: 5 of judgment, the thrones of the house of **D**. 1732
124: T A Song of degrees of **D**. 1732
131: T A Song of degrees of **D**. 1732
132: 1 remember **D**, *and* all his afflictions: 1732
132:11 The LORD hath sworn *in* truth unto **D**; 1732
132:17 There will I make the horn of **D** to bud: 1732
133: T A Song of degrees of **D**. 1732
138: T *A Psalm* of **D**. 1732
139: T To the chief Musician, A Psalm of **D**. 1732
140: T To the chief Musician, A Psalm of **D**. 1732
141: T A Psalm of **D**. 1732
142: T Maschil of **D**; A Prayer when he was in 1732
143: T A Psalm of **D**. 1732
144: T *A Psalm* of **D**. 1732
144:10 who delivereth **D** his servant from 1732
Pr 1: 1 The proverbs of Solomon the son of **D**, 1732
Ecc 1: 1 the son of **D**, king in Jerusalem. 1732
SS 4: 4 Thy neck *is* like the tower of **D** builded for 1732
Isa 7: 2 it was told the house of **D**, saying, Syria is 1732
7:13 he said, Hear ye now, O house of **D**; *Is it* a 1732
9: 7 upon the throne of **D**, and upon his 1732
16: 5 sit upon it in truth in the tabernacle of **D**, 1732
22: 9 seen also the breaches of the city of **D**, 1732
22:22 the key of the house of **D** will I lay upon 1732
29: 1 to Ariel, to Ariel, the city *where* **D** dwelt! 1732
38: 5 saith the LORD, the God of **D** thy father, 1732
55: 3 with you, *even* the sure mercies of **D**. 1732
Jer 17:25 and princes sitting upon the throne of **D**, 1732
21:12 O house of **D**, thus saith the LORD; 1732
22: 2 that sittest upon the throne of **D**, thou, and 1732
22: 4 house kings sitting upon the throne of **D**, 1732
22:30 sitting upon the throne of **D**, and ruling any 1732
23: 5 that I will raise unto **D** a righteous Branch, 1732
29:16 the king that sitteth upon the throne of **D**, 1732
30: 9 **D** their king, whom I will raise up unto 1732
33:15 Branch of righteousness to grow up unto **D**; 1732
33:17 **D** shall never want a man to sit upon 1732
33:21 my covenant be broken with **D** my servant, 1732
33:22 so will I multiply the seed of **D** my servant, 1732
33:26 **D** my servant, *so* that *I* will not take *any* of 1732
36:30 shall have none to sit upon the throne of **D**: 1732
Eze 34:23 and he shall feed them, *even* my servant **D**; 1732
34:24 and my servant **D** a prince among them; 1732
37:24 **D** my servant *shall be* king over them; and 1732
Eze 37:25 my servant **D** *shall be* their prince for ever. 1732
Hos 3: 5 the LORD their God, and **D** their king; 1732
Am 6: 5 themselves instruments of musick, like **D**; 1732
9:11 I raise up the tabernacle of **D** that is fallen, 1732
Zec 12: 7 that the glory of the house of **D** and 1732
12: 8 among them at that day shall be as **D**; 1732
12: 8 the house of **D** *shall be* as God, as the angel 1732
12:10 I will pour upon the house of **D**, and 1732
12:12 the family of the house of **D** apart, and 1732
13: 1 be a fountain opened to the house of **D** 1732
Mt 1: 1 the son of **D**, the son of Abraham. *1138*
1: 6 And Jesse begat **D** the king; and David *1138*
1: 6 **D** the king begat Solomon of *her that had* *1138*
1:17 So all the generations from Abraham to **D** *1138*
1:17 from **D** until the carrying away into *1138*
1:20 saying, Joseph, *thou* son of **D**, fear not to *1138*
9:27 crying, and saying, *Thou* Son of **D**, *1138*
12: 3 unto them, Have ye not read what **D** did, *1138*
12:23 were amazed, and said, Is this the son of **D**? *1138*
15:22 Have mercy on me, O Lord, *thou* Son of **D**; *1138*
20:30 Have mercy on us, O Lord, *thou* Son of **D**. *1138*
20:31 Have mercy on us, O Lord, *thou* Son of **D**. *1138*
21: 9 cried, saying, Hosanna to the Son of **D**: *1138*
21:15 and saying, Hosanna to the Son of **D**; *1138*
22:42 is he? They say unto him, *The Son* of **D**. *1138*
22:43 How then doth **D** in spirit call him Lord, *1138*
22:45 If **D** then call him Lord, how is he his son? *1138*
Mk 2:25 Have ye never read what **D** did, when he *1138*
10:47 and say, Jesus, *thou* Son of **D**, have mercy *1138*
10:48 *Thou* Son of **D**, have mercy on me. *1138*
11:10 Blessed *be* the kingdom of our father **D**, *1138*
12:35 say the scribes that Christ is the Son of **D**? *1138*
12:36 For **D** himself said by the Holy Ghost, *1138*
12:37 **D** therefore himself calleth him Lord; and *1138*
Lk 1:27 whose name was Joseph, of the house of **D**; *1138*
1:32 give unto him the throne of his father **D**: *1138*
1:69 for us in the house of his servant **D**; *1138*
2: 4 of Nazareth, into Judea, unto the city of **D**, *1138*
2: 4 he was of the house and lineage of **D**:) *1138*
2:11 is born this day in the city of **D** a Saviour, *1138*
3:31 *the son* of Nathan, which was *the son* of **D**, *1138*
6: 3 ye not read so much as this, what **D** did, *1138*
18:38 And he cried, saying, Jesus, *thou* Son of **D**, *1138*
18:39 he cried *so* much the more, *Thou* Son of **D**, *1138*
20:42 And **D** himself saith in the book of Psalms, *1138*
20:44 **D** therefore calleth him Lord, how is he *1138*
Jn 7:42 That Christ cometh of the seed of **D**, and *1138*
7:42 of the town of Bethlehem, where **D** was? *1138*
Ac 1:16 which the Holy Ghost by the mouth of **D** *1138*
2:25 For **D** speaketh concerning him, I foresaw *1138*
2:29 freely speak unto you of the patriarch **D**, *1138*
2:34 For **D** is not ascended into the heavens: but *1138*
4:25 Who by the mouth of thy servant **D** hast *1138*
7:45 the face of our fathers, unto the days of **D**; *1138*
13:22 he raised up unto them **D** to be their king; *1138*
13:22 and said, I have found **D** the *son* of Jesse, *1138*
13:34 I will give you the sure mercies of **D**. *1138*
13:36 For **D**, after he had served his own *1138*
15:16 and will build again the tabernacle of **D**, *1138*
Ro 1: 3 which was made of the seed of **D** according *1138*
4: 6 Even as **D** also describeth the blessedness *1138*
11: 9 And **D** saith, Let their table be made a *1138*
2Ti 2: 8 that Jesus Christ of the seed of **D** *1138*
Heb 4: 7 saying in **D**, To day, after so long a time; *1138*
11:32 *of* **D** also, and Samuel, and *of* the prophets: *1138*
Rev 3: 7 he *that is* true, he that hath the key of **D**, *1138*
5: 5 the Lion of the tribe of Juda, the root of **D**, *1138*
22:16 I am the root and the offspring of **D**, *and* *1138*

DAVID'S (54) [DAVID]

1Sa 18:29 and Saul became **D** enemy continually. 1732
19:11 Saul also sent messengers unto **D** house, 1732
19:11 Michal **D** wife told him, saying, If thou 1732
20:16 even require *it* at the hand of **D** enemies. 1732
20:25 sat by Saul's side, and **D** place was empty. 1732
20:27 *day* of the month, that **D** place was empty: 1732
23: 3 **D** men said unto him, Behold, we *be* afraid 1732
24: 5 that **D** heart smote him, because he had cut 1732
25: 9 when **D** young men came, they spake to 1732
25:10 Nabal answered **D** servants, and said, 1732
25:12 So **D** young men turned their way, and 1732
25:44 **D** wife, to Phalti the son of Laish, 1732
26:17 Saul knew **D** voice, and said, *Is* this thy 1732
30: 5 **D** two wives were taken captives, 1732
30:20 those *other* cattle, and said, This *is* **D** spoil. 1732
2Sa 2:30 there lacked of **D** servants nineteen men 1732
3: 5 the sixth, Ithream, by Eglah **D** wife. 1732
5: 8 and the blind, *that are* hated of **D** soul, 1732
8: 2 *so* the Moabites became **D** servants, and 1732
8:14 and all they of Edom became **D** servants. 1732
8:18 the Pelethites; and **D** sons were chief rulers. 1732
10: 2 **D** servants came *into* the land of 1732
10: 4 Wherefore Hanun took **D** servants, and 1732
12: 5 **D** anger was greatly kindled against 1732
12:30 it was *set* on **D** head. And he brought forth 1732
13: 3 the son of Shimeah **D** brother: 1732
13:32 the son of Shimeah **D** brother, answered 1732
15:12 **D** counseller, from his city, *even* from 1732
15:37 So Hushai **D** friend came *into* the city, and 1732
16:16 **D** friend, was come unto Absalom, 1732
19:41 and all **D** men with him, over Jordan? 1732
24:10 **D** heart smote him after that he had 1732
24:11 came unto the prophet Gad, **D** seer, saying, 1732
1Ki 1:38 caused Solomon to ride upon king **D** mule, 1732
11:32 shall have one tribe for my servant **D** sake, 1732
15: 4 Nevertheless for **D** sake did the LORD his 1732
2Ki 11:10 hundreds did the priest give king **D** spears 1732
19:34 mine own sake, and for my servant **D** sake. 1732
20: 6 mine own sake, and for my servant **D** sake. 1732
1Ch 18: 2 the Moabites became **D** servants, and 1732
18: 6 the Syrians became **D** servants, and 1732
18:13 and all the Edomites became **D** servants. 1732
19: 4 Wherefore Hanun took **D** servants, and 1732
20: 2 stones in it; and it was *set* upon **D** head: 1732
20: 7 Jonathan the son of Shimea **D** brother slew 1732
1Ch 21: 9 LORD spake unto Gad, **D** seer, saying, 1732
27:31 of the substance which *was* king **D**. 1732+3807.1
27:32 Also Jonathan **D** uncle *was* a counseller, 1732
2Ch 23: 9 and shields, that *had been* king **D**, 1732+3807.1
Ps 132:10 For thy servant **D** sake turn not away 1732
145: T **D** *Psalm of* praise. 1732
Isa 37:35 mine own sake, and for my servant **D** sake. 1732
Jer 13:13 even the kings that sit upon **D** 1732+3807.1
Lk 20:41 How say they that Christ is **D** son? *1138*

DAWN (2) [DAWNING]

Mt 28: 1 as it began to **d** towards the first *day* of *2020*
2Pe 1:19 until the day **d**, and the day star arise in *1306*

DAWNING (5) [DAWN]

Jos 6:15 that they rose early about the **d** of the day, 5927
Jdg 19:26 came the woman in the **d** of the day, and 6437
Job 3: 9 neither let it see the **d** of the day: 6079
7: 4 *of* tossings to and fro unto the **d of the day**. 5399
Ps 119:147 I prevented the **d of the morning**, and 5399

DAY (1732) [BIRTHDAY, DAILY, DAY'S, DAYS, DAYS', DAYSMAN, DAYSPRING, DAYTIME, HOLYDAY, MIDDAY, NOONDAY, NOONDAYS, YESTERDAY]

Ge 1: 5 God called the light **D**, and the darkness he 3117
1: 5 and the morning were the first **d**. 3117
1: 8 and the morning were the second **d**. 3117
1:13 and the morning were the third **d**. 3117
1:14 the heaven to divide the **d** from the night; 3117
1:16 the greater light to rule the **d**, and the lesser 3117
1:18 to rule over the **d** and over the night, and 3117
1:19 and the morning were the fourth **d**. 3117
1:23 and the morning were the fifth **d**. 3117
1:31 and the morning were the sixth **d**. 3117
2: 2 on the seventh **d** God ended his work 3117
2: 2 he rested on the seventh **d** from all his work 3117
2: 3 God blessed the seventh **d**, and 3117
2: 4 in the **d** that the LORD God made 3117
2:17 for in the **d** that thou eatest thereof thou 3117
3: 5 For God doth know that in the **d** ye eat 3117
3: 8 walking in the garden in the cool of the **d**: 3117
4:14 thou hast driven me out *this* **d** from the face 3117
5: 1 In the **d** that God created man, in 3117
5: 2 in the **d** when they were created. 3117
7:11 the seventeenth **d** of the month, 3117
7:11 the same **d** were all the fountains of 3117
7:13 In the selfsame **d** entered Noah, and Shem, 3117
8: 4 on the seventeenth **d** of the month, upon 3117
8: 5 in the tenth *month*, on the first *d* of NIH
8:13 in the first *month*, the first *d* of the month, NIH
8:14 on the seven and twentieth **d** of the month, 3117
8:22 and winter, and **d** and night shall not cease. 3117
15:18 In the same **d** the LORD made a covenant 3117
17:23 the flesh of their foreskin in the selfsame **d**, 3117
17:26 In the selfsame **d** was Abraham 3117
18: 1 he sat *in* the tent door in the heat of the **d**; 3117
19:37 *is* the father of the Moabites unto *this* **d**. 3117
19:38 of the children of Ammon unto *this* **d**. 3117
21: 8 Abraham made a great feast the *same* **d** that 3117
21:26 neither yet heard I *of it*, but to **d**. 3117+1886.1
22: 4 on the third **d** Abraham lift up his eyes, 3117
22:14 as it is said *to this* **d**, In the mount of 3117
24:12 send me good speed *this* **d**, and 3117
24:42 I came this **d** unto the well, and said, 3117
25:31 Jacob said, Sell me *this* **d** thy birthright. 3117
25:33 Jacob said, Swear to me *this* **d**; and 3117
26:32 it came to pass the same **d**, that Isaac's 3117
26:33 name of the city *is* Beer-sheba unto this **d**. 3117
27: 2 I am old, I know not the **d** of my death: 3117
27:45 I be deprived also of you both *in* one **d**? 3117
29: 7 he said, Lo, *it is* yet high **d**, neither *is it* 3117
30:32 will pass through all thy flock to **d**, 3117+1886.1
30:35 he removed that **d** the he goats that were 3117
31:22 it was told Laban on the third **d** that Jacob 3117
31:39 *whether* stolen by **d**, or stolen by night. 3117
31:40 *Thus* I was in the **d**, the drought consumed 3117
31:43 what can I do *this* **d** unto these my 3117
31:48 *is* a witness between me and thee *this* **d**. 3117
32:24 a man with him until the breaking of the **d**. 7837
32:26 he said, Let me go, for the **d** breaketh. 7837
32:32 *is* upon the hollow of the thigh, unto this **d**: 3117
33:13 if *men* should overdrive them one **d**, all 3117
33:16 So Esau returned that **d** on his way unto 3117
34:25 it came to pass on the third **d**, when they 3117
35: 3 who answered me in the **d** of my distress, 3117
35:20 *is* the pillar of Rachel's grave unto *this* **d**. 3117
39:10 to pass, as she spake to Joseph **d** by day, 3117
39:10 to pass, as she spake to Joseph day by **d**, 3117
40: 7 Wherefore look ye *so* sadly **to d**? 3117+1886.1
40:20 it came to pass the third **d**, *which was* 3117
41: 9 I do remember my faults *this* **d**: 3117
42:13 the youngest *is this* **d** with our father, and 3117
42:18 Joseph said unto them the third **d**, This do, 3117
42:32 the youngest *is this* **d** with our father in 3117
47:23 I have bought you *this* **d** and your land for 3117
47:26 it a law over the land of Egypt unto this **d**, 3117
48:15 which fed me all my life long unto this **d**, 3117
48:20 he blessed them that **d**, saying, In thee shall 3117
50:20 it unto good, to bring to pass, as *it is* this **d**, 3117
Ex 2:13 when he went out the second **d**, behold, 3117
2:18 *is it that* you are come so soon **to d**? 3117+1886.1
5: 6 Pharaoh commanded the same **d** 3117
5:14 brick both yesterday and **to d**, 3117+1886.1
6:28 it came to pass on the **d** *when* the LORD 3117
8:22 I will sever in that **d** the land of Goshen, 3117
10: 6 since the **d** that they were upon the earth 3117
10: 6 that they were upon the earth unto this **d**. 3117
10:13 an east wind upon the land all that **d**, 3117
10:28 for in *that* **d** thou seest my face thou shalt 3117
12: 3 In the tenth *d* of this month they shall take NIH
12: 6 ye shall keep it *up* until the fourteenth **d** of 3117
12:14 this **d** shall be unto you for a memorial; 3117
12:15 even the first **d** ye shall put away leaven 3117

Ex 12:15 bread from the first **d** until the seventh day, 3117
12:15 bread from the first day until the seventh **d**, 3117
12:16 in the first **d** *there shall be* a holy 3117
12:16 in the seventh **d** there shall be a holy 3117
12:17 for in this selfsame **d** have I brought your 3117
12:17 shall ye observe this **d** in your generations 3117
12:18 In the first *month*, on the fourteenth **d** of 3117
12:18 and twentieth **d** of the month at even. 3117
12:41 even the selfsame **d** it came to pass, 3117
12:51 it came to pass the selfsame **d**, *that* 3117
13: 3 said unto the people, Remember this **d**, 3117
13: 4 *This* **d** came ye out in the month Abib. 3117
13: 6 in the seventh **d** *shall be* a feast to 3117
13: 8 thou shalt shew thy son in that **d**, saying, 3117
13:21 the LORD went before them **by d** in a 3119
13:21 to give them light; to go **by d** and night: 3119
13:22 took not away the pillar of the cloud **by d**, 3119
14:13 which he will shew to you **to d**: 3117+1886.1
14:13 Egyptians whom ye have seen **to d**, 3117+1886.1
14:30 Thus the LORD saved Israel that **d** out of 3117
16: 1 on the fifteenth **d** of the second month after 3117
16: 4 gather a certain rate **every d**, 3117+3117+871.1
16: 5 that on the sixth **d** they shall prepare *that* 3117
16:22 *that* on the sixth **d** they gathered twice as 3117
16:23 bake *that* which ye will bake *to* **d**, and NIH
16:25 Moses said, Eat that **to d**; for to 3117+1886.1
16:25 **to d** *is* a sabbath unto the LORD: 3117+1886.1
16:25 *is* a sabbath unto the LORD: **to d** 3117+1886.1
16:26 on the seventh **d**, *which is* the sabbath, in it 3117
16:27 of the people on the seventh **d** for to gather, 3117
16:29 he giveth you on the sixth **d** the bread of 3117
16:29 man go out of his place on the seventh **d**. 3117
16:30 So the people rested on the seventh **d**. 3117
19: 1 the same **d** came they *into* the wilderness of 3117
19:10 sanctify them **to d** and to morrow, 3117+1886.1
19:11 be ready against the third **d**: for the third 3117
19:11 for the third **d** the LORD will come down 3117
19:15 the people, Be ready against the third **d**: 3117
19:16 it came to pass on the third **d** in 3117
20: 8 Remember the sabbath **d**, to keep it holy. 3117
20:10 the seventh **d** *is* the sabbath of the LORD 3117
20:11 all that in them *is*, and rested the seventh **d**: 3117
20:11 the LORD blessed the sabbath **d**, 3117
21:21 Notwithstanding, if he continue a **d** or two, 3117
22:30 on the eighth **d** thou shalt give it me. 3117
23:12 and on the seventh **d** thou shalt rest: 3117
24:16 the seventh **d** he called unto Moses out of 3117
29:36 thou shalt offer every **d** a bullock *for* a sin 3117
29:38 year **d by day** continually. 3117+1886.1+3807.1
29:38 year **day by d** continually. 3117+1886.1+3807.1
31:15 doeth *any* work in the sabbath **d**, 3117
31:17 on the seventh **d** he rested, and 3117
32:28 there fell of the people that **d** about three 3117
32:29 yourselves **to d** to the LORD, 3117+1886.1
32:29 he may bestow upon you a blessing *this* **d**. 3117
32:34 nevertheless in the **d** when I visit, I will 3117
34:11 thou that which I command thee *this* **d**: 3117
34:21 but on the seventh **d** thou shalt rest: 3117
35: 2 on the seventh **d** there shall be to you a 3117
35: 2 a holy *d*, a sabbath of rest to the LORD: NIH
35: 3 your habitations upon the sabbath **d**. 3117
40: 2 On the first **d** of the first month shalt thou 3117
40:17 on the first *d* of the month, *that* NIH
40:37 they journeyed not till the **d** that it was 3117
40:38 the LORD *was* upon the tabernacle **by d**, 3119
Lev 6: 5 in the **d** of his trespass offering. 3117
6:20 the LORD in the **d** when he is anointed; 3117
7:15 shall be eaten the same **d** that it is offered; 3117
7:16 it shall be eaten the *same* **d** that he offereth 3117
7:17 on the third **d** shall be burnt with fire. 3117
7:18 offerings be eaten at all on the third **d**, 3117
7:35 in the **d** *when* he presented them to minister 3117
7:36 in the **d** that he anointed them, *by* a statute 3117
7:38 in the **d** that he commanded the children of 3117
8:34 As he hath done this **d**, *so* the LORD hath 3117
8:35 door of the tabernacle of the congregation **d** 3119
9: 1 it came to pass on the eighth **d**, *that* Moses 3117
9: 4 **to d** the LORD will appear unto 3117+1886.1
10:19 *this* **d** have they offered their sin offering 3117
10:19 *if* I had eaten the sin offering **to d**, 3117+1886.1
12: 3 in the eighth **d** the flesh of his foreskin 3117
13: 5 the priest shall look on him the seventh **d**: 3117
13: 6 shall look on him again the seventh **d**: 3117
13:27 priest shall look upon him the seventh **d**: 3117
13:32 in the seventh **d** the priest shall look on 3117
13:34 in the seventh **d** the priest shall look on 3117
13:51 shall look on the plague on the seventh **d**: 3117
14: 2 This shall be the law of the leper in the **d** of 3117
14: 9 it shall be on the seventh **d**, *that* he shall 3117
14:10 on the eighth **d** he shall take two he lambs 3117
14:23 he shall bring them on the eighth **d** for his 3117
14:39 the priest shall come again the seventh **d**, 3117
15:14 on the eighth **d** he shall take to him two 3117
15:29 on the eighth **d** she shall take unto her two 3117
16:29 on the tenth *d* of the month, ye shall afflict NIH
16:30 For on that **d** shall *the priest* make an 3117
19: 6 It shall be eaten the *same* **d** ye offer it, and 3117
19: 6 if ought remain until the third **d**, it shall be 3117
19: 7 if it be eaten at all on the third **d**, it *is* 3117
22:27 from the eighth **d** and thenceforth it shall 3117
22:28 shall not kill it and her young both in one **d**. 3117
22:30 On the same **d** it shall be eaten up; ye shall 3117
23: 3 the seventh **d** *is* the sabbath of rest, a holy 3117
23: 5 In the fourteenth *d* of the first month at even NIH
23: 6 on the fifteenth **d** of the same month *is* 3117
23: 7 In the first **d** ye shall have a holy 3117
23: 8 in the seventh **d** *is* a holy convocation: 3117
23:12 ye shall offer that **d** when ye wave 3117
23:14 until the selfsame **d** that ye have brought an 3117
23:15 from the **d** that ye brought the sheaf of 3117
23:21 ye shall proclaim on the selfsame **d**, *that* it 3117
23:24 seventh month, in the first *d* of the month, NIH
23:27 Also on the tenth *d* of this seventh month NIH
23:27 month *there shall be* a **d** of atonement: 3117
23:28 ye shall do no work in that same **d**: for it *is* 3117
Lev 23:28 for it *is* a **d** of atonement, to make an 3117
23:29 *be* that shall not be afflicted in that same **d**, 3117
23:30 *it be* that doeth any work in that same **d**, 3117
23:32 in the ninth *d* of the month at even, NIH
23:34 The fifteenth **d** of this seventh month *shall* 3117
23:35 On the first **d** *shall be* a holy convocation: 3117
23:36 on the eighth **d** shall be a holy convocation 3117
23:37 every thing **upon** his **d**: 3117+3117+871.1
23:39 Also in the fifteenth **d** of the seventh 3117
23:39 on the first **d** *shall be* a sabbath, and on 3117
23:39 and on the eighth **d** *shall be* a sabbath. 3117
23:40 ye shall take you on the first **d** the boughs 3117
25: 9 sound on the tenth *d* of the seventh month, NIH
25: 9 in the **d** of atonement shall ye make 3117
27:23 he shall give thine estimation in that **d**, *as* a 3117
Nu 1: 1 on the first *d* of the second month, NIH
1:18 together on the first *d* of the second month, NIH
3: 1 Moses in the **d** that the LORD spake with 3117
3:13 *for* on the **d** that I smote all the firstborn in 3117
6: 9 he shall shave his head in the **d** of his 3117
6: 9 on the seventh **d** shall he shave it. 3117
6:10 on the eighth **d** he shall bring two turtles, 3117
6:11 and shall hallow his head that *same* **d**. 3117
7: 1 it came to pass on the **d** that Moses had 3117
7:10 of the altar in the **d** that it was anointed, 3117
7:11 each prince on *his* **d**, for the dedicating of 3117
7:12 he that offered his offering the first **d** was 3117
7:18 On the second **d** Nethaneel the son of Zuar, 3117
7:24 On the third **d** Eliab the son of Helon, 3117
7:30 On the fourth **d** Elizur the son of Shedeur, 3117
7:36 On the fifth **d** Shelumiel the son of 3117
7:42 On the sixth **d** Eliasaph the son of Deuel, 3117
7:48 On the seventh **d** Elishama the son of 3117
7:54 On the eighth **d** *offered* Gamaliel the son of 3117
7:60 On the ninth **d** Abidan the son of Gideoni, 3117
7:66 On the tenth **d** Ahiezer the son of 3117
7:72 On the eleventh **d** Pagiel the son of Ocran, 3117
7:78 On the twelfth **d** Ahira the son of Enan, 3117
7:84 in the **d** when it was anointed, by 3117
8:17 on the **d** that I smote every firstborn in 3117
9: 3 In the fourteenth **d** of this month, at even, 3117
9: 5 they kept the passover on the fourteenth **d** 3117
9: 6 they could not keep the passover on that **d**: 3117
9: 6 before Moses and before Aaron on that **d**: 3117
9:11 The fourteenth **d** of the second month at 3117
9:15 on the **d** that the tabernacle was reared up, 3117
9:16 the cloud covered it *by* **d**, and NIH
9:21 whether *it was* **by d** or by night that 3119
10:10 Also in the **d** of your gladness, and in your 3117
10:11 it came to pass on the twentieth *d* of NIH
10:34 cloud of the LORD *was* upon them **by d**, 3119
11:19 Ye shall not eat one **d**, nor two days, 3117
11:32 the people stood up all that **d**, and all *that* 3117
11:32 all the next **d**, and they gathered the quails: 3117
14:14 **by d time** in a pillar of a cloud, and in a 3119
14:34 *even* forty days, each **d** for a year, shall ye 3117
15:23 from the **d** that the LORD commanded 3117
15:32 that gathered sticks upon the sabbath **d**. 3117
19:12 shall purify himself with it on the third **d**, 3117
19:12 and on the seventh **d** he shall be clean: 3117
19:12 if he purify not himself the third **d**, then 3117
19:12 then the seventh **d** he shall not be clean. 3117
19:19 sprinkle upon the unclean on the third **d**, 3117
19:19 on the third day, and on the seventh **d**: 3117
19:19 on the seventh **d** he shall purify him*self*, 3117
22:30 ridden ever since *I was* thine unto this **d**? 3117
25:18 which was slain in the **d** of the plague for 3117
28: 3 without spot **d by day**, 3117+1886.1+3807.1
28: 3 without spot **day by d**, 3117+1886.1+3807.1
28: 9 on the sabbath **d** two lambs of the first year 3117
28:16 in the fourteenth **d** of the first month *is* 3117
28:17 in the fifteenth **d** of this month *is* the feast: 3117
28:18 In the first **d** *shall be* a holy convocation; 3117
28:25 on the seventh **d** ye shall have a holy 3117
28:26 Also in the **d** of the firstfruits, when ye 3117
29: 1 seventh month, on the first *d* of the month, NIH
29: 1 it is a **d** of blowing the trumpets unto you. 3117
29: 7 ye shall have on the tenth *d* of this seventh NIH
29:12 on the fifteenth **d** of the seventh month ye 3117
29:17 on the second **d** *ye shall offer* twelve young 3117
29:20 on the third **d** eleven bullocks, two rams, 3117
29:23 And on the fourth **d** ten bullocks, two rams, 3117
29:26 on the fifth **d** nine bullocks, two rams, *and* 3117
29:29 on the sixth **d** eight bullocks, two rams, 3117
29:32 on the seventh **d** seven bullocks, two rams, 3117
29:35 On the eighth **d** ye shall have a solemn 3117
30: 5 if her father disallow her in the **d** that he 3117
30: 7 held his peace at her in the **d** that he heard 3117
30: 8 if her husband disallow her on the **d** that he 3117
30:12 made them void on the **d** he heard *them;* 3117
30:14 hold his peace at her from **d** to day; 3117
30:14 hold his peace at her from day to **d**; 3117
30:14 he held his peace at her in the **d** that he 3117
31:19 and your captives on the third **d**, 3117
31:19 on the third day, and on the seventh **d**. 3117
31:24 shall wash your clothes on the seventh **d**, 3117
33: 3 on the fifteenth **d** of the first month; 3117
33:38 of Egypt, in the first *d* of the fifth month. NIH
Dt 1: 3 eleventh month, on the first *d* of the month, NIH
1:10 you *are this* **d** as the stars of heaven for 3117
1:33 way ye should go, and in a cloud **by d**. 3119
1:39 which *in that* **d** had no knowledge between 3117
2:18 over *through* Ar, the coast of Moab, *this* **d**: 3117
2:22 and dwelt in their stead *even* unto this **d**: 3117
2:25 This **d** will I begin to put the dread of thee 3117
2:30 him into thy hand, as *appeareth* this **d**. 3117
3:14 own name, Bashan-havoth-jair, unto this **d**. 3117
4: 4 your God *are* alive every one of you *this* **d**. 3117
4: 8 all this law, which I set before you *this* **d**? 3117
4:10 *Specially* the **d** that thou stoodest before 3117
4:15 for ye saw no *manner of* similitude on the **d** 3117
4:20 a people of inheritance, as *ye are* this **d**. 3117
4:26 and earth to witness against you *this* **d**, 3117
4:32 since the **d** that God created man upon 3117
4:38 their land *for* an inheritance, as *it is* this **d**. 3117
Dt 4:39 Know therefore *this* **d**, and consider *it* in 3117
4:40 which I command thee *this* **d**, 3117
5: 1 which I speak in your ears *this* **d**, 3117
5: 3 *even* us, who *are* all of us here alive *this* **d**. 3117
5:12 Keep the sabbath **d** to sanctify it, as 3117
5:14 the seventh **d** *is* the sabbath of the LORD 3117
5:15 commanded thee to keep the sabbath **d**. 3117
5:24 we have seen this **d** that God doth talk with 3117
6: 6 these words, which I command thee *this* **d**, 3117
6:24 he might preserve us alive, as *it is at* this **d**. 3117
7:11 which I command thee *this* **d**, to do them. 3117
8: 1 command thee *this* **d** shall ye observe to do, 3117
8:11 his statutes, which I command thee *this* **d**: 3117
8:18 he sware unto thy fathers, as *it is* this **d**. 3117
8:19 I testify against you *this* **d** that ye shall 3117
9: 1 Thou art to pass over Jordan *this* **d**, to go in 3117
9: 3 Understand therefore *this* **d**, that 3117
9: 7 from the **d** that thou didst depart out of 3117
9:10 midst of the fire in the **d** of the assembly. 3117
9:24 the LORD from the **d** that I knew you. 3117
10: 4 midst of the fire in the **d** of the assembly: 3117
10: 8 and to bless in his name, unto this **d**. 3117
10:13 which I command thee *this* **d** for thy good? 3117
10:15 *even* you above all people, as *it is* this **d**. 3117
11: 2 know you *this* **d**: for *I speak* not with your 3117
11: 4 LORD hath destroyed them unto this **d**; 3117
11: 8 which I command you *this* **d**, 3117
11:13 which I command you *this* **d**, 3117
11:26 I set before you *this* **d** a blessing and 3117
11:27 your God, which I command you *this* **d**: 3117
11:28 of the way which I command you *this* **d**, 3117
11:32 judgments which I set before you *this* **d**. 3117
12: 8 after all *the things* that we do here *this* **d**, 3117
13:18 which I command thee *this* **d**, 3117
15: 5 which I command thee *this* **d**. 3117
15:15 I command thee this thing **to d**. 3117+1886.1
16: 3 that thou mayest remember the **d** when 3117
16: 4 which thou sacrificedst the first **d** at even, 3117
16: 8 on the seventh **d** *shall be* a solemn 3117
18:16 thy God in Horeb in the **d** of the assembly, 3117
19: 9 which I command thee *this* **d**, to love 3117
20: 3 you approach *this* **d** unto battle against your 3117
21:23 but thou shalt in any wise bury him that **d**; 3117
24:15 At his **d** thou shalt give *him* his hire, 3117
26: 3 I profess *this* **d** unto the LORD thy God, 3117
26:16 This **d** the LORD thy God hath 3117
26:17 Thou hast avouched the LORD *this* **d** to 3117
26:18 the LORD hath avouched thee *this* **d** to be 3117
27: 1 which I command you *this* **d**. 3117
27: 2 it shall be on the **d** when ye shall pass 3117
27: 4 which I command you *this* **d**, in mount 3117
27: 9 this **d** thou art become the people of 3117
27:10 his statutes, which I command thee *this* **d**. 3117
27:11 Moses charged the people the same **d**, 3117
28: 1 which I command thee *this* **d**, 3117
28:13 which I command thee *this* **d**, to observe 3117
28:14 of the words which I command thee *this* **d**, 3117
28:15 his statutes which I command thee *this* **d**; 3117
28:32 fail *with longing* for them all the **d** long: 3117
28:66 thou shalt fear **d** and night, and shalt have 3119
29: 4 eyes to see, and ears to hear, unto this **d**. 3117
29:10 Ye stand *this* **d** all of you before 3117
29:12 LORD thy God maketh with thee *this* **d**: 3117
29:13 That he may establish thee **to d** for 3117+1886.1
29:15 with *him* that standeth here with us *this* **d** 3117
29:15 also with *him* that *is* not here with us *this* **d**: 3117
29:18 whose heart turneth away *this* **d** from 3117
29:28 cast them into another land, as *it is* this **d**. 3117
30: 2 according to all that I command thee *this* **d**, 3117
30: 8 which I command thee *this* **d**. 3117
30:11 which I command thee *this* **d**, 3117
30:15 I have set before thee *this* **d** life and good, 3117
30:16 In that I command thee *this* **d** to love 3117
30:18 I denounce unto you *this* **d**, that ye shall 3117
30:19 and earth to record *this* **d** against you, 3117
31: 2 *am* an hundred and twenty years old *this* **d**; 3117
31:17 shall be kindled against them in that **d**, 3117
31:17 so that they will say in that **d**, Are not these 3117
31:18 I will surely hide my face in that **d** for all 3117
31:22 wrote this song the same **d**, 3117
31:27 while I am yet alive with you *this* **d**, 3117
32:35 for the **d** of their calamity *is* at hand, and 3117
32:46 the words which I testify among you *this* **d**, 3117
32:48 LORD spake unto Moses that selfsame **d**, 3117
33:12 *the LORD* shall cover him all the **d** long, 3117
34: 6 man knoweth of his sepulchre unto this **d**. 3117
Jos 1: 8 thou shalt meditate therein **d** and night, that 3119
3: 7 This **d** will I begin to magnify thee in 3117
4: 9 and they are there unto this **d**. 3117
4:14 On that **d** the LORD magnified Joshua in 3117
4:19 of Jordan on the tenth *d* of the first month, NIH
5: 9 *This* **d** have I rolled away the reproach of 3117
5: 9 of the place is called Gilgal unto this **d**. 3117
5:10 kept the passover on the fourteenth **d** of 3117
5:11 and parched *corn* in the selfsame **d**. 3117
6: 4 the seventh **d** ye shall compass the city 3117
6:10 of your mouth, until the **d** I bid you shout; 3117
6:14 the second **d** they compassed the city once, 3117
6:15 it came to pass on the seventh **d**, that they 3117
6:15 they rose early about the dawning of the **d**, 7837
6:15 only on that **d** they compassed the city 3117
6:25 she dwelleth in Israel *even* unto this **d**; 3117
7:25 the LORD shall trouble thee this **d**. 3117
7:26 over him a great heap of stones unto this **d**. 3117
7:26 The valley of Achor, unto this **d**. 3117
8:25 *so* it was, *that* all that fell that **d**, both of 3117
8:28 heap for ever, *even* a desolation unto this **d**. 3117
8:29 heap of stones, *that remaineth* unto this **d**. 3117
9:12 on the **d** we came forth to go unto you; 3117
9:17 and came unto their cities on the third **d**. 3117
9:27 Joshua made them that **d** hewers of wood 3117
9:27 the altar of the LORD, *even* unto this **d**, 3117
10:12 spake Joshua to the LORD in the **d** when 3117
10:13 and hasted not to go down about a whole **d**. 3117
10:14 there was no **d** like that before it or after it, 3117

Jos 10:27 *which remain* until this very **d**. 3117
10:28 that **d** Joshua took Makkedah, and smote it 3117
10:32 which took it on the second **d**, and smote it 3117
10:35 they took it on that **d**, and smote it with 3117
10:35 *were* therein he utterly destroyed that **d**, 3117
13:13 dwell among the Israelites until this **d**.) 3117
14: 9 Moses sware on that **d**, saying, Surely 3117
14:10 *I am this* **d** fourscore and five years old. 3117
14:11 As yet I *am as* strong *this* **d** as *I was* in 3117
14:11 day as *I was* in the **d** that Moses sent me: 3117
14:12 whereof the LORD spake in that **d**; 3117
14:12 for thou heardest in that **d** how 3117
14:14 son of Jephunneh the Kenezite unto this **d**, 3117
15:63 children of Judah at Jerusalem unto this **d**. 3117
16:10 dwell among the Ephraimites unto this **d**, 3117
22: 3 your brethren these many days unto this **d**, 3117
22:16 to turn away *this* **d** from following 3117
22:16 that ye might rebel *this* **d** against 3117
22:17 from which we are not cleansed until this **d**, 3117
22:18 that ye must turn away *this* **d** from 3117
22:18 ye rebel **to d** against the LORD, 3117+1886.1
22:22 against the LORD, (save us not this **d**,) 3117
22:29 turn *this* **d** from following the LORD, 3117
22:31 *This* **d** we perceive that the LORD *is* 3117
23: 8 your God, as ye have done unto this **d**. 3117
23: 9 *been able to* stand before you unto this **d**. 3117
23:14 *this* **d** I am going the way of all the earth: 3117
24:15 choose you *this* **d** whom you will serve; 3117
24:25 made a covenant with the people that **d**, 3117
Jdg 1:21 of Benjamin in Jerusalem unto this **d**. 3117
1:26 which *is* the name thereof unto this **d**. 3117
3:30 So Moab was subdued that **d** under 3117
4:14 for this *is* the **d** in which the LORD hath 3117
4:23 So God subdued on that **d** Jabin the king of 3117
5: 1 and Barak the son of Abinoam on that **d**, 3117
6:24 unto this **d** it *is* yet in Ophrah of 3117
6:27 of the city, that *he* could not do *it* **by d**, 3119
6:32 Therefore on that **d** he called him 3117
9:18 risen up against my father's house *this* **d**, 3117
9:19 with Jerubbaal and with his house this **d**, 3117
9:45 fought against the city all that **d**; 3117
10: 4 which are called Havoth-jair unto this **d**, 3117
10:15 deliver us only, we pray thee, this **d**. 3117
11:27 the LORD the Judge be judge *this* **d** 3117
12: 3 are ye come up unto me this **d**, 3117
13: 7 God from the womb to the **d** of his death. 3117
13:10 unto me, that came unto me the *other* **d**. 3117
14:15 it came to pass on the seventh **d**, that they 3117
14:17 it came to pass on the seventh **d**, that he 3117
14:18 on the seventh **d** before the sun went down, 3117
15:19 which *is* in Lehi unto this **d**. 3117
16: 2 saying, In the morning, when it is **d**, we shall 216
18: 1 **d** *all their* inheritance had not fallen unto 3117
18:12 called that place Mahaneh-dan unto this **d**: 3117
18:30 Dan until the **d** of the captivity of the land. 3117
19: 5 it came to pass on the fourth **d**, when they 3117
19: 8 he arose early in the morning on the fifth **d** 3117
19: 9 the **d** draweth towards evening, 3117
19: 9 behold, the **d** groweth to an end, 3117
19:11 they *were* by Jebus, the **d** was far spent; 3117
19:25 when the **d began** to spring, they let her go. 7837
19:26 came the woman in the dawning of the **d**, 1242
19:30 **d** that the children of Israel came up out of 3117
19:30 up out of the land of Egypt unto this **d**: 3117
20:21 to the ground of the Israelites that **d** twenty 3117
20:22 they put *themselves* in array the first **d**. 3117
20:24 the children of Benjamin the second **d**. 3117
20:25 against them out of Gibeah the second **d**, 3117
20:26 fasted that **d** until even, and offered burnt 3117
20:30 the children of Benjamin on the third **d**, 3117
20:35 destroyed of the Benjamites that **d** twenty 3117
20:46 So that all which fell that **d** of Benjamin 3117
21: 3 that there should be **to d** one tribe 3117+1886.1
21: 6 There is one tribe cut off from Israel *this* **d**. 3117
Ru 2:19 Where hast thou gleaned **to d**? 3117+1886.1
2:19 with whom I wrought **to d** *is* Boaz. 3117+1886.1
3:18 until he have finished the thing *this* **d**. 3117
4: 5 What **d** thou buyest the field of the hand of 3117
4: 9 *unto* all the people, Ye *are* witnesses *this* **d**, 3117
4:10 gate of his place: ye *are* witnesses *this* **d**. 3117
4:14 which hath not left thee *this* **d** without a 3117
1Sa 2:34 in one **d** they shall die both of them. 3117
3:12 In that **d** I will perform against Eli all 3117
4: 3 us **to d** before the Philistines? 3117+1886.1
4:12 came *to* Shiloh the same **d** with his clothes 3117
4:16 and I fled **to d** out of the army. 3117+1886.1
5: 5 threshold of Dagon in Ashdod unto this **d**. 3117
6:15 sacrificed sacrifices the same **d** unto 3117
6:16 seen *it*, they returned *to* Ekron the same **d**. 3117
6:18 *which stone remaineth* unto this **d** in 3117
7: 6 and fasted on that **d**, and said there, 3117
7:10 great thunder on that **d** upon the Philistines, 3117
8: 8 **d** that I brought them up out of Egypt even 3117
8: 8 them up out of Egypt even unto this **d**, 3117
8:18 ye shall cry out in that **d** because of your 3117
8:18 and the LORD will not hear you in that **d**. 3117
9:12 for he came **to d** to the city; 3117+1886.1
9:12 the people **to d** in the high place: 3117+1886.1
9:15 Samuel in his ear a **d** before Saul came, 3117
9:19 for ye shall eat with me **to d**, and 3117+1886.1
9:24 So Saul did eat with Samuel that **d**. 3117
9:26 it came to pass about the spring of the **d**, 7837
10: 2 thou art departed from me **to d**, 3117+1886.1
10: 9 and all those signs came to pass that **d**. 3117
10:19 ye have *this* **d** rejected your God, 3117
11:11 slew the Ammonites until the heat of the **d**: 3117
11:13 shall not a man be put to death this **d**: 3117
11:13 for **to d** the LORD hath wrought 3117+1886.1
12: 2 before you from my childhood unto this **d**. 3117
12: 5 and his anointed *is* witness this **d**, 3117
12:17 *Is it* not wheat harvest **to d**? I will 3117+1886.1
12:18 the LORD sent thunder and rain that **d**: 3117
13:22 So it came to pass in the **d** of battle, 3117
14: 1 Now it came to pass upon a **d**, 3117
14:23 So the LORD saved Israel that **d**: and 3117

1Sa 14:24 the men of Israel were distressed that **d**: 3117
14:28 *be* the man that eateth *any* food *this* **d**. 3117
14:30 **to d** of the spoil of their enemies 3117+1886.1
14:31 they smote the Philistines that **d** from 3117
14:33 roll a great stone unto me *this* **d**. 3117
14:37 of Israel? But he answered him not that **d**. 3117
14:38 and see wherein this sin hath been *this* **d**. 3117
14:45 for he hath wrought with God this **d**. 3117
15:28 rent the kingdom of Israel from thee *this* **d**, 3117
15:35 no more to see Saul until the **d** of his death: 3117
16:13 came upon David from that **d** forward. 3117
17:10 I defy the armies of Israel this **d**; 3117
17:46 This **d** will the LORD deliver thee into 3117
17:46 Philistines this **d** unto the fowls of the air, 3117
18: 2 Saul took him that **d**, and would let him go 3117
18: 9 Saul eyed David from that **d** and forward. 3117
18:21 Thou shalt *this* **d** be my son in law in 3117
19:24 lay down naked all that **d** and all *that* night. 3117
20: 5 myself in the fields unto the third *d* at even. NIH
20:12 *or* the third *d*, and behold, *if there be* good NIH
20:26 Saul spake not any thing that **d**: 3117
20:27 *which was* the second *d* of the month, NIH
20:27 neither yesterday, nor **to d**? 3117+1886.1
20:34 did eat no meat the second **d** of the month: 3117
21: 5 though it were sanctified *this* **d** in 3117
21: 6 to put hot bread in the **d** when it was taken 3117
21: 7 of the servants of Saul *was* there that **d**, 3117
21:10 fled that **d** for fear of Saul, and went to 3117
22: 8 against me, to lie in wait, as at this **d**? 3117
22:13 rise against me, to lie in wait, as at this **d**? 3117
22:18 slew on that **d** fourscore and five persons 3117
22:22 David said unto Abiathar, I knew *it* that **d**, 3117
23:14 Saul sought him every **d**, but God delivered 3117
24: 4 Behold the **d** of which the LORD said 3117
24:10 this **d** thine eyes have seen how that 3117
24:10 **to d** into mine hand in the cave: 3117+1886.1
24:18 thou hast shewed *this* **d** how that thou hast 3117
24:19 good for that thou hast done unto me this **d**. 3117
25: 8 for we come in a good **d**: give, I pray thee, 3117
25:16 were a wall unto us both by night and **d**, 3119
25:32 of Israel, which sent thee this **d** to meet me: 3117
25:33 which hast kept me this **d** from coming to 3117
26: 8 thine enemy into thine hand *this* **d**: 3117
26:10 or his **d** shall come to die; or he shall 3117
26:19 for they have driven me out *this* **d** from 3117
26:21 my soul was precious in thine eyes this **d**: 3117
26:23 delivered thee into *my* hand **to d**, 3117+1886.1
26:24 as thy life was much set by this **d** in mine 3117
27: 1 I shall now perish one **d** by the hand of 3117
27: 6 Achish gave him Ziklag that **d**: wherefore 3117
27: 6 unto the kings of Judah unto this **d**. 3117
27:10 Whither have ye made a road **to d**? 3117+1886.1
28:18 the LORD done this thing unto thee this **d**. 3117
28:20 for he had eaten no bread all the **d**, nor all 3117
29: 3 in him since he fell *unto me* unto this **d**? 3117
29: 6 for I have not found evil in thee since the **d** 3117
29: 6 the day of thy coming unto me unto this **d**: 3117
29: 8 so long as I have been with thee unto this **d**, 3117
30: 1 his men were come *to* Ziklag on the third **d**, 3117
30:17 even unto the evening of the **next d**: 4283
30:25 it was *so* from that **d** forward, that he made 3117
30:25 and an ordinance for Israel unto this **d**. 3117
31: 6 all his men, that *same* **d** together. 3117
2Sa 1: 2 It came even to pass on the third **d**, that 3117
2:17 there was a very sore battle that **d**; 3117
2:32 and they came to Hebron **at break of d**. 215
3: 8 *this* **d** unto the house of Saul thy father, 3117
3: 8 that thou chargest me **to d** with a 3117+1886.1
3:35 cause David to eat meat while it was yet **d**, 3117
3:37 all Israel understood that **d** that it was not 3117
3:38 and a great *man* fallen this **d** in Israel? 3117
3:39 I *am this* **d** weak, though anointed king; 3117
4: 3 and were sojourners there until this **d**.) 3117
4: 5 came about the heat of the **d** to the house of 3117
4: 8 avenged my lord the king this **d** of Saul, 3117
5: 8 David said on that **d**, Whosoever getteth up 3117
6: 8 *the name* of the place Perez-uzzah to this **d**. 3117
6: 9 David was afraid of the LORD that **d**, 3117
6:20 was the king of Israel **to d**, 3117+1886.1
6:20 who uncovered himself **to d** in 3117+1886.1
6:23 Saul had no child unto the **d** of her death. 3117
7: 6 even to this **d**, but have walked in a tent 3117
11:12 Tarry here **to d** also, and 3117+1886.1
11:12 So Uriah abode in Jerusalem that **d**, and 3117
12:18 it came to pass on the seventh **d**, that 3117
13: 4 *being* the king's son, lean from day to **d**? 1242
13: 4 *being* the king's son, lean from **d** to day? 1242
13:32 from the **d** that he forced his sister Tamar. 3117
13:37 And *David* mourned for his son every **d**. 3117
14:22 **To d** thy servant knoweth that I 3117+1886.1
15:20 should I *this* **d** make thee go up and 3117
16: 3 for he said, **To d** shall the house of 3117+1886.1
16:12 will requite me good for his cursing this **d**. 3117
18: 7 there was there a great slaughter that **d** *of* 3117
18: 8 the wood devoured more people that **d** than 3117
18:18 it is called unto this **d**, Absalom's place. 3117
18:20 Thou *shalt* not bear tidings this **d**, but 3117
18:20 but thou shalt bear tidings another **d**: 3117
18:20 this **d** thou shalt bear no tidings, because 3117
18:31 for the LORD hath avenged thee *this* **d** of 3117
19: 2 the victory that **d** was *turned* into mourning 3117
19: 2 for the people heard say that **d** *how* 3117
19: 3 the people gat them by stealth that **d** *into* 3117
19: 5 Thou hast shamed *this* **d** the faces of all thy 3117
19: 5 which *this* **d** have saved thy life, and 3117
19: 6 for thou hast declared *this* **d**, that thou 3117
19: 6 for *this* **d** I perceive, that if Absalom had 3117
19: 6 all we had died *this* **d**, then it had pleased 3117
19:19 **d** that my lord the king went out of 3117
19:20 I am come the first *this* **d** of all the house of 3117
19:22 that ye should *this* **d** be adversaries unto 3117
19:22 shall there any man be put to death *this* **d** in 3117
19:22 for do not I know that I *am this* **d** king over 3117
19:24 from the **d** the king departed until the day 3117
19:24 from the day the king departed until the **d** 3117

2Sa 19:35 I *am this* **d** fourscore years old: *and* can I 3117
20: 3 So they were shut up unto the **d** of their 3117
21:10 the birds of the air to rest on them **by d**, 3119
22: 1 **d** *that* the LORD had delivered him out of 3117
22:19 They prevented me in the **d** of my 3117
23:10 the LORD wrought a great victory that **d**; 3117
24:18 Gad came that **d** to David, and said unto 3117
1Ki 1:25 For he is gone down *this* **d**, and hath slain 3117
1:30 my stead; even so will I certainly do this **d**. 3117
1:48 hath given *one* to sit on my throne *this* **d**, 3117
1:51 **to d** that he will not slay his 3117+1886.1
2: 8 curse in the **d** when I went *to* Mahanaim: 3117
2:24 Adonijah shall be put to death *this* **d**. 3117
2:37 *that* on the **d** thou goest out, and 3117
2:42 on the **d** thou goest out, and walkest *abroad* 3117
3: 6 him a son to sit on his throne, as *it is* this **d**. 3117
3:18 it came to pass the third **d** after that I was 3117
4:22 Solomon's provision for one **d** was thirty 3117
5: 7 and said, Blessed *be* the LORD *this* **d**, 3117
8: 8 seen without: and there they are unto this **d**. 3117
8:16 Since the **d** that I brought forth my people 3117
8:24 fulfilled *it* with thine hand, as *it is* this **d**. 3117
8:28 servant prayeth before thee **to d**: 3117+1886.1
8:29 may be open toward this house night and **d**, 3117
8:59 be nigh unto the LORD our God **d** and 3119
8:61 to keep his commandments, as at this **d**. 3117
8:64 The same **d** did the king hallow the middle 3117
8:66 On the eighth **d** he sent the people away: 3117
9:13 called them the land of Cabul unto this **d**. 3117
9:21 levy a tribute of bondservice unto this **d**. 3117
10:12 such almug trees, nor were seen unto this **d**. 3117
12: 7 wilt be a servant unto this people *this* **d**, 3117
12:12 the people came to Rehoboam the third **d**, 3117
12:12 saying, Come to me again the third **d**. 3117
12:19 against the house of David unto this **d**. 3117
12:32 on the fifteenth **d** of the month, like unto 3117
12:33 Beth-el the fifteenth **d** of the eighth month, 3117
13: 3 he gave a sign the same **d**, saying, This *is* 3117
13:11 the man of God had done *that* **d** in Beth-el: 3117
14:14 shall cut off the house of Jeroboam that **d**: 3117
16:16 king over Israel that **d** in the camp. 3117
17:14 until the **d** *that* the LORD sendeth rain 3117
18:15 surely shew myself unto him **to d**. 3117+1886.1
18:36 let it be known *this* **d** that thou *art* God in 3117
20:13 I will deliver it into thine hand *this* **d**; 3117
20:29 that in the seventh **d** the battle was joined: 3117
20:29 an hundred thousand footmen in one **d**. 3117
22: 5 at the word of the LORD **to d**. 3117+1886.1
22:25 Behold, thou shalt see in that **d**, 3117
22:35 the battle increased that **d**: and the king was 3117
2Ki 2: 3 thy master from thy head **to d**? 3117+1886.1
2: 5 thy master from thy head **to d**? 3117+1886.1
2:22 So the waters were healed unto this **d**, 3117
4: 8 it fell on a **d**, that Elisha passed to Shunem, 3117
4:11 it fell on a **d**, that he came thither, and 3117
4:18 when the child was grown, it fell on a **d**, 3117
4:23 wilt thou go to him **to d**? 3117+1886.1
6:28 that we may eat him **to d**, and we 3117+1886.1
6:29 I said unto her on the next **d**, Give thy son, 3117
6:31 son of Shaphat shall stand on him *this* **d**. 3117
7: 9 this **d** *is* a day of good tidings, and we hold 3117
7: 9 this day *is* a **d** of good tidings, and we hold 3117
8: 6 all the fruits of the field since the **d** that she 3117
8:22 from under the hand of Judah unto this **d**. 3117
10:27 and made it a draught house unto *this* **d**. 3117
14: 7 called the name of it Joktheel unto this **d**. 3117
15: 5 that he was a leper unto the **d** of his death, 3117
16: 6 came *to* Elath, and dwelt there unto this **d**. 3117
17:23 out of their own land to Assyria unto this **d**. 3117
17:34 Unto this **d** they do after the former 3117
17:41 as did their fathers, *so* do they unto this **d**. 3117
19: 3 This **d** *is* a day of trouble, and of rebuke, 3117
19: 3 This day *is* a **d** of trouble, and of rebuke, 3117
20: 5 on the third **d** thou shalt go up *unto* 3117
20: 8 *into* the house of the LORD the third **d**? 3117
20:17 thy fathers have laid up in store unto this **d**, 3117
21:15 since the **d** their fathers came forth out of 3117
21:15 came forth out of Egypt, even unto this **d**. 3117
25: 1 the tenth month, in the tenth *d* of the month, NIH
25: 3 on the ninth *d* of the *fourth* month NIH
25: 8 fifth month, on the seventh *d* of the month, NIH
25:27 on the seven and twentieth *d* of the month, NIH
25:30 a daily rate for every **d**, all the days of his 3117
1Ch 4:41 destroyed them utterly unto this **d**, and 3117
4:43 were escaped, and dwelt there unto this **d**. 3117
5:26 Hara, and to the river Gozan, unto this **d**. 3117
9:33 for they were employed in *that* work **d** and 3119
11:22 and slew a lion in a pit in a snowy **d**. 3117
12:22 For at *that* time **d** by day there came to 3117
12:22 For at *that* time day by **d** there came to 3117
13:11 that place is called Perez-uzza to this **d**. 3117
13:12 David was afraid of God that **d**, saying, 3117
16: 7 on that **d** David delivered first *this psalm* to 3117
16:23 shew forth from **d** to day his salvation. 3117
16:23 shew forth from day to **d** his salvation. 3117
17: 5 For I have not dwelt in a house since the **d** 3117
17: 5 the day that I brought up Israel unto this **d**; 3117
26:17 northward four a **d**, southward four a day, 3117
26:17 southward four a **d**, and toward Asuppim 3117
28: 7 and my judgments, as *at* this **d**. 3117
29: 5 is willing to consecrate his service *this* **d** 3117
29:21 on the morrow after that **d**, *even* a thousand 3117
29:22 drink before the LORD on that **d** with 3117
2Ch 3: 2 he began to build in the second *d* of NIH
5: 9 not seen without. And there it is unto this **d**. 3117
6: 5 Since the **d** that I brought forth my people 3117
6:15 fulfilled *it* with thine hand, as *it is* this **d**. 3117
6:20 thine eyes may be open upon this house **d** 3119
7: 9 in the eighth **d** they made a solemn 3117
7:10 twentieth **d** of the seventh month he sent 3117
8: 8 Solomon make to pay tribute until this **d**. 3117
8:13 after a certain rate **every d**, 3117+3117+871.1
8:14 the duty of **every d** required: 3117+3117+871.1
8:16 **d** of the foundation of the house of 3117
10:12 people came to Rehoboam on the third **d**, 3117

D

2Ch 10:12 saying, Come again to me on the third **d**. 3117
10:19 against the house of David unto this **d**. 3117
18: 4 at the word of the LORD **to d**. 3117+1886.1
18:24 thou shalt see on that **d** when thou shalt go 3117
18:34 the battle increased that **d**: howbeit the king 3117
20:26 on the fourth **d** they assembled themselves 3117
20:26 The valley of Berachah, unto *this* **d**. 3117
21:10 from under the hand of Judah unto this **d**. 3117
21:15 fall out by reason of the sickness **d** by day. 3117
21:15 fall out by reason of the sickness day by **d**. 3117
24:11 Thus they did **d** by day, and 3117
24:11 Thus they did day by **d**, and 3117
26:21 Uzziah the king was a leper unto the **d** of 3117
28: 6 an hundred and twenty thousand in one **d**, 3117
29:17 Now they began on the first ***d*** of the first NIH
29:17 on the eighth **d** of the month came they to 3117
29:17 in the sixteenth **d** of the first month they 3117
30:15 they killed the passover on the fourteenth ***d*** NIH
30:21 the priests praised the LORD **d** by day, 3117
30:21 the priests praised the LORD day by **d**, 3117
35: 1 they killed the passover on the fourteenth ***d*** NIH
35:16 of the LORD was prepared the same **d**, 3117
35:21 *I come* not against thee *this* **d**, but 3117
35:25 of Josiah in their lamentations to *this* **d**, 3117
Ezr 3: 4 the duty of **every d** required; 3117+3117+871.1
3: 6 From the first **d** of the seventh month 3117
6: 9 let *it* be given them **d** by day without fail: 3118
6: 9 let *it* be given them day by **d** without fail: 3118
6:15 this house was finished on the third **d** of 3118
6:19 upon the fourteenth ***d*** of the first month. NIH
7: 9 For upon the first ***d*** of the first month began NIH
7: 9 on the first ***d*** of the fifth month came he to NIH
8:31 of Ahava on the twelfth ***d*** of the first month, NIH
8:33 Now on the fourth **d** was the silver and 3117
9: 7 we *been* in a great trespass unto this **d**; 3117
9: 7 and to confusion of face, as *it is* this **d**. 3117
9:15 for we remain *yet* escaped, as *it is* this **d**: 3117
10: 9 on the twentieth ***d*** of the month; NIH
10:13 neither *is this* a work of one **d** or two: 3117
10:16 sat down in the first **d** of the tenth month to 3117
10:17 wives by the first **d** of the first month. 3117
Ne 1: 6 which I pray before thee now, **d** and night, 3119
1:11 thy servant *this* **d**, and grant him mercy in 3117
4: 2 will they make an end in a **d**? will they 3117
4: 9 set a watch against them **d** and night, 3119
4:22 may be a guard to us, and labour on the **d**. 3117
5:11 Restore, I pray you, to them, even *this* **d**, 3117
6:15 in the twenty and fifth ***d*** of *the month* Elul, NIH
8: 2 upon the first **d** of the seventh month. 3117
8: 9 *This* **d** *is* holy unto the LORD your God; 3117
8:10 for *this* **d** *is* holy unto our Lord: neither be 3117
8:11 Hold your peace, for the **d** *is* holy; 3117
8:13 on the second **d** were gathered together 3117
8:17 **d** had not the children of Israel done so. 3117
8:18 Also **d** by day, from the first day unto 3117
8:18 Also day by **d**, from the first day unto 3117
8:18 by day, from the first **d** unto the last day, 3117
8:18 by day, from the first day unto the last **d**, 3117
8:18 and on the eighth **d** *was* a solemn assembly, 3117
9: 1 fourth **d** of this month the children of Israel 3117
9: 3 LORD their God *one* fourth *part* of the **d**; 3117
9:10 So didst thou get thee a name, as *it is* this **d**. 3117
9:12 Moreover thou leddest them in the **d** by a 3119
9:19 of the cloud departed not from them by **d**, 3119
9:32 the time of the kings of Assyria unto this **d**. 3117
9:36 we *are* servants *this* **d**, and *for* the land that 3117
10:31 or any victuals on the sabbath **d** to sell, 3117
10:31 *it* of them on the sabbath, or on the holy **d**: 3117
11:23 the singers, due **for every d**. 3117+3117+871.1
12:43 Also that **d** they offered great sacrifices, 3117
12:47 **every d** his portion: 3117+3117+871.1
13: 1 On that **d** they read in the book of Moses in 3117
13:15 brought *into* Jerusalem on the sabbath **d**: 3117
13:15 I testified *against them* in the **d** wherein 3117
13:17 this that ye do, and profane the sabbath **d**? 3117
13:19 no burden be brought in on the sabbath **d**. 3117
13:22 keep the gates, to sanctify the sabbath **d**. 3117
Est 1:10 On the seventh **d**, when the heart of 3117
1:18 Media say this **d** unto all the king's princes, 3117
2:11 **every d** before 3117+3117+3605+2050.1
3: 7 before Haman from **d** to day, and 3117
3: 7 before Haman from day to **d**, and 3117
3:12 called on the thirteenth **d** of the first month, 3117
3:13 little children and women, in one **d**, 3117
3:13 *even* upon the thirteenth ***d*** of the twelfth NIH
3:14 that *they* should be ready against that **d**. 3117
4:16 neither eat nor drink three days, night or **d**; 3117
5: 1 Now it came to pass on the third **d**, 3117
5: 4 Haman come *this* **d** unto the banquet that I 3117
5: 9 went Haman forth that **d** joyful and with a 3117
7: 2 on the second **d** at the banquet of wine, 3117
8: 1 On that **d** did the king Ahasuerus give 3117
8: 9 on the three and twentieth ***d*** thereof; NIH
8:12 Upon one **d** in all the provinces of king 3117
8:12 *namely,* upon the thirteenth ***d*** of the twelfth NIH
8:13 that the Jews should be ready against that **d** 3117
8:17 had joy and gladness, a feast and a good **d**. 3117
9: 1 on the thirteenth **d** of the same, 3117
9: 1 in the **d** that the enemies of the Jews hoped 3117
9:11 On that **d** the number of those that were 3117
9:15 on the fourteenth **d** also of the month Adar, 3117
9:17 On the thirteenth **d** of the month Adar; and 3117
9:17 on the fourteenth **d** of the same rested they, NIH
9:17 and made it a **d** of feasting and gladness. 3117
9:18 together on the thirteenth ***d*** thereof, NIH
9:18 on the fifteenth ***d*** of the same they rested, NIH
9:18 and made it a **d** of feasting and gladness. 3117
9:19 made the fourteenth **d** of the month Adar *a* 3117
9:19 day of the month Adar *a* ***d*** *of* gladness NIH
9:19 a good **d**, and *of* sending portions one to 3117
9:21 that they should keep the fourteenth **d** of 3117
9:21 and the fifteenth **d** of the same, yearly, 3117
9:22 to joy, and from mourning into a good **d**: 3117
Job 1: 4 and feasted *in their* houses, every one his **d**; 3117
1: 6 Now there was a **d** when the sons of God 3117
1:13 there was a **d** when his sons and 3117
2: 1 Again there was a **d** when the sons of God 3117
3: 1 opened Job his mouth, and cursed his **d**. 3117
3: 3 Let the **d** perish wherein I was born, and 3117
3: 4 Let that **d** be darkness; let not God regard it 3117
3: 5 upon it; let the blackness of the **d** terrify it. 3117
3: 8 Let them curse it that curse the **d**, who are 3117
3: 9 neither let it see the dawning of the **d**: 7837
7: 4 and fro unto the **dawning of the d**. 5399
14: 6 till he shall accomplish, as a hireling, his **d**. 3117
15:23 *saying,* Where *is it?* he knoweth that the **d** 3117
17:12 They change the night into **d**: the light *is* 3117
18:20 come after *him* shall be astonied at his **d**, 3117
19:25 *that* he shall stand *at* the latter ***d*** upon NIH
20:28 *his goods shall* flow away in the **d** of his 3117
21:30 That the wicked is reserved to the **d** of 3117
21:30 they shall be brought forth to the **d** of 3117
23: 2 Even **to d** *is* my complaint bitter: 3117+1886.1
26:10 until the **d** and night come to an end. 216
38:23 of trouble, against the **d** of battle and war? 3117
Ps 1: 2 and in his law doth he meditate **d** and night. 3119
2: 7 *art* my Son; *this* **d** have I begotten thee. 3117
7:11 and God is angry *with the wicked* every **d**. 3117
18: T **d** *that* the LORD delivered him from 3117
18:18 They prevented me in the **d** of my 3117
19: 2 **D** unto day uttereth speech, and night unto 3117
19: 2 Day unto **d** uttereth speech, and night unto 3117
20: 1 The LORD hear thee in the **d** of trouble; 3117
25: 5 of my salvation; on thee do I wait all the **d**. 3117
32: 3 old through my roaring all the **d** long. 3117
32: 4 For **d** and night thy hand was heavy upon 3119
35:28 *and* of thy praise all the **d** long. 3117
37:13 at him: for he seeth that his **d** is coming. 3117
38: 6 down greatly; I go mourning all the **d** long. 3117
38:12 and imagine deceits all the **d** long. 3117
42: 3 My tears have been my meat **d** and night, 3119
44: 8 In God we boast all the **d** long, and 3117
44:22 for thy sake are we killed all the **d** long; 3117
50:15 call upon me in the **d** of trouble: I will 3117
55:10 **D** and night they go about it upon the walls 3119
56: 5 Every **d** they wrest my words: all their 3117
59:16 and refuge in the **d** of my trouble. 3117
71: 8 thy praise *and with* thy honour all the **d**. 3117
71:15 *and* thy salvation all the **d**; 3117
71:24 talk of thy righteousness all the **d** long: 3117
73:14 For all the **d** long have I been plagued, and 3117
74:16 The **d** *is* thine, the night also *is* thine: 3117
77: 2 In the **d** of my trouble I sought the Lord: 3117
78: 9 turned *back* in the **d** of battle. 3117
78:42 *nor* the **d** when he delivered them from 3117
81: 3 the time appointed, on our solemn feast **d**. 3117
84:10 For a **d** in thy courts *is* better than a 3117
86: 7 In the **d** of my trouble I will call upon thee: 3117
88: 1 I have cried **d** *and* night before thee: 3117
89:16 In thy name shall they rejoice all the **d**: and 3117
91: 5 by night; *nor* for the arrow *that* flieth **by d**; 3119
92: T A Psalm *or* Song for the sabbath **d**. 3117
95: 7 **To d** if ye will hear his voice, 3117+1886.1
95: 8 as *in* the **d** of temptation in the wilderness: 3117
96: 2 shew forth his salvation from **d** to day. 3117
96: 2 shew forth his salvation from day to **d**. 3117
102: 2 Hide not thy face from me in the **d** *when* I 3117
102: 2 in the **d** *when* I call answer me speedily. 3117
102: 8 Mine enemies reproach me all the **d**; *and* 3117
110: 3 Thy people *shall be* willing in the **d** of thy 3117
110: 5 strike through kings in the **d** of his wrath. 3117
118:24 This *is* the **d** *which* the LORD hath made; 3117
119:91 They continue *this* **d** according to thine 3117
119:97 love I thy law! it *is* my meditation all the **d**. 3117
119:164 Seven *times* a **d** do I praise thee because 3117
121: 6 The sun shall not smite thee **by d**, nor 3119
136: 8 The sun to rule by **d**: for his mercy 3117
137: 7 the children of Edom *in* the **d** of Jerusalem; 3117
138: 3 In the **d** when I cried thou answeredst me, 3117
139:12 from thee; but the night shineth as the **d**: 3117
140: 7 thou hast covered my head in the **d** of 3117
145: 2 Every **d** will I bless thee; and I will praise 3117
146: 4 his earth; in that *very* **d** his thoughts perish. 3117
Pr 4:18 shineth more and more unto the perfect **d**. 3117
6:34 he will not spare in the **d** of vengeance. 3117
7:14 with me; *this* **d** have I payed my vows. 3117
7:20 will come home at the **d** appointed. 3117
11: 4 Riches profit not in the **d** of wrath: but 3117
16: 4 even the wicked for the **d** of evil. 3117
21:26 He coveteth greedily all the **d** long: but 3117
21:31 The horse *is* prepared against the **d** of 3117
22:19 I have made known to thee *this* **d**, even *to* 3117
23:17 *be thou* in the fear of the LORD all the **d** 3117
24:10 *If* thou faint in the **d** of adversity, 3117
27: 1 for thou knowest not what a **d** may bring 3117
27:10 neither go *into* thy brother's house in the **d** 3117
27:15 A continual dropping in a very rainy **d** and 3117
Ecc 7: 1 the **d** of death than the day of one's birth. 3117
7: 1 the day of death than the **d** of one's birth. 3117
7:14 In the **d** of prosperity be joyful, but in 3117
7:14 be joyful, but in the **d** of adversity consider: 3117
8: 8 neither *hath he* power in the **d** of death: 3117
8:16 (for also *there is that* neither **d** nor night 3117
12: 3 In the **d** when the keepers of the house shall 3117
SS 2:17 Until the **d** break, and the shadows flee 3117
3:11 crowned him in the **d** of his espousals, 3117
3:11 and in the **d** of the gladness of his heart. 3117
4: 6 Until the **d** break, and the shadows flee 3117
8: 8 what shall we do for our sister in the **d** 3117
Isa 2:11 the LORD alone shall be exalted in that **d**. 3117
2:12 For the **d** of the LORD of hosts *shall be* 3117
2:17 the LORD alone shall be exalted in that **d**. 3117
2:20 In that **d** a man shall cast his idols of silver, 3117
3: 7 In that **d** shall he swear, saying, I will not 3117
3:18 In that **d** the Lord will take away 3117
4: 1 in that **d** seven women shall take hold of 3117
4: 2 In that **d** shall the branch of the LORD be 3117
4: 5 a cloud and smoke **by d**, and the shining of 3119
5:30 in that **d** they shall roar against them like 3117
7:17 from the **d** that Ephraim departed from 3117
7:18 it shall come to pass in that **d**, *that* 3117
7:20 In the same **d** shall the Lord shave with a 3117
7:21 it shall come to pass in that **d**, *that* a man 3117
7:23 it shall come to pass in that **d**, *that* every 3117
9: 4 rod of his oppressor, as *in* the **d** of Midian. 3117
9:14 and tail, branch and rush, *in* one **d**. 3117
10: 3 what will ye do in the **d** of visitation, and 3117
10:17 devour his thorns and his briers in one **d**; 3117
10:20 it shall come to pass in that **d**, *that* 3117
10:27 it shall come to pass in that **d**, *that* his 3117
10:32 As yet shall *he* remain at Nob *that* **d**: 3117
11:10 in that **d** there shall be a root of Jesse, 3117
11:11 it shall come to pass in that **d**, *that* the Lord 3117
11:16 like as it was to Israel in the **d** that he came 3117
12: 1 in that **d** thou shalt say, O LORD, I will 3117
12: 4 in that **d** shall ye say, Praise the LORD, 3117
13: 6 for the **d** of the LORD *is* at hand; 3117
13: 9 Behold, the **d** of the LORD cometh, 3117
13:13 of hosts, and in the **d** of his fierce anger. 3117
14: 3 it shall come to pass in the **d** that 3117
17: 4 in that **d** it shall come to pass, *that* the glory 3117
17: 7 At that **d** shall a man look to his Maker, 3117
17: 9 In that **d** shall his strong cities be as a 3117
17:11 In the **d** shalt thou make thy plant to grow, 3117
17:11 the harvest *shall be* a heap in the **d** of grief 3117
19:16 In that **d** shall Egypt be like unto women: 3117
19:18 In that **d** shall five cities in the land of 3117
19:19 In that **d** shall there be an altar to 3117
19:21 Egyptians shall know the LORD in that **d**, 3117
19:23 In that **d** shall there be a highway out of 3117
19:24 In that **d** shall Israel be the third with Egypt 3117
20: 6 the inhabitant of this isle shall say in that **d**, 3117
22: 5 For *it is* a **d** of trouble, and of treading 3117
22: 8 thou didst look in that **d** to the armour of 3117
22:12 in that **d** did the Lord GOD of hosts call to 3117
22:20 it shall come to pass in that **d**, that I will 3117
22:25 In that **d**, saith the LORD of hosts, 3117
23:15 it shall come to pass in that **d**, that Tyre 3117
24:21 it shall come to pass in that **d**, *that* 3117
25: 9 it shall be said in that **d**, Lo, this *is* our 3117
26: 1 In that **d** shall this song be sung in the land 3117
27: 1 In that **d** the LORD with his sore and 3117
27: 2 In that **d** sing ye unto her, A vineyard of 3117
27: 3 lest *any* hurt it, I will keep it night and **d**. 3117
27: 8 he stayeth his rough wind in the **d** of 3117
27:12 it shall come to pass in that **d**, *that* 3117
27:13 it shall come to pass in that **d**, *that* the great 3117
28: 5 In that **d** shall the LORD of hosts be for a 3117
28:19 shall it pass over, by **d** and by night: 3117
28:24 Doth the plowman plow all **d** to sow? 3117
29:18 in that **d** shall the deaf hear the words of 3117
30:23 in that **d** shall thy cattle feed *in* large 3117
30:25 streams of waters in the **d** of the great 3117
30:26 in the **d** that the LORD bindeth up 3117
31: 7 For in that **d** every man shall cast away his 3117
34: 8 For *it is* the **d** of the LORD'S vengeance, 3117
34:10 It shall not be quenched night nor **d**; 3119
37: 3 This **d** *is* a day of trouble, and of rebuke, 3117
37: 3 This day *is* a **d** of trouble, and of rebuke, 3117
38:12 from **d** *even* to night wilt thou make an end 3117
38:13 from **d** *even* to night wilt thou make an end 3117
38:19 he shall praise thee, as I *do this* **d**: 3117
39: 6 thy fathers have laid up in store until this **d**, 3117
43:13 Yea, before the **d** *was* I *am* he; and *there is* 3117
47: 9 shall come to thee *in* a moment in one **d**, 3117
48: 7 even before the **d** when thou heardest them 3117
49: 8 and in a **d** of salvation have I helped thee: 3117
51:13 hast feared continually every **d** because of 3117
52: 5 my name continually every **d** *is* 3117
52: 6 *they shall know* in that **d** that I *am* he that 3117
56:12 to morrow shall be as this **d**, *and* 3117
58: 3 in the **d** of your fast you find pleasure, and 3117
58: 4 ye shall not fast as *ye do this* **d**, to make 3117
58: 5 a **d** for a man to afflict his soul? *is it* to bow 3117
58: 5 a fast, and an acceptable **d** to the LORD? 3117
58:13 *from* doing thy pleasure on my holy **d**; 3117
60:11 they shall not be shut **d** nor night; 3119
60:19 The sun shall be no more thy light **by d**; 3119
61: 2 and the **d** of vengeance of our God; 3117
62: 6 *which* shall never hold their peace **d** nor 3117
63: 4 For the **d** of vengeance *is* in mine heart, 3117
65: 2 I have spread out mine hands all the **d** unto 3117
65: 5 in my nose, a fire that burneth all the **d**. 3117
66: 8 the earth be made to bring forth in one **d**? 3117
Jer 1:10 I have this **d** set thee over the nations and 3117
1:18 I have made thee *this* **d** a defenced city, and 3117
3:25 from our youth even unto this **d**, and 3117
4: 9 it shall come to pass at that **d**, saith 3117
6: 4 for the **d** goeth away, for the shadows of 3117
7:22 nor commanded them in the **d** that I 3117
7:25 Since the **d** that your fathers came forth out 3117
7:25 forth out of the land of Egypt unto this **d**, 3117
9: 1 that I might weep **d** and night for the slain 3119
11: 4 Which I commanded your fathers in the **d** 3117
11: 5 flowing with milk and honey, as *it is* this **d**. 3117
11: 7 **d** that I brought them up out of the land of 3117
11: 7 *even* unto this **d**, rising early and 3117
12: 3 and prepare them for the **d** of slaughter. 3117
14:17 mine eyes run down *with* tears night and **d**, 3119
15: 9 her sun is gone down while *it was* yet **d**: 3119
16:13 there shall ye serve other gods **d** and night; 3119
16:19 and my refuge in the **d** of affliction, 3117
17:16 neither have I desired the woeful **d**; 3117
17:17 unto me: thou *art* my hope in the **d** of evil. 3117
17:18 bring upon them the **d** of evil, and 3117
17:21 bear no burden on the sabbath **d**, 3117
17:22 burden out of your houses on the sabbath **d**, 3117
17:22 ye any work, but hallow ye the sabbath **d**, 3117
17:24 the gates of this city on the sabbath **d**, 3117
17:24 hallow the sabbath **d**, to do no work 3117
17:27 hearken unto me to hallow the sabbath **d**, 3117
17:27 at the gates of Jerusalem on the sabbath **d**; 3117
18:17 and not the face, in the **d** of their calamity. 3117
20:14 Cursed *be the* **d** wherein I was born: let not 3117
20:14 let not the **d** wherein my mother bare me be 3117

Jer 25: 3 even unto this **d**, that *is* the three and 3117
25:18 a hissing, and a curse; as *it is* this **d**; 3117
25:33 the slain of the LORD shall be at that **d** 3117
27:22 there shall they be until the **d** that I visit 3117
30: 7 for that **d** *is* great, so that none *is* like it: 3117
30: 8 For it shall come to pass in that **d**, saith 3117
31: 6 For there shall be a **d**, *that* the watchmen 3117
31:32 in the **d** *that* I took them by the hand, 3117
31:35 which giveth the sun for a light **by d**, *and* 3119
32:20 *even* unto this **d**, and in Israel, and 3117
32:20 and hast made thee a name, as *at* this **d**; 3117
32:31 of my fury from the **d** that they built it even 3117
32:31 the day that they built it even unto this **d**; 3117
33:20 If you can break my covenant of the **d**, and 3117
33:20 that there should not be **d** and night in their 3119
33:25 If my covenant *be* not with **d** and night, *and* 3119
34:13 made a covenant with your fathers in the **d** 3117
35:14 for unto this **d** they drink none, but 3117
36: 2 the nations, from the **d** I spake unto thee, 3117
36: 2 from the days of Josiah, even unto this **d**. 3117
36: 6 *in* the LORD'S house upon the fasting **d**: 3117
36:30 his dead body shall be cast out in the **d** to 3117
38:28 prison until the **d** that Jerusalem was taken: 3117
39: 2 the fourth month, the ninth ***d*** of the month, NIH
39:16 they shall be *accomplished* in that **d** before 3117
39:17 I will deliver thee in that **d**, saith 3117
40: 4 I loose thee *this* **d** from the chains which 3117
41: 4 it came to pass the second **d** after *he* had 3117
42:19 certainly that I have admonished you *this* **d**. 3117
42:21 *now* I have *this* **d** declared *it* to you; but 3117
44: 2 this **d** they *are* a desolation, and no man 3117
44: 6 they are wasted *and* desolate, as *at* this **d**. 3117
44:10 They are not humbled *even* unto this **d**, 3117
44:22 a curse, without an inhabitant, as *at* this **d**. 3117
44:23 this evil is happened unto you, as *at* this **d**. 3117
46:10 For this *is* the **d** of the Lord GOD of hosts, 3117
46:10 a **d** of vengeance, that *he* may avenge him 3117
46:21 the **d** of their calamity was come upon 3117
47: 4 Because of the **d** that cometh to spoil all 3117
48:41 the mighty *men's* hearts in Moab at that **d** 3117
49:22 at that **d** shall the heart of the mighty *men* 3117
49:26 all the men of war shall be cut off in that **d**, 3117
50:27 for their **d** is come, the time of their 3117
50:30 all her men of war shall be cut off in that **d**, 3117
50:31 for thy **d** is come, the time *that* I will visit 3117
51: 2 for in the **d** of trouble they shall be against 3117
52: 4 the tenth month, in the tenth ***d*** of the month, NIH
52: 6 fourth month, in the ninth ***d*** of the month, NIH
52:11 and put him in prison till the **d** of his death. 3117
52:12 the fifth month, in the tenth ***d*** of the month, NIH
52:31 in the five and twentieth ***d*** of the month, NIH
52:34 **every d** a portion until 3117+3117+871.1
52:34 every day a portion until the **d** of his death, 3117
La 1:12 afflicted *me* in the **d** of his fierce anger. 3117
1:13 hath made me desolate *and* faint all the **d**. 3117
1:21 thou wilt bring the **d** *that* thou hast called, 3117
2: 1 remembered not his footstool in the **d** of his 3117
2: 7 the LORD, as *in* the **d** of a solemn feast. 3117
2:16 certainly this *is* the **d** that we looked for; 3117
2:18 let tears run down like a river **d** and night: 3119
2:21 thou hast slain *them* in the **d** of thine anger; 3117
2:22 Thou hast called as *in* a solemn **d** my 3117
2:22 that in the **d** of the LORD'S anger none 3117
3: 3 he turneth his hand *against me* all the **d**. 3117
3:14 to all my people; *and* their song all the **d**. 3117
3:57 Thou drewest near in the **d** *that* I called 3117
3:62 and their device against me all the **d**. 3117
Eze 1: 1 in the fourth *month*, in the fifth ***d*** of NIH
1: 2 In the fifth ***d*** of the month, which *was* NIH
1:28 the bow that is in the cloud in the **d** of rain, 3117
2: 3 against me, *even* unto this very **d**. 3117
4: 6 appointed thee **each d** for a year. 3117+3117
4:10 eat *shall be* by weight, twenty shekels a **d**: 3117
7: 7 the **d** of trouble *is* near, and not 3117
7:10 Behold the **d**, behold, it is come: 3117
7:12 The time is come, the **d** draweth near: 3117
7:19 them in the **d** of the wrath of the LORD: 3117
8: 1 in the sixth *month*, in the fifth ***d*** of NIH
12: 3 and remove **by d** in their sight; 3119
12: 4 shalt thou bring forth thy stuff **by d** in their 3119
12: 7 I brought forth my stuff **by d**, as stuff for 3119
13: 5 stand in the battle in the **d** of the LORD. 3117
16: 4 in the **d** thou wast born thy navel was not 3117
16: 5 of thy person, in the **d** that thou wast born. 3117
16:56 by thy mouth in the **d** of thy pride, 3117
20: 1 in the fifth *month*, the tenth ***d*** of the month, NIH
20: 5 In the **d** when I chose Israel, and lifted up 3117
20: 6 In the **d** *that* I lifted up mine hand unto 3117
20:29 name thereof is called Bamah unto this **d**. 3117
20:31 with all your idols, *even* unto *this* **d**: 3117
21:25 wicked prince of Israel, whose **d** is come, 3117
21:29 whose **d** is come, when *their* iniquity *shall* 3117
22:24 nor rained upon in the **d** of indignation. 3117
23:38 have defiled my sanctuary in the same **d**, 3117
23:39 they came the same **d** into my sanctuary to 3117
24: 1 the tenth month, in the tenth **d** of the month, NIH
24: 2 Son of man, write thee the name of the **d**, 3117
24: 2 the name of the day, *even* of this same **d**: 3117
24: 2 set himself against Jerusalem this same **d**. 3117
24:25 *shall it* not *be* in the **d** when I take from 3117
24:26 *That* he that escapeth in that **d** shall come 3117
24:27 In that **d** shall thy mouth be opened to him 3117
26: 1 eleventh year, in the first ***d*** of the month, NIH
26:18 Now shall the isles tremble *in* the **d** of thy 3117
27:27 shall fall into the midst of the seas in the **d** 3117
28:13 of thy pipes was prepared in thee in the **d** 3117
28:15 Thou *wast* perfect in thy ways from the **d** 3117
29: 1 in the tenth *month*, in the twelfth ***d*** of NIH
29:17 in the first *month*, in the first ***d*** of NIH
29:21 In that **d** will I cause the horn of the house 3117
30: 2 Lord GOD; Howl ye, Woe worth the **d**! 3117
30: 3 For the **d** *is* near, even the day of 3117
30: 3 even the **d** of the LORD *is* near, a cloudy 3117
30: 3 the day of the LORD *is* near, a cloudy **d**; 3117
30: 9 In that **d** shall messengers go forth from me 3117

Eze 30: 9 shall come upon them, as *in* the **d** of Egypt: 3117
30:18 At Tehaphnehes also the **d** shall be 3117
30:20 in the first *month*, in the seventh ***d*** of NIH
31: 1 in the third *month*, in the first ***d*** of NIH
31:15 In the **d** when he went down to the grave I 3117
32: 1 twelfth month, in the first ***d*** of the month, NIH
32:10 man for his own life, in the **d** of thy fall. 3117
32:17 twelfth year, in the fifteenth ***d*** of the month, NIH
33:12 deliver him in the **d** of his transgression: 3117
33:12 he shall not fall thereby in the **d** that he 3117
33:12 his *righteousness* in the **d** that he sinneth. 3117
33:21 in the tenth *month*, in the fifth ***d*** of NIH
34:12 As a shepherd seeketh out his flock in the **d** 3117
34:12 been scattered in the cloudy and dark **d**. 3117
36:33 In the **d** that I shall have cleansed you from 3117
38:14 In that **d** when my people of Israel dwelleth 3117
38:19 Surely in that **d** there shall be a great 3117
39: 8 this *is* the **d** whereof I have spoken. 3117
39:11 it shall come to pass in that **d**, *that* I will 3117
39:13 it shall be to them a renown the **d** that I 3117
39:22 that I *am* the LORD their God from that **d** 3117
40: 1 of the year, in the tenth ***d*** of the month, NIH
40: 1 in the selfsame **d** the hand of the LORD 3117
43:18 the altar in the **d** when *they* shall make it, 3117
43:22 on the second **d** thou shalt offer a kid of 3117
43:25 Seven days shalt thou prepare every **d** a 3117
43:27 *that* upon the eight **d**, and *so* forward, 3117
44:27 in the **d** that he goeth into the sanctuary, 3117
45:18 In the first *month*, in the first ***d*** of NIH
45:20 thou shalt do the seventh ***d*** of the month for NIH
45:21 In the first *month*, in the fourteenth **d** of 3117
45:22 upon that **d** shall the prince prepare for 3117
45:25 In the seventh *month*, in the fifteenth **d** of 3117
46: 1 in the **d** of the new moon it shall be opened. 3117
46: 4 **d** *shall be* six lambs without blemish, 3117
46: 6 in the **d** of the new moon *it shall be* a 3117
46:12 peace offerings, as he did on the sabbath **d**: 3117
48:35 the name of the city from *that* **d** *shall be*, 3117
Da 6:10 he kneeled upon his knees three times a **d**, 3118
6:13 but maketh his petition three times a **d**. 3118
9: 7 but unto us confusion of faces, as *at* this **d**; 3117
9:15 and hast gotten thee renown, as *at* this **d**; 3117
10: 4 the four and twentieth **d** of the first month, 3117
10:12 for from the first **d** that thou didst set thine 3117
Hos 1: 5 it shall come to pass at that **d**, that I will 3117
1:11 the land: for great *shall be* the **d** of Jezreel. 3117
2: 3 set her as *in* the **d** that she was born, and 3117
2:15 as *in* the **d** when she came up out of 3117
2:16 it shall be at that **d**, saith the LORD, 3117
2:18 in that **d** will I make a covenant for them 3117
2:21 it shall come to pass in that **d**, I will hear, 3117
4: 5 Therefore shalt thou fall *in* the **d**, and 3117
5: 9 Ephraim shall be desolate in the **d** of 3117
6: 2 in the third **d** he will raise us up, and 3117
7: 5 *In* the **d** of our king the princes have made 3117
9: 5 What will ye do in the solemn **d**, and in 3117
9: 5 and in the **d** of the feast of the LORD? 3117
10:14 as Shalman spoiled Beth-arbel in the **d** of 3117
Joel 1:15 Alas for the **d**! for the day of the LORD *is* 3117
1:15 for the **d** of the LORD *is* at hand, and as a 3117
2: 1 for the **d** of the LORD cometh, for *it is* 3117
2: 2 A **d** of darkness and of gloominess, a day 3117
2: 2 a **d** of clouds and of thick darkness, 3117
2:11 for the **d** of the LORD *is* great and 3117
2:31 and the terrible **d** of the LORD come. 3117
3:14 for the **d** of the LORD *is* near in the valley 3117
3:18 it shall come to pass in that **d**, *that* 3117
Am 1:14 with shouting in the **d** of battle, 3117
1:14 with a tempest in the **d** of the whirlwind: 3117
2:16 the mighty shall flee away naked in that **d**, 3117
3:14 That in the **d** that I shall visit 3117
5: 8 and maketh the **d** dark *with* night: 3117
5:18 Woe unto *you* that desire the **d** of 3117
5:18 the **d** of the LORD *is* darkness, and 3117
5:20 *Shall* not the **d** of the LORD *be* darkness, 3117
6: 3 Ye that put far away the evil **d**, and 3117
8: 3 of the temple shall be howlings in that **d**, 3117
8: 9 it shall come to pass in that **d**, saith 3117
8: 9 and I will darken the earth in the clear **d**: 3117
8:10 only *son*, and the end thereof as a bitter **d**. 3117
8:13 In that **d** shall the fair virgins and young 3117
9:11 In that **d** will I raise up the tabernacle of 3117
Ob 1: 8 Shall I not in that **d**, saith the LORD, 3117
1:11 In the **d** that thou stoodest on the other side, 3117
1:11 in the **d** that the strangers carried away 3117
1:12 thou shouldest not have looked on the **d** of 3117
1:12 brother in the **d** that he became a stranger; 3117
1:12 of Judah in the **d** of their destruction; 3117
1:12 have spoken proudly in the **d** of distress. 3117
1:13 of my people in the **d** of their calamity: 3117
1:13 on their affliction in the **d** of their calamity, 3117
1:13 on their substance in the **d** of their calamity; 3117
1:14 of his that did remain in the **d** of distress. 3117
1:15 For the **d** of the LORD *is* near upon all 3117
Jnh 4: 7 a worm when the morning rose the **next d**, 4283
Mic 2: 4 In that **d** shall *one* take up a parable against 3117
3: 6 and the **d** shall be dark over them. 3117
4: 6 In that **d**, saith the LORD, will I assemble 3117
5:10 it shall come to pass in that **d**, saith 3117
7: 4 the **d** of thy watchmen *and* thy visitation 3117
7:11 *In* the **d** that thy walls are *to be* built, *in* that 3117
7:11 *in* that **d** shall the decree be far removed. 3117
7:12 *In* that **d** *also* he shall come even to thee 3117
Na 1: 7 *is* good, a strong hold in the **d** of trouble; 3117
2: 3 flaming torches in the **d** of his preparation, 3117
3:17 which camp in the hedges in the cold **d**, *but* 3117
Hab 3:16 that I might rest in the **d** of trouble: 3117
Zep 1: 7 for the **d** of the LORD *is* at hand: for 3117
1: 8 it shall come to pass in the **d** of 3117
1: 9 In the same **d** also will I punish all those 3117
1:10 it shall come to pass in that **d**, saith 3117
1:14 The great **d** of the LORD *is* near, *it is* 3117
1:14 *even* the voice of the **d** of the LORD: 3117
1:15 That **d** *is* a day of wrath, a day of trouble 3117
1:15 That day *is* a **d** of wrath, a day of trouble 3117

Zep 1:15 a **d** of trouble and distress, a day of 3117
1:15 distress, a **d** of wasteness and desolation, 3117
1:15 desolation, a **d** of darkness and gloominess, 3117
1:15 a **d** of clouds and thick darkness, 3117
1:16 A **d** of the trumpet and alarm against 3117
1:18 them in the **d** of the LORD'S wrath; 3117
2: 2 bring forth, *before* the **d** pass as the chaff, 3117
2: 2 before the **d** of the LORD'S anger come 3117
2: 3 it may be ye shall be hid in the **d** of 3117
2: 4 they shall drive out Ashdod at the **noon d**, 6672
3: 8 until the **d** that I rise up to the prey: 3117
3:11 In that **d** shalt thou not be ashamed for all 3117
3:16 In that **d** it shall be said to Jerusalem, 3117
Hag 1: 1 the sixth month, in the first **d** of the month, 3117
1:15 the four and twentieth **d** of the sixth month, 3117
2: 1 in the one and twentieth ***d*** of the month, NIH
2:10 twentieth ***d*** of the ninth *month*, in NIH
2:15 pray you, consider from this **d** and upward, 3117
2:18 Consider now from this **d** and upward, 3117
2:18 twentieth **d** of the ninth *month*, *even* from 3117
2:18 **d** that the foundation of the LORD'S 3117
2:19 brought forth: from this **d** will I bless *you*. 3117
2:20 in the four and twentieth ***d*** of the month, NIH
2:23 In that **d**, saith the LORD of hosts, will I 3117
Zec 1: 7 and twentieth **d** of the eleventh month, 3117
2:11 shall be joined to the LORD in that **d**, 3117
3: 9 remove the iniquity of that land in one **d**. 3117
3:10 In that **d**, saith the LORD of hosts, 3117
4:10 For who hath despised the **d** of small 3117
6:10 come thou the same **d**, and go *into* 3117
7: 1 in the fourth ***d*** of the ninth month, NIH
8: 9 which *were* in the **d** *that* the foundation of 3117
9:12 even **to d** do I declare *that* I will 3117+1886.1
9:16 them in that **d** as the flock of his people: 3117
11:11 it was broken in that **d**: and so the poor of 3117
12: 3 in that **d** will I make Jerusalem a 3117
12: 4 In that **d**, saith the LORD, I will smite 3117
12: 6 In that **d** will I make the governors of Judah 3117
12: 8 In that **d** shall the LORD defend 3117
12: 8 he that is feeble among them at that **d** shall 3117
12: 9 it shall come to pass in that **d**, *that* I will 3117
12:11 In that **d** shall there be a great mourning in 3117
13: 1 In that **d** there shall be a fountain opened to 3117
13: 2 it shall come to pass in that **d**, saith 3117
13: 4 it shall come to pass in that **d**, *that* 3117
14: 1 the **d** of the LORD cometh, and thy spoil 3117
14: 3 as when he fought in the **d** of battle. 3117
14: 4 his feet shall stand in that **d** upon the mount 3117
14: 6 it shall come to pass in that **d**, *that* the light 3117
14: 7 it shall be one **d** which shall be known to 3117
14: 7 be known to the LORD, not **d**, nor night: 3117
14: 8 it shall be in that **d**, *that* living waters shall 3117
14: 9 in that **d** shall there be one LORD, and 3117
14:13 it shall come to pass in that **d**, *that* a great 3117
14:20 In that **d** shall there be upon the bells of 3117
14:21 in that **d** there shall be no more 3117
Mal 3: 2 who *may* abide the **d** of his coming? and 3117
3:17 in that **d** when I make *up my* jewels; 3117
4: 1 For behold, the **d** cometh, that *shall* burn as 3117
4: 1 the **d** that cometh shall burn them up, saith 3117
4: 3 **d** that I *shall* do *this*, saith the LORD of 3117
4: 5 of the great and dreadful **d** of the LORD: 3117
Mt 6:11 Give us **this d** our daily bread. *4594*
6:30 which **to d** is, and to morrow is cast into *4594*
6:34 Sufficient unto the **d** *is* the evil thereof. *2250*
7:22 Many will say to me in that **d**, Lord, Lord, *2250*
10:15 and Gomorrha in the **d** of judgment, *2250*
11:22 for Tyre and Sidon at the **d** of judgment, *2250*
11:23 it would have remained until **this d**. *4594*
11:24 for the land of Sodom in the **d** of judgment, *2250*
12: 1 At that time Jesus went on the sabbath **d** NIG
12: 2 is not lawful to do upon the sabbath **d**. NIG
12: 8 Son of man is Lord even of the sabbath **d**. NIG
12:11 and if it fall into a pit on the sabbath **d**, NIG
12:36 they shall give account thereof in the **d** of *2250*
13: 1 The same **d** went Jesus out of the house, *2250*
16: 3 in the morning, *It will be* foul weather **to d**: *4594*
16:21 be killed, and be raised *again* the third **d**. *2250*
17:23 the third **d** he shall be raised *again*. And *2250*
20: 2 agreed with the labourers for a penny a **d**, *2250*
20: 6 Why stand ye here all the **d** idle? *2250*
20:12 have borne the burden and heat of the **d**. *2250*
20:19 and the third **d** he shall rise again. *2250*
21:28 said, Son, go work **to d** in my vineyard. *4594*
22:23 The same **d** came to him *the* Sadducees, *2250*
22:46 neither durst any *man* from that **d** forth ask *2250*
24:20 not in the winter, neither on the sabbath **d**: NIG
24:36 But of that **d** and hour knoweth no *man*, no, *2250*
24:38 until the **d** that Noe entered into the ark, *2250*
24:50 The lord of that servant shall come in a **d** *2250*
25:13 for ye know neither the **d** nor the hour *2250*
26: 5 Not on the feast ***d***, lest there be an uproar NIG
26:17 Now the first ***d*** of the *feast of* unleavened NIG
26:29 until that **d** when I drink it new with you in *2250*
27: 8 was called, The field of blood, unto **this d**. *4594*
27:19 suffered many *things* **this d** in a dream *4594*
27:62 Now the **next d**, that followed the *day of* *1887*
27:62 that followed the ***d*** *of the* preparation, NIG
27:64 the sepulchre be made sure until the third **d**, *2250*
28: 1 as it began to dawn towards the first ***d*** of NIG
28:15 reported among the Jews until **this d**. *4594*
Mk 1:21 straightway on the sabbath **d** he entered into NIG
1:35 rising up a great while **before d**, he went *1773*
2:23 through the corn fields on the sabbath **d**; NIG
2:24 why do they on the sabbath **d** *that* which is NIG
3: 2 he would heal him on the sabbath **d**; NIG
4:27 and rise night and **d**, and the seed should *2250*
4:35 And the same **d**, when the even was come, *2250*
5: 5 And always, night and **d**, he was in *2250*
6: 2 And when the sabbath **d** was come, NIG
6:11 and Gomorrha in the **d** of judgment, *2250*
6:21 And when a convenient **d** was come, *2250*
6:35 And when the **d** was now far spent, *5610*
9:31 that he is killed, he shall rise the third **d**. *2250*
10:34 kill him: and the third **d** he shall rise again. *2250*

D

Mk 13:32 But of that **d** and *that* hour knoweth no 2250
14: 2 Not on the feast ***d***, lest there be an uproar of NIG
14:12 And the first **d** of unleavened bread, 2250
14:25 until that **d** that I drink it new in 2250
14:30 unto thee, That **this d**, *even* in this night, 4594
15:42 that is, the **d before the sabbath**, 4315
16: 2 And very early in the morning the first ***d*** of NIG
16: 9 Now when *Jesus* was risen early the first ***d*** NIG
Lk 1:20 until the **d** that these *things* shall be 2250
1:59 *that* on the eighth **d** they came to 2250
1:80 was in the deserts till the **d** of his shewing 2250
2:11 For unto you is born **this d** in the city of 4594
2:37 *God* with fastings and prayers night and **d**. 2250
4:16 went into the synagogue on the sabbath **d**, 2250
4:21 **This d** is this scripture fulfilled in your 4594
4:42 And when it was **d**, he departed and 2250
5:17 And it came to pass on a certain **d**, as he 2250
5:26 saying, We have seen strange *things* **to d**. 4594
6: 7 whether he would heal on the sabbath **d**; NIG
6:13 And when it was **d**, he called unto *him* his 2250
6:23 Rejoice ye in that **d**, and leap *for joy*: for 2250
7:11 And it came to pass the ***d*** after, *that* he went NIG
8:22 Now it came to pass on a certain **d**, that he 2250
9:12 And *when* the **d** began to wear away, then 2250
9:22 and be slain, and be raised the third **d**. 2250
9:37 And it came to pass, *that* on the next **d**, 2250
10:12 that it shall be more tolerable in that **d** for 2250
11: 3 Give us **d by day** our daily bread. 2250+2596
11: 3 Give us **day by d** our daily bread. 2250+2596
12:28 which is **to d** in the field, and to morrow is 4594
12:46 The lord of that servant will come in a **d** 2250
13:14 that Jesus had healed on the sabbath **d**, NIG
13:14 and be healed, and not on the sabbath **d**. 2250
13:16 be loosed from this bond on the sabbath **d**? 2250
13:31 The same **d** there came certain *of* 2250
13:32 and I do cures **to d** and to morrow, and 4594
13:32 and the third ***d*** I shall be perfected. NIG
13:33 Nevertheless I must walk **to d**, and 4594
13:33 to day, and to morrow, and the ***d*** following: NIG
14: 1 Pharisees to eat bread on the sabbath **d**, NIG
14: 3 saying, Is it lawful to heal on the sabbath **d**? NIG
14: 5 straightway pull him out on the sabbath **d**? 2250
16:19 fine linen, and fared sumptuously every **d**: 2250
17: 4 he trespass against thee seven times in a **d**, 2250
17: 4 and seven times in a **d** turn again to thee, 2250
17:24 so shall also the Son of man be in his **d**. 2250
17:27 until the **d** that Noe entered into the ark, 2250
17:29 But the *same* **d** that Lot went out of Sodom 2250
17:30 Even thus shall it be in the **d** when the Son 2250
17:31 In that **d**, he which shall be upon 2250
18: 7 which cry **d** and night unto him, though he 2250
18:33 to death: and the third **d** he shall rise again. 2250
19: 5 for **to d** I must abide at thy house. 4594
19: 9 **This d** is salvation come to this house, 4594
19:42 even thou, at least in this thy **d**, 2250
21:34 and *so* that **d** come upon you unawares. 2250
21:37 And in the **d time** he was teaching in 2250
22: 7 Then came the **d** of unleavened bread, 2250
22:34 Peter, *the* cock shall not crow **this d**, 4594
22:66 And as soon as it was **d**, the elders of 2250
23:12 And the same **d** Pilate and Herod were 2250
23:43 **To d** shalt thou be with me in paradise. 4594
23:54 And *that* **d** was the preparation, and 2250
23:56 rested the sabbath **d** according to NIG
24: 1 Now upon the first ***d*** of the week, very early NIG
24: 7 and be crucified, and the third **d** rise again. 2250
24:13 two of them went *that* same **d** to a village 2250
24:21 **to d** is the third day since these *things* were 4594
24:21 to day is the third **d** since these *things* were 2250
24:29 it is towards evening, and the **d** is far spent. 2250
24:46 and to rise from the dead the third **d**: 2250
Jn 1:29 The **next d** John seeth Jesus coming unto 1887
1:35 Again the **next d** *after* John stood, and 1887
1:39 where he dwelt, and abode with him that **d**: 2250
1:43 The **d following** Jesus would go forth into 1887
2: 1 And the third **d** there was a marriage in 2250
2:23 in the feast ***d***, many believed in his name, NIG
5: 9 walked: and on the same **d** was the sabbath. 2250
5:10 unto him that was cured, It is the sabbath **d**: NIG
5:16 he had done these *things* on the sabbath **d**. NIG
6:22 The **d following**, when the people which 1887
6:39 but should raise it up *again* at the last **d**. 2250
6:40 and I will raise him up *at* the last **d**. 2250
6:44 and I will raise him up *at* the last **d**. 2250
6:54 and I will raise him up *at* the last **d**. 2250
7:22 and ye on the sabbath **d** circumcise a man. NIG
7:23 If a man on the sabbath **d** receive NIG
7:23 a man every whit whole on the sabbath **d**? NIG
7:37 In the last **d**, *that* great *day* of the feast, 2250
7:37 *that* great ***d*** of the feast, Jesus stood and NIG
8:56 Your father Abraham rejoiced to see my **d**: 2250
9: 4 the works of him that sent me, while it is **d**: 2250
9:14 And it was the sabbath **d** when Jesus made 2250
9:16 because he keepeth not the sabbath **d**. NIG
11: 9 Are there not twelve hours in the **d**? 2250
11: 9 If any *man* walk in the **d**, he stumbleth not, 2250
11:24 rise again in the resurrection at the last **d**. 2250
11:53 Then from that **d** forth they took counsel 2250
12: 7 against the **d** of my burying hath she kept 2250
12:12 On the **next d** much people that were come 1887
12:48 the same shall judge him in the last **d**. 2250
14:20 At that **d** ye shall know that I *am* in my 2250
16:23 And in that **d** ye shall ask me nothing. 2250
16:26 At that **d** ye shall ask in my name: and I say 2250
19:31 not remain upon the cross on the sabbath **d**, NIG
19:31 (for that sabbath **d** was a high day,) NIG
19:31 (for that sabbath day was a high **d**,) 2250
19:42 of the Jews' preparation ***d***; for the sepulchre NIG
20: 1 The first ***d*** of the week cometh Mary NIG
20:19 Then the same **d** at evening, being the first 2250
20:19 at evening, being the first ***d*** of the week, NIG
Ac 1: 2 Until the **d** *in* which he was taken up, 2250
1:22 unto *that same* **d** that he was taken up from 2250
2: 1 And when the **d** of Pentecost was fully 2250
2:15 seeing it is *but* the third hour of the **d**. 2250
Ac 2:20 *that* great and notable **d** of the Lord come: 2250
2:29 and his sepulchre is with us unto this **d**. 2250
2:41 the same **d** there were added *unto them* 2250
4: 3 and put *them* in hold unto the **next d**: 839
4: 9 If we **this d** be examined of the good deed 4594
7: 8 and circumcised him the eighth **d**; 2250
7:26 And the next **d** he shewed himself unto 2250
9:24 And they watched the gates **d** and night to 2250
10: 3 about the ninth hour of the **d**, 2250
10:40 Him God raised up the third **d**, and 2250
12:18 Now as soon as it was **d**, there was no 2250
12:21 And upon a set **d** Herod, arrayed in royal 2250
13:14 went into the synagogue on the sabbath **d**, 2250
13:27 prophets which are read every sabbath **d**, NIG
13:33 art my Son, **this d** have I begotten thee. 4594
13:44 And the next sabbath **d** came almost NIG
14:20 the **next d** he departed with Barnabas to 1887
15:21 read in the synagogues every sabbath **d**. NIG
16:11 to Samothracia, and the next ***d*** to Neapolis; NIG
16:35 And when it was **d**, the magistrates sent 2250
17:31 Because he hath appointed a **d**, in 2250
20: 7 And upon the first ***d*** of the week, when NIG
20:11 *even* till **break of d**, so he departed. 827
20:15 and came the next ***d*** over against Chios; NIG
20:15 and the next ***d*** we arrived at Samos, and NIG
20:15 and the next ***d*** we came to Miletus. NIG
20:16 to be at Jerusalem the **d** of Pentecost. 2250
20:18 from the first **d** that I came into Asia, 2250
20:26 I take you to record **this d**, 2250+4594
20:31 to warn every one night and **d** with tears. 2250
21: 1 and the ***d*** following unto Rhodes, and from NIG
21: 7 the brethren, and abode with them one **d**. 2250
21: 8 And the **next d** we that were of Paul's 1887
21:18 And the ***d*** following Paul went in with us NIG
21:26 the next **d** purifying himself with them 2250
22: 3 zealous towards God, as ye all are **this d**. 4594
23: 1 all good conscience before God until this **d**. 2250
23:12 And when it was **d**, certain of the Jews 2250
24:21 dead I am called in question by you **this d**. 4594
25: 6 and the **next d** sitting in the judgment seat, 1887
26: 2 I shall answer for myself **this d** before thee 4594
26: 7 instantly serving *God* **d** and night, hope to 2250
26:22 help of God, I continue unto this **d**, 2250
26:29 but also all that hear me **this d**, were both 4594
27: 3 And the next ***d*** we touched at Sidon. NIG
27:18 the next ***d*** they lightened the ship; NIG
27:19 And the third ***d*** we cast *out* with our own NIG
27:29 out of the stern, and wished for the **d**. 2250
27:33 And while the **d** was coming on, Paul 2250
27:33 **This d** is the fourteenth day that ye have 4594
27:33 This day is the fourteenth **d** that ye have 2250
27:39 And when it was **d**, they knew not the land: 2250
28:13 and after one **d** the south wind blew, and 2250
28:13 and we came the **next d** to Puteoli: 1206
28:23 And when they had appointed him a **d**, 2250
Ro 2: 5 up unto thyself wrath against the **d** of wrath 2250
2:16 In the **d** when God shall judge the secrets 2250
8:36 For thy sake we are killed all the **d** long; 2250
10:21 All **d** long have I stretched forth my hands 2250
11: 8 that *they* should not hear;) unto **this d**. 2250+4594
13:12 The night is far spent, the **d** is at hand: 2250
13:13 Let us walk honestly, as in the **d**; not in 2250
14: 5 One man esteemeth one **d** above another: 2250
14: 5 another esteemeth every **d** *alike*. Let every 2250
14: 6 He that regardeth the **d**, regardeth *it* unto 2250
14: 6 and he that regardeth not the **d**, to the Lord 2250
1Co 1: 8 *that ye may be* blameless in the **d** of our 2250
3:13 for the **d** shall declare *it*, because it shall be 2250
4:13 *are* the offscouring of all *things* unto **this d**. 737
5: 5 that the spirit may be saved in the **d** of 2250
10: 8 and fell in one **d** three and twenty thousand. 2250
15: 4 that he rose *again* the third **d** according to 2250
16: 2 Upon the first ***d*** of the week let every one of NIG
2Co 1:14 even as ye also *are* ours in the **d** of the Lord 2250
3:14 for until **this d** remaineth the same 2250+4594
3:15 But *even* unto **this d**, when Moses is read, 4594
4:16 yet the inward *man* is renewed **d** by day. 2250
4:16 yet the inward *man* is renewed day by **d**. 2250
6: 2 in the **d** of salvation have I succoured thee: 2250
6: 2 behold, now *is* the **d** of salvation.) 2250
11:25 **a night and a d** I have been in the deep; 3574
Eph 4:30 whereby ye are sealed unto the **d** of 2250
6:13 ye may be able to withstand in the evil **d**, 2250
Php 1: 5 in the gospel from the first **d** until now; 2250
1: 6 will perform *it* until the **d** of Jesus Christ: 2250
1:10 and without offence till the **d** of Christ; 2250
2:16 that I may rejoice in the **d** of Christ, that I 2250
3: 5 Circumcised the **eighth d**, of the stock of 3637
Col 1: 6 since the **d** ye heard of *it*, and knew 2250
1: 9 since the **d** we heard *it*, do not cease to pray 2250
1Th 2: 9 for labouring night and **d**, because *we* 2250
3:10 **d** praying exceedingly that *we* might see 2250
5: 2 For yourselves know perfectly that the **d** of 2250
5: 4 that *that* **d** should overtake you as a thief. 2250
5: 5 children of light, and the children of the **d**: 2250
5: 8 But let us, who are of the **d**, be sober, 2250
2Th 1:10 among you was believed) in that **d**. 2250
2: 2 from us, as that the **d** of Christ is at hand. 2250
2: 3 for *that d shall not come*, except there come NIG
3: 8 with labour and travail night and **d**, 2250
1Ti 5: 5 in supplications and prayers night and **d**. 2250
2Ti 1: 3 of thee in my prayers night and **d**; 2250
1:12 I have committed unto *him* against that **d**. 2250
1:18 *he* may find mercy of the Lord in that **d**: 2250
4: 8 the righteous judge, shall give me at that **d**: 2250
Heb 1: 5 art my Son, **this d** have I begotten thee? 4594
3: 7 Ghost saith, **To d** if ye will hear his voice, 4594
3: 8 in the **d** of temptation in the wilderness: 2250
3:13 one another daily, while it is called **To d**; 4594
3:15 it is said, **To d** if ye will hear his voice, 4594
4: 4 a certain place of the seventh ***d*** on this wise, NIG
4: 4 And God did rest the seventh **d** from all his 2250
4: 7 Again he limiteth a certain **d**, saying in 2250
4: 7 saying in David, **To d**, after so long a time; 4594
4: 7 as it is said, **To d** if ye will hear his voice, 4594
Heb 4: 8 he not afterward have spoken of another **d**. 2250
5: 5 Thou art my Son, **to d** have I begotten thee. 4594
8: 9 **d** when I took them by the hand to lead 2250
10:25 the more, as ye see the **d** approaching. 2250
13: 8 the same yesterday, and **to d**, and for ever. 4594
Jas 4:13 **To d** or to morrow we will go into such a 4594
5: 5 your hearts, as in a **d** of slaughter. 2250
1Pe 2:12 glorify God in the **d** of visitation. 2250
2Pe 1:19 until the **d** dawn, and the day star arise in 2250
1:19 and the **d star** arise in your hearts: 5459
2: 8 vexed *his* righteous soul from **d** to day with 2250
2: 8 vexed *his* righteous soul from day to **d** with 2250
2: 9 to reserve the unjust unto the **d** of judgment 2250
2:13 *as* they that count it pleasure to riot in the **d** 2250
3: 7 reserved unto fire against the **d** of judgment 2250
3: 8 be not ignorant of this one *thing*, that one **d** 2250
3: 8 and a thousand years as one **d**. 2250
3:10 But the **d** of the Lord will come as a thief in 2250
3:12 hasting *unto* the coming of the **d** of God, 2250
1Jn 4:17 that we may have boldness in the **d** of 2250
Jude 1: 6 darkness unto the judgment of the great **d**. 2250
Rev 1:10 I was in the spirit on the Lord's **d**, and 2250
4: 8 and they rest not **d** and night, saying, Holy, 2250
6:17 For the great **d** of his wrath is come; and 2250
7:15 and serve him **d** and night in his temple: 2250
8:12 and the **d** shone not for a third *part* of it, 2250
9:15 and a **d**, and a month, and a year, for to slay 2250
12:10 which accused them before our God **d** and 2250
14:11 and they have no rest **d** nor night, 2250
16:14 to gather them to the battle of that great **d** 2250
18: 8 Therefore shall her plagues come in one **d**, 2250
20:10 and shall be tormented **d** and night for ever 2250
21:25 the gates of it shall not be shut at all by **d**: 2250

DAY'S (9) [DAY]

Nu 11:31 as it were a **d** journey on this side, and as it 3117
11:31 as it were a **d** journey on the other side, 3117
1Ki 19: 4 he himself went a **d** journey into 3117
1Ch 16:37 as **every d** work required: 3117+3117+871.1
Est 9:13 morrow also according unto *this* **d** decree, 3117
Jnh 3: 4 Jonah began to enter into the city a **d** 3117
Lk 2:44 been in the company, went a **d** journey; 2250
Ac 1:12 a **sabbath d journey**. 2192+3598+4521
19:40 to be called in question for **this d** uproar, 4594

DAYS (855) [DAY]

Ge 1:14 and for seasons, and for **d**, and years: 3117
3:14 and dust shalt thou eat all the **d** of thy life: 3117
3:17 in sorrow shalt thou eat *of* it all the **d** of thy 3117
5: 4 the **d** of Adam after he had begotten Seth 3117
5: 5 all the **d** that Adam lived were nine 3117
5: 8 all the **d** of Seth were nine hundred 3117
5:11 all the **d** of Enos were nine hundred 3117
5:14 all the **d** of Cainan were nine hundred 3117
5:17 all the **d** of Mahalaleel were eight hundred 3117
5:20 all the **d** of Jared were nine hundred sixty 3117
5:23 all the **d** of Enoch were three hundred sixty 3117
5:27 all the **d** of Methuselah were nine hundred 3117
5:31 all the **d** of Lamech were seven hundred 3117
6: 3 yet his **d** shall be an hundred and 3117
6: 4 There were giants in the earth in those **d**; 3117
7: 4 For yet seven **d**, *and* I will cause it to rain 3117
7: 4 I will cause it to rain upon the earth forty **d** 3117
7:10 it came to pass after seven **d**, that 3117
7:12 the rain was upon the earth forty **d** and 3117
7:17 the flood was forty **d** upon the earth; and 3117
7:24 upon the earth an hundred and fifty **d**. 3117
8: 3 and fifty **d** the waters were abated. 3117
8: 6 it came to pass at the end of forty **d**, 3117
8:10 he stayed yet other seven **d**; and again he 3117
8:12 he stayed yet other seven **d**; and sent forth 3117
9:29 all the **d** of Noah were nine hundred and 3117
10:25 for in his **d** was the earth divided; and 3117
11:32 the **d** of Terah were two hundred and 3117
14: 1 it came to pass in the **d** of Amraphel king 3117
17:12 he that is eight **d** old shall be circumcised 3117
21: 4 circumcised his son Isaac being eight **d** old, 3117
21:34 sojourned in the Philistines' land many **d**. 3117
24:55 Let the damsel abide with us *a few* **d**, at 3117
25: 7 these *are* the **d** of the years of Abraham's 3117
25:24 when her **d** to be delivered were fulfilled, 3117
26: 1 besides the first famine that was in the **d** of 3117
26:15 had digged in the **d** of Abraham his father, 3117
26:18 which they had digged in the **d** of Abraham 3117
27:41 The **d** of mourning for my father are at 3117
27:44 tarry with him a few **d**, until thy brother's 3117
29:20 they seemed unto him *but* a few **d**, for 3117
29:21 Give *me* my wife, for my **d** are fulfilled, 3117
30:14 Reuben went in the **d** of wheat harvest, 3117
35:28 the **d** of Isaac were an hundred 3117
35:29 unto his people, *being* old and full of **d**: 3117
37:34 his loins, and mourned for his son many **d**. 3117
40:12 of it: The three branches *are* three **d**: 3117
40:13 Yet within three **d** shall Pharaoh lift up 3117
40:18 The three baskets *are* three **d**: 3117
40:19 Yet within three **d** shall Pharaoh lift up thy 3117
42:17 he put them all together into ward three **d**. 3117
47: 9 The **d** of the years of my pilgrimage *are* an 3117
47: 9 evil have the **d** of the years of my life been, 3117
47: 9 have not attained unto the **d** of the years of 3117
47: 9 of my fathers in the **d** of their pilgrimage. 3117
49: 1 you *that* which shall befall you in the last **d**. 3117
50: 3 forty **d** were fulfilled for him; for so 3117
50: 3 are fulfilled the **d** of those which are 3117
50: 3 mourned for him threescore and ten **d**. 3117
50: 4 when the **d** of his mourning were past, 3117
50:10 he made a mourning for his father seven **d**. 3117
Ex 2:11 it came to pass in those **d**, when Moses was 3117
7:25 seven **d** were fulfilled, after *that* 3117
10:22 darkness in all the land of Egypt three **d**: 3117
10:23 neither rose any from his place for three **d**: 3117
12:15 Seven **d** shall ye eat unleavened bread; 3117
12:19 Seven **d** shall there be no leaven found in 3117
13: 6 Seven **d** thou shalt eat unleavened bread, 3117
13: 7 Unleavened bread shall be eaten seven **d**; 3117

Ex 15:22 they went three **d** in the wilderness, and 3117
16:26 Six **d** ye shall gather it; but on the seventh 3117
16:29 you on the sixth day the bread of **two d**; 3117
20: 9 Six **d** shalt thou labour, and do all thy 3117
20:11 For *in* six **d** the LORD made heaven and 3117
20:12 that thy **d** may be long upon the land which 3117
22:30 seven **d** it shall be with his dam; on 3117
23:12 Six **d** thou shalt do thy work, and on 3117
23:15 thou shalt eat unleavened bread seven **d**, 3117
23:26 thy land: the number of thy **d** I will fulfil. 3117
24:16 mount Sinai, and the cloud covered it six **d**: 3117
24:18 Moses was in the mount forty **d** and 3117
29:30 in his stead shall put them on seven **d**, 3117
29:35 seven **d** shalt thou consecrate them. 3117
29:37 Seven **d** thou shalt make an atonement for 3117
31:15 Six **d** may work be done; but in the seventh 3117
31:17 for *in* six **d** the LORD made heaven and 3117
34:18 seven **d** thou shalt eat unleavened bread, 3117
34:21 Six **d** thou shalt work, but on the seventh 3117
34:28 he was there with the LORD forty **d** and 3117
35: 2 Six **d** shall work be done, but on 3117
Lev 8:33 tabernacle of the congregation *in* seven **d**, 3117
8:33 until the **d** of your consecration be at an 3117
8:33 an end: for seven **d** shall he consecrate you. 3117
8:35 of the congregation day and night seven **d**, 3117
12: 2 she shall be unclean seven **d**; according to 3117
12: 2 according to the **d** of the separation for her 3117
12: 4 blood of her purifying three and thirty **d**; 3117
12: 4 until the **d** of her purifying be fulfilled. 3117
12: 5 blood of her purifying threescore and six **d**. 3117
12: 6 when the **d** of her purifying are fulfilled, 3117
13: 4 shut up *him that hath* the plague seven **d**: 3117
13: 5 the priest shall shut him up seven **d** more: 3117
13:21 then the priest shall shut him up seven **d**: 3117
13:26 then the priest shall shut him up seven **d**: 3117
13:31 *that hath* the plague of the scall seven **d**: 3117
13:33 up *him that hath* the scall seven **d** more: 3117
13:46 All the **d** wherein the plague *shall be* in him 3117
13:50 and shut up *it that hath* the plague seven **d**: 3117
13:54 and he shall shut it up seven **d** more: 3117
14: 8 shall tarry abroad out of his tent seven **d**. 3117
14:38 the house, and shut up the house seven **d**: 3117
15:13 he shall number to himself seven **d** for his 3117
15:19 be put apart seven **d**: and 3117
15:24 be upon him, he shall be unclean seven **d**; 3117
15:25 many **d** out of the time of her separation, 3117
15:25 all the **d** of the issue of her uncleanness 3117
15:25 shall be as the **d** of her separation: 3117
15:26 Every bed whereon she lieth all the **d** of her 3117
15:28 she shall number to herself seven **d**, and 3117
22:27 then it shall be seven **d** under the dam; 3117
23: 3 Six **d** shall work be done: but the seventh 3117
23: 6 seven **d** ye must eat unleavened bread. 3117
23: 8 made by fire unto the LORD seven **d**: 3117
23:16 the seventh sabbath shall ye number fifty **d**; 3117
23:34 of tabernacles *for* seven **d** unto the LORD. 3117
23:36 Seven **d** ye shall offer an offering made by 3117
23:39 shall keep a feast unto the LORD seven **d**: 3117
23:40 before the LORD your God seven **d**. 3117
23:41 feast unto the LORD seven **d** in the year. 3117
23:42 Ye shall dwell in booths seven **d**; all that 3117
Nu 6: 4 All the **d** of his separation shall he eat 3117
6: 5 All the **d** of the vow of his separation there 3117
6: 5 until the **d** be fulfilled, *in* the which he 3117
6: 6 All the **d** that he separateth *himself* unto 3117
6: 8 All the **d** of his separation he *is* holy unto 3117
6:12 he shall consecrate unto the LORD the **d** 3117
6:12 the **d** that were before shall be lost, because 3117
6:13 when the **d** of his separation are fulfilled: 3117
9:19 tarried long upon the tabernacle many **d**, 3117
9:20 when the cloud was a few **d** upon 3117
9:22 Or *whether it were* **two d**, or a month, or 3117
10:10 in your **solemn d**, and in the beginnings of 4150
11:19 nor **two d**, nor five days, neither ten days, 3117
11:19 nor two days, nor five **d**, neither ten days, 3117
11:19 nor two days, nor five days, neither ten **d**, 3117
11:19 five days, neither ten days, nor twenty **d**; 3117
12:14 should she not be ashamed seven **d**? 3117
12:14 let her be shut out from the camp seven **d**, 3117
12:15 was shut out from the camp seven **d**: 3117
13:25 from searching of the land after forty **d**. 3117
14:34 After the number of the **d** *in* which ye 3117
14:34 *even* forty **d**, each day for a year, shall ye 3117
19:11 *body* of any man shall be unclean seven **d**. 3117
19:14 that *is* in the tent, shall be unclean seven **d**. 3117
19:16 a man, or a grave, shall be unclean seven **d**. 3117
20:29 they mourned for Aaron thirty **d**, *even* all 3117
24:14 people shall do to thy people in the latter **d**. 3117
28:17 seven **d** shall unleavened bread be eaten. 3117
28:24 ye shall offer daily, *throughout* the seven **d**, 3117
29:12 shall keep a feast unto the LORD seven **d**: 3117
31:19 do ye abide without the camp seven **d**: 3117
Dt 1:46 So ye abode in Kadesh many **d**, 3117
1:46 according unto the **d** that ye abode *there*. 3117
2: 1 and we compassed mount Seir many **d**. 3117
4: 9 lest they depart from thy heart all the **d** of 3117
4:10 that they may learn to fear me all the **d** that 3117
4:26 ye shall not prolong *your* **d** upon it, but 3117
4:30 *even* in the latter **d**, if thou turn to 3117
4:32 For ask now of the **d** that are past, 3117
4:40 that thou mayest prolong *thy* **d** upon 3117
5:13 Six **d** thou shalt labour, and do all thy 3117
5:16 that thy **d** may be prolonged, and that it 3117
5:33 *that* ye may prolong *your* **d** in the land 3117
6: 2 and thy son's son, all the **d** of thy life; 3117
6: 2 thy life; and that thy **d** may be prolonged. 3117
9: 9 I abode in the mount forty **d** and 3117
9:11 it came to pass at the end of forty **d** and 3117
9:18 as at the first, forty **d** and forty nights: 3117
9:25 Thus I fell down before the LORD forty **d** 3117
10:10 to the first time, forty **d** and forty nights; 3117
11: 9 that ye may prolong *your* **d** in the land, 3117
11:21 That your **d** may be multiplied, and 3117
11:21 be multiplied, and the **d** of your children, 3117
11:21 as the **d** of heaven upon the earth. 3117

Dt 12: 1 all the **d** that ye live upon the earth. 3117
16: 3 seven **d** shalt thou eat unleavened bread 3117
16: 3 out of the land of Egypt all the **d** of thy life. 3117
16: 4 seen with thee in all thy coast seven **d**; 3117
16: 8 Six **d** thou shalt eat unleavened bread: and 3117
16:13 observe the feast of tabernacles seven **d**, 3117
16:15 Seven **d** shalt thou keep a solemn feast unto 3117
17: 9 unto the judge that shall be in those **d**, 3117
17:19 he shall read therein all the **d** of his life: 3117
17:20 to the end that he may prolong *his* **d** in his 3117
19:17 and the judges, which shall be in those **d**; 3117
22: 7 and *that* thou mayest prolong *thy* **d**. 3117
22:19 his wife; he may not put her away all his **d**. 3117
22:29 he may not put her away all his **d**. 3117
23: 6 peace nor their prosperity all thy **d** for ever. 3117
25:15 that thy **d** may be lengthened in the land 3117
26: 3 go unto the priest that shall be in those **d**, 3117
30:18 *that* ye shall not prolong *your* **d** upon 3117
30:20 for he *is* thy life, and the length of thy **d**: 3117
31:14 Behold, thy **d** approach that *thou* must die: 3117
31:29 evil will befall you in the latter **d**; because 3117
32: 7 Remember the **d** of old, consider the years 3117
32:47 through this thing ye shall prolong *your* **d** 3117
33:25 and as thy **d**, *so shall* thy strength *be*. 3117
34: 8 for Moses in the plains of Moab thirty **d**: 3117
34: 8 so the **d** of weeping *and* mourning for 3117
Jos 1: 5 *to* stand before thee all the **d** of thy life: 3117
1:11 for within three **d** ye shall pass over this 3117
2:16 hide yourselves there three **d**, until 3117
2:22 unto the mountain, and abode there three **d**, 3117
3: 2 it came to pass after three **d**, that 3117
4:14 as they feared Moses, all the **d** of his life. 3117
6: 3 the city once. Thus shalt thou do six **d**. 3117
6:14 returned *into* the camp: so they did six **d**. 3117
9:16 it came to pass at the end of three **d** after 3117
20: 6 of the high priest that shall be in those **d**: 3117
22: 3 have not left your brethren these many **d** 3117
24:31 Israel served the LORD all the **d** of 3117
24:31 all the **d** of the elders that overlived Joshua, 3117
Jdg 2: 7 the people served the LORD all the **d** of 3117
2: 7 all the **d** of the elders that outlived Joshua, 3117
2:18 hand of their enemies all the **d** of the judge: 3117
5: 6 In the **d** of Shamgar the son of Anath, 3117
5: 6 in the **d** of Jael, the highways were 3117
8:28 in quietness forty years in the **d** of Gideon. 3117
11:40 of Jephthah the Gileadite four **d** in a year. 3117
14:12 it me *within* the seven **d** of the feast, 3117
14:14 they could not *in* three **d** expound 3117
14:17 she wept before him the seven **d**, 3117
15:20 he judged Israel in the **d** of the Philistines 3117
17: 6 In those **d** *there was* no king in Israel, *but* 3117
18: 1 In those **d** *there was* no king in Israel: and 3117
18: 1 in those **d** the tribe of the Danites sought 3117
19: 1 it came to pass in those **d**, when *there was* 3117
19: 4 and he abode with him three **d**: 3117
20:27 the covenant of God *was* there in those **d**, 3117
20:28 son of Aaron, stood before it in those **d**,) 3117
21:25 In those **d** *there was* no king in Israel: 3117
Ru 1: 1 Now it came to pass in the **d** when 3117
1Sa 1:11 I will give him unto the LORD all the **d** of 3117
2:31 Behold, the **d** come, that I will cut off thine 3117
3: 1 of the LORD was precious in those **d**; 3117
7:13 against the Philistines all the **d** of Samuel. 3117
7:15 Samuel judged Israel all the **d** of his life. 3117
9:20 as for thine asses that were lost three **d** ago, 3117
10: 8 seven **d** shalt thou tarry, till I come to thee, 3117
13: 8 he tarried seven **d**, according to the set time 3117
13:11 *that* thou camest not within the **d** 3117
14:52 war against the Philistines all the **d** of Saul: 3117
17:12 among men *for* an old man in the **d** of Saul. 3117
17:16 and evening, and presented himself forty **d**. 3117
18:26 son in law: and the **d** were not expired. 3117
20:19 *when* thou hast **stayed three d**, *then* 8027
21: 5 kept from us about **these three d**, 8032+8543
25:10 there be many servants **now a d** 3117+1886.1
25:28 evil hath not been found in thee *all* thy **d**. 3117
25:38 it came to pass about ten **d** *after*, that 3117
28: 1 it came to pass in those **d**, that 3117
29: 3 which hath been with me these **d**, or 3117
30:12 drunk *any* water, three **d** and three nights. 3117
30:13 left me, because three **d** agone I fell sick. 3117
31:13 under a tree at Jabesh, and fasted seven **d**. 3117
2Sa 1: 1 and David had abode two **d** in Ziklag; 3117
7:12 when thy **d** be fulfilled, and thou shalt sleep 3117
16:23 which he counselled in those **d**, 3117
20: 4 me the men of Judah *within* three **d**, 3117
21: 1 there was a famine in the **d** of David three 3117
21: 9 and were put to death in the **d** of harvest, 3117
21: 9 in the first *d*, in the beginning of barley NIH
24: 8 at the end of nine months and twenty **d**. 3117
1Ki 2: 1 Now the **d** of David drew nigh that *he* 3117
2:11 the **d** that David reigned over Israel *were* 3117
2:38 And Shimei dwelt in Jerusalem many **d**. 3117
3: 2 unto the name of the LORD, until those **d**. 3117
3:13 among the kings like unto thee all thy **d**. 3117
3:14 David did walk, then I will lengthen thy **d**. 3117
4:21 and served Solomon all the **d** of his life. 3117
4:25 even to Beer-sheba, all the **d** of Solomon. 3117
8:40 That they may fear thee all the **d** that they 3117
8:65 seven **d** and seven days, *even* fourteen 3117
8:65 seven days and seven **d**, *even* fourteen 3117
8:65 and seven days, *even* fourteen **d**. 3117
10:21 it was nothing accounted of in the **d** of 3117
11:12 Notwithstanding in thy **d** I will not do it for 3117
11:25 he was an adversary to Israel all the **d** of 3117
11:34 I will make him prince all the **d** of his life 3117
12: 5 Depart yet *for* three **d**, then come again to 3117
14:20 the **d** which Jeroboam reigned *were* two 3117
14:30 and Jeroboam all *their* **d**. 3117
15: 5 that he commanded him all the **d** of his life, 3117
15: 6 and Jeroboam all the **d** of his life. 3117
15:14 heart was perfect with the LORD all his **d**. 3117
15:16 and Baasha king of Israel all their **d**. 3117
15:32 and Baasha king of Israel all their **d**. 3117
16:15 of Judah did Zimri reign seven **d** in Tirzah. 3117

1Ki 16:34 In his **d** did Hiel the Bethelite build 3117
17:15 she, and he, and her house, did eat *many* **d**. 3117
18: 1 it came to pass *after* many **d**, that the word 3117
19: 8 went in the strength of that meat forty **d** 3117
20:29 pitched one over against the other seven **d**. 3117
21:29 before me, I will not bring the evil in his **d**: 3117
21:29 in his son's **d** will I bring the evil upon his 3117
22:46 which remained in the **d** of his father Asa, 3117
2Ki 2:17 and they sought three **d**, but found him not. 3117
8:20 In his **d** Edom revolted from under 3117
10:32 In those **d** the LORD began to cut Israel 3117
12: 2 **d** where*in* Jehoiada the priest instructed 3117
13: 3 of Ben-hadad the son of Hazael, all *their* **d**. 3117
13:22 oppressed Israel all the **d** of Jehoahaz. 3117
15:18 he departed not all his **d** from the sins of 3117
15:29 In the **d** of Pekah king of Israel came 3117
15:37 In those **d** the LORD began to send 3117
18: 4 for unto those **d** the children of Israel did 3117
20: 1 In those **d** was Hezekiah sick unto death. 3117
20: 6 I will add unto thy **d** fifteen years; and 3117
20:17 Behold, the **d** come, that all that *is* in thine 3117
20:19 *it* not *good*, if peace and truth be in my **d**? 3117
23:22 from the **d** of the judges that judged Israel, 3117
23:22 nor *in* all the **d** of the kings of Israel, nor of 3117
23:29 In his **d** Pharaoh-nechoh king of Egypt 3117
24: 1 In his **d** Nebuchadnezzar king of Babylon 3117
25:29 continually before him all the **d** of his life. 3117
25:30 daily rate for every day, all the **d** of his life. 3117
1Ch 1:19 because in his **d** the earth was divided: 3117
4:41 these written by name came in the **d** of 3117
5:10 in the **d** of Saul they made war with 3117
5:17 in the **d** of Jotham king of Judah, 3117
5:17 and in the **d** of Jeroboam king of Israel. 3117
7: 2 whose number *was* in the **d** of David two 3117
7:22 Ephraim their father mourned many **d**, and 3117
9:25 *were* to come after seven **d** from time to 3117
10:12 under the oak in Jabesh, and fasted seven **d**. 3117
12:39 there they were with David three **d**, eating 3117
13: 3 for we inquired not *at* it in the **d** of Saul. 3117
17:11 when thy **d** be expired that *thou* must go *to* 3117
21:12 or else three **d** the sword of the LORD, 3117
22: 9 and quietness unto Israel in his **d**. 3117
23: 1 So when David was old and full *of* **d**, 3117
29:15 our **d** on the earth *are* as a shadow, and 3117
29:28 good old age, full of **d**, riches, and honour: 3117
2Ch 7: 8 same time Solomon kept the feast seven **d**, 3117
7: 9 kept the dedication of the altar seven **d**, 3117
7: 9 the altar seven days, and the feast seven **d**. 3117
9:20 it was *not* any thing accounted of in the **d** 3117
10: 5 Come again unto me after three **d**. 3117
13:20 recover strength again in the **d** of Abijah: 3117
14: 1 In his **d** the land was quiet ten years. 3117
15:17 the heart of Asa was perfect all his **d**. 3117
20:25 they were three **d** in gathering of the spoil, 3117
21: 8 In his **d** the Edomites revolted from under 3117
24: 2 the LORD all the **d** of Jehoiada the priest. 3117
24:14 LORD continually all the **d** of Jehoiada. 3117
24:15 waxed old, and was full *of* **d** when he died; 3117
26: 5 he sought God in the **d** of Zechariah, 3117
29:17 the house of the LORD in eight **d**; 3117
30:21 bread seven **d** with great gladness: 3117
30:22 they did eat throughout the feast seven **d**, 3117
30:23 took counsel to keep other seven **d**: 3117
30:23 and they kept *other* seven **d** *with* gladness. 3117
32:24 In those **d** Hezekiah was sick to the death, 3117
32:26 came not upon them in the **d** of Hezekiah. 3117
34:33 *And* all his **d** they departed not from 3117
35:17 the feast of unleavened bread seven **d**. 3117
35:18 kept in Israel from the **d** of Samuel 3117
36: 9 three months and ten **d** in Jerusalem: 3117
Ezr 4: 2 we do sacrifice unto him since the **d** of 3117
4: 5 all the **d** of Cyrus king of Persia, 3117
4: 7 in the **d** of Artaxerxes wrote Bishlam, 3117
6:22 kept the feast of unleavened bread seven **d** 3117
8:15 and there abode we in tents three **d**: 3117
8:32 came *to* Jerusalem, and abode there three **d**. 3117
9: 7 Since the **d** of our fathers *have* we *been* in a 3117
10: 8 whosoever would not come within three **d**, 3117
10: 9 together *unto* Jerusalem within three **d**. 3117
Ne 1: 4 mourned *certain* **d**, and fasted, and 3117
2:11 I came to Jerusalem, and was there three **d**. 3117
5:18 and once in ten **d** store of all *sorts of* wine: 3117
6:15 *day* of *the month* Elul, in fifty and two **d**. 3117
6:17 Moreover in those **d** the nobles of Judah 3117
8:17 for since the **d** of Jeshua the son of Nun 3117
8:18 they kept the feast seven **d**; and on 3117
12: 7 and of their brethren in the **d** of Jeshua. 3117
12:12 in the **d** of Joiakim were priests, the chief 3117
12:22 The Levites in the **d** of Eliashib, Joiada, 3117
12:23 even until the **d** of Johanan the son of 3117
12:26 These *were* in the **d** of Joiakim the son of 3117
12:26 in the **d** of Nehemiah the governor, and 3117
12:46 For in the **d** of David and Asaph of old 3117
12:47 all Israel in the **d** of Zerubbabel, and in 3117
12:47 in the **d** of Nehemiah, gave the portions of 3117
13: 6 after certain **d** obtained I *leave* of the king: 3117
13:15 In those **d** saw I in Judah *some* treading 3117
13:23 In those **d** also saw I Jews *that* had married 3117
Est 1: 1 Now it came to pass in the **d** of Ahasuerus, 3117
1: 2 *That* in those **d**, when the king Ahasuerus 3117
1: 4 the honour of his excellent majesty many **d**, 3117
1: 4 *even* an hundred and fourscore **d**. 3117
1: 5 when these **d** were expired, the king made a 3117
1: 5 both unto great and small, seven **d**, in 3117
2:12 were the **d** of their purifications 3117
2:21 In those **d**, while Mordecai sat in the king's 3117
4:11 to come in unto the king these thirty **d**. 3117
4:16 neither eat nor drink three **d**, night or day; 3117
9:22 As the **d** wherein the Jews rested from their 3117
9:22 that *they* should make them **d** of feasting 3117
9:26 Wherefore they called these **d** Purim after 3117
9:27 that they would keep these two **d** according 3117
9:28 *that* these **d** *should be* remembered and 3117
9:28 *that* these **d** of Purim should not fail from 3117
9:31 To confirm these **d** of Purim in their times 3117

D

Job 1:5 when the **d** of *their* feasting were gone 3117
2:13 sat down with him upon the ground seven **d** 3117
3:6 let it not be joined unto the **d** of the year, 3117
7:1 *are not* his **d** also like the days of a 3117
7:1 *are not* his days also like the **d** of a 3117
7:6 My **d** are swifter than a weaver's shuttle, 3117
7:16 let me alone; for my **d** *are* vanity. 3117
8:9 because our **d** upon earth *are* a shadow:) 3117
9:25 Now my **d** are swifter than a post: they flee 3117
10:5 *Are* thy **d** as the days of man? *are* thy years 3117
10:5 *Are* thy days as the **d** of man? *are* thy years 3117
10:5 the days of man? *are* thy years as man's **d**, 3117
10:20 *Are* not my **d** few? cease then, and let me 3117
12:12 and *in* length of **d** understanding. 3117
14:1 Man *that is* born of a woman *is* of few **d**, 3117
14:5 Seeing his **d** *are* determined, the number of 3117
14:14 shall he live *again?* all the **d** of my 3117
15:20 wicked *man* travaileth with pain all his **d**, 3117
17:1 My breath is corrupt, my **d** are extinct, 3117
17:11 My **d** are past, my purposes are broken off, 3117
21:13 They spend their **d** in wealth, and in a 3117
24:1 do they that know him not see his **d**? 3117
29:2 as *in* the **d** *when* God preserved me; 3117
29:4 As I was in the **d** of my youth, when 3117
29:18 and I shall multiply *my* **d** as the sand. 3117
30:16 the **d** of affliction have taken hold upon me. 3117
30:27 rested not: the **d** of affliction prevented me. 3117
32:7 **D** should speak, and multitude of years 3117
33:25 he shall return to the **d** of his youth: 3117
36:11 serve *him,* they shall spend their **d** in 3117
38:12 thou commanded the morning since thy **d**; 3117
38:21 or *because* the number of thy **d** *is* great? 3117
42:17 So Job died, *being* old and full of **d**. 3117
Ps 21:4 *it* him, *even* length of **d** for ever and ever. 3117
23:6 mercy shall follow me all the **d** of my life: 3117
27:4 house of the LORD all the **d** of my life, 3117
34:12 *and* loveth *many* **d**, that *he* may see good? 3117
37:18 The LORD knoweth the **d** of the upright: 3117
37:19 in the **d** of famine they shall be satisfied. 3117
39:4 know mine end, and the measure of my **d**, 3117
39:5 thou hast made my **d** *as* a handbreadth; 3117
44:1 *what* work thou didst in their **d**, in the times 3117
49:5 Wherefore should I fear in the **d** of evil, 3117
55:23 deceitful men shall not live out half their **d**; 3117
72:7 In his **d** shall the righteous flourish; and 3117
77:5 I have considered the **d** of old, the years of 3117
78:33 Therefore their **d** did he consume in vanity, 3117
89:29 for ever, and his throne as the **d** of heaven. 3117
89:45 The **d** of his youth hast thou shortened: 3117
90:9 For all our **d** are passed away in thy wrath: 3117
90:10 The **d** of our years *are* threescore years and 3117
90:12 So teach *us* to number our **d**, that we may 3117
90:14 that we may rejoice and be glad all our **d**. 3117
90:15 Make us glad according to the **d** *wherein* 3117
94:13 That *thou* mayest give him rest from the **d** 3117
102:3 For my **d** are consumed like smoke, and 3117
102:11 My **d** *are* like a shadow that declineth; and 3117
102:23 my strength in the way; he shortened my **d**. 3117
102:24 take me not away in the midst of my **d**: 3117
103:15 *As for* man, his **d** *are* as grass: as a flower 3117
109:8 Let his **d** be few; *and* let another take his 3117
119:84 How many *are* the **d** of thy servant? 3117
128:5 the good of Jerusalem all the **d** of thy life. 3117
143:5 I remember the **d** of old; I meditate on all 3117
144:4 his **d** *are* as a shadow that passeth away. 3117
Pr 3:2 For length of **d**, and long life, and peace, 3117
3:16 Length of **d** *is* in her right hand; and in her 3117
9:11 For by me thy **d** shall be multiplied, and 3117
10:27 The fear of the LORD prolongeth **d**: but 3117
15:15 All the **d** of the afflicted *are* evil: but 3117
28:16 hateth covetousness shall prolong *his* **d**. 3117
31:12 him good and not evil all the **d** of her life. 3117
Ecc 2:3 do under the heaven all the **d** of their life. 3117
2:16 seeing *that* which now *is,* in the **d** to come 3117
2:23 For all his **d** *are* sorrows, and his travail 3117
5:17 All his **d** also he eateth in darkness, and 3117
5:18 he taketh under the sun all the **d** of his life, 3117
5:20 For he shall not much remember the **d** of 3117
6:3 so that the **d** of his years be many, and 3117
6:12 all the **d** of his vain life which he spendeth 3117
7:10 What is *the cause* that the former **d** were 3117
7:15 All *things* have I seen in the **d** of my 3117
8:12 an hundred *times,* and his **d** be prolonged, NIH
8:13 neither shall he prolong *his* **d**, *which are* as 3117
8:15 with him of his labour the **d** of his life, 3117
9:9 lovest all the **d** of the life of thy vanity, 3117
9:9 thee under the sun, all the **d** of thy vanity: 3117
11:1 for thou shalt find it after many **d**. 3117
11:8 yet let him remember the **d** of darkness; 3117
11:9 let thy heart cheer thee in the **d** of thy 3117
12:1 Remember now thy Creator in the **d** of thy 3117
12:1 while the evil **d** come not, nor the years 3117
Isa 1:1 and Jerusalem in the **d** of Uzziah, 3117
2:2 it shall come to pass in the last **d**, *that* 3117
7:1 it came to pass in the **d** of Ahaz the son of 3117
7:17 thy father's house, **d** that have not come, 3117
13:22 to come, and her **d** shall not be prolonged. 3117
23:7 *city,* whose antiquity *is* of ancient **d**? 3117
23:15 according to the **d** of one king: 3117
24:22 and after many **d** shall they be visited. 3117
30:26 shall be sevenfold, as the light of seven **d**, 3117
32:10 Many **d** and years shall ye be troubled, 3117
38:1 In those **d** was Hezekiah sick unto death. 3117
38:5 behold, I will add unto thy **d** fifteen years. 3117
38:10 I said, in the cutting off of my **d**, I shall go 3117
38:20 **d** of our life in the house of the LORD. 3117
39:6 Behold, the **d** come, that all that *is* in thine 3117
39:8 For there shall be peace and truth in my **d**. 3117
51:9 awake, as *in* the ancient **d**, *in* 3117
53:10 he shall prolong *his* **d**, and the pleasure of 3117
60:20 and the **d** of thy mourning shall be ended. 3117
63:9 bare them, and carried them all the **d** of old. 3117
63:11 he remembered the **d** of old, Moses, *and* 3117
65:20 shall be no more thence an infant of **d**, 3117
65:20 nor an old man that hath not filled his **d**: 3117
Isa 65:22 for as the **d** of a tree *are* the days of my 3117
65:22 for as the days of a tree *are* the **d** of my 3117
Jer 1:2 **d** of Josiah the son of Amon king of Judah, 3117
1:3 It came also in the **d** of Jehoiakim the son 3117
2:32 yet my people have forgotten me **d** without 3117
3:6 The LORD said also unto me in the **d** of 3117
3:16 in the land, in those **d**, saith the LORD, 3117
3:18 In those **d** the house of Judah shall walk 3117
5:18 Nevertheless in those **d**, saith the LORD, 3117
6:11 be taken, the aged with *him that is* full of **d**. 3117
7:32 Therefore, behold, the **d** come, saith 3117
9:25 Behold, the **d** come, saith the LORD, 3117
13:6 it came to pass after many **d**, that 3117
16:9 in your **d**, the voice of mirth, and the voice 3117
16:14 the **d** come, saith the LORD, 3117
17:11 shall leave them in the midst of his **d**, and 3117
19:6 the **d** come, saith the LORD, 3117
20:18 that my **d** should be consumed with shame? 3117
22:30 a man *that* shall not prosper in his **d**: 3117
23:5 Behold, the **d** come, saith the LORD, 3117
23:6 In his **d** Judah shall be saved, and 3117
23:7 the **d** come, saith the LORD, 3117
23:20 in the latter **d** ye shall consider it perfectly. 3117
25:34 for the **d** of your slaughter and of your 3117
26:18 Micah the Morasthite prophesied in the **d** 3117
30:3 For lo, the **d** come, saith the LORD, that I 3117
30:24 his heart: in the latter **d** ye shall consider it. 3117
31:27 Behold, the **d** come, saith the LORD, 3117
31:29 In those **d** they shall say no more, 3117
31:31 Behold, the **d** come, saith the LORD, 3117
31:33 After those **d**, saith the LORD, I will put 3117
31:38 Behold, the **d** come, saith the LORD, 3117
32:14 that they may continue many **d**. 3117
33:14 Behold, the **d** come, saith the LORD, 3117
33:15 In those **d**, and at that time, will I cause 3117
33:16 In those **d** shall Judah be saved, and 3117
35:1 **d** of Jehoiakim the son of Josiah king of 3117
35:7 but all your **d** ye shall dwell in tents; 3117
35:7 that ye may live many **d** in the land where 3117
35:8 to drink no wine all our **d**, we, our wives, 3117
36:2 from the **d** of Josiah, even unto this day. 3117
37:16 and Jeremiah had remained there many **d**; 3117
42:7 it came to pass after ten **d**, that the word of 3117
46:26 as *in* the **d** of old, saith the LORD. 3117
48:12 the **d** come, saith the LORD, 3117
48:47 again the captivity of Moab in the latter **d**, 3117
49:2 the **d** come, saith the LORD, 3117
49:39 it shall come to pass in the latter **d**, *that* I 3117
50:4 In those **d**, and in that time, saith 3117
50:20 In those **d**, and in that time, saith 3117
51:47 Therefore behold, the **d** come, that I will do 3117
51:52 the **d** come, saith the LORD, 3117
52:33 eat bread before him all the **d** of his life. 3117
52:34 the day of his death, all the **d** of his life. 3117
La 1:7 Jerusalem remembered in the **d** of her 3117
1:7 pleasant things that she had in the **d** of old, 3117
2:17 that he had commanded in the **d** of old: 3117
4:18 our end is near, our **d** are fulfilled; for our 3117
5:21 we shall be turned; renew our **d** as of old. 3117
Eze 3:15 there astonished among them seven **d**. 3117
3:16 it came to pass at the end of seven **d**, 3117
4:4 *according to* the number of the **d** that thou 3117
4:5 according to the number of the **d**, 3117
4:5 of the days, three hundred and ninety **d**: 3117
4:6 the iniquity of the house of Judah forty **d**: 3117
4:8 till thou hast ended the **d** of thy siege. 3117
4:9 *according to* the number of the **d** that thou 3117
4:9 and ninety **d** shalt thou eat thereof. 3117
5:2 when the **d** of the siege are fulfilled: 3117
12:22 The **d** are prolonged, and every vision 3117
12:23 The **d** are at hand, and the effect of every 3117
12:25 for in your **d**, O rebellious house, will I say 3117
12:27 The vision that he seeth *is* for many **d** *to* 3117
16:22 hast not remembered the **d** of thy youth, 3117
16:43 Because thou hast not remembered the **d** of 3117
16:60 covenant with thee in the **d** of thy youth, 3117
22:4 thou hast caused thy **d** to draw near, and 3117
22:14 in the **d** that I shall deal with thee? 3117
23:19 in calling to remembrance the **d** of her 3117
38:8 After many **d** thou shalt be visited: in 3117
38:16 it shall be in the latter **d**, and I will bring 3117
38:17 which prophesied in those **d** *many* years, 3117
43:25 Seven **d** shalt thou prepare every day a goat 3117
43:26 Seven **d** shall they purge the altar and 3117
43:27 when *these* **d** are expired, it shall be, 3117
44:26 they shall reckon unto him seven **d**. 3117
45:21 shall have the passover, a feast of seven **d**; 3117
45:23 seven **d** of the feast he shall prepare a burnt 3117
45:23 rams without blemish daily the seven **d**; 3117
45:25 he do the like in the feast *of* the seven **d**, 3117
46:1 the east shall be shut the six working **d**; 3117
Da 1:12 Prove thy servants, I beseech thee, ten **d**; 3117
1:14 them in this matter, and proved them ten **d**. 3117
1:15 at the end of ten **d** their countenances 3117
1:18 Now at the end of the **d** that the king had 3117
2:28 what shall be in the latter **d**. 3118
2:44 in the **d** of these kings shall the God of 3118
4:34 at the end of the **d** I Nebuchadnezzar lift up 3118
5:11 in the **d** of thy father light and 3118
6:7 a petition of any God or man for thirty **d**, 3118
6:12 *petition* of any God or man within thirty **d**, 3118
7:9 cast *down,* and the Ancient of **d** did sit, 3118
7:13 came to the Ancient of **d**, and they brought 3118
7:22 Until the Ancient of **d** came, and 3118
8:14 two thousand and three hundred **d**; 1242+6153
8:26 up the vision; for *it shall be* for many **d**. 3117
8:27 I Daniel fainted, and was sick *certain* **d**; 3117
10:2 In those **d** I Daniel was mourning three full 3117
10:13 of Persia withstood me one and twenty **d**: 3117
10:14 what shall befall thy people in the latter **d**: 3117
10:14 latter days: for yet the vision *is* for *many* **d**. 3117
11:20 within few **d** he shall be destroyed, 3117
11:33 by captivity, and by spoil, *many* **d**. 3117
12:11 *be* a thousand two hundred and ninety **d**. 3117
12:12 three hundred *and* five and thirty **d**. 3117
Da 12:13 and stand in thy lot at the end of the **d**. 3117
Hos 1:1 in the **d** of Uzziah, Jotham, Ahaz, *and* 3117
1:1 in the **d** of Jeroboam the son of Joash, 3117
2:11 her feast **d**, her new moons, and NIH
2:13 I will visit upon her the **d** of Baalim, 3117
2:15 as *in* the **d** of her youth, and as *in* the day 3117
3:3 unto her, Thou shalt abide for me many **d**; 3117
3:4 of Israel shall abide many **d** without a king, 3117
3:5 and his goodness in the latter **d**. 3117
6:2 After **two d** will he revive us: in the third 3117
9:7 The **d** of visitation are come, the days of 3117
9:7 are come, the **d** of recompence are come; 3117
9:9 *themselves,* as *in* the **d** of Gibeah: 3117
10:9 thou hast sinned from the **d** of Gibeah: 3117
12:9 as *in* the **d** of the solemn feast. 3117
Joel 1:2 Hath this been in your **d**, or even in 3117
1:2 your days, or even in the **d** of your fathers? 3117
2:29 upon the handmaids in those **d** will I pour 3117
3:1 For behold, in those **d**, and in that time, 3117
Am 1:1 which he saw concerning Israel in the **d** of 3117
1:1 in the **d** of Jeroboam the son of Joash king 3117
4:2 that lo, the **d** shall come upon you, that he 3117
5:21 I despise your feast **d**, and I will not smell NIH
8:11 Behold, the **d** come, saith the Lord GOD, 3117
9:11 and I will build it as *in* the **d** of old: 3117
9:13 Behold, the **d** come, saith the LORD, 3117
Jnh 1:17 Jonah was in the belly of the fish three **d** 3117
3:4 Yet forty **d**, and Nineveh *shall be* 3117
Mic 1:1 to Micah the Morasthite in the **d** of Jotham, 3117
4:1 in the last **d** it shall come to pass, *that* 3117
7:14 *in* Bashan and Gilead, as *in* the **d** of old. 3117
7:15 According to the **d** of thy coming out of 3117
7:20 sworn unto our fathers from the **d** of old. 3117
Hab 1:5 for *I will* work a work in your **d**, *which* ye 3117
Zep 1:1 in the **d** of Josiah the son of Amon, king of 3117
Hag 2:16 Since those **d** were, when *one* came to a NIH
Zec 8:6 of the remnant of this people in these **d**, 3117
8:9 ye that hear in these **d** these words by 3117
8:10 For before these **d** there was no hire for 3117
8:11 residue of this people as *in* the former **d**, 3117
8:15 So again have I thought in these **d** to do 3117
8:23 In those **d** *it shall come to pass,* that ten 3117
14:5 in the **d** of Uzziah king of Judah: 3117
Mal 3:4 as *in* the **d** of old, and as *in* former years. 3117
3:7 Even from the **d** of your fathers ye are gone 3117
Mt 2:1 of Judea in the **d** of Herod the king, *2250*
3:1 In those **d** came John the Baptist, *2250*
4:2 And when he had fasted forty **d** and *2250*
9:15 but the **d** will come, when the bridegroom *2250*
11:12 And from the **d** of John the Baptist until *2250*
12:5 how that on the sabbath **d** the priests in NIG
12:10 saying, Is it lawful to heal on the sabbath **d**? NIG
12:12 it is lawful to do well on the sabbath **d**. NIG
12:40 For as Jonas was three **d** and three nights in *2250*
12:40 so shall the Son of man be three **d** and *2250*
15:32 they continue with me now three **d**, *2250*
17:1 And after six **d** Jesus taketh Peter, James, *2250*
23:30 If we had been in the **d** of our fathers, *2250*
24:19 and to them that give suck in those **d**. *2250*
24:22 And except those **d** should be shortened, *2250*
24:22 for the elect's sake those **d** shall be *2250*
24:29 Immediately after the tribulation of those **d** *2250*
24:37 But as the **d** of Noe *were,* so shall also *2250*
24:38 For as in the **d** that were before the flood *2250*
26:2 Ye know that after two **d** is *the feast of* *2250*
26:61 temple of God, and to build it in three **d**. *2250*
27:40 and buildest *it* in three **d**, save thyself. *2250*
27:63 yet alive, After three **d** I will rise *again.* *2250*
Mk 1:9 And it came to pass in those **d**, *that* Jesus *2250*
1:13 And he was there in the wilderness forty **d**, *2250*
2:1 he entered into Capernaum after *some* **d**; *2250*
2:20 But the **d** will come, when the bridegroom *2250*
2:20 and then shall they fast in those **d**. *2250*
2:26 of God **in the d of** Abiathar the high priest, *1909*
3:4 Is it lawful to do good on the sabbath **d**, or NIG
8:1 In those **d** the multitude being very great, *2250*
8:2 they have now been with me three **d**, *2250*
8:31 and be killed, and after three **d** rise again. *2250*
9:2 And after six **d** Jesus taketh with *him* Peter, *2250*
13:17 and to them that give suck in those **d**. *2250*
13:19 For *in* those **d** shall be affliction, such as *2250*
13:20 except that the Lord had shortened *those* **d**, *2250*
13:20 he hath chosen, he hath shortened the **d**. *2250*
13:24 But in those **d**, after that tribulation, the sun *2250*
14:1 After two **d** was *the feast of* the passover, *2250*
14:58 within three **d** I will build another made *2250*
15:29 the temple, and buildest *it* in three **d**, *2250*
Lk 1:5 There was in the **d** of Herod, the king of *2250*
1:23 And it came to pass *that,* as soon as the **d** of *2250*
1:24 And after those **d** his wife Elisabeth *2250*
1:25 Thus hath the Lord dealt with me in the **d** *2250*
1:39 And Mary arose in those **d**, and went into *2250*
1:75 before him, all the **d** of our life. *2250*
2:1 And it came to pass in those **d**, *that* there *2250*
2:6 the **d** were accomplished that she should be *2250*
2:21 And when eight **d** were accomplished for *2250*
2:22 And when the **d** of her purification *2250*
2:43 And when they had fulfilled the **d**, as they *2250*
2:46 *that* after three **d** they found him in *2250*
4:2 Being forty **d** tempted of the devil. And in *2250*
4:2 And in those **d** he did eat nothing: and *2250*
4:25 many widows were in Israel in the **d** of *2250*
4:31 and taught them on the sabbath **d**. NIG
5:35 But the **d** will come, when the bridegroom *2250*
5:35 and then shall they fast in those **d**. *2250*
6:2 which is not lawful to do on the sabbath **d**? NIG
6:9 Is it lawful on the sabbath **d** to do good, NIG
6:12 And it came to pass in those **d**, *that* he went *2250*
9:28 And it came to pass about an eight **d** after *2250*
9:36 told no *man* in those **d** any of *those things* *2250*
13:14 There are six **d** in which *men* ought to *2250*
15:13 And not many **d** after the younger son *2250*
17:22 he said unto the disciples, The **d** will come, *2250*
17:22 when ye shall desire to see one of the **d** of *2250*
17:26 And as it was in the **d** of Noe, so shall it be *2250*

Lk 17:26 shall it be also in the **d** of the Son of man. 2250
17:28 Likewise also as it was in the **d** of Lot; 2250
19:43 For the **d** shall come upon thee, that thine 2250
20: 1 And it came to pass, *that* on one of those **d**, 2250
21: 6 *things* which ye behold, the **d** will come, 2250
21:22 For these be *the* **d** of vengeance, that all 2250
21:23 and to them that give suck, in those **d**, 2250
23:29 For behold, the **d** are coming, in the which 2250
24:18 which are come to pass there in these **d**? 2250
Jn 2:12 and they continued there not many **d**. 2250
2:19 this temple, and in three **d** I will raise it up. 2250
2:20 and wilt thou rear it up in three **d**? 2250
4:40 tarry with them: and he abode there two **d**. 2250
4:43 Now after two **d** he departed thence, and 2250
11: 6 he abode two **d** *still* in the *same* place 2250
11:17 that he had *lien* in the grave four **d** already. 2250
11:39 he stinketh: for he hath been *dead* **four d**. 5066
12: 1 Then Jesus six **d** before the passover came 2250
20:26 And after eight **d** again his disciples were 2250
Ac 1: 3 being seen of them forty **d**, and speaking of 2250
1: 5 with the Holy Ghost not many **d** hence. 2250
1:15 And in those **d** Peter stood up in the midst 2250
2:17 And it shall come to pass in the last **d**, 2250
2:18 I will pour out in those **d** of my Spirit; 2250
3:24 have likewise foretold of these **d**. 2250
5:36 For before these **d** rose up Theudas, 2250
5:37 up Judas of Galilee in the **d** of the taxing, 2250
6: 1 And in those **d**, when the number of 2250
7:41 And they made a calf in those **d**, and 2250
7:45 the face of our fathers, unto the **d** of David; 2250
9: 9 And he was three **d** without sight, and 2250
9:19 Then was Saul certain **d** with the disciples 2250
9:23 And after that many **d** were fulfilled, 2250
9:37 And it came to pass in those **d**, that she was 2250
9:43 that he tarried many **d** in Joppa with one 2250
10:30 Four **d** ago I was fasting until this hour; 2250
10:48 Then prayed they him to tarry certain **d**. 2250
11:27 And in these **d** came prophets from 2250
11:28 which came to pass in the **d** of Claudius NIG
12: 3 (Then were the **d** of unleavened bread.) 2250
13:31 And he was seen many **d** of them which 2250
13:41 for I work a work in your **d**, a work which 2250
15:36 And some **d** after Paul said unto Barnabas, 2250
16:12 and we were in that city abiding certain **d**. 2250
16:18 And this did she many **d**. But Paul, 2250
17: 2 three sabbath **d** reasoned with them out of NIG
20: 6 Philippi after the **d** of unleavened bread, 2250
20: 6 and came unto them to Troas in five **d**, 2250
20: 6 in five days; where we abode seven **d**. 2250
21: 4 finding disciples, we tarried there seven **d**: 2250
21: 5 And when we had accomplished *those* **d**, 2250
21:10 And as we tarried *there* many **d**, there came 2250
21:15 And after those **d** we took up our carriages, 2250
21:26 to signify the accomplishment of the **d** of 2250
21:27 And when the seven **d** were almost ended, 2250
21:38 which before these **d** madest an uproar, and 2250
24: 1 And after five **d** Ananias the high priest 2250
24:11 twelve **d** since I went up to Jerusalem for to 2250
24:24 And after certain **d**, when Felix came with 2250
25: 1 after three **d** he ascended from Cesarea to 2250
25: 6 he had tarried among them more than ten **d**, 2250
25:13 And after certain **d** king Agrippa and 2250
25:14 And when they had been there many **d**, 2250
27: 7 And when we had sailed slowly many **d**, 2250
27:20 And when neither sun nor stars in many **d** 2250
28: 7 and lodged *us* three **d** courteously. 2250
28:12 at Syracuse, we tarried *there* three **d**. 2250
28:14 were desired to tarry with them seven **d**: 2250
28:17 that after three **d** Paul called the chief of 2250
Gal 1:18 to see Peter, and abode with him fifteen **d**. 2250
4:10 Ye observe **d**, and months, and times, and 2250
Eph 5:16 Redeeming the time, because the **d** are evil. 2250
Col 2:16 or of the new moon, or of the **sabbath d**: 4521
2Ti 3: 1 that in the last **d** perilous times shall come. 2250
Heb 1: 2 Hath in these last **d** spoken unto us by *his* 2250
5: 7 Who in the **d** of his flesh, when he had 2250
7: 3 having neither beginning of **d**, nor end of 2250
8: 8 *he* saith, Behold, the **d** come, saith 2250
8:10 make with the house of Israel after those **d**, 2250
10:16 that I will make with them after those **d**, 2250
10:32 But call to remembrance the former **d**, 2250
11:30 after they were compassed about seven **d**. 2250
12:10 For they verily for a few **d** chastened *us* 2250
Jas 5: 3 have heaped treasure together for the last **d**. 2250
1Pe 3:10 For he that will love life, and see good **d**, 2250
3:20 of God waited in the **d** of Noah, 2250
2Pe 3: 3 that there shall come in the last **d** scoffers, 2250
Rev 2:10 be tried; and ye shall have tribulation ten **d**: 2250
2:13 even in *those* **d** wherein Antipas *was* my 2250
9: 6 And in those **d** shall men seek death, and 2250
10: 7 But in the **d** of the voice of the seventh 2250
11: 3 a thousand two hundred *and* threescore **d**, 2250
11: 6 that it rain not in the **d** of their prophecy: 2250
11: 9 nations shall see their dead bodies three **d** 2250
11:11 And after three **d** and a half the spirit of life 2250
12: 6 a thousand two hundred *and* threescore **d**. 2250

DAYS' (13) [DAY]
Ge 30:36 he set three **d** journey betwixt himself and 3117
31:23 and pursued after him seven **d** journey; 3117
Ex 3:18 three **d** journey into the wilderness, 3117
5: 3 three **d** journey into the desert, and 3117
8:27 We will go three **d** journey into 3117
Nu 10:33 the mount of the LORD three **d** journey: 3117
10:33 went before them *in* the three **d** journey, 3117
33: 8 went three **d** journey in the wilderness of 3117
Dt 1: 2 (*There are* eleven **d** *journey* from Horeb *by* 3117
1Sa 11: 3 said unto him, Give us seven **d** respite, 3117
2Sa 24:13 that there be three **d** pestilence in thy land? 3117
2Ki 3: 9 they fetcht a compass of seven **d** journey: 3117
Jnh 3: 3 an exceeding great city of three **d** journey. 3117

DAYSMAN (1) [DAY, MAN]
Job 9:33 Neither is there *any* **d** betwixt us, 3198

DAYSPRING (2) [DAY, SPRING]
Job 38:12 *and* caused the **d** to know his place; 7837
Lk 1:78 whereby the **d** from on high hath visited us, 395

DAYTIME (7) [DAY, TIME]
Job 5:14 They meet with darkness **in** the **d**, and 3119
24:16 they had marked for themselves **in** the **d**: 3119
Ps 22: 2 I cry in the **d**, but thou hearest not; 3119
42: 8 will command his lovingkindness in the **d**, 3119
78:14 In the **d** also he led them with a cloud, and 3119
Isa 4: 6 for a shadow **in** the **d** from the heat, 3119
21: 8 continually upon the watchtower **in** the **d**, 3119

DEACON (2) [DEACONS]
1Ti 3:10 then let them **use the office of a d**, 1247
3:13 For they that have **used the office of** a **d** 1247

DEACONS (3) [DEACON]
Php 1: 1 are at Philippi, with the bishops and **d**: 1249
1Ti 3: 8 Likewise *must* the **d** *be* grave, 1249
3:12 Let the **d** be the husbands of one wife, 1249

DEAD (364) [DIE]
Ge 20: 3 said to him, Behold, thou *art but* a **d** man, 4191
23: 3 Abraham stood up from before his **d**, and 4191
23: 4 that I may bury my **d** out of my sight. 4191
23: 6 in the choice of our sepulchres bury thy **d**; 4191
23: 6 but that thou mayest bury thy **d**. 4191
23: 8 If it be your mind that I should bury my **d** 4191
23:11 sons of my people give I it thee: bury thy **d**. 4191
23:13 take *it* of me, and I will bury my **d** there. 4191
23:15 betwixt me and thee? bury therefore thy **d**. 4191
42:38 for his brother is **d**, and he is left alone: 4191
44:20 his brother is **d**, and he alone is left of his 4191
50:15 brethren saw that their father was **d**, 4191
Ex 4:19 for all the men are **d** which sought thy life. 4191
9: 7 was not one of the cattle of the Israelites **d**. 4191
12:30 *was* not a house where *there was* not one **d**. 4191
12:33 in haste; for they said, We *be* all **d** *men*. 4191
14:30 Israel saw the Egyptians **d** upon the sea 4191
21:34 owner of them; and the **d** *beast* shall be his. 4191
21:35 of it; and the **d** *ox* also they shall divide. 4191
21:36 pay ox for ox; and the **d** shall be his own. 4191
Lev 11:31 doth touch them, when they be **d**, 4194
11:32 when they are **d**, doth fall, it shall be 4194
19:28 make any cuttings in your flesh for the **d**, 5315
21: 1 There shall none be defiled for the **d** among 5315
21:11 Neither shall he go in to any **d** body, 5315
22: 4 toucheth any *thing that is* unclean *by* the **d**, 5315
Nu 5: 2 an issue, and whosoever is defiled by the **d**: 5315
6: 6 the LORD he shall come at no **d** body. 4191
6:11 for that he sinned by the **d**, and shall hallow 5315
9: 6 who were defiled by the **d body** of a man, 5315
9: 7 We *are* defiled by the **d body** of a man: 5315
9:10 shall be unclean by reason of a **d body**, 5315
12:12 Let her not be as one **d**, of whom the flesh 4191
16:48 he stood between the **d** and the living; and 4191
19:11 He that toucheth the **d** *body* of any man 4191
19:13 Whosoever toucheth the **d** *body* of *any* man 4191
19:13 the dead *body* of *any* man that is **d**, 4191
19:16 or a **d** *body*, or a bone of a man, or a grave, 4191
19:18 a bone, or one slain, or one **d**, or a grave: 4191
20:29 all the congregation saw that Aaron was **d**, 1478
Dt 2:16 and **d** from among the people, 4191
14: 1 *any* baldness between your eyes for the **d**. 4191
14: 8 eat of their flesh, nor touch their **d carcase**. 5038
25: 5 The wife of the **d** shall not marry without 4191
25: 6 in the name of his brother which is **d**, 4191
26:14 *use*, nor given *ought* thereof for the **d**: 4191
Jos 1: 2 Moses my servant is **d**; now therefore arise, 4191
Jdg 2:19 when the judge was **d**, *that* they returned, 4194
3:25 their lord *was* fallen down **d** on the earth. 4191
4: 1 the sight of the LORD, when Ehud was **d**. 4191
4:22 Sisera lay **d**, and the nail *was* in his 4191
5:27 where he bowed, there he fell down **d**. 7703
8:33 it came to pass, as soon as Gideon was **d**, 4191
9:55 men of Israel saw that Abimelech was **d**, 4191
16:30 So the **d** which he slew at his death were 4191
20: 5 concubine have they forced, that she is **d**. 4191
Ru 1: 8 as ye have dealt with the **d**, and with me. 4191
2:20 off his kindness to the living and to the **d**. 4191
4: 5 of Ruth the Moabitess, the wife of the **d**, 4191
4: 5 to raise up the name of the **d** upon his 4191
4:10 to raise up the name of the **d** upon his 4191
4:10 that the name of the **d** be not cut off from 4191
1Sa 4:17 are **d**, and the ark of God is taken. 4191
4:19 her father in law and her husband were **d**, 4191
17:51 the Philistines saw their champion was **d**, 4191
24:14 dost thou pursue? after a **d** dog, after a flea. 4191
25:39 when David heard that Nabal was **d**, 4191
28: 3 Now Samuel was **d**, and all Israel had 4191
31: 5 his armourbearer saw that Saul was **d**, 4191
31: 7 that Saul and his sons were **d**, they forsook 4191
2Sa 1: 4 many of the people also are fallen and **d**; 4191
1: 4 and Saul and Jonathan his son are **d** also. 4191
1: 5 thou that Saul and Jonathan his son be **d**? 4191
2: 7 for your master Saul is **d**, and also 4191
4: 1 when Saul's son heard that Abner was **d** in 4191
4:10 one told me, saying, Behold, Saul is **d**, 4191
9: 8 that thou shouldest look upon such a **d** dog 4191
11:21 Thy servant Uriah the Hittite is **d** also. 4191
11:24 *some* of the king's servants be **d**, and 4191
11:24 and thy servant Uriah the Hittite is **d** also. 4191
11:26 Uriah heard that Uriah her husband was **d**, 4191
12:18 feared to tell him that the child was **d**: 4191
12:18 if we tell him *that* the child is **d**? 4191
12:19 David perceived that the child was **d**: 4191
12:19 David said unto his servants, Is the child **d**? 4191
12:19 Is the child dead? And they said, He is **d**. 4191
12:21 when the child was **d**, thou didst rise and 4191
12:23 now he is **d**, wherefore should I fast? can I 4191
13:32 men the king's sons; for Amnon only is **d**: 4191
13:33 to think *that* all the king's sons are **d**: 4191
13:33 king's sons are dead: for Amnon only is **d**. 4191
2Sa 13:39 concerning Amnon, seeing he was **d**. 4191
14: 2 *that had* a long time mourned for the **d**: 4191
14: 5 a widow woman, and mine husband is **d**. 4191
16: 9 Why should this **d** dog curse my lord 4191
18:20 bear no tidings, because the king's son is **d**. 4191
19:10 whom we anointed over us, is **d** in battle. 4191
19:28 but **d** men before my lord the king: 4194
1Ki 3:20 and laid her **d** child in my bosom. 4191
3:21 to give my child suck, behold, it was **d**: 4191
3:22 the living *is* my son, and the **d** *is* thy son. 4191
3:22 the **d** *is* thy son, and the living *is* my son. 4191
3:23 *is* my son that liveth, and thy son *is* the **d**: 4191
3:23 thy son *is* the **d**, and my son *is* the living. 4191
11:21 that Joab the captain of the host was **d**, 4191
13:31 When I am **d**, then bury me in 4191
21:14 saying, Naboth is stoned, and is **d**. 4191
21:15 and was **d**, that Jezebel said to Ahab, Arise, 4191
21:15 for money: for Naboth is not alive, but **d**. 4191
21:16 when Ahab heard that Naboth was **d**, 4191
2Ki 3: 5 it came to pass, when Ahab was **d**, that 4194
4: 1 Thy servant my husband is **d**; 4191
4:32 the child was **d**, *and* laid upon his bed. 4191
8: 5 king how he had restored a **d** *body* to life, 4191
11: 1 mother of Ahaziah saw that her son was **d**, 4191
19:35 behold, they *were* all **d** corpses. 4191
23:30 his servants carried him *in a chariot* **d** from 4191
1Ch 1:44 when Bela was **d**, Jobab the son of Zerah of 4191
1:45 when Jobab was **d**, Husham of the land of 4191
1:46 when Husham was **d**, Hadad the son of 4191
1:47 when Hadad was **d**, Samlah of Masrekah 4191
1:48 when Samlah was **d**, Shaul of Rehoboth *by* 4191
1:49 when Shaul was **d**, Baal-hanan the son of 4191
1:50 when Baal-hanan was **d**, Hadad reigned in 4191
2:19 when Azubah was **d**, Caleb took unto him 4191
2:24 after that Hezron was **d** in Caleb-ephratah, 4194
10: 5 his armourbearer saw that Saul was **d**, 4191
10: 7 that Saul and his sons were **d**, then 4191
2Ch 20:24 they *were* **d bodies** fallen to the earth, and 6297
20:25 in abundance both riches with the **d bodies**, 6297
22:10 mother of Ahaziah saw that her son was **d**, 4191
Est 2: 7 when her father and mother were **d**, 4194
Job 1:19 it fell upon the young men, and they are **d**; 4191
26: 5 **D** *things* are formed from under the waters, 7496
Ps 31:12 I am forgotten as a **d man** out of mind: 4191
76: 6 and horse *are* **cast into a d sleep**. 7290
79: 2 The **d bodies** of thy servants have they 5038
88: 5 Free among the **d**, like the slain that lie in 4191
88:10 Wilt thou shew wonders to the **d**? shall 4191
88:10 shall the **d** arise *and* praise thee? Selah. 7496
106:28 and ate the sacrifices of the **d**. 4191
110: 6 he shall fill *the places with* the **d bodies**; 1472
115:17 The **d** praise not the LORD, neither any 4191
143: 3 in darkness, as those that have been long **d**. 4191
Pr 2:18 unto death, and her paths unto the **d**. 7496
9:18 But he knoweth not that the **d** *are* there; *and* 7496
21:16 shall remain in the congregation of the **d**. 7496
Ecc 4: 2 Wherefore I praised the **d** which are 4191
4: 2 **d** more than the living which are yet alive. 4191
9: 3 they live, and after that *they go* to the **d**. 4191
9: 4 for a living dog *is* better than a **d** lion. 4191
9: 5 the **d** know not any thing, neither have they 4191
10: 1 **D** flies cause the ointment of 4194
Isa 8:19 seek unto their God? for the living to the **d**? 4191
14: 9 it stirreth up the **d** for thee, *even* all 7496
22: 2 *are* not slain with the sword, nor **d** in battle. 4191
26:14 *They are* **d**, they shall not live; *they are* 4191
26:19 Thy **d** *men* shall live, *together with* my 4191
26:19 *together with* my **d body** shall they arise. 5038
26:19 of herbs, and the earth shall cast out the **d**. 7496
37:36 behold, they *were* all **d** corpses. 4191
59:10 *we are* in desolate places as **d** *men*. 4191
Jer 16: 7 in mourning, to comfort them for the **d**; 4191
22:10 Weep ye not for the **d**, neither bemoan him: 4191
26:23 cast his **d body** into the graves of 5038
31:40 the whole valley of the **d bodies**, and of 6297
33: 5 *it is* to fill them with the **d bodies** of men, 6297
34:20 their **d bodies** shall be for meat unto 5038
36:30 his **d body** shall be cast out in the day to 5038
41: 9 had cast all the **d bodies** of the men, 6297
La 3: 6 me in dark places, as they that be **d** of old. 4191
Eze 6: 5 I will lay the **d carcases** of the children of 6297
24:17 to cry, make no mourning *for* the **d**, 4191
44:25 they shall come at no **d** person to defile 4191
44:31 shall not eat *of* any thing **that is d of itself**, 5038
Am 8: 3 *there shall be* many **d bodies** in every 6297
Hag 2:13 If *one that is* unclean *by* a **d body** touch 5315
Mt 2:19 But when Herod was **d**, behold, an angel of 5053
2:20 for they are **d** which sought the young 2348
8:22 Follow me; and let the **d** bury their dead. 3498
8:22 Follow me; and let the dead bury their **d**. 3498
9:18 saying, My daughter is even now **d**: 5053
9:24 for the maid is not **d**, but sleepeth. And they 599
10: 8 the lepers, raise the **d**, cast out devils: 3498
11: 5 the **d** are raised up, and the poor have 3498
14: 2 he is risen from the **d**; and therefore mighty 3498
17: 9 the Son of man be risen again from the **d**. 3498
22:31 But as touching the resurrection of the **d**, 3498
22:32 God is not the God of the **d**, but of 3498
23:27 but are within full of **d** *men's* bones, and 3498
27:64 say unto the people, He is risen from the **d**: 3498
28: 4 keepers did shake, and became as **d** *men*. 3498
28: 7 tell his disciples that he is risen from the **d**; 3498
Mk 5:35 *house certain* which said, Thy daughter is **d**: 599
5:39 and weep? the damsel is not **d**, but sleepeth. 599
6:14 That John the Baptist was risen from the **d**, 3498
6:16 whom I beheaded: he is risen from the **d**. 3498
9: 9 till the Son of man were risen from the **d**. 3498
9:10 what the rising from the **d** should mean. 3498
9:26 and came out of *him*: and he was as **one d**; 3498
9:26 one dead; insomuch that many said, He is **d**. 599
12:25 For when they shall rise from the **d**, 3498
12:26 And as touching the **d**, that they rise: 3498
12:27 He is not the God of the **d**, but the God of 3498
15:44 And Pilate marvelled if he were already **d**: 2348
15:44 asked him whether he had been any while **d**. 599

Lk 7:12 behold, there was a **d man** carried out, 2348
7:15 And he that was **d** sat up, and began to 3498
7:22 are cleansed, the deaf hear, the **d** are raised, 3498
8:49 *house,* saying to him, Thy daughter is **d**; 2348
8:52 he said, Weep not; she is not **d**, but sleepeth. 599
8:53 him to scorn, knowing that she was **d**. 599
9: 7 of some, that John was risen from the **d**; 3498
9:60 said unto him, Let the **d** bury their dead: 3498
9:60 said unto him, Let the dead bury their **d**: 3498
10:30 and departed, leaving *him* **half d**. 2253
15:24 For this my son was **d**, and is alive again; 3498
15:32 for this thy brother was **d**, and is alive 3498
16:30 but if one went unto them from the **d**, 3498
16:31 be persuaded, though one rose from the **d**. 3498
20:35 and the resurrection from the **d**, 3498
20:37 Now that the **d** are raised, even Moses 3498
20:38 For he is not a God of the **d**, but of 3498
24: 5 Why seek ye the living among the **d**? 3498
24:46 and to rise from the **d** the third day: 3498
Jn 2:22 When therefore he was risen from the **d**, 3498
5:21 For as the Father raiseth up the **d**, and 3498
5:25 when the **d** shall hear the voice of the Son 3498
6:49 did eat manna in the wilderness, and are **d**. 599
6:58 not as your fathers did eat manna, and are **d**: 599
8:52 Abraham is **d**, and the prophets; and 599
8:53 greater than our father Abraham, which is **d**? 599
8:53 and the prophets are **d**: whom makest thou 599
11:14 said Jesus unto them plainly, Lazarus is **d**. 599
11:25 in me, though he were **d**, *yet* shall he live: 599
11:39 Martha, the sister of him that was **d**, saith 2348
11:39 he stinketh: for he hath been ***d*** four days. NIG
11:41 stone *from the place* where the **d** was laid. 2348
11:44 And he that was **d** came forth, bound hand 2348
12: 1 where Lazarus was which had been **d**, 2348
12: 1 had been dead, whom he raised from the **d**. 3498
12: 9 whom he had raised from the **d**. 3498
12:17 and raised him from the **d**, bare record. 3498
19:33 and saw that he was **d** already, they brake 2348
20: 9 that he must rise again from the **d**. 3498
21:14 after that he was risen from the **d**. 3498
Ac 2:29 that he is both **d** and buried, and 5053
3:15 of life, whom God hath raised from the **d**; 3498
4: 2 through Jesus the resurrection from the **d**. 3498
4:10 ye crucified, whom God raised from the **d**, 3498
5:10 and found her **d**, and, carrying *her* forth, 3498
7: 4 and from thence, when his father was **d**, 599
10:41 and drink with him after he rose from the **d**. 3498
10:42 of God *to be* the Judge of quick and **d**. 3498
13:30 But God raised him from the **d**: 3498
13:34 that he raised him up from the **d**, 3498
14:19 out of the city, supposing he had been **d**. 2348
17: 3 have suffered, and risen again from the **d**; 3498
17:31 *men,* in that he hath raised him from the **d**. 3498
17:32 they heard of the resurrection of the **d**, 3498
20: 9 from the third loft, and was taken up **d**. 3498
23: 6 resurrection of the **d** I am called in 3498
24:15 that there shall be a resurrection of the **d**, 3498
24:21 Touching the resurrection of the **d** I am 3498
25:19 and of one Jesus, *which was* **d**, whom Paul 2348
26: 8 with you, that God should raise the **d**? 3498
26:23 *be* the first *that* should rise from the **d**, 3498
28: 6 have swollen, or fallen down **d** suddenly: 3498
Ro 1: 4 of holiness, by the resurrection from the **d**: 3498
4:17 who quickeneth the **d**, and calleth those 3498
4:19 he considered not his own body now **d**, 3499
4:24 that raised up Jesus our Lord from the **d**; 3498
5:15 For if through the offence of one many be **d**, 599
6: 2 How shall we, that are **d** to sin, live any 599
6: 4 that like as Christ was raised up from the **d** 3498
6: 7 For he that is **d** is freed from sin. 599
6: 8 Now if we be **d** with Christ, we believe that 599
6: 9 being raised from the **d** dieth no more; 3498
6:11 Likewise reckon ye also yourselves to be **d** 3498
6:13 as *those that are* alive from the **d**, and 3498
7: 2 but if the husband be **d**, she is loosed from 599
7: 3 but if *her* husband be **d**, she is free from *that* 599
7: 4 ye also are become **d** to the law by 2289
7: 4 *even* to him who is raised from the **d**, 3498
7: 6 the law, *that* being **d** wherein we were held; 599
7: 8 For without the law sin *was* **d**. 3498
8:10 *be* in you, the body *is* **d** because of sin; 3498
8:11 raised up Jesus from the **d** dwell in you, 3498
8:11 he that raised up Christ from the **d** shall 3498
10: 7 to bring up Christ again from the **d**.) 3498
10: 9 heart that God hath raised him from the **d**, 3498
11:15 receiving *of them be*, but life from the **d**? 3498
14: 9 that he might be Lord both of the **d** and 3498
1Co 7:39 but if her husband be **d**, she is at liberty to 2837
15:12 Christ be preached that he rose from the **d**, 3498
15:12 you that there is no resurrection of the **d**? 3498
15:13 But if there be no resurrection of the **d**, 3498
15:15 he raised not up, if so be that the **d** rise not. 3498
15:16 For if the **d** rise not, then is not Christ 3498
15:20 But now is Christ risen from the **d**, *and* 3498
15:21 by man *came* also the resurrection of the **d**. 3498
15:29 shall they do which are baptized for the **d**, 3498
15:29 for the dead, if the **d** rise not at all? 3498
15:29 at all? why are they then baptized for the **d**? 3498
15:32 what advantageth it me, if the **d** rise not? 3498
15:35 *man* will say, How are the **d** raised up? 3498
15:42 So also *is* the resurrection of the **d**. It is 3498
15:52 and the **d** shall be raised incorruptible, and 3498
2Co 1: 9 but in God which raiseth the **d**: 3498
5:14 that if one died for all, then were all **d**: 599
Gal 1: 1 the Father, who raised him from the **d**;) 3498
2:19 For I through the law am **d** to the law, that I 599
2:21 *come* by the law, then Christ is **d** in vain. 599
Eph 1:20 when he raised him from the **d**, and 3498
2: 1 And you *hath he quickened,* who were **d** in 3498
2: 5 Even when we were **d** in sins, 3498
5:14 and arise from the **d**, and Christ shall give 3498
Php 3:11 I might attain unto the resurrection of the **d**. 3498
Col 1:18 is the beginning, the firstborn from the **d**; 3498
2:12 of God, who hath raised him from the **d**. 3498
2:13 being **d** in *your* sins and the uncircumcision 3498
2:20 Wherefore if ye be **d** with Christ from 599
3: 3 For ye are **d**, and your life is hid with Christ 599
1Th 1:10 whom he raised from the **d**, *even* Jesus, 3498
4:16 of God: and the **d** in Christ shall rise first: 3498
1Ti 5: 6 But she that liveth in pleasure is **d** while 2348
2Ti 2: 8 raised from the **d** according to my gospel: 3498
2:11 For if we be **d with** *him,* we shall also live 4880
4: 1 and the **d** at his appearing and his kingdom; 3498
Heb 6: 1 the foundation of repentance from **d** works, 3498
6: 2 and of resurrection of the **d**, and of eternal 3498
9:14 purge your conscience from **d** works to 3498
9:17 For a testament *is* of force after *men* are **d**: 3498
11: 4 his gifts: and by it he being **d** yet speaketh. 599
11:12 and him **as good as d**, *so many* as the stars 3499
11:19 *was* able to raise *him* up, even from the **d**; 3498
11:35 Women received their **d** raised to life 3498
13:20 that brought again from the **d** our Lord 3498
Jas 2:17 if it hath not works, is **d**, *being* alone. 3498
2:20 O vain man, that faith without works is **d**? 3498
2:26 For as the body without the spirit is **d**, so 3498
2:26 is dead, so faith without works is **d** also. 3498
1Pe 1: 3 the resurrection of Jesus Christ from the **d**, 3498
1:21 that raised him up from the **d**, and gave him 3498
2:24 that we, being **d** to sins, should live unto 581
4: 5 that is ready to judge the quick and the **d**. 3498
4: 6 the gospel preached also to *them that are* **d**, 3498
Jude 1:12 without fruit, twice **d**, plucked up by 599
Rev 1: 5 *and* the first begotten of the **d**, and 3498
1:17 And when I saw him, I fell at his feet as **d**. 3498
1:18 I am he that liveth, and was **d**; and behold, 3498
2: 8 and the last, which was **d**, and is alive; 3498
3: 1 thou hast a name that thou livest, and art **d**. 3498
11: 8 And their **d bodies** *shall lie* in the street of 4430
11: 9 nations shall see their **d bodies** three days 4430
11: 9 shall not suffer their **d bodies** to be put in 4430
11:18 thy wrath is come, and the time of the **d**, 3498
14:13 Blessed *are* the **d** which die in the Lord 3498
16: 3 and it became as the blood of a **d** *man:* and 3498
20: 5 But the rest of the **d** lived not again until 3498
20:12 And I saw the **d**, small and great, stand 3498
20:12 the **d** were judged out of those *things* which 3498
20:13 And the sea gave up the **d** which were in it; 3498
20:13 hell delivered up the **d** which were in them: 3498

DEADLY (7) [DIE]
1Sa 5:11 for there was a **d** destruction throughout all 4194
Ps 17: 9 *from* my **d** enemies, *who* compass 5315+871.1
Eze 30:24 *with* the groanings of a **d wounded** *man.* 2491
Mk 16:18 if they drink any **d** *thing,* it shall not hurt 2286
Jas 3: 8 *it is* an unruly evil, full of **d** poison. 2287
Rev 13: 3 to death; and his **d** wound was healed: 2288
13:12 the first beast, whose **d** wound was healed. 2288

DEADNESS (1) [DIE]
Ro 4:19 year old, neither *yet* the **d** of Sara's womb: 3500

DEAF (15)
Ex 4:11 the dumb, or **d**, or the seeing, or the blind? 2795
Lev 19:14 Thou shalt not curse the **d**, nor put a 2795
Ps 38:13 I, as a **d** *man,* heard not; and *I was* as a 2795
58: 4 *they are* like the **d** adder *that* stoppeth her 2795
Isa 29:18 in that day shall the **d** hear the words of 2795
35: 5 and the ears of the **d** shall be unstopped. 2795
42:18 Hear, ye **d**; and look, ye blind, that *ye* may 2795
42:19 or **d**, as my messenger *that* I sent? who *is* 2795
43: 8 that have eyes, and the **d** that have ears. 2795
Mic 7:16 upon *their* mouth, their ears shall be **d**. 2790
Mt 11: 5 and the **d** hear, the dead are raised up, and 2974
Mk 7:32 And they bring unto him one *that was* **d**, 2974
7:37 he maketh both the **d** to hear, and the dumb 2974
9:25 *Thou* dumb and **d** spirit, I charge thee, 2974
Lk 7:22 the **d** hear, the dead are raised, 2974

DEAL (60) [DEALER, DEALERS, DEALEST, DEALETH, DEALING, DEALINGS, DEALS, DEALT]
Ge 19: 9 now will we **d worse** with thee, than with 7489
21:23 God that thou wilt not **d falsely** with me, 8266
24:49 now if ye will **d** kindly and truly with my 6213
32: 9 to thy kindred, and I will **d well** with thee: 3190
34:31 Should he **d with** our sister as with a 6213
47:29 my thigh, and **d** kindly and truly with me; 6213
Ex 1:10 Come on, let us **d wisely** with them; 2449
8:29 let not Pharaoh **d deceitfully** any more in 2048
21: 9 he shall **d** with her after the manner of 6213
23:11 In like manner thou shalt **d** with thy 6213
29:40 with the one lamb a **tenth d** of flour 6241
Lev 14:21 **one tenth d** of fine flour mingled with 259+6241
19:11 Ye shall not steal, neither **d falsely**, 3584
Nu 11:15 if thou **d** thus **with** me, kill me, I pray thee, 6213
15: 4 **tenth d** *of* flour mingled with the fourth 6241
28:13 a **several tenth d** of flour mingled 6241+6241
28:21 A **several tenth d** shalt thou offer 6241+6241
28:29 A **several tenth d** unto one lamb, 6241+6241
29: 4 one **tenth d** for one lamb, throughout 6241
29:10 A **several tenth d** for one lamb, 6241+6241
29:15 a **several tenth d** to each lamb of 6241+6241
Dt 7: 5 thus shall ye **d** with them; ye shall destroy 6213
Jos 2:14 that we will **d** kindly and truly with thee. 6213
Ru 1: 8 the LORD **d** kindly with you, as ye have 6213
1Sa 20: 8 Therefore thou shalt **d** kindly with thy 6213
2Sa 18: 5 **D** gently for my sake with the young man, NIH
2Ch 2: 3 As thou didst **d** with David my father, and 6213
2: 3 house to dwell therein, *even so d with me.* NIH
19:11 **D** courageously, and the LORD shall be 6213
Job 42: 8 lest *I* **d** with you *after your* folly, in that ye 6213
Ps 75: 4 I said unto the fools, **D** not **foolishly**: and 1984
105:25 his people, to **d subtilly** with his servants. 5230
119:17 **D bountifully** with thy servant, *that* I may 1580
119:124 **D** with thy servant according unto thy 6213
142: 7 for thou shalt **d bountifully** with me. 1580
Pr 12:22 but they that **d** truly *are* his delight. 6213
Isa 26:10 the land of uprightness will he **d unjustly**, 5765
33: 1 thou shalt make an end to **d treacherously**, 898
33: 1 they shall **d treacherously** with thee. 898
48: 8 thou wouldest **d very treacherously**, 898+898
52:13 Behold, my servant shall **d prudently**, 7919
58: 7 *Is it* not to **d** thy bread to the hungry, and 6536
Jer 12: 1 they happy that **d very treacherously**? 898+899
18:23 **d** *thus* with them in the time of thine anger. 6213
21: 2 be that the LORD will **d** with us 6213
Eze 8:18 Therefore will I also **d** in fury: mine eye 6213
16:59 I will even **d** with thee as thou hast done, 6213
18: 9 and hath kept my judgments, to **d** truly; 6213
22:14 in the days that I shall **d** with thee? 6213
23:25 and they shall **d** furiously with thee: 6213
23:29 they shall **d** with thee hatefully, and 6213
31:11 he shall **surely d** with him: 6213+6213
Da 1:13 and as thou seest, **d** with thy servants. 6213
11: 7 and shall **d** against them, and shall prevail: 6213
Hab 1:13 thou upon them that **d treacherously**, 898
Mal 2:10 why do we **d treacherously** every man 898
2:15 let none **d treacherously** against the wife of 898
2:16 to your spirit, that ye **d** not **treacherously**. 898
Mk 7:36 much the more a **great d** they published *it;* 4054
10:48 but he cried the more a **great d**, *Thou* Son 4183

DEALER (1) [DEAL]
Isa 21: 2 the **treacherous d** dealeth treacherously, and 898

DEALERS (2) [DEAL]
Isa 24:16 the **treacherous d** have dealt treacherously; 898
24:16 the **treacherous d** have dealt very 898

DEALEST (2) [DEAL]
Ex 5:15 Wherefore **d** thou thus with thy servants? 6213
Isa 33: 1 **d treacherously**, and they dealt not 898

DEALETH (10) [DEAL]
Jdg 18: 4 Thus and thus **d** Micah with me, and 6213
1Sa 23:22 it is told me *that* he **d very subtilly**. 6191+6191
Pr 10: 4 *He becometh* poor that **d** *with* a slack hand: 6213
13:16 Every prudent *man* **d** with knowledge: but 6213
14:17 *He that is* soon angry **d** foolishly: and 6213
21:24 scorner *is* his name, who **d** in proud wrath. 6213
Isa 21: 2 the treacherous dealer **d treacherously**, and 898
Jer 6:13 even unto the priest every one **d** falsely. 6213
8:10 even unto the priest every one **d** falsely. 6213
Heb 12: 7 God **d** with you as with sons; 4374

DEALING (1) [DEAL]
Ps 7:16 his **violent d** shall come down upon his 2555

DEALINGS (2) [DEAL]
1Sa 2:23 for I hear of your evil **d** by all this people. 1697
Jn 4: 9 For the Jews **have** no **d with** 4798

DEALS (19) [DEAL]
Lev 14:10 **three tenth d** of fine flour *for* a meat 6241+7969
23:13 two **tenth d** *of* fine flour mingled with oil, 6241
23:17 two wave loaves of two **tenth d**: 6241
24: 5 two **tenth d** shall be *in* one cake. 6241
Nu 15: 6 **tenth d** *of* flour mingled with the third *part* 6241
15: 9 **tenth d** *of* flour mingled with half a hin of 6241
28: 9 two **tenth d** *of* flour *for* a meat offering, 6241
28:12 three **tenth d** *of* flour *for* a meat offering, 6241
28:12 two **tenth d** *of* flour *for* a meat offering, 6241
28:20 three **tenth d** shall ye offer for a bullock, 6241
28:20 for a bullock, and two **tenth d** for a ram; 6241
28:28 three **tenth d** unto one bullock, two tenth 6241
28:28 one bullock, two **tenth d** unto one ram, 6241
29: 3 three **tenth d** for a bullock, *and* two tenth 6241
29: 3 for a bullock, *and* two **tenth d** for a ram, 6241
29: 9 three **tenth d** to a bullock, *and* two tenth 6241
29: 9 to a bullock, *and* two **tenth d** to one ram, 6241
29:14 three **tenth d** unto every bullock of 6241
29:14 two **tenth d** to each ram of the two rams, 6241

DEALT (57) [DEAL]
Ge 16: 6 when Sarai **d hardly with** her, she fled 6031
33:11 because God hath **d graciously** with me, 2603
43: 6 Israel said, Wherefore **d** ye *so* **ill** with me, 7489
Ex 1:20 Therefore God **d well** with the midwives: 3190
14:11 wherefore hast thou **d** thus with us, to carry 6213
18:11 for in the thing wherein they **d proudly** *he* 2102
21: 8 seeing he hath **d deceitfully** with her. 898
Jdg 9:16 if ye have **d** well with Jerubbaal and his 6213
9:19 If ye then have **d** truly and sincerely with 6213
9:23 the men of Shechem **d treacherously** with 898
Ru 1: 8 as ye have **d** with the dead, and with me. 6213
1:20 for the Almighty hath **d** very **bitterly** with 4843
1Sa 24:18 *this* day how that thou hast **d** well with me: 6213
25:31 when the LORD shall have **d well** with 3190
2Sa 6:19 he **d** among all the people, *even* among 2505
2Ki 12:15 on workmen: for they **d** faithfully. 6213
21: 6 and **d** with familiar spirits and wizards: 6213
22: 7 into their hand, because they **d** faithfully. 6213
1Ch 16: 3 he **d** to every one of Israel, both man and 2505
20: 3 **d** David with all the cities of the children of 6213
2Ch 6:37 we have done amiss, and have **d wickedly**; 7561
11:23 he **d wisely**, and dispersed of all his children 995
33: 6 **d** with a familiar spirit, and with wizards: 6213
Ne 1: 7 We have **d very corruptly** against 2254+2254
9:10 for thou knewest that they **d proudly** 2102
9:16 they and our fathers **d proudly**, and 2102
9:29 yet they **d proudly**, and hearkened not unto 2102
Job 6:15 My brethren have **d deceitfully** as a brook, 898
Ps 13: 6 because he hath **d bountifully** with me. 1580
44:17 neither have we **d falsely** in thy covenant. 8266
78:57 and **d unfaithfully** like their fathers: 898
103:10 He hath not **d with** us after our sins; 6213
116: 7 for the LORD hath **d bountifully** with 1580
119:65 Thou hast **d** well with thy servant, 6213
119:78 for they **d perversely with** me without a 5791
147:20 He hath not **d** so with any nation: and *as for* 6213
Isa 24:16 treacherous dealers have **d treacherously**; 898
24:16 dealers have **d very treacherously**. 898+899
33: 1 and they **d** not **treacherously** with thee! 898
Jer 3:20 so have you **d treacherously** with me, 898

Jer 5:11 have **d very treacherously** against me, 898+898
12: 6 even they have **d treacherously** with thee; 898
La 1: 2 her friends have **d treacherously** with her, 898
Eze 22: 7 in the midst of thee have they **d** by 6213
25:12 Because that Edom hath **d** against 6213
25:15 Because the Philistines have **d** by revenge, 6213
Hos 5: 7 They have **d treacherously** against 898
6: 7 there have they **d treacherously** against me. 898
Joel 2:26 that hath **d** wondrously with you: 6213
Zec 1: 6 to our doings, so hath he **d** with us. 6213
Mal 2:11 Judah hath **d treacherously**, and 898
2:14 against whom thou hast **d treacherously**: 898
Lk 1:25 Thus hath the Lord **d** with me in the days *4160*
2:48 Son, why hast thou thus **d** with us? *4160*
Ac 7:19 The same **d subtilly with** our kindred, and *2686*
25:24 the multitude of the Jews have **d with** me, *1793*
Ro 12: 3 according as God hath **d** to every man *3307*

DEAR (7) [DEARLY]

Jer 31:20 *Is* Ephraim my **d** son? *is he* a pleasant 3357
Lk 7: 2 who was **d** unto him, was sick, and ready to *1784*
Ac 20:24 neither count I my life **d** unto myself, so *5093*
Eph 5: 1 therefore followers of God, as **d** children; *27*
Col 1: 7 As ye also learned of Epaphras our **d** *27*
1:13 hath translated *us* into the kingdom of his **d** *26*
1Th 2: 8 our own souls, because ye were **d** unto us. *27*

DEARLY (10) [DEAR]

Jer 12: 7 I have given the **d beloved** of my soul into 3033
Ro 12:19 **D beloved**, avenge not yourselves, but *27*
1Co 10:14 Wherefore, my **d beloved**, flee from idolatry. *27*
2Co 7: 1 Having therefore these promises, **d beloved**, *27*
12:19 but *we do* all *things*, **d beloved**, for your *27*
Php 4: 1 my brethren **d beloved** and longed for, my joy *27*
4: 1 so stand fast in the Lord, *my* **d beloved**. *27*
2Ti 1: 2 To Timothy, *my* **d beloved** son: Grace, *27*
Phm 1: 1 unto Philemon *our* **d beloved**, and *27*
1Pe 2:11 **D beloved**, I beseech *you* as strangers and *27*

DEARTH (8)

Ge 41:54 the seven years of **d** began to come, 7458
41:54 the **d** was in all lands; but in all the land of 7458
2Ki 4:38 *there was* a **d** in the land; and the sons of 7458
2Ch 6:28 If there be **d** in the land, if there be 7458
Ne 5: 3 that we might buy corn, because of the **d**. 7458
Jer 14: 1 that came to Jeremiah concerning the **d**. 1226
Ac 7:11 Now there came a **d** over all the land of *3042*
11:28 should be great **d** throughout all the world: *3042*

DEATH (372) [DIE]

Ge 21:16 she said, Let me not see the **d** of the child. 4194
24:67 Isaac was comforted after his mother's *d*. NIH
25:11 And it came to pass after the **d** of Abraham, 4194
26:11 his wife shall **surely be put to d**. 4191+4191
26:18 had stopped them after the **d** of Abraham: 4194
27: 2 I am old, I know not the day of my **d**: 4194
27: 7 bless thee before the LORD before my **d**. 4194
27:10 and that he may bless thee before his **d**. 4194
Ex 10:17 that he may take away from me this **d** only. 4194
19:12 the mount shall be **surely put to d**: 4191+4191
21:12 that he die, shall be **surely put to d**. 4191+4191
21:15 his mother, shall be **surely put to d**. 4191+4191
21:16 his hand, he shall **surely be put to d**. 4191+4191
21:17 his mother, shall **surely be put to d**. 4191+4191
21:29 and his owner also shall be **put to d**. 4191
22:19 with a beast shall **surely be put to d**. 4191+4191
31:14 defileth it shall **surely be put to d**: 4191+4191
31:15 he shall **surely be put to d**. 4191+4191
35: 2 doeth work therein shall be **put to d**. 4191
Lev 16: 1 the LORD spake unto Moses after the **d** of 4194
19:20 they shall not be **put to d**, because she was 4191
20: 2 he shall **surely be put to d**: 4191+4191
20: 9 his mother shall be **surely put to d**: 4191+4191
20:10 adulteress shall **surely be put to d**. 4191+4191
20:11 of them shall **surely be put to d**; 4191+4191
20:12 of them shall **surely be put to d**: 4191+4191
20:13 they shall **surely be put to d**; their 4191+4191
20:15 a beast, he shall **surely be put to d**: 4191+4191
20:16 they shall **surely be put to d**; their 4191+4191
20:27 is a wizard, shall **surely be put to d**: 4191+4191
24:16 he shall **surely be put to d**, *and* 4191+4191
24:16 the name *of the LORD*, shall be **put to d**. 4191
24:17 any man shall **surely be put to d**. 4191+4191
24:21 he that killeth a man, he shall be **put to d**. 4191
27:29 *but* shall **surely be put to d**. 4191+4191
Nu 1:51 stranger that cometh nigh shall be **put to d**. 4191
3:10 stranger that cometh nigh shall be **put to d**. 4191
3:38 stranger that cometh nigh shall be **put to d**. 4191
15:35 The man shall be **surely put to d**: 4191+4191
16:29 If these *men* die the common **d** of all men, 4194
18: 7 stranger that cometh nigh shall be **put to d**. 4191
23:10 Let me die the **d** of the righteous, and 4194
35:16 murderer shall **surely be put to d**. 4191+4191
35:17 murderer shall **surely be put to d**. 4191+4191
35:18 murderer shall **surely be put to d**. 4191+4191
35:21 smote *him* shall **surely be put to d**; 4191+4191
35:25 he shall abide in it unto the **d** of the high 4194
35:28 of his refuge until the **d** of the high priest: 4194
35:28 after the **d** of the high priest the slayer shall 4194
35:30 the murderer shall be **put to d** by the mouth 7523
35:31 the life of a murderer, which *is* guilty of **d**: 4191
35:31 but he shall be **surely put to d**. 4191+4191
35:32 dwell in the land, until the **d** of the priest. 4194
Dt 13: 5 that dreamer of dreams, shall be **put to d**; 4191
13: 9 shall be first upon him to **put** him **to d**, 4191
17: 6 shall he that is *worthy* of **d** be put to death; 4191
17: 6 shall he that is *worthy* of death be **put to d**; 4191
17: 6 of one witness he shall not be **put to d**. 4191
17: 7 shall be first upon him to **put** him **to d**, 4191
19: 6 whereas he *was* not worthy of **d**, 4194
21:22 if a man have committed a sin worthy of **d**, 4194
21:22 he be *to be* **put to d**, and thou hang him on 4191
22:26 *there is* in the damsel no sin *worthy* of **d**: 4194
24:16 The fathers shall not be **put to d** for 4191

Dt 24:16 neither shall the children be **put to d** for 4191
24:16 every man shall be **put to d** for his own sin. 4191
30:15 thee *this* day life and good, and **d** and evil; 4194
30:19 *that* I have set before you life and **d**, 4194
31:27 and how much more after my **d**? 4194
31:29 For I know that after my **d** ye will utterly 4194
33: 1 blessed the children of Israel before his **d**. 4194
Jos 1: 1 Now after the **d** of Moses the servant of 4194
1:18 thou commandest him, he shall be **put to d**: 4191
2:13 that they have, and deliver our lives from **d**. 4194
20: 6 until the **d** of the high priest that shall be in 4194
Jdg 1: 1 Now after the **d** of Joshua it came to pass, 4194
5:18 unto the **d** in the high places of the field. 4191
6:31 let him be **put to d** whilst *it is yet* morning: 4191
13: 7 to God from the womb to the day of his **d**. 4194
16:16 *so* that his soul was vexed unto **d**; 4191
16:30 So the dead which he slew at his **d** were 4194
20:13 that we may **put** them **to d**, and put away 4191
21: 5 He shall **surely be put to d**. 4191+4191
Ru 1:17 more also, *if ought* but **d** part thee and me. 4194
2:11 mother in law since the **d** of thine husband: 4194
1Sa 4:20 about the time of her **d** the *women* that 4191
11:12 bring the men, that we may **put** them **to d**. 4191
11:13 There shall not a man be **put to d** this day: 4191
15:32 Surely the bitterness of **d** is past. 4194
15:35 no more to see Saul until the day of his **d**: 4194
20: 3 *there is* but a step between me and **d**. 4194
22:22 I have occasioned *the* **d** of all the persons of NIH
2Sa 1: 1 Now it came to pass after the **d** of Saul, 4194
1:23 and in their **d** they were not divided: 4194
6:23 of Saul had no child unto the day of her **d**. 4194
8: 2 *with* two lines measured he to **put to d**, 4191
15:21 whether in **d** or life, even there *also* will thy 4194
19:21 said, Shall not Shimei be **put to d** for this, 4191
19:22 shall there any man be **put to d** *this* day in 4191
20: 3 they were shut up unto the day of their **d**, 4191
21: 9 and were **put to d** in the days of harvest, 4191
22: 5 When the waves of **d** compassed me, 4194
22: 6 me about; the snares of **d** prevented me: 4194
1Ki 2: 8 I will not **put** thee **to d** with the sword. 4191
2:24 Adonijah shall be **put to d** *this* day. 4191
2:26 thine own fields; for thou *art* worthy of **d**: 4194
2:26 I will not at this time **put** thee **to d**, because 4191
11:40 and was in Egypt until the **d** of Solomon. 4194
2Ki 1: 1 Moab rebelled against Israel after the **d** of 4194
2:21 there shall not be from thence any more **d** 4194
4:40 O thou man of God, *there is* **d** in the pot. 4194
14: 6 The fathers shall not be **put to d** for 4191
14: 6 nor the children be **put to d** for the fathers; 4191
14: 6 every man shall be **put to d** for his own sin. 4191
14:17 **d** of Jehoash son of Jehoahaz king of Israel 4194
15: 5 so that he was a leper unto the day of his **d**, 4194
20: 1 In those days was Hezekiah sick unto **d**. 4191
1Ch 22: 5 So David prepared abundantly before his **d**. 4194
2Ch 15:13 LORD God of Israel should be **put to d**, 4191
22: 4 for they were his counsellers after the **d** of 4194
23: 7 cometh into the house, he shall be **put to d**: 4191
24:17 Now after the **d** of Jehoiada came 4194
25:25 **d** of Joash son of Jehoahaz king of Israel 4194
26:21 the king was a leper unto the day of his **d**, 4194
32:24 In those days Hezekiah was sick to the **d**, 4191
32:33 of Jerusalem did him honour at his **d**. 4194
Ezr 7:26 whether *it be* unto **d**, or to banishment, or 4193
Est 4:11 *there is* one law of his to **put** *him* **to d**, 4191
Job 3: 5 Let darkness and the **shadow of d** stain it; 6757
3:21 Which long for **d**, but it *cometh* not; and 4194
5:20 In famine he shall redeem thee from **d**: and 4194
7:15 *and* **d** rather than my life. 4194
10:21 the land of darkness and the **shadow of d**; 6757
10:22 and *of* the **shadow of d**, without any order, 6757
12:22 and bringeth out to light the **shadow of d**. 6757
16:16 and on mine eyelids *is* the **shadow of d**; 6757
18:13 *even* the firstborn of **d** shall devour his 4194
24:17 *is* to them even as the **shadow of d**: 6757
24:17 *they are in* the terrors of the **shadow of d**. 6757
27:15 that remain of him shall be buried in **d**: 4194
28: 3 stones of darkness, and the **shadow of d**. 6757
28:22 Destruction and **d** say, We have heard 4194
30:23 For I know *that* thou wilt bring me *to* **d**, 4194
34:22 *There is* no darkness, nor **shadow of d**, 6757
38:17 Have the gates of **d** been opened unto thee? 4194
38:17 thou seen the doors of the **shadow of d**? 6757
Ps 6: 5 For in **d** *there is* no remembrance of thee: 4194
7:13 also prepared for him the instruments of **d**; 4194
9:13 thou that liftest me up from the gates of **d**: 4194
13: 3 mine eyes, lest I sleep the *sleep of* **d**; 4194
18: 4 The sorrows of **d** compassed me, and 4194
18: 5 me about: the snares of **d** prevented me. 4194
22:15 and thou hast brought me into the dust of **d**. 4194
23: 4 through the valley of the **shadow of d**, 6757
33:19 To deliver their soul from **d**, and to keep 4194
44:19 and covered us with the **shadow of d**. 6757
48:14 and ever: he will be our guide *even* unto **d**. 4191
49:14 **d** shall feed *on* them; and the upright shall 4194
55: 4 and the terrors of **d** are fallen upon me. 4194
55:15 Let **d** seize upon them, *and* let them go 4194
56:13 For thou hast delivered my soul from **d**: 4194
68:20 GOD the Lord *belong* the issues from **d**. 4194
73: 4 For *there are* no bands in their **d**: but 4194
78:50 he spared not their soul from **d**, but 4194
89:48 man *is he that* liveth, and shall not see **d**? 4194
102:20 loose those that are **appointed to d**; 1121+8546
107:10 as sit in darkness and in the **shadow of d**, 6757
107:14 them out of darkness and the **shadow of d**, 6757
107:18 and they draw near unto the gates of **d**. 4194
116: 3 The sorrows of **d** compassed me, and 4194
116: 8 For thou hast delivered my soul from **d**, 4194
116:15 Precious in the sight of the LORD *is* the **d** 4194
118:18 but he hath not given me over unto **d**. 4194
Pr 2:18 For her house inclineth unto **d**, and 4194
5: 5 Her feet go down *to* **d**; her steps take hold 4194
7:27 to hell, going down to the chambers of **d**. 4194
8:36 his own soul: all they that hate me love **d**. 4194
10: 2 but righteousness delivereth from **d**. 4194
11: 4 but righteousness delivereth from **d**. 4194

Pr 11:19 that pursueth evil *pursueth it* to his own **d**. 4194
12:28 and *in the* pathway *thereof there is* no **d**. 4194
13:14 of life, to depart from the snares of **d**. 4194
14:12 but the end thereof *are* the ways of **d**. 4194
14:27 of life, to depart from the snares of **d**. 4194
14:32 but the righteous hath hope in his **d**. 4194
16:14 The wrath of a king *is as* messengers of **d**: 4194
16:25 but the end thereof *are* the ways of **d**. 4194
18:21 **D** and life *are* in the power of the tongue: 4194
21: 6 vanity tossed to and fro of them that seek **d**. 4194
24:11 to deliver *them that are* drawn unto **d**, 4194
26:18 *man* who casteth firebrands, arrows, and **d**, 4194
Ecc 7: 1 and the day of **d** than the day of one's birth. 4194
7:26 I find more bitter than **d** the woman, 4194
8: 8 neither *hath he* power in the day of **d**: 4194
SS 8: 6 for love *is* strong as **d**; jealousy *is* cruel as 4194
Isa 9: 2 that dwell in the land of the **shadow of d**, 6757
25: 8 He will swallow up **d** in victory; and 4194
28:15 We have made a covenant with **d**, and 4194
28:18 your covenant with **d** shall be disannulled, 4194
38: 1 In those days was Hezekiah sick unto **d**. 4191
38:18 cannot praise thee, **d** can *not* celebrate thee: 4194
53: 9 with the wicked, and with the rich in his **d**; 4194
53:12 because he hath poured out his soul unto **d**: 4194
Jer 2: 6 a land of drought, and of the **shadow of d**, 6757
8: 3 **d** shall be chosen rather than life by all 4194
9:21 For **d** is come up into our windows, *and* 4194
13:16 he turn it into the **shadow of d**, *and* make *it* 6757
15: 2 Such as *are* for **d**, to death; and such as *are* 4194
15: 2 Such as *are* for death, to **d**; and such as *are* 4194
18:21 and let their men be **put to d**; 2026+4194
21: 8 you the way of life, and the way of **d**. 4194
26:15 know ye for certain, that if ye **put** me **to d**, 4191
26:19 and all Judah **put** him **at all to d**? 4191+4191
26:21 his words, the king sought to **put** him **to d**: 4191
26:24 into the hand of the people to **put** him **to d**. 4191
38: 4 We beseech thee, let this man be **put to d**: 4191
38:15 wilt thou not **surely put** me **to d**? 4191+4191
38:16 made us this soul, I will not **put** thee **to d**, 4191
38:25 not from us, and we will not **put** thee **to d**; 4191
43: 3 that *they* might **put** us **to d**, and carry us 4191
43:11 *and deliver* such *as are* for **d** to death; 4194
43:11 *and deliver* such *as are* for death to **d**; 4194
52:11 and put him in prison till the day of his **d**. 4194
52:27 **put** them **to d** in Riblah in the land of 4191
52:34 every day a portion until the day of his **d**, 4194
La 1:20 the sword bereaveth, at home *there is* as **d**. 4194
Eze 18:32 For I have no pleasure in the **d** of him that 4194
31:14 for they are all delivered unto **d**, to 4194
33:11 I have no pleasure in the **d** of the wicked; 4194
Hos 13:14 of the grave; I will redeem them from **d**: 4194
13:14 O **d**, I will be thy plagues; O grave, I will 4194
Am 5: 8 turneth the **shadow of d** into the morning, 6757
Jnh 4: 9 he said, I do well to be angry, *even* unto **d**. 4194
Hab 2: 5 *is* as **d**, and cannot be satisfied, but 4194
Mt 2:15 And was there until the **d** of Herod: that it *5054*
4:16 and shadow of **d** light is sprung up. *2288*
10:21 the brother shall deliver up the brother to **d**, *2288*
10:21 and cause them to be **put to d**. *2289*
14: 5 And when he would have **put** him **to d**, *615*
15: 4 curseth father or mother, let him die the **d**. *2288*
16:28 standing here, which shall not taste of **d**, *2288*
20:18 and they shall condemn him to **d**, *2288*
26:38 soul is exceeding sorrowful, *even* unto **d**: *2288*
26:59 false witness against Jesus, to **put** him **to d**; *2289*
26:66 They answered and said, He is guilty of **d**. *2288*
27: 1 took counsel against Jesus to **put** him **to d**: *2289*
Mk 5:23 daughter **lieth at the point of d**: *2079+2192*
7:10 curseth father or mother, let him die the **d**. *2288*
9: 1 that stand here, which shall not taste of **d**, *2288*
10:33 and they shall condemn him to **d**, and *2288*
13:12 the brother shall betray the brother to **d**, *2288*
13:12 and shall cause them to be **put to d**. *2289*
14: 1 might take him by craft, and **put** *him* **to d**. *615*
14:34 My soul is exceeding sorrowful unto **d**: *2288*
14:55 for witness against Jesus to **put** him **to d**; *2289*
14:64 they all condemned him to be guilty of **d**. *2288*
Lk 1:79 that sit in darkness and *in* the shadow of **d**, *2288*
2:26 that *he* should not see **d**, before he had seen *2288*
9:27 standing here, which shall not taste of **d**, *2288*
18:33 they shall scourge *him*, and **put** him **to d**: *615*
21:16 *some* of you shall they cause to be **put to d**. *2289*
22:33 to go with thee, both into prison, and to **d**. *2288*
23:15 lo, nothing worthy of **d** is done unto him. *2288*
23:22 I have found no cause of **d** in him: I will *2288*
23:32 malefactors, led with him to be **put to d**. *337*
24:20 rulers delivered him to be condemned to **d**, *2288*
Jn 4:47 and heal his son: for he was at the point of **d**. *599*
5:24 but is passed from **d** unto life. *2288*
8:51 a man keep my saying, he shall never see **d**. *2288*
8:52 keep my saying, he shall never taste of **d**. *2288*
11: 4 This sickness is not unto **d**, but for *2288*
11:13 Howbeit Jesus spake of his **d**: but *2288*
11:53 took counsel together for to **put** him **to d**. *615*
12:10 that they might **put** Lazarus also **to d**; *615*
12:33 he said, signifying what **d** he should die. *2288*
18:31 It is not lawful for us to **put** any *man* **to d**: *615*
18:32 he spake, signifying what **d** he should die. *2288*
21:19 signifying by what **d** he should glorify *2288*
Ac 2:24 raised up, having loosed the pains of **d**: *2288*
8: 1 And Saul was consenting unto his **d**. And at *336*
12:19 commanded that *they* should be **put to d**. *520*
13:28 And though they found no cause of **d** *in* *2288*
22: 4 And I persecuted this way unto the **d**, *2288*
22:20 and consenting unto his **d**, and kept *336*
23:29 have nothing laid to his charge worthy of **d** *2288*
25:11 or have committed any *thing* worthy of **d**, *2288*
25:25 that he had committed nothing worthy of **d**, *2288*
26:10 and when they were **put to d**, I gave my *337*
26:31 This man doeth nothing worthy of **d** or *2288*
28:18 because there was no cause of **d** in me. *2288*
Ro 1:32 which commit such *things* are worthy of **d**, *2288*
5:10 we were reconciled to God by the **d** of his *2288*
5:12 sin entered into the world, and **d** by sin; *2288*
5:12 and so **d** passed upon all men, for that all *2288*

Jn 5:14 Nevertheless **d** reigned from Adam to *2288*
5:17 For if by one man's offence **d** reigned by *2288*
5:21 That as sin hath reigned unto **d**, even so *2288*
6: 3 into Jesus Christ were baptized into his **d**? *2288*
6: 4 we are buried with him by baptism into **d**: *2288*
6: 5 planted together in the likeness of his **d**, *2288*
6: 9 **d** hath no more dominion over him. *2288*
6:16 whether of sin unto **d**, or of obedience unto *2288*
6:21 for the end of those *things is* **d**. *2288*
6:23 For the wages of sin *is* **d**; but the gift of *2288*
7: 5 in our members to bring forth fruit unto **d**. *2288*
7:10 was *ordained* to life, I found *to be* unto **d**. *2288*
7:13 then that which is good made **d** unto me? *2288*
7:13 working **d** in me by that which is good; *2288*
7:24 shall deliver me from the body of this **d**? *2288*
8: 2 made me free from the law of sin and **d**. *2288*
8: 6 For to be carnally minded *is* **d**; *2288*
8:38 that neither **d**, nor life, nor angels, *2288*
1Co 3:22 or **d**, or *things* present, or *things* to come; *2288*
4: 9 the apostles last, as *it were* **appointed to d**: *1935*
11:26 ye do shew the Lord's **d** till he come. *2288*
15:21 For since by man *came* **d**, by man *came* *2288*
15:26 The last enemy *that* shall be destroyed *is* **d**. *2288*
15:54 is written, **D** is swallowed up in victory. *2288*
15:55 O **d**, where *is* thy sting? O grave, where *is* *2288*
15:56 The sting of **d** *is* sin; *2288*
2Co 1: 9 But we had the sentence of **d** in ourselves, *2288*
1:10 Who delivered us from so great a **d**, and *2288*
2:16 To the one *we are* the savour of **d** unto *2288*
2:16 the one *we are* the savour of death unto **d**; *2288*
3: 7 But if the ministration of **d**, written *and* *2288*
4:11 are alway delivered unto **d** for Jesus' sake, *2288*
4:12 So then **d** worketh in us, but life in you. *2288*
7:10 but the sorrow of the world worketh **d**. *2288*
Php 1:20 in my body, whether *it be* by life, or by **d**. *2288*
2: 8 and became obedient unto **d**, *2288*
2: 8 unto death, even the **d** of the cross. *2288*
2:27 For indeed he was sick nigh unto **d**: but *2288*
2:30 for the work of Christ he was nigh unto **d**, *2288*
3:10 being made conformable unto his **d**; *2288*
Col 1:22 In the body of his flesh through **d**, *2288*
2Ti 1:10 who hath abolished **d**, and hath brought life *2288*
Heb 2: 9 for the suffering of **d**, crowned with glory *2288*
2: 9 that he by the grace of God should taste **d** *2288*
2:14 that through **d** he might destroy him that *2288*
2:14 might destroy him that had the power of **d**, *2288*
2:15 And deliver them who through fear of **d** *2288*
5: 7 unto him that was able to save him from **d**, *2288*
7:23 not suffered to continue by reason of **d**: *2288*
9:15 of the new testament, that by means of **d**, *2288*
9:16 also of necessity be the **d** of the testator. *2288*
11: 5 was translated that *he* should not see **d**; *2288*
Jas 1:15 when it is finished, bringeth forth **d**. *2288*
5:20 error of his way shall save a soul from **d**, *2288*
1Pe 3:18 being **put to d** in the flesh, but *2289*
1Jn 3:14 We know that we have passed from **d** unto *2288*
3:14 He that loveth not *his* brother abideth in **d**. *2288*
5:16 see his brother sin a sin *which is* not unto **d**, *2288*
5:16 give him life for them that sin not unto **d**. *2288*
5:16 There is a sin unto **d**: I do not say that he *2288*
5:17 is sin: and there is a sin not unto **d**. *2288*
Rev 1:18 and have the keys of hell and of **d**. *2288*
2:10 be thou faithful unto **d**, and I will give thee *2288*
2:11 shall not be hurt of the second **d**. *2288*
2:23 And I will kill her children with **d**; and *2288*
6: 8 and his name that sat on him *was* **D**, and *2288*
6: 8 and with **d**, and with the beasts of the earth. *2288*
9: 6 And in those days shall men seek **d**, and *2288*
9: 6 desire to die, and **d** shall flee from them. *2288*
12:11 and they loved not their lives unto the **d**. *2288*
13: 3 one of his heads as *it were* wounded to **d**; *2288*
18: 8 in one day, **d**, and mourning, and famine; *2288*
20: 6 on such the second **d** hath no power, but *2288*
20:13 and **d** and hell delivered up the dead which *2288*
20:14 And **d** and hell were cast into the lake of *2288*
20:14 into the lake of fire. This is the second **d**. *2288*
21: 4 and there shall be no more **d**, *2288*
21: 8 and brimstone: which is the second **d**. *2288*

DEATHS (4) [DIE]
Jer 16: 4 They shall die of grievous **d**; they shall not 4463
Eze 28: 8 thou shalt die the **d** of *them that are* slain in 4463
28:10 Thou shalt die the **d** of the uncircumcised 4194
2Co 11:23 in prisons more frequent, in **d** oft. *2288*

DEBASE (1)
Isa 57: 9 far off, and didst **d** *thyself even* unto hell. 8213

DEBATE (4) [DEBATES]
Pr 25: 9 **D** thy cause with thy neighbour *himself;* 7378
Isa 27: 8 when it shooteth forth, thou wilt **d with** it: 7378
58: 4 ye fast for strife and **d**, and to smite with 4683
Ro 1:29 full of envy, murder, **d**, deceit, malignity; *2054*

DEBATES (1) [DEBATE]
2Co 12:20 lest *there be* **d**, envyings, wraths, strifes, *2054*

DEBAUCHERY See LASCIVIOUSNESS

DEBIR (14) [KIRJATH-SANNAH, KIRJATH-SEPHER]
Jos 10: 3 and unto **D** king of Eglon, saying, 1688
10:38 and all Israel with him, to **D**; 1688
10:39 so he did to **D**, and to the king thereof; 1688
11:21 from **D**, from Anab, and from all 1688
12:13 The king of **D**, one; the king of Geder, one; 1688
13:26 and from Mahanaim unto the border of **D**; 1688
15: 7 the border went up toward **D** from 1688
15:15 he went up thence to the inhabitants of **D**: 1688
15:15 the name of **D** before *was* Kirjath-sepher. 1688
15:49 and Kirjath-sannah, which *is* **D**, 1688
21:15 with her suburbs, and **D** with her suburbs, 1688
Jdg 1:11 thence he went against the inhabitants of **D**: 1688
1:11 the name of **D** before *was* Kirjath-sepher. 1688
1Ch 6:58 Hilen with her suburbs, **D** with her suburbs, 1688

DEBORAH (10)
Ge 35: 8 **D** Rebekah's nurse died, and she was 1683
Jdg 4: 4 **D**, a prophetess, the wife of Lapidoth, 1683
4: 5 she dwelt under the palm tree of **D** between 1683
4: 9 **D** arose, and went with Barak to Kedesh. 1683
4:10 men at his feet: and **D** went up with him. 1683
4:14 **D** said unto Barak, Up; for this *is* the day in 1683
5: 1 sang **D** and Barak the son of Abinoam on 1683
5: 7 they ceased in Israel, until that I **D** arose, 1683
5:12 Awake, awake, **D**: awake, awake, utter a 1683
5:15 the princes of Issachar *were* with **D**; 1683

DEBT (7) [DEBTOR, DEBTORS, DEBTS, INDEBTED]
1Sa 22: 2 every one that was in **d**, and every one *that* 5378
2Ki 4: 7 pay thy **d**, and live thou and thy children of 5386
Ne 10:31 and the **exaction** of every **d**. 3027+4853
Mt 18:27 and loosed him, and forgave him the **d**. *1156*
18:30 him into prison, till he should pay the **d**. *3784*
18:32 I forgave thee all that **d**, because *3782*
Ro 4: 4 the reward not reckoned of grace, but of **d**. *3783*

DEBTOR (4) [DEBT]
Eze 18: 7 *but* hath restored *to* the **d** his pledge, 2326
Mt 23:16 swear by the gold of the temple, he is a **d**. *3784*
Ro 1:14 I am **d** both to the Greeks, and to *3781*
Gal 5: 3 that he is a **d** to do the whole law. *3781*

DEBTORS (5) [DEBT]
Mt 6:12 forgive us our debts, as we forgive our **d**. *3781*
Lk 7:41 was a certain creditor which had two **d**: *5533*
16: 5 So he called every one of his lord's **d** unto *5533*
Ro 8:12 Therefore, brethren, we are **d**, not to *3781*
15:27 pleased them verily; and their **d** they are. *3781*

DEBTS (2) [DEBT]
Pr 22:26 *or* of them that are sureties for **d**. 4859
Mt 6:12 And forgive us our **d**, as we forgive our *3783*

DECAPOLIS (3)
Mt 4:25 and *from* **D**, and *from* Jerusalem, and *1179*
Mk 5:20 began to publish in **D** how great *things* *1179*
7:31 through the midst of the coasts of **D**. *1179*

DECAY (1) [DECAYED, DECAYETH]
Lev 25:35 and **fallen in d** with thee; 3027+4131

DECAYED (2) [DECAY]
Ne 4:10 The strength of the bearers of burdens is **d**, 3782
Isa 44:26 and I will raise up the **d places** thereof: 2723

DECAYETH (3) [DECAY]
Job 14:11 from the sea, and the flood **d** and drieth up: 2717
Ecc 10:18 By much slothfulness the building **d**; and 4355
Heb 8:13 Now that which **d** and waxeth old *is* ready *3822*

DECEASE (2) [DECEASED]
Lk 9:31 spake of his **d** which he should accomplish *1841*
2Pe 1:15 **d** to have these *things* always in *1841*

DECEASED (2) [DECEASE]
Isa 26:14 shall not live; *they are* **d**, they shall not rise: 7496
Mt 22:25 when he had married a *wife*, **d**, and, *5053*

DECEIT (34) [DECEIVE]
Job 15:35 forth vanity, and their belly prepareth **d**. 4820
27: 4 speak wickedness, nor my tongue utter **d**. 7423
31: 5 with vanity, or *if* my foot hath hasted to **d**; 4820
Ps 10: 7 mouth is full *of* cursing and **d** and fraud: 4820
36: 3 The words of his mouth *are* iniquity and **d**: 4820
50:19 mouth to evil, and thy tongue frameth **d**. 4820
55:11 **d** and guile depart not from her streets. 8496
72:14 He shall redeem their soul from **d** and 8496
101: 7 He that worketh **d** shall not dwell within 7423
119:118 from thy statutes: for their **d** *is* falsehood. 8649
Pr 12: 5 *but* the counsels of the wicked *are* **d**. 4820
12:17 forth righteousness: but a false witness **d**. 4820
12:20 **D** *is* in the heart of them that imagine evil: 4820
14: 8 his way: but the folly of fools *is* **d**. 4820
20:17 Bread of **d** *is* sweet to a man; but 8267
26:24 with his lips, and layeth up **d** within him; 4820
26:26 *Whose* hatred is covered by **d**, 4860
Isa 53: 9 neither *was any* **d** in his mouth. 4820
Jer 5:27 *is* full *of* birds, so *are* their houses full *of* **d**: 4820
8: 5 they hold fast **d**, they refuse to return. 8649
9: 6 Thine habitation *is* in the midst of **d**; 4820
9: 6 through **d** they refuse to know me, saith 4820
9: 8 *is as* an arrow shot out; it speaketh **d**: 4820
14:14 a thing of nought, and the **d** of their heart. 8649
23:26 *they are* prophets of the **d** of their own 8649
Hos 11:12 with lies, and the house of Israel with **d**: 4820
12: 7 the balances of **d** *are* in his hand: 4820
Am 8: 5 and falsifying the balances by **d**? 4820
Zep 1: 9 their masters' houses *with* violence and **d**. 4820
Mk 7:22 Thefts, covetousness, wickedness, **d**, *1388*
Ro 1:29 full of envy, murder, debate, **d**, malignity; *1388*
3:13 with their tongues they have **used d**; *1387*
Col 2: 8 spoil you through philosophy and vain **d**, *539*
1Th 2: 3 For our exhortation *was* not of **d**, nor of *4106*

DECEITFUL (21) [DECEIVE]
Ps 5: 6 LORD will abhor the bloody and **d** man. 4820
35:20 they devise **d** matters against *them that are* 4820
43: 1 O deliver me from the **d** and unjust man. 4820
52: 4 all devouring words, O thou **d** tongue. 4820
55:23 and **d** men shall not live out half their days; 4820
78:57 they were turned aside like a **d** bow. 7423
109: 2 the mouth of the **d** are opened against me: 4820
120: 2 from lying lips, *and* from a **d** tongue. 7423
Pr 11:18 The wicked worketh a **d** work: but *to* him 8267
14:25 but a **d** *witness* speaketh lies. 4820
23: 3 desirous of his dainties: for they *are* **d** meat. 3577
27: 6 a friend; but the kisses of an enemy *are* **d**. 6280
29:13 The poor and the **d** man meet together: 8501
31:30 Favour *is* **d**, and beauty *is* vain: *but* 8267
Jer 17: 9 The heart *is* **d** above all *things*, and 6121
Hos 7:16 they are like a **d** bow: their princes shall 7423
Mic 6:11 and with the bag of **d** weights? 4820
6:12 and their tongue *is* **d** in their mouth. 7423
Zep 3:13 neither shall a **d** tongue be found in their 8649
2Co 11:13 For such *are* false apostles, **d** workers, *1386*
Eph 4:22 which is corrupt according to the **d** lusts; *539*

DECEITFULLY (11) [DECEIVE]
Ge 34:13 and Hamor his father **d**, 4820+871.1
Ex 8:29 let not Pharaoh **deal d** any more in not 2048
21: 8 no power, seeing he hath **dealt d** with her. 898
Lev 6: 4 or the thing which he hath **d gotten**, 6231+6233
Job 6:15 My brethren have **dealt d** as a brook, *and* 898
13: 7 wickedly for God? and talk **d** for him? 7423
Ps 24: 4 his soul unto vanity, nor sworn **d**. 4820+3807.1
52: 2 like a sharp razor, working **d**. 7423
Jer 48:10 *be* he that doeth the work of the LORD **d**, 7423
Da 11:23 the league *made* with him he shall work **d**: 4820
2Co 4: 2 nor **handling** the word of God **d**; *1389*

DECEITFULNESS (3) [DECEIVE]
Mt 13:22 and the **d** of riches, choke the word, and *539*
Mk 4:19 and the **d** of riches, and the lusts of other *539*
Heb 3:13 lest any of you be hardened through the **d** of *539*

DECEITS (2) [DECEIVE]
Ps 38:12 and imagine **d** all the day long. 4820
Isa 30:10 speak unto us smooth *things*, prophesy **d**: 4123

DECEIVABLENESS (1) [DECEIVE]
2Th 2:10 And with all **d** of unrighteousness in them *539*

DECEIVE (27) [DECEIT, DECEITFUL, DECEITFULLY, DECEITFULNESS, DECEITS, DECEIVABLENESS, DECEIVED, DECEIVER, DECEIVERS, DECEIVETH, DECEIVING, DECEIVINGS]
2Sa 3:25 that he came to **d** thee, and to know thy 6601
2Ki 4:28 son of my lord? did I not say, Do not **d** me? 7952
18:29 saith the king, Let not Hezekiah **d** you: 5377
19:10 Let not thy God in whom thou trustest **d** 5377
2Ch 32:15 Now therefore let not Hezekiah **d** you, 5377
Pr 24:28 without cause; and **d** not with thy lips. 6601
Isa 36:14 saith the king, Let not Hezekiah **d** you: 5377
37:10 in whom thou trustest, **d** thee, saying, 5377
Jer 9: 5 they will **d** every one his neighbour, and 2048
29: 8 that *be* in the midst of you, **d** you, 5377
37: 9 **D** not yourselves, saying, The Chaldeans 5377
Zec 13: 4 shall they wear a rough garment to **d**: 3584
Mt 24: 4 unto them, Take heed that no *man* **d** you. *4105*
24: 5 saying, I am Christ; and shall **d** many. *4105*
24:11 false prophets shall rise, and shall **d** many. *4105*
24:24 *it were* possible, *they shall* **d** the very elect. *4105*
Mk 13: 5 to say, Take heed lest any *man* **d** you: *4105*
13: 6 saying, I am *Christ*; and shall **d** many. *4105*
Ro 16:18 and fair speeches **d** the hearts of the simple. *1818*
1Co 3:18 Let no *man* **d** himself. If any *man* among *1818*
Eph 4:14 whereby they lie in wait to **d**; *4106*
5: 6 Let no *man* **d** you with vain words: for *538*
2Th 2: 3 Let no *man* **d** you by any means: for *that* *1818*
1Jn 1: 8 we **d** ourselves, and the truth is not in us. *4105*
3: 7 Little children, let no *man* **d** you: he that *4105*
Rev 20: 3 that he should **d** the nations no more, *4105*
20: 8 And shall go out to **d** the nations which are *4105*

DECEIVED (34) [DECEIVE]
Ge 31: 7 your father hath **d** me, and changed my 2048
Lev 6: 2 away by violence, or hath **d** his neighbour; 6231
Dt 11:16 that your heart be not **d**, and ye turn aside, 6601
1Sa 19:17 Why hast thou **d** me so, and sent away 7411
28:12 spake to Saul, saying, Why hast thou **d** me? 7411
2Sa 19:26 My lord, O king, my servant **d** me: 7411
Job 12:16 and wisdom: the **d** and the deceiver *are* his. 7683
15:31 Let not him that is **d** trust in vanity: 8582
31: 9 If mine heart have been **d** by a woman, or 6601
Pr 20: 1 and whosoever is **d** thereby is not wise. 7686
Isa 19:13 become fools, the princes of Noph are **d**; 5377
44:20 a **d** heart hath turned him aside, that he 2048
Jer 4:10 surely thou hast **greatly d** this people 5377+5377
20: 7 thou hast **d** me, and I was deceived: 6601
20: 7 thou hast deceived me, and I was **d**: 6601
49:16 Thy terribleness hath **d** thee, *and* the pride 5377
La 1:19 I called for my lovers, *but* they **d** me: 7411
Eze 14: 9 if the prophet be **d** when he hath spoken a 6601
14: 9 I the LORD have **d** that prophet, and 6601
Ob 1: 3 The pride of thine heart hath **d** thee, 5377
1: 7 the men that were at peace with thee have **d** 5377
Lk 21: 8 And he said, Take heed that ye be not **d**: *4105*
Jn 7:47 them the Pharisees, Are ye also **d**? *4105*
Ro 7:11 **d** me, and by it slew *me*. *1818*
1Co 6: 9 Be not **d**: neither fornicators, nor idolaters, *4105*
15:33 Be not **d**: evil communications corrupt *4105*
Gal 6: 7 Be not **d**; God is not mocked: *4105*
1Ti 2:14 And Adam was not **d**, but the woman being *538*
2:14 the woman being **d** was in the transgression. *538*
2Ti 3:13 and worse, deceiving, and being **d**. *4105*
Tit 3: 3 disobedient, **d**, serving divers lusts and *4105*
Rev 18:23 for by thy sorceries were all nations **d**. *4105*
19:20 with which he **d** them that had received *4105*
20:10 And the devil that **d** them was cast into *4105*

DECEIVER (5) [DECEIVE]
Ge 27:12 will feel me, and I shall seem to him as a **d**; 8591
Job 12:16 and wisdom: the deceived and the **d** *are* his. 7686
Mal 1:14 cursed *be* the **d**, which hath in his flock a 5230
Mt 27:63 Saying, Sir, we remember that that **d** said, *4108*
2Jn 1: 7 in the flesh. This is a **d** and an antichrist. *4108*

DECEIVERS (3) [DECEIVE]
2Co 6: 8 and good report: as **d**, and *yet* true; *4108*
Tit 1:10 are many unruly and vain talkers and **d**, *5423*
2Jn 1: 7 For many **d** are entered into the world, *4108*

DECEIVETH (6) [DECEIVE]
Pr 26:19 So *is* the man *that* **d** his neighbour, and 7411
Jn 7:12 *man:* others said, Nay; but he **d** the people. *4105*
Gal 6: 3 when he is nothing, he **d** himself. *5422*
Jas 1:26 bridleth not his tongue, but **d** his own heart, *538*
Rev 12: 9 and Satan, which **d** the whole world: *4105*
13:14 And **d** them that dwell on the earth by *4105*

DECEIVING (2) [DECEIVE]
2Ti 3:13 and worse, **d**, and being deceived. *4105*
Jas 1:22 and not hearers only, **d** your own selves. *3884*

DECEIVINGS (1) [DECEIVE]
2Pe 2:13 sporting themselves with their own **d** while *539*

DECENCY See SHAMEFACEDNESS

DECENTLY (1)
1Co 14:40 Let all *things* be done **d** and in order. *2156*

DECIDE See REPROOF; REPROVE

DECIDED (1) [DECISION]
1Ki 20:40 So *shall* thy judgment *be;* thyself hast **d** *it.* 2782

DECISION (2) [DECIDED]
Joel 3:14 Multitudes, multitudes in the valley of **d**: 2742
3:14 of the LORD *is* near in the valley of **d**. 2742

DECK (2) [DECKED, DECKEDST, DECKEST, DECKETH, DECKT]
Job 40:10 **D** thyself now with majesty and excellency; 5710
Jer 10: 4 They **d** it with silver and with gold; 3302

DECKED (5) [DECK]
Eze 16:11 I **d** thee also *with* ornaments, and I put 5710
16:13 Thus wast thou **d** *with* gold and silver; and 5710
Hos 2:13 she **d** herself with her earrings and 5710
Rev 17: 4 and **d with gold** and precious stone *5557+5558*
18:16 and **d** with gold, and precious stones, and *5558*

DECKEDST (2) [DECK]
Eze 16:16 **d** thy high places with divers colours, and 6213
23:40 and **d** thyself **with ornaments**, 5710+5716

DECKEST (1) [DECK]
Jer 4:30 though thou **d** thee **with** ornaments of gold, 5710

DECKETH (1) [DECK]
Isa 61:10 as a bridegroom **d** *himself* **with** ornaments, 3547

DECKT (1) [DECK]
Pr 7:16 I have **d** my bed *with* coverings of tapestry, 7234

DECLARATION (4) [DECLARE]
Est 10: 2 and the **d** of the greatness of Mordecai, 6575
Job 13:17 my speech, and my **d** with your ears. 262
Lk 1: 1 **d** of those things which are most surely *1335*
2Co 8:19 of the same Lord, and *d of* your ready mind: NIG

DECLARE (95) [DECLARATION, DECLARED, DECLARETH, DECLARING]
Ge 41:24 but *there was* none that could **d** *it* to me. 5046
Dt 1: 5 of Moab, began Moses to **d** this law, saying, 874
Jos 20: 4 shall **d** his cause in the ears of the elders of 1696
Jdg 14:12 if you can **certainly d** it me *within* 5046+5046
14:13 if ye cannot **d** *it* me, then shall ye give me 5046
14:15 that he may **d** unto us the riddle, lest we 5046
1Ki 22:13 the words of the prophets **d** good unto NIH
1Ch 16:24 **D** his glory among the heathen; 5608
2Ch 18:12 the words of the prophets **d** good to the king NIH
Est 4: 8 to **d** *it* unto her, and to charge her that *she* 5046
Job 12: 8 and the fishes of the sea shall **d** unto thee. 5608
15:17 and that which I have seen I will **d**; 5608
21:31 Who shall **d** his way to his face? and 5046
28:27 did he see it, and **d** it; he prepared it, yea, 5608
31:37 I would **d** unto him the number of my 5046
38: 4 of the earth? **d**, if thou hast understanding. 5046
38:18 of the earth? **d** if thou knowest it all. 5046
40: 7 I will demand of thee, and **d** thou unto me. 3045
42: 4 I will demand of thee, and **d** thou unto me. 3045
Ps 2: 7 I will **d** the decree: the LORD hath said 5608
9:11 in Zion: **d** among the people his doings. 5046
19: 1 The heavens **d** the glory of God; and 5608
22:22 I will **d** thy name unto my brethren: in 5608
22:31 shall **d** his righteousness unto a people that 5046
30: 9 the dust praise thee? shall it **d** thy truth? 5046
38:18 For I will **d** mine iniquity; I will be sorry 5046
40: 5 *if* I would **d** and speak *of them,* they are 5046
50: 6 the heavens shall **d** his righteousness: 5046
50:16 What hast thou to do to **d** my statutes, or 5608
64: 9 shall fear, and shall **d** the work of God; 5046
66:16 and I will **d** what he hath done for my soul. 5608
73:28 the Lord GOD, that *I* may **d** all thy works. 5608
75: 1 thy name *is* near thy wondrous works **d**. 5608
75: 9 I will **d** for ever; I will sing *praises* to 5046
78: 6 should arise and **d** *them* to their children: 5608
96: 3 **D** his glory among the heathen, 5608
97: 6 The heavens **d** his righteousness, and 5046
102:21 To **d** the name of the LORD in Zion, and 5608
107:22 and **d** his works with rejoicing. 5608
118:17 but live, and **d** the works of the LORD. 5608
145: 4 to another, and shall **d** thy mighty acts. 5046
145: 6 thy terrible acts: and I will **d** thy greatness. 5608
Ecc 9: 1 all this I considered in my heart even to **d** 952
Isa 3: 9 they **d** their sin as Sodom, they hide *it* not. 5046
12: 4 his name, **d** his doings among the people, 3045
21: 6 set a watchman, let him **d** what he seeth. 5046
41:22 end of them; or **d** us *things* for to come. 8085
42: 9 are come to pass, and new *things* do I **d**: 5046
42:12 the LORD, and **d** his praise in the islands. 5046
43: 9 who among them can **d** this, and shew us 5046
43:26 **d** thou, that thou mayest be justified. 5608
Isa 44: 7 and shall **d** it, and set it in order for me, 5046
45:19 I **d** things that are right. 5046
48: 6 will not ye **d** *it?* I have shewed thee new 5046
48:20 with a voice of singing **d** ye, tell this, 5046
53: 8 who shall **d** his generation? for he was cut 7878
57:12 I will **d** thy righteousness, and thy works; 5046
66:19 they shall **d** my glory among the Gentiles. 5046
Jer 4: 5 **D** ye in Judah, and publish in Jerusalem; 5046
5:20 **D** this in the house of Jacob, and publish it 5046
9:12 that he may **d** it, for what the land perisheth 5046
31:10 and **d** *it* in the isles afar off, and say, 5046
38:15 said unto Zedekiah, If I **d** *it* unto thee, 5046
38:25 **D** unto us now what thou hast said unto 5046
42: 4 shall answer you, I will **d** *it* unto you; 5046
42:20 shall say, so **d** unto us, and we will do *it.* 5046
46:14 **D** ye in Egypt, and publish in Migdol, and 5046
50: 2 **D** ye among the nations, and publish, and 5046
50:28 to **d** in Zion the vengeance of the LORD 5046
51:10 let us **d** in Zion the work of the LORD our 5608
Eze 12:16 that they may **d** all their abominations 5608
23:36 yea, **d** unto them their abominations; 5046
40: 4 **d** all that thou seest to the house of Israel. 5046
Da 4:18 O Belteshazzar, **d** the interpretation thereof, 560
Mic 1:10 **D** ye *it* not at Gath, weep ye not at all: 5046
3: 8 to **d** unto Jacob his transgression, and 5046
Zec 9:12 even to day do I **d** *that* I will render double 5046
Mt 13:36 **D** unto us the parable of the tares of *5419*
15:15 and said unto him, **D** unto us this parable. *5419*
Jn 17:26 will **d** *it:* that the love where*with* thou hast *1107*
Ac 8:33 and who shall **d** his generation? for his life *1334*
13:32 And we **d** unto you **glad tidings**, how that *2097*
13:41 wise believe, though a man **d** it unto you. *1555*
17:23 ye ignorantly worship, him **d** I unto you. *2605*
20:27 For I have not shunned to **d** unto you all *312*
Ro 3:25 to **d** his righteousness for the remission of *1732*
3:26 To **d**, *I say,* at this time his righteousness: *1732*
1Co 3:13 for the day shall **d** *it,* because it shall be *1213*
11:17 Now in this that I **d** *unto you* I praise *you* *3853*
15: 1 I **d** unto you the gospel which I preached *1107*
Col 4: 7 All my state shall Tychicus **d** unto you, *1107*
Heb 2:12 Saying, I will **d** thy name unto my brethren, *518*
11:14 For they that say such *things* **d plainly** that *1718*
1Jn 1: 3 we have seen and heard **d** we unto you, *518*
1: 5 and **d** unto you, that God is light, and in him *312*

DECLARED (41) [DECLARE]
Ex 9:16 that my name may be **d** throughout all 5608
Lev 23:44 Moses **d** unto the children of Israel 1696
Nu 1:18 they **d** their **pedigrees** after their families, 3205
15:34 it was not **d** what should be done to him. 6567
Dt 4:13 he **d** unto you his covenant, which he 5046
2Sa 19: 6 for thou hast **d** *this* day, that thou regardest 5046
Ne 8:12 they had understood the words that were **d** 3045
Job 26: 3 *how* hast thou plentifully **d** the thing as it 3045
Ps 40:10 I have **d** thy faithfulness and thy salvation: 559
71:17 and hitherto have I **d** thy wondrous works. 5046
77:14 thou hast **d** thy strength among the people. 3045
88:11 Shall thy lovingkindness be **d** in the grave? 5608
119:13 With my lips have I **d** all the judgments of 5608
119:26 I have **d** my ways, and thou heardest me: 5608
Isa 21: 2 A grievous vision is **d** unto me; 5046
21:10 the God of Israel, have I **d** unto you. 5046
41:26 Who hath **d** from the beginning, that we 5046
43:12 I have **d**, and have saved, and I have 5046
44: 8 and have **d** *it?* ye *are* even my witnesses. 5046
45:21 who hath **d** this from ancient time? 8085
48: 3 I have **d** the former *things* from 5046
48: 5 I have even from the beginning **d** *it* to thee; 5046
48:14 which among them hath **d** these *things?* 5046
Jer 36:13 Michaiah **d** unto them all the words that he 5046
42:21 *now* I have *this* day **d** *it* to you; but ye have 5046
Lk 8:47 she **d** unto him before all the people for what *518*
Jn 1:18 in the bosom of the Father, he hath **d** *him.* *1834*
17:26 And I have **d** unto them thy name, and *1107*
Ac 9:27 **d** unto them how he had seen the Lord in *1334*
10: 8 And when he had **d** all *these things* unto *1834*
12:17 **d** unto them how the Lord had brought him *1334*
15: 4 they **d** all *things* that God had done with *312*
15:14 Simeon hath **d** how God at the first did visit *1834*
21:19 he **d** particularly what *things* God had *1834*
25:14 Festus **d** Paul's cause unto the king, saying, *394*
Ro 1: 4 *And* **d** *to be* the Son of God with power, *3724*
9:17 that my name might be **d** throughout all *1229*
1Co 1:11 For it hath been **d** unto me of you, *1213*
2Co 3: 3 Forasmuch as ye are **manifestly d** to be *5319*
Col 1: 8 Who also **d** unto us your love in the Spirit. *1213*
Rev 10: 7 as he hath **d** to his servants the prophets. *2097*

DECLARETH (4) [DECLARE]
Isa 41:26 that sheweth, yea, *there is* none that **d**, yea, 8085
Jer 4:15 For a voice **d** from Dan, and 5046
Hos 4:12 at their stocks, and their staff **d** unto them: 5046
Am 4:13 and **d** unto man what *is* his thought, 5046

DECLARING (4) [DECLARE]
Isa 46:10 **D** the end from the beginning, and 5046
Ac 15: 3 Samaria, **d** the conversion of the Gentiles: *1555*
15:12 **d** what miracles and wonders God had *1834*
1Co 2: 1 **d** unto you the testimony of God. *2605*

DECLINE (5) [DECLINED, DECLINETH]
Ex 23: 2 neither shalt thou speak in a cause to **d** 5186
Dt 17:11 thou shalt not **d** from the sentence which 5493
Ps 119:157 *yet* do I not **d** from thy testimonies. 5186
Pr 4: 5 neither **d** from the words of my mouth. 5186
7:25 Let not thine heart **d** to her ways, go not 7847

DECLINED (4) [DECLINE]
2Ch 34: 2 **d** neither *to* the right hand, nor *to* the left. 5493
Job 23:11 his steps, his way have I kept, and not **d**. 5186
Ps 44:18 neither have our steps **d** from thy way; 5186
119:51 in derision: *yet* have I not **d** from thy law. 5186

DECLINETH (2) [DECLINE]
Ps 102:11 My days *are* like a shadow that **d**; and I am 5186
109:23 I am gone like the shadow when it **d**: I am 5186

DECREASE (2) [DECREASED]
Ps 107:38 and **suffereth** not their cattle **to d**. 4591
Jn 3:30 He must increase, but I *must* **d**. *1642*

DECREASED (1) [DECREASE]
Ge 8: 5 the waters **d** continually until the tenth 2637

DECREE (49) [DECREED, DECREES]
2Ch 30: 5 So they established a **d** to make 1697
Ezr 5:13 Cyrus made a **d** to build this house of God. 2942
5:17 that a **d** *was* made of Cyrus the king to 2942
6: 1 Darius the king made a **d**, and search was 2942
6: 3 **d** *concerning* the house of God at 2942
6: 8 Moreover I make a **d** what ye shall do to 2942
6:11 Also I have made a **d**, that whosoever shall 2942
6:12 I Darius have made a **d**; let it be done with 2942
7:13 I make a **d**, that all they of the people of 2942
7:21 do make a **d** to all the treasurers which *are* 2942
Est 1:20 when the king's **d** which he shall make 6599
2: 8 king's commandment and his **d** was heard, 1881
3:15 and the **d** was given in Shushan the palace. 1881
4: 3 the king's commandment and his **d** came, 1881
4: 8 **d** that was given at Shushan to destroy 1881
8:14 and the **d** was given at Shushan the palace. 1881
8:17 the king's commandment and his **d** came, 1881
9: 1 and his **d** drew near to be put in execution, 1881
9:13 to morrow also according unto *this* day's **d**, 1881
9:14 the **d** was given at Shushan; and they 1881
9:32 the **d** of Esther confirmed these matters of 3982
Job 22:28 Thou shalt also **d** a thing, and it shall be 1504
28:26 When he made a **d** for the rain, and a way 2706
Ps 2: 7 I will declare the **d**: the LORD hath said 2706
148: 6 he hath made a **d** which shall not pass. 2706
Pr 8:15 By me kings reign, and princes **d** justice. 2710
8:29 When he gave to the sea his **d**, that 2706
Isa 10: 1 Woe unto them that **d** unrighteous decrees, 2710
Jer 5:22 *for* the bound of the sea *by* a perpetual **d**, 2706
Da 2: 9 me the dream, *there is but* one **d** for you: 1882
2:13 the **d** went forth that the wise *men* should 1882
2:15 Why *is* the **d** *so* hasty from the king? 1882
3:10 Thou, O king, hast made a **d**, that every 2942
3:29 Therefore I make a **d**, That every people, 2942
4: 6 Therefore made I a **d** to bring in all 2942
4:17 *This* matter *is* by the **d** of the watchers, and 1510
4:24 O king, and this *is* the **d** of the most High, 1510
6: 7 to make a firm **d**, that whosoever shall ask a 633
6: 8 O king, establish the **d**, and sign the writing, 633
6: 9 king Darius signed the writing and the **d**. 633
6:12 before the king concerning the king's **d**; 633
6:12 Hast thou not signed a **d**, that every man that 633
6:13 nor the **d** that thou hast signed, but 633
6:15 Persians *is,* That no **d** nor statute which 633
6:26 I make a **d**, That in every dominion of my 2942
Jnh 3: 7 published through Nineveh by the **d** of 2940
Mic 7:11 *in* that day shall the **d** be far removed. 2706
Zep 2: 2 Before the **d** bring forth, *before* the day 2706
Lk 2: 1 *that* there went out a **d** from Cesar *1378*

DECREED (5) [DECREE]
Est 2: 1 she had done, and what was **d** against her. 1504
9:31 as they had **d** for themselves and for their 6965
Job 38:10 And brake up for it my **d** *place,* and set bars 2706
Isa 10:22 the consumption **d** shall overflow *with* 2782
1Co 7:37 so **d** in his heart that *he* will keep his virgin, *2919*

DECREES (3) [DECREE]
Isa 10: 1 Woe unto them that decree unrighteous **d**, 2711
Ac 16: 4 they delivered them the **d** for to keep, *1378*
17: 7 and these all do contrary to the **d** of Cesar, *1378*

DEDAN (11) [DEDANIM]
Ge 10: 7 and the sons of Raamah; Sheba, and **D**. 1719
25: 3 Jokshan begat Sheba, and **D**. And the sons 1719
25: 3 the sons of **D** were Asshurim, and 1719
1Ch 1: 9 And the sons of Raamah; Sheba, and **D**. 1719
1:32 And the sons of Jokshan; Sheba, and **D**. 1719
Jer 25:23 **D**, and Tema, and Buz, and all *that are* in 1719
49: 8 turn back, dwell deep, O inhabitants of **D**; 1719
Eze 25:13 and they of **D** shall fall by the sword. 1719
27:15 The men of **D** *were* thy merchants; 1719
27:20 **D** *was* thy merchant in precious clothes for 1719
38:13 and **D**, and the merchants of Tarshish, 1719

DEDANIM (1) [DEDAN]
Isa 21:13 ye lodge, O ye travelling companies of **D**. 1720

DEDANITES See DEDANIM

DEDICATE (11) [DEDICATED, DEDICATING, DEDICATION]
Dt 20: 5 he die in the battle, and another man **d** it. 2596
2Sa 8:11 Which also king David did **d** unto 6942
2Ki 12:18 had **d**, and his own hallowed *things,* and all 6942
1Ch 26:20 and over the treasures of the **d** *things.* 6944
26:26 of the **d** *things,* which David the king, 6944
26:27 Out of the spoils won in battles did they **d** 6942
28:12 and of the treasuries of the **d** *things:* 6944
2Ch 2: 4 to **d** *it* to him, *and* to burn before him sweet 6942
24: 7 also all the **d** *things* of the house of 6944
31:12 and the tithes and the **d** *things* faithfully: 6944
Eze 44:29 and every **d thing** in Israel shall be theirs. 2764

DEDICATED (17) [DEDICATE]
Dt 20: 5 hath built a new house, and hath not **d** it? 2596
Jdg 17: 3 I had **wholly d** the silver unto 6942+6942
2Sa 8:11 gold that he had **d** of all nations which he 6942
1Ki 7:51 in the *things* which David his father had **d**; 6944
8:63 all the children of Israel **d** the house of 2596
15:15 in *the things* which his father had **d**, 6944

1Ki 15:15 *the things* which himself had **d**, *into* 6944
2Ki 12: 4 All the money of the **d** *things* that is 6944
1Ch 18:11 Them also king David **d** unto the LORD, 6942
26:26 and the captains of the host, had **d**. 6942
26:28 of Ner, and Joab the son of Zeruiah, had **d**; 6942
26:28 whosoever had **d** *anything, it was* under 6942
2Ch 5: 1 in *all the things* that David his father had **d**; 6944
7: 5 and all the people **d** the house of God. 2596
15:18 of God *the things* that his father had **d**, 6944
15:18 that he himself had **d**, silver, and gold, and 6944
Heb 9:18 the first *testament* was **d** without blood. *1457*

DEDICATING (2) [DEDICATE]
Nu 7:10 the princes offered *for* **d** of the altar in 2598
7:11 prince on *his* day, for the **d** of the altar. 2598

DEDICATION (11) [DEDICATE]
Nu 7:84 This *was* the **d** of the altar, in the day when 2598
7:88 This *was* the **d** of the altar, after *that* it was 2598
2Ch 7: 9 for they kept the **d** of the altar seven days, 2598
Ezr 6:16 kept the **d** of this house of God with joy, 2597
6:17 offered at the **d** of this house of God an 2597
Ne 12:27 at the **d** of the wall of Jerusalem they 2598
12:27 to keep the **d** with gladness, both with 2598
Ps 30: T *and* Song *at* the **d** of the house of David. 2598
Da 3: 2 to come to the **d** of the image which 2597
3: 3 were gathered together unto the **d** of 2597
Jn 10:22 And it was at Jerusalem *the feast of* the **d**, *1456*

DEED (19) [DEEDS]
Ge 44:15 What **d** *is* this that ye have done? 4639
Ex 9:16 **in very d** for this cause have I raised thee 199
Jdg 19:30 There was no such *d* done nor seen from NIH
1Sa 25:34 For **in very d**, *as* the LORD God of Israel 199
26: 4 understood that Saul was come in **very d**. 3559
2Sa 12:14 by this **d** thou hast given great occasion to 1697
2Ch 6:18 will God **in very d** dwell with men on 552
Est 1:17 For *this* **d** of the queen shall come abroad 1697
1:18 which have heard of the **d** of the queen. 1697
Lk 23:51 consented to the counsel and **d** of them;) *4234*
24:19 which was a prophet mighty in **d** and *2041*
Ac 4: 9 If we this day be examined of the **good d** *2108*
Ro 15:18 make the Gentiles obedient, by word and **d**, *2041*
1Co 5: 2 that he that hath done this **d** might be taken *2041*
5: 3 *concerning* him that hath so done this *d*, NIG
2Co 10:11 such *will we be* also in **d** when we are *2041*
Col 3:17 And whatsoever ye do in word or **d**, *do* all *2041*
Jas 1:25 the work, this *man* shall be blessed in his **d**. *4162*
1Jn 3:18 neither in tongue; but in **d** and in truth. *2041*

DEEDS (33) [DEED]
Ge 20: 9 thou hast done **d** unto me that ought not to 4639
1Ch 16: 8 make known his **d** among the people. 5949
2Ch 35:27 his **d**, first and last, behold, they *are* written 1697
Ezr 9:13 after all that is come upon us for our evil **d**, 4639
Ne 6:19 Also they reported his **good d** before me, 2896
13:14 wipe not out my **good d** that I have done 2617
Ps 28: 4 Give them according to their **d**, and 6467
105: 1 make known his **d** among the people. 5949
Isa 59:18 According to *their* **d**, accordingly he will 1578
Jer 5:28 yea, they overpass the **d** of the wicked: 1697
25:14 will recompense them according to their **d**, 6467
Lk 11:48 Truly ye bear witness that ye allow the **d** of *2041*
23:41 for we receive the due reward of our **d**: *4238*
Jn 3:19 rather than light, because their **d** were evil. *2041*
3:20 to the light, lest his **d** should be reproved. *2041*
3:21 that his **d** may be made manifest, that they *2041*
8:41 Ye do the **d** of your father. Then said they *2041*
Ac 7:22 and was mighty in words and in **d**. *2041*
19:18 and confessed, and shewed their **d**. *4234*
24: 2 that **very worthy d** are done unto this *2735*
Ro 2: 6 will render to every *man* according to his **d**: *2041*
3:20 Therefore by the **d** of the law there shall no *2041*
3:28 justified by faith without the **d** of the law. *2041*
8:13 if ye through the Spirit do mortify the **d** of *4234*
2Co 12:12 in signs, and wonders, and **mighty d**. *1411*
Col 3: 9 that ye have put off the old man with his **d**; *4234*
2Pe 2: 8 from day to day with *their* unlawful **d**;) *2041*
2Jn 1:11 him God speed is partaker of his evil **d**. *2041*
3Jn 1:10 I will remember his **d** which he doeth, *2041*
Jude 1:15 **d** which they have ungodly committed, *2041*
Rev 2: 6 that thou hatest the **d** of the Nicolaitans, *2041*
2:22 except they repent of their **d**. *2041*
16:11 and their sores, and repented not of their **d**. *2041*

DEEMED (1)
Ac 27:27 about midnight the shipmen **d** that they *5282*

DEEP (65) [DEEPER, DEEPLY, DEEPNESS, DEEPS, DEPTH, DEPTHS]
Ge 1: 2 and darkness *was* upon the face of the **d**. 8415
2:21 the LORD God caused a **d sleep** to fall 8639
7:11 all the fountains of the great **d** broken up, 8415
8: 2 The fountains also of the **d** and 8415
15:12 going down, a **d sleep** fell upon Abram; 8639
49:25 blessings of the **d** that lieth under, 8415
Dt 33:13 and for the **d** that coucheth beneath, 8415
1Sa 26:12 a **d sleep** from the LORD was fallen upon 8639
Job 4:13 of the night, when **d sleep** falleth on men. 8639
12:22 He discovereth **d** *things* out of darkness, 6013
33:15 the night, when **d sleep** falleth upon men, 8639
38:30 *with* a stone, and the face of the **d** is frozen. 8415
41:31 He maketh the **d** to boil like a pot: 4688
41:32 *one* would think the **d** to be hoary. 8415
Ps 36: 6 thy judgments *are* a great **d**: 8415
42: 7 **D** calleth unto deep at the noise of thy 8415
42: 7 Deep calleth unto **d** at the noise of thy 8415
64: 6 of every one *of them*, and the heart, *is* **d**. 6013
69: 2 I sink in **d** mire, where *there is* no standing: 4688
69: 2 I am come into **d** waters, where the floods 4615
69:14 them that hate me, and out of the **d** waters. 4615
69:15 neither let the **d** swallow me up, and let not 4688
80: 9 didst **cause** it **to take d root**, and 8327+8328
92: 5 are thy works! *and* thy thoughts are very **d**. 6009
Ps 95: 4 In his hand *are* the **d places** of the earth: 4278
104: 6 Thou coveredst it *with* the **d** as *with* a 8415
107:24 of the LORD, and his wonders in the **d**. 4688
135: 6 and in earth, in the seas, and all **d places**. 8415
140:10 into **d pits**, *that* they rise not up again. 4113
Pr 8:28 *he* strengthened the fountains of the **d**: 8415
18: 4 The words of a man's mouth *are as* **d** 6013
19:15 Slothfulness casteth into a **d sleep**; and 8639
20: 5 Counsel in the heart of man *is like* **d** water; 6013
22:14 The mouth of strange *women is* a **d** pit: 6013
23:27 For a whore *is* a **d** ditch; and a strange 6013
Ecc 7:24 **exceeding d**, who can find it out? 6013+6013
Isa 29:10 poured out upon you the spirit of **d sleep**, 8639
29:15 Woe unto them that **seek d** to hide *their* 6009
30:33 it is prepared; he hath **made** *it* **d** *and* large: 6009
44:27 That saith to the **d**, Be dry, and I will dry 6683
51:10 hath dried the sea, the waters of the great **d**; 8415
63:13 That led them through the **d**, as a horse in 8415
Jer 49: 8 Flee ye, turn back, dwell **d**, O inhabitants 6009
49:30 Flee, get you far off, dwell **d**, O ye 6009
Eze 23:32 Thou shalt drink *of* thy sister's cup **d** and 6013
26:19 when *I* shall bring up the **d** upon thee, 8415
31: 4 the **d** set him up on high with her rivers 8415
31:15 I covered the **d** for him, and I restrained 8415
32:14 will I **make** their waters **d**, and cause their 8257
34:18 to have drunk of the **d** waters, but ye must 4950
Da 2:22 He revealeth the **d** and secret *things*: he 5994
8:18 I was **in a d sleep** on my face toward 7290
10: 9 was I **in a d sleep** on my face, and my face 7290
Am 7: 4 it devoured the great **d**, and did eat up a 8415
Jnh 2: 3 For thou hadst cast me *into* the **d**, in 4688
Hab 3:10 the **d** uttered his voice, *and* lift up his hands 8415
Lk 5: 4 Launch out into the **d**, and let down your *899*
6:48 and digged **d**, and laid the foundation on a *900*
8:31 not command them to go out into the **d**. *12*
Jn 4:11 hast nothing to draw with, and the well is **d**: *901*
Ac 20: 9 named Eutychus, being fallen into a **d** sleep: *901*
Ro 10: 7 Or, Who shall descend into the **d**? (that is, *12*
1Co 2:10 all *things*, yea, the **d things** of God. *899*
2Co 8: 2 their **d** poverty abounded unto *899+2596*
11:25 a night and a day I have been in the **d**; *1037*

DEEPER (9) [DEEP]
Lev 13: 3 the plague in sight *be* **d** than the skin of his 6013
13: 4 in sight *be* not **d** than the skin, and the hair 6013
13:25 and it *be* in sight **d** than the skin; 6013
13:30 behold, *if* it *be* in sight **d** than the skin; and 6013
13:31 it *be* not in sight **d** than the skin, and 6013
13:32 and the scall *be* not in sight **d** than the skin; 6013
13:34 in the skin, nor *be* in sight **d** than the skin; 6013
Job 11: 8 **d** than hell; what canst thou know? 6013
Isa 33:19 a people of a **d** speech than *thou* canst 6012

DEEPLY (3) [DEEP]
Isa 31: 6 the children of Israel have **d** revolted. 6009
Hos 9: 9 They have **d** corrupted *themselves*, as *in* 6009
Mk 8:12 And he **sighed d** in his spirit, and saith, *389*

DEEPNESS (1) [DEEP]
Mt 13: 5 sprung up, because *they* had no **d** of earth: *899*

DEEPS (4) [DEEP]
Ne 9:11 their persecutors thou threwest into the **d**, 4688
Ps 88: 6 me in the lowest pit, in darkness, in the **d**. 4688
148: 7 from the earth, ye dragons, and all **d**: 8415
Zec 10:11 and all the **d** of the river shall dry up: 4688

DEER (1)
Dt 14: 5 the **fallow d**, and the wild goat, and 3180

DEFAMED (1) [DEFAMING]
1Co 4:13 Being **d**, we intreat: we are made as the filth *987*

DEFAMING (1) [DEFAMED]
Jer 20:10 For I heard the **d** of many, fear on every 1681

DEFEAT (2)
2Sa 15:34 mayest thou for me **d** the counsel of 6565
17:14 For the LORD had appointed to **d** 6565

DEFENCE (22) [DEFEND]
Nu 14: 9 their **d** is departed from them, and 6738
2Ch 11: 5 in Jerusalem, and built cities for **d** in Judah. 4692
Job 22:25 the Almighty shall be thy **d**, and thou shalt 1220
Ps 7:10 My **d** *is* of God, which saveth the upright in 4043
31: 2 strong rock, for a house of **d** to save me. 4686
59: 9 will I wait upon thee: for God *is* my **d**. 4869
59:16 for thou hast been my **d** and refuge in 4869
59:17 for God *is* my **d**, *and* the God of my mercy. 4869
62: 2 *is* my rock and my salvation; *he is* my **d**; 4869
62: 6 *he is* my **d**; I shall not be moved. 4869
89:18 For the LORD *is* our **d**; and the Holy One 4043
94:22 the LORD is my **d**; and my God *is* 4869
Ecc 7:12 For wisdom *is* a **d**, *and* money *is* a defence: 6738
7:12 For wisdom *is* a defence, *and* money *is* a **d**: 6738
Isa 4: 5 by night: for upon all the glory *shall be* a **d**. 2646
19: 6 *and* the brooks of **d** shall be emptied and 4693
33:16 his **place of d** *shall be* the munitions of 4869
Na 2: 5 wall thereof, and the **d** shall be prepared. 5526
Ac 19:33 and would have **made** *his* **d** unto the people. *626*
22: 1 hear ye my **d** *which I make* now unto you. *627*
Php 1: 7 and *in* the **d** and confirmation of the gospel, *627*
1:17 knowing that I am set for the **d** of the gospel. *627*

DEFENCED (9) [DEFEND]
Isa 25: 2 made of a city a heap; *of* a **d** city a ruin: 1219
27:10 Yet the **d** city *shall be* desolate, *and* 1219
36: 1 came up against all the **d** cities of Judah, 1219
37:26 that thou shouldest be to lay waste **d** cities 1219
Jer 1:18 I have made thee *this* day a **d** city, and 4013
4: 5 and let us go into the **d** cities. 4013
8:14 let us enter into the **d** cities, and let us be 4013
34: 7 for these **d** cities remained of the cities of 4013
Eze 21:20 to Judah in Jerusalem the **d**. 1219

DEFEND (11) [DEFENCE, DEFENCED, DEFENDED, DEFENDEST, DEFENDING]
Jdg 10: 1 after Abimelech there arose to **d** Israel Tola 3467
2Ki 19:34 For I will **d** this city, to save it, for mine 1598
20: 6 I will **d** this city for mine own sake, and 1598
Ps 20: 1 the name of the God of Jacob **d** thee; 7682
59: 1 **d** me from them that rise up against me. 7682
82: 3 **D** the poor and fatherless: do justice to 8199
Isa 31: 5 so will the LORD of hosts **d** Jerusalem; 1598
37:35 For I will **d** this city to save it for mine own 1598
38: 6 of the king of Assyria: and I will **d** this city. 1598
Zec 9:15 The LORD of hosts shall **d** them; and 1598
12: 8 In that day shall the LORD **d** 1598

DEFENDED (2) [DEFEND]
2Sa 23:12 and **d** it, and slew the Philistines: 5337
Ac 7:24 he **d** *him*, and avenged him that was *292*

DEFENDEST (1) [DEFEND]
Ps 5:11 shout for joy, because thou **d** them: 5526+5921

DEFENDING (1) [DEFEND]
Isa 31: 5 **d** also he will deliver *it*; *and* passing over 1598

DEFER (3) [DEFERRED, DEFERRETH]
Ecc 5: 4 thou vowest a vow unto God, **d** not to pay it; 309
Isa 48: 9 For my name's sake will I **d** mine anger, and 748
Da 9:19 do; **d** not, for thine own sake, O my God: 309

DEFERRED (3) [DEFER]
Ge 34:19 the young man **d** not to do the thing, because 309
Pr 13:12 Hope **d** maketh the heart sick: but *when* 4900
Ac 24:22 he **d** them, and said, When Lysias the chief *306*

DEFERRETH (1) [DEFER]
Pr 19:11 The discretion of a man **d** his anger; and *it is* 748

DEFIED (6) [DEFY]
Nu 23: 8 shall I defy, *whom* the LORD hath not **d**? 2194
1Sa 17:36 seeing he hath **d** the armies of the living 2778
17:45 of the armies of Israel, whom thou hast **d**. 2778
2Sa 21:21 when he **d** Israel, Jonathan the son of 2778
23: 9 when they **d** the Philistines *that* were there 2778
1Ch 20: 7 when he **d** Israel, Jonathan the son of 2778

DEFILE (39) [DEFILED, DEFILEDST, DEFILETH, UNDEFILED]
Lev 11:44 neither shall ye **d** yourselves with any 2930
15:31 when they **d** my tabernacle that *is* among 2930
18:20 thy neighbour's wife, to **d** *thyself* with her. 2930
18:23 Neither shalt thou lie with any beast to **d** 2930
18:24 **D** not you yourselves in any of these 2930
18:28 land spue not you out also, when ye **d** it, 2930
18:30 and that ye **d** not **yourselves** therein: 2930
20: 3 to **d** my sanctuary, and to profane my holy 2930
21: 4 *But* he shall not **d** himself, *being* a chief 2930
21:11 nor **d** himself for his father, or for his 2930
22: 8 is torn *with beasts*, he shall not eat to **d** 2930
Nu 5: 3 that they **d** not their camps, in the midst 2930
35:34 **D** not therefore the land which ye shall 2930
2Ki 23:13 of the children of Ammon, did the king **d**. 2930
SS 5: 3 I have washed my feet; how shall I **d** them? 2936
Isa 30:22 Ye shall **d** also the covering of thy graven 2930
Jer 32:34 which is called by my name, to **d** it. 2930
Eze 7:22 for the robbers shall enter into it, and **d** it. 2490
9: 7 **D** the house, and fill the courts *with* 2930
20: 7 **d** not yourselves with the idols of Egypt: 2930
20:18 nor **d** yourselves with their idols: 2930
22: 3 maketh idols against herself to **d** *herself*. 2930
28: 7 and they shall **d** thy brightness. 2490
33:26 and ye **d** every one his neighbour's wife: 2930
37:23 Neither shall they **d** themselves any more 2930
43: 7 shall the house of Israel no more **d**, 2930
44:25 they shall come at no dead person to **d** 2930
44:25 had no husband, they may **d** themselves. 2930
Da 1: 8 **d** himself with the portion of the king's 1351
1: 8 of the eunuchs that he might not **d** himself. 1351
Mt 15:18 forth from the heart; and they **d** the man. *2840*
15:20 These are *the things* which **d** a man: but *2840*
Mk 7:15 a man, that entering into him can **d** him: *2840*
7:15 out of him, those are they that **d** the man. *2840*
7:18 entereth into the man, *it* cannot **d** him; *2840*
7:23 *things* come from within, and **d** the man. *2840*
1Co 3:17 If any *man* **d** the temple of God, him shall *5351*
1Ti 1:10 for **them that d** themselves **with mankind**, *733*
Jude 1: 8 Likewise also these *filthy* dreamers **d** *3392*

DEFILED (71) [DEFILE]
Ge 34: 2 he took her, and lay with her, and **d** her. 6031
34: 5 Jacob heard that he had **d** Dinah his 2930
34:13 said, because he had **d** Dinah their sister: 2930
34:27 the city, because they had **d** their sister. 2930
Lev 5: 3 *it be* that a man shall be **d** withal, 2930
11:43 with them, that ye should be **d** thereby. 2930
13:46 the plague *shall be* in him he shall be **d**; 2930
15:32 seed goeth from him, and is **d** therewith; 2930
18:24 nations are **d** which I cast out before you: 2930
18:25 the land is **d**: therefore I do visit 2930
18:27 which *were* before you, and the land is **d**;) 2930
19:31 neither seek after wizards, to be **d** by them: 2930
21: 1 There shall none be **d** for the dead among 2930
21: 3 hath had no husband; for her may he be **d**. 2930
Nu 5: 2 an issue, and whosoever is **d** by the dead: 2931
5:13 she be **d**, and *there be* no witness against 2930
5:14 and he be jealous of his wife, and she be **d**: 2930
5:14 he be jealous of his wife, and she be not **d**: 2930
5:20 if thou be **d**, and *some* man hath lain with 2930
5:27 *that*, if she be **d**, and have done trespass 2930
5:28 if the woman be not **d**, but *be* clean; then 2930
5:29 *to another* instead of her husband, and is **d**; 2930
6: 9 and he hath **d** the head of his consecration; 2930
6:12 shall be lost, because his separation was **d**. 2930
9: 6 who were **d** by the dead body of a man, 2931

Nu 9: 7 We *are* **d** by the dead body of a man: 2931
19:20 he hath **d** the sanctuary of the LORD: 2930
Dt 21:23 that thy land be not **d**, which the LORD 2930
22: 9 and the fruit of thy vineyard, be **d**. 6942
24: 4 her again to be his wife, after that she is **d**; 2930
2Ki 23: 8 **d** the high places where the priests had 2930
23:10 he **d** Topheth, which *is* in the valley of 2930
1Ch 5: 1 but, forasmuch as he **d** his father's bed, 2490
Ne 13:29 because they have **d** the priesthood, and 1352
Job 16:15 upon my skin, and **d** my horn in the dust. 5953
Ps 74: 7 they have **d** *by casting down* the dwelling 2490
79: 1 thy holy temple have they **d**; they have laid 2930
106:39 Thus were they **d** with their own works, 2930
Isa 24: 5 The earth also is **d** under the inhabitants 2610
59: 3 For your hands are **d** with blood, and 1351
Jer 2: 7 ye **d** my land, and made mine heritage an 2930
3: 9 that she **d** the land, and committed adultery 2610
16:18 because they have **d** my land, they have 2490
19:13 shall be **d** as the place of Tophet, because 2931
Eze 4:13 Israel eat their **d** bread among the Gentiles, 2931
5:11 thou hast **d** my sanctuary with all thy 2930
7:24 to cease; and their holy places shall be **d**. 2490
18: 6 neither hath **d** his neighbour's wife, 2930
18:11 the mountains, and **d** his neighbour's wife, 2930
18:15 of Israel, hath not **d** his neighbour's wife, 2930
20:43 all your doings, wherein ye have been **d**; 2930
22: 4 hast **d** *thyself* in thine idols which thou hast 2930
22:11 another hath lewdly **d** his daughter in law; 2930
23: 7 she doted: with all their idols she **d** herself. 2930
23:13 I saw that she was **d**, *that* they took both 2930
23:17 they **d** her with their whoredom, and 2930
23:38 they have **d** my sanctuary in the same day, 2930
28:18 Thou hast **d** thy sanctuaries by 2490
36:17 they **d** it by their own way and by their 2930
43: 8 they have even **d** my holy name by their 2930
Hos 5: 3 thou committest whoredom, *and* Israel is **d**. 2930
6:10 *is* the whoredom of Ephraim, Israel is **d**. 2930
Mic 4:11 Let her be **d**, and let our eye look upon 2610
Mk 7: 2 saw some of his disciples eat bread with **d**, *2839*
Jn 18:28 the judgment hall, lest they should be **d**; *3392*
1Co 8: 7 and their conscience being weak is **d**. *3435*
Tit 1:15 but unto them that are **d** and unbelieving *is* *3392*
1:15 but even their mind and conscience is **d**. *3392*
Heb 12:15 up trouble *you*, and thereby many be **d**; *3392*
Rev 3: 4 in Sardis, which have not **d** their garments; *3435*
14: 4 These are they which were not **d** with *3435*

DEFILEDST (1) [DEFILE]
Ge 49: 4 then **d** thou *it*: he went up to my couch. 2490

DEFILETH (9) [DEFILE]
Ex 31:14 *every* one that **d** it shall surely be put to 2490
Nu 19:13 **d** the tabernacle of the LORD; 2930
35:33 land wherein ye *are*: for blood it **d** the land: 2610
Mt 15:11 Not that which goeth into the mouth **d** a *2840*
15:11 cometh out of the mouth, this **d** a man. *2840*
15:20 to eat with unwashen hands **d** not a man. *2840*
Mk 7:20 cometh out of the man, that **d** the man. *2840*
Jas 3: 6 that it **d** the whole body, and setteth on fire *4695*
Rev 21:27 in no wise enter into it any *thing* that **d**, *2840*

DEFORMED See CORRUPTION; SUPERFLUOUS

DEFRAUD (5) [DEFRAUDED]
Lev 19:13 Thou shalt not **d** thy neighbour, neither rob 6231
Mk 10:19 **D** not, Honour thy father and mother. *650*
1Co 6: 8 you do wrong, and **d**, and that *your* brethren. *650*
7: 5 **D** you not one the other, except *it be* with *650*
1Th 4: 6 go beyond and **d** his brother in *any* matter: *4122*

DEFRAUDED (4) [DEFRAUD]
1Sa 12: 3 or whom have I **d**? whom have I 6231
12: 4 they said, Thou hast not **d** us, 6231
1Co 6: 7 do ye not rather *suffer yourselves to* be **d**? *650*
2Co 7: 2 have corrupted no *man*, we have **d** no *man*. *4122*

DEFY (5) [DEFIED]
Nu 23: 7 curse me Jacob, and come, **d** Israel. 2194
23: 8 or how shall I **d**, *whom* the LORD hath 2194
1Sa 17:10 I **d** the armies of Israel this day; 2778
17:25 surely to **d** Israel is he come up: and it shall 2778
17:26 that he should **d** the armies of the living 2778

DEGENERATE (1)
Jer 2:21 art thou turned *into* the **d** plant of a strange 5494

DEGREE (7) [DEGREES]
1Ch 15:18 with them their brethren of the **second d**, 4932
17:17 according to the estate of a man of **high d**, 4609
Ps 62: 9 Surely **men of low d** *are* vanity, *and* 120+1121
62: 9 *and* **men of high d** *are* a lie: 376+1121
Lk 1:52 from *their* seats, and exalted them of **low d**. *5011*
1Ti 3:13 well purchase to themselves a good **d**, *898*
Jas 1: 9 Let the brother of **low d** rejoice in that he is *5011*

DEGREES (24) [DEGREE]
2Ki 20: 9 shall the shadow go forward ten **d**, or 4609
20: 9 go forward ten degrees, or go back ten **d**? 4609
20:10 thing for the shadow to go down ten **d**: 4609
20:10 but let the shadow return backward ten **d**. 4609
20:11 he brought the shadow ten **d** backward, 4609
Ps 120: T A Song of **d**. 4609
121: T A Song of **d**. 4609
122: T A Song of **d** of David. 4609
123: T A Song of **d**. 4609
124: T A Song of **d** of David. 4609
125: T A Song of **d**. 4609
126: T A Song of **d**. 4609
127: T A Song of **d** for Solomon. 4609
128: T A Song of **d**. 4609
129: T A Song of **d**. 4609
130: T A Song of **d**. 4609
Ps 131: T A Song of **d** of David. 4609
132: T A Song of **d**. 4609
133: T A Song of **d** of David. 4609
134: T A Song of **d**. 4609
Isa 38: 8 I will bring again the shadow of the **d**, 4609
38: 8 in the sun dial of Ahaz, ten **d** backward. 4609
38: 8 So the sun returned ten **d**, by which degrees 4609
38: 8 ten degrees, by which **d** it was gone down. 4609

DEHAVITES (1)
Ezr 4: 9 the Susanchites, the **D**, *and* the Elamites, 1723

DEITY See GODHEAD

DEKAR (1)
1Ki 4: 9 The son of **D**, in Makaz, and in Shaalbim, 1857

DELAIAH (6)
1Ch 24:18 The three and twentieth to **D**, the four and 1806
Ezr 2:60 The children of **D**, the children of Tobiah, 1806
Ne 6:10 the son of **D** the son of Mehetabeel, 1806
7:62 The children of **D**, the children of Tobiah, 1806
Jer 36:12 **D** the son of Shemaiah, and Elnathan 1806
36:25 Nevertheless Elnathan and **D** and 1806

DELAY (3) [DELAYED, DELAYETH]
Ex 22:29 Thou shalt not **d** *to offer the first of* thy ripe 309
Ac 9:38 desiring *him* that *he* would not **d** to come to *3635*
25:17 they were come hither, without any **d**, *311+4160*

DELAYED (2) [DELAY]
Ex 32: 1 when the people saw that Moses **d** to come 954
Ps 119:60 and **d** not to keep thy commandments. 4102

DELAYETH (2) [DELAY]
Mt 24:48 say in his heart, My lord **d** his coming; *5549*
Lk 12:45 say in his heart, My lord **d** his coming; *5549*

DELECTABLE (1)
Isa 44: 9 their **d** *things* shall not profit; and they *are* 2530

DELEGATION See AMBASSAGE

DELICACIES (1)
Rev 18: 3 waxed rich through the abundance of her **d**. *4764*

DELICATE (5) [DELICATELY, DELICATENESS, DELICATES, DELICIOUSLY]
Dt 28:54 very **d**, his eye shall be evil toward his 6028
28:56 The tender and **d** *woman* among you, 6028
Isa 47: 1 thou shalt no more be called tender and **d**. 6028
Jer 6: 2 of Zion *to* a comely and **d** *woman*. 6026
Mic 1:16 thee bald, and poll thee for thy **d** children; 8588

DELICATELY (4) [DELICATE]
1Sa 15:32 Agag came unto him **d**. And Agag said, 4574
Pr 29:21 He that **d bringeth up** his servant from a 6445
La 4: 5 They that did feed **d** are desolate in 4574+3807.1
Lk 7:25 and live **d**, are in kings' courts. *5172*

DELICATENESS (1) [DELICATE]
Dt 28:56 the sole of her foot upon the ground for **d** 6026

DELICATES (1) [DELICATE]
Jer 51:34 he hath filled his belly with my **d**, he hath 5730

DELICIOUSLY (2) [DELICATE]
Rev 18: 7 and **lived d**, so much torment and *4763*
18: 9 committed fornication and **lived d** with her, *4763*

DELIGHT (51) [DELIGHTED, DELIGHTEST, DELIGHTETH, DELIGHTS, DELIGHTSOME]
Ge 34:19 because he had **d** in Jacob's daughter: 2654
Nu 14: 8 If the LORD **d** in us, then he will bring us 2654
Dt 10:15 Only the LORD **had** a **d** in thy fathers to 2836
21:14 if thou have no **d** in her, then thou shalt let 2654
1Sa 15:22 Hath the LORD *as great* **d** in burnt 2656
18:22 the king hath **d** in thee, and all his servants 2654
2Sa 15:26 if he thus say, I have no **d** in thee; behold, 2654
24: 3 why doth my lord the king **d** in this thing? 2654
Est 6: 6 To whom would the king **d** to do honour 2654
Job 22:26 then shalt thou **have** thy **d** in the Almighty, 6026
27:10 Will he **d** himself in the Almighty? will he 6026
34: 9 It profiteth a man nothing that he should **d** 7521
Ps 1: 2 his **d** *is* in the law of the LORD; and in his 2656
16: 3 *to* the excellent, in whom *is* all my **d**. 2656
37: 4 **D** thyself also in the LORD; and he shall 6026
37:11 shall **d** themselves in the abundance of 6026
40: 8 I **d** to do thy will, O my God: yea, thy law 2654
62: 4 they **d in** lies: they bless with their mouth, 7521
68:30 scatter thou the people *that* **d in** war. 2654
94:19 thoughts within me thy comforts **d** my soul. 8173
119:16 I will **d** myself in thy statutes: I will not 8173
119:24 Thy testimonies also *are* my **d** *and* 8191
119:35 of thy commandments; for therein do I **d**. 2654
119:47 I will **d** myself in thy commandments, 8173
119:70 heart is as fat as grease; *but* I **d** in thy law. 8173
119:77 that I may live: for thy law *is* my **d**. 8191
119:174 O LORD; and thy law *is* my **d**. 8191
Pr 1:22 the scorners **d in** their scorning, and 2530
2:14 *and* **d** in the frowardness of the wicked; 1523
8:30 brought up *with him*: and I was daily *his* **d**, 8191
11: 1 to the LORD: but a just weight *is* his **d**. 7522
11:20 *such as are* upright in *their* way *are* his **d**. 7522
12:22 but they that deal truly *are* his **d**. 7522
15: 8 but the prayer of the upright *is* his **d**. 7522
16:13 Righteous lips *are* the **d** of kings; and 7522
18: 2 A fool hath no **d** in understanding, but that 2654
19:10 **D** *is* not seemly for a fool; much less for a 8588
24:25 to them that rebuke *him* shall be **d**, and 5276
29:17 thee rest; yea, he shall give **d** unto thy soul. 4574
SS 2: 3 I sat down under his shadow **with great d**, 2530
Isa 1:11 I **d** not in the blood of bullocks, or 2654
Isa 13:17 and *as for* gold, they shall not **d** in it. 2654
55: 2 *is* good, and let your soul **d** itself in fatness. 6026
58: 2 seek me daily, and **d** to know my ways, 2654
58: 2 they **take** in **d** in approaching to God. 2654
58:13 call the sabbath a **d**, the holy of 6027
58:14 shalt thou **d** thyself in the LORD; and 6026
Jer 6:10 unto them a reproach; they have no **d** in it. 2654
9:24 for in these *things* I **d**, saith the LORD. 2654
Mal 3: 1 messenger of the covenant, whom ye **d** in: 2655
Ro 7:22 For I **d in** the law of God after the inward *4913*

DELIGHTED (12) [DELIGHT]
1Sa 19: 2 Jonathan Saul's son **d** much in David: and 2654
2Sa 22:20 he delivered me, because he **d** in me. 2654
1Ki 10: 9 be the LORD thy God, which **d** in thee, 2654
2Ch 9: 8 which **d** in thee to set thee on his throne, 2654
Ne 9:25 and **d** themselves in thy great goodness. 5727
Est 2:14 except the king **d** in her, and *that* she were 2654
Ps 18:19 he delivered me, because he **d** in me. 2654
22: 8 let him deliver him, seeing he **d** in him. 2654
109:17 as he **d** not in blessing, so let it be far from 2654
Isa 65:12 and did choose *that* wherein I **d** not. 2654
66: 4 mine eyes, and chose *that* in which I **d** not. 2654
66:11 and be **d** with the abundance of her glory. 6026

DELIGHTEST (1) [DELIGHT]
Ps 51:16 else would I give *it*: thou **d** not **in** burnt 7521

DELIGHTETH (14) [DELIGHT]
Est 6: 6 unto the man whom the king **d** to honour? 2654
6: 7 *For* the man whom the king **d** to honour, 2654
6: 9 the man *withal* whom the king **d** to honour, 2654
6: 9 to the man whom the king **d** to honour. 2654
6:11 unto the man whom the king **d** to honour. 2654
Ps 37:23 by the LORD: and he **d** in his way. 2654
112: 1 *that* **d** greatly in his commandments. 2654
147:10 He **d** not in the strength of the horse: 2654
Pr 3:12 even as a father the son *in whom* he **d**. 7521
Isa 42: 1 I uphold; mine elect, *in whom* my soul **d**; 7521
62: 4 for the LORD **d** in thee, and thy land shall 2654
66: 3 and their soul **d** in their abominations. 2654
Mic 7:18 his anger for ever, because he **d** in mercy. 2654
Mal 2:17 the sight of the LORD, and he **d** in them; 2654

DELIGHTFUL See GOODLIER; GOODLIEST; GOODLY

DELIGHTS (6) [DELIGHT]
2Sa 1:24 who clothed you in scarlet, with *other* **d**, 5730
Ps 119:92 Unless thy law *had been* my **d**, I should 8191
119:143 on me: *yet* thy commandments *are* my **d**. 8191
Pr 8:31 and my **d** *were* with the sons of men. 8191
Ecc 2: 8 and the **d** of the sons of men, 8588
SS 7: 6 and how pleasant art thou, O love, for **d**! 8588

DELIGHTSOME (1) [DELIGHT]
Mal 3:12 for ye shall be a **d** land, saith the LORD of 2656

DELILAH (6)
Jdg 16: 4 in the valley of Sorek, whose name *was* **D**. 1807
16: 6 **D** said to Samson, Tell me, I pray thee, 1807
16:10 **D** said unto Samson, Behold, thou hast 1807
16:12 **D** therefore took new ropes, and bound him 1807
16:13 **D** said unto Samson, Hitherto thou hast 1807
16:18 when **D** saw that he had told her all his 1807

DELIVER (296) [DELIVERANCE, DELIVERANCES, DELIVERED, DELIVEREDST, DELIVERER, DELIVEREST, DELIVERETH, DELIVERING, DELIVERY]
Ge 32:11 **D** me, I pray thee, from the hand of my 5337
37:22 their hands, to **d** him to his father again. 3807.1
40:13 thou shalt **d** Pharaoh's cup into his hand, 5414
42:34 *are* true *men: so* will I **d** you your brother, 5414
42:37 **d** him into my hand, and I will bring him to 5414
Ex 3: 8 I am come down to **d** them out of the hand 5337
5:18 given you, yet shall ye **d** the tale of bricks. 5414
21:13 lie not in wait, but God **d** *him* into his hand; 579
22: 7 If a man shall **d** unto his neighbour money 5414
22:10 If a man **d** unto his neighbour an ass, or 5414
22:26 thou shalt **d** it unto him by that the sun 7725
23:31 for I will **d** the inhabitants of the land into 5414
Lev 26:26 they shall **d** *you* your bread **again** by 7725
Nu 21: 2 If thou wilt **indeed d** this people into 5414+5414
35:25 the congregation shall **d** the slayer out of 5337
Dt 1:27 to **d** us into the hand of the Amorites, 5414
2:30 that he might **d** him into thy hand, 5414
3: 2 for I will **d** him, and all his people, and 5414
7: 2 when the LORD thy God shall **d** them 5414
7:16 which the LORD thy God shall **d** thee; 5414
7:23 the LORD thy God shall **d** them unto thee, 5414
7:24 he shall **d** their kings into thine hand, and 5414
19:12 **d** him into the hand of the avenger of 5414
23:14 to **d** thee, and to give up thine enemies 5337
23:15 Thou shalt not **d** unto his master the servant 5462
24:13 **In any case** thou shalt **d** him the pledge **again** 7725+7725
25:11 the wife of the one draweth near for to **d** 5337
32:39 neither *is there any* that can **d** out of my 5337
Jos 2:13 that they have, and **d** our lives from death. 5337
7: 7 to **d** us into the hand of the Amorites, 5414
8: 7 for the LORD your God will **d** it into your 5414
11: 6 time will I **d** them **up** all slain before Israel: 5414
20: 5 they shall not **d** the slayer **up** into his hand; 5462
Jdg 4: 7 and I will **d** him into thine hand. 5414
7: 7 and **d** the Midianites into thine hand: 5414
10:11 *Did* not *I* **d** *you* from the Egyptians, and NIH
10:13 other gods: wherefore I will **d** you no more. 3467
10:14 let them **d** you in the time of your 3467
10:15 unto thee; **d** us only, we pray thee, this day. 5337
11: 9 the LORD **d** them before me, shall I be 5414
11:30 If thou shalt **without fail d** 5414+5414
13: 5 he shall begin to **d** Israel out of the hand of 3467

Jdg 15:12 that we may **d** thee into the hand of 5414
15:13 bind thee fast, and **d** thee into their hand: 5414
20:13 Now therefore **d** *us* the men, the children of 5414
20:28 for to morrow I will **d** them into thine hand. 5414
1Sa 4: 8 who shall **d** us out of the hand of these 5337
7: 3 he will **d** you out of the hand of 5337
7:14 the coasts thereof did Israel **d** out of 5337
12:10 now **d** us out of the hand of our enemies, 5337
12:21 after vain *things,* which cannot profit nor **d**; 5337
14:37 wilt thou **d** them into the hand of Israel? 5414
17:37 he will **d** me out of the hand of this 5337
17:46 This day will the LORD **d** thee into mine 5462
23: 4 for I will **d** the Philistines into thine hand. 5414
23:11 Will the men of Keilah **d** me **up** into his 5462
23:12 Will the men of Keilah **d** me and my men 5462
23:12 And the LORD said, They will **d** *thee* **up**. 5462
23:20 our part *shall be* to **d** him into the king's 5462
24: 4 I will **d** thine enemy into thine hand, 5414
24:15 my cause, and **d** me out of thine hand. 8199
26:24 and let him **d** me out of all tribulation. 5337
28:19 Moreover the LORD will also **d** Israel 5414
28:19 the LORD also shall **d** the host of Israel 5414
30:15 nor **d** me into the hands of my master, and 5462
2Sa 3:14 Saul's son, saying, **D** *me* my wife Michal, 5414
5:19 wilt thou **d** them into mine hand? And 5414
5:19 for I will **doubtless d** the Philistines 5414+5414
14: 7 and they said, **D** him that smote his brother, 5414
14:16 to **d** his handmaid out of the hand of 5337
20:21 **d** him only, and I will depart from the city. 5414
1Ki 8:46 **d** them to the enemy, so that they carry 5414
18: 9 that thou wouldest **d** thy servant into 5414
20: 5 Thou shalt **d** me thy silver, and thy gold, 5414
20:13 behold, I will **d** it into thine hand *this* day; 5414
20:28 will I **d** all this great multitude into thine 5414
22: 6 for the Lord shall **d** *it* into the hand of 5414
22:12 for the LORD shall **d** *it* into the king's 5414
22:15 for the LORD shall **d** *it* into the hand of 5414
2Ki 3:10 *together,* to **d** them into the hand of Moab. 5414
3:13 *together,* to **d** them into the hand of Moab. 5414
3:18 he will **d** the Moabites also into your hand. 5414
12: 7 but **d** it for the breaches of the house. 5414
17:39 he shall **d** you out of the hand of all your 5337
18:23 and I will **d** thee two thousand horses, 5414
18:29 for he shall not be able to **d** you out of his 5337
18:30 The LORD will **surely d** us, and 5337+5337
18:32 saying, The LORD will **d** us. 5337
18:35 that the LORD should **d** Jerusalem out of 5337
20: 6 I will **d** thee and this city out of the hand of 5337
21:14 and **d** them into the hand of their enemies; 5414
22: 5 let them **d** it into the hand of the doers of 5414
1Ch 14:10 wilt thou **d** them into mine hand? And 5414
14:10 Go up; for I will **d** them into thine hand. 5414
16:35 us together, and **d** us from the heathen, 5337
2Ch 6:36 **d** them *over* before *their* enemies, and 5414
18: 5 for God will **d** *it* into the king's hand. 5414
18:11 for the LORD shall **d** *it* into the hand of 5414
25:15 which could not **d** their own people out of 5337
25:20 that *he* might **d** them into the hand *of their* 5414
28:11 me therefore, and **d** the captives **again**, 7725
32:11 The LORD our God shall **d** us out of 5337
32:13 able to **d** their lands out of mine hand? 5337
32:14 that could **d** his people out of mine hand, 5337
32:14 that your God should be able to **d** you out 5337
32:15 kingdom was able to **d** his people out of 5337
32:15 how much less shall your God **d** you out of 5337
32:17 shall not the God of Hezekiah **d** his people 5337
Ezr 7:19 *those* **d** thou before the God of Jerusalem. 8000
Ne 9:28 many times didst thou **d** them according to 5337
Job 5: 4 in the gate, neither *is there* any to **d** *them.* 5337
5:19 He shall **d** thee in six troubles: yea, 5337
6:23 Or, **D** me from the enemy's hand? or, 4422
10: 7 *there is* none that can **d** out of thine hand. 5337
22:30 He shall **d** the island of the innocent: and 4422
33:24 saith, **D** him from going down *to* the pit: 6308
33:28 He will **d** his soul from going into the pit, 6299
36:18 then a great ransom cannot **d** thee. 5186
Ps 6: 4 Return, O LORD, **d** my soul: O save me 2502
7: 1 from all them that persecute me, and **d** me: 5337
7: 2 *it* in pieces, while *there is* none to **d**. 5337
17:13 **d** my soul from the wicked, *which is* thy 6403
22: 4 in thee: they trusted, and thou didst **d** them. 6403
22: 8 He trusted on the LORD *that* he would **d** 6403
22: 8 let him **d** him, seeing he delighted in him. 5337
22:20 **D** my soul from the sword; my darling 5337
25:20 O keep my soul, and **d** me: let me not be 5337
27:12 **D** me not **over** unto the will of mine 5414
31: 1 be ashamed: **d** me in thy righteousness. 6403
31: 2 Bow down thine ear to me; **d** me speedily: 5337
31:15 **d** me from the hand of mine enemies, and 5337
33:17 neither shall he **d** *any* by his great strength. 4422
33:19 To **d** their soul from death, and to keep 5337
37:40 the LORD shall help them, and **d** them: 6403
37:40 he shall **d** them from the wicked, and 6403
39: 8 **D** me from all my transgressions: make me 5337
40:13 Be pleased, O LORD, to **d** me: O LORD, 5337
41: 1 the LORD will **d** him in time of trouble. 4422
41: 2 thou wilt not **d** him unto the will of his 5414
43: 1 O **d** me from the deceitful and unjust man. 6403
50:15 I will **d** thee, and thou shalt glorify me. 2502
50:22 I tear *you* in pieces, and *there be* none to **d**. 5337
51:14 **D** me from bloodguiltiness, O God, 5337
56:13 *wilt* not *thou* **d** my feet from falling, that *I* NIH
59: 1 **D** me from mine enemies, O my God: 5337
59: 2 **D** me from the workers of iniquity, and 5337
69:14 **D** me out of the mire, and let me not sink: 5337
69:18 redeem it: **d** me because of mine enemies. 6299
70: 1 *Make haste,* O God, to **d** me; make haste to 5337
71: 2 **D** me in thy righteousness, and cause me to 5337
71: 4 **D** me, O my God, out of the hand of 6403
71:11 and take him; for *there is* none to **d** *him.* 5337
72:12 For he shall **d** the needy when he crieth; 5337
74:19 O **d** not the soul of thy turtledove unto 5414
79: 9 **d** us, and purge away our sins, for thy 5337
82: 4 **D** the poor and needy: rid *them* out of 6403
89:48 shall he **d** his soul from the hand of 4422
Ps 91: 3 Surely he shall **d** thee from the snare of 5337
91:14 his love upon me, therefore will I **d** him: 6403
91:15 in trouble; I will **d** him, and honour him. 2502
106:43 Many times did he **d** them; but 5337
109:21 because thy mercy *is* good, **d** thou me. 5337
116: 4 O LORD, I beseech thee, **d** my soul. 4422
119:134 **D** me from the oppression of man: so will I 6299
119:153 Consider mine affliction, and **d** me: for I do 2502
119:154 Plead my cause, and **d** me: quicken me 1350
119:170 before thee: **d** me according to thy word. 5337
120: 2 **D** my soul, O LORD, from lying lips, *and* 5337
140: 1 **D** me, O LORD, from the evil man: 2502
142: 6 **d** me from my persecutors; for they are 5337
143: 9 **D** me, O LORD, from mine enemies: 5337
144: 7 rid me, and **d** me out of great waters, 5337
144:11 and **d** me from the hand of strange children, 5337
Pr 2:12 To **d** thee from the way of the evil *man,* 5337
2:16 To **d** thee from the strange woman, 5337
4: 9 a crown of glory shall she **d** *to* thee. 4042
6: 3 Do this now, my son, and **d** thyself, 5337
6: 5 **D** thyself as a roe from the hand *of* 5337
11: 6 The righteousness of the upright shall **d** 5337
12: 6 but the mouth of the upright shall **d** them. 5337
19:19 for if thou **d** *him,* yet thou must do *it* again. 5337
23:14 with the rod, and shalt **d** his soul from hell. 5337
24:11 If thou forbear to **d** *them that are* drawn 5337
Ecc 8: 8 neither shall wickedness **d** those that are 4422
Isa 5:29 carry *it* away safe, and none shall **d** *it.* 5337
19:20 and a great one, and he shall **d** them. 5337
29:11 which *men* **d** to one that is learned, saying, 5414
31: 5 defending also he will **d** *it;* and 5337
36:14 for he shall not be able to **d** you. 5337
36:15 The LORD will **surely d** us: 5337+5337
36:18 saying, The LORD will **d** us. 5337
36:20 that the LORD should **d** Jerusalem out of 5337
38: 6 I will **d** thee and this city out of the hand of 5337
43:13 *there is* none that can **d** out of my hand: 5337
44:17 and prayeth unto it, and saith, **D** me; 5337
44:20 that he cannot **d** his soul, nor say, *Is there* 5337
46: 2 they could not **d** the burden, but 4422
46: 4 will bear; even I will carry, and will **d** *you.* 4422
47:14 they shall not **d** themselves from the power 5337
50: 2 or have I no power to **d**? behold, at my 5337
57:13 When thou criest, let thy companies **d** thee; 5337
Jer 1: 8 for I *am* with thee to **d** thee, saith 5337
1:19 I *am* with thee, saith the LORD, to **d** thee. 5337
15: 9 the residue of them will I **d** to the sword 5414
15:20 I *am* with thee to save thee and to **d** thee, 5337
15:21 I will **d** thee out of the hand of the wicked, 5337
18:21 Therefore **d up** their children to the famine, 5414
20: 5 Moreover I will **d** all the strength of this 5414
21: 7 I will **d** Zedekiah king of Judah, and his 5414
21:12 **d** *him that is* spoiled out of the hand of 5337
22: 3 **d** the spoiled out of the hand of 5337
24: 9 I will **d** them to be removed into all 5414
29:18 will **d** them to be removed to all 5414
29:21 I will **d** them into the hand of 5414
38:19 lest they **d** me into their hand, and 5414
38:20 They shall not **d** *thee.* Obey, I beseech thee, 5414
39:17 I will **d** thee in that day, saith the LORD: 5337
39:18 For I will **surely d** thee, and 4422+4422
42:11 to save you, and to **d** you from his hand. 5337
43: 3 for to **d** us into the hand of the Chaldeans, 5414
43:11 *and* **d** such *as are* for death to death; NIH
46:26 I will **d** them into the hand of those that 5414
51: 6 of Babylon, and **d** every man his soul: 4422
51:45 **d** ye every man his soul from the fierce 4422
La 5: 8 *there is* none that doth **d** *us* out of their 6561
Eze 7:19 their gold shall not be able to **d** them in 5337
11: 9 **d** you into the hands of strangers, and 5414
13:21 **d** my people out of your hand, and 5337
13:23 for I will **d** my people out of your hand: 5337
14:14 they should **d** *but* their own souls by their 5337
14:16 they shall **d** neither sons nor daughters; 5337
14:18 they shall **d** neither sons nor daughters, but 5337
14:20 they shall **d** neither son nor daughter; 5337
14:20 **d** their own souls by their righteousness. 5337
21:31 **d** thee into the hand of brutish men, *and* 5414
23:28 I *will* **d** thee into the hand *of them* whom 5414
25: 4 I *will* **d** thee to the men of the east for a 5414
25: 7 and will **d** thee for a spoil to the heathen; 5414
33: 5 But he that taketh warning shall **d** his soul. 4422
33:12 not **d** him in the day of his transgression: 5337
34:10 for I will **d** my flock from their mouth, 5337
34:12 will **d** them out of all places where they 5337
Da 3:15 who *is* that God that shall **d** you out of my 7804
3:17 our God whom we serve *is* able to **d** us 7804
3:17 and he will **d** *us* out of thine hand, O king. 7804
3:29 there is no other God that can **d** after this 5338
6:14 and set *his* heart on Daniel to **d** him: 7804
6:14 till the going down of the sun to **d** him. 5338
6:16 thou servest continually, he will **d** thee. 7804
6:20 able to **d** thee from the lions? 7804
8: 4 neither *was there any* that could **d** out of his 5337
8: 7 there was none that could **d** the ram out of 5337
Hos 2:10 and none shall **d** her out of mine hand, 5337
11: 8 *how* shall I **d** thee, Israel? how shall I make 4042
Am 1: 6 the whole captivity, to **d** *them* **up** to Edom: 5462
2:14 neither shall the mighty **d** himself: 4422
2:15 *he that is* swift of foot shall not **d** *himself:* 4422
2:15 shall he that rideth the horse **d** himself. 4422
6: 8 will I **d up** the city with all that is therein. 5462
Jnh 4: 6 over his head, to **d** him from his grief. 5337
Mic 5: 6 thus shall he **d** *us* from the Assyrian, 5337
5: 8 and teareth in pieces, and none can **d**. 5337
6:14 thou shalt take hold, but shalt not **d**; and 6403
Zep 1:18 **d** them in the day of the LORD'S wrath; 5337
Zec 2: 7 **D** thyself, O Zion, that dwellest *with* 4422
11: 6 I *will* **d** the men every one into his 4672
11: 6 and out of their hand I will not **d** *them.* 5337
Mt 5:25 lest at any time the adversary **d** thee to *3860*
5:25 and the judge **d** thee to the officer, and *3860*
6:13 us not into temptation, but **d** us from evil: *4506*
10:17 for they will **d** you **up** to the councils, and *3860*
10:19 But when they **d** you **up**, take no thought *3860*
Mt 10:21 And the brother shall **d up** the brother to *3860*
20:19 And shall **d** him to the Gentiles to mock, *3860*
24: 9 Then shall they **d** you **up** to be afflicted, *3860*
26:15 will ye give me, and I will **d** him unto you? *3860*
27:43 let him **d** him now, if he will have him: *4506*
Mk 10:33 to death, and shall **d** him to the Gentiles: *3860*
13: 9 for they shall **d** you **up** to councils; and *3860*
13:11 when they shall lead *you,* and **d** you **up**, *3860*
Lk 11: 4 us not into temptation; but **d** us from evil. *4506*
12:58 and the judge **d** thee to the officer, and *3860*
20:20 *so they* might **d** him unto the power and *3860*
Ac 7:25 that God by his hand would **d** them: *1325+4991*
7:34 and am come down to **d** them. *1807*
21:11 shall **d** *him* into the hands of the Gentiles. *3860*
25:11 accuse me, no *man* may **d** me unto them. *5483*
25:16 It is not the manner of the Romans to **d** any *5483*
Ro 7:24 who shall **d** me from the body of this *4506*
1Co 5: 5 To **d** such a one unto Satan for *3860*
2Co 1:10 us from so great a death, and doth **d**: *4506*
1:10 in whom we trust that he will yet **d** *us;* *4506*
Gal 1: 4 that he might **d** us from *this* present evil *1807*
2Ti 4:18 And the Lord shall **d** me from every evil *4506*
Heb 2:15 And **d** them who through fear of death were *525*
2Pe 2: 9 The Lord knoweth *how* to **d** the godly out *4506*

DELIVERANCE (16) [DELIVER]

Ge 45: 7 and to save your lives by a great **d**. 6413
Jdg 15:18 Thou hast given this great **d** into the hand 8668
2Ki 5: 1 by him the LORD had given **d** unto Syria: 8668
13:17 The arrow of the LORD'S **d**, and 8668
13:17 and the arrow of **d** from Syria: 8668
1Ch 11:14 and the LORD saved *them* by a great **d**. 8668
2Ch 12: 7 destroy them, but I will grant them some **d**; 6413
Ezr 9:13 and hast given us *such* **d** as this; 6413
Est 4:14 and **d** arise to the Jews from another place; 2020
Ps 18:50 Great **d** giveth he to his king; and 3444
32: 7 shalt compass me about *with* songs of **d**. 6405
Isa 26:18 we have not wrought any **d** *in* the earth; 3444
Joel 2:32 in mount Zion and in Jerusalem shall be **d**, 6413
Ob 1:17 upon mount Zion shall be **d**, and there shall 6413
Lk 4:18 to preach **d** to the captives, and recovering of *859*
Heb 11:35 and others were tortured, not accepting **d**; *629*

DELIVERANCES (1) [DELIVER]

Ps 44: 4 *art* my King, O God: command **d** for Jacob. 3444

DELIVERED (291) [DELIVER]

Ge 9: 2 fishes of the sea; into your hand **are** they **d**. 5414
14:20 which hath **d** thine enemies into thy hand. 4042
25:24 when her days to be **d** were fulfilled, 3205
32:16 he **d** *them* into the hand of his servants, 5414
37:21 heard *it,* and he **d** him out of their hands; 5337
Ex 1:19 are **d** ere the midwives come in unto them. 3205
2:19 An Egyptian **d** us out of the hand of 5337
5:23 neither hast thou **d** thy people **at all**. 5337+5337
12:27 he smote the Egyptians, and **d** our houses. 5337
18: 4 and **d** me from the sword of Pharaoh: 5337
18: 8 by the way, and *how* the LORD **d** them. 5337
18: 9 whom he had **d** out of the hand of 5337
18:10 who hath **d** you out of the hand of 5337
18:10 who hath **d** the people from under the hand 5337
Lev 6: 2 in **that which was d** him **to keep**, 6487
6: 4 that which was **d** him **to keep**, 854+6485+6487
26:25 ye shall be **d** into the hand of the enemy. 5414
Nu 21: 3 voice of Israel, and **d up** the Canaanites; 5414
21:34 for I have **d** him into thy hand, and all his 5414
31: 5 So there were **d** out of the thousands of 4560
Dt 2:33 the LORD our God **d** him before us; and 5414
2:36 for us: the LORD our God **d** all unto us: 5414
3: 3 So the LORD our God **d** into our hands 5414
5:22 in two tables of stone, and **d** them unto me. 5414
9:10 the LORD **d** unto me two tables of stone 5414
20:13 when the LORD thy God hath **d** it into 5414
21:10 the LORD thy God hath **d** them into thine 5414
31: 9 **d** it unto the priests the sons of Levi, 5414
Jos 2:24 Truly the LORD hath **d** into our hands all 5414
9:26 **d** them out of the hand of the children of 5337
10: 8 for I have **d** them into thine hand; 5414
10:12 **d up** the Amorites before the children of 5414
10:19 for the LORD your God hath **d** them into 5414
10:30 the LORD **d** it also, and the king thereof, 5414
10:32 the LORD **d** Lachish into the hand of 5414
11: 8 the LORD **d** them into the hand of Israel, 5414
21:44 the LORD **d** all their enemies into their 5414
22:31 now ye have **d** the children of Israel out of 5337
24:10 blessed you still: so I **d** you out of his hand. 5337
24:11 the Jebusites; and I **d** them into your hand. 5414
Jdg 1: 2 behold, I have **d** the land into his hand. 5414
1: 4 the LORD **d** the Canaanites and 5414
2:14 he **d** them into the hands of spoilers that 5414
2:16 which **d** them out of the hand of those that 3467
2:18 **d** them out of the hand of their enemies all 3467
2:23 neither **d** he them into the hand of Joshua. 5414
3: 9 who **d** them, *even* Othniel the son of 3467
3:10 the LORD **d** Chushan-rishathaim king of 5414
3:28 for the LORD hath **d** your enemies 5414
3:31 men with an ox goad: and he also **d** Israel. 3467
4:14 the LORD hath **d** Sisera into thine hand: 5414
5:11 *They that are* **d** from the noise of archers in NIH
6: 1 the LORD **d** them into the hand of Midian 5414
6: 9 I **d** you out of the hand of the Egyptians, 5337
6:13 and **d** us into the hands of the Midianites. 5414
7: 9 the host; for I have **d** it into thine hand. 5414
7:14 *for* into his hand hath God **d** Midian, and 5414
7:15 for the LORD hath **d** into your hand 5414
8: 3 God hath **d** into your hands the princes of 5414
8: 7 Therefore when the LORD hath **d** Zebah 5414
8:22 for thou hast **d** us from the hand of Midian. 3467
8:34 who had **d** them out of the hands of all their 5337
9:17 and **d** you out of the hand of Midian: 5337
10:12 cried to me, and I **d** you out of their hand. 3467
11:21 the LORD God of Israel **d** Sihon and all 5414
11:32 and the LORD **d** them into his hands. 5414
12: 2 I called you, ye **d** me not out of their hands. 3467

Jdg 12: 3 when I saw that ye d me not, I put my life 3467
12: 3 and the LORD d them into my hand: 5414
13: 1 the LORD d them into the hand of 5414
16:23 Our god hath d Samson our enemy into our 5414
16:24 Our god hath d into our hands our enemy, 5414
1Sa 4:19 was with child, near to be d: 3205
10:18 d you out of the hand of the Egyptians, and 5337
12:11 d you out of the hand of your enemies on 5337
14:10 for the LORD hath d them into our hand: 5414
14:12 for the LORD hath d them into the hand 5414
14:48 d Israel out of the hands of them that 5337
17:35 and smote him, and d it out of his mouth: 5337
17:37 The LORD that d me out of the paw of 5337
23: 7 Saul said, God hath d him into mine hand; 5234
23:14 every day, but God d him not into his hand. 5414
24:10 d thee to day into mine hand in the cave: 5414
24:18 forasmuch as when the LORD had d me 5462
26: 8 God hath d thine enemy into thine hand 5462
26:23 for the LORD d thee into my hand to day, 5414
30:23 d the company that came against us into 5414
2Sa 3: 8 and have not d thee into the hand of David, 4672
10:10 the rest of the people he d into the hand of 5414
12: 7 and I d thee out of the hand of Saul; 5337
16: 8 the LORD hath d the kingdom into 5414
18:28 which hath d up the men that lift up their 5462
19: 9 he d us out of the hand of the Philistines; 4422
21: 6 Let seven men of his sons be d unto us, and 5414
21: 9 he d them into the hands of the Gibeonites, 5414
22: 1 d him out of the hand of all his enemies, 5337
22:18 He d me from my strong enemy, and 5337
22:20 he d me, because he delighted in me. 2502
22:44 Thou also hast d me from the strivings of 6403
22:49 thou hast d me from the violent man. 5337
1Ki 3:17 I was d of a child with her in the house. 3205
3:18 to pass the third day after that I was d, 3205
3:18 was delivered, that this woman was d also: 3205
13:26 the LORD hath d him unto the lion, 5414
15:18 and d them into the hand of his servants: 5414
17:23 into the house, and d him unto his mother: 5414
2Ki 12:15 into whose hand they d the money to be 5414
13: 3 he d them into the hand of Hazael king of 5414
17:20 and d them into the hand of spoilers, 5414
18:30 this city shall not be d into the hand of 5414
18:33 d at all his land out of the hand of 5337+5337
18:34 have they d Samaria out of mine hand? 5337
18:35 that have d their country out of mine hand, 5337
19:10 Jerusalem shall not be d into the hand of 5414
19:11 them utterly: and shalt thou be d? 5337
19:12 Have the gods of the nations d them which 5337
22: 7 of the money that was d into their hand, 5414
22: 9 have d it into the hand of them that do 5414
22:10 saying, Hilkiah the priest hath d me a book. 5414
1Ch 5:20 the Hagarites were d into their hand, and 5414
11:14 and d it, and slew the Philistines; 5337
16: 7 on that day David d first this psalm to 5414
19:11 the rest of the people he d unto the hand of 5414
2Ch 13:16 and God d them into their hand. 5414
16: 8 on the LORD, he d them into thine hand. 5414
18:14 prosper, and they shall be d into your hand. 5414
23: 9 Moreover Jehoiada the priest d to 5414
24:24 the LORD d a very great host into their 5414
28: 5 Wherefore the LORD his God d him into 5414
28: 5 he was also d into the hand of the king of 5414
28: 9 he hath d them into your hand, and ye have 5414
29: 8 Jerusalem, and he hath d them to trouble, 5414
32:17 have not d their people out of mine hand, 5337
34: 9 they d the money that was brought into 5414
34:15 And Hilkiah d the book to Shaphan. 5414
34:17 and have d it into the hand of the overseers, 5414
Ezr 5:14 they were d unto one, whose name was 3052
8:31 he d us from the hand of the enemy, and 5337
8:36 they d the king's commissions unto 5414
9: 7 been d into the hand of the kings of 5414
Est 6: 9 horse be d to the hand of one of the king's 5414
Job 16:11 God hath d me to the ungodly, and 5462
22:30 and it is d by the pureness of thine hands. 4422
23: 7 so should I be d for ever from my judge. 6403
29:12 Because I d the poor that cried, and 4422
Ps 7: 4 I have d him that without cause is mine 2502
18: T d him from the hand of all his enemies, 5337
18:17 He d me from my strong enemy, and 5337
18:19 he d me, because he delighted in me. 2502
18:43 Thou hast d me from the strivings of 6403
18:48 thou hast d me from the violent man. 5337
22: 5 They cried unto thee, and were d: 4422
33:16 a mighty man is not d by much strength. 5337
34: 4 he heard me, and d me from all my fears. 5337
54: 7 For he hath d me out of all trouble: and 5337
55:18 He hath d my soul in peace from the battle 6299
56:13 For thou hast d my soul from death: wilt 5337
60: 5 That thy beloved may be d; save with thy 2502
69:14 let me be d from them that hate me, and 5337
78:42 nor the day when he d them from 6299
78:61 d his strength into captivity, and his glory 5414
81: 6 the burden: his hands were d from the pots. 5674
81: 7 Thou calledst in trouble, and I d thee; 2502
86:13 thou hast d my soul from the lowest hell. 5337
107: 6 and he d them out of their distresses. 5337
107:20 and d them from their destructions. 4422
108: 6 That thy beloved may be d: save with thy 2502
116: 8 For thou hast d my soul from death, mine 2502
Pr 11: 8 The righteous is d out of trouble, and 2502
11: 9 but through knowledge shall the just be d. 2502
11:21 but the seed of the righteous shall be d. 4422
28:26 but whoso walketh wisely, he shall be d. 4422
Ecc 9:15 wise man, and he by his wisdom d the city; 4422
Isa 20: 6 whither we flee for help to be d from 5337
29:12 the book is d to him that is not learned, 5414
34: 2 he hath d them to the slaughter. 5414
36:15 this city shall not be d into the hand of 5414
36:18 Hath any of the gods of the nations d his 5337
36:19 and have they d Samaria out of my hand? 5337
36:20 that have d their land out of my hand, 5337
37:11 them utterly; and shalt thou be d? 5337
37:12 Have the gods of the nations d them which 5337

Isa 38:17 thou hast in love to my soul d it from the pit NIH
49:24 from the mighty, or the lawful captive d? 4422
49:25 and the prey of the terrible shall be d: 4422
66: 7 her pain came, she was d of a man child. 4422
Jer 7:10 say, We are d to do all these abominations? 5337
20:13 for he hath d the soul of the poor from 5337
32: 4 shall surely be d into the hand of the king 5414
32:16 Now when I had d the evidence of 5414
32:36 It shall be d into the hand of the king of 5414
34: 3 shalt surely be taken, and d into his hand; 5414
37:17 thou shalt be d into the hand of the king of 5414
46:24 she shall be d into the hand of the people of 5414
La 1:14 to fall, the Lord hath d me into their hands, 5414
Eze 3:19 die in his iniquity; but thou hast d thy soul. 5337
3:21 he is warned; also thou hast d thy soul. 5337
14:16 they only shall be d, but the land shall be 5337
14:18 but they only shall be d themselves. 5337
16:21 d them to cause them to pass through 5414
16:27 d thee unto the will of them that hate thee, 5414
17:15 or shall he break the covenant, and be d? 4422
23: 9 Wherefore I have d her into the hand of her 5414
31:11 d him into the hand of the mighty one of 5414
31:14 for they are all d unto death, to the nether 5414
32:20 she is d to the sword: draw her and all her 5414
33: 9 die in his iniquity; but thou hast d thy soul. 5337
34:27 d them out of the hand of those that served 5337
Da 3:28 d his servants that trusted in him, and 7804
6:27 who hath d Daniel from the power of 7804
12: 1 at that time thy people shall be d, every one 4422
Joel 2:32 call on the name of the LORD shall be d: 4422
Am 1: 9 they d up the whole captivity to Edom, 5462
9: 1 and he that escapeth of them shall not be d. 4422
Ob 1:14 neither shouldest thou have d up those of 5462
Mic 4:10 go even to Babylon; there shalt thou be d; 5337
Hab 2: 9 that he may be d from the power of evil! 5337
Mal 3:15 set up; yea, they that tempt God are even d. 4422
Mt 11:27 All things are d unto me of my Father: and 3860
18:34 was wroth, and d him to the tormentors, 3860
25:14 own servants, and d unto them his goods. 3860
27: 2 and d him to Pontius Pilate the governor. 3860
27:18 For he knew that for envy they had d him. 3860
27:26 scourged Jesus, he d him to be crucified. 3860
27:58 Then Pilate commanded the body to be d. 591
Mk 7:13 through your tradition, which ye have d: 3860
9:31 The Son of man is d into the hands of men, 3860
10:33 the Son of man shall be d unto the chief 3860
15: 1 and carried him away, and d him to Pilate. 3860
15:10 For he knew that the chief priests had d 3860
15:15 released Barabbas unto them, and d Jesus, 3860
Lk 1: 2 Even as they d them unto us, which from 3860
1:57 full time came that she should be d; 5088
1:74 that we being d out of the hand of our 4506
2: 6 were accomplished that she should be d. 5088
4: 6 for that is d unto me; and to whomsoever I 3860
4:17 And there was d unto him the book of 1929
7:15 to speak. And he d him to his mother. 1325
9:42 the child, and d him again to his father. 591
9:44 for the Son of man shall be d into the hands 3860
10:22 All things are d to me of my Father: and 3860
12:58 give diligence that thou mayest be d from 525
18:32 For he shall be d unto the Gentiles, and 3860
19:13 and d them ten pounds, and said unto them, 1325
23:25 had desired; but he d Jesus to their will. 3860
24: 7 The Son of man must be d into the hands of 3860
24:20 our rulers d him to be condemned to death, 3860
Jn 16:21 but as soon as she is d of the child, 1080
18:30 we would not have d him up unto thee. 3860
18:35 and the chief priests have d thee unto me: 3860
18:36 that I should not be d to the Jews: 3860
19:11 he that d me unto thee hath the greater sin. 3860
19:16 Then d he him therefore unto them to be 3860
Ac 2:23 being d by the determinate counsel and 1560
3:13 whom ye d up, and denied him in 3860
6:14 shall change the customs which Moses d 3860
7:10 And d him out of all his afflictions, and 1807
12: 4 d him to four quaternions of soldiers to 3860
12:11 and hath d me out of the hand of Herod, 1807
15:30 the multitude together, they d the epistle: 1929
16: 4 they d them the decrees for to keep, 3860
23:33 to Cesarea, and d the epistle to the governor, 325
27: 1 they d Paul and certain other prisoners unto 3860
28:16 the centurion d the prisoners to the captain 3860
28:17 yet was I d prisoner from Jerusalem into 3860
Ro 4:25 Who was d for our offences, and was raised 3860
6:17 that form of doctrine which was d you. 3860
7: 6 But now we are d from the law, that being 2673
8:21 Because the creature itself also shall be d 1659
8:32 not his own Son, but d him up for us all, 3860
15:31 That I may be d from them that do not 4506
1Co 11: 2 keep the ordinances, as I d them to you. 3860
11:23 of the Lord that which also I d unto you, 3860
15: 3 For I d unto you first of all that which I 3860
15:24 when he shall have d up the kingdom to 3860
2Co 1:10 Who d us from so great a death, and 4506
4:11 For we which live are alway d unto death 3860
Col 1:13 Who hath d us from the power of darkness, 4506
1Th 1:10 which d us from the wrath to come. 4506
2Th 3: 2 And that we may be d from unreasonable 4506
1Ti 1:20 whom I have d unto Satan, that they may 3860
2Ti 3:11 but out of them all the Lord d me. 4506
4:17 and I was d out of the mouth of the lion. 4506
Heb 11:11 was d of a child when she was past age, 5088
2Pe 2: 4 to hell, and d them into chains of darkness, 3860
2: 7 And d just Lot, vexed with the filthy 4506
2:21 from the holy commandment d unto them. 3860
Jude 1: 3 the faith which was once d unto the saints. 3860
Rev 12: 2 travailing in birth, and pained to be d. 5088
12: 4 before the woman which was ready to be d, 5088
20:13 and hell d up the dead which were in them: 1325

DELIVEREDST (3) [DELIVER]
Ne 9:27 Therefore thou d them into the hand of 5414
Mt 25:20 saying, Lord, thou d unto me five talents: 3860
25:22 and said, Lord, thou d unto me two talents: 3860

DELIVERER (10) [DELIVER]
Jdg 3: 9 the LORD raised up a d to the children of 3467
3:15 the LORD raised them up a d, Ehud 3467
18:28 there was no d, because it was far from 5337
2Sa 22: 2 is my rock, and my fortress, and my d; 6403
Ps 18: 2 is my rock, and my fortress, and my d; 6403
40:17 thou art my help and my d; make no 6403
70: 5 thou art my help and my d; O LORD, 6403
144: 2 my high tower, and my d; my shield, and 6403
Ac 7:35 a d by the hand of the angel which 3086
Ro 11:26 There shall come out of Sion the D, and 4506

DELIVEREST (2) [DELIVER]
Ps 35:10 which d the poor from him that is too 5337
Mic 6:14 that which thou d will I give up to 6403

DELIVERETH (13) [DELIVER]
Job 36:15 He d the poor in his affliction, and 2502
Ps 18:48 He d me from mine enemies: yea, 6403
34: 7 about them that fear him, and d them. 2502
34:17 and d them out of all their troubles. 5337
34:19 but the LORD d him out of them all. 5337
97:10 he d them out of the hand of the wicked. 5337
144:10 who d David his servant from the hurtful 6475
Pr 10: 2 but righteousness d from death. 5337
11: 4 of wrath: but righteousness d from death. 5337
14:25 A true witness d souls: but a deceitful 5337
31:24 selleth it; and d girdles unto the merchant. 5414
Isa 42:22 they are for a prey, and none d; for a spoil, 5337
Da 6:27 He d and rescueth, and he worketh signs 7804

DELIVERING (3) [DELIVER]
Lk 21:12 persecute you, d you up to the synagogues, 3860
Ac 22: 4 binding and d into prisons both men and 3860
26:17 D thee from the people, and from 1807

DELIVERY (1) [DELIVER]
Isa 26:17 that draweth near the time of her d, is in 3205

DELUSION (1) [DELUSIONS]
2Th 2:11 for this cause God shall send them strong d, 4106

DELUSIONS (1) [DELUSION]
Isa 66: 4 I also will choose their d, and will bring 8586

DEMAND (4) [DEMANDED]
Job 38: 3 for I will d of thee, and answer thou me. 7592
40: 7 I will d of thee, and declare thou unto me. 7592
42: 4 I will d of thee, and declare thou unto me. 7592
Da 4:17 and the d by the word of the holy ones: 7595

DEMANDED (7) [DEMAND]
Ex 5:14 had set over them, were beaten, and d, 559
2Sa 11: 7 David d of him how Joab did, and how 7592
Da 2:27 The secret which the king hath d cannot 7593
Mt 2: 4 he d of them where Christ should be born. 4441
Lk 3:14 And the soldiers likewise d of him, saying, 1905
17:20 And when he was d of the Pharisees, 1905
Ac 21:33 and d who he was, and what he had done. 4441

DEMAS (3)
Col 4:14 the beloved physician, and D, greet you. 1214
2Ti 4:10 For D hath forsaken me, having loved this 1214
Phm 1:24 Marcus, Aristarchus, D, Lucas, 1214

DEMETRIUS (3)
Ac 19:24 For a certain man named D, a silversmith, 1216
19:38 Wherefore if D, and the craftsmen which 1216
3Jn 1:12 D hath good report of all men, and of 1216

DEMON; DEMONS See DEVIL; DEVILS

DEMONSTRATION (1)
1Co 2: 4 but in d of the Spirit and of power: 585

DEN (19) [DENS]
Ps 10: 9 He lieth in wait secretly as a lion in his d: 5520
Isa 11: 8 shall put his hand on the cockatrice' d. 3975
Jer 7:11 become a d of robbers in your eyes? 4631
9:11 make Jerusalem heaps, and a d of dragons; 4583
10:22 cities of Judah desolate, and a d of dragons. 4583
Da 6: 7 O king, he shall be cast into the d of lions. 1358
6:12 O king, shall be cast into the d of lions? 1358
6:16 and cast him into the d of lions. 1358
6:17 and laid upon the mouth of the d; 1358
6:19 and went in haste unto the d of lions. 1358
6:20 when he came to the d, he cried with a 1358
6:23 they should take Daniel up out of the d. 1358
6:23 So Daniel was taken up out of the d, and 1358
6:24 and they cast them into the d of lions, them, 1358
6:24 or ever they came at the bottom of the d. 1358
Am 3: 4 will a young lion cry out of his d, if he 4585
Mt 21:13 but ye have made it a d of thieves. 4693
Mk 11:17 but ye have made it a d of thieves. 4693
Lk 19:46 but ye have made it a d of thieves. 4693

DENARII See PENCE

DENARIUS See PENNY

DENIED (19) [DENY]
Ge 18:15 Sarah d, saying, I laughed not; for she was 3584
1Ki 20: 7 and for my gold; and I d him not. 4513
Job 31:28 for I should have d the God that is above. 3584
Mt 26:70 But he d before them all, saying, I know not 720
26:72 And again he d with an oath, I do not know 720
Mk 14:68 But he d, saying, I know not, neither 720
14:70 And he d it again. And a little after, they that 720
Lk 8:45 When all d, Peter and they that were with 720
12: 9 But he that denieth me before men shall be d 533
22:57 And he d him, saying, Woman, I know him 720
Jn 1:20 And he confessed, and d not; but confessed, 720
13:38 shall not crow, till thou hast d me thrice. 533

Jn 18:25 of his disciples? He **d** *it,* and said, I am not. 720
18:27 Peter then **d** again: and immediately *the* cock 720
Ac 3:13 and **d** him in the presence of Pilate, 720
3:14 But ye **d** the Holy One and the Just, and 720
1Ti 5: 8 he hath **d** the faith, and is worse than an 720
Rev 2:13 fast my name, and hast not **d** my faith, 720
3: 8 hast kept my word, and hast not **d** my name. 720

DENIETH (4) [DENY]
Lk 12: 9 But he that **d** me before men shall be denied 720
1Jn 2:22 is a liar but he that **d** that Jesus is the Christ? 720
2:22 is antichrist, that **d** the Father and the Son. 720
2:23 Whosoever **d** the Son, the same hath not 720

DENOUNCE (1)
Dt 30:18 I **d** unto you *this* day, that ye shall surely 5046

DENOUNCED See UPBRAID; UPBRAIDED; UPBRAIDETH

DENS (9) [DEN]
Jdg 6: 2 them the **d** which *are* in the mountains, 4492
Job 37: 8 the beasts go into **d**, and remain in their 695
38:40 When they couch in *their* **d**, *and* abide in 4585
Ps 104:22 and lay them down in their **d**. 4585
SS 4: 8 of Shenir and Hermon, from the lions' **d**, 4585
Isa 32:14 the forts and towers shall be for **d** for ever, 4631
Na 2:12 his holes *with* prey, and his **d** *with* ravin. 4585
Heb 11:38 and *in* **d** and caves of the earth. 4693
Rev 6:15 every free *man,* hid themselves in the **d** and 4693

DENY (24) [DENIED, DENIETH, DENYING]
Jos 24:27 a witness unto you, lest ye **d** your God. 3584
1Ki 2:16 I ask one petition of thee, **d** me not. 6440+7725
Job 8:18 *it* shall **d** him, *saying,* I have not seen thee. 3584
Pr 30: 7 of thee; **d** me *them* not before I die: 4513
30: 9 Lest I be full, and **d** *thee,* and say, Who *is* 3584
Mt 10:33 But whosoever shall **d** me before men, 720
10:33 him will I also **d** before my Father which is 720
16:24 let him **d** himself, and take up his cross, and 533
26:34 before *the* cock crow, thou shalt **d** me thrice. 533
26:35 I should die with thee, *yet* will I not **d** thee. 533
26:75 Before *the* cock crow, thou shalt **d** me thrice. 533
Mk 8:34 let him **d** himself, and take up his cross, and 533
14:30 *the* cock crow twice, thou shalt **d** me thrice. 533
14:31 die with thee, I will not **d** thee in any wise. 533
14:72 *the* cock crow twice, thou shalt **d** me thrice. 533
Lk 9:23 let him **d** himself, and take up his cross 533
20:27 which **d** that there is any resurrection; 483
22:34 before that thou shalt thrice **d** that *thou* 533
22:61 Before *the* cock crow, thou shalt **d** me thrice. 533
Ac 4:16 that dwell in Jerusalem; and we cannot **d** *it.* 720
2Ti 2:12 we shall also reign with *him:* if we **d** *him,* he 720
2:12 with *him:* if we deny *him,* he also will **d** us: 720
2:13 *yet* he abideth faithful: he cannot **d** himself. 720
Tit 1:16 but in works they **d** *him,* being abominable, 720

DENYING (4) [DENY]
2Ti 3: 5 a form of godliness, but **d** the power thereof: 720
Tit 2:12 Teaching us that **d** ungodliness and worldly 720
2Pe 2: 1 even **d** the Lord that bought them, and 720
Jude 1: 4 and **d** the only Lord God, and our Lord Jesus 720

DEPART (125) [DEPARTED, DEPARTETH, DEPARTING, DEPARTURE]
Ge 13: 9 or if *thou* **d** *to* the right hand, then I will go NIH
49:10 The sceptre shall not **d** from Judah, nor a 5493
Ex 8:11 the frogs shall **d** from thee, and from thy 5493
8:29 the swarms *of flies* may **d** from Pharaoh, 5493
18:27 Moses let his father in law **d**; and he went 7971
21:22 so that her fruit **d** *from her,* and yet no 3318
33: 1 **D**, *and* go up hence, thou and 1980+4480
Lev 25:41 *then* shall he **d** from thee, *both* he and 3318
Nu 10:30 I will **d** to mine own land, and to my 1980
16:26 saying, **D**, I pray you, from the tents of 5493
Dt 4: 9 lest they **d** from thy heart all the days of thy 5493
9: 7 from the day that thou didst **d** out of 3318
Jos 1: 8 This book of the law shall not **d** out of thy 4185
24:28 So Joshua **let** the people **d**, every man unto 7971
Jdg 6:18 **D** not hence, I pray thee, until I come unto 4185
7: 3 him return and **d early** from mount Gilead. 6852
19: 5 early in the morning, that he rose up to **d**: 1980
19: 7 when the man rose up to **d**, his father in law 1980
19: 8 early in the morning on the fifth day to **d**: 1980
19: 9 when the man rose up to **d**, he, and 1980
1Sa 15: 6 Saul said unto the Kenites, Go, **d**, get you 5493
22: 5 **d**, and get thee *into* the land of Judah. 1980
29:10 up early in the morning, and have light, **d**. 1980
29:11 his men rose up early to **d** in the morning, 1980
30:22 that they may lead *them* away, and **d**. 1980
2Sa 7:15 my mercy shall not **d away** from him, as I 5493
11:12 to day also, and to morrow I will let thee **d**. 7971
12:10 the sword shall never **d** from thine house, 5493
15:14 make speed to **d**, lest he overtake us 1980
20:21 deliver him only, and I will **d** from the city. 1980
22:23 *as for* his statutes, I did not **d** from them. 5493
1Ki 11:21 Hadad said to Pharaoh, **Let** me **d**, that I 7971
12: 5 **D** yet *for* three days, then come again to 1980
12:24 the word of the LORD, and returned to **d**, 1980
15:19 king of Israel, that he may **d** from me. 5927
2Ch 16: 3 king of Israel, that he may **d** from me. 5927
18:31 and God moved them *to* **d** from him. NIH
35:15 they might not **d** from their service; 5493
Job 7:19 How long wilt thou not **d** from me, nor let 8159
15:30 He shall not **d** out of darkness; the flame 5493
20:28 The increase of his house shall **d**, *and* 1540
21:14 Therefore they say unto God, **D** from us; 5493
22:17 Which said unto God, **D** from us: and 5493
28:28 and to **d** from evil *is* understanding. 5493
Ps 6: 8 **D** from me, all ye workers of iniquity; 5493
34:14 **D** from evil, and do good; seek peace, and 5493
37:27 **D** from evil, and do good; and dwell for 5493
55:11 and guile **d** not from her streets. 4185
101: 4 A froward heart shall **d** from me: I will not 5493
Ps 119:115 **D** from me, ye evildoers: for I will keep 5493
139:19 **d** from me therefore, ye bloody men. 5493
Pr 3: 7 fear the LORD, and **d** from evil. 5493
3:21 My son, let not them **d** from thine eyes: 3868
4:21 Let them not **d** from thine eyes; keep them 3868
5: 7 and **d** not from the words of my mouth. 5493
13:14 of life, to **d** from the snares of death. 5493
13:19 but *it is* abomination to fools to **d** from evil. 5493
14:27 of life, to **d** from the snares of death. 5493
15:24 the wise, that *he* may **d** from hell beneath. 5493
16: 6 by the fear of the LORD *men* **d** from evil. 5493
16:17 The highway of the upright *is* to **d** from 5493
17:13 for good, evil shall not **d** from his house. 4185
22: 6 and when he is old, he will not **d** from it. 5493
27:22 *yet* will not his foolishness **d** from him. 5493
Isa 11:13 The envy also of Ephraim shall **d**, and 5493
14:25 shall his yoke **d** from off them, and 5493
14:25 and his burden **d** from off their shoulders. 5493
52:11 **D** ye, depart ye, go ye out from thence, 5493
52:11 Depart ye, **d** ye, go ye out from thence, 5493
54:10 For the mountains shall **d**, and the hills be 4185
54:10 my kindness shall not **d** from thee, 4185
59:21 shall not **d** out of thy mouth, nor out of 4185
Jer 6: 8 O Jerusalem, lest my soul **d** from thee; 3363
17:13 they that **d** from me shall be written in 5493
31:36 If those ordinances **d** from before me, 4185
32:40 their hearts, that *they* shall not **d** from me. 5493
37: 9 Chaldeans shall **surely d** from us: 1980+1980
37: 9 surely depart from us: for they shall not **d**. 1980
50: 3 they shall **d**, both man and beast. 1980
La 4:15 They cried unto them, **D** ye; *it is* unclean; 5493
4:15 **d**, depart, touch not, when they fled away 5493
4:15 depart, **d**, touch not, when they fled away 5493
Eze 16:42 my jealousy shall **d** from thee, and I will be 5493
Hos 9:12 woe also to them when I **d** from them! 5493
Mic 2:10 Arise ye, and **d**; for this *is* not *your* rest: 1980
Zec 10:11 and the sceptre of Egypt shall **d away**. 5493
Mt 7:23 knew you: **d** from me, ye that work iniquity. 672
8:18 he gave commandment to **d** unto the other 565
8:34 they besought *him* that he would **d** out of 3327
10:14 when ye **d** out of that house or city, 1831
14:16 But Jesus said unto them, They need not **d**; 565
25:41 **D** from me, ye cursed, into everlasting fire, 4198
Mk 5:17 And they began to pray him to **d out** of their 565
6:10 there abide till ye **d** from that place. 1831
6:11 nor hear you, when ye **d** thence, 1607
Lk 2:29 now lettest thou thy servant **d** in peace, 630
4:42 stayed him, that *he* should not **d** from them. 4198
5: 8 down at Jesus' knees, saying, **D** from me; 1831
8:37 round about besought him to **d** from them; 565
9: 4 ye enter into, there abide, and thence **d**. 1831
12:59 I tell thee, thou shalt not **d** thence, till thou 1831
13:27 **d** from me, all *ye* workers of iniquity. 868
13:31 saying unto him, Get *thee* out, and **d** hence: 4198
21:21 let them which are in the midst of it **d out**; 1633
Jn 7: 3 said unto him, **D** hence, and go into Judea, 3327
13: 1 should **d** out of this world unto the Father, 3327
16: 7 but if I **d**, I will send him unto you. 4198
Ac 1: 4 commanded them that *they* should not **d** 5563
16:36 you go: now therefore **d**, and go in peace. 1831
16:39 and desired *them* to **d out** of the city. 1831
18: 2 that Claudius had commanded all Jews to **d** 5563
20: 7 unto them, ready to **d** on the morrow; 1826
22:21 And he said unto me, **D**: for I will send thee 4198
23:22 the chief captain then **let** the young man **d**, 630
25: 4 and that he himself would **d** shortly *thither.* 1607
27:12 the more part advised to **d** thence also, 321
1Co 7:10 Let not the wife **d** from *her* husband: 5563
7:11 But and if she **d**, let her remain unmarried, 5563
7:15 But if the unbelieving **d**, let him depart. 5563
7:15 But if the unbelieving depart, let him **d**. 5563
2Co 12: 8 the Lord thrice, that it might **d** from me. 868
Php 1:23 having a desire to **d**, and to be with Christ; 360
1Ti 4: 1 that in the latter times some shall **d from** 868
2Ti 2:19 nameth the name of Christ **d** from iniquity. 868
Jas 2:16 **D** in peace, be you warmed and filled; 5217

DEPARTED (217) [DEPART]
Ge 12: 4 So Abram **d**, as the LORD had spoken 1980
12: 4 and five years old when he **d** out of Haran. 3318
14:12 who dwelt in Sodom, and his goods, and **d**. 1980
21:14 she **d**, and wandered in the wilderness of 1980
24:10 camels of the camels of his master, and **d**; 1980
26:17 Isaac **d** thence, and pitched his tent in 1980
26:31 them away, and they **d** from him in peace. 1980
31:40 by night; and my sleep **d** from mine eyes. 5074
31:55 and Laban **d**, and returned unto his place. 1980
37:17 the man said, They are **d** hence; for I heard 5265
42:26 their asses with the corn, and **d** thence. 1980
45:24 So he sent his brethren away, and they **d**: 1980
Ex 19: 2 For they were **d** from Rephidim, and 5265
33:11 a young man, **d** not out of the tabernacle. 4185
35:20 of Israel **d** from the presence of Moses. 3318
Lev 13:58 if the plague be **d** from them, then it shall 5493
Nu 10:33 they **d** from the mount of the LORD three 5265
12: 9 was kindled against them; and he **d**. 1980
12:10 the cloud **d** from off the tabernacle; and 5493
14: 9 their defence is **d** from them, and 5493
14:44 and Moses, **d** not out of the camp. 4185
22: 7 the elders of Midian **d** with the rewards of 1980
33: 3 they **d** from Rameses in the first month, 5265
33: 6 they **d** from Succoth, and pitched in Etham, 5265
33: 8 they **d** from before *Pi*-hahiroth, and 5265
33:13 they **d** from Dophkah, and encamped in 5265
33:15 they **d** from Rephidim, and pitched in 5265
33:17 they **d** from Kibroth-hattaavah, and 5265
33:18 they **d** from Hazeroth, and pitched in 5265
33:19 they **d** from Rithmah, and pitched at 5265
33:20 they **d** from Rimmon-parez, and pitched in 5265
33:27 they **d** from Tahath, and pitched at Tarah. 5265
33:30 they **d** from Hashmonah, and encamped at 5265
33:31 they **d** from Moseroth, and pitched in 5265
33:35 they **d** from Ebronah, and encamped at 5265
33:41 they **d** from mount Hor, and pitched in 5265
33:42 they **d** from Zalmonah, and pitched in 5265
Nu 33:43 they **d** from Punon, and pitched in Oboth. 5265
33:44 they **d** from Oboth, and pitched in 5265
33:45 they **d** from Iim, and pitched in Dibon-gad. 5265
33:48 they **d** from the mountains of Abarim, and 5265
Dt 1:19 when we **d** from Horeb, we went *through* 5265
24: 2 when she is **d** out of his house, she may go 3318
Jos 2:21 she sent them away, and they **d**: and 1980
22: 9 **d** from the children of Israel out of Shiloh, 1980
Jdg 6:21 the angel of the LORD **d** out of his sight. 1980
9:55 was dead, they **d** every man unto his place. 1980
16:20 he wist not that the LORD was **d** from 5493
17: 8 the man **d** out of the city from 1980
18: 7 the five men **d**, and came to Laish, and 1980
18:21 So they turned and **d**, and put the little ones 1980
19:10 he rose up and **d**, and came over against 1980
21:24 the children of Israel **d** thence at that 1980+4480
1Sa 4:21 saying, The glory is **d** from Israel: 1540
4:22 she said, The glory is **d** from Israel: for 1540
6: 6 did they not let the people go, and they **d**? 1980
10: 2 When thou art **d** from me to day, then 1980
15: 6 So the Kenites **d** from among 5493
16:14 the spirit of the LORD **d** from Saul, and 5493
16:23 was well, and the evil spirit **d** from him. 5493
18:12 was with him, and was **d** from Saul. 5493
20:42 he arose and **d**: and Jonathan went *into* 1980
22: 1 David therefore **d** thence, and 1980+4480
22: 5 David **d**, and came *into* the forest of 1980
23:13 arose and **d** out of Keilah, and 3318
28:15 God is **d** from me, and answereth me no 5493
28:16 seeing the LORD is **d** from thee, and 5493
2Sa 6:19 a flagon *of wine.* So all the people **d** every 1980
11: 8 Uriah **d** out of the king's house, and 3318
12:15 Nathan **d** unto his house. And the LORD 1980
17:21 it came to pass, after they were **d**, that they 1980
19:24 from the day the king **d** until the day he 1980
22:22 and have not **wickedly d** from my God. 7561
1Ki 12: 5 then come again to me. And the people **d**. 1980
12:16 David. So Israel **d** unto their tents. 1980
14:17 wife arose, and **d**, and came to Tirzah: 1980
19:19 So he **d** thence, and found Elisha the son of 1980
20: 9 the messengers **d**, and brought him word 1980
20:36 behold, as soon as thou art **d** from me, a 1980
20:36 as soon as he was **d** from him, a lion found 1980
20:38 So the prophet **d**, and waited for the king 1980
2Ki 1: 4 gone up, but shalt surely die. And Elijah **d**. 1980
3: 3 made Israel to sin; he **d** not therefrom. 5493
3:27 they **d** from him, and returned to *their own* 5265
5: 5 he **d**, and took with him ten talents of 1980
5:19 Go in peace. So he **d** from him a little way. 1980
5:24 and he let the men go, and they **d**. 1980
8:14 So he **d** from Elisha, and came to his 1980
10:12 he arose and **d**, and came *to* Samaria. *And* as 935
10:15 when he was **d** thence, he lighted on 1980+4480
10:29 Israel to sin, Jehu **d** not from after them, 5493
10:31 *for* he **d** not from the sins of Jeroboam, 5493
13: 2 made Israel to sin; he **d** not therefrom. 5493
13: 6 Nevertheless they **d** not from the sins of 5493
13:11 he **d** not from all the sins of Jeroboam 5493
14:24 he **d** not from all the sins of Jeroboam 5493
15: 9 he **d** not from the sins of Jeroboam the son 5493
15:18 he **d** not all his days from the sins of 5493
15:24 he **d** not from the sins of Jeroboam the son 5493
15:28 he **d** not from the sins of Jeroboam the son 5493
17:22 which he did; they **d** not from them; 5493
18: 6 *and* **d** not from following him, but kept his 5493
19: 8 for he had heard that he was **d** from 5265
19:36 So Sennacherib king of Assyria **d**, and 5265
1Ch 16:43 all the people **d** every man to his house: 1980
21: 4 Wherefore Joab **d**, and went throughout all 3318
2Ch 8:15 they **d** not *from* the commandment of 5493
10: 5 unto me after three days. And the people **d**. 1980
20:32 the way of Asa his father, and **d** not from it, 5493
21:20 eight years, and **d** without being desired. 1980
24:25 when they were **d** from him, (for they left 1980
34:33 *And* all his days they **d** not from following 5493
Ezr 8:31 we **d** from the river of Ahava on the twelfth 5265
Ne 9:19 the pillar of the cloud **d** not from them by 5493
Ps 18:21 and have not **wickedly d** from my God. 7561
34: T who drove him away, and he **d**. 1980
105:38 Egypt was glad when they **d**: for the fear of 3318
119:102 I have not **d** from thy judgments: for thou 5493
Isa 7:17 from the day that Ephraim **d** from Judah; 5493
37: 8 for he had heard that he was **d** from 5265
37:37 So Sennacherib king of Assyria **d**, and 5265
38:12 Mine age is **d**, and is removed from me as a 5265
Jer 29: 2 and the smiths, were **d** from Jerusalem;) 3318
37: 5 tidings of them, they **d** from Jerusalem. 5927
41:10 and **d** to go over to the Ammonites. 1980
41:17 they **d**, and dwelt in the habitation of 1980
La 1: 6 the daughter of Zion all her beauty is **d**: 3318
Eze 6: 9 which hath **d** from me, and with their eyes, 5493
10:18 the glory of the LORD **d** from off 3318
Da 4:31 it is spoken; The kingdom is **d** from thee. 5709
Hos 10: 5 for the glory thereof, because it is **d** from it. 1540
Mal 2: 8 ye are **d** out of the way; ye have caused 5493
Mt 2: 9 When they had heard the king, they **d**; and 4198
2:12 they **d** into their own country another way. 402
2:13 And when they were **d**, behold, *the* angel of 402
2:14 and his mother by night, and **d** into Egypt: 402
4:12 John was cast into prison, he **d** into Galilee; 402
9: 7 And he arose, and **d** to his house. 565
9:27 And when Jesus **d** thence, two blind men 3855
9:31 But they, when they were **d**, spread abroad 1831
11: 1 he **d** thence to teach and to preach in their 3327
11: 7 And as they **d**, Jesus began to say unto 4198
12: 9 And when he was **d** thence, he went into 3327
13:53 had finished these parables, he **d** thence. 3332
14:13 When Jesus heard *of it,* he **d** thence by ship 402
15:21 and **d** into the coasts of Tyre and Sidon. 402
15:29 And Jesus **d** from thence, and came nigh 3327
16: 4 the prophet Jonas. And he left them, and **d**. 565
17:18 rebuked the devil; and he **d** out of him: 1831
19: 1 he **d** from Galilee, and came into the coasts 3332
19:15 he laid *his* hands on them, and **d** thence. 4198
20:29 And as they **d** from Jericho, a great 1607

Mt 24: 1 And Jesus went out, and **d** from the temple: *4198*
27: 5 and **d**, and went and hanged himself. *402*
27:60 stone to the door of the sepulchre, and **d**. *565*
28: 8 And they **d** quickly from the sepulchre with *1831*
Mk 1:35 and **d** into a solitary place, and there prayed. *565*
1:42 immediately the leprosy **d** from him, and *565*
5:20 And he **d**, and began to publish in Decapolis *565*
6:32 And they **d** into a desert place by ship *565*
6:46 them away, he **d** into a mountain to pray. *565*
8:13 entering into the ship again **d** to the other *565*
9:30 And they **d** thence, and passed through *1831*
Lk 1:23 were accomplished, he **d** to his own house. *565*
1:38 to thy word. And the angel **d** from her. *565*
2:37 which **d** not from the temple, but served *God* *868*
4:13 the temptation, he **d** from him for a season. *868*
4:42 was day, he **d** and went into a desert place: *1831*
5:13 And immediately the leprosy **d** from him. *565*
5:25 and **d** to his own house, glorifying God. *565*
7:24 And when the messengers of John were **d**, *565*
8:35 the man, out of whom the devils were **d**, *1831*
8:38 **d** besought him that *he* might be with him: *1831*
9: 6 And they **d**, and went through the towns, *1831*
9:33 And it came to pass, as they **d** from him, *1316*
10:30 and wounded *him,* and **d**, leaving *him* half *565*
10:35 And on the morrow when he **d**, he took out *1831*
24:12 the linen clothes laid by themselves, and **d**, *565*
Jn 4: 3 He left Judea, and **d** again into Galilee. *565*
4:43 Now after two days he **d** thence, and *1831*
5:15 The man **d**, and told the Jews that it was *565*
6:15 he **d** again into a mountain himself alone. *402*
12:36 and **d**, and did hide himself from them. *565*
Ac 5:41 And they **d** from the presence of *4198*
10: 7 the angel which spake unto Cornelius was **d**, *565*
11:25 Then **d** Barnabas to Tarsus, for to seek *1831*
12:10 and forthwith the angel **d** from him. *868*
12:17 And he **d**, and went into another place. *1831*
13: 4 forth by the Holy Ghost, **d** unto Seleucia; *2718*
13:14 But when they **d** from Perga, they came to *1330*
14:20 the next day he **d** with Barnabas to Derbe. *1831*
15:38 *them,* who **d** from them from Pamphylia, *868*
15:39 sharp *between them,* that they **d asunder** *673*
15:40 And Paul chose Silas, and **d**, *1831*
16:40 the brethren, they comforted them, and **d**. *1831*
17:15 for to come to him with all speed, they **d**. *1826*
17:33 So Paul **d** from among them. *1831*
18: 1 After these *things* Paul **d** from Athens, and *5563*
18: 7 And he **d** thence, and entered into a certain *3327*
18:23 after he had spent some time *there,* he **d**, *1831*
19: 9 he **d** from them, and separated the disciples, *868*
19:12 and the diseases **d** from them, and the evil *525*
20: 1 and **d** for to go into Macedonia. *1831*
20:11 a long while, *even* till break of day, so he **d**. *1831*
21: 5 we **d** and went *our way;* and *they* all *1831*
21: 8 next day we that were of Paul's company **d**, *1831*
22:29 Then straightway they **d** from him which *868*
28:10 and when we **d**, they laded *us* with such *321*
28:11 And after three months we **d** in a ship of *321*
28:25 they **d**, after that Paul had spoken one word, *630*
28:29 when he had said these *words,* the Jews **d**, *565*
Php 4:15 of the gospel, when I **d** from Macedonia, *1831*
2Ti 4:10 present world, and is **d** unto Thessalonica; *4198*
Phm 1:15 For perhaps he therefore **d** for a season, *5563*
Rev 6:14 And the heaven **d** as a scrole when it is *673*
18:14 And the fruits that thy soul lusted after are **d** *565*
18:14 *were* dainty and goodly are **d** from thee, *565*

DEPARTETH (8) [DEPART]
Job 27:21 The east wind carrieth him away, and he **d**: 1980
Pr 14:16 A wise *man* feareth, and **d** from evil: but 5493
Ecc 6: 4 **d** in darkness, and his name shall be 1980
Isa 59:15 he *that* **d** from evil maketh himself a prey: 5493
Jer 3:20 Surely *as* a wife treacherously **d from** her 4480
17: 5 and whose heart **d** from the LORD. 5493
Na 3: 1 all full *of* lies *and* robbery; the prey **d** not; 4185
Lk 9:39 and bruising him hardly **d** from him. *672*

DEPARTING (12) [DEPART]
Ge 35:18 to pass, as her soul was **in d** (for she died) 3318
Ex 16: 1 month after their **d** out of the land of Egypt. 3318
Isa 59:13 **d away** from our God, speaking oppression 5253
Da 9: 5 even by **d** from thy precepts and from thy 5493
9:11 even by **d**, that *they* might not obey thy 5493
Hos 1: 2 great whoredom, *d* from the LORD. NIH
Mk 6:33 And the people saw them **d**, and *5217*
7:31 **d** from the coasts of Tyre and Sidon, *1831*
Ac 13:13 and John **d** from them returned to Jerusalem. *672*
20:29 that after my **d** shall grievous wolves enter *867*
Heb 3:12 heart of unbelief, in **d** from the living God. *868*
11:22 made mention of the **d** of the children of *1841*

DEPARTURE (2) [DEPART]
Eze 26:18 that *are* in the sea shall be troubled at thy **d**. 3318
2Ti 4: 6 be offered, and the time of my **d** is at hand. *359*

DEPOSED (1)
Da 5:20 he was **d** from his kingly throne, and 5182

DEPRAVED See REPROBATE; REPROBATES

DEPRIVE See SUBVERT

DEPRIVED (3)
Ge 27:45 why should I be **d** also of you both *in* one 7921
Job 39:17 Because God hath **d** her of wisdom, 5382
Isa 38:10 I am **d** of the residue of my years. 6485

DEPTH (12) [DEEP]
Job 28:14 The **d** saith, It *is* not in me: and the sea 8415
38:16 or hast thou walked in the search of the **d**? 8415
Ps 33: 7 as a heap: he layeth up the **d** in storehouses. 8415
Pr 8:27 he set a compass upon the face of the **d**: 8415
25: 3 the earth for **d**, and the heart of kings *is* 6011
Isa 7:11 ask it either in the **d**, or in the height above. 6009
Jnh 2: 5 the **d** closed me round about, the weeds 8415
Mt 18: 6 *that* he were drowned in the **d** of the sea. *3989*
Mk 4: 5 it sprang up, because *it* had no **d** of earth: *899*
Ro 8:39 Nor height, nor **d**, nor any other creature, *899*
11:33 O the **d** of the riches both of the wisdom and *899*
Eph 3:18 *is* the breadth, and length, and **d**, and height; *899*

DEPTHS (17) [DEEP]
Ex 15: 5 The **d** have covered them: they sank into 8415
15: 8 the **d** were congealed in the heart of 8415
Dt 8: 7 **d** that spring out of the valleys and hills; 8415
Ps 68:22 I will bring *my people* again from the **d** of 4688
71:20 shalt bring me up again from the **d** of 8415
77:16 they were afraid: the **d** also were troubled. 8415
78:15 and gave *them* drink as *out of* the great **d**. 8415
106: 9 so he led them through the **d**, as *through* 8415
107:26 *to* the heaven, they go down *again to* the **d**: 8415
130: 1 Out of the **d** have I cried unto thee, 4615
Pr 3:20 By his knowledge the **d** are broken up, and 8415
8:24 When *there were* no **d**, I was brought forth; 8415
9:18 *and that* her guests *are* in the **d** of hell. 6012
Isa 51:10 that hath made the **d** of the sea a way for 4615
Eze 27:34 *be* broken by the seas in the **d** of the waters, 4615
Mic 7:19 thou wilt cast all their sins into the **d** of 4688
Rev 2:24 and which have not known the **d** of Satan, *899*

DEPUTED (1) [DEPUTY]
2Sa 15: 3 *there is* no man *d* of the king to hear thee. NIH

DEPUTIES (3) [DEPUTY]
Est 8: 9 the **d** and rulers of the provinces which *are* 6346
9: 3 and the **d**, and officers of the king, 6346
Ac 19:38 any *man,* the law is open, and there are **d**: *446*

DEPUTY (5) [DEPUTED, DEPUTIES]
1Ki 22:47 then no king in Edom: a **d** *was* king. 5324
Ac 13: 7 Which was with the **d** *of the country,* *446*
13: 8 seeking to turn away the **d** from the faith. *446*
13:12 Then the **d**, when he saw what was done, *446*
18:12 And when Gallio was the **d** of Achaia, *445*

DERBE (4)
Ac 14: 6 were ware of *it,* and fled unto Lystra and **D**, *1191*
14:20 next day he departed with Barnabas to **D**. *1191*
16: 1 Then came he to **D** and Lystra: and behold, *1191*
20: 4 and Gaius **of D**, and Timotheus; and *1190*

DERIDE (1) [DERIDED, DERISION]
Hab 1:10 they shall **d** every strong hold; for they 7832

DERIDED (2) [DERIDE]
Lk 16:14 heard all these *things:* and they **d** him. *1592*
23:35 And the rulers also with them **d** *him,* *1592*

DERISION (15) [DERIDE]
Job 30: 1 *they that are* younger than I have me in **d**, 7832
Ps 2: 4 the LORD shall have them in **d**. 3932
44:13 and a **d** to them that are round about us. 7047
59: 8 thou shalt **have** all the heathen **in d**. 3932
79: 4 and **d** to them that are round about us. 7047
119:51 The proud have **had** me greatly **in d**: 3887
Jer 20: 7 I am in **d** daily, every one mocketh me. 7814
20: 8 made a reproach unto me, and a **d**, daily. 7047
48:26 in his vomit, and he also shall be in **d**. 7814
48:27 For was not Israel a **d** unto thee? was he 7814
48:39 so shall Moab be a **d** and a dismaying to all 7814
La 3:14 I was a **d** to all my people; *and* their song 7814
Eze 23:32 thou shalt be laughed to scorn and had in **d**; 3933
36: 4 **d** to the residue of the heathen that *are* 3933
Hos 7:16 this *shall be* their **d** in the land of Egypt. 3933

DESCEND (10) [DESCENDED, DESCENDETH, DESCENDING, DESCENT]
Nu 34:11 the border shall **d**, and shall reach unto 3381
1Sa 26:10 to die; or he shall **d** into battle, and perish. 3381
Ps 49:17 his glory shall not **d** after him. 3381
Isa 5:14 and he that rejoiceth, shall **d** into it. 3381
Eze 26:20 thee down with them that **d** into the pit, 3381
31:16 down to hell with them that **d** into the pit: 3381
Mk 15:32 Let Christ the King of Israel **d** now from *2597*
Ac 11: 5 a trance I saw a vision, A certain vessel **d**, *2597*
Ro 10: 7 Or, Who shall **d** into the deep? (that is, *2597*
1Th 4:16 For the Lord himself shall **d** from heaven *2597*

DESCENDED (19) [DESCEND]
Ex 19:18 the LORD **d** upon it in fire: 3381
33: 9 the cloudy pillar **d**, and stood *at* the door of 3381
34: 5 the LORD **d** in the cloud, and stood with 3381
Dt 9:21 I cast the dust thereof into the brook that **d** 3381
Jos 2:23 **d** from the mountain, and passed over, and 3381
17: 9 the coast **d** *unto* the river Kanah, 3381
18:13 the border **d** *to* Ataroth-adar, near the hill 3381
18:16 **d** *to* the valley of Hinnom, to the side of 3381
18:16 of Jebusi on the south, and **d** *to* En-rogel, 3381
18:17 **d** *to* the stone of Bohan the son of Reuben, 3381
Ps 133: 3 *as the dew* that **d** upon the mountains of 3381
Pr 30: 4 Who hath ascended up *into* heaven, or **d**? 3381
Mt 7:25 And the rain **d**, and the floods came, and *2597*
7:27 And the rain **d**, and the floods came, and *2597*
28: 2 for *the* angel of the Lord **d** from heaven, *2597*
Lk 3:22 And the Holy Ghost **d** in a bodily shape *2597*
Ac 24: 1 Ananias the high priest **d** with the elders, *2597*
Eph 4: 9 that he also **d** first into the lower parts of *2597*
4:10 He that **d** is the same also that ascended up *2597*

DESCENDETH (1) [DESCEND]
Jas 3:15 This wisdom **d** not from above, but *2718*

DESCENDING (8) [DESCEND]
Ge 28:12 the angels of God ascending and **d** on it. 3381
Mt 3:16 and he saw the Spirit of God **d** like a dove, *2597*
Mk 1:10 and the Spirit like a dove **d** upon him: *2597*
Jn 1:32 I saw the Spirit **d** from heaven like a dove, *2597*
1:33 Upon whom thou shalt see the Spirit **d**, and *2597*
1:51 God ascending and **d** upon the Son of man. *2597*
Ac 10:11 and a certain vessel **d** unto him, *2597*
Rev 21:10 holy Jerusalem, **d** out of heaven from God, *2597*

DESCENT (3) [DESCEND]
Lk 19:37 *even* now at the **d** of the mount of Olives, *2600*
Heb 7: 3 Without father, without mother, **without d**, *35*
7: 6 But he whose **d** is not **counted** from them *1075*

DESCRIBE (4) [DESCRIBED, DESCRIBETH, DESCRIPTION]
Jos 18: 4 **d** it according to the inheritance of them; 3789
18: 6 therefore **d** the land *into* seven parts, 3789
18: 8 Joshua charged them that went to **d** 3789
18: 8 the land, and **d** it, and come again to me, 3789

D

DESCRIBED (2) [DESCRIBE]
Jos 18: 9 **d** it by cities into seven parts in a book, and 3789
Jdg 8:14 he **d** unto him the princes of Succoth, and 3789

DESCRIBETH (2) [DESCRIBE]
Ro 4: 6 Even as David also **d** the blessedness of *3004*
10: 5 For Moses **d** the righteousness which is of *1125*

DESCRIPTION (1) [DESCRIBE]
Jos 18: 6 seven parts, and bring *the* **d** hither to me, NIH

DESCRY (1)
Jdg 1:23 the house of Joseph **sent to d** Beth-el. 8446

DESERT (42) [DESERTS]
Ex 3: 1 he led the flock to the backside of the **d**, 4057
5: 3 three days' journey into the **d**, and 4057
19: 2 were come *to* the **d** of Sinai, and 4057
23:31 and from the **d** unto the river: 4057
Nu 20: 1 *into* the **d** of Zin in the first month: 4057
27:14 against my commandment in the **d** of Zin, 4057
33:16 they removed from the **d** of Sinai, and 4057
Dt 32:10 He found him in a **d** land, and in the waste 4057
2Ch 26:10 Also he built towers in the **d**, and 4057
Job 24: 5 Behold, *as* wild asses in the **d**, go they forth 4057
Ps 28: 4 work of their hands; render to them their **d**. 1576
78:40 in the wilderness, *and* grieve him in the **d**! 3452
102: 6 of the wilderness: I am like an owl of the **d**. 2723
106:14 the wilderness, and tempted God in the **d**. 3452
Isa 13:21 **wild beasts of the d** shall lie there; and 6728
21: 1 The burden of the **d** of the sea. 4057
21: 1 *so* it cometh from the **d**, from a terrible 4057
34:14 The **wild beasts of the d** shall also meet 6728
35: 1 the **d** shall rejoice, and blossom as the rose. 6160
35: 6 shall waters break out, and streams in the **d**. 6160
40: 3 make straight in the **d** a highway for our 6160
41:19 I will set in the **d** the fir tree, *and* the pine, 6160
43:19 a way in the wilderness, *and* rivers in the **d**. 3452
43:20 *and* rivers in the **d**, to give drink to my 3452
51: 3 and her **d** like the garden of the LORD; 6160
Jer 17: 6 For he shall be like the heath in the **d**, and 6160
25:24 of the mingled people that dwell in the **d**, 4057
50:12 *shall be* a wilderness, a dry land, and a **d**. 6160
50:39 Therefore the **wild beasts of the d** with 6728
Eze 47: 8 and go down into the **d**, and go into the sea: 6160
Mt 14:13 thence by ship into a **d** place apart: *2048*
14:15 *This* is a **d** place, and the time is now past; *2048*
24:26 shall say unto you, Behold, he is in the **d**; *2048*
Mk 1:45 into the city, but was without in **d** places: *2048*
6:31 Come ye yourselves apart into a **d** place, *2048*
6:32 And they departed into a **d** place by ship *2048*
6:35 *This* is a **d** place, and now the time *is* far *2048*
Lk 4:42 he departed and went into a **d** place: *2048*
9:10 went aside privately into a **d** place *2048*
9:12 get victuals: for we are here in a **d** place. *2048*
Jn 6:31 Our fathers did eat manna in the **d**; as it is *2048*
Ac 8:26 from Jerusalem unto Gaza, which is **d**. *2048*

DESERTS (6) [DESERT]
Isa 48:21 not *when* he led them through the **d**: 2723
Jer 2: 6 through a land of **d** and of pits, through a 6160
Eze 7:27 and according to their **d** will I judge them; 4941
13: 4 thy prophets are like the foxes in the **d**. 2723
Lk 1:80 was in the **d** till the day of his shewing unto *2048*
Heb 11:38 they wandered in **d**, and *in* mountains, and *2047*

DESERVE (1) [DESERVETH, DESERVING]
Ezr 9:13 hast punished us less than our iniquities *d*, NIH

DESERVETH (1) [DESERVE]
Job 11: 6 exacteth of thee *less* than thine iniquity *d*. NIH

DESERVING (1) [DESERVE]
Jdg 9:16 have done unto him according to the **d** of 1576

DESIRABLE (3) [DESIRE]
Eze 23: 6 and rulers, all of them **d** young men, 2531
23:12 upon horses, all of them **d** young men. 2531
23:23 all of them **d** young men, captains and 2531

DESIRE (111) [DESIRABLE, DESIRED, DESIREDST, DESIRES, DESIREST, DESIRETH, DESIRING, DESIROUS]
Ge 3:16 thy **d** *shall be* to thy husband, and he shall 8669
4: 7 unto thee *shall be* his **d**, and thou shalt rule 8669
Ex 10:11 and serve the LORD; for that you did **d**. 1245
34:24 neither shall any man **d** thy land, when thou 2530
Dt 5:21 Neither shalt thou **d** thy neighbour's wife, 2530
7:25 thou shalt not **d** the silver or gold *that is* on 2530
18: 6 come with all the **d** of his mind unto 185
21:11 **hast a d** unto her, that thou wouldest have 2836
Jdg 8:24 I would **d a request** of you, 7592+7596
1Sa 9:20 on whom *is* all the **d** of Israel? *Is it* not on 2532
23:20 come down according to all the **d** of thy soul 185
2Sa 23: 5 for *this is* all my salvation, and all my *d*, 2656
1Ki 2:20 she said, I **d** one small petition of thee; 7592
5: 8 I will do all thy **d** concerning timber of 2656

1Ki 5: 9 and thou shalt accomplish my **d**, 2656
5:10 and fir trees *according to* all his **d**. 2656
9: 1 all Solomon's **d** which he was pleased to 2837
9:11 and with gold, according to all his **d**,) 2656
10:13 gave unto the queen of Sheba all her **d**, 2656
2Ki 4:28 she said, Did I **d** a son of my lord? did I not 7592
2Ch 9:12 gave to the queen of Sheba all her **d**, 2656
15:15 and sought him with their whole **d**; 7522
Ne 1:11 of thy servants, who **d** to fear thy name: 2655
Job 13: 3 the Almighty, and I **d** to reason with God. 2654
14:15 thou wilt **have** a **d** to the work of thine 3700
21:14 for we **d** not the knowledge of thy ways. 2654
31:16 If I have withheld the poor from *their* **d**, or 2656
31:35 my **d** *is, that* the Almighty would answer 8420
33:32 answer me: speak, for I **d** to justify thee. 2654
34:36 **My d** *is that* Job may be tried unto the end 15
36:20 **D** not the night, when people are cut off in 7602
Ps 10: 3 For the wicked boasteth of his heart's **d**, 8378
10:17 thou hast heard the **d** of the humble: 8378
21: 2 Thou hast given him his heart's **d**, and 8378
38: 9 Lord, all my **d** *is* before thee; and 8378
40: 6 Sacrifice and offering thou didst not **d**; 2654
45:11 So shall the king **greatly d** thy beauty: for he 183
54: 7 mine eye hath seen *his* **d** upon mine NIH
59:10 God shall let me see *my* **d** upon mine NIH
70: 2 and put to confusion, that **d** my hurt. 2655
73:25 *there is* none upon earth *that* I **d** beside 2654
78:29 well filled: for he gave them their own **d**; 8378
92:11 Mine eye also shall see *my* **d** on mine NIH
92:11 mine ears shall hear *my* **d** of the wicked that NIH
112: 8 until he see *his* **d** upon his enemies. NIH
112:10 melt away: the **d** of the wicked shall perish. 8378
118: 7 shall I see *my* **d** upon them that hate me. NIH
145:16 and satisfiest the **d** of every living thing. 7522
145:19 He will fulfil the **d** of them that fear him: 7522
Pr 3:15 all the things thou canst **d** are not to be 2656
10:24 but the **d** of the righteous shall be granted. 8378
11:23 The **d** of the righteous *is* only good: *but* 8378
13:12 but *when* the **d** cometh, *it is* a tree of life. 8378
13:19 The **d** accomplished is sweet to the soul: 8378
18: 1 Through **d** a man, having separated 8378
19:22 The **d** of a man *is* his kindness: and a poor 8378
21:25 The **d** of the slothful killeth him; for his 8378
23: 6 an evil eye, neither **d** thou his dainty meats: 183
24: 1 against evil men, neither **d** to be with them. 183
Ecc 6: 9 of the eyes than the wandering of the **d**: 5315
12: 5 shall be a burden, and **d** shall fail: 35
SS 7:10 *am* my beloved's, and his **d** *is* towards me. 8669
Isa 26: 8 the **d** of *our* soul *is* to thy name, and to 8378
53: 2 *there is* no beauty that we should **d** him. 2530
Jer 22:27 to the land whereunto they **d** to 5315+5375
42:22 in the place whither ye **d** to go *and* 2654
44:14 to the which they **have a d** to return 5315+5375
Eze 24:16 I take away from thee the **d** of thine eyes 4261
24:21 the **d** of your eyes, and that which your 4261
24:25 the **d** of their eyes, and that whereupon they 4261
Da 2:18 That *they* would **d** mercies of the God of 1156
11:37 nor the **d** of women, nor regard any god: 2532
Hos 10:10 *It is* in my **d** that I should chastise them; and 185
Am 5:18 Woe unto *you* that **d** the day of the LORD! 183
Mic 7: 3 great *man,* he uttereth his mischievous **d**: 5315
Hab 2: 5 who enlargeth his **d** as hell, and *is* as death, 5315
Hag 2: 7 and the **d** of all nations shall come: 2532
Mk 9:35 saith unto them, If any *man* **d** to be first, *2309*
10:35 shouldest do for us whatsoever we shall **d**. *154*
11:24 What *things* soever ye **d**, when ye pray, *154*
15: 8 And the multitude crying aloud began to **d** *154*
Lk 17:22 when ye shall **d** to see one of the days of *1937*
20:46 which **d** to walk in long robes, and *2309*
22:15 With **d** I have desired to eat this passover *1939*
Ac 23:20 The Jews have agreed to **d** thee that thou *2065*
28:22 But we **d** to hear of thee what thou thinkest: *515*
Ro 10: 1 my heart's **d** and prayer to God for Israel *2107*
15:23 having a **great d** these many years to come *1974*
1Co 14: 1 and **d** spiritual *gifts,* but rather that ye may *2206*
2Co 7: 7 when he told us your **earnest d**, your *1972*
7:11 yea, *what* fear, yea, *what* **vehement d**, yea, *1972*
11:12 off occasion from them which **d** occasion; *2309*
12: 6 For though I would **d** to glory, I shall not *2309*
Gal 4: 9 whereunto ye **d** again to be in bondage? *2309*
4:20 I **d** to be present with you now, and *2309*
4:21 Tell me, ye that **d** to be under the law, *2309*
6:12 As many as **d** to make a fair shew in *2309*
6:13 but **d** to have you circumcised, that they *2309*
Eph 3:13 Wherefore I **d** that *ye* faint not at my *154*
Php 1:23 having a **d** to depart, and to be with Christ; *1939*
4:17 Not because I **d** a gift: but I desire fruit that *1934*
4:17 I **d** fruit that *may* abound to your account. *1934*
Col 1: 9 to **d** that ye might be filled *with* *154*
1Th 2:17 abundantly to see your face with great **d**. *1939*
1Ti 3: 1 If a man **d** the office of a bishop, *3713*
Heb 6:11 And we **d** that every one of you do shew *1937*
11:16 But now they **d** a better *country,* that is, *3713*
Jas 4: 2 ye kill, and **d** *to have,* and cannot obtain: *2206*
1Pe 1:12 which *things* the angels **d** to look into. *1937*
2: 2 **d** the sincere milk of the word, *1971*
Rev 9: 6 and shall **d** to die, and death shall flee from *1937*

DESIRED (50) [DESIRE]

Ge 3: 6 a tree to be **d** to make *one* wise, she took of 2530
1Sa 12:13 ye have chosen, *and* whom ye have **d**: 7592
1Ki 9:19 that which Solomon **d** to build in 2836+2837
2Ch 8: 6 Solomon **d** to build in Jerusalem, 2836+2837
11:23 in abundance. And he **d** many wives. 7592
21:20 eight years, and departed without being **d**. 2532
Est 2:13 whatsoever she **d** was given her to go with 559
Job 20:20 he shall not save of that which he **d**. 2530
Ps 19:10 More to be **d** *are they* than gold, yea, 2530
27: 4 One *thing* have I **d** of the LORD, that will 7592
107:30 so he bringeth them unto their **d** haven. 2656
132:13 chosen Zion; he hath **d** *it* for his habitation. 183
132:14 for ever: here will I dwell; for I have **d** it. 183
Pr 8:11 all the things that may be **d** are not to be 2656
21:20 *There is* treasure to be **d** and oil in 2530
Ecc 2:10 whatsoever mine eyes **d** I kept not from 7592

Isa 1:29 be ashamed of the oaks which ye have **d**, 2530
26: 9 *With* my soul have I **d** thee in the night; yea, 183
Jer 17:16 neither have I **d** the woeful day; 183
Da 2:16 **d** of the king that he would give him time, 1156
2:23 hast made known unto me now what we **d** 1156
Hos 6: 6 For I **d** mercy, and not sacrifice; and 2654
Mic 7: 1 no cluster to eat: my soul **d** the firstripe fruit. 183
Zep 2: 1 yea, gather together, O nation not **d**; 3700
Mt 13:17 righteous *men* have **d** to see *those things* *1937*
16: 1 tempting **d** him that *he* would shew them a *1905*
Mk 15: 6 unto them one prisoner, whomsoever they **d**. *154*
Lk 7:36 And one of the Pharisees **d** him that he *2065*
9: 9 of whom I hear such *things?* And he **d** to *2212*
10:24 kings have **d** to see *those things* which ye *2309*
22:15 With desire I have **d** to eat this passover *1937*
22:31 Simon, behold, Satan hath **d** *to have* you, *1809*
23:25 was cast into prison, whom they had **d**; *154*
Jn 12:21 and **d** him, saying, Sir, we would see Jesus. *2065*
Ac 3:14 and **d** a murderer to be granted unto you; *154*
7:46 **d** to find a tabernacle for the God of Jacob. *154*
8:31 And he **d** Philip that *he* would come up and *3870*
9: 2 And **d** of him letters to Damascus to *154*
12:20 the king's chamberlain their friend, **d** peace; *154*
13: 7 and Saul, and **d** to hear the word of God. *1934*
13:21 And afterward they **d** a king: and God gave *154*
13:28 *him, yet* **d** they Pilate that he should be slain. *154*
16:39 and **d** *them* to depart out of the city. *2065*
18:20 When they **d** *him* to tarry longer time with *2065*
25: 3 And **d** favour against him, that he would *154*
28:14 and were **d** to tarry with them seven days: *3870*
1Co 16:12 I greatly **d** him to come unto you with *3870*
2Co 8: 6 Insomuch that we **d** Titus, that as he had *3870*
12:18 I **d** Titus, and with *him* I sent a brother. *3870*
1Jn 5:15 we know that we have the petitions that we **d** *154*

DESIREDST (2) [DESIRE]

Dt 18:16 According to all that thou **d** of the LORD 7592
Mt 18:32 thee all that debt, because thou **d** me: *3870*

DESIRES (3) [DESIRE]

Ps 37: 4 and he shall give thee the **d** of thine heart. 4862
140: 8 Grant not, O LORD, the **d** of the wicked: 3970
Eph 2: 3 fulfilling the **d** of the flesh and of the mind; *2307*

DESIREST (2) [DESIRE]

Ps 51: 6 Behold, thou **d** truth in the inward parts: 2654
51:16 For thou **d** not sacrifice; else would I give 2654

DESIRETH (17) [DESIRE]

Dt 14:26 strong drink, or for whatsoever thy soul **d**: 7592
1Sa 2:16 *then* take *as much* as thy soul **d**; 183
18:25 The king **d** not *any* dowry, but an hundred 2656
20: 4 Whatsoever thy soul **d**, I will even do *it* for 559
2Sa 3:21 thou mayest reign over all that thine heart **d**. 183
1Ki 11:37 shalt reign according to all that thy soul **d**, 183
Job 7: 2 As a servant **earnestly d** the shadow, and 7602
23:13 and *what* his soul **d**, even *that* he doeth. 183
Ps 34:12 What man *is he that* **d** life, *and* loveth *many* 2655
68:16 *this is* the hill *which* God **d** to dwell in; yea, 2530
Pr 12:12 The wicked **d** the net of evil *men:* but 2530
13: 4 The soul of the sluggard **d**, and *hath* nothing: 183
21:10 The soul of the wicked **d** evil: his neighbour 183
Ecc 6: 2 wanteth nothing for his soul of all that he **d**, 183
Lk 5:39 having drunk old *wine* straightway **d** new: *2309*
14:32 an ambassage, and **d** conditions of peace. *2065*
1Ti 3: 1 the office of a bishop, he **d** a good work. *1937*

DESIRING (12) [DESIRE]

Mt 12:46 stood without, **d** to speak with him. *2212*
12:47 stand without, **d** to speak with thee. *2212*
20:20 and **d** a certain *thing* of him. *154*
Lk 8:20 thy brethren stand without, **d** to see thee. *2309*
16:21 And **d** to be fed with the crumbs which fell *1937*
Ac 9:38 **d** *him* that *he* would not delay to come to *3870*
19:31 **d** *him* that *he* would not adventure himself *3870*
25:15 the elders of the Jews informed *me,* **d** *to* *154*
2Co 5: 2 **earnestly d** to be clothed upon with our *1971*
1Th 3: 6 **d greatly** to see us, as we also *to see* you: *1971*
1Ti 1: 7 **D** to be teachers of the law; *2309*
2Ti 1: 4 **Greatly d** to see thee, being mindful of thy *1971*

DESIROUS (6) [DESIRE]

Pr 23: 3 Be not **d** of his dainties: for they *are* 183
Lk 23: 8 for he was **d** to see him of a long *season,* *2309*
Jn 16:19 Now Jesus knew that they were **d** to ask *2309*
2Co 11:32 *with a garrison,* **d** to apprehend me: *2309*
Gal 5:26 Let us not be **d** of vain glory, provoking one NIG
1Th 2: 8 So being **affectionately d** of you, we were *2442*

DESOLATE (148) [DESOLATION, DESOLATIONS]

Ge 47:19 and not die, that the land be not **d**. 3456
Ex 23:29 lest the land become **d**, and the beast of 8077
Lev 26:22 in number; and your *high* ways shall be **d**. 8074
26:33 your land shall be **d**, and your cities waste. 8077
26:34 as long as it **lieth d**, and ye *be* in your 8074
26:35 As long as it **lieth d** it shall rest; because 8074
26:43 while she **lieth d** without them: 8074
2Sa 13:20 So Tamar remained **d** *in* her brother 8074
2Ch 36:21 *for* as long as *she* **lay d** she kept sabbath, 8074
Job 3:14 which built **d places** for themselves; 2723
15:28 he dwelleth in **d** cities, *and* in houses which 3582
15:34 the congregation of hypocrites *shall be* **d**, 1565
16: 7 thou hast **made d** all my company. 8074
30: 3 flying *into* the wilderness in former time **d** 7722
38:27 To satisfy the **d** and waste *ground;* and 7722
Ps 25:16 mercy upon me; for I *am* **d** and afflicted. 3173
34:21 and they that hate the righteous shall be **d**. 816
34:22 and none of them that trust in him shall be **d**. 816
40:15 Let them be **d** for a reward of their shame 8074
69:25 Let their habitation be **d**; *and* let none dwell 8074
109:10 seek *their bread* also out of their **d places**. 2723
143: 4 within me; my heart within me is **d**. 8074
Isa 1: 7 Your country *is* **d**, your cities *are* burnt 8077
1: 7 and *it is* **d**, as overthrown by strangers. 8077

Isa 3:26 and she *being* **d** shall sit upon the ground. 5352
5: 9 Of a truth many houses shall be **d**, 8047
6:11 without man, and the land be utterly **d**, 7582
7:19 shall rest all of them in the **d** valleys, and 1327
13: 9 and fierce anger, to lay the land **d**: 8047
13:22 of the islands shall cry in their **d houses**, 490
15: 6 For the waters of Nimrim shall be **d**: for 4923
24: 6 the earth, and they that dwell therein are **d**: 816
27:10 Yet the defenced city *shall be* **d**, *and* 910
49: 8 the earth, to cause to inherit the **d** heritages; 8074
49:19 For thy waste and thy **d places**, and 8074
49:21 *am* **d**, a captive, and removing to and fro? 1565
54: 1 for more *are* the children of the **d** than 8074
54: 3 and make the **d** cities to be inhabited. 8074
59:10 the night; *we are* in **d places** as dead *men.* 820
62: 4 shall thy land any more be termed **D**: 8077
Jer 2:12 be ye very **d**, saith the LORD. 2717
4: 7 forth from his place to make thy land **d**; 8047
4:27 LORD said, The whole land shall be **d**; 8077
6: 8 lest I make thee **d**, a land not inhabited. 8077
7:34 voice of the bride: for the land shall be **d**. 2723
9:11 I will make the cities of Judah **d**, 8077
10:22 to make the cities of Judah **d**, *and* a den of 8077
10:25 and have **made** his habitation **d**. 8074
12:10 they have made my pleasant portion a **d** 8077
12:11 They have made it **d**, *and being* desolate it 8076
12:11 *and being* **d** it mourneth unto me; 8077
12:11 the whole land is **made d**, because no man 8074
18:16 To make their land **d**, *and* a perpetual 8047
19: 8 I will make this city **d**, and a hissing; 8047
25:38 for their land is **d** because of the fierceness 8047
26: 9 this city shall be **d** without an inhabitant? 2717
32:43 ye say, *It is* **d** without man or beast; 8077
33:10 which ye say *shall be* **d** without man and 2720
33:10 that are **d**, without man, and without 8074
33:12 *which is* **d** without man and without beast, 2720
44: 6 and they are wasted *and* **d**, as *at* this day. 8077
46:19 shall be waste and **d** without an inhabitant. 3341
48: 9 for the cities thereof shall be **d**, without any 8047
48:34 for the waters also of Nimrim shall be **d**. 4923
49: 2 it shall be a **d** heap, and her daughters shall 8077
49:20 surely he shall **make** their habitations **d** 8074
50: 3 which shall make her land **d**, and none shall 8047
50:13 not be inhabited, but it shall be wholly **d**: 8077
50:45 surely he shall **make** *their* habitation **d** with 8074
51:26 thou shalt be **d** for ever, saith the LORD. 8077
51:62 nor beast, but that it shall be **d** for ever. 8077
La 1: 4 all her gates are **d**: her priests sigh: 8074
1:13 he hath made me **d** *and* faint all the day. 8074
1:16 my children are **d**, because the enemy 8074
3:11 pulled me in pieces: he hath made me **d**. 8074
4: 5 They that did feed delicately are **d** in 8074
5:18 of Zion, which is **d**, the foxes walk upon it. 8074
Eze 6: 4 your altars shall be **d**, and your images 8074
6: 6 laid waste, and the high places shall be **d**; 3456
6: 6 your altars may be laid waste and **made d**, 816
6:14 hand upon them, and make the land **d**, yea, 8077
6:14 more **d** than the wilderness toward Diblath, 4923
12:19 that her land may be **d** from all that is 3456
12:20 shall be laid waste, and the land shall be **d**; 8077
14:15 they spoil it, so that it be **d**, that no man 8077
14:16 shall be delivered, but the land shall be **d**. 8077
15: 8 I will make the land **d**, because they have 8077
19: 7 he knew their **d palaces**, and he laid waste 490
19: 7 the land was **d**, and the fulness thereof, 3456
20:26 that I might **make** them **d**, to the end that 8074
25: 3 against the land of Israel, when it was **d**; 8074
25:13 I will make it **d** from Teman; and they of 2723
26:19 When I shall make thee a **d** city, like 2717
26:20 in **places d** of old, with them that go down 2723
29: 9 And the land of Egypt shall be **d** and waste; 8077
29:10 make the land of Egypt utterly waste *and* **d**, 8077
29:12 I will make the land of Egypt **d** in the midst 8077
29:12 in the midst of the countries *that are* **d**, 8074
29:12 *that are* laid waste shall be **d** forty years: 8077
30: 7 they shall be **d** in the midst of the countries 8074
30: 7 in the midst of the countries *that are* **d**, 8074
30:14 I will **make** Pathros **d**, and will set fire in 8074
32:15 When I shall make the land of Egypt **d**, and 8077
33:28 I will lay the land **most d**, 4923+8077+2050.1
33:28 the mountains of Israel shall be **d**, that none 8074
33:29 I have laid the land **most d** 4923+8077+2050.1
35: 3 and I will make thee **most d**. 4923+8077+2050.1
35: 4 thou shalt be **d**, and thou shalt know that I 8077
35: 7 I make mount Seir **most d**, 8077+8077+2050.1
35:12 saying, They are **laid d**, they are given us 8074
35:14 whole earth rejoiceth, I will make thee **d**. 8077
35:15 because it was **d**, so will I do unto thee: 8074
35:15 thou shalt be **d**, O mount Seir, and 8077
36: 3 Because *they* have **made** *you* **d**, and 8074
36: 4 to the **d** wastes, and to the cities that are 8074
36:34 the **d** land shall be tilled, whereas it lay 8074
36:34 whereas it lay **d** in the sight of all that 8077
36:35 This land that was **d** is become like 8074
36:35 the waste and **d** and ruined cities *are* 8074
36:36 the ruined *places, and* plant that that was **d**: 8074
38:12 to turn thine hand upon the **d places** *that* 2723
Da 9:17 face to shine upon thy sanctuary that is **d**, 8076
9:27 of abominations he *shall* **make** it **d**, 8074
9:27 that determined shall be poured upon the **d**. 8074
11:31 shall place the abomination that **maketh d**. 8074
12:11 the abomination that **maketh d** set up, 8074
Hos 5: 9 Ephraim shall be **d** in the day of rebuke: 8047
13:16 Samaria shall become **d**; for she hath 816
Joel 1:17 the garners are **laid d**, the barns are broken 8074
1:18 yea, the flocks of sheep are **made d**. 816
2: 3 and behind them a **d** wilderness; 8077
2:20 and will drive him into a land barren and **d**, 8077
3:19 and Edom shall be a **d** wilderness, 8077
Am 7: 9 the high places of Isaac shall be **d**, and 8074
Mic 1: 7 and all the idols thereof will I lay **d**: 8077
6:13 in **making** *thee* **d** because of thy sins. 8074
7:13 Notwithstanding the land shall be **d** 8077
Zep 3: 6 their towers are **d**; I made their streets 8074
Zec 7:14 thus the land was **d** after them, that no man 8074

Zec 7:14 for they laid the pleasant land **d**. 8047
Mal 1: 4 but we will return and build the **d places**; 2723
Mt 23:38 Behold, your house is left unto you **d**. *2048*
Lk 13:35 Behold, your house is left unto you **d**: and *2048*
Ac 1:20 Let his habitation be **d**, and let no man *2048*
Gal 4:27 for the **d** hath many moe children than she *2048*
1Ti 5: 5 and **d**, trusteth in God, and continueth in *3443*
Rev 17:16 and shall make her **d** and naked, and shall *2049*
18:19 for in one hour is she **made d**. *2049*

DESOLATION (46) [DESOLATE]
Lev 26:31 **bring** your sanctuaries **unto d**, and I will 8074
26:32 I will **bring** the land **into d**: and 8074
Jos 8:28 it a heap for ever, *even* a **d** unto this day. 8077
2Ki 22:19 that *they* should become a **d** and a curse, 8047
2Ch 30: 7 *who* therefore gave them up to **d**, as ye see. 8047
Job 30:14 in the **d** they rolled themselves *upon me*. 7722
Ps 73:19 How are they *brought* into **d**, as *in* a 8047
Pr 1:27 When your fear cometh as **d**, and 7722
3:25 neither of the **d** of the wicked, when it 7722
Isa 10: 3 and in the **d** *which* shall come from far? 7722
17: 9 the children of Israel: and there shall be **d**. 8077
24:12 In the city is left **d**, and the gate is smitten 8047
47:11 **d** shall come upon thee suddenly, 7722
51:19 **d**, and destruction, and the famine, and 7701
64:10 Zion is a wilderness, Jerusalem a **d**. 8077
Jer 22: 5 that this house shall become a **d**. 2723
25:11 this whole land shall be a **d**, *and* 2723
25:18 to make them a **d**, an astonishment, a 2723
34:22 I will make the cities of Judah a **d** without 8077
44: 2 this day they *are* a **d**, and no man dwelleth 2723
44:22 therefore is your land a **d**, and an 2723
49:13 that Bozrah shall become a **d**, a reproach, a 8047
49:17 Also Edom shall be a **d**: every one that 8047
49:33 be a dwelling for dragons, *and* a **d** for ever: 8077
50:23 how is Babylon become a **d** among 8047
51:29 to make the land of Babylon a **d** without an 8047
51:43 Her cities are a **d**, a dry land, and 8047
La 3:47 a snare is come upon us, **d** and destruction. 7612
Eze 7:27 the prince shall be clothed with **d**, and 8077
23:33 sorrow, *with* the cup of astonishment and **d**, 8077
Da 8:13 daily *sacrifice*, and the transgression of **d**, 8074
Hos 12: 1 he daily increaseth lies and **d**; and they do 7701
Joel 3:19 Egypt shall be a **d**, and Edom shall be a 8077
Mic 6:16 that I should make thee a **d**, and 8047
Zep 1:13 shall become a booty, and their houses a **d**: 8077
1:15 and distress, a day of wasteness and **d**, 4875
2: 4 Gaza shall be forsaken, and Ashkelon a **d**: 8077
2: 9 of nettles, and saltpits, and a perpetual **d**: 8077
2:13 will make Nineveh a **d**, *and* dry like a 8077
2:14 the windows; **d** *shall be* in the thresholds: 2721
2:15 how is she become a **d**, a place for beasts to 8047
Mt 12:25 divided against itself is **brought to d**; *2049*
24:15 therefore shall see the abomination of **d**, *2050*
Mk 13:14 But when ye shall see the abomination of **d**, *2050*
Lk 11:17 divided against itself is **brought to d**; *2049*
21:20 then know that the **d** thereof is nigh. *2050*

DESOLATIONS (11) [DESOLATE]
Ezr 9: 9 to repair the **d** thereof, and to give us a wall 2723
Ps 46: 8 what **d** he hath made in the earth. 8047
74: 3 Lift up thy feet unto the perpetual **d**; 4876
Isa 61: 4 they shall raise up the former **d**, and 8074
61: 4 the waste cities, the **d** of many generations. 8074
Jer 25: 9 and a hissing, and perpetual **d**. 2723
25:12 and will make it perpetual **d**. 8077
Eze 35: 9 I will make thee perpetual **d**, and thy cities 8077
Da 9: 2 seventy years in the **d** of Jerusalem. 2723
9:18 behold our **d**, and the city which is called 8074
9:26 unto the end of the war **d** *are* determined. 8074

DESPAIR (3) [DESPAIRED]
1Sa 27: 1 Saul shall **d** of me, to seek me any more in 2976
Ecc 2:20 **cause** my heart **to d** of all the labour which 2976
2Co 4: 8 *we are* perplexed, but not **in d**; *1820*

DESPAIRED (1) [DESPAIR]
2Co 1: 8 insomuch that we **d** even of life: *1820*

DESPERATE (2) [DESPERATELY]
Job 6:26 the speeches of one that is **d**, *which are* as 2976
Isa 17:11 *be* a heap in the day of grief and of **d** sorrow. 605

DESPERATELY (1) [DESPERATE]
Jer 17: 9 *is* deceitful above all *things*, and **d wicked**: 605

DESPISE (37) [DESPISED, DESPISERS, DESPISEST, DESPISETH, DESPISING]
Lev 26:15 if ye shall **d** my statutes, or if your soul 3988
1Sa 2:30 and they that **d** me shall be lightly esteemed. 959
2Sa 19:43 why then did ye **d** us, that our advice 7043
Est 1:17 that *they* shall **d** their husbands in their eyes, 959
Job 5:17 **d** not thou the chastening of the Almighty: 3988
9:21 I not know my soul: I would **d** my life. 3988
10: 3 that thou shouldest **d** the work of thine 3988
31:13 If I did **d** the cause of my manservant or 3988
Ps 51:17 and a contrite heart, O God, thou wilt not **d**. 959
73:20 when thou awakest, thou shalt **d** their image. 959
102:17 of the destitute, and not **d** their prayer. 959
Pr 1: 7 *but* fools **d** wisdom and instruction. 936
3:11 **d** not the chastening of the LORD; 3988
6:30 *Men* do not **d** a thief, if he steal to satisfy his 936
23: 9 for he will **d** the wisdom of thy words. 936
23:22 and **d** not thy mother when she is old. 936
Isa 30:12 Because ye **d** this word, and trust in 3988
Jer 4:30 *thy* lovers will **d** thee, they will seek thy 3988
23:17 They say still unto them that **d** me, 5006
La 1: 8 all that honoured her **d** her, because 2107
Eze 16:57 the Philistines, which **d** thee round about. 7590
28:26 all those that **d** them round about them; 7590
Am 5:21 I **d** your feast *days*, and I will not smell in 3988
Mal 1: 6 of hosts unto you, O priests, that **d** my name. 959
Mt 6:24 else he will hold to the one, and **d** the other. *2706*
18:10 Take heed that ye **d** not one of these little *2706*
Lk 16:13 else he will hold to the one, and **d** the other. *2706*
Ro 14: 3 Let not him that eateth **d** him that eateth *1848*
1Co 11:22 and to drink *in?* or **d** ye the church of God, *2706*
16:11 Let no *man* therefore **d** him: but *1848*
1Th 5:20 **D** not prophesyings. *1848*
1Ti 4:12 Let no *man* **d** thy youth; but be thou an *2706*
6: 2 let them not **d** *them*, because they are *2706*
Tit 2:15 with all authority. Let no *man* **d** thee. *4065*
Heb 12: 5 **d** not thou the chastening of the Lord, *3643*
2Pe 2:10 the lust of uncleanness, and **d** government. *2706*
Jude 1: 8 **d** dominion, and speak evil of dignities. *114*

DESPISED (60) [DESPISE]
Ge 16: 4 her mistress was **d** in her eyes. 7043
16: 5 that she had conceived, I was **d** in her eyes: 7043
25:34 and went his way: thus Esau **d** *his* birthright. 959
Lev 26:43 even because they **d** my judgments, and 3988
Nu 11:20 that ye have **d** the LORD which *is* among 3988
14:31 they shall know the land which ye have **d**. 3988
15:31 Because he hath **d** the word of the LORD, 959
Jdg 9:38 *is* not this the people that thou hast **d**? go 3988
1Sa 10:27 they **d** him, and brought him no presents. 959
2Sa 6:16 the LORD; and she **d** him in her heart. 959
12: 9 Wherefore hast thou **d** the commandment of 959
12:10 because thou hast **d** me, and hast taken 959
2Ki 19:21 The virgin the daughter of Zion hath **d** thee, 959
1Ch 15:29 and playing: and she **d** him in her heart. 959
2Ch 36:16 and **d** his words, and misused his prophets, 959
Ne 2:19 **d** us, and said, What *is* this thing that ye do? 959
4: 4 Hear, O our God; for we are **d**: and turn their 939
Job 12: 5 a lamp **d** in the thought of him that is at ease. 937
19:18 Yea, young children **d** me; I arose, and 3988
Ps 22: 6 a reproach of men, and **d** of the people. 959
22:24 For he hath not **d** nor abhorred the affliction 959
53: 5 *them* to shame, because God hath **d** them. 3988
106:24 Yea, they **d** the pleasant land, they believed 3988
119:141 I *am* small and **d**: *yet* do not I forget thy 959
Pr 1:30 none of my counsel: they **d** all my reproof. 5006
5:12 I hated instruction, and my heart **d** reproof; 5006
12: 8 but he that is of a perverse heart shall be **d**. 937
12: 9 *He that is* **d**, and hath a servant, *is* better 7034
Ecc 9:16 nevertheless the poor *man's* wisdom *is* **d**, 959
SS 8: 1 I would kiss thee; yea, I should not be **d**. 936
Isa 5:24 and **d** the word of the Holy One of Israel. 5006
33: 8 he hath **d** the cities, he regardeth no man. 3988
37:22 hath **d** thee, *and* laughed thee to scorn; 959
53: 3 He is **d** and rejected of men; a man of 959
53: 3 he was **d**, and we esteemed him not. 959
60:14 all they that **d** thee shall bow themselves 5006
Jer 22:28 *Is* this man Coniah a **d** broken idol? *is he* a 959
33:24 thus they have **d** my people, that *they* 5006
49:15 small among the heathen, *and* **d** among men. 959
La 2: 6 hath **d** in the indignation of his anger 5006
Eze 16:59 which hast **d** the oath in breaking 959
17:16 whose oath he **d**, and whose covenant he 959
17:18 Seeing he **d** the oath by breaking 959
17:19 surely mine oath that he hath **d**, and 959
20:13 they **d** my judgments, which *if* a man do, 3988
20:16 Because they **d** my judgments, and walked 3988
20:24 had **d** my statutes, and had polluted my 3988
22: 8 Thou hast **d** mine holy *things*, and hast 959
28:24 all *that are* round about them, that **d** them; 7590
Am 2: 4 because they have **d** the law of the LORD, 3988
Ob 1: 2 small among the heathen: thou *art* greatly **d**. 959
Zec 4:10 For who hath **d** the day of small *things*? for 936
Mal 1: 6 And ye say, Wherein have we **d** thy name? 959
Lk 18: 9 that they were righteous, and **d** other: *1848*
Ac 19:27 goddess Diana should be **d**, *1519+3049+3762*
1Co 1:28 and *things* which are **d**, hath God chosen, *1848*
4:10 *are* strong; ye *are* honourable, but we *are* **d**. *820*
Gal 4:14 temptation which was in my flesh ye **d** not, *1848*
Heb 10:28 He that **d** Moses' law died without mercy *114*
Jas 2: 6 But ye have **d** the poor. Do not rich *men* *818*

DESPISERS (2) [DESPISE]
Ac 13:41 Behold *ye* **d**, and wonder, and perish: for I *2707*
2Ti 3: 3 incontinent, fierce, **d of** *those that are* **good**, *865*

DESPISEST (1) [DESPISE]
Ro 2: 4 Or **d** thou the riches of his goodness and *2706*

DESPISETH (19) [DESPISE]
Job 36: 5 **d** not *any: he is* mighty in strength *and* 3988
Ps 69:33 heareth the poor, and **d** not his prisoners. 959
Pr 11:12 He that is void of wisdom **d** his neighbour: 936
13:13 Whoso **d** the word shall be destroyed: but 936
14: 2 but he that is perverse in his ways **d** him. 959
14:21 He that **d** his neighbour sinneth: but he that 936
15: 5 A fool **d** his father's instruction: but he that 5006
15:20 a glad father: but a foolish man **d** his mother. 959
15:32 He that refuseth instruction **d** his own soul: 3988
19:16 own soul; *but* he that **d** his ways shall die. 959
30:17 at *his* father, and **d** to obey *his* mother, 936
Isa 33:15 he that **d** the gain of oppressions, 3988
49: 7 *and* his Holy One, to him whom man **d**, 960
Lk 10:16 and he that **d** you despiseth me; and he that *114*
10:16 and he that despiseth you **d** me; and he that *114*
10:16 and he that **d** me despiseth him that sent me. *114*
10:16 and he that despiseth me **d** him that sent me. *114*
1Th 4: 8 He therefore that **d**, despiseth not man, but *114*
4: 8 therefore that despiseth, **d** not man, but God, *114*

DESPISING (1) [DESPISE]
Heb 12: 2 **d** the shame, and is set down at the right *2706*

DESPITE (2) [DESPITEFUL, DESPITEFULLY]
Eze 25: 6 rejoiced in heart with all thy **d** against 7589
Heb 10:29 and hath **done d unto** the Spirit of grace? *1796*

DESPITEFUL (3) [DESPITE]
Eze 25:15 have taken vengeance with a **d** heart, 7589
36: 5 with **d** minds, to cast it out for a prey. 7589
Ro 1:30 haters of God, **d**, proud, boasters, *5197*

DESPITEFULLY (3) [DESPITE]
Mt 5:44 and pray for them which **d use** you, and *1908*
Lk 6:28 and pray for them which **d use** you. *1908*
Ac 14: 5 to **use** *them* **d**, and to stone them, *5195*

DESTINY See END; EVENT; NUMBER; PATHS

DESTITUTE (8)
Ge 24:27 who hath not **left d** my master of his mercy 5800
Ps 102:17 He will regard the prayer of the **d**, and 6199
141: 8 in thee is my trust; **leave** not my soul **d**. 6168
Pr 15:21 Folly *is* joy to *him that is* **d** of wisdom: but 2638
Eze 32:15 the country shall be **d** of that whereof it 8074
1Ti 6: 5 and **d** of the truth, supposing that gain is *650*
Heb 11:37 being **d**, afflicted, tormented; *5302*
Jas 2:15 or sister be naked, and **d** of daily food, *3007*

D

DESTROY (261) [DESTROYED, DESTROYER, DESTROYERS, DESTROYEST, DESTROYETH, DESTROYING, DESTRUCTION, DESTRUCTIONS]
Ge 6: 7 I will **d** man whom I have created from 4229
6:13 and behold, I will **d** them with the earth. 7843
6:17 to **d** all flesh, wherein *is* the breath of life, 7843
7: 4 made will I **d** from off the face of the earth. 4229
9:11 neither shall there any more be a flood to **d** 7843
9:15 shall no more become a flood to **d** all flesh. 7843
18:23 Wilt thou also **d** the righteous with 5595
18:24 wilt thou also **d** and not spare the place for 5595
18:28 wilt thou **d** all the city for *lack of* five? And 7843
18:28 If I find there forty and five, I will not **d** *it*. 7843
18:31 he said, I will not **d** *it* for twenty's sake. 7843
18:32 And he said, I will not **d** *it* for ten's sake. 7843
19:13 For we will **d** this place, because the cry of 7843
19:13 and the LORD hath sent us to **d** it. 7843
19:14 this place; for the LORD will **d** this city. 7843
Ex 8: 9 to **d** the frogs from thee and thy houses, 3772
12:13 the plague shall not be upon you to **d** *you*, 4889
15: 9 will draw my sword, my hand shall **d** them. 3423
23:27 will **d** all the people to whom thou shalt 2000
34:13 ye shall **d** their altars, break their images, 5422
Lev 23:30 the same soul will I **d** from among his people. 6
26:22 **d** your cattle, and make you few in number; 3772
26:30 I will **d** your high places, and cut down 8045
26:44 to **d** them **utterly**, and to break my 3615
Nu 21: 2 my hand, then I will **utterly d** their cities. 2763
24:17 of Moab, and **d** all the children of Sheth. 6979
24:19 and shall **d** him that remaineth of the city. 6
32:15 and ye shall **d** all this people. 7843
33:52 **d** all their pictures, and destroy all their molten 6
33:52 **d** all their molten images, and quite pluck 6
Dt 1:27 us into the hand of the Amorites, to **d** us. 8045
2:15 to **d** them from among the host, until they 2000
4:31 he will not forsake thee, neither **d** thee, 7843
6:15 and **d** thee from off the face of the earth. 8045
7: 2 thou shalt smite them, *and* **utterly d** 2763+2763
7: 4 kindled against you, and **d** thee suddenly. 8045
7: 5 ye shall **d** their altars, and break down their 5422
7:10 them that hate him to their face, to **d** them: 6
7:23 shall **d** them *with* a mighty destruction, 1949
7:24 and thou shalt **d** their name from under heaven: 6
9: 3 *as* a consuming fire he shall **d** them, and 8045
9: 3 shalt thou drive them out, and **d** them quickly, 6
9:14 that I may **d** them, and blot out their name 8045
9:19 LORD was wroth against you to **d** you. 8045
9:25 the LORD had said he would **d** you. 8045
9:26 **d** not thy people and thine inheritance, 7843
10:10 *and* the LORD would not **d** thee. 7843
12: 2 Ye shall **utterly d** all the places, wherein 6+6
12: 3 and **d** the names of them out of that place. 6
20:17 thou shalt **utterly d** them; 2763+2763
20:19 thou shalt not **d** the trees thereof by forcing 7843
20:20 for meat, thou shalt **d** and cut them down; 7843
28:63 so the LORD will rejoice over you to **d** you, 6
31: 3 he will **d** these nations from before thee, 8045
32:25 shall **d** both the young man and the virgin, 7921
33:27 from before thee; and shall say, **D** *them*. 8045
Jos 7: 7 us into the hand of the Amorites, to **d** us? 6
7:12 except ye **d** the accursed from amongst 8045
9:24 to **d** all the inhabitants of the land from 8045
11:20 that *he* might **d** them **utterly**, *and* that they 2763
11:20 have no favour, but that *he* might **d** them, 8045
22:33 to **d** the land wherein the children of 7843
Jdg 6: 5 and they entered into the land to **d** it. 7843
21:11 Ye shall **utterly d** every male, and 2763
1Sa 15: 3 **utterly d** all that they have, and spare them 2763
15: 6 the Amalekites, lest I **d** you with them: 622
15: 9 *was* good, and would not **utterly d** them: 2763
15:18 and **utterly d** the sinners the Amalekites, 2763
23:10 come to Keilah, to **d** the city for my sake. 7843
24:21 that thou wilt not **d** my name out of my 8045
26: 9 David said to Abishai, **D** him not: for who 7843
26:15 for there came one of the people in to **d** 7843
2Sa 1:14 thine hand to **d** the LORD'S anointed? 7843
14: 7 whom he slew; and we will **d** the heir also: 8045
14:11 the revengers of blood to **d** any more, 7843
14:11 to destroy any more, lest they **d** my son. 8045
14:16 out of the hand of the man *that would* **d** me 8045
20:19 thou seekest to **d** a city and a mother in 4191
20:20 it from me, that I should swallow up or **d**. 7843
22:41 that I might **d** them that hate me. 6789
24:16 out his hand *upon* Jerusalem to **d** it, 7843
1Ki 9:21 of Israel also were not able **utterly** to **d**, 2763
13:34 and to **d** *it* from off the face of the earth. 8045
16:12 Thus did Zimri **d** all the house of Baasha, 8045
2Ki 8:19 Yet the LORD would not **d** Judah for 7843
10:19 to the intent that *he* might **d** the worshippers of 6
13:23 Isaac, and Jacob, and would not **d** them, 7843
18:25 the LORD against this place to **d** it? 7843
18:25 to me, Go up against this land, and **d** it. 7843
24: 2 of Ammon, and sent them against Judah to **d** it, 6
1Ch 21:15 God sent an angel unto Jerusalem to **d** it: 7843
2Ch 12: 7 *therefore* I will not **d** them, but I will grant 7843
12:12 that *he* would not **d** *him* altogether: 7843
20:23 utterly to slay and **d** *them*: and when they 8045

2Ch 20:23 of Seir, every one helped to d another. 4889
21: 7 Howbeit the LORD would not d the house 7843
25:16 I know that God hath determined to d thee, 7843
35:21 who is with me, that he d thee not. 7843
Ezr 6:12 caused his name to dwell there d all kings 4049
6:12 to d this house of God which is at 2255
Est 3: 6 wherefore Haman sought to d all the Jews 8045
3:13 to d, to kill, and to cause to perish, all Jews, 8045
4: 7 to the king's treasuries for the Jews, to d them. 6
4: 8 decree that was given at Shushan to d them, 8045
8: 5 which he wrote to d the Jews which are in all 6
8:11 to d, to slay, and to cause to perish, 8045
9:24 had devised against the Jews to d them, and 6
9:24 that is, the lot, to consume them, and to d them; 6
Job 2: 3 me against him, to d him without cause. 1104
6: 9 Even that it would please God to d me; 1792
8:18 If he d him from his place, then it shall 1104
10: 8 together round about; yet thou dost d me. 1104
19:26 though after my skin worms d this body, 5362
Ps 5: 6 Thou shalt d them that speak leasing: 6
5:10 D thou them, O God; let them fall by their 816
18:40 that I might d them that hate me. 6789
21:10 Their fruit shalt thou d from the earth, and 6
28: 5 he shall d them, and not build them up. 2040
40:14 together that seek after my soul to d it; 5595
52: 5 God shall likewise d thee for ever, he shall 5422
55: 9 D, O Lord, and divide their tongues: for I 1104
63: 9 to d it, shall go into the lower parts of 7722
69: 4 they that would d me, being mine enemies 6789
74: 8 said in their hearts, Let us d them together: 3238
101: 8 I will early d all the wicked of the land; 6789
106:23 Therefore he said that he would d them, 8045
106:23 turn away his wrath, lest he should d them. 7843
106:34 They did not d the nations, 8045
118:10 in the name of the LORD will I d them. 4135
118:11 in the name of the LORD I will d them. 4135
118:12 for in the name of the LORD I will d 4135
119:95 The wicked have waited for me to d me: but 6
143:12 and d all them that afflict my soul: 6
144: 6 shoot out thine arrows, and d them. 2000
145:20 that love him: but all the wicked will he d. 8045
Pr 1:32 and the prosperity of fools shall d them. 6
11: 3 the perverseness of transgressors shall d 7703
15:25 The LORD will d the house of the proud: 5255
21: 7 The robbery of the wicked shall d them; 1641
Ecc 5: 6 at thy voice, and d the work of thine hands? 2254
7:16 over wise: why shouldest thou d thyself? 8074
Isa 3:12 thee to err, and d the way of thy paths. 1104
10: 7 it is in his heart to d and cut off nations not 8045
11: 9 They shall not hurt nor d in all my holy 7843
11:15 the LORD shall utterly d the tongue of 2763
13: 5 of his indignation, to d the whole land. 2254
13: 9 and he shall d the sinners thereof out of it. 8045
19: 3 and I will d the counsel thereof: 1104
23:11 merchant city, to d the strong holds thereof. 8045
25: 7 he will d in this mountain the face of 1104
32: 7 he deviseth wicked devices to d the poor 2254
36:10 the LORD against this land to d it? 7843
36:10 unto me, Go up against this land, and d it. 7843
42:14 I will d and devour at once. 5395
51:13 of the oppressor, as if he were ready to d? 7843
54:16 and I have created the waster to d. 2254
65: 8 found in the cluster, and one saith, D it not; 7843
65: 8 servants' sakes, that I may not d them all. 7843
65:25 They shall not hurt nor d in all my holy 7843
Jer 1:10 to d, and to throw down, to build, and to plant. 6
5:10 Go ye up upon her walls, and d; but 7843
6: 5 let us go by night, and let us d her palaces. 7843
11:19 saying, Let us d the tree with the fruit 7843
12:17 I will utterly pluck up and d that nation, saith 6
13:14 nor spare, nor have mercy, but d them. 7843
15: 3 and the beasts of the earth, to devour and d. 7843
15: 6 out my hand against thee, and d thee; 7843
15: 7 bereave them of children, I will d my people, 6
17:18 of evil, and d them with double destruction. 7665
18: 7 to pluck up, and to pull down, and to d it; 6
23: 1 Woe be unto the pastors that d and scatter 6
25: 9 will utterly d them, and make them an 2763
31:28 and to throw down, and to d, and to afflict; 6
36:29 shall certainly come and d this land, 7843
46: 8 I will d the city and the inhabitants thereof. 6
48:18 upon thee, and he shall d thy strong holds. 7843
49: 9 by night, they will d till they have enough. 7843
49:38 will d from thence the king and the princes, 6
50:21 waste and utterly d after them, saith 2763
50:26 cast her up as heaps, and d her utterly: 2763
51: 3 her young men; d ye utterly all her host. 2763
51:11 for his device is against Babylon, to d it; 7843
51:20 and with thee will I d kingdoms: 7843
La 2: 8 The LORD hath purposed to d the wall of 7843
3:66 d them in anger from under the heavens of 8045
Eze 5:16 and which I will send to d you: 7843
6: 3 sword upon you, and I will d your high places. 6
9: 8 wilt thou d all the residue of Israel in thy 7843
14: 9 will d him from the midst of my people 8045
21:31 the hand of brutish men, and skilful to d. 4889
22:27 to shed blood, and to d souls, to get dishonest 6
22:30 me for the land, that I should not d it: 7843
25: 7 I will d thee; and thou shalt know that I am 8045
25:15 a despiteful heart, to d it for the old hatred; 4889
25:16 and d the remnant of the sea coast. 6
26: 4 they shall d the walls of Tyrus, and 7843
26:12 down thy walls, and d thy pleasant houses: 5422
28:16 I will d thee, O covering cherub, from 6
30:11 the nations, shall be brought to d the land: 7843
30:13 I will also d the idols, and I will cause their 6
32:13 I will d also all the beasts thereof from besides 6
34:16 I will d the fat and the strong; I will feed 8045
43: 3 vision that I saw when I came to d the city: 7843
Da 2:12 commanded to d all the wise men of Babylon. 7
2:24 whom the king had ordained to d the wise men 7
2:24 thus unto him; D not the wise men of Babylon: 7
4:23 saying, Hew the tree down, and d it; 2255
7:26 to consume and to d it unto the end. 7
8:24 he shall d wonderfully, and shall prosper, 7843
Da 8:24 and shall d the mighty and the holy people. 7843
8:25 in his heart, and by peace shall d many: 7843
9:26 of the prince that shall come shall d the city 7843
11:26 feed of the portion of his meat shall d him, 7665
11:44 he shall go forth with great fury to d, 8045
Hos 2:12 I will d her vines and her fig trees, 8074
4: 5 thee in the night, and I will d thy mother. 1820
11: 9 mine anger, I will not return to d Ephraim: 7843
Am 9: 8 and I will d it from off the face of the earth; 8045
9: 8 saving that I will not utterly d 8045+8045
Ob 1: 8 even d the wise men out of Edom, and 6
Mic 2:10 it shall d you, even with a sore destruction. 2254
5:10 of the midst of thee, and I will d thy chariots: 6
5:14 of the midst of thee: so will I d thy cities. 8045
Zep 2: 5 the land of the Philistines, I will even d thee, 6
2:13 out his hand against the north, and d Assyria; 6
Hag 2:22 I will d the strength of the kingdoms of 8045
Zec 12: 9 that I will seek to d all the nations that 8045
Mal 3:11 and he shall not d the fruits of your ground; 7843
Mt 2:13 for Herod will seek the young child to d 622
5:17 Think not that I am come to d the law, or 2647
5:17 I am not come to d, but to fulfil. 2647
10:28 rather fear him which is able to d both soul 622
12:14 council against him, how they might d him. 622
21:41 He will miserably d those wicked men, and 622
26:61 I am able to d the temple of God, and 2647
27:20 that they should ask Barabbas, and d Jesus. 622
Mk 1:24 art thou come to d us? I know thee who thou 622
3: 6 against him, how they might d him. 622
9:22 into the fire, and into the waters, to d him: 622
11:18 heard it, and sought how they might d him: 622
12: 9 he will come and d the husbandmen, and 622
14:58 I will d this temple that is made with hands, 2647
Lk 4:34 art thou come to d us? I know thee who thou 622
6: 9 or to do evil? to save life, or to d it? 622
9:56 For the Son of man is not come to d men's 622
19:47 and the chief of the people sought to d him, 622
20:16 He shall come and d these husbandmen, and 622
Jn 2:19 D this temple, and in three days I will raise 3089
10:10 but for to steal, and to kill, and to d: 622
Ac 6:14 that this Jesus of Nazareth shall d this 2647
Ro 14:15 D not him with thy meat, for whom Christ 622
14:20 For meat d not the work of God. All things 2647
1Co 1:19 I will d the wisdom of the wise, and 622
3:17 defile the temple of God, him shall God d; 5351
6:13 but God shall d both it and them. Now 2673
2Th 2: 8 shall d with the brightness of his coming: 2673
Heb 2:14 that through death he might d him that had 2673
Jas 4:12 is one lawgiver, who is able to save and to d: 622
1Jn 3: 8 that he might d the works of the devil. 3089
Rev 11:18 shouldest d them which destroy the earth. 1311
11:18 shouldest destroy them which d the earth. 1311

DESTROYED (167) [DESTROY]

Ge 7:23 every living substance was d which was 4229
7:23 the heaven; and they were d from the earth: 4229
13:10 before the LORD d Sodom and 7843
19:29 to pass, when God d the cities of the plain, 7843
34:30 slay me; and I shall be d, I and my house. 8045
Ex 10: 7 knowest thou not yet that Egypt is d? 6
22:20 the LORD only, he shall be utterly d. 2763
Nu 21: 3 and they utterly d them and their cities: 2763
Dt 1:44 chased you, as bees do, and d you in Seir, 3807
2:12 when they had d them from before them, 8045
2:21 the LORD d them before them; and 8045
2:22 when he d the Horims from before them; 8045
2:23 d them, and dwelt in their stead.) 8045
2:34 utterly d the men, and the women, and 2763
3: 6 we utterly d them, as we did unto Sihon 2763
4: 3 the LORD thy God hath d them from 8045
4:26 days upon it, but shall utterly be d. 8045+8045
7:20 are left, and hide themselves from thee, be d. 6
7:23 with a mighty destruction, until they be d. 8045
7:24 stand before thee, until thou have d them. 8045
9: 8 LORD was angry with you to have d you. 8045
9:20 was very angry with Aaron to have d him: 8045
11: 4 and how the LORD hath d them unto this day; 6
12:30 after that they be d from before thee; 8045
28:20 until thou be d, and until thou perish 8045
28:24 it come down upon thee, until thou be d. 8045
28:45 and overtake thee, till thou be d; 8045
28:48 of iron upon thy neck, until he have d thee. 8045
28:51 and the fruit of thy land, until thou be d: 8045
28:51 or flocks of thy sheep, until he have d thee. 6
28:61 LORD bring upon thee, until thou be d. 8045
31: 4 and unto the land of them, whom he d. 8045
Jos 2:10 Sihon and Og, whom ye utterly d. 2763
6:21 they utterly d all that was in the city, 2763
8:26 until he had utterly d all the inhabitants of 2763
10: 1 Joshua had taken Ai, and had utterly d it; 2763
10:28 the king thereof he utterly d, them, 2763
10:35 all the souls that were therein he utterly d 2763
10:37 d it utterly, and all the souls that were 2763
10:39 utterly d all the souls that were therein; 2763
10:40 but utterly d all that breathed, 2763
11:12 edge of the sword, and he utterly d them, 2763
11:14 until they had d them, neither left they any 8045
11:21 Joshua d them utterly with their cities. 2763
23:15 until he have d you from off this good land 8045
24: 8 their land; and I d them from before you. 8045
Jdg 1:17 that inhabited Zephath, and utterly d it: 2763
4:24 until they had d Jabin king of Canaan. 3772
6: 4 d the increase of the earth, till thou come 7843
20:21 d down to the ground of the Israelites that 7843
20:25 d down to the ground of the children of 7843
20:35 the children of Israel d of the Benjamites 7843
20:42 them which came out of the cities they d in 7843
21:16 seeing the women are d out of Benjamin? 8045
21:17 that a tribe be not d out of Israel. 4229
1Sa 5: 6 he d them, and smote them with emerods, 8074
15: 8 utterly d all the people with the edge of 2763
15: 9 was vile and refuse, that they d utterly. 2763
15:15 thy God; and the rest we have utterly d. 2763
15:20 and have utterly d the Amalekites. 2763
15:21 things which should have been utterly d, 2764
2Sa 11: 1 they d the children of Ammon, and 7843
21: 5 that devised against us that we should be d 8045
22:38 I have pursued mine enemies, and d them; 8045
24:16 said to the angel that d the people, It is 7843
1Ki 15:13 Asa d her idol, and burnt it by the brook 3772
15:29 until he had d him, according unto 8045
2Ki 10:17 till he had d him, according to the saying of 8045
10:28 Thus Jehu d Baal out of Israel. 8045
11: 1 was dead, she arose and d all the seed royal. 6
13: 7 for the king of Syria had d them, and had made 6
19:12 delivered them which my fathers have d; 7843
19:17 the kings of Assyria have d the nations and 2717
19:18 wood and stone: therefore they have d them. 6
21: 3 high places which Hezekiah his father had d; 6
21: 9 the LORD d before the children of Israel. 8045
1Ch 4:41 d them utterly unto this day, and dwelt in 2763
5:25 of the land, whom God d before them. 8045
20: 1 And Joab smote Rabbah, and d it. 2040
21:12 or three months to be d before thy foes, 5595
21:15 said to the angel that d, It is enough, 7843
2Ch 14:13 for they were d before the LORD, and 7665
15: 6 nation was d of nation, and city of city: 3807
20:10 but they turned from them, and d them not; 8045
22:10 d all the seed royal of the house of Judah. 1696
24:23 d all the princes of the people from among 7843
31: 1 until they had utterly d them all. Then all 3615
32:14 of those nations that my fathers utterly d, 2763
33: 9 whom the LORD had d before 8045
34:11 the houses which the kings of Judah had d. 7843
36:19 and d all the goodly vessels thereof. 7843
Ezr 4:15 of old time: for which cause was this city d. 2718
5:12 who d this house, and carried the people 5642
Est 3: 9 the king, let it be written that they may be d: 6
4:14 but thou and thy father's house shall be d: 6
7: 4 to be d, to be slain, and to perish. 8045
9: 6 palace the Jews slew and d five hundred men. 6
9:12 and d five hundred men in Shushan the palace, 6
Job 4:20 They are d from morning to evening: 3807
19:10 He hath d me on every side, and I am gone: 5422
34:25 them in the night, so that they are d. 1792
Ps 9: 5 rebuked the heathen, thou hast d the wicked, 6
9: 6 thou hast d cities; their memorial is 5428
11: 3 If the foundations be d, what can 2040
37:38 the transgressors shall be d together: 8045
73:27 thou hast d all them that go a whoring from 6789
78:38 forgave their iniquity, and d them not: 7843
78:45 devoured them; and frogs, which d them. 7843
78:47 He d their vines with hail, and 2026
92: 7 it is that they shall be d for ever: 8045
137: 8 O daughter of Babylon, who art to be d; 7703
Pr 13:13 Whoso despiseth the word shall be d: 2254
13:20 but a companion of fools shall be d. 7489
13:23 but there is that is d for want of judgment. 5595
29: 1 shall suddenly be d, and that without 7665
Isa 9:16 to err; and they that are led of them are d. 1104
10:27 the yoke shall be d because of 2254
14:17 as a wilderness, and d the cities thereof; 2040
14:20 because thou hast d thy land, and slain thy 7843
26:14 therefore hast thou visited and d them, and 8045
34: 2 he hath utterly d them, he hath delivered 2763
37:12 delivered them which my fathers have d, 7843
37:19 wood and stone: therefore they have d them. 6
48:19 his name should not have been cut off nor d 8045
Jer 12:10 Many pastors have d my vineyard, 7843
22:20 from the passages: for all thy lovers are d. 7665
48: 4 Moab is d; her little ones have caused a cry 7665
48: 8 also shall perish, and the plain shall be d, 8045
48:42 Moab shall be d from being a people, 8045
51: 8 Babylon is suddenly fallen and d: howl for 7665
51:55 and d out of her the great voice; 6
La 2: 5 he hath d his strong holds, and 7843
2: 6 he hath d his places of the assembly: 7843
2: 9 into the ground; he hath d and broken her bars: 6
Eze 26:17 say to thee, How art thou d, that wast inhabited 6
27:32 like the d in the midst of the sea? 1822
30: 8 and when all her helpers shall be d. 7665
32:12 and all the multitude thereof shall be d. 8045
Da 2:44 set up a kingdom, which shall never be d: 2255
6:26 his kingdom that which shall not be d, and 2255
7:11 and his body d, and given to the burning flame. 7
7:14 and his kingdom that which shall not be d. 2255
11:20 within few days he shall be d, neither in 7665
Hos 4: 6 My people are d for lack of knowledge, 1820
10: 8 also of Aven, the sin of Israel, shall be d: 8045
13: 9 O Israel, thou hast d thyself; but in me is 7843
Am 2: 9 Yet d I the Amorite before them, 8045
2: 9 yet I d his fruit from above, and his roots 8045
Zep 3: 6 their cities are d, so that there is no man, 6658
Mt 22: 7 and d those murderers, and burnt up their 622
Lk 17:27 the ark, and the flood came, and d them all. 622
17:29 and brimstone from heaven, and d them all. 622
Ac 3:23 shall be d from among the people. 1842
9:21 Is not this he that d them which called on 4199
13:19 And when he had d seven nations in 2507
19:27 and her magnificence should be d, 2507
Ro 6: 6 with him, that the body of sin might be d, 2673
1Co 10: 9 them also tempted, and were d of serpents. 622
10:10 also murmured, and were d of the destroyer. 622
15:26 The last enemy that shall be d is death. 2673
2Co 4: 9 but not forsaken; cast down, but not d; 622
Gal 1:23 now preacheth the faith which once he d. 4199
2:18 For if I build again the things which I d, 2647
Heb 11:28 lest he that d the firstborn should touch 3645
2Pe 2:12 brute beasts, made to be taken and d, 5356
Jude 1: 5 of Egypt, afterward d them that believed not. 622
Rev 8: 9 died; and the third part of the ships were d. 1311

DESTROYER (7) [DESTROY]

Ex 12:23 will not suffer the d to come in unto your 7843
Jdg 16:24 the d of our country, which slew many of 2717
Job 15:21 in prosperity the d shall come upon him. 7703
Ps 17: 4 lips I have kept me from the paths of the d. 6530
Pr 28:24 the same is the companion of a d. 376+4889
Jer 4: 7 and the d of the Gentiles is on his way; 7843
1Co 10:10 and were destroyed of the d. 3644

DESTROYERS (4) [DESTROY]
Job 33:22 near unto the grave, and his life to the **d**. 4191
Isa 49:17 thy **d** and they that made thee waste shall 2040
Jer 22: 7 I will prepare **d** against thee, every one 7843
50:11 O ye **d** of mine heritage, because ye are 8154

DESTROYEST (4) [DESTROY]
Job 14:19 dust of the earth; and thou **d** the hope of man. 6
Jer 51:25 saith the LORD, which **d** all the earth: 7843
Mt 27:40 *Thou* that **d** the temple, and buildest *it* in *2647*
Mk 15:29 *thou* that **d** the temple, and buildest *it* in *2647*

DESTROYETH (8) [DESTROY]
Dt 8:20 As the nations which the LORD **d** before your 6
Job 9:22 therefore I said *it,* He **d** the perfect and 3615
12:23 He increaseth the nations, and **d** them: 6
Pr 6:32 he *that* doeth it **d** his own soul. 7843
11: 9 A hypocrite with *his* mouth **d** his 7843
31: 3 nor thy ways to *that which* **d** kings. 4229
Ecc 7: 7 maketh a wise *man* mad; and a gift **d** the heart. 6
9:18 weapons of war: but one sinner **d** much good. 6

DESTROYING (14) [DESTROY]
Dt 3: 6 **utterly d** the men, women, and children, 2763
13:15 **d** it **utterly**, and all that *is* therein, and 2763
Jos 11:11 **utterly d** *them:* there was not any left to 2763
2Ki 19:11 have done to all lands, by **d** them **utterly**: 2763
1Ch 21:12 the angel of the LORD **d** throughout all 7843
21:15 as *he* was **d**, the LORD beheld, and 7843
Isa 28: 2 *which* as a tempest of hail *and* a **d** storm, 6986
37:11 have done to all lands by **d** them **utterly**; 2763
Jer 2:30 hath devoured your prophets, like a **d** lion. 7843
51: 1 of them that rise up against me, a **d** wind; 7843
51:25 Behold, I *am* against thee, O **d** mountain, 4889
La 2: 8 he hath not withdrawn his hand from **d**: 1104
Eze 9: 1 even every man *with* his **d** weapon in his 4892
20:17 Nevertheless mine eye spared them from **d** 7843

DESTRUCTION (94) [DESTROY]
Dt 7:23 shall destroy them *with* a mighty **d**, 4103
32:24 with burning heat, and with bitter **d**: 6986
1Sa 5: 9 was against the city *with* a very great **d**: 4103
5:11 for there was a deadly **d** throughout all 4103
1Ki 20:42 hand a man whom I **appointed to utter d**, 2764
2Ch 22: 4 after the death of his father to his **d**. 4889
22: 7 the **d** of Ahaziah was of God by coming to 8395
26:16 was strong, his heart was lifted up to *his* **d**: 7843
Est 8: 6 how can I endure to see the **d** of my kindred? 13
9: 5 **d**, and did what they would unto those that 12
Job 5:21 neither shalt thou be afraid of **d** when it 7701
5:22 At **d** and famine thou shalt laugh: 7701
18:12 and **d** *shall be* ready at his side. 343
21:17 *how oft* cometh their **d** upon them! 343
21:20 His eyes shall see his **d**, and he shall drink 3589
21:30 That the wicked is reserved to the day of **d**? 343
26: 6 *is* naked before him, and **d** hath no covering. 11
28:22 **D** and death say, We have heard the fame 11
30:12 they raise up against me the ways of their **d**. 343
30:24 hand to the grave, though *they* cry in his **d**. 6365
31: 3 *Is* not **d** to the wicked? and a strange 343
31:12 For it *is* a fire *that* consumeth to **d**, and 11
31:23 For **d** from God *was* a terror to me, and 343
31:29 If I rejoiced at the **d** of him that hated me, 6365
Ps 35: 8 Let **d** come upon him at unawares; and 7722
35: 8 catch himself: into that *very* **d** let him fall. 7722
55:23 shalt bring them down into the pit of **d**: 7845
73:18 *places:* thou castedst them down into **d**. 4876
88:11 in the grave? *or* thy faithfulness in **d**? 11
90: 3 Thou turnest man to **d**; and sayest, Return, 1793
91: 6 *nor* for the **d** *that* wasteth at noonday. 6986
103: 4 Who redeemeth thy life from **d**; 7845
Pr 1:27 and your **d** cometh as a whirlwind; 343
10:14 but the mouth of the foolish *is* near **d**. 4288
10:15 the **d** of the poor *is* their poverty. 4288
10:29 but **d** *shall be* to the workers of iniquity. 4288
13: 3 he that openeth wide his lips shall have **d**. 4288
14:28 in the want of people *is* the **d** of the prince. 4288
15:11 Hell and **d** *are* before the LORD: how much 11
16:18 Pride *goeth* before **d**, and a haughty spirit 7667
17:19 *and* he that exalteth his gate seeketh **d**. 7667
18: 7 A fool's mouth *is* his **d**, and his lips *are* 4288
18:12 Before **d** the heart of man is haughty, and 7667
21:15 but **d** *shall be* to the workers of iniquity. 4288
24: 2 For their heart studieth **d**, and their lips talk 7701
27:20 Hell and **d** are never full; so the eyes of man 10
31: 8 of all such as are **appointed to d**. 1121+2475
Isa 1:28 the **d** of the transgressors and of the sinners 7667
10:25 shall cease, and mine anger in their **d**. 8399
13: 6 it shall come as a **d** from the Almighty. 7701
14:23 I will sweep it with the besom of **d**, 8045
15: 5 of Horonaim they shall raise up a cry of **d**. 7667
19:18 of hosts: one shall be called, The city of **d**. 2041
24:12 and the gate is smitten *with* **d**. 7591
49:19 thy desolate places, and the land of thy **d**, 2035
51:19 and **d**, and the famine, and the sword: 7667
59: 7 of iniquity; wasting and **d** *are* in their paths. 7667
60:18 thy land, wasting nor **d** within thy borders; 7667
Jer 4: 6 bring evil from the north, and a great **d**. 7667
4:20 **D** upon destruction is cried; for the whole 7667
4:20 Destruction upon **d** is cried; for the whole 7667
6: 1 evil appeareth out of the north, and great **d**. 7667
17:18 of evil, and destroy them *with* double **d**. 7670
46:20 *is like* a very fair heifer, *but* **d** cometh; 7171
48: 3 *be* from Horonaim, spoiling and great **d**. 7667
48: 5 the enemies have heard a cry of **d**. 7667
50:22 of battle *is* in the land, and of great **d**. 7667
51:54 and great **d** from the land of the Chaldeans: 7667
La 2:11 for the **d** of the daughter of my people; 7667
3:47 a snare is come upon us, desolation and **d**. 7667
3:48 for the **d** of the daughter of my people. 7667
4:10 they were their meat in the **d** of 7667
Eze 5:16 which shall be for *their* **d**, *and* which I will 4889
7:25 **D** cometh; and they shall seek peace, and 7089
32: 9 when I shall bring thy **d** among the nations, 7667
Hos 7:13 **d** unto them! because they have 7701
9: 6 For lo, they are gone because of **d**: 7701
13:14 be thy plagues; O grave, I will be thy **d**: 6987
Joel 1:15 and as a **d** from the Almighty shall it come. 7701
Ob 1:12 over the children of Judah in the day of their **d**; 6
Mic 2:10 it shall destroy *you,* even *with* a sore **d**. 2256
Zec 14:11 in it, and there shall be no more **utter d**; 2764
Mt 7:13 that leadeth to **d**, and many there be which *684*
Ro 3:16 **D** and misery *are* in their ways: *4938*
9:22 longsuffering *the* vessels of wrath fitted to **d**: *684*
1Co 5: 5 To deliver such a one unto Satan for the **d** *3639*
2Co 10: 8 and not for your **d**, I should not be *2506*
13:10 hath given me to edification, and not to **d**. *2506*
Php 3:19 Whose end *is* **d**, whose God *is their* belly, *684*
1Th 5: 3 then sudden **d** cometh upon them, as travail *3639*
2Th 1: 9 Who shall be punished *with* everlasting **d** *3639*
1Ti 6: 9 which drown men in **d** and perdition. *3639*
2Pe 2: 1 and bring upon themselves swift **d**. *684*
3:16 also the other scriptures, unto their own **d**. *684*

DESTRUCTIONS (3) [DESTROY]
Ps 9: 6 thou enemy, **d** are come to a perpetual end: 2723
35:17 rescue my soul from their **d**, my darling 7722
107:20 and delivered *them* from their **d**. 7825

DETAIN (2) [DETAINED]
Jdg 13:15 I pray thee, let us **d** thee, until we shall 6113
13:16 Though thou **d** me, I will not eat of thy 6113

DETAINED (1) [DETAIN]
1Sa 21: 7 *was* there that day, **d** before the LORD; 6113

DETER See FORBAD

DETERMINATE (1) [DETERMINE]
Ac 2:23 being delivered by the **d** counsel and *3724*

DETERMINATION (1) [DETERMINE]
Zep 3: 8 for my **d** *is* to gather the nations, that I may 4941

DETERMINE (1) [DETERMINATE, DETERMINATION, DETERMINED]
Ex 21:22 upon him; and he shall pay as the judges **d**. NIH

DETERMINED (30) [DETERMINE]
1Sa 20: 7 *then* be sure that evil is **d** by him. 3615
20: 9 for if I knew certainly that evil were **d** by 3615
20:33 whereby Jonathan knew that it was **d** of his 3617
25:17 for evil is **d** against our master, and 3615
2Sa 13:32 **d** from the day that he forced his 1961+7760
2Ch 2: 1 Solomon **d** to build a house for the name of 559
25:16 I know that God hath **d** to destroy thee, 3289
Est 7: 7 for he saw that there was evil **d** against him 3615
Job 14: 5 Seeing his days *are* **d**, the number of his 2782
Isa 10:23 even **d**, *in* the midst of all *the land.* 2782
19:17 of hosts, which he hath **d** against it. 3289
28:22 even **d** upon the whole earth. 2782
Da 9:24 Seventy weeks are **d** upon thy people and 2852
9:26 unto the end of the war desolations *are* **d**. 2782
9:27 that **d** shall be poured upon the desolate. 2782
11:36 for that that is **d** shall be done. 2782
Lk 22:22 truly the Son of man goeth, as it was **d**: *3724*
Ac 3:13 of Pilate, when he was **d** to let *him* go. *2919*
4:28 and thy counsel **d before** to be done. *4309*
11:29 **d** to send relief unto the brethren which *3724*
15: 2 they **d** that Paul and Barnabas, and *5021*
15:37 And Barnabas **d** to take with *them* John, *1011*
17:26 and hath **d** the times before appointed, and *3724*
19:39 *matters,* it shall be **d** in a lawful assembly. *1956*
20:16 For Paul had **d** to sail by Ephesus, because *2919*
25:25 appealed to Augustus, I have **d** to send him. *2919*
27: 1 And when it was **d** that we should sail into *2919*
1Co 2: 2 For I **d** not to know any *thing* among you, *2919*
2Co 2: 1 But I **d** this with myself, that *I* would not *2919*
Tit 3:12 to Nicopolis: for I have **d** there to winter. *2919*

DETEST (1) [DETESTABLE]
Dt 7:26 *but* thou shalt **utterly d** it, and 8262+8262

DETESTABLE (6) [DETEST]
Jer 16:18 inheritance with the carcases of their **d** 8251
Eze 5:11 defiled my sanctuary with all thy **d things**, 8251
7:20 *and* of their **d things** therein: 8251
11:18 they shall take away all the **d things** 8251
11:21 walketh after the heart of their **d things** 8251
37:23 nor with their **d things**, nor with any of 8251

DEUEL (4) [REUEL]
Nu 1:14 Of Gad; Eliasaph the son of **D**. 1845
7:42 On the sixth day Eliasaph the son of **D**, 1845
7:47 *was* the offering of Eliasaph the son of **D**. 1845
10:20 children of Gad *was* Eliasaph the son of **D**. 1845

DEVICE (10) [DEVICES]
2Ch 2:14 to find out every **d** which shall be put to 4284
Est 8: 3 his **d** that he had devised against the Jews. 4284
9:25 he commanded by letters *that* his wicked **d**, 4284
Ps 21:11 they imagined a **mischievous d**, 4209
140: 8 further not his **wicked d**; *lest* they exalt 2162
Ecc 9:10 nor **d**, nor knowledge, nor wisdom, in 2808
Jer 18:11 against you, and devise a **d** against you: 4284
51:11 for his **d** *is* against Babylon, to destroy it; 4209
La 3:62 and their **d** against me all the day. 1902
Ac 17:29 silver, or stone, graven by art and man's **d**. *1761*

DEVICES (16) [DEVICE]
Job 5:12 He disappointeth the **d** of the crafty, so 4284
21:27 the **d** *which* ye wrongfully imagine against 4209
Ps 10: 2 let them be taken in the **d** that they have 4209
33:10 he maketh the **d** of the people of none 4284
37: 7 of the man who bringeth **wicked d** to pass. 4209
Pr 1:31 own way, and be filled with their own **d**. 4156
12: 2 but a man of **wicked d** will he condemn. 4209
14:17 and a man of **wicked d** is hated. 4209
19:21 *There are* many **d** in a man's heart; 4284
Isa 32: 7 he deviseth **wicked d** to destroy the poor 2154
Jer 11:19 I knew not that they had devised **d** against 4284
18:12 we will walk after our own **d**, and we will 4284
18:18 Come, and let us devise **d** against Jeremiah; 4284
Da 11:24 he shall forecast his **d** against the strong 4284
11:25 for they shall forecast **d** against him. 4284
2Co 2:11 of us: for we are not ignorant of his **d**. *3540*

DEVIL (61) [DEVILISH, DEVILS]
Mt 4: 1 into the wilderness to be tempted of the **d**. *1228*
4: 5 Then the **d** taketh him *up* into the holy city, *1228*
4: 8 the **d** taketh him *up* into an exceeding high *1228*
4:11 Then the **d** leaveth him, and behold, *1228*
9:32 to him a dumb man **possessed with a d**. *1139*
9:33 And when the **d** was cast out, the dumb *1140*
11:18 nor drinking, and they say, He hath a **d**. *1140*
12:22 brought unto him **one possessed with a d**, *1139*
13:39 The enemy that sowed them is the **d**; *1228*
15:22 my daughter is grievously **vexed with a d**. *1139*
17:18 And Jesus rebuked the **d**; and he departed *1140*
25:41 prepared for the **d** and his angels: *1228*
Mk 5:15 and see him that was **possessed with the d**, *1139*
5:16 to him that was **possessed with the d**, *1139*
5:18 he that had been **possessed with the d** *1139*
7:26 would cast forth the **d** out of her daughter. *1140*
7:29 thy way; the **d** is gone out of thy daughter. *1140*
7:30 she found the **d** gone out, and *her* daughter *1140*
Lk 4: 2 Being forty days tempted of the **d**. And in *1228*
4: 3 And the **d** said unto him, If thou be the Son *1228*
4: 5 And the **d**, taking him up into a high *1228*
4: 6 And the **d** said unto him, All this power *1228*
4:13 And when the **d** had ended all *1228*
4:33 which had a spirit of an unclean **d**, and *1140*
4:35 And when the **d** had thrown him in *1140*
7:33 nor drinking wine; and ye say, He hath a **d**. *1140*
8:12 then cometh the **d**, and taketh away *1228*
8:29 was driven of the **d** into the wilderness.) *1142*
9:42 the **d** threw him down, and tare *him.* And *1140*
11:14 And he was casting out a **d**, and it was *1140*
11:14 when the **d** was gone out, the dumb spake; *1140*
Jn 6:70 I chosen you twelve, and one of you is a **d**? *1228*
7:20 people answered and said, Thou hast a **d**: *1140*
8:44 Ye are of *your* father the **d**, and the lusts of *1228*
8:48 well that thou art a Samaritan, and hast a **d**? *1140*
8:49 Jesus answered, I have not a **d**; but *1140*
8:52 unto him, Now we know that thou hast a **d**. *1140*
10:20 of them said, He hath a **d**, and is mad; *1140*
10:21 are not the words of him that **hath a d**. *1139*
10:21 a devil. Can a **d** open the eyes of the blind? *1140*
13: 2 the **d** having now put into the heart of Judas *1228*
Ac 10:38 healing all that were oppressed of the **d**; *1228*
13:10 and all mischief, *thou* child of the **d**, *1228*
Eph 4:27 Neither give place to the **d**. *1228*
6:11 be able to stand against the wiles of the **d**. *1228*
1Ti 3: 6 he fall into the condemnation of the **d**. *1228*
3: 7 he fall into reproach and the snare of the **d**. *1228*
2Ti 2:26 themselves out of the snare of the **d**, *1228*
Heb 2:14 that had the power of death, that is, the **d**; *1228*
Jas 4: 7 Resist the **d**, and he will flee from you. *1228*
1Pe 5: 8 because your adversary the **d**, as a roaring *1228*
1Jn 3: 8 He that committeth sin is of the **d**; for *1228*
3: 8 for the **d** sinneth from the beginning. *1228*
3: 8 that he might destroy the works of the **d**. *1228*
3:10 God are manifest, and the children of the **d**: *1228*
Jude 1: 9 when contending with the **d** he disputed *1228*
Rev 2:10 the **d** shall cast *some* of you into prison, *1228*
12: 9 called the **d**, and Satan, which deceiveth *1228*
12:12 for the **d** is come down unto you, *1228*
20: 2 which is the **d**, and Satan, and bound him a *1228*
20:10 And the **d** that deceived them was cast into *1228*

DEVILISH (1) [DEVIL]
Jas 3:15 not from above, but *is* earthly, sensual, **d**. *1141*

DEVILS (55) [DEVIL]
Lev 17: 7 shall no more offer their sacrifices unto **d**, 8163
Dt 32:17 They sacrificed unto **d**, not *to* God; *to* gods 7700
2Ch 11:15 for the **d**, and for the calves which he had 8163
Ps 106:37 their sons and their daughters unto **d**, 7700
Mt 4:24 and those which were **possessed with d**, *1139*
7:22 thy name? and in thy name have cast out **d**? *1140*
8:16 unto him many *that were* **possessed with d**: *1139*
8:28 there met him two **possessed with d**, *1139*
8:31 So the **d** besought him, saying, If thou cast *1142*
8:33 was befallen to the **possessed of the d**. *1139*
9:34 He casteth out the **d** through the prince of *1140*
9:34 out the devils through the prince of the **d**. *1140*
10: 8 the lepers, raise the dead, cast out **d**: *1140*
12:24 This *fellow* doth not cast out **d**, but by *1140*
12:24 but by Beelzebub the prince of the **d**. *1140*
12:27 And if I by Beelzebub cast out **d**, by whom *1140*
12:28 But if I cast out **d** by the Spirit of God, then *1140*
Mk 1:32 and them that were **possessed with d**. *1139*
1:34 of divers diseases, and cast out many **d**; *1140*
1:34 and suffered not the **d** to speak, because *1140*
1:39 throughout all Galilee, and cast out **d**. *1140*
3:15 power to heal sicknesses, and to cast out **d**: *1140*
3:22 by the prince of the **d** casteth he out devils. *1140*
3:22 by the prince of the devils casteth he out **d**. *1140*
5:12 And all the **d** besought him, saying, *1142*
6:13 And they cast out many **d**, and *1140*
9:38 we saw one casting out **d** in thy name, and *1140*
16: 9 out of whom he had cast seven **d**. *1140*
16:17 In my name shall they cast out **d**; they shall *1140*
Lk 4:41 And **d** also came out of many, crying out, *1140*
8: 2 out of whom went seven **d**, *1140*
8:27 which had **d** long time, and ware no *1140*
8:30 because many **d** were entered into him. *1140*
8:33 Then went the **d** out of the man, and *1140*
8:35 the man, out of whom the **d** were departed, *1140*
8:36 he that was **possessed of the d** was healed. *1139*
8:38 Now the man out of whom the **d** were *1140*

Lk 9: 1 gave them power and authority over all **d**, *1140*
9:49 we saw one casting out **d** in thy name; *1140*
10:17 even the **d** are subject unto us through thy *1140*
11:15 He casteth out **d** through Beelzebub *1140*
11:15 devils through Beelzebub the chief of the **d**. *1140*
11:18 ye say that I cast out **d** through Beelzebub. *1140*
11:19 And if I by Beelzebub cast out **d**, by whom *1140*
11:20 But if I with the finger of God cast out **d**, *1140*
13:32 I cast out **d**, and I do cures to day and *1140*
1Co 10:20 they sacrifice to **d**, and not to God: *1140*
10:20 not that ye should have fellowship with **d**. *1140*
10:21 drink the cup of the Lord, and the cup of **d**: *1140*
10:21 of the Lord's table, and of the table of **d**. *1140*
1Ti 4: 1 heed to seducing spirits, and doctrines of **d**; *1140*
Jas 2:19 doest well: the **d** also believe, and tremble. *1140*
Rev 9:20 that they should not worship **d**, and idols of *1140*
16:14 For they are the spirits of **d**, working *1142*
18: 2 is fallen, and is become the habitation of **d**, *1142*

D

DEVIOUS See FROWARD

DEVISE (16) [DEVISED, DEVISETH]
Ex 31: 4 To **d** cunning works, to work in gold, and 2803
35:32 to **d** curious works, to work in gold, and 2803
35:35 and of **those that d cunning work**. 2803+4284
2Sa 14:14 yet doth he **d** means, that *his* banished be 2803
Ps 35: 4 and brought to confusion that **d** my hurt. 2803
35:20 they **d** deceitful matters against *them that* 2803
41: 7 against me: against me do they **d** my hurt. 2803
Pr 3:29 **D** not evil against thy neighbour, seeing he 2790
14:22 Do they not err that **d** evil? but mercy and 2790
14:22 and truth *shall be* to them that **d** good. 2790
16:30 He shutteth his eyes to **d** froward things: 2803
Jer 18:11 against you, and **d** a device against you: 2803
18:18 and let us **d** devices against Jeremiah; 2803
Eze 11: 2 these *are* the men that **d** mischief, and give 2803
Mic 2: 1 Woe to them that **d** iniquity, and work evil 2803
2: 3 Behold, against this family do I **d** an evil, 2803

DEVISED (12) [DEVISE]
2Sa 21: 5 that **d** against us *that* we should be 1819
1Ki 12:33 *even* in the month which he had **d** of his own 908
Est 8: 3 his device that he had **d** against the Jews. 2803
8: 5 let it be written to reverse the letters **d** by 4284
9:24 had **d** against the Jews to destroy them, and 2803
9:25 which he **d** against the Jews, should return 2803
Ps 31:13 against me, they **d** to take away my life. 2161
Jer 11:19 I knew not that they had **d** devices against 2803
48: 2 in Heshbon they have **d** evil against it; 2803
51:12 for the LORD hath both **d** and done that 2161
La 2:17 LORD hath done *that* which he had **d**; 2161
2Pe 1:16 For we have not followed **cunningly d** *4679*

DEVISETH (8) [DEVISE]
Ps 36: 4 He **d** mischief upon his bed; he setteth 2803
52: 2 Thy tongue **d** mischiefs; like a sharp rasor, 2803
Pr 6:14 *is* in his heart, he **d** mischief continually; 2790
6:18 A heart that **d** wicked imaginations, 2790
16: 9 A man's heart **d** his way: but the LORD 2803
24: 8 He that **d** to do evil shall be called a 2803
Isa 32: 7 he **d** wicked devices to destroy the poor 3289
32: 8 the liberal **d** liberal *things;* and by liberal 3289

DEVOTE (1) [DEVOTED, DEVOTIONS]
Lev 27:28 that a man shall **d** unto the LORD of all 2763

DEVOTED (7) [DEVOTE]
Lev 27:21 shall be holy unto the LORD, as a field **d**; 2764
27:28 Notwithstanding no **d thing**, that a man 2764
27:28 every **d thing** *is* most holy unto 2764
27:29 None **d**, which shall be devoted of men, 2764
27:29 None devoted, which shall be **d** of men, 2763
Nu 18:14 Every thing **d** in Israel shall be thine. 2764
Ps 119:38 word unto thy servant, who *is* **d** to thy fear. NIH

DEVOTIONS (1) [DEVOTE]
Ac 17:23 For as I passed by, and beheld your **d**, *4574*

DEVOUR (71) [DEVOURED, DEVOURER, DEVOUREST, DEVOURETH, DEVOURING]
Ge 49:27 in the morning he shall **d** the prey, and 398
Dt 32:42 with blood, and my sword shall **d** flesh; 398
Jdg 9:15 of the bramble, and **d** the cedars of Lebanon. 398
9:20 **d** the men of Shechem, and the house of 398
9:20 from the house of Millo, and **d** Abimelech. 398
2Sa 2:26 to Joab, and said, Shall the sword **d** for ever? 398
2Ch 7:13 or if I command the locusts to **d** the land, or 398
Job 18:13 It shall **d** the strength of his skin: *even* 398
18:13 *even* the firstborn of death shall **d** his 398
Ps 21: 9 up in his wrath, and the fire shall **d** them. 398
50: 3 a fire shall **d** before him, and it shall be very 398
80:13 and the wild beast of the field doth **d** it. 7462
Pr 30:14 to **d** the poor from off the earth, and 398
Isa 1: 7 strangers **d** it in your presence, and *it is* 398
9:12 they shall **d** Israel with open mouth. 398
9:18 it shall **d** the briers and thorns, and 398
10:17 it shall burn and **d** his thorns and his briers 398
26:11 yea, the fire of thine enemies shall **d** them. 398
31: 8 the sword, not of a mean man, shall **d** him: 398
33:11 your breath, *as* fire, shall **d** you. 398
42:14 I will destroy and **d** at once. 7602
56: 9 All ye beasts of the field, come to **d**, *yea,* all 398
Jer 2: 3 all that **d** him shall offend; evil shall come 398
5:14 and this people wood, and it shall **d** them. 398
12: 9 all the beasts of the field, come to **d**. 402
12:12 for the sword of the LORD *shall* **d** from 398
15: 3 and the beasts of the earth, to **d** and destroy. 398
17:27 it shall **d** the palaces of Jerusalem, and 398
21:14 and it shall **d** all things round about it. 398
30:16 Therefore all they that **d** thee shall be 398
46:10 the sword shall **d**, and it shall be satiate and 398
46:14 for the sword shall **d** round about thee. 398
48:45 shall **d** the corner of Moab, and the crown of 398
50:32 his cities, and it shall **d** all round about him. 398
Eze 7:15 the city, famine and pestilence shall **d** him. 398
15: 7 from *one* fire, and *another* fire shall **d** them; 398
20:47 it shall **d** every green tree in thee, and 398
23:37 to pass for them through *the fire,* to **d** *them.* 402
28:18 it shall **d** thee, and I will bring thee to ashes 398
34:28 neither shall the beast of the land **d** them; 398
36:14 Therefore thou shalt **d** men no more, 398
Da 7: 5 they said thus unto it, Arise, **d** much flesh. 399
7:23 shall **d** the whole earth, and shall tread it 399
Hos 5: 7 now shall a month **d** them with their 398
8:14 his cities, and it shall **d** the palaces thereof. 398
11: 6 and **d** *them,* because of their own counsels. 398
13: 8 and there will I **d** them like a lion: 398
Am 1: 4 which shall **d** the palaces of Ben-hadad. 398
1: 7 of Gaza, which shall **d** the palaces thereof: 398
1:10 of Tyrus, which shall **d** the palaces thereof. 398
1:12 which shall **d** the palaces of Bozrah. 398
1:14 it shall **d** the palaces thereof, with shouting 398
2: 2 and it shall **d** the palaces of Kerioth: 398
2: 5 and it shall **d** the palaces of Jerusalem. 398
5: 6 **d** *it,* and *there be* none to quench *it* in 398
Ob 1:18 and they shall kindle in them, and **d** them; 398
Na 2:13 and the sword shall **d** thy young lions: 398
3:13 unto thine enemies: the fire shall **d** thy bars. 398
3:15 There shall the fire **d** thee; the sword shall 398
Hab 3:14 their rejoicing *was* as to **d** the poor secretly. 398
Zec 9:15 they shall **d**, and subdue *with* sling stones; 398
11: 1 O Lebanon, that the fire may **d** thy cedars. 398
12: 6 they shall **d** all the people round about, 398
Mt 23:14 for ye **d** widows' houses, and for a pretence *2719*
Mk 12:40 Which **d** widows' houses, and for a *2719*
Lk 20:47 Which **d** widows' houses, and for a shew *2719*
2Co 11:20 if a man **d** *you,* if a man take *of you,* if a *2719*
Gal 5:15 But if ye bite and **d** one another, take heed *2719*
Heb 10:27 which shall **d** the adversaries. *2068*
1Pe 5: 8 walketh about, seeking whom he may **d**: *2666*
Rev 12: 4 for to **d** her child as soon as it was born. *2719*

DEVOURED (53) [DEVOUR]
Ge 31:15 and hath **quite d** also our money. 398+398
37:20 and we will say, *Some* evil beast hath **d** him: 398
37:33 *It is* my son's coat; an evil beast hath **d** him; 398
41: 7 the seven thin ears **d** the seven rank and 1104
41:24 the thin ears **d** the seven good ears: 1104
Lev 10: 2 **d** them, and they died before the LORD. 398
Nu 26:10 what time the fire **d** two hundred and 398
Dt 31:17 they shall be **d**, and many evils and 398
32:24 **d** with burning heat, and with bitter 3898
2Sa 18: 8 the wood **d** more people that day than 398
18: 8 more people that day than the sword **d**. 398
22: 9 of his nostrils, and fire out of his mouth **d**: 398
Ps 18: 8 of his nostrils, and fire out of his mouth **d**: 398
78:45 sorts *of flies* among them, which **d** them; 398
79: 7 For they have **d** Jacob, and laid waste his 398
105:35 in their land, and **d** the fruit of their ground. 398
Isa 1:20 and rebel, ye shall be **d** *with* the sword: 398
24: 6 Therefore hath the curse **d** the earth, and 398
Jer 2:30 your own sword hath **d** your prophets, like a 398
3:24 For shame hath **d** the labour of our fathers 398
8:16 and have **d** the land, and all that is in it; 398
10:25 **d** him, and consumed him, and have made 398
30:16 all they that devour thee shall be **d**; 398
50: 7 All that found them have **d** them: and 398
50:17 first the king of Assyria hath **d** him; and last 398
51:34 Nebuchadrezzar the king of Babylon hath **d** 398
La 4:11 and it hath **d** the foundations thereof. 398
Eze 15: 5 when the fire hath **d** it, and it is burned? 398
16:20 these hast thou sacrificed unto them to be **d**. 398
19: 3 and it learned to catch the prey; it **d** men. 398
19: 6 and learned to catch the prey, *and* **d** men. 398
19:14 *which* hath **d** her fruit, so that she hath no 398
22:25 they have **d** souls; they have taken 398
23:25 and thy residue shall be **d** by the fire. 398
33:27 open field will I give to the beasts to be **d**, 398
39: 4 and *to* the beasts of the field to be **d**. 402
Da 7: 7 it **d** and brake in pieces, and stamped 399
7:19 *which* **d**, brake in pieces, and stamped 399
Hos 7: 7 all hot as an oven, and have **d** their judges; 398
7: 9 Strangers have **d** his strength, and 398
Joel 1:19 for the fire hath **d** the pastures of 398
1:20 the fire hath **d** the pastures of the wilderness. 398
Am 4: 9 the palmerworm **d** *them:* yet have ye not 398
7: 4 and it **d** the great deep, and did eat up a part. 398
Na 1:10 they shall be **d** as stubble fully dry. 398
Zep 1:18 the whole land shall be **d** by the fire of his 398
3: 8 for all the earth shall be **d** with the fire of my 398
Zec 9: 4 in the sea; and she shall be **d** with fire. 398
Mt 13: 4 and the fowls came and **d** them **up**: *2719*
Mk 4: 4 and the fowls of the air came and **d** it **up**. *2719*
Lk 8: 5 trodden down, and the fowls of the air **d** it. *2719*
15:30 which hath **d** thy living with harlots, *2719*
Rev 20: 9 down from God out of heaven, and **d** them. *2719*

DEVOURER (1) [DEVOUR]
Mal 3:11 I will rebuke the **d** for your sakes, and 398

DEVOUREST (1) [DEVOUR]
Eze 36:13 Thou *land* **d up** men, and hast bereaved thy 398

DEVOURETH (10) [DEVOUR]
2Sa 11:25 for the sword **d** one as well as another: 398
Pr 19:28 and the mouth of the wicked **d** iniquity. 1104
20:25 *It is* a snare to the man *who* **d** *that which is* 3216
Isa 5:24 Therefore as the fire **d** the stubble, and 398
La 2: 3 like a flaming fire, *which* **d** round about. 398
Eze 15: 4 the fire **d** both the ends of it, and the midst 398
Joel 2: 3 A fire **d** before them; and behind them a 398
2: 5 like the noise of a flame of fire that **d** 398
Hab 1:13 holdest thy tongue when the wicked **d** 1104
Rev 11: 5 out of their mouth, and **d** their enemies: *2719*

DEVOURING (6) [DEVOUR]
Ex 24:17 **d** fire on the top of the mount in the eyes of 398
Ps 52: 4 Thou lovest all **d** words, O thou deceitful 1105
Isa 29: 6 and tempest, and the flame of **d** fire. 398
30:27 *of* indignation, and his tongue as a **d** fire: 398
30:30 *with* the flame of a **d** fire, *with* scattering, 398
33:14 Who among us shall dwell *with* the **d** fire? 398

DEVOUT (9)
Lk 2:25 and the same man *was* just and **d**, *2126*
Ac 2: 5 **d** men, out of every nation under heaven. *2126*
8: 2 And **d** men carried Stephen *to his burial,* *2126*
10: 2 A **d** *man,* and one that feared God with all *2152*
10: 7 a **d** soldier of them that waited on him *2152*
13:50 But the Jews stirred up the **d** and *4576*
17: 4 and of the **d** Greeks a great multitude, and *4576*
17:17 and with the **d** *persons,* and in the market *4576*
22:12 one Ananias, a **d** man according to the law, *2152*

DEW (37)
Ge 27:28 Therefore God give thee of the **d** of heaven, 2919
27:39 and of the **d** of heaven from above; 2919
Ex 16:13 in the morning the **d** lay round about 2919
16:14 when the **d** that lay was gone up, behold, 2919
Nu 11: 9 when the **d** fell upon the camp in the night, 2919
Dt 32: 2 as the rain, my speech shall distil as the **d**, 2919
33:13 for the **d**, and for the deep that coucheth 2919
33:28 wine; also his heavens shall drop down **d**. 2919
Jdg 6:37 *and* if the **d** be on the fleece only, and *it be* 2919
6:38 wringed the **d** out of the fleece, a bowl full 2919
6:39 upon all the ground let there be **d**. 2919
6:40 and there was **d** on all the ground. 2919
2Sa 1:21 Ye mountains of Gilboa, *let there be* no **d**, 2919
17:12 we *will light* upon him as the **d** falleth on 2919
1Ki 17: 1 there shall not be **d** nor rain these years, but 2919
Job 29:19 and the **d** lay all night upon my branch. 2919
38:28 or who hath begotten the drops of **d**? 2919
Ps 110: 3 the morning: thou hast the **d** of thy youth. 2919
133: 3 As the **d** of Hermon, *and as the dew* that 2919
133: 3 *as the* **d** that descended upon the mountains NIH
Pr 3:20 broken up, and the clouds drop down the **d**. 2919
19:12 a lion; but his favour *is* as **d** upon the grass. 2919
SS 5: 2 for my head is filled *with* **d**, *and* my locks 2919
Isa 18: 4 *and* like a cloud of **d** in the heat of harvest. 2919
26:19 for thy **d** *is as* the dew of herbs, and 2919
26:19 for thy dew *is as* the **d** of herbs, and 2919
Da 4:15 let it be wet with the **d** of heaven, and 2920
4:23 let it be wet with the **d** of heaven, and 2920
4:25 they *shall* wet thee with the **d** of heaven, 2920
4:33 and his body was wet with the **d** of heaven, 2920
5:21 and his body was wet with the **d** of heaven; 2920
Hos 6: 4 and as the early **d** *it* goeth away. 2919
13: 3 and as the early **d** that passeth away, 2919
14: 5 I will be as the **d** unto Israel: he shall grow 2919
Mic 5: 7 of many people as a **d** from the LORD, 2919
Hag 1:10 the heaven over you is stayed from **d**, 2919
Zec 8:12 and the heavens shall give their **d**; 2919

DIADEM (4)
Job 29:14 my judgment *was* as a robe and a **d**. 6797
Isa 28: 5 for a **d** of beauty, unto the residue of his 6843
62: 3 and a royal **d** in the hand of thy God. 6797
Eze 21:26 Remove the **d**, and take off the crown: 4701

DIAL (2)
2Ki 20:11 by which it had gone down in the **d** of 4609
Isa 38: 8 which is gone down in the sun **d** of Ahaz, 4609

DIAMOND (4)
Ex 28:18 *shall be* an emerald, a sapphire, and a **d**. 3095
39:11 an emerald, a sapphire, and a **d**. 3095
Jer 17: 1 a pen of iron, *and* with the point of a **d**: 8068
Eze 28:13 topaz, and the **d**, the beryl, the onyx, and 3095

DIANA (5)
Ac 19:24 which made silver shrines for **D**, *735*
19:27 also that the temple of the great goddess **D** *735*
19:28 saying, Great *is* **D** of the Ephesians. *735*
19:34 hours cried out, Great *is* **D** of the Ephesians. *735*
19:35 is a worshipper of the great goddess **D**, *735*

DIBLAH See DIBLATH

DIBLAIM (1)
Hos 1: 3 he went and took Gomer the daughter of **D**; 1691

DIBLATH (1)
Eze 6:14 desolate than the wilderness toward **D**, 1689

DIBON (9) [DIBON-GAD]
Nu 21:30 Heshbon is perished even unto **D**, and 1769
32: 3 **D**, and Jazer, and Nimrah, and Heshbon, 1769
32:34 the children of Gad built **D**, and Ataroth, 1769
Jos 13: 9 and all the plain of Medeba unto **D**; 1769
13:17 **D**, and Bamoth-baal, and Beth-baal-meon, 1769
Ne 11:25 at **D**, and *in* the villages thereof, and 1769
Isa 15: 2 and *to* **D**, the high places, to weep: 1769
Jer 48:18 Thou daughter that dost inhabit **D**, 1769
48:22 upon **D**, and upon Nebo, and 1769

DIBON-GAD (2) [DIBON, GAD]
Nu 33:45 they departed from Iim, and pitched in **D**. 1769
33:46 they removed from **D**, and encamped in 1769

DIBRI (1)
Lev 24:11 the daughter of **D**, of the tribe of Dan:) 1704

DID (1006) [DO]
Ge 3: 6 **d** eat, and gave also unto her husband with NIH
3: 6 unto her husband with her; and he **d** eat. NIH
3:12 she gave me of the tree, and I **d** eat. NIH
3:13 The serpent beguiled me, and I **d** eat. NIH
3:21 to his wife **d** the LORD God make coats of NIH
6:22 Thus **d** Noah; according to all that God 6213
6:22 to all that God commanded him, so **d** he. 6213
7: 5 Noah **d** according unto all that the LORD 6213

Ge 7:20 Fifteen cubits upward **d** the waters prevail; NIH
11: 9 the LORD **d** there confound the language NIH
11: 9 from thence **d** the LORD scatter them NIH
18: 8 stood by them under the tree, and they **d** eat. NIH
18:13 Wherefore **d** Sarah laugh, saying, NIH
19: 3 **d** bake unleavened bread, and they did eat. NIH
19: 3 did bake unleavened bread, and they **d** eat. NIH
21: 1 the LORD **d** unto Sarah as he had spoken. 6213
22: 1 that God **d** tempt Abraham, and said unto NIH
22:23 these eight Milcah **d** bear to Nahor, NIH
24:54 they **d** eat and drink, he and the men that NIH
25:28 loved Esau, because he **d** eat of *his* venison: NIH
25:34 he **d** eat and drink, and rose up, and NIH
26:20 the herdmen of Gerar **d** strive with Isaac's NIH
26:30 made them a feast, and they **d** eat and drink. NIH
27:25 And he brought *it* near to him, and he **d** eat: NIH
29:25 **d** not I serve with thee for Rachel? NIH
29:28 Jacob **d** so, and fulfilled her week: and 6213
30:40 Jacob **d** separate the lambs, and set the faces NIH
30:41 whensoever the stronger cattle **d** conceive, NIH
31:46 a heap: and they **d** eat there upon the heap. NIH
31:54 they **d** eat bread, and tarried all night in NIH
35: 5 they **d** not pursue after the sons of Jacob. NIH
38:10 *the thing* which he **d** displeased 6213
38:11 as his brethren **d**. And Tamar went and NIH
39: 3 *that* the LORD made all that he **d** to 6213
39: 6 ought he had, save the bread which he **d** eat. NIH
39:19 After this manner **d** thy servant to me; 6213
39:22 whatsoever they **d** there, he was the doer 6213
39:23 LORD *was* with him, and *that* which he **d**, 6213
40:17 the birds **d** eat them out of the basket upon NIH
40:23 Yet **d** not the chief butler remember Joseph, NIH
41: 4 leanfleshed kine **d** eat up the seven well NIH
41:12 to each man according to his dream he **d** NIH
41:20 the ill favoured kine **d** eat up the first seven NIH
42:20 and ye shall not die. And they **d** so. 6213
42:25 for the way: and thus **d** he unto them. 6213
43: 3 The man **d** solemnly protest unto us, saying, NIH
43:17 the man **d** as Joseph bade; and the man 6213
43:30 for his bowels **d** yern upon his brother: NIH
43:32 which **d** eat with him, by themselves: NIH
44: 2 he **d** according to the word that Joseph had 6213
45: 5 for God **d** send me before you to preserve NIH
45:21 the children of Israel **d** so: and Joseph gave 6213
47:22 **d** eat their portion which Pharaoh gave NIH
48:15 my fathers Abraham and Isaac **d** walk, NIH
50:12 his sons **d** unto him according as he 6213
50:15 requite us all the evil which we **d** unto him. 1580
50:16 Thy father **d** command before he died, NIH
50:17 and their sin; for they **d** unto thee evil: 1580
Ex 1:11 Therefore they **d** set over them taskmasters NIH
1:17 **d** not as the king of Egypt commanded 6213
2:13 he said to **him that d** the **wrong**, 7563
4:30 and **d** the signs in the sight of the people. 6213
5: 8 which they **d** make heretofore, you shall lay NIH
5:19 the officers of the children of Israel **d** see NIH
6: 8 *concerning* the which I **d** swear to give it to NIH
7: 6 Aaron **d** as the LORD commanded them, 6213
7: 6 as the LORD commanded them, so **d** they. 6213
7:10 they **d** so as the LORD had commanded: 6213
7:11 they also **d** in like manner with their 6213
7:20 Moses and Aaron **d** so, as the LORD 6213
7:22 the magicians of Egypt **d** so with their 6213
7:22 neither **d** he hearken unto them; NIH
7:23 neither **d** he set his heart to this also. NIH
8: 7 the magicians **d** so with their enchantments, 6213
8:13 the LORD **d** according to the word of 6213
8:17 they **d** so; for Aaron stretched out his hand 6213
8:18 the magicians **d** so with their enchantments 6213
8:24 the LORD **d** so; and there came a 6213
8:31 the LORD **d** according to the word of 6213
9: 6 the LORD **d** that thing on the morrow, 6213
9: 7 and he **d** not let the people go. NIH
10:11 and serve the LORD; for that you **d** desire. NIH
10:15 they **d** eat every herb of the land, and all NIH
11:10 Aaron **d** all these wonders before Pharaoh: 6213
12:28 **d** as the LORD had commanded Moses 6213
12:28 commanded Moses and Aaron, so **d** they. 6213
12:35 the children of Israel **d** according to 6213
12:50 Thus **d** all the children of Israel; as 6213
12:50 commanded Moses and Aaron, so **d** they. 6213
12:51 *that* the LORD **d** bring the children of NIH
13: 8 of that *which* the LORD **d** unto me when I 6213
14: 4 know that I *am* the LORD. And they **d** so. 6213
14:12 *Is* not this the word that we **d** tell thee in NIH
14:31 which the LORD **d** upon the Egyptians: 6213
16: 3 *and* when we **d** eat bread to the full; NIH
16:17 the children of Israel **d** so, and gathered, 6213
16:18 when they **d** mete *it* with an omer, he that NIH
16:24 it **d** not stink, neither was there any worm NIH
16:35 the children of Israel **d** eat manna forty NIH
16:35 they **d** eat manna, until they came unto NIH
17: 2 Wherefore the people **d** chide with Moses, NIH
17: 6 Moses **d** so in the sight of the elders of 6213
17:10 So Joshua **d** as Moses had said to him, and 6213
18: 7 in law, and **d obeisance**, and kissed him; 7812
18:14 when Moses' father in law saw all that he **d** 6213
18:24 his father in law, and **d** all that he had said. 6213
19: 4 Ye have seen what I **d** unto the Egyptians, 6213
24:11 also they saw God, and **d** eat and drink. NIH
32:12 say, For mischief **d** he bring them out, NIH
32:21 What **d** this people unto thee, that thou hast 6213
32:28 the children of Levi **d** according to 6213
33: 4 and no man **d** put on him his ornaments. NIH
34:28 he **d** neither eat bread, nor drink water. NIH
35:24 Every one that **d** offer an offering of silver NIH
35:25 all the women that were wise hearted **d** spin NIH
36:22 thus **d** he make for all the boards of NIH
36:29 thus he **d** to both of them in both 6213
39: 3 they **d** beat the gold into thin plates, and NIH
39:21 they **d** bind the breastplate by his rings unto NIH
39:32 the children of Israel **d** according to all that 6213
39:32 the LORD commanded Moses, so **d** they. 6213
39:43 Moses **d** look upon all the work, and NIH
40:16 Thus **d** Moses: according to all that 6213
Ex 40:16 that the LORD commanded him, so **d** he. 6213
Lev 4:20 he shall do with the bullock as he **d** with 6213
8: 4 Moses **d** as the LORD commanded him; 6213
8: 9 **d** he put the golden plate, the holy crown; NIH
8:36 his sons **d** all things which the LORD 6213
9:14 he **d** wash the inwards and the legs, and NIH
10: 7 they **d** according to the word of Moses. 6213
16:15 do with that blood as he **d** with the blood of 6213
16:34 he **d** as the LORD commanded Moses. 6213
24:23 the children of Israel **d** as the LORD 6213
26:35 because it **d** not rest in your sabbaths, NIH
27:24 whom the possession of the land **d** *belong.* NIH
Nu 1:54 the children of Israel **d** according to all that 6213
1:54 the LORD commanded Moses, so **d** they. 6213
2:34 the children of Israel **d** according to all that 6213
4:37 Aaron **d** number according to NIH
4:41 Aaron **d** number according to NIH
5: 4 the children of Israel **d** so, and put them out 6213
5: 4 unto Moses, so **d** the children of Israel. 6213
7:18 the son of Zuar, prince of Issachar, **d** offer: NIH
7:24 prince of the children of Zebulun, ***d** offer:* NIH
7:30 prince of the children of Reuben, ***d** offer:* NIH
7:36 prince of the children of Simeon, ***d** offer:* NIH
8: 3 Aaron **d** so; he lighted the lamps thereof 6213
8:20 **d** to the Levites according unto all that 6213
8:20 so **d** the children of Israel unto them. 6213
8:22 the Levites, so **d** they unto them. 6213
9: 5 so **d** the children of Israel. 6213
10:21 *the other* **d** set up the tabernacle against NIH
11: 5 the fish, which we **d** eat in Egypt freely; NIH
11:25 they prophesied, and **d** not cease. NIH
14:22 which I **d** in Egypt and in the wilderness, 6213
14:37 Even *those* men that **d** bring up the evil NIH
17:11 Moses **d** *so:* as the LORD commanded 6213
17:11 as the LORD commanded him, so **d** he. 6213
20:27 Moses **d** as the LORD commanded: and 6213
21:14 **What he d** in the Red sea, and *in* 2052
22:37 **D** I not earnestly send unto thee to call thee? NIH
23: 2 Balak **d** as Balaam had spoken; and Balak 6213
23:30 Balak **d** as Balaam had said, and offered a 6213
25: 2 the people **d** eat, and bowed down to their NIH
27:22 Moses **d** as the LORD commanded him: 6213
31:31 Eleazar the priest **d** as the LORD 6213
32: 8 Thus **d** your fathers, when I sent them from 6213
36:10 so **d** the daughters of Zelophehad: 6213
Dt 1:30 according to all that he **d** for you in Egypt 6213
1:32 Yet in this thing ye **d** not believe NIH
2:12 as Israel **d** unto the land of his possession, 6213
2:22 As he **d** to the children of Esau, 6213
2:29 Moabites which dwell in Ar, **d** unto me;) 6213
3: 6 as we **d** unto Sihon king of Heshbon, 6213
4: 3 Your eyes have seen what the LORD **d** 6213
4: 4 ye that **d** cleave unto the LORD your God NIH
4:33 **D** *ever* people hear the voice of God NIH
4:34 God **d** for you in Egypt before your eyes? 6213
5:23 (for the mountain **d** burn with fire,) NIH
7: 7 The LORD **d** not set his love upon you, NIH
7:18 what the LORD thy God **d** unto Pharaoh, 6213
8: 3 knewest not, neither **d** thy fathers know; NIH
8: 4 neither **d** thy foot swell, these forty years. NIH
9: 9 I neither **d** eat bread nor drink water: NIH
9:18 I **d** neither eat bread, nor drink water, NIH
11: 3 which he **d** in the midst of Egypt unto 6213
11: 4 what he **d** unto the army of Egypt, 6213
11: 5 what he **d** unto you in the wilderness, 6213
11: 6 what he **d** unto Dathan and Abiram, 6213
11: 7 all the great acts of the LORD which he **d**. 6213
12:30 How **d** these nations serve their gods? NIH
24: 9 Remember what the LORD thy God **d** 6213
25:17 Remember what Amalek **d** unto thee by 6213
29: 2 Ye have seen all that the LORD **d** before 6213
31: 4 the LORD shall do unto them as he **d** to 6213
32:12 *So* the LORD alone **d** lead him, and NIH
32:38 Which **d** eat the fat of their sacrifices, *and* NIH
33: 9 neither **d** he acknowledge his brethren, NIH
34: 9 and **d** as the LORD commanded Moses. 6213
Jos 2:10 what you **d** unto the two kings of 6213
2:11 had heard *these things,* our hearts **d** melt, NIH
2:11 neither **d** there remain any more courage in NIH
4: 8 the children of Israel **d** so as Joshua 6213
4:18 flowed over all his banks, as *they* **d** before. NIH
4:20 took out of Jordan, **d** Joshua pitch in Gilgal. NIH
4:23 as the LORD your God **d** to the Red sea, 6213
5: 4 this *is* the cause why Joshua **d** circumcise: NIH
5:11 they **d** eat of the old corn of the land on NIH
5:12 they **d** eat of the fruit of the land of Canaan NIH
5:14 **d** worship, and said unto him, What saith NIH
5:15 thou standest *is* holy. And Joshua **d** so. 6213
6:14 returned *into* the camp: so they **d** six days. 6213
9: 4 They **d** work wilily, and went and made as NIH
9: 9 the fame of him, and all that he **d** in Egypt, 6213
9:10 all that he **d** to the two kings of 6213
9:26 so **d** he unto them, and delivered them out 6213
10:23 they **d** so, and brought forth those five 6213
10:28 he **d** to the king of Makkedah as he did 6213
10:28 he did to the king of Makkedah as he **d** 6213
10:30 **d** unto the king thereof as he did unto 6213
10:30 did unto the king thereof as he **d** unto 6213
10:39 so he **d** to Debir, and to the king thereof; 6213
10:42 and their land **d** Joshua take *at* one time, NIH
11: 9 Joshua **d** unto them as the LORD bade 6213
11:12 **d** Joshua take, and smote them with NIH
11:13 save Hazor only; *that* **d** Joshua burn. NIH
11:15 so **d** Moses command Joshua, and so NIH
11:15 Moses command Joshua, and so **d** Joshua; 6213
12: 6 Them **d** Moses the servant of the LORD NIH
13:12 for these **d** Moses smite, and cast them out. NIH
13:22 **d** the children of Israel slay with the sword NIH
13:32 These *are the countries* which Moses **d** NIH
14: 5 so the children of Israel **d**, and they divided 6213
17:13 to tribute; but **d** not utterly drive them out. NIH
22:20 **D** not Achan the son of Zerah commit a NIH
22:33 **d** not intend to go up against them in battle, NIH
24: 5 according to *that* which I **d** amongst them: 6213
24:13 I have given you a land for which ye **d** not NIH
Jos 24:17 which **d** those great signs in our sight, and 6213
Jdg 1:21 the children of Benjamin **d** not drive out NIH
1:27 Neither **d** Manasseh drive out NIH
1:28 to tribute, and **d** not utterly drive them out. NIH
1:29 Neither **d** Ephraim drive out the Canaanites NIH
1:30 Neither **d** Zebulun drive out the inhabitants NIH
1:31 Neither **d** Asher drive out the inhabitants of NIH
1:32 of the land: for they **d** not drive them out. NIH
1:33 Neither **d** Naphtali drive out the inhabitants NIH
2: 7 works of the LORD, that he **d** for Israel. 6213
2:11 the children of Israel **d** evil in the sight of 6213
2:17 of the LORD; *but* they **d** not so. 6213
2:22 as their fathers **d** keep *it,* or not. NIH
3: 7 the children of Israel **d** evil in the sight of 6213
3:12 the children of Israel **d** evil again in 6213
3:16 he **d** gird it under his raiment upon his right NIH
4: 1 the children of Israel again **d** evil in 6213
5:17 why **d** Dan remain *in* ships? NIH
6: 1 the children of Israel **d** evil in the sight of 6213
6:13 **D** not the LORD bring us up from Egypt? NIH
6:20 and pour out the broth. And he **d** so. 6213
6:27 and **d** as the LORD had said unto him: 6213
6:27 could not do *it* by day, that he **d** *it* by night. 6213
6:40 God **d** so that night: for it was dry upon 6213
8: 1 And they **d** chide with him sharply. NIH
8:15 with whom ye **d** upbraid me, saying, NIH
8:25 **d** cast therein every man the earrings of his NIH
9:27 and **d** eat and drink, and cursed Abimelech. NIH
9:56 which he **d** unto his father, in slaying his 6213
9:57 all the evil of the men of Shechem **d** God NIH
10: 6 the children of Israel **d** evil again in 6213
10:11 ***D*** not *I deliver you* from the Egyptians, and NIH
10:12 and the Maonites, **d** oppress you; NIH
11: 7 **D** ye not hate me, and expel me out of my NIH
11:25 **d** he ever strive against Israel, or did he ever NIH
11:25 or **d** he ever fight against them, NIH
11:26 **d** ye not recover *them* within that time? NIH
11:39 who **d** with her *according to* his vow which 6213
13: 1 the children of Israel **d** evil again in 6213
13:19 *the angel* **d** wondrously; and Manoah and 6213
13:21 the angel of the LORD **d** no more appear NIH
14: 9 and he gave them, and they **d** eat: NIH
15:11 As they **d** unto me, so have I done unto 6213
16:21 of brass; and he **d** grind in the prison house. 1961
17: 6 every man **d** *that* which *was* right in his 6213
19: 4 so they **d** eat and drink, and lodged there. NIH
19: 6 and **d** eat and drink both of them together: NIH
19: 8 until afternoon, and they **d** eat both of them. NIH
19:21 they washed their feet, and **d** eat and drink. NIH
21:22 for ye **d** not give unto them at *this* time, NIH
21:23 the children of Benjamin **d** so, and 6213
21:25 every man **d** *that* which *was* right in his 6213
Ru 2:14 he reached her parched *corn,* and she **d** eat, NIH
2:19 blessed be he that **d** take knowledge of thee. NIH
3: 6 **d** according to all that her mother in law 6213
4:11 which two **d** build the house of Israel: NIH
1Sa 1: 7 *as* he **d** so year by year, when she went up 6213
1: 7 therefore she wept, and **d** not eat. NIH
1:18 **d** eat, and her countenance was no more NIH
2:11 the child **d** minister unto the LORD before 1961
2:14 So they **d** in Shiloh unto all the Israelites 6213
2:22 and heard all that his sons **d** unto all Israel; 6213
2:27 **D** I plainly appear unto the house of thy NIH
2:28 **d** I choose him out of all the tribes of Israel NIH
2:28 **d** I give unto the house of thy father all NIH
3: 7 Now Samuel **d** not yet know the LORD, NIH
3:19 **d** let none of his words fall to the ground. NIH
4:20 she answered not, neither **d** she regard *it.* NIH
6: 6 **d** they not let the people go, and NIH
6:10 the men **d** so; and took two milch kine, 6213
7: 4 the children of Israel **d** put away Baalim NIH
7:14 the coasts thereof **d** Israel deliver out of NIH
9:24 So Saul **d** eat with Samuel that day. NIH
12: 7 which he **d** to you and to your fathers. 6213
13: 6 the people **d** hide themselves in caves, and NIH
14:32 and the people **d** eat *them* with the blood. NIH
14:43 I **d but taste** a little honey with 2938+2938
15: 2 I remember *that* which Amalek **d** to Israel, 6213
16: 4 Samuel **d** *that* which the LORD spake, 6213
19: 5 For he **d** put his life in his hand, and NIH
20:34 **d** eat no meat the second day of the month: NIH
21:11 **d** they not sing one to another of him in NIH
22:15 **D** I then begin to inquire of God for him? NIH
22:17 knew when he fled, and **d** not shew it to me. NIH
22:18 and five persons that **d** wear a linen ephod. NIH
25: 4 David heard in the wilderness that Nabal **d** NIH
27:11 So **d** David, and so *will be* his manner all 6213
28:24 and **d** bake unleavened bread thereof: NIH
28:25 and before his servants; and they **d** eat. NIH
30:11 to David, and gave him bread, and he **d** eat; NIH
2Sa 1: 2 that he fell to the earth, and **d** obeisance. NIH
2: 3 his men that *were* with him **d** David bring NIH
3:36 as whatsoever the king **d**, pleased all 6213
5:25 David **d** so, as the LORD had commanded 6213
7:17 this vision, so **d** Nathan speak unto David. NIH
8:11 Which also king David **d** dedicate unto NIH
9: 6 he fell on his face, and **d** reverence. NIH
9:13 for he **d** eat continually at the king's table; NIH
11: 7 demanded *of him* **how** Joab **d**, 7965+3807.1
11: 7 **how** the people **d**, and how the war 7965+3807.1
11:13 called him, he **d** eat and drink before him; NIH
11:20 *so* nigh unto the city when *ye* **d** fight? NIH
11:21 **d** not a woman cast a piece of a millstone NIH
12: 3 it **d** eat of his own meat, and drank of his NIH
12: 6 because he **d** this thing, and because he had 6213
12:17 would not, neither **d** he eat bread with them. NIH
12:20 they set bread before him, and he **d** eat. NIH
12:31 thus **d** he unto all the cities of the children 6213
13: 8 cakes in his sight, and **d** bake the cakes. NIH
13:29 the servants of Absalom **d** unto Amnon as 6213
14: 4 and **d** obeisance, and said, Help, O king. NIH
15: 6 on this manner **d** Absalom to all Israel that 6213
17:15 and thus **d** Ahithophel counsel Absalom and NIH
19:19 **d perversely** the day that my lord the king 5753
19:28 among them that **d** eat at thine own table. NIH

2Sa 19:43 why then **d** ye despise us, that our advice NIH
20: 6 of Bichri do us more harm than **d** Absalom: NIH
21: 6 of Saul, whom the LORD **d** choose. NIH
22: 7 he **d** hear my voice out of his temple, and NIH
22: 7 his temple, and my cry **d** *enter* into his ears. NIH
22:11 he rode upon a cherub, and **d** fly: and NIH
22:23 *as for* his statutes, I **d** not depart from them. NIH
22:37 steps under me; so that my feet **d** not slip. NIH
22:43 **d** I beat them *as* small as the dust of NIH
22:43 I **d** stamp them as the mire of the street, *and* NIH
22:43 of the street, *and* **d** spread them abroad. NIH
23:17 These *things* **d** *these* three mighty *men*. 6213
23:22 These *things* **d** Benaiah the son of 6213
24:23 All *these things* **d** Araunah, *as* a king, NIH
1Ki 1:16 and **d obeisance** unto the king. 7812
1:31 **d reverence** to the king, and said, Let my 7812
2: 5 also what Joab the son of Zeruiah **d** to me, 6213
2: 5 what he **d** to the two captains of the hosts 6213
2:35 Zadok the priest **d** the king put in the room NIH
2:42 **D** I not make thee to swear by the LORD, NIH
3: 4 a thousand burnt offerings **d** Solomon offer NIH
3:14 as thy father David **d** walk, then I will NIH
3:21 it was not my son, which I **d** bear. NIH
5:18 Hiram's builders **d** hew *them*, and NIH
7:15 a line of twelve cubits **d** compass either of NIH
7:18 and so **d** he for the other chapiter. 6213
7:23 a line of thirty cubits **d** compass it round NIH
7:46 In the plain of Jordan **d** the king cast them, NIH
7:51 **d** he put among the treasures of the house of NIH
8: 4 even those **d** the priests and the Levites NIH
8:64 The same day **d** the king hallow the middle NIH
9:21 upon those **d** Solomon levy a tribute of NIH
9:22 of the children of Israel **d** Solomon make no NIH
9:24 had built for her: then **d** he build Millo. NIH
9:25 three times in a year **d** Solomon offer burnt NIH
10:29 **d** they bring *them* out by their means. NIH
11: 6 Solomon **d** evil in the sight of the LORD, 6213
11: 6 after the LORD, as *d* David his father. NIH
11: 7 **d** Solomon build a high place for Chemosh, NIH
11: 8 likewise **d** he for all his strange wives, 6213
11:16 (For six months **d** Joab remain there with all NIH
11:25 beside the mischief that Hadad *d*: and NIH
11:33 and my judgments, as *d* David his father. NIH
11:38 as David my servant **d**; 6213
11:41 and all that he **d**, and his wisdom, 6213
12: 9 Make the yoke which thy father **d** put upon NIH
12:11 now whereas my father **d** lade you with a NIH
12:32 offered upon the altar (so **d** he in Beth-el,) 6213
13:19 **d** eat bread in his house, and drank water. NIH
13:22 of the which *the LORD* **d** say to thee, NIH
14: 4 Jeroboam's wife **d** so, and arose, and 6213
14:16 who **d** sin, and who made Israel to sin. NIH
14:21 the city which the LORD **d** choose out of NIH
14:22 Judah **d** evil in the sight of the LORD, 6213
14:24 they **d** according to all the abominations of 6213
14:29 of the acts of Rehoboam, and all that he **d**, 6213
15: 4 Nevertheless for David's sake **d** the LORD NIH
15: 5 Because David **d** *that* which *was* right in 6213
15: 7 rest of the acts of Abijam, and all that he **d**, 6213
15:11 Asa **d** *that* which *was* right in the eyes of 6213
15:11 eyes of the LORD, as *d* David his father. NIH
15:23 all that he **d**, and the cities which he built, 6213
15:26 he **d** evil in the sight of the LORD, and 6213
15:28 of Asa king of Judah **d** Baasha slay him, NIH
15:31 rest of the acts of Nadab, and all that he **d**, 6213
15:34 he **d** evil in the sight of the LORD, and 6213
16: 5 of Baasha, and what he **d**, and his might, 6213
16: 7 even for all the evil that he **d** in the sight of 6213
16:12 Thus **d** Zimri destroy all the house of NIH
16:14 rest of the acts of Elah, and all that he **d**, 6213
16:15 seventh year of Asa king of Judah **d** Zimri NIH
16:19 in his sin which he **d**, to make Israel sin. 6213
16:25 and **d** worse than all that *were* before him. NIH
16:27 the rest of the acts of Omri which he **d**, 6213
16:30 Ahab the son of Omri **d** evil in the sight of 6213
16:33 Ahab **d** more to provoke the LORD God 6213
16:34 In his days **d** Hiel the Bethelite build NIH
17: 5 **d** according unto the word of the LORD: 6213
17:15 and **d** according to the saying of Elijah: 6213
17:15 she, and he, and her house, **d** eat *many* days. NIH
17:16 wasted not, neither **d** the cruse of oil fail, NIH
18:13 Was it not told my lord what I **d** when 6213
18:34 they **d** *it* **the second time.** And he said, 8138
18:34 the third time. And they **d** *it* **the third time.** 8027
19: 6 he **d** eat and drink, and laid him down NIH
19: 8 **d** eat and drink, and went in the strength of NIH
19:21 and gave unto the people, and they **d** eat. NIH
20:25 he hearkened unto their voice, and **d** so. 6213
20:33 Now the men **d** diligently observe whether NIH
20:33 **d** hastily catch *it*: and they said, Thy brother NIH
21:11 **d** as Jezebel had sent unto them, *and* as *it* 6213
21:13 Naboth **d** blaspheme God and the king. NIH
21:25 which **d** sell himself to work wickedness in NIH
21:26 he **d** very abominably in following idols, NIH
21:26 according to all *things* as **d** the Amorites, 6213
22:18 **D** I not tell thee that he would prophesy no NIH
22:39 all that he **d**, and the ivory house which he 6213
22:52 he **d** evil in the sight of the LORD, and 6213
2Ki 1:18 the rest of the acts of Ahaziah which he **d**, 6213
2:18 unto them, **D** I not say unto you, Go not? NIH
4: 1 thou knowest that thy servant **d** fear 1961
4:28 she said, **D** I desire a son of my lord? did I NIH
4:28 of my lord? **d** I not say, Do not deceive me? NIH
4:44 they **d** eat, and left *thereof*, according to NIH
6: 6 and cast *it* in thither; and the iron **d** swim. NIH
6:29 So we boiled my son, and **d** eat him: and NIH
7: 8 **d** eat and drink, and carried thence silver, NIH
8: 2 and **d** after the saying of the man of God: 6213
8:18 the kings of Israel, as **d** the house of Ahab: 6213
8:18 and he **d** evil in the sight of the LORD. 6213
8:23 rest of the acts of Joram, and all that he **d**, 6213
8:25 **d** Ahaziah the son of Jehoram king of Judah NIH
8:27 **d** evil in the sight of the LORD, as *did* 6213
8:27 of the LORD, as *d* the house of Ahab: NIH
9:27 *And they d so* at the going up to Gur, NIH
2Ki 9:34 come in, he **d** eat and drink, and said, Go, NIH
10:19 Jehu **d** *it* in subtilty, to the intent that *he* 6213
10:34 of Jehu, and all that he **d**, and all his might, 6213
11: 3 And Athaliah **d** reign over the land. NIH
11: 9 the captains over the hundreds **d** according 6213
11:10 to the captains over hundreds **d** the priest NIH
12: 2 Jehoash **d** *that* which *was* right in the sight 6213
12:11 into the hands of *them* that **d** the work, 6213
12:19 rest of the acts of Joash, and all that he **d**, 6213
13: 2 he **d** *that* which *was* evil in the sight of 6213
13: 7 Neither **d** he leave *of* the people to Jehoahaz NIH
13: 8 and all that he **d**, and his might, 6213
13:11 he **d** *that* which *was* evil in the sight of 6213
13:12 all that he **d**, and his might where*with* he 6213
13:25 Three times **d** Joash beat him, and NIH
14: 3 he **d** *that* which *was* right in the sight of 6213
14: 3 he **d** according to all *things* as Joash his 6213
14: 3 according to all *things* as Joash his father **d**. 6213
14: 4 as yet the people **d** sacrifice and NIH
14:15 the rest of the acts of Jehoash which he **d**, 6213
14:24 he **d** *that* which *was* evil in the sight of 6213
14:28 all that he **d**, and his might, how he warred, 6213
15: 3 he **d** *that* which *was* right in the sight of 6213
15: 6 rest of the acts of Azariah, and all that he **d**, 6213
15: 8 eighth year of Azariah king of Judah **d** NIH
15: 9 he **d** *that* which *was* evil in the sight of 6213
15:18 he **d** *that* which *was* evil in the sight of 6213
15:21 of the acts of Menahem, and all that he **d**, 6213
15:24 he **d** *that* which *was* evil in the sight of 6213
15:26 acts of Pekahiah, and all that he **d**, behold, 6213
15:28 he **d** *that* which *was* evil in the sight of 6213
15:31 the acts of Pekah, and all that he **d**, behold, 6213
15:34 he **d** *that* which *was* right in the sight of 6213
15:34 he **d** according to all that his father Uzziah 6213
15:36 rest of the acts of Jotham, and all that he **d**, 6213
16: 2 **d** not *that* which *was* right in the sight of 6213
16:16 Thus **d** Urijah the priest, according to all 6213
16:19 the rest of the acts of Ahaz which he **d**, 6213
17: 2 he **d** *that* which *was* evil in the sight of 6213
17: 9 the children of Israel **d** secretly *those* things NIH
17:11 as *d* the heathen whom the LORD carried NIH
17:14 that **d** not believe in the LORD their God. NIH
17:22 in all the sins of Jeroboam which he **d**; 6213
17:40 Howbeit they **d** not hearken, but they did NIH
17:40 but they **d** after their former manner. 6213
17:41 as **d** their fathers, *so* do they unto this day. 6213
18: 3 he **d** *that* which *was* right in the sight of 6213
18: 3 according to all that David his father **d**. 6213
18: 4 for unto those days the children of Israel **d** 1961
18:11 the king of Assyria **d** carry away Israel unto NIH
18:13 **d** Sennacherib king of Assyria come up NIH
18:16 At that time **d** Hezekiah cut off *the gold* NIH
21: 2 he **d** *that* which *was* evil in the sight of 6213
21: 3 and made a grove, as **d** Ahab king of Israel; 6213
21: 9 **d** the nations whom the LORD destroyed NIH
21:11 wickedly above all that the Amorites **d**, 6213
21:17 and all that he **d**, and his sin that he sinned, 6213
21:20 he **d** *that* which *was* evil in the sight of 6213
21:20 of the LORD, as his father Manasseh **d**. 6213
21:25 the rest of the acts of Amon which he **d**, 6213
22: 2 he **d** *that* which *was* right in the sight of 6213
23: 9 they **d** eat of the unleavened bread among NIH
23:12 **d** the king beat down, and brake *them* down NIH
23:13 of the children of Ammon, **d** the king defile. NIH
23:19 **d** to them according to all the acts that he 6213
23:24 and in Jerusalem, **d** Josiah put away, NIH
23:28 rest of the acts of Josiah, and all that he **d**, 6213
23:32 he **d** *that* which *was* evil in the sight of 6213
23:37 he **d** *that* which *was* evil in the sight of 6213
24: 3 of Manasseh, according to all that he **d**; 6213
24: 5 of the acts of Jehoiakim, and all that he **d**, 6213
24: 9 he **d** *that* which *was* evil in the sight of 6213
24:11 the city, and his servants *d* besiege it. NIH
24:19 he **d** *that* which *was* evil in the sight of 6213
25:11 **d** Nebuzar-adan the captain of the guard NIH
25:13 **d** the Chaldees break *in pieces*, and NIH
25:27 **d** lift up the head of Jehoiachin king of NIH
25:29 he **d** eat bread continually before him all NIH
1Ch 4:27 neither **d** all their family multiply, like to NIH
9:22 Samuel the seer **d** ordain in their set office. NIH
11:19 These *things* **d** *these* three mightiest. 6213
11:24 These *things* **d** Benaiah the son of 6213
14:16 David therefore **d** as God commanded him: 6213
15:13 For because ye *d it* not at the first, NIH
15:24 **d** blow with the trumpets before the ark of NIH
17:15 this vision, so **d** Nathan speak unto David. NIH
23:24 that **d** the work for the service of the house 6213
26:27 Out of the spoils won in battles **d** they NIH
27:26 over them that **d** the work of the field for 6213
29:22 **d** eat and drink before the LORD on that NIH
2Ch 1: 7 In that night **d** God appear unto Solomon, NIH
2: 7 whom David my father **d** provide. NIH
4: 2 a line of thirty cubits **d** compass it round NIH
4: 3 of oxen, which **d** compass it round about: NIH
4:16 **d** Huram his father make to king Solomon NIH
4:17 In the plain of Jordan **d** the king cast them, NIH
5: 5 these **d** the priests *and* the Levites bring up. NIH
5:11 *and* **d** not *then* wait by course: NIH
8: 8 them **d** Solomon make to pay tribute until NIH
8: 9 of the children of Israel **d** Solomon make no NIH
10: 9 Ease somewhat the yoke that thy father **d** NIH
12:14 he **d** evil, because he prepared not his heart 6213
13:20 Neither **d** Jeroboam recover strength again NIH
14: 2 Asa **d** *that* which *was* good and right in 6213
15: 4 when they in their trouble **d** turn unto NIH
15: 6 for God **d** vex them with all adversity. NIH
18:16 I **d** see all Israel scattered upon NIH
18:17 **D** I not tell thee *that* he would not prophesy NIH
19: 8 Moreover in Jerusalem **d** Jehoshaphat set of NIH
20:35 after this **d** Jehoshaphat king of Judah join NIH
20:35 king of Israel, who **d** very wickedly: 6213
21: 6 kings of Israel, like as **d** the house of Ahab: 6213
21:10 The same time also **d** Libnah revolt from NIH
22: 4 Wherefore he **d** evil in the sight of 6213
23: 8 all Judah **d** according to all *things* that 6213
2Ch 24: 2 Joash **d** *that* which *was* right in the sight of 6213
24: 7 of the LORD **d** they bestow upon Baalim. NIH
24:11 Thus they **d** day by day, and 6213
24:12 Jehoiada gave it to such as **d** the work of 6213
25: 2 he **d** *that* which *was* right in the sight of 6213
25: 4 *d* as it is written in the law in the book of NIH
25:12 *other* ten thousand *left* alive **d** the children NIH
25:27 Now after the time that Amaziah **d** turn NIH
26: 4 he **d** *that* which *was* right in the sight of 6213
26: 4 according to all that his father Amaziah **d**. 6213
26:22 first and last, **d** Isaiah the prophet, the son NIH
27: 2 he **d** *that* which *was* right in the sight of 6213
27: 2 according to all that his father Uzziah **d**: 6213
27: 2 the LORD. And the people **d** yet corruptly. NIH
27: 5 So much **d** the children of Ammon pay unto NIH
28: 1 he **d** not *that* which *was* right in the sight of 6213
28:16 At that time **d** king Ahaz send unto NIH
28:22 in the time of his distress **d** he trespass yet NIH
29: 2 he **d** *that* which *was* right in the sight of 6213
29:19 which king Ahaz in his reign **d** cast away in NIH
29:34 wherefore their brethren the Levites **d** help NIH
30:18 yet **d** they eat the passover otherwise than it NIH
30:22 they **d** eat throughout the feast seven days, NIH
30:24 For Hezekiah king of Judah **d** give to NIH
31:20 thus **d** Hezekiah throughout all Judah, and 6213
31:21 he **d** *it* with all his heart, and prospered. 6213
32: 3 *were* without the city: and they **d** help him. NIH
32: 9 After this **d** Sennacherib king of Assyria NIH
32:33 the inhabitants of Jerusalem **d** him honour 6213
33: 2 **d** *that* which *was* evil in the sight of 6213
33:17 Nevertheless the people **d** sacrifice still in NIH
33:22 he **d** *that* which *was* evil in the sight of 6213
33:22 of the LORD, as **d** Manasseh his father: 6213
34: 2 he **d** *that* which *was* right in the sight of 6213
34: 6 *so d he* in the cities of Manasseh, and NIH
34:12 the men **d** the work faithfully: and 6213
34:32 **d** according to the covenant of God, 6213
35: 3 the son of David king of Israel **d** build; NIH
35:12 of Moses. And so *d they* with the oxen. NIH
35:18 neither **d** all the kings of Israel keep such a NIH
36: 5 he **d** *that* which *was* evil in the sight of 6213
36: 8 his abominations which he **d**, and 6213
36: 9 he **d** *that* which *was* evil in the sight of 6213
36:12 he **d** *that* which *was* evil in the sight of 6213
Ezr 1: 8 Even those **d** Cyrus king of Persia bring NIH
1:11 All *these* **d** Sheshbazzar bring up with *them* NIH
5:14 those **d** Cyrus the king take out of NIH
6:13 the king had sent, so they **d** speedily. 5648
6:21 to seek the LORD God of Israel, **d** eat, NIH
10: 6 he **d** eat no bread, nor drink water: NIH
10:16 the children of the captivity **d** so. And Ezra 6213
Ne 2:16 rulers knew not whither I went, or what I **d**; 6213
2:16 to the rulers, nor to the rest that **d** the work. 6213
3: 3 the fish gate **d** the sons of Hassenaah build, NIH
5:13 And the people **d** according to this promise. 6213
5:15 but so **d** not I, because of the fear of God. 6213
9:25 so they **d** eat, and were filled, and NIH
9:28 they had rest, they **d** evil again before thee: 6213
11:12 their brethren that **d** the work of the house 6213
13: 7 understood of the evil that Eliashib **d** for 6213
13:10 the Levites and the singers, that **d** the work, 6213
13:18 **D** not your fathers thus, and *did not* our 6213
13:18 *d not* our God bring all this evil upon us, NIH
13:26 **D** not Solomon king of Israel sin by these NIH
13:26 *nevertheless* even him **d** outlandish women NIH
Est 1: 8 *was* according to the law; none **d** compel: NIH
1:21 the king **d** according to the word of 6213
2: 4 the thing pleased the king; and he **d** so. 6213
2:11 to know how Esther **d**, and what should 7965
2:20 for Esther **d** the commandment of 6213
3: 1 After these things **d** king Ahasuerus NIH
3: 2 Mordecai bowed not, nor **d** *him* reverence. NIH
3: 5 nor **d** him reverence, *then* was Haman full NIH
4:17 **d** according to all that Esther had 6213
5:12 Esther the queen **d** let no *man* come in with NIH
8: 1 On that day **d** the king Ahasuerus give NIH
9: 5 **d** what they would unto those that hated 6213
Job 1: 5 God in their hearts. Thus **d** Job continually. 6213
2:10 In all this **d** not Job sin with his lips. NIH
3:11 *why* **d** I not give up the ghost when I came NIH
3:12 Why **d** the knees prevent me? or why NIH
6:22 **D** I say, Bring unto me? or, Give a reward NIH
28:27 **d** he see it, and declare it; he prepared it, NIH
30:25 **D** not I weep for him that was in trouble? NIH
31:13 If I **d** despise the cause of my manservant or NIH
31:15 **D** not he that made me in the womb make NIH
31:15 and **d** not one fashion us in the womb? NIH
31:32 The stranger **d** not lodge in the street: *but* NIH
31:34 **D** I fear a great multitude, or did NIH
31:34 or **d** the contempt of families terrify me, NIH
42: 9 **d** according as the LORD commanded 6213
42:11 and **d** eat bread with him in his house: NIH
Ps 14: 2 to see if there were *any* that **d** understand, NIH
18:10 he rode upon a cherub, and **d** fly: yea, NIH
18:10 yea, he **d** fly upon the wings of the wind. NIH
18:22 and I **d** not put away his statutes from me. NIH
18:36 my steps under me, that my feet **d** not slip. NIH
18:37 neither **d** I turn again till they were NIH
18:42 **d** I beat them small as the dust before NIH
18:42 I **d** cast them out as the dirt in the streets. NIH
31:11 they that **d** see me without fled from me. NIH
35:11 False witnesses **d** rise up; they laid to my NIH
35:15 knew *it* not; they **d** tear *me*, and ceased not: NIH
41: 9 in whom I trusted, which **d** eat *of* my bread, NIH
44: 3 neither **d** their own arm save them: NIH
45: 9 hand **d** stand the queen in gold of Ophir. NIH
51: 5 and in sin **d** my mother conceive me. NIH
53: 2 to see if there were *any* that **d** understand, NIH
53: 2 *any* that did understand, that **d** seek God. NIH
55:12 me *that* **d** magnify *himself* against me; NIH
66: 6 the flood on foot: there **d** we rejoice in him. NIH
68:12 Kings of armies **d** flee apace: and she that NIH
78:12 Marvellous things **d** he in the sight of their 6213
78:25 Man **d** eat angels' food: he sent them meat NIH
78:29 So they **d** eat, and were well filled: for he NIH

Ps 78:33 Therefore their days **d** he consume in NIH
78:36 Nevertheless they **d** flatter him with their NIH
78:38 anger away, and **d** not stir up all his wrath. NIH
78:40 How oft **d** they provoke him in NIH
102:19 from heaven **d** the LORD behold the earth; NIH
105:35 **d** eat up all the herbs in their land, and NIH
106:34 They **d** not destroy the nations, NIH
106:43 Many times **d** he deliver them; but NIH
119:23 Princes also **d** sit *and* speak against me: *but* NIH
119:23 *but* thy servant **d** meditate in thy statutes. NIH
135: 6 *that* **d** he in heaven, and in earth, in 6213
139:16 Thine eyes **d** see my substance, yet being NIH
142: 1 *with* my voice unto the LORD **d** I make NIH
Pr 1:29 and **d** not choose the fear of the LORD: NIH
Isa 5:25 the hills **d** tremble, and their carcases were NIH
6: 2 he covered his feet, and with twain he **d** fly. NIH
9: 1 afterward **d** more grievously afflict *her by* NIH
10:10 whose graven images **d** excel *them of* NIH
13: 1 which Isaiah the son of Amoz **d** see. NIH
14:16 the earth to tremble, that **d** shake kingdoms; NIH
20: 2 And he **d** so, walking naked and barefoot. 6213
22:12 in that day **d** the Lord GOD of hosts call to NIH
38:14 Like a crane *or* a swallow, so **d** I chatter: NIH
38:14 I **d** mourn as a dove: mine eyes fail *with* NIH
42:24 **d** not the LORD, he against whom we NIH
48: 3 I **d** *them* suddenly, and they came to pass. 6213
53: 4 yet we **d** esteem him stricken, smitten of NIH
58: 2 as a nation that **d** righteousness, and 6213
65:12 because when I called, ye **d** not answer; NIH
65:12 when I spake, ye **d** not hear; but did evil NIH
65:12 **d** evil before mine eyes, and did choose 6213
65:12 and **d** choose *that* wherein I delighted not. NIH
66: 4 because when I called, none **d** answer; NIH
66: 4 did answer; when I spake, they **d** not hear: NIH
66: 4 they **d** evil before mine eyes, and chose *that* 6213
Jer 7:12 see what I **d** to it for the wickedness of my 6213
7:26 their neck: they **d** **worse** than their fathers. 7489
11: 8 *them* to do; but they **d** *them* not. 6213
14: 6 the wild asses **d** stand in the high places, NIH
14: 6 their eyes **d** fail, because *there was* no grass. NIH
15: 4 of Judah, for *that* which he **d** in Jerusalem. 6213
15:16 Thy words were found, and I **d** eat them; NIH
22:15 **d** not thy father eat and drink, and NIH
26:19 **D** Hezekiah king of Judah and all Judah put NIH
26:19 **d** he not fear the LORD, and besought NIH
31:19 because I **d** bear the reproach of my youth. NIH
36: 8 Baruch the son of Neriah **d** according to all 6213
37: 2 **d** hearken unto the words of the LORD. NIH
38:12 under the cords. And Jeremiah **d** so. 6213
41: 1 there they **d** eat bread together in Mizpah. NIH
44:19 **d** we make her cakes to worship her, and NIH
44:21 **d** not the LORD remember them, and NIH
46:15 because the LORD **d** drive them. NIH
46:17 They **d** cry there, Pharaoh king of Egypt *is* NIH
46:21 they **d** not stand, because the day of their NIH
52: 2 he **d** *that* which *was* evil in the eyes of 6213
52:21 a fillet of twelve cubits **d** compass it; and NIH
52:33 he **d** continually eat bread before him all NIH
La 1: 7 the hand of the enemy, and none **d** help her: NIH
1: 7 saw her, *and* **d** mock at her sabbaths. NIH
4: 5 They that **d** feed delicately are desolate in NIH
Eze 3: 3 **d** I eat *it;* and it was in my mouth as honey NIH
6:13 the place where they **d** offer sweet savour to NIH
11:22 **d** the cherubims lift up their wings, and NIH
12: 7 I **d** so as I was commanded: I brought forth 6213
16:49 neither **d** she strengthen the hand of NIH
17: 7 this vine **d** bend her roots toward him, and NIH
18:18 **d** *that* which *is* not good among his people, 6213
20: 8 they **d** not every man cast away NIH
20: 8 neither **d** they forsake the idols of Egypt: NIH
20:17 neither **d** I make an end of them in NIH
24:18 I **d** in the morning as I was commanded. 6213
27:25 The ships of Tarshish **d** sing of thee *in* thy NIH
31: 6 under his branches **d** all the beasts of NIH
34: 6 and none **d** search or seek *after them.* NIH
34: 8 neither **d** my shepherds search for my flock, NIH
43:22 as they **d** cleanse *it* with the bullock. NIH
46:12 peace offerings, as he **d** on the sabbath day: 6213
Da 1:15 fatter in flesh than all the children which **d** NIH
3:24 **D** not we cast three men bound into NIH
4: 7 they **d** not make known unto me NIH
4:33 **d** eat grass as oxen, and his body was wet NIH
6:10 thanks before his God, as he **d** aforetime. 5648
7: 9 cast *down,* and the Ancient of days **d** sit, NIH
8: 4 he **d** according to his will, and 6213
8:27 I rose up, and **d** the king's business; 6213
10: 3 neither **d** I anoint myself at all, till three NIH
Hos 2: 8 For she **d** not know that I gave her corn, and NIH
9:17 because they **d** not hearken unto him: NIH
10: 9 the children of iniquity **d** not overtake them. NIH
13: 5 I **d** know thee in the wilderness, in the land NIH
Am 1:11 he **d** pursue his brother with the sword, NIH
1:11 **d** cast off all pity, and his anger did tear NIH
1:11 his anger **d** tear perpetually, and he kept his NIH
5:19 As if a man **d** flee from a lion, and a bear NIH
7: 4 devoured the great deep, and **d** eat up a part. NIH
Ob 1:14 to cut off those of his that **d** escape; NIH
1:14 of his that **d** remain in the day of distress. NIH
Jnh 3:10 that he would do unto them; and he **d** *it* not. 6213
4: 8 it came to pass, when the sun **d** arise, NIH
Na 2:12 The lion **d** tear in pieces enough for his NIH
Hab 1: 1 The burden which Habakkuk the prophet **d** NIH
3: 6 were scattered, the perpetual hills **d** bow: NIH
3: 7 the curtains of the land of Midian **d** tremble. NIH
Hag 1: 9 when ye brought *it* home, I **d** blow upon it. NIH
1:12 and the people **d** fear before the LORD. NIH
1:14 **d** work in the house of the LORD of 6213
Zec 1: 4 they **d** not hear, nor hearken unto me, NIH
1: 6 **d** they not take hold of your fathers? NIH
1:21 so that no man **d** lift up his head: NIH
7: 5 **d** ye at all fast *unto* me, *even to* me? NIH
7: 6 when ye **d** eat, and when ye did drink, did NIH
7: 6 when ye did eat, and when ye **d** drink, did NIH
7: 6 **d** not ye eat *for yourselves,* and drink *for* NIH
9: 3 And Tyrus **d** build herself a strong hold, and NIH

Mal 2: 6 equity, and **d** turn many away from iniquity. NIH
2:15 **d** not he make one? Yet had he the residue NIH
Mt 1:24 Then Joseph being raised from sleep **d** as 4160
2:22 But when he heard that Archelaus **d** reign in NIG
9:19 and followed him, and *so* **d** his disciples. NIG
12: 3 unto them, Have ye not read what David **d**, 4160
12: 4 and **d** eat the shewbread, which was not NIG
13:58 And he **d** not many mighty works there, 4160
14:20 And they **d** all eat, and were filled: and NIG
15: 7 well **d** Esaias prophesy of you, saying, NIG
15:37 And they **d** all eat, and were filled: and NIG
15:38 And they that **d** eat were four thousand NIG
17: 2 and his face **d** shine as the sun, and NIG
19: 7 Why **d** Moses then command to give a NIG
20: 5 the sixth and ninth hour, and **d** likewise. 4160
21: 6 and **d** as Jesus commanded them, 4160
21:15 scribes saw the wonderful *things* that he **d**, 4160
21:25 unto us, Why **d** ye not then believe him? NIG
21:31 Whether of *them* twain **d** the will of *his* 4160
21:36 the first: and they **d** unto them likewise. 4160
21:42 unto them, **D** ye never read in the scriptures, NIG
25:44 or in prison, and **d** not minister unto thee? NIG
25:45 Inasmuch as ye **d** *it* not to one of the least 4160
25:45 one of the least of these, ye **d** *it* not to me. 4160
26:12 on my body, she **d** *it* for my burial. 4160
26:19 And the disciples **d** as Jesus had appointed 4160
26:21 And as they **d** eat, he said, Verily I say unto NIG
26:67 Then **d** they spit in his face, and NIG
27: 9 whom they of the children of Israel **d** value; NIG
27:35 and upon my vesture **d** they cast lots. NIG
27:51 and the earth **d** quake, and the rocks rent; NIG
28: 4 And for fear of him the keepers **d** shake, NIG
28: 8 and **d** run to bring his disciples word. NIG
28:15 took the money, and **d** as they were taught: 4160
Mk 1: 4 John **d** baptize in the wilderness, and 1096
1: 6 and he **d** eat locusts and wild honey; NIG
1:32 And at even, when the sun **d** set, NIG
2:25 Have ye never read what David **d**, when he 4160
2:26 and **d** eat the shewbread, which is not NIG
3: 8 they had heard what great *things* he **d**, 4160
4: 8 and **d** yield fruit that sprang up and NIG
5:20 had done for him: and all *men* **d** marvel. NIG
6:20 he **d** many *things,* and heard him gladly. 4160
6:42 And they **d** all eat, and were filled. NIG
6:44 And they that **d** eat *of* the loaves were about NIG
8: 6 and they **d** set *them* before the people. NIG
8: 8 So they **d** eat, and were filled: and they took NIG
10: 3 unto them, What **d** Moses command you? NIG
11:31 will say, Why then **d** ye not believe him? NIG
12:44 For all *they* **d** cast in of their abundance; NIG
12:44 she of her want **d** cast in all that she had, NIG
14:18 And as they sat and **d** eat, Jesus said, NIG
14:22 And as they **d** eat, Jesus took bread, and NIG
14:59 so **d** their witness agree together. NIG
14:65 the servants **d** strike him with the palms of NIG
15:19 and **d** spit upon him, and bowing *their* knees NIG
Lk 4: 2 And in those days he **d** eat nothing: and NIG
6: 1 and **d** eat, rubbing *them* in *their* hands. NIG
6: 3 ye not read so much as this, what David **d**, 4160
6: 4 of God, and **d** take and eat the shewbread, NIG
6:10 And he **d** so: and his hand was restored 4160
6:23 for in the like manner **d** their fathers unto 4160
6:26 for so **d** their fathers to the false prophets. 4160
6:49 against which the stream **d** beat vehemently, NIG
7:38 and **d** wipe *them* with the hairs of her head, NIG
9:15 And they **d** so, and made *them* all sit down. 4160
9:17 And they **d** eat, and were all filled: and NIG
9:43 every one at all *things* which Jesus **d**, 4160
9:53 And they **d** not receive him, because his NIG
9:54 and consume them, even as Elias **d**? 4160
11:40 **d** not he that made that *which is* without NIG
12:47 prepared not *himself,* neither **d** according to 4160
12:48 and **d** commit *things* worthy of stripes, NIG
15:16 his belly with the husks that the swine **d** eat: NIG
17: 9 he **d** the *things* that were commanded him? 4160
17:27 They **d** eat, they drank, they married *wives,* NIG
17:28 they **d** eat, they drank, they bought, NIG
19:22 laid not down, and reaping that I **d** not sow: NIG
24:32 to another, **D** not our heart burn within us, 1510
24:43 And he took *it,* and **d** eat before them. NIG
Jn 1:45 and the prophets, **d** write, Jesus of Nazareth, NIG
2:11 This beginning of miracles **d** Jesus in Cana 4160
2:23 when they saw the miracles which he **d**. 4160
2:24 But Jesus **d** not commit himself unto them, NIG
4:29 which told me all *things* that ever I **d**: 4160
4:39 which testified, He told me all that ever I **d**. 4160
4:45 having seen all *the things* that he **d** at 4160
4:54 *is* again the second miracle *that* Jesus **d**, 4160
5:16 And therefore **d** the Jews persecute Jesus, NIG
6: 2 they saw his miracles which he **d** on them 4160
6:14 they had seen the miracle that Jesus **d**, 4160
6:23 nigh unto the place where they **d** eat bread, NIG
6:26 but because ye **d** eat of the loaves, and NIG
6:31 Our fathers **d** eat manna in the desert; as it NIG
6:49 Your fathers **d** eat manna in the wilderness, NIG
6:58 not as your fathers **d** eat manna, and NIG
7: 5 For neither **d** his brethren believe in him. NIG
7:19 **D** not Moses give you the law, and *yet* none NIG
8:40 I have heard of God: this **d** not Abraham. 4160
9: 2 saying, Master, who **d** sin, this *man,* or NIG
9:18 But the Jews **d** not believe concerning him, NIG
9:22 that if any *man* **d** confess that he *was* Christ, NIG
9:26 said they to him again, What **d** he to thee? 4160
9:27 I have told you already, and ye **d** not hear: NIG
10: 8 and robbers: but the sheep **d** not hear them. NIG
10:41 unto him, and said, John **d** no miracle: 4160
11:45 and had seen *the things* which Jesus **d**, 4160
12:36 and departed, and **d** hide himself from them. NIG
12:42 of the Pharisees they **d** not confess *him,* lest NIG
15:24 them the works which none other *man* **d**, 4160
18:15 followed Jesus, and *so* **d** another disciple: NIG
18:26 **D** not I see thee in the garden with him? NIG
18:34 of thyself, or **d** others tell *it* thee of me? NIG
19:24 and for my vesture they **d** cast lots. NIG
19:24 These *things* therefore the soldiers **d**. 4160

Jn 20: 4 and the other disciple **d** outrun Peter, and NIG
20:30 And many other signs truly **d** Jesus in 4160
21: 7 was naked,) and **d** cast himself into the sea. NIG
21:25 are also many other *things* which Jesus **d**, 4160
Ac 2:22 which God **d** by him in the midst of you, 4160
2:26 Therefore **d** my heart rejoice, and NIG
2:31 in hell, neither his flesh **d** see corruption. NIG
2:40 And with many other words **d** he testify and NIG
2:46 **d** eat *their* meat with gladness and NIG
3:17 I wot that through ignorance ye **d** *it,* as *did* 4238
3:17 I wot that through ignorance ye did *it,* as **d** NIG
4:25 Why **d** the heathen rage, and the people NIG
5:28 **D** not we straitly command you that *you* NIG
6: 8 **d** great wonders and miracles among 4160
7:27 But he that **d** his neighbour **wrong** thrust him 91
7:35 the same **d** God send *to be* a ruler and NIG
7:51 the Holy Ghost: as your fathers **d**, so *do* ye. NIG
8: 6 and seeing the miracles which he **d**. 4160
9: 9 without sight, and neither **d** eat nor drink. NIG
9:36 of good works and almsdeeds which she **d**. 4160
10:39 which he **d** both in the land of the Jews, 4160
10:41 who **d** eat and drink with him after he rose NIG
11:17 as God gave them the like gift as *he* **d** unto NIG
11:30 Which also they **d**, and sent it to the elders 4160
12: 8 And so he **d**. And he saith unto him, 4160
14:17 himself without witness, in that he **d** **good**, 15
15: 8 them the Holy Ghost, even as *he* **d** unto us; NIG
15:14 Simeon hath declared how God at the first **d** NIG
16:18 And this **d** she many days. But Paul, 4160
19:14 a Jew, *and* chief of the priests, which **d** so. 4160
21: 9 four daughters, virgins, which **d** prophesy. NIG
26:10 Which *thing* I also **d** in Jerusalem: and 4160
26:10 and many of the saints **d** I shut up in prison, NIG
26:22 the prophets and Moses **d** say should come: NIG
Ro 1:26 for even their women **d** change the natural NIG
1:28 And even as they **d** not like to retain God in NIG
3: 3 For what if some **d** not believe? shall their NIG
5:20 sin abounded, grace **d** much more abound: NIG
7: 5 **d** work in our members to bring forth fruit NIG
8:29 For whom he **d** foreknow, he also did NIG
8:29 he also **d** predestinate *to be* conformed to NIG
8:30 Moreover whom he **d** predestinate, them he NIG
10:19 But I say, **D** not Israel know? First Moses NIG
1Co 4: 8 and I would *to God* ye **d** reign, that we also 1065
10: 3 And **d** all eat the same spiritual meat; NIG
10: 4 And **d** all drink the same spiritual drink: NIG
15:27 which **d** put all *things* under him. NIG
2Co 1:17 was thus minded, **d** I use lightness? NIG
2: 9 For to this end also **d** I write, that I might NIG
5:20 as though God **d** beseech *you* by us: NIG
7: 8 a letter, I do not repent, though I **d** repent: NIG
7:12 *I* **d** *it* not for his cause that had done NIG
8: 5 And *this they* **d**, not as we hoped, but NIG
12:16 But be it so, I **d** not burden you: NIG
12:17 **D** I make a gain of you by any of them NIG
12:18 **D** Titus make a gain of you? walked we not NIG
Gal 2:12 from James, he **d** eat with the Gentiles: NIG
4: 8 ye **d** **service** unto them which by nature 1398
5: 7 Ye **d** run well; who did hinder you that *ye* NIG
5: 7 who **d** hinder you that *ye* should not obey NIG
Php 4:14 that ye **d** communicate with my affliction. NIG
2Th 3: 8 Neither **d** we eat any *man's* bread for NIG
1Ti 1:13 because I **d** *it* ignorantly in unbelief. 4160
2Ti 4:14 Alexander the coppersmith **d** me much 1731
Heb 3:16 For some, when they had heard, **d** provoke: NIG
4: 2 but the word preached **d** not profit them, NIG
4: 4 And God **d** rest the seventh day from all his NIG
4:10 from his own works, as God **d** from his. NIG
7:19 the bringing in of a better hope **d**; by NIG
7:27 for this he **d** once, when he offered up 4160
9: 9 that could not make him that **d** the service NIG
1Pe 1:11 of Christ which was in them **d** signify, NIG
1:12 but unto us they **d** minister the things, NIG
2:22 Who **d** no sin, neither was guile found in 4160
Rev 12: 4 of heaven, and **d** cast them to the earth: NIG
13:14 had the wound by a sword, and **d** live. NIG
19: 2 which **d** corrupt the earth with her NIG
21:23 for the glory of God **d** lighten it, and NIG

DIDST (123) [DO]

Ge 12:18 why **d** thou not tell me that she *was* thy NIH
18:15 And he said, Nay; but thou **d** laugh. NIH
20: 6 I know that thou **d** this in the integrity of 6213
21:26 neither **d** thou tell me, neither yet heard I *of* NIH
31:27 Wherefore **d** thou flee away secretly, NIH
31:27 **d** not tell me, that I might have sent thee NIH
31:39 of my hand **d** thou require it, *whether* stolen NIH
Ex 15:10 Thou **d** blow with thy wind, the sea covered NIH
40:15 anoint them, as thou **d** anoint their father, NIH
Nu 21:34 thou shalt do to him as thou **d** unto Sihon 6213
Dt 3: 2 thou shalt do unto him as thou **d** unto Sihon 6213
9: 7 from the day that thou **d** depart out of NIH
32:14 thou **d** drink the pure blood of the grape. NIH
33: 8 whom thou **d** prove at Massah, *and* NIH
33: 8 *with* whom thou **d** strive at the waters of NIH
Jos 2:18 in the window which thou **d** let us down by: NIH
8: 2 her king as thou **d** unto Jericho and 6213
Jdg 12: 1 and **d** not call us to go with thee? NIH
13: 8 let the man of God which thou **d** send come NIH
1Sa 3: 6 and said, Here *am* I; for thou **d** call me. NIH
3: 8 and said, Here *am* I; for thou **d** call me. NIH
15:19 **d** thou not obey the voice of the LORD, NIH
15:19 **d** fly upon the spoil, and didst evil in NIH
15:19 and **d** evil in the sight of the LORD? 6213
19: 5 thou sawest *it,* and **d** rejoice: wherefore then NIH
20:19 come to the place where thou **d** hide thyself NIH
25:25 young men of my lord, whom thou **d** send. NIH
2Sa 11:10 *then* **d** thou not go down unto thine house? NIH
12:12 For thou **d** *it* secretly: but I will do this 6213
12:21 thou **d** fast and weep for the child, *while it* NIH
12:21 child was dead, thou **d** rise and eat bread. NIH
13:16 greater than the other that thou **d** unto me. 6213
18:11 why **d** thou not smite him there to NIH
19:28 yet **d** thou set thy servant among them that NIH
1Ki 1:13 say unto him, **D** not thou, my lord O king, NIH

1Ki 2:44 is privy to, that thou **d** to David my father: 6213
8:18 thou **d well** that it was in thine heart. 2895
8:53 For thou **d** separate them from among all NIH
20: 9 All that thou **d** send for to thy servant at NIH
21:10 Thou **d** blaspheme God and the king. NIH
1Ch 17:22 For thy people Israel **d** thou make thine own NIH
2Ch 2: 3 As thou **d** deal with David my father, and NIH
2: 3 **d** send him cedars to build him a house to NIH
6: 8 thou **d well** *in* that it was in thine heart: 2895
16: 8 yet, because thou **d** rely on the LORD, NIH
20: 7 who **d** drive out the inhabitants of this land NIH
34:27 and thou **d** humble thyself before God, NIH
34:27 and **d** rend thy clothes, and weep before me; NIH
Ne 9: 7 who **d** choose Abram, and broughtest him NIH
9: 9 **d** see the affliction of our fathers in Egypt, NIH
9:10 So **d** thou get thee a name, as *it is* this day. NIH
9:11 thou **d** divide the sea before them, so NIH
9:17 of thy wonders that thou **d** among them; 6213
9:21 forty years **d** thou sustain them in NIH
9:22 and nations, and **d** divide them into corners: NIH
9:28 many times **d** thou deliver them according NIH
9:30 Yet many years **d** thou forbear them, and NIH
9:31 sake thou **d** not utterly consume them, 6213
9:34 where*with* thou **d** testify against them. NIH
Ps 22: 4 they trusted, and thou **d** deliver them. NIH
22: 9 thou **d** make me hope *when I was* upon my NIH
30: 7 thou **d** hide thy face, *and* I was troubled. NIH
39: 9 I opened not my mouth; because thou **d** *it.* 6213
40: 6 Sacrifice and offering thou **d** not desire; NIH
44: 1 *what* work thou **d** in their days, in the times 6466
44: 2 *How* thou **d** drive out the heathen *with* thy NIH
44: 2 *how* thou **d** afflict the people, and cast them NIH
60:10 O God, *which* **d** not go out with our armies? NIH
68: 7 when thou **d** march through the wilderness; NIH
68: 9 Thou, O God, **d** send a plentiful rain, NIH
68: 9 whereby thou **d** confirm thine inheritance, NIH
73:18 Surely thou **d** set them in slippery *places:* NIH
74:13 Thou **d** divide the sea by thy strength: NIH
74:15 Thou **d** cleave the fountain and the flood: NIH
76: 8 Thou **d** cause judgment to be heard from NIH
80: 9 **d** cause it to take deep root, and it filled NIH
Isa 14:12 to the ground, which **d** weaken the nations! NIH
22: 8 thou **d** look in that day to the armour of NIH
47: 6 thou **d** shew them no mercy; upon NIH
47: 7 that thou **d** not lay these *things* to thy heart, NIH
47: 7 neither **d** remember the latter end of it. NIH
48: 6 hidden *things,* and thou **d** not know them. NIH
54: 1 Sing, O barren, thou *that* **d** not bear; NIH
54: 1 cry aloud, thou *that* **d** not travail with child: NIH
57: 9 **d** increase thy perfumes, and didst send thy NIH
57: 9 **d** send thy messengers far off, and NIH
57: 9 far off, and **d** debase *thyself even* unto hell. NIH
63:14 so **d** thou lead thy people, to make thyself a NIH
64: 3 When thou **d** terrible things *which* we 6213
Jer 32:22 which thou **d** swear to their fathers to give NIH
36:17 How **d** thou write all these words at his NIH
45: 3 Thou **d** say, Woe is me now! for NIH
La 1:10 whom thou **d** command *that* they should not NIH
Eze 16:13 thou **d** eat fine flour, and honey, and oil: NIH
16:13 and thou **d** prosper into a kingdom. NIH
16:15 thou **d** trust in thine own beauty, and NIH
16:16 of thy garments thou **d** take, and NIH
16:17 and **d** commit whoredom with them, NIH
16:36 thy children, which thou **d** give unto them; NIH
23:40 for whom thou **d** wash *thyself,* paintedst thy NIH
27:33 thou **d** enrich the kings of the earth with NIH
29: 7 thou **d** break, and rent all their shoulder: NIH
35:15 As thou **d** rejoice at the inheritance of NIH
Da 10:12 for from the first day that thou **d** set thine NIH
Hos 10:13 because thou **d** trust in thy way, in NIH
Hab 3: 8 that thou **d** ride upon thine horses *and* NIH
3: 9 Selah. Thou **d** cleave the earth *with* rivers. NIH
3:12 Thou **d** march through the land in NIH
3:12 thou **d** thresh the heathen in anger. NIH
3:14 Thou **d** strike through with his staves NIH
3:15 Thou **d** walk through the sea *with* thine NIH
Mt 13:27 Sir, **d** not thou sow good seed in thy field? NIG
14:31 thou of little faith, wherefore **d** thou doubt? NIG
20:13 **d** not thou agree with me for a penny? NIG
Lk 7:46 Mine head with oil thou **d** not anoint: but NIG
19:21 not down, and reapest that thou **d** not sow. NIG
Jn 17: 8 and they have believed that thou **d** send me. NIG
Ac 7:28 kill me, as thou **d** the Egyptian yesterday? *337*
11: 3 to men uncircumcised, and **d** eat with them. NIG
1Co 4: 7 and what hast thou that thou **d** not receive? NIG
4: 7 now if thou **d** receive *it,* why dost thou NIG
Heb 2: 7 and **d** set him over the works of thy hands: NIG
Rev 17: 7 said unto me, Wherefore **d** thou marvel? NIG

DIDYMUS (3)

Jn 11:16 Then said Thomas, which is called **D**, *1324*
20:24 But Thomas, one of the twelve, called **D**, *1324*
21: 2 and Thomas called **D**, and Nathanael of *1324*

DIE (321) [DEAD, DEADLY, DEADNESS, DEATH, DEATHS, DIED, DIEST, DIETH]

Ge 2:17 eatest thereof thou shalt **surely d**. 4191+4191
3: 3 eat of it, neither shall ye touch it, lest ye **d**. 4191
3: 4 the woman, Ye shall not **surely d**: 4191+4191
6:17 *and* every *thing* that *is* in the earth shall **d**. 1478
19:19 lest *some* evil take me, and I **d**: 4191
20: 7 know thou that thou shalt **surely d**, 4191+4191
25:32 Esau said, Behold, I *am* at the point to **d**: 4191
26: 9 unto him, Because I said, Lest I **d** for her. 4191
27: 4 that my soul may bless thee before I **d**. 4191
30: 1 unto Jacob, Give me children, or else I **d**. 4191
33:13 them one day, all the flock will **d**. 4191
38:11 for he said, Lest peradventure he **d** also, 4191
42: 2 from thence; that we may live, and not **d**. 4191
42:20 your words be verified, and ye shall not **d**. 4191
43: 8 not **d**, both we, and thou, *and* also our little 4191
44: 9 both let him **d**, and we also will be my 4191
44:22 should leave his father, *his father* would **d**. 4191
44:31 that the lad *is* not *with us,* that he will **d**: 4191
Ge 45:28 yet alive: I will go and see him before I **d**. 4191
46:30 Now let me **d**, since I have seen thy face, 4191
47:15 for why should we **d** in thy presence? 4191
47:19 Wherefore shall we **d** before thine eyes, 4191
47:19 give *us* seed, that we may live, and not **d**, 4191
47:29 the time drew nigh that Israel must **d**: and 4191
48:21 Israel said unto Joseph, Behold, I **d**: but 4191
50: 5 My father made me swear, saying, Lo, I **d**: 4191
50:24 Joseph said unto his brethren, I **d**: and 4191
Ex 7:18 the fish that *is* in the river shall **d**, and 4191
9: 4 there shall nothing **d** of all *that is* 4191
9:19 come down upon them, and they shall **d**. 4191
10:28 in *that* day thou seest my face thou shalt **d**. 4191
11: 5 all the firstborn in the land of Egypt shall **d**, 4191
14:11 hast thou taken us away to **d** in 4191
14:12 than that we should **d** in the wilderness. 4191
20:19 but let not God speak with us, lest we **d**. 4191
21:12 He that smiteth a man, so that he **d**, shall be 4191
21:14 take him from mine altar, that he may **d**. 4191
21:18 *his* fist, and he **d** not, but keepeth *his* bed: 4191
21:20 with a rod, and he **d** under his hand; 4191
21:28 an ox gore a man or a woman, that they **d**: 4191
21:35 if one man's ox hurt another's, that he **d**; 4191
22: 2 breaking up, and be smitten that he **d**, 4191
22:10 it **d**, or be hurt, or driven away, no man 4191
22:14 it be hurt, or **d**, the owner thereof *being* not 4191
28:35 and when he cometh out, that he **d** not. 4191
28:43 *place;* that they bear not iniquity, and **d**: 4191
30:20 they shall wash *with* water, that they **d** not; 4191
30:21 their hands and their feet, that they **d** not: 4191
Lev 8:35 the charge of the LORD, that ye **d** not: 4191
10: 6 lest you **d**, and lest wrath come upon all 4191
10: 7 tabernacle of the congregation, lest you **d**: 4191
10: 9 tabernacle of the congregation, lest ye **d**: 4191
11:39 if any beast, of which ye may eat, **d**; he that 4191
15:31 that they **d** not in their uncleanness, 4191
16: 2 which *is* upon the ark; that he **d** not: 4191
16:13 that *is* upon the Testimony, that he **d** not: 4191
20:20 shall bear their sin; they shall **d** childless. 4191
22: 9 sin for it, and **d** therefore, if they profane it: 4191
Nu 4:15 shall not touch *any* holy *thing,* lest they **d**. 4191
4:19 do unto them, that they may live, and not **d**, 4191
4:20 the holy *things* are covered, lest they **d**. 4191
6: 7 his brother, or for his sister, when they **d**: 4194
6: 9 if any man **d** very suddenly by him, 4191+4191
14:35 shall be consumed, and there they shall **d**. 4191
16:29 If these *men* **d** the common death of all 4191
17:10 their murmurings from me, that they **d** not. 4191
17:12 saying, Behold, we **d**, we perish, we all 1478
17:13 unto the tabernacle of the LORD shall **d**: 4191
18: 3 the altar, that neither they, nor you also, **d**. 4191
18:22 the congregation, lest they bear sin, and **d**. 4191
18:32 *things* of the children of Israel, lest ye **d**. 4191
20: 4 that we and our cattle should **d** there? 4191
20:26 gathered *unto his people,* and shall **d** there. 4191
21: 5 us up out of Egypt to **d** in the wilderness? 4191
23:10 Let me **d** the death of the righteous, and 4191
26:65 shall **surely d** in the wilderness. 4191+4191
27: 8 If a man **d**, and have no son, then ye shall 4191
35:12 that the manslayer **d** not, until he stand 4191
35:16 of iron, so that he **d**, he *is* a murderer: 4191
35:17 wherewith he may **d**, and he die, he *is* a 4191
35:17 he may die, and he **d**, he *is* a murderer: 4191
35:18 wherewith he may **d**, and he die, he *is* a 4191
35:18 he may die, and he **d**, he *is* a murderer: 4191
35:20 or hurl at him by laying of wait, that he **d**; 4191
35:21 enmity smite him with his hand, that he **d**: 4191
35:23 wherewith *a man* may **d**, seeing *him* not, 4191
35:23 that he **d**, and *was* not his enemy, 4191
35:30 testify against *any* person *to cause him* to **d**. 4191
Dt 4:22 I *must* **d** in this land, I *must* not go over 4191
5:25 Now therefore why should we **d**? for this 4191
5:25 our God any more, then we shall **d**. 4191
13:10 thou shalt stone him with stones, that he **d**; 4191
17: 5 shalt stone them with stones, till they **d**. 4191
17:12 or unto the judge, even that man shall **d**: 4191
18:16 me see this great fire any more, that I **d** not. 4191
18:20 of other gods, even that prophet shall **d**. 4191
19: 5 and lighteth upon his neighbour, that he **d**; 4191
19:11 smite him mortally that he **d**, and 4191
19:12 of the avenger of blood, that he may **d**. 4191
20: 5 lest he **d** in the battle, and another man 4191
20: 6 lest he **d** in the battle, and another man eat 4191
20: 7 lest he **d** in the battle, and another man take 4191
21:21 city shall stone him with stones, that he **d**: 4191
22:21 city shall stone her with stones that she **d**: 4191
22:22 they shall both of them **d**, *both* the man that 4191
22:24 ye shall stone them with stones that they **d**; 4191
22:25 then the man only that lay with her shall **d**: 4191
24: 3 or if the latter husband **d**, which took her *to* 4191
24: 7 that thief shall **d**; and thou shalt put evil 4191
25: 5 and one of them **d**, and have no child, 4191
31:14 thy days approach that *thou* must **d**: 4191
32:50 **d** in the mount whither thou goest up, and 4191
33: 6 Let Reuben live, and not **d**; and let *not* his 4191
Jos 20: 9 not **d** by the hand of the avenger of blood, 4191
Jdg 6:23 *be* unto thee; fear not: thou shalt not **d**. 4191
6:30 Bring out thy son, that he may **d**: 4191
13:22 We shall **surely d**, because we have 4191+4191
15:18 now shall I **d** for thirst, and fall into 4191
16:30 Samson said, Let me **d** with the Philistines. 4191
Ru 1:17 will I **d**, and there will I be buried: 4191
1Sa 2:33 all the increase of thine house shall **d** in 4191
2:34 in one day they shall **d** both of them. 4191
12:19 unto the LORD thy God, that we **d** not: 4191
14:39 Jonathan my son, he shall **surely d**. 4191+4191
14:43 rod that *was* in mine hand, *and* lo, I must **d**. 4191
14:44 for thou shalt **surely d**, Jonathan. 4191+4191
14:45 the people said unto Saul, Shall Jonathan **d**, 4191
20: 2 said unto him, God forbid; thou shalt not **d**: 4191
20:14 the kindness of the LORD, that I **d** not: 4191
20:31 him unto me, for he shall **surely d**. 1121+4194
22:16 Thou shalt **surely d**, Ahimelech, 4191+4191
26:10 or his day shall come to **d**; or he shall 4191
26:16 ye *are* **worthy to d**, because ye have 1121+4194
1Sa 28: 9 thou a snare for my life, to **cause** me **to d**? 4191
2Sa 11:15 ye from him, that he may be smitten, and **d**. 4191
12: 5 hath done this *thing* shall **surely d**: 1121+4194
12:13 also hath put away thy sin; thou shalt not **d**. 4191
12:14 that is born unto thee shall **surely d**. 4191+4191
14:14 For we **must needs d**, and *are* as 4191+4191
18: 3 neither if half of us **d**, will they care for us: 4191
19:23 the king said unto Shimei, Thou shalt not **d**. 4191
19:37 that I may **d** in mine own city, *and* 4191
1Ki 1:52 shall be found in him, he shall **d**. 4191
2: 1 days of David drew nigh that *he* should **d**; 4191
2:30 he said, Nay; but I will **d** here. 4191
2:37 for certain that thou shalt **surely d**: 4191+4191
2:42 that thou shalt **surely d**? 4191+4191
14:12 thy feet enter into the city, the child shall **d**. 4191
17:12 and my son, that we may eat it, and **d**. 4191
19: 4 he requested for himself that he might **d**; 4191
21:10 him out, and stone him, that he may **d**. 4191
2Ki 1: 4 thou art gone up, but shalt **surely d**. 4191+4191
1: 6 thou art gone up, but shalt **surely d**. 4191+4191
1:16 thou art gone up, but shalt **surely d**. 4191+4191
7: 3 one to another, Why sit we here until we **d**? 4191
7: 4 famine *is* in the city, and we shall **d** there: 4191
7: 4 if we sit still here, we **d** also. Now therefore 4191
7: 4 shall live; and if they kill us, we shall but **d**. 4191
8:10 shewed me that he shall **surely d**. 4191+4191
18:32 and of honey, that ye may live, and not **d**: 4191
20: 1 in order; for thou shalt **d**, and not live. 4191
2Ch 25: 4 The fathers shall not **d** for the children, 4191
25: 4 neither shall the children **d** for the fathers, 4191
25: 4 but every man shall **d** for his own sin. 4191
32:11 you to give over yourselves to **d** by famine 4191
Job 2: 9 retain thine integrity? curse God, and **d**. 4191
4:21 go away? they **d**, even without wisdom. 4191
12: 2 the people, and wisdom shall **d** with you. 4191
14: 8 and the stock thereof **d** in the ground; 4191
14:14 If a man **d**, shall he live *again?* all the days 4191
27: 5 till I **d** I will not remove my integrity from 1478
29:18 I shall **d** in my nest, and I shall multiply *my* 1478
34:20 *In* a moment shall they **d**, and the people 4191
36:12 and they shall **d** without knowledge. 1478
36:14 They **d** in youth, and their life *is* among 4191
Ps 41: 5 When shall he **d**, and his name perish? 4191
49:10 For he seeth *that* wise *men* **d**, likewise 4191
79:11 thou those that are **appointed to d**; 1121+8546
82: 7 ye shall **d** like men, and fall like one of 4191
88:15 **ready to d** from *my* youth *up: while* I 1478
104:29 their breath, they **d**, and return to their dust. 1478
118:17 I shall not **d**, but live, and declare the works 4191
Pr 5:23 He shall **d** without instruction; and in 4191
10:21 feed many: but fools **d** for want of wisdom. 4191
15:10 the way: *and* he that hateth reproof shall **d**. 4191
19:16 *but* he that despiseth his ways shall **d**. 4191
23:13 beatest him with the rod, he shall not **d**. 4191
30: 7 of thee; deny me *them* not before I **d**: 4191
Ecc 3: 2 A time to be born, and a time to **d**; a time to 4191
7:17 why shouldest thou **d** before thy time? 4191
9: 5 For the living know that they shall **d**: but 4191
Isa 22:13 us eat and drink; for to morrow we shall **d**. 4191
22:14 shall not be purged from you till ye **d**, 4191
22:18 there shalt thou **d**, and there the chariots of 4191
38: 1 in order: for thou shalt **d**, and not live. 4191
51: 6 they that dwell therein shall **d** in like 4191
51:12 shouldest be afraid of a man *that* shall **d**, 4191
51:14 that he should not **d** in the pit, nor that his 4191
65:20 for the child shall **d** an hundred years old; 4191
66:24 for their worm shall not **d**, neither shall 4191
Jer 11:21 of the LORD, that thou **d** not by our hand: 4191
11:22 the young men shall **d** by the sword; 4191
11:22 and their daughters shall **d** by famine: 4191
16: 4 They shall **d** of grievous deaths; they shall 4191
16: 6 the great and the small shall **d** in this land: 4191
20: 6 there thou shalt **d**, and shalt be buried there, 4191
21: 6 and beast: they shall **d** of a great pestilence. 4191
21: 9 He that abideth in this city shall **d** by 4191
22:12 he shall **d** in the place whither they have 4191
22:26 ye were not born; and there shall ye **d**. 4191
26: 8 saying, Thou shalt **surely d**. 4191+4191
26:11 saying, This man *is* worthy to **d**; 4194
26:16 the prophets; This man *is* not worthy to **d**: 4194
27:13 Why will ye **d**, thou and thy people, by 4191
28:16 *this* year thou *shalt* **d**, because thou hast 4191
31:30 every one shall **d** for his own iniquity: 4191
34: 4 of thee, Thou shalt not **d** by the sword: 4191
34: 5 *But* thou shalt **d** in peace: and with 4191
37:20 house of Jonathan the scribe, lest I **d** there. 4191
38: 2 He that remaineth in this city shall **d** by 4191
38: 9 he is like to **d** for hunger in the place where 4191
38:10 prophet out of the dungeon, before he **d**. 4191
38:24 know of these words, and thou shalt not **d**. 4191
38:26 to return to Jonathan's house, to **d** there. 4191
42:16 you there *in* Egypt; and there ye shall **d**. 4191
42:17 they shall **d** by the sword, by the famine, 4191
42:22 know certainly that ye shall **d** by the sword, 4191
44:12 they shall **d**, from the least even unto 4191
Eze 3:18 the wicked, Thou shalt **surely d**; 4191+4191
3:18 the same wicked *man* shall **d** in his 4191
3:19 his wicked way, he shall **d** in his iniquity; 4191
3:20 a stumblingblock before him, he shall **d**: 4191
3:20 he shall **d** in his sin, and his righteousness 4191
5:12 A third *part* of thee shall **d** with 4191
6:12 *He* that *is* far off shall **d** of the pestilence; 4191
6:12 and is besieged shall **d** by the famine: 4191
7:15 he that *is* in the field shall **d** with 4191
12:13 shall he not see it, though he shall **d** there. 4191
13:19 to slay the souls that should not **d**, and 4191
17:16 him in the midst of Babylon he shall **d**. 4191
18: 4 son *is* mine: the soul that sinneth, it shall **d**. 4191
18:13 he shall **surely d**; his blood shall be 4191+4191
18:17 he shall not **d** for the iniquity of his father, 4191
18:18 lo, even he shall **d** in his iniquity. 4191
18:20 The soul that sinneth, it shall **d**. The son 4191
18:21 right, he shall surely live, he shall not **d**. 4191
18:23 pleasure at all that the wicked should **d**? 4194
18:24 sin that he hath sinned, in them shall he **d**. 4191

Eze 18:26 for his iniquity that he hath done shall he **d**. 4191
18:28 he shall surely live, he shall not **d**. 4191
18:31 for why will ye **d**, O house of Israel? 4191
28: 8 thou shalt **d** the deaths of *them that are* 4191
28:10 Thou shalt **d** the deaths of 4191
33: 8 O wicked *man,* thou shalt **surely d**; 4191+4191
33: 8 that wicked *man* shall **d** in his iniquity; 4191
33: 9 from his way, he shall **d** in his iniquity; 4191
33:11 for why will ye **d**, O house of Israel? 4191
33:13 that he hath committed, he shall **d** for it. 4191
33:14 the wicked, Thou shalt **surely d**; 4191+4191
33:15 he shall surely live, he shall not **d**. 4191
33:18 he shall even **d** thereby. 4191
33:27 and in the caves shall **d** of the pestilence. 4191
Am 2: 2 Moab shall **d** with tumult, with shouting, 4191
6: 9 ten men in one house, that they shall **d**. 4191
7:11 Jeroboam shall **d** by the sword, and 4191
7:17 by line; and thou shalt **d** in a polluted land: 4191
9:10 All the sinners of my people shall **d** by 4191
Jnh 4: 3 for *it is* better for me to **d** than to live. 4194
4: 8 and wished in himself to **d**, and said, 4191
4: 8 and said, *It is* better for me to **d** than to live. 4194
Hab 1:12 we shall not **d**. O LORD, thou hast 4191
Zec 11: 9 that that dieth, let it **d**; and that that is to be 4191
13: 8 two parts therein shall be cut off *and* **d**; 1478
Mt 15: 4 or mother, let him **d** the death. *5053*
22:24 Saying, Master, Moses said, If a man **d**, *599*
26:35 said unto him, Though I should **d** with thee, *599*
Mk 7:10 or mother, let him **d** the death. *5053*
12:19 If a man's brother **d**, and leave *his* wife *599*
14:31 If I should **d with** thee, I will not deny thee *4880*
Lk 7: 2 dear unto him, was sick, and ready to **d**. *5053*
20:28 If any *man's* brother **d**, having a wife, and *599*
20:28 having a wife, and he **d** without children, *599*
20:36 Neither can they **d** any more: for they are *599*
Jn 4:49 unto him, Sir, come down ere my child **d**. *599*
6:50 that a man may eat thereof, and not **d**. *599*
8:21 ye shall seek me, and shall **d** in your sins: *599*
8:24 unto you, that ye shall **d** in your sins: *599*
8:24 for if ye believe not that I am *he,* ye shall **d** *599*
11:16 Let us also go, that we may **d** with him. *599*
11:26 and believeth in me shall never **d**. *599*
11:50 that one man should **d** for the people, and *599*
11:51 he prophesied that Jesus should **d** for *that* *599*
12:24 a corn of wheat fall into the ground and **d**, *599*
12:24 but if it **d**, it bringeth forth much fruit. *599*
12:33 he said, signifying what death he should **d**. *599*
18:14 that it was expedient that one man should **d** *622*
18:32 he spake, signifying what death he should **d**. *599*
19: 7 and by our law he ought to **d**, because *599*
21:23 the brethren, that that disciple should not **d**: *599*
21:23 yet Jesus said not unto him, He shall not **d**; *599*
Ac 21:13 also to **d** at Jerusalem for the name of *599*
25:11 any *thing* worthy of death, I refuse not to **d**: *599*
25:16 of the Romans to deliver any man to **d**, *684*
Ro 5: 7 For scarcely for a righteous *man* will one **d**: *599*
5: 7 for a good *man* some would even dare to **d**. *599*
8:13 For if ye live after the flesh, ye shall **d**: but *599*
14: 8 and whether we **d**, we die unto the Lord: *599*
14: 8 and whether we die, we **d** unto the Lord: *599*
14: 8 we live therefore, or **d**, we are the Lord's. *599*
1Co 9:15 for *it were* better for me to **d**, than that any *599*
15:22 For as in Adam all **d**, even so in Christ shall *599*
15:31 I have in Christ Jesus our Lord, I **d** daily. *599*
15:32 let us eat and drink; for to morrow we **d**. *599*
15:36 thou sowest is not quickened, except it **d**: *599*
2Co 7: 3 that you are in our hearts to **d** and live with *4880*
Php 1:21 For to me to live *is* Christ, and to **d** *is* gain. *599*
Heb 7: 8 And here men that **d** receive tithes; but *599*
9:27 And as it is appointed unto men once to **d**, *599*
Rev 3: 2 the *things* which remain, that are ready to **d**: *599*
9: 6 and shall desire to **d**, and death shall flee *599*
14:13 Blessed *are* the dead which **d** in the Lord *599*

DIED (201) [DIE]

Ge 5: 5 nine hundred and thirty years: and he **d**. 4191
5: 8 nine hundred and twelve years: and he **d**. 4191
5:11 were nine hundred and five years: and he **d**. 4191
5:14 were nine hundred and ten years: and he **d**. 4191
5:17 hundred ninety and five years: and he **d**. 4191
5:20 nine hundred sixty and two years: and he **d**. 4191
5:27 hundred sixty and nine years: and he **d**. 4191
5:31 hundred seventy and seven years: and he **d**. 4191
7:21 all flesh **d** that moved upon the earth, 1478
7:22 of life, of all that *was* in the dry *land,* **d**. 4191
9:29 nine hundred and fifty years: and he **d**. 4191
11:28 Haran **d** before his father Terah in the land 4191
11:32 five years: and Terah **d** in Haran. 4191
23: 2 Sarah **d** in Kirjath-arba; the same *is* Hebron 4191
25: 8 **d** in a good old age, an old man, and full *of* 4191
25:17 he gave up the ghost and **d**; and 4191
25:18 *and* he **d** in the presence of all his brethren. 5307
35: 8 Deborah Rebekah's nurse **d**, and she was 4191
35:18 as her soul was in departing (for she **d**) 4191
35:19 Rachel **d**, and was buried in the way to 4191
35:29 **d**, and was gathered unto his people, 4191
36:33 Bela **d**, and Jobab the son of Zerah of 4191
36:34 Jobab **d**, and Husham of the land of Temani 4191
36:35 Husham **d**, and Hadad the son of Bedad, 4191
36:36 Hadad **d**, and Samlah of Masrekah reigned 4191
36:37 Samlah **d**, and Saul of Rehoboth *by* 4191
36:38 Saul **d**, and Baal-hanan the son of Achbor 4191
36:39 Baal-hanan the son of Achbor **d**, and 4191
38:12 time the daughter of Shuah Judah's wife **d**; 4191
46:12 Er and Onan **d** in the land of Canaan. 4191
48: 7 Rachel **d** by me in the land of Canaan in 4191
50:16 Thy father did command before he **d**, 4194
50:26 So Joseph **d**, *being* an hundred and 4191
Ex 1: 6 Joseph **d**, and all his brethren, and all that 4191
2:23 in process of time, that the king of Egypt **d**: 4191
7:21 the fish that *was* in the river **d**; and the river 4191
8:13 the frogs **d** out of the houses, out of 4191
9: 6 the morrow, and all the cattle of Egypt **d**: 4191
9: 6 of the cattle of the children of Israel **d** not 4191
16: 3 Would to God we had **d** by the hand of 4191
Lev 10: 2 and they **d** before the LORD. 4191
16: 1 they offered before the LORD, and **d**; 4191
17:15 soul that eateth **that which d of itself**, 5038
Nu 3: 4 and Abihu **d** before the LORD, 4191
14: 2 Would God that we had **d** in the land of 4191
14: 2 or would God we had **d** in this wilderness! 4191
14:37 **d** by the plague before the LORD. 4191
15:36 and stoned him with stones, and he **d**; 4191
16:49 Now they that **d** in the plague were 4191
16:49 beside them that **d** about the matter of 4191
20: 1 and Miriam **d** there, and was buried there. 4191
20: 3 Would God that we had **d** when our 1478
20: 3 when our brethren **d** before the LORD! 1478
20:28 and Aaron **d** there in the top of the mount: 4191
21: 6 bit the people; and much people of Israel **d**. 4191
25: 9 those that **d** in the plague were twenty and 4191
26:10 when that company **d**, what time the fire 4194
26:11 Notwithstanding the children of Korah **d** 4191
26:19 and Er and Onan **d** in the land of Canaan. 4191
26:61 Nadab and Abihu **d**, when they offered 4191
27: 3 Our father **d** in the wilderness, and he was 4191
27: 3 but **d** in his own sin, and had no sons. 4191
33:38 **d** there, in the fortieth year after 4191
33:39 three years old when he **d** in mount Hor. 4194
Dt 10: 6 there Aaron **d**, and there he was buried; and 4191
32:50 as Aaron thy brother **d** in mount Hor, 4191
34: 5 So Moses the servant of the LORD **d** 4191
34: 7 and twenty years old when he **d**: 4194
Jos 5: 4 men of war, **d** in the wilderness by the way, 4191
10:11 upon them unto Azekah, and they **d**: 4191
10:11 *they were* moe which **d** with hailstones 4191
24:29 **d**, *being* an hundred and ten years old. 4191
24:33 Eleazar the son of Aaron **d**; and they buried 4191
Jdg 1: 7 brought him *to* Jerusalem, and there he **d**. 4191
2: 8 **d**, *being* an hundred and ten years old. 4191
2:21 of the nations which Joshua left when he **d**: 4191
3:11 And Othniel the son of Kenaz **d**. 4191
4:21 for he was fast asleep and weary. So he **d**. 4191
8:32 Gideon the son of Joash **d** in a good old 4191
9:49 that all the men of the tower of Shechem **d** 4191
9:54 young man thrust him through, and he **d**. 4191
10: 2 and **d**, and was buried in Shamir. 4191
10: 5 And Jair **d**, and was buried in Camon. 4191
12: 7 **d** Jephthah the Gileadite, and was buried in 4191
12:10 **d** Ibzan, and was buried at Beth-lehem. 4191
12:12 Elon the Zebulonite **d**, and was buried in 4191
12:15 Abdon the son of Hillel the Pirathonite **d**, 4191
Ru 1: 3 Elimelech Naomi's husband **d**; and she was 4191
1: 5 and Chilion **d** also both of them; 4191
1Sa 4:18 of the gate, and his neck brake, and he **d**: 4191
5:12 the men that **d** not were smitten with 4191
14:45 the people rescued Jonathan, that he **d** not. 4191
25: 1 Samuel **d**; and all the Israelites were 4191
25:37 that his heart **d** within him, and he became 4191
25:38 that the LORD smote Nabal, that he **d**. 4191
31: 5 likewise upon his sword, and **d** with him. 4191
31: 6 So Saul **d**, and his three sons, and 4191
2Sa 1:15 fall upon him. And he smote him that he **d**. 4191
2:23 he fell down there, and **d** in the same place: 4191
2:23 where Asahel fell down and **d** stood still. 4191
2:31 *so that* three hundred and threescore men **d**. 4191
3:27 him there *under* the fifth *rib,* that he **d**, 4191
3:33 and said, **D** Abner as a fool dieth? 4191
6: 7 *his* error; and there he **d** by the ark of God. 4191
10: 1 that the king of the children of Ammon **d**, 4191
10:18 the captain of their host, who **d** there. 4191
11:17 of David; and Uriah the Hittite **d** also. 4191
11:21 him from the wall, that he **d** in Thebez? 4191
12:18 to pass on the seventh day, that the child **d**. 4191
17:23 **d**, and was buried in the sepulchre of his 4191
18:33 would God I had **d** for thee, O Absalom, 4191
19: 6 all we had **d** *this* day, then it had pleased 4191
20:10 and strake him not again; and he **d**. 4191
24:15 there **d** of the people from Dan even to 4191
1Ki 2:25 of Jehoiada; and he fell upon him that he **d**. 4191
2:46 went out, and fell upon him, that he **d**. 4191
3:19 this woman's child **d** in the night; because 4191
12:18 all Israel stoned him with stones, that he **d**. 4191
14:17 to the threshold of the door, the child **d**; 4191
16:18 the king's house over him with fire, and **d**, 4191
16:22 of Ginath: so Tibni **d**, and Omri reigned. 4191
21:13 and stoned him with stones, that he **d**. 4191
22:35 chariot against the Syrians, and **d** at even: 4191
22:37 So the king **d**, and was brought *to* Samaria; 4191
2Ki 1:17 So he **d** according to the word of 4191
4:20 he sat on her knees till noon, and *then* **d**. 4191
7:17 and he **d**, as the man of God had said, 4191
7:20 trode upon him in the gate, and he **d**. 4191
8:15 and spread *it* on his face, so that he **d**: 4191
9:27 And he fled *to* Megiddo, and **d** there. 4191
12:21 his servants, smote him, and he **d**; 4191
13:14 fallen sick of his sickness whereof he **d**. 4191
13:20 Elisha **d**, and they buried him. And 4191
13:24 So Hazael king of Syria **d**; and 4191
23:34 and he came *to* Egypt, and **d** there. 4191
25:25 that he **d**, and the Jews and the Chaldees 4191
1Ch 1:51 Hadad **d** also. And the dukes of Edom 4191
2:30 and Appaim: but Seled **d** without children. 4191
2:32 Jonathan: and Jether **d** without children. 4191
10: 5 he fell likewise on the sword, and **d**. 4191
10: 6 So Saul **d**, and his three sons, and all his 4191
10: 6 his three sons, and all his house **d** together. 4191
10:13 So Saul **d** for his transgression which he 4191
13:10 hand to the ark: and there he **d** before God. 4191
19: 1 the king of the children of Ammon **d**, 4191
23:22 Eleazar **d**, and had no sons, but daughters: 4191
24: 2 Nadab and Abihu **d** before their father, and 4191
29:28 he **d** in a good old age, full of days, riches, 4191
2Ch 10:18 of Israel stoned him with stones, that he **d**. 4191
13:20 and the LORD struck him, and he **d**. 4191
16:13 **d** in the one and fortieth year of his reign. 4191
18:34 about the time of the sun going down he **d**. 4191
21:19 so he **d** of sore diseases. And his people 4191
24:15 waxed old, and was full *of* days when he **d**; 4191
24:15 and thirty years old *was he* when he **d**. 4194
2Ch 24:22 when he **d**, he said, The LORD look upon 4194
24:25 and slew him on his bed, and he **d**: 4191
35:24 he **d**, and was buried in *one of* 4191
Job 3:11 Why **d** I not from the womb? *why* did I *not* 4191
42:17 So Job **d**, *being* old and full of days. 4191
Isa 6: 1 In the year that king Uzziah **d** I saw also 4194
14:28 In the year that king Ahaz **d** was this 4194
Jer 28:17 So Hananiah the prophet **d** the same year in 4191
Eze 11:13 that Pelatiah the son of Benaiah **d**. 4191
24:18 at even my wife **d**; and I did in the morning 4191
Hos 13: 1 but when he offended in Baal, he **d**. 4191
Mt 22:27 And last of all the woman **d** also. *599*
Mk 12:21 took her, and **d**, neither left he *any* seed: *599*
12:22 left no seed: last of all the woman **d** also. *599*
Lk 16:22 And it came to pass that the beggar **d**, and *599*
16:22 the rich *man* also **d**, and was buried; *599*
20:29 the first took a wife, and **d** without children. *599*
20:30 second took her to wife, and he **d** childless. *599*
20:31 seven also: and they left no children, and **d**. *599*
20:32 Last of all the woman **d** also. *599*
Jn 11:21 thou hadst been here, my brother had not **d**. *2348*
11:32 thou hadst been here, my brother had not **d**. *599*
11:37 that even this *man* should not have **d**? *599*
Ac 7:15 into Egypt, and **d**, he, and our fathers, *5053*
9:37 pass in those days, that she was sick, and **d**: *599*
Ro 5: 6 in due time Christ **d** for the ungodly. *599*
5: 8 while we were yet sinners, Christ **d** for us. *599*
6:10 For in that he **d**, he died unto sin once: but *599*
6:10 For in that he died, he **d** unto sin once: but *599*
7: 9 commandment came, sin revived, and I **d**. *599*
8:34 *It is* Christ that **d**, yea rather, that is risen *599*
14: 9 For to this end Christ both **d**, and rose, *599*
14:15 not him with thy meat, for whom Christ **d**. *599*
1Co 8:11 the weak brother perish, for whom Christ **d**? *599*
15: 3 how that Christ **d** for our sins according to *599*
2Co 5:14 that if one **d** for all, then were all dead: *599*
5:15 And *that* he **d** for all, that they which live *599*
5:15 but unto him which **d** for them, and *599*
1Th 4:14 For if we believe that Jesus **d** and rose again, *599*
5:10 Who **d** for us, that, whether we wake or *599*
Heb 10:28 He that despised Moses' law **d** without *599*
11:13 These all **d** in faith, not having received *599*
11:22 By faith Joseph, when he **d**, made mention *5053*
Rev 8: 9 which were in the sea, and had life, **d**; *599*
8:11 and many men **d** of the waters, because *599*
16: 3 dead *man:* and every living soul **d** in the sea. *599*

DIEST (1) [DIE]

Ru 1:17 Where thou **d**, will I die, and there will I be 4191

DIET (2)

Jer 52:34 *for* his **d**, there was a continual diet given 737
52:34 there was a continual **d** given him of 737

DIETH (30) [DIE]

Lev 7:24 the fat of the **beast that d of itself**, and 5038
22: 8 **That which d of itself**, or is torn *with* 5038
Nu 19:14 This *is* the law, when a man **d** in a tent: 4191
Dt 14:21 Ye shall not eat of any thing that **d of itself**: 5038
2Sa 3:33 and said, Died Abner as a fool **d**? 4194
1Ki 14:11 Him that **d** of Jeroboam in the city shall 4191
14:11 him that **d** in the field shall the fowls of 4191
16: 4 Him that **d** of Baasha in the city shall 4191
16: 4 him that **d** of his in the fields shall 4191
21:24 Him that **d** of Ahab in the city the dogs 4191
21:24 him that **d** in the field shall the fowls of 4191
Job 14:10 man **d**, and wasteth away: yea, man giveth 4191
21:23 One **d** in his full strength, *being* wholly at 4191
21:25 another **d** in the bitterness of his soul, and 4191
Ps 49:17 For when he **d** he shall carry nothing away: 4194
Pr 11: 7 When a wicked man **d**, *his* expectation 4194
Ecc 2:16 And how **d** the wise *man?* as the fool. 4191
3:19 as the one **d**, so dieth the other; yea, 4194
3:19 as the one dieth, so **d** the other; yea, 4194
Isa 50: 2 because *there is* no water, and **d** for thirst. 4191
59: 5 he that eateth of their eggs **d**, and 4191
Eze 4:14 have I not eaten *of* that which **d of itself**, 5038
18:26 and committeth iniquity, and **d** in them; 4191
18:32 have no pleasure in the death of him that **d**, 4191
Zec 11: 9 that that **d**, let it die; and that that is to be 4191
Mk 9:44 Where their worm **d** not, and the fire is not *5053*
9:46 Where their worm **d** not, and the fire is not *5053*
9:48 Where their worm **d** not, and the fire is not *5053*
Ro 6: 9 Christ being raised from the dead **d** no more; *599*
14: 7 liveth to himself, and no *man* **d** to himself. *599*

DIFFER (1) [DIFFERENCE, DIFFERENCES, DIFFERETH, DIFFERING]

1Co 4: 7 For who **maketh** thee **to d** *from another?* *1252*

DIFFERENCE (12) [DIFFER]

Ex 11: 7 doth **put a d** between the Egyptians 6395
Lev 10:10 that *ye* may **put d** between holy and unholy, 914
11:47 To **make a d** between the unclean and 914
20:25 **put d** between clean beasts and unclean, 914
Eze 22:26 *things:* they have **put** no **d** between the holy 914
22:26 neither have they shewed ***d*** between NIH
44:23 they shall teach my people *the* ***d*** between NIH
Ac 15: 9 And **put** no **d** between us and them, *1252*
Ro 3:22 upon all them that believe: for there is no **d**: *1293*
10:12 For there is no **d** between the Jew and *1293*
1Co 7:34 There is **d** *also* **between** a wife and a *3307*
Jude 1:22 of some have compassion, **making a d**: *1252*

DIFFERENCES (1) [DIFFER]

1Co 12: 5 And there are **d** of administrations, but *1243*

DIFFERENT See DIVERS; DIVERSE

DIFFERETH (2) [DIFFER]

1Co 15:41 for *one* star **d from** *another* star in glory. *1308*
Gal 4: 1 as he is a child, **d** nothing **from** a servant, *1308*

DIFFERING (1) [DIFFER]
Ro 12: 6 gifts **d** according to the grace that is given *1313*

DIG (13) [DIGGED, DIGGEDST, DIGGETH]
Ex 21:33 or if a man shall **d** a pit, and not cover it, 3738
Dt 8: 9 and out of whose hills thou mayest **d** brass. 2672
23:13 thou shalt **d** therewith, and shalt turn back 2658
Job 3:21 and **d** for it more than for hid treasures; 2658
6:27 and you **d** *a pit* for your friend. 3738
11:18 thou shalt **d** *about thee, and* thou shalt take 2658
24:16 In the dark *they* **d** *through* houses, 2864
Eze 8: 8 he unto me, Son of man, **d** now in the wall: 2864
12: 5 **D** thou through the wall in their sight, and 2864
12:12 they shall **d** through the wall to carry out 2864
Am 9: 2 Though they **d** into hell, thence shall mine 2864
Lk 13: 8 year also, till I shall **d** about it, and dung *it:* *4626*
16: 3 I cannot **d**; to beg I am ashamed. *4626*

DIGGED (37) [DIG]
Ge 21:30 a witness unto me, that I have **d** this well. 2658
26:15 had **d** in the days of Abraham his father, 2658
26:18 Isaac **d** again the wells of water, which they 2658
26:18 which they had **d** in the days of Abraham 2658
26:19 Isaac's servants **d** in the valley, and 2658
26:21 they **d** another well, and strove for that 2658
26:22 removed from thence, and **d** another well; 2658
26:25 and there Isaac's servants **d** a well. 3738
26:32 him concerning the well which they had **d**, 2658
49: 6 and in their selfwill they **d down** a wall. 6131
50: 5 in my grave which I have **d** for me in 3738
Ex 7:24 all the Egyptians **d** round about the river 2658
Nu 21:18 The princes **d** the well, the nobles of 2658
21:18 the well, the nobles of the people **d** it, 3738
Dt 6:11 wells **d**, which thou diggedst not, vineyards 2672
2Ki 19:24 I have **d** and drunk strange waters, and 6979
2Ch 26:10 towers in the desert, and **d** many wells: 2672
Ne 9:25 wells **d**, vineyards, and oliveyards, and 2672
Ps 7:15 **d** it, and is fallen into the ditch *which* he 2658
35: 7 *which* without cause they have **d** for my 2658
57: 6 they have **d** a pit before me, into the midst 3738
94:13 until the pit be **d** for the wicked. 3738
119:85 The proud have **d** pits for me, which *are* 3738
Isa 5: 6 it shall not be pruned, nor **d**; but there shall 5737
7:25 *on* all hills that shall be **d** with the mattock, 5737
37:25 I have **d**, and drunk water; and with 6979
51: 1 and to the hole of the pit *whence* ye are **d**. 5365
Jer 13: 7 **d**, and took the girdle from the place where 2658
18:20 for they have **d** a pit for my soul. 3738
18:22 for they have **d** a pit to take me, and 3738
Eze 8: 8 when I had **d** in the wall, behold a door. 2864
12: 7 in the even I **d** through the wall with mine 2864
Mt 21:33 and **d** a winepress in it, and built a tower, *3736*
25:18 had received one went and **d** in the earth, *3736*
Mk 12: 1 about *it,* and **d** *a place for* the winefat, *3736*
Lk 6:48 and **d** deep, and laid the foundation on a *4626*
Ro 11: 3 thy prophets, and **d down** thine altars; *2679*

DIGGEDST (1) [DIG]
Dt 6:11 which thou **d** not, vineyards and olive trees, 2672

DIGGETH (3) [DIG]
Pr 16:27 An ungodly man **d up** evil: and in his lips 3738
26:27 Whoso **d** a pit shall fall therein: and he that 3738
Ecc 10: 8 He that **d** a pit shall fall into it; and 2658

DIGNITIES (2) [DIGNITY]
2Pe 2:10 they are not afraid to speak evil of **d**. *1391*
Jude 1: 8 despise dominion, and speak evil of **d**. *1391*

DIGNITY (4) [DIGNITIES]
Ge 49: 3 the excellency of **d**, and the excellency of 7613
Est 6: 3 and **d** hath been done to Mordecai for this? 1420
Ecc 10: 6 Folly is set in great **d**, and the rich sit in 4791
Hab 1: 7 and their **d** shall proceed of themselves. 7613

DIKLAH (2)
Ge 10:27 And Hadoram, and Uzal, and **D**, 1853
1Ch 1:21 Hadoram also, and Uzal, and **D**, 1853

DILEAN (1)
Jos 15:38 And **D**, and Mizpeh, and Joktheel, 1810

DILIGENCE (10) [DILIGENT]
Pr 4:23 Keep thy heart with all **d**; for out of it *are* 4929
Lk 12:58 give **d** that *thou* mayest be delivered from *2039*
Ro 12: 8 he that ruleth, with **d**; he that sheweth *4710*
2Co 8: 7 and *in* all **d**, and *in* your love to us, *4710*
2Ti 4: 9 **Do** thy **d** to come shortly unto me: *4704*
4:21 **Do** thy **d** to come before winter. *4704*
Heb 6:11 **d** to the full assurance of hope unto the end: *4710*
2Pe 1: 5 And beside this, giving all **d**, add to your *4710*
1:10 **give d** to make your calling and *4704*
Jude 1: 3 when I gave all **d** to write unto you of *4710*

DILIGENT (15) [DILIGENCE, DILIGENTLY]
Dt 19:18 the judges shall make **d** inquisition: and 3190
Jos 22: 5 take **d** heed to do the commandment and 3966
Ps 64: 6 out iniquities; they accomplish a **d** search: 2664
77: 6 own heart: and my spirit **made d search**. 2664
Pr 10: 4 but the hand of the **d** maketh rich. 2742
12:24 The hand of the **d** shall bear rule: but 2742
12:27 but the substance of a **d** man *is* precious. 2742
13: 4 but the soul of the **d** shall be made fat. 2742
21: 5 The thoughts of the **d** *tend* only to 2742
22:29 Seest thou a man **d** in his business? he shall 4106
27:23 Be thou **d to know** the state of thy 3045+3045
2Co 8:22 whom we have oftentimes proved **d** in *4707*
8:22 in many *things,* but now much more **d**, *4705*
Tit 3:12 be **d** to come unto me to Nicopolis: *4704*
2Pe 3:14 seeing that ye look for such *things,* be **d** *4704*

DILIGENTLY (37) [DILIGENT]
Ex 15:26 If thou wilt **d hearken** to the voice 8085+8085
Lev 10:16 Moses **d sought** the goat of the sin 1875+1875
Dt 4: 9 take heed to thyself, and keep thy soul **d**, 3966
6: 7 thou shalt **teach** them **d** unto thy children, 8150
6:17 You shall **d keep** the commandments 8104+8104
11:13 if you shall **hearken d** unto my 8085+8085
11:22 For if ye shall **d keep** all these 8104+8104
13:14 thou inquire, and make search, and ask **d**; 3190
17: 4 thou hast heard *of it,* and inquired **d**, and 3190
24: 8 that *thou* observe **d**, and do according to all 3966
28: 1 if thou shalt **hearken d** unto 8085+8085
1Ki 20:33 Now the men did **d observe** whether *any* 5172
Ezr 7:23 let it be **d** done for the house of the God of 149
Job 13:17 **Hear d** my speech, and 8085+8085
21: 2 **Hear d** my speech, and let this be 8085+8085
Ps 37:10 thou shalt **d consider** his place, and it *shall* 995
119: 4 hast commanded *us* to keep thy precepts **d**. 3966
Pr 7:15 **d** to **seek** thy face, and I have found thee. 7836
11:27 He that **d seeketh** good procureth favour: 7836
23: 1 a ruler, **consider d** what *is* before thee: 995+995
Isa 21: 7 he **hearkened d** *with* much heed: 7181+7182
55: 2 **hearken d** unto me, and eat ye *that which* 8085
Jer 2:10 consider **d**, and see if there be such a *thing.* 3966
12:16 if they will **d learn** the ways of my 3925+3925
17:24 **d hearken** unto me, saith 8085+8085
Zec 6:15 if ye will **d obey** the voice of 8085+8085
Mt 2: 7 **inquired** of them **d** what time the star *198*
2: 8 said, Go and search **d** for the young child; *199*
2:16 which he had **d inquired** of the wise men. *198*
Lk 15: 8 the house, and seek **d** till she find *it?* *1960*
Ac 18:25 he spake and taught **d** the *things* of the Lord, *199*
1Ti 5:10 if she have **d followed** every good work. *1872*
2Ti 1:17 he was in Rome, he sought me out **very d**, *4706*
Tit 3:13 the lawyer and Apollos on their journey **d**, *4709*
Heb 11: 6 *that* he is a rewarder of them that **d seek** *1567*
12:15 **Looking d** lest any *man* fail of the grace of *1983*
1Pe 1:10 the prophets have inquired and **searched d**, *1830*

DILL See ANISE

DIM (9) [DIMNESS]
Ge 27: 1 his eyes were **d**, so that he could not see, 3543
48:10 Now the eyes of Israel were **d** for age, *so* 3513
Dt 34: 7 his eye was not **d**, nor his natural force 3543
1Sa 3: 2 his eyes began *to wax* **d**, *that* he could not 3544
4:15 and his eyes were **d**, that he could not see. 6965
Job 17: 7 Mine eye also is **d** by reason of sorrow, and 3543
Isa 32: 3 the eyes of them that see shall not be **d**, 8159
La 4: 1 How is the gold **become d**! *how* is the most 6004
5:17 is faint; for these *things* our eyes are **d**. 2821

DIMINISH (8) [DIMINISHED, DIMINISHING]
Ex 5: 8 upon them; you shall not **d** *ought* thereof: 1639
21:10 and her duty of marriage, shall he not **d**. 1639
Lev 25:16 fewness of years thou shalt **d** the price of it: 4591
Dt 4: 2 neither shall you **d** *ought* from it, 1639
12:32 thou shalt not add thereto, nor **d** from it. 1639
Jer 26: 2 thee to speak unto them; **d** not a word: 1639
Eze 5:11 will I also **d** *thee;* neither shall mine eye 1639
29:15 for I will **d** them, that *they* shall no more 4591

DIMINISHED (5) [DIMINISH]
Ex 5:11 *it:* yet not ought of your work *shall be* **d**. 1639
Pr 13:11 Wealth *gotten* by vanity shall be **d**: but 4591
Isa 21:17 *men* of the children of Kedar, shall be **d**: 4591
Jer 29: 6 that ye may be increased there, and not **d**. 4591
Eze 16:27 have **d** thine ordinary *food,* and 1639

DIMINISHING (1) [DIMINISH]
Ro 11:12 and the **d** of them the riches of the Gentiles; *2275*

DIMNAH (1)
Jos 21:35 **D** with her suburbs, Nahalal with her 1829

DIMNESS (2) [DIM]
Isa 8:22 behold trouble and darkness, **d** of anguish; 4588
9: 1 Nevertheless the **d** *shall* not *be* such as *was* 4155

DIMON (2)
Isa 15: 9 For the waters of **D** shall be full *of* blood: 1775
15: 9 for I will bring more upon **D**, lions upon 1775

DIMONAH (1)
Jos 15:22 And Kinah, and **D**, and Adadah, 1776

DINAH (7) [DINAH'S]
Ge 30:21 she bare a daughter, and called her name **D**. 1783
34: 1 **D** the daughter of Leah, which she bare 1783
34: 3 his soul clave unto **D** the daughter of Jacob, 1783
34: 5 Jacob heard that he had defiled **D** his 1783
34:13 said, because he had defiled **D** their sister: 1783
34:26 took **D** out of Shechem's house, and 1783
46:15 Jacob in Padan-aram, with his daughter **D**: 1783

DINAH'S (1) [DINAH]
Ge 34:25 Simeon and Levi, **D** brethren, took each 1783

DINAITES (1)
Ezr 4: 9 the **D**, the Apharsathchites, the Tarpelites, 1784

DINE (3) [DINED, DINNER]
Ge 43:16 for *these* men shall **d** with me at noon. 398
Lk 11:37 a certain Pharisee besought him to **d** with *709*
Jn 21:12 Jesus saith unto them, Come *and* **d**. *709*

DINED (1) [DINE]
Jn 21:15 So when they had **d**, Jesus saith to Simon *709*

DINHABAH (2)
Ge 36:32 in Edom: and the name of his city *was* **D**. 1838
1Ch 1:43 of Beor: and the name of his city *was* **D**. 1838

DINNER (4) [DINE]
Pr 15:17 Better *is* a **d** of herbs where love is, than a 737
Mt 22: 4 are bidden, Behold, I have prepared my **d**: *712*
Lk 11:38 that he had not first washed before **d**. *712*
14:12 When thou makest a **d** or a supper, call not *712*

DIONYSIUS (1)
Ac 17:34 among the which *was* **D** the Areopagite, *1354*

DIOTREPHES (1)
3Jn 1: 9 but **D**, who loveth to have the preeminence *1361*

DIP (10) [DIPPED, DIPPETH, DIPT]
Ex 12:22 **d** *it* in the blood that *is* in the bason, and 2881
Lev 4: 6 the priest shall **d** his finger in the blood, 2881
4:17 the priest shall **d** his finger *in some of* 2881
14: 6 shall **d** them and the living bird in the blood 2881
14:16 the priest shall **d** his right finger in the oil 2881
14:51 **d** them in the blood of the slain bird, 2881
Nu 19:18 **d** *it* in the water, and sprinkle *it* upon 2881
Dt 33:24 to his brethren, and let him **d** his foot in oil. 2881
Ru 2:14 the bread, and **d** thy morsel in the vinegar. 2881
Lk 16:24 that he may **d** the tip of his finger in water, *911*

DIPPED (6) [DIP]
Ge 37:31 of the goats, and **d** the coat in the blood; 2881
Jos 3:15 the ark were **d** in the brim of the water, 2881
2Ki 5:14 and **d** *himself* seven times in Jordan, 2881
Ps 68:23 That thy foot may be **d** in the blood of *thine* 4272
Jn 13:26 when I have **d** *it.* And when he had dipped *911*
13:26 when I have dipped *it.* And when he had **d** *1686*

DIPPETH (2) [DIP]
Mt 26:23 He that **d** *his* hand with me in the dish, *1686*
Mk 14:20 of the twelve, that **d** with me in the dish. *1686*

DIPT (4) [DIP]
Lev 9: 9 he **d** his finger in the blood, and put *it* upon 2881
1Sa 14:27 **d** it in a honeycomb, and put his hand to his 2881
2Ki 8:15 **d** *it* in water, and spread *it* on his face, so 2881
Rev 19:13 And he *was* clothed with a vesture **d** in *911*

DIRECT (10) [DIRECTED, DIRECTETH, DIRECTION, DIRECTLY]
Ge 46:28 him unto Joseph, to **d** his face unto Goshen; 3384
Ps 5: 3 *in* the morning will I **d** *my prayer* unto 6186
Pr 3: 6 acknowledge him, and he shall **d** thy paths. 3474
11: 5 The righteousness of the perfect shall **d** his 3474
Ecc 10:10 but wisdom *is* profitable to **d**. 3787
Isa 45:13 in righteousness, and I will **d** all his ways: 3474
61: 8 I will **d** their work in truth, and I will make 5414
Jer 10:23 *it is* not in man that walketh to **d** his steps. 3559
1Th 3:11 our Lord Jesus Christ, **d** our way unto you. *2720*
2Th 3: 5 And the Lord **d** your hearts into the love of *2720*

DIRECTED (3) [DIRECT]
Job 32:14 Now he hath not **d** *his* words against me: 6186
Ps 119: 5 O that my ways were **d** to keep thy statutes! 3559
Isa 40:13 Who hath **d** the spirit of the LORD, or 8505

DIRECTETH (3) [DIRECT]
Job 37: 3 He **d** it under the whole heaven, and 3474
Pr 16: 9 his way: but the LORD **d** his steps. 3559
21:29 his face: but *as for* the upright, he **d** his way. 995

DIRECTION (1) [DIRECT]
Nu 21:18 **by the d of** the lawgiver, with their staves. 871.1

DIRECTLY (2) [DIRECT]
Nu 19: 4 sprinkle of her blood **d** before 413+5227
Eze 42:12 *even* the way **d** before the wall toward 1903

DIRT (3)
Jdg 3:22 dagger out of his belly; and the **d** came out. 6574
Ps 18:42 I did cast them out as the **d** in the streets. 2916
Isa 57:20 whose waters cast up mire and **d**. 2916

DISABLED See IMPOTENT

DISALLOW (2) [DISALLOWED]
Nu 30: 5 if her father **d** her in the day that he 5106
30: 8 if her husband **d** her on the day that he 5106

DISALLOWED (4) [DISALLOW]
Nu 30: 5 shall forgive her, because her father **d** her. 5106
30:11 and held his peace at her, *and* **d** her not: 5106
1Pe 2: 4 **d** indeed of men, but chosen of God, *and* *593*
2: 7 the stone which the builders **d**, *593*

DISANNUL (3) [DISANNULLED, DISANNULLETH, DISANNULLING]
Job 40: 8 Wilt thou also **d** my judgment? wilt thou 6565
Isa 14:27 who shall **d** *it?* and his hand *is* stretched 6565
Gal 3:17 hundred and thirty years after, cannot **d**, *208*

DISANNULLED (1) [DISANNUL]
Isa 28:18 your covenant with death shall be **d**, and 3722

DISANNULLETH (1) [DISANNUL]
Gal 3:15 *it be* confirmed, no *man* **d**, or added thereto. *114*

DISANNULLING (1) [DISANNUL]
Heb 7:18 For there is verily a **d** of the commandment *115*

DISAPPOINT (1) [DISAPPOINTED, DISAPPOINTETH]
Ps 17:13 Arise, O LORD, **d** him, cast him 6440+6923

DISAPPOINTED (1) [DISAPPOINT]
Pr 15:22 Without counsel purposes *are* **d**: but in 6565

DISAPPOINTETH (1) [DISAPPOINT]
Job 5:12 He **d** the devices of the crafty, so that their 6565

DISCERN (17) [DISCERNED, DISCERNER, DISCERNETH, DISCERNING]
Ge 31:32 before our brethren **d** thou what *is* thine 5234
38:25 she said, **D**, I pray thee, whose *are* these, 5234
2Sa 14:17 so *is* my lord the king to **d** good and bad: 8085
19:35 *and* can I **d** between good and evil? can thy 3045
1Ki 3: 9 that *I* may **d** between good and bad: 995
3:11 hast asked for thyself understanding to **d** 8085
Ezr 3:13 So that the people could not **d** the noise of 5234
Job 4:16 but I could not **d** the form thereof: 5234
6:30 cannot my taste **d** perverse things? 995
Eze 44:23 **cause** them **to d** between the unclean and 3045
Jnh 4:11 that cannot **d** between their right hand 3045
Mal 3:18 **d** between the righteous and the wicked, 7200
Mt 16: 3 *ye* hypocrites, ye can **d** the face of the sky; *1252*
16: 3 but can ye not *d* the signs of the times? NIG
Lk 12:56 ye can **d** the face of the sky and of *1381*
12:56 how *is it that* ye do not **d** this time? *1381+1492*
Heb 5:14 have their senses exercised to **d** both good *1253*

DISCERNED (4) [DISCERN]
Ge 27:23 he **d** him not, because his hands were hairy, 5234
1Ki 20:41 the king of Israel **d** him that he *was* of 5234
Pr 7: 7 the simple ones, I **d** among the youths, 995
1Co 2:14 know *them,* because they are spiritually **d**. *350*

DISCERNER (1) [DISCERN]
Heb 4:12 and *is* a **d** of the thoughts and intents of *2924*

DISCERNETH (1) [DISCERN]
Ecc 8: 5 a wise *man's* heart **d** *both* time and 3045

DISCERNING (2) [DISCERN]
1Co 11:29 to himself, not **d** the Lord's body. *1252*
12:10 to another prophecy; to another **d** of spirits; *1253*

DISCHARGE (1) [DISCHARGED]
Ecc 8: 8 *there is* no **d** in *that* war; neither shall 4917

DISCHARGED (1) [DISCHARGE]
1Ki 5: 9 will **cause** them **to be d** there, and 5310

DISCIPLE (29) [DISCIPLES, DISCIPLES', FELLOW-DISCIPLES]
Mt 10:24 The **d** is not above *his* master, nor *3101*
10:25 *It is* enough for the **d** that he be as his *3101*
10:42 a cup of cold *water* only in the name of a **d**, *3101*
27:57 who also himself was Jesus' **d**: *3100*
Lk 6:40 The **d** is not above his master: but *3101*
14:26 and his own life also, he cannot be my **d**. *3101*
14:27 and come after me, cannot be my **d**. *3101*
14:33 not all that he hath, he cannot be my **d**. *3101*
Jn 9:28 they reviled him, and said, Thou art his **d**; *3101*
18:15 Peter followed Jesus, and *so did* another **d**: *3101*
18:15 that **d** was known unto the high priest, and *3101*
18:16 Then went out *that* other **d**, which was *3101*
19:26 saw *his* mother, and the **d** standing by, *3101*
19:27 Then saith he to the **d**, Behold thy mother. *3101*
19:27 And from that hour *that* **d** took her unto his *3101*
19:38 being a **d** of Jesus, but secretly for fear of *3101*
20: 2 and to the other **d**, whom Jesus loved, and *3101*
20: 3 and *that* other **d**, and came to the sepulchre. *3101*
20: 4 and the other **d** did outrun Peter, and *3101*
20: 8 Then went in also *that* other **d**, which came *3101*
21: 7 Therefore that **d** whom Jesus loved saith *3101*
21:20 seeth the **d** whom Jesus loved following; *3101*
21:23 the brethren, that that **d** should not die: *3101*
21:24 This is the **d** which testifieth of these *3101*
Ac 9:10 And there was a certain **d** at Damascus, *3101*
9:26 of him, and believed not that he was a **d**. *3101*
9:36 Now there was at Joppa a certain **d** named *3102*
16: 1 and behold, a certain **d** was there, *3101*
21:16 an old **d**, with whom we should lodge. *3101*

DISCIPLES (243) [DISCIPLE]
Isa 8:16 up the testimony, seal the law among my **d**. 3928
Mt 5: 1 and when he was set, his **d** came unto him: *3101*
8:21 And another of his **d** said unto him, Lord, *3101*
8:23 was entered into a ship, his **d** followed him. *3101*
8:25 And his **d** came to *him,* and awoke him, *3101*
9:10 and sat down with him and his **d**. *3101*
9:11 the Pharisees saw *it,* they said unto his **d**, *3101*
9:14 Then came to him the **d** of John, saying, *3101*
9:14 the Pharisees fast oft, but thy **d** fast not? *3101*
9:19 and followed him, and *so did* his **d**. *3101*
9:37 Then saith he unto his **d**, The harvest truly *3101*
10: 1 when he had called unto *him* his twelve **d**, *3101*
11: 1 made an end of commanding his twelve **d**, *3101*
11: 2 the works of Christ, he sent two of his **d**, *3101*
12: 1 and his **d** were a hungred, and began to *3101*
12: 2 thy **d** do *that* which is not lawful to do upon *3101*
12:49 he stretched forth his hand toward his **d**, *3101*
13:10 And the **d** came, and said unto him, *3101*
13:36 and his **d** came unto him, saying, *3101*
14:12 And his **d** came, and took up the body, *3101*
14:15 his **d** came to him, saying, *This* is a desert *3101*
14:19 and gave the loaves to *his* **d**, and *3101*
14:19 to *his* disciples, and the **d** to the multitude. *3101*
14:22 And straightway Jesus constrained his **d** to *3101*
14:26 And when the **d** saw him walking on *3101*
15: 2 Why do thy **d** transgress the tradition of *3101*
15:12 Then came his **d**, and said unto him, *3101*
15:23 And his **d** came and besought him, saying, *3101*
15:32 Then Jesus called his **d** unto *him,* and said, *3101*
15:33 And his **d** say unto him, Whence should we *3101*
15:36 and brake *them,* and gave to his **d**, and *3101*
15:36 to his disciples, and the **d** to the multitude. *3101*
16: 5 And when his **d** were come to the other *3101*
16:13 he asked his **d**, saying, Whom do men say *3101*
16:20 Then charged he his **d** that they should tell *3101*
16:21 time forth began Jesus to shew unto his **d**, *3101*
16:24 Then said Jesus unto his **d**, If any *man* will *3101*
17: 6 And when the **d** heard *it,* they fell on their *3101*
Mt 17:10 And his **d** asked him, saying, Why then *3101*
17:13 Then the **d** understood that he spake unto *3101*
17:16 And I brought him to thy **d**, and they could *3101*
17:19 Then came the **d** to Jesus apart, *3101*
18: 1 At the same time came the **d** unto Jesus, *3101*
19:10 His **d** say unto him, If the case of the man *3101*
19:13 on them, and pray: and the **d** rebuked them. *3101*
19:23 Then said Jesus unto his **d**, Verily I say *3101*
19:25 When his **d** heard *it,* they were exceedingly *3101*
20:17 took the twelve **d** apart in the way, *3101*
21: 1 the mount of Olives, then sent Jesus two **d**, *3101*
21: 6 And the **d** went, and did as Jesus *3101*
21:20 And when the **d** saw *it,* they marvelled, *3101*
22:16 And they sent out unto him their **d** with *3101*
23: 1 spake Jesus to the multitude, and to his **d**, *3101*
24: 1 his **d** came to *him* for to shew him *3101*
24: 3 the **d** came unto him privately, saying, *3101*
26: 1 all these sayings, he said unto his **d**, *3101*
26: 8 But when his **d** saw *it,* they had *3101*
26:17 *of* unleavened bread the **d** came to Jesus, *3101*
26:18 keep the passover at thy house with my **d**. *3101*
26:19 And the **d** did as Jesus had appointed them; *3101*
26:26 blessed *it,* and brake *it,* and gave *it* to the **d**, *3101*
26:35 not deny thee. Likewise also said all the **d**. *3101*
26:36 and saith unto the **d**, Sit ye here, while I go *3101*
26:40 And he cometh unto the **d**, and *3101*
26:45 Then cometh he to his **d**, and saith unto *3101*
26:56 Then all the **d** forsook him, and fled. *3101*
27:64 lest his **d** come by night, and steal him *3101*
28: 7 and tell his **d** that he is risen from the dead; *3101*
28: 8 great joy; and did run to bring his **d** word. *3101*
28: 9 And as they went to tell his **d**, behold, Jesus *3101*
28:13 His **d** came by night, and stole him *away* *3101*
28:16 Then the eleven **d** went *away* into Galilee, *3101*
Mk 2:15 sat also together with Jesus and his **d**: *3101*
2:16 and sinners, they said unto his **d**, *3101*
2:18 And the **d** of John and of the Pharisees used *3101*
2:18 Why do the **d** of John and of the Pharisees *3101*
2:18 and of the Pharisees fast, but thy **d** fast not? *3101*
2:23 and his **d** began, as they went, to pluck *3101*
3: 7 But Jesus withdrew himself with his **d** to *3101*
3: 9 And he spake to his **d**, that a small ship *3101*
4:34 he expounded all *things* to his **d**. *3101*
5:31 And his **d** said unto him, Thou seest *3101*
6: 1 into his own country; and his **d** follow him. *3101*
6:29 And when his **d** heard *of it,* they came and *3101*
6:35 his **d** came unto him, and said, *This* is a *3101*
6:41 and gave *them* to his **d** to set before them; *3101*
6:45 And straightway he constrained his **d** to get *3101*
7: 2 And when they saw some of his **d** eat bread *3101*
7: 5 Why walk not thy **d** according to *3101*
7:17 his **d** asked him concerning the parable. *3101*
8: 1 Jesus called his **d** unto *him,* and saith unto *3101*
8: 4 And his **d** answered him, From whence can *3101*
8: 6 and gave to his **d** to set before *them;* and *3101*
8:10 he entered into a ship with his **d**, *3101*
8:14 Now *the d* had forgotten to take bread, NIG
8:27 And Jesus went out, and his **d**, into *3101*
8:27 and by the way he asked his **d**, saying unto *3101*
8:33 he had turned about and looked on his **d**, *3101*
8:34 called the people unto *him* with his **d** also, *3101*
9:14 And when he came to *his* **d**, he saw a great *3101*
9:18 I spake to thy **d** that they should cast him *3101*
9:28 his **d** asked him privately, Why could not *3101*
9:31 For he taught his **d**, and said unto them, *3101*
10:10 And in the house his **d** asked him again of *3101*
10:13 *his* **d** rebuked those that brought *them.* *3101*
10:23 looked round about, and saith unto his **d**, *3101*
10:24 And the **d** were astonished at his words. *3101*
10:46 as he went out of Jericho with his **d** and *3101*
11: 1 of Olives, he sendeth forth two of his **d**, *3101*
11:14 thee hereafter for ever. And his **d** heard *it.* *3101*
12:43 And he called unto *him* his **d**, and *3101*
13: 1 one of his **d** saith unto him, Master, *3101*
14:12 his **d** said unto him, Where wilt thou *that* *3101*
14:13 And he sendeth forth two of his **d**, and *3101*
14:14 where I shall eat the passover with my **d**? *3101*
14:16 And his **d** went forth, and came into *3101*
14:32 and he saith to his **d**, Sit ye here, while I *3101*
16: 7 tell his **d** and Peter that he goeth before you *3101*
Lk 5:30 and Pharisees murmured against his **d**, *3101*
5:33 Why do the **d** of John fast often, and *3101*
5:33 and likewise the *d* of the Pharisees; NIG
6: 1 and his **d** plucked the ears of corn, and *3101*
6:13 when it was day, he called unto *him* his **d**: *3101*
6:17 and the company of his **d**, and a great *3101*
6:20 And he lifted up his eyes on his **d**, and said, *3101*
7:11 and many of his **d** went with him, and *3101*
7:18 And the **d** of John shewed him of all these *3101*
7:19 And John calling unto *him* two of his **d** sent *3101*
8: 9 And his **d** asked him, saying, What might *3101*
8:22 that he went into a ship with his **d**: *3101*
9: 1 Then he called his twelve **d** together, and *3101*
9:14 And he said to his **d**, Make them sit down *3101*
9:16 gave to the **d** to set before the multitude. *3101*
9:18 he was alone praying, *his* **d** were with him: *3101*
9:40 And I besought thy **d** to cast him out; and *3101*
9:43 *things* which Jesus did, he said unto his **d**, *3101*
9:54 And when his **d** James and John saw *this,* *3101*
10:23 And he turned him unto *his* **d**, and *3101*
11: 1 he ceased, one of his **d** said unto him, Lord, *3101*
11: 1 teach us to pray, as John also taught his **d**. *3101*
12: 1 he began to say unto his **d** first *of all,* *3101*
12:22 And he said unto his **d**, Therefore I say *3101*
16: 1 And he said also unto his **d**, There was a *3101*
17: 1 Then said he unto the **d**, It is impossible but *3101*
17:22 And he said unto the **d**, The days will *3101*
18:15 but when *his* **d** saw *it,* they rebuked them. *3101*
19:29 *the mount* of Olives, he sent two of his **d**, *3101*
19:37 the whole multitude of the **d** began to *3101*
19:39 said unto him, Master, rebuke thy **d**. *3101*
20:45 of all the people he said unto his **d**, *3101*
22:11 where I shall eat the passover with my **d**? *3101*
22:39 of Olives; and his **d** also followed him. *3101*
22:45 rose up from prayer, and was come to his **d**, *3101*
Jn 1:35 next day *after* John stood, and two of his **d**; *3101*
1:37 And the two **d** heard him speak, and *3101*
2: 2 Jesus was called, and his **d**, to the marriage. *3101*
2:11 forth his glory; and his **d** believed on him. *3101*
2:12 and his mother, and his brethren, and his **d**: *3101*
2:17 And his **d** remembered that it was written, *3101*
2:22 his **d** remembered that he had said this unto *3101*
3:22 came Jesus and his **d** into the land of Judea; *3101*
3:25 arose a question between *some* of John's **d** *3101*
4: 1 Jesus made and baptized moe **d** than John, *3101*
4: 2 Jesus himself baptized not, but his **d**,) *3101*
4: 8 (For his **d** were gone away unto the city to *3101*
4:27 And upon this came his **d**, and *3101*
4:31 In the mean while *his* **d** prayed him, saying, *3101*
4:33 Therefore said the **d** one to another, *3101*
6: 3 into a mountain, and there he sat with his **d**. *3101*
6: 8 One of his **d**, Andrew, Simon Peter's *3101*
6:11 he distributed to the **d**, and the disciples to *3101*
6:11 and the **d** to them that were set down; *3101*
6:12 When they were filled, he said unto his **d**, *3101*
6:16 *now* come, his **d** went down unto the sea, *3101*
6:22 save that one whereinto his **d** were entered, *3101*
6:22 that Jesus went not with his **d** into the boat, *3101*
6:22 but *that* his **d** were gone away alone; *3101*
6:24 neither his **d**, they also took shipping, *3101*
6:60 Many therefore of his **d**, when they had *3101*
6:61 When Jesus knew in himself that his **d** *3101*
6:66 From that *time* many of his **d** went back, *3101*
7: 3 that thy **d** also may see the works that thou *3101*
8:31 in my word, *then* are ye my **d** indeed; *3101*
9: 2 And his **d** asked him, saying, Master, *3101*
9:27 you hear *it* again? will ye also be his **d**? *3101*
9:28 Thou art his disciple; but we are Moses' **d**. *3101*
11: 7 Then after that saith he to *his* **d**, Let us go *3101*
11: 8 *His* **d** say unto him, Master, the Jews of late *3101*
11:12 Then said his **d**, Lord, if he sleep, he shall *3101*
11:54 and there continued with his **d**. *3101*
12: 4 Then saith one of his **d**, Judas Iscariot, *3101*
12:16 These *things* understood not his **d** at *3101*
13:22 Then the **d** looked one on another, *3101*
13:23 was leaning on Jesus' bosom one of his **d**, *3101*
13:35 this shall all *men* know that ye are my **d**, *3101*
15: 8 ye bear much fruit; so shall ye be my **d**. *3101*
16:17 Then said *some* of his **d** among themselves, *3101*
16:29 His **d** said unto him, Lo, now speakest thou *3101*
18: 1 forth with his **d** over the brook Cedron, *3101*
18: 1 into the which he entered, and his **d**. *3101*
18: 2 Jesus ofttimes resorted thither with his **d**. *3101*
18:17 Art not thou also *one* of this man's **d**? *3101*
18:19 The high priest then asked Jesus of his **d**, *3101*
18:25 unto him, Art not thou also *one* of his **d**? *3101*
20:10 Then the **d** went away again unto their own *3101*
20:18 and told the **d** that she had seen the Lord, *3101*
20:19 when the doors were shut where the **d** were *3101*
20:20 Then were the **d** glad, when they saw *3101*
20:25 The other **d** therefore said unto him, *3101*
20:26 And after eight days again his **d** were *3101*
20:30 truly did Jesus in the presence of his **d**, *3101*
21: 1 himself again to the **d** at the sea of Tiberias; *3101*
21: 2 the *sons* of Zebedee, and two other of his **d**. *3101*
21: 4 but the **d** knew not that it was Jesus. *3101*
21: 8 And the other **d** came in a little ship; *3101*
21:12 And none of the **d** durst ask him, Who art *3101*
21:14 time *that* Jesus shewed himself to his **d**, *3101*
Ac 1:15 days Peter stood up in the midst of the **d**, *3101*
6: 1 when the number of the **d** was multiplied, *3101*
6: 2 called the multitude of the **d** unto *them,* *3101*
6: 7 the number of the **d** multiplied in Jerusalem *3101*
9: 1 and slaughter against the **d** of the Lord, *3101*
9:19 Then was Saul certain days with the **d** *3101*
9:25 Then the **d** took him by night, and let *him* *3101*
9:26 he assayed to join himself to the **d**: *3101*
9:38 and the **d** had heard that Peter was there, *3101*
11:26 the **d** were called Christians first in *3101*
11:29 Then the **d**, every man according to his *3101*
13:52 And the **d** were filled with joy, and with *3101*
14:20 Howbeit, as the **d** stood round about him, *3101*
14:22 Confirming the souls of the **d**, *and* *3101*
14:28 And there they abode long time with the **d**. *3101*
15:10 to put a yoke upon the neck of the **d**, *3101*
18:23 Phrygia in order, strengthening all the **d**. *3101*
18:27 exhorting the **d** to receive him: *3101*
19: 1 came to Ephesus: and finding certain **d**, *3101*
19: 9 he departed from them, and separated the **d**, *3101*
19:30 in unto the people, the **d** suffered him not. *3101*
20: 1 Paul called unto *him* the **d**, and embraced *3101*
20: 7 when the **d** came together to break bread, *3101*
20:30 speaking perverse *things,* to draw away **d** *3101*
21: 4 And finding **d**, we tarried there seven days: *3101*
21:16 There went with us also *certain* of the **d** of *3101*

DISCIPLES' (1) [DISCIPLE]
Jn 13: 5 and began to wash the **d** feet, and to wipe *3101*

DISCIPLINE (1)
Job 36:10 He openeth also their ear to **d**, and 4148

DISCLOSE (1)
Isa 26:21 the earth also shall **d** her blood, and 1540

DISCOMFITED (9) [DISCOMFITURE]
Ex 17:13 Joshua **d** Amalek and his people with 2522
Nu 14:45 smote them, and **d** them, *even* unto 3807
Jos 10:10 the LORD **d** them before Israel, and 2000
Jdg 4:15 the LORD **d** Sisera, and all *his* chariots, 2000
8:12 and Zalmunna, and **d** all the host. 2729
1Sa 7:10 that day upon the Philistines, and **d** them; 2000
2Sa 22:15 and scattered them; lightning, and **d** them. 2000
Ps 18:14 and he shot out lightnings, and **d** them. 2000
Isa 31: 8 the sword, and his young men shall be **d**. 4522

DISCOMFITURE (1) [DISCOMFITED]
1Sa 14:20 his fellow, *and there was* a very great **d**. 4103

D

D

DISCONTENTED (1)
1Sa 22: 2 in debt, and every one *that was* **d**, 4751+5315

DISCONTINUE (1)
Jer 17: 4 shalt **d** from thine heritage that I gave thee; 8058

DISCORD (2)
Pr 6:14 deviseth mischief continually; he soweth **d**. 4066
6:19 and he that soweth **d** among brethren. 4066

DISCOURAGE (1) [DISCOURAGED]
Nu 32: 7 wherefore **d** ye the heart of the children of 5106

DISCOURAGED (6) [DISCOURAGE]
Nu 21: 4 the soul of the people was much **d** because 7114
32: 9 they **d** the heart of the children of Israel, 5106
Dt 1:21 hath said unto thee; fear not, neither be **d**. 2865
1:28 our brethren have **d** our heart, saying, 4549
Isa 42: 4 He shall not fail nor be **d**, till he have set 7533
Col 3:21 not your children *to anger*, lest they be **d**. *120*

DISCOVER (12) [DISCOVERED, DISCOVERETH, DISCOVERING]
Dt 22:30 his father's wife, nor **d** his father's skirt. 1540
1Sa 14: 8 and we will **d** ourselves unto them. 1540
Job 41:13 Who can **d** the face of his garment? *or* 1540
Pr 18: 2 but that his heart may **d** itself. 1540
25: 9 and **d** not a secret *to* another: 1540
Isa 3:17 and the LORD will **d** their secret parts. 6168
Jer 13:26 Therefore will I **d** thy skirts upon thy face, 2834
La 4:22 O daughter of Edom; he will **d** thy sins. 1540
Eze 16:37 will **d** thy nakedness unto them, that they 1540
Hos 2:10 now will I **d** her lewdness in the sight of 1540
Mic 1: 6 and I will **d** the foundations thereof. 1540
Na 3: 5 I will **d** thy skirts upon thy face, and I will 1540

DISCOVERED (22) [DISCOVER]
Ex 20:26 that thy nakedness be not **d** thereon. 1540
Lev 20:18 he hath **d** her fountain, and she hath 6168
1Sa 14:11 both of them **d** themselves unto 1540
22: 6 When Saul heard that David was **d**, and 3045
2Sa 22:16 the foundations of the world were **d**, at 1540
Ps 18:15 the foundations of the world were **d** at thy 1540
Isa 22: 8 he **d** the covering of Judah, and thou didst 1540
57: 8 for thou hast **d** *thyself to another* than me, 1540
Jer 13:22 greatness of thine iniquity are thy skirts **d**, 1540
La 2:14 they have not **d** thine iniquity, to turn away 1540
Eze 13:14 so that the foundation thereof shall be **d**, 1540
16:36 thy nakedness **d** through thy whoredoms 1540
16:57 Before thy wickedness was **d**, as *at* the time 1540
21:24 in that your transgressions are **d**, so that in 1540
22:10 In thee have they **d** their father's 1540
23:10 These **d** her nakedness: they took her sons 1540
23:18 So she **d** her whoredoms, and 1540
23:18 her whoredoms, and **d** her nakedness: 1540
23:29 the nakedness of thy whoredoms shall be **d**, 1540
Hos 7: 1 the iniquity of Ephraim was **d**, and 1540
Ac 21: 3 Now when we had **d** Cyprus, we left it on *398*
27:39 but they **d** a certain creek with a shore, *2657*

DISCOVERETH (2) [DISCOVER]
Job 12:22 He **d** deep *things* out of darkness, and 1540
Ps 29: 9 the hinds to calve, and **d** the forests: 2834

DISCOVERING (1) [DISCOVER]
Hab 3:13 by **d** the foundation unto the neck. 6168

DISCREDIT See DISANNUL; DISANNULLED

DISCREET (3) [DISCREETLY, DISCRETION]
Ge 41:33 let Pharaoh look out a man **d** and wise, 995
41:39 *there is* none so **d** and wise as thou *art*: 995
Tit 2: 5 *To be* **d**, chaste, keepers at home, good, *4998*

DISCREETLY (1) [DISCREET]
Mk 12:34 And when Jesus saw that he answered **d**, *3562*

DISCRETION (9) [DISCREET]
Ps 112: 5 lendeth: he will guide his affairs with **d**. 4941
Pr 1: 4 to the young man knowledge and **d**. 4209
2:11 **D** shall preserve thee, understanding shall 4209
3:21 from thine eyes: keep sound wisdom and **d**: 4209
5: 2 That *thou* mayest regard **d**, and *that* thy lips 4209
11:22 *so is* a fair woman which is without **d**. 2940
19:11 The **d** of a man deferreth his anger; and *it is* 7922
Isa 28:26 For his God doth instruct him to **d**, *and* 4941
Jer 10:12 and hath stretched out the heavens by his **d**. 8394

DISDAINED (2)
1Sa 17:42 looked about, and saw David, he **d** him: 959
Job 30: 1 whose fathers I would have **d** to have set 3988

DISEASE (15) [DISEASED, DISEASES]
2Ki 1: 2 of Ekron whether I shall recover of this **d**. 2483
8: 8 by him, saying, Shall I recover of this **d**? 2483
8: 9 to thee, saying, Shall I recover of this **d**? 2483
2Ch 16:12 until his **d** *was* exceeding *great*: yet in his 2483
16:12 yet in his **d** he sought not *to* the LORD, 2483
21:15 thou *shalt* have great sickness by **d** of thy 4245
21:18 him in his bowels with an incurable **d**. 2483
Job 30:18 By the great force *of my* **d** is my garment NIH
Ps 38: 7 For my loins are filled *with* a loathsome *d*: NIH
41: 8 An evil **d**, *say they*, cleaveth fast unto him: 1697
Ecc 6: 2 eateth it: this *is* vanity, and it *is* an evil **d**. 2483
Mt 4:23 and all *manner of* **d** among the people. *3119*
9:35 and every **d** among the people. *3119*
10: 1 all *manner of* sickness and all *manner of* **d**. *3119*
Jn 5: 4 was made whole of whatsoever **d** he had. *3553*

DISEASED (8) [DISEASE]
1Ki 15:23 the time of his old age he was **d** in his feet. 2470
2Ch 16:12 and ninth year of his reign was **d** in his feet, 2456
Eze 34: 4 The **d** have ye not strengthened, 2470
34:21 and pusht all the **d** with your horns, 2470
Mt 9:20 which was **d with an issue of blood** twelve *131*
14:35 and brought unto him all that were **d**; *2192+2560*
Mk 1:32 they brought unto him all that were **d**, and *2560*
Jn 6: 2 miracles which he did on them that were **d**. *770*

DISEASES (13) [DISEASE]
Ex 15:26 I will put none of *these* **d** upon thee, 4245
Dt 7:15 will put none of the evil **d** of Egypt, 4064
28:60 Moreover he will bring upon thee all the **d** 4064
2Ch 21:19 so he died of sore **d**. And his people made 8463
24:25 from him, (for they left him in great **d**,) 4251
Ps 103: 3 all thine iniquities; who healeth all thy **d**; 8463
Mt 4:24 sick people that were taken with divers **d** *3554*
Mk 1:34 he healed many *that were* sick of divers **d**, *3554*
Lk 4:40 all they that had *any* sick with divers **d** *3554*
6:17 to hear him, and to be healed of their **d**; *3554*
9: 1 and authority over all devils, and to cure **d**. *3554*
Ac 19:12 and the **d** departed from them, and the evil *3554*
28: 9 which had **d** in the island, came, and *769*

DISFIGURE (1)
Mt 6:16 for they **d** their faces, that they may appear *853*

DISGRACE (1)
Jer 14:21 do not **d** the throne of thy glory: 5034

DISGUISE (3) [DISGUISED, DISGUISETH]
1Ki 14: 2 his wife, Arise, I pray thee, and **d** thyself, 8138
22:30 I will **d** myself, and enter into the battle; 2664
2Ch 18:29 I will **d** myself, and will go to the battle; 2664

DISGUISED (5) [DISGUISE]
1Sa 28: 8 Saul **d** himself, and put on other raiment, 2664
1Ki 20:38 and **d** himself with ashes upon his face. 2664
22:30 the king of Israel **d** himself, and went into 2664
2Ch 18:29 So the king of Israel **d** himself; and 2664
35:22 **d** himself, that *he* might fight with him, and 2664

DISGUISETH (1) [DISGUISE]
Job 24:15 No eye shall see me: and **d** *his* face. 5643

DISH (4) [DISHES, SNUFFDISHES]
Jdg 5:25 she brought forth butter in a lordly **d**. 5602
2Ki 21:13 I will wipe Jerusalem as *a man* wipeth a **d**, 6747
Mt 26:23 He that dippeth *his* hand with me in the **d**, *5165*
Mk 14:20 of the twelve, that dippeth with me in the **d**. *5165*

DISHAN (5)
Ge 36:21 Dishon, and Ezer, and **D**: these *are* 1789
36:28 The children of **D** *are* these; Uz, and Aran. 1789
36:30 Duke Dishon, duke Ezer, duke **D**: these *are* 1789
1Ch 1:38 and Anah, and Dishon, and Ezer, and **D**. 1789
1:42 *and* Jakan. The sons of **D**; Uz, and Aran. 1789

DISHES (3) [DISH]
Ex 25:29 thou shalt make the **d** thereof, and 7086
37:16 his **d**, and his spoons, and his bowls, and 7086
Nu 4: 7 put thereon the **d**, and the spoons, and 7086

DISHON (7)
Ge 36:21 **D**, and Ezer, and Dishan: these *are* 1787
36:25 **D**, and Aholibamah the daughter of Anah. 1787
36:26 these *are* the children of **D**; Hemdan, and 1789
36:30 Duke **D**, duke Ezer, duke Dishan: these *are* 1787
1Ch 1:38 and Anah, and **D**, and Ezer, and Dishan. 1787
1:41 The sons of Anah; **D**. And the sons of 1787
1:41 the sons of **D**; Amram, and Eshban, and 1787

DISHONEST (2) [DISHONESTY]
Eze 22:13 I have smitten mine hand at thy **d gain** 1215
22:27 *and* to destroy souls, to **get d gain**. 1214+1215

DISHONESTY (1) [DISHONEST]
2Co 4: 2 But have renounced the hidden *things* of **d**, *152*

DISHONOUR (11) [DISHONOUREST, DISHONOURETH]
Ezr 4:14 *it was* not meet for us to see the king's **d**, 6173
Ps 35:26 and **d** that magnify *themselves* against me. 3639
69:19 my reproach, and my shame, and my **d**: 3639
71:13 *with* reproach and **d** that seek my hurt. 3639
Pr 6:33 A wound and **d** shall he get; and 7036
Jn 8:49 but I honour my Father, and ye do **d** me. *818*
Ro 1:24 to **d** their own bodies between themselves: *818*
9:21 one vessel unto honour, and another unto **d**? *819*
1Co 15:43 It is sown in **d**; it is raised in glory: it is *819*
2Co 6: 8 By honour and **d**, by evil report and *819*
2Ti 2:20 of earth; and some to honour, and some to **d**. *819*

DISHONOUREST (1) [DISHONOUR]
Ro 2:23 through breaking the law **d** thou God? *818*

DISHONOURETH (3) [DISHONOUR]
Mic 7: 6 For the son **d** the father, the daughter riseth 5034
1Co 11: 4 having *his* head covered, **d** his head. *2617*
11: 5 prophesieth with *her* head uncovered **d** her *2617*

DISINHERIT (1)
Nu 14:12 **d** them, and will make of thee a greater 3423

DISMAYED (31) [DISMAYING]
Dt 31: 8 neither forsake thee: fear not, neither be **d**. 2865
Jos 1: 9 be not afraid, neither be thou **d**: 2865
8: 1 unto Joshua, Fear not, neither be thou **d**: 2865
10:25 Fear not, nor be **d**, be strong and of good 2865
1Sa 17:11 they were **d**, and greatly afraid. 2865
2Ki 19:26 small power, they were **d** and confounded; 2865
1Ch 22:13 and of good courage; dread not, nor be **d**. 2865
28:20 good courage, and do *it*: fear not, nor be **d**: 2865
2Ch 20:15 Be not afraid nor **d** by reason of this great 2865
20:17 fear not, nor be **d**; to morrow go out against 2865
32: 7 be not afraid nor **d** for the king of Assyria, 2865
Isa 21: 3 the hearing *of it*; I was **d** at the seeing *of it*. 926
37:27 small power, they were **d** and confounded: 2865
41:10 be not **d**; for I *am* thy God: I will 8159
41:23 that we may be **d**, and behold *it* together. 8159
Jer 1:17 be not **d** at their faces, lest I confound thee 2865
8: 9 *men* are ashamed, they are **d** and taken: 2865
10: 2 and be not **d** at the signs of heaven; 2865
10: 2 of heaven; for the heathen are **d** at them. 2865
17:18 let them be **d**, but let not me be dismayed: 2865
17:18 let them be dismayed, but let not me be **d**: 2865
23: 4 they shall fear no more, nor be **d**, neither 2865
30:10 saith the LORD; neither be **d**, O Israel: 2865
46: 5 Wherefore have I seen them **d** *and* 2844
46:27 O my servant Jacob, and be not **d**, O Israel: 2865
48: 1 *and* taken: Misgab is confounded and **d**. 2865
49:37 For I will **cause** Elam **to be d** before their 2865
50:36 upon her mighty *men*; and they shall be **d**. 2865
Eze 2: 6 of their words, nor be **d** at their looks, 2865
3: 9 fear them not, neither be **d** at their looks, 2865
Ob 1: 9 thy mighty *men*, O Teman, shall be **d**, 2865

DISMAYING (1) [DISMAYED]
Jer 48:39 be a derision and a **d** to all them about him. 4288

DISMISSED (3)
2Ch 23: 8 for Jehoiada the priest **d** not the courses. 6362
Ac 15:30 So when they were **d**, they came to Antioch: *630*
19:41 when he had thus spoken, he **d** the assembly. *630*

DISOBEDIENCE (6) [DISOBEDIENT, DISOBEYED]
Ro 5:19 For as by one man's **d** many were made *3876*
2Co 10: 6 And having in a readiness to revenge all **d**, *3876*
Eph 2: 2 spirit that now worketh in the children of **d**: *543*
5: 6 the wrath of God upon the children of **d**. *543*
Col 3: 6 wrath of God cometh on the children of **d**: *543*
Heb 2: 2 **d** received a just recompence of reward; *3876*

DISOBEDIENT (13) [DISOBEDIENCE]
1Ki 13:26 who was **d** unto the word of the LORD: 4784
Ne 9:26 Nevertheless they were **d**, and 4784
Lk 1:17 and the **d** to the wisdom of the just; *545*
Ac 26:19 I was not **d** unto the heavenly vision: *545*
Ro 1:30 inventors of evil *things*, **d** to parents, *545*
10:21 have I stretched forth my hands unto a **d** *544*
1Ti 1: 9 a righteous *man*, but for the lawless and **d**, *506*
2Ti 3: 2 **d** to parents, unthankful, unholy, *545*
Tit 1:16 and **d**, and unto every good work reprobate. *545*
3: 3 **d**, deceived, serving divers lusts and *545*
1Pe 2: 7 but unto them which be **d**, the stone which *544*
2: 8 *to them* which stumble at the word, being **d**: *544*
3:20 Which sometime were **d**, when once *544*

DISOBEYED (1) [DISOBEDIENCE]
1Ki 13:21 Forasmuch as thou hast **d** the mouth of 4784

DISORDERLY (3)
2Th 3: 6 from every brother that walketh **d**, *814*
3: 7 for we **behaved** not ourselves **d** among you; *812*
3:11 *there are* some which walk among you **d**, *814*

DISPATCH (1)
Eze 23:47 with stones, and **d** them with their swords; 1254

DISPENSATION (4)
1Co 9:17 a **d** *of the gospel* is committed unto me. *3622*
Eph 1:10 That in the **d** of the fulness of times *he* *3622*
3: 2 If ye have heard of the **d** of the grace of *3622*
Col 1:25 according to the **d** of God which is given to *3622*

DISPERSE (8) [DISPERSED, DISPERSIONS]
1Sa 14:34 **D** yourselves among the people, and 6327
Pr 15: 7 The lips of the wise **d** knowledge: but 2219
Eze 12:15 the nations, and **d** them in the countries. 2219
20:23 and **d** them through the countries; 2219
22:15 **d** thee in the countries, and will consume 2219
29:12 and will **d** them through the countries. 2219
30:23 and will **d** them through the countries. 2219
30:26 and **d** them among the countries; 2219

DISPERSED (10) [DISPERSE]
2Ch 11:23 **d** of all his children throughout all 6555
Est 3: 8 **d** among the people in all the provinces of 6504
Ps 112: 9 He hath **d**, he hath given to the poor; 6340
Pr 5:16 Let thy fountains be **d** abroad, *and* rivers of 6327
Isa 11:12 gather together the **d** of Judah from the four 5310
Eze 36:19 and they were **d** through the countries: 2219
Zep 3:10 *even* the daughter of my **d**, shall bring mine 6327
Jn 7:35 will he go unto the **d among** the Gentiles, *1290*
Ac 5:37 all, *even* as many as obeyed him, were **d**. *1287*
2Co 9: 9 (As it is written, He hath **d abroad**; he hath *4650*

DISPERSIONS (1) [DISPERSE]
Jer 25:34 and of your **d** are accomplished. 8600

DISPLAYED (1)
Ps 60: 4 that *it* may be **d** because of the truth. 5127

DISPLEASE (5) [DISPLEASED, DISPLEASURE]
Ge 31:35 Let it not **d** my lord that I 2734+5869+871.1
Nu 22:34 now therefore, if it **d** thee, 5869+7489+871.1
1Sa 29: 7 **d** not the lords of 5869+6213+7451+871.1
2Sa 11:25 Let not this thing **d** thee, 3415+7489+871.1
Pr 24:18 the LORD see *it*, and it **d** 5869+7489+871.1

DISPLEASED (25) [DISPLEASE]
Ge 38:10 *the thing* which he did **d** 3415+5869+871.1
48:17 the head of Ephraim, it **d** him: 3415+5869+871.1
Nu 11: 1 it **d** the LORD: 241+7451+871.1
11:10 Moses also was **d**. 5869+7489+871.1
1Sa 8: 6 the thing **d** Samuel, 3415+5869+871.1
18: 8 and the saying **d** him; 3415+5869+871.1
2Sa 6: 8 David was **d**, because the LORD had 2734
11:27 had done **d** the LORD. 3415+7489+871.1

1Ki 1: 6 his father had not **d** him at any time in 6087
20:43 of Israel went to his house heavy and **d**, 2198
21: 4 came into his house heavy and **d** because 2198
1Ch 13:11 David was **d**, because the LORD had 2734
21: 7 God was **d** with this thing; 3415+5869+871.1
Ps 60: 1 thou hast scattered us, thou hast been **d**; 599
Isa 59:15 **d** him that *there was* no 3415+5869+871.1
Da 6:14 was sore **d** with himself, and set *his* heart on 888
Jnh 4: 1 it **d** Jonah **exceedingly**, and he 1419+3415+7451
Hab 3: 8 Was the LORD **d** against the rivers? 2734
Zec 1: 2 The LORD hath been **sore d** with 7107+7110
1:15 I am very **sore d** with the heathen 7107+7110
1:15 for I was *but* a little **d**, and they helped 7107
Mt 21:15 to the Son of David; they were **sore d**, *23*
Mk 10:14 But when Jesus saw *it*, he was **much d**, and *23*
10:41 heard *it*, they began to be **much d** with James *23*
Ac 12:20 And Herod was **highly d** with them of Tyre *2371*

DISPLEASURE (5) [DISPLEASE]
Dt 9:19 For I was afraid of the anger and **hot d**, 2534
Jdg 15: 3 than the Philistines, though I do them a **d**. 7451
Ps 2: 5 in his wrath, and vex them in his **sore d**. 2740
6: 1 neither chasten me in thy **hot d**. 2534
38: 1 thy wrath: neither chasten me in thy **hot d**. 2534

DISPOSED (4) [DISPOSITION]
Job 34:13 the earth? or who hath **d** the whole world? 7760
37:15 Dost thou know when God **d** them, and 7760
Ac 18:27 And when he was **d** to pass into Achaia, *1014*
1Co 10:27 not bid you *to a feast*, and ye be **d** to go; *2309*

DISPOSING (1) [DISPOSITION]
Pr 16:33 but the whole **d** thereof *is* of the LORD. 4941

DISPOSITION (1) [DISPOSED, DISPOSING]
Ac 7:53 Who have received the law by the **d** of *1296*

DISPOSSESS (2) [DISPOSSESSED]
Nu 33:53 ye shall **d** *the inhabitants of* the land, and 3423
Dt 7:17 nations *are* moe than I; how can I **d** them? 3423

DISPOSSESSED (2) [DISPOSSESS]
Nu 32:39 took it, and **d** the Amorite which *was* in it. 3423
Jdg 11:23 So now the LORD God of Israel hath **d** 3423

DISPUTATION (1) [DISPUTE]
Ac 15: 2 had no small dissension and **d** with them, *4803*

DISPUTATIONS (1) [DISPUTE]
Ro 14: 1 the faith receive you, *but* not to doubtful **d**. *1253*

DISPUTE (1) [DISPUTATION, DISPUTATIONS, DISPUTED, DISPUTER, DISPUTING, DISPUTINGS]
Job 23: 7 There the righteous *might* **d** with him; so 3198

DISPUTED (5) [DISPUTE]
Mk 9:33 What *was it that* ye **d** among yourselves by *1260*
9:34 for by the way they had **d** among *1256*
Ac 9:29 the Lord Jesus, and **d** against the Grecians: *4802*
17:17 Therefore **d** he in the synagogue with *1256*
Jude 1: 9 when contending with the devil he **d** about *1256*

DISPUTER (1) [DISPUTE]
1Co 1:20 where *is* the **d** of this world? hath not God *4804*

DISPUTING (5) [DISPUTE]
Ac 6: 9 of Cilicia and of Asia, **d** with Stephen. *4802*
15: 7 And when there had been much **d**, Peter *4803*
19: 8 **d** and persuading the *things* concerning *1256*
19: 9 **d** daily in the school of one Tyrannus. *1256*
24:12 And they neither found me in the temple **d** *1256*

DISPUTINGS (2) [DISPUTE]
Php 2:14 Do all *things* without murmurings and **d**: *1261*
1Ti 6: 5 **Perverse d** of men of corrupt minds, and *3859*

DISQUALIFIED See CASTAWAY

DISQUALIFY See BEGUILE; BEGUILED; BEGUILING

DISQUIET (1) [DISQUIETED, DISQUIETNESS]
Jer 50:34 the land, and **d** the inhabitants of Babylon. 7264

DISQUIETED (6) [DISQUIET]
1Sa 28:15 Why hast thou **d** me, to bring me up? 7264
Ps 39: 6 surely they are **d** in vain: he heapeth up 1993
42: 5 *why* art thou **d** in me? hope thou in God: 1993
42:11 why art thou **d** within me? hope thou in 1993
43: 5 why art thou **d** within me? hope in God: 1993
Pr 30:21 For three *things* the earth is **d**, and for four 7264

DISQUIETNESS (1) [DISQUIET]
Ps 38: 8 I have roared by reason of the **d** of my 5100

DISSEMBLED (3) [DISSEMBLERS, DISSEMBLETH]
Jos 7:11 **d** also, and they have put *it* even amongst 3584
Jer 42:20 For ye **d** in your hearts, when ye sent me 8582
Gal 2:13 And the other Jews **d** likewise **with** him; *4942*

DISSEMBLERS (1) [DISSEMBLED]
Ps 26: 4 vain persons, neither will I go in with **d**. 5956

DISSEMBLETH (1) [DISSEMBLED]
Pr 26:24 He that hateth **d** with his lips, and layeth up 5234

DISSENSION (3)
Ac 15: 2 and Barnabas had no small **d** and *4714*
23: 7 there arose a **d** between the Pharisees and *4714*
23:10 And when there arose a great **d**, the chief *4714*

DISSENSIONS See SEDITIONS

DISSIMULATION (2)
Ro 12: 9 *Let* love *be* **without d**. Abhor *that which is* *505*
Gal 2:13 also was carried away with their **d**. *5272*

DISSIPATION See SURFEITING

DISSOLVE (1) [DISSOLVED, DISSOLVEST, DISSOLVING]
Da 5:16 canst make interpretations, and **d** doubts: 8271

DISSOLVED (8) [DISSOLVE]
Ps 75: 3 and all the inhabitants thereof *are* **d**: 4127
Isa 14:31 cry, O city; thou, whole Palestina, *art* **d**: 4127
24:19 the earth is **clean d**, the earth is 6565+6565
34: 4 all the host of heaven shall be **d**, and 4743
Na 2: 6 shall be opened, and the palace shall be **d**. 4127
2Co 5: 1 our earthly house of *this* tabernacle were **d**, *2647*
2Pe 3:11 Seeing then that all these *things shall* be **d**, *3089*
3:12 the heavens being on fire shall be **d**, *3089*

DISSOLVEST (1) [DISSOLVE]
Job 30:22 me to ride *upon it*, and **d** my substance. 4127

DISSOLVING (1) [DISSOLVE]
Da 5:12 shewing of hard sentences, and **d** of doubts, 8271

DISTAFF (1)
Pr 31:19 to the spindle, and her hands hold the **d**. 6418

DISTANT (1)
Ex 36:22 two tenons, **equally d** one from another: 7947

DISTIL (2)
Dt 32: 2 as the rain, my speech shall **d** as the dew, 5140
Job 36:28 do drop *and* **d** upon man abundantly. 7491

DISTINCTION (1) [DISTINCTLY]
1Co 14: 7 or harp, except they give a **d** in the sounds, *1293*

DISTINCTLY (1) [DISTINCTION]
Ne 8: 8 they read in the book in the law of God **d**, 6567

DISTORT See WREST

DISTRACTED (1) [DISTRACTION]
Ps 88:15 youth *up: while* I suffer thy terrors I am **d**. 6323

DISTRACTION (1) [DISTRACTED]
1Co 7:35 you may attend upon the Lord **without d**. *563*

DISTRESS (33) [DISTRESSED, DISTRESSES]
Ge 35: 3 who answered me in the day of my **d**, and 6869
42:21 not hear; therefore is this **d** come upon us. 6869
Dt 2: 9 LORD said unto me, **D** not the Moabites, 6696
2:19 **d** them not, nor meddle with them: 6696
28:53 wherewith thine enemies shall **d** thee: 6693
28:55 wherewith thine enemies shall **d** thee in all 6693
28:57 wherewith thine enemy shall **d** thee in thy 6693
Jdg 11: 7 ye come unto me now when ye are in **d**? 6887
1Sa 22: 2 every one *that was* in **d**, and every one that 4689
2Sa 22: 7 In my **d** I called upon the LORD, and 6862
1Ki 1:29 that hath redeemed my soul out of all **d**, 6869
2Ch 28:22 in the time of his **d** did he trespass yet more 6887
Ne 2:17 I unto them, Ye see the **d** that we *are* in, 7451
9:37 at their pleasure, and we *are* in great **d**. 6869
Ps 4: 1 thou hast enlarged me *when I was* in **d**; 6862
18: 6 In my **d** I called upon the LORD, and 6862
118: 5 I called upon the LORD in **d**: the LORD 4712
120: 1 In my **d** I cried unto the LORD, and 6869
Pr 1:27 when **d** and anguish cometh upon you: 6869
Isa 25: 4 a strength to the needy in his **d**, a refuge 6862
29: 2 Yet I will **d** Ariel, and there shall be 6693
29: 7 and her munition, and that **d** her, 6693
Jer 10:18 and will **d** them, that they may find *it so*. 6887
La 1:20 Behold, O LORD; for I *am* **in d**: my 6887
Ob 1:12 thou have spoken proudly in the day of **d**. 6869
1:14 those of his that did remain in the day of **d**. 6869
Zep 1:15 a day of trouble and **d**, a day of wasteness 4691
1:17 I will **bring d** upon men, that they shall 6887
Lk 21:23 for there shall be great **d** in the land, and *318*
21:25 and upon the earth **d** of nations, *4928*
Ro 8:35 or **d**, or persecution, or famine, or *4730*
1Co 7:26 therefore that this is good for the present **d**, *318*
1Th 3: 7 over you in all our affliction and **d**, *318*

DISTRESSED (11) [DISTRESS]
Ge 32: 7 Jacob was greatly afraid and **d**: and he 3334
Nu 22: 3 Moab was **d** because of the children of 6973
Jdg 2:15 sworn unto them: and they were greatly **d**. 3334
10: 9 house of Ephraim; so that Israel was sore **d**. 3334
1Sa 13: 6 were in a strait, (for the people were **d**,) 5065
14:24 the men of Israel were **d** that day: for Saul 5065
28:15 Saul answered, I am sore **d**; for 6887
30: 6 David was greatly **d**; for the people spake 3334
2Sa 1:26 I am **d** for thee, my brother Jonathan: 6887
2Ch 28:20 and **d** him, but strengthened him not. 6696
2Co 4: 8 *We are* troubled on every *side*, yet not **d**; *4729*

DISTRESSES (8) [DISTRESS]
Ps 25:17 are enlarged: O bring thou me out of my **d**. 4691
107: 6 *and* he delivered them out of their **d**. 4691
107:13 *and* he saved them out of their **d**. 4691
107:19 their trouble, he saveth them out of their **d**. 4691
107:28 and he bringeth them out of their **d**. 4691
Eze 30:16 rent asunder, and Noph *shall have* **d** daily. 6862
2Co 6: 4 in afflictions, in necessities, in **d**, *4730*
12:10 in persecutions, in **d** for Christ's sake: *4730*

DISTRIBUTE (5) [DISTRIBUTED, DISTRIBUTETH, DISTRIBUTING, DISTRIBUTION]
Jos 13:32 **d for inheritance** in the plains of Moab, 5157
2Ch 31:14 to **d** the oblations of the LORD, and 5414
Ne 13:13 their office *was* to **d** unto their brethren. 2505
Lk 18:22 and **d** unto the poor, and thou shalt have *1239*
1Ti 6:18 **ready to d**, willing to communicate; *2130*

DISTRIBUTED (6) [DISTRIBUTE]
Jos 14: 1 of Israel, **d for inheritance** to them. 5157
1Ch 24: 3 David **d** them, both Zadok of the sons of 2505
2Ch 23:18 whom David had **d** in the house of 2505
Jn 6:11 he **d** to the disciples, and the disciples to *1239*
1Co 7:17 But as God hath **d** to every man, as *3307*
2Co 10:13 measure of the rule which God hath **d** to us, *3307*

DISTRIBUTETH (1) [DISTRIBUTE]
Job 21:17 upon them! *God* **d** sorrows in his anger. 2505

DISTRIBUTING (1) [DISTRIBUTE]
Ro 12:13 **D** to the necessity of saints; given to *2841*

DISTRIBUTION (2) [DISTRIBUTE]
Ac 4:35 **d** was made unto every man according as *1239*
2Co 9:13 and *for your* liberal **d** unto them, and unto *2842*

DITCH (6) [DITCHES]
Job 9:31 Yet shalt thou plunge me in the **d**, and 7845
Ps 7:15 and is fallen into the **d** *which* he made. 7845
Pr 23:27 For a whore *is* a deep **d**; and a strange 7745
Isa 22:11 Ye made also a **d** between the two walls for 4724
Mt 15:14 blind lead the blind, both shall fall into the **d**. *999*
Lk 6:39 the blind? shall they not both fall into the **d**? *999*

DITCHES (1) [DITCH]
2Ki 3:16 Make this valley **full of d**. 1356+1356

DIVERS (37) [DIVERSE]
Dt 22: 9 Thou shalt not sow thy vineyard with **d** 3610
22:11 Thou shalt not wear a **garment of d sorts**, 8162
25:13 not have in thy bag **d weights**, 68+68+2050.1
25:14 in thine house **d measures**, 374+374+2050.1
Jdg 5:30 to Sisera a prey of **d colours**, a prey of 6648
5:30 a prey of **d colours** of needlework, 6648
5:30 of **d colours** of needlework on both sides, 6648
2Sa 13:18 *she had* a garment of **d colours** upon her: 6446
13:19 rent her garment of **d colours** that *was* on 6446
1Ch 29: 2 of **d colours**, and all *manner of* precious 7553
2Ch 16:14 **d kinds** *of spices* prepared by 2177
21: 4 and ***d*** also of the princes of Israel. NIH
30:11 Nevertheless **d** of Asher and Manasseh and 376
Ps 78:45 He sent **d sorts** *of flies* among them, 6157
105:31 there came **d sorts** *of flies, and* lice in all 6157
Pr 20:10 **D weights**, *and* divers measures, 68+68+2050.1
20:10 *and* **d measures**, 374+374+2050.1
20:23 **D weights** *are* an abomination 68+68+2050.1
Ecc 5: 7 and many words *there are* also ***d*** vanities: NIH
Eze 16:16 deckedst thy high places with **d colours**, 2921
17: 3 full *of* feathers, which had **d colours**, 7553
Mt 4:24 sick people that were taken with **d** diseases *4164*
24: 7 pestilences, and earthquakes **in d** places. *2596*
Mk 1:34 And he healed many *that were* sick of **d** *4164*
8: 3 by the way: for **d** of them came from far. *5100*
13: 8 and there shall be earthquakes **in d** places, *2596*
Lk 4:40 all they that had *any* sick with **d** diseases *4164*
21:11 And great earthquakes shall be **in d places**, *2596*
Ac 19: 9 But when **d** were hardened, and *5100*
1Co 12:10 of spirits; to another ***d*** kinds of tongues; NIG
2Ti 3: 6 laden with sins, led away with **d** lusts, *4164*
Tit 3: 3 deceived, serving **d** lusts and pleasures, *4164*
Heb 1: 1 **in d** manners spake in time past unto **the** *3588*
2: 4 and with **d** miracles, and gifts of the Holy *4164*
9:10 and **d** washings, and carnal ordinances, *1313*
13: 9 Be not carried about with **d** and *4164*
Jas 1: 2 count *it* all joy when ye fall into **d** *4164*

DIVERSE (8) [DIVERS, DIVERSITIES]
Lev 19:19 shalt not let thy cattle gender with a **d kind**: 3610
Est 1: 7 (the vessels being **d** one from another,) 8138
3: 8 their laws *are* **d** from all people; 8138
Da 7: 3 came up from the sea, **d** one from another. 8133
7: 7 it *was* **d** from all the beasts that *were* before 8133
7:19 which was **d** from all the others, 8133
7:23 which shall be **d** from all kingdoms, 8133
7:24 he shall be **d** from the first, and he shall 8133

DIVERSITIES (3) [DIVERSE]
1Co 12: 4 Now there are **d** of gifts, but the same *1243*
12: 6 And there are **d** of operations, but it is *1243*
12:28 helps, governments, **d** of tongues. *1085*

DIVIDE (49) [DIVIDED, DIVIDER, DIVIDETH, DIVIDING, DIVISION, DIVISIONS]
Ge 1: 6 let it **d** the waters from the waters. 914
1:14 of the heaven to **d** the day from the night; 914
1:18 and to **d** the light from the darkness: 914
49: 7 I will **d** them in Jacob, and scatter them in 2505
49:27 the prey, and at night he shall **d** the spoil. 2505
Ex 14:16 stretch out thine hand over the sea, and **d** it: 1234
15: 9 I will overtake, I will **d** the spoil; 2505
21:35 shall sell the live ox, and **d** the money of it; 2673
21:35 of it; and the dead *ox* also they shall **d**. 2673
26:33 the vail shall **d** unto you between the holy 914
Lev 1:17 the wings thereof, *but* shall not **d** *it* **asunder**: 914
5: 8 from his neck, but shall not **d** *it* **asunder**: 914
11: 4 chew the cud, or of them that **d** the hoof: 6536
11: 7 though he **d** the hoof, and *be* clovenfooted, 6536
Nu 31:27 **d** the prey **into two parts**; between them 2673
33:54 **d** the land by lot for **an inheritance among** 5157
34:17 of the men which shall **d** the land unto you: 5157
34:18 of every tribe, to **d** the land **by inheritance**. 5157
34:29 **d** the **inheritance unto** the children of 5157
Dt 14: 7 the cud, or of them that **d** the cloven hoof; 6536
14: 7 for they chew the cud, but **d** not the hoof; 6536
19: 3 **d** the coasts of thy land, which the LORD thy God giveth thee to inherit, **into three parts**, 8027
Jos 1: 6 shalt thou **d for an inheritance** the land, 5157

Jos 13: 6 only d thou it by lot unto the Israelites for 5307
13: 7 d this land for an inheritance unto the nine 2505
18: 5 they shall d it into seven parts: Judah shall 2505
22: 8 d the spoil of your enemies with your 2505
2Sa 19:29 I have said, Thou and Ziba d the land. 2505
1Ki 3:25 D the living child in two, and give half to 1504
3:26 Let it be neither mine nor thine, but d it. 1504
Ne 9:11 thou didst d the sea before them, so 1234
9:22 and nations, and didst d them into corners: 2505
Job 27:17 put it on, and the innocent shall d the silver. 2505
Ps 55: 9 Destroy, O Lord, and d their tongues: for I 6385
60: 6 I will d Shechem, and mete out the valley 2505
74:13 Thou didst d the sea by thy strength: 6565
108: 7 I will d Shechem, and mete out the valley 2505
Pr 16:19 than to d the spoil with the proud. 2505
Isa 9: 3 and as men rejoice when they d the spoil. 2505
53:12 Therefore will I d him a portion with 2505
53:12 and he shall d the spoil with the strong; 2505
Eze 5: 1 take thee balances to weigh, and d the hair. 2505
45: 1 when ye shall d by lot the land for 5307
47:21 So shall ye d this land unto you according 2505
47:22 that ye shall d it by lot for an inheritance 5307
48:29 This is the land which ye shall d by lot unto 5307
Da 11:39 over many, and shall d the land for gain. 2505
Lk 12:13 that he d the inheritance with me. 3307
22:17 said, Take this, and d it among yourselves: 1266

DIVIDED (69) [DIVIDE]

Ge 1: 4 and God d the light from the darkness. 914
1: 7 d the waters which were under 914
10: 5 By these were the isles of the Gentiles d in 6504
10:25 for in his days was the earth d; and 6385
10:32 by these were the nations d in the earth 6504
14:15 he d himself against them, he and 2505
15:10 d them in the midst, and laid each piece 1334
15:10 one against another: but the birds d he not. 1334
32: 7 he d the people that was with him, and 2673
33: 1 he d the children unto Leah, and 2673
Ex 14:21 the sea dry land, and the waters were d. 1234
Nu 26:53 Unto these the land shall be d for an 2505
26:55 Notwithstanding the land shall be d by lot: 2505
26:56 the possession thereof be d between many 2505
31:42 which Moses d from the men that warred, 2673
Dt 4:19 which the LORD thy God hath d unto all 2505
32: 8 High d to the nations their inheritance, 5157
Jos 14: 5 children of Israel did, and they d the land. 2505
18:10 there Joshua d the land unto the children of 2505
19:51 d for an inheritance by lot in Shiloh 5157
23: 4 I have d unto you by lot these nations that 5307
Jdg 5:30 have they not d the prey; to every man a 2505
7:16 he d the three hundred men into three 2673
9:43 d them into three companies, and laid wait 2673
19:29 d her, together with her bones, into twelve 5408
2Sa 1:23 and in their death they were not d: 6504
1Ki 16:21 were the people of Israel d into two parts: 2505
18: 6 So they d the land between them to pass 2505
2Ki 2: 8 they were d hither and thither, so that they 2673
1Ch 1:19 because in his days the earth was d: 6385
23: 6 David d them into courses among the sons 2505
24: 4 the sons of Ithamar; and thus were they d. 2505
24: 5 Thus were they d by lot, one sort with 2505
2Ch 35:13 and d them speedily among all the people. 7323
Job 38:25 Who hath d a watercourse for 6385
Ps 68:12 she that tarried at home d the spoil. 2505
78:13 He d the sea, and caused them to pass 1234
78:55 d them an inheritance by line, and made 5307
136:13 To him which d the Red sea into parts: 1504
Isa 33:23 is the prey of a great spoil d; the lame take 2505
34:17 and his hand hath d it unto them by line: 2505
51:15 that d the sea, whose waves roared: 7280
La 4:16 The anger of the LORD hath d them; 2505
Eze 37:22 neither shall they be d into two kingdoms 2673
Da 2:41 and part of iron, the kingdom shall be d; 6386
5:28 Thy kingdom is d, and given to the Medes 6537
11: 4 shall be d toward the four winds of heaven; 2673
Hos 10: 2 Their heart is d; now shall they be found 2505
Am 7:17 the sword, and thy land shall be d by line; 2505
Mic 2: 4 from me! turning away he hath d our fields. 2505
Zec 14: 1 and thy spoil shall be d in the midst of thee. 2505
Mt 12:25 Every kingdom d against itself is brought 3307
12:25 or house d against itself shall not stand: 3307
12:26 cast out Satan, he is d against himself; 3307
Mk 3:24 And if a kingdom be d against itself, 3307
3:25 And if a house be d against itself, 3307
3:26 and be d, he cannot stand, but hath an end. 3307
6:41 and the two fishes d he among them all. 3307
Lk 11:17 Every kingdom d against itself is brought 1266
11:17 and a house d against a house falleth. NIG
11:18 If Satan also be d against himself, 1266
12:52 there shall be five in one house d, 1266
12:53 The father shall be d against the son, and 1266
15:12 to me. And he d unto them his living. 1244
Ac 13:19 of Canaan, he d their land to them by lot. 2624
14: 4 But the multitude of the city was d: and 4977
23: 7 the Sadducees: and the multitude was d. 4977
1Co 1:13 Is Christ d? was Paul crucified for you? or 3307
Rev 16:19 And the great city was d into three parts, NIG

DIVIDER (1) [DIVIDE]

Lk 12:14 who made me a judge or a d over you? 3312

DIVIDETH (10) [DIVIDE]

Lev 11: 4 he cheweth the cud, but d not the hoof; 6536
11: 5 he cheweth the cud, but d not the hoof; 6536
11: 6 he cheweth the cud, but d not the hoof; 6536
11:26 The carcases of every beast which d 6536
Dt 14: 8 the swine, because it d the hoof, 6536
Job 26:12 He d the sea with his power, and by his 7280
Ps 29: 7 The voice of the LORD d the flames of 2672
Jer 31:35 which d the sea when the waves thereof 7280
Mt 25:32 as a shepherd d his sheep from the goats: 873
Lk 11:22 armour wherein he trusted, and d his spoils. 1239

DIVIDING (7) [DIVIDE]

Jos 19:49 d the land for inheritance by their coasts, 5157
19:51 So they made an end of d the country. 2505
Isa 63:12 d the water before them, to make himself 1234
Da 7:25 until a time and times and the d of time. 6387
1Co 12:11 d to every man severally as he will. 1244
2Ti 2:15 to be ashamed, rightly d the word of truth. 3718
Heb 4:12 piercing even to the d asunder of soul and 3311

DIVINATION (12) [DIVINE]

Nu 22: 7 with the rewards of d in their hand; 7081
23:23 neither is there any d against Israel: 7081
Dt 18:10 or that useth d, or an observer of 7080+7081
2Ki 17:17 used d and enchantments, and 7080+7081
Jer 14:14 prophesy unto you a false vision and d, 7081
Eze 12:24 nor flattering d within the house of Israel. 4738
13: 6 They have seen vanity and lying d, saying, 7081
13: 7 have ye not spoken a lying d, whereas ye 4738
21:21 at the head of the two ways, to use d: 7080+7081
21:22 At his right hand was the d for Jerusalem, 7081
21:23 it shall be unto them as a false d in their 7080
Ac 16:16 certain damsel possessed with a spirit of d 4436

DIVINATIONS (1) [DIVINE]

Eze 13:23 ye shall see no more vanity, nor divine d: 7081

DIVINE (11) [DIVINATION, DIVINATIONS, DIVINERS, DIVINETH, DIVINING]

Ge 44:15 that such a man as I can certainly d? 5172+5172
1Sa 28: 8 d unto me by the familiar spirit, and 7080
Pr 16:10 A d sentence is in the lips of the king: 7081
Eze 13: 9 the prophets that see vanity, and that d lies: 7080
13:23 shall see no more vanity, nor d divinations: 7080
21:29 unto thee, whiles they d a lie unto thee, 7080
Mic 3: 6 shall be dark unto you, that ye shall not d; 7080
3:11 and the prophets thereof d for money: 7080
Heb 9: 1 covenant had also ordinances of d service, 2999
2Pe 1: 3 According as his d power hath given unto 2304
1: 4 you might be partakers of the d nature, 2304

DIVINE BEING See GODHEAD

DIVINERS (7) [DIVINE]

Dt 18:14 unto observers of times, and unto d: 7080
1Sa 6: 2 Philistines called for the priests and the d, 7080
Isa 44:25 the tokens of the liars, and maketh d mad; 7080
Jer 27: 9 nor to your d, nor to your dreamers, nor to 7080
29: 8 Let not your prophets and your d, that be in 7080
Mic 3: 7 seers be ashamed, and the d confounded: 7080
Zec 10: 2 the d have seen a lie, and have told false 7080

DIVINETH (1) [DIVINE]

Ge 44: 5 and whereby indeed he d? 5172+5172

DIVINING (1) [DIVINE]

Eze 22:28 d lies unto them, saying, Thus saith 7080

DIVISION (6) [DIVIDE]

Ex 8:23 I will put a d between my people and thy 6304
2Ch 35: 5 after the d of the families of the Levites. 2515
Lk 12:51 on earth? I tell you, Nay; but rather d: 1267
Jn 7:43 So there was a d among the people because 4978
9:16 And there was a d among them. 4978
10:19 There was a d therefore again among 4978

DIVISIONS (17) [DIVIDE]

Jos 11:23 Israel according to their d by their tribes. 4256
12: 7 Israel for a possession according to their d; 4256
18:10 the children of Israel according to their d. 4256
Jdg 5:15 For the d of Reuben there were great 6390
5:16 For the d of Reuben there were great 6390
1Ch 24: 1 Now these are the d of the sons of Aaron. 4256
26: 1 Concerning the d of the porters: Of 4256
26:12 Among these were the d of the porters, 4256
26:19 These are the d of the porters among 4256
2Ch 35: 5 stand in the holy place according to the d of 6391
35:12 that they might give according to the d of 4653
Ezr 6:18 they set the priests in their d, and 6392
Ne 11:36 of the Levites were d in Judah, and 4256
Ro 16:17 mark them which cause d and offences 1370
1Co 1:10 and that there be no d among you; 4978
3: 3 and strife, and d, are ye not carnal, and 1370
11:18 I hear that there be d among you; 4978

DIVISIVE PERSON See HERETICK

DIVORCE (1) [DIVORCED, DIVORCEMENT]

Jer 3: 8 had put her away, and given her a bill of d; 3748

DIVORCED (4) [DIVORCE]

Lev 21:14 or a d woman, or profane, or a harlot, 1644
22:13 or d, and have no child, and is returned 1644
Nu 30: 9 every vow of a widow, and of her that is d, 1644
Mt 5:32 whosoever shall marry her that is d 630

DIVORCEMENT (6) [DIVORCE]

Dt 24: 1 let him write her a bill of d, and give it in 3748
24: 3 write her a bill of d, and giveth it in her 3748
Isa 50: 1 Where is the bill of your mother's d, 3748
Mt 5:31 his wife, let him give her a writing of d: 647
19: 7 then command to give a writing of d, 647
Mk 10: 4 Moses suffered to write a bill of d, and 647

DIZAHAB (1)

Dt 1: 1 and Laban, and Hazeroth, and D. 1774

DO (1368) [DID, DIDST, DOER, DOERS, DOEST, DOETH, DOING, DOINGS, DONE, DOST, DOTH, UNDO]

Ge 6:17 d bring a flood of waters upon the earth, NIH
9:13 I d set my bow in the cloud, and it shall be NIH
11: 6 all one language; and this they begin to d: 6213
11: 6 from them, which they have imagined to d. 6213
16: 6 is in thy hand; d to her as it pleaseth thee. 6213
18: 5 And they said, So d, as thou hast said. 6213
18:17 I hide from Abraham that thing which I d; 6213
18:19 of the LORD, to d justice and judgment; 6213
18:25 That be far from thee to d after this 6213
18:25 Shall not the Judge of all the earth d right? 6213
18:29 And he said, I will not d it for forty's sake. 6213
18:30 he said, I will not d it, if I find thirty there. 6213
19: 7 I pray you, brethren, d not so wickedly. 7489
19: 8 and d ye to them as is good in your eyes: 6213
19: 8 only unto these men d nothing; for 6213
19:22 for I cannot d any thing till thou be come 6213
21:23 thou shalt d unto me, and to the land 6213
22:12 the lad, neither d thou any thing unto him: 6213
24:42 if now thou d prosper my way which I go: 3426
25:32 and what profit shall this birthright d to me? NIH
26:29 That thou wilt d us no hurt, as we have not 6213
27:37 and what shall I d now unto thee, my son? 6213
27:46 of the land, what good shall my life d me? NIH
30:31 if thou wilt d this thing for me, I will again 6213
31:16 whatsoever God hath said unto thee, d. 6213
31:29 It is in the power of my hand to d you hurt: 6213
31:43 what can I d this day unto these my 6213
32:12 I will surely d thee good, and 3190+3190
34:14 said unto them, We cannot d this thing, 6213
34:19 the young man deferred not to d the thing, 6213
37:13 D not thy brethren feed the flock in NIH
39: 9 how then can I d this great wickedness, and 6213
39:11 that Joseph went into the house to d his 6213
40: 8 D not interpretations belong to God? NIH
41: 9 I d remember my faults this day: NIH
41:25 hath shewed Pharaoh what he is about to d. 6213
41:28 What God is about to d he sheweth unto 6213
41:34 Let Pharaoh d this, and let him appoint 6213
41:55 Go unto Joseph; what he saith to you, d. 6213
42: 1 his sons, Why d ye look one upon another? NIH
42:18 unto them the third day, This d, and live; 6213
42:22 saying, D not sin against the child; NIH
43:11 said unto them, If it must be so now, d this; 6213
44: 7 God forbid that thy servants should d 6213
44:17 he said, God forbid that I should d so: but 6213
45:17 Say unto thy brethren, This d ye; 6213
45:19 Now thou art commanded, this d ye; 6213
47:30 And he said, I will d as thou hast said. 6213
Ex 1:16 When ye d the office of a midwife to 3205
3:20 which I will d in the midst thereof: 6213
4:15 and will teach you what ye shall d. 6213
4:17 in thine hand, wherewith thou shalt d signs. 6213
4:21 see that thou d all those wonders before 6213
5: 4 Wherefore d ye, Moses and Aaron, let NIH
5:17 Let us go and d sacrifice to the LORD. 2076
6: 1 Now shalt thou see what I will d to 6213
8: 8 that they may d sacrifice unto the LORD. 2076
8:26 Moses said, It is not meet so to d; for we 6213
9: 5 To morrow the LORD shall d this thing in 6213
15:26 wilt d that which is right in his sight, and 6213
17: 2 wherefore d ye tempt the LORD? NIH
17: 4 What shall I d unto this people? 6213
18:16 I d make them know the statutes of God, NIH
18:20 must walk, and the work that they must d. 6213
18:23 If thou shalt d this thing, and 6213
19: 8 All that the LORD hath spoken we will d. 6213
20: 9 days shalt thou labour, and d all thy work: 6213
20:10 in it thou shalt not d any work, thou, 6213
21: 7 she shall not go out as the menservants d[S]. 3318
21:11 if he d not these three unto her, then 6213
22:30 Likewise shalt thou d with thine oxen, and 6213
23: 2 Thou shalt not follow a multitude to d evil; NIH
23:12 Six days thou shalt d thy work, and on 6213
23:22 obey his voice, and d all that I speak; 6213
23:24 nor serve them, nor d after their works: 6213
24: 3 which the LORD hath said will we d. 6213
24: 7 All that the LORD hath said will we d, 6213
24:14 if any man have any matters to d, let him NIH
29: 1 this is the thing that thou shalt d unto them 6213
29:35 thus shalt thou d unto Aaron, and to his 6213
29:41 shalt d thereto according to the meat 6213
31:11 that I have commanded thee shall they d. 6213
32:14 evil which he thought to d unto his people. 6213
32:18 but the noise of them that sing d I hear. NIH
33: 5 that I may know what to d unto thee. 6213
33:17 I will d this thing also that thou hast 6213
34:10 before all thy people I will d marvels, 6213
34:10 for it is a terrible thing that I will d with 6213
34:15 d sacrifice unto their gods, and one call NIH
35: 1 hath commanded, that ye should d them. 6213
35:19 to d service in the holy place, the holy 8334
35:35 even of them that d any work, and of those 6213
36: 2 him up to come unto the work to d it: 6213
39: 1 to d service in the holy place, and made NIH
39:41 The clothes of service to d service in NIH
Lev 4: 2 be done), and shall d against any of them: 6213
4: 3 If the priest that is anointed d sin according NIH
4:20 he shall d with the bullock as he did with 6213
4:20 for a sin offering, so shall he d with this: 6213
5: 1 or known of it; if he d not utter it, then NIH
5: 4 pronouncing with his lips to d evil, or to do 7489
5: 4 with his lips to do evil, or to d good, 3190
8:34 so the LORD hath commanded to d, 6213
9: 6 the LORD commanded that ye should d: 6213
10: 9 D not drink wine nor strong drink, thou, NIH
16:15 d with that blood as he did with the blood 6213
16:16 shall he d for the tabernacle of 6213
16:29 d no work at all, whether it be one of your 6213
18: 3 of Egypt, wherein ye dwelt, shall ye not d: 6213
18: 3 whither I bring you, shall ye not d: 6213
18: 4 Ye shall d my judgments, and keep mine 6213
18: 5 which if a man d, he shall live in them: 6213
18:25 I d visit the iniquity thereof upon it, NIH
19:15 Ye shall d no unrighteousness in judgment: 6213
19:29 D not prostitute thy daughter, to cause her NIH
19:35 Ye shall d no unrighteousness in judgment, 6213
19:37 and all my judgments, and d them: 6213
20: 4 if the people of the land d any ways hide NIH
20: 8 ye shall keep my statutes, and d them: I am 6213

Lev 20:22 and all my judgments, and **d** them: 6213
21: 6 *and* the bread of their God, they **d** offer: NIH
21:15 his people: for I the LORD **d** sanctify him. NIH
21:23 for I the LORD **d** sanctify them. NIH
22: 9 profane it: I the LORD **d** sanctify them. NIH
22:16 *things:* for I the LORD **d** sanctify them. NIH
22:31 ye keep my commandments, and **d** them: 6213
23: 3 ye shall **d** no work *therein:* it *is* the sabbath 6213
23: 7 ye shall **d** no servile work *therein.* 6213
23: 8 ye shall **d** no servile work *therein.* 6213
23:21 ye shall **d** no servile work *therein: it shall* 6213
23:25 Ye shall **d** no servile work *therein:* but 6213
23:28 ye shall **d** no work in that same day: for it 6213
23:31 Ye shall **d** no *manner of* work: *it shall be* a 6213
23:35 ye shall **d** no servile work *therein.* 6213
23:36 *and* ye shall **d** no servile work *therein.* 6213
25:18 Wherefore ye shall **d** my statutes, and keep 6213
25:18 and keep my judgments, and **d** them; 6213
25:45 of the strangers that **d** sojourn among you, NIH
26: 3 and keep my commandments, and **d** them; 6213
26:14 and will not **d** all these commandments; 6213
26:15 so that *ye* will not **d** all my commandments, 6213
26:16 I also will **d** this unto you; I will even 6213
27:11 of which they **d** not offer a sacrifice unto NIH
Nu 2: 5 those that **d** pitch next unto him *shall be* NIH
3: 7 to **d** the service of the tabernacle. 5647
3: 8 of Israel, to **d** the service of the tabernacle. 5647
4: 3 to **d** the work in the tabernacle of 6213
4:19 thus **d** unto them, that they may live, and 6213
4:23 to **d** the work in the tabernacle of 5647
4:30 to **d** the work of the tabernacle of 5647
4:37 all that *might* **d service** in the tabernacle of 5647
4:41 of all that *might* **d service** in the tabernacle 5647
4:47 every one that came to **d** the service of 5647
5: 6 to **d a trespass** against the LORD, 4603+4604
6:21 so he must **d** after the law of 6213
7: 5 that they may be to **d** the service of 5647
8: 7 thus shalt thou **d** unto them, to cleanse 6213
8:15 **d** the **service** of the tabernacle of 5647
8:19 to **d** the service of the children of Israel in 5647
8:22 after that went the Levites in to **d** their 5647
8:26 to keep the charge, and shall **d** no service. 5647
8:26 Thus shalt thou **d** unto the Levites touching 6213
9:14 to the manner thereof, so shall he **d**: 6213
10:29 thou with us, and we will **d** thee **good**: 2895
10:32 *that* what goodness the LORD shall **d** unto 2895
10:32 do unto us, the same will we **d** unto thee. 3190
11:27 Eldad and Medad **d** prophesy in the camp. NIH
14:28 spoken in mine ears, so will I **d** to you: 6213
14:35 I will surely **d** it unto all this evil 6213
14:41 Wherefore now **d** ye transgress NIH
15:12 shall ye **d** to *every* one according to their 6213
15:13 All that are born of the country shall **d** 6213
15:14 unto the LORD; as ye **d**, so he shall do. 6213
15:14 unto the LORD; as ye do, so he shall **d**. 6213
15:20 as *ye d* the heave offering of NIH
15:39 of the LORD, and **d** them; 6213
15:40 **d** all my commandments, and be holy unto 6213
16: 6 This **d**; Take you censers, Korah, and 6213
16: 9 to bring you near to himself to **d** the service 5647
16:28 LORD hath sent me to **d** all these works; 6213
18: 6 to **d** the service of the tabernacle of 5647
18:23 the Levites shall **d** the service of 5647
21:34 thou shalt **d** to him as thou didst unto Sihon 6213
22:17 I will **d** whatsoever thou sayest unto me: 6213
22:18 of the LORD my God, to **d** less or more. 6213
22:20 I shall say unto thee, that shalt thou **d**. 6213
22:30 was I ever wont to **d** so unto thee? And he 6213
23:19 shall he not **d** *it?* or hath he spoken, and 6213
23:26 that the LORD speaketh, that I must **d**? 6213
24:13 to **d** *either* good or bad of mine own mind; 6213
24:14 will advertise thee what this people shall **d** 6213
24:18 for his enemies; and Israel shall **d** valiantly. 6213
28:18 ye shall **d** no *manner of* servile work 6213
28:25 ye shall **d** no servile work. 6213
28:26 ye shall **d** no servile work: 6213
29: 1 ye shall **d** no servile work: 6213
29: 7 ye shall not **d** any work *therein:* 6213
29:12 ye shall **d** no servile work, and ye shall 6213
29:35 ye shall **d** no servile work *therein:* 6213
29:39 These *things* ye shall **d** unto the LORD in 6213
30: 2 he shall **d** according to all that proceedeth 6213
31:19 **d** ye abide without the camp seven days: NIH
32:20 said unto them, If ye will **d** this thing, 6213
32:23 if ye will not **d** so, behold, ye have sinned 6213
32:24 **d** that which hath proceeded out of your 6213
32:25 Thy servants will **d** as my lord 6213
32:31 hath said unto thy servants, so will we **d**. 6213
33:56 *that* I shall **d** unto you, as I thought to do 6213
33:56 do unto you, as I thought to **d** unto them. 6213
Dt 1:14 which thou hast spoken *is* good *for us* to **d**. 6213
1:18 that time all the things which ye should **d**. 6213
1:44 as bees **d**, and destroyed you in Seir, 6213
3: 2 thou shalt **d** unto him as thou didst unto 6213
3:21 shall the LORD **d** unto all the kingdoms 6213
3:24 that can **d** according to thy works, and 6213
4: 1 for to **d** *them,* that ye may live, and go in 6213
4: 5 that *ye* should **d** so in the land whither ye 6213
4: 6 and **d** *them;* for this *is* your wisdom and 6213
4:14 that ye might **d** them in the land whither ye 6213
4:25 shall **d** evil in the sight of the LORD thy 6213
5: 1 ye may learn them, and keep, and **d** them. 6213
5:13 days thou shalt labour, and **d** all thy work: 6213
5:14 *in it* thou shalt not **d** any work, thou, 6213
5:27 unto thee; and we will hear *it,* and **d** *it.* 6213
5:31 that they may **d** *them* in the land which I 6213
5:32 Ye shall observe to **d** therefore as 6213
6: 1 that ye might **d** *them* in the land whither ye 6213
6: 3 observe to **d** *it;* that it may be well with 6213
6:18 thou shalt **d** *that which is* right and good in 6213
6:24 the LORD commanded us to **d** all these 6213
6:25 if we observe to **d** all these commandments 6213
7:11 which I command thee *this* day, to **d** them. 6213
7:12 to these judgments, and keep, and **d** them, 6213
7:19 shall the LORD thy God **d** unto all 6213

Dt 8: 1 thee *this* day shall ye observe to **d**, 6213
8:16 prove thee, to **d** thee **good** at thy latter end; 3190
8:19 if thou **d at all forget** the LORD 7911+7911
11:22 to **d** them, to love the LORD your God, 6213
11:32 ye shall observe to **d** all the statutes and 6213
12: 1 which ye shall observe to **d** in the land, 6213
12: 4 Ye shall not **d** so unto the LORD your 6213
12: 8 Ye shall not **d** after all *the things* that we do 6213
12: 8 Ye shall not do after all *the things* that we **d** 6213
12:14 there thou shalt **d** all that I command thee. 6213
12:25 when thou shalt **d** *that which is* right in 6213
12:30 serve their gods? even so will I **d** likewise. 6213
12:31 Thou shalt not **d** so unto the LORD thy 6213
12:32 soever I command you, observe to **d** it: 6213
13:11 shall **d** no more any such wickedness as 6213
13:18 to **d** *that which is* right in the eyes of 6213
15: 5 to observe to **d** all these commandments 6213
15:17 also unto thy maidservant thou shalt **d** 6213
15:19 thou shalt **d** no **work** with the firstling of 5647
16: 8 thy God: thou shalt **d** no work *therein.* 6213
16:12 and thou shalt observe and **d** these statutes. 6213
17:10 thou shalt **d** according to the sentence, 6213
17:10 thou shalt observe to **d** according to all that 6213
17:11 which they shall tell thee, thou shalt **d**: 6213
17:12 the man that will **d** presumptuously, 6213
17:13 and fear, and **d** no more presumptuously. NIH
17:19 of this law and these statutes, to **d** them: 6213
18: 7 as all his brethren the Levites *d,* which NIH
18: 9 thou shalt not learn to **d** after 6213
18:12 For all that **d** these *things are* an 6213
18:14 thy God hath not suffered thee so *to d.* NIH
19: 9 keep all these commandments to **d** them, 6213
19:19 shall ye **d** unto him, as he had thought to 6213
20: 3 fear not, and **d** not tremble, neither be ye NIH
20:15 Thus shalt thou **d** unto all the cities *which* 6213
20:18 That they teach you not to **d** after all their 6213
21: 9 when thou shalt **d** *that which is* right in 6213
22: 3 In like manner shalt thou **d** with his ass; 6213
22: 3 so shalt thou **d** with his raiment; and with 6213
22: 3 thou hast found, shalt thou **d** likewise: 6213
22: 5 for all that **d** so *are* abomination unto 6213
22:26 unto the damsel thou shalt **d** nothing; *there* 6213
24: 8 **d** according to all that the priests 6213
24: 8 commanded them, *so* ye shall observe to **d**. 6213
24:18 I command thee to **d** this thing. 6213
24:22 I command thee to **d** this thing. 6213
25:16 For all that **d** such *things, and* all that do 6213
25:16 do such *things, and* all that **d** unrighteously, 6213
26:16 hath commanded thee to **d** these statutes 6213
26:16 keep and **d** them with all thine heart, 6213
27:10 **d** his commandments and his statutes, 6213
27:26 not *all* the words of this law to **d** them. 6213
28: 1 to **d** all his commandments which I 6213
28:13 thee *this* day, to observe and to **d** *them:* 6213
28:15 to observe to **d** all his commandments and 6213
28:20 all that thou settest thine hand unto for to **d**, 6213
28:58 If thou wilt not observe to **d** all the words 6213
28:63 LORD rejoiced over you to **d** you **good**, 3190
29: 9 the words of this covenant, and **d** them, 6213
29: 9 that ye may prosper *in* all that ye **d**. 6213
29:14 Neither with you only **d** I make this NIH
29:29 that *we* may **d** all the words of this law. 6213
30: 5 he will **d** thee **good**, and multiply thee 3190
30: 8 **d** all his commandments which I command 6213
30:12 it unto us, that we may hear it, and **d** it? 6213
30:13 it unto us, that we may hear it, and **d** it? 6213
30:14 and in thy heart, that *thou* mayest **d** it. 6213
31: 4 the LORD shall **d** unto them as he did to 6213
31: 5 that ye may **d** unto them according unto all 6213
31:12 and observe to **d** all the words of this law: 6213
31:29 ye will **d** evil in the sight of the LORD, 6213
32: 6 **D** ye thus requite the LORD, O foolish NIH
32:46 command your children to observe to **d**, 6213
34:11 which the LORD sent him to **d** in the land 6213
Jos 1: 2 unto the land which I **d** give to them, NIH
1: 7 that *thou* mayest observe to **d** according to 6213
1: 8 that thou mayest observe to **d** according to 6213
1:16 All that thou commandest us we will **d**, and 6213
2:24 for even all the inhabitants of the country **d** NIH
3: 5 for to morrow the LORD will **d** wonders 6213
6: 3 the city once. Thus shalt thou **d** six days. 6213
7: 9 and what wilt thou **d** unto thy great name? 6213
8: 2 thou shalt **d** to Ai and her king as thou didst 6213
8: 8 commandment of the LORD shall ye **d**. 6213
9:20 This we will **d** to them; we will even let 6213
9:25 and right unto thee to **d** unto us, 6213
9:25 and right unto thee to do unto us, **d**. 6213
10:25 for thus shall the LORD **d** to all your 6213
22: 5 take diligent heed to **d** the commandment 6213
22:24 What **have** you **to d with** the LORD 3807.1
22:27 that *we* might **d** the service of the LORD 5647
23: 6 to **d** all that is written in the book of the law 6213
23:12 Else if ye **d** in any wise go back, and NIH
24:13 oliveyards which ye planted not **d** ye eat. NIH
24:20 he will turn and **d** you **hurt**, and 7489
Jdg 6:27 of the city, that *he* could not **d** *it* by day, 6213
7:17 unto them, Look on me, and **d** likewise: 6213
7:17 it shall be *that,* as I **d**, so shall ye do. 6213
7:17 it shall be *that,* as I do, so shall ye **d**. 6213
8: 3 what was I able to **d** in comparison of you? 6213
9:33 mayest thou **d** to them as thou shalt find 6213
9:48 What ye have seen me **d**, make haste, *and* 6213
9:48 me do, make haste, *and* **d** as I *have done.* 6213
10:15 **d** thou unto us whatsoever seemeth good 6213
11:10 if we **d** not so according to thy words. 6213
11:12 saying, What hast thou to **d** with me, NIH
11:36 **d** to me according to that which hath 6213
13: 8 teach us what we shall **d** unto the child that 6213
13:12 the child, and *how* shall we **d** unto him? 4639
13:17 come to pass we may **d** thee **honour**? 3513
14:10 a feast; for so **used** the young men **to d**. 6213
15: 3 though I **d** them a displeasure. 6213
15:10 come up, to **d** to him as he hath done to us. 6213
17:13 know I that the LORD will **d** me **good**, 3190
18:14 **D** ye know that there is in these houses an NIH

Jdg 18:14 now therefore consider what ye have to **d**. 6213
18:18 Then said the priest unto them, What **d** ye? 6213
19:23 *nay,* I pray you, **d** not *so* wickedly; NIH
19:23 is come into mine house, **d** not this folly. 6213
19:24 **d** with them what seemeth good unto you: 6213
19:24 but unto this man **d** not so vile a thing. 6213
20: 9 now this *shall be* the thing which we will **d** 6213
20:10 victual for the people, that *they* may **d**, 6213
21: 7 How shall we **d** for wives for them that 6213
21:11 this *is* the thing that ye shall **d**, Ye shall 6213
21:16 How shall we **d** for wives for them that 6213
Ru 1:17 the LORD **d** so to me, and more also, 6213
2: 9 *Let* thine eyes *be* on the field that they **d** NIH
3: 4 and he will tell thee what thou shalt **d**. 6213
3: 5 All that thou sayest unto me I will **d**. 6213
3:11 I will **d** to thee all that thou requirest: 6213
3:13 well; let him **d the kinsman's part**: 1350
3:13 if he will not **d the part of a kinsman** to 1350
3:13 then will I **d the part of a kinsman** to thee, 1350
4:11 **d** thou worthily in Ephratah, and be famous 6213
1Sa 1:23 said unto her, **D** what seemeth thee good; 6213
2:23 he said unto them, Why **d** ye such things? 6213
2:35 *that* shall **d** according to *that* which *is* in my 6213
3:11 Behold, I will **d** a thing in Israel, 6213
3:17 God **d** so to thee, and more also, if thou 6213
3:18 let him **d** what seemeth him good. 6213
5: 8 What shall we **d** with the ark of the God of 6213
6: 2 What shall we **d** to the ark of the LORD? 6213
6: 6 Wherefore then **d** ye harden your hearts, NIH
7: 3 If ye **d** return unto the LORD with all your NIH
8: 8 served other gods, so **d** they also unto thee. 6213
10: 2 for you, saying, What shall I **d** for my son? 6213
10: 7 *that* thou **d** as occasion serve thee; 6213
10: 8 to thee, and shew thee what thou shalt **d**. 6213
11:10 ye shall **d** with us all that seemeth good 6213
12:16 which the LORD will **d** before your eyes. 6213
12:25 if ye shall **still d wickedly**, ye shall 7489+7489
14: 7 said unto him, **D** all that *is* in thine heart: 6213
14:36 **D** whatsoever seemeth good unto thee. 6213
14:40 unto Saul, **D** what seemeth good unto thee. 6213
14:44 Saul answered, God **d** so and more also: 6213
16: 3 and I will shew thee what thou shalt **d**: 6213
20: 2 my father will **d** nothing *either* great or 6213
20: 4 thy soul desireth, I will even **d** *it* for thee. 6213
20:13 The LORD **d** so and much more to 6213
20:13 *but* if it please my father *to* **d** thee evil, then NIH
20:30 **d** not I know that thou hast chosen the son NIH
22: 3 till I know what God will **d** for me. 6213
24: 4 that thou mayest **d** to him as it shall seem 6213
24: 6 The LORD forbid that I should **d** this 6213
25:17 know and consider what thou wilt **d**; 6213
25:22 more also **d** God unto the enemies of 6213
26:21 for I will no more **d** thee **harm**, because 7489
26:25 thou shalt both **d great things**, and 6213+6213
28: 2 thou shalt know what thy servant can **d**. 6213
28:15 make known unto me what I shall **d**. 6213
29: 3 What *d* these Hebrews *here?* And Achish NIH
30:23 said David, Ye shall not **d** so, my brethren, 6213
2Sa 3: 8 which against Judah **d** shew kindness *this* NIH
3: 9 So **d** God to Abner, and more also, except, 6213
3: 9 hath sworn to David, even so I **d** to him; 6213
3:18 **d** *it:* for the LORD hath spoken of David, 6213
3:35 So **d** God to me, and more also, 6213
7: 3 to the king, Go, **d** all that *is* in thine heart; 6213
7:23 to **d** for you great things and terrible, 6213
7:25 establish *it* for ever, and **d** as thou hast said. 6213
9:11 his servant, so shall thy servant **d**. 6213
10:12 the LORD **d** that which seemeth him 6213
11:11 *as* thy soul liveth, I will not **d** this thing. 6213
12: 9 of the LORD, to **d** evil in his sight? 6213
12:12 I will **d** this thing before all Israel, and 6213
13: 2 Amnon thought it hard for him to **d** any 6213
13:12 Nay, my brother, **d** not force me; NIH
13:12 to be done in Israel: **d** not thou this folly. 6213
15: 4 come unto me, and I would **d** him justice. NIH
15: 5 that when any man came nigh *to him* to **d** NIH
15:15 thy servants *are ready to* **d** whatsoever my NIH
15:26 let him **d** to me as seemeth good unto him. 6213
16:10 the king said, What have I to **d** with you, NIH
16:11 how much more now *may this* Benjamite **d** NIH
16:20 Give counsel among you what we shall **d**. 6213
17: 6 shall we **d** *after* his saying? if not; 6213
18: 4 unto them, What seemeth you best I will **d**. 6213
18:32 all that rise against thee to **d** *thee* hurt, NIH
19:13 God **d** so to me, and more also, if thou be 6213
19:18 and to **d** what he thought good. 6213
19:19 neither **d** thou remember *that* which thy NIH
19:22 And David said, What have I to **d** with you, NIH
19:22 for **d** not I know that I *am this* day king over NIH
19:27 **d** therefore what *is* good in thine eyes. 6213
19:37 **d** to him what shall seem good unto thee. 6213
19:38 I will **d** to him *that* which shall seem good 6213
19:38 shalt require of me, *that* will I **d** for thee. 6213
20: 6 Bichri **d** us more **harm** than *did* Absalom: 3415
20:17 thine handmaid. And he answered, I **d** hear. NIH
21: 3 the Gibeonites, What shall I **d** for you? 6213
21: 4 What you shall say, *that* will I **d** for you. 6213
23:17 from me, O LORD, that I should **d** this: 6213
24:12 thee one of them, that I may **d** *it* unto thee. 6213
1Ki 1:30 even so will I certainly **d** this day. 6213
2: 6 **D** therefore according to thy wisdom, and 6213
2: 9 knowest what thou oughtest to **d** unto him; 6213
2:23 God **d** so to me, and more also, 6213
2:31 **D** as he hath said, and fall upon him, and 6213
2:38 the king hath said, so will thy servant **d**. 6213
3:28 wisdom of God *was* in him, to **d** judgment. 6213
5: 8 I will **d** all thy desire concerning timber of 6213
8:32 **d**, and judge thy servants, condemning 6213
8:39 **d**, and give to every man according to his 6213
8:43 **d** according to all that the stranger calleth 6213
8:43 to fear thee, as **d** thy people Israel; NIH
9: 1 desire which he was pleased to **d**, 6213
9: 4 to **d** according to all that I have 6213
10: 9 he thee king, to **d** judgment and justice. 6213
11:12 Notwithstanding in thy days I will not **d** it 6213

D

1Ki 11:33 to **d** *that* which *is* right in mine eyes, and 6213
11:38 **d** that *is* right in my sight, to keep my 6213
12: 6 How **d** you advise that *I* may answer this NIH
12:27 If this people go up to **d** sacrifice in 6213
14: 8 to **d** *that* only which *was* right in mine eyes; 6213
17:13 Fear not; go *and* **d** as thou hast said: 6213
17:18 What have I to **d** with thee, O thou man of NIH
18:34 he said, **D** *it* **the second time**. And they did 8138
18:34 he said, **D** *it* **the third time**. And they did *it* 8027
19: 2 So let the gods **d** *to me,* and more also, 6213
20: 9 send for to thy servant at the first I will **d**: 6213
20: 9 this thing I may not **d**. And the messengers 6213
20:10 The gods **d** so unto me, and more also, 6213
20:24 **d** this thing, Take the kings away, 6213
22:22 and prevail also: go forth, and **d** so. 6213
2Ki 2: 9 unto Elisha, Ask what I shall **d** for thee, 6213
3:13 king of Israel, What have I to **d** with thee? NIH
4: 2 said unto her, What shall I **d** for thee? 6213
4:16 man of God, **d** not lie unto thine handmaid. NIH
4:28 my lord? did I not say, **D** not deceive me? NIH
5:13 *if* the prophet had bid thee ***d** some* great NIH
6:15 Alas, my master, how shall we **d**? 6213
6:27 he said, *If* the LORD **d** not help thee, NIH
6:31 he said, God **d** so and more also to me, 6213
7: 9 they said one to another, We **d** not well: 6213
8:12 Because I know the evil that thou wilt **d** 6213
8:13 a dog, that he should **d** this great thing? 6213
9:18 Jehu said, What hast thou to **d** with peace? NIH
9:19 What hast thou to **d** with peace? NIH
10: 5 and will **d** all that thou shalt bid us; 6213
10: 5 **d** thou *that* which *is* good in thine eyes. 6213
10:19 for I have a great sacrifice *to* **d** to Baal; NIH
11: 5 This *is* the thing that ye shall **d**; 6213
17:12 said unto them, Ye shall not **d** this thing. 6213
17:15 that *they* should not **d** like them. 6213
17:17 sold themselves to **d** evil in the sight of 6213
17:34 Unto this day they **d** after the former 6213
17:34 neither **d** they after their statutes, or 6213
17:36 ye worship, and to him shall ye **d** sacrifice. NIH
17:37 for you, ye shall observe to **d** for evermore; 6213
17:41 as did their fathers, *so* **d** they unto this day. 6213
18:12 and would not hear *them,* nor **d** *them.* 6213
19:31 the zeal of the LORD *of hosts* shall **d** this. 6213
20: 9 that the LORD will **d** the thing that he 6213
21: 8 only if they will observe to **d** according to 6213
21: 9 Manasseh seduced them to **d** more evil than 6213
22: 9 it into the hand of them that **d** the work, 6213
22:13 to **d** according unto all that which is written 6213
1Ch 11:19 that *I* should **d** this *thing:* shall I drink 6213
12:32 the times, to know what Israel ought to **d**; 6213
13: 4 all the congregation said that *they* would **d** 6213
16:21 He suffered no man to **d** them **wrong**: yea, 6231
16:22 and **d** my prophets no **harm**. 7489
16:40 *to* **d** according to all that is written in NIH
17: 2 said unto David, **D** all that *is* in thine heart; 6213
17:23 for ever, and **d** as thou hast said. 6213
19:13 let the LORD **d** *that* which *is* good in his 6213
21: 8 **d away** the iniquity of thy servant; 5674
21:10 thee one of them, that I may **d** *it* unto thee. 6213
21:23 let my lord the king **d** *that* which *is* good in 6213
28: 7 if he be constant to **d** my commandments 6213
28:10 house for the sanctuary: be strong, and **d** *it.* 6213
28:20 and of good courage, and **d** *it:* fear not, 6213
29:19 to **d** all *these things,* and to build 6213
2Ch 6:23 **d**, and judge thy servants, by requiting 6213
6:33 **d** according to all that the stranger calleth 6213
7:17 **d** according to all that I have commanded 6213
9: 8 king over them, to **d** judgment and justice. 6213
14: 4 and to **d** the law and the commandment. 6213
18:21 shalt also prevail: go out, and **d** *even* so. 6213
19: 6 said to the judges, Take heed what ye **d**: 6213
19: 7 **d** *it:* for *there is* no iniquity with 6213
19: 9 Thus shall ye **d** in the fear of the LORD, 6213
19:10 this **d**, and ye shall not trespass. 6213
20:12 against us; neither know we what to **d**: 6213
22: 3 mother was his counsellor to **d wickedly**. 7561
23: 4 This *is* the thing that ye shall **d**; A third *part* 6213
25: 8 if thou *wilt* go, **d** *it,* be strong for the battle: 6213
25: 9 what *shall we* **d** for the hundred talents 6213
30:12 heart to **d** the commandment of the king 6213
32:10 Whereon **d** ye trust, that ye abide in NIH
33: 8 that they will take heed to **d** all that I have 6213
33: 9 to err, *and* to **d** worse than the heathen, 6213
34:16 was committed to thy servants, they **d** *it.* 6213
34:21 to **d** after all that is written in this book. 6213
35: 6 that *they* may **d** according to the word of 6213
35:21 saying, What have I to **d** with thee, NIH
Ezr 4: 2 as ye ***d***; and we do sacrifice unto him since NIH
4: 2 we **d sacrifice** unto him since the days of 2076
4: 3 You have nothing to **d** with us to build a NIH
4:22 Take heed now that ye fail not to **d** this: 5648
6: 8 Moreover I make a decree what ye shall **d** 5648
7:10 to **d** *it,* and to teach in Israel statutes and 6213
7:18 to **d** with the rest of the silver and gold, 5648
7:18 and gold, *that* **d** after the will of your God. 5648
7:21 **d** make a decree to all the treasurers which NIH
7:26 whosoever will not **d** the law of thy God, 5648
10: 4 *be* with thee: be of good courage, and **d** *it.* 6213
10: 5 to swear that *they* should **d** according to 6213
10:11 God of your fathers, and **d** his pleasure: 6213
10:12 As thou hast said, so must we **d**. 6213
Ne 1: 9 and keep my commandments, and **d** them; 6213
2:12 God had put in my heart to **d** at Jerusalem: 6213
2:19 and said, What *is* this thing that ye **d**? 6213
4: 2 and said, What **d** *these* feeble Jews? 6213
5: 9 Also I said, It *is* not good that ye **d**: ought 6213
5:12 of them; so will we **d** as thou sayest. 6213
5:12 that *they* should **d** according to this 6213
6: 2 of Ono. But they thought to **d** me mischief. 6213
6:13 **d** so, and sin, and *that* they might have 6213
9:24 that *they* might **d** with them as they would. 6213
9:29 (which if a man **d**, he shall live in them;) 6213
10:29 **d** all the commandments of the LORD our 6213
13:17 What evil thing *is* this that ye **d**, and 6213
13:21 if ye **d** *so* **again**, I will lay hands on you. 8138

Ne 13:27 hearken unto you to **d** all this great evil, 6213
Est 1: 8 that *they* should **d** according to every man's 6213
1:15 What shall *we* **d** unto the queen Vashti 6213
3:11 to **d** with them as it seemeth good to thee. 6213
4:11 **d** know, that whosoever, *whether* man or NIH
5: 5 that *he* may **d** as Esther hath said. 6213
5: 8 I will **d** to morrow as the king hath said. 6213
6: 6 To whom would the king delight to **d** 6213
6:10 and **d** *even* so to Mordecai the Jew, 6213
7: 5 that durst presume in his heart to **d** so? 6213
9:13 **d** to morrow also according unto *this* day's 6213
9:23 the Jews undertook to **d** as they had begun, 6213
Job 6: 4 the terrors of God **d** set *themselves* in array NIH
6:26 **D** ye imagine to reprove words, and NIH
7:20 what shall I **d** unto thee, O thou preserver 6466
9:13 the proud helpers **d** stoop under him. NIH
10: 2 I will say unto God, **D** not condemn me; NIH
11: 8 *It is* as high as heaven; what canst thou **d**? 6466
13: 2 What ye know, *the same* **d** I know also. NIH
13: 9 man mocketh another, **d** ye *so* mock him? NIH
13:10 reprove you, if ye **d** secretly accept persons. NIH
13:14 Wherefore **d** I take my flesh in my teeth, NIH
13:20 Only **d** not two *things* unto me: then will I 6213
15: 3 speeches wherewith he can **d** no **good**? 3276
15:12 thee away? and what **d** thine eyes wink at, NIH
16: 4 I also could speak as ye ***d***: if your soul were NIH
17:10 *as for* you all, **d** you return, and come now: NIH
19:22 Why **d** ye persecute me as God, and are not NIH
20: 2 Therefore **d** my thoughts cause me to NIH
21: 7 Wherefore **d** the wicked live, become old, NIH
21:29 by the way? and **d** ye not know their tokens, NIH
22:17 and what can the Almighty **d** for them? 6466
24: 1 **d** they that know him not see his days? NIH
31:14 What then shall I **d** when God riseth up? 6213
32: 9 neither **d** the aged understand judgment. NIH
34:10 it from God, *that he should* **d** wickedness; NIH
34:12 Yea, surely God will not **d wickedly**, 7561
34:32 if I have done iniquity, I will **d** no **more**. 3254
36:28 Which the clouds **d** drop *and* distil upon NIH
37:12 that they may **d** whatsoever he 6467
37:24 Men **d** therefore fear him: he respecteth not NIH
39: 1 *or* canst thou mark when the hinds **d** calve? NIH
41: 8 upon him, remember the battle, **d** no **more**. 3254
42: 2 I know that thou **canst d** every *thing,* and 3201
Ps 2: 1 Why **d** the heathen rage, and the people NIH
7: 1 O LORD my God, in thee **d** I put my trust: NIH
11: 3 be destroyed, what can the righteous **d**? 6466
12: 2 *and* with a double heart **d** they speak. NIH
16: 1 O God: for in thee **d** I put my trust. NIH
25: 1 Unto thee, O LORD, **d** I lift up my soul. NIH
25: 5 of my salvation; on thee **d** I wait all the day. NIH
31: 1 In thee, O LORD, **d** I put my trust; let me NIH
34:10 The young lions **d** lack, and suffer hunger: NIH
34:14 Depart from evil, and **d** good; seek peace, 6213
34:16 of the LORD *is* against them that **d** evil, 6213
36: 3 he hath left off to be wise, *and* to **d good**. 3190
37: 3 Trust in the LORD, and **d** good; *so* 6213
37: 8 fret not thyself in any wise to **d evil**. 7489
37:27 Depart from evil, and **d** good; and dwell for 6213
38:15 For in thee, O LORD, **d** I hope: thou wilt NIH
40: 8 I delight to **d** thy will, O my God: yea, 6213
41: 7 against me **d** they devise my hurt. NIH
50:16 What hast thou to **d** to declare my 3807.1
51:18 **D good** in thy good pleasure unto Zion: 3190
56: 4 I will not fear what flesh can **d** unto me. 6213
56:11 I will not be afraid what man can **d** unto 6213
58: 1 **D** ye indeed speak righteousness, NIH
58: 1 **d** ye judge uprightly, O ye sons of men? NIH
60:12 Through God we shall **d** valiantly: for he *it* 6213
64: 4 suddenly **d** they shoot at him, and fear not. NIH
71: 1 In thee, O LORD, **d** I put my trust: let me NIH
75: 1 Unto thee, O God, **d** we give thanks, NIH
75: 1 we give thanks, *unto thee* **d** we give thanks: NIH
80:12 that all they which pass by the way **d** pluck NIH
82: 3 **d justice** to the afflicted and needy. 6663
83: 9 **D** unto them as *unto* the Midianites; as *to* 6213
86: 4 for unto thee, O Lord, **d** I lift up my soul. NIH
89:50 *how* I **d** bear in my bosom *the reproach of* NIH
92: 7 when all the workers of iniquity **d** flourish; NIH
95:10 It *is* a people that **d** err in *their* heart, and NIH
103:18 remember his commandments to **d** them. 6213
103:20 in strength, that **d** his commandments, 6213
103:21 ye ministers of his, that **d** his pleasure. 6213
104:20 wherein all the beasts of the forest **d** creep NIH
105:14 He suffered no man to **d** them **wrong**: yea, 6231
105:15 and **d** my prophets no **harm**. 7489
107:23 sea in ships, that **d** business in great waters; 6213
108:13 Through God we shall **d** valiantly: for he *it* 6213
109:21 **d** thou for me, O GOD the Lord, for thy 6213
111:10 a good understanding have all they that **d** 6213
118: 6 I will not fear: what can man **d** unto me? 6213
119: 3 They also **d** no iniquity: they walk in his 6466
119:21 which **d** err from thy commandments. NIH
119:35 thy commandments; for therein **d** I delight. NIH
119:83 in the smoke; *yet* **d** I not forget thy statutes. NIH
119:109 in my hand: yet **d** I not forget thy law. NIH
119:113 I hate *vain* thoughts: but thy law **d** I love. NIH
119:132 as thou **usest to d** unto those that love thy 4941
119:141 and despised: *yet* **d** not I forget thy precepts. NIH
119:153 and deliver me: for I **d** not forget thy law. NIH
119:157 *yet* **d** I not decline from thy testimonies. NIH
119:163 I hate and abhor lying: *but* thy law **d** I love. NIH
119:164 Seven *times* a day **d** I praise thee because NIH
119:176 for I **d** not forget thy commandments. NIH
125: 4 **D good**, O LORD, unto *those that be* 2895
129: 8 Neither **d** they which go by say, NIH
130: 5 my soul doth wait, and in his word **d** I hope. NIH
131: 1 neither **d** I exercise myself in great *matters,* NIH
137: 6 If I **d** not remember thee, let my tongue NIH
139:21 **D** not I hate them, O LORD, that hate NIH
143: 8 in the morning; for in thee **d** I trust: NIH
143:10 Teach me to **d** thy will; for thou *art* my 6213
Pr 2:14 Who rejoice to **d** evil, *and* delight in 6213
3:27 when it is in the power of thine hand to **d** 6213
6: 3 **D** this now, my son, and deliver thyself, 6213

Pr 6:30 *Men* **d** not despise a thief, if he steal to NIH
8:13 evil way, and the froward mouth, **d** I hate. NIH
10:23 *It is* as sport to a fool to **d** mischief: but a 6213
14:22 **D** they not err that devise evil? but mercy NIH
17: 7 not a fool: much less **d** lying lips a prince. NIH
19: 7 All the brethren of the poor **d** hate him: NIH
19: 7 how much more **d** his friends go far from NIH
19:19 deliver *him,* yet thou must **d** *it* **again**. 3254+5750
20:30 so ***d*** stripes the inward parts of the belly. NIH
21: 3 To **d** justice and judgment *is* more 6213
21: 7 because they refuse to **d** judgment. 6213
21:15 *It is* joy to the just to **d** judgment: but 6213
24: 8 He that deviseth to **d evil** shall be called a 7489
24:29 I will **d** so to him as he hath done to me: 6213
25: 8 lest *thou know not* what to **d** in the end 6213
28:12 When righteous *men* **d** rejoice, *there is* great NIH
31:12 She will **d** him good and not evil all 1580
Ecc 2: 3 which they should **d** under the heaven all 6213
2:11 and on the labour that I had laboured to **d**: 6213
2:12 for what *can* the man ***d*** that cometh after NIH
3:12 *a man* to rejoice, and to **d** good in his life. 6213
4: 8 neither *saith he,* For whom **d** I labour, and NIH
5: 1 for they consider not that *they* **d** evil. 6213
6: 6 he seen no good: **d** not all go to one place? NIH
8:11 sons of men is fully set in them to **d** evil. 6213
8:12 Though a sinner **d** evil an hundred *times,* 6213
9:10 Whatsoever thy hand findeth to **d**, do *it* 6213
9:10 thy hand findeth to do, **d** *it* with thy might; 6213
10:10 he **d** not whet the edge, then must he put to NIH
11: 5 *nor* how the bones ***d** grow* in the womb of NIH
SS 1: 3 therefore **d** the virgins love thee. NIH
8: 8 what shall we **d** for our sister in the day 6213
Isa 1:16 from before mine eyes; cease to **d evil**; 7489
1:17 Learn to **d well**; seek judgment, relieve 3190
5: 5 I will tell you what I *will* **d** to my vineyard: 6213
9:13 neither **d** they seek the LORD of hosts. NIH
10: 3 what will ye **d** in the day of visitation, and 6213
10:11 her idols, so **d** to Jerusalem and her idols? 6213
14:21 *that* they **d** not rise, nor possess the land, NIH
19:15 the head or tail, branch or rush, may **d**. 6213
19:21 that day, and shall **d** sacrifice and oblation; 5647
23: 4 neither **d** I nourish up young men, *nor* bring NIH
24: 4 the haughty people of the earth **d** languish. NIH
24: 7 all the merryhearted **d** sigh. NIH
24:18 and the foundations of the earth **d** shake. NIH
27: 3 I the LORD **d** keep it; I will water it every NIH
28:21 that *he* may **d** his work, his strange work; 6213
29:13 with their lips **d** honour me, but NIH
29:14 I will proceed to **d a marvellous work** 6381
37:32 the zeal of the LORD of hosts shall **d** this. 6213
38: 7 that the LORD will **d** this thing that he 6213
38:19 he shall praise thee, as I ***d** this* day: NIH
41:23 yea, **d good**, or do evil, that we may be 3190
41:23 yea, do good, or **d evil**, that we may be 7489
42: 9 come to pass, and new *things* **d** I declare: NIH
42:16 These things will I **d** unto them, and 6213
43:19 I will **d** a new *thing;* now it shall spring 6213
45: 7 create evil: I the LORD **d** all these *things.* 6213
46:10 shall stand, and I will **d** all my pleasure: 6213
46:11 to pass; I have purposed *it,* I will also **d** it. 6213
48:11 will I **d** *it:* for how should *my name* be 6213
48:14 he will **d** his pleasure on Babylon, and 6213
55: 2 Wherefore **d** ye spend money for *that which* NIH
56: 1 Keep ye judgment, and **d** justice: 6213
57: 4 Against whom **d** ye sport yourselves? NIH
58: 4 ye shall not fast as *ye **d** this* day, to make NIH
64: 6 we all **d** fade as a leaf; and our iniquities, NIH
65: 8 so will I **d** for my servants' sakes, that *I* 6213
Jer 2: 8 and walked after *things that* **d** not profit. NIH
2:18 now what hast thou to **d** in the way of NIH
2:18 or what hast thou to **d** in the way of Assyria, NIH
4:22 they *are* wise to **d evil**, but to do good they 7489
4:22 but to **d good** they have no knowledge. 3190
4:30 when thou art spoiled, what wilt thou **d**? 6213
5:28 and the right of the needy **d** they not judge. NIH
5:31 *it* so: and what will ye **d** in the end thereof? 6213
7:10 We are delivered to **d** all these 6213
7:14 Therefore will I **d** unto *this* house, which is 6213
7:17 Seest thou not what they **d** in the cities of 6213
7:19 **D** they provoke me to anger? saith NIH
7:19 ***d** they* not *provoke* themselves to NIH
8: 8 How **d** ye say, We *are* wise, and the law of NIH
8:14 Why **d** we sit still? assemble yourselves, NIH
9: 7 for how shall I **d** for the daughter of my 6213
10: 5 for they cannot **d evil**, neither also *is it* in 7489
10: 5 do evil, neither also *is it* in them to **d good**. 3190
11: 4 Obey my voice, and **d** them, 6213
11: 6 ye the words of this covenant, and **d** them. 6213
11: 8 which I commanded *them* to **d**; 6213
11:15 What **hath** my beloved to **d** in mine 3807.1
12: 5 how wilt thou **d** in the swelling of Jordan? 6213
13:12 **D** we not certainly know that every bottle NIH
13:23 *then* may ye also **d good**, that are 3190
13:23 also do good, that are accustomed to **d evil**. 7489
14: 7 against us, **d** thou *it* for thy name's sake: 6213
14:21 **D** not abhor *us,* for thy name's sake, do not NIH
14:21 **d** not disgrace the throne of thy glory: NIH
17:22 neither **d** ye any work, but hallow ye 6213
17:24 the sabbath day, to **d** no work therein; 6213
18: 6 of Israel, cannot I **d** with you as this potter? 6213
18: 8 I will repent of the evil that I thought to **d** 6213
18:10 If it **d** evil in my sight, that *it* obey not my 6213
18:12 we will every one **d** the imagination of his 6213
19:12 Thus will I **d** unto this place, saith 6213
22: 3 **d no wrong**, do no violence, to 3238
22: 3 do no wrong, **d** no **violence**, to the stranger, 2554
22: 4 For if ye **d** this thing **indeed**, then 6213+6213
22:15 **d** judgment and justice, *and* then *it was* 6213
22:17 for oppression, and for violence, to **d** *it.* 6213
23:24 **D** not I fill heaven and earth? saith NIH
23:32 **d** tell them, and cause my people to err by NIH
25: 6 of your hands; and I will **d** you no hurt. NIH
26: 3 which I purpose to **d** unto them because of 6213
26:14 **d** with me as seemeth good and meet unto 6213
28: 6 the LORD **d** so: the LORD perform thy 6213

Jer 29:32 behold the good that I will **d** for my people, 6213
30: 6 wherefore **d** I see every man *with* his hands NIH
31:20 I **d** earnestly remember him still: NIH
32:23 of all that thou commandedst them to **d**: 6213
32:35 that *they* should **d** this abomination, to 6213
32:40 not turn away from them, to **d** them **good**; 3190
32:41 I will rejoice over them to **d** them **good**, 2895
33: 9 which shall hear all the good that I **d** unto 6213
33:18 and to **d** sacrifice continually. 6213
36: 3 all the evil which I purpose to **d** unto them; 6213
38: 5 for the king *is* not *he that* **can d** *any* thing 3201
39:12 and look well to him, and **d** him no harm; 6213
39:12 **d** unto him even as he shall say unto thee. 6213
40:16 son of Kareah, Thou shalt not **d** this thing: 6213
42: 2 a few of many, as thine eyes **d** behold us:) NIH
42: 3 we may walk, and the thing that we may **d**. 6213
42: 5 if we **d** not even according to all things *for* 6213
42:20 so declare unto us, and we will **d** *it*. 6213
44: 4 Oh, **d** not this abominable thing that I hate. 6213
44:17 we will **certainly d** whatsoever thing 6213+6213
50:15 upon her; as she hath done, **d** unto her. 6213
50:21 **d** according to all that I have commanded 6213
50:29 to all that she hath done, **d** unto her: 6213
51:47 that I will **d judgment** upon the graven 6485
51:52 that I will **d judgment** upon her graven 6485
51:55 when her waves **d** roar like great waters, NIH
La 1: 4 The ways of Zion **d** mourn, because NIH
1:22 **d** unto them, as thou hast done unto me for 5953
2:11 Mine eyes **d** fail with tears, my bowels are NIH
Eze 2: 4 I **d** send thee unto them; and thou shalt say NIH
5: 9 I will **d** in thee that which I have not done, 6213
5: 9 whereunto I will not **d** any more the like, 6213
6:10 *that* I have not said in vain that *I* would **d** 6213
7:27 I will **d** unto them after their way, and 6213
8: 6 Son of man, seest thou what they **d**? 6213
8: 9 behold the wicked abominations that they **d** 6213
8:12 ancients of the house of Israel **d** in the dark, 6213
8:13 shalt see great*er* abominations that they **d**. 6213
11:20 and keep mine ordinances, and **d** them: 6213
15: 3 Shall wood be taken thereof to **d** *any* work? 6213
16: 5 eye pitied thee, to **d** any of these unto thee, 6213
18: 5 and **d** that which is lawful and right, 6213
18:21 **d** that which is lawful and right, he shall 6213
20:11 which *if* a man **d**, he shall even live in 6213
20:13 which *if* a man **d**, he shall even live in 6213
20:19 and keep my judgments, and **d** them; 6213
20:21 neither kept my judgments to **d** them, 6213
20:21 which *if* a man **d**, he shall even live in 6213
21:24 so that in all your doings your sins **d** appear; NIH
22:14 I the LORD have spoken *it*, and will **d** *it*. 6213
23:30 *I will* **d** these *things* unto thee, because 6213
23:48 that all women may be taught not to **d** after 6213
24:14 I will **d** *it*; I will not go back, neither will I 6213
24:22 ye shall **d** as I have done: ye shall not cover 6213
24:24 to all that he hath done shall ye **d**: 6213
25: 8 Because that Moab and Seir **d** say, Behold, NIH
25:14 they shall **d** in Edom according to mine 6213
33: 9 if he **d** not turn from his way, he shall die in NIH
33:14 and **d** that which is lawful and right; 6213
33:19 **d** that which is lawful and right, he shall 6213
33:31 hear thy words, but they will not **d** them: 6213
33:32 they hear thy words, but they **d** them not. 6213
34: 2 Woe *be* to the shepherds of Israel that **d** 1961
35:11 I will even **d** according to thine anger, and 6213
35:15 it was desolate, so will I **d** unto thee: 6213
36:11 will **d better** *unto you* than at your 2895
36:22 I **d** not *this* for your sakes, O house of 6213
36:27 ye shall keep my judgments, and **d** *them*. 6213
36:32 Not for your sakes **d** I *this*, saith the Lord 6213
36:36 the LORD have spoken *it*, and I will **d** *it*. 6213
36:37 of by the house of Israel, to **d** *it* for them; 6213
37:24 and observe my statutes, and **d** them. 6213
37:28 the heathen shall know that I the LORD **d** NIH
39:17 to my sacrifice that I **d** sacrifice for you, NIH
43:11 and all the ordinances thereof, and **d** them. 6213
44:13 to **d the office of a priest** unto me, 3547
45:20 thou shalt **d** the seventh *day* of the month 6213
45:25 shall he **d** the like in the feast *of* the seven 6213
Da 3:14 and Abed-nego, **d** not ye serve my gods, NIH
4:26 shalt have known that the heavens **d** rule. NIH
9:18 for we **d** not present our supplications NIH
9:19 O Lord, forgive; O Lord, hearken and **d**; 6213
11: 3 great dominion, and **d** according to his will. 6213
11:16 he that cometh against him shall **d** 6213
11:17 and upright ones with him; thus shall he **d**: 6213
11:24 he shall **d** *that* which his fathers have not 6213
11:27 these kings' hearts *shall be* to **d mischief**, 4827
11:28 he shall **d** *exploits*, and return to his own 6213
11:30 so shall he **d**; he shall even return, and 6213
11:32 such as **d wickedly** against the covenant 7561
11:32 the people that **d** know their God shall be NIH
11:32 their God shall be strong, and **d** *exploits*. 6213
11:36 the king shall **d** according to his will; 6213
11:39 Thus shall he **d** in the most strong holds 6213
12:10 and tried; but the wicked shall **d wickedly**: 7561
Hos 4:18 her rulers *with* shame **d** love, Give ye. NIH
6: 4 O Ephraim, what shall I **d** unto thee? 6213
6: 4 O Judah, what shall I **d** unto thee? for your 6213
7:10 they **d** not return to the LORD their God, NIH
7:15 yet **d** they imagine mischief against me. NIH
9: 5 What will ye **d** in the solemn day, and 6213
10: 3 what then should a king **d** to us? 6213
10:15 So shall Beth-el **d** unto you because of your 6213
12: 1 they **d** make a covenant with the Assyrians, NIH
14: 8 What **have** I **to d** any more **with** idols? 3807.1
Joel 1:18 How **d** the beasts groan! the herds of cattle NIH
2:21 rejoice: for the LORD will **d** great things. 6213
2:22 for the pastures of the wilderness **d** spring, NIH
2:22 fig tree and the vine **d** yield their strength. NIH
3: 4 Yea, and what have ye to **d** with me, NIH
Am 3: 7 Surely the Lord GOD will **d** nothing, 6213
3:10 For they know not to **d** right, saith 6213
4:12 Therefore thus will I **d** unto thee, O Israel: 6213
4:12 *and* because I will **d** this unto thee, 6213
Jnh 1:11 they unto him, What shall we **d** unto thee, 6213
3:10 that he had said that he would **d** unto them; 6213
4: 9 he said, I **d well** to be angry, *even* unto 3190
Mic 2: 3 against this family **d** I devise an evil, NIH
2: 7 **d** not my words do good to him that walketh NIH
2: 7 do not my words **d good** to him that 3190
2:11 walking *in* the spirit and falsehood **d** lie, NIH
6: 8 to **d** justly, and to love mercy, and to walk 6213
7: 3 That *they* may **d** evil with both hands NIH
Na 1: 9 What **d** ye imagine against the LORD? NIH
Zep 1:12 in their heart, The LORD will not **d good**, 3190
1:12 will not do good, neither will he **d evil**. 7489
3: 5 in the midst thereof; he will not **d** iniquity: 6213
3:13 The remnant of Israel shall not **d** iniquity, 6213
Hag 2: 3 how **d** ye see it now? *is it* not in your eyes NIH
2:12 with his skirt **d** touch bread, or pottage, or NIH
Zec 1: 5 and the prophets, **d** they live for ever? NIH
1: 6 Like as the LORD of hosts thought to **d** 6213
1:21 said I, What come these to **d**? And he 6213
5:10 with me, Whither **d** these bear the ephah? NIH
8:15 in these days to **d well** unto Jerusalem 3190
8:16 These *are* the things that ye shall **d**; 6213
9:12 even to day **d** I declare *that* I will render NIH
12: 7 the glory of the inhabitants of Jerusalem **d** NIH
Mal 1:10 **d** ye kindle *fire* on mine altar for nought. NIH
2: 2 because ye **d** not lay *it* to heart. NIH
2:10 why **d** we deal treacherously every man NIH
4: 1 all the proud, yea, and all that **d** wickedly, 6213
4: 3 I *shall* **d** *this*, saith the LORD of hosts. 6213
Mt 5: 6 Blessed *are* they which **d** hunger and NIG
5:15 Neither **d** men light a candle, and put it NIG
5:19 but whosoever shall **d** and teach *them*, 4160
5:44 **d** good to them that hate you, and pray for 4160
5:46 **d** not even the publicans the same? 4160
5:47 what **d** ye more *than others?* do not even 4160
5:47 what do ye more *than others?* **d** not even 4160
6: 1 Take heed that *ye* **d** not your alms before 4160
6: 2 **d** not sound a trumpet before thee, NIG
6: 2 as the hypocrites **d** in the synagogues and 4160
6: 7 as the heathen **d**: for they think that they NIG
6:20 where thieves **d** not break through nor steal: NIG
6:26 for they sow not, neither **d** they reap, NIG
6:28 they grow; they toil not, neither **d** they spin: NIG
6:32 (For after all these *things* **d** the Gentiles NIG
7:12 ye would that men should **d** to you, 4160
7:12 should do to you, **d** ye even so to them: 4160
7:16 **D** *men* gather grapes of thorns, or figs of NIG
8: 9 and to my servant, **D** this, and he doeth *it*. 4160
8:29 saying, What have we to **d** with thee, Jesus, NIG
9:14 Why **d** we and the Pharisees fast oft, but NIG
9:17 Neither **d** *men* put new wine into old NIG
9:28 Believe ye that I am able to **d** this? 4160
11: 3 that should come, or **d** we look for another? NIG
11: 4 shew John again *those things* which ye **d** NIG
12: 2 thy disciples **d** *that* which is not lawful to 4160
12: 2 is not lawful to **d** upon the sabbath day. 4160
12:12 Wherefore it is lawful to **d** well on 4160
12:27 by whom **d** your children cast *them* out? NIG
12:50 For whosoever shall **d** the will of my 4160
13:13 they hear not, neither **d** they understand. NIG
13:41 that offend, and them which **d** iniquity; 4160
14: 2 mighty works **d** shew forth themselves in NIG
15: 2 Why **d** thy disciples transgress the tradition NIG
15: 3 Why **d** you also transgress NIG
15: 9 But in vain they **d** worship me, teaching for NIG
15:17 **D** not ye yet understand, that whatsoever NIG
16: 9 **D** ye not yet understand, neither remember NIG
16:11 How *is it that* ye **d** not understand that I NIG
16:13 Whom **d** men say that I the Son of man am? NIG
17:25 of whom **d** the kings of the earth take NIG
18:10 That in heaven their angels **d** always behold NIG
18:35 So likewise shall my heavenly Father **d** 4160
19:16 Good Master, what good *thing* shall I **d**, 4160
19:18 Jesus said, Thou shalt **d** no murder, NIG
20:13 and said, Friend, I **d** thee no wrong: NIG
20:15 Is it not lawful for me to **d** what I will with 4160
20:32 said, What will ye *that* I shall **d** unto you? 4160
21:21 ye shall not only **d** this which is done to 4160
21:24 tell you by what authority I **d** these *things*. 4160
21:27 Neither tell I you by what authority I **d** 4160
21:40 what will he **d** unto those husbandmen? 4160
22:29 and said unto them, Ye **d** err, NIG
23: 3 they bid you observe, *that* observe and **d**; 4160
23: 3 and do; but **d** not ye after their works: 4160
23: 3 ye after their works: for they say, and **d** not. 4160
23: 5 But all their works they **d** for to be seen of 4160
26:72 denied with an oath, I **d** not know the man. NIG
27:19 Have thou nothing to **d** with that just *man*: NIG
27:22 What shall I **d** then with Jesus which is 4160
Mk 1:24 what have we to **d** with thee, *thou* Jesus of NIG
1:27 the unclean spirits, and they **d** obey him. NIG
2:18 Why **d** the disciples of John and of NIG
2:24 why **d** they on the sabbath day *that* which is 4160
3: 4 Is it lawful to **d good** on the sabbath days, or *15*
3: 4 do good on the sabbath days, or to **d evil**? *2554*
3:35 For whosoever shall **d** the will of God, 4160
5: 7 and said, What have I to **d** with thee, Jesus, NIG
6: 5 And he could there **d** no mighty work, 4160
6:14 mighty works **d** shew forth themselves in NIG
7: 7 Howbeit in vain **d** they worship me, NIG
7: 8 cups: and many other such like *things* ye **d**. 4160
7:12 And ye suffer him no more to **d** ought for 4160
7:13 and many such like *things* **d** ye. 4160
7:18 **D** ye not perceive, that whatsoever *thing* NIG
8:18 hear ye not? and **d** ye not remember? NIG
8:21 How *is it that* ye **d** not understand? NIG
8:27 unto them, Whom **d** men say that I am? NIG
9:22 if thou canst **d** any *thing*, have compassion NIG
9:39 for there is no *man* which shall **d** a miracle 4160
10:17 what shall I **d** that I may inherit eternal 4160
10:19 **D** not commit adultery, Do not kill, Do not NIG
10:19 commit adultery, **D** not kill, Do not steal, NIG
10:19 commit adultery, Do not kill, **D** not steal, NIG
10:19 **D** not bear false witness, Defraud not, NIG
10:35 we would that thou shouldest **d** for us 4160
10:36 What would ye that I should **d** for you? 4160
Mk 10:51 What wilt thou *that* I should **d** unto thee? 4160
11: 3 if any *man* say unto you, Why **d** ye this? 4160
11: 5 unto them, What **d** ye, loosing the colt? 4160
11:26 But if ye **d** not forgive, neither will your NIG
11:28 who gave thee this authority to **d** these 4160
11:29 I will tell you by what authority I **d** these 4160
11:33 Neither **d** I tell you by what authority I do NIG
11:33 Neither do I tell you by what authority I **d** 4160
12: 9 therefore the lord of the vineyard **d**? 4160
12:24 **D** ye not therefore err, because ye know not NIG
12:27 God of the living: ye therefore **d** greatly err. NIG
13:11 ye shall speak, neither **d** ye premeditate: NIG
14: 7 whensoever ye will ye may **d** them good: 4160
15: 8 *him to* **d** as he had ever done unto them. NIG
15:12 *that* I shall **d** *unto him* whom ye call 4160
Lk 2:27 to **d** for him after the custom of the law, 4160
3:10 asked him, saying, What shall we **d** then? 4160
3:11 and he that hath meat, let him **d** likewise. 4160
3:12 said unto him, Master, what shall we **d**? 4160
3:14 of him, saying, And what shall we **d**? 4160
3:14 he said unto them, **D** violence to no man, NIG
4:23 in Capernaum, **d** also here in thy country. 4160
4:34 what have we to **d** with thee, *thou* Jesus of NIG
5:30 Why **d** ye eat and drink with publicans and NIG
5:33 Why **d** the disciples of John fast often, and NIG
6: 2 Why **d** ye *that* which is not lawful to do on 4160
6: 2 Why do ye *that* which is not lawful to **d** on 4160
6: 9 Is it lawful on the sabbath days to **d good**, *15*
6: 9 the sabbath days to do good, or to **d evil**? *2554*
6:11 with another what they might **d** to Jesus. 4160
6:27 **d** good to them which hate you, 4160
6:31 And as ye would that men should **d** to you, 4160
6:31 do to you, **d** ye also to them likewise. 4160
6:33 And if ye **d good** to them which do good to *15*
6:33 And if ye do good to them which **d good** to *15*
6:33 have ye? for sinners also **d** *even* the same. 4160
6:35 and **d good**, and lend, hoping for nothing *15*
6:44 For of thorns *men* **d** not gather figs, nor of a NIG
6:46 Lord, and **d** not *the things* which I say? 4160
7: 4 That he was worthy for whom he should **d** *3930*
7: 8 and to my servant, **D** this, and he doeth *it*. 4160
8:21 these which hear the word of God, and **d** it. 4160
8:28 What have I to **d** with thee, Jesus, NIG
10:11 cleaveth on us, we **d** wipe off against you: NIG
10:25 what shall I **d** to inherit eternal life? 4160
10:28 answered right: this **d**, and thou shalt live. 4160
10:37 Jesus unto him, Go, and **d** thou likewise. 4160
11:19 by whom **d** your sons cast *them* out? NIG
11:39 Now **d** ye Pharisees make clean the outside NIG
12: 4 and after that have no more that *they* can **d**. 4160
12:17 saying, What shall I **d**, because I have no 4160
12:18 And he said, This will I **d**: I will pull down 4160
12:26 be not able *to* **d** *that thing which is* least, NIG
12:30 For all these *things* **d** the nations of NIG
12:56 but how *is it that* ye **d** not discern this time? NIG
13:32 and I **d** cures to day and to morrow, and *2005*
15:29 Lo, these many years **d** I serve thee, NIG
16: 3 said within himself, What shall I **d**? 4160
16: 4 I am resolved what to **d**, that, when I am 4160
17:10 we have done *that* which was our duty to **d**. 4160
18:18 what shall I **d** to inherit eternal life? 4160
18:20 **D** not commit adultery, Do not kill, Do not NIG
18:20 commit adultery, **D** not kill, Do not steal, NIG
18:20 commit adultery, Do not kill, **D** not steal, NIG
18:20 Do not steal, **D** not bear false witness, NIG
18:41 What wilt thou *that* I shall **d** unto thee? 4160
19:31 Why **d** ye loose *him?* thus shall ye say unto NIG
19:48 And could not find what they might **d**: 4160
20: 8 Neither tell I you by what authority I **d** 4160
20:13 the lord of the vineyard, What shall I **d**? 4160
20:15 shall the lord of the vineyard **d** unto them? 4160
22:19 for you: this **d** in remembrance of me. 4160
22:23 which of them it was that should **d** this *4238*
23:31 For if they **d** these *things* in a green tree, 4160
23:34 for they know not what they **d**. 4160
24:38 and why **d** thoughts arise in your hearts? NIG
Jn 2: 4 Woman, what have I to **d** with thee? NIG
2: 5 Whatsoever he saith unto you, **d** *it*. 4160
3: 2 for no *man* can **d** these miracles that thou 4160
3:11 We speak that we **d** know, and testify that NIG
4:34 My meat is to **d** the will of him that sent 4160
5:19 The Son can **d** nothing of himself, but 4160
5:19 of himself, but what he seeth the Father **d**: 4160
5:30 I can of mine own self **d** nothing: as I hear, 4160
5:36 the same works that I **d**, bear witness of 4160
5:45 **D** not think that I will accuse you to NIG
6: 6 for he himself knew what he would **d**. 4160
6:28 Then said they unto him, What shall we **d**, 4160
6:38 not to **d** mine own will, but the will of him 4160
7: 4 If thou **d** these *things*, shew thyself to 4160
7:17 If any *man* will **d** his will, he shall know of 4160
7:26 **D** the rulers know indeed that this is NIG
7:31 will he **d** moe miracles than these which 4160
8:11 said unto her, Neither **d** I condemn thee: NIG
8:28 that I am *he*, and *that* I **d** nothing of myself; 4160
8:29 for I **d** always those *things* that please him. 4160
8:38 ye **d** *that* which ye have seen with your 4160
8:39 ye would **d** the works of Abraham. 4160
8:41 Ye **d** the deeds of your father. Then said 4160
8:43 Why **d** ye not understand my speech? *even* NIG
8:44 and the lusts of your father ye will **d**. 4160
8:46 if I say the truth, why **d** ye not believe me? NIG
8:49 I honour my Father, and ye **d** dishonour me. NIG
9:15 upon mine eyes, and I washed, and **d** see. NIG
9:16 How can a man *that is* a sinner **d** such 4160
9:33 *man* were not of God, he could **d** nothing. 4160
10:25 the works that I **d** in my Father's name, 4160
10:32 for which of those works **d** ye stone me? NIG
10:37 If I **d** not the works of my Father, 4160
10:38 But if I **d**, though ye believe not me, 4160
11:12 Lord, if he sleep, he shall **d well**. *4982*
11:47 Pharisees a council, and said, What **d** we? 4160
13: 7 unto him, What I **d** thou knowest not now; 4160
13:15 that ye should **d** as I have done to you. 4160
13:17 these *things*, happy are ye if ye **d** them. 4160

Jn 13:27 Jesus unto him, That thou doest, d quickly. 4160
14:12 on me, the works that I d shall he do also; 4160
14:12 on me, the works that I do shall he d also; 4160
14:12 and greater *works* than these shall he d; 4160
14:13 ye shall ask in my name, that will I d, 4160
14:14 shall ask any *thing* in my name, I will d *it.* 4160
14:31 Father gave me commandment, *even* so I d. 4160
15: 5 for without me ye can d nothing. 4160
15:14 if ye d whatsoever I command you. 4160
15:21 But all these *things* will they d unto you for 4160
16: 3 And these *things* will they d unto you, 4160
16:19 D ye inquire among yourselves of that I NIG
16:31 Jesus answered them, D ye now believe? NIG
17: 4 the work which thou gavest me to d. 4160
21:21 to Jesus, Lord, and what *shall* this *man* d? NIG
Ac 1: 1 of all that Jesus began both to d and teach, 4160
2:11 we d hear them speak in our tongues NIG
2:37 Men *and* brethren, what shall we d? 4160
4:16 Saying, What shall we d to these men? 4160
4:28 For to d whatsoever thy hand and 4160
5:35 take heed to yourselves what ye intend to d 4238
7:26 why d ye wrong one to another? NIG
7:51 and ears, ye d always resist the Holy Ghost: NIG
7:51 the Holy Ghost: as your fathers *did,* so d ye. NIG
9: 6 Lord, what wilt thou have me to d? 4160
9: 6 and it shall be told thee what thou must d. 4160
10: 6 he shall tell thee what thou oughtest to d. 4160
14:15 why d ye these *things?* We also are men of 4160
15:29 if ye keep yourselves, ye shall d well. 4238
15:36 the word of the Lord, *and see* how they d. 2192
16:20 being Jews, d exceedingly trouble our city, NIG
16:28 a loud voice, saying, D thyself no harm: 4238
16:30 and said, Sirs, what must I d to be saved? 4160
16:37 and now d they thrust us out privily? NIG
17: 7 these all d contrary to the decrees of Cesar, 4238
19:36 ought to be quiet, and to d nothing rashly. 4238
21:23 D therefore this that we say to thee: 4160
22:10 And I said, What shall I d, Lord? And 4160
22:10 all *things* which are appointed for thee to d. 4160
23:21 But d not thou yield unto them: for there lie NIG
24:10 I d the more cheerfully answer for myself: NIG
24:16 And herein d I exercise myself, to have NIG
25: 9 willing to d the Jews a pleasure, 2698
26: 9 that I ought to d many *things* contrary to 4238
26:20 to God, and d works meet for repentance. 4238
Ro 1:28 to d those *things* which are not convenient; 4160
1:32 not only d the same, but have pleasure in 4160
1:32 but have pleasure in them that d *them.* 4238
2: 3 that judgest them which d such *things,* and 4238
2: 8 and d not obey the truth, but NIG
2:14 d by nature the *things* contained in the law, 4160
3: 8 Let us d evil, that good may come? 4160
3:31 D we then make void the law through faith? NIG
7:15 For *that* which I d I allow not: for what I 2716
7:15 for what I would, that d I not; but what I 4238
7:15 that do I not; but what I hate, that d I. 4160
7:16 If then I d that which I would not, I consent 4160
7:17 Now then it is no more I that d it, but 2716
7:19 For the good that I would I d not: but 4160
7:19 but the evil which I would not, that I d. 4238
7:20 Now if I d that I would not, it is no more I 4160
7:20 it is no more I that d it, but sin that 2716
7:21 then a law, that, when I would d good, 4160
8: 3 For what the law could not d, in that it was 102
8: 5 For they that are after the flesh d mind NIG
8:13 if ye through the Spirit d mortify the deeds NIG
8:25 see not, *then* d we with patience wait for *it.* NIG
12: 8 he that giveth, *let him d it* with simplicity; NIG
12:15 Rejoice with them that d rejoice, and NIG
13: 3 d *that which is* good, and thou shalt have 4160
13: 4 But if thou d *that which is* evil, be afraid; 4160
15:31 That I may be delivered from them that d NIG
1Co 5:12 For what have I to d to judge them 1473+5101
5:12 d not ye judge them that are within? NIG
6: 2 D ye not know that the saints shall judge NIG
6: 7 Why d ye not rather take wrong? why do ye NIG
6: 7 why d ye not rather *suffer yourselves to* be NIG
6: 8 you d wrong, and defraud, and that *your* NIG
7:36 need so require, let him d what he will, 4160
9: 3 Mine answer to them that d examine me is NIG
9:13 D ye not know that they which minister NIG
9:17 For if I d this *thing* willingly, I have a 4238
9:23 And this I d for the gospel's sake, that I 4160
9:25 Now they *d it* to obtain a corruptible crown; NIG
10:22 D we provoke the Lord to jealousy? are we NIG
10:31 ye eat, or drink, or whatsoever ye d, 4160
10:31 whatsoever ye do, d all to the glory of God. 4160
11:24 for you: this d in remembrance of me. 4160
11:25 this d ye, as oft as ye drink *it,* in 4160
11:26 ye d shew the Lord's death till he come. NIG
12:30 d all speak with tongues? do all interpret? NIG
12:30 do all speak with tongues? d all interpret? NIG
15:29 Else what shall they d which are baptized 4160
15:35 and with what body d they come? NIG
16: 1 to the churches of Galatia, even so d ye. 4160
16: 5 for I d pass through Macedonia. NIG
16:10 worketh the work of the Lord, as I also *d.* NIG
2Co 1:17 d I purpose according to the flesh, NIG
3: 1 D we begin again to commend ourselves? or NIG
5: 4 For we that are in *this* tabernacle d groan, NIG
7: 8 a letter, I d not repent, though I did repent: NIG
8: 1 we d you to wit of the grace of God NIG
8:10 not only to d, but also to be forward a year 4160
8:23 Whether *any d inquire* of Titus, *he is* my NIG
10: 3 in the flesh, we d not war after the flesh: NIG
10: 7 D ye look on *things* after the outward NIG
11: 8 taking wages *of them,* to d you service. 4314
11:12 But what I d, that I will do, that I may cut 4160
11:12 But what I do, that I will d, that I may cut 4160
12:19 but *we d* all *things,* dearly beloved, for your NIG
13: 7 Now I pray to God that ye d no evil; 4160
13: 7 but that ye should d *that which is* honest, 4160
13: 8 For we can d nothing against the truth, but 1410
Gal 1:10 For d I now persuade men, or God? or do I NIG
1:10 or d I seek to please men? for if I yet NIG
Gal 2:10 the same which I also was forward to d. 4160
2:14 manner of Gentiles, and not as d the Jews, 2452
2:14 thou the Gentiles to live as d the Jews? 2450
2:21 I d not frustrate the grace of God: for if NIG
3:10 written in the book of the law to d them. 4160
4:21 to be under the law, d ye not hear the law? NIG
5: 3 that he is a debtor to d the whole law. 4160
5:11 why d I yet suffer persecution? NIG
5:17 that ye cannot d the *things* that ye would. 4160
5:21 that they which d such *things* shall not 4238
6:10 let us d good unto all *men,* especially unto 2038
Eph 3:20 Now unto him that is able to d exceeding 4160
6: 9 ye masters, d the same *things* unto them, 4160
6:21 *and* how I d, Tychicus, a beloved brother 4238
Php 1:18 and I therein d rejoice, yea, and will rejoice. NIG
2:13 both to will and to d of *his* good pleasure. 1754
2:14 D all *things* without murmurings and 4160
2:18 *For* the same *cause* also d ye joy, and NIG
3: 8 of all *things,* and d count *them but* dung, NIG
3:13 *this* one *thing I d,* forgetting those *things* NIG
4: 9 and received, and heard, and seen in me, d: 4238
4:13 I can d all *things* through Christ which 2480
Col 1: 9 since the day we heard *it,* d not cease to NIG
3:13 even as Christ forgave you, so also *d* ye. NIG
3:17 And whatsoever ye d in word or deed, 4160
3:17 or deed, *d* all in the name of the Lord Jesus, NIG
3:23 And whatsoever ye d, do *it* heartily, as to 4160
3:23 d *it* heartily, as to the Lord, and not unto 2038
1Th 3:12 towards all *men,* even as we *d* towards you: NIG
4:10 And indeed ye d it towards all the brethren 4160
4:11 and to d your own *business,* and to work 4238
5: 6 Therefore let us not sleep, as *d* others; but NIG
5:11 and edify one another, even as also ye d. 4160
5:24 *is* he that calleth you, who also will d *it.* 4160
2Th 3: 4 that ye both d and will do *the things* which 4160
3: 4 will d *the things* which we command you. 4160
1Ti 1: 4 than godly edifying which is in faith: *so d.* NIG
6: 2 but rather d *them* service, because they are 1398
6:18 That *they* d good, that *they* be rich in good 14
2Ti 2:23 knowing that they d gender strifes. NIG
3: 8 so d these also resist the truth: NIG
4: 5 d the work of an evangelist, make full 4160
4: 9 D thy diligence to come shortly unto me: 4704
4:21 D thy diligence to come before winter. 4704
Phm 1:14 But without thy mind would I d nothing; 4160
1:19 I will repay *it:* albeit I d not say to thee how NIG
1:21 knowing that thou wilt also d more than I 4160
Heb 3:10 and said, They d alway err in *their* heart; NIG
4: 3 For we which have believed d enter into NIG
4:13 the eyes of him with whom we have to d. 3056
6: 3 And this will we d, if God permit. 4160
6:10 ministered to the saints, and d minister. NIG
6:11 And we desire that every one of you d shew NIG
10: 7 it is written of me,) to d thy will, O God. 4160
10: 9 said he, Lo, I come to d thy will, O God. 4160
11: 3 were not made of *things* which d appear. NIG
11:29 the Egyptians assaying to d were drowned. 2983
13: 6 I will not fear what man shall d unto me. 4160
13:16 But to d good and to communicate forget 2140
13:17 that they may d it with joy, and not with 4160
13:19 But I beseech *you* the rather to d this, that I 4160
13:21 Make you perfect in every good work to d 4160
Jas 1:16 D not err, my beloved brethren. NIG
2: 6 D not rich *men* oppress you, and draw you NIG
2: 7 D not they blaspheme *that* worthy name by NIG
2: 8 love thy neighbour as thyself, ye d well: 4160
2:11 D not commit adultery, said also, Do not NIG
2:11 not commit adultery, said also, D not kill. NIG
2:12 So speak ye, and so d, as they that shall be 4160
4: 5 D ye think that the scripture saith in vain, NIG
4:15 Lord will, we shall live, and d this, or that. 4160
4:17 Therefore to him that knoweth to d good, 4160
5:19 if any of you d err from the truth, and NIG
1Pe 1:21 Who by him d believe in God, that raised NIG
2:14 and *for* the praise of them that d well. 17
2:20 but if, when ye d well, and suffer *for it,* ye 15
3: 6 as long as ye d well, and are not afraid *with* 15
3:11 Let him eschew evil, and d good; let him 4160
3:12 the face of the Lord *is* against them that d 4160
4:11 *let him d it* as of the ability which God NIG
2Pe 1:10 for if ye d these *things,* ye shall never fall: 4160
1:19 whereunto ye d well that ye take heed, 4160
3:16 as *they d* also the other scriptures, NIG
1Jn 1: 6 in darkness, we lie, and d not the truth: 4160
2: 3 And hereby we d know that we know him, NIG
3:22 d those *things* that are pleasing in his sight. 4160
4:14 d testify that the Father sent the Son *to be* NIG
5:16 I d not say that he shall pray for it. NIG
3Jn 1: 6 journey after a godly sort, thou shalt d well: 4160
Rev 2: 5 art fallen, and repent, and d the first works; 4160
3: 9 say they are Jews, and are not, but d lie; NIG
3:18 *that* the shame of thy nakedness d not NIG
9:19 and had heads, and with them they d hurt. NIG
13:14 he had power to d in the sight of the beast; 4160
14:13 and their works d follow them. NIG
19:10 And he said unto me, See *thou d it* not: I am NIG
21:24 the kings of the earth d bring their glory and NIG
22: 9 Then saith he unto me, See *thou d it* not: NIG
22:14 Blessed *are* they that d his commandments, 4160

DO BEST See STUDY

DOCTOR (1) [DOCTORS]

Ac 5:34 a Pharisee, named Gamaliel, a d of law, 3547

DOCTORS (2) [DOCTOR]

Lk 2:46 sitting in the midst of the d, both hearing 1320
5:17 d of the law sitting *by,* which were come 3547

DOCTRINE (51) [DOCTRINES]

Dt 32: 2 My d shall drop as the rain, my speech 3948
Job 11: 4 My d *is* pure, and I am clean in thine eyes. 3948
Pr 4: 2 For I give you good d, forsake you not my 3948
Isa 28: 9 whom shall he make to understand d? 8052
Isa 29:24 and they that murmured shall learn d. 3948
Jer 10: 8 and foolish: the stock *is* a d of vanities. 4148
Mt 7:28 the people were astonished at his d: 1322
16:12 but of the d of the Pharisees and of 1322
22:33 heard *this,* they were astonished at his d. 1322
Mk 1:22 And they were astonished at his d: for he 1322
1:27 what new d *is* this? for with authority 1322
4: 2 by parables, and said unto them in his d, 1322
11:18 all the people was astonished at his d. 1322
12:38 And he said unto them in his d, Beware of 1322
Lk 4:32 And they were astonished at his d: for his 1322
Jn 7:16 said, My d is not mine, but his that sent me. 1322
7:17 he shall know of the d, whether it be of 1322
18:19 asked Jesus of his disciples, and of his d. 1322
Ac 2:42 they continued stedfastly in the apostles' d 1322
5:28 ye have filled Jerusalem with your d, and 1322
13:12 being astonished at the d of the Lord. 1322
17:19 saying, May we know what this new d, 1322
Ro 6:17 *that* form of d which was delivered you. 1322
16:17 offences contrary to the d which ye have 1322
1Co 14: 6 by knowledge, or by prophesying, or by d? 1322
14:26 hath a d, hath a tongue, hath a revelation, 1322
Eph 4:14 fro, and carried about with every wind of d, 1319
1Ti 1: 3 charge some that *they* teach no other d, 2085
1:10 any other *thing that* is contrary to sound d; 1319
4: 6 up in the words of faith and of good d, 1319
4:13 attendance to reading, to exhortation, to d. 1319
4:16 Take heed unto thyself, and unto the d; 1319
5:17 they who labour in the word and d. 1319
6: 1 name of God and *his* d be not blasphemed. 1319
6: 3 to the d which is according to godliness; 1319
2Ti 3:10 But thou hast fully known my d, manner of 1319
3:16 and *is* profitable for d, for reproof, 1319
4: 2 rebuke, exhort with all longsuffering and d. 1322
4: 3 come when they will not endure sound d; 1319
Tit 1: 9 that he may be able by sound d both to 1319
2: 1 thou *the things* which become sound d: 1319
2: 7 in d *shewing* uncorruptness, gravity, 1319
2:10 that they may adorn the d of God our 1319
Heb 6: 1 Therefore leaving the principles of the d of 3056
6: 2 Of the d of baptisms, and of laying on of 1322
2Jn 1: 9 and abideth not in the d of Christ, hath not 1322
1: 9 He that abideth in the d of Christ, he hath 1322
1:10 come any unto you, and bring not this d, 1322
Rev 2:14 thou hast there them that hold the d of 1322
2:15 So hast thou also them that hold the d of 1322
2:24 as many as have not this d, and which have 1322

DOCTRINES (5) [DOCTRINE]

Mt 15: 9 teaching *for* d the commandments of men. 1319
Mk 7: 7 teaching *for* d the commandments of men. 1319
Col 2:22 after the commandments and d of men? 1319
1Ti 4: 1 heed to seducing spirits, and d of devils; 1319
Heb 13: 9 not carried about with divers and strange d. 1322

DODAI (1)

1Ch 27: 4 over the course of the second month *was* D 1737

DODANIM (2)

Ge 10: 4 Elishah, and Tarshish, Kittim, and D. 1721
1Ch 1: 7 Elishah, and Tarshish, Kittim, and D. 1721

DODAVAH (1)

2Ch 20:37 Eliezer the son of D of Mareshah 1735

DODAVAHU See DODAVAH

DODO (5)

Jdg 10: 1 of Puah, the son of D, a man of Issachar; 1734
2Sa 23: 9 after him *was* Eleazar the son of D 1734
23:24 Elhanan the son of D *of* Beth-lehem, 1734
1Ch 11:12 after him *was* Eleazar the son of D, 1734
11:26 Elhanan the son of D of Beth-lehem, 1734

DOE See HIND

DOEG (6)

1Sa 21: 7 his name *was* D, an Edomite, the chiefest 1673
22: 9 answered D the Edomite, which *was* set 1673
22:18 the king said to D, Turn thou, and fall upon 1673
22:18 D the Edomite turned, and he fell upon 1673
22:22 *it* that day, when D the Edomite *was* there, 1673
Ps 52: T when D the Edomite came and told Saul, 1673

DOER (8) [DO]

Ge 39:22 they did there, he was the d *of it.* 6213
2Sa 3:39 the LORD shall reward the d of evil 6213
Ps 31:23 and plentifully rewardeth the proud d. 6213
Pr 17: 4 A wicked d giveth heed to false lips; *and* 7489
2Ti 2: 9 as an evil d, *even* unto bonds; 2557
Jas 1:23 if any be a hearer of the word, and not a d, 4163
1:25 but a d of the work, this *man* shall be 4163
4:11 thou art not a d of the law, but a judge. 4163

DOERS (6) [DO]

2Ki 22: 5 let them deliver it into the hand of the d of 6213
22: 5 let them give it to the d of the work which 6213
Job 8:20 perfect *man,* neither will he help the evil d: 7489
Ps 101: 8 that *I* may cut off all wicked d from the city 6466
Ro 2:13 but the d of the law shall be justified. 4163
Jas 1:22 But be ye d of the word, and not hearers 4163

DOEST (45) [DO]

Ge 4: 7 If thou d well, *shalt thou* not be accepted? NIH
4: 7 if thou d not well, sin lieth at the door. NIH
21:22 God *is* with thee in all that thou d: 6213
Ex 18:14 What *is* this thing that thou d to the people? 6213
18:17 unto him, The thing that thou d *is* not good. 6213
Dt 12:28 when thou d *that which is* good and right in 6213
14:29 in all the work of thine hand which thou d. 6213
15:18 thy God shall bless thee in all that thou d. 6213
Jdg 11:27 but thou d me wrong to war against me: 6213
2Sa 3:25 thy coming in, and to know all that thou d. 6213
1Ki 2: 3 that thou mayest prosper *in* all that thou d, 6213

1Ki 19: 9 said unto him, What **d** thou here, Elijah? 3807.1
19:13 and said, What **d** thou here, Elijah? 3807.1
20:22 and mark, and see what thou **d**: 6213
Job 9:12 who will say unto him, What **d** thou? 6213
35: 6 If thou sinnest, what **d** thou against him? or 6466
35: 6 be multiplied, what **d** thou unto him? 6213
Ps 49:18 praise thee, when thou **d well** to thyself. 3190
77:14 Thou *art* the God that **d** wonders: thou hast 6213
86:10 and **d** wondrous *things:* thou *art* God alone. 6213
119:68 Thou *art* good, and **d good**; teach me thy 2895
Ecc 8: 4 and who may say unto him, What **d** thou? 6213
Jer 11:15 when thou **d evil**, then thou rejoicest. 7451
15: 5 shall go aside to ask **how** thou **d**? 7965+3807.1
Eze 12: 9 said unto thee, What **d** thou? 6213
16:30 seeing thou **d** all these *things,* the work of 6213
24:19 what these *things are* to us, that thou **d** *so?* 6213
Da 4:35 his hand, or say unto him, What **d** thou? 5648
Jnh 4: 4 said the LORD, **D** thou well to be angry? NIH
4: 9 **D** thou well to be angry for the gourd? NIH
Mt 6: 2 Therefore when thou **d** *thine* alms, do not *4160*
6: 3 But when thou **d** alms, let not thy left hand *4160*
21:23 By what authority **d** thou these *things?* and *4160*
Mk 11:28 By what authority **d** thou these *things?* and *4160*
Lk 20: 2 by what authority **d** thou these *things?* or *4160*
Jn 2:18 unto us, seeing that thou **d** these *things?* *4160*
3: 2 no *man* can do these miracles that thou **d**, *4160*
7: 3 also may see the works that thou **d**. *4160*
13:27 Jesus unto him, That thou **d**, do quickly. *4160*
Ac 22:26 saying, Take heed what thou **d**: *4160*
Ro 2: 1 for thou that judgest **d** the same *things.* *4238*
2: 3 them which do such *things,* and **d** the same, *4160*
Jas 2:19 believest that there is one God; thou **d** well: *4160*
3Jn 1: 5 thou **d** faithfully whatsoever thou doest to *4160*
1: 5 thou doest faithfully whatsoever thou **d** to *2038*

DOETH (93) [DO]

Ge 31:12 for I have seen all that Laban **d** unto thee. 6213
Ex 31:14 for whosoever **d** *any* work therein, that soul 6213
31:15 whosoever **d** *any* work in the sabbath day, 6213
35: 2 whosoever **d** work therein shall be put to 6213
Lev 4:27 while he **d** somewhat against *any of* 6213
6: 3 in any of all *these* that a man **d**, sinning 6213
23:30 whatsoever soul *it be* that **d** any work in 6213
Nu 15:30 the soul that **d** *ought* presumptuously, 6213
24:23 said, Alas, who shall live when God **d** this! 7760
Job 5: 9 Which **d** great *things* and unsearchable; 6213
9:10 Which **d** great *things* past finding out; yea, 6213
23:13 and *what* his soul desireth, even *that* he **d**. 6213
24:21 beareth not: and **d** not **good** to the widow. 3190
37: 5 great *things* **d** he, which we cannot 6213
Ps 1: 3 and whatsoever he **d** shall prosper. 6213
14: 1 *there is* none that **d** good. 6213
14: 3 *there is* none that **d** good, no, not one. 6213
15: 3 with his tongue, nor **d** evil to his neighbour, 6213
15: 5 He that **d** these *things* shall never be 6213
53: 1 *there is* none that **d** good. 6213
53: 3 *there is* none that **d** good, no, not one. 6213
72:18 of Israel, who only **d** wondrous *things.* 6213
106: 3 *and* he that **d** righteousness at all times. 6213
118:15 the right hand of the LORD **d** valiantly. 6213
118:16 the right hand of the LORD **d** valiantly. 6213
136: 4 To him who alone **d** great wonders: for his 6213
Pr 6:32 he *that* **d** it destroyeth his own soul. 6213
11:17 The merciful man **d good** to his own soul: 1580
15: 7 but the heart of the foolish *d* not so. NIH
17:21 He that begetteth a fool *d it* to his sorrow: NIH
17:22 A merry heart **d good** *like* a medicine: but 3190
28:17 A man that **d violence** to the blood of *any* 6231
Ecc 2: 2 *It is* mad: and of mirth, What **d** it? 6213
3:14 I know that, whatsoever God **d**, it shall be 6213
3:14 God **d** *it,* that *men* should fear before him. 6213
7:20 upon earth, that **d** good, and sinneth not. 6213
8: 3 for he **d** whatsoever pleaseth him. 6213
Isa 56: 2 Blessed *is* the man *that* **d** this, and the son 6213
Jer 48:10 Cursed *be* he that **d** the work of the LORD 6213
Eze 17:15 shall he escape that **d** such *things?* or 6213
18:10 *that* **d** the like to *any* one of these *things,* 6213
18:11 that **d** not any of those *duties,* but even hath 6213
18:14 and considereth, and **d** not such like, 6213
18:24 **d** according to all the abominations that 6213
18:24 all the abominations that the wicked *man* **d**, 6213
18:27 **d** that which is lawful and right, he shall 6213
Da 4:35 he **d** according to his will in the army of 5648
9:14 *is* righteous in all his works which he **d**: 6213
Am 9:12 by my name, saith the LORD that **d** this. 6213
Mal 2:17 Every one that **d** evil *is* good in the sight of 6213
Mt 6: 3 thy left hand know what thy right hand **d**: *4160*
7:21 he that **d** the will of my Father which is in *4160*
7:24 and **d** them, I will liken him unto a wise *4160*
7:26 and **d** them not, shall be likened unto a *4160*
8: 9 and to my servant, Do this, and he **d** *it.* *4160*
Lk 6:47 to me, and heareth my sayings, and **d** them, *4160*
6:49 But he that heareth, and **d** not, is like a man *4160*
7: 8 and to my servant, Do this, and he **d** *it.* *4160*
Jn 3:20 For every one that **d** evil hateth the light, *4238*
3:21 But he that **d** truth cometh to the light, *4160*
5:19 for what *things* soever he **d**, these also *4160*
5:19 he doeth, these also **d** the Son likewise. *4160*
5:20 and sheweth him all *things* that himself **d**: *4160*
7: 4 For *there is* no *man that* **d** any *thing* in *4160*
7:51 before it hear him, and know what he **d**? *4160*
9:31 of God, and **d** his will, him he heareth. *4160*
11:47 What do we? for this man **d** many miracles. *4160*
14:10 Father that dwelleth in me, he **d** the works. *4160*
15:15 for the servant knoweth not what his lord **d**: *4160*
16: 2 killeth you will think that he **d** God service. *4374*
Ac 15:17 saith the Lord, who **d** all these *things.* *4160*
26:31 This man **d** nothing worthy of death or *4238*
Ro 2: 9 upon every soul of man that **d** evil, *2716*
3:12 there is none that **d** good, no, not one. *4160*
10: 5 That the man which **d** those *things* shall *4160*
13: 4 to *execute* wrath upon him that **d** evil. *4238*
1Co 6:18 Every sin that a man **d** is without the body; *4160*
7:37 heart that *he* will keep his virgin, **d** well. *4160*
7:38 then he that giveth *her* in marriage **d** well; *4160*
1Co 7:38 he that giveth *her* not in marriage **d** better. *4160*
Gal 3: 5 *d he it* by the works of the law, or by NIG
3:12 but, The man that **d** them shall live in them. *4160*
Eph 6: 8 that whatsoever good *thing* any man **d**, *4160*
Col 3:25 But he that **d wrong** shall receive *for* *91*
Jas 4:17 to do good, and **d** *it* not, to him it is sin. *4160*
1Jn 2:17 he that **d** the will of God abideth for ever. *4160*
2:29 ye know that every one which **d** *4160*
3: 7 he that **d** righteousness is righteous, even as *4160*
3:10 whosoever **d** not righteousness is not of *4160*
3Jn 1:10 I will remember his deeds which he **d**, *4160*
1:11 He that **d good** is of God: but he that doeth *15*
1:11 but he that **d evil** hath not seen God. *2554*
Rev 13:13 And he **d** great wonders, so that he maketh *4160*

DOG (15) [DOG'S, DOGS]

Ex 11: 7 of Israel shall not a **d** move his tongue, 3611
Dt 23:18 the hire of a whore, or the price of a **d**, 3611
Jdg 7: 5 as a **d** lappeth, him shalt thou set by 3611
1Sa 17:43 the Philistine said unto David, *Am* I a **d**, 3611
24:14 thou pursue? after a dead **d**, after a flea. 3611
2Sa 9: 8 thou shouldest look upon such a dead **d** 3611
16: 9 Why should this dead **d** curse my lord 3611
2Ki 8:13 Hazael said, But what, *is* thy servant a **d**, 3611
Ps 22:20 my darling from the power of the **d**. 3611
59: 6 they make a noise like a **d**, and go round 3611
59:14 *and* let them make a noise like a **d**, and 3611
Pr 26:11 As a **d** returneth to his vomit, *so* a fool 3611
26:17 *is like* one that taketh a **d** by the ears. 3611
Ecc 9: 4 for a living **d** *is* better than a dead lion. 3611
2Pe 2:22 The **d** *is* turned to his own vomit again; *2965*

DOG'S (2) [DOG]

2Sa 3: 8 of Ish-bosheth, and said, *Am* I a **d** head, 3611
Isa 66: 3 sacrificeth a lamb, *as if* he cut off a **d** neck; 3611

DOGS (24) [DOG]

Ex 22:31 *beasts* in the field; ye shall cast it to the **d**. 3611
1Ki 14:11 dieth of Jeroboam in the city shall the **d** eat; 3611
16: 4 dieth of Baasha in the city shall the **d** eat; 3611
21:19 In the place where **d** licked the blood of 3611
21:19 the blood of Naboth shall **d** lick thy blood, 3611
21:23 The **d** shall eat Jezebel by the wall of 3611
21:24 Him that dieth of Ahab in the city the **d** 3611
22:38 the **d** licked up his blood; and they washed 3611
2Ki 9:10 the **d** shall eat Jezebel in the portion of 3611
9:36 In the portion of Jezreel shall **d** eat the flesh 3611
Job 30: 1 to have set with the **d** of my flock. 3611
Ps 22:16 For **d** have compassed me: the assembly of 3611
68:23 *and* the tongue of thy **d** in the same. 3611
Isa 56:10 they *are* all dumb **d**, they cannot bark; 3611
56:11 *they are* greedy **d** *which* can never have 3611
Jer 15: 3 the **d** to tear, and the fowls of the heaven, 3611
Mt 7: 6 *Give* not that which is holy unto the **d**, *2965*
15:26 take the children's bread, and to cast *it* to **d**. *2952*
15:27 yet the **d** eat of the crumbs which fall from *2952*
Mk 7:27 children's bread, and to cast *it* unto the **d**. *2952*
7:28 yet the **d** under the table eat of *2952*
Lk 16:21 moreover the **d** came and licked his sores. *2965*
Php 3: 2 Beware of **d**, beware of evil workers, *2965*
Rev 22:15 For without *are* **d**, and sorcerers, and *2965*

DOING (39) [DO]

Ge 31:28 thou hast now done foolishly in *so* **d**. 6213
44: 5 he divineth? ye have done evil in *so* **d**. 6213
Ex 15:11 in holiness, fearful *in* praises, **d** wonders? 6213
Nu 20:19 without *d any* thing *else,* go through on my NIH
Dt 9:18 in **d** wickedly in the sight of the LORD, 6213
1Ki 7:40 So Hiram made an end of **d** all the work 6213
16:19 For his sins which he sinned in **d** evil in 6213
22:43 **d** *that* which *was* right in the eyes of 6213
2Ki 21:16 in **d** *that* which *was* evil in the sight of 6213
1Ch 22:16 Arise *therefore,* and be **d**, and the LORD 6213
2Ch 20:32 **d** *that* which *was* right in the sight of 6213
Ezr 9: 1 *d* according to their abominations, *even* of NIH
Ne 6: 3 I *am* **d** a great work, so that I cannot come 6213
Job 32:22 *so d* my Maker would soon take me away. NIH
Ps 64: 9 for they shall wisely consider of his **d**. 4639
66: 5 *he is* terrible *in his d* toward the children of 5949
118:23 This is the LORD'S **d**; it *is* 854+4480
Isa 56: 2 and keepeth his hand from **d** any evil. 6213
58:13 *from* **d** thy pleasure on my holy day; 6213
58:13 shalt honour him, not **d** thine own ways, 6213
Mt 21:42 this is the Lord's **d**, and it is marvellous in *1096*
24:46 his lord when he cometh shall find so **d**. *4160*
Mk 12:11 This was the Lord's **d**, and it is marvellous *1096*
Lk 12:43 his lord when he cometh shall find so **d**. *4160*
Ac 10:38 who went about **d good**, and healing all *2109*
24:20 *here* say, if they have found any **evil d** in me, *92*
Ro 2: 7 patient continuance in well **d** seek for glory *2041*
12:20 **d** thou shalt heap coals of fire on his head. *4160*
2Co 8:11 perform the **d** *of it;* that as *there was* a *4160*
Gal 6: 9 And let us not be weary in well **d**: for in *4160*
Eph 6: 6 of Christ, **d** the will of God from the heart; *4160*
6: 7 With good will **d service**, as to the Lord, *1398*
2Th 3:13 But ye, brethren, be not weary in **well d**. *2569*
1Ti 4:16 for in **d** this thou shalt both save thyself, *4160*
5:21 *one before another,* **d** nothing by partiality. *4160*
1Pe 2:15 that with **well d** *ye* may put to silence *15*
3:17 that *ye* suffer for **well d**, than for evil doing. *15*
3:17 *ye* suffer for well doing, than for **evil d**. *2554*
4:19 the keeping of their souls *to him* in **well d**, *16*

DOINGS (51) [DO]

Lev 18: 3 After the **d** of the land of Egypt, wherein ye 4639
18: 3 after the **d** of the land of Canaan, whither I 4639
Dt 28:20 because of the wickedness of thy **d**, 4611
Jdg 2:19 they ceased not from their own **d**, nor from 4611
1Sa 25: 3 the man *was* churlish and evil *in* his **d**; and 4611
2Ch 17: 4 and not after the **d** of Israel. 4639
Ps 9:11 in Zion: declare among the people his **d**. 5949
77:12 also of all thy work, and talk of thy **d**. 5949
Pr 20:11 Even a child is known by his **d**, whether his 4611
Isa 1:16 put away the evil of your **d** from before 4611
Isa 3: 8 and their **d** *are* against the LORD, 4611
3:10 *him:* for they shall eat the fruit of their **d**. 4611
12: 4 his name, declare his **d** among the people, 5949
Jer 4: 4 can quench *it,* because of the evil of your **d**. 4611
4:18 thy **d** have procured these *things* unto thee; 4611
7: 3 Amend your ways and your **d**, and I will 4611
7: 5 throughly amend your ways and your **d**; 4611
11:18 I know *it:* then thou shewedst me their **d**. 4611
17:10 *and* according to the fruit of his **d**. 4611
18:11 and make your ways and your **d** good. 4611
21:12 can quench *it,* because of the evil of your **d**. 4611
21:14 punish you according to the fruit of your **d**, 4611
23: 2 I will visit upon you the evil of your **d**, 4611
23:22 their evil way, and from the evil of their **d**. 4611
25: 5 from the evil of your **d**, and dwell in 4611
26: 3 do unto them because of the evil of their **d**. 4611
26:13 now amend your ways and your **d**, 4611
32:19 and according to the fruit of his **d**: 4611
35:15 amend your **d**, and go not after other gods 4611
44:22 because of the evil of your **d**, *and* because 4611
Eze 14:22 and ye shall see their way and their **d**: 5949
14:23 when ye see their ways and their **d**: 5949
20:43 all your **d**, wherein ye have been defiled; 5949
20:44 nor according to your corrupt **d**, O ye house 5949
21:24 so that in all your **d** your sins do appear; 5949
24:14 according to thy **d**, shall they judge thee, 5949
36:17 defiled it by their own way and by their **d**: 5949
36:19 and according to their **d** I judged them. 5949
36:31 your **d** that *were* not good, and shall lothe 4611
Hos 4: 9 for their ways, and reward them their **d**. 4611
5: 4 They will not frame their **d** to turn unto 4611
7: 2 now their own **d** have beset them about; 4611
9:15 for the wickedness of their **d** I will drive 4611
12: 2 according to his **d** will he recompense him. 4611
Mic 2: 7 *are* these his **d**? do not my words do good 4611
3: 4 they have behaved themselves ill in their **d**. 4611
7:13 that dwell therein, for the fruit of their **d**. 4611
Zep 3: 7 they rose early, *and* corrupted all their **d**. 5949
3:11 day shalt thou not be ashamed for all thy **d**, 5949
Zec 1: 4 from your evil ways, and *from* your evil **d**: 4611
1: 6 according to our **d**, so hath he dealt with us. 4611

DOLEFUL (2)

Isa 13:21 and their houses shall be full *of* **d creatures**; 255
Mic 2: 4 lament with a **d lamentation**, *and* say, 5093

DOMINION (62) [DOMINIONS]

Ge 1:26 and let them **have d** over the fish of the sea, 7287
1:28 **have d** over the fish of the sea, and over 7287
27:40 come to pass when thou shalt have the **d**, 7300
37: 8 or shalt thou **indeed have d** over us? 4910+4910
Nu 24:19 of Jacob shall come *he* that shall have **d**, 7287
Jdg 5:13 he **made** him that remaineth **have d over** 7287
5:13 the LORD **made** me **have d over** 7287
14: 4 for at that time the Philistines **had d** over 4910
1Ki 4:24 For he had **d** over all *the region* on *this* side 7287
9:19 and in Lebanon, and in all the land of his **d**. 4475
2Ki 20:13 was nothing in his house, nor in all his **d**, 4475
1Ch 4:22 who had the **d** in Moab, and Jashubi-lehem. 1166
18: 3 as he went to stablish his **d** by the river 3027
2Ch 8: 6 and throughout all the land of his **d**. 4475
21: 8 revolted from under the **d** of Judah, 3027
Ne 9:28 so that they had the **d** over them: 7287
9:37 also they **have d** over our bodies, and 4910
Job 25: 2 **D** and fear *are* with him, he maketh peace 4910
38:33 canst thou set the **d** thereof in the earth? 4896
Ps 8: 6 Thou **madest** him **to have d** over the works 4910
19:13 *sins;* let them not **have d** over me: 4910
49:14 the upright shall have **d** over them in 7287
72: 8 He shall have **d** also from sea to sea, and 7287
103:22 all his works in all places of his **d**: 4475
114: 2 Judah was his sanctuary, *and* Israel his **d**. 4475
119:133 and let not any iniquity **have d** over me. 7980
145:13 thy **d** *endureth* throughout all generations. 4475
Isa 26:13 *other* lords besides thee have **had d over** 1166
39: 2 was nothing in his house, nor in all his **d**, 4475
Jer 34: 1 the kingdoms of the earth of his **d**, 3027+4475
51:28 the rulers thereof, and all the land of his **d**. 4475
Da 4: 3 and his **d** *is* from generation to generation. 7985
4:22 and thy **d** to the end of the earth. 7985
4:34 whose **d** *is* an everlasting dominion, and 7985
4:34 whose dominion *is* an everlasting **d**, and 7985
6:26 That in every **d** of my kingdom *men* 7985
6:26 and his **d** *shall be even* unto the end. 7985
7: 6 had also four heads; and **d** *was* given to it. 7985
7:12 of the beasts, they had their **d** taken away: 7985
7:14 there *was* given him **d**, and glory, and 7985
7:14 his **d** *is* an everlasting dominion, 7985
7:14 his dominion *is* an everlasting **d**, 7985
7:26 they shall take away his **d**, to consume and 7985
7:27 the kingdom and **d**, and the greatness of 7985
11: 3 that shall rule *with* great **d**, and 4474
11: 4 nor according to his **d** which he ruled: 4915
11: 5 he shall be strong above him, and **have d**; 4910
11: 5 his **d** *shall be* a great dominion. 4475
11: 5 his dominion *shall be* a great **d**. 4474
Mic 4: 8 unto thee shall it come, even the first **d**; 4475
Zec 9:10 his **d** *shall be* from sea *even* to sea, and 4915
Mt 20:25 of the Gentiles **exercise d over** them, *2634*
Ro 6: 9 no more; death hath no more **d over** him. *2961*
6:14 For sin shall not have **d** over you: for ye are NIG
7: 1 how that the law **hath d over** a man, *2961*
2Co 1:24 Not for that we **have d over** your faith, but *2961*
Eph 1:21 and **d**, and every name that is named, *2963*
1Pe 4:11 to whom be praise and **d** for ever and ever. *2904*
5:11 To him *be* glory and **d** for ever and ever. *2904*
Jude 1: 8 despise **d**, and speak evil of dignities. *2963*
1:25 *be* glory and majesty, **d** and power, *2904*
Rev 1: 6 to him *be* glory and **d** for ever and ever. *2904*

DOMINIONS (2) [DOMINION]

Da 7:27 and all **d** shall serve and obey him. 7985
Col 1:16 or **d**, or principalities, or powers: *2963*

D

DONE (565) [DO]

Ge 3:13 the woman, What *is* this *that* thou hast **d**? 6213
3:14 Because thou hast **d** this, thou *art* cursed 6213
4:10 he said, What hast thou **d**? the voice of thy 6213
8:21 any more every *thing* living, as I have **d**. 6213
9:24 knew what his younger son had **d** unto him. 6213
12:18 said, What *is* this *that* thou hast **d** unto me? 6213
18:21 see whether they have **d** altogether 6213
20: 5 and innocency of my hands have I **d** this. 6213
20: 9 said unto him, What hast thou **d** unto us? 6213
20: 9 thou hast **d** deeds unto me that ought not to 6213
20: 9 done deeds unto me that ought not to be **d**. 6213
20:10 sawest thou, that thou hast **d** this thing? 6213
21:23 according to the kindness that I have **d** unto 6213
21:26 I wot not who hath **d** this thing: 6213
22:16 for because thou hast **d** this thing, and 6213
24:15 before he had **d** speaking, that behold, 3615
24:19 when she had **d** giving him drink, she said, 3615
24:19 thy camels also, until they have **d** drinking. 3615
24:22 came to pass, as the camels had **d** drinking, 3615
24:45 before I had **d** speaking in mine heart, 3615
24:66 servant told Isaac all things that he had **d**. 6213
26:10 What *is* this thou hast **d** unto us? 6213
26:29 as we have **d** unto thee nothing but good, 6213
27:19 I have **d** according as thou badest me: 6213
27:45 and he forget *that* which thou hast **d** to him: 6213
28:15 until I have **d** *that* which I have spoken to 6213
29:25 to Laban, What *is* this thou hast **d** unto me? 6213
29:26 It must not be so **d** in our country, 6213
30:26 knowest my service which I have **d** thee. 5647
31:26 And Laban said to Jacob, What hast thou **d**, 6213
31:28 thou hast now **d foolishly** in *so* doing. 5528
34: 7 which thing ought not to be **d**. 6213
40:15 here also have I **d** nothing that they should 6213
42:28 What *is* this *that* God hath **d** unto us? 6213
44: 5 he divineth? ye have **d evil** in *so* doing. 7489
44:15 What deed *is* this that ye have **d**? 6213
Ex 1:18 Why have ye **d** this thing, and have saved 6213
2: 4 afar off, to wit what would be **d** to him. 6213
3:16 and *seen* that which is **d** to you in Egypt: 6213
5:23 in thy name, he hath **d evil** to this people; 7489
10: 2 my signs which I have **d** amongst them; 7760
12:16 no *manner of* work shall be **d** in them, 6213
12:16 man must eat, that only may be **d** of you. 6213
13: 8 *This is* **d** because of that *which* the LORD NIH
14: 5 they said, Why have we **d** this, that we 6213
18: 1 heard of all that God had **d** for Moses, and 6213
18: 8 law all that the LORD had **d** unto Pharaoh 6213
18: 9 which the LORD had **d** to Israel, 6213
21:31 according to this judgment shall it be **d** 6213
31:15 Six days may work be **d**; but in the seventh 6213
34:10 such as have not been **d** in all the earth, 1254
34:33 *till* Moses had **d** speaking with them, he put 3615
35: 2 Six days shall work be **d**, but on 6213
39:43 they had **d** it as the LORD had 6213
39:43 had commanded, *even* so had they **d** it: 6213
Lev 4: 2 *things* which ought not to be **d**), 6213
4:13 they have **d** somewhat against any of 6213
4:13 *concerning things* which should not be **d**, 6213
4:22 **d** somewhat through ignorance against any 6213
4:22 *concerning things* which should not be **d**, 6213
4:27 *concerning things* which ought not to be **d**, 6213
5:16 the **harm** that he hath **d** in the holy *thing*, 2398
5:17 be **d** by the commandments of the LORD; 6213
6: 7 of all that he hath **d** in trespassing therein. 6213
8: 5 which the LORD commanded to be **d**. 6213
8:34 As he hath **d** this day, *so* the LORD hath 6213
11:32 vessel *it be*, wherein *any* work is **d**, 6213
18:27 abominations have the men of the land **d**, 6213
19:22 the LORD for his sin which he hath **d**: 2398
19:22 the sin which he hath **d** shall be forgiven 2398
23: 3 Six days shall work be **d**: but the seventh 6213
24:19 as he hath **d**, so shall it be done to him; 6213
24:19 as he hath done, so shall it be **d** to him; 6213
24:20 in a man, so shall it be **d** to him *again*. 5414
Nu 5: 7 shall confess their sin which they have **d**: 6213
5:27 have **d trespass** against her husband, 4603+4604
12:11 wherein we have **d foolishly**, and 2973
15:11 Thus shall it be **d** for one bullock, or 6213
15:34 it was not declared what should be **d** to 6213
16:28 for *I have* not **d** *them* of mine own mind. NIH
22: 2 saw all that Israel had **d** to the Amorites. 6213
22:28 said unto Balaam, What have I **d** unto thee, 6213
23:11 unto Balaam, What hast thou **d** unto me? 6213
27: 4 father be **d away** from among his family, 1639
32:13 that had **d** evil in the sight of the LORD, 6213
Dt 3:21 your God hath **d** unto these two kings: 6213
10:21 that hath **d** for thee these great and terrible 6213
12:31 he hateth, have they **d** unto their gods; 6213
19:19 as he had thought to have **d** unto his 6213
20:18 which they have **d** unto their gods; 6213
25: 9 So shall it be **d** unto *that* man that will not 6213
26:14 have **d** according to all that thou hast 6213
29:24 Wherefore hath the LORD **d** thus unto 6213
32:27 is high, and the LORD hath not **d** all this. 6466
Jos 5: 8 when they had **d** circumcising all 8552
7:19 tell me now what thou hast **d**; hide *it* not 6213
7:20 God of Israel, and thus and thus have I **d**: 6213
9: 3 heard what Joshua had **d** unto Jericho 6213
9:24 because of you, and have **d** this thing. 6213
10: 1 as he had **d** to Jericho and her king, so 6213
10: 1 her king, so he had **d** to Ai and her king; 6213
10:32 according to all that he had **d** to Libnah. 6213
10:35 according to all that he had **d** to Lachish. 6213
10:37 according to all that he had **d** to Eglon; 6213
10:39 as he had **d** to Hebron, so he did to Debir, 6213
10:39 as he had **d** also to Libnah, and to her king. 6213
22:24 if we have not *rather* **d** it for fear of *this* 6213
23: 3 your God hath **d** unto all these nations 6213
23: 8 your God, as ye have **d** unto this day. 6213
24: 7 your eyes have seen what I have **d** in 6213
24:20 after that he hath **d** you **good**. 3190
24:31 of the LORD, that he had **d** for Israel. 6213
Jdg 1: 7 as I have **d**, so God hath requited me. 6213
2: 2 not obeyed my voice: why have ye **d** this? 6213
2:10 nor yet the works which he had **d** for Israel. 6213
3:12 they had **d** evil in the sight of the LORD. 6213
6:29 said one to another, Who hath **d** this thing? 6213
6:29 Gideon the son of Joash hath **d** this thing. 6213
8: 2 What have I **d** now in comparison of you? 6213
9:16 if ye have **d** truly and sincerely, 6213
9:16 have **d** unto him according to the deserving 6213
9:24 That the cruelty **d** to the threescore and NIH
9:48 seen me do, make haste, *and* do as I *have* **d**. NIH
11:37 unto her father, Let this thing be **d** for me: 6213
14: 6 not his father or his mother what he had **d**. 6213
15: 6 the Philistines said, Who hath **d** this? 6213
15: 7 Though ye have **d** this, yet will I be 6213
15:10 come up, to do to him as he hath **d** to us. 6213
15:11 what *is* this *that* thou hast **d** unto us? 6213
15:11 As they did unto me, so have I **d** unto them. 6213
19:30 There was no such *deed* **d** nor seen from 1961
20:12 What wickedness *is* this that is **d** among 1961
Ru 2:11 all that thou hast **d** unto thy mother in law 6213
3: 3 until he shall have **d** eating and drinking. 3615
3:16 she told her all that the man had **d** to her. 6213
1Sa 4:16 And he said, What is there **d**, my son? 1961
6: 9 *then* he hath **d** us this great evil: 6213
8: 8 **d** since the day that I brought them up out 6213
11: 7 after Samuel, so shall it be **d** unto his oxen. 6213
12:17 which ye have **d** in the sight of the LORD, 6213
12:20 ye have **d** all this wickedness: yet turn not 6213
12:24 for consider how **great things** he hath **d** for 1431
13:11 Samuel said, What hast thou **d**? And Saul 6213
13:13 Samuel said to Saul, Thou hast **d foolishly**: 5528
14:43 said to Jonathan, Tell me what thou hast **d**. 6213
17:26 What shall be **d** to the man that killeth this 6213
17:27 So shall it be **d** to the man that killeth him. 6213
17:29 David said, What have I now **d**? *Is there* 6213
19:18 and told him all that Saul had **d** to him. 6213
20: 1 and said before Jonathan, What have I **d**? 6213
20:32 shall he be slain? what hath he **d**? 6213
20:34 because his father had **d** him **shame**. 3637
24:19 good for that thou hast **d** unto me this day. 6213
25:30 when the LORD shall have **d** to my lord 6213
26:16 This thing *is* not good that thou hast **d**. 6213
26:18 for what have I **d**? or what evil *is* in mine 6213
28: 9 Behold, thou knowest what Saul hath **d**, 6213
28:17 the LORD hath **d** to him, as he spake by 6213
28:18 hath the LORD **d** this thing unto thee this 6213
29: 8 David said unto Achish, But what have I **d**? 6213
31:11 of that which the Philistines had **d** to Saul, 6213
2Sa 2: 6 this kindness, because ye have **d** this thing. 6213
3:24 to the king, and said, What hast thou **d**? 6213
7:21 hast thou **d** all these great things, 6213
11:27 the thing that David had **d** displeased 6213
12: 5 the man that hath **d** this *thing* shall surely 6213
12:21 What thing *is* this that thou hast **d**? 6213
13:12 for no such thing ought to be **d** in Israel: 6213
14:20 speech hath thy servant Joab **d** this thing: 6213
14:21 unto Joab, Behold now, I have **d** this thing: 6213
15:24 until all the people had **d** passing out of 8552
16:10 then say, Wherefore hast thou **d** so? 6213
21:11 of Aiah, the concubine of Saul, had **d**. 6213
23:20 of Kabzeel, who had **d** many **acts**, 6467
24:10 I have sinned greatly *in* that I have **d**: 6213
24:10 of thy servant; for I have **d** very **foolishly**. 5528
24:17 Lo, I have sinned, and I have **d wickedly**: 5753
24:17 these sheep, what have they **d**? let thine 6213
1Ki 1: 6 at any time in saying, Why hast thou **d** so? 6213
1:27 Is this thing **d** by my lord the king, and 1961
3:12 Behold, I have **d** according to thy word: lo, 6213
8:47 We have sinned, and have **d perversely**, 5753
8:66 the LORD had **d** for David his servant, 6213
9: 8 Why hath the LORD **d** thus unto this land, 6213
11:11 Forasmuch as this is **d** of thee, and 1961
13:11 the man of God had **d** *that* day in Beth-el: 6213
14: 9 hast **d** evil above all that were before thee: 6213
14:22 above all that their fathers had **d**. 6213
15: 3 of his father, which he had **d** before him: 6213
18:36 *that* I have **d** all these things at thy word. 6213
19: 1 And Ahab told Jezebel all that Elijah had **d**, 6213
19:20 Go back again: for what have I **d** to thee? 6213
22:53 according unto all that his father had **d**. 6213
2Ki 4:13 with all this care; what *is* to be **d** for thee? 6213
4:14 he said, What then *is* to be **d** for her? 6213
5:13 wouldest thou not have **d** *it?* how much 6213
7:12 shew you what the Syrians have **d** to us. 6213
8: 4 all the great *things* that Elisha hath **d**. 6213
10:10 for the LORD hath **d** *that* which he spake 6213
10:30 Because thou hast **d well** in executing *that* 2895
10:30 hast **d** unto the house of Ahab according to 6213
15: 3 to all that his father Amaziah had **d**; 6213
15: 9 sight of the LORD, as his fathers had **d**: 6213
15:34 to all that his father Uzziah had **d**. 6213
17: 4 king of Assyria, as *he had* **d** year by year: NIH
19:11 the kings of Assyria have **d** to all lands, 6213
19:25 Hast thou not heard long ago *how* I have **d** 6213
20: 3 and have **d** *that* which *is* good in thy sight. 6213
21:11 Because Manasseh king of Judah hath **d** 6213
21:11 hath **d wickedly** above all that 7489
21:15 Because they have **d** *that* which *was* evil in 6213
23:17 proclaimed these things that thou hast **d** 6213
23:19 to all the acts that he had **d** in Beth-el. 6213
23:32 according to all that his fathers had **d**. 6213
23:37 according to all that his fathers had **d**. 6213
24: 9 according to all that his father had **d**. 6213
24:19 according to all that Jehoiakim had **d**. 6213
1Ch 10:11 heard all that the Philistines had **d** to Saul, 6213
11:22 man of Kabzeel, who had **d** many **acts**; 6467
16:12 his marvellous works that he hath **d**, 6213
17:19 own heart, hast thou **d** all this greatness, 6213
21: 8 sinned greatly, because I have **d** this thing: 6213
21: 8 of thy servant; for I have **d** very **foolishly**. 5528
21:17 that have sinned and **d evil indeed**; 7489+7489
21:17 *as for* these sheep, what have they **d**? 6213
2Ch 6:37 we have **d amiss**, and have dealt wickedly; 5753
7:21 Why hath the LORD **d** thus unto this land, 6213
11: 4 man to his house, for this thing is **d** of me. 1961
2Ch 16: 9 Herein thou hast **d foolishly**: therefore 5528
24:16 because he had **d** good in Israel, 6213
24:22 which Jehoiada his father had **d** to him, 6213
25:16 because thou hast **d** this, and hast not 6213
29: 2 according to all that David his father had **d**. 6213
29: 6 **d** *that* which *was* evil in the eyes of 6213
29:36 the people: for the thing was **d** suddenly. NIH
30: 5 for they had not **d** *it* of a long *time in such* 6213
32:13 my fathers have **d** unto all the people of 6213
32:25 again according to the benefit **d** unto him; NIH
32:31 inquire of the wonder that was **d** in the land, NIH
Ezr 6:12 have made a decree; let it be **d** with speed. 5648
7:21 shall require of you, *it* be **d** speedily, 5648
7:23 let it be diligently **d** for the house of 5648
9: 1 Now when these *things* were **d**, the princes 3615
10: 3 and let it be **d** according to the law. 6213
Ne 5:19 *according to* all that I have **d** for this 6213
6: 8 There are no such things **d** as thou sayest, NIH
6: 9 weakened from the work, that it be not **d**. 6213
8:17 that day had not the children of Israel **d** so. 6213
9:33 for thou hast **d** right, but we have done 6213
9:33 hast done right, but we have **d wickedly**: 7561
13:14 wipe not out my good deeds that I have **d** 6213
Est 1:16 Vashti the queen hath not **d wrong** to 5753
2: 1 what she had **d**, and what was decreed 6213
4: 1 When Mordecai perceived all that was **d**, 6213
6: 3 dignity hath been **d** to Mordecai for this? 6213
6: 3 unto him, There is nothing **d** for him. 6213
6: 6 What shall be **d** unto the man whom 6213
6: 9 Thus shall it be **d** to the man whom 6213
6:11 Thus shall it be **d** unto the man whom 6213
9:12 what have they **d** in the rest of the king's 6213
9:12 *is* thy request further? and it shall be **d**. 6213
9:14 the king commanded it so to be **d**: and 6213
Job 21:31 and who shall repay him *what* he hath **d**? 6213
34:29 whether *it be* **d** against a nation, or against a NIH
34:32 if I have **d** iniquity, I will do no more. 6466
Ps 7: 3 O LORD my God, if I have **d** this; if there 6213
14: 1 they have **d abominable** works, 8581
22:31 that *shall be* born, that he hath **d** *this*. 6213
33: 4 *is* right; and all his works *are* **d** in truth. NIH
33: 9 it was **d**; he commanded, and it stood fast. NIH
40: 5 *are* thy wonderful works *which* thou hast **d**, 6213
50:21 These *things* hast thou **d**, and I kept silence; 6213
51: 4 have I sinned, and **d** *this* evil in thy sight: 6213
52: 9 because thou hast **d** *it:* and I will wait on 6213
53: 1 are they, and have **d abominable** iniquity: 8581
66:16 I will declare what he hath **d** for my soul. 6213
71:19 very high, who hast **d** great *things:* O God, 6213
74: 3 *even* all *that* the enemy hath **d wickedly** in 7489
78: 4 and his wonderful works that he hath **d**. 6213
98: 1 for he hath **d** marvellous *things:* his right 6213
105: 5 his marvellous works that he hath **d**; 6213
106: 6 committed iniquity, we have **d wickedly**. 7561
106:21 which had **d** great *things* in Egypt; 6213
109:27 *is* thy hand; *that* thou, LORD, hast **d** it. 6213
111: 8 *and are* **d** in truth and uprightness. 6213
115: 3 he hath **d** whatsoever he pleased. 6213
119:121 I have **d** judgment and justice: leave me not 6213
119:166 thy salvation, and **d** thy commandments. 6213
120: 3 or what shall be **d** unto thee, thou false 3254
126: 2 The LORD hath **d** great things for them. 6213
126: 3 The LORD hath **d** great things for us; 6213
Pr 3:30 without cause, if he have **d** thee no harm. 1580
4:16 sleep not, except they have **d mischief**; 7489
24:29 I will do so to him as he hath **d** to me: 6213
30:20 and saith, I have **d** no wickedness. 6466
30:32 If thou hast **d foolishly** in lifting up thyself, 5034
31:29 Many daughters have **d** virtuously, but 6213
Ecc 1: 9 that which is **d** *is* that which shall be done: 6213
1: 9 that which is done *is* that which shall be **d**: 6213
1:13 all *things* that are **d** under heaven: 6213
1:14 I have seen all the works that are **d** under 6213
2:12 *even* that which hath been already **d**. 6213
4: 1 considered all the oppressions that *are* **d** 6213
4: 3 who hath not seen the evil work that is **d** 6213
8: 9 applied my heart unto every work that is **d** 6213
8:10 forgotten in the city where they had so **d**: 6213
8:14 There is a vanity which is **d** upon the earth; 6213
8:16 to see the business that is **d** upon the earth: 6213
8:17 find out the work that is **d** under the sun: 6213
9: 3 This *is* an evil among all *things* that are **d** 6213
9: 6 for ever in any *thing* that is **d** under the sun. 6213
Isa 5: 4 What could have been **d** more to my 6213
5: 4 to my vineyard, that I have not **d** in it? 6213
10:11 as I have **d** unto Samaria and her idols, so 6213
10:13 By the strength of my hand I have **d** *it*, and 6213
12: 5 the LORD; for he hath **d** excellent things: 6213
24:13 the gleaning grapes when the vintage is **d**. 3615
25: 1 thy name; for thou hast **d** wonderful things; 6213
33:13 Hear, ye *that are* far off, what I have **d**; and 6213
37:11 **d** to all lands by destroying them utterly; 6213
37:26 thou not heard long ago, *how* I have **d** it; 6213
38: 3 and have **d** *that* which *is* good in thy sight. 6213
38:15 himself hath **d** *it:* I shall go softly all my 6213
41: 4 **d** *it*, calling the generations from 6213
41:20 that the hand of the LORD hath **d** this, 6213
44:23 for the LORD hath **d** *it:* shout, ye lower 6213
46:10 ancient times *the things* that are not *yet* **d**, 6213
48: 5 Mine idol hath **d** them, and my graven 6213
53: 9 because he had **d** no violence, neither *was* 6213
Jer 2:23 way in the valley, know what thou hast **d**: 6213
3: 5 and **d** evil *things* as thou couldest. 6213
3: 6 seen *that* which backsliding Israel hath **d**? 6213
3: 7 I said after she had **d** all these *things*, Turn 6213
3:16 visit *it;* neither shall *that* be **d** any more. 6213
5:13 *is* not in them: thus shall it be **d** unto them. 6213
7:13 because ye have **d** all these works, 6213
7:14 and to your fathers, as I have **d** to Shiloh. 6213
7:30 For the children of Judah have **d** evil in my 6213
8: 6 of his wickedness, saying, What have I **d**? 6213
11:17 which they have **d** against themselves to 6213
16:12 ye have **d** worse than your fathers; 6213
18:13 virgin of Israel hath **d** a very horrible thing. 6213
22: 8 Wherefore hath the LORD **d** thus unto 6213

Jer 30:15 I have **d** these things unto thee. 6213
30:24 until he have **d** *it,* and until he have 6213
31:37 the seed of Israel for all that they have **d**, 6213
32:23 they have **d** nothing of all that thou 6213
32:30 the children of Judah have only **d** evil 6213
32:32 which they have **d** to provoke me to anger, 6213
34:15 now turned, and had **d** right in my sight, 6213
35:10 **d** according to all that Jonadab our father 6213
35:18 **d** according unto all that he hath 6213
38: 9 these men have **d evil** in all that they have 7489
38: 9 all that they have **d** to Jeremiah the prophet, 6213
40: 3 brought *it,* and **d** according as he hath said: 6213
41:11 that Ishmael the son of Nethaniah had **d**, 6213
42:10 for I repent me of the evil that I have **d** unto 6213
44:17 as we have **d**, we, and our fathers, 6213
48:19 and her that escapeth, *and* say, What is **d**? 1961
50:15 upon her; as she hath **d**, do unto her. 6213
50:29 according to all that she hath **d**, do unto 6213
51:12 **d** that which he spake against 6213
51:24 evil that they have **d** in Zion in your sight, 6213
51:35 The violence **d** to me and *to* my flesh *be* NIH
52: 2 according to all that Jehoiakim had **d**. 6213
La 1:12 like unto my sorrow, which is **d** unto me, 5953
1:21 they are glad that thou hast **d** *it:* thou wilt 6213
1:22 as thou hast **d** unto me for all my 5953
2:17 The LORD hath **d** *that* which he had 6213
2:20 and consider to whom thou hast **d** this. 5953
Eze 3:20 his righteousness which he hath **d** shall not 6213
5: 7 neither have **d** according to the judgments 6213
5: 9 I will do in thee that which I have not **d**, 6213
9: 4 that cry for all the abominations that be **d** in 6213
9:11 I have **d** as thou hast commanded me. 6213
11:12 have **d** after the manners of the heathen that 6213
12:11 like as I have **d**, so shall it be done unto 6213
12:11 as I have done, so shall it be **d** unto them: 6213
12:28 the word which I have spoken shall be **d**, 6213
14:23 ye shall know that I have not **d** without 6213
14:23 done without cause all that I have **d** in it, 6213
16:47 their ways, nor **d** after their abominations: 6213
16:48 Lord GOD, Sodom thy sister hath not **d**, 6213
16:48 as thou hast **d**, thou and thy daughters. 6213
16:51 in all thine abominations which thou hast **d**. 6213
16:54 be confounded in all that thou hast **d**, 6213
16:59 I will even deal with thee as thou hast **d**, 6213
16:63 pacified toward thee for all that thou hast **d**, 6213
17:18 hath **d** all these *things,* he shall not escape. 6213
17:24 I the LORD have spoken and have **d** *it.* 6213
18:13 he hath **d** all these abominations; he shall 6213
18:14 seeth all his father's sins which he hath **d**, 6213
18:19 When the son hath **d** that which is lawful 6213
18:19 and hath **d** them, he shall surely live. 6213
18:22 in his righteousness that he hath **d** he shall 6213
18:24 All his righteousness that he hath **d** shall 6213
18:26 for his iniquity that he hath **d** shall he die. 6213
23:38 Moreover this they have **d** unto me: 6213
23:39 thus have they **d** in the midst of mine 6213
24:22 ye shall do as I have **d**: ye shall not cover 6213
24:24 according to all that he hath **d** shall ye do: 6213
33:16 he hath **d** that which is lawful and right; 6213
39: 8 Behold, it is come, and it is **d**, saith 1961
39:24 according to their transgressions have I **d** 6213
43:11 if they be ashamed of all that they have **d**, 6213
44:14 and for all that shall be **d** therein. 6213
Da 6:22 also before thee, O king, have I **d** no hurt. 5648
9: 5 and have **d wickedly**, and have rebelled, 7561
9:12 for under the whole heaven hath not been **d** 6213
9:12 been done as hath been **d** upon Jerusalem. 6213
9:15 we have sinned, we have **d wickedly**. 7561
11:24 shall do *that* which his fathers have not **d**, 6213
11:36 for that that is determined shall be **d**. 6213
Hos 2: 5 she that conceived them hath **d shamefully**: 954
Joel 2:20 come up, because he hath **d** great things. 6213
Am 3: 6 in a city, and the LORD hath not **d** *it?* 6213
Ob 1:15 as thou hast **d**, it shall be done unto thee; 6213
1:15 as thou hast done, it shall be **d** unto thee; 6213
Jnh 1:10 said unto him, Why hast thou **d** this? 6213
1:14 O LORD, hast **d** as it pleased thee. 6213
Mic 6: 3 O my people, what have I **d** unto thee? and 6213
Zep 3: 4 they have **d violence** to the law. 2554
Zec 7: 3 as I have **d** these so many years? 6213
Mal 2:13 this have ye **d** again, covering the altar of 6213
Mt 1:22 Now all this was **d**, that it might be fulfilled *1096*
6:10 Thy will be **d** in earth, as *it is* in heaven. *1096*
7:22 and in thy name **d** many wonderful works? *4160*
8:13 as thou hast believed, *so* be it **d** unto thee. *1096*
11:20 wherein most of his mighty works were **d**, *1096*
11:21 for if the mighty works which were **d** in *1096*
11:21 had been **d** in Tyre and Sidon they would *1096*
11:23 mighty works, which have been **d** in thee, *1096*
11:23 been done in thee, had been **d** in Sodom, *1096*
13:28 He said unto them, An enemy hath **d** this. *4160*
17:12 but have **d** unto him whatsoever they listed. *4160*
18:19 it shall be **d** for them of my Father which is *1096*
18:31 when his fellowservants saw what was **d**, *1096*
18:31 came and told unto their lord all that was **d**. *1096*
21: 4 All this was **d**, that it might be fulfilled *1096*
21:21 ye shall not only do this which is **d** to NIG
21:21 and be thou cast into the sea; it shall be **d**. *1096*
23:23 these ought *ye* to have **d**, and not to leave *4160*
25:21 Well **d**, *thou* good and faithful servant: NIG
25:23 unto him, Well **d**, good and faithful servant; NIG
25:40 Inasmuch as ye have **d** *it* unto one of *4160*
25:45 of these my brethren, ye have **d** *it* unto me. *4160*
26:13 shall also *this,* that this *woman* hath **d**, *4160*
26:42 from me, except I drink it, thy will be **d**. *1096*
26:56 But all this was **d**, that the scriptures of *1096*
27:23 governor said, Why, what evil hath he **d**? *4160*
27:54 and *those things* that were **d**, they feared *1096*
28:11 the chief priests all the *things* that were **d**. *1096*
Mk 4:11 all *these things* are **d** in parables: *1096*
5:14 they went out to see what it was that was **d**. *1096*
5:19 tell them how great *things* the Lord hath **d** *4160*
5:20 how great *things* Jesus had **d** for him: *4160*
5:32 about to see her that had **d** this *thing.* *4160*
5:33 knowing what was **d** in her, came and *1096*
Mk 6:30 told him all *things,* both what they had **d**, *4160*
7:37 saying, He hath **d** all *things* well: *4160*
9:13 they have **d** unto him whatsoever they *4160*
13:30 shall not pass, till all these *things* be **d**. *1096*
14: 8 She hath **d** what she could: she is come *4160*
14: 9 *this* also that she hath **d** shall be spoken of *4160*
15: 8 *him to do* as he had ever **d** unto them. *4160*
15:14 said unto them, Why, what evil hath he **d**? *4160*
Lk 1:49 For he *that is* mighty hath **d** to me great *4160*
3:19 and for all the evils which Herod had **d**, *4160*
4:23 whatsoever we have heard **d** in Capernaum, *1096*
5: 6 And when they had this **d**, they inclosed a *4160*
8:34 When they that fed *them* saw what was **d**, *1096*
8:35 Then they went out to see what was **d**; and *1096*
8:39 shew how great *things* God hath **d** unto *4160*
8:39 city how great *things* Jesus had **d** unto him. *4160*
8:56 that they should tell no *man* what was **d**. *1096*
9: 7 the tetrarch heard of all that was **d** by him: *1096*
9:10 were returned, told him all that they had **d**. *4160*
10:13 for if the mighty works had been **d** in Tyre *1096*
10:13 and Sidon, which have been **d** in you, *1096*
11: 2 Thy will be **d**, as in heaven, so in earth. *1096*
11:42 these ought *ye* to have **d**, and not to leave *4160*
13:17 all the glorious *things* that were **d** by him. *1096*
14:22 it is **d** as thou hast commanded, and *1096*
16: 8 unjust steward, because he had **d** wisely: *4160*
17:10 when ye shall have **d** all those *things* which *4160*
17:10 we have **d** *that* which was our duty to do. *4160*
22:42 nevertheless not my will, but thine, be **d**. *1096*
23: 8 he hoped to have seen some miracle **d** by *1096*
23:15 lo, nothing worthy of death is **d** unto him. *4238*
23:22 the third time, Why, what evil hath he **d**? *4160*
23:31 in a green tree, what shall be **d** in the dry? *1096*
23:41 but this *man* hath **d** nothing amiss. *4238*
23:47 Now when the centurion saw what was **d**, *1096*
23:48 beholding the *things* which were **d**, *1096*
24:21 is the third day since these *things* were **d**. *1096*
24:35 And they told what *things were* **d** in NIG
Jn 1:28 These *things* were **d** in Bethabara beyond *1096*
5:16 he had **d** these *things* on the sabbath day. *4160*
5:29 they that have **d** good, unto the resurrection *4160*
5:29 and they that have **d** evil, unto *4238*
7:21 I have **d** one work, and ye all marvel. *4160*
7:31 miracles than these which this *man* hath **d**? *4160*
11:46 and told them what *things* Jesus had **d**. *4160*
12:16 and *that* they had **d** these *things* unto him. *4160*
12:18 for that they heard that he had **d** this *4160*
12:37 But though he had **d** so many miracles *4160*
13:12 unto them, Know ye what I have **d** to you? *4160*
13:15 that ye should do as I have **d** to you. *4160*
15: 7 ask what ye will, and it shall be **d** unto you. *1096*
15:24 If I had not **d** among them the works which *4160*
18:35 delivered thee unto me: what hast thou **d**? *4160*
19:36 For these *things* were **d**, that the scripture *1096*
Ac 2:43 and signs were **d** by the apostles. *1096*
4: 7 or by what name, have ye **d** this? *4160*
4: 9 of the good deed **d** to the impotent man, NIG
4:16 **d** by them *is* manifest to all them that dwell *1096*
4:21 all *men* glorified God for that which was **d**. *1096*
4:28 and thy counsel determined before to be **d**. *1096*
4:30 wonders may be **d** by the name of thy holy *1096*
5: 7 his wife, not knowing what was **d**, came in. *1096*
8:13 *the* miracles and signs *which were* **d**. *1096*
9:13 how much evil he hath **d** to thy saints at *4160*
10:16 This was **d** thrice: and the vessel was *1096*
10:33 and thou hast well **d** that thou art come. *4160*
11:10 And this was **d** three times: and all were *1096*
12: 9 wist not that it was true which was **d** by *1096*
13:12 when he saw what was **d**, believed, *1096*
14: 3 and wonders to be **d** by their hands. *1096*
14:11 And when the people saw what Paul had **d**, *4160*
14:13 and would have **d** sacrifice with the people. NIG
14:18 that *they* had not **d sacrifice** unto them. *2380*
14:27 they rehearsed all that God had **d** with *4160*
15: 4 they declared all *things* that God had **d** with *4160*
21:14 saying, The will of the Lord be **d**. *1096*
21:33 demanded who he was, and what he had **d**. *4160*
24: 2 that very worthy deeds are **d** unto this *1096*
25:10 to the Jews have I **d** no **wrong**, as thou very *91*
26:26 for this *thing* was not **d** in a corner. *4238*
28: 9 So when this was **d**, others also, which had *1096*
Ro 9:11 yet born, neither having **d** any good or evil, *4238*
1Co 5: 2 that he that hath **d** this deed might be taken *4160*
5: 3 *concerning* him that hath so **d** this *deed,* *2716*
9:15 these *things,* that it should be so **d** unto me: *1096*
13:10 then that which is in part shall be **d away**. *2673*
14:26 Let all *things* be **d** unto edifying. *1096*
14:40 Let all *things* be **d** decently and in order. *1096*
16:14 Let all your *things* be **d** with charity. *1096*
2Co 3: 7 which *glory* was to be **d away**: *2673*
3:11 For if that which is **d away** *was* glorious, *2673*
3:14 which *vail* is **d away** in Christ. *2673*
5:10 that every one may receive the *things* **d** in NIG
5:10 according to that he hath **d**, whether *it be* *4238*
7:12 *I did it* not for his cause that had **d** the **wrong**, *91*
Eph 5:12 those *things* which are **d** of them in secret. *1096*
6:13 in the evil day, and having **d** all, to stand. *2716*
Php 2: 3 *Let* nothing *be* **d** through strife or vainglory; NIG
4:14 Notwithstanding ye have well **d**, that ye did *4160*
Col 3:25 shall receive *for* the **wrong** which he hath **d**: *91*
4: 9 known unto you all *things* which *are* **d** here. NIG
Tit 3: 5 works of righteousness which we have **d**, *4160*
Heb 10:29 and hath **d despite unto** the Spirit of grace? *1796*
10:36 that, after ye have **d** the will of God, *4160*
Rev 16:17 of heaven, from the throne, saying, It is **d**. *1096*
21: 6 And he said unto me, It is **d**. I am Alpha *1096*
22: 6 *the things* which must shortly be **d**. *1096*

DONKEY; DONKEYS See ASS; ASS'S; ASSES

DOOR (189) [DOORKEEPER, DOORKEEPERS, DOORS]

Ge 4: 7 if thou doest not well, sin lieth at the **d**. 6607
6:16 the **d** of the ark shalt thou set in the side 6607
18: 1 he sat *in* the tent **d** in the heat of the day; 6607
Ge 18: 2 *them,* he ran to meet them from the tent **d**, 6607
18:10 Sarah heard *it in* the tent **d**, which *was* 6607
19: 6 Lot went out at the **d** unto them, and 6607
19: 6 door unto them, and shut the **d** after him, 1817
19: 9 *even* Lot, and came near to break the **d**. 1817
19:10 into the house to them, and shut to the **d**. 1817
19:11 they smote the men that *were at* the **d** of 6607
19:11 that they wearied themselves to find the **d**. 6607
43:19 they communed with him *at* the **d** of 6607
Ex 12: 7 and on the **upper d post** of the houses, 4947
12:22 and none of you shall go out at the **d** of his 6607
12:23 the LORD will pass over the **d**, and 6607
21: 6 he shall also bring him to the **d**, or unto 1817
21: 6 bring him to the door, or unto the **d post**; 4201
26:36 thou shalt make a hanging for the **d** of 6607
29: 4 his sons thou shalt bring unto the **d** of 6607
29:11 *by* the **d** of the tabernacle of 6607
29:32 *by* the **d** of the tabernacle of 6607
29:42 **d** of the tabernacle of the congregation 6607
33: 8 stood every man *at* his tent **d**, and 6607
33: 9 stood *at* the **d** of the tabernacle, and 6607
33:10 the cloudy pillar stand *at* the tabernacle **d**: 6607
33:10 and worshipped, every man *in* his tent **d**. 6607
35:15 the hanging for the **d** at the entering in of 6607
35:17 and the hanging for the **d** of the court, 8179
36:37 he made a hanging for the tabernacle **d** *of* 6607
38: 8 which assembled *at* the **d** of the tabernacle 6607
38:30 therewith he made the sockets to the **d** of 6607
39:38 and the hanging for the tabernacle **d**, 6607
40: 5 put the hanging of the **d** to the tabernacle. 6607
40: 6 **d** of the tabernacle of the tent of 6607
40:12 his sons unto the **d** of the tabernacle of 6607
40:28 he set up the hanging at the **d** of 6607
40:29 he put the altar of burnt offering *by* the **d** of 6607
Lev 1: 3 **d** of the tabernacle of the congregation 6607
1: 5 the **d** of the tabernacle of the congregation. 6607
3: 2 kill it *at* the **d** of the tabernacle of 6607
4: 4 he shall bring the bullock unto the **d** of 6607
4: 7 which *is at* the **d** of the tabernacle of 6607
4:18 which *is at* the **d** of the tabernacle of 6607
8: 3 the **d** of the tabernacle of the congregation. 6607
8: 4 the **d** of the tabernacle of the congregation. 6607
8:31 Boil the flesh *at* the **d** of the tabernacle of 6607
8:33 ye shall not go out of the **d** of 6607
8:35 Therefore shall ye abide *at* the **d** of 6607
10: 7 ye shall not go out from the **d** of 6607
12: 6 unto the **d** of the tabernacle of 6607
14:11 *at* the **d** of the tabernacle of 6607
14:23 unto the **d** of the tabernacle of 6607
14:38 the priest shall go out of the house to the **d** 6607
15:14 come before the LORD unto the **d** of 6607
15:29 to the **d** of the tabernacle of 6607
16: 7 present them before the LORD *at* the **d** of 6607
17: 4 bringeth it not unto the **d** of the tabernacle 6607
17: 5 unto the **d** of the tabernacle of 6607
17: 6 the **d** of the tabernacle of the congregation, 6607
17: 9 bringeth it not unto the **d** of the tabernacle 6607
19:21 unto the **d** of the tabernacle of 6607
Nu 3:25 the hanging for the **d** of the tabernacle of 6607
3:26 the curtain for the **d** of the court, which *is* 6607
4:25 the hanging for the **d** of the tabernacle 6607
4:26 the hanging for the **d** of the gate of 6607
6:10 to the **d** of the tabernacle of 6607
6:13 he shall be brought unto the **d** of 6607
6:18 the **d** of the tabernacle of the congregation, 6607
10: 3 the **d** of the tabernacle of the congregation. 6607
11:10 every man in the **d** of his tent: 6607
12: 5 stood *in* the **d** of the tabernacle, and 6607
16:18 stood *in* the **d** of the tabernacle of 6607
16:19 the **d** of the tabernacle of the congregation: 6607
16:27 stood *in* the **d** of their tents, and 6607
16:50 Aaron returned unto Moses unto the **d** of 6607
20: 6 the **d** of the tabernacle of the congregation, 6607
25: 6 who *were* weeping *before* the **d** of 6607
27: 2 *by* the **d** of the tabernacle of 6607
Dt 11:20 thou shalt write them upon the **d posts** of 4201
15:17 thrust *it* through his ear unto the **d**, and 1817
22:21 they shall bring out the damsel to the **d** of 6607
31:15 the pillar of the cloud stood over the **d** of 6607
Jos 19:51 *at* the **d** of the tabernacle of 6607
Jdg 4:20 Stand *in* the **d** of the tent, and it shall be, 6607
9:52 went hard unto the **d** of the tower to burn it 6607
19:22 *and* beat at the **d**, and spake to the master of 1817
19:26 fell down *at* the **d** of the man's house where 6607
19:27 *was* fallen down *at* the **d** of the house, 6607
1Sa 2:22 the **d** of the tabernacle of the congregation. 6607
2Sa 11: 9 Uriah slept *at* the **d** of the king's house with 6607
13:17 out from me, and bolt the **d** after her. 1817
13:18 brought her out, and bolted the **d** after her. 1817
1Ki 6: 8 The **d** for the middle chamber *was* in 6607
6:33 So also made he for the **d** of the temple 6607
6:34 the two leaves of the one **d** *were* folding, 1817
6:34 the two leaves of the other **d** *were* folding. 1817
14: 6 as she came in at the **d**, that he said, 6607
14:17 when she came to the threshold of the **d**, 1004
14:27 which kept the **d** of the king's house. 6607
2Ki 4: 4 thou shalt shut the **d** upon thee and 1817
4: 5 and shut the **d** upon her and upon her sons, 1817
4:15 when he had called her, she stood in the **d**. 6607
4:21 and shut *the* **d** upon him, and went out. NIH
4:33 shut the **d** upon them twain, and 1817
5: 9 and stood *at* the **d** of the house of Elisha. 6607
6:32 shut the **d**, and hold him fast at the door: 1817
6:32 shut the door, and hold him fast at the **d**: 1817
9: 3 Then open the **d**, and flee, and tarry not. 1817
9:10 *be* none to bury *her.* And he opened the **d**, 1817
12: 9 the priests that kept the **d** put therein all 5592
22: 4 which the keepers of the **d** have gathered of 5592
23: 4 the keepers of the **d**, to bring forth out of 5592
25:18 and the three keepers of the **d**: 5592
1Ch 9:21 the **d** of the tabernacle of the congregation. 6607
Ne 3:20 from the turning *of the wall* unto the **d** of 6607
3:21 from the **d** of the house of Eliashib even to 6607
Est 2:21 and Teresh, of those which kept the **d**, 5592
6: 2 king's chamberlains, the keepers of the **d**, 5592

Job 31: 9 or *if* I have laid wait at my neighbour's **d**; 6607
31:34 I kept silence, *and* went not out *of* the **d**? 6607
Ps 141: 3 before my mouth; keep the **d** of my lips. 1817
Pr 5: 8 and come not nigh the **d** of her house: 6607
9:14 For she sitteth at the **d** of her house, on a 6607
26:14 *As* the **d** turneth upon his hinges, so 1817
SS 5: 4 beloved put in his hand by the hole *of the* **d**, NIH
8: 9 if she *be* a **d**, we will inclose her with 1817
Isa 6: 4 the posts of the **d** moved at the voice of 5592
Jer 35: 4 the son of Shallum, the keeper of the **d**: 5592
52:24 and the three keepers of the **d**: 5592
Eze 8: 3 to the **d** of the inner gate that looketh 6607
8: 7 he brought me to the **d** of the court; and 6607
8: 8 when I had digged in the wall, behold a **d**. 6607
8:14 he brought me to the **d** of the gate of 6607
8:16 *at* the **d** of the temple of the LORD, 6607
10:19 *every one* stood *at* the **d** of the east gate of 6607
11: 1 behold at the **d** of the gate five and 6607
40:13 *was* five and twenty cubits, **d** against door. 6607
40:13 *was* five and twenty cubits, door against **d**. 6607
41: 2 the breadth of the **d** *was* ten cubits; and 6607
41: 2 the sides of the **d** *were* five cubits on 6607
41: 3 measured the post of the **d**, two cubits; 6607
41: 3 the **d**, six cubits; and the breadth of 6607
41: 3 and the breadth of the **d**, seven cubits. 6607
41:11 one **d** toward the north, and another door 6607
41:11 the north, and another **d** toward the south: 6607
41:16 The **d posts**, and the narrow windows, and 5592
41:16 on their three *stories*, over against the **d**, 5592
41:17 To *that* above the **d**, even unto the inner 6607
41:20 From the ground unto above the **d** *were* 6607
41:24 two *leaves* for the one **d**, and two leaves 1817
41:24 one door, and two leaves for the other *d*. NIH
42: 2 of an hundred cubits *was* the north **d**, 6607
42:12 the south *was* a **d** in the head of the way, 6607
46: 3 **d** of this gate before the LORD in 6607
47: 1 Afterward he brought me again unto the **d** 6607
Hos 2:15 and the valley of Achor for a **d** of hope: 6607
Am 9: 1 he said, Smite the **lintel of the d**, that 3730
Mt 6: 6 thy closet, and when thou hast shut thy **d**, 2374
25:10 him to the marriage: and the **d** was shut. 2374
27:60 he rolled a great stone to the **d** of 2374
28: 2 came and rolled back the stone from the **d**, 2374
Mk 1:33 all the city was gathered together at the **d**. 2374
2: 2 *them*, no, not so much as about the **d**: 2374
11: 4 found the colt tied by the **d** without in a 2374
15:46 rolled a stone unto the **d** of the sepulchre. 2374
16: 3 Who shall roll us away the stone from the **d** 2374
Lk 11: 7 the **d** is now shut, and my children are with 2374
13:25 and hath shut to the **d**, and ye begin to 2374
13:25 and to knock at the **d**, saying, Lord, Lord, 2374
Jn 10: 1 He that entereth not by the **d** into 2374
10: 2 But he that entereth in by the **d** is 2374
10: 7 I say unto you, I am the **d** of the sheep. 2374
10: 9 I am the **d**: by me if any *man* enter in, 2374
18:16 But Peter stood at the **d** without. Then went 2374
18:16 and spake unto her that **kept the d**, and 2377
18:17 Then saith the damsel that **kept the d** unto 2377
Ac 5: 9 which have buried thy husband *are* at the **d**, 2374
12: 6 *the* keepers before the **d** kept the prison. 2374
12:13 And as Peter knocked at the **d** of the gate, 2374
12:16 and when they had opened *the d*, and NIG
14:27 how he had opened *the* **d** of faith unto 2374
1Co 16: 9 For a great **d** and effectual is opened unto 2374
2Co 2:12 and a **d** was opened unto me of the Lord, 2374
Col 4: 3 that God would open unto us a **d** of 2374
Jas 5: 9 the judge standeth before the **d**. 2374
Rev 3: 8 I have set before thee an open **d**, and no 2374
3:20 Behold, I stand at the **d**, and knock: if any 2374
3:20 and open the **d**, I will come in to him, and 2374
4: 1 and behold, a **d** *was* opened in heaven: 2374

DOORKEEPER (1) [DOOR, KEEP]

Ps 84:10 I had rather be a **d** in the house of my God, 5605

DOORKEEPERS (2) [DOOR, KEEP]

1Ch 15:23 and Elkanah *were* **d** for the ark. 7778
15:24 Obed-edom and Jehiah *were* **d** for the ark. 7778

DOORS (71) [DOOR]

Jos 2:19 *that* whosoever shall go out of the **d** of thy 1817
Jdg 3:23 shut the **d** of the parlour upon him, and 1817
3:24 the **d** of the parlour *were* locked, they said, 1817
3:25 behold, he opened not the **d** of the parlour; 1817
11:31 that whatsoever cometh forth of the **d** of 1817
16: 3 took the **d** of the gate of the city, and 1817
19:27 opened the **d** of the house, and went out to 1817
1Sa 3:15 opened the **d** of the house of the LORD. 1817
21:13 scrabled on the **d** of the gate, and let his 1817
1Ki 6:31 for the entering of the oracle he made **d** of 1817
6:32 The two **d** also *were of* olive tree; and 1817
6:34 the two **d** *were* of fir tree: the two leaves of 1817
7: 5 all the **d** and posts *were* square, *with* 6607
7:50 *of* gold, *both* for the **d** of the inner house, 1817
7:50 most holy *place*, *and* for the **d** of the house, 1817
2Ki 18:16 *from* the **d** of the temple of the LORD, 1817
1Ch 22: 3 for the nails for the **d** of the gates, 1817
2Ch 3: 7 walls thereof, and the **d** thereof, with gold; 1817
4: 9 **d** for the court, and overlaid the doors of 1817
4: 9 and overlaid the **d** of them with brass. 1817
4:22 the inner **d** thereof for the most holy *place*, 1817
4:22 and the **d** of the house of the temple, 1817
23: 4 and of the Levites, *shall be* porters of the **d**; 5592
28:24 shut up the **d** of the house of the LORD, 1817
29: 3 opened the **d** of the house of the LORD, 1817
29: 7 Also they have shut up the **d** of the porch, 1817
34: 9 which the Levites that kept the **d** had 5592
Ne 3: 1 they sanctified it, and set up the **d** of it; 1817
3: 3 set up the **d** thereof, the locks thereof, and 1817
3: 6 set up the **d** thereof, and the locks thereof, 1817
3:13 they built it, and set up the **d** thereof, 1817
3:14 he built it, and set up the **d** thereof, 1817
3:15 and covered it, and set up the **d** thereof, 1817
6: 1 (though at that time I had not set up the **d** 1817
Ne 6:10 and let us shut the **d** of the temple: 1817
7: 1 I had set up the **d**, and the porters and 1817
7: 3 let them shut the **d**, and bar *them*: and 1817
Job 3:10 Because it shut not up the **d** of my *mother's* 1817
31:32 *but* I opened my **d** to the traveller. 1817
38: 8 Or *who* shut up the sea with **d**, when it 1817
38:10 for it my decreed *place*, and set bars and **d**, 1817
38:17 hast thou seen the **d** of the shadow of 8179
41:14 Who can open the **d** of his face? his teeth 1817
Ps 24: 7 be ye lift up, ye everlasting **d**; and the King 6607
24: 9 even lift *them* up, ye everlasting **d**; and 6607
78:23 from above, and opened the **d** of heaven, 1817
Pr 8: 3 entry of the city, *at* the coming in at the **d**. 6607
8:34 at my gates, waiting at the posts of my **d**. 6607
Ecc 12: 4 the **d** shall be shut in the streets, when 1817
Isa 26:20 thy chambers, and shut thy **d** about thee: 1817
57: 8 Behind the **d** also and the posts hast thou 1817
Eze 33:30 thee by the walls and in the **d** of the houses, 6607
41:11 the **d** of the side chambers *were* toward 6607
41:23 the temple and the sanctuary had two **d**. 1817
41:24 the **d** had two leaves *apiece*, two turning 1817
41:25 on the **d** of the temple, cherubims and 1817
42: 4 of one cubit; and their **d** toward the north. 6607
42:11 to their fashions, and according to their **d**. 6607
42:12 according to the **d** of the chambers that 6607
Mic 7: 5 keep the **d** of thy mouth from her that lieth 6607
Zec 11: 1 Open thy **d**, O Lebanon, that the fire may 1817
Mal 1:10 **d** *for nought?* neither do ye kindle *fire* on 1817
Mt 24:33 *things*, know that it is near, *even* at the **d**. 2374
Mk 13:29 to pass, know that it is nigh, *even* at the **d**. 2374
Jn 20:19 when the **d** were shut where the disciples 2374
20:26 *then* came Jesus, the **d** being shut, 2374
Ac 5:19 of the Lord by night opened the prison **d**, 2374
5:23 the keepers standing without before the **d**: 2374
16:26 and immediately all the **d** were opened, and 2374
16:27 and seeing the prison **d** open, he drew out 2374
21:30 the temple: and forthwith the **d** were shut. 2374

DOPHKAH (2)

Nu 33:12 the wilderness of Sin, and encamped in **D**. 1850
33:13 they departed from **D**, and encamped in 1850

DOR (7) [HAMMOTH-DOR]

Jos 11: 2 and in the borders of **D** on the west, 1756
12:23 The king of **D** in the coast of Dor, one; 1756
12:23 The king of Dor in the coast of **D**, one; 1756
17:11 the inhabitants of **D** and her towns, and 1756
Jdg 1:27 nor the inhabitants of **D** and her towns, 1756
1Ki 4:11 The son of Abinadab, *in* all the region of **D**; 1756
1Ch 7:29 Megiddo and her towns, **D** and her towns. 1756

DORCAS (2)

Ac 9:36 which by interpretation is called **D**: 1393
9:39 the coats and garments which **D** made, 1393

DOST (56) [DO]

Ge 32:29 Wherefore *is* it *that* thou **d** ask after my NIH
44: 4 when thou **d** overtake them, say unto them, NIH
Dt 9: 5 thine heart, **d** thou go to possess their land: NIH
24:10 When thou **d** lend thy brother any thing, NIH
24:11 the man to whom thou **d** lend shall bring out NIH
Jdg 14:16 said, Thou **d** but hate me, and lovest me not: NIH
1Sa 24:14 after whom **d** thou pursue? after a dead dog, NIH
28:16 Wherefore then **d** thou ask of me, NIH
1Ki 2:22 why **d** thou now ask Abishag the Shunammite NIH
21: 7 **D** thou now govern the kingdom of Israel? NIH
2Ki 18:20 Now on whom **d** thou trust, that thou NIH
2Ch 6:26 from their sin, when thou **d** afflict them; NIH
Ne 2: 4 unto me, For what **d** thou make request? NIH
Job 2: 9 unto him, **D** thou still retain thine integrity? NIH
7:21 why **d** thou not pardon my transgression, NIH
10: 8 round about; yet thou **d** destroy me. NIH
14: 3 **d** thou open thine eyes upon such a one, NIH
14:16 my steps: **d** thou not watch over my sin? NIH
15: 8 and **d** thou restrain wisdom to thyself? NIH
30:20 I cry unto thee, and thou **d** not hear me: NIH
33:13 Why **d** thou strive against him? for he NIH
37:15 **D** thou know when God disposed them, and NIH
37:16 **D** thou know the balancings of the clouds, NIH
Ps 39:11 When thou with rebukes **d** correct man for NIH
43: 2 why **d** thou cast me off? why go I mourning NIH
44:12 and **d** not increase *thy wealth* by their price. NIH
99: 4 thou **d** establish equity, thou executest NIH
Pr 4: 8 thee to honour, when thou **d** embrace her. NIH
Ecc 7:10 for thou **d** not inquire wisely concerning NIH
SS 5: 9 *another* beloved, that thou **d** so charge us? NIH
Isa 26: 7 most upright, **d** weigh the path of the just. NIH
36: 5 now on whom **d** thou trust, that thou NIH
Jer 32: 3 Wherefore **d** thou prophesy, and say, NIH
40:14 **D** thou certainly know that Baalis the king NIH
48:18 Thou daughter that **d** inhabit Dibon, NIH
La 5:20 Wherefore **d** thou forget us for ever, *and* NIH
Eze 2: 6 and thou **d** dwell among scorpions: NIH
32:19 Whom **d** thou pass in beauty? go down, and NIH
33: 8 if thou **d** not speak to warn the wicked from NIH
Mic 4: 9 Now why **d** thou cry out aloud? *is there* no NIH
Hab 1: 3 Why **d** thou shew me iniquity, and cause *me* NIH
Lk 10:40 **d** thou not care that my sister hath left me to NIG
23:40 rebuked him, saying, **D** not thou fear God, NIG
Jn 6:30 and believe thee? what **d** thou work? NIG
9:34 altogether born in sins, and **d** thou teach us? NIG
9:35 **D** thou believe on the Son of God? NIG
10:24 How long **d** thou make us to doubt? NIG
13: 6 saith unto him, Lord, **d** thou wash my feet? NIG
Ro 2:21 *a man* should not steal, **d** thou steal? NIG
2:22 commit adultery, **d** thou commit adultery? NIG
2:22 abhorrest idols, **d** thou commit sacrilege? NIG
2:27 and circumcision **d** transgress the law? NIG
14:10 But why **d** thou judge thy brother? or why NIG
14:10 or why **d** thou set at nought thy brother? NIG
1Co 4: 7 now if thou didst receive *it*, why **d** thou NIG
Rev 6:10 **d** thou not judge and avenge our blood on NIG

DOTE (1) [DOTED, DOTING]

Jer 50:36 A sword *is* upon the liars; and they shall **d**: 2973

DOTED (6) [DOTE]

Eze 23: 5 she **d** on her lovers, on the Assyrians *her* 5689
23: 7 of Assyria, and with all *on* whom she **d**: 5689
23: 9 hand of the Assyrians, upon whom she **d**. 5689
23:12 She **d** upon the Assyrians *her* neighbours, 5689
23:16 she **d** upon them, and sent messengers unto 5689
23:20 For she **d** upon their paramours, 5689

DOTH (210) [DO]

Ge 3: 5 For God **d** know that in the day ye eat NIH
27:42 as touching thee, **d** comfort himself, NIH
45: 3 I *am* Joseph; **d** my father yet live? NIH
Ex 11: 7 that ye may know how that the LORD **d** NIH
31:13 that I *am* the LORD that **d** sanctify you. NIH
32:11 why **d** thy wrath wax hot against thy people, NIH
Lev 11:31 whosoever **d** touch them, when they be NIH
11:32 they are dead, **d** fall, it shall be unclean; NIH
25:16 *of the years* of the fruits **d** he sell unto thee. NIH
Nu 5:21 when the LORD **d** make thy thigh to rot, NIH
16: 7 it shall be *that* the man whom the LORD **d** NIH
36: 6 This *is* the thing which the LORD **d** NIH
Dt 1:20 which the LORD our God **d** give unto us. NIH
1:25 land which the LORD our God **d** give us. NIH
1:31 as a man **d** bear his son, in all the way that NIH
5:24 we have seen this day that God **d** talk with NIH
8: 3 that he might make thee know that man **d** NIH
8: 3 out of the mouth of the LORD **d** man live. NIH
9: 4 LORD **d** drive them out from before thee. NIH
9: 5 thy God **d** drive them out from before thee, NIH
10:12 what **d** the LORD thy God require of thee, NIH
10:18 He **d** execute the judgment of the fatherless NIH
16:19 for a gift **d** blind the eyes of the wise, and NIH
18:12 these abominations the LORD thy God **d** NIH
20:16 which the LORD thy God **d** give thee *for* NIH
31: 6 thy God, he *it is* that **d** go with thee; NIH
31: 8 the LORD, he *it is* that **d** go before thee; NIH
Jos 1:18 Whosoever *he be* that **d** rebel against thy NIH
20: 4 when he that **d** flee unto one of those cities NIH
Jdg 4:20 when any man **d** come and inquire of thee, NIH
Ru 3:11 for all the city of my people **d** know that NIH
1Sa 9:13 he come, because he **d** bless the sacrifice; NIH
23:19 **D** not David hide himself with us in strong NIH
26: 1 **D** not David hide himself in the hill of NIH
26:18 Wherefore **d** my lord thus pursue after his NIH
26:20 as when *one* **d** hunt a partridge in NIH
2Sa 10: 3 Thinkest thou that David **d** honour thy NIH
14:13 for the king **d** speak this thing as one which NIH
14:13 in that the king **d** not fetch *home* again his NIH
14:14 up *again*; neither **d** God respect *any* person: NIH
14:14 yet **d** he devise means, that *his* banished be NIH
19: 8 Behold, the king **d** sit in the gate. NIH
19:20 For thy servant **d** know that I have sinned: NIH
24: 3 why **d** my lord the king delight in this NIH
24:24 my God of that which **d** cost me nothing. NIH
1Ki 1:11 that Adonijah the son of Haggith **d** reign, NIH
1:13 my throne? why then **d** Adonijah reign? NIH
22: 8 for he **d** not prophesy good concerning me, NIH
2Ki 2:15 The spirit of Elijah **d** rest on Elisha. NIH
5: 7 that this *man* **d** send unto me to recover a NIH
1Ch 19: 3 Thinkest thou that David **d** honour thy NIH
21: 3 **d** my lord require this *thing?* why will he be NIH
2Ch 6:33 as **d** thy people Israel, and may know that NIH
32:11 **D** not Hezekiah persuade you to give over NIH
Job 1: 9 and said, **D** Job fear God for nought? NIH
4:21 **D** not their excellency *which is* in them go NIH
5: 6 neither **d** trouble spring out of the ground; NIH
6: 5 **D** the wild ass bray when he hath grass? or NIH
6:25 but what **d** your arguing reprove? NIH
8: 3 **D** God pervert judgment? or doth NIH
8: 3 or **d** the Almighty pervert justice? NIH
12:11 **D** not the ear try words? and the mouth taste NIH
15:12 Why **d** thine heart carry thee away? and NIH
16:13 cleaveth my reins asunder, and **d** not spare; NIH
17: 2 *d not* mine eye continue in their NIH
22:13 thou sayest, How **d** God know? can he NIH
23: 9 where he **d** work, but I cannot behold *him*: NIH
24:19 *so* **d** the grave *those which* have sinned. NIH
25: 3 and upon whom **d** not his light arise? NIH
31: 4 **D** not he see my ways, and count all my NIH
35:16 Therefore **d** Job open his mouth in vain; NIH
36: 7 he **d** establish them for ever, and they are NIH
39:26 **D** the hawk fly by thy wisdom, *and* NIH
39:27 **D** the eagle mount up at thy command, and NIH
41:18 *By* his neesings a light **d** shine, and his eyes NIH
Ps 1: 2 and in his law **d** he meditate day and night. NIH
10: 2 The wicked in *his* pride **d** persecute NIH
10: 8 in the secret places **d** he murder NIH
10: 9 he **d** catch the poor, when he draweth him NIH
10:13 Wherefore **d** the wicked contemn God? NIH
11: 7 his countenance **d** behold the upright. NIH
29: 9 in his temple **d** every one speak of *his* glory. NIH
41:11 mine enemy **d** not triumph over me. NIH
54: T to Saul, **D** not David hide himself with us? NIH
59: 7 *are* in their lips: for who, *say they*, **d** hear? NIH
68:33 lo, he **d** send out his voice, *and that* a NIH
73:11 they say, How **d** God know? and is there NIH
74: 1 *why* **d** thine anger smoke against the sheep NIH
77: 8 for ever? **d** *his* promise fail for evermore? NIH
80:13 The boar out of the wood **d** waste it, and NIH
80:13 and the wild beast of the field **d** devour it. NIH
92: 6 neither **d** a fool understand this. NIH
119:129 therefore **d** my soul keep them. NIH
130: 5 my soul **d** wait, and in his word do I hope. NIH
147: 2 The LORD **d** build up Jerusalem: NIH
Pr 6:16 These six *things* **d** the LORD hate: yea, NIH
8: 1 **D** not wisdom cry? and understanding put NIH
14:10 a stranger **d** not intermeddle with his joy. NIH
22: 5 he that **d** keep his soul shall be far from NIH
24:12 **d** not he that pondereth the heart consider NIH
24:12 **d** *not* he know *it?* and shall *not* he render to NIH

Pr 25:23 **d** an angry countenance a backbiting NIH
26:14 his hinges, so **d** the slothful upon his bed. NIH
27: 9 **d** the sweetness of a man's friend by hearty NIH
27:24 **d** the crown *endure* to every generation? NIH
29: 6 a snare: but the righteous **d** sing and rejoice. NIH
30:11 their father, and **d** not bless their mother. NIH
31:11 The heart of her husband **d** *safely* trust in NIH
Ecc 10: 1 **d** a little folly *him that is* in reputation for NIH
SS 2: 6 my head, and his right hand **d** embrace me. NIH
Isa 1: 3 *but* Israel **d** not know, my people doth not NIH
1: 3 doth not know, my people **d** not consider. NIH
1:23 neither **d** the cause of the widow come unto NIH
3: 1 **d** take away from Jerusalem and from Judah NIH
3: 9 The shew of their countenance **d** witness NIH
10: 7 meaneth not so, neither **d** his heart think so; NIH
28:24 **D** the plowman plow all day to sow? NIH
28:24 **d** he open and break the clods of his NIH
28:25 **d** he not cast abroad the fitches, and NIH
28:26 For his God **d** instruct him to discretion, *and* NIH
28:26 instruct him to discretion, *and* **d** teach him. NIH
30:33 like a stream of brimstone, **d** kindle it. NIH
42:11 *voice,* the villages *that* Kedar **d** inhabit: NIH
44:14 he planteth an ash, and the rain **d** nourish *it.* NIH
49:18 and bind them *on thee,* as a bride **d**. NIH
52: 6 *know* in that day that I *am* he that **d** speak: NIH
59: 9 far from us, neither **d** justice overtake us: NIH
Jer 2:11 their glory for *that which* **d** not profit. NIH
5:19 Wherefore **d** the LORD our God all these 6213
10: 7 for to thee **d** it appertain: forasmuch as NIH
12: 1 Wherefore **d** the way of the wicked NIH
14:10 therefore the LORD **d** not accept them; NIH
15:10 on usury; *yet* every one of them **d** curse me. NIH
23:14 that none **d** return from his wickedness: NIH
30: 6 and see whether a man **d** travail with child? NIH
31:10 and keep him as a shepherd **d** his flock. NIH
49: 1 why *then* **d** their king inherit Gad, and NIH
51:43 neither **d** *any* son of man pass thereby. NIH
La 1: 1 How **d** the city sit solitary, *that was* full of NIH
3:33 For he **d** not afflict willingly nor grieve NIH
3:39 Wherefore **d** a living man complain, a man NIH
5: 8 *there is* none that **d** deliver *us* out of their NIH
Eze 3:20 When a righteous *man* **d** turn from his NIH
3:21 he **d** not sin, he shall surely live, because NIH
18:19 **d** not the son bear the iniquity of the father? NIH
20:49 they say of me, **D** he not speak parables? NIH
Hos 4:14 the people *that* **d** not understand shall fall. NIH
5: 5 the pride of Israel **d** testify to his face: NIH
Mic 6: 8 what **d** the LORD require of thee, but to NIH
Hab 1: 4 is slacked, and judgment **d** never go forth: NIH
1: 4 for the wicked **d** compass about NIH
Zep 3: 5 every morning **d** he bring his judgment to NIH
Mal 2:12 The LORD will cut off the man that **d** 6213
Mt 6:19 where moth and rust **d** corrupt, and NIG
6:20 where neither moth nor rust **d** corrupt, and NIG
12:24 This *fellow* **d** not cast out devils, but by NIG
17:24 and said, **D** not your master pay tribute? NIG
18:12 **d** he not leave the ninety and nine, and NIG
19: 9 whoso marrieth her *which is* put away **d** NIG
22:43 How then **d** David in spirit call him Lord, NIG
24:42 for ye know not what hour your Lord **d** NIG
26:46 behold, he is at hand that **d** betray me. NIG
Mk 2: 7 Why **d** this *man* thus speak blasphemies? NIG
2:22 else the new wine **d** burst the bottles, and NIG
8:12 Why **d** this generation seek after a sign? NIG
Lk 1:46 Mary said, My soul **d** magnify the Lord, NIG
6:43 neither **d** a corrupt tree bring forth good NIG
11:36 as when the bright shining of a candle **d** NIG
13:15 **d** not each one of you on the sabbath loose NIG
13:34 as a hen **d** *gather* her brood under *her* NIG
14:27 And whosoever **d** not bear his cross, and NIG
15: 4 **d** not leave the ninety and nine in NIG
15: 8 **d** not light a candle, and sweep the house, NIG
17: 9 **D** he thank that servant because he did NIG
22:26 and he that is chief, as he that **d** serve. NIG
Jn 2:10 Every man at the beginning **d** set forth good NIG
6:61 at it, he said unto them, **D** this offend you? NIG
7:51 **D** our law judge any man, before it hear NIG
9:19 was born blind? how then **d** he now see? NIG
10:17 Therefore **d** *my* Father love me, because NIG
Ac 4:10 *even* by him **d** this *man* stand here before NIG
8:36 *is* water; what **d** hinder me to be baptized? NIG
22: 5 As also the high priest **d** bear me witness, NIG
26:24 much learning **d** make thee mad. NIG
Ro 8:24 what a man seeth, why **d** he yet hope for? NIG
9:19 then unto me, Why **d** he yet find fault? NIG
14: 6 to the Lord he **d** not regard *it.* He that NIG
1Co 9: 9 out the corn. **D** God take care for oxen? NIG
11:14 **D** not even nature itself teach you, that, if a NIG
13: 5 **D** not behave itself unseemly, seeketh not NIG
15:50 neither **d** corruption inherit incorruption. NIG
2Co 1:10 us from so great a death, and **d** deliver: NIG
3: 9 much more **d** the ministration of NIG
Eph 5:13 for whatsoever **d** make manifest is light. NIG
Col 1: 6 and bringeth forth fruit, as *it* **d** also in you, NIG
1Th 2:11 every one of you, as a father **d** his children, NIG
2Th 2: 7 For the mystery of iniquity **d** already work: NIG
2Ti 2:17 And their word will eat as **d** a canker: NIG
Heb 1:11 and they all shall wax old as **d** a garment; NIG
12: 1 and the sin which **d** so easily beset *us,* and NIG
Jas 2:14 What **d** *it* profit, my brethren, though a man NIG
2:16 *are* needful to the body; what **d** *it* profit? NIG
3:11 **D** a fountain send forth at the same place *3385*
5: 6 *and* killed the just; *and* he **d** not resist you. NIG
1Pe 3:21 The like figure whereunto *even* baptism **d** NIG
5:13 *you,* saluteth you; and *so* **d** Marcus my son. NIG
1Jn 3: 2 and it **d** not yet appear what we shall be: NIG
3: 9 Whosoever is born of God **d** not commit NIG
3Jn 1:10 neither **d** he himself receive the brethren, NIG
Rev 19:11 and in righteousness he **d** judge and NIG

DOTHAN (3)

Ge 37:17 for I heard *them* say, Let us go to **D**. 1886
37:17 after his brethren, and found them in **D**. 1886
2Ki 6:13 it was told him, saying, Behold, *he is* in **D**. 1886

DOTING (1) [DOTE]

1Ti 6: 4 but **d** about questions and strifes of words, *3552*

DOUBLE (26) [DOUBLED, DOUBLETONGUED]

Ge 43:12 take **d** money in your hand; and the money 4932
43:15 they took **d** money in their hand, and 4932
Ex 22: 4 it be ox, or ass, or sheep; he shall restore **d**. 8147
22: 7 if the thief be found, let him pay **d**. 8147
22: 9 he shall pay **d** unto his neighbour. 8147
26: 9 shalt **d** the sixth curtain in the forefront of 3717
39: 9 they made the breastplate **d**: 3717
Dt 15:18 for he hath been worth a **d** hired servant *to* 4932
21:17 by giving him a **d** portion of all that he 8147
2Ki 2: 9 let a **d** portion of thy spirit be upon me. 8147
1Ch 12:33 *they were* not of **d heart**. 3820+3820+2050.1
Job 11: 6 of wisdom, that *they are* **d** to that which is. 3718
41:13 *or* who can come *to him* with his **d** bridle? 3718
Ps 12: 2 a **d heart** do they speak. 3820+3820+2050.1
Isa 40: 2 of the LORD'S hand **d** for all her sins. 3718
61: 7 For your shame *you shall have* **d**; and 4932
61: 7 in their land they shall possess the **d**: 4932
Jer 16:18 recompense their iniquity and their sin **d**; 4932
17:18 and destroy them *with* **d** destruction. 4932
Zec 9:12 even to day do I declare *that* I will render **d** 4932
1Ti 5:17 rule well be counted worthy of **d** honour, *1362*
Jas 1: 8 A **d minded** man *is* unstable in all his *1374*
4: 8 and purify *your* hearts, *ye* **d minded.** *1374*
Rev 18: 6 **d** unto her double according to her works: *1363*
18: 6 double unto her **d** according to her works: *1362*
18: 6 in the cup which she hath filled fill to her **d**. *1362*

DOUBLED (4) [DOUBLE]

Ge 41:32 for that the dream was **d** unto Pharaoh 8138
Ex 28:16 Foursquare it shall be *being* **d**; a span *shall* 3717
39: 9 and a span the breadth thereof, *being* **d**. 3717
Eze 21:14 let the sword be **d** the third time, the sword 3717

DOUBLE-EDGED See TWOEDGED

DOUBLETONGUED (1) [DOUBLE, TONGUE]

1Ti 3: 8 not **d**, not given to much wine, not greedy *1351*

DOUBT (13) [DOUBTED, DOUBTETH, DOUBTFUL, DOUBTING, DOUBTLESS, DOUBTS]

Ge 37:33 Joseph is **without d rent in pieces**. 2963+2963
Dt 28:66 thy life shall **hang in d** before thee; and 8511
Job 12: 2 **No d** but ye *are* the people, and 551
Mt 14:31 thou of little faith, wherefore didst thou **d**? *1365*
21:21 I say unto you, If ye have faith, and **d** not, *1252*
Mk 11:23 and shall not **d** in his heart, but *1252*
Lk 11:20 **no d** the kingdom of God is come upon you. *686*
Jn 10:24 long dost thou **make** us to **d**? *142+3588+5590*
Ac 2:12 and were in **d**, saying one to another, *1280*
28: 4 **No d** this man is a murderer, whom, *3843*
1Co 9:10 For our sakes, **no d**, *this* is written: that he *1063*
Gal 4:20 to change my voice; for I **stand in d** of you. *639*
1Jn 2:19 they would *no* **d** have continued with us: NIG

DOUBTED (4) [DOUBT]

Mt 28:17 saw him, they worshipped him: but some **d**. *1365*
Ac 5:24 they **d** of them whereunto this would grow. *1280*
10:17 Now while Peter **d** in himself what *this* *1280*
25:20 because I **d** of such *manner of* questions, *639*

DOUBTETH (1) [DOUBT]

Ro 14:23 And he that **d** is damned if he eat, because *1252*

DOUBTFUL (2) [DOUBT]

Lk 12:29 ye shall drink, neither be ye of **d mind.** *3349*
Ro 14: 1 faith receive you, *but* not to **d** disputations. *1261*

DOUBTING (4) [DOUBT]

Jn 13:22 looked one on another, **d** of whom he spake. *639*
Ac 10:20 *thee* down, and go with them, **d** nothing: *1252*
11:12 the Spirit bade me go with them, nothing **d**. *1252*
1Ti 2: 8 lifting up holy hands, without wrath and **d**. *1261*

DOUBTLESS (7) [DOUBT]

Nu 14:30 **D** ye shall **not** come into the land, 518
2Sa 5:19 for I will **d deliver** the Philistines 5414+5414
Ps 126: 6 shall **d come again** with rejoicing, 935+935
Isa 63:16 **D** thou *art* our father, though Abraham be 3588
1Co 9: 2 apostle unto others, **yet d** I am to you: *235+1065*
2Co 12: 1 It is not expedient for me **d** to glory. I will *1211*
Php 3: 8 Yea **d**, and I count all *things but* loss for *3304*

DOUBTS (2) [DOUBT]

Da 5:12 of hard sentences, and dissolving of **d**, 7001
5:16 canst make interpretations, and dissolve **d**: 7001

DOUGH (8)

Ex 12:34 the people took their **d** before it was 1217
12:39 they baked unleavened cakes of the **d** 1217
Nu 15:20 *of* the first of your **d** *for* a heave offering: 6182
15:21 Of the first of your **d** ye shall give unto 6182
Ne 10:37 *that* we should bring the firstfruits of our **d**, 6182
Jer 7:18 the fire, and the women knead *their* **d**, 1217
Eze 44:30 also give unto the priest the first of your **d**, 6182
Hos 7: 4 from raising after *he* hath kneaded the **d**, 1217

DOVE (18) [DOVE'S, DOVES, DOVES']

Ge 8: 8 Also he sent forth a **d** from him, to see if 3123
8: 9 the **d** found no rest for the sole of her foot, 3123
8:10 and again he sent forth the **d** out of the ark; 3123
8:11 the **d** came in to him in the evening; and 3123
8:12 yet other seven days; and sent forth the **d**; 3123
Ps 55: 6 O that I had wings like a **d**, *for then* 3123
68:13 *yet shall ye be as* the wings of a **d** covered 3123
SS 2:14 O my **d**, *that art* in the clefts of the rock, 3123
5: 2 my sister, my love, my **d**, my undefiled: 3123
6: 9 My **d**, my undefiled *is but* one; she *is* 3123
Isa 38:14 I did mourn as a **d**: mine eyes fail *with* 3123
Jer 48:28 be like the **d** *that* maketh her nest in 3123
Hos 7:11 Ephraim also is like a silly **d**, without heart: 3123
11:11 and as a **d** out of the land of Assyria: 3123
Mt 3:16 saw the Spirit of God descending like a **d**, *4058*
Mk 1:10 the Spirit like a **d** descending upon him: *4058*
Lk 3:22 in a bodily shape like a **d** upon him, *4058*
Jn 1:32 the Spirit descending from heaven like a **d**, *4058*

DOVE'S (1) [DOVE]

2Ki 6:25 the fourth part of a kab of **d dung** for five 1686

DOVES (10) [DOVE]

SS 5:12 His eyes *are* as *the eyes of* **d** by the rivers 3123
Isa 59:11 roar all like bears, and mourn sore like **d**: 3123
60: 8 as a cloud, and as the **d** to their windows? 3123
Eze 7:16 shall be on the mountains like **d** of 3123
Na 2: 7 maids *shall* lead *her* as *with* the voice of **d**, 3123
Mt 10:16 wise as serpents, and harmless as **d.** *4058*
21:12 and the seats of them that sold **d**, *4058*
Mk 11:15 and the seats of them that sold **d**; *4058*
Jn 2:14 those that sold oxen and sheep and **d**, *4058*
2:16 And said unto them that sold **d**, Take these *4058*

DOVES' (2) [DOVE]

SS 1:15 behold, thou *art* fair; thou *hast* **d** eyes. 3123
4: 1 *art* fair; thou *hast* **d** eyes within thy locks: 3123

DOWN (1125) [DOWNSITTING, DOWNWARD]

Ge 11: 5 the LORD **came d** to see the city and 3381
11: 7 let us **go d**, and there confound their 3381
12:10 Abram **went d** into Egypt to sojourn there; 3381
15:11 when the fowls **came d** upon the carcases, 3381
15:12 when the sun was **going d**, a deep sleep fell 935
15:17 that, when the sun **went d**, and it was dark, 935
18:21 I will **go d** now, and see whether they have 3381
19: 4 before they **lay d**, the men of the city, 7901
19:33 he perceived not when she **lay d**, nor when 7901
19:35 he perceived not when she **lay d**, nor when 7901
21:16 **sat** her **d** over against *him* a good way off, 3427
23:12 Abraham **bowed d** himself before 7812
24:11 he **made** *his* camels **to kneel d** without 1288
24:14 **Let d** thy pitcher, I pray thee, that I may 5186
24:16 she **went d** to the well, and filled her 3381
24:18 **let d** her pitcher upon her hand, and 3381
24:26 the man **bowed d** his **head**, and 6915
24:45 she **went d** unto the well, and drew *water:* 3381
24:46 **let d** her pitcher from her *shoulder,* and 3381
24:48 I **bowed d** my **head**, and worshipped 6915
26: 2 unto him, and said, **Go** not **d** into Egypt; 3381
27:29 serve thee, and nations **bow d** to thee: 7812
27:29 and let thy mother's sons **bow d** to thee: 7812
28:11 his pillows, and **lay d** in that place **to sleep.** 7901
37:10 thy brethren indeed come to **bow d** 7812
37:25 they **sat d** to eat bread: and they lift up 3427
37:25 and myrrh, going to **carry** *it* **d** to Egypt. 3381
37:35 For I will **go d** into the grave unto my son 3381
38: 1 that Judah **went d** from his brethren, and 3381
39: 1 Joseph was **brought d** to Egypt; and 3381
39: 1 which had **brought** him **d** thither. 3381
42: 2 **get** you **d** thither, and buy for us from 3381
42: 3 Joseph's ten brethren **went d** to buy corn in 3381
42: 6 **bowed d** themselves before him *with* their 7812
42:38 he said, My son shall not **go d** with you; 3381
42:38 shall ye **bring d** my gray hairs with sorrow 3381
43: 4 with us, we will **go d** and buy thee food: 3381
43: 5 if thou wilt not send *him,* we will not **go d**: 3381
43: 7 that he would say, **Bring** your brother **d**? 3381
43:11 **carry d** the man a present, a little balm, 3381
43:15 **went d** *to* Egypt, and stood before Joseph. 3381
43:20 we **came indeed d** at the first time to 3381+3381
43:22 other money have we **brought d** in our 3381
43:28 they **bowed d** their **heads**, and 6915
44:11 they speedily **took d** every man his sack to 3381
44:21 unto thy servants, **Bring** him **d** unto me, 3381
44:23 Except your youngest brother **come d** with 3381
44:26 we said, We cannot **go d**: if our youngest 3381
44:26 brother be with us, then will we **go d**: 3381
44:29 ye shall **bring d** my gray hairs with sorrow 3381
44:31 thy servants shall **bring d** the gray hairs of 3381
45: 9 of all Egypt: **come d** unto me, tarry not: 3381
45:13 ye shall haste and **bring d** my father hither. 3381
46: 3 fear not to **go d** into Egypt; for I will there 3381
46: 4 I will **go d** with thee into Egypt; and I will 3381
49: 6 and in their selfwill they **digged d** a wall. 6131
49: 8 thy father's children shall **bow d** before 7812
49: 9 he **stooped d**, he couched as a lion, and 3766
49:14 Issachar *is* a strong ass **couching d** between 7257
50:18 also went and **fell d** before his face; 5307
Ex 2: 5 the daughter of Pharaoh **came d** to wash 3381
2:15 the land of Midian: and he **sat d** by a well. 3427
3: 8 I am **come d** to deliver them out of 3381
7:10 Aaron **cast d** his rod before Pharaoh, and 7993
7:12 For they **cast d** every man his rod, and 7993
9:19 the hail shall **come d** upon them, and 3381
11: 8 all these thy servants shall **come d** unto me, 3381
11: 8 **bow d** themselves unto me, saying, 7812
17:11 when he **let d** his hand, Amalek prevailed. 5117
17:12 his hands were steady until the **going d** of 935
19:11 for the third day the LORD will **come d** in 3381
19:14 Moses **went d** from the mount unto 3381
19:20 And the LORD **came d** upon mount Sinai, 3381
19:21 said unto Moses, **Go d**, charge the people, 3381
19:24 **get** thee **d**, and thou shalt come up, thou, 3381
19:25 So Moses **went d** unto the people, and 3381
20: 5 Thou shalt not **bow d** thyself to them, 7812
22:26 deliver it unto him by that the sun **goeth d**: 935
23:24 Thou shalt not **bow d** to their gods, 7812
23:24 and **quite break d** their images. 7665+7665
32: 1 Moses delayed to **come d** out of the mount, 3381
32: 6 and the people **sat d** to eat and to drink, and 3427
32: 7 LORD said unto Moses, Go, **get** thee **d**; 3381
32:15 **went d** from the mount, and the two tables 3381
34:13 break their images, and **cut d** their groves: 3772
34:29 when Moses **came d** from mount Sinai 3381

Ex 34:29 when he **came d** from the mount, 3381
Lev 9:22 **came d** from offering of the sin offering, 3381
11:35 or ranges for pots, they shall be **broken d**: 5422
14:45 he shall **break d** the house, the stones of it, 5422
18:23 woman stand before a beast to **lie d** thereto: 7250
19:16 Thou shalt not **go up and d** *as* a talebearer 1980
20:16 **lie d** thereto, thou shalt kill the woman and 7250
22: 7 And when the sun is **d**, he shall be clean, and 935
26: 1 of stone in your land, to **bow d** unto it: 7812
26: 6 ye shall **lie d**, and none shall make *you* 7901
26:30 **cut d** your images, and cast your carcases 3772
Nu 1:51 setteth forward, the Levites shall **take** it **d**: 3381
4: 5 they shall **take d** the covering vail, and 3381
10:17 the tabernacle was **taken d**; and the sons of 3381
11:17 I will **come d** and talk with thee there: and 3381
11:25 the LORD **came d** in a cloud, and 3381
12: 5 the LORD **came d** in the pillar of 3381
13:23 **cut d** from thence a branch with one cluster 3772
13:24 the children of Israel **cut d** from thence. 3772
14:45 the Amalekites **came d**, and the Canaanites 3381
16:30 unto them, and they **go d** quick into the pit; 3381
16:33 **went d** alive into the pit, and the earth 3381
20:15 How our fathers **went d** into Egypt, and 3381
20:28 Moses and Eleazar **came d** from the mount. 3381
21:15 *at* the stream of the brooks that **goeth d** to 5186
22:27 of the LORD, she **fell d** under Balaam: 7257
22:31 he **bowed d** his **head**, and fell flat on his 6915
23:24 he shall not **lie d** until he eat *of* the prey, 7901
24: 9 he **lay d** as a lion, and as a great lion: 7901
25: 2 people did eat, and **bowed d** to their gods. 7812
33:52 and **quite pluck d** all their high places: 8045
34:11 the coast shall **go d** from Shepham *to* 3381
34:12 the border shall **go d** to Jordan, and 3381
Dt 1:25 **brought** *it* **d** unto us, and brought us word 3381
5: 9 Thou shalt not **bow d** thyself unto them, 7812
6: 7 when thou **liest d**, and when thou risest up. 7901
7: 5 **break d** their images, and cut down their 7665
7: 5 **cut d** their groves, and burn their graven 1438
9: 3 and he shall **bring** them **d** before thy face: 3665
9:12 Arise, **get** thee **d** quickly from hence; 3381
9:15 So I turned and **came d** from the mount, 3381
9:18 I **fell d** before the LORD, as at the first, 5307
9:25 Thus I **fell d** before the LORD forty days 5307
9:25 as I **fell d** *at the first;* because the LORD 5307
10: 5 turned myself and **came d** from the mount, 3381
10:22 Thy fathers **went d** into Egypt with 3381
11:19 when thou **liest d**, and when thou risest up. 7901
11:30 by the way where the sun **goeth d**, in 3996
12: 3 you shall **hew d** the graven images of their 1438
16: 6 at the **going d** of the sun, *at* the season that 935
19: 5 a stroke with the axe to **cut d** the tree, 3772
20:19 thou shalt not **cut** them **d** (for the tree of 3772
20:20 for meat, thou shalt destroy and **cut** them **d**; 3772
21: 4 the elders of that city shall **bring d** 3381
22: 4 brother's ass or his ox **fall d** by the way, 5307
23:11 when the sun is **d**, he shall come into 935
24:13 him the pledge again when the sun **goeth d**, 935
24:15 his hire, neither shall the sun **go d** upon it; 935
24:19 When thou **cuttest d** thine **harvest** in 7105+7114
25: 2 that the judge shall **cause** him **to lie d**, and 5307
26: 4 **set** it **d** before the altar of the LORD thy 3240
26: 5 he **went d** into Egypt, and sojourned there 3381
26:15 **Look d** from thy holy habitation, 8259
28:24 from heaven shall it **come d** upon thee, 3381
28:43 very high; and thou shalt **come d** very low. 3381
28:52 until thy high and fenced walls **come d**, 3381
33: 3 they **sat d** at thy feet; *every one* shall 8497
33:28 wine; also his heavens shall **drop d** dew. 6201
Jos 1: 4 unto the great sea *toward* the **going d** of 3996
2: 8 before they were **laid d**, she came up unto 7901
2:15 she **let** them **d** by a cord through 3381
2:18 in the window which thou didst **let** us **d** by: 3381
3:13 *from* the waters that **come d** from above; 3381
3:16 That the waters which **came d** from above 3381
3:16 those that **came d** toward the sea of 3381
4: 8 where they lodged, and **laid** them **d** there. 3240
6: 5 the wall of the city shall **fall d** flat, and 5307
6:20 that the wall **fell d** flat, so that the people 5307
7: 5 and smote them in the **going d**: 4174
8:29 as soon as the sun was **d**, 935
8:29 should **take** his carcase **d** from the tree, 3381
10:11 *and* were in the **going d** to Beth-horon, 4174
10:11 that the LORD **cast d** great stones from 7993
10:13 and hasted not to **go d** about a whole day. 935
10:27 it came to pass at the time of the **going d** of 935
10:27 they **took** them **d** off the trees, and 3381
15:10 **went d** *to* Beth-shemesh, and passed on *to* 3381
16: 3 **goeth d** westward to the coast of Japhleti, 3381
16: 7 it **went d** from Janohah *to* Ataroth, and 3381
17:15 **cut d** for thyself there in the land of 1254
17:18 for it *is* a wood, and thou shalt **cut** it **d**: 1254
18:16 the border **came d** to the end of 3381
18:18 and **went d** unto Arabah: 3381
24: 4 Jacob and his children **went d** *into* Egypt. 3381
Jdg 1: 9 afterward the children of Judah **went d** to 3381
1:34 for they would not suffer them to **come d** to 3381
2: 2 of this land; you shall **throw d** their altars: 5422
2:19 to serve them, and to **bow d** unto them; 7812
3:25 their lord *was* **fallen d** dead on the earth. 5307
3:27 the children of Israel **went d** with him from 3381
3:28 they **went d** after him, and took the fords of 3381
4:14 So Barak **went d** from mount Tabor, and 3381
4:15 so that Sisera **lighted d** off *his* chariot, and 3381
5:11 shall the people of the LORD **go d** to 3381
5:14 out of Machir **came d** governors, and out of 3381
5:21 O my soul, thou hast **trodden d** strength. 1869
5:27 At her feet he bowed, he fell, he **lay d**: 7901
5:27 where he bowed, there he **fell d** dead. 5307
6:25 **throw d** the altar of Baal that thy father 2040
6:25 and **cut d** the grove that *is* by it: 3772
6:26 wood of the grove which thou shalt **cut d**. 3772
6:28 the altar of Baal was **cast d**, and the grove 5422
6:28 the grove was **cut d** that *was* by it, and 3772
6:30 because he hath **cast d** the altar of Baal, 5422
6:30 he hath **cut d** the grove that *was* by it. 3772
Jdg 6:31 because *one* hath **cast d** his altar. 5422
6:32 because he hath **thrown d** his altar. 5422
7: 4 **bring** them **d** unto the water, and I will try 3381
7: 5 So he **brought d** the people unto the water: 3381
7: 5 likewise every one that **boweth d** upon his 3766
7: 6 all the rest of the people **bowed d** upon 3766
7: 9 unto him, Arise, **get** thee **d** unto the host; 3381
7:10 if thou fear to **go d**, go thou with Phurah 3381
7:10 **go** thou with Phurah thy servant **d** to 3381
7:11 be strengthened to **go d** unto the host. 3381
7:11 **went** he **d** with Phurah his servant unto 3381
7:24 **Come d** against the Midianites, and 3381
8: 9 again in peace, I will **break d** this tower. 5422
8:17 he **beat d** the tower of Penuel, and slew 5422
9:36 there **come** people **d** from the top of 3381
9:37 See there **come** people **d** by the middle of 3381
9:45 **beat d** the city, and sowed it *with* salt. 5422
9:48 **cut d** a bough from the trees, and took it, 3772
9:49 all the people likewise **cut d** every man his 3772
11:37 that I may go up and **d** upon the mountains, 3381
14: 1 Samson **went d** *to* Timnath, and saw a 3381
14: 5 **went** Samson **d**, and his father and 3381
14: 7 he **went d**, and talked with the woman; 3381
14:10 So his father **went d** unto the woman: and 3381
14:18 on the seventh day before the sun **went d**, 935
14:19 he **went d** *to* Ashkelon, and slew thirty men 3381
15: 8 he **went d** and dwelt in the top of the rock 3381
15:12 said unto him, We are **come d** to bind thee, 3381
16:21 **brought** him **d** to Gaza, and bound him 3381
16:31 and all the house of his father **came d**, 3381
19: 6 they **sat d**, and did eat and drink both of 3427
19:14 the sun **went d** upon them *when they were* 935
19:15 went in, he **sat** him **d** in a street of the city: 3427
19:26 **fell d** *at* the door of the man's house where 5307
19:27 the woman his concubine *was* **fallen d** *at* 5307
20:21 destroyed ***d*** to the ground of the Israelites NIH
20:25 destroyed ***d*** to the ground of the children of NIH
20:32 They *are* **smitten d** before us, as at the first. 5062
20:39 Surely they are **smitten d** before us, 5062+5062
20:43 **trode** them **d** with ease over against Gibeah 1869
Ru 3: 3 upon thee, and **get** thee **d** *to* the floor: 3381
3: 4 it shall be, when he **lieth d**, that thou shalt 7901
3: 4 go in, and uncover his feet, and **lay** thee **d**; 7901
3: 6 she **went d** *unto* the floor, and 3381
3: 7 he went to **lie d** at the end of the heap *of* 7901
3: 7 and uncovered his feet, and **laid** her **d**. 7901
3:13 the LORD liveth: **lie d** until the morning. 7901
4: 1 Boaz up *to* the gate, and **sat** him **d** there: 3427
4: 1 *Ho,* such a one, turn aside, **sit d** here. 3427
4: 1 down here. And he turned aside, and **sat d**. 3427
4: 2 elders of the city, and said, **Sit** ye **d** here. 3427
4: 2 and said, Sit ye down here. And they **sat d**. 3427
1Sa 2: 6 he **bringeth d** *to* the grave, and 3381
3: 2 when Eli *was* **laid d** in his place, and 7901
3: 3 God *was,* and Samuel was **laid d** *to sleep;* 7901
3: 5 he said, I called not; **lie d** again. And he 7901
3: 5 lie down again. And he went and **lay d**. 7901
3: 6 I called not, my son; **lie d** again. 7901
3: 9 Therefore Eli said unto Samuel, Go, **lie d**: 7901
3: 9 So Samuel went and **lay d** in his place. 7901
6:15 the Levites **took d** the ark of the LORD, 3381
6:18 whereon they **set d** the ark of the LORD: 3240
6:21 **come** ye **d**, *and* fetch it up to you. 3381
9:25 when they were **come d** from the high 3381
9:27 *And* as they were **going d** to the end of 3381
10: 5 **coming d** from the high place with a 3381
10: 8 thou shalt **go d** before me *to* Gilgal; and 3381
10: 8 behold, I will **come d** unto thee, to offer 3381
13:12 The Philistines will **come d** now upon me 3381
13:20 all the Israelites **went d** *to* the Philistines, 3381
14:16 and they went on **beating d** *one another.* 1986
14:36 Let us **go d** after the Philistines by night, 3381
14:37 of God, Shall I **go d** after the Philistines? 3381
15: 6 **get** you **d** from among the Amalekites, 3381
15:12 and passed on, and **gone d** *to* Gilgal. 3381
16:11 for we will not **sit d** till he come hither. 5437
17: 8 a man for you, and let him **come d** to me. 3381
17:28 and he said, Why **camest** thou **d** hither? 3381
17:28 for thou art **come d** that *thou* mightest see 3381
17:52 the wounded of the Philistines **fell d** by 5307
19:12 So Michal **let** David **d** through a window: 3381
19:24 **lay d** naked all that day and all *that* night. 5307
20:19 *then* thou shalt **go d** quickly, and come to 3381
20:24 was come, the king **sat** him **d** to eat meat. 3427
21:13 and **let** his spittle **fall d** upon his beard. 3381
22: 1 all his father's house heard *it,* they **went d** 3381
23: 4 and said, Arise, **go d** *to* Keilah; 3381
23: 6 *that* he **came d** *with* an ephod in his hand. 3381
23: 8 to **go d** *to* Keilah, to besiege David and his 3381
23:11 Will Saul **come d**, as thy servant hath 3381
23:11 And the LORD said, He will **come d**. 3381
23:20 **come d** according to all the desire of thy 3381
23:20 to all the desire of thy soul to **come d**; 3381
23:25 wherefore he **came d** *into* a rock, and 3381
25: 1 and **went d** to the wilderness of Paran. 3381
25:20 that she **came d** by the covert of the hill, 3381
25:20 David and his men **came d** against her; 3381
26: 2 and **went d** to the wilderness of Ziph, 3381
26: 6 Who will **go d** with me to Saul to 3381
26: 6 And Abishai said, I will **go d** with thee. 3381
29: 4 and let him not **go d** with us to battle, 3381
30:15 Canst thou **bring** me **d** to this company? 3381
30:15 and I will **bring** thee **d** to this company. 3381
30:16 when he had **brought** him **d**, behold *they* 3381
30:24 as his part *is* that **goeth d** to the battle, so 3381
31: 1 and **fell d** slain in mount Gilboa. 5307
2Sa 2:13 they **sat d**, the one on the one side of 3427
2:16 in his fellow's side; so they **fell d** together: 5307
2:23 he **fell d** there, and died in the same place: 5307
2:23 as came to the place where Asahel **fell d** 5307
2:24 the sun **went d** when they were come to 935
3:35 I taste bread, or ought else, till the sun be **d**. 935
5:17 David heard *of it,* and **went d** to the hold. 3381
8: 2 with a line, **casting** them **d** to the ground; 7901
11: 8 **Go d** to thy house, and wash thy feet. 3381
2Sa 11: 9 of his lord, and **went** not **d** to his house. 3381
11:10 saying, Uriah **went** not **d** unto his house, 3381
11:10 *then* didst thou not **go d** unto thine house? 3381
11:13 of his lord, but **went** not **d** to his house. 3381
13: 5 **Lay** *thee* **d** on thy bed, and make thyself 7901
13: 6 So Amnon **lay d**, and made himself sick: 7901
13: 8 brother Amnon's house; and he was **laid d**. 7901
15:20 should I *this* day make thee **go up and d** 1980
15:24 they **set d** the ark of God; and 3332
17:18 a well in his court; whither they **went d**. 3381
18:28 he **fell d** to the earth upon his face before 7812
19:16 **came d** with the men of Judah to meet king 3381
19:18 Shimei the son of Gera **fell d** before 5307
19:20 of Joseph to **go d** to meet my lord the king. 3381
19:24 Mephibosheth the son of Saul **came d** to 3381
19:31 Barzillai the Gileadite **came d** from 3381
20:15 with Joab battered the wall, to **throw** *it* **d**. 5307
21:15 David **went d**, and his servants with him, 3381
22:10 He bowed the heavens also, and **came d**; 3381
22:28 *that* thou mayest **bring** *them* **d**. 8213
22:48 and that **bringeth d** the people under me, 3381
23:13 three of the thirty chief **went d**, and 3381
23:20 he **went d** also and slew a lion in the midst 3381
23:21 he **went d** to him with a staff, and 3381
1Ki 1:25 For he is **gone d** *this* day, and hath slain 3381
1:33 mine own mule, and **bring** him **d** to Gihon: 3381
1:38 **went d**, and caused Solomon to ride upon 3381
1:53 and they **brought** him **d** from the altar. 3381
2: 6 let not his hoar head **go d** *to* the grave in 3381
2: 8 he **came d** to meet me *at* Jordan, and 3381
2: 9 his hoar head **bring** thou **d** *to* the grave 3381
2:19 **sat d** on his throne, and caused a seat to be 3427
5: 9 My servants shall **bring** *them* **d** from 3381
8:33 When thy people Israel be **smitten d** before 5062
17:23 **brought** him **d** out of the chamber into 3381
18:30 the altar of the LORD that was **broken d**. 2040
18:40 Elijah **brought** them **d** to the brook 3381
18:42 he **cast** himself **d** upon the earth, and 1457
18:44 Prepare *thy chariot,* and **get** thee **d**, 3381
19: 4 and came and **sat d** under a juniper tree: 3427
19: 6 he did eat and drink, and **laid** him **d** again. 7901
19:10 **thrown d** thine altars, and slain thy 2040
19:14 **thrown d** thine altars, and slain thy 2040
21: 4 he **laid** him **d** upon his bed, and 7901
21:16 that Ahab rose up to **go d** to the vineyard of 3381
21:18 Arise, **go d** to meet Ahab king of Israel, 3381
21:18 whither he is **gone d** to possess it. 3381
22: 2 that Jehoshaphat the king of Judah **came d** 3381
22:36 the host about the **going d** of the sun, 935
2Ki 1: 2 Ahaziah **fell d** through a lattice in his upper 5307
1: 4 Thou shalt not **come d** from *that* bed on 3381
1: 6 thou shalt not **come d** from *that* bed on 3381
1: 9 man of God, the king hath said, **Come d**. 3381
1:10 let fire **come d** from heaven, and 3381
1:10 there **came d** fire from heaven, and 3381
1:11 thus hath the king said, **Come d** quickly. 3381
1:12 let fire **come d** from heaven, and 3381
1:12 the fire of God **came d** from heaven, and 3381
1:14 there **came** fire **d** from heaven, and 3381
1:15 LORD said unto Elijah, **Go d** with him: 3381
1:15 and **went d** with him unto the king. 3381
1:16 thou shalt not **come d** off *that* bed on which 3381
2: 2 not leave thee. So they **went d** *to* Beth-el. 3381
3:12 and the king of Edom **went d** to him. 3381
3:25 they **beat d** the cities, and *on* every good 2040
5:14 **went** he **d**, and dipped *himself* seven times 3381
5:18 when I **bow d** myself *in* the house of 7812
5:21 he **lighted d** from the chariot to meet him, 5307
6: 4 they came to Jordan, they **cut d** wood. 1504
6: 6 he **cut d** a stick, and cast *it* in thither; 7094
6: 9 a place; for thither the Syrians are **come d**. 5185
6:18 when they **came d** to him, Elisha prayed 3381
6:33 the messenger **came d** unto him: 3381
7:17 who spake when the king **came d** to him. 3381
8:29 **went d** to see Joram the son of Ahab in 3381
9:16 Ahaziah king of Judah was **come d** to see 3381
9:24 at his heart, and he **sunk d** in his chariot. 3766
9:33 he said, **Throw** her **d**. So they threw her 8058
9:33 So they **threw** her **d**: and *some* of her blood 8058
10:13 we **go d** to salute the children of the king 3381
10:27 they **brake d** the image of Baal, and 5422
10:27 **brake d** the house of Baal, and made it a 5422
11: 6 watch of the house, that it be **not broken d**. 4535
11:18 went *into* the house of Baal, and **brake** it **d**; 5422
11:19 they **brought d** the king from the house of 3381
12:20 the house of Millo, which **goeth d** *to* Silla. 3381
13:14 Joash the king of Israel **came d** unto him, 3381
13:21 when the man was **let d**, and touched 1980
14: 9 *was* in Lebanon, and **trode d** the thistle. 7429
14:13 **brake d** the wall of Jerusalem from 6555
16:17 **took d** the sea from off the brasen oxen that 3381
18: 4 **cut d** the groves, and brake in pieces 3772
19:16 LORD, **bow d** thine ear, and hear: open, 5186
19:23 will **cut d** the tall cedar trees thereof, *and* 3772
20:10 It is a light thing for the shadow to **go d** ten 5186
20:11 by which it had **gone d** in the dial of Ahaz. 3381
21:13 wiping *it,* and turning *it* **upside d**. 5921+6440
23: 5 he **put d** the idolatrous priests, whom 7673
23: 7 he **brake d** the houses of the sodomites, 5422
23: 8 **brake d** the high places of the gates that 5422
23:12 did the king **beat d**, and brake *them* down 5422
23:12 **brake** *them* **d** from thence, and cast 7323
23:14 **cut d** the groves, and filled their places 3772
23:15 that altar and the high place he **brake d**, 5422
25:10 **brake d** the walls of Jerusalem round 5422
1Ch 5:22 For there **fell d** many slain, because the war 5307
7:21 they **came d** to take *away* their cattle. 3381
10: 1 and **fell d** slain in mount Gilboa. 5307
11:15 Now three of the thirty captains **went d** to 3381
11:22 also he **went d** and slew a lion in a pit in a 3381
11:23 he **went d** to him with a staff, and 3381
29:20 **bowed d** their **heads**, and worshipped 6915
2Ch 6:13 kneeled ***d*** upon his knees before all NIH
7: 1 the fire **came d** from heaven, and 3381
7: 3 children of Israel saw how the fire **came d**, 3381

2Ch 13:17 there **fell d** slain of Israel five hundred 5307
14: 3 **brake d** the images, and cut down 7665
14: 3 down the images, and **cut d** the groves: 1438
15:16 Asa **cut d** her idol, and stamped *it,* and 3772
18: 2 after *certain* years he **went d** to Ahab to 3381
18:34 about the time of the sun **going d** he died. 935
20:16 To morrow **go ye d** against them: behold, 3381
22: 6 **went d** to see Jehoram the son of Ahab at 3381
23:17 **brake** it **d**, and brake his altars and his 5422
23:20 **brought d** the king from the house of 3381
25: 8 for God hath power to help, and to **cast d**. 3782
25:12 **cast** them **d** from the top of the rock, 7993
25:14 **bowed d** himself before them, and 7812
25:18 *was* in Lebanon, and **trode d** the thistle. 7429
25:23 **brake d** the wall of Jerusalem from 6555
26: 6 **brake d** the wall of Gath, and the wall of 6555
31: 1 the images *in pieces,* and **cut d** the groves, 1438
31: 1 **threw d** the high places and the altars out 5422
32:30 brought it straight **d** to the west 4295+3807.1
33: 3 which Hezekiah his father had **broken d**, 5422
34: 4 they **brake d** the altars of Baalim in his 5422
34: 4 that *were* on high above them, he **cut d**; 1438
34: 7 when he had **broken d** the altars and 5422
34: 7 **cut d** all the idols throughout all the land of 1438
36: 3 the king of Egypt **put** him **d** at Jerusalem, 5493
36:19 **brake d** the wall of Jerusalem, and 5422
Ezr 6:11 let timber be **pulled d** from his house, and 5256
9: 3 and of my beard, and **sat d** astonied. 3427
10: 1 **casting** himself **d** before the house of God, 5307
10:16 **sat d** in the first day of the tenth month to 3427
Ne 1: 3 the wall of Jerusalem also *is* **broken d**, and 6555
1: 4 *that* I **sat d** and wept, and mourned *certain* 3427
2:13 which were **broken d**, and the gates thereof 6555
3:15 unto the stairs that **go d** from the city of 3381
4: 3 he shall even **break d** their stone wall. 6555
6: 3 a great work, so that I cannot **come d**: 3381
6: 3 whilst I leave it, and **come d** to you? 3381
6:16 they were much **cast d** in their own eyes: 5307
9:13 Thou **camest d** also upon mount Sinai, and 3381
Est 3:15 And the king and Haman **sat d** to drink; but 3427
8: 3 **fell d** at his feet, and besought him with 5307
Job 1: 7 the earth, and from **walking up and d** in it. 1980
1:20 **fell d** upon the ground, and worshipped, 5307
2: 2 the earth, and from **walking up and d** in it. 1980
2: 8 and he **sat d** among the ashes. 3427
2:13 So they **sat d** with him upon the ground 3427
6:21 ye see *my* **casting d**, and are afraid. 2866
7: 4 When I **lie d**, I say, When shall I arise, and 7901
7: 9 he that **goeth d** *to* the grave shall come up 3381
7:19 nor let me alone till I **swallow d** my spittle? 1104
8:12 it *is* yet in his greenness, *and* not **cut d**, 6998
11:19 Also thou shalt **lie d**, and none shall make 7257
12:14 he **breaketh d**, and it cannot be built *again:* 2040
14: 2 He cometh forth like a flower, and is **cut d**: 5243
14: 7 if it be **cut d**, that it will sprout again, and 3772
14:12 So man **lieth d**, and riseth not: till 7901
17: 3 **Lay d** now, put me in a surety with thee; 7760
17:16 They shall **go d** *to* the bars of the pit, 3381
18: 7 and his own counsel shall **cast** him **d**. 7993
20:11 which shall **lie d** with him in the dust. 7901
20:15 He hath **swallowed d** riches, and he shall 1104
20:18 shall he restore, and shall not **swallow** *it* **d**: 1104
21:13 and in a moment **go d** *to* the grave. 2865
21:26 They shall **lie d** alike in the dust, and 7901
22:16 Which were **cut d** out of time, 7059
22:20 Whereas our substance is not **cut d**, but 3582
22:29 When *men* are **cast d**, then thou shalt say, 8213
27:19 The rich *man* shall **lie d**, but he shall not be 7901
29:24 light of my countenance they **cast** not **d**. 5307
31:10 and let others **bow d** upon her. 3766
32:13 God **thrusteth** him **d**, not man. 5086
33:24 saith, Deliver him from **going d** *to* the pit: 3381
36:27 they **pour d** rain according to the vapour 2212
40:12 and **tread d** the wicked in their place. 1915
41: 1 tongue with a cord *which* thou **lettest d**? 8257
41: 9 shall *not one* be **cast d** even at the sight of 2904
Ps 3: 5 **I laid** me **d** and slept; I awaked; for 7901
4: 8 I will both **lay** me **d** in peace, and sleep: 7901
7: 5 let him **tread d** my life upon the earth, and 7429
7:16 his violent dealing shall **come d** upon his 3381
9:15 The heathen are **sunk d** in the pit *that* they 2883
14: 2 The LORD **looked d** from heaven upon 8259
17:11 they have set their eyes **bowing d** to 5186
17:13 O LORD, disappoint him, **cast** him **d**: 3766
18: 9 He bowed the heavens also, and **came d**: 3381
18:27 but wilt **bring d** high looks. 8213
20: 8 They are **brought d** and fallen: but we are 3766
22:29 all they that **go d** to the dust shall bow 3381
23: 2 He **maketh** me **to lie d** in green pastures: 7257
28: 1 I become like them that **go d** into the pit. 3381
30: 3 me alive, that I should not **go d** *to* the pit. 3381
30: 9 *is there* in my blood, when I **go d** to the pit? 3381
31: 2 **Bow d** thine ear to me; deliver me speedily: 5186
35:14 I **bowed d** heavily, as one that mourneth 7817
36:12 they are **cast d**, and shall not be able to 1760
37: 2 For they shall soon be **cut d** like the grass, 5243
37:14 to **cast d** the poor and needy, *and* to slay 5307
37:24 he fall, he shall not be **utterly cast d**: 2904
38: 6 I am troubled; I am **bowed d** greatly; I go 7817
42: 5 Why art thou **cast d**, O my soul? and 7817
42: 6 O my God, my soul is **cast d** within me: 7817
42:11 Why art thou **cast d**, O my soul? and 7817
43: 5 Why art thou **cast d**, O my soul? and 7817
44: 5 Through thee will we **push d** our enemies: 5055
44:25 For our soul is **bowed d** to the dust: 7743
50: 1 rising of the sun unto the **going d** thereof. 3996
53: 2 God **looked d** from heaven upon 8259
55:15 *and* let them **go d** quick *into* hell: 3381
55:23 shalt **bring** them **d** into the pit of 3381
56: 7 in *thine* anger **cast d** the people, O God. 3381
57: 6 a net for my steps; my soul is **bowed d**: 3721
59:11 and **bring** them **d**, O Lord our shield. 3381
59:15 Let them **wander up and d** for meat, and 5128
60:12 for he *it is that* shall **tread d** our enemies. 947
62: 4 They only consult to **cast** *him* **d** from his 5080
Ps 72: 6 He shall **come d** like rain upon the mown 3381
72:11 Yea, all kings shall **fall d** before him: 7812
73:18 thou **castedst** them **d** into destruction. 5307
74: 6 now they **break d** the carved work thereof 1986
74: 7 they have defiled *by casting* **d** the dwelling NIH
75: 7 he **putteth d** one, and setteth up another. 8213
78:16 and **caused** waters **to run d** like rivers. 3381
78:24 had **rained d** manna upon them to eat, and 4305
78:31 and **smote d** the chosen *men* of Israel. 3766
80:12 Why hast thou *then* **broken d** her hedges, 6555
80:14 **look d** from heaven, and behold, and 5027
80:16 *It is* burnt with fire, *it is* **cut d**: they perish 3683
85:11 righteousness shall **look d** from heaven. 8259
86: 1 **Bow d** thine ear, O LORD, hear me: for I 5186
88: 4 I am counted with them that **go d** into 3381
89:23 I will **beat d** his foes before his face, and 3807
89:40 Thou hast **broken d** all his hedges; 6555
89:44 and **cast** his throne **d** to the ground. 4048
90: 6 in the evening it is **cut d**, and withereth. 4135
95: 6 O come, let us worship and **bow d**: let us 3766
102:10 for thou hast lifted me up, and **cast** me **d**. 7993
102:19 For he hath **looked d** from the height of his 8259
104: 8 they **go d** *by* the valleys unto the place 3381
104:19 for seasons: the sun knoweth his **going d**. 3996
104:22 and **lay** them **d** in their dens. 7257
107:12 Therefore he **brought d** their heart with 3665
107:12 they **fell d**, and *there was* none to help. 3782
107:23 They that **go d** to the sea in ships, that do 3381
107:26 the heaven, they **go d** *again to* the depths: 3381
108:13 for he *it is that* shall **tread d** our enemies. 947
109:23 I am **tossed up and d** as the locust. 5287
113: 3 From the rising of the sun unto the **going d** 3996
115:17 neither any that **go d** into silence. 3381
119:118 Thou hast **trodden d** all them that err from 5541
119:136 Rivers of waters **run d** mine eyes, because 3381
133: 2 that **ran d** upon the beard, *even* Aaron's 3381
133: 2 that **went d** to the skirts of his garments; 3381
137: 1 of Babylon, there we **sat d**, yea, we wept, 3427
139: 3 Thou compassest my path and my **lying d**, 7252
143: 3 he hath **smitten** my life **d** to the ground; 1792
143: 7 lest I be like unto them that **go d** into 3381
144: 5 Bow thy heavens, O LORD, and **come d**: 3381
145:14 and raiseth up all those that be **bowed d**. 3721
146: 8 the LORD raiseth them that are **bowed d**: 3721
146: 9 the way of the wicked he **turneth upside d**. 5791
147: 6 he **casteth** the wicked **d** to the ground. 8213
Pr 1:12 and whole, as those that **go d** into the pit: 3381
3:20 broken up, and the clouds **drop d** the dew. 7491
3:24 When thou **liest d**, thou shalt not be afraid: 7901
3:24 thou shalt **lie d**, and thy sleep shall be 7901
5: 5 Her feet **go d** *to* death; her steps take hold 3381
7:26 For she hath **cast d** many wounded: yea, 5307
7:27 to hell, **going d** to the chambers of death. 3381
14: 1 the foolish **plucketh** it **d** with her hands. 2040
18: 8 they **go d** *into* the innermost parts of 3381
21:22 **casteth d** the strength of the confidence 3381
22:17 **Bow d** thine ear, and hear the words of 5186
23:34 thou shalt be as he that **lieth d** in the midst 7901
24:31 and the stone wall thereof was **broken d**. 2040
25:26 A righteous *man* **falling d** before 4131
25:28 own spirit *is like* a city *that is* **broken d**, 6555
26:22 they **go d** *into* the innermost parts of 3381
Ecc 1: 5 The sun **goeth d**, and hasteth to his place 935
3: 3 a time to **break d**, and a time to build *up;* 6555
SS 2: 3 I **sat d** under his shadow with great delight, 3427
6: 2 My beloved is **gone d** into his garden, 3381
6:11 I **went d** into the garden of nuts to see 3381
7: 9 for my beloved, that goeth *d* sweetly, NIH
Isa 2: 9 the mean man **boweth d**, and the great man 7817
2:11 the haughtiness of men shall be **bowed d**, 7817
2:17 the loftiness of man shall be **bowed d**, and 7817
5: 5 *and* **break d** the wall thereof, and it shall 6555
5: 5 the wall thereof, and it shall be **trodden d**: 4823
5:15 the mean man shall be **brought d**, and 7817
9:10 The bricks are **fallen d**, but we will build 5307
9:10 the sycomores are **cut d**, but we will 1438
10: 4 Without me they shall **bow d** under 3766
10: 6 **tread** them **d** like the mire of 4823+7760
10:13 I have **put d** the inhabitants like a valiant 3381
10:33 the high ones of stature *shall be* **hewn d**, 1438
10:34 he shall **cut d** the thickets of the forest with 5362
11: 6 and the leopard shall **lie d** with the kid; 7257
11: 7 their young ones shall **lie d** together: 7257
14: 8 of Lebanon, *saying,* Since thou art **laid d**, 7901
14:11 Thy pomp is **brought d** *to* the grave, *and* 3381
14:12 *how* art thou **cut d** to the ground, 1438
14:15 Yet thou shalt be **brought d** to hell, to 3381
14:19 a sword, that **go d** to the stones of the pit; 3381
14:30 and the needy shall **lie d** in safety: 7257
16: 8 the lords of the heathen have **broken d** 1986
17: 2 which shall **lie d**, and none shall make *them* 7257
18: 2 a nation meted out and **trodden d**, 4001
18: 5 and take away *and* **cut d** the branches. 8456
21: 3 I was **bowed d** at the hearing *of it;* I was 5753
22: 5 of **treading d**, and of perplexity by 4001
22: 5 **breaking d** the walls, and of crying to 6979
22:10 the houses have ye **broken d** to fortify 5422
22:19 and from thy state shall he **pull** thee **d**. 2040
22:25 place be removed, and be **cut d**, and fall; 1438
24: 1 turneth it **upside d**, and scattereth abroad 6440
24:10 The city of confusion is **broken d**: 7665
24:19 The earth is **utterly broken d**, 7489+7489
25: 5 Thou shalt **bring d** the noise of strangers, 3665
25:10 Moab shall be **trodden d** under him, 1758
25:10 *even* as straw is **trodden d** for the dunghill. 1758
25:11 he shall **bring d** their pride together with 8213
25:12 the high fort of thy walls shall he **bring d**, 7817
26: 5 For he **bringeth d** them that dwell on high; 7817
26: 6 The foot shall **tread** it **d**, *even* the feet of 7429
27:10 there shall he **lie d**, and consume 7257
28: 2 shall **cast d** to the earth with the hand. 3240
28:18 then ye shall be **trodden d** by it. 4823
29: 4 thou shalt be **brought d**, *and* shalt speak 8213
29:16 Surely your **turning** *of things* **upside d** 2017
30: 2 That walk to **go d** *into* Egypt, and have not 3381
Isa 30:30 shall shew the **lighting d** of his arm, 5183
30:31 the LORD shall the Assyrian be **beaten d**, 2865
31: 1 Woe to them that **go d** *to* Egypt for help; 3381
31: 3 he that is holpen shall **fall d**, and they all 5307
31: 4 shall the LORD of hosts **come d** to fight 3381
32:19 When it shall hail, **coming d** *on* the forest; 3381
33: 9 Lebanon is ashamed *and* **hewn d**: Sharon is 7060
33:20 a tabernacle *that* shall not be **taken d**; 6813
34: 4 all their host shall **fall d**, as the leaf falleth 5034
34: 5 it shall **come d** upon Idumea, and upon 3381
34: 7 the unicorns shall **come d** with them, and 3381
37:24 I will **cut d** the tall cedars thereof, *and* 3772
38: 8 which is **gone d** in the sun dial of Ahaz, 3381
38: 8 by which degrees it was **gone d**. 3381
38:18 they that **go d** into the pit cannot hope for 3381
42:10 ye that **go d** to the sea, and all that is 3381
43:14 have **brought d** all their nobles, and 3381
43:17 they shall **lie d** together, they shall not rise: 7901
44:14 *He* **heweth** him **d** cedars, and taketh 3772
44:15 it a graven image, and **falleth d** thereto. 5456
44:17 he **falleth d** unto it, and worshippeth *it,* and 5456
44:19 shall I **fall d** to the stock of a tree? 5456
45: 8 **Drop d**, ye heavens, from above, and 7491
45: 8 and let the skies **pour d** righteousness: 5140
45:14 come over, and they shall **fall d** unto thee, 7812
46: 1 Bel **boweth d**, Nebo stoopeth, their idols 3766
46: 2 They stoop, they **bow d** together; 3766
46: 6 it a god: they **fall d**, yea, they worship. 5456
47: 1 **Come d**, and sit in the dust, O virgin 3381
49:23 they shall **bow d** to thee *with their* face 7812
50:11 have of mine hand; ye shall **lie d** in sorrow. 7901
51:23 to thy soul, **Bow d**, that we may go over: 7812
52: 2 from the dust; arise, *and* **sit d**, O Jerusalem: 3427
52: 4 My people **went d** aforetime *into* Egypt to 3381
55:10 For as the rain **cometh d**, and the snow 3381
56:10 sleeping, **lying d**, loving to slumber. 7901
58: 5 *is it* to **bow d** his head as a bulrush, and 3721
60:14 **bow** themselves **d** at the soles of thy feet; 7812
60:20 Thy sun shall no more **go d**; neither shall thy 935
63: 6 And I will **tread d** the people in mine anger, 947
63: 6 I will **bring d** their strength to the earth. 3381
63:14 As a beast **goeth d** into the valley, 3381
63:15 **Look d** from heaven, and behold from 5027
63:18 our adversaries have **trodden d** thy 947
64: 1 the heavens, that thou wouldest **come d**, 3381
64: 1 that the mountains might **flow d** at thy 2151
64: 3 thou **camest d**, the mountains flowed down 3381
64: 3 the mountains **flowed d** at thy presence. 2151
65:10 of Achor a **place** for the herds **to lie d in**, 7258
65:12 and ye shall all **bow d** to the slaughter: 3766
Jer 1:10 to **pull d**, and to destroy, and to throw 5422
1:10 and to **throw d**, to build, and to plant. 2040
3:25 We **lie d** in our shame, and our confusion 7901
4:26 all the cities thereof were **broken d** at 5422
6: 6 **Hew** ye **d** trees, and cast a mount against 3772
6:15 time *that* I visit them they shall be **cast d**, 3782
8:12 time of their visitation they shall be **cast d**, 3782
9:18 that our eyes may **run d** *with* tears, and 3381
13:17 **run d** *with* tears, because the LORD'S 3381
13:18 and to the queen, Humble yourselves, **sit d**: 3427
13:18 for your principalities shall **come d**, 3381
14:17 Let mine eyes **run d** *with* tears night and 3381
15: 9 her sun is **gone d** while *it was* yet day: 935
18: 2 **go d** *to* the potter's house, and there I will 3381
18: 3 I **went d** *to* the potter's house, and behold, 3381
18: 7 pluck up, and to **pull d**, and to destroy *it;* 5422
21:13 which say, Who shall **come d** against us? 5181
22: 1 **Go d** *to* the house of the king of Judah, and 3381
22: 7 they shall **cut d** thy choice cedars, and 3772
24: 6 I will build them, and not **pull** *them* **d**; and 2040
25:37 the peaceable habitations are **cut d** because 1826
26:10 **sat d** in the entry of the new gate of 3427
31:28 to **break d**, and to throw down, and 5422
31:28 to **throw d**, and to destroy, and to afflict; 2040
31:40 nor **thrown d** any more for ever. 2040
33: 4 which are **thrown d** by the mounts, and 5422
33:12 of shepherds **causing** *their* flocks **to lie d**. 7257
36:12 he **went d** *into* the king's house, into 3381
36:15 unto him, **Sit d** now, and read it in our ears. 3427
38: 6 they **let d** Jeremiah with cords. And in 7971
38:11 **let** them **d** by cords into the dungeon to 7971
39: 8 and **brake d** the walls of Jerusalem. 5422
42:10 not **pull** *you* **d**, and I will plant you, and 2040
45: 4 *that* which I have built *will* I **break d**, and 2040
46: 5 their mighty ones are **beaten d**, and are fled 3807
46:23 They shall **cut d** her forest, saith 3772
48: 2 Also thou shalt be **cut d**, O Madmen; 1826
48: 5 for in the **going d** of Horonaim the enemies 4174
48:15 his chosen young men are **gone d** to 3381
48:18 **come d** from *thy* glory, and sit in thirst; 3381
48:20 Moab is confounded; for it is **broken d**: 2865
48:39 shall howl, *saying,* How is it **broken d**! 2865
49:16 I will **bring** thee **d** from thence, saith 3381
50:15 are fallen, her walls are **thrown d**: 2040
50:27 her bullocks; let them **go d** to the slaughter: 3381
51:25 **roll** thee **d** from the rocks, and will make 1556
51:40 I will **bring** them **d** like lambs to 3381
52:14 **brake d** all the walls of Jerusalem round 5422
La 1: 9 last end; therefore she **came d** wonderfully: 3381
1:16 mine eye **runneth d** *with* water, because 3381
2: 1 **cast d** from heaven *unto* the earth 7993
2: 2 he hath **thrown d** in his wrath the strong 2040
2: 2 he hath **brought** *them* **d** to the ground: 5060
2:10 the virgins of Jerusalem **hang d** their heads 3381
2:17 he hath **thrown d**, and hath not pitied: and 2040
2:18 let tears **run d** like a river day and night: 3381
3:48 Mine eye **runneth d** *with* rivers of water 3381
3:49 Mine eye **trickleth d**, and ceaseth not, 5064
3:50 Till the LORD **look d**, and behold from 8259
3:63 Behold their **sitting d**, and their rising up; 3427
Eze 1:13 it **went up and d** among the living 1980
1:24 when they stood, they **let d** their wings. 7503
1:25 when they stood, *and* had **let d** their wings. 7503
6: 4 I will **cast d** your slain *men* before your 5307
6: 6 your images may be **cut d**, and your works 1438

D

Eze 11:13 **fell** I **d** upon my face, and cried *with* a loud 5307
13:14 So will I **break d** the wall that ye have 2040
13:14 and **bring** it **d** to the ground, 5060
16:39 and they shall **throw d** thine eminent place, 2040
16:39 and shall **break d** thy high places: 5422
17:24 I the LORD have **brought d** the high tree, 8213
19: 2 she **lay d** among lions, she nourished her 7257
19: 6 he **went up and d** among the lions, 1980
19:12 she was **cast d** to the ground, and the east 7993
24:16 nor weep, neither shall thy tears **run d**. 935
26: 4 the walls of Tyrus, and **break d** her towers: 2040
26: 9 with his axes he shall **break d** thy towers. 5422
26:11 of his horses shall he **tread d** all thy streets: 7429
26:11 thy strong garrisons shall **go d** to 3381
26:12 they shall **break d** thy walls, and 2040
26:16 all the princes of the sea shall **come d** from 3381
26:20 When I shall **bring** thee **d** with them that 3381
26:20 of old, with them that **go d** to the pit, 3381
27:29 of the sea, shall **come d** from their ships, 3381
28: 8 They shall **bring** thee **d** to the pit, and 3381
28:14 thou hast **walked up and d** in the midst of 1980
30: 4 and her foundations shall be **broken d**. 2040
30: 6 and the pride of her power shall **come d**: 3381
30:25 and the arms of Pharaoh shall **fall d**; 5307
31:12 all the people of the earth are **gone d** from 3381
31:14 of men, with them that **go d** to the pit. 3381
31:15 In the day when he **went d** to the grave I 3381
31:16 when I **cast** him **d** to hell with them that 3381
31:17 They also **went d** into hell with him unto 3381
31:18 yet shalt thou be **brought d** with the trees 3381
32:18 **cast** them **d**, *even* her, and the daughters of 3381
32:18 the earth, with them that **go d** into the pit. 3381
32:19 **go d**, and be thou laid with 3381
32:21 they are **gone d**, they lie uncircumcised, 3381
32:24 which are **gone d** uncircumcised into 3381
32:24 their shame with them that **go d** to the pit. 3381
32:25 their shame with them that **go d** to the pit: 3381
32:27 which are **gone d** *to* hell with their 3381
32:29 and with them that **go d** to the pit. 3381
32:30 which are **gone d** with the slain; 3381
32:30 bear their shame with them that **go d** to 3381
34:15 my flock, and I will **cause** them **to lie d**, 7257
34:18 ye must **tread d** with your feet the residue 7429
34:26 I will **cause** the shower **to come d** in his 3381
37: 1 **set** me **d** in the midst of the valley which 5117
38:20 the mountains shall be **thrown d**, and 2040
39:10 neither **cut d** *any* out of the forests; 2404
47: 1 the waters **came d** from under from 3381
47: 8 **go d** into the desert, and go into the sea: 3381
Da 3: 5 ye **fall d** and worship the golden image that 5308
3: 6 whoso **falleth** not **d** and worshippeth shall 5308
3: 7 **fell d** *and* worshipped the golden image 5308
3:10 shall **fall d** and worship the golden image: 5308
3:11 whoso **falleth** not **d** and worshippeth, 5308
3:15 ye **fall d** and worship the image which I 5308
3:23 **fell d** bound into the midst of the burning 5308
4:13 and a holy one **came d** from heaven; 5182
4:14 **Hew d** the tree, and cut off his branches, 1414
4:23 and a holy one **coming d** from heaven, 5182
4:23 saying, **Hew** the tree **d**, and destroy it; 1414
5:19 he set up; and whom he would he **put d**. 8214
6:14 he laboured till the **going d** of the sun to 4606
7: 9 I beheld till the thrones were cast *d*, and NIH
7:23 and shall **tread** it **d**, and break it in pieces. 1759
8: 7 he **cast** him **d** to the ground, and 7993
8:10 it **cast d** *some* of the host and of the stars to 5307
8:11 and the place of his sanctuary was **cast d**. 7993
8:12 and it **cast d** the truth to the ground; 7993
11:12 and he shall **cast d** *many* ten thousands: 5307
11:26 shall overflow: and many shall **fall d** slain. 5307
Hos 2:18 and will **make** them **to lie d** safely. 7901
7:12 I will **bring** them **d** as the fowls of 3381
10: 2 he shall **break d** their altars, he shall spoil 6202
Joel 1:17 are laid desolate, the barns are **broken d**; 2040
2:23 he will **cause to come d** for you the rain, 3381
3: 2 will **bring** them **d** into the valley of 3381
3:11 thither **cause** thy mighty ones **to come d**, 5181
3:13 come, **get** you **d**; for the press is full, 3381
3:18 *that* the mountains shall **drop d** new wine, 5197
Am 2: 8 they **lay** *themselves* **d** upon clothes laid to 5186
3:11 and he shall **bring d** thy strength from thee, 3381
5:24 let judgment **run d** as waters, and 1556
6: 2 **go d** *to* Gath of the Philistines: *be they* 3381
8: 9 that I will **cause** the sun **to go d** at noon, and 935
9: 2 up *to* heaven, thence will I **bring** them **d**: 3381
Ob 1: 3 Who shall **bring** me **d** *to* the ground? 3381
1: 4 thence will I **bring** thee **d**, saith 3381
1:16 they shall **swallow d**, and they shall be as 3886
Jnh 1: 3 of the LORD, and **went d** *to* Joppa; 3381
1: 3 he paid the fare thereof, and **went d** into it, 3381
1: 5 Jonah was **gone d** into the sides of the ship; 3381
2: 6 I **went d** to the bottoms of the mountains; 3381
Mic 1: 3 will **come d** and tread upon the high places 3381
1: 4 as the waters *that are* poured **d** a steep 871.1
1: 6 I will **pour d** the stones thereof into 5064
1:12 evil **came d** from the LORD unto the gate 3381
3: 6 and the sun shall **go d** over the prophets, and 935
5: 8 both **treadeth d**, and teareth in pieces, and 7429
5:11 thy land, and **throw d** all thy strong holds: 2040
6:14 thy **casting d** *shall be* in the midst of thee; 3445
7:10 now shall she be **trodden d** as the mire of 4823
Na 1: 6 and the rocks are **thrown d** by him. 5422
1:12 likewise many, yet thus shall they be **cut d**, 1494
Zep 1:11 for all the merchant people are **cut d**; 1820
2: 7 in the houses of Ashkelon shall they **lie d** in 7257
2:14 flocks shall **lie d** in the midst of her, all 7257
2:15 a desolation, a **place** for beasts **to lie d in**! 4769
3:13 for they shall feed and **lie d**, and none shall 7257
Hag 2:22 the horses and their riders shall **come d**, 3381
Zec 10: 5 they shall be as mighty *men*, which **tread d** 947
10:11 the pride of Assyria shall be **brought d**, 3381
10:12 they shall **walk up and d** in his name, 1980
11: 2 for the forest of the vintage is **come d**. 3381
Mal 1: 4 They shall build, but I will **throw d**; 2040
1:11 **going d** of the same my name *shall be* great 3996

Mal 4: 3 ye shall **tread d** the wicked; for they shall 6072
Mt 2:11 his mother, and **fell d**, and worshipped him: 4098
3:10 bringeth not forth good fruit is **hewn d**, 1581
4: 6 If thou be the Son of God, cast thyself **d**: 2736
4: 9 if thou wilt **fall d** and worship me. 4098
7:19 that bringeth not forth good fruit is **hewn d**, 1581
8: 1 When he was **come d** from the mountain, 2597
8:11 and shall **sit d** with Abraham, and Isaac, and 347
8:32 the whole herd of swine ran violently **d** a 2596
9:10 and **sat d with** him and his disciples. 4873
11:23 unto heaven, shalt be **brought d** to hell: 2601
13:48 and **sat d**, and gathered the good into 2523
14:19 And he commanded the multitude to **sit d** on 347
14:29 And when Peter was **come d** out of 2597
15:29 went up into a mountain, and **sat d** there. 2521
15:30 many others, and cast them *d* at Jesus' feet; NIG
15:35 And he commanded the multitude to **sit d** on 377
17: 9 And as they **came d** from the mountain, 2597
17:14 *certain* man, **kneeling d** to him, and saying, 1120
18:26 The servant therefore **fell d**, and 4098
18:29 And his fellowservant **fell d** at his feet, and 4098
21: 8 others **cut d** branches from the trees, and 2875
24: 2 upon another, that shall not be **thrown d**. 2647
24:17 **come d** to take any *thing* out of his house: 2597
26:20 the even was come, he **sat d** with the twelve. 345
27: 5 And he **cast d** the pieces of silver in 4496
27:19 When he was **set d** on the judgment seat, 2521
27:36 And **sitting d** they watched him there; 2521
27:40 be the Son of God, **come d** from the cross. 2597
27:42 let him now **come d** from the cross, and 2597
Mk 1: 7 of whose shoes I am not worthy to **stoop d** 2955
1:40 and **kneeling d** to him, and saying unto 1120
2: 4 they **let d** the bed wherein the sick of 5465
3:11 **fell d before** him, and cried, saying, 4363
3:22 And the scribes which **came d** from 2597
5:13 the herd ran violently **d** a steep place into 2596
5:33 came and **fell d before** him, and told him 4363
6:39 And he commanded them to **make** all **sit d** 347
6:40 And they **sat d** in ranks, by hundreds, and 377
8: 6 And he commanded the people to **sit d** on 377
9: 9 And as they **came d** from the mountain, 2597
9:35 And he **sat d**, and called the twelve, and 2523
11: 8 and others **cut d** branches off the trees, 2875
13: 2 upon another, that shall not be **thrown d**. 2647
13:15 is on the housetop not **go d** into the house, 2597
15:30 Save thyself, and **come d** from the cross. 2597
15:36 see whether Elias will come to **take** him **d**. 2507
15:46 and **took** him **d**, and wrapped *him* in 2507
Lk 1:52 He hath **put d** the mighty from *their* seats, 2507
2:51 And he **went d** with them, and came to 2597
3: 9 bringeth not forth good fruit is **hewn d**, 1581
4: 9 the Son of God, cast thyself **d** from hence: 2736
4:20 he gave *it* again to the minister, and **sat d**. 2523
4:29 that *they* might **cast** him **d headlong**. 2630
4:31 And **came d** to Capernaum, a city of 2718
5: 3 And he **sat d**, and taught the people out of 2523
5: 4 the deep, and **let d** your nets for a draught. 5465
5: 5 nevertheless at thy word I will **let d** the net. 5465
5: 8 When Simon Peter saw *it*, he **fell d at** 4363
5:19 **let** him **d** through the tiling with *his* couch 2524
5:29 and of others that sat **d** with them. 1510
6:17 And he **came d** with them, and stood in 2597
6:38 **pressed d**, and shaken *together*, and 4085
7:36 the Pharisee's house, and **sat d to meat**. 347
8: 5 and it was **trodden d**, and the fowls of 2662
8:23 there **came d** a storm of wind on the lake; 2597
8:28 and **fell d before** him, and with a loud 4363
8:33 the herd ran violently **d** a steep place into 2596
8:41 and he **fell d** at Jesus' feet, and 4098
8:47 came trembling, and **falling d before** him, 4363
9:14 **Make** them **sit d** by fifties in a company. 2625
9:15 And they did so, and **made** *them* all **sit d**. 347
9:37 when they were **come d** from the hill, 2718
9:42 the devil **threw** him **d**, and tare *him*. And 4486
9:44 Let these sayings **sink d** into your ears: 5087
9:54 wilt thou *that* we command fire to **come d** 2597
10:15 exalted to heaven, shalt be **thrust d** to hell. 2601
10:30 A certain man **went d** from Jerusalem to 2597
10:31 And by chance there **came d** a certain 2597
11:37 with him: and he went in, and **sat d to meat**. 377
12:18 I will **pull d** my barns, and build greater; 2507
12:37 and **make** them to **sit d to meat**, and 347
13: 7 **cut** it **d**; why cumbereth it the ground? 1581
13: 9 and if not, *then* after that thou shalt **cut** it **d**. 1581
13:29 and shall **sit d** in the kingdom of God. 347
14: 8 to a wedding, **sit** not **d** in the highest room; 2625
14:10 art bidden, go and **sit d** in the lowest room; 377
14:28 **sitteth** not **d** first, and counteth the cost, 2523
14:31 **sitteth** not **d** first, and consulteth whether 2523
16: 6 thy bill, and **sit d** quickly, and write fifty. 2523
17: 7 come from the field, Go and **sit d to meat**? 377
17:16 And **fell d** on *his* face at his feet, 4098
17:31 let him not **come d** to take it away: 2597
18:14 this man **went d** to his house justified 2597
19: 5 Zaccheus, make haste, and **come d**; 2597
19: 6 and **came d**, and received him joyfully. 2597
19:21 thou takest up that thou **layedst** not **d**, and 5087
19:22 taking up that I **laid** not **d**, and reaping that 5087
21: 6 upon another, that shall not be **thrown d**. 2647
21:24 Jerusalem shall be **trodden d** of 3961
22:14 he **sat d**, and the twelve apostles with him. 377
22:41 a stone's cast, and **kneeled d**, 1119+3588+5087
22:44 drops of blood **falling d** to the ground. 2597
22:55 and were **set d together**, Peter sat down 4776
22:55 set down together, Peter **sat d** among them. 2521
23:53 And he **took** it **d**, and wrapped it in linen, 2507
24: 5 and **bowed d** *their* faces to the earth, 2827
24:12 and **stooping d**, he beheld the linen clothes 3879
Jn 2:12 After this he **went d** to Capernaum, he, and 2597
3:13 but he that **came d** from heaven, *even* 2597
4:47 and besought him that he would **come d**, 2597
4:49 unto him, Sir, **come d** ere my child die. 2597
4:51 And as he was now **going d**, his servants 2597
5: 4 For an angel **went d** at a *certain* season into 2597
5: 7 am coming, another **steppeth d** before me. 2597

Jn 6:10 And Jesus said, Make the men **sit d**. 377
6:10 So the men **sat d**, *in* number about five 377
6:11 and the disciples to them that were **set d**; 345
6:16 his disciples **went d** unto the sea, 2597
6:33 For the bread of God is he which **cometh d** 2597
6:38 For I **came d** from heaven, not to do mine 2597
6:41 I am the bread which **came d** from heaven. 2597
6:42 then *that* he saith, I **came d** from heaven? 2597
6:50 This is the bread which **cometh d** from 2597
6:51 I am the living bread which **came d** from 2597
6:58 This is *that* bread which **came d** from 2597
8: 2 unto him; and he **sat d**, and taught them. 2523
8: 6 But Jesus stooped **d**, and with *his* finger 2736
8: 8 And again he stooped **d**, and wrote on 2736
10:15 and I **lay d** my life for the sheep. 5087
10:17 because I **lay d** my life, that I might take it 5087
10:18 taketh it from me, but I **lay** it **d** of myself. 5087
10:18 I have power to **lay** it **d**, and I have power 5087
11:32 and saw him, she **fell d** at his feet, 4098
13:12 and was **set d** again, he said unto them, 377
13:37 thee now? I will **lay d** my life for thy sake. 5087
13:38 Wilt thou **lay d** thy life for my sake? 5087
15:13 that a man **lay d** his life for his friends. 5087
19:13 **sat d** in the judgment seat in a place *that is* 2523
20: 5 And he **stooping d, and looking** in, 3879
20:11 she **stooped d, and looked** into 3879
Ac 4:35 And laid *them* *d* at the apostles' feet: and NIG
5: 5 And Ananias hearing these words **fell d**, 4098
5:10 Then **fell** she **d** straightway at his feet, and 4098
7:15 So Jacob **went d** into Egypt, and died, he, 2597
7:34 and am **come d** to deliver them. 2597
7:58 the witnesses **laid d** their clothes at a young 659
7:60 And he **kneeled d**, 1119+3588+5087
8: 5 Then Philip **went d** to the city of Samaria, 2718
8:15 Who, when they were **come d**, prayed for 2597
8:26 that **goeth d** from Jerusalem unto Gaza, 2597
8:38 and they **went d** both into the water, 2597
9:25 and **let** *him* **d** by the wall in a basket. 2524+5465
9:30 they **brought** him **d** to Cesarea, and 2609
9:32 **came d** also to the saints which dwelt at 2718
9:40 and **kneeled d**, and prayed; 1119+3588+5087
10:11 at the four corners, and **let d** to the earth: 2524
10:20 and **get** *thee* **d**, and go with them, 2597
10:21 Then Peter **went d** to the men which were 2597
10:25 and **fell d** at *his* feet, and worshipped *him*. 4098
11: 5 **let d** from heaven by four corners; 2524
12:19 And he **went d** from Judea to Cesarea, and 2718
13:14 synagogue on the sabbath day, and **sat d**. 2523
13:29 they **took** *him* **d** from the tree, and laid *him* 2507
14:11 The gods are **come d** to us in the likeness 2597
14:25 in Perga, they **went d** into Attalia: 2597
15: 1 And certain *men* which **came d** from Judea 2718
15:16 the tabernacle of David, which is **fallen d**; 4098
16: 8 And they passing by Mysia **came d** to 2597
16:13 and we **sat d**, and spake unto the women 2523
16:29 and **fell d before** Paul and Silas, 4363
17: 6 These that have **turned** the world **upside d** 387
18:22 saluted the church, he **went d** to Antioch. 2597
19:35 of the *image* which **fell d from Jupiter**? 1356
20: 9 he **sunk d** with sleep, and fell down from 2702
20: 9 and fell **d** from the third loft, and was taken 2736
20:10 And Paul **went d**, and fell on him, and 2597
20:36 **kneeled d**, and prayed with 1119+3588+5087
21: 5 and we **kneeled d** on 1119+3588+5087
21:10 there **came d** from Judea a certain prophet, 2718
21:32 and centurions, and **ran d** unto them: 2701
22:30 and **brought** Paul **d**, and set *him* before 2609
23:10 commanded the soldiers to **go d**, and 2597
23:15 that he **bring** him **d** unto you to morrow, 2609
23:20 **bring d** Paul to morrow into the council, 2609
24:22 Lysias the chief captain shall **come d**, 2597
25: 5 **go d with** *me*, and accuse this man, 4782
25: 6 than ten days, he **went d** unto Cesarea; 2597
25: 7 the Jews which **came d** from Jerusalem 2597
27:27 as we were **driven up and d** in Adria, 1308
27:30 when they had **let d** the boat into the sea, 5465
28: 6 have swollen, or **fallen d** dead suddenly: 2667
Ro 10: 6 (that is, to **bring** Christ **d** *from above*:) 2609
11: 3 thy prophets, and **digged d** thine altars; 2679
11:10 may not see, and **bow d** their back alway. 4781
16: 4 Who have for my life **laid d** their own 5294
1Co 10: 7 The people **sat d** to eat and drink, and 2523
14:25 **falling d** on *his* face he will worship God, 4098
15:24 when he shall have **put d** all rule and 2673
2Co 4: 9 but not forsaken; **cast d**, but not destroyed; 2598
7: 6 that comforteth *those that are* **cast d**, 5011
10: 4 mighty through God to the **pulling d** of 2506
10: 5 **Casting d** imaginations, and every high 2507
11:33 window in a basket was I **let d** by the wall, 5465
Eph 2:14 hath **broken d** the middle wall of partition 3089
4:26 let not the sun **go d** upon your wrath: 1931
Heb 1: 3 **sat d** on the right hand of the Majesty on 2523
10:12 for ever, **sat d** on the right hand of God; 2523
11:30 By faith the walls of Jericho **fell d**, 4098
12: 2 is **set d** at the right hand of the throne of 2523
12:12 Wherefore lift up the hands which **hang d**, 3935
Jas 1:17 and **cometh d** from the Father of lights, 2597
5: 4 labourers which have reaped *d* your fields, NIG
1Pe 1:12 with the Holy Ghost sent *d* from heaven; NIG
2Pe 2: 4 but **cast** *them* **d to hell**, and delivered *them* 5020
1Jn 3:16 *of God*, because he **laid d** his life for us: 5087
3:16 we ought to **lay d** *our* lives for the brethren. 5087
Rev 1:13 clothed with a garment **d to the foot**, and 4158
3:12 which **cometh d** out of heaven from my 2597
3:21 and am **set d** with my Father in his throne. 2523
4:10 twenty elders **fall d** before him that sat on 4098
5: 8 *and* twenty elders **fell d** before the Lamb, 4098
5:14 And the four *and* twenty elders **fell d** and 4098
10: 1 And I saw another mighty angel **come d** 2597
12:10 for the accuser of our brethren is **cast d**, 2598
12:12 for the devil is **come d** unto you, 2597
13:13 that he maketh fire **come d** from heaven on 2597
18: 1 I saw another angel **come d** from heaven, 2597
18:21 shall *that* great city Babylon be thrown **d**, NIG
19: 4 twenty elders and the four beasts **fell d** and 4098

Rev 20: 1 And I saw an angel **come d** from heaven, *2597*
20: 9 and fire **came d** from God out of heaven, *2597*
21: 2 **coming d** from God out of heaven, *2597*
22: 8 I **fell d** to worship before the feet of *4098*

DOWNSITTING (1) [DOWN, SIT]
Ps 139: 2 Thou knowest my **d** and mine uprising, 3427

DOWNWARD (5) [DOWN]
2Ki 19:30 Judah shall *yet* again take root **d**, 4295+3807.1
Ecc 3:21 the spirit of the beast that goeth **d** 4295+3807.1
Isa 37:31 of Judah shall again take root **d**, 4295+3807.1
Eze 1:27 the appearance of his loins even **d**, 4295+3807.1
8: 2 the appearance of his loins even **d**, 4295+3807.1

DOWRY (4)
Ge 30:20 God hath endued me with a good **d**; 2065
34:12 Ask me never so much **d** and gift, and 4119
Ex 22:17 he shall pay money according to the **d** of 4119
1Sa 18:25 The king desireth not *any* **d**, but an hundred 4119

DRACHMAS See DRAMS

DRAG (2) [DRAGGING]
Hab 1:15 in their net, and gather them in their **d**: 4365
1:16 their net, and burn incense unto their **d**; 4365

DRAGGING (1) [DRAG]
Jn 21: 8 two hundred cubits,) **d** the net with fishes. *4951*

DRAGON (19) [DRAGONS]
Ne 2:13 even before the **d** well, and to the dung 8577
Ps 91:13 and the **d** shalt thou trample under feet. 8577
Isa 27: 1 and he shall slay the **d** that *is* in the sea. 8577
51: 9 it that hath cut Rahab, *and* wounded the **d**? 8577
Jer 51:34 he hath swallowed me up like a **d**, 8577
Eze 29: 3 the great **d** that lieth in the midst of his 8577
Rev 12: 3 and behold a great red **d**, having seven *1404*
12: 4 the **d** stood before the woman which was *1404*
12: 7 and his angels fought against the **d**; *1404*
12: 7 the dragon; and the **d** fought and his angels, *1404*
12: 9 And the great **d** was cast *out, that* old *1404*
12:13 And when the **d** saw that he was cast unto *1404*
12:16 swallowed up the flood which the **d** cast *1404*
12:17 And the **d** was wroth with the woman, and *1404*
13: 2 and the **d** gave him his power, and his seat, *1404*
13: 4 And they worshipped the **d** which gave *1404*
13:11 two horns like a lamb, and he spake as a **d**. *1404*
16:13 like frogs *come* out of the mouth of the **d**, *1404*
20: 2 And he laid hold on the **d**, *that* old serpent, *1404*

DRAGONS (16) [DRAGON]
Dt 32:33 Their wine *is* the poison of **d**, and the cruel 8577
Job 30:29 I am a brother to **d**, and a companion to 8577
Ps 44:19 thou hast sore broken us in the place of **d**, 8577
74:13 thou brakest the heads of the **d** in 8577
148: 7 LORD from the earth, ye **d**, and all deeps: 8577
Isa 13:22 and **d** in *their* pleasant palaces: 8577
34:13 it shall be a habitation of **d**, *and* a court for 8577
35: 7 in the habitation of **d**, where each lay, 8577
43:20 field shall honour me, the **d** and the owls: 8577
Jer 9:11 will make Jerusalem heaps, *and* a den of **d**; 8577
10:22 the cities of Judah desolate, *and* a den of **d**. 8577
14: 6 they snuffed up the wind like **d**; 8577
49:33 Hazor shall be a dwelling for **d**, *and* 8577
51:37 a dwelling place for **d**, an astonishment, 8577
Mic 1: 8 I will make a wailing like the **d**, and 8577
Mal 1: 3 his heritage waste for the **d** of 8577

DRAMS (6)
1Ch 29: 7 five thousand talents and ten thousand **d**, 150
Ezr 2:69 and one thousand **d** *of* gold, 1871
8:27 Also twenty basons of gold, of a thousand **d**; 150
Ne 7:70 gave to the treasure a thousand **d** *of* gold, 1871
7:71 of the work twenty thousand **d** *of* gold, 1871
7:72 gave *was* twenty thousand **d** *of* gold, 1871

DRANK (18) [DRINK]
Ge 9:21 he **d** of the wine, and was drunken; and 8354
24:46 so I **d**, and she made the camels drink also. 8354
27:25 did eat: and he brought him wine, and he **d**. 8354
Nu 20:11 the congregation **d**, and their beasts *also*. 8354
Dt 32:38 *and* **d** the wine of their drink offerings? 8354
2Sa 12: 3 **d** of his own cup, and lay in his bosom, and 8354
1Ki 13:19 and did eat bread in his house, and **d** water. 8354
17: 6 flesh in the evening; and he **d** of the brook. 8354
Da 1: 5 king's meat, and of the wine which he **d**: 4960
1: 8 king's meat, nor with the wine which he **d**: 4960
5: 1 his lords, and **d** wine before the thousand. 8355
5: 3 his wives, and his concubines, **d** in them. 8355
5: 4 They **d** wine, and praised the gods of gold, 8355
Mk 14:23 he gave *it* to them: and they all **d** of it. *4095*
Lk 17:27 They did eat, they **d**, they married *wives*, *4095*
17:28 they did eat, they **d**, they bought, they sold, *4095*
Jn 4:12 and **d** thereof himself, and his children, and *4095*
1Co 10: 4 for they **d** of *that* spiritual Rock that *4095*

DRAUGHT (5)
2Ki 10:27 and made it a **d house** unto *this* day. 4280
Mt 15:17 into the belly, and is cast out into the **d**? *856*
Mk 7:19 but into the belly, and goeth out into the **d**, *856*
Lk 5: 4 into the deep, and let down your nets for a **d**. *61*
5: 9 at the **d** of the fishes which they had taken: *61*

DRAVE (13) [DRIVE]
Ex 14:25 chariot wheels, that they **d** them heavily: 5090
Jos 16:10 they **d** not **out** the Canaanites that dwelt in 3423
24:12 which **d** them **out** from before you, 1644
24:18 the LORD **d out** from before us all 1644
Jdg 1:19 he **d out** *the inhabitants of* the mountain; 3423
6: 9 **d** them **out** from before you, and gave you 1644
1Sa 30:20 *which* they **d** before those *other* cattle, and 5090
2Sa 6: 3 Ahio, the sons of Abinadab, **d** the new cart. 5090
2Ki 16: 6 Elath to Syria, and **d** the Jews from Elath: 5394
2Ki 17:21 Jeroboam **d** Israel from following 5080
1Ch 13: 7 of Abinadab: and Uzza and Ahio **d** the cart. 5090
Ac 7:45 whom God **d out** before the face of our *1856*
18:16 And he **d** them from the judgment seat. *556*

DRAW (76) [DRAWER, DRAWERS, DRAWETH, DRAWING, DRAWN, DREW, DREWEST]
Ge 24:11 *even* the time that *women* go out to **d** 7579
24:13 of the men of the city come out to **d** water: 7579
24:19 she said, I will **d** *water* for thy camels also, 7579
24:20 ran again unto the well to **d** *water*, and 7579
24:43 *that when* the virgin cometh forth to **d** 7579
24:44 drink thou, and I will also **d** for thy camels: 7579
Ex 3: 5 he said, **D** not **nigh** hither: put off thy shoes 7126
12:21 **D out** and take you a lamb according to 4900
15: 9 I will **d** my sword, my hand shall destroy 7324
Lev 26:33 and will **d out** a sword after you: 7324
Jdg 3:22 that he could not **d** the dagger out of his 8025
4: 6 *saying*, Go and **d** toward mount Tabor, and 4900
4: 7 I will **d** unto thee to the river Kishon 4900
9:54 said unto him, **D** thy sword, and slay me, 8025
19:13 let us **d near** to one of *these* places to lodge 7126
20:32 **d** them from the city unto the highways. 5423
1Sa 9:11 they found young maidens going out to **d** 7579
14:36 the priest, Let us **d near** hither unto God. 7126
14:38 Saul said, **D** ye **near** hither, all the chief of 5066
31: 4 **D** thy sword, and thrust me through 8025
2Sa 17:13 to that city, and we will **d** it into the river, 5498
1Ch 10: 4 **D** thy sword, and thrust me through 8025
Job 21:33 every man shall **d** after him, as *there are* 4900
40:23 he trusteth that he can **d up** Jordan into his 1518
41: 1 Canst thou **d out** leviathan with a hook? or 4900
Ps 28: 3 **D** me not **away** with the wicked, and 4900
35: 3 **D out** also the spear, and stop *the way* 7324
69:18 **D nigh** unto my soul, *and* redeem it: 7126
73:28 *it is* good for me to **d near** to God: I have 7132
85: 5 wilt thou **d out** thine anger to all 4900
107:18 and they **d near** unto the gates of death. 5060
119:150 They **d nigh** that follow after mischief: 7126
Pr 20: 5 but a man of understanding will **d** it **out**. 1802
Ecc 12: 1 nor the years **d nigh**, when thou shalt say, 5060
SS 1: 4 **D** me, we will run after thee: the king hath 4900
Isa 5:18 Woe unto them that **d** iniquity with cords 4900
5:19 counsel of the Holy One of Israel **d nigh** 7126
12: 3 Therefore with joy shall ye **d** water out of 7579
29:13 Forasmuch as this people **d near** *me* with 5066
45:20 **d near** together, ye *that are* escaped of 5066
57: 3 **d near** hither, ye sons of the sorceress, 7126
57: 4 ye a wide mouth, *and* **d out** the tongue? 748
58:10 *if* thou **d out** thy soul to the hungry, and 6329
66:19 Pul, and Lud, that **d** the bow, *to* Tubal, and 4900
Jer 30:21 I will **cause** him to **d near**, and he shall 7126
46: 3 the buckler and shield, and **d near** to battle. 5066
49:20 the least of the flock shall **d** them **out**: 5498
50:45 the least of the flock shall **d** them **out**: 5498
La 4: 3 Even the sea monsters **d out** the breast, 2502
Eze 5: 2 and I will **d out** a sword after them. 7324
5:12 and I will **d out** a sword after them. 7324
9: 1 **Cause** them that have charge over the city **to d near**, 7126
12:14 and I will **d out** the sword after them. 7324
21: 3 will **d forth** my sword out of his sheath, 3318
22: 4 thou hast **caused** thy days **to d near**, and 7126
28: 7 they shall **d** their swords against the beauty 7324
30:11 and they shall **d** their swords against Egypt, 7324
32:20 *to* the sword: **d** her and all her multitudes. 4900
Joel 3: 9 mighty *men*, let all the men of war **d near**; 5066
Na 3:14 **D** thee waters for the siege, fortify thy 7579
Hag 2:16 when *one* came to the pressfat for to **d out** 2834
Jn 2: 8 **D out** now, and bear unto the governor of *501*
4: 7 There cometh a woman of Samaria to **d** *501*
4:11 Sir, thou hast nothing to **d with**, and the well *502*
4:15 that I thirst not, neither come hither to **d**. *501*
6:44 except the Father which hath sent me **d** *1670*
12:32 up from the earth, will **d** all *men* unto me. *1670*
21: 6 now they were not able to **d** it for *1670*
Ac 20:30 speaking perverse *things*, to **d away** *645*
Heb 7:19 *did*; by the which we **d nigh** unto God. *1448*
10:22 Let us **d near** with a true heart in full *4334*
10:38 but if *any man* **d back**, my soul shall have *5288*
10:39 But we are not of *them* who **d back** unto *5289*
Jas 2: 6 and **d** you before the judgment seats? *1670*
4: 8 **D nigh** to God, and he will draw nigh to *1448*
4: 8 nigh to God, and he will **d nigh** to you. *1448*

DRAWER (1) [DRAW]
Dt 29:11 from the hewer of thy wood unto the **d** of 7579

DRAWERS (3) [DRAW]
Jos 9:21 and **d** of water unto all the congregation; 7579
9:23 and **d** of water for the house of my God. 7579
9:27 and **d** of water for the congregation, 7579

DRAWETH (12) [DRAW]
Dt 25:11 the wife of the one **d near** for to deliver her 7126
Jdg 19: 9 Behold now, the day **d** towards evening, 7503
Job 24:22 He **d** also the mighty with his power: 4900
33:22 his soul **d near** unto the grave, and his life 7126
Ps 10: 9 catch the poor, when he **d** him into his net. 4900
88: 3 and my life **d nigh** unto the grave. 5060
Isa 26:17 *that* **d near the time** of her delivery, is in 7126
Eze 7:12 The time is come, the day **d near**: let not 5060
Mt 15: 8 This people **d nigh** unto me with their *1448*
Lk 21: 8 saying, I am *Christ;* and the time **d near**: *1448*
21:28 up your heads; for your redemption **d nigh**. *1448*
Jas 5: 8 for the coming of the Lord **d nigh**. *1448*

DRAWING (2) [DRAW]
Jdg 5:11 **places of d** *water*, there shall they rehearse 4857
Jn 6:19 on the sea, and **d** nigh unto the ship: *1096*

DRAWN (28) [DRAW]
Nu 22:23 in the way, and his sword **d** in his hand: 8025
22:31 in the way, and his sword **d** in his hand: 8025
Dt 21: 3 *and* which hath not **d** in the yoke; 4900
30:17 shalt be **d away**, and worship other gods, 5080
Jos 5:13 against him with his sword **d** in his hand: 8025
8: 6 till we have **d** them from the city; for they 5423
8:16 and were **d away** from the city. 5423
15: 9 the border was **d** from the top of the hill 8388
15: 9 the border was **d** *to* Baalah, which *is* 8388
15:11 the border was **d** to Shicron, and 8388
18:14 the border was **d** *thence*, and 8388
18:17 was **d** from the north, and went forth *to* 8388
Jdg 20:31 the people, *and* were **d away** from the city; 5423
Ru 2: 9 drink of *that* which the young men have **d**. 7579
1Ch 21:16 having a **d** sword in his hand stretched out 8025
Job 20:25 It is **d**, and cometh out of the body; yea, 8025
Ps 37:14 The wicked have **d out** the sword, and 6605
55:21 softer than oil, yet *were* they **d swords**. 6609
Pr 24:11 to deliver *them that are* **d unto** death, 3947
Isa 21:15 from the **d** sword, and from the bent bow, 5203
28: 9 from the milk, *and* **d** from the breasts. 6267
Jer 22:19 **d** and cast forth beyond the gates of 5498
31: 3 *with* lovingkindness have I **d** thee. 4900
La 2: 3 he hath **d** back his right hand from before 7725
Eze 21: 5 have **d forth** my sword out of his sheath: 3318
21:28 even say thou, The sword, the sword *is* **d**: 6605
Ac 11:10 and all were **d up** again into heaven. *385*
Jas 1:14 when he is **d away** of his own lust, and *1828*

DREAD (9) [DREADFUL]
Ge 9: 2 the **d** of you shall be upon every beast of 2844
Ex 15:16 Fear and **d** shall fall upon them; by 6343
Dt 1:29 I said unto you, **D** not, neither be afraid of 6206
2:25 This day will I begin to put the **d** of thee 6343
11:25 the **d** of you upon all the land that ye shall 4172
1Ch 22:13 of good courage; **d** not, nor be dismayed. 3372
Job 13:11 make you afraid? and his **d** fall upon you? 6343
13:21 from me: and let not thy **d** make me afraid. 367
Isa 8:13 *let* him *be* your fear, and *let* him *be* your **d**. 6206

DREADFUL (9) [DREAD]
Ge 28:17 was afraid, and said, How **d** *is* this place! 3372
Job 15:21 A **d** sound *is* in his ears: in prosperity 6343
Eze 1:18 they were so high that they were **d**; 3374
Da 7: 7 **d** and terrible, and strong exceedingly; 1763
7:19 exceeding **d**, whose teeth *were of* iron, and 1763
9: 4 and said, O Lord, the great and **d** God, 3372
Hab 1: 7 They *are* terrible and **d**: their judgment and 3372
Mal 1:14 and my name *is* **d** among the heathen. 3372
4: 5 of the great and **d** day of the LORD: 3372

DREAM (74) [DREAMED, DREAMER, DREAMERS, DREAMETH, DREAMS]
Ge 20: 3 God came to Abimelech in a **d** by night, 2472
20: 6 God said unto him in a **d**, Yea, I know that 2472
31:10 up mine eyes, and saw in a **d**, and beheld, 2472
31:11 the angel of God spake unto me in a **d**, 2472
31:24 God came to Laban the Syrian in a **d** by 2472
37: 5 Joseph **dreamed** a **d**, and he told *it* his 2472
37: 6 I pray you, this **d** which I have dreamed: 2472
37: 9 he dreamed yet another **d**, and told it his 2472
37: 9 and said, Behold, I have dreamed a **d** more; 2472
37:10 What *is* this **d** that thou hast dreamed? 2472
40: 5 they dreamed a **d** both of them, each man 2472
40: 5 both of them, each man his **d** in one night, 2472
40: 5 according to the interpretation of his **d**, 2472
40: 8 We have dreamed a **d**, and *there is* no 2472
40: 9 the chief butler told his **d** to Joseph, and 2472
40: 9 said to him, In my **d**, behold, a vine *was* 2472
40:16 I also *was* in my **d**, and, behold, 2472
41: 7 Pharaoh awoke, and behold, *it was* a **d**. 2472
41: 8 Pharaoh told them his **d**; but *there was* 2472
41:11 we dreamed a **d** in one night, I and he; 2472
41:11 according to the interpretation of his **d**. 2472
41:12 to each man according to his **d** he did 2472
41:15 I have dreamed a **d**, and *there is* none that 2472
41:15 *that* thou canst understand a **d** to interpret 2472
41:17 Pharaoh said unto Joseph, In my **d**, behold, 2472
41:22 I saw in my **d**, and behold, seven ears came 2472
41:25 said unto Pharaoh, The **d** of Pharaoh *is* one: 2472
41:26 good ears *are* seven years: the **d** *is* one. 2472
41:32 for that the **d** was doubled unto Pharaoh 2472
Nu 12: 6 in a vision, *and* will speak unto him in a **d**. 2472
Jdg 7:13 *there was* a man that told a **d** unto his 2472
7:13 and said, Behold, I dreamed a **d**, and lo, 2472
7:15 *so*, when Gideon heard the telling of the **d**, 2472
1Ki 3: 5 appeared to Solomon in a **d** by night: 2472
3:15 Solomon awoke; and, behold, *it was* a **d**. 2472
Job 20: 8 He shall fly away as a **d**, and shall not be 2472
33:15 In a **d**, *in* a vision of the night, when deep 2472
Ps 73:20 As a **d** when *one* awaketh; *so*, O Lord, 2472
126: 1 captivity of Zion, we were like them that **d**. 2492
Ecc 5: 3 For a **d** cometh through the multitude of 2472
Isa 29: 7 shall be as a **d** of a night vision. 2472
Jer 23:28 The prophet that hath a **d**, let him tell a 2472
23:28 prophet that hath a dream, let him tell a **d**; 2472
Da 2: 3 I have dreamed a **d**, and my spirit was 2472
2: 3 and my spirit was troubled to know the **d**. 2472
2: 4 tell thy servants the **d**, and we will shew 2493
2: 5 if ye will not make known unto me the **d**, 2493
2: 6 if ye shew the **d**, and the interpretation 2493
2: 6 therefore shew me the **d**, and 2493
2: 7 Let the king tell his servants the **d**, and 2493
2: 9 if ye will not make known unto me the **d**, 2493
2: 9 therefore tell me the **d**, and I shall know 2493
2:26 Art thou able to make known unto me the **d** 2493
2:28 Thy **d**, and the visions of thy head upon thy 2493
2:36 This *is* the **d**; and we will tell 2493
2:45 the **d** *is* certain, and the interpretation 2493
4: 5 I saw a **d** which made me afraid, and 2493
4: 6 known unto me the interpretation of the **d**. 2493
4: 7 I told the **d** before them; but they *did* not 2493
4: 8 and before him I told the **d**, *saying*, 2493
4: 9 tell *me* the visions of my **d** that I have seen, 2493
4:18 This **d** I king Nebuchadnezzar have seen. 2493
4:19 let not the **d**, or the interpretation thereof, 2493

D

Da 4:19 the **d** *be* to them that hate thee, and 2493
7: 1 Belshazzar king of Babylon Daniel had a **d** 2493
7: 1 he wrote the **d**, *and* told the sum of 2493
Joel 2:28 your old men shall **d** dreams, 2492
Mt 1:20 angel of the Lord appeared unto him in a **d**, *3677*
2:12 And being warned of God in a **d** that *they* *3677*
2:13 of the Lord appeareth to Joseph in a **d**, *3677*
2:19 an angel of the Lord appeareth in a **d** to *3677*
2:22 being warned of God in a **d**, *3677*
27:19 I have suffered many *things* this day in a **d** *3677*
Ac 2:17 and your old men shall **d** dreams: *1797*

DREAMED (20) [DREAM]

Ge 28:12 he **d**, and behold a ladder set up on 2492
37: 5 Joseph **d** a dream, and he told *it* his 2492
37: 6 I pray you, this dream which I have **d**: 2492
37: 9 he **d** yet another dream, and told it his 2492
37: 9 and said, Behold, I have **d** a dream more; 2492
37:10 What *is* this dream that thou hast **d**? 2492
40: 5 they **d** a dream both of them, each man his 2492
40: 8 We have **d** a dream, and *there is* no 2492
41: 1 at the end of two full years, that Pharaoh **d**: 2492
41: 5 he slept and **d** the second time: and behold, 2492
41:11 we **d** a dream in one night, I and he; 2492
41:11 we **d** each man according to 2492
41:15 I have **d** a dream, and *there is* none that can 2492
42: 9 Joseph remembered the dreams which he **d** 2492
Jdg 7:13 and said, Behold, I **d** a dream, and lo, 2492
Jer 23:25 my name, saying, I have **d**, I have dreamed. 2492
23:25 my name, saying, I have dreamed, I have **d**. 2492
29: 8 to your dreams which ye **cause to be d**. 2492
Da 2: 1 Nebuchadnezzar **d** dreams, wherewith his 2492
2: 3 I have **d** a dream, and my spirit was 2492

DREAMER (4) [DREAM]

Ge 37:19 this **d** cometh. 1167+2472+1886.1
Dt 13: 1 or a **d** of dreams, and giveth thee a sign or 2492
13: 3 words of that prophet, or that **d** of dreams: 2492
13: 5 that prophet, or that **d** of dreams, shall be 2492

DREAMERS (2) [DREAM]

Jer 27: 9 nor to your diviners, nor to your **d**, nor to 2472
Jude 1: 8 Likewise also these *filthy* **d** defile the flesh, *1797*

DREAMETH (2) [DREAM]

Isa 29: 8 It shall even be as when a hungry *man* **d**, 2492
29: 8 or as when a thirsty *man* **d**, and behold, 2492

DREAMS (21) [DREAM]

Ge 37: 8 they hated him yet the more for his **d**, and 2472
37:20 and we shall see what will become of his **d**. 2472
41:12 we told him, and he interpreted to us our **d**; 2472
42: 9 Joseph remembered the **d** which he 2472
Dt 13: 1 or a dreamer of **d**, and giveth thee a sign or 2472
13: 3 words of that prophet, or that dreamer of **d**: 2472
13: 5 that prophet, or that dreamer of **d**, shall be 2472
1Sa 28: 6 neither by **d**, nor by Urim, nor by prophets. 2472
28:15 me no more, neither by prophets, nor by **d**: 2472
Job 7:14 thou scarest me with **d**, and terrifiest me 2472
Ecc 5: 7 For in the multitude of **d** and many words 2472
Jer 23:27 **d** which they tell every man to his 2472
23:32 I *am* against them that prophesy false **d**, 2472
29: 8 neither hearken to your **d** which ye cause to 2472
Da 1:17 had understanding in all visions and **d**. 2472
2: 1 Nebuchadnezzar dreamed **d**, wherewith his 2472
2: 2 the Chaldeans, for to shew the king his **d**. 2472
5:12 interpreting of **d**, and shewing of hard 2493
Joel 2:28 shall prophesy, your old men shall dream **d**, 2472
Zec 10: 2 have seen a lie, and have told false **d**; 2472
Ac 2:17 and your old men shall dream **d**: *1798*

DREGS (3)

Ps 75: 8 the **d** thereof, all the wicked of the earth 8105
Isa 51:17 thou hast drunken the **d** of the cup of 6907
51:22 *even* the **d** of the cup of my fury; 6907

DRESS (9) [DRESSED, DRESSER, DRESSETH, UNDRESSED, VINEDRESSERS]

Ge 2:15 put him into the garden of Eden to **d** it and 5647
18: 7 *it* unto a young man; and he hasted to **d** it. 6213
Dt 28:39 **d** *them*, but shalt neither drink *of* the wine, 5647
2Sa 12: 4 to **d** for the wayfaring man that was come 6213
13: 5 give me meat, and **d** the meat in my sight, 6213
13: 7 brother Amnon's house, and **d** him meat. 6213
1Ki 17:12 I may go in and **d** it for me and my son, 6213
18:23 fire *under*: and I will **d** the other bullock, 6213
18:25 one bullock for yourselves, and **d** *it* first; 6213

DRESSED (7) [DRESS]

Ge 18: 8 the calf which he had **d**, and set *it* before 6213
Lev 7: 9 all *that is* **d** in the fryingpan, and in the pan, 6213
1Sa 25:18 five sheep **ready d**, and five measures of 6213
2Sa 12: 4 and **d** it for the man that was come to him. 6213
19:24 had neither **d** his feet, nor trimmed his 6213
1Ki 18:26 they **d** *it*, and called on the name of Baal 6213
Heb 6: 7 forth herbs meet for them by whom it is **d**, *1090*

DRESSER (1) [DRESS]

Lk 13: 7 Then said he unto the **d** of his **vineyard**, *289*

DRESSETH (1) [DRESS]

Ex 30: 7 when he **d** the lamps, he shall burn incense 3190

DREW (85) [DRAW]

Ge 18:23 Abraham **d near**, and said, Wilt thou also 5066
24:20 well to draw *water*, and **d** for all his camels. 7579
24:45 **d** *water*: and I said unto her, Let me drink, 7579
37:28 they **d** and lift up Joseph out of the pit, and 4900
38:29 to pass, as he **d back** his hand, that, behold, 7725
47:29 the time **d nigh** that Israel must die: and 7126
Ex 2:10 she said, Because I **d** him out of the water. 4871
2:16 they came and **d water**, and filled 1802
2:19 also **d water enough** for us, and 1802+1802
14:10 when Pharaoh **d nigh**, the children of Israel 7126
20:21 Moses **d near** unto the thick darkness 5066
Lev 9: 5 all the congregation **d near** and 7126
Jos 8:11 **d nigh**, and came before the city, and 5066
8:26 For Joshua **d** not his hand **back**, 7725
Jdg 8:10 and twenty thousand men that **d** sword. 8025
8:20 the youth **d** not his sword: for he feared, 8025
20: 2 four hundred thousand footmen that **d** 8025
20:15 and six thousand men that **d** sword, 8025
20:17 four hundred thousand men that **d** sword: 8025
20:25 thousand men; all these **d** the sword. 8025
20:35 and an hundred men: all these **d** the sword. 8025
20:37 the liers in wait **d** *themselves* **along**, and 4900
20:46 and five thousand men that **d** the sword; 8025
Ru 4: 8 Buy *it* for thee. So he **d off** his shoe. 8025
1Sa 7: 6 **d** water, and poured *it* out before 7579
7:10 the Philistines **d near** to battle against 5066
9:18 Saul **d near** to Samuel in the gate, and 5066
17:16 the Philistine **d near** morning and evening, 5066
17:40 in his hand: and he **d near** to the Philistine. 5066
17:41 Philistine came on and **d near** unto David; 7131
17:48 came and **d nigh** to meet David, that David 7126
17:51 **d** it out of the sheath thereof, and slew him, 8025
2Sa 10:13 Joab **d nigh**, and the people that *were* with 5066
18:25 his mouth. And he came apace, and **d near**. 7131
22:17 he took me; he **d** me **out** of many waters; 4871
23:16 **d** water out of the well of Beth-lehem, 7579
24: 9 thousand valiant men that **d** the sword; 8025
1Ki 2: 1 Now the days of David **d nigh** that *he* 7126
8: 8 they **d out** the staves, that the ends of 748
22:34 a *certain* man **d** a bow at a venture, 4900
2Ki 3:26 he took with him seven hundred men that **d** 8025
9:24 **d** a bow with his **full strength**, 3027+4390+871.1
1Ch 11:18 **d** water out of the well of Beth-lehem, 7579
19:14 the people that *were* with him **d nigh** 5066
19:16 **d forth** the Syrians that *were* beyond 3318
21: 5 and an hundred thousand men that **d** sword: 8025
21: 5 and ten thousand men that **d** sword. 8025
2Ch 5: 9 they **d out** the staves *of the ark*, that the ends 748
14: 8 that bare shields and **d** bows, two hundred 1869
18:33 a *certain* man **d** a bow at a venture, 4900
Est 5: 2 So Esther **d near**, and touched the top of 7126
9: 1 his decree **d near** to be put in execution, 5060
Ps 18:16 he took me, he **d** me **out** of many waters. 4871
Isa 41: 5 of the earth were afraid, **d near**, and came. 7126
Jer 38:13 So they **d up** Jeremiah with cords, and 4900
Hos 11: 4 I **d** them with cords of a man, with bands of 4900
Zep 3: 2 in the LORD; she **d** not **near** to her God. 7126
Mt 13:48 they **d** to shore, and sat down, and *307*
21: 1 And when they **d nigh** unto Jerusalem, and *1448*
21:34 And when the time of the fruit **d near**, *1448*
26:51 and **d** his sword, and stroke a servant of *645*
Mk 6:53 the land of Genesaret, and **d to the shore**. *4358*
14:47 And one of them that stood by **d** a sword, *4685*
Lk 15: 1 Then **d near** unto him all the publicans and *1448*
15:25 and as he came and **d nigh** to the house, *1448*
22: 1 Now the feast of unleavened bread **d nigh**, *1448*
22:47 and **d near** unto Jesus to kiss him. *1448*
23:54 was the preparation, and the sabbath **d on**. *2020*
24:15 Jesus himself **d near**, and went with them. *1448*
24:28 And they **d nigh** unto the village, *1448*
Jn 2: 9 (but the servants which **d** the water knew;) *501*
18:10 Then Simon Peter having a sword **d** it, and *1670*
21:11 and **d** the net to land full of great fishes, *1670*
Ac 5:37 and **d away** much people after him: *868*
7:17 But when the time of the promise **d nigh**, *1448*
7:31 as he **d near** to behold *it*, the voice of *4334*
10: 9 on their journey, and **d nigh** unto the city, *1448*
14:19 having stoned Paul, **d** *him* out of the city, *4951*
16:19 **d** *them* into the market-place unto *1670*
16:27 he **d out** his sword, and would have killed *4685*
17: 6 they **d** Jason and certain brethren unto *4951*
19:33 And they **d** Alexander out of the multitude, *4264*
21:30 took Paul, and **d** him **out** of the temple: *1670*
27:27 deemed that they **d near** to some country; *4317*
Rev 12: 4 And his tail **d** the third *part* of the stars of *4951*

DREWEST (1) [DRAW]

La 3:57 Thou **d near** in the day *that* I called upon 7126

DRIED (39) [DRY]

Ge 8: 7 until the waters were **d up** from off 3001
8:13 the waters were **d up** from off the earth: 2717
8:14 day of the month, was the earth **d**. 3001
Lev 2:14 firstfruits green ears of corn **d** by the fire, 7033
Nu 6: 3 liquor of grapes, nor eat moist grapes, or **d**. 3002
11: 6 now our soul *is* **d away**: *there is* nothing at 3002
Jos 2:10 For we have heard how the LORD **d up** 3001
4:23 For the LORD your God **d up** the waters 3001
4:23 which he **d up** from before us, until we 3001
5: 1 heard that the LORD had **d up** the waters 3001
Jdg 16: 7 with seven green withs that were never **d**, 2717
16: 8 seven green withs which had not been **d**, 2717
1Ki 13: 4 **d up**, so that he could not pull it in again to 3001
17: 7 that the brook **d up**, because there had been 3001
2Ki 19:24 with the sole of my feet have I **d up** all 2717
Job 18:16 His roots shall be **d up** beneath, and 3001
28: 4 they are **d up**, they are gone away from 1809
Ps 22:15 My strength is **d up** like a potsherd; and 3001
69: 3 my throat is **d**: mine eyes fail while *I* wait 2787
106: 9 rebuked the Red sea also, and it was **d up**: 2717
Isa 5:13 and their multitude **d up** with thirst. 6704
19: 5 and the river shall be wasted and **d up**. 3001
19: 6 of defence shall be emptied and **d up**: 2717
37:25 with the sole of my feet have I **d up** all 2717
51:10 *Art* thou not it which hath **d** the sea, 2717
Jer 23:10 pleasant places of the wilderness are **d up**, 3001
50:38 *is* upon her waters; and they shall be **d up**: 3001
Eze 17:24 have **d up** the green tree, and have made 3001
19:12 and the east wind **d up** her fruit: 3001
37:11 Our bones are **d**, and our hope is lost: 3001
Hos 9:16 Ephraim is smitten, their root is **d up**, 3001
13:15 become dry, and his fountain shall be **d up**: 2717
Joel 1:10 the new wine is **d up**, the oil languisheth. 3001
1:12 The vine is **d up**, and the fig tree 3001
Joel 1:20 for the rivers of waters are **d up**, and 3001
Zec 11:17 his arm shall be **clean d up**, and 3001+3001
Mk 5:29 the fountain of her blood was **d up**; *3583*
11:20 they saw the fig tree **d up** from the roots. *3583*
Rev 16:12 and the water thereof was **d up**, that *3583*

DRIEDST (1) [DRY]

Ps 74:15 and the flood: thou **d up** mighty rivers. 3001

DRIETH (3) [DRY]

Job 14:11 the sea, and the flood decayeth and **d up**: 3001
Pr 17:22 a medicine: but a broken spirit **d** the bones. 3001
Na 1: 4 and maketh it dry, and **d up** all the rivers: 2717

DRINK (369) [DRANK, DRINKERS, DRINKETH, DRINKING, DRINKS, DRUNK, DRUNKARD, DRUNKARDS, DRUNKEN, DRUNKENNESS]

Ge 19:32 let us **make** our father **d** wine, and we will 8248
19:33 they **made** their father **d** wine that night: 8248
19:34 let us **make** him **d** wine this night also; and 8248
19:35 they **made** their father **d** wine that night 8248
21:19 the bottle *with* water, and **gave** the lad **d**. 8248
24:14 down thy pitcher, I pray thee, that I may **d**; 8354
24:14 **D**, and I will give thy camels drink also: 8354
24:14 Drink, and I will **give** thy camels **d** also: 8248
24:17 I pray thee, **d** a little water of thy pitcher. 1572
24:18 she said, **D**, my lord: and she hasted, and 8354
24:18 her pitcher upon her hand, and **gave** him **d**. 8248
24:19 when she had done **giving** him **d**, she said, 8248
24:43 **Give** me, I pray thee, a little water of thy pitcher **to d**; 8248
24:44 Both **d** thou, and I will also draw for thy 8354
24:45 and I said unto her, Let me **d**, I pray thee. 8248
24:46 **D**, and I will give thy camels drink also: 8354
24:46 Drink, and I will **give** thy camels **d** also: 8248
24:46 so I drank, and she **made** the camels **d** also. 8248
24:54 they did eat and **d**, he and the men that 8354
25:34 he did eat and **d**, and rose up, and went his 8354
26:30 made them a feast, and they did eat and **d**. 8354
30:38 troughs when the flocks came to **d**, 8354
30:38 they should conceive when they came to **d**. 8354
35:14 he poured a **d offering** thereon, and 5262
Ex 7:18 the Egyptians shall lothe to **d** of the water 8354
7:21 the Egyptians could not **d** of the water of 8354
7:24 digged round about the river *for* water to **d**; 8354
7:24 for they could not **d** of the water of 8354
15:23 they could not **d** of the waters of Marah, 8354
15:24 against Moses, saying, What shall we **d**? 8354
17: 1 and *there was* no water for the people to **d**. 8354
17: 2 and said, Give us water that we may **d**. 8354
17: 6 come water out of it, that the people may **d**. 8354
24:11 also they saw God, and did eat and **d**. 8354
29:40 *part* of a hin of wine *for* a **d offering**. 5262
29:41 according to the **d offering** thereof, for a 5262
30: 9 neither shall ye pour **d offering** thereon. 5262
32: 6 and the people sat down to eat and to **d**, and 8354
32:20 and **made** the children of Israel **d** *of it*. 8248
34:28 he did neither eat bread, nor **d** water. 8354
Lev 10: 9 Do not **d** wine nor strong drink, thou, 8354
10: 9 Do not drink wine nor **strong d**, thou, 7941
11:34 all **d** that may be drunk in every *such* vessel 4945
23:13 the **d offering** thereof *shall be of* wine, 5262
23:18 their meat offering, and their **d offerings**, 5262
23:37 meat offering, a sacrifice, and **d offerings**, 5262
Nu 5:24 he shall **cause** the woman **to d** the bitter 8248
5:26 afterward shall **cause** the woman **to d** 8248
5:27 And when he hath **made** her **to d** the water, 8248
6: 3 separate *himself* from wine and **strong d**, 7941
6: 3 *and* shall **d** no vinegar of wine, or 8354
6: 3 no vinegar of wine, or vinegar of **strong d**, 7941
6: 3 neither shall he **d** any liquor of grapes, 8354
6:15 their meat offering, and their **d offerings**. 5262
6:17 also his meat offering, and his **d offering**. 5262
6:20 and after *that* the Nazarite may **d** wine. 8354
15: 5 **d offering** shalt thou prepare with the burnt 5262
15: 7 for a **d offering** thou shalt offer the third 5262
15:10 thou shalt bring for a **d offering** half a hin 5262
15:24 with his meat offering, and his **d offering**, 5262
20: 5 neither *is there any* water to **d**. 8354
20: 8 **give** the congregation and their beasts **d**. 8248
20:17 neither will we **d** *of* the water of the wells: 8354
20:19 if I and my cattle **d** *of* thy water, then I will 8354
21:22 we will not **d** *of* the waters of the well: 8354
23:24 eat *of* the prey, and **d** the blood of the slain. 8354
28: 7 the **d offering** thereof *shall be* the fourth 5262
28: 7 poured unto the LORD *for* a **d offering**. 5262
28: 8 the morning, and as the **d offering** thereof, 5262
28: 9 with oil, and the **d offering** thereof: 5262
28:10 burnt offering, and his **d offering**. 5262
28:14 their **d offerings** shall be half a hin of wine 5262
28:15 burnt offering, and his **d offering**. 5262
28:24 burnt offering, and his **d offering**. 5262
28:31 you without blemish) and their **d offerings**. 5262
29: 6 his meat offering, and their **d offerings**, 5262
29:11 meat offering of it, and their **d offerings**. 5262
29:16 his meat offering, and his **d offering**. 5262
29:18 and their **d offerings** for the bullocks, 5262
29:19 offering thereof, and their **d offerings**. 5262
29:21 and their **d offerings** for the bullocks, 5262
29:22 and his meat offering, and his **d offering**. 5262
29:24 and their **d offerings** for the bullocks, 5262
29:25 his meat offering, and his **d offering**. 5262
29:27 and their **d offerings** for the bullocks, 5262
29:28 and his meat offering, and his **d offering**. 5262
29:30 and their **d offerings** for the bullocks, 5262
29:31 his meat offering, and his **d offering**. 5262
29:33 and their **d offerings** for the bullocks, 5262
29:34 his meat offering, and his **d offering**. 5262
29:37 and their **d offerings** for the bullock, 5262
29:38 and his meat offering, and his **d offering**. 5262
29:39 for your **d offerings**, and for your peace 5262
33:14 where was no water for the people to **d**. 8354
Dt 2: 6 water of them for money, that ye may **d**. 8354
2:28 and give me water for money, that I may **d**: 8354

Dt 9: 9 I neither did eat bread nor **d** water: 8354
9:18 nor **d** water, because of all your sins which 8354
14:26 or for **strong d**, or for whatsoever thy soul 7941
28:39 dress *them,* but shalt neither **d** *of* the wine, 8354
29: 6 neither have you drunk wine or **strong d**: 7941
32:14 thou didst **d** the pure blood of the grape. 8354
32:38 *and* drank the wine of their **d offerings**? 5257
Jdg 4:19 **Give** me, I pray thee, a little water **to d**; 8248
4:19 of milk, and **gave** him **d**, and covered him. 8248
7: 5 one that boweth down upon his knees to **d**. 8354
7: 6 bowed down upon their knees to **d** water. 8354
9:27 and did eat and **d**, and cursed Abimelech. 8354
13: 4 **d** not wine nor strong drink, and eat not 8354
13: 4 drink not wine nor **strong d**, and eat not 7941
13: 7 now **d** no wine nor strong drink, neither eat 8354
13: 7 now drink no wine nor **strong d**, neither eat 7941
13:14 neither let her **d** wine or strong drink, 8354
13:14 neither let her drink wine or **strong d**, 7941
19: 4 so they did eat and **d**, and lodged there. 8354
19: 6 and did eat and **d** both of them together: 8354
19:21 they washed their feet, and did eat and **d**. 8354
Ru 2: 9 **d** of *that* which the young men have drawn. 8354
1Sa 1:15 I have drunk neither wine nor **strong d**, but 7941
30:11 and he did eat; and they **made** him **d** water; 8248
2Sa 11:11 to eat and to **d**, and to lie with my wife? 8354
11:13 called him, he did eat and **d** before him; 8354
16: 2 such as be faint in the wilderness may **d**. 8354
19:35 can thy servant taste what I eat or what I **d**? 8354
23:15 Oh that one would **give** me **d** *of* the water 8248
23:16 nevertheless he would not **d** thereof, but 8354
23:17 therefore he would not **d** it. These *things* 8354
1Ki 1:25 behold, they eat and **d** before him, and say, 8354
13: 8 neither will I eat bread nor **d** water in this 8354
13: 9 saying, Eat no bread, nor **d** water, 8354
13:16 neither will I eat bread nor **d** water with 8354
13:17 Thou shalt eat no bread nor **d** water there, 8354
13:18 that he may eat bread and **d** water. 8354
13:22 say to thee, Eat no bread, and **d** no water; 8354
17: 4 it shall be, *that* thou shalt **d** of the brook; 8354
17:10 a little water in a vessel, that I may **d**. 8354
18:41 said unto Ahab, Get thee up, eat and **d**; 8354
18:42 So Ahab went up to eat and to **d**. 8354
19: 6 he did eat and **d**, and laid him down again. 8354
19: 8 did eat and **d**, and went in the strength of 8354
2Ki 3:17 that ye may **d**, *both* ye, and your cattle, and 8354
6:22 that they may eat and **d**, and go to their 8354
7: 8 did eat and **d**, and carried thence silver, and 8354
9:34 come in, he did eat and **d**, and said, Go, 8354
16:13 poured his **d offering**, and sprinkled 5262
16:15 their meat offering, and their **d offerings**; 5262
18:27 own dung, and **d** their own piss with you? 8354
18:31 **d** ye every one the waters of his cistern: 8354
1Ch 11:17 Oh that one would **give** me **d** *of* the water 8248
11:18 David would not **d** *of* it, but poured it out to 8354
11:19 that *I* should do this *thing:* shall I **d** 8354
11:19 Therefore he would not **d** it. These *things* 8354
29:21 with their **d offerings**, and sacrifices in 5262
29:22 **d** before the LORD on that day with great 8354
2Ch 28:15 gave them to eat and to **d**, and 8248
29:35 the **d offerings** for *every* burnt offering. 5262
Ezr 3: 7 meat, and **d**, and oil, unto them of Zidon, 4960
7:17 their meat offerings and their **d offerings**, 5261
10: 6 he did eat no bread, nor **d** water: 8354
Ne 8:10 **d** the sweet, and send portions unto *them* 8354
8:12 to **d**, and to send portions, and to make 8354
Est 1: 7 *they* **gave** *them* **d** in vessels of gold, 8248
3:15 And the king and Haman sat down to **d**; but 8354
4:16 neither eat nor **d** three days, night or day; 8354
Job 1: 4 their three sisters to eat and to **d** with them. 8354
21:20 and he shall **d** of the wrath of the Almighty. 8354
22: 7 hast not **given** water to the weary **to d**, 8248
Ps 16: 4 their **d offerings** of blood will I not offer, 5262
36: 8 thou shalt **make** them **d** *of* the river of thy 8248
50:13 the flesh of bulls, or **d** the blood of goats? 8354
60: 3 **made** us **to d** the wine *of* astonishment. 8248
69:21 and in my thirst they **gave** me vinegar **to d**. 8248
75: 8 the earth shall wring *them* out, *and* **d** *them.* 8354
78:15 and **gave** *them* **d** as *out of* the great depths. 8248
78:44 and their floods, *that* they could not **d**. 8354
80: 5 and **givest** them tears **to d** *in great* measure. 8248
102: 9 and mingled my **d** with weeping, 8249
104:11 They **give d** to every beast of the field: 8248
110: 7 He shall **d** of the brook in the way: 8354
Pr 4:17 of wickedness, and **d** the wine of violence. 8354
5:15 **D** waters out of thine own cistern, and 8354
9: 5 and **d** of the wine *which* I have mingled. 8354
20: 1 Wine *is* a mocker, **strong d** *is* raging: and 7941
23: 7 Eat and **d**, saith he to thee; but his heart *is* 8354
25:21 and if he *be* thirsty, **give** him water **to d**: 8248
31: 4 O Lemuel, *it is* not for kings to **d** wine; 8354
31: 4 to drink wine; nor for princes **strong d**: 7941
31: 5 Lest they **d**, and forget the law, and 8354
31: 6 Give **strong d** unto him that is ready to 7941
31: 7 Let him **d**, and forget his poverty, and 8354
Ecc 2:24 *than* that he should eat and **d**, and *that* he 8354
3:13 also that every man should eat and **d**, and 8354
5:18 *is* good and comely *for one* to eat and to **d**, 8354
8:15 than to eat, and to **d**, and to be merry: 8354
9: 7 and **d** thy wine with a merry heart; 8354
SS 5: 1 **d**, yea, drink abundantly, O beloved. 8354
5: 1 drink, yea, **d abundantly**, O beloved. 7937
8: 2 I would **cause** thee to **d** of spiced wine, 8248
Isa 5:11 *that* they may follow **strong d**; 7941
5:22 Woe unto *them that are* mighty to **d** wine, 8354
5:22 and men of strength to mingle **strong d**: 7941
21: 5 the table, watch *in* the watchtower, eat, **d**: 8354
22:13 let us eat and **d**; for to morrow we shall die. 8354
24: 9 They shall not **d** wine with a song; 8354
24: 9 **strong d** shall be bitter to them that drink 7941
24: 9 strong drink shall be bitter to them that **d** it. 8354
28: 7 and through **strong d** are out of the way; 7941
28: 7 the prophet have erred through **strong d**, 7941
28: 7 they are out of the way through **strong d**; 7941
29: 9 they stagger, but not *with* **strong d**. 7941
32: 6 and he will cause the **d** of the thirsty to fail. 4945

Isa 36:12 own dung, and **d** their own piss with you? 8354
36:16 **d** ye every one the waters of his own 8354
43:20 to **give d** to my people, my chosen. 8248
51:22 of my fury; thou shalt no more **d** it again: 8354
56:12 and we will fill ourselves with **strong d**; 7941
57: 6 even to them hast thou poured a **d offering**, 5262
62: 8 the sons of the stranger shall not **d** thy 8354
62: 9 they that have brought it together shall **d** it 8354
65:11 that furnish the **d offering** unto *that* 4469
65:13 my servants shall **d**, but ye shall be thirsty: 8354
Jer 2:18 the way of Egypt, to **d** the waters of Sihor? 8354
2:18 of Assyria, to **d** the waters of the river? 8354
7:18 to pour out **d offerings** unto other gods, 5262
8:14 **given** us water of gall **to d**, because 8248
9:15 and **give** them water of gall **to d**. 8248
16: 7 and **give** them the cup of consolation **to d** for 8248
16: 8 of feasting, to sit with them to eat and to **d**. 8354
19:13 have poured out **d offerings** unto other 5262
22:15 did not thy father eat and **d**, and 8354
23:15 and **make** them **d** the water of gall: 8248
25:15 **cause** all the nations, to whom I send thee, **to d** 8248
25:16 they shall **d**, and be moved, and be mad, 8354
25:17 **made** all the nations **to d**, unto whom 8248
25:26 and the king of Sheshach shall **d** after them. 8354
25:27 **D** ye, and be drunken, and spue, and fall, 8354
25:28 refuse to take the cup at thine hand to **d**, 8354
25:28 of hosts; Ye shall **certainly d**. 8354+8354
32:29 and poured out **d offerings** unto other gods, 5262
35: 2 of the chambers, and **give** them wine **to d**. 8248
35: 5 and cups, and I said unto them, **D** ye wine. 8354
35: 6 they said, We will **d** no wine: for Jonadab 8354
35: 6 saying, Ye shall **d** no wine, *neither* ye, 8354
35: 8 to **d** no wine all our days, we, our wives, 8354
35:14 that he commanded his sons not to **d** wine, 8354
35:14 for unto this day they **d** none, but 8354
44:17 to pour out **d offerings** unto her, as we 5262
44:18 to pour out **d offerings** unto her, we have 5262
44:19 poured out **d offerings** unto her, did we 5262
44:19 pour out **d offerings** unto her, without our 5262
44:25 and to pour out **d offerings** unto her: 5262
49:12 they whose judgment *was* not to **d** of 8354
49:12 but thou shalt **surely d** *of it.* 8354+8354
Eze 4:11 Thou shalt **d** also water by measure, 8354
4:11 of a hin: from time to time shalt thou **d**. 8354
4:16 they shall **d** water by measure, and 8354
12:18 **d** thy water with trembling and 8354
12:19 and **d** their water with astonishment, 8354
20:28 and poured out there their **d offerings**. 5262
23:32 Thou shalt **d** *of* thy sister's cup deep and 8354
23:34 Thou shalt even **d** it and suck *it* out, and 8354
25: 4 shall eat thy fruit, and they shall **d** thy milk. 8354
31:14 stand up in their height, all that **d** water: 8354
31:16 and best of Lebanon, all that **d** water, 8354
34:19 they **d** that which ye have fouled with your 8354
39:17 that ye may eat flesh, and **d** blood. 8354
39:18 **d** the blood of the princes of the earth, 8354
39:19 *ye* be full, and **d** blood till *ye* be drunken, 8354
44:21 Neither shall any priest **d** wine, when they 8354
45:17 **d offerings**, in the feasts, and in the new 5262
Da 1:10 who hath appointed your meat and your **d**: 4960
1:12 them give us pulse to eat, and water to **d**. 8354
1:16 their meat, and the wine that they should **d**; 4960
5: 2 and his concubines, might **d** therein. 8355
Hos 2: 5 my wool and my flax, mine oil and my **d**. 8250
4:18 Their **d** is sour; they have committed 5435
Joel 1: 9 the **d offering** is cut off from the house of 5262
1:13 the **d offering** is withholden from the house 5262
2:14 a **d offering** unto the LORD your God? 5262
3: 3 and sold a girl for wine, that they might **d**. 8354
Am 2: 8 they **d** the wine of the condemned *in* 8354
2:12 ye **gave** the Nazarites wine **to d**; 8248
4: 1 say to their masters, Bring, and let us **d**. 8354
4: 8 cities wandered unto one city, to **d** water; 8354
5:11 but ye shall not **d** wine of them. 8354
6: 6 That **d** wine in bowls, and 8354
9:14 plant vineyards, and **d** the wine thereof; 8354
Ob 1:16 *so* shall all the heathen **d** continually, yea, 8354
1:16 they shall **d**, and they shall swallow down, 8354
Jnh 3: 7 any thing: let them not feed, nor **d** water: 8354
Mic 2:11 unto thee of wine and of **strong d**; 7941
6:15 and sweet wine, but shalt not **d** wine. 8354
Hab 2:15 Woe unto him that **giveth** his neighbour **d**, 8248
2:16 **d** thou also, and let thy foreskin be 8354
Zep 1:13 plant vineyards, but not **d** the wine thereof. 8354
Hag 1: 6 *ye* **d**, but ye are not filled with drink; 8354
1: 6 *ye* drink, but ye are not **filled with d**; 7937
Zec 7: 6 when ye did eat, and when ye did **d**, did not 8354
7: 6 eat *for yourselves*, and **d** *for yourselves?* 8354
9:15 they shall **d**, *and* make a noise as *through* 8354
Mt 6:25 what ye shall eat, or what ye shall **d**; 4095
6:31 or, What shall we **d**? or, Wherewithal shall 4095
10:42 And whosoever shall **give to d** unto one of 4222
20:22 Are ye able to **d** *of* the cup that I shall drink 4095
20:22 Are ye able to drink *of* the cup that I shall **d** 4095
20:23 Ye shall **d** indeed *of* my cup, and 4095
24:49 and to eat and **d** with the drunken; 4095
25:35 I was thirsty, and ye **gave** me **d**: I was a 4222
25:37 and fed *thee?* or thirsty, and **gave** *thee* **d**? 4222
25:42 I was thirsty, and ye **gave** me no **d**: 4222
26:27 and gave *it* to them, saying, **D** ye all of it; 4095
26:29 I will not **d** henceforth of this fruit of 4095
26:29 until that day when I **d** it new with you in 4095
26:42 from me, except I **d** it, thy will be done. 4095
27:34 They gave him vinegar to **d** mingled with 4095
27:34 when he had tasted *thereof,* he would not **d**. 4095
27:48 and put *it* on a reed, and **gave** him **to d**. 4222
Mk 9:41 **give** you a cup of water **to d** in my name, 4222
10:38 can ye **d** *of* the cup that I drink *of?* and be 4095
10:38 can ye drink *of* the cup that I **d** *of?* and be 4095
10:39 Ye shall indeed **d** *of* the cup that I drink *of;* 4095
10:39 Ye shall indeed drink *of* the cup that I **d** *of;* 4095
14:25 I will **d** no more of the fruit of the vine, 4095
14:25 until that day that I **d** it new in the kingdom 4095
15:23 And they gave him to **d** wine mingled with 4095

Mk 15:36 and **gave** him **to d**, saying, Let alone; 4222
16:18 if they **d** any deadly *thing,* it shall not hurt 4095
Lk 1:15 and shall **d** neither wine nor strong drink; 4095
1:15 and shall drink neither wine nor **strong d**; 4608
5:30 do ye eat and **d** with publicans and sinners? 4095
5:33 of the Pharisees; but thine eat and **d**? 4095
12:19 take thine ease, eat, **d**, *and* be merry. 4095
12:29 or what ye shall **d**, neither be ye of doubtful 4095
12:45 and to eat and **d**, and to be drunken; 4095
17: 8 and afterward thou shalt eat and **d**? 4095
22:18 I will not **d** of the fruit of the vine, 4095
22:30 may eat and **d** at my table in my kingdom, 4095
Jn 4: 7 Jesus saith unto her, Give me to **d**. 4095
4: 9 *is it that* thou, being a Jew, askest **d** of me, 4095
4:10 who it is that saith to thee, Give me to **d**; 4095
6:53 and **d** his blood, ye have no life in you. 4095
6:55 is meat indeed, and my blood is **d** indeed. 4213
7:37 *man* thirst, let him come unto me, and **d**. 4095
18:11 my Father hath given me, shall I not **d** it? 4095
Ac 9: 9 without sight, and neither did eat nor **d**. 4095
10:41 and **d with** him after he rose from the dead. 4844
23:12 saying that *they* would neither eat nor **d** till 4095
23:21 that *they* will neither eat nor **d** till they have 4095
Ro 12:20 feed him; if he thirst, **give** him **d**: 4222
14:17 For the kingdom of God is not meat and **d**; 4213
14:21 *It is* good neither to eat flesh, nor to **d** wine, 4095
1Co 9: 4 Have we not power to eat and to **d**? 4095
10: 4 And did all **d** the same spiritual drink: 4095
10: 4 And did all drink the same spiritual **d**: 4188
10: 7 The people sat down to eat and **d**, and 4095
10:21 Ye cannot **d** the cup of the Lord, and 4095
10:31 therefore ye eat, or **d**, or whatsoever ye do, 4095
11:22 have ye not houses to eat and to **d** *in?* or 4095
11:25 as oft as ye **d** *it,* in remembrance of me. 4095
11:26 as often as ye eat this bread, and **d** this cup, 4095
11:27 and **d** *this* cup of the Lord unworthily, 4095
11:28 let him eat of *that* bread, and **d** of *that* cup. 4095
12:13 have been all **made to d** into one Spirit. 4222
15:32 let us eat and **d**; for to morrow we die. 4095
Col 2:16 or in **d**, or in respect of a holyday, or of 4213
1Ti 5:23 **D** no longer **water**, but use a little wine for 5202
Rev 14: 8 she **made** all nations **d** of the wine of 4222
14:10 The same shall **d** of the wine of the wrath 4095
16: 6 and thou hast given them blood to **d**; 4095

DRINKERS (1) [DRINK]

Joel 1: 5 howl, all ye **d** of wine, because of the new 8354

DRINKETH (17) [DRINK]

Ge 44: 5 *Is* not this *it* in which my lord **d**, and 8354
Dt 11:11 valleys, *and* **d** water of the rain of heaven: 8354
Job 6: 4 the poison whereof **d up** my spirit: 8354
15:16 filthy *is* man, which **d** iniquity like water? 8354
34: 7 *Is* like Job, *who* **d up** scorning like water? 8354
40:23 Behold, he **d up** a river, *and* hasteth not: 6231
Pr 26: 6 of a fool cutteth off the feet, *and* **d** damage. 8354
Isa 29: 8 a thirsty *man* dreameth, and behold, he **d**; 8354
44:12 strength faileth: he **d** no water, and is faint. 8354
Mk 2:16 he eateth and **d** with publicans and sinners? 4095
Jn 4:13 Whosoever **d** of this water shall thirst 4095
4:14 But whosoever **d** of the water that I shall 4095
6:54 my flesh, and **d** my blood, hath eternal life; 4095
6:56 and **d** my blood, dwelleth in me, and I in 4095
1Co 11:29 For he that eateth and **d** unworthily, eateth 4095
11:29 eateth and **d** damnation to himself, 4095
Heb 6: 7 For the earth which **d** *in* the rain that 4095

DRINKING (21) [DRINK]

Ge 24:19 for thy camels also, until they have done **d**. 8354
24:22 it came to pass, as the camels had done **d**, 8354
Ru 3: 3 until he shall have done eating and **d**. 8354
1Sa 30:16 eating and **d**, and dancing, because of all 8354
1Ki 4:20 eating and **d**, and making merry. 8354
10:21 all king Solomon's **d** vessels *were of* gold, 4945
16: 9 **d** *himself* drunk *in* the house of Arza 8354
20:12 as he *was* **d**, he and the kings in 8354
20:16 Ben-hadad *was* **d** *himself* drunk in 8354
1Ch 12:39 were with David three days, eating and **d**: 8354
2Ch 9:20 all the **d** vessels of king Solomon *were of* 4945
Est 1: 8 the **d** *was* according to the law; none did 8360
Job 1:13 and **d** wine in their eldest brother's house: 8354
1:18 and **d** wine in their eldest brother's house: 8354
Isa 22:13 and killing sheep, eating flesh, and **d** wine: 8354
Mt 11:18 For John came neither eating nor **d**, and 4095
11:19 The Son of man came eating and **d**, and 4095
24:38 before the flood they were eating and **d**, 4095
Lk 7:33 came neither eating bread nor **d** wine; 4095
7:34 The Son of man is come eating and **d**; and 4095
10: 7 eating and **d** such *things* as they give: 4095

DRINKS (1) [DRINK]

Heb 9:10 *Which stood* only in meats and **d**, and 4188

DRIVE (57) [DRAVE, DRIVEN, DRIVER, DRIVETH, DRIVING, DROVE, OVERDRIVE]

Ex 6: 1 with a strong hand shall he **d** them **out** of 1644
23:28 which shall **d out** the Hivite, the Canaanite, 1644
23:29 I will not **d** them **out** from before thee in 1644
23:30 little I will **d** them **out** from before thee, 1644
23:31 thou shalt **d** them out before thee. 1644
33: 2 and I will **d out** the Canaanite, the Amorite, 1644
34:11 I **d out** before thee the Amorite, and 1644
Nu 22: 6 and *that* I may **d** them **out** of the land: 1644
22:11 be able to overcome them, and **d** them **out**. 1644
33:52 ye shall **d out** all the inhabitants of the land 3423
33:55 if ye will not **d out** the inhabitants of 3423
Dt 4:38 To **d out** nations from before thee greater 3423
9: 3 so shalt thou **d** them **out**, and destroy them 3423
9: 4 LORD doth **d** them **out** from before thee. 3423
9: 5 thy God doth **d** them **out** from before thee, 3423
11:23 will the LORD **d out** all these nations 3423
18:12 thy God doth **d** them **out** from before thee. 3423
Jos 3:10 *that* he will **without fail d out** from 3423+3423
13: 6 them will I **d out** from before the children 3423

D

Jos 14:12 I shall *be able to* **d** them **out**, as the LORD 3423
15:63 the children of Judah could not **d** them **out**: 3423
17:12 the children of Manasseh could not **d out** 3423
17:13 but did not **utterly d** them **out**. 3423+3423
17:18 for thou shalt **d out** the Canaanites, 3423
23: 5 and **d** them from out of your sight; 3423
23:13 **d out** *any of* these nations from before you; 3423
Jdg 1:19 could not **d out** the inhabitants of 3423
1:21 the children of Benjamin did not **d out** 3423
1:27 Neither did Manasseh **d out** *the inhabitants* 3423
1:28 and did not **utterly d** them **out**. 3423+3423
1:29 Neither did Ephraim **d out** the Canaanites 3423
1:30 Neither did Zebulun **d out** the inhabitants 3423
1:31 Neither did Asher **d out** the inhabitants of 3423
1:32 of the land: for they did not **d** them **out**. 3423
1:33 Neither did Naphtali **d out** the inhabitants 3423
2: 3 I will not **d** them **out** from before you; 1644
2:21 I also will not henceforth **d out** any from 3423
2Ki 4:24 our God shall **d out** from before us, 3423
4:24 **D**, and go *forward;* slack not *thy* riding for 5090
2Ch 20: 7 who didst **d out** the inhabitants of this land 3423
Job 18:11 on every side, and shall **d** him to his feet. 6327
24: 3 They **d away** the ass of the fatherless, 5090
Ps 44: 2 *How* thou didst **d out** the heathen *with* thy 3423
68: 2 As smoke is driven away, *so* **d** *them* **away**: 5086
Pr 22:15 the rod of correction shall **d** it **far** from 7368
Isa 22:19 I will **d** thee from thy station, and from thy 1920
Jer 24: 9 a curse, in all places whither I shall **d** them. 5080
27:10 *that* I should **d** you **out**, and ye should 5080
27:15 that I might **d** you **out**, and that ye might 5080
46:15 stood not, because the LORD did **d** them. 1920
Eze 4:13 among the Gentiles, whither I will **d** them. 5080
Da 4:25 That they *shall* **d** thee from men, and 2957
4:32 they *shall* **d** thee from men, and 2957
Hos 9:15 doings I will **d** them **out** of mine house, 1644
Joel 2:20 will **d** him into a land barren and desolate, 5080
Zep 2: 4 they shall **d out** Ashdod at the noon day, 1644
Ac 27:15 bear up into the wind, we **let** *her* **d**. *1929+5342*

DRIVEN (49) [DRIVE]

Ge 4:14 thou hast **d** me **out** *this* day from the face 1644
Ex 10:11 they were **d out** from Pharaoh's presence. 1644
22:10 it die, or be hurt, or **d away**, no man seeing 7617
Nu 32:21 until he hath **d out** his enemies from before 3423
Dt 4:19 shouldest be **d** to worship them, and 5080
30: 1 whither the LORD thy God hath **d** thee, 5080
30: 4 If *any* of thine be **d out** unto the outmost 5080
Jos 23: 9 For the LORD hath **d out** from before you 3423
1Sa 26:19 for they have **d** me **out** *this* day from 1644
Job 6:13 in me? and is wisdom **d** *quite* from me? 5080
13:25 Wilt thou break a leaf **d to and fro**? and 5086
18:18 He shall be **d** from light into darkness, and 1920
30: 5 They were **d forth** from among men, 1644
Ps 40:14 let them be **d** backward and put to shame 5472
68: 2 As smoke is **d away**, *so* drive *them* away: 5086
114: 3 sea saw *it*, and fled: Jordan was **d** back. 5437
114: 5 thou Jordan, *that* thou wast **d** back? 5437
Pr 14:32 The wicked is **d away** in his wickedness: 1760
Isa 8:22 of anguish; and *they shall be* **d** *to* darkness. 5080
19: 7 shall wither, be **d away**, and *be* no *more*. 5086
41: 2 *to* his sword, *and* as **d** stubble *to* his bow. 5086
Jer 8: 3 in all the places whither I have **d** them, 5080
16:15 from all the lands whither he had **d** them: 5080
23: 2 **d** them **away**, and have not visited them: 5080
23: 3 out of all countries whither I have **d** them, 5080
23: 8 from all countries whither I had **d** them; 5080
23:12 they shall be **d on**, and fall therein: for I 1760
29:14 from all the places whither I have **d** you, 5080
29:18 among all the nations whither I have **d** 5080
32:37 whither I have **d** them in mine anger, and 5080
40:12 out of all places whither they were **d**, 5080
43: 5 whither they had been **d**, to dwell in 5080
46:28 end of all the nations whither I have **d** thee: 5080
49: 5 ye shall be **d out** every man right forth; 5080
50:17 scattered sheep; the lions have **d** *him* **away**: 5080
Eze 31:11 I have **d** him **out** for his wickedness. 1644
34: 4 ye brought again that which was **d away**, 5080
34:16 bring again that which was **d away**, and 5080
Da 4:33 he *was* **d** from men, and did eat grass as 2957
5:21 he *was* **d** from the sons of men; and 2957
9: 7 all the countries whither thou hast **d** them, 5080
Hos 13: 3 as the chaff *that* is **d with a whirlwind** out 5590
Mic 4: 6 I will gather her that is **d out**, and *her* that I 5080
Zep 3:19 that halteth, and gather her that was **d out**; 5080
Lk 8:29 and was **d** of the devil into the wilderness.) *1643*
Ac 27:17 the quicksands, strake sail, and so were **d**. *5342*
27:27 as we were **d up and down** in Adria, *1308*
Jas 1: 6 is like a wave of the sea **d with the wind** *416*
3: 4 they be so great, and are **d** of fierce winds, *1643*

DRIVER (2) [DRIVE]

1Ki 22:34 wherefore he said unto the **d of** his **chariot**, 7395
Job 39: 7 neither regardeth he the crying of the **d**. 5065

DRIVETH (4) [DRIVE]

2Ki 9:20 Jehu the son of Nimshi; for he **d** furiously. 5090
Ps 1: 4 *are* like the chaff which the wind **d away**. 5086
Pr 25:23 The north wind **d away** rain: so *doth* an 2342
Mk 1:12 And immediately the Spirit **d** him into *1544*

DRIVING (4) [DRIVE]

Jdg 2:23 those nations, without **d** them **out** hastily; 3423
2Ki 9:20 the **d** *is* like the driving of Jehu the son of 4491
9:20 the driving *is* like the **d** of Jehu the son of 4491
1Ch 17:21 by **d out** nations from before thy people, 1644

DROMEDARIES (3) [DROMEDARY]

1Ki 4:28 **d** brought they unto the place where 7409
Est 8:10 *and* riders on mules, camels, *and* young **d**: 7424
Isa 60: 6 cover thee, the **d** of Midian and Ephah; 1070

DROMEDARY (1) [DROMEDARIES]

Jer 2:23 *thou art* a swift **d** traversing her ways; 1072

DROP (15) [DROPPED, DROPPETH, DROPPING, DROPS]

Dt 32: 2 My doctrine shall **d** as the rain, my speech 6201
33:28 wine; also his heavens shall **d down** dew. 6201
Job 36:28 Which the clouds do **d** *and* distil upon man 5140
Ps 65:11 with thy goodness; and thy paths **d** fatness. 7491
65:12 They **d** *upon* the pastures of the wilderness: 7491
Pr 3:20 broken up, and the clouds **d down** the dew. 7491
5: 3 For the lips of a strange *woman* **d** *as* a 5197
SS 4:11 O *my* spouse, **d** *as* the honeycomb: 5197
Isa 40:15 the nations *are* as a **d** of a bucket, and 4752
45: 8 **D down**, ye heavens, from above, and 7491
Eze 20:46 **d** *thy word* toward the south, and 5197
21: 2 **d** *thy word* toward the holy places, and 5197
Joel 3:18 *that* the mountains shall **d down** new wine, 5197
Am 7:16 **d** not *thy word* against the house of Isaac. 5197
9:13 the mountains shall **d** sweet wine, and 5197

DROPPED (7) [DROP]

Jdg 5: 4 the earth trembled, and the heavens **d**, 5197
5: 4 heavens dropped, the clouds also **d** water. 5197
1Sa 14:26 come into the wood, behold the honey **d**; 1982
2Sa 21:10 from the beginning of harvest until water **d** 5413
Job 29:22 not again; and my speech **d** upon them. 5197
Ps 68: 8 the heavens also **d** at the presence of God: 5197
SS 5: 5 my hands **d** *with* myrrh, and my fingers 5197

DROPPETH (1) [DROP]

Ecc 10:18 idleness of the hands the house **d through**. 1811

DROPPING (3) [DROP]

Pr 19:13 the contentions of a wife *are* a continual **d**. 1812
27:15 A **continual d** in a very rainy day 1812+2956
SS 5:13 his lips *like* lilies, **d** sweet smelling myrrh. 5197

DROPS (4) [DROP]

Job 36:27 For he maketh small the **d** of water: 5198
38:28 a father? or who hath begotten the **d** of dew? 96
SS 5: 2 *and* my locks *with* the **d** of the night. 7447
Lk 22:44 his sweat was as it were great **d** of blood *2361*

DROPSY (1)

Lk 14: 2 a certain man before him, which **had the d**. *5203*

DROSS (8)

Ps 119:119 away all the wicked of the earth *like* **d**: 5509
Pr 25: 4 Take away the **d** from the silver, and 5509
26:23 *are like* a potsherd covered with silver **d**. 5509
Isa 1:22 Thy silver is become **d**, thy wine mixt with 5509
1:25 purely purge away thy **d**, and take away all 5509
Eze 22:18 the house of Israel is to me become **d**: 5509
22:18 of the furnace; they are *even the* **d** *of* silver. 5509
22:19 Because ye are all become **d**, 5509

DROUGHT (10)

Ge 31:40 the **d** consumed me, and the frost by night; 2721
Dt 8:15 scorpions, and **d**, where *there was* no water; 6774
Job 24:19 **D** and heat consume the snow waters: *so* 6723
Ps 32: 4 my moisture is turned into the **d** of 2725
Isa 58:11 satisfy thy soul in **d**, and make fat thy 6710
Jer 2: 6 through a land of **d**, and of the shadow of 6723
17: 8 shall not be careful in the year of **d**, 1226
50:38 A **d** *is* upon her waters; and they shall be 2721
Hos 13: 5 in the wilderness, in the land of **great d**. 8514
Hag 1:11 I called *for* a **d** upon the land, and upon 2721

DROVE (13) [DRIVE, DROVES]

Ge 3:24 So he **d out** the man; and he placed at 1644
15:11 upon the carcases, Abram **d** them **away**. 5380
32:16 his servants, **every d** by themselves; 5739+5739
32:16 and put a space betwixt **d** and drove. 5739
32:16 and put a space betwixt drove and **d**. 5739
33: 8 What meanest thou by all this **d** which I 4264
Ex 2:17 the shepherds came and **d** them **away**: but 1644
Nu 21:32 and **d out** the Amorites that *were* there. 3423
Jos 15:14 Caleb **d** thence the three sons of Anak, 3423
1Ch 8:13 who **d away** the inhabitants of Gath: 1272
Ps 34: T who **d** him **away**, and he departed. 1644
Hab 3: 6 he beheld, and **d asunder** the nations; and 5425
Jn 2:15 he **d** *them* all **out** of the temple, and *1544*

DROVES (1) [DROVE]

Ge 32:19 and all that followed the **d**, saying, 5739

DROWN (2) [DROWNED]

SS 8: 7 quench love, neither can the floods **d** it: 7857
1Ti 6: 9 which **d** men in destruction and perdition. *1036*

DROWNED (5) [DROWN]

Ex 15: 4 his chosen captains also are **d** in the Red 2883
Am 8: 8 it shall be cast out and **d**, as *by* the flood of 8257
9: 5 and shall be **d**, as *by* the flood of Egypt. 8257
Mt 18: 6 and *that* he were **d** in the depth of the sea. *2670*
Heb 11:29 which the Egyptians assaying to do were **d**. *2666*

DROWSINESS (1)

Pr 23:21 and **d** shall clothe *a man* with rags. 5124

DRUNK (31) [DRINK]

Ge 43:34 And they **d**, and were merry with him. 8354
Lev 11:34 all drink that may be **d** in every *such* vessel 8354
Dt 29: 6 neither have you **d** wine or strong drink: 8354
32:42 I will **make** mine arrows **d** with blood, and 7937
Jdg 15:19 when he had **d**, his spirit came again, and 8354
Ru 3: 7 when Boaz had eaten and **d**, and his heart 8354
1Sa 1: 9 had eaten in Shiloh, and after *they* had **d**. 8354
1:15 I have **d** neither wine nor strong drink, but 8354
30:12 nor **d** *any* water, three days and 8354
2Sa 11:13 and drink before him; and he **made** him **d**: 7937
1Ki 13:22 hast eaten bread and **d** water in the place, 8354
13:23 after he had eaten bread, and after he had **d**, 8354
16: 9 drinking *himself* **d** *in* the house of Arza 7910
20:16 Ben-hadad *was* drinking *himself* **d** in 7910
2Ki 6:23 when they had eaten and **d**, he sent them 8354
19:24 I have digged and **d** strange waters, and 8354
SS 5: 1 my honey; I have **d** my wine with my milk: 8354
Isa 37:25 I have digged, and **d** water; and with 8354
51:17 which hast **d** at the hand of the LORD 8354
63: 6 **make** them **d** in my fury, and I will bring 7937
Jer 46:10 be satiate and **made d** with their blood: 7301
51:57 I will **make d** her princes, and her wise 7937
Eze 34:18 to have **d** of the deep waters, but ye must 8354
Da 5:23 and thy concubines, *have* **d** wine in them; 8355
Ob 1:16 For as ye have **d** upon my holy mountain, 8354
Lk 5:39 No *man* also having **d** old *wine* straightway *4095*
13:26 We have eaten and **d** in thy presence, and *4095*
Jn 2:10 and when *men* have **well d**, then that which *3182*
Eph 5:18 And be not **d** with wine, wherein is excess; *3182*
Rev 17: 2 **made d** with the wine of her fornication. *3184*
18: 3 For all nations have **d** of the wine of *4095*

DRUNKARD (5) [DRINK]

Dt 21:20 not obey our voice; *he is* a glutton, and a **d**. 5433
Pr 23:21 For the **d** and the glutton shall come to 5433
26: 9 *As* a thorn goeth up into the hand of a **d**, so 7910
Isa 24:20 The earth shall reel to and fro like a **d**, and 7910
1Co 5:11 or a railer, or a **d**, or an extortioner; *3183*

DRUNKARDS (6) [DRINK]

Ps 69:12 and *I was* the song of the **d**. 7941+8354
Isa 28: 1 to the crown of pride, to the **d** of Ephraim, 7910
28: 3 The crown of pride, the **d** of Ephraim, 7910
Joel 1: 5 Awake, ye **d**, and weep; and howl, all ye 7910
Na 1:10 while they be drunken *as* **d**, they shall be 5435
1Co 6:10 nor covetous, nor **d**, nor revilers, *3183*

DRUNKEN (33) [DRINK]

Ge 9:21 he drank of the wine, and was **d**; and 7937
1Sa 1:13 therefore Eli thought she had been **d**. 7910
1:14 Eli said unto her, How long wilt thou be **d**? 7937
25:36 *was* merry within him, for he *was* very **d**: 7910
Job 12:25 he maketh them to stagger like a **d** *man*. 7910
Ps 107:27 stagger like a **d** *man*, and are at their wit's 7910
Isa 19:14 as a **d** *man* staggereth in his vomit. 7910
29: 9 they are **d**, but not *with* wine; they stagger, 7937
49:26 they shall be **d** with their own blood, 7937
51:17 thou hast **d** the dregs of the cup of 8354
51:21 thou afflicted, and **d**, but not with wine: 7937
Jer 23: 9 I am like a **d** man, and like a man whom 7910
25:27 be **d**, and spue, and fall, and rise no more, 7937
48:26 **Make** ye him **d**: for he magnified *himself* 7937
49:12 to drink of the cup have **assuredly d**; 8354+8354
51: 7 LORD'S hand, that **made** all the earth **d**: 7937
51: 7 the nations have **d** of her wine; therefore 8354
51:39 I will **make** them **d**, that they may rejoice, 7937
La 3:15 he hath **made** me **d** *with* wormwood. 7301
4:21 thou shalt be **d**, and shalt make thyself 7937
5: 4 We have **d** our water for money; our wood 8354
Eze 39:19 till *ye* be full, and drink blood till *ye* be **d**, 7943
Na 1:10 while they be **d** *as* drunkards, they shall be 5433
3:11 Thou also shalt be **d**: thou shalt be hid, 7937
Hab 2:15 thy bottle to *him*, and **makest** *him* **d** also, 7937
Mt 24:49 and to eat and drink with the **d**; *3184*
Lk 12:45 and to eat and drink, and to be **d**; *3182*
17: 8 and serve me, till I have eaten and **d**; *4095*
Ac 2:15 For these are not **d**, as ye suppose, seeing it *3184*
1Co 11:21 and one is hungry, and another is **d**. *3184*
1Th 5: 7 and they that be **d** are drunken in the night. *3182*
5: 7 and they that be drunken are **d** in the night. *3184*
Rev 17: 6 And I saw the woman **d** with the blood of *3184*

DRUNKENNESS (7) [DRINK]

Dt 29:19 of mine heart, to add **d** *to* thirst: 7302
Ecc 10:17 in due season, for strength, and not for **d**. 8358
Jer 13:13 and all the inhabitants of Jerusalem, *with* **d**. 7943
Eze 23:33 Thou shalt be filled *with* **d** and sorrow, 7943
Lk 21:34 and **d**, and cares of *this* life, and *so* that day *3178*
Ro 13:13 not in rioting and **d**, not in chambering and *3178*
Gal 5:21 Envyings, murders, **d**, revellings, and *3178*

DRUSILLA (1)

Ac 24:24 when Felix came with his wife **D**, *1409*

DRY (71) [DRIED, DRIEDST, DRIETH, DRYSHOD]

Ge 1: 9 unto one place, and let the **d** *land* appear: 3004
1:10 God called the **d** *land* Earth; and 3004
7:22 of life, of all that *was* in the **d** *land*, died. 2724
8:13 and behold, the face of the ground was **d**. 2717
Ex 4: 9 pour *it upon the* **d** *land*: and the water 3004
4: 9 river shall become blood upon the **d** *land*. 3006
14:16 the children of Israel shall go on **d** *ground* 3004
14:21 made the sea **d** *land*, and the waters were 2724
14:22 into the midst of the sea upon the **d** *ground*: 3004
14:29 the children of Israel walked upon **d** *land* in 3004
15:19 the children of Israel went on **d** *land* in 3004
Lev 7:10 meat offering, mingled with oil, and **d**, 2720
13:30 it *is* a **d scall**, *even* a leprosy upon the head 5424
Jos 3:17 firm on **d** *ground* in the midst of Jordan, 2724
3:17 all the Israelites passed over on **d** *ground*, 2724
4:18 **d** *land*, that the waters of Jordan returned 2724
4:22 Israel came over this Jordan on **d** *land*. 3004
9: 5 all the bread of their provision was **d** *and* 3001
9:12 but now, behold, it is **d**, and it is mouldy: 3001
Jdg 6:37 *it be* **d** upon all the earth *beside*, then shall I 2721
6:39 let it now be **d** only upon the fleece, 2721
6:40 for it was **d** upon the fleece only, and 2721
2Ki 2: 8 so that they two went over on **d** *ground*. 2724
Ne 9:11 through the midst of the sea on the **d** *land*; 3004
Job 12:15 he withholdeth the waters, and they **d up**: 3001
13:25 fro? and wilt thou pursue the **d** stubble? 3002
15:30 the flame shall **d up** his branches, and 3001
Ps 63: 1 in a **d** and thirsty land, where no water is; 6723
66: 6 He turned the sea into **d** *land*: they went 3004
68: 6 but the rebellious dwell *in* a **d** *land*. 6707
95: 5 made it: and his hands formed the **d** *land*. 3006
105:41 they ran in the **d** *places like* a river. 6723
107:33 and the watersprings into **d ground**; 6774

Ps 107:35 and d ground into watersprings; 6723
Pr 17: 1 Better *is* a d morsel, and 2720
Isa 25: 5 noise of strangers, as the heat in a d place; 6724
32: 2 as rivers of water in a d place, as 6724
41:18 of water, and the d land springs of water. 6723
42:15 and hills, and d up all their herbs; 3001
42:15 the rivers islands, and I will d up the pools. 3001
44: 3 floods upon the d *ground:* I will pour my 3004
44:27 the deep, Be d, and I will dry up thy rivers: 2717
44:27 the deep, Be dry, and I will d up thy rivers: 3001
50: 2 behold, at my rebuke I d up the sea, I make 2717
53: 2 and as a root out of a d ground: 6723
56: 3 let the eunuch say, Behold, I *am* a d tree. 3002
Jer 4:11 A d wind of the high places in 6703
50:12 *be* a wilderness, a d land, and a desert. 6723
51:36 I will d up her sea, and make her springs 2717
51:36 dry up her sea, and make her springs d. 3001
51:43 are a desolation, a d land, and a wilderness, 6723
Eze 17:24 and have made the d tree to flourish: 3002
19:13 in the wilderness, in a d and thirsty ground. 6723
20:47 every green tree in thee, and every d tree: 3002
30:12 I will make the rivers d, and sell the land 2724
37: 2 the open valley; and lo, *they were* very d. 3002
37: 4 and say unto them, O ye d bones, 3002
Hos 2: 3 set her like a d land, and slay her with 6723
9:14 them a miscarrying womb and d breasts. 6784
13:15 his spring shall become d, and his fountain 3001
Jnh 1: 9 which hath made the sea and the d *land.* 3004
2:10 and it vomited out Jonah upon the d *land.* 3004
Na 1: 4 maketh it d, and drieth up all the rivers: 3001
1:10 they shall be devoured as stubble fully d. 3002
Zep 2:13 a desolation, *and* d like a wilderness. 6723
Hag 2: 6 and the earth, and the sea, and the d *land;* 2724
Zec 10:11 and all the deeps of the river shall d up: 3001
Mt 12:43 he walketh through d places, seeking rest, *504*
Lk 11:24 he walketh through d places, seeking rest; *504*
23:31 in a green tree, what shall be done in the d? *3584*
Heb 11:29 d *land:* which the Egyptians assaying to do *3584*

DRYSHOD (1) [DRY]

Isa 11:15 seven streams, and make *men* go over d. 5275

DUE (31) [DUES]

Lev 10:13 because it *is* thy d, and thy sons' due, 2706
10:13 because it *is* thy due, and thy sons' d, 2706
10:14 for *they be* thy d, and thy sons' due, 2706
10:14 for *they be* thy due, and thy sons' d, 2706
26: 4 I will give you rain in d season, and 6256
Nu 28: 2 observe to offer unto me in their d season. 4150
Dt 11:14 *you* the rain of your land in his d season, 6256
18: 3 this shall be the priest's d from the people, 4941
32:35 recompence; their foot shall slide in d time: NIH
1Ch 15:13 that we sought him not after the d order. 4941
16:29 Give unto the LORD the glory d unto his NIH
Ne 11:23 *should be* for the singers, d for every day. 1697
Ps 29: 2 Give unto the LORD the glory d unto his NIH
96: 8 Give unto the LORD the glory d unto his NIH
104:27 mayest give *them* their meat in d season. 6256
145:15 thou givest them their meat in d season. 6256
Pr 3:27 not good from them to whom it is d, 1167
15:23 a word *spoken* in d season, how 6256+2050.2
Ecc 10:17 thy princes eat in d season, for strength, 6256
Mt 18:34 till he should pay all that was d unto him. *3784*
24:45 to give them meat in d season? *2540*
Lk 12:42 *them their* portion of meat in d season? *2540*
23:41 for we receive the d reward of our deeds: *514*
Ro 5: 6 in d time Christ died for the ungodly. *2596*
13: 7 tribute to whom tribute *is d;* custom to NIG
1Co 7: 3 Let the husband render unto the wife d *3784*
15: 8 of me also, as of one born out of d time. *1626*
Gal 6: 9 for in d season we shall reap, if we faint *2398*
1Ti 2: 6 a ransom for all, to be testified in d time. *2398*
Tit 1: 3 But hath in d times manifested his word *2398*
1Pe 5: 6 of God, that he may exalt you in d time: *2540*

DUES (1) [DUE]

Ro 13: 7 Render therefore to all *their* d: tribute to *3782*

DUKE (43) [DUKES]

Ge 36:15 d Teman, duke Omar, duke Zepho, 441
36:15 d Omar, duke Zepho, duke Kenaz, 441
36:15 duke Omar, d Zepho, duke Kenaz, 441
36:15 duke Omar, duke Zepho, d Kenaz, 441
36:16 D Korah, duke Gatam, *and* duke Amalek: 441
36:16 Duke Korah, d Gatam, *and* duke Amalek: 441
36:16 Duke Korah, duke Gatam, *and* d Amalek: 441
36:17 d Nahath, duke Zerah, duke Shammah, 441
36:17 duke Nahath, d Zerah, duke Shammah, 441
36:17 duke Nahath, duke Zerah, d Shammah, 441
36:17 duke Zerah, duke Shammah, d Mizzah: 441
36:18 d Jeush, duke Jaalam, duke Korah: 441
36:18 duke Jeush, d Jaalam, duke Korah: 441
36:18 duke Jeush, duke Jaalam, d Korah: 441
36:29 d Lotan, duke Shobal, duke Zibeon, 441
36:29 duke Lotan, d Shobal, duke Zibeon, 441
36:29 duke Shobal, d Zibeon, duke Anah, 441
36:29 duke Shobal, duke Zibeon, d Anah, 441
36:30 D Dishon, duke Ezer, duke Dishan: these *are* 441
36:30 Duke Dishon, d Ezer, duke Dishan: these *are* 441
36:30 Duke Dishon, duke Ezer, d Dishan: these *are* 441
36:40 d Timnah, duke Alvah, duke Jetheth, 441
36:40 duke Timnah, d Alvah, duke Jetheth, 441
36:40 duke Timnah, duke Alvah, d Jetheth, 441
36:41 D Aholibamah, duke Elah, duke Pinon, 441
36:41 Duke Aholibamah, d Elah, duke Pinon, 441
36:41 Duke Aholibamah, duke Elah, d Pinon, 441
36:42 D Kenaz, duke Teman, duke Mibzar, 441
36:42 Duke Kenaz, d Teman, duke Mibzar, 441
36:42 Duke Kenaz, duke Teman, d Mibzar, 441
36:43 D Magdiel, duke Iram: these *be* the dukes of 441
36:43 Duke Magdiel, d Iram: these *be* the dukes of 441
1Ch 1:51 d Timnah, duke Aliah, duke Jetheth, 441
1:51 duke Timnah, d Aliah, duke Jetheth, 441
1:51 duke Timnah, duke Aliah, d Jetheth, 441
1Ch 1:52 D Aholibamah, duke Elah, duke Pinon, 441
1:52 Duke Aholibamah, d Elah, duke Pinon, 441
1:52 Duke Aholibamah, duke Elah, d Pinon, 441
1:53 D Kenaz, duke Teman, duke Mibzar, 441
1:53 Duke Kenaz, d Teman, duke Mibzar, 441
1:53 Duke Kenaz, duke Teman, d Mibzar, 441
1:54 D Magdiel, duke Iram. These *are* the dukes 441
1:54 Duke Magdiel, d Iram. These *are* the dukes 441

DUKES (15) [DUKE]

Ge 36:15 These *were* d of the sons of Esau: the sons 441
36:16 these *are* the d *that came* of Eliphaz in 441
36:17 these *are* the d *that came* of Reuel in the land 441
36:18 these *were* the d *that came* of Aholibamah 441
36:19 of Esau, who *is* Edom, and these *are* their d. 441
36:21 these *are* the d of the Horites, the children of 441
36:29 These *are* the d *that came* of the Horites; 441
36:30 these *are* the d *that came* of Hori, 441
36:30 of Hori, among their d in the land of Seir. 441
36:40 these *are* the names of the d *that came* of 441
36:43 these *be* the d of Edom, according to their 441
Ex 15:15 the d of Edom shall be amazed; the mighty 441
Jos 13:21 Hur, and Reba, *which were* d of Sihon, 5257
1Ch 1:51 the d of Edom were; duke Timnah, 441
1:54 duke Iram. These *are* the d of Edom. 441

DULCIMER (3)

Da 3: 5 psaltery, d, and all kinds of musick, 5481
3:10 psaltery, and d, and all kinds of musick, 5481
3:15 psaltery, and d, and all kinds of musick, 5481

DULL (3)

Mt 13:15 and *their* ears are d of hearing, and their eyes *917*
Ac 28:27 and *their* ears are d of hearing, and their eyes *917*
Heb 5:11 to be uttered, seeing ye are d of hearing. *3576*

DUMAH (4)

Ge 25:14 And Mishma, and D, and Massa, 1746
Jos 15:52 Arab, and D, and Eshean, 1746
1Ch 1:30 Mishma, and D, Massa, Hadad, and Tema, 1746
Isa 21:11 The burden of D. He calleth to me out of 1746

DUMB (29)

Ex 4:11 or who maketh the d, or deaf, or the seeing, 483
Ps 38:13 *I was* as a d *man that* openeth not his mouth. 483
39: 2 I was d *with* silence, I held my peace, 481
39: 9 I was d, I opened not my mouth; because 481
Pr 31: 8 Open thy mouth for the d in the cause of all 483
Isa 35: 6 leap as a hart, and the tongue of the d sing: 483
53: 7 as a sheep before her shearers is d, so 481
56:10 they *are* all d dogs, they cannot bark; 483
Eze 3:26 that thou shalt be d, and shalt not be to them 481
24:27 and thou shalt speak, and be no more d: 481
33:22 my mouth was opened, and I was no more d. 481
Da 10:15 my face toward the ground, and I became d. 481
Hab 2:18 of his work trusteth therein, to make d idols? 483
2:19 Awake; to the d stone, Arise, it shall teach! 1748
Mt 9:32 they brought to him a d man possessed *2974*
9:33 when the devil was cast out, the d spake: *2974*
12:22 one possessed with a devil, blind, and d: *2974*
12:22 that the blind and d both spake and saw. *2974*
15:30 blind, d, maimed, and many others, and *2974*
15:31 when they saw the d to speak, the maimed *2974*
Mk 7:37 both the deaf to hear, and the d to speak. *216*
9:17 unto thee my son, which hath a d spirit: *216*
9:25 *Thou* d and deaf spirit, I charge thee, *216*
Lk 1:20 thou shalt be d, and not able to speak, *4623*
11:14 he was casting out a devil, and it was d. *2974*
11:14 when the devil was gone out, the d spake; *2974*
Ac 8:32 and like a lamb d before his shearer, so *880*
1Co 12: 2 carried away unto *these* d idols, *even* as ye *880*
2Pe 2:16 the d ass speaking with man's voice forbad *880*

DUNG (28) [DUNGHILL, DUNGHILLS]

Ex 29:14 flesh of the bullock, and his skin, and his d, 6569
Lev 4:11 with his legs, and his inwards, and his d, 6569
8:17 and his hide, his flesh, and his d, 6569
16:27 fire their skins, and their flesh, and their d. 6569
Nu 19: 5 and her flesh, and her blood, with her d, 6569
1Ki 14:10 as *a man* taketh away d, till it be all gone. 1557
2Ki 6:25 the fourth part of a kab of dove's d for five 1686
9:37 the carcase of Jezebel shall be as d upon 1828
18:27 that *they* may eat their own d, and drink 6675
Ne 2:13 to the d port, and viewed the walls of 830
3:13 a thousand cubits on the wall unto the d 830
3:14 the d gate repaired Malchiah the son of 830
12:31 right hand upon the wall toward the d gate: 830
Job 20: 7 *Yet* he shall perish for ever like his own d: 1561
Ps 83:10 at En-dor: they became *as* d for the earth. 1828
Isa 36:12 that *they* may eat their own d, and drink 6675
Jer 8: 2 they shall be for d upon the face of 1828
9:22 Even the carcases of men shall fall as d 1828
16: 4 they shall be as d upon the face of 1828
25:33 nor buried; they shall be d upon the ground. 1828
Eze 4:12 thou shalt bake it with d that cometh out of 1561
4:15 I have given thee cow's d for man's dung, 6832
4:15 I have given thee cow's dung for man's d, 1561
Zep 1:17 poured out as dust, and their flesh as the d. 1561
Mal 2: 3 your seed, and spread d upon your faces, 6569
2: 3 *even* the d of your solemn feasts; 6569
Lk 13: 8 till I shall dig about it, and d *it:* *906+2874*
Php 3: 8 loss of all *things,* and do count *them but* d, *4657*

DUNGEON (13)

Ge 40:15 nothing that they should put me into the d. 953
41:14 and they brought him hastily out of the d: 953
Ex 12:29 of the captive that *was* in the d; 953+1004
Jer 37:16 was entered into the d, 953+1004+1886.1
38: 6 cast him into the d of Malchiah the son of 953
38: 6 And in the d *there was* no water, but mire: so 953
38: 7 heard that they had put Jeremiah in the d; 953
38: 9 the prophet, whom they have cast into the d; 953
38:10 take up Jeremiah the prophet out of the d, 953
38:11 let them down by cords into the d to 953
Jer 38:13 with cords, and took him up out of the d: 953
La 3:53 They have cut off my life in the d, and cast a 953
3:55 upon thy name, O LORD, out of the low d. 953

DUNGHILL (7) [DUNG, HILL]

1Sa 2: 8 *and* lifteth up the beggar from the d, to set 830
Ezr 6:11 let his house be made a d for this. 5122
Ps 113: 7 of the dust, *and* lifteth the needy out of the d; 830
Isa 25:10 *even* as straw is trodden down for the d. 4087
Da 2: 5 and your houses shall be made a d. 5122
3:29 and their houses shall be made a d: 5122
Lk 14:35 is neither fit for the land, nor yet for the d; *2874*

DUNGHILLS (1) [DUNG, HILL]

La 4: 5 that were brought up in scarlet embrace d. 830

DURA (1)

Da 3: 1 he set it up in the plain of D, in 1757

DURABLE (2) [DURETH]

Pr 8:18 with me; *yea,* d riches and righteousness. 6276
Isa 23:18 to eat sufficiently, and for d clothing. 6266

DURETH (1) [DURABLE]

Mt 13:21 he not root in himself, but d for a while: *1510*

DURST (9) [DARE]

Est 7: 5 *is* he, that d presume in his heart to do so? 4390
Job 32: 6 and d not shew you mine opinion. 3372
Mt 22:46 neither d any *man* from that day forth ask *5111*
Mk 12:34 And no *man* after that d ask him *any* *5111*
Lk 20:40 And after that they d not ask him any *5111*
Jn 21:12 And none of the disciples d ask him, *5111*
Ac 5:13 And of the rest d no *man* join himself to *5111*
7:32 Then Moses trembled, and d not behold. *5111*
Jude 1: 9 d not bring against *him* a railing *5111*

DUST (108)

Ge 2: 7 the LORD God formed man *of* the d of 6083
3:14 and d shalt thou eat all the days of thy life: 6083
3:19 for d thou *art,* and unto dust shalt thou 6083
3:19 dust thou *art,* and unto d shalt thou return. 6083
13:16 I will make thy seed as the d of the earth: 6083
13:16 that if a man can number the d of the earth, 6083
18:27 unto the Lord, which *am but* d and ashes: 6083
28:14 thy seed shall be as the d of the earth, and 6083
Ex 8:16 out thy rod, and smite the d of the land, 6083
8:17 smote the d of the earth, and it became lice 6083
8:17 all the d of the land became lice throughout 6083
9: 9 it shall become small d in all the land of 80
Lev 14:41 they shall pour out the d that they scrape 6083
17:13 out the blood thereof, and cover it with d. 6083
Nu 5:17 of the d that is in the floor of the tabernacle 6083
23:10 Who can count the d of Jacob, and 6083
Dt 9:21 very small, *even* until *it was as* small as d: 6083
9:21 I cast the d thereof into the brook that 6083
28:24 make the rain of thy land powder and d: 6083
32:24 with the poison of serpents of the d. 6083
Jos 7: 6 elders of Israel, and put d upon their heads. 6083
1Sa 2: 8 He raiseth up the poor out of the d, *and* 6083
2Sa 16:13 and threw stones at him, and cast d. 6083
22:43 did I beat them *as* small as the d of 6083
1Ki 16: 2 Forasmuch as I exalted thee out of the d, 6083
18:38 the d, and licked up the water that *was* in 6083
20:10 if the d of Samaria shall suffice for 6083
2Ki 13: 7 and had made them like the d by threshing. 6083
23:12 cast the d of them into the brook Kidron. 6083
2Ch 1: 9 a people like the d of the earth in multitude. 6083
34: 4 brake *in pieces,* and made d *of them,* 1854
Job 2:12 sprinkled d upon their heads toward 6083
4:19 whose foundation *is* in the d, which are 6083
5: 6 affliction cometh not forth of the d, 6083
7: 5 flesh is clothed with worms and clods of d; 6083
7:21 for now shall I sleep in the d; and 6083
10: 9 and wilt thou bring me into d again? 6083
14:19 things which grow out of the d of the earth; 6083
16:15 upon my skin, and defiled my horn in the d. 6083
17:16 of the pit, when *our* rest together *is* in the d. 6083
20:11 which shall lie down with him in the d. 6083
21:26 They shall lie down alike in the d, and 6083
22:24 shalt thou lay up gold as d, and *the gold of* 6083
27:16 Though he heap up silver as the d, and 6083
28: 6 place of sapphires: and it hath d of gold. 6083
30:19 the mire, and I am become like d and ashes. 6083
34:15 and man shall turn again unto d. 6083
38:38 When the d groweth into hardness, and 6083
39:14 eggs in the earth, and warmeth them in d, 6083
40:13 Hide them in the d together; *and* bind their 6083
42: 6 I abhor *myself,* and repent in d and ashes. 6083
Ps 7: 5 the earth, and lay mine honour in the d. 6083
18:42 did I beat them small as the d before 6083
22:15 thou hast brought me into the d of death. 6083
22:29 all they that go down to the d shall bow 6083
30: 9 Shall the d praise thee? shall it declare thy 6083
44:25 For our soul is bowed down to the d: 6083
72: 9 and his enemies shall lick the d. 6083
78:27 He rained flesh also upon them as d, and 6083
102:14 in her stones, and favour the d thereof. 6083
103:14 our frame; he remembereth that we *are* d. 6083
104:29 their breath, they die, and return to their d. 6083
113: 7 He raiseth up the poor out of the d, *and* 6083
119:25 My soul cleaveth unto the d: quicken thou 6083
Pr 8:26 nor the highest part of the d of the world. 6083
Ecc 3:20 all are of the d, and all turn to dust again. 6083
3:20 all are of the dust, and all turn to d again. 6083
12: 7 shall the d return to the earth as it was: 6083
Isa 2:10 Enter into the rock, and hide thee in the d, 6083
5:24 and their blossom shall go up as d: 80
25:12 *and* bring to the ground, *even* to the d. 6083
26: 5 to the ground; he bringeth it *even* to the d. 6083
26:19 Awake and sing, ye that dwell in d: for thy 6083
29: 4 thy speech shall be low out of the d, and 6083
29: 4 and thy speech shall whisper out of the d. 6083
29: 5 of thy strangers shall be like small d, 80

Isa 34: 7 and their **d** made fat with fatness. 6083
34: 9 the **d** thereof into brimstone, and the land 6083
40:12 comprehended the **d** of the earth in a 6083
40:15 are counted as the **small d** of the balance: 7834
41: 2 he gave *them* as the **d** *to* his sword, *and* 6083
47: 1 Come down, and sit in the **d**, O virgin 6083
49:23 the earth, and lick up the **d** of thy feet; 6083
52: 2 Shake thyself from the **d**; arise, *and* 6083
65:25 **d** *shall be* the serpent's meat. They shall 6083
La 2:10 they have cast up **d** upon their heads; 6083
3:29 He putteth his mouth in the **d**; if so be there 6083
Eze 24: 7 it not upon the ground, to cover it with **d**; 6083
26: 4 I will also scrape her **d** from her, and 6083
26:10 of his horses their **d** shall cover thee: 80
26:12 and thy **d** in the midst of the water. 6083
27:30 and shall cast up **d** upon their heads, 6083
Da 12: 2 many of them that sleep in the **d** of the earth 127
Am 2: 7 That pant after the **d** of the earth on 6083
Mic 1:10 in the house of Aphrah roll thyself *in* the **d**. 6083
7:17 They shall lick the **d** like a serpent, 6083
Na 1: 3 the storm, and the clouds *are* the **d** of his feet. 80
3:18 thy nobles shall dwell *in the d*: thy people is NIH
Hab 1:10 for they shall heap **d**, and take it. 6083
Zep 1:17 their blood shall be poured out as **d**, and 6083
Zec 9: 3 heaped up silver as the **d**, and fine gold as 6083
Mt 10:14 or city, shake off the **d** of your feet. *2868*
Mk 6:11 shake off the **d** under your feet for a *5522*
Lk 9: 5 shake off the very **d** from your feet for a *2868*
10:11 Even the *very* **d** of your city, *2868*
Ac 13:51 But they shook off the **d** of their feet *2868*
22:23 *off their* clothes, and threw **d** into the air, *2868*
Rev 18:19 And they cast **d** on their heads, and cried, *5522*

DUTIES (1) [DUTY]

Eze 18:11 that doeth not any of those **d**, but even hath NIH

DUTY (8) [DUTIES]

Ex 21:10 her raiment, and her **d of marriage**, 5772
Dt 25: 5 **perform the d of a husband's brother** 2992
25: 7 **perform the d of** my **husband's brother**. 2992
2Ch 8:14 the priests, as the **d** of every day **required**: 1697
Ezr 3: 4 the custom, as the **d** of every day required; 1697
Ecc 12:13 for this *is* the whole **d** *of* man. NIH
Lk 17:10 we have done *that* which was our **d** to do. *3784*
Ro 15:27 **d** is also to minister unto them in carnal *3784*

DWARF (1)

Lev 21:20 or a **d**, or that hath a blemish in his eye, or 1851

DWELL (338) [DWELLED, DWELLERS, DWELLEST, DWELLETH, DWELLING, DWELLINGS, DWELT]

Ge 4:20 he was the father of such as **d in** tents, and 3427
9:27 and he shall **d** in the tents of Shem; 7931
13: 6 to bear them, that they might **d** together: 3427
13: 6 was great, so that they could not **d** together. 3427
16:12 he shall **d** in the presence of all his 7931
19:30 with him; for he feared to **d** in Zoar: 3427
20:15 *is* before thee: **d** where it pleaseth thee. 3427
24: 3 of the Canaanites, amongst whom I **d**: 3427
24:37 of the Canaanites, in whose land I **d**: 3427
26: 2 **d** in the land which I shall tell thee of: 7931
30:20 now will my husband **d with** me, because 2082
34:10 ye shall **d** with us: and the land shall be 3427
34:10 **d** and trade you therein, and get you 3427
34:16 we will **d** with you, and we will become 3427
34:21 therefore let them **d** in the land, and 3427
34:22 the men consent unto us for to **d** with us, 3427
34:23 consent unto them, and they will **d** with us. 3427
35: 1 Arise, go up to Beth-el, and **d** there: 3427
36: 7 were more than that they might **d** together; 3427
45:10 And thou shalt **d** in the land of Goshen, and 3427
46:34 that ye may **d** in the land of Goshen; 3427
47: 4 let thy servants **d** in the land of Goshen. 3427
47: 6 the land **make** thy father and brethren **to d**; 3427
47: 6 to dwell; in the land of Goshen let them **d**: 3427
49:13 Zebulun shall **d** at the haven of the sea; and 7931
Ex 2:21 Moses was content to **d** with the man: and 3427
8:22 in which my people **d**, that no swarms *of* 5975
15:17 *which* thou hast made for thee to **d in**, 3427
23:33 They shall not **d** in thy land, lest they make 3427
25: 8 me a sanctuary; that I may **d** amongst them. 7931
29:45 I will **d** amongst the children of Israel, and 7931
29:46 land of Egypt, that I may **d** amongst them: 7931
Lev 13:46 he shall **d** alone; without the camp *shall* his 3427
20:22 the land, whither I bring you to **d** therein, 3427
23:42 Ye shall **d** in booths seven days; all that are 3427
23:42 all that are Israelites born shall **d** in booths: 3427
23:43 I **made** the children of Israel **to d** in booths, 3427
25:18 and ye shall **d** in the land in safety. 3427
25:19 shall eat *your* fill, and **d** therein in safety. 3427
26: 5 bread to the full, and **d** in your land safely. 3427
26:32 your enemies which **d** therein shall be 3427
Nu 5: 3 not their camps, in the midst whereof I **d**. 7931
13:19 what the land *is* that they **d** in, whether it *be* 3427
13:19 what cities *they be* that they **d** in, whether 3427
13:28 Nevertheless the people *be* strong that **d** in 3427
13:29 The Amalekites **d** in the land of the south: 3427
13:29 and the Amorites, **d** in the mountains: 3427
13:29 the Canaanites **d** by the sea, and by 3427
14:30 *concerning* which I sware to **make** you **d** 7931
23: 9 lo, the people shall **d** alone, and shall not be 7931
32:17 our little ones shall **d** in the fenced cities 3427
33:53 *the inhabitants of* the land, and **d** therein: 3427
33:55 and shall vex you in the land wherein ye **d**. 3427
35: 2 of their possession cities to **d in**; 3427
35: 3 the cities shall they have to **d in**; and 3427
35:32 that he should come again to **d** in the land, 3427
35:34 land which ye shall inhabit, wherein I **d**: 7931
35:34 for I the LORD **d** among the children of 7931
Dt 2: 4 the children of Esau, which **d** in Seir; 3427
2:29 (As the children of Esau which **d** in Seir, 3427
2:29 the Moabites which **d** in Ar, did unto me;) 3427
11:30 which **d** in the champaign over against 3427
11:31 and ye shall possess it, and **d** therein. 3427

Dt 12:10 **d** in the land which the LORD your God 3427
12:10 enemies round about, so that ye **d** in safety; 3427
12:11 shall choose to **cause** his name **to d** there; 7931
13:12 LORD thy God hath given thee to **d** there, 3427
17:14 and shalt **d** therein, and shalt say, 3427
23:16 He shall **d** with thee, *even* among you, 3427
25: 5 If brethren **d** together, and one of them die, 3427
28:30 build a house, and thou shalt not **d** therein: 3427
30:20 that thou mayest **d** in the land which 3427
33:12 The beloved of the LORD shall **d** in 7931
33:12 and he shall **d** between his shoulders. 7931
33:28 Israel then shall **d** *in* safety alone: 7931
Jos 9: 7 the Hivites, Peradventure ye **d** among us; 3427
9:22 very far from you; when ye **d** among us? 3427
10: 6 for all the kings of the Amorites that **d** in 3427
13:13 the Maachathites **d** among the Israelites 3427
14: 4 save cities to **d** *in*, with their suburbs for 3427
15:63 the Jebusites **d** with the children of Judah at 3427
16:10 the Canaanites **d** among the Ephraimites 3427
17:12 but the Canaanites would **d** in that land. 3427
17:16 all the Canaanites that **d** in the land of 3427
20: 4 him a place, that he may **d** among them. 3427
20: 6 he shall **d** in that city, until he stand before 3427
21: 2 the hand of Moses to give us cities to **d in**, 3427
24:13 cities which ye built not, and ye **d** in them; 3427
24:15 gods of the Amorites, in whose land ye **d**: 3427
Jdg 1:21 the Jebusites **d** with the children of 3427
1:27 but the Canaanites would **d** in that land. 3427
1:35 the Amorites would **d** in mount Heres in 3427
6:10 gods of the Amorites, in whose land ye **d**: 3427
9:41 that *they* should not **d** in Shechem. 3427
17:10 **D** with me, and be unto me a father and 3427
17:11 the Levite was content to **d** with the man; 3427
18: 1 **d** *in;* for unto that day *all their* inheritance 3427
1Sa 12: 8 of Egypt, and **made** them **d** in this place. 3427
27: 5 town in the country, that I may **d** there: 3427
27: 5 for why should thy servant **d** in the royal 3427
2Sa 7: 2 I **d** in a house of cedar, but the ark of God 3427
7: 5 Shalt thou build me a house for me to **d in**? 3427
7:10 that they may **d** in a place of their own, and 7931
1Ki 2:36 **d** there, and go not forth thence any 3427
3:17 my lord, I and this woman **d** in one house; 3427
6:13 I will **d** among the children of Israel, and 7931
8:12 The LORD said that *he* would **d** in 7931
8:13 I have surely built thee a house to **d in**, 2073
8:27 But will God indeed **d** on the earth? behold, 3427
17: 9 which *belongeth* to Zidon, and **d** there: 3427
2Ki 4:13 she answered, I **d** among mine own people. 3427
6: 1 the place where we **d** with thee is too strait 3427
6: 2 us make us a place there, where we may **d**. 3427
17:27 let them go and **d** there, and let him teach 3427
25:24 **d** in the land, and serve the king of 3427
1Ch 17: 1 I **d** in a house of cedars, but the ark of 3427
17: 4 Thou shalt not build me a house to **d in**: 3427
17: 9 they shall **d** in their place, and shall be 7931
23:25 that they may **d** in Jerusalem for ever: 7931
2Ch 2: 3 cedars to build him a house to **d** therein, 3427
6: 1 The LORD hath said that *he* would **d** in 7931
6:18 will God in very deed **d** with men on 3427
8: 2 and **caused** the children of Israel **to d** there. 3427
8:11 My wife shall not **d** in the house of David 3427
19:10 to you of your brethren that **d** in their cities, 3427
Ezr 4:17 *to* the rest of their companions that **d** in 3488
6:12 the God that hath **caused** his name **to d** 7932
Ne 8:14 that the children of Israel should **d** in 3427
11: 1 to bring one of ten to **d** in Jerusalem 3427
11: 1 holy city, and nine parts *to* **d** in *other* cities. NIH
11: 2 that willingly offered themselves to **d** at 3427
Job 3: 5 of death stain it; let a cloud **d** upon it; 7931
4:19 How much less *in* them that **d in** houses of 7931
11:14 and let not wickedness **d** in thy tabernacles. 7931
18:15 It shall **d** in his tabernacle, because *it is* 7931
19:15 They that **d** in mine house, and 1481
30: 6 To **d** in the clifts of the valleys, *in* caves of 7931
Ps 4: 8 LORD, only **makest** me **d** in safety. 3427
5: 4 neither shall evil **d** *with* thee. 1481
15: 1 who shall **d** in thy holy hill? 7931
23: 6 I will **d** in the house of the LORD for 3427
24: 1 the world, and they that **d** therein. 3427
25:13 His soul shall **d** at ease; and his seed shall 3885
27: 4 that I may **d** in the house of the LORD all 3427
37: 3 *so* shalt thou **d** in the land, and verily thou 7931
37:27 and do good; and **d** for evermore. 7931
37:29 inherit the land, and **d** therein for ever. 7931
65: 4 *unto thee, that* he may **d** in thy courts: 7931
65: 8 They also that **d** in the uttermost parts are 3427
68: 6 but the rebellious **d** *in* a dry *land.* 7931
68:16 *this is* the hill *which* God desireth to **d in**; 3427
68:16 yea, the LORD will **d** *in it* for ever. 7931
68:18 that the LORD God might **d** *among them.* 7931
69:25 be desolate; *and* let none **d** in their tents. 3427
69:35 that they may **d** there, and have it in 3427
69:36 and they that love his name shall **d** therein. 7931
72: 9 They **that d in the wilderness** shall bow 6728
78:55 **made** the tribes of Israel **to d** in their tents. 7931
84: 4 Blessed *are* they that **d in** thy house: 3427
84:10 than to **d** in the tents of wickedness. 1752
85: 9 that fear him; that glory may **d** in our land. 7931
98: 7 the world, and they that **d** therein. 3427
101: 6 of the land, that *they* may **d** with me: 3427
101: 7 He that worketh deceit shall not **d** within 3427
107: 4 a solitary way; they found no city to **d in**. 4186
107:34 for the wickedness of them that **d** therein. 3427
107:36 there he **maketh** the hungry **to d**, that they 3427
120: 5 *in* Mesech, *that* I **d** in the tents of Kedar! 7931
132:14 for ever: here will I **d**; for I have desired it. 3427
133: 1 how pleasant *it is* for brethren to **d** together 3427
139: 9 *and* **d** in the uttermost parts of the sea; 7931
140:13 the upright shall **d** in thy presence. 3427
143: 3 he hath **made** me **to d** in darkness, as those 3427
Pr 1:33 whoso hearkeneth unto me shall **d** safely, 7931
2:21 For the upright shall **d** *in* the land, and 7931
8:12 I wisdom **d** *with* prudence, and find out 7931
21: 9 *It is* better to **d** in a corner of the housetop, 3427
21:19 *It is* better to **d** in the wilderness, than with 3427

Pr 25:24 *It is* better to **d** in a corner of the housetop, 3427
Isa 6: 5 I **d** in the midst of a people of unclean lips: 3427
9: 2 they that **d** in the land of the shadow of 3427
11: 6 The wolf also shall **d** with the lamb, and 1481
13:21 owls shall **d** there, and satyrs shall dance 7931
16: 4 Let mine outcasts **d** with thee, Moab; 1481
23:13 it for **them that d in the wilderness**: 6728
23:18 for her merchandise shall be for them that **d** 3427
24: 6 and they that **d** therein are desolate: 3427
26: 5 For he bringeth down them that **d** on high; 3427
26:19 Awake and sing, ye that **d in** dust: for thy 7931
30:19 For the people shall **d** in Zion at Jerusalem: 3427
32:16 judgment shall **d** in the wilderness, and 7931
32:18 my people shall **d** in a peaceable habitation, 3427
33:14 Who among us shall **d** *with* the devouring 1481
33:14 who amongst us shall **d** *with* everlasting 1481
33:16 He shall **d** on high: his place of defence 7931
33:24 the people that **d** therein *shall be* forgiven 3427
34:11 the owl also and the raven shall **d** in it: 7931
34:17 from generation to generation shall they **d** 7931
40:22 and spreadeth them out as a tent to **d in**: 3427
49:20 strait for me: give place to me that I may **d**. 3427
51: 6 they that **d** therein shall die in like manner: 3427
57:15 I **d** *in* the high and holy *place*, with him 7931
58:12 of the breach, The restorer of paths to **d in**. 3427
65: 9 inherit it, and my servants shall **d** there. 7931
Jer 4:29 *shall be* forsaken, and not a man **d** therein. 3427
7: 3 and I will **cause** you **to d** in this place. 7931
7: 7 will I **cause** you **to d** in this place, in 7931
8:16 is in it; the city, and those that **d** therein. 3427
8:19 because of them that **d** in a far country: NIH
9:26 the utmost corners, that **d** in the wilderness: 3427
12: 4 for the wickedness of them that **d** therein? 3427
20: 6 all that **d in** thine house shall go into 3427
23: 6 shall be saved, and Israel shall **d** safely: 7931
23: 8 and they shall **d** in their own land. 3427
24: 8 and them that **d** in the land of Egypt: 3427
25: 5 **d** in the land that the LORD hath given 3427
25:24 all the kings of the mingled people that **d** in 7931
27:11 and they shall till it, and **d** therein. 3427
29: 5 **d** *in them;* and plant gardens, and eat 3427
29:28 **d** *in them;* and plant gardens, and eat 3427
29:32 he shall not have a man to **d** among this 3427
31:24 there shall **d** in Judah itself, and *in* all 3427
32:37 and I will **cause** them **to d** safely: 3427
33:16 be saved, and Jerusalem shall **d** safely: 7931
35: 7 but all your days ye shall **d** in tents; 3427
35: 9 Nor to build houses for us to **d in**: 3427
35:11 army of the Syrians: so we **d** at Jerusalem. 3427
35:15 ye shall **d** in the land which I have given to 3427
40: 5 and **d** with him among the people: 3427
40: 9 **d** in the land and serve the king of Babylon, 3427
40:10 I *will* **d** at Mizpah to serve the Chaldeans, 3427
40:10 and **d** in your cities that ye have taken. 3427
42:13 if ye say, We will not **d** in this land, neither 3427
42:14 have hunger of bread; and there will we **d**: 3427
43: 4 of the LORD, to **d** in the land of Judah. 3427
43: 5 had been driven, to **d** in the land of Judah: 1481
44: 1 all the Jews which **d** in the land of Egypt, 3427
44: 1 which **d** at Migdol, and at Tahpanhes, and 3427
44: 8 whither ye be gone to **d**, that ye might cut 1481
44:13 For I will punish them that **d** in the land of 3427
44:14 they have a desire to return to **d** there: 3427
44:26 all Judah that **d** in the land of Egypt; 3427
47: 2 is therein; the city, and them that **d** therein: 3427
48: 9 shall be desolate, without any to **d** therein. 3427
48:28 O ye that **d** in Moab, leave the cities, and 3427
48:28 **d** in the rock, and be like the dove *that* 7931
49: 1 inherit Gad, and his people **d** in his cities? 3427
49: 8 Flee ye, turn back, **d** deep, O inhabitants of 3427
49:18 neither shall a son of man **d** in it. 1481
49:30 Flee, get you far off, **d** deep, O ye 3427
49:31 have neither gates nor bars, *which* **d** alone. 7931
49:33 man abide there, nor *any* son of man **d** in it. 1481
50: 3 her land desolate, and none shall **d** therein: 3427
50:39 the wild beasts of the islands shall **d** *there*, 3427
50:39 dwell *there*, and the owls shall **d** therein: 3427
50:40 neither shall any son of man **d** therein. 1481
51: 1 against them that **d** in the midst of them 3427
Eze 2: 6 and thou dost **d** among scorpions: 3427
12:19 of the violence of all them that **d** therein. 3427
16:46 and her daughters that **d** at thy left hand: 3427
17:23 under it shall **d** all fowl of every wing; 7931
17:23 of the branches thereof shall they **d**. 7931
28:25 shall they **d** in their land that I have given 3427
28:26 they shall **d** safely therein, and shall build 3427
28:26 yea, they shall **d** with confidence, when I 3427
32:15 when I shall smite all them that **d** therein, 3427
34:25 they shall **d** safely in the wilderness, and 3427
34:28 they shall **d** safely, and none shall make 3427
36:28 ye shall **d** in the land that I gave to your 3427
36:33 I will also **cause** *you* **to d in** the cities, and 3427
37:25 they shall **d** in the land that I have given 3427
37:25 they shall **d** therein, *even* they, and 3427
38: 8 and they shall **d** safely all of them. 3427
38:11 go *to* them that are at rest, that **d** safely, 3427
38:12 and goods, that **d** in the midst of the land. 3427
39: 6 among them that **d** carelessly **in** the isles: 3427
39: 9 they that **d in** the cities of Israel shall go 3427
43: 7 where I will **d** in the midst of the children 7931
43: 9 and I will **d** in the midst of them for ever. 7931
Da 2:38 wheresoever the children of men **d**, 1753
4: 1 languages, that **d** in all the earth; 1753
6:25 languages, that **d** in all the earth; 1753
Hos 9: 3 They shall not **d** in the LORD'S land; but 3427
12: 9 will yet **make** thee **to d** in tabernacles, 3427
14: 7 They that **d** under his shadow shall return; 3427
Joel 3:20 Judah shall **d** for ever, and Jerusalem from 3427
Am 3:12 out that **d** in Samaria in the corner of a bed, 3427
5:11 of hewn stone, but ye shall not **d** in them; 3427
9: 5 and all that **d** therein shall mourn: 3427
Mic 4:10 thou shalt **d** in the field, and thou shalt go 7931
7:13 be desolate because of them that **d** therein, 3427
7:14 which **d** solitarily *in* the wood, in the midst 7931
Na 1: 5 yea, the world, and all that **d** therein. 3427

Na 3:18 thy nobles shall **d** *in the dust:* thy people is 7931
Hab 2: 8 *of* the city, and *of* all that **d** therein. 3427
2:17 *of* the city, and *of* all that **d** therein. 3427
Zep 1:18 riddance of all them that **d** in the land. 3427
Hag 1: 4 to **d** in your cieled houses, and this house 3427
Zec 2:10 I come, and I will **d** in the midst of thee, 7931
2:11 I will **d** in the midst of thee, and thou shalt 7931
8: 3 and will **d** in the midst of Jerusalem: 7931
8: 4 old women **d** in the streets of Jerusalem, 3427
8: 8 and they shall **d** in the midst of Jerusalem: 7931
9: 6 a bastard shall **d** in Ashdod, and I will cut 3427
14:11 *men* shall **d** in it, and there shall be no more 3427
Mt 12:45 than himself, and they enter in and **d** there: 2730
Lk 11:26 than himself; and they enter in, and **d** there: 2730
21:35 them that **d** on the face of the whole earth. 2521
Ac 1:20 be desolate, and let no man **d** therein: 2730
2:14 of Judea, and all *ye* that **d** at Jerusalem, 2730
4:16 *is* manifest to all them that **d** in Jerusalem; 2730
7: 4 him into this land, wherein ye now **d**. 2730
13:27 For they that **d** at Jerusalem, and 2730
17:26 of men for to **d** on all the face of the earth, 2730
28:16 Paul was suffered to **d** by himself with a 3306
Ro 8: 9 if so be that the Spirit of God **d** in you. 3611
8:11 that raised up Jesus from the dead **d** in you, 3611
1Co 7:12 and she be pleased to **d** with him, let him 3611
7:13 and *if* he be pleased to **d** with her, let her 3611
2Co 6:16 I will **d** in them, and walk in *them;* and 1774
Eph 3:17 That Christ may **d** in your hearts by faith; 2730
Col 1:19 *the Father* that in him should all fulness **d**; 2730
3:16 Let the word of Christ **d** in you richly in all 1774
1Pe 3: 7 **d with** *them* according to knowledge, 4924
1Jn 4:13 Hereby know we that we **d** in him, and 3306
Rev 3:10 the world, to try them that **d** upon the earth. 2730
6:10 avenge our blood on them that **d** on 2730
7:15 he that sitteth on the throne shall **d** among 4637
11:10 And they that **d** upon the earth shall rejoice 2730
12:12 ye heavens, and ye that **d** in them. 4637
13: 6 his tabernacle, and them that **d** in heaven. 4637
13: 8 And all that **d** upon the earth shall worship 2730
13:12 them which **d** therein to worship the first 2730
13:14 And deceiveth them that **d** on the earth by 2730
13:14 saying to them that **d** on the earth, that *they* 2730
14: 6 to preach unto them that **d** on the earth, 2730
17: 8 and they that **d** on the earth shall wonder, 2730
21: 3 and he will **d** with them, and they shall be 4637

DWELLED (6) [DWELL]

Ge 13: 7 and the Perizzite **d** then in the land. 3427
13:12 Abram **d** in the land of Canaan, and 3427
13:12 Lot **d** in the cities of the plain, and 3427
20: 1 **d** between Kadesh and Shur, and 3427
Ru 1: 4 and they **d** there about ten years. 3427
1Sa 12:11 your enemies on every side, and ye **d** safe. 3427

DWELLERS (3) [DWELL]

Isa 18: 3 of the world, and **d** on the earth, see ye, 7931
Ac 1:19 And it was known unto all the **d** at 2730
2: 9 and the **d** in Mesopotamia, and in Judea, 2730

DWELLEST (19) [DWELL]

Dt 12:29 thou succeedest them, and **d** in their land; 3427
19: 1 and **d** in their cities, and in their houses; 3427
26: 1 and possessest it, and **d** therein; 3427
2Ki 19:15 which **d** *between* the cherubims, thou *art* 3427
Ps 80: 1 thou that **d** *between* the cherubims, 3427
123: 1 up mine eyes, O thou that **d** in the heavens. 3427
SS 8:13 Thou that **d** in the gardens, the companions 3427
Isa 10:24 O my people that **d in** Zion, be not afraid of 3427
37:16 of Israel, that **d** *between* the cherubims, 3427
47: 8 that **d** carelessly, that sayest in thine heart, 3427
Jer 49:16 O thou that **d** in the clefts of the rock, 7931
51:13 O thou that **d** upon many waters, 7931
La 4:21 daughter of Edom, that **d** in the land of Uz; 3427
Eze 7: 7 come unto thee, O thou that **d in** the land: 3427
12: 2 thou **d** in the midst of a rebellious house, 3427
Ob 1: 3 thou that **d** in the clefts of the rock, 7931
Zec 2: 7 that **d** *with* the daughter of Babylon. 3427
Jn 1:38 being interpreted, Master,) where **d** thou? 3306
Rev 2:13 I know thy works, and where thou **d**, 2730

DWELLETH (58) [DWELL]

Lev 19:34 *But* the stranger that **d** with you shall be 1481
25:39 if thy brother *that* **d** by thee be waxen poor, NIH
25:47 and thy brother *that* **d** by him wax poor, and NIH
Nu 13:18 what it *is;* and the people that **d** therein, 3427
Dt 33:20 he **d** as a lion, and teareth the arm with 7931
Jos 6:25 she **d** in Israel *even* unto this day; because 3427
22:19 wherein the LORD'S tabernacle **d**, and 7931
1Sa 4: 4 of hosts, which **d** *between* the cherubims: 3427
27:11 *will be* his manner all the while he **d** in 3427
2Sa 6: 2 of hosts that **d** *between* the cherubims. 3427
7: 2 but the ark of God **d** within curtains. 3427
1Ch 13: 6 that **d** *between* the cherubims, whose name 3427
Job 15:28 he **d in** desolate cities, *and* in houses which 7931
38:19 Where *is* the way *where* light **d**? and *as for* 7931
39:28 She **d** and abideth on the rock, upon 7931
Ps 9:11 *praises* to the LORD, which **d** in Zion: 3427
26: 8 and the place **where** thine honour **d**. 4908
91: 1 He that **d** in the secret place of the most 3427
113: 5 unto the LORD our God, who **d** on high, 3427
135:21 LORD out of Zion, which **d** *at* Jerusalem. 7931
Pr 3:29 seeing he **d** securely by thee. 3427
Isa 8:18 LORD of hosts, which **d** in mount Zion. 7931
33: 5 The LORD *is* exalted; for he **d** on high: 7931
Jer 29:16 of all the people that **d** in this city, *and* 3427
44: 2 they *are* a desolation, and no man **d** therein, 3427
49:31 that **d** without care, saith the LORD, 3427
51:43 and a wilderness, a land wherein no man **d**, 3427
La 1: 3 she **d** among the heathen, she findeth no 3427
Eze 16:46 that **d** at thy right hand, *is* Sodom and 3427
17:16 surely in the place *where* the king *d* that NIH
38:14 In that day when my people of Israel **d** 3427
Da 2:22 *is* in the darkness, and the light **d** with him. 8271
Hos 4: 3 every one that **d** therein shall languish, 3427
Joel 3:21 not cleansed: for the LORD **d** in Zion. 7931
Am 8: 8 and every one mourn that **d** therein? 3427
Mt 23:21 sweareth by it, and by him that **d** therein. 2730
Jn 6:56 drinketh my blood, **d** in me, and I in him. 3306
14:10 but the Father that **d** in me, he doeth 3306
14:17 for he **d** with you, and shall be in you. 3306
Ac 7:48 Howbeit the most High **d** not in temples 2730
17:24 earth, **d** not in temples made with hands; 2730
Ro 7:17 is no more I that do it, but sin that **d** in me. 3611
7:18 **d** no good *thing:* for to will is present with 3611
7:20 is no more I that do it, but sin that **d** in me. 3611
8:11 mortal bodies by his Spirit that **d** in you. 1774
1Co 3:16 of God, and *that* the Spirit of God **d** in you? 3611
Col 2: 9 For in him **d** all the fulness of the Godhead 2730
2Ti 1:14 *thee* keep by the Holy Ghost which **d** in us. 1774
Jas 4: 5 the spirit that **d** in us lusteth to envy? 2730
2Pe 3:13 and a new earth, wherein **d** righteousness. 2730
1Jn 3:17 from him, how **d** the love of God in him? 3306
3:24 And he that keepeth his commandments **d** 3306
4:12 God **d** in us, and his love is perfected in us. 3306
4:15 Son of God, God **d** in him, and he in God. 3306
4:16 and he that **d** in love dwelleth in God, and 3306
4:16 and he that dwelleth in love **d** in God, and 3306
2Jn 1: 2 which **d** in us, and shall be with us for ever. 3306
Rev 2:13 who was slain among you, where Satan **d**. 2730

DWELLING (60) [DWELL]

Ge 10:30 their **d** was from Mesha, as thou goest unto 4186
25:27 and Jacob *was* a plain man, **d** in tents. 3427
27:39 thy **d** shall be the fatness of the earth, and 4186
Lev 25:29 if a man sell a **d** house in a walled city, 4186
Nu 21:15 the brooks that goeth down to the **d** of Ar, 3427
24:21 Strong *is* thy **d place**, and thou puttest thy 4186
Jos 13:21 *were* dukes of Sihon, **d in** the country. 3427
1Ki 8:30 hear thou in heaven thy **d** place: and 3427
8:39 hear thou *in* heaven thy **d** place, and 3427
8:43 Hear thou *in* heaven thy **d** place, and 3427
8:49 their supplication *in* heaven thy **d** place, 3427
21: 8 nobles that *were* in his city, **d** with Naboth. 3427
2Ki 17:25 *so* it was at the beginning of their **d** there, 3427
1Ch 6:32 they ministered before the **d place** of 4908
6:54 Now these *are* their **d places** throughout 4186
2Ch 6: 2 for thee, and a place for thy **d** for ever. 3427
6:21 hear thou from thy **d** place, *even* from 3427
6:30 hear thou from heaven thy **d** place, and 3427
6:33 *even* from thy **d** place, and do according to 3427
6:39 *even* from thy **d** place, their prayer and 3427
30:27 their prayer came *up* to his **holy d** place, 6944
36:15 on his people, and on his **d place**: 4583
Job 8:22 the **d place** of the wicked shall come to 168
21:28 and where *are* the **d** places of the wicked? 4908
Ps 49:11 *and* their **d places** to all generations; 4908
49:14 shall consume *in* the grave from their **d**. 2073
52: 5 pluck thee out of *thy* **d place**, and root thee 168
74: 7 the **d place** of thy name to the ground. 4908
76: 2 is his tabernacle, and his **d place** in Zion. 4585
79: 7 devoured Jacob, and laid waste his **d place**. 5116
90: 1 thou hast been our **d place** in all 4583
91:10 neither shall *any* plague come nigh thy **d**. 168
Pr 21:20 to be desired and oil in the **d** of the wise, 5116
24:15 O wicked *man,* against the **d** of 5116
Isa 4: 5 the LORD will create upon every **d place** 4349
18: 4 I will consider in my **d place** like a clear 4349
Jer 30:18 and have mercy on his **d places**; 4908
46:19 O thou daughter **d** in Egypt, furnish thyself 3427
49:33 Hazor shall be a **d** for dragons, *and* 4583
51:30 they have burnt her **d places**; her bars are 4908
51:37 a **d place** for dragons, an astonishment, and 4583
Eze 6: 6 In all your **d places** the cities shall be laid 4186
37:23 I will save them out of all their **d places**, 4186
38:11 all of them **d** without walls, and 3427
48:15 *place* for the city, for **d**, and for suburbs: 4186
Da 2:11 except the gods, whose **d** is not with flesh. 4070
4:25 thy **d** shall be with the beasts of the field, 4070
4:32 thy **d** *shall be* with the beasts of the field: 4070
5:21 and his **d** *was* with the wild asses: 4070
Joel 3:17 that I *am* the LORD your God **d** in Zion, 7931
Na 2:11 Where *is* the **d** of the lions, and the feeding 4583
Hab 1: 6 to possess the **d places** *that are* not theirs. 4908
Zep 3: 7 so their **d** should not be cut off, 4583
Mk 5: 3 Who had *his* **d** among the tombs; 2731
Ac 2: 5 And there were **d** at Jerusalem Jews, 2730
19:17 all the Jews and Greeks also **d** at Ephesus; 2730
1Co 4:11 are buffeted, and **have no certain d place**; 790
1Ti 6:16 **d** in the light which no *man* can approach 3611
Heb 11: 9 as *in* a strange *country,* **d** in tabernacles 2730
2Pe 2: 8 (For *that* righteous *man* **d** among them, 1460

DWELLINGS (17) [DWELL]

Ex 10:23 all the children of Israel had light in their **d**. 4186
Lev 3:17 for your generations throughout all your **d**, 4186
7:26 *it be* of fowl or of beast, in any of your **d**. 4186
23: 3 *is* the sabbath of the LORD in all your **d**. 4186
23:14 throughout your generations in all your **d**. 4186
23:21 in all your **d** throughout your generations. 4186
23:31 throughout your generations in all your **d**. 4186
Nu 35:29 throughout your generations in all your **d**. 4186
Job 18:19 his people, nor *any* remaining in his **d**. 4033
18:21 Surely such *are* the **d** of the wicked, and 4908
39: 6 the wilderness, and the barren *land* his **d**. 4908
Ps 55:15 for wickedness *is* in their **d**, *and* 4033
87: 2 gates of Zion more than all the **d** of Jacob. 4908
Isa 32:18 and in sure **d**, and in quiet resting places; 4908
Jer 9:19 the land, because our **d** have cast *us* out. 4908
Eze 25: 4 palaces in thee, and make their **d** in thee: 4908
Zep 2: 6 the sea coast shall be **d** *and* cottages for 5116

DWELT (226) [DWELL]

Ge 4:16 **d** in the land of Nod, on the east of Eden. 3427
11: 2 in the land of Shinar; and they **d** there. 3427
11:31 and they came unto Haran, and **d** there. 3427
13:18 came and **d** in the plain of Mamre, which *is* 3427
14: 7 also the Amorites, that **d** in Hazezon-tamar. 3427
14:12 who **d** in Sodom, and his goods, and 3427
14:13 for he **d** in the plain of Mamre the Amorite, 7931
16: 3 after Abram had **d** ten years in the land of 3427
19:29 he overthrew the cities in the which Lot **d**. 3427
19:30 **d** in the mountain, and his two daughters 3427
19:30 he **d** in a cave, he and his two daughters. 3427
21:20 **d** in the wilderness, and became an archer. 3427
21:21 he **d** in the wilderness of Paran: and 3427
22:19 and Abraham **d** at Beer-sheba. 3427
23:10 Ephron **d** amongst the children of Heth: 3427
24:62 for he **d** in the south country. 3427
25:11 and Isaac **d** by the well Lahai-roi. 3427
25:18 they **d** from Havilah unto Shur, that *is* 7931
26: 6 And Isaac **d** in Gerar: 3427
26:17 his tent in the valley of Gerar, and **d** there. 3427
35:22 when Israel **d** in that land, that Reuben 7931
36: 8 Thus **d** Esau in mount Seir: Esau *is* Edom. 3427
37: 1 Jacob **d** in the land wherein his father was a 3427
38:11 Tamar went and **d** *in* her father's house. 3427
47:27 Israel **d** in the land of Egypt, in the country 3427
50:22 Joseph **d** in Egypt, he, and his father's 3427
Ex 2:15 of Pharaoh, and **d** in the land of Midian: 3427
12:40 who **d** in Egypt, *was* four hundred and 3427
Lev 18: 3 of Egypt, wherein ye **d**, shall ye not do: 3427
26:35 rest in your sabbaths, when ye **d** upon it. 3427
Nu 14:25 and the Canaanites **d** in the valley.) 3427
14:45 the Canaanites which **d** in that hill, 3427
20:15 and we have **d** in Egypt a long time; 3427
21: 1 Arad the Canaanite, which **d** *in* the south, 3427
21:25 Israel **d** in all the cities of the Amorites, 3427
21:31 Thus Israel **d** in the land of the Amorites. 3427
21:34 king of the Amorites, which **d** at Heshbon. 3427
31:10 they burnt all their cities wherein they **d**, 4186
32:40 the son of Manasseh; and he **d** therein. 3427
33:40 which **d** in the south in the land of Canaan, 3427
Dt 1: 4 which **d** in Heshbon, and Og the king of 3427
1: 4 of Bashan, which **d** at Astaroth in Edrei: 3427
1: 6 Ye have **d** long enough in this mount: 3427
1:44 the Amorites, which **d** in that mountain, 3427
2: 8 which **d** in Seir, through the way of 3427
2:10 (The Emims **d** therein in times past, 3427
2:12 The Horims also **d** in Seir beforetime; but 3427
2:12 from before them, and **d** in their stead; 3427
2:20 giants **d** therein in old time; and 3427
2:21 they succeeded them, and **d** in their stead: 3427
2:22 did to the children of Esau, which **d** in Seir, 3427
2:22 and **d** in their stead *even* unto this day: 3427
2:23 the Avims which **d** in Hazerim, *even* unto 3427
2:23 destroyed them, and **d** in their stead.) 3427
3: 2 king of the Amorites, which **d** at Heshbon. 3427
4:46 who **d** at Heshbon, whom Moses and 3427
8:12 hast built goodly houses, and **d** *therein;* 3427
29:16 (For ye know how we have **d** in the land of 3427
33:16 *for* the good will of him that **d in** the bush: 7931
Jos 2:15 the town wall, and she **d** upon the wall. 3427
7: 7 and **d** on the *other* side Jordan! 3427
9:16 and *that* they **d** among them. 3427
12: 2 who **d** in Heshbon, *and* ruled from Aroer, 3427
12: 4 the giants, that **d** at Ashtaroth and at Edrei, 3427
16:10 they drave not out the Canaanites that **d** in 3427
19:47 and **d** therein, and called Leshem, Dan, 3427
19:50 and he built the city, and **d** therein. 3427
21:43 and they possessed it, and **d** therein. 3427
22:33 wherein the children of Reuben and Gad **d**. 3427
24: 2 Your fathers **d** on the *other* side of 3427
24: 7 and ye **d** in the wilderness a long season. 3427
24: 8 which **d** on the *other* side Jordan; 3427
24:18 even the Amorites which **d in** the land: 3427
Jdg 1: 9 that **d in** the mountain, and in the south, 3427
1:10 Judah went against the Canaanites that **d** in 3427
1:16 and they went and **d** among the people. 3427
1:29 drive out the Canaanites that **d** in Gezer; 3427
1:29 but the Canaanites **d** in Gezer among them. 3427
1:30 the Canaanites **d** among them, and 3427
1:32 the Asherites **d** among the Canaanites, 3427
1:33 he **d** among the Canaanites, the inhabitants 3427
3: 3 and the Hivites that **d in** mount Lebanon, 3427
3: 5 the children of Israel **d** among 3427
4: 2 which **d** in Harosheth of the Gentiles. 3427
4: 5 she **d** under the palm tree of Deborah 3427
8:11 Gideon went up *by the* way of them that **d** 7931
8:29 son of Joash went and **d** in his own house. 3427
9:21 and fled, and went to Beer, and **d** there, 3427
9:41 Abimelech **d** at Arumah: and Zebul thrust 3427
10: 1 and he **d** in Shamir in mount Ephraim. 3427
11: 3 from his brethren, and **d** in the land of Tob: 3427
11:26 While Israel **d** in Heshbon and her towns, 3427
15: 8 and **d** in the top of the rock Etam. 3427
18: 7 that *were* therein, how they **d** careless, 3427
18:28 And they built a city, and **d** therein, 3427
21:23 and repaired the cities, and **d** in them. 3427
Ru 2:23 and **d** with her mother in law. 3427
1Sa 19:18 And he and Samuel went and **d** in Naioth. 3427
22: 4 they **d** with him all the while that David 3427
23:29 and **d** in strong holds at En-gedi. 3427
27: 3 David **d** with Achish at Gath, he and 3427
27: 7 the time that David **d** in the country of 3427
31: 7 and the Philistines came and **d** in them. 3427
2Sa 2: 3 and they **d** in the cities of Hebron. 3427
5: 9 So David **d** in the fort, and called it the city 3427
7: 6 Whereas I have not **d** in *any* house since 3427
9:12 all that **d** in the house of Ziba *were* servants 4186
9:13 So Mephibosheth **d** in Jerusalem: for he did 3427
14:28 So Absalom **d** two full years in Jerusalem, 3427
1Ki 2:38 And Shimei **d** in Jerusalem many days. 3427
4:25 Judah and Israel **d** safely, every man under 3427
7: 8 his house where he **d** *had* another court 3427
9:16 slain the Canaanites that **d** in the city, and 3427
11:24 and **d** therein, and reigned in Damascus. 3427
12: 2 king Solomon, and Jeroboam **d** in Egypt;) 3427
12:17 *as for* the children of Israel which **d** in 3427
12:25 Shechem in mount Ephraim, and **d** therein; 3427
13:11 Now there **d** an old prophet in Beth-el; and 3427
13:25 told *it* in the city where the old prophet **d**. 3427
15:18 king of Syria, that **d** at Damascus, saying, 3427
15:21 left off building of Ramah, and **d** in Tirzah. 3427

1Ki 17: 5 for he went and **d** by the brook Cherith, 3427
2Ki 13: 5 the children of Israel **d** in their tents, 3427
15: 5 day of his death, and **d** in a several house. 3427
16: 6 came *to* Elath, and **d** there unto this day. 3427
17:24 and **d** in the cities thereof. 3427
17:28 away from Samaria came and **d** in Beth-el, 3427
17:29 every nation in their cities wherein they **d**. 3427
19:36 and went and returned, and **d** at Nineveh. 3427
22:14 (now she **d** in Jerusalem in the college;) 3427
1Ch 2:55 the families of the scribes which **d at** 3427
4:23 those that **d amongst** plants and hedges: 3427
4:23 there they **d** with the king for his work. 3427
4:28 they **d** at Beer-sheba, and Moladah, and 3427
4:40 for *they* of Ham had **d** there of old. 3427
4:41 utterly unto this day, and **d** in their rooms: 3427
4:43 were escaped, and **d** there unto this day. 3427
5: 8 the son of Joel, who **d** in Aroer, even unto 3427
5:10 they **d** in their tents throughout all the east 3427
5:11 the children of Gad **d** over against them, 3427
5:16 they **d** in Gilead in Bashan, and in her 3427
5:22 they **d** in their steads until the captivity. 3427
5:23 the children of the half tribe of Manasseh **d** 3427
7:29 In these **d** the children of Joseph the son of 3427
8:28 chief *men*. These **d** in Jerusalem. 3427
8:29 at Gibeon **d** the father of Gibeon; 3427
8:32 these also **d** with their brethren in 3427
9: 2 Now the first inhabitants that *d* in their NIH
9: 3 in Jerusalem **d** of the children of Judah, 3427
9:16 that **d** in the villages of the Netophathites. 3427
9:34 their generations; these **d** at Jerusalem. 3427
9:35 in Gibeon **d** the father of Gibeon, Jehiel, 3427
9:38 they also **d with** their brethren at 3427
10: 7 and the Philistines came and **d** in them. 3427
11: 7 David **d** in the castle; therefore they called 3427
17: 5 For I have not **d** in a house since the day 3427
2Ch 10:17 *as for* the children of Israel that **d** in 3427
11: 5 Rehoboam **d** in Jerusalem, and built cities 3427
16: 2 king of Syria, that **d** at Damascus, saying, 3427
19: 4 Jehoshaphat **d** at Jerusalem: and he went 3427
20: 8 they **d** therein, and have built thee a 3427
26: 7 and against the Arabians that **d** in Gur-baal, 3427
26:21 and **d** *in* a several house, *being* a leper; 3427
28:18 and the villages thereof: and they **d** there. 3427
30:25 land of Israel, and that **d** in Judah, rejoiced. 3427
31: 4 **d in** Jerusalem to give the portion of 3427
31: 6 and Judah, that **d** in the cities of Judah, 3427
34:22 (now she **d** in Jerusalem in the college:) 3427
Ezr 2:70 **d** in their cities, and all Israel in their cities. 3427
Ne 3:26 Moreover the Nethinims **d** in Ophel, 3427
4:12 that when the Jews which **d** by them came, 3427
7:73 and all Israel, **d** in their cities; 3427
11: 1 And the rulers of the people **d** at Jerusalem: 3427
11: 3 chief of the province that **d** in Jerusalem: 3427
11: 3 in the cities of Judah **d** every one in his 3427
11: 4 at Jerusalem **d** *certain* of the children of 3427
11: 6 All the sons of Perez that **d** at Jerusalem 3427
11:21 the Nethinims **d** in Ophel: and Ziha and 3427
11:25 *some* of the children of Judah **d** at 3427
11:30 they **d** from Beer-sheba unto the valley of 2583
11:31 The children also of Benjamin from Geba *d* NIH
13:16 There **d** men of Tyre also therein, which 3427
Est 9:19 the villages, that **d** in the unwalled towns, 3427
Job 22: 8 the earth; and the honourable *man* **d** in it. 3427
29:25 and sat chief, and **d** as a king in the army, 7931
Ps 68:10 Thy congregation hath **d** therein: thou, 3427
74: 2 this mount Zion, wherein thou hast **d**. 7931
94:17 my help, my soul had almost **d** *in* silence. 7931
120: 6 My soul hath long **d** with him that hateth 7931
Isa 13:20 neither shall it be **d in** from generation to 7931
29: 1 to Ariel, to Ariel, the city *where* David **d**! 2583
37:37 and went and returned, and **d** at Nineveh. 3427
Jer 2: 6 man passed through, and where no man **d**? 3427
35:10 we have **d** in tents, and have obeyed, and 3427
39:14 carry him home: so he **d** among the people. 3427
40: 6 **d** with him among the people that were left 3427
41:17 and **d** in the habitation of Chimham, 3427
44:15 even all the people that **d** in the land of 3427
50:39 neither shall it be **d in** from generation to 7931
Eze 3:15 that **d** by the river of Chebar, and I sat 3427
31: 6 and under his shadow **d** all great nations. 3427
31:17 *that* **d** under his shadow in the midst of 3427
36:17 when the house of Israel **d** in their own 3427
37:25 my servant, wherein your fathers have **d**; 3427
39:26 when they **d** safely in their land, and 3427
Da 4:12 the fowls of the heaven **d** in the boughs 1753
4:21 under which the beasts of the field **d**, and 1753
Zep 2:15 This *is* the rejoicing city that **d** carelessly, 3427
Mt 2:23 he came and **d** in a city called Nazareth: *2730*
4:13 he came and **d** in Capernaum, *2730*
Lk 1:65 And fear came on all that **d round about** *4039*
13: 4 sinners above all men that **d** in Jerusalem? *2730*
Jn 1:14 and **d** among us, (and we beheld his glory, *4637*
1:39 They came and saw where he **d**, and *3306*
Ac 7: 2 in Mesopotamia, before he **d** in Charran, *2730*
7: 4 land of the Chaldeans, and **d** in Charran: *2730*
9:22 confounded the Jews which **d** at Damascus, *2730*
9:32 down also to the saints which **d** at Lydda. *2730*
9:35 And all that **d** at Lydda and Saron saw him, *2730*
11:29 relief unto the brethren which **d** in Judea: *2730*
13:17 *they* **d as strangers** in the land of Egypt, *3940*
19:10 that all they which **d in** Asia heard *2730*
22:12 a good report of all the Jews which **d** *there*, *2730*
28:30 And Paul **d** two whole years in his own *3306*
2Ti 1: 5 which **d** first in thy grandmother Lois, and *1774*
Rev 11:10 these two prophets tormented them that **d** *2730*

DYED (7) [DYING]

Ex 25: 5 rams' skins **d red**, and badgers' skins, and 119
26:14 a covering for the tent *of* rams' skins **d red**, 119
35: 7 rams' skins **d red**, and badgers' skins, and 119
36:19 a covering for the tent *of* rams' skins **d red**, 119
39:34 the covering of rams' skins **d red**, and 119
Isa 63: 1 from Edom, with **d** garments from Bozrah? 2556
Eze 23:15 **exceeding in d attire** upon their 2871+5628

DYING (6) [DYED]

Nu 17:13 shall die: shall we be consumed with **d**? 1478
Mk 12:20 and the first took a wife, and **d** left no seed. *599*
Lk 8:42 about twelve years of age, and she lay a **d**. *599*
2Co 4:10 Always bearing about in the body the **d** of *3500*
6: 9 as **d**, and behold, we live; as chastened, and *599*
Heb 11:21 By faith Jacob, when he was a **d**, *599*

DYSENTERY See FLUX

E

EACH (51)

Ge 15:10 and laid **e** piece one against another: 376
34:25 took **e man** his sword, and came upon 376
40: 5 both of them, **e man** his dream in one night, 376
40: 5 **e man** according to the interpretation of his 376
41:11 we dreamed **e man** according to 376
41:12 to **e man** according to his dream he did 376
45:22 To all of them he gave **e man** changes of 376
Ex 18: 7 they asked **e** other of *their* welfare; and 376
30:34 of **e** shall there be **a like** *weight:* 905+905+871.1
Lev 24: 7 thou shalt put pure frankincense upon **e** NIH
Nu 1:44 **e** one was for the house of his fathers. 376+376
7: 3 for two of the princes, and for *e* one an ox: NIH
7:11 **e** prince on *his* day, for the dedicating of 259
7:85 **E** charger of silver *weighing* an hundred and 259
7:85 and thirty *shekels*, **e** bowl seventy: 259
14:34 *even* forty days, **e**[S] day for a year, shall ye 3117
16:17 thou also, and Aaron, **e** *of you* his censer. 376
17: 6 **for e** prince one, according to their 3807.1
29:14 two tenth deals to **e** ram of the two rams, 259
29:15 a several tenth deal to **e** lamb of the fourteen 259
Jos 18: 4 Give out from among you three men for *e* NIH
22:14 of **e** chief house a prince throughout all 259
22:14 **e one** *was* a head of the house of their 376
Jdg 8:18 *e* one resembled the children of a king. NIH
21:22 we reserved not to **e man** his wife in 376
Ru 1: 8 in law, Go, return **e** to her mother's house: 802
1: 9 **e** *of you in* the house of her husband. 802
1Ki 4: 7 **e man** *his* month in a year made provision. 259
6:23 cherubims *of* olive tree, **e** ten cubits high. 2050.2
22:10 Jehoshaphat the king of Judah sat **e** on his 376
2Ki 9:21 **e** in his chariot, and they went out against 376
15:20 of **e** man fifty shekels *of* silver, to give to 259
1Ch 20: 6 six *on e hand*, and six *on each foot:* and NIH
20: 6 six *on each hand*, and six *on e foot:* and NIH
2Ch 3:15 the chapiter that *was* on the top *of* **e** of them NIH
4:13 two rows *of* pomegranates on **e** wreath, to 259
9:18 stays **on e side** 2088+2088+4480+4480+2050.1
Ne 13:24 to the language of **e people**. 5971+5971+2050.1
Ps 85:10 and peace have kissed *e other.* NIH
Isa 2:20 which they made *e one* for himself to NIH
6: 2 **e one** had six wings; with twain he covered 259
35: 7 where **e** lay, *shall be* grass with reeds and 1886.3
57: 2 their beds, *e one* walking *in* his uprightness. NIH
Eze 4: 6 have appointed thee **e day** for a year. 3117+3117
40:16 and upon *e* post *were* palm trees. NIH
40:48 measured *e* post of the porch, five cubits on NIH
Lk 13:15 doth not **e one** of you on the sabbath loose *1538*
Ac 2: 3 as of fire, and it sat upon **e** of them. *1520+1538*
Php 2: 3 in lowliness of mind *let* **e** esteem **other** *240*
2Th 1: 3 one of you all towards **e other** aboundeth; *240*
Rev 4: 8 And the four beasts had **e** of them six wings *1527*

EAGERNESS See FORWARDNESS

EAGLE (23) [EAGLE'S, EAGLES, EAGLES']

Lev 11:13 the **e**, and the ossifrage, and the ospray, 5404
11:18 the swan, and the pelican, and the **gier e**, 7360
Dt 14:12 the **e**, and the ossifrage, and the ospray, 5404
14:17 and the **gier e**, and the cormorant, 7360
28:49 the end of the earth, *as swift* as the **e** flieth; 5404
32:11 As an **e** stirreth up her nest, fluttereth over 5404
Job 9:26 swift ships: as the **e** *that* hasteth to the prey. 5404
39:27 Doth the **e** mount up at thy command, and 5404
Pr 23: 5 they fly away as an **e** *toward* heaven. 5404
30:19 The way of an **e** in the air; the way of a 5404
Jer 48:40 he shall fly as an **e**, and shall spread his 5404
49:16 shouldest make thy nest as high as the **e**, 5404
49:22 he shall come up and fly as the **e**, and 5404
Eze 1:10 left side; they four also had the face of an **e**. 5404
10:14 of a lion, and the fourth the face of an **e**. 5404
17: 3 A great **e** with great wings, longwinged, 5404
17: 7 There was also another great **e** with great 5404
Hos 8: 1 *He shall come* as an **e** against the house of 5404
Ob 1: 4 Though thou exalt *thyself* as the **e**, and 5404
Mic 1:16 enlarge thy baldness as the **e**; 5404
Hab 1: 8 they shall fly as the **e** *that* hasteth to eat. 5404
Rev 4: 7 and the fourth beast *was* like a flying **e**. *105*
12:14 woman were given two wings of a great **e**, *105*

EAGLE'S (2) [EAGLE]

Ps 103: 5 *so that* thy youth is renewed like the **e**. 5404
Da 7: 4 The first *was* like a lion, and had **e** wings: I 5403

EAGLES (7) [EAGLE]

2Sa 1:23 they were swifter than **e**, they were stronger 5404
Pr 30:17 pick it out, and the young **e** shall eat it. 5404
Isa 40:31 they shall mount up *with* wings as **e**; 5404
Jer 4:13 his horses are swifter than **e**. Woe unto us! 5404
La 4:19 Our persecutors are swifter than the **e** of 5404
Mt 24:28 there will the **e** be gathered together. *105*
Lk 17:37 Wheresoever the body *is*, thither will the **e** *105*

EAGLES' (2) [EAGLE]

Ex 19: 4 *how* I bare you on **e** wings, and 5404
Da 4:33 till his hairs were grown like **e** *feathers*, and 5403

EAR (120) [EARED, EARING, EARRING, EARRINGS, EARS]

Ex 9:31 for the barley *was* **in the e**, and the flax *was* 24
15:26 wilt **give e** to his commandments, and 238
21: 6 his master shall bore his **e** through with an 241
29:20 put *it* upon the tip of the *right* **e** of Aaron, 241
29:20 upon the tip of the right **e** of his sons, and 241
Lev 8:23 put *it* upon the tip of Aaron's right **e**, and 241
8:24 put of the blood upon the tip of their right **e**, 241
14:14 of the right **e** of him that is to be cleansed, 241
14:17 of the right **e** of him that is to be cleansed, 241
14:25 put *it* upon the tip of the right **e** of him that is 241
14:28 of the right **e** of him that is to be cleansed, 241
Dt 1:45 hearken to your voice, nor **give e** unto you. 238
15:17 and thrust *it* through his **e** unto the door, and 241
32: 1 **Give e**, O ye heavens, and I will speak; and 238
Jdg 5: 3 **give e**, O ye princes; I, *even* I, will sing unto 238
1Sa 8:12 *will set them* to **e** his ground, and to reap 2790
9:15 Now the LORD had told Samuel in his **e** a 241
2Ki 19:16 LORD, bow down thine **e**, and hear: open, 241
2Ch 24:19 against them: but they would not **give e**. 238
Ne 1: 6 Let thine **e** now be attentive, and thine eyes 241
1:11 let now thine **e** be attentive to the prayer of 241
9:30 yet would they not **give e**: therefore 238
Job 4:12 to me, and mine **e** received a little thereof. 241
12:11 Doth not the **e** try words? and the mouth 241
13: 1 mine eye hath seen all *this*, mine **e** hath 241
29:11 When the **e** heard *me*, then it blessed me; 241
29:21 Unto me *men* **gave e**, and waited, and 8085
32:11 I **gave e** to your reasons, whilst you searched 238
34: 2 ye wise *men*; and **give e** unto me, 238
34: 3 For the **e** trieth words, as the mouth tasteth 241
36:10 He openeth also their **e** to discipline, and 241
42: 5 I have heard of thee by the hearing of the **e**: 241
Ps 5: 1 **Give e** to my words, O LORD, consider my 238
10:17 their heart, thou wilt cause thine **e** to hear: 241
17: 1 attend unto my cry, **give e** unto my prayer, 238
17: 6 incline thine **e** unto me, *and* hear my speech. 241
31: 2 Bow down thine **e** to me; deliver me 241
39:12 O LORD, and **give e** unto my cry; 238
45:10 and consider, and incline thine **e**; 241
49: 1 **give e**, all ye inhabitants of the world: 238
49: 4 I will incline mine **e** to a parable: I will open 241
54: 2 O God; **give e** to the words of my mouth. 238
55: 1 **Give e** to my prayer, O God; and hide not 238
58: 4 *are* like the deaf adder *that* stoppeth her **e**; 241
71: 2 incline thine **e** unto me, and save me. 241
77: 1 God *with* my voice; and he **gave e** unto me. 238
78: 1 **Give e**, O my people, to my law: 238
80: 1 **Give e**, O Shepherd of Israel, thou that 238
84: 8 my prayer: **give e**, O God of Jacob. Selah. 238
86: 1 Bow down thine **e**, O LORD, hear me: for I 241
86: 6 **Give e**, O LORD, unto my prayer; and 238
88: 2 before thee: incline thine **e** unto my cry; 241
94: 9 He that planted the **e**, shall he not hear? he 241
102: 2 I am in trouble; incline thine **e** unto me: 241
116: 2 Because he hath inclined his **e** unto me, 241
141: 1 **give e** unto my voice, when I cry unto thee. 238
143: 1 O LORD, **give e** to my supplications: 238
Pr 2: 2 So that *thou* incline thine **e** unto wisdom, 241
4:20 my words; incline thine **e** unto my sayings. 241
5: 1 *and* bow thine **e** to my understanding: 241
5:13 nor inclined mine **e** to them that instructed 241
15:31 The **e** that heareth the reproof of life abideth 241
17: 4 *and* a liar **giveth e** to a naughty tongue. 238
18:15 and the **e** of the wise seeketh knowledge. 241
20:12 The hearing **e**, and the seeing eye, 241
22:17 Bow down thine **e**, and hear the words of 241
25:12 *so is* a wise reprover upon an obedient **e**. 241
28: 9 He that turneth away his **e** from hearing 241
Ecc 1: 8 with seeing, nor the **e** filled with hearing. 241
Isa 1: 2 Hear, O heavens, and **give e**, O earth: for 238
1:10 **give e** unto the law of our God, ye people of 238
8: 9 in pieces; and **give e**, all ye of far countries: 238
28:23 **Give** ye **e**, and hear my voice; hearken, and 238
30:24 the young asses that **e** the ground shall eat 5647
32: 9 careless daughters, **give e** unto my speech. 238
37:17 Incline thine **e**, O LORD, and hear; 241
42:23 Who among you will **give e** to this? *who* will 238
48: 8 from that time *that* thine **e** was not opened: 241
50: 4 he wakeneth mine **e** to hear as the learned. 241
50: 5 The Lord GOD hath opened mine **e**, and 241
51: 4 and **give e** unto me, O my nation: 238
55: 3 Incline your **e**, and come unto me: hear, and 241
59: 1 neither his **e** heavy, that *it* cannot hear: 241
64: 4 nor **perceived by the e**, neither hath the eye 238
Jer 6:10 their **e** *is* uncircumcised, and they cannot 241
7:24 nor inclined their **e**, but walked in 241
7:26 nor inclined their **e**, but hardened their neck: 241
9:20 and let your **e** receive the word of his mouth, 241
11: 8 nor inclined their **e**, but walked every one in 241
13:15 Hear ye, and **give e**; be not proud: for 238
17:23 neither inclined their **e**, but made their neck 241
25: 4 not hearkened, nor inclined your **e** to hear. 241
34:14 not unto me, neither inclined their **e**. 241
35:15 ye have not inclined your **e**, nor hearkened 241
44: 5 nor inclined their **e** to turn from their 241
La 3:56 hide not thine **e** at my breathing, at my cry. 241
Da 9:18 O my God, incline thine **e**, and hear; 241
Hos 5: 1 of Israel; and **give** ye **e**, O house of the king; 238
Joel 1: 2 Hear this, ye old men, and **give e**, all ye 238
Am 3:12 of the lion two legs, or a piece of an **e**; 241
Mt 10:27 and what ye hear in the **e**, *that* preach ye *3775*
26:51 of the high priest's, and smote off his **e**. *5621*
Mk 4:28 first the blade, then the **e**, after that the full *4719*
4:28 then the ear, after that the full corn in the **e**. *4719*
14:47 servant of the high priest, and cut off his **e**. *5621*
Lk 12: 3 *that* which ye have spoken in the **e** in *3775*

Lk 22:50 of the high priest, and cut off his right **e**. *3775*
22:51 And he touched his **e**, and healed him. *5621*
Jn 18:10 high priest's servant, and cut off his right **e**. *5621*
18:26 being *his* kinsman whose **e** Peter cut off, *5621*
1Co 2: 9 it is written, Eye hath not seen, nor **e** heard, *3775*
12:16 And if the **e** shall say, Because I am not *3775*
Rev 2: 7 He that hath an **e**, let him hear what *3775*
2:11 He that hath an **e**, let him hear what *3775*
2:17 He that hath an **e**, let him hear what *3775*
2:29 He that hath an **e**, let him hear what *3775*
3: 6 He that hath an **e**, let him hear what *3775*
3:13 He that hath an **e**, let him hear what *3775*
3:22 He that hath an **e**, let him hear what *3775*
13: 9 If any *man* have an **e**, let him hear. *3775*

EARED (1) [EAR]
Dt 21: 4 which is neither **e** nor sown, and shall strike 5647

EARING (2) [EAR]
Ge 45: 6 *in* the which *there shall* neither *be* **e** nor 2758
Ex 34:21 in **e time** and in harvest thou shalt rest. 2758

EARLIER See HERETOFORE

EARLY (86)
Ge 19: 2 ye shall **rise up e**, and go on your ways. 7925
19:27 Abraham **gat up e** in the morning to 7925
20: 8 Therefore Abimelech **rose e** in 7925
21:14 Abraham **rose up e** in the morning, and 7925
22: 3 Abraham **rose up e** in the morning, and 7925
28:18 Jacob **rose up e** in the morning, and 7925
31:55 **e** in the morning Laban **rose up**, and 7925
Ex 8:20 **Rise up e** in the morning, and stand before 7925
9:13 **Rise up e** in the morning, and stand before 7925
24: 4 **rose up e** in the morning, and builded an 7925
32: 6 they **rose up e** on the morrow, and 7925
34: 4 Moses **rose up e** in the morning, and 7925
Nu 14:40 they **rose up e** in the morning, and 7925
Jos 3: 1 Joshua **rose e** in the morning; and 7925
6:12 Joshua **rose e** in the morning, and 7925
6:15 that they **rose e** about the dawning of 7925
7:16 So Joshua **rose up e** in the morning, and 7925
8:10 Joshua **rose up e** in the morning, and 7925
8:14 of Ai saw *it*, that they hasted and **rose up e**, 7925
Jdg 6:28 when the men of the city **arose e** in 7925
6:38 for he **rose up e** on the morrow, and 7925
7: 1 **rose up e**, and pitched beside the well of 7925
7: 3 and **depart e** from mount Gilead. 6852
9:33 thou shalt **rise e**, and set upon the city: 7925
19: 5 when they **arose e** in the morning, that he 7925
19: 8 he **arose e** in the morning on the fifth day 7925
19: 9 to morrow **get** you **e** on your way, that thou 7925
21: 4 that the people **rose e**, and built there an 7925
1Sa 1:19 they **rose up** in the morning **e**, and 7925
5: 3 when they of Ashdod **arose e** on 7925
5: 4 when they **arose e** on the morrow morning, 7925
9:26 they **arose e**: and it came to pass about 7925
15:12 when Samuel **rose e** to meet Saul in 7925
17:20 David **rose up e** in the morning, and 7925
29:10 Wherefore now **rise up e** in the morning 7925
29:10 as soon as ye **be up e** in the morning, and 7925
29:11 his men **rose up e** to depart in the morning, 7925
2Sa 15: 2 Absalom **rose up e**, and stood beside 7925
2Ki 3:22 they **rose up e** in the morning, and the sun 7925
6:15 the servant of the man of God was risen **e**, 7925
19:35 when they **arose e** in the morning, behold, 7925
2Ch 20:20 they **rose e** in the morning, and went forth 7925
29:20 Hezekiah the king **rose e**, and gathered 7925
Job 1: 5 **rose up e** in the morning, and offered burnt 7925
Ps 46: 5 God shall help her, *and that* right **e**. 1242
57: 8 and harp: I *myself* will awake **e**. 7837
63: 1 O God, thou *art* my God; **e** will I **seek** thee: 7836
78:34 they returned and **inquired e after** God. 7836
90:14 O satisfy us **e** *with* thy 1242+871.1+1886.1
101: 8 I will **e** destroy all 1242+1886.1+3807.1
108: 2 and harp: I *myself* will awake **e**. 7837
127: 2 *It is* vain for you to rise up **e**, to sit up late, 7925
Pr 1:28 they shall **seek** me **e**, but they shall not find 7836
8:17 and those that **seek** me **e** shall find me. 7836
27:14 **rising e** in the morning, it shall be counted 7925
SS 7:12 Let us **get up e** to the vineyards; let us see 7925
Isa 5:11 Woe unto them that **rise up e** in 7925
26: 9 *with* my spirit within me will I **seek** thee **e**: 7836
37:36 when they **arose e** in the morning, behold, 7925
Jer 7:13 **rising up e** and speaking, but ye heard not; 7925
7:25 daily **rising up e** and sending *them*: 7925
11: 7 **rising e** and protesting, saying, Obey my 7925
25: 3 spoken unto you, **rising e** and speaking; 7925
25: 4 **rising e** and sending *them*; but ye have not 7925
26: 5 both **rising up e**, and sending *them*, but 7925
29:19 **rising up e** and sending *them*; but ye would 7925
32:33 **rising up e** and teaching *them*, yet they 7925
35:14 spoken unto you, **rising e** and speaking; 7925
35:15 **rising up e** and sending *them*, saying, 7925
44: 4 **rising e** and sending *them*, saying, Oh, 7925
Da 6:19 the king arose **very e** in the morning, and 8238
Hos 5:15 in their affliction they will **seek** me **e**. 7836
6: 4 and as the **e** dew *it* goeth away. 7925
13: 3 and as the **e** dew that passeth away, 7925
Zep 3: 7 they **rose e**, *and* corrupted all their doings. 7925
Mt 20: 1 which went out **e in the morning** to *260+4404*
Mk 16: 2 And very **e in the morning** the first *day* of *4404*
16: 9 Now when *Jesus* was risen **e** the first *day* of *4404*
Lk 21:38 And all the people **came e in the morning** *3719*
24: 1 **very e in the morning**, they came *901+3722*
24:22 which were **e** at the sepulchre; *3721*
Jn 8: 2 And **e in the morning** he came again into *3722*
18:28 unto the hall of judgment: and it was **e**; *4405*
20: 1 of the week cometh Mary Magdalene **e**, *4404*
Ac 5:21 the temple **e in the morning**, *3588+3722+5259*
Jas 5: 7 for it, until he receive the **e** and latter rain. *4406*

EARNEST (8) [EARNESTLY]
Ro 8:19 For the **e expectation** of the creature waiteth *603*
2Co 1:22 and given the **e** of the Spirit in our hearts. *728*
5: 5 who also hath given unto us the **e** of *728*
7: 7 when he told us your **e desire**, your *1972*
8:16 which put the same **e care** into the heart of *4710*
Eph 1:14 Which is the **e** of our inheritance, until *728*
Php 1:20 According to my **e expectation** and *603*
Heb 2: 1 Therefore we ought to give the **more e** *4056*

EARNESTLY (16) [EARNEST]
Nu 22:37 I not **e send** unto thee to call thee? 7971+7971
1Sa 20: 6 David **e asked** *leave* of me that *he* 7592+7592
20:28 David **e asked** *leave* of me *to go* to 7592+7592
Ne 3:20 After him Baruch the son of Zabbai **e** 2734
Job 7: 2 As a servant **e desireth** the shadow, and 7602
Jer 11: 7 For I **e protested** unto your fathers 5749+5749
31:20 I do **e remember** him still: 2142+2142
Mic 7: 3 may do evil with both hands **e**, 3190+3807.1
Lk 22:44 And being in an agony he prayed **more e**: *1617*
22:56 and **e looked** upon him, and said, This *man* *816*
Ac 3:12 or why **look** ye *so* **e** on us, as though by our *816*
23: 1 **e beholding** the council, said, Men *and* *816*
1Co 12:31 But **covet e** the best gifts: and yet shew I *2206*
2Co 5: 2 **e desiring** to be clothed upon with our *1971*
Jas 5:17 he **prayed e** that it might not rain: *4335+4336*
Jude 1: 3 exhort *you* that *ye* should **e contend for** *1864*

EARNESTNESS See FORWARDNESS

EARNETH (2)
Hag 1: 6 he that **e wages** earneth wages *to put it* into 7936
1: 6 he that earneth wages **e wages** *to put it* into 7936

EARRING (5) [EAR, RING]
Ge 24:22 that the man took a golden **e** of half a 5141
24:30 when he saw the **e** and bracelets upon his 5141
24:47 I put the **e** upon her face, and the bracelets 5141
Job 42:11 piece of money, and every one an **e** of gold. 5141
Pr 25:12 *As* an **e** of gold, and an ornament of fine 5141

EARRINGS (12) [EAR, RING]
Ge 35: 4 and *all their* **e** which *were* in their ears; 5141
Ex 32: 2 said unto them, Break off the golden **e**, 5141
32: 3 all the people brake off the golden **e** which 5141
35:22 and **e**, and rings, and tablets, 5141
Nu 31:50 chains, and bracelets, rings, **e**, and tablets, 5694
Jdg 8:24 that you would give me every man the **e** of 5141
8:24 (For they had golden **e**, because they *were* 5141
8:25 did cast therein every man the **e** of his prey. 5141
8:26 the weight of the golden **e** that he requested 5141
Isa 3:20 the headbands, and the tablets, and the **e**, 3908
Eze 16:12 **e** in thine ears, and a beautiful crown upon 5694
Hos 2:13 she decked herself with her **e** and 5141

EARS (151) [EAR]
Ge 20: 8 and told all these things in their **e**: 241
35: 4 and *all their* earrings which *were* in their **e**; 241
41: 5 seven **e of corn** came up upon one stalk, 7641
41: 6 seven thin **e** and blasted with the east wind 7641
41: 7 the seven thin **e** devoured the seven rank 7641
41: 7 ears devoured the seven rank and full **e**. 7641
41:22 seven **e** came up in one stalk, full and good: 7641
41:23 seven **e**, withered, thin, *and* blasted with 7641
41:24 the thin **e** devoured the seven good ears: 7641
41:24 the thin ears devoured the seven good **e**: 7641
41:26 the seven good **e** *are* seven years: 7641
41:27 the seven empty **e** blasted with the east 7641
44:18 speak a word in my lord's **e**, and let not thine 241
50: 4 I pray you, in the **e** of Pharaoh, saying, 241
Ex 10: 2 And that thou mayest tell in the **e** of thy son, 241
11: 2 Speak now in the **e** of the people, and 241
17:14 in a book, and rehearse *it* in the **e** of Joshua: 241
32: 2 which *are* in the **e** of your wives, of your 241
32: 3 off the golden earrings which *were* in their **e**, 241
Lev 2:14 firstfruits **green e of corn** dried by the fire, 24
2:14 by the fire, *even* **corn** beaten out of **full e**. 3759
23:14 nor parched *corn*, nor **green e**, 3759
Nu 11:18 for you have wept in the **e** of the LORD, 241
14:28 as ye have spoken in mine **e**, so will I do to 241
Dt 5: 1 judgments which I speak in your **e** *this* day, 241
23:25 thou mayest pluck the **e** with thine hand; 4425
29: 4 and eyes to see, and **e** to hear, unto this day. 241
31:28 that I may speak these words in their **e**, 241
31:30 Moses spake in the **e** of all the congregation 241
32:44 spake all the words of this song in the **e** of 241
Jos 20: 4 shall declare his cause in the **e** of the elders 241
Jdg 7: 3 go to, proclaim in the **e** of the people, 241
9: 2 pray you, in the **e** of all the men of Shechem, 241
9: 3 his mother's brethren spake of him in the **e** 241
17: 2 spakest of also in mine **e**, behold, the silver 241
Ru 2: 2 glean **e of corn** after *him* in whose sight I 7641
1Sa 3:11 *at* which both the **e** of every one that heareth 241
8:21 he rehearsed them in the **e** of the LORD. 241
11: 4 and told the tidings in the **e** of the people: 241
15:14 then this bleating of the sheep in mine **e**, 241
18:23 Saul's servants spake those words in the **e** of 241
2Sa 3:19 And Abner also spake in the **e** of Benjamin: 241
3:19 Abner went also to speak in the **e** of David 241
7:22 to all that we have heard with our **e**. 241
22: 7 his temple, and my cry *did enter* into his **e**. 241
2Ki 4:42 and **full e of corn** in the husk thereof. 3759
18:26 in the **e** of the people that *are* on the wall. 241
19:28 and thy tumult is come up into mine **e**, 241
21:12 heareth of it, both his **e** shall tingle. 241
23: 2 he read in their **e** all the words of the book of 241
1Ch 17:20 to all that we have heard with our **e**. 241
2Ch 6:40 *let* thine **e** *be* attent unto the prayer *that is* 241
7:15 mine **e** attent unto the prayer *that is made* in 241
34:30 he read in their **e** all the words of the book of 241
Ne 8: 3 the **e** of all the people *were attentive* unto 241
Job 13:17 my speech, and my declaration with your **e**. 241
15:21 A dreadful sound *is* in his **e**: in prosperity 241
24:24 and cut off as the tops of the **e of corn**. 7641
28:22 We have heard the fame thereof with our **e**. 241
33:16 he openeth the **e** of men, and sealeth their 241
36:15 and openeth their **e** in oppression. 241
Ps 18: 6 and my cry came before him, *even* into his **e**. 241
34:15 and his **e** *are open* unto their cry. 241
40: 6 didst not desire; mine **e** hast thou opened: 241
44: 1 We have heard with our **e**, O God, 241
78: 1 incline your **e** to the words of my mouth. 241
92:11 mine **e** shall hear *my desire* of the wicked 241
115: 6 They have **e**, but they hear not: noses have 241
130: 2 let thine **e** be attentive to the voice of my 241
135:17 They have **e**, but they hear not; neither is 241
Pr 21:13 Whoso stoppeth his **e** at the cry of the poor, 241
23: 9 Speak not in the **e** of a fool: for he will 241
23:12 and thine **e** to the words of knowledge. 241
26:17 to him, *is like* one that taketh a dog by the **e**. 241
Isa 5: 9 In mine **e** *said* the LORD of hosts, Of a 241
6:10 and make their **e** heavy, and shut their eyes; 241
6:10 hear with their **e**, and understand *with* their 241
11: 3 neither reprove after the hearing of his **e**: 241
17: 5 the corn, and reapeth the **e** *with* his arm; 7641
17: 5 it shall be as he that gathereth **e** in 7641
22:14 it was revealed in mine **e** *by* the LORD of 241
30:21 thine **e** shall hear a word behind thee, saying, 241
32: 3 and the **e** of them that hear shall hearken. 241
33:15 that stoppeth his **e** from hearing of blood, 241
35: 5 and the **e** of the deaf shall be unstopped. 241
36:11 in the **e** of the people that *are* on the wall. 241
37:29 is come up into mine **e**, therefore will I put 241
42:20 opening the **e**, but he heareth not. 241
43: 8 that have eyes, and the deaf that have **e**. 241
49:20 hast lost the other, shall say again in thine **e**, 241
Jer 2: 2 Go and cry in the **e** of Jerusalem, saying, 241
5:21 and see not; which have **e**, and hear not: 241
19: 3 which whosoever heareth, his **e** shall tingle. 241
26:11 this city, as ye have heard with your **e**. 241
26:15 unto you to speak all these words in your **e**. 241
28: 7 thou now this word that I speak in thine **e**, 241
28: 7 in thine ears, and in the **e** of all the people. 241
29:29 Zephaniah the priest read this letter in the **e** 241
36: 6 the words of the LORD in the **e** of 241
36: 6 also thou shalt read them in the **e** of all 241
36:10 LORD'S house, in the **e** of all the people. 241
36:13 when Baruch read the book in the **e** of 241
36:14 wherein thou hast read in the **e** of the people, 241
36:15 unto him, Sit down now, and read it in our **e**. 241
36:15 it in our ears. So Baruch read *it* in their **e**. 241
36:20 and told all the words in the **e** of the king. 241
36:21 Jehudi read it in the **e** of the king, and in 241
36:21 in the **e** of all the princes which stood beside 241
Eze 3:10 receive in thine heart, and hear with thine **e**. 241
8:18 though they cry in mine **e** *with* a loud voice, 241
9: 1 He cried also in mine **e** *with* a loud voice, 241
12: 2 see not; they have **e** to hear, and hear not: 241
16:12 earrings in thine **e**, and a beautiful crown 241
23:25 they shall take away thy nose and thine **e**; 241
24:26 to cause *thee* to hear *it* with *thine* **e**? 241
40: 4 hear with thine **e**, and set thine heart upon all 241
44: 5 hear with thine **e** all that I say unto thee 241
Mic 7:16 hand upon *their* mouth, their **e** shall be deaf. 241
Zec 7:11 stopped their **e**, that *they* should not hear. 241
Mt 11:15 He that hath **e** to hear, let him hear. *3775*
12: 1 and began to pluck the **e of corn**, and *4719*
13: 9 Who hath **e** to hear, let him hear. *3775*
13:15 and *their* **e** are dull of hearing, and *3775*
13:15 see with *their* eyes, and hear with *their* **e**, *3775*
13:16 for they see: and your **e**, for they hear. *3775*
13:43 Who hath **e** to hear, let him hear. *3775*
28:14 And if this **come to** the governor's **e**, *191+1909*
Mk 2:23 as they went, to pluck the **e of corn**. *4719*
4: 9 He that hath **e** to hear, let him hear. *3775*
4:23 If any *man* have **e** to hear, let him hear. *3775*
7:16 If any *man* have **e** to hear, let him hear. *3775*
7:33 and put his fingers into his **e**, and he spit, *3775*
7:35 And straightway his **e** were opened, *189*
8:18 and having **e**, hear ye not? and do ye not *3775*
Lk 1:44 voice of thy salutation sounded in mine **e**, *3775*
4:21 This day is this scripture fulfilled in your **e**. *3775*
6: 1 and his disciples plucked the **e of corn**, and *4719*
8: 8 He that hath **e** to hear, let him hear. *3775*
9:44 Let these sayings sink down into your **e**: *3775*
14:35 it out. He that hath **e** to hear, let him hear *3775*
Ac 7:51 and uncircumcised in heart and **e**, *3775*
7:57 and stopped their **e**, and ran upon him with *3775*
11:22 the **e** of the church which was in Jerusalem: *3775*
17:20 thou bringest certain strange *things* to our **e**: *189*
28:27 and *their* **e** are dull of hearing, *3775*
28:27 and hear with *their* **e**, and understand with *3775*
Ro 11: 8 not see, and **e** that *they* should not hear;) *3775*
2Ti 4: 3 to themselves teachers, having itching **e**; *189*
4: 4 And they shall turn away *their* **e** from *189*
Jas 5: 4 entered into the **e** of the Lord of sabaoth. *3775*
1Pe 3:12 and his **e** *are open* unto their prayers: *3775*

EARTH (987) [EARTHEN, EARTHLY, EARTHQUAKE, EARTHQUAKES, EARTHY]
Ge 1: 1 beginning God created the heaven and the **e**. 776
1: 2 the **e** was without form, and void; and 776
1:10 God called the dry *land* **E**; and the gathering 776
1:11 God said, Let the **e** bring forth grass, 776
1:11 his kind, whose seed *is* in itself, upon the **e**: 776
1:12 the **e** brought forth grass, *and* herb yielding 776
1:15 of the heaven to give light upon the **e**: 776
1:17 of the heaven to give light upon the **e**, 776
1:20 fowl *that* may fly above the **e** in the open 776
1:22 in the seas, and let fowl multiply in the **e**. 776
1:24 Let the **e** bring forth the living creature after 776
1:24 and beast of the **e** after his kind: 776
1:25 God made the beast of the **e** after his kind, 776
1:25 every thing that creepeth upon the **e** after his 127
1:26 over all the **e**, and over every creeping thing 776
1:26 creeping thing that creepeth upon the **e**. 776
1:28 multiply, and replenish the **e**, and subdue it: 776
1:28 every living thing that moveth upon the **e**. 776
1:29 which *is* upon the face of all the **e**, and every 776
1:30 to every beast of the **e**, and to every fowl of 776
1:30 to every *thing* that creepeth upon the **e**, 776

Ge 2: 1 Thus the heavens and the **e** were finished, 776
2: 4 and of the **e** when they were created, 776
2: 4 in the day that the LORD God made the **e** 776
2: 5 every plant of the field before it was in the **e**, 776
2: 5 God had not caused it to rain upon the **e**, 776
2: 6 there went up a mist from the **e**, and 776
4:11 now *art* thou cursed from the **e**, which hath 127
4:12 and a vagabond shalt thou be in the **e**. 776
4:14 driven me out *this* day from the face of the **e**; 127
4:14 I shall be a fugitive and a vagabond in the **e**; 776
6: 1 men began to multiply on the face of the **e**, 127
6: 4 There were giants in the **e** in those days; and 776
6: 5 the wickedness of man *was* great in the **e**, 776
6: 6 the LORD that he had made man on the **e**, 776
6: 7 whom I have created from the face of the **e**; 127
6:11 The **e** also was corrupt before God, and 776
6:11 and the **e** was filled *with* violence. 776
6:12 God looked upon the **e**, and behold, it was 776
6:12 all flesh had corrupted his way upon the **e**. 776
6:13 for the **e** is filled *with* violence through 776
6:13 and behold, I will destroy them with the **e**. 776
6:17 even I, do bring a flood of waters upon the **e**, 776
6:17 *and* every *thing* that *is* in the **e** shall die. 776
6:20 of every creeping thing of the **e** after his 127
7: 3 to keep seed alive upon the face of all the **e**. 776
7: 4 I will cause it to rain upon the **e** forty days 776
7: 4 will I destroy from off the face of the **e**. 127
7: 6 old when the flood of waters was upon the **e**. 776
7: 8 and of every *thing* that creepeth upon the **e**, 127
7:10 that the waters of the flood were upon the **e**. 776
7:12 the rain was upon the **e** forty days and 776
7:14 every creeping thing that creepeth upon the **e** 776
7:17 And the flood was forty days upon the **e**; and 776
7:17 up the ark, and it was lift up above the **e**. 776
7:18 and were increased greatly upon the **e**; 776
7:19 the waters prevailed exceedingly upon the **e**; 776
7:21 all flesh died that moved upon the **e**, *both* of 776
7:21 creeping thing that creepeth upon the **e**, 776
7:23 and they were destroyed from the **e**: 776
7:24 the waters prevailed upon the **e** an hundred 776
8: 1 and God made a wind to pass over the **e**, and 776
8: 3 the waters returned from off the **e** 776
8: 7 until the waters were dried up from off the **e**. 776
8: 9 the waters *were* on the face of the whole **e**: 776
8:11 that the waters were abated from off the **e**. 776
8:13 the waters were dried up from off the **e**: 776
8:14 twentieth day of the month, was the **e** dried. 776
8:17 creeping thing that creepeth upon the **e**; 776
8:17 that they may breed abundantly in the **e**, and 776
8:17 and be fruitful, and multiply upon the **e**. 776
8:19 *and* whatsoever creepeth upon the **e**, 776
8:22 While the **e** remaineth, seedtime and harvest, 776
9: 1 Be fruitful, and multiply, and replenish the **e**. 776
9: 2 of you shall be upon every beast of the **e**, 776
9: 2 upon all that moveth *upon* the **e**, and 127
9: 7 bring forth abundantly in the **e**, and 776
9:10 and of every beast of the **e** with you; 776
9:10 that go out of the ark, to every beast of the **e**. 776
9:11 there any more be a flood to destroy the **e**. 776
9:13 a token of a covenant between me and the **e**. 776
9:14 to pass, when I bring a cloud over the **e**, 776
9:16 living creature of all flesh that *is* upon the **e**. 776
9:17 between me and all flesh that *is* upon the **e**. 776
9:19 and of them was the whole **e** overspread. 776
10: 8 he began to be a mighty *one* in the **e**. 776
10:25 for in his days was the **e** divided; and 776
10:32 by these were the nations divided in the **e** 776
11: 1 the whole **e** was of *one* language, and *of* one 776
11: 4 abroad upon the face of the whole **e**. 776
11: 8 from thence upon the face of all the **e**: 776
11: 9 did there confound the language of all the **e**: 776
11: 9 them abroad upon the face of all the **e**. 776
12: 3 in thee shall all families of the **e** be blessed. 127
13:16 And I will make thy seed as the dust of the **e**: 776
13:16 so that if a man can number the dust of the **e**, 776
14:19 most high God, possessor of heaven and **e**: 776
14:22 high God, the possessor of heaven and **e**, 776
18:18 all the nations of the **e** shall be blessed in 776
18:25 Shall not the Judge of all the **e** do right? 776
19:23 The sun was risen upon the **e** when Lot 776
19:31 *there is* not a man in the **e** to come in unto us 776
19:31 come in unto us after the manner of all the **e**: 776
22:18 in thy seed shall all the nations of the **e** be 776
24: 3 the God of heaven, and the God of the **e**, 776
24:52 the LORD, *bowing himself* to the **e**. 776
26: 4 in thy seed shall all the nations of the **e** be 776
26:15 had stopped them, and filled them *with* **e**. 6083
27:28 the fatness of the **e**, and plenty of corn and 776
27:39 thy dwelling shall be the fatness of the **e**, and 776
28:12 behold a ladder set up on the **e**, and the top 776
28:14 thy seed shall be as the dust of the **e**, and 776
28:14 in thy seed shall all the families of the **e** be 127
37:10 to bow down ourselves to thee to the **e**? 776
41:47 in the seven plenteous years the **e** brought 776
41:56 the famine was over all the face of the **e**: 776
42: 6 before him *with* their faces to the **e**. 776
43:26 and bowed themselves to him to the **e**. 776
45: 7 you to preserve you a posterity in the **e**, 776
48:12 and he bowed himself with his face to the **e**. 776
48:16 grow into a multitude in the midst of the **e**. 776
Ex 8:17 smote the dust of the **e**, and it became lice in 776
8:22 that I *am* the LORD in the midst of the **e**. 776
9:14 know that *there is* none like me in all the **e**. 776
9:15 and thou shalt be cut off from the **e**. 776
9:16 name may be declared throughout all the **e**. 776
9:29 that thou mayest know how that the **e** *is* 776
9:33 and the rain was not poured upon the **e**. 776
10: 5 they shall cover the face of the **e**, that *one* 776
10: 5 that *one* cannot be able to see the **e**: 776
10: 6 since the day that they were upon the **e** unto 127
10:15 For they covered the face of the whole **e**, so 776
15:12 out thy right hand, the **e** swallowed them. 776
19: 5 me above all people: for all the **e** *is* mine: 776
20: 4 or that *is* in the **e** beneath, or that *is* in 776
20: 4 or that *is* in the water under the **e**: 776

Ex 20:11 *in* six days the LORD made heaven and **e**, 776
20:24 An altar of **e** thou shalt make unto me, and 127
31:17 *in* six days the LORD made heaven and **e**, 776
32:12 and to consume them from the face of the **e**? 127
33:16 all the people that *are* upon the face of the **e**. 127
34: 8 bowed his head toward the **e**, and 776
34:10 such as have not been done in all the **e**, 776
Lev 11: 2 eat among all the beasts that *are* on the **e**. 776
11:21 above their feet, to leap withal upon the **e**; 776
11:29 the creeping things that creep upon the **e**; 776
11:41 every creeping thing that creepeth upon the **e** 776
11:42 all creeping things that creep upon the **e**, 776
11:44 *of* creeping thing that creepeth upon the **e**. 776
11:46 of every creature that creepeth upon the **e**: 776
15:12 the vessel of **e**, that he toucheth which hath 2789
26:19 your heaven as iron, and your **e** as brass: 776
Nu 11:31 were two cubits *high* upon the face of the **e**. 776
12: 3 the men which *were* upon the face of the **e**.) 127
14:21 all the **e** shall be filled *with* the glory of 776
16:30 the **e** open her mouth, and swallow them up, 127
16:32 the **e** opened her mouth, and 776
16:33 into the pit, and the **e** closed upon them: 776
16:34 for they said, Lest the **e** swallow us up *also*. 776
22: 5 they cover the face of the **e**, and they abide 776
22:11 of Egypt, which covereth the face of the **e**: 776
26:10 the **e** opened her mouth, and 776
Dt 3:24 for what God *is there* in heaven or in **e**, 776
4:10 all the days that they shall live upon the **e**, 127
4:17 The likeness of any beast that *is* on the **e**, 776
4:18 any fish that *is* in the waters beneath the **e**: 776
4:26 and **e** to witness against you *this* day, 776
4:32 the day that God created man upon the **e**, 776
4:36 and upon **e** he shewed thee his great fire; and 776
4:39 in heaven above, and upon the **e** beneath: 776
4:40 thou mayest prolong *thy* days upon the **e**, 127
5: 8 or that *is* in the **e** beneath, or that *is* in 776
5: 8 or that *is* in the waters beneath the **e**: 776
6:15 and destroy thee from off the face of the **e**. 127
7: 6 all people that *are* upon the face of the **e**. 127
10:14 thy God, the **e** *also*, with all that therein *is*. 776
11: 6 how the **e** opened her mouth, and 776
11:21 give them, as the days of heaven upon the **e**. 776
12: 1 all the days that ye live upon the **e**. 127
12:16 ye shall pour it upon the **e** as water. 776
12:19 the Levite as long as thou livest upon the **e**. 127
12:24 eat it; thou shalt pour it upon the **e** as water. 776
13: 7 from the *one* end of the **e** even unto the *other* 776
13: 7 of the earth even unto the *other* end of the **e**; 776
14: 2 above all the nations that *are* upon the **e**. 127
26: 2 shalt take of the first of all the fruit of the **e**, 127
28: 1 set thee on high above all nations of the **e**: 776
28:10 all people of the **e** shall see that thou art 776
28:23 and the **e** that *is* under thee *shall be* iron. 776
28:25 be removed into all the kingdoms of the **e**. 776
28:26 unto the beasts of the **e**, and no man shall 776
28:49 from the end of the **e**, *as swift* as the eagle 776
28:64 from the *one* end of the **e** even unto 776
30:19 and **e** to record *this* day against you, 776
31:28 and call heaven and **e** to record against them. 776
32: 1 and hear, O **e**, the words of my mouth. 776
32:13 made him ride on the high places of the **e**, 776
32:22 shall consume the **e** with her increase, and 776
33:16 for the precious things of the **e** and 776
33:17 push the people together *to* the ends of the **e**: 776
Jos 2:11 he *is* God in heaven above, and in **e** beneath. 776
3:11 *even* the Lord of all the **e** passeth over before 776
3:13 the Lord of all the **e**, shall rest in the waters 776
4:24 That all the people of the **e** might know 776
5:14 Joshua fell on his face to the **e**, and 776
7: 6 fell to the **e** upon his face before the ark of 776
7: 9 us round, and cut off our name from the **e**: 776
7:21 they *are* hid in the **e** in the midst of my tent, 776
23:14 *this* day I am going the way of all the **e**: 776
Jdg 3:25 their lord *was* fallen down dead on the **e**. 776
5: 4 the **e** trembled, and the heavens dropped, 776
6: 4 destroyed the increase of the **e**, till thou 776
6:37 *it be* dry upon all the **e** *beside*, then shall I 776
18:10 *there is* no want of any thing that *is* in the **e**. 776
1Sa 2: 8 for the pillars of the **e** *are* the LORD'S, and 776
2:10 the LORD shall judge the ends of the **e**; and 776
4: 5 *with* a great shout, so that the **e** rang again. 776
4:12 his clothes rent, and *with* **e** upon his head. 127
5: 3 Dagon *was* fallen upon his face to the **e** 776
14:15 they also trembled, and the **e** quaked: 776
17:46 of the air, and to the wild beasts of the **e**; 776
17:46 that all the **e** may know that there is a God in 776
17:49 and he fell upon his face to the **e**. 776
20:15 of David every one from the face of the **e**. 127
24: 8 David stooped *with his* face to the **e**, and 776
25:41 bowed herself *on her* face to the **e**, and said, 776
26: 8 with the spear even to the **e** at once, and 776
26:20 let not my blood fall to the **e** before the face 776
28:13 unto Saul, I saw gods ascending out of the **e**. 776
28:20 Then Saul fell straightway all along on the **e**, 776
28:23 So he arose from the **e**, and sat upon the bed. 776
30:16 *they were* spread abroad upon all the **e**, 776
2Sa 1: 2 with his clothes rent, and **e** upon his head: 127
1: 2 that he fell to the **e**, and did obeisance. 776
4:11 of your hand, and take you away from the **e**? 776
7: 9 the name of the great *men* that *are* in the **e**. 776
7:23 what one nation in the **e** *is* like thy people, 776
12:16 and went in, and lay all night upon the **e**. 776
12:17 *and went* to him, to raise him up from the **e**: 776
12:20 David arose from the **e**, and washed, and 776
13:31 and tare his garments, and lay on the **e**; 776
14: 7 *neither* name nor remainder upon the **e**. 127
14:11 shall not one hair of thy son fall to the **e**. 776
14:20 of God, to know all *things* that *are* in the **e**. 776
15:32 him with his coat rent, and **e** upon his head: 127
18: 9 was taken up between the heaven and the **e**; 776
18:28 he fell down to the **e** upon his face before 776
22: 8 the **e** shook and trembled; the foundations of 776
22:43 did I beat them *as* small as the dust of the **e**, 776
23: 4 *as* the tender grass *springing* out of the **e** by 776
1Ki 1:31 Bath-sheba bowed *with her* face *to* the **e**, 776

1Ki 1:40 so that the **e** rent with the sound of them. 776
1:52 there shall not a hair of him fall to the **e**: 776
2: 2 I go the way of all the **e**: be thou strong 776
4:34 from all kings of the **e**, which had heard of 776
8:23 in heaven above, or on **e** beneath, 776
8:27 But will God indeed dwell on the **e**? behold, 776
8:43 that all people of the **e** may know thy name, 776
8:53 them from among all the people of the **e**, 776
8:60 That all the people of the **e** may know that 776
10:23 exceeded all the kings of the **e** for riches 776
10:24 all the **e** sought to Solomon, to hear his 776
13:34 and to destroy *it* from off the face of the **e**. 127
17:14 day *that* the LORD sendeth rain upon the **e**. 127
18: 1 unto Ahab; and I will send rain upon the **e**. 127
18:42 he cast himself down upon the **e**, and put his 776
2Ki 5:15 now I know that *there is* no God in all the **e**, 776
5:17 given to thy servant two mules' burden of **e**? 127
10:10 Know now that there shall fall unto the **e** 776
19:15 thou alone, of all the kingdoms of the **e**; 776
19:15 of the earth; thou hast made heaven and **e**. 776
19:19 that all the kingdoms of the **e** may know that 776
1Ch 1:10 he began to be mighty upon the **e**. 776
1:19 because in his days the **e** was divided: 776
16:14 our God; his judgments *are* in all the **e**. 776
16:23 Sing unto the LORD, all the **e**; shew forth 776
16:30 Fear before him, all the **e**: the world also 776
16:31 Let the heavens be glad, and let the **e** rejoice: 776
16:33 because he cometh to judge the **e**. 776
17: 8 the name of the great *men* that *are* in the **e**. 776
17:21 what one nation in the **e** *is* like thy people 776
21:16 the angel of the LORD stand between the **e** 776
22: 8 thou hast shed much blood upon the **e** in my 776
29:11 and in the **e** *is thine;* thine *is* the kingdom, 776
29:15 our days on the **e** *are* as a shadow, and 776
2Ch 1: 9 a people like the dust of the **e** in multitude. 776
2:12 God of Israel, that made heaven and **e**, 776
6:14 no God like thee in the heaven, nor in the **e**; 776
6:18 God in very deed dwell with men on the **e**? 776
6:33 that all people of the **e** may know thy name, 776
9:22 king Solomon passed all the kings of the **e** in 776
9:23 all the kings of the **e** sought the presence of 776
16: 9 run to and fro throughout the whole **e**, 776
20:24 they *were* dead bodies fallen to the **e**, and 776
32:19 as against the gods of the people of the **e**, 776
36:23 All the kingdoms of the **e** hath the LORD 776
Ezr 1: 2 hath given me all the kingdoms of the **e**; 776
5:11 are the servants of the God of heaven and **e**, 772
Ne 9: 1 and with sackclothes, and **e** upon them. 127
9: 6 the **e**, and all *things* that *are* therein, the seas, 776
Job 1: 7 From going to and fro in the **e**, and 776
1: 8 that *there is* none like him in the **e**, a perfect 776
2: 2 From going to and fro in the **e**, and 776
2: 3 that *there is* none like him in the **e**, a perfect 776
3:14 With kings and counsellers of the **e**, 776
5:10 Who giveth rain upon the **e**, and 776
5:22 shalt thou be afraid of the beasts of the **e**. 776
5:25 and thine offspring as the grass of the **e**. 776
7: 1 *there* not an appointed time to man upon **e**? 776
8: 9 because our days upon **e** *are* a shadow:) 776
8:19 his way, and out of the **e** shall others grow. 6083
9: 6 Which shaketh the **e** out of her place, and 776
9:24 The **e** is given into the hand of the wicked: 776
11: 9 The measure thereof *is* longer than the **e**, and 776
12: 8 Or speak to the **e**, and it shall teach thee: and 776
12:15 he sendeth them out, and they overturn the **e**. 776
12:24 the heart of the chief of the people of the **e**, 776
14: 8 Though the root thereof wax old in the **e**, 776
14:19 things which grow out of the dust of the **e**; 776
15:19 Unto whom alone the **e** was given, and 776
15:29 he prolong the perfection thereof upon the **e**. 776
16:18 O **e**, cover not thou my blood, and let my cry 776
18: 4 shall the **e** be forsaken for thee? and shall 776
18:17 His remembrance shall perish from the **e**, 776
19:25 he shall stand *at the* latter *day* upon the **e**: 6083
20: 4 *not* this of old, since man was placed upon **e**, 776
20:27 and the **e** shall rise up against him. 776
22: 8 But *as for* the mighty man, he had the **e**; and 776
24: 4 the poor of the **e** hide themselves together. 776
24:18 as the waters; their portion is cursed in the **e**: 776
26: 7 *and* hangeth the **e** upon nothing. 776
28: 2 Iron is taken out of the **e**, and brass *is* 6083
28: 5 *As for* the **e**, out of it cometh bread: and 776
28:24 For he looketh to the ends of the **e**, *and* 776
30: 6 *in* caves of the **e**, and *in* the rocks. 6083
30: 8 of base men: they were viler than the **e**. 776
34:13 Who hath given him a charge over the **e**? or 776
35:11 teacheth us more than the beasts of the **e**, 776
37: 3 and his lightning unto the ends of the **e**. 776
37: 6 For he saith to the snow, Be thou *on* the **e**; 776
37:12 them upon the face of the world in the **e**. 776
37:17 when he quieteth the **e** by the south *wind?* 776
38: 4 thou when I laid the foundations of the **e**? 776
38:13 That *it* might take hold of the ends of the **e**, 776
38:18 Hast thou perceived the breadth of the **e**? 776
38:24 *which* scattereth the east wind upon the **e**? 776
38:26 To cause it to rain on the **e**, *where* no man *is;* 776
38:33 canst thou set the dominion thereof in the **e**? 776
39:14 Which leaveth her eggs in the **e**, and 776
41:33 Upon **e** there is not his like, who is made 6083
Ps 2: 2 The kings of the **e** set themselves, and 776
2: 8 the uttermost parts of the **e** *for* thy 776
2:10 O ye kings: be instructed, ye judges of the **e**. 776
7: 5 let him tread down my life upon the **e**, and 776
8: 1 how excellent *is* thy name in all the **e**! 776
8: 9 how excellent *is* thy name in all the **e**! 776
10:18 that the man of the **e** may no more oppress. 776
12: 6 *as* silver tried in a furnace of **e**, 776
16: 3 *But* to the saints that *are* in the **e**, and *to* 776
17:11 have set their eyes bowing down to the **e**; 776
18: 7 the **e** shook and trembled; the foundations 776
19: 4 Their line is gone out through all the **e**, and 776
21:10 Their fruit shalt thou destroy from the **e**, and 776
22:29 All *they that be* fat upon **e** shall eat and 776
24: 1 The **e** *is* the LORD'S, and the fulness 776
25:13 dwell at ease; and his seed shall inherit the **e**. 776

Ps 33: 5 the **e** is full *of* the goodness of the LORD. 776
33: 8 Let all the **e** fear the LORD: let all 776
33:14 he looketh upon all the inhabitants of the **e**. 776
34:16 cut off the remembrance of them from the **e**. 776
37: 9 upon the LORD, they shall inherit the **e**. 776
37:11 the meek shall inherit the **e**; and shall delight 776
37:22 such as be blessed of him shall inherit the **e**; 776
41: 2 *and* he shall be blessed upon the **e**: 776
44:25 to the dust: our belly cleaveth unto the **e**. 776
45:16 whom thou mayest make princes in all the **e**. 776
46: 2 though the **e** be removed, and though 776
46: 6 he uttered his voice, the **e** melted. 776
46: 8 what desolations he hath made in the **e**. 776
46: 9 maketh wars to cease unto the end of the **e**; 776
46:10 among the heathen, I will be exalted in the **e**. 776
47: 2 *is* terrible; *he is* a great King over all the **e**. 776
47: 7 For God *is* the King of all the **e**: sing ye 776
47: 9 for the shields of the **e** *belong* unto God: 776
48: 2 the joy of the whole **e**, *is* mount Zion, 776
48:10 so *is* thy praise unto the ends of the **e**: 776
50: 1 called the **e** from the rising of the sun unto 776
50: 4 and to the **e**, that *he* may judge his people. 776
57: 5 the heavens; *let* thy glory *be* above all the **e**. 776
57:11 the heavens: *let* thy glory *be* above all the **e**. 776
58: 2 weigh the violence of your hands in the **e**. 776
58:11 verily he is a God that judgeth in the **e**. 776
59:13 God ruleth in Jacob unto the ends of the **e**. 776
60: 2 Thou hast made the **e** to tremble; thou hast 776
61: 2 From the end of the **e** will I cry unto thee, 776
63: 9 *it*, shall go into the lower parts of the **e**. 776
65: 5 *art* the confidence of all the ends of the **e**, 776
65: 9 Thou visitest the **e**, and waterest it: 776
66: 4 All the **e** shall worship thee, and shall sing 776
67: 2 That thy way may be known upon **e**, 776
67: 4 and govern the nations upon **e**. 776
67: 6 *Then* shall the **e** yield her increase; *and* God, 776
67: 7 and all the ends of the **e** shall fear him. 776
68: 8 The **e** shook, the heavens also dropped at 776
68:32 Sing unto God, ye kingdoms of the **e**; O sing 776
69:34 Let the heaven and **e** praise him, the seas, 776
71:20 bring me up again from the depths of the **e**. 776
72: 6 the mown grass: *as* showers *that* water the **e**. 776
72: 8 and from the river unto the ends of the **e**. 776
72:16 There shall be a handful of corn in the **e** 776
72:16 of the city shall flourish like grass of the **e**. 776
72:19 let the whole **e** be filled *with* his glory; 776
73: 9 and their tongue walketh through the **e**. 776
73:25 *there is* none upon **e** *that* I desire beside thee. 776
74:12 working salvation in the midst of the **e**. 776
74:17 Thou hast set all the borders of the **e**: 776
74:20 for the dark places of the **e** are full *of* 776
75: 3 The **e** and all the inhabitants thereof *are* 776
75: 8 all the wicked of the **e** shall wring *them* out, 776
76: 8 from heaven; the **e** feared, and was still, 776
76: 9 to judgment, to save all the meek of the **e**. 776
76:12 of princes: *he is* terrible to the kings of the **e**. 776
77:18 the world: the **e** trembled and shook. 776
78:69 like the **e** which he hath established for ever. 776
79: 2 flesh of thy saints unto the beasts of the **e**. 776
82: 5 all the foundations of the **e** are out of course. 776
82: 8 Arise, O God, judge the **e**: for thou shalt 776
83:10 at En-dor: they became *as* dung for the **e**. 127
83:18 *art* the most High over all the **e**. 776
85:11 Truth shall spring out of the **e**; and 776
89:11 The heavens *are* thine, the **e** also *is* thine: 776
89:27 *my* firstborn, higher than the kings of the **e**. 776
90: 2 or ever thou hadst formed the **e** and 776
94: 2 Lift up thyself, thou judge of the **e**: render a 776
95: 4 In his hand *are* the deep places of the **e**: 776
96: 1 a new song: sing unto the LORD, all the **e**. 776
96: 9 beauty of holiness: fear before him, all the **e**. 776
96:11 Let the heavens rejoice, and let the **e** be glad; 776
96:13 for he cometh, for he cometh to judge the **e**: 776
97: 1 The LORD reigneth; let the **e** rejoice; 776
97: 4 the world: the **e** saw, and trembled. 776
97: 5 at the presence of the Lord of the whole **e**. 776
97: 9 For thou, LORD, *art* High above all the **e**: 776
98: 3 all the ends of the **e** have seen the salvation 776
98: 4 a joyful noise unto the LORD, all the **e**: 776
98: 9 the LORD; for he cometh to judge the **e**: 776
99: 1 *between* the cherubims; let the **e** be moved. 776
102:15 and all the kings of the **e** thy glory. 776
102:19 from heaven did the LORD behold the **e**; 776
102:25 Of old hast thou laid the foundation of the **e**: 776
103:11 For as the heaven is high above the **e**, *so* 776
104: 5 *Who* laid the foundations of the **e**, *that* it 776
104: 9 *that* they turn not again to cover the **e**. 776
104:13 the **e** is satisfied with the fruit of thy works. 776
104:14 that *he* may bring forth food out of the **e**; 776
104:24 made them all: the **e** is full *of* thy riches. 776
104:30 and thou renewest the face of the **e**. 127
104:32 He looketh on the **e**, and it trembleth: 776
104:35 Let the sinners be consumed out of the **e**, 776
105: 7 our God: his judgments *are* in all the **e**. 776
106:17 The **e** opened and swallowed up Dathan, and 776
108: 5 the heavens: and thy glory above all the **e**. 776
109:15 may cut off the memory of them from the **e**. 776
112: 2 His seed shall be mighty upon **e**: 776
113: 6 *the things that are* in heaven, and in the **e**? 776
114: 7 Tremble, thou **e**, at the presence of the Lord, 776
115:15 of the LORD which made heaven and **e**. 776
115:16 the **e** hath he given to the children of men. 776
119:19 I *am* a stranger in the **e**: hide not thy 776
119:64 The **e**, O LORD, is full *of* thy mercy; 776
119:87 They had almost consumed me upon **e**; but 776
119:90 thou hast established the **e**, and it abideth. 776
119:119 Thou puttest away all the wicked of the **e** 776
121: 2 from the LORD, which made heaven and **e**. 776
124: 8 of the LORD, who made heaven and **e**. 776
134: 3 made heaven and **e** bless thee out of Zion. 776
135: 6 and in **e**, in the seas, and all deep places. 776
135: 7 the vapours to ascend from the ends of the **e**; 776
136: 6 To him that stretched out the **e** above 776
138: 4 All the kings of the **e** shall praise thee, 776
139:15 wrought in the lowest parts of the **e**. 776
Ps 140:11 not an evil speaker be established in the **e**: 776
141: 7 one cutteth and cleaveth *wood* upon the **e**. 776
146: 4 His breath goeth forth, he returneth to his **e**; 127
146: 6 and **e**, the sea, and all that therein is: 776
147: 8 with clouds, who prepareth rain for the **e**, 776
147:15 He sendeth forth his commandment *upon* **e**: 776
148: 7 Praise the LORD from the **e**, ye dragons, 776
148:11 Kings of the **e**, and all people; princes, and 776
148:11 all people; princes, and all judges of the **e**: 776
148:13 his glory *is* above the **e** and heaven. 776
Pr 2:22 the wicked shall be cut off from the **e**, and 776
3:19 The LORD by wisdom hath founded the **e**; 776
8:16 and nobles, *even* all the judges of the **e**. 776
8:23 from the beginning, or ever the **e** was. 776
8:26 While as yet he had not made the **e**, nor 776
8:29 when he appointed the foundations of the **e**: 776
8:31 Rejoicing in the habitable part of his **e**; and 776
10:30 but the wicked shall not inhabit the **e**. 776
11:31 the righteous shall be recompensed in the **e**: 776
17:24 but the eyes of a fool *are* in the ends of the **e**. 776
25: 3 the **e** for depth, and the heart of kings *is* 776
30: 4 who hath established all the ends of the **e**? 776
30:14 to devour the poor from off the **e**, and 776
30:16 the **e** *that* is not filled *with* water; and the fire 776
30:21 For three *things* the **e** is disquieted, and 776
30:24 be four *things which are* little upon the **e**, 776
Ecc 1: 4 but the **e** abideth for ever. 776
3:21 of the beast that goeth downward to the **e**? 776
5: 2 for God *is* in heaven, and thou upon **e**: 776
5: 9 Moreover the profit of the **e** *is* for all: 776
7:20 For *there is* not a just man upon **e**, that doeth 776
8:14 There is a vanity which is done upon the **e**; 776
8:16 to see the business that is done upon the **e**: 776
10: 7 and princes walking as servants upon the **e**. 776
11: 2 knowest not what evil shall be upon the **e**. 776
11: 3 *of* rain, they empty *themselves* upon the **e**: 776
12: 7 shall the dust return to the **e** as it was: and 776
SS 2:12 The flowers appear on the **e**; the time of 776
Isa 1: 2 Hear, O heavens, and give ear, O **e**: for 776
2:19 into the caves of the **e**, for fear of 6083
2:19 when he ariseth to shake terribly the **e**. 776
2:21 when he ariseth to shake terribly the **e**. 776
4: 2 the fruit of the **e** *shall be* excellent and 776
5: 8 may be placed alone in the midst of the **e**! 776
5:26 will hiss unto them from the end of the **e**: 776
6: 3 of hosts: the whole **e** *is* full of his glory. 776
8:22 they shall look unto the **e**; and 776
10:14 eggs *that are* left, have I gathered all the **e**; 776
11: 4 reprove with equity for the meek of the **e**: 776
11: 4 he shall smite the **e** with the rod of his 776
11: 9 for the **e** shall be full *of* the knowledge of 776
11:12 of Judah from the four corners of the **e**. 776
12: 5 excellent things: this *is* known in all the **e**. 776
13:13 and the **e** shall remove out of her place, 776
14: 7 The whole **e** is at rest, *and* is quiet: 776
14: 9 for thee, *even* all the chief ones of the **e**; 776
14:16 *saying, Is* this the man that made the **e** to 776
14:26 purpose that is purposed upon the whole **e**: 776
18: 3 of the world, and dwellers on the **e**, see ye, 776
18: 6 of the mountains, and to the beasts of the **e**: 776
18: 6 all the beasts of the **e** shall winter upon 776
23: 8 traffickers *are* the honourable of the **e**? 776
23: 9 into contempt all the honourable of the **e**. 776
23:17 of the world upon the face of the **e**. 127
24: 1 the LORD maketh the **e** empty, and 776
24: 4 The **e** mourneth *and* fadeth away, the world 776
24: 4 the haughty people of the **e** do languish. 776
24: 5 The **e** also is defiled under the inhabitants 776
24: 6 Therefore hath the curse devoured the **e**, and 776
24: 6 therefore the inhabitants of the **e** are burned, 776
24:16 From the uttermost part of the **e** have we 776
24:17 *are* upon thee, O inhabitant of the **e**. 776
24:18 and the foundations of the **e** do shake. 776
24:19 The **e** is utterly broken down, the earth is 776
24:19 the **e** is clean dissolved, the earth is moved 776
24:19 clean dissolved, the **e** is moved exceedingly. 776
24:20 The **e** shall reel to and fro like a drunkard, 776
24:21 and the kings of the **e** upon the earth. 127
24:21 and the kings of the earth upon the **e**. 127
25: 8 people shall he take away from off all the **e**: 776
26: 9 for when thy judgments *are* in the **e**, 776
26:15 removed *it* far *unto* all the ends of the **e**. 776
26:18 have not wrought any deliverance *in* the **e**; 776
26:19 of herbs, and the **e** shall cast out the dead. 776
26:21 the inhabitants of the **e** for their iniquity: 776
26:21 the **e** also shall disclose her blood, and 776
28: 2 shall cast down to the **e** with the hand. 776
28:22 even determined upon the whole **e**. 776
30:23 bread of the increase of the **e**, and it shall be 127
33: 9 The **e** mourneth *and* languisheth: Lebanon is 776
34: 1 let the **e** hear, and all that is therein; 776
37:16 thou alone, of all the kingdoms of the **e**: 776
37:16 of the earth: thou hast made heaven and **e**. 776
37:20 that all the kingdoms of the **e** may know that 776
40:12 comprehended the dust of the **e** in a measure, 776
40:21 understood *from* the foundations of the **e**? 776
40:22 *It is* he that sitteth upon the circle of the **e**, 776
40:23 he maketh the judges of the **e** as vanity. 776
40:24 yea, their stock shall not take root in the **e**: 776
40:28 the Creator of the ends of the **e**, fainteth not, 776
41: 5 the ends of the **e** were afraid, drew near, and 776
41: 9 whom I have taken from the ends of the **e**, 776
42: 4 till he have set judgment in the **e**: 776
42: 5 he that spread forth the **e**, and that which 776
42:10 *and* his praise from the end of the **e**, ye that 776
43: 6 and my daughters from the ends of the **e**; 776
44:23 hath done *it*: shout, ye lower parts of the **e**: 776
44:24 that spreadeth abroad the **e** by myself; 776
45: 8 let the **e** open, and let them bring forth 776
45: 9 potsherd *strive* with the potsherds of the **e**. 127
45:12 I have made the **e**, and created man upon it: 776
45:18 God himself that formed the **e** and made it; 776
45:19 not spoken in secret, in a dark place of the **e**: 776
45:22 and be ye saved, all the ends of the **e**: 776
48:13 hand also hath laid the foundation of the **e**, 776
Isa 48:20 tell this, utter it *even* to the end of the **e**; 776
49: 6 be my salvation unto the end of the **e**. 776
49: 8 a covenant of the people, to establish the **e**, 776
49:13 be joyful, O **e**; and break forth *into* singing, 776
49:23 down to thee *with their* face *toward* the **e**, 776
51: 6 to the heavens, and look upon the **e** beneath: 776
51: 6 the **e** shall wax old like a garment, and 776
51:13 and laid the foundations of the **e**; 776
51:16 lay the foundations of the **e**, and say unto 776
52:10 all the ends of the **e** shall see the salvation of 776
54: 5 The God of the whole **e** shall he be called. 776
54: 9 of Noah should no more go over the **e**; 776
55: 9 For *as* the heavens are higher than the **e**, so 776
55:10 but watereth the **e**, and maketh it bring forth 776
58:14 thee to ride upon the high places of the **e**, 776
60: 2 the darkness shall cover the **e**, and 776
61:11 For as the **e** bringeth forth her bud, and 776
62: 7 and till he make Jerusalem a praise in the **e**. 776
63: 6 and I will bring down their strength to the **e**. 776
65:16 That he who blesseth himself in the **e** shall 776
65:16 he that sweareth in the **e** shall swear by 776
65:17 behold, I create new heavens and a new **e**: 776
66: 1 *is* my throne, and the **e** *is* my footstool: 776
66: 8 the **e** be made to bring forth in one day? 776
66:22 For as the new heavens and the new **e**, which 776
Jer 4:23 I beheld the **e**, and lo, *it was* without form, 776
4:28 For this shall the **e** mourn, and the heavens 776
6:19 Hear, O **e**: behold, I will bring evil upon this 776
6:22 nation shall be raised from the sides of the **e**. 776
7:33 of the heaven, and for the beasts of the **e**; 776
8: 2 they shall be for dung upon the face of the **e**. 127
9: 3 they are not valiant for the truth upon the **e**; 776
9:24 judgment, and righteousness, in the **e**: 776
10:10 at his wrath the **e** shall tremble, and 776
10:11 that have not made the heavens and the **e**, 778
10:11 *even* they shall perish from the **e**, and 772
10:12 He hath made the **e** by his power, he hath 776
10:13 the vapours to ascend from the ends of the **e**; 776
14: 4 for there was no rain in the **e**, the plowmen 776
15: 3 the beasts of the **e**, to devour and destroy. 776
15: 4 to be removed into all kingdoms of the **e**, 776
15:10 and a man of contention to the whole **e**! 776
16: 4 they shall be as dung upon the face of the **e**: 127
16: 4 fowls of heaven, and for the beasts of the **e**. 776
16:19 shall come unto thee from the ends of the **e**, 776
17:13 that depart from me shall be written in the **e**, 776
19: 7 of the heaven, and for the beasts of the **e**. 776
22:29 O **e**, earth, earth, hear the word of 776
22:29 O earth, **e**, earth, hear the word of 776
22:29 O earth, earth, **e**, hear the word of 776
23: 5 shall execute judgment and justice in the **e**. 776
23:24 Do not I fill heaven and **e**? saith the LORD. 776
24: 9 into all the kingdoms of the **e** for *their* hurt, 776
25:26 the world, which *are* upon the face of the **e**. 127
25:29 for a sword upon all the inhabitants of the **e**, 776
25:30 *grapes*, against all the inhabitants of the **e**. 776
25:31 A noise shall come *even* to the ends of the **e**; 776
25:32 shall be raised up from the coasts of the **e**. 776
25:33 of the **e** even unto the *other* end of the earth: 776
25:33 of the earth even unto the *other* end of the **e**. 776
26: 6 this city a curse to all the nations of the **e**. 776
27: 5 I have made the **e**, the man and the beast that 776
28:16 I will cast thee from off the face of the **e**: 127
29:18 to be removed to all the kingdoms of the **e**, 776
31: 8 and gather them from the coasts of the **e**, *and* 776
31:22 LORD hath created a new *thing* in the **e**, 776
31:37 the foundations of the **e** searched out 776
32:17 the **e** by thy great power and stretched out 776
33: 9 and an honour before all the nations of the **e**, 776
33:25 appointed the ordinances of heaven and **e**; 776
34: 1 all the kingdoms of the **e** of his dominion, 776
34:17 to be removed into all the kingdoms of the **e**. 776
34:20 of the heaven, and to the beasts of the **e**. 776
44: 8 a reproach among all the nations of the **e**? 776
46: 8 he saith, I will go up, *and* will cover the **e**; 776
49:21 The **e** is moved at the noise of their fall, 776
50:23 How is the hammer of the whole **e** cut 776
50:41 shall be raised up from the coasts of the **e**. 776
50:46 At the noise of the taking of Babylon the **e** is 776
51: 7 LORD'S hand, that made all the **e** drunken: 776
51:15 He hath made the **e** by his power, he hath 776
51:16 the vapours to ascend from the ends of the **e**: 776
51:25 saith the LORD, which destroyest all the **e**: 776
51:41 *how* is the praise of the whole **e** surprised! 776
51:48 the heaven and the **e**, and all that *is* therein, 776
51:49 so at Babylon shall fall the slain of all the **e**. 776
La 2: 1 cast down from heaven *unto* the **e** the beauty 776
2:11 are troubled, my liver is poured upon the **e**, 776
2:15 perfection of beauty, The joy of the whole **e**? 776
3:34 crush under his feet all the prisoners of the **e**, 776
4:12 The kings of the **e**, and all the inhabitants of 776
Eze 1:15 behold one wheel upon the **e** by the living 776
1:19 the living creatures were lift up from the **e**, 776
1:21 when those were lifted up from the **e**, 776
7:21 a prey, and to the wicked of the **e** for a spoil; 776
8: 3 the spirit lift me up between the **e** and 776
8:12 seeth us not; the LORD hath forsaken the **e**. 776
9: 9 The LORD hath forsaken the **e**, and 776
10:16 lift up their wings to mount up from the **e**, 776
10:19 and mounted up from the **e** in my sight: 776
26:20 shall set thee in the low parts of the **e**, 776
27:33 thou didst enrich the kings of the **e** with 776
28:18 I will bring thee to ashes upon the **e** in 776
31:12 all the people of the **e** are gone down from 776
31:14 to the nether parts of the **e**, in the midst of 776
31:16 be comforted in the nether parts of the **e**. 776
31:18 trees of Eden unto the nether parts of the **e**: 776
32: 4 I will fill the beasts of the whole **e** with thee. 776
32:18 unto the nether parts of the **e**, with them that 776
32:24 uncircumcised into the nether parts of the **e**, 776
34: 6 flock was scattered upon all the face of the **e**, 776
34:27 the **e** shall yield her increase, and they shall 776
35:14 When the whole **e** rejoiceth, I will make thee 776
38:20 and all creeping things that creep upon the **e**, 127
38:20 all the men that *are* upon the face of the **e**, 127

Eze 39:14 those that remain upon the face of the e, 776
39:18 drink the blood of the princes of the e, 776
43: 2 and the e shined with his glory. 776
Da 2:10 There is not a man upon the e that can shew 3007
2:35 a great mountain, and filled the whole e. 772
2:39 of brass, which shall bear rule over all the e. 772
4: 1 languages, that dwell in all the e; 772
4:10 a tree in the midst of the e, and the height 772
4:11 the sight thereof to the end of all the e: 772
4:15 leave the stump of his roots in the e, 772
4:15 *be* with the beasts in the grass of the e: 772
4:20 the heaven, and the sight thereof to all the e; 772
4:22 and thy dominion to the end of the e. 772
4:23 leave the stump of the roots thereof in the e, 772
4:35 all the inhabitants of the e *are* reputed as 772
4:35 and *among* the inhabitants of the e: 772
6:25 languages, that dwell in all the e; 772
6:27 and wonders in heaven and in e, 772
7: 4 it was lifted up from the e, and made stand 772
7:17 *are* four kings, *which* shall arise out of the e. 772
7:23 beast shall be the fourth kingdom upon e, 772
7:23 shall devour the whole e, and shall tread it 772
8: 5 from the west on the face of the whole e, 776
12: 2 many of them that sleep in the dust of the e 6083
Hos 2:18 and the sword and the battle out of the e, 776
2:21 hear the heavens, and they shall hear the e; 776
2:22 the e shall hear the corn, and the wine, and 776
2:23 I will sow her unto me in the e; and I will 776
6: 3 as the latter *and* former rain *unto* the e. 776
Joel 2:10 The e shall quake before them; the heavens 776
2:30 shew wonders in the heavens and in the e, 776
3:16 and the heavens and the e shall shake: 776
Am 2: 7 That pant after the dust of the e on the head 776
3: 2 have I known of all the families of the e: 127
3: 5 Can a bird fall in a snare upon the e, 776
3: 5 shall *one* take up a snare from the e, and 127
4:13 treadeth upon the high places of the e, 776
5: 7 and leave off righteousness in the e, 776
5: 8 and poureth them out upon the face of the e: 776
8: 9 and I will darken the e in the clear day: 776
9: 6 and hath founded his troop in the e; 776
9: 6 and poureth them out upon the face of the e: 776
9: 8 I will destroy it from off the face of the e; 127
9: 9 yet shall not the least grain fall *upon* the e. 776
Jnh 2: 6 the e *with* her bars *was* about me for ever: 776
Mic 1: 2 hearken, O e, and all that therein is: 776
1: 3 and tread upon the high places of the e. 776
4:13 their substance unto the Lord of the whole e. 776
5: 4 now shall he be great unto the ends of the e. 776
6: 2 and ye strong foundations of the e: 776
7: 2 The good *man* is perished out of the e: and 776
7:17 move out of their holes like worms of the e: 776
Na 1: 5 the e is burnt at his presence, yea, the world, 776
2:13 I will cut off thy prey from the e, and 776
Hab 2:14 For the e shall be filled with the knowledge 776
2:20 let all the e keep silence before him. 776
3: 3 the heavens, and the e was full *of* his praise. 776
3: 6 He stood, and measured the e: he beheld, 776
3: 9 Selah. Thou didst cleave the e *with* rivers. 776
Zep 2: 3 Seek ye the LORD, all ye meek of the e, 776
2:11 for he will famish all the gods of the e; and 776
3: 8 for all the e shall be devoured with the fire 776
3:20 and a praise among all people of the e, 776
Hag 1:10 from dew, and the e is stayed *from* her fruit. 776
2: 6 and the e, and the sea, and the dry *land;* 776
2:21 I *will* shake the heavens and the e; 776
Zec 1:10 hath sent to walk to and fro through the e. 776
1:11 We have walked to and fro through the e, 776
1:11 behold, all the e sitteth still, and is at rest. 776
4:10 which run to and fro through the whole e. 776
4:14 that stand by the Lord of the whole e. 776
5: 3 that goeth forth over the face of the whole e: 776
5: 6 This *is* their resemblance through all the e. 776
5: 9 and they lift up the ephah between the e and 776
6: 5 from standing before the Lord of all the e. 776
6: 7 *they* might walk to and fro through the e: 776
6: 7 Get ye *hence,* walk to and fro through the e. 776
6: 7 So they walked to and fro through the e. 776
9:10 and from the river *even* to the ends of the e. 776
12: 1 layeth the foundation of the e, and 776
12: 3 though all the people of the e be gathered 776
14: 9 And the LORD shall be king over all the e: 776
14:17 of the e unto Jerusalem to worship the King, 776
Mal 4: 6 lest I come and smite the e *with* a curse. 776
Mt 5: 5 *are* the meek: for they shall inherit the e. 1093
5:13 Ye are the salt of the e: but if the salt have 1093
5:18 Till heaven and e pass, one jot or one tittle 1093
5:35 Nor by the e; for it is his footstool: neither 1093
6:10 Thy will be done in e, as *it is* in heaven. 1093
6:19 Lay not up for yourselves treasures upon e, 1093
9: 6 Son of man hath power on e to forgive sins, 1093
10:34 not that I am come to send peace on e: 1093
11:25 Lord of heaven and e, because thou hast hid 1093
12:40 and three nights in the heart of the e. 1093
12:42 of the e to hear the wisdom of Solomon; 1093
13: 5 stony *places,* where they had not much e: 1093
13: 5 because *they* had no deepness of e: 1093
16:19 whatsoever thou shalt bind on e shall be 1093
16:19 whatsoever thou shalt loose on e shall be 1093
17:25 of whom do the kings of the e take custom 1093
18:18 Whatsoever ye shall bind on e shall be 1093
18:18 whatsoever ye shall loose on e shall be 1093
18:19 That if two of you shall agree on e as 1093
23: 9 And call no *man* your father upon the e: 1093
23:35 all the righteous blood shed upon the e, 1093
24:30 and then shall all the tribes of the e mourn, 1093
24:35 Heaven and e shall pass away, but 1093
25:18 had received one went and digged in the e, 1093
25:25 and went and hid thy talent in the e: 1093
27:51 and the e did quake, and the rocks rent; 1093
28:18 power is given unto me in heaven and in e. 1093
Mk 2:10 Son of man hath power on e to forgive sins, 1093
4: 5 on stony ground, where it had not much e; 1093
4: 5 it sprang up, because *it* had no depth of e: 1093
4:28 For the e bringeth forth fruit of herself; 1093
Mk 4:31 which, when it is sown in the e, 1093
4:31 is less than all the seeds that be in the e: 1093
9: 3 so as no fuller on e can white *them.* 1093
13:27 from the uttermost part of the e to 1093
13:31 Heaven and e shall pass away: but 1093
Lk 2:14 and on e peace, good will towards men. 1093
5:24 of man hath power upon e to forgive sins, 1093
6:49 a foundation built a house upon the e; 1093
10:21 thank thee, O Father, Lord of heaven and e, 1093
11: 2 Thy will be done, as in heaven, so in e. 1093
11:31 for she came from the utmost parts of the e 1093
12:49 I am come to send fire on the e; and 1093
12:51 ye that I am come to give peace on e? 1093
12:56 can discern the face of the sky and of the e; 1093
16:17 And it is easier for heaven and e to pass, 1093
18: 8 of man cometh, shall he find faith on the e? 1093
21:25 and upon the e distress of nations, 1093
21:26 those *things* which are coming on the e: 3625
21:33 Heaven and e shall pass away: but 1093
21:35 them that dwell on the face of the whole e. 1093
23:44 there was a darkness over all the e until 1093
24: 5 and bowed down *their* faces to the e, 1093
Jn 3:31 is above all: he that is of the e is earthly, 1093
3:31 the earth is earthly, and speaketh of the e: 1093
12:32 And I, if I be lifted up from the e, will draw 1093
17: 4 I have glorified thee on the e: I have 1093
Ac 1: 8 and unto the uttermost part of the e. 1093
2:19 in heaven above, and signs in the e beneath; 1093
3:25 shall all the kindreds of the e be blessed. 1093
4:24 and e, and the sea, and all that in them is: 1093
4:26 The kings of the e stood up, and the rulers 1093
7:49 Heaven *is* my throne, and e *is* my footstool: 1093
8:33 for his life is taken from the e. 1093
9: 4 And he fell to the e, and heard a voice 1093
9: 8 And Saul arose from the e; and when his 1093
10:11 at the four corners, and let down to the e: 1093
10:12 all *manner of* fourfooted beasts of the e, 1093
11: 6 and saw fourfooted beasts of the e, and 1093
13:47 be for salvation unto the ends of the e. 1093
14:15 and e, and the sea, and all *things* that are 1093
17:24 seeing that he is Lord of heaven and e, 1093
17:26 of men for to dwell on all the face of the e, 1093
22:22 said, Away with such *a fellow* from the e: 1093
26:14 And when we were all fallen to the e, 1093
Ro 9:17 might be declared throughout all the e. 1093
9:28 a short work will the Lord make upon the e. 1093
10:18 their sound went into all the e, and 1093
1Co 8: 5 whether in heaven or in e, (as there be gods 1093
10:26 For the e *is* the Lord's, and the fulness 1093
10:28 *for* conscience *sake:* for the e *is* the Lord's, 1093
15:47 The first man *is* of the e, earthy: the second 1093
Eph 1:10 which are in heaven, and which are on e; 1093
3:15 the whole family in heaven and e is named, 1093
4: 9 first into the lower parts of the e? 1093
6: 3 and thou mayest live long on the e. 1093
Php 2:10 and *things* **in** e, and *things* under the earth; 1919
2:10 and *things* in earth, and *things* **under the** e; 2709
Col 1:16 and that are in e, visible and invisible, 1093
1:20 *I say,* whether *they be things* in e, or 1093
3: 2 on *things* above, not on *things* on the e. 1093
3: 5 your members which are upon the e; 1093
2Ti 2:20 and of silver, but also of wood and **of** e; 3749
Heb 1:10 beginning hast laid the foundation of the e; 1093
6: 7 For the e which drinketh *in* the rain that 1093
8: 4 For if he were on e, he should not be a 1093
11:13 they were strangers and pilgrims on the e. 1093
11:38 and *in* dens and caves of the e. 1093
12:25 not who refused him that spake on e, 1093
12:26 Whose voice then shook the e: but now he 1093
12:26 Yet once *more* I shake not the e only, but 1093
Jas 5: 5 Ye have lived in pleasure on the e, and 1093
5: 7 waiteth for the precious fruit of the e, 1093
5:12 neither by heaven, neither by the e, 1093
5:17 it rained not on the e *by the space of* three 1093
5:18 gave rain, and the e brought forth her fruit. 1093
2Pe 3: 5 and the e standing out of the water and 1093
3: 7 But the heavens and the e, which are now, 1093
3:10 the e also and the works that are therein 1093
3:13 look for new heavens and a new e, 1093
1Jn 5: 8 And there are three that bear witness in e, 1093
Rev 1: 5 and the prince of the kings of the e. 1093
1: 7 and all kindreds of the e shall wail because 1093
3:10 the world, to try them that dwell upon the e. 1093
5: 3 in heaven, nor in e, neither under the earth, 1093
5: 3 in heaven, nor in earth, neither under the e, 1093
5: 6 seven spirits of God sent forth into all the e. 1093
5:10 and priests: and we shall reign on the e. 1093
5:13 and on the e, and under the earth, and 1093
5:13 and under the e, and such as are in the sea, 1093
6: 4 that sat thereon to take peace from the e, 1093
6: 8 unto them over the fourth *part* of the e, 1093
6: 8 and with death, and with the beasts of the e. 1093
6:10 our blood on them that dwell on the e? 1093
6:13 And the stars of heaven fell unto the e, 1093
6:15 And the kings of the e, and the great men, 1093
7: 1 angels standing on the four corners of the e, 1093
7: 1 holding the four winds of the e, that 1093
7: 1 that the wind should not blow on the e, 1093
7: 2 to whom it was given to hurt the e and 1093
7: 3 Saying, Hurt not the e, neither the sea, 1093
8: 5 with fire of the altar, and cast *it* into the e: 1093
8: 7 with blood, and they were cast upon the e: 1093
8:13 to the inhabiters of the e by reason of 1093
9: 1 and I saw a star fall from heaven unto the e: 1093
9: 3 came out of the smoke locusts upon the e: 1093
9: 3 as the scorpions of the e have power. 1093
9: 4 that they should not hurt the grass of the e, 1093
10: 2 foot upon the sea, and *his* left *foot* on the e, 1093
10: 5 and upon the e lifted up his hand to heaven, 1093
10: 6 and the e, and the *things* that therein are, 1093
10: 8 standeth upon the sea and upon the e. 1093
11: 4 standing before the God of the e. 1093
11: 6 and to smite the e with all plagues, as often 1093
11:10 And they that dwell upon the e shall rejoice 1093
11:10 tormented them that dwelt on the e. 1093
Rev 11:18 shouldest destroy them which destroy the e. 1093
12: 4 stars of heaven, and did cast them to the e: 1093
12: 9 he was cast *out* into the e, and his angels 1093
12:12 Woe to the inhabiters of the e and of 1093
12:13 the dragon saw that he was cast unto the e, 1093
12:16 And the e helped the woman, and the earth 1093
12:16 and the e opened her mouth, and 1093
13: 8 And all that dwell upon the e shall worship 1093
13:11 another beast coming up out of the e; 1093
13:12 and causeth the e and them which dwell 1093
13:13 from heaven on the e in the sight of men, 1093
13:14 And deceiveth them that dwell on the e by 1093
13:14 saying to them that dwell on the e, that *they* 1093
14: 3 which were redeemed from the e. 1093
14: 6 to preach unto them that dwell on the e, 1093
14: 7 and e, and the sea, and the fountains of 1093
14:15 thee to reap; for the harvest of the e is ripe. 1093
14:16 sat on the cloud thrust in his sickle on the e; 1093
14:16 sickle on the earth; and the e was reaped. 1093
14:18 and gather the clusters of the vine of the e; 1093
14:19 And the angel thrust in his sickle into the e, 1093
14:19 and gathered the vine of the e, and cast *it* 1093
16: 1 the vials of the wrath of God upon the e. 1093
16: 2 and poured out his vial upon the e; 1093
16:14 which go forth unto the kings of the e and 1093
16:18 such as was not since men were upon the e, 1093
17: 2 With whom the kings of the e have 1093
17: 2 the inhabiters of the e have been made 1093
17: 5 AND ABOMINATIONS OF THE E. 1093
17: 8 and they that dwell on the e shall wonder, 1093
17:18 which reigneth over the kings of the e. 1093
18: 1 and the e was lightened with his glory. 1093
18: 3 the kings of the e have committed 1093
18: 3 the merchants of the e are waxed rich 1093
18: 9 And the kings of the e, who have 1093
18:11 And the merchants of the e *shall* weep and 1093
18:23 thy merchants were the great men of the e; 1093
18:24 and of all that were slain upon the e. 1093
19: 2 which did corrupt the e with her 1093
19:19 and the kings of the e, and their armies, 1093
20: 8 which are in the four quarters of the e, 1093
20: 9 And they went up on the breadth of the e, 1093
20:11 from whose face the e and the heaven fled 1093
21: 1 And I saw a new heaven and a new e: 1093
21: 1 and the first e were passed away; 1093
21:24 the kings of the e do bring their glory and 1093

EARTHEN (10) [EARTH]

Lev 6:28 the e vessel wherein it is sodden shall be 2789
11:33 every e vessel, whereinto *any* of them 2789
14: 5 be killed in an e vessel over running water: 2789
14:50 he shall kill the one of the birds in an e 2789
Nu 5:17 the priest shall take holy water in an e 2789
2Sa 17:28 e vessels, and wheat, and barley, and flour, 3335
Jer 19: 1 Go and get a potter's e bottle, and *take* of 2789
32:14 put them in an e vessel, that they may 2789
La 4: 2 how are they esteemed as e pitchers, 2789
2Co 4: 7 But we have this treasure in e vessels, 3749

EARTHLY (5) [EARTH]

Jn 3:12 If I have told you e *things,* and ye believe 1919
3:31 he that is of the earth is e, 1093+1537+3588
2Co 5: 1 For we know that if our e house of *this* 1919
Php 3:19 glory *is* in their shame, who mind e *things.*) 1919
Jas 3:15 not from above, but *is* e, sensual, devilish. 1919

EARTHQUAKE (16) [EARTH, QUAKE]

1Ki 19:11 after the wind an e; *but* the LORD *was* not 7494
19:11 *but* the LORD *was* not in the e: 7494
19:12 after the e a fire; *but* the LORD *was* not in 7494
Isa 29: 6 with e, and great noise, *with* storm and 7494
Am 1: 1 Joash king of Israel, two year before the e. 7494
Zec 14: 5 like as ye fled from before the e in the days 7494
Mt 27:54 saw the e, and *those things* that were done, 4578
28: 2 And behold, there was a great e: for 4578
Ac 16:26 And suddenly there was a great e, so 4578
Rev 6:12 the sixth seal, and lo, there was a great e; 4578
8: 5 and thunderings, and lightnings, and an e. 4578
11:13 And the same hour was there a great e, and 4578
11:13 in the e were slain of men seven thousand: 4578
11:19 and thunderings, and an e, and great hail. 4578
16:18 and there was a great e, such as was not 4578
16:18 the earth, so mighty an e, *and* so great. 4578

EARTHQUAKES (3) [EARTH, QUAKE]

Mt 24: 7 and pestilences, and e in divers places. 4578
Mk 13: 8 and there shall be e in divers places, and 4578
Lk 21:11 And great e shall be in divers places, and 4578

EARTHY (4) [EARTH]

1Co 15:47 The first man *is* of the earth, e: the second 5517
15:48 As *is* the e, such *are they* also *that are* 5517
15:48 *is* the earthy, such *are they* also *that are* e: 5517
15:49 And as we have borne the image of the e, 5517

EASE (20) [EASED, EASIER, EASILY, EASY]

Dt 23:13 it shall be, when thou wilt e thyself abroad, 3427
28:65 among these nations shalt thou **find** no e, 7280
Jdg 20:43 trode them down **with** e over against 4496
2Ch 10: 4 e thou **somewhat** the grievous servitude of 7043
10: 9 **E somewhat** the yoke that thy father did 7043
Job 7:13 my couch shall e my complaint; 5375
12: 5 despised in the thought of him that is **at** e. 7600
16:12 I was **at** e, but he hath broken me asunder: 7961
21:23 full strength, *being* wholly **at** e and quiet. 7946
Ps 25:13 His soul shall dwell **at** e; and his seed shall 2896
123: 4 *with* the scorning of those that are **at** e, 7600
Isa 1:24 I will e me of mine adversaries, and 5162
32: 9 Rise up, ye women that are **at** e, hear my 7600
32:11 Tremble, ye *women* that are **at** e; 7600
Jer 46:27 be in rest and **at** e, and none shall make 7599
48:11 Moab hath been **at** e from his youth, and 7599
Eze 23:42 a voice of a multitude being **at** e *was* with 7961
Am 6: 1 Woe to them *that are* **at** e in Zion, and trust 7600

Zec 1:15 displeased with the heathen *that are* **at e**: 7600
Lk 12:19 **take** thine **e**, eat, drink, *and* be merry. *373*

EASED (2) [EASE]

Job 16: 6 *though* I forbear, what am I **e**? 4480+1980
2Co 8:13 For *I mean* not that other *men* be **e**, and *425*

EASIER (8) [EASE]

Ex 18:22 so shall it be **e** for thyself, and 4480+7043
Mt 9: 5 For whether is **e**, to say, *Thy* sins be *2123*
19:24 It is **e** for a camel to go through the eye of a *2123*
Mk 2: 9 Whether is it **e** to say to the sick of *2123*
10:25 It is **e** for a camel to go through the eye of a *2123*
Lk 5:23 Whether is **e**, to say, Thy sins be forgiven *2123*
16:17 And it is **e** for heaven and earth to pass, *2123*
18:25 For it is **e** for a camel to go through a *2123*

EASILY (2) [EASE]

1Co 13: 5 is not **e provoked**, thinketh no evil; *3947*
Heb 12: 1 and the sin which doth so **e beset** *us,* and *2139*

EAST (157) [EASTWARD]

Ge 2:14 that *is it* which goeth **toward** the **e** of 6926
3:24 he placed at the **e** of the garden of Eden 6924
4:16 dwelt in the land of Nod, on the **e** of Eden. 6926
10:30 as thou goest unto Sephar, a mount of the **e**. 6924
11: 2 came to pass, as they journeyed from the **e**, 6924
12: 8 thence unto a mountain on the **e** of Beth-el, 6924
12: 8 Beth-el on the west, and Hai on the **e**: 6924
13:11 all the plain of Jordan; and Lot journeyed **e**: 6924
25: 6 he yet lived, eastward, unto the **e** country. 6924
28:14 to the **e**, and to the north, and to the south: 6924
29: 1 came into the land of the people of the **e**. 6924
41: 6 blasted with the **e wind** sprang up after 6921
41:23 withered, thin, *and* blasted with the **e wind**, 6921
41:27 the **e wind** shall be seven years of famine. 6921
Ex 10:13 the LORD brought an **e** wind upon 6921
10:13 the **e** wind brought the locusts. 6921
14:21 to go *back* by a strong **e** wind all *that* night, 6921
27:13 the breadth of the court on the **e** side 6924
38:13 for the **e** side eastward fifty cubits. 6924+1886.5
Lev 1:16 cast it beside the altar on the **e part**, by 6924
Nu 2: 3 on the **e side** toward the rising of the sun 6924
3:38 encamp before the tabernacle toward the **e**, 6924
10: 5 the camps that lie on the **e parts** shall go 6924
23: 7 out of the mountains of the **e**, 6924
34:10 ye shall point out your **e** border 6924+1886.5
34:11 Shepham *to* Riblah, on the **e side** of Ain; 6924
35: 5 the city *on* the **e** side two thousand cubits, 6924
Jos 4:19 in Gilgal, in the **e** border of Jericho. 4217
7: 2 on the **e side** of Beth-el, and spake unto 6924
11: 3 *And to* the Canaanite on the **e** and on 4217
12: 1 mount Hermon, and all the plain on the **e**: 4217
12: 3 the plain to the sea of Cinneroth on the **e**, 4217
12: 3 sea of the plain, *even* the salt sea on the **e**, 4217
15: 5 the **e** border *was* the salt sea, 6924+1886.5
16: 1 unto the water of Jericho on the **e**, 4217
16: 5 on the **e side** was Ataroth-addar, 4217
16: 6 and passed by it on the **e** *to* Janohah; 4217
17:10 on the north, and in Issachar on the **e**. 4217
18: 7 their inheritance beyond Jordan on the **e**, 4217
18:20 Jordan was the border of it on the **e** 6924+1886.5
19:13 on the **e** to Gittah-hepher, 4217+6924+1886.5
Jdg 6: 3 the Amalekites, and the children of the **e**, 6924
6:33 the children of the **e** were gathered 6924
7:12 all the children of the **e** lay along in 6924
8:10 left of all the hosts of the children of the **e**: 6924
8:11 them that dwelt in tents on the **e** of Nobah 6924
11:18 by the **e side** of the land of Moab, 4217+8121
21:19 on **the e side** of the highway 4217+8121+1886.1
1Ki 4:30 wisdom of all the children of the **e country**, 6924
7:25 the south, and three looking toward the **e**: 4217
1Ch 4:39 *even* unto the **e** *side* of the valley, to seek 4217
5:10 they dwelt in their tents throughout all the **e** 4217
6:78 Jordan *by* Jericho, on the **e** *side* of Jordan, 4217
9:24 toward the **e**, west, north, and south. 4217
12:15 *both* toward the **e**, and toward the west. 4217
2Ch 4: 4 the south, and three looking toward the **e**: 4217
4:10 he set the sea on the right side of the **e end**, 6924
5:12 stood *at* the **e** *end* of the altar, and 4217
29: 4 and gathered them together into the **e** street, 4217
31:14 Imnah the Levite, the porter toward the **e**, 4217
Ne 3:26 over against the water gate toward the **e**, 4217
3:29 son of Shechaniah, the keeper of the **e** gate. 4217
Job 1: 3 was the greatest of all the men of the **e**. 6924
15: 2 and fill his belly *with* the **e wind**? 6921
27:21 The **e wind** carrieth him away, and 6921
38:24 *which* scattereth the **e wind** upon the earth? 6921
Ps 48: 7 the ships of Tarshish with an **e** wind. 6921
75: 6 For promotion *cometh* neither from the **e**, 4161
78:26 He caused an **e wind** to blow in the heaven: 6921
103:12 As far as the **e** is from the west, *so* far hath 4217
107: 3 from the **e**, and from the west, from 4217
Isa 2: 6 because they be replenished from the **e**, and 6924
11:14 they shall spoil them of the **e** together: 6924
27: 8 his rough wind in the day of the **e wind**. 6921
41: 2 raised up the righteous *man* from the **e**, 4217
43: 5 I will bring thy seed from the **e**, and 4217
46:11 Calling a ravenous bird from the **e**, the man 4217
Jer 18:17 I will scatter them as *with* an **e** wind before 6921
19: 2 which *is by* the entry of the **e** gate, and 2777
31:40 the corner of the horse gate towards the **e**, 4217
49:28 go up to Kedar, and spoil the men of the **e**. 6924
Eze 8:16 the LORD, and their faces towards the **e**; 6924
8:16 and they worshipped the sun towards the **e**. 6924
10:19 *every one* stood *at* the door of the **e** gate of 6931
11: 1 brought me unto the **e** gate of 6931
11:23 mountain which *is* on the **e side** of the city. 6924
17:10 utterly wither, when the **e** wind toucheth it? 6921
19:12 and the **e** wind dried up her fruit: 6921
25: 4 I *will* deliver thee to the men of the **e** for a 6924
25:10 Unto the men of the **e** with the Ammonites, 6924
27:26 the **e** wind hath broken thee in the midst of 6921
39:11 the valley of the passengers *on* the **e** of 6926
Eze 40: 6 gate which looketh toward the **e**, 6921+1886.5
40:22 of the gate that looketh towards the **e**; 6921
40:23 the gate toward the north, and toward the **e**; 6921
40:32 me into the inner court toward the **e**: 6921
40:44 one at the side of the **e** gate *having* 6921
41:14 of the separate place toward the **e**, 6921
42: 9 these chambers *was* the entry on the **e side**, 6921
42:10 of the wall of the court toward the **e**, 6921
42:12 way directly before the wall toward the **e**, 6921
42:15 the gate whose prospect *is* toward the **e**, 6921
42:16 He measured the **e** side with the measuring 6921
43: 1 *even* the gate that looketh toward the **e**: 6921
43: 2 God of Israel came from the way of the **e**: 6921
43: 4 of the gate whose prospect *is* toward the **e**. 6921
43:17 and his stairs *shall* look toward the **e**. 6921
44: 1 sanctuary which looketh *toward* the **e**; 6921
45: 7 from the west side eastward: 6924+1886.5
45: 7 the west border unto the **e** border. 6921+1886.5
46: 1 the **e** shall be shut the six working days; 6921
46:12 open him the gate that looketh *toward* the **e**, 6921
47: 1 forefront of the house *stood toward* the **e**, 6921
47: 8 These waters issue out toward the **e** 6930
47:18 the **e** side ye shall measure from Hauran, 6921
47:18 *by* Jordan, from the border unto the **e** sea. 6931
47:18 the east sea. And *this is* the **e** side. 6921+1886.5
48: 1 for these are his sides **e** *and* west; a *portion* 6921
48: 2 from the **e** side unto the west side, a *portion* 6921
48: 3 from the **e** side even unto the west 6921+1886.5
48: 4 from the **e** side unto the west side, 6921+1886.5
48: 5 from the **e** side unto the west side, 6921+1886.5
48: 6 from the **e** side even unto the west side, 6921
48: 7 from the **e** side unto the west side, a *portion* 6921
48: 8 of Judah, from the **e** side unto the west side, 6921
48: 8 from the **e** side unto the west side: 6921+1886.5
48:10 toward the **e** ten thousand *in* breadth, and 6921
48:16 on the **e** side four thousand and 6921
48:17 and toward the **e** two hundred and fifty, and 6921
48:21 of the oblation toward the **e** border, 6921+1886.5
48:23 from the **e** side unto the west side, 6921+1886.5
48:24 from the **e** side unto the west side, 6921+1886.5
48:25 from the **e** side unto the west side, 6921+1886.5
48:26 from the **e** side unto the west side, 6921+1886.5
48:27 from the **e** side unto the west side, 6921+1886.5
48:32 at the **e** side four thousand and 6921+1886.5
Da 8: 9 toward the **e**, and toward the pleasant *land*. 4217
11:44 tidings out of the **e** and out of the north 4217
Hos 12: 1 on wind, and followeth after the **e wind**: 6921
13:15 among *his* brethren, an **e** wind shall come, 6921
Joel 2:20 with his face toward the **e** sea, and 6931
Am 8:12 from the north even to the **e**, they shall run 4217
Jnh 4: 5 sat on the **e side** of the city, and there made 6924
4: 8 that God prepared a vehement **e** wind; 6921
Hab 1: 9 their faces shall sup up *as* the **e wind**, and 6921
Zec 8: 7 I *will* save my people from the **e** country, 4217
14: 4 which *is* before Jerusalem on the **e**, and 6924
14: 4 cleave in the midst thereof toward the **e** 4217
Mt 2: 1 there came wise men from the **e** to *395*
2: 2 for we have seen his star in the **e**, and *395*
2: 9 and lo, the star, which they saw in the **e**, *395*
8:11 That many shall come from the **e** and west, *395*
24:27 For as the lightning cometh out of the **e**, and *395*
Lk 13:29 And they shall come from the **e**, and *395*
Rev 7: 2 another angel ascending from the **e**, *395+2246*
16:12 that the way of the kings of the **e** *395+2246*
21:13 On the **e** three gates; on the north three *395*

EASTER (1)

Ac 12: 4 intending after **E** to bring him forth to *3957*

EASTWARD (40) [EAST]

Ge 2: 8 the LORD God planted a garden **e** 4480+6924
13:14 southward, and **e**, and westward: 6924+1886.5
25: 6 while he yet lived, **e**, unto the east country. 6924
Ex 27:13 the east side *shall be* fifty cubits. 4217+1886.5
38:13 And for the east side **e** fifty cubits. 4217+1886.5
Lev 16:14 his finger upon the mercy seat **e**; 6924+1886.5
Nu 3:38 tabernacle of the congregation **e**, 4217+1886.5
32:19 is fallen to us on *this* side Jordan **e**. 4217+1886.5
34: 3 the outmost coast of the salt sea **e**: 6924+1886.5
34:11 the side of the sea of Chinnereth **e**: 6924+1886.5
34:15 on *this* side Jordan *near* Jericho **e**, 6924+1886.5
Dt 3:17 salt sea, under Ashdoth-pisgah **e**. 4217+1886.5
3:27 **e**, and behold *it* with thine eyes: 4217+1886.5
4:49 all the plain on *this* side Jordan **e**, 4217+1886.5
Jos 11: 8 and unto the valley of Mizpeh **e**; 4217+1886.5
13: 8 gave them, beyond Jordan **e**, 4217+1886.5
13:27 on the *other* side Jordan **e**. 4217+1886.5
13:32 the *other* side Jordan, *by* Jericho, **e**. 4217+1886.5
16: 6 the border went about **e** *unto* 4217+1886.5
19:12 turned from Sarid **e** *toward* 6924+1886.5
20: 8 the *other* side Jordan *by* Jericho **e**, 4217+1886.5
1Sa 13: 5 pitched in Michmash, **e** from Beth aven. 6926
1Ki 7:39 the house **e** over against the south. 6924+1886.5
17: 3 turn thee **e**, and hide thyself by 6924+1886.5
2Ki 10:33 From Jordan **e**, all the land 4217+8121+1886.1
13:17 he said, Open the window **e**. And 6924+1886.5
1Ch 5: 9 **e** he inhabited unto the entering in of 4217
7:28 **e** Naaran, and westward 4217+1886.1+3807.1
9:18 hitherto *waited* in the king's gate **e**: 4217+1886.5
26:14 the lot **e** fell to Shelemiah. 4217+1886.5
26:17 **E** *were* six Levites, northward four a day, 4217
Ne 12:37 of David, even unto the water gate **e**. 4217
Eze 11: 1 LORD'S house, which looketh **e**: 6921+1886.5
40:10 **e** *were* three on this side, 1870+6921+1886.1
40:19 an hundred cubits **e** and north*ward*. 6921
45: 7 and from the east side **e**: 6921+1886.5
47: 1 under the threshold of the house **e**: 6921+1886.5
47: 2 utter gate *by* the way that looketh **e**; 6921
47: 3 **e**, he measured a thousand cubits, 6921
48:18 *portion shall be* ten thousand **e**, 6921+1886.5

EASY (4) [EASE]

Pr 14: 6 knowledge *is* **e** unto him that 7043
Mt 11:30 For my yoke *is* **e**, and my burden is light. *5543*
1Co 14: 9 by the tongue words **e to be understood**, *2154*
Jas 3:17 peaceable, gentle, *and* **e to be intreated**, *2138*

EAT (655) [ATE, EATEN, EATER, EATERS, EATEST, EATETH, EATING, MOTHEATEN, MOTH-EATEN]

Ge 2:16 tree of the garden thou mayest **freely e**: 398+398
2:17 of good and evil, thou shalt not **e** of it: 398
3: 1 Ye shall not **e** of every tree of the garden? 398
3: 2 We may **e** of the fruit of the trees of 398
3: 3 God hath said, Ye shall not **e** of it, 398
3: 5 For God doth know that in the day ye **e** 398
3: 6 did **e**, and gave also unto her husband with 398
3: 6 also unto her husband with her; and he did **e**. 398
3:11 I commanded thee that thou shouldest not **e**? 398
3:12 with me, she gave me of the tree, and I did **e**. 398
3:13 The serpent beguiled me, and I did **e**. 398
3:14 and dust shalt thou **e** all the days of thy life: 398
3:17 saying, Thou shalt not **e** of it: 398
3:17 in sorrow shalt thou **e** *of* it all the days of thy 398
3:18 to thee; and thou shalt **e** the herb of the field; 398
3:19 In the sweat of thy face shalt thou **e** bread, 398
3:22 of the tree of life, and **e**, and live for ever: 398
9: 4 *which is* the blood thereof, shall you not **e**. 398
18: 8 stood by them under the tree, and they did **e**. 398
19: 3 did bake unleavened bread, and they did **e**. 398
24:33 there was set *meat* before him to **e**: but 398
24:33 he said, I will not **e**, until I have told mine 398
24:54 they did **e** and drink, he and the men that 398
25:28 because he did **e** of *his* venison: 6310+871.1
25:34 he did **e** and drink, and rose up, and went his 398
26:30 made them a feast, and they did **e** and drink. 398
27: 4 as I love, and bring *it* to me, that I may **e**; 398
27: 7 that I may **e**, and bless thee before 398
27:10 that he may **e**, and that he may bless thee 398
27:19 arise, I pray thee, sit and **e** of my venison, 398
27:25 near to me, and I will **e** of my son's venison, 398
27:25 And he brought *it* near to him, and he did **e**: 398
27:31 my father arise, and **e** of his son's venison, 398
28:20 will give me bread to **e**, and raiment to put 398
31:46 a heap: and they did **e** there upon the heap. 398
31:54 the mount, and called his brethren to **e** bread: 398
31:54 they did **e** bread, and tarried all night in 398
32:32 Therefore the children of Israel **e** not *of* 398
37:25 they sat down to **e** bread: and they lift up 398
39: 6 ought he had, save the bread which he did **e**. 398
40:17 the birds did **e** them out of the basket upon 398
40:19 and the birds shall **e** thy flesh from off thee. 398
41: 4 leanfleshed kine did **e up** the seven well 398
41:20 the ill favoured kine did **e up** the first seven 398
43:25 for they heard that they should **e** bread there. 398
43:32 which did **e** with him, by themselves: 398
43:32 the Egyptians might not **e** bread with 398
45:18 of Egypt, and ye shall **e** the fat of the land. 398
47:22 did **e** their portion which Pharaoh gave them: 398
Ex 2:20 left the man? call him, that he may **e** bread. 398
10: 5 they shall **e** the residue of that which is 398
10: 5 shall **e** every tree which groweth for you out 398
10:12 **e every** herb of the land, *even* all that the hail 398
10:15 they did **e** every herb of the land, and all 398
12: 7 post of the houses, wherein they shall **e** it. 398
12: 8 they shall **e** the flesh in that night, roast with 398
12: 8 *and* with bitter *herbs* they shall **e** it. 398
12: 9 **E** not of it raw, nor sodden at all with water, 398
12:11 thus shall ye **e** it; *with* your loins girded, 398
12:11 staff in your hand; and ye shall **e** it in haste: 398
12:15 Seven days shall ye **e** unleavened bread; 398
12:16 save *that* which every man must **e**, that only 398
12:18 ye shall **e** unleavened bread, until the one 398
12:20 Ye shall **e** nothing leavened; in all your 398
12:20 in all your habitations shall ye **e** unleavened 398
12:43 There shall no stranger **e** thereof: 398
12:44 hast circumcised him, then shall he **e** thereof. 398
12:45 and a hired servant shall not **e** thereof. 398
12:48 for no uncircumcised person shall **e** thereof. 398
13: 6 Seven days thou shalt **e** unleavened bread, 398
16: 3 *and* when we did **e** bread to the full; 398
16: 8 shall give you in the evening flesh to **e**, 398
16:12 At even ye shall **e** flesh, and in the morning 398
16:15 bread which the LORD hath given you to **e**. 402
16:25 Moses said, **E** that to day; for to day *is* a 398
16:35 the children of Israel did **e** manna forty 398
16:35 they did **e** manna, until they came unto 398
18:12 to **e** bread with Moses' father in law before 398
22:31 neither shall ye **e** *any* flesh *that is* torn *of* 398
23:11 lie still; that the poor of thy people may **e**: 398
23:11 they leave the beasts of the field shall **e**. 398
23:15 thou shalt **e** unleavened bread seven days, 398
24:11 also they saw God, and did **e** and drink. 398
29:32 and his sons shall **e** the flesh of the ram, 398
29:33 they shall **e** those *things* wherewith 398
29:33 a stranger shall not **e** *thereof,* because 398
32: 6 the people sat down to **e** and to drink, and 398
34:15 and *one* call thee, and thou **e** of his sacrifice; 398
34:18 seven days thou shalt **e** unleavened bread, 398
34:28 he did neither **e** bread, nor drink water. 398
Lev 3:17 *that* ye **e** neither fat nor blood. 398
6:16 thereof shall Aaron and his sons **e**: 398
6:16 tabernacle of the congregation they shall **e** it. 398
6:18 among the children of Aaron shall **e** of it. 398
6:26 The priest that offereth it for sin shall **e** it: 398
6:29 All the males among the priests shall **e** 398
7: 6 Every male among the priests shall **e** thereof: 398
7:19 *for* the flesh, all that be clean shall **e** thereof. 398
7:21 **e** of the flesh of the sacrifice of peace 398
7:23 Ye shall **e** no *manner* fat, of ox, or of sheep, 398
7:24 but ye shall **in no wise e** of it. 398+398+3808
7:26 Moreover ye shall **e** no *manner of* blood, 398
8:31 there **e** it with the bread that *is* in the basket 398
8:31 Aaron and his sons shall **e** it. 398
10:12 and **e** it without leaven beside the altar: 398
10:13 ye shall **e** it in the holy place, because it *is* 398
10:14 heave shoulder shall ye **e** in a clean place; 398
11: 2 These *are* the beasts which ye shall **e** among 398
11: 3 among the beasts, that shall ye **e**. 398
11: 4 Nevertheless these shall ye not **e** of them 398

Lev 11: 8 Of their flesh shall ye not **e**, and 398
11: 9 These shall ye **e** of all that *are* in the waters: 398
11: 9 in the seas, and in the rivers, them shall ye **e**. 398
11:11 ye shall not **e** of their flesh, but you shall 398
11:21 Yet these may ye **e** of every flying creeping 398
11:22 *Even* these of them ye may **e**; the locust after 398
11:39 if any beast, of which ye may **e**, die; he that 402
11:42 creep upon the earth, them ye shall not **e**; 398
17:12 of you shall **e** blood, No soul of you shall **e** blood, 398
17:12 stranger that sojourneth among you **e** blood. 398
17:14 Ye shall **e** the blood of no *manner of* flesh: 398
19:25 in the fifth year shall ye **e** of the fruit thereof, 398
19:26 Ye shall not **e** *any thing* with the blood: 398
21:22 He shall **e** the bread of his God, *both* of 398
22: 4 he shall not **e** of the holy *things*, until he be 398
22: 6 shall not **e** of the holy *things*, unless he wash 398
22: 7 shall afterward **e** of the holy *things*; because 398
22: 8 is torn *with beasts*, he shall not **e** to defile 398
22:10 There shall no stranger **e** *of* the holy *thing*: a 398
22:10 a hired servant, shall not **e** *of* the holy *thing*. 398
22:11 he shall **e** of it, and he that is born in his 398
22:11 is born in his house: they shall **e** of his meat. 398
22:12 she may not **e** of an offering of the holy 398
22:13 *in* her youth, she shall **e** of her father's meat: 398
22:13 but there shall no stranger **e** thereof. 398
22:14 And if a man **e** *of* the holy *thing* unwittingly, 398
22:16 when they **e** their holy *things*: for I 398
23: 6 seven days ye must **e** unleavened bread. 398
23:14 ye shall **e** neither bread, nor parched *corn*, 398
24: 9 and they shall **e** it in the holy place: 398
25:12 ye shall **e** the increase thereof out of 398
25:19 ye shall **e** *your* fill, and dwell therein in 398
25:20 shall say, What shall we **e** the seventh year? 398
25:22 and **e** *yet* of old fruit until the ninth year; 398
25:22 until her fruits come in ye shall **e** *of* the old 398
26: 5 ye shall **e** your bread to the full, and dwell in 398
26:10 ye shall **e** old store, and bring forth the old 398
26:16 your seed in vain, for your enemies shall **e** it. 398
26:26 and ye shall **e**, and not be satisfied. 398
26:29 ye shall **e** the flesh of your sons, and 398
26:29 and the flesh of your daughters shall ye **e**. 398
26:38 and the land of your enemies shall **e** you **up**. 398
Nu 6: 3 liquor of grapes, nor **e** moist grapes, or dried. 398
6: 4 All the days of his separation shall he **e** 398
9:11 *and* **e** it with unleavened bread and 398
11: 4 and said, Who shall **give** us flesh **to e**? 398
11: 5 the fish, which we did **e** in Egypt freely; 398
11:13 saying, Give us flesh, that we may **e**. 398
11:18 against to morrow, and ye shall **e** flesh: 398
11:18 Who shall **give** us flesh **to e**? 398
11:18 LORD will give you flesh, and ye shall **e**. 398
11:19 Ye shall not **e** one day, nor two days, 398
11:21 them flesh, that they may **e** a whole month. 398
15:19 *that* when ye **e** of the bread of the land, 398
18:10 In the most holy *place* shalt thou **e** it; 398
18:10 *place* shalt thou eat it; every male shall **e** it: 398
18:11 every one *that is* clean in thy house shall **e** of 398
18:13 every one *that is* clean in thine house shall **e** 398
18:31 ye shall **e** it in every place, ye and 398
23:24 he shall not lie down until he **e** *of* the prey, 398
24: 8 he shall **e up** the nations his enemies, and 398
25: 2 the people did **e**, and bowed down to their 398
Dt 2: 6 buy meat of them for money, that ye may **e**; 398
2:28 shalt sell me meat for money, that I may **e**; 398
4:28 which neither see, nor hear, nor **e**, nor smell. 398
8: 9 A land wherein thou shalt **e** bread without 398
9: 9 I neither did **e** bread nor drink water: 398
9:18 I did neither **e** bread, nor drink water, 398
11:15 for thy cattle, that thou mayest **e** and be full. 398
12: 7 there ye shall **e** before the LORD your God, 398
12:15 thou mayest kill and **e** flesh in all thy gates, 398
12:15 the unclean and the clean may **e** thereof, 398
12:16 Only ye shall not **e** the blood; ye shall pour it 398
12:17 Thou mayest not **e** within thy gates the tithe 398
12:18 thou must **e** them before the LORD thy 398
12:20 I will **e** flesh, because thy soul longeth to eat 398
12:20 eat flesh, because thy soul longeth to **e** flesh; 398
12:20 thou mayest **e** flesh, whatsoever thy soul 398
12:21 thou shalt **e** in thy gates whatsoever thy soul 398
12:22 and the hart is eaten, so thou shalt **e** them: 398
12:22 and the clean shall **e** of them alike. 398
12:23 Only be sure that thou **e** not the blood: 398
12:23 and thou mayest not **e** the life with the flesh. 398
12:24 Thou shalt not **e** it; thou shalt pour it upon 398
12:25 Thou shalt not **e** it; that it may go well with 398
12:27 LORD thy God, and thou shalt **e** the flesh. 398
14: 3 Thou shalt not **e** any abominable *thing*. 398
14: 4 These *are* the beasts which ye shall **e**: the ox, 398
14: 6 the cud amongst the beasts: that ye shall **e**. 398
14: 7 Nevertheless these ye shall not **e** of them 398
14: 8 ye shall not **e** of their flesh, nor touch their 398
14: 9 These ye shall **e** of all that *are* in the waters: 398
14: 9 all that have fins and scales shall ye **e**: 398
14:10 hath not fins and scales ye may not **e**; 398
14:11 *Of* all clean birds ye shall **e**. 398
14:12 these *are they* of which ye shall not **e**: 398
14:20 *But* of all clean fowls ye may **e**. 398
14:21 Ye shall not **e** of any thing that dieth of 398
14:21 stranger that *is* in thy gates, that he may **e** it; 398
14:23 And thou shalt **e** before the LORD thy God, 398
14:26 thou shalt **e** there before the LORD thy 398
14:29 shall come, and shall **e** and be satisfied; 398
15:20 Thou shalt **e** it before the LORD thy God 398
15:22 Thou shalt **e** it within thy gates: the unclean 398
15:22 and the clean *person shall* **e** *it* alike, NIH
15:23 Only thou shalt not **e** the blood thereof; 398
16: 3 Thou shalt **e** no leavened bread with it; 398
16: 3 seven days shalt thou **e** unleavened bread 398
16: 7 **e** *it* in the place which the LORD thy God 398
16: 8 Six days thou shalt **e** unleavened bread: and 398
18: 1 they shall **e** the offerings of the LORD 398
18: 8 They shall have like portions to **e**, beside 398
20: 6 he die in the battle, and another man **e** of it. 2490
20:14 thou shalt **e** the spoil of thine enemies, 398
20:19 for thou mayest **e** of them, and thou shalt not 398
Dt 23:24 thou mayest **e** grapes thy fill at thine own 398
26:12 that they may **e** within thy gates, and 398
27: 7 shalt **e** there, and rejoice before the LORD 398
28:31 thine eyes, and thou shalt not **e** thereof: 398
28:33 shall a nation which thou knowest not **e up**; 398
28:39 nor gather *the grapes*; for the worms shall **e** 398
28:51 he shall **e** the fruit of thy cattle, and the fruit 398
28:53 And thou shalt **e** the fruit of thine own body, 398
28:55 of the flesh of his children whom he shall **e**: 398
28:57 for she shall **e** them for want of all *things* 398
32:13 that he might **e** the increase of the fields; 398
32:38 Which did **e** the fat of their sacrifices, *and* 398
Jos 5:11 they did **e** of the old corn of the land on 398
5:12 they did **e** of the fruit of the land of Canaan 398
24:13 and oliveyards which ye planted not do ye **e**. 398
Jdg 9:27 and did **e** and drink, and cursed Abimelech. 398
13: 4 strong drink, and **e** not any unclean *thing*: 398
13: 7 neither **e** any unclean *thing*: for the child 398
13:14 She may not **e** of any *thing* that cometh of 398
13:14 nor **e** any unclean *thing*: all that I 398
13:16 thou detain me, I will not **e** of thy bread: 398
14: 9 and he gave them, and they did **e**: 398
19: 4 so they did **e** and drink, and lodged there. 398
19: 6 and did **e** and drink both of them together: 398
19: 8 until afternoon, and they did **e** both of them. 398
19:21 they washed their feet, and did **e** and drink. 398
Ru 2:14 **e** of the bread, and dip thy morsel in 398
2:14 he reached her parched *corn*, and she did **e**, 398
1Sa 1: 7 therefore she wept, and did not **e**. 398
1:18 did **e**, and her countenance was no more 398
2:36 priests' offices, that *I* may **e** a piece of bread. 398
9:13 before he go up to the high place to **e**: 398
9:13 for the people will not **e** until he come, 398
9:13 *and* afterwards they **e** that be bidden. 398
9:19 for ye shall **e** with me to day, and to morrow 398
9:24 that which is left; set *it* before thee, *and* **e**: 398
9:24 So Saul did **e** with Samuel that day. 398
14:32 and the people did **e** *them* with the blood. 398
14:33 the LORD, in that they **e** with the blood. 398
14:34 man his sheep, and slay *them* here, and **e**; 398
20:24 was come, the king sat him down to **e** meat. 398
20:34 did **e** no meat the second day of the month: 398
28:22 **e**, that thou mayest have strength, when thou 398
28:23 he refused, and said, I will not **e**. But his 398
28:25 and before his servants; and they did **e**. 398
30:11 to David, and gave him bread, and he did **e**; 398
2Sa 3:35 **cause** David **to e** meat while it was yet day, 1262
9: 7 thou shalt **e** bread at my table continually. 398
9:10 that thy master's son may have food to **e**: 398
9:10 Mephibosheth thy master's son shall **e** bread 398
9:11 *said the king*, he shall **e** at my table, 398
9:13 for he did **e** continually at the king's table; 398
11:11 to **e** and to drink, and to lie with my wife? 398
11:13 called him, he did **e** and drink before him; 398
12: 3 it did **e** of his own meat, and drank of his 398
12:17 neither did he **e** bread with them. 1262
12:20 they set bread before him, and he did **e**. 398
12:21 child was dead, thou didst rise and **e** bread. 398
13: 5 that I may see *it*, and **e** *it* at her hand. 398
13: 6 cakes in my sight, that I may **e** at her hand. 1262
13: 9 *them* out before him; but he refused to **e**. 398
13:10 the chamber, that I may **e** of thine hand. 1262
13:11 when she had brought *them* unto him to **e**, 398
16: 2 and summer fruit for the young men to **e**; 398
17:29 and for the people that *were* with him, to **e**: 398
19:28 among them that did **e** at thine own table. 398
19:35 can thy servant taste what I **e** or what I 398
1Ki 1:25 behold, they **e** and drink before him, and say, 398
2: 7 and let them be of *those* that **e** at thy table: 398
13: 8 neither will I **e** bread nor drink water in this 398
13: 9 **E** no bread, nor drink water, 398
13:15 unto him, Come home with me, and **e** bread. 398
13:16 neither will I **e** bread nor drink water with 398
13:17 Thou shalt **e** no bread nor drink water there, 398
13:18 that he may **e** bread and drink water. 398
13:19 did **e** bread in his house, and drank water. 398
13:22 say to thee, **E** no bread, and drink no water; 398
14:11 of Jeroboam in the city shall the dogs **e**; 398
14:11 dieth in the field shall the fowls of the air **e**: 398
16: 4 dieth of Baasha in the city shall the dogs **e**; 398
16: 4 his in the fields shall the fowls of the air **e**. 398
17:12 for me and my son, that we may **e** it, and die. 398
17:15 she, and he, and her house, did **e** *many* days. 398
18:19 four hundred, which **e** *at* Jezebel's table. 398
18:41 said unto Ahab, Get thee up, **e** and drink; 398
18:42 So Ahab went up to **e** and to drink. 398
19: 5 touched him, and said unto him, Arise *and* **e**. 398
19: 6 he did **e** and drink, and laid him down again. 398
19: 7 and touched him, and said, Arise *and* **e**; 398
19: 8 did **e** and drink, and went in the strength of 398
19:21 and gave unto the people, and they did **e**. 398
21: 4 turned away his face, and would **e** no bread. 398
21: 7 *and* **e** bread, and let thine heart be merry: 398
21:23 The dogs shall **e** Jezebel by the wall of 398
21:24 dieth of Ahab in the city the dogs shall **e**; 398
21:24 dieth in the field shall the fowls of the air **e**. 398
2Ki 4: 8 and she constrained him to **e** bread. 398
4: 8 he passed by, he turned in thither to **e** bread. 398
4:40 So they poured out for the men to **e**. And it 398
4:40 in the pot. And they could not **e** *thereof*. 398
4:41 Pour out for the people, that they may **e**. 398
4:42 Give unto the people, that they may **e**. 398
4:43 said again, Give the people, that they may **e**: 398
4:43 They shall **e**, and shall leave *thereof*. 398
4:44 they did **e**, and left *thereof*, according to 398
6:22 that they may **e** and drink, and go to their 398
6:28 that we may **e** him to day, and we will eat 398
6:28 him to day, and we will **e** my son to morrow. 398
6:29 So we boiled my son, and did **e** him: and 398
6:29 next day, Give thy son, that we may **e** him: 398
7: 2 see *it* with thine eyes, but shalt not **e** thereof. 398
7: 8 did **e** and drink, and carried thence silver, 398
7:19 see *it* with thine eyes, but shalt not **e** thereof. 398
9:10 the dogs shall **e** Jezebel in the portion of 398
9:34 come in, he did **e** and drink, and said, Go, 398
2Ki 9:36 In the portion of Jezreel shall dogs **e** 398
18:27 that *they* may **e** their own dung, and drink 398
18:31 *then* **e** ye every man of his own vine, and 398
19:29 Ye shall **e** *this* year such things as grow of 398
19:29 and plant vineyards, and **e** the fruits thereof. 398
23: 9 they did **e** of the unleavened bread among 398
25:29 he did **e** bread continually before him all 398
1Ch 29:22 did **e** and drink before the LORD on that 398
2Ch 28:15 **gave** them **to e** and to drink, and 398
30:18 yet did they **e** the passover otherwise than it 398
30:22 they did **e** throughout the feast seven days, 398
31:10 *we* have had enough to **e**, and have left 398
Ezr 2:63 that they should not **e** of the most holy *things* 398
6:21 to seek the LORD God of Israel, did **e**, 398
9:12 **e** the good of the land, and leave *it* for an 398
10: 6 he did **e** no bread, nor drink water: 398
Ne 5: 2 we take up corn *for them*, that we may **e**, 398
7:65 that they should not **e** of the most holy 398
8:10 Go *your way*, **e** the fat, and drink the sweet, 398
8:12 all the people went *their way* to **e**, and 398
9:25 so they did **e**, and were filled, and 398
9:36 gavest unto our fathers to **e** the fruit thereof 398
Est 4:16 neither **e** nor drink three days, night or day; 398
Job 1: 4 sent and called for their three sisters to **e** and 398
3:24 For my sighing cometh before I **e**, and 3899
31: 8 *Then* let me sow, and let another **e**; yea, 398
42:11 and did **e** bread with him in his house: 398
Ps 14: 4 who **e up** my people *as* they eat bread, *and* 398
14: 4 who eat up my people *as* they **e** bread, *and* 398
22:26 The meek shall **e** and be satisfied: they shall 398
22:29 All *they that be* fat upon earth shall **e** and 398
27: 2 my foes, came upon me to **e up** my flesh, 398
41: 9 in whom I trusted, which did **e** *of* my bread, 398
50:13 Will I **e** the flesh of bulls, or drink the blood 398
53: 4 who **e up** my people *as* they eat bread: 398
53: 4 who eat up my people *as* they **e** bread: 398
78:24 And had rained down manna upon them to **e**, 398
78:25 Man did **e** angels' food: he sent them meat to 398
78:29 So they did **e**, and were well filled: for he 398
102: 4 like grass; so that I forget to **e** my bread. 398
105:35 did **e up** all the herbs in their land, and 398
127: 2 to sit up late, to **e** the bread of sorrows: 398
128: 2 For thou shalt **e** the labour of thine hands: 398
141: 4 and let me not **e** of their dainties. 3898
Pr 1:31 Therefore shall they **e** of the fruit of their 398
4:17 For they **e** the bread of wickedness, and 3898
9: 5 **e** of my bread, and drink of the wine *which* 3898
13: 2 A man shall **e** good by the fruit of *his* mouth: 398
13: 2 the soul of the transgressors *shall* **e** NIH
18:21 and they that love it shall **e** the fruit thereof. 398
23: 1 When thou sittest to **e** with a ruler, 3898
23: 6 **E** thou not the bread of *him that hath* an 3898
23: 7 **E** and drink, saith he to thee; but his heart *is* 398
24:13 My son, **e** thou honey, because *it is* good; 398
25:16 **e** so much as is sufficient for thee, lest thou 398
25:21 thine enemy *be* hungry, **give** him bread **to e**; 398
25:27 *It is* not good to **e** much honey: so *for men* to 398
27:18 Whoso keepeth the fig tree shall **e** the fruit 398
30:17 pick it out, and the young eagles shall **e** it. 398
Ecc 2:24 *than* that he should **e** and drink, and *that* he 398
2:25 For who can **e**, or who else can hasten 398
3:13 And also that every man should **e** and drink, 398
5:11 they are increased that **e** them: 398
5:12 *man is* sweet, whether he **e** little or much: 398
5:18 *is* good and comely *for one* to **e** and to drink, 398
5:19 hath given him power to **e** thereof, and 398
6: 2 yet God giveth him not power to **e** thereof, 398
8:15 than to **e**, and to drink, and to be merry: 398
9: 7 Go *thy way*, **e** thy bread with joy, and 398
10:16 *is* a child, and thy princes **e** in the morning. 398
10:17 and thy princes **e** in due season, for strength, 398
SS 4:16 into his garden, and **e** his pleasant fruits. 398
5: 1 **e**, O friends; drink, yea, drink abundantly, 398
Isa 1:19 and obedient, ye shall **e** the good of the land: 398
3:10 that *it shall be* well *with him*: for they shall **e** 398
4: 1 We will **e** our own bread, and wear our own 398
5:17 waste places of the fat ones shall strangers **e**. 398
7:15 Butter and honey shall he **e**, that he may 398
7:22 of milk *that they* shall give he shall **e** butter: 398
7:22 honey shall every one **e** that is left in 398
9:20 he shall **e** on the left hand, and they shall not 398
9:20 they shall **e** every man the flesh of his own 398
11: 7 and the lion shall **e** straw like the ox. 398
21: 5 the table, watch *in* the watchtower, **e**, drink: 398
22:13 let us **e** and drink; for to morrow we shall 398
23:18 to **e** sufficiently, and for durable clothing. 398
30:24 the young asses that ear the ground shall **e** 398
36:12 that *they* may **e** their own dung, and drink 398
36:16 **e** ye every one *of* his vine, and every one *of* 398
37:30 Ye shall **e** *this* year such as groweth of itself; 398
37:30 and plant vineyards, and **e** the fruit thereof. 398
50: 9 old as a garment; the moth shall **e** them **up**. 398
51: 8 For the moth shall **e** them **up** like a garment, 398
51: 8 and the worm shall **e** them like wool: 398
55: 1 come ye, buy, and **e**; yea, come, buy wine 398
55: 2 **e** ye *that which is* good, and let your soul 398
61: 6 ye shall **e** the riches of the Gentiles, and 398
62: 9 they that have gathered it shall **e** it, and 398
65: 4 which **e** swine's flesh, and broth of 398
65:13 my servants shall **e**, but ye shall be hungry: 398
65:21 shall plant vineyards, and **e** the fruit of them. 398
65:22 they shall not plant, and another **e**: 398
65:25 and the lion shall **e** straw like the bullock: 398
Jer 2: 7 to **e** the fruit thereof and the goodness 398
5:17 they shall **e up** thine harvest, and thy bread, 398
5:17 *which* thy sons and thy daughters should **e**: 398
5:17 they shall **e up** thy flocks and thine herds: 398
5:17 they shall **e up** thy vines and thy fig trees: 398
7:21 offerings unto your sacrifices, and **e** flesh. 398
15:16 Thy words were found, and I did **e** them; and 398
16: 8 of feasting, to sit with them to **e** and to drink. 398
19: 9 I will **cause** them **to e** the flesh of their sons 398
19: 9 they shall **e** every one the flesh of his friend 398
22:15 did not thy father **e** and drink, and 398
22:22 The wind shall **e up** all thy pastors, and 7462

Jer 29: 5 and plant gardens, and e the fruit of them; 398
29:28 and plant gardens, and e the fruit of them. 398
31: 5 and shall e them as common things. 2490
41: 1 there they did e bread together in Mizpah. 398
52:33 he did continually e bread before him all 398
La 2:20 Shall the women e their fruit, and children of 398
Eze 2: 8 open thy mouth, and e that I give thee. 398
3: 1 unto me, Son of man, e that thou findest; 398
3: 1 e this roll, and go speak unto the house of 398
3: 2 my mouth, and he caused me to e that roll. 398
3: 3 cause thy belly to e, and fill thy bowels with 398
3: 3 did I e it; and it was in my mouth as honey 398
4: 9 and ninety days shalt thou e thereof. 398
4:10 thy meat which thou shalt e shall be by 398
4:10 a day: from time to time shalt thou e it. 398
4:12 thou shalt e it as barley cakes, and thou shalt 398
4:13 Even thus shall the children of Israel e their 398
4:16 they shall e bread by weight, and with care; 398
5:10 Therefore the fathers shall e the sons in 398
5:10 of thee, and the sons shall e their fathers; 398
12:18 e thy bread with quaking, and drink thy 398
12:19 They shall e their bread with carefulness, 398
16:13 thou didst e fine flour, and honey, and oil: 398
22: 9 in thee they e upon the mountains: in 398
24:17 not thy lips, and e not the bread of men. 398
24:22 not cover your lips, nor e the bread of men. 398
25: 4 they shall e thy fruit, and they shall drink thy 398
33:25 Ye e with the blood, and lift up your eyes 398
34: 3 Ye e the fat, and ye clothe you with 398
34:19 they e that which ye have trodden with 7462
39:17 that ye may e flesh, and drink blood. 398
39:18 Ye shall e the flesh of the mighty, and 398
39:19 ye shall e fat till ye be full, and drink blood 398
42:13 e the most holy things: there shall they lay 398
44: 3 he shall sit in it to e bread before 398
44:29 They shall e the meat offering, and the sin 398
44:31 The priests shall not e of any thing that is 398
Da 1:12 let them give us pulse to e, and water to 398
1:13 the countenance of the children that e of 398
1:15 which did e the portion of the king's meat. 398
4:25 they shall make thee to e grass as oxen, 2939
4:32 they shall make thee to e grass as oxen, 2939
4:33 did e grass as oxen, and his body was wet 399
Hos 2:12 and the beasts of the field shall e them. 398
4: 8 They e up the sin of my people, and they set 398
4:10 For they shall e, and not have enough: 398
8:13 and e it; but the LORD accepteth them not; 398
9: 3 and they shall e unclean things in Assyria. 398
9: 4 all that e thereof shall be polluted: 398
Joel 2:26 ye shall e in plenty, and be satisfied, 398+398
Am 6: 4 e the lambs out of the flock, and the calves 398
7: 4 devoured the great deep, and did e up a part. 398
7:12 and there e bread, and prophesy there: 398
9:14 also make gardens, and e the fruit of them. 398
Ob 1: 7 they that e thy bread have laid a wound NIH
Mic 3: 3 Who also e the flesh of my people, and 398
6:14 Thou shalt e, but not be satisfied; and 398
7: 1 there is no cluster to e: my soul desired 398
Na 3:15 it shall e thee up like the cankerworm: 398
Hab 1: 8 they shall fly as the eagle that hasteth to e. 398
Hag 1: 6 ye e, but ye have not enough; ye drink, but 398
Zec 7: 6 when ye did e, and when ye did drink, did 398
7: 6 did not ye e for yourselves, and drink for 398
11: 9 let the rest e every one the flesh of another. 398
11:16 he shall e the flesh of the fat, and tear their 398
Mt 6:25 what ye shall e, or what ye shall drink; 5315
6:31 take no thought, saying, What shall we e? 5315
12: 1 began to pluck the ears of corn, and to e. 2068
12: 4 and did e the shewbread, which was not 5315
12: 4 which was not lawful for him to e, 5315
14:16 They need not depart; give ye them to e. 5315
14:20 And they did all e, and were filled: and 5315
15: 2 for they wash not their hands when they e 2068
15:20 to e with unwashen hands defileth not a 5315
15:27 yet the dogs e of the crumbs which fall 2068
15:32 me now three days, and have nothing to e: 5315
15:37 And they did all e, and were filled: and 5315
15:38 And they that did e were four thousand 2068
24:49 and to e and drink with the drunken; 2068
26:17 that we prepare for thee to e the passover? 5315
26:21 And as they did e, he said, Verily I say unto 2068
26:26 gave it to the disciples, and said, Take, e; 5315
Mk 1: 6 and he did e locusts and wild honey; 2068
2:16 and Pharisees saw him e with publicans and 2068
2:26 and did e the shewbread, which is not 5315
2:26 which is not lawful to e but for the priests, 5315
3:20 so that they could not so much as e bread. 5315
5:43 that something should be given her to e. 5315
6:31 and they had no leisure so much as to e. 5315
6:36 for they have nothing to e. 5315
6:37 and said unto them, Give ye them to e. 5315
6:37 pennyworth of bread, and give them to e? 5315
6:42 And they did all e, and were filled. 5315
6:44 And they that did e of the loaves were 5315
7: 2 And when they saw some of his disciples e 2068
7: 3 except they wash their hands oft, e not, 2068
7: 4 the market, except they wash, they e not. 2068
7: 5 but e bread with unwashen hands? 2068
7:28 yet the dogs under the table e of 2068
8: 1 and having nothing to e, Jesus called his 5315
8: 2 with me three days, and have nothing to e: 5315
8: 8 So they did e, and were filled: and 5315
11:14 No man e fruit of thee hereafter for ever. 5315
14:12 prepare that thou mayest e the passover? 5315
14:14 where I shall e the passover with my 5315
14:18 And as they sat and did e, Jesus said, 2068
14:22 And as they did e, Jesus took bread, and 2068
14:22 and gave to them, and said, Take, e: 5315
Lk 4: 2 And in those days he did e nothing: and 5315
5:30 Why do ye e and drink with publicans and 2068
5:33 of the Pharisees; but thine e and drink? 2068
6: 1 and did e, rubbing them in their hands. 2068
6: 4 of God, and did take and e the shewbread, 5315
6: 4 which it is not lawful to e but for the priests 5315
7:36 desired him that he would e with him. 5315
Lk 9:13 But he said unto them, Give ye them to e. 5315
9:17 And they did e, and were all filled: and 5315
10: 8 e such things as are set before you: 2068
12:19 take thine ease, e, drink, and be merry. 5315
12:22 no thought for your life, what ye shall e; 5315
12:29 And seek not ye what ye shall e, or what ye 5315
12:45 and to e and drink, and to be drunken; 2068
14: 1 Pharisees to e bread on the sabbath day, 5315
14:15 Blessed is he that shall e bread in 5315
15:16 belly with the husks that the swine did e: 2068
15:23 and kill it; and let us e, and be merry: 5315
17: 8 and afterward thou shalt e and drink? 5315
17:27 They did e, they drank, they married wives, 2068
17:28 they did e, they drank, they bought, 2068
22: 8 and prepare us the passover, that we may e. 5315
22:11 where I shall e the passover with my 5315
22:15 With desire I have desired to e this 5315
22:16 say unto you, I will not any more e thereof, 5315
22:30 That ye may e and drink at my table in my 2068
24:43 And he took it, and did e before them. 5315
Jn 4:31 his disciples prayed him, saying, Master, e. 5315
4:32 I have meat to e that ye know not of. 5315
4:33 Hath any man brought him ought to e? 5315
6: 5 shall we buy bread, that these may e? 5315
6:23 nigh unto the place where they did e bread, 5315
6:26 but because ye did e of the loaves, and 5315
6:31 Our fathers did e manna in the desert; as it 5315
6:31 He gave them bread from heaven to e. 5315
6:49 Your fathers did e manna in the wilderness, 5315
6:50 from heaven, that a man may e thereof, 5315
6:51 if any man e of this bread, he shall live for 5315
6:52 How can this man give us his flesh to e? 5315
6:53 Except ye e the flesh of the Son of man, 5315
6:58 not as your fathers did e manna, and 5315
18:28 but that they might e the passover. 5315
Ac 2:46 did e their meat with gladness and 3335
9: 9 without sight, and neither did e nor drink. 5315
10:13 a voice to him, Rise, Peter; kill, and e. 5315
10:41 who did e and drink with him after he rose 4906
11: 3 men uncircumcised, and didst e with them. 4906
11: 7 saying unto me, Arise, Peter; slay and e. 5315
23:12 saying that they would neither e nor drink 5315
23:14 that we will e nothing until we have slain 1089
23:21 that they will neither e nor drink till they 5315
27:35 and when he had broken it, he began to e. 2068
Ro 14: 2 For one believeth that he may e all things: 5315
14:21 It is good neither to e flesh, nor to drink 5315
14:23 And he that doubteth is damned if he e, 5315
1Co 5:11 an extortioner; with such a one no not to e. 4906
8: 7 e it as a thing offered unto an idol; 2068
8: 8 for neither, if we e, are we the better; 5315
8: 8 neither, if we e not, are we the worse. 5315
8:10 to e those things which are offered to idols; 2068
8:13 I will e no flesh while the world standeth, 5315
9: 4 Have we not power to e and to drink? 5315
10: 3 And did all e the same spiritual meat; 5315
10: 7 The people sat down to e and drink, and 5315
10:18 are not they which e of the sacrifices 2068
10:25 Whatsoever is sold in the shambles, that e, 2068
10:27 whatsoever is set before you, e, asking no 2068
10:28 e not for his sake that shewed it, and 2068
10:31 Whether therefore ye e, or drink, or 2068
11:20 one place, this is not to e the Lord's supper. 5315
11:22 have ye not houses to e and to drink in? or 2068
11:24 given thanks, he brake it, and said, Take, e: 5315
11:26 For as often as ye e this bread, and 2068
11:27 Wherefore whosoever shall e this bread, 2068
11:28 and so let him e of that bread, and drink of 2068
11:33 my brethren, when ye come together to e, 5315
11:34 And if any man hunger, let him e at home; 2068
15:32 let us e and drink; for to morrow we die. 5315
Gal 2:12 from James, he did e with the Gentiles: 4906
2Th 3: 8 Neither did we e any man's bread for 5315
3:10 if any would not work, neither should he e. 2068
3:12 quietness they work, and e their own bread. 2068
2Ti 2:17 And their word will e as doth a 2192+3542
Heb 13:10 whereof they have no right to e which serve 5315
Jas 5: 3 and shall e your flesh as it were fire: 5315
Rev 2: 7 To him that overcometh will I give to e of 5315
2:14 to e things sacrificed unto idols, and 5315
2:17 To him that overcometh will I give to e of 5315
2:20 and to e things sacrificed unto idols. 5315
10: 9 And he said unto me, Take it, and e it up; 2719
17:16 and shall e her flesh, and burn her with fire. 5315
19:18 That ye may e the flesh of kings, and 5315

EATEN (104) [EAT]

Ge 3:11 Hast thou e of the tree, whereof I 398
3:17 hast e of the tree, of which I commanded 398
6:21 And take thou unto thee of all food that is e, 398
14:24 Save only that which the young men have e, 398
27:33 I have e of all before thou camest, and 398
31:38 and the rams of thy flock have I not e. 398
41:21 when they had e them up, it 413+935+7130
41:21 be known that they had e them; 413+935+7130
43: 2 when they had e up the corn which they had 398
Ex 12:46 In one house shall it be e; thou shalt not 398
13: 3 place: there shall no leavened bread be e. 398
13: 7 Unleavened bread shall be e seven days; and 398
21:28 be surely stoned, and his flesh shall not be e; 398
22: 5 man shall cause a field or vineyard to be e, 1197
29:34 with fire: it shall not be e, because it is holy. 398
Lev 6:16 with unleavened bread shall it be e in 398
6:23 priest shall be wholly burnt: it shall not be e. 398
6:26 in the holy place shall it be e, in the court of 398
6:30 reconcile withal in the holy place, shall be e: 398
7: 6 it shall be e in the holy place: it is most holy. 398
7:15 shall be e the same day that it is offered; 398
7:16 it shall be e the same day that he offereth his 398
7:16 morrow also the remainder of it shall be e: 398
7:18 offerings be e at all on the third day, 398+398
7:19 toucheth any unclean thing shall not be e; 398
10:17 Wherefore have ye not e the sin offering in 398
10:18 indeed have e it in the holy place, as I 398+398
10:19 if I had e the sin offering to day, should it 398
Lev 11:13 they shall not be e, they are an abomination: 398
11:34 Of all meat which may be e, that on which 398
11:41 shall be an abomination; it shall not be e. 398
11:47 between the beast that may be e and 398
11:47 be eaten and the beast that may not be e. 398
17:13 and catcheth any beast or fowl that may be e; 398
19: 6 It shall be e the same day ye offer it, and 398
19: 7 if it be e at all on the third day, it is 398+398
19:23 uncircumcised unto you: it shall not be e of. 398
22:30 On the same day it shall be e up; ye shall 398
Nu 28:17 seven days shall unleavened bread be e. 398
Dt 6:11 when thou shalt have e and be full; 398
8:10 When thou hast e and art full, then thou shalt 398
8:12 Lest when thou hast e and art full, and 398
12:22 Even as the roebuck and the hart is e, so 398
14:19 is unclean unto you: they shall not be e. 398
20: 6 planted a vineyard, and hath not yet e of it? 2490
26:14 I have not e thereof in my mourning, 398
29: 6 Ye have not e bread, neither have you drunk 398
31:20 they shall have e and filled themselves, and 398
Jos 5:12 after they had e of the old corn of the land; 398
Ru 3: 7 when Boaz had e and drunk, and his heart 398
1Sa 1: 9 So Hannah rose up after they had e in 398
14:30 if haply the people had e freely to day 398+398
28:20 for he had e no bread all the day, nor all 398
30:12 when he had e, his spirit came again to him: 398
30:12 for he had e no bread, nor drunk any water, 398
2Sa 19:42 have we e at all of the king's cost? or 398+398
1Ki 13:22 hast e bread and drunk water in the place, 398
13:23 after he had e bread, and after he had drunk, 398
13:28 the lion had not e the carcase, nor torn 398
2Ki 6:23 when they had e and drunk, he sent them 398
Ne 5:14 my brethren have not e the bread of 398
Job 6: 6 Can that which is unsavoury be e without 398
31:17 Or have e my morsel myself alone, and 398
31:17 and the fatherless hath not e thereof; 398
31:39 If I have e the fruits thereof without money, 398
Ps 69: 9 For the zeal of thine house hath e me up; 398
102: 9 For I have e ashes like bread, and 398
Pr 9:17 are sweet, and bread e in secret is pleasant. NIH
23: 8 The morsel which thou hast e shalt thou 398
SS 5: 1 I have e my honeycomb with my honey; 398
Isa 3:14 for ye have e up the vineyard; the spoil of 1197
5: 5 the hedge thereof, and it shall be e up; 1197
6:13 a tenth, and it shall return, and shall be e: 1197
44:19 e it: and shall I make the residue thereof an 398
Jer 10:25 for they have e up Jacob, and devoured him, 398
24: 2 which could not be e, they were so bad. 398
24: 3 very evil, that cannot be e, they are so evil. 398
24: 8 evil figs, which cannot be e, they are so evil; 398
29:17 vile figs, that cannot be e, they are so evil. 398
31:29 The fathers have e a sour grape, and 398
Eze 4:14 now have I not e of that which dieth of itself, 398
18: 2 The fathers have e sour grapes, and 398
18: 6 And hath not e upon the mountains, 398
18:11 but even hath e upon the mountains, 398
18:15 That hath not e upon the mountains, 398
34:18 unto you to have e up the good pasture, 7462
45:21 of seven days; unleavened bread shall be e. 398
Hos 10:13 reaped iniquity; ye have e the fruit of lies. 398
Joel 1: 4 the palmerworm hath left hath the locust e; 398
1: 4 the locust hath left hath the cankerworm e; 398
1: 4 cankerworm hath left hath the caterpillar e. 398
2:25 to you the years that the locust hath e, 398
Mt 14:21 And they that had e were about five 2068
Mk 8: 9 And they that had e were about four 5315
Lk 13:26 We have e and drunk in thy presence, and 5315
17: 8 and serve me, till I have e and drunken; 5315
Jn 2:17 The zeal of thine house hath e me up. 2719
6:13 and above unto them that had e. 977
Ac 10:10 he became very hungry, and would have e: 1089
10:14 for I have never e any thing that is common 5315
12:23 and he was e of worms, and gave up 4662
20:11 and e, and talked a long while, 1089
27:38 And when they had e enough, 2880+5160
Rev 10:10 and as soon as I had e it, my belly was 5315

EATER (3) [EAT]

Jdg 14:14 Out of the e came forth meat, and out of 398
Isa 55:10 give seed to the sower, and bread to the e: 398
Na 3:12 they shall even fall into the mouth of the e. 398

EATERS (1) [EAT]

Pr 23:20 amongst riotous e of flesh: 2151

EATEST (3) [EAT]

Ge 2:17 for in the day that thou e thereof thou shalt 398
1Sa 1: 8 why e thou not? and why is thy heart 398
1Ki 21: 5 is thy spirit so sad, that thou e no bread? 398

EATETH (56) [EAT]

Ex 12:15 for whosoever e leavened bread from 398
12:19 for whosoever e that which is leavened, 398
Lev 7:18 the soul that e of it shall bear his iniquity. 398
7:20 the soul that e of the flesh of the sacrifice of 398
7:25 For whosoever e the fat of the beast, 398
7:25 even the soul that e it shall be cut off from 398
7:27 Whatsoever soul it be that e any manner of 398
11:40 he that e of the carcase of it shall wash his 398
14:47 he that e in the house shall wash his clothes. 398
17:10 among you, that e any manner of blood; 398
17:10 will even set my face against that soul that e 398
17:14 whosoever e it shall be cut off. 398
17:15 every soul that e that which died of itself, 398
19: 8 Therefore every one that e it shall bear his 398
Nu 13:32 is a land that e up the inhabitants thereof; 398
1Sa 14:24 Cursed be the man that e any food until 398
14:28 Cursed be the man that e any food this day. 398
Job 5: 5 Whose harvest the hungry e up, and taketh it 398
21:25 of his soul, and never e with pleasure. 398
40:15 which I made with thee; he e grass as an ox. 398
Ps 106:20 into the similitude of an ox that e grass. 398
Pr 13:25 The righteous e to the satisfying of his soul: 398
30:20 she e, and wipeth her mouth, and saith, 398

E

Pr 31:27 and e not the bread of idleness. 398
Ecc 4: 5 his hands together, and e his own flesh. 398
5:17 All his days also he e in darkness, and 398
6: 2 not power to eat thereof, but a stranger e it: 398
Isa 28: 4 while it is yet in his hand he e it up. 1104
29: 8 a hungry man dreameth, and behold, he e; 398
44:16 with part thereof he e flesh; he roasteth roast, 398
59: 5 he that e of their eggs dieth, and that which 398
Jer 31:30 every man that e the sour grape, his teeth 398
Mt 9:11 Why e your Master with publicans and 2068
Mk 2:16 How is it that he e and drinketh with 2068
14:18 One of you which e with me shall betray 2068
Lk 15: 2 man receiveth sinners, and e with them. 4906
Jn 6:54 Whoso e my flesh, and drinketh my blood, 5176
6:56 He that e my flesh, and drinketh my blood, 5176
6:57 so he that e me, even he shall live by me. 5176
6:58 he that e of this bread shall live for ever. 5176
13:18 He that e bread with me hath lift up his heel 5176
Ro 14: 2 all things: another, who is weak, e herbs. 2068
14: 3 Let not him that e despise him that eateth 2068
14: 3 Let not him that eateth despise him that e 2068
14: 3 let not him which e not judge him that 2068
14: 3 not him which eateth not judge him that e: 2068
14: 6 to the Lord he doth not regard it. He that e, 2068
14: 6 e to the Lord, for he giveth God thanks; 2068
14: 6 and he that e not, to the Lord he eateth not, 2068
14: 6 to the Lord he e not, and giveth God 2068
14:20 it is evil for that man who e with offence. 2068
14:23 damned if he eat, because he e not of faith: NIG
1Co 9: 7 a vineyard, and e not of the fruit thereof? 2068
9: 7 a flock, and e not of the milk of the flock? 2068
11:29 For he that e and drinketh unworthily, 2068
11:29 e and drinketh damnation to himself, 2068

EATING (27) [EAT]

Ex 12: 4 every man according to his e shall make 400
16:16 Gather of it every man according to his e, 400
16:18 they gathered every man according to his e. 400
16:21 every man according to his e: 400
Jdg 14: 9 went on e, and came to his father and 398
Ru 3: 3 until he shall have done e and drinking. 398
1Sa 14:34 sin not against the LORD in e with 398
30:16 e and drinking, and dancing, because of all 398
1Ki 1:41 him heard it as they had made an end of e. 398
4:20 e and drinking, and making merry. 398
2Ki 4:40 as they were e of the pottage, that they cried 398
1Ch 12:39 were with David three days, e and drinking: 398
Job 1:13 when his sons and his daughters were e and 398
1:18 Thy sons and thy daughters were e and 398
20:23 and shall rain it upon him while he is e. 3894
Isa 22:13 and killing sheep, e flesh, and drinking wine: 398
66:17 e swine's flesh, and the abomination, and 398
Am 7: 2 that when they had made an end of e 398
Mt 11:18 For John came neither e nor drinking, and 2068
11:19 The Son of man came e and drinking, and 2068
24:38 days that were before the flood they were e 5176
26:26 And as they were e, Jesus took bread, and 2068
Lk 7:33 For John the Baptist came neither e bread 2068
7:34 The Son of man is come e and drinking; 2068
10: 7 e and drinking such things as they give: 2068
1Co 8: 4 the e of those things that are offered in 1035
11:21 For in e every one taketh before other his 5315

EBAL (8)

Ge 36:23 and Manahath, and E, Shepho, and Onam. 5858
Dt 11:29 and the curse upon mount E. 5858
27: 4 in mount E, and thou shalt plaister them 5858
27:13 these shall stand upon mount E to curse; 5858
Jos 8:30 unto the LORD God of Israel in mount E, 5858
8:33 and half of them over against mount E; 5858
1Ch 1:22 And E, and Abimael, and Sheba, 5858
1:40 and Manahath, and E, Shephi, and Onam. 5858

EBED (6)

Jdg 9:26 Gaal the son of E came with his brethren, 5651
9:28 Gaal the son of E said, Who is Abimelech, 5651
9:30 city heard the words of Gaal the son of E, 5651
9:31 Gaal the son of E and his brethren be come 5651
9:35 Gaal the son of E went out, and stood in 5651
Ezr 8: 6 E the son of Jonathan, and with him fifty 5651

EBED-MELECH (6)

Jer 38: 7 Now when E the Ethiopian, one of 5663
38: 8 E went forth out of the king's house, and 5663
38:10 the king commanded E the Ethiopian, 5663
38:11 So E took the men with him, and went into 5663
38:12 E the Ethiopian said unto Jeremiah, 5663
39:16 Go and speak to E the Ethiopian, saying, 5663

EBEN-EZER (3)

1Sa 4: 1 the Philistines to battle, and pitched beside E: 72
5: 1 of God, and brought it from E unto Ashdod. 72
7:12 and Shen, and called the name of it E, 72

EBENY (1)

Eze 27:15 thee for a present horns of ivory and e. 1894

EBER (13) [HEBER]

Ge 10:21 the father of all the children of E, 5677
10:24 Arphaxad begat Salah; and Salah begat E. 5677
10:25 unto E were born two sons: the name of 5677
11:14 And Salah lived thirty years, and begat E: 5677
11:15 Salah lived after he begat E four hundred 5677
11:16 E lived four and thirty years, and 5677
11:17 E lived after he begat Peleg four hundred 5677
Nu 24:24 shall afflict E, and he also shall perish for 5677
1Ch 1:18 begat Shelah, and Shelah begat E. 5677
1:19 unto E were born two sons: the name of 5677
1:25 E, Peleg, Rehu, 5677
8:12 E, and Misham, and Shamed, who built 5677
Ne 12:20 Of Sallai, Kallai; of Amok, E; 5677

EBEZ See ABEZ

EBIASAPH (3)

1Ch 6:23 his son, and E his son, and Assir his son, 43
6:37 the son of Assir, the son of E, the son of 43
9:19 the son of E, the son of Korah, and 43

EBRONAH (2)

Nu 33:34 from Jotbathah, and encamped at E. 5684
33:35 they departed from E, and encamped at 5684

ECBATANA See ACHMETHA

ED (1)

Jos 22:34 the children of Gad called the altar E: for it NIH

EDAR (1)

Ge 35:21 and spread his tent beyond the tower of E. 5740

EDEN (20)

Ge 2: 8 God planted a garden eastward in E; 5731
2:10 a river went out of E to water the garden; 5731
2:15 put him into the garden of E to dress it and 5731
3:23 God sent him forth from the garden of E, 5731
3:24 he placed at the east of the garden of E 5731
4:16 dwelt in the land of Nod, on the east of E. 5731
2Ki 19:12 the children of E which were in Thelasar? 5729
2Ch 29:12 the son of Zimmah, and E the son of Joah: 5731
31:15 next him were E, and Miniamin, and 5731
Isa 37:12 the children of E which were in Telassar? 5729
51: 3 and he will make her wilderness like E, and 5731
Eze 27:23 Haran, and Canneh, and E, the merchants 5729
28:13 Thou hast been in E the garden of God; 5731
31: 9 so that all the trees of E, that were in 5731
31:16 all the trees of E, the choice and best of 5731
31:18 and in greatness among the trees of E? 5731
31:18 trees of E unto the nether parts of the earth: 5731
36:35 desolate is become like the garden of E; 5731
Joel 2: 3 the land is as the garden of E before them, 5731
Am 1: 5 holdeth the sceptre from the house of E: 5729

EDER (3)

Jos 15:21 southward were Kabzeel, and E, and Jagur, 5740
1Ch 23:23 Mahli, and E, and Jeremoth, three. 5740
24:30 also of Mushi; Mahli, and E, and Jerimoth. 5740

EDGE (56) [EDGES, TWOEDGED]

Ge 34:26 Shechem his son with the e of the sword, 6310
Ex 13:20 in Etham, in the e of the wilderness. 7097
17:13 and his people with the e of the sword. 6310
26: 4 thou shalt make loops of blue upon the e of 8193
26: 4 likewise shalt thou make in the uttermost e 8193
26: 5 fifty loops shalt thou make in the e of 7097
26:10 thou shalt make fifty loops on the e of 8193
26:10 fifty loops in the e of the curtain which 8193
36:11 he made loops of blue on the e of one 8193
36:12 fifty loops made he in the e of the curtain 7097
36:17 he made fifty loops upon the uttermost e of 8193
36:17 fifty loops made he upon the e of 8193
Nu 21:24 Israel smote him with the e of the sword, 6310
33: 6 which is in the e of the wilderness. 7097
33:37 in mount Hor, in the e of the land of Edom. 7097
Dt 13:15 of that city with the e of the sword, 6310
13:15 the cattle thereof, with the e of the sword. 6310
20:13 every male thereof with the e of the sword: 6310
Jos 6:21 and sheep, and ass, with the e of the sword. 6310
8:24 when they were all fallen on the e of 6310
8:24 and smote it with the e of the sword. 6310
10:28 smote it with the e of the sword, and 6310
10:30 he smote it with the e of the sword, and all 6310
10:32 smote it with the e of the sword, and all 6310
10:35 smote it with the e of the sword, and all 6310
10:37 smote it with the e of the sword, and 6310
10:39 they smote them with the e of the sword, 6310
11:11 that were therein with the e of the sword, 6310
11:12 smote them with the e of the sword, and 6310
11:14 every man they smote with the e of 6310
13:27 even unto the e of the sea of Cinnereth on 7097
19:47 smote it with the e of the sword, and 6310
Jdg 1: 8 smitten it with the e of the sword, and set 6310
1:25 they smote the city with the e of the sword; 6310
4:15 with the e of the sword before Barak; 6310
4:16 all the host of Sisera fell upon the e of 6310
18:27 they smote them with the e of the sword, 6310
20:37 smote all the city with the e of the sword. 6310
20:48 smote them with the e of the sword, as well 6310
21:10 of Jabesh-gilead with the e of the sword, 6310
1Sa 15: 8 utterly destroyed all the people with the e 6310
22:19 smote he with the e of the sword, both men 6310
22:19 asses, and sheep, with the e of the sword. 6310
2Sa 15:14 and smite the city with the e of the sword. 6310
2Ki 10:25 they smote them with the e of the sword; 6310
Job 1:15 they have slain the servants with the e of 6310
1:17 slain the servants with the e of the sword; 6310
Ps 89:43 Thou hast also turned the e of his sword, 6697
Ecc 10:10 he do not whet the e, then must he put to 6440
Jer 21: 7 he shall smite them with the e of the sword; 6310
31:29 and the children's teeth are set on e. 6949
31:30 the sour grape, his teeth shall be set on e. 6949
Eze 18: 2 and the children's teeth are set on e? 6949
43:13 the border thereof by the e thereof round 8193
Lk 21:24 And they shall fall by the e of the sword, 4750
Heb 11:34 violence of fire, escaped the e of the sword, 4750

EDGES (4) [EDGE]

Ex 28: 7 thereof joined at the two e thereof; 7098
39: 4 by the two e was it coupled together. 7098
Jdg 3:16 Ehud made him a dagger which had two e, 6310
Rev 2:12 he which hath the sharp sword with two e; 1366

EDIFICATION (4) [EDIFY]

Ro 15: 2 of us please his neighbour for his good to e. 3619
1Co 14: 3 he that prophesieth speaketh unto men to e, 3619
2Co 10: 8 which the Lord hath given us for e, and 3619
13:10 power which the Lord hath given me to e, 3619

EDIFIED (2) [EDIFY]

Ac 9:31 and Galilee and Samaria, and were e; 3618
1Co 14:17 givest thanks well, but the other is not e. 3618

EDIFIETH (3) [EDIFY]

1Co 8: 1 Knowledge puffeth up, but charity e. 3618
14: 4 He that speaketh in an unknown tongue e 3618
14: 4 but he that prophesieth e the church. 3618

EDIFY (3) [EDIFICATION, EDIFIED, EDIFIETH, EDIFYING]

Ro 14:19 and things wherewith one may e another. 3619
1Co 10:23 are lawful for me, but all things e not. 3618
1Th 5:11 and e one another, even as also ye do. 3618

EDIFYING (8) [EDIFY]

1Co 14: 5 he interpret, that the church may receive e. 3619
14:12 that ye may excel to the e of the church. 3619
14:26 Let all things be done unto e. 3619
2Co 12:19 we do all things, dearly beloved, for your e. 3619
Eph 4:12 the ministry, for the e of the body of Christ: 3619
4:16 maketh increase of the body unto the e of 3619
4:29 but that which is good to the use of e, that it 3619
1Ti 1: 4 rather than godly e which is in faith: 3622

EDOM (87) [EDOMITE, EDOMITES, ESAU]

Ge 25:30 I am faint: therefore was his name called E. 123
32: 3 unto the land of Seir, the country of E. 123
36: 1 these are the generations of Esau, who is E. 123
36: 8 Thus dwelt Esau in mount Seir: Esau is E. 123
36:16 dukes that came of Eliphaz in the land of E; 123
36:17 dukes that came of Reuel in the land of E; 123
36:19 of Esau, who is E, and these are their dukes. 123
36:21 the children of Seir in the land of E. 123
36:31 are the kings that reigned in the land of E, 123
36:32 Bela the son of Beor reigned in E: and 123
36:43 these be the dukes of E, according to their 123
Ex 15:15 the dukes of E shall be amazed; the mighty 123
Nu 20:14 messengers from Kadesh unto the king of E, 123
20:18 E said unto him, Thou shalt not pass by me, 123
20:20 E came out against him with much people, 123
20:21 Thus E refused to give Israel passage 123
20:23 by the coast of the land of E, saying, 123
21: 4 of the Red sea, to compass the land of E: 123
24:18 E shall be a possession, Seir also shall be a 123
33:37 in mount Hor, in the edge of the land of E. 123
34: 3 wilderness of Zin along by the coast of E, 123
Jos 15: 1 even to the border of E, the wilderness of 123
15:21 the coast of E southward were Kabzeel, 123
Jdg 5: 4 when thou marchedst out of the field of E, 123
11:17 Israel sent messengers unto the king of E, 123
11:17 the king of E would not hearken thereto. 123
11:18 compassed the land of E, and the land of 123
1Sa 14:47 against E, and against the kings of Zobah, 123
2Sa 8:14 he put garrisons in E; throughout all Edom 123
8:14 throughout all E put he garrisons, and 123
8:14 and all they of E became David's servants. 123
1Ki 9:26 on the shore of the Red sea, in the land of E. 123
11:14 the Edomite: he was of the king's seed in E. 123
11:15 when David was in E, and Joab the captain 123
11:15 after he had smitten every male in E; 123
11:16 until he had cut off every male in E:) 123
22:47 There was then no king in E: a deputy was 123
2Ki 3: 8 The way through the wilderness of E. 123
3: 9 and the king of Judah, and the king of E: 123
3:12 and the king of E went down to him. 123
3:20 there came water by the way of E, and 123
3:26 to break through even unto the king of E: 123
8:20 In his days E revolted from under the hand 123
8:22 Yet E revolted from under the hand of Judah 123
14: 7 He slew of E in the valley of salt ten 123
14:10 Thou hast indeed smitten E, and thine heart 123
1Ch 1:43 E before any king reigned over the children 123
1:51 the dukes of E were; duke Timnah, 123
1:54 duke Iram. These are the dukes of E. 123
18:11 from E, and from Moab, and from 123
18:13 he put garrisons in E; and all the Edomites 123
2Ch 8:17 and to Eloth, at the sea side in the land of E. 123
25:20 because they sought after the gods of E. 123
Ps 60: T smote of E in the valley of salt twelve 123
60: 8 my washpot; over E will I cast out my shoe: 123
60: 9 the strong city? who will lead me into E? 123
83: 6 The tabernacles of E, and the Ishmaelites; 123
108: 9 my washpot; over E will I cast out my shoe; 123
108:10 the strong city? who will lead me into E? 123
137: 7 the children of E in the day of Jerusalem; 123
Isa 11:14 they shall lay their hand upon E and Moab; 123
63: 1 Who is this that cometh from E, with dyed 123
Jer 9:26 E, and the children of Ammon, and Moab, 123
25:21 E, and Moab, and the children of Ammon, 123
27: 3 send them to the king of E, and to the king 123
40:11 in E, and that were in all the countries, 123
49: 7 Concerning E, thus saith the LORD of 123
49:17 Also E shall be a desolation: every one that 123
49:20 of the LORD, that he hath taken against E; 123
49:22 E be as the heart of a woman in her pangs. 123
La 4:21 Rejoice and be glad, O daughter of E, 123
4:22 he will visit thine iniquity, O daughter of E; 123
Eze 25:12 Because that E hath dealt against the house 123
25:13 I will also stretch out mine hand upon E, and 123
25:14 I will lay my vengeance upon E by the hand 123
25:14 they shall do in E according to mine anger 123
32:29 There is E, her kings, and all her princes, 123
Da 11:41 even E, and Moab, and the chief of 123
Joel 3:19 and E shall be a desolate wilderness, 123
Am 1: 6 the whole captivity, to deliver them up to E: 123
1: 9 they delivered up the whole captivity to E, 123
1:11 For three transgressions of E, and for four, 123
2: 1 he burnt the bones of the king of E into lime: 123
9:12 That they may possess the remnant of E, and 123
Ob 1: 1 Thus saith the Lord GOD concerning E; 123
1: 8 even destroy the wise men out of E, and 123
Mal 1: 4 Whereas E saith, We are impoverished, but 123

EDOMITE (7) [EDOM]
Dt 23: 7 Thou shalt not abhor an **E**; for he *is* thy 130
1Sa 21: 7 his name *was* Doeg, an **E**, the chiefest of 130
22: 9 answered Doeg the **E**, which *was* set over 130
22:18 Doeg the **E** turned, and he fell upon 130
22:22 *it* that day, when Doeg the **E** *was* there, 130
1Ki 11:14 up an adversary unto Solomon, Hadad the **E**: 130
Ps 52: T when Doeg the **E** came and told Saul, and 130

EDOMITES (13) [EDOM]
Ge 36: 9 of Esau the father of the **E** in mount Seir: 123
36:43 he *is* Esau the father of the **E**. 123
1Ki 11: 1 Ammonites, **E**, Zidonians, *and* Hittites; 130
11:17 certain **E** of his father's servants with him, 130
2Ki 8:21 smote the **E** which compassed him about, 123
1Ch 18:12 the **E** in the valley of salt eighteen thousand. 123
18:13 and all the **E** became David's servants. 123
2Ch 21: 8 In his days the **E** revolted from under 123
21: 9 smote the **E** which compassed him in, and 123
21:10 So the **E** revolted from under the hand of 123
25:14 was come from the slaughter of the **E**, 130
25:19 Thou sayest, Lo, thou hast smitten the **E**; 123
28:17 For again the **E** had come and smitten Judah, 130

EDREI (8)
Nu 21:33 he, and all his people, to the battle *at* **E**. 154
Dt 1: 4 of Bashan, which dwelt at Astaroth in **E**: 154
3: 1 he and all his people, to battle *at* **E**. 154
3:10 and all Bashan, unto Salchah and **E**, 154
Jos 12: 4 the giants, that dwelt at Ashtaroth and at **E**, 154
13:12 which reigned in Ashtaroth and in **E**, 154
13:31 half Gilead, and Ashtaroth, and **E**, cities of 154
19:37 And Kedesh, and **E**, and En-hazor, 154

EFFECT (14) [EFFECTED, EFFECTUAL, EFFECTUALLY]
Nu 30: 8 wherewith she bound her soul, of **none e**: 6565
2Ch 34:22 the college:) and they spake to her to that **e**. NIH
Ps 33:10 **maketh** the devices of the people **of none e**. 5106
Isa 32:17 the **e** of righteousness quietness and 5656
Jer 48:30 *it shall* not *be* so; his lies shall not so **e** *it*. 6213
Eze 12:23 days are at hand, and the **e** of every vision. 1697
Mt 15: 6 **made** the commandment of God **of none e** *208*
Mk 7:13 **Making** the word of God **of none e** through *208*
Ro 3: 3 unbelief **make** the faith of God **without e**? *2673*
4:14 and the promise **made of none e**: *2673*
9: 6 though the word of God hath **taken none e**. *1601*
1Co 1:17 cross of Christ should be **made of none e**. *2758*
Gal 3:17 that *it* should **make** the promise **of none e**. *2673*
5: 4 Christ is **become of no e** unto you, *2673*

EFFECTED (1) [EFFECT]
2Ch 7:11 and in his own house, he **prosperously e**. 6743

EFFECTUAL (6) [EFFECT]
1Co 16: 9 For a great door and **e** is opened unto me, *1756*
2Co 1: 6 which is **e** in the enduring of the same *1754*
Eph 3: 7 unto me by the **e working** of his power. *1753*
4:16 according to the **e working** in the measure *1753*
Phm 1: 6 **e** by the acknowledging of every good *1756*
Jas 5:16 The **e fervent** prayer of a righteous *man* *1754*

EFFECTUALLY (2) [EFFECT]
Gal 2: 8 (For he that **wrought e in** Peter to *1754*
1Th 2:13 which **e worketh** also in you that believe. *1754*

EFFEMINATE (1)
1Co 6: 9 nor idolaters, nor adulterers, nor **e**, *3120*

EGG (2) [EGGS]
Job 6: 6 or is there *any* taste in the white of an **e**? 2495
Lk 11:12 Or if he shall ask an **e**, will he offer him a *5609*

EGGS (7) [EGG]
Dt 22: 6 or **e**, and the dam sitting upon the young, or 1000
22: 6 dam sitting upon the young, or upon the **e**, 1000
Job 39:14 Which leaveth her **e** in the earth, and 1000
Isa 10:14 as *one* gathereth **e** *that are* left, have I 1000
59: 5 They hatch cockatrice' **e**, and weave 1000
59: 5 he that eateth of their **e** dieth, and 1000
Jer 17:11 *As* the partridge sitteth *on* **e**, and NIH

EGLAH (2)
2Sa 3: 5 the sixth, Ithream, by **E** David's wife. 5698
1Ch 3: 3 of Abital: the sixth, Ithream by **E** his wife. 5698

EGLAIM (1)
Isa 15: 8 the howling thereof unto **E**, and the howling 97

EGLON (13)
Jos 10: 3 and unto Debir king of **E**, saying, 5700
10: 5 the king of Lachish, the king of **E**, 5700
10:23 the king of Lachish, *and* the king of **E**. 5700
10:34 from Lachish Joshua passed unto **E**, and 5700
10:36 Joshua went up from **E**, and all Israel with 5700
10:37 according to all that he had done to **E**; 5700
12:12 The king of **E**, one; the king of Gezer, one; 5700
15:39 Lachish, and Bozkath, and **E**, 5700
Jdg 3:12 the LORD strengthened **E** the king of 5700
3:14 So the children of Israel served **E** the king 5700
3:15 sent a present unto **E** the king of Moab. 5700
3:17 he brought the present unto **E** king of 5700
3:17 king of Moab: and **E** *was* a very fat man. 5700

EGYPT (611) [EGYPTIAN, EGYPTIAN'S, EGYPTIANS]
Ge 12:10 Abram went down into **E** to sojourn there; 4714
12:11 when he was come near to enter into **E**, 4714
12:14 that, when Abram was come into **E**, 4714
13: 1 Abram went up out of **E**, he, and his wife, 4714
13:10 like the land of **E**, as thou comest unto 4714
15:18 from the river of **E** unto the great river, 4714
21:21 took him a wife out of the land of **E**. 4714
25:18 that *is* before **E**, as thou goest towards 4714
Ge 26: 2 unto him, and said, Go not down into **E**; 4714
37:25 and myrrh, going to carry *it* down to **E**. 4714
37:28 of silver: and they brought Joseph into **E**. 4714
37:36 the Medanites sold him into **E** unto 4714
39: 1 Joseph was brought down to **E**; and 4714
40: 1 *that* the butler of the king of **E** and *his* 4714
40: 1 baker had offended their lord the king of **E**. 4714
40: 5 the butler and the baker of the king of **E**, 4714
41: 8 and called for all the magicians of **E**, 4714
41:19 such as I never saw in all the land of **E** for 4714
41:29 of great plenty throughout all the land of **E**: 4714
41:30 plenty shall be forgotten in the land of **E**; 4714
41:33 and wise, and set him over the land of **E**. 4714
41:34 take up the fifth *part* of the land of **E** in 4714
41:36 of famine, which shall be in the land of **E**; 4714
41:41 See, I have set thee over all the land of **E**. 4714
41:43 he made him *ruler* over all the land of **E**. 4714
41:44 lift up his hand or foot in all the land of **E**. 4714
41:45 And Joseph went out over *all* the land of **E**. 4714
41:46 when he stood before Pharaoh king of **E**. 4714
41:46 and went throughout all the land of **E**. 4714
41:48 which were in the land of **E**, and laid up 4714
41:53 that was in the land of **E**, were ended. 4714
41:54 but in all the land of **E** there was bread. 4714
41:55 when all the land of **E** was famished, 4714
41:56 and the famine waxed sore in the land of **E**. 4714
41:57 all countries came into **E** to Joseph for to 4714
42: 1 when Jacob saw that there was corn in **E**, 4714
42: 2 Behold, I have heard that there is corn in **E**: 4714
42: 3 ten brethren went down to buy corn in **E**. 4714
43: 2 the corn which they had brought out of **E**, 4714
43:15 went down *to* **E**, and stood before Joseph. 4714
45: 4 Joseph your brother, whom ye sold into **E**. 4714
45: 8 and a ruler throughout all the land of **E**. 4714
45: 9 God hath made me lord of all **E**: 4714
45:13 shall tell my father of all my glory in **E**, 4714
45:18 I will give you the good of the land of **E**, 4714
45:19 take you wagons out of the land of **E** for 4714
45:20 for the good of all the land of **E** *is* yours. 4714
45:23 ten asses laden with the good things of **E**, 4714
45:25 they went up out of **E**, and came *into* 4714
45:26 and he *is* governor over all the land of **E**. 4714
46: 3 fear not to go down into **E**; for I will there 4714
46: 4 I will go down with thee into **E**; and I will 4714
46: 6 came into **E**, Jacob, and all his seed with 4714
46: 7 and all his seed brought he with him into **E**. 4714
46: 8 which came into **E**, Jacob and his sons: 4714
46:20 unto Joseph in the land of **E** were born 4714
46:26 All the souls that came with Jacob into **E**, 4714
46:27 which were born him in **E**, *were* two souls: 4714
46:27 which came into **E**, *were* threescore and 4714
47: 6 The land of **E** *is* before thee; in the best of 4714
47:11 gave them a possession in the land of **E**, 4714
47:13 so that the land of **E** and *all* the land of 4714
47:14 the money that was found in the land of **E**, 4714
47:15 when money failed in the land of **E**, and 4714
47:20 Joseph bought all the land of **E** for 4714
47:21 borders of **E** even to the *other* end thereof. 4714
47:26 Joseph made it a law over the land of **E** 4714
47:27 Israel dwelt in the land of **E**, in the country 4714
47:28 Jacob lived in the land of **E** seventeen 4714
47:29 with me; bury me not, I pray thee, in **E**: 4714
47:30 thou shalt carry me out of **E**, and bury me 4714
48: 5 which were born unto thee in the land of **E** 4714
48: 5 of Egypt before I came unto thee into **E**, 4714
50: 7 and all the elders of the land of **E**, 4714
50:14 Joseph returned into **E**, he, and 4714
50:22 Joseph dwelt in **E**, he, and his father's 4714
50:26 and he was put in a coffin in **E**. 4714
Ex 1: 1 the children of Israel, which came into **E**; 4714
1: 5 seventy souls: for Joseph was in **E** *already*. 4714
1: 8 Now there arose up a new king over **E**, 4714
1:15 the king of **E** spake to the Hebrew 4714
1:17 did not as the king of **E** commanded them, 4714
1:18 the king of **E** called for the midwives, and 4714
2:23 in process of time, that the king of **E** died: 4714
3: 7 the affliction of my people which *are* in **E**, 4714
3:10 my people the children of Israel out of **E**. 4714
3:11 bring forth the children of Israel out of **E**? 4714
3:12 thou hast brought forth the people out of **E**, 4714
3:16 and *seen* that which is done to you in **E**: 4714
3:17 I will bring you up out of the affliction of **E** 4714
3:18 unto the king of **E**, and you shall say unto 4714
3:19 I am sure that the king of **E** will not let you 4714
3:20 smite **E** with all my wonders which I will 4714
4:18 and return unto my brethren which *are* in **E**, 4714
4:19 unto Moses in Midian, Go, return *into* **E**: 4714
4:20 an ass, and he returned to the land of **E**: 4714
4:21 When thou goest to return into **E**, 4714
5: 4 the king of **E** said unto them, Wherefore do 4714
5:12 land of **E** to gather stubble instead of straw. 4714
6:11 Go in, speak unto Pharaoh king of **E**, 4714
6:13 of Israel, and unto Pharaoh king of **E**, 4714
6:13 the children of Israel out of the land of **E**. 4714
6:26 the land of **E** according to their armies. 4714
6:27 *are* they which spake to Pharaoh king of **E**, 4714
6:27 to bring out the children of Israel from **E**: 4714
6:28 LORD spake unto Moses in the land of **E**, 4714
6:29 speak thou unto Pharaoh king of **E** all that I 4714
7: 3 my signs and my wonders in the land of **E**. 4714
7: 4 that I may lay my hand upon **E**, and 4714
7: 4 out of the land of **E** by great judgments. 4714
7: 5 when I stretch forth mine hand upon **E**, and 4714
7:11 now the magicians of **E**, they also did in 4714
7:19 stretch out thine hand upon the waters of **E**, 4714
7:19 may be blood throughout all the land of **E**, 4714
7:21 was blood throughout all the land of **E**. 4714
7:22 the magicians of **E** did so with their 4714
8: 5 cause frogs to come up upon the land of **E**. 4714
8: 6 stretched out his hand over the waters of **E**; 4714
8: 6 frogs came up, and covered the land of **E**. 4714
8: 7 and brought up frogs upon the land of **E**. 4714
8:16 become lice throughout all the land of **E**. 4714
8:17 became lice throughout all the land of **E**. 4714
8:24 servants' houses, and into all the land of **E**: 4714
Ex 9: 4 the cattle of Israel and the cattle of **E**: 4714
9: 6 on the morrow, and all the cattle of **E** died: 4714
9: 9 shall become small dust in all the land of **E**, 4714
9: 9 upon beast, throughout all the land of **E**. 4714
9:18 such as hath not been in **E** since 4714
9:22 that there may be hail in all the land of **E**, 4714
9:22 herb of the field, throughout the land of **E**. 4714
9:23 the LORD rained hail upon the land of **E**. 4714
9:24 in all the land of **E** since it became a nation. 4714
9:25 the hail smote throughout all the land of **E** 4714
10: 2 what things I have wrought in **E**, and my 4714
10: 7 knowest thou not yet that **E** is destroyed? 4714
10:12 Stretch out thine hand over the land of **E** 4714
10:12 that they may come up upon the land of **E**, 4714
10:13 stretched forth his rod over the land of **E**, 4714
10:14 the locusts went up over all the land of **E**, 4714
10:14 of Egypt, and rested in all the coasts of **E**: 4714
10:15 herbs of the field, through all the land of **E**. 4714
10:19 not one locust in all the coasts of **E**. 4714
10:21 there may be darkness over the land of **E**, 4714
10:22 darkness in all the land of **E** three days: 4714
11: 1 plague *more* upon Pharaoh, and upon **E**; 4714
11: 3 man Moses *was* very great in the land of **E**, 4714
11: 4 midnight will I go out into the midst of **E**: 4714
11: 5 all the firstborn in the land of **E** shall die, 4714
11: 6 be a great cry throughout all the land of **E**, 4714
11: 9 may be multiplied in the land of **E**. 4714
12: 1 unto Moses and Aaron in the land of **E**, 4714
12:12 For I will pass through the land of **E** this 4714
12:12 will smite all the firstborn in the land of **E**, 4714
12:12 against all the gods of **E** I will execute 4714
12:13 to destroy *you*, when I smite the land of **E**. 4714
12:17 I brought your armies out of the land of **E**: 4714
12:27 the houses of the children of Israel in **E**, 4714
12:29 smote all the firstborn in the land of **E**, 4714
12:30 and there was a great cry in **E**; 4714
12:39 dough which they brought forth out of **E**, 4714
12:39 because they were thrust out of **E**, and 4714
12:40 who dwelt in **E**, *was* four hundred and 4714
12:41 of the LORD went out from the land of **E**. 4714
12:42 for bringing them out from the land of **E**: 4714
12:51 Israel out of the land of **E** by their armies. 4714
13: 3 this day, *in* which ye came out from **E**, 4714
13: 8 did unto me when I came forth out of **E**. 4714
13: 9 hath the LORD brought thee out of **E**. 4714
13:14 of hand the LORD brought us out from **E**, 4714
13:15 slew all the firstborn in the land of **E**, 4714
13:16 hand the LORD brought us forth out of **E**. 4714
13:17 when they see war, and they return to **E**: 4714
13:18 went up harnessed out of the land of **E**. 4714
14: 5 it was told the king of **E** that the people 4714
14: 7 all the chariots of **E**, and captains over 4714
14: 8 hardened the heart of Pharaoh king of **E**, 4714
14:11 Because *there were* no graves in **E**, 4714
14:11 thus with us, to carry us forth out of **E**? 4714
14:12 not this the word that we did tell thee in **E**, 4714
16: 1 after their departing out of the land of **E**. 4714
16: 3 by the hand of the LORD in the land of **E**, 4714
16: 6 hath brought you out from the land of **E**: 4714
16:32 I brought you forth from the land of **E**. 4714
17: 3 *Is* this *that* thou hast brought us up out of **E**, 4714
18: 1 the LORD had brought Israel out of **E**; 4714
19: 1 Israel were gone forth out of the land of **E**, 4714
20: 2 have brought thee out of the land of **E**, 4714
22:21 for ye were strangers in the land of **E**. 4714
23: 9 seeing ye were strangers in the land of **E**. 4714
23:15 for in it thou camest out from **E**: 4714
29:46 brought them forth out of the land of **E**, 4714
32: 1 man that brought us up out of the land of **E**, 4714
32: 4 which brought thee up out of the land of **E**. 4714
32: 7 which thou broughtest out of the land of **E**, 4714
32: 8 have brought thee up out of the land of **E**. 4714
32:11 forth out of the land of **E** with great power, 4714
32:23 man that brought us up out of the land of **E**, 4714
33: 1 thou hast brought up out of the land of **E**, 4714
34:18 in the month Abib thou camest out from **E**. 4714
Lev 11:45 that bringeth you up out of the land of **E**, 4714
18: 3 After the doings of the land of **E**, 4714
19:34 for ye were strangers in the land of **E**: 4714
19:36 which brought you out of the land of **E**. 4714
22:33 That brought you out of the land of **E**, to be 4714
23:43 when I brought them out of the land of **E**: 4714
25:38 brought you forth out of the land of **E**, 4714
25:42 which I brought forth out of the land of **E**: 4714
25:55 whom I brought forth out of the land of **E**: 4714
26:13 brought you forth out of the land of **E**, 4714
26:45 whom I brought forth out of the land of **E** 4714
Nu 1: 1 after they were come out of the land of **E**, 4714
3:13 **E** I hallowed unto me all the firstborn in 4714
8:17 I smote every firstborn in the land of **E**, 4714
9: 1 after they were come out of the land of **E**, 4714
11: 5 the fish, which we did eat in **E** freely; 4714
11:18 for *it was* well with us in **E**: therefore 4714
11:20 saying, Why came we forth out of **E**? 4714
13:22 was built seven years before Zoan in **E**.) 4714
14: 2 God that we had died in the land of **E**! 4714
14: 3 were it not better for us to return into **E**? 4714
14: 4 us make a captain, and let us return into **E**. 4714
14:19 this people, from **E** even until now. 4714
14:22 which I did in **E** and in the wilderness, and 4714
15:41 which brought you out of the land of **E**, 4714
20: 5 have ye made us to come up out of **E**, 4714
20:15 How our fathers went down into **E**, and 4714
20:15 and we have dwelt in **E** a long time; 4714
20:16 and hath brought us forth out of **E**: 4714
21: 5 Wherefore have ye brought us up out of **E** 4714
22: 5 Behold, there is a people come out from **E**: 4714
22:11 Behold, *there is* a people come out of **E**, 4714
23:22 God brought them out of **E**; he hath as it 4714
24: 8 God brought him forth out of **E**; he hath as 4714
26: 4 which went forth out of the land of **E**. 4714
26:59 whom *her mother* bare to Levi in **E**: 4714
32:11 none of the men that came up out of **E**, 4714
33: 1 which went forth out of the land of **E** with 4714
33:38 of Israel were come out of the land of **E**, 4714

E

Nu 34: 5 a compass from Azmon unto the river of E, 4714
Dt 1:27 hath brought us forth out of the land of E, 4714
1:30 according to all that he did for you in E 4714
4:20 *even* out of E, to be unto him a people of 4714
4:34 God did for you in E before your eyes? 4714
4:37 in his sight with his mighty power out of E; 4714
4:45 of Israel, after they came forth out of E, 4714
4:46 after they were come forth out of E: 4714
5: 6 which brought thee out of the land of E, 4714
5:15 that thou wast a servant in the land of E, 4714
6:12 brought thee forth out of the land of E, 4714
6:21 thy son, We were Pharaoh's bondmen in E; 4714
6:21 the LORD brought us out of E with a 4714
6:22 and wonders, great and sore, upon E, 4714
7: 8 from the hand of Pharaoh king of E. 4714
7:15 will put none of the evil diseases of E, 4714
7:18 thy God did unto Pharaoh, and unto all E; 4714
8:14 brought thee forth out of the land of E, 4714
9: 7 that thou didst depart out of the land of E, 4714
9:12 E have corrupted *themselves;* they are 4714
9:26 which thou hast brought forth out of E with 4714
10:19 for ye were strangers in the land of E. 4714
10:22 Thy fathers went down into E with 4714
11: 3 which he did in the midst of E unto 4714
11: 3 midst of Egypt unto Pharaoh the king of E, 4714
11: 4 what he did unto the army of E, unto their 4714
11:10 *is* not as the land of E, from whence ye 4714
13: 5 which brought you out of the land of E, and 4714
13:10 which brought thee out of the land of E, 4714
15:15 that thou wast a bondman in the land of E, 4714
16: 1 God brought thee forth out of E by night. 4714
16: 3 for thou camest forth out of the land of E in 4714
16: 3 out of the land of E all the days of thy life. 4714
16: 6 the season that thou camest forth out of E. 4714
16:12 remember that thou wast a bondman in E: 4714
17:16 nor cause the people to return to E, to 4714
20: 1 which brought thee up out of the land of E. 4714
23: 4 in the way, when ye came forth out of E; 4714
24: 9 after that ye were come forth out of E. 4714
24:18 remember that thou wast a bondman in E, 4714
24:22 that thou wast a bondman in the land of E: 4714
25:17 when ye were come forth out of E; 4714
26: 5 he went down into E, and sojourned there 4714
26: 8 the LORD brought us forth out of E with 4714
28:27 LORD will smite thee with the botch of E, 4714
28:60 will bring upon thee all the diseases of E, 4713
28:68 the LORD shall bring thee *into* E again 4714
29: 2 your eyes in the land of E unto Pharaoh, 4714
29:16 know how we have dwelt in the land of E; 4714
29:25 he brought them forth out of the land of E: 4714
34:11 sent him to do in the land of E to Pharaoh, 4714
Jos 2:10 Red sea for you, when you came out of E; 4714
5: 4 All the people that came out of E, *that were* 4714
5: 4 by the way, after they came out of E. 4714
5: 5 by the way as they came forth out of E, 4714
5: 6 which came out of E, were consumed, 4714
5: 9 rolled away the reproach of E from off you. 4714
9: 9 the fame of him, and all that he did in E, 4714
13: 3 From Sihor, which *is* before E, even unto 4714
15: 4 and went out *unto* the river of E; 4714
15:47 unto the river of E, and the great sea, and 4714
24: 4 Jacob and his children went down *into* E. 4714
24: 5 Moses also and Aaron, and I plagued E, 4714
24: 6 I brought your fathers out of E: and 4714
24: 7 your eyes have seen what I have done in E: 4713
24:14 on the *other* side of the flood, and in E; 4714
24:17 us up and our fathers out of the land of E, 4714
24:32 the children of Israel brought up out of E, 4714
Jdg 2: 1 I made you to go up out of E, and 4714
2:12 which brought them out of the land of E, 4714
6: 8 I brought you up from E, and brought you 4714
6:13 Did not the LORD bring us up from E? 4714
11:13 when they came up out of E, from Arnon 4714
11:16 when Israel came up from E, and 4714
19:30 came up out of the land of E unto this day: 4714
1Sa 2:27 when they were in E in Pharaoh's house? 4714
8: 8 them up out of E even unto this day, 4714
10:18 I brought up Israel out of E, and 4714
12: 6 your fathers up out of the land of E. 4714
12: 8 When Jacob was come *into* E, and 4714
12: 8 which brought forth your fathers out of E, 4714
15: 2 him in the way, when he came up from E. 4714
15: 6 of Israel, when they came up out of E. 4714
15: 7 thou comest *to* Shur, that *is* over against E. 4714
27: 8 thou goest to Shur, even unto the land of E. 4714
30:13 I *am* a young man of E, servant to 4713
2Sa 7: 6 I brought up the children of Israel out of E, 4714
7:23 which thou redeemedst to thee from E, 4714
1Ki 3: 1 made affinity with Pharaoh king of E, 4714
4:21 of the Philistines, and unto the border of E: 4714
4:30 the east country, and all the wisdom of E. 4714
6: 1 of Israel were come out of the land of E, 4714
8: 9 when they came out of the land of E. 4714
8:16 I brought forth my people Israel out of E, 4714
8:21 when he brought them out of the land of E. 4714
8:51 which thou broughtest forth out of E, 4714
8:53 when thou broughtest our fathers out of E, 4714
8:65 entering in of Hamath unto the river of E, 4714
9: 9 forth their fathers out of the land of E, 4714
9:16 *For* Pharaoh king of E had gone up, and 4714
10:28 Solomon had horses brought out of E, and 4714
10:29 went out of E for six hundred *shekels* of 4714
11:17 his father's servants with him, to go *into* E; 4714
11:18 they came *to* E, unto Pharaoh king of 4714
11:18 came *to* Egypt, unto Pharaoh king of E, 4714
11:21 when Hadad heard in E that David slept 4714
11:40 Jeroboam arose, and fled *into* E, 4714
11:40 unto Shishak king of E, and was in Egypt 4714
11:40 and was in E until the death of Solomon. 4714
12: 2 the son of Nebat, who was yet in E, 4714
12: 2 king Solomon, and Jeroboam dwelt in E;) 4714
12:28 which brought thee up out of the land of E. 4714
14:25 *that* Shishak king of E came up against 4714
2Ki 17: 4 for he had sent messengers to So king of E, 4714
17: 7 had brought them up out of the land of E, 4714
2Ki 17: 7 from under the hand of Pharaoh king of E, 4714
17:36 who brought you up out of the land of E 4714
18:21 *even* upon E, on which if a man lean, it will 4714
18:21 *is* Pharaoh king of E unto all that trust on 4714
18:24 put thy trust on E for chariots and 4714
21:15 the day their fathers came forth out of E, 4714
23:29 In his days Pharaoh-nechoh king of E went 4714
23:34 took Jehoahaz *away:* and he came *to* E, and 4714
24: 7 the king of E came not again any more out 4714
24: 7 E unto the river Euphrates all that pertained 4714
24: 7 all that pertained to the king of E. 4714
25:26 of the armies, arose, and came *to* E: 4714
1Ch 13: 5 from Shihor of E even unto the entering of 4714
17:21 whom thou hast redeemed out of E? 4714
2Ch 1:16 Solomon had horses brought out of E, and 4714
1:17 brought forth out of E a chariot for six 4714
5:10 of Israel, when they came out of E. 4714
6: 5 E I chose no city among all the tribes of 4714
7: 8 entering in of Hamath unto the river of E. 4714
7:22 brought them forth out of the land of E, 4714
9:26 of the Philistines, and to the border of E. 4714
9:28 they brought unto Solomon horses out of E, 4714
10: 2 Jeroboam the son of Nebat, who *was* in E, 4714
10: 2 heard *it,* that Jeroboam returned out of E. 4714
12: 2 king of E came up against Jerusalem, 4714
12: 3 number that came with him out of E; 4714
12: 9 So Shishak king of E came up against 4714
20:10 when they came out of the land of E, but 4714
26: 8 spread abroad even to the entering in of E: 4714
35:20 Necho king of E came up to fight against 4714
36: 3 the king of E put him down at Jerusalem, 4714
36: 4 the king of E made Eliakim his brother 4714
36: 4 Jehoahaz his brother, and carried him to E. 4714
Ne 9: 9 didst see the affliction of our fathers in E, 4714
9:18 *is* thy God that brought thee up out of E, 4714
Ps 68:31 Princes shall come out of E; Ethiopia shall 4714
78:12 in the land of E, *in* the field of Zoan. 4714
78:43 How he had wrought his signs in E, and 4714
78:51 smote all the firstborn in E; the chief of 4714
80: 8 Thou hast brought a vine out of E: 4714
81: 5 when he went out through the land of E: 4714
81:10 which brought thee out of the land of E: 4714
105:23 Israel also came *into* E; and 4714
105:38 E was glad when they departed: for the fear 4714
106: 7 fathers understood not thy wonders in E; 4714
106:21 which had done great *things* in E; 4714
114: 1 When Israel went out of E, the house of 4714
135: 8 Who smote the firstborn of E, both of man 4714
135: 9 O E, upon Pharaoh, and upon all his 4714
136:10 To him that smote E in their firstborn: 4714
Pr 7:16 *with* carved *works, with* fine linen of E. 4714
Isa 7:18 *is* in the uttermost part of the rivers of E, 4714
10:24 his staff against thee, after the manner of E. 4714
10:26 so shall he lift it up after the manner of E. 4714
11:11 from E, and from Pathros, and from Cush, 4714
11:16 day that he came up out of the land of E. 4714
19: 1 The burden of E. Behold, the LORD 4714
19: 1 upon a swift cloud, and shall come *into* E: 4714
19: 1 the idols of E shall be moved at his 4714
19: 1 the heart of E shall melt in the midst of it. 4714
19: 3 the spirit of E shall fail in the midst thereof; 4714
19:12 the LORD of hosts hath purposed upon E. 4714
19:13 they have also seduced E, *even they that* 4714
19:14 they have caused E to err in every work 4714
19:15 Neither shall there be *any* work for E, 4714
19:16 In that day shall E be like unto women: and 4714
19:17 the land of Judah shall be a terror unto E, 4714
19:18 In that day shall five cities in the land of E 4714
19:19 to the LORD in the midst of the land of E, 4714
19:20 unto the LORD of hosts in the land of E: 4714
19:21 the LORD shall be known to E, and 4714
19:22 the LORD shall smite E: *he* shall smite 4714
19:23 there be a highway out of E to Assyria, 4714
19:23 the Assyrian shall come into E, and 4714
19:24 In that day shall Israel be the third with E 4714
19:25 Blessed *be* E my people, and Assyria 4714
20: 3 and wonder upon E and upon Ethiopia; 4714
20: 4 buttocks uncovered, *to* the shame of E. 4714
20: 5 their expectation, and of E their glory. 4714
23: 5 As *at* the report concerning E, so shall they 4714
27:12 channel of the river unto the stream of E, 4714
27:13 the outcasts in the land of E, and 4714
30: 2 That walk to go down *into* E, and have not 4714
30: 2 of Pharaoh, and to trust in the shadow of E. 4714
30: 3 the trust in the shadow of E *your* confusion. 4714
31: 1 Woe to them that go down *to* E for help; 4714
36: 6 in the staff of this broken reed, on E; 4714
36: 6 *is* Pharaoh king of E to all that trust in him. 4714
36: 9 put thy trust on E for chariots and 4714
43: 3 I gave E *for* thy ransom, Ethiopia and 4714
45:14 The labour of E, and merchandise of 4714
52: 4 My people went down aforetime *into* E to 4714
Jer 2: 6 that brought us up out of the land of E, 4714
2:18 now what hast thou to do in the way of E, 4714
2:36 thou also shalt be ashamed of E, as thou 4714
7:22 that I brought them out of the land of E, 4714
7:25 forth out of the land of E unto this day, 4714
9:26 E, and Judah, and Edom, and the children 4714
11: 4 I brought them forth out of the land of E, 4714
11: 7 that I brought them up out of the land of E, 4714
16:14 the children of Israel out of the land of E; 4714
23: 7 the children of Israel out of the land of E; 4714
24: 8 and them that dwell in the land of E: 4714
25:19 Pharaoh king of E, and his servants, and his 4714
26:21 *it,* he was afraid, and fled, and went *into* E; 4714
26:22 Jehoiakim the king sent men *into* E, 4714
26:22 and *certain* men with him into E. 4714
26:23 they fet forth Urijah out of E, and 4714
31:32 to bring them out of the land of E; 4714
32:20 hast set signs and wonders in the land of E, 4714
32:21 Israel out of the land of E with signs, 4714
34:13 I brought them forth out of the land of E, 4714
37: 5 Pharaoh's army was come forth out of E: 4714
37: 7 shall return *to* E into their own land. 4714
41:17 *is* by Beth-lehem, to go to enter *into* E, 4714
Jer 42:14 we will go *into* the land of E, where we 4714
42:15 If ye wholly set your faces to enter *into* E, 4714
42:16 shall overtake you there in the land of E, 4714
42:16 shall follow close after you there *in* E; 4714
42:17 set their faces to go *into* E to sojourn there; 4714
42:18 forth upon you, when ye shall enter *into* E: 4714
42:19 O ye remnant of Judah; Go ye not *into* E: 4714
43: 2 thee to say, Go not *into* E to sojourn there: 4714
43: 7 So they came *into* the land of E: for they 4714
43:11 he shall smite the land of E, *and* 4714
43:12 kindle a fire in the houses of the gods of E; 4714
43:12 he shall array himself with the land of E, 4714
43:13 of Beth-shemesh, that *is* in the land of E; 4714
44: 1 all the Jews which dwell in the land of E, 4714
44: 8 incense unto other gods in the land of E, 4714
44:12 to go *into* the land of E to sojourn there, 4714
44:12 all be consumed, *and* fall in the land of E; 4714
44:13 punish them that dwell in the land of E, 4714
44:14 which are gone into the land of E to 4714
44:15 all the people that dwelt in the land of E, 4714
44:24 all Judah that *are* in the land of E: 4714
44:26 all Judah that dwell in the land of E; 4714
44:26 of any man of Judah in all the land of E, 4714
44:27 land of E shall be consumed by the sword 4714
44:28 out of the land of E *into* the land of Judah, 4714
44:28 that are gone into the land of E to sojourn 4714
44:30 I *will* give Pharaoh-hophra king of E into 4714
46: 2 Against E, against the army of 4714
46: 2 the army of Pharaoh-necho king of E, 4714
46: 8 E riseth up like a flood, and *his* waters are 4714
46:11 and take balm, O virgin, the daughter of E: 4714
46:13 should come and smite the land of E. 4714
46:14 Declare ye in E, and publish in Migdol, and 4714
46:17 cry there, Pharaoh king of E *is but* a noise; 4714
46:19 O thou daughter dwelling in E, 4714
46:20 E *is like* a very fair heifer, *but* 4714
46:24 The daughter of E shall be confounded; 4714
46:25 Pharaoh, and E, with their gods, and their 4714
Eze 17:15 him in sending his ambassadors *into* E, 4714
19: 4 brought him with chains unto the land of E. 4714
20: 5 myself known unto them in the land of E, 4714
20: 6 to bring them forth of the land of E into a 4714
20: 7 defile not yourselves with the idols of E: 4714
20: 8 neither did they forsake the idols of E: 4714
20: 8 against them in the midst of the land of E. 4714
20: 9 in bringing them forth out of the land of E. 4714
20:10 them to go forth out of the land of E, 4714
20:36 fathers in the wilderness of the land of E, 4714
23: 3 they committed whoredoms in E; 4714
23: 8 left she her whoredoms *brought* from E: 4714
23:19 she had played the harlot in the land of E. 4714
23:27 thy whoredom *brought* from the land of E: 4714
23:27 eyes unto them, nor remember E any more. 4714
27: 7 Fine linen with broidered work from E was 4714
29: 2 set thy face against Pharaoh king of E, and 4714
29: 2 prophesy against him, and against all E: 4714
29: 3 I *am* against thee, Pharaoh king of E, 4714
29: 6 all the inhabitants of E shall know that I *am* 4714
29: 9 the land of E shall be desolate and waste; 4714
29:10 I will make the land of E utterly waste *and* 4714
29:12 I will make the land of E desolate in 4714
29:14 I will bring again the captivity of E, and 4714
29:19 I *will* give the land of E unto 4714
29:20 I have given him the land of E *for* his 4714
30: 4 the sword shall come upon E, and 4714
30: 4 when the slain shall fall in E, and they shall 4714
30: 6 They also that uphold E shall fall; and 4714
30: 8 when I have set a fire in E, and *when* all 4714
30: 9 shall come upon them, as *in* the day of E: 4714
30:10 I will also make the multitude of E to cease 4714
30:11 they shall draw their swords against E, and 4714
30:13 shall be no more a prince of the land of E: 4714
30:13 and I will put a fear in the land of E. 4714
30:15 pour my fury upon Sin, the strength of E; 4714
30:16 I will set fire in E: Sin shall have great 4714
30:18 when I shall break there the yokes of E: 4714
30:19 Thus will I execute judgments in E: and 4714
30:21 have broken the arm of Pharaoh king of E; 4714
30:22 I *am* against Pharaoh king of E, and 4714
30:25 he shall stretch it out upon the land of E. 4714
31: 2 speak unto Pharaoh king of E, and to his 4714
32: 2 up a lamentation for Pharaoh king of E, 4714
32:12 they shall spoil the pomp of E, and all 4714
32:15 When I shall make the land of E desolate, 4714
32:16 *even* for E, and for all her multitude, 4714
32:18 wail for the multitude of E, and cast them 4714
Da 9:15 out of the land of E with a mighty hand, 4714
11: 8 shall also carry captives *into* E their gods, 4714
11:42 and the land of E shall not escape. 4714
11:43 and over all the precious *things* of E: 4714
Hos 2:15 day when she came up out of the land of E. 4714
7:11 they call *to* E, they go *to* Assyria. 4714
7:16 this *shall be* their derision in the land of E. 4714
8:13 and visit their sins: they shall return *to* E. 4714
9: 3 Ephraim shall return *to* E, and they shall 4714
9: 6 E shall gather them up, Memphis shall bury 4714
11: 1 I loved him, and called my son out of E. 4714
11: 5 He shall not return into the land of E, but 4714
11:11 They shall tremble as a bird out of E, and 4714
12: 1 the Assyrians, and oil is carried into E. 4714
12: 9 E will yet make thee to dwell in 4714
12:13 the LORD brought Israel out of E, 4714
13: 4 *am* the LORD thy God from the land of E, 4714
Joel 3:19 E shall be a desolation, and Edom shall be 4714
Am 2:10 Also I brought you up from the land of E, 4714
3: 1 which I brought up from the land of E, 4714
3: 9 and in the palaces in the land of E, and say, 4714
4:10 you the pestilence after the manner of E: 4714
8: 8 cast out and drowned, as *by* the flood of E. 4714
9: 5 and shall be drowned, as *by* the flood of E. 4714
9: 7 not I brought up Israel out of the land of E? 4714
Mic 6: 4 For I brought thee up out of the land of E, 4714
7:15 E will I shew unto him marvellous *things.* 4714
Na 3: 9 Ethiopia and E *were* her strength, and 4714
Hag 2: 5 with you when ye came out of E, 4714

Zec 10:10 bring them again also out of the land of E, 4714
10:11 and the sceptre of E shall depart away. 4714
14:18 if the family of E go not up, and come not, 4714
14:19 This shall be the punishment of E, and 4714
Mt 2:13 and flee into E, and be thou there until I 125
2:14 his mother by night, and departed into E: 125
2:15 saying, Out of E have I called my son. 125
2:19 Lord appeareth in a dream to Joseph in E, 125
Ac 2:10 in E, and in the parts of Libya about Cyrene, 125
7: 9 moved with envy, sold Joseph into E: 125
7:10 wisdom in the sight of Pharaoh king of E; 125
7:10 and he made him governor over E and all his 125
7:11 there came a dearth over all the land of E 125
7:12 when Jacob heard that there was corn in E, 125
7:15 So Jacob went down into E, and died, he, 125
7:17 the people grew and multiplied in E, 125
7:34 the affliction of my people which is in E, 125
7:34 And now come, I will send thee into E. 125
7:36 shewed wonders and signs in the land of E, 125
7:39 and in their hearts turned *back again* into E, 125
7:40 which brought us out of the land of E, 125
13:17 *they* dwelt as strangers in the land of E, 125
Heb 3:16 howbeit not all that came out of E by Moses. 125
8: 9 the hand to lead them out of the land of E; 125
11:26 Christ greater riches than the treasures in E: 125
11:27 By faith he forsook E, not fearing the wrath 125
Jude 1: 5 having saved the people out of the land of E, 125
Rev 11: 8 which spiritually is called Sodom and E, 125

EGYPTIAN (23) [EGYPT]

Ge 16: 1 no *children*: and she had a handmaid, an E, 4713
16: 3 Abram's wife took Hagar her maid the E, 4713
21: 9 Sarah saw the son of Hagar the E, 4713
25:12 Abraham's son, whom Hagar the E, 4713
39: 1 of Pharaoh, captain of the guard, an E, 4713
39: 2 and he was in the house of his master the E. 4713
Ex 1:19 Hebrew women *are* not as the E women; 4713
2:11 he spied an E smiting a Hebrew, *one* of his 4713
2:12 he slew the E, and hid him in the sand. 4713
2:14 thou to kill me, as thou killedst the E? 4713
2:19 An E delivered us out of the hand of 4713
Lev 24:10 Israelitish woman, whose father *was* an E, 4713
Dt 23: 7 thou shalt not abhor an E; because 4713
1Sa 30:11 they found an E in the field, and 376+4713
2Sa 23:21 he slew an E, a goodly man: and 4713
23:21 the E had a spear in his hand; but he went 4713
1Ch 2:34 had a servant, an E, whose name *was* Jarha. 4713
11:23 he slew an E, a man of *great* 376+4713+1886.1
Isa 11:15 utterly destroy the tongue of the E sea; 4714
19:23 the E into Assyria, and the Egyptians shall 4714
Ac 7:24 him that was oppressed, and smote the E: 124
7:28 thou kill me, as thou didst the E yesterday? 124
21:38 Art not thou *that* E, which before these days 124

EGYPTIAN'S (4) [EGYPT]

Ge 39: 5 that the LORD blessed the E house for 4713
2Sa 23:21 plucked the spear out of the E hand, and 4713
1Ch 11:23 in the E hand *was* a spear like a weaver's 4713
11:23 pluckt the spear out of the E hand, and 4713

EGYPTIANS (98) [EGYPT]

Ge 12:12 when the E shall see thee, that they shall 4714
12:14 the E beheld the woman that she *was* very 4713
41:55 Pharaoh said unto all the E, Go unto 4714
41:56 all the storehouses, and sold unto the E; 4714
43:32 for the E, which did eat with him, by 4713
43:32 the E might not eat bread with 4713
43:32 for that *is* an abomination unto the E. 4714
45: 2 and the E and the house of Pharaoh heard. 4714
46:34 shepherd *is* an abomination unto the E. 4714
47:15 all the E came unto Joseph, and said, 4714
47:20 for the E sold every man his field, because 4714
50: 3 the E mourned for him threescore and 4714
50:11 This *is* a grievous mourning to the E: 4714
Ex 1:13 the E made the children of Israel to serve 4714
3: 8 to deliver them out of the hand of the E, 4714
3: 9 oppression wherewith the E oppress them. 4714
3:21 this people favour in the sight of the E: 4714
3:22 your daughters; and ye shall spoil the E. 4714
6: 5 of Israel, whom the E keep in bondage; 4714
6: 6 you out from under the burdens of the E, 4714
6: 7 you out from under the burdens of the E. 4714
7: 5 the E shall know that I *am* the LORD, 4714
7:18 the E shall lothe to drink of the water of 4714
7:21 the E could not drink of the water of 4714
7:24 all the E digged round about the river *for* 4714
8:21 the houses of the E shall be full of swarms 4714
8:26 of the E to the LORD our God: 4714
8:26 shall we sacrifice the abomination of the E 4714
9:11 upon the magicians, and upon all the E. 4714
10: 6 all thy servants, and the houses of all the E; 4714
11: 3 gave the people favour in the sight of the E. 4714
11: 7 doth put a difference between the E 4714
12:23 LORD will pass through to smite the E; 4714
12:27 when he smote the E, and delivered our 4714
12:30 he, and all his servants, and all the E; 4714
12:33 the E were urgent upon the people, that 4714
12:35 and they borrowed of the E jewels of silver, 4714
12:36 gave the people favour in the sight of the E, 4714
12:36 *as they required*. And they spoiled the E. 4714
14: 4 that the E may know that I *am* the LORD. 4714
14: 9 the E pursued after them (all the horses *and* 4714
14:10 and behold, the E marched after them; 4714
14:12 Let us alone, that we may serve the E? 4714
14:12 For *it had been* better for us to serve the E, 4714
14:13 for the E whom ye have seen to day, 4714
14:17 I will harden the hearts of the E, and 4714
14:18 the E shall know that I *am* the LORD, 4714
14:20 And it came between the camp of the E and 4714
14:23 the E pursued, and went in after them to 4714
14:24 the host of the E through the pillar of fire 4714
14:24 of the cloud, and troubled the host of the E, 4714
14:25 so that the E said, Let us flee from the face 4714
14:25 the LORD fighteth for them against the E. 4714
Ex 14:26 that the waters may come again upon the E, 4714
14:27 the E fled against it; and the LORD 4714
14:27 the LORD overthrew the E in the midst of 4714
14:30 Israel that day out of the hand of the E; 4714
14:30 Israel saw the E dead upon the sea shore. 4714
14:31 work which the LORD did upon the E: 4714
15:26 which I have brought upon the E: 4714
18: 8 unto Pharaoh and to the E for Israel's sake, 4714
18: 9 he had delivered out of the hand of the E. 4714
18:10 hath delivered you out of the hand of the E, 4714
18:10 the people from under the hand of the E. 4714
19: 4 Ye have seen what I did unto the E, and 4714
32:12 Wherefore should the E speak, and say, 4714
Nu 14:13 the E shall hear *it*, (for thou broughtest up 4714
20:15 and the E vexed us, and our fathers: 4714
33: 3 with a high hand in the sight of all the E. 4714
33: 4 For the E buried all *their* firstborn, which 4714
Dt 26: 6 the E evil entreated us, and afflicted us, 4713
Jos 24: 6 the E pursued after your fathers with 4714
24: 7 he put darkness between you and the E, and 4714
Jdg 6: 9 I delivered you out of the hand of the E, 4714
10:11 *Did* not *I deliver you* from the E, and 4714
1Sa 4: 8 these *are* the Gods that smote the E with all 4714
6: 6 as the E and Pharaoh hardened their hearts? 4714
10:18 delivered you out of the hand of the E, and 4714
2Ki 7: 6 and the kings of the E, to come upon us. 4714
Ezr 9: 1 the Moabites, the E, and the Amorites. 4713
Isa 19: 2 I will set the E against the Egyptians: and 4714
19: 2 I will set the Egyptians against the E: and 4714
19: 4 the E will I give over into the hand of a 4714
19:21 the E shall know the LORD in that day, 4714
19:23 and the E shall serve *with* the Assyrians. 4714
20: 4 king of Assyria lead away the E prisoners, 4714
30: 7 For the E shall help in vain, and to no 4714
31: 3 Now the E *are* men, and not God; and 4714
Jer 43:13 the houses of the gods of the E shall he 4714
La 5: 6 We have given the hand *to* the E, *and to* 4714
Eze 16:26 with the E thy neighbours, 1121+4714
23:21 in bruising thy teats by the E for the paps 4714
29:12 I will scatter the E among the nations, and 4714
29:13 At the end of forty years will I gather the E 4714
30:23 I will scatter the E among the nations, and 4714
30:26 I will scatter the E among the nations, and 4714
Ac 7:22 was learned in all the wisdom of the E, 124
Heb 11:29 which the E assaying to do were drowned. 124

EHI (1)

Ge 46:21 Ashbel, Gera, and Naaman, E, and Rosh, 278

EHUD (10)

Jdg 3:15 E the son of Gera, a Benjamite, a man 164
3:16 E made him a dagger which had two edges, 164
3:20 E came unto him; and he was sitting in a 164
3:20 E said, I have a message from God unto 164
3:21 E put forth his left hand, and took the dagger 164
3:23 E went forth through the porch, and shut 164
3:26 E escaped while they tarried, and passed 164
4: 1 the sight of the LORD, when E was dead. 164
1Ch 7:10 E, and Chenaanah, and Zethan, and 164
8: 6 these *are* the sons of E: these *are* the heads 261

EIGHT (81) [EIGHTH]

Ge 5: 4 he had begotten Seth were e hundred years: 8083
5: 7 Seth lived after he begat Enos e hundred 8083
5:10 Enos lived after he begat Cainan e hundred 8083
5:13 Cainan lived after he begat Mahalaleel e 8083
5:16 Mahalaleel lived after he begat Jared e 8083
5:17 all the days of Mahalaleel were e hundred 8083
5:19 Jared lived after he begat Enoch e hundred 8083
17:12 he that is e days old shall be circumcised 8083
21: 4 Abraham circumcised his son Isaac being e 8083
22:23 these e Milcah did bear to Nahor, 8083
Ex 26: 2 The length of one curtain *shall be* e and 8083
26:25 they shall be e boards, and their sockets *of* 8083
36: 9 of one curtain *was* twenty and e cubits, 8083
36:30 there were e boards; and their sockets *were* 8083
Nu 2:24 and e thousand and an hundred, 8083
3:28 upward, *were* e thousand and six hundred, 8083
4:48 were e thousand and five hundred and 8083
7: 8 and e oxen he gave unto the sons of Merari, 8083
29:29 on the sixth day e bullocks, two rams, *and* 8083
35: 7 to the Levites *shall be* forty and e cities: 8083
Dt 2:14 the brook Zered, *was* thirty and e years; 8083
Jos 21:41 *were* forty and e cities with their suburbs. 8083
Jdg 3: 8 Israel served Chushan-rishathaim e years. 8083
12:14 ten ass colts: and he judged Israel e years. 8083
1Sa 4:15 Now Eli *was* ninety and e years old; and 8083
17:12 whose name *was* Jesse; and he had e sons: 8083
2Sa 23: 8 *he lift up his spear* against e hundred, 8083
24: 9 there were in Israel e hundred thousand 8083
1Ki 7:10 stones of ten cubits, and stones of e cubits. 8083
2Ki 8:17 and he reigned e years in Jerusalem. 8083
10:36 Israel in Samaria *was* twenty and e years. 8083
22: 1 Josiah *was* e years old when he *began* to 8083
1Ch 12:24 and spear *were* six thousand and e hundred, 8083
12:30 of Ephraim twenty thousand and e hundred, 8083
12:35 and e thousand and six hundred. 8083
16:38 with their brethren, threescore and e; 8083
23: 3 man by man, was thirty and e thousand. 8083
24: 4 e among the sons of Ithamar according to 8083
25: 7 was two hundred fourscore and e. 8083
2Ch 11:21 begat twenty and e sons, and 8083
13: 3 him with e hundred thousand chosen men, 8083
21: 5 and he reigned e years in Jerusalem. 8083
21:20 he reigned in Jerusalem e years, and 8083
29:17 the house of the LORD in e days; 8083
34: 1 Josiah *was* e years old when he *began* to 8083
36: 9 Jehoiachin *was* e years old when he *began* 8083
Ezr 2: 6 Joab, two thousand e hundred and twelve. 8083
2:16 children of Ater of Hezekiah, ninety and e. 8083
2:23 men of Anathoth, an hundred twenty and e. 8083
2:41 of Asaph, an hundred twenty and e. 8083
8:11 of Bebai, and with him twenty and e males. 8083
Ne 7:11 two thousand and e hundred *and* eighteen. 8083
Ne 7:13 children of Zattu, e hundred forty and five. 8083
7:15 children of Binnui, six hundred forty and e. 8083
7:16 of Bebai, six hundred twenty and e. 8083
7:21 children of Ater of Hezekiah, ninety and e. 8083
7:22 of Hashum, three hundred twenty and e. 8083
7:26 and Netophah, an hundred fourscore and e. 8083
7:27 men of Anathoth, an hundred twenty and e. 8083
7:44 children of Asaph, an hundred forty and e. 8083
7:45 children of Shobai, an hundred thirty and e. 8083
11: 6 four hundred threescore and e valiant men. 8083
11: 8 Sallai, nine hundred twenty and e. 8083
11:12 work of the house *were* e hundred twenty 8083
11:14 *men* of valour, an hundred twenty and e: 8083
Ecc 11: 2 Give a portion to seven, and also to e; 8083
Jer 41:15 escaped from Johanan with e men, 8083
52:29 captive from Jerusalem e hundred thirty 8083
Eze 40: 9 measured he the porch of the gate, e cubits; 8083
40:31 and the going up to it *had* e steps. 8083
40:34 that side: and the going up to it *had* e steps. 8083
40:37 that side: and the going up to it *had* e steps. 8083
40:41 e tables, whereupon they slew *their* 8083
43:27 *that* upon the e day, and *so* forward, 8066
Mic 5: 5 him seven shepherds, and e principal men. 8083
Lk 2:21 And when e days were accomplished for 3638
9:28 And it came to pass about an e days after 3638
Jn 5: 5 which had an infirmity thirty *and* e years. 3638
20:26 And after e days again his disciples were 3638
Ac 9:33 which had kept his bed e years, and was 3638
1Pe 3:20 that is, e souls were saved by water. 3638

EIGHTEEN (22) [EIGHTEENTH]

Ge 14:14 three hundred and e, and 6240+8083
Jdg 3:14 Eglon the king of Moab e years. 6240+8083
10: 8 e years, all the children of Israel that 6240+8083
20:25 of Israel again e thousand men; 6240+8083
20:44 there fell of Benjamin e thousand 6240+8083
2Sa 8:13 valley of salt, *being* e thousand *men*. 6240+8083
1Ki 7:15 *of* brass, of e cubits high apiece: 6240+8083
2Ki 24: 8 Jehoiachin *was* e years old when he 6240+8083
25:17 The height of the one pillar *was* e 6240+8083
1Ch 12:31 of the half tribe of Manasseh e 6240+8083
18:12 in the valley of salt e thousand. 6240+8083
26: 9 had sons and brethren, strong men, e. 6240+8083
29: 7 *of* brass e **thousand** 505+7239+8083+2050.1
2Ch 11:21 (for he took e wives, and 6240+8083
Ezr 8: 9 with him two hundred and e males. 6240+8083
8:18 with his sons and his brethren, e; 6240+8083
Ne 7:11 and eight hundred *and* e. 6240+8083
Jer 52:21 the height of one pillar *was* e cubits; 6240+8083
Eze 48:35 *It was* round about e thousand 6240+8083
Lk 13: 4 Or those e, upon whom the tower 1176+2532+3638
13:11 a spirit of infirmity e years, 1176+2532+3638
13:16 Satan hath bound, lo *these* e 1176+2532+3638

EIGHTEENTH (11) [EIGHTEEN]

1Ki 15: 1 Now in the e year of king Jeroboam 6240+8083
2Ki 3: 1 e year of Jehoshaphat king of Judah, 6240+8083
22: 3 it came to pass in the e year of king 6240+8083
23:23 in the e year of king Josiah, 6240+8083
1Ch 24:15 to Hezir, the e to Aphses, 6240+8083
25:25 The e to Hanani, *he*, his sons, and 6240+8083
2Ch 13: 1 Now in the e year of king Jeroboam 6240+8083
34: 8 Now in the e year of his reign, 6240+8083
35:19 In the e year of the reign of Josiah 6240+8083
Jer 32: 1 *was* the e year of Nebuchadrezzar. 6240+8083
52:29 In the e year of Nebuchadrezzar he 6240+8083

EIGHTH (38) [EIGHT]

Ex 22:30 his dam; on the e day thou shalt give it me. 8066
Lev 9: 1 it came to pass on the e day, *that* Moses 8066
12: 3 in the e day the flesh of his foreskin shall 8066
14:10 on the e day he shall take two he lambs 8066
14:23 he shall bring them on the e day for his 8066
15:14 on the e day he shall take to him two 8066
15:29 on the e day she shall take unto her two 8066
22:27 from the e day and thenceforth it shall be 8066
23:36 on the e day shall be a holy convocation 8066
23:39 and on the e day *shall be* a sabbath. 8066
25:22 ye shall sow the e year, and eat *yet* of old 8066
Nu 6:10 on the e day he shall bring two turtles, or 8066
7:54 On the e day *offered* Gamaliel the son of 8066
29:35 On the e day ye shall have a solemn 8066
1Ki 6:38 in the month Bul, which *is* the e month, 8066
8:66 On the e day he sent the people away: and 8066
12:32 Jeroboam ordained a feast in the e month, 8066
12:33 in Beth-el the fifteenth day of the e month, 8066
16:29 e year of Asa king of Judah *began* Ahab 8083
2Ki 15: 8 e year of Azariah king of Judah did 8083
24:12 the king of Babylon took him in the e year 8083
1Ch 12:12 Johanan the e, Elzabad the ninth, 8066
24:10 The seventh to Hakkoz, the e to Abijah, 8066
25:15 The e *to* Jeshaiah, *he*, his sons, and 8066
26: 5 Issachar the seventh, Peulthai the e: 8066
27:11 The e *captain* for the eighth month *was* 8066
27:11 The eighth *captain* for the e month *was* 8066
2Ch 7: 9 in the e day they made a solemn assembly: 8066
29:17 on the e day of the month came they to 8083
34: 3 For in the e year of his reign, while he was 8083
Ne 8:18 on the e day *was* a solemn assembly, 8066
Zec 1: 1 In the e month, in the second year of 8066
Lk 1:59 *that* on the e day they came to circumcise 3590
Ac 7: 8 begat Isaac, and circumcised him the e day; 3590
Php 3: 5 Circumcised the e **day**, of the stock of 3637
2Pe 2: 5 saved Noah the e *person*, a preacher of 3590
Rev 17:11 even he is the e, and is of the seven, and 3590
21:20 the e, beryl; the ninth, a topaz; the tenth, 3590

EIGHTIETH (1) [EIGHTY]

1Ki 6: 1 e year after the children of Israel were 8084

EIGHTY (3) [EIGHTIETH, FOURSCORE]

Ge 5:25 Methuselah lived an hundred e and seven 8084
5:26 after he begat Lamech seven hundred e 8084
5:28 Lamech lived an hundred e and two years, 8084

EITHER (41)
Ge 31:24 Take heed that thou speak not to Jacob e 4480
31:29 heed that thou speak not to Jacob e good 4480
Lev 10: 1 took e[S] of them his censer, and put fire 376
13:49 e in the warp, or in the woof, or in any thing 176
13:51 e in the warp, or in the woof, or in a skin, or 176
13:53 e in the warp, or in the woof, or in any thing 176
13:57 e in the warp, or in the woof, or in any thing 176
13:58 e warp, or woof, or whatsoever thing of skin 176
13:59 e in the warp, or woof, or any thing of skins, 176
22:23 E a bullock or a lamb that hath any thing 2050.1
25:49 E his uncle, or his uncle's son, may redeem 176
Nu 6: 2 When e man or woman shall separate NIH
22:26 where was no way to turn e to the right NIH
24:13 to do e good or bad of mine own mind; NIH
Dt 17: 3 e the sun, or moon, or any of the host of 2050.1
28:51 which also shall not leave thee e corn, wine, NIH
Jdg 9: 2 e that all the sons of Jerubbaal, which are 518
1Sa 20: 2 my father will do nothing e great or small, NIH
25:31 e that thou hast shed blood causeless, or 2050.1
30: 2 e great or small, but carried them away, and 4480
1Ki 7:15 a line of twelve cubits did compass e of 8145
10:19 on e side on 2088+2088+4480+4480+2050.1
18:27 e he is talking, or he is pursuing, or he is in 3588
1Ch 21:12 E three years' famine; or three months to be 518
2Ch 18: 9 Jehoshaphat king of Judah sat e[S] of them on 376
Ecc 9: 1 no man knoweth e love or hatred by all that 1571
11: 6 e this or that, or whether they both shall 1886.2
Isa 7:11 ask it e in the depth, or in the height above. NIH
17: 8 have made, e the groves, or the images. 2050.1
Eze 21:16 or other, e on the right hand, or on the left, NIH
Mt 6:24 for e he will hate the one, and love 2228
12:33 E make the tree good, and his fruit good; or 2228
Lk 6:42 E how canst thou say to thy brother, 2228
15: 8 E what woman having ten pieces of silver, 2228
16:13 for e he will hate the one, and love 2228
Jn 19:18 other with him, on e side one, 1782+1782+2532
Ac 17:21 but e to tell, or to hear some new thing.) NIG
1Co 14: 6 except I shall speak to you e by revelation, 2228
Php 3:12 already attained, e were already perfect: 2228
Jas 3:12 e a vine, figs? so can no fountain both yield 2228
Rev 22: 2 and of e side of the river, 1782+1782+2532

EKER (1)
1Ch 2:27 Jerahmeel were, Maaz, and Jamin, and E. 6134

EKRON (22) [EKRONITES]
Jos 13: 3 even unto the borders of E northward, 6138
15:11 the border went out unto the side of E 6138
15:45 E, with her towns and her villages: 6138
15:46 From E even unto the sea, all that lay near 6138
19:43 And Elon, and Thimnathah, and E, 6138
Jdg 1:18 coast thereof, and E with the coast thereof. 6138
1Sa 5:10 Therefore they sent the ark of God to E. 6138
5:10 came to pass, as the ark of God came to E, 6138
6:16 seen it, they returned to E the same day. 6138
6:17 for Askelon one, for Gath one, for E one; 6138
7:14 restored to Israel, from E even unto Gath; 6138
17:52 come to the valley, and to the gates of E. 6138
17:52 to Shaaraim, even unto Gath, and unto E. 6138
2Ki 1: 2 inquire of Baal-zebub the god of E whether 6138
1: 3 go to inquire of Baal-zebub the god of E? 6138
1: 6 to inquire of Baal-zebub the god of E? 6138
1:16 to inquire of Baal-zebub the god of E, 6138
Jer 25:20 and E, and the remnant of Ashdod: 6138
Am 1: 8 and I will turn mine hand against E: 6138
Zep 2: 4 at the noon day, and E shall be rooted up. 6138
Zec 9: 5 shall see it, and be very sorrowful, and E; 6138
9: 7 as a governor in Judah, and E as a Jebusite. 6138

EKRONITES (2) [EKRON]
Jos 13: 3 the Eshkalonites, the Gittites, and the E; 6139
1Sa 5:10 came to Ekron, that the E cried out, saying, 6139

ELADAH (1)
1Ch 7:20 his son, and E his son, and Tahath his son, 497

ELAH (17)
Ge 36:41 Duke Aholibamah, duke E, duke Pinon, 425
1Sa 17: 2 pitched by the valley of E, and set the battle 425
17:19 all the men of Israel, were in the valley of E, 425
21: 9 whom thou slewest in the valley of E, 425
1Ki 4:18 Shimei the son of E, in Benjamin: 414
16: 6 in Tirzah: and E his son reigned in his stead. 425
16: 8 sixth year of Asa king of Judah began E 425
16:13 the sins of E his son, by which they sinned, 425
16:14 Now the rest of the acts of E, and all that he 425
2Ki 15:30 Hoshea the son of E made a conspiracy 425
17: 1 E to reign in Samaria over Israel nine years. 425
18: 1 third year of Hoshea son of E king of Israel, 425
18: 9 year of Hoshea son of E king of Israel, 425
1Ch 1:52 Duke Aholibamah, duke E, duke Pinon, 425
4:15 the son of Jephunneh; Iru, E, and Naam: 425
4:15 and Naam: and the sons of E, even Kenaz. 425
9: 8 and E the son of Uzzi, the son of Michri, and 425

ELAM (28) [ELAMITES]
Ge 10:22 E, and Asshur, and Arphaxad, and Lud, and 5867
14: 1 Chedorlaomer king of E, and Tidal king of 5867
14: 9 With Chedorlaomer the king of E, and 5867
1Ch 1:17 E, and Asshur, and Arphaxad, and Lud, and 5867
8:24 And Hananiah, and E, and Antothijah, 5867
26: 3 E the fifth, Jehohanan the sixth, 5867
Ezr 2: 7 The children of E, a thousand two hundred 5867
2:31 The children of the other E, a thousand two 5867
8: 7 of the sons of E; Jeshaiah the son of 5867
10: 2 one of the sons of E, answered and 5867
10:26 of the sons of E; Mattaniah, Zechariah, 5867
Ne 7:12 The children of E, a thousand two hundred 5867
7:34 The children of the other E, a thousand two 5867
10:14 Parosh, Pahath-moab, E, Zatthu, Bani, 5867
12:42 and Malchijah, and E, and Ezer. 5867
Isa 11:11 from E, and from Shinar, and 5867
21: 2 Go up, O E: besiege, O Media; all 5867
22: 6 E bare the quiver with chariots of men and 5867
Jer 25:25 all the kings of E, and all the kings of 5867
49:34 E in the beginning of the reign of Zedekiah 5867
49:35 Behold, I will break the bow of E, the chief 5867
49:36 upon E will I bring the four winds from 5867
49:36 whither the outcasts of E shall not come. 5867
49:37 For I will cause E to be dismayed before 5867
49:38 I will set my throne in E, and will destroy 5867
49:39 that I will bring again the captivity of E, 5867
Eze 32:24 There is E and all her multitude round 5867
Da 8: 2 in the palace, which is in the province of E; 5867

ELAMITES (2) [ELAM]
Ezr 4: 9 the Susanchites, the Dehavites, and the E, 5962
Ac 2: 9 and E, and the dwellers in Mesopotamia, 1639

ELAPSED See EXPIRED

ELASAH (2)
Ezr 10:22 Ishmael, Nethaneel, Jozabad, and E. 501
Jer 29: 3 By the hand of E the son of Shaphan, and 501

ELATH (5) [ELOTH]
Dt 2: 8 through the way of the plain from E, and 359
2Ki 14:22 He built E, and restored it to Judah, after that 359
16: 6 At that time Rezin king of Syria recovered E 359
16: 6 Elath to Syria, and drave the Jews from E: 359
16: 6 the Syrians came to E, and dwelt there unto 359

EL-BERITH See BERITH; GOD

EL-BETH-EL (1) [BETH-EL]
Ge 35: 7 built there an altar, and called the place E: 416

ELDAAH (2)
Ge 25: 4 and Epher, and Hanoch, and Abidah, and E. 420
1Ch 1:33 and Epher, and Henoch, and Abida, and E. 420

ELDAD (2)
Nu 11:26 the name of the one was E, and the name of 419
11:27 said, E and Medad do prophesy in the camp. 419

ELDER (20) [OLD]
Ge 10:21 the brother of Japheth the e, even to him 1419
25:23 and the e shall serve the younger. 7227
27:42 these words of Esau her e son were told to 1419
29:16 the name of the e was Leah, and the name 1419
1Sa 18:17 to David, Behold my e daughter Merab, 1419
1Ki 2:22 for he is mine e brother; even for 1419+4480
Job 15:10 and very aged men, much e than thy father. 3117
32: 4 because they were e than he. 2205+3117+3807.1
Eze 16:46 thine e sister is Samaria, she and 1419
16:61 receive thy sisters, thine e and thy younger: 1419
23: 4 the names of them were Aholah the e, and 1419
Lk 15:25 Now his e son was in the field: and as he 4245
Ro 9:12 unto her, The e shall serve the younger. 3187
1Ti 5: 1 Rebuke not an e, but intreat him as a father; 4245
5: 2 The e women as mothers; the younger as 4245
5:19 Against an e receive not an accusation, but 4245
1Pe 5: 1 who am also an e, and a witness of 4850
5: 5 ye younger, submit yourselves unto the e. 4245
2Jn 1: 1 The e unto the elect lady and her children, 4245
3Jn 1: 1 The e unto the wellbeloved Gaius, whom I 4245

ELDERS (179) [OLD]
Ge 50: 7 the e of his house, and all the elders of 2205
50: 7 and all the e of the land of Egypt, 2205
Ex 3:16 gather the e of Israel together, and say unto 2205
3:18 thou shalt come, thou and the e of Israel, 2205
4:29 gathered together all the e of the children of 2205
12:21 Moses called for all the e of Israel, and 2205
17: 5 and take with thee of the e of Israel; 2205
17: 6 Moses did so in the sight of the e of Israel. 2205
18:12 Aaron came, and all the e of Israel, to eat 2205
19: 7 and called for the e of the people, 2205
24: 1 and Abihu, and seventy of the e of Israel; 2205
24: 9 and Abihu, and seventy of the e of Israel: 2205
24:14 he said unto the e, Tarry ye here for us, 2205
Lev 4:15 the e of the congregation shall lay their 2205
9: 1 and his sons, and the e of Israel; 2205
Nu 11:16 Gather unto me seventy men of the e of 2205
11:16 whom thou knowest to be the e of 2205
11:24 gathered the seventy men of the e of 2205
11:25 upon him, and gave it unto the seventy e: 2205
11:30 him into the camp, he and the e of Israel. 2205
16:25 Abiram; and the e of Israel followed him. 2205
22: 4 Moab said unto the e of Midian, Now shall 2205
22: 7 the e of Moab and the elders of Midian 2205
22: 7 the e of Midian departed with the rewards 2205
Dt 5:23 all the heads of your tribes, and your e; 2205
19:12 the e of his city shall send and fetch him 2205
21: 2 thy e and thy judges shall come forth, and 2205
21: 3 even the e of that city shall take a heifer, 2205
21: 4 the e of that city shall bring down the heifer 2205
21: 6 all the e of that city, that are next unto 2205
21:19 and bring him out unto the e of his city, and 2205
21:20 they shall say unto the e of his city, 2205
22:15 virginity unto the e of the city in the gate: 2205
22:16 the damsel's father shall say unto the e, 2205
22:17 they shall spread the cloth before the e of 2205
22:18 the e of that city shall take that man and 2205
25: 7 brother's wife go up to the gate unto the e, 2205
25: 8 the e of his city shall call him, and 2205
25: 9 come unto him in the presence of the e, 2205
27: 1 Moses with the e of Israel commanded 2205
29:10 your e, and your officers, with all the men 2205
31: 9 of the LORD, and unto all the e of Israel. 2205
31:28 Gather unto me all the e of your tribes, and 2205
32: 7 shew thee; thy e, and they will tell thee. 2205
Jos 7: 6 he and the e of Israel, and put dust upon 2205
8:10 and went up, he and the e of Israel, 2205
8:33 and their e, and officers, and their judges, 2205
9:11 Wherefore our e and all the inhabitants of 2205
20: 4 shall declare his cause in the ears of the e 2205
Jos 23: 2 and for their e, and for their heads, and 2205
24: 1 called for the e of Israel, and for their 2205
24:31 all the days of the e that overlived Joshua, 2205
Jdg 2: 7 all the days of the e that outlived Joshua, 2205
8:14 the e thereof, even threescore 2205
8:16 he took the e of the city, and thorns of 2205
11: 5 the e of Gilead went to fetch Jephthah out 2205
11: 7 Jephthah said unto the e of Gilead, Did not 2205
11: 8 the e of Gilead said unto Jephthah, 2205
11: 9 Jephthah said unto the e of Gilead, If ye 2205
11:10 the e of Gilead said unto Jephthah, 2205
11:11 Jephthah went with the e of Gilead, and 2205
21:16 the e of the congregation said, How shall 2205
Ru 4: 2 he took ten men of the e of the city, and 2205
4: 4 and before the e of my people. 2205
4: 9 Boaz said unto the e, and unto all 2205
4:11 the gate, and the e, said, We are witnesses. 2205
1Sa 4: 3 come into the camp, the e of Israel said, 2205
8: 4 all the e of Israel gathered themselves 2205
11: 3 the e of Jabesh said unto him, Give us 2205
15:30 before the e of my people, and 2205
16: 4 the e of the town trembled at his coming, 2205
30:26 he sent of the spoil unto the e of Judah, 2205
2Sa 3:17 Abner had communication with the e of 2205
5: 3 So all the e of Israel came to the king to 2205
12:17 the e of his house arose, and went to him, 2205
17: 4 Absalom well, and all the e of Israel. 2205
17:15 counsel Absalom and the e of Israel; 2205
19:11 Speak unto the e of Judah, saying, 2205
1Ki 8: 1 Solomon assembled the e of Israel, 2205
8: 3 all the e of Israel came, and the priests took 2205
20: 7 the king of Israel called all the e of 2205
20: 8 all the e and all the people said unto him, 2205
21: 8 sent the letters unto the e and to the nobles 2205
21:11 even the e and the nobles who were 2205
2Ki 6:32 sat in his house, and the e sat with him; 2205
6:32 messenger came to him, he said to the e, 2205
10: 1 to the e, and to them that brought up 2205
10: 5 the e also, and the bringers up of 2205
19: 2 Shebna the scribe, and the e of the priests, 2205
23: 1 they gathered unto him all the e of Judah 2205
1Ch 11: 3 Therefore came all the e of Israel to 2205
15:25 the e of Israel, and the captains over 2205
21:16 the e of Israel, who were clothed in 2205
2Ch 5: 2 Solomon assembled the e of Israel, and 2205
5: 4 all the e of Israel came; and the Levites 2205
34:29 gathered together all the e of Judah and 2205
Ezr 5: 5 the eye of their God was upon the e of 7868
5: 9 asked we those e, and said unto them thus, 7868
6: 7 the e of the Jews build this house of God in 7868
6: 8 e of these Jews for the building of this 7868
6:14 the e of the Jews builded, and 7868
10: 8 to the counsel of the princes and the e, 2205
10:14 with them the e of every city, and 2205
Ps 107:32 and praise him in the assembly of the e. 2205
Pr 31:23 when he sitteth among the e of the land. 2205
Isa 37: 2 the e of the priests covered with sackcloth, 2205
Jer 26:17 rose up certain of the e of the land, and 2205
29: 1 of the e which were carried away captives, 2205
La 1:19 and mine e gave up the ghost in the city, 2205
2:10 The e of the daughter of Zion sit upon 2205
4:16 of the priests, they favoured not the e. 2205
5:12 the faces of e were not honoured. 2205
5:14 The e have ceased from the gate, the young 2205
Eze 8: 1 and the e of Judah sat before me, 2205
14: 1 came certain of the e of Israel unto me, 2205
20: 1 that certain of the e of Israel came to 2205
20: 3 speak unto the e of Israel, and say unto 2205
Joel 1:14 gather the e and all the inhabitants of 2205
2:16 assemble the e, gather the children, and 2205
Mt 15: 2 disciples transgress the tradition of the e? 4245
16:21 and suffer many things of the e and 4245
21:23 the e of the people came unto him as he 4245
26: 3 and the scribes, and the e of the people, 4245
26:47 from the chief priests and e of the people. 4245
26:57 the scribes and the e were assembled. 4245
26:59 the chief priests, and e, and all the council, 4245
27: 1 e of the people took counsel against Jesus 4245
27: 3 pieces of silver to the chief priests and e, 4245
27:12 he was accused of the chief priests and e, 4245
27:20 e persuaded the multitude that they should 4245
27:41 priests mocking him, with the scribes and e, 4245
28:12 And when they were assembled with the e, 4245
Mk 7: 3 eat not, holding the tradition of the e. 4245
7: 5 disciples according to the tradition of the e, 4245
8:31 suffer many things, and be rejected of the e, 4245
11:27 the chief priests, and the scribes, and the e, 4245
14:43 the chief priests and the scribes and the e. 4245
14:53 the chief priests and the e and the scribes. 4245
15: 1 chief priests held a consultation with the e 4245
Lk 7: 3 of Jesus, he sent unto him the e of the Jews, 4245
9:22 and be rejected of the e and chief priests 4245
20: 1 and the scribes came upon him with the e, 4245
22:52 and captains of the temple, and the e, 4245
22:66 the e of the people and the chief priests and 4244
Ac 4: 5 that their rulers, and e, and scribes, 4245
4: 8 Ye rulers of the people, and e of Israel, 4245
4:23 the chief priests and e had said unto them. 4245
6:12 and the e, and the scribes, and came upon 4245
11:30 sent it to the e by the hands of Barnabas 4245
14:23 And when they had ordained them e in 4245
15: 2 unto the apostles and e about this question. 4245
15: 4 and of the apostles and e, and they declared 4245
15: 6 e came together for to consider of this 4245
15:22 Then pleased it the apostles and e, with 4245
15:23 The apostles and e and brethren send 4245
16: 4 the apostles and e which were at Jerusalem. 4245
20:17 to Ephesus, and called the e of the church. 4245
21:18 us unto James; and all the e were present. 4245
22: 5 bear me witness, and all the estate of the e: 4244
23:14 And they came to the chief priests and e, 4245
24: 1 the high priest descended with the e, 4245
25:15 the e of the Jews informed me, desiring to 4245
1Ti 5:17 Let the e that rule well be counted worthy 4245
Tit 1: 5 and ordain e in every city, as I had 4245

Heb 11: 2 For by it the **e** obtained a good report. *4245*
Jas 5:14 let him call for the **e** of the church; and *4245*
1Pe 5: 1 The **e** which are among you I exhort, *4245*
Rev 4: 4 the seats I saw four and twenty **e** sitting, *4245*
4:10 twenty **e** fall down before him that sat on *4245*
5: 5 And one of the **e** saith unto me, Weep not: *4245*
5: 6 of the four beasts, and in the midst of the **e**, *4245*
5: 8 *and* twenty **e** fell down before the Lamb, *4245*
5:11 about the throne and the beasts and the **e**: *4245*
5:14 And the four *and* twenty **e** fell down and *4245*
7:11 and *about* the **e** and the four beasts, and *4245*
7:13 And one of the **e** answered, saying unto me, *4245*
11:16 And the four and twenty **e**, which sat before *4245*
14: 3 and before the four beasts, and the **e**: *4245*
19: 4 And the four and twenty **e** and the four *4245*

ELDEST (14) [OLD]
Ge 24: 2 Abraham said unto his **e** servant of his 2205
27: 1 he called Esau his **e** son, and said unto him, 1419
27:15 Rebekah took goodly raiment of her **e** son 1419
44:12 *and* began at the **e**, and left at the youngest: 1419
Nu 1:20 Israel's **e son**, *by* their generations, 1060
26: 5 Reuben, the **e son** of Israel: the children of 1060
1Sa 17:13 the three **e** sons of Jesse went *and* 1419
17:14 the youngest: and the three **e** followed Saul. 1419
17:28 Eliab his **e** brother heard when he spake 1419
2Ki 3:27 he took his **e** son that should have reigned 1060
2Ch 22: 1 the Arabians to the camp had slain all the **e**. 7223
Job 1:13 drinking wine in their **e** brother's house: 1060
1:18 drinking wine in their **e** brother's house: 1060
Jn 8: 9 beginning at the **e**, *even* unto the last: *4245*

ELEAD (1)
1Ch 7:21 and Shuthelah his son, and Ezer, and **E**, 496

ELEADAH See ELADAH

ELEALEH (5)
Nu 32: 3 and **E**, and Shebam, and Nebo, and Beon, 500
32:37 built Heshbon, and **E**, and Kirjathaim, 500
Isa 15: 4 Heshbon shall cry, and **E**: their voice shall 500
16: 9 water thee *with* my tears, O Heshbon, and **E**: 500
Jer 48:34 From the cry of Heshbon *even* unto **E**, *and* 500

ELEASAH (4)
1Ch 2:39 Azariah begat Helez, and Helez begat **E**, 501
2:40 **E** begat Sisamai, and Sisamai begat 501
8:37 Rapha *was* his son, **E** his son, Azel his son: 501
9:43 Rephaiah his son, **E** his son, Azel his son. 501

ELEAZAR (74)
Ex 6:23 bare him Nadab, and Abihu, **E**, and Ithamar. 499
6:25 **E** Aaron's son took him *one* of the daughters 499
28: 1 Nadab and Abihu, **E** and Ithamar, 499
Lev 10: 6 unto **E** and unto Ithamar his sons, 499
10:12 unto **E** and unto Ithamar his sons that were 499
10:16 he was angry with **E** and Ithamar the sons of 499
Nu 3: 2 the firstborn, and Abihu, **E**, and Ithamar. 499
3: 4 **E** and Ithamar ministered in the priest's 499
3:32 **E** the son of Aaron the priest *shall be* chief 499
4:16 *to* the office of **E** the son of Aaron the priest 499
16:37 Speak unto **E** the son of Aaron the priest, 499
16:39 **E** the priest took the brasen censers, 499
19: 3 ye shall give her unto **E** the priest, that he 499
19: 4 **E** the priest shall take of her blood with his 499
20:25 Take Aaron and **E** his son, and bring them 499
20:26 his garments, and put them upon **E** his son: 499
20:28 his garments, and put them upon **E** his son; 499
20:28 Moses and **E** came down from the mount. 499
25: 7 when Phinehas, the son of **E**, the son of 499
25:11 Phinehas, the son of **E**, the son of Aaron 499
26: 1 and unto **E** the son of Aaron the priest, 499
26: 3 **E** the priest spake with them in the plains of 499
26:60 was born Nadab, and Abihu, **E**, and Ithamar. 499
26:63 were numbered by Moses and **E** the priest, 499
27: 2 before **E** the priest, and before the princes 499
27:19 set him before **E** the priest, and before all 499
27:21 he shall stand before **E** the priest, who shall 499
27:22 set him before **E** the priest, and before all 499
31: 6 them and Phinehas the son of **E** the priest, 499
31:12 **E** the priest, and unto the congregation of 499
31:13 **E** the priest, and all the princes of 499
31:21 **E** the priest said unto the men of war which 499
31:26 **E** the priest, and the chief fathers of 499
31:29 *it* of their half, and give *it* unto **E** the priest, 499
31:31 **E** the priest did as the LORD commanded 499
31:41 unto **E** the priest, as the LORD commanded 499
31:51 and **E** the priest took the gold of them, 499
31:54 **E** the priest took the gold of the captains of 499
32: 2 to **E** the priest, and unto the princes of 499
32:28 So concerning them Moses commanded **E** 499
34:17 **E** the priest, and Joshua the son of Nun. 499
Dt 10: 6 **E** his son ministered in the priest's office in 499
Jos 14: 1 which **E** the priest, and Joshua the son of 499
17: 4 And they came near before **E** the priest, and 499
19:51 which **E** the priest, and Joshua the son of 499
21: 1 the fathers of the Levites unto **E** the priest, 499
22:13 of Gilead, Phinehas the son of **E** the priest, 499
22:31 Phinehas the son of **E** the priest said unto 499
22:32 Phinehas the son of **E** the priest, and 499
24:33 **E** the son of Aaron died; and they buried 499
Jdg 20:28 Phinehas, the son of **E**, the son of Aaron, 499
1Sa 7: 1 sanctified **E** his son to keep the ark of 499
2Sa 23: 9 after him *was* **E** the son of Dodo 499
1Ch 6: 3 Nadab, and Abihu, **E**, and Ithamar. 499
6: 4 **E** begat Phinehas, Phinehas begat Abishua, 499
6:50 **E** his son, Phinehas his son, Abishua his son, 499
9:20 Phinehas the son of **E** was the ruler over 499
11:12 after him *was* **E** the son of Dodo, 499
23:21 and Mushi. The sons of Mahli; **E**, and Kish. 499
23:22 And **E** died, and had no sons, but daughters: 499
24: 1 Nadab, and Abihu, **E**, and Ithamar. 499
24: 2 therefore **E** and Ithamar executed the priest's 499
24: 3 both Zadok of the sons of **E**, and 499
1Ch 24: 4 of the sons of **E** than of the sons of Ithamar; 499
24: 4 Among the sons of **E** *there were* sixteen 499
24: 5 were of the sons of **E**, and of the sons of 499
24: 6 one principal household being taken for **E**, 499
24:28 Of Mahli *came* **E**, who had no sons. 499
Ezr 7: 5 the son of Phinehas, the son of **E**, 499
8:33 and with him *was* **E** the son of Phinehas; and 499
10:25 Miamin, and **E**, and Malchijah, and Benaiah. 499
Ne 12:42 **E**, and Uzzi, and Jehohanan, and Malchijah, 499
Mt 1:15 And Eliud begat **E**; and Eleazar begat *1648*
1:15 and **E** begat Matthan; and Matthan begat *1648*

ELECT (17) [ELECT'S, ELECTED, ELECTION, ELECTS']
Isa 42: 1 mine **e**, *in whom* my soul delighteth; 972
45: 4 Jacob my servant's sake, and Israel mine **e**, 972
65: 9 mine **e** shall inherit it, and my servants shall 972
65:22 mine **e** shall long enjoy the work of their 972
Mt 24:24 *were* possible, *they shall* deceive the very **e**. *1588*
24:31 they shall gather together his **e** from *1588*
Mk 13:22 to seduce, if *it were* possible, even the **e**. *1588*
13:27 shall gather together his **e** from the four *1588*
Lk 18: 7 And shall not God avenge his own **e**, *1588*
Ro 8:33 lay any thing to the charge of God's **e**? *1588*
Col 3:12 as the **e** of God, holy and beloved, *1588*
1Ti 5:21 and the Lord Jesus Christ, and the **e** angels, *1588*
Tit 1: 1 according to the faith of God's **e**, and *1588*
1Pe 1: 2 **E** according to the foreknowledge of God *1588*
2: 6 lay in Sion a chief corner stone, **e**, precious: *1588*
2Jn 1: 1 The elder unto the **e** lady and her children, *1588*
1:13 The children of thy **e** sister greet thee. *1588*

ELECT'S (2) [ELECT]
Mt 24:22 for the **e** sake those days shall be shortened. *1588*
Mk 13:20 but for the **e** sake, whom he hath chosen, *1588*

ELECTED (1) [ELECT]
1Pe 5:13 **e together with** *you,* saluteth you; *4899*

ELECTION (6) [ELECT]
Ro 9:11 that the purpose of God according to **e** *1589*
11: 5 is a remnant according to the **e** of grace. *1589*
11: 7 but the **e** hath obtained *it,* and the rest were *1589*
11:28 but as touching the **e**, *they are* beloved for *1589*
1Th 1: 4 Knowing, brethren beloved, your **e** of God. *1589*
2Pe 1:10 diligence to make your calling and **e** sure: *1589*

ELECTS' (1) [ELECT]
2Ti 2:10 Therefore I endure all *things* for the **e** *1588*

ELEGANT See GORGEOUS

EL-ELOHE-ISRAEL (1) [ISRAEL]
Ge 33:20 And he erected there an altar, and called it **E**. 415

ELEMENTS (4)
Gal 4: 3 were in bondage under the **e** of the world: *4747*
4: 9 turn ye again to the weak and beggarly **e**, *4747*
2Pe 3:10 and the **e** shall melt with fervent heat, *4747*
3:12 and the **e** shall melt with fervent heat? *4747*

ELEPH (1)
Jos 18:28 Zelah, **E**, and Jebusi, which *is* Jerusalem, 507

ELEUZAI (1)
1Ch 12: 5 **E**, and Jerimoth, and Bealiah, and 498

ELEVEN (24) [ELEVENTH]
Ge 32:22 his **e** sons, and passed over the ford 259+6240
37: 9 and the **e** stars made obeisance to me. 259+6240
Ex 26: 7 **e** curtains shalt thou make. 6240+6249
26: 8 **e** curtains *shall be all* of one 6240+6249
36:14 **e** curtains he made them. 6240+6249
36:15 the **e** curtains *were* of one size. 6240+6249
Nu 29:20 on the third day **e** bullocks, 6240+6249
Dt 1: 2 (*There are* **e** days' *journey* from Horeb 259+6240
Jos 15:51 and Giloh; **e** cities with their villages. 259+6240
Jdg 16: 5 *us* **e hundred** *pieces* of silver. 505+3967+2050.1
17: 2 The **e hundred** *shekels* of 505+3967+2050.1
17: 3 **e hundred** *shekels* of silver to 505+3967+2050.1
2Ki 23:36 and he reigned **e** years in Jerusalem. 259+6240
24:18 and he reigned **e** years in Jerusalem. 259+6240
2Ch 36: 5 and he reigned **e** years in Jerusalem: 259+6240
36:11 and reigned **e** years in Jerusalem. 259+6240
Jer 52: 1 and he reigned **e** years in Jerusalem. 259+6240
Eze 40:49 and the breadth **e** cubits; 6240+6249
Mt 28:16 Then the **e** disciples went *away* into *1733*
Mk 16:14 Afterward he appeared unto the **e** as they *1733*
Lk 24: 9 and told all these *things* unto the **e**, and *1733*
24:33 and found the **e** gathered together, and *1733*
Ac 1:26 and he was numbered with the **e** apostles. *1733*
2:14 But Peter, standing up with the **e**, lift up his *1733*

ELEVENTH (20) [ELEVEN]
Nu 7:72 On the **e** day Pagiel the son of Ocran, 6240+6249
Dt 1: 3 in the **e** month, on the first *day* of 6240+6249
1Ki 6:38 in the **e** year, in the month Bul, 259+6240
2Ki 9:29 in the **e** year of Joram the son of Ahab 259+6240
25: 2 the city was besieged unto the **e** year 6240+6249
1Ch 12:13 Jeremiah the tenth, Machbanai the **e**. 6240+6249
24:12 The **e** to Eliashib, the twelfth to 6240+6249
25:18 The **e** *to* Azareel, *he,* his sons, and 6240+6249
27:14 The **e** *captain* for the eleventh month 6240+6249
27:14 The eleventh *captain* for the **e** month 6240+6249
Jer 1: 3 unto the end of the **e** year of 6240+6249
39: 2 *And* in the **e** year of Zedekiah, in 6240+6249
52: 5 So the city was besieged unto the **e** 6240+6249
Eze 26: 1 it came to pass in the **e** year, in 6240+6249
30:20 it came to pass in the **e** year, in 259+6240
31: 1 it came to pass in the **e** year, in 259+6240
Zec 1: 7 and twentieth day of the **e** month, 6240+6249
Mt 20: 6 And about the **e** hour he went out, and *1734*
20: 9 they came that *were hired* about the **e** hour, *1734*
Rev 21:20 the **e**, a jacinth; the twelfth, an amethyst. *1734*

ELHANAN (4)
2Sa 21:19 where **E** the son of Jaare-oregim, 445
23:24 the thirty; **E** the son of Dodo *of* Beth-lehem, 445
1Ch 11:26 of Joab, **E** the son of Dodo of Beth-lehem, 445
20: 5 **E** the son of Jair slew Lahmi the brother of 445

ELI (34) [ELI'S, ELOI]
1Sa 1: 3 the two sons of **E**, Hophni and Phinehas, 5941
1: 9 Now **E** the priest sat upon a seat by a post 5941
1:12 the LORD, that **E** marked her mouth. 5941
1:13 therefore **E** thought she had been drunken. 5941
1:14 **E** said unto her, How long wilt thou be 5941
1:17 **E** answered and said, Go in peace: and 5941
1:25 slew a bullock, and brought the child to **E**. 5941
2:11 unto the LORD before **E** the priest. 5941
2:12 Now the sons of **E** *were* sons of Belial; 5941
2:20 **E** blessed Elkanah and his wife, and said, 5941
2:22 Now **E** was very old, and heard all that his 5941
2:27 there came a man of God unto **E**, and said 5941
3: 1 ministered unto the LORD before **E**. 5941
3: 2 when **E** *was* laid down in his place, and 5941
3: 5 he ran unto **E**, and said, Here *am* I; for thou 5941
3: 6 Samuel arose and went to **E**, and said, 5941
3: 8 he arose and went to **E**, and said, Here *am* 5941
3: 8 **E** perceived that the LORD had called 5941
3: 9 Therefore **E** said unto Samuel, Go, 5941
3:12 In that day I will perform against **E** all 5941
3:14 I have sworn unto the house of **E**, 5941
3:15 And Samuel feared to shew **E** the vision. 5941
3:16 **E** called Samuel, and said, Samuel, my son. 5941
4: 4 the two sons of **E**, Hophni and Phinehas, 5941
4:11 the two sons of **E**, Hophni and Phinehas, 5941
4:13 **E** sat upon a seat *by* the wayside watching: 5941
4:14 when **E** heard the noise of the crying, he 5941
4:14 And the man came in hastily, and told **E**. 5941
4:15 Now **E** *was* ninety and eight years old; and 5941
4:16 the man said unto **E**, I *am* he that came out 5941
14: 3 the son of Phinehas, the son of **E**, 5941
1Ki 2:27 which he spake concerning the house of **E** 5941
Mt 27:46 saying, **E**, ELI, LAMA SABACHTHANI? *2241*
27:46 saying, ELI, **E**, LAMA SABACHTHANI? *2241*

ELI'S (1) [ELI]
1Sa 3:14 that the iniquity of **E** house shall not be 5941

ELIAB (20) [ELIAB'S]
Nu 1: 9 Of Zebulun; **E** the son of Helon. 446
2: 7 **E** the son of Helon *shall be* captain of 446
7:24 On the third day **E** the son of Helon, 446
7:29 this *was* the offering of **E** the son of Helon. 446
10:16 children of Zebulun *was* **E** the son of Helon. 446
16: 1 Dathan and Abiram, the sons of **E**, and On, 446
16:12 to call Dathan and Abiram, the sons of **E**: 446
26: 8 And the sons of Pallu; **E**. 446
26: 9 And the sons of **E**; Nemuel, and Dathan, and 446
Dt 11: 6 did unto Dathan and Abiram, the sons of **E**, 446
1Sa 16: 6 were come, that he looked on **E**, and said, 446
17:13 that went to the battle *were* **E** the firstborn, 446
17:28 **E** his eldest brother heard when he spake 446
1Ch 2:13 Jesse begat his firstborn **E**, and Abinadab 446
6:27 **E** his son, Jeroham his son, Elkanah his son. 446
12: 9 the first, Obadiah the second, **E** the third, 446
15:18 **E**, and Benaiah, and Maaseiah, and 446
15:20 Unni, and **E**, and Maaseiah, and Benaiah, 446
16: 5 and **E**, and Benaiah, and Obed-edom: 446
2Ch 11:18 Abihail the daughter of **E** the son of Jesse; 446

ELIAB'S (1) [ELIAB]
1Sa 17:28 and **E** anger was kindled against David, and 446

ELIADA (3)
2Sa 5:16 And Elishama, and **E**, and Eliphalet. 450
1Ch 3: 8 And Elishama, and **E**, and Eliphelet, nine. 450
2Ch 17:17 **E** a mighty *man* of valour, and with him 450

ELIADAH (1)
1Ki 11:23 up *another* adversary, Rezon the son of **E**, 450

ELIAH (2)
1Ch 8:27 Jaresiah, and **E**, and Zichri, the sons of 452
Ezr 10:26 and Jehiel, and Abdi, and Jeremoth, and **E**. 452

ELIAHBA (2)
2Sa 23:32 **E** the Shaalbonite, *of* the sons of Jashen, 455
1Ch 11:33 the Baharumite, **E** the Shaalbonite, 455

ELIAKIM (15) [JEHOIAKIM]
2Ki 18:18 there came out to them **E** the son of Hilkiah, 471
18:26 Then said **E** the son of Hilkiah, and Shebna, 471
18:37 came **E** the son of Hilkiah, which *was* over 471
19: 2 he sent **E**, which *was* over the household, 471
23:34 Pharaoh-nechoh made **E** the son of Josiah 471
2Ch 36: 4 the king of Egypt made **E** his brother king 471
Ne 12:41 **E**, Maaseiah, Miniamin, Michaiah, Elioenai, 471
Isa 22:20 that I will call my servant **E** the son of 471
36: 3 came forth unto him **E**, Hilkiah's son, 471
36:11 said **E** and Shebna and Joah unto 471
36:22 came **E**, the son of Hilkiah, that *was* over 471
37: 2 And he sent **E**, who *was* over the household, 471
Mt 1:13 and Abiud begat **E**; and Eliakim begat *1662*
1:13 Abiud begat Eliakim; and **E** begat Azor; *1662*
Lk 3:30 *the son* of Jonan, which was *the son* of **E**, *1662*

ELIAM (2)
2Sa 11: 3 *Is* not this Bath-sheba, the daughter of **E**, 463
23:34 **E** the son of Ahithophel the Gilonite, 463

ELIAS (30) [ELIJAH]
Mt 11:14 And if ye will receive *it,* this is **E**, *2243*
16:14 some, **E**; and others, Jeremias, or one of *2243*
17: 3 unto them Moses and **E** talking with him. *2243*
17: 4 for thee, and one for Moses, and one for **E**. *2243*
17:10 then say the scribes that **E** must first come? *2243*

Mt 17:11 E truly shall first come, and restore all 2243
17:12 That E is come already, and they knew him 2243
27:47 heard *that*, said, This *man* calleth for E. 2243
27:49 let us see whether E will come to save him. 2243
Mk 6:15 Others said, That it is E. And others said, 2243
8:28 but some *say*, E; and others, One of 2243
9: 4 And there appeared unto them E with 2243
9: 5 for thee, and one for Moses, and one for E. 2243
9:11 Why say the scribes that E must first 2243
9:12 E verily cometh first, and restoreth all 2243
9:13 That E is indeed come, and they have done 2243
15:35 they heard *it*, said, Behold, he calleth E. 2243
15:36 let us see whether E will come to take him 2243
Lk 1:17 go before him in the spirit and power of E, 2243
4:25 widows were in Israel in the days of E, 2243
4:26 But unto none of them was E sent, 2243
9: 8 And of some, that E had appeared; and 2243
9:19 but some *say*, E; and others *say*, that one of 2243
9:30 him two men, which were Moses and E: 2243
9:33 for thee, and one for Moses, and one for E: 2243
9:54 and consume them, even as E did? 2243
Jn 1:21 Art thou E? And he saith, I am not. 2243
1:25 not *that* Christ, nor E, neither *that* prophet? 2243
Ro 11: 2 Wot ye not what the scripture saith of E? 2243
Jas 5:17 E was a man subject to like passions as we 2243

ELIASAPH (6)
Nu 1:14 Of Gad; E the son of Deuel. 460
2:14 the captain of the sons of Gad *shall be* E 460
3:24 of the Gershonites *shall be* E the son of Lael. 460
7:42 On the sixth day E the son of Deuel, 460
7:47 this *was* the offering of E the son of Deuel. 460
10:20 the children of Gad *was* E the son of Deuel. 460

ELIASHIB (17)
1Ch 3:24 E, and Pelaiah, and Akkub, and Johanan, 475
24:12 The eleventh to E, the twelfth to Jakim, 475
Ezr 10: 6 into the chamber of Johanan the son of E: 475
10:24 Of the singers also; E: and of the porters; 475
10:27 Elioenai, E, Mattaniah, and Jeremoth, and 475
10:36 Vaniah, Meremoth, E, 475
Ne 3: 1 E the high priest rose up with his brethren 475
3:20 the door of the house of E the high priest. 475
3:21 from the door of the house of E even to 475
3:21 of Eliashib even to the end of the house of E. 475
12:10 Joiakim also begat E, and Eliashib begat 475
12:10 also begat Eliashib, and E begat Joiada, 475
12:22 The Levites in the days of E, Joiada, and 475
12:23 even until the days of Johanan the son of E. 475
13: 4 before this, E the priest, having the oversight 475
13: 7 understood of the evil that E did for Tobiah, 475
13:28 sons of Joiada, the son of E the high priest, 475

ELIATHAH (2)
1Ch 25: 4 Hanani, E, Giddalti, and Romamti-ezer, 448
25:27 The twentieth to E, *he*, his sons, and 448

ELIDAD (1)
Nu 34:21 the tribe of Benjamin, E the son of Chislon. 449

ELIEHOENAI See ELIHOENAI

ELIEL (10)
1Ch 5:24 E, and Azriel, and Jeremiah, and Hodaviah, 447
6:34 of Jeroham, the son of E, the son of Toah, 447
8:20 And Elienai, and Zilthai, and E, 447
8:22 And Ishpan, and Heber, and E, 447
11:46 E the Mahavite, and Jeribai, and Joshaviah, 447
11:47 E, and Obed, and Jasiel the Mesobaite. 447
12:11 Attai the sixth, E the seventh, 447
15: 9 E the chief, and his brethren fourscore: 447
15:11 and Joel, Shemaiah, and E, and Amminadab, 447
2Ch 31:13 E, and Ismachiah, and Mahath, and Benaiah, 447

ELIENAI (1)
1Ch 8:20 And E, and Zilthai, and Eliel, 462

ELIEZER (15)
Ge 15: 2 the steward of my house *is* this E of 461
Ex 18: 4 the name of the other *was* E; for the God of 461
1Ch 7: 8 E, and Elioenai, and Omri, and Jerimoth, 461
15:24 Amasai, and Zechariah, and Benaiah, and E, 461
23:15 The sons of Moses *were*, Gershom, and E. 461
23:17 And the sons of E *were*, Rehabiah the chief. 461
23:17 E had none other sons; but the sons of 461
26:25 his brethren by E; Rehabiah his son, and 461
27:16 the ruler of the Reubenites *was* E the son of 461
2Ch 20:37 E the son of Dodavah of Mareshah 461
Ezr 8:16 sent I for E, for Ariel, for Shemaiah, and 461
10:18 Maaseiah, and E, and Jarib, and Gedaliah. 461
10:23 same *is* Kelita,) Pethahiah, Judah, and E. 461
10:31 E, Ishijah, Malchiah, Shemaiah, Shimeon, 461
Lk 3:29 *the son* of Jose, which was *the son* of E, 1663

ELIHOENAI (1)
Ezr 8: 4 E the son of Zerahiah, and with him two 454

ELIHOREPH (1)
1Ki 4: 3 E and Ahiah, the sons of Shisha, scribes; 456

ELIHU (11)
1Sa 1: 1 the son of E, the son of Tohu, the son of 453
1Ch 12:20 Michael, and Jozabad, and E, and Zilthai, 453
26: 7 *were* strong men, E, and Semachiah. 453
27:18 Of Judah, E, *one* of the brethren of David: 453
Job 32: 2 was kindled the wrath of E the son of 453
32: 4 Now E had waited till Job had spoken, 453
32: 5 When E saw that *there was* no answer in 453
32: 6 E the son of Barachel the Buzite answered 453
34: 1 Furthermore E answered and said, 453
35: 1 E spake moreover, and said, 453
36: 1 E also proceeded, and said, 453

ELIJAH (69) [ELIAS]
1Ki 17: 1 E the Tishbite, *who was* of the inhabitants of 452
17:13 E said unto her, Fear not; go *and* do as thou 452
17:15 and did according to the saying of E: 452
17:16 word of the LORD, which he spake by E. 452
17:18 she said unto E, What have I to do with thee, 452
17:22 the LORD heard the voice of E; and 452
17:23 E took the child, and brought him down out 452
17:23 his mother: and E said, See, thy son liveth. 452
17:24 the woman said to E, Now *by* this I know 452
18: 1 that the word of the LORD came to E in 452
18: 2 E went to shew himself unto Ahab. 452
18: 7 Obadiah was in the way, behold E met him: 452
18: 7 his face, and said, *Art* thou that my lord E? 452
18: 8 I *am*: go, tell thy lord, Behold, E *is here*. 452
18:11 Go, tell thy lord, Behold, E *is here*. 452
18:14 Behold, E *is here*: and he shall slay me. 452
18:15 E said, *As* the LORD of hosts liveth, before 452
18:16 and told him: and Ahab went to meet E. 452
18:17 it came to pass, when Ahab saw E, 452
18:21 E came unto all the people, and said, How 452
18:22 said E unto the people, I, *even* I only, 452
18:25 E said unto the prophets of Baal, 452
18:27 that E mocked them, and said, Cry aloud: 452
18:30 E said unto all the people, Come near unto 452
18:31 E took twelve stones, according to 452
18:36 that E the prophet came near, and said, 452
18:40 E said unto them, Take the prophets of Baal; 452
18:40 E brought them down to the brook Kishon, 452
18:41 E said unto Ahab, Get thee up, eat and drink; 452
18:42 E went up to the top of Carmel; and he cast 452
18:46 the hand of the LORD was on E; and 452
19: 1 Ahab told Jezebel all that E had done, and 452
19: 2 Jezebel sent a messenger unto E, saying, 452
19: 9 he said unto him, What doest thou here, E? 452
19:13 when E heard *it*, that he wrapped his face in 452
19:13 unto him, and said, What doest thou here, E? 452
19:19 E passed by him, and cast his mantle upon 452
19:20 ran after E, and said, Let me, I pray thee, 452
19:21 and went after E, and ministered unto him. 452
21:17 the word of the LORD came to E 452
21:20 Ahab said to E, Hast thou found me, O mine 452
21:28 the word of the LORD came to E 452
2Ki 1: 3 the angel of the LORD said to E 452
1: 4 but shalt surely die. And E departed. 452
1: 8 his loins. And he said, It *is* E the Tishbite. 452
1:10 E answered and said to the captain of fifty, 452
1:12 E answered and said unto them, If I *be* a 452
1:13 and came and fell on his knees before E, and 452
1:15 the angel of the LORD said unto E, 452
1:17 word of the LORD which E had spoken. 452
2: 1 when the LORD would take up E *into* 452
2: 1 that E went with Elisha from Gilgal. 452
2: 2 E said unto Elisha, Tarry here, I pray thee; 452
2: 4 E said unto him, Elisha, tarry here, I pray 452
2: 6 E said unto him, Tarry, I pray thee, here; 452
2: 8 E took his mantle, and wrapt *it* together, 452
2: 9 they were gone over, that E said unto Elisha, 452
2:11 and E went up by a whirlwind *into* heaven. 452
2:13 He took up also the mantle of E that fell 452
2:14 he took the mantle of E that fell from him, 452
2:14 and said, Where *is* the LORD God of E? 452
2:15 they said, The spirit of E doth rest on Elisha. 452
3:11 which poured water on the hands of E. 452
9:36 which he spake by his servant E 452
10:10 done *that* which he spake by his servant E. 452
10:17 saying of the LORD, which he spake to E. 452
2Ch 21:12 there came a writing to him from E 452
Ezr 10:21 E, and Shemaiah, and Jehiel, and Uzziah. 452
Mal 4: 5 I *will* send you E the prophet before 452

ELIKA (1)
2Sa 23:25 Shammah the Harodite, E the Harodite, 470

ELIM (6) [BEER-ELIM]
Ex 15:27 they came to E, where *were* twelve wells of 362
16: 1 they took their journey from E, and all 362
16: 1 of Sin, which *is* between E and Sinai, 362
Nu 33: 9 they removed from Marah, and came unto E: 362
33: 9 and in E *were* twelve fountains of water, and 362
33:10 they removed from E, and encamped by 362

ELIMELECH (4) [ELIMELECH'S]
Ru 1: 2 the name of the man *was* E, and the name of 458
1: 3 E Naomi's husband died; and she was left, 458
2: 1 a mighty man of wealth, of the family of E; 458
2: 3 unto Boaz, who *was* of the kindred of E. 458

ELIMELECH'S (2) [ELIMELECH]
Ru 4: 3 a parcel of land, which *was* our brother E: 458
4: 9 that I have bought all that *was* E, and all that 458

ELIOENAI (8)
1Ch 3:23 E, and Hezekiah, and Azrikam, three. 454
3:24 the sons of E *were*, Hodaiah, and Eliashib, 454
4:36 E, and Jaakobah, and Jeshohaiah, and 454
7: 8 E, and Omri, and Jerimoth, and Abiah, and 454
26: 3 the fifth, Jehohanan the sixth, E the seventh. 454
Ezr 10:22 E, Maaseiah, Ishmael, Nethaneel, Jozabad, 454
10:27 E, Eliashib, Mattaniah, and Jeremoth, and 454
Ne 12:41 Eliakim, Maaseiah, Miniamin, Michaiah, E, 454

ELIPHAL (1)
1Ch 11:35 son of Sacar the Hararite, E the son of Ur, 465

ELIPHALET (2)
2Sa 5:16 And Elishama, and Eliada, and E. 467
1Ch 14: 7 And Elishama, and Beeliada, and E. 467

ELIPHAZ (15)
Ge 36: 4 Adah bare to Esau E; and Bashemath bare 464
36:10 E the son of Adah the wife of Esau, 464
36:11 the sons of E were Teman, Omar, Zepho, 464
36:12 And Timna was concubine to E Esau's son; 464
36:12 Esau's son; and she bare to E Amalek: 464
36:15 the sons of E the firstborn *son* of Esau; 464
36:16 these *are* the dukes *that came* of E in 464
1Ch 1:35 E, Reuel, and Jeush, and Jaalam, and Korah. 464
1:36 The sons of E; Teman, and Omar, Zephi, 464
Job 2:11 E the Temanite, and Bildad the Shuhite, and 464
4: 1 Then E the Temanite answered and said, 464
15: 1 Then answered E the Temanite, and said, 464
22: 1 Then E the Temanite answered and said, 464
42: 7 the LORD said to E the Temanite, 464
42: 9 So E the Temanite and Bildad the Shuhite 464

ELIPHELEH (2)
1Ch 15:18 E, and Mikneiah, and Obed-edom, and Jeiel, 466
15:21 E, and Mikneiah, and Obed-edom, and Jeiel, 466

ELIPHELEHU See ELIPHELEH

ELIPHELET (6)
2Sa 23:34 E the son of Ahasbai, the son of 467
1Ch 3: 6 Ibhar also, and Elishama, and E, 467
3: 8 And Elishama, and Eliada, and E, nine. 467
8:39 Jehush the second, and E the third. 467
Ezr 8:13 E, Jeiel, and Shemaiah, and with them 467
10:33 Zabad, E, Jeremai, Manasseh, *and* Shimei. 467

ELISABETH (8) [ELISABETH'S]
Lk 1: 5 daughters of Aaron, and her name *was* E. 1665
1: 7 because that E was barren, and they both 1665
1:13 and thy wife E shall bear thee a son, and 1665
1:24 And after those days his wife E conceived, 1665
1:36 And behold, thy cousin E, she hath also 1665
1:40 into the house of Zacharias, and saluted E. 1665
1:41 And it came to pass *that*, when E heard 1665
1:41 and E was filled with the Holy Ghost: 1665

ELISABETH'S (1) [ELISABETH]
Lk 1:57 Now E full time came that she should be 1665

ELISEUS (1) [ELISHA]
Lk 4:27 were in Israel in the time of E the prophet; 1666

ELISHA (58) [ELISEUS]
1Ki 19:16 E the son of Shaphat of Abel-meholah shalt 477
19:17 from the sword of Jehu shall E slay. 477
19:19 and found E the son of Shaphat, 477
2Ki 2: 1 that Elijah went with E from Gilgal. 477
2: 2 Elijah said unto E, Tarry here, I pray thee; 477
2: 2 And E said *unto him*, *As* the LORD liveth, 477
2: 3 that *were at* Beth-el came forth to E, 477
2: 4 said unto him, E, tarry here, I pray thee; 477
2: 5 the prophets that *were* at Jericho came to E, 477
2: 9 they were gone over, that Elijah said unto E, 477
2: 9 E said, I pray thee, let a double portion of 477
2:12 E saw *it*, and he cried, My father, my father, 477
2:14 parted hither and thither: and E went over. 477
2:15 they said, The spirit of Elijah doth rest on E. 477
2:19 And the men of the city said unto E, Behold, 477
2:22 according to the saying of E which he spake. 477
3:11 and said, Here *is* E the son of Shaphat, 477
3:13 E said unto the king of Israel, What have I to 477
3:14 E said, *As* the LORD of hosts liveth, before 477
4: 1 the wives of the sons of the prophets unto E, 477
4: 2 E said unto her, What shall I do for thee? 477
4: 8 it fell on a day, that E passed to Shunem, 477
4:17 bare a son at that season that E had said unto 477
4:32 when E was come into the house, behold, 477
4:38 E came again to Gilgal: and *there was* a 477
5: 8 when E the man of God had heard that 477
5: 9 and stood *at* the door of the house of E. 477
5:10 E sent a messenger unto him, saying, Go 477
5:20 the servant of E the man of God, said, 477
5:25 E said unto him, Whence *comest thou*, 477
6: 1 the sons of the prophets said unto E, 477
6:12 E, the prophet that *is* in Israel, telleth 477
6:17 E prayed, and said, LORD, I pray thee, 477
6:17 *of* horses and chariots of fire round about E. 477
6:18 E prayed unto the LORD, and said, 477
6:18 with blindness according to the word of E. 477
6:19 E said unto them, This *is* not the way, 477
6:20 come *into* Samaria, that E said, LORD, 477
6:21 the king of Israel said unto E, when he saw 477
6:31 if the head of E the son of Shaphat shall 477
6:32 E sat in his house, and the elders sat with 477
7: 1 E said, Hear ye the word of the LORD; 477
8: 1 spake E unto the woman, whose son he had 477
8: 4 all the great *things* that E hath done. 477
8: 5 and this *is* her son, whom E restored to life. 477
8: 7 E came *to* Damascus; and Ben-hadad 477
8:10 E said unto him, Go, say unto him, 477
8:13 E answered, The LORD hath shewed me 477
8:14 So he departed from E, and came to his 477
8:14 who said to him, What said E to thee? 477
9: 1 E the prophet called one of the children of 477
13:14 Now E was fallen sick of his sickness 477
13:15 And E said unto him, Take bow and arrows. 477
13:16 and E put his hands upon the king's hands. 477
13:17 he opened *it*. Then E said, Shoot. And he 477
13:20 E died, and they buried him. And the bands 477
13:21 they cast the man into the sepulchre of E: 477
13:21 and touched the bones of E, he revived, and 477

ELISHAH (3)
Ge 10: 4 E, and Tarshish, Kittim, and Dodanim. 473
1Ch 1: 7 E, and Tarshish, Kittim, and Dodanim. 473
Eze 27: 7 purple from the isles of E was that which 473

ELISHAMA (17)
Nu 1:10 of Ephraim; E the son of Ammihud: 476
2:18 the captain of the sons of Ephraim *shall be* E 476
7:48 On the seventh day E the son of Ammihud, 476
7:53 this *was* the offering of E the son of 476
10:22 over his host *was* E the son of Ammihud. 476

2Sa 5:16 And **E**, and Eliada, and Eliphalet. 476
2Ki 25:25 the son of **E**, of the seed royal, came, and 476
1Ch 2:41 begat Jekamiah, and Jekamiah begat **E**. 476
3: 6 Ibhar also, and **E**, and Eliphelet, 476
3: 8 And **E**, and Eliada, and Eliphelet, nine. 476
7:26 Laadan his son, Ammihud his son, **E** his son, 476
14: 7 And **E**, and Beeliada, and Eliphalet. 476
2Ch 17: 8 and with them **E** and Jehoram, priests. 476
Jer 36:12 *even* **E** the scribe, and Delaiah the son of 476
36:20 they laid up the roll in the chamber of **E** 476
36:21 and he took it out of **E** the scribe's chamber. 476
41: 1 Ishmael the son of Nethaniah the son of **E**, 476

ELISHAPHAT (1)
2Ch 23: 1 **E** the son of Zichri, into covenant with him. 478

ELISHEBA (1)
Ex 6:23 Aaron took him **E**, daughter of Amminadab, 472

ELISHUA (2)
2Sa 5:15 Ibhar also, and **E**, and Nepheg, and Japhia, 474
1Ch 14: 5 And Ibhar, and **E**, and Elpalet, 474

ELIUD (2)
Mt 1:14 Sadoc begat Achim; and Achim begat **E**; *1664*
1:15 And **E** begat Eleazar; and Eleazar begat *1664*

ELIZABETH See ELISABETH

ELIZAPHAN (4)
Nu 3:30 the Kohathites *shall be* **E** the son of Uzziel. 469
34:25 children of Zebulun, **E** the son of Parnach. 469
1Ch 15: 8 Of the sons of **E**; Shemaiah the chief, and 469
2Ch 29:13 And of the sons of **E**; Shimri, and Jeiel: and 469

ELIZUR (5)
Nu 1: 5 of *the tribe of* Reuben; **E** the son of Shedeur. 468
2:10 of Reuben *shall be* **E** the son of Shedeur. 468
7:30 On the fourth day **E** the son of Shedeur, 468
7:35 this *was* the offering of **E** the son of 468
10:18 and over his host *was* **E** the son of Shedeur. 468

ELKANAH (21)
Ex 6:24 sons of Korah; Assir, and **E**, and Abiasaph: 511
1Sa 1: 1 of mount Ephraim, and his name *was* **E**, 511
1: 4 when the time was that **E** offered, he gave to 511
1: 8 said **E** her husband to her, Hannah, why 511
1:19 **E** knew Hannah his wife; and the LORD 511
1:21 the man **E**, and all his house, went up to 511
1:23 **E** her husband said unto her, Do what 511
2:11 **E** went to Ramah to his house. And the child 511
2:20 Eli blessed **E** and his wife, and said, 511
1Ch 6:23 **E** his son, and Ebiasaph his son, and 511
6:25 And the sons of **E**; Amasai, and Ahimoth. 511
6:26 *As for* **E**: the sons of Elkanah; Zophai his 511
6:26 the sons of **E**; Zophai his son, and 511
6:27 Eliab his son, Jeroham his son, **E** his son. 511
6:34 The son of **E**, the son of Jeroham, the son of 511
6:35 The son of Zuph, the son of **E**, the son of 511
6:36 The son of **E**, the son of Joel, the son of 511
9:16 and Berechiah the son of Asa, the son of **E**, 511
12: 6 **E**, and Jesiah, and Azareel, and Joezer, and 511
15:23 and **E** *were* doorkeepers for the ark. 511
2Ch 28: 7 of the house, and **E** *that was* next to the king. 511

ELKOSHITE (1)
Na 1: 1 The book of the vision of Nahum the **E**. 512

ELLASAR (2)
Ge 14: 1 Arioch king of **E**, Chedorlaomer king of 495
14: 9 king of Shinar, and Arioch king of **E**; 495

ELMADAM See ELMODAM

ELMODAM (1)
Lk 3:28 which was *the son* of **E**, which was *the son* *1678*

ELMS (1)
Hos 4:13 under oaks and poplars and **e**, because 424

ELNAAM (1)
1Ch 11:46 the sons of **E**, and Ithmah the Moabite, 493

ELNATHAN (7)
2Ki 24: 8 the daughter of **E** of Jerusalem. 494
Ezr 8:16 for **E**, and for Jarib, and for Elnathan, and 494
8:16 for **E**, and for Nathan, and for Zechariah, 494
8:16 for Joiarib, and for **E**, *men* of understanding. 494
Jer 26:22 *namely*, **E** the son of Achbor, and 494
36:12 **E** the son of Achbor, and Gemariah the son 494
36:25 Nevertheless **E** and Delaiah and 494

ELOI (2) [ELI]
Mk 15:34 saying, **E**, ELOI, *1682*
15:34 saying, ELOI, **E**, *1682*

ELON (7) [ELON-BETH-HANAN, ELONITES]
Ge 26:34 and Bashemath the daughter of **E** the Hittite: 356
36: 2 Adah the daughter of **E** the Hittite, and 356
46:14 sons of Zebulun; Sered, and **E**, and Jahleel. 440
Nu 26:26 of **E**, the family of the Elonites: of Jahleel, 356
Jos 19:43 And **E**, and Thimnathah, and Ekron, 356
Jdg 12:11 And after him **E**, a Zebulonite, judged Israel; 356
12:12 **E** the Zebulonite died, and was buried in 356

ELON-BETH-HANAN (1) [ELON, HANAN]
1Ki 4: 9 and in Shaalbim, and Beth-shemesh, and **E**: 358

ELONITES (1) [ELON]
Nu 26:26 of Elon, the family of the **E**: of Jahleel, 440

ELOQUENT (3)
Ex 4:10 I *am* not **e**, neither heretofore, 376+1697
Isa 3: 3 and the cunning artificer, and the **e** orator. 995
Ac 18:24 an **e** man, *and* mighty in the scriptures, *3052*

ELOTH (3) [ELATH]
1Ki 9:26 which *is* beside **E**, on the shore of the Red 359
2Ch 8:17 and to **E**, at the sea side in the land of Edom. 359
26: 2 He built **E**, and restored it to Judah, after that 359

ELPAAL (3)
1Ch 8:11 And of Hushim he begat Abitub, and **E**. 508
8:12 The sons of **E**; Eber, and Misham, and 508
8:18 and Jezliah, and Jobab, the sons of **E**; 508

ELPALET (1)
1Ch 14: 5 And Ibhar, and Elishua, and **E**, 467

EL-PARAN (1) [PARAN]
Ge 14: 6 unto **E**, which *is* by the wilderness. 364

ELPELET See ELPALET

ELSE (48)
Ge 30: 1 said unto Jacob, Give me children, or **e** I die. 369
42:16 **e** by the life of Pharaoh surely ye *are* 518+3808
Ex 8:21 **E**, if thou wilt not let my people go, behold, 3588
10: 4 **E**, if thou refuse to let my people go, 3588
Nu 20:19 without *doing any* thing **e**, go through on NIH
Dt 4:35 he *is* God; *there is* none **e** besides him. 5750
4:39 and upon the earth beneath: *there is* none **e**. 5750
Jos 23:12 **E** if ye do in any wise go back, and 3588
Jdg 7:14 This *is* **nothing e** save the sword of 369+1115
2Sa 3:35 if I taste bread, or **ought e**, 3605+3972
15:14 for we shall not **e** escape from Absalom: NIH
1Ki 8:60 the LORD *is* God, *and that there is* none **e**. 5750
20:39 his life, **or e** thou shalt pay a talent of silver. 176
21: 6 or **e**, if it please thee, I will give thee NIH
1Ch 21:12 **or e** three days the sword of 518+2050.1
2Ch 23: 7 whosoever **e** cometh into the house, he shall NIH
Ne 2: 2 this *is* nothing **e** but sorrow of heart. Then I NIH
Ps 51:16 **e** would I give *it*: thou delightest not in 2050.1
Ecc 2:25 or **who e** can hasten *hereunto*, more than I? 4310
Isa 45: 5 I *am* the LORD, and *there is* none **e**, 5750
45: 6 I *am* the LORD, and *there is* none **e**. 5750
45:14 and *there is* none **e**, *there is* no God. 5750
45:18 I *am* the LORD; and *there is* none **e**. 5750
45:21 *there is* no God **e beside** me; 1107+4480+5750
45:22 the earth: for I *am* God, and *there is* none **e**. 5750
46: 9 for I *am* God, and *there is* none **e**; I *am* 5750
47: 8 in thine heart, I *am*, and **none e** besides me; 657
47:10 in thine heart, I *am*, and **none e** besides me. 657
Joel 2:27 I *am* the LORD your God, and none **e**: 5750
Mt 6:24 **or e** he will hold to the one, and despise *2228*
9:17 **e** the bottles break, and the wine runneth *1490*
12:29 **Or e** how can one enter into a strong *man's* *2228*
12:33 **or e** make the tree corrupt, and his fruit *2228*
Mk 2:21 **e** the new piece that filled it up taketh away *1490*
2:22 **e** the new wine doth burst the bottles, and *1490*
Lk 5:37 **e** the new wine will burst the bottles, and *1490*
14:32 **Or e**, while the other is yet a great way off, *1490*
16:13 **or e** he will hold to the one, and despise *2228*
Jn 14:11 **or e** believe me for the very works' sake. *1490*
Ac 17:21 were there spent their time in nothing **e**, *2087*
24:20 **Or e** let these same *here* say, if they have *2228*
Ro 2:15 while accusing or **e** excusing one another;) *2532*
1Co 7:14 **e** were your children unclean; but *686+1893*
14:16 **E** when thou shalt bless with the spirit, *1893*
15:29 **E** what shall they do which are baptized for *1893*
Php 1:27 whether I come and see you, or **e** be absent, NIG
Rev 2: 5 **or e** I *will* come unto thee quickly, and *1490*
2:16 **or e** I *will* come unto thee quickly, and *1490*

ELTEKEH (2)
Jos 19:44 And **E**, and Gibbethon, and Baalath, 514
21:23 out of the tribe of Dan, **E** with her suburbs, 514

ELTEKON (1)
Jos 15:59 Maarath, and Beth-anoth, and **E**; six cities 515

ELTOLAD (2)
Jos 15:30 And **E**, and Chesil, and Hormah, 513
19: 4 And **E**, and Bethul, and Hormah, 513

ELUL (1)
Ne 6:15 in the twenty and fifth *day* of *the month* **E**, 435

ELYMAS (1)
Ac 13: 8 But **E** the sorcerer (for so is his name by *1681*

ELZABAD (2)
1Ch 12:12 Johanan the eighth, **E** the ninth, 443
26: 7 Othni, and Rephael, and Obed, **E**, 443

ELZAPHAN (2)
Ex 6:22 sons of Uzziel; Mishael, and **E**, and Zithri. 469
Lev 10: 4 Moses called Mishael and **E**, the sons of 469

EMBALM (1) [EMBALMED]
Ge 50: 2 his servants the physicians to **e** his father: 2590

EMBALMED (3) [EMBALM]
Ge 50: 2 his father: and the physicians **e** Israel. 2590
50: 3 are fulfilled the days of those which are **e**: 2590
50:26 they **e** him, and he was put in a coffin in 2590

EMBOLDENED (1) [BOLD]
1Co 8:10 **e** to eat those things which are offered to *3618*

EMBOLDENETH (1) [BOLD]
Job 16: 3 an end? or what **e** thee that thou answerest? 4834

EMBRACE (8) [EMBRACED, EMBRACING]
2Ki 4:16 to the time of life, thou shalt **e** a son. 2263
Job 24: 8 and **e** the rock for want of a shelter. 2263
Pr 4: 8 bring thee to honour, when thou dost **e** her. 2263
5:20 and **e** the bosom of a stranger? 2263
Ecc 3: 5 a time to **e**, and a time to refrain from 2263
SS 2: 6 my head, and his right hand doth **e** me. 2263
8: 3 my head, and his right hand should **e** me. 2263
La 4: 5 they that were brought up in scarlet **e** 2263

EMBRACED (5) [EMBRACE]
Ge 29:13 **e** him, and kissed him, and brought him to 2263
33: 4 **e** him, and fell on his neck, and kissed him: 2263
48:10 unto him; and he kissed them, and **e** them. 2263
Ac 20: 1 and **e** *them*, and departed for to go into *782*
Heb 11:13 were persuaded of *them*, and **e** *them*, and *782*

EMBRACING (2) [EMBRACE]
Ecc 3: 5 to embrace, and a time to refrain from **e**; 2263
Ac 20:10 went down, and fell on him, and **e** *him* said, *4843*

EMBROIDER (1) [EMBROIDERER]
Ex 28:39 thou shalt **e** the coat of fine linen, and 7660

E

EMBROIDERED See DIVERS; DIVERSE

EMBROIDERER (2) [EMBROIDER]
Ex 35:35 of the **e**, in blue, and in purple, in scarlet, 7551
38:23 an **e** in blue, and in purple, and in scarlet, 7551

EMERALD (5) [EMERALDS]
Ex 28:18 the second row *shall be* an **e**, a sapphire, 5306
39:11 an **e**, a sapphire, and a diamond. 5306
Eze 28:13 the **e**, and the carbuncle, and gold: 5306
Rev 4: 3 about the throne, in sight like unto an **e**. *4664*
21:19 the third, a chalcedony; the fourth, an **e**; *4665*

EMERALDS (1) [EMERALD]
Eze 27:16 they occupied in thy fairs with **e**, purple, 5306

EMERODS (8)
Dt 28:27 with the **e**, and with the scab, and with 6076
1Sa 5: 6 smote them with **e**, *even* Ashdod and 2914
5: 9 and they had **e** in their secret parts. 2914
5:12 men that died not were smitten with the **e**: 2914
6: 4 Five golden **e**, and five golden mice, 2914
6: 5 Wherefore ye shall make images of your **e**, 2914
6:11 the mice of gold and the images of their **e**. 2914
6:17 these *are* the golden **e** which the Philistines 2914

EMIMS (3)
Ge 14: 5 in Ham, and the **E** in Shaveh Kiriathaim, 368
Dt 2:10 (The **E** dwelt therein in times past, a people 368
2:11 the Anakims; but the Moabites call them **E**. 368

EMINENT (4) [PREEMINENCE]
Eze 16:24 thou hast also built unto thee an **e place**, 1354
16:31 In that thou buildest thine **e place** in 1354
16:39 they shall throw down thine **e place**, and 1354
17:22 will plant *it* upon a high mountain and **e**: 8524

EMISSION See COPULATION

EMITES See EMIMS

EMMANUEL (1) [IMMANUEL]
Mt 1:23 forth a son, and they shall call his name **E**, *1694*

EMMAUS (1)
Lk 24:13 went *that* same day to a village called **E**, *1695*

EMMOR (1) [HAMOR]
Ac 7:16 of the sons of **E** the *father* of Sychem. *1697*

EMPIRE (1)
Est 1:20 shall be published throughout all his **e**, 4438

EMPLOY (1) [EMPLOYED, EMPLOYMENT]
Dt 20:19 to **e** *them* in the siege: 935+4480+6440

EMPLOYED (2) [EMPLOY]
1Ch 9:33 for they were **e** in *that* work day and night 5921
Ezr 10:15 Jahaziah the son of Tikvah were **e** about 5975

EMPLOYMENT (1) [EMPLOY]
Eze 39:14 they shall sever out men of **continual e**, 8548

EMPTIED (8) [EMPTY]
Ge 24:20 **e** her pitcher into the trough, and ran again 6168
42:35 it came to pass as they **e** their sacks, 7324
2Ch 24:11 high priest's officer came and **e** the chest, 6168
Ne 5:13 even thus be he shaken out, and **e**. 7386
Isa 19: 6 *and* the brooks of defence shall be **e** and 1809
24: 3 The land shall be **utterly e**, 1238+1238
Jer 48:11 and hath not been **e** from vessel to vessel, 7324
Na 2: 2 for the emptiers have **e** them **out**, and 1238

EMPTIERS (1) [EMPTY]
Na 2: 2 for the **e** have emptied them out, and 1238

EMPTINESS (1) [EMPTY]
Isa 34:11 it the line of confusion, and the stones of **e**. 922

EMPTY (38) [EMPTIED, EMPTIERS, EMPTINESS]
Ge 31:42 surely thou hadst sent me away now **e**. 7387
37:24 and the pit *was* **e**, *there was* no water in it. 7386
41:27 the seven **e** ears blasted with the east wind 7386
Ex 3:21 to pass, that, when ye go, ye shall not go **e**: 7387
23:15 and none shall appear before me **e**: 7387
34:20 and none shall appear before me **e**. 7387
Lev 14:36 the priest shall command that they **e** 6437
Dt 15:13 from thee, thou shalt not let him go away **e**: 7387
16:16 they shall not appear before the LORD **e**: 7387
Jdg 7:16 with **e** pitchers, and lamps within 7386
Ru 1:21 the LORD hath brought me *home* again **e**: 7387
3:17 to me, Go not **e** unto thy mother in law. 7387

1Sa 6: 3 the ark of the God of Israel, send it not **e**. 7387
20:18 shalt be missed, because thy seat will be **e**. 6485
20:25 sat by Saul's side, and David's place was **e**. 6485
20:27 *day* of the month, that David's place was **e**: 6485
2Sa 1:22 and the sword of Saul returned not **e**. 7387
2Ki 4: 3 of all thy neighbours, *even* **e** vessels; 7386
Job 22: 9 Thou hast sent widows away **e**, and 7387
26: 7 He stretcheth out the north over the **e place**, 8414
Ecc 11: 3 *of* rain, they **e** *themselves* upon the earth: 7324
Isa 24: 1 the LORD **maketh** the earth **e**, and 1238
29: 8 he eateth; but he awaketh, and his soul *is* **e**: 7386
32: 6 to **make e** the soul of the hungry, and 7324
Jer 14: 3 no water; they returned *with* their vessels **e**; 7387
48:12 shall **e** his vessels, and break their bottles. 7324
51: 2 that shall fan her, and shall **e** her land: 1238
51:34 crushed me, he hath made me an **e** vessel, 7385
Eze 24:11 set it **e** upon the coals thereof, that the brass 7386
Hos 10: 1 Israel *is* an **e** vine, he bringeth forth fruit 1238
Na 2:10 She *is* **e**, and void, and waste: and the heart 950
Hab 1:17 Shall they therefore **e** their net, and 7324
Zec 4:12 pipes **e** the golden *oil* out of themselves? 7324
Mt 12:44 he findeth *it* **e**, swept, and garnished. *4980*
Mk 12: 3 and beat *him*, and sent *him* away **e**. *2756*
Lk 1:53 and the rich he hath sent **e** away. *2756*
20:10 beat him, and sent *him* away **e**. *2756*
20:11 *him* shamefully, and sent *him* away **e**. *2756*

EMULATION (1) [EMULATIONS]
Ro 11:14 If by any means I may **provoke to e** *them* *3863*

EMULATIONS (1) [EMULATION]
Gal 5:20 hatred, variance, **e**, wrath, strife, seditions, *2205*

ENABLED (1)
1Ti 1:12 who hath **e** me, for that he counted me *1743*

ENAM (1)
Jos 15:34 and En-gannim, Tappuah, and **E**, 5879

ENAN (5) [HAZAR-ENAN]
Nu 1:15 Of Naphtali; Ahira the son of **E**. 5881
2:29 of Naphtali *shall be* Ahira the son of **E**. 5881
7:78 On the twelfth day Ahira the son of **E**, 5881
7:83 this *was* the offering of Ahira the son of **E**. 5881
10:27 of Naphtali *was* Ahira the son of **E**. 5881

ENCAMP (11) [CAMP]
Ex 14: 2 that they turn and **e** before Pi-hahiroth, 2583
14: 2 before it shall ye **e** by the sea. 2583
Nu 1:50 and shall **e** round about the tabernacle. 2583
2:17 as they **e**, so shall they set forward, 2583
2:27 those that **e** by him *shall be* the tribe of 2583
3:38 those that **e** before the tabernacle toward 2583
10:31 forasmuch as thou knowest how we are to **e** 2583
2Sa 12:28 and **e** against the city, and take it: 2583
Job 19:12 and **e** round about my tabernacle. 2583
Ps 27: 3 Though a host should **e** against me, 2583
Zec 9: 8 I will **e about** mine house because of 2583

ENCAMPED (33) [CAMP]
Ex 13:20 **e** in Etham, in the edge of the wilderness. 2583
15:27 palm trees: and they **e** there by the waters. 2583
18: 5 where he **e** *at* the mount of God: 2583
Nu 33:10 removed from Elim, and **e** by the Red sea. 2583
33:11 the Red sea, and **e** in the wilderness of Sin. 2583
33:12 of the wilderness of Sin, and **e** in Dophkah. 2583
33:13 departed from Dophkah, and **e** in Alush. 2583
33:14 removed from Alush, and **e** at Rephidim, 2583
33:17 from Kibroth-hattaavah, and **e** at Hazeroth. 2583
33:24 from mount Shapher, and **e** in Haradah. 2583
33:26 removed from Makheloth, and **e** at Tahath. 2583
33:30 from Hashmonah, and **e** at Moseroth. 2583
33:32 from Bene-jaakan, and **e** at Hor-hagidgad. 2583
33:34 removed from Jotbathah, and **e** at Ebronah. 2583
33:35 from Ebronah, and **e** at Ezion-gaber. 2583
33:46 and **e** in Almon-diblathaim. 2583
Jos 4:19 **e** in Gilgal, in the east border of Jericho. 2583
5:10 the children of Israel **e** in Gilgal, and 2583
10: 5 **e** before Gibeon, and made war against it. 2583
10:31 and **e** against it, and fought against it: 2583
10:34 and they **e** against it, and fought against it: 2583
Jdg 6: 4 they **e** against them, and destroyed 2583
9:50 and **e** against Thebez, and took it. 2583
10:17 were gathered together, and **e** in Gilead. 2583
10:17 themselves together, and **e** in Mizpeh. 2583
20:19 up in the morning, and **e** against Gibeah. 2583
1Sa 11: 1 came up, and **e** against Jabesh-gilead: 2583
13:16 but the Philistines **e** in Michmash. 2583
2Sa 11:11 of my lord, are **e** in the open fields; 2583
1Ki 16:15 the people *were* **e** against Gibbethon, 2583
16:16 the people *that were* **e** heard say, Zimri hath 2583
1Ch 11:15 the host of the Philistines **e** in the valley of 2583
2Ch 32: 1 **e** against the fenced cities, and thought to 2583

ENCAMPETH (2) [CAMP]
Ps 34: 7 The angel of the LORD **e** round about 2583
53: 5 the bones of him that **e** *against* thee: 2583

ENCAMPING (1) [CAMP]
Ex 14: 9 overtook them **e** by the sea, 2583

ENCHANTER (1) [ENCHANTERS, ENCHANTMENT, ENCHANTMENTS]
Dt 18:10 an observer of times, or an **e**, or a witch, 5172

ENCHANTERS (1) [ENCHANTER]
Jer 27: 9 nor to your **e**, nor to your sorcerers, 6049

ENCHANTMENT (3) [ENCHANTER]
Lev 19:26 neither shall ye **use e**, nor observe times. 5172
Nu 23:23 Surely *there is* no **e** against Jacob, neither *is* 5173
Ecc 10:11 Surely the serpent will bite without **e**; and 3908

ENCHANTMENTS (10) [ENCHANTER]
Ex 7:11 they also did in like manner with their **e**. 3858
7:22 the magicians of Egypt did so with their **e**: 3909
8: 7 the magicians did so with their **e**, and 3909
8:18 so with their **e** to bring forth lice, 3909
Nu 24: 1 to seek for **e**, but he set his face toward 5173
2Ki 17:17 used divination and **e**, and sold themselves 5172
21: 6 **used e**, and dealt with familiar spirits and 5172
2Ch 33: 6 **used e**, and used witchcraft, and dealt with 5172
Isa 47: 9 *and* for the great abundance of thine **e**. 2267
47:12 Stand now with thine **e**, and with 2267

ENCLOSE See INCLOSE

ENCOUNTERED (1)
Ac 17:18 the Epicureans, and of the Stoicks, **e** him. *4820*

ENCOURAGE (4) [ENCOURAGED]
Dt 1:38 **e** him: for he shall cause Israel to inherit it. 2388
3:28 and **e** him, and strengthen him: 2388
2Sa 11:25 the city, and overthrow it: and **e** thou him. 2388
Ps 64: 5 They **e** themselves *in* an evil matter: 2388

ENCOURAGED (5) [ENCOURAGE]
Jdg 20:22 the people the men of Israel **e** themselves, 2388
1Sa 30: 6 but David **e** himself in the LORD his God. 2388
2Ch 31: 4 that they might be **e** in the law of 2388
35: 2 **e** them to the service of the house of 2388
Isa 41: 7 So the carpenter **e** the goldsmith, *and* 2388

END (307) [ENDED, ENDETH, ENDING, ENDLESS, ENDS]
Ge 6:13 The **e** of all flesh is come before me; 7093
8: 3 after the **e** of the hundred and fifty days 7097
8: 6 it came to pass at the **e** of forty days, 7093
23: 9 which he hath, which *is* in the **e** of his field; 7097
27:30 as soon as Isaac had **made an e** of blessing 3615
41: 1 it came to pass at the **e** of two full years, 7093
47:21 he removed them to cities from *one* **e** of 7097
47:21 of Egypt even to the *other* **e** thereof. 7097
49:33 when Jacob had **made an e** of commanding 3615
Ex 8:22 *of flies* shall be there; **to the e** 4616+3807.1
12:41 it came to pass at the **e** of the four hundred 7093
23:16 of ingathering, *which is* in the **e** of the year, 3318
25:19 make one cherub on the one **e**, and 7098
25:19 and the other cherub on the other **e**: 7098
26:28 of the boards shall reach from **e** to end. 7097
26:28 of the boards shall reach from end to **e**. 7097
31:18 when he had **made an e** of communing 3615
34:22 and the feast of ingathering *at* the year's **e**. 8622
36:33 the boards from the one **e** to the other. 7097
37: 8 One cherub on the **e** on this side, and 7098
37: 8 another cherub on the *other* **e** on that side: 7098
Lev 8:33 the days of your consecration be **at an e**: 4390
16:20 when he hath **made an e** of reconciling 3615
17: 5 **To the e** that the children of Israel 4616+3807.1
Nu 4:15 his sons have **made an e** of covering 3615
16:31 as he had **made an e** of speaking all these 3615
23:10 the righteous, and let my **last e** be like his! 319
24:20 his **latter e** *shall be* that he perish for ever. 319
Dt 8:16 prove thee, to do thee good at thy **latter e**; 319
9:11 it came to pass at the **e** of forty days and 7093
11:12 of the year even unto the **e** of the year. 319
13: 7 from the *one* **e** of the earth even unto 7097
13: 7 the earth even unto the *other* **e** of the earth; 7097
14:28 At the **e** of three years thou shalt bring forth 7097
15: 1 At the **e** of *every* seven years thou shalt 7093
17:16 to return to Egypt, **to the e that** 4616+3807.1
17:20 *to* the left: **to the e that** he may 4616+3807.1
20: 9 when the officers have **made an e** of 3615
26:12 When thou hast **made an e** of tithing all 3615
28:49 from the **e** of the earth, *as swift* as the eagle 7097
28:64 from the *one* **e** of the earth even unto 7097
31:10 saying, At the **e** of *every* seven years, 7093
31:24 when Moses had **made an e** of writing 3615
32:20 I will see what their **e** *shall be*: for they *are* a 319
32:29 *that* they would consider their **latter e**! 319
32:45 Moses **made an e** of speaking all these 3615
Jos 8:24 when Israel had **made an e** of slaying all 3615
9:16 it came to pass at the **e** of three days after 7097
10:20 the children of Israel had **made an e** of 3615
15: 5 *was* the salt sea, *even* unto the **e** of Jordan. 7097
15: 8 which *is* at the **e** of the valley of the giants 7097
18:15 the south quarter *was* from the **e** of 7097
18:16 the border came down to the **e** of 7097
18:19 bay of the salt sea at the south **e** of Jordan: 7097
19:49 When they had **made an e** of dividing 3615
19:51 So they **made an e** of dividing the country. 3615
Jdg 3:18 when he had **made an e** to offer 3615
6:21 the angel of the LORD put forth the **e** of 7097
11:39 it came to pass at the **e** of two months, 7093
15:17 when he had **made an e** of speaking, 3615
19: 9 behold, the day **groweth to an e**, 2583
Ru 2:23 Boaz to glean unto the **e** of barley harvest 3615
3: 7 he went to lie down at the **e** of the heap *of* 7097
3:10 in the **latter e** than at the beginning, 314
1Sa 3:12 when I begin, I will also **make an e**. 3615
9:27 *And* as they were going down to the **e** of 7097
10:13 when he had **made an e** of prophesying, 3615
13:10 that as soon as he had **made an e** of 3615
14:27 wherefore he put forth the **e** of the rod that 7097
14:43 taste a little honey with the **e** of the rod that 7097
18: 1 when he **made an e** of speaking unto Saul, 3615
24:16 when David had **made an e** of speaking 3615
2Sa 2:23 wherefore Abner with the **hinder e** of 310
2:26 not that it will be bitterness in the **latter e**? 314
6:18 as soon as David had **made an e** of offering 3615
11:19 When thou hast **made an e** of telling 3615
13:36 as soon as he had **made an e** of speaking, 3615
14:26 (for it was at every year's **e** that he polled 7093
24: 8 they came *to* Jerusalem at the **e** of nine 7097
1Ki 1:41 heard *it* as they had **made an e** of eating. 3615
2:39 it came to pass at the **e** of three years, 7093
3: 1 until he had **made an e** of building his own 3615
7:40 So Hiram **made an e** of doing all the work 3615
8:54 *that* when Solomon had **made an e** of 3615
9:10 it came to pass at the **e** of twenty years, 7097
2Ki 8: 3 it came to pass at the seven years' **e**, 7097
10:21 the house of Baal was full from **one e** to 6310
10:25 as soon as he had **made an e** of offering 3615
18:10 at the **e** of three years they took it: *even* in 7097
21:16 till he had filled Jerusalem from **one e** to 6310
1Ch 16: 2 when David had **made an e** of offering 3615
2Ch 4:10 he set the sea on the right side of the **east e**, 6924
5:12 stood *at* the east **e** of the altar, and NIH
7: 1 Now when Solomon had **made an e** of 3615
8: 1 it came to pass at the **e** of twenty years, 7093
20:16 ye shall find them at the **e** of the brook, 5490
20:23 when they had **made an e** of 3615
21:19 in process of time, after the **e** of two years, 7093
24:10 into the chest, until *they* had **made an e**. 3615
24:23 it came to pass at the **e** of the year, *that* 8622
29:17 day of the first month they **made an e**. 3615
29:29 when *they* had **made an e** of offering, 3615
Ezr 9:11 which have filled it from one **e** to another 6310
10:17 they **made an e** with all the men that had 3615
Ne 3:21 even to the **e** of the house of Eliashib. 8503
4: 2 will they **make an e** in a day? will they 3615
Job 6:11 what *is* mine **e**, that I should prolong my 7093
8: 7 yet thy **latter e** should greatly increase. 319
16: 3 Shall vain words **have an e**? or 7093
18: 2 How long *will it be ere* you make an **e** of 7078
26:10 until the day and night **come to an e**. 8503
28: 3 He setteth an **e** to darkness, and searcheth 7093
34:36 desire *is that* Job may be tried unto the **e** 5331
42:12 So the LORD blessed the **latter e** of Job 319
Ps 7: 9 wickedness of the wicked **come to an e**; 1584
9: 6 destructions are **come to** a perpetual **e**: 8552
19: 4 and their words to the **e** of the world. 7097
19: 6 His going forth *is* from the **e** of the heaven, 7097
30:12 **To the e that** *my* glory may sing 4616+3807.1
37:37 the upright: for the **e** of *that* man *is* peace. 319
37:38 the **e** of the wicked shall be cut off. 319
39: 4 make me to know mine **e**, and the measure 7093
46: 9 He maketh wars to cease unto the **e** of 7097
61: 2 From the **e** of the earth will I cry unto thee, 7097
73:17 sanctuary of God; *then* understood I their **e**. 319
102:27 *art* the same, and thy years shall have no **e**. 8552
107:27 and are **at** their **wit's e**. 1104+2451+3605
119:33 thy statutes; and I shall keep it *unto* the **e**. 6118
119:96 I have seen an **e** of all perfection: *but* 7093
119:112 perform thy statutes alway, *even unto* the **e**. 6118
Pr 5: 4 her **e** is bitter as wormwood, sharp as a 319
14:12 but the **e** thereof *are* the ways of death. 319
14:13 and the **e** of that mirth *is* heaviness. 319
16:25 but the **e** thereof *are* the ways of death. 319
19:20 that thou mayest be wise in thy **latter e**. 319
20:21 but the **e** thereof shall not be blessed. 319
23:18 For surely there is an **e**; and 319
25: 8 lest *thou know not* what to do in the **e** 319
Ecc 3:11 God maketh from the beginning to the **e**. 5490
4: 8 yet *is there* no **e** of all his labour; neither is 7093
4:16 *There is* no **e** of all the people, *even* of all 7093
7: 2 for that *is* the **e** of all men; and the living 5490
7: 8 Better *is* the **e** of a thing than the beginning 319
7:14 to the **e** that man should find nothing after 1700
10:13 and the **e** of his talk *is* mischievous madness. 319
12:12 of making many books *there is* no **e**; and 7093
Isa 2: 7 neither *is there any* **e** of their treasures; 7097
2: 7 neither *is there any* **e** of their chariots: 7097
5:26 will hiss unto them from the **e** of the earth: 7097
7: 3 at the **e** of the conduit of the upper pool in 7097
9: 7 and peace *there shall be* no **e**, 7093
13: 5 from the **e** of the heaven, *even* the LORD, 7097
16: 4 for the extortioner is **at an e**, the spoiler 656
23:15 after the **e** of seventy years shall Tyre sing 7093
23:17 it shall come to pass after the **e** of seventy 7093
33: 1 when thou shalt **make an e** to deal 5239
38:12 from day *even* to night wilt thou **make an e** 7999
38:13 from day *even* to night wilt thou **make an e** 7999
41:22 and know the **latter e** of them; 319
42:10 *and* his praise from the **e** of the earth, 7097
45:17 confounded **world without e**. 5703+5704+5769
46:10 Declaring the **e** from the beginning, and 319
47: 7 neither didst remember the **latter e** of it. 319
48:20 tell this, utter it *even* to the **e** of the earth; 7097
49: 6 that *thou* mayest be my salvation unto the **e** 7097
62:11 the LORD hath proclaimed unto the **e** of 7097
Jer 1: 3 unto the **e** of the eleventh year of Zedekiah 8552
3: 5 will he keep *it* to the **e**? Behold, thou hast 5331
4:27 be desolate; yet will I not make a **full e**. 3617
5:10 and destroy; but make not a **full e**: 3617
5:18 I will not make a **full e** with you. 3617
5:31 *it* so: and what will ye do in the **e** thereof? 319
12: 4 they said, He shall not see our **last e**. 319
12:12 **e** of the land even to the *other* end of 7097
12:12 of the land even to the *other* **e** of the land: 7097
17:11 midst of his days, and at his **e** shall be a fool. 319
25:33 **e** of the earth even unto the *other* end of 7097
25:33 the earth even unto the *other* **e** of the earth: 7097
26: 8 when Jeremiah had **made an e** of speaking 3615
29:11 and not of evil, to give you an expected **e**. 319
30:11 though I make a **full e** of all nations 3617
30:11 yet will I not make a **full e** of thee: 3617
31:17 there is hope in thine **e**, saith the LORD, 319
34:14 At the **e** of seven years let ye go every man 7093
43: 1 *that* when Jeremiah had **made an e** of 3615
44:27 by the famine, until there be an **e** of them. 3615
46:28 for I will make a **full e** of all the nations 3617
46:28 I will not make a **full e** of thee, but 3617
51:13 thine **e** is come, *and* the measure of thy 7093
51:31 of Babylon that his city is taken at *one* **e**, 7097
51:63 when thou hast **made an e** of reading this 3615
La 1: 9 she remembereth not her **last e**; therefore 319
4:18 our **e** is near, our days are fulfilled; for our 7093
4:18 our days are fulfilled; for our **e** is come. 7093
Eze 3:16 it came to pass at the **e** of seven days, 7097
7: 2 An **e**, the end is come upon the four corners 7093
7: 2 the **e** is come upon the four corners of 7093

Eze 7: 3 Now *is* the e *come* upon thee, and I will 7093
7: 6 An e is come, the end is come: it watcheth 7093
7: 6 An end is come, the e is come: it watcheth 7093
11:13 *wilt* thou make a **full e** of the remnant of 3617
20:17 neither did I make an e of them in 3617
20:26 might make them desolate, **to the e** 4616+3807.1
21:25 day is come, when iniquity *shall have* an e, 7093
21:29 when *their* iniquity *shall have* an e. 7093
29:13 At the e of forty years will I gather 7093
31:14 **To the e** that none of all the trees 4616+3807.1
35: 5 in the time *that their* iniquity *had* an e: 7093
39:14 after the e of seven months shall they 7097
41:12 e toward the west *was* seventy cubits broad; 6285
42:15 Now when he had **made an e** of measuring 3615
43:23 When thou hast **made an e** of cleansing *it,* 3615
48: 1 From the north e to the coast of the way of 7097
Da 1: 5 that at the e thereof they might stand before 7117
1:15 at the e of ten days their countenances 7117
1:18 Now at the e of the days that the king had 7117
4:11 the sight thereof to the e of all the earth: 5491
4:22 thy dominion to the e of the earth. 5491
4:29 At the e of twelve months he walked in 7118
4:34 at the e of the days I Nebuchadnezzar lift 7118
6:26 and his dominion *shall be even* unto the e. 5491
7:26 to consume and to destroy *it* unto the e. 5491
7:28 Hitherto *is* the e of the matter. *As for* me 5491
8:17 for at the time of the e *shall be* the vision. 7093
8:19 what shall be in the **last e** of the indignation: 319
8:19 for at the time appointed the e *shall be.* 7093
9:24 to **make an e** of sins, and to make 8552
9:26 the e thereof *shall be* with a flood, and 7093
9:26 unto the e of the war desolations *are* 7093
11: 6 in the e of years they shall join themselves 7093
11:27 for yet the e *shall be* at the time appointed. 7093
11:35 make *them* white, *even* to the time of the e: 7093
11:40 at the time of the e shall the king of 7093
11:45 yet he shall come to his e, and none shall 7093
12: 4 and seal the book, *even* to the time of the e: 7093
12: 6 How long *shall it be to* the e of *these* 7093
12: 8 my lord, what *shall be* the e of these *things?* 319
12: 9 closed up and sealed till the time of the e. 7093
12:13 go thou thy way till the e *be:* for thou shalt 7093
12:13 and stand in thy lot at the e of the days. 7093
Am 3:15 the great houses shall **have an e**, saith 5486
5:18 **to what e** *is* it for you? the day of 4100+3807.1
7: 2 *that* when they had **made an e** of eating 3615
8: 2 The e is come upon my people *of* Israel; 7093
8:10 an only *son,* and the e thereof as a bitter day. 319
Ob 1: 9 **to the e that** every one of 4616+3807.1
Na 1: 8 will make an **utter** e of the place thereof, 3617
1: 9 he *will* make an **utter** e: affliction shall not 3617
2: 9 for *there is* none e of the store *and* glory out 7097
3: 3 and *there is* none e of *their* corpses; 7097
Hab 2: 3 but at the e it shall speak, and not lie: 7093
Mt 10:22 but he that endureth to the e shall be saved. *5056*
11: 1 when Jesus had **made an e** of commanding *5055*
13:39 the harvest is the e of the world; and *4930*
13:40 the fire; so shall it be in the e of this world. *4930*
13:49 So shall it be at the e of the world: *4930*
24: 3 of thy coming, and of the e of the world? *4930*
24: 6 must come to pass, but the e is not yet. *5056*
24:13 But he that shall endure unto the e, *5056*
24:14 unto all nations; and then shall the e come. *5056*
24:31 from one e of heaven to the other. *206*
26:58 and sat with the servants, to see the e. *5056*
28: 1 **In the e** of the sabbath, as it began to dawn *3796*
28:20 you alway, *even* unto the e of the world. *4930*
Mk 3:26 be divided, he cannot stand, but hath an e. *5056*
13: 7 must needs be; but the e *shall* not *be* yet. *5056*
13:13 but he that shall endure unto the e, the same *5056*
Lk 1:33 and of his kingdom there shall be no e. *5056*
18: 1 And he spake a parable unto them *to this* e, NIG
21: 9 come to pass; but the e *is* not by and by. *5056*
22:37 for the *things* concerning me have an e. *5056*
Jn 13: 1 in the world, he loved them unto the e. *5056*
18:37 **To this** e was I born, and for this cause *1519*
Ac 7:19 **to the e** *they* might not live. *1519+3588*
Ro 1:11 **to the e** you may be established; *1519+3588*
4:16 **to the e** the promise might be sure to *1519+3588*
6:21 for the e of those *things is* death. *5056*
6:22 unto holiness, and the e everlasting life. *5056*
10: 4 For Christ *is* the e of the law for *5056*
14: 9 For **to this e** Christ both died, and *1519+3778*
1Co 1: 8 Who shall also confirm you unto the e, *5056*
15:24 Then *cometh* the e, when he shall have *5056*
2Co 1:13 I trust you shall acknowledge even to the e; *5056*
2: 9 For **to this e** also did I write, that I *1519+3778*
3:13 look to the e of that which is abolished: *5056*
11:15 whose e shall be according to their works. *5056*
Eph 3:21 all ages, **world without e.** *165+165+3588+3588*
Php 3:19 Whose e *is* destruction, whose God *is their* *5056*
1Th 3:13 **To the e** *he* may stablish your hearts *1519+3588*
1Ti 1: 5 Now the e of the commandment is charity *5056*
Heb 3: 6 the rejoicing of the hope firm unto the e. *5056*
3:14 of *our* confidence stedfast unto the e; *5056*
6: 8 nigh unto cursing; whose e *is* to be burned. *5056*
6:11 to the full assurance of hope unto the e: *5056*
6:16 an oath for confirmation *is* to them an e of *4009*
7: 3 neither beginning of days, nor e of life; *5056*
9:26 now once in the e of the world hath he *4930*
13: 7 considering the e of *their* conversation. *1545*
Jas 5:11 of Job, and have seen the e of the Lord; *5056*
1Pe 1: 9 Receiving the e of your faith, *even* *5056*
1:13 hope to the e for the grace that is *to be* *5049*
4: 7 But the e of all *things* is at hand: be ye *5056*
4:17 what *shall* the e *be* of them that obey not *5056*
2Pe 2:20 the latter e is worse with them than NIG
Rev 2:26 and keepeth my works unto the e, *5056*
21: 6 and Omega, the beginning and the e. *5056*
22:13 the beginning and the e, the first and *5056*

ENDAMAGE (1) [DAMAGE]
Ezr 4:13 and *so* thou shalt e the revenue of the kings. 5142

ENDANGER (1) [ENDANGERED]
Da 1:10 shall ye **make** *me* e my head to the king. 2325

ENDANGERED (1) [ENDANGER]
Ecc 10: 9 he that cleaveth wood shall be e thereby. 5533

ENDEAVOUR (1) [ENDEAVOURED, ENDEAVOURING, ENDEAVOURS]
2Pe 1:15 Moreover I will e that you may be able *4704*

ENDEAVOURED (2) [ENDEAVOUR]
Ac 16:10 immediately we e to go into Macedonia, *2212*
1Th 2:17 e the more abundantly to see your face with *4704*

ENDEAVOURING (1) [ENDEAVOUR]
Eph 4: 3 E to keep the unity of the Spirit in the bond *4704*

ENDEAVOURS (1) [ENDEAVOUR]
Ps 28: 4 and according to the wickedness of their e: 4611

ENDED (21) [END]
Ge 2: 2 on the seventh day God e his work which 3615
41:53 that was in the land of Egypt, were e. 3615
47:18 When that year was e, they came unto him 8552
Dt 31:30 the words of this song, until they were e. 8552
34: 8 *and* mourning for Moses were e. 8552
Ru 2:21 until they have e all my harvest. 3615
2Sa 20:18 *counsel* at Abel: and so they e *the matter.* 8552
1Ki 7:51 So was e all the work that king Solomon 7999
2Ch 29:34 till the work was e, and until the *other* 3615
Job 31:40 instead of barley. The words of Job are e. 8552
Ps 72:20 The prayers of David the son of Jesse are e. 3615
Isa 60:20 and the days of thy mourning shall be e. 7999
Jer 8:20 the summer is e, and we are not saved. 3615
Eze 4: 8 till thou hast e the days of thy siege. 3615
Mt 7:28 to pass, when Jesus had e these sayings, *4931*
Lk 4: 2 and when they were e, he afterward *4931*
4:13 And when the devil had e all *4931*
7: 1 Now when he had e all his sayings in *4137*
Jn 13: 2 And supper being e, the devil having now *1096*
Ac 19:21 After these *things* were e, Paul purposed in *4137*
21:27 And when the seven days were almost e, *4931*

ENDETH (1) [END]
Isa 24: 8 the noise of them that rejoice e, the joy of 2308

ENDING (1) [END]
Rev 1: 8 and Omega, the beginning and the e, *5056*

ENDLESS (2) [END]
1Ti 1: 4 give heed to fables and e genealogies, *562*
Heb 7:16 but after the power of an e life. *179*

ENDOR, EN-DOR (3) [ENDOR]
Jos 17:11 the inhabitants of E and her towns, and 5874
1Sa 28: 7 *is* a woman that hath a familiar spirit at E. 5874
Ps 83:10 *Which* perished at E: they became *as* dung 5874

ENDOW (1)
Ex 22:16 he shall **surely** e her to be his wife. 4117+4117

ENDS (51) [END]
Ex 25:18 make them, in the two e of the mercy seat. 7098
25:19 make the cherubims on the two e thereof. 7098
28:14 two chains *of* pure gold at the e; 4020
28:22 at the e *of* wreathen work *of* pure gold. 1383
28:23 shalt put the two rings on the two e of 7098
28:24 rings *which are* on the e of the breastplate. 7098
28:25 *the other* two e of the two wreathen *chains* 7098
28:26 thou shalt put them upon the two e of 7098
37: 7 he them, on the two e of the mercy seat; 7098
37: 8 he the cherubims on the two e thereof. 7098
38: 5 he cast four rings for the four e of the grate 7099
39:15 made upon the breastplate chains **at the e**, 1383
39:16 put the two rings in the two e of 7098
39:17 in the two rings on the e of the breastplate. 7098
39:18 the two e of the two wreathen *chains* they 7098
39:19 put *them* on the two e of the breastplate, 7098
Dt 33:17 push the people together *to* the e of the earth: 657
1Sa 2:10 the LORD shall judge the e of the earth; 657
1Ki 8: 8 that the e of the staves were seen out in 7218
2Ch 5: 9 e of the staves were seen from the ark 7218
Job 28:24 For he looketh to the e of the earth, *and* 7098
37: 3 and his lightning unto the e of the earth. 3671
38:13 That *it* might take hold of the e of the earth, 3671
Ps 19: 6 the heaven, and his circuit unto the e of it: 7098
22:27 All the e of the world shall remember and 657
48:10 so *is* thy praise unto the e of the earth: 7099
59:13 God ruleth in Jacob unto the e of the earth. 657
65: 5 *who art* the confidence of all the e of 7099
67: 7 and all the e of the earth shall fear him. 657
72: 8 and from the river unto the e of the earth. 657
98: 3 all the e of the earth have seen the salvation 657
135: 7 vapours to ascend from the e of the earth; 7097
Pr 17:24 the eyes of a fool *are* in the e of the earth. 7097
30: 4 who hath established all the e of the earth? 657
Isa 26:15 thou hadst removed *it* far *unto* all the e of 7099
40:28 the Creator of the e of the earth, 7098
41: 5 the e of the earth were afraid, drew near, 7098
41: 9 *Thou* whom I have taken from the e of 7098
43: 6 and my daughters from the e of the earth; 7097
45:22 and be ye saved, all the e of the earth: 657
52:10 all the e of the earth shall see the salvation of 657
Jer 10:13 he causeth the vapours to ascend from the e 7097
16:19 the Gentiles shall come unto thee from the e 657
25:31 A noise shall come *even* to the e of 7097
51:16 he causeth the vapours to ascend from the e 7097
Eze 15: 4 the fire devoureth both the e of it, and 7098
Mic 5: 4 for now shall he be great unto the e of 657
Zec 9:10 and from the river *even* to the e of the earth. 657
Ac 13:47 be for salvation unto the e of the earth. *2078*
Ro 10:18 and their words unto the e of the world. *4009*
1Co 10:11 upon whom the e of the world are come. *5056*

ENDUED (5)
Ge 30:20 God hath e me with a good dowry; 2064
2Ch 2:12 e with prudence and understanding, 3045
2:13 e with understanding, of Huram my 3045
Lk 24:49 until ye be **e with** power from on high. *1746*
Jas 3:13 and e with knowledge amongst you? NIG

ENDURE (29) [ENDURED, ENDURETH, ENDURING]
Ge 33:14 and the children be **able to e**, 7272+3807.1
Ex 18:23 *so,* then thou shalt be able to e, 5975
Est 8: 6 For how can I e to see the evil that shall 3201
8: 6 how can I e to see the destruction of my 3201
Job 8:15 he shall hold it fast, but it shall not e. 6965
31:23 and by reason of his highness I **could** not e. 3201
Ps 9: 7 the LORD shall e for ever: he hath 3427
30: 5 weeping may e for a night, but joy *cometh* 3885
72: 5 thee as long as the sun and moon e, 6440+3807.1
72:17 His name shall e for ever: his name shall be 1961
89:29 His seed also will I make *to* e for ever, and NIH
89:36 His seed shall e for ever, and his throne as 1961
102:12 thou, O LORD, shalt e for ever; and 3427
102:26 They shall perish, but thou shalt e: yea, 5975
104:31 The glory of the LORD shall e for ever: 1961
Pr 27:24 and doth the crown e to every generation? NIH
Eze 22:14 Can thine heart e, or can thine hands be 5975
Mt 24:13 But he that shall e unto the end, the same *5278*
Mk 4:17 root in themselves, and so e but for a time; *1510*
13:13 but he that shall e unto the end, the same *5278*
2Th 1: 4 your persecutions and tribulations that ye e: *430*
2Ti 2: 3 Thou therefore e **hardness**, as a good *2553*
2:10 Therefore I e all *things* for the elects' sakes, *5278*
4: 3 For the time will come when they will not e *430*
4: 5 But watch thou in all *things,* e **afflictions**, *2553*
Heb 12: 7 If ye e chastening, God dealeth with you as *5278*
12:20 (For they could not e that which was *5342*
Jas 5:11 Behold, we count them happy which e. *5278*
1Pe 2:19 if a man for conscience toward God e grief, *5297*

ENDURED (8) [ENDURE]
Ps 81:15 but their time should have e for ever. 1961
Ro 9:22 e with much longsuffering *the* vessels of *5342*
2Ti 3:11 at Lystra; what persecutions I e: *5297*
Heb 6:15 And so, after he had **patiently** e, *3114*
10:32 ye e a great fight of afflictions; *5278*
11:27 for he e, as seeing *him who is* invisible. *2594*
12: 2 who for the joy that was set before him e *5278*
12: 3 For consider him that e such contradiction *5278*

ENDURETH (59) [ENDURE]
1Ch 16:34 for *he is* good; for his mercy *e* for ever. NIH
16:41 the LORD, because his mercy *e* for ever; NIH
2Ch 5:13 For *he is* good; for his mercy *e* for ever: NIH
7: 3 For *he is* good; for his mercy *e* for ever. NIH
7: 6 because his mercy *e* for ever, when David NIH
20:21 Praise the LORD; for his mercy *e* for ever. NIH
Ezr 3:11 for his mercy *e* for ever towards Israel. NIH
Ps 30: 5 For his anger *e but* a moment; in his favour NIH
52: 1 O mighty *man?* the goodness of God *e* NIH
72: 7 of peace **so long as** the moon e. 1097+5704
100: 5 his truth *e* to all generations. NIH
106: 1 for *he is* good: for his mercy *e* for ever. NIH
107: 1 for *he is* good: for his mercy *e* for ever. NIH
111: 3 glorious: and his righteousness e for ever. 5975
111:10 *his commandments:* his praise e for ever. 5975
112: 3 his house: and his righteousness e for ever. 5975
112: 9 to the poor; his righteousness e for ever; 5975
117: 2 the truth of the LORD *e* for ever. Praise ye NIH
118: 1 for *he is* good: because his mercy *e* for ever. NIH
118: 2 Israel now say, that his mercy *e* for ever. NIH
118: 3 of Aaron now say, that his mercy *e* for ever. NIH
118: 4 the LORD say, that his mercy *e* for ever. NIH
118:29 for *he is* good: for his mercy *e* for ever. NIH
119:160 every one of thy righteous judgments *e* for NIH
135:13 Thy name, O LORD, *e* for ever; *and* NIH
136: 1 for *he is* good: for his mercy *e* for ever. NIH
136: 2 the God of gods: for his mercy *e* for ever. NIH
136: 3 the Lord of lords: for his mercy *e* for ever. NIH
136: 4 great wonders: for his mercy *e* for ever. NIH
136: 5 made the heavens: for his mercy *e* for ever. NIH
136: 6 above the waters: for his mercy *e* for ever. NIH
136: 7 made great lights: for his mercy *e* for ever: NIH
136: 8 sun to rule by day: for his mercy *e* for ever: NIH
136: 9 to rule by night: for his mercy *e* for ever. NIH
136:10 in their firstborn: for his mercy *e* for ever: NIH
136:11 from among them: for his mercy *e* for ever: NIH
136:12 stretched out arm: for his mercy *e* for ever: NIH
136:13 Red sea into parts: for his mercy *e* for ever: NIH
136:14 the midst of it: for his mercy *e* for ever: NIH
136:15 host in the Red sea: for his mercy *e* for ever. NIH
136:16 the wilderness: for his mercy *e* for ever. NIH
136:17 smote great kings: for his mercy *e* for ever: NIH
136:18 slew famous kings: for his mercy *e* for ever: NIH
136:19 of the Amorites: for his mercy *e* for ever: NIH
136:20 the king of Bashan: for his mercy *e* for ever: NIH
136:21 for an heritage: for his mercy *e* for ever: NIH
136:22 Israel his servant: for his mercy *e* for ever. NIH
136:23 in our low estate: for his mercy *e* for ever: NIH
136:24 from our enemies: for his mercy *e* for ever. NIH
136:25 food to all flesh: for his mercy *e* for ever. NIH
136:26 the God of heaven: for his mercy *e* for ever. NIH
138: 8 thy mercy, O LORD, *e* for ever: NIH
145:13 thy dominion *e* throughout all generations. NIH
Jer 33:11 LORD *is* good; for his mercy *e* for ever: NIH
Mt 10:22 but he that e to the end shall be saved. *5278*
Jn 6:27 for *that* meat which e unto everlasting life, *3306*
1Co 13: 7 all *things,* hopeth all *things,* e all *things.* *5278*
Jas 1:12 Blessed *is* the man that e temptation: *5278*
1Pe 1:25 But the word of the Lord e for ever. And *3306*

ENDURING (3) [ENDURE]
Ps 19: 9 The fear of the LORD *is* clean, e for ever: 5975
2Co 1: 6 which is effectual in the e of the same *5281*
Heb 10:34 have in heaven a better and an e substance. *3306*

EN-EGLAIM (1)

Eze 47:10 stand upon it from En-gedi even unto E; 5882

ENEMIES (267) [ENEMY]

Ge 14:20 which hath delivered thine e into thy hand. 6862
22:17 and thy seed shall possess the gate of his e; 341
49: 8 thy hand *shall be* in the neck of thine e; 341
Ex 1:10 they join also unto our e, and fight against 8130
23:22 I will be an enemy unto thine e, and 341
23:27 I will make all thine e turn their backs unto 341
32:25 naked unto *their* shame amongst their e:) 6965
Lev 26: 7 ye shall chase your e, and they shall fall 341
26: 8 your e shall fall before you by the sword. 341
26:16 sow your seed in vain, for your e shall eat it. 341
26:17 and ye shall be slain before your e; 341
26:32 your e which dwell therein shall be 341
26:36 into their hearts in the lands of their e; 341
26:37 shall have no power to stand before your e. 341
26:38 and the land of your e shall eat you up. 341
26:41 have brought them into the land of their e; 341
26:44 all that, when they be in the land of their e, 341
Nu 10: 9 your God, and ye shall be saved from your e. 341
10:35 LORD, and let thine e be scattered; 341
14:42 that ye be not smitten before your e. 341
23:11 I took thee to curse mine e, and behold, 341
24: 8 he shall eat up the nations his e, and 6862
24:10 I called thee to curse mine e, and behold, 341
24:18 Seir also shall be a possession for his e; 341
32:21 until he hath driven out his e from before 341
Dt 1:42 among you; lest ye be smitten before your e. 341
6:19 To cast out all thine e from before thee, 341
12:10 *when* he giveth you rest from all your e 341
20: 1 When thou goest out to battle against thine e, 341
20: 3 approach *this* day unto battle against your e: 341
20: 4 to fight for you against your e, to save you. 341
20:14 thou shalt eat the spoil of thine e, which 341
21:10 When thou goest forth to war against thine e, 341
23: 9 When the host goeth forth against thine e, 341
23:14 and to give up thine e before thee; 341
25:19 given thee rest from all thine e round about, 341
28: 7 The LORD shall cause thine e that rise up 341
28:25 shall cause thee *to be* smitten before thine e: 341
28:31 thy sheep *shall be* given unto thine e, and 341
28:48 Therefore shalt thou serve thine e which 341
28:53 wherewith thine e shall distress thee: 341
28:55 wherewith thine e shall distress thee in all 341
28:68 there ye shall be sold unto your e for 341
30: 7 God will put all these curses upon thine e, 341
32:31 even our e themselves *being* judges. 341
32:41 I will render vengeance to mine e, and 6862
33: 7 and be thou a help *to him* from his e. 6862
33:29 thine e shall be found liars unto thee; and 341
Jos 7: 8 Israel turneth *their* backs before their e! 341
7:12 of Israel could not stand before their e, 341
7:12 *but* turned *their* backs before their e, because 341
7:13 thou canst not stand before thine e, until ye 341
10:13 people had avenged themselves upon their e. 341
10:19 *but* pursue after your e, and smite 341
10:25 for thus shall the LORD do to all your e 341
21:44 there stood not a man of all their e before 341
21:44 the LORD delivered all their e into their 341
22: 8 divide the spoil of your e with your brethren. 341
23: 1 rest unto Israel from all their e round about, 341
Jdg 2:14 he sold them into the hands of their e round 341
2:14 could not any longer stand before their e. 341
2:18 delivered them out of the hand of their e all 341
3:28 for the LORD hath delivered your e 341
5:31 So let all thine e perish, O LORD: but 341
8:34 out of the hands of all their e on every side: 341
11:36 hath taken vengeance for thee of thine e, 341
1Sa 2: 1 my mouth is enlarged over mine e; because 341
4: 3 it may save us out of the hand of our e. 341
12:10 now deliver us out of the hand of our e, and 341
12:11 delivered you out of the hand of your e on 341
14:24 that I may be avenged on mine e. 341
14:30 day of the spoil of their e which they found? 341
14:47 fought against all his e on every side, 341
18:25 the Philistines, to be avenged of the king's e. 341
20:15 not when the LORD hath cut off the e of 341
20:16 even require *it* at the hand of David's e. 341
25:22 and more also do God unto the e of David, 341
25:26 now let thine e, and they that seek evil to my 341
25:29 the souls of thine e, them shall he sling out 341
29: 8 that I may not go fight against the e of my 341
30:26 Behold a present for you of the spoil of the e 341
2Sa 3:18 and out of the hand of all their e. 341
5:20 The LORD hath broken forth upon mine e 341
7: 1 given him rest round about from all his e; 341
7: 9 have cut off all thine e out of thy sight, and 341
7:11 and have caused thee to rest from all thine e. 341
12:14 to the e of the LORD to blaspheme, 341
18:19 that the LORD hath avenged him of his e. 341
18:32 The e of my lord the king, and all that rise 341
19: 6 In that thou lovest thine e, and hatest thy 8130
19: 9 The king saved us out of the hand of our e, 341
22: 1 delivered him out of the hand of all his e, 341
22: 4 be praised: so shall I be saved from mine e. 341
22:38 I have pursued mine e, and destroyed them; 341
22:41 Thou hast also given me the necks of mine e, 341
22:49 that bringeth me forth from mine e: thou also 341
24:13 wilt thou flee three months before thine e, 6862
1Ki 3:11 for thyself, nor hast asked the life of thine e; 341
8:48 and with all their soul, in the land of their e, 341
2Ki 17:39 deliver you out of the hand of all your e. 341
21:14 and deliver them into the hand of their e; 341
21:14 shall become a prey and a spoil to all their e; 341
1Ch 12:17 if *ye be come* to betray me to mine e, 6862
14:11 God hath broken in upon mine e by mine 341
17: 8 and have cut off all thine e from before thee, 341
17:10 Moreover I will subdue all thine e. 341
21:12 while that the sword of thine e overtaketh 341
22: 9 I will give him rest from all his e round 341
2Ch 1:11 wealth, or honour, nor the life of thine e, 8130
6:28 if their e besiege them in the cities of their 341
2Ch 6:34 If thy people go out to war against their e by 341
6:36 deliver them *over* before *their* e, and 341
20:27 had made them to rejoice over their e. 341
20:29 the LORD fought against the e of Israel. 341
25:20 might deliver them into the hand *of their* e, NIH
Ne 4:15 when our e heard that it was known unto us, 341
5: 9 of the reproach of the heathen our e? 341
6: 1 Geshem the Arabian, and the rest of our e, 341
6:16 that when all our e heard *thereof*, and all 341
9:27 deliveredst them into the hand of their e, 6862
9:27 who saved them out of the hand of their e. 6862
9:28 leftest thou them in the hand of their e, 341
Est 8:13 that day to avenge themselves on their e. 341
9: 1 in the day that the e of the Jews hoped to 341
9: 5 Thus the Jews smote all their e *with* 341
9:16 had rest from their e, and slew of their foes 341
9:22 days wherein the Jews rested from their e, 341
Job 19:11 he counteth me unto him as *one of* his e. 6862
Ps 3: 7 for thou hast smitten all mine e *upon* 341
5: 8 in thy righteousness because of mine e; 8324
6: 7 it waxeth old because of all mine e. 6887
6:10 Let all mine e be ashamed and sore vexed: 341
7: 6 up thyself because of the rage of mine e: 6887
8: 2 thou ordained strength because of thine e, 6887
9: 3 When mine e are turned back, they shall fall 341
10: 5 his sight: *as for* all his e, he puffeth at them. 6887
17: 9 *from* my deadly e, *who* compass me about. 341
18: T delivered him from the hand of all his e, 341
18: 3 be praised: so shall I be saved from mine e. 341
18:37 I have pursued mine e, and overtaken them: 341
18:40 Thou hast also given me the necks of mine e; 341
18:48 He delivereth me from my e: yea, 341
21: 8 Thine hand shall find out all thine e: 341
23: 5 a table before me in the presence of mine e: 6887
25: 2 be ashamed, let not mine e triumph over me. 341
25:19 Consider mine e; for they are many; and 341
27: 2 the wicked, *even* mine e and my foes, 6862
27: 6 be lifted up above mine e round about me: 341
27:11 lead me in a plain path, because of mine e. 8324
27:12 me not over unto the will of mine e: 6862
31:11 I was a reproach among all mine e, but 6887
31:15 deliver me from the hand of mine e, and 341
35:19 Let not them that are mine e wrongfully 341
37:20 the e of the LORD *shall be* as the fat of 341
38:19 mine e *are* lively, *and* they are strong: and 341
41: 2 wilt not deliver him unto the will of his e. 341
41: 5 Mine e speak evil of me, When shall he die, 341
42:10 a sword in my bones, mine e reproach me; 6887
44: 5 Through thee will we push down our e: 6862
44: 7 thou hast saved us from our e, and hast put 6862
45: 5 arrows *are* sharp in the heart of the king's e; 341
54: 5 He shall reward evil unto mine e: cut them 8324
54: 7 mine eye hath seen *his desire* upon mine e. 341
56: 2 Mine e would daily swallow *me* up: 8324
56: 9 I cry *unto thee*, then shall mine e turn back: 341
59: 1 Deliver me from mine e, O my God: 341
59:10 shall let me see *my desire* upon mine e. 8324
60:12 for he *it is that* shall tread down our e. 6862
66: 3 shall thine e submit themselves unto thee. 341
68: 1 Let God arise, let his e be scattered: let them 341
68:21 God shall wound the head of his e, *and* 341
68:23 foot may be dipped in the blood of *thine* e, 341
69: 4 *being* mine e wrongfully, are mighty: 341
69:18 *and* redeem it: deliver me because of mine e. 341
71:10 For mine e speak against me; and they that 341
72: 9 bow before him; and his e shall lick the dust. 341
74: 4 Thine e roar in the midst of thy 6887
74:23 Forget not the voice of thine e: the tumult 6887
78:53 feared not: but the sea overwhelmed their e. 341
78:66 he smote his e in the hinder parts: he put 6862
80: 6 and our e laugh among themselves. 341
81:14 I should soon have subdued their e, and 341
83: 2 For lo, thine e make a tumult: and they that 341
89:10 thou hast scattered thine e with thy strong 341
89:42 thou hast made all his e to rejoice. 341
89:51 Wherewith thine e have reproached, 341
92: 9 For lo, thine e, O LORD, for lo, 341
92: 9 O LORD, for lo, thine e shall perish; 341
92:11 eye also shall see *my desire* on mine e, 7790
97: 3 and burneth up his e round about. 6862
102: 8 Mine e reproach me all the day; *and* 341
105:24 and made them stronger than their e. 6862
106:11 the waters covered their e: there was not 6862
106:42 Their e also oppressed them, and they were 341
108:13 for he *it is that* shall tread down our e. 6862
110: 1 right hand, until I make thine e thy footstool. 341
110: 2 out of Zion: rule thou in the midst of thine e. 341
112: 8 be afraid, until he see *his desire* upon his e. 6862
119:98 hast made me wiser than mine e: 341
119:139 because mine e have forgotten thy words. 6862
119:157 Many *are* my persecutors and mine e; 6862
127: 5 but they shall speak with the e in the gate. 341
132:18 His e will I clothe with shame: but 341
136:24 hath redeemed us from our e: for his mercy 6862
138: 7 forth thine hand against the wrath of mine e, 341
139:20 *and* thine e take *thy name* in vain. 6145
139:22 *with* perfect hatred: I count them mine e. 341
143: 9 Deliver me, O LORD, from mine e: I flee 341
143:12 of thy mercy cut off mine e, and destroy all 341
Pr 16: 7 he maketh even his e to be at peace with 341
Isa 1:24 mine adversaries, and avenge me of mine e: 341
9:11 of Rezin against him, and join his e together; 341
26:11 yea, the fire of thine e shall devour them. 6862
42:13 yea, roar; he shall prevail against his e. 341
59:18 fury to his adversaries, recompence to his e; 341
62: 8 no more give thy corn *to be* meat for thine e; 341
66: 6 LORD that rendereth recompence to his e. 341
66:14 and *his* indignation towards his e. 341
Jer 12: 7 beloved of my soul into the hand of her e. 341
15: 9 will I deliver to the sword before their e, 341
15:14 I will make *thee* to pass with thine e into a 341
17: 4 I will cause thee to serve thine e in the land 341
19: 7 them to fall by the sword before their e, 341
19: 9 wherewith their e, and they that seek their 341
20: 4 they shall fall by the sword of their e, and 341
Jer 20: 5 of Judah will I give into the hand of their e, 341
21: 7 into the hand of their e, and into the hand of 341
34:20 I will even give them into the hand of their e, 341
34:21 princes will I give into the hand of their e, 341
44:30 king of Egypt into the hand of his e, 341
48: 5 for in the going down of Horonaim the e 6862
49:37 cause Elam to be dismayed before their e, 341
La 1: 2 with her, they are become her e. 341
1: 5 Her adversaries are the chief, her e prosper; 341
1:21 all mine e have heard of my trouble; they are 341
2:16 All thine e have opened their mouth against 341
3:46 All our e have opened their mouths against 341
3:52 Mine e chased me sore, like a bird, 341
Eze 39:23 and gave them into the hand of their e: 6862
Da 4:19 and the interpretation thereof to thine e. 6146
Am 9: 4 though they go into captivity before their e, 341
Mic 4:10 shall redeem thee from the hand of thine e. 341
5: 9 and all thine e shall be cut off. 341
7: 6 a man's e *are* the men of his own house. 341
Na 1: 2 and he reserveth *wrath* for his e. 341
1: 8 and darkness shall pursue his e. 341
3:13 thy land shall be set wide open unto thine e: 341
Zec 10: 5 *their* e in the mire of the streets in the battle: NIH
Mt 5:44 But I say unto you, Love your e, bless them 2190
22:44 right hand, till I make thine e thy footstool? 2190
Mk 12:36 right hand, till I make thine e thy footstool. 2190
Lk 1:71 That *we* should be saved from our e, and 2190
1:74 hand of our e might serve him without fear, 2190
6:27 I say unto you which hear, Love your e, 2190
6:35 But love ye your e, and do good, and lend, 2190
19:27 But those mine e, which would not that I 2190
19:43 that thine e shall cast a trench about thee, 2190
20:43 Till I make thine e thy footstool. 2190
Ro 5:10 For if, when we were e, we were reconciled 2190
11:28 the gospel, *they are* e for your sakes: 2190
1Co 15:25 till he hath put all e under his feet. 2190
Php 3:18 *that they are* the e of the cross of Christ: 2190
Col 1:21 and e in *your* mind by wicked works, 2190
Heb 1:13 until I make thine e thy footstool? 2190
10:13 From henceforth expecting till his e be 2190
Rev 11: 5 out of their mouth, and devoureth their e: 2190
11:12 heaven in a cloud; and their e beheld them. 2190

ENEMIES' (3) [ENEMY]

Lev 26:34 as it lieth desolate, and ye *be* in your e land; 341
26:39 pine away in their iniquity in your e lands; 341
Eze 39:27 gathered them out of their e lands, and 341

ENEMY (107) [ENEMIES, ENEMIES', ENEMY'S]

Ex 15: 6 O LORD, hath dashed in pieces the e. 341
15: 9 The e said, I will pursue, I will overtake, 341
23:22 I will be an e unto thine enemies, and 340
Lev 26:25 ye shall be delivered into the hand of the e. 341
Nu 10: 9 if ye go *to* war in your land against the e 6862
35:23 *it* upon him, that he die, and *was* not his e, 341
Dt 28:57 wherewith thine e shall distress thee in thy 341
32:27 Were it not that I feared the wrath of the e, 341
32:42 from the beginning of revenges upon the e. 341
33:27 he shall thrust out the e from before thee; 341
Jdg 16:23 Our god hath delivered Samson our e into 341
16:24 Our god hath delivered into our hands our e, 341
1Sa 2:32 thou shalt see an e *in my* habitation, in all 6862
18:29 and Saul became David's e continually. 341
19:17 and sent away mine e, that he is escaped? 341
24: 4 Behold, I will deliver thine e into thine hand, 341
24:19 For if a man find his e, will he let him go 341
26: 8 God hath delivered thine e into thine hand 341
28:16 departed from thee, and is become thine e? 6145
2Sa 4: 8 head of Ish-bosheth the son of Saul thine e, 341
22:18 He delivered me from my strong e, *and* 341
1Ki 8:33 people Israel be smitten down before the e, 341
8:37 if their e besiege them in the land of their 341
8:44 If thy people go out to battle against their e, 341
8:46 deliver them to the e, so that they carry them 341
8:46 them away captives unto the land of the e, 341
21:20 to Elijah, Hast thou found me, O mine e? 341
2Ch 6:24 Israel be put to the worse before the e, 341
25: 8 God shall make thee fall before the e: 341
26:13 mighty power, to help the king against the e. 341
Ezr 8:22 horsemen to help us against the e in the way: 341
8:31 he delivered us from the hand of the e, and 341
Est 3:10 of Hammedatha the Agagite, the Jews' e. 6887
7: 4 although the e could not countervail 6862
7: 6 The adversary and e *is* this wicked Haman. 341
8: 1 Haman the Jews' e unto Esther the queen. 6887
9:10 the e of the Jews, slew they; 6887
9:24 the Agagite, the e of all the Jews, 6887
Job 13:24 thou thy face, and holdest me for thine e? 341
16: 9 mine e sharpeneth his eyes upon me. 6862
27: 7 Let mine e be as the wicked, and he that 341
33:10 against me, he counteth me for his e, 341
Ps 7: 4 delivered him that without cause is mine e:) 6887
7: 5 Let the e persecute my soul, and take *it*; yea, 341
8: 2 that *thou* mightest still the e and the avenger. 341
9: 6 O thou e, destructions are come to a 341
13: 2 how long shall mine e be exalted over me? 341
13: 4 Lest mine e say, I have prevailed against 341
18:17 He delivered me from my strong e, and 341
31: 8 hast not shut me up into the hand of the e: 341
41:11 because mine e doth not triumph over me. 341
42: 9 because of the oppression of the e? 341
43: 2 because of the oppression of the e? 341
44:10 Thou makest us to turn back from the e: 6862
44:16 blasphemeth; by reason of the e and avenger. 341
55: 3 Because of the voice of the e, because of 341
55:12 For *it was* not an e *that* reproached me; then 341
61: 3 shelter for me, *and* a strong tower from the e. 341
64: 1 preserve my life from fear of the e. 341
74: 3 *even* all *that* the e hath done wickedly in 341
74:10 shall the e blaspheme thy name for ever? 341
74:18 *that* the e hath reproached, O LORD, and 341
78:42 the day when he delivered them from the e. 6862
89:22 The e shall not exact upon him; nor the son 341
106:10 and redeemed them from the hand of the e. 341
107: 2 he hath redeemed from the hand of the e; 6862

Ps 143: 3 For the e hath persecuted my soul; he hath 341
Pr 24:17 Rejoice not when thine e falleth, and let not 341
25:21 If thine e *be* hungry, give him bread to eat; 8130
27: 6 a friend; but the kisses of an e *are* deceitful. 8130
Isa 59:19 When the e shall come in like a flood, 6862
63:10 therefore he was turned to be their e, *and* 341
Jer 6:25 for the sword of the e *and* fear *is* on every 341
15:11 verily I will cause the e to entreat thee *well* 341
18:17 them as *with* an east wind before the e; 341
30:14 I have wounded thee *with* the wound of an e, 341
31:16 they shall come again from the land of the e. 341
44:30 of Babylon, his e, and that sought his life. 341
La 1: 5 are gone *into* captivity before the e. 6862
1: 7 when her people fell into the hand of the e, 6862
1: 9 for the e hath magnified *himself.* 341
1:16 are desolate, because the e prevailed. 341
2: 3 drawn back his right hand from before the e, 341
2: 4 He hath bent his bow like an e: *he* stood *with* 341
2: 5 The Lord was as an e: he hath swallowed up 341
2: 7 he hath given up into the hand of the e 341
2:17 he hath caused *thine* e to rejoice over thee, 341
2:22 and brought up hath mine e consumed. 341
4:12 the e should have entered into the gates of 341
Eze 36: 2 Because the e hath said against you, Aha, 341
Hos 8: 3 *the thing that is* good: the e shall pursue him. 341
Mic 2: 8 Even of late my people is risen up as an e: 341
7: 8 Rejoice not against me, O mine e: when I 341
7:10 she *that is* mine e shall see *it,* and 341
Na 3:11 also shalt seek strength because of the e. 341
Zep 3:15 away thy judgments, he hath cast out thine e: 341
Mt 5:43 shalt love thy neighbour, and hate thine e. *2190*
13:25 his e came and sowed tares among *2190*
13:28 He said unto them, An e hath done *444+2190*
13:39 The e that sowed them is the devil; *2190*
Lk 10:19 scorpions, and over all the power of the e: *2190*
Ac 13:10 of the devil, *thou* e of all righteousness, *2190*
Ro 12:20 Therefore if thine e hunger, feed him; if he *2190*
1Co 15:26 The last e *that* shall be destroyed *is* death. *2190*
Gal 4:16 Am I therefore become your e, because *2190*
2Th 3:15 Yet count *him* not as an e, but *2190*
Jas 4: 4 will be a friend of the world is the e of *2190*

ENEMY'S (3) [ENEMY]
Ex 23: 4 If thou meet thine e ox or his ass going 341
Job 6:23 Or, Deliver me from the e hand? or, 6862
Ps 78:61 into captivity, and his glory into the e hand. 6862

ENGAGED (1)
Jer 30:21 for who *is* this that e his heart to approach 6148

EN-GANNIM (3)
Jos 15:34 And Zanoah, and E, Tappuah, and Enam, 5873
19:21 and E, and En-haddah, and Beth-pazzez; 5873
21:29 with her suburbs, E with her suburbs; 5873

EN-GEDI (6)
Jos 15:62 Nibshan, and the city of salt, and E; 5872
1Sa 23:29 from thence, and dwelt in strong holds at E. 5872
24: 1 Behold, David *is* in the wilderness of E. 5872
2Ch 20: 2 they *be* in Hazazon-tamar, which *is* E. 5872
SS 1:14 a cluster of camphire in the vineyards of E. 5872
Eze 47:10 *that* the fishers shall stand upon it from E 5872

ENGINES (2)
2Ch 26:15 he made in Jerusalem e, invented by 2810
Eze 26: 9 he shall set e of war against thy walls, and 4239

ENGRAFTED (1)
Jas 1:21 and receive with meekness the e word, *1721*

ENGRAVE (2) [ENGRAVEN, ENGRAVER, ENGRAVINGS]
Ex 28:11 shalt thou e the two stones with the names 6605
Zec 3: 9 behold, I *will* e the graving thereof, 6605

ENGRAVED See GRAVED; GRAVEN

ENGRAVEN (1) [ENGRAVE]
2Co 3: 7 written *and* e in stones, was glorious, *1795*

ENGRAVER (3) [ENGRAVE]
Ex 28:11 *With* the work of an e in stone, *like* 2796
35:35 of the e, and of the cunning workman, and 2796
38:23 an e, and a cunning workman, and 2796

ENGRAVINGS (5) [ENGRAVE]
Ex 28:11 an engraver in stone, *like* the e of a signet, 6603
28:21 to their names, *like* the e of a signet; 6603
28:36 grave upon it, *like* the e of a signet, 6603
39:14 *like* the e of a signet, every one with his 6603
39:30 upon it a writing, *like to* the e of a signet, 6603

EN-HADDAH (1)
Jos 19:21 and En-gannim, and E, and Beth-pazzez; 5876

EN-HAKKORE (1)
Jdg 15:19 wherefore he called the name thereof E, 5875

ENHANCE See ABOUNDED; ABOUNDETH

EN-HAZOR (1)
Jos 19:37 And Kedesh, and Edrei, and E, 5877

ENJOIN (1) [ENJOINED]
Phm 1: 8 though I might be much bold in Christ to e *2004*

ENJOINED (3) [ENJOIN]
Est 9:31 and Esther the queen had e them, 5921+6965
Job 36:23 Who hath e him his way? or who can say, 6485
Heb 9:20 the testament which God hath e unto you. *1781*

ENJOY (14) [ENJOYED]
Lev 26:34 shall the land e her sabbaths, as long as it 7521
26:34 then shall the land rest, and e her sabbaths. 7521
26:43 be left of them, and shall e her sabbaths, 7521
Nu 36: 8 that the children of Israel may e every man 3423
Dt 28:41 but thou shalt not e them; 1961+3807.1
Jos 1:15 unto the land of your possession, and e it, 3423
Ecc 2: 1 prove thee with mirth, therefore e pleasure: 7200
2:24 *that* he should **make** his soul e good in his 7200
3:13 and drink, and e the good of all his labour, 7200
5:18 to e the good of all his labour that he taketh 7200
Isa 65:22 mine elect shall **long** e the work of their 1086
Ac 24: 2 Seeing that by thee we e great quietness, *5177*
1Ti 6:17 who giveth us richly all *things* to e; *619*
Heb 11:25 than to e the pleasures of sin for a season; *2192*

ENJOYED (1) [ENJOY]
2Ch 36:21 until the land had e her sabbaths: 7521

ENLARGE (10) [ENLARGED, ENLARGEMENT, ENLARGETH, ENLARGING]
Ge 9:27 God shall e Japheth, and he shall dwell in 6601
Ex 34:24 the nations before thee, and e thy borders: 7337
Dt 12:20 When the LORD thy God shall e thy 7337
19: 8 if the LORD thy God e thy coast, as he 7337
1Ch 4:10 e my coast, and that thine hand might be 7235
Ps 119:32 when thou shalt e my heart. 7337
Isa 54: 2 E the place of thy tent, and let them stretch 7337
Am 1:13 at Gilead, that *they* might e their border: 7337
Mic 1:16 e thy baldness as the eagle; 7337
Mt 23: 5 and e the borders of their garments, *3170*

ENLARGED (11) [ENLARGE]
1Sa 2: 1 my mouth is e over mine enemies; because 7337
2Sa 22:37 Thou hast e my steps under me; so that my 7337
Ps 4: 1 thou hast e me *when I was* in distress; 7337
18:36 Thou hast e my steps under me, that my 7337
25:17 The troubles of my heart are e: O bring 7337
Isa 5:14 Therefore hell hath e herself, and 7337
57: 8 thou hast e thy bed, and made thee *a* 7337
60: 5 and thine heart shall fear, and be e; 7337
2Co 6:11 our mouth is open unto you, our heart is e. *4115*
6:13 (I speak as unto *my* children,) be ye also e. *4115*
10:15 that *we* shall be e by you according to our *3170*

ENLARGEMENT (1) [ENLARGE]
Est 4:14 *then* shall there e and deliverance arise to 7305

ENLARGETH (3) [ENLARGE]
Dt 33:20 of Gad he said, Blessed *be* he that e Gad: 7337
Job 12:23 he e the nations, and straiteneth them 7849
Hab 2: 5 who e his desire as hell, and *is* as death, 7337

ENLARGING (1) [ENLARGE]
Eze 41: 7 *there was* an e, and a winding about still 7337

ENLIGHTEN (1) [LIGHT]
Ps 18:28 the LORD my God will e my darkness. 5050

ENLIGHTENED (6) [LIGHT]
1Sa 14:27 his hand to his mouth; and his eyes were e. 215
14:29 how mine eyes have been e, because I tasted 215
Job 33:30 the pit, to be e with the light of the living. 215
Ps 97: 4 His lightnings e the world: the earth saw, 215
Eph 1:18 The eyes of your understanding being e; *5461*
Heb 6: 4 *it is* impossible for those who were once e, *5461*

ENLIGHTENING (1) [LIGHT]
Ps 19: 8 of the LORD *is* pure, e the eyes. 215

EN-MISHPAT (1)
Ge 14: 7 came to E, which *is* Kadesh, and smote all 5880

ENMITY (8)
Ge 3:15 I will put e between thee and the woman, 342
Nu 35:21 Or in e smite him with his hand, that he die: 342
35:22 if he thrust him suddenly without e, or 342
Lk 23:12 for before they were at e between *2189*
Ro 8: 7 Because the carnal mind *is* e against God: *2189*
Eph 2:15 Having abolished in his flesh the e, *2189*
2:16 by the cross, having slain the e thereby: *2189*
Jas 4: 4 the friendship of the world is e with God? *2189*

ENOCH (12) [HENOCH]
Ge 4:17 his wife; and she conceived, and bare E: 2585
4:17 of the city, after the name of his son, E. 2585
4:18 unto E was born Irad: and Irad begat 2585
5:18 and two years, and he begat E: 2585
5:19 Jared lived after he begat E eight hundred 2585
5:21 E lived sixty and five years, and 2585
5:22 E walked with God after he begat 2585
5:23 all the days of E were three hundred sixty 2585
5:24 E walked with God: and he *was* not; 2585
Lk 3:37 which was *the son* of E, which was *the son* *1802*
Heb 11: 5 By faith E was translated that *he* should not *1802*
Jude 1:14 And E also, the seventh from Adam, *1802*

ENOS (7) [ENOSH]
Ge 4:26 he called his name E; then began *men* to call 583
5: 6 an hundred and five years, and begat E: 583
5: 7 Seth lived after he begat E eight hundred 583
5: 9 And E lived ninety years, and begat Cainan: 583
5:10 E lived after he begat Cainan eight hundred 583
5:11 And all the days of E were nine hundred and 583
Lk 3:38 Which was *the son* of E, which was *the son* *1800*

ENOSH (1) [ENOS]
1Ch 1: 1 Adam, Sheth, E, 583

ENOUGH (32)
Ge 24:25 We have both straw and provender e, and 7227
33: 9 Esau said, I have e, my brother; keep that 7227
33:11 graciously with me, and because I have e. 3605
34:21 behold, *it is* **large** e for them; 3027+7342
45:28 Israel said, *It is* e; Joseph my son *is* yet 7227
Ex 2:19 also **drew water** e for us, and 1802+1802
9:28 Intreat the LORD (for *it is* e) that there be 7227
36: 5 The people bring much more than e for 1767
Dt 1: 6 Ye have dwelt **long** e in this mount: 7227
2: 3 Ye have compassed this mountain **long** e: 7227
Jos 17:16 of Joseph said, The hill is not e for us: 4672
2Sa 24:16 the angel that destroyed the people, *It is* e: 7227
1Ki 19: 4 said, *It is* e; now, O LORD, take away my 7227
1Ch 21:15 that destroyed, *It is* e, stay now thine hand. 7227
2Ch 31:10 *we* have **had** e to eat, and have left plenty: 7646
Pr 27:27 *thou shalt have* goats' milk e for thy food, 1767
28:19 after vain *persons* shall **have** poverty e. 7646
30:15 *yea,* four *things* say not, *It is* e: 1952
30:16 and the fire *that* saith not, *It is* e. 1952
Isa 56:11 *are* greedy dogs *which* can never have e, 7654
Jer 49: 9 by night, they will destroy till they have e. 1767
Hos 4:10 For they shall eat, and not **have** e: 7646
Ob 1: 5 would they not have stolen till they had e? 1767
Na 2:12 The lion did tear in pieces e for his whelps, 1767
Hag 1: 6 *ye* eat, but ye have not e; *ye* drink, but 7654
Mal 3:10 that *there shall* not *be room* e *to receive it.* 1767
Mt 10:25 *It is* e for the disciple that he be as his *713*
25: 9 *Not so;* lest there be not e for us and you: *714*
Mk 14:41 it is e, the hour is come; behold, the Son of *568*
Lk 15:17 of my father's **have** bread e **and to spare,** *4052*
22:38 two swords. And he said unto them, It is e. *2425*
Ac 27:38 And when they had **eaten** e, *2880+5160*

ENRICH (2) [RICH]
1Sa 17:25 the king will e him *with* great riches, and 6238
Eze 27:33 thou didst e the kings of the earth with 6238

ENRICHED (2) [RICH]
1Co 1: 5 That in every *thing* ye are e by him, in all *4148*
2Co 9:11 Being e in every *thing* to all bountifulness, *4148*

ENRICHEST (1) [RICH]
Ps 65: 9 thou greatly e it *with* the river of God, 6238

EN-RIMMON (1)
Ne 11:29 And at E, and at Zareah, and at Jarmuth, 5884

EN-ROGEL (4)
Jos 15: 7 and the goings out thereof were at E: 5883
18:16 of Jebusi on the south, and descended *to* E, 5883
2Sa 17:17 Now Jonathan and Ahimaaz stayed by E; 5883
1Ki 1: 9 which *is* by E, and called all his brethren 5883

ENSAMPLE (3) [ENSAMPLES]
Php 3:17 them which walk so as ye have us for an e. *5179*
2Th 3: 9 to make ourselves an e unto you to follow *5179*
2Pe 2: 6 making *them* an e unto those that after *5262*

ENSAMPLES (3) [ENSAMPLE]
1Co 10:11 all these *things* happened unto them for e: *5179*
1Th 1: 7 So that ye were e to all that believe in *5179*
1Pe 5: 3 *God's* heritage, but being e to the flock. *5179*

EN-SHEMESH (2)
Jos 15: 7 the border passed towards the waters of E, 5885
18:17 went forth *to* E, and went forth toward 5885

ENSIGN (8) [ENSIGNS]
Nu 2: 2 with the e of their father's house: 226
Isa 5:26 he will lift up an e to the nations from far, 5251
11:10 which shall stand for an e of the people; 5251
11:12 And he shall set up an e for the nations, and 5251
18: 3 when *he* lifteth up an e *on* the mountains; 5251
30:17 the top of a mountain, and as an e on a hill. 5251
31: 9 his princes shall be afraid of the e, saith 5251
Zec 9:16 of a crown, **lifted up as an** e upon his land. 5264

ENSIGNS (1) [ENSIGN]
Ps 74: 4 they set up their e *for* signs. 226

ENSNARED (1) [SNARE]
Job 34:30 the hypocrite reign not, lest the people be e. 4170

ENSUE (1)
1Pe 3:11 and do good; let him seek peace, and e it. *1377*

ENSURE See SURETY

ENTANGLE (1) [ENTANGLED, ENTANGLETH]
Mt 22:15 took counsel how they might e him in *his* *3802*

ENTANGLED (3) [ENTANGLE]
Ex 14: 3 They *are* e in the land, the wilderness hath 943
Gal 5: 1 be not e again with the yoke of bondage. *1758*
2Pe 2:20 they are again e therein, and overcome, *1707*

ENTANGLETH (1) [ENTANGLE]
2Ti 2: 4 No *man* that warreth e himself **with** *1707*

EN-TAPPUAH (1)
Jos 17: 7 on the right hand unto the inhabitants of E. 5887

ENTER (149) [ENTERED, ENTERETH, ENTERING, ENTRANCE, ENTRANCES]
Ge 12:11 when he was come near to e into Egypt, 935
Ex 40:35 Moses was not able to e into the tent of 935
Nu 4: 3 until fifty years old, all that e into the host, 935
4:23 all that e **in** to perform the service, to do 935
5:24 the water that causeth the curse shall e into 935
5:27 that the water that causeth the curse shall e 935
20:24 for he shall not e into the land which I have 935
Dt 23: 1 shall not e into the congregation of 935
23: 2 A bastard shall not e into the congregation of 935
23: 2 even *to* his tenth generation shall he not e 935
23: 3 Moabite shall not e into the congregation of 935
23: 3 e **into** the congregation of the LORD for 935
23: 8 children that are begotten of them shall e 935
29:12 That thou shouldest e into covenant with 5674

E

Jos 10:19 of them; suffer them not to e into their cities: 935
Jdg 18: 9 slothful to go, and to e to possess the land. 935
2Sa 22: 7 of his temple, and my cry did e into his ears. NIH
1Ki 14:12 and when thy feet e into the city, the child 935
22:30 I will disguise myself, and e into the battle; 935
2Ki 7: 4 We will e into the city, then the famine is in 935
11: 5 A third part of you that e in on the sabbath 935
19:23 and I will e into the lodgings of his borders, 935
2Ch 7: 2 the priests could not e into the house of 935
23:19 which was unclean in any thing should e in. 935
30: 8 e into his sanctuary, which he hath sanctified 935
Ne 2: 8 the city, and for the house that I shall e into. 935
Est 4: 2 for none might e into the king's gate clothed 935
Job 22: 4 of thee? will he e with thee into judgment? 935
34:23 that he should e into judgment with God. 1980
Ps 37:15 Their sword shall e into their own heart, and 935
45:15 they shall e into the king's palace. 935
95:11 my wrath that they should not e into my rest. 935
100: 4 E into his gates with thanksgiving, and 935
118:20 the LORD, into which the righteous shall e. 935
143: 2 e not into judgment with thy servant: for in 935
Pr 4:14 E not into the path of the wicked, and 935
18: 6 A fool's lips e into contention, and 935
23:10 and e not into the fields of the fatherless: 935
Isa 2:10 E into the rock, and hide thee in the dust, 935
3:14 The LORD will e into judgment with 935
26: 2 nation which keepeth the truth may e in. 935
26:20 e thou into thy chambers, and shut thy doors 935
37:24 and I will e into the height of his border, and 935
57: 2 He shall e into peace: they shall rest in their 935
59:14 is fallen in the street, and equity cannot e. 935
Jer 7: 2 that e in at these gates to worship 935
8:14 let us e into the defenced cities, and let us be 935
14:18 if I e into the city, then behold them that are 935
16: 5 E not into the house of mourning, 935
17:20 of Jerusalem, that e in by these gates: 935
17:25 shall there e into the gates of this city kings 935
21:13 or who shall e into our habitations? 935
22: 2 and thy people that e in by these gates: 935
22: 4 shall there e in by the gates of this house 935
41:17 is by Beth-lehem, to go to e into Egypt, 935
42:15 If ye wholly set your faces to e into Egypt, 935
42:18 forth upon you, when ye shall e into Egypt: 935
La 1:10 that they should not e into thy congregation. 935
3:13 He hath caused the arrows of his quiver to e 935
Eze 7:22 secret place: for the robbers shall e into it, 935
13: 9 neither shall they e into the land of Israel; 935
20:38 and they shall not e into the land of Israel: 935
26:10 the chariots, when he shall e into thy gates, 935
26:10 as men e into a city wherein is made a 3996
37: 5 I will cause breath to e into you, and ye shall 935
42:14 When the priests e therein, then shall they 935
44: 2 not be opened, and no man shall e in by it; 935
44: 3 he shall e by the way of the porch of that 935
44: 9 in flesh, shall e into my sanctuary, 935
44:16 They shall e into my sanctuary, and 935
44:17 that when they e in at the gates of the inner 935
44:21 drink wine, when they e into the inner court. 935
46: 2 the prince shall e by the way of the porch of 935
46: 8 when the prince shall e, he shall go in by 935
Da 11: 7 shall e into the fortress of the king of 935
11:17 He shall also set his face to e with 935
11:24 He shall e peaceably even upon the fattest 935
11:40 he shall e into the countries, and 935
11:41 He shall e also into the glorious land, and 935
Hos 11: 9 midst of thee: and I will not e into the city. 935
Joel 2: 9 they shall e in at the windows like a thief. 935
Am 5: 5 nor e into Gilgal, and pass not to Beer-sheba: 935
Jnh 3: 4 Jonah began to e into the city a day's 935
Zec 5: 4 and it shall e into the house of the thief, and 935
Mt 5:20 ye shall in no case e into the kingdom of 1525
6: 6 e into thy closet, and when thou hast shut 1525
7:13 E ye in at the strait gate: for wide is 1525
7:21 Lord, shall e into the kingdom of heaven; 1525
10: 5 into any city of the Samaritans e ye not: 1525
10:11 into whatsoever city or town ye shall e, 1525
12:29 Or else how can one e into a strong man's 1525
12:45 than himself, and they e in and dwell there: 1525
18: 3 ye shall not e into the kingdom of heaven. 1525
18: 8 it is better for thee to e into life halt or 1525
18: 9 it is better for thee to e into life with one 1525
19:17 but if thou wilt e into life, keep 1525
19:23 That a rich man shall hardly e into 1525
19:24 than for a rich man to e into the kingdom of 1525
25:21 many things: e thou into the joy of thy lord. 1525
25:23 many things: e thou into the joy of thy lord. 1525
26:41 and pray, that ye e not into temptation: 1525
Mk 1:45 Jesus could no more openly e into the city, 1525
3:27 No man can e into a strong man's house, 1525
5:12 us into the swine, that we may e into them. 1525
6:10 In what place soever ye e into a house, 1525
9:25 come out of him, and e no more into him. 1525
9:43 it is better for thee to e into life maimed, 1525
9:45 it is better for thee to e halt into life, 1525
9:47 it is better for thee to e into the kingdom of 1525
10:15 God as a little child, he shall not e therein. 1525
10:23 How hardly shall they that have riches e 1525
10:24 in riches to e into the kingdom of God! 1525
10:25 than for a rich man to e into the kingdom of 1525
13:15 neither e therein, to take any thing out of 1525
14:38 and pray, lest ye e into temptation. 1525
Lk 7: 6 for I am not worthy that thou shouldest e 1525
8:16 that they which e in may see the light. 1531
8:32 that he would suffer them to e into them. 1525
9: 4 And whatsoever house ye e into, 1525
10: 5 And into whatsoever house ye e, first say, 1525
10: 8 And into whatsoever city ye e, and 1525
10:10 But into whatsoever city ye e, and 1525
11:26 and they e in, and dwell there: 1525
13:24 Strive to e in at the strait gate: for many, 1525
13:24 will seek to e in, and shall not be able. 1525
18:17 as a little child shall in no wise e therein. 1525
18:24 How hardly shall they that have riches e 1525
18:25 than for a rich man to e into the kingdom of 1525
21:21 let not them that are in the countries e 1525
Lk 22:40 Pray that ye e not into temptation. 1525
22:46 rise and pray, lest ye e into temptation. 1525
24:26 these things, and to e into his glory? 1525
Jn 3: 4 can he e the second time into his mother's 1525
3: 5 he cannot e into the kingdom of God. 1525
10: 9 by me if any man e in, he shall be saved, 1525
Ac 14:22 that we must through much tribulation e 1525
20:29 shall grievous wolves e in among you, 1525
Heb 3:11 in my wrath, They shall not e into my rest. 1525
3:18 sware he that they should not e into his rest, 1525
3:19 So we see that they could not e in because 1525
4: 3 For we which have believed do e into rest, 1525
4: 3 in my wrath, if they shall e into my rest: 1525
4: 5 this place again, If they shall e into my rest. 1525
4: 6 it remaineth that some must e therein, 1525
4:11 Let us labour therefore to e into that rest, 1525
10:19 boldness to e into the holiest by the blood 1529
Rev 15: 8 and no man was able to e into the temple, 1525
21:27 And there shall in no wise e into it any 1525
22:14 may e in through the gates into the city. 1525

ENTERED (107) [ENTER]

Ge 7:13 In the selfsame day e Noah, and Shem, and 935
19: 3 turned in unto him, and e into his house; 935
19:23 The sun was risen upon the earth when Lot e 935
31:33 out of Leah's tent, and e into Rachel's tent. 935
43:30 and he e into his chamber, and wept there. 935
Ex 33: 9 came to pass, as Moses e into the tabernacle, 935
Jos 2: 3 come to thee, which are e into thine house: 935
8:19 they e into the city, and took it, and hasted 935
10:20 that the rest which remained of them e into 935
Jdg 6: 5 and they e into the land to destroy it. 935
9:46 e into a hold of the house of the god Berith. 935
2Sa 10:14 they also before Abishai, and e into the city. 935
2Ki 7: 8 e into another tent, and carried thence also, 935
9:31 as Jehu e in at the gate, she said, Had Zimri 935
1Ch 19:15 Abishai his brother, and e into the city. 935
2Ch 12:11 when the king e into the house of 935
15:12 they e into a covenant to seek the LORD 935
27: 2 howbeit he e not into the temple of 935
32: 1 e into Judah, and encamped against 935
Ne 2:15 e by the gate of the valley, and so returned. 935
10:29 and e into a curse, and into an oath, 935
Job 38:16 Hast thou e into the springs of the sea? or 935
38:22 Hast thou e into the treasures of the snow? or 935
Jer 2: 7 when ye e, ye defiled my land, and 935
9:21 and is e into our palaces, to cut off 935
34:10 the people, which had e into the covenant, 935
37:16 When Jeremiah was e into the dungeon, and 935
La 1:10 for she hath seen that the heathen e into her 935
4:12 the enemy should have e into the gates of 935
Eze 2: 2 the spirit e into me when he spake unto me, 935
3:24 the spirit e into me, and set me upon my feet, 935
16: 8 unto thee, and e into a covenant with thee, 935
36:20 when they e unto the heathen, whither they 935
41: 6 they e into the wall which was of the house 935
44: 2 hath e in by it, therefore it shall be shut. 935
Ob 1:11 foreigners e into his gates, and cast lots upon 935
1:13 Thou shouldest not have e into the gate of 935
Hab 3:16 rottenness e into my bones, and I trembled in 935
Mt 8: 5 And when Jesus was e into Capernaum, 1525
8:23 And when he was e into a ship, 1684
9: 1 And he e into a ship, and passed over, and 1684
12: 4 How he e into the house of God, and 1525
24:38 until the day that Noe e into the ark, 1525
Mk 1:21 straightway on the sabbath day he e into 1525
1:29 they e into the house of Simon and 2064
2: 1 And again he e into Capernaum after some 1525
3: 1 And he e again into the synagogue; and 1525
4: 1 so that he e into a ship, and sat in the sea; 1684
5:13 spirits went out, and e into the swine: 1525
6:56 And whithersoever he e, into villages, or 1531
7:17 And when he was e into the house from 1525
7:24 and e into a house, and would have no man 1525
8:10 And straightway he e into a ship with his 1684
11: 2 and as soon as ye be e into it, ye shall find a 1531
11:11 And Jesus e into Jerusalem, and into 1525
Lk 1:40 And e into the house of Zacharias, and 1525
4:38 the synagogue, and e into Simon's house. 1525
5: 3 And he e into one of the ships, which was 1684
6: 6 that he e into the synagogue and taught: 1525
7: 1 of the people, he e into Capernaum. 1525
7:44 I e into thine house, thou gavest me no 1525
8:30 because many devils were e into him. 1525
8:33 devils out of the man, and e into the swine: 1525
9:34 and they feared as they e into the cloud. 1525
9:52 and e into a village of the Samaritans, 1525
10:38 they went, that he e into a certain village: 1525
11:52 ye e not in yourselves, and them that were 1525
17:12 And as he e into a certain village, there met 1525
17:27 until the day that Noe e into the ark, and 1525
19: 1 And Jesus e and passed through Jericho. 1525
22: 3 Then e Satan into Judas surnamed Iscariot, 1525
22:10 Behold, when ye are e into the city, 1525
24: 3 And they e in, and found not the body of 1525
Jn 4:38 and ye are e into their labours. 1525
6:17 And e into a ship, and went over the sea 1684
6:22 that one whereinto his disciples were e, 1684
13:27 And after the sop Satan e into him. 1525
18: 1 into the which he e, and his disciples. 1525
18:33 Then Pilate e into the judgment hall again, 1525
21: 3 went forth, and e into a ship immediately; 305
Ac 3: 2 to ask alms of them that e into the temple; 1531
3: 8 walked, and e with them into the temple, 1525
5:21 And when they heard that, they e into 1525
9:17 Ananias went his way, and e into the house; 1525
10:24 And the morrow after they e into Cesarea. 1525
11: 8 unclean hath at any time e into my mouth. 1525
11:12 and we e into the man's house: 1525
16:40 of the prison, and e into the house of Lydia: 1525
18: 7 and e into a certain man's house, 2064
18:19 but he himself e into the synagogue, and 1525
19:30 And when Paul would have e in unto 1525
21: 8 we e into the house of Philip the evangelist, 1525
21:26 the next day purifying himself with them e 1524
Ac 23:16 he went and e into the castle, and told Paul. 1525
25:23 and were e into the place of hearing, 1525
28: 8 to whom Paul e in, and prayed, and laid his 1525
Ro 5:12 as by one man sin e into the world, and 1525
5:20 Moreover the law e, that the offence might 3922
1Co 2: 9 neither have e into the heart of man, 305
Heb 4: 6 they to whom it was first preached e not in 1525
4:10 For he that is e into his rest, he also hath 1525
6:20 Whither the forerunner is for us e, 1525
9:12 by his own blood he e in once into the holy 1525
9:24 For Christ is not e into the holy places 1525
Jas 5: 4 the cries of them which have reaped are e 1525
2Jn 1: 7 For many deceivers are e into the world, 1525
Rev 11:11 a half the spirit of life from God e into 1525

ENTERETH (20) [ENTER]

Nu 4:30 every one that e into the service, to do 935
4:35 years old, every one that e into the service, 935
4:39 years old, every one that e into the service, 935
4:43 years old, every one that e into the service, 935
2Ch 31:16 even unto every one that e into the house of 935
Pr 2:10 When wisdom e into thine heart, and 935
17:10 A reproof e more into a wise man than an 5181
Eze 21:14 which e into their privy chambers. 2314
42:12 the wall toward the east, as one e into them. 935
46: 9 he that e in by the way of the north gate to 935
46: 9 he that e by the way of the south gate shall 935
Mt 15:17 that whatsoever e in at the mouth goeth into 1531
Mk 5:40 and e in where the damsel was lying. 1531
7:18 that whatsoever thing from without e into 1531
7:19 Because it e not into his heart, but into 1531
Lk 22:10 follow him into the house where he e in. 1531
Jn 10: 1 He that e not by the door into 1525
10: 2 But he that e in by the door is the shepherd 1525
Heb 6:19 and which e into that within the vail; 1525
9:25 as the high priest e into the holy place 1525

ENTERING (46) [ENTER]

Ex 35:15 the hanging for the door at the e in of 6607
Jos 8:29 cast it at the e of the gate of the city, and 6607
13: 5 mount Hermon unto the e into Hamath. 935
20: 4 shall stand at the e of the gate of the city, 6607
Jdg 3: 3 from mount Baal-hermon unto the e in of 935
9:35 and stood in the e of the gate of the city: 6607
9:40 and wounded, even unto the e of the gate. 6607
9:44 and stood in the e of the gate of the city: 6607
18:16 children of Dan, stood by the e of the gate. 6607
18:17 the priest stood in the e of the gate with 6607
1Sa 23: 7 by e into a town that hath gates and bars. 935
2Sa 10: 8 put the battle in array at the e in of the gate: 6607
11:23 we were upon them even unto the e of 6607
1Ki 6:31 for the e of the oracle he made doors of 6607
8:65 from the e in of Hamath unto the river of 935
19:13 went out, and stood in the e in of the cave. 6607
2Ki 7: 3 there were four leprous men at the e in of 6607
10: 8 Lay ye them in two heaps at the e in of 6607
14:25 He restored the coast of Israel from the e of 935
23: 8 e in of the gate of Joshua the governor of 6607
23:11 at the e in of the house of the LORD, by 935
1Ch 5: 9 eastward he inhabited unto the e in of 935
13: 5 from Shihor of Egypt even unto the e of 935
2Ch 7: 8 from the e in of Hamath unto the river of 935
18: 9 they sat in a void place at the e in of 6607
23: 4 A third part of you e on the sabbath, of 935
23:13 the king stood at his pillar at the e in, and 3996
23:15 when she was come to the e of the horse 3996
26: 8 his name spread abroad even to the e in of 935
33:14 even to the e in at the fish gate, and 935
Isa 23: 1 laid waste, so that there is no house, no e in: 935
Jer 1:15 they shall set every one his throne at the e 6607
17:27 even e in at the gates of Jerusalem on 935
Eze 44: 5 mark well the e in of the house, with every 3996
Am 6:14 they shall afflict you from the e in of 935
Mt 23:13 neither suffer ye them that are e to go in. 1525
Mk 4:19 and the lusts of other things e in, choke 1531
7:15 a man, that e into him can defile him: 1531
8:13 e into the ship again departed to the other 1684
16: 5 And e into the sepulchre, they saw a young 1525
Lk 11:52 and them that were e in ye hindered. 1525
19:30 the which at your e ye shall find a colt tied, 1531
Ac 8: 3 havock of the church, e into every house, 1531
27: 2 And e into a ship of Adramyttium, 1910
1Th 1: 9 of us what manner of e in we had unto you, 1529
Heb 4: 1 a promise being left us of e into his rest, 1525

ENTERPRISE (1)

Job 5:12 so that their hands cannot perform their e. 8454

ENTERTAIN (1) [ENTERTAINED]

Heb 13: 2 Be not forgetful to e strangers: for thereby 5381

ENTERTAINED (1) [ENTERTAIN]

Heb 13: 2 for thereby some have e angels unawares. 3579

ENTICE (8) [ENTICED, ENTICETH, ENTICING]

Ex 22:16 if a man e a maid that is not betrothed, and 6601
Dt 13: 6 e thee secretly, saying, Let us go and 5496
Jdg 14:15 said unto Samson's wife, E thy husband, 6601
16: 5 E him, and see wherein his great strength 6601
2Ch 18:19 Who shall e Ahab king of Israel, that he 6601
18:20 before the LORD, and said, I will e him. 6601
18:21 Thou shalt e him, and thou shalt also 6601
Pr 1:10 My son, if sinners e thee, consent thou not. 6601

ENTICED (3) [ENTICE]

Job 31:27 my heart hath been secretly e, or my mouth 6601
Jer 20:10 saying, Peradventure he will be e, and 6601
Jas 1:14 he is drawn away of his own lust, and e. 1185

ENTICETH (1) [ENTICE]

Pr 16:29 A violent man e his neighbour, and 6601

ENTICING (2) [ENTICE]

1Co 2: 4 my preaching was not with e words of 3981

Col 2: 4 any *man* should beguile you with e words. *4086*

ENTIRE (1)
Jas 1: 4 that ye may be perfect and e, *3648*

ENTRANCE (11) [ENTER]
Nu 34: 8 point out *your border* unto the e of Hamath; 935
Jdg 1:24 the e into the city, and we will shew thee 3996
1:25 when he shewed them the e into the city, 3996
1Ki 18:46 and ran before Ahab to the e of Jezreel. 935
22:10 in a void place *in* the e of the gate of 6607
1Ch 4:39 they went to the e of Gedor, *even* unto 3996
2Ch 12:10 that kept the e of the king's house. 6607
Ps 119:130 The e of thy words giveth light; it giveth 6608
Eze 40:15 from the face of the gate of the e unto 2978
1Th 2: 1 brethren, know our e in unto you, *1529*
2Pe 1:11 an e shall be ministered unto you *1529*

ENTRANCES (1) [ENTER]
Mic 5: 6 and the land of Nimrod in the e thereof: 6607

ENTREAT (2) [ENTREATED, ENTREATETH, INTREAT]
Jer 15:11 verily I will cause the enemy to e thee *well* 6293
Ac 7: 6 and e *them* evil four hundred years. *2559*

ENTREATED (9) [ENTREAT]
Ge 12:16 he e Abram well for her sake: and he had 3190
Ex 5:22 wherefore hast thou *so* evil e this people? 7489
Dt 26: 6 the Egyptians evil e us, and afflicted us, 7489
Mt 22: 6 and e *them* spitefully, and slew *them.* *5195*
Lk 18:32 be mocked, and spitefully e, and spitted on: *5195*
20:11 and e *him* shamefully, and sent *him* away *818*
Ac 7:19 and evil e our fathers, so that *they* cast out *2559*
27: 3 And Julius courteously e Paul, and *5530*
1Th 2: 2 and were shamefully e, as ye know, *5195*

ENTREATETH (1) [ENTREAT]
Job 24:21 He evil e the barren *that* beareth not: and 7462

ENTREATY See INTREAT; INTREATED; INTREATIES; INTREATY

ENTRIES (1) [ENTRY]
Eze 40:38 the e thereof *were* by the posts of the gates, 6607

ENTRY (15) [ENTRIES]
2Ki 16:18 built in the house, and the king's e without, 3996
1Ch 9:19 host of the LORD, *were* keepers of the e. 3996
2Ch 4:22 the e of the house, the inner doors thereof 6607
Pr 8: 3 She crieth at the gates, at the e of the city, 6310
Jer 19: 2 which *is by* the e of the east gate, and 6607
26:10 sat down in the e of the new gate of 6607
36:10 in the higher court *at* the e of the new gate 6607
38:14 third e that *is* in the house of the LORD: 3996
43: 9 which *is* at the e of Pharaoh's house in 6607
Eze 8: 5 of the altar this image of jealousy in the e. 872
27: 3 O thou that art situate at the e of the sea, 3997
40:11 he measured the breadth of the e of 6607
40:40 as one goeth up to the e of the north gate, 6607
42: 9 from under these chambers *was* the e on 3996
46:19 After, he brought me through the e, 3996

ENVIED (6) [ENVY]
Ge 26:14 store of servants: and the Philistims e him. 7065
30: 1 bare Jacob no *children,* Rachel e her sister; 7065
37:11 his brethren e him; but his father observed 7065
Ps 106:16 They e Moses also in the camp, *and* 7065
Ecc 4: 4 that for this a man is e of his neighbour. 7068
Eze 31: 9 that *were* in the garden of God, e him. 7065

ENVIES (1) [ENVY]
1Pe 2: 1 hypocrisies, and e, and all evil speakings, *5355*

ENVIEST (1) [ENVY]
Nu 11:29 Moses said unto him, E thou for my sake? 7065

ENVIETH (1) [ENVY]
1Co 13: 4 suffereth long, *and* is kind; charity e not; *2206*

ENVIOUS (4) [ENVY]
Ps 37: 1 neither be thou e against the workers of 7065
73: 3 For I was e at the foolish, *when* I saw 7065
Pr 24: 1 Be not thou e against evil men, 7065
24:19 of evil *men,* neither be thou e at 7065

ENVIRON (1)
Jos 7: 9 land shall hear *of it,* and shall e us round, 5437

ENVY (20) [ENVIED, ENVIES, ENVIEST, ENVIETH, ENVIOUS, ENVYING, ENVYINGS]
Job 5: 2 the foolish man, and e slayeth the silly one. 7068
Pr 3:31 E thou not the oppressor, and choose none 7065
14:30 the flesh: but e the rottenness of the bones. 7068
23:17 Let not thine heart e sinners: but *be thou* in 7065
27: 4 but who is able to stand before e? 7068
Ecc 9: 6 their love, and their hatred, and their e, 7068
Isa 11:13 The e also of Ephraim shall depart, and 7068
11:13 Ephraim shall not e Judah, and Judah shall 7065
26:11 and be ashamed for *their* e at the people; 7068
Eze 35:11 according to thine e which thou hast used 7068
Mt 27:18 For he knew that for e they had delivered *5355*
Mk 15:10 the chief priests had delivered him for e. *5355*
Ac 7: 9 And the patriarchs, moved with e, *2206*
13:45 they were filled with e, and spake against *2205*
17: 5 Jews which believed not, moved with e, *2206*
Ro 1:29 full of e, murder, debate, deceit, malignity; *5355*
Php 1:15 Some indeed preach Christ even of e and *5355*
1Ti 6: 4 whereof cometh e, strife, railings, *5355*
Tit 3: 3 living in malice and e, hateful, *and* *5355*
Jas 4: 5 the spirit that dwelleth in us lusteth to e? *5355*

ENVYING (5) [ENVY]
Ro 13:13 and wantonness, not in strife and e. *2205*
1Co 3: 3 for whereas *there is* among you e, and *2205*
Gal 5:26 provoking one another, e one another. *5354*
Jas 3:14 But if ye have bitter e and strife in your *2205*
3:16 For where e and strife *is,* there *is* confusion *2205*

ENVYINGS (2) [ENVY]
2Co 12:20 e, wraths, strifes, backbitings, whisperings, *2205*
Gal 5:21 E, murders, drunkenness, revellings, and *5355*

EPAPHRAS (3)
Col 1: 7 As ye also learned of E our dear *1889*
4:12 E, who is *one* of you, a servant of Christ, *1889*
Phm 1:23 There salute thee E, my fellowprisoner in *1889*

EPAPHRODITUS (3)
Php 2:25 I supposed it necessary to send to you E, *1891*
4:18 having received of E the *things which were* *1891*
4: S written to the Philippians from Rome by E. *1891*

EPENETUS (1)
Ro 16: 5 Salute my wellbeloved E, who is *1866*

EPHAH (39)
Ge 25: 4 E, and Epher, and Hanoch, and Abidah, 5891
Ex 16:36 Now an omer *is* the tenth *part* of an e. 374
Lev 5:11 *part* of an e of fine flour for a sin offering; 374
6:20 the tenth *part* of an e of fine flour *for* a meat 374
19:36 just weights, a just e, and a just hin, shall ye 374
Nu 5:15 for her, the tenth *part* of an e of barley meal; 374
28: 5 a tenth *part* of an e *of* flour for a meat 374
Jdg 6:19 a kid, and unleavened *cakes of* an e of flour: 374
Ru 2:17 had gleaned: and it was about an e of barley. 374
1Sa 1:24 and one e of flour, and a bottle of wine, and 374
17:17 Take now for thy brethren an e of this 374
1Ch 1:33 E, and Epher, and Henoch, and Abida, and 5891
2:46 E, Caleb's concubine, bare Haran, and 5891
2:47 and Geshan, and Pelet, and E, and Shaaph. 5891
Isa 5:10 and the seed of a homer shall yield an e. 374
60: 6 the dromedaries of Midian and E; 5891
Eze 45:10 just balances, and a just e, and a just bath. 374
45:11 The e and the bath shall be of one measure, 374
45:11 a homer, and the e the tenth *part* of a homer: 374
45:13 the sixth *part* of an e of a homer of wheat, 374
45:13 ye shall give the sixth part of an e of a homer 374
45:24 he shall prepare a meat offering *of* an e for a 374
45:24 an e for a ram, and a hin of oil for an ephah. 374
45:24 an ephah for a ram, and a hin of oil for an e. 374
46: 5 the meat offering *shall be* an e for a ram, 374
46: 5 shall be able to give, and a hin of oil to an e. 374
46: 7 an e for a bullock, and an ephah for a ram, 374
46: 7 an e for a ram, and for the lambs according 374
46: 7 shall attain unto, and a hin of oil to an e. 374
46:11 the meat offering shall be an e to a bullock, 374
46:11 an e to a ram, and to the lambs as he is able 374
46:11 as he is able to give, and a hin of oil to an e. 374
46:14 the sixth *part* of an e, and the third *part* of a 374
Am 8: 5 making the e small, and the shekel great, and 374
Zec 5: 6 he said, This *is* an e that goeth forth. He said 374
5: 7 *is* a woman that sitteth in the midst of the e. 374
5: 8 he cast it into the midst of the e; and he cast 374
5: 9 they lift up the e between the earth and 374
5:10 talked with me, Whither do these bear the e? 374

EPHAI (1)
Jer 40: 8 the sons of E the Netophathite, and 5778

EPHER (4)
Ge 25: 4 E, and Hanoch, and Abidah, and Eldaah. 6081
1Ch 1:33 and E, and Henoch, and Abida, and Eldaah. 6081
4:17 *were,* Jether, and Mered, and E, and Jalon: 6081
5:24 even E, and Ishi, and Eliel, and Azriel, and 6081

EPHES-DAMMIM (1)
1Sa 17: 1 pitched between Shochoh and Azekah, in E. 658

EPHESIAN (1) [EPHESUS]
Ac 21:29 with him in the city Trophimus an E, *2180*

EPHESIANS (5) [EPHESUS]
Ac 19:28 cried out, saying, Great *is* Diana of the E. *2180*
19:34 hours cried out, Great *is* Diana of the E. *2180*
19:35 of the E is a worshipper of the great *2180*
Eph 6: S Written from Rome unto the E by *2180*
2Ti 4: S the first bishop of the church of the E, *2180*

EPHESUS (17) [EPHESIAN, EPHESIANS]
Ac 18:19 And he came to E, and left them there: but *2181*
18:21 if God will. And he sailed from E. *2181*
18:24 *and* mighty in the scriptures, came to E. *2181*
19: 1 passed through the upper coasts came to E: *2181*
19:17 all the Jews and Greeks also dwelling at E; *2181*
19:26 that not alone at E, but almost throughout *2181*
19:35 appeased the people, he said, *Ye* men of E, *2180*
20:16 For Paul had determined to sail by E, *2181*
20:17 And from Miletus he sent to E, and *2181*
1Co 15:32 of men I have fought with beasts at E, *2181*
16: 8 But I will tarry at E until Pentecost. *2181*
Eph 1: 1 to the saints which are at E, and to *2181*
1Ti 1: 3 As I besought thee to abide *still* at E, *2181*
2Ti 1:18 many *things* he ministered *unto me* at E, *2181*
4:12 And Tychicus have I sent to E. *2181*
Rev 1:11 unto E, and unto Smyrna, and *2181*
2: 1 Unto the angel of the church of E write; *2179*

EPHLAL (2)
1Ch 2:37 And Zabad begat E, and Ephlal begat Obed, 654
2:37 And Zabad begat Ephlal, and E begat Obed, 654

EPHOD (52)
Ex 25: 7 stones to be set in the e, and in 646
28: 4 an e, and a robe, and a broidered coat, 646
28: 6 they shall make the e *of* gold, *of* blue, and 646
28: 8 the curious girdle of the e, which *is* upon it, 642
28:12 e *for* stones of memorial unto the children of 646
28:15 after the work of the e thou shalt make it; 646
28:25 put *them* on the shoulderpieces of the e 646
28:26 which *is* in the side of the e inward. 646
28:27 shalt put them on the two sides of the e 646
28:27 above the curious girdle of the e. 646
28:28 unto the rings of the e with a lace of blue, 646
28:28 *it* may be above the curious girdle of the e, 646
28:28 that the breastplate be not loosed from the e. 646
28:31 thou shalt make the robe of the e all of blue. 646
29: 5 the robe of the e, and the ephod, and 646
29: 5 the e, and the breastplate, and gird him with 646
29: 5 and gird him with the curious girdle of the e: 646
35: 9 stones to be set for the e, and for 646
35:27 to be set, for the e, and for the breastplate; 646
39: 2 And he made the e *of* gold, blue, and purple, 646
39: 5 the curious girdle of his e, that *was* upon it, 642
39: 7 he put them on the shoulders of the e, 646
39: 8 *of* cunning work, like the work of the e; 646
39:18 and put them on the shoulderpieces of the e, 646
39:19 of it, which *was* on the side of the e inward. 646
39:20 put them on the two sides of the e 646
39:20 above the curious girdle of the e. 646
39:21 unto the rings of the e with a lace of blue, 646
39:21 *it* might be above the curious girdle of the e, 646
39:21 breastplate might not be loosed from the e; 646
39:22 he made the robe of the e *of* woven work, 646
Lev 8: 7 put the e upon him, and he girded him with 646
8: 7 girded him with the curious girdle of the e, 646
Nu 34:23 children of Manasseh, Hanniel the son of E. 641
Jdg 8:27 Gideon made an e thereof, and put it in his 646
17: 5 made an e, and teraphim, and 646
18:14 ye know that there is in these houses an e, 646
18:17 the e, and the teraphim, and the molten 646
18:18 the e, and the teraphim, and the molten 646
18:20 he took the e, and the teraphim, and 646
1Sa 2:18 *being* a child, girded *with* a linen e. 646
2:28 to burn incense, to wear an e before me? 646
14: 3 the LORD'S priest in Shiloh, wearing an e. 646
21: 9 it *is here* wrapt in a cloth behind the e: 646
22:18 and five persons that did wear a linen e. 646
23: 6 *that* he came down *with* an e in his hand. 646
23: 9 to Abiathar the priest, Bring hither the e. 646
30: 7 I pray thee, bring me hither the e. 646
30: 7 And Abiathar brought thither the e to David. 646
2Sa 6:14 and David *was* girded *with* a linen e. 646
1Ch 15:27 David also *had* upon him an e of linen. 646
Hos 3: 4 and without an e, and *without* teraphim: 646

EPHPHATHA (1)
Mk 7:34 and saith unto him, E, that is, Be opened. *2188*

EPHRAIM (172) [EPHRAIM'S, EPHRAIMITE, EPHRAIMITES]
Ge 41:52 the name of the second called he E: For God 669
46:20 land of Egypt were born Manasseh and E, 669
48: 1 with him his two sons, Manasseh and E. 669
48: 5 now thy two sons, E and Manasseh, 669
48:13 E in his right hand toward Israel's left hand, 669
48:17 father laid his right hand upon the head of E, 669
48:20 God make thee as E and as Manasseh: 669
48:20 as Manasseh: and he set E before Manasseh. 669
Nu 1:10 of E; Elishama the son of Ammihud: 669
1:32 *namely,* of the children of E, *by* their 669
1:33 *even* of the tribe of E, *were* forty thousand 669
2:18 of the camp of E according to their armies: 669
2:18 the captain of the sons of E *shall be* 669
2:24 All that were numbered of the camp of E 669
7:48 prince of the children of E, *offered:* 669
10:22 the standard of the camp of the children of E 669
13: 8 Of the tribe of E, Oshea the son of Nun. 669
26:28 after their families *were* Manasseh and E. 669
26:35 These *are* the sons of E after their families: 669
26:37 These *are* the families of the sons of E 669
34:24 the prince of the tribe of the children of E, 669
Dt 33:17 they *are* the ten thousands of E, and they *are* 669
34: 2 the land of E, and Manasseh, and all the land 669
Jos 14: 4 of Joseph were two tribes, Manasseh and E: 669
16: 4 Manasseh and E, took their inheritance. 669
16: 5 the border of the children of E according to 669
16: 8 tribe of the children of E by their families. 669
16: 9 the separate cities for the children of E *were* 669
17: 8 of Manasseh *belonged* to the children of E; 669
17: 9 these cities of E *are* among the cities of 669
17:15 the giants, if mount E be too narrow for thee. 669
17:17 *even* to E and to Manasseh, saying, Thou *art* 669
19:50 he asked, *even* Timnath-serah in mount E: 669
20: 7 Shechem in mount E, and Kirjath-arba, 669
21: 5 by lot out of the families of the tribe of E, 669
21:20 the cities of their lot out of the tribe of E. 669
21:21 them Shechem with her suburbs in mount E, 669
24:30 which *is* in mount E, on the north side of 669
24:33 his son, which was given him in mount E. 669
Jdg 1:29 Neither did E drive out the Canaanites that 669
2: 9 in the mount of E, on the north side of 669
3:27 that he blew a trumpet in the mountain of E, 669
4: 5 between Ramah and Beth-el in mount E: 669
5:14 Out of E *was there* a root of them against 669
7:24 sent messengers throughout all mount E, 669
7:24 all the men of E gathered themselves 669
8: 1 the men of E said unto him, Why hast thou 669
8: 2 *Is* not the gleaning of the grapes of E better 669
10: 1 and he dwelt in Shamir in mount E. 669
10: 9 and against the house of E; 669
12: 1 the men of E gathered themselves together, 669
12: 4 all the men of Gilead, and fought with E: 669
12: 4 the men of Gilead smote E, because 669
12: 4 Ye Gileadites *are* fugitives of E among 669
12:15 was buried in Pirathon in the land of E, 669
17: 1 there was a man of mount E, whose name 669
17: 8 he came *to* mount E to the house of Micah, 669
18: 2 who when they came *to* mount E, to 669

Jdg 18:13 they passed thence *unto* mount **E**, and 669
19: 1 Levite sojourning on the side of mount **E**, 669
19:16 field at even, which *was* also of mount **E**; 669
19:18 toward the side of mount **E**; 669
1Sa 1: 1 of mount **E**, and his name *was* Elkanah, 669
9: 4 he passed through mount **E**, and 669
14:22 Israel which had hid themselves in mount **E**, 669
2Sa 2: 9 over **E**, and over Benjamin, and over all 669
13:23 in Baal-hazor, which *is* beside **E**: 669
18: 6 and the battle was in the wood of **E**; 669
20:21 a man of mount **E**, Sheba the son of Bichri 669
1Ki 4: 8 *are* their names: The son of Hur, in mount **E**: 669
12:25 Jeroboam built Shechem in mount **E**, and 669
2Ki 5:22 **E** two young men of the sons of 669
14:13 from the gate of **E** unto the corner gate, 669
1Ch 6:66 had cities of their coasts out of the tribe of **E**. 669
6:67 Shechem in mount **E** with her suburbs; 669
7:20 the sons of **E**; Shuthelah, and Bered his son, 669
7:22 And **E** their father mourned many days, and 669
9: 3 and of the children of **E**, and Manasseh; 669
12:30 of the children of **E** twenty thousand and 669
27:10 *was* Helez the Pelonite, of the children of **E**: 669
27:14 Benaiah the Pirathonite, of the children of **E**: 669
27:20 Of the children of **E**, Hoshea the son of 669
2Ch 13: 4 which *is* in mount **E**, and said, Hear me, 669
15: 8 the cities which he had taken from mount **E**, 669
15: 9 the strangers with them out of **E** and 669
17: 2 in the cities of **E**, which Asa his father had 669
19: 4 the people from Beer-sheba to mount **E**, 669
25: 7 with Israel, *to wit, with* all the children of **E**. 669
25:10 the army that was come to him out of **E**, 669
25:23 from the gate of **E** to the corner gate, 669
28: 7 Zichri, a mighty *man* of **E**, slew Maaseiah 669
28:12 certain of the heads of the children of **E**, 669
30: 1 and wrote letters also to **E** and Manasseh, 669
30:10 from city to city through the country of **E** 669
30:18 *even* many of **E**, and Manasseh, Issachar, 669
31: 1 and Benjamin, in **E** also and Manasseh, 669
34: 6 and **E**, and Simeon, even unto Naphtali, 669
34: 9 had gathered of the hand of Manasseh and **E**, 669
Ne 8:16 water gate, and in the street of the gate of **E**. 669
12:39 from above the gate of **E**, and above the old 669
Ps 60: 7 *is* mine; **E** also *is* the strength of mine head; 669
78: 9 The children of **E**, *being* armed, *and* 669
78:67 of Joseph, and chose not the tribe of **E**: 669
80: 2 Before **E** and Benjamin and Manasseh stir 669
108: 8 *is* mine; **E** also *is* the strength of mine head; 669
Isa 7: 2 saying, Syria is confederate with **E**. 669
7: 5 Because Syria, **E**, and the son of Remaliah, 669
7: 8 and five years shall **E** be broken, 669
7: 9 the head of **E** *is* Samaria, and the head of 669
7:17 from the day that **E** departed from Judah; 669
9: 9 *even* **E** and the inhabitant of Samaria, 669
9:21 Manasseh, **E**; and Ephraim, Manasseh: *and* 669
9:21 Manasseh, Ephraim; and **E**, Manasseh: *and* 669
11:13 The envy also of **E** shall depart, and 669
11:13 **E** shall not envy Judah, and Judah shall not 669
11:13 not envy Judah, and Judah shall not vex **E**. 669
17: 3 The fortress also shall cease from **E**, and 669
28: 1 to the crown of pride, to the drunkards of **E**, 669
28: 3 The crown of pride, the drunkards of **E**, 669
Jer 4:15 and publisheth affliction from mount **E**. 669
7:15 all your brethren, *even* the whole seed of **E**. 669
31: 6 *that* the watchmen upon the mount **E** shall 669
31: 9 I am a father to Israel, and **E** *is* my firstborn. 669
31:18 I have surely heard **E** bemoaning himself 669
31:20 *Is* **E** my dear son? *is he* a pleasant child? 669
50:19 his soul shall be satisfied upon mount **E** and 669
Eze 37:16 the stick of **E**, and *for* all the house of Israel 669
37:19 which *is* in the hand of **E**, and the tribes of 669
48: 5 east side unto the west side, a *portion for* **E**. 669
48: 6 by the border of **E**, from the east side even 669
Hos 4:17 **E** *is* joined to idols: let him alone. 669
5: 3 I know **E**, and Israel is not hid from me: 669
5: 3 for now, O **E**, thou committest whoredom, 669
5: 5 shall Israel and **E** fall in their iniquity; 669
5: 9 **E** shall be desolate in the day of rebuke: 669
5:11 **E** *is* oppressed *and* broken in judgment, 669
5:12 Therefore *will* I *be* unto **E** as a moth, and 669
5:13 When **E** saw his sickness, and Judah *saw* his 669
5:13 went **E** to the Assyrian, and sent to king 669
5:14 For I *will be* unto **E** as a lion, and as a young 669
6: 4 O **E**, what shall I do unto thee? O Judah, 669
6:10 there *is* the whoredom of **E**, Israel is defiled. 669
7: 1 the iniquity of **E** was discovered, and 669
7: 8 **E**, he hath mixed himself among the people; 669
7: 8 among the people; **E** is a cake not turned. 669
7:11 **E** also is like a silly dove, without heart: 669
8: 9 ass alone by himself: **E** hath hired lovers. 669
8:11 Because **E** hath made many altars to sin, 669
9: 3 **E** shall return *to* Egypt, and they shall eat 669
9: 8 The watchman of **E** *was* with my God: *but* 669
9:11 *As for* **E**, their glory shall fly away like a 669
9:13 **E**, as I saw Tyrus, *is* planted in a pleasant 669
9:13 **E** *shall* bring forth his children to 669
9:16 **E** is smitten, their root is dried up, they shall 669
10: 6 **E** shall receive shame, and Israel shall be 669
10:11 **E** *is as* a heifer *that is* taught, *and* loveth to 669
10:11 I will make **E** to ride; Judah shall plow, *and* 669
11: 3 I taught **E** also to go, taking them by their 669
11: 8 How shall I give thee up, **E**? *how* shall I 669
11: 9 of mine anger, I will not return to destroy **E**: 669
11:12 **E** compasseth me about with lies, and 669
12: 1 **E** feedeth on wind, and followeth after 669
12: 8 **E** said, Yet I am become rich, I have found 669
12:14 **E** provoked *him* to anger most bitterly: 669
13: 1 When **E** spake trembling, he exalted *himself* 669
13:12 The iniquity of **E** *is* bound up; his sin *is* hid. 669
14: 8 **E** *shall say*, What have I to do any more with 669
Ob 1:19 they shall possess the fields of **E**, and 669
Zec 9:10 I will cut off the chariot from **E**, and 669
9:13 filled the bow *with* **E**, and raised up thy 669
10: 7 *they of* **E** shall be like a mighty *man*, and 669
Jn 11:54 into a city called **E**, and there continued *2187*

EPHRAIM'S (4) [EPHRAIM]
Ge 48:14 laid *it* upon **E** head, who *was* the younger, 669
48:17 to remove it from **E** head unto Manasseh's 669
50:23 Joseph saw **E** children of the third 669
Jos 17:10 Southward *it was* **E**, and 669+3807.1

EPHRAIMITE (1) [EPHRAIM]
Jdg 12: 5 men of Gilead said unto him, *Art* thou an **E**? 673

EPHRAIMITES (5) [EPHRAIM]
Jos 16:10 the Canaanites dwell among the **E** unto this 669
Jdg 12: 4 *are* fugitives of Ephraim among the **E**, 669
12: 5 took the passages of Jordan before the **E**: 669
12: 5 that when those **E** which were escaped said, 669
12: 6 there fell at that time of the **E** forty and 669

EPHRAIN (1)
2Ch 13:19 and **E** with the towns thereof. 6085

EPHRATAH (5) [CALEB-EPHRATAH, EPHRATH]
Ru 4:11 do thou worthily in **E**, and be famous in 672
1Ch 2:50 of Caleb the son of Hur, the firstborn of **E**; 672
4: 4 the firstborn of **E**, the father of Beth-lehem. 672
Ps 132: 6 Lo, we heard *of* it at **E**: we found it in 672
Mic 5: 2 thou, Beth-lehem **E**, *though thou* be little 672

EPHRATH (5) [EPHRATAH, EPHRATHITE, EPHRATHITES]
Ge 35:16 and there was but a little way to come to **E**: 672
35:19 Rachel died, and was buried in the way to **E**, 672
48: 7 *there was* but a little way to come unto **E**: 672
48: 7 I buried her there in the way of **E**; the same 672
1Ch 2:19 Caleb took unto him **E**, which bare him Hur. 672

EPHRATHITE (3) [EPHRATH]
1Sa 1: 1 the son of Tohu, the son of Zuph, an **E**: 673
17:12 Now David *was* the son of that **E** of 673
1Ki 11:26 an **E** of Zereda, Solomon's servant, 673

EPHRATHITES (1) [EPHRATH]
Ru 1: 2 and Chilion, **E** of Beth-lehem-judah. 673

EPHRON (13)
Ge 23: 8 and intreat for me to **E** the son of Zohar, 6085
23:10 **E** dwelt amongst the children of Heth: and 6085
23:10 **E** the Hittite answered Abraham in 6085
23:13 he spake unto **E** in the audience of 6085
23:14 **E** answered Abraham, saying unto him, 6085
23:16 Abraham hearkened unto **E**; and 6085
23:16 Abraham weighed to **E** the silver, which he 6085
23:17 the field of **E**, which *was* in Machpelah, 6085
25: 9 in the field of **E** the son of Zohar 6085
49:29 the cave that *is* in the field of **E** the Hittite, 6085
49:30 which Abraham bought with the field of **E** 6085
50:13 of a buryingplace of **E** the Hittite, 6085
Jos 15: 9 and went out to the cities of mount **E**; 6085

EPICUREANS (1)
Ac 17:18 Then certain philosophers of the **E**, and *1946*

EPISTLE (19) [EPISTLES]
Ac 15:30 the multitude together, they delivered the **e**: *1992*
23:33 and delivered the **e** to the governor, *1992*
Ro 16:22 I Tertius, who wrote *this* **e**, salute you in *1992*
1Co 5: 9 I wrote unto you in an **e** not to company *1992*
16: S The first **e** to the Corinthians was written NIG
2Co 3: 2 Ye are our **e** written in our hearts, known *1992*
3: 3 to be the **e** of Christ ministered by us, *1992*
7: 8 for I perceive that the same **e** hath made *1992*
13: S The second **e** to the Corinthians was written NIG
Col 4:16 And when *this* **e** is read amongst you, *1992*
4:16 that ye likewise read the **e** from Laodicea. NIG
1Th 5:27 I charge you by the Lord that *this* **e** be read *1992*
5: S The first **e** unto the Thessalonians was NIG
2Th 2:15 been taught, whether by word, or by our **e**. *1992*
3:14 if any *man* obey not our word by *this* **e**, *1992*
3:17 own hand, which is the token in every **e**: *1992*
3: S The second **e** to the Thessalonians was NIG
2Ti 4: S The second **e** unto Timotheus, ordained NIG
2Pe 3: 1 This second **e**, beloved, I now write unto *1992*

EPISTLES (2) [EPISTLE]
2Co 3: 1 as some *others*, **e** of commendation to you, *1992*
2Pe 3:16 As also in all *his* **e**, speaking in them of *1992*

EQUAL (21) [EQUALITY, EQUALLY, EQUALS, UNEQUAL]
Job 28:17 The gold and the crystal cannot **e** it: and 6186
28:19 The topaz of Ethiopia shall not **e** it, 6186
Ps 17: 2 let thine eyes behold the **things that are e**. 4339
55:13 a man mine **e**, my guide, and 6187+3509.1
Pr 26: 7 The legs of the lame are **not e**: so *is* a 1809
Isa 40:25 then will ye liken me, or shall I be **e**? 7737
46: 5 **make** *me* **e**, and compare me, that we may 7737
La 2:13 what shall I **e** to thee, that I may comfort 7737
Eze 18:25 Yet ye say, The way of the Lord is not **e**. 8505
18:25 O house of Israel; Is not my way **e**? 8505
18:29 of Israel, The way of the Lord is not **e**. 8505
18:29 O house of Israel, are not my ways **e**? 8505
33:17 people say, The way of the Lord is not **e**: 8505
33:17 but *as for* them, their way is not **e**. 8505
33:20 Yet ye say, The way of the Lord is not **e**. 8505
Mt 20:12 and thou hast made them **e** unto us, *2470*
Lk 20:36 for they are **e unto** *the* **angels**; and are *2465*
Jn 5:18 was his Father, making himself **e** with God. *2470*
Php 2: 6 thought it not robbery to be **e** with God: *2470*
Col 4: 1 unto *your* servants that which is just and **e**; *2471*
Rev 21:16 and the breadth and the height of it are **e**. *2470*

EQUALITY (2) [EQUAL]
2Co 8:14 But by an **e**, *that* now at *this* time your *2471*
8:14 *a supply* for your want: that there may be **e**: *2471*

EQUALLY (1) [EQUAL]
Ex 36:22 two tenons, **e distant** one from another: 7947

EQUALS (1) [EQUAL]
Gal 1:14 above many *my* **e** in mine own nation, *4915*

EQUITY (10)
Ps 98: 9 he judge the world, and the people with **e**. 4339
99: 4 thou dost establish **e**, thou executest 4339
Pr 1: 3 of wisdom, justice, and judgment, and **e**; 4339
2: 9 and judgment, and **e**; 4339
17:26 just *is* not good, *nor* to strike princes for **e**. 3476
Ecc 2:21 *is* in wisdom, and in knowledge, and in **e**; 3788
Isa 11: 4 reprove with **e** for the meek of the earth: 4334
59:14 is fallen in the street, and **e** cannot enter. 5229
Mic 3: 9 that abhor judgment, and pervert all **e**. 3477
Mal 2: 6 he walked with me in peace and **e**, and 4334

ER (11)
Ge 38: 3 and bare a son; and he called his name **E**. 6147
38: 6 Judah took a wife for **E** his firstborn, 6147
38: 7 **E**, Judah's firstborn, was wicked in 6147
46:12 **E**, and Onan, and Shelah, and Pharez, and 6147
46:12 **E** and Onan died in the land of Canaan. 6147
Nu 26:19 The sons of Judah *were* **E** and Onan: and 6147
26:19 and **E** and Onan died in the land of Canaan. 6147
1Ch 2: 3 sons of Judah; **E**, and Onan, and Shelah: 6147
2: 3 **E**, the firstborn of Judah, was evil in 6147
4:21 son of Judah *were*, **E** the father of Lecah, 6147
Lk 3:28 *son* of Elmodam, which was *the son* of **E**, *2262*

ERAN (1) [ERANITES]
Nu 26:36 of **E**, the family of the Eranites. 6197

ERANITES (1) [ERAN]
Nu 26:36 of Shuthelah: of Eran, the family of the **E**. 6198

ERASTUS (3)
Ac 19:22 that ministered unto him, Timotheus and **E**; *2037*
Ro 16:23 **E** the chamberlain of the city saluteth you, *2037*
2Ti 4:20 **E** abode at Corinth: but Trophimus have I *2037*

ERE (10)
Ex 1:19 are delivered **e** the midwives come 2962+871.1
Nu 11:33 yet between their teeth, **e** it was chewed, 2962
14:11 how long will it be **e** they believe me, 3808
1Sa 3: 3 **e** the lamp of God went out in the temple of 2962
2Sa 2:26 **e** thou bid the people return from following 3808
2Ki 6:32 **but e** the messenger came to him, he 2962+871.1
Job 18: 2 How long *will it be* **e** you make an end of NIH
Jer 47: 6 how long *will it be* **e** thou be quiet? 3808
Hos 8: 5 how long *will it be* **e** they attain to 3808
Jn 4:49 unto him, Sir, come down **e** my child die. *4250*

ERECH (1)
Ge 10:10 **E**, and Accad, and Calneh, in the land of 751

ERECTED (1)
Ge 33:20 he **e** there an altar, and called it 5324

ERI (2) [ERITES]
Ge 46:16 Shuni, and Ezbon, **E**, and Arodi, and Areli. 6179
Nu 26:16 the Oznites: of **E**, the family of the Erites: 6179

ERITES (1) [ERI]
Nu 26:16 of the Oznites: of Eri, the family of the **E**: 6180

ERR (24) [ERRED, ERRETH, ERROR, ERRORS]
2Ch 33: 9 **made** Judah and the inhabitants of Jerusalem **to e**, 8582
Ps 95:10 It *is* a people that do **e** in *their* heart, and 8582
119:21 which do **e** from thy commandments. 7686
119:118 Thou hast trodden down all them that **e** 7686
Pr 14:22 Do they not **e** that devise evil? but mercy 8582
19:27 to hear the instruction *that causeth* to **e** 7686
Isa 3:12 they which lead thee **cause** *thee* **to e**, and 8582
9:16 the leaders of this people **cause** *them* **to e**; 8582
19:14 they have **caused** Egypt **to e** in every work 8582
28: 7 they **e** in vision, they stumble *in* judgment. 7686
30:28 the jaws of the people, **causing** *them* **to e**. 8582
35: 8 though fools, shall not **e** *therein*. 8582
63:17 why hast thou **made** us **to e** from thy ways, 8582
Jer 23:13 in Baal, and **caused** my people Israel **to e**. 8582
23:32 **cause** my people **to e** by their lies, and 8582
Hos 4:12 spirit of whoredoms hath **caused** *them* **to e**, 8582
Am 2: 4 and their lies **caused** them **to e**, 8582
Mic 3: 5 the prophets that **make** my people **e**, 8582
Mt 22:29 and said unto them, Ye do **e**, *4105*
Mk 12:24 Do ye not therefore **e**, because ye know not *4105*
12:27 God of the living: ye therefore do greatly **e**. *4105*
Heb 3:10 and said, They do alway **e** in *their* heart; *4105*
Jas 1:16 Do not **e**, my beloved brethren. *4105*
5:19 if any of you do **e** from the truth, and *4105*

ERRAND (3)
Ge 24:33 I will not eat, until I have told mine **e**. 1697
Jdg 3:19 said, I have a secret **e** unto thee, O king: 1697
2Ki 9: 5 and he said, I have an **e** to thee, O captain. 1697

ERRED (12) [ERR]
Lev 5:18 him concerning his ignorance wherein he **e** 7683
Nu 15:22 if ye have **e**, and not observed all these 7686
1Sa 26:21 played the fool, and have **e** exceedingly. 7686
Job 6:24 cause me to understand wherein I have **e**. 7686
19: 4 be it indeed *that* I have **e**, mine error 7686
Ps 119:110 snare for me: yet I **e** not from thy precepts. 8582
Isa 28: 7 they also have **e** through wine, and 7686
28: 7 the prophet have **e** through strong drink, 7686
29:24 They also that **e** in spirit shall come to 8582
1Ti 6:10 they have **e** from the faith, and *635*
6:21 Which some professing have **e** concerning *795*
2Ti 2:18 Who concerning the truth have **e**, saying that *795*

ERRETH (2) [ERR]
Pr 10:17 but he that refuseth reproof e. 8582
Eze 45:20 *day* of the month for every one that e, 7686

ERROR (13) [ERR]
2Sa 6: 7 God smote him there for *his* e; and there he 7944
Job 19: 4 I have erred, mine e remaineth with myself. 4879
Ecc 5: 6 say thou before the angel, that it *was* an e: 7684
10: 5 as an e *which* proceedeth from the ruler: 7684
Isa 32: 6 and to utter e against the LORD, 8442
Da 6: 4 neither was there any e or fault found in 7960
Mt 27:64 so the last e shall be worse than the first. 4106
Ro 1:27 *that* recompence of their e which was meet. 4106
Jas 5:20 e of his way shall save a soul from death, 4106
2Pe 2:18 clean escaped from them who live in e. 4106
3:17 being led away with the e of the wicked, 4106
1Jn 4: 6 we the spirit of truth, and the spirit of e. 4106
Jude 1:11 ran greedily after the e of Balaam for 4106

ERRORS (4) [ERR]
Ps 19:12 Who can understand *his* e? cleanse thou 7691
Jer 10:15 They *are* vanity, *and* the work of e: in 8595
51:18 They *are* vanity, the work of e: in the time 8595
Heb 9: 7 for himself, and *for* the e of the people: 51

ESAI (1) [ISAIAH]
2Ki 19: 2 to E the prophet the son of Amoz. 3470

ESAIAS (21) [ISAIAH]
Mt 3: 3 is he that was spoken of by the prophet E, 2268
4:14 which was spoken by E the prophet, 2268
8:17 which was spoken by E the prophet, 2268
12:17 which was spoken by E the prophet, 2268
13:14 And in them is fulfilled the prophecy of E, 2268
15: 7 well did E prophesy of you, saying, 2268
Mk 7: 6 Well hath E prophesied of you hypocrites, 2268
Lk 3: 4 in the book of the words of E the prophet, 2268
4:17 unto him the book of the prophet E. 2268
Jn 1:23 the way of the Lord, as said the prophet E. 2268
12:38 That the saying of E the prophet might be 2268
12:39 not believe, because that E said again, 2268
12:41 These *things* said E, when he saw his glory, 2268
Ac 8:28 and sitting in his chariot read E the prophet. 2268
8:30 to *him,* and heard him read the prophet E, 2268
28:25 Well spake the Holy Ghost by E 2268
Ro 9:27 E also crieth concerning Israel, Though 2268
9:29 And as E said before, Except the Lord of 2268
10:16 For E saith, Lord, who hath believed our 2268
10:20 But E is very bold, and saith, I was found 2268
15:12 And again E saith, There shall be a root of 2268

ESARHADDON, ESAR-HADDON (3) [ESARHADDON]
2Ki 19:37 And E his son reigned in his stead. 634
Ezr 4: 2 we do sacrifice unto him since the days of E 634
Isa 37:38 and E his son reigned in his stead. 634

ESAU (88) [EDOM, ESAU'S]
Ge 25:25 hairy garment; and they called his name E. 6215
25:27 E was a cunning hunter, a man of the field; 6215
25:28 Isaac loved E, because he did eat of *his* 6215
25:29 E came from the field, and he *was* faint: 6215
25:30 E said to Jacob, Feed me, I pray thee, 6215
25:32 E said, Behold, I *am* at the point to die: 6215
25:34 Jacob gave E bread and pottage of lentiles; 6215
25:34 his way: thus E despised *his* birthright. 6215
26:34 E was forty years old when he took to wife 6215
27: 1 he called E his eldest son, and said unto 6215
27: 5 Rebekah heard when Isaac spake to E his 6215
27: 5 And E went to the field to hunt for venison, 6215
27: 6 I heard thy father speak unto E thy brother, 6215
27:11 E my brother *is* a hairy man, and I *am* a 6215
27:15 took goodly raiment of her eldest son E, 6215
27:19 said unto his father, I *am* E thy firstborn; 6215
27:21 whether thou *be* my very son E or not. 6215
27:22 but the hands *are* the hands of E. 6215
27:24 he said, *Art* thou my very son E? And he 6215
27:30 that E his brother came in from his hunting. 6215
27:32 And he said, I *am* thy son, thy firstborn E. 6215
27:34 when E heard the words of his father, he 6215
27:37 Isaac answered and said unto E, Behold, 6215
27:38 E said unto his father, Hast thou but one 6215
27:38 And E lift up his voice, and wept. 6215
27:41 E hated Jacob because of the blessing 6215
27:41 E said in his heart, The days of mourning 6215
27:42 these words of E her elder son were told to 6215
27:42 said unto him, Behold, thy brother E, 6215
28: 6 When E saw that Isaac had blessed Jacob, 6215
28: 8 E seeing that the daughters of Canaan 6215
28: 9 went E unto Ishmael, and took unto 6215
32: 3 Jacob sent messengers before him to E his 6215
32: 4 saying, Thus shall ye speak unto my lord E; 6215
32: 6 We came to thy brother E, and also he 6215
32: 8 If E come to the one company, and smite it, 6215
32:11 the hand of my brother, from the hand of E: 6215
32:13 to his hand a present for E his brother; 6215
32:17 When E my brother meeteth thee, and 6215
32:18 it *is* a present sent unto my lord E: 6215
32:19 On this manner shall you speak unto E, 6215
33: 1 E came, and with him four hundred men. 6215
33: 4 E ran to meet him, and embraced him, and 6215
33: 9 E said, I have enough, my brother; 6215
33:15 E said, Let me now leave with thee *some* of 6215
33:16 So E returned that day on his way unto 6215
35: 1 fleddest from the face of E thy brother. 6215
35:29 and his sons E and Jacob buried him. 6215
36: 1 Now these *are* the generations of E, who *is* 6215
36: 2 E took his wives of the daughters of 6215
36: 4 Adah bare to E Eliphaz; and 6215
36: 5 these *are* the sons of E, which were born 6215
36: 6 E took his wives, and his sons, and his 6215
36: 8 Thus dwelt E in mount Seir: Esau *is* Edom. 6215
36: 8 Thus dwelt Esau in mount Seir: E *is* Edom. 6215
Ge 36: 9 these *are* the generations of E the father of 6215
36:10 Eliphaz the son of Adah the wife of E, 6215
36:10 Reuel the son of Bashemath the wife of E. 6215
36:14 she bare to E Jeush, and Jaalam, and 6215
36:15 These *were* dukes of the sons of E: the sons 6215
36:15 the sons of Eliphaz the firstborn *son* of E; 6215
36:19 These *are* the sons of E, who *is* Edom, and 6215
36:40 *are* the names of the dukes *that came* of E, 6215
36:43 he *is* E the father of the Edomites. 6215
Dt 2: 4 the coast of your brethren the children of E, 6215
2: 5 I have given mount Seir unto E *for* a 6215
2: 8 by from our brethren the children of E, 6215
2:12 the children of E succeeded them, 6215
2:22 As he did to the children of E, which dwelt 6215
2:29 (As the children of E which dwell in Seir, 6215
Jos 24: 4 I gave unto Isaac Jacob and E: and I gave 6215
24: 4 I gave unto E mount Seir, to possess it; 6215
1Ch 1:34 begat Isaac. The sons of Isaac; E and Israel. 6215
1:35 The sons of E; Eliphaz, Reuel, and Jeush, 6215
Jer 49: 8 for I will bring the calamity of E upon him, 6215
49:10 I have made E bare, I have uncovered his 6215
Ob 1: 6 How are *the things of* E searched out! 6215
1: 8 and understanding out of the mount of E? 6215
1: 9 to the end that every one of the mount of E 6215
1:18 the house of E for stubble, and they shall 6215
1:18 not be *any* remaining of the house of E; 6215
1:19 *of* the south shall possess the mount of E; 6215
1:21 up on mount Zion to judge the mount of E; 6215
Mal 1: 2 *was* not E Jacob's brother? saith 6215
1: 3 I hated E, and laid his mountains and his 6215
Ro 9:13 Jacob have I loved, but E have I hated. 2269
Heb 11:20 and E concerning *things* to come. 2269
12:16 *be* any fornicator, or profane *person,* as E, 2269

ESAU'S (12) [ESAU]
Ge 25:26 and his hand took hold on E heel; 6215
27:23 hands were hairy, as his brother E hands: 6215
28: 5 brother of Rebekah, Jacob's and E mother. 6215
36:10 These *are* the names of E sons; Eliphaz 6215
36:12 Timna was concubine to Eliphaz E son; 6215
36:12 these *were* the sons of Adah E wife. 6215
36:13 these were the sons of Bashemath E wife. 6215
36:14 of Anah, daughter of Zibeon, E wife: 6215
36:17 these *are* the sons of Reuel E son; 6215
36:17 these *are* the sons of Bashemath E wife. 6215
36:18 these *are* the sons of Aholibamah E wife; 6215
36:18 Aholibamah the daughter of Anah, E wife. 6215

ESCAPE (59) [ESCAPED, ESCAPETH, ESCAPING]
Ge 19:17 forth abroad, that he said, E for thy life; 4422
19:17 e to the mountain, lest thou be consumed. 4422
19:19 I cannot e to the mountain, lest *some* evil 4422
19:20 Oh, let me e thither, (*is* it not a little one?) 4422
19:22 Haste thee, e thither; for I cannot do any 4422
32: 8 the *other* company which is left shall e. 6413
Jos 8:22 so that *they* let none of them remain or e. 6412
1Sa 27: 1 **speedily e** into the land of 4422+4422
27: 1 coast of Israel: so shall I e out of his hand. 4422
2Sa 15:14 we shall not *else* e from Absalom: 1961+6413
20: 6 he get him fenced cities, and e us. 5337+5869
1Ki 18:40 the prophets of Baal; let not one of them e. 4422
2Ki 9:15 let none go forth *nor* e out of the city to go 6412
10:24 whom I *have* brought into your hands e, 4422
19:31 and **they that** e out of mount Zion: 6413
Ezr 9: 8 to leave us a **remnant to e**, and to give us a 6413
Est 4:13 Think not with thyself that *thou* shalt e *in* 4422
Job 11:20 they shall not e, and their hope *shall be as* 4498
Ps 55: 8 I would hasten my e from the windy storm 4655
56: 7 *Shall* they e by iniquity? in *thine* anger cast 6405
71: 2 me in thy righteousness, and **cause** me **to e**: 6403
141:10 into their own nets, whilst that I withal e. 5674
Pr 19: 5 and *he that* speaketh lies shall not e. 4422
Ecc 7:26 whoso pleaseth God shall e from her; but 4422
Isa 20: 6 the king of Assyria: and how shall we e? 4422
37:32 and **they that** e out of mount Zion: 6413
66:19 I will send those that e of them unto 6412
Jer 11:11 which they shall not be able to e; 3318
25:35 to flee, nor the principal of the flock to e. 6413
32: 4 Zedekiah king of Judah shall not e out of 4422
34: 3 thou shalt not e out of his hand, but 4422
38:18 and thou shalt not e out of their hand. 4422
38:23 thou shalt not e out of their hand, but 4422
42:17 e from the evil that I *will* bring upon them. 6412
44:14 shall e or remain, that *they* should 1961+6412
44:14 for none shall return but such as shall e. 6405
44:28 Yet a small number that e the sword shall 6412
46: 6 the swift flee away, nor the mighty *man* e; 4422
48: 8 come upon every city, and no city shall e: 4422
50:28 that flee and e out of the land of Babylon, 6405
50:29 against it round about; let none thereof e: 6413
Eze 6: 8 that ye may have *some* that shall e 6412
6: 9 they that e of you shall remember me 6412
7:16 they that e of them shall escape, and 6412
7:16 they that escape of them shall e, and 6403
17:15 shall he e that doeth such *things?* or 4422
17:18 hath done all these *things,* he shall not e. 4422
Da 11:41 these shall e out of his hand, *even* Edom, 4422
11:42 and the land of Egypt shall not e. 6413
Joel 2: 3 and nothing shall e them. 1961+6413
Ob 1:14 to cut off those of his that did e; 6412
Mt 23:33 how can ye e the damnation of hell? 5343
Lk 21:36 that ye may be accounted worthy to e all 1628
Ac 27:42 lest any *of them* should swim out, and e. 1309
Ro 2: 3 that thou shalt e the judgment of God? 1628
1Co 10:13 with the temptation also make a **way to e**, 1545
1Th 5: 3 a *woman* with child; and they shall not e. 1628
Heb 2: 3 How shall we e, if we neglect so 1628
12:25 much more *shall not* we e, if we turn away NIG

ESCAPED (58) [ESCAPE]
Ge 14:13 there came one that had e, and told Abram 6412
Ex 10: 5 they shall eat the residue of that **which is e** 6413
Nu 21:29 he hath given his sons that e, and 6412
Dt 23:15 which is e from his master unto thee: 5337
Jdg 3:26 Ehud e while they tarried, and passed 4422
3:26 beyond the quarries, and e unto Seirath. 4422
3:29 all men of valour; and there e not a man. 4422
12: 5 that when those Ephraimites which were e 6412
21:17 for **them that be e** of Benjamin, 6413
1Sa 14:41 and Jonathan were taken: but the people e. 3318
19:10 the wall: and David fled, and e that night. 4422
19:12 a window: and he went, and fled, and e. 4422
19:17 and sent away mine enemy, that he is e? 4422
19:18 e, and came to Samuel to Ramah, and 4422
22: 1 departed thence, and e to the cave Adullam: 4422
22:20 named Abiathar, e, and fled after David. 4422
23:13 it was told Saul that David was e from 4422
30:17 there e not a man of them, save four 4422
2Sa 1: 3 unto him, Out of the camp of Israel am I e. 4422
4: 6 and Rechab and Baanah his brother e. 4422
1Ki 20:20 Ben-hadad the king of Syria e on a horse 4422
2Ki 19:30 the remnant **that is e** of the house of Judah 6413
19:37 they e *into* the land of Armenia. 4422
1Ch 4:43 the rest of the Amalekites that were e, 6413
2Ch 16: 7 is the host of the king of Syria e out of 4422
20:24 dead bodies fallen to the earth, and none e. 6413
30: 6 **that are e** out of the hand of the kings of 6413
36:20 them that had e from the sword carried he 7611
Ezr 9:15 for we remain *yet* e, as *it is* this day: 6413
Ne 1: 2 asked them concerning the Jews that had e, 6413
Job 1:15 and I only am e alone to tell thee. 4422
1:16 and I only am e alone to tell thee. 4422
1:17 and I only am e alone to tell thee. 4422
1:19 are dead; and I only am e alone to tell thee. 4422
19:20 and I am e with the skin of my teeth. 4422
Ps 124: 7 Our soul is e as a bird out of the snare of 4422
124: 7 the snare is broken, and we are e. 4422
Isa 4: 2 and comely for **them that are** e of Israel. 6413
10:20 and **such as are** e of the house of Jacob, 6413
37:31 the remnant **that is** e of the house of Judah 6413
37:38 and they e *into* the land of Armenia: 4422
45:20 near together, ye *that are* e of the nations: 6412
Jer 41:15 Ishmael the son of Nethaniah e from 4422
51:50 Ye that have e the sword, go *away,* stand 6405
La 2:22 the LORD'S anger none e nor remained: 6412
Eze 24:27 thy mouth be opened to him which is e, 6412
33:21 *that* **one that** had e out of Jerusalem came 6412
33:22 in the evening, afore he **that** was e came; 6412
Jn 10:39 to take him: but he e out of their hand, 1831
Ac 27:44 it came to pass, that *they* e all **safe** to land. 1295
28: 1 And when they were e, then they knew that 1295
28: 4 whom, though he hath e the sea, 1295
2Co 11:33 was I let down by the wall, and e his hands. 1628
Heb 11:34 violence of fire, e the edge of the sword, 5343
12:25 for if they e not who refused him that spake 5343
2Pe 1: 4 having e the corruption that is in the world 668
2:18 those that were clean e **from** them who live 668
2:20 For if after they have e the pollutions of 668

ESCAPETH (6) [ESCAPE]
1Ki 19:17 *that* him that e the sword of Hazael shall 4422
19:17 him that e from the sword of Jehu shall 4422
Isa 15: 9 lions upon **him that** e of Moab, and 6413
Jer 48:19 and her that e, *and* say, What is done? 4422
Eze 24:26 *That* he that e in that day shall come unto 6412
Am 9: 1 and he that e of them shall not be delivered. 6412

ESCAPING (1) [ESCAPE]
Ezr 9:14 so that *there should be* no remnant nor e? 6413

ESCHEW (1) [ESCHEWED, ESCHEWETH]
1Pe 3:11 Let him e evil, and do good; let him seek 1578

ESCHEWED (1) [ESCHEW]
Job 1: 1 and one that feared God, and e evil. 5493

ESCHEWETH (2) [ESCHEW]
Job 1: 8 one that feareth God, and e evil? 5493
2: 3 one that feareth God, and e evil? 5493

ESCORT See FETCH; FETCHED

ESEK (1)
Ge 26:20 he called the name of the well E; because 6230

ESHAN See ESHEAN

ESHBAAL (2) [ISH-BOSHETH]
1Ch 8:33 and Malchishua, and Abinadab, and E. 792
9:39 and Malchishua, and Abinadab, and E. 792

ESHBAN (2)
Ge 36:26 Hemdan, and E, and Ithran, and Cheran. 790
1Ch 1:41 Amram, and E, and Ithran, and Cheran. 790

ESHCOL (6)
Ge 14:13 brother of E, and brother of Aner: 812
14:24 which went with me, Aner, E, and Mamre; 812
Nu 13:23 they came unto the brook of E, and cut down 812
13:24 The place was called the brook E, because 812
32: 9 For when they went up unto the valley of E, 812
Dt 1:24 came unto the valley of E, and searched it 812

ESHEAN (1)
Jos 15:52 Arab, and Dumah, and E, 824

ESHEK (1)
1Ch 8:39 the sons of E his brother *were,* Ulam his 6232

ESHKALONITES (1) [ASHKELON]
Jos 13: 3 the E, the Gittites, and the Ekronites; 832

ESHTAOL (7)
Jos 15:33 in the valley, E, and Zoreah, and Ashnah, 847
19:41 was Zorah, and E, and Ir-shemesh, 847
Jdg 13:25 in the camp of Dan, between Zorah and E. 847
16:31 E in the buryingplace of Manoah his father. 847

Jdg 18: 2 men of valour, from Zorah and from E, 847
18: 8 came unto their brethren to Zorah and E: 847
18:11 out of Zorah and out of E, six hundred men 847

ESHTAOLITES See ESHTAULITES

ESHTAULITES (1)
1Ch 2:53 of them came the Zareathites, and the E. 848

ESHTEMOA (5)
Jos 21:14 with her suburbs, and E with her suburbs, 851
1Sa 30:28 in Siphmoth, and to them which were in E, 851
1Ch 4:17 and Shammai, and Ishbah the father of E. 851
4:19 Keilah the Garmite, and E the Maachathite. 851
6:57 and Jattir, and E, with their suburbs, 851

ESHTEMOH (1)
Jos 15:50 And Anab, and E, and Anim, 851

ESHTON (2)
1Ch 4:11 begat Mehir, which was the father of E. 850
4:12 E begat Beth-rapha, and Paseah, and 850

ESLI (1)
Lk 3:25 the son of Naum, which was the son of E, 2069

ESPECIALLY (5) [SPECIAL]
Ps 31:11 e among my neighbours, and a fear to mine 3966
Ac 26: 3 E because I know thee to be expert in all 3122
Gal 6:10 let us do good unto all men, e unto them 3122
1Ti 5:17 e they who labour in the word and doctrine. 3122
2Ti 4:13 and the books, but e the parchments. 3122

ESPIED (2) [SPY]
Ge 42:27 ass provender in the inn, he e his money; 7200
Eze 20: 6 of Egypt into a land that I had e for them, 8446

ESPOUSALS (2) [ESPOUSED]
SS 3:11 his mother crowned him in the day of his e, 2861
Jer 2: 2 kindness of thy youth, the love of thine e, 3623

ESPOUSED (5) [ESPOUSALS]
2Sa 3:14 which I e to me for an hundred foreskins of 781
Mt 1:18 When as his mother Mary was e to Joseph, 3423
Lk 1:27 To a virgin e to a man whose name was 3423
2: 5 To be taxed with Mary his e wife, 3423
2Co 11: 2 for I have e you to one husband, that I may 718

ESPY (2) [SPY]
Jos 14: 7 me from Kadesh-barnea to e out the land; 7270
Jer 48:19 inhabitant of Aroer, stand by the way and e; 6822

ESROM (3) [HEZRON]
Mt 1: 3 and Phares begat E; and Esrom begat 2074
1: 3 Phares begat Esrom; and E begat Aram; 2074
Lk 3:33 the son of Aram, which was the son of E, 2074

ESTABLISH (41) [ESTABLISHED, ESTABLISHETH, ESTABLISHMENT]
Ge 6:18 with thee will I e my covenant; and 6965
9: 9 behold I e my covenant with you and 6965
9:11 I will e my covenant with you; neither shall 6965
17: 7 I will e my covenant between me and thee 6965
17:19 I will e my covenant with him for an 6965
17:21 my covenant will I e with Isaac, 6965
Lev 26: 9 multiply you, and e my covenant with you. 6965
Nu 30:13 her husband may e it, or her husband may 6965
Dt 8:18 that he may e his covenant which he sware 6965
28: 9 The LORD shall e thee a holy people unto 6965
29:13 That he may e thee to day for a people unto 6965
1Sa 1:23 weaned him; only the LORD e his word. 6965
2Sa 7:12 out of thy bowels, and I will e his kingdom. 3559
7:25 e it for ever, and do as thou hast said. 6965
1Ki 9: 5 I will e the throne of thy kingdom upon 6965
15: 4 set up his son after him, and to e Jerusalem: 5975
1Ch 22:10 I will e the throne of his kingdom over 3559
28: 7 Moreover I will e his kingdom for ever, 3559
2Ch 9: 8 to e them for ever, therefore made he thee 5975
Job 36: 7 he doth e them for ever, and they are 3427
Ps 7: 9 the wicked come to an end; but e the just: 3559
48: 8 of our God: God will e it for ever. Selah. 3559
87: 5 in her: and the Highest himself shall e her. 3559
89: 2 thy faithfulness shalt thou e in the very 3559
90:17 e thou the work of our hands upon us; yea, 3559
90:17 yea, the work of our hands e thou it. 3559
99: 4 thou dost e equity, thou executest judgment 3559
Pr 15:25 but he will e the border of the widow. 5324
Isa 49: 8 for a covenant of the people, to e the earth, 6965
62: 7 till he e, and till he make Jerusalem a praise 3559
Jer 33: 2 the LORD that formed it, to e it; 3559
Eze 16:60 I will e unto thee an everlasting covenant. 6965
16:62 I will e my covenant with thee; and 6965
Da 6: 7 have consulted together to e a royal statute, 6966
6: 8 O king, e the decree, and sign the writing, 6966
11:14 shall exalt themselves to e the vision; 5975
Am 5:15 love the good, and e judgment in the gate: 3322
Ro 3:31 God forbid: yea, we e the law. 2476
10: 3 going about to e their own righteousness, 2476
1Th 3: 2 to e you, and to comfort you concerning 4741
Heb 10: 9 away the first, that he may e the second. 2476

ESTABLISHED (68) [ESTABLISH]
Ge 9:17 which I have e between me and all flesh 6965
41:32 it is because the thing is e by God, and God 3559
Ex 6: 4 I have also e my covenant with them, 6965
15:17 O Lord, which thy hands have e. 3559
Dt 32: 6 hath he not made thee, and e thee? 3559
1Sa 3:20 Samuel was e to be a prophet of the LORD. 539
13:13 for now would the LORD have e thy 3559
24:20 that the kingdom of Israel shall be e in 6965
2Sa 5:12 David perceived that the LORD had e him 3559
7:26 let the house of thy servant David be e 3559
1Ki 2:12 his father; and his kingdom was e greatly. 3559
1Ki 2:24 which hath e me, and set me on the throne 3559
2:45 the throne of David shall be e before 3559
2:46 the kingdom was e in the hand of Solomon. 3559
1Ch 17:14 and his throne shall be e for evermore. 3559
17:23 and concerning his house be e for ever, 539
17:24 Let it even be e, that thy name may be 539
17:24 let the house of David thy servant be e 3559
2Ch 1: 9 let thy promise unto David my father be e: 539
12: 1 when Rehoboam had e the kingdom, and 3559
20:20 in the LORD your God, so shall you be e; 539
25: 3 to pass, when the kingdom was e to him, 2388
30: 5 So they e a decree to make proclamation 5975
Job 21: 8 Their seed is e in their sight with them, and 3559
22:28 decree a thing, and it shall be e unto thee: 6965
Ps 24: 2 it upon the seas, and e it upon the floods. 3559
40: 2 set my feet upon a rock, and e my goings. 3559
78: 5 For he e a testimony in Jacob, and 6965
78:69 like the earth which he hath e for ever. 3245
89:21 With whom my hand shall be e: mine arm 3559
89:37 It shall be e for ever as the moon, and as a 3559
93: 2 Thy throne is e of old: thou art from 3559
96:10 the world also shall be e that it shall not be 3559
102:28 and their seed shall be e before thee. 3559
112: 8 His heart is e, he shall not be afraid, 5564
119:90 thou hast e the earth, and it abideth. 3559
140:11 Let not an evil speaker be e in the earth: 3559
Pr 3:19 by understanding hath he e the heavens. 3559
4:26 path of thy feet, and let all thy ways be e. 3559
8:28 When he e the clouds above: when he 553
12: 3 A man shall not be e by wickedness: but 3559
12:19 The lip of truth shall be e for ever: but 3559
15:22 in the multitude of counsellers they are e. 6965
16: 3 the LORD, and thy thoughts shall be e. 3559
16:12 for the throne is e by righteousness. 3559
20:18 Every purpose is e by counsel: and 3559
24: 3 house builded; and by understanding it is e: 3559
25: 5 and his throne shall be e in righteousness. 3559
29:14 the poor, his throne shall be e for ever. 3559
30: 4 who hath e all the ends of the earth? what is 6965
Isa 2: 2 shall be e in the top of the mountains, 3559
7: 9 ye will not believe, surely ye shall not be e. 539
16: 5 in mercy shall the throne be e: and he shall 3559
45:18 he hath e it, he created it not in vain, 3559
54:14 In righteousness shalt thou be e: thou shalt 3559
Jer 10:12 he hath e the world by his wisdom, and 3559
30:20 and their congregation shall be e before me, 3559
51:15 he hath e the world by his wisdom, and 3559
Da 4:36 I was e in my kingdom, and 8627
Mic 4: 1 shall be e in the top of the mountains, 3559
Hab 1:12 thou hast e them for correction. 3245
Zec 5:11 it shall be e, and set there upon her own 3559
Mt 18:16 or three witnesses every word may be e. 2476
Ac 16: 5 And so were the churches e in the faith, and 4732
Ro 1:11 spiritual gift, to the end you may be e; 4741
2Co 13: 1 or three witnesses shall every word be e. 2476
Heb 8: 6 which was e upon better promises. 3549
13: 9 For it is a good thing that the heart be e with 950

ESTABLISHETH (2) [ESTABLISH]
Nu 30:14 he e all her vows, or all her bonds, 6965
Da 6:15 statute which the king e may be changed. 6966

ESTABLISHMENT (1) [ESTABLISH]
2Ch 32: 1 the e thereof, Sennacherib king of Assyria 571

ESTATE (17) [ESTATES]
1Ch 17:17 hast regarded me according to the e of a 8448
Est 1:19 let the king give her royal e unto another 4438
Ps 136:23 Who remembered us in our low e: for his 8216
Ecc 1:16 Lo, I am come to great e, and have gotten 1431
3:18 I said in my heart concerning the e of 1700
Eze 16:55 shall return to their former e, and Samaria 6927
16:55 her daughters shall return to their former e, 6927
16:55 thy daughters shall return to your former e. 6927
Da 11: 7 of her roots shall one stand up in his e, 3653
11:20 shall stand up in his e a raiser of taxes in 3653
11:21 in his e shall stand up a vile person, to 3653
11:38 in his e shall he honour the God of forces: 3653
Lk 1:48 For he hath regarded the low e of his 5014
Ac 22: 5 bear me witness, and all the e of the elders: 4244
Ro 12:16 things, but condescend to men of low e. 5011
Col 4: 8 that he might know your e, and 4012
Jude 1: 6 And the angels which kept not their first e, 746

ESTATES (2) [ESTATE]
Eze 36:11 I will settle you after your old e, and 6927
Mk 6:21 high captains, and chief e of Galilee; NIG

ESTEEM (5) [ESTEEMED, ESTEEMETH, ESTEEMING]
Job 36:19 Will he e thy riches? no, not gold, nor all 6186
Ps 119:128 e all thy precepts concerning all things to be right; 3474
Isa 53: 4 yet we did e him stricken, smitten of God, 2803
Php 2: 3 in lowliness of mind let each e other better 2233
1Th 5:13 And to e them very highly in love for their 2233

ESTEEMED (11) [ESTEEM]
Dt 32:15 and lightly e the Rock of his salvation. 5034
1Sa 2:30 and they that despise me shall be lightly e. 7043
18:23 seeing that I am a poor man, and lightly e? 7034
Job 23:12 I have e the words of his mouth more than 6845
Pr 17:28 he that shutteth his lips is e a man of NIH
Isa 29:16 upside down shall be e as the potter's clay: 2803
29:17 and the fruitful field shall be e as a forest? 2803
53: 3 he was despised, and we e him not. 2803
La 4: 2 how are they e as earthen pitchers, 2803
Lk 16:15 for that which is highly e amongst men is 5308
1Co 6: 4 set them to judge who are least e in 1848

ESTEEMETH (4) [ESTEEM]
Job 41:27 He e iron as straw, and brass as rotten 2803
Ro 14: 5 One man e one day above another: 2919
14: 5 another e every day alike. Let every man be 2919
14:14 but to him that e any thing to be unclean, 3049

ESTEEMING (1) [ESTEEM]
Heb 11:26 E the reproach of Christ greater riches than 2233

ESTHER (53) [ESTHER'S, HADASSAH]
Est 2: 7 up Hadassah, that is, E, his uncle's daughter: 635
2: 8 that E was brought also unto the king's 635
2:10 E had not shewed her people nor her 635
2:11 to know how E did, and what should become 635
2:15 Now when the turn of E, the daughter of 635
2:15 E obtained favour in the sight of all them 635
2:16 So E was taken unto king Ahasuerus into his 635
2:17 the king loved E above all the women, and 635
2:20 E had not yet shewed her kindred nor her 635
2:20 for E did the commandment of Mordecai, 635
2:22 to Mordecai, who told it unto E the queen; 635
2:22 E certified the king thereof in Mordecai's 635
4: 5 called E for Hatach, one of the king's 635
4: 8 to shew it unto E, and to declare it unto her, 635
4: 9 and told E the words of Mordecai. 635
4:10 Again E spake unto Hatach, and gave him 635
4:13 Mordecai commanded to answer E, 635
4:15 E bade them return Mordecai this answer: 635
4:17 did according to all that E had commanded 635
5: 1 that E put on her royal apparel, and stood in 635
5: 2 when the king saw E the queen standing in 635
5: 2 the king held out to E the golden sceptre that 635
5: 2 So E drew near, and touched the top of 635
5: 3 the king unto her, What wilt thou, queen E? 635
5: 4 E answered, If it seem good unto the king, 635
5: 5 to make haste, that he may do as E hath said. 635
5: 5 Haman came to the banquet that E had 635
5: 6 the king said unto E at the banquet of wine, 635
5: 7 Then answered E, and said, My petition and 635
5:12 E the queen did let no man come in with 635
6:14 unto the banquet that E had prepared. 635
7: 1 Haman came to banquet with E the queen. 635
7: 2 the king said again unto E on the second day 635
7: 2 of wine, What is thy petition, queen E? 635
7: 3 E the queen answered and said, If I have 635
7: 5 and said unto E the queen, 635
7: 6 E said, The adversary and enemy is this 635
7: 7 to make request for his life to E the queen; 635
7: 8 Haman was fallen upon the bed whereon E 635
8: 1 Haman the Jews' enemy unto E the queen. 635
8: 1 for E had told what he was unto her. 635
8: 2 E set Mordecai over the house of Haman. 635
8: 3 E spake yet again before the king, and 635
8: 4 king held out the golden sceptre toward E. 635
8: 4 So E arose, and stood before the king, 635
8: 7 the king Ahasuerus said unto E the queen 635
8: 7 I have given E the house of Haman, and him 635
9:12 the king said unto E the queen, The Jews 635
9:13 said E, If it please the king, let it be granted 635
9:25 when E came before the king, NIH
9:29 E the queen, the daughter of Abihail, and 635
9:31 the Jew and E the queen had enjoined them, 635
9:32 the decree of E confirmed these matters of 635

ESTHER'S (3) [ESTHER]
Est 2:18 all his princes and his servants, even E feast; 635
4: 4 So E maids and her chamberlains came and 635
4:12 And they told to Mordecai E words. 635

ESTIMATE (2) [ESTIMATION, ESTIMATIONS]
Lev 27:14 the priest shall e it, whether it be good or 6186
27:14 as the priest shall e it, so shall it stand. 6186

ESTIMATION (23) [ESTIMATE]
Lev 5:15 with thy e by shekels of silver, after 6187
5:18 with thy e, for a trespass offering, unto 6187
6: 6 with thy e, for a trespass offering, unto 6187
27: 2 persons shall be for the LORD by thy e. 6187
27: 3 thy e shall be, of the male from twenty 6187
27: 3 even thy e shall be fifty shekels of silver, 6187
27: 4 a female, then thy e shall be thirty shekels. 6187
27: 5 thy e shall be of the male twenty shekels, 6187
27: 6 thy e shall be of the male five shekels of 6187
27: 6 for the female thy e shall be three shekels 6187
27: 7 thy e shall be fifteen shekels, and for 6187
27: 8 if he be poorer than thy e, then he shall 6187
27:13 he shall add a fifth part thereof unto thy e. 6187
27:15 the fifth part of the money of thy e unto it, 6187
27:16 thy e shall be according to the seed thereof: 6187
27:17 of jubile, according to thy e it shall stand. 6187
27:18 the jubile, and it shall be abated from thy e. 6187
27:19 the fifth part of the money of thy e unto it, 6187
27:23 shall reckon unto him the worth of thy e, 6187
27:23 he shall give thine e in that day, as a holy 6187
27:27 he shall redeem it according to thine e, and 6187
27:27 then it shall be sold according to thy e. 6187
Nu 18:16 according to thine e, for the money of five 6187

ESTIMATIONS (1) [ESTIMATE]
Lev 27:25 all thy e shall be according to the shekel of 6187

ESTRANGED (5)
Job 19:13 mine acquaintance are verily e from me. 2114
Ps 58: 3 The wicked are e from the womb: they go 2114
78:30 They were not e from their lust. But while 2114
Jer 19: 4 have e this place, and have burnt incense in 5234
Eze 14: 5 they are all e from me through their idols. 2114

ETAM (5)
Jdg 15: 8 and dwelt in the top of the rock E. 5862
15:11 men of Judah went to the top of the rock E, 5862
1Ch 4: 3 these were of the father of E; Jezreel, and 5862
4:32 their villages were, E, and Ain, Rimmon, 5862
2Ch 11: 6 built even Beth-lehem, and E, and Tekoa, 5862

ETERNAL (47) [ETERNITY]
Dt 33:27 The e God is thy refuge, and underneath are 6924
Isa 60:15 thee, I will make thee an e excellency, 5769
Mt 19:16 good thing shall I do, that I may have e life? 166

Mt 25:46 but the righteous into life e. 166
Mk 3:29 but is in danger of e damnation. 166
10:17 what shall I do that I may inherit e life? 166
10:30 and in the world to come e life. 166
Lk 10:25 Master, what shall I do to inherit e life? 166
18:18 what shall I do to inherit e life? 166
Jn 3:15 in him should not perish, but have e life. 166
4:36 and gathereth fruit unto life e: 166
5:39 for in them ye think ye have e life: 166
6:54 my flesh, and drinketh my blood, hath e life; 166
6:68 shall we go? thou hast the words of e life. 166
10:28 And I give unto them e life; and they shall 166
12:25 his life in this world shall keep it unto life e. 166
17: 2 that he should give e life to as many as thou 166
17: 3 And this is life e, that they might know thee 166
Ac 13:48 as many as were ordained to e life believed. 166
Ro 1:20 are made, *even* his e power and Godhead; 126
2: 7 for glory and honour and immortality, e life: 166
5:21 unto e life by Jesus Christ our Lord. 166
6:23 the gift of God *is* e life through Jesus Christ 166
2Co 4:17 a far more exceeding *and* e weight of glory; 166
4:18 but the *things* which are not seen *are* e. 166
5: 1 house not made with hand, e in the heavens. 166
Eph 3:11 According to the e purpose which he 165
1Ti 1:17 Now unto the King e, immortal, invisible, 165
6:12 the good fight of faith, lay hold on e life, 166
6:19 to come, that they may lay hold on e life. 166
2Ti 2:10 which is in Christ Jesus with e glory. 166
Tit 1: 2 In hope of e life, which God, that cannot lie, 166
3: 7 be made heirs according to the hope of e life. 166
Heb 5: 9 he became the author of e salvation unto all 166
6: 2 resurrection of the dead, and of e judgment. 166
9:12 *place,* having obtained e redemption *for us.* 166
9:14 who through the e Spirit offered himself 166
9:15 might receive the promise of e inheritance. 166
1Pe 5:10 who hath called us into his e glory by Christ 166
1Jn 1: 2 bear witness, and shew unto you *that* e life, 166
2:25 that he hath promised us, *even* e life. 166
3:15 ye know that no murderer hath e life abiding 166
5:11 that God hath given to us e life, and this life 166
5:13 that ye may know that ye have e life, and 166
5:20 Jesus Christ. This is the true God, and e life. 166
Jude 1: 7 suffering the vengeance of e fire. 166
1:21 mercy of our Lord Jesus Christ unto e life. 166

ETERNITY (1) [ETERNAL]
Isa 57:15 the high and lofty One that inhabiteth e, 5703

ETH KAZIN See ITTAH-KAZIN

ETHAM (4)
Ex 13:20 encamped in E, in the edge of 864
Nu 33: 6 departed from Succoth, and pitched in E, 864
33: 7 they removed from E, and turned again unto 864
33: 8 three days' journey in the wilderness of E, 864

ETHAN (8)
1Ki 4:31 than E the Ezrahite, and Heman, and 387
1Ch 2: 6 and E, and Heman, and Calcol, and Dara: 387
2: 8 And the sons of E; Azariah. 387
6:42 The son of E, the son of Zimmah, the son of 387
6:44 E the son of Kishi, the son of Abdi, the son 387
15:17 Merari their brethren, E the son of Kushaiah; 387
15:19 So the singers, Heman, Asaph, and E, 387
Ps 89: T Maschil of E the Ezrahite. 387

ETHANIM (1)
1Ki 8: 2 king Solomon at the feast in the month E, 388

ETHBAAL (1)
1Ki 16:31 the daughter of E king of the Zidonians, 856

ETHER (2)
Jos 15:42 Libnah, and E, and Ashan, 6281
19: 7 Ain, Remmon, and E, and Ashan; 6281

ETHIOPIA (20) [ETHIOPIAN, ETHIOPIANS]
Ge 2:13 *is it* that compasseth the whole land of E. 3568
2Ki 19: 9 when he heard say of Tirhakah king of E, 3568
Est 1: 1 from India even unto E, *over* an hundred 3568
8: 9 the provinces which *are* from India unto E, 3568
Job 28:19 The topaz of E shall not equal it, 3568
Ps 68:31 E shall soon stretch out her hands unto 3568
87: 4 behold Philistia, and Tyre, with E; this *man* 3568
Isa 18: 1 which *is* beyond the rivers of E: 3568
20: 3 a sign and wonder upon Egypt and upon E; 3568
20: 5 and ashamed of E their expectation, 3568
37: 9 heard say concerning Tirhakah king of E, 3568
43: 3 Egypt *for* thy ransom, E and Seba for thee. 3568
45:14 merchandise of E and of the Sabeans, 3568
Eze 29:10 tower of Syene even unto the border of E. 3568
30: 4 great pain shall be in E, when the slain 3568
30: 5 E, and Libya, and Lydia, and all 3568
38: 5 Persia, E, and Libya with them; all of them 3568
Na 3: 9 E and Egypt *were* her strength, and *it was* 3568
Zep 3:10 From beyond the rivers of E my suppliants, 3568
Ac 8:27 and behold, a man of E, an eunuch of great 128

ETHIOPIAN (8) [ETHIOPIA]
Nu 12: 1 of the E woman whom he had married: 3569
12: 1 for he had married an E woman. 3569
2Ch 14: 9 there came out against them Zerah the E 3569
Jer 13:23 Can the E change his skin, or the leopard 3569
38: 7 Now when Ebed-melech the E, one of 3569
38:10 the king commanded Ebed-melech the E, 3569
38:12 Ebed-melech the E said unto Jeremiah, 3569
39:16 Go and speak to Ebed-melech the E, 3569

ETHIOPIANS (13) [ETHIOPIA]
2Ch 12: 3 the Lubims, the Sukkiims, and the E. 3569
14:12 So the LORD smote the E before Asa, and 3569
14:12 and before Judah; and the E fled. 3569
14:13 the E were overthrown, that they could not 3569
16: 8 Were not the E and the Lubims a huge 3569
21:16 and of the Arabians, that *were* near the E: 3569
Isa 20: 4 the E captives, young and old, naked and 3568
Jer 46: 9 the E and the Libyans, that handle 3568
Eze 30: 9 me in ships to make the careless E afraid, 3568
Da 11:43 the Libyans and the E *shall be* at his steps. 3569
Am 9: 7 *Are* ye not as children of the E unto me, 3569
Zep 2:12 Ye E also, ye *shall be* slain by my sword. 3569
Ac 8:27 authority under Candace queen of the E, 128

ETHNAN (1)
1Ch 4: 7 of Helah *were,* Zereth, and Jezoar, and E. 869

ETHNI (1)
1Ch 6:41 The son of E, the son of Zerah, the son of 867

EUBULUS (1)
2Ti 4:21 E greeteth thee, and Pudens, and Linus, and 2103

EUNICE (1)
2Ti 1: 5 in thy grandmother Lois, and thy mother E; 2131

EUNUCH (7) [EUNUCHS]
Isa 56: 3 neither let the e say, Behold, I *am* a dry 5631
Jer 52:25 He took also out of the city an e, which had 5631
Ac 8:27 an e of great authority under Candace 2135
8:34 And the e answered Philip, and said, I pray 2135
8:36 and the e said, See, *here is* water; what doth 2135
8:38 both into the water, both Philip and the e; 2135
8:39 away Philip, that the e saw him no more: 2135

EUNUCHS (20) [EUNUCH]
2Ki 9:32 And there looked out to him two *or* three e. 5631
20:18 they shall be e in the palace of the king of 5631
Isa 39: 7 they shall be e in the palace of the king of 5631
56: 4 For thus saith the LORD unto the e that 5631
Jer 29: 2 the queen, and the e, the princes of Judah 5631
34:19 the e, and the priests, and all the people of 5631
38: 7 one of the e which *was* in the king's house, 5631
41:16 and the women, and the children, and the e, 5631
Da 1: 3 spake unto Ashpenaz the master of his e, 5631
1: 7 Unto whom the prince of the e gave names: 5631
1: 8 he requested of the prince of the e that he 5631
1: 9 and tender love with the prince of the e. 5631
1:10 the prince of the e said unto Daniel, I fear 5631
1:11 whom the prince of the e had set over 5631
1:18 the prince of the e brought them in before 5631
Mt 19:12 For there are *some* e, which were so 2135
19:12 and there are *some* e, which were made 2135
19:12 *some* eunuchs, which were **made** e of men: 2134
19:12 and there be e, which have made 2135
19:12 which have **made** themselves e for 2134

EUODIAS (1)
Php 4: 2 I beseech E, and beseech Syntyche, 2136

EUPHRATES (21)
Ge 2:14 east of Assyria. And the fourth river *is* E. 6578
15:18 of Egypt unto the great river, the river E: 6578
Dt 1: 7 unto the great river, the river E. 6578
11:24 and Lebanon, from the river, the river E, 6578
Jos 1: 4 the river E, all the land of the Hittites, and 6578
2Sa 8: 3 he went to recover his border at the river E. 6578
2Ki 23:29 against the king of Assyria to the river E: 6578
24: 7 E all that pertained to the king of Egypt. 6578
1Ch 5: 9 in of the wilderness from the river E: 6578
18: 3 to stablish his dominion by the river E. 6578
2Ch 35:20 came up to fight against Carchemish by E: 6578
Jer 13: 4 go to E, and hide it there in a hole of 6578
13: 5 So I went, and hid it by E, as the LORD 6578
13: 6 go to E, and take the girdle from thence, 6578
13: 7 I went to E, and digged, and took the girdle 6578
46: 2 which was by the river E in Carchemish, 6578
46: 6 and fall toward the north by the river E. 6578
46:10 sacrifice in the north country by the river E. 6578
51:63 a stone to it, and cast it into the midst of E: 6578
Rev 9:14 angels which are bound in the great river E. 2166
16:12 poured out his vial upon the great river E; 2166

EUROCLYDON (1)
Ac 27:14 against it a tempestuous wind, called E. 2148

EUTYCHUS (1)
Ac 20: 9 in a window a certain young man named E, 2161

EVANGELIST (2) [EVANGELISTS]
Ac 21: 8 we entered into the house of Philip the e, 2099
2Ti 4: 5 do the work of an e, make full proof of thy 2099

EVANGELISTS (1) [EVANGELIST]
Eph 4:11 and some, e; and some, pastors and 2099

EVE (4)
Ge 3:20 Adam called his wife's name E; because 2332
4: 1 Adam knew E his wife; and she conceived, 2332
2Co 11: 3 as the serpent beguiled E through his 2096
1Ti 2:13 For Adam was first formed, then E. 2096

EVEN (1395) [EVENING, EVENINGS, EVENINGTIDE, EVENTIDE]
Ge 6:17 behold, I, e I, do bring a flood of waters NIH
9: 3 e as the green herb have I given you all NIH
10: 9 E as Nimrod the mighty hunter before NIH
10:19 and Admah, and Zeboim, e **unto** Lasha. 5704
10:21 the elder, e to him were *children* born. 1571
13: 3 he went on his journeys from the south e 2050.1
13:10 e as the garden of the LORD, NIH
14:23 That I will not *take* from a thread e to a 2050.1
19: 1 there came two angels to Sodom at e; and 6153
19: 4 the men of the city, e the men of Sodom, NIH
19: 9 e Lot, and came near to break the door. NIH
20: 5 she, e she herself said, He *is* my brother: 1571
21:10 shall not be heir with my son, e with Isaac. NIH
23: 7 people of the land, e to the children of Heth. NIH
23:10 e of all that went in *at* the gate of his city, NIH
24:11 e the time that *women* go out to draw NIH
26:28 e betwixt us and thee, and let us make a NIH
27:34 his father, Bless me, e me also, O my father. NIH
27:38 bless me, e me also, O my father. And Esau NIH
34:29 and spoiled e all that *was* in the house. 2050.1
35:14 he talked with him, e a pillar of stone: NIH
37:18 afar off, e before he came near unto them, 2050.1
42:28 is restored; and lo, *it is* e in my sack: 1571
44:18 thy servant: for thou *art* e as Pharaoh. 3644
46:18 these she bare unto Jacob, e sixteen souls. NIH
46:34 about cattle from our youth e until now, 2050.1
47: 2 e five men, and presented them unto NIH
47:21 of Egypt e to the *other* end thereof. 2050.1
49:22 fruitful bough, e a fruitful bough by a well; NIH
49:25 E by the God of thy father, who shall help NIH
Ex 3: 1 came to the mountain of God, e to Horeb. NIH
4:16 e he shall be to thee instead of a mouth, and NIH
4:22 Israel *is* my son, e my firstborn: NIH
4:23 behold, I will slay thy son, e thy firstborn. NIH
9:18 since the foundation thereof e until now. 2050.1
10:12 herb of the land, e all that the hail hath left. NIH
10:21 of Egypt, e darkness *which* may be felt. 2050.1
11: 5 e unto the firstborn of the maidservant that NIH
12:15 e the first day ye shall put away leaven out 389
12:18 on the fourteenth day of the month at e, 6153
12:18 the one and twentieth day of the month at e. 6153
12:19 e that soul shall be cut off from 2050.1
12:38 and flocks, and herds, e very much cattle. NIH
12:41 e the selfsame day it came to pass, 871.1
14:23 e all Pharaoh's horses, his chariots, and NIH
16: 6 At e, then ye shall know that the LORD 6153
16:12 **At** e ye shall eat flesh, and 996+6153+1886.1
16:13 that at e the quails came up, and 6153
18:14 people stand by thee from morning unto e? 6153
23:31 I will set thy bounds from the Red sea e 2050.1
25: 9 e so shall ye make *it.* 2050.1
25:19 e of the mercy seat shall ye make NIH
27: 5 that the net may be e **to** the midst of 5704
28: 1 e Aaron, Nadab and Abihu, Eleazar and NIH
28: 8 e *of* gold, *of* blue, and purple, and scarlet, NIH
28:17 it settings of stones, e four rows of stones: NIH
28:42 from the loins e unto the thighs they shall 2050.1
29:27 e of *that* which *is* for Aaron, and of *that* NIH
29:28 e their heave offering unto the LORD. NIH
29:39 lamb thou shalt offer **at** e: 996+6153+1886.1
29:41 lamb thou shalt offer **at** e, 996+6153+1886.1
30: 8 Aaron lighteth the lamps **at** e, 996+6153+1886.1
30:21 e to him and to his seed throughout their NIH
30:23 e two hundred and fifty *shekels,* and NIH
30:33 shall e be cut off from his people. 2050.1
30:38 shall e be cut off from his people. 2050.1
32:29 e every man upon his son, and upon his 3588
35:35 e of them that do any work, and of those NIH
36: 2 e every one whose heart stirred him up to NIH
37: 3 e two rings upon the one side of it, and 2050.1
37: 9 e to the mercy seatward were the faces of NIH
38:21 e of the tabernacle of Testimony, as it was NIH
38:24 the holy *place,* e the gold of the offering, 2050.1
39:37 e with the lamps to be set in order, and all NIH
39:43 had commanded, e so had they done it: NIH
Lev 1: 2 of the cattle, e of the herd, and of the flock. NIH
2:14 by the fire, e corn beaten out of full ears. NIH
3:14 e an offering made by fire unto the LORD; NIH
4:12 E the whole bullock shall he carry forth 2050.1
4:17 times before the LORD, e before the vail. NIH
5:12 e a memorial thereof, and burn *it* on NIH
6: 5 he shall e restore it in the principal, and 2050.1
6:15 e the memorial of it, unto the LORD. NIH
7: 8 e the priest shall have to himself the skin of NIH
7:20 e that soul shall be cut off from his 2050.1
7:21 e that soul shall be cut off from his 2050.1
7:25 e the soul that eateth *it* shall be cut off 2050.1
7:27 e that soul shall be cut off from his 2050.1
8: 9 also upon the mitre, e upon his forefront, NIH
11:11 They shall be e an abomination unto you: 2050.1
11:22 E these of them ye may eat; the locust after NIH
11:24 carcase of them shall be unclean until the e. 6153
11:25 wash his clothes, and be unclean until the e. 6153
11:27 their carcase shall be unclean until the e. 6153
11:28 wash his clothes, and be unclean until the e: 6153
11:31 they be dead, shall be unclean until the e. 6153
11:32 and it shall be unclean until the e; 6153
11:39 carcase thereof shall be unclean until the e. 6153
11:40 wash his clothes, and be unclean until the e: 6153
11:40 wash his clothes, and be unclean until the e. 6153
13:12 the plague from his head e to his foot, 2050.1
13:18 in which, e in the skin thereof, was a boil, NIH
13:30 e a leprosy upon the head or beard. NIH
13:38 their flesh bright spots, e white bright spots; NIH
14: 9 e all his hair he shall shave off: 2050.1
14:31 E such as he is able to get, the one *for* a sin NIH
14:46 that it is shut up shall be unclean until the e. 6153
15: 5 *himself* in water, and be unclean until the e. 6153
15: 6 *himself* in water, and be unclean until the e. 6153
15: 7 *himself* in water, and be unclean until the e. 6153
15: 8 *himself* in water, and be unclean until the e. 6153
15:10 was under him shall be unclean until the e: 6153
15:10 *himself* in water, and be unclean until the e. 6153
15:11 *himself* in water, and be unclean until the e. 6153
15:16 flesh in water, and be unclean until the e. 6153
15:17 with water, and be unclean until the e. 6153
15:18 in water, and be unclean until the e. 6153
15:19 toucheth her shall be unclean until the e. 6153
15:21 *himself* in water, and be unclean until the e. 6153
15:22 *himself* in water, and be unclean until the e. 6153
15:23 toucheth it, he shall be unclean until the e. 6153
15:27 *himself* in water, and be unclean until the e. 6153
16:32 on the linen clothes, e the holy garments: NIH
17: 5 e **that** they may bring them unto 2050.1
17: 9 e that man shall be cut off from among 2050.1
17:10 I will e set my face against *that* soul that 2050.1
17:13 he shall e pour out the blood thereof, and 2050.1
17:15 *himself* in water, and be unclean until the e: 6153
18: 9 e their nakedness thou shalt not uncover. NIH

E

Lev 18:10 e their nakedness thou shalt not uncover: NIH
18:29 e the souls that commit *them* shall be cut 2050.1
19:21 e a ram for a trespass offering. NIH
20: 6 I will e set my face against that soul, and 2050.1
20:10 e *he* that committeth adultery with his NIH
22: 6 touched *any* such shall be unclean until e, 6153
23: 2 *be* holy convocations, e these *are* my feasts. NIH
23: 4 feasts of the LORD, e holy convocations, NIH
23: 5 In the fourteenth *day* of the first month at e 6153
23:16 E unto the morrow after the seventh 5704
23:18 drink offerings, e an offering made by fire, NIH
23:32 in the ninth *day* of the month at e, 6153
23:32 from e unto even, shall ye celebrate your 6153
23:32 from even unto e, shall ye celebrate your 6153
24: 7 e an offering made by fire unto the LORD. NIH
26:16 I will e appoint over you terror, 2050.1
26:28 I, e I, will chastise you seven *times* for your 637
26:34 e then shall the land rest, and enjoy her NIH
26:43 e because they despised my judgments, 2050.1
27: 3 of the male from twenty years old e unto 2050.1
27: 3 e thy estimation shall be fifty shekels of 2050.1
27: 5 if *it be* from five years old e unto twenty 2050.1
27: 6 if *it be* from a month old e unto five years 2050.1
27:18 e unto the year of the jubile, and it shall be NIH
27:23 thy estimation, e unto the year of the jubile: NIH
27:24 e to him to whom the possession of NIH
27:32 e *of* whatsoever passeth under the rod, NIH
Nu 1:21 e of the tribe of Reuben, *were* forty and NIH
1:23 e of the tribe of Simeon, *were* fifty and NIH
1:25 e of the tribe of Gad, *were* forty and NIH
1:27 e of the tribe of Judah, *were* threescore and NIH
1:29 e of the tribe of Issachar, *were* fifty and NIH
1:31 e of the tribe of Zebulun, *were* fifty and NIH
1:33 e of the tribe of Ephraim, *were* forty NIH
1:35 e of the tribe of Manasseh, *were* thirty and NIH
1:37 e of the tribe of Benjamin, *were* thirty and NIH
1:39 e of the tribe of Dan, *were* threescore and NIH
1:41 e of the tribe of Asher, *were* forty and NIH
1:43 e of the tribe of Naphtali, *were* fifty and NIH
1:46 E all they that were numbered were six 2050.1
3:22 e those that were numbered of them *were* NIH
3:38 e before the tabernacle of the congregation NIH
3:47 Thou shalt e take five shekels apiece by 2050.1
4: 3 and upward e until fifty years old, 2050.1
4:14 e the censers, the fleshhooks, and NIH
4:30 upward e unto fifty years old shalt thou 2050.1
4:35 and upward e unto fifty years old, 2050.1
4:39 and upward e unto fifty years old, 2050.1
4:40 E those that were numbered of them, 2050.1
4:43 and upward e unto fifty years old, 2050.1
4:44 E those that were numbered of them after 2050.1
4:47 and upward e unto fifty years old, 2050.1
4:48 E those that were numbered of them, 2050.1
5: 8 unto the LORD, e to the priest; NIH
5:26 e the memorial thereof, and burn *it* upon NIH
6: 4 vine tree, from the kernels e to the husk. 2050.1
7:10 e the princes offered their offering before 2050.1
8: 8 e fine flour mingled with oil, and NIH
8:16 e *instead of* the firstborn of all the children NIH
9: 3 In the fourteenth day of this month, at e, 6153
9: 5 first month at e in the wilderness of Sinai: 6153
9:11 fourteenth day of the second month at e 6153
9:13 e the same soul shall be cut off from 2050.1
9:15 at e there was upon the tabernacle as it 6153
9:21 when the cloud abode from e unto 6153
11:20 *But* e a whole month, until it come out at 5704
12: 8 e apparently, and not in dark speeches; 2050.1
14:19 this people, from Egypt e until now. 2050.1
14:34 e forty days, each day for a year, shall ye NIH
14:34 e forty years, and ye shall know my breach NIH
14:37 E *those* men that did bring up the evil 2050.1
14:45 and discomfited them, e unto Hormah. NIH
15:23 E all that the LORD hath commanded you NIH
16: 5 E to morrow the LORD will shew who *are* NIH
16: 5 e *him* whom he hath chosen will he cause 2050.1
17: 6 to their fathers' houses, e twelve rods: NIH
18:21 e the service of the tabernacle of NIH
18:26 it for the LORD, e a tenth *part* of the tithe. NIH
18:29 e the hallowed *part* thereof out of it. NIH
19: 7 and the priest shall be unclean until the e. 6153
19: 8 in water, and shall be unclean until the e. 6153
19:10 wash his clothes, and be unclean until the e: 6153
19:19 *himself* in water, and shall be clean at e. 6153
19:21 water of separation shall be unclean until e. 6153
19:22 that toucheth *it* shall be unclean until e. 6153
20: 1 children of Israel, e the whole congregation, NIH
20:22 e the whole congregation, journeyed from NIH
20:29 Aaron thirty days, e all the house of Israel. NIH
21:24 unto Jabbok, e unto the children of Ammon: NIH
21:26 all his land out of his hand, e unto Arnon. NIH
21:30 Heshbon is perished **e unto** Dibon, and 5704
21:30 we have laid *them* waste **e unto** Nophah, 5704
25:13 e the covenant of an everlasting priesthood; NIH
25:14 e that was slain with the Midianitish NIH
27:21 of Israel with him, e all the congregation. 2050.1
28: 4 lamb shalt thou offer **at e**; 996+6153+1886.1
28: 8 lamb shalt thou offer **at e**: 996+6153+1886.1
31:12 E of the children of Israel's half, 2050.1
31:51 took the gold of them, e all wrought jewels. NIH
32: 4 E the country which the LORD smote NIH
32:33 e to the children of Gad, and to the children NIH
32:33 e the cities of the country round about. NIH
33:49 from Beth-jesimoth e unto Abel-shittim in NIH
34: 2 e the land of Canaan with the coasts NIH
34: 6 shall e have the great sea for a border: 2050.1
36:10 **E as** the LORD commanded 834+3509.1
Dt 1:44 destroyed you in Seir, e unto Hormah. NIH
2:22 and dwelt in their stead e unto this day: NIH
2:23 e unto Azzah, the Caphtorims, which came NIH
2:36 the city that *is* by the river, e unto Gilead, 2050.1
3:16 unto the Gadites I gave from Gilead e 2050.1
3:16 and the border, e unto the river Jabbok, 2050.1
3:17 the coast *thereof*, from Chinnereth e unto 2050.1
3:17 e the salt sea, under Ashdoth-pisgah NIH
4: 5 **e as** the LORD my God 834+3509.1
Dt 4:13 you to perform, e ten commandments; NIH
4:19 and the stars, e all the host of heaven, NIH
4:20 e out of Egypt, to be unto him a people of NIH
4:24 God *is* a consuming fire, e a jealous God. NIH
4:30 e in the latter days, if thou turn to NIH
4:48 e unto mount Sion, which *is* Hermon, 2050.1
4:49 e unto the sea of the plain, under 2050.1
5: 3 with us, e us, who *are* all of us here alive NIH
5:23 e all the heads of your tribes, and NIH
9: 9 e the tables of the covenant which NIH
9:11 tables of stone, e the tables of the covenant. NIH
9:21 *it* very small, e until *it was as* small as dust: NIH
10:15 e you above all people, as *it is* this day. NIH
11:12 from the beginning of the year e unto 2050.1
11:24 e unto the uttermost sea shall your coast 2050.1
12: 5 e unto his habitation shall ye seek, and NIH
12:22 E as the roebuck and the hart is eaten, so 389
12:30 serve their gods? e so will I do likewise. 2050.1
12:31 for e their sons and their daughters they 1571
13: 7 from the *one* end of the earth e unto 2050.1
16: 3 bread therewith, e the bread of affliction; NIH
16: 4 which thou sacrificedst the first day at e, 6153
16: 6 there thou shalt sacrifice the passover at e, 6153
17: 5 e *that* man or *that* woman, and shalt stone NIH
17:12 or unto the judge, e that man shall die: 2050.1
18:20 of other gods, e that prophet shall die. 2050.1
20:14 all that is in the city, e all the spoil thereof, NIH
21: 3 e the elders of that city shall take a heifer, 2050.1
22:26 and slayeth him, **e so** *is* this matter: 3651
23: 2 e *to* his tenth generation shall he not enter 1571
23: 3 e *to* their tenth generation shall they not 1571
23:16 He shall dwell with thee, e among you, NIH
23:18 for e both these *are* abomination unto 1571
23:23 e a freewill offering, according as thou hast NIH
25:18 e all that were feeble behind thee, NIH
26: 9 e a land that floweth with milk and honey. NIH
28:59 e great plagues, and of long continuance, NIH
28:64 from the *one* end of the earth e unto 2050.1
28:64 thy fathers have known, e wood and stone. NIH
28:67 thou shalt say, Would God it were e! 6153
28:67 at e thou shalt say, Would God it were 6153
29:24 E all nations shall say, Wherefore hath 2050.1
31:21 imagination which they go about, e now, NIH
32:31 e our enemies themselves *being* judges. 2050.1
32:39 e I, *am* he, and *there is* no god with me: NIH
33: 4 e the inheritance of the congregation of NIH
Jos 1: 2 I do give to them, e to the children of Israel. NIH
1: 4 and this Lebanon e unto the great river, 2050.1
2: 1 Go view the land, e Jericho. 2050.1
2:24 for e all the inhabitants of the country do 1571
3:11 e the Lord of all the earth passeth over NIH
3:16 e the salt sea, failed, *and* were cut off: NIH
5: 4 *that were* males, e all the men of war, NIH
5:10 of the month at e in the plains of Jericho. 6153
6:17 e it, and all that *are* therein, to the LORD: NIH
6:25 she dwelleth in Israel e unto this day; NIH
7: 5 for they chased them *from* before the gate e NIH
7:11 for they have e taken of the accursed thing, 1571
7:11 they have put *it* e amongst their own stuff. 1571
8: 4 lie in wait against the city, e behind the city: NIH
8:11 e *the people* of war that *were* with him, NIH
8:13 e all the host that *was* on the north of NIH
8:25 *were* twelve thousand, e all the men of Ai. NIH
8:28 a heap for ever, e a desolation unto this day. NIH
9:20 we will e let them live, lest wrath be upon 2050.1
9:27 for the altar of the LORD, e unto this day, NIH
10:41 Joshua smote them from Kadesh-barnea e 2050.1
10:41 all the country of Goshen, e unto Gibeon. 2050.1
11: 4 e as the sand that *is* upon the sea shore in NIH
11:17 E from the mount Halak, that goeth up *to* NIH
11:17 e unto Baal-gad in the valley of Lebanon 2050.1
12: 2 *from* half Gilead, e unto the river Jabbok, 2050.1
12: 3 sea of the plain, e the salt sea on the east, NIH
12: 7 from Baal-gad in the valley of Lebanon e 2050.1
13: 3 e unto the borders of Ekron northward, 2050.1
13: 8 e as Moses the servant of the LORD gave NIH
13:24 e unto the children of Gad according to their NIH
13:27 e unto the edge of the sea of Cinnereth on NIH
13:31 e to the one half of the children of Machir NIH
14:10 e since the LORD spake this word unto NIH
14:11 e so *is* my strength now, for war, both to 2050.1
15: 1 e to the border of Edom, the wilderness of NIH
15: 5 *was* the salt sea, e unto the end of Jordan. NIH
15:13 e the city of Arba the father of Anak, NIH
15:46 From Ekron e unto the sea, all that *lay* 2050.1
16: 5 e the border of their inheritance on 2050.1
17:11 and her towns, e three countries. NIH
17:17 e to Ephraim and to Manasseh, saying, NIH
19: 1 e for the tribe of the children of Simeon NIH
19:28 Hammon, and Kanah, e unto great Zidon; NIH
19:32 e for the children of Naphtali according to NIH
19:50 e Timnath-serah in mount Ephraim: NIH
21:20 e they had the cities of their lot out of 2050.1
23: 4 cut off, e *unto* the great sea westward. 2050.1
23:12 e these that remain among you, and NIH
24: 2 e Terah, the father of Abraham, and NIH
24:12 before you, e the two kings of the Amorites; NIH
24:18 e the Amorites which dwelt in the land: 2050.1
Jdg 3: 1 e as many *of Israel* as had not known all NIH
3: 9 delivered them, e Othniel the son of Kenaz, NIH
4:13 e nine hundred chariots of iron, and all NIH
5: 3 ye princes; I, e I, will sing unto the LORD; NIH
5: 5 e that Sinai from before the LORD God of NIH
5:11 e the righteous acts *towards the inhabitants* NIH
5:15 with Deborah; e Issachar, *and* also Barak: 2050.1
6: 3 of the east, e they came up against them; 2050.1
6:25 e the second bullock of seven years old, 2050.1
7:22 his fellow, e throughout all the host: 2050.1
8:14 e threescore and seventeen men. NIH
8:19 *were* my brethren, e the sons of my mother: NIH
8:27 and put it in his city, e in Ophrah: NIH
9:40 wounded, e unto the entering of the gate. NIH
11:13 from Arnon e unto Jabbok, and 2050.1
11:22 from Arnon e unto Jabbok, and from 2050.1
11:22 and from the wilderness e unto Jordan. 2050.1
Jdg 11:33 e till thou come *to* Minnith, *even* twenty 2050.1
11:33 e twenty cities, and unto the plain of NIH
11:36 thine enemies, e of the children of Ammon. NIH
18:15 e *unto* the house of Micah, and saluted him. NIH
19:16 old man from his work out of the field at e, 6153
20: 1 from Dan e to Beer-sheba, with the land 2050.1
20: 2 of all the people, e of all the tribes of Israel, NIH
20:23 and wept before the LORD until e, 6153
20:26 fasted that day until e, and offered burnt 6153
20:33 e out of the meadows of Gibeah. NIH
21: 2 abode there till e before God, and lift up 6153
Ru 2: 7 hath continued **e from** the morning 227+4480
2:15 Let her glean e among the sheaves, and 1571
2:17 So she gleaned in the field until e, and 6153
1Sa 3:20 all Israel from Dan e to Beer-sheba knew 2050.1
5: 6 e Ashdod and the coasts thereof. NIH
6:18 e unto the great *stone of* Abel, 2050.1
6:19 e he smote of the people fifty thousand 2050.1
7:14 to Israel, from Ekron e unto Gath; 2050.1
8: 8 them up out of Egypt e unto this day, 2050.1
8:14 e the best *of them*, and give *them* to his NIH
14:21 e they also *turned* to be with the Israelites 2050.1
14:22 e they also followed hard after them in 2050.1
17:40 shepherd's bag which he had, e in a scrip; 2050.1
17:52 e unto Gath, and unto Ekron. 2050.1
18: 4 e to his sword, and to his bow, and to his 2050.1
18:11 I will smite David e to the wall *with it*. 2050.1
19:10 Saul sought to smite David e to the wall 2050.1
20: 4 thy soul desireth, I will e do *it* for thee. 2050.1
20: 5 myself in the fields unto the third *day* at e. 6153
20:16 *saying*, Let the LORD e require *it* at 2050.1
20:25 as at other times, e upon a seat by the wall: NIH
25:25 regard this man of Belial, e Nabal: 5921
25:27 let it e be given unto the young men that 2050.1
26: 8 with the spear e to the earth at once, and 2050.1
27: 3 e David with his two wives, Ahinoam NIH
27: 8 goest to Shur, e unto the land of Egypt. 2050.1
28: 3 buried him in Ramah, e in his own city. 2050.1
28:17 and given it to thy neighbour, e to David: NIH
30:17 David smote them from the twilight e 2050.1
30:26 the elders of Judah, e to his friends, saying, NIH
2Sa 1: 2 It came e to pass on the third day, that 2050.1
1:12 wept, and fasted until e, for Saul, and 6153
2: 5 your lord, e unto Saul, and have buried him. NIH
3: 9 hath sworn to David, e so I do to him; 3588
3:10 over Judah, from Dan e to Beer-sheba. 2050.1
3:15 e from Phaltiel the son of Laish. NIH
6: 5 e on harps, and on psalteries, and 2050.1
6:19 e among the whole multitude of Israel, NIH
7: 6 e to this day, but have walked in a tent 2050.1
7:23 e like Israel, whom God went to redeem for NIH
8: 2 e *with* two lines measured he to put to 2050.1
10: 4 e to their buttocks, and sent them away. NIH
11:13 at e he went out to lie on his bed with 6153
11:23 we were upon them e unto the entering of NIH
14:25 from the sole of his foot e to the crown of 2050.1
15:12 from his city, e from Giloh, NIH
15:21 or life, e there *also* will thy servant be. 3588
17:11 from Dan e to Beer-sheba, as the sand 2050.1
18: 5 sake with the young man, e with Absalom. NIH
19:11 all Israel is come to the king, e to his house. NIH
19:14 the men of Judah, e as *the heart of* one man; NIH
19:32 was a very aged man, e fourscore years old: NIH
20: 2 their king, from Jordan e to Jerusalem. 2050.1
20:21 his hand against the king, e against David: NIH
22:42 e unto the LORD, but he answered them NIH
23: 4 the sun riseth, e a morning without clouds; NIH
24: 2 from Dan e to Beer-sheba, and number ye 2050.1
24: 7 out to the south of Judah, e *to* Beer-sheba. NIH
24:15 from the morning e to the time appointed: 2050.1
24:15 there died of the people from Dan e to 2050.1
1Ki 1:26 e me thy servant, and Zadok the priest, and NIH
1:30 E as I sware unto thee by the LORD God 3588
1:30 my stead; e so will I certainly do this day. 3588
1:37 e so be he with Solomon, and make his 3651
1:48 my throne *this* day, mine eyes e seeing *it*. 2050.1
2:22 e for him, and for Abiathar the priest, and 2050.1
4:12 e unto *the place that is* beyond Jokneam: NIH
4:24 from Tiphsah e to Azzah, over all 2050.1
4:25 his fig tree, from Dan e to Beer-sheba, 2050.1
4:29 e as the sand that *is* on the sea shore. NIH
4:33 from the cedar tree that *is* in Lebanon e 2050.1
6:16 he e built *them* for it within, *even* for 2050.1
6:16 e for the oracle, *even* for the most holy NIH
6:16 for the oracle, e for the most holy *place*. NIH
7: 7 he might judge, e the porch of judgment: NIH
7: 9 e from the foundation unto the coping, 2050.1
7:10 e great stones, stones of ten cubits, and NIH
7:42 e two rows *of* pomegranates for one NIH
7:51 e the silver, and the gold, and the vessels, NIH
8: 4 e those did the priests and the Levites 2050.1
8: 6 to the most holy *place*, e under the wings of NIH
8:29 e toward the place of which thou hast said, NIH
8:39 (for thou, e thou only, knowest the hearts of NIH
8:65 seven days and seven days, e fourteen days. NIH
11:26 e he lift up *his* hand against the king. 2050.1
11:35 and will give it unto thee, e ten tribes. NIH
12:27 e unto Rehoboam king of Judah, and NIH
12:30 went *to worship* before the one, e unto Dan. NIH
12:33 e in the month which he had devised of his NIH
13:34 e to cut *it* off, and to destroy *it* from off 2050.1
14:14 of Jeroboam that day: but what? e now. 1571
14:26 of the king's house; he e took away all: 2050.1
15:13 e her he removed from *being* queen, 2050.1
15:28 E in the third year of Asa king of Judah 2050.1
16: 7 e for all the evil that he did in the sight of 2050.1
18:22 I, e I only, remain a prophet of the LORD; NIH
18:26 name of Baal from morning e until noon, 2050.1
19:10 I, e I only, am left; and they seek my life, NIH
19:14 I, e I only, am left; and they seek my life, NIH
20: 3 and thy children, e the goodliest, *are* mine. NIH
20:14 E by the young men of the princes of NIH
20:15 e all the children of Israel, *being* seven NIH
21:11 e the elders and the nobles who *were* NIH
21:13 e against Naboth, in the presence of NIH

1Ki 21:19 of Naboth shall dogs lick thy blood, e thine. 1571
22:35 chariot against the Syrians, and died at e: 6153
2Ki 3:24 smiting the Moabites, e in their country. 2050.1
3:26 to break through e unto the king of Edom: NIH
4: 3 of all thy neighbours, e empty vessels; NIH
5:22 e now there be come to me from 2088+6258
7: 6 a noise of horses, e the noise of a great host: NIH
7: 7 e the camp as it was, and fled for their life. NIH
7:13 I say, they are e as all the multitude of NIH
8: 6 the day that she left the land, e until now. 2050.1
8: 9 e of every good thing of Damascus, 2050.1
9: 4 young man, e the young man the prophet, NIH
9: 6 the people of the LORD, e over Israel. NIH
9:20 He came e unto them, and cometh not 5704
10: 3 Look e out the best and meetest of your 2050.1
10:14 of the shearing house, e two and forty men; NIH
10:33 by the river Arnon, e Gilead and Bashan. 2050.1
11: 2 they hid him, e him and his nurse, in NIH
11: 5 e be keepers of the watch of the king's 2050.1
11: 7 e they shall keep the watch of the house 2050.1
12: 4 e the money of every one that passeth NIH
14:10 shouldest fall, e thou, and Judah with thee? NIH
14:29 with his fathers, e with the kings of Israel; NIH
15:20 e of all the mighty men of wealth, of each NIH
17:16 e two calves, and made a grove, and NIH
18: 8 e unto Gaza, and the borders thereof, NIH
18:10 e in the sixth year of Hezekiah, that is NIH
18:21 e upon Egypt, on which if a man lean, it NIH
19:15 thou art the God, e thou alone, of all NIH
19:19 that thou art the LORD God, e thou only. NIH
19:22 on high? e against the Holy One of Israel. NIH
20:14 come from a far country, e from Babylon. NIH
21:15 came forth out of Egypt, e unto this day. 2050.1
22:16 e all the words of the book which the king NIH
24:14 e ten thousand captives, and all NIH
24:16 e seven thousand, and craftsmen and smiths NIH
24:16 e them the king of Babylon brought 2050.1
25:22 e over them he made Gedaliah the son of 2050.1
25:23 e Ishmael the son of Nethaniah, and 2050.1
1Ch 2:23 and the towns thereof, e threescore cities. NIH
4:15 and Naam: and the sons of Elah, e Kenaz. 2050.1
4:39 e unto the east side of the valley, to seek NIH
4:42 e of the sons of Simeon, five hundred men, NIH
5: 8 in Aroer, e unto Nebo and Baal-meon: 2050.1
5:24 e Epher, and Ishi, and Eliel, and Azriel, 2050.1
5:26 e the Reubenites, and the Gadites, and 3807.1
6:39 e Asaph the son of Berachiah, the son of NIH
10:13 e against the word of the LORD, which he NIH
11: 2 in time past, e when Saul was king, 1571
11: 8 e from Millo round about: 5704+2050.1
12: 2 of a bow, e of Saul's brethren of Benjamin. NIH
12:40 e unto Issachar and Zebulun and Naphtali, NIH
13: 5 from Shihor of Egypt e unto the entering 2050.1
14:16 Philistines from Gibeon e to Gazer. 5704+2050.1
16:16 E of the covenant which he made with NIH
16:19 but few, e a few, and strangers in it. 3509.1
17: 7 the sheepcote, e from following the sheep, NIH
17:24 Let it e be established, that thy name may 2050.1
17:24 hosts is the God of Israel, e a God to Israel: NIH
20: 3 E so dealt David with all the cities of 2050.1
21: 2 number Israel from Beer-sheba e to Dan; 2050.1
21:12 e the pestilence, in the land, and the angel 2050.1
21:17 e I it is that have sinned and done evil 2050.1
23:24 e the chief of the fathers, as they were NIH
23:30 and praise the LORD, and likewise at e; 6153
24:31 e the principal fathers over against their NIH
25: 7 e all that were cunning, was two hundred NIH
26:12 e among the chief men, having wards one NIH
26:21 e of Laadan the Gershonite, were Jehieli. NIH
26:31 e among the Hebronites, according to NIH
28:15 E the weight for the candlesticks of gold, 2050.1
28:19 upon me, e all the works of this pattern. NIH
28:20 LORD God, e my God, will be with thee; NIH
28:21 e they shall be with thee for all the service NIH
29: 4 E three thousand talents of gold, of the gold NIH
29:21 e a thousand bullocks, a thousand rams, and NIH
2Ch 2: 3 a house to dwell therein, e so deal with me. NIH
2: 9 E to prepare me timber in abundance: 2050.1
5: 7 into the most holy place, e under the wings NIH
5:13 It came e to pass, as the trumpeters and 2050.1
5:13 with a cloud, e the house of the LORD; NIH
6:21 from thy dwelling place, e from heaven; NIH
6:33 e from thy dwelling place, and do according NIH
6:39 e from thy dwelling place, their prayer and NIH
8:10 e two hundred and fifty, that bare rule over NIH
8:13 E after a certain rate every day, offering 2050.1
8:13 e in the feast of unleavened bread, and NIH
9:26 the river e unto the land of the Philistines, 2050.1
11: 6 He built e Beth-lehem, and Etam, and 2050.1
13: 3 e four hundred thousand chosen men: NIH
13: 5 e to him and to his sons by a covenant of NIH
17: 7 e to Ben-hail, and to Obadiah, and NIH
17: 8 e Shemaiah, and Nethaniah, and Zebadiah, NIH
18:13 e what my God saith, that will I speak. 3588
18:21 thou shalt also prevail: go out, and do e so. NIH
18:34 in his chariot against the Syrians until the e: 6153
19:10 ye shall e warn them that they trespass 2050.1
20: 4 e out of all the cities of Judah they came to 1571
24:14 e vessels to minister, and to offer withal, NIH
25:13 from Samaria e unto Beth-horon, and 2050.1
25:19 shouldest fall, e thou, and Judah with thee? NIH
26: 8 his name spread abroad e to the entering in 5704
26:19 e the leprosy e rose up in his forehead 2050.1
28:10 are there not with you, e with you, NIH
28:27 they buried him in the city, e in Jerusalem: NIH
30: 5 all Israel, from Beer-sheba e to Dan, 2050.1
30:10 and Manasseh e unto Zebulun: 2050.1
30:18 e many of Ephraim, and Manasseh, NIH
30:27 to his holy dwelling place, e unto heaven. NIH
31:16 e unto every one that entereth into the house NIH
33:14 e to the entering in at the fish gate, and 2050.1
34: 6 Ephraim, and Simeon, e unto Naphtali, 2050.1
34:11 E to the artificers and builders gave they 2050.1
34:24 e all the curses that are written in the book NIH
34:27 have e heard thee also, saith the LORD. 2050.1

2Ch 34:33 to serve, e to serve the LORD their God. NIH
Ezr 1: 8 E those did Cyrus king of Persia bring 2050.1
3: 3 e burnt offerings morning and evening. NIH
4: 5 e until the reign of Darius king of Persia. 2050.1
4:11 sent unto him, e unto Artaxerxes the king: NIH
5: 1 the name of the God of Israel, e unto them. NIH
5:16 since that time e until now hath it been in 2050.3
6: 8 e of the tribute beyond the river, NIH
7:11 e a scribe of the words of NIH
7:21 I, e I Artaxerxes the king, do make a decree NIH
8:25 e the offering of the house of our God, NIH
8:26 I e weighed unto their hand six hundred 2050.1
9: 1 e of the Canaanites, the Hittites, NIH
Ne 2:13 e before the dragon well, and to the dung 2050.1
3: 1 e unto the tower of Meah they sanctified 2050.1
3:10 of Harumaph, e over against his house. 2050.1
3:21 from the door of the house of Eliashib e 2050.1
3:24 the turning of the wall, e unto the corner. 2050.1
3:27 that lieth out, e unto the wall of Ophel. 2050.1
4: 3 he said, E that which they build, if a fox go 1571
4: 3 he shall e break down their stone wall. 2050.1
4:13 I e set the people after their families with 2050.1
5: 8 and will you e sell your brethren? 1571
5:11 Restore, I pray you, to them, e this day, 3509.1
5:13 e thus be he shaken out, and emptied. 2050.1
5:14 from the twentieth year e unto the two 2050.1
5:15 yea, e their servants bare rule over 1571
8:13 e to understand the words of the law. 2050.1
9: 6 Thou, e thou, art LORD alone; thou hast NIH
12:23 e until the days of Johanan the son of 2050.1
12:37 of David, e unto the water gate eastward. 2050.1
12:38 from beyond the tower of the furnaces e 2050.1
12:39 the tower of Meah, e unto the sheep gate: 2050.1
12:43 of Jerusalem was heard e afar off. 4480+7350
13:26 nevertheless e him did outlandish women 1571
Est 1: 1 from India e unto Ethiopia, over an 2050.1
1: 4 e an hundred and fourscore days. NIH
2:18 and his servants, e Esther's feast; NIH
3: 6 of Ahasuerus, e the people of Mordecai. NIH
3:13 e upon the thirteenth day of the twelfth NIH
4: 2 came e before the king's gate: for none 5704
5: 3 it shall be e given thee to the half of 2050.1
5: 6 e to the half of the kingdom it shall be 5704
6:10 hast said, and do e so to Mordecai the Jew, NIH
7: 2 be performed, e to the half of the kingdom. NIH
Job 4: 8 E as I have seen, they that plow 834+3509.1
4:21 go away? they die, e without wisdom. 2050.1
5: 5 taketh it e out of the thorns, and the robber NIH
6: 9 E that it would please God to destroy me: 2050.1
10:21 e to the land of darkness and the shadow of NIH
15:26 He runneth upon him, e on his neck, NIH
17: 5 e the eyes of his children shall fail. 2050.1
17:11 are broken off, e the thoughts of my heart. NIH
18:13 e the firstborn of death shall devour his NIH
21: 6 E when I remember I am afraid, and 2050.1
23: 2 E to day is my complaint bitter: my stroke 1571
23: 3 find him! that I might come e to his seat! NIH
23:13 what his soul desireth, e that he doeth. 2050.1
24:17 For the morning is to them e as the shadow 3162
25: 5 Behold e to the moon, and it shineth not; NIH
28: 4 e the waters forgotten of the foot: NIH
31: 6 Let me be weighed in an e balance, 6664
34:17 Shall e he that hateth right govern? and wilt 637
36:16 E so would he have removed thee out of 2050.1
41: 9 shall not one be cast down e at the sight of 1571
42:16 and his sons' sons, e four generations. NIH
Ps 18: 6 and my cry came before him, e into his ears. NIH
18:41 there was none to save them: e unto NIH
21: 4 it him, e length of days for ever and ever. NIH
24: 9 e lift them up, ye everlasting doors; and 2050.1
26:12 My foot standeth in an e place: in 4334
27: 2 the wicked, e mine enemies and my foes, NIH
35:23 e unto my cause, my God and my Lord. NIH
39: T e to Jeduthun, A Psalm of David. NIH
39: 2 with silence, I held my peace, e from good; NIH
40: 3 song in my mouth, e praise unto our God: NIH
45:12 e the rich among the people shall intreat thy NIH
47: 9 e the people of the God of Abraham: NIH
48:14 and ever: he will be our guide e unto death. NIH
50: 1 e the LORD, hath spoken, and called NIH
50: 7 testify against thee: I am God, e thy God. NIH
55:19 and afflict them, e he that abideth of old. 2050.1
57: 4 and I lie e among them that are set on fire, NIH
57: 4 e the sons of men, whose teeth are spears NIH
59:12 the words of their lips let them e be taken 2050.1
64: 3 bows to shoot their arrows, e bitter words: NIH
65: 4 goodness of thy house, e of thy holy temple. NIH
67: 6 and God, e our own God, shall bless us. NIH
68: 8 e Sinai itself was moved at the presence of NIH
68:17 are twenty thousand, e thousands of angels: NIH
68:19 who daily loadeth us with benefits, e NIH
68:24 e the goings of my God, my King, in NIH
68:26 e the Lord, from the fountain of Israel. NIH
71:16 of thy righteousness, e of thine only. NIH
71:22 with the psaltery, e thy truth, O my God: NIH
73: 1 to Israel, e to such as are of a clean heart. NIH
74: 3 e all that the enemy hath done wickedly in NIH
74:11 thou thy hand, e thy right hand? 2050.1
76: 7 Thou, e thou, art to be feared: and who may NIH
77: 1 with my voice, e unto God with my voice; NIH
78: 6 them, e the children which should be born; NIH
78:54 e to this mountain, which his right hand had NIH
84: 2 yea, e fainteth for the courts of the LORD: 1571
84: 3 e thine altars, O LORD of hosts, my King, NIH
90: 2 e from everlasting to everlasting, 2050.1
90:11 e according to thy fear, so is thy wrath. 2050.1
91: 9 my refuge, e the most High, thy habitation; NIH
105:17 e Joseph, who was sold for a servant: NIH
105:20 e the ruler of the people, and let him go NIH
106: 7 provoked him at the sea, e at the Red sea. NIH
106:38 e the blood of their sons and of their NIH
107:43 will observe these things, e they shall 2050.1
108: 1 I will sing and give praise, e with my glory. 637
109:16 that he might e slay the broken in heart. 2050.1
113: 8 e with the princes of his people. NIH

Ps 115:16 The heaven, e the heavens, are NIH
118:27 with cords, e unto the horns of the altar. NIH
119:41 O LORD, e thy salvation, according to thy NIH
119:112 perform thy statutes alway, e unto the end. NIH
121: 8 in from this time forth, and e for evermore. NIH
125: 2 his people from henceforth e for ever. 2050.1
131: 2 his mother: my soul is e as a weaned child. NIH
133: 2 ran down upon the beard, e Aaron's beard: NIH
133: 3 the blessing, e life for evermore. NIH
136:22 E an heritage unto Israel his servant: for his NIH
137: 7 Rase it, rase it, e to the foundation thereof. NIH
139:10 E there shall thy hand lead me, and 1571
139:11 e the night shall be light about me. 2050.1
146:10 e thy God, O Zion, unto all generations. NIH
148:14 e of the children of Israel, a people near NIH
Pr 2:16 e from the stranger which flattereth with her NIH
3:12 e as a father the son in whom he 2050.1
8:16 and nobles, e all the judges of the earth. NIH
14:13 E in laughter the heart is sorrowful; and 1571
14:20 The poor is hated e of his own neighbour: 1571
16: 4 e the wicked for the day of evil. 1571
16: 7 he maketh e his enemies to be at peace with 1571
17:15 e they both are abomination to the LORD. 1571
17:28 E a fool, when he holdeth his peace, 1571
20:11 E a child is known by his doings, 1571
20:12 the LORD hath made e both of them. 1571
22:19 have made known to thee this day, e to thee. 637
23:15 be wise, my heart shall rejoice, e mine. 1571
28: 9 the law, e his prayer shall be abomination. 1571
30: 1 of Agur the son of Jakeh, e the prophecy: NIH
30: 1 spake unto Ithiel, e unto Ithiel and Ucal. NIH
Ecc 2:12 e that which hath been already done. NIH
2:15 to the fool, so it happeneth e to me; NIH
3:19 e one thing befalleth them: 2050.1
4:16 e of all that have been before them: NIH
7:25 of folly, e of foolishness and madness: 2050.1
9: 1 For all this I considered in my heart e to 2050.1
11: 5 e so thou knowest not the works of God 3602
12:10 was written was upright, e words of truth. NIH
SS 4: 2 are like a flock of sheep that are e shorn, 7094
Isa 1: 6 From the sole of the foot e unto the head 2050.1
1:13 it is iniquity, e the solemn meeting. 2050.1
4: 3 e every one that is written among the living NIH
5: 9 e great and fair, without inhabitant. NIH
7: 6 a king in the midst of it, e the son of Tabeal: NIH
7:17 departed from Judah; e the king of Assyria. NIH
7:23 it shall e be for briers and thorns. NIH
8: 7 e the king of Assyria, and all his glory: NIH
8: 8 and go over, he shall reach e to the neck; NIH
9: 7 with justice from henceforth e for ever. 2050.1
9: 9 e Ephraim and the inhabitant of Samaria, NIH
10:21 e the remnant of Jacob, unto the mighty NIH
10:23 e determined, in the midst of all the land. 2050.1
13: 3 e them that rejoice in my highness. NIH
13: 5 e the LORD, and the weapons of his NIH
13:12 e a man than the golden wedge of Ophir. 2050.1
14: 9 for thee, e all the chief ones of the earth; NIH
14:18 of the nations, e all of them, lie in glory, NIH
15: 4 their voice shall be heard e unto Jahaz: NIH
16: 6 e of his haughtiness, and his pride, and NIH
16: 8 they are come e unto Jazer, they wandered NIH
18: 2 e in vessels of bulrushes upon the waters, 2050.1
19:13 e they that are the stay of the tribes thereof. NIH
19:22 and they shall return e to the LORD, NIH
19:24 e a blessing in the midst of the land: NIH
20: 4 barefoot, e with their buttocks uncovered, 2050.1
22:15 e unto Shebna, which is over the house, and NIH
22:24 of cups, e to all the vessels of flagons. 2050.1
23: 4 e the strength of the sea, saying, I travail NIH
24:15 e the name of the LORD God of Israel in NIH
24:16 we heard songs, e glory to the righteous. NIH
25: 5 e the heat with the shadow of a cloud: NIH
25:10 e as straw is trodden down for the dunghill. NIH
25:12 and bring to the ground, e to the dust. NIH
26: 5 it low; he layeth it low, e to the ground; NIH
26: 5 to the ground; he bringeth it e to the dust. NIH
26: 6 e the feet of the poor, and the steps of NIH
27: 1 e leviathan that crooked serpent; 2050.1
28:22 e determined upon the whole earth. 2050.1
29: 7 e all that fight against her and 2050.1
29: 8 It shall e be as when a hungry man 2050.1
29:14 e a marvellous work and a wonder: NIH
32: 7 e when the needy speaketh right. 2050.1
35: 2 rejoice e with joy and singing: 637
35: 4 with vengeance, e God with a recompence; NIH
37:16 thou art the God, e thou alone, of all NIH
37:20 know that thou art the LORD, e thou only. NIH
37:23 on high? e against the Holy One of Israel. NIH
38:11 e the LORD, in the land of the living: NIH
38:12 from day e to night wilt thou make an end NIH
38:13 from day e to night wilt thou make an end NIH
39: 3 a far country unto me, e from Babylon. NIH
40:30 E the youths shall faint and be weary, and 2050.1
41: 3 e by the way that he had not gone with his NIH
41:12 find them, e them that contended with thee: NIH
41:28 e amongst them, and there was no 2050.1
43: 7 E every one that is called by my name: for I NIH
43:11 I, e I, am the LORD; and beside me there NIH
43:19 I will e make a way in the wilderness, and 637
43:25 I, e I, am he that blotteth out thy NIH
44: 8 have declared it? ye are e my witnesses. 2050.1
44:17 he maketh a god, e his graven image: NIH
44:28 e saying to Jerusalem, Thou shalt be 2050.1
45: 4 I have e called thee by thy name: 2050.1
45:12 I, e my hands, have stretched out NIH
45:24 e to him shall men come; and all that are NIH
46: 4 e to your old age I am he; and even to hoar NIH
46: 4 e to hoar hairs will I carry you: I have made, NIH
46: 4 e I will carry, and will deliver you. 2050.1
47:15 e thy merchants, from thy youth: NIH
48: 5 I have e from the beginning declared it to 2050.1
48: 6 e hidden things, and thou didst not know 2050.1
48: 7 e before the day when thou heardest them 2050.1
48:11 For mine own sake, e for mine own sake, NIH
48:15 I, e I, have spoken; yea, I have called him: NIH

E

Isa 48:20 tell this, utter it e to the end of the earth; NIH
49:10 e by the springs of water shall he guide 2050.1
49:19 shall e now be too narrow by reason of 3588
49:25 E the captives of the mighty shall be taken 1571
51:12 I, e I, am he that comforteth you: who art NIH
51:22 e the dregs of the cup of my fury; NIH
55: 3 with you, e the sure mercies of David. NIH
56: 5 E unto them will I give in mine house 2050.1
56: 7 E them will I bring to my holy mountain, 2050.1
57: 6 e to them hast thou poured a drink offering, 1571
57: 7 e thither wentest thou up to offer sacrifice. 1571
57: 9 far off, and didst debase thyself e unto hell. NIH
57:11 have not I held my peace e of old, and 2050.1
65: 6 e recompense into their bosom, 2050.1
66: 2 e to him that is poor and of a contrite spirit, NIH
Jer 3:25 from our youth e unto this day, and 2050.1
4:12 E a full wind from those places shall come NIH
6:11 for e the husband with the wife shall be 1571
6:13 For from the least of them e unto 2050.1
6:13 from the prophet e unto the priest every 2050.1
6:19 e the fruit of their thoughts, because NIH
7:11 Behold, e I have seen it, saith the LORD. 1571
7:15 your brethren, e the whole seed of Ephraim. NIH
7:25 I have e sent unto you all my servants 2050.1
8:10 e unto the greatest is given to 2050.1
8:10 from the prophet e unto the priest every 2050.1
9:15 Behold, I will feed them, e this people, with NIH
9:22 E the carcases of men shall fall as dung 2050.1
10:11 e they shall perish from the earth, and NIH
11: 7 e unto this day, rising early and protesting, NIH
11:13 e altars to burn incense unto Baal. NIH
11:23 of Anathoth, e the year of their visitation. NIH
12: 6 For e thy brethren, and the house of thy 1571
12: 6 e they have dealt treacherously with thee; 1571
12:12 of the land e to the other end of the land: 2050.1
13:10 to worship them, shall e be as this girdle, 2050.1
13:13 e the kings that sit upon David's throne, 2050.1
13:14 e the fathers and the sons together, 2050.1
13:18 shall come down, e the crown of your glory. NIH
15:13 that for all thy sins, e in all thy borders. 2050.1
16: 5 the LORD, e lovingkindness and mercies. NIH
17: 4 thou, e thyself, shalt discontinue from 2050.1
17:10 e to give every man according to his 2050.1
17:27 e entering in at the gates of Jerusalem on 2050.1
19:11 E so will I break this people and this city, 3602
19:12 and e make this city as Tophet: NIH
21: 5 e in anger, and in fury, and in great wrath. 2050.1
22:25 e into the hand of Nebuchadrezzar king 2050.1
23:12 e the year of their visitation, saith NIH
23:19 forth in fury, e a grievous whirlwind: 2050.1
23:33 I will e forsake you, saith the LORD. 2050.1
23:34 I will e punish that man and his house. 2050.1
23:39 Therefore behold, I, e I, will utterly forget 2050.1
24: 2 good figs, e like the figs that are first ripe: NIH
25: 3 e unto this day, that is the three and 2050.1
25:13 e all that is written in this book, which NIH
25:31 A noise shall come e to the ends of NIH
25:33 the earth e unto the other end of the earth: 2050.1
28: 6 E the prophet Jeremiah said, Amen: 2050.1
28:11 E so will I break the yoke of 3602
29:23 e I know, and am a witness, saith 2050.1
30: 7 it is e the time of Jacob's trouble; but 2050.1
31: 2 e Israel when I went to cause him to rest. NIH
31:19 yea, e confounded, because I did bear 2050.1
31:21 the highway, e the way which thou wentest: NIH
32: 9 the money, e seventeen shekels of silver. NIH
32:20 e unto this day, and in Israel, and NIH
32:31 my fury from the day that they built it e 2050.1
33:10 e in the cities of Judah, and in the streets of NIH
33:24 hath chosen, he hath e cast them off? 2050.1
34:20 I will e give them into the hand of their 2050.1
36: 2 from the days of Josiah, e unto this day. 2050.1
36:12 e Elishama the scribe, and Delaiah the son NIH
39: 3 e Nergal-sharezer, Samgar-nebo, NIH
39:12 e as he shall say unto thee. 834+3651+3509.1
39:14 E they sent, and took Jeremiah out of 2050.1
40: 7 were in the fields, e they and their men, NIH
40: 8 e Ishmael the son of Nethaniah, and 2050.1
40:12 E all the Jews returned out of all places 2050.1
41: 1 princes of the king, e ten men with him, 2050.1
41: 3 e with Gedaliah at Mizpah, and NIH
41: 5 and from Samaria, e fourscore men, NIH
41:10 e the king's daughters, and all the people NIH
41:16 e mighty men of war, and the women, and NIH
42: 1 all the people from the least e unto 2050.1
42: 2 the LORD thy God, e for all this remnant; NIH
42: 5 if we do not e according to all things for 3808
42: 8 all the people from the least e to 2050.1
43: 1 had sent him to them, e all these words; NIH
43: 6 E men, and women, and children, and NIH
43: 7 the LORD: thus came they e to Tahpanhes. NIH
44:10 They are not humbled e unto this day, NIH
44:12 they shall e be consumed by the sword, and NIH
44:12 from the least e unto the greatest, by 2050.1
44:15 e all the people that dwelt in the land of 2050.1
45: 4 planted I will pluck up, e this whole land. 2050.1
46:25 e Pharaoh, and all them that trust in him: 2050.1
48:32 over the sea, they reach e to the sea of Jazer: NIH
48:34 From the cry of Heshbon e unto Elealeh, NIH
48:34 and e unto Jahaz, have they uttered their NIH
48:34 from Zoar e unto Horonaim, as a heifer of NIH
48:44 for I will bring upon it, e upon Moab, NIH
49:37 e my fierce anger, saith the LORD; NIH
50: 7 the habitation of justice, e the LORD, 2050.1
50:21 e against it, and against the inhabitants of NIH
51: 9 unto heaven, and is lifted up e to the skies. NIH
51:56 e upon Babylon, and her mighty men are NIH
51:60 e all these words that are written against NIH
La 4: 3 E the sea monsters draw out the breast, 1571
Eze 1:27 from the appearance of his loins e 2050.1
1:27 from the appearance of his loins e 2050.1
2: 3 against me, e unto this very day. NIH
4: 1 and pourtray upon it the city, e Jerusalem: NIH
4:13 E thus shall the children of Israel eat their 3602
4:14 for from my youth up e till now have I 2050.1

Eze 5: 8 Behold, I, e I, am against thee, and 1571
6: 3 Behold, I, e I, will bring a sword upon you, NIH
7:14 blown the trumpet, e to make all ready; 2050.1
8: 2 from the appearance of his loins e 2050.1
8: 2 from his loins e upward, as 2050.1
8: 6 e the great abominations that the house of NIH
9: 1 e every man with his destroying weapon 2050.1
10: 2 e under the cherub, and fill thine hand with NIH
10: 5 wings was heard e to the utter court, NIH
10:12 e the wheels that they four had. NIH
11:15 Son of man, thy brethren, e thy brethren, NIH
11:17 I will e gather you from the people, and 2050.1
12: 4 thou shalt go forth at e in their sight, 6153
12: 7 in the e I digged through the wall with mine 6153
13:10 e because they have seduced my people, 2050.1
13:13 I will e rent it with a stormy wind in my 2050.1
13:20 e the souls that ye hunt to make them fly. NIH
14:10 e as the punishment of him that seeketh 3509.1
14:22 e concerning all that I have brought upon it. NIH
16:19 thou hast e set it before them for a sweet 2050.1
16:37 I will e gather them round about against 2050.1
16:59 I will e deal with thee as thou hast done, 2050.1
17: 9 e without great power or many people to 2050.1
17:16 e with him in the midst of Babylon he shall NIH
17:19 e it will I recompense upon his own head. 2050.1
18:11 but e hath eaten upon the mountains, 1571
18:18 lo, e he shall die in his iniquity. 2050.1
20:11 which if a man do, he shall e live in them. 2050.1
20:13 which if a man do, he shall e live in them; 2050.1
20:21 which if a man do, he shall e live in them; 2050.1
20:31 with all your idols, e unto this day: NIH
21:13 and what if the sword contemn e the rod? 1571
21:28 e say thou, The sword, the sword is 2050.1
22: 4 to draw near, and art come e unto thy years: NIH
22:18 of the furnace; they are e the dross of silver. NIH
23:34 Thou shalt e drink it and suck it out, and 2050.1
24: 2 thee the name of the day, e of this same day: NIH
24: 4 e every good piece, the thigh, and NIH
24: 9 I will e make the pile for fire great. 1571
24:18 at e my wife died; and I did in the morning 6153
29:10 from the tower of Syene e unto the border 2050.1
30: 3 e the day of the LORD is near, a cloudy 2050.1
32: 6 wherein thou swimmest, e to the mountains; NIH
32:16 e for Egypt, and for all her multitude, NIH
32:18 e her, and the daughters of the famous NIH
32:31 e Pharaoh and all his army slain by NIH
32:32 e Pharaoh and all his multitude, saith NIH
33:18 he shall e die thereby. 2050.1
34:11 Behold, I, e I, will both search my sheep, NIH
34:20 Behold, I, e I, will judge between the fat NIH
34:23 and he shall feed them, e my servant David; NIH
34:30 that they, e the house of Israel, are my NIH
35: 6 hated blood, e blood shall pursue thee. 2050.1
35:11 I will e do according to thine anger, and 2050.1
35:15 O mount Seir, and all Idumea, e all of it: NIH
36: 2 e the ancient high places are ours in 2050.1
36:10 upon you, all the house of Israel, e all of it: NIH
36:12 men to walk upon you, e my people Israel; NIH
37:19 e with the stick of Judah, and make them NIH
37:25 e they, and their children, and NIH
38: 4 of armour, e a great company with bucklers NIH
39:17 e a great sacrifice upon the mountains of NIH
40:14 e unto the post of the court round about 2050.1
41:17 e unto the inner house, and without, 2050.1
42:12 e the way directly before the wall toward NIH
43: 1 e the gate that looketh toward the east: NIH
43: 3 e according to the vision that I saw when I NIH
43: 8 they have e defiled my holy name by 2050.1
43:13 e the bottom shall be a cubit, and 2050.1
43:14 from the bottom upon the ground e to NIH
43:14 from the lesser settle e to the greater settle NIH
44: 6 e to the house of Israel, Thus saith the Lord NIH
44: 7 in my sanctuary, to pollute it, e my house, NIH
44:10 their idols; they shall e bear their iniquity. 2050.1
44:19 e into the utter court to the people, NIH
47:10 upon it from En-gedi e unto En-eglaim; 2050.1
47:19 from Tamar e to the waters of strife in NIH
48: 3 from the east side e unto the west side, 2050.1
48: 6 from the east side e unto the west side, 2050.1
48:10 for them, e for the priests, shall be this holy NIH
48:28 the border shall be e from Tamar unto 2050.1
Da 1:21 Daniel continued e unto the first year of NIH
2:43 to another, e as iron is not mixed with clay. 1888
4:15 e with a band of iron and brass, in 2050.3
4:23 e with a band of iron and brass, in 2050.3
5:14 I have e heard of thee, that the spirit of 2050.3
6:26 and his dominion shall be e unto the end. NIH
7:11 I beheld e till the beast was slain, and NIH
7:18 the kingdom for ever, e for ever and ever. 2050.3
7:20 e of that horn that had eyes, and a mouth 2050.3
8: 1 e unto me Daniel, after that which appeared NIH
8:10 it waxed great, e to the host of heaven; and NIH
8:11 he magnified himself e to the prince of NIH
8:15 when I, e I Daniel, had seen the vision, and NIH
9: 5 e by departing from thy precepts and 2050.1
9:11 e by departing, that they might not obey 2050.1
9:21 speaking in prayer, e the man Gabriel, 2050.1
9:25 and the wall, e in troublous times. 2050.1
9:27 e until the consummation, and 2050.1
11: 1 e I, stood to confirm and to strengthen him. NIH
11: 4 be plucked up, e for others besides those. 2050.1
11:10 he return, and be stirred up, e to his fortress. NIH
11:11 fight with him, e with the king of the north: NIH
11:24 He shall enter peaceably e upon 2050.1
11:24 against the strong holds, e for a time. 2050.1
11:30 he shall e return, and have intelligence 2050.1
11:35 make them white, e to the time of the end: NIH
11:41 e Edom, and Moab, and the chief of NIH
12: 1 such as never was since there was a nation e NIH
12: 4 and seal the book, e to the time of the end: NIH
Hos 2:20 I will e betroth thee unto me in 2050.1
5:14 I, e I, will tear and go away; I will take NIH
9:16 yet will I slay e the beloved fruit of their NIH
12: 5 E the LORD God of hosts; the LORD 2050.1
Joel 1: 2 your days, or e in the days of your fathers? 518

Joel 1:12 e all the trees of the field, are withered: NIH
2: 2 after it, e to the years of many generations. NIH
2:12 turn ye e to me with all your heart, and NIH
2:14 e a meat offering and a drink offering unto NIH
Am 2:11 Is it not e thus, O ye children of Israel? 637
3:11 An adversary there shall be e round about 2050.1
5: 1 e a lamentation, O house of Israel. NIH
5:20 e very dark, and no brightness in it? 2050.1
8: 4 e to make the poor of the land to fail, 2050.1
8:12 from the north e to the east, they shall run 2050.1
8:14 e they shall fall, and never rise up again. 2050.1
Ob 1: 7 have brought thee e to the border: NIH
1: 8 e destroy the wise men out of Edom, and 2050.1
1:11 e thou wast as one of them. 1571
1:20 that of the Canaanites, e unto Zarephath; NIH
Jnh 2: 5 waters compassed me about, e to the soul: NIH
3: 5 from the greatest of them e to the least of 2050.1
4: 9 he said, I do well to be angry, e unto death. NIH
Mic 1: 9 unto the gate of my people, e to Jerusalem. NIH
2: 2 and his house, e a man and his heritage. 2050.1
2: 8 E of late my people is risen up as an 2050.1
2:10 it shall destroy you, e with a sore 2050.1
2:11 he shall e be the prophet of this people. 2050.1
3: 4 he will e hide his face from them at that 2050.1
3: 5 they e prepare war against him. 2050.1
4: 7 mount Zion from henceforth, e for ever. 2050.1
4: 8 thee shall it come, e the first dominion; 2050.1
4:10 in the field, and thou shalt go e to Babylon; NIH
7:12 In that day also he shall come e to thee 2050.1
7:12 from the fortress e to the river, and 2050.1
Na 2:11 e the old lion, walked, and the lion's whelp, NIH
3:12 shall e fall into the mouth of the eater. 2050.1
Hab 1: 2 e cry out unto thee of violence, and NIH
3: 9 to the oaths of the tribes, e thy word. NIH
3:13 e for salvation with thine anointed; NIH
Zep 1:14 e the voice of the day of the LORD: NIH
1:18 for he shall make e a speedy riddance of all 389
2: 5 of the Philistines, I will e destroy thee, 2050.1
2: 9 e the breeding of nettles, and saltpits, and NIH
2:11 from his place, e all the isles of the heathen. NIH
3: 8 mine indignation, e all my fierce anger: NIH
3:10 e the daughter of my dispersed, shall bring NIH
3:15 the king of Israel, e the LORD, is in NIH
3:20 At that time will I bring you again, e in 2050.1
Hag 2:18 twentieth day of the ninth month, e from NIH
Zec 3: 2 e the LORD that hath chosen Jerusalem 2050.1
6:10 e of Heldai, of Tobijah, and of Jedaiah, NIH
6:13 E he shall build the temple of 2050.1
7: 1 fourth day of the ninth month, e in Chisleu; NIH
7: 5 and seventh month, e those seventy years, 2050.1
7: 5 did ye at all fast unto me, e to me? NIH
8:23 e shall take hold of the skirt of him that is 2050.1
9: 7 he that remaineth, e he, shall be for our 1571
9:10 and his dominion shall be from sea e to sea, NIH
9:10 and from the river e to the ends of the earth. NIH
9:12 e to day do I declare that I will render 1571
11: 7 of slaughter, e you, O poor of the flock. NIH
11:10 I took my staff, e Beauty, and cut it asunder, NIH
11:14 I cut asunder mine other staff, e Bands, NIH
12: 6 again in her own place, e in Jerusalem. NIH
14:16 e go up from year to year to worship 2050.1
14:17 of hosts, e upon them shall be no rain. 2050.1
Mal 1:10 Who is there e among you that would shut 1571
1:11 For from the rising of the sun e unto 2050.1
1:12 the fruit thereof, e his meat, is contemptible. NIH
2: 2 I will e send a curse upon you, and 2050.1
2: 3 e the dung of your solemn feasts; NIH
3: 1 e the messenger of the covenant, 2050.1
3: 7 E from the days of your fathers ye are 3807.1
3: 9 for ye have robbed me, e this whole nation. NIH
3:15 yea, they that tempt God are e delivered. 2050.1
Mt 5:46 have ye? do not e the publicans the same? 2532
5:47 what do ye more than others? do not e 2532
5:48 e as your Father which is in heaven is 5618
6:29 That e Solomon in all his glory was not 3761
7:12 men should do to you, do ye e so to them: 2532
7:17 E so every good tree bringeth forth good NIG
8:16 When the e was come, they brought unto 3798
8:27 that e the winds and the sea obey him? 2532
9:18 saying, My daughter is e now dead: 737
11:26 E so, Father: for so it seemed good in thy 3483
12: 8 For the Son of man is Lord e of the sabbath 2532
12:45 E so shall it be also unto this wicked NIG
13:12 from him shall be taken away e that he 2532
15:28 be it unto thee e as thou wilt. And her NIG
18:14 E so it is not the will of your Father which NIG
18:33 thy fellowservant, e as I had pity on thee? 2504
20: 8 So when e was come, the lord of 3798
20:14 I will give unto this last, e as unto thee. 2532
20:28 E as the Son of man came not to be 5618
23: 8 for one is your Master, e Christ; NIG
23:10 for one is your Master, e Christ. NIG
23:28 E so ye also outwardly appear righteous NIG
23:37 e as a hen gathereth her chickens 3739+5158
24:27 out of the east, and shineth e unto the west; NIG
24:33 things, know that it is near, e at the doors. NIG
25:29 shall be taken away e that which he hath. 2532
26:20 Now when the e was come, he sat down 3798
26:38 soul is exceeding sorrowful, e unto death: NIG
27:57 When the e was come, there came a rich 3798
28:20 with you alway, e unto the end of the world. NIG
Mk 1:27 for with authority commandeth he e 2532
1:32 And at e, when the sun did set, 1096+3798
4:25 from him shall be taken e that which he 2532
4:35 And the same day, when the e was come, 3798
4:36 they took him e as he was in the ship. NIG
4:41 that e the wind and the sea obey him? 2532
6: 2 that e such mighty works are wrought by 2532
6:47 And when e was come, the ship was in 3798
10:45 For e the Son of man came not to be 2532
11: 6 And they said unto them e as Jesus had 2531
11:19 And when e was come, he went out of 3796
12:44 did cast in all that she had, e all her living. NIG
13:22 to seduce, if it were possible, e the elect. 2532
13:29 to pass, know that it is nigh, e at the doors. NIG

Mk 13:35 at e, or at midnight, or at the cockcrowing, 3796
14:30 I say unto thee, That this day, e in this night, NIG
14:54 afar off, e into the palace of the high priest: 2193
15:42 And now when the e was come, because 3798
Lk 1: 2 E as they delivered them unto us, 2531
1:15 the Holy Ghost, e from his mother's womb. 2089
2:15 Let us now go e unto Bethlehem, and NIG
6:33 have ye? for sinners also do e the same. NIG
8:18 from him shall be taken e that which he 2532
8:25 for he commandeth e the winds and water, 2532
9:54 and consume them, e as Elias did? 2532
10:11 E the very dust of your city, which cleaveth 2532
10:17 e the devils are subject unto us through thy 2532
10:21 e so, Father; for so it seemed good in thy 3483
12: 7 But e the very hairs of your head are all 2532
12:41 thou this parable unto us, or e to all? 2532
12:57 why e of yourselves judge ye not what is 2532
17:30 E thus shall it be in the day when 2596+5024
18:11 unjust, adulterers, or e as this publican. 2532
19:26 e that he hath shall be taken away from 2532
19:32 and found e as he had said unto them. 2531
19:37 e now at the descent of the mount of Olives, NIG
19:42 Saying, If thou hadst known, e thou, at least 2532
19:44 And shall lay thee e with the ground, and 1474
20:37 are raised, e Moses shewed at the bush, 2532
24:24 and found it e so as the women had said: 2532
Jn 1:12 of God, e to them that believe on his name: NIG
3:13 e the Son of man which is in heaven. NIG
3:14 e so must the Son of man be lifted up: NIG
5:21 and quickeneth them; e so the Son 2532
5:23 the Son, e as they honour the Father. 2531
5:45 accuseth you, e Moses, in whom ye trust. NIG
6:16 And when e was now come, his disciples 3798
6:57 so he that eateth me, e he shall live by me. 2548
8: 9 beginning at the eldest, e unto the last: NIG
8:25 E the same that I said unto you from 2532
8:41 of fornication; we have one Father, e God. NIG
8:43 e because ye cannot hear my word. NIG
10:15 Father knoweth me, e so know I the Father: NIG
11:22 But I know, that e now, whatsoever thou 2532
11:37 have caused that e this man should not have 2532
12:50 e as the Father said unto me, so I speak. 2531
14:17 E the Spirit of truth; whom the world NIG
14:31 Father gave me commandment, e so I do. NIG
15:10 e as I have kept my Father's 2531
15:26 e the Spirit of truth, which proceedeth from NIG
17:14 not of the world, e as I am not of the world. 2531
17:16 not of the world, e as I am not of the world. 2531
17:18 e so have I also sent them into the world. 2504
17:22 that they may be one, e as we are one: 2531
20:21 as my Father hath sent me, e so send I you. 2504
21:25 I suppose that e the world itself could not NIG
Ac 2:39 e as many as the Lord our God shall call. NIG
4:10 e by him doth this man stand here before NIG
5:37 and all, e as many as obeyed him, NIG
5:39 lest haply ye be found e to fight against 2532
9:17 on him said, Brother Saul, the Lord, e Jesus, NIG
10:41 e to us, who did eat and drink with him after NIG
11: 5 heaven by four corners; and it came e to me: NIG
12:15 But she constantly affirmed that it was e so. NIG
15: 8 them the Holy Ghost, e as he did unto us; 2532
15:11 Jesus Christ we shall be saved, e as they. 2548
20:11 e till break of day, so he departed. NIG
22:17 e while I prayed in the temple, I was in a 2532
26:11 persecuted them e unto strange cities. 2193+2532
27:25 be e as it was told me. 2596+3739+3779+5158
Ro 1:13 among you also, e as among other Gentiles. 2532
1:20 are made, e his eternal power and Godhead; NIG
1:26 for e their women did change the natural 5037
1:28 And e as they did not like to retain God in 2531
3:22 E the righteousness of God which is by 1161
4: 6 E as David also describeth the blessedness 2509
4:17 e God, who quickeneth the dead, and NIG
5: 7 for a good man some would e dare to die. 2532
5:14 e over them that had not sinned after 2532
5:18 e so by the righteousness of one the free 2532
5:21 e so might grace reign through 2532
6: 4 e so we also should walk in newness of life. NIG
6:19 e so now yield your members servants to NIG
7: 4 e to him who is raised from the dead, NIG
8:23 e we ourselves groan within ourselves, 2532
8:34 that is risen again, who is e at the right 2532
9:10 had conceived by one, e by our father Isaac; NIG
9:17 E for this same purpose have I raised thee NIG
9:24 E us, whom he hath called, not of the Jews 2532
9:30 e the righteousness which is of faith. 1161
10: 8 nigh thee, e in thy mouth, and in thy heart: NIG
11: 5 E so then at this present time also there is a NIG
11:31 E so have these also now not believed, NIG
15: 3 For e Christ pleased not himself; but, as it 2532
15: 6 e the Father of our Lord Jesus Christ. 2532
1Co 1: 6 E as the testimony of Christ was confirmed 2531
2: 7 e the hidden wisdom, which God ordained NIG
2:11 e so the things of God knoweth no man, but 2532
3: 1 but as unto carnal, e as unto babes in Christ. NIG
3: 5 e as the Lord gave to every man? 2532
4:11 E unto this present hour we both hunger, 891
5: 7 For e Christ our passover is sacrificed for 2532
7: 7 For I would that all men were e as I myself. 2532
7: 8 It is good for them if they abide e as I. 2504
9:14 E so hath the Lord ordained that they 2532
10:33 E as I please all men in all things, not 2504
11: 1 ye followers of me, e as I also am of Christ. 2531
11: 5 e all one as if she were 846+1520+2532+3588
11:12 the man, e so is the man also by the woman; NIG
11:14 Doth not e nature itself teach you, that, if a 3761
12: 2 unto these dumb idols, e as ye were led. NIG
13:12 but then shall I know e as also I am known. 2531
14: 7 And e things without life giving sound, 3676
14:12 E so ye, forasmuch as ye are zealous of 2532
15:22 e so in Christ shall all be made alive. 2532
15:24 up the kingdom to God, e the Father; 2532
16: 1 order to the churches of Galatia, e so do ye. 2532
2Co 1: 3 e the Father of our Lord Jesus Christ, 2532
1: 8 insomuch that we despaired e of life: 2532
2Co 1:13 I trust you shall acknowledge e to the end; 2532
1:14 e as ye also are ours in the day of the Lord 2509
1:19 e by me and Silvanus and Timotheus, NIG
3:10 For e that which was made glorious had no 2532
3:15 But e unto this day, when Moses is read, NIG
3:18 glory to glory, e as by the Spirit of the Lord. NIG
7:14 e so our boasting, which I made before 2532
10: 7 that, as he is Christ's, e so are we Christ's. 2532
10:13 to us, a measure to reach e unto you. 2532
11:12 they glory, they may be found e as we. 2532
13: 9 and this also we wish, e your perfection. NIG
Gal 2:16 e we have believed in Jesus Christ, 2532
3: 6 E as Abraham believed God, and it was 2531
4: 3 E so we, when we were children, were in 2532
4:14 me as an angel of God, e as Christ Jesus. NIG
4:29 that was born after the Spirit, e so it is now. 2532
5:12 I would they were e cut off which trouble 2532
5:14 e in this; Thou shalt love thy neighbour as NIG
Eph 1:10 in heaven, and which are on earth; e in him: NIG
2: 3 by nature the children of wrath, e as others. 2532
2: 5 E when we were dead in sins, 2532
2:15 e the law of commandments contained in NIG
4: 4 e as ye are called in one hope of your 2531
4:15 in all things, which is the head, e Christ: NIG
4:32 e as God for Christ's sake hath forgiven 2531
5:12 For it is a shame e to speak of those things 2532
5:23 e as Christ is the head of the church: 2532
5:25 e as Christ also loved the church, and 2531
5:29 and cherisheth it, e as the Lord the church: 2531
5:33 in particular so love his wife e as himself; 5613
Php 1: 7 E as it is meet for me to think this of you 2531
1:15 Some indeed preach Christ e of envy and 2532
2: 8 unto death, e the death of the cross. 1161
3:15 God shall reveal e this unto you. 2532
3:18 told you often, and now tell you e weeping, 2532
3:21 is able e to subdue all things unto himself. 2532
4:16 For e in Thessalonica ye sent once and 2532
Col 1:14 through his blood, e the forgiveness of sins: NIG
1:26 E the mystery which hath been hid from NIG
3:13 e as Christ forgave you, so also do ye. 2531
1Th 1:10 whom he raised from the dead, e Jesus, NIG
2: 2 But e after that we had suffered before, and 2532
2: 4 put in trust with the gospel, e so we speak; NIG
2: 7 e as a nurse cherisheth her children: NIG
2:14 e as they have of the Jews: 2531
2:18 come unto you, e I Paul, once and again; 3303
2:19 Are not e ye in the presence of our Lord 2532
3: 4 e as it came to pass, and ye know. 2532
3:12 towards all men, e as we do towards you: 2532
3:13 e our Father, at the coming of our Lord 2532
4: 3 this is the will of God, e your sanctification, NIG
4: 5 e as the Gentiles which know not God: 2532
4:13 e as others which have no hope. 2531
4:14 e so them also which sleep in Jesus will NIG
5:11 and edify one another, e as also ye do. 2531
2Th 2: 9 E him, whose coming is after the working NIG
2:16 and God, e our Father, which hath loved us, 2532
3: 1 and be glorified, e as it is with you: 2532
3:10 For e when we were with you, this we 2532
1Ti 3:11 E so must their wives be grave, 5615
6: 3 e the words of our Lord Jesus Christ, and NIG
2Ti 2: 9 suffer trouble, as an evil doer, e unto bonds; NIG
Tit 1:12 e a prophet of their own, said, NIG
1:15 but e their mind and conscience is defiled. 2532
Phm 1:19 owest unto me e thine own self besides. 2532
Heb 1: 9 therefore God, e thy God, hath anointed NIG
4:12 piercing e to the dividing asunder of soul 891
5:14 e those who by reason of use have their NIG
6:20 the forerunner is for us entered, e Jesus, NIG
7: 4 e the patriarch Abraham gave the tenth of 2532
11:12 Therefore sprang there e of one, and him as 2532
11:19 was able to raise him up, e from the dead; 2532
Jas 2:17 E so faith, if it hath not works, is dead, 2532
3: 5 E so the tongue is a little member, and 2532
3: 9 Therewith bless we God, e the Father; and 2532
4: 1 e of your lusts that war in your members? NIG
4:14 It is e a vapour, that appeareth for a little 1063
1Pe 1: 9 of your faith, e the salvation of your souls. NIG
2: 8 e to them which stumble at the word, NIG
2:21 For e hereunto were ye called: because NIG
3: 4 e the ornament of a meek and quiet spirit, NIG
3: 6 E as Sara obeyed Abraham, calling him NIG
3:21 The like figure whereunto e baptism doth NIG
4:10 e so minister the same one to another, NIG
2Pe 1:14 e as our Lord Jesus Christ hath shewed me. 2532
2: 1 e as there shall be false teachers among 2532
2: 1 e denying the Lord that bought them, and 2532
3:15 e as our beloved brother Paul also 2531
1Jn 2: 6 himself also so to walk, e as he walked. 2531
2: 9 his brother, is in darkness e until now. NIG
2:18 e now are there many antichrists; 2532
2:25 that he hath promised us, e eternal life. NIG
2:27 and is no lie, and e as it hath taught you, 2531
3: 3 in him purifieth himself, e as he is pure. 2531
3: 7 is righteous, e as he is righteous. 2531
4: 3 and e now already is it in the world. NIG
5: 4 that overcometh the world, e our faith. NIG
5: 6 came by water and blood, e Jesus Christ; NIG
5:20 in him that is true, e in his Son Jesus Christ. NIG
3Jn 1: 2 and be in health, e as thy soul prospereth. 2531
1: 3 is in thee, e as thou walkest in the truth. 2531
Jude 1: 7 E as Sodom and Gomorrha, and the cities NIG
1:23 hating e the garment spotted by the flesh. 2532
Rev 1: 7 shall wail because of him. E so, Amen. 3483
2:13 e where Satan's seat is: and thou holdest NIG
2:13 e in those days wherein Antipas was my 2532
2:27 to shivers: e as I received of my Father. 2504
3: 4 Thou hast a few names e in Sardis, 2532
3:21 e as I also overcame, and am set down with NIG
6:13 e as a fig tree casteth her untimely figs, NIG
14:20 e unto the horse bridles, by the space of a NIG
16: 7 E so, Lord God Almighty, true and 3483
17:11 e he is the eighth, and is of the seven, and 2532
18: 6 Reward her e as she rewarded you, and 2532
21:11 e like a jasper stone, clear as crystal; NIG
Rev 22:20 Amen. E so, come, Lord Jesus. 3483

EVENING (60) [EVEN]

Ge 1: 5 the e and the morning were the first day. 6153
1: 8 the e and the morning were the second day. 6153
1:13 the e and the morning were the third day. 6153
1:19 the e and the morning were the fourth day. 6153
1:23 the e and the morning were the fifth day. 6153
1:31 the e and the morning were the sixth day. 6153
8:11 the dove came in to him in the e; and lo, 6153
24:11 city by a well of water at the time of the e, 6153
29:23 it came to pass in the e, that he took Leah 6153
30:16 Jacob came out of the field in the e, and 6153
Ex 12: 6 congregation of Israel shall kill it in the e. 6153
16: 8 LORD shall give you in the e flesh to eat, 6153
18:13 by Moses from the morning unto the e. 6153
27:21 his sons shall order it from e to morning 6153
Lev 24: 3 shall Aaron order it from the e unto 6153
Dt 23:11 it shall be, when e cometh on, he shall wash 6153
Jos 10:26 were hanging upon the trees until the e. 6153
Jdg 19: 9 Behold now, the day draweth towards e, 6150
1Sa 14:24 be the man that eateth any food until e, 6153
17:16 the Philistine drew near morning and e, 6150
30:17 the twilight even unto the e of the next day: 6153
1Ki 17: 6 the morning, and bread and flesh in the e; 6153
18:29 the time of the offering of the e sacrifice, NIH
18:36 at the time of the offering of the e sacrifice, NIH
2Ki 16:15 the e meat offering, and the king's burnt 6153
1Ch 16:40 burnt offering continually morning and e, 6153
2Ch 2: 4 for the burnt offerings morning and e, 6153
13:11 every morning and every e
6153+6153+871.1+871.1+1886.1+1886.1
13:11 to burn every e:
6153+6153+871.1+871.1+1886.1+1886.1
31: 3 wit, for the morning and e burnt offerings, 6153
Ezr 3: 3 even burnt offerings morning and e. 6153
9: 4 and I sat astonied until the e sacrifice. 6153
9: 5 at the e sacrifice I arose up from my 6153
Est 2:14 In the e she went, and on the morrow she 6153
Job 4:20 They are destroyed from morning to e: 6153
Ps 55:17 E, and morning, and at noon, will I pray, 6153
59: 6 They return at e: they make a noise like a 6153
59:14 at e let them return; and let them make a 6153
65: 8 outgoings of the morning and e to rejoice. 6153
90: 6 in the e it is cut down, and withereth. 6153
104:23 unto his work and to his labour until the e. 6153
141: 2 the lifting up of my hands as the e sacrifice. 6153
Pr 7: 9 in the e, in the black and dark night: 6153
Ecc 11: 6 and in the e withhold not thine hand: 6153
Jer 6: 4 for the shadows of the e are stretched out. 6153
Eze 33:22 hand of the LORD was upon me in the e, 6153
46: 2 but the gate shall not be shut until the e. 6153
Da 8:26 the vision of the e and the morning which 6153
9:21 touched me about the time of the e 6153
Hab 1: 8 and are more fierce than the e wolves: 6153
Zep 2: 7 of Ashkelon shall they lie down in the e: 6153
3: 3 are roaring lions; her judges are e wolves; 6153
Zec 14: 7 come to pass, that at e time it shall be light. 6153
Mt 14:15 And when it was e, his disciples came to 3798
14:23 and when the e was come, he was there 3798
16: 2 and said unto them, When it is e, ye say, 3798
Mk 14:17 And in the e he cometh with the twelve. 3798
Lk 24:29 for it is towards e, and the day is far spent. 2073
Jn 20:19 Then the same day at e, being the first day 3798
Ac 28:23 out of the prophets, from morning till e. 2073

EVENINGS (1) [EVEN]

Jer 5: 6 and a wolf of the e shall spoil them, 6160

EVENINGTIDE (2) [EVEN]

2Sa 11: 2 it came to pass in an e, that David 6153+6256
Isa 17:14 behold at e trouble; and before 6153+6256

EVENT (3)

Ecc 2:14 I myself perceived also that one e 4745
9: 2 there is one e to the righteous, and to 4745
9: 3 under the sun, that there is one e unto all: 4745

EVENTIDE (5) [EVEN]

Ge 24:63 out to meditate in the field at the e: 6153+6437
Jos 7: 6 before the ark of the LORD until the e, 6153
8:29 he hanged on a tree until e: 6153+6256+1886.1
Mk 11:11 and now the e was come, 3588+3798+5610
Ac 4: 3 in hold unto the next day: for it was now e. 2073

EVER (476) [EVERLASTING, EVERMORE, HOWSOEVER, SOEVER, WHATSOEVER, WHENSOEVER, WHEREINSOEVER, WHERESOEVER, WHITHERSOEVER, WHOMSOEVER, WHOSOEVER]

Ge 3:22 of the tree of life, and eat, and live for e: 5769
13:15 to thee will I give it, and to thy seed for e. 5769
43: 9 let me bear the blame for e: 3117+3605+1886.1
44:32 the blame to my father for e. 3117+3605+1886.1
Ex 3:15 this is my name for e, and this is my 5769
12:14 shall keep it a feast by an ordinance for e. 5769
12:17 in your generations by an ordinance for e. 5769
12:24 an ordinance to thee and to thy sons for e. 5769
14:13 ye shall see them again no more for e. 5769
15:18 The LORD shall reign for e and ever. 5769
15:18 The LORD shall reign for ever and e. 5703
19: 9 I speak with thee, and believe thee for e. 5769
21: 6 with an aul; and he shall serve him for e. 5769
27:21 it shall be a statute for e unto their 5769
28:43 it shall be a statute for e unto him and his 5769
29:28 his sons' by a statute for e from 5769
30:21 it shall be a statute for e to them, even to 5769
31:17 between me and the children of Israel for e: 5769
32:13 your seed, and they shall inherit it for e. 5769
Lev 6:13 The fire shall e be burning upon the altar; 8548
6:18 It shall be a statute for e in your 5769
6:22 it is a statute for e unto the LORD; it shall 5769
7:34 unto his sons by a statute for e from among 5769
7:36 by a statute for e throughout their 5769

Lev 10: 9 *it shall be* a statute **for e throughout** your 5769
10:15 and thy sons' with thee, by a statute **for e**; 5769
16:29 *this* shall be a statute **for e** unto you: *that* in 5769
16:31 shall afflict your souls, *by* a statute **for e**. 5769
17: 7 This shall be a statute **for e** unto them 5769
23:14 *it shall be* a statute **for e** throughout your 5769
23:21 **for e** in all your dwellings throughout your 5769
23:31 *it shall be* a statute **for e** throughout your 5769
23:41 *It shall be* a statute **for e** in your 5769
24: 3 *it shall be* a statute **for e** in your 5769
25:23 The land shall not be sold for **e**: for the land 6783
25:30 **e** to him that bought it throughout his 6783
25:46 they shall be your bondmen for **e**: 5769
Nu 10: 8 they shall be to you for an ordinance **for e** 5769
15:15 an ordinance **for e** in your generations: 5769
18: 8 and to thy sons, by an ordinance **for e**. 5769
18:11 thy daughters with thee, by a statute **for e**: 5769
18:19 thy daughters with thee, by a statute **for e**: 5769
18:19 it *is* a covenant of salt **for e** before 5769
18:23 *it shall be* a statute **for e** throughout your 5769
19:10 sojourneth among them, for a statute **for e**. 5769
22:30 upon which thou hast ridden **e since** 4480+5750
22:30 was I **e wont** to do so unto thee? 5532+5532
24:20 his latter end *shall be* that he perish **for e**. 5703
24:24 afflict Eber, and he also shall perish **for e**. 5703
Dt 4:33 Did **e** people hear the voice of God NIH
4:40 thy God giveth thee, **for e**. 3117+3605+1886.1
5:29 and with their children **for e**! 5769+3807.1
12:28 and with thy children after thee for **e**, 5769
13:16 it shall be a heap for **e**; it shall not be built 5769
15:17 the door, and he shall be thy servant **for e**. 5769
18: 5 him and his sons **for e**. 3117+3605+1886.1
19: 9 and to walk **e** in his ways; 3117+3605+1886.1
23: 3 into the congregation of the LORD for **e**: 5769
23: 6 peace nor their prosperity all thy days for **e**. 5769
28:46 and for a wonder, and upon thy seed for **e**. 5769
29:29 *belong* unto us and to our children for **e**, 5769
32:40 up my hand to heaven, and say, I live for **e**. 5769
Jos 4: 7 a memorial unto the children of Israel for **e**. 5769
4:24 the LORD your God **for e**. 3117+3605+1886.1
8:28 Joshua burnt Ai, and made it a heap **for e**, 5769
14: 9 thy children's for **e**, because thou hast 5769
Jdg 11:25 did he **e strive** against Israel; or 7378+7378
11:25 or did he **e fight** against them, 3898+3898
1Sa 1:22 before the LORD, and there abide for **e**. 5769
2:30 of thy father, should walk before me for **e**: 5769
2:32 old man in thine house **for e**. 3117+3605+1886.1
2:35 before mine anointed **for e**. 3117+3605+1886.1
3:13 for **e** for the iniquity which he knoweth; 5769
3:14 be purged with sacrifice nor offering for **e**. 5769
13:13 established thy kingdom upon Israel for **e**. 5769
20:15 cut off thy kindness from my house for **e**: 5769
20:23 the LORD *be* between thee and me for **e**. 5769
20:42 and between my seed and thy seed for **e**. 5769
27:12 therefore he shall be my servant **for e**. 5769
28: 2 keeper of mine head **for e**. 3117+3605+1886.1
2Sa 2:26 and said, Shall the sword devour for **e**? 5331
3:28 **e** from the blood of Abner the son of Ner: 5769
7:13 stablish the throne of his kingdom for **e**. 5769
7:16 thy kingdom shall be established for **e** before 5769
7:16 thy throne shall be established for **e**. 5769
7:24 people Israel to be a people unto thee for **e**; 5769
7:25 establish *it* for **e**, and do as thou hast said. 5769
7:26 let thy name be magnified for **e**, saying, 5769
7:29 that *it* may continue for **e** before thee: 5769
7:29 let the house of thy servant be blessed for **e**. 5769
1Ki 1:31 and said, Let my lord king David live for **e**. 5769
2:33 and upon the head of his seed for **e**: 5769
2:33 shall there be peace for **e** from the LORD. 5769
2:45 be established before the LORD for **e**. 5769
5: 1 was **e** a lover of David. 3117+3605+1886.1
8:13 a settled place for thee to abide in **for e**. 5769
9: 3 thou hast built, to put my name there for **e**; 5769
9: 5 the throne of thy kingdom upon Israel for **e**, 5769
10: 9 because the LORD loved Israel for **e**, 5769
11:39 seed of David, but not **for e**. 3117+3605+1886.1
12: 7 will be thy servants **for e**. 3117+3605+1886.1
2Ki 5:27 cleave unto thee, and unto thy seed for **e**. 5769
21: 7 of Israel, will I put my name **for e**: 5769+3807.1
1Ch 15: 2 ark of God, and to minister unto him for **e**. 5769
16:34 for *he is* good; for his mercy *endureth* for **e**. 5769
16:36 Blessed *be* the LORD God of Israel for **e** 5769
16:36 *be* the LORD God of Israel for ever and **e**. 5703
16:41 because his mercy *endureth* for **e**; 5769
17:12 a house, and I will stablish his throne for **e**. 5769
17:14 in mine house and in my kingdom for **e**: 5769
17:22 didst thou make thine own people for **e**; 5769
17:23 concerning his house be established for **e**, 5769
17:24 that thy name may be magnified for **e**, 5769
17:27 thy servant, that *it* may be before thee for **e**: 5769
17:27 O LORD, and *it shall be* blessed for **e**. 5769
22:10 the throne of his kingdom over Israel for **e**. 5769
23:13 the most holy *things*, he and his sons for **e**, 5769
23:13 unto him, and to bless in his name for **e**. 5769
23:25 they may dwell in Jerusalem for **e**: 5769+3807.1
28: 4 of my father to be king over Israel for **e**: 5769
28: 7 I will establish his kingdom for **e**, 5769
28: 8 for your children after you for **e**. 5769
28: 9 thou forsake him, he will cast thee off for **e**. 5703
29:10 God of Israel our father, for **e** and ever. 5769
29:10 God of Israel our father, for ever and **e**. 5769
29:18 keep this for **e** in the imagination of 5769
2Ch 2: 4 This *is an ordinance* for **e** to Israel. 5769
5:13 *he is* good; for his mercy *endureth* for **e**: 5769
6: 2 for thee, and a place for thy dwelling **for e**. 5769
7: 3 *he is* good; for his mercy *endureth* for **e**. 5769
7: 6 because his mercy *endureth* for **e**, 5769
7:16 that my name may be there for **e**: 5769
9: 8 to establish them for **e**, therefore made he 5769
10: 7 will be thy servants **for e**. 3117+3605+1886.1
13: 5 the kingdom over Israel to David for **e**, 5769
20: 7 it to the seed of Abraham thy friend for **e**? 5769
20:21 the LORD; for his mercy *endureth* for **e**. 5769
21: 7 to him and to his sons **for e**. 3117+3605+1886.1
30: 8 which he hath sanctified for **e**: 5769
2Ch 33: 4 In Jerusalem shall my name be for **e**. 5769
33: 7 tribes of Israel, will I put my name for **e**: 5865
Ezr 3:11 for his mercy *endureth* for **e** towards Israel. 5769
9:12 nor seek their peace or their wealth for **e**: 5769
9:12 *it* for an inheritance to your children for **e**. 5769
Ne 2: 3 said unto the king, Let the king live for **e**: 5769
9: 5 *and* bless the LORD your God for **e** and 5769
9: 5 bless the LORD your God for ever and **e**: 5769
13: 1 come into the congregation of God for **e**; 5769
Job 4: 7 Remember, I pray thee, who **e** perished, NIH
4:20 they perish for **e** without *any* regarding *it*. 5331
14:20 Thou prevailest for **e** against him, and 5331
19:24 with an iron pen and lead in the rock for **e**! 5703
20: 7 *Yet* he shall perish for **e** like his own dung: 5331
23: 7 should I be delivered for **e** from my judge. 5331
36: 7 he doth establish them for **e**, and they are 5331
41: 4 wilt thou take him for a servant **for e**? 5769
Ps 5:11 let them **e** shout for joy, because 5769+3807.1
9: 5 thou hast put out their name for **e** and ever. 5769
9: 5 thou hast put out their name for ever and **e**. 5703
9: 7 the LORD shall endure for **e**: he hath 5769
9:18 of the poor shall *not* perish for **e**. 5703
10:16 The LORD *is* King **for e** and ever: 5769
10:16 The LORD *is* King for ever and **e**: 5703
12: 7 preserve them from this generation for **e**. 5769
13: 1 **for e**? how long wilt thou hide thy face 5331
19: 9 fear of the LORD *is* clean, enduring for **e**: 5703
21: 4 *it* him, *even* length of days **for e** and ever. 5769
21: 4 *it* him, *even* length of days for ever and **e**. 5703
21: 6 For thou hast made him most blessed for **e**: 5703
22:26 that seek him: your heart shall live for **e**. 5703
23: 6 in the house of the LORD for **e**. 753+3117
25: 6 for they *have been* **e of old**. 4480+5769
25:15 Mine eyes *are* **e** towards the LORD; for he 8548
28: 9 feed them also, and lift them up for **e**. 5769
29:10 yea, the LORD sitteth King for **e**. 5769
30:12 my God, I will give thanks unto thee for **e**. 5769
33:11 The counsel of the LORD standeth for **e**, 5769
37:18 and their inheritance shall be for **e**. 5769
37:26 *He is* **e** merciful, and 3117+3605+1886.1
37:28 not his saints; they are preserved for **e**: 5769
37:29 inherit the land, and dwell therein for **e**. 5703
41:12 and settest me before thy face for **e**. 5769
44: 8 all the day long, and praise thy name for **e**. 5769
44:23 O Lord? arise, cast *us* not off for **e**. 5331
45: 2 therefore God hath blessed thee for **e**. 5769
45: 6 Thy throne, O God, *is* **for e** and ever: 5769
45: 6 Thy throne, O God, *is* for ever and **e**: 5703
45:17 shall the people praise thee for **e** and ever. 5769
45:17 shall the people praise thee for ever and **e**. 5703
48: 8 our God: God will establish it for **e**. Selah. 5769
48:14 For this God *is* our God **for e** and ever: 5769
48:14 For this God *is* our God for ever and **e**: 5703
49: 8 their soul is precious, and it ceaseth for **e**:) 5769
49: 9 That he should still live for **e**, *and* not see 5331
49:11 *is, that* their houses *shall continue* for **e**, 5769
51: 3 and my sin *is* **e** before me. 8548
52: 5 God shall likewise destroy thee for **e**, 5331
52: 8 I trust in the mercy of God **for e** and ever. 5769
52: 8 I trust in the mercy of God for ever and **e**. 5703
52: 9 I will praise thee for **e**, because thou hast 5769
61: 4 I will abide in thy tabernacle **for e**: I will 5769
61: 7 He shall abide before God **for e**: O prepare 5769
61: 8 So will I sing *praise* unto thy name for **e**, 5703
66: 7 He ruleth by his power **for e**; his eyes 5769
68:16 yea, the LORD will dwell *in it* for **e**. 5331
72:17 His name shall endure for **e**: his name shall 5769
72:19 And blessed *be* his glorious name for **e**: and 5769
73:26 strength of my heart, and my portion for **e**. 5769
74: 1 O God, why hast thou cast *us* off for **e**? 5331
74:10 shall the enemy blaspheme thy name for **e**? 5331
74:19 not the congregation of thy poor for **e**. 5331
75: 9 I will declare for **e**; I will sing *praises* to 5769
77: 7 Will the Lord cast off for **e**? and will he be 5769
77: 8 Is his mercy clean gone for **e**? doth *his* 5331
78:69 the earth which he hath established for **e**. 5769
79: 5 wilt thou be angry, for **e**? shall thy jealousy 5331
79:13 of thy pasture will give thee thanks for **e**: 5769
81:15 but their time should have endured for **e**. 5769
83:17 Let them be confounded and troubled for **e**; 5703
85: 5 Wilt thou be angry with us for **e**? wilt thou 5769
89: 1 sing of the mercies of the LORD **for e**: 5769
89: 2 I have said, Mercy shall be built up **for e**: 5769
89: 4 Thy seed will I stablish for **e**, and build up 5769
89:29 His seed also will I make *to endure* for **e**, 5703
89:36 His seed shall endure for **e**, and his throne 5769
89:37 It shall be established for **e** as the moon, 5769
89:46 wilt thou hide thyself, for **e**? shall thy wrath 5331
90: 2 or **e** thou hadst formed the earth and NIH
92: 7 *it is* that they shall be destroyed for **e**: 5703
93: 5 thine house, O LORD, for **e**. 753+3117
102:12 thou, O LORD, shalt endure for **e**; and 5769
103: 9 neither will he keep *his anger* for **e**. 5769
104: 5 should not be removed **for e**. 5703+5769+2050.1
104:31 The glory of the LORD shall endure for **e**: 5769
105: 8 He hath remembered his covenant for **e**, 5769
106: 1 for *he is* good: for his mercy *endureth* for **e**. 5769
107: 1 for *he is* good: for his mercy *endureth* for **e**. 5769
110: 4 Thou *art* a priest for **e** after the order of 5769
111: 3 and his righteousness endureth for **e**. 5703
111: 5 will **e** be mindful of his covenant. 5769+3807.1
111: 8 They stand fast for **e** and ever, *and are* done 5703
111: 8 They stand fast for ever and **e**, *and* 5769+3807.1
111: 9 he hath commanded his covenant for **e**: 5769
111:10 *commandments*: his praise endureth for **e**. 5703
112: 3 and his righteousness endureth for **e**. 5703
112: 6 Surely he shall not be moved for **e**: 5769
112: 9 the poor; his righteousness endureth for **e**; 5703
117: 2 the truth of the LORD *endureth* for **e**. 5769
118: 1 *is* good: because his mercy *endureth* for **e**. 5769
118: 2 now say, that his mercy *endureth* for **e**. 5769
118: 3 now say, that his mercy *endureth* for **e**. 5769
118: 4 LORD say, that his mercy *endureth* for **e**. 5769
118:29 for *he is* good: for his mercy *endureth* for **e**. 5769
119:44 So shall I keep thy law continually for **e** 5769
Ps 119:44 I keep thy law continually for ever and **e**. 5703
119:89 For **e**, O LORD, thy word *is* settled in 5769
119:98 for they *are* **e** with me. 5769+3807.1
119:111 have I taken as an heritage for **e**: 5769
119:152 of old that thou hast founded them for **e**. 5769
119:160 of thy righteous judgments *endureth* for **e**. 5769
125: 1 cannot be removed, *but* abideth for **e**. 5769
125: 2 his people from henceforth even for **e**. 5769
131: 3 in the LORD from henceforth and for **e**. 5769
132:14 This *is* my rest for **e**: here will I dwell; for I 5703
135:13 Thy name, O LORD, *endureth* for **e**; *and* 5769
136: 1 for *he is* good: for his mercy *endureth* for **e**. 5769
136: 2 God of gods: for his mercy *endureth* for **e**. 5769
136: 3 Lord of lords: for his mercy *endureth* for **e**. 5769
136: 4 for his mercy *endureth* for **e**. 5769
136: 5 the heavens: for his mercy *endureth* for **e**. 5769
136: 6 the waters: for his mercy *endureth* for **e**. 5769
136: 7 great lights: for his mercy *endureth* for **e**: 5769
136: 8 to rule by day: for his mercy *endureth* for **e**: 5769
136: 9 rule by night: for his mercy *endureth* for **e**. 5769
136:10 their firstborn: for his mercy *endureth* for **e**: 5769
136:11 among them: for his mercy *endureth* for **e**: 5769
136:12 out arm: for his mercy *endureth* for **e**. 5769
136:13 sea into parts: for his mercy *endureth* for **e**: 5769
136:14 the midst of it: for his mercy *endureth* for **e**: 5769
136:15 the Red sea: for his mercy *endureth* for **e**. 5769
136:16 for his mercy *endureth* for **e**. 5769
136:17 great kings: for his mercy *endureth* for **e**: 5769
136:18 famous kings: for his mercy *endureth* for **e**: 5769
136:19 the Amorites: for his mercy *endureth* for **e**: 5769
136:20 of Bashan: for his mercy *endureth* for **e**: 5769
136:21 an heritage: for his mercy *endureth* for **e**: 5769
136:22 his servant: for his mercy *endureth* for **e**. 5769
136:23 low estate: for his mercy *endureth* for **e**: 5769
136:24 our enemies: for his mercy *endureth* for **e**. 5769
136:25 to all flesh: for his mercy *endureth* for **e**. 5769
136:26 of heaven: for his mercy *endureth* for **e**. 5769
138: 8 thy mercy, O LORD, *endureth* for **e**: 5769
145: 1 and I will bless thy name for **e** and ever. 5769
145: 1 and I will bless thy name for ever and **e**. 5703
145: 2 and I will praise thy name for **e** and ever. 5769
145: 2 and I will praise thy name for ever and **e**. 5703
145:21 let all flesh bless his holy name for **e** and 5769
145:21 all flesh bless his holy name for ever and **e**. 5703
146: 6 all that therein is: which keepeth truth for **e**: 5769
146:10 The LORD shall reign for **e**, *even* thy 5769
148: 6 He hath also stablished them for **e** and ever: 5703
148: 6 He hath also stablished them for ever and **e**: 5703
Pr 8:23 the beginning, **or e** the earth **was**. 4480+6924
12:19 The lip of truth shall be established for **e**: 5703
27:24 For riches *are* not for **e**: and doth the crown 5769
29:14 his throne shall be established for **e**. 5703
Ecc 1: 4 but the earth abideth for **e**. 5769
2:16 of the wise more than of the fool for **e**; 5769
3:14 whatsoever God doeth, it shall be for **e**: 5769
9: 6 neither have they any more a portion for **e** 5769
12: 6 **Or e** the silver cord be loosed, 834+3808+5704
SS 6:12 **Or e** I was aware, my soul made me *like* 3808
Isa 9: 7 and with justice from henceforth even for **e**. 5769
26: 4 Trust ye in the LORD for **e**: for in 5703
28:28 because he will not **e** be threshing 5331+3807.1
30: 8 that it may be for the time to come for **e** 5703
30: 8 may be for the time to come for ever and **e**: 5769
32:14 the forts and towers shall be for dens for **e**, 5769
32:17 and assurance for **e**. 5769
33:20 not one of the stakes thereof shall **e** 5331+3807.1
34:10 the smoke thereof shall go up for **e**: 5769
34:10 none shall pass through it for **e** and ever. 5331
34:10 none shall pass through it for ever and **e**. 5331
34:17 they shall possess it for **e**, from generation 5769
40: 8 but the word of our God shall stand for **e**. 5769
47: 7 thou saidst, I shall be a lady for **e**: *so* 5703+5769
51: 6 my salvation shall be for **e**, and 5769
51: 8 my righteousness shall be for **e**, and 5769
57:16 For I will not contend for **e**, neither will I 5769
59:21 the LORD, from henceforth and for **e**. 5769
60:21 they shall inherit the land for **e**, the branch 5769
64: 9 O LORD, neither remember iniquity for **e**: 5703
65:18 and rejoice for **e** *in that* which I create: 5703
Jer 3: 5 Will he reserve *his anger* for **e**? will he 5769
3:12 the LORD, *and* I will not keep *anger* for **e**. 5769
7: 7 I gave to your fathers, for **e** and ever. 4480+5769
7: 7 I gave to your fathers, for ever and **e**. 5704+5769
17: 4 a fire in mine anger, *which* shall burn for **e**. 5769
17:25 and this city shall remain for **e**. 5769
25: 5 unto you and to your fathers for **e** and ever: 5769
25: 5 and to your fathers for ever and **e**: 5704+5769
31:36 a nation before me **for e**. 3117+3605+1886.1
31:40 nor thrown down any more for **e**. 5769
32:39 that *they* may fear me **for e**, 3117+3605+1886.1
33:11 *is* good; for his mercy *endureth* for **e**: 5769
35: 6 no wine, *neither* ye, nor your sons for **e**: 5769
35:19 to stand before me **for e**. 3117+3605+1886.1
49:33 for dragons, *and* a desolation for **e**: 5769
50:39 it shall be no more inhabited for **e**; 5331
51:26 thou shalt be desolate **for e**, saith 5769
51:62 nor beast, but that it shall be desolate **for e**. 5769
La 3:31 For the Lord will not cast off for **e**: 5769
5:19 Thou, O LORD, remainest for **e**; 5769
5:20 Wherefore dost thou forget us for **e**, *and* 5331
Eze 37:25 and their children's children for **e**: 5769
37:25 servant David *shall be* their prince for **e**. 5769
43: 7 in the midst of the children of Israel for **e**, 5769
43: 9 and I will dwell in the midst of them for **e**. 5769
Da 2: 4 to the king in Syriack, O king, live for **e**: 5957
2:20 be the name of God for **e** and ever: 0.2+5957
2:20 the name of God for ever and **e**: 0.2+5705+5957
2:44 all these kingdoms, and it shall stand for **e**. 5957
3: 9 king Nebuchadnezzar, O king, live for **e**. 5957
4:34 and honoured him that liveth for **e**, 0.2+5957
5:10 the queen spake and said, O king, live for **e**: 5957
6: 6 said thus unto him, King Darius, live for **e**. 5957
6:21 Daniel unto the king, O king, live for **e**. 5957
6:24 or **e** they came at the bottom of the den. 3809
6:26 stedfast for **e**, and his kingdom *that* which 5957

Da 7:18 possess the kingdom for e, even for ever 5957
7:18 the kingdom for ever, even for e and ever. 5957
7:18 the kingdom for ever, even for ever and e. 5957
12: 3 turn many to righteousness as the stars for e 5769
12: 3 to righteousness as the stars for ever and e. 5703
12: 7 sware by him that liveth for e that it shall 5769
Hos 2:19 I will betroth thee unto me for e; yea, I will 5769
Joel 2: 2 there hath not been e 4480+5769+1886.1
3:20 Judah shall dwell for e, and Jerusalem from 5769
Am 1:11 and he kept his wrath for e: 5331
Ob 1:10 cover thee, and thou shalt be cut off for e. 5769
Jnh 2: 6 the earth with her bars was about me for e: 5769
Mic 2: 9 have ye taken away my glory for e. 5769
4: 5 in the name of the LORD our God for e 5769
4: 5 of the LORD our God for ever and e. 5703
4: 7 in mount Zion from henceforth, even for e. 5769
7:18 he retaineth not his anger for e, because 5703
Zec 1: 5 and the prophets, do they live for e? 5769
Mal 1: 4 whom the LORD hath indignation for e. 5769
Mt 6:13 and the power, and the glory, for e. 165
21:19 no fruit grow on thee henceforward for e. 165
24:21 of the world to this time, no, nor e shall be. 3364
Mk 11:14 No man eat fruit of thee hereafter for e. 165
15: 8 desire him to do as he had e done unto them. 104
Lk 1:33 he shall reign over the house of Jacob for e; 165
1:55 to Abraham, and to his seed for e. 165
15:31 thou art e with me, and all that I have is 3842
Jn 4:29 which told me all things that e I did: 3745
4:39 which testified, He told me all that e I did. 3745
6:51 any man eat of this bread, he shall live for e: 165
6:58 he that eateth of this bread shall live for e. 165
8:35 the servant abideth not in the house for e: 165
8:35 for ever: but the son abideth e. 165+1519+3588
10: 8 All that e came before me are thieves and 3745
12:34 heard out of the law that Christ abideth for e: 165
14:16 that he may abide with you for e; 165
18:20 I e taught in the synagogue, and in 3842
Ac 23:15 and we, or e he come near, are ready 3588+4253
Ro 1:25 more than the Creator, who is blessed for e. 165
9: 5 came, who is over all, God blessed for e. 165
11:36 are all things: to whom be glory for e. 165
16:27 be glory through Jesus Christ for e. 165
2Co 9: 9 the poor: his righteousness remaineth for e. 165
Gal 1: 5 To whom be glory for e and ever. Amen. 165
1: 5 To whom be glory for ever and e. Amen. 165
Eph 5:29 For no man e yet hated his own flesh; but 4218
Php 4:20 and our Father be glory for e and ever. 165
4:20 and our Father be glory for ever and e. 165
1Th 4:17 the air: and so shall we e be with the Lord. 3842
5:15 any man; but e follow that which is good, 3842
1Ti 1:17 be honour and glory for e and ever. 165
1:17 be honour and glory for ever and e. 165
2Ti 3: 7 E learning, and never able to come to 3842
4:18 to whom be glory for e and ever. Amen. 165
4:18 to whom be glory for ever and e. Amen. 165
Phm 1:15 that thou shouldest receive him for e; 166
Heb 1: 8 saith, Thy throne, O God, is for e and ever: 165
1: 8 saith, Thy throne, O God, is for ever and e: 165
5: 6 a priest for e after the order of Melchisedec. 165
6:20 made a high priest for e after the order of 165
7:17 Thou art a priest for e after the order of 165
7:21 Thou art a priest for e after the order of 165
7:24 because he continueth e, 165+1519+3588
7:25 seeing he e liveth to make intercession for 3842
10:12 one sacrifice for sins for e, 1336+1519+3588
10:14 for e them that are sanctified. 1336+1519+3588
13: 8 the same yesterday, and to day, and for e. 165
13:21 to whom be glory for e and ever. 165
13:21 to whom be glory for ever and e. 165
1Pe 1:23 word of God, which liveth and abideth for e. 165
1:25 But the word of the Lord endureth for e. And 165
4:11 be praise and dominion for e and ever. 165
4:11 be praise and dominion for ever and e. 165
5:11 him be glory and dominion for e and ever. 165
5:11 him be glory and dominion for ever and e. 165
2Pe 2:17 whom the mist of darkness is reserved for e. 165
3:18 be glory both now and for e. Amen. 165+2250
1Jn 2:17 he that doeth the will of God abideth for e. 165
2Jn 1: 2 dwelleth in us, and shall be with us for e. 165
Jude 1:13 is reserved the blackness of darkness for e. 165
1:25 power, both now and e. 165+1519+3588+3056
Rev 1: 6 to him be glory and dominion for e and ever. 165
1: 6 to him be glory and dominion for ever and e. 165
4: 9 sat on the throne, who liveth for e and ever, 165
4: 9 sat on the throne, who liveth for ever and e, 165
4:10 and worship him that liveth for e and ever, 165
4:10 and worship him that liveth for ever and e, 165
5:13 the throne, and unto the Lamb for e and ever. 165
5:13 the throne, and unto the Lamb for ever and e. 165
5:14 and worshipped him that liveth for e and 165
5:14 worshipped him that liveth for ever and e. 165
7:12 and might, be unto our God for e and ever. 165
7:12 and might, be unto our God for ever and e. 165
10: 6 And sware by him that liveth for e and ever, 165
10: 6 And sware by him that liveth for ever and e, 165
11:15 his Christ; and he shall reign for e and ever. 165
11:15 his Christ; and he shall reign for ever and e. 165
14:11 smoke of their torment ascendeth up for e 165
14:11 of their torment ascendeth up for ever and e: 165
15: 7 the wrath of God, who liveth for e and ever. 165
15: 7 the wrath of God, who liveth for ever and e. 165
19: 3 And her smoke rose up for e and ever. 165
19: 3 And her smoke rose up for ever and e. 165
20:10 be tormented day and night for e and ever. 165
20:10 be tormented day and night for ever and e. 165
22: 5 and they shall reign for e and ever. 165
22: 5 and they shall reign for ever and e. 165

EVERLASTING (97) [EVER]

Ge 9:16 that I may remember the e covenant 5769
17: 7 thee in their generations for an e covenant, 5769
17: 8 all the land of Canaan, for an e possession; 5769
17:13 my covenant shall be in your flesh for an e 5769
17:19 my covenant with him for an e covenant, 5769
21:33 on the name of the LORD, the e God. 5769
48: 4 to thy seed after thee for an e possession. 5769
49:26 unto the utmost bound of the e hills: 5769
Ex 40:15 for their anointing shall surely be an e 5769
Lev 16:34 this shall be an e statute unto you, to make 5769
24: 8 the children of Israel by an e covenant. 5769
Nu 25:13 even the covenant of an e priesthood; 5769
Dt 33:27 thy refuge, and underneath are the e arms: 5769
2Sa 23: 5 yet he hath made with me an e covenant, 5769
1Ch 16:17 for a law, and to Israel for an e covenant, 5769
Ps 24: 7 be ye lift up, ye e doors; and the King of 5769
24: 9 even lift them up, ye e doors; and the King 5769
41:13 be the LORD God of Israel from e, 5769
41:13 God of Israel from everlasting, and to e. 5769
90: 2 and the world, even from e to everlasting, 5769
90: 2 and the world, even from everlasting to e, 5769
93: 2 throne is established of old: thou art from e. 5769
100: 5 his mercy is e; and his truth 5769+3807.1
103:17 the mercy of the LORD is from e to 5769
103:17 everlasting to e upon them that fear him, 5769
105:10 for a law, and to Israel for an e covenant: 5769
106:48 be the LORD God of Israel from e 5769
106:48 LORD God of Israel from everlasting to e: 5769
112: 6 the righteous shall be in e remembrance. 5769
119:142 Thy righteousness is an e 5769+3807.1
119:144 of thy testimonies is e: 5769+3807.1
139:24 way in me, and lead me in the way e. 5769
145:13 Thy kingdom is an e kingdom, and 3605+5769
Pr 8:23 I was set up from e, from the beginning, or 5769
10:25 but the righteous is an e foundation. 5769
Isa 9: 6 Counseller, The mighty God, The e Father, 5703
24: 5 the ordinance, broken the e covenant. 5769
26: 4 for in the LORD JEHOVAH is e strength: 5769
33:14 who amongst us shall dwell with e 5769
35:10 Zion with songs and e joy upon their heads: 5769
40:28 thou not heard, that the e God, the LORD, 5769
45:17 be saved in the LORD with an e salvation: 5769
51:11 and e joy shall be upon their head: 5769
54: 8 with e kindness will I have mercy on thee, 5769
55: 3 I will make an e covenant with you, 5769
55:13 for an e sign that shall not be cut off. 5769
56: 5 I will give them an e name, that shall not be 5769
60:19 the LORD shall be unto thee an e light, 5769
60:20 for the LORD shall be thine e light, and 5769
61: 7 the double: e joy shall be unto them. 5769
61: 8 and I will make an e covenant with them. 5769
63:12 before them, to make himself an e name? 5769
63:16 our redeemer; thy name is from e. 5769
Jer 10:10 he is the living God, and an e king: 5769
20:11 their e confusion shall never be forgotten. 5769
23:40 I will bring an e reproach upon you, and 5769
31: 3 I have loved thee with an e love; 5769
32:40 I will make an e covenant with them, that I 5769
Eze 16:60 and I will establish unto thee an e covenant. 5769
37:26 it shall be an e covenant with them: 5769
Da 4: 3 his kingdom is an e kingdom, and 5957
4:34 whose dominion is an e dominion, and 5957
7:14 his dominion is an e dominion, which shall 5957
7:27 whose kingdom is an e kingdom, and 5957
9:24 to bring in e righteousness, and to seal up 5769
12: 2 some to e life, and some to shame and 5769
12: 2 and some to shame and e contempt. 5769
Mic 5: 2 forth have been from of old, from e. 3117+5769
Hab 1:12 Art thou not from e, O LORD my God, 6924
3: 6 the e mountains were scattered, 5703
3: 6 the perpetual hills did bow: his ways are e. 5769
Mt 18: 8 two hands or two feet to be cast into e fire. 166
19:29 an hundredfold, and shall inherit e life. 166
25:41 Depart from me, ye cursed, into e fire, 166
25:46 And these shall go away into e punishment: 166
Lk 16: 9 they may receive you into e habitations. 166
18:30 present time, and in the world to come life e. 166
Jn 3:16 in him should not perish, but have e life. 166
3:36 He that believeth on the Son hath e life: and 166
4:14 him a well of water springing up into e life. 166
5:24 hath e life, and shall not come into 166
6:27 but for that meat which endureth unto e life, 166
6:40 and believeth on him, may have e life: 166
6:47 unto you, He that believeth on me hath e life. 166
12:50 And I know that his commandment is life e: 166
Ac 13:46 and judge yourselves unworthy of e life, 166
Ro 6:22 your fruit unto holiness, and the end e life. 166
16:26 according to the commandment of the e 166
Gal 6: 8 to the Spirit shall of the Spirit reap life e. 166
2Th 1: 9 Who shall be punished with e destruction 166
2:16 and hath given us e consolation and 166
1Ti 1:16 should hereafter believe on him to life e. 166
6:16 to whom be honour and power e. Amen. 166
Heb 13:20 through the blood of the e covenant, 166
2Pe 1:11 abundantly into the e kingdom of our Lord 166
Jude 1: 6 he hath reserved in e chains under darkness 126
Rev 14: 6 having the e gospel to preach unto them that 166

EVERMORE (26) [EVER]

Dt 28:29 and spoiled e, 3117+3605+1886.1
2Sa 22:51 unto David, and to his seed for e. 5769
2Ki 17:37 ye shall observe to do for e; 3117+3605+1886.1
1Ch 17:14 and his throne shall be established for e. 5769
Ps 16:11 at thy right hand there are pleasures for e. 5331
18:50 to David, and to his seed for e. 5769
37:27 from evil, and do good; and dwell for e. 5769
77: 8 doth his promise fail for e? 1755+1755+2050.1
86:12 my heart: and I will glorify thy name for e. 5769
89:28 My mercy will I keep for him for e, and 5769
89:52 Blessed be the LORD for e. Amen, and 5769
92: 8 But thou, LORD, art most high for e. 5769
105: 4 and his strength: seek his face e. 8548
106:31 for righteousness unto all generations for e. 5769
113: 2 the LORD from this time forth and for e. 5769
115:18 the LORD from this time forth and for e. 5769
121: 8 in from this time forth, and even for e. 5769
132:12 children also shall sit upon thy throne for e. 5703
133: 3 commanded the blessing, even life for e. 5769
Eze 37:26 set my sanctuary in the midst of them for e. 5769
37:28 shall be in the midst of them for e. 5769
Jn 6:34 they unto him, Lord, e give us this bread. 3842
2Co 11:31 which is blessed for e, knoweth that I lie not. 165
1Th 5:16 Rejoice e. 3842
Heb 7:28 maketh the Son, who is consecrated for e. 165
Rev 1:18 and behold, I am alive for e, Amen; 165+165

EVERY (1238)

Ge 1:21 and e living creature that moveth, 3605
1:21 their kind, and e winged fowl after his kind: 3605
1:25 e thing that creepeth upon the earth after 3605
1:26 over e creeping thing that creepeth upon 3605
1:28 over e living thing that moveth upon 3605
1:29 I have given you e herb bearing seed, 3605
1:29 is upon the face of all the earth, and e tree, 3605
1:30 to e beast of the earth, and to every fowl of 3605
1:30 to e fowl of the air, and to every thing that 3605
1:30 to e thing that creepeth upon the earth, 3605
1:30 is life, I have given e green herb for meat: 3605
1:31 God saw e thing that he had made, and 3605
2: 5 e plant of the field before it was in 3605
2: 5 and e herb of the field before it grew: 3605
2: 9 to grow e tree that is pleasant to the sight, 3605
2:16 Of e tree of the garden thou mayest freely 3605
2:19 LORD God formed e beast of the field, 3605
2:19 beast of the field, and e fowl of the air; 3605
2:19 Adam called e living creature, 2050.2
2:20 fowl of the air, and to e beast of the field; 3605
3: 1 Ye shall not eat of e tree of the garden? 3605
3:14 all cattle, and above e beast of the field; 3605
3:24 a flaming sword which turned e way, 2015
4:14 that e one that findeth me shall slay me. 3605
4:22 an instructor of e artificer in brass and iron: 3605
6: 5 that e imagination of the thoughts of his 3605
6:17 and e thing that is in the earth shall die. 3605
6:19 of e living thing of all flesh, two of every 3605
6:19 two of e sort shalt thou bring into the ark, 3605
6:20 of e creeping thing of the earth after his 3605
6:20 two of e sort shall come unto thee, to keep 3605
7: 2 Of e clean beast thou shalt take to thee by 3605
7: 4 e living substance that I have made will I 3605
7: 8 and of e thing that creepeth upon the earth, 3605
7:14 e beast after his kind, and all the cattle after 3605
7:14 e creeping thing that creepeth upon 3605
7:14 e fowl after his kind, every bird of every 3605
7:14 fowl after his kind, e bird of every sort. 3605
7:14 fowl after his kind, every bird of e sort. 3605
7:21 of e creeping thing that creepeth upon 3605
7:21 that creepeth upon the earth, and e man: 3605
7:23 e living substance was destroyed which 3605
8: 1 e living thing, and all the cattle that was 3605
8:17 Bring forth with thee e living thing that is 3605
8:17 of e creeping thing that creepeth upon 3605
8:19 E beast, every creeping thing, and 3605
8:19 e creeping thing, and every fowl, and 3605
8:19 e fowl, and whatsoever creepeth upon 3605
8:20 took of e clean beast, and of every clean 3605
8:20 of e clean fowl, and offered burnt offerings 3605
8:21 neither will I again smite any more e thing 3605
9: 2 the dread of you shall be upon e beast of 3605
9: 2 upon e fowl of the air, upon all that moveth 3605
9: 3 E moving thing that liveth shall be meat for 3605
9: 5 at the hand of e beast will I require it, and 3605
9: 5 at the hand of e[S] man's brother will I 2050.2
9:10 with e living creature that is with you, 3605
9:10 and of e beast of the earth with you; 3605
9:10 go out of the ark, to e beast of the earth. 3605
9:12 and e living creature that is with you, 3605
9:15 and you and e living creature of all flesh; 3605
9:16 e living creature of all flesh that is upon 3605
10: 5 e one after his tongue, after their families, 376
13:10 of Jordan, that it was well watered e where, 3605
16:12 his hand will be against e man, and 3605
16:12 every man, and e man's hand against him; 3605
17:10 E man child among you shall be 3605
17:12 e man child in your generations, he that is 3605
17:23 e male among the men of Abraham's 3605
19: 4 and young, all the people from e quarter: 7097
20:13 at e place whither we shall come, say of 3605
27:29 cursed be e one that curseth thee, and NIH
30:33 e one that is not speckled and 3605
30:35 and e one that had some white in it, and 3605
32:16 his servants, e drove by themselves; 5739+5739
34:15 If ye will be as we be, that e male of you be 3605
34:22 if e male among us be circumcised, 3605
34:23 and e beast of theirs be ours? 3605
34:24 e male was circumcised, all that went out of 3605
41:48 the field, which was round about e[S] city, 1886.1
42:25 to restore e[S] man's money into his sack, 1992.1
42:35 e[S] man's bundle of money was in his 2050.2
43:21 e man's money was in the mouth of his NIH
44: 1 and put e man's money in his sack's mouth. 376
44:11 they speedily took down e man his sack to 376
44:11 to the ground, and opened e man his sack. 376
44:13 laded e man his ass, and returned to the city. 376
45: 1 he cried, Cause e man to go out from me. 3605
46:34 for e shepherd is an abomination unto 3605
47:20 for the Egyptians sold e man his field, 376
49:28 e one according to his blessing he blessed 376
Ex 1: 1 e man and his household came with Jacob. 376
1:22 E son that is born ye shall cast into 3605
1:22 the river, and e daughter ye shall save alive. 3605
3:22 But e woman shall borrow of her neighbour, NIH
7:12 For they cast down e man his rod, and 376
9:19 for upon e man and beast which shall be 3605
9:22 upon beast, and upon e herb of the field, 3605
9:25 the hail smote e herb of the field, and brake 3605
9:25 of the field, and brake e tree of the field. 3605
10: 5 shall eat e tree which groweth for you out 3605
10:12 eat e herb of the land, even all that the hail 3605
10:15 they did eat e herb of the land, and all 3605
11: 2 let e man borrow of his neighbour, and 376
11: 2 e woman of her neighbour, jewels of silver, 802
12: 3 month they shall take to them e man a lamb, 376
12: 4 e man according to his eating shall make 376
12:16 save that which e man must eat, that only 3605
12:44 e man's servant that is bought for money, 3605

Ex 13:12 **e** firstling that cometh of a beast which 3605
13:13 **e** firstling of an ass thou shalt redeem with 3605
14: 7 of Egypt, and captains over **e one** of them. 3605
16: 4 gather a certain rate **e day**, 3117+3117+871.1
16:16 Gather of it **e man** according to his eating, 376
16:16 an omer for **e man**, *according to* 1538
16:16 take ye **e man** for *them* which *are* in his 376
16:18 they gathered **e man** according to his eating. 376
16:21 they gathered it **e morning**,
1242+1242+871.1+871.1+1886.1+1886.1
16:21 **e man** according to his eating: 376
16:29 abide ye **e man** in his place, let no man go 376
18:22 *that* **e** great matter they shall bring unto 3605
18:22 but **e** small matter they shall judge: 3605
18:26 but **e** small matter they judged themselves. 3605
25: 2 of **e** man that giveth it willingly with his 3605
26: 2 **e** one of the curtains shall have one 3605
27:18 breadth **fifty e where**, 2572+2572+871.1+1886.1
28:21 **e one** with his name shall they be according 376
29:36 thou shalt offer **e** day a bullock *for* a sin 3807.1
30: 7 burn thereon sweet incense **e morning**:
1242+1242+871.1+871.1+1886.1+1886.1
30:12 shall they give **e man** a ransom for his soul 376
30:13 **e one** that passeth among them that are 3605
30:14 **E one** that passeth among them that are 3605
31:14 *e* one that defileth it shall surely be put to NIH
32:27 Put **e man** his sword by his side, *and* go in 376
32:27 slay **e man** his brother, and every man his 376
32:27 **e man** his companion, and every man his 376
32:27 his companion, and **e man** his neighbour. 376
32:29 even **e man** upon his son, and upon his 376
33: 7 *that* **e one** which sought the LORD went 3605
33: 8 stood **e man** *at* his tent door, and 376
33:10 and worshipped, **e man** *in* his tent door. 376
34:19 **e** firstling amongst thy cattle, *whether* ox 3605
35:10 **e** wise hearted among you shall come, and 3605
35:21 **e** one whose heart stirred him up, and 3605
35:21 **e one** whom his spirit made willing, *and* 3605
35:22 **e** man that offered *offered* an offering of 3605
35:23 **e** man, with whom was found blue, and 3605
35:24 **E one** that did offer an offering of silver 3605
35:24 **e man**, with whom was found shittim wood 3605
35:29 **e** man and woman, whose heart made them 3605
36: 1 and Aholiab, and **e** wise hearted man, 3605
36: 2 and Aholiab, and **e** wise hearted man, 3605
36: 2 *even* **e one** whose heart stirred him up to 3605
36: 3 free offerings **e morning**.
1242+1242+871.1+871.1+1886.1+1886.1
36: 4 came **e man** from his work which they 376+376
36: 8 **e** wise hearted *man* among them that 3605
36:30 sockets *of* silver, under **e** board two sockets. 259
38:26 A bekah for **e** man, *that is*, half a shekel, 1886.1
38:26 for **e one** that went to be numbered, 3605
39:14 **e one** with his name, according to the twelve 376
Lev 2:13 **e** oblation of thy meat offering shalt thou 3605
6:12 burn wood on it **e morning**,
1242+1242+871.1+871.1+1886.1+1886.1
6:18 **e one** that toucheth them shall be holy. 3605
6:23 For **e** meat offering for the priest shall be 3605
7: 6 **E** male among the priests shall eat thereof: 3605
7:10 **e** meat offering, mingled with oil, and dry, 3605
11:15 **E** raven after his kind; 3605
11:21 Yet these may ye eat of **e** flying creeping 3605
11:26 *The carcases* of **e** beast which divideth 3605
11:26 **e one** that toucheth them shall be unclean. 3605
11:33 **e** earthen vessel, whereinto *any* of them 3605
11:34 all drink that may be drunk in **e** *such* vessel 3605
11:35 **e** *thing* whereupon *any part* of their carcase 3605
11:41 **e** creeping thing that creepeth upon 3605
11:46 of **e** living creature that moveth in 3605
11:46 of **e** creature that creepeth upon the earth: 3605
15: 4 **E** bed, whereon he lieth that hath the issue, 3605
15: 4 **e** thing, whereon he sitteth, shall be 3605
15:12 **e** vessel of wood shall be rinsed in water. 3605
15:17 **e** garment, and every skin, whereon is 3605
15:17 every garment, and **e** skin, whereon is 3605
15:20 **e** *thing* that she lieth upon in her separation 3605
15:20 **e** *thing* also that she sitteth upon shall be 3605
15:26 **E** bed whereon she lieth all the days of her 3605
17:15 **e** soul that eateth that which died of itself, 3605
19: 3 Ye shall fear **e man** his mother, and 376
19: 8 Therefore *e one* that eateth it shall bear his NIH
19:10 neither shalt thou gather *e* grape of thy NIH
20: 9 For **e one** that curseth his father or his 376+376
23:37 and drink offerings, **e thing** upon his day: 1697
24: 8 **E sabbath** he shall set it in order
3117+3117+7676+7676+
871.1+871.1+1886.1+1886.1
25:10 ye shall return **e man** unto his possession, 376
25:10 and ye shall return **e man** unto his family. 376
25:13 ye shall return **e man** unto his possession. 376
27:28 **e** devoted thing *is* most holy unto 3605
Nu 1: 2 of *their* names, **e** male by their polls; 3605
1: 4 with you there shall be a man of **e**^{S} tribe; 1886.1
1: 4 **e** one head of the house of his fathers. NIH
1:20 **e** male from twenty years old and upward, 3605
1:22 **e** male from twenty years old and upward, 3605
1:52 **e man** by his own camp, and every man by 376
1:52 **e man** by his own standard, throughout their 376
2: 2 **E man** of the children of Israel shall pitch by 376
2:17 **e man** in his place by their standards. 376
2:34 they set forward, **e one** after their families, 376
3:15 **e** male from a month old and upward shalt 3605
4:19 appoint them **e one** to his service and 376+376
4:30 **e one** that entereth into the service, to do 3605
4:35 **e one** that entereth into the service, 3605
4:39 **e one** that entereth into the service, 3605
4:43 **e one** that entereth into the service, 3605
4:47 **e one** that came to do the service of 3605
4:49 **e one** according to his service, and 376+376
5: 2 that they put out of the camp **e** leper, and 3605
5: 2 **e one** that hath an issue, and whosoever is 3605
5: 9 **e** offering of all the holy *things* of 3605
5:10 **e man's** hallowed *things* shall be his: 376
7: 5 to **e man** according to his service. 376

Nu 8:16 instead of such as open **e** womb, 3605
8:17 on the day that I smote **e** firstborn in 3605
11:10 their families, **e man** in the door of his tent: 376
13: 2 of **e** tribe of their fathers shall ye send a NIH
13: 2 ye send a man, **e one** a ruler among them. 3605
15:12 shall ye do to **e one** according to their NIH
16: 3 **e one** of them, and the LORD *is* among 3605
16:17 take **e man** his censer, and put incense in 376
16:17 bring ye before the LORD **e man** his 376
16:18 they took **e man** his censer, and put fire in 376
16:27 of Korah, Dathan, and Abiram, on **e side**: 5439
17: 2 take of **e** one of them a rod according to NIH
17: 2 write thou **e man's** name upon his rod. 376
17: 6 **e one** of their princes gave him a rod 3605
17: 9 and they looked, and took **e man** his rod. 376
18: 7 your priest's office for **e** thing of the altar, 3605
18: 9 **e** oblation of theirs, every meat offering of 3605
18: 9 **e** meat offering of theirs, and every sin 3605
18: 9 **e** sin offering of theirs, and every trespass 3605
18: 9 of theirs, and **e** trespass offering of theirs, 3605
18:10 *place* shalt thou eat it; **e** male shall eat it: 3605
18:11 **e one** *that is* clean in thy house shall eat of 3605
18:13 **e one** *that is* clean in thine house shall eat 3605
18:14 **E thing** devoted in Israel shall be thine. 3605
18:15 **E thing** that openeth the matrix in all flesh, 3605
18:29 Out of all your gifts ye shall offer **e** heave 3605
18:31 ye shall eat it in **e** place, ye and 3605
19:15 **e** open vessel, which hath no covering 3605
21: 8 shall come to pass, that **e one** that is bitten, 3605
23: 2 and Balaam offered on *e* altar a bullock and NIH
23: 4 I have offered upon *e* altar a bullock and NIH
23:14 and offered a bullock and a ram on *e* altar. NIH
23:30 and offered a bullock and a ram on *e* altar. NIH
25: 5 Slay ye **e one** his men that were joined unto 376
26:54 *to* **e one** shall his inheritance be given 376
28:10 burnt offering of **e sabbath**, 7676+7676+871.1
28:14 **e month** throughout 2320+2320+871.1
28:21 A several tenth deal shalt thou offer for **e** 259
29:14 three tenth deals unto **e** bullock of 259
30: 4 **e** bond wherewith she hath bound her soul 3605
30: 9 **e** vow of a widow, and of her that is 3605
30:11 **e** bond wherewith she bound her soul shall 3605
30:13 **E** vow, and every binding oath to afflict 3605
30:13 and **e** binding oath to afflict the soul, 3605
31: 4 Of **e** tribe a thousand, throughout all 1886.1
31: 5 a thousand of *e* tribe, twelve thousand NIH
31: 6 a thousand of *e* tribe, them and Phinehas NIH
31:17 therefore kill **e** male among the little ones, 3605
31:17 kill **e** woman that hath known man by lying 3605
31:23 **E** thing that may abide the fire, ye shall 3605
31:50 what **e man** hath gotten, *of* jewels of gold, 376
31:53 of war had taken spoil, **e man** for himself.) 376
32:18 Israel have inherited **e man** his inheritance. 376
32:27 **e man** armed for war, before the LORD to 3605
32:29 **e man** armed to battle, before the LORD, 3605
33:54 **e** man's *inheritance* shall be in the place 834
34:18 ye shall take one prince of **e** tribe, to divide 259
35: 8 **e one** shall give of his cities unto the Levites 376
35:15 that **e one** that killeth *any* person unawares 3605
36: 7 for **e one** of the children of Israel shall keep 376
36: 8 **e** daughter, that possesseth an inheritance in 3605
36: 8 that the children of Israel may enjoy **e man** 376
36: 9 **e one** of the tribes of the children of Israel 376
Dt 1:16 judge righteously between **e** man and his NIH
1:22 ye came near unto me **e one** of you, and 3605
1:41 when ye had girded on **e man** his weapons 376
2:34 the women, and the little ones, of **e** city, 3605
3: 6 the men, women, and children, of **e** city. 3605
3:20 shall ye return **e man** unto his possession, 376
4: 4 your God *are* alive **e one** of you *this* day. 3605
8: 3 by **e** *word* that proceedeth out of the mouth 3605
11:24 **E** place whereon the soles of your feet shall 3605
12: 2 and upon the hills, and under **e** green tree: 3605
12: 8 **e man** whatsoever *is* right in his own eyes. 376
12:13 burnt offerings in **e** place that thou seest: 3605
12:31 for **e** abomination to the LORD, which he 3605
13:16 all the spoil thereof **e whit**, for the LORD 3632
14: 6 **e** beast that parteth the hoof, and 3605
14:14 And **e** raven after his kind, 3605
14:19 **e** creeping thing that flieth *is* unclean unto 3605
15: 1 At the end of *e* seven years thou shalt make NIH
15: 2 **E** creditor that lendeth *ought* unto his 3605
16:17 **E man** *shall give* as he is able, according to 376
19: 3 three parts, that **e** slayer may flee thither. 3605
20:13 thou shalt smite **e** male thereof with 3605
21: 5 by their word shall **e** controversy and 3605
21: 5 every controversy and **e** stroke be *tried:* 3605
23: 9 then keep thee from **e** wicked thing. 3605
24:16 **e man** shall be put to death for his own sin. 376
26:11 thou shalt rejoice in **e** good *thing* which 3605
28:61 Also **e** sickness, and every plague, which *is* 3605
28:61 Also every sickness, and **e** plague, which *is* 3605
30: 9 thee plenteous in **e** work of thine hand, 3605
31:10 saying, At the end of *e* seven years, NIH
33: 3 at thy feet; *e one* shall receive of thy words. NIH
Jos 1: 3 **E** place that the sole of your foot shall tread 3605
3:12 the tribes of Israel, out of **e** tribe a man. 3807.1
4: 2 men out of the people, out of **e** tribe a man, NIH
4: 4 the children of Israel, out of **e** tribe a man: NIH
4: 5 take ye up **e man** of you a stone upon his 376
4:10 until **e** thing was finished that the LORD 3605
6: 5 the people shall ascend up **e man** straight 376
6:20 **e man** straight before him, and they took 376
11:14 **e** man they smote with the edge of 3605
21:42 These **cities** were **e one** with their 5892+5892
24:28 people depart, **e man** unto his inheritance. 376
Jdg 2: 6 the children of Israel went **e man** unto his 376
5:30 divided the prey; to **e** man a damsel *or* two; 7218
7: 5 **E one** that lappeth of the water with his 3605
7: 5 likewise **e one** that boweth down upon his 3605
7: 7 let all the *other* people go **e man** unto his 376
7: 8 he sent all the *rest of* Israel **e man** unto his 376
7:16 he put a trumpet in **e** man's hand, 3605
7:18 blow ye the trumpets also **on e side** of all 5439
7:21 they stood **e man** in his place round about 376

Jdg 7:22 the LORD set **e man's** sword against his 376
8:24 that you would give me **e man** the earrings 376
8:25 did cast therein **e man** the earrings of his 376
8:34 hands of all their enemies **on e side**: 4480+5439
9:49 all the people likewise cut down **e man** his 376
9:55 they departed **e man** unto his place. 376
16: 5 we will give thee **e one** *of us* eleven hundred 376
17: 6 **e man** did *that* which *was* right in his own 376
20:16 **e** one could sling stones at a hair *breadth*, 3605
20:48 as well the men of *e* city, as the beast, and NIH
21:11 Ye shall utterly destroy **e** male, and 3605
21:11 and **e** woman that hath lien by man. 3605
21:21 catch you **e man** his wife of the daughters of 376
21:24 **e man** to his tribe and to his family, and 376
21:24 they went out from thence **e man** to his 376
21:25 **e man** did *that* which *was* right in his own 376
1Sa 2:36 *that* **e one** that is left in thine house shall 3605
3:11 *at* which both the ears of **e one** that heareth 3605
3:18 Samuel told him **e** whit, and hid nothing 3605
4:10 and they fled **e man** into his tent: 376
8:22 the men of Israel, Go ye **e man** unto his city. 376
10:25 sent all the people away, **e man** to his house. 376
12:11 out of the hand of your enemies on **e side**, 5439
13: 2 the rest of the people he sent **e man** to his 376
13:20 to sharpen **e man** his share, and his coulter, 376
14:20 **e man's** sword was against his fellow, *and* 376
14:34 Bring me hither **e man** his ox, and 376
14:34 **e man** his sheep, and slay *them* here, and 376
14:34 all the people brought **e man** his ox with him 376
14:47 fought against all his enemies **on e side**, 5439
15: 9 **e** thing *that was* vile and refuse, that they 3605
20:15 of David **e one** from the face of the earth. 376
22: 2 **e** one *that was* in distress, and every one 3605
22: 2 **e** one that was in debt, and every one *that* 3605
22: 2 in debt, and **e** one *that was* discontented, 3605
22: 7 will the son of Jesse give **e one** of you 3605
23:14 Saul sought him **e** day, but God delivered 3605
25:10 days that break away **e man** from his master. 376
25:13 unto his men, Gird you on **e man** his sword. 376
25:13 they girded on **e man** his sword; and 376
26:23 The LORD render to **e man** his 376
27: 3 he and his men, **e man** with his household, 376
30: 6 **e man** for his sons and for his daughters: 376
30:22 save *to* **e man** his wife and his children, 376
2Sa 2: 3 David bring up, **e man** with his household: 376
2:16 they caught **e one** his fellow by the head, 376
2:27 in the morning the people had gone up **e one** 376
6:19 to **e one** a cake of bread, and a good piece *of* 376
6:19 all the people departed **e one** to his house. 376
13: 9 And they went out **e** man from him. 3605
13:29 **e man** gat him up upon his mule, and fled. 376
13:37 And *David* mourned for his son **e** day. 3605
14:26 (for it was at **e year's** end 3117+3117+3807.1
15: 4 that **e** man which hath *any* suit or 3605
15:30 that *was* with him covered **e man** his head, 376
15:36 by them ye shall send unto me **e** thing that 3605
18:17 and all Israel fled **e one** to his tent. 376
19: 8 for Israel had fled **e man** to his tent. 376
20: 1 the son of Jesse: **e man** to his tents, O Israel. 376
20: 2 So **e** man of Israel went up from after 3605
20:12 when he saw that **e one** that came by him 3605
20:22 they retired from the city, **e man** to his tent. 376
21:20 that had on **e**^{S} hand six fingers, and 2050.2
21:20 on **e**^{S} foot six toes, four and twenty *in* 2050.2
1Ki 1:49 and rose up, and went **e man** his way. 376
4:25 **e man** under his vine and under his fig tree, 376
4:27 king Solomon's table, **e man** *in* his month: 376
4:28 **e man** according to his charge. 376
5: 3 the wars which were **about** him **on e side**, 5437
5: 4 my God hath given me rest **on e side**, 5439
7:30 **e** base had four brasen wheels, and plates of 259
7:30 undersetters molten, at the side of **e** addition. 376
7:36 according to the proportion of **e one**, and 376
7:38 *and* **e** laver was four cubits: *and* upon every 259
7:38 **e**^{S} one of the ten bases one laver. 4350+1886.1
8:38 which shall know **e man** the plague of his 376
8:39 do, and give to **e man** according to his ways, 376
9: 8 **e one** that passeth by it shall be astonished, 3605
10:25 they brought **e man** his present, vessels of 376
11:15 after he had smitten **e** male in Edom; 3605
11:16 until he had cut off **e** male in Edom:) 3605
12:24 return **e man** to his house; for this thing is 376
14:23 on **e** high hill, and under every green tree. 3605
14:23 on every high hill, and under **e** green tree. 3605
19:18 and **e** mouth which hath not kissed him. 3605
20:20 they slew **e one** his man: and the Syrians 376
20:24 **e man** out of his place, and put captains in 376
22:17 let them return **e man** to his house in peace. 376
22:28 he said, Hearken, O people, **e one** of you. 3605
22:36 **E man** to his city, and every man to his own 376
22:36 to his city, and **e man** to his own country. 376
2Ki 3:19 ye shall smite **e** fenced city, and 3605
3:19 **e** choice city, and shall fell every good tree, 3605
3:19 shall fell **e** good tree, and stop all wells of 3605
3:19 and mar **e** good piece of land with stones. 3605
3:25 *on* **e** good piece of land cast every man his 3605
3:25 *on* every good piece of land cast **e man** his 376
6: 2 take thence **e man** a beam, and let us make 376
8: 9 even *of* **e** good thing of Damascus, 3605
9:13 took **e man** his garment, and put *it* under 376
11: 8 **e man** with his weapons in his hand: 376
11: 9 they took **e man** his men that were to come 376
11:11 **e man** with his weapons in his hand, 376
12: 4 *even* the money of **e one** that passeth 376
12: 4 *the account*, the money that **e** man is set at, NIH
12: 5 take *it* to them, **e man** of his acquaintance: 376
14: 6 **e man** shall be put to death for his own sin. 376
14:12 and they fled **e man** to their tents. 376
16: 4 and on the hills, and under **e** green tree. 3605
17:10 them up images and groves in **e** high hill, 3605
17:10 in every high hill, and under **e** green tree: 3605
17:29 Howbeit **e nation** made gods of their 1471+1471
17:29 **e nation** in their cities wherein they 1471+1471
18:31 *then* eat ye **e man** of his own vine, and 376
18:31 **e one** of his fig tree, and drink ye every one 376

2Ki 18:31 and drink ye **e one** the waters of his cistern: 376
23:35 of **e one** according to his taxation, to give *it* 376
25: 9 and **e** great *man's* house burnt he with fire. 3605
25:30 a daily rate for **e** day, all the days of his 871.1
1Ch 9:27 the opening *thereof* **e morning**
1242+1242+1886.1+1886.1+3807.1+3807.1
9:32 to prepare *it* **e sabbath.** 7676+7676
13: 1 and hundreds, *and* with **e** leader. 3605
13: 2 us send **abroad** unto our brethren **e where,** 6555
16: 3 he dealt to **e** one of Israel, both man and 3605
16: 3 to **e one** a loaf of bread, and a good piece *of* 376
16:37 as **e day's** work required: 3117+3117+871.1
16:43 all the people departed **e man** to his house: 376
22:15 all *manner of* cunning *men* for **e** *manner of* 3605
22:18 hath he *not* given you rest **on e side?** 4480+5439
23:30 **e morning** to thank and praise the LORD,
1242+1242+871.1+871.1+1886.1+1886.1
26:13 of their fathers, for **e gate.** 8179+8179+2050.1
26:32 for **e** matter pertaining to God, and 3605
27: 1 *of* **e** course *were* twenty and four thousand. 259
28:14 of **e kind of service:** 5656+5656+2050.1
28:15 by weight for **e candlestick,** 4501+4501+2050.1
28:15 to the use of **e candlestick.** 4501+4501+2050.1
28:16 of shewbread, for **e table;** 7979+7979+2050.1
28:17 *gold* by weight for **e bason;** 3713+3713+2050.1
28:17 weight for **e bason** of silver: 3713+3713+2050.1
28:21 **e** willing skilful *man,* for any *manner of* 3605
2Ch 1: 2 the judges, and to **e** governor in all Israel, 3605
2:14 to find out **e** device which shall be put to 3605
6:29 when **e one** shall know his own sore and 376
6:30 render unto **e man** according unto all his 376
7:21 shall be an astonishment to **e one** that 3605
8:13 after a certain rate **e day,** 3117+3117+871.1
8:14 as the duty of **e day** required: 3117+3117+871.1
8:14 by their courses at **e gate:** 8179+8179+2050.1
9:21 **e** three years once came the ships of 3807.1
9:24 they brought **e man** his present, vessels of 376
10:16 **e man** to your tents, O Israel: *and* now, 376
11: 4 return **e man** to his house, for this thing is 376
11:12 in **e** several city *he put* shields and spears, 3605
11:23 of Judah and Benjamin, unto **e** fenced city: 3605
13:11 burn unto the LORD **e morning**
1242+1242+871.1+871.1+1886.1+1886.1
13:11 **e evening** burnt sacrifices
6153+6153+871.1+871.1+1886.1+1886.1
13:11 to burn **e evening:**
6153+6153+871.1+871.1+1886.1+1886.1
14: 7 and he hath given us rest **on e side.** 4480+5439
18:16 *therefore* **e man** to his house in peace. 376
20:23 of Seir, **e one** helped to destroy another. 376
20:27 **e** man of Judah and Jerusalem, and 3605
23: 7 **e man** with his weapons in his hand; 376
23: 8 took **e man** his men that were to come in on 376
23:10 **e man** having his weapon in his hand, 376
25: 4 but **e man** shall die for his own sin. 376
25:22 before Israel, and they fled **e man** to his tent. 376
28: 4 and on the hills, and under **e** green tree. 3605
28:24 he made him altars in **e** corner of 3605
28:25 in **e** several city of Judah he made high 3605
29:35 and the drink offerings for **e** burnt offering. NIH
30:17 the passovers for **e one** *that was* not clean, 3605
30:18 The good LORD pardon **e one** 3605
31: 1 **e man** to his possession, into their own 376
31: 2 **e man** according to his service, the priests 376
31:16 *even* unto **e one** that entereth into the house 3605
31:19 in **e** several city, the men that were 3605
31:21 in **e** work that he began in the service of 3605
32:22 all *other,* and guided them **on e side.** 4480+5439
35:15 the porters *waited* at **e gate;** 8179+8179+2050.1
Ezr 2: 1 and Judah, **e one** unto his city; 376
3: 4 as the duty of **e day** required; 3117+3117+871.1
3: 5 of **e one** that willingly offered a freewill 3605
6: 5 *e one* to his place, and place *them* in NIH
8:34 By number *and* by weight of **e one:** and 3605
9: 4 were assembled unto me **e one** that 3605
10:14 them the elders of **e city,** 5892+5892+2050.1
Ne 3:28 the priests, **e one** over against his house. 376
4:15 all of us to the wall, **e one** unto his work. 376
4:17 *e one* with one of his hands wrought in NIH
4:18 **e one** had his sword girded by his side, and 376
4:22 Let **e one** with his servant lodge within 376
4:23 *saving that* **e one** put them off *for* washing. 376
5: 7 You exact usury, **e one** of his brother. 376
5:13 So God shake out **e** man from his house, 3605
7: 3 **e one** in his watch, and every one *to be* over 376
7: 3 and **e one** *to be* over against his house. 376
7: 6 and to Judah, **e one** unto his city; 376
8:16 **e one** upon the roof of his house, and in their 376
10:28 **e one** having knowledge, *and* 3605
10:31 the seventh year, and the exaction of **e** debt. 3605
11: 3 in the cities of Judah dwelt **e one** in his 376
11:20 the cities of Judah, **e one** in his inheritance. 376
11:23 for the singers, due **for e day.** 3117+3117+871.1
12:47 the porters, **e day** his portion: 3117+3117+871.1
13:10 did the work, were fled **e one** to his field. 376
13:30 and the Levites, **e one** in his business; 376
Est 1: 8 according to **e man's** pleasure. 376+376+2050.1
1:22 into **e province** according to 4082+4082+2050.1
1:22 to **e people** after their 5971+5971+2050.1
1:22 that **e** man should bear rule in his own 3605
1:22 according to the language of **e** people. 2050.2
2:11 walked **e day** 3117+3117+3605+2050.1
2:12 Now when **e maid's** turn 5291+5291+2050.1
2:13 thus came **e** maiden unto the king; NIH
3:12 that *were* over **e province,** 4082+4082+2050.1
3:12 to the rulers of **e people** of 5971+5971+2050.1
3:12 **e province** according to 4082+4082+2050.1
3:12 **e people** after their 5971+5971+2050.1
3:14 **e province** *was* 3605+4082+4082+2050.1
4: 3 in **e province,** 3605+4082+4082+2050.1
6:13 all his friends **e** *thing* that had befallen him. 3605
8: 9 *unto* **e province** according to 4082+4082+2050.1
8: 9 *unto* **e people** after their 5971+5971+2050.1
8:11 **e city** to gather 3605+5892+5892+2050.1
8:13 **e province** *was* 3605+4082+4082+2050.1
Est 8:17 in **e province,** and 3605+4082+4082+2050.1
8:17 in **e city,** 3605+5892+5892+2050.1
9:27 *appointed* time **e year;** 3605+8141+8141+2050.1
9:28 **e generation,** 1755+1755+3605+2050.1
9:28 **e family,** every province, 4940+4940+2050.1
9:28 **e province,** and every city; 4082+4082+2050.1
9:28 every province, and **e city;** 5892+5892+2050.1
Job 1: 4 and feasted *in their* houses, **e one** his day; 376
1:10 and about all that he hath **on e side?** 4480+5439
2:11 they came **e one** from his own place; 376
2:12 they rent **e one** his mantle, and 376
7:18 *that* thou shouldest visit him **e** morning, 3807.1
7:18 every morning, *and* try him **e** moment? 3807.1
12:10 In whose hand *is* the soul of **e** living *thing,* 3605
18:11 Terrors shall make him afraid **on e side,** 5439
19:10 He hath destroyed me **on e side,** and I am 5439
20:22 **e** hand of the wicked shall come *upon* him. 3605
21:33 **e** man shall draw after him, as *there are* 3605
24: 6 They reap *e one* his corn in the field: and NIH
28:10 and his eye seeth **e** precious thing. 3605
34:11 cause **e man** to find according to *his* ways. 376
36:25 **E** man may see it; man may behold *it* afar 3605
37: 7 He sealeth up the hand of **e** man; that all 3605
39: 8 and he searcheth after **e** green thing. 3605
40:11 behold **e one** *that is* proud, and abase him. 3605
40:12 Look on **e one** *that is* proud, *and* bring him 3605
42: 2 I know that thou canst do **e** *thing,* and 3605
42:11 **e man** also gave him a piece of money, and 376
42:11 of money, and **e one** an earring of gold. 376
Ps 7:11 and God is angry *with the wicked* **e** day. 3605
12: 2 They speak vanity **e one** with his neighbour: 376
12: 8 The wicked walk **on e side,** when the vilest 5439
29: 9 in his temple doth **e** one speak of *his* glory. 3605
31:13 fear *was* **on e side:** while they took 4480+5439
32: 6 For this shall **e one** *that is* godly pray unto 3605
39: 5 verily **e** man at his best state *is* altogether 3605
39: 6 Surely **e man** walketh in a vain shew: 376
39:11 like a moth: surely **e** man *is* vanity. Selah. 3605
50:10 For **e** beast of the forest *is* mine, *and* 3605
53: 3 **E one** of them is gone back, they are 3605
56: 5 **E** day they wrest my words: all their 3605
58: 8 *which* melteth, let *e one of them* pass away: NIH
62:12 for thou renderest to *e* man according to his NIH
63:11 **e one** that sweareth by him shall glory: 3605
64: 6 both the inward *thought* of **e one** *of them,* 376
65:12 and the little hills rejoice **on e side.** 2296
68:30 *till e one* submit himself with pieces of NIH
69:34 the seas, and **e** *thing* that moveth therein. 3605
71:18 *and* thy power to **e one** *that is* to come. 3605
71:21 my greatness, and comfort me **on e side.** 5437
73:14 I been plagued, and chastened **e** morning. 3807.1
84: 7 *e one of them* in Zion appeareth before God. NIH
92: 2 the morning, and thy faithfulness **e** night, 871.1
104:11 They give drink to **e** beast of the field: 3605
115: 8 unto them; *so is* **e one** that trusteth in them. 3605
119:101 I have refrained my feet from **e** evil way, 3605
119:104 therefore I hate **e** false way. 3605
119:128 all *things* to be right; *and* I hate **e** false way. 3605
119:160 **e one** of thy righteous judgments *endureth* 3605
128: 1 Blessed *is* **e one** that feareth the LORD; 3605
135:18 unto them: *so is* **e one** that trusteth in them. 3605
145: 2 **E** day will I bless thee; and I will praise thy 3605
145:16 and satisfiest the desire of **e** living thing. 3605
150: 6 Let **e** *thing that hath* breath praise 3605
Pr 1:19 So *are* the ways of **e one** that is greedy of 3605
2: 9 and judgment, and equity; *yea,* **e** good path. 3605
3:18 and happy *is* **e** one that retaineth her. NIH
7:12 in the streets, and lieth in wait at **e** corner.) 3605
13:16 **E** prudent *man* dealeth with knowledge: but 3605
14: 1 **E** wise woman buildeth her house: but NIH
14:15 The simple believeth **e** word: but 3605
15: 3 The eyes of the LORD *are* in **e** place, 3605
16: 5 **E one** *that is* proud in heart *is* an 3605
19: 6 *e man is* a friend to him that giveth gifts. 3605
20: 3 from strife: but **e** fool will be meddling. 3605
20: 6 Most men will proclaim **e one** his own 376
20:18 **E** purpose is established by counsel: and NIH
21: 2 **E** way of a man *is* right in his own eyes: 3605
21: 5 but *of* **e one** that is hasty only to want. 3605
24:12 shall *not* he render to **e** man according to his NIH
24:26 *E man* shall kiss *his* lips that giveth a right NIH
27: 7 *to the* hungry soul **e** bitter *thing is* sweet. 3605
27:24 *endure* to **e generation?** 1755+1755+2050.1
29:26 **e** man's judgment *cometh* from the LORD. NIH
30: 5 **E** word of God *is* pure: he *is* a shield unto 3605
Ecc 3: 1 To **e** *thing there is* a season, and a time to 3605
3: 1 and a time to **e** purpose under the heaven: 3605
3:11 He hath made **e** *thing* beautiful in his time: 3605
3:13 also that **e** man should eat and drink, and 3605
3:17 for *there is* a time there for **e** purpose and 3605
3:17 there for every purpose and for **e** work. 3605
4: 4 I considered all travail, and **e** right work, 3605
5:19 **E** man also to whom God hath given riches 3605
8: 6 Because to **e** purpose there is time and 3605
8: 9 applied my heart unto **e** work that is done 3605
10: 3 and he saith to **e one** *that* he *is* a fool. 3605
10:15 of the foolish wearieth **e one of them,** 5105.2
12:14 For God shall bring **e** work into judgment, 3605
12:14 with **e** secret *thing,* whether *it be* good, or 3605
SS 3: 8 **e man** *hath* his sword upon his thigh because 376
4: 2 whereof **e one** beareth twins, and none *is* 3605
6: 6 whereof **e one** beareth twins, and *there is* 3605
8:11 **e one** for the fruit thereof was to bring a 376
Isa 1:23 **e one** loveth gifts, and followeth after 3605
2:12 of hosts *shall be* upon **e one** *that is* proud 3605
2:12 and lofty, and upon **e one** that is lifted up; 3605
2:15 upon **e** high tower, and upon every fenced 3605
2:15 every high tower, and upon **e** fenced wall, 3605
3: 5 **e one** by another, and every one by his 376
3: 5 one by another, and **e one** by his neighbour: 376
4: 3 *even* **e one** that is written among the living 3605
4: 5 the LORD will create upon **e** dwelling 3605
7:22 honey shall **e** one eat that is left in the land. 3605
7:23 to pass in that day, *that* **e** place shall be, 3605
9: 5 For **e** battle of the warrior *is* with confused 3605
Isa 9:17 for **e one** *is* a hypocrite and an evildoer, 3605
9:17 an evildoer, and **e** mouth speaketh folly. 3605
9:20 they shall eat **e man** the flesh of his own 376
13: 7 be faint, and **e** man's heart shall melt: 3605
13:14 they shall **e man** turn to his own people, and 376
13:14 and flee **e one** into his own land. 376
13:15 **E one** that is found shall be thrust through; 3605
13:15 **e one** that is joined *unto them* shall fall by 3605
14:18 of them, lie in glory, **e one** in his own house. 376
15: 2 heads *shall be* baldness, *and* **e** beard cut off. 3605
15: 3 in their streets, **e** one shall howl, weeping 3605
16: 7 Moab howl for Moab, **e** one shall howl: 3605
19: 2 and they shall fight **e one** against his brother, 376
19: 2 his brother, and **e one** against his neighbour; 376
19: 7 **e thing** sown by the brooks, shall wither, 3605
19:14 they have caused Egypt to err in **e** work 3605
19:17 **e one** that maketh mention thereof shall be 3605
24:10 **e** house is shut up, that no *man may* come 3605
27: 3 keep it; I will water it **e moment:** 7281+3807.1
30:25 there shall be upon **e** high mountain, and 3605
30:25 upon **e** high hill, rivers *and* streams of 3605
30:32 *in* **e** *place* where the grounded staff shall 3605
31: 7 For in that day **e man** shall cast away his 376
33: 2 be thou their arm **e** morning, 3807.1
34:15 also be gathered, **e one** *with* her mate. 802
36:16 eat ye **e one** *of* his vine, and every one *of* his 376
36:16 **e one** *of* his fig tree, and drink ye every one 376
36:16 drink ye **e one** the waters of his own cistern; 376
40: 4 **E** valley shall be exalted, and 3605
40: 4 and **e** mountain and hill shall be made low: 3605
41: 6 They helped **e one** his neighbour; and 376
41: 6 *e one* said to his brother, Be of good NIH
43: 7 *Even* **e one** that is called by my name: for I 3605
44:23 ye mountains, O forest, and **e** tree therein: 3605
45:23 not return, That unto me **e** knee shall bow, 3605
45:23 every knee shall bow, **e** tongue shall swear. 3605
47:15 they shall wander **e one** to his quarter; 376
51:13 hast feared continually **e** day because of 3605
52: 5 my name continually **e** day *is* blasphemed. 3605
53: 6 we have turned **e one** to his own way; and 376
54:17 **e** tongue *that* shall rise against thee in 3605
55: 1 Ho, **e one** that thirsteth, come ye to 3605
56: 6 **e one** that keepeth the sabbath from 3605
56:11 **e one** for his gain, from his quarter. 376
57: 5 Inflaming yourselves with idols under **e** 3605
58: 6 go free, and *that* ye break **e** yoke? 3605
Jer 1:15 they shall set **e one** his throne *at* the entering 376
2:20 when upon **e** high hill and under every 3605
2:20 and under **e** green tree thou wanderest, 3605
3: 6 she is gone up upon **e** high mountain and 3605
3: 6 high mountain and under **e** green tree, 3605
3:13 ways to the strangers under **e** green tree, 3605
4:29 **e** city *shall be* forsaken, and not a man 3605
5: 6 **e one** that goeth out thence shall be torn in 3605
5: 8 **e one** neighed after his neighbour's wife. 376
6: 3 they shall feed **e one** *in* his place. 376
6:13 of them **e one** *is* given to covetousness; 3605
6:13 from the prophet even unto the priest **e** one 3605
6:25 of the enemy *and* fear *is* **on e side.** 4480+5439
8: 6 **e one** turned to his course, as the horse 3605
8:10 **e one** from the least even unto the greatest 3605
8:10 from the prophet even unto the priest **e one** 3605
9: 4 Take ye heed **e one** of his neighbour, and 376
9: 4 for **e** brother will utterly supplant, 3605
9: 4 **e** neighbour will walk *with* slanders. 3605
9: 5 they will deceive **e one** his neighbour, and 376
9:20 and **e one** her neighbour lamentation. 802
10:14 **E** man is brutish in *his* knowledge: 3605
10:14 **e** founder is confounded by the graven 3605
11: 8 walked **e one** in the imagination of their evil 376
12: 4 land mourn, and the herbs of **e** field wither, 3605
12:15 **e man** to his heritage, and every man to his 376
12:15 man to his heritage, and **e man** to his land. 376
13:12 of Israel, **E** bottle shall be filled *with* wine: 3605
13:12 Do we not certainly know that **e** bottle shall 3605
15:10 on usury; *yet* **e one** of them doth curse me. 3605
16:12 ye walk **e one** after the imagination of his 376
16:16 they shall hunt them from **e** mountain, and 3605
16:16 from **e** hill, and out of the holes of 3605
17:10 even to give **e man** according to his ways, 376
18:11 return ye now **e one** from his evil way, and 376
18:12 we will **e one** do the imagination of his evil 376
18:16 **e one** that passeth thereby shall be 3605
19: 8 **e one** that passeth thereby shall be 3605
19: 9 they shall eat **e one** the flesh of his friend in 376
20: 7 I am in derision daily, **e one** mocketh me. 3605
20:10 defaming of many, fear **on e side.** 4480+5439
22: 7 against thee, **e one** with his weapons: 376
22: 8 they shall say **e man** to his neighbour, 376
23:17 they say *unto* **e one** that walketh after 3605
23:27 which they tell **e man** to his neighbour, 376
23:30 that steal my words **e one** from his 376
23:35 Thus shall ye say **e one** to his neighbour, and 376
23:35 **e one** to his brother, What hath the LORD 376
23:36 for **e man's** word shall be his 376+3807.1
25: 5 Turn ye again now **e one** from his evil way, 376
26: 3 and turn **e man** from his evil way, 376
29:26 for **e** man *that is* mad, and maketh himself a 3605
30: 6 wherefore do I see **e** man *with* his hands on 3605
30:16 all thine adversaries, **e one** of them, 3605
31:25 and I have replenished **e** sorrowful soul. 3605
31:30 **e one** shall die for his own iniquity: 376
31:30 **e** man that eateth the sour grape, his teeth 3605
31:34 they shall teach no more **e man** his 376
31:34 **e man** his brother, saying, Know 376
32:19 to give **e one** according to his ways, and 376
34: 9 That **e man** should let his manservant, and 376
34: 9 and **e man** his maidservant, *being* a Hebrew 376
34:10 heard that **e one** should let his manservant, 376
34:10 and **e one** his maidservant, go free, 376
34:14 At the end of seven years let ye go **e man** his 376
34:15 in proclaiming liberty **e man** to his 376
34:16 caused **e man** his servant, and every man his 376
34:16 man his servant, and **e man** his handmaid, 376
34:17 **e one** to his brother, and every man to his 376

Jer 34:17 to his brother, and e man to his neighbour: 376
35:15 Return ye now e man from his evil way, and 376
36: 3 that they may return e man from his evil 376
36: 7 and will return e one from his evil way: 376
37:10 yet should they rise up e man in his tent, and 376
43: 6 e person that Nebuzar-adan the captain of 3605
47: 4 and Zidon e helper that remaineth: 3605
48: 8 the spoiler shall come upon e city, and 3605
48:37 For e head shall be bald, and every beard 3605
48:37 every head shall be bald, and e beard clipt: 3605
49: 5 and ye shall be driven out e man right forth; 376
49:17 e one that goeth by it shall be astonished, 3605
49:29 cry unto them, Fear is on e side. 4480+5439
50:13 e one that goeth by Babylon shall be 3605
50:16 sword they shall turn e one to his people, 376
50:16 and they shall flee e one to his own land. 376
50:42 e one put in array, like a man to the battle, NIH
51: 6 of Babylon, and deliver e man his soul: 376
51: 9 and let us go e one into his own country: 376
51:17 E man is brutish by his knowledge; 3605
51:17 e founder is confounded by the graven 3605
51:29 for e purpose of the LORD shall be NIH
51:45 deliver ye e man his soul from the fierce 376
51:56 are taken, e one of their bows is broken: NIH
52:34 e day a portion until the day 3117+3117+871.1
La 2:19 that faint for hunger in the top of e street. 3605
3:23 They are new e morning: great is thy 3807.1
4: 1 are poured out in the top of e street. 3605
Eze 1: 6 e one had four faces, and every one had four NIH
1: 6 had four faces, and e one had four wings. 259
1: 9 they went; they went e one straight forward. 376
1:11 two wings of e one were joined one to 376
1:12 they went e one straight forward: whither 376
1:23 e one had two, which covered on this side, 376
1:23 covered on this side, and e one had two, 376
6:13 upon e high hill, in all the tops of 3605
6:13 under e green tree, and under every thick 3605
6:13 every green tree, and under e thick oak, 3605
7:16 all of them mourning, e one for his iniquity. 376
8:10 behold e form of creeping things, and 3605
8:11 with e man his censer in his hand; 376
8:12 e man in the chambers of his imagery? 376
9: 1 even e man with his destroying weapon in 376
9: 2 and e man a slaughter weapon in his hand; 376
10:14 e one had four faces: the first face was NIH
10:19 e one stood at the door of the east gate of NIH
10:21 E one had four faces apiece, and every one 259
10:21 had four faces apiece, and e one four wings; 259
10:22 they went e one straight forward. 376
11: 5 that come into your mind, e one of them. NIH
12:14 I will scatter toward e wind all that are 3605
12:22 days are prolonged, and e vision faileth? 3605
12:23 days are at hand, and the effect of e vision. 3605
13:18 make kerchiefs upon the head of e stature 3605
14: 4 E man of the house of Israel that 376+376
14: 7 For e one of the house of Israel, or 376+376
16:15 pouredst out thy fornications on e one that 3605
16:24 and hast made thee a high place in e street. 3605
16:25 Thou hast built thy high place at e head of 3605
16:25 hast opened thy feet to e one that passed 3605
16:31 thine eminent place in the head of e way, 3605
16:31 and makest thine high place in e street; 3605
16:33 thee on e side for thy whoredom. 4480+5439
16:44 e one that useth proverbs shall use this 3605
17:23 under it shall dwell all fowl of e wing; 3605
18:30 house of Israel, e one according to his ways, 376
19: 8 the nations set against him on e side from 5439
20: 7 Cast ye away e man the abominations of his 376
20: 8 they did not e man cast away 376
20:28 they saw e high hill, and all the thick trees, 3605
20:39 serve ye e one his idols, and hereafter also, if 376
20:47 it shall devour e green tree in thee, and 3605
20:47 every green tree in thee, and e dry tree: 3605
21: 7 e heart shall melt, and all hands shall be 3605
21: 7 e spirit shall faint, and all knees shall be 3605
21:10 it contemneth the rod of my son, as e tree. 3605
22: 6 e one were in thee to their power to shed 376
23:22 bring them against thee on e side; 4480+5439
24: 4 even e good piece, the thigh, and 3605
26:16 shall tremble at e moment, and NIH
28:13 e precious stone was thy covering, 3605
28:23 her by the sword upon her on e side; 4480+5439
29:18 e head was made bald, and every shoulder 3605
29:18 was made bald, and e shoulder was peeled: 3605
32:10 they shall tremble at e moment, every man NIH
32:10 e man for his own life, in the day of thy fall. 376
33:20 I will judge you e one after his ways. 376
33:26 and ye defile e one his neighbour's wife: 376
33:30 e one to his brother, saying, Come, I pray 376
34: 6 all the mountains, and upon e high hill: 3605
34: 8 my flock became meat to e beast of 3605
36: 3 and swallowed you up on e side, 4480+5439
37:21 will gather them on e side, and 4480+5439
38:20 and e wall shall fall to the ground. 3605
38:21 e man's sword shall be against his brother. 376
39: 4 I will give thee unto the ravenous birds of e 3605
39:17 Speak unto e feathered fowl, and to every 3605
39:17 to e beast of the field, 3605
39:17 gather yourselves on e side to my 4480+5439
40: 7 And e little chamber was one reed long, and NIH
41: 5 the breadth of e side chamber, four cubits, NIH
41: 5 round about the house on e side. 5439
41:10 round about the house on e side. 5439+5439
41:18 and a cherub; and e cherub had two faces; NIH
43:25 Seven days shalt thou prepare e day a 3807.1
44: 5 with e going forth of the sanctuary. 3605
44:29 and e dedicate thing in Israel shall be theirs. 3605
44:30 firstfruits of all things, and e oblation of all, 3605
44:30 of e sort of your oblations, shall be 3605
45:20 day of the month for e one that erreth, 376
46:13 thou shalt prepare it e morning. 1242+1242+871.1+871.1+1886.1+1886.1
46:14 a meat offering for it e morning, 1242+1242+871.1+871.1+1886.1+1886.1
Eze 46:15 e morning for a continual burnt offering. 1242+1242+871.1+871.1+1886.1+1886.1
46:18 that my people be not scattered e man from 376
46:21 e corner of the court there was a 4740+4740
47: 9 that e thing that liveth, which moveth, 3605
47: 9 e thing shall live whither the river cometh. 3605
Da 3:10 that e man that shall hear the sound of 3606
3:29 That e people, nation, and language, 3606
6:12 that e man that shall ask a petition of any 3606
6:26 That in e dominion of my kingdom men 3606
11:36 magnify himself above e god, and 3605
12: 1 e one that shall be found written in 3605
Hos 4: 3 e one that dwelleth therein shall languish, 3605
9: 1 thou hast loved a reward upon e cornfloor. 3605
Joel 2: 7 and they shall march e one on his ways, and 376
2: 8 they shall walk e one in his path: 1397
Am 2: 8 down upon clothes laid to pledge by e altar, 3605
4: 3 e cow at that which is before her; 802
4: 4 bring your sacrifices e morning, and NIH
8: 3 there shall be many dead bodies in e place; 3605
8: 8 and e one mourn that dwelleth therein? 3605
8:10 upon all loins, and baldness upon e head; 3605
Ob 1: 9 to the end that e one of the mount of Esau 376
Jnh 1: 5 cried e man unto his god, and cast forth 376
1: 7 And they said e one to his fellow, Come, and 376
3: 8 let them turn e one from his evil way, and 376
Mic 4: 4 they shall sit e man under his vine and 376
4: 5 For all people will walk e one in the name of 376
7: 2 they hunt e man his brother with a net. 376
Hab 1:10 they shall deride e strong hold; for they 3605
Zep 2:11 men shall worship him, e one from his place, 376
2:15 e one that passeth by her shall hiss, and 3605
3: 5 e morning doth he bring his judgment 1242+1242+871.1+871.1+1886.1+1886.1
3:19 fame in e land where they have been put to 3605
Hag 1: 9 and ye run e man unto his own house. 376
2:14 so is e work of their hands; and that which 3605
2:22 e one by the sword of his brother. 376
Zec 3:10 shall ye call e man his neighbour, under 376
5: 3 for e one that stealeth shall be cut off as on 3605
5: 3 e one that sweareth shall be cut off as on 3605
7: 9 and compassions e man to his brother: 376
8: 4 e man with his staff in his hand for very age. 376
8:10 for I set all men e one against his neighbour. 376
8:16 Speak ye e man the truth to his neighbour; 376
10: 1 showers of rain, to e one grass in the field. 376
10: 4 battle bow, out of him e oppressor together. 3605
11: 6 I will deliver the men e one into his 376
11: 9 and let the rest eat e one the flesh of another. 802
12: 4 I will smite e horse with astonishment, and 3605
12: 4 will smite e horse of the people with 3605
12:12 the land shall mourn, e family apart; 4940+4940
12:14 e family apart, and their wives apart. 4940+4940
13: 4 that the prophets shall be ashamed e one of 376
14:13 they shall lay hold e one on the hand of his 376
14:16 that e one that is left of all the nations 3605
14:21 e pot in Jerusalem and in Judah shall be 3605
Mal 1:11 in e place incense shall be offered unto my 3605
2:10 why do we deal treacherously e man against 376
2:17 E one that doeth evil is good in the sight of 3605
Mt 3:10 e tree which bringeth not forth good fruit is 3956
4: 4 by e word that proceedeth out of the mouth 3956
7: 8 For e one that asketh receiveth; and he that 3956
7:17 so e good tree bringeth forth good fruit; 3956
7:19 E tree that bringeth not forth good fruit is 3956
7:21 Not e one that saith unto me, Lord, Lord, 3956
7:26 And e one that heareth these sayings of 3956
8:33 and told e thing, and what was befallen to 3956
9:35 and healing e sickness and every disease 3956
9:35 and e disease among the people. 3956
12:25 E kingdom divided against itself is brought 3956
12:25 and e city or house divided against itself 3956
12:36 That e idle word that men shall speak, 3956
13:47 cast into the sea, and gathered of e kind: 3956
13:52 Therefore e scribe which is instructed unto 3956
15:13 But he answered and said, E plant, 3956
16:27 he shall reward e man according to his 1538
18:16 three witnesses e word may be established. 3956
18:35 if ye from your hearts forgive not e one his 1538
19: 3 for a man to put away his wife for e cause? 3956
19:29 And e one that hath forsaken houses, or 3956
20: 9 eleventh hour, they received e man a penny. 303
20:10 and they likewise received e man a penny. 303
25:15 to e man according to his several ability; 1538
25:29 For unto e one that hath shall be given, and 3956
26:22 and began e one of them to say unto him, 1538
Mk 1:45 and they came to him from e quarter. 3836
7:14 Hearken unto me e one of you, and 3956
8:25 and he was restored, and saw e man clearly. 537
9:49 For e one shall be salted with fire, and 3956
9:49 and e sacrifice shall be salted with salt. 3956
13:34 and to e man his work, and commanded 1538
15:24 lots upon them, what e man should take. 5101
16:15 and preach the gospel to e creature. 3956
16:20 they went forth, and preached e where, 3837
Lk 2: 3 went to be taxed, e one into his own city. 1538
2:23 E male that openeth the womb shall be 3956
2:41 Now his parents went to Jerusalem e year 2596
3: 5 E valley shall be filled, and every mountain 3956
3: 5 and e mountain and hill shall be brought 3956
3: 9 e tree therefore which bringeth not forth 3956
4: 4 live by bread alone, but by e word of God. 3956
4:37 And the fame of him went out into e place 3956
4:40 and he laid his hands on e one of them, and 1538
5:17 which were come out of e town of Galilee, 3956
6:30 Give to e man that asketh of thee; and 3956
6:40 e one that is perfect shall be as his master. 3956
6:44 For e tree is known by his own fruit. For of 1538
8: 1 that he went throughout e city and village, 2596
8: 4 and were come to him out of e city, 2596
9: 6 preaching the gospel, and healing e where. 3837
9:43 But while they wondered e one at all things 3956
10: 1 and two before his face into e city and 3956
11: 4 for we also forgive e one that is indebted to 3956
11:10 For e one that asketh receiveth; and he that 3956
Lk 11:17 E kingdom divided against itself is brought 3956
16: 5 So he called e one of his lord's debtors unto 1538
16:16 God is preached, and e man presseth into it. 3956
16:19 fine linen, and fared sumptuously e day: 2596
18:14 for e one that exalteth himself shall be 3956
19:15 that he might know how much e man had 5101
19:26 That unto e one which hath shall be given; 3956
19:43 thee round, and keep thee in on e side, 3840
Jn 1: 9 which lighteth e man that cometh into 3956
2:10 E man at the beginning doth set forth good 3956
3: 8 so is e one that is born of the Spirit. 3956
3:20 For e one that doeth evil hateth the light, 3956
6: 7 that e one of them may take a little. 1538
6:40 that e one which seeth the Son, and 3956
6:45 E man therefore that hath heard, and 3956
7:23 I have made a man e whit whole on 3650
7:53 And e man went unto his own house. 1538
13:10 save to wash his feet, but is clean e whit: 3650
15: 2 E branch in me that beareth not fruit he 3956
15: 2 and e branch that beareth fruit, he purgeth 3956
16:32 e man to his own, and shall leave me alone: 1538
18:37 E one that is of the truth heareth my voice. 3956
19:23 and made four parts, to e soldier a part; 1538
21:25 the which, if they should be written e one, 2596
Ac 2: 5 devout men, out of e nation under heaven. 3956
2: 6 that e man heard them speak in his own 1538
2: 8 And how hear we e man in our own 1538
2:38 be baptized e one of you in the name of 1538
2:43 And fear came upon e soul: and 3956
2:45 parted them to all men, as e man had need. 5100
3:23 And it shall come to pass, that e soul, 3956
3:26 in turning away e one of you from his 1538
4:35 distribution was made unto e man 1538
5:16 unclean spirits: and they were healed e one. 537
5:42 and in e house, they ceased not to 2596+3624
8: 3 of the church, entering into e house, 2596+3624
8: 4 abroad went e where preaching the word. 1330
10:35 But in e nation he that feareth him, and 3956
11:29 e man according to his ability, 1538
13:27 which are read e sabbath day, 2596+3956
14:23 ordained them elders in e church, 1577+2596
15:21 For Moses of old time hath in e city them 2596
15:21 being read in the synagogues e 2596+3956
15:36 visit our brethren in e city where we have 3956
16:26 and e one's bands were loosed. 3956
17:27 find him, though he be not far from e one 1538
17:30 now commandeth all men e where to 3837
18: 4 And he reasoned in the synagogue e 2596+3956
20:23 Save that the Holy Ghost witnesseth in e 2596
20:31 three years I ceased not to warn e one night 1538
21:26 should be offered for e one of them. 1538
21:28 that teacheth all men e where against 3837
22:19 beat in e synagogue them that believed on 2596
26:11 And I punished them oft in e synagogue, 3956
28: 2 and received us e one, because of 3956
28:22 we know that e where it is spoken against. 3837
Ro 1:16 God unto salvation to e one that believeth; 3956
2: 6 Who will render to e man according to his 1538
2: 9 anguish, upon e soul of man that doeth evil, 3956
2:10 and peace, to e man that worketh good, 3956
3: 2 Much e way: chiefly, because that unto 3956
3: 4 yea, let God be true, but e man a liar; as it 3956
3:19 that e mouth may be stopped, and all 3956
10: 4 for righteousness to e one that believeth. 3956
12: 3 given unto me, to e man that is among you, 3956
12: 3 according as God hath dealt to e man 1538
12: 5 and e one members one of another. 2596+3588
13: 1 Let e soul be subject unto the higher 3956
14: 5 another esteemeth e day alike. Let every 3956
14: 5 e man be fully persuaded in his own mind. 1538
14:11 e knee shall bow to me, and every tongue 3956
14:11 to me, and e tongue shall confess to God. 3956
14:12 e one of us shall give account of himself to 1538
15: 2 Let e one of us please his neighbour for his 1538
1Co 1: 2 with all that in e place call upon the name 3956
1: 5 That in e thing ye are enriched by him, 3956
1:12 I say, that e one of you saith, I am of Paul; 1538
3: 5 even as the Lord gave to e man? 1538
3: 8 e man shall receive his own reward 1538
3:10 But let e man take heed how he buildeth 1538
3:13 E man's work shall be made manifest: 1538
3:13 the fire shall try e man's work of what sort 1538
4: 5 and then shall e man have praise of God. 1538
4:17 as I teach e where in every church. 3837
4:17 as I teach every where in e church. 3956
6:18 E sin that a man doeth is without the body; 3956
7: 2 let e man have his own wife, and let every 1538
7: 2 and let e woman have her own husband. 1538
7: 7 But e man hath his proper gift of God, 1538
7:17 But as God hath distributed to e man, 1538
7:17 as the Lord hath called e one, so let him 1538
7:20 Let e man abide in the same calling 1538
7:24 Brethren, let e man, wherein he is called, 1538
8: 7 Howbeit there is not in e man that 3956
9:25 And e man that striveth for the mastery is 3956
10:24 seek his own, but e man another's wealth. 1538
11: 3 you know, that the head of e man is Christ; 3956
11: 4 E man praying or prophesying, having his 3956
11: 5 But e woman that prayeth or 3956
11:21 For in eating e one taketh before other his 1538
12: 7 the Spirit is given to e man to profit withal. 1538
12:11 dividing to e man severally as he will. 1538
12:18 But now hath God set the members e one of 1538
14:26 e one of you hath a psalm, hath a doctrine, 1538
15:23 But e man in his own order: Christ 1538
15:30 And why stand we in jeopardy e hour? 3956
15:38 pleased him, and to e seed his own body. 1538
16: 2 Upon the first day of the week let e one of 1538
16:16 and to e one that helpeth with us, and 3956
2Co 2:14 savour of his knowledge by us in e place. 3956
4: 2 to e man's conscience in the sight of God. 3956
4: 8 We are troubled on e side, yet not 3956
5:10 that e one may receive the things done in 1538
7: 5 we were troubled on e side; without were 3956
8: 7 as ye abound in e thing, in faith, and 3956

2Co 9: 7 E man according as he purposeth in his 1538
9: 8 in all things, may abound to e good work: 3956
9:11 Being enriched in e thing to all 3956
10: 5 e high thing that exalteth itself against 3956
10: 5 bringing into captivity e thought to 3956
13: 1 three witnesses shall e word be established. 3956
Gal 3:10 Cursed is e one that continueth not in all 3956
3:13 Cursed is e one that hangeth on a tree: 3956
5: 3 For I testify again to e man that is 3956
6: 4 But let e man prove his own work, and 1538
6: 5 For e man shall bear his own burden. 1538
Eph 1:21 and dominion, and e name that is named, 3956
4: 7 But unto e one of us is given grace 1538
4:14 and carried about with e wind of doctrine, 3956
4:16 compacted by that which e joint supplieth, 3956
4:16 working in the measure of e part, 1520+1538
4:25 speak e man truth with his neighbour: 1538
5:24 let the wives be to their own husbands in e 3956
5:33 Nevertheless let e one of you in particular 1538
Php 1: 3 I thank my God upon e remembrance of 3956
1: 4 Always in e prayer of mine for you all 3956
1:18 notwithstanding, e way, whether in 3956
2: 4 Look not e man on his own things, but 1538
2: 4 but e man also on the things of others. 1538
2: 9 given him a name which is above e name: 3956
2:10 That at the name of Jesus e knee should 3956
2:11 And that e tongue should confess that Jesus 3956
4: 6 but in e thing by prayer and supplication 3956
4:12 e where and in all things I am instructed 3956
4:21 Salute e saint in Christ Jesus. The brethren 3956
Col 1:10 being fruitful in e good work, and 3956
1:15 invisible God, the firstborn of e creature: 3956
1:23 which was preached to e creature which is 3956
1:28 warning e man, and teaching every man in 3956
1:28 and teaching e man in all wisdom; 3956
1:28 that we may present e man perfect in Christ 3956
4: 6 may know how ye ought to answer e man. 1538
1Th 1: 8 also in e place your faith to God-ward is 3956
2:11 and comforted and charged e one of you, 1538
4: 4 That e one of you should know how to 1538
5:18 In e thing give thanks: for this is the will of 3956
2Th 1: 3 the charity of e one of you all towards each 1538
2:17 and stablish you in e good word and work. 3956
3: 6 that ye withdraw yourselves from e brother 3956
3:17 own hand, which is the token in e epistle: 3956
1Ti 2: 8 I will therefore that men pray e where, 3956
4: 4 For e creature of God is good, and 3956
5:10 if she have diligently followed e good 3956
2Ti 2:19 Let e one that nameth the name of Christ 3956
2:21 and prepared unto e good work. 3956
4:18 And the Lord shall deliver me from e evil 3956
Tit 1: 5 and ordain elders in e city, as I had 2596
1:16 and unto e good work reprobate. 3956
3: 1 to be ready to e good work, 3956
Phm 1: 6 e good thing which is in you in Christ 3956
Heb 2: 2 and e transgression and 3956
2: 9 grace of God should taste death for e man. 3956
3: 4 For e house is builded by some man; but 3956
5: 1 For e high priest taken from among men is 3956
5:13 For e one that useth milk is unskilful in 3956
6:11 And we desire that e one of you do shew 1538
8: 3 For e high priest is ordained to offer gifts 3956
8:11 And they shall not teach e man his 1538
8:11 and e man his brother, saying, Know 1538
9: 7 went the high priest alone once e year, NIG
9:19 For when Moses had spoken e precept to 3956
9:25 the holy place e year with blood of others; 2596
10: 3 a remembrance again made of sins e year. 2596
10:11 And e priest standeth daily ministering and 3956
12: 1 let us lay aside e weight, and the sin which 3956
12: 6 and scourgeth e son whom he receiveth. 3956
13:21 Make you perfect in e good work to do his 3956
Jas 1:14 But e man is tempted, when he is drawn 1538
1:17 E good gift and every perfect gift is from 3956
1:17 good gift and e perfect gift is from above, 3956
1:19 let e man be swift to hear, slow to speak, 3956
3: 7 For e kind of beasts, and of birds, and 3956
3:16 strife is, there is confusion and e evil work. 3956
1Pe 1:17 judgeth according to e man's work, 1538
2:13 Submit yourselves to e ordinance of man 3956
3:15 be ready always to give an answer to e man 3956
4:10 As e man hath received the gift, even so 1538
1Jn 2:29 ye know that e one which doeth 3956
3: 3 And e man that hath this hope in him 3956
4: 1 believe not e spirit, but try the spirits 3956
4: 2 E spirit that confesseth that Jesus Christ is 3956
4: 3 And e spirit that confesseth not that Jesus 3956
4: 7 and e one that loveth is born of God, and 3956
5: 1 e one that loveth him that begat loveth him 3956
Rev 1: 7 and e eye shall see him, and they also 3956
2:23 I will give unto e one of you according to 1538
5: 8 having e one of them harps, and 1538
5: 9 us to God by thy blood out of e kindred, 3956
5:13 And e creature which is in heaven, and 3956
6:11 And white robes were given unto e one of 1538
6:14 and e mountain and island were moved out 3956
6:15 and the mighty men, and e bondman, and e 3956
6:15 e free man, hid themselves in the dens and 3956
14: 6 and to e nation, and kindred, and tongue, 3956
16: 3 dead man: and e living soul died in the sea. 3956
16:20 And e island fled away, and the mountains 3956
16:21 e stone about the weight of a talent: NIG
18: 2 and the hold of e foul spirit, and a cage of 3956
18: 2 and a cage of e unclean and hateful bird. 3956
18:17 And e shipmaster, and all the company in 3956
20:13 they were judged e man according to their 1538
21:21 e several gate was of one pearl: 1538
22: 2 and yielded her fruit e month: 1520+1538+2596
22:12 to give e man according as his work shall 1538
22:18 For I testify unto e man that heareth 3956

EVI (2)

Nu 31: 8 namely, E, and Rekem, and Zur, and Hur, 189
Jos 13:21 E, and Rekem, and Zur, and Hur, and Reba, 189

EVIDENCE (7) [EVIDENCES]

Jer 32:10 I subscribed the e, and sealed it, and 5612
32:11 So I took the e of the purchase, both that 5612
32:12 I gave the e of the purchase unto Baruch 5612
32:14 this e of the purchase, both which is sealed, 5612
32:14 which is sealed, and this e which is open; 5612
32:16 Now when I had delivered the e of 5612
Heb 11: 1 things hoped for, the e of things not seen. 1650

EVIDENCES (2) [EVIDENCE]

Jer 32:14 Take these e, this evidence of the purchase, 5612
32:44 subscribe e, and seal them, and 5612

EVIDENT (5) [EVIDENTLY]

Job 6:28 look upon me; for it is e unto you if I lie. 6440
Gal 3:11 by the law in the sight of God, it is e: 1212
Php 1:28 which is to them an e token of perdition, 1732
Heb 7:14 For it is e that our Lord sprang out of Juda; 4271
7:15 And it is yet far more e: for that after 2612

EVIDENTLY (2) [EVIDENT]

Ac 10: 3 He saw in a vision e, about the ninth hour 5320
Gal 3: 1 eyes Jesus Christ hath been e set forth, 4270

EVIL (613) [EVILDOER, EVILDOERS, EVILS]

Ge 2: 9 and the tree of knowledge of good and e. 7451
2:17 of the tree of the knowledge of good and e, 7451
3: 5 ye shall be as gods, knowing good and e. 7451
3:22 become as one of us, to know good and e: 7451
6: 5 of his heart was only e continually. 7451
8:21 for the imagination of man's heart is e from 7451
19:19 lest some e take me, and I die: 7451
37: 2 Joseph brought unto his father their e 7451
37:20 will say, Some e beast hath devoured him: 7451
37:33 son's coat; an e beast hath devoured him; 7451
44: 4 Wherefore have ye rewarded e for good? 7451
44: 5 he divineth? ye have done e in so doing. 7489
44:34 lest peradventure I see the e that shall come 7451
47: 9 e have the days of the years of my life 7451
48:16 The Angel which redeemed me from all e, 7451
50:15 will certainly requite us all the e which we 7451
50:17 and their sin; for they did unto thee e: 7451
50:20 But as for you, ye thought e against me; but 7451
Ex 5:19 that they were in e case, after it was said, 7451
5:22 hast thou so e entreated this people? 7489
5:23 in thy name, he hath done e to this people; 7489
10:10 little ones: look to it; for e is before you. 7451
23: 2 Thou shalt not follow a multitude to do e; 7451
32:12 and repent of this e against thy people. 7451
32:14 the LORD repented of the e which he 7451
33: 4 when the people heard these e tidings, they 7451
Lev 5: 4 pronouncing with his lips to do e, or to do 7489
26: 6 I will rid e beasts out of the land, 7451
Nu 13:32 they brought up an e report of the land 1681
14:27 How long shall I bear with this e 7451
14:35 I will surely do it unto all this e 7451
14:37 Even those men that did bring up the e 7451
20: 5 of Egypt, to bring us in unto this e place? 7451
32:13 that had done e in the sight of the LORD, 7451
Dt 1:35 men of this e generation see that good land, 7451
1:39 day had no knowledge between good and e, 7451
4:25 shall do e in the sight of the LORD thy 7451
7:15 will put none of the e diseases of Egypt, 7451
13: 5 So shalt thou put the e away from the midst 7451
15: 9 thine eye be e against thy poor brother, and 7489
17: 1 is blemish, or any e favouredness: 1697+7451
17: 7 So thou shalt put the e away from among 7451
17:12 and thou shalt put away the e from Israel. 7451
19:19 shalt thou put the e away from among you. 7451
19:20 henceforth commit no more any such e 7451
21:21 so shalt thou put e away from among you; 7451
22:14 bring up an e name upon her, and say, I 7451
22:19 he hath brought up an e name upon a virgin 7451
22:21 so shalt thou put e away from among you. 7451
22:22 so shalt thou put away e from Israel. 7451
22:24 so thou shalt put away e from among you. 7451
24: 7 and thou shalt put e away from among you. 7451
26: 6 the Egyptians e entreated us, and 7489
28:54 his eye shall be e toward his brother, and 3415
28:56 her eye shall be e towards the husband of 3415
29:21 the LORD shall separate him unto e out of 7451
30:15 this day life and good, and death and e; 7451
31:29 e will befall you in the latter days; because 7451
31:29 ye will do e in the sight of the LORD, 7451
Jos 23:15 shall the LORD bring upon you all e 7451
24:15 if it seem e unto you to serve the LORD, 7489
Jdg 2:11 the children of Israel did e in the sight of 7451
2:15 hand of the LORD was against them for e, 7451
3: 7 the children of Israel did e in the sight of 7451
3:12 the children of Israel did e again in 7451
3:12 they had done e in the sight of the LORD. 7451
4: 1 the children of Israel again did e in 7451
6: 1 the children of Israel did e in the sight of 7451
9:23 God sent an e spirit between Abimelech 7451
9:57 all the e of the men of Shechem did God 7451
10: 6 the children of Israel did e again in 7451
13: 1 the children of Israel did e again in 7451
20:13 them to death, and put away e from Israel. 7451
20:34 but they knew not that e was near them. 7451
20:41 for they saw that e was come upon them. 7451
1Sa 2:23 for I hear of your e dealings by all this 7451
6: 9 then he hath done us this great e: 7451
12:19 for we have added unto all our sins this e, 7451
15:19 and didst e in the sight of the LORD? 7451
16:14 an e spirit from the LORD troubled him. 7451
16:15 an e spirit from God troubleth thee. 7451
16:16 when the e spirit from God is upon thee, 7451
16:23 when the e spirit from God was upon Saul, NIH
16:23 and the e spirit departed from him. 7451
18:10 that the e spirit from God came upon Saul, 7451
19: 9 the e spirit from the LORD was upon 7451
20: 7 be sure that e is determined by him. 7451
20: 9 for if I knew certainly that e were 7451
20:13 but if it please my father to do thee e, then 7451
1Sa 24:11 see that there is neither e nor transgression 7451
24:17 me good, whereas I have rewarded thee e. 7451
25: 3 the man was churlish and e in his doings; 7451
25:17 for e is determined against our master, and 7451
25:21 and he hath requited me e for good. 7451
25:26 they that seek e to my lord, be as Nabal. 7451
25:28 e hath not been found in thee all thy days. 7451
25:39 of Nabal, and hath kept his servant from e: 7451
26:18 have I done? or what e is in mine hand? 7451
29: 6 for I have not found e in thee since the day 7451
2Sa 3:39 the LORD shall reward the doer of e 7451
12: 9 of the LORD, to do e in his sight? 7451
12:11 I will raise up e against thee out of thine 7451
13:16 this e in sending me away is greater than 7451
15:14 bring e upon us, and smite the city with 7451
17:14 to the intent that the LORD might bring e 7451
19: 7 that will be worse unto thee than all the e 7451
19:35 and can I discern between good and e? can 7451
24:16 the LORD repented him of the e, and 7451
1Ki 5: 4 that there is neither adversary nor e 7451
9: 9 the LORD brought upon them all this e. 7451
11: 6 Solomon did e in the sight of the LORD, 7451
13:33 Jeroboam returned not from his e way, 7451
14: 9 hast done e above all that were before thee: 7489
14:10 I will bring e upon the house of Jeroboam, 7451
14:22 And Judah did e in the sight of the LORD, 7451
15:26 he did e in the sight of the LORD, and 7451
15:34 he did e in the sight of the LORD, and 7451
16: 7 even for all the e that he did in the sight of 7451
16:19 For his sins which he sinned in doing e in 7451
16:25 Omri wrought e in the eyes of the LORD, 7451
16:30 Ahab the son of Omri did e in the sight of 7451
17:20 hast thou also brought e upon the widow 7489
21:20 thou hast sold thyself to work e in the sight 7451
21:21 I will bring e upon thee, and will take away 7451
21:29 before me, I will not bring the e in his days: 7451
21:29 in his son's days will I bring the e upon his 7451
22: 8 not prophesy good concerning me, but e. 7451
22:18 prophesy no good concerning me, but e? 7451
22:23 the LORD hath spoken e concerning thee. 7451
22:52 he did e in the sight of the LORD, and 7451
2Ki 3: 2 he wrought e in the sight of the LORD; 7451
6:33 he said, Behold, this e is of the LORD; 7451
8:12 Because I know the e that thou wilt do unto 7451
8:18 and he did e in the sight of the LORD. 7451
8:27 did e in the sight of the LORD, as did 7451
13: 2 he did that which was e in the sight of 7451
13:11 he did that which was e in the sight of 7451
14:24 he did that which was e in the sight of 7451
15: 9 he did that which was e in the sight of 7451
15:18 he did that which was e in the sight of 7451
15:24 he did that which was e in the sight of 7451
15:28 he did that which was e in the sight of 7451
17: 2 he did that which was e in the sight of 7451
17:13 Turn ye from your e ways, and keep my 7451
17:17 sold themselves to do e in the sight of 7451
21: 2 he did that which was e in the sight of 7451
21: 9 Manasseh seduced them to do more e than 7451
21:12 I am bringing such e upon Jerusalem and 7451
21:15 Because they have done that which was e 7451
21:16 in doing that which was e in the sight of 7451
21:20 he did that which was e in the sight of 7451
22:16 I will bring e upon this place, and upon 7451
22:20 thine eyes shall not see all the e which I 7451
23:32 he did that which was e in the sight of 7451
23:37 he did that which was e in the sight of 7451
24: 9 he did that which was e in the sight of 7451
24:19 he did that which was e in the sight of 7451
1Ch 2: 3 of Judah, was e in the sight of the LORD; 7451
4:10 that thou wouldest keep me from e, that it 7451
7:23 because it went e with his house. 7451
21:15 he repented him of the e, and said to 7451
21:17 that have sinned and done e indeed; 7489+7489
2Ch 7:22 hath he brought all this e upon them. 7451
12:14 he did e, because he prepared not his heart 7451
18: 7 prophesied good unto me, but always e: 7451
18:17 would not prophesy good unto me, but e? 7451
18:22 and the LORD hath spoken e against thee. 7451
20: 9 If, when e cometh upon us, as the sword, 7451
21: 6 he wrought that which was e in the eyes of 7451
22: 4 Wherefore he did e in the sight of 7451
29: 6 done that which was e in the eyes of 7451
33: 2 did that which was e in the sight of 7451
33: 6 he wrought much e in the sight of 7451
33:22 he did that which was e in the sight of 7451
34:24 I will bring e upon this place, and upon 7451
34:28 neither shall thine eyes see all the e that I 7451
36: 5 he did that which was e in the sight of 7451
36: 9 he did that which was e in the sight of 7451
36:12 he did that which was e in the sight of 7451
Ezr 9:13 after all that is come upon us for our e 7451
Ne 6:13 that they might have matter for an e report, 7451
9:28 they had rest, they did e again before thee: 7451
13: 7 understood of the e that Eliashib did for 7451
13:17 What e thing is this that ye do, and 7451
13:18 did not our God bring all this e upon us, 7451
13:27 then hearken unto you to do all this great e, 7451
Est 7: 7 for he saw that there was e determined 7451
8: 6 For how can I endure to see the e that shall 7451
Job 1: 1 and one that feared God, and eschewed e. 7451
1: 8 one that feareth God, and escheweth e? 7451
2: 3 one that feareth God, and escheweth e? 7451
2:10 hand of God, and shall we not receive e? 7451
2:11 heard of all this e that was come upon him, 7451
5:19 yea, in seven there shall no e touch thee. 7451
8:20 man, neither will he help the e doers: 7489
24:21 He e entreateth the barren that beareth not: 7462
28:28 and to depart from e is understanding. 7451
30:26 e came unto me: and when I waited for 7451
31:29 or lift up myself when e found him: 7451
35:12 because of the pride of e men. 7451
42:11 comforted him over all the e that 7451
Ps 5: 4 neither shall e dwell with thee. 7451
7: 4 If I have rewarded e unto him that was at 7451
10:15 the e man: seek out his wickedness till thou 7451

E

Ps 15: 3 his tongue, nor doeth **e** to his neighbour, 7451
21:11 For they intended **e** against thee: 7451
23: 4 of the shadow of death, I will fear no **e**: 7451
34:13 Keep thy tongue from **e**, and thy lips from 7451
34:14 Depart from **e**, and do good; seek peace, 7451
34:16 of the LORD *is* against them that do **e**, 7451
34:21 **E** shall slay the wicked: and they that hate 7451
35:12 They rewarded me **e** for good *to* 7451
36: 4 a way *that is* not good; he abhorreth not **e**. 7451
37: 8 fret not thyself in any wise to **do e**. 7489
37:19 They shall not be ashamed in the **e** time: 7451
37:27 Depart from **e**, and do good; and dwell for 7451
38:20 They also that render **e** for good are mine 7451
40:14 and put to shame that wish me **e**. 7451
41: 5 Mine enemies speak **e** of me, When shall 7451
41: 8 An **e** disease, *say they,* cleaveth fast unto 1100
49: 5 Wherefore should I fear in the days of **e**, 7451
50:19 Thou givest thy mouth to **e**, and thy tongue 7451
51: 4 have I sinned, and done *this* **e** in thy sight: 7451
52: 3 Thou lovest **e** more than good; *and* 7451
54: 5 He shall reward **e** unto mine enemies: 7451
56: 5 all their thoughts *are* against me for **e**. 7451
64: 5 They encourage themselves *in* an **e** matter: 7451
78:49 trouble, *by* sending **e** angels *among them.* 7451
90:15 *and* the years *wherein* we have seen **e**. 7451
91:10 There shall no **e** befall thee, neither shall 7451
97:10 Ye that love the LORD, hate **e**: 7451
109: 5 And they have rewarded me **e** for good, and 7451
109:20 and of them that speak **e** against my soul. 7451
112: 7 He shall not be afraid of **e** tidings: his heart 7451
119:101 I have refrained my feet from every **e** way, 7451
121: 7 The LORD shall preserve thee from all **e**: 7451
140: 1 Deliver me, O LORD, from the **e** man: 7451
140:11 Let not an **e speaker** be established in 376+3956
140:11 **e** shall hunt the violent man to overthrow 7451
141: 4 Incline not my heart to *any* **e** thing, 7451
Pr 1:16 For their feet run to **e**, and make haste to 7451
1:33 and shall be quiet from fear of **e**. 7451
2:12 To deliver thee from the way of the **e** *man,* 7451
2:14 Who rejoice to do **e**, *and* delight in 7451
3: 7 fear the LORD, and depart from **e**. 7451
3:29 Devise not **e** against thy neighbour, 7451
4:14 and go not in the way of **e** *men.* 7451
4:27 nor *to* the left: remove thy foot from **e**. 7451
5:14 I was almost in all **e** in the midst of 7451
6:24 To keep thee from the **e** woman, from 7451
8:13 The fear of the LORD *is* to hate **e**: pride, 7451
8:13 the **e** way, and the froward mouth, do I 7451
11:19 he that pursueth **e** *pursueth it* to his own 7451
12:12 The wicked desireth the net of **e** *men:* but 7451
12:20 *is* in the heart of them that imagine **e**: 7451
12:21 There shall no **e** happen to the just: but 205
13:19 *it is* abomination to fools to depart from **e**. 7451
13:21 **E** pursueth sinners: but to the righteous 7451
14:16 A wise *man* feareth, and departeth from **e**: 7451
14:19 The **e** bow before the good; and the wicked 7451
14:22 Do they not err that devise **e**? but mercy 7451
15: 3 every place, beholding the **e** and the good. 7451
15:15 All the days of the afflicted *are* **e**: but 7451
15:28 the mouth of the wicked poureth out **e** 7451
16: 4 even the wicked for the day of **e**. 7451
16: 6 the fear of the LORD *men* depart from **e**. 7451
16:17 highway of the upright *is* to depart from **e**: 7451
16:27 An ungodly man diggeth up **e**: and in his 7451
16:30 moving his lips he bringeth **e** to pass. 7451
17:11 An **e** *man* seeketh only rebellion: therefore 7451
17:13 Whoso rewardeth **e** for good, evil shall not 7451
17:13 for good, **e** shall not depart from his house. 7451
19:23 he shall not be visited *with* **e**. 7451
20: 8 scattereth *away* all **e** with his eyes. 7451
20:22 Say not thou, I will recompense **e**; *but* 7451
20:30 The blueness of a wound cleanseth away **e**: 7451
21:10 The soul of the wicked desireth **e**: 7451
22: 3 A prudent *man* foreseeth the **e**, and 7451
23: 6 Eat thou not the bread of *him that hath* an **e** 7451
24: 1 Be not thou envious against **e** men, 7451
24: 8 He that deviseth to **do e** shall be called a 7489
24:19 of **e** *men,* neither be thou envious at 7489
24:20 For there shall be no reward to the **e** *man;* 7451
27:12 A prudent *man* foreseeth the **e**, *and* 7451
28: 5 **E** men understand not judgment: but 7451
28:10 the righteous to go astray in an **e** way, 7451
28:22 He that hasteth to be rich *hath* an **e** eye, and 7451
29: 6 In the transgression of an **e** man *there is* a 7451
30:32 or if thou hast **thought e**, *lay thine* hand 2161
31:12 him good and not **e** all the days of her life. 7451
Ecc 2:21 This also *is* vanity and a great **e**. 7451
4: 3 who hath not seen the **e** work that is done 7451
5: 1 for they consider not that *they* do **e**. 7451
5:13 There is a sore **e** *which* I have seen under 7451
5:14 those riches perish by **e** travail: and 7451
5:16 this also *is* a sore **e**, *that* in all points as he 7451
6: 1 There is an **e** which I have seen under 7451
6: 2 this *is* vanity, and it *is* an **e** disease. 7451
8: 3 stand not in an **e** thing; for he doeth 7451
8: 5 the commandment shall feel no **e** thing: 7451
8:11 Because sentence *against* an **e** work is not 7451
8:11 the sons of men is fully set in them to do **e**. 7451
8:12 Though a sinner do **e** an hundred *times,* and 7451
9: 3 This *is* an **e** among all *things* that are done 7451
9: 3 also the heart of the sons of men is full *of* **e**, 7451
9:12 as the fishes that are taken in an **e** net, and 7451
9:12 so *are* the sons of men snared in an **e** time, 7451
10: 5 There is an **e** *which* I have seen under 7451
11: 2 for thou knowest not what **e** shall be upon 7451
11:10 thy heart, and put away **e** from thy flesh: 7451
12: 1 while the **e** days come not, nor the years 7451
12:14 whether *it be* good, or whether *it be* **e**. 7451
Isa 1:16 put away the **e** of your doings from before 7455
1:16 from before mine eyes; cease to **do e**; 7489
3: 9 for they have rewarded **e** unto themselves. 7451
5:20 Woe unto them that call **e** good, and good 7451
5:20 unto them that call evil good, and good **e**; 7451
7: 5 have taken **e** counsel against thee, saying, 7451
7:15 that he may know to refuse the **e**, and 7451
Isa 7:16 before the child shall know to refuse the **e**, 7451
13:11 I will punish the world for *their* **e**, and 7451
31: 2 will bring **e**, and will not call back his 7451
32: 7 The instruments also of the churl *are* **e**: 7451
33:15 and shutteth his eyes from seeing **e**; 7451
41:23 yea, do good, or **do e**, that we may be 7489
45: 7 I make peace, and create **e**: I the LORD 7451
47:11 Therefore shall **e** come upon thee; 7451
56: 2 and keepeth his hand from doing any **e**. 7451
57: 1 is taken away from the **e** *to come.* 7451
59: 7 Their feet run to **e**, and they make haste to 7451
59:15 he *that* departeth from **e** maketh himself a 7451
65:12 did **e** before mine eyes, and did choose *that* 7451
66: 4 they did **e** before mine eyes, and chose *that* 7451
Jer 1:14 Out of the north an **e** shall break forth upon 7451
2: 3 **e** shall come upon them, saith the LORD. 7451
2:19 and see that *it is* an **e** *thing* and bitter, 7451
3: 5 and done **e** *things* as thou couldest. 7451
3:17 more after the imagination of their **e** heart. 7451
4: 4 quench *it,* because of the **e** of your doings. 7455
4: 6 for I will bring **e** from the north, and a great 7451
4:22 they *are* wise to **do e**, but to do good they 7489
5:12 *It is* not he; neither shall **e** come upon us; 7451
6: 1 for **e** appeareth out of the north, and 7451
6:19 behold, I will bring **e** upon this people, 7451
7:24 *and* in the imagination of their **e** heart, 7451
7:30 For the children of Judah have done **e** in 7451
8: 3 residue of them that remain of this **e** family, 7451
9: 3 for they proceed from **e** to evil, and they 7451
9: 3 for they proceed from evil to **e**, and they 7451
10: 5 for they cannot **do e**, neither also *is it* in 7489
11: 8 one in the imagination of their **e** heart: 7451
11:11 Behold, I *will* bring **e** upon them, 7451
11:15 when thou **doest e**, then thou rejoicest. 7451
11:17 hath pronounced **e** against thee, 7451
11:17 for the **e** of the house of Israel and of 7451
11:23 for I will bring **e** upon the men of 7451
12:14 Thus saith the LORD against all mine **e** 7451
13:10 This **e** people, which refuse to hear my 7451
13:23 also do good, that are accustomed to **do e**. 7489
15:11 enemy to entreat thee *well* in the time of **e**, 7451
16:10 pronounced all this great **e** against us? 7451
16:12 one after the imagination of his **e** heart, 7451
17:17 unto me: thou *art* my hope in the day of **e**. 7451
17:18 bring upon them the day of **e**, and 7451
18: 8 whom I have pronounced, turn from their **e**, 7451
18: 8 I will repent of the **e** that I thought to do 7451
18:10 If it do **e** in my sight, that *it* obey not my 7451
18:11 I frame **e** against you, and devise a device 7451
18:11 return ye now every one from his **e** way, 7451
18:12 every one do the imagination of his **e** heart. 7451
18:20 Shall **e** be recompensed for good? for they 7451
19: 3 Behold, I *will* bring **e** upon this place, 7451
19:15 upon all her towns all the **e** that I have 7451
21:10 I have set my face against this city for **e**, 7451
21:12 quench *it,* because of the **e** of your doings. 7455
23: 2 I will visit upon you the **e** of your doings, 7455
23:10 their course is **e**, and their force *is* not right. 7451
23:12 for I will bring **e** upon them, *even* the year 7451
23:17 his own heart, No **e** shall come upon you. 7451
23:22 they should have turned them from their **e** 7451
23:22 evil way, and from the **e** of their doings. 7455
24: 3 the **e**, very evil, that cannot be eaten, 7451
24: 3 the evil, very **e**, that cannot be eaten, 7451
24: 3 that cannot be eaten, they are so **e**. 7455
24: 8 as the **e** figs, which cannot be eaten, 7451
24: 8 which cannot be eaten, they are so **e**; 7455
25: 5 Turn ye again now every one from his **e** 7451
25: 5 from the **e** of your doings, and dwell in 7455
25:29 I begin to **bring e** on the city which is 7489
25:32 **e** *shall* go forth from nation to nation, and 7451
26: 3 and turn every man from his **e** way, 7451
26: 3 that I may repent me of the **e**, which I 7451
26: 3 unto them because of the **e** of their doings. 7455
26:13 the LORD will repent him of the **e** that he 7451
26:19 the LORD repented him of the **e** which he 7451
26:19 Thus *might* we procure great **e** against our 7451
28: 8 of war, and of **e**, and of pestilence. 7451
29:11 thoughts of peace, and not of **e**, 7451
29:17 vile figs, that cannot be eaten, they are so **e**. 7455
32:23 thou hast caused all this **e** to come upon 7451
32:30 the children of Judah have only done **e** 7451
32:32 Because of all the **e** of the children of Israel 7451
32:42 Like as I have brought all this great **e** upon 7451
35:15 Return ye now every man from his **e** way, 7451
35:17 the **e** that I have pronounced against them: 7451
36: 3 all the **e** which I purpose to do unto them; 7451
36: 3 that they may return every man from his **e** 7451
36: 7 and will return every one from his **e** way: 7451
36:31 all the **e** that I have pronounced against 7451
38: 9 these men have **done e** in all that they have 7489
39:16 I *will* bring my words upon this city for **e**, 7451
40: 2 LORD thy God hath pronounced this **e** 7451
41:11 heard of all the **e** that Ishmael the son of 7451
42: 6 Whether *it be* good, or whether *it be* **e**, 7451
42:10 for I repent me of the **e** that I have done 7451
42:17 escape from the **e** that I *will* bring upon 7451
44: 2 Ye have seen all the **e** that I have brought 7451
44: 7 Wherefore commit ye *this* great **e** against 7451
44:11 I will set my face against you for **e**, and 7451
44:17 of victuals, and were well, and saw no **e**. 7451
44:22 because of the **e** of your doings, *and* 7455
44:23 therefore this **e** is happened unto you, as *at* 7451
44:27 I *will* watch over them for **e**, and not for 7451
44:29 words shall surely stand against you for **e**: 7451
45: 5 for behold, I *will* bring **e** upon all flesh, 7451
48: 2 in Heshbon they have devised **e** against it; 7451
49:23 for they have heard **e** tidings: they are 7451
49:37 I will bring **e** upon them, *even* my fierce 7451
51:24 unto all the inhabitants of Chaldea all their **e** 7451
51:60 So Jeremiah wrote in a book all the **e** that 7451
51:64 shall not rise from the **e** that I *will* bring 7451
52: 2 he did *that which was* **e** in the eyes of 7451
La 3:38 mouth of the most High proceedeth not **e** 7451
Eze 5:16 When I shall send upon them the **e** arrows 7451
Eze 5:17 will I send upon you famine and **e** beasts, 7451
6:10 in vain that *I* would do this **e** unto them. 7451
6:11 Alas for all the **e** abominations of the house 7451
7: 5 An **e**, an only evil, behold, is come. 7451
7: 5 An evil, an only **e**, behold, is come. 7451
14:22 ye shall be comforted concerning the **e** that 7451
33:11 turn ye, turn ye from your **e** ways; for why 7451
34:25 will cause the **e** beasts to cease out of 7451
36:31 shall ye remember your own **e** ways, and 7451
38:10 thy mind, and thou shalt think an **e** thought: 7451
Da 9:12 judged us, by bringing upon us a great **e**: 7451
9:13 law of Moses, all this **e** is come upon us: 7451
9:14 hath the LORD watched upon the **e**, 7451
Joel 2:13 great kindness, and repenteth him of the **e**. 7451
Am 3: 6 shall there be **e** in a city, and the LORD 7451
5:13 keep silence in that time; for it *is* an **e** time. 7451
5:14 Seek good, and not **e**, that ye may live: and 7451
5:15 Hate the **e**, and love the good, and 7451
6: 3 Ye that put far away the **e** day, and 7451
9: 4 I will set mine eyes upon them for **e**, and 7451
9:10 The **e** shall not overtake nor prevent us. 7451
Jnh 1: 7 that we may know for whose cause this **e** *is* 7451
1: 8 for whose cause this **e** *is* upon us; 7451
3: 8 let them turn every one from his **e** way, and 7451
3:10 that they turned from their **e** way; 7451
3:10 God repented of the **e**, that he had said that 7451
4: 2 great kindness, and repentest thee of the **e**. 7451
Mic 1:12 **e** came down from the LORD unto 7451
2: 1 and work **e** upon their beds! 7451
2: 3 Behold, against this family do I devise an **e**, 7451
2: 3 shall ye go haughtily: for this time *is* **e**. 7451
3: 2 Who hate the good, and love the **e**; 7451
3:11 among us? none **e** can come upon us. 7451
7: 3 That *they* may do **e** with both hands 7451
Na 1:11 that imagineth **e** against the LORD, 7451
Hab 1:13 *Thou art* of purer eyes than to behold **e**, and 7451
2: 9 Woe to him that coveteth an **e** covetousness 7451
2: 9 *he* may be delivered from the power of **e**! 7451
Zep 1:12 will not do good, neither will he **do e**. 7489
3:15 of thee: thou shalt not see **e** any more. 7451
Zec 1: 4 Turn ye now from your **e** ways, and 7451
1: 4 your evil ways, and *from* your **e** doings: 7451
7:10 let none of you imagine **e** against his 7451
8:17 let none of you imagine **e** in your hearts 7451
Mal 1: 8 if ye offer the blind for sacrifice, *is it* not **e**? 7451
1: 8 and if ye offer the lame and sick, *is it* not **e**? 7451
2:17 Every one that doeth **e** *is* good in the sight 7451
Mt 5:11 shall say all manner of **e** against you *4190*
5:37 whatsoever is more than these cometh of **e**. *4190*
5:39 But I say unto you, That *ye* resist not **e**: but *4190*
5:45 for he maketh his sun to rise on the **e** and *4190*
6:13 not into temptation, but deliver us from **e**: *4190*
6:23 But if thine eye be **e**, thy whole body shall *4190*
6:34 Sufficient unto the day *is* the **e** thereof. *2549*
7:11 If ye then, being **e**, know how to give good *4190*
7:17 but a corrupt tree bringeth forth **e** fruit. *4190*
7:18 A good tree cannot bring forth **e** fruit, *4190*
9: 4 Wherefore think ye **e** in your hearts? *4190*
12:34 generation of vipers, how can ye, being **e**, *4190*
12:35 an **e** man out of the evil treasure bringeth *4190*
12:35 an evil man out of the **e** treasure bringeth *4190*
12:35 of the evil treasure bringeth forth **e** *things.* *4190*
12:39 An **e** and adulterous generation seeketh *4190*
15:19 For out of the heart proceed **e** thoughts, *4190*
20:15 what I will with mine own? Is thine eye **e**, *4190*
24:48 *and* if that **e** servant shall say in his heart, *2556*
27:23 governor said, Why, what **e** hath he done? *2556*
Mk 3: 4 to do good on the sabbath days, or to **do e**? *2554*
7:21 proceed **e** thoughts, adulteries, fornications, *2556*
7:22 an **e** eye, blasphemy, pride, foolishness: *4190*
7:23 All these **e** *things* come from within, and *4190*
9:39 in my name, that can lightly **speak e** of me. *2551*
15:14 said unto them, Why, what **e** hath he done? *2556*
Lk 6: 9 on the sabbath days to do good, or to **do e**? *2554*
6:22 reproach *you,* and cast out your name as **e**, *4190*
6:35 he is kind unto the unthankful and *to the* **e**. *4190*
6:45 an **e** man out of the evil treasure of his *4190*
6:45 an evil man out of the **e** treasure of his *4190*
6:45 of his heart bringeth forth that which is **e**: *4190*
7:21 and plagues, and of **e** spirits; *4190*
8: 2 which had been healed of **e** spirits and *4190*
11: 4 not into temptation; but deliver us from **e**. *4190*
11:13 If ye then, being **e**, know how to give good *4190*
11:29 he began to say, This is an **e** generation: *4190*
11:34 but when *thine eye* is **e**, thy body also *is* *4190*
16:25 and likewise Lazarus **e** *things:* but now he *2556*
23:22 the third time, Why, what **e** hath he done? *2556*
Jn 3:19 than light, because their deeds were **e**. *4190*
3:20 For every one that doeth **e** hateth the light, *5337*
5:29 and they that have done **e**, unto *5337*
7: 7 I testify of it, that the works thereof are **e**. *4190*
17:15 that thou shouldest keep them from the **e**. *4190*
18:23 Jesus answered him, If I have spoken **e**, *2560*
18:23 If I have spoken evil, bear witness of the **e**: *2556*
Ac 7: 6 and **entreat** *them* **e** four hundred years. *2559*
7:19 and **e entreated** our fathers, so that *they* *2559*
9:13 how much **e** he hath done to thy saints at *2556*
14: 2 **made** their minds **e affected** against *2559*
19: 9 **spake e** of *that* way before the multitude, *2551*
19:12 and the **e** spirits went out of them. *4190*
19:13 had **e** spirits the name of the Lord Jesus, *4190*
19:15 And the **e** spirit answered and said, Jesus I *4190*
19:16 And the man in whom the **e** spirit was leapt *4190*
23: 5 Thou shalt not speak **e** of the ruler of thy *2560*
23: 9 strove, saying, We find no **e** in this man: *2556*
24:20 if they have found any **e doing** in me, *92*
Ro 1:30 inventors of **e** *things,* disobedient to *2556*
2: 9 upon every soul of man that doeth **e**, *2556*
3: 8 we say,) Let us do **e**, that good may come? *2556*
7:19 but the **e** which I would not, that I do. *2556*
7:21 I would do good, **e** is present with me. *2556*
9:11 neither having done any good or **e**, *2556*
12: 9 Abhor *that which is* **e**; cleave to *that which* *4190*
12:17 Recompense to no *man* **e** for evil. *2556*
12:17 Recompense to no *man* evil for **e**. *2556*

Ro 12:21 Be not overcome of **e**, but overcome evil 2556
12:21 of evil, but overcome **e** with good. 2556
13: 3 are not a terror to good works, but to the **e**. 2556
13: 4 But if thou do *that which is* **e**, be afraid; 2556
13: 4 to *execute* wrath upon him that doeth **e**. 2556
14:16 Let not then your good be **e spoken of**: 987
14:20 *it is* **e** for *that* man who eateth with offence. 2556
16:19 *which is* good, and simple concerning **e**. 2556
1Co 10: 6 to the intent we should not lust after **e** 2556
10:30 why am I **e spoken of** for *that for* which I 987
13: 5 is not easily provoked, thinketh no **e**; 2556
15:33 **e** communications corrupt good manners. 2556
2Co 6: 8 dishonour, by **e report** and good report: 1426
13: 7 Now I pray to God that ye do no **e**; not that 2556
Gal 1: 4 that he might deliver us from *this* present **e** 4190
Eph 4:31 and anger, and clamour, and **e speaking**, 988
5:16 the time, because the days are **e**. 4190
6:13 that ye may be able to withstand in the **e** 4190
Php 3: 2 Beware of dogs, beware of **e** workers, 2556
Col 3: 5 **e** concupiscence, and covetousness, 2556
1Th 5:15 See that none render **e** for evil unto any 2556
5:15 See that none render evil for **e** unto any 2556
5:22 Abstain from all appearance of **e**. 4190
2Th 3: 3 shall stablish you, and keep *you* from **e**. 4190
1Ti 6: 4 cometh envy, strife, railings, **e** surmisings, 4190
6:10 For the love of money is the root of all **e**: 2556
2Ti 2: 9 as an **e doer**, *even* unto bonds; 2557
3:13 But **e** men and seducers shall wax worse 4190
4:14 Alexander the coppersmith did me much **e**: 2556
4:18 And the Lord shall deliver me from every **e** 4190
Tit 1:12 *are* alway liars, **e** beasts, slow bellies. 2556
2: 8 having no **e** *thing* to say of you. 5337
3: 2 To **speak e** of no *man*, to be no brawlers, *but* 987
Heb 3:12 lest there be in any of you an **e** heart of 4190
5:14 exercised to discern both good and **e**. 2556
10:22 having *our* hearts sprinkled from an **e** 4190
Jas 1:13 for God cannot be tempted with **e**, 2556
2: 4 and are become judges of **e** thoughts? 4190
3: 8 *it is* an unruly **e**, full of deadly poison. 2556
3:16 *is*, there *is* confusion and every **e** work. 5337
4:11 **Speak** not **e** one of another, brethren. 2635
4:11 He that **speaketh e** of *his* brother, and 2635
4:11 **speaketh e** of the law, and judgeth the law: 2635
4:16 in your boastings: all such rejoicing is **e**. 4190
1Pe 2: 1 and envies, and all **e speakings**, 2636
3: 9 Not rendering **e** for evil, or railing for 2556
3: 9 Not rendering evil for **e**, or railing for 2556
3:10 let him refrain his tongue from **e**, and 2556
3:11 Let him eschew **e**, and do good; let him 2556
3:12 face of the Lord *is* against them that do **e**. 2556
3:16 that, whereas they **speak e** of you, as of 2635
3:17 *ye* suffer for well doing, than for **e doing**. 2554
4: 4 the same excess of riot, **speaking e** *of you*: 987
4:14 on their part he is **e spoken of**, but on your 987
2Pe 2: 2 whom the way of truth shall be **e spoken of**. 987
2:10 they are not afraid to **speak e** of dignities. 987
2:12 **speak e** of *the things* that they understand 987
1Jn 3:12 Because his own works were **e**, and his 4190
2Jn 1:11 him God speed is partaker of his **e** deeds. 4190
3Jn 1:11 follow not *that which is* **e**, but *that which is* 2556
1:11 but he that **doeth e** hath not seen God. 2554
Jude 1: 8 despise dominion, and **speak e** of dignities. 987
1:10 But these **speak e** of those *things* which they 987
Rev 2: 2 how thou canst not bear *them which are* **e**: 2556

EVILDOER (2) [EVIL]

Isa 9:17 for every one *is* a hypocrite and an **e**, and 7489
1Pe 4:15 or *as* an **e**, or as a busybody in other men's 2555

EVILDOERS (13) [EVIL]

Ps 26: 5 I have hated the congregation of **e**; and 7489
37: 1 Fret not thyself because of **e**, neither be 7489
37: 9 For **e** shall be cut off: but those that wait 7489
94:16 Who will rise up for me against the **e**? *or* 7489
119:115 Depart from me, ye **e**: for I will keep 7489
Isa 1: 4 a seed of **e**, children that are corrupters: 7489
14:20 the seed of **e** shall never be renowned. 7489
31: 2 but will arise against the house of the **e**, and 7489
Jer 20:13 the soul of the poor from the hand of **e**. 7489
23:14 they strengthen also the hands of **e**, 7489
1Pe 2:12 that, whereas they speak against you as **e**, 2555
2:14 are sent by him for the punishment of **e**, 2555
3:16 whereas they speak evil of you, as of **e**, 2555

EVIL-MERODACH (2)

2Ki 25:27 *day* of the month, *that* **E** king of Babylon, 192
Jer 52:31 *that* **E** king of Babylon in the *first* year of his 192

EVILS (9) [EVIL]

Dt 31:17 and many **e** and troubles shall befall them; 7451
31:17 Are not these **e** come upon us, because our 7451
31:18 for all the **e** which they shall have wrought, 7451
31:21 when many **e** and troubles are befallen 7451
Ps 40:12 For innumerable **e** have compassed me 7451
Jer 2:13 For my people have committed two **e**; 7451
Eze 6: 9 they shall lothe themselves for the **e** which 7451
20:43 sight for all your **e** that ye have committed. 7451
Lk 3:19 and for all the **e** which Herod had done, 4190

EWE (7) [EWES]

Ge 21:28 Abraham set seven **e lambs** of the flock by 3535
21:29 What *mean* these seven **e lambs** which 3535
21:30 For *these* seven **e lambs** shalt thou take of 3535
Lev 14:10 one **e lamb** of the first year without 3535
22:28 *whether it be* cow or **e**, ye shall not kill it 7716
Nu 6:14 one **e lamb** of the first year without 3535
2Sa 12: 3 save one little **e lamb**, which he had bought 3535

EWES (3) [EWE]

Ge 31:38 thy **e** and thy she goats have not cast their 7353
32:14 he goats, two hundred **e**, and twenty rams, 7353
Ps 78:71 From following the **e** great with young he NIH

EXACT (8) [EXACTED, EXACTETH, EXACTION, EXACTIONS, EXACTORS]

Dt 15: 2 release *it;* he shall not **e** *it* of his neighbour, 5065
15: 3 Of a foreigner thou mayest **e** *it again:* but 5065
Ne 5: 7 the rulers, and said unto them, You **e** usury, 5378
5:10 *might* **e** of them money and corn: 5383
5:11 the wine, and the oil, that ye **e** of them. 5383
Ps 89:22 The enemy shall not **e** upon him; nor 5378
Isa 58: 3 you find pleasure, and **e** all your labours. 5065
Lk 3:13 **E** no more than that which is appointed 4238

EXACTED (2) [EXACT]

2Ki 15:20 Menahem **e** the money of Israel, *even* of all 3318
23:35 he **e** the silver and the gold of the people of 5065

EXACTETH (1) [EXACT]

Job 11: 6 that God **e** of thee *less* than thine iniquity 5382

EXACTION (1) [EXACT]

Ne 10:31 and the **e of** every **debt**. 3027+4853

EXACTIONS (1) [EXACT]

Eze 45: 9 justice, take away your **e** from my people, 1646

EXACTORS (1) [EXACT]

Isa 60:17 officers peace, and thine **e** righteousness. 5065

EXALT (26) [EXALTED, EXALTEST, EXALTETH]

Ex 15: 2 my father's God, and I will **e** him. 7311
1Sa 2:10 his king, and **e** the horn of his anointed. 7311
Job 17: 4 shalt thou not **e** *them.* 7311
Ps 34: 3 with me, and let us **e** his name together. 7311
37:34 and he shall **e** thee to inherit the land: 7311
66: 7 let not the rebellious **e** themselves. Selah. 7311
92:10 my horn shalt thou **e** like *the horn of* an 7311
99: 5 **E** ye the LORD our God, and worship at 7311
99: 9 **E** the LORD our God, and worship at his 7311
107:32 Let them **e** him also in the congregation of 7311
118:28 praise thee: *thou art* my God, I will **e** thee. 7311
140: 8 his wicked device; *lest* they **e** themselves. 7311
Pr 4: 8 **E** her, and she shall promote thee: she shall 5549
Isa 13: 2 **e** the voice unto them, shake the hand, 7311
14:13 I will **e** my throne above the stars of God: 7311
25: 1 I will **e** thee, I will praise thy name; 7311
Eze 21:26 **e** *him that is* low, and abase *him that is* 1361
29:15 neither shall it **e** itself any more above 5375
31:14 by the waters **e** themselves for their height, 1361
Da 11:14 also the robbers of thy people shall **e** 5375
11:36 he shall **e** himself, and magnify himself 7311
Hos 11: 7 to the most High, none at all would **e** *him.* 7311
Ob 1: 4 Though thou **e** *thyself* as the eagle, and 1361
Mt 23:12 And whosoever shall **e** himself shall be 5312
2Co 11:20 if a man take *of you,* if a man **e** himself, 1869
1Pe 5: 6 of God, that he may **e** you in due time: 5312

EXALTED (64) [EXALT]

Nu 24: 7 than Agag, and his kingdom shall be **e**. 5375
1Sa 2: 1 the LORD, mine horn is **e** in the LORD: 7311
2Sa 5:12 that he had **e** his kingdom for his people 5375
22:47 be the God of the rock of my salvation. 7311
1Ki 1: 5 Adonijah the son of Haggith **e** himself, 5375
14: 7 Forasmuch as I **e** thee from among 7311
16: 2 Forasmuch as I **e** thee out of the dust, and 7311
2Ki 19:22 against whom hast thou **e** *thy* voice, and 7311
1Ch 29:11 and *thou* art **e** as head **above** all. 5375
Ne 9: 5 which *is* **e** above all blessing and praise. 7311
Job 5:11 that those which mourn may be **e** *to* safety. 7682
24:24 They are **e** for a little while, but are gone 7426
36: 7 doth establish them for ever, and they are **e**. 1361
Ps 12: 8 on every side, when the vilest men are **e**. 7311
13: 2 how long shall mine enemy be **e** over me? 7311
18:46 and let the God of my salvation be **e**. 7311
21:13 Be thou **e**, LORD, in thine own strength: 7311
46:10 I will be **e** among the heathen, I will be 7311
46:10 among the heathen, I will be **e** in the earth. 7311
47: 9 the earth *belong* unto God: he is greatly **e**. 5927
57: 5 Be thou **e**, O God, above the heavens; 7311
57:11 Be thou **e**, O God, above the heavens: 7311
75:10 *but* the horns of the righteous shall be **e**. 7311
89:16 and in thy righteousness shall they be **e**. 7311
89:17 and in thy favour our horn shall be **e**. 7311
89:19 I have **e** *one* chosen out of the people. 7311
89:24 and in my name shall his horn be **e**. 7311
97: 9 all the earth: thou art **e** far above all gods. 5927
108: 5 Be thou **e**, O God, above the heavens: and 7311
112: 9 for ever; his horn shall be **e** with honour. 7311
118:16 The right hand of the LORD is **e**: the right 7426
Pr 11:11 By the blessing of the upright the city is **e**: 7311
Isa 2: 2 and *shall be* **e** above the hills; 5375
2:11 and the LORD alone shall be **e** in that day. 7682
2:17 and the LORD alone shall be **e** in that day. 7682
5:16 the LORD of hosts shall be **e** in judgment, 1361
12: 4 make mention that his name *is* **e**. 7682
30:18 unto you, and therefore will he be **e**, 7311
33: 5 The LORD *is* **e**; for he dwelleth on high: 7682
33:10 I rise, saith the LORD; now will I be **e**; 7426
37:23 against whom hast thou **e** *thy* voice, and 7311
40: 4 Every valley shall be **e**, and every mountain 5375
49:11 a way, and my highways shall be **e**. 7311
52:13 he shall be **e** and extolled, and be very high. 7311
Eze 17:24 have **e** the low tree, have dried up the green 1361
19:11 her stature was **e** among the thick branches, 1361
31: 5 Therefore his height was **e** above all 1361
Hos 13: 1 spake trembling, he **e** *himself* in Israel; 5375
13: 6 they were filled, and their heart was **e**; 7311
Mic 4: 1 and *it shall be* **e** above the hills; 5375
Mt 11:23 Capernaum, which art **e** unto heaven, 5312
23:12 and he that shall humble himself shall be **e**. 5312
Lk 1:52 from *their* seats, and **e** them of low degree. 5312
10:15 Capernaum, which art **e** to heaven, 5312
14:11 and he that humbleth himself shall be **e**. 5312
18:14 and he that humbleth himself shall be **e**. 5312
Ac 2:33 Therefore being by the right hand of God **e**, 5312
5:31 Him hath God **e** with his right hand *to be* a 5312
13:17 **e** the people when *they* dwelt as strangers 5312
2Co 11: 7 in abasing myself that you might be **e**, 5312
12: 7 And lest I should be **e above measure** 5229
12: 7 lest I should be **e above measure**. 5229
Php 2: 9 Wherefore God also hath **highly e** him, and 5251
Jas 1: 9 brother of low degree rejoice in that he is **e**: 5311

EXALTEST (1) [EXALT]

Ex 9:17 As yet **e** thou thyself against my people, 5549

EXALTETH (9) [EXALT]

Job 36:22 Behold, God **e** by his power: who teacheth 7682
Ps 148:14 He also **e** the horn of his people, the praise 7311
Pr 14:29 but *he that is* hasty of spirit **e** folly. 7311
14:34 Righteousness **e** a nation: but sin *is* a 7311
17:19 *and* he that **e** his gate seeketh destruction. 1361
Lk 14:11 For whosoever **e** himself shall be abased; 5312
18:14 for every one that **e** himself shall be 5312
2Co 10: 5 every high thing that **e** itself against 1869
2Th 2: 4 and **e** himself above all that is called God, 5229

EXAMINATION (1) [EXAMINE]

Ac 25:26 O king Agrippa, that, after **e** had, 351

EXAMINE (5) [EXAMINATION, EXAMINED, EXAMINING]

Ezr 10:16 first day of the tenth month to **e** the matter. 1875
Ps 26: 2 **E** me, O LORD, and prove me; try my 974
1Co 9: 3 Mine answer to them that do **e** me is this: 350
11:28 But let a man **e** himself, and so let him eat 1381
2Co 13: 5 **E** yourselves, whether ye be in the faith; 3985

EXAMINED (6) [EXAMINE]

Lk 23:14 and behold, I, having **e** *him* before you, 350
Ac 4: 9 If we this day be **e** of the good deed done to 350
12:19 he **e** the keepers, and commanded that *they* 350
22:24 and bade that he should be **e** by scourging; 426
22:29 departed from him which should have **e** him: 426
28:18 Who, when they had **e** me, would have let 350

EXAMINING (1) [EXAMINE]

Ac 24: 8 by **e** of whom thyself mayest take 350

EXAMPLE (8) [EXAMPLES]

Mt 1:19 and not willing to **make** her **a publick e**, 3856
Jn 13:15 For I have given you an **e**, that ye should do 5262
1Ti 4:12 but be thou an **e** of the believers, in word, 5179
Heb 4:11 lest any *man* fall after the same **e** of 5262
8: 5 Who serve unto the **e** and shadow of 5262
Jas 5:10 for an **e** of suffering affliction, and 5262
1Pe 2:21 Christ also suffered for us, leaving us an **e**, 5261
Jude 1: 7 after strange flesh, are set forth for an **e**, 1164

EXAMPLES (1) [EXAMPLE]

1Co 10: 6 Now these *things* were our **e**, to the intent 5179

EXCEED (4) [EXCEEDED, EXCEEDEST, EXCEEDETH, EXCEEDING, EXCEEDINGLY]

Dt 25: 3 Forty stripes he may give him, *and* not **e**: 3254
25: 3 *if* he should **e**, and beat him above these 3254
Mt 5:20 **e** *the righteousness* of the scribes 4052+4183
2Co 3: 9 the ministration of righteousness **e** in glory. 4052

EXCEEDED (3) [EXCEED]

1Sa 20:41 wept one with another, until David **e**. 1431
1Ki 10:23 So king Solomon **e** all the kings of 1431+4480
Job 36: 9 and their transgressions that they have **e**. 1396

EXCEEDEST (1) [EXCEED]

2Ch 9: 6 told me: *for* thou **e** the fame that I heard. 3254

EXCEEDETH (1) [EXCEED]

1Ki 10: 7 and prosperity **e** the fame which I heard. 3254

EXCEEDING (59) [EXCEED]

Ge 15: 1 I *am* thy shield, *and* thy **e** great reward. 3966
17: 6 I will make thee **e** fruitful, and 3966+3966+871.1
27:34 he cried with a great and **e** bitter cry, 3966+5704
Ex 1: 7 and waxed **e** mighty, 3966+3966+871.1
19:16 and the voice of the trumpet **e** loud; 3966
Nu 14: 7 to search it, *is* an **e** good land. 3966+3966
1Sa 2: 3 Talk no more *so* **e proudly**; let *not* 1364+1364
2Sa 8: 8 king David took **e** much brass. 3966
12: 2 The rich *man* had **e** many flocks and herds: 3966
1Ki 4:29 and understanding **e** much, 3966
7:47 because they were **e** many: 3966+3966
1Ch 20: 2 he brought also **e** much spoil *out* of 3966
22: 5 the LORD *must be* **e** magnifical, 4605+1886.5
2Ch 11:12 and spears, and made them **e** strong, 3966+7235
14:14 for there was **e** much spoil in them. NIH
16:12 until his disease *was* **e** 4605+1886.5+3807.1
32:27 Hezekiah had **e** much riches and honour: 3966
Ps 21: 6 thou hast made him **e** glad with thy 871.1
43: 4 unto the altar of God, unto God my **e** joy: 8057
119:96 *but* thy commandment *is* **e** broad. 3966
Pr 30:24 upon the earth, but they *are* **e wise**: 2449+2450
Ecc 7:24 and **e deep**, who can find it out? 6013+6013
Jer 48:29 heard the pride of Moab; *he is* **e** proud: 3966
Eze 9: 9 of Israel and Judah *is* **e** great, 3966+3966+871.1
16:13 thou wast **e** beautiful, and 3966+3966+871.1
23:15 **e in dyed attire** upon their heads, 2871+5628
37:10 up upon their feet, an **e** great army. 3966+3966
47:10 as the fish of the great sea, **e** many. 3966
Da 3:22 *was* urgent, and the furnace **e** hot, 3493
6:23 was the king **e** glad for him, and 7690
7:19 **e** dreadful, whose teeth *were of* iron, and 3493
8: 9 which waxed **e** great, toward the south, and 3499
Jnh 3: 3 Now Nineveh was an **e** great city of 430+3807.1
4: 6 Jonah was **e glad** of the gourd. 1419+8055+8057
Mt 2:10 saw the star, they rejoiced *with* **e** great joy. 4970
2:16 was **e** wroth, and sent forth, and slew all 3029
4: 8 the devil taketh him *up* into an **e** high 3029

Mt 5:12 Rejoice, and be **e glad**: for great *is* your *21*
8:28 e fierce, so that no *man* might pass by that *3029*
17:23 be raised *again*. And they were **e** sorry. *4970*
26:22 And they were **e** sorrowful, and *4970*
26:38 My soul is **e sorrowful**, *even* unto death: *4036*
Mk 6:26 And the king was **e sorry**; *yet* for his oaths' *4036*
9: 3 raiment became shining, **e** white as snow; *3029*
14:34 My soul is **e sorrowful** unto death: *4036*
Lk 23: 8 And when Herod saw Jesus, he was **e** glad: *3029*
Ac 7:20 was born, and was **e fair**, *791+2316+3588*
Ro 7:13 might become **e** sinful. *2596+5236*
2Co 4:17 for us a **far more e** *1519+2596+5236+5236*
7: 4 I am **e** joyful in all our tribulation. *5248*
9:14 which long after you for the **e** grace of God *5235*
Eph 1:19 And what *is* the **e** greatness of his power to *5235*
2: 7 **e** riches of his grace in *his* kindness *5235*
3:20 Now unto him that is able to do **e** *5228*
1Ti 1:14 And the grace of our Lord was **e abundant** *5250*
1Pe 4:13 be revealed, ye may be glad also with **e joy**. *21*
2Pe 1: 4 Whereby are given unto us **e great** and *3176*
Jude 1:24 before the presence of his glory with **e joy**, *20*
Rev 16:21 the hail; for the plague thereof was **e** great. *4970*

EXCEEDINGLY (39) [EXCEED]

Ge 7:19 the waters prevailed **e** upon the earth; 3966+3966
13:13 and sinners before the LORD **e**. 3966
16:10 I will **multiply** thy seed **e**, that it 7235+7235
17: 2 and will multiply thee **e**. 3966+3966+871.1
17:20 will multiply him **e**; 3966+3966+871.1
27:33 Isaac trembled very **e**, and said, Who? 1419
30:43 the man increased **e**, and had much 3966+3966
47:27 and grew, and multiplied **e**. 3966
1Sa 26:21 played the fool, and have erred **e**. 3966+7235
2Sa 13:15 Amnon **hated** her **e**; so 1419+3966+8130+8135
2Ki 10: 4 they were **e** afraid, and said, Behold, 3966+3966
1Ch 29:25 **e** in the sight of all Israel, 4605+1886.5+3807.1
2Ch 1: 1 and magnified him **e**. 4605+1886.5+3807.1
17:12 waxed great **e**; 4605+5704+1886.5+3807.1
26: 8 *himself* **e**. 4605+5704+1886.5+3807.1
Ne 2:10 heard *of it*, it **grieved** them **e** 1419+7451+7489
Est 4: 4 was the queen **e** grieved; and she sent 3966
Job 3:22 Which **rejoice e**, *and* are glad, 413+1524+8056
Ps 68: 3 yea, let them **e rejoice**. 7797+8057+871.1
106:14 **lusted e** in the wilderness, and 183+8378
119:167 kept thy testimonies; and *I* love them **e**. 3966
123: 3 upon us: for we are **e** filled *with* contempt. 7227
123: 4 Our soul is **e** filled *with* the scorning of 7227
Isa 24:19 the earth is **moved e**. 4131+4131
Da 7: 7 dreadful and terrible, and strong **e**; 3493
Jnh 1:10 were the men **e afraid**, 1419+3372+3374
1:16 the men **feared** the LORD **e**, 1419+3372+3374
4: 1 it **displeased** Jonah **e**, and he 1419+3415+7451
Mt 19:25 When his disciples heard *it*, they were **e** *4970*
Mk 4:41 And they feared **e**, and said one to another, *3173*
15:14 And they cried out the **more e**, Crucify *4056*
Ac 16:20 being Jews, do **e trouble** our city, *1613*
26:11 and being **e** mad against them, I persecuted *4057*
27:18 And we being **e** tossed with a tempest, *4971*
2Co 7:13 **e** the more joyed we for the joy of Titus, *4056*
Gal 1:14 being **more e** zealous of the traditions of *4056*
1Th 3:10 **e** that *we* might see your face, *1537+4053+5228*
2Th 1: 3 because that your faith **groweth e**, and *5232*
Heb 12:21 *that* Moses said, I **e fear** and quake;) *1510+1630*

EXCEL (5) [EXCELLED, EXCELLENCY, EXCELLENT, EXCELLEST, EXCELLETH]

Ge 49: 4 Unstable as water, thou shalt not **e**; because 3498
1Ch 15:21 Azaziah, with harps on the Sheminith to **e**. 5329
Ps 103:20 ye his angels, that **e** in strength, 1368
Isa 10:10 whose graven images did **e** *them of* 4480
1Co 14:12 that ye may **e** to the edifying of the church. *4052*

EXCELLED (1) [EXCEL]

1Ki 4:30 Solomon's wisdom **e** the wisdom of all 7235

EXCELLENCY (26) [EXCEL]

Ge 49: 3 the **e** of dignity, and the excellency of 3499
49: 3 excellency of dignity, and the **e** of power: 3499
Ex 15: 7 in the greatness of thine **e** thou hast 1347
Dt 33:26 heaven in thy help, and in his **e** *on* the sky. 1346
33:29 of thy help, and who *is* the sword of thy **e**! 1346
Job 4:21 Doth not their **e** *which is* in them go away? 3499
13:11 Shall not his **e** make you afraid? and 7613
20: 6 Though his **e** mount up to the heavens, and 7863
37: 4 he thundereth with the voice of his **e**; and 1347
40:10 Deck thyself now with majesty and **e**; and 1363
Ps 47: 4 for us, the **e** of Jacob whom he loved. 1347
62: 4 only consult to cast *him* down from his **e**: 7613
68:34 his **e** *is* over Israel, and his strength *is* in 1346
Ecc 7:12 the **e** of knowledge *is, that* wisdom giveth 3504
Isa 13:19 of kingdoms, the beauty of the Chaldees' **e**, 1347
35: 2 the **e** of Carmel and Sharon, they shall see 1926
35: 2 glory of the LORD, *and* the **e** of our God. 1926
60:15 through *thee*, I will make thee an eternal **e**, 1347
Eze 24:21 the **e** of your strength, the desire of your 1347
Am 6: 8 I abhor the **e** of Jacob, and hate his palaces: 1347
8: 7 The LORD hath sworn by the **e** of Jacob, 1347
Na 2: 2 For the LORD hath turned *away* the **e** of 1347
2: 2 the excellency of Jacob, as the **e** of Israel: 1347
1Co 2: 1 came not with **e** of speech or of wisdom, *5247*
2Co 4: 7 that the **e** of the power may be of God, and *5236*
Php 3: 8 loss for the **e** of the knowledge of Christ *5242*

EXCELLENT (34) [EXCEL]

Est 1: 4 and the honour of his **e** majesty many days, 8597
Job 37:23 *he is* **e** in power, and *in* judgment, and 7689
Ps 8: 1 our Lord, how **e** *is* thy name in all the earth! 117
8: 9 our Lord, how **e** *is* thy name in all the earth! 117
16: 3 *to* the **e**, in whom *is* all my delight. 117
36: 7 How **e** *is* thy lovingkindness, O God! 3368
76: 4 *and* **e** than the mountains of prey. 117
141: 5 *it shall be* an **e** oil, *which* shall not break 7218
148:13 for his name alone *is* **e**; his glory *is* above 7682
150: 2 praise him according to his **e** greatness. 7230
Pr 8: 6 Hear, for I will speak of **e things**; and 5057
12:26 The righteous *is* more **e** than his neighbour: 8446
17: 7 **E** speech becometh not a fool: much less 3499
17:27 *and* a man of understanding is of an **e** spirit. 3368
22:20 Have not I written to thee **e things** in 7991
SS 5:15 countenance *is* as Lebanon, **e** as the cedars. 977
Isa 4: 2 the fruit of the earth *shall be* **e** and comely 1347
12: 5 the LORD; for he hath done **e things**: 1348
28:29 is wonderful in counsel, *and* **e** in working. 1431
Eze 16: 7 and thou art come to **e ornaments**: 5716+5716
Da 2:31 This great image, whose brightness *was* **e**, 3493
4:36 and **e** majesty was added unto me. 3493
5:12 Forasmuch as an **e** spirit, and knowledge, 3493
5:14 and **e** wisdom is found in thee. 3493
6: 3 and princes, because an **e** spirit *was* in him; 3493
Lk 1: 3 unto thee in order, **most e** Theophilus, *2903*
Ac 23:26 Claudius Lysias unto the **most e** governor *2903*
Ro 2:18 and approvest the *things* that are **more e**, *1308*
1Co 12:31 yet shew I unto you a **more e** way. *2596+5236*
Php 1:10 That ye may approve *things* that are **e**; *1308*
Heb 1: 4 as he hath by inheritance obtained a **more e** *1313*
8: 6 But now hath he obtained a **more e** *1313*
11: 4 By faith Abel offered unto God a **more e** *4183*
2Pe 1:17 came such a voice to him from the **e** glory, *3169*

EXCELLEST (1) [EXCEL]

Pr 31:29 have done virtuously, but thou **e** them all. 5927

EXCELLETH (3) [EXCEL]

Ecc 2:13 I saw that wisdom **e** folly, as far as light 3504
2:13 excelleth folly, as far as light **e** darkness. 3504
2Co 3:10 in this respect, by reason of the glory that **e**. *5235*

EXCEPT (74) [EXCEPTED]

Ge 31:42 **E** the God of my father, the God of 3884
32:26 I will not let thee go, **e** thou bless me. 518+3588
42:15 **e** your youngest brother come hither. 518+3588
43: 3 see my face, **e** your brother *be* with you. 1115
43: 5 see my face, **e** your brother *be* with you. 1115
43:10 For **e** we had lingered, surely now we had 3884
44:23 **E** your youngest brother come down 518+3808
44:26 **e** our youngest brother *be* with us. 369
47:26 *that* Pharaoh should have the fifth *part*; **e** 7535
Nu 16:13 **e** thou make thyself altogether a 1571+3588
Dt 32:30 **e** their Rock had sold them, and 518+3588+3808
Jos 7:12 **e** ye destroy the accursed from 518+3808
1Sa 25:34 kept me back from hurting thee, **e** 3588+3884
2Sa 3: 9 So do God to Abner, and more also, **e**, 3588
3:13 **e** thou first bring Michal Saul's 518+3588
5: 6 **E** thou take away the blind and 518+3588
2Ki 4:24 not *thy* riding for me, **e** I bid thee. 518+3588
Est 2:14 **e** the king delighted in her, and 518+3588
4:11 **e** such to whom the king shall hold 905+3807.1
Ps 127: 1 **E** the LORD build the house, 518+3808
127: 1 **e** the LORD keep the city, 518+3808
Pr 4:16 sleep not, **e** they have done mischief; 518+3808
Isa 1: 9 **E** the LORD of hosts had left unto us a 3884
Da 2:11 **e** the gods, whose dwelling is not with 3861
3:28 nor worship any god, **e** their own God. 3861
6: 5 **e** we find *it* against him concerning the law 3861
Am 3: 3 two walk together, **e** they be agreed? 518+1115
Mt 5:20 That **e** your righteousness shall exceed *3362*
12:29 **e** he first bind the strong *man*? and then *3362*
18: 3 **E** ye be converted, and become as little *3362*
19: 9 **e** *it be* for fornication, and shall marry *1508*
24:22 And **e** those days should be shortened, *1508*
26:42 from me, **e** I drink it, thy will be done. *3362*
Mk 3:27 **e** he will first bind the strong *man*; and then *3362*
7: 3 **e** they wash *their* hands oft, eat not, *3362*
7: 4 from the market, **e** they wash, they eat not. *3362*
13:20 And **e** that the Lord had shortened *those* *1508*
Lk 9:13 **e** we should go and buy meat for all this *1509*
13: 3 but, **e** ye repent, ye shall all likewise perish. *3362*
13: 5 but **e** ye repent, ye shall all likewise perish. *3362*
Jn 3: 2 that thou doest, **e** God be with him. *3362*
3: 3 I say unto thee, **E** a man be born again, *3362*
3: 5 **E** a man be born of water and *of* the Spirit, *3362*
3:27 **e** it be given him from heaven. *3362*
4:48 **E** ye see signs and wonders, ye will not *3362*
6:44 **e** the Father which hath sent me draw him: *3362*
6:53 **E** ye eat the flesh of the Son of man, and *3362*
6:65 **e** it were given unto him of my Father. *3362*
12:24 **E** a corn of wheat fall into the ground and *3362*
15: 4 bear fruit of itself, **e** it abide in the vine; *3362*
15: 4 the vine; no more can ye, **e** ye abide in me. *3362*
19:11 **e** it were given thee from above: *1508*
20:25 **E** I shall see in his hands the print of *3362*
Ac 8: 1 of Judea and Samaria, **e** the apostles. *4133*
8:31 How can I, **e** some *man* should guide me? *3362*
15: 1 *said*, **E** ye be circumcised after the manner *3362*
24:21 **E** *it be* for this one voice, that I cried *2228*
26:29 and altogether such as I am, **e** these bonds. *3924*
27:31 to the soldiers, **E** these abide in the ship, *3362*
Ro 7: 7 **e** the law had said, Thou shalt not covet. *1508*
9:29 **E** the Lord of sabaoth had left us a seed, *1508*
10:15 And how shall they preach, **e** they be sent? *3362*
1Co 7: 5 **e** *it be* with consent for a time, *302+1509*
14: 5 **e** he interpret, that the church *1487+1622+3361*
14: 6 **e** I shall speak to you either by revelation, *3362*
14: 7 **e** they give a distinction in *1437+3361*
14: 9 **e** ye utter by the tongue words easy to be *3362*
15:36 thou sowest is not quickened, **e** it die: *3362*
2Co 12:13 **e** *it be* that I myself was not burdensome to *1508*
13: 5 Jesus Christ is in you, **e** ye be reprobates? *1509*
2Th 2: 3 for *that day shall not come*, **e** there come a *3362*
2Ti 2: 5 *yet* is he not crowned, **e** he strive lawfully. *3362*
Rev 2: 5 candlestick out of his place, **e** thou repent. *3362*
2:22 **e** they repent of their deeds. *3362*

EXCEPTED (1) [EXCEPT]

1Co 15:27 are put under *him*, *it is* manifest that he is **e**, *1622*

EXCESS (4)

Mt 23:25 but within they are full of extortion and **e**. *192*
Eph 5:18 And be not drunk with wine, wherein is **e**; *810*
1Pe 4: 3 lusts, **e of wine**, revellings, banquetings, *3632*
4: 4 you run not with *them* to the same **e** of riot, *401*

EXCESSIVE See OVERMUCH

EXCHANGE (6) [EXCHANGERS]

Ge 47:17 Joseph gave them bread *in* **e** for horses, and NIH
Lev 27:10 then it and the **e** thereof shall be holy. 8545
Job 28:17 the **e** of it *shall not be for* jewels of fine 8545
Eze 48:14 they shall not sell of it, neither **e**, 4171
Mt 16:26 or what shall a man give **in e for** his soul? *465*
Mk 8:37 Or what shall a man give **in e for** his soul? *465*

EXCHANGERS (1) [EXCHANGE]

Mt 25:27 therefore to have put my money to the **e**, *5133*

EXCLUDE (1) [EXCLUDED]

Gal 4:17 yea, they would **e** you, that you might *1576*

EXCLUDED (1) [EXCLUDE]

Ro 3:27 It is **e**. By what law? of works? Nay: but *1576*

EXCUSE (3) [EXCUSED, EXCUSING]

Lk 14:18 they all with one *consent* began to **make e**. *3868*
Ro 1:20 and Godhead; so that they are **without e**: *379*
2Co 12:19 think you that we **e ourselves** unto you? *626*

EXCUSED (2) [EXCUSE]

Lk 14:18 needs go and see it: I pray thee have me **e**. *3868*
14:19 I go to prove them: I pray thee have me **e**. *3868*

EXCUSING (1) [EXCUSE]

Ro 2:15 mean while accusing or else **e** one another;) *626*

EXECRATION (2)

Jer 42:18 ye shall be an **e**, and an astonishment, and 423
44:12 and they shall be an **e**, *and* an astonishment, 423

EXECUTE (32) [EXECUTED, EXECUTEDST, EXECUTEST, EXECUTETH, EXECUTING, EXECUTION, EXECUTIONER]

Ex 12:12 against all the gods of Egypt I will **e** 6213
Nu 5:30 and the priest shall **e** upon her all this law. 6213
8:11 that they may **e** the service of the LORD. 5647
Dt 10:18 He doth **e** the judgment of the fatherless 6213
1Ki 6:12 **e** my judgments, and keep all my 6213
Ps 119:84 when wilt thou **e** judgment on them that 6213
149: 7 To **e** vengeance upon the heathen, *and* 6213
149: 9 To **e** upon them the judgment written: 6213
Isa 16: 3 Take counsel, **e** judgment; make thy 6213
Jer 7: 5 if you **throughly e** judgment 6213+6213
21:12 **E** judgment in the morning, and 1777
22: 3 **E** ye judgment and righteousness, and 6213
23: 5 shall **e** judgment and justice in the earth. 6213
33:15 he shall **e** judgment and righteousness in 6213
Eze 5: 8 will **e** judgments in the midst of thee in 6213
5:10 I will **e** judgments in thee, and the whole 6213
5:15 when I shall **e** judgments in thee in anger 6213
11: 9 and will **e** judgments among you. 6213
16:41 **e** judgments upon thee in the sight of many 6213
25:11 I will **e** judgments upon Moab; and 6213
25:17 I will **e** great vengeance upon them with 6213
30:14 fire in Zoan, and will **e** judgments in No. 6213
30:19 Thus will I **e** judgments in Egypt: and 6213
45: 9 and spoil, and **e** judgment and justice, 6213
Hos 11: 9 I will not **e** the fierceness of mine anger, 6213
Mic 5:15 I will **e** vengeance in anger and fury upon 6213
7: 9 he plead my cause, and **e** judgment for me: 6213
Zec 7: 9 **E** true judgment, and shew mercy and 8199
8:16 **e the judgment** of truth and peace in 4941+8199
Jn 5:27 And hath given him authority to **e** judgment *4160*
Ro 13: 4 a revenger to **e** wrath upon him that doeth NIG
Jude 1:15 To **e** judgment upon all, and to convince all *4160*

EXECUTED (20) [EXECUTE]

Nu 33: 4 upon their gods also the LORD **e** 6213
Dt 33:21 he **e** the justice of the LORD, and 6213
2Sa 8:15 David **e** judgment and justice unto all his 6213
1Ch 6:10 (he *it is* that **e the priest's office** in 3547
18:14 **e** judgment and justice among all his 6213
24: 2 Eleazar and Ithamar **e the priest's office**. 3547
2Ch 24:24 So they **e** judgment against Joash. 6213
Ezr 7:26 let judgment be **e** speedily upon him, 5648
Ps 106:30 stood up Phinehas, and **e judgment**: and 6419
Ecc 8:11 *against* an evil work is not **e** speedily, 6213
Jer 23:20 until he have **e**, and till he have performed 6213
Eze 11:12 neither **e** my judgments, but have done 6213
18: 8 hath **e** true judgment between man and 6213
18:17 hath **e** my judgments, hath walked in my 6213
20:24 Because they had not **e** my judgments, but 6213
23:10 for they had **e** judgment upon her. 6213
28:22 when I shall have **e** judgments in her, and 6213
28:26 when I have **e** judgments upon all those 6213
39:21 shall see my judgment that I have **e**, 6213
Lk 1: 8 *that* while he **e the priest's office** before *2407*

EXECUTEDST (1) [EXECUTE]

1Sa 28:18 nor **e** his fierce wrath upon Amalek, 6213

EXECUTEST (1) [EXECUTE]

Ps 99: 4 thou **e** judgment and righteousness in 6213

EXECUTETH (6) [EXECUTE]

Ps 9:16 is known *by* the judgment *which* he **e**: 6213
103: 6 The LORD **e** righteousness and 6213
146: 7 Which **e** judgment for the oppressed: 6213
Isa 46:11 the man that **e** my counsel from a far NIH
Jer 5: 1 find a man, if there be *any* that **e** judgment, 6213
Joel 2:11 for *he is* strong that **e** his word: for the day 6213

EXECUTING (3) [EXECUTE]

2Ki 10:30 Because thou hast done well in **e** *that* which 6213

2Ch 11:14 from **e the priest's office** unto the LORD: 3547
22: 8 that when Jehu was **e judgment** upon 8199

EXECUTION (1) [EXECUTE]
Est 9: 1 and his decree drew near to be **put in e**, 6213

EXECUTIONER (1) [EXECUTE]
Mk 6:27 And immediately the king sent an **e**, and *4688*

EXEMPTED (1)
1Ki 15:22 throughout all Judah; none *was* **e**: 5355

EXERCISE (11) [EXERCISED, EXERCISETH]
Ps 131: 1 neither do I **e** myself in great *matters*, or 1980
Jer 9:24 that I *am* the LORD which **e** 6213
Mt 20:25 of the Gentiles **e dominion over** them, *2634*
20:25 they *that are* great **e authority upon** them. *2715*
Mk 10:42 over the Gentiles **e lordship over** them; *2634*
10:42 their great ones **e authority upon** them. *2715*
Lk 22:25 The kings of the Gentiles **e lordship over** *2961*
22:25 they that **e authority upon** them are called *1850*
Ac 24:16 And herein do I **e** myself, to have always a *778*
1Ti 4: 7 and **e** thyself *rather* unto godliness. *1128*
4: 8 For bodily **e** profiteth little: *1129*

EXERCISED (6) [EXERCISE]
Ecc 1:13 given to the sons of man to be **e** therewith. 6031
3:10 hath given to the sons of men to be **e** in it. 6031
Eze 22:29 **e robbery**, and have vexed the poor 1497+1498
Heb 5:14 use have their senses **e** to discern both good *1128*
12:11 unto them which are **e** thereby. *1128*
2Pe 2:14 a heart they have **e** with covetous practices; *1128*

EXERCISETH (1) [EXERCISE]
Rev 13:12 And he **e** all the power of the first beast *4160*

EXHORT (16) [EXHORTATION, EXHORTED, EXHORTETH, EXHORTING]
Ac 2:40 with many other words did he testify and **e**, *3870*
27:22 And now I **e** you to be of good cheer: *3867*
2Co 9: 5 Therefore I thought it necessary to **e** *3870*
1Th 4: 1 brethren, and **e** *you* by the Lord Jesus, *3870*
5:14 Now we **e** you, brethren, warn *them that* *3870*
2Th 3:12 and **e** by our Lord Jesus Christ, *3870*
1Ti 2: 1 I **e** therefore that, first of all, supplications, *3870*
6: 2 of the benefit. These *things* teach and **e**. *3870*
2Ti 4: 2 **e** with all longsuffering and doctrine. *3870*
Tit 1: 9 he may be able by sound doctrine both to **e** *3870*
2: 6 Young *men* likewise **e** to be sober minded. *3870*
2: 9 ***E*** servants to be obedient unto their own NIG
2:15 and **e**, and rebuke with all authority. *3870*
Heb 3:13 But **e** one another daily, while it is called *3870*
1Pe 5: 1 The elders which are among you I **e**, *3870*
Jude 1: 3 **e** *you* that *ye* should earnestly contend for *3870*

EXHORTATION (10) [EXHORT]
Lk 3:18 And many other *things* in his **e** preached he *3870*
Ac 13:15 if ye have *any* word of **e** for the people, *3874*
20: 2 and had **given** them much **e**, he came *3056+3870*
Ro 12: 8 Or he that exhorteth, on **e**: he that giveth, *3874*
1Co 14: 3 unto men *to* edification, and **e**, and comfort. *3874*
2Co 8:17 For indeed he accepted the **e**; but *3874*
1Th 2: 3 For our **e** *was* not of deceit, nor of *3874*
1Ti 4:13 give attendance to reading, to **e**, to doctrine. *3874*
Heb 12: 5 And ye have forgotten the **e** which speaketh *3874*
13:22 beseech you, brethren, suffer the word of **e**: *3874*

EXHORTED (3) [EXHORT]
Ac 11:23 the grace of God, was glad, and **e** *them* all, *3870*
15:32 **e** the brethren with many words, and *3870*
1Th 2:11 As you know how we **e** and comforted and *3870*

EXHORTETH (1) [EXHORT]
Ro 12: 8 Or he that **e**, on exhortation: he that giveth, *3870*

EXHORTING (4) [EXHORT]
Ac 14:22 *and* **e** *them* to continue in the faith, and *3870*
18:27 **e** the disciples to receive him: *4389*
Heb 10:25 but **e** *one another:* and so much the more, *3870*
1Pe 5:12 **e**, and testifying that this is the true grace of *3870*

EXILE (2)
2Sa 15:19 for thou *art* a stranger, and also an **e**. 1540
Isa 51:14 The **captive e** hasteneth that *he* may be 6808

EXORCISTS (1)
Ac 19:13 Then certain of the vagabond Jews, **e**, *1845*

EXPANSE See FIRMAMENT

EXPECTATION (14) [EXPECTED, EXPECTING]
Ps 9:18 the **e** of the poor shall *not* perish for ever. 8615
62: 5 thou only upon God; for my **e** *is* from him. 8615
Pr 10:28 but the **e** of the wicked shall perish. 8615
11: 7 a wicked man dieth, *his* **e** shall perish: 8615
11:23 only good: *but* the **e** of the wicked *is* wrath. 8615
23:18 is an end; and thine **e** shall not be cut off. 8615
24:14 be a reward, and thy **e** shall not be cut off. 8615
Isa 20: 5 be afraid and ashamed of Ethiopia their **e**, 4007
20: 6 shall say in that day, Behold, such *is* our **e**, 4007
Zec 9: 5 for her **e** shall be ashamed; and the king 4007
Lk 3:15 And as the people were **in e**, and all *men* *4328*
Ac 12:11 and *from* all the **e** of the people of the Jews. *4329*
Ro 8:19 For the **earnest e** of the creature waiteth for *603*
Php 1:20 According to my **earnest e** and *my* hope, *603*

EXPECTED (1) [EXPECTATION]
Jer 29:11 and not of evil, to give you an **e** end. 8615

EXPECTING (2) [EXPECTATION]
Ac 3: 5 unto them, **e to** receive something of them. *4328*
Heb 10:13 From henceforth **e** till his enemies be made *1551*

EXPEDIENT (7)
Jn 11:50 Nor consider that it is **e** for us, that one man *4851*
16: 7 you the truth; It is **e** for you that I go away: *4851*
18:14 that it was **e** that one man should die for *4851*
1Co 6:12 are lawful unto me, but all *things* are not **e**: *4851*
10:23 are lawful for me, but all *things* are not **e**: *4851*
2Co 8:10 for this is **e** for you, who have begun *4851*
12: 1 It is not **e** for me doubtless to glory. I will *4851*

EXPEL (2) [EXPELLED]
Jos 23: 5 he shall **e** them from before you, and 1920
Jdg 11: 7 and **e** me out of my father's house? 1644

EXPELLED (4) [EXPEL]
Jos 13:13 (Nevertheless the children of Israel **e** not 3423
Jdg 1:20 and he **e** thence the three sons of Anak. 3423
2Sa 14:14 that *his* banished be not **e** from him. 5080
Ac 13:50 Barnabas, and **e** them out of their coasts. *1544*

EXPENCES (2)
Ezr 6: 4 let the **e** be given out of the king's house: 5313
6: 8 forthwith **e** be given unto these men, 5313

EXPERIENCE (4)
Ge 30:27 *tarry: for* I have **learned by e** that 5172
Ecc 1:16 my heart **had** great **e** of wisdom and 7200
Ro 5: 4 And patience, **e**; and experience, hope: *1382*
5: 4 And patience, experience; and **e**, hope: *1382*

EXPERIMENT (1)
2Co 9:13 Whiles by the **e** of this ministration they *1382*

EXPERT (6)
1Ch 12:33 **e** in war, with all instruments of war, 6186
12:35 of the Danites **e** in war twenty and 6186
12:36 forth to battle, **e** in war, forty thousand. 6186
SS 3: 8 They all hold swords, *being* **e** in war: 3925
Jer 50: 9 their arrows *shall be* as of a mighty **e** *man;* 7919
Ac 26: 3 *I know* thee to be **e** in all customs and *1109*

EXPERT BUILDER See MASTERBUILDER

EXPIRED (9)
1Sa 18:26 king's son in law: and the days were not **e**. 4390
2Sa 11: 1 it came to pass, after the year was **e**, at 8666
1Ch 17:11 when thy days be **e** that *thou* must go *to be* 4390
20: 1 it came to pass, that after the year was **e**, 8666
2Ch 36:10 when the year was **e**, king Nebuchadnezzar 8666
Est 1: 5 when these days were **e**, the king made a 4390
Eze 43:27 when *these* days are **e**, it shall be, *that* upon 3615
Ac 7:30 And when forty years were **e**, *4137*
Rev 20: 7 And when the thousand years are **e**, Satan *5055*

EXPLOITS (2)
Da 11:28 he shall do **e**, and return to his own land. NIH
11:32 know their God shall be strong, and do ***e***. NIH

EXPLORE See ESPIED; ESPY

EXPOSE See REPROOF; REPROVE

EXPOUND (1) [EXPOUNDED]
Jdg 14:14 they could not *in* three days **e** the riddle. 5046

EXPOUNDED (6) [EXPOUND]
Jdg 14:19 *of garments* unto them which **e** the riddle. 5046
Mk 4:34 *were* alone, he **e** all *things* to his disciples. *1956*
Lk 24:27 he **e** unto them in all the scriptures *1329*
Ac 11: 4 *and* **e** *it* by order unto them, saying, *1620*
18:26 **e** unto him the way of God more perfectly. *1620*
28:23 to whom he **e** and testified the kingdom of *1620*

EXPRESS (1) [EXPRESSED, EXPRESSLY]
Heb 1: 3 and the **e image** of his person, and *5481*

EXPRESSED (6) [EXPRESS]
Nu 1:17 Aaron took these men which are **e** by *their* 5344
1Ch 12:31 which were **e** by name, to come and make 5344
16:41 rest that were chosen, who were **e** by name, 5344
2Ch 28:15 the men which were **e** by name rose up, 5344
31:19 several city, the men that were **e** by name, 5344
Ezr 8:20 all of them were **e** by name. 5344

EXPRESSLY (3) [EXPRESS]
1Sa 20:21 If I **e say** unto the lad, Behold, 559+559
Eze 1: 3 The word of the LORD **came e** 1961+1961
1Ti 4: 1 Now the Spirit speaketh **e**, that in the latter *4490*

EXTEND (2) [EXTENDED, EXTENDETH]
Ps 109:12 Let there be none to **e** mercy **unto** him: 4900
Isa 66:12 I will **e** peace to her like a river, and 5186

EXTENDED (2) [EXTEND]
Ezr 7:28 hath **e** mercy unto me before the king, and 5186
9: 9 hath **e** mercy unto us in the sight of 5186

EXTENDETH (1) [EXTEND]
Ps 16: 2 *art* my Lord: my goodness ***e*** not to thee; NIH

EXTINCT (2)
Job 17: 1 My breath is corrupt, my days are **e**, 2193
Isa 43:17 they are **e**, they are quenched as tow. 1846

EXTINGUISHED See EXTINCT

EXTOL (4) [EXTOLLED]
Ps 30: 1 I will **e** thee, O LORD; for thou hast lifted 7311
68: 4 **e** him that rideth upon the heavens by his 5549
145: 1 I will **e** thee, my God, O king; and I will 7311
Da 4:37 and **e** and honour the King of heaven, 7313

EXTOLLED (2) [EXTOL]
Ps 66:17 my mouth, and *he was* **e** with my tongue. 7311
Isa 52:13 he shall be exalted and **e**, and be very high. 5375

EXTORTION (2) [EXTORTIONER, EXTORTIONERS]
Eze 22:12 hast greedily gained of thy neighbours by **e**, 6233
Mt 23:25 but within they are full of **e** and excess. *724*

EXTORTIONER (3) [EXTORTION]
Ps 109:11 Let the **e** catch all that he hath; and let 5383
Isa 16: 4 for the **e** is at an end, the spoiler ceaseth, 4160
1Co 5:11 an idolater, or a railer, or a drunkard, or an **e**; *727*

EXTORTIONERS (3) [EXTORTION]
Lk 18:11 that I am not as other men *are*, **e**, unjust, *727*
1Co 5:10 or with the covetous, or **e**, or with idolaters; *727*
6:10 nor drunkards, nor revilers, nor **e**, *727*

EXTREME (1) [EXTREMITY]
Dt 28:22 with an **e burning**, and with the sword, and 2746

EXTREMITY (1) [EXTREME]
Job 35:15 his anger; yet he knoweth *it* not in great **e**: 6580

EYE (116) [EYE'S, EYEBROWS, EYED, EYELIDS, EYES, EYESALVE, EYESERVICE, EYESIGHT, EYEWITNESSES]
Ex 21:24 **E** for eye, tooth for tooth, hand for hand, 5869
21:24 Eye for **e**, tooth for tooth, hand for hand, 5869
21:26 if a man smite the **e** of his servant, or 5869
21:26 or the **e** of his maid, that it perish; 5869
Lev 21:20 or that hath a blemish in his **e**, or be scurvy, 5869
24:20 for breach, **e** for eye, tooth for tooth: 5869
24:20 for breach, eye for **e**, tooth for tooth: 5869
Dt 7:16 thine **e** shall have no pity upon them: 5869
13: 8 neither shall thine **e** pity him, neither shalt 5869
15: 9 thine **e** be evil against thy poor brother, and 5869
19:13 Thine **e** shall not pity him, but thou shalt 5869
19:21 thine **e** shall not pity; *but* life *shall go* for 5869
19:21 **e** for eye, tooth for tooth, hand for hand, 5869
19:21 eye for **e**, tooth for tooth, hand for hand, 5869
25:12 cut off her hand, thine **e** shall not pity *her.* 5869
28:54 his **e** shall be evil toward his brother, and 5869
28:56 her **e** shall be evil towards the husband of 5869
32:10 he kept him as the apple of his **e**. 5869
34: 7 his **e** was not dim, nor his natural force 5869
1Sa 24:10 *mine* **e** spared thee; and I said, I will not put NIH
2Sa 22:25 according to my cleanness in his **e sight**. 5869
Ezr 5: 5 the **e** of their God was upon the elders of 5870
Job 7: 7 life *is* wind: mine **e** shall no more see good. 5869
7: 8 The **e** of him that hath seen me shall see me 5869
10:18 given up the ghost, and no **e** had seen me! 5869
13: 1 mine **e** hath seen all *this,* mine ear hath 5869
16:20 *but* mine **e** poureth out *tears* unto God. 5869
17: 2 *doth not* mine **e** continue in their 5869
17: 7 Mine **e** also is dim by reason of sorrow, and 5869
20: 9 The **e** also *which* saw him shall *see him* no 5869
24:15 The **e** also of the adulterer waiteth for 5869
24:15 for the twilight, saying, No **e** shall see me: 5869
28: 7 and which the vulture's **e** hath not seen: 5869
28:10 and his **e** seeth every precious thing. 5869
29:11 when the **e** saw *me*, it gave witness to me: 5869
42: 5 of the ear: but now mine **e** seeth thee. 5869
Ps 6: 7 Mine **e** is consumed because of grief; 5869
17: 8 Keep me as the apple of the **e**, hide me 5869
31: 9 mine **e** is consumed with grief, *yea*, my 5869
32: 8 thou shalt go: I will guide thee with mine **e**. 5869
33:18 the **e** of the LORD *is* upon them that fear 5869
35:19 *neither* let them wink *with* the **e** that hate 5869
35:21 *and* said, Aha, aha, our **e** hath seen *it.* 5869
54: 7 mine **e** hath seen *his desire* upon mine 5869
88: 9 Mine **e** mourneth by reason of affliction: 5869
92:11 Mine **e** also shall see *my desire* on mine 5869
94: 9 he that formed the **e**, shall he not see? 5869
Pr 7: 2 live; and my law as the apple of thine **e**. 5869
10:10 He that winketh *with* the **e** causeth sorrow: 5869
20:12 The hearing ear, and the seeing **e**, 5869
22: 9 He that hath a bountiful **e** shall be blessed; 5869
23: 6 not the bread of *him that hath* an evil **e**, 5869
28:22 He that hasteth to be rich *hath* an evil **e**, and 5869
30:17 The **e** *that* mocketh at *his* father, and 5869
Ecc 1: 8 man cannot utter *it:* the **e** is not satisfied 5869
4: 8 neither is his **e** satisfied *with* riches; 5869
Isa 13:18 the womb; their **e** shall not spare children. 5869
52: 8 for they shall see **e** to eye, when 5869
52: 8 for they shall see eye to **e**, when 5869
64: 4 neither hath the **e** seen, O God, 5869
Jer 13:17 mine **e** shall weep sore, and run down *with* 5869
La 1:16 mine **e**, mine eye runneth down *with* water, 5869
1:16 mine **e** runneth down *with* water, because 5869
2: 4 slew all *that were* pleasant to the **e**, in 5869
2:18 no rest; let not the apple of thine **e** cease. 5869
3:48 Mine **e** runneth down *with* rivers of water 5869
3:49 Mine **e** trickleth down, and ceaseth not, 5869
3:51 Mine **e** affecteth mine heart because of all 5869
Eze 5:11 diminish *thee;* neither shall mine **e** spare, 5869
7: 4 mine **e** shall not spare thee, neither will I 5869
7: 9 mine **e** shall not spare, neither will I have 5869
8:18 mine **e** shall not spare, neither will I have 5869
9: 5 let not your **e** spare, neither have ye pity: 5869
9:10 *as for* me also, mine **e** shall not spare, 5869
16: 5 None **e** pitied thee, to do any of these unto 5869
20:17 Nevertheless mine **e** spared them from 5869
Mic 4:11 be defiled, and let our **e** look upon Zion. 5869
Zec 2: 8 toucheth you toucheth the apple of his **e**. 5869
11:17 *shall be* upon his arm, and upon his right **e**: 5869
11:17 and his right **e** shall be utterly darkened. 5869
Mt 5:29 And if thy right **e** offend thee, pluck it out, *3788*
5:38 An **e** for an eye, and a tooth for a tooth: *3788*
5:38 An eye for an **e**, and a tooth for a tooth: *3788*
6:22 The light of the body is the **e**: if therefore *3788*
6:22 if therefore thine **e** be single, thy whole *3788*
6:23 But if thine **e** be evil, thy whole body shall *3788*

Mt 7: 3 thou the mote that is in thy brother's **e**, 3788
7: 3 not the beam that is in thine own **e**? 3788
7: 4 Let me pull out the mote out of thine **e**; 3788
7: 4 and behold, a beam *is* in thine own **e**? 3788
7: 5 first cast out the beam out of thine own **e**; 3788
7: 5 to cast out the mote out of thy brother's **e**. 3788
18: 9 And if thine **e** offend thee, pluck it out, and 3788
18: 9 better for thee to enter into life with **one e**, 3442
19:24 It is easier for a camel to go through the **e** 5169
20:15 what I will with mine own? Is thine **e** evil, 3788
Mk 7:22 an evil **e**, blasphemy, pride, foolishness: 3788
9:47 And if thine **e** offend thee, pluck it out: it is 3788
9:47 enter into the kingdom of God with **one e**, 3442
10:25 It is easier for a camel to go through the **e** 5168
Lk 6:41 thou the mote that is in thy brother's **e**, 3788
6:41 not the beam that is in thine own **e**? 3788
6:42 let me pull out the mote that is in thine **e**, 3788
6:42 not the beam that is in thine own **e**? 3788
6:42 cast out first the beam out of thine own **e**, 3788
6:42 pull out the mote that is in thy brother's **e**. 3788
11:34 The light of the body is the **e**: 3788
11:34 therefore when thine **e** is single, thy whole 3788
11:34 but when *thine* **e** is evil, thy body also *is* full NIG
18:25 for a camel to go through a needle's **e**, 5168
1Co 2: 9 it is written, **E** hath not seen, nor ear heard, 3788
12:16 Because I am not the **e**, I am not of 3788
12:17 If the whole body *were* an **e**, where *were* 3788
12:21 And the **e** cannot say unto the hand, I have 3788
15:52 In a moment, in the twinkling of an **e**, at 3788
Rev 1: 7 and every **e** shall see him, and they *also* 3788

EYE'S (1) [EYE]

Ex 21:26 he shall let him go free for his **e** sake. 5869

EYEBROWS (1) [EYE, BROW]

Lev 14: 9 off his head and his beard and his **e**, 1354+5869

EYED (2) [EYE]

Ge 29:17 Leah was tender **e**; but Rachel was 5869
1Sa 18: 9 Saul **e** David from that day and forward. 5770

EYELIDS (9) [EYE]

Job 16:16 and on mine **e** *is* the shadow of death; 6079
41:18 and his eyes *are* like the **e** of the morning. 6079
Ps 11: 4 his eyes behold, his **e** try, the children of 6079
132: 4 sleep to mine eyes, *or* slumber to mine **e**, 6079
Pr 4:25 and let thine **e** look straight before thee. 6079
6: 4 sleep to thine eyes, nor slumber to thine **e**. 6079
6:25 neither let her take thee with her **e**. 6079
30:13 are their eyes! and their **e** are lifted up. 6079
Jer 9:18 *with* tears, and our **e** gush out with waters. 6079

EYES (501) [EYE]

Ge 3: 5 your **e** shall be opened, and ye shall be as 5869
3: 6 that it *was* pleasant to the **e**, and a tree to be 5869
3: 7 the **e** of them both were opened, and 5869
6: 8 Noah found grace in the **e** of the LORD. 5869
13:10 Lot lifted up his **e**, and beheld all the plain 5869
13:14 Lift up now thine **e**, and look from 5869
16: 4 her mistress was despised in her **e**. 5869
16: 5 she had conceived, I was despised in her **e**: 5869
18: 2 he lift up his **e** and looked, and lo, 5869
19: 8 and do ye to them as *is* good in your **e**: 5869
20:16 behold, he *is* to thee a covering of the **e**, 5869
21:19 God opened her **e**, and she saw a well of 5869
22: 4 on the third day Abraham lift up his **e**, 5869
22:13 Abraham lifted up his **e**, and looked, and 5869
24:63 he lift up his **e**, and saw, and behold, 5869
24:64 Rebekah lift up her **e**, and when she saw 5869
27: 1 his **e** were dim, so that he could not see, 5869
30:27 pray thee, if I have found favour in thine **e**, 5869
30:41 that Jacob laid the rods before the **e** of 5869
31:10 that I lifted up mine **e**, and saw in a dream, 5869
31:12 he said, Lift up now thine **e**, and see, all 5869
31:40 and my sleep departed from mine **e**. 5869
33: 1 Jacob lifted up his **e**, and looked, and 5869
33: 5 he lift up his **e**, and saw the women and 5869
34:11 Let me find grace in your **e**, and what ye 5869
37:25 they lift up their **e** and looked, and behold, 5869
39: 7 that his master's wife cast her **e** upon 5869
41:37 the thing was good in the **e** of Pharaoh, 5869
41:37 of Pharaoh, and in the **e** of all his servants. 5869
42:24 and bound him before their **e**. 5869
43:29 he lift up his **e**, and saw his brother 5869
44:21 unto me, that I may set mine **e** upon him. 5869
45:12 your **e** see, and the eyes of my brother 5869
45:12 eyes see, and the **e** of my brother Benjamin, 5869
46: 4 and Joseph shall put his hand upon thine **e**. 5869
47:19 Wherefore shall we die before thine **e**, 5869
48:10 Now the **e** of Israel were dim for age, *so* 5869
49:12 *His* **e** *shall be* red with wine, and *his* teeth 5869
50: 4 If now I have found grace in your **e**, speak, 5869
Ex 5:21 savour to be abhorred in the **e** of Pharaoh, 5869
5:21 in the **e** of his servants, to put a sword in 5869
8:26 of the Egyptians before their **e**, 5869
13: 9 for a memorial between thine **e**, that 5869
13:16 and for frontlets between thine **e**: 5869
14:10 the children of Israel lift up their **e**, and 5869
24:17 the mount in the **e** of the children of Israel. 5869
Lev 4:13 the thing be hid from the **e** of the assembly, 5869
20: 4 do any ways hide their **e** from the man, 5869
26:16 that shall consume the **e**, and cause sorrow 5869
Nu 5:13 it be hid from the **e** of her husband, and 5869
10:31 and thou mayest be to us instead of **e**. 5869
11: 6 at all, beside *this* manna, *before* our **e**. 5869
15:39 not after your own heart and your own **e**, 5869
16:14 wilt thou put out the **e** of these men? 5869
20: 8 and speak ye unto the rock before their **e**; 5869
20:12 to sanctify me in the **e** of the children of 5869
22:31 the LORD opened the **e** of Balaam, and 5869
24: 2 Balaam lift up his **e**, and he saw Israel 5869
24: 3 and the man whose **e** are open hath said: 5869
24: 4 falling *into a trance*, but having his **e** open: 5869
24:15 and the man whose **e** are open hath said: 5869
Nu 24:16 falling *into a trance*, but having his **e** open: 5869
27:14 to sanctify me at the water before their **e**: 5869
33:55 let remain of them *shall be* pricks in your **e**, 5869
Dt 1:30 that he did for you in Egypt before your **e**; 5869
3:21 Thine **e** have seen all that the LORD your 5869
3:27 lift up thine **e** westward, and northward, 5869
3:27 eastward, and behold *it* with thine **e**: 5869
4: 3 Your **e** have seen what the LORD did 5869
4: 9 lest thou forget the things which thine **e** 5869
4:19 lest thou lift up thine **e** unto heaven, and 5869
4:34 God did for you in Egypt before your **e**? 5869
6: 8 they shall be as frontlets between thine **e**. 5869
6:22 and upon all his household, before our **e**: 5869
7:19 The great temptations which thine **e** saw, 5869
9:17 two hands, and brake them before your **e**. 5869
10:21 and terrible *things*, which thine **e** have seen. 5869
11: 7 your **e** have seen all the great acts of 5869
11:12 the **e** of the LORD thy God *are* always 5869
11:18 they may be as frontlets between your **e**. 5869
12: 8 every man whatsoever *is* right in his own **e**. 5869
13:18 to do *that which is* right in the **e** of 5869
14: 1 nor make *any* baldness between your **e** for 5869
16:19 for a gift doth blind the **e** of the wise, and 5869
21: 7 shed this blood, neither have our **e** seen *it*. 5869
24: 1 to pass that she find no favour in his **e**, 5869
28:31 Thine ox *shall be* slain before thine **e**, and 5869
28:32 thine **e** shall look, and fail *with longing* for 5869
28:34 for the sight of thine **e** which thou shalt see. 5869
28:65 and failing of **e**, and sorrow of mind: 5869
28:67 for the sight of thine **e** which thou shalt see. 5869
29: 2 your **e** in the land of Egypt unto Pharaoh, 5869
29: 3 The great temptations which thine **e** have 5869
29: 4 and **e** to see, and ears to hear, unto this day. 5869
34: 4 I have caused thee to see *it* with thine **e**, but 5869
Jos 5:13 that he lift up his **e** and looked, and behold, 5869
23:13 in your sides, and thorns in your **e**, 5869
24: 7 your **e** have seen what I have done in 5869
Jdg 16:21 put out his **e**, and brought him down to 5869
16:28 avenged of the Philistines for my two **e**. 5869
17: 6 man did *that which was* right in his own **e**. 5869
19:17 when he had lift up his **e**, he saw a 5869
21:25 man did *that* which *was* right in his own **e**. 5869
Ru 2: 9 *Let* thine **e** *be* on the field that they do reap, 5869
2:10 Why have I found grace in thine **e**, 5869
1Sa 2:33 *shall be* to consume thine **e**, and to grieve 5869
3: 2 his **e** began *to wax* dim, *that* he could not 5869
4:15 and his **e** were dim, that he could not see. 5869
6:13 they lifted up their **e**, and saw the ark, and 5869
11: 2 that *I* may thrust out all your right **e**, and 5869
12: 3 *any* bribe to blind mine **e** therewith? 5869
12:16 which the LORD will do before your **e**. 5869
14:27 to his mouth; and his **e** were enlightened. 5869
14:29 how mine **e** have been enlightened, because 5869
20: 3 knoweth that I have found grace in thine **e**; 5869
20:29 and now, if I have found favour in thine **e**, 5869
24:10 this day thine **e** have seen how that 5869
25: 8 let the young men find favour in thine **e**: 5869
26:21 my soul was precious in thine **e** this day: 5869
26:24 thy life was much set by this day in mine **e**, 5869
26:24 let my life be much set by in the **e** of 5869
27: 5 If I have now found grace in thine **e**, 5869
2Sa 6:20 who uncovered himself to day in the **e** of 5869
12:11 and I will take thy wives before thine **e**, and 5869
13:34 young man that kept the watch lift up his **e**, 5869
15:25 if I shall find favour in the **e** of the LORD, 5869
18:24 lift up his **e**, and looked, and behold a man 5869
19:27 do therefore what *is* good in thine **e**. 5869
22:28 thine **e** *are* upon the haughty, *that* thou 5869
24: 3 *that* the **e** of my lord the king may see *it*: 5869
1Ki 1:20 O king, the **e** of all Israel *are* upon thee, 5869
1:48 my throne *this* day, mine **e** even seeing *it*. 5869
8:29 That thine **e** may be open toward this house 5869
8:52 That thine **e** may be open unto 5869
9: 3 mine **e** and mine heart shall be there 5869
10: 7 I came, and mine **e** had seen *it*: and behold, 5869
11:33 to do *that* which *is* right in mine **e**, and 5869
14: 4 for his **e** were set by reason of his age. 5869
14: 8 to do *that* only which *was* right in mine **e**; 5869
15: 5 which *was* right in the **e** of the LORD, 5869
15:11 Asa did *that* which *was* right in the **e** of 5869
16:25 Omri wrought evil in the **e** of the LORD, 5869
20: 6 *that* whatsoever *is* pleasant in thine **e**, 5869
22:43 doing *that* which *was* right in the **e** of 5869
2Ki 4:34 his **e** upon his eyes, and his hands upon his 5869
4:34 his eyes upon his **e**, and his hands upon his 5869
4:35 seven times, and the child opened his **e**. 5869
6:17 said, LORD, I pray thee, open his **e**, 5869
6:17 the LORD opened the **e** of the young man; 5869
6:20 open the **e** of these *men*, that they may see. 5869
6:20 the LORD opened their **e**, and they saw; 5869
7: 2 thou shalt see *it* with thine **e**, but shalt not 5869
7:19 thou shalt see *it* with thine **e**, but shalt not 5869
10: 5 do thou *that* which *is* good in thine **e**. 5869
10:30 in executing *that* which *is* right in mine **e**, 5869
19:16 open, LORD, thine **e**, and see: and 5869
19:22 *thy* voice, and lift up thine **e** on high? 5869
22:20 thine **e** shall not see all the evil which I will 5869
25: 7 they slew the sons of Zedekiah before his **e**, 5869
25: 7 put out the **e** of Zedekiah, and bound him 5869
1Ch 13: 4 for the thing was right in the **e** of all 5869
17:17 *yet* this was a small thing in thine **e**, O God; 5869
21:16 David lift up his **e**, and saw the angel of 5869
21:23 lord the king do *that* which *is* good in his **e**: 5869
2Ch 6:20 That thine **e** may be open upon this house 5869
6:40 thine **e** be open, and *let* thine ears *be* attent 5869
7:15 Now mine **e** shall be open, and mine ears 5869
7:16 mine **e** and mine heart shall be there 5869
9: 6 I came, and mine **e** had seen *it*: and behold, 5869
14: 2 and right in the **e** of the LORD his God: 5869
16: 9 For the **e** of the LORD run to and 5869
20:12 we what to do: but our **e** *are* upon thee. 5869
21: 6 he wrought *that* which *was* evil in the **e** of 5869
29: 6 done *that* which *was* evil in the **e** of 5869
29: 8 and to hissing, as ye see with your **e**. 5869
34:28 neither shall thine **e** see all the evil that I 5869
Ezr 3:12 of this house was laid before their **e**, 5869
9: 8 that our God may lighten our **e**, and give us 5869
Ne 1: 6 ear now be attentive, and thine **e** open, 5869
6:16 they were much cast down in their own **e**: 5869
Est 1:17 *they* shall despise their husbands in their **e**, 5869
8: 5 before the king, and I *be* pleasing in his **e**, 5869
Job 2:12 when they lift up their **e** afar off, and 5869
3:10 nor hid sorrow from mine **e**. 5869
4:16 an image *was* before mine **e**, *there was* 5869
7: 8 shall see me no *more*: thine **e** *are* upon me, 5869
10: 4 Hast thou **e** of flesh? or seest thou as man 5869
11: 4 doctrine *is* pure, and I am clean in thine **e**. 5869
11:20 the **e** of the wicked shall fail, and they shall 5869
14: 3 dost thou open thine **e** upon such a one, 5869
15:12 thee away? and what do thine **e** wink at, 5869
16: 9 mine enemy sharpeneth his **e** upon me. 5869
17: 5 even the **e** of his children shall fail. 5869
19:27 and mine **e** shall behold, and not another; 5869
21: 8 and their offspring before their **e**. 5869
21:20 His **e** shall see his destruction, and he shall 5869
24:23 he resteth; yet his **e** *are* upon their ways. 5869
27:19 be gathered: he openeth his **e**, and he *is* not. 5869
28:21 Seeing it is hid from the **e** of all living, and 5869
29:15 I was **e** to the blind, and feet *was* I to 5869
31: 1 I made a covenant with mine **e**; why then 5869
31: 7 mine heart walked after mine **e**, and *if any* 5869
31:16 or have caused the **e** of the widow to fail; 5869
32: 1 because he *was* righteous in his own **e**. 5869
34:21 For his **e** *are* upon the ways of man, and 5869
36: 7 He withdraweth not his **e** from 5869
39:29 seeketh the prey, *and* her **e** behold afar off. 5869
40:24 He taketh it with his **e**: *his* nose pierceth 5869
41:18 his **e** *are* like the eyelids of the morning. 5869
Ps 10: 8 his **e** are privily set against the poor. 5869
11: 4 his **e** behold, his eyelids try, the children of 5869
13: 3 lighten mine **e**, lest I sleep the *sleep of* 5869
15: 4 In whose **e** a vile *person* is contemned; but 5869
17: 2 let thine **e** behold the things that are equal. 5869
17:11 they have set their **e** bowing down to 5869
19: 8 of the LORD *is* pure, enlightening the **e**. 5869
25:15 Mine **e** *are* ever towards the LORD; for he 5869
26: 3 For thy lovingkindness *is* before mine **e**: 5869
31:22 my haste, I am cut off from before thine **e**: 5869
34:15 The **e** of the LORD *are* upon 5869
36: 1 *that there is* no fear of God before his **e**. 5869
36: 2 For he flattereth himself in his own **e**, 5869
38:10 as for the light of mine **e**, it also is gone 5869
50:21 and set *them* in order before thine **e**. 5869
66: 7 his power for ever; his **e** behold the nations: 5869
69: 3 mine **e** fail while *I* wait for my God. 5869
69:23 Let their **e** be darkened, that *they* see not; 5869
73: 7 Their **e** stand out with fatness: they have 5869
77: 4 Thou holdest mine **e** waking: I am *so* 5869
91: 8 Only with thine **e** shalt thou behold and 5869
101: 3 I will set no wicked thing before mine **e**: 5869
101: 6 Mine **e** *shall be* upon the faithful of 5869
115: 5 speak not: **e** have they, but they see not: 5869
116: 8 mine **e** from tears, *and* my feet from falling. 5869
118:23 LORD'S doing; it is marvellous in our **e**. 5869
119:18 Open thou mine **e**, that I may behold 5869
119:37 Turn away mine **e** from beholding vanity; 5869
119:82 Mine **e** fail for thy word, saying, When wilt 5869
119:123 Mine **e** fail for thy salvation, and for 5869
119:136 Rivers of waters run down mine **e**, because 5869
119:148 Mine **e** prevent the *night* watches, that *I* 5869
121: 1 I will lift up mine **e** unto the hills, 5869
123: 1 Unto thee lift I up mine **e**, O thou that 5869
123: 2 as the **e** of servants *look* unto the hand of 5869
123: 2 as the **e** of a maiden unto the hand of her 5869
123: 2 so our **e** *wait* upon the LORD our God, 5869
131: 1 my heart is not haughty, nor mine **e** lofty: 5869
132: 4 I will not give sleep to mine **e**, *or* 5869
135:16 speak not; **e** have they, but they see not; 5869
139:16 Thine **e** did see my substance, yet being 5869
141: 8 mine **e** *are* unto thee, O GOD the Lord: 5869
145:15 The **e** of all wait upon thee; and thou givest 5869
146: 8 The LORD openeth *the* **e** *of* the blind: NIH
Pr 3: 7 Be not wise in thine own **e**: fear 5869
3:21 My son, let not them depart from thine **e**: 5869
4:21 Let them not depart from thine **e**; 5869
4:25 Let thine **e** look right on, and let thine 5869
5:21 For the ways of man *are* before the **e** of 5869
6: 4 Give not sleep to thine **e**, nor slumber to 5869
6:13 He winketh with his **e**, he speaketh with his 5869
10:26 as smoke to the **e**, so *is* the sluggard to 5869
12:15 The way of a fool *is* right in his own **e**: but 5869
15: 3 The **e** of the LORD *are* in every place, 5869
15:30 The light of the **e** rejoiceth the heart: *and* 5869
16: 2 the ways of a man *are* clean in his own **e**; 5869
16:30 He shutteth his **e** to devise froward things: 5869
17: 8 A gift *is as* a precious stone in the **e** of him 5869
17:24 the **e** of a fool *are* in the ends of the earth. 5869
20: 8 scattereth *away* all evil with his **e**. 5869
20:13 open thine **e**, *and* thou shalt be satisfied 5869
21: 2 Every way of a man *is* right in his own **e**: 5869
21:10 his neighbour findeth no favour in his **e**. 5869
22:12 The **e** of the LORD preserve knowledge, 5869
23: 5 Wilt thou set thine **e** upon that which is 5869
23:26 and let thine **e** observe my ways. 5869
23:29 without cause? who hath redness of **e**? 5869
23:33 Thine **e** shall behold strange *women*, and 5869
25: 7 of the prince whom thine **e** have seen. 5869
27:20 so the **e** of man are never satisfied. 5869
28:27 he that hideth his **e** shall have many a 5869
29:13 the LORD lighteneth both their **e**. 5869
30:12 *is* a generation *that are* pure in their own **e**, 5869
30:13 *is* a generation, O how lofty are their **e**! 5869
Ecc 2:10 whatsoever mine **e** desired I kept not from 5869
2:14 The wise *man's* **e** *are* in his head; but 5869
5:11 saving the beholding *of them* with their **e**? 5869
6: 9 Better *is* the sight of the **e** than 5869
8:16 day nor night seeth sleep with his **e**:) 5869
11: 7 a pleasant *thing it is* for the **e** to behold 5869
11: 9 of thine heart, and in the sight of thine **e**: 5869
SS 1:15 behold, thou *art* fair; thou *hast* doves' **e**. 5869

SS 4: 1 art fair; thou hast doves' e within thy locks: 5869
4: 9 hast ravished my heart with one of thine e, 5869
5:12 His e are as the eyes of doves by the rivers 5869
5:12 His eyes are as the e of doves by the rivers NIH
6: 5 Turn away thine e from me, for they have 5869
7: 4 thine e like the fishpools in Heshbon, 5869
8:10 then was I in his e as one that found favour. 5869
Isa 1:15 your hands, I will hide mine e from you: 5869
1:16 the evil of your doings from before mine e; 5869
3: 8 the LORD, to provoke the e of his glory. 5869
3:16 with stretched forth necks and wanton e, 5869
5:15 and the e of the lofty shall be humbled: 5869
5:21 Woe unto them that are wise in their own e, 5869
6: 5 for mine e have seen the King, the LORD 5869
6:10 and make their ears heavy, and shut their e 5869
6:10 lest they see with their e, and hear with 5869
11: 3 he shall not judge after the sight of his e, 5869
13:16 shall be dashed to pieces before their e; 5869
17: 7 his e shall have respect to the Holy One of 5869
29:10 spirit of deep sleep, and hath closed your e: 5869
29:18 the e of the blind shall see out of obscurity, 5869
30:20 any more, but thine e shall see thy teachers: 5869
32: 3 the e of them that see shall not be dim, and 5869
33:15 and shutteth his e from seeing evil; 5869
33:17 Thine e shall see the king in his beauty: 5869
33:20 thine e shall see Jerusalem a quiet 5869
35: 5 Then the e of the blind shall be opened, and 5869
37:17 and hear; open thine e, O LORD, and see: 5869
37:23 thy voice, and lifted up thine e on high? 5869
38:14 mine e fail with looking upward: 5869
40:26 Lift up your e on high, and behold who 5869
42: 7 To open the blind e, to bring out 5869
43: 8 Bring forth the blind people that have e, 5869
44:18 for he hath shut their e, that they cannot 5869
49: 5 yet shall I be glorious in the e of 5869
49:18 Lift up thine e round about, and behold: 5869
51: 6 Lift up your e to the heavens, and 5869
52:10 bare his holy arm in the e of all the nations; 5869
59:10 the blind, and we grope as if we had no e: 5869
60: 4 Lift up thine e round about, and see: 5869
65:12 did evil before mine e, and did choose that 5869
65:16 and because they are hid from mine e. 5869
66: 4 they did evil before mine e, and chose that 5869
Jer 3: 2 Lift up thine e unto the high places, and 5869
5: 3 O LORD, are not thine e upon the truth? 5869
5:21 which have e, and see not; which have ears, 5869
7:11 become a den of robbers in your e? 5869
9: 1 mine e a fountain of tears, that I might 5869
9:18 that our e may run down with tears, and 5869
13:20 Lift up your e, and behold them that come 5869
14: 6 their e did fail, because there was no grass. 5869
14:17 Let mine e run down with tears night and 5869
16: 9 cause to cease out of this place in your e, 5869
16:17 For mine e are upon all their ways: they are 5869
16:17 neither is their iniquity hid from mine e. 5869
20: 4 thine e shall behold it; and I will give all 5869
22:17 thine e and thine heart are not but for thy 5869
24: 6 For I will set mine e upon them for good, 5869
29:21 and he shall slay them before your e; 5869
31:16 voice from weeping, and thine e from tears: 5869
32: 4 to mouth, and his e shall behold his eyes; 5869
32: 4 to mouth, and his eyes shall behold his e: 5869
32:19 for thine e are open upon all the ways of 5869
34: 3 thine e shall behold the eyes of the king of 5869
34: 3 thine eyes shall behold the e of the king of 5869
39: 6 the sons of Zedekiah in Riblah before his e: 5869
39: 7 Moreover he put out Zedekiah's e, and 5869
42: 2 but a few of many, as thine e do behold us:) 5869
52: 2 he did that which was evil in the e of 5869
52:10 slew the sons of Zedekiah before his e: 5869
52:11 he put out the e of Zedekiah; and the king 5869
La 2:11 Mine e do fail with tears, my bowels are 5869
4:17 for us, our e as yet failed for our vain help: 5869
5:17 heart is faint; for these things our e are dim. 5869
Eze 1:18 their rings were full of e round about them 5869
6: 9 hath departed from me, and with their e, 5869
8: 5 lift up thine e now the way towards 5869
8: 5 So I lift up mine e the way toward 5869
10:12 and the wheels, were full of e round about, 5869
12: 2 which have e to see, and see not; 5869
12:12 that he see not the ground with his e. 5869
18: 6 neither hath lift up his e to the idols of 5869
18:12 and hath lift up his e to the idols, 5869
18:15 neither hath lift up his e to the idols of 5869
20: 7 away every man the abominations of his e, 5869
20: 8 man cast away the abominations of their e, 5869
20:24 and their e were after their fathers' idols. 5869
21: 6 and with bitterness sigh before their e. 5869
22:26 have hid their e from my sabbaths, and 5869
23:16 as soon as she saw them with her e, 5869
23:27 that thou shalt not lift up thine e unto them, 5869
23:40 thou didst wash thyself, paintedst thy e, 5869
24:16 I take away from thee the desire of thine e 5869
24:21 the desire of your e, and that which your 5869
24:25 the desire of their e, and that whereupon 5869
33:25 lift up your e toward your idols, and 5869
36:23 I shall be sanctified in you before their e. 5869
37:20 writest shall be in thine hand before their e. 5869
38:16 be sanctified in thee, O Gog, before their e. 5869
38:23 I will be known in the e of many nations, 5869
40: 4 behold with thine e, and hear with thine 5869
44: 5 behold with thine e, and hear with thine 5869
Da 4:34 lift up mine e unto heaven, 5870
7: 8 in this horn were e like the eyes of man, 5870
7: 8 in this horn were eyes like the e of man, 5870
7:20 even of that horn that had e, and a mouth 5870
8: 3 I lifted up mine e, and saw, and behold, 5869
8: 5 the goat had a notable horn between his e. 5869
8:21 the great horn that is between his e is 5869
9:18 open thine e, and behold our desolations, 5869
10: 5 I lift up mine e, and looked, and behold, 5869
10: 6 his e as lamps of fire, and his arms and 5869
Hos 13:14 repentance shall be hid from mine e. 5869
Joel 1:16 Is not the meat cut off before our e, yea, joy 5869
Am 9: 4 I will set mine e upon them for evil, and 5869
Am 9: 8 the e of the Lord GOD are upon the sinful 5869
Mic 7:10 mine e shall behold her: now shall she be 5869
Hab 1:13 Thou art of purer e than to behold evil, and 5869
Zep 3:20 I turn back your captivity before your e, 5869
Hag 2: 3 is it not in your e in comparison of it as 5869
Zec 1:18 lift I up mine e, and saw, and behold four 5869
2: 1 I lift up mine e again, and looked, and 5869
3: 9 upon one stone shall be seven e: 5869
4:10 they are the e of the LORD, which run to 5869
5: 1 lift up mine e, and looked, and behold, 5869
5: 5 Lift up now thine e, and see what is this 5869
5: 9 lift I up mine e, and looked, and behold, 5869
6: 1 and lift up mine e, and looked, and behold, 5869
8: 6 If it be marvellous in the e of the remnant 5869
8: 6 should it also be marvellous in my e? 5869
9: 1 when the e of man, as of all the tribes of 5869
9: 8 any more: for now have I seen with mine e. 5869
12: 4 I will open mine e upon the house of Judah, 5869
14:12 their e shall consume away in their holes, 5869
Mal 1: 5 your e shall see, and ye shall say, 5869
Mt 9:29 Then touched he their e, saying, 3788
9:30 And their e were opened; and Jesus straitly 3788
13:15 of hearing, and their e they have closed; 3788
13:15 lest at any time they should see with their e, 3788
13:16 But blessed are your e, for they see: and 3788
17: 8 And when they had lift up their e, they saw 3788
18: 9 rather than having two e to be cast into hell 3788
20:33 unto him, Lord, that our e may be opened. 3788
20:34 compassion on them, and touched their e: 3788
20:34 and immediately their e received sight, and 3788
21:42 Lord's doing, and it is marvellous in our e? 3788
26:43 them asleep again: for their e were heavy. 3788
Mk 8:18 Having e, see ye not? and having ears, 3788
8:23 and when he had spit on his e, and put his 3659
8:25 that he put his hands again upon his e, 3788
9:47 than having two e to be cast into hell fire: 3788
12:11 Lord's doing, and it is marvellous in our e? 3788
14:40 them asleep again, (for their e were heavy,) 3788
Lk 2:30 For mine e have seen thy salvation, 3788
4:20 And the e of all them that were in 3788
6:20 And he lifted up his e on his disciples, and 3788
10:23 Blessed are the e which see the things that 3788
16:23 And in hell he lift up his e, being in 3788
18:13 not lift up so much as his e unto heaven, 3788
19:42 but now they are hid from thine e. 3788
24:16 But their e were holden that they should not 3788
24:31 And their e were opened, and they knew 3788
Jn 4:35 Lift up your e, and look on the fields; 3788
6: 5 When Jesus then lift up his e, 3788
9: 6 he anointed the e of the blind man with 3788
9:10 they unto him, How were thine e opened? 3788
9:11 and anointed mine e, and said unto me, Go 3788
9:14 Jesus made the clay, and opened his e. 3788
9:15 He put clay upon mine e, and I washed, 3788
9:17 thou of him, that he hath opened thine e? 3788
9:21 or who hath opened his e, we know not: 3788
9:26 did he to thee? how opened he thine e? 3788
9:30 he is, and yet he hath opened mine e. 3788
9:32 opened the e of one that was born blind. 3788
10:21 a devil. Can a devil open the e of the blind? 3788
11:37 Could not this man, which opened the e of 3788
11:41 And Jesus lift up his e, and said, Father, 3788
12:40 He hath blinded their e, and hardened their 3788
12:40 that they should not see with their e, 3788
17: 1 and lift up his e to heaven, and said, Father, 3788
Ac 3: 4 fastening his e upon him with John, said, 816
9: 8 and when his e were opened, he saw no 3788
9:18 And immediately there fell from his e as it 3788
9:40 And she opened her e: and when she saw 3788
11: 6 Upon the which when I had fastened mine e, 816
13: 9 filled with the Holy Ghost, set his e on him, 816
26:18 To open their e, and to turn them from 3788
28:27 of hearing, and their e have they closed; 3788
28:27 lest they should see with their e, and 3788
Ro 3:18 There is no fear of God before their e. 3788
11: 8 e that they should not see, and ears that 3788
11:10 Let their e be darkened, that they may not 3788
Gal 3: 1 before whose e Jesus Christ hath been 3788
4:15 ye would have plucked out your own e, and 3788
Eph 1:18 The e of your understanding being 3788
Heb 4:13 opened unto the e of him with whom we 3788
1Pe 3:12 For the e of the Lord are over the righteous, 3788
2Pe 2:14 Having e full of adultery and that cannot 3788
1Jn 1: 1 have heard, which we have seen with our e, 3788
2:11 because that darkness hath blinded his e. 3788
2:16 and the lust of the e, and the pride of life, 3788
Rev 1:14 as snow; and his e were as a flame of fire; 3788
2:18 who hath his e like unto a flame of fire, and 3788
3:18 and anoint thine e with eyesalve, that thou 3788
4: 6 were four beasts full of e before and 3788
4: 8 about him; and they were full of e within: 3788
5: 6 been slain, having seven horns and seven e, 3788
7:17 God shall wipe away all tears from their e. 3788
19:12 His e were as a flame of fire, and on his 3788
21: 4 God shall wipe away all tears from their e; 3788

EYESALVE (1) [EYE]
Rev 3:18 and anoint thine eyes with e, that thou 2854

EYESERVICE (2) [EYE, SERVE]
Eph 6: 6 Not with e, as menpleasers; but as 3787
Col 3:22 not with e, as menpleasers; but 3787

EYESIGHT (1) [EYE, SEE]
Ps 18:24 to the cleanness of my hands in his e. 5869

EYEWITNESSES (2) [EYE, WITNESS]
Lk 1: 2 which from the beginning were e, and 845
2Pe 1:16 Jesus Christ, but were e of his majesty. 2030

EZBAI (1)
1Ch 11:37 Hezro the Carmelite, Naarai the son of E, 229

EZBON (2)
Ge 46:16 Shuni, and E, Eri, and Arodi, and Areli. 675
1Ch 7: 7 E, and Uzzi, and Uzziel, and Jerimoth, and 675

EZEKIAS (2) [HEZEKIAH]
Mt 1: 9 Joatham begat Achaz; and Achaz begat E; 1478
1:10 And E begat Manasses; and 1478

EZEKIEL (2)
Eze 1: 3 LORD came expressly unto E the priest, 3168
24:24 Thus E is unto you a sign: according to all 3168

EZEL (1) [BETH-EZEL]
1Sa 20:19 in hand, and shalt remain by the stone E. 237

EZEM (1)
1Ch 4:29 And at Bilhah, and at E, and at Tolad, 6107

EZER (10)
Ge 36:21 Dishon, and E, and Dishan: these are 687
36:27 The children of E are these; Bilhan, and 687
36:30 Duke Dishon, duke E, duke Dishan: 687
1Ch 1:38 and Anah, and Dishon, and E, and Dishan. 687
1:42 The sons of E; Bilhan, and Zavan, and 687
4: 4 of Gedor, and E the father of Hushah. 5829
7:21 and Shuthelah his son, and E, and Elead, 5827
12: 9 E the first, Obadiah the second, Eliab 5829
Ne 3:19 next to him repaired E the son of Jeshua, 5829
12:42 and Malchijah, and Elam, and E. 5829

EZION-GABER (3) [EZION-GEBER]
Nu 33:35 from Ebronah, and encamped at E. 6100
33:36 they removed from E, and pitched in 6100
Dt 2: 8 from E, we turned and passed by the way 6100

EZION-GEBER (4) [EZION-GABER]
1Ki 9:26 king Solomon made a navy of ships in E, 6100
22:48 went not; for the ships were broken at E. 6100
2Ch 8:17 went Solomon to E, and to Eloth, at the sea 6100
20:36 to Tarshish: and they made the ships in E. 6100

EZNITE (1)
2Sa 23: 8 the captains; the same was Adino the E: 6112

EZRA (26)
1Ch 4:17 the sons of E were, Jether, and Mered, and 5834
Ezr 7: 1 E the son of Seraiah, the son of Azariah, 5830
7: 6 This E went up from Babylon; and he was 5830
7:10 For E had prepared his heart to seek 5830
7:11 the king Artaxerxes gave unto E the priest, 5830
7:12 Artaxerxes, king of kings, unto E the priest, 5831
7:21 that whatsoever E the priest, the scribe of 5831
7:25 thou, E, after the wisdom of thy God, 5831
10: 1 Now when E had prayed, and when he had 5830
10: 2 sons of Elam, answered and said unto E, 5830
10: 5 arose E, and made the chief priests, 5830
10: 6 E rose up from before the house of God, 5830
10:10 E the priest stood up, and said unto them, 5830
10:16 E the priest, with certain chief of 5830
Ne 8: 1 they spake unto E the scribe to bring 5830
8: 2 E the priest brought the law before 5830
8: 4 E the scribe stood upon a pulpit of wood, 5830
8: 5 E opened the book in the sight of all 5830
8: 6 E blessed the LORD, the great God. 5830
8: 9 E the priest the scribe, and the Levites that 5830
8:13 and the Levites, unto E the scribe, 5830
12: 1 and Jeshua: Seraiah, Jeremiah, E, 5830
12:13 Of E, Meshullam; of Amariah, Jehohanan; 5830
12:26 the governor, and of E the priest, the scribe. 5830
12:33 And Azariah, E, and Meshullam, 5830
12:36 man of God, and E the scribe before them. 5830

EZRAHITE (3)
1Ki 4:31 than Ethan the E, and Heman, and Chalcol, 250
Ps 88: T Maschil of Heman the E. 250
89: T Maschil of Ethan the E. 250

EZRI (1)
1Ch 27:26 of the ground was E the son of Chelub: 5836

F

FABLES (5)
1Ti 1: 4 Neither give heed to f and 3454
4: 7 But refuse profane and old wives' f, and 3454
2Ti 4: 4 from the truth, and shall be turned unto f. 3454
Tit 1:14 Not giving heed to Jewish f, and 3454
2Pe 1:16 we have not followed cunningly devised f, 3454

FACE (416) [FACES]
Ge 1: 2 and darkness was upon the f of the deep. 6440
1: 2 the Spirit of God moved upon the f of 6440
1:29 which is upon the f of all the earth, and 6440
2: 6 and watered the whole f of the ground. 6440
3:19 In the sweat of thy f shalt thou eat bread, 639
4:14 thou hast driven me out this day from the f 6440
4:14 from thy f shall I be hid; and I shall be a 6440
6: 1 when men began to multiply on the f of 6440
6: 7 I have created from the f of the earth; 6440
7: 3 to keep seed alive upon the f of all 6440
7: 4 will I destroy from off the f of the earth. 6440
7:18 and the ark went upon the f of the waters. 6440

Ge 7:23 which *was* upon the f of the ground, 6440
8: 8 were abated from off the f of the ground; 6440
8: 9 for the waters *were* on the f of the whole 6440
8:13 and behold, the f of the ground was dry. 6440
11: 4 lest we be scattered abroad upon the f of 6440
11: 8 from thence upon the f of all the earth: 6440
11: 9 them abroad upon the f of all the earth. 6440
16: 6 dealt hardly with her, she fled from her f. 6440
16: 8 I flee from the f of my mistress Sarai. 6440
17: 3 Abram fell on his f: and God talked with 6440
17:17 Abraham fell upon his f, and laughed, and 6440
19: 1 he bowed himself with his f toward 639
19:13 the cry of them is waxen great before the f 6440
24:47 I put the earring upon her f, and the bracelets 639
30:33 when it shall come for my hire before thy f: 6440
31:21 and set his f *toward* the mount Gilead. 6440
32:20 before me, and afterward I will see his f; 6440
32:30 for I have seen God f to face, and my life is 6440
32:30 for I have seen God face to f, and my life is 6440
33:10 for therefore I have seen thy f, as though I 6440
33:10 as though I had seen the f of God, and 6440
35: 1 fleddest from the f of Esau thy brother. 6440
35: 7 when he fled from the f of his brother. 6440
36: 6 went into the country from the f of his 6440
38:15 be a harlot; because she had covered her f. 6440
41:56 the famine was over all the f of the earth: 6440
43: 3 saying, Ye shall not see my f, except your 6440
43: 5 the man said unto us, Ye shall not see my f, 6440
43:31 he washed his f, and went out, and 6440
44:23 down with you, ye shall see my f no more. 6440
44:26 for we may not see the man's f, except our 6440
46:28 unto Joseph, to direct his f unto Goshen; 6440
46:30 since I have seen thy f, because thou *art* yet 6440
48:11 unto Joseph, I had not thought to see thy f: 6440
48:12 and he bowed himself with his f to the earth. 639
50: 1 Joseph fell upon his father's f, and 6440
50:18 also went and fell down before his f; 6440
Ex 2:15 Moses fled from the f of Pharaoh, and 6440
3: 6 Moses hid his f; for he was afraid to look 6440
10: 5 they shall cover the f of the earth, that *one* 5869
10:15 For they covered the f of the whole earth, 5869
10:28 take heed to thyself, see my f no more; 6440
10:28 for in *that* day thou seest my f thou shalt 6440
10:29 spoken well, I will see thy f again no more. 6440
14:19 pillar of the cloud went from **before** their f, 6440
14:25 Let us flee from the f of Israel; 6440
16:14 upon the f of the wilderness *there lay* a 6440
32:12 to consume them from the f of the earth? 6440
33:11 the LORD spake unto Moses f to face, 6440
33:11 the LORD spake unto Moses face to f, 6440
33:16 from all the people that *are* upon the f of 6440
33:20 he said, Thou canst not see my f: for there 6440
33:23 my back parts: but my f shall not be seen. 6440
34:29 that Moses wist not that the skin of his f 6440
34:30 saw Moses, behold, the skin of his f shone; 6440
34:33 speaking with them, he put a vail on his f. 6440
34:35 the children of Israel saw the f of Moses, 6440
34:35 of Moses, that the skin of Moses' f shone: 6440
34:35 Moses put the vail upon his f again, until he 6440
Lev 13:41 off from the part of *his head toward* his f, 6440
17:10 I will even set my f against *that* soul that 6440
19:32 honour the f of the old man, and fear thy 6440
20: 3 I will set my f against that man, and 6440
20: 5 I will set my f against that man, and 6440
20: 6 I will even set my f against that soul, and 6440
26:17 I will set my f against you, and ye shall be 6440
Nu 6:25 The LORD make his f shine upon thee, 6440
11:31 as it were two cubits *high* upon the f of 6440
12: 3 above all the men which *were* upon the f of 6440
12:14 If her father had but spit in her f, 6440
14:14 that thou LORD *art* seen f to face, and 5869
14:14 that thou LORD *art* seen face to f, and 5869
16: 4 when Moses heard *it,* he fell upon his f: 6440
19: 3 and *one* shall slay her before his f: 6440
22: 5 they cover the f of the earth, and they abide 5869
22:11 of Egypt, which covereth the f of the earth: 5869
22:31 bowed down his head, and fell flat on his f. 639
24: 1 but he set his f toward the wilderness. 6440
Dt 1:17 you shall not be afraid of the f of man; 6440
5: 4 The LORD talked with you f to face in 6440
5: 4 The LORD talked with you face to f in 6440
6:15 and destroy thee from off the f of the earth. 6440
7: 6 above all people that *are* upon the f of 6440
7:10 repayeth them that hate him to their f, 6440
7:10 that hateth him, he will repay him to his f. 6440
8:20 which the LORD destroyeth before your f, 6440
9: 3 and he shall bring them down before thy f: 6440
25: 2 to be beaten before his f, according to his 6440
25: 9 and spit in his f, and shall answer and say, 6440
28: 7 up against thee *to be* smitten before thy f: 6440
28:31 *be* violently taken away from before thy f, 6440
31: 5 LORD shall give them up before your f, 6440
31:17 I will hide my f from them, and they shall 6440
31:18 I will surely hide my f in that day for all 6440
32:20 he said, I will hide my f from them, I will 6440
34:10 whom the LORD knew f to face, 6440
34:10 whom the LORD knew face to f, 6440
Jos 5:14 Joshua fell on his f to the earth, and 6440
7: 6 fell to the earth upon his f before the ark of 6440
7:10 wherefore liest thou thus upon thy f? 6440
Jdg 6:22 I have seen an angel of the LORD f to 6440
6:22 have seen an angel of the LORD face to f. 6440
Ru 2:10 she fell on her f, and bowed herself to 6440
1Sa 5: 3 Dagon *was* fallen upon his f to the earth 6440
5: 4 Dagon *was* fallen upon his f to the ground 6440
17:49 and he fell upon his f to the earth. 6440
20:15 of David every one from the f of the earth. 6440
20:41 fell on his f to the ground, and 639
24: 8 David stooped *with his* f to the earth, and 639
25:23 fell before David on her f, and 6440
25:41 bowed herself *on her* f to the earth, and said, 639
26:20 fall to the earth before the f of the LORD: 6440
28:14 and he stooped *with his* f to the ground, and 639
2Sa 2:22 should I hold up my f to Joab thy brother? 6440
3:13 of thee, that is, Thou shalt not see my f, 6440
2Sa 3:13 when thou comest to see my f. 6440
9: 6 he fell on his f, and did reverence. 6440
14: 4 she fell on her f to the ground, and 639
14:22 Joab fell to the ground on his f, and 6440
14:24 to his own house, and let him not see my f. 6440
14:24 to his own house, and saw not the king's f. 6440
14:28 in Jerusalem, and saw not the king's f. 6440
14:32 now therefore let me see the king's f; and 6440
14:33 bowed himself on his f to the ground before 639
18: 8 For the battle was there scattered over the f 6440
18:28 he fell down to the earth upon his f before 639
19: 4 the king covered his f, and the king cried 6440
24:20 bowed himself before the king *on* his f upon 639
1Ki 1:23 he bowed himself before the king with his f 639
1:31 Bath-sheba bowed *with her* f *to* the earth, 639
8:14 the king turned his f about, and blessed all 6440
13: 6 Intreat now the f of the LORD thy God, 6440
13:34 and to destroy *it* from off the f of the earth. 6440
18: 7 he knew him, and fell on his f, and said, 6440
18:42 the earth, and put his f between his knees, 6440
19:13 when Elijah heard *it,* that he wrapped his f 6440
20:38 disguised himself with ashes upon his f. 5869
20:41 and took the ashes away from his f; 5869
21: 4 turned away his f, and would eat no bread. 6440
2Ki 4:29 and lay my staff upon the f of the child. 6440
4:31 and laid the staff upon the f of the child; 6440
8:15 and spread *it* on his f, so that he died: 6440
9:30 Jezebel heard *of it;* and she painted her f, 5869
9:32 he lift up his f to the window, and said, 6440
9:37 the f of the field *in* the portion of Jezreel; 6440
12:17 and Hazael set his f to go up to Jerusalem. 6440
13:14 wept over his f, and said, O my father, 6440
14: 8 Come, let us look one another *in* the f. 6440
14:11 one another *in* the f at Beth-shemesh, 6440
18:24 wilt thou turn away the f of one captain of 6440
20: 2 he turned his f to the wall, and prayed unto 6440
1Ch 16:11 and his strength, seek his f continually. 6440
21:21 bowed himself to David *with his* f to 639
2Ch 6: 3 the king turned his f, and blessed the whole 6440
6:42 turn not away the f of thine anointed: 6440
7:14 seek my f, and turn from their wicked 6440
20:18 Jehoshaphat bowed his head *with his* f to 639
25:17 Come, let us see one another *in* the f. 6440
25:21 they saw one another *in* the f, *both* he and 6440
30: 9 and will not turn away *his* f from you, 6440
32:21 So he returned with shame of f to his own 6440
35:22 Nevertheless Josiah would not turn his f 6440
Ezr 9: 6 and blush to lift up my f to thee, 6440
9: 7 and to a spoil, and to confusion of f, 6440
Est 1:14 which saw the king's f, *and* which sat 6440
7: 8 the king's mouth, they covered Haman's f. 6440
Job 1:11 that he hath, and he will curse thee to thy f. 6440
2: 5 his flesh, and he will curse thee to thy f. 6440
4:15 a spirit passed before my f; the hair of my 6440
11:15 then shalt thou lift up thy f without spot; 6440
13:24 Wherefore hidest thou thy f, and 6440
15:27 Because he covereth his f with his fatness, 6440
16: 8 rising up in me beareth witness to my f. 6440
16:16 My f is foul with weeping, and on mine 6440
21:31 Who shall declare his way to his f? and 6440
22:26 and shalt lift up thy f unto God. 6440
23:17 hath he covered the darkness from my f. 6440
24:15 No eye shall see me: and disguiseth *his* f. 6440
26: 9 He holdeth back the f of *his* throne, *and* 6440
30:10 far from me, and spare not to spit in my f. 6440
33:26 he shall see his f with joy: for he will 6440
34:29 when he hideth *his* f, who then can behold 6440
37:12 them upon the f of the world in the earth. 6440
38:30 *with* a stone, and the f of the deep is frozen. 6440
41:13 Who can discover the f of his garment? *or* 6440
41:14 Who can open the doors of his f? his teeth 6440
Ps 5: 8 make thy way straight before my f. 6440
10:11 he hideth his f; he will never see *it.* 6440
13: 1 how long wilt thou hide thy f from me? 6440
17:15 *for* me, I will behold thy f in righteousness: 6440
21:12 upon thy strings against the f of them. 6440
22:24 neither hath he hid his f from him; but 6440
24: 6 that seek him, that seek thy f, O Jacob. 6440
27: 8 *When thou saidst,* Seek ye my f; my heart 6440
27: 8 said unto thee, Thy f, LORD, will I seek. 6440
27: 9 Hide not thy f *far* from me; put not thy 6440
30: 7 thou didst hide thy f, *and* I was troubled. 6440
31:16 Make thy f to shine upon thy servant: 6440
34:16 The f of the LORD *is* against them that do 6440
41:12 and settest me before thy f for ever. 6440
44:15 and the shame of my f hath covered me, 6440
44:24 Wherefore hidest thou thy f, *and* 6440
51: 9 Hide thy f from my sins, and blot out all 6440
67: 1 *and* cause his f to shine upon us; Selah. 6440
69: 7 borne reproach; shame hath covered my f. 6440
69:17 hide not thy f from thy servant; for I am in 6440
80: 3 us again, O God, and cause thy f to shine; 6440
80: 7 O God *of* hosts, and cause thy f to shine; 6440
80:19 LORD God *of* hosts, cause thy f to shine; 6440
84: 9 and look upon the f of thine anointed. 6440
88:14 my soul? *why* hidest thou thy f from me? 6440
89:14 mercy and truth shall go before thy f. 6440
89:23 I will beat down his foes before his f, and 6440
102: 2 Hide not thy f from me in the day *when* I 6440
104:15 *and* oil to make *his* f to shine, and 6440
104:29 Thou hidest thy f, they are troubled: 6440
104:30 and thou renewest the f of the earth. 6440
105: 4 and his strength: seek his f evermore. 6440
119:135 Make thy f to shine upon thy servant; and 6440
132:10 sake turn not away the f of thine anointed. 6440
143: 7 hide not thy f from me, lest I be like unto 6440
Pr 7:13 and with an impudent f said unto him, 6440
7:15 diligently to seek thy f, and I have found 6440
8:27 when he set a compass upon the f of 6440
21:29 A wicked man hardeneth his f: but *as for* 6440
24:31 *and* nettles had covered the f thereof, and 6440
27:19 As *in* water f *answereth* to face, so the heart 6440
27:19 As *in* water face *answereth* to the f, so the heart 6440
Ecc 8: 1 a man's wisdom maketh his f to shine, and 6440
8: 1 and the boldness of his f shall be changed. 6440
Isa 6: 2 with twain he covered his f, and with twain 6440
8:17 that hideth his f from the house of Jacob, 6440
14:21 nor fill the f of the world *with* cities. 6440
16: 4 be thou a covert to them from the f of 6440
23:17 of the world upon the f of the earth. 6440
25: 7 he will destroy in this mountain the f of 6440
27: 6 bud, and fill the f of the world *with* fruit. 6440
28:25 When he hath made plain the f thereof, 6440
29:22 neither shall his f now wax pale. 6440
36: 9 wilt thou turn away the f of one captain of 6440
38: 2 Hezekiah turned his f toward the wall, 6440
49:23 they shall bow down to thee *with their* f 639
50: 6 I hid not my f from shame and spitting. 6440
50: 7 therefore have I set my f like a flint, and 6440
54: 8 In a little wrath I hid my f from thee for a 6440
59: 2 and your sins have hid *his* f from you, 6440
64: 7 for thou hast hid thy f from us, and 6440
65: 3 provoketh me to anger continually to my f; 6440
Jer 1:13 and the f thereof *is* towards the north. 6440
2:27 turned *their* back unto me, and not *their* f: 6440
4:30 though thou rentest thy f with painting, 5869
8: 2 they shall be for dung upon the f of 6440
13:26 will I discover thy skirts upon thy f, 6440
16: 4 they shall be as dung upon the f of the 6440
16:17 they are not hid from my f, neither is their 6440
18:17 I will shew them the back, and not the f, 6440
21:10 For I have set my f against this city for evil, 6440
22:25 into the hand *of them* whose f thou fearest, 6440
25:26 which *are* upon the f of the earth: 6440
28:16 I will cast thee from off the f of the earth: 6440
32:31 that *I* should remove it from before my f, 6440
32:33 turned unto me the back, and not the f: 6440
33: 5 for all whose wickedness I have hid my f 6440
44:11 I will set my f against you for evil, and 6440
La 2:19 pour out thine heart like water before the f 6440
3:35 To turn aside the right of a man before the f 6440
Eze 1:10 they four had the f of a man, and the face of 6440
1:10 a man, and the f of a lion, on the right side: 6440
1:10 they four had the f of an ox on the left side; 6440
1:10 they four also had the f of an eagle. 6440
1:28 when I saw *it,* I fell upon my f, and I heard 6440
3: 8 I have made thy f strong against their faces, 6440
3:23 by the river of Chebar: and I fell on my f. 6440
4: 3 set thy f against it, and it shall be besieged, 6440
4: 7 Therefore thou shalt set thy f toward 6440
6: 2 set thy f towards the mountains of Israel, 6440
7:22 My f will I turn also from them, and 6440
9: 8 that I fell upon my f, and cried, and said, 6440
10:14 the first f *was* the face of a cherub, and 6440
10:14 the first face *was* the f of a cherub, and 6440
10:14 the second f *was* the face of a man, and 6440
10:14 the second face *was* the f of a man, and 6440
10:14 the third the f of a lion, and the fourth 6440
10:14 of a lion, and the fourth the f of an eagle. 6440
11:13 fell I down upon my f, and cried *with* a 6440
12: 6 thou shalt cover thy f, that thou see not 6440
12:12 he shall cover his f, that he see not 6440
13:17 set thy f against the daughters of thy 6440
14: 3 of their iniquity before their f: 6440
14: 4 stumblingblock of his iniquity before his f, 6440
14: 7 stumblingblock of his iniquity before his f, 6440
14: 8 I will set my f against that man, and 6440
15: 7 I will set my f against them; they shall go 6440
15: 7 the LORD, when I set my f against them. 6440
20:35 and there will I plead with you f to face. 6440
20:35 and there will I plead with you face to f. 6440
20:46 set thy f toward the south, and drop *thy* 6440
21: 2 set thy f toward Jerusalem, and drop *thy* 6440
21:16 on the left, whithersoever thy f *is* set. 6440
25: 2 set thy f against the Ammonites, 6440
28:21 set thy f against Zidon, and 6440
29: 2 set thy f against Pharaoh king of Egypt, and 6440
34: 6 my flock was scattered upon all the f of 6440
35: 2 set thy f against mount Seir, and 6440
38: 2 Son of man, set thy f against Gog, the land 6440
38:18 *that* my fury shall come up in my f. 639
38:20 all the men that *are* upon the f of the earth, 6440
39:14 those that remain upon the f of the earth, 6440
39:23 therefore hid I my f from them, and 6440
39:24 I done unto them, and hid my f from them. 6440
39:29 Neither will I hide my f any more from 6440
40:15 from the f of the gate of the entrance unto 6440
40:15 f of the porch of the inner gate *were* fifty 6440
41:14 Also the breadth of the f of the house, and 6440
41:19 So that the f of a man *was* toward the palm 6440
41:19 the f of a young lion toward the palm tree 6440
41:21 *were* squared, *and* the f of the sanctuary; 6440
41:25 *there were* thick planks upon the f of 6440
43: 3 by the river Chebar; and I fell upon my f. 6440
44: 4 house of the LORD: and I fell upon my f. 6440
Da 2:46 the king Nebuchadnezzar fell upon his f, 600
8: 5 a he goat came from the west on the f of 6440
8:17 he came, I was afraid, and fell upon my f: 6440
8:18 I was in a deep sleep on my f toward 6440
9: 3 I set my f unto the Lord God, to seek *by* 6440
9: 8 O Lord, to us *belongeth* confusion of f, 6440
9:17 cause thy f to shine upon thy sanctuary that 6440
10: 6 his f as the appearance of lightning, and 6440
10: 9 was I in a deep sleep on my f, and my face 6440
10: 9 on my face, and my f toward the ground. 6440
10:15 I set my f toward the ground, and I became 6440
11:17 He shall also set his f to enter with 6440
11:18 After this shall he turn his f unto the isles, 6440
11:19 he shall turn his f towards the fort of his 6440
Hos 5: 5 the pride of Israel doth testify to his f: 6440
5:15 acknowledge their offence, and seek my f: 6440
7: 2 beset them about; they are before my f. 6440
7:10 the pride of Israel testifieth to his f: and 6440
Joel 2: 6 Before their f *the* people shall be much 6440
2:20 with his f toward the east sea, and 6440
Am 5: 8 poureth them out upon the f of the earth: 6440
9: 6 poureth them out upon the f of the earth: 6440
9: 8 I will destroy it from off the f of the earth; 6440
Mic 3: 4 he will even hide his f from them at that 6440
Na 2: 1 dasheth in pieces is come up before thy f: 6440

Na 3: 5 I will discover thy skirts upon thy f, and 6440
Zec 5: 3 This is the curse that goeth forth over the f 6440
Mt 6:17 anoint thine head, and wash thy f; 4383
11:10 Behold, I send my messenger before thy f, 4383
16: 3 ye can discern the f of the sky; 4383
17: 2 and his f did shine as the sun, and 4383
17: 6 the disciples heard it, they fell on their f, 4383
18:10 the f of my Father which is in heaven. 4383
26:39 and fell on his f, and prayed, saying, O my 4383
26:67 Then did they spit in his f, and 4383
Mk 1: 2 Behold, I send my messenger before thy f, 4383
14:65 and to cover his f, and to buffet him, and 4383
Lk 1:76 for thou shalt go before the f of the Lord to 4383
2:31 Which thou hast prepared before the f of all 4383
5:12 who seeing Jesus fell on his f, and 4383
7:27 Behold, I send my messenger before thy f, 4383
9:51 he stedfastly set his f to go to Jerusalem, 4383
9:52 And sent messengers before his f: and 4383
9:53 his f was as though he would go to 4383
10: 1 and two before his f into every city and 4383
12:56 ye can discern the f of the sky and of 4383
17:16 And fell down on his f at his feet, 4383
21:35 them that dwell on the f of the whole earth. 4383
22:64 they stroke him on the f, and asked him, 4383
Jn 11:44 and his f was bound about with a napkin. 3799
Ac 2:25 I foresaw the Lord always before my f, 1799
6:15 saw his f as it had been the face of an 4383
6:15 saw his face as it had been the f of an 4383
7:45 whom God drave out before the f of our 4383
17:26 of men for to dwell on all the f of the earth, 4383
20:25 kingdom of God, shall see my f no more. 4383
20:38 that they should see his f no more. 4383
25:16 accused have the accusers f to face, 2596+4383
25:16 accused have the accusers face to f, 2596+4383
1Co 13:12 through a glass, darkly; but then f to face: 4383
13:12 through a glass, darkly; but then face to f: 4383
14:25 falling down on his f he will worship God, 4383
2Co 3: 7 f of Moses for the glory of his countenance; 4383
3:13 not as Moses, which put a vail over his f, 4383
3:18 with open f beholding as in a glass 4383
4: 6 of the glory of God in the f of Jesus Christ. 4383
11:20 exalt himself, if a man smite you on the f. 4383
Gal 1:22 And was unknown by f unto the churches 4383
2:11 I withstood him to the f, because he was to 4383
Col 2: 1 for as many as have not seen my f in 4383
1Th 2:17 abundantly to see your f with great desire. 4383
3:10 exceedingly that we might see your f, 4383
Jas 1:23 he is like unto a man beholding his natural f 4383
1Pe 3:12 the f of the Lord is against them that do 4383
2Jn 1:12 and speak f to face, that our joy may be 4750
1:12 and speak face to f, that our joy may be 4750
3Jn 1:14 see thee, and we shall speak f to face. 4750
1:14 see thee, and we shall speak face to f. 4750
Rev 4: 7 and the third beast had a f as a man, and 4383
6:16 hide us from the f of him that sitteth on 4383
10: 1 and his f was as it were the sun, and his feet 4383
12:14 and half a time, from the f of the serpent. 4383
20:11 from whose f the earth and the heaven fled 4383
22: 4 And they shall see his f; and his name shall 4383

FACES (73) [FACE]
Ge 9:23 their f were backward, and they saw not 6440
18:22 the men turned their f from thence, and 6437
30:40 set the f of the flocks toward 6440
42: 6 before him with their f to the earth. 639
Ex 19: 7 laid before their f all these words which 6440
20:20 that his fear may be before your f, that ye 6440
25:20 and their f shall look one to another; 6440
25:20 toward the mercy seat shall the f of 6440
37: 9 the mercy seat, with their f one to another; 6440
37: 9 even to the mercy seatward were the f of 6440
Lev 9:24 they shouted, and fell on their f. 6440
Nu 14: 5 Aaron fell on their f before all the assembly 6440
16:22 they fell upon their f, and said, O God, 6440
16:45 as in a moment. And they fell upon their f. 6440
20: 6 the congregation, and they fell upon their f: 6440
Jdg 13:20 on it, and fell on their f to the ground. 6440
18:23 they turned their f, and said unto Micah, 6440
2Sa 19: 5 Thou hast shamed this day the f of all thy 6440
1Ki 2:15 that all Israel set their f on me, that I should 6440
18:39 all the people saw it, they fell on their f: 6440
1Ch 12: 8 whose f were like the faces of lions, and 6440
12: 8 whose faces were like the f of lions, and 6440
21:16 were clothed in sackcloth, fell upon their f. 6440
2Ch 3:13 stood on their feet, and their f were inward. 6440
7: 3 they bowed themselves with their f to 639
29: 6 have turned away their f from 6440
Ne 8: 6 worshipped the LORD with their f to 639
Job 9:24 he covereth the f of the judges thereof; 6440
40:13 the dust together; and bind their f in secret. 6440
Ps 34: 5 and their f were not ashamed. 6440
83:16 Fill their f with shame; that they may seek 6440
Isa 3:15 to pieces, and grind the f of the poor? 6440
13: 8 one at another; their f shall be as flames. 6440
25: 8 GOD will wipe away tears from off all f; 6440
53: 3 we hid as it were our f from him; he was 6440
Jer 1: 8 Be not afraid of their f: for I am with thee 6440
1:17 be not dismayed at their f, lest I confound 6440
5: 3 they have made their f harder than a rock; 6440
7:19 themselves to the confusion of their own f? 6440
30: 6 in travail, and all f are turned into paleness? 6440
42:15 If ye wholly set your f to enter into Egypt, 6440
42:17 set their f to go into Egypt to sojourn there; 6440
44:12 that have set their f to go into the land of 6440
50: 5 They shall ask the way to Zion with their f 6440
51:51 shame hath covered our f: for strangers are 6440
La 5:12 the f of elders were not honoured. 6440
Eze 1: 6 every one had four f, and every one had 6440
1: 8 and they four had their f and their wings. 6440
1:10 As for the likeness of their f, they four had 6440
1:11 Thus were their f: and their wings were 6440
1:15 by the living creatures, with his four f. 6440
3: 8 I have made thy face strong against their f, 6440
7:18 shame shall be upon all f, and 6440
8:16 of the LORD, and their f towards the east; 6440
Eze 10:14 every one had four f: the first face was 6440
10:21 Every one had four f apiece, and every one 6440
10:22 the likeness of their f was the same faces 6440
10:22 the likeness of their faces was the same f 6440
14: 6 turn away your f from all your 6440
20:47 all f from the south to the north shall be 6440
41:18 and a cherub; and every cherub had two f; 6440
Da 1:10 for why should he see your f worse liking 6440
9: 7 but unto us confusion of f, as at this day; 6440
Joel 2: 6 much pained: all f shall gather blackness. 6440
Na 2:10 the f of them all gather blackness. 6440
Hab 1: 9 their f shall sup up as the east wind, and 6440
Mal 2: 3 your seed, and spread dung upon your f, 6440
Mt 6:16 for they disfigure their f, that they may 4383
Lk 24: 5 and bowed down their f to the earth, 4383
Rev 7:11 and fell before the throne on their f, and 4383
9: 7 and their f were as the faces of men. 4383
9: 7 and their faces were as the f of men. 4383
11:16 fell upon their f, and worshipped God, 4383

FADE (6) [FADETH, FADING]
2Sa 22:46 Strangers shall f away, and they shall be 5034
Ps 18:45 The strangers shall f away, and be afraid 5034
Isa 64: 6 we all do f as a leaf; and our iniquities, 5034
Jer 8:13 nor figs on the fig tree, and the leaf shall f; 5034
Eze 47:12 all trees for meat, whose leaf shall not f, 5034
Jas 1:11 also shall the rich man f away in his ways. 3133

FADETH (7) [FADE]
Isa 1:30 For ye shall be as an oak whose leaf f, and 5034
24: 4 The earth mourneth and f away, the world 5034
24: 4 the world languisheth and f away, 5034
40: 7 The grass withereth, the flower f: because 5034
40: 8 The grass withereth, the flower f: but 5034
1Pe 1: 4 and undefiled, and that f not away, 263
5: 4 receive a crown of glory that f not away. 262

FADING (2) [FADE]
Isa 28: 1 whose glorious beauty is a f flower, 5034
28: 4 shall be a f flower, and as the hasty fruit 5034

FAIL (64) [FAILED, FAILETH, FAILING]
Ge 47:16 I will give you for your cattle, if money f. 656
Dt 28:32 f with longing for them all the day long: 3616
31: 6 he will not f thee, nor forsake thee. 7503
31: 8 he will be with thee, he will not f thee, 7503
Jos 1: 5 with thee: I will not f thee, nor forsake thee. 7503
3:10 that he will without f drive out from 3423+3423
Jdg 11:30 If thou shalt without f deliver 5414+5414
1Sa 2:16 Let them not f to burn the fat 6999+6999
17:32 Let no man's heart f because of him; 5307
20: 5 I should not f to sit with the king at meat: 3427
30: 8 and without f recover all. 5337+5337
2Sa 3:29 let there not f from the house of Joab one 3772
1Ki 2: 4 all their soul, there shall not f thee (said he) 3772
8:25 There shall not f thee a man in my sight to 3772
9: 5 There shall not f thee a man upon 3772+3807.1
17:14 not waste, neither shall the cruse of oil f, 2637
17:16 wasted not, neither did the cruse of oil f, 2638
1Ch 28:20 he will not f thee, nor forsake thee, 7503
2Ch 6:16 There shall not f thee a man in my sight to 3772
7:18 There shall not f thee a man to be ruler in 3772
Ezr 4:22 Take heed now that ye f not to do this: why 7960
6: 9 let it be given them day by day without f: 7960
Est 6:10 let nothing f of all that thou hast spoken. 5307
9:27 themselves unto them, so as it should not f, 5674
9:28 that these days of Purim should not f from 5674
Job 11:20 the eyes of the wicked shall f, and 3615
14:11 As the waters f from the sea, and the flood 235
17: 5 even the eyes of his children shall f. 3615
31:16 or have caused the eyes of the widow to f; 3615
Ps 12: 1 for the faithful f from among the children 6461
69: 3 mine eyes f while I wait for my God. 3615
77: 8 for ever? doth his promise f for evermore? 1584
89:33 from him, nor suffer my faithfulness to f. 8266
119:82 Mine eyes f for thy word, saying, 3615
119:123 Mine eyes f for thy salvation, and for 3615
Pr 22: 8 reap vanity: and the rod of his anger shall f. 3615
Ecc 12: 5 shall be a burden, and desire shall f: 6565
Isa 19: 3 the spirit of Egypt shall f in the midst 1238
19: 5 the waters shall f from the sea, and the river 5405
21:16 and all the glory of Kedar shall f: 3615
31: 3 fall down, and they all shall f together. 3615
32: 6 he will cause the drink of the thirsty to f. 2637
32:10 ye careless women: for the vintage shall f, 3615
34:16 no one of these shall f, none shall want her 5737
38:14 mine eyes f with looking upward: 1809
42: 4 He shall not f nor be discouraged, till he 3543
51:14 die in the pit, nor that his bread should f. 2637
57:16 for the spirit should f before me, and 5848
58:11 like a spring of water, whose waters f not. 3576
Jer 14: 6 their eyes did f, because there was no grass. 3615
15:18 unto me as a liar, and as waters that f? 539+3808
48:33 I have caused wine to f from the wine 7673
La 2:11 Mine eyes do f with tears, my bowels are 3615
3:22 because his compassions f not. 3615
Hos 9: 2 feed them, and the new wine shall f in her. 3584
Am 8: 4 even to make the poor of the land to f, 7673
Hab 3:17 the labour of the olive shall f, and the fields 3584
Lk 16: 9 that, when ye f, they may receive you into 1587
16:17 earth to pass, than one tittle of the law to f. 4098
22:32 I have prayed for thee, that thy faith f not: 1587
1Co 13: 8 whether there be prophecies, they shall f; 2673
Heb 1:12 thou art the same, and thy years shall not f. 1587
11:32 for the time would f me to tell of Gedeon, 1952
12:15 Looking diligently lest any man f of 5302

FAILED (12) [FAIL]
Ge 42:28 and their heart f them, and they were afraid, 3318
47:15 when money f in the land of Egypt, and 8552
Jos 3:16 even the salt sea, f, and were cut off: 8552
21:45 There f not ought of any good thing which 5307
23:14 that not one thing hath f of all the good 5307
23:14 unto you, and not one thing hath f thereof. 5307
1Ki 8:56 there hath not f one word of all his good 5307
Job 19:14 My kinsfolk have f, and my familiar friends 2308
Ps 142: 4 refuge f me; no man cared for my soul. 6+4480
SS 5: 6 my soul f when he spake: I sought him, but 3318
Jer 51:30 their might hath f; they became as women: 5405
La 4:17 for us, our eyes as yet f for our vain help: 3615

FAILETH (19) [FAIL]
Ge 47:15 we die in thy presence? for the money f. 656
Job 21:10 Their bull gendereth, and f not; their cow 1602
Ps 31:10 my strength f because of mine iniquity, and 3782
38:10 My heart panteth, my strength f me: as for 5800
40:12 of mine head: therefore my heart f me. 5800
71: 9 forsake me not when my strength f. 3615
73:26 My flesh and my heart f: but God is 3615
109:24 through fasting; and my flesh f of fatness. 3584
143: 7 my spirit f: hide not thy face from me, lest I 3615
Ecc 10: 3 his wisdom f him, and he saith to every one 2638
Isa 15: 6 the grass f, there is no green thing. 3615
40:26 for that he is strong in power; not one f. 5737
41:17 there is none, and their tongue f for thirst, 5405
44:12 yea, he is hungry, and his strength f: 369
59:15 Yea, truth f; and he that departeth from evil 5737
Eze 12:22 The days are prolonged, and every vision f? 6
Zep 3: 5 he bring his judgment to light, he f not; 5737
Lk 12:33 a treasure in the heavens that f not, where no 413
1Co 13: 8 Charity never f: 1601

FAILING (2) [FAIL]
Dt 28:65 and f of eyes, and sorrow of mind: 3631
Lk 21:26 Men's hearts f them for fear, and 674

FAIN (2)
Job 27:22 he would f flee out of his hand. 1272+1272
Lk 15:16 And he would f have filled his belly with 1937

FAINT (41) [FAINTED, FAINTEST, FAINTETH, FAINTHEARTED, FAINTNESS]
Ge 25:29 and Esau came from the field, and he was f: 5889
25:30 with that same red pottage; for I am f: 5889
Dt 20: 3 let not your hearts f, fear not, and do not 7401
20: 8 lest his brethren's heart f as well as his 4549
25:18 behind thee, when thou wast f and weary; 5889
Jos 2: 9 that all the inhabitants of the land f because 4127
2:24 even all the inhabitants of the country do f 4127
Jdg 8: 4 that were with him, f, yet pursuing them. 5889
8: 5 for they be f, and I am pursuing after Zebah 5889
1Sa 14:28 any food this day. And the people were f. 5774
14:31 to Aijalon: and the people were very f. 5774
30:10 so f that they could not go over the brook 6296
30:21 so f that they could not follow David, 6296
2Sa 16: 2 that such as be f in the wilderness may 3287
21:15 against the Philistines: and David waxed f. 5774
Pr 24:10 If thou f in the day of adversity, 7503
Isa 1: 5 whole head is sick, and the whole heart f. 1742
13: 7 Therefore shall all hands be f, and 7503
29: 8 behold, he is f, and his soul hath appetite: 5889
40:29 He giveth power to the f; and to them that 3287
40:30 Even the youths shall f and be weary, and 3286
40:31 be weary; and they shall walk, and not f. 3286
44:12 he drinketh no water, and is f. 3286
Jer 8:18 myself against sorrow, my heart is f in me. 1742
51:46 lest your heart f, and ye fear for the rumour 7401
La 1:13 he hath made me desolate and f all the day. 1739
1:22 for my sighs are many, and my heart is f. 1742
2:19 that f for hunger in the top of every street. 5848
5:17 For this our heart is f; for these things our 1739
Eze 21: 7 every spirit shall f, and all knees shall be 3543
21:15 that their heart may f, and their ruins be 4127
Am 8:13 the fair virgins and young men f for thirst. 5968
Mt 15:32 them away fasting, lest they f in the way. 1590
Mk 8: 3 to their own houses, they will f by the way: 1590
Lk 18: 1 men ought always to pray, and not to f; 1573
2Co 4: 1 as we have received mercy, we f not; 1573
4:16 For which cause we f not; but though our 1573
Gal 6: 9 for in due season we shall reap, if we f not. 1590
Eph 3:13 Wherefore I desire that ye f not at my 1573
Heb 12: 3 lest ye be wearied and f in your minds. 1590
12: 5 nor f when thou art rebuked of him: 1590

FAINTED (12) [FAINT]
Ge 45:26 Jacob's heart f, for he believed them not. 6313
47:13 all the land of Canaan f by reason of 3856
Ps 27:13 I had f, unless I had believed to see NIH
107: 5 Hungry and thirsty, their soul f in them. 5848
Isa 51:20 Thy sons have f, they lie at the head of all 5968
Jer 45: 3 I f in my sighing, and I find no rest. 3021
Eze 31:15 and all the trees of the field f for him. 5969
Da 8:27 I Daniel f, and was sick certain days; 1961
Jnh 2: 7 When my soul f within me I remembered 5848
4: 8 that he f, and wished in himself to die, and 5968
Mt 9:36 with compassion on them, because they f, 1590
Rev 2: 3 name's sake hast laboured, and hast not f. 2577

FAINTEST (1) [FAINT]
Job 4: 5 now it is come upon thee, and thou f; 3811

FAINTETH (4) [FAINT]
Ps 84: 2 yea, even f for the courts of the LORD: 3615
119:81 My soul f for thy salvation: but I hope in 3615
Isa 10:18 they shall be as when a standard-bearer f. 4549
40:28 ends of the earth, f not, neither is weary? 3286

FAINTHEARTED (3) [FAINT, HEART]
Dt 20: 8 is there that is fearful and f? 3824+7390+1886.1
Isa 7: 4 neither be f for the two tails of these 3824+7401
Jer 49:23 they are f; there is sorrow on the sea; 4127

FAINTNESS (1) [FAINT]
Lev 26:36 f into their hearts in the lands of their 4816

FAIR (53) [FAIRER, FAIREST, FAIRS]
Ge 6: 2 saw the daughters of men that they were f; 2896
12:11 I know that thou art a f woman to look 3303

Ge 12:14 beheld the woman that she *was* very **f**. 3303
24:16 the damsel *was* very **f** to look upon, 2896
26: 7 because she *was* **f** to look upon. 2896
1Sa 17:42 a youth, and ruddy, and of a **f** countenance. 3303
2Sa 13: 1 that Absalom the son of David had a **f** 3303
14:27 she was a woman of a **f** countenance. 3303
1Ki 1: 3 So they sought for a **f** damsel throughout 3303
1: 4 the damsel *was* very **f**, and cherished 3303
Est 1:11 princes her beauty: for she *was* **f** to look on. 2896
2: 2 Let there be **f** young virgins sought 2896+4758
2: 3 **f** young virgins unto Shushan 2896+4758
2: 7 and the maid *was* **f** and beautiful; 3303+8389
Job 37:22 **F weather** cometh out of the north: 2091
42:15 women found *so* **f** as the daughters of Job: 3303
Pr 7:21 With her much **f speech** she caused him to 3948
11:22 *is* a **f** woman which is without discretion. 3303
26:25 When he speaketh **f**, believe him not: 2603
SS 1:15 Behold, thou *art* **f**, my love; behold, 3303
1:15 thou *art* fair, my love; behold, thou *art* **f**; 3303
1:16 Behold, thou *art* **f**, my beloved, yea, 3303
2:10 my love, my **f one**, and come away. 3303
2:13 Arise, my love, my **f one**, and come away. 3303
4: 1 Behold, thou *art* **f**, my love; behold, 3303
4: 1 thou *art* fair, my love; behold, thou *art* **f**; 3303
4: 7 Thou *art* all **f**, my love; *there is* no spot in 3303
4:10 How **f** is thy love, my sister, *my* spouse! 3302
6:10 **f** as the moon, clear as the sun, *and* 3303
7: 6 How **f** and how pleasant art thou, O love, 3302
Isa 5: 9 *even* great and **f**, without inhabitant. 2896
54:11 I will lay thy stones with **f colours**, and 6320
Jer 4:30 in vain shalt thou **make** thyself **f**; 3302
11:16 A green olive tree, **f**, *and* of goodly fruit: 3303
12: 6 though they speak **f** *words* unto thee. 2896
46:20 Egypt *is like* a **very f** heifer, *but* 3304
Eze 16:17 Thou hast also taken thy **f** jewels of my 8597
16:39 shall take thy **f** jewels, and leave thee naked 8597
23:26 of thy clothes, and take away thy **f** jewels. 8597
31: 3 the Assyrian *was* a cedar in Lebanon with **f** 3303
31: 7 Thus was he **f** in his greatness, in the length 3302
31: 9 I have made him **f** by the multitude of his 3303
Da 4:12 The leaves thereof *were* **f**, and the fruit 8209
4:21 Whose leaves *were* **f**, and the fruit thereof 8209
Hos 10:11 *the corn;* but I passed over upon her **f** neck: 2898
Am 8:13 In that day shall the **f** virgins and young 3303
Zec 3: 5 I said, Let them set a **f** mitre upon his head. 2889
3: 5 So they set a **f** mitre upon his head, and 2889
Mt 16: 2 it is evening, ye say, *It will be* **f weather**: *2105*
Ac 7:20 was born, and was **exceeding f**, *791+2316+3588*
27: 8 unto a place *which is* called The **f havens**; *2568*
Ro 16:18 **f speeches** deceive the hearts of the simple. *2129*
Gal 6:12 As many as desire to **make a f shew** in *2146*

FAIRER (3) [FAIR]

Jdg 15: 2 *is* not her younger sister **f** than she? 2896
Ps 45: 2 Thou art **f** than the children of men: 3302
Da 1:15 of ten days their countenances appeared **f** 2896

FAIREST (3) [FAIR]

SS 1: 8 If thou know not, O thou **f** among women, 3303
5: 9 *another* beloved, O thou **f** among women? 3303
6: 1 thy beloved gone, O thou **f** among women? 3303

FAIRS (6) [FAIR]

Eze 27:12 iron, tin, and lead, they traded in thy **f**. 5801
27:14 of Togarmah traded in thy **f** with horses 5801
27:16 they occupied in thy **f** with emeralds, 5801
27:19 Javan going to and fro occupied in thy **f**: 5801
27:22 they occupied in thy **f** with chief of all 5801
27:27 Thy riches, and thy **f**, thy merchandise, 5801

FAITH (246) [FAITHFUL, FAITHFULLY, FAITHFULNESS, FAITHLESS, UNFAITHFUL]

Dt 32:20 children in whom *is* no **f**. 529
Hab 2: 4 in him: but the just shall live by his **f**. 530
Mt 6:30 not much more *clothe* you, O ye **of little f**? *3640*
8:10 I have not found so great **f**, no not in Israel. *4102*
8:26 Why are ye fearful, O ye **of little f**? *3640*
9: 2 Jesus seeing their **f** said unto the sick of *4102*
9:22 good comfort; thy **f** hath made thee whole. *4102*
9:29 saying, According to your **f** be it unto you. *4102*
14:31 and said unto him, O thou **of little f**, *3640*
15:28 and said unto her, O woman, great *is* thy **f**: *4102*
16: 8 he said unto them, O ye **of little f**, *3640*
17:20 If ye have **f** as a grain of mustard seed, *4102*
21:21 I say unto you, If ye have **f**, and doubt not, *4102*
23:23 *matters* of the law, judgment, mercy, and **f**: *4102*
Mk 2: 5 When Jesus saw their **f**, he said unto *4102*
4:40 ye so fearful? how *is it that* you have no **f**? *4102*
5:34 Daughter, thy **f** hath made thee whole; *4102*
10:52 Go thy way; thy **f** hath made thee whole. *4102*
11:22 answering saith unto them, Have **f** in God. *4102*
Lk 5:20 And when he saw their **f**, he said unto him, *4102*
7: 9 I have not found so great **f**, no, not in Israel. *4102*
7:50 said to the woman, Thy **f** hath saved thee; *4102*
8:25 And he said unto them, Where is your **f**? *4102*
8:48 thy **f** hath made thee whole; go in peace.) *4102*
12:28 more *will he clothe* you, O ye **of little f**? *3640*
17: 5 apostles said unto the Lord, Increase our **f**. *4102*
17: 6 If ye had **f** as a grain of mustard seed, *4102*
17:19 go *thy way:* thy **f** hath made thee whole. *4102*
18: 8 of man cometh, shall he find **f** on the earth? *4102*
18:42 Receive thy sight: thy **f** hath saved thee. *4102*
22:32 I have prayed for thee, that thy **f** fail not: *4102*
Ac 3:16 And his name through **f** in his name hath *4102*
3:16 the **f** which is by him hath given him this *4102*
6: 5 a man full of **f** and of the Holy Ghost, and *4102*
6: 7 of the priests were obedient to the **f**. *4102*
6: 8 And Stephen, full of **f** and power, did great *4102*
11:24 and full of the Holy Ghost and of **f**: *4102*
13: 8 seeking to turn away the deputy from the **f**. *4102*
14: 9 and perceiving that he had **f** to be healed, *4102*
14:22 *and* exhorting *them* to continue in the **f**, and *4102*
14:27 how he had opened *the* door of **f** unto *4102*
15: 9 and them, purifying their hearts by **f**. *4102*
Ac 16: 5 so were the churches established in the **f**, *4102*
20:21 and **f** toward our Lord Jesus Christ. *4102*
24:24 and heard him concerning the **f** in Christ. *4102*
26:18 them which are sanctified by **f** that is in me. *4102*
Ro 1: 5 for obedience to the **f** among all nations, *4102*
1: 8 that your **f** is spoken of throughout *4102*
1:12 with you by the mutual **f** both of you *4102*
1:17 of God revealed from **f** to faith: *4102*
1:17 of God revealed from faith to **f**: *4102*
1:17 as it is written, The just shall live by **f**. *4102*
3: 3 shall their unbelief make the **f** of God *4102*
3:22 God *which is* by **f** of Jesus Christ unto all *4102*
3:25 *to be* a propitiation through **f** in his blood, *4102*
3:27 of works? Nay: but by the law of **f**. *4102*
3:28 justified by **f** without the deeds of the law. *4102*
3:30 which shall justify the circumcision by **f**, *4102*
3:30 by faith, and uncircumcision through **f**. *4102*
3:31 Do we then make void the law through **f**? *4102*
4: 5 his **f** is counted for righteousness. *4102*
4: 9 for we say that **f** was reckoned to Abraham *4102*
4:11 a seal of the righteousness of the **f** which he *4102*
4:12 who also walk in the steps of *that* **f** of our *4102*
4:13 the law, but through the righteousness of **f**. *4102*
4:14 **f** is made void, and the promise made of *4102*
4:16 Therefore *it is* of **f**, that *it might be* by *4102*
4:16 to that also which is of the **f** of Abraham; *4102*
4:19 And being not weak in **f**, he considered not *4102*
4:20 but was strong in **f**, giving glory to God; *4102*
5: 1 Therefore being justified by **f**, we have *4102*
5: 2 By whom also we have access by **f** into this *4102*
9:30 even the righteousness which is of **f**. *4102*
9:32 Because *they sought it* not by **f**, but as *it* *4102*
10: 6 But the righteousness which is of **f** *4102*
10: 8 that is, the word of **f**, which we preach; *4102*
10:17 So then **f** *cometh* by hearing, *4102*
11:20 were broken off, and thou standest by **f**. *4102*
12: 3 hath dealt to every man the measure of **f**. *4102*
12: 6 *prophesy* according to the proportion of **f**; *4102*
14: 1 Him that is weak in the **f** receive ye, *but* *4102*
14:22 Hast thou **f**? have *it* to thyself before God. *4102*
14:23 if he eat, because *he eateth* not of **f**: *4102*
14:23 of faith: for whatsoever *is* not of **f** is sin. *4102*
16:26 known to all nations for the obedience of **f**: *4102*
1Co 2: 5 That your **f** should not stand in the wisdom *4102*
12: 9 To another **f** by the same Spirit; to another *4102*
13: 2 and though I have all **f**, so that *I* could *4102*
13:13 And now abideth **f**, hope, charity, *4102*
15:14 our preaching vain, and your **f** *is* also vain. *4102*
15:17 And if Christ be not raised, your **f** *is* vain; *4102*
16:13 Watch ye, stand fast in the **f**, quit you like *4102*
2Co 1:24 Not for that we have dominion over your **f**, *4102*
1:24 are helpers of your joy: for by **f** ye stand. *4102*
4:13 We having the same spirit of **f**, *4102*
5: 7 (For we walk by **f**, not by sight:) *4102*
8: 7 as ye abound in every *thing, in* **f**, and *4102*
10:15 but having hope, when your **f** is increased, *4102*
13: 5 Examine yourselves, whether ye be in the **f**; *4102*
Gal 1:23 preacheth the **f** which once he destroyed. *4102*
2:16 but by the **f** of Jesus Christ, even we have *4102*
2:16 that we might be justified by the **f** of Christ, *4102*
2:20 the flesh I live by the **f** of the Son of God, *4102*
3: 2 the works of the law, or by the hearing of **f**? *4102*
3: 5 the works of the law, or by the hearing of **f**? *4102*
3: 7 Know ye therefore that they which are of **f**, *4102*
3: 8 God would justify the heathen through **f**, *4102*
3: 9 they which be of **f** are blessed with faithful *4102*
3:11 *it is* evident: for, The just shall live by **f**. *4102*
3:12 And the law is not of **f**: but, The man that *4102*
3:14 receive the promise of the Spirit through **f**. *4102*
3:22 that the promise by **f** of Jesus Christ might *4102*
3:23 But before **f** came, we were kept under *4102*
3:23 shut up unto the **f** which should afterwards *4102*
3:24 unto Christ, that we might be justified by **f**. *4102*
3:25 But after that **f** is come, we are no longer *4102*
3:26 For ye are all the children of God by **f** in *4102*
5: 5 wait for the hope of righteousness by **f**. *4102*
5: 6 but **f** which worketh by love. *4102*
5:22 longsuffering, gentleness, goodness, **f**, *4102*
6:10 unto them who are of the household of **f**. *4102*
Eph 1:15 after I heard of your **f** in the Lord Jesus, *4102*
2: 8 For by grace are ye saved through **f**; and *4102*
3:12 and access with confidence by the **f** of him. *4102*
3:17 That Christ may dwell in your hearts by **f**; *4102*
4: 5 One Lord, one **f**, one baptism, *4102*
4:13 Till we all come in the unity of the **f**, and *4102*
6:16 Above all, taking the shield of **f**, *4102*
6:23 and love with **f**, from God the Father and *4102*
Php 1:25 you all for your furtherance and joy of **f**; *4102*
1:27 with one mind striving together for the **f** of *4102*
2:17 upon the sacrifice and service of your **f**, *4102*
3: 9 but that which is through the **f** of Christ, *4102*
3: 9 the righteousness which is of God by **f**: *4102*
Col 1: 4 Since we heard of your **f** in Christ Jesus, *4102*
1:23 If ye continue in the **f** grounded and settled, *4102*
2: 5 and the stedfastness of your **f** in Christ. *4102*
2: 7 and built up in him, and stablished in the **f**, *4102*
2:12 *him* through the **f** of the operation of God, *4102*
1Th 1: 3 without ceasing your work of **f**, *4102*
1: 8 also in every place your **f** to God-ward is *4102*
3: 2 and to comfort you concerning your **f**: *4102*
3: 5 no longer forbear, I sent to know your **f**, *4102*
3: 6 and brought us good tidings of your **f** and *4102*
3: 7 in all our affliction and distress, by your **f**: *4102*
3:10 perfect that which is lacking in your **f**? *4102*
5: 8 putting on the breastplate of **f** and love; *4102*
2Th 1: 3 because that your **f** groweth exceedingly, *4102*
1: 4 and **f** in all your persecutions and *4102*
1:11 *his* goodness, and the work of **f** with power: *4102*
3: 2 and wicked men: for all *men* have not **f**. *4102*
1Ti 1: 2 Unto Timothy, *my* own son in the **f**: Grace, *4102*
1: 4 rather than godly edifying which is in **f**: *4102*
1: 5 *of* a good conscience, and *of* **f** unfeigned: *4102*
1:14 of our Lord was exceeding abundant with **f** *4102*
1:19 Holding **f**, and a good conscience; *4102*
1:19 concerning **f** have made shipwrack: *4102*
1Ti 2: 7 a teacher of the Gentiles in **f** and verity. *4102*
2:15 if they continue in **f** and charity and *4102*
3: 9 Holding the mystery of the **f** in a pure *4102*
3:13 great boldness in the **f** which is in Christ *4102*
4: 1 latter times some shall depart from the **f**, *4102*
4: 6 nourished up in the words of **f** and of good *4102*
4:12 in charity, in spirit, in **f**, in purity. *4102*
5: 8 he hath denied the **f**, and is worse than an *4102*
5:12 because they have cast off *their* first **f**. *4102*
6:10 they have erred from the **f**, and *4102*
6:11 godliness, **f**, love, patience, meekness. *4102*
6:12 Fight the good fight of **f**, lay hold on *4102*
6:21 professing have erred concerning the **f**. *4102*
2Ti 1: 5 the unfeigned **f** that is in thee, *4102*
1:13 in **f** and love which is in Christ Jesus. *4102*
2:18 past already; and overthrow the **f** of some. *4102*
2:22 but follow righteousness, **f**, charity, peace, *4102*
3: 8 corrupt minds, reprobate concerning the **f**. *4102*
3:10 **f**, longsuffering, charity, patience, *4102*
3:15 salvation through **f** which is in Christ Jesus. *4102*
4: 7 have finished *my* course, I have kept the **f**: *4102*
Tit 1: 1 according to the **f** of God's elect, and *4102*
1: 4 *mine* own son after the common **f**: *4102*
1:13 that they may be sound in the **f**; *4102*
2: 2 grave, temperate, sound in **f**, in charity, *4102*
3:15 Greet them that love us in the **f**. Grace *be* *4102*
Phm 1: 5 Hearing of thy love and **f**, which thou hast *4102*
1: 6 That the communication of thy **f** may *4102*
Heb 4: 2 not being mixed with **f** in them that heard *4102*
6: 1 from dead works, and of **f** towards God, *4102*
6:12 but followers of them who through **f** and *4102*
10:22 near with a true heart in full assurance of **f**, *4102*
10:38 Now the just shall live by **f**: but if *any man* *4102*
11: 1 Now **f** is the substance of *things* hoped for, *4102*
11: 3 Through **f** we understand that the worlds *4102*
11: 4 By **f** Abel offered unto God a more *4102*
11: 5 By **f** Enoch was translated that *he* should *4102*
11: 6 But without **f** *it is* impossible to please *him:* *4102*
11: 7 By **f** Noah, being warned of God of *things* *4102*
11: 7 heir of the righteousness which is by **f**. *4102*
11: 8 By **f** Abraham, when he was called to go *4102*
11: 9 By **f** he sojourned in the land of promise, *4102*
11:11 Through **f** also Sara herself received *4102*
11:13 These all died in **f**, not having received *4102*
11:17 By **f** Abraham, when he was tried, *4102*
11:20 By **f** Isaac blessed Jacob and Esau *4102*
11:21 By **f** Jacob, when he was a dying, *4102*
11:22 By **f** Joseph, when he died, made mention *4102*
11:23 By **f** Moses, when he was born, was hid *4102*
11:24 By **f** Moses, when he was come to years, *4102*
11:27 By **f** he forsook Egypt, not fearing *4102*
11:28 Through **f** he kept the passover, and *4102*
11:29 By **f** they passed through the Red sea as by *4102*
11:30 By **f** the walls of Jericho fell down, *4102*
11:31 By **f** the harlot Rahab perished not with *4102*
11:33 Who through **f** subdued kingdoms, *4102*
11:39 having obtained a good report through **f**, *4102*
12: 2 unto Jesus the author and finisher of *our* **f**; *4102*
13: 7 whose **f** follow, considering the end of *their* *4102*
Jas 1: 3 Knowing *this*, that the trying of your **f** *4102*
1: 6 But let him ask in **f**, nothing wavering: *4102*
2: 1 have not the **f** of our Lord Jesus Christ, *4102*
2: 5 God chosen the poor of this world rich in **f**, *4102*
2:14 though a man say *he* hath **f**, and have not *4102*
2:14 and have not works? can **f** save him? *4102*
2:17 Even so **f**, if it hath not works, is dead, *4102*
2:18 may say, Thou hast **f**, and I have works: *4102*
2:18 shew me thy **f** without thy works, and I will *4102*
2:18 and I will shew thee my **f** by my works. *4102*
2:20 O vain man, that **f** without works is dead? *4102*
2:22 Seest thou how **f** wrought with his works, *4102*
2:22 and by works was **f** made perfect? *4102*
2:24 works a man is justified, and not by **f** only. *4102*
2:26 is dead, so **f** without works is dead also. *4102*
5:15 And the prayer of **f** shall save the sick, and *4102*
1Pe 1: 5 **f** unto salvation ready to be revealed in *4102*
1: 7 That the trial of your **f**, *being* much more *4102*
1: 9 Receiving the end of your **f**, *even* *4102*
1:21 that your **f** and hope might be in God. *4102*
5: 9 Whom resist stedfast in the **f**, knowing that *4102*
2Pe 1: 1 to them that have obtained like precious **f** *4102*
1: 5 giving all diligence, add to your **f** virtue; *4102*
1Jn 5: 4 that overcometh the world, *even* our **f**. *4102*
Jude 1: 3 **f** which was once delivered unto the saints. *4102*
1:20 building up yourselves on your most holy **f**, *4102*
Rev 2:13 fast my name, and hast not denied my **f**, *4102*
2:19 thy works, and charity, and service, and **f**, *4102*
13:10 Here is the patience and the **f** of the saints. *4102*
14:12 commandments of God, and the **f** of Jesus. *4102*

FAITHFUL (82) [FAITH]

Nu 12: 7 Moses *is* not so, who *is* **f** in all mine house. 539
Dt 7: 9 he *is* God, the **f** God, which keepeth 539
1Sa 2:35 I will raise me up a **f** priest, *that* shall do 539
22:14 who *is so* **f** among all thy servants as David, 539
2Sa 20:19 *of them that are* peaceable *and* **f** in Israel: 539
Ne 7: 2 for he *was* a **f** man, and feared God above 571
9: 8 foundest his heart **f** before thee, and 539
13:13 for they were counted **f**, and their office *was* 539
Ps 12: 1 for the **f** fail from among the children of 539
31:23 *for* the LORD preserveth the **f**, and 529
89:37 as the moon, and *as* a **f** witness in heaven. 539
101: 6 Mine eyes *shall be* upon the **f** of the land, 539
119:86 All thy commandments *are* **f**: they persecute 530
119:138 hast commanded *are* righteous and very **f**. 530
Pr 11:13 he that is of a **f** spirit concealeth the matter. 539
13:17 into mischief: but a **f** ambassador *is* health. 529
14: 5 A **f** witness will not lie: but a false witness 529
20: 6 his own goodness: but a **f** man who can find? 529
25:13 *so is* a **f** messenger to them that send him: 539
27: 6 **F** *are* the wounds of a friend; but the kisses 539
28:20 A **f** man shall abound with blessings: but 530
Isa 1:21 How is the **f** city become a harlot! *it was* full 539
1:26 The city of righteousness, the **f** city. 539
8: 2 I took unto me **f** witnesses to record, Uriah 539

F

Isa 49: 7 because of the LORD that is f, and 539
Jer 42: 5 LORD be a true and f witness between us, 539
Da 6: 4 forasmuch as he was f, neither was there any 540
Hos 11:12 yet ruleth with God, and is f with the saints. 539
Mt 24:45 Who then is a f and wise servant, whom his 4103
25:21 Well done, thou good and f servant: 4103
25:21 thou hast been f over a few things, I will 4103
25:23 unto him, Well done, good and f servant; 4103
25:23 thou hast been f over a few things, I will 4103
Lk 12:42 Who then is that f and wise steward, 4103
16:10 He that is f in that which is least is faithful 4103
16:10 He that is faithful in that which is least is f 4103
16:11 ye have not been f in the unrighteous 4103
16:12 And if ye have not been f in that which is 4103
19:17 because thou hast been f in a very little, 4103
Ac 16:15 If ye have judged me to be f to the Lord, 4103
1Co 1: 9 God is f, by whom ye were called unto 4103
4: 2 required in stewards, that a man be found f. 4103
4:17 who is my beloved son, and f in the Lord, 4103
7:25 hath obtained mercy of the Lord to be f. 4103
10:13 but God is f, who will not suffer you to be 4103
Gal 3: 9 they which be of faith are blessed with f 4103
Eph 1: 1 are at Ephesus, and to the f in Christ Jesus: 4103
6:21 beloved brother and f minister in the Lord, 4103
Col 1: 2 f brethren in Christ which are at Colosse: 4103
1: 7 who is for you a f minister of Christ; 4103
4: 7 and a f minister and fellowservant in 4103
4: 9 With Onesimus, a f and beloved brother, 4103
1Th 5:24 F is he that calleth you, who also will do it. 4103
2Th 3: 3 But the Lord is f, who shall stablish you, 4103
1Ti 1:12 hath enabled me, for that he counted me f, 4103
1:15 This is a f saying, and worthy of all 4103
3:11 not slanderers, sober, f in all things. 4103
4: 9 This is a f saying and worthy of all 4103
6: 2 because they are f and beloved, 4103
2Ti 2: 2 the same commit thou to f men, who shall 4103
2:11 It is a f saying: For if we be dead with him, 4103
2:13 If we believe not, yet he abideth f: 4103
Tit 1: 6 having f children not accused of riot or 4103
1: 9 Holding fast the f word as he hath been 4103
3: 8 This is a f saying, and these things I will 4103
Heb 2:17 f high priest in things pertaining to God, 4103
3: 2 Who was f to him that appointed him, 4103
3: 2 as also Moses was f in all his house. NIG
3: 5 And Moses verily was f in all his house, 4103
10:23 (for he is f that promised;) 4103
11:11 she judged him f who had promised. 4103
1Pe 4:19 to him in well doing, as unto a f Creator. 4103
5:12 By Silvanus, a f brother unto you, as I 4103
1Jn 1: 9 he is f and just to forgive us our sins, and 4103
Rev 1: 5 who is the f witness, and the first begotten 4103
2:10 be thou f unto death, and I will give thee a 4103
2:13 days wherein Antipas was my f martyr, 4103
3:14 saith the Amen, the f and true witness, 4103
17:14 are with him are called, and chosen, and f. 4103
19:11 and he that sat upon him was called F and 4103
21: 5 Write: for these words are true and f. 4103
22: 6 said unto me, These sayings are f and true: 4103

FAITHFULLY (8) [FAITH]

2Ki 12:15 on workmen: for they dealt f. 530+871.1
22: 7 into their hand, because they dealt f. 530+871.1
2Ch 19: 9 ye do in the fear of the LORD, f, 530+871.1
31:12 the tithes and the dedicate things f: 530+871.1
34:12 the men did the work f: and 530+871.1
Pr 29:14 The king that f judgeth the poor, his throne 571
Jer 23:28 that hath my word, let him speak my word f. 571
3Jn 1: 5 thou doest f whatsoever thou doest to 4103

FAITHFULNESS (19) [FAITH]

1Sa 26:23 to every man his righteousness and his f: 530
Ps 5: 9 For there is no f in their mouth; 3559
36: 5 and thy f reacheth unto the clouds. 530
40:10 I have declared thy f and thy salvation: 530
88:11 in the grave? or thy f in destruction? 530
89: 1 with my mouth will I make known thy f to 530
89: 2 thy f shalt thou establish in the very heavens. 530
89: 5 thy f also in the congregation of the saints. 530
89: 8 like unto thee? or to thy f round about thee? 530
89:24 my f and my mercy shall be with him: and 530
89:33 utterly take from him, nor suffer my f to fail. 530
92: 2 in the morning, and thy f every night, 530
119:75 are right, and that thou in f hast afflicted me. 530
119:90 Thy f is unto all generations: thou hast 530
143: 1 in thy f answer me, and in thy righteousness. 530
Isa 11: 5 of his loins, and f the girdle of his reins. 530
25: 1 thy counsels of old are f and truth. 530
La 3:23 They are new every morning: great is thy f. 530
Hos 2:20 I will even betroth thee unto me in f: and 530

FAITHLESS (4) [FAITH]

Mt 17:17 and said, O f and perverse generation, 571
Mk 9:19 He answereth him, and saith, O f generation, 571
Lk 9:41 answering said, O f and perverse generation, 571
Jn 20:27 it into my side: and be not f, but believing. 571

FALL (252) [FALLEN, FALLEST, FALLETH, FALLING, FELL]

Ge 2:21 the LORD God caused a deep sleep to f 5307
43:18 f upon us, and take us for bondmen, and 5307
45:24 unto them, See that ye f not out by the way. 7264
49:17 so that his rider shall f backward. 5307
Ex 5: 3 lest he f upon us with pestilence, or 6293
15:16 Fear and dread shall f upon them; by 5307
21:33 not cover it, and an ox or an ass f therein; 5307
Lev 11:32 they are dead, doth f, it shall be unclean; 5307
11:37 if any part of their carcase f upon any 5307
11:38 any part of their carcase f thereon, it shall 5307
19:29 lest the land f to whoredom, and the land 2181
26: 7 and they shall f before you by the sword. 5307
26: 8 your enemies shall f before you by 5307
26:36 and they shall f when none pursueth. 5307
26:37 they shall f one upon another, as it were 3782
Nu 11:31 from the sea, and let them f by the camp, 5203
Nu 14: 3 to f by the sword, that our wives and 5307
14:29 Your carcases shall f in this wilderness; and 5307
14:32 they shall f in this wilderness. 5307
14:43 before you, and ye shall f by the sword: 5307
34: 2 (this is the land that shall f unto you for an 5307
Dt 22: 4 brother's ass or his ox f down by the way, 5307
22: 8 upon thine house, if any man f from thence. 5307
Jos 6: 5 the wall of the city shall f down flat, 5307
Jdg 8:21 Zalmunna said, Rise thou, and f upon us: 6293
15:12 that ye will not f upon me yourselves. 6293
15:18 and f into the hand of the uncircumcised? 5307
Ru 2:16 let f also some of the handfuls
of purpose 7997+7997
3:18 until thou know how the matter will f: 5307
1Sa 3:19 did let none of his words f to the ground. 5307
14:45 there shall not one hair of his head f to 5307
18:25 Saul thought to make David f by the hand 5307
21:13 and let his spittle f down upon his beard. 3381
22:17 hand to f upon the priests of the LORD. 6293
22:18 to Doeg, Turn thou, and f upon the priests. 6293
26:20 let not my blood f to the earth before 5307
2Sa 1:15 and said, Go near, and f upon him. 6293
14:11 there shall not one hair of thy son f to 5307
24:14 let us f now into the hand of the LORD; 5307
24:14 and let me not f into the hand of man. 5307
1Ki 1:52 there shall not a hair of him f to the earth: 5307
2:29 son of Jehoiada, saying, Go, f upon him. 6293
2:31 he hath said, and f upon him, and bury him; 6293
22:20 that he may go up and f at Ramoth-gilead? 5307
2Ki 7: 4 and let us f unto the host of the Syrians: 5307
10:10 Know now that there shall f unto the earth 5307
14:10 that thou shouldest f, even thou, and 5307
19: 7 I will cause him to f by the sword in his 5307
1Ch 12:19 He will f to his master Saul to the jeopardy 5307
21:13 let me f now into the hand of the LORD; 5307
21:13 but let me not f into the hand of man. 5307
2Ch 18:19 that he may go up and f at Ramoth-gilead? 5307
21:15 until thy bowels f out by reason of 3318
25: 8 God shall make thee f before the enemy: 3782
25:19 that thou shouldest f, even thou, and 5307
Est 6:13 before whom thou hast begun to f, 5307
6:13 but shalt surely f before him. 5307+5307
Job 13:11 make you afraid? and his dread f upon you? 5307
31:22 Then let mine arm f from my shoulder 5307
Ps 5:10 O God; let them f by their own counsels; 5307
9: 3 they shall f and perish at thy presence. 3782
10:10 that the poor may f by his strong ones. 5307
35: 8 into that very destruction let him f. 5307
37:24 Though he f, he shall not be utterly cast 5307
45: 5 whereby the people f under thee. 5307
63:10 They shall f by the sword: they shall be a 5064
64: 8 So they shall make their own tongue to f 3782
72:11 Yea, all kings shall f down before him: 7812
78:28 he let it f in the midst of their camp, 5307
82: 7 die like men, and f like one of the princes. 5307
91: 7 A thousand shall f at thy side, and 5307
118:13 Thou hast thrust sore at me that I might f: 5307
140:10 Let burning coals f upon them: let them be 4131
141:10 Let the wicked f into their own nets, 5307
145:14 The LORD upholdeth all that f, and 5307
Pr 4:16 is taken away, unless they cause some to f. 3782
10: 8 but a prating fool shall f. 3832
10:10 causeth sorrow: but a prating fool shall f. 3832
11: 5 the wicked shall f by his own wickedness. 5307
11:14 Where no counsel is, the people f: but 5307
11:28 He that trusteth in his riches shall f: but 5307
16:18 and a haughty spirit before a f. 3783
22:14 he that is abhorred of the LORD shall f 5307
24:16 but the wicked shall f into mischief. 3782
26:27 Whoso diggeth a pit shall f therein: and 5307
28:10 he shall f himself into his own pit: 5307
28:14 he that hardeneth his heart shall f into 5307
28:18 he that is perverse in his ways shall f at 5307
29:16 but the righteous shall see their f. 4658
Ecc 4:10 For if they f, the one will lift up his fellow: 5307
10: 8 He that diggeth a pit shall f into it; and 5307
11: 3 if the tree f toward the south, or toward 5307
Isa 3:25 Thy men shall f by the sword, and 5307
8:15 f, and be broken, and be snared, and 5307
10: 4 and they shall f under the slain. 5307
10:34 and Lebanon shall f by a mighty one. 5307
13:15 every one that is joined unto them shall f by 5307
22:25 place be removed, and be cut down, and f; 5307
24:18 the noise of the fear shall f into the pit; 5307
24:20 upon it; and it shall f, and not rise again. 5307
28:13 f backward, and be broken, and snared, and 3782
30:13 shall be to you as a breach ready to f, 5307
30:25 of the great slaughter, when the towers f. 5307
31: 3 both he that helpeth shall f, and he that is 3782
31: 3 he that is holpen shall f down, and they all 5307
31: 8 shall the Assyrian f with the sword, not of a 5307
34: 4 all their host shall f down, as the leaf 5034
37: 7 I will cause him to f by the sword in his 5307
40:30 and the young men shall utterly f: 3782+3782
44:19 shall I f down to the stock of a tree? 5456
45:14 and they shall f down unto thee, 7812
46: 6 it a god: they f down, yea, they worship. 5456
47:11 mischief shall f upon thee; thou shalt not be 5307
54:15 together against thee shall f for thy sake. 5307
Jer 3:12 I will not cause mine anger to f upon you: 5307
6:15 therefore they shall f among them that fall: 5307
6:15 therefore they shall fall among them that f: 5307
6:21 and the sons together shall f upon them; 3782
8: 4 the LORD; Shall they f, and not arise? 5307
8:12 therefore shall they f among them that fall: 5307
8:12 therefore shall they fall among them that f: 5307
9:22 Even the carcases of men shall f as dung 5307
15: 8 I have caused him to f upon it suddenly, 5307
19: 7 I will cause them to f by the sword before 5307
20: 4 they shall f by the sword of their enemies, 5307
23:12 they shall be driven on, and f therein: for I 5307
23:19 it shall f grievously upon the head of 2342
25:27 spue, and f, and rise no more, because 5307
25:34 And ye shall f like a pleasant vessel. 5307
30:23 it shall f with pain upon the head of 2342
Jer 37:14 It is false; I f not away to the Chaldeans. 5307
39:18 thou shalt not f by the sword, but thy life 5307
44:12 all be consumed, and f in the land of Egypt; 5307
46: 6 f toward the north by the river Euphrates. 5307
46:16 He made many to f, yea, one fell upon 3782
48:44 He that fleeth from the fear shall f into 5307
49:21 The earth is moved at the noise of their f, 5307
49:26 Therefore her young men shall f in her 5307
50:30 Therefore shall her young men f in 5307
50:32 the most proud shall stumble and f, and 5307
51: 4 Thus the slain shall f in the land of 5307
51:44 unto him: yea, the wall of Babylon shall f. 5307
51:47 and all her slain shall f in the midst of her. 5307
51:49 Babylon hath caused the slain of Israel to f, 5307
51:49 at Babylon shall f the slain of all the earth. 5307
La 1:14 he hath made my strength to f, the Lord 3782
Eze 5:12 a third part shall f by the sword round about 5307
6: 7 the slain shall f in the midst of you, and 5307
6:11 for they shall f by the sword, by the famine, 5307
6:12 he that is near shall f by the sword; and 5307
11:10 Ye shall f by the sword; I will judge you in 5307
13:11 it with untempered morter, that it shall f: 5307
13:11 ye, O great hailstones, shall f; and a stormy 5307
13:14 it shall f, and ye shall be consumed in 5307
17:21 all his fugitives with all his bands shall f by 5307
23:25 and thy remnant shall f by the sword: 5307
24: 6 it out piece by piece; let no lot f upon it. 5307
24:21 your daughters whom ye have left shall f 5307
25:13 and they of Dedan shall f by the sword. 5307
26:15 not the isles shake at the sound of thy f, 4658
26:18 shall the isles tremble in the day of thy f; 4658
27:27 shall f into the midst of the seas in the day 5307
27:34 all thy company in the midst of thee shall f. 5307
29: 5 thou shalt f upon the open fields; thou shalt 5307
30: 4 when the slain shall f in Egypt, and 5307
30: 5 is in league, shall f with them by the sword. 5307
30: 6 They also that uphold Egypt shall f; and 5307
30: 6 from the tower of Syene shall they f in it by 5307
30:17 and of Phi-beseth shall f by the sword: 5307
30:22 I will cause the sword to f out of his hand. 5307
30:25 and the arms of Pharaoh shall f down; 5307
31:16 the nations to shake at the sound of his f, 4658
32:10 man for his own life, in the day of thy f. 4658
32:12 the mighty will I cause thy multitude to f, 5307
32:20 They shall f in the midst of them that are 5307
33:12 he shall not f thereby in the day that he 3782
33:27 surely they that are in the wastes shall f by 5307
35: 8 shall they f that are slain with the sword. 5307
36:15 neither shalt thou cause thy nations to f any 3782
38:20 the steep places shall f, and every wall shall 5307
38:20 and every wall shall f to the ground. 5307
39: 3 will cause thine arrows to f out of thy right 5307
39: 4 Thou shalt f upon the mountains of Israel, 5307
39: 5 Thou shalt f upon the open field: for I have 5307
44:12 caused the house of Israel to f into 4383
47:14 this land shall f unto you for inheritance. 5307
Da 3: 5 ye f down and worship the golden image 5308
3:10 shall f down and worship the golden 5308
3:15 ye f down and worship the image which I 5308
11:14 to establish the vision; but they shall f. 3782
11:19 he shall stumble and f, and not be found. 5307
11:26 and many shall f down slain. 5307
11:33 yet they shall f by the sword, and by flame, 3782
11:34 Now when they shall f, they shall be holpen 3782
11:35 some of them of understanding shall f, 3782
Hos 4: 5 Therefore shalt thou f in the day, and 3782
4: 5 the prophet also shall f with thee in 3782
4:14 the people that doth not understand shall f. 3832
5: 5 shall Israel and Ephraim f in their iniquity; 3782
5: 5 their iniquity; Judah also shall f with them. 3782
7:16 their princes shall f by the sword for 5307
10: 8 Cover us; and to the hills, F on us. 5307
13:16 they shall f by the sword: their infants shall 5307
14: 9 but the transgressors shall f therein. 3782
Joel 2: 8 when they f upon the sword, they shall not 5307
Am 3: 5 Can a bird f in a snare upon the earth, 5307
3:14 altar shall be cut off, and f to the ground. 5307
7:17 and thy daughters shall f by the sword, 5307
8:14 even they shall f, and never rise up again. 5307
9: 9 yet shall not the least grain f upon the earth. 5307
Mic 7: 8 when I f, I shall arise; when I sit in 5307
Na 3:12 they shall even f into the mouth of 5307
Mt 4: 9 if thou wilt f down and worship me. 4098
7:27 and it fell: and great was the f of it. 4431
10:29 one of them shall not f on the ground 4098
12:11 and if it f into a pit on the sabbath day, 1706
15:14 lead the blind, both shall f into the ditch. 4098
15:27 yet the dogs eat of the crumbs which f from 4098
21:44 And whosoever shall f on this stone shall 4098
21:44 but on whomsoever it shall f, it will grind 4098
24:29 and the stars shall f from heaven, and 4098
Mk 13:25 And the stars of heaven shall f, 1601
Lk 2:34 this child is set for the f and rising again of 4431
6:39 shall they not both f into the ditch? 4098
8:13 and in time of temptation f away. 868
10:18 I beheld Satan as lightning f from heaven. 4098
20:18 Whosoever shall f upon that stone shall be 4098
20:18 but on whomsoever it shall f, it will grind 4098
21:24 And they shall f by the edge of the sword, 4098
23:30 they begin to say to the mountains, F on us; 4098
Jn 12:24 Except a corn of wheat f into the ground 4098
Ac 27:17 fearing lest they should f into 1601
27:32 off the ropes of the boat, and let her f off. 1601
27:34 for there shall not a hair f from the head of 4098
Ro 11:11 Have they stumbled that they should f? 4098
11:11 rather through their f salvation is come unto 3900
11:12 Now if the f of them be the riches of 3900
14:13 or an occasion to f in his brother's way. 4625
1Co 10:12 that thinketh he standeth take heed lest he f. 4098
1Ti 3: 6 lest being lifted up with pride he f into 1706
3: 7 lest he f into reproach and the snare of 1706
6: 9 But they that will be rich f into temptation 1706
Heb 4:11 lest any man f after the same example of 4098
6: 6 If they shall f away, to renew them again 3895
10:31 It is a fearful thing to f into the hands of 1706

F

F

Jas 1: 2 count *it* all joy when ye **f into** divers 4045
5:12 *your* nay, nay; lest ye **f** into condemnation. 4098
2Pe 1:10 for if ye do these *things,* ye shall never **f**: 4417
3:17 the wicked, **f from** your own stedfastness. 1601
Rev 4:10 twenty elders **f down** before him that sat on 4098
6:16 **F** on us, and hide us from the face of him 4098
9: 1 I saw a star **f** from heaven unto the earth: 4098

FALLEN (79) [FALL]

Ge 4: 6 thou wroth? and why is thy countenance **f**? 5307
Lev 13:40 the man whose **hair** is **f off** his head, he *is* 4803
13:41 he that hath his **hair f off** from the part of 4803
25:35 and **f in decay** with thee; 3027+4131
Nu 32:19 our inheritance is **f** to us on *this* side Jordan 935
Jos 2: 9 that your terror is **f** upon us, and that all 5307
8:24 *when* they were all **f** on the edge of 5307
Jdg 3:25 their lord *was* **f down** dead on the earth. 5307
18: 1 not **f** unto them among the tribes of Israel. 5307
19:27 the woman his concubine *was* **f down** *at* 5307
1Sa 5: 3 Dagon *was* **f** upon his face to the earth 5307
5: 4 Dagon *was* **f** upon his face to the ground 5307
26:12 a deep sleep from the LORD was **f** upon 5307
31: 8 and his three sons **f** in mount Gilboa. 5307
2Sa 1: 4 and many of the people also are **f** and dead; 5307
1:10 that he could not live after *that* he was **f**: 5307
1:12 of Israel; because they were **f** by the sword. 5307
1:19 upon thy high places: how are the mighty **f**! 5307
1:25 How are the mighty **f** in the midst of 5307
1:27 How are the mighty **f**, and the weapons of 5307
3:38 and a great *man* **f** this day in Israel? 5307
22:39 not arise: yea, they are **f** under my feet. 5307
2Ki 13:14 Now Elisha was **f sick** of his sickness 2470
1Ch 10: 8 found Saul and his sons **f** in mount Gilboa. 5307
2Ch 20:24 they *were* dead bodies **f** to the earth, and 5307
29: 9 our fathers have **f** by the sword, and 5307
Est 7: 8 Haman was **f** upon the bed whereon Esther 5307
Job 1:16 The fire of God is **f** from heaven, and 5307
Ps 7:15 and is **f** into the ditch *which* he made. 5307
16: 6 The lines are **f** unto me in pleasant *places;* 5307
18:38 not able to rise: they are **f** under my feet. 5307
20: 8 They are brought down and **f**: but we are 5307
36:12 There are the workers of iniquity **f**: they are 5307
55: 4 and the terrors of death are **f** upon me. 5307
57: 6 into the midst whereof they are **f** 5307
69: 9 of them that reproached thee are **f** upon me. 5307
Isa 3: 8 For Jerusalem is ruined, and Judah is **f**: 5307
9:10 The bricks are **f down**, but we will build 5307
14:12 How art thou **f** from heaven, O Lucifer, 5307
16: 9 thy summer fruits and for thy harvest is **f**. 5307
21: 9 he answered and said, Babylon is **f**, 5307
21: 9 and said, Babylon is fallen, is **f**; 5307
26:18 neither have the inhabitants of the world **f**. 5307
59:14 for truth is **f** in the street, and equity cannot 3782
Jer 38:19 I am afraid of the Jews that are **f** to 5307
46:12 the mighty, *and* they are **f** both together. 5307
48:32 the spoiler is **f** upon thy summer fruits and 5307
50:15 her foundations are **f**, her walls are thrown 5307
51: 8 Babylon is suddenly **f** and destroyed: 5307
La 2:21 and my young men are **f** by the sword; 5307
5:16 The crown is **f** *from* our head: woe unto us, 5307
Eze 13:12 Lo, when the wall is **f**, shall it not be said 5307
31:12 and in all the valleys his branches are **f**, 5307
32:22 about him: all of them slain, **f** by the sword: 5307
32:23 all of them slain, **f** by the sword, 5307
32:24 her grave, all of them slain, **f** by the sword, 5307
32:27 they shall not lie with the mighty *that are* **f** 5307
Hos 7: 7 devoured their judges; all their kings are **f**: 5307
14: 1 thy God; for thou hast **f** by thine iniquity. 3782
Am 5: 2 The virgin of Israel is **f**; she shall no more 5307
9:11 I raise up the tabernacle of David that is **f**, 5307
Zec 11: 2 Howl, fir tree; for the cedar is **f**; because 5307
Lk 14: 5 you shall have an ass or an ox **f** into a pit, *1706*
Ac 8:16 (For as yet he was **f upon** none of *1968*
15:16 the tabernacle of David, which is **f down**; *4098*
20: 9 named Eutychus, being **f into** a deep sleep: *2702*
26:14 And when we were all **f** to the earth, *2667*
27:29 Then fearing lest we should have **f** upon *1601*
28: 6 have swollen, or **f down** dead suddenly: *2667*
1Co 15: 6 unto this present, but some are **f asleep**. *2837*
15:18 Then they also which are **f asleep** in Christ *2837*
Gal 5: 4 justified by the law; ye are **f from** grace. *1601*
Php 1:12 **f out** rather unto the furtherance of *2064*
Rev 2: 5 therefore from whence thou art **f**, *1601*
14: 8 saying, Babylon is **f**, is fallen, *that* great *4098*
14: 8 Babylon is fallen, is **f**, *that* great city, *4098*
17:10 five are **f**, and one is, *and* the other is not *4098*
18: 2 saying, Babylon the great is **f**, is fallen, and *4098*
18: 2 is **f**, and is become the habitation of devils, *4098*

FALLEST (1) [FALL]

Jer 37:13 Thou **f away** to the Chaldeans. 5307

FALLETH (28) [FALL]

Ex 1:10 to pass, that, when there **f out** any war, 7122
Lev 11:33 earthen vessel, whereinto *any* of them **f**, 5307
11:35 *any part* of their carcase **f** shall be unclean; 5307
Nu 33:54 shall be in the place where his lot **f**; 3318
2Sa 3:29 or that **f** on the sword, or that lacketh bread. 5307
3:34 as *a man* **f** before wicked men, *so* 5307
17:12 we *will light* upon him as the dew **f** on 5307
Job 4:13 of the night, when deep sleep **f** on men. 5307
33:15 of the night, when deep sleep **f** upon men, 5307
Pr 13:17 A wicked messenger **f** into mischief: but 5307
17:20 he that hath a perverse tongue **f** into 5307
24:16 For a just *man* **f** seven *times,* and riseth up 5307
24:17 Rejoice not when thine enemy **f**, and let not 5307
Ecc 4:10 woe to him *that is* alone when he **f**; for *he* 5307
9:12 an evil time, when it **f** suddenly upon them. 5307
11: 3 *in* the place where the tree **f**, there it shall 5307
Isa 34: 4 as the leaf **f off** from the vine, and as a 5034
44:15 it a graven image, and **f down** thereto. 5456
44:17 he **f down** unto it, and worshippeth *it,* and 5456
Jer 21: 9 **f** to the Chaldeans that besiege you, he shall 5307
Da 3: 6 whoso **f** not **down** and worshippeth shall 5308
Da 3:11 whoso **f** not **down** and worshippeth, *that* he 5308
Mt 17:15 for ofttimes he **f** into the fire, and oft into *4098*
Lk 11:17 and a house *divided* against a house **f**. *4098*
15:12 give me the portion of goods that **f to** *me.* *1911*
Ro 14: 4 to his own master he standeth or **f**. Yea, *4098*
Jas 1:11 and the flower thereof **f**, and the grace of *1601*
1Pe 1:24 and the flower thereof **f away**: *1601*

FALLING (15) [FALL]

Nu 24: 4 **f** *into a trance,* but having his eyes open: 5307
24:16 **f** *into a trance,* but having his eyes open: 5307
Job 4: 4 Thy words have upholden him that was **f**, 3782
14:18 surely the mountain **f** cometh to nought, 5307
Ps 56:13 *wilt* not *thou deliver* my feet from **f**, that *I* 1762
116: 8 mine eyes from tears, *and* my feet from **f**. 1762
Pr 25:26 A righteous *man* **f down** before the wicked 4131
Isa 34: 4 the vine, and as a **f** *fig* from the fig tree. 5034
Lk 8:47 came trembling, and **f down before** him, *4363*
22:44 great drops of blood **f down** to the ground. *2597*
Ac 1:18 and **f headlong**, he burst asunder in *1096+4248*
27:41 And **f** into a place where two seas met, *4045*
1Co 14:25 so **f down** on *his* face he will worship God, *4098*
2Th 2: 3 *not come,* except there come a **f away** first, *646*
Jude 1:24 unto him that is able to keep you from **f**, *679*

FALLOW (3)

Dt 14: 5 the **f deer**, and the wild goat, and 3180
Jer 4: 3 Break up your **f ground**, and sow not 5215
Hos 10:12 reap in mercy; break up your **f ground**: 5215

FALLOWDEER (1)

1Ki 4:23 and roebucks, and **f**, and fatted fowl. 3180

FALSE (64) [FALSEHOOD, FALSELY, FALSIFYING]

Ex 20:16 Thou shalt not bear **f** witness against thy 8267
23: 1 Thou shalt not raise a **f** report: put not thine 7723
23: 7 Keep thee far from a **f** matter; and 8267
Dt 5:20 Neither shalt thou bear **f** witness against thy 7723
19:16 If a **f** witness rise up against any man to 2555
19:18 *if* the witness *be* a **f** witness, *and* 8267
2Ki 9:12 they said, *It is* **f**; tell us now. And he said, 8267
Job 36: 4 For truly my words *shall* not *be* **f**: *he that is* 8267
Ps 27:12 for **f** witnesses are risen up against me, and 8267
35:11 **F** witnesses did rise up; they laid to my 2555
119:104 therefore I hate every **f** way. 8267
119:128 *things* to be right; *and* I hate every **f** way. 8267
120: 3 shall be done unto thee, thou **f** tongue? 7423
Pr 6:19 A **f** witness *that* speaketh lies, and he that 8267
11: 1 A **f** balance *is* abomination to the LORD: 4820
12:17 forth righteousness: but a **f** witness deceit. 8267
14: 5 will not lie: but a **f** witness will utter lies. 8267
17: 4 A wicked doer giveth heed to **f** lips; *and* 205
19: 5 A **f** witness shall not be unpunished, and 8267
19: 9 A **f** witness shall not be unpunished, and 8267
20:23 the LORD; and a **f** balance *is* not good. 4820
21:28 A **f** witness shall perish: but the man that 3577
25:14 Whoso boasteth himself of a **f** gift *is like* 8267
25:18 A man that beareth **f** witness against his 8267
Jer 14:14 they prophesy unto you a **f** vision and 8267
23:32 I *am* against them that prophesy **f** dreams, 8267
37:14 said Jeremiah, *It is* **f**; I fall not away to 8267
La 2:14 have seen for thee **f** burdens and causes of 7723
Eze 21:23 it shall be unto them as a **f** divination in 7723
Zec 8:17 against his neighbour; and love no **f** oath: 8267
10: 2 have seen a lie, and have told **f** dreams; 7723
Mal 3: 5 against **f** swearers, and against those that 8267
Mt 7:15 Beware of **f prophets**, which come to you *5578*
15:19 adulteries, fornications, thefts, **f witness**, *5577*
19:18 not steal, Thou shalt not **bear f witness**, *5576*
24:11 And many **f prophets** shall rise, and *5578*
24:24 For there shall arise **f Christs**, and *5580*
24:24 and **f prophets**, and shall shew great signs *5578*
26:59 the council, sought **f witness** against Jesus, *5577*
26:60 yea, though many **f witnesses** came, *5575*
26:60 At the last came two **f witnesses**, *5575*
Mk 10:19 Do not **bear f witness**, Defraud not, *5576*
13:22 For **f Christs** and false prophets shall rise, *5580*
13:22 For false Christs and **f prophets** shall rise, *5578*
14:56 For many **bare f witness** against him, but *5576*
14:57 and **bare f witness** against him, saying, *5576*
Lk 6:26 for so did their fathers to the **f prophets**. *5578*
18:20 Do not steal, Do not **bear f witness**, *5576*
19: 8 **taken** any *thing* from any *man*
by f accusation, *4811*
Ac 6:13 And set up **f** witnesses, which said, *5571*
13: 6 a **f prophet**, a Jew, whose name *was* *5578*
Ro 13: 9 not steal, Thou shalt not **bear f witness**, *5576*
1Co 15:15 Yea, and we are found **f witnesses** of God; *5575*
2Co 11:13 For such *are* **f apostles**, deceitful workers, *5570*
11:26 in the sea, *in* perils among **f brethren**; *5569*
Gal 2: 4 because of **f brethren** unawares brought in, *5569*
2Ti 3: 3 **f accusers**, incontinent, fierce, *1228*
Tit 2: 3 not **f accusers**, not given to much wine, *1228*
2Pe 2: 1 But there were **f prophets** also among *5578*
2: 1 even as there shall be **f teachers** among *5572*
1Jn 4: 1 many **f prophets** are gone out into *5578*
Rev 16:13 and out of the mouth of the **f prophet**. *5578*
19:20 with him the **f prophet** that wrought *5578*
20:10 where the beast and the **f prophet** *are,* and *5578*

FALSEHOOD (14) [FALSE]

2Sa 18:13 Otherwise I should have wrought **f** against 8267
Job 21:34 seeing *in* your answers there remaineth **f**? 4604
Ps 7:14 conceived mischief, and brought forth **f**. 8267
119:118 err from thy statutes: for their deceit *is* **f**. 8267
144: 8 and their right hand *is* a right hand of **f**. 8267
144:11 and their right hand *is* a right hand of **f**: 8267
Isa 28:15 and under **f** have we hid ourselves: 8267
57: 4 ye not children of transgression, a seed of **f**, 8267
59:13 and uttering from the heart words of **f**. 8267
Jer 10:14 for his molten image *is* **f**, and *there is* no 8267
13:25 thou hast forgotten me, and trusted in **f**. 8267
51:17 for his molten image *is* **f**, and *there is* no 8267
Hos 7: 1 for they commit **f**; and the thief cometh in, 8267
Mic 2:11 If a man walking *in* the spirit and **f** do lie, 8267

FALSELY (21) [FALSE]

Ge 21:23 by God that thou wilt not **deal f** with me, 8266
Lev 6: 3 lieth concerning it, and sweareth **f**; 5921+8267
6: 5 which he hath sworn **f**; 8267+1886.1+3807.1
19:11 Ye shall not steal, neither **deal f**, neither lie 3584
19:12 not swear by my name **f**, 8267+1886.1+3807.1
Dt 19:18 *and* hath testified **f** against his brother; 8267
Ps 44:17 neither have we **dealt f** in thy covenant. 8266
Jer 5: 2 surely they swear **f**. 8267+1886.1+3807.1
5:31 The prophets prophesy **f**, 8267+871.1+1886.1
6:13 even unto the priest every one dealeth **f**. 8267
7: 9 swear **f**, and burn incense 8267+1886.1+3807.1
8:10 even unto the priest every one dealeth **f**. 8267
29: 9 For they prophesy **f** unto you in my name: 8267
40:16 this thing: for thou speakest **f** of Ishmael. 8267
43: 2 saying unto Jeremiah, Thou speakest **f**: 8267
Hos 10: 4 swearing **f** in making a covenant: 7723
Zec 5: 4 into the house of him that sweareth **f** by my 8267
Mt 5:11 shall say all manner of evil against you **f**, *5574*
Lk 3:14 violence to no man, neither **accuse** *any* **f**; *4811*
1Ti 6:20 and oppositions of science **f** so **called**: *5581*
1Pe 3:16 they may be ashamed that **f accuse** your *1908*

FALSIFYING (1) [FALSE]

Am 8: 5 shekel great, and **f** the balances by deceit? 5791

FALTERS See PANTED; PANTETH

FAME (24) [FAMOUS]

Ge 45:16 the **f** *thereof* was heard *in* Pharaoh's house, 6963
Nu 14:15 the nations which have heard the **f** of thee 8088
Jos 6:27 his **f** was *noised* throughout all the country. 8089
9: 9 for we have heard the **f** of him, and all that 8089
1Ki 4:31 and his **f** was in all nations round about. 8034
10: 1 when the queen of Sheba heard of the **f** of 8088
10: 7 prosperity exceedeth the **f** which I heard. 8052
1Ch 14:17 the **f** of David went out into all lands; and 8034
22: 5 of **f** and of glory throughout all countries: 8034
2Ch 9: 1 when the queen of Sheba heard of the **f** of 8088
9: 6 *for* thou exceedest the **f** that I heard. 8052
Est 9: 4 his **f** went out throughout all the provinces: 8089
Job 28:22 We have heard the **f** thereof with our ears. 8088
Isa 66:19 the isles afar off, that have not heard my **f**, 8088
Jer 6:24 We have heard the **f** thereof: our hands wax 8089
Zep 3:19 **f** in every land where they have been put to 8034
Mt 4:24 And his **f** went throughout all Syria: and *189*
9:26 And the **f** hereof went abroad into all that *5345*
9:31 **spread abroad** his **f** in all that country. *1310*
14: 1 At that time Herod the tetrarch heard of the **f** *189*
Mk 1:28 And immediately his **f** spread abroad *189*
Lk 4:14 there went out a **f** of him through all *5345*
4:37 And the **f** of him went out into every place *2279*
5:15 *much* the more went there a **f** abroad of *3056*

FAMILIAR (18) [FAMILIARS]

Lev 19:31 Regard not them that have **f spirits**, 178
20: 6 soul that turneth after such as have **f spirits**, 178
20:27 A man also or woman that hath a **f spirit**, or 178
Dt 18:11 or a consulter with **f spirits**, or a wizard, or 178
1Sa 28: 3 Saul had put away those that had **f spirits**, 178
28: 7 Seek me a woman that hath a **f spirit**, that I 178
28: 7 *there is* a woman that hath a **f spirit** at 178
28: 8 divine unto me by the **f spirit**, and bring me 178
28: 9 how he hath cut off those that have **f spirits**, 178
2Ki 21: 6 and dealt with **f spirits** and wizards: 178
23:24 Moreover the *workers with* **f spirits**, and 178
1Ch 10:13 for asking *counsel* of *one that had* a **f spirit**, 178
2Ch 33: 6 and dealt with a **f spirit**, and with wizards: 178
Job 19:14 and my **f friends** have forgotten me. 3045
Ps 41: 9 Yea, mine own **f friend**, in whom I 376+7965
Isa 8:19 Seek unto them that have **f spirits**, and 178
19: 3 to them that have **f spirits**, and to 178
29: 4 as of one that hath a **f spirit**, out of 178

FAMILIARS (1) [FAMILIAR]

Jer 20:10 All my **f** watched for my halting, 582+7965

FAMILIES (174) [FAMILY]

Ge 10: 5 his tongue, after their **f**, in their nations. 4940
10:18 afterward were the **f** of the Canaanites 4940
10:20 after their **f**, after their tongues, in their 4940
10:31 after their **f**, after their tongues, in their 4940
10:32 These *are* the **f** of the sons of Noah, 4940
12: 3 in thee shall all **f** of the earth be blessed. 4940
28:14 in thy seed shall all the **f** of the earth be 4940
36:40 according to their **f**, after their places, 4940
47:12 *with* bread, according to *their* **f**. 2945
Ex 6:14 and Carmi: these *be* the **f** of Reuben. 4940
6:15 these *are* the **f** of Simeon. 4940
6:17 Libni, and Shimi, according to their **f**. 4940
6:19 these *are* the **f** of Levi according to their 4940
6:24 Abiasaph: these *are* the **f** of the Korhites. 4940
6:25 fathers of the Levites according to their **f**. 4940
12:21 and take you a lamb according to your **f**, 4940
Lev 25:45 ye buy, and of their **f** that *are* with you, 4940
Nu 1: 2 after their **f**, by the house of their fathers, 4940
1:18 they declared their pedigrees after their **f**, 4940
1:20 *by* their generations, after their **f**, 4940
1:22 *by* their generations, after their **f**, 4940
1:24 of Gad, *by* their generations, after their **f**, 4940
1:26 of Judah, *by* their generations, after their **f**, 4940
1:28 *by* their generations, after their **f**, 4940
1:30 *by* their generations, after their **f**, 4940
1:32 *by* their generations, after their **f**, by 4940
1:34 *by* their generations, after their **f**, by 4940
1:36 *by* their generations, after their **f**, by 4940
1:38 of Dan, *by* their generations, after their **f**, 4940
1:40 of Asher, *by* their generations, after their **f**, 4940
1:42 after their **f**, by the house of their fathers, 4940
2:34 so they set forward, every one after their **f**, 4940
3:15 after the house of their fathers, by their **f**: 4940
3:18 the names of the sons of Gershon by their **f**; 4940

Nu 3:19 the sons of Kohath by their **f**; Amram, and 4940
3:20 the sons of Merari by their **f**; Mahli, and 4940
3:20 These *are* the **f** of the Levites according to 4940
3:21 these *are* the **f** of the Gershonites. 4940
3:23 The **f** of the Gershonites shall pitch behind 4940
3:27 these *are* the **f** of the Kohathites. 4940
3:29 The **f** of the sons of Kohath shall pitch on 4940
3:30 the chief of the house of the father of the **f** 4940
3:33 of the Mushites: these *are* the **f** of Merari. 4940
3:35 the chief of the house of the father of the **f** 4940
3:39 throughout their **f**, all the males from a 4940
4: 2 after their **f**, by the house of their fathers, 4940
4:18 Cut ye not off the tribe of the **f** of 4940
4:22 the houses of their fathers, by their **f**; 4940
4:24 This *is* the service of the **f** of 4940
4:28 This *is* the service of the **f** of the sons of 4940
4:29 thou shalt number them after their **f**, 4940
4:33 This *is* the service of the **f** of the sons of 4940
4:34 the sons of the Kohathites after their **f**, 4940
4:36 those that were numbered of them by their **f** 4940
4:37 were numbered of the **f** of the Kohathites, 4940
4:38 throughout their **f**, and by the house of their 4940
4:40 throughout their **f**, by the house of their 4940
4:41 These *are* they that were numbered of the **f** 4940
4:42 those that were numbered of the **f** of 4940
4:42 throughout their **f**, by the house of their 4940
4:44 that were numbered of them after their **f**, 4940
4:45 These *be* those that were numbered of the **f** 4940
4:46 after their **f**, and after the house of their 4940
11:10 heard the people weep throughout their **f**, 4940
26: 7 These *are* the **f** of the Reubenites: and 4940
26:12 The sons of Simeon after their **f**: 4940
26:14 These *are* the **f** of the Simeonites, twenty 4940
26:15 The children of Gad after their **f**: 4940
26:18 These *are* the **f** of the children of Gad 4940
26:20 the sons of Judah after their **f** were, 4940
26:22 These *are* the **f** of Judah according to those 4940
26:23 *Of* the sons of Issachar after their **f**: 4940
26:25 These *are* the **f** of Issachar according to 4940
26:26 *Of* the sons of Zebulun after their **f**: 4940
26:27 These *are* the **f** of the Zebulunites 4940
26:28 The sons of Joseph after their **f** *were* 4940
26:34 These *are* the **f** of Manasseh, and those that 4940
26:35 These *are* the sons of Ephraim after their **f**: 4940
26:37 These *are* the **f** of the sons of Ephraim 4940
26:37 These *are* the sons of Joseph after their **f**. 4940
26:38 The sons of Benjamin after their **f**: of Bela, 4940
26:41 *are* the sons of Benjamin after their **f**: 4940
26:42 These *are* the sons of Dan after their **f**: 4940
26:42 These *are* the **f** of Dan after their families. 4940
26:42 These *are* the families of Dan after their **f**. 4940
26:43 All the **f** of the Shuhamites, according to 4940
26:44 *Of* the children of Asher after their **f**: 4940
26:47 These *are* the **f** of the sons of Asher 4940
26:48 *Of* the sons of Naphtali after their **f**: 4940
26:50 These *are* the **f** of Naphtali according to 4940
26:50 families of Naphtali according to their **f**: 4940
26:57 were numbered of the Levites after their **f**: 4940
26:58 These *are* the **f** of the Levites: the family of 4940
27: 1 of the **f** of Manasseh the son of Joseph: 4940
33:54 land by lot for an inheritance among your **f**: 4940
36: 1 the chief fathers of the **f** of the children of 4940
36: 1 of the **f** of the sons of Joseph, came near, 4940
36:12 *And* they were married into the **f** of 4940
Jos 7:14 shall come according to the **f** *thereof*; 4940
13:15 of Reuben *inheritance* according to their **f**. 4940
13:23 of the children of Reuben after their **f**, 4940
13:24 the children of Gad according to their **f**. 4940
13:28 of the children of Gad after their **f**, 4940
13:29 tribe of the children of Manasseh by their **f**. 4940
13:31 half of the children of Machir by their **f**. 4940
15: 1 the tribe of the children of Judah by their **f**; 4940
15:12 of Judah round about according to their **f**. 4940
15:20 the children of Judah according to their **f**. 4940
16: 5 **f** was *thus:* even the border of their 4940
16: 8 tribe of the children of Ephraim by their **f**. 4940
17: 2 rest of the children of Manasseh by their **f**; 4940
17: 2 of Manasseh the son of Joseph by their **f**. 4940
18:11 of Benjamin came up according to their **f**: 4940
18:20 thereof round about, according to their **f**. 4940
18:21 Benjamin according to their **f** were Jericho 4940
18:28 children of Benjamin according to their **f**. 4940
19: 1 the children of Simeon according to their **f**: 4940
19: 8 the children of Simeon according to their **f**. 4940
19:10 the children of Zebulun according to their **f**: 4940
19:16 the children of Zebulun according to their **f**, 4940
19:17 the children of Issachar according to their **f**. 4940
19:23 the children of Issachar according to their **f**, 4940
19:24 the children of Asher according to their **f**. 4940
19:31 the children of Asher according to their **f**, 4940
19:32 children of Naphtali according to their **f**. 4940
19:39 children of Naphtali according to their **f**, 4940
19:40 of the children of Dan according to their **f**. 4940
19:48 of the children of Dan according to their **f**, 4940
21: 4 the lot came out for the **f** of the Kohathites: 4940
21: 5 by lot out of the **f** of the tribe of Ephraim, 4940
21: 6 by lot out of the **f** of the tribe of Issachar, 4940
21: 7 The children of Merari by their **f** *had* out of 4940
21:10 of Aaron, *being* of the **f** of the Kohathites, 4940
21:20 the **f** of the children of Kohath, the Levites 4940
21:26 **f** of the children of Kohath that remained. 4940
21:27 children of Gershon, of the **f** of the Levites, 4940
21:33 **f** *were* thirteen cities with their suburbs. 4940
21:34 unto the **f** of the children of Merari, the rest 4940
21:40 cities for the children of Merari by their **f**, 4940
21:40 which were remaining of the **f** of 4940
1Sa 9:21 my family the least of all the **f** of the tribe 4940
10:21 tribe of Benjamin to come near by their **f**, 4940
1Ch 2:53 the **f** of Kirjath-jearim; the Ithrites, and 4940
2:55 the **f** of the scribes which dwelt at Jabez; 4940
4: 2 These *are* the **f** of the Zorathites. 4940
4: 8 and the **f** of Aharhel the son of Harum. 4940
4:21 the **f** of the house of them that wrought fine 4940
4:38 by *their* names *were* princes in their **f**: 4940
5: 7 his brethren by their **f**, when the genealogy 4940

1Ch 6:19 these *are* the **f** of the Levites according to 4940
6:54 sons of Aaron, of the **f** of the Kohathites: 4940
6:60 All their cities throughout their **f** *were* 4940
6:62 to the sons of Gershom throughout their **f** 4940
6:63 throughout their **f**, out of the tribe of 4940
6:66 *the residue* of the **f** of the sons of Kohath 4940
7: 5 their brethren among all the **f** of Issachar 4940
2Ch 35: 5 **f** of the fathers of your brethren the people, 1004
35: 5 *after* the division of the **f** of the Levites. 1+1004
35:12 to the divisions of the **f** of the people, 1+1004
Ne 4:13 I even set the people after *their* **f** with their 4940
Job 31:34 or did the contempt of **f** terrify me, that I 4940
Ps 68: 6 God setteth the solitary in **f**: he bringeth out 1004
107:41 and maketh *him* **f** like a flock. 4940
Jer 1:15 I will call all the **f** of the kingdoms of 4940
2: 4 of Jacob, and all the **f** of the house of Israel: 4940
10:25 and upon the **f** that call not on thy name: 4940
25: 9 I will send and take all the **f** of the north, 4940
31: 1 will I be the God of all the **f** of Israel, and 4940
33:24 The two **f** which the LORD hath chosen, 4940
Eze 20:32 as the **f** of the countries, to serve wood and 4940
Am 3: 2 You only have I known of all the **f** of 4940
Na 3: 4 and **f** through her witchcrafts. 4940
Zec 12:14 All the **f** that remain, every family apart, 4940
14:17 *that* whoso will not come up of *all* the **f** of 4940

FAMILY (123) [FAMILIES]

Lev 20: 5 against his **f**, and will cut him off, and all 4940
25:10 and ye shall return every man unto his **f**. 4940
25:41 shall return unto his own **f**, and unto 4940
25:47 by thee, or to the stock of the stranger's **f**: 4940
25:49 *any* that is nigh of kin unto him of his **f** 4940
Nu 3:21 Of Gershon *was* the **f** of the Libnites, and 4940
3:21 of the Libnites, and the **f** of the Shimites: 4940
3:27 of Kohath *was* the **f** of the Amramites, and 4940
3:27 the **f** of the Izeharites, and the family of 4940
3:27 the **f** of the Hebronites, and the family of 4940
3:27 the Hebronites, and the **f** of the Uzzielites: 4940
3:33 Of Merari *was* the **f** of the Mahlites, and 4940
3:33 of the Mahlites, and the **f** of the Mushites: 4940
26: 5 *of whom cometh* the **f** of the Hanochites: 4940
26: 5 of Pallu, the **f** of the Palluites: 4940
26: 6 Of Hezron, the **f** of the Hezronites: 4940
26: 6 of Carmi, the **f** of the Carmites. 4940
26:12 of Nemuel, the **f** of the Nemuelites: 4940
26:12 of Jamin, the **f** of the Jaminites: of Jachin, 4940
26:12 of Jachin, the **f** of the Jachinites: 4940
26:13 Of Zerah, the **f** of the Zarhites: of Shaul, 4940
26:13 of Shaul, the **f** of the Shaulites. 4940
26:15 of Zephon, the **f** of the Zephonites: 4940
26:15 of Haggi, the **f** of the Haggites: of Shuni, 4940
26:15 of Shuni, the **f** of the Shunites: 4940
26:16 Of Ozni, the **f** of the Oznites: of Eri, 4940
26:16 of the Oznites: of Eri, the **f** of the Erites: 4940
26:17 Of Arod, the **f** of the Arodites: of Areli, 4940
26:17 the Arodites: of Areli, the **f** of the Arelites. 4940
26:20 of Shelah, the **f** of the Shelanites: 4940
26:20 of Pharez, the **f** of the Pharzites: of Zerah, 4940
26:20 of Zerah, the **f** of the Zarhites. 4940
26:21 of Hezron, the **f** of the Hezronites: 4940
26:21 of Hamul, the **f** of the Hamulites. 4940
26:23 *of* Tola, the **f** of the Tolaites: of Pua, 4940
26:23 of the Tolaites: of Pua, the **f** of the Punites: 4940
26:24 Of Jashub, the **f** of the Jashubites: 4940
26:24 of Shimron, the **f** of the Shimronites. 4940
26:26 of Sered, the **f** of the Sardites: of Elon, 4940
26:26 of Elon, the **f** of the Elonites: of Jahleel, 4940
26:26 of Jahleel, the **f** of the Jahleelites. 4940
26:29 of Machir, the **f** of the Machirites: and 4940
26:29 of Gilead *come* the **f** of the Gileadites. 4940
26:30 *of* Jeezer, the **f** of the Jeezerites: of Helek, 4940
26:30 of Helek, the **f** of the Helekites: 4940
26:31 *of* Asriel, the **f** of the Asrielites: and 4940
26:31 and *of* Shechem, the **f** of the Shechemites: 4940
26:32 *of* Shemida, the **f** of the Shemidaites: and 4940
26:32 and *of* Hepher, the **f** of the Hepherites. 4940
26:35 of Shuthelah, the **f** of the Shuthalhites: 4940
26:35 of Becher, the **f** of the Bachrites: of Tahan, 4940
26:35 of Tahan, the **f** of the Tahanites. 4940
26:36 of Shuthelah: of Eran, the **f** of the Eranites. 4940
26:38 of Bela, the **f** of the Belaites: of Ashbel, 4940
26:38 of Ashbel, the **f** of the Ashbelites: 4940
26:38 of Ahiram, the **f** of the Ahiramites: 4940
26:39 Of Shupham, the **f** of the Shuphamites: 4940
26:39 of Hupham, the **f** of the Huphamites. 4940
26:40 *of* Ard, the **f** of the Ardites: *and* of Naaman, 4940
26:40 *and* of Naaman, the **f** of the Naamites. 4940
26:42 of Shuham, the **f** of the Shuhamites. 4940
26:44 of Jimna, the **f** of the Jimnites: of Jesui, 4940
26:44 of Jesui, the **f** of the Jesuites: of Beriah, 4940
26:44 the Jesuites: of Beriah, the **f** of the Beriites. 4940
26:45 of Heber, the **f** of the Heberites: 4940
26:45 of Malchiel, the **f** of the Malchielites. 4940
26:48 of Jahzeel, the **f** of the Jahzeelites: of Guni, 4940
26:48 of Guni, the **f** of the Gunites: 4940
26:49 Of Jezer, the **f** of the Jezerites: of Shillem, 4940
26:49 of Shillem, the **f** of the Shillemites. 4940
26:57 of Gershon, the **f** of the Gershonites: 4940
26:57 of Kohath, the **f** of the Kohathites: 4940
26:57 of Merari, the **f** of the Merarites. 4940
26:58 the **f** of the Libnites, the family of 4940
26:58 of the Libnites, the **f** of the Hebronites, 4940
26:58 the **f** of the Mahlites, the family of 4940
26:58 of the Mahlites, the **f** of the Mushites, 4940
26:58 of the Mushites, the **f** of the Korahites. 4940
27: 4 our father be done away from among his **f**, 4940
27:11 his kinsman that is next to him of his **f**, 4940
36: 6 only to the **f** of the tribe of their father shall 4940
36: 8 shall be wife unto one of the **f** of the tribe 4940
36:12 remained in the tribe of the **f** of their father. 4940
Dt 29:18 among you man, or woman, or **f**, or tribe, 4940
Jos 7:14 the **f** which the LORD shall take shall 4940
7:17 he brought the **f** of Judah; and he took 4940
7:17 of Judah; and he took the **f** of the Zarhites: 4940
7:17 he brought the **f** of the Zarhites man by 4940

Jdg 1:25 but they let go the man and all his **f**. 4940
6:15 my **f** *is* poor in Manasseh, and I *am* the least 504
9: 1 with all the **f** of the house of his mother's 4940
13: 2 of the **f** of the Danites, whose name *was* 4940
17: 7 out of Beth-lehem-judah of the **f** of Judah, 4940
18: 2 the children of Dan sent of their **f** five men 4940
18:11 there went from thence of the **f** of 4940
18:19 be a priest unto a tribe and a **f** in Israel? 4940
21:24 every man to his tribe and to his **f**, and 4940
Ru 2: 1 man of wealth, of the **f** of Elimelech; 4940
1Sa 9:21 my **f** the least of all the families of the tribe 4940
10:21 the **f** of Matri was taken, and Saul the son 4940
18:18 what *is* my life, *or* my father's **f** in Israel, 4940
20: 6 *there is* a yearly sacrifice there for all the **f**. 4940
20:29 for our **f** hath a sacrifice in the city; and 4940
2Sa 14: 7 the whole **f** is risen against thine handmaid, 4940
16: 5 thence came out a man of the **f** of the house 4940
1Ch 4:27 neither did all their **f** multiply, like to 4940
6:61 which were left of the **f** of *that* tribe, 4940
6:70 for the **f** of the remnant of the sons of 4940
6:71 out of the **f** of the half tribe of Manasseh, 4940
13:14 the ark of God remained with the **f** of 1004
Est 9:28 **every f**, every province, 4940+4940+2050.1
Jer 3:14 and two of a **f**, and I will bring you *to* Zion: 4940
8: 3 residue of them that remain of this evil **f**, 4940
Am 3: 1 against the whole **f** which I brought up 4940
Mic 2: 3 Behold, against this **f** do I devise an evil, 4940
Zec 12:12 the land shall mourn, **every f** apart; 4940+4940
12:12 the **f** of the house of David apart, and 4940
12:12 the **f** of the house of Nathan apart, and 4940
12:13 The **f** of the house of Levi apart, and 4940
12:13 the **f** of Shimei apart, and their wives apart; 4940
12:14 **every f** apart, and their wives apart. 4940+4940
14:18 if the **f** of Egypt go not up, and come not, 4940
Eph 3:15 Of whom the whole **f** in heaven and earth is *3965*

FAMINE (96) [FAMINES]

Ge 12:10 there was a **f** in the land: and Abram went 7458
12:10 for the **f** *was* grievous in the land. 7458
26: 1 there was a **f** in the land, besides the first 7458
26: 1 besides the first **f** that was in the days of 7458
41:27 with the east wind shall be seven years of **f**. 7458
41:30 there shall arise after them seven years of **f**; 7458
41:30 of Egypt; and the **f** shall consume the land; 7458
41:31 in the land by reason of that **f** following; 7458
41:36 to the land against the seven years of **f**, 7458
41:36 that the land perish not through the **f**. 7458
41:50 born two sons before the years of **f** came, 7458
41:56 the **f** was over all the face of the earth: 7458
41:56 and the **f** waxed sore in the land of Egypt. 7458
41:57 because that the **f** was *so* sore in all lands. 7458
42: 5 for the **f** was in the land of Canaan. 7458
42:19 go ye, carry corn *for* the **f** of your houses: 7459
42:33 take *food for* the **f** of your households, and 7459
43: 1 And the **f** *was* sore in the land. 7458
45: 6 For these two years *hath* the **f** *been* in 7458
45:11 for yet *there are* five years of **f**; lest thou, 7458
47: 4 for the **f** *is* sore in the land of Canaan: 7458
47:13 for the **f** *was* very sore, so that the land of 7458
47:13 land of Canaan fainted by reason of the **f**. 7458
47:20 his field, because the **f** prevailed over them: 7458
Ru 1: 1 judges ruled, that there was a **f** in the land. 7458
2Sa 21: 1 there was a **f** in the days of David three 7458
24:13 Shall seven years of **f** come unto thee in thy 7458
1Ki 8:37 If there be in the land **f**, if there be 7458
18: 2 And *there was* a sore **f** in Samaria. 7458
2Ki 6:25 there was a great **f** in Samaria: and behold, 7458
7: 4 the **f** *is* in the city, and we shall die there: 7458
8: 1 for the LORD hath called for a **f**; and 7458
25: 3 on the ninth *day* of the *fourth* month the **f** 7458
1Ch 21:12 Either three years' **f**; or three months to be 7458
2Ch 20: 9 *as* the sword, judgment, or pestilence, or **f**, 7458
32:11 you to give over yourselves to die by **f** 7458
Job 5:20 In **f** he shall redeem thee from death: and 7458
5:22 At destruction and **f** thou shalt laugh: 3720
30: 3 For want and **f** *they were* solitary; flying 3720
Ps 33:19 from death, and to keep them alive in **f**. 7458
37:19 and in the days of **f** they shall be satisfied. 7459
105:16 Moreover, he called *for* a **f** upon the land: 7458
Isa 14:30 I will kill thy root with **f**, and he shall slay 7458
51:19 and destruction, and the **f**, and the sword: 7458
Jer 5:12 upon us; neither shall we see sword nor **f**: 7458
11:22 their sons and their daughters shall die by **f**: 7458
14:12 and by the **f**, and by the pestilence. 7458
14:13 not see the sword, neither shall ye have **f**; 7458
14:15 Sword and **f** shall not be in this land; 7458
14:15 and **f** shall those prophets be consumed. 7458
14:16 because of the **f** and the sword; 7458
14:18 then behold them that are sick with **f**: 7458
15: 2 such as *are* for the **f**, to the famine; and 7458
15: 2 such as *are* for the famine, to the **f**; and 7458
16: 4 shall be consumed by the sword, and by **f**; 7458
18:21 Therefore deliver up their children to the **f**, 7458
21: 7 from the sword, and from the **f**, 7458
21: 9 and by the **f**, and by the pestilence: 7458
24:10 the **f**, and the pestilence, among them, 7458
27: 8 and with the **f**, and with the pestilence, 7458
27:13 the sword, by the **f**, and by the pestilence, 7458
29:17 the **f**, and the pestilence, and will make 7458
29:18 with the **f**, and with the pestilence, and 7458
32:24 and *of* the **f**, and *of* the pestilence: 7458
32:36 and by the **f**, and by the pestilence; 7458
34:17 to the sword, to the pestilence, and to the **f**; 7458
38: 2 the sword, by the **f**, and by the pestilence: 7458
42:16 the **f**, whereof ye were afraid, shall follow 7458
42:17 the sword, by the **f**, and by the pestilence: 7458
42:22 by the **f**, and by the pestilence, in the place 7458
44:12 be consumed by the sword, *and* by the **f**: 7458
44:12 unto the greatest, by the sword and by the **f**: 7458
44:13 the sword, by the **f**, and by the pestilence: 7458
44:18 been consumed by the sword and by the **f**. 7458
44:27 be consumed by the sword and by the **f**, 7458
52: 6 the **f** was sore in the city, so that there was 7458
La 5:10 black like an oven because of the terrible **f**. 7458
Eze 5:12 with **f** shall they be consumed in the midst 7458

Eze 5:16 I shall send upon them the evil arrows of f, 7458
5:16 I *will* increase the f upon you, and 7458
5:17 So will I send upon you f and evil beasts, 7458
6:11 the sword, by the f, and by the pestilence. 7458
6:12 and is besieged shall die by the f: 7458
7:15 and the pestilence and the f within: 7458
7:15 the city, f and pestilence shall devour him. 7458
12:16 from the f, and from the pestilence; 7458
14:13 and will send f upon it, and will cut off man 7458
14:21 the f, and the noisome beast, and 7458
36:29 and will increase it, and lay no f upon you. 7458
36:30 that ye shall receive no more reproach of f 7458
Am 8:11 Lord GOD, that I will send a f in the land, 7458
8:11 not a f of bread, nor a thirst for water, but 7458
Lk 4:25 when great f was throughout all the land; *3042*
15:14 there arose a mighty f in that land; *3042*
Ro 8:35 or f, or nakedness, or peril, or sword? *3042*
Rev 18: 8 in one day, death, and mourning, and f; *3042*

FAMINES (3) [FAMINE]
Mt 24: 7 and there shall be f, and pestilences, and *3042*
Mk 13: 8 and there shall be f and troubles: *3042*
Lk 21:11 be in divers places, and f, and pestilences; *3042*

F

FAMISH (2) [FAMISHED]
Pr 10: 3 not **suffer** the soul of the righteous **to f**: 7456
Zep 2:11 for he will f all the gods of the earth; and 7329

FAMISHED (2) [FAMISH]
Ge 41:55 when all the land of Egypt was f, 7456
Isa 5:13 their honourable men *are* f, and 7458

FAMOUS (10) [FAME]
Nu 16: 2 f in the congregation, men of renown: 7148
26: 9 Abiram, *which were* f in the congregation, 7148
Ru 4:11 in Ephratah, and be f in Beth-lehem: 7121+8034
4:14 a kinsman, that his name may be f in Israel. 7121
1Ch 5:24 f men, *and* heads of the house of their 8034
12:30 mighty *men* of valour, f throughout 376+8034
Ps 74: 5 *A man* was f according as he had lifted up 3045
136:18 slew f kings: for his mercy *endureth* for 117
Eze 23:10 she became f among women; for they had 8034
32:18 *even* her, and the daughters of the f nations, 117

FAN (8) [FANNERS]
Isa 30:24 winnowed with the shovel and with the f. 4214
41:16 Thou shalt f them, and the wind shall carry 2219
Jer 4:11 of my people, not to f, nor to cleanse, 2219
15: 7 I will f them with a fan in the gates of 2219
15: 7 I will fan them with a f in the gates of 4214
51: 2 that shall f her, and shall empty her land: 2219
Mt 3:12 Whose f *is* in his hand, and he will *4425*
Lk 3:17 Whose f *is* in his hand, and he will *4425*

FANNERS (1) [FAN]
Jer 51: 2 will send unto Babylon f, that shall fan her, 2114

FAR (173) [AFAR, FURTHER]
Ge 18:25 **That be f** from thee to do after this manner, 2486
18:25 be as the wicked, **that be f** from thee: 2486
44: 4 *and* not *yet* **f off**, Joseph said unto his 7368
Ex 8:28 only you shall not go **very f away**: 7368+7368
23: 7 **Keep** thee f from a false matter; and 7368
Nu 2: 2 **f off** about the tabernacle of 4480+5048
Dt 12:21 to put his name there be too f from thee, 7368
13: 7 nigh unto thee, or **f off** from thee, 7350
14:24 *or* if the place be too f from thee, which 7368
20:15 all the cities *which are* very **f off** from thee, 7350
28:49 shall bring a nation against thee from f, 7350
29:22 the stranger that shall come from a f land, 7350
30:11 it *is* not hidden from thee, neither *is* it **f off**. 7350
Jos 3:16 *and* rose up *upon* a heap very f, 7368
8: 4 **go** not very f from the city, but be ye all 7368
9: 6 of Israel, We be come from a f country: 7350
9: 9 From a very f country thy servants are 7350
9:22 saying, We *are* very f from you; 7350
Jdg 9:17 adventured his life f, and 4480+5048
18: 7 they *were* f from the Zidonians, and had no 7350
18:28 because it *was* f from Zidon, and they had 7350
19:11 they *were* by Jebus, the day was f spent; 3966
1Sa 2:30 now the LORD saith, **Be it f** from me; 2486
20: 9 Jonathan said, **F be it** from thee: for if I 2486
22:15 **be it f** from me: let not the king impute *any* 2486
2Sa 15:17 and tarried *in* a place that *was* **f off**. 4801
20:20 Joab answered and said, **F be it**, far be it 2486
20:20 and said, Far be it, **f be it** from me, 2486
23:17 he said, **Be it f** from me, O LORD, that I 2486
1Ki 8:41 cometh out of a f country for thy name's 7350
8:46 unto the land of the enemy, f or near; 7350
2Ki 20:14 They are come from a f country, 7350
2Ch 6:32 is come from a f country for thy great 7350
6:36 carry them away captives unto a land **f off** 7350
26:15 spread **f abroad**; 4480+5704+7350+3807.1
Ezr 6: 6 *are* beyond the river, be ye f from thence: 7352
Ne 4:19 upon the wall, one f from another. 7350
Est 9:20 of the king Ahasuerus, *both* nigh and f, 7350
Job 5: 4 His children are f from safety, and they are 7368
11:14 **put** it **f away**, and let not wickedness dwell 7368
13:21 **Withdraw** thine hand f from me: and 7368
19:13 He hath **put** my brethren f from me, and 7368
21:16 the counsel of the wicked is f from me. 7368
22:18 but the counsel of the wicked is f from me. 7368
22:23 **put away** iniquity f from thy tabernacles. 7368
30:10 they **flee** f from me, and spare not to spit in 7368
34:10 **f be it** from God, *that he should do* 2486
Ps 10: 5 thy judgments *are* **f above** out of his sight: 4791
22: 1 *why art thou so* f from helping me, *and* 7350
22:11 Be not f from me; for trouble *is* near; 7368
22:19 be not thou f *from me,* O LORD: O my 7368
27: 9 Hide not thy face *f* from me; put not thy NIH
35:22 keep not silence: O Lord, be not f from me. 7368
38:21 O LORD: O my God, be not f from me. 7368
55: 7 Lo, *then* would I wander **f off**, and 7368
71:12 O God, be not f from me: O my God, 7368

Ps 73:27 they that are **f from** thee shall perish: 7369
88: 8 Thou hast **put away** mine acquaintance f 7368
88:18 Lover and friend hast thou **put** f from me, 7368
97: 9 the earth: thou art exalted f above all gods. 3966
103:12 As f as the east is from the west, *so* far hath 7368
103:12 f hath he **removed** our transgressions from 7368
109:17 not in blessing, so let it be f from him. 7368
119:150 after mischief: they are f from thy law. 7368
119:155 Salvation *is* f from the wicked: for they 7350
Pr 4:24 and perverse lips **put** f from thee. 7368
5: 8 **Remove** thy way f from her, and come not 7368
15:29 The LORD *is* f from the wicked: but 7350
19: 7 how much more do his friends **go** f from 7368
22: 5 he that doth keep his soul shall be f from 7368
22:15 the rod of correction shall **drive** it f from 7368
25:25 so *is* good news from a f country. 4801
27:10 a neighbour *that is* near than a brother **f off**. 7350
30: 8 **Remove** f from me vanity and lies: give me 7368
31:10 for her price *is* f above rubies. 7350
Ecc 2:13 **as f as** light excelleth darkness. 3509.1
7:23 I said, I will be wise; but it *was* f from me. 7350
7:24 That which is **f off**, and exceeding deep, 7350
Isa 5:26 will lift up an ensign to the nations from f, 7350
6:12 the LORD have **removed** men **f away**, 7368
8: 9 in pieces; and give ear, all ye of f countries: 4801
10: 3 in the desolation *which* shall come from f? 4801
13: 5 They come from a f country, from the end 4801
17:13 they shall flee **f off**, and shall be 4480+4801
19: 6 they shall **turn** the rivers **f away**; *and* 2186
22: 3 are bound together, *which* have fled from f. 7350
26:15 thou hadst **removed** *it* f *unto* all the ends of 7368
29:13 have **removed** their heart f from me, and 7368
30:27 the name of the LORD cometh from f, 4801
33:13 Hear, ye *that are* **f off**, what I have done; 7350
33:17 they shall behold the land that is **very f off**. 4801
39: 3 They are come from a f country unto me, 7350
43: 6 bring my sons from f, and my daughters 7350
46:11 the man that executeth my counsel from a f 4801
46:12 that *are* f from righteousness: 7350
46:13 it shall not be **f off**, and my salvation shall 7368
49:12 Behold, these shall come from f: and lo, 7350
49:19 that swallowed thee up shall be **f away**. 7368
54:14 thou shalt be f from oppression; for thou 7368
57: 9 didst send thy messengers **f off**, and 4480+7350
57:19 peace to *him that is* **f off**, and to *him that is* 7350
59: 9 Therefore is judgment f from us, 7368
59:11 *is* none; for salvation, *but it* is **f off** from us. 7368
60: 4 thy sons shall come from f, and 7350
60: 9 to bring thy sons from f, their silver and 7350
Jer 2: 5 that they are **gone** f from me, and 7368
4:16 *that* watchers come from a f country, and 4801
5:15 Lo, I will bring a nation upon you from f, 4801
6:20 and the sweet cane from a f country? 4801
8:19 because of them that dwell in a f country: 4801
12: 2 near in their mouth, and f from their reins. 7350
25:26 f and near, one with another, and all 7350
27:10 unto you, to **remove** you f from your land; 7368
48:24 all the cities of the land of Moab, f or near. 7350
48:47 **Thus f** *is* the judgment of Moab. 2008+5704
49:30 Flee, get you **f off**, dwell deep, O ye 3966
51:64 **Thus f** *are* the words of Jeremiah. 2008+5704
La 1:16 that *should* relieve my soul is f from me: 7368
3:17 thou hast **removed** my soul **f off** from 2186
Eze 6:12 *He* that *is* **f off** shall die of the pestilence; 7350
7:20 therefore have I set it f from them. 5079
8: 6 that *I* should **go f off** from my sanctuary? 7368
11:15 have said, Get ye f from the LORD: 7368
11:16 Although I have **cast** them **f off** among 7368
12:27 he prophesieth of the times *that are* **f off**. 7350
22: 5 *those that be* f from thee, shall mock thee, 7350
23:40 that ye have sent for men to come from f, 4801
43: 9 **put away** their whoredom, and the carcases of their kings, f 7368
44:10 the Levites that are **gone away** f from me, 7368
Da 9: 7 all Israel, *that are* near, and *that are* **f off**, 7350
11: 2 and the fourth shall be f richer than *they* all: 1419
Joel 2:20 I will **remove f off** from you the northern 7368
3: 6 that *ye* might **remove** them f from their 7368
3: 8 sell them to the Sabeans, to a people **f off**: 7350
Am 6: 3 Ye that **put** f **away** the evil day, and 5077
Mic 4: 7 and her that was **cast f off** a strong nation: 1972
7:11 *in* that day shall the decree be **f removed**. 7368
Hab 1: 8 and their horsemen shall come from f; 7350
Zec 6:15 *they that are* **f off** shall come and build in 7350
10: 9 they shall remember me in **f countries**; and 4801
Mt 15: 8 with *their* lips; but their heart is f from me. *4206*
16:22 saying, **Be it f from** thee, Lord: *2436*
21:33 to husbandmen, and **went into a f country**: *589*
25:14 *is* as a man **travelling into a f country**, *589*
Mk 6:35 And when the day was now f spent, *4183*
6:35 desert place, and now the time *is* **f passed**: *4183*
7: 6 with *their* lips, but their heart is f from me. *4206*
8: 3 the way: for divers of them came **from f**. *3113*
12: 1 to husbandmen, and **went into a f country**. *589*
12:34 Thou art not f from the kingdom of God. *3112*
13:34 *Son of man is* as a man **taking a f journey**, *590*
Lk 7: 6 And when he was now not f from *3112*
15:13 and took his journey into a f country, and *3117*
19:12 A certain nobleman went into a f country to *3117*
20: 9 and **went into a f country** for a long time. *589*
22:51 and said, Suffer ye **thus f**. *2193+3778*
24:29 and the day is **f spent**. *2235+2827*
24:50 And he led them out **as f as** to Bethany, and *2193*
Jn 21: 8 (for they were not f from land, but as it *3112*
Ac 11:19 about Stephen travelled **as f as** Phenice, *2193*
11:22 that *he* should go **as f as** Antioch. *2193*
17:27 find *him,* though he be not f from every one *3112*
22:21 for I will send thee **f hence** unto *3112*
28:15 they came to meet us **as f as** Appii forum, *891*
Ro 13:12 The night is **f spent**, the day is at hand: *4298*
2Co 4:17 us a **f more exceeding** *1519+2596+5236+5236*
10:14 for we are come **as f as** to you also in *891*
Eph 1:21 **F above** all principality, and power, and *5231*
2:13 **f off** are made nigh by the blood of Christ. *3112*
4:10 also that ascended up **f above** all heavens, *5231*

Php 1:23 to be with Christ; *which is* f better: *3123+4183*
Heb 7:15 And it is yet **f more** evident: for that after *4054*
2Pe 1: 9 and **cannot see f off**, and hath forgotten *3467*

FARE (3) [FARED, FAREWELL, SEAFARING, WAYFARING]
1Sa 17:18 look how thy brethren f, and take their 7965
Jnh 1: 3 so he paid the f thereof, and went down 7939
Ac 15:29 ye shall do well. **F** ye **well**. *4517*

FARED (1) [FARE]
Lk 16:19 fine linen, and f sumptuously every day: *2165*

FAREWELL (4) [FARE]
Lk 9:61 but let me first go **bid** them f, which are *at* *657*
Ac 18:21 But **bade** them f, saying, I must by all means *657*
23:30 before them what *they had* against him. **F.** *4517*
2Co 13:11 Finally, brethren, f. Be perfect, be of good *5463*

FARM (1)
Mt 22: 5 light of *it,* and went their ways, one to his f, *68*

FARMED See TILLAGE

FARMER See HUSBANDMAN

FARTHER (1)
Mk 10: 1 into the coasts of Judea by the **f side** *4008*

FARTHEST See OUTGOINGS; UTTERMOST

FARTHING (3) [FARTHINGS]
Mt 5:26 till thou hast paid the uttermost f. *2835*
10:29 Are not two sparrows sold for a f? and *787*
Mk 12:42 she threw in two mites, which make a f. *2835*

FARTHINGS (1) [FARTHING]
Lk 12: 6 Are not five sparrows sold for two f, and *787*

FASHION (13) [FASHIONED, FASHIONETH, FASHIONING, FASHIONS]
Ge 6:15 this *is the f* which thou shalt make it *of:* NIH
Ex 26:30 f thereof which was shewed thee in 4941
37:19 Three bowls **made after the f of almonds** 8246
1Ki 6:38 and according to all the f of it. 4941
2Ki 16:10 king Ahaz sent to Urijah the priest the f of 1823
Job 31:15 and did not one f us in the womb? 3559
Eze 43:11 the f thereof, and the goings out thereof, 8498
Mk 2:12 saying, We never saw *it* **on this f**. *3779*
Lk 9:29 the f of his countenance was altered, and *1491*
Ac 7:44 that *he* should make it according to the f *5179*
1Co 7:31 as not abusing *it:* for the f of this world *4976*
Php 2: 8 And being found **in** f as a man, he humbled *4976*
Jas 1:11 and the grace of the f of it perisheth: *4383*

FASHIONED (7) [FASHION]
Ex 32: 4 f it with a graving tool, after he had made it 6696
Job 10: 8 made me and f me together round about; 6213
Ps 119:73 Thy hands have made me and f me: 3559
139:16 *which* in continuance were f, when *as yet* 3335
Isa 22:11 neither had respect unto him that f it long 3335
Eze 16: 7 *thy* breasts are f, and thine hair is grown, 3559
Php 3:21 that it may be **f like unto** his glorious body, *4832*

FASHIONETH (3) [FASHION]
Ps 33:15 He f their hearts alike; he considereth all 3335
Isa 44:12 f it with hammers, and worketh it with 3335
45: 9 Shall the clay say to him that f it, 3335

FASHIONING (1) [FASHION]
1Pe 1:14 not f yourselves **according to** the former *4964*

FASHIONS (1) [FASHION]
Eze 42:11 goings out *were* both according to their f, 4941

FAST (85) [FASTED, FASTEST, FASTING, FASTINGS]
Ge 20:18 For the LORD had **f closed up** all 6113+6113
Jdg 4:21 for he was **f asleep** and weary. So he died. 7290
15:13 we will **bind** thee f, and deliver thee 631+631
16:11 If they **bind** me f with new ropes that 631+631
Ru 2: 8 but **abide** here f by my maidens: 1692
2:21 Thou shalt **keep** f by my young men, 1692
2:23 So she **kept** f by the maidens of Boaz to 1692
2Sa 12:21 thou didst f and weep for the child, *while it* 6684
12:23 now he is dead, wherefore should I f? can I 6684
1Ki 21: 9 Proclaim a f, and set Naboth on high 6685
21:12 They proclaimed a f, and set Naboth on 6685
2Ki 6:32 shut the door, and **hold** him f at the door: 3905
2Ch 20: 3 and proclaimed a f throughout all Judah. 6685
Ezr 5: 8 this work goeth f on, and prospereth in their 629
8:21 I proclaimed a f there, at the river Ahava, 6685
Est 4:16 f ye for me, and neither eat nor drink three 6684
4:16 I also and my maidens will f likewise; and 6684
Job 2: 3 still he **holdeth** f his integrity, 2388
8:15 he shall **hold** it f, but it shall not endure. 2388
27: 6 My righteousness I **hold** f, and will not let 2388
38:38 and the clods **cleave** f **together**? 1692
Ps 33: 9 it was *done;* he commanded, and it **stood** f. 5975
38: 2 For thine arrows **stick** f in me, and 5181
41: 8 evil disease, *say they,* **cleaveth** f unto him: 3332
65: 6 Which by his strength **setteth** f 3559
89:28 and my covenant *shall* **stand** f with him. 539
111: 8 They **stand** f for ever and ever, *and* 5564
Pr 4:13 **Take** f **hold** of instruction; let *her* not go: 2388
Isa 58: 3 in the day of your f you find pleasure, and 6685
58: 4 ye f for strife and debate, and to smite with 6684
58: 4 ye shall not f as *ye do this* day, to make 6684
58: 5 Is it such a f that I have chosen? a day for a 6685
58: 5 and ashes *under him?* wilt thou call this a f, 6685
58: 6 *Is* not this the f that I have chosen? to loose 6685
Jer 8: 5 they **hold** f deceit, they refuse to return. 2388
14:12 When they f, I will not hear their cry; and 6684
36: 9 *that* they proclaimed a f before the LORD 6685

Jer 46:14 say ye, **Stand** f, and prepare thee; for 3320
48:16 is near to come, and his affliction hasteth f. 3966
50:33 all that took them captives **held** them f; 2388
Joel 1:14 Sanctify ye a f, call a solemn assembly, 6685
2:15 sanctify a f, call a solemn assembly: 6685
Jnh 1: 5 of the ship; and he lay, and was f **asleep**. 7290
3: 5 and proclaimed a f, and put on sackcloth, 6685
Zec 7: 5 did ye **at all** f unto me, even to me? 6684+6684
8:19 The f of the fourth month, and the fast of 6685
8:19 of the fourth month, and the f of the fifth, 6685
8:19 the f of the seventh, and the fast of 6685
8:19 fast of the seventh, and the f of the tenth, 6685
Mt 6:16 Moreover when ye f, be not as 3522
6:16 that they may appear unto men to f. 3522
6:18 That thou appear not unto men to f, but 3522
9:14 Why do we and the Pharisees f oft, but 3522
9:14 Pharisees fast oft, but thy disciples f not? 3522
9:15 be taken from them, and then shall they f. 3522
26:48 I shall kiss, that same is he: **hold** him f. 2902
Mk 2:18 of John and of the Pharisees used to f: 3522
2:18 the disciples of John and of the Pharisees f, 3522
2:18 the Pharisees fast, but thy disciples f not? 3522
2:19 Can the children of the bridechamber f, 3522
2:19 the bridegroom with them, they cannot f. 3522
2:20 and then shall they f in those days. 3522
Lk 5:33 Why do the disciples of John f often, and 3522
5:34 ye make the children of the bridechamber f, 3522
5:35 and then shall they f in those days. 3522
18:12 I f twice in the week, I give tithes of all that 3522
Ac 16:24 and **made** their feet f in the stocks. 805
27: 9 because the f was now already past, Paul 3521
27:41 and the forepart **stuck** f, and 2043
1Co 16:13 Watch ye, **stand** f in the faith, quit you like 4739
Gal 5: 1 **Stand** f therefore in the liberty wherewith 4739
Php 1:27 of your affairs, that ye **stand** f in one spirit, 4739
4: 1 my joy and crown, so **stand** f in the Lord, 4739
1Th 3: 8 For now we live, if ye **stand** f in the Lord. 4739
5:21 Prove all things; **hold** f that which is good. 2722
2Th 2:15 **stand** f, and hold the traditions which ye 4739
2Ti 1:13 **Hold** f the form of sound words, 2192
Tit 1: 9 **Holding** f the faithful word as he hath been 472
Heb 3: 6 if we **hold** f the confidence and 2722
4:14 Son of God, let us **hold** f our profession. 2902
10:23 Let us **hold** f the profession of our hope 2722
Rev 2:13 seat is: and thou **holdest** f my name, 2902
2:25 But that which ye have already hold f till I 2902
3: 3 and heard, and **hold** f, and repent. 5083
3:11 **hold** that f which thou hast, that no man 2902

FASTED (15) [FAST]
Jdg 20:26 f that day until even, and offered burnt 6684
1Sa 7: 6 and f on that day, and said there, 6684
31:13 under a tree at Jabesh, and f seven days. 6684
2Sa 1:12 wept, and f until even, for Saul, and 6684
12:16 David f, and went in, and lay all 6684+6685
12:22 While the child was yet alive, I f and wept: 6684
1Ki 21:27 and f, and lay in sackcloth, and went softly. 6684
1Ch 10:12 under the oak in Jabesh, and f seven days. 6684
Ezr 8:23 So we f and besought our God for this: and 6684
Ne 1: 4 f, and prayed before the God of heaven, 6684
Isa 58: 3 Wherefore have we f, say they, and 6684
Zec 7: 5 When ye f and mourned in the fifth and 6684
Mt 4: 2 And when he had f forty days and 3522
Ac 13: 2 and f, the Holy Ghost said, Separate me 3522
13: 3 And when they had f and prayed, and 3522

FASTEN (5) [FASTENED, FASTENING]
Ex 28:14 and f the wreathen chains to the ouches. 5414
28:25 chains thou shalt f in the two ouches, 5414
39:31 lace of blue, to f it on high upon the mitre; 5414
Isa 22:23 I will f him as a nail in a sure place; and 8628
Jer 10: 4 they f it with nails and with hammers, 2388

FASTENED (18) [FASTEN]
Ex 39:18 wreathen chains they f in the two ouches, 5414
40:18 f his sockets, and set up the boards thereof, 5414
Jdg 4:21 into his temples, and f it into the ground: 6795
16:14 she f it with the pin, and said unto him, 8628
1Sa 31:10 they f his body to the wall of Beth-shan. 8628
2Sa 20: 8 upon it a girdle with a sword f upon his 6775
1Ki 6: 6 that the beams should not be f in the walls of 270
1Ch 10:10 and f his head in the temple of Dagon. 8628
2Ch 9:18 which were f to the throne, and stays on each 270
Est 1: 6 blue hangings, f with cords of fine linen and 270
Job 38: 6 Whereupon are the foundations thereof f? 2883
Ecc 12:11 and as nails f by the masters of assemblies, 5193
Isa 22:25 shall the nail that is f in the sure place be 8628
41: 7 he f it with nails, that it should not be 2388
Eze 40:43 were hooks, a hand broad, f round about: 3559
Lk 4:20 that were in the synagogue were f on him. 816
Ac 11: 6 Upon the which when I had f mine **eyes**, 816
28: 3 a viper out of the heat, and f on his hand. 2510

FASTENING (1) [FASTEN]
Ac 3: 4 f his **eyes** upon him with John, said, 816

FASTEST (1) [FAST]
Mt 6:17 But thou, when thou f, anoint thine head, 3522

FASTING (17) [FAST]
Ne 9: 1 children of Israel were assembled with f, 6685
Est 4: 3 the Jews, and f, and weeping, and wailing; 6685
Ps 35:13 I humbled my soul with f; and my prayer 6685
69:10 I wept, and chastened my soul with f, 6685
109:24 My knees are weak through f; and my flesh 6685
Jer 36: 6 in the LORD'S house upon the f day: 6685
Da 6:18 went to his palace, and passed the night f: 2908
9: 3 with f, and sackcloth, and ashes: 6685
Joel 2:12 with f, and with weeping, and 6685
Mt 15:32 and I will not send them away f, lest they 3523
17:21 this kind goeth not out but by prayer and f. 3521
Mk 8: 3 And if I send them away f to their own 3523
9:29 come forth by nothing, but by prayer and f. 3521
Ac 10:30 Four days ago I was f until this hour; 3522
14:23 and had prayed with f, they commended 3521
27:33 day that ye have tarried and continued f, 777
1Co 7: 5 that ye may give yourselves to f and 3521

FASTINGS (4) [FAST]
Est 9:31 their seed, the matters of the f and their cry. 6685
Lk 2:37 but served God with f and prayers night 3521
2Co 6: 5 in tumults, in labours, in watchings, in f; 3521
11:27 in hunger and thirst, in f often, in cold and 3521

FAT (130) [FATFLESHED, FATLING, FATLINGS, FATNESS, FATS, FATTED, FATTER, FATTEST]
Ge 4: 4 firstlings of his flock and of the f thereof. 2459
41: 4 eat up the seven well favoured and f kine. 1277
41:20 kine did eat up the first seven f kine: 1277
45:18 of Egypt, and ye shall eat the f of the land. 2459
49:20 Out of Asher his bread shall be f, and 8082
Ex 23:18 neither shall the f of my sacrifice remain 2459
29:13 thou shalt take all the f that covereth 2459
29:13 the f that is upon them, and burn them upon 2459
29:22 Also thou shalt take of the ram the f and 2459
29:22 the f that covereth the inwards, and the caul 2459
29:22 the f that is upon them, and the right 2459
Lev 1: 8 shall lay the parts, the head, and the f, 6309
1:12 it into his pieces, with his head and his f: 6309
3: 3 the f that covereth the inwards, and all 2459
3: 3 and all the f that is upon the inwards, 2459
3: 4 the two kidneys, and the f that is on them, 2459
3: 9 the f thereof, and the whole rump, it shall 2459
3: 9 the f that covereth the inwards, and all 2459
3: 9 and all the f that is upon the inwards, 2459
3:10 two kidneys, and the f that is upon them, 2459
3:14 the f that covereth the inwards, and all 2459
3:14 and all the f that is upon the inwards, 2459
3:15 two kidneys, and the f that is upon them, 2459
3:16 a sweet savour: all the f is the LORD'S. 2459
3:17 that ye eat neither f nor blood. 2459
4: 8 he shall take off from it all the f of 2459
4: 8 the f that covereth the inwards, and all 2459
4: 8 and all the f that is upon the inwards, 2459
4: 9 two kidneys, and the f that is upon them, 2459
4:19 he shall take all his f from him, and burn it 2459
4:26 he shall burn all his f upon the altar, as 2459
4:26 as the f of the sacrifice of peace offerings: 2459
4:31 he shall take away all the f thereof, as 2459
4:31 as the f is taken away from off the sacrifice 2459
4:35 he shall take away all the f thereof, as 2459
4:35 as the f of the lamb is taken away from 2459
6:12 he shall burn thereon the f of the peace 2459
7: 3 he shall offer of it all the f thereof; 2459
7: 3 and the f that covereth the inwards, 2459
7: 4 the two kidneys, and the f that is on them, 2459
7:23 Ye shall eat no manner f, of ox, or of sheep, 2459
7:24 the f of the beast that dieth of itself, and 2459
7:24 the f of that which is torn with beasts, may 2459
7:25 For whosoever eateth the f of the beast, 2459
7:30 the f with the breast, it shall he bring, 2459
7:31 the priest shall burn the f upon the altar: 2459
7:33 the f, shall have the right shoulder for his 2459
8:16 he took all the f that was upon the inwards, 2459
8:16 their f, and Moses burned it upon the altar. 2459
8:20 burnt the head, and the pieces, and the f. 6309
8:25 he took the f, and the rump, and all the fat 2459
8:25 all the f that was upon the inwards, and 2459
8:25 and their f, and the right shoulder: 2459
8:26 put them on the f, and upon the right 2459
9:10 the f, and the kidneys, and the caul above 2459
9:19 the f of the bullock and of the ram, 2459
9:20 they put the f upon the breasts, and he burnt 2459
9:20 and he burnt the f upon the altar: 2459
9:24 upon the altar the burnt offering and the f: 2459
10:15 with the offerings made by fire of the f, 2459
16:25 the f of the sin offering shall he burn upon 2459
17: 6 burn the f for a sweet savour unto 2459
Nu 13:20 what the land is, whether it be f or lean, 8082
18:17 shalt burn their f for an offering made by 2459
Dt 31:20 and filled themselves, and **waxen** f; 1878
32:14 with f of lambs, and rams of the breed of 2459
32:14 and goats, with the f of kidneys of wheat; 2459
32:15 Jeshurun **waxed** f, and kicked: thou art 8080
32:15 thou art **waxed** f, thou art grown thick, 8080
32:38 Which did eat the f of their sacrifices, and 2459
Jdg 3:17 king of Moab: and Eglon was a very f man. 1277
3:22 the f closed upon the blade, so that he could 2459
1Sa 2:15 Also before they burnt the f, the priest's 2459
2:16 Let them not fail to burn the f presently, 2459
2:29 to **make** yourselves f with the chiefest of 1254
15:22 and to hearken than the f of rams. 2459
28:24 the woman had a f calf in the house; and 4770
2Sa 1:22 blood of the slain, from the f of the mighty, 2459
1Ki 1: 9 oxen and f **cattle** by the stone of Zoheleth, 4806
1:19 and f **cattle** and sheep in abundance, 4806
1:25 hath slain oxen and f **cattle** and sheep in 4806
4:23 Ten f oxen, and twenty oxen out of 1277
8:64 and the f of the peace offerings: 2459
8:64 and the f of the peace offerings. 2459
1Ch 4:40 they found f pasture and good, and the land 8082
2Ch 7: 7 the f of the peace offerings, because 2459
7: 7 and the meat offerings, and the f. 2459
29:35 with the f of the peace offerings, and 2459
35:14 of burnt offerings and the f until night; 2459
Ne 8:10 Go your way, eat the f, and drink the sweet, 4924
9:25 a f land, and possessed houses full of all 8082
9:25 **became** f, and delighted themselves in thy 8080
9:35 and f land which thou gavest before them, 8082
Job 15:27 and maketh **collops of** f on his flanks. 6371
Ps 17:10 They are inclosed in their own f: with their 2459
22:29 All they that be f upon earth shall eat and 1879
37:20 the enemies of the LORD shall be as the f 3368
92:14 in old age; they shall be f and flourishing; 1879
119:70 Their heart is as f as grease; but I delight in 2954
Pr 11:25 The liberal soul shall be **made** f: and 1878
13: 4 but the soul of the diligent shall be **made** f. 1878
15:30 and a good report **maketh** the bones f. 1878
28:25 his trust in the LORD shall be **made** f. 1878
Isa 1:11 offerings of rams, and the f of fed beasts; 2459
5:17 the waste places of the f **ones** shall 4220
6:10 **Make** the heart of this people f, and 8080
10:16 of hosts, send among his f **ones** leanness; 4924
25: 6 make unto all people a feast of f **things**, 8081
25: 6 on the lees, of f **things** full of marrow, 8081
28: 1 which are on the head of the f valleys of 8081
28: 4 which is on the head of the f valley, 8081
30:23 of the earth, and it shall be f and plenteous: 1879
34: 6 it is **made** f with fatness, and with 1878
34: 6 goats, with the f of the kidneys of rams: 2459
34: 7 and their dust **made** f with fatness. 1878
43:24 neither hast thou filled me with the f of thy 2459
58:11 thy soul in drought, and **make** f thy bones: 2502
Jer 5:28 They are **waxen** f, they shine: yea, 8080
50:11 ye are **grown** f as the heifer at grass, 6335
Eze 34: 3 Ye eat the f, and ye clothe you with 2459
34:14 in a f pasture shall they feed upon 8082
34:16 I will destroy the f and the strong; I will 8082
34:20 will judge between the f cattle and 1274
39:19 ye shall eat f till ye be full, and drink blood 2459
44: 7 the f and the blood, and they have broken 2459
44:15 shall stand before me to offer unto me the f 2459
45:15 out of the f **pastures** of Israel; 4945
Am 5:22 regard the peace offerings of your f **beasts**. 4806
Hab 1:16 because by them their portion is f, and 8082
Zec 11:16 he shall eat the flesh of the f, and tear their 1277

FATAL MISTAKE See DISSEMBLED; DISSIMULATION

FATE See END; EVENT; WAY

FATFLESHED (2) [FAT, FLESH]
Ge 41: 2 river seven well favoured kine and f; 1277+1320
41:18 river seven kine, f and well favoured; 1277+1320

FATHER (979) [FATHER'S, FATHERLESS, FATHERS, FATHERS', FOREFATHERS]
Ge 2:24 Therefore shall a man leave his f and his 1
4:20 he was the f of such as dwell in tents, and 1
4:21 he was the f of all such as handle the harp and 1
9:18 Ham, and Japheth: and Ham is the f of Canaan. 1
9:22 Ham, the f of Canaan, saw the nakedness of his 1
9:22 saw the nakedness of his f, and told his two 1
9:23 and covered the nakedness of their f; 1
10:21 Shem also, the f of all the children of Eber, 1
11:28 Haran died before his f Terah in the land of his 1
11:29 the f of Milcah, and the father of Iscah. 1
11:29 the father of Milcah, and the f of Iscah. 1
17: 4 and thou shalt be a f of many nations. 1
17: 5 for a f of many nations have I made thee. 1
19:31 Our f is old, and there is not a man in the earth 1
19:32 let us make our f drink wine, and we will lie 1
19:32 with him, that we may preserve seed of our f. 1
19:33 And they made their f drink wine that night: 1
19:33 and the firstborn went in, and lay with her f; 1
19:34 Behold, I lay yesternight with my f: 1
19:34 with him, that we may preserve seed of our f. 1
19:35 they made their f drink wine that night also: 1
19:36 both the daughters of Lot with child by their f. 1
19:37 the same is the f of the Moabites unto this day. 1
19:38 the same is the f of the children of Ammon 1
20:12 she is the daughter of my f, but not 1
22: 7 And Isaac spake unto Abraham his f, and said, 1
22: 7 spake unto Abraham his father, and said, My f: 1
22:21 Buz his brother, and Kemuel the f of Aram, 1
26: 3 the oath which I sware unto Abraham thy f; 1
26:15 had digged in the days of Abraham his f, 1
26:18 they had digged in the days of Abraham his f; 1
26:18 after the names by which his f had called them. 1
26:24 and said, I am the God of Abraham thy f: 1
27: 6 I heard thy f speak unto Esau thy brother, 1
27: 9 and I will make them savoury meat for thy f, 1
27:10 And thou shalt bring it to thy f, that he may eat, 1
27:12 My f peradventure will feel me, and I shall 1
27:14 mother made savoury meat, such as his f loved. 1
27:18 And he came unto his f, and said, My father: 1
27:18 And he came unto his father, and said, My f. 1
27:19 Jacob said unto his f, I am Esau thy firstborn; 1
27:22 Jacob went near unto Isaac his f; and he felt 1
27:26 And his f Isaac said unto him, Come near now, 1
27:30 gone out from the presence of Isaac his f, 1
27:31 brought it unto his f, and said unto his father, 1
27:31 said unto his f, Let my father arise, and eat of 1
27:31 Let my f arise, and eat of his son's venison, 1
27:32 And Isaac his f said unto him, Who art thou? 1
27:34 when Esau heard the words of his f, he cried 1
27:34 said unto his f, Bless me, even me also, O my 1
27:34 his father, Bless me, even me also, O my f. 1
27:38 Esau said unto his f, Hast thou but one 1
27:38 his father, Hast thou but one blessing, my f? 1
27:38 bless me, even me also, O my f. And Esau lift 1
27:39 And Isaac his f answered and said unto him, 1
27:41 of the blessing wherewith his f blessed him: 1
27:41 The days of mourning for my f are at hand; 1
28: 2 to the house of Bethuel thy mother's f; 1
28: 7 And that Jacob obeyed his f and his mother, 1
28: 8 the daughters of Canaan pleased not Isaac his f; 1
28:13 I am the LORD God of Abraham thy f, and 1
29:12 was Rebekah's son: and she ran and told her f. 1
31: 5 but the God of my f hath been with me. 1
31: 6 that with all my power I have served your f. 1
31: 7 your f hath deceived me, and changed my 1
31: 9 Thus God hath taken away the cattle of your f, 1
31:16 all the riches which God hath taken from our f, 1
31:18 for to go to Isaac his f in the land of Canaan. 1
31:29 the God of your f spake unto me yesternight, 1
31:35 she said to her f, Let it not displease my lord 1
31:42 Except the God of my f, the God of Abraham, 1
31:53 of Nahor, the God of their f, judge betwixt us. 1
31:53 And Jacob sware by the fear of his f Isaac. 1
32: 9 O God of my f Abraham, and God of my father 1

Ge 32: 9 of my father Abraham, and God of my **f** Isaac, 1
33:19 Shechem's **f**, for an hundred pieces of money. 1
34: 4 And Shechem spake unto his **f** Hamor, saying, 1
34: 6 Hamor the **f** of Shechem went out unto Jacob 1
34:11 Shechem said unto her **f** and unto her brethren, 1
34:13 and Hamor his **f** deceitfully, 1
34:19 more honourable than all the house of his **f**. 1
35:18 name Ben-oni: but his **f** called him Benjamin. 1
35:27 And Jacob came unto Isaac his **f** unto Mamre, 1
36: 9 these *are* the generations of Esau the **f** of 1
36:24 as he fed the asses of Zibeon his **f**. 1
36:43 he *is* Esau the **f** of the Edomites. 1
37: 1 Jacob dwelt in the land wherein his **f** was a 1
37: 2 and Joseph brought unto his **f** their evil report. 1
37: 4 when his brethren saw that their **f** loved him 1
37:10 And he told *it* to his **f**, and to his brethren: and 1
37:10 his **f** rebuked him, and said unto him, What *is* 1
37:11 envied him; but his **f** observed the saying. 1
37:22 out of their hands, to deliver him to his **f** again. 1
37:32 of many colours, and they brought *it* to their **f**; 1
37:35 my son mourning. Thus his **f** wept for him. 1
38:13 Behold thy **f in law** goeth up to Timnath to 2524
38:25 she sent to her **f in law**, saying, By 2524
42:13 the youngest *is this* day with our **f**, and one *is* 1
42:29 they came unto Jacob their **f** unto the land of 1
42:32 We *be* twelve brethren, sons of our **f**; one *is* 1
42:32 the youngest *is this* day with our **f** in the land 1
42:35 *both* they and their **f** saw the bundles of money, 1
42:36 Jacob their **f** said unto them, Me have ye 1
42:37 Reuben spake unto his **f**, saying, Slay my two 1
43: 2 their **f** said unto them, Go again, buy us a little 1
43: 7 and of our kindred, saying, *Is* your **f** yet alive? 1
43: 8 Judah said unto Israel his **f**, Send the lad with 1
43:11 And their **f** Israel said unto them, If *it must be* 1
43:23 your God, and the God of your **f**, hath given 1
43:27 said, *Is* your **f** well, the old man of whom ye 1
43:28 Thy servant our **f** *is* in good health, he *is* yet 1
44:17 and as for you, get you up in peace unto your **f**. 1
44:19 his servants, saying, Have ye a **f**, or a brother? 1
44:20 We have a **f**, an old man, and a child of *his* old 1
44:20 alone is left of his mother, and his **f** loveth him. 1
44:22 said unto my lord, The lad cannot leave his **f**: 1
44:22 for *if* he should leave his **f**, *his father* would 1
44:22 *if* he should leave his father, *his* **f** would die. NIH
44:24 pass when we came up unto thy servant my **f**, 1
44:25 our **f** said, Go again, *and* buy us a little food. 1
44:27 thy servant my **f** said unto us, Ye know that 1
44:30 therefore when I come to thy servant my **f**, 1
44:31 of thy servant our **f** with sorrow to the grave. 1
44:32 servant became surety for the lad unto my **f**, 1
44:32 then I shall bear the blame to my **f** for ever. 1
44:34 For how shall I go up to my **f**, and the lad *be* 1
44:34 I see the evil that shall come on my **f**. 1
45: 3 his brethren, I *am* Joseph; doth my **f** yet live? 1
45: 8 he hath made me a **f** to Pharaoh, and lord of all 1
45: 9 and go up to my **f**, and say unto him, 1
45:13 you shall tell my **f** of all my glory in Egypt, 1
45:13 and ye shall haste and bring down my **f** hither. 1
45:18 take your **f** and your households, and 1
45:19 for your wives, and bring your **f**, and come. 1
45:23 to his **f** he sent after this manner; ten asses 1
45:23 and bread and meat for his **f** by the way. 1
45:25 *into* the land of Canaan unto Jacob their **f**, 1
45:27 to carry him, the spirit of Jacob their **f** revived: 1
46: 1 offered sacrifices unto the God of his **f** Isaac. 1
46: 3 he said, I *am* God, the God of thy **f**: fear not to 1
46: 5 and the sons of Israel carried Jacob their **f**, and 1
46:29 went up to meet Israel his **f**, to Goshen, and 1
47: 1 My **f** and my brethren, and their flocks, and 1
47: 5 Thy **f** and thy brethren are come unto thee: 1
47: 6 in the best of the land make thy **f** and brethren 1
47: 7 Joseph brought in Jacob his **f**, and set him 1
47:11 And Joseph placed his **f** and his brethren, and 1
47:12 And Joseph nourished his **f**, and his brethren, 1
48: 1 that *one* told Joseph, Behold, thy **f** *is* sick: 1
48: 9 And Joseph said unto his **f**, They *are* my sons, 1
48:17 when Joseph saw that his **f** laid his right hand 1
48:18 And Joseph said unto his **f**, Not so, my father: 1
48:18 And Joseph said unto his father, Not so, my **f**: 1
48:19 And his **f** refused, and said, I know *it*, my son, 1
49: 2 sons of Jacob; and hearken unto Israel your **f**. 1
49:25 *Even* by the God of thy **f**, who shall help thee; 1
49:26 The blessings of thy **f** have prevailed above 1
49:28 and this *is it* that their **f** spake unto them, and 1
50: 2 his servants the physicians to embalm his **f**: 1
50: 5 My **f** made me swear, saying, Lo, I die: in my 1
50: 5 and bury my **f**, and I will come again. 1
50: 6 Pharaoh said, Go up, and bury thy **f**, 1
50: 7 Joseph went up to bury his **f**: and with him 1
50:10 and he made a mourning for his **f** seven days. 1
50:14 and all that went up with him to bury his **f**, 1
50:14 him to bury his father, after he had buried his **f**. 1
50:15 when Joseph's brethren saw that their **f** was 1
50:16 Thy **f** did command before he died, saying, 1
50:17 the trespass of the servants of the God of thy **f**. 1
Ex 2:18 And when they came to Reuel their **f**, he said, 1
3: 1 Moses kept the flock of Jethro his **f in law**, 2859
3: 6 Moreover he said, I *am* the God of thy **f**, 1
4:18 and returned to Jethro his **f in law**, 2859
18: 1 the priest of Midian, Moses' **f in law**, 2859
18: 2 Jethro, Moses' **f in law**, took Zipporah, 2859
18: 4 for the God of my **f**, *said he, was* mine help, 1
18: 5 Jethro, Moses' **f in law**, came with his sons 2859
18: 6 I thy **f in law** Jethro am come unto thee, 2859
18: 7 Moses went out to meet his **f in law**, and 2859
18: 8 Moses told his **f in law** all that the LORD 2859
18:12 Jethro, Moses' **f in law**, took a burnt 2859
18:12 to eat bread with Moses' **f in law** before 2859
18:14 when Moses' **f in law** saw all that he did to 2859
18:15 Moses said unto his **f in law**, Because 2859
18:17 Moses' **f in law** said unto him, The thing 2859
18:24 hearkened to the voice of his **f in law**, 2859
18:27 Moses let his **f in law** depart; and he went 2859
20:12 Honour thy **f** and thy mother: that thy days may 1
21:15 he that smiteth his **f**, or his mother, shall be 1

Ex 21:17 he that curseth his **f**, or his mother, shall surely 1
22:17 If her **f** utterly refuse to give her unto him, 1
40:15 shalt anoint them, as thou didst anoint their **f**, 1
Lev 18: 7 The nakedness of thy **f**, or the nakedness of thy 1
18: 9 the daughter of thy **f**, or daughter of thy 1
18:11 begotten of thy **f**, she *is* thy sister, thou shalt 1
19: 3 his mother, and his **f**, and keep my sabbaths: 1
20: 9 For every one that curseth his **f** or his mother 1
20: 9 he hath cursed his **f** or his mother; his blood 1
21: 2 for his **f**, and for his son, and for his daughter, 1
21: 9 by playing the whore, she profaneth her **f**: 1
21:11 nor defile himself for his **f**, or for his mother; 1
24:10 whose **f**[S] *was* an Egyptian, 1121
Nu 3: 4 the priest's office in the sight of Aaron their **f**. 1
3:24 the chief of the house of the **f** of 1
3:30 the chief of the house of the **f** of the families of 1
3:35 the chief of the house of the **f** of the families of 1
6: 7 He shall not make himself unclean for his **f**, 1
10:29 of Raguel the Midianite, Moses' **f in law**, 2859
11:12 as a **nursing f** beareth the sucking child, 539
12:14 unto Moses, If her **f** had but spit in her face, 1
18: 2 the tribe of thy **f**, bring thou with thee, that they 1
27: 3 Our **f** died in the wilderness, and he was not in 1
27: 4 Why should the name of our **f** be done away 1
27: 4 a possession among the brethren of our **f**. 1
27: 7 thou shalt cause the inheritance of their **f** to 1
27:11 if his **f** have no brethren, then ye shall give his 1
30: 4 her **f** hear her vow, and her bond wherewith 1
30: 4 her soul, and her **f** shall hold his peace at her: 1
30: 5 if her **f** disallow her in the day that he heareth; 1
30: 5 shall forgive her, because her **f** disallowed her. 1
30:16 and his wife, between the **f** and his daughter, 1
36: 6 only to the family of the tribe of their **f** shall 1
36: 8 wife unto one of the family of the tribe of her **f**, 1
36:12 remained in the tribe of the family of their **f**. 1
Dt 5:16 Honour thy **f** and thy mother, as the LORD 1
21:13 and bewail her **f** and her mother a full month: 1
21:18 which will not obey the voice of his **f**, or 1
21:19 shall his **f** and his mother lay hold on him, 1
22:15 Then shall the **f** of the damsel, and her mother, 1
22:16 And the damsel's **f** shall say unto the elders, 1
22:19 and give *them* unto the **f** of the damsel, because 1
22:29 give unto the damsel's **f** fifty *shekels* of silver, 1
26: 5 A Syrian ready to perish *was* my **f**, and he went 1
27:16 Cursed *be* he that setteth light by his **f** or 1
27:22 the daughter of his **f**, or the daughter of his 1
32: 6 *is* not he thy **f** *that* hath bought thee? hath he 1
32: 7 ask thy **f**, and he will shew thee; thy elders, and 1
33: 9 Who said unto his **f** and to his mother, I have 1
Jos 2:13 *that* ye will save alive my **f**, and my mother, 1
2:18 and thou shalt bring thy **f**, and thy mother, and 1
6:23 her **f**, and her mother, and her brethren, and 1
15:13 *even* the city of Arba the **f** of Anak, which *city* 1
15:18 *him*, that she moved him to ask of her **f** a field: 1
17: 1 the firstborn of Manasseh, the **f** of Gilead: 1
17: 4 an inheritance among the brethren of their **f**. 1
19:47 Dan, after the name of Dan their **f**. 1
21:11 they gave them the city of Arbah the **f** of Anak, 1
24: 2 the **f** of Abraham, and the father of Nachor: 1
24: 2 the father of Abraham, and the **f** of Nachor: 1
24: 3 I took your **f** Abraham from the *other* side of 1
24:32 **f** of Shechem for an hundred pieces of silver: 1
Jdg 1:14 *him*, that she moved him to ask of her **f** a field: 1
1:16 the children of the Kenite, Moses' **f in law**, 2859
4:11 children of Hobab the **f in law** of Moses, 2859
6:25 throw down the altar of Baal that thy **f** hath, 1
8:32 and was buried in the sepulchre of Joash his **f**, 1
9: 1 all the family of the house of his mother's **f**, 1
9:17 (For my **f** fought for you, and adventured his 1
9:28 serve the men of Hamor the **f** of Shechem: 1
9:56 which he did unto his **f**, in slaying his seventy 1
11:36 she said unto him, My **f**, *if* thou hast opened 1
11:37 she said unto her **f**, Let this thing be done for 1
11:39 end of two months, that she returned unto her **f**, 1
14: 2 and told his **f** and his mother, and said, 1
14: 3 his **f** and his mother said unto him, *Is there* 1
14: 3 And Samson said unto his **f**, Get her for me; 1
14: 4 his **f** and his mother knew not that it *was* of 1
14: 5 his **f** and his mother, *to* Timnath, and came to 1
14: 6 he told not his **f** or his mother what he had 1
14: 9 came to his **f** and mother, and he gave them, 1
14:10 So his **f** went down unto the woman: and 1
14:16 I have not told *it* my **f** nor my mother, and shall 1
15: 1 But her **f** would not suffer him to go in. 1
15: 2 her **f** said, I verily thought that thou hadst 1
15: 6 came up, and burnt her and her **f** with fire. 1
16:31 and all the house of his **f** came down, 1
16:31 Eshtaol in the buryingplace of Manoah his **f**. 1
17:10 be unto me a **f** and a priest, and I will give thee 1
18:19 and go with us, and be to us a **f** and a priest: 1
18:29 after the name of Dan their **f**, who was born 1
19: 3 when the **f** of the damsel saw him, he rejoiced 1
19: 4 his **f in law**, the damsel's father, 2859
19: 4 his father in law, the damsel's **f**, retained him; 1
19: 5 the damsel's **f** said unto his son in law, 1
19: 6 for the damsel's **f** had said unto the man, 1
19: 7 rose up to depart, his **f in law** urged him: 2859
19: 8 and the damsel's **f** said, Comfort thine heart, 1
19: 9 his concubine, and his servant, his **f in law**, 2859
19: 9 the damsel's **f**, said unto him, Behold now, 1
Ru 2:11 and *how* thou hast left thy **f** and thy mother, 1
4:17 he *is* the **f** of Jesse, the father of David. 1
4:17 he *is* the father of Jesse, the **f** of David. 1
1Sa 2:25 they hearkened not unto the voice of their **f**, 1
2:27 Did I plainly appear unto the house of thy **f**, 1
2:28 did I give unto the house of thy **f** all 1
2:30 indeed *that* thy house, and the house of thy **f**, 1
4:19 that her **f in law** and her husband were 2524
4:21 because of her **f in law** and her husband. 2524
9: 3 the asses of Kish Saul's **f** were lost. And Kish 1
9: 5 lest my **f** leave *caring* for the asses, and 1
10: 2 and lo, thy **f** hath left the care of the asses, and 1
10:12 place answered and said, But who *is* their **f**? 1
14: 1 that *is* on the other side. But he told not his **f**. 1
14:27 Jonathan heard not when his **f** charged 1

1Sa 14:28 Thy **f** straitly charged the people with an oath, 1
14:29 said Jonathan, My **f** hath troubled the land: 1
14:51 Kish *was* the **f** of Saul; and Ner the father of 1
14:51 and Ner the **f** of Abner *was* the son of Abiel. 1
19: 2 saying, Saul my **f** seeketh to kill thee: 1
19: 3 stand beside my **f** in the field where thou *art*, 1
19: 3 thou *art*, and I will commune with my **f** of thee; 1
19: 4 Jonathan spake good of David unto Saul his **f**, 1
20: 1 what *is* my sin before thy **f**, that he seeketh my 1
20: 2 my **f** will do nothing *either* great or small, but 1
20: 2 and why should my **f** hide this thing from me? 1
20: 3 Thy **f** certainly knoweth that I have found 1
20: 6 If thy **f** at all miss me, then say, 1
20: 8 for why shouldest thou bring me to thy **f**? 1
20: 9 were determined by my **f** to come upon thee, 1
20:10 tell me? or what *if* thy **f** answer thee roughly? 1
20:12 when I have sounded my **f** about to morrow 1
20:13 *but* if it please my **f** *to do* thee evil, then I will 1
20:13 be with thee, as he hath been with my **f**. 1
20:32 Jonathan answered Saul his **f**, and said unto 1
20:33 that it was determined of his **f** to slay David. 1
20:34 for David, because his **f** had done him shame. 1
22: 3 Let my **f** and my mother, I pray thee, 1
22:15 unto his servant, *nor* to all the house of my **f**: 1
23:17 for the hand of Saul my **f** shall not find thee; 1
23:17 unto thee; and that also Saul my **f** knoweth. 1
24:11 Moreover, my **f**, see, yea see the skirt of thy 1
2Sa 2:32 and buried him in the sepulchre of his **f**, 1
3: 8 kindness *this* day unto the house of Saul thy **f**, 1
6:21 which chose me before thy **f**, and before all his 1
7:14 I will be his **f**, and he shall be my son. If he 1
9: 7 and will restore thee all the land of Saul thy **f**; 1
10: 2 of Nahash, as his **f** shewed kindness unto me. 1
10: 2 him by the hand of his servants for his **f**. 1
10: 3 Thinkest thou that David doth honour thy **f**, 1
13: 5 when thy **f** cometh to see thee, say unto him, 1
16: 3 house of Israel restore me the kingdom of my **f**. 1
16:21 Israel shall hear that thou art abhorred of thy **f**: 1
17: 8 thou knowest thy **f** and his men, that they *be* 1
17: 8 thy **f** *is* a man of war, and will not lodge with 1
17:10 for all Israel knoweth that thy **f** *is* a mighty 1
17:23 died, and was buried in the sepulchre of his **f**. 1
19:37 *and be buried* by the grave of my **f** and of my 1
21:14 in Zelah, in the sepulchre of Kish his **f**: 1
1Ki 1: 6 his **f** had not displeased him at any time in 1
2:12 sat Solomon upon the throne of David his **f**; 1
2:24 and set me on the throne of David my **f**, and 1
2:26 the ark of the Lord GOD before David my **f**, 1
2:26 thou hast been afflicted in all where*in* my **f** was 1
2:31 from me, and from the house of my **f**. 1
2:32 my **f** David not knowing *thereof, to wit*, Abner 1
2:44 heart is privy to, that thou didst to David my **f**: 1
3: 3 walking in the statutes of David his **f**: 1
3: 6 Thou hast shewed unto thy servant David my **f** 1
3: 7 made thy servant king instead of David my **f**: 1
3:14 as thy **f** David did walk, then I will lengthen 1
5: 1 had anointed him king in the room of his **f**: 1
5: 3 Thou knowest how that David my **f** could not 1
5: 5 as the LORD spake unto David my **f**, saying, 1
6:12 with thee, which I spake unto David thy **f**: 1
7:14 and his **f** *was* a man of Tyre, a worker in brass: 1
7:51 in the *things* which David his **f** had dedicated; 1
8:15 which spake with his mouth unto David my **f**, 1
8:17 it was in the heart of David my **f** to build a 1
8:18 the LORD said unto David my **f**, Whereas it 1
8:20 and I am risen up in the room of David my **f**, 1
8:24 Who hast kept with thy servant David my **f** that 1
8:25 keep with thy servant David my **f** that thou 1
8:26 thou spakest unto thy servant David my **f**. 1
9: 4 as David thy **f** walked, in integrity of heart, and 1
9: 5 as I promised to David thy **f**, saying, 1
11: 4 his God, as *was* the heart of David his **f**. 1
11: 6 not fully after the LORD, as *did* David his **f**. 1
11:27 repaired the breaches of the city of David his **f**. 1
11:33 and my judgments, as *did* David his **f**. 1
11:43 and was buried in the city of David his **f**: 1
12: 4 Thy **f** made our yoke grievous: now therefore 1
12: 4 make thou the grievous service of thy **f**, 1
12: 6 that stood before Solomon his **f** while he *yet* 1
12: 9 Make the yoke which thy **f** did put upon us 1
12:10 Thy **f** made our yoke heavy, but make thou *it* 1
12:11 now whereas my **f** did lade you with a heavy 1
12:11 my **f** hath chastised you with whips, but I will 1
12:14 My **f** made your yoke heavy, and I will add to 1
12:14 my **f** *also* chastised you with whips, but I will 1
13:11 unto the king, them they told also to their **f**. 1
13:12 And their **f** said unto them, What way went he? 1
15: 3 he walked in all the sins of his **f**, which he had 1
15: 3 LORD his God, as the heart of David his **f**. 1
15:11 in the eyes of the LORD, as *did* David his **f**. 1
15:15 he brought in *the things* which his **f** had 1
15:19 and thee, *and* between my **f** and thy father: 1
15:19 and thee, *and* between my father and thy **f**: 1
15:24 with his fathers in the city of David his **f**: 1
15:26 walked in the way of his **f**, and in his sin 1
19:20 kiss my **f** and my mother, and *then* I will 1
20:34 The cities, which my **f** took from thy father, 1
20:34 The cities, which my father took from thy **f**, 1
20:34 thee in Damascus, as my **f** made in Samaria. 1
22:43 he walked in all the ways of Asa his **f**; 1
22:46 which remained in the days of his **f** Asa, 1
22:50 with his fathers in the city of David his **f**: 1
22:52 walked in the way of his **f**, and in the way of 1
22:53 of Israel, according unto all that his **f** had done. 1
2Ki 2:12 Elisha saw *it*, and he cried, My **f**, my father, 1
2:12 Elisha saw *it*, and he cried, My father, my **f**, 1
3: 2 but not like his **f**, and like his mother: 1
3: 2 for he put away the image of Baal that his **f** had 1
3:13 get thee to the prophets of thy **f**, and to 1
4:18 a day, that he went out to his **f** to the reapers. 1
4:19 he said unto his **f**, My head, my head. And he 1
5:13 came near, and spake unto him, and said, My **f**, 1
6:21 said unto Elisha, when he saw them, My **f**, 1
9:25 when I and thou rode together after Ahab his **f**, 1
13:14 wept over his face, and said, O my **f**, my father, 1

2Ki 13:14 wept over his face, and said, O my father, my **f**, 1
13:25 taken out of the hand of Jehoahaz his **f** by war. 1
14: 3 sight of the LORD, yet not like David his **f**: 1
14: 3 he did according to all *things* as Joash his **f** did. 1
14: 5 slew his servants which had slain the king his **f**. 1
14:21 and made him king instead of his **f** Amaziah. 1
15: 3 according to all that his **f** Amaziah had done; 1
15:34 he did according to all that his **f** Uzziah had 1
15:38 with his fathers in the city of David his **f**. 1
16: 2 sight of the LORD his God, like David his **f**. 1
18: 3 according to all that David his **f** did. 1
20: 5 Thus saith the LORD, the God of David thy **f**, 1
21: 3 places which Hezekiah his **f** had destroyed; 1
21:20 the sight of the LORD, as his **f** Manasseh did. 1
21:21 he walked in all the way that his **f** walked *in*, 1
21:21 and served the idols that his **f** served, 1
22: 2 and walked in all the way of David his **f**, and 1
23:34 son of Josiah king in the room of Josiah his **f**, 1
24: 9 according to all that his **f** had done. 1
1Ch 2:17 and the **f** of Amasa *was* Jether the Ishmeelite. 1
2:21 in to the daughter of Machir the **f** of Gilead, 1
2:23 All these *belonged to* the sons of Machir the **f** 1
2:24 Abiah Hezron's wife bare him Ashur the **f** of 1
2:42 Mesha his firstborn, which *was* the **f** of Ziph; 1
2:42 and the sons of Mareshah the **f** of Hebron. 1
2:44 And Shema begat Raham, the **f** of Jorkoam: 1
2:45 *was* Maon: and Maon *was* the **f** of Beth-zur. 1
2:49 She bare also Shaaph the **f** of Madmannah, 1
2:49 Sheva the **f** of Machbenah, and the father of 1
2:49 the father of Machbenah, and the **f** of Gibea: 1
2:50 of Ephratah; Shobal the **f** of Kirjath-jearim, 1
2:51 Salma the **f** of Beth-lehem, Hareph the father 1
2:51 of Beth-lehem, Hareph the **f** of Beth-gader. 1
2:52 And Shobal the **f** of Kirjath-jearim had sons; 1
2:55 came of Hemath, the **f** of the house of Rechab. 1
4: 3 And these *were of* the **f** of Etam; Jezreel, and 1
4: 4 Penuel the **f** of Gedor, and Ezer the father of 1
4: 4 the father of Gedor, and Ezer the **f** of Hushah. 1
4: 4 the firstborn of Ephratah, the **f** of Beth-lehem. 1
4: 5 Ashur the **f** of Tekoa had two wives, Helah 1
4:11 Shuah begat Mehir, which *was* the **f** of Eshton. 1
4:12 and Paseah, and Tehinnah the **f** of Irnahash. 1
4:14 begat Joab, the **f** of the valley of Charashim; 1
4:17 and Shammai, and Ishbah the **f** of Eshtemoa. 1
4:18 his wife Jehudijah bare Jered the **f** of Gedor, 1
4:18 Heber the **f** of Socho, and Jekuthiel the father 1
4:18 father of Socho, and Jekuthiel the **f** of Zanoah. 1
4:19 the **f** of Keilah the Garmite, and Eshtemoa 1
4:21 the son of Judah *were*, Er the **f** of Lecah, 1
4:21 Laadah the **f** of Mareshah, and the families of 1
7:14 his concubine the Aramitess bare Machir the **f** 1
7:22 And Ephraim their **f** mourned many days, and 1
7:31 Heber, and Malchiel, who *is* the **f** of Birzavith. 1
8:29 at Gibeon dwelt the **f** of Gibeon; whose wife's 1
9:19 his brethren, of the house of his **f**, 1
9:35 And in Gibeon dwelt the **f** of Gibeon, Jehiel, 1
17:13 I will be his **f**, and he shall be my son: and 1
19: 2 because his **f** shewed kindness to me. 1
19: 2 messengers to comfort him concerning his **f**. 1
19: 3 Thinkest thou that David doth honour thy **f**, 1
22:10 and he shall be my son, and I *will be* his **f**; and 1
24: 2 But Nadab and Abihu died before their **f**, and 1
24:19 according to their manner, under Aaron their **f**, 1
25: 3 six, under the hands of their **f** Jeduthun, 1
25: 6 All these *were* under the hands of their **f** for 1
26: 6 that ruled throughout the house of their **f**: 1
26:10 not the firstborn, yet his **f** made him the chief;) 1
28: 4 house of my **f** to be king over Israel for ever: 1
28: 4 and of the house of Judah, the house of my **f**; 1
28: 4 among the sons of my **f** he liked me to make 1
28: 6 chosen him to be my son, and I will be his **f**. 1
28: 9 know thou the God of thy **f**, and serve him with 1
29:10 LORD God of Israel our **f**, for ever and ever. 1
29:23 of the LORD as king instead of David his **f**, 1
2Ch 1: 8 hast shewed great mercy unto David my **f**, 1
1: 9 let thy promise unto David my **f** be established: 1
2: 3 As thou didst deal with David my **f**, and 1
2: 7 in Jerusalem, whom David my **f** did provide. 1
2:14 his **f** *was* a man of Tyre, skilful to work in 1
2:14 with the cunning *men* of my lord David thy **f**. 1
2:17 after the numbering where *with* David his **f** had 1
3: 1 where *the LORD* appeared unto David his **f**, 1
4:16 did Huram his **f** make to king Solomon for 1
5: 1 in *all the things* that David his **f** had dedicated; 1
6: 4 which he spake with his mouth to my **f** David, 1
6: 7 Now it was in the heart of David my **f** to build 1
6: 8 the LORD said to David my **f**, Forasmuch as 1
6:10 for I am risen up in the room of David my **f**, 1
6:15 David my **f** *that* which thou hast promised him; 1
6:16 keep with thy servant David my **f** *that* which 1
7:17 as David thy **f** walked, and do according to all 1
7:18 as I have covenanted with David thy **f**, 1
8:14 according to the order of David his **f**, 1
9:31 and he was buried in the city of David his **f**: 1
10: 4 Thy **f** made our yoke grievous: now therefore 1
10: 4 thou somewhat the grievous servitude of thy **f**, 1
10: 6 stood before Solomon his **f** while he *yet* lived, 1
10: 9 Ease somewhat the yoke that thy **f** did put upon 1
10:10 Thy **f** made our yoke heavy, but make thou *it* 1
10:11 For whereas my **f** put a heavy yoke upon you, 1
10:11 my **f** chastised you with whips, but I *will* 1
10:14 My **f** made your yoke heavy, but I will add 1
10:14 my **f** chastised you with whips, but I *will* 1
15:18 of God *the things* that his **f** had dedicated, 1
16: 3 thee, as *there was* between my **f** and thy father: 1
16: 3 thee, as *there was* between my father and thy **f**: 1
17: 2 cities of Ephraim, which Asa his **f** had taken. 1
17: 3 he walked in the first ways of his **f** David, 1
17: 4 sought to the *LORD* God of his **f**, and 1
20:32 he walked in the way of Asa his **f**, and 1
21: 3 And their **f** gave them great gifts of silver, and 1
21: 4 Jehoram was risen up to the kingdom of his **f**, 1
21:12 Thus saith the LORD God of David thy **f**, 1
21:12 not walked in the ways of Jehoshaphat thy **f**, 1
22: 4 after the death of his **f** to his destruction. 1

2Ch 24:22 kindness which Jehoiada his **f** had done to him, 1
25: 3 slew his servants that had killed the king his **f**. 1
26: 1 made him king in the room of his **f** Amaziah. 1
26: 4 according to all that his **f** Amaziah did. 1
27: 2 according to all that his **f** Uzziah did: 1
28: 1 in the sight of the LORD, like David his **f**: 1
29: 2 according to all that David his **f** had done. 1
33: 3 places which Hezekiah his **f** had broken down, 1
33:22 the sight of the LORD, as did Manasseh his **f**: 1
33:22 carved images which Manasseh his **f** had made, 1
33:23 as Manasseh his **f** had humbled himself; 1
34: 2 walked in the ways of David his **f**, and 1
34: 3 he began to seek after the God of David his **f**: 1
Est 2: 7 for she had neither **f** nor mother, and the maid 1
2: 7 when her **f** and mother were dead, 1
Job 15:10 and very aged men, much elder than thy **f**. 1
17:14 I have said to corruption, Thou *art* my **f**: to 1
29:16 I *was* a **f** to the poor: and the cause *which* I 1
31:18 as *with* a **f**, and I have guided her from my 1
38:28 Hath the rain a **f**? or who hath begotten 1
42:15 their **f** gave them inheritance among their 1
Ps 27:10 When my **f** and my mother forsake me, then 1
68: 5 A **f** of the fatherless, and a judge of 1
89:26 Thou *art* my **F**, my God, and the rock of my 1
103:13 Like as a **f** pitieth *his* children, *so* the LORD 1
Pr 1: 8 hear the instruction of thy **f**, and forsake not 1
3:12 even as a **f** the son *in whom* he delighteth. 1
4: 1 the instruction of a **f**, and attend to know 1
10: 1 A wise son maketh a glad **f**: but a foolish son *is* 1
15:20 A wise son maketh a glad **f**: but a foolish man 1
17:21 *it* to his sorrow: and the **f** of a fool hath no joy. 1
17:25 A foolish son *is* a grief to his **f**, and 1
19:13 A foolish son *is* the calamity of his **f**: and 1
19:26 He that wasteth *his* **f**, *and* chaseth away *his* 1
20:20 Whoso curseth his **f** or his mother, his lamp 1
23:22 Hearken unto thy **f** that begat thee, and 1
23:24 The **f** of the righteous shall greatly rejoice: and 1
23:25 Thy **f** and thy mother shall be glad, and she that 1
28: 7 is a companion of riotous *men* shameth his **f**. 1
28:24 Whoso robbeth his **f** or his mother, and saith, 1
29: 3 Whoso loveth wisdom rejoiceth his **f**: but 1
30:11 *There is* a generation *that* curseth their **f**, and 1
30:17 The eye *that* mocketh at *his* **f**, and despiseth to 1
Isa 3: 6 take hold of his brother *of* the house of his **f**, 1
8: 4 My **f**, and my mother, the riches of Damascus 1
9: 6 The mighty God, The everlasting **F**, 1
22:21 he shall be a **f** to the inhabitants of Jerusalem, 1
38: 5 Thus saith the LORD, the God of David thy **f**, 1
38:19 the **f** to the children shall make known thy 1
43:27 Thy first **f** hath sinned, and thy teachers have 1
45:10 Woe unto him that saith unto *his* **f**, 1
51: 2 Look unto Abraham your **f**, and unto Sarah *that* 1
58:14 and feed thee with the heritage of Jacob thy **f**: 1
63:16 Doubtless thou *art* our **f**, though Abraham be 1
63:16 thou, O LORD, *art* our **f**, our redeemer; 1
64: 8 now, O LORD, thou *art* our **f**; we *are* the clay, 1
Jer 2:27 Saying to a stock, Thou *art* my **f**; and to a 1
3: 4 unto me, My **f**, thou *art* the guide of my youth? 1
3:19 I said, Thou shalt call me, My **f**; and shalt not 1
12: 6 For even thy brethren, and the house of thy **f**, 1
16: 7 them the cup of consolation to drink for their **f** 1
20:15 *be* the man who brought tidings to my **f**, 1
22:11 which reigned instead of Josiah his **f**, 1
22:15 did not thy **f** eat and drink, and do judgment 1
31: 9 for I am a **f** to Israel, and Ephraim *is* my 1
35: 6 for Jonadab the son of Rechab our **f** 1
35: 8 of Rechab our **f** in all that he hath charged us, 1
35:10 done according to all that Jonadab our **f** 1
35:16 have performed the commandment of their **f**, 1
35:18 obeyed the commandment of Jonadab your **f**, 1
Eze 16: 3 thy **f** *was* an Amorite, and thy mother a Hittite. 1
16:45 mother *was* a Hittite, and your **f** an Amorite. 1
18: 4 as the soul of the **f**, so also the soul of the son 1
18:17 he shall not die for the iniquity of his **f**, he shall 1
18:18 *As for* his **f**, because he cruelly oppressed, 1
18:19 doth not the son bear the iniquity of the **f**? 1
18:20 The son shall not bear the iniquity of the **f**, 1
18:20 neither shall the **f** bear the iniquity of the son: 1
22: 7 In thee have they set light by **f** and mother: 1
44:25 no dead person to defile *themselves:* but for **f**, 1
Da 5: 2 silver vessels which his **f** Nebuchadnezzar had 2
5:11 and in the days of thy **f** light and understanding 2
5:11 whom the king Nebuchadnezzar thy **f**, the king, 2
5:11 the king, *I say*, thy **f**, made master of 2
5:13 whom the king my **f** brought out of Jewry? 2
5:18 the most high God gave Nebuchadnezzar thy **f** 2
Am 2: 7 a man and his **f** will go in unto the *same* maid, 1
Mic 7: 6 For the son dishonoureth the **f**, the daughter 1
Zec 13: 3 his **f** and his mother that begat him shall say 1
13: 3 his **f** and his mother that begat him shall thrust 1
Mal 1: 6 A son honoureth *his* **f**, and a servant his master: 1
1: 6 if then I *be* a **f**, where *is* mine honour? and if I 1
2:10 Have we not all one **f**? hath not one God 1
Mt 2:22 reign in Judea in the room of his **f** Herod, 3962
3: 9 We have Abraham to *our* **f**: 3962
4:21 his brother, in a ship with Zebedee their **f**, 3962
4:22 they immediately left the ship and their **f**, 3962
5:16 and glorify your **F** which is in heaven. 3962
5:45 That ye may be the children of your **F** 3962
5:48 even as your **F** which is in heaven is 3962
6: 1 otherwise ye have no reward of your **F** 3962
6: 4 thy **F** which seeth in secret himself shall 3962
6: 6 thy door, pray to thy **F** which is in secret; 3962
6: 6 thy **F** which seeth in secret shall reward 3962
6: 8 for your **F** knoweth what *things* ye have 3962
6: 9 Our **F** which art in heaven, Hallowed be 3962
6:14 your heavenly **F** will also forgive you: 3962
6:15 neither will your **F** forgive your trespasses. 3962
6:18 to fast, but unto thy **F** which is in secret: 3962
6:18 and thy **F**, which seeth in secret, 3962
6:26 yet your heavenly **F** feedeth them. 3962
6:32 for your heavenly **F** knoweth that ye have 3962
7:11 how much more shall your **F** which is in 3962
7:21 he that doeth the will of my **F** which is in 3962
8:21 Lord, suffer me first to go and bury my **f**. 3962

Mt 10:20 the Spirit of your **F** which speaketh in you. 3962
10:21 up the brother to death, and the **f** the child: 3962
10:29 shall not fall on the ground without your **F**. 3962
10:32 him will I confess also before my **F** which 3962
10:33 him will I also deny before my **F** which is 3962
10:35 come to set a man at variance against his **f**, 3962
10:37 He that loveth **f** or mother more than me is 3962
11:25 Jesus answered and said, I thank thee, O **F**, 3962
11:26 Even so, **F**: for so it seemed good in thy 3962
11:27 All *things* are delivered unto me of my **F**: 3962
11:27 and no *man* knoweth the Son, but the **F**; 3962
11:27 neither knoweth any *man* the **F**, save 3962
12:50 For whosoever shall do the will of my **F** 3962
13:43 forth as the sun in the kingdom of their **F**. 3962
15: 4 saying, Honour thy **f** and mother: 3962
15: 4 and, He that curseth **f** or mother, let him die 3962
15: 5 Whosoever shall say to *his* **f** or *his* mother, 3962
15: 6 And honour not his **f** or his mother, *he shall* 3962
15:13 which my heavenly **F** hath not planted, 3962
16:17 *it* unto thee, but my **F** which is in heaven. 3962
16:27 come in the glory of his **F** with his angels; 3962
18:10 behold the face of my **F** which is in heaven. 3962
18:14 it is not the will of your **F** which is in 3962
18:19 it shall be done for them of my **F** which is 3962
18:35 So likewise shall my heavenly **F** do *also* 3962
19: 5 For this cause shall a man leave **f** and 3962
19:19 Honour thy **f** and *thy* mother: and, 3962
19:29 or **f**, or mother, or wife, or children, or 3962
20:23 *to them* for whom it is prepared of my **F**. 3962
21:31 Whether of *them* twain did the will of *his* **f**? 3962
23: 9 And call no *man* your **f** upon the earth: 3962
23: 9 for one is your **F**, which is in heaven. 3962
24:36 not the angels of heaven, but my **F** only. 3962
25:34 his right hand, Come, ye blessed of my **F**, 3962
26:39 on his face, and prayed, saying, O my **F**, 3962
26:42 second time, and prayed, saying, O my **F**, 3962
26:53 thou that I cannot now pray to my **F**, 3962
28:19 baptizing them in the name of the **F**, and 3962
Mk 1:20 they left their **f** Zebedee in the ship with 3962
5:40 he taketh the **f** and the mother of 3962
7:10 Moses said, Honour thy **f** and thy mother; 3962
7:10 and, Whoso curseth **f** or mother, let him die 3962
7:11 ye say, If a man shall say to *his* **f** or mother, 3962
7:12 ye suffer him no more to do ought for his **f** 3962
8:38 when he cometh in the glory of his **F** with 3962
9:21 And he asked his **f**, How long is it ago 3962
9:24 And straightway the **f** of the child cried out, 3962
10: 7 For this cause shall a man leave his **f** and 3962
10:19 Defraud not, Honour thy **f** and mother. 3962
10:29 or **f**, or mother, or wife, or children, or 3962
11:10 Blessed *be* the kingdom of our **f** David, 3962
11:25 that your **F** also which is in heaven may 3962
11:26 neither will your **F** which is in heaven 3962
13:12 the brother to death, and the **f** the son; 3962
13:32 are in heaven, neither the Son, but the **F**. 3962
14:36 And he said, Abba, **F**, all *things are* 3962
15:21 the **f** of Alexander and Rufus, to bear his 3962
Lk 1:32 give unto him the throne of his **f** David: 3962
1:59 him Zacharias, after the name of his **f**. 3962
1:62 And they made signs to his **f**, how he 3962
1:67 And his **f** Zacharias was filled with 3962
1:73 The oath which he sware to our **f** Abraham, 3962
2:48 thy **f** and I have sought thee sorrowing. 3962
3: 8 We have Abraham to *our* **f**: 3962
6:36 merciful, as your **F** also is merciful. 3962
8:51 and the **f** and the mother of the maiden. 3962
9:42 the child, and delivered him again to his **f**. 3962
9:59 Lord, suffer me first to go and bury my **f**. 3962
10:21 and said, I thank thee, O **F**, Lord of heaven 3962
10:21 even so, **F**; for so it seemed good in thy 3962
10:22 All *things* are delivered to me of my **F**: and 3962
10:22 no *man* knoweth who the Son is, but the **F**; 3962
10:22 and who the **F** is, but the Son, and *he* to 3962
11: 2 ye pray, say, Our **F** which art in heaven, 3962
11:11 son shall ask bread of any of you that is a **f**, 3962
11:13 how much more shall *your* heavenly **F** give 3962
12:30 your **F** knoweth that ye have need of these 3962
12:53 The **f** shall be divided against the son, and 3962
12:53 against the son, and the son against the **f**; 3962
14:26 and hate not his **f**, and mother, and wife, 3962
15:12 And the younger of them said to his **f**, 3962
15:12 the younger of them said to *his* father, **F**, 3962
15:18 I will arise and go to my **f**, and will say 3962
15:18 go to my father, and will say unto him, **F**, 3962
15:20 And he arose, and came to his **f**. But when 3962
15:20 his **f** saw him, and had compassion, and 3962
15:21 And the son said unto him, **F**, I have sinned 3962
15:22 But the **f** said to his servants, Bring forth 3962
15:27 and thy **f** hath killed the fatted calf, 3962
15:28 therefore came his **f** out and intreated him. 3962
15:29 And he answering said to *his* **f**, Lo, 3962
16:24 And he cried and said, **F** Abraham, 3962
16:27 Then he said, I pray thee therefore, **f**, 3962
16:30 And he said, Nay, **f** Abraham: but if one 3962
18:20 false witness, Honour thy **f** and thy mother. 3962
22:29 as my **F** hath appointed unto me; 3962
22:42 Saying, **F**, if thou be willing, remove this 3962
23:34 Then said Jesus, **F**, forgive them; for they 3962
23:46 he said, **F**, into thy hands I commend my 3962
24:49 I send the promise of my **F** upon you: 3962
Jn 1:14 the glory as of the only begotten of the **F**,) 3962
1:18 which is in the bosom of the **F**, he hath 3962
3:35 The **F** loveth the Son, and hath given all 3962
4:12 Art thou greater than our **f** Jacob, 3962
4:21 nor *yet* at Jerusalem, worship the **F**. 3962
4:23 worshippers shall worship the **F** in spirit 3962
4:23 for the **F** seeketh such to worship him. 3962
4:53 So the **f** knew that *it was* at the same hour, 3962
5:17 answered them, My **F** worketh hitherto, 3962
5:18 but said also that God was his **F**, 3962
5:19 of himself, but what he seeth the **F** do: 3962
5:20 For the **F** loveth the Son, and sheweth him 3962
5:21 For as the **F** raiseth up the dead, and 3962
5:22 For the **F** judgeth no *man*, but 3962
5:23 honour the Son, even as they honour the **F**. 3962

F

Jn 5:23 honoureth not the F which hath sent him. 3962
5:26 For as the F hath life in himself; so hath he 3962
5:30 but the will of the F which hath sent me. 3962
5:36 for the works which the F hath given me to 3962
5:36 bear witness of me, that the F hath sent me. 3962
5:37 And the F himself, which hath sent me, 3962
5:45 Do not think that I will accuse you to the F: 3962
6:27 unto you: for him hath God the F sealed. 3962
6:32 my F giveth you the true bread from 3962
6:37 All that the F giveth me shall come to me; 3962
6:42 of Joseph, whose f and mother we know? 3962
6:44 except the F which hath sent me draw him: 3962
6:45 that hath heard, and hath learned of the F, 3962
6:46 Not that any *man* hath seen the F, save he 3962
6:46 he which is of God, he hath seen the F. 3962
6:57 As the living F hath sent me, and I live by 3962
6:57 Father hath sent me, and I live by the F: 3962
6:65 except it were given unto him of my F. 3962
8:16 I am not alone, but I and the F that sent me. 3962
8:18 the F that sent me beareth witness of me. 3962
8:19 Then said they unto him, Where is thy F? 3962
8:19 Ye neither know me, nor my F: 3962
8:19 ye should have known my F also. 3962
8:27 not that he spake to them of the F. 3962
8:28 but as my F hath taught me, I speak these 3962
8:29 the F hath not left me alone; for I do 3962
8:38 I speak *that* which I have seen with my F: 3962
8:38 ye do *that* which ye have seen with your f. 3962
8:39 and said unto him, Abraham is our f. 3962
8:41 Ye do the deeds of your f. Then said they to 3962
8:41 of fornication; we have one F, *even* God. 3962
8:42 If God were your F, ye would love me: 3962
8:44 Ye are of *your* f the devil, and the lusts of 3962
8:44 the devil, and the lusts of your f ye will do. 3962
8:44 of his own: for he is a liar, and the f of it. 3962
8:49 but I honour my F, and ye do dishonour 3962
8:53 Art thou greater than our f Abraham, 3962
8:54 it is my F that honoureth me; of whom ye 3962
8:56 Your f Abraham rejoiced to see my day: 3962
10:15 As the F knoweth me, *even* so know I 3962
10:15 Father knoweth me, *even* so know I the F: 3962
10:17 Therefore doth *my* F love me, because I lay 3962
10:18 commandment have I received of my F. 3962
10:29 My F, which gave *them* me, is greater than 3962
10:30 I and *my* F are one. 3962
10:32 good works have I shewed you from my F; 3962
10:36 Say ye *of him*, whom the F hath sanctified, 3962
10:37 If I do not the works of my F, believe me 3962
10:38 believe, that the F *is* in me, and I in him. 3962
11:41 And Jesus lift up *his* eyes, and said, F, 3962
12:26 any *man* serve me, him will *my* F honour. 3962
12:27 F, save me from this hour: but for this 3962
12:28 F, glorify thy name. Then came there a 3962
12:49 but the F which sent me, he gave me a 3962
12:50 even as the F said unto me, so I speak. 3962
13:1 should depart out of this world unto the F, 3962
13:3 Jesus knowing that the F had given all 3962
14:6 no *man* cometh unto the F, but by me. 3962
14:7 ye should have known my F also: 3962
14:8 Lord, shew us the F, and it sufficeth us. 3962
14:9 he that hath seen me hath seen the F; and 3962
14:9 and how sayest thou *then*, Shew us the F? 3962
14:10 Believest thou not that I am in the F, and 3962
14:10 that I am in the Father, and the F in me? 3962
14:10 but the F that dwelleth in me, he doeth 3962
14:11 Believe me that I *am* in the F, and 3962
14:11 me that I *am* in the Father, and the F in me: 3962
14:12 these shall he do; because I go unto my F. 3962
14:13 I do, that the F may be glorified in the Son. 3962
14:16 And I will pray the F, and he shall give you 3962
14:20 that day ye shall know that I *am* in my F, 3962
14:21 he that loveth me shall be loved of my F, 3962
14:23 and my F will love him, and we will come 3962
14:26 whom the F will send in my name, 3962
14:28 because I said, I go unto the F: 3962
14:28 unto the Father: for my F is greater than I. 3962
14:31 that the world may know that I love the F; 3962
14:31 and as the F gave me commandment, *even* 3962
15:1 the true vine, and my F is the husbandman. 3962
15:8 Herein is my F glorified, that ye bear much 3962
15:9 As the F hath loved me, so have I loved 3962
15:15 for all *things* that I have heard of my F I 3962
15:16 that whatsoever ye shall ask of the F in my 3962
15:23 He that hateth me hateth my F also. 3962
15:24 both seen and hated both me and my F. 3962
15:26 whom I will send unto you from the F, 3962
15:26 which proceedeth from the F, he shall 3962
16:3 because they have not known the F, 3962
16:10 because I go to my F, and ye see me no 3962
16:15 All *things* that the F hath are mine: 3962
16:16 and ye shall see me, because I go to the F. 3962
16:17 ye shall see me: and, Because I go to the F? 3962
16:23 Whatsoever ye shall ask the F in my name, 3962
16:25 but I shall shew you plainly of the F. 3962
16:26 not unto you, that I will pray the F for you: 3962
16:27 For the F himself loveth you, because 3962
16:28 I came forth from the F, and am come into 3962
16:28 again, I leave the world, and go to the F. 3962
16:32 I am not alone, because the F is with me. 3962
17:1 to heaven, and said, F, the hour is come; 3962
17:5 And now, O F, glorify thou me with thine 3962
17:11 Holy F, keep through thine own name 3962
17:21 as thou, F, *art* in me, and I in thee, that they 3962
17:24 F, I will that they also, whom thou hast 3962
17:25 O righteous F, the world hath not known 3962
18:11 the cup which my F hath given me, shall I 3962
18:13 for he was **f in law** to Caiaphas, which was 3995
20:17 me; for I am not yet ascended to my F: 3962
20:17 I ascend unto my F, and your Father; 3962
20:17 I ascend unto my Father, and your F; 3962
20:21 as *my* F hath sent me, even *so* send I you. 3962
Ac 1:4 but wait for the promise of the F, which, 3962
1:7 which the F hath put in his own power. 3962
2:33 having received of the F the promise of 3962
7:2 The God of glory appeared unto our f 3962
Ac 7:4 and from thence, when his f was dead, 3962
7:14 and called his f Jacob to *him*, and all his 3962
7:16 of the sons of Emmor the *f* of Sychem. NIG
16:1 and believed; but his f *was* a Greek: 3962
16:3 for they knew all that his f was a Greek. 3962
28:8 that the f of Publius lay sick of a fever and 3962
Ro 1:7 Grace to you and peace from God our F, 3962
4:1 What shall we say then that Abraham our f, 3962
4:11 that he might be the f of all them that 3962
4:12 And the f of circumcision to them who are 3962
4:12 in the steps of *that* faith of our f Abraham, 3962
4:16 the faith of Abraham; who is the f of us all, 3962
4:17 I have made thee a f of many nations,) 3962
4:18 that he might become the f of many 3962
6:4 up from the dead by the glory of the F, 3962
8:15 of adoption, whereby we cry, Abba, F. 3962
9:10 had conceived by one, *even* by our f Isaac; 3962
15:6 even the F of our Lord Jesus Christ. 3962
1Co 1:3 from God our F, and *from* the Lord Jesus 3962
8:6 But to us *there is but* one God, the F, 3962
15:24 up the kingdom to God, even the F; 3962
2Co 1:2 Grace *be* to you and peace from God our F, 3962
1:3 even the F of our Lord Jesus Christ, 3962
1:3 the F of mercies, and the God of all 3962
6:18 And will be a F unto you, and ye shall be 3962
11:31 The God and F of our Lord Jesus Christ, 3962
Gal 1:1 by man, but by Jesus Christ, and God the F, 3962
1:3 Grace *be* to you and peace from God the F, 3962
1:4 according to the will of God and our F: 3962
4:2 governors until the time appointed of the f. 3962
4:6 his Son into your hearts, crying, Abba, F. 3962
Eph 1:2 from God our F, and *from* the Lord Jesus 3962
1:3 *be* the God and F of our Lord Jesus Christ, 3962
1:17 of our Lord Jesus Christ, the F of glory, 3962
2:18 both have access by one Spirit unto the F. 3962
3:14 For this cause I bow my knees unto the F 3962
4:6 One God and F of all, who *is* above all, and 3962
5:20 the F in the name of our Lord Jesus Christ; 3962
5:31 For this cause shall a man leave his f and 3962
6:2 Honour thy f and mother; (which is the first 3962
6:23 from God the F and the Lord Jesus Christ. 3962
Php 1:2 from God our F, and *from* the Lord Jesus 3962
2:11 Christ *is* Lord, to the glory of God the F. 3962
2:22 the proof of him, that, as a son *with the* f, 3962
4:20 and our F *be* glory for ever and ever. 3962
Col 1:2 from God our F and the Lord Jesus Christ. 3962
1:3 to God and the F of our Lord Jesus Christ, 3962
1:12 Giving thanks unto the F, which hath made 3962
1:19 For it pleased *the F* that in him should all NIG
2:2 of the mystery of God and of the F, 3962
3:17 giving thanks to God and the F by him. 3962
1Th 1:1 of the Thessalonians *which is* in God the F 3962
1:1 from God our F, and the Lord Jesus Christ. 3962
1:3 Jesus Christ, in the sight of God and our F; 3962
2:11 every one of you, as a f *doth* his children, 3962
3:11 Now God himself and our F, and our Lord 3962
3:13 even our F, at the coming of our Lord Jesus 3962
2Th 1:1 church of the Thessalonians in God our F 3962
1:2 from God our F and the Lord Jesus Christ. 3962
2:16 and God, even our F, which hath loved us, 3962
1Ti 1:2 from God our F and Jesus Christ our Lord. 3962
5:1 Rebuke not an elder, but intreat *him* as a f; 3962
2Ti 1:2 from God the F and Christ Jesus our Lord. 3962
Tit 1:4 from God the F and the Lord Jesus Christ 3962
Phm 1:3 from God our F and the Lord Jesus Christ. 3962
Heb 1:5 I will be to him a F, and he shall be to me a 3962
7:3 **Without f**, without mother, without descent, 540
7:10 For he was yet in the loins of his f, 3962
12:7 for what son is *he* whom the f chasteneth 3962
12:9 rather be in subjection unto the F of spirits, 3962
Jas 1:17 and cometh down from the F of lights, 3962
1:27 and undefiled before God and the F is this, 3962
2:21 Was not Abraham our f justified by works, 3962
3:9 Therewith bless we God, even the F; and 3962
1Pe 1:2 to the foreknowledge of God the F, 3962
1:3 *be* the God and F of our Lord Jesus Christ, 3962
1:17 And if ye call on the F, who without 3962
2Pe 1:17 For he received from God the F honour and 3962
1Jn 1:2 which was with the F, and was manifested 3962
1:3 and truly our fellowship *is* with the F, and 3962
2:1 *man* sin, we have an advocate with the F, 3962
2:13 because ye have known the F. 3962
2:15 the world, the love of the F is not in him. 3962
2:16 of life, is not of the F, but is of the world. 3962
2:22 is antichrist, that denieth the F and the Son. 3962
2:23 denieth the Son, the same hath not the F: 3962
2:23 *he that acknowledgeth the Son hath the F* NIG
2:24 also shall continue in the Son, and in the F. 3962
3:1 what manner of love the F hath bestowed 3962
4:14 do testify that the F sent the Son *to be* 3962
5:7 the F, the Word, and the Holy Ghost: 3962
2Jn 1:3 from God the F, and from the Lord Jesus 3962
1:3 the Son of the F, in truth and love. 3962
1:4 have received a commandment from the F. 3962
1:9 of Christ, he hath both the F and the Son. 3962
Jude 1:1 to them that are sanctified by God the F, 3962
Rev 1:6 us kings and priests unto God and his F; 3962
2:27 to shivers: even as I received of my F. 3962
3:5 but I will confess his name before my F, 3962
3:21 and am set down with my F in his throne. 3962

FATHER'S (144) [FATHER]

Ge 9:23 and they saw not their f nakedness. 1
12:1 and from thy kindred, and from thy f house, 1
20:13 when God caused me to wander from my f 1
24:7 which took me from my f house, and from 1
24:23 is there room *in* thy f house for us to lodge in? 1
24:38 thou shalt go unto my f house, and to my 1
24:40 for my son of my kindred, and of my f house: 1
26:15 For all the wells which his f servants had 1
28:21 So that I come again to my f house in peace; 1
29:9 Rachel came with her f sheep: 1+3807.1
29:12 Jacob told Rachel that he *was* her f brother, 1
31:1 hath taken away all that *was* our f; 1+3807.1
31:1 of *that* which *was* of our f hath he 1+3807.1
31:5 And said unto them, I see your f countenance, 1
31:14 or inheritance for us in our f house? 1
31:19 had stolen the images that *were* her f. 1+3807.1
31:30 because thou sore longedst after thy f house, 1
35:22 and lay with Bilhah his f concubine: 1
37:2 and with the sons of Zilpah, his f wives: 1
37:12 his brethren went to feed their f flock in 1
38:11 Remain a widow *at* thy f house, till Shelah my 1
38:11 *did*. And Tamar went and dwelt *in* her f house. 1
41:51 made me forget all my toil, and all my f house. 1
46:31 unto his f house, I will go up, and 1
46:31 say unto him, My brethren, and my f house, 1
47:12 and all his f household, *with* bread, 1
48:17 he held up his f hand, to remove it from 1
49:4 because thou wentest up to thy f bed; then 1
49:8 thy f children shall bow down before thee. 1
50:1 Joseph fell upon his f face, and wept upon him, 1
50:8 of Joseph, and his brethren, and his f house: 1
50:22 And Joseph dwelt in Egypt, he, and his f house: 1
Ex 2:16 and filled the troughs to water their f flock. 1
6:20 Amram took him Jochebed his **f sister** to 1733
15:2 a habitation; my f God, and I will exalt him. 1
Lev 16:32 to minister in the priest's office in his f stead, 1
18:8 The nakedness of thy f wife shalt thou not 1
18:8 shalt thou not uncover: it *is* thy f nakedness. 1
18:11 The nakedness of thy f wife's daughter, 1
18:12 Thou shalt not uncover the nakedness of thy f 1
18:12 thy father's sister: she *is* thy f near kinswoman. 1
18:14 Thou shalt not uncover the nakedness of thy f 1
20:11 the man that lieth with his f wife hath 1
20:11 father's wife hath uncovered his f nakedness: 1
20:17 his f daughter, or his mother's daughter, and 1
20:19 of thy mother's sister, nor of thy f sister: 1
22:13 have no child, and is returned unto her f house, 1
22:13 as *in* her youth, she shall eat of her f meat: 1
Nu 2:2 own standard, with the ensign of their f house: 1
18:1 thy f house with thee shall bear the iniquity of 1
27:7 of an inheritance among their f brethren; 1
27:10 ye shall give his inheritance unto his f brethren. 1
30:3 *by* a bond, *being* in her f house in her youth; 1
30:16 *being yet* in her youth *in* her f house. 1
36:11 were married unto their **f brothers'** sons: 1730
Dt 22:21 bring out the damsel to the door of her f house, 1
22:21 folly in Israel, to play the whore *in* her f house: 1
22:30 A man shall not take his f wife, nor discover 1
22:30 take his father's wife, nor discover his f skirt. 1
27:20 Cursed *be* he that lieth with his f wife; because 1
27:20 father's wife; because he uncovereth his f skirt. 1
Jos 2:12 that ye will also shew kindness unto my f 1
2:18 and thy brethren, and all thy f household, 1
6:25 and her f household, and all that she had; 1
Jdg 6:15 in Manasseh, and I *am* the least in my f house. 1
6:25 said unto him, Take thy f young bullock, 1
6:27 because he feared his f household, and the men 1
9:5 And he went unto his f house at Ophrah, and 1
9:18 ye are risen up against my f house *this* day, 1
11:2 unto him, Thou shalt not inherit in our f house; 1
11:7 ye hate me, and expel me out of my f house? 1
14:15 lest we burn thee and thy f house with fire: 1
14:19 was kindled, and he went up *to* his f house. 1
19:2 went away from him unto her f house to 1
19:3 she brought him *into* her f house: and when 1
1Sa 2:31 cut off thine arm, and the arm of thy f house, 1
9:20 *Is it* not on thee, and on all thy f house? 1
17:15 returned from Saul to feed his f sheep *at* 1
17:25 and make his f house free in Israel. 1
17:34 Thy servant kept his f sheep, and 1+3807.1
18:2 would let him go no more home *to* his f house. 1
18:18 and what *is* my life, *or* my f family in Israel, 1
22:1 all his f house heard *it*, they went down thither 1
22:11 the son of Ahitub, and all his f house, 1
22:16 Ahimelech, thou, and all thy f house. 1
22:22 *the death* of all the persons of thy f house. 1
24:21 that thou wilt not destroy my name out of my f 1
2Sa 3:7 Wherefore hast thou gone in unto my f 1
3:29 rest on the head of Joab, and on all his f house; 1
9:7 shew thee kindness for Jonathan thy f sake, 1
14:9 the iniquity *be* on me, and on my f house: 1
15:34 as I *have been* thy f servant hitherto, so *will* I 1
16:19 as I have served in thy f presence, so will I be 1
16:21 unto Absalom, Go in unto thy f concubines, 1
16:22 Absalom went in unto his f concubines in 1
19:28 For all *of* my f house were but dead men before 1
24:17 be against me, and against my f house. 1
1Ki 11:12 in thy days I will not do it for David thy f sake: 1
11:17 certain Edomites of his f servants with him, 1
12:10 My little *finger* shall be thicker than my f loins. 1
18:18 thou, and thy f house, in that ye have forsaken 1
2Ki 10:3 set *him* on his f throne, and fight for your 1
23:30 anointed him, and made him king in his f stead. 1
24:17 Mattaniah his **f brother** king in his stead, 1730
1Ch 5:1 but, forasmuch as he defiled his f bed, 1
12:28 and *of* his f house twenty and two captains. 1
21:17 LORD my God, be on me, and on my f house; 1
23:11 in one reckoning, according to *their* f house. 1
2Ch 2:13 endued with understanding, of Huram my f, 1
10:10 My little *finger* shall be thicker than my f loins. 1
21:13 and also hast slain thy brethren of thy f house, 1
36:1 and made him king in his f stead in Jerusalem. 1
Ne 1:6 both I and my f house have sinned. 1
Est 4:14 but thou and thy f house shall be destroyed: 1
Ps 45:10 forget also thine own people, and thy f house; 1
Pr 4:3 For I was my f son, tender and 1+3807.1
6:20 keep thy f commandment, and forsake not 1
13:1 A wise son *heareth his* f instruction: but 1
15:5 A fool despiseth his f instruction: but he that 1
27:10 Thine own friend, and thy f friend, forsake not; 1
Isa 7:17 upon thy people, and upon thy f house, 1
22:23 he shall be for a glorious throne to his f house. 1
22:24 they shall hang upon him all the glory of his f 1
Jer 35:14 drink none, but obey their f commandment: 1
Eze 18:14 that seeth all his f sins which he hath done, and 1
22:10 In thee have they discovered their f nakedness: 1
22:11 in thee hath humbled his sister, his f daughter. 1
Mt 26:29 I drink it new with you in my F kingdom. 3962

Lk 2:49 wist ye not that I must be about my **F** *3962*
9:26 and *in his* **F**, and of the holy angels. *3962*
12:32 for it is your **F** good pleasure to give you *3962*
15:17 How many hired *servants* of my **f** have *3962*
16:27 that thou wouldest send him to my **f** house: *3962*
Jn 2:16 make not my **F** house a house of *3962*
5:43 I am come in my **F** name, and ye receive *3962*
6:39 And this is the **F** will which hath sent me, *3962*
10:25 the works that I do in my **F** name, they bear *3962*
10:29 no *man* is able to pluck *them* out of my **F** *3962*
14: 2 In my **F** house are many mansions: if *it* *3962*
14:24 hear is not mine, but the **F** which sent me. *3962*
15:10 even as I have kept my **F** commandments, *3962*
Ac 7:20 nourished up in his **f** house three months: *3962*
1Co 5: 1 that one should have *his* **f** wife. *3962*
Rev 14: 1 having his **F** name written in their *3962*

FATHERLESS (43) [FATHER]
Ex 22:22 Ye shall not afflict any widow, or **f child**. 3490
22:24 wives shall be widows, and your children **f**. 3490
Dt 10:18 He doth execute the judgment of the **f** and 3490
14:29 the stranger, and the **f**, and the widow, 3490
16:11 the stranger, and the **f**, and the widow, 3490
16:14 the stranger, and the **f**, and the widow, 3490
24:17 the judgment of the stranger, *nor* of the **f**; 3490
24:19 the stranger, for the **f**, and for the widow: 3490
24:20 the stranger, for the **f**, and for the widow. 3490
24:21 the stranger, for the **f**, and for the widow. 3490
26:12 the stranger, the **f**, and the widow, 3490
26:13 the stranger, to the **f**, and to the widow, 3490
27:19 the judgment of the stranger, **f**, and widow. 3490
Job 6:27 ye overwhelm the **f**, and you dig *a pit* for 3490
22: 9 and the arms of the **f** have been broken. 3490
24: 3 They drive away the ass of the **f**, they take 3490
24: 9 They pluck the **f** from the breast, and take a 3490
29:12 the **f**, and *him that had* none to help him. 3490
31:17 and the **f** hath not eaten thereof; 3490
31:21 If I have lift up my hand against the **f**, 3490
Ps 10:14 unto thee; thou art the helper of the **f**. 3490
10:18 To judge the **f** and the oppressed, that 3490
68: 5 A father of the **f**, and a judge of 3490
82: 3 Defend the poor and **f**: do justice to 3490
94: 6 and the stranger, and murder the **f**. 3490
109: 9 Let his children be **f**, and his wife a widow. 3490
109:12 let there be any to favour his **f children**. 3490
146: 9 the strangers; he relieveth the **f** and widow: 3490
Pr 23:10 and enter not into the fields of the **f**: 3490
Isa 1:17 judge the **f**, plead for the widow. 3490
1:23 they judge not the **f**, neither doth the cause 3490
9:17 neither shall have mercy on their **f** and 3490
10: 2 be their prey, and *that* they may rob the **f**. 3490
Jer 5:28 the cause of the **f**, yet they prosper; 3490
7: 6 the **f**, and the widow, and shed not innocent 3490
22: 3 to the stranger, the **f**, nor the widow, 3490
49:11 Leave thy **f children**, I will preserve *them* 3490
La 5: 3 We are orphans and **f**, our mothers *are* as 1+369
Eze 22: 7 in thee have they vexed the **f** and 3490
Hos 14: 3 our gods: for in thee the **f** findeth mercy. 3490
Zec 7:10 nor the **f**, the stranger, nor the poor; 3490
Mal 3: 5 the **f**, and that turn aside the stranger *from* 3490
Jas 1:27 To visit the **f** and widows in their affliction, *3737*

FATHERS (538) [FATHER]
Ge 15:15 thou shalt go to thy **f** in peace; thou shalt be 1
31: 3 Return unto the land of thy **f**, and to thy 1
46:34 youth even until now, both we, *and* also our **f**: 1
47: 3 servants *are* shepherds, both we, *and* also our **f**. 1
47: 9 the life of my **f** in the days of their pilgrimage. 1
47:30 I will lie with my **f**, and thou shalt carry me out 1
48:15 before whom my **f** Abraham and Isaac did 1
48:16 and the name of my **f** Abraham and Isaac; 1
48:21 and bring you again unto the land of your **f**. 1
49:29 bury me with my **f** in the cave that *is* in 1
Ex 3:13 The God of your **f** hath sent me unto you; 1
3:15 The LORD God of your **f**, the God of 1
3:16 and say unto them, The LORD God of your **f**, 1
4: 5 may believe that the LORD God of their **f**, 1
6:25 these *are* the heads of the **f** of the Levites 1
10: 6 which neither thy **f**, nor thy fathers' fathers 1
10: 6 neither thy fathers, nor thy fathers' **f** have seen, 1
12: 3 according to the house of *their* **f**, a lamb for a 1
13: 5 which he sware unto thy **f** to give thee, 1
13:11 as he sware unto thee and to thy **f**, and 1
20: 5 visiting the iniquity of the **f** upon the children 1
34: 7 visiting the iniquity of the **f** upon the children, 1
Lev 25:41 and unto the possession of his **f** shall he return. 1
26:39 also in the iniquities of their **f** shall they pine 1
26:40 their iniquity, and the iniquity of their **f**, 1
Nu 1: 2 after their families, by the house of their **f**, 1
1: 4 every one head of the house of his **f**. 1
1:16 princes of the tribes of their **f**, heads of 1
1:18 by the house of their **f**, according to the number 1
1:20 after their families, by the house of their **f**, 1
1:22 after their families, by the house of their **f**, 1
1:24 after their families, by the house of their **f**, 1
1:26 after their families, by the house of their **f**, 1
1:28 after their families, by the house of their **f**, 1
1:30 after their families, by the house of their **f**, 1
1:32 after their families, by the house of their **f**, 1
1:34 after their families, by the house of their **f**, 1
1:36 after their families, by the house of their **f**, 1
1:38 after their families, by the house of their **f**, 1
1:40 after their families, by the house of their **f**, 1
1:42 after their families, by the house of their **f**, 1
1:44 each one was for the house of his **f**. 1
1:45 by the house of their **f**, from twenty years old 1
1:47 the Levites after the tribe of their **f** were not 1
2:32 of the children of Israel by the house of their **f**: 1
2:34 their families, according to the house of their **f**. 1
3:15 the children of Levi after the house of their **f**, 1
3:20 of the Levites according to the house of their **f**. 1
4: 2 after their families, by the house of their **f**, 1
4:22 throughout the houses of their **f**, by their 1
4:29 after their families, by the house of their **f**; 1
4:34 their families, and after the house of their **f**, 1
Nu 4:38 their families, and by the house of their **f**, 1
4:40 by the house of their **f**, were two thousand and 1
4:42 their families, by the house of their **f**, 1
4:46 their families, and after the house of their **f**, 1
7: 2 princes of Israel, heads of the house of their **f**, 1
11:12 unto the land which thou swarest unto their **f**? 1
13: 2 of every tribe of their **f** shall ye send a man, 1
14:18 of the **f** upon the children unto the third 1
14:23 not see the land which I sware unto their **f**, 1
17: 2 of them a rod according to the house of *their* **f**, 1
17: 2 according to the house of their **f** twelve rods: 1
17: 3 rod *shall be* for the head of the house of their **f**. 1
20:15 How our **f** went down into Egypt, and we have 1
20:15 and the Egyptians vexed us, and our **f**: 1
26:55 according to the names of the tribes of their **f** 1
31:26 the priest, and the chief **f** of the congregation: 1
32: 8 Thus did your **f**, when I sent them from 1
32:28 the chief **f** of the tribes of the children of Israel: 1
33:54 according to the tribes of your **f** ye shall 1
34:14 of Reuben according to the house of their **f**, 1
34:14 of Gad according to the house of their **f**, 1
36: 1 the chief **f** of the families of the children of 1
36: 1 the princes, the chief **f** of the children of Israel: 1
36: 3 be taken from the inheritance of our **f**, 1
36: 4 away from the inheritance of the tribe of our **f**. 1
36: 7 himself to the inheritance of the tribe of his **f**. 1
36: 8 may enjoy every man the inheritance of his **f**. 1
Dt 1: 8 the land which the LORD sware unto your **f**, 1
1:11 (The LORD God of your **f** make you a 1
1:21 possess *it*, as the LORD God of thy **f** hath said 1
1:35 good land, which I sware to give unto your **f**, 1
4: 1 which the LORD God of your **f** giveth you. 1
4:31 nor forget the covenant of thy **f** which he sware 1
4:37 because he loved thy **f**, therefore he chose their 1
5: 3 The LORD made not this covenant with our **f**, 1
5: 9 visiting the iniquity of the **f** upon the children 1
6: 3 as the LORD God of thy **f** hath promised thee, 1
6:10 thee into the land which he swore unto thy **f**, 1
6:18 good land which the LORD sware unto thy **f**, 1
6:23 to give us the land which he sware unto our **f**. 1
7: 8 keep the oath which he had sworn unto your **f**, 1
7:12 and the mercy which he sware unto thy **f**: 1
7:13 in the land which he sware unto thy **f** to give 1
8: 1 the land which the LORD sware unto your **f**. 1
8: 3 thou knewest not, neither did thy **f** know; 1
8:16 which thy **f** knew not, that he might humble 1
8:18 his covenant which he sware unto thy **f**, 1
9: 5 the word which the LORD sware unto thy **f**, 1
10:11 which I sware unto their **f** to give unto them. 1
10:15 Only the LORD had a delight in thy **f** to love 1
10:22 Thy **f** went down into Egypt with threescore 1
11: 9 which the LORD sware unto your **f** to give 1
11:21 the land which the LORD sware unto your **f** 1
12: 1 which the LORD God of thy **f** giveth thee to 1
13: 6 which thou hast not known, thou, nor thy **f**; 1
13:17 and multiply thee, as he hath sworn unto thy **f**; 1
19: 8 as he hath sworn unto thy **f**, and give thee all 1
19: 8 the land which he promised to give unto thy **f**; 1
24:16 The **f** shall not be put to death for the children, 1
24:16 shall the children be put to death for the **f**: 1
26: 3 the LORD sware unto our **f** for to give us. 1
26: 7 when we cried unto the LORD God of our **f**, 1
26:15 as thou swarest unto our **f**, a land that floweth 1
27: 3 as the LORD God of thy **f** hath promised thee. 1
28:11 in the land which the LORD sware unto thy **f** 1
28:36 unto a nation which neither thou nor thy **f** have 1
28:64 which neither thou nor thy **f** have known, 1
29:13 and as he hath sworn unto thy **f**, to Abraham, 1
29:25 the covenant of the LORD God of their **f**, 1
30: 5 bring thee into the land which thy **f** possessed, 1
30: 5 do thee good, and multiply thee above thy **f**. 1
30: 9 over thee for good, as he rejoiced over thy **f**: 1
30:20 in the land which the LORD sware unto thy **f**, 1
31: 7 LORD hath sworn unto their **f** to give them; 1
31:16 Behold, thou shalt sleep with thy **f**; 1
31:20 them into the land which I sware unto their **f**, 1
32:17 *that* came newly up, whom your **f** feared not. 1
Jos 1: 6 which I sware unto their **f** to give them. 1
4: 6 *that* when your children ask *their* **f** in time NIH
4:21 When your children shall ask their **f** in time to 1
5: 6 which the LORD sware unto their **f** that he 1
14: 1 the heads of the **f** of the tribes of the children of 1
18: 3 which the LORD God of your **f** hath given 1
19:51 the heads of the **f** of the tribes of the children of 1
21: 1 came near the heads of the **f** of the Levites unto 1
21: 1 unto the heads of the **f** of the tribes of 1
21:43 all the land which he sware to give unto their **f**; 1
21:44 according to all that he sware unto their **f**: 1
22:14 each one *was* a head of the house of their **f** 1
22:28 which our **f** made, not for burnt offerings, 1
24: 2 Your **f** dwelt on the *other* side of the flood in 1
24: 6 I brought your **f** out of Egypt: and you came 1
24: 6 the Egyptians pursued after your **f** with chariots 1
24:14 put away the gods which your **f** served on 1
24:15 whether the gods which your **f** served that *were* 1
24:17 us up and our **f** out of the land of Egypt, 1
Jdg 2: 1 you unto the land which I sware unto your **f**; 1
2:10 all that generation were gathered unto their **f**: 1
2:12 And they forsook the LORD God of their **f**, 1
2:17 quickly out of the way which their **f** walked in, 1
2:19 and corrupted *themselves* more than their **f**, 1
2:20 my covenant which I commanded their **f**, 1
2:22 to walk therein, as their **f** did keep *it*, or not. 1
3: 4 which he commanded their **f** by the hand of 1
6:13 where *be* all his miracles which our **f** told us of, 1
21:22 when their **f** or their brethren come unto us to 1
1Sa 12: 6 that brought your **f** up out of the land of Egypt. 1
12: 7 the LORD, which he did to you and to your **f**. 1
12: 8 your **f** cried unto the LORD, then the LORD 1
12: 8 which brought forth your **f** out of Egypt, and 1
12:15 be against you, as *it was* against your **f**. 1
2Sa 7:12 thou shalt sleep with thy **f**, I will set up thy 1
1Ki 1:21 when my lord the king shall sleep with his **f**, 1
2:10 So David slept with his **f**, and was buried in 1
8: 1 the chief of the **f** of the children of Israel, 1
1Ki 8:21 of the LORD, which he made with our **f**, 1
8:34 unto the land which thou gavest unto their **f**. 1
8:40 live in the land which thou gavest unto our **f**. 1
8:48 which thou gavest unto their **f**, the city which 1
8:53 when thou broughtest our **f** out of Egypt, 1
8:57 our God be with us, as he was with our **f**: 1
8:58 and his judgments, which he commanded our **f**. 1
9: 9 who brought forth their **f** out of the land of 1
11:21 heard in Egypt that David slept with his **f**, 1
11:43 Solomon slept with his **f**, and was buried in 1
13:22 shall not come unto the sepulchre of thy **f**. 1
14:15 which he gave to their **f**, and shall scatter them 1
14:20 he slept with his **f**, and Nadab his son reigned 1
14:22 had committed, above all that their **f** had done. 1
14:31 Rehoboam slept with his **f**, and was buried with 1
14:31 and was buried with his **f** in the city of David. 1
15: 8 Abijam slept with his **f**; and they buried him in 1
15:12 and removed all the idols that his **f** had made. 1
15:24 Asa slept with his **f**, and was buried with his 1
15:24 was buried with his **f** in the city of David his 1
16: 6 So Baasha slept with his **f**, and was buried in 1
16:28 So Omri slept with his **f**, and was buried in 1
19: 4 away my life; for I *am* not better than my **f**. 1
21: 3 that I should give the inheritance of my **f** unto 1
21: 4 I will not give thee the inheritance of my **f**. 1
22:40 So Ahab slept with his **f**; and Ahaziah his son 1
22:50 Jehoshaphat slept with his **f**, and was buried 1
22:50 was buried with his **f** in the city of David his 1
2Ki 8:24 Joram slept with his **f**, and was buried with his 1
8:24 and was buried with his **f** in the city of David: 1
9:28 buried him in his sepulchre with his **f** in 1
10:35 Jehu slept with his **f**: and they buried him in 1
12:18 Jehoram, and Ahaziah, his **f**, kings of Judah, 1
12:21 they buried him with his **f** in the city of David: 1
13: 9 Jehoahaz slept with his **f**; and they buried him 1
13:13 Joash slept with his **f**; and Jeroboam sat upon 1
14: 6 The **f** shall not be put to death for the children, 1
14: 6 nor the children be put to death for the **f**; 1
14:16 Jehoash slept with his **f**, and was buried in 1
14:20 he was buried at Jerusalem with his **f** in the city 1
14:22 it to Judah, after that the king slept with his **f**. 1
14:29 Jeroboam slept with his **f**, *even* with the kings 1
15: 7 So Azariah slept with his **f**; and they buried 1
15: 7 they buried him with his **f** in the city of David: 1
15: 9 in the sight of the LORD, as his **f** had done: 1
15:22 Menahem slept with his **f**; and Pekahiah his 1
15:38 Jotham slept with his **f**, and was buried with his 1
15:38 was buried with his **f** in the city of David his 1
16:20 Ahaz slept with his **f**, and was buried with his 1
16:20 and was buried with his **f** in the city of David: 1
17:13 to all the law which I commanded your **f**, 1
17:14 hardened their necks, like to the neck of their **f**, 1
17:15 and his covenant that he made with their **f**, and 1
17:41 as did their **f**, *so* do they unto this day. 1
19:12 delivered them which my **f** have destroyed; 1
20:17 *that* which thy **f** have laid up in store unto this 1
20:21 Hezekiah slept with his **f**: and Manasseh his 1
21: 8 any more out of the land which I gave their **f**; 1
21:15 since the day their **f** came forth out of Egypt, 1
21:18 Manasseh slept with his **f**, and was buried in 1
21:22 And he forsook the LORD God of his **f**, and 1
22:13 our **f** have not hearkened unto the words of this 1
22:20 I will gather thee unto thy **f**, and thou shalt be 1
23:32 according to all that his **f** had done. 1
23:37 according to all that his **f** had done. 1
24: 6 So Jehoiakim slept with his **f**: and 1
1Ch 4:38 and the house of their **f** increased greatly. 1
5:13 their brethren of the house of their **f** *were*, 1
5:15 the son of Guni, chief of the house of their **f**. 1
5:24 these *were* the heads of the house of their **f**, 1
5:24 famous men, *and* heads of the house of their **f**. 1
5:25 they transgressed against the God of their **f**, 1
6:19 the families of the Levites according to their **f**. 1
7: 4 by their generations, after the house of their **f**, 1
7: 7 heads of the house of *their* **f**, mighty *men* of 1
7: 9 heads of the house of their **f**, mighty *men* of 1
7:11 by the heads of *their* **f**, mighty *men* of valour, 1
8: 6 these *are* the heads of the **f** of the inhabitants of 1
8:10 These *were* his sons, heads of the **f**. 1
8:13 who *were* heads of the **f** of the inhabitants of 1
8:28 These *were* heads of the **f**, by their generations, 1
9: 9 All these men *were* chief of the **f** in the house 1
9: 9 *were* chief of the fathers in the house of their **f**. 1
9:13 heads of the house of their **f**, a thousand and 1
9:19 and their **f**, *being* over the host of the LORD, 1
9:33 *are* the singers, chief of the **f** of the Levites, 1
9:34 These chief **f** of the Levites *were* chief 1
12:17 the God of our **f** look *thereon*, and rebuke *it*. 1
12:30 famous throughout the house of their **f**. 1
15:12 Ye *are* the chief of the **f** of the Levites: 1
17:11 be expired that *thou* must go *to be* with thy **f**, 1
23: 9 three. These *were* the chief of the **f** of Laadan. 1
23:24 *were* the sons of Levi after the house of their **f**; 1
23:24 *even* the chief of the **f**, as they were counted by 1
24: 4 *were* sixteen chief *men* of the house of *their* **f**, 1
24: 4 of Ithamar according to the house of their **f**. 1
24: 6 and *before* the chief of the **f** of the priests and 1
24:30 sons of the Levites after the house of their **f**. 1
24:31 and the chief of the **f** of the priests and Levites, 1
24:31 *even* the principal **f** over against their younger 1
26:13 according to the house of their **f**, for every gate. 1
26:21 chief **f**, *even* of Laadan the Gershonite, 1
26:26 and the chief **f**, the captains over thousands and 1
26:31 according to the generations of his **f**. 1
26:32 *were* two thousand and seven hundred chief **f**, 1
27: 1 *to wit*, the chief **f** and captains of thousands 1
29: 6 the chief of the **f** and princes of the tribes of 1
29:15 before thee, and sojourners, as *were* all our **f**: 1
29:18 God of Abraham, Isaac, and of Israel, our **f**, 1
29:20 blessed the LORD God of their **f**, 1
2Ch 1: 2 every governor in all Israel, the chief of the **f**. 1
5: 2 the chief of the **f** of the children of Israel, 1
6:25 land which thou gavest to them and to their **f**. 1
6:31 live in the land which thou gavest unto our **f**. 1
6:38 which thou gavest unto their **f**, and *toward* 1

F

2Ch 7:22 they forsook the LORD God of their f, 1
9:31 Solomon slept with his f, and he was buried in 1
11:16 to sacrifice unto the LORD God of their f. 1
12:16 Rehoboam slept with his f, and was buried in 1
13:12 fight ye not against the LORD God of your f; 1
13:18 they relied upon the LORD God of their f. 1
14: 1 So Abijah slept with his f, and they buried him 1
14: 4 Judah to seek the LORD God of their f, 1
15:12 the LORD God of their f with all their heart 1
16:13 And Asa slept with his f, and died in the one 1
17:14 of them according to the house of their f: 1
19: 4 them back unto the LORD God of their f. 1
19: 8 *of* the priests, and of the chief of the f of Israel, 1
20: 6 said, O LORD God of our f, *art* not thou God 1
20:33 prepared their hearts unto the God of their f. 1
21: 1 Now Jehoshaphat slept with his f, and 1
21: 1 and was buried with his f in the city of David. 1
21:10 he had forsaken the LORD God of his f. 1
21:19 no burning for him, like the burning of his f. 1
23: 2 the chief of the f of Israel, and they came to 1
24:18 left the house of the LORD God of their f, 1
24:24 they had forsaken the LORD God of their f. 1
25: 4 saying, The f shall not die for the children, 1
25: 4 neither shall the children die for the f, but 1
25: 5 according to the houses of *their* f, 1
25:28 and buried him with his f in the city of Judah. 1
26: 2 it to Judah, after that the king slept with his f. 1
26:12 The whole number of the chief of the f of 1
26:23 So Uzziah slept with his f, and they buried him 1
26:23 they buried him with his f in the field of 1
27: 9 Jotham slept with his f, and they buried him in 1
28: 6 they had forsaken the LORD God of their f. 1
28: 9 the LORD God of your f was wroth with 1
28:25 provoked to anger the LORD God of his f. 1
28:27 Ahaz slept with his f, and they buried him in 1
29: 5 the house of the LORD God of your f, 1
29: 6 For our f have trespassed, and done *that* which 1
29: 9 our f have fallen by the sword, and our sons 1
30: 7 be not ye like your f, and like your brethren, 1
30: 7 trespassed against the LORD God of their f, 1
30: 8 as your f *were, but* yield yourselves unto 1
30:19 his heart to seek God, the LORD God of his f, 1
30:22 confession to the LORD God of their f. 1
31:17 genealogy of the priests by the house of their f, 1
32:13 my f have done unto all the people of *other* 1
32:14 of those nations that my f utterly destroyed, 1
32:15 out of mine hand, and out of the hand of my f: 1
32:33 Hezekiah slept with his f, and they buried him 1
33: 8 of the land which I have appointed for your f; 1
33:12 himself greatly before the God of his f, 1
33:20 So Manasseh slept with his f, and they buried 1
34:21 our f have not kept the word of the LORD, 1
34:28 I will gather thee to thy f, and thou shalt be 1
34:32 to the covenant of God, the God of their f. 1
34:33 from following the LORD, the God of their f. 1
35: 4 prepare *yourselves* by the houses of your f, 1
35: 5 families of the f of your brethren the people, 1
35:24 was buried in *one of the* sepulchres of his f. 1
36:15 the LORD God of their f sent to them by his 1
Ezr 1: 5 rose up the chief of the f of Judah and 1
2:68 *some* of the chief of the f, when they came to 1
3:12 of the priests and Levites and chief of the f, 1
4: 2 and to the chief of the f, and said unto them, 1
4: 3 and the rest of the chief of the f of Israel, 1
4:15 be made in the book of the records of thy f: 2
5:12 after that our f had provoked the God of heaven 2
7:27 Blessed *be* the LORD God of our f, 1
8: 1 These *are* now the chief of their f, and *this is* 1
8:28 offering unto the LORD God of your f. 1
8:29 and the Levites, and chief of the f of Israel, 1
9: 7 Since the days of our f *have* we *been* in a great 1
10:11 confession unto the LORD God of your f, 1
10:16 And Ezra the priest, *with* certain chief of the f, 1
10:16 after the house of their f, and all of them by 1
Ne 7:70 some of the chief of the f gave unto the work. 1
7:71 *some* of the chief of the f gave to the treasure 1
8:13 together the chief of the f of all the people, 1
9: 2 their sins, and the iniquities of their f. 1
9: 9 And didst see the affliction of our f in Egypt, 1
9:16 they and our f dealt proudly, and hardened their 1
9:23 which thou hadst promised to their f, 1
9:32 and on our f, and on all thy people, 1
9:34 our princes, our priests, nor our f, kept thy law, 1
9:36 *for* the land that thou gavest unto our f to eat 1
10:34 after the houses of our f, at times appointed 1
11:13 his brethren, chief of the f, two hundred forty 1
12:12 days of Joiakim were priests, the chief of the f: 1
12:22 and Jaddua, *were* recorded chief of the f: 1
12:23 The sons of Levi, the chief of the f, 1
13:18 Did not your f thus, and *did not* our God bring 1
Job 8: 8 and prepare *thyself* to the search of their f: 1
15:18 Which wise *men* have told from their f, and 1
30: 1 whose f I would have disdained to have set 1
Ps 22: 4 Our f trusted in thee: they trusted, and 1
39:12 with thee, *and* a sojourner, as all my f *were*. 1
44: 1 heard with our ears, O God, our f have told us, 1
45:16 Instead of thy f shall be thy children, 1
49:19 He shall go to the generation of his f; they shall 1
78: 3 have heard and known, and our f have told us. 1
78: 5 a law in Israel, which he commanded our f, 1
78: 8 might not be as their f, a stubborn and 1
78:12 Marvellous things did he in the sight of their f, 1
78:57 turned *back*, and dealt unfaithfully like their f: 1
95: 9 When your f tempted me, proved me, and 1
106: 6 We have sinned with our f, we have committed 1
106: 7 Our f understood not thy wonders in Egypt; 1
109:14 Let the iniquity of his f be remembered with 1
Pr 17: 6 old men; and the glory of children *are* their f. 1
19:14 House and riches *are* the inheritance of f: and 1
22:28 not the ancient landmark, which thy f have set. 1
Isa 14:21 for his children for the iniquity of their f; 1
37:12 delivered them which my f have destroyed, 1
39: 6 *that* which thy f have laid up in store until this 1
49:23 kings shall be thy **nursing** f, and 539
64:11 our beautiful house, where our f praised thee, 1

Isa 65: 7 and the iniquities of your f together, 1
Jer 2: 5 What iniquity have your f found in me, 1
3:18 that I have given for an inheritance unto your f. 1
3:24 For shame hath devoured the labour of our f 1
3:25 we and our f, from our youth even unto this 1
6:21 the f and the sons together shall fall upon them; 1
7: 7 in the land that I gave to your f, for ever and 1
7:14 the place which I gave to you and to your f, 1
7:18 the f kindle the fire, and the women knead *their* 1
7:22 For I spake not unto your f, nor commanded 1
7:25 Since the day that your f came forth out of 1
7:26 their neck: they did worse than their f. 1
9:14 and after Baalim, which their f taught them: 1
9:16 whom neither they nor their f have known: 1
11: 4 Which I commanded your f in the day that I 1
11: 5 the oath which I have sworn unto your f, 1
11: 7 For I earnestly protested unto your f in the day 1
11:10 broken my covenant which I made with their f. 1
13:14 even the f and the sons together, saith 1
14:20 our wickedness, *and* the iniquity of our f: 1
16: 3 concerning their f that begat them in this land; 1
16:11 Because your f have forsaken me, saith 1
16:12 ye have done worse than your f; for behold, 1
16:13 a land that ye know not, *neither* ye nor your f; 1
16:15 again into their land that I gave unto their f. 1
16:19 Surely our f have inherited lies, vanity, and 1
17:22 ye the sabbath day, as I commanded your f. 1
19: 4 whom neither they nor their f have known, nor 1
23:27 as their f have forgotten my name for Baal. 1
23:39 the city that I gave you and your f, *and cast you* 1
24:10 off the land that I gave unto them and to their f. 1
25: 5 given unto you and to your f for ever and ever: 1
30: 3 them to return to the land that I gave to their f, 1
31:29 The f have eaten a sour grape, and 1
31:32 their f in the day *that* I took them by the hand, 1
32:18 recompensest the iniquity of the f into 1
32:22 which thou didst swear to their f to give them, 1
34: 5 with the burnings of thy f, the former kings 1
34:13 I made a covenant with your f in the day that I 1
34:14 your f hearkened not unto me, neither inclined 1
35:15 land which I have given to you and to your f: 1
44: 3 they knew not, *neither* they, you, nor your f. 1
44: 9 Have ye forgotten the wickedness of your f, 1
44:10 that I set before you and before your f. 1
44:17 we, and our f, our kings, and our princes, 1
44:21 ye, and your f, your kings, and your princes, 1
47: 3 the f shall not look back to *their* children for 1
50: 7 of justice, even the LORD, the hope of their f. 1
La 5: 7 Our f have sinned, *and are* not; *and* we have 1
Eze 2: 3 they and their f have transgressed against me, 1
5:10 Therefore the f shall eat the sons in the midst 1
5:10 the midst of thee, and the sons shall eat their f; 1
18: 2 The f have eaten sour grapes, and 1
20: 4 them to know the abominations of their f: 1
20:18 Walk ye not in the statutes of your f, 1
20:27 Yet *in* this your f have blasphemed me, in that 1
20:30 Are ye polluted after the manner of your f? 1
20:36 Like as I pleaded with your f in the wilderness 1
20:42 which I lifted up mine hand to give it to your f. 1
36:28 ye shall dwell in the land that I gave to your f; 1
37:25 Jacob my servant, wherein your f have dwelt; 1
47:14 I lifted up mine hand to give it unto your f: 1
Da 2:23 and praise thee, O thou God of my f, 2
9: 6 and our f, and to all the people of the land. 1
9: 8 to our f, because we have sinned against thee. 1
9:16 and for the iniquities of our f, Jerusalem and 1
11:24 and he shall do *that* which his f have not done, 1
11:24 his fathers have not done, nor his fathers' f; 1
11:37 Neither shall he regard the God of his f, nor 1
11:38 a god whom his f knew not shall he honour 1
Hos 9:10 I saw your f as the firstripe in the fig tree at her 1
Joel 1: 2 in your days, or even in the days of your f? 1
Am 2: 4 to err, after the which their f have walked: 1
Mic 7:20 which thou hast sworn unto our f from the days 1
Zec 1: 2 LORD hath been sore displeased with your f. 1
1: 4 Be ye not as your f, unto whom the former 1
1: 5 Your f, where *are* they? and the prophets, do 1
1: 6 the prophets, did they not take hold of your f? 1
8:14 when your f provoked me to wrath, saith 1
Mal 2:10 his brother, by profaning the covenant of our f? 1
3: 7 Even from the days of your f ye are gone away 1
4: 6 he shall turn the heart of the f to the children, 1
4: 6 the heart of the children to their f, lest I come 1
Mt 23:30 If we had been in the days of our f, *3962*
23:32 Fill ye up then the measure of your f. *3962*
Lk 1:17 to turn the hearts of the f to the children, *3962*
1:55 (As he spake to our f), to Abraham, and *3962*
1:72 To perform the mercy *promised* to our f, *3962*
6:23 for in the like manner did their f unto *3962*
6:26 for so did their f to the false prophets. *3962*
11:47 of the prophets, and your f killed them. *3962*
11:48 witness that ye allow the deeds of your f: *3962*
Jn 4:20 Our f worshipped in this mountain; and *3962*
6:31 Our f did eat manna in the desert; as it is *3962*
6:49 Your f did eat manna in the wilderness, and *3962*
6:58 not as your f did eat manna, and are dead: *3962*
7:22 not because it is of Moses, but of the f; *3962*
Ac 3:13 and of Isaac, and of Jacob, the God of our f, *3962*
3:22 For Moses truly said unto the f, A prophet *3962*
3:25 the covenant which God made with our f, *3962*
5:30 The God of our f raised up Jesus, whom ye *3962*
7: 2 And he said, Men, brethren, and f, hearken; *3962*
7:11 and our f found no sustenance. *3962*
7:12 was corn in Egypt, he sent out our f first. *3962*
7:15 down into Egypt, and died, he, and our f, *3962*
7:19 and evil entreated our f, so that *they* cast *3962*
7:32 *Saying*, I *am* the God of thy f, the God of *3962*
7:38 to him in the mount Sina, and *with* our f: *3962*
7:39 To whom our f would not obey, *3962*
7:44 Our f had the tabernacle of Witness in *3962*
7:45 Which also our f that came after brought in *3962*
7:45 God drave out before the face of our f, *3962*
7:51 the Holy Ghost: as your f *did*, so *do* ye. *3962*
7:52 Which of the prophets have not your f *3962*
13:17 God of this people of Israel chose our f, *3962*

Ac 13:32 the promise which was made unto the f, *3962*
13:36 and was laid unto his f, and saw corruption: *3962*
15:10 which neither our f nor we were able to *3962*
22: 1 Men, brethren, and f, hear ye my defence *3962*
22: 3 to the perfect manner of the law of the f, *3971*
22:14 he said, The God of our f hath chosen thee, *3962*
24:14 call heresy, so worship I the God of my f, *3971*
26: 6 of the promise made of God unto *our* f: *3962*
28:17 against the people, or customs of our f, *3971*
28:25 Ghost by Esaias the prophet unto our f, *3962*
Ro 9: 5 Whose *are* the f, and of whom as *3962*
15: 8 to confirm the promises made unto the f: *3962*
1Co 4:15 in Christ, yet *have ye* not many f: *3962*
10: 1 how that all our f were under the cloud, and *3962*
Gal 1:14 zealous of the traditions of my f. *3967*
Eph 6: 4 And, ye f, provoke not your children to *3962*
Col 3:21 F, provoke not your children *to anger*, lest *3962*
1Ti 1: 9 for **murderers of** f and murderers of *3964*
Heb 1: 1 in time past unto the f by the prophets, *3962*
3: 9 When your f tempted me, proved me, and *3962*
8: 9 f in the day when I took them by the hand *3962*
12: 9 Furthermore we have had f of our flesh *3962*
1Pe 1:18 **received by tradition from** your f; *3970*
2Pe 3: 4 for since the f fell asleep, all *things* *3962*
1Jn 2:13 f, because ye have known him that is from *3962*
2:14 f, because ye have known him that is from *3962*

FATHERS' (14) [FATHER]

Ex 6:14 These *be* the heads of their f houses: The sons 1
10: 6 neither thy fathers, nor thy f fathers have seen, 1
Nu 17: 6 according to their f houses, *even* twelve rods: 1
26: 2 years old and upward, throughout their f house, 1
32:14 behold, ye are risen up in your f stead, 1
1Ch 7: 2 Jibsam, and Shemuel, heads of their f house, 1
7:40 heads of *their* f house, choice *and* mighty *men* 1
Ezr 2:59 they could not shew their f house, and 1
Ne 2: 3 the place of my f sepulchres, *lieth* waste, and 1
2: 5 unto the city of my f sepulchres, that I may 1
7:61 they could not shew their f house, nor their 1
Eze 20:24 and their eyes were after their f idols. 1
Da 11:24 his fathers have not done, nor his f fathers; 1
Ro 11:28 *they are* beloved for the f sakes. *3962*

FATHOMS (2)

Ac 27:28 And sounded, and found *it* twenty f: and *3712*
27:28 they sounded again, and found *it* fifteen f. *3712*

FATLING (1) [FAT]

Isa 11: 6 and the young lion and the f together; 4806

FATLINGS (5) [FAT]

1Sa 15: 9 of the f, and the lambs, and all *that was* 4932
2Sa 6:13 gone six paces, he sacrificed oxen and f. 4806
Ps 66:15 I will offer unto thee burnt sacrifices of f, 4220
Eze 39:18 of bullocks, all of them f of Bashan. 4806
Mt 22: 4 my oxen and *my* f *are* killed, and all *things* *4619*

FATNESS (17) [FAT]

Ge 27:28 the f of the earth, and plenty of corn and 4924
27:39 thy dwelling shall be the f of the earth, and 4924
Dt 32:15 thou art covered *with* f, then he forsook NIH
Jdg 9: 9 tree said unto them, Should I leave my f, 1880
Job 15:27 Because he covereth his face with his f, and 2459
36:16 be set on thy table *should be* full *of* f. 1880
Ps 36: 8 abundantly satisfied with the f of thy house; 1880
63: 5 shall be satisfied as *with* marrow and f; 1880
65:11 with thy goodness; and thy paths drop f. 1880
73: 7 Their eyes stand out with f: they have more 2459
109:24 through fasting; and my flesh faileth of f. 8081
Isa 17: 4 and the f of his flesh shall wax lean. 4924
34: 6 it is made fat with f, *and* with the blood of 2459
34: 7 with blood, and their dust made fat with f. 2459
55: 2 *is* good, and let your soul delight itself in f. 1880
Jer 31:14 I will satiate the soul of the priests with f, 1880
Ro 11:17 partakest of the root and f of the olive tree; *4096*

FATS (2) [FAT]

Joel 2:24 and the f shall overflow *with* wine and oil. 3342
3:13 for the press is full, the f overflow; 3342

FATTED (5) [FAT]

1Ki 4:23 and roebucks, and fallowdeer, and f fowl. 75
Jer 46:21 men *are* in the midst of her like f bullocks; 4770
Lk 15:23 And bring hither the f calf, and kill *it*; and *4618*
15:27 and thy father hath killed the f calf, *4618*
15:30 thou hast killed for him the f calf. *4618*

FATTER (1) [FAT]

Da 1:15 f in flesh than all the children which did eat 1277

FATTEST (2) [FAT]

Ps 78:31 slew the f of them, and smote down 4924
Da 11:24 even upon the f **places** of the province; 4924

FAULT (19) [FAULTLESS, FAULTS, FAULTY]

Ex 5:16 *are* beaten; but the f *is* in thine own people. 2398
Dt 25: 2 according to his f, by a *certain* number. 7564
1Sa 29: 3 I have found no f in him since he fell *unto* NIH
2Sa 3: 8 that thou chargest me to day with a f 5771
Ps 59: 4 and prepare themselves without *my* f: 5771
Da 6: 4 they could find none occasion nor f; 7844
6: 4 was there any error or f found in him. 7844
Mt 18:15 go and **tell** him his f between thee and *1651*
Mk 7: 2 to say, with unwashen, hands, they **found** f. *3201*
Lk 23: 4 and *to* the people, I find no f in this man. *158*
23:14 have found no f in this man *touching those* *158*
Jn 18:38 and saith unto them, I find in him no f *at all*. *156*
19: 4 that ye may know that I find no f in him. *156*
19: 6 and crucify *him*: for I find no f in him. *156*
Ro 9:19 then unto me, Why doth he yet **find** f? *3201*
1Co 6: 7 therefore there is utterly a f among you, *2275*
Gal 6: 1 Brethren, if a man be overtaken in a f, *3900*
Heb 8: 8 For **finding** f **with** them, he saith, Behold, *3201*
Rev 14: 5 for they are **without** f before the throne of *299*

FAULTLESS (2) [FAULT]
Heb 8: 7 For if that first *covenant* had been **f**, *then* *273*
Jude 1:24 to present *you* **f** before the presence of his *299*

FAULTS (4) [FAULT]
Ge 41: 9 I do remember my **f** *this* day: 2399
Ps 19:12 *his* errors? cleanse thou me from secret *f.* NIH
Jas 5:16 Confess *your* **f** one to another, and pray one *3900*
1Pe 2:20 glory *is it,* if, when ye be buffeted for your **f**, *264*

FAULTY (2) [FAULT]
2Sa 14:13 king doth speak this thing as one **which is f**, 818
Hos 10: 2 heart is divided; now shall they be **found f**: 816

FAVORITISM See RESPECTER

FAVOUR (70) [FAVOURABLE, FAVOURED, FAVOUREDNESS, FAVOUREST, FAVOURETH, WELLFAVOURED]
Ge 18: 3 My Lord, if now I have found **f** in thy sight, 2580
30:27 I pray thee, if I have found **f** in thine eyes, 2580
39:21 gave him **f** in the sight of the keeper of 2580
Ex 3:21 I will give this people **f** in the sight of 2580
11: 3 the LORD gave the people **f** in the sight of 2580
12:36 the LORD gave the people **f** in the sight of 2580
Nu 11:11 wherefore have I not found **f** in thy sight, 2580
11:15 out of hand, if I have found **f** in thy sight; 2580
Dt 24: 1 it come to pass that she find no **f** in his 2580
28:50 person of the old, nor **shew f** to the young: 2603
33:23 satisfied with **f**, and full *with* the blessing 7522
Jos 11:20 *and* that they might have no **f**, but that *he* 8467
Ru 2:13 Let me find **f** in thy sight, my lord; 2580
1Sa 2:26 was **in f** both with the LORD, and 2896
16:22 before me; for he hath found **f** in my sight. 2580
20:29 and now, if I have found **f** in thine eyes, 2580
25: 8 Wherefore let the young men find **f** in thine 2580
29: 6 the lords **f** thee not. 2896+5869+871.1
2Sa 15:25 if I shall find **f** in the eyes of the LORD, 2580
1Ki 11:19 Hadad found great **f** in the sight of Pharaoh, 2580
Ne 2: 5 and if thy servant have **found f** in thy sight, 3190
Est 2:15 Esther obtained **f** in the sight of all them 2580
2:17 and **f** in his sight more than all the virgins; 2617
5: 2 in the court, *that* she obtained **f** in his sight: 2580
5: 8 If I have found **f** in the sight of the king, 2580
7: 3 and said, If I have found **f** in thy sight, 2580
8: 5 if I have found **f** in his sight, and the thing 2580
Job 10:12 Thou hast granted me life and **f**, and 2617
Ps 5:12 *with* **f** wilt thou compass him as *with* a 7522
30: 5 *but* a moment; in his **f** *is* life: 7522
30: 7 by thy **f** thou hast made my mountain to 7522
35:27 and be glad, that **f** my righteous cause: 2655
44: 3 because thou **hadst a f** unto them. 7521
45:12 among the people shall **intreat** thy **f**. 2470+6440
89:17 and in thy **f** our horn shall be exalted. 7522
102:13 for the time to **f** her, yea, the set time, 2603
102:14 in her stones, and **f** the dust thereof. 2603
106: 4 with the **f** *that thou bearest* unto thy people: 7522
109:12 neither let there be any to **f** his fatherless 2603
112: 5 A good man **sheweth f**, and lendeth: 2603
119:58 I intreated thy **f** with *my* whole heart: 6440
Pr 3: 4 So shalt thou find **f** and good understanding 2580
8:35 and shall obtain **f** of the LORD. 7522
11:27 He that diligently seeketh good procureth **f**: 7522
12: 2 A good *man* obtaineth **f** of the LORD: but 7522
13:15 Good understanding giveth **f**: but the way 2580
14: 9 at sin: but among the righteous *there is* **f**. 7522
14:35 The king's **f** *is* toward a wise servant: but 7522
16:15 and his **f** *is* as a cloud of the latter rain. 7522
18:22 good *thing,* and obtaineth **f** of the LORD. 7522
19: 6 Many will intreat the **f** of the prince: and 6440
19:12 of a lion; but his **f** *is* as dew upon the grass. 7522
21:10 his neighbour **findeth** no **f** in his eyes. 2603
22: 1 *and* loving **f** rather than silver and gold. 2580
28:23 afterwards shall find more **f** than he that 2580
29:26 Many seek the ruler's **f**; but *every* man's 6440
31:30 **F** *is* deceitful, and beauty *is* vain: *but* 2580
Ecc 9:11 of understanding, nor yet **f** to men of skill; 2580
SS 8:10 then was I in his eyes as one that found **f**. 7965
Isa 26:10 Let **f** be **shewed** to the wicked, *yet* will he 2603
27:11 he that formed them will **shew** them no **f**. 2603
60:10 but in my **f** have I had mercy on thee. 7522
Jer 16:13 and night; where I will not shew you **f**. 2594
Da 1: 9 Now God had brought Daniel into **f** and 2617
Lk 1:30 Mary: for thou hast found **f** with God. *5485*
2:52 and stature, and in **f** with God and man. *5485*
Ac 2:47 and having **f** with all the people. *5485*
7:10 and gave him **f** and wisdom in the sight of *5485*
7:46 Who found **f** before God, and desired to *5485*
25: 3 And desired **f** against him, that he would *5485*

FAVOURABLE (4) [FAVOUR]
Jdg 21:22 unto them, Be **f** unto them for our sakes: 2603
Job 33:26 pray unto God, and he will be **f** unto him: 7521
Ps 77: 7 cast off for ever? and will he be **f** no more? 7521
85: 1 LORD, thou hast been **f** unto thy land: 7521

FAVOURED (14) [FAVOUR]
Ge 29:17 but Rachel was beautiful and well **f**. 4758
39: 6 Joseph was *a* goodly *person,* and well **f**. 4758
41: 2 there came up out of the river seven well **f** 4758
41: 3 them out of the river, ill **f** and leanfleshed; 4758
41: 4 the ill **f** and leanfleshed kine did eat up 4758
41: 4 leanfleshed kine did eat up the seven well **f** 4758
41:18 the river seven kine, fatfleshed and well **f**; 8389
41:19 poor and very ill **f** and leanfleshed, 8389
41:20 the **ill f** kine did eat up the first seven fat 7451
41:21 but they *were still* ill **f**, as at the beginning. 4758
41:27 **ill f** kine that came up after them *are* seven 7451
La 4:16 persons of the priests, they **f** not the elders. 2603
Da 1: 4 well **f**, and skilful in all wisdom, and 4758
Lk 1:28 and said, Hail, *thou that art* **highly f**, *5487*

FAVOUREDNESS (1) [FAVOUR]
Dt 17: 1 wherein is blemish, *or* any **evil f**: 1697+7451

FAVOUREST (1) [FAVOUR]
Ps 41:11 By this I know that thou **f** me, because 2654

FAVOURETH (1) [FAVOUR]
2Sa 20:11 He that **f** Joab, and he that *is* for David, 2654

FEAR (400) [AFRAID, FEARED, FEAREST, FEARETH, FEARFUL, FEARFULLY, FEARFULNESS, FEARING, FEARS]
Ge 9: 2 the **f** of you and the dread of you shall be 4172
15: 1 Abram in a vision, saying, **F** not, Abram: 3372
20:11 Surely the **f** of God *is* not in this place; 3374
21:17 **f** not; for God hath heard the voice of 3372
26:24 **f** not, for I *am* with thee, and will bless 3372
31:42 and the **f** of Isaac, had been with me, 6343
31:53 Jacob sware by the **f** of his father Isaac. 6343
32:11 for I **f** him, lest he will come and smite me, 3373
35:17 that the midwife said unto her, **F** not; 3372
42:18 the third day, This do, and live; *for* I **f** God: 3373
43:23 he said, Peace *be* to you, **f** not: your God, 3372
46: 3 **f** not to go down into Egypt; for I will there 3372
50:19 Joseph said unto them, **F** not: for *am* I in 3372
50:21 Now therefore **f** ye not: I will nourish you 3372
Ex 9:30 I know that ye will not yet **f** the LORD 3372
14:13 **F** ye not, stand still, and see the salvation of 3372
15:16 **F** and dread shall fall upon them; by 367
18:21 such as **f** God, men of truth, 3373
20:20 Moses said unto the people, **F** not: for God 3372
20:20 that his **f** may be before your faces, that ye 3374
23:27 I will send my **f** before thee, and will destroy 367
Lev 19: 3 Ye shall **f** every man his mother, and 3372
19:14 before the blind, but shalt **f** thy God: 3372
19:32 the face of the old man, and **f** thy God: 3372
25:17 one another; but thou shalt **f** thy God: 3372
25:36 **f** thy God; that thy brother may live with 3372
25:43 over him with rigour; but shalt **f** thy God. 3372
Nu 14: 9 neither **f** ye the people of the land; 3372
14: 9 and the LORD *is* with us: **f** them not. 3372
21:34 the LORD said unto Moses, **F** him not: 3372
Dt 1:21 unto thee; **f** not, neither be discouraged. 3372
2:25 the **f** of thee upon the nations *that are* under 3374
3: 2 the LORD said unto me, **F** him not: for I 3372
3:22 Ye shall not **f** them: for the LORD your 3372
4:10 that they may learn to **f** me all the days that 3372
5:29 that they would **f** me, and keep all my 3372
6: 2 That thou mightest **f** the LORD thy God, 3372
6:13 Thou shalt **f** the LORD thy God, and 3372
6:24 to **f** the LORD our God, for our good 3372
8: 6 thy God, to walk in his ways, and to **f** him. 3372
10:12 to **f** the LORD thy God, to walk in all his 3372
10:20 Thou shalt **f** the LORD thy God; him shalt 3372
11:25 *for* the LORD your God shall lay the **f** of 6343
13: 4 **f** him, and keep his commandments, and 3372
13:11 **f**, and shall do no more any such 3372
14:23 that thou mayest learn to **f** the LORD thy 3372
17:13 and **f**, and do no more presumptuously. 3372
17:19 that he may learn to **f** the LORD his God, 3372
19:20 **f**, and shall henceforth commit no more any 3372
20: 3 **f** not, and do not tremble, neither be ye 3372
21:21 among you; and all Israel shall hear, and **f**. 3372
28:58 that *thou* mayest **f** this glorious and fearful 3372
28:66 thou shalt **f** day and night, and shalt have 6342
28:67 for the **f** of thine heart where*with* thou shalt 6343
28:67 fear of thine heart where*with* thou shalt **f**, 6342
31: 6 Be strong and of a good courage, **f** not, 3372
31: 8 forsake thee: **f** not, neither be dismayed. 3372
31:12 **f** the LORD your God, and observe to do 3372
31:13 and learn to **f** the LORD your God, 3372
Jos 4:24 that ye might **f** the LORD your God for 3372
8: 1 **F** not, neither be thou dismayed: 3372
10: 8 the LORD said unto Joshua, **F** them not: 3372
10:25 **F** not, nor be dismayed, be strong and 3372
22:24 if we have not *rather* done it for **f** of *this* 1674
24:14 Now therefore **f** the LORD, and serve him 3372
Jdg 4:18 Turn in, my lord, turn in to me; **f** not. 3372
6:10 **f** not the gods of the Amorites, in whose 3372
6:23 said unto him, Peace *be* unto thee; **f** not: 3372
7:10 If thou **f** to go down, go thou with Phurah 3373
9:21 **for f** of Abimelech his brother. 4480+6440
Ru 3:11 now, my daughter, **f** not; I will do to thee 3372
1Sa 4:20 that stood by her said *unto her,* **F** not; 3372
11: 7 the **f** of the LORD fell on the people, and 6343
12:14 If ye will **f** the LORD, and serve him, and 3372
12:20 Samuel said unto the people, **F** not: ye have 3372
12:24 Only **f** the LORD, and serve him in truth 3372
21:10 fled that day for **f** of Saul, and went to 6440
22:23 Abide thou with me, **f** not: for he that 3372
23:17 he said unto him, **F** not: for the hand of 3372
23:26 David made haste to get away for **f** of Saul; 6440
2Sa 9: 7 David said unto him, **F** not: for I will surely 3372
13:28 Smite Amnon; then kill him, **f** not: 3372
23: 3 men *must be* just, ruling *in* the **f** of God. 3374
1Ki 8:40 That they may **f** thee all the days that they 3372
8:43 thy name, to **f** thee, as *do* thy people Israel; 3372
17:13 Elijah said unto her, **F** not; go *and* do as 3372
18:12 *I* thy servant **f** the LORD from my youth. 3372
2Ki 4: 1 thou knowest that thy servant did **f** 3373
6:16 he answered, **F** not: for *they* that *be* with us 3372
17:28 taught them how they should **f** the LORD. 3372
17:34 they **f** not the LORD, neither do they after 3373
17:35 saying, Ye shall not **f** other gods, 3372
17:36 him shall ye **f**, and him shall ye worship, 3372
17:37 for evermore; and ye shall not **f** other gods. 3372
17:38 not forget; neither shall ye **f** other gods. 3372
17:39 the LORD your God ye shall **f**; and 3372
25:24 **F** not to be the servants of the Chaldees: 3372
1Ch 14:17 the LORD brought the **f** of him upon all 6343
16:30 **F** before him, all the earth: the world also 2342
28:20 and of good courage, and do *it:* **f** not, 3372
2Ch 6:31 That they may **f** thee, to walk in thy ways, 3372
6:33 **f** thee, as *doth* thy people Israel, and may 3372
14:14 for the **f** of the LORD came upon them: 6343
17:10 the **f** of the LORD fell upon all 6343
19: 7 Wherefore now let the **f** of the LORD be 6343
19: 9 Thus shall ye do in the **f** of the LORD, 3374
20:17 **f** not, nor be dismayed; to morrow go out 3372
20:29 the **f** of God was on all the kingdoms of 6343
Ezr 3: 3 for **f** *was* upon them because of the people of 367
Ne 1:11 of thy servants, who desire to **f** thy name: 3372
5: 9 ought ye not to walk in the **f** of our God 3374
5:15 but so did not I, because of the **f** of God. 3374
6:14 the prophets, that would have **put** me **in f**. 3372
6:19 *And* Tobiah sent letters to **put** me **in f**. 3372
Est 8:17 for the **f** of the Jews fell upon them. 6343
9: 2 for the **f** of them fell upon all people. 6343
9: 3 because the **f** of Mordecai fell upon them. 6343
Job 1: 9 and said, Doth Job **f** God for nought? 3372
4: 6 *Is* not *this* thy **f**, thy confidence, thy hope; 3374
4:14 **F** came upon me, and trembling, 6343
6:14 but he forsaketh the **f** of the Almighty. 3374
9:34 away from me, and let not his **f** terrify me: 367
9:35 *Then* would I speak, and not **f** him; but *it is* 3372
11:15 yea, thou shalt be steadfast, and shalt not **f**. 3372
15: 4 thou castest off **f**, and restrainest prayer 3374
21: 9 Their houses *are* safe from **f**, neither *is* 6343
22: 4 Will he reprove thee for **f** of thee? will he 3374
22:10 about thee, and sudden **f** troubleth thee; 6343
25: 2 Dominion and **f** *are* with him, he maketh 6343
28:28 Behold, the **f** of the Lord, that *is* wisdom; 3374
31:34 Did I **f** a great multitude, or did 6206
37:24 Men do therefore **f** him: he respecteth not 3372
39:16 not hers: her labour *is* in vain without **f**; 6343
39:22 He mocketh at **f**, and is not affrighted; 6343
41:33 there is not his like, who is made without **f**. 2844
Ps 2:11 Serve the LORD with **f**, and rejoice with 3374
5: 7 in thy **f** will I worship toward thy holy 3374
9:20 Put them in **f**, O LORD: *that* the nations 4172
14: 5 There were they **in great f**: for God 6342+6343
15: 4 but he honoureth them that **f** the LORD. 3373
19: 9 The **f** of the LORD *is* clean, enduring for 3374
22:23 Ye that **f** the LORD, praise him; all ye 3373
22:23 and **f** him, all ye the seed of Israel. 1481
22:25 I will pay my vows before them that **f** him. 3373
23: 4 of the shadow of death, I will **f** no evil: 3372
25:14 of the LORD *is* with them that **f** him; 3373
27: 1 my light and my salvation; whom shall I **f**? 3372
27: 3 encamp against me, my heart shall not **f**: 3372
31:11 and a **f** to mine acquaintance: 6343
31:13 **f** *was* on every side: while they took 4032
31:19 which thou hast laid up for them that **f** thee; 3373
33: 8 Let all the earth **f** the LORD: let all 3372
33:18 the eye of the LORD *is* upon them that **f** 3373
34: 7 encampeth round about them that **f** him, 3373
34: 9 O **f** the LORD, ye his saints: for *there is* 3372
34: 9 for *there is* no want to them that **f** him. 3373
34:11 I will teach you the **f** of the LORD. 3374
36: 1 *that there is* no **f** of God before his eyes. 6343
40: 3 many shall see *it,* and **f**, and shall trust in 3372
46: 2 Therefore will not we **f**, though the earth be 3372
48: 6 **F** took hold upon them there, *and* pain, 7461
49: 5 Wherefore should I **f** in the days of evil, 3372
52: 6 also shall see, and **f**, and shall laugh at him: 3372
53: 5 There were they **in great f**, *where* no 6342+6343
53: 5 were they in great fear, *where* no **f** was: 6343
55:19 have no changes, therefore they **f** not God. 3372
56: 4 I will not **f** what flesh can do unto me. 3372
60: 4 Thou hast given a banner to them that **f** 3373
61: 5 *me* the heritage of those that **f** thy name. 3373
64: 1 preserve my life from **f** of the enemy. 6343
64: 4 suddenly do they shoot at him, and **f** not. 3372
64: 9 all men shall **f**, and shall declare the work 3372
66:16 all ye that **f** God, and I will declare what he 3373
67: 7 and all the ends of the earth shall **f** him. 3372
72: 5 They shall **f** thee as long as the sun and 3372
85: 9 Surely his salvation *is* nigh them that **f** him; 3373
86:11 in thy truth: unite my heart to **f** thy name. 3372
90:11 even according to thy **f**, *so is* thy wrath. 3374
96: 9 of holiness: **f** before him, all the earth. 2342
102:15 So the heathen shall **f** the name of 3372
103:11 great is his mercy toward them that **f** him. 3373
103:13 *so* the LORD pitieth them that **f** him. 3373
103:17 to everlasting upon them that **f** him, 3373
105:38 for the **f** of them that fell upon them. 6343
111: 5 He hath given meat unto them that **f** him: 3373
111:10 The **f** of the LORD *is* the beginning of 3374
115:11 Ye that **f** the LORD, trust in the LORD: 3373
115:13 He will bless them that **f** the LORD, *both* 3373
118: 4 Let them now that **f** the LORD say, 3373
118: 6 The LORD *is* on my side; I will not **f**: 3372
119:38 unto thy servant, who *is devoted* to thy **f**. 3374
119:39 Turn away my reproach which I **f**: for thy 3025
119:63 I *am* a companion of all *them* that **f** thee, 3372
119:74 They that **f** thee will be glad when they see 3373
119:79 Let those that **f** thee turn unto me, and 3373
119:120 My flesh trembleth for **f** of thee; and I am 6343
135:20 ye that **f** the LORD, bless the LORD. 3373
145:19 He will fulfil the desire of them that **f** him: 3373
147:11 The LORD taketh pleasure in them that **f** 3373
Pr 1: 7 The **f** of the LORD *is* the beginning of 3374
1:26 I will mock when your **f** cometh; 6343
1:27 When your **f** cometh as desolation, and 6343
1:29 and did not choose the **f** of the LORD: 3374
1:33 and shall be quiet from **f** of evil. 6343
2: 5 shalt thou understand the **f** of the LORD, 3374
3: 7 **f** the LORD, and depart from evil. 3372
3:25 Be not afraid of sudden **f**, neither of 6343
8:13 The **f** of the LORD *is* to hate evil: pride, 3374
9:10 The **f** of the LORD *is* the beginning of 3374
10:24 The **f** of the wicked, it shall come *upon* 4034
10:27 The **f** of the LORD prolongeth days: but 3374
14:26 In the **f** of the LORD *is* strong confidence: 3374
14:27 The **f** of the LORD *is* a fountain of life, 3374
15:16 Better *is* little with the **f** of the LORD than 3374
15:33 The **f** of the LORD *is* the instruction of 3374
16: 6 by the **f** of the LORD *men* depart from 3374
19:23 The **f** of the LORD *tendeth* to life: and 3374

Pr 20: 2 The f of a king is as the roaring of a lion: 367
22: 4 and the f of the LORD are riches, 3374
23:17 be thou in the f of the LORD all the day 3374
24:21 My son, f thou the LORD and the king: 3372
29:25 The f of man bringeth a snare: but 2731
Ecc 3:14 God doeth it, that men should f before him. 3372
5: 7 are also divers vanities: but f thou God. 3372
8:12 that it shall be well with them that f God, 3373
8:12 them that fear God, which f before him: 3372
12:13 F God, and keep his commandments: 3372
SS 3: 8 upon his thigh because of f in the night. 6343
Isa 2:10 for f of the LORD, and for the glory of his 6343
2:19 for f of the LORD, and for the glory of his 6343
2:21 for f of the LORD, and for the glory of his 6343
7: 4 f not, neither be fainthearted for the two 3372
7:25 there shall not come thither the f of briers 3374
8:12 neither f ye their fear, nor be afraid. 3372
8:12 neither fear ye their f, nor be afraid. 4172
8:13 let him be your f, and let him be your 4172
11: 2 of knowledge and of the f of the LORD; 3374
11: 3 quick understanding in the f of the LORD: 3374
14: 3 from thy f, and from the hard bondage 7267
19:16 it shall be afraid and f because of 6342
21: 4 my pleasure hath he turned into f unto me. 2731
24:17 F, and the pit, and the snare, are upon thee, 6343
24:18 that he who fleeth from the noise of the f 6343
25: 3 the city of the terrible nations shall f thee. 3372
29:13 their f towards me is taught by the precept 3374
29:23 One of Jacob, and shall f the God of Israel. 6206
31: 9 he shall pass over to his strong hold for f, 4032
33: 6 the f of the LORD is his treasure. 3374
35: 4 that are of a fearful heart, Be strong, f not: 3372
41:10 F thou not; for I am with thee: be not 3372
41:13 thy right hand, saying unto thee, F not; 3372
41:14 F not, thou worm Jacob, and ye men of 3372
43: 1 and he that formed thee, O Israel, F not: 3372
43: 5 F not: for I am with thee: I will bring thy 3372
44: 2 F not, O Jacob, my servant; and 3372
44: 8 F ye not, neither be afraid: have not I told 6342
44:11 let them stand up; yet they shall f, and 6342
51: 7 f ye not the reproach of men, neither be ye 3372
54: 4 F not; for thou shalt not be ashamed: 3372
54:14 be far from oppression; for thou shalt not f: 3372
59:19 So shall they f the name of the LORD 3372
60: 5 flow together, and thine heart shall f, and 6342
63:17 and hardened our heart from thy f? 3374
Jer 2:19 that my f is not in thee, saith the Lord 6345
5:22 F ye not me? saith the LORD: will ye not 3372
5:24 Let us now f the LORD our God, 3372
6:25 sword of the enemy and f is on every side. 4032
10: 7 Who would not f thee, O King of nations? 3372
20:10 the defaming of many, f on every side. 4032
23: 4 they shall f no more, nor be dismayed, 3372
26:19 did he not f the LORD, and besought 3373
30: 5 a voice of trembling, of f, and not of peace. 6343
30:10 Therefore f thou not, O my servant Jacob, 3372
32:39 one way, that they may f me for ever, for 3372
32:40 I will put my f in their hearts, that they 3374
33: 9 they shall f and tremble for all the goodness 6342
35:11 let us go to Jerusalem for f of the army of 6440
35:11 and for f of the army of the Syrians: 6440
37:11 up from Jerusalem for f of Pharaoh's army, 6440
40: 9 saying, F not to serve the Chaldeans: 3372
41: 9 was it which Asa the king had made for f of 6440
46: 5 for f was round about, saith the LORD. 4032
46:27 f not thou, O my servant Jacob, and be not 3372
46:28 F thou not, O Jacob my servant, saith 3372
48:43 F, and the pit, and the snare, shall be upon 6343
48:44 He that fleeth from the f shall fall into 6343
49: 5 Behold, I will bring a f upon thee, saith 6343
49:24 f hath seized on her: anguish and 7374
49:29 they shall cry unto them, F is on every side. 4032
50:16 for f of the oppressing sword they shall turn 6440
51:46 ye f for the rumour that shall be heard in 3372
La 3:47 F and a snare is come upon us, desolation 6343
3:57 that I called upon thee: thou saidst, F not. 3372
Eze 3: 9 f them not, neither be dismayed at their 3372
30:13 and I will put a f in the land of Egypt. 3374
Da 1:10 I f my lord the king, who hath appointed 3373
6:26 and f before the God of Daniel: 1763
10:12 said he unto me, F not, Daniel: for from 3372
10:19 said, O man greatly beloved, f not: 3372
Hos 3: 5 shall f the LORD and his goodness in 6342
10: 5 The inhabitants of Samaria shall f because 1481
Joel 2:21 F not, O land; be glad and rejoice: for 3372
Am 3: 8 The lion hath roared, who will not f? 3372
Jnh 1: 9 I f the LORD, the God of heaven, 3373
Mic 7:17 our God, and shall f because of thee. 3372
Zep 3: 7 I said, Surely thou wilt f me, thou wilt 3372
3:16 it shall be said to Jerusalem, F thou not: 3372
Hag 1:12 and the people did f before the LORD. 3372
2: 5 so my spirit remaineth among you: f ye not. 3372
Zec 8:13 f not, but let your hands be strong. 3372
8:15 and to the house of Judah: f ye not. 3372
9: 5 Ashkelon shall see it, and f; Gaza also shall 3372
Mal 1: 6 if I be a master, where is my f? saith 4172
2: 5 I gave them to him for the f wherewith he 4172
3: 5 the stranger from his right, and f not me, 3372
4: 2 unto you that f my name shall the Sun of 3373
Mt 1:20 f not to take unto thee Mary thy wife: 5399
10:26 F them not therefore: for there is nothing 5399
10:28 And f not them which kill the body, but 5399
10:28 rather f him which is able to destroy both 5399
10:31 F ye not therefore, ye are of more value 5399
14:26 It is a spirit; and they cried out for f. 5401
21:26 if we shall say, Of men; we f the people; 5399
28: 4 And for f of him the keepers did shake, 5401
28: 5 and said unto the women, F not ye: 5399
28: 8 departed quickly from the sepulchre with f 5401
Lk 1:12 him, he was troubled, and f fell upon him. 5401
1:13 the angel said unto him, F not, Zacharias: 5399
1:30 And the angel said unto her, F not, Mary: 5399
1:50 And his mercy is on them that f him from 5399
1:65 And f came on all that dwelt round about 5401
1:74 of our enemies might serve him without f, 870
Lk 2:10 And the angel said unto them, F not: 5399
5:10 And Jesus said unto Simon, F not; 5399
5:26 and were filled with f, saying, 5401
7:16 And there came a f on all: 5401
8:37 for they were taken with great f: 5401
8:50 heard it, he answered him, saying, F not: 5399
12: 5 But I will forewarn you whom you shall f: 5399
12: 5 F him, which after he hath killed hath 5399
12: 5 to cast into hell; yea, I say unto you, F him. 5399
12: 7 F not therefore: ye are of more value than 5399
12:32 F not, little flock; for it is your Father's 5399
18: 4 Though I f not God, nor regard man; 5399
21:26 Men's hearts failing them for f, and 5401
23:40 rebuked him, saying, Dost not thou f God, 5399
Jn 7:13 Howbeit no man spake openly of him for f 5401
12:15 F not, daughter of Sion: behold, thy King 5399
19:38 of Jesus, but secretly for f of the Jews, 5401
20:19 disciples were assembled for f of the Jews, 5401
Ac 2:43 And f came upon every soul: and 5401
5: 5 great f came on all them that heard these 5401
5:11 And great f came upon all the church, and 5401
9:31 and walking in the f of the Lord, and in 5401
13:16 Men of Israel, and ye that f God, 5399
19:17 and f fell on them all, and the name of 5401
27:24 Saying, F not, Paul; thou must be brought 5399
Ro 3:18 There is no f of God before their eyes. 5401
8:15 received the spirit of bondage again to f; 5401
11:20 by faith. Be not high-minded, but f: 5399
13: 7 f to whom fear; honour to whom honour. 5401
13: 7 fear to whom f; honour to whom honour. 5401
1Co 2: 3 and in f, and in much trembling. 5401
16:10 see that he may be with you without f: 870
2Co 7: 1 spirit, perfecting holiness in the f of God. 5401
7:11 yea, what indignation, yea, what f, yea, 5401
7:15 how with f and trembling you received 5401
11: 3 But I f, lest by any means, as the serpent 5399
12:20 For I f, lest, when I come, I shall not find 5399
Eph 5:21 yourselves one to another in the f of God. 5401
6: 5 with f and trembling, in singleness of your 5401
Php 1:14 more bold to speak the word without f. 870
2:12 work out your own salvation with f and 5401
1Ti 5:20 before all, that others also may f. 2192+5401
2Ti 1: 7 For God hath not given us the spirit of f; 1167
Heb 2:15 And deliver them who through f of death 5401
4: 1 Let us therefore f, lest, a promise being left 5399
11: 7 moved with f, prepared an ark to 2125
12:21 I exceedingly f and quake;) 1510+1630
12:28 God acceptably with reverence and godly f: 2124
13: 6 and I will not f what man shall do unto me. 5399
1Pe 1:17 pass the time of your sojourning here in f: 5401
2:17 the brotherhood. F God. Honour the king. 5399
2:18 be subject to your masters with all f; 5401
3: 2 your chaste conversation coupled with f. 5401
3:15 the hope that is in you with meekness and f: 5401
1Jn 4:18 There is no f in love; but perfect love 5401
4:18 fear in love; but perfect love casteth out f: 5401
4:18 because f hath torment. He that feareth is 5401
Jude 1:12 with you, feeding themselves without f: 870
1:23 And others save with f, pulling them out of 5401
Rev 1:17 right hand upon me, saying unto me, F not; 5399
2:10 F none of those things which thou shalt 5399
11:11 and great f fell upon them which saw them. 5401
11:18 and them that f thy name, small and great; 5399
14: 7 a loud voice, F God, and give glory to him; 5399
15: 4 Who shall not f thee, O Lord, and 5399
18:10 Standing afar off for the f of her torment, 5401
18:15 shall stand afar off for the f of her torment, 5401
19: 5 and ye that f him, both small and great. 5399

FEARED (74) [FEAR]

Ge 19:30 with him; for he f to dwell in Zoar: 3372
26: 7 for he f to say, She is my wife; lest, said he, 3372
Ex 1:17 the midwives f God, and did not as the king 3372
1:21 came to pass, because the midwives f God, 3372
2:14 Moses f, and said, Surely this thing is 3372
9:20 He that f the word of the LORD amongst 3373
14:31 the people f the LORD, and believed 3372
Dt 25:18 wast faint and weary; and he f not God. 3373
32:17 came newly up, whom your fathers f not. 8175
32:27 Were it not that I f the wrath of the enemy, 1481
Jos 4:14 they f him, as they feared Moses, all 3372
4:14 they feared him, as they f Moses, all 3372
10: 2 That they f greatly, because Gibeon was a 3372
Jdg 6:27 because he f his father's household, and 3372
8:20 for he f, because he was yet a youth. 3372
1Sa 3:15 And Samuel f to shew Eli the vision. 3372
12:18 all the people greatly f the LORD and 3372
14:26 hand to his mouth: for the people f the oath. 3372
15:24 because I f the people, and obeyed their 3372
2Sa 3:11 Abner a word again, because he f him. 3372
10:19 So the Syrians f to help the children of 3372
12:18 the servants of David f to tell him that 3372
1Ki 1:50 Adonijah f because of Solomon, and arose, 3372
3:28 the king had judged; and they f the king: 3372
18: 3 (Now Obadiah f the LORD greatly: 3373
2Ki 17: 7 king of Egypt, and had f other gods, 3372
17:25 dwelling there, that they f not the LORD: 3372
17:32 So they f the LORD, and made unto 3373
17:33 They f the LORD, and served their own 3373
17:41 So these nations f the LORD, and served 3373
1Ch 16:25 be praised: he also is to be f above all gods. 3372
2Ch 20: 3 Jehoshaphat f, and set himself to seek 3372
Ne 7: 2 was a faithful man, and f God above many. 3372
Job 1: 1 and one that f God, and eschewed evil. 3373
3:25 For the thing which I greatly f is come 6343
Ps 76: 7 Thou, even thou, art to be f: and who may 3372
76: 8 from heaven; the earth f, and was still, 3372
76:11 bring presents unto him that ought to be f. 4172
78:53 he led them on safely, so that they f not: 6342
89: 7 God is greatly to be f in the assembly of 6206
96: 4 to be praised: he is to be f above all gods. 3372
130: 4 with thee, that thou mayest be f. 3372
Isa 41: 5 The isles saw it, and f; the ends of the earth 3372
51:13 hast f continually every day because of 6342
57:11 of whom hast thou been afraid or f, 3372
Jer 3: 8 yet her treacherous sister Judah f not, but 3372
42:16 come to pass, that the sword, which ye f, 3373
44:10 neither have they f, nor walked in my law, 3372
Eze 11: 8 Ye have f the sword; and I will bring a 3372
Da 5:19 languages, trembled and f before him: 1763
Hos 10: 3 have no king, because we f not the LORD; 3372
Jnh 1:16 f the LORD exceedingly, 1419+3372+3374
Mal 2: 5 them to him for the fear wherewith he f me, 3372
3:16 they that f the LORD spake often one to 3373
3:16 before him for them that f the LORD, 3373
Mt 14: 5 he f the multitude, because they counted 5399
21:46 they f the multitude, because they took him 5399
27:54 that were done, they f greatly, saying, 5399
Mk 4:41 And they f exceedingly, and said one 5399+5401
6:20 For Herod f John, knowing that he was a 5399
11:18 for they f him, because all the people was 5399
11:32 if we shall say, Of men; they f the people: 5399
12:12 sought to lay hold on him, but f the people: 5399
Lk 9:34 and they f as they entered into the cloud. 5399
9:45 it not: and they f to ask him of that saying. 5399
18: 2 which f not God, neither regarded man: 5399
19:21 For I f thee, because thou art an austere 5399
20:19 to lay hands on him; and they f the people: 5399
22: 2 they might kill him; for they f the people. 5399
Jn 9:22 spake his parents, because they f the Jews: 5399
Ac 5:26 for they f the people, lest they should have 5399
10: 2 and one that f God with all his house, 5399
16:38 and they f, when they heard that they were 5399
Heb 5: 7 him from death, and was heard in that he f; 2124

FEAREST (3) [FEAR]

Ge 22:12 for now I know that thou f God, 3373
Isa 57:11 my peace even of old, and thou f me not? 3372
Jer 22:25 into the hand of them whose face thou f, 3016

FEARETH (20) [FEAR]

1Ki 1:51 Behold, Adonijah f king Solomon: 3372
Job 1: 8 one that f God, and escheweth evil? 3373
2: 3 one that f God, and escheweth evil? 3373
Ps 25:12 What man is he that f the LORD? 3373
112: 1 Blessed is the man that f the LORD, 3372
128: 1 Blessed is every one that f the LORD; 3373
128: 4 that thus shall the man be blessed that f 3373
Pr 13:13 he that f the commandment shall be 3373
14: 2 He that walketh in his uprightness f 3373
14:16 A wise man f, and departeth from evil: but 3373
28:14 Happy is the man that f alway: but he that 6342
31:30 but a woman that f the LORD, she shall 3373
Ecc 7:18 for he that f God shall come forth of them 3373
8:13 as a shadow; because he f not before God. 3373
9: 2 and he that sweareth, as he that f an oath. 3373
Isa 50:10 Who is among you that f the LORD, 3373
Ac 10:22 and one that f God, and of good report 5399
10:35 But in every nation he that f him, and 5399
13:26 and whosoever among you f God, 5399
1Jn 4:18 He that f is not made perfect in love. 5399

FEARFUL (11) [FEAR]

Ex 15:11 in holiness, f in praises, doing wonders? 3372
Dt 20: 8 What man is there that is f and 3373
28:58 thou mayest fear this glorious and f name, 3372
Jdg 7: 3 saying, Whosoever is f and afraid, let him 3373
Isa 35: 4 Say to them that are of a f heart, Be strong, 4116
Mt 8:26 Why are ye f, O ye of little faith? 1169
Mk 4:40 And he said unto them, Why are ye so f? 1169
Lk 21:11 and f sights and great signs shall there be 5400
Heb 10:27 But a certain f looking for of judgment and 5398
10:31 It is a f thing to fall into the hands of 5398
Rev 21: 8 But the f, and unbelieving, and 1169

FEARFULLY (1) [FEAR]

Ps 139:14 for I am f and wonderfully made: 3372

FEARFULNESS (3) [FEAR]

Ps 55: 5 F and trembling are come upon me, and 3374
Isa 21: 4 My heart panted, f affrighted me: the night 6427
33:14 are afraid; f hath surprised the hypocrites. 7461

FEARING (8) [FEAR]

Jos 22:25 our children cease from f the LORD: 3372
Mk 5:33 But the woman f and trembling, 5399
Ac 23:10 f lest Paul should have been pulled in 2125
27:17 f lest they should fall into the quicksands, 5399
27:29 Then f lest we should have fallen upon 5399
Gal 2:12 f them which were of the circumcision. 5399
Col 3:22 but in singleness of heart, f God: 5399
Heb 11:27 forsook Egypt, not f the wrath of the king: 5399

FEARS (4) [FEAR]

Ps 34: 4 heard me, and delivered me from all my f. 4035
Ecc 12: 5 f shall be in the way, and the almond tree 2849
Isa 66: 4 and will bring their f upon them; 4035
2Co 7: 5 side; without were fightings, within were f. 5401

FEAST (123) [FEASTED, FEASTING, FEASTS]

Ge 19: 3 he made them a f, and did bake unleavened 4960
21: 8 Abraham made a great f the same day that 4960
26:30 he made them a f, and they did eat and 4960
29:22 all the men of the place, and made a f. 4960
40:20 that he made a f unto all his servants: 4960
Ex 5: 1 that they may hold a f unto me in 2287
10: 9 for we must hold a f unto the LORD. 2282
12:14 you shall keep it a f to the LORD 2282
12:14 you shall keep it a f by an ordinance for 2287
12:17 ye shall observe the f of unleavened bread; NIH
13: 6 in the seventh day shall be a f to 2282
23:14 Three times thou shalt keep a f unto me in 2287
23:15 Thou shalt keep the f of unleavened bread: 2282
23:16 the f of harvest, the firstfruits of thy 2282
23:16 the f of ingathering, which is in the end of 2282
32: 5 and said, To morrow is a f to the LORD. 2282
34:18 The f of unleavened bread shalt thou keep: 2282
34:22 thou shalt observe the f of weeks, of 2282
34:22 and the f of ingathering at the year's end. 2282

Ex 34:25 neither shall the sacrifice of the **f** of 2282
Lev 23: 6 the **f** of unleavened bread unto the LORD: 2282
23:34 **f** of tabernacles *for* seven days unto 2282
23:39 ye shall keep a **f** unto the LORD seven 2282
23:41 ye shall **keep** it **a f** unto the LORD 2282+2287
Nu 28:17 in the fifteenth day of this month *is* the **f**: 2282
29:12 ye shall **keep a f** unto the LORD 2282+2287
Dt 16:10 thou shalt keep the **f** of weeks unto 2282
16:13 Thou shalt observe the **f** of tabernacles 2282
16:14 thou shalt rejoice in thy **f**, thou, and 2282
16:15 Seven days shalt thou **keep a solemn f** unto 2287
16:16 in the **f** of unleavened bread, and in 2282
16:16 in the **f** of weeks, and in the feast of 2282
16:16 feast of weeks, and in the **f** of tabernacles: 2282
31:10 the year of release, in the **f** of tabernacles, 2282
Jdg 14:10 Samson made there a **f**; for so used 4960
14:12 declare it me *within* the seven days of the **f**, 4960
14:17 him the seven days, while their **f** lasted: 4960
21:19 *there is* a **f** of the LORD in Shiloh yearly 2282
1Sa 25:36 behold, he held a **f** in his house, like 4960
25:36 a feast in his house, like the **f** of a king; 4960
2Sa 3:20 and the men that *were* with him a **f**. 4960
1Ki 3:15 and made a **f** to all his servants. 4960
8: 2 Solomon at the **f** in the month Ethanim, 2282
8:65 at that time Solomon held a **f**, and all Israel 2282
12:32 Jeroboam ordained a **f** in the eighth month, 2282
12:32 like unto the **f** that *is* in Judah, and 2282
12:33 and ordained a **f** unto the children of Israel: 2282
2Ch 5: 3 in the **f** which *was in* the seventh month. 2282
7: 8 Also at the same time Solomon kept the **f** 2282
7: 9 the altar seven days, and the **f** seven days. 2282
8:13 *even* in the **f** of unleavened bread, and 2282
8:13 in the **f** of weeks, and in the feast of 2282
8:13 feast of weeks, and in the **f** of tabernacles. 2282
30:13 **f** of unleavened bread in the second month, 2282
30:21 **f** of unleavened bread seven days with great 2282
30:22 they did eat throughout the **f** seven days, 4150
35:17 the **f** of unleavened bread seven days. 2282
Ezr 3: 4 They kept also the **f** of tabernacles, as it is 2282
6:22 kept the **f** of the unleavened bread seven days 2282
Ne 8:14 in booths in the **f** of the seventh month: 2282
8:18 they kept the **f** seven days; and on 2282
Est 1: 3 he made a **f** unto all his princes and 4960
1: 5 the king made a **f** unto all the people that 4960
1: 9 Also Vashti the queen made a **f** for 4960
2:18 the king made a great **f** unto all his princes 4960
2:18 and his servants, *even* Esther's **f**; 4960
8:17 had joy and gladness, a **f** and a good day. 4960
Ps 81: 3 in the time appointed, on our **solemn f** day. 2282
Pr 15:15 *that is* of a merry heart *hath* a continual **f**. 4960
Ecc 10:19 A **f** is made for laughter, and wine maketh 3899
Isa 25: 6 hosts make unto all people a **f** of fat things, 4960
25: 6 a **f** of wines on the lees, of fat things full of 4960
La 2: 7 of the LORD, as *in* the day of a **solemn f**. 4150
Eze 45:21 shall have the passover, a **f** of seven days; 2282
45:23 seven days of the **f** he shall prepare a burnt 2282
45:25 shall he do the like in the **f** *of* the seven 2282
Da 5: 1 Belshazzar the king made a great **f** to a 3900
Hos 2:11 her **f** *days*, her new moons, and 2282
9: 5 and in the day of the **f** of the LORD? 2282
12: 9 as *in* the days of the **solemn f**. 4150
Am 5:21 I despise your **f** *days*, and I will not smell in 2282
Zec 14:16 of hosts, and to keep the **f** of tabernacles. 2282
14:18 come not up to keep the **f** of tabernacles. 2282
14:19 come not up to keep the **f** of tabernacles. 2282
Mt 26: 2 Ye know that after two days is *the f of* NIG
26: 5 Not on the **f** *day*, lest there be an uproar *1859*
26:17 Now the first *day* of the *f of* unleavened NIG
27:15 Now at *that* **f** the governor was wont to *1859*
Mk 14: 1 After two days was *the f of* the passover, NIG
14: 2 Not on the **f** *day*, lest there be an uproar of *1859*
15: 6 Now at *that* **f** he released unto them one *1859*
Lk 2:41 every year at the **f** of the passover. *1859*
2:42 up to Jerusalem after the custom of the **f**. *1859*
5:29 And Levi made him a great **f** in his own *1403*
14:13 But when thou makest a **f**, call the poor, *1403*
22: 1 Now the **f** of unleavened bread drew nigh, *1859*
23:17 he must release one unto them at the **f**.) *1859*
Jn 2: 8 and bear unto the **governor of the f**. *755*
2: 9 When the **ruler of the f** had tasted the water *755*
2: 9 the **governor of the f** called the bridegroom, *755*
2:23 in the **f** *day*, many believed in his name, *1859*
4:45 *the things* that he did at Jerusalem at the **f**: *1859*
4:45 at the feast: for they also went unto the **f**. *1859*
5: 1 After this there was a **f** of the Jews; and *1859*
6: 4 And the passover, a **f** of the Jews, was nigh. *1859*
7: 2 Now the Jews' **f** of tabernacles was at hand. *1859*
7: 8 Go ye up unto this **f**: I go not up yet unto *1859*
7: 8 I go not up yet unto this **f**; for my time is *1859*
7:10 then went he also up unto the **f**, not openly, *1859*
7:11 Then the Jews sought him at the **f**, and said, *1859*
7:14 Now about the midst of the **f** Jesus went up *1859*
7:37 *that* great *day* of the **f**, Jesus stood and *1859*
10:22 And it was at Jerusalem *the f of* NIG
11:56 think ye, that he will not come to the **f**? *1859*
12:12 day much people that were come to the **f**, *1859*
12:20 them that came up to worship at the **f**: *1859*
13: 1 Now before the **f** of the passover, *1859*
13:29 *things* that we have need of against the **f**; *1859*
Ac 18:21 I must by all means keep *this* **f** that cometh *1859*
1Co 5: 8 Therefore let us **keep the f**, not with old *1858*
10:27 any of them that believe not bid you *to a f*, NIG
2Pe 2:13 their own deceivings while they **f with** you; *4910*
Jude 1:12 **f with** *you*, feeding themselves without *4910*

FEASTED (1) [FEAST]
Job 1: 4 his sons went and **f** *in their* houses, 4960+6213

FEASTING (7) [FEAST]
Est 9:17 and made it a day of **f** and gladness. 4960
9:18 and made it a day of **f** and gladness. 4960
9:19 of the month Adar *a day of* gladness and **f**, 4960
9:22 that *they* should make them days of **f** and 4960
Job 1: 5 when the days of *their* **f** were gone about, 4960
Ecc 7: 2 of mourning, than to go to the house of **f**: 4960
Jer 16: 8 Thou shalt not also go *into* the house of **f**, 4960

FEASTS (32) [FEAST]
Lev 23: 2 unto them, *Concerning* the **f** of the LORD, 4150
23: 2 *be* holy convocations, *even* these *are* my **f**. 4150
23: 4 These *are* the **f** of the LORD, *even* holy 4150
23:37 These *are* the **f** of the LORD, which ye 4150
23:44 the children of Israel the **f** of the LORD. 4150
Nu 15: 3 in a freewill offering, or in your **solemn f**, 4150
29:39 ye shall do unto the LORD in your **set f**, 4150
1Ch 23:31 new moons, and on the **set f**, by number, 4150
2Ch 2: 4 on the **solemn f** of the LORD our God. 4150
8:13 on the new moons, and on the **solemn f**, 4150
31: 3 and for the new moons, and for the **set f**, 4150
Ezr 3: 5 of all the **set f** of the LORD that were 4150
Ne 10:33 for the **set f**, and for the holy *things*, and 4150
Ps 35:16 With hypocritical mockers in **f**, 4580
Isa 1:14 and your **appointed f** my soul hateth: 4150
5:12 the tabret, and pipe, and wine, are *in* their **f**: 4960
Jer 51:39 In their heat I will make their **f**, and I will 4960
La 1: 4 because none come to the **solemn f**: 4150
2: 6 the LORD hath caused the **solemn f** and 4150
Eze 36:38 as the flock of Jerusalem in her **solemn f**; 4150
45:17 in the **f**, and in the new moons, and in 2282
46: 9 come before the LORD in the **solemn f**, 4150
46:11 in the **f** and in the solemnities the meat 2282
Hos 2:11 and her sabbaths, and all her **solemn f**. 4150
Am 8:10 I will turn your **f** into mourning, and 2282
Na 1:15 O Judah, keep thy **solemn f**, perform thy 2282
Zec 8:19 of Judah joy and gladness, and cheerful **f**; 4150
Mal 2: 3 your faces, *even* the dung of your **solemn f**; 2282
Mt 23: 6 And love the uppermost rooms at **f**, and *1173*
Mk 12:39 and the uppermost rooms at **f**: *1173*
Lk 20:46 in the synagogues, and the chief rooms at **f**; *1173*
Jude 1:12 These are spots in your **f of charity** when *26*

FEATHERED (2) [FEATHERS]
Ps 78:27 and **f** fowls like as the sand of the sea: 3671
Eze 39:17 Speak unto every **f** fowl, and to every beast 3671

FEATHERS (7) [FEATHERED]
Lev 1:16 he shall pluck away his crop with his **f**, 5133
Job 39:13 or wings and **f** *unto* the ostrich? 5133
Ps 68:13 with silver, and her **f** with yellow gold. 84
91: 4 He shall cover thee with his **f**, and under his 84
Eze 17: 3 longwinged, full *of* **f**, which had divers 5133
17: 7 great eagle with great wings and many **f**: 5133
Da 4:33 till his hairs were grown like eagles' *f*, and NIH

FED (31) [FEED]
Ge 30:36 and Jacob **f** the rest of Laban's flocks. 7462
36:24 as he **f** the asses of Zibeon his father. 7462
41: 2 and fatfleshed; and they **f** in a meadow. 7462
41:18 well favoured; and they **f** in a meadow: 7462
47:17 he **f** them with bread for all their cattle for 5095
48:15 the God which **f** me all my life long unto 7462
Ex 16:32 wherewith I have **f** you in the wilderness, 398
Dt 8: 3 thee to hunger, and **f** thee with manna, 398
8:16 Who **f** thee in the wilderness with manna, 398
2Sa 20: 3 **f** them, but went not in unto them. 3557
1Ki 18: 4 in a cave, and **f** them *with* bread and water.) 3557
18:13 in a cave, and **f** them *with* bread and water? 3557
1Ch 27:29 over the herds that **f** in Sharon *was* Shitrai 7462
Ps 37: 3 dwell in the land, and verily thou shalt be **f**. 7462
78:72 So he **f** them according to the integrity of 7462
81:16 He should have **f** them also with the finest of 398
Isa 1:11 offerings of rams, and the fat of **f beasts**; 4806
Jer 5: 7 when I had **f** them **to the full**, they then 7650
5: 8 They were *as* **f** horses in the morning: 2109
Eze 16:19 and oil, and honey, *wherewith* I **f** thee, 398
34: 3 you with the wool, ye kill them that are **f**: 1277
34: 8 the shepherds **f** themselves, and fed not my 7462
34: 8 fed themselves, and **f** not my flock; 7462
Da 4:12 the boughs thereof, and all flesh was **f** of it. 2110
5:21 they **f** him with grass like oxen, and 2939
Zec 11: 7 the other I called Bands; and I **f** the flock. 7462
Mt 25:37 and **f** *thee?* or thirsty, and gave *thee* drink? *5142*
Mk 5:14 And they that **f** the swine fled, and told *it* in *1006*
Lk 8:34 When they that **f** *them* saw what was done, *1006*
16:21 And desiring to be **f** with the crumbs which *5526*
1Co 3: 2 I have **f** you with milk, and not with meat: *4222*

FEEBLE (20) [FEEBLEMINDED, FEEBLENESS, FEEBLER]
Ge 30:42 when the cattle were **f**, he put *them* not in: 5848
Dt 25:18 *even* all that were **f** behind thee, when thou 2826
1Sa 2: 5 and she that hath many children is **waxed f**. 535
2Sa 4: 1 his hands were **f**, and all the Israelites were 7503
2Ch 28:15 carried all the **f** of them upon asses, 3782
Ne 4: 2 of Samaria, and said, What do *these* **f** Jews? 537
Job 4: 4 and thou hast strengthened the **f** knees. 3766
Ps 38: 8 I am **f** and sore broken: I have roared by 6313
105:37 *there was* not *one* **f** *person* among their 3782
Pr 30:26 The conies *are but* a **f** folk, yet make 3808+6099
Isa 16:14 remnant *shall be* very small *and* **f**. 3524+3808
35: 3 ye the weak hands, and confirm the **f** knees. 3782
Jer 6:24 our hands **wax f**: anguish hath taken hold 7503
49:24 Damascus is **waxed f**, *and* turneth herself 7503
50:43 the report of them, and his hands **waxed f**: 7503
Eze 7:17 All hands shall be **f**, and all knees shall be 7503
21: 7 all hands shall be **f**, and every spirit shall 7503
Zec 12: 8 he that is **f** among them at that day shall be 3782
1Co 12:22 which seem to be **more f**, are necessary: *772*
Heb 12:12 hands which hang down, and the **f** knees; *3886*

FEEBLEMINDED (1) [FEEBLE, MIND]
1Th 5:14 *are* unruly, comfort the **f**, support the weak, *3642*

FEEBLENESS (1) [FEEBLE]
Jer 47: 3 look back to *their* children for **f** of hands; 7510

FEEBLER (1) [FEEBLE]
Ge 30:42 so the **f** were Laban's, and the stronger 5848

FEED (81) [FED, FEEDEST, FEEDETH, FEEDING, FOOD]
Ge 25:30 Esau said to Jacob, **F** me, I pray thee, 3938
29: 7 water ye the sheep, and go *and* **f** *them.* 7462
30:31 for me, I will again **f** *and* keep thy flock: 7462
37:12 his brethren went to **f** their father's flock in 7462
37:13 Do not thy brethren **f** *the flock* in 7462
37:16 I pray thee, where they **f** *their flocks.* 7462
46:32 for their **trade** hath been **to f cattle**; 376+4735
Ex 22: 5 his beast, and shall **f** in another man's field; 1197
34: 3 neither let the flocks nor herds **f** before that 7462
1Sa 17:15 returned from Saul to **f** his father's sheep *at* 7462
2Sa 5: 2 Thou shalt **f** my people Israel, and 7462
7: 7 whom I commanded to **f** my people Israel, 7462
19:33 and I will **f** thee with me in Jerusalem. 3557
1Ki 17: 4 I have commanded the ravens to **f** thee 3557
22:27 **f** him with bread of affliction and with water 398
1Ch 11: 2 Thou shalt **f** my people Israel, and 7462
17: 6 whom I commanded to **f** my people, 7462
2Ch 18:26 **f** him with bread of affliction and with water 398
Job 24: 2 violently take away flocks, and **f** *thereof.* 7462
24:20 the worm shall **f sweetly on** him; 4988
Ps 28: 9 **f** them also, and lift them up for ever. 7462
49:14 death shall **f** *on* them; and the upright shall 7462
78:71 young he brought him to **f** Jacob his people, 7462
Pr 10:21 The lips of the righteous **f** many: but 7462
30: 8 **f** me with food convenient for me: 2963
SS 1: 8 and **f** thy kids beside the shepherds' tents. 7462
4: 5 *that are* twins, which **f** among the lilies. 7462
6: 2 to **f** in the gardens, and to gather lilies. 7462
Isa 5:17 shall the lambs **f** after their manner, and 7462
11: 7 the cow and the bear shall **f**; their young 7462
14:30 the firstborn of the poor shall **f**, and 7462
27:10 there shall the calf **f**, and there shall he lie 7462
30:23 in that day shall thy cattle **f** *in* large 7462
40:11 He shall **f** his flock like a shepherd: he shall 7462
49: 9 They shall **f** in the ways, and their pastures 7462
49:26 I will **f** them that oppress thee with their own 398
58:14 **f** thee with the heritage of Jacob thy father: 398
61: 5 strangers shall stand and **f** your flocks, and 7462
65:25 The wolf and the lamb shall **f** together, and 7462
Jer 3:15 which shall **f** you with knowledge and 7462
6: 3 they shall **f** every one *in* his place. 7462
9:15 Behold, I *will* **f** them, *even* this people, with 398
23: 2 Israel against the pastors that **f** my people; 7462
23: 4 up shepherds over them which shall **f** them: 7462
23:15 I will **f** them with wormwood, and 398
50:19 he shall **f** on Carmel and Bashan, and 7462
La 4: 5 They that did **f** delicately are desolate in 398
Eze 34: 2 Woe *be* to the shepherds of Israel that do **f** 7462
34: 2 should not the shepherds **f** the flocks? 7462
34: 3 kill them that are fed: *but* ye **f** not the flock. 7462
34:10 neither shall the shepherds **f** themselves 7462
34:13 **f** them upon the mountains of Israel by 7462
34:14 I will **f** them in a good pasture, and 7462
34:14 *in* a fat pasture shall they **f** upon 7462
34:15 I will **f** my flock, and I will cause them to 7462
34:16 and the strong; I will **f** them with judgment. 7462
34:23 he shall **f** them, *even* my servant David; 7462
34:23 he shall **f** them, and he shall be their 7462
Da 11:26 they that **f** of the portion of his meat shall 398
Hos 4:16 now the LORD will **f** them as a lamb in a 7462
9: 2 and the winepress shall not **f** them, 7462
Jnh 3: 7 any thing: let them not **f**, nor drink water: 7462
Mic 5: 4 and **f** in the strength of the LORD, 7462
7:14 **F** thy people with thy rod, the flock of thine 7462
7:14 let them **f** *in* Bashan and Gilead, as *in* 7462
Zep 2: 7 the house of Judah; they shall **f** thereupon: 7462
3:13 for they shall **f** and lie down, and none shall 7462
Zec 11: 4 my God; **F** the flock of the slaughter; 7462
11: 7 I will **f** the flock of slaughter, *even* you, 7462
11: 9 said I, I will not **f** you: that that dieth, let it 7462
11:16 that is broken, nor **f** that that standeth still: 3557
Lk 15:15 and he sent him into his fields to **f** swine. *1006*
Jn 21:15 I love thee. He saith unto him, **F** my lambs. *1006*
21:16 I love thee. He saith unto him, **F** my sheep. *4165*
21:17 Jesus saith unto him, **F** my sheep. *1006*
Ac 20:28 to **f** the church of God, which he hath *4165*
Ro 12:20 Therefore if thine enemy hunger, **f** him; *5595*
1Co 13: 3 And though I **bestow** all my goods **to f** *5595*
1Pe 5: 2 **F** the flock of God which is among you, *4165*
Rev 7:17 is in the midst of the throne shall **f** them, *4165*
12: 6 that they should **f** her there a thousand two *5142*

FEEDEST (2) [FEED]
Ps 80: 5 Thou **f** them with the bread of tears; and 398
SS 1: 7 O thou whom my soul loveth, where thou **f**, 7462

FEEDETH (8) [FEED]
Pr 15:14 but the mouth of fools **f on** foolishness. 7462
SS 2:16 *is* mine, and I *am* his: he **f** among the lilies. 7462
6: 3 my beloved *is* mine: he **f** among the lilies. 7462
Isa 44:20 He **f on** ashes: a deceived heart hath turned 7462
Hos 12: 1 Ephraim **f on** wind, and followeth after 7462
Mt 6:26 into barns; yet your heavenly Father **f** them. *5142*
Lk 12:24 have storehouse nor barn; and God **f** them: *5142*
1Co 9: 7 or who **f** a flock, and eateth not of the milk *4165*

FEEDING (9) [FEED]
Ge 37: 2 years old, was **f** the flock with his brethren; 7462
Job 1:14 were plowing, and the asses **f** beside them: 7462
Eze 34:10 and cause them to cease from **f** the flock; 7462
Na 2:11 the **f place** of the young lions, where 4829
Mt 8:30 way off from them a herd of many swine **f**. *1006*
Mk 5:11 unto the mountains a great herd of swine **f**. *1006*
Lk 8:32 And there was there a herd of many swine **f** *1006*
17: 7 having a servant plowing or **f cattle**, *4165*
Jude 1:12 feast with *you*, **f** themselves without fear: *4165*

FEEL (7) [FEELING, FELT]
Ge 27:12 My father peradventure will **f** me, and 4959
27:21 I pray thee, that I may **f** thee, my son, 4184
Jdg 16:26 Suffer me that I may **f** the pillars 4184
Job 20:20 Surely he shall not **f** quietness in his belly, 3045

Ps 58: 9 Before your pots can **f** the thorns, he shall 995
Ecc 8: 5 Whoso keepeth the commandment shall **f** 3045
Ac 17:27 if haply they might **f after** him, and *5584*

FEELING (2) [FEEL]
Eph 4:19 Who being **past f** have given themselves *524*
Heb 4:15 be **touched with the f** of our infirmities; *4834*

FEET (256) [FOOT]
Ge 18: 4 wash your **f**, and rest yourselves under 7272
19: 2 wash your **f**, and ye shall rise up early, and 7272
24:32 water to wash his **f**, and the men's feet that 7272
24:32 and the men's **f** that *were* with him. 7272
43:24 gave *them* water, and they washed their **f**; 7272
49:10 nor a lawgiver from between his **f**, 7272
49:33 he gathered up his **f** into the bed, and 7272
Ex 3: 5 put off thy shoes from off thy **f**, for 7272
4:25 of her son, and cast *it* at his **f**, and said, 7272
12:11 your shoes on your **f**, and your staff in your 7272
24:10 *there was* under his **f** as it were a paved 7272
25:26 four corners that *are* on the four **f** thereof. 7272
30:19 shall wash their hands and their **f** thereat: 7272
30:21 So they shall wash their hands and their **f**, 7272
37:13 four corners that *were* in the four **f** thereof. 7272
40:31 sons washed their hands and their **f** thereat: 7272
Lev 8:24 and upon the great toes of their right **f**: 7272
11:21 which have legs above their **f**, to leap 7272
11:23 which have four **f**, *shall be* an abomination 7272
11:42 whatsoever hath more **f** among all creeping 7272
Nu 20:19 *doing any* thing *else*, go through on my **f**. 7272
Dt 2:28 only I will pass through on my **f**; 7272
11:24 Every place whereon the soles of your **f** 7272
28:57 one that cometh out from between her **f**, 7272
33: 3 they sat down at thy **f**; *every one* shall 7272
Jos 3:13 as soon as the soles of the **f** of the priests 7272
3:15 the **f** of the priests that bare the ark were 7272
4: 3 out of the place where the priests' **f** stood 7272
4: 9 in the place where the **f** of the priests which 7272
4:18 the soles of the priests' **f** were lift up unto 7272
9: 5 old shoes and clouted upon their **f**, and 7272
10:24 put your **f** upon the necks of these kings. 7272
10:24 and put their **f** upon the necks of them. 7272
14: 9 Surely the land whereon thy **f** have trodden 7272
Jdg 3:24 Surely he covereth his **f** in *his* summer 7272
4:10 he went up with ten thousand men at his **f**: 7272
4:15 off *his* chariot, and fled away on his **f**. 7272
4:17 Howbeit Sisera fled away on his **f** to 7272
5:27 At her **f** he bowed, he fell, he lay down: 7272
5:27 at her **f** he bowed, he fell: where he bowed, 7272
19:21 they washed their **f**, and did eat and drink. 7272
Ru 3: 4 go in, and uncover his **f**, and lay thee down; 4772
3: 7 and uncovered his **f**, and laid her down. 4772
3: 8 and behold, a woman lay *at* his **f**. 4772
3:14 she lay *at* his **f** until the morning: and 4772
1Sa 2: 9 He will keep the **f** of his saints, and 7272
14:13 climbed up upon his hands and upon his **f**, 7272
24: 3 *was* a cave; and Saul went in to cover his **f**: 7272
25:24 fell at his **f**, and said, Upon me, my lord, 7272
25:41 to wash the **f** of the servants of my lord. 7272
2Sa 3:34 *were* not bound, nor thy **f** put into fetters: 7272
4: 4 had a son *that was* lame of *his* **f**, and 7272
4:12 cut off their hands and their **f**, and 7272
9: 3 hath yet a son, *which is* lame on *his* **f**. 7272
9:13 king's table; and *was* lame on both his **f**. 7272
11: 8 Go down to thy house, and wash thy **f**. 7272
19:24 had neither dressed his **f**, nor trimmed his 7272
22:10 came down; and darkness *was* under his **f**. 7272
22:34 He maketh my **f** like hinds' *feet:* and 7272
22:34 He maketh my feet like hinds' *f:* and NIH
22:37 steps under me; so that my **f** did not slip. 7166
22:39 not arise: yea, they are fallen under my **f**. 7272
1Ki 2: 5 and in his shoes that *were* on his **f**. 7272
5: 3 LORD put them under the soles of his **f**. 7272
14: 6 *so*, when Ahijah heard the sound of her **f**, 7272
14:12 *and* when thy **f** enter into the city, the child 7272
15:23 time of his old age he was diseased in his **f**. 7272
2Ki 4:27 of God to the hill, she caught him by the **f**: 7272
4:37 fell at his **f**, and bowed herself to 7272
6:32 *is* not the sound of his master's **f** behind 7272
9:35 and the **f**, and the palms of *her* hands. 7272
13:21 of Elisha, he revived, and stood up on his **f**. 7272
19:24 with the sole of my **f** have I dried up all 6471
21: 8 Neither will I make the **f** of Israel move any 7272
1Ch 28: 2 David the king stood up upon his **f**, and 7272
2Ch 3:13 they stood on their **f**, and their faces *were* 7272
16:12 ninth year of his reign was diseased in his **f**, 7272
Ne 9:21 waxed not old, and their **f** swelled not. 7272
Est 8: 3 fell down at his **f**, and besought him with 7272
Job 12: 5 He that is ready to slip with *his* **f** *is as* a 7272
13:27 Thou puttest my **f** also in the stocks, and 7272
13:27 thou settest a print upon the heels of my **f**. 7272
18: 8 For he is cast into a net by his own **f**, and 7272
18:11 on every side, and shall drive him to his **f**. 7272
29:15 eyes to the blind, and **f** *was* I to the lame. 7272
30:12 they push away my **f**, and they raise up 7272
33:11 He putteth my **f** in the stocks, he marketh 7272
Ps 8: 6 thou hast put all *things* under his **f**: 7272
18: 9 came down: and darkness *was* under his **f**. 7272
18:33 He maketh my **f** like hinds' *feet*, and 7272
18:33 He maketh my feet like hinds' *f*, and NIH
18:36 my steps under me, that my **f** did not slip. 7166
18:38 not able to rise: they are fallen under my **f**. 7272
22:16 they pierced my hands and my **f**. 7272
25:15 for he shall pluck my **f** out of the net. 7272
31: 8 thou hast set my **f** in a large room. 7272
40: 2 set my **f** upon a rock, *and* established my 7272
47: 3 under us, and the nations under our **f**. 7272
56:13 *wilt* not *thou deliver* my **f** from falling, 7272
58:10 he shall wash his **f** in the blood of 6471
66: 9 in life, and suffereth not our **f** to be moved. 7272
73: 2 *as for* me, my **f** were almost gone; my steps 7272
74: 3 Lift up thy **f** unto the perpetual desolations; 6471
91:13 and the dragon shalt thou **trample under f**. 7429
105:18 Whose **f** they hurt with fetters: he was laid 7272
115: 7 **f** *have* they, but they walk not: 7272
Ps 116: 8 eyes from tears, *and* my **f** from falling. 7272
119:59 and turned my **f** unto thy testimonies. 7272
119:101 I have refrained my **f** from every evil way, 7272
119:105 Thy word *is* a lamp unto my **f**, and a light 7272
122: 2 Our **f** shall stand within thy gates, 7272
Pr 1:16 For their **f** run to evil, and make haste to 7272
4:26 Ponder the path of thy **f**, and let all thy 7272
5: 5 Her **f** go down *to* death; her steps take hold 7272
6:13 with his eyes, he speaketh with his **f**, 7272
6:18 **f** that be swift in running to mischief, 7272
6:28 go upon hot coals, and his **f** not be burnt? 7272
7:11 and stubborn; her **f** abide not in her house: 7272
19: 2 and he that hasteth with *his* **f**, sinneth. 7272
26: 6 by the hand of a fool cutteth off the **f**, 7272
29: 5 his neighbour spreadeth a net for his **f**. 6471
SS 5: 3 I have washed my **f**; how shall I defile 7272
7: 1 How beautiful are thy **f** with shoes, 6471
Isa 3:16 they go, and making a tinkling with their **f**: 7272
3:18 of *their* tinkling ornaments *about their f*, NIH
6: 2 with twain he covered his **f**, and with twain 7272
7:20 of Assyria, the head, and the hair of the **f**: 7272
14:19 of the pit; as a carcase **trodden under f**. 947
23: 7 her own **f** shall carry her afar off to sojourn. 7272
26: 6 *even* the **f** of the poor, *and* the steps of 7272
28: 3 of Ephraim, shall be trodden under **f**: 7272
32:20 that send forth *thither* the **f** of the ox and 7272
37:25 with the sole of my **f** have I dried up all 6471
41: 3 *by* the way *that* he had not gone with his **f**. 7272
49:23 the earth, and lick up the dust of thy **f**; 7272
52: 7 How beautiful upon the mountains are the **f** 7272
59: 7 Their **f** run to evil, and they make haste to 7272
60:13 and I will make the place of my **f** glorious. 7272
60:14 bow themselves down at the soles of thy **f**; 7272
Jer 13:16 before your **f** stumble upon the dark 7272
14:10 they have not refrained their **f**, therefore 7272
18:22 a pit to take me, and hid snares for my **f**. 7272
38:22 thy **f** are sunk in the mire, *and* they are 7272
La 1:13 he hath spread a net for my **f**, he hath 7272
3:34 To crush under his **f** all the prisoners of 7272
Eze 1: 7 their **f** *were* straight feet; and the sole of 7272
1: 7 their feet *were* straight **f**; and the sole of 7272
1: 7 the sole of their **f** *was* like the sole of a 7272
2: 1 stand upon thy **f**, and I will speak unto thee. 7272
2: 2 set me upon my **f**, that I heard him that 7272
3:24 set me upon my **f**, and spake with me, and 7272
16:25 hast opened thy **f** to every one that passed 7272
24:17 put on thy shoes upon thy **f**, and cover not 7272
24:23 your heads, and your shoes upon your **f**: 7272
25: 6 stamped with the **f**, and rejoiced in heart 7272
32: 2 troubledst the waters with thy **f**, and 7272
34:18 ye must tread down with your **f** the residue 7272
34:18 but ye must foul the residue with your **f**? 7272
34:19 eat that which ye have trodden with your **f**; 7272
34:19 that which ye have fouled with your **f**. 7272
37:10 they lived, and stood up upon their **f**, 7272
43: 7 and the place of the soles of my **f**, 7272
Da 2:33 of iron, his **f** part of iron and part of clay. 7271
2:34 which smote the image upon his **f** *that were* 7271
2:41 whereas thou sawest the **f** and toes, part of 7271
2:42 *as* the toes of the **f** *were* part of iron, and 7271
7: 4 made stand upon the **f** as a man, and 7271
7: 7 and stamped the residue with the **f** of it: 7271
7:19 and stamped the residue with his **f**; 7271
10: 6 and his **f** like in colour to polished brass, 4772
Na 1: 3 and the clouds *are* the dust of his **f**. 7272
1:15 Behold upon the mountains the **f** of him 7272
Hab 3: 5 and burning coals went forth at his **f**. 7272
3:19 he will make my **f** like hinds' *feet*, and 7272
3:19 he will make my feet like hinds' *f*, and NIH
Zec 14: 4 his **f** shall stand in that day upon the mount 7272
14:12 away while they stand upon their **f**, 7272
Mal 4: 3 **f** in the day that I *shall* do *this*, saith 7272
Mt 7: 6 lest they trample them under their **f**, and *4228*
10:14 or city, shake off the dust of your **f**. *4228*
15:30 and cast them *down* at Jesus' **f**; *4228*
18: 8 or two **f** to be cast into everlasting fire. *4228*
18:29 And his fellowservant fell down at his **f**, *4228*
28: 9 And they came and held him by the **f**, and *4228*
Mk 5:22 and when he saw him, he fell at his **f**, *4228*
6:11 shake off the dust under your **f** for a *4228*
7:25 heard of him, and came and fell at his **f**: *4228*
9:45 than having two **f** to be cast into hell, *4228*
Lk 1:79 to guide our **f** into the way of peace. *4228*
7:38 And stood at his **f** behind *him* weeping, and *4228*
7:38 and began to wash his **f** with tears, and *4228*
7:38 and kissed his **f**, and anointed *them* with *4228*
7:44 thou gavest me no water for my **f**: *4228*
7:44 but she hath washed my **f** with tears, and *4228*
7:45 time I came in hath not ceased to kiss my **f**. *4228*
7:46 this *woman* hath anointed my **f** with *4228*
8:35 sitting at the **f** of Jesus, clothed, and in his *4228*
8:41 and he fell down at Jesus' **f**, and *4228*
9: 5 shake off the very dust from your **f** for a *4228*
10:39 which also sat at Jesus' **f**, and heard his *4228*
15:22 put a ring on his hand, and shoes on *his* **f**: *4228*
17:16 And fell down on *his* face at his **f**, *4228*
24:39 Behold my hands and my **f**, that it is I *4228*
24:40 he shewed them *his* hands and *his* **f**. *4228*
Jn 11: 2 and wiped his **f** with her hair, *4228*
11:32 and saw him, she fell down at his **f**, *4228*
12: 3 and anointed the **f** of Jesus, and wiped his *4228*
12: 3 feet of Jesus, and wiped his **f** with her hair: *4228*
13: 5 and began to wash the disciples' **f**, and *4228*
13: 6 saith unto him, Lord, dost thou wash my **f**? *4228*
13: 8 unto him, Thou shalt never wash my **f**. *4228*
13: 9 not my **f** only, but also *my* hands and *4228*
13:10 is washed needeth not save to wash *his* **f**, *4228*
13:12 So after he had washed their **f**, and *4228*
13:14 *your* Lord and Master, have washed your **f**; *4228*
13:14 ye also ought to wash one another's **f**. *4228*
20:12 the one at the head, and the other at the **f**, *4228*
Ac 3: 7 and immediately his **f** and ankle bones *939*
4:35 And laid *them down* at the apostles' **f**: and *4228*
4:37 the money, and laid *it* at the apostles' **f**. *4228*
5: 2 a certain part, and laid *it* at the apostles' **f**. *4228*
Ac 5: 9 the **f** of them which have buried thy *4228*
5:10 Then fell she down straightway at his **f**, and *4228*
7:33 Lord to him, Put off *thy* shoes from thy **f**: *4228*
7:58 laid down their clothes at a young man's **f**, *4228*
10:25 and fell down at *his* **f**, and *4228*
13:25 whose shoes of *his* **f** I am not worthy to *4228*
13:51 But they shook off the dust of their **f** *4228*
14: 8 a certain man at Lystra, impotent in *his* **f**, *4228*
14:10 with a loud voice, Stand upright on thy **f**. *4228*
16:24 and made their **f** fast in the stocks. *4228*
21:11 and bound his *own* hands and **f**, and said, *4228*
22: 3 yet brought up in this city at the **f** of *4228*
26:16 But rise, and stand upon thy **f**: for I have *4228*
Ro 3:15 Their **f** *are* swift to shed blood: *4228*
10:15 How beautiful *are* the **f** of them that preach *4228*
16:20 shall bruise Satan under your **f** shortly. *4228*
1Co 12:21 nor again the head to the **f**, I have no need *4228*
15:25 till he hath put all enemies under his **f**. *4228*
15:27 For he hath put all *things* under his **f**. *4228*
Eph 1:22 And hath put all *things* under his **f**, and *4228*
6:15 And *your* **f** shod with the preparation of *4228*
1Ti 5:10 if she have washed the saints' **f**, *4228*
Heb 2: 8 hast put all *things* in subjection under his **f**. *4228*
12:13 And make straight paths for your **f**, lest *that* *4228*
Rev 1:15 And his **f** like unto fine brass, as if they *4228*
1:17 And when I saw him, I fell at his **f** as dead. *4228*
2:18 a flame of fire, and his **f** *are* like fine brass; *4228*
3: 9 them to come and worship before thy **f**, *4228*
10: 1 *it were* the sun, and his **f** as pillars of fire: *4228*
11:11 into them, and they stood upon their **f**; *4228*
12: 1 and the moon under her **f**, and upon her *4228*
13: 2 and his **f** *were* as *the feet* of a bear, and *4228*
13: 2 and his feet *were* as *the f* of a bear, and NIG
19:10 And I fell at his **f** to worship him. And he *4228*
22: 8 I fell down to worship before the **f** of *4228*

FEIGN (3) [FEIGNED, FEIGNEDLY, FEIGNEST, UNFEIGNED]
2Sa 14: 2 **f** thyself **to be a mourner**, and put on now 56
1Ki 14: 5 that she shall **f** herself **to be another** 5234
Lk 20:20 which *should* **f** themselves just *men*, that *5271*

FEIGNED (3) [FEIGN]
1Sa 21:13 **f** himself **mad** in their hands, and 1984
Ps 17: 1 unto my prayer, *that goeth* not out of **f** lips. 4820
2Pe 2: 3 And through covetousness shall they with **f** *4112*

FEIGNEDLY (1) [FEIGN]
Jer 3:10 whole heart, but **f**, saith the LORD. 8267+871.1

FEIGNEST (2) [FEIGN]
1Ki 14: 6 why **f** thou thyself **to be another**? 5234
Ne 6: 8 but thou **f** them out of thine own heart. 908

FELIX (8) [FELIX']
Ac 23:24 and bring *him* safe unto **F** the governor. *5344*
23:26 excellent governor **F** *sendeth* greeting. *5344*
24: 3 *it* always, and in all places, most noble **F**, *5344*
24:22 And when **F** heard these *things*, having *5344*
24:24 when **F** came with his wife Drusilla, *5344*
24:25 and judgment to come, **F** trembled, *5344*
24:27 and **F**, willing to shew the Jews a pleasure, *5344*
25:14 There is a certain man left in bonds by **F**: *5344*

FELIX' (1) [FELIX]
Ac 24:27 two years Porcius Festus came into **F** room: *5344*

FELL (243) [FALL, FELLED, FELLER, FELLEST, FELLING]
Ge 4: 5 was very wroth, and his countenance **f**. 5307
14:10 of Sodom and Gomorrah fled, and **f** there; 5307
15:12 going down, a deep sleep **f** upon Abram; 5307
15:12 lo, a horror of great darkness **f** upon him. 5307
17: 3 Abram **f** on his face: and God talked with 5307
17:17 Abraham **f** upon his face, and laughed, 5307
33: 4 and **f** on his neck, and kissed him: 5307
44:14 and they **f** before him on the ground. 5307
45:14 And he **f** upon his brother Benjamin's neck, 5307
46:29 he **f** on his neck, and wept on his neck a 5307
50: 1 Joseph **f** upon his father's face, and 5307
50:18 also went and **f down** before his face; 5307
Ex 32:28 there **f** of the people that day about three 5307
Lev 9:24 they shouted, and **f** on their faces. 5307
16: 9 the goat upon which the LORD'S lot **f**, 5927
16:10 on which the lot **f** to be the scapegoat, 5927
Nu 11: 4 that *was* among them **f a lusting**: 183+8378
11: 9 when the dew **f** upon the camp in the night, 3381
11: 9 the camp in the night, the manna **f** upon it. 3381
14: 5 Aaron **f** on their faces before all 5307
16: 4 when Moses heard *it*, he **f** upon his face: 5307
16:22 they **f** upon their faces, and said, O God, 5307
16:45 in a moment. And they **f** upon their faces. 5307
20: 6 and they **f** upon their faces: 5307
22:27 of the LORD, she **f down** under Balaam: 7257
22:31 down his head, and **f flat** on his face. 7812
Dt 9:18 I **f down** before the LORD, as at the first, 5307
9:25 Thus I **f down** before the LORD forty 5307
9:25 as I **f down** *at the first;* because the LORD 5307
Jos 5:14 Joshua **f** on his face to the earth, and 5307
6:20 that the wall **f down** flat, so that the people 5307
7: 6 **f** to the earth upon his face before the ark of 5307
8:25 *so* it was, *that* all that **f** that day, both of 5307
11: 7 of Merom suddenly; and they **f** upon them. 5307
16: 1 the lot of the children of Joseph **f** from 3318
17: 5 there **f** ten portions to Manasseh, beside 5307
22:20 wrath **f** on all the congregation of Israel? 1961
Jdg 4:16 all the host of Sisera **f** upon the edge of 5307
5:27 At her feet he bowed, he **f**, he lay down: 5307
5:27 at her feet he bowed, he **f**: where he bowed, 5307
5:27 where he bowed, there he **f down** dead. 5307
7:13 and smote it that it **f**, and overturned it, 5307
8:10 for there **f** an hundred and twenty thousand 5307
12: 6 there **f** at that time of the Ephraimites forty 5307
13:20 on *it*, and **f** on their faces to the ground. 5307

Jdg 16:30 the house f upon the lords, and upon all 5307
19:26 f down at the door of the man's house 5307
20:44 there f of Benjamin eighteen thousand men; 5307
20:46 So that all which f that day of Benjamin 5307
Ru 2:10 she f on her face, and bowed herself to 5307
1Sa 4:10 for there f of Israel thirty thousand 5307
4:18 that he f from off the seat backward by 5307
11: 7 And the fear of the LORD f on the people, 5307
14:13 they f before Jonathan; and 5307
17:49 and he f upon his face to the earth. 5307
17:52 the wounded of the Philistines f down by 5307
20:41 f on his face to the ground, and 5307
22:18 he f upon the priests, and slew on that day 6293
25:23 f before David on her face, and 5307
25:24 f at his feet, and said, Upon me, my lord, 5307
28:20 Saul f straightway all along on the earth, 5307
29: 3 I have found no fault in him since he f unto 5307
30:13 left me, because three days agone I f sick. 2470
31: 1 and f down slain in mount Gilboa. 5307
31: 4 therefore Saul took a sword, and f upon it. 5307
31: 5 he f likewise upon his sword, and died with 5307
2Sa 1: 2 that he f to the earth, and did obeisance. 5307
2:16 his fellow's side; so they f down together: 5307
2:23 he f down there, and died in the same 5307
2:23 as came to the place where Asahel f down 5307
4: 4 haste to flee, that he f, and became lame. 5307
9: 6 he f on his face, and did reverence. 5307
11:17 there f some of the people of the servants of 5307
13: 2 so vexed, that he f sick for his sister Tamar; 2470
14: 4 she f on her face to the ground, and 5307
14:22 Joab f to the ground on his face, and 5307
18:28 he f down to the earth upon his face before 7812
19:18 Shimei the son of Gera f down before 5307
20: 8 sheath thereof; and as he went forth it f out. 5307
21: 9 they f all seven together, and were put to 5307
21:22 f by the hand of David, and by the hand of 5307
1Ki 2:25 of Jehoiada; and he f upon him that he died. 6293
2:32 who f upon two men more righteous and 6293
2:34 went up, and f upon him, and slew him: 6293
2:46 went out, and f upon him, that he died. 6293
14: 1 that time Abijah the son of Jeroboam f sick. 2470
17:17 the mistress of the house, f sick; 2470
18: 7 he knew him, and f on his face, and said, 5307
18:38 the fire of the LORD f, and consumed 5307
18:39 when all the people saw it, they f on their 5307
20:30 there a wall f upon twenty and 5307
2Ki 1: 2 Ahaziah f down through a lattice in his 5307
1:13 came and f on his knees before Elijah, and 3766
2:13 He took up also the mantle of Elijah that f 5307
2:14 he took the mantle of Elijah that f from 5307
3:19 shall f every good tree, and stop all wells of 5307
4: 8 it f on a day, that Elisha passed to Shunem, 1961
4:11 it f on a day, that he came thither, and 1961
4:18 when the child was grown, it f on a day, 1961
4:37 f at his feet, and bowed herself to 5307
6: 5 a beam, the axe head f into the water: 5307
6: 6 the man of God said, Where f it? And he 5307
7:20 so it f out unto him: for the people trode 1961
25:11 the fugitives that f away to the king of 5307
1Ch 5:10 with the Hagarites, who f by their hand: 5307
5:22 For there f down many slain, because 5307
10: 1 and f down slain in mount Gilboa. 5307
10: 4 So Saul took a sword, and f upon it. 5307
10: 5 he f likewise on the sword, and died. 5307
12:19 there f some of Manasseh to David, 5307
12:20 there f to him of Manasseh, Adnah, and 5307
20: 8 they f by the hand of David, and by 5307
21:14 and there f of Israel seventy thousand men. 5307
21:16 clothed in sackcloth, f upon their faces. 5307
26:14 the lot eastward f to Shelemiah. Then for 5307
27:24 because there f wrath for it against Israel; 1961
2Ch 13:17 there f down slain of Israel five hundred 5307
15: 9 for they f to him out of Israel in abundance, 5307
17:10 the fear of the LORD f upon all 1961
20:18 the inhabitants of Jerusalem f before 5307
21:19 his bowels f out by reason of his sickness: 3318
25:13 f upon the cities of Judah, from Samaria 6584
Ezr 9: 5 I f upon my knees, and spread out my 3766
Est 8: 3 f down at his feet, and besought him with 5307
8:17 for the fear of the Jews f upon them. 5307
9: 2 for the fear of them f upon all people. 5307
9: 3 because the fear of Mordecai f upon them. 5307
Job 1:15 the Sabeans f upon them, and took them 5307
1:17 f upon the camels, and have carried them 6584
1:19 it f upon the young men, and they are dead; 5307
1:20 f down upon the ground, and worshipped, 5307
Ps 27: 2 me to eat up my flesh, they stumbled and f. 5307
78:64 Their priests f by the sword; and 5307
105:38 for the fear of them f upon them. 5307
107:12 they f down, and there was none to help. 3782
Jer 39: 9 those that f away, that fell to him, with 5307
39: 9 those that fell away, that f to him, with 5307
46:16 made many to fall, yea, one f upon another: 5307
52:15 those that f away, that fell to the king of 5307
52:15 that f to the king of Babylon, and the rest of 5307
La 1: 7 when her people f into the hand of 5307
5:13 to grind, and the children f under the wood. 3782
Eze 1:28 when I saw it, I f upon my face, and I heard 5307
3:23 by the river of Chebar: and I f on my face. 5307
8: 1 that the hand of the Lord GOD f there 5307
9: 8 that I f upon my face, and cried, and said, 5307
11: 5 the Spirit of the LORD f upon me, and 5307
11:13 f I down upon my face, and cried with a 5307
39:23 of their enemies: so f they all by the sword. 5307
43: 3 by the river Chebar; and I f upon my face. 5307
44: 4 house of the LORD: and I f upon my face. 5307
Da 2:46 the king Nebuchadnezzar f upon his face, 5308
3: 7 f down and worshipped the golden image 5308
3:23 f down bound into the midst of the burning 5308
4:31 there f a voice from heaven, saying, O king 5308
7:20 which came up, and before whom three f; 5308
8:17 he came, I was afraid, and f upon my face: 5307
10: 7 a great quaking f upon them, so that they 5307
Jnh 1: 7 So they cast lots, and the lot f upon Jonah. 5307
Mt 2:11 and f down, and worshipped him: 4098
7:25 and beat upon that house; and it f not: 4098
7:27 and beat upon that house; and it f: 4098
13: 4 some seeds f by the way side, and the fowls 4098
13: 5 Some f upon stony places, where they had 4098
13: 7 And some f among thorns; and the thorns 4098
13: 8 But other f into good ground, and 4098
17: 6 And when the disciples heard it, they f on 4098
18:26 The servant therefore f down, and 4098
18:29 And his fellowservant f down at his feet, 4098
26:39 and f on his face, and prayed, saying, O my 4098
Mk 3:11 f down before him, and cried, saying, 4363
4: 4 some f by the way side, and the fowls of 4098
4: 5 And some f on stony ground, where it had 4098
4: 7 And some f among thorns, and the thorns 4098
4: 8 And other f on good ground, and did yield 4098
5:22 and when he saw him, he f at his feet, 4098
5:33 came and f down before him, and told him 4363
7:25 heard of him, and came and f at his feet: 4363
9:20 and he f on the ground, and 4098
14:35 and f on the ground, and prayed that, if it 4098
Lk 1:12 was troubled, and fear f upon him. 1968
5: 8 When Simon Peter saw it, he f down at 4363
5:12 who seeing Jesus f on his face, and 4098
6:49 did beat vehemently, and immediately it f; 4098
8: 5 and as he sowed, some f by the way side; 4098
8: 6 And some f upon a rock; and as soon as it 4098
8: 7 And some f among thorns; and the thorns 4098
8: 8 And other f on good ground, and sprang up, 4098
8:14 And that which f among thorns are they, 4098
8:23 But as they sailed he f asleep: and 879
8:28 and f down before him, and with a loud 4363
8:41 and he f down at Jesus' feet, and 4098
10:30 and f among thieves, which stripped him of 4045
10:36 was neighbour unto him that f among 1706
13: 4 upon whom the tower in Siloam f, and 4098
15:20 and ran, and f on his neck, and kissed him. 1968
16:21 crumbs which f from the rich man's table: 4098
17:16 And f down on his face at his feet, 4098
Jn 11:32 and saw him, she f down at his feet, 4098
18: 6 they went backward, and f to the ground. 4098
Ac 1:25 from which Judas by transgression f, 3845
1:26 and the lot f upon Matthias; and he was 4098
5: 5 And Ananias hearing these words f down, 4098
5:10 Then f she down straightway at his feet, 4098
7:60 And when he had said this, he f asleep. 2837
9: 4 And he f to the earth, and heard a voice 4098
9:18 And immediately there f from his eyes as it 634
10:10 while they made ready, he f into a trance, 1968
10:25 and f down at his feet, and 4098
10:44 the Holy Ghost f on all them which 1968
11:15 to speak, the Holy Ghost f on them, 1968
12: 7 And his chains f off from his hands. 1601
13:11 And immediately there f on him a 1968
13:36 f on sleep, and was laid unto his fathers, 2837
16:29 and f down before Paul and Silas, 4363
19:17 and fear f on them all, and the name 1968
19:35 of the image which f down from Jupiter? 1356
20: 9 and f down from the third loft, and 4098
20:10 and f on him, and embracing him said, 1968
20:37 and f on Paul's neck, and kissed him, 1968
22: 7 And I f unto the ground, and heard a voice 4098
Ro 11:22 on them which f, severity; but toward thee, 4098
15: 3 of them that reproached thee f on me. 1968
1Co 10: 8 and f in one day three and twenty thousand. 4098
Heb 3:17 whose carcases f in the wilderness? 4098
11:30 By faith the walls of Jericho f down, 4098
2Pe 3: 4 for since the fathers f asleep, all things 2837
Rev 1:17 And when I saw him, I f at his feet as dead. 4098
5: 8 and twenty elders f down before the Lamb, 4098
5:14 And the four and twenty elders f down and 4098
6:13 And the stars of heaven f unto the earth, 4098
7:11 and f before the throne on their faces, and 4098
8:10 and there f a great star from heaven, 4098
8:10 and it f upon the third part of the rivers, and 4098
11:11 and great fear f upon them which saw them. 4098
11:13 and the tenth part of the city f, and in 4098
11:16 f upon their faces, and worshipped God, 4098
16: 2 and there f a noisome and grievous sore 1096
16:19 three parts, and the cities of the nations f: 4098
16:21 And there f upon men a great hail out of 2597
19: 4 and the four beasts f down and 4098
19:10 And I f at his feet to worship him. And he 4098
22: 8 I f down to worship before the feet of 4098

FELLED (1) [FELL]
2Ki 3:25 the wells of water, and f all the good trees: 5307

FELLER (1) [FELL]
Isa 14: 8 art laid down, no f is come up against us. 3772

FELLEST (1) [FELL]
2Sa 3:34 a man falleth before wicked men, so f thou. 5307

FELLING (1) [FELL]
2Ki 6: 5 as one was f a beam, the axe head fell into 5307

FELLOES (1)
1Ki 7:33 their naves, and their f, and their spokes, 2839

FELLOW (27) [FELLOW'S, FELLOW-DISCIPLES, FELLOWCITIZENS, FELLOWHEIRS, FELLOWHELPER, FELLOWHELPERS, FELLOWLABOURER, FELLOWLABOURERS, FELLOWPRISONER, FELLOWPRISONERS, FELLOWS, FELLOWSERVANT, FELLOWSERVANTS, FELLOWSHIP, FELLOWSOLDIER, FELLOWWORKERS, WORKFELLOW, YOKEFELLOW]
Ge 19: 9 they said again, This one f came in to NIH
Ex 2:13 the wrong, Wherefore smitest thou thy f? 7453
Jdg 7:13 was a man that told a dream unto his f, 7453
7:14 his f answered and said, This is nothing 7453
7:22 set every man's sword against his f, 7453
1Sa 14:20 every man's sword was against his f, and 7453
21:15 that ye have brought this f to play the mad NIH
21:15 shall this f come into my house? NIH
25:21 Surely in vain have I kept all that this f hath NIH
29: 4 Make this f return, that he may go again to 376
2Sa 2:16 they caught every one his f by the head, 7453
1Ki 22:27 Put this f in the prison, and feed him with NIH
2Ki 9:11 wherefore came this mad f to thee? And he NIH
2Ch 18:26 Put this f in the prison, and feed him with NIH
Ecc 4:10 For if they fall, the one will lift up his f: but 2270
Isa 34:14 of the island, and the satyr shall cry to his f; 7453
Jnh 1: 7 And they said every one to his f, Come, and 7453
Zec 13: 7 and against the man that is my f, 5997
Mt 12:24 This f doth not cast out devils, but by NIG
26:61 And said, This f said, I am able to destroy NIG
26:71 This f was also with Jesus of Nazareth. NIG
Lk 22:59 saying, Of a truth this f also was with him: NIG
23: 2 We found this f perverting the nation, and NIG
Jn 9:29 as for this f, we know not from whence he NIG
Ac 18:13 This f persuadeth men to worship God NIG
22:22 and said, Away with such a f from the earth: NIG
24: 5 For we have found this man a pestilent f, NIG

FELLOW'S (1) [FELLOW]
2Sa 2:16 the head, and thrust his sword in his f side; 7453

FELLOWCITIZENS (1) [FELLOW, CITIZEN]
Eph 2:19 but f with the saints, and of the household 4847

FELLOW-DISCIPLES (1) [DISCIPLE, FELLOW]
Jn 11:16 called Didymus, unto his f, Let us also go, 4827

FELLOWHEIRS (1) [FELLOW, HEIR]
Eph 3: 6 That the Gentiles should be f, and of 4789

FELLOWHELPER (1) [FELLOW, HELP]
2Co 8:23 he is my partner and f concerning you: 4904

FELLOWHELPERS (1) [FELLOW, HELP]
3Jn 1: 8 that we might be f to the truth. 4904

FELLOWLABOURER (2) [FELLOW, LABOUR]
1Th 3: 2 and our f in the gospel of Christ, 4904
Phm 1: 1 unto Philemon our dearly beloved, and f, 4904

FELLOWLABOURERS (2) [FELLOW, LABOUR]
Php 4: 3 with Clement also, and with other my f, 4904
Phm 1:24 Marcus, Aristarchus, Demas, Lucas, my f. 4904

FELLOWPRISONER (2) [FELLOW, PRISON]
Col 4:10 Aristarchus my f saluteth you, and Marcus, 4869
Phm 1:23 salute thee Epaphras, my f in Christ Jesus; 4869

FELLOWPRISONERS (1) [FELLOW, PRISON]
Ro 16: 7 and Junia, my kinsmen, and my f, 4869

FELLOWS (13) [FELLOW]
Jdg 11:37 and bewail my virginity, I and my f. 7464
18:25 lest angry f run upon thee, and thou lose thy 376
2Sa 6:20 as one of the vain f shamelessly uncovereth NIH
Ps 45: 7 thee with the oil of gladness above thy f. 2270
Isa 44:11 Behold, all his f shall be ashamed: and 2270
Eze 37:19 the tribes of Israel his f, and will put them 2270
Da 2:13 and they sought Daniel and his f to be slain. 2269
2:18 his f should not perish with the rest of 2269
7:20 whose look was more stout than his f. 2273
Zec 3: 8 thou, and thy f that sit before thee: 7453
Mt 11:16 in the markets, and calling unto their f, 2083
Ac 17: 5 took unto them certain lewd f of the baser 435
Heb 1: 9 thee with the oil of gladness above thy f. 3353

FELLOWSERVANT (6) [FELLOW, SERVE]
Mt 18:29 And his f fell down at his feet, and 4889
18:33 not thou also have had compassion on thy f, 4889
Col 1: 7 As ye also learned of Epaphras our dear f, 4889
4: 7 and a faithful minister and f in the Lord: 4889
Rev 19:10 I am thy f, and of thy brethren that have 4889
22: 9 for I am thy f, and of thy brethren 4889

FELLOWSERVANTS (4) [FELLOW, SERVE]
Mt 18:28 servant went out, and found one of his f, 4889
18:31 So when his f saw what was done, 4889
24:49 And shall begin to smite his f, and to eat 4889
Rev 6:11 until their f also and their brethren, 4889

FELLOWSHIP (17) [FELLOW]
Lev 6: 2 or in f, or in a thing taken away by 3027+8667
Ps 94:20 Shall the throne of iniquity have f with 2266
Ac 2:42 stedfastly in the apostles' doctrine and f, 2842
1Co 1: 9 by whom ye were called unto the f of his 2842
10:20 I would not that ye should have f with 2844
2Co 6:14 for what f hath righteousness with 3352
8: 4 take upon us the f of the ministering to 2842
Gal 2: 9 to me and Barnabas the right hands of f; 2842
Eph 3: 9 And to make all men see what is the f of 2842
5:11 And have no f with the unfruitful works of 4790
Php 1: 5 For your f in the gospel from the first day 2842
2: 1 if any f of the Spirit, if any bowels and 2842
3:10 his resurrection, and the f of his sufferings, 2842
1Jn 1: 3 unto you, that ye also may have f with us: 2842
1: 3 and truly our f is with the Father, and with 2842
1: 6 If we say that we have f with him, and 2842
1: 7 we have f one with another, and the blood 2842

FELLOWSOLDIER (2) [FELLOW, SOLDIER]
Php 2:25 and f, but your messenger, and the fellow 4961
Phm 1: 2 and Archippus our f, and to the church in 4961

FELLOWWORKERS (1) [FELLOW, WORK]
Col 4:11 These only are my f unto the kingdom of 4904

FELT (5) [FEEL]
Ge 27:22 he f him, and said, The voice is Jacob's 4959

Ex 10:21 of Egypt, even darkness *which* may be **f**. 4959
Pr 23:35 not sick; they have beaten me, *and* I **f** *it* not: 3045
Mk 5:29 she **f** in *her* body that she was healed of *that* *1097*
Ac 28: 5 off the beast into the fire, and **f** no harm. *3958*

FEMALE (24)
Ge 1:27 created he him; male and **f** created he them. 5347
5: 2 Male and **f** created he them; and 5347
6:19 alive with thee; they shall be male and **f**. 5347
7: 2 take to thee by sevens, the male and his **f**: 802
7: 2 that *are* not clean by two, the male and his **f**. 802
7: 3 also of the air by sevens, the male and the **f**; 5347
7: 9 unto Noah into the ark, the male and the **f**, 5347
7:16 that went in, went in male and **f** of all flesh, 5347
Lev 3: 1 whether *it be* a male or **f**, he shall offer it 5347
3: 6 male or **f**, he shall offer it without blemish. 5347
4:28 a kid of the goats, a **f** without blemish, 5347
4:32 he shall bring it a **f** without blemish. 5347
5: 6 a **f** from the flock, a lamb or a kid of 5347
12: 7 the law for her that hath born a male or a **f**. 5347
27: 4 if it *be* a **f**, then thy estimation shall be 5347
27: 5 twenty shekels, and for the **f** ten shekels. 5347
27: 6 for the **f** thy estimation *shall be* three 5347
27: 7 be fifteen shekels, and for the **f** ten shekels. 5347
Nu 5: 3 Both male and **f** shall ye put out, without 5347
Dt 4:16 of any figure, the likeness of male or **f**, 5347
7:14 shall not be male or **f barren** among you, 6135
Mt 19: 4 at the beginning made them male and **f**, *2338*
Mk 10: 6 of the creation God made them male and **f**. *2338*
Gal 3:28 bond nor free, there is neither male nor **f**: *2338*

FEMALE SLAVES See WOMENSERVANTS

FENCE (1) [FENCED]
Ps 62: 3 wall *shall ye be, and as* a tottering **f**. 1447

FENCED (38) [FENCE]
Nu 32:17 our little ones shall dwell in the **f** cities 4013
32:36 Beth-nimrah, and Beth-haran, **f** cities: and 4013
Dt 3: 5 All these cities *were* **f** *with* high walls, 1219
9: 1 than thyself, cities great and **f** up to heaven, 1219
28:52 until thy high and **f** walls come down, 1219
Jos 10:20 remained of them entered into **f** cities. 4013
14:12 and *that* the cities *were* great *and* **f**: 1219
19:35 the **f** cities *are* Ziddim, Zer, and Hammath, 4013
1Sa 6:18 *both* of **f** cities, and of country villages, 4013
2Sa 20: 6 lest he get him **f** cities, and escape us. 1219
23: 7 the man *that* shall touch them must be **f** 4390
2Ki 3:19 ye shall smite every **f** city, and every choice 4013
10: 2 and horses, a **f** city also, and armour; 4013
17: 9 from the tower of the watchmen to the **f** 4013
18: 8 from the tower of the watchmen to the **f** 4013
18:13 come up against all the **f** cities of Judah, 1219
19:25 that thou shouldest be to lay waste **f** cities 1219
2Ch 8: 5 **f** cities, *with* walls, gates, and bars; 4692
11:10 *are* in Judah and in Benjamin, **f** cities. 4694
11:23 of Judah and Benjamin, unto every **f** city: 4694
12: 4 he took the **f** cities which *pertained* to 4694
14: 6 he built **f** cities in Judah: for the land had 4694
17: 2 he placed forces in all the **f** cities of Judah, 1219
17:19 besides *those* whom the king put in the **f** 4013
19: 5 he set judges in the land throughout all the **f** 1219
21: 3 of precious things, with **f** cities in Judah: 4694
32: 1 encamped against the **f** cities, and 1219
33:14 put captains of war in all the **f** cities of 1219
Job 10:11 flesh, and hast **f** me with bones and sinews. 7753
19: 8 He hath **f up** my way that I cannot pass, 1443
Isa 2:15 every high tower, and upon every **f** wall, 1219
5: 2 he **f** it, and gathered out the stones thereof, 5823
Jer 5:17 they shall impoverish thy **f** cities, 4013
15:20 I will make thee unto this people a **f** brasen 1219
Eze 36:35 and desolate and ruined cities *are become* **f**, 1219
Da 11:15 cast up a mount, and take the **most** **f** cities: 4013
Hos 8:14 and Judah hath multiplied **f** cities: 1219
Zep 1:16 the trumpet and alarm against the **f** cities, 1219

FENS (1)
Job 40:21 shady trees, in the covert of the reed, and **f**. 1207

FERRET (1)
Lev 11:30 And the **f**, and the chameleon, and the lizard, 604

FERRY (1)
2Sa 19:18 there went over a **f boat** to carry over 5679

FERVENT (7) [FERVENTLY]
Ac 18:25 and being **f** in the spirit, he spake and *2204*
Ro 12:11 in business; **f** in spirit; serving the Lord; *2204*
2Co 7: 7 your mourning, your **f mind** toward me; *2205*
Jas 5:16 The **effectual** **f** prayer of a righteous *man* *1754*
1Pe 4: 8 And above all *things* have **f** charity among *1618*
2Pe 3:10 and the elements shall melt with **f heat**, *2741*
3:12 and the elements shall melt with **f heat**? *2741*

FERVENTLY (2) [FERVENT]
Col 4:12 always **labouring f** for you in prayers, *75*
1Pe 1:22 *that ye* love one another with a pure heart **f**: *1619*

FESTERING See BLAINS; SCAB; SCABBED; SCURVY

FESTIVAL; FESTIVALS See SOLEMNITIES; SOLEMNITY

FESTUS (12) [FESTUS']
Ac 24:27 But after two years Porcius **F** came into *5347*
25: 1 Now when **F** was come into the province, *5347*
25: 4 But **F** answered, that Paul should be kept at *5347*
25: 9 But **F**, willing to do the Jews a pleasure, *5347*
25:12 Then **F**, when he had conferred with *5347*
25:13 and Bernice came unto Cesarea to salute **F**. *5347*
25:14 **F** declared Paul's cause unto the king, *5347*
25:22 Then Agrippa said unto **F**, I would also *5347*
Ac 25:24 And **F** said, King Agrippa, and all men *5347*
26:24 **F** said with a loud voice, Paul, thou art *5347*
26:25 But he said, I am not mad, most noble **F**; *5347*
26:32 Then said Agrippa unto **F**, This man might *5347*

FESTUS' (1) [FESTUS]
Ac 25:23 at **F** commandment Paul was brought *5347*

FET (9) [FETCH]
2Sa 9: 5 **f** him out of the house of Machir, the son of 3947
11:27 David sent and **f** her to his house, and 622
1Ki 7:13 king Solomon sent and **f** Hiram out of Tyre. 3947
9:28 **f** from thence gold, four hundred and 3947
2Ki 11: 4 and **f** the rulers over hundreds, 3947
2Ch 12:11 the guard came and **f** them, and 5375
Jer 26:23 they **f forth** Urijah out of Egypt, and 3318
36:21 So the king sent Jehudi to **f** the roll: and 3947
Ac 28:13 And from thence we **f a compass**, *4022*

FETCH (30) [FET, FETCHED, FETCHETH, FETCHT]
Ge 18: 5 I will **f** a morsel of bread, and comfort ye 3947
27: 9 **f** me from thence two good kids of 3947
27:13 only obey my voice, and go **f** me *them*. 3947
27:45 I will send, and **f** thee from thence: why 3947
42:16 let him **f** your brother, and ye shall be kept 3947
Ex 2: 5 among the flags, she sent her maid to **f** it. 3947
Nu 20:10 must we **f** you water out of this rock? 3318
34: 5 the border shall **f a compass** from Azmon 5437
Dt 19:12 of his city shall send and **f** him thence, 3947
24:10 thou shalt not go into his house to **f** his 5670
24:19 in the field, thou shalt not go again to **f** it: 3947
30: 4 gather thee, and from thence will he **f** thee: 3947
Jdg 11: 5 the elders of Gilead went to **f** Jephthah out 3947
20:10 to **f** victual for the people, that *they* may do, 3947
1Sa 4: 3 Let us **f** the ark of the covenant of 3947
6:21 come ye down, *and* **f** it **up** to you. 5927
16:11 Samuel said unto Jesse, Send and **f** him: 3947
20:31 Wherefore now send and **f** him unto me, 3947
26:22 one of the young men come over and **f** it. 3947
2Sa 5:23 *but* **f a compass** behind them, and 5437
14:13 in that the king doth not **f** *home* **again** his 7725
14:20 To **f about** *this* form of speech hath thy 5437
1Ki 17:10 he called to her, and said, **F** me, I pray thee, 3947
17:11 as she was going to **f** *it*, he called to her, and 3947
2Ki 6:13 spy where he *is*, that I may send and **f** him. 3947
2Ch 18: 8 said, **F quickly** Micaiah the son of Imla. 4116
Ne 8:15 and **f** olive branches, and pine branches, and 935
Job 36: 3 I will **f** my knowledge from afar, and 5375
Isa 56:12 *say they*, I will **f** wine, and we will fill 3947
Ac 16:37 but let them come themselves and **f** us **out**. *1806*

FETCHED (7) [FETCH]
Ge 18: 4 be **f**, and wash your feet, and 3947
27:14 and **f**, and brought *them* to his mother: 3947
Jos 15: 3 up to Adar, and **f a compass** to Karkaa: 5437
Jdg 18:18 **f** the carved image, the ephod, and 3947
1Sa 7: 1 **f up** the ark of the LORD, and brought it 5927
10:23 they ran and **f** him thence: and when he 3947
2Sa 4: 6 *as though* they would have **f** wheat; 3947

FETCHETH (1) [FETCH]
Dt 19: 5 his hand **f a stroke** with the axe to cut 5080

FETCHT (4) [FETCH]
Ge 18: 7 **f** a calf tender and good, and gave *it* unto a 3947
2Sa 14: 2 **f** thence a wise woman, and said unto her, 3947
2Ki 3: 9 they **f a compass** of seven days' journey: 5437
2Ch 1:17 they **f up**, and brought forth out of Egypt a 5927

FETTERS (11)
Jdg 16:21 to Gaza, and bound him with **f of brass**; 5178
2Sa 3:34 *were* not bound, nor thy feet put into **f**: 5178
2Ki 25: 7 bound him with **f of brass**, and carried him 5178
2Ch 33:11 bound him with **f**, and carried him to 5178
36: 6 bound him in **f**, to carry him to Babylon. 5178
Job 36: 8 if *they be* bound in **f**, *and* be holden in 2131
Ps 105:18 Whose feet they hurt with **f**: he was laid *in* 3525
149: 8 with chains, and their nobles with **f** of iron; 3525
Mk 5: 4 that he had been often bound with **f** *3976*
5: 4 asunder by him, and the **f** broken in pieces: *3976*
Lk 8:29 and he was kept bound with chains and in **f**; *3976*

FEVER (9)
Dt 28:22 and with a **f**, and with an inflammation, and 6920
Mt 8:14 saw his wife's mother laid, and **sick of a f**. *4445*
8:15 And he touched her hand, and the **f** left her: *4446*
Mk 1:30 But Simon's wife's mother lay **sick of a f**, *4445*
1:31 and immediately the **f** left her, and *4446*
Lk 4:38 wife's mother was taken with a great **f**; *4446*
4:39 And he stood over her, and rebuked the **f**; *4446*
Jn 4:52 Yesterday at the seventh hour the **f** left him. *4446*
Ac 28: 8 that the father of Publius lay sick of a **f** and *4446*

FEW (65) [FEWER, FEWEST, FEWNESS]
Ge 24:55 Let the damsel abide with us *a* **f** days, at NIH
27:44 tarry with him a **f** days, until thy brother's 259
29:20 they seemed unto him *but* a **f** days, for 259
34:30 I *being* **f** in number, they shall gather 4962
47: 9 **f** and evil have the days of the years of my 4592
Lev 25:52 but **f** years unto the year of jubile, 4592
26:22 your cattle, and **make** you **f in number**; 4591
Nu 9:20 when the cloud was a **f** days upon 4557
13:18 whether they *be* strong or weak, **f** or many; 4592
26:54 to **f** thou shalt give the less inheritance: 4592
26:56 thereof be divided between many and **f**. 4592
35: 8 but from *them that have* **f** ye shall give few: 4592
35: 8 but from *them that have* few ye shall **give f**: 4591
Dt 4:27 ye shall be left **f** in number among 4962
26: 5 sojourned there with a **f**, and 4592+4962
28:62 ye shall be left **f** in number, whereas ye 4592
33: 6 and not die; and let *not* his men be **f**. 4557
Jos 7: 3 people to labour thither; for they *are but* **f**. 4592
1Sa 14: 6 to the LORD to save by many or by **f**. 4592
17:28 with whom hast thou left those **f** sheep in 4592
2Ki 4: 3 *even* empty vessels; borrow not a **f**. 4591
1Ch 16:19 When ye were *but* **f**, even a few, and 4557+4962
16:19 *but* few, even a **f**, and strangers in it. 4592
2Ch 29:34 the priests were *too* **f**, so that they could not 4592
Ne 2:12 in the night, I and *some* **f** men with me; 4592
7: 4 the people *were* **f** therein, and the houses 4592
Job 10:20 *Are* not my days **f**? cease then, and let me 4592
14: 1 Man *that is* born of a woman *is* of **f** days, 7116
16:22 When a **f** years are come, then I shall go 4557
Ps 105:12 When they were *but a* **f** men in number; NIH
105:12 in number; yea, *very* **f**, and strangers in it. 4592
109: 8 Let his days be **f**; *and* let another take his 4592
Ecc 5: 2 upon earth: therefore let thy words be **f**. 4592
9:14 *There was* a little city, and **f** men within it; 4592
12: 3 the grinders cease because they are **f**, and 4591
Isa 10: 7 heart to destroy and cut off nations not a **f**. 4592
10:19 the rest of the trees of his forest shall be **f**, 4557
24: 6 of the earth are burned, and **f** men left. 4213
Jer 30:19 will multiply them, and they shall not be **f**; 4591
42: 2 (for we are left *but* a **f** of many, as thine 4592
Eze 5: 3 Thou shalt also take thereof a **f** in number, 4592
12:16 I will leave a **f** men of them from 4557
Da 11:20 within **f** days he shall be destroyed, 259
Mt 7:14 leadeth unto life, and **f** there be that find it. *3641*
9:37 truly is plenteous, but the labourers *are* **f**; *3641*
15:34 And they said, Seven, and a **f** little fishes. *3641*
20:16 first last: for many be called, but **f** chosen. *3641*
22:14 For many are called, but **f** *are* chosen. *3641*
25:21 thou hast been faithful over a **f** *things*, I *3641*
25:23 thou hast been faithful over a **f** *things*, I *3641*
Mk 6: 5 save that he laid *his* hands upon a **f** sick *3641*
8: 7 And they had a **f** small fishes: and *3641*
Lk 10: 2 truly *is* great, but the labourers *are* **f**: *3641*
12:48 shall be beaten with **f** *stripes*. For unto *3641*
13:23 unto him, Lord, are there **f** that be saved? *3641*
Ac 17: 4 and of the chief women not a **f**. *3641*
17:12 which were Greeks, and of men, not a **f**. *3641*
24: 4 hear us of thy clemency a **f words**. *4935*
Eph 3: 3 the mystery; (as I wrote afore in **f** *words*, *3641*
Heb 12:10 For they verily for a **f** days chastened *us* *3641*
13:22 for I have written a letter unto you in **f** *1024*
1Pe 3:20 the ark was a preparing, wherein **f**, that is, *3641*
Rev 2:14 But I have a **f** *things* against thee, because *3641*
2:20 Notwithstanding I have a **f** *things* against *3641*
3: 4 Thou hast a **f** names even in Sardis, *3641*

FEWER (1) [FEW]
Nu 33:54 to the **f** ye shall give the less inheritance: 4592

FEWEST (1) [FEW]
Dt 7: 7 any people; for ye *were* the **f** of all people: 4592

FEWNESS (1) [FEW]
Lev 25:16 according to the **f** of years thou shalt 4591

FIDELITY (1)
Tit 2:10 Not purloining, but shewing all good **f**; *4102*

FIELD (290) [FIELDS]
Ge 2: 5 every plant of the **f** before it was in 7704
2: 5 and every herb of the **f** before it grew: 7704
2:19 LORD God formed every beast of the **f**, 7704
2:20 fowl of the air, and to every beast of the **f**; 7704
3: 1 of the **f** which the LORD God had made. 7704
3:14 all cattle, and above every beast of the **f**; 7704
3:18 to thee; and thou shalt eat the herb of the **f**; 7704
4: 8 it came to pass, when they were in the **f**, 7704
23: 9 which he hath, which *is* in the end of his **f**; 7704
23:11 the **f** give I thee, and the cave that *is* 7704
23:13 I will give *thee* money for the **f**; take *it* of 7704
23:17 the **f** of Ephron, which *was* in Machpelah, 7704
23:17 the **f**, and the cave which *was* therein, 7704
23:17 and all the trees that *were* in the **f**, 7704
23:19 cave of the **f** of Machpelah before Mamre: 7704
23:20 the **f**, and the cave that *is* therein, were 7704
24:63 Isaac went out to meditate in the **f** at 7704
24:65 What man *is* this that walketh in the **f** to 7704
25: 9 in the **f** of Ephron the son of Zohar 7704
25:10 The **f** which Abraham purchased of 7704
25:27 Esau was a cunning hunter, a man of the **f**; 7704
25:29 and Esau came from the **f**, and he *was* faint: 7704
27: 3 go out to the **f**, and take me *some* venison; 7704
27: 5 Esau went to the **f** to hunt for venison, *and* 7704
27:27 the smell of my son *is* as the smell of a **f** 7704
29: 2 and behold a well in the **f**, and lo, 7704
30:14 found mandrakes in the **f**, and brought them 7704
30:16 Jacob came out of the **f** in the evening, and 7704
31: 4 and Leah to the **f** unto his flock, 7704
33:19 he bought a parcel of a **f**, where he had 7704
34: 5 now his sons were with his cattle in the **f**: 7704
34: 7 the sons of Jacob came out of the **f** when 7704
34:28 *was* in the city, and that which *was* in the **f**, 7704
36:35 who smote Midian in the **f** of Moab, 7704
37: 7 we *were* binding sheaves in the **f**, and lo, 7704
37:15 and behold, *he was* wandering in the **f**: 7704
39: 5 all that he had in the house, and in the **f**. 7704
41:48 the food of the **f**, which *was* round about 7704
47:20 for the Egyptians sold every man his **f**, 7704
47:24 for seed of the **f**, and for your food, and 7704
49:29 cave that *is* in the **f** of Ephron the Hittite, 7704
49:30 In the cave that *is* in the **f** of Machpelah, 7704
49:30 which Abraham bought with the **f** of 7704
49:32 The purchase of the **f** and of the cave that *is* 7704
50:13 buried him in the cave of the **f** of 7704
50:13 which Abraham bought with the **f** for a 7704
Ex 1:14 and in all manner of service in the **f**: 7704
9: 3 LORD is upon thy cattle which *is* in the **f**, 7704
9:19 thy cattle, and all that thou hast in the **f**; 7704
9:19 and beast which shall be found in the **f**, 7704
9:21 left his servants and his cattle in the **f**. 7704
9:22 upon beast, and upon every herb of the **f**, 7704
9:25 all the land of Egypt all that *was* in the **f**, 7704
9:25 the hail smote every herb of the **f**, and 7704
9:25 of the field, and brake every tree of the **f**. 7704

Ex 10: 5 tree which groweth for you out of the f: 7704
10:15 or in the herbs of the f, through all the land 7704
16:25 to day ye shall not find it in the f. 7704
22: 5 If a man shall cause a f or vineyard to be 7704
22: 5 his beast, and shall feed in another man's f; 7704
22: 5 of the best of his own f, and of the best of 7704
22: 6 of corn, or the standing corn, or the f, 7704
22:31 eat any flesh that is torn of beasts in the f; 7704
23:11 what they leave the beasts of the f shall eat. 7704
23:16 thy labours, which thou hast sown in the f: 7704
23:16 hast gathered in thy labours out of the f. 7704
23:29 and the beast of the f multiply against thee. 7704
Lev 14: 7 let the living bird loose into the open f. 7704
17: 5 which they offer in the open f, even that 7704
19: 9 shalt not wholly reap the corners of thy f, 7704
19:19 thou shalt not sow thy f with mingled seed: 7704
23:22 of the corners of thy f when thou reapest, 7704
25: 3 Six years thou shalt sow thy f, and six years 7704
25: 4 thou shalt neither sow thy f, nor prune thy 7704
25:12 ye shall eat the increase thereof out of the f. 7704
25:34 the f of the suburbs of their cities may not 7704
26: 4 and the trees of the f shall yield their fruit. 7704
27:16 LORD some part of a f of his possession, 7704
27:17 If he sanctify his f from the year of jubile, 7704
27:18 if he sanctify his f after the jubile, then 7704
27:19 if he that sanctified the f will in any wise 7704
27:20 if he will not redeem the f, or if he have 7704
27:20 or if he have sold the f to another man, 7704
27:21 the f, when it goeth out in the jubile, 7704
27:21 be holy unto the LORD, as a f devoted; 7704
27:22 if a man sanctify unto the LORD a f 7704
27:24 In the year of the jubile the f shall return 7704
27:28 and beast, and of the f of his possession, 7704
Nu 22: 4 as the ox licketh up the grass of the f. 7704
22:23 aside out of the way, and went into the f: 7704
23:14 he brought him into the f of Zophim, to 7704
Dt 5:21 his f, or his manservant, or his maidservant, 7704
7:22 lest the beasts of the f increase upon thee. 7704
14:22 that the f bringeth forth year by year. 7704
20:19 down (for the tree of the f is man's life) 7704
21: 1 lying in the f, and it be not known who hath 7704
22:25 if a man find a betrothed damsel in the f, 7704
22:27 For he found her in the f, and the betrothed 7704
24:19 thou cuttest down thine harvest in thy f, 7704
24:19 hast forgot a sheaf in the f, thou shalt not 7704
28: 3 the city, and blessed shalt thou be in the f. 7704
28:16 in the city, and cursed shalt thou be in the f. 7704
28:38 Thou shalt carry much seed out into the f, 7704
Jos 8:24 of slaying all the inhabitants of Ai in the f, 7704
15:18 that she moved him to ask of her father a f: 7704
Jdg 1:14 that she moved him to ask of her father a f: 7704
5: 4 when thou marchedst out of the f of Edom, 7704
5:18 unto the death in the high places of the f. 7704
9:32 that is with thee, and lie in wait in the f: 7704
9:42 that the people went out into the f; 7704
9:43 laid wait in the f, and looked, and behold, 7704
13: 9 again unto the woman as she sat in the f: 7704
19:16 old man from his work out of the f at even, 7704
20:31 the other to Gibeah in the f, about thirty 7704
Ru 2: 2 Let me now go to the f, and glean ears of 7704
2: 3 came, and gleaned in the f after the reapers: 7704
2: 3 her hap was to light on a part of the f 7704
2: 8 Go not to glean in another f, neither go 7704
2: 9 Let thine eyes be on the f that they do reap, 7704
2:17 So she gleaned in the f until even, and 7704
2:22 that they meet thee not in any other f. 7704
4: 5 What day thou buyest the f of the hand of 7704
1Sa 4: 2 they slew of the army in the f about four 7704
6:14 the cart came into the f of Joshua, 7704
6:18 which stone remaineth unto this day in the f 7704
11: 5 Saul came after the herd out of the f; 7704
14:15 the host, in the f, and among all the people: 7704
17:44 fowls of the air, and to the beasts of the f. 7704
19: 3 stand beside my father in the f where thou 7704
20:11 Come, and let us go out into the f. 7704
20:11 And they went out both of them into the f. 7704
20:24 So David hid himself in the f: and when 7704
20:35 that Jonathan went out into the f at the time 7704
30:11 they found an Egyptian in the f, and 7704
2Sa 10: 8 and Maacah, were by themselves in the f. 7704
11:23 came out unto us into the f, and we were 7704
14: 6 they two strove together in the f, and 7704
14:30 Joab's f is near mine, and he hath barley 2513
14:30 And Absalom's servants set the f on fire. 2513
14:31 Wherefore have thy servants set my f on 2513
17: 8 as a bear robbed of her whelps in the f: 7704
18: 6 So the people went out into the f against 7704
20:12 Amasa out of the highway into the f, 7704
21:10 by day, nor the beasts of the f by night. 7704
1Ki 11:29 and they two were alone in the f: 7704
14:11 him that dieth in the f shall the fowls of 7704
21:24 him that dieth in the f shall the fowls of 7704
2Ki 4:39 one went out into the f to gather herbs, and 7704
7:12 out of the camp to hide themselves in the f, 7704
8: 6 all the fruits of the f since the day that she 7704
9:25 cast him in the portion of the f of Naboth 7704
9:37 the face of the f in the portion of Jezreel; 7704
18:17 which is in the highway of the fuller's f. 7704
19:26 they were as the grass of the f, and as 7704
1Ch 1:46 which smote Midian in the f of Moab, 7704
19: 9 that were come were by themselves in the f. 7704
27:26 over them that did the work of the f for 7704
2Ch 26:23 they buried him with his fathers in the f of 7704
31: 5 and honey, and of all the increase of the f; 7704
Ne 13:10 did the work, were fled every one to his f. 7704
Job 5:23 shalt be in league with the stones of the f: 7704
5:23 the beasts of the f shall be at peace with 7704
24: 6 They reap every one his corn in the f: and 7704
40:20 where all the beasts of the f play. 7704
Ps 8: 7 and oxen, yea, and the beasts of the f; 7704
50:11 and the wild beasts of the f are mine. 7704
78:12 in the land of Egypt, in the f of Zoan. 7704
78:43 in Egypt, and his wonders in the f of Zoan: 7704
80:13 and the wild beast of the f doth devour it. 7704
96:12 Let the f be joyful, and all that is therein: 7704
Ps 103:15 as a flower of the f, so he flourisheth. 7704
104:11 They give drink to every beast of the f: 7704
Pr 24:27 and make it fit for thyself in the f; 7704
24:30 I went by the f of the slothful, and by 7704
27:26 and the goats are the price of the f. 7704
31:16 She considereth a f, and buyeth it: with 7704
Ecc 5: 9 for all: the king himself is served by the f. 7704
SS 2: 7 by the roes, and by the hinds of the f, 7704
3: 5 by the roes, and by the hinds of the f, 7704
7:11 my beloved, let us go forth into the f; 7704
Isa 5: 8 that lay f to field, till there be no place, 7704
5: 8 that lay field to f, till there be no place, 7704
7: 3 upper pool in the highway of the fuller's f; 7704
10:18 and of his **fruitful** f, both soul and body: 3759
16:10 taken away, and joy out of the **plentiful** f; 3759
29:17 Lebanon shall be turned into a **fruitful** f, 3759
29:17 the **fruitful** f shall be esteemed as a forest? 3759
32:15 the wilderness be a **fruitful** f, and 3759
32:15 and the **fruitful** f be counted for a forest. 3759
32:16 and righteousness remain in the **fruitful** f. 3759
36: 2 upper pool in the highway of the fuller's f. 7704
37:27 they were as the grass of the f, and as 7704
40: 6 goodliness thereof is as the flower of the f: 7704
43:20 The beast of the f shall honour me, 7704
55:12 all the trees of the f shall clap their hands. 7704
56: 9 All ye beasts of the f, come to devour, 7704
Jer 4:17 As keepers of a f, are they against her 7704
6:25 Go not forth into the f, nor walk by 7704
7:20 upon the trees of the f, and upon the fruit of 7704
9:22 of men shall fall as dung upon the open f, 7704
12: 4 and the herbs of every f wither, 7704
12: 9 come ye, assemble all the beasts of the f, 7704
14: 5 the hind also calved in the f, and forsook it, 7704
14:18 If I go forth into the f, then behold the slain 7704
17: 3 O my mountain in the f, I will give thy 7704
18:14 which cometh from the rock of the f? 7704
26:18 Zion shall be plowed like a f, and 7704
27: 6 the beasts of the f have I given him also to 7704
28:14 I have given him the beasts of the f also. 7704
32: 7 Buy thee my f that is in Anathoth: 7704
32: 8 said unto me, Buy my f, I pray thee, that is 7704
32: 9 I bought the f of Hanameel my uncle's son, 7704
32:25 Buy thee the f for money, and 7704
35: 9 neither have we vineyard, nor f, nor seed: 7704
41: 8 for we have treasures in the f, of wheat, and 7704
48:33 and gladness is taken from the **plentiful** f, 3759
La 4: 9 through for want of the fruits of the f. 7704
Eze 7:15 he that is in the f shall die with the sword; 7704
16: 5 thou wast cast out in the open f, to 7704
16: 7 caused thee to multiply as the bud of the f, 7704
17: 5 of the land, and planted it in a fruitful f; 7704
17:24 all the trees of the f shall know that I 7704
20:46 prophesy against the forest of the south f; 7704
26: 6 her daughters which are in the f shall be 7704
26: 8 slay with the sword thy daughters in the f: 7704
29: 5 given thee for meat to the beasts of the f 776
31: 4 her little rivers unto all the trees of the f. 7704
31: 5 was exalted above all the trees of the f, 7704
31: 6 under his branches did all the beasts of the f 7704
31:13 all the beasts of the f shall be upon his 7704
31:15 and all the trees of the f fainted for him. 7704
32: 4 I will cast thee forth upon the open f, and 7704
33:27 him that is in the open f will I give to 7704
34: 5 they became meat to all the beasts of the f, 7704
34: 8 flock became meat to every beast of the f, 7704
34:27 the tree of the f shall yield her fruit, and 7704
36:30 fruit of the tree, and the increase of the f, 7704
38:20 the beasts of the f, and all creeping things 7704
39: 4 and to the beasts of the f to be devoured. 7704
39: 5 Thou shalt fall upon the open f: for I have 7704
39:10 So that they shall take no wood out of the f, 7704
39:17 to every beast of the f, 7704
Da 2:38 the beasts of the f and the fowls of 1251
4:12 the beasts of the f had shadow under it, and 1251
4:15 and brass, in the tender grass of the f; 1251
4:21 under which the beasts of the f dwelt, and 1251
4:23 and brass, in the tender grass of the f; 1251
4:23 let his portion be with the beasts of the f, 1251
4:25 dwelling shall be with the beasts of the f, 1251
4:32 dwelling shall be with the beasts of the f: 1251
Hos 2:12 and the beasts of the f shall eat them. 7704
2:18 a covenant for them with the beasts of the f, 7704
4: 3 with the beasts of the f, and with the fowls 7704
10: 4 up as hemlock in the furrows of the f. 7704
Joel 1:10 The f is wasted, the land mourneth; for 7704
1:11 because the harvest of the f is perished. 7704
1:12 even all the trees of the f, are withered: 7704
1:19 the flame hath burnt all the trees of the f. 7704
1:20 The beasts of the f cry also unto thee: 7704
2:22 Be not afraid, ye beasts of the f: for 7704
Mic 1: 6 I will make Samaria as a heap of the f, 7704
3:12 shall Zion for your sake be plowed as a f, 7704
4:10 thou shalt dwell in the f, and thou shalt go 7704
Zec 10: 1 showers of rain, to every one grass in the f. 7704
Mal 3:11 vine cast her fruit before the time in the f, 7704
Mt 6:28 Consider the lilies of the f, how they grow; *68*
6:30 Wherefore, if God so clothe the grass of the f, *68*
13:24 unto a man which sowed good seed in his f: *68*
13:27 Sir, didst not thou sow good seed in thy f? *68*
13:31 which a man took, and sowed in his f: *68*
13:36 unto us the parable of the tares of the f. *68*
13:38 The f is the world; the good seed are *68*
13:44 of heaven is like unto treasure hid in a f; *68*
13:44 and selleth all that he hath, and buyeth that f. *68*
24:18 Neither let him which is in the f return back to *68*
24:40 Then shall two be in the f; the one shall be *68*
27: 7 and bought with them the potter's f, to bury *68*
27: 8 Wherefore that f was called, The field of *68*
27: 8 field was called, The f of blood, unto this day. *68*
27:10 And gave them for the potter's f, as the Lord *68*
Mk 13:16 And let him that is in the f not turn back again *68*
Lk 2: 8 same country shepherds abiding in the f, *5561*
12:28 which is to day in the f, and to morrow is cast *68*
15:25 Now his elder son was in the f: and as he *68*
17: 7 when he is come from the f, Go and sit down *68*
Lk 17:31 and he that is in the f, let him likewise not *68*
17:36 Two men shall be in the f; the one shall be *68*
Ac 1:18 Now this man purchased a f with *5564*
1:19 insomuch as that f is called in their proper *5564*
1:19 Aceldama, that is to say, The f of blood. *5564*

FIELD COMMANDER See RABSHAKEH

FIELDS (60) [FIELD]

Ex 8:13 out of the villages, and out of the f. 7704
Lev 14:53 living bird out of the city into the open f, 7704
25:31 shall be counted as the f of the country: 7704
27:22 which is not of the f of his possession; 7704
Nu 16:14 or given us inheritance of f and vineyards: 7704
19:16 one that is slain with a sword in the open f, 7704
20:17 we will not pass through the f, or 7704
21:22 we will not turn into the f, or into 7704
Dt 11:15 I will send grass in thy f for thy cattle, 7704
32:13 that he might eat the increase of the f; 7704
32:32 vine of Sodom, and of the f of Gomorrah: 7709
Jos 21:12 the f of the city, and the villages thereof, 7704
Jdg 9:27 they went out into the f, and gathered their 7704
9:44 ran upon all the people that were in the f, 7704
1Sa 8:14 he will take your f, and your vineyards, 7704
20: 5 that I may hide myself in the f unto 7704
22: 7 the son of Jesse give every one of you f 7704
25:15 with them, when we were in the f: 7704
2Sa 1:21 there be rain upon you, nor f of offerings: 7704
11:11 of my lord, are encamped in the open f; 7704
1Ki 2:26 Get thee to Anathoth, unto thine own f; 7704
16: 4 him that dieth of his in the f shall the fowls 7704
2Ki 23: 4 he burnt them without Jerusalem in the f of 7709
1Ch 6:56 the f of the city, and the villages thereof, 7704
16:32 let the f rejoice, and all that is therein. 7704
27:25 over the storehouses in the f, in the cities, 7704
2Ch 31:19 which were in the f of the suburbs of their 7704
Ne 11:25 for the villages, with their f, some of 7704
11:30 the f thereof, at Azekah, and in the villages 7704
12:29 and out of the f of Geba and Azmaveth: 7704
12:44 to gather into them out of the f of the cities 7704
Job 5:10 the earth, and sendeth waters upon the f: 2351
Ps 107:37 sow the f, and plant vineyards, which may 7704
132: 6 we found it in the f of the wood. 7704
Pr 8:26 as yet he had not made the earth, nor the f, 2351
23:10 and enter not into the f of the fatherless: 7704
Isa 16: 8 For the f of Heshbon languish, and the vine 7709
32:12 for the pleasant f, for the fruitful vine. 7704
Jer 6:12 unto others, with their f and wives together: 7704
8:10 their f to them that shall inherit them: for 7704
13:27 and thine abominations on the hills in the f. 7704
31:40 and all the f unto the brook of Kidron, 7709
32:15 Houses and f and vineyards shall be 7704
32:43 f shall be bought in this land, whereof ye 7704
32:44 Men shall buy f for money, and 7704
39:10 gave them vineyards and f at the same time. 3010
40: 7 captains of the forces which were in the f, 7704
40:13 the captains of the forces that were in the f, 7704
Eze 29: 5 thou shalt fall upon the open f; thou shalt 7704
Hos 12:11 altars are as heaps in the furrows of the f. 7704
Ob 1:19 and they shall possess the f of Ephraim, and 7704
1:19 the fields of Ephraim, and the f of Samaria: 7704
Mic 2: 2 they covet f, and take them by violence; 7704
2: 4 turning away he hath divided our f. 7704
Hab 3:17 shall fail, and the f shall yield no meat; 7709
Mk 2:23 that he went through the **corn** f on *4702*
Lk 6: 1 the first, that he went through the **corn** f; *4702*
15:15 and he sent him into his f to feed swine. *68*
Jn 4:35 Lift up your eyes, and look on the f; *5561*
Jas 5: 4 labourers which have reaped down your f, *5561*

FIERCE (41) [FIERCENESS, FIERCER, FIERY]

Ge 49: 7 Cursed be their anger, for it was f; and 5794
Ex 32:12 Turn from thy f wrath, and repent of this 2740
Nu 25: 4 that the f anger of the LORD may be 2740
32:14 to augment yet the f anger of the LORD 2740
Dt 28:50 A nation of f countenance, which shall not 5794
1Sa 20:34 So Jonathan arose from the table in f anger, 2750
28:18 nor executedst his f wrath upon Amalek, 2740
2Ch 28:11 for the f wrath of the LORD is upon you. 2740
28:13 is great, and there is f wrath against Israel. 2740
29:10 that his f wrath may turn away from us. 2740
Ezr 10:14 until the f wrath of our God for this matter 2740
Job 4:10 the voice of the f **lion**, and the teeth of 7826
10:16 Thou huntest me as a f **lion**: and again thou 7826
28: 8 not trodden it, nor the f **lion** passed by it. 7826
41:10 None is so f that dare stir him up: who then 393
Ps 88:16 Thy f **wrath** goeth over me; thy terrors 2740
Isa 7: 4 for the f anger of Rezin with Syria, and 2750
13: 9 cruel both with wrath and f anger, to lay 2740
13:13 of hosts, and in the day of his f anger. 2740
19: 4 a f king shall rule over them, saith the Lord, 5794
33:19 Thou shalt not see a f people, a people of a 3267
Jer 4: 8 for the f anger of the LORD is not turned 2740
4:26 presence of the LORD, and by his f anger. 2740
12:13 because of the f anger of the LORD. 2740
25:37 because of the f anger of the LORD. 2740
25:38 the oppressor, and because of his f anger. 2740
30:24 The f anger of the LORD shall not return, 2740
49:37 even my f anger, saith the LORD; 2740
51:45 deliver ye every man his soul from the f 2740
La 1:12 hath afflicted me in the day of his f anger. 2740
2: 3 He hath cut off in his f anger all the horn of 2750
4:11 he hath poured out his f anger, and 2740
Da 8:23 a king of f countenance, and 5794
Jnh 3: 9 and repent, and turn away from his f anger, 2740
Hab 1: 8 and are more f than the evening wolves: 2300
Zep 2: 2 before the f anger of the LORD come 2740
3: 8 them mine indignation, even all my f anger: 2740
Mt 8:28 exceeding f, so that no man might pass by *5467*
Lk 23: 5 And they were the **more** f, saying, He *2001*
2Ti 3: 3 trucebreakers, false accusers, incontinent, f, *434*
Jas 3: 4 they be so great, and are driven of f winds, *4642*

FIERCENESS (12) [FIERCE]

Dt 13:17 that the LORD may turn from the **f** of his 2740
Jos 7:26 So the LORD turned from the **f** of his 2740
2Ki 23:26 turned not from the **f** of his great wrath, 2740
2Ch 30: 8 that the **f** of his wrath may turn away from 2740
Job 39:24 He swalloweth the ground with **f** and rage: 7494
Ps 78:49 He cast upon them the **f** of his anger, wrath, 2740
85: 3 thou hast turned *thyself* from the **f** of thine 2740
Jer 25:38 because of the **f** of the oppressor, 2740
Hos 11: 9 I will not execute the **f** of mine anger, I will 2740
Na 1: 6 who can abide in the **f** of his anger? 2740
Rev 16:19 to give unto her the cup of the wine of the **f** *2372*
19:15 and he treadeth the winepress of the **f** and *2372*

FIERCER (1) [FIERCE]

2Sa 19:43 the words of the men of Judah were **f** than 7185

FIERY (20) [FIERCE]

Nu 21: 6 the LORD sent **f** serpents among 8314
21: 8 Make thee a **f** *serpent*, and set it upon a 8314
Dt 8:15 *wherein were* **f** serpents, and scorpions, and 8314
33: 2 from his right hand *went* a **f** law for them. 784
Ps 21: 9 Thou shalt make them as a **f** oven in the time 784
Isa 14:29 and his fruit *shall be* a **f** flying **serpent**. 8314
30: 6 and old lion, the viper and **f** flying **serpent**, 8314
Da 3: 6 cast into the midst of a burning **f** furnace. 5135
3:11 cast into the midst of a burning **f** furnace. 5135
3:15 hour into the midst of a burning **f** furnace; 5135
3:17 to deliver us from the burning **f** furnace, 5135
3:20 *and* to cast *them* into the burning **f** furnace. 5135
3:21 were cast into the midst of the burning **f** 5135
3:23 into the midst of the burning **f** furnace. 5135
3:26 near to the mouth of the burning **f** furnace, 5135
7: 9 his throne *was like* the **f** flame, *and* 5135
7:10 A **f** stream issued and came forth from 5135
Eph 6:16 able to quench all the **f** darts of the wicked. *4448*
Heb 10:27 looking for of judgment and **f** indignation, *4442*
1Pe 4:12 think it not strange concerning the **f trial** *4451*

FIFTEEN (24) [FIFTEENTH]

Ge 5:10 Cainan eight hundred and **f** years, 2568+6240
7:20 **F** cubits upward did the waters 2568+6240
25: 7 **threescore and f** years. 2568+7657+2050.1
Ex 27:14 *one* side *of the gate shall be* **f** cubits: 2568+6240
27:15 **f** *cubits:* their pillars three, and 2568+6240
38:14 the *one* side *of the gate were* **f** cubits; 2568+6240
38:15 that hand, *were* hangings of **f** cubits; 2568+6240
38:25 **threescore and f** 2568+7657+2050.1+2050.1
Lev 27: 7 thy estimation shall be **f** shekels, and 2568+6240
Nu 31:37 *and* **threescore and f**. 2568+7657+2050.1
Jdg 8:10 about **f** thousand *men*, all that were 2568+6240
2Sa 9:10 Ziba had **f** sons and twenty servants. 2568+6240
19:17 his **f** sons and his twenty servants 2568+6240
1Ki 7: 3 *lay* on forty five pillars, **f** *in* a row. 2568+6240
2Ki 14:17 of Jehoahaz king of Israel **f** years. 2568+6240
20: 6 I will add unto thy days **f** years; and 2568+6240
2Ch 25:25 of Jehoahaz king of Israel **f** years. 2568+6240
Isa 38: 5 I will add unto thy days **f** years. 2568+6240
Eze 45:12 twenty shekels, **f** shekels, 2568+6235+2050.1
Hos 3: 2 So I bought her to me for **f** *pieces* of 2568+6240
Jn 11:18 nigh unto Jerusalem, about **f** furlongs off: *1178*
Ac 7:14 his kindred, **threescore and f** souls. *1440+4002*
27:28 they sounded again, and found *it* **f** fathoms. *1178*
Gal 1:18 to see Peter, and abode with him **f** days. *1178*

FIFTEENTH (18) [FIFTEEN]

Ex 16: 1 on the **f** day of the second month 2568+6240
Lev 23: 6 on the **f** day of the same month *is* 2568+6240
23:34 The **f** day of this seventh month *shall* 2568+6240
23:39 Also in the **f** day of the seventh 2568+6240
Nu 28:17 in the **f** day of this month *is* the feast: 2568+6240
29:12 on the **f** day of the seventh month ye 2568+6240
33: 3 on the **f** day of the first month; 2568+6240
1Ki 12:32 on the **f** day of the month, like unto 2568+6240
12:33 the **f** day of the eighth month, 2568+6240
2Ki 14:23 In the **f** year of Amaziah the son of 2568+6240
1Ch 24:14 The **f** to Bilgah, the sixteenth to 2568+6240
25:22 The **f** to Jeremoth, *he*, his sons, and 2568+6240
2Ch 15:10 in the **f** year of the reign of Asa. 2568+6240
Est 9:18 on the **f** *day* of the same they rested, 2568+6240
9:21 and the **f** day of the same, yearly, 2568+6240
Eze 32:17 in the **f** *day* of the month, 2568+6240
45:25 In the seventh *month*, in the **f** day of 2568+6240
Lk 3: 1 Now in the **f** year of the reign of Tiberius *4003*

FIFTH (61) [FIVE]

Ge 1:23 and the morning were the **f** day. 2549
30:17 she conceived, and bare Jacob the **f** son. 2549
41:34 **take up the f** *part* of the land of Egypt in 2567
47:24 that you shall give the **f** *part* unto Pharaoh, 2549
47:26 *that* Pharaoh should have the **f** *part;* except 2569
Lev 5:16 holy *thing*, and shall add the **f** *part* thereto, 2549
6: 5 shall add the **f** *part* more thereto, *and* give it 2549
19:25 in the **f** year shall ye eat of the fruit thereof, 2549
22:14 he shall put the **f** *part* thereof unto it, and 2549
27:13 he shall add a **f** *part* thereof unto thy 2549
27:15 he shall add the **f** *part* of the money of thy 2549
27:19 he shall add the **f** *part* of the money of thy 2549
27:27 and shall add a **f** *part* of it thereto: 2549
27:31 he shall add thereto the **f** *part* thereof. 2549
Nu 5: 7 add unto it the **f** *part* thereof, and give *it* 2549
7:36 On the **f** day Shelumiel the son of 2549
29:26 on the **f** day nine bullocks, two rams, *and* 2549
33:38 of Egypt, in the first *day* of the **f** month. 2549
Jos 19:24 the **f** lot came out for the tribe of 2549
Jdg 19: 8 he arose early in the morning on the **f** day 2549
2Sa 2:23 **f** *rib*, that the spear came out behind him; 2570
3: 4 and the **f**, Shephatiah the son of Abital; 2549
3:27 smote him there *under* the **f** *rib*, that he 2570
4: 6 they smote him under the **f** *rib:* and Rechab 2570
20:10 so he smote him therewith in the **f** *rib*, and 2570
1Ki 6:31 *and* side posts *were* a **f** *part of the wall.* 2549
14:25 it came to pass in the **f** year of king 2549
2Ki 8:16 in the **f** year of Joram the son of Ahab king 2568
2Ki 25: 8 in the **f** month, on the seventh *day* of 2549
1Ch 2:14 Nethaneel the fourth, Raddai the **f**, 2549
3: 3 The **f**, Shephatiah of Abital: the sixth, 2549
8: 2 Nohah the fourth, and Rapha the **f**. 2549
12:10 Mishmannah the fourth, Jeremiah the **f**, 2549
24: 9 The **f** to Malchijah, the sixth to Mijamin, 2549
25:12 The **f** *to* Nethaniah, *he*, his sons, and 2549
26: 3 Elam the **f**, Jehohanan the sixth, 2549
26: 4 and Sacar the fourth, and Nethaneel the **f**, 2549
27: 8 The **f** captain for the fifth month *was* 2549
27: 8 The fifth captain for the **f** month *was* 2549
2Ch 12: 2 *that* in the **f** year of king Rehoboam 2549
Ezr 7: 8 he came *to* Jerusalem in the **f** month, 2549
7: 9 on the first *day* of the **f** month came he to 2549
Ne 6: 5 the **f** time with an open letter in his hand; 2549
6:15 in the twenty and **f** *day of the month* Elul, 2568
Jer 1: 3 away of Jerusalem captive in the **f** month. 2549
28: 1 in the fourth year, *and* in the **f** month, 2549
36: 9 it came to pass in the **f** year of Jehoiakim 2549
52:12 Now in the **f** month, in the tenth *day* of 2549
Eze 1: 1 in the fourth *month*, in the **f** *day* of 2568
1: 2 In the **f** *day* of the month, which *was* 2568
1: 2 which *was* the **f** year of king Jehoiachin's 2549
8: 1 in the sixth *month*, in the **f** *day* of 2568
20: 1 in the **f** *month*, the tenth *day* of the month, 2549
33:21 in the tenth *month*, in the **f** *day* of 2568
Zec 7: 3 Should I weep in the **f** month, 2549
7: 5 When ye fasted and mourned in the **f** and 2549
8:19 of the fourth *month*, and the fast of the **f**, 2549
Rev 6: 9 And when he had opened the **f** seal, I saw *3991*
9: 1 And the **f** angel sounded, and I saw a star *3991*
16:10 And the **f** angel poured out his vial upon *3991*
21:20 The **f**, sardonyx; the sixth, sardius; *3991*

FIFTIES (8) [FIFTY]

Ex 18:21 of hundreds, rulers of **f**, and rulers of tens: 2572
18:25 of hundreds, rulers of **f**, and rulers of tens. 2572
Dt 1:15 captains over **f**, and captains over tens, and 2572
1Sa 8:12 over thousands, and captains over **f**; 2572
2Ki 1:14 burnt up the two captains of the former **f** 2572
1:14 captains of the former fifties with their **f**: 2572
Mk 6:40 sat down in ranks, by hundreds, and by **f**. *4004*
Lk 9:14 Make them sit down by **f** in a company. *4004*

FIFTIETH (4) [FIFTY]

Lev 25:10 ye shall hallow the **f** year, and 2572
25:11 A jubile shall that **f** year be unto you: 2572
2Ki 15:23 In the **f** year of Azariah king of Judah 2572
15:27 **f** year of Azariah king of Judah Pekah 2572

FIFTY (157) [FIFTIES, FIFTIETH]

Ge 6:15 the breadth of it **f** cubits, and the height of 2572
7:24 upon the earth an hundred and **f** days. 2572
8: 3 and **f** days the waters were abated. 2572
9:28 after the flood three hundred and **f** years. 2572
9:29 of Noah were nine hundred and **f** years: 2572
18:24 Peradventure there be **f** righteous within 2572
18:24 not spare the place for the **f** righteous that 2572
18:26 If I find in Sodom **f** righteous within 2572
18:28 Peradventure there shall lack five of the **f** 2572
Ex 26: 5 **F** loops shalt thou make in the one curtain, 2572
26: 5 **f** loops shalt thou make in the edge of 2572
26: 6 thou shalt make **f** taches of gold, and 2572
26:10 thou shalt make **f** loops on the edge of 2572
26:10 **f** loops in the edge of the curtain which 2572
26:11 thou shalt make **f** taches of brass, and 2572
27:12 the west side *shall be* hangings of **f** cubits: 2572
27:13 on the east side eastward *shall be* **f** cubits. 2572
27:18 **f every where**, 2572+2572+871.1+1886.1
30:23 *even* two hundred and **f** *shekels*, and 2572
30:23 sweet calamus two hundred and **f** *shekels*, 2572
36:12 **F** loops made he in one curtain, and 2572
36:12 **f** loops made he in the edge of the curtain 2572
36:13 he made **f** taches of gold, and coupled 2572
36:17 he made **f** loops upon the uttermost edge of 2572
36:17 **f** loops made he upon the edge of 2572
36:18 he made **f** taches of brass to couple the tent 2572
38:12 for the west side *were* hangings of **f** cubits, 2572
38:13 And for the east side eastward **f** cubits. 2572
38:26 and five hundred and **f** *men*. 2572
Lev 23:16 the seventh sabbath shall ye number **f** days; 2572
27: 3 even thy estimation shall be **f** shekels of 2572
27:16 a homer of barley seed *shall be valued* at **f** 2572
Nu 1:23 *were* **f** and nine thousand and 2572
1:25 and five thousand six hundred and **f**. 2572
1:29 *were* **f** and four thousand and four hundred. 2572
1:31 *were* **f** and seven thousand and 2572
1:43 *were* **f** and three thousand and 2572
1:46 and three thousand and five hundred and **f**. 2572
2: 6 *were* **f** and four thousand and four hundred. 2572
2: 8 *were* **f** and seven thousand and 2572
2:13 *were* **f** and nine thousand and 2572
2:15 and five thousand and six hundred and **f**. 2572
2:16 **f** and one thousand and four hundred and 2572
2:16 and one thousand and four hundred and **f**, 2572
2:30 *were* **f** and three thousand and 2572
2:31 and **f** and seven thousand and six hundred. 2572
2:32 and three thousand and five hundred and **f**. 2572
4: 3 years old and upward even until **f** years old, 2572
4:23 upward until **f** years old shalt thou number 2572
4:30 upward even unto **f** years old shalt thou 2572
4:35 years old and upward even unto **f** years old, 2572
4:36 were two thousand seven hundred and **f**. 2572
4:39 years old and upward even unto **f** years old, 2572
4:43 years old and upward even unto **f** years old, 2572
4:47 years old and upward even unto **f** years old, 2572
8:25 from the age of **f** years they shall cease 2572
16: 2 two hundred and **f** princes of the assembly, 2572
16:17 man his censer, two hundred and **f** censers; 2572
16:35 and **f** men that offered incense. 2572
26:10 the fire devoured two hundred and **f** men: 2572
26:34 **f** and two thousand and seven hundred. 2572
26:47 *who were* **f** and three thousand and 2572
31:30 thou shalt take one portion of **f**, of 2572
Nu 31:47 Moses took one portion of **f**, *both* of man 2572
31:52 thousand seven hundred and **f** shekels. 2572
Dt 22:29 unto the damsel's father **f** *shekels* of silver, 2572
Jos 7:21 a wedge of gold of **f** shekels weight, then 2572
1Sa 6:19 even he smote of the people **f** thousand 2572
2Sa 15: 1 and horses, and **f** men to run before him. 2572
24:24 and the oxen for **f** shekels of silver. 2572
1Ki 1: 5 and horsemen, and **f** men to run before him. 2572
7: 2 the breadth thereof **f** cubits, and the height 2572
7: 6 the length thereof *was* **f** cubits, and 2572
9:23 five hundred and **f**, which bare rule over 2572
10:29 of silver, and a horse for an hundred and **f**: 2572
18: 4 hid them *by* **f** in a cave, and fed them *with* 2572
18:13 LORD'S prophets **by f** in a cave, 2572+2572
18:19 the prophets of Baal four hundred and **f**, 2572
18:22 prophets *are* four hundred and **f** men. 2572
2Ki 1: 9 the king sent unto him a captain of **f** with 2572
1: 9 sent unto him a captain of fifty with his **f**. 2572
1:10 Elijah answered and said to the captain of **f**, 2572
1:10 from heaven, and consume thee and thy **f**. 2572
1:10 from heaven, and consumed him and his **f**. 2572
1:11 unto him another captain of **f** with his fifty. 2572
1:11 unto him another captain of fifty with his **f**. 2572
1:12 from heaven, and consume thee and thy **f**. 2572
1:12 from heaven, and consumed him and his **f**. 2572
1:13 he sent again a captain of the third **f** with 2572
1:13 again a captain of the third fifty with his **f**. 2572
1:13 the third captain of **f** went up, and came 2572
1:13 my life, and the life of these **f** thy servants, 2572
2: 7 And **f** men of the sons of the prophets went, 2572
2:16 there be with thy servants **f** strong men; 2572
2:17 They sent therefore **f** men; and they sought 2572
13: 7 *of* the people to Jehoahaz but **f** horsemen, 2572
15: 2 he reigned two and **f** years in Jerusalem. 2572
15:20 of each man **f** shekels *of* silver, to give to 2572
15:25 and with him **f** men of the Gileadites: 2572
21: 1 and reigned **f** and five years in Jerusalem. 2572
1Ch 5:21 *of* their camels **f** thousand, and *of* sheep 2572
5:21 *of* sheep two hundred and **f** thousand, and 2572
8:40 and sons' sons, an hundred and **f**. 2572
9: 9 nine hundred and **f** and six. 2572
12:33 of war, **f** thousand, which could keep rank: 2572
2Ch 1:17 of silver, and a horse for an hundred and **f**: 2572
2:17 **f** thousand and three thousand and 2572
3: 9 the weight of the nails *was* **f** shekels of 2572
8:10 *even* two hundred and **f**, that bare rule over 2572
8:18 thence four hundred and **f** talents of gold, 2572
26: 3 he reigned **f** and two years in Jerusalem. 2572
33: 1 he reigned **f** and five years in Jerusalem: 2572
Ezr 2: 7 a thousand two hundred **f** and four. 2572
2:14 children of Bigvai, two thousand **f** and six. 2572
2:15 children of Adin, four hundred **f** and four. 2572
2:22 The men of Netophah, **f** and six. 2572
2:29 The children of Nebo, **f** and two. 2572
2:30 children of Magbish, an hundred **f** and six. 2572
2:31 a thousand two hundred **f** and four. 2572
2:37 children of Immer, a thousand **f** and two. 2572
2:60 children of Nekoda, six hundred **f** and two. 2572
8: 3 genealogy of the males an hundred and **f**. 2572
8: 6 the son of Jonathan, and with him **f** males. 2572
8:26 hand six hundred and **f** talents *of* silver, 2572
Ne 5:17 an hundred and **f** of the Jews and rulers, 2572
6:15 *day of the month* Elul, in **f** and two days. 2572
7:10 children of Arah, six hundred **f** and two. 2572
7:12 a thousand two hundred **f** and four. 2572
7:20 children of Adin, six hundred **f** and five. 2572
7:33 The men of the other Nebo, **f** and two. 2572
7:34 a thousand two hundred **f** and four. 2572
7:40 children of Immer, a thousand **f** and two. 2572
7:70 **f** basons, five hundred and thirty priests' 2572
Est 5:14 Let a gallows be made of **f** cubits high, and 2572
7: 9 Behold also, the gallows **f** cubits high, 2572
Isa 3: 3 The captain of **f**, and the honourable *man*, 2572
Eze 40:15 of the porch of the inner gate *were* **f** cubits. 2572
40:21 the length thereof *was* **f** cubits, and 2572
40:25 the length *was* **f** cubits, and the breadth five 2572
40:29 *it was* **f** cubits long, and five and 2572
40:33 *it was* **f** cubits long, and five and 2572
40:36 the length *was* **f** cubits, and the breadth five 2572
42: 2 north door, and the breadth *was* **f** cubits. 2572
42: 7 the length thereof *was* **f** cubits. 2572
42: 8 that *were* in the utter court *was* **f** cubits: 2572
45: 2 **f** cubits round about *for* the suburbs 2572
48:17 be toward the north two hundred and **f**, 2572
48:17 toward the south two hundred and **f**, and 2572
48:17 toward the east two hundred and **f**, and 2572
48:17 and toward the west two hundred and **f**. 2572
Hag 2:16 for to draw out **f** *vessels out of* the press, 2572
Lk 7:41 ought five hundred pence, and the other **f**. *4004*
16: 6 thy bill, and sit down quickly, and write **f**. *4004*
Jn 8:57 Thou art not yet **f** years old, and hast thou *4004*
21:11 of great fishes, an hundred and **f** *and* three: *4004*
Ac 13:20 about *the space of* four hundred and **f** years, *4004*
19:19 found *it* **f thousand** *pieces* of silver. *3461+4002*

FIG (41) [FIGS]

Ge 3: 7 they sewed **f** leaves together, and 8384
Dt 8: 8 and vines, and **f trees**, and pomegranates; 8384
Jdg 9:10 the trees said to the **f tree**, Come thou, *and* 8384
9:11 the **f tree** said unto them, Should I forsake 8384
1Ki 4:25 man under his vine and under his **f tree**, 8384
2Ki 18:31 every one of his **f tree**, and drink ye every 8384
Ps 105:33 He smote their vines also and their **f trees**; 8384
Pr 27:18 Whoso keepeth the **f tree** shall eat the fruit 8384
SS 2:13 The **f tree** putteth forth her green figs, and 8384
Isa 34: 4 the vine, and as a falling *f* from the fig tree. NIH
34: 4 the vine, and as a falling *fig* from the **f tree**. 8384
36:16 every one *of* his **f tree**, and drink ye every 8384
Jer 5:17 they shall eat up thy vines and thy **f trees**: 8384
8:13 nor figs on the **f tree**, and the leaf shall 8384
Hos 2:12 And I will destroy her vines and her **f trees**, 8384
9:10 as the firstripe in the **f tree** at her first time: 8384
Joel 1: 7 laid my vine waste, and barked my **f tree**: 8384
1:12 vine is dried up, and the **f tree** languisheth; 8384
2:22 the **f tree** and the vine do yield their 8384

Am 4: 9 and your vineyards and your **f trees** and 8384
Mic 4: 4 man under his vine and under his **f tree**; 8384
Na 3:12 All thy strong holds *shall be like* **f trees** 8384
Hab 3:17 Although the **f tree** shall not blossom, 8384
Hag 2:19 the **f tree**, and the pomegranate, and 8384
Zec 3:10 under the vine and under the **f tree**. 8384
Mt 21:19 And when he saw a **f tree** in the way, *4808*
21:19 And presently the **f tree** withered away. *4808*
21:20 How soon is the **f tree** withered away! *4808*
21:21 not only do this which is done to the **f tree**, *4808*
24:32 Now learn a parable of the **f tree**; When his *4808*
Mk 11:13 And seeing a **f tree** afar off having leaves, *4808*
11:20 they saw the **f tree** dried up from the roots. *4808*
11:21 the **f tree** which thou cursedst is withered *4808*
13:28 Now learn a parable of the **f tree**; When her *4808*
Lk 13: 6 A certain *man* had a **f tree** planted in his *4808*
13: 7 years I come seeking fruit on this **f tree**, *4808*
21:29 Behold the **f tree**, and all the trees; *4808*
Jn 1:48 when thou wast under the **f tree**, I saw thee. *4808*
1:50 I saw thee under the **f tree**, believest thou? *4808*
Jas 3:12 Can the **f tree**, my brethren, bear olive *4808*
Rev 6:13 *even* as a **f tree** casteth her untimely figs, *4808*

FIGHT (107) [FIGHTETH, FIGHTING, FIGHTINGS, FOUGHT]

Ex 1:10 f against us, and *so* get them up out of 3898
14:14 The LORD shall f for you, and ye shall 3898
17: 9 us out men, and go out, f with Amalek: 3898
Dt 1:30 which goeth before you, he shall f for you, 3898
1:41 against the LORD, we will go up and f, 3898
1:42 Say unto them, Go not up, neither f; 3898
2:32 he and all his people, to f *at* Jahaz. 4421
3:22 for the LORD your God he shall f for you. 3898
20: 4 to f for you against your enemies, to save 3898
20:10 When thou comest nigh unto a city to f 3898
Jos 9: 2 to f with Joshua and with Israel, *with* one 3898
10:25 do to all your enemies against whom ye f. 3898
11: 5 at the waters of Merom, to f against Israel. 3898
19:47 the children of Dan went up to f against 3898
Jdg 1: 1 the Canaanites first, to f against them? 3898
1: 3 that we may f against the Canaanites; 3898
1: 9 went down to f against the Canaanites, 3898
8: 1 when thou wentest to f with the Midianites? 3898
9:38 go out, I pray now, and f with them. 3898
9:39 passed over Jordan to f also against Judah, 3898
10:18 What man *is he* that will begin to f against 3898
11: 6 that we may f with the children of Ammon. 3898
11: 8 f against the children of Ammon, and 3898
11: 9 If ye bring me *home* again to f against 3898
11:12 that thou art come against me to f in my 3898
11:25 or did he **ever** f against them, 3898+3898
11:32 the children of Ammon to f against them; 3898
12: 1 Wherefore passedst thou over to f against 3898
12: 3 come up unto me this day, to f against me? 3898
20:20 in array to f against them at Gibeah. 4421
1Sa 4: 9 to you: quit yourselves like men, and f. 3898
8:20 and go out before us, and f our battles. 3898
13: 5 themselves together to f with Israel, 3898
15:18 and f against them until they be consumed. 3898
17: 9 If he be able to f with me, and *to* kill me, 3898
17:10 give me a man, that we may f together. 3898
17:20 as the host was going forth to the f, and 4634
17:32 servant will go and f with this Philistine. 3898
17:33 to go against this Philistine to f with him: 3898
18:17 valiant for me, and f the LORD'S battles. 3898
23: 1 the Philistines f against Keilah, and 3898
28: 1 armies together for warfare, to f with Israel. 3898
29: 8 that I may not go f against the enemies of 3898
2Sa 11:20 *so* nigh unto the city when *ye* did f? 3898
1Ki 12:21 to f against the house of Israel, 3898
12:24 nor f against your brethren the children of 3898
20:23 let us f against them in the plain, and 3898
20:25 we will f against them in the plain, *and* 3898
20:26 and went up to Aphek, to f against Israel. 4421
22:31 saying, F neither with small nor great, 3898
22:32 they turned aside to f against him: and 3898
2Ki 3:21 the kings were come up to f against them, 3898
10: 3 and f for your master's house. 3898
19: 9 Behold, he is come out to f against thee: 3898
2Ch 11: 1 to f against Israel, that *he* might bring 3898
11: 4 shall not go up, nor f against your brethren: 3898
13:12 f ye not against the LORD God of your 3898
18:30 saying, F ye not with small or great, 3898
18:31 Therefore they compassed about him to f: 3898
20:17 Ye shall not need to f in this *battle:* set 3898
32: 2 that he was purposed to f against 4421
32: 8 our God to help us, and to f our battles. 3898
35:20 Necho king of Egypt came up to f against 3898
35:22 that *he* might f with him, and hearkened not 3898
35:22 and came to f in the valley of Megiddo. 3898
Ne 4: 8 to come *and* to f against Jerusalem, 3898
4:14 and terrible, and f for your brethren, 3898
4:20 ye thither unto us: our God shall f for us. 3898
Ps 35: 1 f against them that fight against me. 3898
35: 1 fight against them that f against me. 3898
56: 2 for *they be* many that f against me, O thou 3898
144: 1 my hands to war, *and* my fingers to f: 4421
Isa 19: 2 they shall f every one against his brother, 3898
29: 7 the multitude of all the nations that f 6633
29: 7 even all that f against her and her munition, 6638
29: 8 the nations be, that f against mount Zion. 6633
30:32 and in battles of shaking will he f with it. 3898
31: 4 shall the LORD of hosts come down to f 6633
Jer 1:19 they shall f against thee; but they shall not 3898
15:20 they shall f against thee, but they shall not 3898
21: 4 wherewith ye f against the king of Babylon, 3898
21: 5 I myself will f against you with an 3898
32: 5 though ye f with the Chaldeans, ye shall not 3898
32:24 that f against it, because of the sword, and 3898
32:29 that f against this city, shall come and 3898
33: 5 They come to f with the Chaldeans, but *it is* 3898
34:22 they shall f against it, and take it, and 3898
37: 8 f against this city, and take it, and burn it 3898
37:10 army of the Chaldeans that f against you, 3898
41:12 went to f with Ishmael the son of 3898
Jer 51:30 mighty *men* of Babylon have forborn to f, 3898
Da 10:20 now will I return to f with the prince of 3898
11:11 shall come forth and f with him, *even* with 3898
Zec 10: 5 they shall f, because the LORD *is* with 3898
14: 3 go forth, and f against those nations, 3898
14:14 Judah also shall f at Jerusalem; and 3898
Jn 18:36 were of this world, then would my servants f, *75*
Ac 5:39 haply ye be found even to f **against God**. *2314*
23: 9 spoken to him, let us not f **against God**. *2313*
1Co 9:26 so f I, not as one that beateth the air: *4438*
1Ti 6:12 F the good fight of faith, lay hold on eternal *75*
6:12 Fight the good f of faith, lay hold on eternal *73*
2Ti 4: 7 I have fought a good f, I have finished *my* *73*
Heb 10:32 ye endured a great f of afflictions; *119*
11:34 were made strong, waxed valiant in f, *4171*
Jas 4: 2 ye f and war, yet ye have not, because ye *3164*
Rev 2:16 will f against them with the sword of my *4170*

FIGHTETH (3) [FIGHT]

Ex 14:25 for the LORD f for them against 3898
Jos 23:10 he *it is* that f for you, as he hath promised 3898
1Sa 25:28 my lord f the battles of the LORD, 3898

FIGHTING (3) [FIGHT]

1Sa 17:19 in the valley of Elah, f with the Philistines. 3898
2Ch 26:11 Moreover Uzziah had a host of f 4421+6213
Ps 56: 1 swallow me up; he f daily oppresseth me. 3898

FIGHTINGS (2) [FIGHT]

2Co 7: 5 troubled on every *side;* without *were* f, *3163*
Jas 4: 1 From whence *come* wars and f among you? *3163*

FIGS (25) [FIG]

Nu 13:23 *brought* of the pomegranates, and of the f. 8384
20: 5 or of f, or vines, or of pomegranates; 8384
1Sa 25:18 two hundred cakes *of f,* and laid *them* on NIH
30:12 they gave him a piece of a cake *of f,* and NIH
2Ki 20: 7 Isaiah said, Take a lump of f. And they 8384
1Ch 12:40 cakes *of f,* and bunches of raisins, and wine, NIH
Ne 13:15 grapes, and f, and all *manner of* burdens, 8384
SS 2:13 The fig tree putteth forth her **green f**, and 6291
Isa 38:21 Let them take a lump of f, and lay *it* for a 8384
Jer 8:13 nor f on the fig tree, and the leaf shall fade; 8384
24: 1 two baskets of f *were* set before the temple 8384
24: 2 One basket *had* very good f, *even* like 8384
24: 2 good figs, *even* like the f *that are* first ripe: 8384
24: 2 the other basket *had* very naughty f, 8384
24: 3 And I said, F; the good figs, very good; and 8384
24: 3 the good f, very good; and the evil, 8384
24: 5 Like these good f, so will I acknowledge 8384
24: 8 as the evil f, which cannot be eaten, 8384
29:17 and will make them like vile f, 8384
Na 3:12 *shall be like* fig trees with the **firstripe** f: 1061
Mt 7:16 gather grapes of thorns, or f of thistles? *4810*
Mk 11:13 but leaves; for the time of f was not *yet.* *4810*
Lk 6:44 For of thorns *men* do not gather f, nor of a *4810*
Jas 3:12 either a vine, f? so *can* no fountain *both* *4810*
Rev 6:13 *even* as a fig tree casteth her **untimely** f, *3653*

FIGURE (7) [FIGURES]

Dt 4:16 the similitude of any f, the likeness of male 5566
Isa 44:13 maketh it after the f of a man, according to 8403
Ro 5:14 who is the f of *him* that was to come. *5179*
1Co 4: 6 I have **in a f transferred** to myself and *3345*
Heb 9: 9 Which *was* a f for the time *then* present, *3850*
11:19 from whence also he received him in a f. *3850*
1Pe 3:21 The **like** f whereunto *even* baptism doth also *499*

FIGURES (3) [FIGURE]

1Ki 6:29 about *with* **carved** f of cherubims 4734+6603
Ac 7:43 f which ye made to worship them: *5179*
Heb 9:24 made with hands, *which are* the f of the true; *499*

FILE (1)

1Sa 13:21 Yet they had a f for the mattocks, 6310+6477

FILIGREE See OUCHES

FILL (49) [FILLED, FILLEDST, FILLEST, FILLING, FULL, FULLY, FULNESS]

Ge 1:22 f the waters in the seas, and let fowl 4390
42:25 Joseph commanded to f their sacks *with* 4390
44: 1 saying, F the men's sacks *with* food, 4390
Ex 10: 6 they shall f thy houses, and the houses of 4390
16:32 F an omer of it to be kept for your 4393
Lev 25:19 ye shall eat *your* f, and dwell therein in 7648
Dt 23:24 thou mayest eat grapes thy f at thine own 7648
1Sa 16: 1 f thine horn *with* oil, and go, I will send 4390
1Ki 18:33 F four barrels *with* water, and pour *it* on 4390
Job 8:21 Till he f thy mouth *with* laughing, and 4390
15: 2 and f his belly *with* the east wind? 4390
20:23 *When* he is about to f his belly, *God* shall 4390
23: 4 and f my mouth *with* arguments. 4390
38:39 or f the appetite of the young lions, 4390
41: 7 Canst thou f his skin with barbed irons? or 4390
Ps 81:10 open thy mouth wide, and I will f it. 4390
83:16 F their faces *with* shame; that they may 4390
110: 6 he shall f *the places* with the dead bodies; 4390
Pr 1:13 we shall f our houses *with* spoil: 4390
7:18 let us **take** our f of love until the morning: 7301
8:21 and I will f their treasures. 4390
Isa 8: 8 the stretching out of his wings shall f 4393
14:21 nor f the face of the world *with* cities. 4390
27: 6 bud, and f the face of the world *with* fruit. 4390
56:12 and we will f ourselves with strong drink; 5433
Jer 13:13 I *will* f all the inhabitants of this land, 4390
23:24 Do not I f heaven and earth? saith 4392
33: 5 *it is* to f them with the dead bodies of men, 4390
51:14 *saying,* Surely I will f thee *with* men, 4390
Eze 3: 3 f thy bowels with this roll that I give thee. 4390
7:19 satisfy their souls, neither f their bowels: 4390
9: 7 the house, and f the courts *with* the slain: 4390
10: 2 f thine hand *with* coals of fire from 4390
24: 4 and the shoulder; f *it with* the choice bones. 4390
Eze 30:11 against Egypt, and f the land *with* the slain. 4390
32: 4 I will f the beasts of the whole earth with 7646
32: 5 and f the valleys *with* thy height. 4390
35: 8 I will f his mountains *with* his slain *men:* in 4390
Zep 1: 9 which f their masters' houses *with* violence 4390
Hag 2: 7 I will f this house *with* glory, saith 4390
Mt 9:16 for that which is **put in to f it up** taketh *4138*
15:33 the wilderness, as to f so great a multitude? *5526*
23:32 F ye **up** then the measure of your fathers. *4137*
Jn 2: 7 unto them, F the waterpots with water. *1072*
Ro 15:13 Now the God of hope f you **with** all joy *4137*
Eph 4:10 all heavens, that he might f all *things.*) *4137*
Col 1:24 f **up** that which is behind of the afflictions of *466*
1Th 2:16 they might be saved, to f **up** their sins alway: *378*
Rev 18: 6 in the cup which she hath filled f to her *2767*

FILLED (159) [FILL]

Ge 6:11 and the earth was f *with* violence. 4390
6:13 for the earth is f *with* violence through 4390
21:19 f the bottle *with* water, and gave the lad 4390
24:16 to the well, and f her pitcher, and came up. 4390
26:15 had stopped them, and f them *with* earth. 4390
Ex 1: 7 and the land was f with them. 4390
2:16 f the troughs to water their father's flock. 4390
16:12 and in the morning ye shall be f *with* bread; 7646
28: 3 whom I have f with the spirit of wisdom, 4390
31: 3 I have f him *with* the spirit of God, 4390
35:31 he hath f him *with* the spirit of God, 4390
35:35 Them hath he f *with* wisdom of heart, 4390
40:34 the glory of the LORD f the tabernacle. 4390
40:35 the glory of the LORD f the tabernacle. 4390
Nu 14:21 all the earth shall be f *with* the glory of 4390
Dt 26:12 that they may eat within thy gates, and be f; 7646
31:20 and f *themselves,* and waxen fat; 7646
Jos 9:13 bottles of wine, which we f, *were* new; 4390
1Ki 7:14 he was f *with* wisdom, and understanding, 4390
8:10 that the cloud f the house of the LORD, 4390
8:11 for the glory of the LORD had f the house 4390
18:35 and he f the trench also *with* water. 4390
20:27 flocks of kids; but the Syrians f the country. 4390
2Ki 3:17 yet that valley shall be f *with* water, that ye 4390
3:20 of Edom, and the country was f with water. 4390
3:25 of land cast every man his stone, and f it; 4390
21:16 till he had f Jerusalem from one end to 4390
23:14 and f their places *with* the bones of men. 4390
24: 4 for he f Jerusalem *with* innocent blood; 4390
2Ch 5:13 that *then* the house was f *with* a cloud, 4390
5:14 for the glory of the LORD had f the house 4390
7: 1 and the glory of the LORD f the house. 4390
7: 2 the glory of the LORD had f 4390
16:14 laid him in the bed which was f *with* sweet 4390
Ezr 9:11 which have f it from one end to another 4390
Ne 9:25 were f, and became fat, and 7646
Job 3:15 had gold, who f their houses *with* silver: 4390
16: 8 thou hast f me **with wrinkles**, *which* is a 7059
22:18 Yet he f their houses *with* good *things:* but 4390
Ps 38: 7 For my loins are f *with* a loathsome 4390
71: 8 Let my mouth be f *with* thy praise *and* 4390
72:19 let the whole earth be f *with* his glory; 4390
78:29 So they did eat, and were well f: for he 7646
80: 9 cause it to take deep root, and it f the land. 4390
104:28 openest thine hand, they are f *with* good. 7646
123: 3 for we are exceedingly f *with* contempt. 7646
123: 4 Our soul is exceedingly f *with* the scorning 7646
126: 2 was our mouth f *with* laughter, and 4390
Pr 1:31 own way, and be f with their own devices. 7646
3:10 So shall thy barns be f *with* plenty, and 4390
5:10 Lest strangers be f *with* thy wealth; and 7646
12:21 but the wicked shall be f *with* mischief. 4390
14:14 The backslider in heart shall be f with his 7646
18:20 *with* the increase of his lips shall he be f. 7646
20:17 afterwards his mouth shall be f *with* gravel. 4390
24: 4 by knowledge shall the chambers be f *with* 4390
25:16 lest thou be f there*with,* and vomit it. 7646
30:16 the earth *that* is not f *with* water; and 7646
30:22 and a fool when he is f *with* meat; 7646
Ecc 1: 8 with seeing, nor the ear f with hearing. 4390
6: 3 his soul be not f with good, and also *that* he 7646
6: 7 for his mouth, and yet the appetite is not f. 4390
SS 5: 2 for my head is f *with* dew, *and* my locks 4390
Isa 6: 1 and lifted up, and his train f the temple. 4392
6: 4 that cried, and the house was f *with* smoke. 4390
21: 3 Therefore are my loins f *with* pain: 4390
33: 5 he hath f Zion *with* judgment and 4390
34: 6 The sword of the LORD is f *with* blood, 4390
43:24 neither hast thou f me *with* the fat of thy 7301
65:20 nor an old man that hath not f his days: 4390
Jer 13:12 of Israel, Every bottle shall be f *with* wine: 4390
13:12 know that every bottle shall be f *with* wine? 4390
15:17 for thou hast f me *with* indignation. 4390
16:18 they have f mine inheritance with 4390
19: 4 have f this place *with* the blood of 4390
41: 9 Ishmael the son of Nethaniah f it *with them* 4390
46:12 *of* thy shame, and thy cry hath f the land: 4390
51: 5 though their land was f *with* sin against 4390
51:34 he hath f his belly with my delicates, 4390
La 3:15 He hath f me with bitterness, he hath made 7646
3:30 that smiteth him: he is **f full** with reproach. 7646
Eze 8:17 for they have f the land *with* violence, and 4390
10: 3 went in; and the cloud f the inner court. 4390
10: 4 the house was f with the cloud, and 4390
11: 6 ye have f the streets thereof *with* the slain. 4390
23:33 Thou shalt be f *with* drunkenness and 4390
28:16 they have f the midst of thee *with* violence, 4390
36:38 shall the waste cities be f *with* flocks of 4392
39:20 Thus ye shall be f at my table *with* horses 7646
43: 5 the glory of the LORD f the house. 4390
44: 4 the glory of the LORD f the house of 4390
Da 2:35 a great mountain, and f the whole earth. 4391
Hos 13: 6 According to their pasture, so were they f; 7646
13: 6 they were f, and their heart was exalted; 7646
Na 2:12 f his holes *with* prey, and his dens *with* 4390
Hab 2:14 For the earth shall be f with the knowledge 4390
2:16 Thou art f *with* shame for glory: drink thou 7646
Hag 1: 6 *ye* drink, but ye are not **f with drink**; 7937

Zec 9:13 f the bow *with* Ephraim, and raised up thy 4390
9:15 they shall be f like bowls, *and* as 4390
Mt 5: 6 after righteousness: for they shall be f. *5526*
14:20 And they did all eat, and were f: and *5526*
15:37 And they did all eat, and were f: and *5526*
27:48 and f *it* with vinegar, and put *it* on a reed, *4130*
Mk 2:21 else the new **piece that** f **it up** taketh away *4138*
6:42 And they did all eat, and were f. *5526*
7:27 said unto her, Let the children first be f: *5526*
8: 8 So they did eat, and were f: and they took *5526*
15:36 And one ran and f a spunge *full* of vinegar, *1072*
Lk 1:15 and he shall be f with the Holy Ghost, *4130*
1:41 and Elisabeth was f with the Holy Ghost: *4130*
1:53 He hath f the hungry with good *things;* and *1705*
1:67 And his father Zacharias was f with *4130*
2:40 and waxed strong in spirit, f with wisdom: *4137*
3: 5 Every valley shall be f, and every mountain *4137*
4:28 when they heard these *things,* were f with *4130*
5: 7 and f both the ships, so that they began to *4130*
5:26 glorified God, and were f with fear, saying, *4130*
6:11 And they were f with madness; and *4130*
6:21 for ye shall be f. Blessed *are ye* that weep *5526*
8:23 and they were f *with water,* and were in *4845*
9:17 And they did eat, and were all f: and *5526*
14:23 *them* to come in, that my house may be f. *1072*
15:16 And he would fain have f his belly with *1072*
Jn 2: 7 with water. And they f them up to the brim. *1072*
6:12 When they were f, he said unto his *1705*
6:13 f twelve baskets with the fragments of *1072*
6:26 ye did eat of the loaves, and were f. *5526*
12: 3 the house was f with the odour of *4137*
16: 6 *things* unto you, sorrow hath f your heart. *4137*
19:29 and they f a spunge with vinegar, and put *it* *4130*
Ac 2: 2 it f all the house where they were sitting. *4137*
2: 4 And they were all f with the Holy Ghost, *4130*
3:10 and they were f with wonder and *4130*
4: 8 Then Peter, f with the Holy Ghost, *4130*
4:31 and they were all f with the Holy Ghost, *4130*
5: 3 why hath Satan f thine heart to lie to *4137*
5:17 and were f with indignation, *4130*
5:28 ye have f Jerusalem with your doctrine, and *4137*
9:17 thy sight, and be f with the Holy Ghost. *4130*
13: 9 f with the Holy Ghost, set his eyes on him, *4130*
13:45 they were f with envy, and spake against *4130*
13:52 And the disciples were f with joy, and *4137*
19:29 And the whole city was f with confusion: *4130*
Ro 1:29 Being **f with** all unrighteousness, *4137*
15:14 are full of goodness, f with all knowledge, *4137*
15:24 if first I be somewhat f with your *1705*
2Co 7: 4 I am f with comfort, I am exceeding joyful *4137*
Eph 3:19 that ye might be f with all the fulness of *4137*
5:18 wherein is excess; but be f with the Spirit; *4137*
Php 1:11 Being f with the fruits of righteousness, *4137*
Col 1: 9 to desire that ye might be f *with* *4137*
2Ti 1: 4 of thy tears, that I may be f with joy; *4137*
Jas 2:16 Depart in peace, be you warmed and f; *5526*
Rev 8: 5 and f it with fire of the altar, and cast *it* into *1072*
15: 1 for in them is f **up** the wrath of God. *5055*
15: 8 And the temple was f with smoke from *1072*
18: 6 in the cup which she hath f fill to her *2767*
19:21 and all the fowls were f with their flesh. *5526*

FILLEDST (2) [FILL]

Dt 6:11 houses full *of* all good *things,* which thou f 4390
Eze 27:33 forth out of the seas, thou f many people; 7646

FILLEST (1) [FILL]

Ps 17:14 whose belly thou f *with* thy hid *treasure:* 4390

FILLET (1) [FILLETED, FILLETH, FILLETS]

Jer 52:21 a f of twelve cubits did compass it; and 2339

FILLETED (3) [FILLET]

Ex 27:17 round about the court *shall be* f *with* silver; 2836
38:17 all the pillars of the court *were* f *with* 2836
38:28 and overlaid their chapiters, and f them. 2836

FILLETH (6) [FILLET]

Job 9:18 to take my breath, but f me *with* bitterness. 7646
Ps 84: 6 make it a well; the rain also f the pools. 5844
107: 9 and f the hungry soul *with* goodness. 4390
129: 7 Where*with* the mower f not his hand; 4390
147:14 *and* f thee *with* the finest of the wheat. 7646
Eph 1:23 his body, the fulness of him that f all in all. *4137*

FILLETS (8) [FILLET]

Ex 27:10 of the pillars and their f *shall be of* silver. 2838
27:11 the hooks of the pillars and their f *of* silver. 2838
36:38 their chapiters and their f with gold: 2838
38:10 of the pillars and their f *were of* silver. 2838
38:11 the hooks of the pillars and their f *of* silver. 2838
38:12 the hooks of the pillars and their f *of* silver. 2838
38:17 the hooks of the pillars and their f *of* silver; 2838
38:19 of their chapiters and their f *of* silver. 2838

FILLING (1) [FILL]

Ac 14:17 f our hearts **with** food and gladness. *1705*

FILTH (4) [FILTHINESS, FILTHY]

Isa 4: 4 washed away the f of the daughters of Zion, 6675
Na 3: 6 I will cast **abominable** f upon thee, and 8251
1Co 4:13 we are made as the f of the world, *and* *4027*
1Pe 3:21 (not the putting away of the f of the flesh, *4509*

FILTHINESS (16) [FILTH]

2Ch 29: 5 and carry forth the f out of the holy *place.* 5079
Ezr 6:21 them from the f of the heathen of the land, 2932
9:11 *is* an unclean land with the f of the people 5079
Pr 30:12 and *yet* is not washed from their f. 6675
Isa 28: 8 For all tables are full *of* vomit *and* f, *so* 6675
La 1: 9 Her f *is* in her skirts; she remembereth not 2932
Eze 16:36 Because thy f was poured out, and 5178
22:15 and will consume thy f out of thee. 2932
24:11 and *that* the f of it may be molten in it, 2932
24:13 In thy f *is* lewdness: because I have purged 2932
24:13 thou shalt not be purged from thy f any 2932
36:25 from all your f, and from all your idols, 2932
2Co 7: 1 let us cleanse ourselves from all f of *3436*
Eph 5: 4 Neither f, nor foolish talking, nor jesting, *151*
Jas 1:21 Wherefore lay apart all f and superfluity of *4507*
Rev 17: 4 full of abominations and f of her fornication: *168*

FILTHY (17) [FILTH]

Job 15:16 How much more abominable and f *is* man, 444
Ps 14: 3 gone aside, they are *all* together become f: 444
53: 3 is gone back, they are altogether become f; 444
Isa 64: 6 and all our righteousnesses *are* as f rags; 5708
Zep 3: 1 Woe to her that is f and polluted, to 4754
Zec 3: 3 Now Joshua was clothed with f garments, 6674
3: 4 Take away the f garments from him. 6674
Col 3: 8 f **communication** out of your mouth. *148*
1Ti 3: 3 to wine, no striker, not **greedy of f lucre;** *146*
3: 8 given to much wine, not **greedy of f lucre;** *146*
Tit 1: 7 to wine, no striker, not **given to f lucre;** *146*
1:11 which *they* ought not, for f lucre's sake. *150*
1Pe 5: 2 not **for f lucre**, but of a ready mind; *147*
2Pe 2: 7 vexed with the f conversation of the wicked: *766*
Jude 1: 8 Likewise also these *f* dreamers defile NIG
Rev 22:11 and he which is f, let him be filthy still: and *4510*
22:11 and he which is filthy, let him be f still: and *4510*

FINALLY (6)

2Co 13:11 F, brethren, farewell. Be perfect, be of *3062*
Eph 6:10 F, my brethren, be strong in *3062+3588*
Php 3: 1 F, my brethren, rejoice in the Lord. *3062+3588*
4: 8 F, brethren, whatsoever *things* are *3062+3588*
2Th 3: 1 F, brethren, pray for us, that *3062+3588*
1Pe 3: 8 F, *be ye* all of one mind, *3588+5056*

FIND (156) [FINDEST, FINDETH, FINDING, FOUND]

Ge 18:26 If I f in Sodom fifty righteous within 4672
18:28 he said, If I f there forty and five, I will not 4672
18:30 he said, I will not do *it,* if I f thirty there. 4672
19:11 that they wearied themselves to f the door. 4672
32: 5 tell my lord, that I may f grace in thy sight. 4672
32:19 shall you speak unto Esau, when you f him. 4672
33: 8 *These are* to f grace in the sight of my lord. 4672
33:15 let me f grace in the sight of my lord. 4672
34:11 Let me f grace in your eyes, and what ye 4672
38:22 returned to Judah, and said, I cannot f her; 4672
41:38 Can we f *such a one* as this *is,* a man in 4672
47:25 let us f grace in the sight of my lord, and 4672
Ex 5:11 get you straw where you can f *it:* yet not 4672
16:25 to day ye shall not f it in the field. 4672
33:13 know thee, that I may f grace in thy sight: 4672
Nu 32:23 and be sure your sin will f you **out**. 4672
35:27 the revenger of blood f him without 4672
Dt 4:29 thou shalt f *him,* if thou seek him with all 4672
22:23 and a man f her in the city, and lie with her; 4672
22:25 if a man f a betrothed damsel in the field, 4672
22:28 If a man f a damsel *that is* a virgin, which is 4672
24: 1 it come to pass that she f no favour in his 4672
28:65 among these nations shalt thou f no **ease**, 7280
Jdg 9:33 thou do to them as thou shalt f **occasion**. 4672
14:12 f *it* **out**, then I will give you thirty sheets 4672
17: 8 to sojourn where he could f *a place:* 4672
17: 9 I go to sojourn where I may f *a place.* 4672
Ru 1: 9 The LORD grant you that you may f rest, 4672
2: 2 after *him* in whose sight I shall f grace. 4672
2:13 Let me f favour in thy sight, my lord; 4672
1Sa 1:18 Let thine handmaid f grace in thy sight. 4672
9:13 *into* the city, ye shall straightway f him, 4672
9:13 you up; for about *this* time ye shall f him. 4672
10: 2 thou shalt f two men by Rachel's sepulchre 4672
20:21 send a lad, *saying,* Go, f **out** the arrows. 4672
20:36 Run, f **out** now the arrows which I shoot. 4672
23:17 for the hand of Saul my father shall not f 4672
24:19 For if a man f his enemy, will he let him go 4672
25: 8 Wherefore let the young men f favour in 4672
2Sa 15:25 if I shall f favour in the eyes of the LORD, 4672
16: 4 I humbly beseech thee *that* I may f grace in 4672
17:20 could not f *them,* they returned *to* 4672
1Ki 18: 5 peradventure we may f grass to save 4672
18:12 I come and tell Ahab, and he cannot f thee, 4672
2Ch 2:14 to f **out** every device which shall be put to 2803
20:16 ye shall f them at the end of the brook, 4672
30: 9 your children *shall f* compassion before NIH
32: 4 kings of Assyria come, and f much water? 4672
Ezr 4:15 so shalt thou f in the book of the records, 7912
7:16 gold that thou canst f in all the province of 7912
Job 3:22 are glad, when they can f the grave? 4672
11: 7 Canst thou *by* searching f **out** God? 4672
11: 7 canst thou f **out** the Almighty unto 4672
17:10 for I cannot f *one* wise *man* among you. 4672
23: 3 O that I knew where I might f him! *that* I 4672
34:11 **cause** every man **to** f according to *his* 4672
37:23 the Almighty, we cannot f him **out**: 4672
Ps 10:15 seek out his wickedness *till* thou f none. 4672
17: 3 thou hast tried me, *and* shalt f nothing; 4672
21: 8 Thine hand shall f **out** all thine enemies: 4672
21: 8 thy right hand shall f **out** those that hate 4672
132: 5 Until I f **out** a place for the LORD, 4672
Pr 1:13 We shall f all precious substance, we shall 4672
1:28 shall seek me early, but they shall not f me: 4672
2: 5 the LORD, and f the knowledge of God. 4672
3: 4 So shalt thou f favour and 4672
4:22 For they *are* life unto those that f them, and 4672
8: 9 and right to them that f knowledge. 4672
8:12 and f **out** knowledge of witty inventions. 4672
8:17 and those that seek me early shall f me. 4672
16:20 He that handleth a matter wisely shall f 4672
19: 8 he that keepeth understanding shall f good. 4672
20: 6 but a faithful man who can f? 4672
28:23 afterwards shall f more favour than he that 4672
31:10 Who can f a virtuous woman? for her price 4672
Ecc 3:11 that no man can f **out** the work that God 4672
7:14 to the end that man should f nothing after 4672
7:24 and exceeding deep, who can f it **out**? 4672
7:26 I f more bitter than death the woman, 4672
7:27 *counting* one by one, to f **out** the account: 4672
7:28 Which yet my soul seeketh, but I f not: 4672
8:17 that a man cannot f **out** the work that is 4672
8:17 seek *it* out, yet he shall not f *it;* yea further, 4672
8:17 to know *it,* yet shall he not be able to f *it.* 4672
11: 1 for thou shalt f it after many days. 4672
12:10 The Preacher sought to f **out** acceptable 4672
SS 5: 6 I sought him, but I could not f him; I called 4672
5: 8 if ye f my beloved, that ye tell him, that I 4672
8: 1 *when* I should f thee without, I would kiss 4672
Isa 34:14 rest there, and f for herself a place of rest. 4672
41:12 Thou shalt seek them, and shalt not f them, 4672
58: 3 in the day of your fast you f pleasure, and 4672
Jer 2:24 in her month they shall f her. 4672
5: 1 the broad places thereof, if ye can f a man, 4672
6:16 and ye shall f rest for your souls. 4672
10:18 and will distress them, that they may f *it so.* 4672
29:13 f *me,* when ye shall search for me with all 4672
45: 3 I fainted in my sighing, and I f no rest. 4672
La 1: 6 her princes are become like harts *that* f no 4672
2: 9 the law *is* no *more;* her prophets also f no 4672
Da 6: 4 princes sought to f occasion against Daniel 7912
6: 4 they could f none occasion nor fault; 7912
6: 5 We shall not f any occasion against this 7912
6: 5 except we f *it* against him concerning 7912
Hos 2: 6 make a wall, that she shall not f her paths. 4672
2: 7 shall not f *them:* then shall she say, I will 4672
5: 6 they shall not f *him;* he hath withdrawn 4672
12: 8 *in* all my labours they shall f none iniquity 4672
Am 8:12 the word of the LORD, and shall not f *it.* 4672
Mt 7: 7 seek, and ye shall f; knock, and it shall be *2147*
7:14 leadeth unto life, and few there be that f it. *2147*
10:39 he that loseth his life for my sake shall f it. *2147*
11:29 in heart: and ye shall f rest unto your souls. *2147*
16:25 will lose his life for my sake shall f it. *2147*
17:27 his mouth, thou shalt f a piece of money: *2147*
18:13 And if so be that he f it, verily I say unto *2147*
21: 2 and straightway ye shall f an ass tied, and *2147*
22: 9 the highways, and as many as ye shall f, *2147*
24:46 whom his lord when he cometh shall f so *2147*
Mk 11: 2 ye shall f a colt tied, whereon never man *2147*
11:13 if haply he might f any *thing* thereon: *2147*
13:36 Lest coming suddenly he f you sleeping. *2147*
Lk 2:12 Ye shall f *the* babe wrapped in swaddling *2147*
5:19 And when they could not f by what *way* *2147*
6: 7 that they might f an accusation against him. *2147*
11: 9 seek, and ye shall f; knock, and it shall be *2147*
12:37 whom the lord when he cometh shall f *2147*
12:38 or come in the third watch, and f *them* so, *2147*
12:43 whom his lord when he cometh shall f so *2147*
13: 7 seeking fruit on this fig tree, and f none: *2147*
15: 4 and go after that which is lost, until he f it? *2147*
15: 8 the house, and seek diligently till she f *it?* *2147*
18: 8 man cometh, shall he f faith on the earth? *2147*
19:30 which at your entering ye shall f a colt tied, *2147*
19:48 And could not f what they might do: for all *2147*
23: 4 and *to* the people, I f no fault in this man. *2147*
Jn 7:34 and shall not f *me:* and where I am, *2147*
7:35 Whither will he go, that we shall not f him? *2147*
7:36 and shall not f *me:* and where I am, *2147*
10: 9 and shall go in and out, and f pasture. *2147*
18:38 saith unto them, I f in him no fault *at all.* *2147*
19: 4 that ye may know that I f no fault in him. *2147*
19: 6 and crucify *him:* for I f no fault in him. *2147*
21: 6 on the right side of the ship, and ye shall f. *2147*
Ac 7:46 desired to f a tabernacle for the God of *2147*
17:27 f *him,* though he be not far from every one *2147*
23: 9 strove, saying, We f no evil in this man: *2147*
Ro 7:18 *how* to perform that which is good I f not. *2147*
7:21 I f then a law, that, when I would do good, *2147*
9:19 then unto me, Why doth he yet f **fault**? *3201*
2Co 9: 4 and f you unprepared, we (that we say not, *2147*
12:20 I shall not f you such as I would, and *that* I *2147*
2Ti 1:18 The Lord grant unto him that *he* may f *2147*
Heb 4:16 and f grace to help in time of need. *2147*
Rev 9: 6 shall men seek death, and shall not f it; *2147*
18:14 and thou shalt f them no more at all. *2147*

FINDEST (2) [FIND]

Ge 31:32 With whomsoever thou f thy gods, let him 4672
Eze 3: 1 said unto me, Son of man, eat that thou f; 4672

FINDETH (27) [FIND]

Ge 4:14 *that* every one that f me shall slay me. 4672
Job 33:10 Behold, he f occasions against me, 4672
Ps 119:162 rejoice at thy word, as one that f great spoil. 4672
Pr 3:13 Happy *is* the man *that* f wisdom, and 4672
8:35 For whoso f me findeth life, and 4672
8:35 For whoso findeth me f life, and 4672
14: 6 A scorner seeketh wisdom, and *f it* not: but NIH
17:20 He that hath a froward heart f no good: and 4672
18:22 *Whoso* f a wife findeth a good *thing,* and 4672
18:22 *Whoso* findeth a wife f a good *thing,* and 4672
21:10 his neighbour f no **favour** in his eyes. 2603
21:21 after righteousness and mercy f life, 4672
Ecc 9:10 Whatsoever thy hand f to do, do *it* with thy 4672
La 1: 3 dwelleth among the heathen, she f no rest: 4672
Hos 14: 3 our gods: for in thee the fatherless f **mercy**. 7355
Mt 7: 8 that asketh receiveth; and he that seeketh f: *2147*
10:39 He that f his life shall lose it: and he that *2147*
12:43 dry places, seeking rest, and f none. *2147*
12:44 he f *it* empty, swept, and garnished. *2147*
26:40 and f them asleep, and saith unto Peter, *2147*
Mk 14:37 and f them sleeping, and saith unto Peter, *2147*
Lk 11:10 and he that seeketh f; and to him that *2147*
11:25 he cometh, he f *it* swept and garnished. *2147*
Jn 1:41 He first f his own brother Simon, and *2147*
1:43 and f Philip, and saith unto him, *2147*
1:45 Philip f Nathanael, and saith unto him, *2147*
5:14 Afterward Jesus f him in the temple, and *2147*

FINDING (10) [FIND]

Ge 4:15 upon Cain, lest any f him should kill him. 4672
Job 9:10 Which doeth great things past f out; yea, 2714
Isa 58:13 thine own ways, nor f thine own pleasure, 4672
Lk 11:24 and f none, he saith, I will return unto my 2147
Ac 4:21 f nothing how they might punish them, 2147
19: 1 came to Ephesus: and f certain disciples, 2147
21: 2 And f a ship sailing over unto Phenicia, 2147
21: 4 And f disciples, we tarried there seven days: 429
Ro 11:33 are his judgments, and his ways past f out! 421
Heb 8: 8 For f fault with them, he saith, Behold, 3201

FINE (113) [FINER, FINEST, FINING]

Ge 18: 6 Make ready quickly three measures of f 5560
41:42 arrayed him in vestures of f linen, and put a 8336
Ex 25: 4 and scarlet, and f linen, and goats' hair, 8336
26: 1 with ten curtains of f twined linen, 8336
26:31 f twined linen of cunning work: 8336
26:36 and purple, and scarlet, and f twined linen, 8336
27: 9 f twined linen of an hundred cubits long for 8336
27:16 and purple, and scarlet, and f twined linen, 8336
27:18 the height five cubits of f twined linen, and 8336
28: 5 and purple, and scarlet, and f linen. 8336
28: 6 of purple, of scarlet, and f twined linen, 8336
28: 8 and purple, and scarlet, and f twined linen. 8336
28:15 and of scarlet, and of f twined linen, 8336
28:39 thou shalt embroider the coat of f linen, 8336
28:39 thou shalt make the mitre of f linen, and 8336
35: 6 and scarlet, and f linen, and goats' hair, 8336
35:23 f linen, and goats' hair, and red skins of 8336
35:25 and of purple, and of scarlet, and of f linen. 8336
35:35 in scarlet, and in f linen, and of the weaver, 8336
36: 8 made ten curtains of f twined linen, 8336
36:35 and purple, and scarlet, and f twined linen: 8336
36:37 purple, and scarlet, and f twined linen, 8336
38: 9 of the court were of f twined linen, 8336
38:16 court round about were of f twined linen. 8336
38:18 and purple, and scarlet, and f twined linen: 8336
38:23 and in purple, and in scarlet, and f linen. 8336
39: 2 and purple, and scarlet, and f twined linen. 8336
39: 3 and in the scarlet, and in the f linen, 8336
39: 5 and purple, and scarlet, and f twined linen; 8336
39: 8 and purple, and scarlet, and f twined linen. 8336
39:27 they made coats of f linen of woven work 8336
39:28 a mitre of f linen, and goodly bonnets of 8336
39:28 goodly bonnets of f linen, and linen 8336
39:28 and linen breeches of f twined linen, 8336
39:29 a girdle of f twined linen, and blue, and 8336
Lev 2: 1 the LORD, his offering shall be of f flour; 5560
2: 4 it shall be unleavened cakes of f flour 5560
2: 5 it shall be of f flour unleavened, 5560
2: 7 it shall be made of f flour with oil. 5560
5:11 of an ephah of f flour for a sin offering; 5560
6:20 the tenth part of an ephah of f flour for a 5560
7:12 cakes mingled with oil, of f flour, fried. 5560
14:10 three tenth deals of f flour for a meat 5560
14:21 one tenth deal of f flour mingled with oil 5560
23:13 two tenth deals of f flour mingled with oil, 5560
23:17 they shall be of f flour; they shall be baken 5560
24: 5 thou shalt take f flour, and bake twelve 5560
Nu 6:15 cakes of f flour mingled with oil, and 5560
7:13 both of them were full of f flour mingled 5560
7:19 both of them full of f flour mingled with 5560
7:25 both of them full of f flour mingled with 5560
7:31 both of them full of f flour mingled with 5560
7:37 both of them full of f flour mingled with 5560
7:43 both of them full of f flour mingled with 5560
7:49 both of them full of f flour mingled with 5560
7:55 both of them full of f flour mingled with 5560
7:61 both of them full of f flour mingled with 5560
7:67 both of them full of f flour mingled with 5560
7:73 both of them full of f flour mingled with 5560
7:79 both of them full of f flour mingled with 5560
8: 8 even f flour mingled with oil, and 5560
1Ki 4:22 for one day was thirty measures of f flour, 5560
2Ki 7: 1 a measure of f flour be sold for a shekel, 5560
7:16 So a measure of f flour was sold for a 5560
7:18 and a measure of f flour for a shekel, 5560
1Ch 4:21 of the house of them that wrought f linen, 948
9:29 the f flour, and the wine, and the oil, and 5560
15:27 David was clothed with a robe of f linen, 948
23:29 for the f flour for meat offering, and for 5560
2Ch 2:14 in blue, and in f linen, and in crimson; 948
3: 5 which he overlaid with f gold, and 2896
3: 8 he overlaid it with f gold, amounting to six 2896
3:14 and f linen, and wrought cherubims thereon. 948
Ezr 8:27 two vessels of f copper, precious as 2896+6668
Est 1: 6 blue hangings, fastened with cords of f linen 948
8:15 and with a garment of f linen and purple: 948
Job 28: 1 and a place for gold where they f it. 2212
28:17 of it shall not be for jewels of f gold. 6337
31:24 or have said to the f gold, Thou art my 3800
Ps 19:10 are they than gold, yea, than much f gold: 6337
119:127 above gold; yea, above f gold. 6337
Pr 3:14 of silver, and the gain thereof than f gold. 2742
7:16 with carved works, with f linen of Egypt. 330
8:19 fruit is better than gold, yea, than f gold; 6337
25:12 an ornament of f gold, so is a wise reprover 3800
31:24 She maketh f linen, and selleth it; and 5466
SS 5:11 His head is as the most f gold, his locks are 6337
5:15 of marble, set upon sockets of f gold: 6337
Isa 3:23 the f linen, and the hoods, and the vails. 5466
13:12 will make a man more precious than f gold; 6337
19: 9 Moreover they that work in f flax, and 8305
La 4: 1 how is the most f gold changed! the stones 3800
4: 2 sons of Zion, comparable to f gold, 6337
Eze 16:10 and I girded thee about with f linen, 8336
16:13 thy raiment was of f linen, and silk, and 8336
16:13 thou didst eat f flour, and honey, and oil: 5560
16:19 f flour, and oil, and honey, wherewith I fed 5560
27: 7 F linen with broidered work from Egypt 8336
27:16 and f linen, and coral, and agate. 948
46:14 of a hin of oil, to temper with the f flour; 5560
Da 2:32 This image's head was of f gold, his breast 2869
10: 5 whose loins were girded with f gold of 3800
Zec 9: 3 and f gold as the mire of the streets. 2742
Mk 15:46 And he bought f linen, and took him down, 4616
Lk 16:19 which was clothed in purple and f linen, 1040
Rev 1:15 And his feet like unto f brass, as if they 5474
2:18 a flame of fire, and his feet are like f brass; 5474
18:12 and f linen, and purple, and silk, and 1040
18:13 and oil, and f flour, and wheat, and beasts, 4585
18:16 that was clothed in f linen, and purple, and 1039
19: 8 that she should be arrayed in f linen, 1039
19: 8 for the f linen is the righteousness of saints. 1039
19:14 clothed in f linen, white and clean. 1039

FINER (1) [FINE]

Pr 25: 4 and there shall come forth a vessel for the f. 6884

FINERY See BRAVERY

FINEST (2) [FINE]

Ps 81:16 He should have fed them also with the f of 2459
147:14 and filleth thee with the f of the wheat. 2459

FINGER (26) [FINGERS]

Ex 8:19 said unto Pharaoh, This is the f of God: 676
29:12 put it upon the horns of the altar with thy f, 676
31:18 tables of stone, written with the f of God. 676
Lev 4: 6 the priest shall dip his f in the blood, and 676
4:17 the priest shall dip his f in some of the blood, 676
4:25 of the blood of the sin offering with his f, 676
4:30 shall take of the blood thereof with his f, 676
4:34 of the blood of the sin offering with his f, 676
8:15 the horns of the altar round about with his f, 676
9: 9 he dipt his f in the blood, and put it upon 676
14:16 the priest shall dip his right f in the oil that is 676
14:16 shall sprinkle of the oil with his f seven 676
14:27 the priest shall sprinkle with his right f some 676
16:14 sprinkle it with his f upon the mercy seat 676
16:14 sprinkle of the blood with his f seven times. 676
16:19 of the blood upon it with his f seven times, 676
Nu 19: 4 the priest shall take of her blood with his f, 676
Dt 9:10 two tables of stone written with the f of God; 676
1Ki 12:10 My little f shall be thicker than my father's NIH
2Ch 10:10 My little f shall be thicker than my father's NIH
Isa 58: 9 the putting forth of the f, and 676
Lk 11:20 But if I with the f of God cast out devils, 1147
16:24 that he may dip the tip of his f in water, and 1147
Jn 8: 6 and with his f wrote on the ground, 1147
20:25 and put my f into the print of the nails, and 1147
20:27 Reach hither thy f, and behold my hands; 1147

FINGERS (15) [FINGER]

2Sa 21:20 that had on every hand six f, and on every 676
1Ch 20: 6 whose f and toes were four and twenty, 676
Ps 8: 3 the work of thy f, the moon and the stars, 676
144: 1 teacheth my hands to war, and my f to fight: 676
Pr 6:13 speaketh with his feet, he teacheth with his f; 676
7: 3 Bind them upon thy f, write them upon 676
SS 5: 5 my f with sweet smelling myrrh, upon 676
Isa 2: 8 that which their own f have made: 676
17: 8 neither shall respect that which his f have 676
59: 3 defiled with blood, and your f with iniquity; 676
Jer 52:21 and the thickness thereof was four f: 676
Da 5: 5 In the same hour came forth f of a man's 677
Mt 23: 4 will not move them with one of their f. 1147
Mk 7:33 and put his f into his ears, and he spit, and 1147
Lk 11:46 touch not the burdens with one of your f. 1147

FINING (2) [FINE]

Pr 17: 3 The f pot is for silver, and the furnace for 4715
27:21 As the f pot for silver, and the furnace for 4715

FINISH (11) [FINISHED, FINISHER]

Ge 6:16 the ark, and in a cubit shalt thou f it above; 3615
Da 9:24 to f the transgression, and to make an end 3607
Zec 4: 9 his hands shall also f it; and thou shalt 1214
Lk 14:28 the cost, whether he have sufficient to f it? 535
14:29 is not able to f it, all that behold it begin to 1615
14:30 man began to build, and was not able to f. 1615
Jn 4:34 will of him that sent me, and to f his work. 5048
5:36 works which the Father hath given me to f, 5048
Ac 20:24 so that I might f my course with joy, and 5048
Ro 9:28 For he will f the work, and cut it short in 4931
2Co 8: 6 he would also f in you the same grace also. 2005

FINISHED (42) [FINISH]

Ge 2: 1 Thus the heavens and the earth were f, and 3615
Ex 39:32 tabernacle of the tent of the congregation f: 3615
40:33 of the court gate. So Moses f the work. 3615
Dt 31:24 of this law in a book, until they were f, 8552
Jos 4:10 until every thing was f that the LORD 8552
Ru 3:18 be in rest, until he have f the thing this day. 3615
1Ki 6: 9 So he built the house, and f it; and 3615
6:14 So Solomon built the house, and f it. 3615
6:22 with gold, until he had f all the house: 8552
6:38 was the house f throughout all the parts 3615
7: 1 house thirteen years, and he f all his house. 3615
7:22 lily work: so was the work of the pillars f. 8552
9: 1 when Solomon had f the building of 3615
9:25 was before the LORD. So he f the house. 7999
1Ch 27:24 he f not, because there fell wrath for it 3615
28:20 until thou hast f all the work for the service 3615
2Ch 4:11 Huram f the work that he was to make for 3615
5: 1 made for the house of the LORD was f: 7999
7:11 Thus Solomon f the house of the LORD, 3615
8:16 the house of the LORD, and until it was f. 3615
24:14 when they had f it, they brought the rest of 3615
29:28 continued until the burnt offering was f. 3615
31: 1 Now when all this was f, all Israel that 3615
31: 7 the heaps, and f them in the seventh month. 3615
Ezr 5:16 hath it been in building, and yet it is not f. 8000
6:14 f it, according to the commandment of 3635
6:15 this house was f on the third day of 3319
Ne 6:15 So the wall was f in the twenty and 7999
Da 5:26 God hath numbered thy kingdom, and f it. 8000
12: 7 the holy people, all these things shall be f. 3615
Mt 13:53 that when Jesus had f these parables, 5055
19: 1 that when Jesus had f these sayings, 5055
26: 1 to pass, when Jesus had f all these sayings, 5055
Jn 17: 4 I have f the work which thou gavest me to 5048
19:30 had received the vinegar, he said, It is f: 5055
Ac 21: 7 And when we had f our course from Tyre, 1274
2Ti 4: 7 I have f my course, I have kept the faith: 5055
Heb 4: 3 although the works were f from 1096
Jas 1:15 and sin, when it is f, bringeth forth death. 658
Rev 10: 7 to sound, the mystery of God should be f, 5055
11: 7 And when they shall have f their testimony, 5055
20: 5 not again until the thousand years were f. 5055

FINISHER (1) [FINISH]

Heb 12: 2 unto Jesus the author and f of our faith; 5051

FINS (5)

Lev 11: 9 whatsoever hath f and scales in the waters, 5579
11:10 all that have not f nor scales in the seas, 5579
11:12 Whatsoever hath no f nor scales in 5579
Dt 14: 9 all that have f and scales shall ye eat: 5579
14:10 whatsoever hath not f and scales ye may 5579

FIR (21)

2Sa 6: 5 all manner of instruments made of f wood, 1265
1Ki 5: 8 timber of cedar, and concerning timber of f. 1265
5:10 and f trees according to all his desire. 1265
6:15 the floor of the house with planks of f. 1265
6:34 the two doors were of f tree: the two leaves 1265
9:11 Solomon with cedar trees and f trees, 1265
2Ki 19:23 trees thereof, and the choice f trees thereof: 1265
2Ch 2: 8 f trees, and algum trees, out of Lebanon: 1265
3: 5 the greater house he cieled with f tree, 1265
Ps 104:17 as for the stork, the f trees are her house. 1265
SS 1:17 of our house are cedar, and our rafters of f. 1266
Isa 14: 8 the f trees rejoice at thee, and the cedars of 1265
37:24 and the choice f trees thereof: 1265
41:19 I will set in the desert the f tree, and 1265
55:13 of the thorn shall come up the f tree, 1265
60:13 the f tree, the pine tree, and the box 1265
Eze 27: 5 made all thy ship boards of f trees of Senir: 1265
31: 8 the f trees were not like his boughs, and 1265
Hos 14: 8 I am like a green f tree. From me is thy 1265
Na 2: 3 and the f trees shall be terribly shaken. 1265
Zec 11: 2 Howl, f tree; for the cedar is fallen; 1265

FIRE (549) [FIREBRAND, FIREBRANDS, FIREPANS, FIRES]

Ge 19:24 and f from the LORD out of heaven; 784
22: 6 he took the f in his hand, and a knife; and 784
22: 7 And he said, Behold the f and the wood: but 784
Ex 3: 2 in a flame of f out of the midst of a bush: 784
3: 2 the bush burned with f, and the bush was not 784
9:23 hail, and the f ran along upon the ground; 784
9:24 and f mingled with the hail, very grievous, 784
12: 8 roast with f, and unleavened bread; 784
12: 9 nor sodden at all with water, but roast with f; 784
12:10 of it until the morning ye shall burn with f. 784
13:21 by night in a pillar of f, to give them light; 784
13:22 nor the pillar of f by night, from before 784
14:24 host of the Egyptians through the pillar of f 784
19:18 the LORD descended upon it in f: 784
22: 6 If f break out, and catch in thorns, so that 784
22: 6 kindled the f shall surely make restitution. 1200
24:17 f on the top of the mount in the eyes of 784
29:14 shalt thou burn with f without the camp: 784
29:18 an offering made by f unto the LORD. 801
29:25 it is an offering made by f unto the LORD. 801
29:34 then thou shalt burn the remainder with f: 784
29:41 an offering made by f unto the LORD. 801
30:20 to burn offering made by f unto 801
32:20 and burnt it in the f, and ground it to powder, 784
32:24 I cast it into the f, and there came out this 784
35: 3 Ye shall kindle no f throughout your 784
40:38 f was on it by night, in the sight of all 784
Lev 1: 7 the sons of Aaron the priest shall put f upon 784
1: 7 and lay the wood in order upon the f: 784
1: 8 in order upon the wood that is on the f which 784
1: 9 be a burnt sacrifice, an offering made by f, 801
1:12 wood that is on the f which is upon the altar: 784
1:13 it is a burnt sacrifice, an offering made by f, 801
1:17 the altar, upon the wood that is upon the f: 784
1:17 it is a burnt sacrifice, an offering made by f, 801
2: 2 to be an offering made by f, of a sweet 801
2: 3 of the offerings of the LORD made by f. 801
2: 9 it is an offering made by f, of a sweet 801
2:10 of the offerings of the LORD made by f. 801
2:11 in any offering of the LORD made by f. 801
2:14 firstfruits green ears of corn dried by the f, 784
2:16 it is an offering made by f unto the LORD. 801
3: 3 an offering made by f unto the LORD; 801
3: 5 which is upon the wood that is on the f: 784
3: 5 it is an offering made by f, of a sweet 801
3: 9 an offering made by f unto the LORD; 801
3:11 it is the food of the offering made by f unto 801
3:14 even an offering made by f unto 801
3:16 it is the food of the offering made by f for a 801
4:12 and burn him on the wood with f: 784
4:35 according to the offerings made by f unto 801
5:12 according to the offerings made by f unto 801
6: 9 and the f of the altar shall be burning in it. 784
6:10 take up the ashes which the f hath consumed 784
6:12 the f upon the altar shall be burning in it; 784
6:13 The f shall ever be burning upon the altar; 784
6:17 for their portion of my offerings made by f; 801
6:18 the offerings of the LORD made by f. 801
6:30 shall be eaten: it shall be burnt in the f. 784
7: 5 for an offering made by f unto the LORD: 801
7:17 on the third day shall be burnt with f. 784
7:19 shall not be eaten; it shall be burnt with f: 784
7:25 of which men offer an offering made by f 801
7:30 the offerings of the LORD made by f, 801
7:35 of the offerings of the LORD made by f, 801

F

Lev 8:17 his dung, he burnt with f without the camp; 784
8:21 *and* an **offering made by f** unto the LORD; 801
8:28 it *is* an **offering made by f** unto the LORD. 801
8:32 and of the bread shall ye burn with f. 784
9:11 the hide he burnt with f without the camp. 784
9:24 there came a f out from before the LORD, 784
10: 1 put f therein, and put incense thereon, 784
10: 1 offered strange f before the LORD, 784
10: 2 there went out f from the LORD, and 784
10:12 of the **offerings** of the LORD **made by f**, 801
10:13 of the **sacrifices** of the LORD **made by f**: 801
10:15 with the **offerings made by f** of the fat, 801
13:52 *is* a fretting leprosy; it shall be burnt in the f. 784
13:55 it *is* unclean; thou shalt burn it in the f; it *is* 784
13:57 shalt burn that wherein the plague *is* with f. 784
16:12 shall take a censer full of burning coals of f 784
16:13 he shall put the incense upon the f before 784
16:27 they shall burn in the f their skins, and their 784
18:21 of thy seed pass through *the f* to Molech, NIH
19: 6 until the third day, it shall be burnt in the f. 784
20:14 they shall be burnt with f, both he and they; 784
21: 6 for the **offerings** of the LORD **made by f**, 801
21: 9 her father: she shall be burnt with f. 784
21:21 the **offerings** of the LORD **made by f**: 801
22:22 nor make an **offering by f** of them upon 801
22:27 **offering made by f** unto the LORD. 801+7133
23: 8 ye shall offer an **offering made by f** unto 801
23:13 an **offering made by f** unto the LORD *for* 801
23:18 drink offerings, *even* an **offering made by f**, 801
23:25 ye shall offer an **offering made by f** unto 801
23:27 offer an **offering made by f** unto 801
23:36 an **offering made by f** unto the LORD: 801
23:36 ye shall offer an **offering made by f** unto 801
23:37 to offer an **offering made by f** unto 801
24: 7 *even* an **offering made by f** unto 801
24: 9 of the **offerings** of the LORD **made by f**, 801
Nu 3: 4 when they offered strange f before 784
6:18 put *it* in the f which *is* under the sacrifice of 784
9:15 the tabernacle as it were the appearance of f, 784
9:16 it *by day*, and the appearance of f by night. 784
11: 1 the f of the LORD burnt among them, and 784
11: 2 unto the LORD, the f was quenched. 784
11: 3 the f of the LORD burnt among them. 784
14:14 pillar of a cloud, and in a pillar of f by night. 784
15: 3 will make an **offering by f** unto the LORD, 801
15:10 *for* an **offering made by f**, of a sweet savour 801
15:13 in offering an **offering made by f**, of a 801
15:14 will offer an **offering made by f**, of a sweet 801
15:25 a **sacrifice made by f** unto the LORD, and 801
16: 7 put f therein, and put incense in them before 784
16:18 put f in them, and laid incense thereon, 784
16:35 there came out a f from the LORD, and 784
16:37 of the burning, and scatter thou the f yonder; 784
16:46 put f therein from off the altar, and put on 784
18: 9 of the most holy *things, reserved* from the f: 784
18:17 burn their fat *for* an **offering made by f**, 801
21:28 For there is a f gone out of Heshbon, a flame 784
26:10 what time the f devoured two hundred and 784
26:61 when they offered strange f before 784
28: 2 *and* my bread for my **sacrifices made by f**, 801
28: 3 This *is* the **offering made by f** which ye 801
28: 6 a **sacrifice made by f** unto the LORD. 801
28: 8 thou shalt offer *it*, a **sacrifice made by f**, 801
28:13 a **sacrifice made by f** unto the LORD. 801
28:19 ye shall offer a **sacrifice made by f** *for* a 801
28:24 the meat of the **sacrifice made by f**, 801
29: 6 a **sacrifice made by f** unto the LORD. 801
29:13 offer a burnt offering, a **sacrifice made by f**, 801
29:36 offer a burnt offering, a **sacrifice made by f**, 801
31:10 and all their goodly castles, with f. 784
31:23 Every thing that may abide the f, ye shall 784
31:23 ye shall make *it* go through the f, and it shall 784
31:23 all that abideth not the f ye shall make go 784
Dt 1:33 a place to pitch your tents *in*, in f by night, 784
4:11 the mountain burnt with f unto the midst of 784
4:12 spake unto you out of the midst of the f: 784
4:15 unto you in Horeb out of the midst of the f: 784
4:24 For the LORD thy God *is* a consuming f, 784
4:33 of God speaking out of the midst of the f, 784
4:36 upon earth he shewed thee his great f; and 784
4:36 heardest his words out of the midst of the f. 784
5: 4 to face in the mount out of the midst of the f, 784
5: 5 for ye were afraid by reason of the f, and 784
5:22 in the mount out of the midst of the f, 784
5:23 (for the mountain did burn with f,) 784
5:24 heard his voice out of the midst of the f: 784
5:25 for this great f will consume us: if we hear 784
5:26 living God speaking out of the midst of the f, 784
7: 5 and burn their graven images with f. 784
7:25 images of their gods shall ye burn with f: 784
9: 3 *as* a consuming f he shall destroy them, and 784
9:10 the midst of the f in the day of the assembly. 784
9:15 the mount, and the mount burned with f: 784
9:21 burnt it with f, and stamped it, *and* ground *it* 784
10: 4 the midst of the f in the day of the assembly: 784
12: 3 their pillars, and burn their groves with f; 784
12:31 their daughters they have burnt in the f to 784
13:16 shalt burn with f the city, and all the spoil 784
18: 1 eat the **offerings** of the LORD **made by f**, 801
18:10 his son or his daughter to pass through the f, 784
18:16 neither let me see this great f any more, 784
32:22 For a f is kindled in my anger, and shall burn 784
32:22 **set on f** the foundations of the mountains. 3857
Jos 6:24 they burnt the city with f, and all that *was* 784
7:15 with the accursed thing shall be burnt with f, 784
7:25 him *with* stones, and burned them with f, 784
8: 8 taken the city, *that* ye shall set the city on f: 784
8:19 and took it, and hasted and set the city on f. 784
11: 6 their horses, and burn their chariots with f. 784
11: 9 their horses, and burnt their chariots with f. 784
11:11 left to breathe: and he burnt Hazor with f. 784
13:14 **sacrifices** of the LORD God of Israel
made by f 801
Jdg 1: 8 the edge of the sword, and set the city on f. 784
6:21 and there rose up f out of the rock, 784
Jdg 9:15 let f come out of the bramble, and devour 784
9:20 let f come out from Abimelech, and 784
9:20 let f come out from the men of Shechem, 784
9:49 to the hold, and set the hold on f upon them; 784
9:52 unto the door of the tower to burn it with f. 784
12: 1 we will burn thine house upon thee with f. 784
14:15 we burn thee and thy father's house with f: 784
15: 5 when he had set the brands on f, he let *them* 784
15: 6 came up, and burnt her and her father with f. 784
15:14 arms became as flax that was burnt with f, 784
16: 9 of tow is broken when it toucheth the f. 784
18:27 edge of the sword, and burnt the city with f. 784
20:48 also they set on f all the cities that they came 784
1Sa 2:28 **offerings made by f** of the children of 801
30: 1 and smitten Ziklag, and burnt it with f; 784
30: 3 to the city, and behold, *it was* burnt with f; 784
30:14 south of Caleb; and we burnt Ziklag with f. 784
2Sa 14:30 and he hath barley there; go and set it on f. 784
14:30 And Absalom's servants set the field on f. 784
14:31 have thy servants set my field on f? 784
22: 9 his nostrils, and f out of his mouth devoured: 784
22:13 before him were coals of f kindled. 784
23: 7 they shall be utterly burnt with f in the same 784
1Ki 9:16 burnt it with f, and slain the Canaanites that 784
16:18 burnt the king's house over him with f, and 784
18:23 put no f *under*: and I will dress the other 784
18:23 and lay *it* on wood, and put no f *under*: 784
18:24 the God that answereth by f, let him be God. 784
18:25 the name of your gods, but put no f *under*. 784
18:38 the f of the LORD fell, and consumed 784
19:12 after the earthquake a f; *but* the LORD *was* 784
19:12 a fire; *but* the LORD *was* not in the f: 784
19:12 in the fire: and after the f a still small voice. 784
2Ki 1:10 let f come down from heaven, and 784
1:10 there came down f from heaven, and 784
1:12 let f come down from heaven, and 784
1:12 the f of God came down from heaven, and 784
1:14 there came f down from heaven, and 784
2:11 *there appeared* a chariot of f, and horses of 784
2:11 horses of f, and parted them both asunder; 784
6:17 and chariots of f round about Elisha. 784
8:12 their strong holds wilt thou set on f, and 784
16: 3 yea, and made his son to pass through the f, 784
17:17 and their daughters to pass through the f, 784
17:31 the Sepharvites burnt their children in f to 784
19:18 have cast their gods into the f: for they *were* 784
21: 6 And he made his son pass through the f, and 784
23:10 his daughter to pass through the f to Molech. 784
23:11 and burnt the chariots of the sun with f. 784
25: 9 and every great *man's* house burnt he with f. 784
1Ch 14:12 a commandment, and they were burnt with f. 784
21:26 he answered him from heaven by f upon 784
2Ch 7: 1 the f came down from heaven, and 784
7: 3 when all the children of Israel saw how the f 784
28: 3 burnt his children in the f after 784
33: 6 he caused his children to pass through the f 784
35:13 they roasted the passover with f according to 784
36:19 burnt all the palaces thereof with f, and 784
Ne 1: 3 and the gates thereof are burnt with f. 784
2: 3 and the gates thereof are consumed with f? 784
2:13 and the gates thereof were consumed with f. 784
2:17 and the gates thereof are burnt with f: 784
9:12 in the night by a pillar of f, to give them 784
9:19 neither the pillar of f by night, to shew them 784
Job 1:16 The f of God is fallen from heaven, and 784
15:34 f shall consume the tabernacles of bribery. 784
18: 5 put out, and the spark of his f shall not shine. 784
20:26 a f not blown shall consume him; it shall go 784
22:20 but the remnant of them the f consumeth. 784
28: 5 and under it is turned up as it were f. 784
31:12 For it *is* a f *that* consumeth to destruction, 784
41:19 go burning lamps, *and* sparks of f leap out. 784
Ps 11: 6 f and brimstone, and a horrible tempest: 784
18: 8 his nostrils, and f out of his mouth devoured: 784
18:12 clouds passed, hail-*stones* and coals of f. 784
18:13 gave his voice; hail-*stones* and coals of f. 784
21: 9 up in his wrath, and the f shall devour them. 784
29: 7 voice of the LORD divideth the flames of f. 784
39: 3 within me, while I was musing the f burned: 784
46: 9 in sunder; he burneth the chariot in the f. 784
50: 3 a f shall devour before him, and it shall be 784
57: 4 *and* I lie *even among* them that are **set on f**, 3857
66:12 we went through f and through water: 784
68: 2 as wax melteth before the f, *so* let 784
74: 7 They have cast f into thy sanctuary, 784
78:14 a cloud, and all the night with a light of f. 784
78:21 so a f was kindled against Jacob, and 784
78:63 The f consumed their young men; and 784
79: 5 for ever? shall thy jealousy burn like f? 784
80:16 *It is* burnt with f, *it is* cut down: they perish 784
83:14 As the f burneth a wood, and as the flame 784
83:14 as the flame **setteth** the mountains **on f**; 3857
89:46 for ever? shall thy wrath burn like f? 784
97: 3 A f goeth before him, and burneth up his 784
104: 4 his angels spirits; his ministers a flaming f: 784
105:32 hail *for* rain, *and* flaming f in their land. 784
105:39 a covering; and f to give light in the night. 784
106:18 a f was kindled in their company; the flame 784
118:12 they are quenched as the f of thorns: 784
140:10 let them be cast into the f; into deep pits, 784
148: 8 F, and hail; snow, and vapour; stormy wind 784
Pr 6:27 Can a man take f in his bosom, and 784
16:27 up evil: and in his lips *there is* as a burning f. 784
25:22 For thou shalt heap **coals of f** upon his 1513
26:20 Where no wood is, *there* the f goeth out: so 784
26:21 *As* coals *are* to burning coals, and wood to f; 784
30:16 and the f *that* saith not, *It is* enough. 784
SS 8: 6 the coals thereof *are* coals of f, *which hath* a 784
Isa 1: 7 *is* desolate, your cities *are* burnt *with* f: 784
4: 5 and the shining of a flaming f by night: 784
5:24 Therefore as the f devoureth 784+3956
9: 5 but *this* shall be with burning *and* fuel of f. 784
9:18 For wickedness burneth as the f: it shall 784
9:19 and the people shall be as the fuel of the f: 784
10:16 shall kindle a burning like the burning of a f. 784
Isa 10:17 the light of Israel shall be for a f, and 784
26:11 the f of thine enemies shall devour them. 784
27:11 the women come, *and* **set** them **on f**: for it *is* 215
29: 6 and tempest, and the flame of devouring f. 784
30:14 of it a sheard to take f from the hearth, 784
30:27 and his tongue as a devouring f: 784
30:30 *with* the flame of a devouring f, 784
30:33 the pile thereof *is* f and much wood; 784
31: 9 whose f *is* in Zion, and his furnace in 217
33:11 your breath, *as* f, shall devour you. 784
33:12 *as* thorns cut up shall they be burnt in the f. 784
33:14 among us shall dwell *with* the devouring f? 784
37:19 have cast their gods into the f: for they *were* 784
42:25 it hath **set** him **on f** round about, yet he 3857
43: 2 when thou walkest through the f, thou shalt 784
44:16 He burneth part thereof in the f; with part 784
44:16 and saith, Aha, I am warm, I have seen the f: 217
44:19 to say, I have burnt part of it in the f; 784
47:14 shall be as stubble; the f shall burn them; 784
47:14 *be* a coal to warm at, *nor* f to sit before it. 217
50:11 Behold, all ye that kindle a f, that compass 784
50:11 walk in the light of your f, and in the sparks 784
54:16 the smith that bloweth the coals in the f, 784
64: 2 As *when* the melting f burneth, the fire 784
64: 2 fire burneth, the f causeth the waters to boil, 784
64:11 our fathers praised thee, is burnt up with f: 784
65: 5 in my nose, a f that burneth all the day. 784
66:15 the LORD will come with f, and with his 784
66:15 with fury, and his rebuke with flames of f. 784
66:16 For by f and by his sword will the LORD 784
66:24 not die, neither shall their f be quenched; 784
Jer 4: 4 lest my fury come forth like f, and burn that 784
5:14 I will make my words in thy mouth f, and 784
6: 1 and set up a **sign of f** in Beth-haccerem: 4864
6:29 are burnt, the lead is consumed of the f; 784
7:18 the fathers kindle the f, and the women 784
7:31 burn their sons and their daughters in the f; 784
11:16 of a great tumult he hath kindled f upon it, 784
15:14 for a f is kindled in mine anger, *which* shall 784
17: 4 for ye have kindled a f in mine anger, 784
17:27 then will I kindle a f in the gates thereof, and 784
19: 5 to burn their sons with f *for* burnt offerings 784
20: 9 *his word* was in mine heart as a burning f 784
21:10 king of Babylon, and he shall burn it with f. 784
21:12 lest my fury go out like f, and burn that none 784
21:14 and I will kindle a f in the forest thereof, and 784
22: 7 thy choice cedars, and cast *them* into the f. 784
23:29 *Is* not my word like as a f? saith the LORD; 784
29:22 whom the king of Babylon roasted in the f; 784
32:29 shall come and set f on this city, and burn it 784
32:35 their daughters to pass through *the f* unto NIH
34: 2 king of Babylon, and he shall burn it with f: 784
34:22 against it, and take it, and burn it with f: 784
36:22 *there was a f on* the hearth burning before NIH
36:23 cast *it* into the f that *was* on the hearth, 784
36:23 until all the roll was consumed in the f that 784
36:32 Jehoiakim king of Judah had burnt in the f: 784
37: 8 this city, and take it, and burn it with f. 784
37:10 man in his tent, and burn this city with f. 784
38:17 and this city shall not be burnt with f; 784
38:18 they shall burn it with f, and thou shalt not 784
38:23 thou shalt cause this city to be burnt with f. 784
39: 8 with f, and brake down the walls of 784
43:12 I will kindle a f in the houses of the gods of 784
43:13 gods of the Egyptians shall he burn with f. 784
48:45 but a f shall come forth out of Heshbon, and 784
49: 2 and her daughters shall be burnt with f: 784
49:27 I will kindle a f in the wall of Damascus, 784
50:32 I will kindle a f in his cities, and it shall 784
51:32 the reeds they have burnt with f, and the men 784
51:58 her high gates shall be burnt with f; 784
51:58 and the folk in the f, and they shall be weary. 784
52:13 the houses of the great *men*, burnt he with f: 784
La 1:13 From above hath he sent f into my bones, 784
2: 3 and he burned against Jacob like a flaming f, 784
2: 4 of Zion: he poured out his fury like f. 784
4:11 hath kindled a f in Zion, and it hath 784
Eze 1: 4 a f infolding itself, and a brightness *was* 784
1: 4 the colour of amber, out of the midst of the f. 784
1:13 their appearance *was* like burning coals of f, 784
1:13 the f was bright, and out of the fire went 784
1:13 and out of the f went forth lightning. 784
1:27 as the appearance of f round about within it, 784
1:27 I saw as it were the appearance of f, and 784
5: 2 Thou shalt burn with f a third *part* in 217
5: 4 cast them into the midst of the f, and 784
5: 4 the midst of the fire, and burn them in the f; 784
5: 4 *for* thereof shall a f come forth into all 784
8: 2 and lo, a likeness as the appearance of f: 784
8: 2 appearance of his loins even downward, f; 784
10: 2 fill thine hand *with* coals of f from between 784
10: 6 saying, Take f from between the wheels, 784
10: 7 unto the f that *was* between the cherubims, 784
15: 4 Behold, it is cast into the f for fuel; the fire 784
15: 4 the f devoureth both the ends of it, and 784
15: 5 when the f hath devoured it, and it is 784
15: 6 which I have given to the f for fuel, so will I 784
15: 7 they shall go out from *one* f, and *another* fire 784
15: 7 *one* fire, and *another* f shall devour them; 784
16:21 cause them to pass through *the f* for them? NIH
16:41 And they shall burn thine houses with f, and 784
19:12 and withered; the f consumed them. 784
19:14 f is gone out of a rod of her branches, 784
20:26 in that they caused to pass through *the f* all NIH
20:31 *ye* make your sons to pass through the f, 784
20:47 I *will* kindle a f in thee, and it shall devour 784
21:31 I will blow against thee in the f of my wrath, 784
21:32 Thou shalt be for fuel to the f; thy blood 784
22:20 to blow the f upon it, to melt *it*; so will I 784
22:21 and blow upon you in the f of my wrath, and 784
22:31 I have consumed them with the f of my 784
23:25 and thy residue shall be devoured by the f. 784
23:37 to pass for them through *the f*, to devour NIH
23:47 and burn up their houses with f. 784
24: 9 I will even make the **pile for f** great. 4071

Eze 24:10 Heap on wood, kindle the f, consume 784
24:12 forth out of her: her scum *shall be* in the f. 784
28:14 and down in the midst of the stones of f. 784
28:16 from the midst of the stones of f. 784
28:18 will I bring forth a f from the midst of thee, 784
30: 8 when I have set a f in Egypt, and *when* all 784
30:14 will set f in Zoan, and will execute 784
30:16 I will set f in Egypt: Sin shall have great 784
36: 5 Surely in the f of my jealousy have I spoken 784
38:19 *and* in the f of my wrath have I spoken, 784
38:22 and great hailstones, f, and brimstone. 784
39: 6 I will send a f on Magog, and among them 784
39: 9 shall **set on** f and burn the weapons, 1197
39: 9 and they shall burn them with f seven years: 784
39:10 for they shall burn the weapons with f 784
Da 3:22 the flame of the f slew those men that took 5135
3:24 three men bound into the midst of the f? 5135
3:25 walking in the midst of the f, and they have 5135
3:26 came forth of the midst of the f. 5135
3:27 upon whose bodies the f had no power, 5135
3:27 nor the smell of f had passed on them. 5135
7: 9 the fiery flame, *and* his wheels *as* burning f. 5135
10: 6 and his eyes as lamps of f, and his arms and 784
Hos 7: 6 *in* the morning it burneth as a flaming f. 784
8:14 I will send a f upon his cities, and it shall 784
Joel 1:19 for the f hath devoured the pastures of 784
1:20 the f hath devoured the pastures of 784
2: 3 A f devoureth before them; and behind them 784
2: 5 like the noise of a flame of f that devoureth 784
2:30 the earth, blood, and f, and pillars of smoke. 784
Am 1: 4 I will send a f into the house of Hazael, 784
1: 7 I will send a f on the wall of Gaza, 784
1:10 I will send a f on the wall of Tyrus, 784
1:12 I will send a f upon the Teman, which shall 784
1:14 I will kindle a f in the wall of Rabbah, and 784
2: 2 I will send a f upon Moab, and it shall 784
2: 5 I will send a f upon Judah, and it shall 784
5: 6 lest he break out like f *in* the house of 784
7: 4 the Lord GOD called to contend by f, and 784
Ob 1:18 the house of Jacob shall be a f, and the house 784
Mic 1: 4 as wax before the f, *and* as the waters *that* 784
1: 7 all the hires thereof shall be burnt with the f, 784
Na 1: 6 his fury is poured out like f, and the rocks 784
3:13 thine enemies: the f shall devour thy bars. 784
3:15 There shall the f devour thee; the sword shall 784
Hab 2:13 that the people shall labour in the very f, 784
Zep 1:18 the whole land shall be devoured by the f of 784
3: 8 for all the earth shall be devoured with the f 784
Zec 2: 5 will be unto her a wall of f round about, and 784
3: 2 *is* not this a brand pluckt out of the f? 784
9: 4 in the sea; and she shall be devoured with f. 784
11: 1 that the f may devour thy cedars. 784
12: 6 of Judah like a hearth of f among the wood, 784
12: 6 the wood, and like a torch of f in a sheaf; 784
13: 9 And I will bring the third *part* through the f, 784
Mal 1:10 do ye kindle *f on* mine altar for nought. NIH
3: 2 for he *is* like a refiner's f, and like fullers' 784
Mt 3:10 fruit is hewn down, and cast into the f. 4442
3:11 you with the Holy Ghost, and *with* f: 4442
3:12 will burn up the chaff with unquenchable f. 4442
5:22 *Thou* fool, shall be in danger of hell f. 4442
7:19 fruit is hewn down, and cast into the f. 4442
13:40 the tares are gathered and burnt in the f; 4442
13:42 And shall cast them into a furnace of f: 4442
13:50 And shall cast them into the furnace of f: 4442
17:15 for ofttimes he falleth into the f, and 4442
18: 8 or two feet to be cast into everlasting f. 4442
18: 9 than having two eyes to be cast into hell f. 4442
25:41 from me, ye cursed, into everlasting f, 4442
Mk 9:22 And ofttimes it hath cast him into the f, and 4442
9:43 into the f that never shall be quenched: 4442
9:44 worm dieth not, and the f is not quenched. 4442
9:45 into the f that never shall be quenched: 4442
9:46 worm dieth not, and the f is not quenched. 4442
9:47 than having two eyes to be cast into hell f: 4442
9:48 worm dieth not, and the f is not quenched. 4442
9:49 For every one shall be salted with f, and 4442
14:54 the servants, and warmed himself at the f. 5457
Lk 3: 9 fruit is hewn down, and cast into the f. 4442
3:16 you with the Holy Ghost and *with* f: 4442
3:17 the chaff he will burn with f unquenchable. 4442
9:54 wilt thou *that* we command f to come down 4442
12:49 I am come to send f on the earth; and 4442
17:29 day that Lot went out of Sodom it rained f 4442
22:55 And when they had kindled a f in the midst 4442
22:56 a certain maid beheld him as he sat by the f, 5457
Jn 15: 6 and cast *them* into the f, and they are 4442
18:18 stood *there,* who had made a **f of coals**; 439
21: 9 they saw a **f of coals** there, and fish laid 439
Ac 2: 3 unto them cloven tongues like as of f, 4442
2:19 blood, and f, and vapour of smoke: 4442
7:30 angel of the Lord in a flame of f in a bush. 4442
28: 2 for they kindled a f, and received us every 4443
28: 3 and laid *them* on the f, there came a viper 4443
28: 5 And he shook off the beast into the f, and 4442
Ro 12:20 doing thou shalt heap coals of f on his 4442
1Co 3:13 declare *it,* because it shall be revealed by f; 4442
3:13 the f shall try every man's work of what 4442
3:15 he himself shall be saved; yet so as by f. 4442
2Th 1: 8 In flaming f, taking vengeance on them that 4442
Heb 1: 7 and his ministers a flame of f. 4442
11:34 Quenched the violence of f, escaped 4442
12:18 and that burned with f, nor unto blackness, 4442
12:29 For our God *is* a consuming f. 4442
Jas 3: 5 how great a matter a little f kindleth. 4442
3: 6 And the tongue *is* a f, a world of iniquity: 4442
3: 6 and **setteth on** f the course of nature; 5394
3: 6 course of nature; and it is **set on** f of hell. 5394
5: 3 and shall eat your flesh as *it were* f: 4442
1Pe 1: 7 though it be tried with f, might be found 4442
2Pe 3: 7 reserved unto f against the day of judgment 4442
3:12 wherein the heavens being **on** f shall be 4448
Jude 1: 7 suffering the vengeance of eternal f. 4442
1:23 save with fear, pulling *them* out of the f; 4442
Rev 1:14 as snow; and his eyes *were* as a flame of f; 4442

Rev 2:18 who hath his eyes like unto a flame of f, 4442
3:18 thee to buy of me gold tried in the f, 4442
4: 5 *there were* seven lamps of f burning before 4442
8: 5 and filled it with f of the altar, and cast *it* 4442
8: 7 followed hail and f mingled with blood, 4442
8: 8 as *it were* a great mountain burning with f 4442
9:17 having breastplates of f, and of jacinth, and 4447
9:17 and out of their mouths issued f and smoke 4442
9:18 by the f, and by the smoke, and by 4442
10: 1 *it were* the sun, and his feet as pillars of f: 4442
11: 5 f proceedeth out of their mouth, and 4442
13:13 that he maketh f come down from heaven 4442
14:10 and he shall be tormented with f and 4442
14:18 out from the altar, which had power over f; 4442
15: 2 as *it were* a sea of glass mingled with f: 4442
16: 8 was given unto him to scorch men with f. 4442
17:16 and shall eat her flesh, and burn her with f. 4442
18: 8 and she shall be utterly burnt with f: 4442
19:12 His eyes *were* as a flame of f, and on his 4442
19:20 *These* both were cast alive into a lake of f 4442
20: 9 and f came down from God out of heaven, 4442
20:10 deceived them was cast into the lake of f 4442
20:14 and hell were cast into the lake of f. 4442
20:15 the book of life was cast into the lake of f. 4442
21: 8 their part in the lake which burneth with f 4442

FIREBRAND (2) [FIRE, BRAND]

Jdg 15: 4 and put a f in the midst between two tails. 3940
Am 4:11 and ye were as a f pluckt out of the burning: 181

FIREBRANDS (3) [FIRE, BRAND]

Jdg 15: 4 took f, and turned tail to tail, and put a 3940
Pr 26:18 As a mad *man* who casteth f, arrows, and 2131
Isa 7: 4 for the two tails of these smoking f, 181

FIREPANS (4) [FIRE, PAN]

Ex 27: 3 his basons, and his fleshhooks, and his f: 4289
38: 3 the basons, *and* the fleshhooks, and the f: 4289
2Ki 25:15 the f, and the bowls, *and* such *things* as 4289
Jer 52:19 the f, and the bowls, and the caldrons, and 4289

FIRES (1) [FIRE]

Isa 24:15 Wherefore glorify ye the LORD in the f, 217

FIRKINS (1)

Jn 2: 6 the Jews, containing two or three f apiece. 3355

FIRM (7)

Jos 3:17 f on dry *ground* in the midst of Jordan, 3559
4: 3 of the place where the priests' feet stood f, 3559
Job 41:23 they are f in themselves; they cannot be 3332
41:24 His heart is as f as a stone; yea, as hard as 3332
Ps 73: 4 bands in their death: but their strength *is* f. 1277
Da 6: 7 to **make** a f decree, that whosoever shall 8631
Heb 3: 6 and the rejoicing of the hope f unto the end. 949

FIRMAMENT (17)

Ge 1: 6 Let there be a f in the midst of the waters, 7549
1: 7 God made the f, and divided the waters 7549
1: 7 divided the waters which *were* under the f 7549
1: 7 from the waters which *were* above the f: 7549
1: 8 God called the f Heaven. And the evening 7549
1:14 Let there be lights in the f of the heaven to 7549
1:15 let them be for lights in the f of the heaven 7549
1:17 God set them in the f of the heaven to give 7549
1:20 fly above the earth in the open f of heaven. 7549
Ps 19: 1 of God; and the f sheweth his handywork. 7549
150: 1 praise him in the f of his power. 7549
Eze 1:22 the likeness of the f upon the heads of 7549
1:23 under the f *were* their wings straight, 7549
1:25 there was a voice from the f that *was* over 7549
1:26 above the f that *was* over their heads *was* 7549
10: 1 in the f that *was* above the head of 7549
Da 12: 3 wise shall shine as the brightness of the f; 7549

FIRST (436) [FIRSTBEGOTTEN, FIRSTBORN, FIRSTFRUIT, FIRSTFRUITS, FIRSTLING, FIRSTLINGS, FIRSTRIPE]

Ge 1: 5 the evening and the morning were the f day. 259
2:11 The name of the f *is* Pison: that *is* it which 259
8: 5 in the tenth *month,* on the f *day* of 259
8:13 came to pass in the six hundredth and f year, 259
8:13 in the f *month,* the first *day* of the month, 7223
8:13 in the first *month,* the f *day* of the month, 259
13: 4 the altar, which he had made there at the f: 7223
25:25 the f came out red, all over like a hairy 7223
26: 1 besides the f famine that was in the days of 7223
28:19 name of *that* city *was called* Luz at the f. 7223
38:28 a scarlet thread, saying, This came out f. 7223
41:20 the ill favoured kine did eat up the f seven 7223
43:18 in our sacks at the **f time** *are* we brought in; 8462
43:20 we came indeed down at the **f time** to buy 8462
Ex 4: 8 neither hearken to the voice of the f sign, 7223
12: 2 it *shall be* the f month of the year to you. 7223
12: 5 be without blemish, a male of the f year: 1121
12:15 even the f day ye shall put away leaven out 7223
12:15 bread from the f day until the seventh day, 7223
12:16 in the f day *there shall be* a holy 7223
12:18 In the f *month,* on the fourteenth day of 7223
22:29 Thou shalt not delay *to offer the f of* thy NIH
23:19 The f of the firstfruits of thy land thou shalt 7225
28:17 *the f* row *shall be* a sardius, a topaz, and NIH
28:17 and a carbuncle: this *shall be* the f row 259
29:38 two lambs of the f year day by day 1121
34: 1 thee two tables of stone like unto the f: 7223
34: 1 tables the words that were in the f tables, 7223
34: 4 hewed two tables of stone like unto the f; 7223
34:26 The f of the firstfruits of thy land thou shalt 7225
39:10 *the f* row *was* a sardius, a topaz, and NIH
39:10 a topaz, and a carbuncle: *this was* the f row. 259
40: 2 On the f day of the first month shalt thou 7223
40: 2 On the first day of the f month shalt thou set 259
40:17 it came to pass in the f month in the second 7223
40:17 on the f *day* of the month, *that* the tabernacle 259

Lev 4:21 and burn him as he burned the f bullock: 7223
5: 8 offer *that* which *is* for the sin offering f, 7223
9: 3 a calf and a lamb, both of the f year, 1121
9:15 and slew it, and offered it for sin, as the f. 7223
12: 6 she shall bring a lamb of the f year for a 1121
14:10 one ewe lamb of the f year without 1323
23: 5 In the fourteenth *day* of the f month at even 7223
23: 7 In the f day ye shall have a holy 7223
23:12 f year for a burnt offering unto the LORD. 1121
23:18 seven lambs without blemish of the f year, 1121
23:19 two lambs of the f year for a sacrifice of 1121
23:24 the seventh month, in the f *day* of the month, 259
23:35 On the f day *shall be* a holy convocation: 7223
23:39 on the f day *shall be* a sabbath, and on 7223
23:40 ye shall take you on the f day the boughs of 7223
Nu 1: 1 on the f *day* of the second month, 259
1:18 together on the f *day* of the second month, 259
2: 9 their armies. *These* shall f set forth. 7223
6:12 shall bring a lamb of the **f year** for a 1121+8141
6:14 one he lamb of the **f year** without 1121+8141
6:14 one ewe lamb of the **f year** without 1323+8141
7:12 he that offered his offering the f day was 7223
7:15 one ram, one lamb of the **f year**, 1121+8141
7:17 he goats, five lambs of the **f year**: 1121+8141
7:21 one ram, one lamb of the **f year**, 1121+8141
7:23 he goats, five lambs of the **f year**: 1121+8141
7:27 one ram, one lamb of the **f year**, 1121+8141
7:29 he goats, five lambs of the **f year**: 1121+8141
7:33 one ram, one lamb of the **f year**, 1121+8141
7:35 he goats, five lambs of the **f year**: 1121+8141
7:39 one ram, one lamb of the **f year**, 1121+8141
7:41 he goats, five lambs of the **f year**: 1121+8141
7:45 one ram, one lamb of the **f year**, 1121+8141
7:47 he goats, five lambs of the **f year**: 1121+8141
7:51 one ram, one lamb of the **f year**, 1121+8141
7:53 he goats, five lambs of the **f year**: 1121+8141
7:57 one ram, one lamb of the **f year**, 1121+8141
7:59 he goats, five lambs of the **f year**: 1121+8141
7:63 one ram, one lamb of the **f year**, 1121+8141
7:65 he goats, five lambs of the **f year**: 1121+8141
7:69 one ram, one lamb of the **f year**, 1121+8141
7:71 he goats, five lambs of the **f year**: 1121+8141
7:75 one ram, one lamb of the **f year**, 1121+8141
7:77 he goats, five lambs of the **f year**: 1121+8141
7:81 one ram, one lamb of the **f year**, 1121+8141
7:83 he goats, five lambs of the **f year**: 1121+8141
7:87 the lambs of the **f year** twelve, 1121+8141
7:88 the lambs of the **f year** sixty. 1121+8141
9: 1 in the f month of the second year after they 7223
9: 5 f month at even in the wilderness of Sinai: 7223
10:13 they f took their journey according to 7223
10:14 In the f *place* went the standard of the camp 7223
13:20 Now the time *was* the time of the **f ripe** 1061
15:20 Ye shall offer up a cake *of* the f of your 7225
15:21 Of the f of your dough ye shall give unto 7225
15:27 he shall bring a she goat of the f year for a 1323
18:13 *And* whatsoever is **f ripe** in the land, 1061
20: 1 *into* the desert of Zin in the f month: 7223
24:20 and said, Amalek *was* the f of the nations; 7225
28: 3 two lambs of the **f year** without spot 1121+8141
28: 9 on the sabbath day two lambs of the f year 1121
28:11 lambs of the **f year** without spot; 1121+8141
28:16 in the fourteenth day of the f month *is* 7223
28:18 In the f day *shall be* a holy convocation; 7223
28:19 and seven lambs of the **f year**: 1121+8141
28:27 one ram, seven lambs of the **f year**; 1121+8141
29: 1 seventh month, on the f *day* of the month, 259
29: 2 lambs of the **f year** without blemish: 1121+8141
29: 8 *and* seven lambs of the **f year**; 1121+8141
29:13 *and* fourteen lambs of the **f year**; 1121+8141
29:17 lambs of the **f year** without spot: 1121+8141
29:20 fourteen lambs of the **f year** without 1121+8141
29:23 fourteen lambs of the **f year** without 1121+8141
29:26 lambs of the **f year** without spot: 1121+8141
29:29 fourteen lambs of the **f year** without 1121+8141
29:32 fourteen lambs of the **f year** without 1121+8141
29:36 lambs of the **f year** without blemish: 1121+8141
33: 3 they departed from Rameses in the f month, 7223
33: 3 on the fifteenth day of the f month; 7223
33:38 land of Egypt, in the f *day* of the fifth month. 259
Dt 1: 3 eleventh month, on the f *day* of the month, 259
9:18 as at the f, forty days and forty nights: 7223
9:25 as I fell down *at the f,* because the LORD NIH
10: 1 thee two tables of stone like unto the f, 7223
10: 2 that were in the f tables which thou brakest, 7223
10: 3 hewed two tables of stone like unto the f, 7223
10: 4 according to the f writing, the ten 7223
10:10 according to the f time, forty days and 7223
11:14 the **f rain** and the latter rain, that thou 3138
13: 9 thine hand shall be f upon him to put him to 7223
16: 4 which thou sacrificedst the f day at even, 7223
17: 7 The hands of the witnesses shall be f upon 7223
18: 4 thy oil, and the f of the fleece of thy sheep, 7225
26: 2 That thou shalt take of the f of all the fruit 7225
33:21 he provided the f *part* for himself, because 7225
Jos 4:19 of Jordan on the tenth *day* of the f month, 7223
8: 5 as at the f, that we will flee before them, 7223
8: 6 will say, *They* flee before us, as at the f: 7223
21:10 of Levi, had: for theirs was the f lot. 7223
Jdg 1: 1 shall go up for us against the Canaanites f, 8462
18:29 the name of the city *was* Laish at the f. 7223
20:18 Which of us shall go up f to 8462+871.1+1886.1
20:18 Judah *shall go up* f. 8462+871.1+1886.1
20:22 they put *themselves* in array the f day 7223
20:32 *are* smitten down before us, as at the f. 7223
20:39 smitten down before us, as *in* the f battle. 7223
1Sa 14:14 *that* f slaughter, which Jonathan and 7223
14:35 the same was the f altar that he built unto 2490
2Sa 3:13 f bring Michal Saul's daughter, 6440+3807.1
17: 9 when *some* of them be overthrown at the f, 8462
19:20 I am come the f *this* day of all the house of 7223
19:43 that our advice should not be f had in 7223
21: 9 in the f *days,* in the beginning of barley 7223
23:19 howbeit he attained not unto the *f* three. NIH
23:23 the thirty, but he attained not to the *f* three. NIH

1Ki 16:23 **f** year of Asa king of Judah *began* Omri to 259
17:13 me thereof a little cake **f**, 7223+871.1+1886.1
18:25 one bullock for yourselves, and dress *it* **f**; 7223
20: 9 send for to thy servant at the **f** I will do: 7223
20:17 of the princes of the provinces went out **f**; 7223
1Ch 9: 2 Now the **f** inhabitants that *dwelt* in their 7223
11: 6 Whosoever smiteth the Jebusites **f** shall be 7223
11: 6 So Joab the son of Zeruiah went **f** up, and 7223
11:21 howbeit he attained not to the *f* three. NIH
11:25 the thirty, but attained not to the *f* three: NIH
12: 9 Ezer the **f**, Obadiah the second, Eliab 7218
12:15 they that went over Jordan in the **f** month, 7223
15:13 For because ye *did it* not at the **f**, 7223
16: 7 on that day David delivered **f** *this psalm* to 7218
23:19 Jeriah the **f**, Amariah the second, 7218
23:20 Michah the **f**, and Jesiah the second. 7218
24: 7 Now the **f** lot came forth to Jehoiarib, 7223
24:21 of the sons of Rehabiah, the **f** *was* Isshiah. 7218
24:23 the sons *of Hebron;* Jeriah *the f,* Amariah NIH
25: 9 Now the **f** lot came forth for Asaph to 7223
27: 2 Over the **f** course for the first month *was* 7223
27: 2 Over the first course for the **f** month *was* 7223
27: 3 all the captains of the host for the **f** month. 7223
29:29 acts of David the king, **f** and last, behold, 7223
2Ch 3: 3 The length *by* cubits after the **f** measure 7223
9:29 the rest of the acts of Solomon, **f** and last, 7223
12:15 Now the acts of Rehoboam, **f** and last, *are* 7223
16:11 behold, the acts of Asa, **f** and last, lo, 7223
17: 3 he walked in the **f** ways of his father David, 7223
20:34 rest of the acts of Jehoshaphat, **f** and last, 7223
25:26 of the acts of Amaziah, **f** and last, behold, 7223
26:22 **f** and last, did Isaiah the prophet, the son of 7223
28:26 and of all his ways, **f** and last, behold, 7223
29: 3 He in the **f** year of his reign, in the first 7223
29: 3 in the first year of his reign, in the **f** month, 7223
29:17 Now they began on the **f** *day* of the first 259
29:17 Now they began on the first *day* of the **f** 7223
29:17 in the sixteenth day of the **f** month they 7223
35: 1 on the fourteenth *day* of the **f** month. 7223
35:27 his deeds, **f** and last, behold, they *are* 7223
36:22 Now in the **f** year of Cyrus king of Persia, 259
Ezr 1: 1 Now in the **f** year of Cyrus king of Persia, 259
3: 6 From the **f** day of the seventh month began 259
3:12 *who were* ancient men that had seen the **f** 7223
5:13 in the **f** year of Cyrus the king of Babylon 2298
6: 3 In the **f** year of Cyrus the king *the same* 2298
6:19 upon the fourteenth *day* of the **f** month. 7223
7: 9 For upon the **f** *day* of the first month began 259
7: 9 For upon the first *day* of the **f** month began 7223
7: 9 on the **f** *day* of the fifth month came he to 259
8:31 of Ahava on the twelfth *day* of the **f** month, 7223
10:16 sat down in the **f** day of the tenth month to 259
10:17 strange wives by the **f** day of the first month. 259
10:17 wives by the first day of the **f** month. 7223
Ne 7: 5 genealogy of them which came up at the **f**, 7223
8: 2 upon the **f** day of the seventh month. 259
8:18 by day, from the **f** day unto the last day, 7223
Est 1:14 *and* which sat the **f** in the kingdom;) 7223
3: 7 In the **f** month, that *is*, the month Nisan, 7223
3:12 called on the thirteenth day of the **f** month, 7223
Job 15: 7 *Art* thou the **f** man *that* was born? or 7223
42:14 he called the name of the **f**, Jemima; and 259
Pr 18:17 *He that is* **f** in his own cause *seemeth* just; 7223
Isa 1:26 And I will restore thy judges as at the **f**, and 7223
9: 1 when at the **f** he lightly afflicted the land of 7223
41: 4 I the LORD, the **f**, and with the last; I *am* 7223
41:27 The **f** *shall say* to Zion, Behold, 7223
43:27 Thy **f** father hath sinned, and thy teachers 7223
44: 6 I *am* the **f**, and I *am* the last; and besides 7223
48:12 I *am* he; I *am* the **f**, I also *am* the last. 7223
60: 9 the ships of Tarshish **f**, to bring thy sons 7223
Jer 4:31 as of her that **bringeth forth** her **f child**, 1069
7:12 where I set my name at the **f**, and see what 7223
16:18 **f** I will recompense their iniquity and 7223
24: 2 good figs, *even* like the figs *that are* **f ripe**: 1073
25: 1 that *was* the **f** year of Nebuchadrezzar king 7224
33: 7 to return, and will build them, as at the **f**. 7223
33:11 to return the captivity of the land as at the **f**, 7223
36:28 all the former words that were in the **f** roll, 7223
50:17 **f** the king of Assyria hath devoured him; 7223
52:31 *that* Evil-merodach king of Babylon in the *f* NIH
Eze 10:14 the **f** face *was* the face of a cherub, and 7223
26: 1 the eleventh year, in the **f** *day* of the month, 259
29:17 in the **f** *month,* in the first *day* of the month, 7223
29:17 in the first *month,* in the **f** *day* of the month, 259
30:20 in the **f** *month,* in the seventh *day* of 7223
31: 1 in the third *month,* in the **f** *day* of the month, 259
32: 1 in the twelfth month, in the **f** *day* of the month, 259
40:21 thereof were after the measure of the **f** gate: 7223
44:30 the **f** of all the firstfruits of all *things,* and 7225
44:30 ye shall also give unto the priest the **f** of 7225
45:18 In the **f** *month,* in the first *day* of 7223
45:18 In the first *month,* in the **f** *day* of the month, 259
45:21 In the **f** *month,* in the fourteenth day of 7223
46:13 *of* a lamb of the **f** year without blemish: 1121
Da 1:21 Daniel continued *even* unto the **f** year of 259
6: 2 three presidents; of whom Daniel *was* **f**: 2298
7: 1 In the **f** year of Belshazzar king of Babylon 2298
7: 4 The **f** *was* like a lion, and had eagle's 6933
7: 8 before whom there were three of the **f** 6933
7:24 he shall be diverse from the **f**, and he shall 6933
8: 1 after that which appeared unto me at the **f**. 8462
8:21 horn that *is* between his eyes *is* the **f** king. 7223
9: 1 In the **f** year of Darius the son of Ahasuerus, 259
9: 2 In the **f** year of his reign I Daniel understood 259
10: 4 the four and twentieth day of the **f** month, 7223
10:12 for from the **f** day that thou didst set thine 7223
11: 1 Also I in the **f** year of Darius the Mede, 259
Hos 2: 7 I will go and return to my **f** husband; 7223
9:10 as the firstripe in the fig tree at her **f time**: 7225
Joel 2:23 and the latter rain in the **f** *month.* 7223
Am 6: 7 they go captive with the **f** that go captive, 7218
Mic 4: 8 thee shall it come, even the **f** dominion; 7223
Hag 1: 1 in the sixth month, in the **f** day of the month, 259
2: 3 you that saw this house in her **f** glory? 7223
Zec 6: 2 In the **f** chariot *were* red horses; and in 7223
12: 7 LORD also shall save the tents of Judah **f**, 7223
14:10 gate unto the place of the **f** gate, 7223
Mt 5:24 **f** be reconciled to thy brother, and then 4412
6:33 But seek ye **f** the kingdom of God, and 4412
7: 5 **f** cast out the beam out of thine own eye; 4412
8:21 Lord, suffer me **f** to go and bury my father. 4412
10: 2 The **f**, Simon, who is called Peter, and 4413
12:29 except he **f** bind the strong *man?* and then 4412
12:45 the last *state* of that man is worse than the **f**. 4413
13:30 Gather ye together **f** the tares, and 4412
17:10 then say the scribes that Elias must **f** come? 4412
17:11 Elias truly shall **f** come, and restore all 4412
17:27 and take up the fish that **f** cometh up; 4412
19:30 But many *that are* **f** shall be last; and 4413
19:30 *are* first shall be last; and *the* last *shall be* **f**. 4413
20: 8 beginning from the last unto the **f**. 4413
20:10 But when the **f** came, they supposed that 4413
20:16 So the last shall be **f**, and the first last: 4413
20:16 So the last shall be first, and the **f** last: 4413
21:28 and he came to the **f**, and said, Son, 4413
21:31 They say unto him, The **f**. Jesus saith unto 4413
21:36 he sent other servants moe than the **f**: 4413
22:25 and the **f**, when he had married *a wife,* 4413
22:38 This is the **f** and great commandment. 4413
23:26 cleanse **f** that *which is* within the cup and 4412
26:17 Now the **f** *day* of the *feast of* unleavened 4413
27:64 so the last error shall be worse than the **f**. 4413
28: 1 as it began to dawn towards the **f** *day* of 1520
Mk 3:27 except he will **f** bind the strong *man;* and 4412
4:28 **f** the blade, then the ear, after that the full 4412
7:27 said unto her, Let the children **f** be filled: 4412
9:11 Why say the scribes that Elias must **f** 4412
9:12 Elias verily cometh **f**, and restoreth all 4412
9:35 saith unto them, If any *man* desire to be **f**, 4413
10:31 But many *that are* **f** shall be last; and 4413
10:31 *that are* first shall be last; and the last **f**. 4413
12:20 and the **f** took a wife, and dying left no 4413
12:28 Which is the **f** commandment of all? 4413
12:29 The **f** of all the commandments *is,* Hear, 4413
12:30 all thy strength: this *is* the **f** commandment. 4413
13:10 And the gospel must **f** be published among 4412
14:12 And the **f** day of unleavened bread, 4413
16: 2 And very early in the morning the **f** *day* of 1520
16: 9 Now when *Jesus* was risen early the **f** *day* 4413
16: 9 he appeared **f** to Mary Magdalene, out of 4412
Lk 1: 3 understanding of all *things* **from the very f**, 509
2: 2 (*And* this taxing was **f** made when Cyrenius 4413
6: 1 to pass on the **second** sabbath **after the f**, 1207
6:42 cast out **f** the beam out of thine own eye, 4412
9:59 Lord, suffer me **f** to go and bury my father. 4412
9:61 but let me **f** go bid them farewell, which are 4412
10: 5 ye enter, **f** say, Peace *be* to this house. 4412
11:26 the last *state* of that man is worse than the **f**. 4413
11:38 that he had not **f** washed before dinner. 4412
12: 1 he began to say unto his disciples **f** *of all,* 4412
13:30 there are last which shall be **f**, and there are 4413
13:30 be first, and there are **f** which shall be last. 4413
14:18 The **f** said unto him, I have bought a piece 4413
14:28 sitteth not down **f**, and counteth the cost, 4412
14:31 sitteth not down **f**, and consulteth whether 4412
16: 5 lord's debtors unto *him,* and said unto the **f**, 4413
17:25 But **f** must he suffer many *things,* and 4412
19:16 Then came the **f**, saying, Lord, thy pound 4413
20:29 and the **f** took a wife, and died without 4413
21: 9 for these *things* must **f** come to pass; but 4412
24: 1 Now upon the **f** *day* of the week, very early 1520
Jn 1:41 He **f** findeth his own brother Simon, and 4413
5: 4 **f** after the troubling of the water stepped in, 4413
8: 7 sin among you, let him **f** cast a stone at her. 4413
10:40 into the place where John **at f** baptized; 4412
12:16 *things* understood not his disciples **at** the **f**: 4412
18:13 And led him away to Annas **f**; for he was 4412
19:32 and brake the legs of the **f**, and of the other 4413
19:39 which at the **f** came to Jesus by night, and 4412
20: 1 The **f** *day* of the week cometh Mary 1520
20: 4 outrun Peter, and came **f** to the sepulchre. 4413
20: 8 which came **f** to the sepulchre, and he saw, 4413
20:19 day at evening, being the **f** *day* of the week, 1520
Ac 3:26 Unto you **f** God, having raised up his Son 4412
7:12 was corn in Egypt, he sent out our fathers **f**. 4412
11:26 the disciples were called Christians **f** in 4412
12:10 When they were past the **f** and the second 4413
13:24 When John had **f preached** before his 4296
13:46 of God should **f** have been spoken to you: 4412
15:14 Simeon hath declared how God at the **f** did 4412
20: 7 And upon the **f** *day* of the week, when 1520
20:18 from the **f** day that I came into Asia, 4413
26: 4 which was at the **f** among mine own nation 746
26:20 But shewed **f** unto them of Damascus, 4412
26:23 that he *should be* the **f** *that* should rise from 4413
27:43 swim should cast *themselves* **f** into the *sea,* 4413
Ro 1: 8 **F**, I thank my God through Jesus Christ for 4412
1:16 to the Jew **f**, and *also* to the Greek. 4412
2: 9 of the Jew **f**, and *also* of the Gentile; 4412
2:10 to the Jew **f**, and *also* to the Gentile: 4412
10:19 **F** Moses saith, I will provoke you to 4413
11:35 Or who hath **f given** to him, and it shall be 4272
15:24 if **f** I be somewhat filled with your 4412
1Co 11:18 For **f of all**, when ye come together in 4412
12:28 **f** apostles, secondarily prophets, 4412
14:30 that sitteth *by,* let the **f** hold his peace. 4413
15: 3 For I delivered unto you **f** *of all* that 1722+4413
15:45 The **f** man Adam was made a living soul; 4413
15:46 Howbeit *that was* not **f** *which is* spiritual, 4412
15:47 The **f** man *is* of the earth, earthy: 4413
16: 2 Upon the **f** *day* of the week let every one of 1520
16: S The **f** *epistle* to the Corinthians was written 4413
2Co 8: 5 but **f** gave their own selves to the Lord, and 4412
8:12 For if there be **f** a willing mind, *it is* 4295
Gal 4:13 I preached the gospel unto you **at** the **f**. 4387
Eph 1:12 praise of his glory, who **f trusted** in Christ: 4276
4: 9 that he also descended **f** into the lower parts 4412
6: 2 (which is the **f** commandment with 4413
Php 1: 5 For your fellowship in the gospel from the **f** 4413
1Th 4:16 of God: and the dead in Christ shall rise **f**: *4412*
5: S The **f** *epistle* unto the Thessalonians was *4413*
2Th 2: 3 *come,* except there come a falling away **f**, *4412*
1Ti 1:16 that in me **f** Jesus Christ might shew forth *4413*
2: 1 I exhort therefore that, **f** of all, *4412*
2:13 For Adam was **f** formed, then Eve. *4413*
3:10 And let these also **f** be proved; then *4412*
5: 4 let them learn **f** to shew piety at home, and *4412*
5:12 because they have cast off *their* **f** faith. *4413*
6: S The **f** to Timothy was written from *4413*
2Ti 1: 5 which dwelt **f** in thy grandmother Lois, and *4412*
2: 6 The husbandman that laboureth must be **f** *4413*
4:16 At my **f** answer no *man* stood with me, but *4413*
4: S ordained the **f** bishop of the church of *4413*
Tit 3:10 A man *that is* a heretick after the **f** and *1520*
3: S ordained the **f** bishop of the church of *4413*
Heb 2: 3 which at the **f** began to be spoken by *746*
4: 6 they to whom it was **f** preached entered not *4387*
5:12 be the **f** principles of the oracles of God; *746*
7: 2 **f** being by interpretation King of *4412*
7:27 **f** for his own sins, *and* then for *4387*
8: 7 For if that **f** *covenant* had been faultless, *4413*
8:13 A new *covenant,* he hath made the **f** old. *4413*
9: 1 Then verily the **f** *covenant* had also *4413*
9: 2 the **f**, wherein *was* the candlestick, and *4413*
9: 6 the priests went always into the **f** *4413*
9: 8 while as the **f** tabernacle was yet standing: *4413*
9:15 that were under the **f** testament, *4413*
9:18 Whereupon neither the **f** *testament* was *4413*
10: 9 He taketh away the **f**, that he may establish *4413*
Jas 3:17 But the wisdom that is from above is **f** *4412*
1Pe 4:17 and if *it* **f** *begin* at us, what *shall* the end *be* *4412*
2Pe 1:20 Knowing this **f**, that no prophecy of *4412*
3: 3 Knowing this **f**, that there shall come in *4412*
1Jn 4:19 We love him, because he **f** loved us. *4413*
Jude 1: 6 And the angels which kept not their **f estate**, *746*
Rev 1: 5 *and* the **f begotten** of the dead, and *4416*
1:11 I am Alpha and Omega, the **f** and the last: *4413*
1:17 unto me, Fear not; I am the **f** and the last: *4413*
2: 4 because thou hast left thy **f** love. *4413*
2: 5 art fallen, and repent, and do the **f** works; *4413*
2: 8 These *things* saith the **f** and the last, *4413*
2:19 and the last *to be* more than the **f**. *4413*
4: 1 the **f** voice which I heard *was* as *it were* of *4413*
4: 7 And the **f** beast *was* like a lion, and *4413*
8: 7 The **f** angel sounded, and there followed *4413*
13:12 And he exerciseth all the power of the **f** *4413*
13:12 them which dwell therein to worship the **f** *4413*
16: 2 And the **f** went, and poured out his vial *4413*
20: 5 were finished. This *is* the **f** resurrection. *4413*
20: 6 holy *is* he that hath part in the **f** *4413*
21: 1 for the **f** heaven and the first earth were *4413*
21: 1 and the **f** earth were passed away; *4413*
21:19 The **f** foundation *was* jasper; the second, *4413*
22:13 and the end, the **f** and the last. *4413*

FIRSTBEGOTTEN (1) [FIRST, BEGET]

Heb 1: 6 when he bringeth in the **f** into the world, *4416*

FIRSTBORN (117) [FIRST, BEAR]

Ge 10:15 And Canaan begat Sidon his **f**, and Heth, 1060
19:31 the **f** said unto the younger, Our father *is* 1067
19:33 the **f** went in, and lay with her father; and 1067
19:34 that the **f** said unto the younger, Behold, 1067
19:37 the **f** bare a son, and called his name Moab: 1067
22:21 Huz his **f**, and Buz his brother, and Kemuel 1060
25:13 the **f** of Ishmael, Nebajoth; and Kedar, and 1060
27:19 Jacob said unto his father, I *am* Esau thy **f**; 1060
27:32 And he said, I *am* thy son, thy **f** Esau. 1060
29:26 to give the younger before the **f**. 1067
35:23 Jacob's **f**, and Simeon, and Levi, and 1060
36:15 the sons of Eliphaz the **f** *son* of Esau; 1060
38: 6 Judah took a wife for Er his **f**, whose name 1060
38: 7 Er, Judah's **f**, was wicked in the sight of 1060
41:51 Joseph called the name of the **f** Manasseh: 1060
43:33 the **f** according to his birthright, and 1060
46: 8 Jacob and his sons: Reuben, Jacob's **f**. 1060
48:14 hands wittingly; for Manasseh *was* the **f**. 1060
48:18 for this *is* the **f**; put thy right hand upon his 1060
49: 3 Reuben, thou *art* my **f**, my might, and 1060
Ex 4:22 the LORD, Israel *is* my son, *even* my **f**: 1060
4:23 behold, I will slay thy son, *even* thy **f**. 1060
6:14 The sons of Reuben the **f** of Israel; Hanoch, 1060
11: 5 all the **f** in the land of Egypt shall die, 1060
11: 5 from the **f** of Pharaoh that sitteth upon his 1060
11: 5 *even* unto the **f** of the maidservant that *is* 1060
11: 5 *is* behind the mill; and all the **f** of beasts. 1060
12:12 will smite all the **f** in the land of Egypt, 1060
12:29 that at midnight the LORD smote all the **f** 1060
12:29 from the **f** of Pharaoh that sat on his throne 1060
12:29 the **f** of the captive that *was* in the dungeon; 1060
12:29 *was* in the dungeon; and all the **f** of cattle. 1060
13: 2 Sanctify unto me all the **f**, 1060
13:13 all the **f** of man amongst thy children shalt 1060
13:15 that the LORD slew all the **f** in the land of 1060
13:15 both the **f** of man, and the firstborn of 1060
13:15 the firstborn of man, and the **f** of beast: 1060
13:15 but all the **f** of my children I redeem. 1060
22:29 the **f** of thy sons shalt thou give unto me. 1060
34:20 All the **f** of thy sons thou shalt redeem: and 1060
Nu 3: 2 Nadab the **f**, and Abihu, Eleazar, and 1060
3:12 **f** that openeth the matrix among 1060
3:13 Because all the **f** *are* mine; *for* on the day 1060
3:13 *for* on the day that I smote all the **f** in 1060
3:13 Egypt I hallowed unto me all the **f** in Israel, 1060
3:40 Number all the **f** of the males of 1060
3:41 instead of all the **f** among the children of 1060
3:42 all the **f** among the children of Israel. 1060
3:43 all the **f** males by the number of names, 1060
3:45 Take the Levites instead of all the **f** among 1060
3:46 thirteen of the **f** of the children of Israel, 1060
3:50 Of the **f** of the children of Israel took he 1060
8:16 *even instead of* the **f** of all the children of 1060
8:17 For all the **f** of the children of Israel *are* 1060
8:17 on the day that I smote every **f** in the land 1060

Nu 8:18 I have taken the Levites for all the f of 1060
18:15 nevertheless the f of man shalt thou surely 1060
33: 4 For the Egyptians buried all *their* f, which 1060
Dt 21:15 and *if* the f son be hers that was hated: 1060
21:16 **make** the son of the beloved f before 1069
21:16 the son of the hated, *which is indeed* the f: 1060
21:17 acknowledge the son of the hated *for* the f, 1060
21:17 of his strength; the right of the f *is* his. 1062
25: 6 *that* the f which she beareth shall succeed 1060
Jos 6:26 he shall lay the foundation thereof in his f, 1060
17: 1 for he *was* the f of Joseph; *to wit,* for 1060
17: 1 *to wit,* for Machir the f of Manasseh, 1060
Jdg 8:20 he said unto Jether his f, Up, *and* slay them. 1060
1Sa 8: 2 Now the name of his f was Joel; and 1060
14:49 *were these;* the name of the f Merab, 1067
17:13 sons that went to the battle *were* Eliab the f, 1060
2Sa 3: 2 his f was Amnon, of Ahinoam 1060
1Ki 16:34 laid the foundation thereof in Abiram his f, 1060
1Ch 1:13 And Canaan begat Zidon his f, and Heth, 1060
1:29 The f of Ishmael, Nebajoth; then Kedar, 1060
2: 3 Er, the f of Judah, was evil in the sight of 1060
2:13 Jesse begat his f Eliab, and Abinadab 1060
2:25 the sons of Jerahmeel the f of Hezron were, 1060
2:25 Ram the f, and Bunah, and Oren, and 1060
2:27 the sons of Ram the f of Jerahmeel were, 1060
2:42 the brother of Jerahmeel *were,* Mesha his f, 1060
2:50 of Caleb the son of Hur, the f of Ephratah; 1060
3: 1 the f Amnon, of Ahinoam the Jezreelitess; 1060
3:15 the sons of Josiah *were,* the f Johanan, 1060
4: 4 the f of Ephratah, the father of Beth-lehem. 1060
5: 1 Now the sons of Reuben the f of Israel, 1060
5: 1 the firstborn of Israel, (for he *was* the f; 1060
5: 3 *I say,* of Reuben the f of Israel *were,* 1060
6:28 sons of Samuel; the f Vashni, and Abiah. 1060
8: 1 Now Benjamin begat Bela his f, Ashbel 1060
8:30 his f son Abdon, and Zur, and Kish, and 1060
8:39 sons of Eshek his brother *were,* Ulam his f, 1060
9: 5 of the Shilonites; Asaiah the f, and his sons. 1060
9:31 who *was* the f of Shallum the Korahite, 1060
9:36 his f son Abdon, then Zur, and Kish, and 1060
26: 2 sons of Meshelemiah *were,* Zechariah the f, 1060
26: 4 sons of Obed-edom *were,* Shemaiah the f, 1060
26:10 the chief, (for *though* he was not the f, 1060
2Ch 21: 3 gave he to Jehoram; because he *was* the f. 1060
Ne 10:36 Also the f of our sons, and of our cattle, 1060
Job 18:13 *even* the f of death shall devour his 1060
Ps 78:51 smote all the f in Egypt; the chief of *their* 1060
89:27 Also I will make him *my* f, higher than 1060
105:36 He smote also all the f in their land, 1060
135: 8 Who smote the f of Egypt, both of man and 1060
136:10 To him that smote Egypt in their f: for his 1060
Isa 14:30 the f of the poor shall feed, and the needy 1060
Jer 31: 9 I am a father to Israel, and Ephraim *is* my f. 1060
Mic 6: 7 shall I give my f *for* my transgression, 1060
Zec 12:10 for him, as one that is in bitterness for *his* f. 1060
Mt 1:25 her not till she had brought forth her f son: *4416*
Lk 2: 7 And she brought forth her f son, and *4416*
Ro 8:29 that he might be the f among many *4416*
Col 1:15 of the invisible God, the f of every creature: *4416*
1:18 who is the beginning, the f from the dead; *4416*
Heb 11:28 lest he that destroyed the f should touch *4416*
12:23 the general assembly, and church of the f, *4416*

FIRSTFRUIT (2) [FIRST, FRUIT]

Dt 18: 4 The f *also* of thy corn, of thy wine, and 7225
Ro 11:16 For if the f *be* holy, the lump *is* also *holy:* *536*

FIRSTFRUITS (32) [FIRST, FRUIT]

Ex 23:16 the feast of harvest, the f of thy labours, 1061
23:19 The first of the f of thy land thou shalt 1061
34:22 of the f of wheat harvest, and the feast of 1061
34:26 The first of the f of thy land thou shalt 1061
Lev 2:12 *As for* the oblation of the f, ye shall offer 7225
2:14 if thou offer a meat offering of *thy* f unto 1061
2:14 of thy f green ears of corn dried by the fire, 1061
23:10 ye shall bring a sheaf of the f of your 7225
23:17 *they are* the f unto the LORD. 1061
23:20 f *for* a wave offering before the LORD, 1061
Nu 18:12 the f of them which they shall offer unto 7225
28:26 Also in the day of the f, when ye bring a 1061
Dt 26:10 I have brought the f of the land, 6529+7225
2Ki 4:42 brought the man of God bread of the f, 1061
2Ch 31: 5 Israel brought in abundance the f of corn, 7225
Ne 10:35 to bring the f of our ground, and 1061
10:35 the f of all fruit of all trees, year by year, 1061
10:37 *that* we should bring the f of our dough, 7225
12:44 the offerings, for the f, and for the tithes, 7225
13:31 at times appointed, and for the f. 1061
Pr 3: 9 and with the f of all thine increase: 7225
Jer 2: 3 unto the LORD, *and* the f of his increase: 7225
Eze 20:40 the f of your oblations, with all your holy 7225
44:30 the first of all the f of all *things,* and 1061
48:14 nor alienate the f of the land: 7225
Ro 8:23 ourselves also, which have the f of the Spirit, *536*
16: 5 who is the f of Achaia unto Christ. *536*
1Co 15:20 *and* become the f of them that slept. *536*
15:23 Christ the f; afterward they that are Christ's *536*
16:15 that it is the f of Achaia, and *that* they have *536*
Jas 1:18 that we should be a kind of f of his creatures. *536*
Rev 14: 4 *being* the f unto God and to the Lamb. *536*

FIRSTLING (14) [FIRST]

Ex 13:12 every f that cometh of a beast which thou 6363
13:13 every f of an ass thou shalt redeem with a 6363
34:19 every f amongst thy cattle, *whether* ox or 6363
34:20 the f of an ass thou shalt redeem with a 6363
Lev 27:26 Only the f of the beasts, which should be 1060
27:26 which should be the LORD'S f, no man 1069
Nu 18:15 the f of unclean beasts shalt thou redeem. 1060
18:17 the f of a cow, or the firstling of a sheep, 1060
18:17 or the f of a sheep, or the firstling of a goat, 1060
18:17 or the f of a goat, thou shalt not redeem; 1060
Dt 15:19 All the f males that come of thy herd and 1060
15:19 thou shalt do no work with the f of thy 1060
15:19 of thy bullock, nor shear the f of thy sheep. 1060
33:17 His glory *is like* the f of his bullock, and 1060

FIRSTLINGS (6) [FIRST]

Ge 4: 4 he also brought of the f of his flock and 1062
Nu 3:41 the cattle of the Levites instead of all the f 1060
Dt 12: 6 and the f of your herds and of your flocks: 1062
12:17 thy oil, or the f of thy herds or of thy flock, 1062
14:23 and the f of thy herds and of thy flocks; 1062
Ne 10:36 and the f of our herds and of our flocks, 1062

FIRSTRIPE (3) [FIRST, RIPE]

Hos 9:10 I saw your fathers as the f in the fig tree at 1063
Mic 7: 1 cluster to eat: my soul desired the f **fruit.** 1063
Na 3:12 holds *shall be like* fig trees with the f **figs:** 1061

FISH (35) [FISH'S, FISHER'S, FISHERMEN, FISHERS, FISHES, FISHHOOKS, FISHING, FISHPOOLS]

Ge 1:26 let them have dominion over the f of 1710
1:28 have dominion over the f of the sea, and 1710
Ex 7:18 the f that *is* in the river shall die, and 1710
7:21 the f that *was* in the river died; and the river 1710
Nu 11: 5 We remember the f, which we did eat in 1710
11:22 shall all the f of the sea be gathered 1709
Dt 4:18 the likeness of any f that *is* in the waters 1710
2Ch 33:14 even to the entering in at the f gate, and 1709
Ne 3: 3 the f gate did the sons of Hassenaah build, 1709
12:39 above the f gate, and the tower of 1709
13:16 which brought f, and all *manner of* ware, 1709
Job 41: 7 barbed irons? or his head with f spears? 1709
Ps 8: 8 the f of the sea, *and whatsoever* passeth 1709
105:29 their waters into blood, and slew their f. 1710
Isa 19:10 all that make sluces *and* ponds for f. 5315
50: 2 their f stinketh, because *there is* no water, 1710
Jer 16:16 saith the LORD, and they shall f them; 1770
Eze 29: 4 I will cause the f of thy rivers to stick unto 1710
29: 4 all the f of thy rivers shall stick unto thy 1710
29: 5 thee and all the f of thy rivers: 1710
47: 9 there shall be a very great multitude of f, 1710
47:10 their f shall be according to their kinds, 1710
47:10 as the f of the great sea, exceeding many. 1710
Jnh 1:17 Now the LORD had prepared a great f to 1709
1:17 Jonah was in the belly of the f three days 1709
2:10 the LORD spake unto the f, and 1709
Zep 1:10 *shall be* the noise of a cry from the f gate, 1709
Mt 7:10 Or if he ask a f, will he give him a serpent? *2486*
17:27 and take up the f that first cometh up; *2486*
Lk 11:11 or if *he ask* a f, will he for a fish give him a *2486*
11:11 a fish, will he for a f give him a serpent? *2486*
24:42 And they gave him a piece of a broiled f, *2486*
Jn 21: 9 of coals there, and f laid thereon, and bread. *3795*
21:10 Bring of the f which ye have now caught. *3795*
21:13 and giveth them, and f likewise. *3795*

FISH'S (1) [FISH]

Jnh 2: 1 unto the LORD his God out of the f belly, 1710

FISHER'S (1) [FISH]

Jn 21: 7 he girt *his* f **coat** unto him, (for he was *1903*

FISHERMEN (1) [FISH, MAN]

Lk 5: 2 but the f were gone out of them, and *231*

FISHERS (7) [FISH]

Isa 19: 8 The f also shall mourn, and all they that 1771
Jer 16:16 Behold, I will send for many f, saith 1771
Eze 47:10 *that* the f shall stand upon it from En-gedi 1728
Mt 4:18 casting a net into the sea: for they were f. *231*
4:19 Follow me, and I will make you f of men. *231*
Mk 1:16 casting a net into the sea: for they were f. *231*
1:17 and I will make you to become f of men. *231*

FISHES (27) [FISH]

Ge 9: 2 *upon* the earth, and upon all the f of the sea; 1709
1Ki 4:33 of fowl, and of creeping things, and of f. 1709
Job 12: 8 and the f of the sea shall declare unto thee. 1709
Ecc 9:12 as the f that are taken in an evil net, and 1709
Eze 38:20 So that the f of the sea, and the fowls of 1709
Hos 4: 3 the f of the sea also shall be taken away. 1709
Hab 1:14 makest men as the f of the sea, as 1709
Zep 1: 3 the f of the sea, and the stumblingblocks 1709
Mt 14:17 We have here but five loaves, and two f. *2486*
14:19 and the two f, and looking up to heaven, *2486*
15:34 And they said, Seven, and a few **little** f. *2485*
15:36 And he took the seven loaves and the f, and *2486*
Mk 6:38 when they knew, they say, Five, and two f. *2486*
6:41 he had taken the five loaves and the two f, *2486*
6:41 and the two f divided he among *them* all. *2486*
6:43 baskets full of the fragments, and of the f. *2486*
8: 7 And they had a few **small** f: and he blessed, *2485*
Lk 5: 6 they inclosed a great multitude of f: *2486*
5: 9 at the draught of the f which they had *2486*
9:13 We have no more but five loaves and two f; *2486*
9:16 Then he took the five loaves and the two f, *2486*
Jn 6: 9 hath five barley loaves, and two **small** f: *3795*
6:11 likewise of the f as much as they would. *3795*
21: 6 not able to draw it for the multitude of f. *2486*
21: 8 hundred cubits,) dragging the net with f. *2486*
21:11 and drew the net to land full of great f, *2486*
1Co 15:39 of beasts, another of f, *and* another of birds. *2486*

FISHHOOKS (1) [FISH, HOOK]

Am 4: 2 and your posterity with f. 1729+5518

FISHING (1) [FISH]

Jn 21: 3 Simon Peter saith unto them, I go a f. *232*

FISHPOOLS (1) [FISH, POOL]

SS 7: 4 thine eyes *like* the f in Heshbon, 1295

FIST (2)

Ex 21:18 or with *his* f, and he die not, but keepeth *his* 106
Isa 58: 4 and to smite with the f of wickedness: 106

FISTS (1) [HOOK]

Pr 30: 4 who hath gathered the wind in his f? 2651

FIT (9) [FITLY, FITTED, FITTETH]

Lev 16:21 shall send *him* away by the hand of a f man 6261
1Ch 7:11 two hundred *soldiers,* f to go out *for* war NIH
12: 8 *and* men of war f for the battle, that could NIH
Job 34:18 *Is it* f to say to a king, *Thou art* wicked? *and* NIH
Pr 24:27 and **make** it f for thyself in the field; 6257
Lk 9:62 looking back, is f for the kingdom of God. *2111*
14:35 It is neither f for the land, nor yet for *2111*
Ac 22:22 the earth: for it is not f that he should live. *2520*
Col 3:18 your own husbands, as it is f in the Lord. *433*

FITCHES (4)

Isa 28:25 doth he not cast abroad the f, and 7100
28:27 For the f are not threshed with a threshing 7100
28:27 the f are beaten out with a staff, and 7100
Eze 4: 9 f, and put them in one vessel, and 3698

FITLY (4) [FIT]

Pr 25:11 A word f spoken *is like* apples of gold 212+5921
SS 5:12 of waters, washed with milk, *and* f set. 4402
Eph 2:21 f **framed together** groweth unto a holy *4883*
4:16 whom the whole body f **joined together** *4883*

FITTED (3) [FIT]

1Ki 6:35 covered *them* with gold f upon the carved 3474
Pr 22:18 they shall withal be f in thy lips. 3559
Ro 9:22 *the* vessels of wrath f to destruction: *2675*

FITTETH (1) [FIT]

Isa 44:13 he f it with planes, and he marketh it out 6213

FITTING See SEEMLY

FIVE (345) [FIFTH]

Ge 5: 6 Seth lived an hundred and f years, and 2568
5:11 of Enos were nine hundred and f years: 2568
5:15 Mahalaleel lived sixty and f years, 2568
5:17 were eight hundred ninety and f years: 2568
5:21 Enoch lived sixty and f years, and 2568
5:23 were three hundred sixty and f years: 2568
5:30 Lamech lived after he begat Noah f 2568
5:30 begat Noah five hundred ninety and f years, 2568
5:32 Noah was f hundred years old: and 2568
11:11 Shem lived after he begat Arphaxad f 2568
11:12 Arphaxad lived f and thirty years, and 2568
11:32 of Terah were two hundred and f years: 2568
12: 4 f years old when he departed out of Haran. 2568
14: 9 Arioch king of Ellasar; four kings with f. 2568
18:28 Peradventure there shall lack f of the fifty 2568
18:28 wilt thou destroy all the city for *lack of* f? 2568
18:28 he said, If I find there forty and f, I will not 2568
43:34 Benjamin's mess was f times so much as 2568
45: 6 yet *there are* f years, *in* the which *there* 2568
45:11 for yet *there are* f years of famine; 2568
45:22 *pieces* of silver, and f changes of raiment. 2568
47: 2 *even* f men, and presented them unto 2568
Ex 22: 1 he shall restore f oxen for an ox, and 2568
26: 3 The f curtains shall be coupled together one 2568
26: 3 *other* f curtains *shall be* coupled one to 2568
26: 9 thou shalt couple f curtains by themselves, 2568
26:26 f for the boards of the one side of 2568
26:27 f bars for the boards of the other side of 2568
26:27 f bars for the boards of the side of 2568
26:37 thou shalt make for the hanging f pillars of 2568
26:37 thou shalt cast f sockets of brass for them. 2568
27: 1 f cubits long, and five cubits broad; 2568
27: 1 five cubits long, and f cubits broad; 2568
27:18 the height f cubits *of* fine twined linen, and 2568
30:23 of pure myrrh f hundred *shekels,* and 2568
30:24 of cassia f hundred *shekels,* after the shekel 2568
36:10 he coupled the f curtains one unto another: 2568
36:10 *the other* f curtains he coupled one unto 2568
36:16 he coupled f curtains by themselves, and 2568
36:31 f for the boards of the one side of 2568
36:32 f bars for the boards of the other side of 2568
36:32 f bars for the boards of the tabernacle for 2568
36:38 the f pillars of it with their hooks: and 2568
36:38 with gold: but their f sockets *were of* brass. 2568
38: 1 f cubits *was* the length thereof, and 2568
38: 1 and f cubits the breadth thereof; 2568
38:18 and the height in the breadth *was* f cubits, 2568
38:26 and f hundred and fifty *men.* 2568
38:28 and f *shekels* he made hooks for the pillars, 2568
Lev 26: 8 f of you shall chase an hundred, and 2568
27: 5 if *it be* from f years old even unto twenty 2568
27: 6 if *it be* from a month old even unto f years 2568
27: 6 thy estimation shall be of the male f shekels 2568
Nu 1:21 *were* forty and six thousand and f hundred. 2568
1:25 and f thousand six hundred and fifty. 2568
1:33 *were* forty thousand and f hundred. 2568
1:37 *were* thirty and f thousand and 2568
1:41 *were* forty and one thousand and f hundred. 2568
1:46 and three thousand and f hundred and fifty. 2568
2:11 *were* forty and six thousand and f hundred. 2568
2:15 *were* forty and f thousand and six hundred 2568
2:19 *were* forty thousand and f hundred. 2568
2:23 *were* thirty and f thousand and 2568
2:28 *were* forty and one thousand and f hundred. 2568
2:32 and three thousand and f hundred and fifty. 2568
3:22 them *were* seven thousand and f hundred. 2568
3:47 Thou shalt even take f shekels **apiece** 2568+2568
3:50 f *shekels,* after the shekel of the sanctuary: 2568
4:48 and f hundred and fourscore. 2568
7:17 two oxen, f rams, five he goats, five lambs 2568
7:17 two oxen, five rams, f he goats, five lambs 2568
7:17 five he goats, f lambs of the first year: 2568
7:23 two oxen, f rams, five he goats, five lambs 2568
7:23 two oxen, five rams, f he goats, five lambs 2568
7:23 five he goats, f lambs of the first year: 2568
7:29 two oxen, f rams, five he goats, five lambs 2568
7:29 two oxen, five rams, f he goats, five lambs 2568

F

Nu 7:29 five he goats, f lambs of the first year: 2568
7:35 two oxen, f rams, five he goats, five lambs 2568
7:35 two oxen, five rams, f he goats, five lambs 2568
7:35 five he goats, f lambs of the first year: 2568
7:41 two oxen, f rams, five he goats, five lambs 2568
7:41 two oxen, five rams, f he goats, five lambs 2568
7:41 five he goats, f lambs of the first year: 2568
7:47 two oxen, f rams, five he goats, five lambs 2568
7:47 two oxen, five rams, f he goats, five lambs 2568
7:47 five he goats, f lambs of the first year: 2568
7:53 two oxen, f rams, five he goats, five lambs 2568
7:53 two oxen, five rams, f he goats, five lambs 2568
7:53 five he goats, f lambs of the first year: 2568
7:59 two oxen, f rams, five he goats, five lambs 2568
7:59 two oxen, five rams, f he goats, five lambs 2568
7:59 five he goats, f lambs of the first year: 2568
7:65 two oxen, f rams, five he goats, five lambs 2568
7:65 two oxen, five rams, f he goats, five lambs 2568
7:65 five he goats, f lambs of the first year: 2568
7:71 two oxen, f rams, five he goats, five lambs 2568
7:71 two oxen, five rams, f he goats, five lambs 2568
7:71 five he goats, f lambs of the first year: 2568
7:77 two oxen, f rams, five he goats, five lambs 2568
7:77 two oxen, five rams, f he goats, five lambs 2568
7:77 five he goats, f lambs of the first year: 2568
7:83 two oxen, f rams, five he goats, five lambs 2568
7:83 two oxen, five rams, f he goats, five lambs 2568
7:83 five he goats, f lambs of the first year: 2568
8:24 from twenty and f years old and 2568
11:19 nor two days, nor f days, neither ten days, 2568
18:16 *for* the money of f shekels, 2568
26:18 of them, forty thousand and f hundred. 2568
26:22 and sixteen thousand and f hundred. 2568
26:27 threescore thousand and f hundred. 2568
26:37 thirty and two thousand and f hundred. 2568
26:41 *were* forty and f thousand and six hundred. 2568
26:50 and f thousand and four hundred. 2568
31:8 and Hur, and Reba, f kings of Midian: 2568
31:28 one soul of f hundred, *both* of the persons, 2568
31:32 and seventy thousand and f thousand sheep, 2568
31:36 and thirty thousand and f hundred sheep: 2568
31:39 asses *were* thirty thousand and f hundred; 2568
31:43 *and* seven thousand and f hundred sheep, 2568
31:45 And thirty thousand asses and f hundred, 2568
Jos 8:12 he took about f thousand men, and set them 2568
10:5 Therefore the f kings of the Amorites, 2568
10:16 these f kings fled, and hid themselves in a 2568
10:17 The f kings are found hid in a cave at 2568
10:22 bring out those f kings unto me out of 2568
10:23 brought forth those f kings unto him out of 2568
10:26 and slew them, and hanged them on f trees: 2568
13:3 f lords of the Philistines; the Gazathites, 2568
14:10 me alive, as he said, these forty and f years, 2568
14:10 I *am this* day fourscore and f years old. 2568
Jdg 3:3 *Namely,* f lords of the Philistines, and 2568
18:2 the children of Dan sent of their family f 2568
18:7 the f men departed, and came to Laish, 2568
18:14 answered the f men that went to spy out 2568
18:17 the f men that went to spy out the land went 2568
20:35 and f thousand and an hundred men: 2568
20:45 they gleaned of them in the highways f 2568
20:46 and f thousand men that drew the sword; 2568
1Sa 6:4 F golden emerods, and five golden mice, 2568
6:4 Five golden emerods, and f golden mice, 2568
6:16 when the f lords of the Philistines had seen 2568
6:18 of the Philistines *belonging* to the f lords, 2568
17:5 the weight of the coat *was* f thousand 2568
17:40 chose him f smooth stones out of the brook, 2568
21:3 give *me* f *loaves of* bread in mine hand, or 2568
22:18 and f persons that did wear a linen ephod. 2568
25:18 f sheep ready dressed, and five measures of 2568
25:18 f measures of parched *corn,* and an hundred 2568
25:42 with f damsels of hers that went after her; 2568
2Sa 4:4 was f years old when the tidings came of 2568
21:8 the f sons of Michal the daughter of Saul, 2568
24:9 the men of Judah *were* f hundred thousand 2568
1Ki 4:32 and his songs were a thousand and f. 2568
6:6 The nethermost chamber *was* f cubits 2568
6:10 against all the house, f cubits high: 2568
6:24 f cubits *was* the one wing of the cherub, 2568
6:24 and f cubits the other wing of the cherub: 2568
7:3 that *lay* on forty f pillars, fifteen *in* a row. 2568
7:16 the height of the one chapiter *was* f cubits, 2568
7:16 the height of the other chapiter *was* f 2568
7:23 round all about, and his height *was* f cubits: 2568
7:39 he put f bases on the right side of the house, 2568
7:39 and f on the left side of the house: 2568
7:49 f on the right side, and five on the left, 2568
7:49 f on the left, before the oracle, with 2568
9:23 f hundred and fifty, which bare rule over 2568
22:42 and f years old when he *began* to reign; 2568
22:42 he reigned twenty and f years in Jerusalem. 2568
2Ki 6:25 the fourth part of a kab of dove's dung for f 2568
7:13 I pray thee, f of the horses that remain, 2568
13:19 *Thou* shouldest have smitten f or six times; 2568
14:2 and f years old when he *began* to reign, 2568
15:33 F and twenty years old was he when he 2568
18:2 f years old was he when he *began* to reign; 2568
19:35 an hundred fourscore and f thousand: 2568
21:1 and reigned fifty and f years in Jerusalem. 2568
23:36 and f year old when he *began* to reign; 2568
25:19 f men of them that were in the king's 2568
1Ch 2:4 and Zerah. All the sons of Judah *were* f. 2568
2:6 and Calcol, and Dara: f of them in all. 2568
3:20 Berechiah, and Hasadiah, Jushabhesed, f. 2568
4:32 Rimmon, and Tochen, and Ashan, f cities: 2568
4:42 f hundred men, went to mount Seir, 2568
7:3 Michael, and Obadiah, and Joel, Ishiah, f: 2568
7:7 Uzzi, and Uzziel, and Jerimoth, and Iri, f; 2568
11:23 f cubits *high;* and in the Egyptian's hand 2568
29:7 the house of God *of* gold f thousand talents 2568
2Ch 3:11 *one* wing of the one *cherub was* f cubits, 2568
3:11 the other wing *was likewise* f cubits, 2568
3:12 *one* wing of the other cherub *was* f cubits, 2568
3:12 the other wing *was* f cubits *also,* joining to 2568

2Ch 3:15 house two pillars of thirty and f cubits high, 2568
3:15 *was* on the top *of each* of them *was* f cubits. 2568
4:2 in compass, and f cubits the height thereof; 2568
4:6 put f on the right hand, and five on the left, 2568
4:6 and f on the left, to wash in them: 2568
4:7 f on the right hand, and five on the left. 2568
4:7 five on the right hand, and f on the left. 2568
4:8 f on the right side, and five on the left. 2568
4:8 five on the right side, and f on the left. 2568
6:13 of f cubits long, and five cubits broad, 2568
6:13 f cubits broad, and three cubits high, 2568
13:17 there fell down slain of Israel f hundred 2568
15:19 there was no *more* war unto the f and 2568
20:31 and f years old when he *began* to reign, 2568
20:31 he reigned twenty and f years in Jerusalem. 2568
25:1 and f years old *when* he *began* to reign, 2568
26:13 and seven thousand and f hundred, 2568
27:1 and f years old when he *began* to reign, 2568
27:8 He was f and twenty years old when he 2568
29:1 Hezekiah *began* to reign *when he was* f and 2568
33:1 he reigned fifty and f years in Jerusalem: 2568
35:9 passover *offerings* f thousand *small cattle,* 2568
35:9 thousand *small cattle,* and f hundred oxen. 2568
36:5 and f years old when he *began* to reign, 2568
Ezr 1:11 of silver *were* f thousand and four hundred. 2568
2:5 of Arah, seven hundred seventy and f. 2568
2:8 children of Zattu, nine hundred forty and f. 2568
2:20 The children of Gibbar, ninety and f. 2568
2:33 and Ono, seven hundred twenty and f. 2568
2:34 of Jericho, three hundred forty and f. 2568
2:66 six; their mules, two hundred forty and f; 2568
2:67 Their camels, four hundred thirty and f; 2568
2:69 f thousand pound *of* silver, and 2568
Ne 7:13 children of Zattu, eight hundred forty and f. 2568
7:20 children of Adin, six hundred fifty and f. 2568
7:25 The children of Gibeon, ninety and f. 2568
7:36 of Jericho, three hundred forty and f. 2568
7:67 and f singing *men* and singing *women.* 2568
7:68 six: their mules, two hundred forty and f: 2568
7:69 *Their* camels, four hundred thirty and f: 2568
7:70 f hundred and thirty priests' garments. 2568
Est 9:6 Jews slew and destroyed f hundred men. 2568
9:12 destroyed f hundred men in Shushan 2568
9:16 slew of their foes seventy and f thousand, 2568
Job 1:3 f hundred yoke of oxen, and five hundred 2568
1:3 f hundred she asses, and a very great 2568
Isa 7:8 and f years shall Ephraim be broken, 2568
17:6 f in the outmost fruitful branches thereof, 2568
19:18 In that day shall f cities in the land of Egypt 2568
30:17 of one; at the rebuke of f shall ye flee: 2568
37:36 an hundred and fourscore and f thousand: 2568
Jer 52:22 the height of one chapiter *was* f cubits, 2568
52:30 the Jews seven hundred forty and f persons: 2568
52:31 in the f and twentieth *day* of the month, 2568
Eze 8:16 and the altar, *were* about f and twenty men, 2568
11:1 behold at the door of the gate f and 2568
40:1 In the f and twentieth year of our captivity, 2568
40:7 between the little chambers *were* f cubits; 2568
40:13 the breadth *was* f and twenty cubits, 2568
40:21 and the breadth f and twenty cubits. 2568
40:25 and the breadth f and twenty cubits. 2568
40:29 cubits long, and f and twenty cubits broad. 2568
40:30 the arches round about *were* f and 2568
40:30 and twenty cubits long, and f cubits broad. 2568
40:33 cubits long, and f and twenty cubits broad. 2568
40:36 and the breadth f and twenty cubits. 2568
40:48 f cubits on this side, and five cubits on that 2568
40:48 cubits on this side, and f cubits on that side: 2568
41:2 the sides of the door *were* f cubits on 2568
41:2 the one side, and f cubits on the other side: 2568
41:9 for the side chamber without, *was* f cubits: 2568
41:11 the breadth of the place that was left *was* f 2568
41:12 the wall of the building *was* f cubits thick 2568
42:16 f hundred reeds, with the measuring reed 2568
42:17 measured the north side, f hundred reeds, 2568
42:18 f hundred reeds, with the measuring reed. 2568
42:19 measured f hundred reeds with 2568
42:20 f hundred *reeds* long, and five hundred 2568
42:20 hundred *reeds* long, and f hundred broad, 2568
45:1 the length *shall be* the length *of* f and 2568
45:2 Of this there shall be for the sanctuary f 2568
45:2 f hundred *in breadth,* square round about; 2568
45:3 measure shalt thou measure the length of f 2568
45:5 *the* f and twenty thousand of length, and 2568
45:6 ye shall appoint the possession of the city f 2568
45:6 and f and twenty thousand long, 2568
45:12 f and twenty shekels, fifteen shekels, 2568
48:8 be the offering which ye shall offer *of* f 2568
48:9 ye shall offer unto the LORD *shall be of* f 2568
48:10 toward the north f and twenty thousand *in* 2568
48:10 toward the south f and twenty thousand *in* 2568
48:13 the Levites *shall have* f and 2568
48:13 all the length *shall be* f and 2568
48:15 the f thousand, that are left in the breadth 2568
48:15 that are left in the breadth over against the f 2568
48:16 the north side four thousand and f hundred, 2568
48:16 the south side four thousand and f hundred, 2568
48:16 the east side four thousand and f hundred, 2568
48:16 the west side four thousand and f hundred. 2568
48:20 All the oblation *shall be* f and 2568
48:20 twenty thousand by f and twenty thousand: 2568
48:21 over against the f and twenty thousand of 2568
48:21 westward over against the f and 2568
48:30 four thousand and f hundred measures. 2568
48:32 the east side four thousand and f hundred: 2568
48:33 side four thousand and f hundred measures: 2568
48:34 the west side four thousand and f hundred, 2568
Da 12:12 three hundred *and* f and thirty days. 2568
Mt 14:17 We have here but f loaves, and two fishes. *4002*
14:19 and took the f loaves, and the two fishes, *4002*
14:21 that had eaten were about f **thousand** men, *4000*
16:9 neither remember the f loaves of the five *4002*
16:9 the five loaves of the f **thousand,** *4000*
25:2 And f of them were wise, and five *were* *4002*
25:2 five of them were wise, and f *were* foolish. *4002*

Mt 25:15 And unto one he gave f talents, to another *4002*
25:16 Then he that had received the f talents *4002*
25:16 the same, and made *them* other f talents. *4002*
25:20 *so* he that had received f talents came and *4002*
25:20 talents came and brought other f talents, *4002*
25:20 Lord, thou deliveredst unto me f talents: *4002*
25:20 I have gained besides them f talents moe. *4002*
Mk 6:38 they knew, they say, F, and two fishes. *4002*
6:41 And when he had taken the f loaves and *4002*
6:44 *of* the loaves were about f **thousand** men. *4000*
8:19 When I brake the f loaves among five *4002*
8:19 I brake the five loaves among f **thousand,** *4000*
Lk 1:24 and hid herself f months, saying, *4002*
7:41 the one ought f **hundred** pence, and *4001*
9:13 have no more but f loaves and two fishes; *4002*
9:14 For they were about f **thousand** men. *4000*
9:16 Then he took the f loaves and the two *4002*
12:6 Are not f sparrows sold for two farthings, *4002*
12:52 For from henceforth there shall be f in one *4002*
14:19 I have bought f yoke of oxen, and I go to *4002*
16:28 For I have f brethren; that he may testify *4002*
19:18 Lord, thy pound hath gained f pounds. *4002*
19:19 likewise to him, Be thou also over f cities. *4002*
Jn 4:18 For thou hast had f husbands; and he whom *4002*
5:2 Hebrew tongue Bethesda, having f porches. *4002*
6:9 which hath f barley loaves, and two small *4002*
6:10 sat down, *in* number about f **thousand.** *4000*
6:13 with the fragments of the f barley loaves, *4002*
6:19 So when they had rowed about f and *4002*
Ac 4:4 the number of the men was about f *4002*
20:6 and came unto them to Troas in f days; *4002*
24:1 And after f days Ananias the high priest *4002*
1Co 14:19 Yet in the church I had rather speak f words *4002*
15:6 he was seen of above f **hundred** brethren at *4001*
2Co 11:24 Of the Jews f **times** received I forty *stripes* *3999*
Rev 9:5 but that they should be tormented f months: *4002*
9:10 and their power *was* to hurt men f months. *4002*
17:10 f are fallen, and one is, *and* the other is not *4002*

FIXED (5)

Ps 57:7 My heart is f, O God, my heart is fixed: 3559
57:7 My heart is fixed, O God, my heart is f: 3559
108:1 O God, my heart is f; I will sing and 3559
112:7 his heart is f, trusting in the LORD. 3559
Lk 16:26 between us and you there is a great gulf f: *4741*

FLAG (1) [FLAGS]

Job 8:11 without mire? can the f grow without water? 260

FLAGON (2) [FLAGONS]

2Sa 6:19 a f *of wine.* So all the people departed every 809
1Ch 16:3 and a good piece *of flesh,* and a f *of wine.* 809

FLAGONS (3) [FLAGON]

SS 2:5 Stay me with f, comfort me with apples: 809
Isa 22:24 vessels of cups, even to all the vessels of f. 5035
Hos 3:1 who look to other gods, and love f of wine. 809

FLAGS (3) [FLAG]

Ex 2:3 she laid *it* in the f by the river's brink. 5488
2:5 when she saw the ark among the f, she sent 5488
Isa 19:6 and dried up: the reeds and f shall wither. 5488

FLAGSTAFF See BEACON

FLAKES (1)

Job 41:23 The f of his flesh are joined together: 4651

FLAME (34) [FLAMES, FLAMING]

Ex 3:2 him in a f of fire out of the midst of a bush: 3827
Nu 21:28 out of Heshbon, a f from the city of Sihon: 3852
Jdg 13:20 when the f went up toward heaven from off 3851
13:20 the LORD ascended in the f of the altar. 3851
20:38 that they should make a great f with smoke 4864
20:40 when the f began to arise up out of the city 4864
20:40 the f of the city ascended up to heaven. 3632
Job 15:30 the f shall dry up his branches, and by 7957
41:21 and a f goeth out of his mouth. 3851
Ps 83:14 and as the f setteth the mountains on fire; 3852
106:18 in their company; the f burnt up the wicked. 3852
SS 8:6 of fire, *which hath* a **most vehement** f. 7957
Isa 5:24 the f consumeth the chaff, *so* their root 3852
10:17 shall be for a fire, and his Holy One for a f: 3852
29:6 and tempest, and the f of devouring fire. 3851
30:30 *with* the f of a devouring fire, 3851
43:2 neither shall the f kindle upon thee. 3852
47:14 deliver themselves from the power of the f: 3852
Jer 48:45 a f from the midst of Sihon, and 3852
Eze 20:47 the flaming f shall not be quenched, and 7957
Da 3:22 the f of the fire slew those men that took up 7631
7:9 his throne *was like* the fiery f, *and* 7631
7:11 body destroyed, and given to the burning f. 785
11:33 by f, by captivity, and by spoil, *many* days. 3852
Joel 1:19 and the f hath burnt all the trees of the field. 3852
2:3 before them; and behind them a f burneth: 3852
2:5 like the noise of a f of fire that devoureth 3851
Ob 1:18 the house of Joseph a f, and the house of 3852
Lk 16:24 my tongue; for I am tormented in this f. *5395*
Ac 7:30 an angel of the Lord in a f of fire in a bush. *5395*
Heb 1:7 angels spirits, and his ministers a f of fire. *5395*
Rev 1:14 as snow; and his eyes *were* as a f of fire; *5395*
2:18 who hath his eyes like unto a f of fire, and *5395*
19:12 His eyes *were* as a f of fire, and on his head *5395*

FLAMES (3) [FLAME]

Ps 29:7 The voice of the LORD divideth the f of 3852
Isa 13:8 one at another; their faces *shall be as* f. 3851
66:15 with fury, and his rebuke with f of fire. 3851

FLAMING (9) [FLAME]

Ge 3:24 a f sword which turned every way, to keep 3858
Ps 104:4 his angels spirits; his ministers a f fire: 3857
105:32 them hail *for* rain, *and* f fire in their land. 3852
Isa 4:5 by day, and the shining of a f fire by night: 3852

La 2: 3 he burned against Jacob like a f fire, 3852
Eze 20:47 the f flame shall not be quenched, and 3852
Hos 7: 6 in the morning it burneth as a f fire. 3852
Na 2: 3 the chariots shall be with f torches in the day 784
2Th 1: 8 In f fire, taking vengeance on them that 5395

FLANKS (6)
Lev 3: 4 which is by the f, and the caul above 3689
3:10 which is by the f, and the caul above 3689
3:15 which is by the f, and the caul above 3689
4: 9 which is by the f, and the caul above 3689
7: 4 which is by the f, and the caul that is above 3689
Job 15:27 and maketh collops of fat on his f. 3689

FLASH (1)
Eze 1:14 as the appearance of a f of lightning. 965

FLASK See BOX; VIAL; VIALS

FLAT (4)
Lev 21:18 or he that hath a f nose, or any thing 2763
Nu 22:31 down his head, and fell f on his face. 7812
Jos 6: 5 the wall of the city shall fall down f, 8478
6:20 that the wall fell down f, so that the people 8478

FLATTER (2) [FLATTERETH, FLATTERIES, FLATTERING, FLATTERY]
Ps 5: 9 an open sepulchre; they f with their tongue. 2505
78:36 Nevertheless they did f him with their 6601

FLATTERETH (6) [FLATTER]
Ps 36: 2 For he f himself in his own eyes, until his 2505
Pr 2:16 even from the stranger which f with her 2505
7: 5 from the stranger which f with her words. 2505
20:19 meddle not with him that f with his lips. 6601
28:23 more favour than he that f with the tongue. 2505
29: 5 A man that f his neighbour spreadeth a net 2505

FLATTERIES (3) [FLATTER]
Da 11:21 in peaceably, and obtain the kingdom by f. 2519
11:32 against the covenant shall he corrupt by f: 2514
11:34 but many shall cleave to them with f. 2519

FLATTERING (8) [FLATTER]
Job 32:21 neither let me give f titles unto man. 3655
32:22 For I know not to give f titles; in so 3655
Ps 12: 2 with f lips and with a double heart do they 2513
12: 3 The LORD shall cut off all f lips, and 2513
Pr 7:21 with the f of her lips she forced him. 2506
26:28 afflicted by it; and a f mouth worketh ruin. 2509
Eze 12:24 nor f divination within the house of Israel. 2509
1Th 2: 5 For neither at any time used we f words, 2850

FLATTERY (2) [FLATTER]
Job 17: 5 He that speaketh f to his friends, 2506+3807.1
Pr 6:24 from the f of the tongue of a strange 2513

FLAWLESS See UNDEFILED

FLAX (11)
Ex 9:31 the f and the barley was smitten: for 6594
9:31 barley was in the ear, and the f was bolled. 6594
Jos 2: 6 hid them with the stalks of f, which she had 6593
Jdg 15:14 arms became as f that was burnt with fire, 6593
Pr 31:13 f, and worketh willingly with her hands. 6593
Isa 19: 9 Moreover they that work in fine f, and 6593
42: 3 and the smoking f shall he not quench: 6594
Eze 40: 3 with a line of f in his hand, and a measuring 6593
Hos 2: 5 my wool and my f, mine oil and my drink. 6593
2: 9 and my f given to cover her nakedness. 6593
Mt 12:20 and smoking f shall he not quench, 3043

FLAY (3) [FLAYED]
Lev 1: 6 he shall f the burnt offering, and cut it into 6584
2Ch 29:34 that they could not f all the burnt offerings: 6584
Mic 3: 3 my people, and f their skin from off them; 6584

FLAYED (1) [FLAY]
2Ch 35:11 from their hands, and the Levites f them. 6584

FLEA (2)
1Sa 24:14 dost thou pursue? after a dead dog, after a f. 6550
26:20 the king of Israel is come out to seek a f, 6550

FLED (148) [FLEE]
Ge 14:10 the kings of Sodom and Gomorrah f, and 5127
14:10 they that remained f to the mountain. 5127
16: 6 dealt hardly with her, she f from her face. 1272
31:20 the Syrian, in that he told him not that he f. 1272
31:21 So he f with all that he had; and he rose up, 1272
31:22 Laban on the third day that Jacob was f. 1272
35: 7 when he f from the face of his brother. 1272
39:12 in her hand, and f, and got him out. 5127
39:13 his garment in her hand, and was f forth, 5127
39:15 garment with me, and f, and got him out. 5127
39:18 that he left his garment with me, and f out. 5127
Ex 2:15 Moses f from the face of Pharaoh, and 1272
4: 3 a serpent; and Moses f from before it. 5127
14: 5 was told the king of Egypt that the people f: 1272
14:27 the Egyptians f against it; and the LORD 5127
Nu 16:34 all Israel that were round about them f at 5127
35:25 to the city of his refuge, whither he was f. 5127
35:26 of the city of his refuge, whither he was f; 5127
35:32 ye shall take no satisfaction for him that is f 5127
Jos 7: 4 and they f before the men of Ai. 5127
8:15 and f by the way of the wilderness. 5127
8:20 the people that f to the wilderness turned 5127
10:11 as they f from before Israel, and were in 5127
10:16 these five kings f, and hid themselves in a 5127
20: 6 own house, unto the city from whence he f. 5127
Jdg 1: 6 Adoni-bezek f; and they pursued after him, 5127
4:15 off his chariot, and f away on his feet. 5127
4:17 Howbeit Sisera f away on his feet to 5127
Jdg 7:21 and all the host ran, and cried, and f. 5127
7:22 the host f to Beth-shittah in Zererath, and 5127
8:12 when Zebah and Zalmunna f, he pursued 5127
9:21 and f, and went to Beer, and dwelt there, 1272
9:40 he f before him, and many were 5127
9:51 thither f all the men and women, and 5127
11: 3 Jephthah f from his brethren, and dwelt in 1272
20:45 f toward the wilderness unto the rock of 5127
20:47 f to the wilderness unto the rock Rimmon, 5127
1Sa 4:10 and they f every man into his tent: 5127
4:16 of the army, and I f to day out of the army. 5127
4:17 Israel is f before the Philistines, and 5127
14:22 when they heard that the Philistines f, 5127
17:24 the man, f from him, and were sore afraid. 5127
17:51 saw their champion was dead, they f. 5127
19: 8 with a great slaughter; and they f from him. 5127
19:10 and David f, and escaped that night. 5127
19:12 a window: and he went, and f, and escaped. 1272
19:18 So David f, and escaped, and came to 1272
20: 1 David f from Naioth in Ramah, and came 1272
21:10 f that day for fear of Saul, and went to 1272
22:17 because they knew when he f, and did not 1272
22:20 escaped, and f after David. 1272
23: 6 when Abiathar the son of Ahimelech f to 1272
27: 4 it was told Saul that David was f to Gath: 1272
30:17 young men, which rode upon camels, and f. 5127
31: 1 the men of Israel f from before 5127
31: 7 saw that the men of Israel f, and that Saul 5127
31: 7 were dead, they forsook the cities, and f; 5127
2Sa 1: 4 That the people are f from the battle, and 5127
4: 3 the Beerothites f to Gittaim, and 1272
4: 4 of Jezreel, and his nurse took him up, and f: 5127
10:13 against the Syrians: and they f before him. 5127
10:14 of Ammon saw that the Syrians were f, 5127
10:14 then f they also before Abishai, and 5127
10:18 the Syrians f before Israel; and David slew 5127
13:29 every man gat him up upon his mule, and f. 5127
13:34 Absalom f. And the young man that kept 1272
13:37 Absalom f, and went to Talmai, the son of 1272
13:38 So Absalom f, and went to Geshur, and 1272
18:17 and all Israel f every one to his tent. 5127
19: 8 for Israel had f every man to his tent. 5127
19: 9 now he is f out of the land for Absalom. 1272
23:11 and the people f from the Philistines. 5127
1Ki 2: 7 for so they came to me when I f because of 1272
2:28 Joab f unto the tabernacle of the LORD, 5127
2:29 it was told king Solomon that Joab was f 5127
11:17 That Hadad f, he and certain Edomites of 1272
11:23 which f from his lord Hadadezer king of 1272
11:40 Jeroboam arose, and f into Egypt, 1272
12: 2 heard of it, (for he was f from the presence 1272
20:20 the Syrians f; and Israel pursued them: and 5127
20:30 the rest f to Aphek, into the city; and 5127
20:30 Ben-hadad f, and came into the city, into an 5127
2Ki 3:24 the Moabites, so that they f before them: 5127
7: 7 Wherefore they arose and f in the twilight, 5127
7: 7 even the camp as it was, and f for their life. 5127
8:21 and the people f into their tents. 5127
9:10 to bury her. And he opened the door, and f. 5127
9:23 f, and said to Ahaziah, There is treachery, 5127
9:27 this, he f by the way of the garden house. 5127
9:27 And he f to Megiddo, and died there. 5127
14:12 and they f every man to their tents. 5127
14:19 he f to Lachish; but they sent after him to 5127
25: 4 all the men of war f by night by the way of NIH
1Ch 10: 1 the men of Israel f from before 5127
10: 7 that were in the valley saw that they f, 5127
10: 7 then they forsook their cities, and f: 5127
11:13 and the people f from before the Philistines. 5127
19:14 unto the battle; and they f before him. 5127
19:15 of Ammon saw that the Syrians were f, 5127
19:15 they likewise f before Abishai his brother, 5127
19:18 the Syrians f before Israel; and David slew 5127
2Ch 10: 2 whither he had f from the presence of 1272
13:16 the children of Israel f before Judah: and 5127
14:12 and before Judah; and the Ethiopians f. 5127
25:22 and they f every man to his tent. 5127
25:27 him in Jerusalem; and he f to Lachish: 5127
Ne 13:10 did the work, were f every one to his field. 1272
Ps 3: T of David, when he f from Absalom his son. 1272
31:11 they that did see me without f from me. 5074
57: T of David, when he f from Saul in the cave. 1272
104: 7 At thy rebuke they f; at the voice of thy 5127
114: 3 The sea saw it, and f: Jordan was driven 5127
Isa 10:29 Ramah is afraid; Gibeah of Saul is f. 5127
21:14 they prevented with their bread him that f. 5074
21:15 For they f from the swords, from the drawn 5074
22: 3 All thy rulers are f together, they are bound 5074
22: 3 are bound together, which have f from far. 1272
33: 3 At the noise of the tumult the people f; 5074
Jer 4:25 and all the birds of the heavens were f. 5074
9:10 the fowl of the heavens and the beast are f; 5074
26:21 he was afraid, and f, and went into Egypt; 1272
39: 4 they f, and went forth out of the city by 1272
46: 5 and are f apace, and look not back: 4498+5127
46:21 are turned back, and are f away together; 5127
48:45 They that f stood under the shadow of 5127
52: 7 all the men of war f, and went forth out of 1272
La 4:15 touch not, when they f away and wandered: 5132
Da 10: 7 so that they f to hide themselves. 1272
Hos 7:13 for they have f from me: destruction unto 5074
12:12 Jacob f into the country of Syria, and 1272
Jnh 1:10 For the men knew that he f from 1272
4: 2 Therefore I f before unto Tarshish: for I 1272
Zec 14: 5 like as ye f from before the earthquake in 5127
Mt 8:33 And they that kept them f, and went their 5343
26:56 Then all the disciples forsook him, and f. 5343
Mk 5:14 And they that fed the swine f, and told it in 5343
14:50 And they all forsook him, and f. 5343
14:52 left the linen cloth, and f from them naked. 5343
16: 8 went out quickly, and f from the sepulchre; 5343
Lk 8:34 they f, and went and told it in the city and 5343
Ac 7:29 Then f Moses at this saying, and was a 5343
14: 6 ware of it, and f unto Lystra and Derbe, 2703
16:27 supposing that the prisoners had been f. 1628
Ac 19:16 so that they f out of that house naked and 1628
Heb 6:18 who have f for refuge to lay hold upon 2703
Rev 12: 6 And the woman f into the wilderness, 5343
16:20 And every island f away, and 5343
20:11 face the earth and the heaven f away; and 5343

FLEDDEST (2) [FLEE]
Ge 35: 1 that appeared unto thee when thou f from 1272
Ps 114: 5 What ailed thee, O thou sea, that thou f? 5127

FLEE (105) [FLED, FLEDDEST, FLEEING, FLEETH]
Ge 16: 8 I f from the face of my mistress Sarai. 1272
19:20 this city is near to f unto, and it is a little 5127
27:43 arise, f thou to Laban my brother to Haran; 1272
31:27 Wherefore didst thou f away secretly, 1272
Ex 9:20 Pharaoh made his servants and his cattle f 5127
14:25 Let us f from the face of Israel; 5127
21:13 will appoint thee a place whither he shall f. 5127
Lev 26:17 and ye shall f when none pursueth you. 5127
26:36 they shall f, as fleeing from a sword; and 5127
Nu 10:35 and let them that hate thee f before thee. 5127
24:11 Therefore now f thou to thy place: 1272
35: 6 for the manslayer, that he may f thither: 5127
35:11 that the slayer may f thither, which killeth 5127
35:15 killeth any person unawares may f thither. 5127
Dt 4:42 That the slayer might f thither, which 5127
19: 3 three parts, that every slayer may f thither. 5127
19: 4 which shall f thither, that he may live: 5127
19: 5 he shall f unto one of those cities, and live: 5127
28: 7 one way, and f before thee seven ways. 5127
28:25 and f seven ways before them: 5127
Jos 8: 5 as at the first, that we will f before them, 5127
8: 6 will say, They f before us, as at the first: 5127
8: 6 at the first: therefore we will f before them. 5127
8:20 they had no power to f this way or 5127
20: 3 and unwittingly may f thither: 5127
20: 4 when he that doth f unto one of those cities 5127
20: 9 any person at unawares might f thither, 5127
Jdg 20:32 Let us f, and draw them from the city unto 5127
2Sa 4: 4 as she made haste to f, that he fell, and 5127
15:14 with him at Jerusalem, Arise, and let us f; 1272
17: 2 all the people that are with him shall f; and 5127
18: 3 for if we f away, they will not care 5127+5127
19: 3 ashamed steal away when they f in battle. 5127
24:13 wilt thou f three months before thine 5127
1Ki 12:18 get him up to his chariot, to f to Jerusalem. 5127
2Ki 9: 3 Then open the door, and f, and tarry not. 5127
2Ch 10:18 get him up to his chariot, to f to Jerusalem. 5127
Ne 6:11 I said, Should such a man as I f? and who is 1272
Job 9:25 than a post: they f away, they see no good. 1272
20:24 He shall f from the iron weapon, and 1272
27:22 he would fain f out of his hand. 1272+1272
30:10 they f far from me, and spare not to spit in 7368
41:28 The arrow cannot make him f: 1272
Ps 11: 1 to my soul, F as a bird to your mountain? 5110
64: 8 all that see them shall f away. 5074
68: 1 let them also that hate him f before him. 5127
68:12 Kings of armies did f apace: and 5074+5074
139: 7 or whither shall I f from thy presence? 1272
143: 9 mine enemies: I f unto thee to hide me. 3680
Pr 28: 1 The wicked f when no man pursueth: but 5127
28:17 to the blood of any person shall f to the pit; 5127
SS 2:17 the shadows f away, turn, my beloved, and 5127
4: 6 the day break, and the shadows f away, 5127
Isa 10: 3 to whom will ye f for help? and where will 5127
10:31 of Gebim gather themselves to f. 5756
13:14 and f every one into his own land. 5127
15: 5 his fugitives shall f unto Zoar, a heifer of NIH
17:13 they shall f far off, and shall be chased as 5127
20: 6 whither we f for help to be delivered from 5127
30:16 ye said, No; for we will f upon horses; 5127
30:16 will flee upon horses; therefore shall ye f: 5127
30:17 One thousand shall f at the rebuke of one; NIH
30:17 of one; at the rebuke of five shall ye f: 5127
31: 8 he shall f from the sword, and his young 5127
35:10 and sorrow and sighing shall f away. 5127
48:20 forth of Babylon, f ye from the Chaldeans, 1272
51:11 joy; and sorrow and mourning shall f away. 5127
Jer 4:29 The whole city shall f for the noise of 1272
6: 1 gather yourselves to f out of the midst of 5756
25:35 the shepherds shall have no way to f, 4498
46: 6 Let not the swift f away, nor the mighty 5127
48: 6 F, save your lives, and be like the heath in 5127
48: 9 unto Moab, that it may f and get away: 5323
49: 8 F ye, turn back, dwell deep, O inhabitants 5127
49:24 and turneth herself to f, and fear hath seized 5127
49:30 F, get you far off, dwell deep, O ye 5127
50:16 and they shall f every one to his own land. 5127
50:28 The voice of them that f and escape out of 5127
51: 6 F out of the midst of Babylon, and 5127
Am 2:16 the mighty shall f away naked in that day, 5127
5:19 As if a man did f from a lion, and a bear 5127
7:12 go, f thee away into the land of Judah, and 1272
9: 1 he that fleeth of them shall not f away, and 5127
Jnh 1: 3 Jonah rose up to f unto Tarshish from 1272
Na 2: 8 yet they shall f away. Stand, stand, 5127
3: 7 that all they that look upon thee shall f from 5074
3:17 but when the sun ariseth they f away, and 5074
Zec 2: 6 and f from the land of the north, 5127
14: 5 ye shall f to the valley of the mountains; 5127
14: 5 yea, ye shall f, like as ye fled from before 5127
Mt 2:13 and f into Egypt, and be thou there until I 5343
3: 7 who hath warned you to f from the wrath to 5343
10:23 persecute you in this city, f ye into another: 5343
24:16 Then let them which be in Judea f into 5343
Mk 13:14 let them that be in Judea f to the mountains: 5343
Lk 3: 7 who hath warned you to f from the wrath to 5343
21:21 Then let them which are in Judea f to 5343
Jn 10: 5 will they not follow, but will f from him: 5343
Ac 27:30 And as the shipmen were about to f out of 5343
1Co 6:18 F fornication. Every sin that a man doeth is 5343
10:14 my dearly beloved, f from idolatry. 5343
1Ti 6:11 f these things; and follow after 5343
2Ti 2:22 F also youthful lusts: but 5343
Jas 4: 7 Resist the devil, and he will f from you. 5343

Rev 9: 6 desire to die, and death shall f from them. 5343

FLEECE (9)

Dt 18: 4 of thy oil, and the first of the f of thy sheep, 1488
Jdg 6:37 Behold, I will put a f of wool in the floor; 1492
6:37 and if the dew be on the f only, and it be 1492
6:38 thrust the f together, and wringed the dew 1492
6:38 wringed the dew out of the f, a bowl full of 1492
6:39 I pray thee, but this once with the f; 1492
6:39 let it now be dry only upon the f, and 1492
6:40 for it was dry upon the f only, and 1492
Job 31:20 if he were not warmed with the f of my 1488

FLEEING (2) [FLEE]

Lev 26:36 they shall flee, as f from a sword; and 4499
Dt 4:42 that f unto one of these cities he might live: 5127

FLEET See NAVY

FLEETH (8) [FLEE]

Dt 19:11 that he die, and f into one of these cities: 5127
Job 14: 2 he f also as a shadow, and continueth not. 1272
Isa 24:18 that he who f from the noise of the fear 5127
Jer 48:19 ask him that f, and her that escapeth, and 5127
48:44 He that f from the fear shall fall into the pit; 5127
Am 9: 1 he that f of them shall not flee away, and 5127
Jn 10:12 wolf coming, and leaveth the sheep, and f: 5343
10:13 The hireling f, because he is a hireling, and 5343

FLEETING See FLEE; FLEETH; FRAIL; VANITIES; VANITY

FLESH (420) [FATFLESHED, FLESHHOOK, FLESHHOOKS, FLESHLY, FLESHY, LEANFLESHED]

Ge 2:21 his ribs, and closed up the f instead thereof; 1320
2:23 now bone of my bones, and f of my flesh: 1320
2:23 now bone of my bones, and flesh of my f: 1320
2:24 unto his wife: and they shall be one f. 1320
6: 3 always strive with man, for that he also is f: 1320
6:12 for all f had corrupted his way upon 1320
6:13 The end of all f is come before me; 1320
6:17 to destroy all f, wherein is the breath of life, 1320
6:19 of every living thing of all f, two of every 1320
7:15 two and two of all f, wherein is the breath 1320
7:16 went in, went in male and female of all f, 1320
7:21 all f died that moved upon the earth, 1320
8:17 of all f, both of fowl, and of cattle, and 1320
9: 4 f with the life thereof, which is the blood 1320
9:11 neither shall all f be cut off any more by 1320
9:15 and you and every living creature of all f; 1320
9:15 no more become a flood to destroy all f. 1320
9:16 every living creature of all f that is upon 1320
9:17 between me and all f that is upon the earth. 1320
17:11 ye shall circumcise the f of your foreskin; 1320
17:13 my covenant shall be in your f for an 1320
17:14 the uncircumcised man child whose f of his 1320
17:23 circumcised the f of their foreskin in 1320
17:24 when he was circumcised in the f of his 1320
17:25 when he was circumcised in the f of his 1320
29:14 to him, Surely thou art my bone and my f. 1320
37:27 upon him; for he is our brother and our f. 1320
40:19 and the birds shall eat thy f from off thee. 1320
Ex 4: 7 behold, it was turned again as his other f. 1320
12: 8 they shall eat the f in that night, roast with 1320
12:46 thou shalt not carry forth ought of the f 1320
16: 3 when we sat by the f pots, and when we did 1320
16: 8 shall give you in the evening f to eat, 1320
16:12 At even ye shall eat f, and in the morning 1320
21:28 surely stoned, and his f shall not be eaten; 1320
22:31 neither shall ye eat any f that is torn of 1320
29:14 the f of the bullock, and his skin, and his 1320
29:31 and seethe his f in the holy place. 1320
29:32 and his sons shall eat the f of the ram, 1320
29:34 if ought of the f of the consecrations, or 1320
30:32 Upon man's f shall it not be poured, 1320
Lev 4:11 all his f, with his head, and with his legs, 1320
6:10 his linen breeches shall he put upon his f, 1320
6:27 Whatsoever shall touch the f thereof shall 1320
7:15 the f of the sacrifice of his peace offerings 1320
7:17 the remainder of the f of the sacrifice on 1320
7:18 if any of the f of the sacrifice of his peace 1320
7:19 the f that toucheth any unclean thing shall 1320
7:19 as for the f, all that be clean shall eat 1320
7:20 the soul that eateth of the f of the sacrifice 1320
7:21 eat of the f of the sacrifice of peace 1320
8:17 and his hide, his f, and his dung, 1320
8:31 Boil the f at the door of the tabernacle of 1320
8:32 that which remaineth of the f and of 1320
9:11 the f and the hide he burnt with fire without 1320
11: 8 Of their f shall ye not eat, and their carcase 1320
11:11 ye shall not eat of their f, but you shall have 1320
12: 3 in the eighth day the f of his foreskin shall 1320
13: 2 When a man shall have in the skin of his f a 1320
13: 2 it be in the skin of his f like the plague of 1320
13: 3 shall look on the plague in the skin of the f: 1320
13: 3 in sight be deeper than the skin of his f, 1320
13: 4 the bright spot be white in the skin of his f, 1320
13:10 and there be quick raw f in the rising; 1320
13:11 It is an old leprosy in the skin of his f, and 1320
13:13 behold, if the leprosy have covered all his f, 1320
13:14 when raw f appeareth in him, he shall be 1320
13:15 the priest shall see the raw f, and 1320
13:15 for the raw f is unclean: it is a leprosy. 1320
13:16 Or if the raw f turn again, and be changed 1320
13:18 The f also, in which, even in the skin 1320
13:24 Or if there be any f, in the skin whereof 1320
13:24 the quick f that burneth have a white bright NIH
13:38 a woman have in the skin of their f bright 1320
13:39 if the bright spots in the skin of their f be 1320
13:43 as the leprosy appeareth in the skin of the f; 1320
14: 9 also he shall wash his f in water, and 1320
15: 2 any man hath a running issue out of his f, 1320
15: 3 whether his f run with his issue, or his flesh 1320
15: 3 or his f be stopped from his issue, it is his 1320
Lev 15: 7 he that toucheth the f of him that hath 1320
15:13 bathe his f in running water, and shall be 1320
15:16 he shall wash all his f in water, and 1320
15:19 an issue, and her issue in her f be blood, 1320
16: 4 he shall have the linen breeches upon his f, 1320
16: 4 therefore shall he wash his f in water, and 1320
16:24 he shall wash his f with water in the holy 1320
16:26 bathe his f in water, and afterward come 1320
16:27 fire their skins, and their f, and their dung. 1320
16:28 bathe his f in water, and afterward he shall 1320
17:11 For the life of the f is in the blood: and 1320
17:14 For it is the life of all f; the blood of it is for 1320
17:14 Ye shall eat the blood of no manner of f: 1320
17:14 for the life of all f is the blood thereof: 1320
17:16 if he wash them not, nor bathe his f; then 1320
19:28 Ye shall not make any cuttings in your f for 1320
21: 5 nor make any cuttings in their f. 1320
22: 6 things, unless he wash his f with water. 1320
26:29 ye shall eat the f of your sons, and the flesh 1320
26:29 and the f of your daughters shall ye eat. 1320
Nu 8: 7 let them shave all their f, and let them wash 1320
11: 4 and said, Who shall give us f to eat? 1320
11:13 Whence should I have f to give unto all this 1320
11:13 unto me, saying, Give us f, that we may eat. 1320
11:18 against to morrow, and ye shall eat f: 1320
11:18 saying, Who shall give us f to eat? 1320
11:18 therefore the LORD will give you f, and 1320
11:21 thou hast said, I will give them f, that they 1320
11:33 while the f was yet between their teeth, 1320
12:12 of whom the f is half consumed when he 1320
16:22 said, O God, the God of the spirits of all f, 1320
18:15 Every thing that openeth the matrix in all f, 1320
18:18 the f of them shall be thine, as the wave 1320
19: 5 her skin, and her f, and her blood, with her 1320
19: 7 he shall bathe his f in water, and 1320
19: 8 bathe his f in water, and shall be unclean 1320
27:16 the LORD, the God of the spirits of all f, 1320
Dt 5:26 For who is there of all f, that hath heard 1320
12:15 thou mayest kill and eat f in all thy gates, 1320
12:20 I will eat f, because thy soul longeth to eat 1320
12:20 eat flesh, because thy soul longeth to eat f; 1320
12:20 thou mayest eat f, whatsoever thy soul 1320
12:23 and thou mayest not eat the life with the f. 1320
12:27 the f and the blood, upon the altar of 1320
12:27 LORD thy God, and thou shalt eat the f. 1320
14: 8 ye shall not eat of their f, nor touch their 1320
16: 4 neither shall there any thing of the f, 1320
28:53 the f of thy sons and of thy daughters, 1320
28:55 of the f of his children whom he shall eat: 1320
32:42 with blood, and my sword shall devour f; 1320
Jdg 6:19 the f he put in a basket, and he put the broth 1320
6:20 Take the f and the unleavened cakes, and 1320
6:21 touched the f and the unleavened cakes; 1320
6:21 consumed the f and the unleavened cakes. 1320
8: 7 I will tear your f with the thorns of 1320
9: 2 also that I am your bone and your f. 1320
1Sa 2:13 servant came, while the f was in seething, 1320
2:15 that sacrificed, Give f to roast for the priest; 1320
2:15 for he will not have sodden f of thee, but 1320
17:44 I will give thy f unto the fowls of the air, 1320
25:11 my f that I have killed for my shearers, and 2878
2Sa 5: 1 Behold, we are thy bone and thy f. 1320
6:19 a good piece of f, and a flagon of wine. So NIH
19:12 are my brethren, ye are my bones and my f: 1320
19:13 Art thou not of my bone, and of my f? 1320
1Ki 17: 6 brought him bread and f in the morning, 1320
17: 6 and bread and f in the evening; 1320
19:21 boiled their f with the instruments of 1320
21:27 put sackcloth upon his f, and fasted, and 1320
2Ki 4:34 and the f of the child waxed warm. 1320
5:10 thy f shall come again to thee, and 1320
5:14 his f came again like unto the flesh of a 1320
5:14 his flesh came again like unto the f of a 1320
6:30 behold, he had sackcloth within upon his f. 1320
9:36 In the portion of Jezreel shall dogs eat the f 1320
1Ch 11: 1 Behold, we are thy bone and thy f. 1320
16: 3 and a good piece of f, and a flagon of wine. NIH
2Ch 32: 8 With him is an arm of f; but with us is 1320
Ne 5: 5 Yet now our f is as the flesh of our 1320
5: 5 Yet now our flesh is as the f of our 1320
Job 2: 5 touch his bone and his f, and he will curse 1320
4:15 before my face; the hair of my f stood up: 1320
6:12 the strength of stones? or is my f of brass? 1320
7: 5 My f is clothed with worms and clods of 1320
10: 4 Hast thou eyes of f? or seest thou as man 1320
10:11 Thou hast clothed me with skin and f, and 1320
13:14 Wherefore do I take my f in my teeth, and 1320
14:22 his f upon him shall have pain, and his soul 1320
19:20 My bone cleaveth to my skin and to my f, 1320
19:22 me as God, and are not satisfied with my f? 1320
19:26 this body, yet in my f shall I see God: 1320
21: 6 and trembling taketh hold on my f. 1320
31:31 tabernacle said not, O that we had of his f! 1320
33:21 His f is consumed away, that it cannot be 1320
33:25 His f shall be fresher than a child's: he shall 1320
34:15 All f shall perish together, and man shall 1320
41:23 The flakes of his f are joined together: 1320
Ps 16: 9 glory rejoiceth: my f also shall rest in hope. 1320
27: 2 and my foes, came upon me to eat up my f, 1320
38: 3 There is no soundness in my f because 1320
38: 7 and there is no soundness in my f. 1320
50:13 Will I eat the f of bulls, or drink the blood 1320
56: 4 I will not fear what f can do unto me. 1320
63: 1 my f longeth for thee, in a dry and 1320
65: 2 hearest prayer, unto thee shall all f come. 1320
73:26 My f and my heart faileth: but God is 7607
78:20 bread also? can he provide f for his people? 7607
78:27 He rained f also upon them as dust, and 7607
78:39 For he remembered that they were but f; 1320
79: 2 the f of thy saints unto the beasts of 1320
84: 2 and my f crieth out for the living God. 1320
109:24 through fasting; and my f faileth of fatness. 1320
119:120 My f trembleth for fear of thee; and I am 1320
136:25 Who giveth food to all f: for his mercy 1320
145:21 let all f bless his holy name for ever and 1320
Pr 4:22 that find them, and health to all their f. 1320
5:11 when thy f and thy body are consumed, 1320
11:17 but he that is cruel troubleth his own f. 7607
14:30 A sound heart is the life of the f: but 1320
23:20 amongst riotous eaters of f: 1320
Ecc 4: 5 his hands together, and eateth his own f. 1320
5: 6 Suffer not thy mouth to cause thy f to sin; 1320
11:10 thy heart, and put away evil from thy f: 1320
12:12 and much study is a weariness of the f. 1320
Isa 9:20 they shall eat every man the f of his own 1320
17: 4 and the fatness of his f shall wax lean. 1320
22:13 killing sheep, eating f, and drinking wine: 1320
31: 3 not God; and their horses f, and not spirit. 1320
40: 5 be revealed, and all f shall see it together: 1320
40: 6 All f is grass, and all the goodliness thereof 1320
44:16 with part thereof he eateth f; he roasteth 1320
44:19 I have roasted f, and eaten it: and shall I 1320
49:26 them that oppress thee with their own f; 1320
49:26 all f shall know that I the LORD am thy 1320
58: 7 that thou hide not thyself from thine own f? 1320
65: 4 which eat swine's f, and broth of 1320
66:16 his sword will the LORD plead with all f: 1320
66:17 eating swine's f, and the abomination, and 1320
66:23 shall all f come to worship before me, 1320
66:24 and they shall be an abhorring unto all f. 1320
Jer 7:21 offerings unto your sacrifices, and eat f. 1320
11:15 and the holy f is passed from thee? 1320
12:12 other end of the land: no f shall have peace. 1320
17: 5 maketh f his arm, and whose heart 1320
19: 9 I will cause them to eat the f of their sons 1320
19: 9 of their sons and the f of their daughters, 1320
19: 9 they shall eat every one the f of his friend 1320
25:31 with the nations, he will plead with all f; 1320
32:27 Behold, I am the LORD, the God of all f: 1320
45: 5 for behold, I will bring evil upon all f, 1320
51:35 done to me and to my f be upon Babylon, 7607
La 3: 4 My f and my skin hath he made old; 1320
Eze 4:14 neither came there abominable f into my 1320
11: 3 this city is the caldron, and we be the f. 1320
11: 7 they are the f, and this city is the caldron: 1320
11:11 neither shall ye be the f in the midst 1320
11:19 I will take the stony heart out of their f, and 1320
11:19 their flesh, and will give them a heart of f: 1320
16:26 the Egyptians thy neighbours, great of f; 1320
20:48 all f shall see that I the LORD have 1320
21: 4 against all f from the south to the north: 1320
21: 5 That all f may know that I the LORD have 1320
23:20 whose f is as the flesh of asses, and 1320
23:20 whose flesh is as the f of asses, and 1320
24:10 consume the f, and spice it well, and let 1320
32: 5 I will lay thy f upon the mountains, and 1320
36:26 will take away the stony heart out of your f, 1320
36:26 your flesh, and I will give you a heart of f. 1320
37: 6 will bring up f upon you, and cover you 1320
37: 8 lo, the sinews and the f came up upon them, 1320
39:17 of Israel, that ye may eat f, and drink blood. 1320
39:18 Ye shall eat the f of the mighty, and 1320
40:43 upon the tables was the f of the offering. 1320
44: 7 uncircumcised in f, to be in my sanctuary, 1320
44: 9 in heart, nor uncircumcised in f, 1320
Da 1:15 fatter in f than all the children which did eat 1320
2:11 the gods, whose dwelling is not with f. 1321
4:12 the boughs thereof, and all f was fed of it. 1321
7: 5 they said thus unto it, Arise, devour much f. 1321
10: 3 neither came f nor wine in my mouth, 1320
Hos 8:13 They sacrifice f for the sacrifices of mine 1320
Joel 2:28 that I will pour out my spirit upon all f; 1320
Mic 3: 2 off them, and their f from off their bones; 7607
3: 3 Who also eat the f of my people, and 7607
3: 3 as for the pot, and as f within the caldron. 1320
Zep 1:17 poured out as dust, and their f as the dung. 3894
Hag 2:12 If one bear holy f in the skirt of his 1320
Zec 2:13 Be silent, O all f, before the LORD: for he 1320
11: 9 let the rest eat every one the f of another. 1320
11:16 he shall eat the f of the fat, and tear their 1320
14:12 Their f shall consume away while they 1320
Mt 16:17 for f and blood hath not revealed it unto 4561
19: 5 to his wife: and they twain shall be one f? 4561
19: 6 they are no more twain, but one f. 4561
24:22 be shortened, there should no f be saved: 4561
26:41 spirit indeed is willing, but the f is weak. 4561
Mk 10: 8 And they twain shall be one f: so then 4561
10: 8 so then they are no more twain, but one f. 4561
13:20 shortened those days, no f should be saved: 4561
14:38 The spirit truly is ready, but the f is weak. 4561
Lk 3: 6 And all f shall see the salvation of God. 4561
24:39 for a spirit hath not f and bones, as ye see 4561
Jn 1:13 not of blood, nor of the will of the f, 4561
1:14 And the Word was made f, and 4561
3: 6 That which is born of the f is flesh; and 4561
3: 6 That which is born of the flesh is f; and 4561
6:51 and the bread that I will give is my f, 4561
6:52 How can this man give us his f to eat? 4561
6:53 Except ye eat the f of the Son of man, and 4561
6:54 Whoso eateth my f, and drinketh my blood, 4561
6:55 For my f is meat indeed, 4561
6:56 He that eateth my f, and drinketh my blood, 4561
6:63 that quickeneth; the f profiteth nothing: 4561
8:15 Ye judge after the f; I judge no man. 4561
17: 2 As thou hast given him power over all f, 4561
Ac 2:17 I will pour out of my Spirit upon all f: 4561
2:26 moreover also my f shall rest in hope: 4561
2:30 of the fruit of his loins, according to the f, 4561
2:31 left in hell, neither his f did see corruption. 4561
Ro 1: 3 of the seed of David according to the f; 4561
2:28 which is outward in the f: 4561
3:20 law there shall no f be justified in his sight: 4561
4: 1 as pertaining to the f, hath found? 4561
6:19 of men because of the infirmity of your f: 4561
7: 5 For when we were in the f, the motions of 4561
7:18 For I know that in me (that is, in my f,) 4561
7:25 law of God; but with the f the law of sin. 4561
8: 1 are in Christ Jesus who walk not after the f, 4561
8: 3 not do, in that it was weak through the f, 4561
8: 3 his own Son in the likeness of sinful f, 4561

Ro 8: 3 and for sin, condemned sin in the f: 4561
8: 4 who walk not after the f, but after 4561
8: 5 For they that are after the f do mind 4561
8: 5 after the flesh do mind the *things* of the f; 4561
8: 8 they that are in the f cannot please God. 4561
8: 9 But ye are not in the f, but in the Spirit, if 4561
8:12 we are debtors, not to the f, 4561
8:12 not to the flesh, to live after the f. 4561
8:13 For if ye live after the f, ye shall die: but 4561
9: 3 my kinsmen according to the f: 4561
9: 5 of whom as concerning the f Christ *came,* 4561
9: 8 *They which are* the children of the f, 4561
11:14 provoke to emulation *them which are* my f, 4561
13:14 and make not provision for the f, to *fulfil* 4561
14:21 *It is* good neither to eat f, nor to drink wine, 2907
1Co 1:26 how that not many wise *men* after the f, 4561
1:29 That no f should glory in his presence. 4561
5: 5 one unto Satan for the destruction of the f, 4561
6:16 one body? for two, saith *he,* shall be one f. 4561
7:28 such shall have trouble in the f: 4561
8:13 I will eat no f while the world standeth, 2907
10:18 Behold Israel after the f: are not they which 4561
15:39 All f *is* not the same flesh: but *there is* one 4561
15:39 All flesh *is* not the same f: but *there is* one 4561
15:39 but *there is* one *kind of* f of men, 4561
15:39 another f of beasts, another of fishes, *and* 4561
15:50 that f and blood cannot inherit the kingdom 4561
2Co 1:17 I purpose, do I purpose according to the f, 4561
4:11 might be made manifest in our mortal f. 4561
5:16 henceforth know we no *man* after the f: 4561
5:16 though we have known Christ after the f, 4561
7: 1 cleanse ourselves from all filthiness of the f 4561
7: 5 our f had no rest, but *we were* troubled on 4561
10: 2 of us as if we walked according to the f. 4561
10: 3 For though we walk in the f, we do not war 4561
10: 3 walk in the flesh, we do not war after the f: 4561
11:18 Seeing that many glory after the f, I will 4561
12: 7 there was given to me a thorn in the f, 4561
Gal 1:16 immediately I conferred not with f and 4561
2:16 for by the works of the law shall no f be 4561
2:20 *the life* which I now live in the f I live by 4561
3: 3 are ye now made perfect by the f? 4561
4:13 Ye know how through infirmity of the f I 4561
4:14 And my temptation which was in my f ye 4561
4:23 of the bondwoman was born after the f; 4561
4:29 he that was born after the f persecuted him 4561
5:13 only *use* not liberty for an occasion to the f, 4561
5:16 and ye shall not fulfil the lust of the f. 4561
5:17 For the f lusteth against the Spirit, and 4561
5:17 the Spirit, and the Spirit against the f: 4561
5:19 Now the works of the f are manifest, 4561
5:24 have crucified the f with the affections 4561
6: 8 For he that soweth to his f shall of the flesh 4561
6: 8 For he that soweth to his flesh shall of the f 4561
6:12 many as desire to make a fair shew in the f, 4561
6:13 that they may glory in your f. 4561
Eph 2: 3 in times past in the lusts of our f, 4561
2: 3 fulfilling the desires of the f and of 4561
2:11 ye *being* in time passed Gentiles in the f, 4561
2:11 the Circumcision in the f made by hands; 4561
2:15 Having abolished in his f the enmity, 4561
5:29 For no *man* ever yet hated his own f; but 4561
5:30 of his body, of his f, and of his bones. 4561
5:31 unto his wife, and they two shall be one f. 4561
6: 5 *that are your* masters according to the f, 4561
6:12 For we wrestle not against f and blood, but 4561
Php 1:22 But if *I* live in the f, this *is* the fruit of my 4561
1:24 Nevertheless to abide in the f *is* more 4561
3: 3 and have no confidence in the f. 4561
3: 4 I *might* also have confidence in the f. 4561
3: 4 that *he hath whereof he* might trust in the f, 4561
Col 1:22 In the body of his f through death, 4561
1:24 of Christ in my f for his body's sake, 4561
2: 1 as many as have not seen my face in the f; 4561
2: 5 For though I be absent in the f, yet am I 4561
2:11 in putting off the body of the sins of the f, 4561
2:13 *your* sins and the uncircumcision of your f, 4561
2:23 not in any honour to the satisfying of the f. 4561
3:22 all *things your* masters according to the f; 4561
1Ti 3:16 God was manifest in the f, justified in 4561
Phm 1:16 unto thee, both in the f, and in the Lord? 4561
Heb 2:14 then as the children are partakers of f and 4561
5: 7 Who in the days of his f, when he had 4561
9:13 sanctifieth to the purifying of the f: 4561
10:20 for us, through the vail, that is to say, his f; 4561
12: 9 Furthermore we have had fathers of our f 4561
Jas 5: 3 and shall eat your f as *it were* fire: 4561
1Pe 1:24 For all f *is* as grass, and all the glory of 4561
3:18 being put to death in the f, but 4561
3:21 us (not the putting away of the filth of the f, 4561
4: 1 then as Christ hath suffered for us in the f, 4561
4: 1 for he that hath suffered in the f hath ceased 4561
4: 2 rest of *his* time in the f to the lusts of men, 4561
4: 6 might be judged according to men in the f, 4561
2Pe 2:10 But chiefly them that walk after the f in 4561
2:18 they allure through the lusts of the f, 4561
1Jn 2:16 the lust of the f, and the lust of the eyes, 4561
4: 2 that Jesus Christ is come in the f is of God: 4561
4: 3 Jesus Christ is come in the f is not of God: 4561
2Jn 1: 7 not that Jesus Christ is come in the f. 4561
Jude 1: 7 and going after strange f, are set forth for 4561
1: 8 also these *filthy* dreamers defile the f, 4561
1:23 hating even the garment spotted by the f. 4561
Rev 17:16 and shall eat her f, and burn her with fire. 4561
19:18 That ye may eat the f of kings, and the flesh 4561
19:18 and the f of captains, and the flesh of 4561
19:18 and the f of mighty *men,* and the flesh of 4561
19:18 flesh of mighty *men,* and the f of horses, 4561
19:18 and the f of all *men, both* free and bond, 4561
19:21 and all the fowls were filled with their f. 4561

FLESHHOOK (2) [FLESH, HOOK]
1Sa 2:13 with a f of three teeth in his hand; 4207
2:14 all that the f brought up the priest took for 4207

FLESHHOOKS (5) [FLESH, HOOK]
Ex 27: 3 and his basons, and his f, and his firepans: 4207
38: 3 and the basons, *and* the f, and the firepans: 4207
Nu 4:14 the f, and the shovels, and the basons, 4207
1Ch 28:17 Also pure gold *for* the f, and the bowls, and 4207
2Ch 4:16 and the f, and all their instruments, 4207

FLESHLY (3) [FLESH]
2Co 1:12 not with f wisdom, but by the grace of God, 4559
Col 2:18 hath not seen, vainly puft up by his f mind, 4561
1Pe 2:11 and pilgrims, abstain from f lusts, 4559

FLESHY (1) [FLESH]
2Co 3: 3 tables of stone, but in f tables of the heart. 4560

FLEW (2) [FLY]
1Sa 14:32 the people f upon the spoil, and took sheep, 5860
Isa 6: 6 f one of the seraphims unto me, having a 5774

FLIES (10) [FLY]
Ex 8:21 I will send swarms *of f* upon thee, and NIH
8:21 the Egyptians shall be full of swarms *of f,* NIH
8:22 that no swarms *of f* shall be there; NIH
8:24 there came a grievous swarm *of f* into NIH
8:24 was corrupted by reason of the swarm *of f.* NIH
8:29 the swarms *of f* may depart from Pharaoh, NIH
8:31 he removed the swarms *of f* from Pharaoh, NIH
Ps 78:45 He sent divers sorts *of f* among them, NIH
105:31 there came divers sorts *of f, and* lice in all NIH
Ecc 10: 1 Dead f cause the ointment of 2070

FLIETH (5) [FLY]
Dt 4:17 the likeness of any winged fowl that f in 5774
14:19 every creeping thing that f *is* unclean unto 5775
28:49 the end of the earth, *as swift* as the eagle f; 1675
Ps 91: 5 by night; *nor* for the arrow *that* f by day; 5774
Na 3:16 the cankerworm spoileth, and f **away**. 5774

FLIGHT (8) [FLY]
Lev 26: 8 hundred of you shall **put** ten thousand **to** f: 7291
Dt 32:30 two **put** ten thousand **to** f, except their 5127
1Ch 12:15 they **put to** f all *them of* the valleys, 1272
Isa 52:12 ye shall not go out with haste, nor go by f: 4499
Am 2:14 Therefore the f shall perish from the swift, 4498
Mt 24:20 But pray ye that your f be not in the winter, 5437
Mk 13:18 And pray ye that your f be not in 5437
Heb 11:34 **turned to** f the armies of the aliens. 2827

FLINT (5) [FLINTY]
Dt 8:15 thee forth water out of the rock of f; 2496
Ps 114: 8 the f into a fountain of waters. 2496
Isa 5:28 their horses' hoofs shall be counted like f, 6864
50: 7 therefore have I set my face like a f, and 2496
Eze 3: 9 As an adamant harder than f have I made 6864

FLINTY (1) [FLINT]
Dt 32:13 out of the rock, and oil out of the f rock; 2496

FLIXE (1)
Ac 28: 8 lay sick of a fever and of a **bloody** f: 1420

FLOAT See FLOTES; SWIM

FLOCK (111) [FLOCKS]
Ge 4: 4 he also brought of the firstlings of his f and 6629
21:28 Abraham set seven ewe lambs of the f by 6629
27: 9 Go now to the f, and fetch me from thence 6629
29:10 watered the f of Laban his mother's 6629
30:31 for me, I will again feed *and* keep thy f: 6629
30:32 I will pass through all thy f to day, 6629
30:40 and all the brown in the f of Laban; 6629
31: 4 and Leah to the field unto his f, 6629
31:38 and the rams of thy f have I not eaten. 6629
33:13 overdrive them one day, all the f will die. 6629
37: 2 was feeding the f with his brethren; 6629
37:12 his brethren went to feed their father's f in 6629
37:13 Do not thy brethren feed *the f* in Shechem? NIH
38:17 he said, I will send *thee* a kid from the f. 6629
Ex 2:16 filled the troughs to water their father's f. 6629
2:17 and helped them, and watered their f. 6629
2:19 water enough for us, and watered the f. 6629
3: 1 Now Moses kept the f of Jethro his father 6629
3: 1 he led the f to the backside of the desert, 6629
Lev 1: 2 of the cattle, *even* of the herd, and of the f. 6629
3: 6 peace offering unto the LORD *be* of the f, 6629
5: 6 a female from the f, a lamb or a kid of 6629
5:18 bring a ram without blemish out of the f, 6629
6: 6 a ram without blemish out of the f, with thy 6629
27:32 *concerning* the tithe of the herd, or of the f, 6629
Nu 15: 3 unto the LORD, of the herd, or of the f: 6629
Dt 12:17 or the firstlings of thy herds or of thy f, 6629
12:21 thou shalt kill of thy herd and of thy f, 6629
15:14 shalt furnish him liberally out of thy f, 6629
15:19 of thy f thou shalt sanctify unto the LORD 6629
16: 2 the LORD thy God, *of* the f and the herd, 6629
1Sa 17:34 and a bear, and took a lamb out of the f: 5739
2Sa 12: 4 he spared to take of his own f and of his 6629
2Ch 35: 7 gave to the people, *of* the f, lambs and kids, 6629
Ezr 10:19 *they offered* a ram of the f for their 6629
Job 21:11 They send forth their little ones like a f, and 6629
30: 1 disdained to have set with the dogs of my f. 6629
Ps 77:20 Thou leddest thy people like a f by the hand 6629
78:52 and guided them in the wilderness like a f. 5739
80: 1 of Israel, thou that leadest Joseph like a f; 6629
107:41 and maketh *him* families like a f. 6629
SS 1: 7 where thou makest *thy f* to rest at noon: NIH
1: 8 go thy way forth by the footsteps of the f, 6629
4: 1 thy hair *is* as a f of goats, that appear from 5739
4: 2 Thy teeth *are* like a f of *sheep that are* even 5739
6: 5 thy hair *is* as a f of goats that appear from 5739
6: 6 Thy teeth *are* as a f of sheep which go up 5739
Isa 40:11 He shall feed his f like a shepherd: he shall 5739
63:11 up out of the sea with the shepherd of his f? 6629
Jer 13:17 the LORD'S f is carried away captive. 5739
13:20 where *is* the f *that* was given thee, 5739
13:20 flock *that* was given thee, thy beautiful f? 6629
23: 2 Ye have scattered my f, and driven them 6629
23: 3 I will gather the remnant of my f out of all 6629
25:34 *in the ashes,* ye principal of the f: 6629
25:35 to flee, nor the principal of the f to escape. 6629
25:36 and a howling of the principal of the f, 6629
31:10 and keep him as a shepherd *doth* his f. 5739
31:12 and for the young of the f and of the herd: 6629
49:20 Surely the least of the f shall draw them 6629
50:45 Surely the least of the f shall draw them 6629
51:23 in pieces with thee the shepherd and his f; 5739
Eze 24: 5 Take the choice of the f, and burn also 6629
34: 3 kill them that are fed: *but* ye feed not the f. 6629
34: 6 my f was scattered upon all the face of 6629
34: 8 surely because my f became a prey, and 6629
34: 8 my f became meat to every beast of 6629
34: 8 neither did my shepherds search for my f, 6629
34: 8 fed themselves, and fed not my f; 6629
34:10 I will require my f at their hand, and 6629
34:10 and cause them to cease from feeding the f; 6629
34:10 for I will deliver my f from their mouth, 6629
34:12 As a shepherd seeketh out his f in the day 5739
34:15 I will feed my f, and I will cause them to lie 6629
34:17 *as for* you, O my f, thus saith the Lord 6629
34:19 *as for* my f, they eat that which ye have 6629
34:22 Therefore will I save my f, and they shall 6629
34:31 ye my f, the flock of my pasture, *are* men, 6629
34:31 the f of my pasture, *are* men, *and* I *am* your 6629
36:37 I will increase them *with* men like a f. 6629
36:38 As the holy f, as the flock of Jerusalem in 6629
36:38 as the f of Jerusalem in her solemn feasts; 6629
43:23 and a ram out of the f without blemish. 6629
43:25 and a ram out of the f, without blemish. 6629
45:15 one lamb out of the f, out of two hundred, 6629
Am 6: 4 eat the lambs out of the f, and the calves 6629
7:15 the LORD took me as I followed the f, 6629
Jnh 3: 7 man nor beast, herd nor f, taste any thing: 6629
Mic 2:12 as the f in the midst of their fold: 5739
4: 8 thou, O tower of the f, the strong hold of 5739
7:14 people with thy rod, the f of thine heritage, 6629
Hab 3:17 the f shall be cut off from the fold, and 6629
Zec 9:16 save them in that day as the f of his people: 6629
10: 2 therefore they went their way as a f, 6629
10: 3 for the LORD of hosts hath visited his f 5739
11: 4 my God; Feed the f of the slaughter; 6629
11: 7 And I will feed the f of slaughter, *even* you, 6629
11: 7 of slaughter, *even* you, O poor of the f. 6629
11: 7 and the other I called Bands; and I fed the f. 6629
11:11 the poor of the f that waited upon me knew 6629
11:17 Woe to the idol shepherd that leaveth the f! 6629
Mal 1:14 which hath in his f a male, and voweth, and 5739
Mt 26:31 the sheep of the f shall be scattered abroad. 4167
Lk 2: 8 keeping watch over their f by night. 4167
12:32 Fear not, little f; for it is your Father's good 4168
Ac 20:28 therefore unto yourselves, and to all the f, 4168
20:29 enter in among you, not sparing the f. 4168
1Co 9: 7 or who feedeth a f, and eateth not of 4167
9: 7 a flock, and eateth not of the milk of the f? 4167
1Pe 5: 2 Feed the f of God which is among you, 4168
5: 3 but being ensamples to the f. 4168

FLOCKS (80) [FLOCK]
Ge 13: 5 with Abram, had f, and herds, and tents. 6629
24:35 he hath given him f, and herds, and silver, 6629
26:14 For he had possession of f, and 6629
29: 2 lo, there *were* three f of sheep lying by it; 5739
29: 2 by it; for out of that well they watered the f: 5739
29: 3 thither were all the f gathered: and 5739
29: 8 until all the f be gathered together, and 5739
30:36 and Jacob fed the rest of Laban's f. 6629
30:38 f in the gutters in the watering troughs 6629
30:38 watering troughs when the f came to drink, 6629
30:39 the f conceived before the rods, and 6629
30:40 set the faces of the f toward the ringstraked, 6629
30:40 he put his own f by themselves, and 5739
32: 5 f, and menservants, and womenservants: 6629
32: 7 the f, and herds, and the camels, into two 6629
33:13 the f and herds with young *are* with me: 6629
37:14 well with thy brethren, and well with the f; 6629
37:16 tell me, I pray thee, where they feed *their f.* NIH
45:10 thy f, and thy herds, and all that thou hast, 6629
46:32 they have brought their f, and their herds, 6629
47: 1 their f, and their herds, and all that they 6629
47: 4 for thy servants have no pasture for their f; 6629
47:17 for the f, and for the cattle of 4735+6629
50: 8 their little ones, and their f, and their herds, 6629
Ex 10: 9 with our f and with our herds will we go; 6629
10:24 only let your f and your herds be stayed: 6629
12:32 Also take your f and your herds, as ye have 6629
12:38 and f, and herds, *even* very much cattle. 6629
34: 3 neither let the f nor herds feed before that 6629
Lev 1:10 if his offering *be* of the f, *namely,* of 6629
5:15 LORD a ram without blemish out of the f, 6629
Nu 11:22 Shall the f and the herds be slain for them, 6629
31: 9 and all their f, and all their goods. 4735
31:30 of the beeves, of the asses, and of the f, 6629
32:26 our wives, our f, and all our cattle, 4735
Dt 7:13 increase of thy kine, and the f of thy sheep, 6251
8:13 *when* thy herds and thy f multiply, and thy 6629
12: 6 the firstlings of your herds and of your f: 6629
14:23 and the firstlings of thy herds and of thy f; 6629
28: 4 increase of thy kine, and the f of thy sheep 6251
28:18 increase of thy kine, and the f of thy sheep. 6251
28:51 the increase of thy kine, or f of thy sheep, 6251
Jdg 5:16 to hear the bleatings of the f? 5739
1Sa 30:20 David took all the f and the herds, 6629
2Sa 12: 2 The rich *man* had exceeding many f and 6629
1Ki 20:27 pitched before them like two **little** f of kids; 2835
1Ch 4:39 of the valley, to seek pasture for their f. 6629
4:41 because *there was* pasture there for their f. 6629
27:31 over the f *was* Jaziz the Hagerite. All these 6629
2Ch 17:11 the Arabians brought him f, seven thousand 6629
32:28 for all *manner of* beasts, and cotes for f. 5739

2Ch 32:29 possessions of f and herds in abundance: 6629
Ne 10:36 and the firstlings of our herds and of our f, 6629
Job 24: 2 they violently take away f, and 5739
Ps 65:13 The pastures are clothed with f; the valleys 6629
78:48 to the hail, and their f to hot thunderbolts. 4735
Pr 27:23 Be thou diligent to know the state of thy f, 6629
SS 1: 7 turneth aside by the f of thy companions? 5739
Isa 17: 2 they shall be for f, which shall lie down, 5739
32:14 for ever, a joy of wild asses, a pasture of f; 5739
60: 7 All the f of Kedar shall be gathered 6629
61: 5 strangers shall stand and feed your f, and 6629
65:10 Sharon shall be a fold of f, and the valley of 6629
Jer 3:24 their f and their herds, their sons and their 6629
5:17 they shall eat up thy f and thine herds: 6629
6: 3 The shepherds with their f shall come unto 5739
10:21 and all their f shall be scattered. 4830
31:24 husbandmen, and they *that* go forth with f. 5739
33:12 of shepherds causing *their* f to lie down. 6629
33:13 shall the f pass again under the hands of 6629
49:29 their f shall they take *away:* they shall take 6629
50: 8 and be as the he goats before the f. 6629
Eze 25: 5 and the Ammonites a couching place for f: 6629
34: 2 should not the shepherds feed the f? 6629
36:38 shall the waste cities be filled *with* f of 6629
Hos 5: 6 They shall go with their f and with their 6629
Joel 1:18 yea, the f of sheep are made desolate. 5739
Mic 5: 8 as a young lion among the f of sheep: 5739
Zep 2: 6 *and* cottages for shepherds, and folds for f. 6629
2:14 f shall lie down in the midst of her, all 5739

FLOG; FLOGGED; FLOGGING; FLOGGINGS
See SCOURGES; SCOURGETH; SCOURGING; SCOURGINGS; STRIPE; STRIPES

FLOOD (43) [FLOODS, WATERFLOOD]
Ge 6:17 do bring a f of waters upon the earth, 3999
7: 6 Noah *was* six hundred years old when the f 3999
7: 7 into the ark, because of the waters of the f. 3999
7:10 that the waters of the f were upon the earth. 3999
7:17 the f was forty days upon the earth; and 3999
9:11 be cut off any more by the waters of a f; 3999
9:11 neither shall there any more be a f to 3999
9:15 the waters shall no more become a f to 3999
9:28 Noah lived after the f three hundred and 3999
10: 1 and unto them were sons born after the f. 3999
10:32 the nations divided in the earth after the f. 3999
11:10 and begat Arphaxad two years after the f: 3999
Jos 24: 2 Your fathers dwelt on the *other* side of the f 5104
24: 3 father Abraham from the *other* side of the f, 5104
24:14 fathers served on the *other* side of the f, 5104
24:15 served that *were* on the *other* side of the f, 5104
Job 14:11 the sea, and the f decayeth and drieth up: 5104
22:16 whose foundation was overflown *with* a f: 5104
28: 4 The f breaketh out from the inhabitant; 5158
Ps 29:10 The LORD sitteth upon the f; yea, 3999
66: 6 dry *land:* they went through the f on foot: 5104
74:15 Thou didst cleave the fountain and the f: 5158
90: 5 Thou **carriest** them **away as with a f;** 2229
Isa 28: 2 as a f of mighty waters overflowing, 2230
59:19 When the enemy shall come in like a f, 5104
Jer 46: 7 Who *is* this *that* cometh up as a f, 2975
46: 8 Egypt riseth up like a f, and *his* waters are 2975
47: 2 shall be an overflowing f, and 5158
Da 9:26 the end thereof *shall be* with a f, and 7858
11:22 *with* the arms of a f shall they be overflown 7858
Am 8: 8 it shall rise up wholly as a f; and it shall be 2975
8: 8 cast out and drowned, as *by* the f of Egypt. 2975
9: 5 it shall rise up wholly like a f; and shall be 2975
9: 5 and shall be drowned, as *by* the f of Egypt. 2975
Na 1: 8 with an overrunning f he will make an utter 7858
Mt 24:38 For as in the days that were before the f *2627*
24:39 And knew not until the f came, and *2627*
Lk 6:48 and when the f arose, the stream beat *4132*
17:27 and the f came, and destroyed *them* all. *2627*
2Pe 2: 5 bringing in the f upon the world of *2627*
Rev 12:15 of his mouth water as a f after the woman, *4215*
12:15 cause her to be **carried away of the f.** *4216*
12:16 swallowed up the f which the dragon cast *4215*

FLOODS (19) [FLOOD]
Ex 15: 8 the f stood upright as a heap, *and* the depths 5140
2Sa 22: 5 the f of ungodly men made me afraid; 5158
Job 20:17 the f, the brooks of honey and butter. 5104
28:11 He bindeth the f from overflowing; and 5104
Ps 18: 4 and the f of ungodly men made me afraid. 5158
24: 2 upon the seas, and established it upon the f. 5104
32: 6 surely in the f of great waters they shall not 7858
69: 2 into deep waters, where the f overflow me. 7641
78:44 and their f, *that* they could not drink. 5140
93: 3 The f have lifted up, O LORD, the floods 5104
93: 3 O LORD, the f have lifted up their voice; 5104
93: 3 up their voice; the f lift up their waves. 5104
98: 8 Let the f clap *their* hands: let the hills be 5104
SS 8: 7 quench love, neither can the f drown it: 5104
Isa 44: 3 f upon the dry *ground:* I will pour my spirit 5140
Eze 31:15 I restrained the f thereof, and the great 5104
Jnh 2: 3 of the seas; and the f compassed me about: 5104
Mt 7:25 and the f came, and the winds blew, and *4215*
7:27 and the f came, and the winds blew, and *4215*

FLOODWATERS See WATERFLOOD

FLOOR (19) [BARNFLOOR, CORNFLOOR, FLOORS, THRESHINGFLOOR, THRESHINGFLOORS]
Ge 50:11 saw the mourning in the f of Atad, they 1637
Nu 5:17 of the dust that is in the f of the tabernacle 7172
Dt 15:14 and out of thy f, and out of thy winepress: 1637
Jdg 6:37 Behold, I will put a fleece of wool in the f; 1637
Ru 3: 3 upon thee, and get thee down *to* the f: 1637
3: 6 she went down *unto* the f, and 1637
3:14 not be known that a woman came *into* the f. 1637
1Ki 6:15 both the f of the house, and the walls of 7172
6:15 covered the f of the house with planks of 7172
6:16 both the f and the walls with boards of 7172
6:30 the f of the house he overlaid with gold, 7172
7: 7 cedar from one side of the f to the other. 7172
2Ch 34:11 to f the houses which the kings of Judah 7136
Isa 21:10 O my threshing, and the corn of my f: 1637
Hos 9: 2 The f and the winepress shall not feed 1637
13: 3 *that* is driven with a whirlwind out of the f, 1637
Mic 4:12 shall gather them as the sheaves into the f. 1637
Mt 3:12 and he will throughly purge his f, and *257*
Lk 3:17 and he will throughly purge his f, and *257*

FLOORS (1) [FLOOR]
Joel 2:24 the f shall be full *of* wheat, and the fats 1637

FLOTES (2)
1Ki 5: 9 I will convey them by sea *in* f unto 1702
2Ch 2:16 we will bring it to thee *in* f by sea *to* Joppa; 7513

FLOUR (58)
Ex 29: 2 *of* wheaten f shalt thou make them. 5560
29:40 with the one lamb a tenth deal of f mingled 5560
Lev 2: 1 the LORD, his offering shall be *of* fine f; 5560
2: 2 he shall take thereout his handful of the f 5560
2: 4 *it shall be* unleavened cakes of fine f 5560
2: 5 it shall be *of* fine f unleavened, 5560
2: 7 it shall be made *of* fine f with oil. 5560
5:11 *part* of an ephah of fine f for a sin offering; 5560
6:15 of the f of the meat offering, and of the oil 5560
6:20 the tenth *part* of an ephah of fine f *for* a 5560
7:12 and cakes mingled with oil, of fine f, fried. 5560
14:10 three tenth deals of fine f *for* a meat 5560
14:21 one tenth deal of fine f mingled with oil for 5560
23:13 two tenth deals *of* fine f mingled with oil, 5560
23:17 they shall be *of* fine f; they shall be baken 5560
24: 5 thou shalt take fine f, and bake twelve 5560
Nu 6:15 cakes *of* fine f mingled with oil, and 5560
7:13 both of them *were* full *of* fine f mingled 5560
7:19 both of them full *of* fine f mingled with oil 5560
7:25 both of them full *of* fine f mingled with oil 5560
7:31 both of them full *of* fine f mingled with oil 5560
7:37 both of them full *of* fine f mingled with oil 5560
7:43 both of them full *of* fine f mingled with oil 5560
7:49 both of them full *of* fine f mingled with oil 5560
7:55 both of them full *of* fine f mingled with oil 5560
7:61 both of them full *of* fine f mingled with oil 5560
7:67 both of them full *of* fine f mingled with oil 5560
7:73 both of them full *of* fine f mingled with oil 5560
7:79 both of them full *of* fine f mingled with oil 5560
8: 8 *even* fine f mingled with oil, and 5560
15: 4 f mingled with the fourth *part* of a hin of 5560
15: 6 f mingled with the third *part* of a hin of oil. 5560
15: 9 deals *of* f mingled with half a hin of oil. 5560
28: 5 a tenth *part* of an ephah *of* f for a meat 5560
28: 9 two tenth deals *of* f *for* a meat offering, 5560
28:12 three tenth deals *of* f *for* a meat offering, 5560
28:12 two tenth deals *of* f *for* a meat offering, 5560
28:13 a several tenth deal of f mingled with oil 5560
28:20 their meat offering *shall be of* f mingled 5560
28:28 their meat offering *of* f mingled with oil, 5560
29: 3 their meat offering *shall be of* f mingled 5560
29: 9 their meat offering *shall be of* f mingled 5560
29:14 their meat offering *shall be of* f mingled 5560
Jdg 6:19 and unleavened *cakes of* an ephah of f: 7058
1Sa 1:24 one ephah of f, and a bottle of wine, and 7058
28:24 took f, and kneaded *it,* and did bake 7058
2Sa 13: 8 she took f, and kneaded *it,* and made cakes 1217
17:28 f, and parched *corn,* and beans, and lentiles, 7058
1Ki 4:22 for one day was thirty measures of fine f, 5560
2Ki 7: 1 a measure of fine f *be sold* for a shekel, 5560
7:16 So a measure of fine f was *sold* for a 5560
7:18 and a measure of fine f for a shekel, 5560
1Ch 9:29 the fine f, and the wine, and the oil, and 5560
23:29 for the fine f for meat offering, and for 5560
Eze 16:13 thou didst eat fine f, and honey, and oil: 5560
16:19 fine f, and oil, and honey, *wherewith* I fed 5560
46:14 of a hin of oil, to temper with the fine f; 5560
Rev 18:13 and oil, and fine f, and wheat, and beasts, *4585*

FLOURISH (13) [FLOURISHED, FLOURISHETH, FLOURISHING]
Ps 72: 7 In his days shall the righteous f; and 6524
72:16 *they* of the city shall f like grass of 6692
92: 7 and when all the workers of iniquity do f; 6692
92:12 The righteous shall f like the palm tree: 6524
92:13 the LORD shall f in the courts of our God. 6524
132:18 but upon himself shall his crown f. 6692
Pr 11:28 but the righteous shall f as a branch. 6524
14:11 but the tabernacle of the upright shall f. 6524
Ecc 12: 5 the almond tree shall f, and the grasshopper 5340
SS 7:12 let us see if the vine f, *whether* the tender 6524
Isa 17:11 the morning shalt thou **make** thy seed **to** f: 6524
66:14 and your bones shall f like an herb: 6524
Eze 17:24 green tree, and have **made** the dry tree **to** f: 6524

FLOURISHED (2) [FLOURISH]
SS 6:11 *and* to see whether the vine f, *and* 6524
Php 4:10 now at the last your care of me hath **f again;** *330*

FLOURISHETH (2) [FLOURISH]
Ps 90: 6 In the morning it f, and groweth up; in 6692
103:15 *are* as grass: as a flower of the field, so he f. 6692

FLOURISHING (2) [FLOURISH]
Ps 92:14 forth fruit in old age; they shall be fat and f; 7488
Da 4: 4 at rest in mine house, and f in my palace: 7487

FLOW (13) [FLOWED, FLOWETH, FLOWING, OVERFLOW]
Job 20:28 *his goods shall* **f away** in the day of his 5064
Ps 147:18 causeth his wind to blow, *and* the waters f. 5140
SS 4:16 *that* the spices thereof may **f out.** 5140
Isa 2: 2 the hills; and all nations shall f unto it. 5102
48:21 he **caused** the waters **to** f out of the rock 5140
60: 5 f *together,* and thine heart shall fear, and 5102
64: 1 that the mountains might **f down** at thy 2151
Jer 31:12 shall f *together* to the goodness of 5102
51:44 the nations shall not f *together* any more 5102
Joel 3:18 the hills shall f *with* milk, and all the rivers 1980
3:18 all the rivers of Judah shall f *with* waters, 1980
Mic 4: 1 above the hills; and people shall f unto it. 5102
Jn 7:38 out of his belly shall f rivers of living *4482*

FLOWED (3) [FLOW]
Jos 4:18 and f over all his banks, as *they did* before. 1980
Isa 64: 3 the mountains **f down** at thy presence. 2151
La 3:54 Waters f over mine head; *then* I said, I am 6687

FLOWER (20) [FLOWERS]
Ex 25:33 *with* a knop and a f in one branch; 6525
25:33 in the other branch, *with* a knop and a f: 6525
37:19 of almonds in one branch, a knop and a f; 6525
37:19 almonds in another branch, a knop and a f: 6525
1Sa 2:33 of thine house shall die **in the f of** their **age.** 376
Job 14: 2 He cometh forth like a f, and is cut down: 6731
15:33 the vine, and shall cast off his f as the olive. 5328
Ps 103:15 as a f of the field, so he flourisheth. 6731
Isa 18: 5 and the sour grape is ripening in the f, 5328
28: 1 whose glorious beauty *is* a fading f, 6731
28: 4 shall be a fading f, *and* as the hasty fruit 6733
40: 6 all the goodliness thereof *is* as the f of 6731
40: 7 The grass withereth, the f fadeth: because 6731
40: 8 The grass withereth, the f fadeth: but 6731
Na 1: 4 Carmel, and the f of Lebanon languisheth. 6525
1Co 7:36 if she **pass the f of** *her* **age,** *1510+5230*
Jas 1:10 as the f of the grass he shall pass away. *438*
1:11 and the f thereof falleth, and the grace of *438*
1Pe 1:24 and all the glory of man as the f of grass. *438*
1:24 and the f thereof falleth away: *438*

FLOWERS (17) [FLOWER]
Ex 25:31 his bowls, his knops, and his f, 6525
25:34 unto almonds, *with* their knops and their f. 6525
37:17 his branch, his bowls, his knops, and his f, 6525
37:20 made like almonds, his knops, and his f: 6525
Lev 15:24 her f be upon him, he shall be unclean 5079
15:33 of her that is sick of her f, and of him that 5079
Nu 8: 4 unto the f thereof, *was* beaten work: 6525
1Ki 6:18 within *was* carved with knops and open f: 6731
6:29 of cherubims and palm trees and open f, 6731
6:32 of cherubims and palm trees and open f, 6731
6:35 and palm trees and open f: 6731
7:26 like the brim of a cup, *with* f of lilies: 6525
7:49 with the f, and the lamps, and the tongs *of* 6525
2Ch 4: 5 work of the brim of a cup, *with* f of lilies; 6525
4:21 the f, and the lamps, and the tongs, *made he* 6525
SS 2:12 The f appear on the earth; the time of 5339
5:13 cheeks *are* as a bed of spices, *as* sweet f: 4026

FLOWETH (12) [FLOW]
Lev 20:24 a land that f with milk and honey: 2100
Nu 13:27 and surely it f with milk and honey; 2100
14: 8 it us; a land which f with milk and honey. 2100
16:13 brought us up out of a land that f with milk 2100
16:14 not brought us into a land that f with milk 2100
Dt 6: 3 *in* the land that f with milk and honey. 2100
11: 9 a land that f with milk and honey. 2100
26: 9 *even* a land that f with milk and honey. 2100
26:15 a land that f with milk and honey. 2100
27: 3 a land that f with milk and honey; 2100
31:20 their fathers, that f with milk and honey; 2100
Jos 5: 6 give us, a land that f with milk and honey. 2100

FLOWING (12) [FLOW]
Ex 3: 8 a large, unto a land f with milk and honey; 2100
3:17 unto a land f with milk and honey. 2100
13: 5 to give thee, a land f with milk and honey, 2100
33: 3 Unto a land f with milk and honey: for I 2100
Pr 18: 4 *and* the wellspring of wisdom *as* a f brook. 5042
Isa 66:12 the glory of the Gentiles like a f stream: 7857
Jer 11: 5 to give them a land f with milk and honey, 2100
18:14 shall the cold f waters that come from 5140
32:22 to give them, a land f with milk and honey; 2100
49: 4 thy f valley, O backsliding daughter? 2100
Eze 20: 6 f with milk and honey, which *is* the glory 2100
20:15 land which I had given *them,* f with milk 2100

FLUTE (4)
Da 3: 5 f, harp, sackbut, psaltery, dulcimer, and 4953
3: 7 f, harp, sackbut, psaltery, and all kinds of 4953
3:10 f, harp, sackbut, psaltery, and dulcimer, and 4953
3:15 f, harp, sackbut, psaltery, and dulcimer, and 4953

FLUTTERETH (1)
Dt 32:11 f over her young, spreadeth abroad her 7363

FLY (25) [FLEW, FLIES, FLIETH, FLIGHT, FLYING]
Ge 1:20 fowl *that* may f above the earth in the open 5774
1Sa 15:19 didst f upon the spoil, and didst evil in 5860
2Sa 22:11 he rode upon a cherub, and did f: and 5774
Job 5: 7 is born unto trouble, as the sparks f upward. 5774
20: 8 He shall **f away** as a dream, and shall not 5774
39:26 Doth the hawk f by thy wisdom, *and* 82
Ps 18:10 he rode upon a cherub, and did f: yea, 5774
18:10 yea, he did f upon the wings of the wind. 1675
55: 6 *for then* would I **f away,** and be at rest. 5774
90:10 for it is soon cut off, and we **f away.** 5774
Pr 23: 5 they **f away** as an eagle *toward* heaven. 5774
Isa 6: 2 he covered his feet, and with twain he did f. 5774
7:18 *that* the LORD shall hiss for the f that *is* in 2070
11:14 they shall f upon the shoulders of 5774
60: 8 Who *are* these *that* f as a cloud, and as 5774
Jer 48:40 he shall f as an eagle, and shall spread his 1675
49:22 he shall come up and f as the eagle, and 1675
Eze 13:20 ye there hunt the souls to **make** *them* f, 6524
13:20 *even* the souls that ye hunt to **make** *them* f. 6524
Da 9:21 at the beginning, being **caused to** f swiftly, 3286

Hos 9:11 their glory shall f away like a bird, 5774
Hab 1: 8 they shall f as the eagle *that* hasteth to eat. 5774
Rev 12:14 that she might f into the wilderness, 4072
14: 6 And I saw another angel f in the midst of 4072
19:17 saying to all the fowls that f in the midst of 4072

FLYING (12) [FLY]
Lev 11:21 Yet these may ye eat of every f creeping 5775
11:23 all *other* f creeping things, which have four 5775
Job 30: 3 f *into* the wilderness in former time 6207
Ps 148:10 all cattle; creeping things, and f fowl: 3671
Pr 26: 2 as the swallow by f, so the curse causeless 5774
Isa 14:29 and his fruit *shall be* a fiery f serpent. 5774
30: 6 and old lion, the viper and fiery f serpent, 5774
31: 5 As birds f, so will the LORD of hosts 5774
Zec 5: 1 mine eyes, and looked, and behold, a f roll. 5774
5: 2 I answered, I see a f roll; the length thereof 5774
Rev 4: 7 and the fourth beast *was* like a f eagle. 4072
8:13 heard an angel f through the midst of 4072

FOAL (3) [FOALS]
Ge 49:11 Binding his f unto the vine, and his ass's 5895
Zec 9: 9 upon an ass, and upon a colt the f of an ass. 1121
Mt 21: 5 upon an ass, and a colt the f of an ass. 5207

FOALS (1) [FOAL]
Ge 32:15 and ten bulls, twenty she asses, and ten f. 5895

FOAM (1) [FOAMETH, FOAMING]
Hos 10: 7 her king is cut off as the f upon the water. 7110

FOAMETH (2) [FOAM]
Mk 9:18 and he f, and gnasheth with his teeth, and 875
Lk 9:39 and it teareth him that he f again, and 876+3326

FOAMING (2) [FOAM]
Mk 9:20 and he fell on the ground, and wallowed f. 875
Jude 1:13 waves of the sea, f out their own shame; 1890

FODDER (1)
Job 6: 5 he hath grass? or loweth the ox over his f? 1098

FOES (7)
1Ch 21:12 three months to be destroyed before thy f, 6862
Est 9:16 slew of their f seventy and five thousand, 8130
Ps 27: 2 the wicked, *even* mine enemies and my f, 341
30: 1 and hast not made my f to rejoice over me. 341
89:23 I will beat down his f before his face, and 6862
Mt 10:36 And a man's f *shall be* they of his own 2190
Ac 2:35 Until I make thy f thy footstool. 2190

FOLD (9) [FOLDEN, FOLDETH, FOLDING, FOLDS, SHEEPFOLD, SHEEPFOLDS]
Isa 13:20 neither shall the shepherds make their f 7257
65:10 Sharon shall be a f of flocks, and the valley 5116
Eze 34:14 the high mountains of Israel shall their f be: 5116
34:14 there shall they lie in a good f, and *in* a fat 5116
Mic 2:12 as the flock in the midst of their f: 1699
Hab 3:17 the flock shall be cut off from the f, and 4356
Jn 10:16 other sheep I have, which are not of this f: 833
10:16 and there shall be one f, *and* one shepherd. 4167
Heb 1:12 And as a vesture shalt thou f them up, and 1667

FOLDEN (1) [FOLD]
Na 1:10 For while *they be* f together *as* thorns, and 5440

FOLDETH (1) [FOLD]
Ecc 4: 5 The fool f his hands together, and 2263

FOLDING (4) [FOLD]
1Ki 6:34 the two leaves of the one door *were* f, and 1550
6:34 and the two leaves of the other door *were* f. 1550
Pr 6:10 a little f of the hands to sleep: 2264
24:33 a little f of the hands to sleep: 2264

FOLDS (5) [FOLD]
Nu 32:24 for your little ones, and f for your sheep; 1448
32:36 fenced cities: and f for sheep. 1448
Ps 50: 9 out of thy house, *nor* he goats out of thy f. 4356
Jer 23: 3 and will bring them again to their f; 5116
Zep 2: 6 *and* cottages for shepherds, and f for flocks. 1448

FOLK (5) [FOLKS, KINSFOLK, KINSFOLKS]
Ge 33:15 Let me now leave with thee *some* of the f 5971
Pr 30:26 The conies *are but* a feeble f, yet make they 5971
Jer 51:58 the f in the fire, and they shall be weary. 3816
Mk 6: 5 that he laid *his* hands upon a few sick *f*, NIG
Jn 5: 3 In these lay a great multitude of impotent *f*, NIG

FOLKS (1) [FOLK]
Ac 5:16 bringing sick *f*, and *them which were* vexed NIG

FOLLOW (86) [FOLLOWED, FOLLOWEDST, FOLLOWERS, FOLLOWETH, FOLLOWING]
Ge 24: 5 not be willing to f me unto this land: 310+1980
24: 8 if the woman will not be willing to f 310+1980
24:39 the woman will not f me. 310+1980
44: 4 said unto his steward, Up, f after the men; 7291
Ex 11: 8 and all the people that f thee: 7272+871.1
14: 4 Pharaoh's heart, that he shall f after them; 7291
14:17 of the Egyptians, and they shall f them: 310+935
21:22 fruit depart *from her*, and yet no mischief f: 1961
21:23 if *any* mischief f, then thou shalt give life 1961
23: 2 Thou shalt not f a multitude to *do* 310+1961
Dt 16:20 That which is altogether just shalt thou f, 7291
18:22 if the thing f not, nor come to pass, that *is* 1961
Jdg 3:28 he said unto them, F after me: for 7291
8: 5 of bread unto the people that f me; 7272+871.1
9: 3 their hearts inclined to f Abimelech; for they 310
1Sa 25:27 the young men that f my lord. 1980+7272+871.1
30:21 so faint that they could not f David, 310+1980
2Sa 17: 9 There is a slaughter among the people that f 310
1Ki 18:21 if the LORD *be* God, f him: but 310+1980
1Ki 18:21 if Baal, *then* f him. And the people 310+1980
19:20 and my mother, and *then* I will f thee. 310+1980
20:10 handfuls for all the people that f me. 7272+871.1
2Ki 6:19 f me, and I will bring you to the man 310+1980
Ps 23: 6 mercy shall f me all the days of my life: 7291
38:20 because I f *the thing that* good *is*. 7291
45:14 the virgins her companions that f her *shall be* 310
94:15 and all the upright in heart shall f it. 310
119:150 They draw nigh that f after mischief: 7291
Isa 5:11 the morning, *that* they may f strong drink; 7291
51: 1 to me, ye that f after righteousness, 7291
Jer 17:16 I have not hastened from *being* a pastor to f 310
42:16 shall f close after you there *in* Egypt; 1692
Eze 13: 3 that f their own spirit, and have seen 310+1980
Hos 2: 7 she shall f after her lovers, but she shall 7291
6: 3 we know, *if* we f on to know the LORD: 7291
Mt 4:19 F me, and I will make you fishers of 1205+3694
8:19 I will f thee whithersoever thou goest. 190
8:22 But Jesus said unto him, F me; and let 190
9: 9 and he saith unto him, F me. And he arose, 190
16:24 and take up his cross, and f me. 190
19:21 have treasure in heaven: and come *and* f me. 190
Mk 2:14 receipt of custom, and said unto him, F me. 190
5:37 And he suffered no *man* to f him, 4870
6: 1 into his own country; and his disciples f him. 190
8:34 and take up his cross, and f me. 190
10:21 and come, take up the cross, and f me. 190
14:13 you a man bearing a pitcher of water: f him. 190
16:17 And these signs shall f them that believe; 3877
Lk 5:27 of custom: and he said unto him, F me. 190
9:23 and take up his cross daily, and f me. 190
9:57 Lord, I will f thee whithersoever thou goest. 190
9:59 And he said unto another, F me. But he said, 190
9:61 And another also said, Lord, I will f thee; but 190
17:23 or, see there: go not after *them*, nor f *them*. 1377
18:22 have treasure in heaven: and come, f me. 190
22:10 f him into the house where he entereth in. 190
22:49 which were about him saw what would f, 1510
Jn 1:43 and findeth Philip, and saith unto him, F me. 190
10: 4 he goeth before them, and the sheep f him: 190
10: 5 And a stranger will they not f, but will flee 190
10:27 my voice, and I know them, and they f me: 190
12:26 If any *man* serve me, let him f me; and 190
13:36 Whither I go, thou canst not f me now; 190
13:36 me now; but thou shalt f me afterwards. 190
13:37 unto him, Lord, why cannot I f thee now? 190
21:19 he had spoken this, he saith unto him, F me. 190
21:22 till I come, what *is that* to thee? f thou me. 190
Ac 3:24 from Samuel and those that f after, 2517
12: 8 Cast thy garment about thee, and f me. 190
Ro 14:19 f *after* the *things* which make for peace, 1377
1Co 14: 1 F after charity, and desire spiritual *gifts*, 1377
Php 3:12 I f *after*, if that I may apprehend *that* for 1377
1Th 5:15 any *man*; but ever f *that which is* good, 1377
2Th 3: 7 For yourselves know how *ye* ought to f us: 3401
3: 9 ourselves an ensample unto you to f us. 3401
1Ti 5:24 to judgment; and some *men* they f after. 1872
6:11 flee these *things*; and f *after* righteousness, 1377
2Ti 2:22 but f righteousness, faith, charity, peace, 1377
Heb 12:14 F peace with all *men*, and holiness, 1377
13: 7 whose faith f, considering the end of *their* 3401
1Pe 1:11 and the glory that should f. 3326+3778
2:21 us an example, that ye should f his steps: 1872
2Pe 2: 2 And many shall f their pernicious ways; 1811
3Jn 1:11 f not *that which is* evil, but *that which is* 3401
Rev 14: 4 These are they which f the Lamb 190
14:13 their labours; and their works do f them. 190

FOLLOWED (108) [FOLLOW]
Ge 24:61 rode upon the camels, and f the man: 310+1980
32:19 and all that f the droves, saying, 310+1980
Nu 14:24 another spirit with him, and hath f me fully, 310
16:25 Abiram; and the elders of Israel f him. 310+1980
32:11 because they have not wholly f me: 310
32:12 of Nun: for they have wholly f the LORD. 310
Dt 1:36 because he hath wholly f the LORD. 310
4: 3 for all the men that f Baal-peor, 310+1980
Jos 6: 8 of the covenant of the LORD f them. 310+1980
14: 8 but I wholly f the LORD my God. 310
14: 9 thou hast wholly f the LORD my God. 310
14:14 that he wholly f the LORD God of Israel. 310
Jdg 2:12 of the land of Egypt, and f other gods, 310+1980
9: 4 and light persons, which f him. 310+1980
9:49 f Abimelech, and put *them* to the hold, 310+1980
1Sa 13: 7 in Gilgal, and all the people f him trembling. 310
14:22 even they also f hard after them in 1692
17:13 of Jesse went *and* f Saul to the battle: 310+1980
17:14 and the three eldest f Saul. 310+1980
31: 2 the Philistines f hard upon Saul and upon 1692
2Sa 1: 6 and horsemen f hard after him. 1692
2:10 But the house of Judah f David. 310+1961
3:31 And king David *himself* f the bier. 310+1980
11: 8 f him a mess *of meat* from the king. 310+3318
17:23 Ahithophel saw that his counsel was not f, 6213
20: 2 after David, *and* f Sheba the son of Bichri: 310
1Ki 12:20 there was none that f the house of David, but 310
14: 8 and who f me with all his heart, 310+1980
16:21 half of the people f Tibni the son of 310+1961
16:21 to make him king; and half f Omri. 310
16:22 the people that f Omri prevailed against 310
16:22 the people that f Tibni the son of Ginath: 310
18:18 the LORD, and thou hast f Baalim. 310+1980
20:19 out of the city, and the army which f them. 310
2Ki 3: 9 and for the cattle that f them. 7272+871.1
4:30 leave thee. And he arose, and f her. 310+1980
5:21 So Gehazi f after Naaman. And when 7291
9:27 Jehu f after him, and said, Smite him also 7291
13: 2 f the sins of Jeroboam the son of 310+1980
17:15 they f vanity, and became vain, and 310+1980
1Ch 10: 2 the Philistines f hard after Saul, and 1692
Ne 4:23 nor the men of the guard which f me, 310
Ps 68:25 the players on instruments *f* after; NIH
Eze 10:11 *to* the place whither the head looked they f 1980
Am 7:15 the LORD took me as I f the flock, and 310
Mt 4:20 they straightway left *their* nets, and f him. 190
Mt 4:22 left the ship and their father, and f him. 190
4:25 And there f him great multitudes *of people* 190
8: 1 from the mountain, great multitudes f him. 190
8:10 and said to them that f, Verily I say unto 190
8:23 was entered into a ship, his disciples f him. 190
9: 9 Follow me. And he arose, and f him. 190
9:19 and f him, and *so did* his disciples. 190
9:27 two blind men f him, crying, and saying, 190
12:15 and great multitudes f him, and he healed 190
14:13 when the people had heard *thereof*, they f 190
19: 2 And great multitudes f him; and he healed 190
19:27 Behold, we have forsaken all, and f thee; 190
19:28 That ye which have f me, in 190
20:29 from Jericho, a great multitude f him. 190
20:34 their eyes received sight, and they f him. 190
21: 9 and that f, cried, saying, Hosanna to the Son 190
26:58 But Peter f him afar off unto the high priest's 190
27:55 which f Jesus from Galilee, ministering unto 190
27:62 that f the *day of the* preparation, 1510+3326
Mk 1:18 they forsook their nets, and f him. 190
1:36 and they that were with him f after him. 2614
2:14 Follow me. And he arose and f him. 190
2:15 for there were many, and they f him. 190
3: 7 and a great multitude from Galilee f him, 190
5:24 and much people f him, and thronged him. 190
10:28 Lo, we have left all, and have f thee. 190
10:32 and as they f, they were afraid. 190
10:52 he received his sight, and f Jesus in the way. 190
11: 9 and they that f, cried, saying, Hosanna; 190
14:51 And there f him a certain young man, 190
14:54 And Peter f him afar off, even into 190
15:41 in Galilee, f him, and ministered unto him;) 190
Lk 5:11 ships to land, they forsook all, and f him. 190
5:28 And he left all, rose up, and f him. 190
7: 9 and said unto the people that f him, 190
9:11 And the people, when they knew *it*, f him: 190
18:28 Peter said, Lo, we have left all, and f thee. 190
18:43 received his sight, and f him, glorifying God: 190
22:39 of Olives; and his disciples also f him. 190
22:54 the high priest's house. And Peter f afar off. 190
23:27 And there f him a great company of people, 190
23:49 and the women that f him from Galilee, 4870
23:55 f after, and beheld the sepulchre, and 2628
Jn 1:37 disciples heard him speak, and they f Jesus. 190
1:40 and f him, was Andrew, Simon Peter's 190
6: 2 And a great multitude f him, because 190
11:31 rose up hastily and went out, f her, saying, 190
18:15 And Simon Peter f Jesus, and *so did* another 190
Ac 12: 9 And he went out, and f him; and wist not 190
13:43 and religious proselytes f Paul and Barnabas: 190
16:17 The same f Paul and us, and cried, saying, 2628
21:36 For the multitude of the people f *after*, 190
Ro 9:30 which f not *after* righteousness, 1377
9:31 which f *after* the law of righteousness, 1377
1Co 10: 4 for they drank of *that* spiritual Rock that f 190
1Ti 5:10 if she have diligently f every good work. 1872
2Pe 1:16 For we have not f cunningly devised fables, 1811
Rev 6: 8 sat on him *was* Death, and Hell f with him. 190
8: 7 and there f hail and fire mingled with 1096
14: 8 And there f another angel, saying, 190
14: 9 And *the* third angel f them, saying with a 190
19:14 And the armies which were in heaven f him 190

FOLLOWEDST (1) [FOLLOW]
Ru 3:10 inasmuch as *thou* f not young men, 310+1980

FOLLOWERS (8) [FOLLOW]
1Co 4:16 Wherefore I beseech you, be ye f of me. 3402
11: 1 Be ye f of me, even as I also *am* of Christ. 3402
Eph 5: 1 Be ye therefore f of God, as dear children; 3402
Php 3:17 be f together of me, and mark them which 4831
1Th 1: 6 And ye became f of us, and of the Lord, 3402
2:14 became f of the churches of God which in 3402
Heb 6:12 but f of them who through faith and 3402
1Pe 3:13 harm you, if ye be f of *that which is* good? 3402

FOLLOWETH (15) [FOLLOW]
2Ki 11:15 him that f her kill with the sword. 310+935
2Ch 23:14 whoso f her, let him be slain with 310+935
Ps 63: 8 My soul f hard after thee: thy right hand 1692
Pr 12:11 he that f vain *persons is* void of 7291
15: 9 he loveth him that f after righteousness. 7291
21:21 He that f after righteousness and 7291
28:19 he that f after vain persons shall have 7291
Isa 1:23 every one loveth gifts, and f after rewards: 7291
Eze 16:34 whereas none f thee to commit whoredoms: 310
Hos 12: 1 feedeth on wind, and f after the east wind: 7291
Mt 10:38 and f after me, is not worthy of me. 190
Mk 9:38 out devils in thy name, and he f not us: 190
9:38 and we forbad him, because he f not us. 190
Lk 9:49 and we forbad him, because he f not with us. 190
Jn 8:12 he that f me shall not walk in darkness, but 190

FOLLOWING (43) [FOLLOW]
Ge 41:31 in the land by reason of that famine f; 310+3651
Dt 7: 4 For they will turn away thy son from f me, 310
12:30 to thyself that thou be not snared by f them, 310
Jos 22:16 to turn away *this* day from f the LORD, 310
22:18 that ye must turn away *this* day from f 310
22:23 That we have built us an altar to turn from f 310
22:29 turn *this* day from f the LORD, to build an 310
Jdg 2:19 in f other gods to serve them, and 310+1980
Ru 1:16 to leave thee, *or* to return from f after thee: 310
1Sa 12:14 over you continue f the LORD your God: 310
12:20 yet turn not aside from f the LORD, but 310
14:46 Saul went up from f the Philistines: and 310
15:11 for he is turned back from f me, and hath not 310
24: 1 when Saul was returned from f 310
2Sa 2:19 to the right hand nor to the left from f Abner. 310
2:21 Asahel would not turn aside from f of him. 310
2:22 again to Asahel, Turn thee aside from f me: 310
2:26 ere thou bid the people return from f their 310
2:27 had gone up every one from f his brother. 310
2:30 Joab returned from f Abner: and when he 310

2Sa 7: 8 from f the sheep, to be ruler over my people, 310
1Ki 1: 7 the priest: and they f Adonijah helped *him.* 310
9: 6 *But* if you shall at all turn from f me, you or 310
21:26 he did very abominably in f idols, 310+1980
2Ki 17:21 Jeroboam drave Israel from f the LORD, 310
18: 6 *and* departed not from f him, but kept his 310
1Ch 17: 7 from the sheepcote, *even* from f the sheep, 310
2Ch 25:27 f the LORD they made a conspiracy against 310
34:33 *And* all his days they departed not from f 310
Ps 48:13 that ye may tell *it* to the generation f. 314
78:71 From f the *ewes* great with young he brought 310
109:13 in the generation f let their name be blotted 312
Mk 16:20 and confirming the word with signs f. *1872*
Lk 13:33 walk to day, and to morrow, and the *day* f: *2192*
Jn 1:38 and saw them f, and saith unto them, *190*
1:43 The **day** f Jesus would go forth into *1887*
6:22 The **day** f, when the people which stood on *1887*
20: 6 Then cometh Simon Peter f him, and *190*
21:20 seeth the disciple whom Jesus loved f; *190*
Ac 21: 1 and the *day* f unto Rhodes, and from thence *1836*
21:18 And the *day* f Paul went in with us unto *1966*
23:11 And the night f the Lord stood by him, and *1966*
2Pe 2:15 f the way of Balaam *the son* of Bosor, *1811*

FOLLY (37) [FOOL]

Ge 34: 7 he had wrought f in Israel in lying with 5039
Dt 22:21 because she hath wrought f in Israel, 5039
Jos 7:15 and because he hath wrought f in Israel. 5039
Jdg 19:23 man is come into mine house, do not this f. 5039
20: 6 have committed lewdness and f in Israel. 5039
20:10 according to all the f that they have 5039
1Sa 25:25 *is* he; Nabal *is* his name, and f *is* with him: 5039
2Sa 13:12 to be done in Israel: do not thou this f. 5039
Job 4:18 and his angels he charged with f: 8417
24:12 crieth out: yet God layeth not f *to them.* 8604
42: 8 lest *I* deal with you *after your* f, in that ye 5039
Ps 49:13 This their way *is* their f: yet their posterity 3689
85: 8 his saints: but let them not turn *again* to f. 3690
Pr 5:23 in the greatness of his f he shall go astray. 200
13:16 with knowledge: but a fool layeth open *his* f. 200
14: 8 his way: but the f of fools *is* deceit. 200
14:18 The simple inherit f: but the prudent are 200
14:24 their riches: *but* the foolishness of fools *is* f. 200
14:29 but *he that is* hasty of spirit exalteth f. 200
15:21 F *is* joy to *him that is* destitute of wisdom: 200
16:22 that hath it: but the instruction of fools *is* f. 200
17:12 meet a man, rather than a fool in his f. 200
18:13 a matter before he heareth *it,* it *is* f 200
26: 4 Answer not a fool according to his f, 200
26: 5 Answer a fool according to his f, lest he be 200
26:11 to his vomit, *so* a fool returneth to his f. 200
Ecc 1:17 know wisdom, and to know madness and f: 5531
2: 3 to lay hold on f, till I might see what *was* 5531
2:12 to behold wisdom, and madness, and f: 5531
2:13 I saw that wisdom excelleth f, as far as 5531
7:25 *of things,* and to know the wickedness of f, 3689
10: 1 *doth* a little f *him that is* in reputation for 5531
10: 6 F is set in great dignity, and the rich sit in 5529
Isa 9:17 an evildoer, and every mouth speaketh f. 5039
Jer 23:13 I have seen f in the prophets of Samaria; 8604
2Co 11: 1 *God* you could bear with me a little in *my* f: *877*
2Ti 3: 9 for their f shall be manifest unto all *men,* as *454*

FOOD (55) [FEED]

Ge 2: 9 that is pleasant to the sight, and good for f; 3978
3: 6 the woman saw that the tree *was* good for f, 3978
6:21 take thou unto thee of all f that is eaten, 3978
6:21 and it shall be for f for thee, and for them. 402
41:35 let them gather all the f of those good years 400
41:35 of Pharaoh, and let them keep f in the cities. 400
41:36 *that* f shall be for store to the land against 400
41:48 he gathered up all the f of the seven years, 400
41:48 land of Egypt, and laid up the f in the cities: 400
41:48 the f of the field, which *was* round about 400
42: 7 they said, From the land of Canaan to buy f. 400
42:10 my lord, but to buy f are thy servants come. 400
42:33 take *f for* the famine of your households, NIH
43: 2 said unto them, Go again, buy us a little f. 400
43: 4 with us, we will go down and buy thee f: 400
43:20 came indeed down at the first time to buy f: 400
43:22 have we brought down in our hands to buy f: 400
44: 1 saying, Fill the men's sacks *with* f, as much 400
44:25 father said, Go again, *and* buy us a little f. 400
47:24 for your f, and for them of your households, 400
47:24 and for f for your little ones. 398
Ex 21:10 If he take him another *wife;* her f, 7607
Lev 3:11 *it is* the f of the offering made by fire unto 3899
3:16 *it is* the f of the offering made by fire for a 3899
19:23 shall have planted all *manner of* trees for f, 3978
22: 7 eat of the holy *things;* because it *is* his f. 3899
Dt 10:18 the stranger, in giving him f and raiment. 3899
1Sa 14:24 Cursed *be* the man that eateth *any* f until 3899
14:24 So none of the people tasted *any* f. 3899
14:28 Cursed *be* the man that eateth *any* f *this* 3899
2Sa 9:10 that thy master's son may have f to eat: 3899
1Ki 5: 9 my desire, in giving f for my household. 3899
5:11 measures of wheat *for* f to his household, 4361
Job 23:12 of his mouth more than my necessary *f.* NIH
24: 5 the wilderness *yieldeth* f for them *and* 3899
38:41 Who provideth for the raven his f? 6718
40:20 Surely the mountains bring him forth f, 944
Ps 78:25 Man did eat angels' f: he sent them meat to 3899
104:14 that *he* may bring forth f out of the earth; 3899
136:25 Who giveth f to all flesh: for his mercy 3899
146: 7 which giveth f to the hungry. The LORD 3899
147: 9 He giveth to the beast his f, *and* to 3899
Pr 6: 8 *and* gathereth her f in the harvest. 3978
13:23 Much f *is in* the tillage of the poor: but 400
27:27 *shalt have* goats' milk enough for thy f, 3899
27:27 for the f of thy household, and *for* 3899
28: 3 *is like* a sweeping rain which leaveth no f. 3899
30: 8 feed me with f convenient for me: 3899
31:14 she bringeth her f from afar. 3899
Eze 16:27 have diminished thine ordinary *f,* and NIH
48:18 the increase thereof shall be for f unto them 3899
Ac 14:17 filling our hearts with f and gladness. *5160*
2Co 9:10 to the sower both minister bread for *your* f, *1035*
1Ti 6: 8 And having f and raiment let us be *1305*
Jas 2:15 or sister be naked, and destitute of daily f, *5160*

FOOL (66) [FOLLY, FOOL'S, FOOLISH, FOOLISHLY, FOOLISHNESS, FOOLS, FOOLS']

1Sa 26:21 I have **played the f**, and have erred 5528
2Sa 3:33 and said, Died Abner as a f dieth? 5036
Ps 14: 1 The f hath said in his heart, *There is* no 5036
49:10 likewise the f and the brutish person perish, 3684
53: 1 The f hath said in his heart, *There is* no 5036
92: 6 neither doth a f understand this. 3684
Pr 7:22 or as a f to the correction of the stocks; 191
10: 8 but a prating f shall fall. 191
10:10 eye causeth sorrow: but a prating f shall fall. 191
10:18 and he that uttereth a slander, *is* a f. 3684
10:23 *It is* as sport to a f to do mischief: but a 3684
11:29 the f *shall be* servant to the wise of heart. 191
12:15 The way of a f *is* right in his own eyes: but 191
13:16 but a f layeth open *his* folly. 3684
14:16 from evil: but the f rageth, and *is* confident. 3684
15: 5 A f despiseth his father's instruction: but 191
17: 7 Excellent speech becometh not a f: 5036
17:10 a wise *man* than an hundred stripes into a f. 3684
17:12 meet a man, rather than a f in his folly. 3684
17:16 Wherefore *is there* a price in the hand of a f 3684
17:21 He that begetteth a f *doeth* it to his sorrow: 3684
17:21 his sorrow: and the father of a f hath no joy. 5036
17:24 the eyes of a f *are* in the ends of the earth. 3684
17:28 Even a f, when he holdeth his peace, 191
18: 2 A f hath no delight in understanding, but 3684
19: 1 *he that is* perverse in his lips, and *is* a f. 3684
19:10 Delight *is* not seemly for a f; much less for 3684
20: 3 from strife: but every f will be meddling. 191
23: 9 Speak not in the ears of a f: for he will 3684
24: 7 Wisdom *is too* high for a f: he openeth not 191
26: 1 in harvest, so honour *is* not seemly for a f. 3684
26: 4 Answer not a f according to his folly, 3684
26: 5 Answer a f according to his folly, lest he be 3684
26: 6 by the hand of a f cutteth off the feet, 3684
26: 8 in a sling, so *is* he that giveth honour to a f. 3684
26:10 that formed all *things* both rewardeth the f, 3684
26:11 to his vomit, *so* a f returneth to his folly. 3684
26:12 *there is* more hope of a f than of him. 3684
27:22 Though thou shouldest bray a f in a mortar 191
28:26 He that trusteth in his own heart *is* a f: but 3684
29:11 A f uttereth all his mind: but a wise *man* 3684
29:20 *there is* more hope of a f than of him. 3684
30:22 and a f when he is filled *with* meat; 5036
Ecc 2:14 in his head; but the f walketh in darkness: 3684
2:15 As it happeneth to the f, so it happeneth 3684
2:16 of the wise more than of the f for ever; 3684
2:16 And how dieth the wise *man? as* the f. 3684
2:19 whether he shall be a wise *man* or a f? 5530
4: 5 The f foldeth his hands together, and 3684
6: 8 For what hath the wise more than the f? 3684
7: 6 under a pot, so *is* the laughter of the f: 3684
10: 3 when he that is a f walketh by the way, 5530
10: 3 and he saith to every one *that* he *is* a f. 5530
10:12 but the lips of a f will swallow up himself. 3684
10:14 A f also is full of words: a man cannot tell 5530
Jer 17:11 of his days, and at his end shall be a f. 5036
Hos 9: 7 Israel shall know *it:* the prophet *is* a f, 191
Mt 5:22 but whosoever shall say, *Thou* f, shall be in *3474*
Lk 12:20 But God said unto him, *Thou* f, this night *878*
1Co 3:18 let him become a f, that he may be wise. *3474*
15:36 *Thou* f, *that* which thou sowest is not *878*
2Co 11:16 I say again, Let no *man* think me a f; *878*
11:16 if otherwise, yet as a f receive me, that I may *878*
11:23 (I speak as a f) I *am* more; in labours more *3912*
12: 6 I would desire to glory, I shall not be a f; *878*
12:11 I am become a f in glorying; ye have *878*

FOOL'S (6) [FOOL]

Pr 12:16 A f wrath is presently known: but a prudent 191
18: 6 A f lips enter into contention, and 3684
18: 7 A f mouth *is* his destruction, and his lips 3684
27: 3 but a f wrath *is* heavier than them both. 191
Ecc 5: 3 a f voice *is known* by multitude of words. 3684
10: 2 *is* at his right hand; but a f heart at his left. 3684

FOOLISH (52) [FOOL]

Dt 32: 6 the LORD, O f people and unwise? 5036
32:21 I will provoke them to anger with a f 5036
Job 2:10 Thou speakest as one of the f *women* 5036
5: 2 For wrath killeth the f **man**, and 191
5: 3 I have seen the f taking root: but suddenly I 191
Ps 5: 5 The f shall not stand in thy sight: 1984
39: 8 make me not the reproach of the f. 5036
73: 3 For I was envious at the f, *when* I saw 1984
73:22 So f *was* I, and ignorant: I was *as* a beast 1198
74:18 *that* the f people have blasphemed thy 5036
74:22 remember how the f *man* reproacheth thee 5036
Pr 9: 6 Forsake the f, and live; and go in the way 6612
9:13 A f woman *is* clamorous: *she is* simple, and 3687
10: 1 but a f son *is* the heaviness of his mother. 3684
10:14 but the mouth of the f *is* near destruction. 191
14: 1 but the f plucketh it down with her hands. 200
14: 3 In the mouth of the f *is* a rod of pride: but 191
14: 7 Go from the presence of a f man, 3684
15: 7 but the heart of the f *doeth* not so. 3684
15:20 but a f man despiseth his mother. 3684
17:25 A f son *is* a grief to his father, and 3684
19:13 A f son *is* the calamity of his father: and 3684
21:20 of the wise; but a f man spendeth it up. 3684
29: 9 If a wise man contendeth with a f man, 191
Ecc 4:13 and a wise child than an old and f king, 3684
7:17 not over much wicked, neither be thou f: 5530
10:15 The labour of the f wearieth every one of 3684
Isa 44:25 and **maketh** their knowledge f; 5528
Jer 4:22 For my people *is* f, they have not known me; 191
5: 4 I said, Surely these *are* poor; they are f: 2973
5:21 O f people, and without understanding; 5530
Jer 10: 8 they are altogether brutish and f: the stock 3688
La 2:14 have seen vain and f **things** for thee: 8602
Eze 13: 3 Woe unto the f prophets, that follow their 5036
Zec 11:15 Take unto thee yet the instruments of a f 196
Mt 7:26 them not, shall be likened unto a f man, *3474*
25: 2 five of them were wise, and five *were* f. *3474*
25: 3 They that *were* f took their lamps, and *3474*
25: 8 And the f said unto the wise, Give us of *3474*
Ro 1:21 and their f heart was darkened. *801*
2:20 An instructor of the f, a teacher of babes, *878*
10:19 no people, *and* by a f nation I will anger you. *801*
1Co 1:20 hath not God **made** f the wisdom of this *3471*
1:27 But God hath chosen the f *things* of *3474*
Gal 3: 1 O f Galatians, who hath bewitched you, *453*
3: 3 Are ye so f? having begun in the Spirit, *453*
Eph 5: 4 Neither filthiness, nor f **talking**, nor jesting, *3473*
1Ti 6: 9 a snare, and *into* many f and hurtful lusts, *453*
2Ti 2:23 But f and unlearned questions avoid, *3474*
Tit 3: 3 For we ourselves also were sometimes f, *453*
3: 9 But avoid f questions, and genealogies, and *3474*
1Pe 2:15 *ye* may put to silence the ignorance of f men: *878*

FOOLISHLY (12) [FOOL]

Ge 31:28 thou hast now **done** f in *so* doing. 5528
Nu 12:11 wherein we have **done** f, and wherein we 2973
1Sa 13:13 And Samuel said to Saul, Thou hast **done** f: 5528
2Sa 24:10 of thy servant; for I have **done** very f. 5528
1Ch 21: 8 of thy servant; for I have **done** very f. 5528
2Ch 16: 9 Herein thou hast **done** f: therefore 5528
Job 1:22 all this Job sinned not, nor charged God f. 8604
Ps 75: 4 I said unto the fools, **Deal** not f: and to 1984
Pr 14:17 *He that is* soon angry dealeth f: and a man of 200
30:32 If thou hast **done** f in lifting up thyself, or 5034
2Co 11:17 *it* not after the Lord, but as *it were* f, 877+1722
11:21 whereinsoever any is bold, (I speak f,) 877+1722

FOOLISHNESS (20) [FOOL]

2Sa 15:31 **turn** the counsel of Ahithophel **into** f. 5528
Ps 38: 5 *and* are corrupt because of my f. 200
69: 5 O God, thou knowest my f; and my sins are 200
Pr 12:23 but the heart of fools proclaimeth f. 200
14:24 wise *is* their riches: *but* the f of fools *is* folly. 200
15: 2 but the mouth of fools poureth out f. 200
15:14 but the mouth of fools feedeth on f. 200
19: 3 The f of man perverteth his way: and 200
22:15 F *is* bound in the heart of a child; *but* the rod 200
24: 9 The thought of f *is* sin: and the scorner *is* an 200
27:22 a pestle, *yet* will not his f depart from him. 200
Ecc 7:25 wickedness of folly, even of f *and* madness: 5531
10:13 beginning of the words of his mouth *is* f: 5531
Mk 7:22 an evil eye, blasphemy, pride, f: *877*
1Co 1:18 of the cross is to them that perish f; *3472*
1:21 it pleased God by the f of preaching to save *3472*
1:23 a stumblingblock, and unto the Greeks f; *3472*
1:25 Because the f of God is wiser than men; *3474*
2:14 for they are f unto him: neither can he *3472*
3:19 For the wisdom of this world is f with God. *3472*

FOOLS (42) [FOOL]

2Sa 13:13 thou shalt be as one of the f in Israel. 5036
Job 12:17 away spoiled, and **maketh** the judges f. 1984
30: 8 *They were* children of f, yea, children of 5036
Ps 75: 4 I said unto the f, Deal not foolishly: and 1984
94: 8 the people: and ye f, when will ye be wise? 3684
107:17 F because of their transgression, and because 191
Pr 1: 7 *but* f despise wisdom and instruction. 191
1:22 in their scorning, and f hate knowledge? 3684
1:32 and the prosperity of f shall destroy them. 3684
3:35 but shame shall be the promotion of f. 3684
8: 5 and, ye f, be ye of an understanding heart. 3684
10:21 feed many: but f die for want of wisdom. 191
12:23 but the heart of f proclaimeth foolishness. 3684
13:19 *it is* abomination to f to depart from evil. 3684
13:20 but a companion of f shall be destroyed. 3684
14: 8 his way: but the folly of f *is* deceit. 3684
14: 9 F make a mock at sin: but among 191
14:24 their riches: *but* the foolishness of f *is* folly. 3684
14:33 *that which is* in the midst of f is made 3684
15: 2 but the mouth of f poureth out foolishness. 3684
15:14 but the mouth of f feedeth on foolishness. 3684
16:22 that hath it: but the instruction of f *is* folly. 191
19:29 for scorners, and stripes for the back of f. 3684
26: 7 not equal: so *is* a parable in the mouth of f. 3684
26: 9 so *is* a parable in the mouth of f. 3684
Ecc 5: 1 ready to hear, than to give the sacrifice of f: 3684
5: 4 not to pay it; for *he hath* no pleasure in f: 3684
7: 4 but the heart of f *is* in the house of mirth. 3684
7: 5 than for a man to hear the song of f. 3684
7: 9 for anger resteth in the bosom of f. 3684
9:17 than the cry of him that ruleth among f. 3684
Isa 19:11 Surely the princes of Zoan *are* f, the counsel 191
19:13 The princes of Zoan are become f, 2973
35: 8 the wayfaring men, though f, shall not err 191
Mt 23:17 *Ye* f and blind: for whether is greater, *3474*
23:19 *Ye* f and blind: for whether *is* greater, *3474*
Lk 11:40 *Ye* f, did not he that made that *which is* *878*
24:25 O f, and slow of heart to believe all that *453*
Ro 1:22 *themselves* to be wise, they became f, *3471*
1Co 4:10 We *are* f for Christ's sake, but ye *are* wise *3474*
2Co 11:19 For ye suffer f gladly, seeing ye *yourselves* *878*
Eph 5:15 ye walk circumspectly, not as f, but as wise, *781*

FOOLS' (1) [FOOL]

Pr 26: 3 a bridle for the ass, and a rod for the f back. 3684

FOOT (95) [AFOOT, BAREFOOT, BROKENFOOTED, CLOVENFOOTED, FEET, FOOTMEN, FOOTSTEPS, FOOTSTOOL, FOURFOOTED]

Ge 8: 9 the dove found no rest for the sole of her f, 7272
41:44 lift up his hand or f in all the land of Egypt. 7272
Ex 12:37 about six hundred thousand **on** f *that were* 7273
21:24 tooth for tooth, hand for hand, foot for f, 7272
21:24 tooth for tooth, hand for hand, foot for f, 7272

Ex 29:20 upon the great toe of their right **f**, and 7272
30:18 his **f** *also of* brass, to wash *withal*: and 3653
30:28 with all his vessels, and the laver and his **f**. 3653
31: 9 all his furniture, and the laver and his **f**, 3653
35:16 and all his vessels, the laver and his **f**, 3653
38: 8 the laver *of* brass, and the **f** of it *of* brass, 3653
39:39 and all his vessels, the laver and his **f**, 3653
40:11 thou shalt anoint the laver and his **f**, and 3653
Lev 8:11 and all his vessels, both the laver and his **f**, 3653
8:23 and upon the great toe of his right **f**. 7272
13:12 *hath* the plague from his head even to his **f**, 7272
14:14 and upon the great toe of his right **f**: 7272
14:17 and upon the great toe of his right **f**, 7272
14:25 and upon the great toe of his right **f**: 7272
14:28 and upon the great toe of his right **f**, 7272
Nu 22:25 and crusht Balaam's **f** against the wall: 7272
Dt 2: 5 no, not so much as a **f** breadth; 3709+7272
8: 4 neither did thy **f** swell, these forty years. 7272
11:10 wateredst *it* with thy **f**, as a garden of herbs: 7272
19:21 tooth for tooth, hand for hand, **f** for foot. 7272
19:21 tooth for tooth, hand for hand, foot for **f**. 7272
25: 9 loose his shoe from off his **f**, and spit in his 7272
28:35 from the sole of thy **f** unto the top of thy 7272
28:56 of her **f** upon the ground for delicateness 7272
28:65 neither shall the sole of thy **f** have rest: 7272
29: 5 and thy shoe is not waxen old upon thy **f**. 7272
32:35 recompence; their **f** shall slide in *due* time: 7272
33:24 to his brethren, and let him dip his **f** in oil. 7272
Jos 1: 3 Every place that the sole of your **f** shall 7272
5:15 unto Joshua, Loose thy shoe from off thy **f**; 7272
Jdg 5:15 he was sent on **f** into the valley. For 7272
2Sa 2:18 and Asahel *was as* light of **f** as a wild roe. 7272
14:25 from the sole of his **f** even to the crown of 7272
21:20 on every **f** six toes, four and twenty *in* 7272
2Ki 9:33 on the horses: and he **trode** her **under f**. 7429
1Ch 20: 6 six *on each hand,* and six *on each f,* and NIH
2Ch 33: 8 Neither will I any more remove the **f** of 7272
Job 2: 7 boils from the sole of his **f** unto his crown. 7272
23:11 My **f** hath held his steps, his way have I 7272
28: 4 *even the waters* forgotten of the **f**: 7272
31: 5 with vanity, or *if* my **f** hath hasted to deceit; 7272
39:15 forgetteth that the **f** may crush them, or 7272
Ps 9:15 in the net which they hid is their own **f** 7272
26:12 My **f** standeth in an even place: in 7272
36:11 Let not the **f** of pride come against me, and 7272
38:16 when my **f** slippeth, they magnify 7272
66: 6 dry *land:* they went through the flood on **f**: 7272
68:23 That thy **f** may be dipped in the blood of 7272
91:12 lest thou dash thy **f** against a stone. 7272
94:18 When I said, My **f** slippeth; thy mercy, 7272
121: 3 He will not suffer thy **f** to be moved: 7272
Pr 1:15 with them; refrain thy **f** from their path: 7272
3:23 thy way safely, and thy **f** shall not stumble. 7272
3:26 and shall keep thy **f** from being taken. 7272
4:27 hand nor *to* the left: remove thy **f** from evil. 7272
25:17 Withdraw thy **f** from thy neighbour's 7272
25:19 *is like* a broken tooth, and a **f** out of joint. 7272
Ecc 5: 1 Keep thy **f** when thou goest to the house of 7272
Isa 1: 6 From the sole of the **f** even unto the head 7272
14:25 and upon my mountains **tread** him **under f**: 947
18: 7 a nation meted out and **trodden under f**, 4001
20: 2 thy loins, and put off thy shoe from thy **f**. 7272
26: 6 The **f** shall tread it down, *even* the feet of 7272
41: 2 called him to his **f**, gave the nations before 7272
58:13 If thou turn away thy **f** from the sabbath, 7272
Jer 2:25 Withhold thy **f** from being unshod, and 7272
12:10 they have **trodden** my portion **under f**, 947
La 1:15 The Lord hath **trodden under f** all my 5541
Eze 1: 7 of their feet *was* like the sole of a calf's **f**: 7272
6:11 thine hand, and stamp with thy **f**, and say, 7272
29:11 No **f** of man shall pass through it, nor foot 7272
29:11 nor **f** of beast shall pass through it, 7272
32:13 neither shall the **f** of man trouble them any 7272
Da 8:13 and the host to be **trodden under f**? 4823
Am 2:15 *he that is* swift of **f** shall not deliver 7272
Mt 4: 6 lest at any time thou dash thy **f** against a *4228*
5:13 cast out, and to be **trodden under f** of men. *2662*
14:13 they followed him **on f** out of the cities. *3979*
18: 8 Wherefore if thy hand or thy **f** offend thee, *4228*
22:13 Bind him hand and **f**, and take him away, *4228*
Mk 9:45 And if thy **f** offend thee, cut it off: it is *4228*
Lk 4:11 lest at any time thou dash thy **f** against a *4228*
Jn 11:44 bound hand and **f** with graveclothes: *4228*
Ac 7: 5 in it, no, not so much as to set his **f** on: *4228*
1Co 12:15 If the **f** shall say, Because I am not *4228*
Heb 10:29 who hath **trodden under f** the Son of God, *2662*
Rev 1:13 clothed with a garment **down to the f**, and *4158*
10: 2 and he set his right **f** upon the sea, and *4228*
10: 2 foot upon the sea, and *his* left *f* on the earth, NIG
11: 2 the holy city shall they **tread under f** forty *3961*

FOOTHILLS See VALE

FOOTMEN (12) [FOOT, MAN]
Nu 11:21 whom I *am, are* six hundred thousand **f**; 7273
Jdg 20: 2 hundred thousand **f** that drew sword. 376+7273
1Sa 4:10 for there fell of Israel thirty thousand **f**. 7273
15: 4 two hundred thousand **f**, and ten thousand 7273
22:17 the king said unto the **f** that stood about 7323
2Sa 8: 4 and twenty thousand **f**: 376+7273
10: 6 twenty thousand **f**, and of king Maacah a 7273
1Ki 20:29 Syrians an hundred thousand **f** in one day. 7273
2Ki 13: 7 and ten chariots, and ten thousand **f**; 7273
1Ch 18: 4 and twenty thousand **f**: 376+7273
19:18 forty thousand **f**, and killed Shophach 376+7273
Jer 12: 5 If thou hast run with the **f**, and they have 7273

FOOTSTEPS (4) [FOOT, STEP]
Ps 17: 5 my goings in thy paths, *that* my **f** slip not. 6471
77:19 the great waters, and thy **f** are not known 6119
89:51 wherewith they have reproached the **f** of 6119
SS 1: 8 go thy way forth by the **f** of the flock, and 6119

FOOTSTOOL (16) [FOOT, STOOL]
1Ch 28: 2 for the **f** of our God, and had made 1916+7272
2Ch 9:18 with a **f** of gold, *which were* fastened to 3534
Ps 99: 5 our God, and worship at his **f**; 1916+7272
110: 1 I make thine enemies thy **f**. 1916+7272+3807.1
132: 7 we will worship at his **f**. 1916+7272
Isa 66: 1 *is* my throne, and the earth *is* my **f**: 1916+7272
La 2: 1 remembered not his **f** in the day of 1916+7272
Mt 5:35 Nor by the earth; for it is his **f**: neither by *5286*
22:44 right hand, till I make thine enemies thy **f**? *5286*
Mk 12:36 right hand, till I make thine enemies thy **f**. *5286*
Lk 20:43 Till I make thine enemies thy **f**. *5286*
Ac 2:35 Until I make thy foes thy **f**. *5286*
7:49 Heaven *is* my throne, and earth *is* my **f**: *5286*
Heb 1:13 until I make thine enemies thy **f**? *5286*
10:13 expecting till his enemies be made his **f**. *5286*
Jas 2: 3 Stand thou there, or sit here under my **f**: *5286*

FOR (8985) [FORASMUCH, FORSOMUCH] See Index of Articles, Etc.

FORAGING See BETIMES

FORASMUCH (42) [AS, FOR, MUCH]
Ge 41:39 **F as** God hath shewed thee all this, *there is* 310
Nu 10:31 **f as** thou knowest how we are 3588+3651+5921
Dt 12:12 **f as** he hath no part nor inheritance with 3588
17:16 **f as** the LORD hath said unto you, 2050.1
Jos 17:14 **f as** the LORD hath blessed me 834+5704
Jdg 11:36 **f as** the LORD hath taken vengeance for 310
1Sa 20:42 **f as** we have sworn both of us in the name of 834
24:18 **f as when** the LORD had delivered me into 834
2Sa 19:30 **f as** my lord the king is come *again* in peace 310
1Ki 11:11 **F as** this is done of thee, and thou hast 834+3282
13:21 **F as** thou hast disobeyed the mouth 3282+3588
14: 7 **F as** I exalted thee from among 834+3282
16: 2 **F as** I exalted thee out of the dust, and 834+3282
2Ki 1:16 **F as** thou hast sent messengers to 834+3282
1Ch 5: 1 but, **f as** he defiled his father's bed, 871.1
2Ch 6: 8 **F as** it was in thine heart to build a 834+3282
Ezr 7:14 **F as** *thou art* sent of the king, 1768+3606+6903
Isa 29:13 **F as** this people draw near *me* with their 3588
Jer 10: 6 **F as** *there is* none like unto thee, 4480
10: 7 **f as** among all the wise *men* of the nations, 3588
Da 2:40 **f as** iron breaketh in pieces 1768+3606+6903
2:41 **f as** thou sawest the iron 1768+3606+6903
2:45 **f as** thou sawest that the stone 1768+3606+6903
4:18 **f as** all the wise *men* of my 1768+3606+6903
5:12 **F as** an excellent spirit, and 1768+3606+6903
6: 4 **f as** he *was* faithful, 1768+3606+6903
6:22 **f as** before him innocency was 1768+3606+6903
Am 5:11 **F** therefore as your treading *is* 3651+3807.1
Mt 18:25 But **f as** he had not to pay, his lord NIG
Lk 1: 1 **F as** many have taken in hand to set forth *1895*
Ac 9:38 **And f as** Lydda was nigh to Joppa, and *1161*
11:17 **F** then as God gave them the like gift as *he* *1487*
15:24 **F as** we have heard, that certain which *1894*
17:29 **F then** as we are the offspring of God, *3767*
24:10 **F as** I know that thou hast been of many NIG
1Co 11: 7 **f as** he is the image and glory of God: NIG
14:12 **f as** ye are zealous of spiritual *gifts*, seek *1893*
15:58 **f as** you know that your labour is not in vain NIG
2Co 3: 3 **F as** ye are manifestly declared to be NIG
Heb 2:14 **F** then as the children are partakers of flesh *1893*
1Pe 1:18 **F as** ye know that ye were not redeemed NIG
4: 1 **F then as** Christ hath suffered for us in *3767*

FORBAD (5) [FORBID]
Dt 2:37 nor *unto* whatsoever the LORD our God **f** 6680
Mt 3:14 But John **f** him, saying, I have need to be *1254*
Mk 9:38 and we **f** him, because he followeth not us. *2967*
Lk 9:49 and we **f** him, because he followeth not *2967*
2Pe 2:16 the dumb ass speaking with man's voice **f** *2967*

FORBARE (3) [FORBEAR]
1Sa 23:13 escaped from Keilah; and he **f** to go forth. 2308
2Ch 25:16 the prophet **f**, and said, I know that God 2308
Jer 41: 8 So he **f**, and slew them not among their 2308

FORBEAR (22) [FORBARE, FORBEARANCE, FORBEARETH, FORBEARING, FORBORN]
Ex 23: 5 wouldest **f** to help him, thou shalt surely 2308
Dt 23:22 if thou shalt **f** to vow, it shall be no sin in 2308
1Ki 22: 6 Ramoth-gilead to battle, or shall I **f**? 2308
22:15 Ramoth-gilead to battle, or shall we **f**? 2308
2Ch 18: 5 go to Ramoth-gilead to battle, or shall I **f**? 2308
18:14 go to Ramoth-gilead to battle, or shall I **f**? 2308
25:16 **f**; why shouldest thou be smitten? Then 2308
35:21 **f** thee from meddling with God, who *is* 2308
Ne 9:30 Yet many years didst thou **f** them, 4900+5921
Job 16: 6 and *though* I **f**, what am I eased? 2308
Pr 24:11 If thou **f** to deliver *them that are* drawn unto 2820
Jer 40: 4 unto thee to come with me *into* Babylon, **f**: 2308
Eze 2: 5 they will hear, or whether they will **f**, 2308
2: 7 they will hear, or whether they will **f**: 2308
3:11 they will hear, or whether they will **f**. 2308
3:27 him hear; and he that forbeareth, let him **f**: 2308
24:17 **F** to cry, make no mourning *for* the dead, 1826
Zec 11:12 think good, give *me* my price; and if not, **f**. 2308
1Co 9: 6 Barnabas, have not we power to **f** working? *3361*
2Co 12: 6 but *now* I **f**, lest any *man* should think of *5339*
1Th 3: 1 Wherefore when we could no longer **f**, *4722*
3: 5 For this cause, when I could no longer **f**, *4722*

FORBEARANCE (2) [FORBEAR]
Ro 2: 4 of his goodness and **f** and longsuffering; *463*
3:25 of sins that are past, through the **f** of God; *463*

FORBEARETH (2) [FORBEAR]
Nu 9:13 not in a journey, and **f** to keep the passover, 2308
Eze 3:27 let him hear; and he that **f**, let him forbear: 2310

FORBEARING (5) [FORBEAR]
Pr 25:15 By long **f** is a prince persuaded, and a soft 639
Jer 20: 9 I was weary with **f**, and I could not stay. 3557
Eph 4: 2 with longsuffering, **f** one another in love; *430*
6: 9 do the same *things* unto them, **f** threatening: *447*
Col 3:13 **F** one another, and forgiving one another, *430*

FORBID (37) [FORBAD, FORBIDDEN, FORBIDDETH, FORBIDDING]
Ge 44: 7 **God f** that thy servants should do according 2486
44:17 he said, **God f** that I should do so: *but* 2486
Nu 11:28 answered and said, My lord Moses, **f** them. 3607
Jos 22:29 **God f** that we should rebel against 2486
24:16 **God f** that we should forsake the LORD, 2486
1Sa 12:23 **God f** that I should sin against the LORD 2486
14:45 **God f**: *as* the LORD liveth, there shall not 2486
20: 2 he said unto him, **God f**; thou shalt not die: 2486
24: 6 The LORD **f** that I should do this thing 2486
26:11 The LORD **f** that *I* should stretch forth 2486
1Ki 21: 3 Naboth said to Ahab, The LORD **f** it me, 2486
1Ch 11:19 said, My God **f it** me, that *I* should do this 2486
Job 27: 5 **God f** that I should justify you: till I die I 2486
Mt 19:14 and **f** them not, to come unto me: *2967*
Mk 9:39 But Jesus said, **F** him not: for there is no *2967*
10:14 children to come unto me, and **f** them not: *2967*
Lk 6:29 him that taketh away thy cloke **f** not *to take* *2967*
9:50 And Jesus said unto him, **F** *him* not: for he *2967*
18:16 children to come unto me, and **f** them not: *2967*
20:16 when they heard *it*, they said, **God f**. *1096+3361*
Ac 10:47 Can any *man* **f** water, that these should not *2967*
24:23 that *he* should **f** none of his acquaintance to *2967*
Ro 3: 4 **God f**: yea, let God be true, but *1096+3361*
3: 6 **God f**: for then how shall God judge *1096+3361*
3:31 **God f**: yea, we establish the law. *1096+3361*
6: 2 **God f**. How shall we, that are dead *1096+3361*
6:15 the law, but under grace? **God f**. *1096+3361*
7: 7 **God f**. Nay, I had not known sin, but *1096+3361*
7:13 **God f**. But sin, that it might appear *1096+3361*
9:14 unrighteousness with God? **God f**. *1096+3361*
11: 1 **God f**. For I also am an Israelite, *1096+3361*
11:11 that they should fall? **God f**: *1096+3361*
1Co 6:15 the members of a harlot? **God f**. *1096+3361*
14:39 and **f** not to speak with tongues. *2967*
Gal 2:17 Christ the minister of sin? **God f**. *1096+3361*
3:21 **God f**: for if there had been a law *1096+3361*
6:14 But **God f** that I should glory, *1096+3361*

FORBIDDEN (3) [FORBID]
Lev 5:17 commit any *of these things* which are **f** to 3808
Dt 4:23 which the LORD thy God hath **f** thee. 6680
Ac 16: 6 were **f** of the Holy Ghost to preach *2967*

FORBIDDETH (1) [FORBID]
3Jn 1:10 and **f** them that would, and casteth *them* out *2967*

FORBIDDING (4) [FORBID]
Lk 23: 2 and **f** to give tribute to Cesar, saying that he *2967*
Ac 28:31 with all confidence, **no** man **f** him. *209*
1Th 2:16 **F** us to speak to the Gentiles that they *2967*
1Ti 4: 3 **F** to marry, *and commanding* to abstain *2967*

FORBORN (1) [FORBEAR]
Jer 51:30 The mighty *men* of Babylon have **f** to fight, 2308

FORCE (19) [FORCED, FORCES, FORCIBLE, FORCING]
Ge 31:31 Peradventure thou wouldest **take by f** thy 1497
Dt 22:25 and the man **f** her, and lie with her: 2388
34: 7 eye was not dim, nor his **natural f** abated. 3893
1Sa 2:16 *it me* now: and if not, I will take *it* by **f**. 2394
2Sa 13:12 Nay, my brother, do not **f** me; 6031
Ezr 4:23 and made them to cease by **f** and power. 153
Est 7: 8 Will he **f** the queen also before me in 3533
Job 30:18 By the great **f** *of my disease* is my garment 3581
40:16 and his **f** *is* in the navel of his belly. 202
Jer 18:21 pour out their *blood* by the **f** of the sword; 3027
23:10 their course is evil, and their **f** *is* not right. 1369
48:45 the shadow of Heshbon because of the **f**: 3581
Eze 34: 4 with **f** and with cruelty have ye ruled them. 2394
35: 5 **f** of the sword in the time of their calamity, 3027
Am 2:14 the strong shall not strengthen his **f**, 3581
Mt 11:12 and the violent **take** it **by f**. *726*
Jn 6:15 that they would come and **take** him **by f**, *726*
Ac 23:10 and to **take** him **by f** from among them, and *726*
Heb 9:17 For a testament *is* of **f** after *men* are dead: *949*

FORCED (7) [FORCE]
Jdg 1:34 the Amorites **f** the children of Dan into 3905
20: 5 my concubine have they **f**, that she is dead. 6031
1Sa 13:12 I **f** myself therefore, and offered a burnt 662
2Sa 13:14 stronger than she, **f** her, and lay with her. 6031
13:22 because he had **f** his sister Tamar. 6031
13:32 from the day that he **f** his sister Tamar. 6031
Pr 7:21 with the flattering of her lips she **f** him. 5080

FORCES (16) [FORCE]
2Ch 17: 2 he placed **f** in all the fenced cities of Judah, 2428
Job 36:19 *no*, not gold, nor all the **f** of strength. 3981
Isa 60: 5 the **f** of the Gentiles shall come unto thee. 2428
60:11 that *men* may bring unto thee the **f** of 2428
Jer 40: 7 *Now* when all the captains of the **f** which 2428
40:13 all the captains of the **f** that *were* in 2428
41:11 all the captains of the **f** that *were* with him, 2428
41:13 all the captains of the **f** that *were* with him, 2428
41:16 all the captains of the **f** that *were* with him, 2428
42: 1 all the captains of the **f**, and Johanan 2428
42: 8 all the captains of the **f** which *were* with 2428
43: 4 all the captains of the **f**, and all the people, 2428
43: 5 all the captains of the **f**, took all 2428
Da 11:10 and shall assemble a multitude of great **f**: 2428
11:38 in his estate shall he honour the God of **f**: 4581
Ob 1:11 the strangers carried away captive his **f**, 2428

F

FORCIBLE (1) [FORCE]
Job 6:25 How **f** are right words! but what doth your 4834

FORCING (2) [FORCE]
Dt 20:19 thou shalt not destroy the trees thereof by **f** 5080
Pr 30:33 so the **f** of wrath bringeth forth strife. 4330

FORD (1) [FORDS]
Ge 32:22 eleven sons, and passed over the **f** Jabbok. 4569

FORDS (3) [FORD]
Jos 2: 7 after them the way to Jordan unto the **f**: 4569
Jdg 3:28 took the **f** of Jordan toward Moab, and 4569
Isa 16: 2 the daughters of Moab shall be *at* the **f** of 4569

FORECAST (2)
Da 11:24 he shall **f** his devices **against** the strong 2803
11:25 for they shall **f** devices against him. 2803

FOREFATHERS (2) [FATHER]
Jer 11:10 turned back to the iniquities of their **f**, 1+7223
2Ti 1: 3 whom I serve from *my* **f** with pure *4269*

FOREFRONT (10) [FRONT]
Ex 26: 9 shalt double the sixth curtain in the **f** 4136+6440
28:37 upon the **f** of the mitre it shall be. 4136+6440
Lev 8: 9 also upon the mitre, *even* upon his **f**, did he 6440
1Sa 14: 5 The **f** of the one *was* situate northward over 8127
2Sa 11:15 Set ye Uriah in the **f** of the hottest 4136+6440
2Ki 16:14 from the **f** of the house, from between 6440
2Ch 20:27 and Jehoshaphat in the **f** of them, 7218
Eze 40:19 he measured the breadth from the **f** 6440+3807.1
40:19 gate unto the **f** of the inner court without, 6440
47: 1 for the **f** of the house *stood toward* the east, 6440

FOREHEAD (16) [HEAD]
Ex 28:38 it shall be upon Aaron's **f**, that Aaron may 4696
28:38 it shall be always upon his **f**, that they may 4696
Lev 13:41 of *his head toward* his face, he *is* **f bald**: 1371
13:42 bald head, or **bald f**, a white reddish sore; 1372
13:42 sprung up in his bald head, or his **bald f**. 1372
13:43 or in his **bald f**, as the leprosy appeareth in 1372
1Sa 17:49 slang *it*, and smote the Philistine in his **f**, 4696
17:49 his forehead, that the stone sunk into his **f**; 4696
2Ch 26:19 the leprosy even rose up in his **f** before 4696
26:20 he *was* leprous in his **f**, and they thrust him 4696
Jer 3: 3 thou hadst a whore's **f**, thou refusedst to be 4696
Eze 3: 8 and thy **f** strong against their foreheads. 4696
3: 9 harder than flint have I made thy **f**: 4696
16:12 I put a jewel on thy **f**, and earrings in thine 639
Rev 14: 9 and receive *his* mark in his **f**, or in his hand, *3359*
17: 5 And upon her **f** *was* a name written, *3359*

FOREHEADS (8) [HEAD]
Eze 3: 8 and thy forehead strong against their **f**. 4696
9: 4 set a mark upon the **f** of the men that sigh 4696
Rev 7: 3 sealed the servants of our God in their **f**. *3359*
9: 4 which have not the seal of God in their **f**. *3359*
13:16 a mark in their right hand, or in their **f**: *3359*
14: 1 having his Father's name written in their **f**. *3359*
20: 4 neither had received *his* mark upon their **f**, *3359*
22: 4 his face; and his name *shall be* in their **f**. *3359*

FOREIGN See OUTLANDISH; STRANGE

FOREIGNER (2) [FOREIGNERS]
Ex 12:45 A **f** and a hired servant shall not eat thereof. 8453
Dt 15: 3 Of a **f** thou mayest exact *it again:* but 5237

FOREIGNERS (2) [FOREIGNER]
Ob 1:11 **f** entered *into* his gates, and cast lots upon 5237
Eph 2:19 therefore ye are no more strangers and **f**, *3941*

FOREKNEW (1) [KNOW]
Ro 11: 2 hath not cast away his people which he **f**. *4267*

FOREKNOW (1) [KNOW]
Ro 8:29 For whom he did **f**, he also did predestinate *4267*

FOREKNOWLEDGE (2) [KNOW]
Ac 2:23 by the determinate counsel and **f** of God, *4268*
1Pe 1: 2 Elect according to the **f** of God the Father, *4268*

FOREMOST (3)
Ge 32:17 he commanded the **f**, saying, When Esau 7223
33: 2 he put the handmaids and their children **f**, 7223
2Sa 18:27 Me thinketh the running of the **f** *is* like 7223

FOREORDAINED (1) [ORDAIN]
1Pe 1:20 Who verily was **f** before the foundation of *4267*

FOREPART (5) [PART]
Ex 28:27 towards the **f** thereof, over against *the other* 6440
39:20 toward the **f** of it, over against 4136+6440
1Ki 6:20 the oracle in the **f** *was* twenty cubits in 6440
Eze 42: 7 towards the utter court on the **f** of 6440
Ac 27:41 and the **f** stuck fast, and *4408*

FORERUNNER (1) [RUN]
Heb 6:20 Whither the **f** is for us entered, *even* Jesus, *4274*

FORESAIL See MAINSAIL

FORESAW (1) [SEE]
Ac 2:25 I **f** the Lord always before my face, for he *4308*

FORESEEING (1) [SEE]
Gal 3: 8 **f** that God would justify the heathen *4275*

FORESEETH (2) [SEE]
Pr 22: 3 A prudent *man* **f** the evil, and 7200
27:12 A prudent *man* **f** the evil, *and* 7200

FORESHIP (1) [SHIP]
Ac 27:30 they would have cast anchors out of the **f**, *4408*

FORESKIN (9) [SKIN]
Ge 17:11 ye shall circumcise the flesh of your **f**; and 6190
17:14 whose flesh of his **f** is not circumcised, 6190
17:23 circumcised the flesh of their **f** in 6190
17:24 he was circumcised *in* the flesh of his **f**. 6190
17:25 he was circumcised in the flesh of his **f**. 6190
Ex 4:25 cut off the **f** of her son, and cast *it* at his 6190
Lev 12: 3 in the eighth day the flesh of his **f** shall be 6190
Dt 10:16 Circumcise therefore the **f** of your heart, 6190
Hab 2:16 drink thou also, and let thy **f** be **uncovered**: 6188

FORESKINS (5) [SKIN]
Jos 5: 3 the children of Israel at the hill of the **f**. 6190
1Sa 18:25 but an hundred **f** of the Philistines, 6190
18:27 David brought their **f**, and they gave them 6190
2Sa 3:14 which I espoused to me for an hundred **f** of 6190
Jer 4: 4 take away the **f** of your heart, ye men of 6190

FOREST (38) [FORESTS]
1Sa 22: 5 and came *into* the **f** of Hareth. 3293
1Ki 7: 2 He built also the house of the **f** of Lebanon; 3293
10:17 the king put them *in* the house of the **f** of 3293
10:21 all the vessels of the house of the **f** of 3293
2Ki 19:23 of his borders, *and into* the **f** of his Carmel. 3293
2Ch 9:16 the king put them in the house of the **f** of 3293
9:20 all the vessels of the house of the **f** of 3293
Ne 2: 8 letter unto Asaph the keeper of the king's **f**, 6508
Ps 50:10 For every beast of the **f** *is* mine, *and* 3293
104:20 wherein all the beasts of the **f** do creep 3293
Isa 9:18 shall kindle in the thickets of the **f**, and 3293
10:18 shall consume the glory of his **f**, and of his 3293
10:19 the rest of the trees of his **f** shall be few, 3293
10:34 he shall cut down the thickets of the **f** with 3293
21:13 In the **f** in Arabia shall ye lodge, O ye 3293
22: 8 that day to the armour of the house of the **f**. 3293
29:17 the fruitful field shall be esteemed as a **f**? 3293
32:15 and the fruitful field be counted for a **f**. 3293
32:19 When it shall hail, coming down *on* the **f**; 3293
37:24 of his border, *and* the **f** of his Carmel. 3293
44:14 for himself among the trees of the **f**: 3293
44:23 ye mountains, O **f**, and every tree therein: 3293
56: 9 come to devour, *yea,* all ye beasts in the **f**. 3293
Jer 5: 6 Wherefore a lion out of the **f** shall slay 3293
10: 3 for *one* cutteth a tree out of the **f**, the work 3293
12: 8 Mine heritage is unto me as a lion in the **f**; 3293
21:14 I will kindle a fire in the **f** thereof, and 3293
26:18 of the house as the high places of a **f**. 3293
46:23 They shall cut down her **f**, saith 3293
Eze 15: 2 a branch which is among the trees of the **f**? 3293
15: 6 As the vine tree among the trees of the **f**, 3293
20:46 prophesy against the **f** of the south field; 3293
20:47 say to the **f** of the south, Hear the word of 3293
Hos 2:12 I will make them a **f**, and the beasts of 3293
Am 3: 4 Will a lion roar in the **f**, when he hath no 3293
Mic 3:12 of the house as the high places of the **f**. 3293
5: 8 people as a lion among the beasts of the **f**, 3293
Zec 11: 2 for the **f** of the vintage is come down. 3293

FORESTS (3) [FOREST]
2Ch 27: 4 and in the **f** he built castles and towers. 2793
Ps 29: 9 the hinds to calve, and discovereth the **f**: 3295
Eze 39:10 the field, neither cut down *any* out of the **f**; 3293

FORETELL (1) [TELL]
2Co 13: 2 **f** *you,* as if I were present the second *time;* *4302*

FORETOLD (2) [TELL]
Mk 13:23 ye heed: behold, I have **f** you all *things.* *4302*
Ac 3:24 have spoken, have likewise **f** of these days. *4293*

FOREWARN (1) [WARN]
Lk 12: 5 But I will **f** you whom you shall fear: *5263*

FOREWARNED (1) [WARN]
1Th 4: 6 all such, as we also have **f** you and testified. *4302*

FORFEITED (1)
Ezr 10: 8 all his substance should be **f**, and 2763

FORGAT (8) [FORGET]
Ge 40:23 chief butler remember Joseph, but **f** him. 7911
Jdg 3: 7 **f** the LORD their God, and served Baalim 7911
1Sa 12: 9 when they **f** the LORD their God, he sold 7911
Ps 78:11 **f** his works, and his wonders that he had 7911
106:13 They soon **f** his works; they waited not for 7911
106:21 They **f** God their saviour, which had done 7911
La 3:17 my soul far off from peace: I **f** prosperity. 5382
Hos 2:13 her lovers, and **f** me, saith the LORD. 7911

FORGAVE (9) [FORGIVE]
Ps 78:38 **f** *their* iniquity, and destroyed *them* not: 3722
Mt 18:27 and loosed him, and **f** him the debt. *863*
18:32 I **f** thee all that debt, because thou desiredst *863*
Lk 7:42 had nothing to pay, he **frankly f** *them* both. *5483*
7:43 said, I suppose that *he,* to whom he **f** most. *5483*
2Co 2:10 for if I **f** any *thing,* to whom I forgave *it,* for *5483*
2:10 for if I forgave any *thing,* to whom I **f** *it,* for *5483*
2:10 for your sakes *f I it* in the person of Christ; NIG
Col 3:13 even as Christ **f** you, so also *do* ye. *5483*

FORGAVEST (2) [FORGIVE]
Ps 32: 5 and thou **f** the iniquity of my sin. 5375
99: 8 thou wast a God that **f** them, though thou 5375

FORGED (1) [FORGERS]
Ps 119:69 The proud have **f** a lie against me: *but* I will 2950

FORGERS (1) [FORGED]
Job 13: 4 ye *are* **f** of lies, ye *are* all physicians of no 2950

FORGET (54) [FORGAT, FORGETFUL, FORGETFULNESS, FORGETTEST, FORGETTETH, FORGETTING]
Ge 27:45 and he **f** *that* which thou hast done to him: 7911
41:51 *said he,* hath **made** me **f** all my toil, and all 5382
Dt 4: 9 lest thou **f** the things which thine eyes have 7911
4:23 lest ye **f** the covenant of the LORD your 7911
4:31 nor **f** the covenant of thy fathers which he 7911
6:12 *Then* beware lest thou **f** the LORD, 7911
8:11 Beware that thou **f** not the LORD thy 7911
8:14 lifted up, and thou **f** the LORD thy God, 7911
8:19 if thou **do at all f** the LORD thy 7911+7911
9: 7 Remember, *and* **f** not, how thou provokedst 7911
25:19 from under heaven; thou shalt not **f** *it.* 7911
1Sa 1:11 not **f** thine handmaid, but wilt give unto 7911
2Ki 17:38 that I have made with you ye shall not **f**; 7911
Job 8:13 So *are* the paths of all that **f** God; and 7911
9:27 If I say, I will **f** my complaint, I will leave 7911
11:16 Because thou shalt **f** *thy* misery, *and* 7911
24:20 The womb shall **f** him; the worm shall feed 7911
Ps 9:17 into hell, *and* all the nations that **f** God. 7913
10:12 O God, lift up thine hand: **f** not the humble. 7911
13: 1 How long wilt thou **f** me, O LORD? 7911
45:10 **f** also thine own people, and thy father's 7911
50:22 Now consider this, ye that **f** God, lest I tear 7911
59:11 Slay them not, lest my people **f**: 7911
74:19 **f** not the congregation of thy poor for ever. 7911
74:23 **F** not the voice of thine enemies: the tumult 7911
78: 7 not **f** the works of God, but keep his 7911
102: 4 like grass; so that I **f** to eat my bread. 7911
103: 2 O my soul, and **f** not all his benefits: 7911
119:16 myself in thy statutes: I will not **f** thy word. 7911
119:83 in the smoke; *yet* do I not **f** thy statutes. 7911
119:93 I will never **f** thy precepts: for with them 7911
119:109 in my hand: yet do I not **f** thy law. 7911
119:141 and despised: *yet* do not I **f** thy precepts. 7911
119:153 and deliver me: for I do not **f** thy law. 7911
119:176 for I do not **f** thy commandments. 7911
137: 5 If I **f** thee, O Jerusalem, let my right hand 7911
137: 5 let my right hand **f** *her cunning.* 7911
Pr 3: 1 My son, **f** not my law; but let thine heart 7911
4: 5 **f** *it* not; neither decline from the words of 7911
31: 5 **f** the law, and pervert the judgment of any 7911
31: 7 **f** his poverty, and remember his misery no 7911
Isa 49:15 Can a woman **f** her sucking child, that *she* 7911
49:15 yea, they may **f**, yet will I not forget thee. 7911
49:15 yea, they may forget, yet will I not **f** thee. 7911
54: 4 for thou shalt **f** the shame of thy youth, and 7911
65:11 that **f** my holy mountain, that prepare a 7913
Jer 2:32 Can a maid **f** her ornaments, *or* a bride her 7911
23:27 Which think to **cause** my people to **f** my 7911
23:39 will **utterly f** you, and I will forsake 5377+5382
La 5:20 Wherefore dost thou **f** us for ever, *and* 7911
Hos 4: 6 law of thy God, I will also **f** thy children. 7911
Am 8: 7 Surely I will never **f** any of their works. 7911
Heb 6:10 For God *is* not unrighteous to **f** your work *1950*
13:16 But to do good and to communicate **f** not: *1950*

FORGETFUL (2) [FORGET]
Heb 13: 2 Be not **f** to entertain strangers: for thereby *1950*
Jas 1:25 continueth *therein,* he being not a **f** hearer, *1953*

FORGETFULNESS (1) [FORGET]
Ps 88:12 and thy righteousness in the land of **f**? 5388

FORGETTEST (2) [FORGET]
Ps 44:24 *and* **f** our affliction and our oppression? 7911
Isa 51:13 **f** the LORD thy Maker, that hath stretched 7911

FORGETTETH (4) [FORGET]
Job 39:15 **f** that the foot may crush them, or *that* 7911
Ps 9:12 he **f** not the cry of the humble. 7911
Pr 2:17 of her youth, and **f** the covenant of her God. 7911
Jas 1:24 straightway **f** what manner of *man* he was. *1950*

FORGETTING (1) [FORGET]
Php 3:13 *this* one *thing I do,* **f** those *things which are* *1950*

FORGIVE (56) [FORGAVE, FORGAVEST, FORGIVEN, FORGIVENESS, FORGIVENESSES, FORGIVETH, FORGIVING, FORGOT, FORGOTTEN]
Ge 50:17 **F**, I pray thee now, the trespass of thy 5375
50:17 **f** the trespass of the servants of the God of 5375
Ex 10:17 Now therefore **f**, I pray thee, my sin only 5375
32:32 Yet now, if thou wilt **f** their sin; and if not, 5375
Nu 30: 5 the LORD shall **f** her, because her father 5545
30: 8 of none effect: and the LORD shall **f** her. 5545
30:12 them void; and the LORD shall **f** her. 5545
Jos 24:19 he will not **f** your transgressions nor your 5375
1Sa 25:28 pray thee, **f** the trespass of thine handmaid: 5375
1Ki 8:30 dwelling place: and when thou hearest, **f**. 5545
8:34 **f** the sin of thy people Israel, and 5545
8:36 **f** the sin of thy servants, and of thy people 5545
8:39 **f**, and do, and give to every man according 5545
8:50 **f** thy people that have sinned against thee, 5545
2Ch 6:21 from heaven; and when thou hearest, **f**. 5545
6:25 **f** the sin of thy people Israel, and 5545
6:27 **f** the sin of thy servants, and of thy people 5545
6:30 **f**, and render unto every man according 5545
6:39 **f** thy people which have sinned against 5545
7:14 and will **f** their sin, and will heal their land. 5545
Ps 25:18 and my pain; and **f** all my sins. 5375
86: 5 For thou, Lord, *art* good, and **ready to f**; 5546
Isa 2: 9 humbleth himself; therefore **f** them not. 5375
Jer 18:23 against me to slay *me:* **f** not their iniquity, 3722
31:34 for I will **f** their iniquity, and I will 5545
36: 3 that I may **f** their iniquity and their sin. 5545
Da 9:19 O Lord, hear; O Lord, **f**; O Lord, hearken 5545
Am 7: 2 I said, O Lord GOD, **f**, I beseech thee: 5545
Mt 6:12 And **f** us our debts, as we forgive our *863*
6:12 forgive us our debts, as we **f** our debtors. *863*
6:14 For if ye **f** men their trespasses, *863*

Mt 6:14 your heavenly Father will also **f** you: *863*
6:15 But if ye **f** not men their trespasses, *863*
6:15 neither will your Father **f** your trespasses. *863*
9: 6 the Son of man hath power on earth to **f** sins, *863*
18:21 shall my brother sin against me, and I **f** him? *863*
18:35 if ye from your hearts **f** not every one his *863*
Mk 2: 7 who can **f** sins but God only? *863*
2:10 the Son of man hath power on earth to **f** sins, *863*
11:25 And when ye stand praying, **f**, if ye have *863*
11:25 is in heaven may **f** you your trespasses. *863*
11:26 But if ye do not **f**, neither will your Father *863*
11:26 neither will your Father which is in heaven **f** *863*
Lk 5:21 Who can **f** sins, but God alone? *863*
5:24 Son of man hath power upon earth to **f** sins, *863*
6:37 be condemned: **f**, and ye shall be forgiven: *630*
11: 4 And **f** us our sins; for we also forgive every *863*
11: 4 for we also **f** every one *that is* indebted to us. *863*
17: 3 rebuke him; and if he repent, **f** him. *863*
17: 4 to thee, saying, I repent; thou shalt **f** him. *863*
23:34 Then said Jesus, Father, **f** them; for they *863*
2Co 2: 7 So that contrariwise ye *ought* rather to **f** *5483*
2:10 To whom ye **f** any *thing,* I *forgive* also: for *5483*
2:10 To whom ye forgive any *thing,* I *f* also: for NIG
12:13 not burdensome to you? **f** me this wrong. *5483*
1Jn 1: 9 he is faithful and just to **f** us *our* sins, and *863*

FORGIVEN (42) [FORGIVE]

Lev 4:20 atonement for them, and it shall be **f** them. 5545
4:26 as concerning his sin, and it shall be **f** him. 5545
4:31 an atonement for him, and it shall be **f** him. 5545
4:35 he hath committed, and it shall be **f** him. 5545
5:10 which he had sinned, and it shall be **f** him. 5545
5:13 sinned in one of these, and it shall be **f** him: 5545
5:16 the trespass offering, and it shall be **f** him. 5545
5:18 and wist *it* not, and it shall be **f** him. 5545
6: 7 it shall be **f** him for any *thing* of all that he 5545
19:22 the sin which he hath done shall be **f** him. 5545
Nu 14:19 as thou hast **f** this people, from Egypt even 5375
15:25 the children of Israel; and it shall be **f** them; 5545
15:26 it shall be **f** all the congregation of 5545
15:28 an atonement for him; and it shall be **f** him. 5545
Dt 21: 8 And the blood shall be **f** them. 3722
Ps 32: 1 Blessed *is* he whose transgression *is* **f**, 5375
85: 2 Thou hast **f** the iniquity of thy people, 5375
Isa 33:24 the people that dwell therein *shall be* **f** *their* 5375
Mt 9: 2 Son, be of good cheer; thy sins be **f** thee. *863*
9: 5 whether is easier, to say, *Thy* sins be **f** thee; *863*
12:31 *of* sin and blasphemy shall be **f** unto men: *863*
12:31 the *Holy* Ghost shall not be **f** unto men. *863*
12:32 against the Son of man, it shall be **f** him: *863*
12:32 it shall not be **f** him, neither in this world, *863*
Mk 2: 5 the sick of the palsy, Son, thy sins be **f** thee. *863*
2: 9 to the sick of the palsy, *Thy* sins be **f** thee; *863*
3:28 All sins shall be **f** unto the sons of men, and *863*
4:12 and *their* sins should be **f** them. *863*
Lk 5:20 he said unto him, Man, thy sins are **f** thee. *863*
5:23 Whether is easier, to say, Thy sins be **f** thee; *863*
6:37 not be condemned: forgive, and ye shall be **f**: *630*
7:47 unto thee, Her sins, which are many, are **f**; *863*
7:47 but to whom little is **f**, *the same* loveth little. *863*
7:48 And he said unto her, Thy sins are **f**. *863*
12:10 against the Son of man, it shall be **f** him: *863*
12:10 against the Holy Ghost it shall not be **f**. *863*
Ac 8:22 if perhaps the thought of thine heart may be **f** *863*
Ro 4: 7 Blessed *are they* whose iniquities are **f**, *863*
Eph 4:32 even as God for Christ's sake hath **f** you. *5483*
Col 2:13 with him, having **f** you all trespasses; *5483*
Jas 5:15 he have committed sins, they shall be **f** him. *863*
1Jn 2:12 *your* sins are **f** you for his name's sake. *863*

FORGIVENESS (7) [FORGIVE]

Ps 130: 4 *there is* **f** with thee, that thou mayest be 5547
Mk 3:29 against the Holy Ghost hath never **f**, *859*
Ac 5:31 for to give repentance to Israel, and **f** of sins. *859*
13:38 this *man* is preached unto you the **f** of sins: *859*
26:18 that they may receive **f** of sins, and *859*
Eph 1: 7 the **f** of sins, according to the riches of his *859*
Col 1:14 through his blood, *even* the **f** of sins: *859*

FORGIVENESSES (1) [FORGIVE]

Da 9: 9 To the Lord our God *belong* mercies and **f**, 5547

FORGIVETH (2) [FORGIVE]

Ps 103: 3 Who **f** all thine iniquities; who healeth all 5545
Lk 7:49 Who is this that **f** sins also? *863*

FORGIVING (4) [FORGIVE]

Ex 34: 7 **f** iniquity and transgression and sin, and 5375
Nu 14:18 **f** iniquity and transgression, and by no 5375
Eph 4:32 to another, tenderhearted, **f** one another, *5483*
Col 3:13 Forbearing one another, and **f** one another, *5483*

FORGOT (1) [FORGIVE]

Dt 24:19 hast **f** a sheaf in the field, thou shalt not go 7911

FORGOTTEN (46) [FORGIVE]

Ge 41:30 all the plenty shall be **f** in the land of 7911
Dt 26:13 thy commandments, neither have I **f** *them:* 7911
31:21 for it shall not be **f** out of the mouths of 7911
32:18 and hast **f** God that formed thee. 7911
Job 19:14 and my familiar friends have **f** me. 7911
28: 4 the inhabitant; *even the waters* **f** of the foot: 7911
Ps 9:18 For the needy shall not alway be **f**: 7911
10:11 He hath said in his heart, God hath **f**: 7911
31:12 I am **f** as a dead man out of mind: I am like 7911
42: 9 unto God my rock, Why hast thou **f** me? 7911
44:17 yet have we not **f** thee, neither have we 7911
44:20 If we have **f** the name of our God, or 7911
77: 9 Hath God **f** to be gracious? hath he in anger 7911
119:61 have robbed me: but I have not **f** thy law. 7911
119:139 because mine enemies have **f** thy words. 7911
Ecc 2:16 now *is, in* the days to come shall all be **f**. 7911
8:10 they were **f** in the city where they had so 7911
9: 5 a reward; for the memory of them is **f**. 7911

Isa 17:10 Because thou hast **f** the God of thy 7911
23:15 that Tyre shall be **f** seventy years, 7911
23:16 about the city, thou harlot that hast been **f**; 7911
44:21 O Israel, thou shalt not be **f** of me. 5382
49:14 hath forsaken me, and my Lord hath **f** me. 7911
65:16 because the former troubles are **f**, and 7911
Jer 2:32 yet my people have **f** me days without 7911
3:21 *and* they have **f** the LORD their God. 7911
13:25 because thou hast **f** me, and trusted in 7911
18:15 Because my people hath **f** me, they have 7911
20:11 *their* everlasting confusion shall never be **f**. 7911
23:27 as their fathers have **f** my name for Baal. 7911
23:40 and a perpetual shame, which shall not be **f**. 7911
30:14 All thy lovers have **f** thee; they seek thee 7911
44: 9 Have ye **f** the wickedness of your fathers, 7911
50: 5 *in* a perpetual covenant *that* shall not be **f**. 7911
50: 6 to hill, they have **f** their resting place. 7911
La 2: 6 **caused** the solemn feasts and sabbaths **to be f** 7911
Eze 22:12 and hast **f** me, saith the Lord GOD. 7911
23:35 Because thou hast **f** me, and cast me behind 7911
Hos 4: 6 seeing thou hast **f** the law of thy God, I will 7911
8:14 For Israel hath **f** his Maker, and 7911
13: 6 heart was exalted; therefore have they **f** me. 7911
Mt 16: 5 to the other side, they had **f** to take bread. *1950*
Mk 8:14 Now *the disciples* had **f** to take bread, *1950*
Lk 12: 6 and not one of them is **f** before God? *1950*
Heb 12: 5 And ye have **f** the exhortation which *1585*
2Pe 1: 9 **f** that *he* was purged from his old *2983+3024*

FORKS (1)

1Sa 13:21 for the **f**, and for the axes, and 7053+7969

FORM (24) [FORMED, FORMER, FORMETH, FORMS]

Ge 1: 2 the earth was **without f**, and void; and 8414
1Sa 28:14 he said unto her, What **f** is he of? And she 8389
2Sa 14:20 To fetch about *this* **f** of speech hath thy 6440
2Ch 4: 7 candlesticks of gold according to their **f**, 4941
Job 4:16 but I could not discern the **f** thereof: 4758
Isa 45: 7 I **f** the light, and create darkness: I make 3335
52:14 and his **f** more than the sons of men: 8389
53: 2 he hath no **f** nor comeliness; and when we 8389
Jer 4:23 and lo, *it was* **without f**, and void; 8414
Eze 8: 3 he put forth the **f** of a hand, and took me by 8403
8:10 behold every **f** of creeping things, and 8403
10: 8 there appeared in the cherubims the **f** of a 8403
43:11 shew them the **f** of the house, and 6699
43:11 that they may keep the whole **f** thereof, and 6699
Da 2:31 before thee; and the **f** thereof *was* terrible. 7299
3:19 the **f** of his visage was changed against 6755
3:25 the **f** of the fourth *is* like the Son of God. 7299
Mk 16:12 After that he appeared in another **f** unto two *3444*
Ro 2:20 which hast the **f** of knowledge and of *3446*
6:17 ye have obeyed from the heart *that* **f** of *5179*
Php 2: 6 Who, being in the **f** of God, thought it not *3444*
2: 7 and took *upon him* the **f** of a servant, and *3444*
2Ti 1:13 Hold fast the **f** of sound words, which thou *5296*
3: 5 Having a **f** of godliness, but denying *3446*

FORMED (33) [FORM]

Ge 2: 7 the LORD God **f** man *of* the dust of 3335
2: 8 and there he put the man whom he had **f**. 3335
2:19 out of the ground the LORD God **f** every 3335
Dt 32:18 and hast forgotten God that **f** thee. 2342
2Ki 19:25 *and* of ancient times that I have **f** it? 3335
Job 26: 5 Dead *things* are **f** from under the waters, 2342
26:13 his hand hath **f** the crooked serpent. 2342
33: 6 in God's stead: I also am **f** out of the clay. 7169
Ps 90: 2 or ever thou hadst **f** the earth and the world, 2342
94: 9 not hear? he that **f** the eye, shall he not see? 3335
95: 5 he made it: and his hands **f** the dry *land.* 3335
Pr 26:10 The great *God* that **f** all *things* both 2342
Isa 27:11 he that **f** them will shew them no favour. 3335
37:26 *and* of ancient times, that I have **f** it? 3335
43: 1 O Jacob, and he that **f** thee, O Israel, 3335
43: 7 created him for my glory; I have **f** him; 3335
43:10 before me there was no God **f**, neither shall 3335
43:21 This people have I **f** for myself; they shall 3335
44: 2 **f** thee from the womb, *which* will help thee; 3335
44:10 Who hath **f** a god, or molten a graven 3335
44:21 I have **f** thee; thou *art* my servant: O Israel, 3335
44:24 and he that **f** thee from the womb, 3335
45:18 God himself that **f** the earth and made it; 3335
45:18 created it not in vain, he **f** it to be inhabited: 3335
49: 5 saith the LORD that **f** me from the womb 3335
54:17 No weapon *that* is **f** against thee shall 3335
Jer 1: 5 Before I **f** thee in the belly I knew thee; and 3335
33: 2 the LORD that **f** it, to establish it; 3335
Am 7: 1 he **f** grasshoppers in the beginning of 3335
Ro 9:20 Shall the thing **f** say to him that formed *it,* *4110*
9:20 Shall the thing formed say to him that **f** *it,* *4111*
Gal 4:19 in birth again until Christ be **f** in you, *3445*
1Ti 2:13 For Adam was first **f**, then Eve. *4111*

FORMER (50) [FORM]

Ge 40:13 after the **f** manner when thou wast his 7223
Nu 21:26 who had fought against the **f** king of Moab, 7223
Dt 24: 4 Her **f** husband, which sent her away, 7223
Ru 4: 7 Now this *was the manner* **in f time** 6440+3807.1
1Sa 17:30 the people answered him again after the **f** 7223
2Ki 1:14 burnt up the two captains of the **f** fifties 7223
17:34 Unto this day they do after the **f** manners: 7223
17:40 but they did after their **f** manner. 7223
Ne 5:15 the **f** governors that *had been* before me 7223
Job 8: 8 of the **f** age, and prepare *thyself* to 7223
30: 3 flying *into* the wilderness **in f time** desolate 570
Ps 79: 8 O remember not against us **f** iniquities: 7223
89:49 Lord, where *are* thy **f** lovingkindnesses, 7223
Ecc 1:11 *There is* no remembrance of **f** *things,* 7223
7:10 What is *the cause* that the **f** days were 7223
Isa 41:22 let them shew the **f** *things,* what they *be,* 7223
42: 9 the **f** *things* are come to pass, and 7223
43: 9 shew us **f** *things?* let them bring forth their 7223
43:18 Remember ye not the **f** *things,* neither 7223

Isa 46: 9 Remember the **f** *things* of old: for I *am* 7223
48: 3 I have declared the **f** *things* from 7223
61: 4 they shall raise up the **f** desolations, and 7223
65: 7 will I measure their **f** work into their 7223
65:16 because the **f** troubles are forgotten, and 7223
65:17 the **f** shall not be remembered, nor come 7223
Jer 5:24 both the **f** and the latter, in his season: 3138
10:16 for he *is* the **f** of all *things;* and Israel *is* 3335
34: 5 the **f** kings which were before thee, so 7223
36:28 write in it all the **f** words that were in 7223
51:19 for he *is* the **f** of all *things:* and *Israel is* 3335
Eze 16:55 shall return to their **f estate**, and Samaria 6927
16:55 her daughters shall return to their **f estate**, 6927
16:55 thy daughters shall return to your **f estate**. 6927
Da 11:13 shall set forth a multitude greater than the **f**, 7223
11:29 but it shall not be as the **f**, or as the latter. 7223
Hos 6: 3 as the latter *and* **f rain** *unto* the earth. 3384
Joel 2:23 for he hath given you the **f rain** 4175
2:23 the **f rain**, and the latter rain in the first 4175
Hag 2: 9 latter house shall be greater than of the **f**, 7223
Zec 1: 4 unto whom the **f** prophets have cried, 7223
7: 7 the LORD hath cried by the **f** prophets, 7223
7:12 hath sent in his spirit by the **f** prophets: 7223
8:11 the residue of this people as *in* the **f** days, 7223
14: 8 half of them toward the **f** sea, and half of 6931
Mal 3: 4 as *in* the days of old, and as *in* **f** years. 6931
Ac 1: 1 The **f** treatise have I made, O Theophilus, *4413*
Eph 4:22 That ye put off concerning the **f** *4387*
Heb 10:32 But call to remembrance the **f** days, *4387*
1Pe 1:14 not fashioning yourselves according to the **f** *4387*
Rev 21: 4 more pain: for the **f** *things* are passed away. *4413*

FORMETH (2) [FORM]

Am 4:13 he that **f** the mountains, and createth 3335
Zec 12: 1 and **f** the spirit of man within him. 3335

FORMS (2) [FORM]

Eze 43:11 all the **f** thereof, and all the ordinances 6699
43:11 all the **f** thereof, and all the laws thereof: 6699

FORNICATION (36) [FORNICATIONS, FORNICATOR, FORNICATORS]

2Ch 21:11 **caused** the inhabitants of Jerusalem **to commit f**, 2181
Isa 23:17 shall **commit f** with all the kingdoms of 2181
Eze 16:26 Thou hast also **committed f** with 2181
16:29 Thou hast moreover multiplied thy **f** in 8457
Mt 5:32 saving for the cause of **f**, causeth her to *4202*
19: 9 except *it be* for **f**, and shall marry another, *4202*
Jn 8:41 Then said they to him, We be not born of **f**; *4202*
Ac 15:20 and *from* **f**, and *from* things strangled, and *4202*
15:29 and from things strangled, and from **f**: *4202*
21:25 from blood, and from strangled, and from **f**. *4202*
Ro 1:29 **f**, wickedness, covetousness, *4202*
1Co 5: 1 It is reported commonly *that there is* **f** *4202*
5: 1 and such **f** as is not so much as named *4202*
6:13 Now the body *is* not for **f**, but for the Lord; *4202*
6:18 Flee **f**. Every sin that a man doeth is *4202*
6:18 he that **committeth f** sinneth against his *4203*
7: 2 Nevertheless, to avoid **f**, let every man have *4202*
10: 8 Neither let us **commit f**, as some of them *4203*
2Co 12:21 not repented of the uncleanness and **f** and *4202*
Gal 5:19 **f**, uncleanness, lasciviousness, *4202*
Eph 5: 3 But **f**, and all uncleanness, or covetousness, *4202*
Col 3: 5 **f**, uncleanness, inordinate affection, *4202*
1Th 4: 3 that ye should abstain from **f**: *4202*
Jude 1: 7 in like manner **giving** themselves **over to f**, *1608*
Rev 2:14 sacrificed unto idols, and to **commit f**. *4203*
2:20 and to seduce my servants to **commit f**, *4203*
2:21 And I gave her space to repent of her **f**; and *4202*
9:21 nor of their **f**, nor of their thefts. *4202*
14: 8 drink of the wine of the wrath of her **f**. *4202*
17: 2 the kings of the earth have **committed f**, *4203*
17: 2 been made drunk with the wine of her **f**. *4202*
17: 4 full of abominations and filthiness of her **f**: *4202*
18: 3 drunk of the wine of the wrath of her **f**, *4202*
18: 3 the kings of the earth have **committed f** *4203*
18: 9 who have **committed f** and *4203*
19: 2 which did corrupt the earth with her **f**, and *4202*

FORNICATIONS (3) [FORNICATION]

Eze 16:15 pouredst out thy **f** on every one that passed 8457
Mt 15:19 murders, adulteries, **f**, thefts, false witness, *4202*
Mk 7:21 evil thoughts, adulteries, **f**, murders, *4202*

FORNICATOR (2) [FORNICATION]

1Co 5:11 if any *man that is* called a brother be a **f**, or *4205*
Heb 12:16 Lest there *be* any **f**, or profane *person,* as *4205*

FORNICATORS (3) [FORNICATION]

1Co 5: 9 you in an epistle not to company with **f**: *4205*
5:10 Yet not altogether with the **f** of this world, *4205*
6: 9 neither **f**, nor idolaters, nor adulterers, *4205*

FORSAKE (58) [FORSAKEN, FORSAKETH, FORSAKING, FORSOOK, FORSOOKEST]

Dt 4:31 he will not **f** thee, neither destroy thee, 7503
12:19 Take heed to thyself that thou **f** not 5800
14:27 *is* within thy gates; thou shalt not **f** him; 5800
31: 6 with thee; he will not fail thee, nor **f** thee. 5800
31: 8 he will not fail thee, neither **f** thee: 5800
31:16 will **f** me, and break my covenant which I 5800
31:17 I will **f** them, and I will hide my face from 5800
Jos 1: 5 be with thee: I will not fail thee, nor **f** thee. 5800
24:16 God forbid that we should **f** the LORD, 5800
24:20 If ye **f** the LORD, and serve strange gods, 5800
Jdg 9:11 Should I **f** my sweetness, and my good 2308
1Sa 12:22 For the LORD will not **f** his people for his 5203
1Ki 6:13 of Israel, and will not **f** my people Israel. 5800
8:57 our fathers: let him not leave us, nor **f** us: 5203
2Ki 21:14 I will **f** the remnant of mine inheritance, 5203
1Ch 28: 9 if thou **f** him, he will cast thee off for ever. 5800
28:20 he will not fail thee, nor **f** thee, until *thou* 5800
2Ch 7:19 and **f** my statutes and my commandments, 5800

2Ch 15: 2 of you; but if ye **f** him, he will forsake you. 5800
15: 2 of you; but if ye forsake him, he will **f** you. 5800
Ezr 8:22 and his wrath *is* against all them that **f** him. 5800
Ne 9:31 didst not utterly consume them, nor **f** them; 5800
10:39 and we will not **f** the house of our God. 5800
Job 20:13 *Though* he spare it, and **f** it not; but keep it 5800
Ps 27: 9 leave me not, neither **f** me, O God of my 5800
27:10 When my father and my mother **f** me, then 5800
37: 8 Cease from anger, and **f** wrath: fret not 5800
38:21 **F** me not, O LORD: O my God, be not far 5800
71: 9 old age; **f** me not when my strength faileth. 5800
71:18 I am old and grayheaded, O God, **f** me not; 5800
89:30 If his children **f** my law, and walk not in 5800
94:14 his people, neither will he **f** his inheritance. 5800
119: 8 I will keep thy statutes: O **f** me not utterly. 5800
119:53 because of the wicked that **f** thy law. 5800
138: 8 **f** not the works of thine own hands. 7503
Pr 1: 8 thy father, and **f** not the law of thy mother: 5203
3: 3 Let not mercy and truth **f** thee: bind them 5800
4: 2 I give you good doctrine, **f** you not my law. 5800
4: 6 **F** her not, and she shall preserve thee: 5800
6:20 and **f** not the law of thy mother: 5203
9: 6 **F** the foolish, and live; and go in the way of 5800
27:10 own friend, and thy father's friend, **f** not; 5800
28: 4 They that **f** the law praise the wicked: but 5800
Isa 1:28 they that **f** the LORD shall be consumed. 5800
41:17 *I* the God of Israel will not **f** them. 5800
42:16 things will I do unto them, and not **f** them. 5800
55: 7 Let the wicked **f** his way, and 5800
65:11 ye *are* they that **f** the LORD, that forget 5800
Jer 17:13 all that **f** thee shall be ashamed, and 5800
23:33 I will even **f** you, saith the LORD. 5203
23:39 and I will **f** you, and the city that I gave you 5203
51: 9 **F** her, and let us go every one into his own 5800
La 5:20 forget us for ever, *and* **f** us so long time? 5800
Eze 20: 8 neither did they **f** the idols of Egypt: 5800
Da 11:30 have intelligence with them that **f** the holy 5800
Jnh 2: 8 They that observe lying vanities **f** their own 5800
Ac 21:21 are among the Gentiles to **f** Moses, *575+646*
Heb 13: 5 hath said, I will never leave thee, nor **f** thee. *1459*

FORSAKEN (76) [FORSAKE]

Dt 28:20 of thy doings, where*by* thou hast **f** me. 5800
29:25 Because they have **f** the covenant of 5800
Jdg 6:13 now the LORD hath **f** us, and delivered us 5203
10:10 both because we have **f** our God, and 5800
10:13 Yet ye have **f** me, and served other gods: 5800
1Sa 8: 8 wherewith they have **f** me, and served other 5800
12:10 because we have **f** the LORD, and 5800
1Ki 11:33 Because that they have **f** me, and 5800
18:18 in that ye have **f** the commandments of 5800
19:10 for the children of Israel have **f** thy 5800
19:14 the children of Israel have **f** thy covenant, 5800
2Ki 22:17 Because they have **f** me, and have burnt 5800
2Ch 12: 5 Ye have **f** me, and *therefore* have I also left 5800
13:10 LORD *is* our God, and we have not **f** him; 5800
13:11 of the LORD our God; but ye have **f** him. 5800
21:10 he had **f** the LORD God of his fathers. 5800
24:20 because ye have **f** the LORD, he hath also 5800
24:20 forsaken the LORD, he hath also **f** you. 5800
24:24 they had **f** the LORD God of their fathers. 5800
28: 6 they had **f** the LORD God of their fathers. 5800
29: 6 have **f** him, and have turned away their 5800
34:25 Because they have **f** me, and have burned 5800
Ezr 9: 9 yet our God hath not **f** us in our bondage, 5800
9:10 for we have **f** thy commandments, 5800
Ne 13:11 and said, Why is the house of God **f**? 5800
Job 18: 4 shall the earth be **f** for thee? and shall 5800
20:19 he hath oppressed *and* hath **f** the poor; 5800
Ps 9:10 LORD, hast not **f** them that seek thee. 5800
22: 1 My God, my God, why hast thou **f** me? 5800
37:25 yet have I not seen the righteous **f**, nor his 5800
71:11 Saying, God hath **f** him: persecute and 5800
Isa 1: 4 they have **f** the LORD, they have 5800
2: 6 Therefore thou hast **f** thy people the house 5203
7:16 the land that thou abhorrest shall be **f** of 5800
17: 2 The cities of Aroer *are* **f**: they shall be for 5800
17: 9 In that day shall his strong cities be as a **f** 5800
27:10 *and* the habitation **f**, and left like a 7971
32:14 Because the palaces shall be **f**; 5203
49:14 The LORD hath **f** me, and my Lord hath 5800
54: 6 the LORD hath called thee as a woman **f** 5800
54: 7 For a small moment have I **f** thee; but 5800
60:15 Whereas thou hast been **f** and hated, so 5800
62: 4 Thou shalt no more be termed **F**; 5800
62:12 shalt be called, Sought out, A city not **f**. 5800
Jer 1:16 who have **f** me, and have burnt incense 5800
2:13 they have **f** me the fountain of living 5800
2:17 in that thou hast **f** the LORD thy God, 5800
2:19 that thou hast **f** the LORD thy God, and 5800
4:29 every city *shall be* **f**, and not a man dwell 5800
5: 7 thy children have **f** me, and sworn by *them* 5800
5:19 Like as ye have **f** me, and served strange 5800
7:29 and **f** the generation of his wrath. 5203
9:13 Because they have **f** my law which I set 5800
9:19 because we have **f** the land, because 5800
12: 7 I have **f** mine house, I have left mine 5800
15: 6 Thou hast **f** me, saith the LORD, thou art 5203
16:11 Because your fathers have **f** me, saith 5800
16:11 and have **f** me, and have not kept my law; 5800
17:13 because they have **f** the LORD, 5800
18:14 waters that come from another place be **f**? 5428
19: 4 Because they have **f** me, and 5800
22: 9 Because they have **f** the covenant of 5800
25:38 He hath **f** his covert, as the lion: for their 5800
51: 5 For Israel *hath* not *been* **f**, nor Judah of his 488
Eze 8:12 seeth us not; the LORD hath **f** the earth. 5800
9: 9 The LORD hath **f** the earth, and 5800
36: 4 to the cities that are **f**, which became a prey 5800
Am 5: 2 she is **f** upon her land; *there is* none to raise 5203
Zep 2: 4 For Gaza shall be **f**, and Ashkelon a 5800
Mt 19:27 Behold, we have **f** all, and followed thee; *863*
19:29 And every one that hath **f** houses, or *863*
27:46 My God, my God, why hast thou **f** me? *1459*
Mk 15:34 My God, my God, why hast thou **f** me? *1459*
2Co 4: 9 Persecuted, but not **f**; cast down, but *1459*
2Ti 4:10 For Demas hath **f** me, having loved *this* *1459*
2Pe 2:15 Which have **f** the right way, and are gone *2641*

FORSAKETH (6) [FORSAKE]

Job 6:14 his friend; but he **f** the fear of the Almighty. 5800
Ps 37:28 loveth judgment, and **f** not his saints; 5800
Pr 2:17 Which **f** the guide of her youth, and 5800
15:10 Correction *is* grievous unto him that **f** 5800
28:13 and **f** *them* shall have mercy. 5800
Lk 14:33 whosoever *he be* of you that **f** not all that he *657*

FORSAKING (2) [FORSAKE]

Isa 6:12 *there be* a great **f** in the midst of the land. 5805
Heb 10:25 Not **f** the assembling of ourselves together, *1459*

FORSOMUCH (2) [FOR, MUCH, SO]

Isa 8: 6 **F as** this people refuseth the waters 3282+3588
Lk 19: 9 **f as** he also is a son of Abraham. *2530*

FORSOOK (24) [FORSAKE]

Dt 32:15 then he **f** God *which* made him, 5203
Jdg 2:12 And they **f** the LORD God of their fathers, 5800
2:13 they **f** the LORD, and served Baal and 5800
10: 6 and **f** the LORD, and served not him. 5800
1Sa 31: 7 sons were dead, they **f** the cities, and fled; 5800
1Ki 9: 9 Because they **f** the LORD their God, 5800
12: 8 he **f** the counsel of the old men, which they 5800
12:13 **f** the old men's counsel that they gave him; 5800
2Ki 21:22 he **f** the LORD God of his fathers, and 5800
1Ch 10: 7 were dead, then they **f** their cities, and fled: 5800
2Ch 7:22 Because they **f** the LORD God of their 5800
10: 8 he **f** the counsel which the old men gave 5800
10:13 king Rehoboam **f** the counsel of the old 5800
12: 1 he **f** the law of the LORD, and all Israel 5800
Ps 78:60 So that he **f** the tabernacle of Shiloh, 5203
119:87 me upon earth; but I **f** not thy precepts. 5800
Isa 58: 2 and **f** not the ordinance of their God: 5800
Jer 14: 5 and **f** *it*, because there was no grass. 5800
Mt 26:56 Then all the disciples **f** him, and fled. *863*
Mk 1:18 And straightway they **f** their nets, and *863*
14:50 And they all **f** him, and fled. *863*
Lk 5:11 had brought *their* ships to land, they **f** all, *863*
2Ti 4:16 no *man* stood with me, but all *men* **f** me: *1459*
Heb 11:27 By faith he **f** Egypt, not fearing the wrath *2641*

FORSOOKEST (2) [FORSAKE]

Ne 9:17 and of great kindness, and **f** them not. 5800
9:19 Yet thou in thy manifold mercies **f** them 5800

FORSWEAR (1) [SWEAR]

Mt 5:33 Thou shalt not **f** thyself, but shalt perform *1964*

FORT (6) [FORTIFIED, FORTIFY, FORTRESS, FORTRESSES, FORTS]

2Sa 5: 9 So David dwelt in the **f**, and called it 4686
Isa 25:12 the fortress of the **high f** of thy walls shall 4869
Eze 4: 2 build a **f** against it, and cast a mount against 1785
21:22 the gates, to cast a mount, *and* to build a **f**. 1785
26: 8 he shall make a **f** against thee, and cast a 1785
Da 11:19 he shall turn his face towards the **f** of his 4581

FORTH (888) [HENCEFORTH]

Ge 1:11 God said, Let the earth **bring f** grass, 1876
1:12 the earth **brought f** grass, *and* herb yielding 3318
1:20 Let the waters **bring f abundantly** 8317+8318
1:21 which the waters **brought f abundantly**, 8317
1:24 Let the earth **bring f** the living creature 3318
3:16 in sorrow thou shalt **bring f** children; and 3205
3:18 and thistles shall it **bring f** to thee; 6779
3:22 lest he **put f** his hand, and take also of 7971
3:23 Therefore the LORD God **sent** him **f** from 7971
8: 7 he **sent f** a raven, which went forth to and 7971
8: 7 sent forth a raven, which **went f** to and fro, 3318
8: 8 Also he **sent f** a dove from him, to see if 7971
8: 9 he **put f** his hand, and took her, and 7971
8:10 and again he **sent f** the dove out of the ark; 7971
8:12 yet other seven days; and **sent f** the dove; 7971
8:16 **Go f** of the ark, thou, and thy wife, and 3318
8:17 **Bring f** with thee every living thing that *is* 3318
8:18 Noah **went f**, and his sons, and his wife, 3318
8:19 after their kinds, **went f** out of the ark. 3318
9: 7 **bring f abundantly** in the earth, and 8317
9:18 that **went f** of the ark, were Shem, and 3318
10:11 Out of that land **went f** Asshur, and 3318
11:31 they **went f** with them from Ur of 3318
12: 5 they **went f** to go into the land of Canaan; 3318
14:18 Melchizedek king of Salem **brought f** 3318
15: 4 he that shall **come f** out of thine own 3318
15: 5 he **brought** him **f** abroad, and said, 3318
19:10 the men **put f** their hand, and pulled Lot 7971
19:16 they **brought** him **f**, and set him without 3318
19:17 when they had **brought** them **f** abroad, that 3318
22:10 Abraham **stretched f** his hand, and took 7971
24:43 *that when* the virgin **cometh f** to draw 3318
24:45 Rebekah **came f** with her pitcher on her 3318
24:53 the servant **brought f** jewels of silver, and 3318
30:39 **brought f** cattle ringstraked, speckled, and 3205
38:24 **Bring** her **f**, and let her be burnt. 3318
38:25 When she *was* **brought f**, she sent to her 3318
38:29 she said, How hast thou **broken f**? 6555
39:13 left his garment in her hand, and was fled **f**, 2351
40:10 though it budded, *and* her blossoms **shot f**; 5927
40:10 the clusters thereof **brought f ripe** grapes: 1310
41:47 years the earth **brought f** by handfuls. 6213
42:15 By the life of Pharaoh ye shall not **go f** 3318
Ex 3:10 that thou mayest **bring f** my people 3318
3:11 that I should **bring f** the children of Israel 3318
3:12 When thou hast **brought f** the people out of 3318
4: 4 **Put f** thine hand, and take it by the tail. 7971
4: 4 he **put f** his hand, and caught it, and 7971
4:14 behold, he **cometh f** to meet thee: 3318
5:20 in the way, as they **came f** from Pharaoh: 3318
7: 4 **bring f** mine armies, *and* my people 3318
Ex 7: 5 when I **stretch f** mine hand upon Egypt, 5186
8: 3 the river shall **bring f** frogs **abundantly**, 8317
8: 5 **Stretch f** thine hand with thy rod over 5186
8:18 so with their enchantments to **bring f** lice, 3318
8:20 lo, he **cometh f** to the water; and say unto 3318
9: 9 shall be a boil **breaking f** *with* blains upon 6524
9:10 it became a boil **breaking f** *with* blains 6524
9:22 **Stretch f** thine hand toward heaven, 5186
9:23 Moses **stretched f** his rod toward heaven: 5186
10:13 Moses **stretched f** his rod over the land of 5186
10:22 Moses **stretched f** his hand toward heaven; 5186
12:31 *and* **get** you **f** from amongst my people, 3318
12:39 dough which they **brought f** out of Egypt, 3318
12:46 thou shalt not **carry f** *ought* of the flesh 3318
13: 8 did unto me when I **came f** out of Egypt. 3318
13:16 the LORD **brought** us **f** out of Egypt. 3318
14:11 thus with us, to **carry** us **f** out of Egypt? 3318
14:27 Moses **stretched f** his hand over the sea, 5186
15: 7 thou **sentest f** thy wrath, *which* consumed 7971
15:13 Thou in thy mercy hast **led f** the people 5148
16: 3 for ye have **brought** us **f** into this 3318
16:32 when I **brought** you **f** from the land of 3318
19: 1 when the children of Israel were **gone f** out 3318
19:17 Moses **brought f** the people out of 3318
19:22 lest the LORD **break f** upon them. 6555
19:24 the LORD, lest he **break f** upon them. 6555
25:20 the cherubims shall **stretch f** *their* wings on 6566
29:46 that **brought** them **f** out of the land of 3318
32:11 which thou hast **brought f** out of the land 3318
Lev 4:12 Even the whole bullock shall he **carry f** 3318
4:21 he shall **carry f** the bullock without 3318
6:11 **carry f** the ashes without the camp unto a 3318
14: 3 the priest shall **go f** out of the camp; and 3318
14:45 he shall **carry** *them* **f** out of the city into an 3318
16:24 **come f**, and offer his burnt offering, and 3318
16:27 *place*, shall *one* **carry f** without the camp; 3318
22:27 is **brought f**, then it shall be seven days 3205
24:14 **Bring f** him that hath cursed without 3318
24:23 that they should **bring f** him that had 3318
25:21 it shall **bring f** fruit for three years. 6213
25:38 which **brought** you **f** out of the land of 3318
25:42 which I **brought f** out of the land of Egypt: 3318
25:55 they *are* my servants whom I **brought f out** 3318
26:10 **bring f** the old because of the new. 3318
26:13 which **brought** you **f** out of the land of 3318
26:45 whom I **brought f** out of the land of Egypt 3318
Nu 1: 3 all that *are able to* **go f** *to* war in Israel: 3318
1:20 upward, all that *were able to* **go f** *to* war; 3318
1:22 upward, all that *were able to* **go f** *to* war; 3318
1:24 upward, all that *were able to* **go f** *to* war; 3318
1:26 upward, all that *were able to* **go f** *to* war; 3318
1:28 upward, all that *were able to* **go f** *to* war; 3318
1:30 upward, all that *were able to* **go f** *to* war; 3318
1:32 upward, all that *were able to* **go f** *to* war; 3318
1:34 upward, all that *were able to* **go f** *to* war; 3318
1:36 upward, all that *were able to* **go f** *to* war; 3318
1:38 upward, all that *were able to* **go f** *to* war; 3318
1:40 upward, all that *were able to* **go f** *to* war; 3318
1:42 upward, all that *were able to* **go f** *to* war; 3318
1:45 all that *were able to* **go f** *to* war in Israel; 3318
2: 9 their armies. *These* shall first **set f**. 5265
2:16 And they shall **set f** in the second rank. 5265
11:20 saying, Why **came** we **f** out of Egypt? 3318
11:31 there **went f** a wind from the LORD, and 5265
12: 5 and Miriam: and they both **came f**. 3318
17: 8 **brought f** buds, and bloomed blossoms, 3318
19: 3 that he may **bring** her **f** without the camp, 3318
20: 8 it shall **give f** his water, and thou shalt 5414
20: 8 thou shalt **bring f** to them water out of 3318
20:16 and hath **brought** us **f** out of Egypt: 3318
24: 6 As the valleys are they **spread f**, as gardens 5186
24: 8 God **brought** him **f** out of Egypt; he hath as 3318
26: 4 which **went f** out of the land of Egypt. 3318
31:13 **went f** to meet them without the camp. 3318
33: 1 which **went f** out of the land of Egypt with 3318
34: 4 the **going f** thereof shall be from the south 8444
34: 8 the **goings f** of the border shall be to Zedad: 8444
Dt 1:27 he hath **brought** us **f** out of the land of 3318
2:23 which **came f** out of Caphtor, 3318
4:20 **brought** you **f** out of the iron furnace, 3318
4:45 of Israel, after they **came f** out of Egypt, 3318
4:46 after they were **come f** out of Egypt: 3318
6:12 which **brought** thee **f** out of the land of 3318
8:14 which **brought** thee **f** out of the land of 3318
8:15 who **brought** thee **f** water out of the rock of 3318
9:12 for thy people which thou hast **brought f** 3318
9:26 which thou hast **brought f** out of Egypt 3318
14:22 that the field **bringeth f** year by year. 3318
14:28 At the end of three years thou shalt **bring f** 3318
16: 1 God **brought** thee **f** out of Egypt by night. 3318
16: 3 for thou **camest f** out of the land of Egypt 3318
16: 3 **camest f** out of the land of Egypt all 3318
16: 6 *at* the season that thou **camest f** out of 3318
17: 5 shalt thou **bring f** that man or that woman, 3318
21: 2 thy elders and thy judges shall **come f**, 3318
21:10 When thou **goest f** to war against thine 3318
22:15 **bring f** *the tokens of* the damsel's virginity 3318
23: 4 in the way, when ye **came f** out of Egypt; 3318
23: 9 When the host **goeth f** against thine 3318
23:12 the camp, whither thou shalt **go f** abroad: 3318
24: 9 after that ye were **come f** out of Egypt. 3318
25:11 **putteth f** her hand, and taketh him by 7971
25:17 when ye were **come f** out of Egypt; 3318
26: 8 the LORD **brought** us **f** out of Egypt with 3318
29:25 he **brought** them **f** out of the land of Egypt: 3318
33: 2 he **shined f** from mount Paran, and he came 3313
33:14 for the precious fruits brought **f** by the sun, NIH
33:14 for the precious things **put f** by the moon, 1645
Jos 2: 3 **Bring f** the men that are come to thee, 3318
5: 5 by the way as they **came f** out of Egypt, 3318
8: 9 Joshua therefore **sent** them **f**: and they went 7971
9:12 on the day we **came f** to go unto you; 3318
10:23 **brought f** those five kings unto him out of 3318
18:11 the coast of their lot **came f** between 3318
18:17 **went f** *to* En-shemesh, and went forth 3318

Jos 18:17 *to* En-shemesh, and **went f** toward Geliloth, 3318
19: 1 the second lot **came f** to Simeon, *even* for 3318
Jdg 1:24 the spies saw a man **come f** out of the city, 3318
3:21 Ehud **put f** his left hand, and took 7971
3:23 Ehud **went f** through the porch, and 3318
5:25 she **brought f** butter in a lordly dish. 7126
5:31 *be* as the sun when he **goeth f** in his might. 3318
6: 8 **brought** you **f** out of the house of bondage; 3318
6:18 **bring f** my present, and set *it* before thee. 3318
6:21 the angel of the LORD **put f** the end of 7971
9: 8 The trees **went f on a time** to anoint 1980+1980
9:43 the people *were* **come f** out of the city; 3318
11:31 that whatsoever **cometh f** of the doors of 3318
14:12 I will now **put f** a riddle unto you: 2330
14:13 **Put f** thy riddle, that we may hear it. 2330
14:14 Out of the eater **came f** meat, and out of 3318
14:14 and out of the strong **came f** sweetness. 3318
14:16 thou hast **put f** a riddle unto the children of 2330
15:15 **put f** his hand, and took it, and slew a 7971
19:22 **Bring f** the man that came into thine house, 3318
19:25 his concubine, and brought *her* **f** unto them; 2351
20:21 the children of Benjamin **came f** out of 3318
20:25 Benjamin **went f** against them out of 3318
20:33 the liers in wait of Israel **came f** out of their 1518
Ru 1: 7 Wherefore she **went f** out of the place 3318
2:18 she **brought f**, and gave to her that she had 3318
1Sa 11: 7 Whosoever **cometh** not **f** after Saul and 3318
12: 8 which **brought f** your fathers out of Egypt, 3318
14:11 the Hebrews **come f** out of the holes where 3318
14:27 wherefore he **put f** the end of the rod that 7971
17:20 as the host was **going f** to the fight, and 3318
17:55 when Saul saw David **go f** against 3318
18:30 the princes of the Philistines **went f**: and 3318
18:30 it came to pass, after they **went f**, 3318
22: 3 I pray thee, **come f**, *and be* with you, 3318
22:17 the servants of the king would not **put f** 7971
23:13 from Keilah; and he forbare to **go f**. 3318
24: 6 to **stretch f** mine hand against him, 7971
24:10 I will not **put f** mine hand against my lord; 7971
26: 9 for who can **stretch f** his hand against 7971
26:11 The LORD forbid that *I* should **stretch f** 7971
26:23 I would not **stretch f** mine hand against 7971
30:21 they **went f** to meet David, and to meet 3318
2Sa 1:14 How wast thou not afraid to **stretch f** thine 7971
5:20 The LORD hath **broken f** upon mine 6555
6: 6 Uzzah **put f** *his hand* to the ark of God, and 7971
11: 1 at the time when kings **go f** *to battle,* that 3318
12:30 he **brought f** the spoil of the city in great 3318
12:31 he **brought f** the people that *were* therein, 3318
13:39 *the soul of* king David longed to **go f** unto 3318
15: 5 he **put f** his hand, and took him, and 7971
15:16 the king **went f**, and all his household after 3318
15:17 the king **went f**, and all the people after 3318
16: 5 he **came f**, and cursed still as he came. 3318
16:11 my son, which **came f** of my bowels, 3318
18: 2 David **sent f** a third part of the people 7971
18: 2 **surely go f** with you myself also. 3318+3318
18: 3 the people answered, Thou shalt not **go f**: 3318
18:12 *yet* would I not **put f** mine hand against 7971
19: 7 **go f**, and speak comfortably unto thy 3318
19: 7 for I swear by the LORD, if thou **go** not **f**, 3318
20: 8 sheath thereof; and as he **went f** it fell out. 3318
22:20 He **brought** me **f** also into a large place: he 3318
22:49 that **bringeth** me **f** from mine enemies: 3318
1Ki 2:30 said unto him, Thus saith the king, **Come f**. 3318
2:36 and **go** not **f** thence any whither. 3318
6:27 they **stretched f** the wings of 6566
8: 7 For the cherubims **spread f** *their* two wings 6566
8:16 Since the day that I **brought f** my people 3318
8:19 thy son that shall **come f** out of thy loins, 3318
8:22 and **spread f** his hands *toward* heaven: 6566
8:38 and **spread f** his hands towards this house: 6566
8:51 which thou **broughtest f** out of Egypt, 3318
9: 9 who **brought f** their fathers out of the land 3318
13: 4 that he **put f** his hand from the altar, 7971
13: 4 which he **put f** against him, dried up, so 7971
19:11 **Go f**, and stand upon the mount before 3318
20:33 Ben-hadad **came f** to him; and he caused 3318
21:13 Then they **carried** him **f** out of the city, and 3318
22:21 there **came f** a spirit, and stood before 3318
22:22 I will **go f**, and I will be a lying spirit in 3318
22:22 and prevail also: **go f**, and do so. 3318
2Ki 2: 3 that *were at* Beth-el **came f** to Elisha, 3318
2:21 he **went f** unto the spring of the waters, 3318
2:23 there **came f** little children out of the city, 3318
2:24 there **came f** two she bears out of the wood, 3318
6:15 **gone f**, behold, a host compassed the city 3318
8: 3 she **went f** to cry unto the king for her 3318
9:11 Jehu **came f** to the servants of his lord: 3318
9:15 let none **go f** *nor* escape out of the city to 3318
10:22 **Bring f** vestments for all the worshippers 3318
10:22 of Baal. And he **brought** them **f** vestments. 3318
10:25 Go in, *and* slay them; let none **come f**. 3318
10:26 they **brought f** the images out of the house 3318
11: 7 two parts of all you that **go f** on 3318
11:12 he **brought f** the king's son, and put 3318
11:15 unto them, **Have** her **f** without the ranges: 3318
18: 7 *and* he prospered whithersoever he **went f**: 3318
19: 3 and *there is* not strength to **bring f**. 3205
19:31 For out of Jerusalem shall **go f** a remnant, 3318
21:15 since the day their fathers **came f** out of 3318
23: 4 to **bring f** out of the temple of the LORD 3318
1Ch 12:33 Of Zebulun, such as **went f** to battle, 3318
12:36 such as **went f** to battle, expert in war, 3318
13: 9 Uzza **put f** his hand to hold the ark; 7971
14:11 by mine hand like the **breaking f** of waters: 6556
14:15 for God is **gone f** before thee to smite 3318
16:23 **shew f** from day to day his salvation. 1319
19:16 **drew f** the Syrians that *were* beyond 3318
20: 1 *to battle,* Joab **led f** the power of the army, 5090
24: 7 Now the first lot **came f** to Jehoiarib, 3318
25: 9 Now the first lot **came f** for Asaph to 3318
26:16 and Hosah *the lot came* ***f*** westward, NIH
2Ch 1:17 **brought f** out of Egypt a chariot for six 3318
3:13 **spread** themselves **f** twenty cubits: 6566

2Ch 5: 8 For the cherubims **spread f** *their* wings 6566
6: 5 Since the day that I **brought f** my people 3318
6: 9 thy son which shall **come f** out of thy loins, 3318
6:12 of Israel, and **spread f** his hands: 6566
6:13 and **spread f** his hands towards heaven, 6566
6:29 and shall **spread f** his hands in this house: 6566
7:22 which **brought** them **f** out of the land of 3318
20:20 and **went f** into the wilderness of Tekoa: 3318
20:20 as they **went f**, Jehoshaphat stood and said, 3318
21: 9 Jehoram **went f** with his princes, and all *his* 5674
23:14 said unto them, **Have** her **f** of the ranges: 3318
25: 5 thousand choice *men, able* to **go f** *to* war, 3318
25:11 **led f** his people, and went *to* the valley of 5090
26: 6 he **went f** and warred against 3318
29: 5 **carry f** the filthiness out of the holy *place.* 3318
29:23 they **brought f** the he goats for the sin 5066
32:21 they that **came f** of his own bowels slew 3329
Ezr 1: 7 Also Cyrus the king **brought f** the vessels 3318
1: 7 which Nebuchadnezzar had **brought f** out 3318
1: 8 Even those did Cyrus king of Persia **bring f** 3318
6: 5 which Nebuchadnezzar **took f** out of 5312
Ne 4:16 it came to pass **from** that time **f**, *that* 4480
8:15 **Go f** *unto* the mount, and fetch olive 3318
8:16 So the people **went f**, and brought *them,* 3318
9: 7 **broughtest** him **f** out of Ur of 3318
9:15 **broughtest f** water for them out of the rock 3318
13: 8 I **cast f** all the household stuff of Tobiah 7993
13:21 **From** that time **f** came they no *more* on 4480
Est 4: 6 So Hatach **went f** to Mordecai unto 3318
5: 9 **went** Haman **f** that day joyful and with a 3318
Job 1:11 **put f** thine hand now, and touch all that he 7971
1:12 only upon himself **put** not **f** thine hand. 7971
1:12 So Satan **went f** from the presence of 3318
2: 5 **put f** thine hand now, and touch his bone 7971
2: 7 So **went** Satan **f** from the presence of 3318
5: 6 Although affliction **cometh** not **f** of 3318
8:16 and his branch **shooteth f** in his garden, 3318
10:18 hast thou **brought** me **f** out of the womb? 3318
11:17 thou shalt **shine f**, thou shalt be as 5774
14: 2 He **cometh f** like a flower, and is cut down: 3318
14: 9 it will bud, and **bring f** boughs like a plant. 6213
15:35 **bring f** vanity, and their belly prepareth 3205
21:11 They **send f** their little ones like a flock, 7971
21:30 they shall be **brought f** to the day of wrath. 2986
23:10 he hath tried me, I shall **come f** as gold. 3318
24: 5 asses in the desert, **go** they **f** to their work; 3318
28: 9 He **putteth f** his hand upon the rock; 7971
28:11 the thing that is hid **bringeth** he **f** *to* light. 3318
30: 5 They were **driven f** from among men, 1644
38: 8 shut up the sea with doors, when it **brake f**, 1518
38:27 **cause** the bud of the tender herb to **spring f**? 6779
38:32 Canst thou **bring f** Mazzaroth in his 3318
39: 1 when the wild goats of the rock **bring f**? 3205
39: 2 knowest thou the time when they **bring f**? 3205
39: 3 they **bring f** their young ones, 6398
39: 4 they **go f**, and return not unto them. 3318
40:20 Surely the mountains **bring** him **f** food, 5375
Ps 1: 3 that **bringeth f** his fruit in his season; 5414
7:14 and **brought f** falsehood. 3205
9: 1 I will **shew f** all thy marvellous works. 5608
9:14 That I may **shew f** all thy praise in the gates 5608
17: 2 Let my sentence **come f** from thy presence; 3318
18:19 He **brought** me **f** also into a large place; 3318
19: 6 His **going f** *is* from the end of the heaven, 4161
37: 6 he shall **bring f** thy righteousness as 3318
44: 9 to shame; and **goest** not **f** with our armies. 3318
51:15 and my mouth shall **shew f** thy praise. 5046
55:20 He hath **put f** his hands against such as be 7971
57: 3 God shall **send f** his mercy and his truth. 7971
66: 2 **Sing f** the honour of his name: make his 2167
68: 7 when thou **wentest f** before thy people, 3318
71:15 My mouth shall **shew f** thy righteousness 5608
78:52 **made** his own people **to go f** like sheep, 5265
79:13 we will **shew f** thy praise to all generations. 5608
80: 1 dwellest *between* the cherubims, **shine f**. 3313
88: 8 *I am* shut up, and I cannot **come f**. 3318
90: 2 Before the mountains were **brought f**, or 3205
92: 2 To **shew f** thy lovingkindness in 5046
92:14 They shall still **bring f fruit** in old age; 5107
96: 2 **shew f** his salvation from day to day. 1319
104:14 that *he* may **bring f** food out of the earth; 3318
104:20 all the beasts of the forest do creep ***f***. NIH
104:23 Man **goeth f** unto his work and to his 3318
104:30 Thou **sendest f** thy spirit, they are created: 7971
105:30 Their land **brought f** frogs **in abundance**, 8317
105:37 He **brought** them **f** also with silver and 3318
105:43 he **brought f** his people with joy, *and* 3318
106: 2 the LORD? *who* can **shew f** all his praise? 8085
107: 7 he **led** them **f** by the right way, that *they* 1869
108:11 wilt not thou, O God, go **f** with our hosts? 3318
113: 2 be the name of the LORD from **this time f** 6258
115:18 we will bless the LORD from **this time f** 6258
121: 8 and thy coming in from **this time f**, 6258
125: 3 lest the righteous **put f** their hands unto 7971
125: 5 the LORD shall **lead** them **f** with 1980
126: 6 He that **goeth f and** weepeth, 1980+1980
138: 7 thou shalt **stretch f** thine hand against 7971
141: 2 Let my prayer be **set f** before thee *as* 3559
143: 6 I **stretch f** my hands unto thee: my soul 6566
144: 6 **Cast f lightning**, and scatter them: 1299+1300
144:13 *that* our sheep may **bring f thousands** and 503
146: 4 His breath **goeth f**, he returneth to his earth; 3318
147:15 He **sendeth f** his commandment *upon* 7971
147:17 He **casteth f** his ice like morsels: who can 7993
Pr 7:15 Therefore **came** I **f** to meet thee, 3318
8: 1 and understanding **put f** her voice? 5414
8:24 *there were* no depths, I was **brought f**; 2342
8:25 before the hills was I **brought f**: 2342
9: 3 She hath **sent f** her maidens: she crieth 7971
10:31 The mouth of the just **bringeth f** wisdom: 5107
12:17 *He that* speaketh truth **sheweth f** 5046
25: 4 and there shall **come f** a vessel for the finer. 3318
25: 6 **Put** not **f** thyself in the presence of 1921
25: 8 **Go** not **f** hastily to strive, lest *thou know* 3318
27: 1 thou knowest not what a day may **bring f**. 3205

Pr 30:27 no king, yet **go** they **f** all of them by bands; 3318
30:33 Surely the churning of milk **bringeth f** 3318
30:33 the wringing of the nose **bringeth f** blood: 3318
30:33 so the forcing of wrath **bringeth f** strife. 3318
31:20 yea, she **reacheth f** her hands to the needy. 7971
Ecc 2: 6 to water therewith the wood that **bringeth f** 6779
5:15 As he **came f** of his mother's womb, 3318
7:18 for he that feareth God shall **come f** of 3318
10: 1 **cause** the ointment of the apothecary
to send f 5042
SS 1: 3 thy name *is as* ointment **poured f**, 7324
1: 8 **go** thy **way f** by the footsteps of the flock, 3318
1:12 my spikenard **sendeth f** the smell thereof. 5414
2: 9 our wall, he looketh **f** at the windows, 4480
2:13 The fig tree **putteth f** her green figs, and 2590
3:11 **Go f**, O ye daughters of Zion, and 3318
6:10 Who *is* she that **looketh f** as the morning, 8259
7:11 my beloved, let us **go f** *into* the field; 3318
7:12 grape appear, *and* the pomegranates **bud f**: 5340
8: 5 there thy mother **brought** thee **f**: there she 2254
8: 5 there she **brought** *thee* **f** *that* bare thee. 2254
Isa 1:15 when ye **spread f** your hands, I will hide 6566
2: 3 for out of Zion shall **go f** the law, and 3318
3:16 walk with **stretched f** necks and 5186
5: 2 he looked that *it* should **bring f** grapes, and 6213
5: 2 forth grapes, and it **brought f** wild grapes. 6213
5: 4 when I looked that *it* should **bring f** grapes, 6213
5: 4 forth grapes, **brought** it **f** wild grapes? 6213
5:25 he hath **stretched f** his hand against them, 5186
7: 3 **Go f** now to meet Ahaz, thou, and 3318
7:25 it shall be for the **sending f** of oxen, and 4916
11: 1 there shall **come f** a rod out of the stem of 3318
13:10 the sun shall be darkened in his **going f**, 3318
14: 7 *and* is quiet: they **break f** *into* singing. 6476
14:29 for out of the serpent's root shall **come f** a 3318
23: 4 I travail not, nor **bring f children**, 3205
25:11 he shall **spread f** his hands in the midst of 6566
25:11 as he that swimmeth **spreadeth f** *his hands* 6566
26:18 in pain, we have as it were **brought f** wind; 3205
27: 8 In measure, when it **shooteth f**, thou wilt 7971
28:19 From the time that it **goeth f** it shall take 5674
28:29 This also **cometh f** from the LORD of 3318
31: 4 when a multitude of shepherds is **called f** 7121
32:20 that **send f** *thither* the feet of the ox and 7971
33:11 conceive chaff, ye shall **bring f** stubble: 3205
34: 1 the world, and all things **that come f** of it. 6631
36: 3 **came f** unto him Eliakim, Hilkiah's son, 3318
37: 3 and *there is* not strength to **bring f**. 3205
37: 9 He is **come f** to make war with thee. 3318
37:32 For out of Jerusalem shall **go f** a remnant, 3318
37:36 the angel of the LORD **went f**, and 3318
41:21 **bring f** your strong *reasons,* saith the King 5066
41:22 Let them **bring** *them* **f**, and shew us what 5066
42: 1 he shall **bring f** judgment to the Gentiles. 3318
42: 3 he shall **bring f** judgment unto truth. 3318
42: 5 he that **spread f** the earth, and that which 7554
42: 9 before they **spring f** I tell you of them. 6779
42:13 The LORD shall **go f** as a mighty *man,* he 3318
43: 8 **Bring f** the blind people that have eyes, and 3318
43: 9 shew us former *things?* let them **bring f** 5414
43:17 Which **bringeth f** the chariot and horse, 3318
43:19 I will do a new *thing;* now it shall **spring f**; 6779
43:21 for myself; they shall **shew f** my praise. 5608
44:23 **break f** *into* singing, ye mountains, 6476
44:24 *things;* that **stretcheth f** the heavens alone; 5186
45: 8 let them **bring f** salvation, and 6509
45:10 to the woman, What hast thou **brought f**? 2342
48: 1 and are **come f** out of the waters of Judah, 3318
48: 3 they **went f** out of my mouth, and I shewed 3318
48:20 **Go** ye **f** of Babylon, flee ye from 3318
49: 9 That *thou* mayest say to the prisoners, **Go f**; 3318
49:13 and **break f** *into* singing, O mountains: 6476
49:17 they that made thee waste shall **go f** of thee. 3318
51: 5 my salvation is **gone f**, and mine arms shall 3318
51:13 that hath **stretched f** the heavens, and 5186
51:18 all the sons *whom* she hath **brought f**; 3205
52: 9 **Break f** into joy, sing together, ye waste 6476
54: 1 **break f** *into* singing, and cry aloud, 6476
54: 2 let them **stretch f** the curtains of thine 5186
54: 3 For thou shalt **break f** *on* the right hand 6555
54:16 that **bringeth f** an instrument for his work; 3318
55:10 the earth, and **maketh** it **bring f** and bud, 3205
55:11 So shall my word be that **goeth f** out of my 3318
55:12 go out with joy, and be **led f** with peace: 2986
55:12 the hills shall **break f** before you *into* 6476
58: 8 Then shall thy light **break f** as the morning, 1234
58: 8 and thine health shall **spring f** speedily: 6779
58: 9 the **putting f** of the finger, and 7971
59: 4 conceive mischief, and **bring f** iniquity. 3205
60: 6 they shall **shew f** the praises of the LORD. 1319
61:11 For as the earth **bringeth f** her bud, and 3318
61:11 **causeth** the things that are sown in it
to spring f 6779
61:11 **cause** righteousness and praise **to spring f** 6779
62: 1 until the righteousness thereof **go f** as 3318
65: 9 I will **bring f** a seed out of Jacob, and 3318
65:23 not labour in vain, nor **bring f** for trouble; 3205
66: 7 Before she travailed, she **brought f**; before 3205
66: 8 the earth be **made to bring f** in one day? 2342
66: 8 Zion travailed, she **brought f** her children. 3205
66: 9 bring to the birth, and not **cause to bring f**? 3205
66: 9 shall I **cause to bring f**, and shut 3205
66:24 they shall **go f**, and look upon the carcases 3318
Jer 1: 5 before thou **camest f** out of the womb I 3318
1: 9 the LORD **put f** his hand, and touched my 7971
1:14 Out of the north an evil shall **break f** upon 6605
2:27 and to a stone, Thou hast **brought** me **f**: 3205
2:37 thou shalt **go f** from him, and thine hands 3318
4: 4 lest my fury **come f** like fire, and burn that 3318
4: 7 he is **gone f** from his place to make thy 3318
4:31 as of her that **bringeth f** her **first child**, 1069
6:25 **Go** not **f** *into* the field, nor walk by 3318
7:25 Since the day that your fathers **came f** out 3318
10:13 **bringeth f** the wind out of his treasures. 3318
10:20 my children are **gone f** *of* me, and they *are* 3318

F

Jer 10:20 *there is* none to **stretch f** my tent any more, 5186
11: 4 I **brought** them **f** out of the land of Egypt, 3318
12: 2 they grow, yea, they **bring f** fruit: thou *art* 6213
14:18 If I **go f** *into* the field, then behold the slain 3318
15: 1 *them* out of my sight, and let them **go f.** 3318
15: 2 they say unto thee, Whither shall we **go f**? 3318
15:19 if thou **take f** the precious from the vile, 3318
17:22 Neither **carry f** a burden **out** of your 3318
19: 2 **go f** unto the valley of the son of Hinnom, 3318
20: 3 that Pashur **brought f** Jeremiah out of 3318
20:18 Wherefore **came** I **f** out of the womb to see 3318
22:11 his father, which **went f** out of this place; 3318
22:19 and **cast f** beyond the gates of Jerusalem. 7993
23:15 is profaneness **gone f** into all the land. 3318
23:19 a whirlwind of the LORD is **gone f** *in* 3318
25:32 evil *shall* **go f** from nation to nation, and 3318
26:23 they **fet f** Urijah out of Egypt, and 3318
29:16 *of* your brethren that are not **gone f** with 3318
30:23 the whirlwind of the LORD **goeth f** *with* 3318
31: 4 shalt **go f** in the dances of them that make 3318
31:24 husbandmen, and they *that* **go f** with flocks. 5265
31:39 the measuring line shall yet **go f** over 3318
32:21 hast **brought f** thy people Israel out of 3318
34:13 I **brought** them **f** out of the land of Egypt, 3318
37: 5 Pharaoh's army was **come f** out of Egypt: 3318
37: 7 which is **come f** to help you, 3318
37:12 Jeremiah **went f** out of Jerusalem to go *into* 3318
38: 2 he that **goeth f** to the Chaldeans shall live; 3318
38: 8 Ebed-melech **went f** out of the king's 3318
38:17 If thou wilt **assuredly go f** unto 3318+3318
38:18 if thou wilt not **go f** to the king of 3318
38:21 if thou refuse to **go f**, this *is* the word that 3318
38:22 **brought f** to the king of Babylon's princes, 3318
39: 4 and **went f** out of the city by night, 3318
41: 6 Ishmael the son of Nethaniah **went f** from 3318
42:18 my fury hath been **poured f** upon 5413
42:18 so shall my fury be **poured f** upon you, 5413
43:12 and he shall **go f** from thence in peace. 3318
44: 6 my fury and mine anger was **poured f**, 5413
44:17 thing **goeth f** out of our own mouth, 3318
46: 4 and **stand f** with *your* helmets; 3320
46: 9 ye chariots; and let the mighty *men* **come f**; 3318
48: 7 Chemosh shall **go f** into captivity *with* his 3318
48:45 a fire shall **come f** out of Heshbon, and 3318
49: 5 be driven out every man **right f**; 6440+3807.1
50: 8 **go f** out of the land of the Chaldeans, and 3318
50:25 hath **brought f** the weapons of his 3318
51:10 The LORD hath **brought f** our 3318
51:16 **bringeth f** the wind out of his treasures. 3318
51:44 I will **bring f** out of his mouth that which 3318
52: 7 **went f** out of the city by night *by* the way 3318
52:31 of Judah, and **brought** him **f** out of prison; 3318
La 1:17 Zion **spreadeth f** her hands, *and there is* 6566
Eze 1:13 and out of the fire **went f** lightning. 3318
1:22 **stretched f** over their heads above. 5186
3:22 **go f** into the plain, and I will there talk with 3318
3:23 I arose, and **went f** into the plain: and 3318
5: 4 *for* thereof shall a fire **come f** into all 3318
7:10 the morning is **gone f**; the rod hath 3318
8: 3 he **put f** the form of a hand, and took me by 7971
9: 7 **go** ye **f**. And they went forth, and slew in 3318
9: 7 And they **went f**, and slew in the city. 3318
10: 7 *one* cherub **stretched f** his hand from 7971
11: 7 but *I* will **bring** you **f** out of the midst of it. 3318
12: 4 shalt thou **bring f** thy stuff by day in their 3318
12: 4 thou shalt **go f** at even in their sight, as they 3318
12: 4 their sight, as they that **go f** into captivity. 4161
12: 6 *thy* shoulders, *and* **carry** *it* **f** in the twilight: 3318
12: 7 I **brought f** my stuff by day, as stuff for 3318
12: 7 I **brought** *it* **f** in the twilight, *and* I bare *it* 3318
12:12 *his* shoulder in the twilight, and shall **go f**: 3318
14:22 be left a remnant that shall be **brought f**: 3318
14:22 they *shall* **come f** unto you, and ye shall see 3318
16:14 thy renown **went f** among the heathen for 3318
17: 2 **put f a riddle**, and speak a parable 2330+2420
17: 6 **brought f** branches, and shot forth sprigs. 6213
17: 6 brought forth branches, and **shot f** sprigs. 7971
17: 7 and **shot f** her branches toward him, 7971
17: 8 that *it* might **bring f** branches, and that *it* 6213
17:23 it shall **bring f** boughs, and bear fruit, and 5375
18: 8 He *that* hath not **given f** upon usury, 5414
18:13 Hath **given f** upon usury, and hath taken 5414
20: 6 to **bring** them **f** of the land of Egypt into a 3318
20: 9 in **bringing** them **f** out of the land of Egypt. 3318
20:10 Wherefore I **caused** them **to go f** out of 3318
20:22 in whose sight I **brought** them **f**. 3318
20:38 I will **bring** them **f** out of the country 3318
21: 3 will **draw f** my sword out of his sheath, 3318
21: 4 shall my sword **go f** out of his sheath 3318
21: 5 have **drawn f** my sword out of his sheath: 3318
21:19 both twain shall **come f** out of one land: 3318
24:12 and her great scum **went** not **f** out of her: 3318
27: 7 that **which** thou **spreadest f** to be thy sail; 4666
27:10 helmet in thee; they **set f** thy comeliness. 5414
27:33 When thy wares **went f** out of the seas, 3318
28:18 will I **bring f** a fire from the midst of thee, 3318
29:21 **cause** the horn of the house of Israel
to bud f, 6779
30: 9 In that day shall messengers **go f** from me 3318
31: 5 of the multitude of waters, when he **shot f**. 7971
31: 6 the beasts of the field **bring f** their **young**, 3205
32: 2 thou **camest f** with thy rivers, and 1518
32: 4 I will **cast** thee **f** upon the open field, and 2904
33:30 hear what *is* the word that **cometh f** from 3318
36: 8 ye shall **shoot f** your branches, and 5414
36:20 the LORD, and are **gone f** out of his land. 3318
38: 4 I will **bring** thee **f**, and all thine army, 3318
38: 8 it is **brought f** out of the nations, and 3318
39: 9 that dwell in the cities of Israel shall **go f**, 3318
42: 1 he **brought** me **f** into the utter court, 3318
42:15 he **brought** me **f** toward the gate whose 3318
44: 5 with every **going f** of the sanctuary. 4161
44:19 when they **go f** into the utter court, 3318
46: 2 he shall **go f**; but the gate shall not be shut 3318
46: 8 and he shall **go f** by the way thereof. 3318
Eze 46: 9 gate shall **go f** *by* the way of the north gate: 3318
46: 9 he came in, but shall **go f** over against it. 3318
46:10 go in; and when they **go f**, shall go forth. 3318
46:10 go in; and when they go forth, shall **go f**. 3318
46:12 he shall **go f**; and after his going forth *one* 3318
46:12 and after his **going f** *one* shall shut the gate. 3318
46:21 he **brought** me **f** into the utter court, 3318
47: 3 **went f** east*ward*, he measured a thousand 3318
47: 8 *which* being **brought f** into the sea, 3318
47:10 they shall be a **place to spread f** nets; 4894
47:12 it shall **bring f new fruit** according to his 1069
Da 2:13 the decree **went f** that the wise *men* should 5312
2:14 which was **gone f** to slay the wise *men* of 5312
3:26 **come f**, and come *hither*. Then Shadrach, 5312
3:26 Abed-nego, **came f** of the midst of the fire. 5312
5: 5 In the same hour **came f** fingers of a man's 5312
7:10 stream issued and **came f** from before him: 5312
8: 9 And out of one of them **came f** a little horn, 3318
9:15 that hast **brought** thy people **f** out of 3318
9:22 I am now **come f** to give thee skill and 3318
9:23 supplications the commandment **came f**, 3318
9:25 *that* from the **going f** of the commandment 4161
10:20 when I am **gone f**, lo, the prince of Grecia 3318
11:11 shall **come f** and fight with him, *even* with 3318
11:11 he shall **set f** a great multitude; but 5975
11:13 shall **set f** a multitude greater than 5975
11:42 He shall **stretch f** his hand also upon 7971
11:44 he shall **go f** with great fury to destroy, 3318
Hos 6: 3 his **going f** *is* prepared as the morning; and 4161
6: 5 thy judgments *are as* the light *that* **goeth f**. 3318
9:13 Ephraim *shall* **bring f** his children to 3318
9:16 yea, though they **bring f**, yet will I slay 3205
10: 1 he **bringeth f** fruit unto himself: 7737
13:13 in *the place of* the **breaking f** of children. 4866
14: 5 as the lily, and **cast f** his roots as Lebanon. 5221
Joel 2:16 let the bridegroom **go f** of his chamber, and 3318
3:18 a fountain shall **come f** of the house of 3318
Am 5: 3 that which **went f** *by* an hundred shall leave 3318
7:17 surely go into captivity **f of** his land. 4480+5921
8: 3 they shall **cast** *them* **f** with silence. 7993
8: 5 the sabbath, that we may **set f** wheat, 6605
Jnh 1: 5 **cast f** the wares that *were* in the ship into 2904
1:12 Take me up, and **cast** me **f** into the sea; 2904
1:15 took up Jonah, and **cast** him **f** into the sea: 2904
Mic 1: 3 the LORD **cometh f** out of his place, and 3318
1:11 the inhabitant of Zaanan **came** not **f** *in* 3318
4: 2 for the law shall **go f** of Zion, and the word 3318
4:10 Be in pain, and **labour to bring f**, 1518
4:10 for now shalt thou **go f** out of the city, and 3318
5: 2 *yet* out of thee shall he **come f** unto me *that* 3318
5: 2 whose **goings f** *have been* from of old, 4163
5: 3 *that* she which travaileth hath **brought f**: 3205
7: 9 he will **bring** me **f** to the light, *and* I shall 3318
Hab 1: 4 is slacked, and judgment doth never **go f**: 3318
3: 5 and burning coals **went f** at his feet. 3318
3:13 Thou **wentest f** for the salvation of thy 3318
Zep 2: 2 Before the decree **bring f**, *before* the day 3205
Hag 1:11 upon *that* which the ground **bringeth f**, and 3318
2:19 and the olive tree, hath not **brought f**: 5375
Zec 1:16 a line shall be **stretched f** upon Jerusalem. 5186
2: 3 the angel that talked with me **went f**, and 3318
2: 6 *come f*, and flee from the land of the north, NIH
3: 8 I *will* **bring f** my servant the BRANCH. 935
4: 7 he shall **bring f** the headstone *thereof with* 3318
5: 3 This *is* the curse that **goeth f** over the face 3318
5: 4 I will **bring** it **f**, saith the LORD of hosts, 3318
5: 5 the angel that talked with me **went f**, and 3318
5: 5 thine eyes, and see what *is* this that **goeth f**. 3318
5: 6 he said, This *is* an ephah that **goeth f**. 3318
6: 5 *which* **go f** from standing before the Lord 3318
6: 6 The black horses which *are* therein **go f** 3318
6: 6 the white **go f** after them; and the grisled go 3318
6: 6 the grisled **go f** toward the south country. 3318
6: 7 the bay **went f**, and sought to go that *they* 3318
9:11 by the blood of thy covenant I have **sent f** 7971
9:14 and his arrow shall **go f** as the lightning: 3318
10: 4 Out of him **came f** the corner, out of him 3318
12: 1 which **stretcheth f** the heavens, and 5186
14: 2 half of the city shall **go f** into captivity, and 3318
14: 3 shall the LORD **go f**, and fight against 3318
Mal 4: 2 ye shall **go f**, and grow up as calves of 3318
Mt 1:21 And she shall **bring f** a son, and thou shalt *5088*
1:23 and shall **bring f** a son, and they shall call *5088*
1:25 And knew her not till she had **brought f** *5088*
2:16 and **sent f**, and slew all the children that *649*
3: 8 **Bring f** therefore fruits meet for *4160*
3:10 every tree which **bringeth** not **f** good fruit *4160*
7:17 so every good tree **bringeth f** good fruit; *4160*
7:17 but a corrupt tree **bringeth f** evil fruit. *4160*
7:18 A good tree cannot **bring f** evil fruit, *4160*
7:18 neither *can* a corrupt tree **bring f** good *4160*
7:19 Every tree that **bringeth** not **f** good fruit is *4160*
8: 3 And Jesus **put f** *his* hand, and touched him, *1614*
9: 9 And as Jesus **passed f** from thence, he saw *3855*
9:25 But when the people were **put f**, he went *1544*
9:38 that he will **send f** labourers into his *1544*
10: 5 These twelve Jesus **sent f**, and *649*
10:16 I **send** you **f** as sheep in the midst of wolves: *649*
12:13 saith he to the man, **Stretch f** thine hand. *1614*
12:13 And he **stretched** *it* **f**; and it was restored *1614*
12:20 till he **send f** judgment unto victory. *1544*
12:35 of the heart **bringeth f** good *things*: *1544*
12:35 of the evil treasure **bringeth f** evil *things*. *1544*
12:49 And he **stretched f** his hand toward his *1614*
13: 3 saying, Behold, a sower **went f** to sow; *1831*
13: 8 fell into good ground, and **brought f** fruit, *1325*
13:23 and **bringeth f**, some an hundred*fold*, some *4160*
13:24 Another parable **put** he **f** unto them, saying, *3908*
13:26 and **brought f** fruit, then appeared the tares *4160*
13:31 Another parable **put** he **f** unto them, saying, *3908*
13:41 The Son of man shall **send f** his angels, and *649*
13:43 Then shall the righteous **shine f** as the sun *1584*
13:49 the angels shall **come f**, and sever *1831*
13:52 which **bringeth f** out of his treasure *things* *1544*
14: 2 works do **shew f** themselves **in** him. *1754*
Mt 14:14 And Jesus **went f**, and saw a great *1831*
14:31 And immediately Jesus **stretched f** *his* *1614*
15:18 out of the mouth **come f** from the heart; *1831*
16:21 From **that time f** began Jesus to shew unto *5119*
21:43 given to a nation **bringing f** the fruits *4160*
22: 3 And **sent f** his servants to call them that *649*
22: 4 Again, he **sent f** other servants, saying, *649*
22: 7 and he **sent f** his armies, and *3992*
22:46 neither durst any *man* from that day **f** ask NIG
24:26 Behold, he is in the desert; **go** not **f**: *1831*
24:32 and **putteth f** leaves, ye know that summer *1631*
25: 1 and **went f** to meet the bridegroom. *1831*
Mk 1:38 preach there also: for therefore **came** I **f**. *1831*
1:41 **put f** *his* hand, and touched him, and *1614*
2:12 up the bed, and **went f** before *them* all; *1715*
2:13 And he **went f** again by the sea side; and *1831*
3: 3 the withered hand, Stand **f**. *1519+3319+3588*
3: 5 he saith unto the man, **Stretch f** thine hand. *1614*
3: 6 And the Pharisees **went f**, and *1831*
3:14 and that he might **send** them **f** to preach, *649*
4: 8 and **brought f**, some thirty, and some sixty, *5342*
4:20 the word, and receive *it*, and **bring f fruit**, *2592*
4:28 For the earth **bringeth f fruit** of herself; *2592*
4:29 But when the fruit is **brought f**, *3860*
6: 7 and began to **send** them **f** by two and two; *649*
6:14 mighty works do **shew f** themselves in him. *1754*
6:17 For Herod himself had **sent f** and laid hold *649*
6:24 And she **went f**, and said unto her mother, *1831*
7:26 she besought him that he would **cast f** *1544*
8:11 And the Pharisees **came f**, and began to *1831*
9:29 This kind can **come f** by nothing, but by *1831*
10:17 And when he was **gone f** into the way, *1607*
11: 1 of Olives, he **sendeth f** two of his disciples, *649*
13:28 and **putteth f** leaves, ye know that summer *1631*
14:13 And he **sendeth f** two of his disciples, and *649*
14:16 And his disciples **went f**, and came into *1831*
16:20 And they **went f**, and preached every *1831*
Lk 1: 1 **set f in order** a declaration of those things *392*
1:31 and **bring f** a son, and shalt call his name *5088*
1:57 be delivered; and she **brought f** a son. *1080*
2: 7 And she **brought f** her firstborn son, and *5088*
3: 7 Then said he to the multitude that **came f** to *1607*
3: 8 **Bring f** therefore fruits worthy of *4160*
3: 9 which **bringeth** not **f** good fruit is hewn *4160*
5:13 And he **put f** *his* hand, and touched him, *1614*
5:27 And after these *things* he **went f**, and saw a *1831*
6: 8 Rise up, and stand *f* in the midst. NIG
6: 8 in the midst. And he arose and stood *f*. NIG
6:10 he said unto the man, **Stretch f** thy hand. *1614*
6:43 For a good tree **bringeth** not **f** corrupt fruit; *4160*
6:43 neither doth a corrupt tree **bring f** good *4160*
6:45 of his heart **bringeth f** that which is good; *4393*
6:45 of his heart **bringeth f** that which is evil: *4393*
7:17 And this rumour of him **went f** throughout *1831*
8:14 go *f*, and are choked with cares and riches NIG
8:15 keep *it*, and **bring f fruit** with patience. *2592*
8:22 other side of the lake. And they **launched f**. *321*
8:27 And when he **went f** to land, there met him *1831*
10: 2 that he would **send f** labourers into his *1544*
10: 3 I **send** you **f** as lambs among wolves. *649*
12:16 of a certain rich man **brought f plentifully**: *2164*
12:37 to meat, and will **come f** and serve them. *3928*
14: 7 And he **put f** a parable to those which were *3004*
15:22 **Bring f** the best robe, and put *it* on him; *1627*
20: 9 and **let** it **f** to husbandmen, and went into a *1554*
20:20 And they watched *him*, and **sent f** spies, *649*
21:30 When they now **shoot f**, ye see and *4261*
22:53 ye **stretched f** no hands against me: *1614*
Jn 1:43 The day following Jesus would **go f** into *1831*
2:10 Every man at the beginning doth **set f** good *5087*
2:11 of Galilee, and **manifested f** his glory; *5319*
5:29 And shall **come f**; they that have done *1607*
8:42 for I **proceeded f** and came from God; *1831*
10: 4 And when he **putteth f** his own sheep, he *1544*
11:43 he cried with a loud voice, Lazarus, **come f**. *1854*
11:44 And he that was dead **came f**, bound hand *1831*
11:53 Then from that day **f** they took counsel NIG
12:13 and **went f** to meet him, and cried, *1831*
12:24 but if it die, it **bringeth f** much fruit. *5342*
15: 2 he purgeth it, that it may **bring f** more fruit. *5342*
15: 5 I in him, the same **bringeth f** much fruit: *5342*
15: 6 he is cast **f** as a branch, and is withered; *1854*
15:16 that you should go and **bring f** fruit, and *5342*
16:28 I **came f** from the Father, and am come into *1831*
16:30 by this we believe that thou **camest f** from *1831*
18: 1 **went f** with his disciples over the brook *1831*
18: 4 **went f**, and said unto them, Whom seek *1831*
19: 4 Pilate therefore went **f** again, and *1854*
19: 4 unto them, Behold, I bring him **f** to you, *1854*
19: 5 Then **came** Jesus **f**, wearing the crown of *1831*
19:13 he brought Jesus **f**, and sat down in *1854*
19:17 And he bearing his cross **went f** into a *1831*
20: 3 Peter therefore **went f**, and *that* other *1831*
21: 3 They **went f**, and entered into a ship *1831*
21:18 thou shalt **stretch f** thy hands, and *1614*
Ac 1:26 And they **gave f** their lots; and the lot fell *1325*
2:33 he hath **shed f** this, which ye now see and *1632*
4:30 By **stretching f** thine hand to heal; and *1614*
5:10 and found her dead, and, **carrying** *her* **f**, *1627*
5:15 Insomuch that *they* **brought f** the sick into *1627*
5:19 prison doors, and **brought** them **f**, and said, *1806*
5:34 commanded to put the apostles **f** a little *1854*
7: 7 and after that shall they **come f**, and *1831*
9:30 down to Cesarea, and **sent** him **f** to Tarsus. *1821*
9:40 But Peter **put** *them* all **f**, *1544*
11:22 and they **sent f** Barnabas, that *he* should go *1821*
12: 1 **stretched f** *his* hands to vex certain of *1911*
12: 4 intending after Easter to **bring** him **f** to *321*
12: 6 when Herod would have **brought** him **f**, *4254*
13: 4 So they, being **sent f** by the Holy Ghost, *1599*
16: 3 Him would Paul have to **go f** with him; and *1831*
17:18 other *some*, He seemeth to be a **setter f** of *2604*
21: 2 unto Phenicia, we went aboard, and **set f**. *321*
23:28 I **brought** him **f** into their council: *2609*
24: 2 And when he was called *f*, Tertullus began NIG

Ac 25:17 and commanded the man to be brought f. NIG
25:23 Festus' commandment Paul was brought f. NIG
25:26 Wherefore I have brought him f before 4254
26:1 Then Paul stretched f the hand, and 1614
26:25 but speak f the words of truth and 669
27:21 But after long abstinence Paul stood f in NIG
Ro 3:25 Whom God hath set f to be a propitiation 4388
7:4 that we should bring f fruit unto God. 2592
7:5 did work in our members to bring f fruit 2592
10:21 All day long have I stretched f my hands 1600
1Co 4:9 For I think that God hath set f us the apostles 584
16:11 but conduct him f in peace, that he may 4311
Gal 3:1 eyes Jesus Christ hath been evidently set f, 4270
4:4 God sent f his Son, made of a woman, 1821
4:6 God hath sent f the Spirit of his Son into 1821
4:27 break f and cry, thou that travailest not: 4486
Php 2:16 Holding f the word of life; that I may 1907
3:13 reaching f unto those things which are 1901
Col 1:6 and bringeth f fruit, as it doth also in you, 2592
1Ti 1:16 that in me first Jesus Christ might shew f 1731
Heb 1:14 sent f to minister for them who shall be heirs 649
6:7 bringeth f herbs meet for them by whom it 5088
13:13 Let us go f therefore unto him without 1831
Jas 1:15 when lust hath conceived, it bringeth f sin: 5088
1:15 when it is finished, bringeth f death. 616
3:11 Doth a fountain send f at the same place 1032
5:18 gave rain, and the earth brought f her fruit. 985
1Pe 2:9 that ye should shew f the praises of him 1804
3Jn 1:7 that for his name's sake they went f, 1831
Jude 1:7 after strange flesh, are set f for an example, 4295
Rev 5:6 which are the seven spirits of God sent f into 649
6:2 and he went f conquering, and to conquer. 1831
12:5 And she brought f a man child, who was to 5088
12:13 he persecuted the woman which brought f 5088
16:14 which go f unto the kings of the earth and 1607

FORTHWITH (10)

Ezr 6:8 f expences be given unto these men, 629
Mt 13:5 and f they sprung up, because they had no 2112
26:49 And f he came to Jesus, and said, Hail, 2112
Mk 1:29 And f, when they were come out of 2112
1:43 straitly charged him, and f sent him away; 2112
5:13 And f Jesus gave them leave. And 2112
Jn 19:34 and f came there out blood and water. 2112
Ac 9:18 and he received sight f, and arose, and 3916
12:10 and f the angel departed from him. 2112
21:30 of the temple: and f the doors were shut. 2112

FORTIETH (4) [FORTY]

Nu 33:38 in the f year after the children of Israel were 705
Dt 1:3 it came to pass in the f year, in the eleventh 705
1Ch 26:31 In the f year of the reign of David they were 705
2Ch 16:13 and died in the one and f year of his reign. 705

FORTIFIED (4) [FORT]

2Ch 11:11 he f the strong holds, and put captains in 2388
26:9 and at the turning of the wall, and f them. 2388
Ne 3:8 and they f Jerusalem unto the broad wall. 5800
Mic 7:12 from the f cities, and from the fortress even 4693

FORTIFY (6) [FORT]

Jdg 9:31 and behold, they f the city against thee. 6696
Ne 4:2 will they f themselves? will they sacrifice? 5800
Isa 22:10 the houses have ye broken down to f 1219
Jer 51:53 though she should f the height of her 1219
Na 2:1 make thy loins strong, f thy power mightily. 553
3:14 thee waters for the siege, f thy strong holds: 2388

FORTRESS (15) [FORT]

2Sa 22:2 is my rock, and my f, and my deliverer; 4686
Ps 18:2 is my rock, and my f, and my deliverer; 4686
31:3 For thou art my rock and my f; therefore 4686
71:3 to save me; for thou art my rock and my f. 4686
91:2 of the LORD, He is my refuge and my f: 4686
144:2 My goodness, and my f; my high tower, 4686
Isa 17:3 The f also shall cease from Ephraim, and 4013
25:12 the f of the high fort of thy walls shall he 4013
Jer 6:27 thee for a tower and a f among my people, 4013
10:17 wares out of the land, O inhabitant of the f. 4692
16:19 my f, and my refuge in the day of affliction, 4581
Da 11:7 shall enter into the f of the king of 4581
11:10 he return, and be stirred up, even to his f. 4581
Am 5:9 so that the spoiled shall come against the f. 4013
Mic 7:12 from the f even to the river, and from sea to 4693

FORTRESSES (2) [FORT]

Isa 34:13 nettles and brambles in the f thereof: 4013
Hos 10:14 thy people, and all thy f shall be spoiled, 4013

FORTS (6) [FORT]

2Ki 25:1 and they built f against it round about. 1785
Isa 29:3 with a mount, and I will raise f against thee. 4694
32:14 the f and towers shall be for dens for ever, 6076
Jer 52:4 against it, and built f against it round about. 1785
Eze 17:17 by casting up mounts, and building f, to cut 1785
33:27 they that be in the f and in the caves shall 4679

FORTUNATUS (2)

1Co 16:17 coming of Stephanas and F and Achaicus: 5415
16: S and F, and Achaicus, and Timotheus. 5415

FORTY (157) [FORTIETH, FORTY'S]

Ge 5:13 begat Mahalaleel eight hundred and f years, 705
7:4 I will cause it to rain upon the earth f days 705
7:4 to rain upon the earth forty days and f nights; 705
7:12 the rain was upon the earth f days and 705
7:12 was upon the earth forty days and f nights. 705
7:17 And the flood was f days upon the earth; and 705
8:6 it came to pass at the end of f days, 705
18:28 he said, If I find there f and five, I will not 705
18:29 Peradventure there shall be f found there. 705
25:20 Isaac was f years old when he took Rebekah 705
26:34 Esau was f years old when he took to wife 705
32:15 f kine, and ten bulls, twenty she asses, and 705
47:28 so the whole age of Jacob was an hundred f 705
50:3 f days were fulfilled for him; for so 705
Ex 16:35 the children of Israel did eat manna f years, 705
24:18 Moses was in the mount f days and 705
24:18 was in the mount forty days and f nights. 705
26:19 thou shalt make f sockets of silver under 705
26:21 their f sockets of silver; two sockets under 705
34:28 he was there with the LORD f days and 705
34:28 with the LORD forty days and f nights; 705
36:24 f sockets of silver he made under the twenty 705
36:26 their f sockets of silver; two sockets under 705
Lev 25:8 seven sabbaths of years shall be unto thee f 705
Nu 1:21 were f and six thousand and five hundred. 705
1:25 were f and five thousand six hundred and 705
1:33 were f thousand and five hundred. 705
1:41 were f and one thousand and five hundred. 705
2:11 were f and six thousand and five hundred. 705
2:15 were f and five thousand and six hundred 705
2:19 of them, were f thousand and five hundred. 705
2:28 were f and one thousand and five hundred. 705
13:25 from searching of the land after f days. 705
14:33 shall wander in the wilderness f years, 705
14:34 even f days, each day for a year, shall ye 705
14:34 even f years, and ye shall know my breach 705
26:7 they that were numbered of them were f and 705
26:18 of them, f thousand and five hundred. 705
26:41 they that were numbered of them were f and 705
26:50 they that were numbered of them were f and 705
32:13 he made them wander in the wilderness f 705
35:6 to them ye shall add f and two cities. 705
35:7 which ye shall give to the Levites shall be f 705
Dt 2:7 these f years the LORD thy God hath been 705
8:2 God led thee these f years in the wilderness, 705
8:4 neither did thy foot swell, these f years. 705
9:9 I abode in the mount f days and forty nights, 705
9:9 I abode in the mount forty days and f nights, 705
9:11 it came to pass at the end of f days and 705
9:11 to pass at the end of forty days and f nights, 705
9:18 as at the first, f days and forty nights: 705
9:18 as at the first, forty days and f nights: 705
9:25 Thus I fell down before the LORD f days 705
9:25 before the LORD forty days and f nights, 705
10:10 to the first time, f days and forty nights; 705
10:10 to the first time, forty days and f nights; 705
25:3 F stripes he may give him, and not exceed: 705
29:5 And I have led you f years in the wilderness: 705
Jos 4:13 About f thousand prepared for war passed 705
5:6 For the children of Israel walked f years in 705
14:7 F years old was I when Moses the servant of 705
14:10 me alive, as he said, these f and five years, 705
21:41 possession of the children of Israel were f 705
Jdg 3:11 the land had rest f years. And Othniel 705
5:8 or spear seen among f thousand in Israel? 705
5:31 in his might. And the land had rest f years. 705
8:28 the country was in quietness f years in 705
12:6 there fell at that time of the Ephraimites f 705
12:14 he had f sons and thirty nephews, that rode 705
13:1 them into the hand of the Philistines f years. 705
1Sa 4:18 and heavy. And he had judged Israel f years. 705
17:16 and evening, and presented himself f days. 705
2Sa 2:10 Ish-bosheth Saul's son was f years old when 705
5:4 he began to reign, and he reigned f years. 705
10:18 f thousand horsemen, and smote Shobach 705
15:7 it came to pass after f years, that Absalom 705
1Ki 2:11 that David reigned over Israel were f years: 705
4:26 Solomon had f thousand stalls of horses for 705
6:17 is, the temple before it, was f cubits long. 705
7:3 that lay on f five pillars, fifteen in a row. 705
7:38 one laver contained f baths: and every laver 705
11:42 in Jerusalem over all Israel was f years. 705
14:21 Rehoboam was f and one years old when he 705
15:10 And f and one years reigned he in Jerusalem. 705
19:8 went in the strength of that meat f days and 705
19:8 and f nights unto Horeb the mount of God. 705
2Ki 2:24 and tare f and two children of them. 705
8:9 f camels' burden, and came and stood before 705
10:14 of the shearing house, even two and f men; 705
12:1 to reign; and f years reigned he in Jerusalem. 705
14:23 in Samaria, and reigned f and one years. 705
1Ch 5:18 were four and f thousand seven hundred and 705
12:36 forth to battle, expert in war, f thousand. 705
19:18 f thousand footmen, and killed Shophach 705
29:27 the time that he reigned over Israel was f 705
2Ch 9:30 reigned in Jerusalem over all Israel f years. 705
12:13 and f years old when he began to reign, 705
22:2 F and two years old was Ahaziah when he 705
24:1 to reign, and he reigned f years in Jerusalem. 705
Ezr 2:8 children of Zattu, nine hundred f and five. 705
2:10 The children of Bani, six hundred f and two. 705
2:24 The children of Azmaveth, f and two. 705
2:25 and Beeroth, seven hundred and f and three. 705
2:34 children of Jericho, three hundred f and five. 705
2:38 a thousand two hundred f and seven. 705
2:64 together was f and two thousand 505+702+7239
2:66 and six; their mules, two hundred f and five; 705
Ne 5:15 and wine, beside f shekels of silver, 705
7:13 children of Zattu, eight hundred f and five. 705
7:15 children of Binnui, six hundred f and eight. 705
7:28 The men of Beth-azmaveth, f and two. 705
7:29 and Beeroth, seven hundred f and three. 705
7:36 children of Jericho, three hundred f and five. 705
7:41 a thousand two hundred f and seven. 705
7:44 children of Asaph, an hundred f and eight. 705
7:62 children of Nekoda, six hundred f and two. 705
7:66 together was f and two thousand 505+702+7239
7:67 they had two hundred f and five singing men 705
7:68 and six: their mules, two hundred f and five: 705
9:21 f years didst thou sustain them in 705
11:13 chief of the fathers, two hundred f and two: 705
Job 42:16 After this lived Job an hundred and f years, 705
Ps 95:10 F years long was I grieved with this 705
Jer 52:30 away captive of the Jews seven hundred f 705
Eze 4:6 the iniquity of the house of Judah f days: 705
29:11 neither shall it be inhabited f years. 705
29:12 that are laid waste shall be desolate f years: 705
29:13 At the end of f years will I gather 705
41:2 and he measured the length thereof, f cubits: 705
46:22 there were courts joined of f cubits long 705
Am 2:10 led you f years through the wilderness, 705
5:25 and offerings in the wilderness f years, 705
Jnh 3:4 Yet f days, and Nineveh shall be 705
Mt 4:2 And when he had fasted f days and 5062
4:2 when he had fasted forty days and f nights, 5062
Mk 1:13 And he was there in the wilderness f days, 5062
Lk 4:2 Being f days tempted of the devil. And in 5062
Jn 2:20 F and six years was this temple in building, 5062
Ac 1:3 being seen of them f days, and speaking of 5062
4:22 For the man was above f years old, 5062
7:23 And when he was full f years old, it came 5063
7:30 And when f years were expired, 5062
7:36 the Red sea, and in the wilderness f years. 5062
7:42 sacrifices by the space of f years in 5062
13:18 And about the time of f years suffered he 5063
13:21 tribe of Benjamin, by the space of f years. 5062
23:13 And they were more than f which had made 5062
23:21 lie in wait for him of them moe than f men, 5062
2Co 11:24 Of the Jews five times received I f stripes 5062
Heb 3:9 proved me, and saw my works f years. 5062
3:17 But with whom was he grieved f years? 5062
Rev 7:4 and there were sealed an hundred and f and 5062
11:2 the holy city shall they tread under foot f 5062
13:5 power was given unto him to continue f 5062
14:1 and with him an hundred f and 5062
14:3 but the hundred and f and four thousand, 5062
21:17 an hundred and f and four cubits, 5062

FORTY'S (1) [FORTY]

Ge 18:29 And he said, I will not do it for f sake. 705

FORUM (1)

Ac 28:15 they came to meet us as far as Appii f, and 5410

FORWARD (47) [FORWARDNESS, HENCEFORWARD]

Ge 26:13 went f, and grew until he became very 1980
Ex 14:15 unto the children of Israel, that they go f: 5265
Nu 1:51 when the tabernacle setteth f, the Levites 5265
2:17 set f with the camp of the Levites in 5265
2:17 as they encamp, so shall they set f, 5265
2:24 And they shall go f in the third rank. 5265
2:34 so they set f, every one after their families, 5265
4:5 when the camp setteth f, Aaron shall come, 5265
4:15 of the sanctuary, as the camp is to set f; 5265
10:5 camps that lie on the east parts shall go f. 5265
10:17 of Gershon and the sons of Merari set f, 5265
10:18 the standard of the camp of Reuben set f 5265
10:21 the Kohathites set f, bearing the sanctuary: 5265
10:22 of Ephraim set f according to their armies: 5265
10:25 of the camp of the children of Dan set f, 5265
10:28 according to their armies, when they set f. 5265
10:35 when the ark set f, that Moses said, 5265
21:10 the children of Israel set f, and pitched in 5265
22:1 the children of Israel set f, and pitched in 5265
32:19 with them on yonder side Jordan, or f; 1973
Jdg 9:44 rushed f, and stood in the entering of 6584
1Sa 10:3 shalt thou go on f from thence, and 1973
16:13 came upon David from that day f. 4605+1886.5
18:9 And Saul eyed David from that day and f. 1973
30:25 it was so from that day f, that he 4605+1886.5
2Ki 3:24 they went f smiting the Moabites, even in 935
4:24 Drive, and go f; slack not thy riding for me, NIH
20:9 shall the shadow go f ten degrees, or 1980
1Ch 23:4 four thousand were to set f the work of 5329
2Ch 34:12 of the sons of the Kohathites, to set it f; 5329
Ezr 3:8 to set f the work of the house of 5329
3:9 to set f the workmen in the house of God: 5329
Job 23:8 I go f, but he is not there; and backward, 6924
30:13 They mar my path, they set f my calamity, 3276
Jer 7:24 and went backward, and not f. 6440+3807.1
Eze 1:9 they went every one straight f. 413+5676+6440
1:12 they went every one straight f. 413+5676+6440
10:22 they went every one straight f. 413+5676+6440
39:22 the LORD their God from that day and f. 1973
43:27 it shall be, that upon the eight day, and so f, 1973
Zec 1:15 and they helped f the affliction. 5826
Mk 14:35 And he went f a little, and fell on 4281
Ac 19:33 of the multitude, the Jews putting him f. 4261
2Co 8:10 not only to do, but also to be f a year ago. 2309
8:17 but being more f, of his own accord he 4707
Gal 2:10 the poor; the same which I also was f to do. 4704
3Jn 1:6 whom if thou bring f on their journey 4311

FORWARDNESS (2) [FORWARD]

2Co 8:8 but by occasion of the f of others, and 4710
9:2 For I know the f of your mind, for which I 4288

FOUGHT (64) [FIGHT]

Ex 17:8 and f with Israel in Rephidim. 3898
17:10 Moses had said to him, and f with Amalek: 3898
Nu 21:1 he f against Israel, and took some of them 3898
21:23 and he came to Jahaz, and f against Israel. 3898
21:26 who had f against the former king of Moab, 3898
Jos 10:14 voice of a man: for the LORD f for Israel. 3898
10:29 unto Libnah, and f against Libnah: 3898
10:31 and encamped against it, and f against it: 3898
10:34 they encamped against it, and f against it: 3898
10:36 unto Hebron; and they f against it: 3898
10:38 Israel with him, to Debir; and f against it: 3898
10:42 the LORD God of Israel f for Israel. 3898
23:3 for the LORD your God is he that hath f 3898
24:8 the other side Jordan; and they f with you: 3898
24:11 the men of Jericho f against you, 3898
Jdg 1:5 they f against him, and they slew 3898
1:8 Now the children of Judah had f against 3898
5:19 The kings came and f, then fought the kings 3898
5:19 f the kings of Canaan in Taanach by 3898
5:20 They f from heaven; the stars in their 3898
5:20 the stars in their courses f against Sisera. 3898
9:17 (For my father f for you, and 3898

Jdg 9:39 men of Shechem, and **f** with Abimelech. 3898
9:45 Abimelech **f** against the city all that day; 3898
9:52 **f** against it, and went hard unto the door of 3898
11:20 and pitched in Jahaz, and **f** against Israel. 3898
12: 4 all the men of Gilead, and **f** with Ephraim: 3898
1Sa 4:10 the Philistines **f**, and Israel was smitten, 3898
12: 9 the king of Moab, and they **f** against them. 3898
14:47 **f** against all his enemies on every side, 3898
19: 8 **f** with the Philistines, and slew them *with* a 3898
23: 5 **f** with the Philistines, and brought away 3898
31: 1 Now the Philistines **f** against Israel: and 3898
2Sa 2:28 Israel no more, neither **f** they any more. 3898
8:10 because he had **f** against Hadadezer, and 3898
10:17 in array against David, and **f** with him. 3898
11:17 men of the city went out, and **f** with Joab: 3898
12:26 Joab **f** against Rabbah of the children of 3898
12:27 I have **f** against Rabbah, and have taken 3898
12:29 to Rabbah, and **f** against it, and took it. 3898
21:15 with him, and **f against** the Philistines: 3898
2Ki 8:29 when he **f** against Hazael king of Syria. 3898
9:15 when he **f** with Hazael king of Syria.) 3898
12:17 went up, and **f** against Gath, and took it: 3898
13:12 his might where*with* he **f** against Amaziah 3898
14:15 and how he **f** with Amaziah king of Judah, 3898
1Ch 10: 1 Now the Philistines **f** against Israel; and 3898
18:10 because he had **f** against Hadarezer, and 3898
19:17 array against the Syrians, they **f** with him. 3898
19:18 seven thousand *men which* **f** *in* chariots, NIH
2Ch 20:29 when they had heard that the LORD **f** 3898
22: 6 when he **f** with Hazael king of Syria. 3898
27: 5 He **f** also with the king of the Ammonites, 3898
Ps 109: 3 of hatred; and **f** against me without a cause. 3898
Isa 20: 1 and **f** against Ashdod, and took it; 3898
63:10 to be their enemy, *and* he **f** against them. 3898
Jer 34: 1 **f** against Jerusalem, and against all 3898
34: 7 When the king of Babylon's army **f** against 3898
Zec 14: 3 as when he **f** in the day of battle. 3898
14:12 all the people that have **f** against Jerusalem; 6633
1Co 15:32 of men I have **f with beasts** at Ephesus, *2341*
2Ti 4: 7 I have **f** a good fight, I have finished *my* *75*
Rev 12: 7 and his angels **f** against the dragon; *4170*
12: 7 the dragon; and the dragon **f** and his angels, *4170*

FOUL (5) [FOULED, FOULEDST]

Job 16:16 My face is **f** with weeping, and on mine 2560
Eze 34:18 but ye must **f** the residue with your feet? 7515
Mt 16: 3 in the morning, *It will be* **f weather** to day: *5494*
Mk 9:25 he rebuked the **f** spirit, saying unto him, *169*
Rev 18: 2 and the hold of every **f** spirit, and a cage of *169*

FOULED (1) [FOUL]

Eze 34:19 they drink **that which** ye have **f** with your 4833

FOULEDST (1) [FOUL]

Eze 32: 2 the waters with thy feet, and **f** their rivers. 7515

FOUND (403) [FIND, FOUNDATION, FOUNDATIONS, FOUNDED, FOUNDER, FOUNDEST]

Ge 2:20 for Adam there was not **f** a help meet for 4672
6: 8 Noah **f** grace in the eyes of the LORD. 4672
8: 9 the dove **f** no rest for the sole of her foot, 4672
11: 2 that they **f** a plain in the land of Shinar; 4672
16: 7 the angel of the LORD **f** her by a fountain 4672
18: 3 if now I have **f** favour in thy sight, 4672
18:29 Peradventure there shall be forty **f** there. 4672
18:30 Peradventure there shall thirty be **f** there. 4672
18:31 Peradventure there shall be twenty **f** there. 4672
18:32 Peradventure ten shall be **f** there. And he 4672
19:19 thy servant hath **f** grace in thy sight, and 4672
26:19 and **f** there a well of springing water. 4672
26:32 and said unto him, We have **f** water. 4672
27:20 How *is it that* thou hast **f** *it so* quickly, my 4672
30:14 **f** mandrakes in the field, and brought them 4672
30:27 I pray thee, if I have **f** favour in thine eyes, 4672
31:33 two maidservants' tents; but he **f** *them* not. 4672
31:34 Laban searched all the tent, but **f** *them* not. 4672
31:35 And he searched, but **f** not the images. 4672
31:37 what hast thou **f** of all thy household stuff? 4672
33:10 if now I have **f** grace in thy sight, then 4672
36:24 this *was that* Anah that **f** the mules in 4672
37:15 a *certain* man **f** him, and behold, *he was* 4672
37:17 after his brethren, and **f** them in Dothan. 4672
37:32 *it* to their father; and said, This have we **f**: 4672
38:20 from the woman's hand: but he **f** her not. 4672
38:23 I sent this kid, and thou hast not **f** her. 4672
39: 4 Joseph **f** grace in his sight, and he served 4672
44: 8 which we **f** in our sacks' mouths, 4672
44: 9 With whom*soever* of thy servants it be **f**, 4672
44:10 he with whom it is **f** shall be my servant; 4672
44:12 and the cup was **f** in Benjamin's sack. 4672
44:16 God hath **f out** the iniquity of thy servants: 4672
44:16 and *he* also with whom the cup is **f**. 4672
44:17 *but* the man in whose hand the cup is **f**, 4672
47:14 Joseph gathered up all the money that was **f** 4672
47:29 If now I have **f** grace in thy sight, put, 4672
50: 4 If now I have **f** grace in your eyes, speak, 4672
Ex 9:19 and beast which shall be **f** in the field, 4672
12:19 Seven days shall there be no leaven **f** in 4672
15:22 days in the wilderness, and **f** no water. 4672
16:27 seventh day for to gather, and they **f** none. 4672
21:16 and selleth him, or if he be **f** in his hand, 4672
22: 2 If a thief be **f** breaking up, and be smitten 4672
22: 4 If the theft be **certainly f** in his hand 4672+4672
22: 7 if the thief be **f**, let him pay double. 4672
22: 8 If the thief be not **f**, then the master of 4672
33:12 and thou hast also **f** grace in my sight. 4672
33:13 I pray thee, if I have **f** grace in thy sight, 4672
33:16 and thy people have **f** grace in thy sight? 4672
33:17 for thou hast **f** grace in my sight, and 4672
34: 9 If now I have **f** grace in thy sight, O Lord, 4672
35:23 with whom was **f** blue, and purple, and 4672
35:24 with whom was **f** shittim wood for any 4672
Lev 6: 3 Or have **f** that which was lost, and 4672
Lev 6: 4 him to keep, or the lost *thing* which he **f**, 4672
Nu 11:11 wherefore have I not **f** favour in thy sight, 4672
11:15 out of hand, if I have **f** favour in thy sight; 4672
15:32 they **f** a man that gathered sticks upon 4672
15:33 they that **f** him gathering sticks brought him 4672
32: 5 said they, if we have **f** grace in thy sight, 4672
Dt 17: 2 If there be **f** among you, within any of thy 4672
18:10 There shall not be **f** among you *any one* 4672
20:11 *that* all the people that is **f** therein shall be 4672
21: 1 If *one* be **f** slain in the land which 4672
22: 3 which he hath lost, and thou hast **f**, shalt 4672
22:14 when I came to her, I **f** her not a maid: 4672
22:17 *her,* saying, I **f** not thy daughter a maid; 4672
22:20 *the tokens of* virginity be not **f** for 4672
22:22 If a man be **f** lying with a woman married 4672
22:27 For he **f** her in the field, *and* the betrothed 4672
22:28 hold on her, and lie with her, and they be **f**; 4672
24: 1 because he hath **f** some uncleanness in her: 4672
24: 7 If a man be **f** stealing any of his brethren of 4672
32:10 He **f** him in a desert land, and in the waste 4672
33:29 and thine enemies shall be **f liars** unto thee; 3584
Jos 2:22 throughout all the way, but **f** *them* not. 4672
10:17 The five kings are **f** hid in a cave at 4672
Jdg 1: 5 they **f** Adoni-bezek in Bezek: and 4672
6:17 If now I have **f** grace in thy sight, then 4672
14:18 with my heifer, ye had not **f out** my riddle. 4672
15:15 he **f** a new jawbone of an ass, and put forth 4672
21:12 they **f** among the inhabitants of 4672
Ru 2:10 unto him, Why have I **f** grace in thine eyes, 4672
1Sa 9: 4 the land of Shalisha, but they **f** *them* not: 4672
9: 4 land of the Benjamites, but they **f** *them* not. 4672
9:11 they **f** young maidens going out to draw 4672
9:20 set not thy mind on them; for they are **f**. 4672
10: 2 The asses which thou wentest to seek are **f**: 4672
10:16 He told us plainly that the asses were **f**. 4672
10:21 when they sought him, he could not be **f**. 4672
12: 5 that ye have not **f** ought in my hand. 4672
13:19 Now there was no smith **f** throughout all 4672
13:22 that there was neither sword nor spear **f** in 4672
13:22 and with Jonathan his son was there **f**. 4672
14:30 of the spoil of their enemies which they **f**? 4672
16:22 before me; for he hath **f** favour in my sight. 4672
20: 3 Thy father certainly knoweth that I have **f** 4672
20:29 and now, if I have **f** favour in thine eyes, 4672
25:28 and evil hath not been **f** in thee *all* thy days. 4672
27: 5 If I have now **f** grace in thine eyes, 4672
29: 3 I have **f** no *fault* in him since he fell *unto* 4672
29: 6 for I have not **f** evil in thee since the day of 4672
29: 8 what hast thou **f** in thy servant so long as I 4672
30:11 they **f** an Egyptian in the field, and 4672
31: 8 that they **f** Saul and his three sons fallen in 4672
2Sa 7:27 hath thy servant **f** in his heart to pray this 4672
14:22 To day thy servant knoweth that I have **f** 4672
17:12 him in some place where he shall be **f**, 4672
17:13 until there be not one small stone **f** there. 4672
1Ki 1: 3 **f** Abishag a Shunammite, and brought her 4672
1:52 if wickedness shall be **f** in him, he shall die. 4672
7:47 neither was the weight of the brass **f out**. 2713
11:19 Hadad **f** great favour in the sight of 4672
11:29 that the prophet Ahijah the Shilonite **f** him 4672
13:14 man of God, and **f** him sitting under an oak: 4672
13:28 he went and **f** his carcase cast in the way, 4672
14:13 in him there is **f** *some* good thing toward 4672
18:10 and nation, that they **f** thee not. 4672
19:19 and **f** Elisha the son of Shaphat, 4672
20:36 from him, a lion **f** him, and slew him. 4672
20:37 he **f** another man, and said, Smite me, 4672
21:20 to Elijah, Hast thou **f** me, O mine enemy? 4672
21:20 I have **f** *thee:* because thou hast sold thyself 4672
2Ki 2:17 and they sought three days, but **f** him not. 4672
4:39 **f** a wild vine, and gathered thereof wild 4672
9:35 but they **f** no more of her than the skull, and 4672
12: 5 wheresoever any breach shall be **f**. 4672
12:10 told the money that was **f** *in* the house of 4672
12:18 all the gold that was **f** in the treasures of 4672
14:14 all the vessels that were **f** *in* the house of 4672
16: 8 gold that was **f** *in* the house of the LORD, 4672
17: 4 the king of Assyria **f** conspiracy in Hoshea: 4672
18:15 Hezekiah gave *him* all the silver that was **f** 4672
19: 8 **f** the king of Assyria warring against 4672
20:13 and all that was **f** in his treasures: 4672
22: 8 I have **f** the book of the law in the house of 4672
22: 9 gathered the money that was **f** in the house, 4672
22:13 concerning the words of this book that is **f**: 4672
23: 2 which was **f** in the house of the LORD. 4672
23:24 the priest **f** *in* the house of the LORD. 4672
25:19 which were **f** in the city, and the principal 4672
25:19 people of the land that were **f** in the city: 4672
1Ch 4:40 they **f** fat pasture and good, and the land 4672
4:41 the habitations that were **f** there, 4672
10: 8 that they **f** Saul and his sons fallen in mount 4672
17:25 thy servant hath **f** *in his heart* to pray before 4672
20: 2 **f** it to weigh a talent of gold, and *there were* 4672
24: 4 there were moe chief men **f** of the sons of 4672
26:31 there were **f** among them mighty *men* of 4672
28: 9 if thou seek him, he will be **f** of thee; but 4672
29: 8 they with whom *precious* stones were **f** 4672
2Ch 2:17 they were **f** an hundred and fifty thousand 4672
4:18 the weight of the brass could not be **f out**. 2713
15: 2 if ye seek him, he will be **f** of you; but if ye 4672
15: 4 of Israel, and sought him, he was **f** of them. 4672
15:15 their whole desire; and he was **f** of them: 4672
19: 3 Nevertheless there are good things **f** in 4672
20:25 they **f** among them in abundance both 4672
21:17 carried away all the substance that was **f** in 4672
22: 8 **f** the princes of Judah, and the sons of 4672
25: 5 **f** them three hundred thousand choice *men,* 4672
25:24 all the vessels that were **f** in the house of 4672
29:16 brought out all the uncleanness that they **f** 4672
34:14 Hilkiah the priest **f** a book of the law of 4672
34:15 I have **f** the book of the law in the house of 4672
34:17 that was **f** in the house of the LORD, 4672
34:21 concerning the words of the book that is **f**: 4672
34:30 that was **f** *in* the house of the LORD. 4672
36: 8 he did, and that which was **f** in him, behold, 4672
Ezr 2:62 by genealogy, but they were not **f**: 4672
4:19 it is **f** that this city of old time *hath* made 7912
6: 2 there was **f** at Achmetha, in the palace that 7912
8:15 and **f** there none of the sons of Levi. 4672
10:18 among the sons of the priests there were **f** 4672
Ne 2: 5 if thy servant have **f favour** in thy sight, 3190
5: 8 they their peace, and **f** nothing *to answer.* 4672
7: 5 I **f** a register of the genealogy of them 4672
7: 5 came up at the first, and **f** written therein, 4672
7:64 reckoned by genealogy, but it was not **f**: 4672
8:14 they **f** written in the law which the LORD 4672
13: 1 therein was **f** written, that the Ammonite 4672
Est 2:23 was made of the matter, it was **f out**; 4672
5: 8 If I have **f** favour in the sight of the king, 4672
6: 2 it was **f** written, that Mordecai had told of 4672
7: 3 and said, If I have **f** favour in thy sight, 4672
8: 5 if I have **f** favour in his sight, and the thing 4672
Job 19:28 seeing the root of the matter is **f** in me; 4672
20: 8 fly away as a dream, and shall not be **f**: 4672
28:12 where shall wisdom be **f**? and where *is* 4672
28:13 neither is it **f** in the land of the living. 4672
31:29 hated me, or lift up myself when evil **f** him: 4672
32: 3 because they had **f** no answer, and *yet* had 4672
32:13 Lest ye should say, We have **f out** wisdom: 4672
33:24 going down *to* the pit: I have **f** a ransom. 4672
42:15 in all the land were no women **f** *so* fair as 4672
Ps 32: 6 unto thee in a time when thou mayest be **f**: 4672
36: 2 until his iniquity be **f** to be hateful. 4672
37:36 yea, I sought him, but he could not be **f**. 4672
69:20 *was* none; and for comforters, but I **f** none. 4672
76: 5 none of the men of might have **f** their 4672
84: 3 the sparrow hath **f** a house, and the swallow 4672
89:20 I have **f** David my servant; with my holy oil 4672
107: 4 in a solitary way; they **f** no city to dwell in. 4672
116: 3 gat hold upon me: I **f** trouble and sorrow. 4672
132: 6 we **f** it in the fields of the wood. 4672
Pr 6:31 *if* he be **f**, he shall restore sevenfold; he 4672
7:15 to seek thy face, and I have **f** thee. 4672
10:13 of him that hath understanding wisdom is **f**: 4672
16:31 *if* it be **f** in the way of righteousness. 4672
24:14 when thou hast **f** *it,* then there shall be a 4672
25:16 Hast thou **f** honey? eat so much as is 4672
30: 6 lest he reprove thee, and thou be **f a liar.** 3576
30:10 lest he curse thee, and thou be **f guilty**. 816
Ecc 7:27 Behold, this have I **f**, saith the Preacher, 4672
7:28 one man among a thousand have I **f**; but 4672
7:28 but a woman among all those have I not **f**. 4672
7:29 Lo, this only have I **f**, that God hath made 4672
9:15 Now there was **f** in it a poor wise man, and 4672
SS 3: 1 soul loveth: I sought him, but I **f** him not. 4672
3: 2 soul loveth: I sought him, but I **f** him not. 4672
3: 3 The watchmen that go about the city **f** me: 4672
3: 4 but I **f** *him* whom my soul loveth: 4672
5: 7 The watchmen that went about the city **f** 4672
8:10 then was I in his eyes as one that **f** favour. 4672
Isa 10:10 As my hand hath **f** the kingdoms of 4672
10:14 my hand hath **f** as a nest the riches of 4672
13:15 Every one that is **f** shall be thrust through; 4672
22: 3 all that are **f** in thee are bound together, 4672
30:14 that there shall not be **f** in the bursting of it 4672
35: 9 shall go up thereon, it shall not be **f** there; 4672
37: 8 **f** the king of Assyria warring against 4672
39: 2 and all that was **f** in his treasures: 4672
51: 3 joy and gladness shall be **f** therein, 4672
55: 6 Seek ye the LORD while he may be **f**, 4672
57:10 thou hast **f** the life of thine hand; therefore 4672
65: 1 *for me:* I am **f** of *them that* sought me not: 4672
65: 8 As the new wine is **f** in the cluster, and 4672
Jer 2: 5 What iniquity have your fathers **f** in me, 4672
2:26 As the thief is ashamed when he is **f**, so 4672
2:34 Also in thy skirts is **f** the blood of the souls 4672
2:34 I have not **f** it by secret search, but upon all 4672
5:26 For among my people are **f** wicked *men:* 4672
11: 9 A conspiracy is **f** among the men of Judah, 4672
14: 3 they came to the pits, *and* **f** no water; 4672
15:16 Thy words were **f**, and I did eat them; and 4672
23:11 yea, in my house have I **f** their wickedness, 4672
29:14 I will be **f** of you, saith the LORD: and 4672
31: 2 The people which were left of the sword **f** 4672
41: 3 the Chaldeans that were **f** there, *and* 4672
41: 8 ten men were **f** among them that said unto 4672
41:12 **f** him by the great waters that *are* in 4672
48:27 was he **f** among thieves? for since thou 4672
50: 7 All that **f** them have devoured them: and 4672
50:20 the sins of Judah, and they shall not be **f**: 4672
50:24 thou art **f**, and also caught, because 4672
52:25 the king's person, which were **f** in the city; 4672
52:25 the land, that were **f** in the midst of the city. 4672
La 2:16 we looked for; we have **f**, we have seen it. 4672
Eze 22:30 that *I* should not destroy it: but I **f** none. 4672
26:21 yet shalt thou never be **f** again, saith 4672
28:15 thou wast created, till iniquity was **f** in thee. 4672
Da 1:19 among them all was **f** none like Daniel, 4672
1:20 he **f** them ten times better than all 4672
2:25 I have **f** a man of the captives of Judah, 7912
2:35 them away, that no place was **f** for them: 7912
5:11 like the wisdom of the gods, was **f** in him; 7912
5:12 of doubts, were **f** in the same Daniel, 7912
5:14 and excellent wisdom is **f** in thee. 7912
5:27 weighed in the balances, and art **f** wanting. 7912
6: 4 neither was there any error or fault **f** in him. 7912
6:11 **f** Daniel praying and making supplication 7912
6:22 forasmuch as before him innocency was **f** 7912
6:23 no manner of hurt was **f** upon him, because 7912
11:19 but he shall stumble and fall, and not be **f**. 4672
12: 1 every one that *shall* be **f** written in 4672
Hos 9:10 I **f** Israel like grapes in the wilderness; 4672
10: 2 heart is divided; now shall they be **f faulty**: 816
12: 4 he **f** him *in* Beth-el, and there he spake with 4672
12: 8 am become rich, I have **f** me **out** substance: 4672
14: 8 like a green fir tree. From me is thy fruit **f**. 4672
Jnh 1: 3 *to* Joppa; and he **f** a ship going to Tarshish: 4672
Mic 1:13 for the transgressions of Israel were **f** in 4672
Zep 3:13 neither shall a deceitful tongue be **f** in their 4672
Zec 10:10 Lebanon; and *place* shall not be **f** for them. 4672

Mal 2: 6 and iniquity was not f in his lips: 4672
Mt 1:18 she was f with child of the Holy Ghost. *2147*
2: 8 when ye have f *him,* bring me word again, *2147*
8:10 I have not f so great faith, no, not in Israel. *2147*
13:44 the which when a man hath f, he hideth, *2147*
13:46 when he had f one pearl of great price, *2147*
18:28 went out, and f one of his fellowservants, *2147*
20: 6 and f others standing idle, and saith unto *2147*
21:19 he came to it, and f nothing thereon, *2147*
22:10 and gathered together all as many as they f, *2147*
26:43 And he came and f them asleep again: *2147*
26:60 But f none: yea, though many false *2147*
26:60 many false witnesses came, *yet* f they none. *2147*
27:32 they f a man of Cyrene, Simon by name: *2147*
Mk 1:37 And when they had f him, they said unto *2147*
7: 2 to say, with unwashen, hands, they f **fault**. *3201*
7:30 she f the devil gone out, and *her* daughter *2147*
11: 4 f the colt tied by the door without in a place *2147*
11:13 when he came to it, he f nothing but leaves; *2147*
14:16 the city, and f as he had said unto them: *2147*
14:40 when he returned, he f them asleep again, *2147*
14:55 Jesus to put him to death; and f none. *2147*
Lk 1:30 Mary: for thou hast f favour with God. *2147*
2:16 and f Mary, and Joseph, and the babe lying *429*
2:45 And when they f him not, they turned back *2147*
2:46 *that* after three days they f him in *2147*
4:17 he f the place where it was written, *2147*
7: 9 I have not f so great faith, no, not in Israel. *2147*
7:10 f the servant whole that had been sick. *2147*
8:35 and came to Jesus, and f the man, out of *2147*
9:36 when the voice was past, Jesus was f alone. *2147*
13: 6 and sought fruit thereon, and f none. *2147*
15: 5 And when he hath f *it,* he layeth *it* on his *2147*
15: 6 for I have f my sheep which was lost. *2147*
15: 9 And when she hath f *it,* she calleth *her* *2147*
15: 9 for I have f the piece which I had lost. *2147*
15:24 and is alive again; he was lost, and is f. *2147*
15:32 and is alive again; and was lost, and is f. *2147*
17:18 There are not f that returned to give glory *2147*
19:32 and f even as he had said unto them. *2147*
22:13 they went, and f as he had said unto them: *2147*
22:45 his disciples, he f them sleeping for sorrow, *2147*
23: 2 We f this *fellow* perverting the nation, and *2147*
23:14 have f no fault in this man *touching those* *2147*
23:22 I have f no cause of death in him: I will *2147*
24: 2 And they f the stone rolled away from *2147*
24: 3 and f not the body of the Lord Jesus. *2147*
24:23 And when they f not his body, they came, *2147*
24:24 and f *it* even so as the women had said: *2147*
24:33 and f the eleven gathered together, and *2147*
Jn 1:41 unto him, We have f the Messias, which is, *2147*
1:45 and saith unto him, We have f him, *2147*
2:14 And f in the temple those that sold oxen *2147*
6:25 And when they had f him on the other side *2147*
9:35 and when he had f him, he said unto him, *2147*
11:17 he f that he had *lien* in the grave four days *2147*
12:14 And Jesus, when he had f a young ass, *2147*
Ac 5:10 and f her dead, and, carrying *her* forth, *2147*
5:22 and f them not in the prison, they returned, *2147*
5:23 The prison truly f we shut with all safety, *2147*
5:23 when we had opened, we f no *man* within. *2147*
5:39 lest haply ye be f even to fight against God. *2147*
7:11 and our fathers f no sustenance. *2147*
7:46 Who f favour before God, and desired to *2147*
8:40 But Philip was f at Azotus: and *2147*
9: 2 that if he f any of *this* way, whether they *2147*
9:33 And there he f a certain man named *2147*
10:27 and f many *that were* come together. *2147*
11:26 And when he had f him, he brought him *2147*
12:19 and f *him* not, he examined the keepers, *2147*
13: 6 they f a certain sorcerer, a false prophet, *2147*
13:22 and said, I have f David the *son* of Jesse, *2147*
13:28 And though they f no cause of death *in* *2147*
17: 6 And when they f them not, they drew Jason *2147*
17:23 I f an altar with this inscription, *2147*
18: 2 And f a certain Jew named Aquila, born in *2147*
19:19 and f *it* fifty thousand *pieces* of silver. *2147*
24: 5 For we have f this man a pestilent *fellow,* *2147*
24:12 And they neither f me in the temple *2147*
24:18 Whereupon certain Jews from Asia f me *2147*
24:20 if they have f any evil doing in me, *2147*
25:25 But when I f that he had committed nothing *2638*
27: 6 And there the centurion f a ship of *2147*
27:28 And sounded, and f *it* twenty fathoms: and *2147*
27:28 sounded again, and f *it* fifteen fathoms. *2147*
28:14 Where we f brethren, and were desired to *2147*
Ro 4: 1 our father, as pertaining to the flesh, hath f? *2147*
7:10 was *ordained* to life, I f *to be* unto death. *2147*
10:20 saith, I was f of them that sought me not; *2147*
1Co 4: 2 in stewards, that a man be f faithful. *2147*
15:15 Yea, and we are f false witnesses of God; *2147*
2Co 2:13 my spirit, because I f not Titus my brother: *2147*
5: 3 be that being clothed we shall not be f *2147*
7:14 which *I made* before Titus, is f a truth. *1096*
11:12 they glory, they may be f even as we. *2147*
12:20 *that* I shall be f unto you such as ye would *2147*
Gal 2:17 we ourselves also are f sinners, *is* therefore *2147*
Php 2: 8 And being f in fashion as a man, *2147*
3: 9 And be f in him, not having mine own *2147*
1Ti 3:10 the office of a deacon, being *f* blameless. NIG
2Ti 1:17 sought me out very diligently, and f *me.* *2147*
Heb 11: 5 and was not f, because God had translated *2147*
12:17 for he f no place of repentance, though he *2147*
1Pe 1: 7 might be f unto praise and honour and *2147*
2:22 did no sin, neither was guile f in his mouth: *2147*
2Pe 3:14 diligent that ye may be f of him in peace, *2147*
2Jn 1: 4 I rejoiced greatly that I f of thy children *2147*
Rev 2: 2 and are not, and hast f them liars: *2147*
3: 2 for I have not f thy works perfect before *2147*
5: 4 because no *man* was f worthy to open and *2147*
12: 8 neither was their place f any more in *2147*
14: 5 And in their mouth was f no guile: for they *2147*
16:20 fled *away,* and the mountains were not f. *2147*
18:21 thrown down, and shall be f no more at all. *2147*
18:22 of whatsoever craft *he be,* shall be f any *2147*
Rev 18:24 And in her was f the blood of prophets, and *2147*
20:11 and there was f no place for them. *2147*
20:15 And whosoever was not f written in *2147*

FOUNDATION (54) [FOUND]

Ex 9:18 such as hath not been in Egypt since the f 3245
Jos 6:26 he shall **lay** the f thereof in his firstborn, 3245
1Ki 5:17 *and* hewed stones, to **lay the** f of the house. 3245
6:37 was the f of the house of the LORD **laid**, 3245
7: 9 even from the f unto the coping, and *so* 4527
7:10 the f *was of* costly stones, *even* great 3245
16:34 he **laid** the f thereof in Abiram his 3245
2Ch 8:16 the day of the f of the house of the LORD, 4143
23: 5 and a third *part* at the gate of the f: 3247
31: 7 In the third month they began to **lay** the f of 3245
Ezr 3: 6 f of the temple of the LORD was not *yet* **laid**. 3245
3:10 when the builders **laid** the f of the temple 3245
3:11 the f of the house of the LORD was **laid**. 3245
3:12 when the f of this house was **laid** before 3245
5:16 laid the f of the house of God which *is* in 787
Job 4:19 whose f *is* in the dust, which are crushed 3247
22:16 whose f was overflown *with* a flood: 3247
Ps 87: 1 His f *is* in the holy mountains. 3248
102:25 Of old hast thou **laid** the f of the earth: and 3245
137: 7 Rase *it,* rase *it, even* to the f thereof. 3247
Pr 10:25 but the righteous *is* an everlasting f. 3247
Isa 28:16 Behold, I **lay** in Zion **for a** f a stone, a tried 3245
28:16 a precious corner *stone,* a **sure** f: 3245+4143
44:28 and *to* the temple, Thy f shall be **laid**. 3245
48:13 Mine hand also hath **laid** the f of the earth, 3245
Eze 13:14 so that the f thereof shall be discovered, 3247
Hab 3:13 by discovering the f unto the neck. 3247
Hag 2:18 that the f of the LORD'S temple was **laid**, 3245
Zec 4: 9 The hands of Zerubbabel have **laid** the f of 3245
8: 9 f of the house of the LORD of hosts was **laid**, 3245
12: 1 **layeth** the f of the earth, and formeth 3245
Mt 13:35 *been* kept secret from the f of the world. *2602*
25:34 prepared for you from the f of the world: *2602*
Lk 6:48 and digged deep, and laid the f on a rock: *2310*
6:49 is like a man that without a f built a house *2310*
11:50 which was shed from the f of the world, *2602*
14:29 after he hath laid the f, and is not able to *2310*
Jn 17:24 for thou lovedst me before the f of *2602*
Ro 15:20 lest I should build upon another *man's* f: *2310*
1Co 3:10 I have laid the f, and another buildeth *2310*
3:11 For other f can no *man* lay than that is laid, *2310*
3:12 Now if any *man* build upon this f gold, *2310*
Eph 1: 4 chosen us in him before the f of the world, *2602*
2:20 And are built upon the f of the apostles and *2310*
1Ti 6:19 Laying up in store for themselves a good f *2310*
2Ti 2:19 Nevertheless the f of God standeth sure, *2310*
Heb 1:10 in the beginning hast **laid the** f of the earth; *2311*
4: 3 although the works were finished from the f *2602*
6: 1 not laying again the f of repentance from *2310*
9:26 must he often have suffered since the f of *2602*
1Pe 1:20 Who verily was foreordained before the f *2602*
Rev 13: 8 of the Lamb slain from the f of the world. *2602*
17: 8 in the book of life from the f of the world, *2602*
21:19 The first f *was* jasper; the second, sapphire; *2310*

FOUNDATIONS (32) [FOUND]

Dt 32:22 and set on fire the f of the mountains. 4144
2Sa 22: 8 the f of heaven moved and shook, because 4146
22:16 the f of the world were discovered, at 4146
Ezr 4:12 set up the walls *thereof,* and joined the f. 787
6: 3 and *let* the f thereof *be* strongly laid; 787
Job 38: 4 Where wast thou when I **laid** the f of 3245
38: 6 Whereupon are the f thereof fastened? or 134
Ps 11: 3 If the f be destroyed, what can the righteous 8356
18: 7 the f also of the hills moved and 4146
18:15 the f of the world were discovered at thy 4146
82: 5 all the f of the earth are out of course. 4144
104: 5 *Who* laid the f of the earth, *that* it should 4349
Pr 8:29 when he appointed the f of the earth: 4144
Isa 16: 7 for the f of Kir-hareseth shall ye mourn; 808
24:18 are open, and the f of the earth do shake. 4146
40:21 have ye not understood *from* the f of 4146
51:13 the heavens, and **laid** the f of the earth; 3245
51:16 **lay** the f of the earth, and say unto Zion, 3245
54:11 fair colours, and **lay** thy f with sapphires. 3245
58:12 thou shalt raise up the f of many 4146
Jer 31:37 and the f of the earth searched out beneath, 4146
50:15 her f are fallen, her walls are thrown down: 803
51:26 thee a stone for a corner, nor a stone for f; 4146
La 4:11 in Zion, and it hath devoured the f thereof. 3247
Eze 30: 4 and her f shall be broken down. 3247
41: 8 the f of the side chambers *were* a full reed 4155
Mic 1: 6 the valley, and I will discover the f thereof. 3247
6: 2 and ye strong f of the earth: 4146
Ac 16:26 so that the f of the prison were shaken: *2310*
Heb 11:10 For he looked for a city which hath f, *2310*
Rev 21:14 And the wall of the city had twelve f, and *2310*
21:19 And the f of the wall of the city *were* *2310*

FOUNDED (10) [FOUND]

Ps 24: 2 For he hath f it upon the seas, and 3245
89:11 and the fulness thereof, thou hast f them. 3245
104: 8 unto the place which thou hast f for them. 3245
119:152 I have known of old that thou hast f them 3245
Pr 3:19 The LORD by wisdom hath f the earth; 3245
Isa 14:32 That the LORD hath f Zion, and the poor 3245
23:13 *till* the Assyrian f it for them that dwell in 3245
Am 9: 6 and hath f his troop in the earth; 3245
Mt 7:25 and it fell not: for it was f upon a rock. *2311*
Lk 6:48 could not shake it: for it was f upon a rock. *2311*

FOUNDER (5) [FOUND]

Jdg 17: 4 gave them to the f, who made thereof a 6884
Jer 6:29 consumed of the fire; the f melteth in vain: 6884
10: 9 of the workman, and of the hands of the f: 6884
10:14 every f is confounded by the graven image: 6884
51:17 every f is confounded by the graven image: 6884

FOUNDEST (1) [FOUND]

Ne 9: 8 f his heart faithful before thee, and 4672

FOUNTAIN (33) [FOUNTAINS]

Ge 16: 7 the angel of the LORD found her by a f of 5869
16: 7 the wilderness, by the f in the way to Shur. 5869
Lev 11:36 Nevertheless a f or pit, *wherein there is* 4599
20:18 he hath discovered her f, and she hath 4726
20:18 and she hath uncovered the f of her blood: 4726
Dt 33:28 the f of Jacob *shall be* upon a land of corn 5869
Jos 15: 9 the hill unto the f of the water of Nephtoah, 4599
1Sa 29: 1 the Israelites pitched by a f which *is* in 5869
Ne 2:14 I went on to the gate of the f, and to 5869
3:15 the gate of the f repaired Shallun the son of 5869
12:37 at the f gate, which *was* over against them, 5869
Ps 36: 9 For with thee *is* the f of life: in thy light 4726
68:26 *even* the Lord, from the f of Israel. 4726
74:15 Thou didst cleave the f and the flood: 4599
114: 8 a standing water, the flint into a f of waters. 4599
Pr 5:18 Let thy f be blessed: and rejoice with 4726
13:14 The law of the wise *is* a f of life, to depart 4726
14:27 The fear of the LORD *is* a f of life, 4726
25:26 down before the wicked *is as* a troubled f, 4599
Ecc 12: 6 or the pitcher be broken at the f, or 4002
SS 4:12 *my* spouse; a spring shut up, a f sealed. 4599
4:15 A f of gardens, a well of living waters, and 4599
Jer 2:13 they have forsaken me the f of living 4726
6: 7 As a f casteth out her waters, so she casteth 953
9: 1 mine eyes a f of tears, that I might weep 4726
17:13 forsaken the LORD, the f of living waters. 4726
Hos 13:15 become dry, and his f shall be dried up: 4599
Joel 3:18 a f shall come forth of the house of 4599
Zec 13: 1 In that day there shall be a f opened to 4726
Mk 5:29 And straightway the f of her blood was *4077*
Jas 3:11 Doth a f send forth at the same place sweet *4077*
3:12 so *can* no f *both* yield salt water and fresh. *4077*
Rev 21: 6 I will give unto him that is athirst of the f of *4077*

FOUNTAINS (15) [FOUNTAIN]

Ge 7:11 the same day were all the f of the great 4599
8: 2 The f also of the deep and the windows of 4599
Nu 33: 9 in Elim *were* twelve f of water, and 5869
Dt 8: 7 of f and depths that spring out of 5869
1Ki 18: 5 unto all f of water, and unto all brooks: 4599
2Ch 32: 3 his mighty *men* to stop the waters of the f 5869
32: 4 who stopt all the f, and the brook that ran 4599
Pr 5:16 Let thy f be dispersed abroad, *and* rivers of 4599
8:24 when *there were* no f abounding with 4599
8:28 when he strengthened the f of the deep: 5869
Isa 41:18 and f in the midst of the valleys: 4599
Rev 7:17 and shall lead them unto living f of waters: *4077*
8:10 *part* of the rivers, and upon the f of waters; *4077*
14: 7 and earth, and the sea, and the f of waters. *4077*
16: 4 out his vial upon the rivers and f of waters; *4077*

FOUR (328) [FOURFOLD, FOURFOOTED, FOURSCORE, FOURSQUARE, FOURTH]

Ge 2:10 it was parted, and became into f heads. 702
11:13 Arphaxad lived after he begat Salah f 702
11:15 Salah lived after he begat Eber f hundred 702
11:16 Eber lived f and thirty years, and 702
11:17 Eber lived after he begat Peleg f hundred 702
14: 9 and Arioch king of Ellasar; f kings with five. 702
15:13 and they shall afflict them f hundred years; 702
23:15 the land *is worth* f hundred shekels of silver; 702
23:16 f hundred shekels of silver, current *money* 702
32: 6 to meet thee, and f hundred men with him. 702
33: 1 Esau came, and with him f hundred men. 702
47:24 f parts shall be your own, for seed of 702
Ex 12:40 in Egypt, *was* f hundred and thirty years. 702
12:41 it came to pass at the end of the f hundred 702
22: 1 five oxen for an ox, and f sheep for a sheep. 702
25:12 And thou shalt cast f rings of gold for it, and 702
25:12 for it, and put *them* in the f corners thereof; 702
25:26 thou shalt make for it f rings of gold, and 702
25:26 put the rings in the f corners that *are* on 702
25:26 the four corners that *are* on the f feet thereof. 702
25:34 in the candlestick *shall be* f bowls made like 702
26: 2 and the breadth of one curtain f cubits: 702
26: 8 and the breadth of one curtain f cubits: 702
26:32 thou shalt hang it upon f pillars of shittim 702
26:32 *shall be of* gold, upon the f sockets of silver. 702
27: 2 thou shalt make the horns of it upon the f 702
27: 4 upon the net shalt thou make f brasen rings 702
27: 4 four brasen rings in the f corners thereof. 702
27:16 *and* their pillars *shall be* f, and their sockets 702
27:16 their pillars *shall be* four, and their sockets f. 702
28:17 in it settings of stones, *even* f rows of stones: 702
36: 9 the breadth of one curtain f cubits: 702
36:15 and f cubits *was* the breadth of one curtain: 702
36:36 he made thereunto f pillars of shittim *wood,* 702
36:36 and he cast for them f sockets of silver. 702
37: 3 he cast for it f rings of gold, *to be set* by 702
37: 3 rings of gold, *to be set* by the f corners of it; 702
37:13 he cast for it f rings of gold, and put 702
37:13 put the rings upon the f corners that *were* in 702
37:13 four corners that *were* in the f feet thereof. 702
37:20 in the candlestick *were* f bowls made like 702
38: 2 he made the horns thereof on the f corners of 702
38: 5 he cast f rings for the four ends of the grate 702
38: 5 he cast four rings for the f ends of the grate 702
38:19 their pillars *were* f, and their sockets *of* brass 702
38:19 pillars *were* four, and their sockets *of* brass f; 702
38:29 and two thousand and f hundred shekels. 702
39:10 they set in it f rows of stones: *the first* row 702
Lev 11:20 All fowls that creep, going upon *all* f, 702
11:21 flying creeping thing that goeth upon *all* f, 702
11:23 which have f feet, *shall be* an abomination 702
11:27 among all *manner of* beasts that go on *all* f, 702
11:42 whatsoever goeth upon *all* f, or 702
Nu 1:29 *were* fifty and four thousand and f hundred. 702
1:29 *were* fifty and f thousand and four hundred. 702
1:31 *were* fifty and seven thousand and f hundred. 702
1:37 *were* thirty and five thousand and f hundred. 702

F

Nu 1:43 *were* fifty and three thousand and f hundred. 702
2: 6 *were* fifty and f thousand and four hundred. 702
2: 6 *were* fifty and four thousand and f hundred. 702
2: 8 *were* fifty and seven thousand and f hundred. 702
2: 9 and six thousand and f hundred, 702
2:16 and one thousand and f hundred and fifty, 702
2:23 *were* thirty and five thousand and f hundred. 702
2:30 *were* fifty and three thousand and f hundred. 702
7: 7 and f oxen he gave unto the sons of Gershon, 702
7: 8 f wagons and eight oxen he gave unto 702
7:85 f hundred *shekels*, after the shekel of 702
7:88 peace offerings *were* twenty and f bullocks, 702
25: 9 in the plague were twenty and f thousand. 702
26:25 threescore and f thousand and three hundred. 702
26:43 and f thousand and four hundred. 702
26:43 and four thousand and f hundred. 702
26:47 *were* fifty and three thousand and f hundred. 702
26:50 *were* forty and five thousand and f hundred. 702
Dt 3:11 f cubits the breadth of it, after the cubit of a 702
22:12 Thou shalt make thee fringes upon the f 702
Jos 19: 7 Ether, and Ashan; f cities and their villages: 702
21:18 and Almon with her suburbs; f cities. 702
21:22 and Beth-horon with her suburbs; f cities. 702
21:24 Gath-rimmon with her suburbs; f cities. 702
21:29 En-gannim with her suburbs; f cities. 702
21:31 and Rehob with her suburbs; f cities. 702
21:35 Nahalal with her suburbs; f cities. 702
21:37 and Mephaath with her suburbs; f cities. 702
21:39 Jazer with her suburbs; f cities in all. 702
Jdg 9:34 they laid wait against Shechem *in* f 702
11:40 of Jephthah the Gileadite f days in a year. 702
19: 2 was there f whole months. 702
20: 2 f hundred thousand footmen that drew 702
20:17 were numbered f hundred thousand men that 702
20:47 and abode in the rock Rimmon f months. 702
21:12 of Jabesh-gilead f hundred young virgins, 702
1Sa 4: 2 they slew of the army in the field about f 702
22: 2 there were with him about f hundred men. 702
25:13 there went up after David about f hundred 702
27: 7 the Philistines was a full year and f months. 702
30:10 David pursued, he and f hundred men: 702
30:17 save f hundred young men, which rode upon 702
2Sa 21:20 every foot six toes, f and twenty *in* number; 702
22:22 These f were born to the giant in Gath, and 702
1Ki 6: 1 it came to pass in the f hundred and 702
7: 2 thirty cubits, upon f rows of cedar pillars, 702
7:19 *were* of lily work in the porch, f cubits). 702
7:27 f cubits *was* the length of one base, and 702
7:27 f cubits the breadth thereof, and three cubits 702
7:30 every base had f brasen wheels, and plates of 702
7:30 the f corners thereof had undersetters: under 702
7:32 under the borders *were* f wheels; and 702
7:34 *there were* f undersetters to the four corners 702
7:34 *there were* four undersetters to the f corners 702
7:38 *and* every laver was f cubits: *and* upon every 702
7:42 f hundred pomegranates for the two 702
9:28 f hundred and twenty talents, and brought *it* 702
10:26 he had a thousand and f hundred chariots, 702
15:33 over all Israel in Tirzah, twenty and f years. 702
18:19 and the prophets of Baal f hundred and fifty, 702
18:19 and the prophets of the groves f hundred, 702
18:22 Baal's prophets *are* f hundred and fifty men. 702
18:33 Fill f barrels *with* water, and pour *it* on 702
22: 6 about f hundred men, and said unto them, 702
2Ki 7: 3 there were f leprous men *at* the entering in of 702
14:13 unto the corner gate, f hundred cubits. 702
1Ch 3: 5 and Shobab, and Nathan, and Solomon, f, 702
5:18 *were* f and forty thousand seven hundred and 702
7: 1 and Puah, Jashub, and Shimron, f. 702
7: 7 and two thousand and thirty and f. 702
9:24 In f quarters were the porters, toward 702
9:26 For these Levites, the f chief porters, *were* in 702
12:26 Of the children of Levi f thousand and 702
20: 6 whose fingers and toes *were* f and twenty, 702
21: 5 Judah *was* f hundred threescore and 702
21:20 and his f sons with him hid themselves. 702
23: 4 f thousand *were* to set forward the work of 702
23: 5 Moreover f thousand *were* porters; and 702
23: 5 f thousand praised the LORD with 702
23:10 and Beriah. These f *were* the sons of Shimei. 702
23:12 Amram, Izhar, Hebron, and Uzziel, f. 702
24:18 to Delaiah, the f and twentieth to Maaziah. 702
25:31 The f and twentieth to Romamti-ezer, *he*, his 702
26:17 northward f a day, southward four a day, and 702
26:17 southward f a day, and toward Asuppim two 702
26:18 f at the causeway, *and* two at Parbar. 702
27: 1 *of* every course *were* twenty and f thousand. 702
27: 2 in his course *were* twenty and f thousand. 702
27: 4 course likewise *were* twenty and f thousand. 702
27: 5 in his course *were* twenty and f thousand. 702
27: 7 in his course *were* twenty and f thousand. 702
27: 8 in his course *were* twenty and f thousand. 702
27: 9 in his course *were* twenty and f thousand. 702
27:10 in his course *were* twenty and f thousand. 702
27:11 in his course *were* twenty and f thousand. 702
27:12 in his course *were* twenty and f thousand. 702
27:13 in his course *were* twenty and f thousand. 702
27:14 in his course *were* twenty and f thousand. 702
27:15 in his course *were* twenty and f thousand. 702
2Ch 1:14 he had a thousand and f hundred chariots, 702
4:13 f hundred pomegranates on the two wreaths; 702
8:18 took thence f hundred and fifty talents of 702
9:25 Solomon had f thousand stalls for horses 702
13: 3 *even* f hundred thousand chosen men: 702
18: 5 gathered together *of* prophets f hundred men, 702
25:23 Ephraim to the corner gate, f hundred cubits. 702
Ezr 1:10 silver basons of a second sort f hundred and 702
1:11 of silver *were* five thousand and f hundred. 702
2: 7 of Elam, a thousand two hundred fifty and f. 702
2:15 children of Adin, f hundred fifty and four. 702
2:15 children of Adin, four hundred fifty and f. 702
2:31 a thousand two hundred fifty and f. 702
2:40 of the children of Hodaviah, seventy and f. 702
2:67 Their camels, f hundred thirty and five; 702
6:17 two hundred rams, f hundred lambs; 703

Ne 6: 4 Yet they sent unto me f times after this sort; 702
7:12 of Elam, a thousand two hundred fifty and f. 702
7:23 of Bezai, three hundred twenty and f. 702
7:34 a thousand two hundred fifty and f. 702
7:43 of the children of Hodevah, seventy and f. 702
7:69 *Their* camels, f hundred thirty and five: 702
11: 6 at Jerusalem *were* f hundred threescore 702
11:18 holy city *were* two hundred fourscore and f. 702
Job 1:19 smote the f corners of the house, and it fell 702
42:16 and his sons' sons, *even* f generations. 702
Pr 30:15 *yea*, f *things* say not, *It is* enough: 702
30:18 wonderful for me, yea, f which I know not: 702
30:21 is disquieted, and for f *which* it cannot bear: 702
30:24 There be f *things which are* little upon 702
30:29 which go well, yea, f are comely in going: 702
Isa 11:12 of Judah from the f corners of the earth. 702
17: 6 f *or* five in the outmost fruitful branches 702
Jer 15: 3 I will appoint over them f kinds, saith 702
36:23 *that* when Jehudi had read three or f leaves, 702
49:36 upon Elam will I bring the f winds from 702
49:36 the four winds from the f quarters of heaven, 702
52:21 and the thickness thereof *was* f fingers: 702
52:30 all the persons *were* f thousand and 702
Eze 1: 5 *came* the likeness of f living creatures. 702
1: 6 *every* one had f faces, and every one had 702
1: 6 had four faces, and every one had f wings. 702
1: 8 of a man under their wings on their f sides; 702
1: 8 and they f had their faces and their wings. 702
1:10 they f had the face of a man, and the face of 702
1:10 they f had the face of an ox on the left side; 702
1:10 left side; they f also had the face of an eagle. 702
1:15 earth by the living creatures, with his f faces. 702
1:16 they f had one likeness: and their appearance 702
1:17 they went, they went upon their f sides: 702
1:18 rings *were* full *of* eyes round about them f. 702
7: 2 the end is come upon the f corners of 702
10: 9 behold the f wheels by the cherubims, 702
10:10 their appearances, they f had one likeness, 702
10:11 they went, they went upon their f sides; 702
10:12 round about, *even* the wheels that they f had. 702
10:14 *every* one had f faces: the first face *was* 702
10:21 Every one had f faces **apiece**, and every 702+702
10:21 had four faces apiece, and every one f wings; 702
14:21 How much more when I send my f sore 702
37: 9 Come from the f winds, O breath, and 702
40:41 F tables *were* on this side, and four tables on 702
40:41 f tables on that side, by the side of the gate; 702
40:42 the f tables *were* of hewn stone for the burnt 702
41: 5 the breadth of *every* side chamber, f cubits, 702
42:20 He measured it by the f sides: it had a wall 702
43:14 *even* to the greater settle *shall be* f cubits, 702
43:15 So the altar *shall be* f cubits; and from 702
43:15 from the altar and upward *shall be* f horns. 702
43:16 twelve broad, square in the f squares thereof. 702
43:17 and fourteen broad in the f squares thereof; 702
43:20 put *it* on the f horns of it, and on the four 702
43:20 on the f corners of the settle, and upon 702
45:19 upon the f corners of the settle of the altar, 702
46:21 caused me to pass by the f corners of 702
46:22 In the f corners of the court *there were* courts 702
46:22 these f corners *were* of one measure. 702
46:23 round about them f, and *it was* made *with* 702
48:16 the north side f thousand and five hundred, 702
48:16 the south side f thousand and five hundred, 505
48:16 on the east side f thousand and five hundred, 702
48:16 the west side f thousand and five hundred. 702
48:30 f thousand and five hundred measures. 702
48:32 at the east side f thousand and five hundred: 702
48:33 *at* the south side f thousand and five hundred 702
48:34 *At* the west side f thousand and 702
Da 1:17 As for these f children, God gave them 702
3:25 He answered and said, Lo, I see f men loose, 703
7: 2 the f winds of the heaven strove upon 703
7: 3 f great beasts came up from the sea, 703
7: 6 which had upon the back of it f wings of a 703
7: 6 the beast had also f heads; and dominion *was* 703
7:17 great beasts, which *are* f, *are* four kings, 703
7:17 great beasts, which *are* four, *are* f kings, 703
8: 8 for it came up f notable ones toward the four 702
8: 8 for it came up four notable ones toward the f 702
8:22 that being broken, whereas f stood up for it, 702
8:22 f kingdoms shall stand up out of the nation, 702
10: 4 in the f and twentieth day of the first month, 702
11: 4 shall be divided toward the f winds of 702
Am 1: 3 three transgressions of Damascus, and for f, 702
1: 6 For three transgressions of Gaza, and for f, 702
1: 9 For three transgressions of Tyrus, and for f, 702
1:11 For three transgressions of Edom, and for f, 702
1:13 for f, I will not turn away *the punishment* 702
2: 1 For three transgressions of Moab, and for f, 702
2: 4 For three transgressions of Judah, and for f, 702
2: 6 For three transgressions of Israel, and for f, 702
Hag 1:15 In the f and twentieth day of the sixth month, 702
2:10 In the f and twentieth *day* of the ninth 702
2:18 from the f and twentieth day of the ninth 702
2:20 of the LORD came unto Haggai in the f 702
Zec 1: 7 Upon the f and twentieth day of the eleventh 702
1:18 I up mine eyes, and saw, and behold f horns. 702
1:20 And the LORD shewed me f carpenters. 702
2: 6 for I have spread you abroad as the f winds 702
6: 1 there came f chariots out from between two 702
6: 5 These *are* the f spirits of the heavens, 702
Mt 15:38 And they that did eat were f **thousand** men, *5070*
16:10 Neither the seven loaves of the f **thousand**, *5070*
24:31 gather together his elect from the f winds, *5064*
Mk 2: 3 one sick of the palsy, *which was* borne of f. *5064*
8: 9 they that had eaten were about f **thousand**: *5070*
8:20 And when the seven among f **thousand**, *5070*
13:27 shall gather together his elect from the f *5064*
Lk 2:37 a widow of about fourscore and f years, *5064*
Jn 4:35 There are yet f **months**, and *then* cometh *5072*
11:17 he found that he had *lien* in the grave f days *5064*
11:39 he stinketh: for he hath been *dead* f **days**. *5066*
19:23 took his garments, and made f parts, *5064*
Ac 5:36 about f **hundred**, joined themselves: *5071*
7: 6 and entreat *them* evil f **hundred** years. *5071*
10:11 as *it had been* a great sheet knit at the f *5064*
10:30 F days ago I was fasting until this hour; *5067*
11: 5 let down from heaven by f corners; *5064*
12: 4 delivered *him* to f quaternions of soldiers to *5064*
13:20 *them* judges about *the space of* f **hundred** *5071*
21: 9 And the same *man* had f daughters, virgins, *5064*
21:23 We have f men which have a vow on them; *5064*
21:38 leddest out into the wilderness f **thousand** *5070*
27:29 they cast f anchors out of the stern, and *5064*
Gal 3:17 which was f **hundred** and thirty years *5071*
Rev 4: 4 And round about the throne *were* f and *5064*
4: 4 and upon the seats I saw f and *5064*
4: 6 *were* f beasts full of eyes before and *5064*
4: 8 And the f beasts had each of them six *5064*
4:10 The f and twenty elders fall down before *5064*
5: 6 the midst of the throne and of the f beasts, *5064*
5: 8 the f beasts and four *and* twenty elders fell *5064*
5: 8 the four beasts and f *and* twenty elders fell *5064*
5:14 And the f beasts said, Amen. And the four *5064*
5:14 And the f *and* twenty elders fell down and *5064*
6: 1 one of the f beasts saying, Come and see. *5064*
6: 6 And I heard a voice in the midst of the f *5064*
7: 1 And after these *things* I saw f angels *5064*
7: 1 standing on the f corners of the earth, *5064*
7: 1 holding the f winds of the earth, that *5064*
7: 2 he cried with a loud voice to the f angels, *5064*
7: 4 f thousand of all the tribes of the children *5064*
7:11 and *about* the elders and the f beasts, and *5064*
9:13 I heard a voice from the f horns of *5064*
9:14 Loose the f angels which are bound in *5064*
9:15 And the f angels were loosed, which were *5064*
11:16 And the f and twenty elders, which sat *5064*
14: 1 with him an hundred forty *and* f thousand, *5064*
14: 3 and before the f beasts, and the elders: *5064*
14: 3 but the hundred *and* forty *and* f thousand, *5064*
15: 7 And one of the f beasts gave unto the seven *5064*
19: 4 And the f and twenty elders and the four *5064*
19: 4 twenty elders and the f beasts fell down and *5064*
20: 8 which are in the f quarters of the earth, *5064*
21:17 an hundred *and* forty *and* f cubits, *5064*

FOURFOLD (2) [FOUR]

2Sa 12: 6 he shall restore the lamb f, because he did 702
Lk 19: 8 *man* by false accusation, I restore *him* f. *5073*

FOURFOOTED (3) [FOUR, FOOT]

Ac 10:12 Wherein were all *manner of* f **beasts** of *5074*
11: 6 and saw f **beasts** of the earth, and *5074*
Ro 1:23 to birds, and f **beasts**, and creeping things. *5074*

FOURSCORE (36) [EIGHTY, FOUR]

Ge 16:16 Abram *was* f and six years old, when Hagar 8084
35:28 days of Isaac were an hundred and f years. 8084
Ex 7: 7 Moses *was* f years old, and 8084
7: 7 Aaron f and three years old, when they 8084
Nu 2: 9 f thousand and six thousand and 8084
4:48 eight thousand and five hundred and f. 8084
Jos 14:10 now lo, I *am this* day f and five years old. 8084
Jdg 3:30 of Israel. And the land had rest f years. 8084
1Sa 22:18 slew on that day f and five persons that did 8084
2Sa 19:32 was a very aged man, *even* f years old: 8084
19:35 I *am this* day f years old: *and* can I discern 8084
1Ki 5:15 and f thousand hewers in the mountains; 8084
12:21 f thousand chosen *men*, which were 8084
2Ki 6:25 until an ass's head was *sold* for f *pieces* of 8084
10:24 Jehu appointed f men without, and said, 8084
19:35 in the camp of the Assyrians an hundred f 8084
1Ch 7: 5 reckoned in all by their genealogies f and 8084
15: 9 Eliel the chief, and his brethren f: 8084
25: 7 were cunning, was two hundred f and eight. 8084
2Ch 2: 2 f thousand to hew in the mountain, and 8084
2:18 f thousand *to be* hewers in the mountain, 8084
11: 1 f thousand chosen *men*, which were 8084
14: 8 drew bows, two hundred and f thousand: 8084
17:15 and with him two hundred and f thousand. 8084
17:18 and f thousand ready prepared for the war. 8084
26:17 with him f priests of the LORD, *that were* 8084
Ezr 8: 8 the son of Michael, and with him f males. 8084
Ne 7:26 and Netophah, an hundred f and eight. 8084
11:18 Levites in the holy city *were* two hundred f 8084
Est 1: 4 many days, *even* an hundred and f days. 8084
Ps 90:10 if by reason of strength *they be* f years, 8084
SS 6: 8 f concubines, and virgins without number. 8084
Isa 37:36 an hundred and f and five thousand: 8084
Jer 41: 5 and from Samaria, *even* f men, 8084
Lk 2:37 And she *was* a widow of about f and *3589*
16: 7 he said unto him, Take thy bill, and write f. *3589*

FOURSQUARE (10) [FOUR, SQUARE]

Ex 27: 1 and five cubits broad; the altar shall be f: 7251
28:16 F it shall be *being* doubled; a span *shall be* 7251
30: 2 and a cubit the breadth thereof; f shall it be: 7251
37:25 *it was* f; and two cubits *was* the height of it; 7251
38: 1 *it was* f; and three cubits the height thereof. 7251
39: 9 It was f; they made the breastplate double: 7251
1Ki 7:31 gravings with their borders, f, not round. 7251
Eze 40:47 cubits long, and an hundred cubits broad, f; 7251
48:20 ye shall offer the holy oblation f, with 7243
Rev 21:16 And the city lieth f, and the length is as *5068*

FOURTEEN (26) [FOURTEENTH]

Ge 31:41 I served thee f years for thy two 702+6240
46:22 born to Jacob: all the souls *were* f. 702+6240
Nu 1:27 *were* **threescore and f** 702+7657+2050.1
2: 4 *were* **threescore and f** 702+7657+2050.1
16:49 died in the plague were f thousand 702+6240
29:13 *and* f lambs of the first year; 702+6240
29:15 tenth deal to each lamb of the f lambs: 702+6240
29:17 f lambs of the first year without spot: 702+6240
29:20 f lambs of the first year without 702+6240
29:23 f lambs of the first year without 702+6240
29:26 f lambs of the first year without spot: 702+6240
29:29 f lambs of the first year without 702+6240

Nu 29:32 **f** lambs of the first year without 702+6240
Jos 15:36 **f** cities with their villages. 702+6240
18:28 *and* Kirjath; **f** cities with their villages. 702+6240
1Ki 8:65 and seven days, *even* **f** days. 702+6240
1Ch 25: 5 God gave to Heman **f** sons and 702+6240
2Ch 13:21 married **f** wives, and begat twenty and 702+6240
Job 42:12 for he had **f** thousand sheep, and 702+6240
Eze 43:17 the settle *shall be* **f** *cubits* long and 702+6240
43:17 **f** broad in the four squares thereof; 702+6240
Mt 1:17 from Abraham to David *are* **f** generations; *1180*
1:17 away into Babylon *are* **f** generations; *1180*
1:17 into Babylon unto Christ *are* **f** generations. *1180*
2Co 12: 2 I knew a man in Christ above **f** years ago, *1180*
Gal 2: 1 Then **f** years after I went up again to *1180*

FOURTEENTH (25) [FOURTEEN]

Ge 14: 5 in the **f** year came Chedorlaomer, and 702+6240
Ex 12: 6 ye shall keep it *up* until the **f** day of 702+6240
12:18 In the first *month,* on the **f** day of 702+6240
Lev 23: 5 In the **f** *day* of the first month at even 702+6240
Nu 9: 3 In the **f** day of this month, at even, 702+6240
9: 5 they kept the passover on the **f** day of 702+6240
9:11 The **f** day of the second month at even 702+6240
28:16 in the **f** day of the first month *is* 702+6240
Jos 5:10 kept the passover on the **f** day of 702+6240
2Ki 18:13 Now in the **f** year of king Hezekiah 702+6240
1Ch 24:13 to Huppah, the **f** to Jeshebeab, 702+6240
25:21 The **f** *to* Mattithiah, *he,* his sons, and 702+6240
2Ch 30:15 they killed the passover on the **f** *day* 702+6240
35: 1 they killed the passover on the **f** *day* 702+6240
Ezr 6:19 upon the **f** *day* of the first month. 702+6240
Est 9:15 on the **f** day also of the month Adar, 702+6240
9:17 on the **f** day of the same rested they, 702+6240
9:18 *day* thereof, and on the **f** thereof; 702+6240
9:19 made the **f** day of the month Adar *a* 702+6240
9:21 that they should keep the **f** day of 702+6240
Isa 36: 1 Now it came to pass in the **f** year of 702+6240
Eze 40: 1 **f** year after that the city was smitten, 702+6240
45:21 In the first *month,* in the **f** day of 702+6240
Ac 27:27 But when the **f** night was come, as we were *5065*
27:33 This day is the **f** day that ye have tarried *5065*

FOURTH (84) [FOUR]

Ge 1:19 and the morning were the **f** day. 7243
2:14 of Assyria. And the **f** river *is* Euphrates. 7243
15:16 *in* the **f** generation they shall come hither 7243
Ex 20: 5 and **f** *generation* of them that hate me; 7256
28:20 the **f** row a beryl, and an onyx, and a jasper: 7243
29:40 with the **f** **part** of a hin of beaten oil; 7253
29:40 the **f** *part* of a hin of wine *for* a drink 7243
34: 7 unto the third and to the **f** *generation.* 7256
39:13 the **f** row, a beryl, an onyx, and a jasper: 7243
Lev 19:24 in the **f** year all the fruit thereof shall be 7243
23:13 thereof *shall be of* wine, the **f** *part* of a hin. 7243
Nu 7:30 On the **f** day Elizur the son of Shedeur, 7243
14:18 children unto the third and **f** *generation.* 7256
15: 4 flour mingled with the **f** *part* of a hin of oil. 7243
15: 5 the **f** *part* of a hin *of* wine for a drink 7243
23:10 and the number *of* the **f** **part** of Israel? 7255
28: 5 mingled with the **f** *part* of a hin of beaten 7243
28: 7 the drink offering thereof *shall be* the **f** *part* 7243
28:14 a ram, and a **f** *part* of a hin unto a lamb: 7243
29:23 on the **f** day ten bullocks, two rams, *and* 7243
Dt 5: 9 and **f** *generation* of them that hate me, 7256
Jos 19:17 *And* the **f** lot came out to Issachar, for 7243
Jdg 19: 5 it came to pass on the **f** day, when they 7243
1Sa 9: 8 I have here at hand the **f** **part** of a shekel of 7253
2Sa 3: 4 the **f**, Adonijah the son of Haggith; and 7243
1Ki 6: 1 in the **f** year of Solomon's reign over Israel, 7243
6:33 posts of olive tree, a **f** *part of the wall.* 7243
6:37 In the **f** year was the foundation of 7243
22:41 Judah in the **f** year of Ahab king of Israel. 702
2Ki 6:25 the **f** **part** of a kab of dove's dung for five 7255
10:30 thy children of the **f** *generation* shall sit on 7243
15:12 throne of Israel unto the **f** *generation.* And 7243
18: 9 it came to pass in the **f** year of king 7243
25: 3 on the ninth *day* of the *f* month the famine NIH
1Ch 2:14 Nethaneel the **f**, Raddai the fifth, 7243
3: 2 the **f**, Adonijah the son of Haggith: 7243
3:15 the third Zedekiah, the **f** Shallum. 7243
8: 2 Nohah the **f**, and Rapha the fifth. 7243
12:10 Mishmannah the **f**, Jeremiah the fifth, 7243
23:19 Jahaziel the third, and Jekameam the **f**. 7243
24: 8 The third to Harim, the **f** to Seorim, 7243
24:23 Jahaziel the third, Jekameam the **f**. 7243
25:11 The **f** to Izri, *he,* his sons, and his brethren, 7243
26: 2 Zebadiah the third, Jathniel the **f**, 7243
26: 4 and Sacar the **f**, and Nethaneel the fifth, 7243
26:11 Tebaliah the third, Zechariah the **f**: 7243
27: 7 The **f** *captain* for the fourth month *was* 7243
27: 7 The fourth *captain* for the **f** month *was* 7243
2Ch 3: 2 the second month, in the **f** year of his reign. 702
20:26 on the **f** day they assembled themselves in 7243
Ezr 8:33 Now on the **f** day was the silver and 7243
Ne 9: 1 **f** day of this month the children of Israel 702
9: 3 the LORD their God *one* **f** *part* of the day; 7243
9: 3 *another* **f** *part* they confessed, and 7243
Jer 25: 1 **f** year of Jehoiakim the son of Josiah king 7243
28: 1 in the **f** year, *and* in the fifth month, 7243
36: 1 it came to pass in the **f** year of Jehoiakim 7243
39: 2 in the **f** month, the ninth *day* of the month, 7243
45: 1 in the **f** year of Jehoiakim the son of Josiah 7243
46: 2 **f** year of Jehoiakim the son of Josiah king 7243
51:59 *into* Babylon in the **f** year of his reign. 7243
52: 6 in the **f** month, in the ninth *day* of 7243
Eze 1: 1 in the **f** *month,* in the fifth *day* of 7243
10:14 face of a lion, and the **f** the face of an eagle. 7243
Da 2:40 the **f** kingdom shall be strong as iron: 7244
3:25 and the form of the **f** *is* like the Son of God. 7244
7: 7 behold, a **f** beast, dreadful and terrible, and 7244
7:19 I would know the truth of the **f** beast, 7244
7:23 The **f** beast shall be the fourth kingdom 7244
7:23 The fourth beast shall be the **f** kingdom 7244
11: 2 and the **f** shall be far richer than *they* all: 7243
Zec 6: 3 and in the **f** chariot grisled *and* bay horses. 7243

Eze 7: 1 it came to pass in the **f** year of king Darius, 702
7: 1 Zechariah in the **f** *day* of the ninth month, 702
8:19 The fast of the **f** *month,* and the fast of 7243
Mt 14:25 And in the **f** watch of the night Jesus went *5067*
Mk 6:48 about the **f** watch of the night he cometh *5067*
Rev 4: 7 and the **f** beast *was* like a flying eagle. *5067*
6: 7 And when he had opened the **f** seal, I heard *5067*
6: 7 I heard the voice of the **f** beast say, Come *5067*
6: 8 And power was given unto them over the **f** *5067*
8:12 And the **f** angel sounded, and the third *part* *5067*
16: 8 And the **f** angel poured out his vial upon *5067*
21:19 the third, a chalcedony; the **f**, an emerald; *5067*

FOWL (31) [FOWLER, FOWLERS, FOWLS]

Ge 1:20 **f** *that* may fly above the earth in the open 5775
1:21 and every winged **f** after his kind: 5775
1:22 in the seas, and let **f** multiply in the earth. 5775
1:26 over the **f** of the air, and over the cattle, and 5775
1:28 over the **f** of the air, and over every living 5775
1:30 to every **f** of the air, and to every *thing* that 5775
2:19 beast of the field, and every **f** of the air; 5775
2:20 to the **f** of the air, and to every beast of 5775
7:14 every **f** after his kind, every bird of every 5775
7:21 *both* of **f**, and of cattle, and of beast, and 5775
7:23 the creeping things, and the **f** of the heaven; 5775
8:17 *both* of **f**, and of cattle, and of every 5775
8:19 every **f**, *and* whatsoever creepeth upon 5775
8:20 of every clean **f**, and offered burnt offerings 5775
9: 2 upon every **f** of the air, upon all that 5775
9:10 of the **f**, of the cattle, and of every beast of 5775
Lev 7:26 *whether it be* of **f** or of beast, in any of your 5775
11:46 of the **f**, and of every living creature that 5775
17:13 catcheth *any* beast or **f** that may be eaten; 5775
20:25 or by **f**, or by any *manner of living thing* 5775
Dt 4:17 the likeness of any winged **f** that flieth in 6833
1Ki 4:23 and roebucks, and fallowdeer, and fatted **f**. 1257
4:33 of **f**, and of creeping things, and of fishes. 5775
Job 28: 7 *There is* a path which no **f** knoweth, and 5861
Ps 8: 8 The **f** of the air, and the fish of the sea, *and* 6833
148:10 all cattle; creeping things, and flying **f**: 6833
Jer 9:10 both the **f** of the heavens and the beast are 5775
Eze 17:23 under it shall dwell all **f** of every wing; 6833
39:17 Speak unto every feathered **f**, and to every 6833
44:31 of itself, or torn, whether it be **f** or beast. 5775
Da 7: 6 had upon the back of it four wings of a **f**; 5776

FOWLER (3) [FOWL]

Ps 91: 3 he shall deliver thee from the snare of the **f**, 3353
Pr 6: 5 and as a bird from the hand of the **f**. 3353
Hos 9: 8 the prophet *is* a snare of a **f** in all his ways, 3352

FOWLERS (1) [FOWL]

Ps 124: 7 is escaped as a bird out of the snare of the **f**: 3369

FOWLS (55) [FOWL]

Ge 6: 7 and the creeping thing, and the **f** of the air; 5775
6:20 Of **f** after their kind, and of cattle after their 5775
7: 3 Of **f** also of the air by sevens, the male and 5775
7: 8 of **f**, and of every *thing* that creepeth upon 5775
15:11 when the **f** came down upon the carcases, 5861
Lev 1:14 for his offering to the LORD *be* of **f**, 5775
11:13 ye shall have in abomination among the **f**; 5775
11:20 All **f** that creep, going upon *all* four, 5775
20:25 and between unclean **f** and clean: 5775
Dt 14:20 *But of* all clean **f** ye may eat. 5775
28:26 thy carcase shall be meat unto all **f** of 5775
1Sa 17:44 I will give thy flesh unto the **f** of the air, 5775
17:46 the Philistines this day unto the **f** of the air, 5775
1Ki 14:11 him that dieth in the field shall the **f** of 5775
16: 4 him that dieth of his in the fields shall the **f** 5775
21:24 him that dieth in the field shall the **f** of 5775
Ne 5:18 also **f** were prepared for me, and once in 6833
Job 12: 7 and the **f** of the air, and they shall tell thee: 5775
28:21 and kept close from the **f** of the air. 5775
35:11 and maketh us wiser than the **f** of heaven? 5775
Ps 50:11 I know all the **f** of the mountains: and 5775
78:27 and feathered **f** like as the sand of the sea: 5775
79: 2 given *to be* meat unto the **f** of the heaven, 5775
104:12 By them shall the **f** of the heaven have their 5775
Isa 18: 6 They shall be left together unto the **f** of 5861
18: 6 the **f** shall summer upon them, and all 5861
Jer 7:33 people shall be meat for the **f** of the heaven, 5775
15: 3 the **f** of the heaven, and the beasts of 5775
16: 4 their carcases shall be meat for the **f** of 5775
19: 7 I give to be meat for the **f** of the heaven, 5775
34:20 shall be for meat unto the **f** of the heaven, 5775
Eze 29: 5 of the field and to the **f** of the heaven. 5775
31: 6 All the **f** of heaven made their nests in his 5775
31:13 Upon his ruin shall all the **f** of the heaven 5775
32: 4 will cause all the **f** of the heaven to remain 5775
38:20 the **f** of the heaven, and the beasts of 5775
Da 2:38 the **f** of the heaven hath he given into thine 5776
4:12 the **f** of the heaven dwelt in the boughs 6853
4:14 from under it, and the **f** from his branches: 6853
4:21 upon whose branches the **f** of the heaven 6853
Hos 2:18 with the **f** of heaven, and *with* the creeping 5775
4: 3 beasts of the field, and with the **f** of heaven; 5775
7:12 I will bring them down as the **f** of 5775
Zep 1: 3 I will consume the **f** of the heaven, and 5775
Mt 6:26 Behold the **f** of the air: for they sow not, *4071*
13: 4 and the **f** came and devoured them up: *4071*
Mk 4: 4 and the **f** of the air came and devoured it *4071*
4:32 that the **f** of the air may lodge under *4071*
Lk 8: 5 and the **f** of the air devoured it. *4071*
12:24 how much more are ye better than the **f**? *4071*
13:19 the **f** of the air lodged in the branches of it. *4071*
Ac 10:12 and creeping things, and **f** of the air. *4071*
11: 6 and creeping things, and **f** of the air. *4071*
Rev 19:17 saying to all the **f** that fly in the midst of *3732*
19:21 and all the **f** were filled with their flesh. *3732*

FOX (2) [FOXES]

Ne 4: 3 Even *that* which they build, if a **f** go up, 7776
Lk 13:32 Go ye, and tell that **f**, Behold, I cast out *258*

FOXES (8) [FOX]

Jdg 15: 4 Samson went and caught three hundred **f**, 7776
Ps 63:10 by the sword: they shall be a portion for **f**. 7776
SS 2:15 Take us the **f**, the little foxes, that spoil 7776
2:15 Take us the foxes, the little **f**, that spoil 7776
La 5:18 which is desolate, the **f** walk upon it. 7776
Eze 13: 4 thy prophets are like the **f** in the deserts. 7776
Mt 8:20 The **f** have holes, and the birds of the air *258*
Lk 9:58 **F** have holes, and birds of the air *have* nests; *258*

FRAGMENT See SHERD; SHERDS

FRAGMENTS (7)

Mt 14:20 they took up of the **f** that remained twelve *2801*
Mk 6:43 they took up twelve baskets full of the **f**, *2801*
8:19 how many baskets full of **f** took ye up? *2801*
8:20 how many baskets full of **f** took ye up? *2801*
Lk 9:17 there was taken up of **f** that remained to *2801*
Jn 6:12 Gather up the **f** that remain, that nothing be *2801*
6:13 filled twelve baskets with the **f** of the five *2801*

FRAGRANT See SWEETSMELLING

FRAIL (1)

Ps 39: 4 what it *is; that* I may know how **f** I *am.* 2310

F

FRAME (5) [FRAMED, FRAMETH]

Jdg 12: 6 for he **could** not **f** to pronounce *it* right. 3559
Ps 103:14 For he knoweth our **f**; he remembereth that 3336
Jer 18:11 I **f** evil against you, and devise a device 3335
Eze 40: 2 by which *was* as the **f** of a city on the south. 4011
Hos 5: 4 They will not **f** their doings to turn unto 5414

FRAMED (4) [FRAME]

Isa 29:16 shall the **thing** **f** say of him that framed it, 3336
29:16 shall the thing framed say of him that **f** it, 3335
Eph 2:21 In whom all the building **fitly** **f** **together** *4883*
Heb 11: 3 that the worlds were **f** by the word of God, *2675*

FRAMETH (2) [FRAME]

Ps 50:19 thy mouth to evil, and thy tongue **f** deceit. 6775
94:20 *with* thee, which **f** mischief by a law? 3335

FRANKINCENSE (17) [INCENSE]

Ex 30:34 galbanum; *these* sweet spices with pure **f**: 3828
Lev 2: 1 he shall pour oil upon it, and put **f** thereon: 3828
2: 2 and of the oil thereof, with all the **f** thereof; 3828
2:15 thou shalt put oil upon it, and lay **f** thereon: 3828
2:16 *part* of the oil thereof, with all the **f** thereof: 3828
5:11 upon it, neither shall he put *any* **f** thereon: 3828
6:15 all the **f** which *is* upon the meat offering, 3828
24: 7 thou shalt put pure **f** upon *each* row, that it 3828
Nu 5:15 shall pour no oil upon it, nor put **f** thereon; 3828
1Ch 9:29 and the oil, and the **f**, and the spices. 3828
Ne 13: 5 the **f**, and the vessels, and the tithes of 3828
13: 9 of God, with the meat offering and the **f**. 3828
SS 3: 6 perfumed *with* myrrh and **f**, with all 3828
4: 6 the mountain of myrrh, and to the hill of **f**. 3828
4:14 calamus and cinnamon, with all trees of **f**; 3828
Mt 2:11 unto him gifts; gold, and **f**, and myrrh. *3030*
Rev 18:13 and **f**, and wine, and oil, and fine flour, and *3030*

FRANKLY (1)

Lk 7:42 had nothing to pay, he **f** **forgave** *them* both. *5483*

FRAUD (2)

Ps 10: 7 mouth is full *of* cursing and deceit and **f**: 8496
Jas 5: 4 which is of you **kept back by** **f**, crieth: *650*

FRAY (3)

Dt 28:26 of the earth, and no man shall **f** *them* **away**. 2729
Jer 7:33 of the earth; and none shall **f** *them* **away**. 2729
Zec 1:21 these are come to **f** them, to cast out 2729

FRECKLED (1)

Lev 13:39 it *is* a **f** **spot** *that* groweth in the skin: 933

FREE (59) [FREED, FREEDOM, FREELY, FREEMAN, FREEWILL, FREEWOMAN]

Ex 21: 2 in the seventh he shall go out **f** for nothing. 2670
21: 5 and my children; I will not go out **f**: 2670
21:11 then shall she go out **f** without money. 2600
21:26 he shall let him go **f** for his eye's sake. 2670
21:27 he shall let him go **f** for his tooth's sake. 2670
36: 3 yet unto him **f** **offerings** every morning. 5071
Lev 19:20 not be put to death, because she was not **f**. 2666
Nu 5:19 be thou **f** from this bitter water that causeth 5352
5:28 then she shall be **f**, and shall conceive seed. 5352
Dt 15:12 in the seventh year thou shalt let him go **f** 2670
15:13 when thou sendest him out **f** from thee, 2670
15:18 when thou sendest him away **f** from thee; 2670
24: 5 *but* he shall be **f** at home one year, and 5355
1Sa 17:25 and make his father's house **f** in Israel. 2670
1Ch 9:33 *who remaining* in the chambers *were* **f**: 6362
2Ch 29:31 as many as were of a **f** heart burnt 5081
Job 3:19 and the servant *is* **f** from his master. 2670
39: 5 Who hath sent out the wild ass **f**? or 2670
Ps 51:12 and uphold me *with thy* **f** spirit. 5081
88: 5 **F** among the dead, like the slain that lie in 2670
105:20 the ruler of the people, and let him **go** **f**. 6605
Isa 58: 6 to let the oppressed go **f**, and *that* ye break 2670
Jer 34: 9 *being* a Hebrew or a Hebrewess, go **f**; 2670
34:10 and every one his maidservant, go **f**, 2670
34:11 whom they had let go **f**, to return, and 2670
34:14 six years, thou shalt let him go **f** from thee: 2670
Am 4: 5 and proclaim *and* publish the **f** **offerings**: 5071
Mt 15: 6 *he shall be f.* Thus have ye made NIG
17:26 saith unto him, Then are the children **f**. *1658*
Mk 7:11 mightest be profited by me; *he shall be f.* NIG
Jn 8:32 the truth, and the truth shall **make** you **f**. *1659*
8:33 *man:* how sayest thou, Ye shall be made **f**? *1658*
8:36 If the Son therefore shall **make** you **f**, *1659*
8:36 shall make you free, ye shall be **f** indeed. *1658*

Ac 22:28 And Paul said, But I was *f* born. NIG
Ro 5:15 But not as the offence, so also *is* the **f gift.** *5486*
5:16 the **f gift** *is* of many offences unto *5486*
5:18 by the righteousness of one *the f gift came* NIG
6:18 Being then **made f** from sin, ye became *1659*
6:20 of sin, ye were **f** from righteousness. *1658*
6:22 But now being **made f** from sin, and *1659*
7: 3 *her* husband be dead, she is **f** from *that* law; *1658*
8: 2 Jesus hath **made** me **f** from the law of sin *1659*
1Co 7:21 but if thou mayest be made **f**, use *it* rather. *1658*
7:22 he that is called, *being* **f**, is Christ's servant. *1658*
9: 1 am I not **f**? have I not seen Jesus Christ our *1658*
9:19 For though I be **f** from all *men,* yet have I *1658*
12:13 or Gentiles, whether *we be* bond or **f**; *1658*
Gal 3:28 Jew nor Greek, there is neither bond nor **f**, *1658*
4:26 But Jerusalem which is above is **f**, which is *1658*
4:31 children of *the* bondwoman, but of the **f**. *1658*
5: 1 liberty wherewith Christ hath **made** us **f**, *1659*
Eph 6: 8 of the Lord, whether *he be* bond or **f**. *1658*
Col 3:11 barbarian, Scythian, bond *nor* **f**: *1658*
2Th 3: 1 that the word of the Lord may have *f* NIG
1Pe 2:16 As **f**, and not using *your* liberty for a cloke *1658*
Rev 6:15 every **f** *man,* hid themselves in the dens and *1658*
13:16 and great, rich and poor, **f** and bond, *1658*
19:18 and the flesh of all *men,* both **f** and bond, *1658*

F

FREED (2) [FREE]
Jos 9:23 there shall none of you be **f** from being 3772
Ro 6: 7 For he that is dead is **f** from sin. *1344*

FREEDMEN See LIBERTINES

FREEDOM (2) [FREE]
Lev 19:20 and not at all redeemed, nor **f** given her; 2668
Ac 22:28 With a great sum obtained I this **f**. *4174*

FREELY (17) [FREE]
Ge 2:16 tree of the garden thou mayest **f eat**: 398+398
Nu 11: 5 the fish, which we did eat in Egypt **f**; 2600
1Sa 14:30 if haply the people had **eaten f** to day 398+398
Ezr 2:68 **offered f** for the house of God to set it up 5068
7:15 his counsellers have **f offered** unto the God 5069
Ps 54: 6 I will **f** sacrifice unto thee: I will 5071+871.1
Hos 14: 4 heal their backsliding, I will love them **f**: 5071
Mt 10: 8 out devils: **f** ye have received, freely give. *1432*
10: 8 out devils: freely ye have received, **f** give. *1432*
Ac 2:29 let *me* **f** speak unto you of *3326+3954*
26:26 of these *things,* before whom also I speak **f**: *3955*
Ro 3:24 Being justified **f** by his grace through *1432*
8:32 how shall he not with him also **f give** us all *5483*
1Co 2:12 the *things* that are **f given** to us of God. *5483*
2Co 11: 7 I have preached to you the gospel of God **f**? *1432*
Rev 21: 6 athirst of the fountain of the water of life **f**. *1432*
22:17 let him take the water of life **f**. *1432*

FREEMAN (1) [FREE, MAN]
1Co 7:22 in the Lord, *being* a servant, is the Lord's **f**: *558*

FREEWILL (17) [FREE, WILL]
Lev 22:18 for all his vows, and for all his **f offerings**, 5071
22:21 or a **f offering** in beeves or sheep, it shall 5071
22:23 that mayest thou offer *for* a **f offering**; 5071
23:38 your vows, and beside all your **f offerings**, 5071
Nu 15: 3 or in a **f offering**, or in your solemn feasts, 5071
29:39 besides your vows, and your **f offerings**, 5071
Dt 12: 6 your **f offerings**, and the firstlings of your 5071
12:17 nor thy **f offerings**, or heave offering of 5071
16:10 *with* a tribute of a **f offering** of thine hand, 5071
23:23 *even* a **f offering**, according as thou hast 5071
2Ch 31:14 the east, *was* over the **f offerings** of God, 5071
Ezr 1: 4 besides the **f offering** for the house of God 5071
3: 5 offered a **f offering** unto the LORD. 5071
7:13 *which are* **minded** of their **own f** to go *up* 5069
7:16 with the **f offering** of the people, and of 5069
8:28 the gold *are* a **f offering** unto the LORD 5071
Ps 119:108 the **f offerings** of my mouth, O LORD, 5071

FREEWOMAN (3) [FREE, WOMAN]
Gal 4:22 the one by a bondmaid, the other by a **f**. *1658*
4:23 the flesh; but he of the **f** *was* by promise. *1658*
4:30 shall not be heir with the son of the **f**. *1658*

FREQUENT (1)
2Co 11:23 in prisons **more f**, in deaths oft. *4056*

FRESH (4) [AFRESH, FRESHER]
Nu 11: 8 and the taste of it was as the taste of **f** oil. 3955
Job 29:20 My glory *was* **f** in me, and my bow was 2319
Ps 92:10 *of* an unicorn: I shall be anointed with **f** oil. 7488
Jas 3:12 *can* no fountain *both* yield salt water and **f**. *1099*

FRESHER (1) [FRESH]
Job 33:25 His flesh shall be **f** than a child's: he shall 7375

FRET (7) [FRETTED, FRETTETH, FRETTING]
Lev 13:55 it *is* **f** inward, *whether* it *be* bare within or 6356
1Sa 1: 6 for to **make** her **f**, because the LORD had 7481
Ps 37: 1 **F** not thyself because of evildoers, 2734
37: 7 **f** not thyself because of him who prospereth 2734
37: 8 **f** not thyself in any wise to do evil. 2734
Pr 24:19 **F** not thyself because of evil *men,* neither 2734
Isa 8:21 they shall **f** themselves, and curse their king 7107

FRETTED (1) [FRET]
Eze 16:43 hast **f** me in all these *things;* behold 7264

FRETTETH (1) [FRET]
Pr 19: 3 his way: and his heart **f** against the LORD. 2196

FRETTING (3) [FRET]
Lev 13:51 the plague *is* a **f** leprosy; it *is* unclean. 3992
13:52 for it *is* a **f** leprosy; it shall be burnt in 3992
14:44 in the house, it *is* a **f** leprosy in the house: 3992

FRIED (2) [FRYINGPAN]
Lev 7:12 and cakes mingled with oil, of fine flour, **f**. 7246
1Ch 23:29 for that which is **f**, and for all *manner of* 7246

FRIEND (53) [FRIENDLY, FRIENDS, FRIENDSHIP]
Ge 38:12 he and his **f** Hirah the Adullamite. 7453
38:20 Judah sent the kid by the hand of his **f** 7453
Ex 33:11 face to face, as a man speaketh unto his **f**. 7453
Dt 13: 6 or the wife of thy bosom, or thy **f**, 7453
Jdg 14:20 his companion, whom he had used as his **f**. 7462
2Sa 13: 3 Amnon had a **f**, whose name *was* Jonadab, 7453
15:37 So Hushai David's **f** came *into* the city, and 7463
16:16 David's **f**, was come unto Absalom, 7463
16:17 said to Hushai, *Is* this thy kindness to thy **f**? 7453
16:17 why wentest thou not with thy **f**? 7453
1Ki 4: 5 *was* principal officer, *and* the king's **f**: 7463
2Ch 20: 7 gavest it to the seed of Abraham thy **f** for 157
Job 6:14 afflicted pity *should be shewed* from his **f**; 7453
6:27 the fatherless, and you dig *a pit* for your **f**. 7453
Ps 35:14 behaved myself as though *he had been* my **f** 7453
41: 9 Yea, mine own **familiar f**, in whom I 376+7965
88:18 Lover and **f** hast thou put far from me, *and* 7453
Pr 6: 1 My son, if thou be surety for thy **f**, *if* thou 7453
6: 3 when thou art come into the hand of thy **f**; 7453
6: 3 go, humble thyself, and make sure thy **f**. 7453
17:17 A **f** loveth at all times, and a brother is born 7453
17:18 becometh surety in the presence of his **f**. 7453
18:24 there is a **f** *that* sticketh closer than a brother. 157
19: 6 every *man is* a **f** to him that giveth gifts. 7453
22:11 the grace of his lips the king *shall be* his **f**. 7453
27: 6 Faithful *are* the wounds of a **f**; but the kisses 157
27: 9 *doth* the sweetness of a man's **f** by hearty 7453
27:10 Thine own **f**, and thy father's friend, 7453
27:10 own friend, and thy father's **f**, forsake not; 7453
27:14 He that blesseth his **f** with a loud voice, 7453
27:17 a man sharpeneth the countenance of his **f**. 7453
SS 5:16 This *is* my beloved, and this *is* my **f**, 7453
Isa 41: 8 I have chosen, the seed of Abraham my **f**. 157
Jer 6:21 the neighbour and his **f** shall perish. 7453
19: 9 they shall eat every one the flesh of his **f** in 7453
Hos 3: 1 Go yet, love a woman beloved of *her* **f**, 7453
Mic 7: 5 Trust ye not in a **f**, put ye not confidence in 7453
Mt 11:19 a winebibber, a **f** of publicans and sinners. *5384*
20:13 of them, and said, **F**, I do thee no wrong: *2083*
22:12 And he saith unto him, **F**, how camest thou *2083*
26:50 And Jesus said unto him, **F**, wherefore art *2083*
Lk 7:34 a winebibber, a **f** of publicans and sinners. *5384*
11: 5 Which of you shall have a **f**, and shall go *5384*
11: 5 and say unto him, **F**, lend me three loaves; *5384*
11: 6 For a **f** of mine in *his* journey is come to *5384*
11: 8 because *he* is his **f**, yet because of his *5384*
14:10 he may say unto thee, **F**, go up higher: *5384*
Jn 3:29 but the **f** of the bridegroom, which standeth *5384*
11:11 he saith unto them, Our **f** Lazarus sleepeth; *5384*
19:12 thou let this *man* go, thou art not Cesar's **f**: *5384*
Ac 12:20 **made** Blastus the king's chamberlain their **f**, *3982*
Jas 2:23 and he was called the **F** of God. *5384*
4: 4 will be a **f** of the world is the enemy of *5384*

FRIENDLY (3) [FRIEND]
Jdg 19: 3 **f** unto her, *and* to bring her again, 3820+5921
Ru 2:13 for that thou hast spoken **f** unto thine 3820+5921
Pr 18:24 man that hath friends must **shew** himself **f**: 7462

FRIENDS (49) [FRIEND]
Ge 26:26 Ahuzzath *one* of his **f**, and Phichol the chief 4828
1Sa 30:26 the elders of Judah, *even* to his **f**, saying, 7453
2Sa 3: 8 to his **f**, and have not delivered thee into 4828
19: 6 thou lovest thine enemies, and hatest thy **f**: 157
1Ki 16:11 a wall, neither *of* his kinsfolks, nor *of* his **f**. 7453
Est 5:10 he sent and called for his **f**, and Zeresh his 157
5:14 said Zeresh his wife and all his **f** unto him, 157
6:13 all his **f** every *thing* that had befallen him. 157
Job 2:11 Now when Job's three **f** heard of all this 7453
16:20 My **f** scorn me: *but* mine eye poureth out 7453
17: 5 He *that* speaketh flattery to *his* **f**, even 7453
19:14 and my **familiar f** have forgotten me. 3045
19:19 All my inward **f** abhorred me: and 4962
19:21 upon me, have pity upon me, O ye my **f**; 7453
32: 3 Also against his three **f** was his wrath 7453
42: 7 kindled against thee, and against thy two **f**: 7453
42:10 captivity of Job, when he prayed for his **f**: 7453
Ps 38:11 and my **f** stand aloof from my sore; 7453
Pr 14:20 his own neighbour: but the rich *hath* many **f**. 157
16:28 and a whisperer separateth **chief f**. 441
17: 9 he that repeateth a matter separateth **very f**. 441
18:24 A man that hath **f** must shew himself 7453
19: 4 Wealth maketh many **f**; but the poor is 7453
19: 7 how much more do his **f** go far from him! 4828
SS 5: 1 eat, O **f**; drink, yea, drink abundantly, 7453
Jer 20: 4 make thee a terror to thyself, and to all thy **f**: 157
20: 6 and shalt be buried there, thou, and all thy **f**, 157
38:22 Thy **f** have set thee on, and 376+7965
La 1: 2 all her **f** have dealt treacherously with her, 7453
Zec 13: 6 which I was wounded *in* the house of my **f**. 157
Mk 3:21 And when his **f** heard *of it,* they went *3588+3844*
5:19 Go home to thy *f,* and tell them how great NIG
Lk 7: 6 the centurion sent **f** to him, saying unto *5384*
12: 4 And I say unto you my **f**, Be not afraid of *5384*
14:12 makest a dinner or a supper, call not thy **f**, *5384*
15: 6 he calleth together *his* **f** and neighbours, *5384*
15: 9 when she hath found *it,* she calleth *her* **f** *5384*
15:29 a kid, that I might make merry with my **f**: *5384*
16: 9 Make to yourselves **f** of the mammon of *5384*
21:16 and brethren, and kinsfolks, and **f**; *5384*
23:12 Pilate and Herod were made **f** together: *5384*
Jn 15:13 that a man lay down his life for his **f**. *5384*
15:14 Ye are my **f**, if ye do whatsoever I *5384*
15:15 but I have called you **f**; for all *things* that I *5384*
Ac 10:24 had called together his kinsmen and near **f**. *5384*
19:31 of Asia, which were his **f**, sent unto him, *5384*
27: 3 gave *him* liberty to go unto *his* **f** to refresh *5384*
3Jn 1:14 *Our* **f** salute thee. Greet the friends by *5384*
1:14 friends salute thee. Greet the **f** by name. *5384*

FRIENDSHIP (2) [FRIEND]
Pr 22:24 **Make** no **f** with an angry man; and with a 7462
Jas 4: 4 know ye not that the **f** of the world is *5373*

FRIGHTENED See ABASE; ABASED; ABASING

FRINGE (2) [FRINGES]
Nu 15:38 that they put upon the **f** of the borders a 6734
15:39 it shall be unto you for a **f**, that ye may look 6734

FRINGES (2) [FRINGE]
Nu 15:38 bid them that they make them **f** in 6734
Dt 22:12 Thou shalt make thee **f** upon the four 1434

FRO (25)
Ge 8: 7 forth a raven, which went forth to and **f**, 7725
2Ki 4:35 and walked in the house to and **f**; 259+2008
2Ch 16: 9 For the eyes of the LORD **run to and f** 7751
Job 1: 7 From **going to and f** in the earth, and 7751
2: 2 From **going to and f** in the earth, and 7751
7: 4 I am full *of* **tossings to and f** unto 5076
13:25 Wilt thou break a leaf **driven to and f**? and 5086
Ps 107:27 They **reel to and f**, and stagger like a 2287
Pr 21: 6 a lying tongue *is* a vanity **tossed to and f** 5086
Isa 24:20 The earth shall **reel to and f** like a 5128+5128
33: 4 as the **running to and f** of locusts shall he 4944
49:21 a captive, and **removing to and f**? 5493
Jer 5: 1 **Run** ye **to and f** through the streets of 7751
49: 3 lament, and **run to and f** by the hedges; 7751
Eze 27:19 **going to and f** occupied in thy fairs: 235+4480
Da 12: 4 many shall **run to and f**, and knowledge 7751
Joel 2: 9 They shall **run to and f** in the city; 8264
Am 8:12 they shall **run to and f** to seek the word of 7751
Zec 1:10 the LORD hath sent to **walk to and f** 1980
1:11 We have **walked to and f** through 1980
4:10 which **run to and f** through the whole 7751
6: 7 sought to go that *they* might **walk to and f** 1980
6: 7 Get ye *hence,* **walk to and f** through 1980
6: 7 So they **walked to and f** through the earth. 1980
Eph 4:14 **tossed to and f**, and carried about with *2831*

FROGS (14)
Ex 8: 2 behold, I will smite all thy borders with **f**: 6854
8: 3 And the river shall bring forth **f** abundantly, 6854
8: 4 the **f** shall come up *both* on thee, and 6854
8: 5 cause **f** to come up upon the land of Egypt. 6854
8: 6 the **f** came up, and covered the land of 6854
8: 7 and brought up **f** upon the land of Egypt. 6854
8: 8 that he may take away the **f** from me, and 6854
8: 9 to destroy the **f** from thee and thy houses, 6854
8:11 the **f** shall depart from thee, and from thy 6854
8:12 of the **f** which he had brought against 6854
8:13 the **f** died out of the houses, out of 6854
Ps 78:45 and **f**, which destroyed them. 6854
105:30 Their land brought forth **f** in abundance, 6854
Rev 16:13 And I saw three unclean spirits like **f** *come* *944*

FROM (3660) [THEREFROM] See Index of Articles, Etc.

FRONT (2) [FOREFRONT]
2Sa 10: 9 When Joab saw that the **f** of the battle was 6440
2Ch 3: 4 the porch that *was* **in** the **f** *of* 5921+6440

FRONTIERS (1)
Eze 25: 9 from his cities *which are* on his **f**, the glory 7097

FRONTLETS (3)
Ex 13:16 thine hand, and for **f** between thine eyes: 2903
Dt 6: 8 and they shall be as **f** between thine eyes. 2903
11:18 that they may be as **f** between your eyes. 2903

FROST (6) [HOARFROST]
Ge 31:40 drought consumed me, and the **f** by night; 7140
Ex 16:14 *as* small as the **hoar f** on the ground. 3713
Job 37:10 By the breath of God **f** is given: and 7140
38:29 the **hoary f** of heaven, who hath gendered 3713
Ps 78:47 with hail, and their sycomore trees with **f**. 2602
Jer 36:30 the day to the heat, and in the night to the **f**. 7140

FROWARD (21) [FROWARDLY, FROWARDNESS]
Dt 32:20 *shall be:* for they *are* a **very f** generation, 8419
2Sa 22:27 with the **f** thou wilt shew thyself 6141
Job 5:13 and the counsel of the **f** is carried headlong. 6617
Ps 18:26 with the **f** thou wilt shew thyself froward. 6141
18:26 with the froward thou wilt **shew** thyself **f**. 6617
101: 4 A **f** heart shall depart from me: I will not 6141
Pr 2:12 *man,* from the man that speaketh **f things**; 8419
2:15 ways *are* crooked, and *they* **f** in their paths: 3868
3:32 For the **f** *is* abomination to the LORD: but 3868
4:24 Put away from thee a **f** mouth, and 6143
6:12 a wicked man, walketh *with* a **f** mouth. 6143
8: 8 *there is* nothing **f** or perverse in them. 6617
8:13 the evil way, and the **f** mouth, do I hate. 8419
10:31 but the **f** tongue shall be cut out. 8419
11:20 *They that are* of a **f** heart *are* abomination 6141
16:28 A **f** man soweth strife: and a whisperer 8419
16:30 He shutteth his eyes to devise **f things**: 8419
17:20 He that hath a **f** heart findeth no good: and 6141
21: 8 The way of man *is* **f** and strange: but *as for* 2019
22: 5 Thorns *and* snares *are* in the way of the **f**: 6141
1Pe 2:18 to the good and gentle, but also to the **f**. *4646*

FROWARDLY (1) [FROWARD]
Isa 57:17 and he went on **f** in the way of his heart. 7726

FROWARDNESS (3) [FROWARD]
Pr 2:14 do evil, *and* delight in the **f** of the wicked; 8419
6:14 **F** *is* in his heart, he deviseth mischief 8419
10:32 but the mouth of the wicked *speaketh* **f**. 8419

FROZEN (1)
Job 38:30 *with* a stone, and the face of the deep is **f**. 3920

FRUIT (208) [FIRSTFRUIT, FIRSTFRUITS, FRUITFUL, FRUITS, UNFRUITFUL]

Ge 1:11 *and* the **f** tree yielding fruit after his kind, 6529
1:11 *and* the fruit tree yielding **f** after his kind, 6529
1:12 the tree yielding **f**, whose seed *was* in itself, 6529
1:29 in the which *is* the **f** of a tree yielding seed; 6529
3: 2 We may eat of the **f** of the trees of 6529
3: 3 of the **f** of the tree which *is* in the midst of 6529
3: 6 she took of the **f** thereof, and did eat, and 6529
4: 3 that Cain brought of the **f** of the ground an 6529
30: 2 who hath withheld from thee the **f** of 6529
Ex 10:15 all the **f** of the trees which the hail had left: 6529
21:22 so that her **f** depart *from her,* and yet no 3206
Lev 19:23 ye shall count the **f** thereof as 6529
19:24 in the fourth year all the **f** thereof shall be 6529
19:25 in the fifth year shall ye eat of the **f** thereof, 6529
23:39 when ye have gathered in the **f** of the land, 8393
25: 3 thy vineyard, and gather in the **f** thereof; 8393
25:19 the land shall yield her **f**, and ye shall eat 6529
25:21 it shall bring forth **f** for three years. 8393
25:22 and eat *yet* of old **f** until the ninth year; 8393
26: 4 and the trees of the field shall yield their **f**. 6529
27:30 *or* of the **f** of the tree, *is* the LORD'S: 6529
Nu 13:20 and bring of the **f** of the land. 6529
13:26 and shewed them the **f** of the land. 6529
13:27 with milk and honey; and this *is* the **f** of it. 6529
Dt 1:25 they took of the **f** of the land in their hands, 6529
7:13 he will also bless the **f** of thy womb, and 6529
7:13 the **f** of thy land, thy corn, and thy wine, 6529
11:17 be no rain, and *that* the land yield not her **f**; 2981
22: 9 lest the **f** of *thy* seed which thou hast sown, 4395
22: 9 and the **f** of thy vineyard, be defiled. 8393
26: 2 That thou shalt take of the first of all the **f** 6529
28: 4 Blessed *shall be* the **f** of thy body, and 6529
28: 4 the **f** of thy ground, and the fruit of thy 6529
28: 4 fruit of thy ground, and the **f** of thy cattle, 6529
28:11 in the **f** of thy body, and in the fruit of thy 6529
28:11 in the **f** of thy cattle, and in the fruit of thy 6529
28:11 of thy cattle, and in the **f** of thy ground, 6529
28:18 Cursed *shall be* the **f** of thy body, and 6529
28:18 the **f** of thy land, the increase of thy kine, 6529
28:33 The **f** of thy land, and all thy labours, 6529
28:40 *with* the oil; for thine olive shall cast *his* **f**. NIH
28:42 and **f** of thy land shall the locust consume. 6529
28:51 he shall eat the **f** of thy cattle, and the fruit 6529
28:51 the **f** of thy land, until thou be destroyed: 6529
28:53 thou shalt eat the **f** of thine own body, 6529
30: 9 in the **f** of thy body, and in the fruit of thy 6529
30: 9 in the **f** of thy cattle, and in the fruit of thy 6529
30: 9 thy cattle, and in the **f** of thy land, for good: 6529
Jos 5:12 they did eat of the **f** of the land of Canaan 8393
Jdg 9:11 my good **f**, and go to be promoted over 8570
2Sa 16: 2 and **summer f** for the young men to eat; 7019
2Ki 19:30 take root downward, and bear **f** upward. 6529
Ne 9:25 and oliveyards, and **f** trees in abundance: 3978
9:36 gavest unto our fathers to eat the **f** thereof 6529
10:35 the firstfruits of all **f** of all trees, year by 6529
10:37 and the **f** of all *manner of* trees, of wine and 6529
Ps 1: 3 that bringeth forth his **f** in his season; 6529
21:10 Their **f** shalt thou destroy from the earth, 6529
72:16 the **f** thereof shall shake like Lebanon: 6529
92:14 They shall still **bring forth f** in old age; 5107
104:13 the earth is satisfied with the **f** of thy 6529
105:35 and devoured the **f** of their ground. 6529
127: 3 *and* the **f** of the womb *is his* reward. 6529
132:11 Of the **f** of thy body will I set upon thy 6529
Pr 1:31 Therefore shall they eat of the **f** of their 6529
8:19 My **f** *is* better than gold, yea, than fine 6529
10:16 *tendeth* to life: the **f** of the wicked to sin. 8393
11:30 The **f** of the righteous *is* a tree of life; and 6529
12:12 but the root of the righteous yieldeth *f*. NIH
12:14 A man shall be satisfied *with* good by the **f** 6529
13: 2 A man shall eat good by the **f** of *his* mouth: 6529
18:20 A man's belly shall be satisfied with the **f** 6529
18:21 and they that love it shall eat the **f** thereof. 6529
27:18 Whoso keepeth the fig tree shall eat the **f** 6529
31:16 with the **f** of her hands she planteth a 6529
31:31 Give her of the **f** of her hands; and let her 6529
SS 2: 3 and his **f** *was* sweet to my taste. 6529
8:11 every one for the **f** thereof was to bring a 6529
8:12 those that keep the **f** thereof two hundred. 6529
Isa 3:10 *him:* for they shall eat the **f** of their doings. 6529
4: 2 the **f** of the earth *shall be* excellent and 6529
10:12 I will punish the **f** of the stout heart of 6529
13:18 they shall have no pity on the **f** of 6529
14:29 and his **f** *shall be* a fiery flying serpent. 6529
27: 6 bud, and fill the face of the world *with* **f**. 8570
27: 9 and this *is* all the **f** to take away his sin; 6529
28: 4 *and* as the **hasty f** before the summer; 1061
37:30 and plant vineyards, and eat the **f** thereof. 6529
37:31 take root downward, and bear **f** upward. 6529
57:19 I create the **f** of the lips; Peace, peace to 5108
65:21 shall plant vineyards, and eat the **f** of them. 6529
Jer 2: 7 to eat the **f** thereof and the goodness 6529
6:19 *even* the **f** of their thoughts, because 6529
7:20 of the field, and upon the **f** of the ground; 6529
11:16 A green olive tree, fair, *and* of goodly **f**: 6529
11:19 *saying,* Let us destroy the tree with the **f** 3899
12: 2 they grow, yea, they bring forth **f**: thou *art* 6529
17: 8 neither shall cease from yielding **f**. 6529
17:10 *and* according to the **f** of his doings. 6529
21:14 I will punish you according to the **f** of your 6529
29: 5 and plant gardens, and eat the **f** of them; 6529
29:28 and plant gardens, and eat the **f** of them. 6529
32:19 and according to the **f** of his doings: 6529
La 2:20 Shall the women eat their **f**, *and* children of 6529
Eze 17: 8 that *it* might bear **f**, that *it* might be a 6529
17: 9 and cut off the **f** thereof, that it wither? 6529
17:23 and bear **f**, and be a goodly cedar: 6529
19:12 and the east wind dried up her **f**: 6529
19:14 *which* hath devoured her **f**, so that she hath 6529
25: 4 they shall eat thy **f**, and they shall drink thy 6529
34:27 the tree of the field shall yield her **f**, and 6529
36: 8 and yield your **f** to my people of Israel; 6529
36:11 beast; and they shall increase and **bring f**: 6509
36:30 I will multiply the **f** of the tree, and 6529
47:12 neither shall the **f** thereof be consumed: 6529
47:12 it shall **bring forth new f** according to his 1069
47:12 the **f** thereof shall be for meat, and the leaf 6529
Da 4:12 the **f** thereof much, and in it *was* meat for all: 4
4:14 shake off his leaves, and scatter his **f**: 4
4:21 the **f** thereof much, and in it *was* meat for all; 4
Hos 9:16 their root is dried up, they shall bear no **f**: 6529
9:16 yet will I slay *even* the beloved *f* of their NIH
10: 1 he bringeth forth **f** unto himself: 6529
10: 1 according to the multitude of his **f** he hath 6529
10:13 reaped iniquity; ye have eaten the **f** of lies: 6529
14: 8 a green fir tree. From me is thy **f** found. 6529
Joel 2:22 for the tree beareth her **f**, the fig tree and 6529
Am 2: 9 yet I destroyed his **f** from above, and 6529
6:12 and the **f** of righteousness into hemlock: 6529
7:14 a herdman, and a gatherer of **sycomore f**: 8256
8: 1 and behold, a basket of **summer f**. 7019
8: 2 I said, A basket of **summer f**. Then said 7019
9:14 also make gardens, and eat the **f** of them. 6529
Mic 6: 7 the **f** of my body *for* the sin of my soul? 6529
7: 1 to eat: my soul desired the **firstripe f**. 1063
7:13 that dwell therein, for the **f** of their doings. 6529
Hab 3:17 not blossom, neither *shall* **f** *be* in the vines; 2981
Hag 1:10 and the earth is stayed *from* her **f**. 2981
Zec 8:12 the vine shall give her **f**, and the ground 6529
Mal 1:12 the **f** thereof, *even* his meat, 5108
3:11 vine **cast** her **f before the time** in the field, 7921
Mt 3:10 every tree which bringeth not forth good **f** 2590
7:17 so every good tree bringeth forth good **f**; 2590
7:17 but a corrupt tree bringeth forth evil **f**. 2590
7:18 A good tree cannot bring forth evil **f**, 2590
7:18 *can* a corrupt tree bring forth good **f**. 2590
7:19 Every tree that bringeth not forth good **f** is 2590
12:33 Either make the tree good, and his **f** good; 2590
12:33 make the tree corrupt, and his **f** corrupt: 2590
12:33 fruit corrupt: for the tree is known by *his* **f**. 2590
13: 8 fell into good ground, and brought forth **f**, 2590
13:23 and understandeth *it;* which also **beareth f**, 2592
13:26 and brought forth **f**, then appeared the tares 2590
21:19 Let no **f** grow on thee henceforward for 2590
21:34 And when the time of the **f** drew near, 2590
26:29 I will not drink henceforth of this **f** of 1081
Mk 4: 7 grew up, and choked it, and it yielded no **f**. 2590
4: 8 and did yield **f** that sprang up and 2590
4:20 the word, and receive *it,* and **bring forth f**, 2592
4:28 For the earth **bringeth forth f** of herself; 2592
4:29 But when the **f** is brought forth, 2590
11:14 No *man* eat **f** of thee hereafter for ever. 2590
12: 2 the husbandmen of the **f** of the vineyard. 2590
14:25 I will drink no more of the **f** of the vine, 1081
Lk 1:42 and blessed *is* the **f** of thy womb. 2590
3: 9 which bringeth not forth good **f** is hewn 2590
6:43 For a good tree bringeth not forth corrupt **f**; 2590
6:43 doth a corrupt tree bring forth good **f**. 2590
6:44 For every tree is known by his own **f**. 2590
8: 8 and sprang up, and bare **f** an hundredfold. 2590
8:14 of *this* life, and bring no **f** to perfection. NIG
8:15 keep *it,* and **bring forth f** with patience. 2592
13: 6 and he came and sought **f** thereon, 2590
13: 7 *these* three years I come seeking **f** on this 2590
13: 9 And if it bear **f**, *well:* and if not, *then* 2590
20:10 that they should give him of the **f** of 2590
22:18 I will not drink of the **f** of the vine, 1081
Jn 4:36 and gathereth **f** unto life eternal: 2590
12:24 but if it die, it bringeth forth much **f**. 2590
15: 2 Every branch in me that beareth not **f** he 2590
15: 2 and every *branch* that beareth **f**, he purgeth 2590
15: 2 he purgeth it, that it may bring forth more **f**. 2590
15: 4 As the branch cannot bear **f** of itself, 2590
15: 5 I in him, the same bringeth forth much **f**: 2590
15: 8 is my Father glorified, that ye bear much **f**; 2590
15:16 that you should go and bring forth **f**, and 2590
15:16 forth fruit, and *that* your **f** should remain: 2590
Ac 2:30 that of the **f** of his loins, according to 2590
Ro 1:13 that I might have some **f** among you also, 2590
6:21 What **f** had ye then *in those things* whereof 2590
6:22 ye have your **f** unto holiness, and the end 2590
7: 4 that we should **bring forth f** unto God. 2592
7: 5 did work in our members to **bring forth f** 2592
15:28 and have sealed to them this **f**, 2590
1Co 9: 7 a vineyard, and eateth not of the **f** thereof? 2590
Gal 5:22 But the **f** of the Spirit is love, joy, peace, 2590
Eph 5: 9 (For the **f** of the Spirit *is* in all goodness 2590
Php 1:22 *I* live in the flesh, this *is* the **f** of my labour: 2590
4:17 I desire **f** that *may* abound to your account. 2590
Col 1: 6 and **bringeth forth f**, as *it doth* also in you, 2592
Heb 12:11 **f** of righteousness unto them which are 2590
13:15 the **f** of *our* lips giving thanks to his name. 2590
Jas 3:18 And the **f** of righteousness is sown in peace 2590
5: 7 the husbandman waiteth for the precious **f** 2590
5:18 gave rain, and the earth brought forth her **f**. 2590
Jude 1:12 trees whose **f withereth**, without fruit, 5352
1:12 **without f**, twice dead, plucked up by 175
Rev 22: 2 *of* fruits, *and* yielded her **f** every month: 2590

FRUITFUL (35) [FRUIT]

Ge 1:22 Be **f**, and multiply, and fill the waters in 6509
1:28 Be **f**, and multiply, and replenish the earth, 6509
8:17 and be **f**, and multiply upon the earth. 6509
9: 1 Be **f**, and multiply, and replenish the earth. 6509
9: 7 you, be ye **f**, and multiply; bring forth 6509
17: 6 I will **make** thee exceeding **f**, and I will 6509
17:20 will **make** him **f**, and will multiply him 6509
26:22 room for us, and we shall be **f** in the land. 6509
28: 3 and **make** thee **f**, and multiply thee, 6509
35:11 be **f** and multiply; a nation and a company 6509
41:52 For God hath **caused** me **to be f** in the land 6509
48: 4 I will **make** thee **f**, and multiply thee, and 6509
49:22 Joseph *is* a **f bough**, *even* a fruitful 1121+6509
49:22 *even* a **f bough** by a well; 1121+6509
Ex 1: 7 the children of Israel were **f**, and 6509
Lev 26: 9 **make** you **f**, and multiply you, and 6509
Ps 107:34 A **f** land into barrenness, for 6529
128: 3 Thy wife *shall be* as a **f** vine by the sides of 6509
148: 9 all hills; **f** trees, and all cedars: 6529
Isa 5: 1 hath a vineyard in a **very f** hill: 1121+8081
10:18 and of his **f field**, both soul and body: 3759
17: 6 *or* five in the outmost **f** branches thereof, 6509
29:17 Lebanon shall be turned into a **f field**, and 3759
29:17 the **f field** shall be esteemed as a forest? 3759
32:12 for the pleasant fields, for the **f** vine. 6509
32:15 the wilderness be a **f field**, and the fruitful 3759
32:15 and the **f field** be counted for a forest. 3759
32:16 and righteousness remain in the **f field**. 3759
Jer 4:26 lo, the **f place** *was* a wilderness, and all 3759
23: 3 their folds; and they shall be **f** and increase. 6509
Eze 17: 5 seed of the land, and planted it in a **f** field; 2233
19:10 she was **f** and full of branches by reason of 6509
Hos 13:15 Though he be **f** among *his* brethren, an east 6500
Ac 14:17 gave us rain from heaven, and **f** seasons, 2593
Col 1:10 being **f** in every good work, and 2592

FRUITS (42) [FRUIT]

Ge 43:11 take of the **best f** in the land in your 2173
Ex 22:29 not delay *to offer the first of* thy **ripe f**, 4395
23:10 thy land, and shalt gather in the **f** thereof: 8393
Lev 25:15 according unto the number of years of the **f** 8393
25:16 *of the years* of the **f** doth he sell unto thee. 8393
25:22 until her **f** come in ye shall eat *of* the old 8393
26:20 shall the trees of the land yield their **f**. 6529
Dt 33:14 for the precious **f** brought forth by the sun, 8393
2Sa 9:10 thou shalt bring in *the f*, that thy master's NIH
16: 1 an hundred of **summer f**, and a bottle of 7019
2Ki 8: 6 all the **f** of the field since the day that she 8393
19:29 and plant vineyards, and eat the **f** thereof. 6529
Job 31:39 If I have eaten the **f** thereof without money, 3581
Ps 107:37 which may yield **f** of increase. 6529
Ecc 2: 5 and I planted trees in them of all *kind of* **f**: 6529
SS 4:13 orchard of pomegranates, with pleasant **f**; 6529
4:16 come into his garden, and eat his pleasant **f**. 6529
6:11 I went down into the garden of nuts to see the **f** 3
7:13 at our gates *are* all *manner of* pleasant *f*, NIH
Isa 16: 9 for the shouting for thy **summer f** and 7019
33: 9 and Bashan and Carmel shake off *their f*. NIH
Jer 40:10 **summer f**, and oil, and put *them* in your 7019
40:12 gathered wine and **summer f** very much. 7019
48:32 the spoiler is fallen upon thy **summer f** and 7019
La 4: 9 stricken through for *want of* the **f** of it. 8570
Mic 7: 1 as when they have gathered the **summer f**, 7019
Mal 3:11 he shall not destroy the **f** of your ground; 6529
Mt 3: 8 Bring forth therefore **f** meet for repentance: 2590
7:16 Ye shall know them by their **f**. Do *men* 2590
7:20 Wherefore by their **f** ye shall know them. 2590
21:34 that *they* might receive the **f** of it. 2590
21:41 which shall render him the **f** in their 2590
21:43 given to a nation bringing forth the **f** 2590
Lk 3: 8 therefore **f** worthy of repentance, 2590
12:17 I have no room where to bestow my **f**? 2590
12:18 and there will I bestow all my **f** and 1081
2Co 9:10 and increase the **f** of your righteousness;) 1081
Php 1:11 Being filled with the **f** of righteousness, 2590
2Ti 2: 6 laboureth must be first partaker of the **f**. 2590
Jas 3:17 full of mercy and good **f**, without partiality, 2590
Rev 18:14 And the **f** that thy soul lusted after are 3703
22: 2 which bare twelve *manner of* **f**, and 2590

FRUSTRATE (2) [FRUSTRATETH]

Ezr 4: 5 to **f** their purpose, all the days of Cyrus 6565
Gal 2:21 I do not **f** the grace of God: for if 114

FRUSTRATED See NOUGHT; VEX; VEXATION; VEXED

FRUSTRATETH (1) [FRUSTRATE]

Isa 44:25 That **f** the tokens of the liars, and 6565

FRUSTRATION See VANITIES; VANITY

FRYINGPAN (2) [FRIED, PAN]

Lev 2: 7 oblation *be* a meat offering *baken* in the **f**, 4802
7: 9 all *that* is dressed in the **f**, and in the pan, 4802

FUEL (5)

Isa 9: 5 but *this* shall be with burning *and* **f** of fire. 3980
9:19 and the people shall be as the **f** of the fire: 3980
Eze 15: 4 Behold, it is cast into the fire for **f**; the fire 402
15: 6 which I have given to the fire for **f**, so will I 402
21:32 Thou shalt be for **f** to the fire; thy blood shall 402

FUGITIVE (2) [FUGITIVES]

Ge 4:12 a **f** and a vagabond shalt thou be in 5128
4:14 I shall be a **f** and a vagabond in the earth; 5128

FUGITIVES (4) [FUGITIVE]

Jdg 12: 4 Ye Gileadites *are* **f** of Ephraim among 6412
2Ki 25:11 the **f** that fell away to the king of Babylon, 5307
Isa 15: 5 his **f** *shall flee* unto Zoar, a heifer of three 1280
Eze 17:21 all his **f** with all his bands shall fall by 4015

FULFIL (24) [FULFILLED, FULFILLING]

Ge 29:27 **F** her week, and we will give thee this also 4390
Ex 5:13 **F** your works, *your* daily tasks, as when 3615
23:26 in thy land: the number of thy days I will **f**. 4390
1Ki 2:27 that *he* might **f** the word of the LORD, 4390
1Ch 22:13 if thou takest heed to **f** the statutes and 6213
2Ch 36:21 To **f** the word of the LORD by the mouth 4390
36:21 kept sabbath, to **f** threescore and ten years. 4390
Job 39: 2 Canst thou number the months *that* they **f**? 4390
Ps 20: 4 to thine own heart, and **f** all thy counsel. 4390
20: 5 *our* banners: the LORD **f** all thy petitions. 4390
145:19 He will **f** the desire of them that fear him: 6213
Mt 3:15 for thus it becometh us to **f** all 4137
5:17 I am not come to destroy, but to **f**. 4137
Ac 13:22 mine own heart, which shall **f** all my will. 4160
Ro 2:27 if it **f** the law, judge thee, who by the letter 5055
13:14 for the flesh, to *f* the lusts *thereof.* NIG
Gal 5:16 and ye shall not **f** the lust of the flesh. 5055

Gal 6: 2 another's burdens, and so **f** the law of Christ. *378*
Php 2: 2 **F** ye my joy, that ye be likeminded, having *4137*
Col 1:25 given to me for you, to **f** the word of God; *4137*
4:17 hast received in the Lord, that thou **f** it. *4137*
2Th 1:11 and **f** all the good pleasure of *his* goodness, *4137*
Jas 2: 8 If ye **f** the royal law according to *5055*
Rev 17:17 For God hath put in their hearts to **f** his *4160*

FULFILLED (82) [FULFIL]

Ge 25:24 when her days to be delivered were **f**, 4390
29:21 Give *me* my wife, for my days are **f**, that I 4390
29:28 Jacob did so, and **f** her week: and he gave 4390
50: 3 forty days were **f** for him; for so 4390
50: 3 are **f** the days of those which are 4390
Ex 5:14 Wherefore have ye not **f** your task in 3615
7:25 seven days were **f**, after *that* the LORD 4390
Lev 12: 4 until the days of her purifying be **f**. 4390
12: 6 when the days of her purifying are **f**, for a 4390
Nu 6: 5 until the days be **f**, *in* the which he 4390
6:13 when the days of his separation are **f**: 4390
2Sa 7:12 when thy days be **f**, and thou shalt sleep 4390
14:22 in that the king hath **f** the request of his 6213
1Ki 8:15 and hath with his hand **f** *it*, saying, 4390
8:24 hast **f** *it* with thine hand, as *it is* this day. 4390
2Ch 6: 4 who hath with his hands **f** *that* which he 4390
6:15 hast **f** *it* with thine hand, as *it is* this day. 4390
Ezr 1: 1 by the mouth of Jeremiah might be **f**, 3615
Job 36:17 thou hast **f** the judgment of the wicked: 4390
Jer 44:25 your mouths, and **f** with your hand, saying, 4390
La 2:17 he hath **f** his word that he had commanded 1214
4:18 our end is near, our days are **f**; for our end 4390
Eze 5: 2 of the city, when the days of the siege are **f**: 4390
Da 4:33 The same hour was the thing **f** upon 5487
10: 3 myself at all, till three whole weeks were **f**. 4390
Mt 1:22 that it might be **f** which was spoken of *4137*
2:15 that it might be **f** which was spoken of *4137*
2:17 Then was **f** that which was spoken by *4137*
2:23 that it might be **f** which was spoken by *4137*
4:14 That it might be **f** which was spoken by *4137*
5:18 in no wise pass from the law, till all be **f**. *1096*
8:17 That it might be **f** which was spoken by *4137*
12:17 That it might be **f** which was spoken by *4137*
13:14 And in them is **f** the prophecy of Esaias, *378*
13:35 That it might be **f** which was spoken by *4137*
21: 4 that it might be **f** which was spoken by *4137*
24:34 shall not pass, till all these *things* be **f**. *1096*
26:54 *But* how then shall the scriptures be **f**, *4137*
26:56 the scriptures of the prophets might be **f**. *4137*
27: 9 Then was **f** that which was spoken by *4137*
27:35 that it might be **f** which was spoken by *4137*
Mk 1:15 And saying, The time is **f**, *4137*
13: 4 *be* the sign when all these *things* shall be **f**? *4931*
14:49 took me not: but the scriptures must be **f**. *4137*
15:28 And the scripture was **f**, which saith, *4137*
Lk 1:20 my words, which shall be **f** in their season. *4137*
2:43 And when they had **f** the days, as they *5048*
4:21 This day is this scripture **f** in your ears. *4137*
21:22 that all *things* which are written may be **f**. *4137*
21:24 until the times of the Gentiles be **f**. *4137*
21:32 generation shall not pass away, till all be **f**. *1096*
22:16 until it be **f** in the kingdom of God. *4137*
24:44 I was yet with you, that all *things* must be **f**, *4137*
Jn 3:29 this my joy therefore is **f**. *4137*
12:38 the saying of Esaias the prophet might be **f**, *4137*
13:18 but that the scripture may be **f**, He that *4137*
15:25 word might be **f** that is written in their law, *4137*
17:12 of perdition; that the scripture might be **f**. *4137*
17:13 that they might have my joy **f** in *4137*
18: 9 That the saying might be **f**, which he spake, *4137*
18:32 That the saying of Jesus might be **f**, *4137*
19:24 that the scripture might be **f**, which saith, *4137*
19:28 that the scripture might be **f**, saith, I thirst. *5048*
19:36 were done, that the scripture should be **f**, *4137*
Ac 1:16 this scripture must needs have been **f**, *4137*
3:18 that Christ should suffer, he hath so **f**. *4137*
9:23 And after that many days were **f**, the Jews *4137*
12:25 when they had **f** *their* ministry, and *4137*
13:25 And as John **f** *his* course, he said, *4137*
13:27 they have **f** *them* in condemning *him*. *4137*
13:29 And when they had **f** all that was written of *5055*
13:33 God hath **f** the same unto us their children, *1603*
14:26 the grace of God for the work which they **f**. *4137*
Ro 8: 4 righteousness of the law might be **f** in us, *4137*
13: 8 for he that loveth another hath **f** the law. *4137*
2Co 10: 6 all disobedience, when your obedience is **f**. *4137*
Gal 5:14 For all the law is **f** in one word, *even* in *4137*
Jas 2:23 And the scripture was **f** which saith, *4137*
Rev 6:11 should be killed as they *were*, should be **f**. *4137*
15: 8 seven plagues of the seven angels were **f**. *5055*
17:17 the beast, until the words of God shall be **f**. *5055*
20: 3 no more, till the thousand years should be **f**: *5055*

FULFILLING (3) [FULFIL]

Ps 148: 8 snow, and vapour; stormy wind **f** his word: 6213
Ro 13:10 therefore love *is* the **f** of the law. *4138*
Eph 2: 3 **f** the desires of the flesh and of the mind; *4160*

FULL (260) [FILL]

Ge 14:10 of Siddim *was* **f of slimepits**; 875+875+2564
15:16 for the iniquity of the Amorites *is* not yet **f**. 8003
25: 8 **f** *of years;* and was gathered to his people. 7649
35:29 unto his people, *being* old and **f** of days: 7649
41: 1 to pass at the end of **two f years**, 3117+8141
41: 7 ears devoured the seven rank and **f** ears. 4392
41:22 ears came up in one stalk, **f** and good: 4392
43:21 mouth of his sack, our money in **f weight**: 4948
Ex 8:21 the houses of the Egyptians shall be **f** of 4390
16: 3 *and* when we did eat bread to the **f**; 7648
16: 8 to eat, and in the morning bread to the **f**; 7646
16:33 put an omer **f** of manna therein, and lay it 4393
22: 3 *for* he should **make f restitution**; if 7999+7999
Lev 2:14 by the fire, *even* **corn** beaten out **of f ears**. 3759
16:12 he shall take a censer **f** of burning coals of 4393
16:12 his hands **f** of sweet incense beaten small, 4393
Lev 19:29 and the land **become f** of wickedness. 4390
25:29 it is sold; *within* a **f year** may he redeem it. 3117
25:30 if it be not redeemed within the space of a **f** 8549
26: 5 ye shall eat your bread to the **f**, and dwell in 7648
Nu 7:13 both of them *were* **f** *of* fine flour mingled 4392
7:14 spoon of ten *shekels* of gold, **f** *of* incense: 4392
7:19 both of them **f** *of* fine flour mingled with 4392
7:20 One spoon of gold of ten *shekels*, **f** *of* 4392
7:25 both of them **f** *of* fine flour mingled with 4392
7:26 One golden spoon of ten *shekels*, **f** *of* 4392
7:31 both of them **f** *of* fine flour mingled with 4392
7:32 One golden spoon *of* ten *shekels*, **f** *of* 4392
7:37 both of them **f** *of* fine flour mingled with 4392
7:38 One golden spoon of ten *shekels*, **f** *of* 4392
7:43 both of them **f** *of* fine flour mingled with 4392
7:44 One golden spoon of ten *shekels*, **f** *of* 4392
7:49 both of them **f** *of* fine flour mingled with 4392
7:50 One golden spoon of ten *shekels*, **f** *of* 4392
7:55 both of them **f** *of* fine flour mingled with 4392
7:56 One golden spoon of ten *shekels*, **f** *of* 4392
7:61 both of them **f** *of* fine flour mingled with 4392
7:62 One golden spoon of ten *shekels*, **f** *of* 4392
7:67 both of them **f** *of* fine flour mingled with 4392
7:68 One golden spoon of ten *shekels*, **f** *of* 4392
7:73 both of them **f** *of* fine flour mingled with 4392
7:74 One golden spoon of ten *shekels*, **f** *of* 4392
7:79 both of them **f** *of* fine flour mingled with 4392
7:80 One golden spoon of ten *shekels*, **f** *of* 4392
7:86 **f** *of* incense, *weighing* ten *shekels* apiece, 4392
22:18 If Balak would give me his house **f** *of* silver 4393
24:13 If Balak would give me his house **f** *of* silver 4393
Dt 6:11 houses **f** *of* all good *things*, which thou 4392
6:11 when thou shalt have eaten and be **f**; 7646
8:10 When thou hast eaten and art **f**, then 7646
8:12 Lest *when* thou hast eaten and art **f**, and 7646
11:15 for thy cattle, that thou mayest eat and be **f**. 7646
21:13 her father and her mother a **f month**: 3117+3391
33:23 and **f** *with* the blessing of the LORD: 4392
34: 9 Joshua the son of Nun was **f** *of* the spirit of 4392
Jdg 6:38 the dew out of the fleece, a bowl **f** *of* water. 4393
16:27 Now the house was **f** *of* men and women; 4390
Ru 1:21 I went out **f**, and the LORD hath brought 4392
2:12 a **f** reward be given thee of the LORD 8003
1Sa 2: 5 *They that were* **f** have hired out themselves 7649
18:27 and they **gave** them **in f tale** to the king, 4390
27: 7 the country of the Philistines was a **f year** 3117
2Sa 8: 2 to death, and *with* one **f** line to keep alive. 4393
13:23 it came to pass after **two f years**, 3117+8141
14:28 So Absalom dwelt **two f years** in 3117+8141
23:11 where was a piece of ground **f** *of* lentiles: 4392
2Ki 3:16 Make this valley **f of ditches**. 1356+1356
4: 4 and thou shalt set aside *that* which *is* **f**. 4392
4: 6 it came to pass, when the vessels were **f**, 4390
4:39 gathered thereof wild gourds his lap **f**, and 4393
4:42 and **f ears of corn** in the husk thereof. 3759
6:17 the mountain was **f** *of* horses and 4390
7:15 all the way *was* **f** *of* garments and vessels, 4392
9:24 **drew** a bow **with** his **f strength**, 3027+4390+871.1
10:21 the house of Baal was **f** from one end to 4390
15:13 and he reigned a **f month** in Samaria. 3117+3391
1Ch 11:13 where was a parcel of ground **f** *of* barley; 4392
21:22 thou shalt grant it me for the **f** price: 4392
21:24 Nay; but I will verily buy *it* for the **f** price: 4392
23: 1 So when David was old and **f** *of* days, 7646
29:28 good old age, **f** of days, riches, and honour: 7649
2Ch 24:15 waxed old, and was **f** *of* days when he died; 7646
Ne 9:25 and possessed houses **f** *of* all goods, 4392
Est 3: 5 him reverence, *then* was Haman **f** *of* wrath. 4390
5: 9 he was **f** *of* indignation against Mordecai. 4390
Job 5:26 Thou shalt come to *thy* grave in a **f age**, 3624
7: 4 I am **f** *of* tossings to and fro unto 7646
10:15 *I am* **f** of confusion; therefore see thou 7649
11: 2 and should a man **f of talk** be justified? 8193
14: 1 of a woman *is* of few days, and **f** of trouble. 7649
20:11 His bones are **f** *of the sin of* his youth, 4390
21:23 One dieth in his **f** strength, *being* wholly at 8537
21:24 His breasts are **f** *of* milk, and his bones are 4390
32:18 For I am **f** *of* matter, the spirit within me 4390
36:16 be set on thy table *should* be **f** *of* fatness. 4390
42:17 So Job died, *being* old and **f** of days. 7649
Ps 10: 7 His mouth is **f** *of* cursing and deceit and 4390
17:14 *with* thy hid *treasure:* they are **f** *of* children, 7646
26:10 and their right hand is **f** *of* bribes. 4390
29: 4 the voice of the LORD *is* **f** of **majesty**. 1926
33: 5 the earth is **f** *of* the goodness of 4390
48:10 thy right hand is **f** *of* righteousness. 4390
65: 9 it *with* the river of God, *which is* **f** *of* water: 4390
69:20 broken my heart; and I am **f** of **heaviness**: 5136
73:10 waters of a **f** *cup* are wrung out to them. 4392
74:20 for the dark places of the earth are **f** *of* 4390
75: 8 it is **f** *of* mixture; and he poureth out of 4392
78:25 eat angels' food: he sent them meat to the **f**. 7648
78:38 he, *being* **f of compassion**, forgave *their* 7349
86:15 *art* a God **f of compassion**, and gracious, 7349
88: 3 For my soul is **f** of troubles: and my life 7646
104:16 The trees of the LORD are **f** *of sap;* 7646
104:24 made them all: the earth is **f** *of* thy riches. 4390
111: 4 LORD *is* gracious and **f of compassion**. 7349
112: 4 and **of compassion**, and righteous. 7349
119:64 The earth, O LORD, is **f** *of* thy mercy: 4390
127: 5 Happy *is* the man that hath his quiver **f** of 4390
144:13 *That* our garners *may be* **f**, affording all 4392
145: 8 LORD *is* gracious, and **f of compassion**; 7349
Pr 17: 1 than a house **f** *of* sacrifices with strife. 4392
27: 7 The **f** soul loatheth a honeycomb; but *to* 7649
27:20 Hell and destruction are never **f**; so the eyes 7646
30: 9 Lest I be **f**, and deny *thee*, and say, Who *is* 7646
Ecc 1: 7 rivers run into the sea; yet the sea *is* not **f**; 4392
1: 8 All things *are* **f** of **labour**; man cannot utter 3023
4: 6 than both the hands **f** *with* travail and 4393
9: 3 also the heart of the sons of men is **f** *of* evil, 4390
10:14 A fool also is **f** of words: a man cannot tell 7235
11: 3 If the clouds be **f** *of* rain, they empty 4390
Isa 1:11 I am **f** *of* the burnt offerings of rams, and 7646
Isa 1:15 I will not hear: your hands are **f** *of* blood. 4390
1:21 *it was* **f** of judgment; righteousness lodged 4392
2: 7 Their land also is **f** *of* silver and gold, 4390
2: 7 their land is also **f** *of* horses, neither *is there* 4390
2: 8 Their land also is **f** *of* idols; they worship 4390
6: 3 of hosts: the whole earth *is* **f** of his glory. 4393
11: 9 for the earth shall be **f** *of* the knowledge of 4390
13:21 their houses shall be **f** *of* doleful creatures; 4390
15: 9 For the waters of Dimon shall be **f** of 4390
22: 2 Thou *that art* **f** *of* stirs, a tumultuous city, 4392
22: 7 *that* thy choicest valleys shall be **f** *of* 4390
25: 6 on the lees, of fat things **f of marrow**, 4229
28: 8 For all tables are **f** *of* vomit *and* filthiness, 4390
30:27 his lips are **f** *of* indignation, and his tongue 4390
51:20 *they are* **f** *of* the fury of the LORD, 4392
Jer 4:12 *Even* a **f** wind from those *places* shall come 4392
4:27 be desolate; yet will I not make a **f end**. 3617
5: 7 when I had **fed** them **to the f**, they then 7650
5:10 and destroy; but make not a **f end**: 3617
5:18 I will not make a **f end** with you. 3617
5:27 As a cage *is* **f** *of* birds, so *are* their houses 4392
5:27 full *of* birds, so *are* their houses **f** *of* deceit: 4392
6:11 Therefore I am **f** *of* the fury of the LORD; 4390
6:11 the aged with *him that is* **f** of days. 4392
23:10 For the land is **f** *of* adulterers; for because 4390
28: 3 Within **two f years** *will* I bring again 3117+8141
28:11 within the space of **two f years**. 3117+8141
30:11 though I make a **f end** of all nations 3617
30:11 yet will I not make a **f end** of thee: 3617
35: 5 the house of the Rechabites pots **f** *of* wine, 4392
46:28 for I will make a **f end** of all the nations 3617
46:28 I will not make a **f end** of thee, but 3617
La 1: 1 the city sit solitary, *that was* **f** of people! 7227
3:30 smiteth him: he is **filled f** with reproach. 7646
Eze 1:18 their rings *were* **f** *of* eyes round about them 4392
7:23 for the land is **f** *of* bloody crimes, and 4390
7:23 bloody crimes, and the city is **f** *of* violence. 4390
9: 9 the land is **f** *of* blood, and the city **full** *of* 4390
9: 9 full *of* blood, and the city **f** *of* perverseness: 4390
10: 4 the court was **f** of the brightness of 4390
10:12 and the wheels, *were* **f** *of* eyes round about, 4392
11:13 *wilt* thou make a **f end** of the remnant of 3617
17: 3 longwinged, **f** *of* feathers, which had divers 4392
19:10 **f of branches** by reason of many waters. 6058
28:12 **f** *of* wisdom, and perfect in beauty. 4392
32: 6 and the rivers shall be **f** of thee. 4390
32:15 shall be destitute of that whereof it was **f**, 4393
37: 1 midst of the valley which *was* **f** *of* bones, 4392
39:19 ye shall eat fat till *ye* be **f**, and drink blood 7654
41: 8 chambers *were* a **f** reed of six great cubits. 4393
Da 3:19 was Nebuchadnezzar **f** *of* fury, and 4391
8:23 when the transgressors are **come to the f**, 8552
10: 2 Daniel was mourning three **f weeks**. 3117+7620
Joel 2:24 the floors shall be **f** *of* wheat, and the fats 4390
3:13 for the press is **f**, the fats overflow; 4390
Am 2:13 as a cart is pressed *that is* **f** *of* sheaves. 4392
Mic 3: 8 truly I am **f** *of* power by the spirit of 4390
6:12 For the rich *men* thereof are **f** *of* violence, 4390
Na 3: 1 it *is* all **f** *of* lies *and* robbery; the prey 4392
Hab 3: 3 and the earth was **f** *of* his praise. 4390
Zec 8: 5 the streets of the city shall be **f** *of* boys and 4390
Mt 6:22 thy whole body shall be **f of light**. *5460*
6:23 thy whole body shall be **f of darkness**. *4652*
13:48 Which, when it was **f**, they drew to shore, *4137*
14:20 fragments that remained twelve baskets **f**. *4134*
15:37 broken *meat* that was left seven baskets **f**. *4134*
23:25 but within they are **f** of extortion and *1073*
23:27 but are within **f** of dead *men's* bones, and *1073*
23:28 but within ye are **f** of hypocrisy and *3324*
Mk 4:28 then the ear, after that the **f** corn in the ear. *4134*
4:37 beat into the ship, so that it was now **f**. *1072*
6:43 And they took up twelve baskets **f** of *4134*
7: 9 **F well** ye reject the commandment of God, *2573*
8:19 how many baskets **f** of fragments took ye *4134*
8:20 how many baskets **f** of fragments took ye *4138*
15:36 one ran and filled a spunge *f* of vinegar, NIG
Lk 1:57 Now Elisabeth's **f** time **came** that she *4130*
4: 1 And Jesus being **f** of the Holy Ghost *4134*
5:12 in a certain city, behold a man **f** of leprosy: *4134*
6:25 Woe unto you that are **f**: for ye shall *1705*
11:34 is single, thy whole body also is **f of light**; *5460*
11:34 *eye* is evil, thy body also *is* **f of darkness**. *4652*
11:36 If thy whole body therefore *be* **f of light**, *5460*
11:36 no part dark, the whole shall be **f of light**, *5460*
11:39 but your inward part is **f** of ravening and *1073*
16:20 which was laid at his gate, **f of sores**, *1669*
Jn 1:14 begotten of the Father,) **f** of grace and truth. *4134*
7: 8 this feast; for my time is not yet **f come**. *4137*
15:11 remain in you, and *that* your joy might be **f**. *4137*
16:24 and ye shall receive, that your joy may be **f**. *4137*
19:29 Now there was set a vessel **f** of vinegar: *3324*
21:11 and drew the net to land **f** of great fishes, *3324*
Ac 2:13 *These men* are **f** of new wine. *3325*
2:28 thou shalt **make** me **f** of joy with thy *4137*
6: 3 **f** of the Holy Ghost and wisdom, whom we *4134*
6: 5 a man **f** of faith and of the Holy Ghost, and *4134*
6: 8 And Stephen, **f** of faith and power, *4134*
7:23 And when he was **f** forty years old, it came *4137*
7:55 But he, being **f** of the Holy Ghost, *4134*
9:36 this *woman* was **f** of good works and *4134*
11:24 and **f** of the Holy Ghost and of faith: *4134*
13:10 O **f** of all subtilty and all mischief, *4134*
19:28 heard *these sayings*, they were **f** of wrath, *4134*
Ro 1:29 **f** of envy, murder, debate, deceit, *3324*
3:14 Whose mouth is **f** of cursing and bitterness: *1073*
15:14 my brethren, that ye also are **f** of goodness, *3324*
1Co 4: 8 Now ye are **f**, now ye are rich, ye have *2880*
Php 2:26 and *was* **f of heaviness**, because that ye had *85*
4:12 in all *things* I am instructed both to be **f** and *5526*
4:18 I am **f**, having received of Epaphroditus *4137*
Col 2: 2 unto all riches of the **f assurance** of *4136*
2Ti 4: 5 **make f proof** of thy ministry. *4135*
Heb 5:14 meat belongeth to *them that* are **of f age**, *5046*
6:11 to the **f assurance** of hope unto the end: *4136*
10:22 with a true heart in **f assurance** of faith, *4136*

F

Jas 3: 8 *it is* an unruly evil, **f** of deadly poison. *3324*
3:17 **f** of mercy and good fruits, *3324*
1Pe 1: 8 rejoice with joy unspeakable and **f of glory**: *1392*
2Pe 2:14 Having eyes **f** of adultery and that cannot *3324*
1Jn 1: 4 write we unto you, that your joy may be **f**. *4137*
2Jn 1: 8 but *that* we receive a **f** reward. *4134*
1:12 speak face to face, that our joy may be **f**. *4137*
Rev 4: 6 *were* four beasts **f** of eyes before and *1073*
4: 8 about *him;* and *they were* **f** of eyes within: *1073*
5: 8 and golden vials **f** of odours, which are *1073*
15: 7 seven golden vials **f** of the wrath of God, *1073*
16:10 and his kingdom was **f of darkness**; and *4656*
17: 3 **f of** names of blasphemy, having seven *1073*
17: 4 having a golden cup in her hand **f of** *1073*
21: 9 the seven vials **f** of the seven last plagues, *1073*

FULLER (1) [FULLER'S, FULLERS']
Mk 9: 3 so as no **f** on earth can white *them.* *1102*

FULLER'S (3) [FULLER]
2Ki 18:17 which *is* in the highway of the **f** field. 3526
Isa 7: 3 the upper pool in the highway of the **f** field; 3526
36: 2 the upper pool in the highway of the **f** field. 3526

FULLERS' (1) [FULLER]
Mal 3: 2 he *is* like a refiner's fire, and like **f** sope: 3526

FULLY (13) [FILL]
Nu 7: 1 it came to pass on the day that Moses had **f** 3615
14:24 spirit with him, and hath followed me **f**, 4390
Ru 2:11 unto her, It hath **f been shewed** me, 5046+5046
1Ki 11: 6 **went** not **f** after the LORD, as *did* David 4390
Ecc 8:11 the heart of the sons of men is **f set** in them 4390
Na 1:10 they shall be devoured as stubble **f** dry. 4392
Ac 2: 1 And when the day of Pentecost was **f come**, *4845*
Ro 4:21 And being **f persuaded** that, what he had *4135*
14: 5 man be **f persuaded** in his own mind. *4135*
15:19 I have **f** preached the gospel of Christ. *4137*
2Ti 3:10 But thou hast **f known** my doctrine, *3877*
4:17 by me the preaching might be **f known**, *4135*
Rev 14:18 vine of the earth; for her grapes are **f ripe**. *187*

FULNESS (25) [FILL]
Nu 18:27 and as the **f** of the winepress. 4395
Dt 33:16 precious things of the earth and **f** thereof, 4393
1Ch 16:32 Let the sea roar, and the **f** thereof: let 4393
Job 20:22 In the **f** of his sufficiency he shall be in 4390
Ps 16:11 in thy presence *is* **f** of joy; at thy right hand 7648
24: 1 earth *is* the LORD'S, and the **f** thereof; 4393
50:12 for the world *is* mine, and the **f** thereof. 4393
89:11 *as for* the world and the **f** thereof, thou hast 4393
96:11 be glad; let the sea roar, and the **f** thereof. 4393
98: 7 Let the sea roar, and the **f** thereof, 4393
Eze 16:49 **f** of bread, and abundance of idleness was 7653
19: 7 and the land was desolate, and the **f** thereof, 4393
Jn 1:16 And of his **f** have all we received, and *4138*
Ro 11:12 of the Gentiles; how much more their **f**? *4138*
11:25 until the **f** of the Gentiles be come in. *4138*
15:29 I shall come in the **f** of the blessing of *4138*
1Co 10:26 the earth *is* the Lord's, and the **f** thereof. *4138*
10:28 for the earth *is* the Lord's, and the **f** thereof: *4138*
Gal 4: 4 But when the **f** of the time was come, *4138*
Eph 1:10 That in the dispensation of the **f** of times *he* *4138*
1:23 his body, the **f** of him that filleth all in all. *4138*
3:19 that ye might be filled with all the **f** of God. *4138*
4:13 unto the measure of the stature of the **f** of *4138*
Col 1:19 *the Father* that in him should all **f** dwell; *4138*
2: 9 For in him dwelleth all the **f** of *4138*

FURBISH (1) [FURBISHED]
Jer 46: 4 **f** the spears, *and* put on the brigandines. 4838

FURBISHED (5) [FURBISH]
Eze 21: 9 A sword, a sword is sharpened, and also **f**: 4803
21:10 a sore slaughter; *it is* **f** that it may glitter: 4803
21:11 he hath given it to be **f**, that *it* may be 4803
21:11 this sword is sharpened, and it *is* **f**, to give 4803
21:28 for the slaughter *it is* **f**, to consume because 4803

FURIOUS (6) [FURY]
Pr 22:24 and with a **f** man thou shalt not go: 2534
29:22 and a **f** man aboundeth in transgression. 2534
Eze 5:15 thee in anger and in fury and in **f** rebukes. 2534
25:17 great vengeance upon them with **f** rebukes, 2534
Da 2:12 this cause the king was angry and very **f**, 7108
Na 1: 2 the LORD revengeth, and *is* **f**; 1167+2534

FURIOUSLY (2) [FURY]
2Ki 9:20 the son of Nimshi; for he driveth **f**. 7697+871.1
Eze 23:25 and they shall deal **f** with thee: 2534+871.1

FURLONGS (5)
Lk 24:13 was from Jerusalem *about* threescore **f**. *4712*
Jn 6:19 had rowed about five and twenty or thirty **f**, *4712*
11:18 nigh unto Jerusalem, about fifteen **f** off: *4712*
Rev 14:20 the space of a thousand *and* six hundred **f**. *4712*
21:16 the city with the reed, twelve thousand **f**. *4712*

FURNACE (30) [FURNACES]
Ge 15:17 behold a smoking **f**, and a burning lamp 8574
19:28 of the country went up as the smoke of a **f**. 3536
Ex 9: 8 Take to you handfuls of ashes of the **f**, and 3536
9:10 they took ashes of the **f**, and stood before 3536
19:18 thereof ascended as the smoke of a **f**, 3536
Dt 4:20 brought you forth out of the iron **f**, *even* out 3564
1Ki 8:51 of Egypt, from the midst of the **f** of iron: 3564
Ps 12: 6 *as* silver tried in a **f** of earth, purified seven 5948
Pr 17: 3 fining pot *is* for silver, and the **f** for gold: 3564
27:21 the fining pot for silver, and the **f** for gold; 3564
Isa 31: 9 fire *is* in Zion, and his **f** in Jerusalem. 8574
48:10 I have chosen thee in the **f** of affliction. 3564
Jer 11: 4 from the iron **f**, saying, Obey my voice, and 3564
Eze 22:18 tin, and iron, and lead, in the midst of the **f**; 3564
22:20 and lead, and tin, into the midst of the **f**, 3564
22:22 As silver is melted in the midst of the **f**, so 3564
Da 3: 6 be cast into the midst of a burning fiery **f**. 861
3:11 be cast into the midst of a burning fiery **f**. 861
3:15 same hour into the midst of a burning fiery **f**; 861
3:17 *is* able to deliver us from the burning fiery **f**, 861
3:19 commanded that *they* should heat the **f** one 861
3:20 *and* to cast *them* into the burning fiery **f**. 861
3:21 cast into the midst of the burning fiery **f**. 861
3:22 *was* urgent, and the **f** exceeding hot, 861
3:23 bound into the midst of the burning fiery **f**. 861
3:26 near to the mouth of the burning fiery **f**, 861
Mt 13:42 And shall cast them into a **f** of fire: *2575*
13:50 And shall cast them into the **f** of fire: *2575*
Rev 1:15 like unto fine brass, as if they burned in a **f**; *2575*
9: 2 out of the pit, as the smoke of a great **f**; *2575*

FURNACES (2) [FURNACE]
Ne 3:11 the other piece, and the tower of the **f**. 8574
12:38 from beyond the tower of the **f** even unto 8574

FURNISH (4) [FURNISHED, FURNITURE]
Dt 15:14 Thou shalt **f** him **liberally** out of thy 6059+6059
Ps 78:19 Can God **f** a table in the wilderness? 6186
Isa 65:11 that **f** the drink offering **unto** *that* number. 4390
Jer 46:19 **f** thyself to go into captivity: 3627+6213

FURNISHED (6) [FURNISH]
1Ki 9:11 (*Now* Hiram the king of Tyre had **f** 5375
Pr 9: 2 mingled her wine; she hath also **f** her table. 6186
Mt 22:10 good: and the wedding was **f** with guests. *4130*
Mk 14:15 And he will shew you a large upper room **f** *4766*
Lk 22:12 he shall shew you a large upper room **f**: *4766*
2Ti 3:17 **throughly f** unto all good works. *1822*

FURNISHINGS See FURNITURE

FURNITURE (8) [FURNISH]
Ge 31:34 put them in the camel's **f**, and sat upon 3733
Ex 31: 7 *is* thereupon, and all the **f** of the tabernacle, 3627
31: 8 the table and his **f**, and the pure candlestick 3627
31: 8 the pure candlestick with all his **f**, and 3627
31: 9 the altar of burnt offering with all his **f**, 3627
35:14 his **f**, and his lamps, with the oil for 3627
39:33 the tent, and all his **f**, his taches, his boards, 3627
Na 2: 9 the store *and* glory out of all the pleasant **f**. 3627

FURROW (1) [FURROWS]
Job 39:10 bind the unicorn *with* his band in the **f**? 8525

FURROWS (8) [FURROW]
Job 31:38 or that the **f** likewise thereof complain; 8525
Ps 65:10 *thou* settlest the **f** thereof: thou makest it 1418
129: 3 upon my back: they made long their **f**. 4618
Eze 17: 7 that *he* might water it by the **f** of her 6170
17:10 it shall wither in the **f** where it grew. 6170
Hos 10: 4 up as hemlock in the **f** of the field. 8525
10:10 *they* shall bind themselves in their two **f**. 5772
12:11 their altars *are* as heaps in the **f** of 8525

FURTHER (24) [FAR, FURTHERANCE, FURTHERED, FURTHERMORE]
Nu 22:26 the angel of the LORD went **f**, and 3254
Dt 20: 8 the officers shall speak **f** unto the people, 3254
1Sa 10:22 Therefore they inquired of the LORD **f**, 5750
Est 9:12 or what *is* thy request **f**? and it shall be 5750
Job 38:11 Hitherto shalt thou come, but no **f**: 3254
40: 5 yea, twice; but I will **proceed** no **f**. 3254
Ps 140: 8 **f** not his wicked device; *lest* they exalt 6329
Ecc 8:17 to seek *it* out, yet he shall not find *it;* yea **f**, 1571
12:12 **f**, by these, my son, be admonished: 3148
Mt 26:39 And he **went** a little **f**, and fell on his face, *4281*
26:65 what **f** need have we of witnesses? *2089*
Mk 1:19 And when he had **gone** a little **f** thence, *4260*
5:35 why troublest thou the Master **any f**? *2089*
14:63 and saith, What need we **any f** witnesses? *2089*
Lk 22:71 they said, What need we **any f** witness? *2089*
24:28 he made as though *he* would have gone **f**. *4208*
Ac 4:17 But that it spread no **f** among *1909+4183*
4:21 So when they had **f threatened** *them,* they *4324*
12: 3 the Jews, he **proceeded f** to take Peter also. *4369*
21:28 and **f** brought Greeks also into the temple, *2089*
24: 4 that I be not **f** tedious unto thee, *1909+4183*
27:28 and when they had **gone** a little **f**, *1339*
2Ti 3: 9 But they shall proceed no **f**: for their *1909+4183*
Heb 7:11 what **f** need *was there* that another priest *2089*

FURTHERANCE (2) [FURTHER]
Php 1:12 fallen out rather unto the **f** of the gospel; *4297*
1:25 and continue with you all for your **f** and *4297*

FURTHERED (1) [FURTHER]
Ezr 8:36 they **f** the people, and the house of God. 5375

FURTHERMORE (14) [FURTHER]
Ex 4: 6 the LORD said **f** unto him, Put now thine 5750
Dt 4:21 **F** the LORD was angry with me for 2050.1
9:13 **F** the LORD spake unto me, saying, 2050.1
1Sa 26:10 David said **f**, *As* the LORD liveth, 2050.1
1Ch 17:10 **F** I tell thee that the LORD will build 2050.1
27:16 **F** over the tribes of Israel: the ruler of 2050.1
29: 1 **F** David the king said unto all 2050.1
2Ch 4: 9 **F** he made the court of the priests, and 2050.1
Job 34: 1 **F** Elihu answered and said, 2050.1
Eze 8: 6 He said **f** unto me, Son of man, seest thou 2050.1
23:40 **f**, that ye have sent for men to come from 637
2Co 2:12 **F**, when I came to Troas to *preach* Christ's *1161*
1Th 4: 1 **F** then we beseech you, brethren, and *3062*
Heb 12: 9 **F** we have had fathers of our *1534+3303+3588*

FURY (70) [FURIOUS, FURIOUSLY]
Ge 27:44 a few days, until thy brother's **f** turn away; 2534
Lev 26:28 I will walk contrary unto you also in **f**; 2534
Job 20:23 *God* shall cast the **f** of his wrath upon him, 2740
Isa 27: 4 **F** *is* not in me: who would set the briers 2534
34: 2 all nations, and *his* **f** upon all their armies: 2534
42:25 Therefore he hath poured upon him the **f** of 2534
51:13 every day because of the **f** of the oppressor, 2534
51:13 and where *is* the **f** of the oppressor? 2534
51:17 at the hand of the LORD the cup of his **f**; 2534
51:20 *they are* full *of* the **f** of the LORD, 2534
51:22 *even* the dregs of the cup of my **f**; 2534
59:18 he will repay, **f** to his adversaries, 2534
63: 3 in mine anger, and trample them in my **f**; 2534
63: 5 salvation unto me; and my **f**, it upheld me. 2534
63: 6 make them drunk in my **f**, and I will bring 2534
66:15 to render his anger with **f**, and his rebuke 2534
Jer 4: 4 lest my **f** come forth like fire, and burn that 2534
6:11 Therefore I am full *of* the **f** of the LORD; 2534
7:20 my **f** *shall be* poured out upon this place, 2534
10:25 Pour out thy **f** upon the heathen that know 2534
21: 5 even in anger, and in **f**, and in great wrath. 2534
21:12 lest my **f** go out like fire, and burn that 2534
23:19 whirlwind of the LORD is gone forth *in* **f**, 2534
25:15 Take the wine cup of this **f** at mine hand, 2534
30:23 of the LORD goeth forth *with* **f**, 2534
32:31 of my **f** from the day that they built it even 2534
32:37 mine anger, and in my **f**, and in great wrath; 2534
33: 5 I have slain in mine anger and in my **f**, 2534
36: 7 the **f** that the LORD hath pronounced 2534
42:18 my **f** hath been poured forth upon 2534
42:18 so shall my **f** be poured forth upon you, 2534
44: 6 Wherefore my **f** and mine anger was 2534
La 2: 4 of Zion: he poured out his **f** like fire. 2534
4:11 The LORD hath accomplished his **f**; 2534
Eze 5:13 and I will cause my **f** to rest upon them, and 2534
5:13 when I have accomplished my **f** in them. 2534
5:15 in anger and in **f** and in furious rebukes. 2534
6:12 thus will I accomplish my **f** upon them. 2534
7: 8 Now will I shortly pour out my **f** upon thee, 2534
8:18 Therefore will I also deal in **f**: mine eye 2534
9: 8 in thy pouring out of thy **f** upon Jerusalem? 2534
13:13 even rent *it with* a stormy wind in my **f**; 2534
13:13 and great hailstones in *my* **f** to consume *it*. 2534
14:19 pour out my **f** upon it in blood, to cut off 2534
16:38 and I will give thee blood in **f** and jealousy. 2534
16:42 So will I make my **f** towards thee to rest, 2534
19:12 she was plucked up in **f**, she was cast down 2534
20: 8 I said, *I* will pour out my **f** upon them, 2534
20:13 *I* would pour out my **f** upon them in 2534
20:21 I said, *I* would pour out my **f** upon them, 2534
20:33 and with **f** poured out, will I rule over you: 2534
20:34 a stretched out arm, and with **f** poured out. 2534
21:17 and I will cause my **f** to rest: 2534
22:20 will I gather *you* in mine anger and in my **f**, 2534
22:22 LORD have poured out my **f** upon you. 2534
24: 8 That *it* might cause **f** to come up to take 2534
24:13 till I have caused my **f** to rest upon thee. 2534
25:14 to mine anger and according to my **f**; 2534
30:15 I will pour my **f** upon Sin, the strength of 2534
36: 6 I have spoken in my jealousy and in my **f**, 2534
36:18 Wherefore I poured my **f** upon them for 2534
38:18 *that* my **f** shall come up in my face. 2534
Da 3:13 and **f** commanded to bring Shadrach, 2528
3:19 was Nebuchadnezzar full *of* **f**, and the form 2528
8: 6 and ran unto him in the **f** of his power. 2534
9:16 thy **f** be turned away from thy city 2534
11:44 he shall go forth with great **f** to destroy, 2534
Mic 5:15 vengeance in anger and **f** upon the heathen, 2534
Na 1: 6 his **f** is poured out like fire, and the rocks 2534
Zec 8: 2 and I was jealous for her *with* great **f**. 2534

FUTILE See VANITIES; VANITY

FUTILITY See VANITIES; VANITY

FUTURE See HEREAFTER

G

GAAL (9)
Jdg 9:26 **G** the son of Ebed came with his brethren, 1603
9:28 **G** the son of Ebed said, Who *is* Abimelech, 1603
9:30 city heard the words of **G** the son of Ebed, 1603
9:31 **G** the son of Ebed and his brethren be come 1603
9:35 **G** the son of Ebed went out, and stood *in* 1603
9:36 when **G** saw the people, he said to Zebul, 1603
9:37 **G** spake again and said, See there come 1603
9:39 **G** went out before the men of Shechem, 1603
9:41 Zebul thrust out **G** and his brethren, 1603

GAASH (4)
Jos 24:30 on the north side of the hill of **G**. 1608
Jdg 2: 9 of Ephraim, on the north side of the hill **G**. 1608
2Sa 23:30 the Pirathonite, Hiddai of the brooks of **G**, 1608
1Ch 11:32 Hurai of the brooks of **G**, Abiel 1608

GABA (2)
Jos 18:24 and Ophni, and **G**; 1387
Ezr 2:26 The children of Ramah and **G**, six hundred 1387

GABBAI (1)
Ne 11: 8 after him **G**, Sallai, nine hundred twenty 1373

GABBATHA (1)
Jn 19:13 called the Pavement, but in the Hebrew, **G**. *1042*

GABRIEL (4)
Da 8:16 which called, and said, **G**, make this *man* to 1403
9:21 I *was* speaking in prayer, even the man **G**, 1403
Lk 1:19 I am **G**, that stand in the presence of God; *1043*
1:26 And in the sixth month the angel **G** was *1043*

GAD (72) [BAAL-GAD, DIBON-GAD, GADITE, GADITES]
Ge 30:11 A troop cometh: and she called his name **G**. 1410
35:26 of Zilpah, Leah's handmaid; **G**, and Asher: 1410
46:16 the sons of **G**; Ziphion, and Haggi, Shuni, 1410
49:19 **G**, a troop shall overcome him: but he shall 1410
Ex 1:4 Dan, and Naphtali, **G**, and Asher. 1410
Nu 1:14 Of **G**; Eliasaph the son of Deuel. 1410
1:24 Of the children of **G**, *by* their generations, 1410
1:25 *even* of the tribe of **G**, *were* forty and 1410
2:14 the tribe of **G**: and the captain of the sons 1410
2:14 the captain of the sons of **G** *shall be* 1410
7:42 prince of the children of **G**, *offered:* 1410
10:20 of **G** *was* Eliasaph the son of Deuel. 1410
13:15 Of the tribe of **G**, Geuel the son of Machi. 1410
26:15 The children of **G** after their families: 1410
26:18 These *are* the families of the children of **G** 1410
32:1 the children of **G** had a very great 1410
32:2 The children of **G** and the children of 1410
32:6 Moses said unto the children of **G** and 1410
32:25 the children of **G** and the children of 1410
32:29 If the children of **G** and the children of 1410
32:31 the children of **G** and the children of 1410
32:33 *even* to the children of **G**, and to 1410
32:34 the children of **G** built Dibon, and Ataroth, 1410
34:14 the tribe of the children of **G** according to 1425
Dt 27:13 **G**, and Asher, and Zebulun, Dan, and 1410
33:20 of **G** he said, Blessed *be* he that enlargeth 1410
33:20 he said, Blessed *be* he that enlargeth **G**: 1410
Jos 4:12 the children of **G**, and half the tribe of 1410
13:24 Moses gave *inheritance* unto the tribe of **G**, 1410
13:24 *even* unto the children of **G** according to 1410
13:28 This *is* the inheritance of the children of **G** 1410
18:7 **G**, and Reuben, and half the tribe of 1410
20:8 Ramoth in Gilead out of the tribe of **G**, and 1410
21:7 out of the tribe of **G**, and out of the tribe of 1410
21:38 out of the tribe of **G**, Ramoth in Gilead 1410
22:9 of Reuben and the children of **G** and 1410
22:10 of Reuben and the children of **G** and 1410
22:11 of Reuben and the children of **G** and 1410
22:13 to the children of **G**, and to the half tribe of 1410
22:15 to the children of **G**, and to the half tribe of 1410
22:21 of Reuben and the children of **G** and 1410
22:25 ye children of Reuben and children of **G**; 1410
22:30 the children of **G** and the children of 1410
22:31 to the children of **G**, and to the children of 1410
22:32 from the children of **G**, out of the land of 1410
22:33 the children of Reuben and **G** dwelt. 1410
22:34 the children of **G** called the altar *Ed:* for it 1410
1Sa 13:7 Hebrews went over Jordan *to* the land of **G** 1410
22:5 the prophet **G** said unto David, Abide not 1410
2Sa 24:5 city that *lieth* in the midst of the river of **G**, 1410
24:11 of the LORD came unto the prophet **G**, 1410
24:13 So **G** came to David, and told him, and 1410
24:14 David said unto **G**, I am in a great strait: 1410
24:18 **G** came that day to David, and said unto 1410
24:19 David, according to the saying of **G**, 1410
1Ch 2:2 and Benjamin, Naphtali, **G**, and Asher. 1410
5:11 the children of **G** dwelt over against them, 1410
6:63 out of the tribe of **G**, and out of the tribe of 1410
6:80 out of the tribe of **G**; Ramoth in Gilead 1410
12:14 These *were* of the sons of **G**, captains of 1410
21:9 the LORD spake unto **G**, David's seer, 1410
21:11 So **G** came to David, and said unto him, 1410
21:13 David said unto **G**, I am in a great strait: 1410
21:18 the angel of the LORD commanded **G** to 1410
21:19 David went up at the saying of **G**, which he 1410
29:29 the prophet, and in the book of **G** the seer, 1410
2Ch 29:25 of **G** the king's seer, and Nathan 1410
Jer 49:1 why *then* doth their king inherit **G**, and 1410
Eze 48:27 east side unto the west side, **G** a *portion.* 1410
48:28 by the border of **G**, at the south side 1410
48:34 one gate of **G**, one gate of Asher, one gate 1410
Rev 7:5 Of the tribe of **G** *were* sealed twelve *1045*

GADARENES (3)
Mk 5:1 side of the sea, into the country of the **G**. *1046*
Lk 8:26 And they arrived at the country of the **G**, *1046*
8:37 **G** round about besought him to depart from *1046*

GADDEST (1)
Jer 2:36 Why **g** thou **about** *so* much to change thy 235

GADDI (1)
Nu 13:11 of the tribe of Manasseh, **G** the son of Susi. 1426

GADDIEL (1)
Nu 13:10 Of the tribe of Zebulun, **G** the son of Sodi. 1427

GADI (2)
2Ki 15:14 For Menahem the son of **G** went up from 1424
15:17 Menahem the son of **G** to reign over Israel, 1424

GADITE (1) [GAD]
2Sa 23:36 the son of Nathan of Zobah, Bani the **G**, 1425

GADITES (14) [GAD]
Dt 3:12 gave I unto the Reubenites and to the **G**. 1425
3:16 unto the **G** I gave from Gilead even unto 1425
4:43 Ramoth in Gilead, of the **G**; and Golan in 1425
29:8 to the **G**, and to the half tribe of Manasseh. 1425
Jos 1:12 to the **G**, and to half the tribe of Manasseh, 1425
12:6 and the **G**, and the half tribe of Manasseh. 1425
13:8 and the **G** have received their inheritance, 1425
22:1 and the **G**, and the half tribe of Manasseh, 1425
2Ki 10:33 the **G**, and the Reubenites, and 1425
1Ch 5:18 the **G**, and half the tribe of Manasseh, 1425
5:26 the **G**, and the half tribe of Manasseh, and 1425
12:8 of the **G** there separated themselves unto 1425
12:37 the **G**, and of the half tribe of Manasseh, 1425
26:32 the **G**, and the half tribe of Manasseh, 1425

GAHAM (1)
Ge 22:24 and **G**, and Thahash, and Maachah. 1514

GAHAR (2)
Ezr 2:47 the children of **G**, the children of Reaiah, 1515
Ne 7:49 the children of Giddel, the children of **G**, 1515

GAIN (30) [GAINED, GAINS]
Jdg 5:19 of Megiddo; they took no **g** of money. 1215
Job 22:3 *is it* **g** *to him,* that thou makest thy ways 1215
Pr 1:19 of every one that is **greedy of g**; 1214+1215
3:14 of silver, and the **g** thereof than fine gold. 8393
15:27 He that is **greedy of g** troubleth his 1214+1215
28:8 and **unjust g** increaseth his substance, 8636
Isa 33:15 he that despiseth the **g** of oppressions, 1215
56:11 every one for his **g**, from his quarter. 1215
Eze 22:13 at thy **dishonest g** which thou hast made, 1215
22:27 to destroy souls, to **get dishonest g**. 1214+1215
Da 2:8 I know of certainty that ye would **g** 2084
11:39 over many, and shall divide the land for **g**. 4242
Mic 4:13 I will consecrate their **g** unto the LORD, 1215
Mt 16:26 if he shall **g** the whole world, and lose his *2770*
Mk 8:36 if he shall **g** the whole world, and lose his *2770*
Lk 9:25 if he **g** the whole world, and lose himself, *2770*
Ac 16:16 which brought her masters much **g** by *2039*
19:24 brought no small **g** unto the craftsmen; *2039*
1Co 9:19 servant unto all, that I might **g** the more. *2770*
9:20 I became as a Jew, that I might **g** *the* Jews; *2770*
9:20 that I might **g** them that are under the law; *2770*
9:21 that I might **g** them *that are* without law. *2770*
9:22 became I as weak, that I might **g** the weak: *2770*
2Co 12:17 Did I **make a g** of you by any of them *4122*
12:18 Did Titus **make a g** of you? walked we not *4122*
Php 1:21 For to me to live *is* Christ, and to die *is* **g**. *2771*
3:7 But what *things* were **g** to me, those I *2771*
1Ti 6:5 of the truth, supposing that **g** is godliness: *4200*
6:6 But godliness with contentment is great **g**. *4200*
Jas 4:13 there a year, and buy and sell, and **get g**: *2770*

GAINED (10) [GAIN]
Job 27:8 though he hath **g**, when God taketh away 1214
Eze 22:12 thou hast **greedily g** of thy neighbours by 1214
Mt 18:15 he shall hear thee, thou hast **g** thy brother. *2770*
25:17 that *had received* two, he also **g** other two. *2770*
25:20 I have **g** besides them five talents moe. *2770*
25:22 I have **g** two other talents besides them. *2770*
Lk 19:15 how much every *man* had **g by trading**. *1281*
19:16 saying, Lord, thy pound hath **g** ten pounds. *4333*
19:18 saying, Lord, thy pound hath **g** five pounds. *4160*
Ac 27:21 and to have **g** this harm and loss. *2770*

GAINS (1) [GAIN]
Ac 16:19 saw that the hope of their **g** was gone, *2039*

GAINSAY (1) [GAINSAYERS, GAINSAYING, SAY]
Lk 21:15 adversaries shall not be able to **g** nor resist. *471*

GAINSAYERS (1) [GAINSAY]
Tit 1:9 both to exhort and to convince the **g**. *483*

GAINSAYING (3) [GAINSAY]
Ac 10:29 Therefore came I *unto you* **without g**, *369*
Ro 10:21 my hands unto a disobedient and **g** people. *483*
Jude 1:11 for reward, and perished in the **g** of Core. *485*

GAIUS (5)
Ac 19:29 and having caught **G** and Aristarchus, *1050*
20:4 and **G** of Derbe, and Timotheus; and *1050*
Ro 16:23 **G** mine host, and of the whole church, *1050*
1Co 1:14 I baptized none of you, but Crispus and **G**; *1050*
3Jn 1:1 The elder unto the wellbeloved **G**, whom I *1050*

GALAL (3)
1Ch 9:15 and **G**, and Mattaniah the son of Micah, 1559
9:16 the son of **G**, the son of Jeduthun, and 1559
Ne 11:17 the son of **G**, the son of Jeduthun. 1559

GALATIA (6) [GALATIANS]
Ac 16:6 throughout Phrygia and the region **of G**, *1054*
18:23 and went over *all* the country **of G** and *1054*
1Co 16:1 as I have given order to the churches of **G**, *1053*
Gal 1:2 which are with me, unto the churches of **G**: *1053*
2Ti 4:10 Crescens to **G**, Titus unto Dalmatia. *1053*
1Pe 1:1 **G**, Cappadocia, Asia, and Bithynia, *1053*

GALATIANS (2) [GALATIA]
Gal 3:1 O foolish **G**, who hath bewitched you, *1052*
6:S Unto the **G** written from Rome. *1052*

GALBANUM (1)
Ex 30:34 sweet spices, stacte, and onycha, and **g**; 2464

GALEED (2)
Ge 31:47 it Jegar-sahadutha: but Jacob called it **G**. 1567
31:48 Therefore was the name of it called **G**; 1567

GALILEAN (3) [GALILEE]
Mk 14:70 for thou art a **G**, and thy speech agreeth *1057*
Lk 22:59 this *fellow* also was with him: for he is a **G**. *1057*
23:6 he asked whether the man were a **G**. *1057*

GALILEANS (5) [GALILEE]
Lk 13:1 at that season some that told him of the **G**, *1057*
13:2 Suppose ye that these **G** were sinners above *1057*
13:2 Galileans were sinners above all the **G**, *1057*
Jn 4:45 was come into Galilee, the **G** received him, *1057*
Ac 2:7 Behold, are not all these which speak **G**? *1057*

GALILEE (72) [GALILEAN, GALILEANS]
Jos 20:7 they appointed Kedesh in **G** in mount 1551
21:32 of Naphtali, Kedesh in **G** with her suburbs, 1551
1Ki 9:11 gave Hiram twenty cities in the land of **G**. 1551
2Ki 15:29 and Kedesh, and Hazor, and Gilead, and **G**, 1551
1Ch 6:76 Kedesh in **G** with her suburbs, and 1551
Isa 9:1 the sea, beyond Jordan, in **G** of the nations. 1551
Mt 2:22 he turned aside into the parts of **G**: *1056*
3:13 Then cometh Jesus from **G** to Jordan unto *1056*
4:12 was cast into prison, he departed into **G**; *1056*
4:15 the sea, beyond Jordan, **G** of the Gentiles; *1056*
4:18 And Jesus, walking by the sea of **G**, *1056*
4:23 And Jesus went about all **G**, teaching in *1056*
4:25 him great multitudes *of people* from **G**, *1056*
15:29 and came nigh unto the sea of **G**; *1056*
17:22 And while they abode in **G**, Jesus said unto *1056*
19:1 he departed from **G**, and came into *1056*
21:11 This is Jesus the prophet of Nazareth of **G**. *1056*
26:32 am risen *again*, I will go before you into **G**. *1056*
26:69 saying, Thou also wast with Jesus **of G**. *1057*
27:55 which followed Jesus from **G**, *1056*
28:7 and behold, he goeth before you into **G**; *1056*
28:10 go tell my brethren that they go into **G**, and *1056*
28:16 the eleven disciples went *away* into **G**, *1056*
Mk 1:9 *that* Jesus came from Nazareth of **G**, and *1056*
1:14 John was put in prison, Jesus came into **G**, *1056*
1:16 Now as he walked by the sea of **G**, he saw *1056*
1:28 throughout all the region round about **G**. *1056*
1:39 in their synagogues throughout all **G**, *1056*
3:7 and a great multitude from **G** followed him, *1056*
6:21 high captains, and chief *estates* of **G**; *1056*
7:31 and Sidon, he came unto the sea of **G**, *1056*
9:30 departed thence, and passed through **G**; *1056*
14:28 that I am risen, I will go before you into **G**. *1056*
15:41 (Who also, when he was in **G**, *1056*
16:7 and Peter that he goeth before you into **G**: *1056*
Lk 1:26 was sent from God unto a city of **G**, *1056*
2:4 And Joseph also went up from **G**, out of *1056*
2:39 they returned into **G**, to their own city *1056*
3:1 and Herod being tetrarch of **G**, and *1056*
4:14 returned in the power of the Spirit into **G**: *1056*
4:31 a city of **G**, and taught them on the sabbath *1056*
4:44 And he preached in the synagogues of **G**. *1056*
5:17 which were come out of every town of **G**, *1056*
8:26 of the Gadarenes, which is over against **G**. *1056*
17:11 passed through the midst of Samaria and **G**. *1056*
23:5 all Jewry, beginning from **G** to this place. *1056*
23:6 When Pilate heard of **G**, he asked whether *1056*
23:49 and the women that followed him from **G**, *1056*
23:55 which came with him from **G**, *1056*
24:6 he spake unto you when he was yet in **G**, *1056*
Jn 1:43 day following Jesus would go forth into **G**, *1056*
2:1 day there was a marriage in Cana of **G**; *1056*
2:11 of miracles did Jesus in Cana of **G**, *1056*
4:3 He left Judea, and departed again into **G**. *1056*
4:43 days he departed thence, and went into **G**. *1056*
4:45 Then when he was come into **G**, *1056*
4:46 So Jesus came again into Cana of **G**, *1056*
4:47 that Jesus was come out of Judea into **G**, *1056*
4:54 when he was come out of Judea into **G**. *1056*
6:1 these *things* Jesus went over the sea of **G**, *1056*
7:1 After these *things* Jesus walked in **G**: for he *1056*
7:9 these *words* unto them, he abode *still* in **G**. *1056*
7:41 But some said, Shall Christ come out of **G**? *1056*
7:52 and said unto him, Art thou also of **G**? *1056*
7:52 and look: for out of **G** ariseth no prophet. *1056*
12:21 which was of Bethsaida of **G**, and *1056*
21:2 and Nathanael of Cana in **G**, and the *sons* *1056*
Ac 1:11 Which also said, Ye men **of G**, why stand *1057*
5:37 After this *man* rose up Judas **of G** *1057*
9:31 throughout all Judea and **G** and Samaria, *1056*
10:37 and began from **G**, after the baptism which *1056*
13:31 came up with him from **G** to Jerusalem, *1056*

GALL (14)
Dt 29:18 should be among you a root that beareth **g** 7219
32:32 their grapes *are* grapes of **g**, their clusters 7219
Job 16:13 he poureth out my **g** upon the ground. 4845
20:14 is turned, *it is* the **g** of asps within him. 4846
20:25 the glistering sword cometh out of his **g**: 4846
Ps 69:21 They gave me also **g** for my meat; and 7219
Jer 8:14 given us water of **g** to drink, because 7219
9:15 and give them water of **g** to drink. 7219
23:15 and make them drink the water of **g**: 7219
La 3:5 and compassed *me* with **g** and travail. 7219
3:19 and my misery, the wormwood and the **g**. 7219
Am 6:12 for ye have turned judgment into **g**, and 7219
Mt 27:34 gave him vinegar to drink mingled with **g**: *5521*
Ac 8:23 For I perceive that thou art in the **g** of *5521*

GALLANT (1)
Isa 33:21 with oars, neither shall **g** ship pass thereby. 117

GALLERIES (4) [GALLERY]
SS 7:5 head like purple; the king *is* held in the **g**. 7298
Eze 41:15 the **g** thereof on the one side and on the other 862
41:16 the **g** round about on their three *stories*, over 862
42:5 for the **g** were higher than these, than 862

GALLERY (2) [GALLERIES]
Eze 42:3 *was* **g** against gallery in three *stories*. 862
42:3 *was* gallery against **g** in three *stories*. 862

GALLEY (1)
Isa 33:21 wherein shall go no **g** with oars, neither shall 590

GALLIM (2)
1Sa 25:44 to Phalti the son of Laish, which *was* of **G**. 1554
Isa 10:30 Lift up thy voice, O daughter of **G**: cause *it* 1530

GALLIO (3)
Ac 18:12 And when **G** was the deputy of Achaia, *1058*
18:14 **G** said unto the Jews, If it were a matter of *1058*
18:17 And **G** cared for none of those *things*. *1058*

G

GALLONS See FIRKINS

GALLOWS (8)
Est 5:14 Let a **g** be made of fifty cubits high, and to 6086
5:14 and he caused the **g** to be made. 6086
6: 4 on the **g** that he had prepared for him. 6086
7: 9 Behold also, the **g** fifty cubits high, 6086
7:10 So they hanged Haman on the **g** that he had 6086
8: 7 him they have hanged upon the **g**, because 6086
9:13 let Haman's ten sons be hanged upon the **g**. 6086
9:25 and his sons should be hanged on the **g**. 6086

GAMALIEL (7)
Nu 1:10 of Manasseh; **G** the son of Pedahzur. 1583
2:20 Manasseh *shall be* **G** the son of Pedahzur. 1583
7:54 On the eighth day *offered* **G** the son of 1583
7:59 this *was* the offering of **G** the son of 1583
10:23 of Manasseh *was* **G** the son of Pedahzur. 1583
Ac 5:34 a Pharisee, named **G**, a doctor of law, *1059*
22: 3 yet brought up in this city at the feet of **G**, *1059*

GAME See VENISON

GAMMAD See GAMMADIMS

GAMMADIMS (1)
Eze 27:11 round about, and the **G** were in thy towers: 1575

GAMUL (1) [BETH-GAMUL]
1Ch 24:17 to Jachin, the two and twentieth to **G**, 1577

GANGRENE See CANKER

GAP (1) [GAPS]
Eze 22:30 stand in the **g** before me for the land, that *I* 6556

GAPED (2)
Job 16:10 They have **g** upon me with their mouth; 6473
Ps 22:13 They **g** upon me *with* their mouths, *as* a 6475

GAPS (1) [GAP]
Eze 13: 5 Ye have not gone up into the **g**, 6556

GARDEN (52) [GARDENER, GARDENS]
Ge 2: 8 the LORD God planted a **g** eastward in 1588
2: 9 the tree of life also in the midst of the **g**, 1588
2:10 a river went out of Eden to water the **g**; 1588
2:15 put him into the **g** of Eden to dress it and 1588
2:16 Of every tree of the **g** thou mayest freely 1588
3: 1 Ye shall not eat of every tree of the **g**? 1588
3: 2 We may eat of the fruit of the trees of the **g**: 1588
3: 3 of the tree which *is* in the midst of the **g**, 1588
3: 8 God walking in the **g** in the cool of the day: 1588
3: 8 the LORD God amongst the trees of the **g**. 1588
3:10 I heard thy voice in the **g**, and I was afraid, 1588
3:23 God sent him forth from the **g** of Eden, 1588
3:24 he placed at the east of the **g** of Eden 1588
13:10 *even* as the **g** of the LORD, 1588
Dt 11:10 wateredst *it* with thy foot, as a **g** of herbs: 1588
1Ki 21: 2 that I may have it for a **g** of herbs, because 1588
2Ki 9:27 saw *this,* he fled *by* the way of the **g** house. 1588
21:18 was buried in the **g** of his own house, in 1588
21:18 garden of his own house, in the **g** of Uzza: 1588
21:26 he was buried in his sepulchre in the **g** of 1588
25: 4 two walls, which *is* by the king's **g**: 1588
Ne 3:15 wall of the pool of Siloah by the king's **g**, 1588
Est 1: 5 in the court of the **g** of the king's palace; 1594
7: 7 of wine in his wrath *went* into the palace **g**: 1594
7: 8 the king returned out of the palace **g** into 1594
Job 8:16 and his branch shooteth forth in his **g**. 1593
SS 4:12 A **g** inclosed *is* my sister, *my* spouse; 1588
4:16 blow upon my **g**, *that* the spices thereof 1588
4:16 Let my beloved come into his **g**, and eat his 1588
5: 1 I am come into my **g**, my sister, *my* spouse: 1588
6: 2 My beloved is gone down into his **g**, to 1588
6:11 I went down into the **g** of nuts to see 1594
Isa 1: 8 as a lodge in a **g of cucumbers**, as a 4750
1:30 leaf fadeth, and as a **g** that hath no water. 1593
51: 3 and her desert like the **g** of the LORD; 1588
58:11 thou shalt be like a watered **g**, and like a 1588
61:11 as the **g** causeth the things that are sown in 1593
Jer 31:12 their soul shall be as a watered **g**; and 1588
39: 4 *by* the way of the king's **g**, by the gate 1588
52: 7 the two walls, which *was* by the king's **g**; 1588
La 2: 6 away his tabernacle, as *if it were of* a **g**: 1588
Eze 28:13 Thou hast been in Eden the **g** of God; 1588
31: 8 The cedars in the **g** of God could not hide 1588
31: 8 nor any tree in the **g** of God was like unto 1588
31: 9 that *were* in the **g** of God, envied him. 1588
36:35 was desolate is become like the **g** of Eden; 1588
Joel 2: 3 the land *is* as the **g** of Eden before them, 1588
Lk 13:19 which a man took, and cast into his **g**; *2779*
Jn 18: 1 where was a **g**, into the which he entered, *2779*
18:26 saith, Did not I see thee in the **g** with him? *2779*
19:41 place where he was crucified there was a **g**; *2779*
19:41 and in the **g** a new sepulchre, wherein was *2779*

GARDENER (1) [GARDEN]
Jn 20:15 She, supposing him to be the **g**, saith unto *2780*

GARDENS (12) [GARDEN]
Nu 24: 6 are they spread forth, as **g** by the river side, 1593
Ecc 2: 5 I made me **g** and orchards, and I planted 1593
SS 4:15 A fountain of **g**, a well of living waters, and 1588
6: 2 to feed in the **g**, and to gather lilies. 1588
8:13 Thou that dwellest in the **g**, the companions 1588
Isa 1:29 ye shall be confounded for the **g** that ye 1593
65: 3 that sacrificeth in **g**, and burneth incense 1593
66:17 purify themselves in the **g** behind one *tree* 1593
Jer 29: 5 dwell *in them;* and plant **g**, and eat the fruit 1593
29:28 dwell *in them;* and plant **g**, and eat the fruit 1593
Am 4: 9 when your **g** and your vineyards and 1593
9:14 they shall also make **g**, and eat the fruit of 1593

GAREB (3)
2Sa 23:38 Ira an Ithrite, **G** an Ithrite, 1619
1Ch 11:40 Ira the Ithrite, **G** the Ithrite, 1619
Jer 31:39 yet go forth over against it upon the hill **G**, 1619

GARLANDS (1)
Ac 14:13 brought oxen and **g** unto the gates, and *4725*

GARLICK (1)
Nu 11: 5 and the leeks, and the onions, and the **g**: 7762

GARMENT (86) [GARMENTS]
Ge 9:23 Shem and Japheth took a **g**, and laid *it* upon 8071
25:25 the first came out red, all over like a hairy **g**; 155
39:12 she caught him by his **g**, saying, Lie with 899
39:12 he left his **g** in her hand, and fled, and 899
39:13 when she saw that he had left his **g** in her 899
39:15 that he left his **g** with me, and fled, and 899
39:16 she laid up his **g** by her, until his lord came 899
39:18 cried, that he left his **g** with me, and fled out. 899
Lev 6:10 the priest shall put on his linen **g**, and 4055
6:27 is sprinkled of the blood thereof upon *any* **g**, 899
13:47 The **g** also that the plague of leprosy is in, 899
13:47 *whether it be* a woollen **g**, or a linen 899
13:47 *it be* a woollen garment, or a linen **g**; 899
13:49 *if* the plague be greenish or reddish in the **g**, 899
13:51 if the plague be spread in the **g**, either in 899
13:52 He shall therefore burn *that* **g**, whether warp 899
13:53 behold, the plague be not spread in the **g**, 899
13:56 he shall rend it out of the **g**, or out of 899
13:57 if it appear still in the **g**, either in the warp, 899
13:58 the **g**, either warp, or woof, or 899
13:59 This *is* the law of the plague of leprosy in a **g** 899
14:55 And for the leprosy of a **g**, and of a house, 899
15:17 every **g**, and every skin, whereon is the seed 899
19:19 neither shall a **g** mingled of linen and 899
Dt 22: 5 neither shall a man put on a woman's **g**: 8071
22:11 Thou shalt not wear a **g of divers sorts**, 8162
Jos 7:21 among the spoils a goodly Babylonish **g**, 155
7:24 the **g**, and the wedge of gold, and his sons, 155
Jdg 8:25 willingly give *them.* And they spread a **g**, 8071
2Sa 13:18 *she had* a **g** of divers colours upon her: 3801
13:19 rent her **g** of divers colours that *was* on her, 3801
20: 8 Joab's **g** that he had put on *was* girded unto 4055
1Ki 11:29 he had clad himself with a new **g**; and 8008
11:30 Ahijah caught the new **g** that *was* on him, 8008
2Ki 9:13 took every man his **g**, and put *it* under him 899
Ezr 9: 3 I rent my **g** and my mantle, and pluckt off 899
9: 5 having rent my **g** and my mantle, I fell upon 899
Est 8:15 and *with* a **g** of fine linen and purple: 8509
Job 13:28 consumeth, as a **g** that is moth-eaten. 899
30:18 By the great force *of my disease* is my **g** 3830
38: 9 When I made the cloud the **g** thereof, and 3830
38:14 as clay *to* the seal; and they stand as a **g**. 3830
41:13 Who can discover the face of his **g**? *or* 3830
Ps 69:11 I made sackcloth also my **g**; and I became a 3830
73: 6 as a chain; violence covereth them *as* a **g**. 7897
102:26 yea, all of them shall wax old like a **g**; as a 899
104: 2 Who coverest *thyself with* light as *with* a **g**: 8008
104: 6 Thou coveredst it *with* the deep as *with* a **g**: 3830
109:18 himself with cursing like as with his **g**, 4055
109:19 Let it be unto him as the **g** *which* covereth 899
Pr 20:16 Take his **g** that is surety *for* a stranger: and 899
25:20 *As* he that taketh away a **g** in cold weather, 899
27:13 Take his **g** that is surety *for* a stranger, and 899
30: 4 who hath bound the waters in a **g**? 8071
Isa 50: 9 lo, they all shall wax old as a **g**; the moth 899
51: 6 the earth shall wax old like a **g**, and they that 899
51: 8 For the moth shall eat them up like a **g**, and 899
61: 3 the **g** of praise for the spirit of heaviness; 4594
Jer 43:12 land of Egypt, as a shepherd putteth on his **g**; 899
Eze 18: 7 and hath covered the naked with a **g**; 899
18:16 and hath covered the naked with a **g**, 899
Da 7: 9 whose **g** *was* white as snow, and the hair of 3831
Mic 2: 8 ye pull off the robe with the **g** from them 8008
Hag 2:12 If one bear holy flesh in the skirt of his **g**, 899
Zec 13: 4 neither shall they wear a rough **g** to deceive: 155
Mal 2:16 for *one* covereth violence with his **g**, 3830
Mt 9:16 putteth a piece of new cloth unto an old **g**; *2440*
9:16 is put in to fill it up taketh from the **g**, *2440*
9:20 behind *him,* and touched the hem of his **g**: *2440*
9:21 If I may but touch his **g**, I shall be whole. *2440*
14:36 that they might only touch the hem of his **g**: *2440*
22:11 there a man which had not on a wedding **g**: *1742*
22:12 thou in hither not having a wedding **g**? *1742*
Mk 2:21 seweth a piece of new cloth on an old **g**: *2440*
5:27 in the press behind, and touched his **g**. *2440*
6:56 touch if it were but the border of his **g**: *2440*
10:50 casting away his **g**, rose, and came to Jesus. *2440*
13:16 not turn back again for to take up his **g**. *2440*
16: 5 on the right side, clothed in a **long** white **g**; *4749*
Lk 5:36 No *man* putteth a piece of a new **g** upon an *2440*
8:44 and touched the border of his **g**: *2440*
22:36 no sword, let him sell his **g**, and buy one. *2440*
Ac 12: 8 Cast thy **g** about thee, and follow me. *2440*
Heb 1:11 and they all shall wax old as *doth* a **g**; *2440*
Jude 1:23 hating even the **g** spotted by the flesh. *5509*
Rev 1:13 **clothed with a g** down to the foot, and *1746*

GARMENTS (103) [GARMENT]
Ge 35: 2 and be clean, and change your **g**: 8071
38:14 And she put her widow's **g** off from her, and 899
38:19 and put on the **g** of her widowhood. 899
49:11 he washed his **g** in wine, and his clothes in 3830
Ex 28: 2 thou shalt make holy **g** for Aaron thy 899
28: 3 that they may make Aaron's **g** to consecrate 899
28: 4 these *are* the **g** which they shall make; 899
28: 4 they shall make holy **g** for Aaron thy 899
29: 5 thou shalt take the **g**, and put upon Aaron 899
29:21 upon his **g**, and upon his sons, and upon 899
29:21 and upon the **g** of his sons with him: 899
29:21 his **g**, and his sons, and his sons' garments 899
29:21 and his sons, and his sons' **g** with him. 899
29:29 the holy **g** of Aaron shall be his sons' after 899
Ex 31:10 the holy **g** for Aaron the priest, and 899
31:10 the **g** of his sons, to minister in the priest's 899
35:19 to do service in the holy *place,* the holy **g** for 899
35:19 the **g** of his sons, to minister in the priest's 899
35:21 and for all his service, and for the holy **g**. 899
39: 1 holy *place,* and made the holy **g** for Aaron; 899
39:41 and the holy **g** for Aaron the priest, 899
39:41 his sons' **g**, to minister in the priest's office. 899
40:13 thou shalt put upon Aaron the holy **g**, and 899
Lev 6:11 he shall put off his **g**, and put on other 899
6:11 put on other **g**, and carry forth the ashes 899
8: 2 the **g**, and the anointing oil, and a bullock *for* 899
8:30 *and* upon his **g**, and upon his sons, and 899
8:30 his sons, and upon his sons' **g** with him; 899
8:30 *and* his **g**, and his sons, and his sons' 899
8:30 and his sons, and his sons' **g** with him. 899
16: 4 these *are* holy **g**; therefore shall he wash his 899
16:23 shall put off the linen **g**, which he put on 899
16:24 put on his **g**, and come forth, and offer his 899
16:32 put on the linen clothes, *even* the holy **g**: 899
21:10 that is consecrated to put on the **g**, shall not 899
Nu 15:38 of their **g** throughout their generations, 899
20:26 strip Aaron of his **g**, and put them upon 899
20:28 Moses stripped Aaron of his **g**, and put them 899
Jos 9: 5 upon their feet, and old **g** upon them; 8008
9:13 these our **g** and our shoes are become old 8008
Jdg 14:12 give you thirty sheets and thirty change of **g**: 899
14:13 give me thirty sheets and thirty change of **g**. 899
14:19 gave change *of* **g** unto them which NIH
1Sa 18: 4 gave it to David, and his **g**, even to his 4055
2Sa 10: 4 cut off their **g** in the middle, *even* to their 4063
13:31 and tare his **g**, and lay on the earth; 899
1Ki 10:25 **g**, and armour, and spices, horses, and 8008
2Ki 5:22 a talent of silver, and two changes of **g**. 899
5:23 with two changes of **g**, and laid *them* upon 899
5:26 to receive **g**, and oliveyards, and vineyards, 899
7:15 and lo, all the way *was* full *of* **g** and vessels, 899
25:29 changed his prison **g**: and he did eat bread 899
1Ch 19: 4 cut off their **g** in the midst hard by *their* 4063
Ezr 2:69 pound *of* silver, and one hundred priests' **g**. 3801
Ne 7:70 five hundred and thirty priests' **g**. 3801
7:72 and threescore and seven priests' **g**. 3801
Job 37:17 How thy **g** *are* warm, when he quieteth 899
Ps 22:18 They part my **g** among them, and cast lots 899
45: 8 All thy **g** *smell of* myrrh, and aloes, *and* 899
133: 2 that went down to the skirts of his **g**; 4060
Ecc 9: 8 Let thy **g** be always white; and let thy head 899
SS 4:11 the smell of thy **g** *is* like the smell of 8008
Isa 9: 5 with confused noise, and **g** rolled in blood; 8071
52: 1 put on thy beautiful **g**, O Jerusalem, the holy 899
59: 6 Their webs shall not become **g**, neither shall 899
59:17 he put on the **g** of vengeance *for* clothing, 899
61:10 for he hath clothed me with the **g** of 899
63: 1 from Edom, with dyed **g** from Bozrah? 899
63: 2 thy **g** like him that treadeth in the winefat? 899
63: 3 their blood shall be sprinkled upon my **g**, 899
Jer 36:24 not afraid, nor rent their **g**, *neither* the king, 899
52:33 changed his prison **g**: and he did continually 899
La 4:14 so that *men* could not touch their **g**. 3830
Eze 16:16 of thy **g** thou didst take, and deckedst thy 899
16:18 tookest thy broidered **g**, and coveredst them: 899
26:16 their robes, and put off their broidered **g**: 899
42:14 there they shall lay their **g** wherein they 899
42:14 shall put on other **g**, and shall approach to 899
44:17 they shall be clothed with linen **g**; 899
44:19 they shall put off their **g** wherein they 899
44:19 holy chambers, and they shall put on other **g**; 899
44:19 shall not sanctify the people with their **g**. 899
Da 3:21 their *other* **g**, and were cast into the midst 3831
Joel 2:13 not your **g**, and turn unto the LORD your 899
Zec 3: 3 Now Joshua was clothed with filthy **g**, and 899
3: 4 Take away the filthy **g** from him 899
3: 5 mitre upon his head, and clothed him with **g**. 899
Mt 21: 8 And a very great multitude spread their **g** in *2440*
23: 5 and enlarge the borders of their **g**, *2440*
27:35 crucified him, and parted his **g**, casting lots: *2440*
27:35 They parted my **g** among them, and *2440*
Mk 11: 7 the colt to Jesus, and cast their **g** on him; *2440*
11: 8 And many spread their **g** in the way: and *2440*
15:24 they parted his **g**, casting lots upon them, *2440*
Lk 19:35 and they cast their **g** upon the colt, and *2440*
24: 4 two men stood by them in shining **g**: *2067*
Jn 13: 4 He riseth from supper, and laid aside *his* **g**; *2440*
13:12 and had taken his **g**, and was set down *2440*
19:23 took his **g**, and made four parts, to every *2440*
Ac 9:39 the coats and **g** which Dorcas made, *2440*
Jas 5: 2 are corrupted, and your **g** are motheaten. *2440*
Rev 3: 4 in Sardis, which have not defiled their **g**; *2440*
16:15 and keepeth his **g**, lest he walk naked, and *2440*

GARMITE (1)
1Ch 4:19 the father of Keilah the **G**, and 1636

GARNER (2) [GARNERS]
Mt 3:12 his floor, and gather his wheat into the **g**; *596*
Lk 3:17 and will gather the wheat into his **g**; *596*

GARNERS (2) [GARNER]
Ps 144:13 *That* our **g** *may be* full, affording all 4200
Joel 1:17 the **g** are laid desolate, the barns are broken 214

GARNISH (1) [GARNISHED]
Mt 23:29 and **g** the sepulchres of the righteous, *2885*

GARNISHED (5) [GARNISH]
2Ch 3: 6 he **g** the house with precious stones for 6823
Job 26:13 By his spirit he hath **g** the heavens; 8235
Mt 12:44 is come, he findeth *it* empty, swept, and **g**. *2885*
Lk 11:25 when he cometh, he findeth *it* swept and **g**. *2885*
Rev 21:19 *were* **g** with all *manner of* precious stones. *2885*

GARRISON (13) [GARRISONS]
1Sa 10: 5 of God, where *is* the **g** of the Philistines: 5333
13: 3 Jonathan smote the **g** of the Philistines that 5333

1Sa 13: 4 that Saul had smitten a g of the Philistines, 5333
13:23 the g of the Philistines went out to 4673
14: 1 and let us go over to the Philistines' g, 4673
14: 4 sought to go over unto the Philistines' g, 4673
14: 6 let us go over unto the g of these 4673
14:11 themselves unto the g of the Philistines: 4673
14:12 the men of the g answered Jonathan and 4675
14:15 the g, and the spoilers, they also trembled, 4673
2Sa 23:14 the g of the Philistines was then 4673
1Ch 11:16 the Philistines' g was then at Beth-lehem. 5333
2Co 11:32 with a g, desirous to apprehend me: NIG

GARRISONS (7) [GARRISON]
2Sa 8: 6 David put g in Syria of Damascus: and 5333
8:14 he put g in Edom; throughout all Edom put 5333
8:14 throughout all Edom put he g, and all they 5333
1Ch 18: 6 David put g in Syria-damascus; and NIH
18:13 he put g in Edom; and all the Edomites 5333
2Ch 17: 2 set g in the land of Judah, and in the cities 5333
Eze 26:11 thy strong g shall go down to the ground. 4676

GASHMU (1) [GESHEM]
Ne 6: 6 G saith it, that thou and the Jews think to 1654

GAT (20) [GET]
Ge 19:27 Abraham g up early in the morning to 7925
Ex 24:18 of the cloud, and g him up into the mount: 5927
Nu 11:30 Moses g him into the camp, he and 622
14:40 g them up into the top of the mountain, 5927
16:27 So they g up from the tabernacle of Korah, 5927
Jdg 9:48 Abimelech g him up to mount Zalmon, 5927
9:51 g them up to the top of the tower. 5927
19:28 the man rose up, and g him unto his place. 1980
1Sa 13:15 g him up from Gilgal unto Gibeah of 5927
24:22 and his men g them up unto the hold. 5927
26:12 they g them away, and no man saw it, nor 1980
2Sa 4: 7 g them away through the plain all night. 1980
8:13 David g him a name when he returned from 6213
13:29 every man g him up upon his mule, and 7392
17:23 arose, and g him home to his house, to his 1980
19: 3 the people g them by stealth that day into 935
1Ki 1: 1 covered him with clothes, but he g no heat. 3179
Ps 116: 3 and the pains of hell g hold upon me: 4672
Ecc 2: 8 I g me men singers and women singers, and 6213
La 5: 9 We g our bread with the peril of our lives 935

GATAM (3)
Ge 36:11 Omar, Zepho, and G, and Kenaz. 1609
36:16 Duke Korah, duke G, and duke Amalek: 1609
1Ch 1:36 Omar, Zephi, and G, Kenaz, and Timna, 1609

GATE (275) [GATES]
Ge 19: 1 at even; and Lot sat in the g of Sodom: 8179
22:17 thy seed shall possess the g of his enemies; 8179
23:10 even of all that went in at the g of his city, 8179
23:18 before all that went in at the g of his city. 8179
24:60 let thy seed possess the g of those which 8179
28:17 house of God, and this is the g of heaven. 8179
34:20 Shechem his son came unto the g of their 8179
34:24 all that went out of the g of his city; 8179
34:24 all that went out of the g of his city. 8179
Ex 27:14 The hangings of one side of the g shall be NIH
27:16 for the g of the court shall be a hanging of 8179
32:26 Then Moses stood in the g of the camp, and 8179
32:27 out from g to gate throughout the camp, 8179
32:27 out from gate to g throughout the camp, 8179
38:14 The hangings of the one side of the g were NIH
38:15 for the other side of the court g, on this 8179
38:18 the hanging for the g of the court was 8179
38:31 the sockets of the court g, and all the pins 8179
39:40 the hanging for the court g, his cords, and 8179
40: 8 and hang up the hanging at the court g. 8179
40:33 and set up the hanging of the court g. 8179
Nu 4:26 the hanging for the door of the g of 8179
Dt 21:19 of his city, and unto the g of his place; 8179
22:15 virginity unto the elders of the city in the g: 8179
22:24 ye shall bring them both out unto the g of 8179
25: 7 let his brother's wife go up to the g unto 8179
Jos 2: 5 to pass about the time of shutting of the g, 8179
2: 7 after them were gone out, they shut the g. 8179
7: 5 for they chased them from before the g 8179
8:29 cast it at the entering of the g of the city, 8179
20: 4 stand at the entering of the g of the city, 8179
Jdg 9:35 stood in the entering of the g of the city: 8179
9:40 wounded, even unto the entering of the g. 8179
9:44 stood in the entering of the g of the city: 8179
16: 2 laid wait for him all night in the g of 8179
16: 3 took the doors of the g of the city, and 8179
18:16 of Dan, stood by the entering of the g. 8179
18:17 the priest stood in the entering of the g with 8179
Ru 4: 1 went Boaz up to the g, and sat him down 8179
4:10 his brethren, and from the g of his place: 8179
4:11 all the people that were in the g, and 8179
1Sa 4:18 off the seat backward by the side of the g, 8179
9:18 Saul drew near to Samuel in the g, and 8179
21:13 scrabled on the doors of the g, and let his 8179
2Sa 3:27 Joab took him aside in the g to speak with 8179
10: 8 battle in array at the entering in of the g: 8179
11:23 upon them even unto the entering of the g. 8179
15: 2 up early, and stood beside the way of the g: 8179
18: 4 the king stood by the g side, and all 8179
18:24 went up to the roof over the g unto the wall, 8179
18:33 went up to the chamber over the g, and 8179
19: 8 the king rose, and sat in the g. And they 8179
19: 8 Behold, the king doth sit in the g. 8179
23:15 the well of Beth-lehem, which is by the g. 8179
23:16 that was by the g, and took it, and 8179
1Ki 17:10 when he came to the g of the city, behold, 6607
22:10 in a void place in the entrance of the g of 8179
2Ki 7: 1 of barley for a shekel, in the g of Samaria. 8179
7: 3 four leprous men at the entering in of the g: 8179
7:17 hand he leaned to have the charge of the g: 8179
7:17 the people trode upon him in the g, and 8179
7:18 shall be to morrow about this time in the g 8179
2Ki 7:20 for the people trode upon him in the g, and 8179
9:31 as Jehu entered in at the g, she said, Had 8179
10: 8 at the entering in of the g until the morning. 8179
11: 6 And a third part shall be at the g of Sur; and 8179
11: 6 and a third part at the g behind the guard: 8179
11:19 came by the way of the g of the guard to 8179
14:13 from the g of Ephraim unto the corner gate, 8179
14:13 from the gate of Ephraim unto the corner g, 8179
15:35 He built the higher g of the house of 8179
23: 8 of the g of Joshua the governor of the city, 8179
23: 8 which were on a man's left hand at the g of 8179
25: 4 by the way of the g between two walls, 8179
1Ch 9:18 Who hitherto waited in the king's g 8179
11:17 of the well of Beth-lehem, that is at the g. 8179
11:18 that was by the g, and took it, and 8179
19: 9 put the battle in array before the g of 6607
26:13 of their fathers, for every g. 8179+8179+2050.1
26:16 with the g Shallecheth, by the causeway of 8179
2Ch 8:14 by their courses at every g: 8179+8179+2050.1
18: 9 place at the entering in of the g of Samaria; 8179
23: 5 and a third part at the g of the foundation: 8179
23:15 entering of the horse g by the king's house, 8179
23:20 they came through the high g into 8179
24: 8 set it without at the g of the house of 8179
25:23 from the g of Ephraim to the corner gate, 8179
25:23 from the gate of Ephraim to the corner g, 8179
26: 9 built towers in Jerusalem at the corner g, 8179
26: 9 at the valley g, and at the turning of 8179
27: 3 He built the high g of the house of 8179
32: 6 to him in the street of the g of the city, 8179
33:14 even to the entering in at the fish g, and 8179
35:15 porters waited at every g; 8179+8179+2050.1
Ne 2:13 I went out by night by the g of the valley, 8179
2:14 I went on to the g of the fountain, and 8179
2:15 entered by the g of the valley, and so 8179
3: 1 the priests, and they built the sheep g; 8179
3: 3 the fish g did the sons of Hassenaah build, 8179
3: 6 Moreover the old g repaired Jehoiada 8179
3:13 The valley g repaired Hanun, and 8179
3:13 cubits on the wall unto the dung g. 8179
3:14 the dung g repaired Malchiah the son of 8179
3:15 the g of the fountain repaired Shallun 8179
3:26 unto the place over against the water g 8179
3:28 From above the horse g repaired the priests, 8179
3:29 son of Shechaniah, the keeper of the east g. 8179
3:31 over against the g Miphkad, and to 8179
3:32 unto the sheep g repaired the goldsmiths 8179
8: 1 into the street that was before the water g; 8179
8: 3 the water g from the morning until midday, 8179
8:16 in the street of the water g, and in the street 8179
8:16 and in the street of the g of Ephraim. 8179
12:31 right hand upon the wall toward the dung g: 8179
12:37 at the fountain g, which was over against 8179
12:37 of David, even unto the water g eastward. 8179
12:39 from above the g of Ephraim, and 8179
12:39 above the old g, and above the fish gate, 8179
12:39 above the fish g, and the tower of 8179
12:39 the tower of Meah, even unto the sheep g: 8179
12:39 and they stood still in the prison g. 8179
Est 2:19 then Mordecai sat in the king's g. 8179
2:21 while Mordecai sat in the king's g, 8179
3: 2 that were in the king's g, bowed, and 8179
3: 3 which were in the king's g, said unto 8179
4: 2 came even before the king's g: for none 8179
4: 2 for none might enter into the king's g 8179
4: 6 of the city, which was before the king's g. 8179
5: 1 over against the g of the house. 6607
5: 9 when Haman saw Mordecai in the king's g, 8179
5:13 see Mordecai the Jew sitting at the king's g. 8179
6:10 the Jew, that sitteth at the king's g: 8179
6:12 Mordecai came again to the king's g. 8179
Job 5: 4 from safety, and they are crushed in the g, 8179
29: 7 When I went out to the g through the city, 8179
31:21 the fatherless, when I saw my help in the g: 8179
Ps 69:12 They that sit in the g speak against me; and 8179
118:20 This g of the LORD, into which 8179
127: 5 they shall speak with the enemies in the g. 8179
Pr 17:19 he that exalteth his g seeketh destruction. 6607
22:22 neither oppress the afflicted in the g: 8179
24: 7 a fool: he openeth not his mouth in the g. 8179
SS 7: 4 in Heshbon, by the g of Bath-rabbim: 8179
Isa 14:31 Howl, O g; cry, O city; thou, 8179
22: 7 shall set themselves in array at the g. 8179
24:12 and the g is smitten with destruction. 8179
28: 6 strength to them that turn the battle to the g. 8179
29:21 lay a snare for him that reproveth in the g, 8179
Jer 7: 2 Stand in the g of the LORD'S house, and 8179
17:19 stand in the g of the children of the people, 8179
19: 2 which is by the entry of the east g, and 8179
20: 2 put him in the stocks that were in the high g 8179
26:10 sat down in the entry of the new g of 8179
31:38 tower of Hananeel unto the g of the corner. 8179
31:40 unto the corner of the horse g towards 8179
36:10 in the higher court at the entry of the new g 8179
37:13 when he was in the g of Benjamin, 8179
38: 7 the king then sitting in the g of Benjamin; 8179
39: 3 sat in the middle g, even Nergal-sharezer, 8179
39: 4 by the g betwixt the two walls: 8179
52: 7 by the way of the g between the two walls, 8179
La 5:14 The elders have ceased from the g, 8179
Eze 8: 3 to the door of the inner g that looketh 8179
8: 5 northward at the g of the altar this image of 8179
8:14 he brought me to the door of the g of 8179
9: 2 six men came from the way of the higher g, 8179
10:19 every one stood at the door of the east g of 8179
11: 1 brought me unto the east g of the LORD'S 8179
11: 1 behold at the door of the g five and 8179
40: 3 a measuring reed; and he stood in the g. 8179
40: 6 came he unto the g which looketh toward 8179
40: 6 and measured the threshold of the g, 8179
40: 6 the other threshold of the g, which was one NIH
40: 7 the threshold of the g by the porch of 8179
40: 7 by the porch of the g within was one reed. 8179
40: 8 He measured also the porch of the g within, 8179
40: 9 measured he the porch of the g, 8179
Eze 40: 9 and the porch of the g was inward. 8179
40:10 the little chambers of the g eastward were 8179
40:11 measured the breadth of the entry of the g, 8179
40:11 and the length of the g, thirteen cubits. 8179
40:13 the g from the roof of one little chamber to 8179
40:14 unto the post of the court round about the g. 8179
40:15 from the face of the g of the entrance unto 8179
40:15 of the porch of the inner g were fifty cubits. 8179
40:16 to their posts within the g round about, 8179
40:19 g unto the forefront of the inner court 8179
40:20 the g of the outward court that looked 8179
40:21 were after the measure of the first g: 8179
40:22 were after the measure of the g that looketh 8179
40:23 the g of the inner court was over against 8179
40:23 was over against the g toward the north, 8179
40:23 he measured from g to gate an hundred 8179
40:23 he measured from gate to g an hundred 8179
40:24 the south, and behold a g toward the south: 8179
40:27 there was a g in the inner court toward 8179
40:27 he measured from g to gate toward 8179
40:27 he measured from gate to g toward 8179
40:28 me to the inner court by the south g: 8179
40:28 he measured the south g according to these 8179
40:32 he measured the g according to these 8179
40:35 he brought me to the north g, and 8179
40:39 in the porch of the g were two tables on this 8179
40:40 as one goeth up to the entry of the north g, 8179
40:40 which was at the porch of the g, were two 8179
40:41 four tables on that side, by the side of the g; 8179
40:44 without the inner g were the chambers of 8179
40:44 which was at the side of the north g; 8179
40:44 one at the side of the east g having 8179
40:48 the breadth of the g was three cubits on this 8179
42:15 he brought me forth toward the g whose 8179
43: 1 Afterward he brought me to the g, even 8179
43: 1 even the g that looketh toward the east: 8179
43: 4 of the g whose prospect is toward the east. 8179
44: 1 he brought me back the way of the g of 8179
44: 2 This g shall be shut, it shall not be opened, 8179
44: 3 enter by the way of the porch of that g, 8179
44: 4 brought he me the way of the north g 8179
45:19 upon the posts of the g of the inner court. 8179
46: 1 The g of the inner court that looketh toward 8179
46: 2 by the way of the porch of that g without, 8179
46: 2 shall stand by the post of the g, and 8179
46: 2 he shall worship at the threshold of the g: 8179
46: 2 but the g shall not be shut until the evening. 8179
46: 3 of this g before the LORD in the sabbaths 8179
46: 8 go in by the way of the porch of that g, 8179
46: 9 he that entereth in by the way of the north g 8179
46: 9 shall go out by the way of the south g; 8179
46: 9 he that entereth by the way of the south g 8179
46: 9 shall go forth by the way of the north g: 8179
46: 9 he shall not return by the way of the g 8179
46:12 open him the g that looketh toward the east, 8179
46:12 after his going forth one shall shut the g. 8179
46:19 the entry, which was at the side of the g, 8179
47: 2 brought he me out of the way of the g 8179
47: 2 utter g by the way that looketh eastward; 8179
48:31 one g of Reuben, one gate of Judah, 8179
48:31 one g of Judah, one gate of Levi. 8179
48:31 one gate of Judah, one g of Levi. 8179
48:32 one g of Joseph, one gate of Benjamin, 8179
48:32 one g of Benjamin, one gate of Dan. 8179
48:32 one gate of Benjamin, one g of Dan. 8179
48:33 one g of Simeon, one gate of Issachar, 8179
48:33 one gate of Simeon, one g of Issachar, 8179
48:33 one gate of Issachar, one g of Zebulun. 8179
48:34 one g of Gad, one gate of Asher, one gate 8179
48:34 one gate of Gad, one g of Asher, one gate 8179
48:34 one gate of Asher, one g of Naphtali. 8179
Da 2:49 but Daniel sat in the g of the king. 8651
Am 5:10 They hate him that rebuketh in the g, and 8179
5:12 they turn aside the poor in the g from their 8179
5:15 the good, and establish judgment in the g: 8179
Ob 1:13 Thou shouldest not have entered into the g 8179
Mic 1: 9 he is come unto the g of my people, even to 8179
1:12 from the LORD unto the g of Jerusalem. 8179
2:13 have passed through the g, and are gone out 8179
Zep 1:10 shall be the noise of a cry from the fish g, 8179
Zec 14:10 from Benjamin's g unto the place of 8179
14:10 gate unto the place of the first g, 8179
14:10 unto the corner g, and from the tower of 8179
Mt 7:13 Enter ye in at the strait g: for wide is 4439
7:13 for wide is the g, and broad is the way, 4439
7:14 Because strait is the g, and narrow is 4439
Lk 7:12 Now when he came nigh to the g of 4439
13:24 Strive to enter in at the strait g: for many, 4439
16:20 which was laid at his g, full of sores, 4440
Ac 3: 2 whom they laid daily at the g of the temple 2374
3:10 for alms at the Beautiful g of the temple: 4439
10:17 for Simon's house, and stood before the g, 4440
12:10 they came unto the iron g that leadeth unto 4439
12:13 And as Peter knocked at the door of the g, 4440
12:14 she opened not the g for gladness, but 4440
12:14 and told how Peter stood before the g. 4440
Heb 13:12 with his own blood, suffered without the g. 4439
Rev 21:21 every several g was of one pearl: 4440

GATES (144) [GATE]
Ex 20:10 nor thy stranger that is within thy g: 8179
Dt 3: 5 were fenced with high walls, g, and bars; 1817
5:14 nor thy stranger that is within thy g; 8179
6: 9 upon the posts of thy house, and on thy g. 8179
11:20 door posts of thine house, and upon thy g: 8179
12:12 and the Levite that is within your g; 8179
12:15 thou mayest kill and eat flesh in all thy g, 8179
12:17 Thou mayest not eat within thy g the tithe 8179
12:18 and the Levite that is within thy g: 8179
12:21 thou shalt eat in thy g whatsoever thy soul 8179
14:21 give it unto the stranger that is in thy g, 8179
14:27 the Levite that is within thy g; thou shalt 8179
14:28 same year, and shalt lay it up within thy g: 8179
14:29 the widow, which are within thy g, 8179
15: 7 g in thy land which the LORD thy God 8179

Dt 15:22 Thou shalt eat it within thy **g**: the unclean 8179
16: 5 sacrifice the passover within any of thy **g**, 8179
16:11 the Levite that *is* within thy **g**, and 8179
16:14 and the widow, that *are* within thy **g**. 8179
16:18 officers shalt thou make thee in all thy **g**, 8179
17: 2 within any of thy **g** which the LORD thy 8179
17: 5 unto thy **g**, *even that* man or *that* woman, 8179
17: 8 *being* matters of controversy within thy **g**: 8179
18: 6 if a Levite come from any of thy **g** out of 8179
23:16 place which he shall choose in one of thy **g**, 8179
24:14 strangers that *are* in thy land within thy **g**: 8179
26:12 that they may eat within thy **g**, and 8179
28:52 he shall besiege thee in all thy **g**, until thy 8179
28:52 he shall besiege thee in all thy **g** throughout 8179
28:55 enemies shall distress thee in all thy **g**. 8179
28:57 thine enemy shall distress thee in thy **g**. 8179
31:12 and thy stranger that *is* within thy **g**, 8179
Jos 6:26 in his youngest *son* shall he set up the **g** of 1817
Jdg 5: 8 chose new gods; then *was* war in the **g**: 8179
5:11 the people of the LORD go down to the **g**. 8179
1Sa 17:52 come *to* the valley, and to the **g** of Ekron. 8179
23: 7 by entering into a town that hath **g** and 1817
2Sa 18:24 David sat between the two **g**: and 8179
1Ki 16:34 set up the **g** thereof in his youngest *son* 1817
2Ki 23: 8 brake down the high places of the **g** that 8179
1Ch 9:19 keepers of the **g** of the tabernacle: 5592
9:22 to be porters in the **g** *were* two hundred 5592
9:23 their children had the oversight of the **g** of 8179
22: 3 for the nails for the doors of the **g**, 8179
2Ch 8: 5 fenced cities, *with* walls, **g**, and bars, 1817
14: 7 about *them* walls, and towers, **g**, and bars, 1817
23:19 he set the porters at the **g** of the house of 8179
31: 2 to praise in the **g** of the tents of 8179
Ne 1: 3 and the **g** thereof are burnt with fire. 8179
2: 3 and the **g** thereof are consumed with fire? 8179
2: 8 **g** of the palace which *appertained* to 8179
2:13 and the **g** thereof were consumed with fire. 8179
2:17 and the **g** thereof are burnt with fire: 8179
6: 1 time I had not set up the doors upon the **g**;) 8179
7: 3 Let not the **g** of Jerusalem be opened until 8179
11:19 Talmon, and their brethren that kept the **g**, 8179
12:25 keeping the ward at the thresholds of the **g**. 8179
12:30 purified the people, and the **g**, and the wall. 8179
13:19 that when the **g** of Jerusalem began to be 8179
13:19 I commanded that the **g** should be shut, and 1817
13:19 *some* of my servants set I at the **g**, 8179
13:22 *that* they should come *and* keep the **g**, 8179
Job 38:17 Have the **g** of death been opened unto thee? 8179
Ps 9:13 thou that liftest me up from the **g** of death: 8179
9:14 That I may shew forth all thy praise in the **g** 8179
24: 7 Lift up your heads, O ye **g**; and be ye lift 8179
24: 9 Lift up your heads, O ye **g**; even lift *them* 8179
87: 2 The LORD loveth the **g** of Zion more than 8179
100: 4 Enter *into* his **g** with thanksgiving, *and* 8179
107:16 For he hath broken the **g** of brass, and 1817
107:18 and they draw near unto the **g** of death. 8179
118:19 Open to me the **g** of righteousness: I will go 8179
122: 2 Our feet shall stand within thy **g**, 8179
147:13 For he hath strengthened the bars of thy **g**; 8179
Pr 1:21 of concourse, in the openings of the **g**: 8179
8: 3 She crieth at the **g**, at the entry of the city, 8179
8:34 watching daily at my **g**, waiting at the posts 1817
14:19 and the wicked at the **g** of the righteous. 8179
31:23 Her husband is known in the **g**, when he 8179
31:31 and let her own works praise her in the **g**. 8179
SS 7:13 at our **g** *are* all *manner of* pleasant *fruits*, 6607
Isa 3:26 her **g** shall lament and mourn; and 6607
13: 2 that they may go *into* the **g** of the nobles. 6607
26: 2 Open ye the **g**, that the righteous nation 8179
38:10 of my days, I shall go to the **g** of the grave: 8179
45: 1 to open before him the **two leaved g**; 1817
45: 1 leaved gates; and the **g** shall not be shut; 8179
45: 2 I will break in pieces the **g** of brass, and 1817
54:12 thy **g** of carbuncles, and all thy borders of 8179
60:11 Therefore thy **g** shall be open continually; 8179
60:18 call thy walls Salvation, and thy **g** Praise. 8179
62:10 Go through, go through the **g**; prepare you 8179
Jer 1:15 throne at the entering of the **g** of Jerusalem, 8179
7: 2 that enter in at these **g** to worship 8179
14: 2 Judah mourneth, and the **g** thereof languish; 8179
15: 7 I will fan them with a fan in the **g** of 8179
17:19 they go out, and in all the **g** of Jerusalem; 8179
17:20 of Jerusalem, that enter in by these **g**: 8179
17:21 nor bring *it* in by the **g** of Jerusalem; 8179
17:24 to bring in no burden through the **g** of this 8179
17:25 shall there enter into the **g** of this city kings 8179
17:27 even entering in at the **g** of Jerusalem on 8179
17:27 will I kindle a fire in the **g** thereof, and 8179
22: 2 and thy people that enter in by these **g**: 8179
22: 4 shall there enter in by the **g** of this house 8179
22:19 and cast forth beyond the **g** of Jerusalem. 8179
49:31 the LORD, which have neither **g** nor bars, 1817
51:58 her high **g** shall be burnt with fire; 8179
La 1: 4 all her **g** are desolate: her priests sigh: 8179
2: 9 Her **g** are sunk into the ground; he hath 8179
4:12 the enemy should have entered into the **g** of 8179
Eze 21:15 set the point of the sword against all their **g**, 8179
21:22 to appoint *battering* rams against the **g**, 8179
26: 2 she is broken *that was* the **g** of the people: 1817
26:10 the chariots, when he shall enter into thy **g**, 8179
38:11 and having neither bars nor **g**, 1817
40:18 the pavement by the side of the **g** over 8179
40:18 the length of the **g** *was* the lower pavement. 8179
40:38 entries thereof *were* by the posts of the **g**, 8179
44:11 *having* charge at the **g** of the house, and 8179
44:17 *that* when they enter in at the **g** of the inner 8179
44:17 whiles they minister in the **g** of the inner 8179
48:31 the **g** of the city *shall be* after the names of 8179
48:31 three **g** northward; one gate of Reuben, 8179
48:32 three **g**; and one gate of Joseph, one gate of 8179
48:33 three **g**; one gate of Simeon, one gate of 8179
48:34 and five hundred, *with* their three **g**; 8179
Ob 1:11 foreigners entered *into* his **g**, and cast lots 8179
Na 2: 6 The **g** of the rivers shall be opened, and 8179
3:13 the **g** of thy land shall be set wide open 8179

Zec 8:16 the judgment of truth and peace in your **g**: 8179
Mt 16:18 and the **g** of hell shall not prevail against it. *4439*
Ac 9:24 And they watched the **g** day and night to *4439*
14:13 brought oxen and garlands unto the **g**, and *4440*
Rev 21:12 and had twelve **g**, and at the gates twelve *4440*
21:12 and at the **g** twelve angels, and *4440*
21:13 On the east three **g**; on the north three *4440*
21:13 the east three gates; on the north three **g**; *4440*
21:13 on the south three **g**; and on the west three *4440*
21:13 south three gates; and on the west three **g**. *4440*
21:15 and the **g** thereof, and the wall thereof. *4440*
21:21 And the twelve **g** *were* twelve pearls; *4440*
21:25 And the **g** of it shall not be shut at all by *4440*
22:14 and may enter in through the **g** into the city. *4440*

GATH (33) [GATH-HEPHER, GATH-RIMMON, GITTITE, GITTITES, MORESHETH-GATH]

Jos 11:22 only in Gaza, in **G**, and in Ashdod, 1661
1Sa 5: 8 the God of Israel be carried about *unto* **G**. 1661
6:17 for Askelon one, for **G** one, for Ekron one; 1661
7:14 restored to Israel, from Ekron even unto **G**; 1661
17: 4 named Goliath, of **G**, whose height *was* six 1661
17:23 the Philistine of **G**, Goliath by name, 1661
17:52 to Shaaraim, even unto **G**, and unto Ekron. 1661
21:10 of Saul, and went to Achish the king of **G**. 1661
21:12 was sore afraid of Achish the king of **G**. 1661
27: 2 unto Achish, the son of Maoch, king of **G**. 1661
27: 3 David dwelt with Achish at **G**, he and 1661
27: 4 it was told Saul that David was fled to **G**: 1661
27:11 to bring *tidings* to **G**, saying, Lest they 1661
2Sa 1:20 Tell *it* not in **G**, publish *it* not in the streets 1661
15:18 men which came after him from **G**, 1661
21:20 there was yet a battle in **G**, where was a 1661
21:22 These four were born to the giant in **G**, and 1661
1Ki 2:39 unto Achish son of Maachah king of **G**. 1661
2:39 Behold, thy servants *be* in **G**. 1661
2:40 went to **G** to Achish to seek his servants: 1661
2:40 and brought his servants from **G**. 1661
2:41 that Shimei had gone from Jerusalem *to* **G**, 1661
2Ki 12:17 went up, and fought against **G**, and took it: 1661
1Ch 7:21 whom the men of **G** that were born in *that* 1661
8:13 who drove away the inhabitants of **G**: 1661
18: 1 took **G** and her towns out of the hand of 1661
20: 6 yet again there was war at **G**, where was a 1661
20: 8 These were born unto the giant in **G**; and 1661
2Ch 11: 8 And **G**, and Mareshah, and Ziph, 1661
26: 6 brake down the wall of **G**, and the wall of 1661
Ps 56: T when the Philistines took him in **G**. 1661
Am 6: 2 go down *to* **G** of the Philistines: *be they* 1661
Mic 1:10 Declare ye *it* not at **G**, weep ye not at all: 1661

GATHER (163) [GATHERED, GATHERER, GATHEREST, GATHERETH, GATHERING, GATHERINGS, GRAPEGATHERER, GRAPEGATHERERS, GRAPE-GATHERERS, INGATHERING]

Ge 6:21 food that is eaten, and thou shalt **g** *it* to thee; 622
31:46 Jacob said unto his brethren, **G** stones; and 3950
34:30 they shall **g** themselves **together** against me, 622
41:35 let them **g** all the food of those good years 6908
49: 1 his sons, and said, **G** yourselves **together**, 622
49: 2 **G** yourselves **together**, and hear, ye sons of 6908
Ex 3:16 **g** the elders of Israel **together**, and say unto 622
5: 7 let them go and **g** straw for themselves. 7197
5:12 Egypt to **g stubble** instead of straw. 7179+7197
9:19 *and* **g** thy cattle, and all that thou hast in 5756
16: 4 shall go out and **g** a certain rate every day, 3950
16: 5 it shall be twice as much as they **g** daily. 3950
16:16 **G** of it every man according to his eating, 3950
16:26 Six days ye shall **g** it; but on the seventh 3950
16:27 of the people on the seventh day for to **g**, 3950
23:10 thy land, and shalt **g** in the fruits thereof: 622
Lev 8: 3 **g** thou all the congregation **together** unto 6950
19: 9 neither shalt thou **g** the gleanings of thy 3950
19:10 neither shalt thou **g** *every* grape of thy 3950
23:22 neither shalt thou **g** *any* gleaning of thy 3950
25: 3 prune thy vineyard, and **g** in the fruit thereof; 622
25: 5 neither **g** the grapes of thy vine undressed: 1219
25:11 nor **g** *the grapes* in it of thy vine undressed. 1219
25:20 we shall not sow, nor **g in** our increase: 622
Nu 8: 9 **g** the whole assembly of the children of Israel **together**: 6950
10: 4 of Israel, shall **g** themselves unto thee. 3259
11:16 **G** unto me seventy men of the elders of 622
19: 9 a man *that is* clean shall **g up** the ashes of 622
20: 8 **g** thou the assembly **together**, thou, and 6950
21:16 **G** the people **together**, and I will give them 622
Dt 4:10 **G** me the people **together**, and I will make 6950
11:14 that thou mayest **g in** thy corn, and thy wine, 622
13:16 thou shalt **g** all the spoil of it into the midst 6908
28:30 and shalt not **g the grapes** thereof. 2490
28:38 out *into* the field, and shalt **g** *but* little **in**; 622
28:39 nor **g** *the grapes;* for the worms shall eat 103
30: 3 will return and **g** thee from all the nations, 6908
30: 4 from thence will the LORD thy God **g** 6908
31:12 **G** the people **together**, men, and women, 6950
31:28 **G** unto me all the elders of your tribes, and 6950
Ru 2: 7 and **g** after the reapers amongst the sheaves: 622
1Sa 7: 5 **G** all Israel to Mizpeh, and I will pray for 6908
2Sa 3:21 and will **g** all Israel unto my lord the king, 6908
12:28 therefore **g** the rest of the people **together**, 622
1Ki 18:19 *and* **g** to me all Israel unto mount Carmel, 6908
2Ki 4:39 one went out into the field to **g** herbs, and 3950
22:20 I will **g** thee unto thy fathers, and thou shalt 622
1Ch 13: 2 that they may **g** themselves unto us: 6908
16:35 **g** us **together**, and deliver us from 6908
22: 2 David commanded to **g together** 3664
2Ch 24: 5 **g** of all Israel money to repair the house of 6908
34:28 I will **g** thee to thy fathers, and thou shalt be 622
Ezr 10: 7 that *they* should **g** themselves **together** 6908
Ne 1: 9 *yet* will I **g** them from thence, and 6908
7: 5 my God put into mine heart to **g together** 6908
12:44 to **g** into them out of the fields of the cities 3664
Est 2: 3 that they may **g together** all the fair young 6908

Est 4:16 **g together** all the Jews that are present in 3664
8:11 in every city to **g** themselves **together**, 6950
Job 11:10 or **g together**, then who can hinder him? 6950
24: 6 and they **g** the vintage of the wicked. 3953
34:14 If he set his heart upon *man, if* he **g** unto 622
39:12 bring home thy seed, and **g** *it into* thy barn? 622
Ps 26: 9 **G** not my soul with sinners, nor my life with 622
39: 6 and knoweth not who shall **g** them. 622
50: 5 **G** my saints together unto me; those that 622
56: 6 They **g** themselves **together**, they hide 1481
94:21 They **g** themselves **together** against 1413
104:22 they **g** themselves **together**, and lay them 622
104:28 *That* thou givest them they **g**: thou openest 3950
106:47 our God, and **g** us from among the heathen, 6908
Pr 28: 8 he shall **g** it for him that will pity the poor. 6908
Ecc 2:26 sinner he giveth travail, to **g** and to heap up, 622
3: 5 and a time to **g** stones **together**; 3664
SS 6: 2 to feed in the gardens, and to **g** lilies. 3950
Isa 10:31 inhabitants of Gebim **g** themselves **to flee**. 5756
11:12 **g together** the dispersed of Judah from 6908
34:15 lay, and hatch, and **g** under her shadow: 1716
40:11 he shall **g** the lambs with his arm, and 6908
43: 5 from the east, and **g** thee from the west; 6908
49:18 all these **g** themselves **together**, *and* 6908
54: 7 but with great mercies will I **g** thee. 6908
54:15 they shall **surely g together**, *but* 1481+1481
54:15 whosoever shall **g together** against thee 1481
56: 8 Yet will I **g** *others* to him, besides those 6908
60: 4 all they **g** themselves **together**, they come 6908
62:10 cast up the highway; **g** out the stones; 5619
66:18 that *I* will **g** all nations and tongues; 6908
Jer 4: 5 cry, **g together**, and say, 4390
6: 1 **g** yourselves **to flee** out of the midst of 5756
7:18 The children **g** wood, and the fathers kindle 3950
9:22 after the harvestman, and none shall **g** *them*. 622
10:17 **G up** thy wares out of the land, O inhabitant 622
23: 3 I will **g** the remnant of my flock out of all 6908
29:14 I will **g** you from all the nations, and 6908
31: 8 and **g** them from the coasts of the earth, *and* 6908
31:10 He that scattered Israel will **g** him, and 6908
32:37 Behold, I *will* **g** them out of all countries, 6908
40:10 ye, **g** ye wine, and summer fruits, and oil, 622
49: 5 none shall **g up** him that wandereth. 6908
49:14 *saying*, **G** ye **together**, and come against 6908
51:11 **g** the shields: the LORD hath raised up 4390
Eze 11:17 I will even **g** you from the people, and 6908
16:37 Behold therefore, I will **g** all thy lovers, 6908
16:37 I will even **g** them round about against thee, 6908
20:34 will **g** you out of the countries wherein ye 6908
20:41 **g** you out of the countries wherein ye have 6908
22:19 I will **g** you into the midst of Jerusalem. 6908
22:20 As *they* **g** silver, and brass, and iron, and 6910
22:20 to melt *it;* so will I **g** *you* in mine anger and 6908
22:21 I will **g** you, and blow upon you in the fire 3664
24: 4 **G** the pieces thereof into it, *even* every good 622
29:13 At the end of forty years will I **g** 6908
34:13 **g** them from the countries, and will bring 6908
36:24 **g** you out of all countries, and will bring 6908
37:21 will **g** them on every side, and bring them 6908
39:17 **g** yourselves on every side to my sacrifice 622
Da 3: 2 the king sent to **g together** 3673
Hos 8:10 now will I **g** them, and they shall sorrow a 6908
9: 6 Egypt shall **g** them **up**, Memphis shall bury 6908
Joel 1:14 **g** the elders *and* all the inhabitants of 622
2: 6 be much pained: all faces shall **g** blackness. 6908
2:16 **G** the people, sanctify the congregation, 622
2:16 **g** the children, and those that suck 622
3: 2 I will also **g** all nations, and will bring them 6908
3:11 and **g** yourselves **together** round about: 6908
Mic 2:12 I will **surely g** the remnant of Israel; 6908+6908
4: 6 I will **g** her that is driven out, and *her* that I 6908
4:12 for he shall **g** them as the sheaves into 6908
5: 1 Now **g** thyself **in troops**, O daughter of 1413
Na 2:10 and the faces of them all **g** blackness. 6908
Hab 1: 9 and they shall **g** the captivity as the sand. 622
1:15 them in their net, and **g** them in their drag: 622
Zep 2: 1 **G** yourselves **together**, yea, 7197
2: 1 yea, **g together**, O nation not desired; 7197
3: 8 for my determination *is* to **g** the nations, 622
3:18 I will **g** *them that are* sorrowful for 622
3:19 that halteth, and **g** her that was driven out; 6908
3:20 you *again*, even in the time that I **g** you: 6908
Zec 10: 8 I will hiss for them, and **g** them; for I have 6908
10:10 land of Egypt, and **g** them out of Assyria; 6908
14: 2 For I will **g** all nations against Jerusalem to 622
Mt 3:12 his floor, and **g** his wheat into the garner; *4863*
6:26 neither do they reap, nor **g** into barns; *4863*
7:16 Do *men* **g** grapes of thorns, or figs of *4816*
13:28 Wilt thou then *that* we go and **g** them **up**? *4816*
13:29 lest while ye **g up** the tares, ye root up also *4816*
13:30 **G** ye **together** first the tares, and bind them *4816*
13:30 to burn them: but **g** the wheat into my barn. *4863*
13:41 they shall **g** out of his kingdom all things *4816*
24:31 they shall **g together** his elect from the four *1996*
25:26 sowed not, and **g** where I have not strawed: *4863*
Mk 13:27 shall **g together** his elect from the four *1996*
Lk 3:17 and will **g** the wheat into his garner; *4863*
6:44 For of thorns *men* do not **g** figs, nor of a *4816*
6:44 nor of a bramble bush **g** they grapes. *5166*
13:34 as a hen *doth* **g** her brood under *her* wings, NIG
Jn 6:12 **G up** the fragments that remain, *4863*
11:52 that also he should **g together** in one *4863*
15: 6 and *men* **g** them, and cast *them* into the fire, *4863*
Eph 1:10 might **g together in one** all *things* in Christ, *346*
Rev 14:18 and **g** the clusters of the vine of the earth; *5166*
16:14 to **g** them to the battle of that great day of *4863*
19:17 **g** yourselves **together** unto the supper of *4863*
20: 8 and Magog, to **g** them **together** to battle: *4863*

GATHERED (267) [GATHER]

Ge 1: 9 the heaven be **g together** unto one place, 6960
12: 5 all their substance that they had **g**, and 7408
25: 8 and full *of years;* and was **g** to his people. 622
25:17 and died; and was **g** unto his people. 622
29: 3 thither were all the flocks **g**: and they rolled 622

Ge 29: 7 *is it* time that the cattle should be **g together**: 622
29: 8 until all the flocks be **g together**, and 622
29:22 Laban **g together** all the men of the place, 622
35:29 died, and was **g** unto his people, *being* old 622
41:48 And he **g up** all the food of the seven years, 6908
41:49 Joseph **g** corn as the sand of the sea, 6651
47:14 Joseph **g up** all the money that was found 3950
49:29 said unto them, I *am to be* **g** unto my people: 622
49:33 he **g up** his feet into the bed, and yielded up 622
49:33 up the ghost, and was **g** unto his people. 622
Ex 4:29 **g together** all the elders of the children of 622
8:14 they **g** them **together** upon heaps: and 6651
15: 8 of thy nostrils the waters were **g together**, 6192
16:17 Israel did so, and **g**, some more, some less. 3950
16:18 he that **g much** had nothing over, and 7235
16:18 and he that **g little** had no lack; 4591
16:18 they **g** every man according to his eating. 3950
16:21 they **g** it every morning, every man 3950
16:22 *that* on the sixth day they **g** twice as much 3950
23:16 when thou hast **g in** thy labours out of 622
32: 1 the people **g** themselves **together** unto 6950
32:26 all the sons of Levi **g** themselves **together** 622
35: 1 **g** all the congregation of the children of Israel
together, 6950
Lev 8: 4 the assembly was **g together** unto the door 6950
23:39 when ye have **g in** the fruit of the land, 622
26:25 when ye are **g together** within your cities, 622
Nu 10: 7 when the congregation is to be **g together**, 6950
11: 8 **g** *it*, and ground *it* in mills, or beat *it* in a 3950
11:22 shall all the fish of the sea be **g together** for 622
11:24 **g** the seventy men of the elders of 622
11:32 and all the next day, and they **g** the quails: 622
11:32 he that **g least** gathered ten homers: and 4591
11:32 he that gathered least **g** ten homers: and 622
14:35 that are **g together** against me: 3259
15:32 they found a man that **g** sticks upon 7197
16: 3 they **g** themselves **together** against Moses 6950
16:11 all thy company *are* **g together** against 3259
16:19 Korah **g** all the congregation against them 6950
16:42 when the congregation was **g** against 6950
20: 2 they **g** themselves **together** against Moses 6950
20:10 Aaron **g** the congregation **together** before 6950
20:24 Aaron shall be **g** unto his people: for he shall 622
20:26 Aaron shall be **g** *unto his people*, and 622
21:23 Sihon **g** all his people **together**, and 622
27: 3 **g** themselves **together** against the LORD 3259
27:13 seen it, thou also shalt be **g** unto thy people, 622
27:13 unto thy people, as Aaron thy brother was **g**. 622
31: 2 afterward shalt thou be **g** unto thy people. 622
Dt 16:13 after that thou hast **g in** thy corn and thy 622
32:50 thou goest up, and be **g** unto thy people; 622
32:50 in mount Hor, and was **g** unto his people: 622
33: 5 *and* the tribes of Israel were **g** together. 622
Jos 9: 2 That they **g** themselves together, to fight 6908
10: 5 **g** themselves **together**, and went up, they 622
10: 6 in the mountains are **g together** against us. 6908
22:12 of Israel **g** themselves **together** *at* Shiloh, 6950
24: 1 Joshua **g** all the tribes of Israel to Shechem, 622
Jdg 1: 7 toes cut off, **g** *their meat* under my table: 3950
2:10 also all that generation were **g** unto their 622
3:13 he **g** unto him the children of Ammon and 622
4:13 Sisera **g together** all his chariots, *even* nine 2199
6:33 and the children of the east were **g** together, 622
6:34 a trumpet; and Abi-ezer was **g** after him. 2199
6:35 all Manasseh; who also was **g** after him: 2199
7:23 the men of Israel **g** themselves **together** out 6817
7:24 the men of Ephraim **g** themselves **together**, 6817
9: 6 And all the men of Shechem **g together**, and 622
9:27 **g** their vineyards, and trode *the grapes*, and 1219
9:47 of the tower of Shechem were **g together**. 6908
10:17 the children of Ammon were **g together**, 6817
11: 3 there were **g** vain men to Jephthah, and 3950
11:20 Sihon **g** all his people **together**, and 622
12: 1 men of Ephraim **g themselves together**, 6817
12: 4 Jephthah **g together** all the men of Gilead, 6908
16:23 the lords of the Philistines **g** them **together** 622
18:22 near to Micah's house were **g together**, 2199
20: 1 the congregation was **g together** as one 6950
20:11 So all the men of Israel were **g** against 622
20:14 **g** themselves **together** out of the cities unto 622
1Sa 5: 8 **g** all the lords of the Philistines unto them, 622
5:11 **g together** all the lords of the Philistines, 622
7: 6 they **g together** to Mizpeh, and drew water, 6908
7: 7 of Israel were **g together** to Mizpeh, 6908
8: 4 the elders of Israel **g** themselves **together**, 6908
13: 5 the Philistines **g** themselves **together** to fight 622
13:11 *that* the Philistines **g** themselves **together** *at* 622
14:48 he **g** a host, and smote the Amalekites, and 6213
15: 4 Saul **g** the people **together**, and 8085
17: 1 Now the Philistines **g together** their armies 622
17: 1 were **g together** *at* Shochoh, 622
17: 2 and the men of Israel were **g together**, 622
20:38 Jonathan's lad **g up** the arrows, and 3950
22: 2 *was* discontented, **g** themselves unto him; 6908
25: 1 all the Israelites were **g together**, and 6908
28: 1 that the Philistines **g** their armies **together** 6908
28: 4 the Philistines **g** themselves **together**, and 6908
28: 4 Saul **g** all Israel **together**, and they pitched 6908
29: 1 Now the Philistines **g together** all their 6908
2Sa 2:25 **g** themselves **together** after Abner, 6908
2:30 when he had **g** all the people **together**, 6908
6: 1 David **g together** all the chosen *men* of 622
10:15 before Israel, they **g** themselves together. 622
10:17 he **g** all Israel **together**, and passed over 622
12:29 David **g** all the people **together**, and went to 622
14:14 which cannot be **g up** *again;* neither doth 622
17:11 *that* all Israel be **generally g** unto thee, 622+622
20:14 they were **g together**, and went also after 6950
21:13 they **g** the bones of them that were hanged. 622
23: 9 that were there **g together** to battle, 622
23:11 the Philistines were **g together** into a troop, 622
1Ki 10:26 Solomon **g together** chariots and horsemen: 622
11:24 he **g** men unto him, and became captain 6908
18:20 **g** the prophets **together** unto mount 6908
20: 1 the king of Syria **g** all his host **together**: 6908
1Ki 22: 6 the king of Israel **g** the prophets **together**, 6908
2Ki 3:21 they **g** all that *were able to* put on armour, 6817
4:39 **g** thereof wild gourds his lap full, and came 3950
6:24 that Ben-hadad king of Syria **g** all his host, 6908
10:18 Jehu **g** all the people **together**, and 6908
22: 4 which the keepers of the door have **g** of 622
22: 9 Thy servants have **g** the money that was 5413
22:20 and thou shalt be **g** into thy grave in peace; 622
23: 1 they **g** unto him all the elders of Judah and 622
1Ch 11: 1 all Israel **g** themselves to David unto 6908
11:13 there the Philistines were **g together** to 622
13: 5 So David **g** all Israel **together**, from Shihor 6950
15: 3 David **g** all Israel **together** to Jerusalem, 6950
19: 7 **g** themselves **together** from their cities, 622
19:17 he **g** all Israel, and passed over Jordan, and 622
23: 2 he **g together** all the princes of Israel, 622
2Ch 1:14 And Solomon **g** chariots and horsemen: and 622
11: 1 he **g** *of* the house of Judah and Benjamin an 6950
12: 5 that were **g together** to Jerusalem because 622
13: 7 there are **g** unto him vain men, the children 6908
15: 9 he **g** all Judah and Benjamin, and 6908
15:10 So they **g** themselves **together** *at* Jerusalem 6908
18: 5 Therefore the king of Israel **g together** *of* 6908
20: 4 Judah **g** themselves **together**, to ask *help* of 6908
23: 2 **g** the Levites out of all the cities of Judah, 6908
24: 5 he **g together** the priests and the Levites, 6908
24:11 did day by day, and **g** money in abundance. 622
25: 5 Moreover Amaziah **g** Judah **together**, and 6908
28:24 Ahaz **g together** the vessels of the house of 622
29: 4 and **g** them **together** into the east street, 622
29:15 they **g** their brethren, and 622
29:20 **g** the rulers of the city, and went up *to* 622
30: 3 people **g** themselves **together** to Jerusalem. 622
32: 4 So there was **g** much people **together**, 6908
32: 6 **g** them **together** to him in the street of 6908
34: 9 which the Levites that kept the doors had **g** 622
34:17 they have **g together** the money that was 5413
34:28 and thou shalt be **g** to thy grave in peace, 622
34:29 **g together** all the elders of Judah and 622
Ezr 3: 1 the people **g** themselves **together** as one 622
7:28 I **g together** out of Israel chief *men* to go 6908
8:15 I **g** them **together** to the river that runneth 6908
10: 9 Benjamin **g** themselves **together** *unto* 6908
Ne 5:16 all my servants *were* **g** thither unto 6908
8: 1 all the people **g** themselves **together** as one 622
8:13 on the second day were **g together** the chief 622
12:28 sons of the singers **g** themselves **together**, 622
13:11 I **g** them **together**, and set them in their 6908
Est 2: 8 when many maidens were **g together** unto 6908
2:19 when the virgins were **g together** 6908
9: 2 The Jews **g** themselves **together** in their 6950
9:15 **g** themselves **together** on the fourteenth 6950
9:16 king's provinces **g** themselves **together**, 6950
Job 16:10 they have **g** themselves together against 4390
27:19 *man* shall lie down, but he shall not be **g**: 622
30: 7 under the nettles they were **g together**. 5596
Ps 35:15 they rejoiced, and **g** themselves **together**: 622
35:15 *yea*, the abjects **g** themselves **together** 622
47: 9 The princes of the people are **g together**, 622
59: 3 the mighty are **g** against me; not *for* my 1481
102:22 When the people are **g** together, and 6908
107: 3 **g** them out of the lands, from the east, and 6908
140: 2 continually are they **g together** *for* war. 1481
Pr 27:25 and herbs of the mountains are **g**. 622
30: 4 who hath **g** the wind in his fists? who hath 622
Ecc 2: 8 I **g** me also silver and gold, and the peculiar 3664
SS 5: 1 I have **g** my myrrh with my spice; I have 717
Isa 5: 2 **g out** the **stones** thereof, and planted it *with* 5619
10:14 eggs *that are* left, have I **g** all the earth; 622
13: 4 noise of the kingdoms of nations **g together**: 622
22: 9 ye **g together** the waters of the lower pool. 6908
24:22 they shall be **g together**, *as* prisoners 622+626
24:22 *as* prisoners are **g** in the pit, and shall be NIH
27:12 ye shall be **g** one by one, O ye children of 3950
33: 4 your spoil shall be **g** *like* the gathering of 622
34:15 there shall the vultures also be **g**, every one 6908
34:16 and his spirit it hath **g** them. 6908
43: 9 Let all the nations be **g** together, and let 6908
44:11 let them all be **g together**, let them stand 6908
49: 5 Jacob again to him, Though Israel be not **g**, 622
56: 8 to him, besides those that are **g** unto him. 6908
60: 7 All the flocks of Kedar shall be **g together** 6908
62: 9 they that have **g** it shall eat it, and praise 622
Jer 3:17 all the nations shall be **g** unto it, to 6960
8: 2 they shall not be **g**, nor be buried; they shall 622
25:33 shall not be lamented, neither **g**, nor buried; 622
26: 9 all the people were **g** against Jeremiah in 6950
40:12 and **g** wine and summer fruits very much. 622
40:15 that all the Jews which are **g** unto thee 6908
Eze 28:25 When I shall have **g** the house of Israel 6908
29: 5 thou shalt not be brought together, nor **g**: 6908
38: 8 *and is* **g** out of many people, against 6908
38:12 upon the people *that are* **g** out of the nations, 622
38:13 hast thou **g** thy company to take a prey? to 6950
39:27 **g** them out of their enemies' lands, and 6908
39:28 I have **g** them unto their own land, and 3664
Da 3: 3 were **g together** unto the dedication of 3673
3:27 being **g together**, saw these men, 3673
Hos 1:11 and the children of Israel be **g** together, 6908
10:10 *the* people shall be **g** against them, 622
Mic 1: 7 for she **g** *it* of the hire of a harlot, and 6908
4:11 Now also many nations are **g** against thee, 622
7: 1 for I am as when they have **g** the summer 625
Zec 12: 3 people of the earth be **g together** against it. 622
14:14 the heathen round about shall be **g together**, 622
Mt 2: 4 **g** all the chief priests and scribes of the people
together, *4863*
13: 2 And great multitudes were **g together** unto *4863*
13:40 As therefore the tares are **g** and burnt in *4816*
13:47 *was* cast into the sea, and **g** of every kind: *4863*
13:48 and **g** the good into vessels, but cast the bad *4816*
18:20 or three are **g together** in my name, *4863*
22:10 and **g together** all as many as they found, *4863*
22:34 Sadducees to silence, they were **g** together. *4863*
22:41 While the Pharisees were **g together**, Jesus *4863*
Mt 23:37 often would I have **g** thy children **together**, *1996*
24:28 there will the eagles be **g together**. *4863*
25:32 And before him shall be **g** all nations: and *4863*
27:17 Therefore when they were **g together**, *4863*
27:27 and **g** unto him the whole band *of soldiers*. *4863*
Mk 1:33 And all the city was **g together** at the door. *1996*
2: 2 And straightway many were **g together**, *4863*
4: 1 and there was **g** unto him a great multitude, *4863*
5:21 the other side, much people **g** unto him: *4863*
6:30 And the apostles **g** themselves **together** *4863*
Lk 8: 4 And when much people were **g together**, *4896*
11:29 when the people were **g thick together**, *1865*
12: 1 when there were **g together** an *1996*
13:34 often would I have **g** thy children **together**, *1996*
15:13 days after the younger son **g** all **together**, *4863*
17:37 *is*, thither will the eagles be **g together**. *4863*
24:33 and found the eleven **g together**, and *4867*
Jn 6:13 Therefore they **g** *them* **together**, and *4863*
11:47 Then **g** the chief priests and the Pharisees a *4863*
Ac 4: 6 high priest, were **g together** at Jerusalem. *4863*
4:26 the rulers were **g** together against the Lord, *4863*
4:27 and the people of Israel, were **g together**, *4863*
12:12 where many were **g together** praying. *4867*
14:27 were come, and had **g** the church **together**, *4863*
15:30 when they had **g** the multitude **together**, *4863*
17: 5 and **g a company**, and set all the city on an *3792*
20: 8 where they were **g together**. *4863*
28: 3 And when Paul had **g** a bundle of sticks, *4962*
1Co 5: 4 when ye are **g together**, and my spirit, *4863*
2Co 8:15 He that *had* **g** much had nothing over; NIG
8:15 and he that *had* **g** little had no lack. NIG
Rev 14:19 and **g** the vine of the earth, and cast *it* into *5166*
16:16 And he **g** them **together** into a place called *4863*
19:19 **g together** to make war against him that sat *4863*

GATHERER (1) [GATHER]

Am 7:14 I *was* a herdman, and a **g** of sycomore fruit: 1103

GATHEREST (1) [GATHER]

Dt 24:21 When thou **g** the **grapes** of thy vineyard, 1219

GATHERETH (17) [GATHER]

Nu 19:10 he that **g** the ashes of the heifer shall wash 622
Ps 33: 7 He **g** the waters of the sea **together** as a 3664
41: 6 his heart **g** iniquity to itself; *when* he goeth 6908
147: 2 he **g together** the outcasts of Israel. 3664
Pr 6: 8 in the summer, *and* **g** her food in the harvest. 103
10: 5 He that **g** in summer *is* a wise son: *but* 103
13:11 but he that **g** by labour shall increase. 6908
Isa 10:14 as *one* **g** eggs *that are* left, have I gathered all 622
17: 5 it shall be as when the harvestman **g** 622
17: 5 it shall be as he that **g** ears in the valley of 3950
56: 8 The Lord GOD which **g** the outcasts of 6908
Na 3:18 upon the mountains, and no man **g** *them*. 6908
Hab 2: 5 **g** unto him all nations, and heapeth unto him 622
Mt 12:30 and he that **g** not with me scattereth abroad. *4863*
23:37 even as a hen **g** her chickens under *her* *1996*
Lk 11:23 and he that **g** not with me scattereth. *4863*
Jn 4:36 and **g** fruit unto life eternal: *4863*

GATHERING (11) [GATHER]

Ge 1:10 the **g together** of the waters called he Seas: 4723
49:10 and unto him *shall* the **g** of the people *be*. 3349
Nu 15:33 they that found him **g** sticks brought him 7197
1Ki 17:10 the widow woman *was* there **g** of sticks: 7197
17:12 behold, I *am* **g** two sticks, that I may go in 7197
2Ch 20:25 they were three days in **g** of the spoil, it was 962
Isa 32:10 the vintage shall fail, the **g** shall not come. 625
33: 4 your spoil shall be gathered *like* the **g** of 625
Mt 25:24 and **g** where thou hast not strawed: *4863*
Ac 16:10 **assuredly g** that the Lord had called us for *4822*
2Th 2: 1 and *by* our **g together** unto him, *1997*

GATHERINGS (1) [GATHER]

1Co 16: 2 that there be no **g** when I come. *3048*

GATH-HEPHER (1) [GATH, GITTAH-HEPHER, HEPHER]

2Ki 14:25 of Amittai, the prophet, which *was* of **G**. 1661

GATH-RIMMON (4) [GATH, RIMMON]

Jos 19:45 And Jehud, and Bene-berak, and **G**, 1667
21:24 with her suburbs, **G** with her suburbs; 1667
21:25 with her suburbs, and **G** with her suburbs; 1667
1Ch 6:69 with her suburbs, and **G** with her suburbs: 1667

GAVE (465) [GIVE]

Ge 2:20 Adam **g** names to all cattle, and to the fowl 7121
3: 6 and **g** also unto her husband with her; 5414
3:12 with me, she **g** me of the tree, and I did eat. 5414
14:20 into thy hand. And he **g** him tithes of all. 5414
16: 3 **g** her to her husband Abram to be his wife. 5414
18: 7 and good, and **g** *it* unto a young man; 5414
20:14 **g** *them* unto Abraham, and restored him 5414
21:14 and a bottle of water, and **g** *it* unto Hagar, 5414
21:19 the bottle *with* water, and **g** the lad **drink**. 8248
21:27 and oxen, and **g** *them* unto Abimelech; 5414
24:18 pitcher upon her hand, and **g** him **drink**. 8248
24:32 **g** straw and provender for the camels, and 5414
24:53 and raiment, and **g** *them* to Rebekah: 5414
24:53 he **g** also to her brother and to her mother 5414
25: 5 And Abraham **g** all that he had unto Isaac. 5414
25: 6 Abraham **g** gifts, and sent them away from 5414
25: 8 Abraham **g up the ghost**, and died in a 1478
25:17 he **g up the ghost** and died; and 1478
25:34 Jacob **g** Esau bread and pottage of lentiles; 5414
27:17 she **g** the savoury meat and the bread, 5414
28: 4 art a stranger, which God **g** unto Abraham. 5414
28: 6 that as he blessed him he **g** him **a charge**, 6680
29:24 Laban **g** unto his daughter Leah Zilpah his 5414
29:28 he **g** him Rachel his daughter to wife *also*. 5414
29:29 Laban **g** to Rachel his daughter Bilhah his 5414
30: 4 she **g** him Bilhah her handmaid to wife: 5414
30: 9 Zilpah her maid, and **g** her Jacob to wife. 5414

Ge 30:35 and **g** *them* into the hand of his sons. 5414
35: 4 they **g** unto Jacob all the strange gods 5414
35:12 the land which I **g** Abraham and Isaac, 5414
35:29 Isaac **g up the ghost**, and died, and 1478
38:18 he **g** *it* her, and came in unto her, and 5414
38:26 because that I **g** her not to Shelah my son. 5414
39:21 **g** him favour in the sight of the keeper of 5414
40:11 and I **g** the cup into Pharaoh's hand. 5414
40:21 and he **g** the cup into Pharaoh's hand: 5414
41:45 he **g** him to wife Asenath the daughter of 5414
43:24 **g** *them* water, and they washed their feet; 5414
43:24 their feet; and he **g** their asses provender. 5414
45:21 Joseph **g** them wagons, according to 5414
45:21 and **g** them provision for the way. 5414
45:22 To all of them he **g** each man changes of 5414
45:22 to Benjamin he **g** three hundred *pieces* of 5414
46:18 whom Laban **g** to Leah his daughter, and 5414
46:25 which Laban **g** unto Rachel his daughter, 5414
47:11 **g** them a possession in the land of Egypt, 5414
47:17 Joseph **g** them bread *in exchange* for 5414
47:22 did eat their portion which Pharaoh **g** them: 5414
Ex 2:21 and he **g** Moses Zipporah his daughter. 5414
6:13 **g** them **a charge** unto the children of Israel, 6680
11: 3 the LORD **g** the people favour in the sight 5414
12:36 the LORD **g** the people favour in the sight 5414
14:20 *to them*, but it **g light** by night *to these:* so 215
31:18 he **g** unto Moses, when he had made an end 5414
32:24 So they **g** *it* me: then I cast it into the fire, 5414
34:32 he **g** them **in commandment** all that 6680
36: 6 Moses **g commandment**, and they caused 6680
Nu 3:51 Moses **g** the money of them that were 5414
7: 6 and the oxen, and **g** them unto the Levites. 5414
7: 7 four oxen he **g** unto the sons of Gershon, 5414
7: 8 eight oxen he **g** unto the sons of Merari, 5414
7: 9 unto the sons of Kohath he **g** none: because 5414
11:25 upon him, and **g** *it* unto the seventy elders: 5414
17: 6 every one of their princes **g** him a rod 5414
27:23 his hands upon him, and **g** him **a charge**, 6680
31:41 Moses **g** the tribute, *which was* 5414
31:47 and of beast, and **g** them unto the Levites, 5414
32:33 Moses **g** unto them, *even* to the children of 5414
32:38 **g** other names unto the cities which they 7121
32:40 Moses **g** Gilead unto Machir the son of 5414
Dt 2:12 which the LORD **g** unto them.) 5414
3:12 **g** I unto the Reubenites and to the Gadites. 5414
3:13 of Og, **g** I unto the half tribe of Manasseh; 5414
3:15 And I **g** Gilead unto Machir. 5414
3:16 unto the Gadites I **g** from Gilead even unto 5414
9:11 *that* the LORD **g** me the two tables of 5414
10: 4 and the LORD **g** them unto me. 5414
22:16 I **g** my daughter unto this man to wife, and 5414
29: 8 **g** it for an inheritance unto the Reubenites, 5414
31:23 he **g** Joshua the son of Nun **a charge**, 6680
Jos 1:14 shall remain in the land which Moses **g** you 5414
1:15 which Moses the LORD'S servant **g** you 5414
11:23 Joshua **g** it for an inheritance unto Israel 5414
12: 6 Moses the servant of the LORD **g** it *for* a 5414
12: 7 which Joshua **g** unto the tribes of Israel *for* 5414
13: 8 which Moses **g** them, beyond Jordan 5414
13: 8 *even* as Moses the servant of the LORD **g** 5414
13:14 Only unto the tribe of Levi he **g** none 5414
13:15 Moses **g** unto the tribe of the children of 5414
13:24 Moses **g** *inheritance* unto the tribe of Gad, 5414
13:29 Moses **g** *inheritance* unto the half tribe of 5414
13:33 unto the tribe of Levi Moses **g** not *any* 5414
14: 3 unto the Levites he **g** none inheritance 5414
14: 4 they **g** no part unto the Levites in the land, 5414
14:13 **g** unto Caleb the son of Jephunneh Hebron 5414
15:13 unto Caleb the son of Jephunneh he **g** a part 5414
15:17 and he **g** him Achsah his daughter to wife. 5414
15:19 he **g** her the upper springs, and the nether 5414
17: 4 **g** them an inheritance among the brethren 5414
18: 7 which Moses the servant of the LORD **g** 5414
19:49 the children of Israel **g** an inheritance to 5414
19:50 to the word of the LORD they **g** 5414
21: 3 the children of Israel **g** unto the Levites out 5414
21: 8 the children of Israel **g** by lot unto 5414
21: 9 they **g** out of the tribe of the children of 5414
21:11 they **g** them the city of Arbah the father of 5414
21:12 **g** they to Caleb the son of Jephunneh for 5414
21:13 Thus they **g** to the children of Aaron 5414
21:21 For they **g** them Shechem with her suburbs 5414
21:27 of the *other* half tribe of Manasseh *they* **g** NIH
21:43 the LORD **g** unto Israel all the land which 5414
21:44 the LORD **g** them **rest** round about, 5117
22: 4 which Moses the servant of the LORD **g** 5414
22: 7 unto the *other* half thereof **g** Joshua among 5414
24: 3 and multiplied his seed, and **g** him Isaac. 5414
24: 4 I **g** unto Isaac Jacob and Esau: and I gave 5414
24: 4 I **g** unto Esau mount Seir, to possess it; 5414
24: 8 I **g** them into your hand, that ye might 5414
Jdg 1:13 and he **g** him Achsah his daughter to wife. 5414
1:15 Caleb **g** her the upper springs and 5414
1:20 they **g** Hebron unto Caleb, as Moses said: 5414
3: 6 **g** their daughters to their sons, and 5414
4:19 of milk, and **g** him **drink**, and covered him. 8248
5:25 He asked water, *and* she **g** *him* milk; 5414
6: 9 out from before you, and **g** you their land; 5414
9: 4 they **g** him threescore and ten *pieces* of 5414
14: 9 and he **g** them, and they did eat: 5414
14:19 **g** change *of garments* unto them which 5414
15: 2 therefore I **g** her to thy companion: 5414
17: 4 **g** them to the founder, who made thereof a 5414
19:21 his house, and **g provender** unto the asses: 1101
20:36 for the men of Israel **g** place to 5414
21:14 they **g** them wives which they had saved 5414
Ru 2:18 **g** to her that she had reserved after she was 5414
3:17 These six *measures* of barley **g** he me; 5414
4: 7 off his shoe, and **g** *it* to his neighbour: 5414
4:13 the LORD **g** her conception, and she bare 5414
4:17 And the *women her* neighbours **g** it a name, 7121
1Sa 1: 4 he **g** to Peninnah his wife, and to all her 5414
1: 5 unto Hannah he **g** a worthy portion; for he 5414
1:23 and **g** her son **suck** until she weaned him. 3243
9:23 Bring the portion which I **g** thee, of which I 5414
1Sa 10: 9 go from Samuel, God **g** him another heart: 2015
18: 4 **g** it to David, and his garments, even to his 5414
18:27 and they **g** them **in full tale** to the king, 4390
18:27 Saul **g** him Michal his daughter to wife. 5414
20:40 Jonathan **g** his artillery unto his lad, and 5414
21: 6 So the priest **g** him hallowed *bread:* for 5414
22:10 **g** him victuals, and gave him the sword of 5414
22:10 **g** him the sword of Goliath the Philistine. 5414
27: 6 Achish **g** him Ziklag that day: wherefore 5414
30:11 to David, and **g** him bread, and he did eat; 5414
30:12 they **g** him a piece of a cake *of figs*, and 5414
2Sa 12: 8 I **g** thee thy master's house, and thy 5414
12: 8 and **g** thee the house of Israel and of Judah; 5414
18: 5 **g** all the captains **charge** concerning 6680
24: 9 Joab **g** *up* the sum of the number of 5414
1Ki 4:29 God **g** Solomon wisdom and 5414
5:10 So Hiram **g** Solomon cedar trees and 5414
5:11 Solomon **g** Hiram twenty thousand 5414
5:11 thus **g** Solomon to Hiram year by year. 5414
5:12 the LORD **g** Solomon wisdom, as he 5414
9:11 king Solomon **g** Hiram twenty cities in 5414
10:10 she **g** the king an hundred and 5414
10:10 the queen of Sheba **g** to king Solomon. 5414
10:13 king Solomon **g** unto the queen of Sheba all 5414
10:13 besides *that* which Solomon **g** her of his 5414
11:18 which **g** him a house, and appointed him 5414
11:18 and appointed him victuals, and **g** him land. 5414
11:19 that he **g** him *to* wife the sister of his own 5414
12:13 old men's **counsel** that they **g** him; 3289+6098
13: 3 he **g** a sign the same day, saying, This *is* 5414
14: 8 from the house of David, and **g** it thee: 5414
14:15 which he **g** to their fathers, and shall scatter 5414
19:21 and **g** unto the people, and they did eat. 5414
2Ki 10:15 he **g** *him* his hand; and he took him up to 5414
11:12 crown upon him, and **g** *him* the Testimony; NIH
12:11 they **g** the money, being told, into the hands 5414
12:14 they **g** that to the workmen, and 5414
13: 5 (And the LORD **g** Israel a saviour, so 5414
15:19 Menahem **g** Pul a thousand talents of silver, 5414
17: 3 became his servant, and **g** him presents. 7725
18:15 Hezekiah **g** *him* all the silver that was 5414
18:16 and **g** it to the king of Assyria. 5414
21: 8 more out of the land which I **g** their fathers; 5414
22: 8 Hilkiah **g** the book to Shaphan, and he read 5414
23:35 Jehoiakim **g** the silver and the gold to 5414
25: 6 to Riblah; and they **g** judgment upon him. 1696
1Ch 2:35 Sheshan **g** his daughter to Jarha his servant 5414
6:55 they **g** them Hebron in the land of Judah, 5414
6:56 they **g** to Caleb the son of Jephunneh. 5414
6:57 to the sons of Aaron they **g** the cities of 5414
6:64 the children of Israel **g** to the Levites *these* 5414
6:65 they **g** by lot out of the tribe of the children 5414
6:67 they **g** unto them, *of* the cities of refuge, 5414
6:67 *they* **g** also Gezer with her suburbs, NIH
14:12 David **g a commandment**, and they were 559
21: 5 Joab **g** the sum of the number of the people 5414
21:25 So David **g** to Ornan for the place six 5414
25: 5 God **g** to Heman fourteen sons and 5414
28:11 David **g** to Solomon his son the pattern of 5414
28:14 *He* **g** of gold by weight for *things of* gold, NIH
28:16 *by* weight *he* **g** gold for the tables of NIH
28:17 for the golden basons *he* **g** *gold* by weight NIH
29: 7 **g** for the service of the house of God *of* 5414
29: 8 **g** *them* to the treasure of the house of 5414
2Ch 9: 9 she **g** the king an hundred and 5414
9: 9 as the queen of Sheba **g** king Solomon. 5414
9:12 king Solomon **g** to the queen of Sheba all 5414
10: 8 **counsel** which the old men **g** him, 3289+6098
11:23 he **g** them victual in abundance. And he 5414
13: 5 **g** the kingdom over Israel to David for 5414
13:15 the men of Judah **g a shout**: and as the men 7321
15:15 and the LORD **g** them **rest** round about. 5117
20:30 for his God **g** him **rest** round about. 5117
21: 3 their father **g** them great gifts of silver, and 5414
21: 3 the kingdom **g** he to Jehoram; because 5414
23:11 **g** *him* the Testimony, and made him king. NIH
24:12 Jehoiada **g** it to such as did the work of 5414
26: 8 the Ammonites **g** gifts to Uzziah: and 5414
27: 5 the children of Ammon **g** him the same 5414
28:15 **g** them **to eat** and to drink, and 398
28:21 and **g** *it* unto the king of Assyria: 5414
30: 7 *who* therefore **g** them **up** to desolation, 5414
30:24 the princes **g** to the congregation a 7311
32:24 and he spake unto him, and he **g** him a sign. 5414
34:10 they **g** it *to* the workmen that wrought in 5414
34:11 and builders **g** they *it*, to buy hewn stone, 5414
35: 7 Josiah **g** to the people, *of* the flock, lambs 7311
35: 8 And his princes **g** willingly unto the people, 7311
35: 8 **g** unto the priests for the passover *offerings* 5414
35: 9 **g** unto the Levites for passover *offerings* 7311
36:17 stooped for age: he **g** *them* all into his hand. 5414
Ezr 2:69 They **g** after their ability unto the treasure 5414
3: 7 They **g** money also unto the masons, and 5414
5:12 he **g** them into the hand of Nebuchadnezzar 3052
7:11 the king Artaxerxes **g** unto Ezra the priest, 5414
10:19 they **g** their hands that *they* would put away 5414
Ne 2: 1 I took up the wine, and **g** *it* unto the king. 5414
2: 9 the river, and **g** them the king's letters. 5414
7: 2 **g** my brother Hanani, and Hananiah the ruler of the palace, **charge** 6680
7:70 some of the chief of the fathers **g** unto 5414
7:70 The Tirshatha **g** to the treasure a thousand 5414
7:71 *some* of the chief of the fathers **g** to 5414
7:72 *that* which the rest of the people **g** *was* 5414
8: 8 **g** the sense, and caused *them* to understand 7760
12:31 two great *companies of them that* **g** thanks, NIH
12:38 the other *company of them that* **g** thanks NIH
12:40 So stood the two *companies of them that* **g** NIH
12:47 **g** the portions of the singers and the porters, 5414
Est 1: 7 *they* **g** *them* **drink** in vessels of gold, 8248
2: 9 he speedily **g** her her things for 5414
2:18 **g** gifts, according to the state of the king. 5414
3:10 **g** it unto Haman the son of Hammedatha 5414
4: 5 **g** him **a commandment** to Mordecai, 6680
4: 8 Also he **g** him the copy of the writing of 5414
Est 4:10 and **g** him **commandment** unto Mordecai: 6680
8: 2 taken from Haman, and **g** it unto Mordecai. 5414
Job 1:21 the LORD **g**, and the LORD hath taken 5414
19:16 called my servant, and he **g** *me* no **answer**; 6030
29:11 when the eye saw *me*, it **g witness to** me: 5749
29:21 Unto me *men* **g ear**, and waited, and 8085
32:11 I **g ear** to your reasons, whilst you searched 238
42:10 also the LORD **g** Job twice as much as he 3254
42:11 every man also **g** him a piece of money, 5414
42:15 their father **g** them inheritance among their 5414
Ps 18:13 in the heavens, and the Highest **g** his voice; 5414
68:11 The Lord **g** the word: great *was* 5414
69:21 They **g** me also gall for my meat; and in my 5414
69:21 in my thirst they **g** me vinegar **to drink**. 8248
77: 1 God *with* my voice; and he **g ear** unto me. 238
78:15 **g** *them* **drink** as *out of* the great depths. 8248
78:29 well filled: for he **g** them their own desire; 935
78:46 He **g** also their increase unto the caterpillar, 5414
78:48 He **g up** their cattle also to the hail, and 5462
78:50 but **g** their life **over** to the pestilence; 5462
78:62 He **g** his people **over** also unto the sword; 5462
81:12 So I **g** them **up** unto their own heart's lust: 7971
99: 7 and the ordinance *that* he **g** them. 5414
105:32 He **g** them hail *for* rain, *and* flaming fire in 5414
105:44 **g** them the lands of the heathen: and 5414
106:15 he **g** them their request; but sent leanness 5414
106:41 And he **g** them into the hand of the heathen; 5414
135:12 **g** their land *for* an heritage, an heritage unto 5414
136:21 **g** their land for an heritage: for his mercy 5414
Pr 8:29 When he **g** to the sea his decree, that 7760
Ecc 1:13 I **g** my heart to seek and search out by 5414
1:17 I **g** my heart to know wisdom, and to know 5414
12: 7 the spirit shall return unto God who **g** it. 5414
12: 9 he **g good heed**, and sought out, *and* set in 239
SS 5: 6 I called him, but he **g** me no **answer**. 6030
Isa 41: 2 **g** the nations before him, and made *him* 5414
41: 2 he **g** *them* as the dust *to* his sword, *and* 5414
42:24 Who **g** Jacob for a spoil, and Israel to 5414
43: 3 I **g** Egypt *for* thy ransom, Ethiopia and 5414
50: 6 I **g** my back to the smiters, and my cheeks 5414
Jer 7: 7 in the land that I **g** to your fathers, for ever 5414
7:14 unto the place which I **g** to you and to your 5414
16:15 into their land that I **g** unto their fathers. 5414
17: 4 discontinue from thine heritage that I **g** 5414
23:39 the city that I **g** you and your fathers, *and* 5414
24:10 from off the land that I **g** unto them 5414
30: 3 to return to the land that I **g** to their fathers, 5414
32:12 I **g** the evidence of the purchase unto 5414
36:32 **g** it to Baruch the scribe, the son of Neriah; 5414
39: 5 of Hamath, where he **g** judgment upon him. 1696
39:10 **g** them vineyards and fields at the same 5414
39:11 **g charge** concerning Jeremiah to 6680
40: 5 So the captain of the guard **g** him victuals 5414
44:30 as I **g** Zedekiah king of Judah into the hand 5414
52: 9 of Hamath; where he **g** judgment upon him. 1696
La 1:19 and mine elders **g up the ghost** in the city, 1478
Eze 16:19 My meat also which I **g** thee, fine flour, and 5414
20:11 I **g** them my statutes, and shewed them my 5414
20:12 Moreover also I **g** them my sabbaths, to be 5414
20:25 Wherefore I **g** them also statutes *that were* 5414
36:28 ye shall dwell in the land that I **g** to your 5414
39:23 and **g** them into the hand of their enemies: 5414
Da 1: 2 the Lord **g** Jehoiakim king of Judah into his 5414
1: 7 Unto whom the prince of the eunuchs **g** 7760
1: 7 for he **g** unto Daniel *the name of* 7760
1:16 that they should drink; and **g** them pulse. 5414
1:17 God **g** them knowledge and skill in all 5414
2:48 **g** him many great gifts, and made him ruler 3052
5:18 the most high God **g** Nebuchadnezzar thy 3052
5:19 for the majesty that he **g** him, all people, 3052
6:10 prayed, and **g thanks** before his God, as he 3029
Hos 2: 8 For she did not know that I **g** her corn, and 5414
13:11 I **g** thee a king in mine anger, and took *him* 5414
Am 2:12 ye **g** the Nazarites wine **to drink**; 8248
Mal 2: 5 I **g** them to him *for* the fear wherewith he 5414
Mt 8:18 he **g commandment** to depart unto *2753*
10: 1 he **g** them power against unclean spirits, *1325*
14:19 and **g** the loaves to *his* disciples, and *1325*
15:36 and **g thanks**, and brake *them*, and gave to *2168*
15:36 and brake *them*, and **g** to his disciples, and *1325*
21:23 these *things?* and who **g** thee this authority? *1325*
25:15 And unto one he **g** five talents, to another *1325*
25:35 For I was a hungred, and ye **g** me meat: *1325*
25:35 I was thirsty, and ye **g** me **drink**: I was a *4222*
25:37 and fed *thee?* or thirsty, and **g** *thee* **drink**? *4222*
25:42 For I was a hungred, and ye **g** me no meat: *1325*
25:42 I was thirsty, and ye **g** me no **drink**: *4222*
26:26 and brake *it*, and **g** *it* to the disciples, *1325*
26:27 and **g thanks**, and gave *it* to them, saying, *2168*
26:27 and gave thanks, and **g** *it* to them, saying, *1325*
26:48 Now he that betrayed him **g** them a sign, *1325*
27:10 And **g** them for the potter's field, as *1325*
27:34 They **g** him vinegar to drink mingled with *1325*
27:48 and put *it* on a reed, and **g** him **to drink**. *4222*
28:12 they **g** large money unto the soldiers, *1325*
Mk 2:26 and **g** also to them which were with him? *1325*
5:13 And forthwith Jesus **g** them **leave**. And *2010*
6: 7 two; and **g** them power over unclean spirits; *1325*
6:28 head in a charger, and **g** it to the damsel: *1325*
6:28 and the damsel **g** it to her mother. *1325*
6:41 **g** *them* to his disciples to set before them; *1325*
8: 6 and **g thanks**, and brake, and gave to his *2168*
8: 6 **g** to his disciples to set before *them;* and *1325*
11:28 who **g** thee this authority to do these *1325*
13:34 and **g** authority to his servants, and to every *1325*
14:22 and brake *it*, and **g** to them, and said, Take, *1325*
14:23 when he had given thanks, he **g** *it* to them: *1325*
15:23 And they **g** him to drink wine mingled with *1325*
15:36 and **g** him **to drink**, saying, Let alone; *4222*
15:37 cried with a loud voice, and **g up the ghost**. *1606*
15:39 so cried out, and **g up the ghost**, he said, *1606*
15:45 *it* of the centurion, he **g** the body to Joseph. *1433*
Lk 2:38 that instant **g thanks** *likewise* **unto** the Lord, *437*
4:20 and he **g** *it* **again** to the minister, and *591*
6: 4 and **g** also to them that were with him; *1325*

Lk 7:21 and unto many *that were* blind he **g** sight. *5483*
9: 1 and **g** them power and authority over all *1325*
9:16 **g** to the disciples to set before *1325*
10:35 and **g** *them* to the host, and said unto him, *1325*
15:16 the swine did eat: and no *man* **g** unto him. *1325*
18:43 when they saw *it*, **g** praise unto God. *1325*
20: 2 or who is he that **g** thee this authority? *1325*
22:17 and **g thanks**, and said, Take this, and *2168*
22:19 and **g thanks**, and brake *it*, and gave unto *2168*
22:19 and brake *it*, and **g** unto them, saying, *1325*
23:24 And Pilate **g sentence** that it should be as *1948*
23:29 and the paps which never **g suck**. *2337*
23:46 and having said thus, he **g up the ghost**. *1606*
24:30 and blessed *it*, and brake, and **g** to them. *1929*
24:42 And they **g** him a piece of a broiled fish, *1929*
Jn 1:12 to them **g** he power to become the sons of *1325*
3:16 the world, that he **g** his only begotten Son, *1325*
4: 5 near to the parcel of ground that Jacob **g** to *1325*
4:12 which **g** us the well, and drank thereof *1325*
6:31 He **g** them bread from heaven to eat. *1325*
6:32 Moses **g** you not *that* bread from heaven; *1325*
7:22 Moses therefore **g** unto you circumcision, *1325*
10:29 My Father, which **g** *them* me, is greater *1325*
12:49 he **g** me a commandment, what I should *1325*
13:26 he **g** *it* to Judas Iscariot, *the son* of Simon. *1325*
14:31 and as the Father **g** me **commandment**, *1781*
18:14 was he, which **g counsel** to the Jews, *4823*
19: 9 art thou? But Jesus **g** him no answer. *1325*
19:30 and he bowed *his* head, and **g up** the ghost. *3860*
19:38 and Pilate **g** *him* **leave**. He came therefore, *2010*
Ac 1:26 And they **g forth** their lots; and the lot fell *1325*
2: 4 as the Spirit **g** them utterance. *1325*
3: 5 And he **g** heed unto them, expecting to NIG
4:33 And with great power **g** the apostles witness *591*
5: 5 these words fell down, and **g up the ghost**: *1634*
7: 5 And he **g** him none inheritance in it, no, not *1325*
7: 8 And he **g** him the covenant of circumcision: *1325*
7:10 and **g** him favour and wisdom in the sight *1325*
7:42 **g** them **up** to worship the host of heaven; *3860*
8: 6 And the people with one accord **g heed** *4337*
8:10 To whom they all **g heed**, from the least to *4337*
9:41 And he **g** her *his* hand, and lift her up, and *1325*
10: 2 which **g** much alms to the people, and *4160*
11:17 as God **g** them the like gift as *he did* unto *1325*
12:22 And the people **g a shout**, *saying*, *It is* *2019*
12:23 smote him, because he **g** not God the glory: *1325*
12:23 he was eaten of worms, and **g up the ghost**. *1634*
13:20 And after that he **g** *unto them* judges about *1325*
13:21 and God **g** unto them Saul the son of Cis, *1325*
13:22 to whom also he **g testimony**, and said, *3140*
14: 3 which **g testimony** unto the word of his *3140*
14:17 and **g** us rain from heaven, and *1325*
15:12 and **g audience** to Barnabas and Paul, *191*
15:24 to whom we **g** no *such* **commandment**: *1291*
22:22 And they **g** him **audience** unto this word, *191*
23:30 **g commandment** to *his* accusers also to *3853*
26:10 put to death, I **g** my voice against *them*. *2702*
27: 3 **g** *him* **liberty** to go unto *his* friends to *2010*
27:35 **g thanks** to God in presence of *them* all: *2168*
Ro 1:24 Wherefore God also **g** them **up** to *3860*
1:26 For this cause God **g** them **up** unto vile *3860*
1:28 God **g** them **over** to a reprobate mind, to do *3860*
1Co 3: 5 even as the Lord **g** to every man? *1325*
3: 6 Apollos watered; but God **g** the **increase**. *837*
2Co 8: 5 but first **g** their own selves to the Lord, and *1325*
Gal 1: 4 Who **g** himself for our sins, that he might *1325*
2: 5 To whom we **g place** by subjection, no, *1502*
2: 9 they **g** to me and Barnabas the right hands *1325*
2:20 who loved me, and **g** himself for me. *3860*
3:18 but God **g** *it* to Abraham by promise. *5483*
Eph 1:22 **g** him *to be* the head over all *things* to *1325*
4: 8 led captivity captive, and **g** gifts unto men. *1325*
4:11 And he **g** some, apostles; and some, *1325*
5:25 also loved the church, and **g** himself for it; *3860*
1Th 4: 2 For ye know what commandments we **g** *1325*
1Ti 2: 6 Who **g** himself a ransom for all, to be *1325*
Tit 2:14 Who **g** himself for us, that he might redeem *1325*
Heb 7: 2 To whom also Abraham **g** a tenth *part* of *3307*
7: 4 patriarch Abraham **g** the tenth of the spoils. *1325*
7:13 of which no *man* **g attendance at** the altar. *4337*
11:22 **g commandment** concerning his bones. *1781*
12: 9 corrected *us*, and we **g** *them* **reverence**: *1788*
Jas 5:18 and the heaven **g** rain, and the earth brought *1325*
1Pe 1:21 him up from the dead, and **g** him glory; *1325*
1Jn 3:23 love one another, as he **g** us commandment. *1325*
5:10 he believeth not the record that God **g** of *3140*
Jude 1: 3 when I **g** all diligence to write unto you of *4160*
Rev 1: 1 of Jesus Christ, which God **g** unto him, *1325*
2:21 And I **g** her space to repent of her *1325*
11:13 and **g** glory to the God of heaven. *1325*
13: 2 and the dragon **g** him his power, and *1325*
13: 4 And they worshipped the dragon which **g** *1325*
15: 7 And one of the four beasts **g** unto the seven *1325*
20:13 And the sea **g up** the dead which were in it; *1325*

GAVEST (34) [GIVE]

Ge 3:12 The woman whom thou **g** *to be* with me, 5414
1Ki 8:34 the land which thou **g** unto their fathers. 5414
8:40 in the land which thou **g** unto our fathers. 5414
8:48 which thou **g** unto their fathers, the city 5414
2Ch 6:25 again unto the land which thou **g** to them 5414
6:31 long as they live in the land which thou **g** 5414
6:38 which thou **g** unto their fathers, and 5414
20: 7 **g** it to the seed of Abraham thy friend for 5414
Ne 9: 7 and **g** him the name of Abraham; 7760
9:13 **g** them right judgments, and true laws, 5414
9:15 **g** them bread from heaven for their hunger, 5414
9:20 Thou **g** also thy good spirit to instruct them, 5414
9:20 and **g** them water for their thirst. 5414
9:22 Moreover thou **g** them kingdoms and 5414
9:24 the Canaanites, and **g** them into their hands, 5414
9:27 according to thy manifold mercies thou **g** 5414
9:30 **g** thou them into the hand of the people of 5414
9:35 in thy great goodness that thou **g** them, and 5414
9:35 and fat land which thou **g** before them, 5414
Ne 9:36 *for* the land that thou **g** unto our fathers to 5414
Job 39:13 *G thou* the goodly wings unto the peacocks? NIH
Ps 21: 4 He asked life of thee, *and* thou **g** *it* him, 5414
74:14 **g** him *to be* meat to the people inhabiting 5414
Lk 7:44 thou **g** me no water for my feet: *1325*
7:45 Thou **g** me no kiss: but this *woman* since *1325*
15:29 and yet thou never **g** me a kid, that I might *1325*
19:23 then **g** not thou my money into the bank, *1325*
Jn 17: 4 I have finished the work which thou **g** me *1325*
17: 6 the men which thou **g** me out of the world: *1325*
17: 6 thine they were, and thou **g** them me; and *1325*
17: 8 unto them the words which thou **g** me; *1325*
17:12 *those* that thou **g** me I have kept, and *1325*
17:22 And the glory which thou **g** me I have *1325*
18: 9 Of them which thou **g** me have I lost none. *1325*

GAY (1)

Jas 2: 3 respect to him that weareth the **g** clothing, *2986*

GAZA (19) [GAZATHITES, GAZITES]

Ge 10:19 as thou comest to Gerar, unto **G**; 5804
Jos 10:41 them from Kadesh-barnea even unto **G**, 5804
11:22 only in **G**, in Gath, and in Ashdod, 5804
15:47 **G** *with* her towns and her villages, 5804
Jdg 1:18 Also Judah took **G** with the coast thereof, 5804
6: 4 till thou come *unto* **G**, and left no 5804
16: 1 went Samson to **G**, and saw there a harlot, 5804
16:21 brought him down to **G**, and bound him 5804
1Sa 6:17 for Ashdod one, for **G** one, for Askelon 5804
2Ki 18: 8 *even* unto **G**, and the borders thereof, 5804
1Ch 7:28 unto **G** and the towns thereof: 5804
Jer 47: 1 before that Pharaoh smote **G**. 5804
47: 5 Baldness is come upon **G**; Ashkelon is cut 5804
Am 1: 6 For three transgressions of **G**, and for four, 5804
1: 7 I will send a fire on the wall of **G**, 5804
Zep 2: 4 For **G** shall be forsaken, and Ashkelon a 5804
Zec 9: 5 **G** also *shall see it*, and be very sorrowful, 5804
9: 5 the king shall perish from **G**, and 5804
Ac 8:26 that goeth down from Jerusalem unto **G**, *1048*

GAZATHITES (1) [GAZA]

Jos 13: 3 the **G**, and the Ashdothites, 5841

GAZE (1) [GAZING, GAZING-STOCK, GAZINGSTOCK, STARGAZERS]

Ex 19:21 they break through unto the LORD to **g**, 7200

GAZELLE See ROEBUCK; ROES

GAZER (2)

2Sa 5:25 Philistines from Geba until thou come *to* **G**. 1507
1Ch 14:16 of the Philistines from Gibeon even to **G**. 1507

GAZEZ (2)

1Ch 2:46 bare Haran, and Moza, and **G**: 1495
2:46 and Moza, and Gazez: and Haran begat **G**. 1495

GAZING (1) [GAZE]

Ac 1:11 of Galilee, why stand ye **g up** into heaven? *1689*

GAZINGSTOCK, GAZING-STOCK (2) [GAZE]

Na 3: 6 and make thee vile, and will set thee as a **g**. 7210
Heb 10:33 whilst ye were **made a g** both by *2301*

GAZITES (1) [GAZA]

Jdg 16: 2 *And it was told* the **G**, saying, Samson is 5841

GAZZAM (2)

Ezr 2:48 the children of Nekoda, the children of **G**, 1502
Ne 7:51 The children of **G**, the children of Uzza, 1502

GE HARASHIM See CHARASHIM

GEBA (13)

Jos 21:17 with her suburbs, **G** with her suburbs, 1387
1Sa 13: 3 the garrison of the Philistines that *was* in **G**, 1387
2Sa 5:25 smote the Philistines from **G** until thou 1387
1Ki 15:22 king Asa built with them **G** of Benjamin, 1387
2Ki 23: 8 from **G** to Beer-sheba, and brake down 1387
1Ch 6:60 **G** with her suburbs, and Alemeth with her 1387
8: 6 heads of the fathers of the inhabitants of **G**, 1387
2Ch 16: 6 and he built therewith **G** and Mizpah. 1387
Ne 7:30 The men of Ramah and **G**, six hundred 1387
11:31 The children also of Benjamin from **G** 1387
12:29 and out of the fields of **G** and Azmaveth: 1387
Isa 10:29 they have taken up their lodging at **G**; 1387
Zec 14:10 from **G** to Rimmon south of Jerusalem: 1387

GEBAL (2) [GIBLITES]

Ps 83: 7 **G**, and Ammon, and Amalek; 1381
Eze 27: 9 The ancients of **G** and the wise *men* thereof 1380

GEBALITES See GIBLITES

GEBER (2)

1Ki 4:13 The son of **G**, in Ramoth-gilead; to him 1398
4:19 **G** the son of Uri *was* in the country of 1398

GEBIM (1)

Isa 10:31 the inhabitants of **G** gather themselves to 1374

GEDALIAH (32)

2Ki 25:22 even over them he made **G** the son of 1436
25:23 heard that the king of Babylon had made **G** 1436
25:23 there came to **G** *to* Mizpah, even Ishmael 1436
25:24 And **G** sware to them, and to their men, and 1436
25:25 and smote **G**, that he died, and the Jews and 1436
1Ch 25: 3 **G**, and Zeri, and Jeshaiah, Hashabiah, and 1436
25: 9 the second *to* **G**, who with his brethren and 1436
Ezr 10:18 Maaseiah, and Eliezer, and Jarib, and **G**. 1436
Jer 38: 1 **G** the son of Pashur, and Jucal the son of 1436
39:14 committed him unto **G** the son of Ahikam 1436
40: 5 *he said*, Go back also to **G** the son of 1436
Jer 40: 6 went Jeremiah unto **G** the son of Ahikam to 1436
40: 7 heard that the king of Babylon had made **G** 1436
40: 8 they came to **G** to Mizpah, even Ishmael 1436
40: 9 **G** the son of Ahikam the son of Shaphan 1436
40:11 that he had set over them **G** the son of 1436
40:12 to **G**, unto Mizpah, and gathered wine and 1436
40:13 *were* in the fields, came to **G** to Mizpah, 1436
40:14 **G** the son of Ahikam believed them not. 1436
40:15 Johanan the son of Kareah spake to **G** in 1436
40:16 **G** the son of Ahikam said unto Johanan 1436
41: 1 came unto **G** the son of Ahikam to Mizpah; 1436
41: 2 smote **G** the son of Ahikam the son of 1436
41: 3 *even* with **G** at Mizpah, and the Chaldeans 1436
41: 4 to pass the second day after *he* had slain **G**, 1436
41: 6 unto them, Come to **G** the son of Ahikam. 1436
41: 9 the men, whom he had slain because of **G**, 1436
41:10 had committed to **G** the son of Ahikam: 1436
41:16 after *that* he had slain **G** the son of Ahikam, 1436
41:18 Ishmael the son of Nethaniah had slain **G** 1436
43: 6 **G** the son of Ahikam the son of Shaphan, 1436
Zep 1: 1 the son of **G**, the son of Amariah, the son 1436

GEDEON (1) [GIDEON]

Heb 11:32 for the time would fail me to tell of **G**, and *1066*

GEDER (1)

Jos 12:13 The king of Debir, one; the king of **G**, one; 1445

GEDERAH (1)

Jos 15:36 and Adithaim, and **G**, and Gederothaim; 1449

GEDERATHITE (1)

1Ch 12: 4 Jahaziel, and Johanan, and Josabad the **G**, 1452

GEDERITE (1)

1Ch 27:28 in the low plains *was* Baal-hanan the **G**: 1451

GEDEROTH (2)

Jos 15:41 **G**, Beth-dagon, and Naamah, and 1450
2Ch 28:18 **G**, and Shocho with the villages thereof, 1450

GEDEROTHAIM (1)

Jos 15:36 and Adithaim, and Gederah, and **G**; 1453

GEDOR (7)

Jos 15:58 Halhul, Beth-zur, and **G**, 1446
1Ch 4: 4 Penuel the father of **G**, and Ezer the father 1446
4:18 wife Jehudijah bare Jered the father of **G**, 1446
4:39 they went to the entrance of **G**, *even* unto 1446
8:31 And **G**, and Ahio, and Zacher. 1446
9:37 **G**, and Ahio, and Zechariah, and Mikloth. 1446
12: 7 and Zebadiah, the sons of Jeroham of **G**. 1446

GEHAZI (12)

2Ki 4:12 he said to **G** his servant, Call this 1522
4:14 **G** answered, Verily she hath no child, and 1522
4:25 that he said to **G** his servant, Behold, 1522
4:27 **G** came near to thrust her away. And 1522
4:29 he said to **G**, Gird up thy loins, and take my 1522
4:31 **G** passed on before them, and laid the staff 1522
4:36 he called **G**, and said, Call this 1522
5:20 **G**, the servant of Elisha the man of God, 1522
5:21 So **G** followed after Naaman. And when 1522
5:25 said unto him, Whence *comest thou*, **G**? 1522
8: 4 the king talked with **G** the servant of 1522
8: 5 **G** said, My lord, O king, this *is* the woman, 1522

GELILOTH (1)

Jos 18:17 *to* En-shemesh, and went forth toward **G**, 1553

GEMALLI (1)

Nu 13:12 Of the tribe of Dan, Ammiel the son of **G**. 1582

GEMARIAH (5)

Jer 29: 3 son of Shaphan, and **G** the son of Hilkiah, 1587
36:10 in the chamber of **G** the son of Shaphan 1587
36:11 When Michaiah the son of **G**, the son of 1587
36:12 **G** the son of Shaphan, and Zedekiah 1587
36:25 **G** had made intercession to the king that *he* 1587

GENDER (2) [GENDERED, GENDERETH]

Lev 19:19 Thou shalt not let thy cattle **g with** a 7250
2Ti 2:23 knowing that they do **g** strifes. *1080*

GENDERED (1) [GENDER]

Job 38:29 the hoary frost of heaven, who hath **g** it? 3205

GENDERETH (2) [GENDER]

Job 21:10 Their bull **g**, and faileth not; their cow 5674
Gal 4:24 which **g** to bondage, which is Agar. *1080*

GENEALOGIES (8) [GENEALOGY]

1Ch 5:17 All these were **reckoned by g** in the days 3187
7: 5 **reckoned** in all **by** their **g** fourscore and 3187
7: 7 were **reckoned by** their **g** twenty and 3187
9: 1 So all Israel were **reckoned by g**; and 3187
2Ch 12:15 and of Iddo the seer concerning **g**? 3187
31:19 to all that were **reckoned by g** among 3187
1Ti 1: 4 Neither give heed to fables and endless **g**, *1076*
Tit 3: 9 and **g**, and contentions, and strivings about *1076*

GENEALOGY (15) [GENEALOGIES]

1Ch 4:33 These *were* their habitations, and their **g**. 3187
5: 1 the **g** is not to be **reckoned** after 3187
5: 7 the **g** of their generations was **reckoned**, 3187
7: 9 the **number** of them, **after** their **g** by their 3187
7:40 the number **throughout** the **g** of them *that* 3187
9:22 These were **reckoned** by their **g** in their 3187
2Ch 31:16 Beside their **g** of males, from three years 3187
31:17 Both *to* the **g** of the priests by the house of 3187
31:18 to the **g** of all their little ones, their wives, 3187
Ezr 2:62 *among* those that were **reckoned by g**, 3187
8: 1 *this is* the **g** of them that went up with me 3187

Ezr 8: 3 with him were **reckoned by g** of the males 3187
Ne 7: 5 that *they* might be **reckoned by g**. 3187
7: 5 I found a register of the **g** of them which 3188
7:64 *among* those that were **reckoned by g**, 3187

GENERAL (2) [GENERALLY]
1Ch 27:34 and the **g** of the king's army *was* Joab. 8269
Heb 12:23 To the **g assembly**, and church of *3831*

GENERALLY (2) [GENERAL]
2Sa 17:11 *that* all Israel be **g gathered** unto thee, 622+622
Jer 48:38 *There shall be* lamentation **g** upon all 3605

GENERATION (107) [GENERATIONS]
Ge 7: 1 have I seen righteous before me in this **g**. 1755
15:16 *in* the fourth **g** they shall come hither again: 1755
50:23 *g*: the children also of Machir the son of NIH
Ex 1: 6 and all his brethren, and all that **g**. 1755
17:16 war with Amalek from **g** *to* generation. 1755
17:16 war with Amalek from generation *to* **g**. 1755
20: 5 the third and fourth *g* of them that hate me; NIH
34: 7 unto the third and to the fourth *g*. NIH
Nu 14:18 the children unto the third and fourth *g*. NIH
32:13 until all the **g**, that had done evil in 1755
Dt 1:35 these men of this evil **g** see that good land, 1755
2:14 until all the **g** of the men of war were 1755
5: 9 the third and fourth *g* of them that hate me, NIH
23: 2 even *to* his tenth **g** shall he not enter into 1755
23: 3 even *to* their tenth **g** shall they not enter 1755
23: 8 congregation of the LORD *in* their third **g**. 1755
29:22 So that the **g** to come of your children that 1755
32: 5 *they are* a perverse and crooked **g**. 1755
32:20 end *shall be*: for they *are* a very froward **g**, 1755
Jdg 2:10 also all that **g** were gathered unto their 1755
2:10 there arose another **g** after them, 1755
2Ki 10:30 thy children of the fourth *g* shall sit on NIH
15:12 the throne of Israel unto the fourth *g*. And NIH
Est 9:28 throughout **every g**, 1755+1755+3605+2050.1
Ps 12: 7 thou shalt preserve them from this **g** for 1755
14: 5 for God *is* in the **g** of the righteous. 1755
22:30 it shall be accounted to the Lord for a **g**. 1755
24: 6 This *is* the **g** of them that seek him, 1755
48:13 that ye may tell *it* to the **g** following. 1755
49:19 He shall go to the **g** of his fathers; 1755
71:18 until I have shewed thy strength unto *this* **g**, 1755
73:15 I should offend *against* the **g** of thy 1755
78: 4 shewing to the **g** to come the praises of 1755
78: 6 That the **g** to come might know *them, even* 1755
78: 8 as their fathers, a stubborn and rebellious **g**; 1755
78: 8 a **g** *that* set not their heart aright, and 1755
95:10 Forty years long was I grieved with *this* **g**, 1755
102:18 This shall be written for the **g** to come: and 1755
109:13 in the **g** following let their name be blotted 1755
112: 2 the **g** of the upright shall be blessed. 1755
145: 4 One **g** shall praise thy works to another, 1755
Pr 27:24 crown *endure* to **every g**? 1755+1755+2050.1
30:11 *There is* a **g** *that* curseth their father, and 1755
30:12 *There is* a **g** *that are* pure in their own eyes, 1755
30:13 *There is* a **g**, O how lofty are their eyes! 1755
30:14 *There is* a **g**, whose teeth *are as* swords, and 1755
Ecc 1: 4 *One* **g** passeth away, and 1755
1: 4 passeth away, and *another* **g** cometh: 1755
Isa 13:20 neither shall it be dwelt in from **g** to 1755
13:20 shall it be dwelt in from generation to **g**: 1755
34:10 from **g** to generation it shall lie waste; 1755
34:10 from generation to **g** it shall lie waste; 1755
34:17 from **g** to generation shall they dwell 1755
34:17 from generation to **g** shall they dwell 1755
51: 8 and my salvation from **g** to generation. 1755
51: 8 and my salvation from generation to **g**. 1755
53: 8 who shall declare his **g**? for he was cut off 1755
Jer 2:31 O **g**, see ye the word of the LORD. Have I 1755
7:29 and forsaken the **g** of his wrath. 1755
50:39 neither shall it be dwelt in from **g** to 1755
50:39 shall it be dwelt in from generation to **g**. 1755
La 5:19 for ever; thy throne from **g** to generation. 1755
5:19 for ever; thy throne from generation to **g**. 1755
Da 4: 3 and his dominion *is* from **g** to generation. 1859
4: 3 and his dominion *is* from generation to **g**. 1859
4:34 and his kingdom *is* from **g** to generation: 1859
4:34 and his kingdom *is* from generation to **g**. 1859
Joel 1: 3 their children, and their children another **g**. 1755
3:20 and Jerusalem from **g** to generation. 1755
3:20 and Jerusalem from generation to **g**. 1755
Mt 1: 1 The book of the **g** of Jesus Christ, the son *1078*
3: 7 he said unto them, O **g** of vipers, *1081*
11:16 But whereunto shall I liken this **g**? It is like *1074*
12:34 O **g** of vipers, how can ye, being evil, *1081*
12:39 and adulterous **g** seeketh after a sign; *1074*
12:41 Nineveh shall rise in judgment with this **g**, *1074*
12:42 shall rise up in the judgment with this **g**, *1074*
12:45 *Even* so shall it be also unto this wicked **g**. *1074*
16: 4 and adulterous **g** seeketh after a sign; *1074*
17:17 and said, O faithless and perverse **g**, *1074*
23:33 *Ye* serpents, *ye* **g** of vipers, how can ye *1081*
23:36 All these *things* shall come upon this **g**. *1074*
24:34 Verily I say unto you, This **g** shall not pass, *1074*
Mk 8:12 saith, Why doth this **g** seek after a sign? *1074*
8:12 There shall no sign be given unto this **g**. *1074*
8:38 of my words in this adulterous and sinful **g**; *1074*
9:19 He answereth him, and saith, O faithless **g**, *1074*
13:30 I say unto you, that this **g** shall not pass, *1074*
Lk 1:50 on them that fear him from **g** to generation. *1074*
1:50 on them that fear him from generation to **g**. *1074*
3: 7 O **g** of vipers, who hath warned you to flee *1081*
7:31 then shall I liken the men of this **g**? *1074*
9:41 answering said, O faithless and perverse **g**, *1074*
11:29 he began to say, This is an evil **g**: *1074*
11:30 so shall also the Son of man be to this **g**. *1074*
11:31 up in the judgment with the men of this **g**, *1074*
11:32 shall rise up in the judgment with this **g**, *1074*
11:50 of the world, may be required of this **g**; *1074*
11:51 I say unto you, It shall be required of this **g**. *1074*
16: 8 for the children of this world are in their **g** *1074*
17:25 many *things*, and be rejected of this **g**. *1074*
21:32 This **g** shall not pass away, till all be *1074*
Ac 2:40 Save yourselves from this untoward **g**. *1074*
8:33 and who shall declare his **g**? for his life is *1074*
13:36 after he had served his own **g** by the will of *1074*
Heb 3:10 Wherefore I was grieved with that **g**, and *1074*
1Pe 2: 9 But ye *are* a chosen **g**, a royal priesthood, *1085*

GENERATIONS (118) [GENERATION]
Ge 2: 4 These *are* the **g** of the heavens and of 8435
5: 1 This *is* the book of the **g** of Adam. In 8435
6: 9 These *are* the **g** of Noah: Noah was a just 8435
6: 9 Noah was a just man *and* perfect in his **g**, 1755
9:12 creature that *is* with you, for perpetual **g**: 1755
10: 1 Now these *are* the **g** of the sons of Noah, 8435
10:32 sons of Noah, after their **g**, in their nations: 8435
11:10 These *are* the **g** of Shem: Shem *was* an 8435
11:27 Now these *are* the **g** of Terah: Terah begat 8435
17: 7 thy seed after thee in their **g** for an 1755
17: 9 thou, and thy seed after thee in their **g**. 1755
17:12 every man *child* in your **g**, he that is born in 1755
25:12 Now these *are* the **g** of Ishmael, 8435
25:13 by their names, according to their **g**: 8435
25:19 these *are* the **g** of Isaac, Abraham's son: 8435
36: 1 Now these *are* the **g** of Esau, who *is* Edom. 8435
36: 9 these *are* the **g** of Esau the father of 8435
37: 2 These *are* the **g** of Jacob. Joseph, 8435
Ex 3:15 and this *is* my memorial unto **all g**. 1755+1755
6:16 of the sons of Levi according to their **g**; 8435
6:19 the families of Levi according to their **g**. 8435
12:14 it a feast to the LORD throughout your **g**; 1755
12:17 shall ye observe this day in your **g** by an 1755
12:42 of all the children of Israel in their **g**. 1755
16:32 Fill an omer of it to be kept for your **g**; 1755
16:33 before the LORD, to be kept for your **g**. 1755
27:21 *it shall be* a statute for ever unto their **g** on 1755
29:42 **g** *at* the door of the tabernacle of 1755
30: 8 before the LORD throughout your **g**. 1755
30:10 make atonement upon it throughout your **g**: 1755
30:21 to him and to his seed throughout their **g**. 1755
30:31 anointing oil unto me throughout your **g**. 1755
31:13 between me and you throughout your **g**; 1755
31:16 to observe the sabbath throughout their **g**, 1755
40:15 everlasting priesthood throughout their **g**. 1755
Lev 3:17 *It shall be* a perpetual statute for your **g** 1755
6:18 *It shall be* a statute for ever in your **g** 1755
7:36 *by* a statute for ever throughout their **g**. 1755
10: 9 *be* a statute for ever throughout your **g**: 1755
17: 7 for ever unto them throughout their **g**. 1755
21:17 Whosoever *he be* of thy seed in their **g** that 1755
22: 3 *he be* of all your seed among your **g**, 1755
23:14 throughout your **g** in all your dwellings 1755
23:21 in all your dwellings throughout your **g**. 1755
23:31 throughout your **g** in all your dwellings. 1755
23:41 *It shall be* a statute for ever in your **g**: 1755
23:43 That your **g** may know that I made 1755
24: 3 *it shall be* a statute for ever in your **g**. 1755
25:30 ever to him that bought it throughout his **g**: 1755
Nu 1:20 Israel's eldest son, *by* their **g**, after their 8435
1:22 of Simeon, *by* their **g**, after their families, 8435
1:24 of Gad, *by* their **g**, after their families, 8435
1:26 of Judah, *by* their **g**, after their families, 8435
1:28 of Issachar, *by* their **g**, after their families, 8435
1:30 of Zebulun, *by* their **g**, after their families, 8435
1:32 *by* their **g**, after their families, by the house 8435
1:34 *by* their **g**, after their families, by the house 8435
1:36 *by* their **g**, after their families, by the house 8435
1:38 of Dan, *by* their **g**, after their families, 8435
1:40 of Asher, *by* their **g**, after their families, 8435
1:42 *throughout* their **g**, after their families, 8435
3: 1 These also *are* the **g** of Aaron and Moses in 8435
10: 8 an ordinance for ever throughout your **g**. 1755
15:14 or whosoever *be* among you in your **g**, and 1755
15:15 *with you*, an ordinance for ever in your **g**: 1755
15:21 unto the LORD a heave offering in your **g**. 1755
15:23 and henceforward among your **g**; 1755
15:38 of their garments throughout their **g**, 1755
18:23 *be* a statute for ever throughout your **g**, 1755
35:29 throughout your **g** in all your dwellings. 1755
Dt 7: 9 keep his commandments to a thousand **g**; 1755
32: 7 the years of **many g**: 1755+1755+2050.1
Jos 22:27 between us, and you, and our **g** after us, 1755
22:28 *so* say to us or to our **g** in time to come, 1755
Jdg 3: 2 Only that the **g** of the children of Israel 1755
Ru 4:18 Now these *are* the **g** of Pharez: 8435
1Ch 1:29 These *are* their **g**: The firstborn of Ishmael, 8435
5: 7 when the genealogy of their **g** was 8435
7: 2 *they were* valiant *men* of might in their **g**; 8435
7: 4 with them, by their **g**, after the house of 8435
7: 9 of them, after their genealogy by their **g**, 8435
8:28 These *were* heads of the fathers, by their **g**, 8435
9: 9 according to their **g**, nine hundred and fifty 8435
9:34 the Levites *were* chief throughout their **g**; 8435
16:15 *which* he commanded to a thousand **g**; 1755
26:31 according to the **g** of his fathers. 8435
Job 42:16 his sons, and his sons' sons, *even* four **g**. 1755
Ps 33:11 thoughts of his heart to **all g**. 1755+1755+2050.1
45:17 remembered in **all g**: 1755+1755+3605+2050.1
49:11 their dwelling places to **all g**; 1755+1755+2050.1
61: 6 *and* his years as **many g**. 1755+1755+2050.1
72: 5 and moon endure, **throughout all g**. 1755+1755
79:13 forth thy praise to **all g**. 1755+1755+2050.1
85: 5 out thine anger to **all g**? 1755+1755+2050.1
89: 1 thy faithfulness to **all g**. 1755+1755+2050.1
89: 4 build up thy throne to **all g**. 1755+1755+2050.1
90: 1 our dwelling place in **all g**. 1755+1755+2050.1
100: 5 his truth *endureth* to **all g**. 1755+1755+2050.1
102:12 thy remembrance unto **all g**. 1755+1755+2050.1
102:24 thy years *are* throughout **all g**. 1755+1755
105: 8 *which* he commanded to a thousand **g**. 1755
106:31 unto **all g** for evermore. 1755+1755+2050.1
119:90 faithfulness *is* unto **all g**: 1755+1755+2050.1
135:13 O LORD, throughout **all g**. 1755+1755+2050.1
145:13 *endureth* throughout all **g**. 1755+1755+2050.1
146:10 thy God, O Zion, unto **all g**. 1755+1755+2050.1
Isa 41: 4 done *it*, calling the **g** from the beginning? 1755
51: 9 as *in* the ancient days, *in* the **g** of old. 1755
58:12 the foundations of **many g**; 1755+1755+2050.1
60:15 a joy of **many g**. 1755+1755+2050.1
61: 4 the desolations of **many g**. 1755+1755+2050.1
Joel 2: 2 *even* to the years of **many g**. 1755+1755+2050.1
Mt 1:17 So all the **g** from Abraham to David *are* *1074*
1:17 from Abraham to David *are* fourteen **g**; *1074*
1:17 carrying away into Babylon *are* fourteen **g**; *1074*
1:17 into Babylon unto Christ *are* fourteen **g**. *1074*
Lk 1:48 from henceforth all **g** shall call me blessed. *1074*
Col 1:26 which hath been hid from ages and from **g**, *1074*

GENESARET (1) [GENNESARET]
Mk 6:53 they came into the land of **G**, and drew to *1082*

GENNESARET (2) [GENESARET]
Mt 14:34 gone over, they came into the land of **G**. *1082*
Lk 5: 1 the word of God, he stood by the lake of **G**, *1082*

GENTILE (2) [GENTILES]
Ro 2: 9 of the Jew first, and *also* of the **G**; *1672*
2:10 to the Jew first, and *also* to the **G**: *1672*

GENTILES (129) [GENTILE]
Ge 10: 5 By these were the isles of the **G** divided in 1471
Jdg 4: 2 which dwelt in Harosheth of the **G**. 1471
4:13 from Harosheth of the **G** unto the river of 1471
4:16 and after the host, unto Harosheth of the **G**: 1471
Isa 11:10 ensign of the people; to it shall the **G** seek: 1471
42: 1 he shall bring forth judgment to the **G**. 1471
42: 6 covenant of the people, for a light of the **G**; 1471
49: 6 I will also give thee for a light to the **G**, 1471
49:22 I will lift up mine hand to the **G**, and set up 1471
54: 3 thy seed shall inherit the **G**, and make 1471
60: 3 the **G** shall come to thy light, and kings to 1471
60: 5 the forces of the **G** shall come unto thee. 1471
60:11 may bring unto thee the forces of the **G**, 1471
60:16 Thou shalt also suck the milk of the **G**, and 1471
61: 6 ye shall eat the riches of the **G**, and in their 1471
61: 9 their seed shall be known among the **G**, 1471
62: 2 the **G** shall see thy righteousness, and 1471
66:12 the glory of the **G** like a flowing stream: 1471
66:19 they shall declare my glory among the **G**. 1471
Jer 4: 7 and the destroyer of the **G** is on his way; 1471
14:22 Are there *any* among the vanities of the **G** 1471
16:19 the **G** shall come unto thee from the ends of 1471
46: 1 to Jeremiah the prophet against the **G**; 1471
La 2: 9 her king and her princes *are* among the **G**: 1471
Eze 4:13 Israel eat their defiled bread among the **G**, 1471
Hos 8: 8 now shall they be among the **G** as a vessel 1471
Joel 3: 9 Proclaim ye this among the **G**; Prepare war, 1471
Mic 5: 8 the remnant of Jacob shall be among the **G** 1471
Zec 1:21 to fray them, to cast out the horns of the **G**, 1471
Mal 1:11 same my name *shall be* great among the **G**; 1471
Mt 4:15 of the sea, beyond Jordan, Galilee of the **G**; *1484*
6:32 (For after all these *things* do the **G** seek): *1484*
10: 5 Go not into the way of the **G**, and into *any* *1484*
10:18 for a testimony against them and the **G**. *1484*
12:18 and he shall shew judgment to the **G**. *1484*
12:21 And in his name shall the **G** trust. *1484*
20:19 And shall deliver him to the **G** to mock, *1484*
20:25 Ye know that the princes of the **G** exercise *1484*
Mk 10:33 to death, and shall deliver him to the **G**: *1484*
10:42 over the **G** exercise lordship over them; *1484*
Lk 2:32 A light to lighten the **G**, and the glory of *1484*
18:32 For he shall be delivered unto the **G**, and *1484*
21:24 Jerusalem shall be trodden down of the **G**, *1484*
21:24 until the times of the **G** be fulfilled. *1484*
22:25 The kings of the **G** exercise lordship over *1484*
Jn 7:35 will he go unto the dispersed among the **G**, *1672*
7:35 among the Gentiles, and teach the **G**? *1672*
Ac 4:27 with the **G**, and the people of Israel, *1484*
7:45 in with Jesus into the possession of the **G**, *1484*
9:15 to bear my name before the **G**, and kings, *1484*
10:45 that on the **G** also was poured out the gift *1484*
11: 1 brethren that were in Judea heard that the **G** *1484*
11:18 Then hath God also to the **G** granted *1484*
13:42 the **G** besought that these words might be *1484*
13:46 of everlasting life, lo, we turn to the **G**. *1484*
13:47 I have set thee to be a light of the **G**, *1484*
13:48 And when the **G** heard *this*, they were glad, *1484*
14: 2 But the unbelieving Jews stirred up the **G**, *1484*
14: 5 there was an assault made both of the **G**, *1484*
14:27 he had opened *the* door of faith unto the **G**. *1484*
15: 3 Samaria, declaring the conversion of the **G**: *1484*
15: 7 that the **G** by my mouth should hear *1484*
15:12 wonders God had wrought among the **G** by *1484*
15:14 how God at the first did visit the **G**, *1484*
15:17 and all the **G**, upon whom my name is *1484*
15:19 which from among the **G** are turned to *1484*
15:23 the brethren which are of the **G** in Antioch *1484*
18: 6 from henceforth I will go unto the **G**. *1484*
21:11 shall deliver *him* into the hands of the **G**. *1484*
21:19 had wrought among the **G** by his ministry. *1484*
21:21 which are among the **G** to forsake Moses, *1484*
21:25 As touching the **G** which believe, we have *1484*
22:21 for I will send thee far hence unto the **G**. *1484*
26:17 and *from* the **G**, unto whom now I send *1484*
26:20 and *then* to the **G**, that *they* should repent *1484*
26:23 shew light unto the people, and to the **G**. *1484*
28:28 that the salvation of God is sent unto the **G**, *1484*
Ro 1:13 among you also, even as among other **G**. *1484*
2:14 For when *the* **G**, which have not the law, *1484*
2:24 is blasphemed among the **G** through you, *1484*
3: 9 we have before proved both Jews and **G**, *1672*
3:29 *is he* not also of the **G**? Yes, of the Gentiles *1484*
3:29 not also of the Gentiles? Yes, of the **G** also: *1484*
9:24 not of the Jews only, but also of the **G**? *1484*
9:30 That the **G**, which followed not *after* *1484*
11:11 their fall salvation *is come* unto the **G**, *1484*
11:12 the diminishing of them the riches of the **G**; *1484*
11:13 For I speak to you **G**, inasmuch as I am *1484*
11:13 inasmuch as I am the apostle of the **G**, *1484*

G

Ro 11:25 until the fulness of the G be come in. 1484
15: 9 And that the G might glorify God for his 1484
15: 9 cause I will confess to thee among the G, 1484
15:10 he saith, Rejoice, ye G, with his people. 1484
15:11 And again, Praise the Lord, all ye G; and 1484
15:12 and he that shall rise to reign over the G; 1484
15:12 over the Gentiles; in him shall the G trust. 1484
15:16 be the minister of Jesus Christ to the G, 1484
15:16 that the offering up of the G might be 1484
15:18 to make the G obedient, by word and deed, 1484
15:27 For if the G have been made partakers of 1484
16: 4 but also all the churches of the G. 1484
1Co 5: 1 as is not so much as named amongst the G, 1484
10:20 But I say, that the things which the G 1484
10:32 neither to the Jews, nor to the G, 1672
12: 2 Ye know that ye were G, carried away unto 1484
12:13 whether we be Jews or G, whether we be 1672
Gal 2: 2 that gospel which I preach among the G, 1484
2: 8 the same was mighty in me towards the G:) 1484
2:12 came from James, he did eat with the G: 1484
2:14 livest **after the manner of G**, and not as do 1483
2:14 why compellest thou the G to live as do 1484
2:15 Jews by nature, and not sinners of the G, 1484
3:14 might come on the G through Jesus Christ; 1484
Eph 2:11 that ye being in time passed G in the flesh, 1484
3: 1 the prisoner of Jesus Christ for you G, 1484
3: 6 That the G should be fellowheirs, and 1484
3: 8 that I should preach among the G 1484
4:17 that ye henceforth walk not as other G 1484
Col 1:27 of the glory of this mystery among the G; 1484
1Th 2:16 Forbidding us to speak to the G that they 1484
4: 5 even as the G which know not God: 1484
1Ti 2: 7 a teacher of the G in faith and verity. 1484
3:16 seen of angels, preached unto the G, 1484
2Ti 1:11 and an apostle, and a teacher of the G. 1484
4:17 fully known, and that all the G might hear: 1484
1Pe 2:12 your conversation honest among the G: 1484
4: 3 us to have wrought the will of the G, 1484
3Jn 1: 7 they went forth, taking nothing of the G. 1484
Rev 11: 2 measure it not; for it is given unto the G: 1484

GENTLE (5) [GENTLENESS, GENTLY]

1Th 2: 7 But we were g among you, even as a nurse 2261
2Ti 2:24 but be g unto all men, apt to teach, patient, 2261
Tit 3: 2 but g, shewing all meekness unto all men. 1933
Jas 3:17 then peaceable, g, and easy to be intreated, 1933
1Pe 2:18 not only to the good and g, but also to 1933

GENTLENESS (4) [GENTLE]

2Sa 22:36 and thy g hath made me great. 6031
Ps 18:35 me up, and thy g hath made me great. 6037
2Co 10: 1 you by the meekness and g of Christ, 1932
Gal 5:22 peace, longsuffering, g, goodness, faith, 5544

GENTLY (2) [GENTLE]

2Sa 18: 5 saying, Deal g for my sake with 328+3807.1
Isa 40:11 and shall **g lead** those that are with young. 5095

GENUBATH (2)

1Ki 11:20 the sister of Tahpenes bare him G his son, 1592
11:20 G was in Pharaoh's household among 1592

GERA (9)

Ge 46:21 Ashbel, G, and Naaman, Ehi, and Rosh, 1617
Jdg 3:15 Ehud the son of G, a Benjamite, a man 1617
2Sa 16: 5 whose name was Shimei, the son of G: 1617
19:16 Shimei the son of G, a Benjamite, 1617
19:18 Shimei the son of G fell down before 1617
1Ki 2: 8 thou hast with thee Shimei the son of G, 1617
1Ch 8: 3 of Bela were, Addar, and G, and Abihud, 1617
8: 5 And G, and Shephuphan, and Huram. 1617
8: 7 Naaman, and Ahiah, and G, he removed 1617

GERAHS (5)

Ex 30:13 (a shekel is twenty g:) a half shekel shall be 1626
Lev 27:25 the sanctuary: twenty g shall be the shekel. 1626
Nu 3:47 thou take them: (the shekel is twenty g:) 1626
18:16 shekel of the sanctuary, which is twenty g. 1626
Eze 45:12 the shekel shall be twenty g: 1626

GERAR (10)

Ge 10:19 as thou comest to G, unto Gaza; 1642
20: 1 and Shur, and sojourned in G. 1642
20: 2 Abimelech king of G sent, and took Sarah. 1642
26: 1 Abimelech king of the Philistims unto G. 1642
26: 6 And Isaac dwelt in G: 1642
26:17 pitched his tent in the valley of G, and 1642
26:20 the herdmen of G did strive with Isaac's 1642
26:26 Abimelech went to him from G, and 1642
2Ch 14:13 that were with him pursued them unto G: 1642
14:14 they smote all the cities round about G; 1642

GERGESENES (1)

Mt 8:28 to the other side into the country of the G, 1086

GERIZIM (3) [GERIZZIM]

Dt 11:29 thou shalt put the blessing upon mount G, 1630
Jos 8:33 half of them over against mount G, and half 1630
Jdg 9: 7 he went and stood in the top of mount G, 1630

GERIZZIM (1) [GERIZIM]

Dt 27:12 These shall stand upon mount G to bless 1630

GERSHOM (14)

Ex 2:22 bare him a son, and he called his name G: 1647
18: 3 of which the name of the one was G; for he 1647
Jdg 18:30 Jonathan, the son of G, the son of 1647
1Ch 6:16 The sons of Levi; G, Kohath, and Merari. 1647
6:17 these be the names of the sons of G; Libni, 1647
6:20 Of G; Libni his son, Jahath his son, 1647
6:43 son of Jahath, the son of G, the son of Levi. 1647
6:62 to the sons of G throughout their families 1647
6:71 Unto the sons of G were given out of 1647
15: 7 Of the sons of G; Joel the chief, and 1647
1Ch 23:15 The sons of Moses were, G, and Eliezer. 1647
23:16 Of the sons of G, Shebuel was the chief. 1647
26:24 Shebuel the son of G, the son of Moses, 1647
Ezr 8: 2 Of the sons of Phinehas; G: of the sons of 1647

GERSHON (18) [GERSHONITE, GERSHONITES]

Ge 46:11 the sons of Levi; G, Kohath, and Merari. 1648
Ex 6:16 G, and Kohath, and Merari: 1648
6:17 The sons of G; Libni, and Shimi, 1648
Nu 3:17 by their names; G, and Kohath, and Merari. 1648
3:18 these are the names of the sons of G by 1648
3:21 Of G was the family of the Libnites, and 1648
3:25 the charge of the sons of G in 1648
4:22 Take also the sum of the sons of G, 1648
4:28 of G in the tabernacle of the congregation: 1649
4:38 those that were numbered of the sons of G, 1648
4:41 numbered of the families of the sons of G, 1648
7: 7 and four oxen he gave unto the sons of G, 1648
10:17 the sons of G and the sons of Merari set 1648
26:57 of G, the family of the Gershonites: 1648
Jos 21: 6 the children of G had by lot out of 1648
21:27 unto the children of G, of the families of 1648
1Ch 6: 1 The sons of Levi; G, Kohath, and Merari. 1648
23: 6 of Levi, namely, G, Kohath, and Merari. 1648

GERSHONITE (3) [GERSHON]

1Ch 26:21 the sons of the G Laadan, chief fathers, 1649
26:21 even of Laadan the G, were Jehieli. 1649
29: 8 of the LORD, by the hand of Jehiel the G. 1649

GERSHONITES (9) [GERSHON]

Nu 3:21 these are the families of the G. 1649
3:23 The families of the G shall pitch behind 1649
3:24 the chief of the house of the father of the G 1649
4:24 This is the service of the families of the G, 1649
4:27 shall be all the service of the sons of the G, 1649
26:57 of Gershon, the family of the G: of Kohath, 1649
Jos 21:33 All the cities of the G according to their 1649
1Ch 23: 7 Of the G were, Laadan, and Shimei. 1649
2Ch 29:12 of the G; Joah the son of Zimmah, and 1649

GESHAN (1)

1Ch 2:47 and G, and Pelet, and Ephah, and Shaaph. 1529

GESHEM (3) [GASHMU]

Ne 2:19 the Ammonite, and G the Arabian, 1654
6: 1 G the Arabian, and the rest of our enemies, 1654
6: 2 That Sanballat and G sent unto me, saying, 1654

GESHUR (8) [GESHURI, GESHURITES]

2Sa 3: 3 Maacah the daughter of Talmai king of G; 1650
13:37 to Talmai, the son of Ammihud, king of G. 1650
13:38 and went to G, and was there three years. 1650
14:23 So Joab arose and went to G, and 1650
14:32 to say, Wherefore am I come from G? 1650
15: 8 vowed a vow while I abode at G in Syria, 1650
1Ch 2:23 he took G, and Aram, with the towns of 1650
3: 2 Maachah the daughter of Talmai king of G: 1650

GESHURI (2) [GESHUR]

Dt 3:14 the country of Argob unto the coasts of G 1651
Jos 13: 2 all the borders of the Philistines, and all G, 1651

GESHURITES (5) [GESHUR]

Jos 12: 5 unto the border of the G and 1651
13:11 the border of the G and Maachathites, and 1651
13:13 the children of Israel expelled not the G, 1651
13:13 the G and the Maachathites dwell among 1650
1Sa 27: 8 invaded the G, and the Gezrites, and 1651

GET (118) [GAT, GETTETH, GETTING, GOT, GOTTEN]

Ge 12: 1 G thee out of thy country, and from thy 1980
19:14 and said, Up, **g** ye **out** of this place; 3318
22: 2 and g thee into the land of Moriah; 1980
31:13 **g** thee **out** from this land, and return unto 3318
34: 4 saying, G me this damsel to wife. 3947
34:10 you therein, and g you **possessions** therein. 270
42: 2 **g** you **down** thither, and buy for us from 3381
44:17 for you, **g** you **up** in peace unto your father. 5927
45:17 and go, g you unto the land of Canaan; 935
Ex 1:10 and so **g** them **up** out of the land. 5927
5: 4 from their works? g you unto your burdens. 1980
5:11 g you straw where you can find it: yet not 3947
7:15 G thee unto Pharaoh in the morning; lo, 1980
10:28 G thee from me, take heed to thyself, 1980
11: 8 **G** thee **out**, and all the people that follow 3318
12:31 and **g** you **forth** from amongst my people, 3318
14:17 I will **g** me **honour** upon Pharaoh, and 3513
19:24 **g** thee **down**, and thou shalt come up, thou, 3381
32: 7 LORD said unto Moses, Go, **g** thee **down**; 3381
Lev 14:21 cannot g so much; then he shall take 3027+5381
14:22 such as he is **able to g**; 3027+5381
14:30 the young pigeons, such as he **can g**; 3027+5381
14:31 Even such as he is **able to g**, the one 3027+5381
14:32 whose **hand is** not **able to g** that 3027+5381
Nu 6:21 besides that that his hand shall **g**: 5381
13:17 **G** you **up** this way southward, and go up 5927
14:25 g you into the wilderness by the way of 5265
16:24 **G** you **up** from about the tabernacle of 5927
16:45 **G** you **up** from among this congregation, 7426
22:13 the princes of Balak, G you into your land: 1980
22:34 if it displease thee, I will **g** me **back again**. 7725
27:12 **G** thee **up** into this mount Abarim, and 5927
Dt 2:13 said I, and g you **over** the brook Zered. 5674
3:27 **G** thee **up** into the top of Pisgah, and lift up 5927
5:30 say to them, G you into your tents **again**. 7725
8:18 for it is he that giveth thee power to **g** 6213
9:12 Arise, **g** thee **down** quickly from hence; 3381
17: 8 **g** thee **up** into the place which the LORD 5927
28:43 The stranger that is within thee shall **g up** 5927
32:49 G thee **up** into this mountain Abarim, 5927
Jos 2:16 she said unto them, G you to the mountain, 1980
7:10 the LORD said unto Joshua, **G** thee **up**; 6965
Jos 17:15 then **g** thee **up** to the wood country, and 5927
22: 4 g ye unto your tents, and unto the land of 1980
Jdg 7: 9 unto him, Arise, **g** thee **down** unto the host; 3381
14: 2 therefore g her for me to wife. 3947
14: 3 Samson said unto his father, G her for me; 3947
19: 9 to morrow **g** you **early** on your way, that 7925
Ru 3: 3 upon thee, and **g** thee **down** to the floor: 3381
1Sa 9:13 Now therefore **g** you **up**; for about this time 5927
15: 6 **g** you **down** from among the Amalekites, 3381
20:29 let me **g away**, I pray thee, and see my 4422
22: 5 depart, and g thee into the land of Judah. 935
23:26 David made haste to **g away** for fear of 1980
25: 5 G you **up** to Carmel, and go to Nabal, and 5927
2Sa 20: 6 lest he g him fenced cities, and escape us. 4672
1Ki 1: 2 that my lord the king may **g heat**. 2552
1:13 Go and g thee **in** unto king David, and 935
2:26 G thee to Anathoth, unto thine own fields; 1980
12:18 made speed to **g** him **up** to his chariot, 5927
14: 2 the wife of Jeroboam; and g thee to Shiloh: 1980
14:12 thou therefore, g thee to thine own house: 1980
17: 3 G thee hence, and turn thee eastward, 1980
17: 9 Arise, g thee to Zarephath, which belongeth 1980
18:41 said unto Ahab, G thee **up**, eat and drink; 5927
18:44 Prepare thy chariot, and g thee **down**, 3381
2Ki 3:13 g thee to the prophets of thy father, and 1980
7:12 we shall catch them alive, and g into the city. 935
2Ch 10:18 king Rehoboam made speed to **g** him **up** to 5927
Ne 9:10 So didst thou g thee a name, as it is this 6213
Ps 119:104 Through thy precepts I g understanding: NIH
Pr 4: 5 G wisdom, get understanding: forget it not; 7069
4: 5 Get wisdom, g understanding: forget it not; 7069
4: 7 is the principal thing; therefore g wisdom: 7069
4: 7 and with all thy getting g understanding. 7069
6:33 A wound and dishonour shall he g; and 4672
16:16 How much better is it to g wisdom than 7069
16:16 to g understanding rather to be chosen than 7069
17:16 a price in the hand of a fool to g wisdom, 7069
22:25 learn his ways, and g a snare to thy soul. 3947
Ecc 3: 6 A time to g, and a time to lose; a time to 1245
SS 4: 6 I will g me to the mountain of myrrh, and 1980
7:12 Let us **g up early** to the vineyards; let us 7925
Isa 22:15 Go, g thee unto this treasurer, even unto 935
30:11 G ye **out** of the way, turn aside out of 5493
30:22 thou shalt say unto it, G thee **hence**. 3318
40: 9 **g** thee **up** into the high mountain; 5927
47: 5 Sit thou silent, and g thee into darkness, 935
Jer 5: 5 I will g me unto the great men, and 1980
13: 1 Go and g thee a linen girdle, and put it 7069
19: 1 Go and g a potter's earthen bottle, and 7069
46: 4 **g up**, ye horsemen, and stand forth with 5927
48: 9 unto Moab, that it may flee and **g away**: 3318
49:30 Flee, g you far off, dwell deep, O ye 5110
49:31 Arise, **g** you **up** unto the wealthy nation, 5927
La 3: 7 hath hedged me about, that I cannot **g out**: 3318
Eze 3: 4 go, g thee unto the house of Israel, and 935
3:11 go, g thee to them of the captivity, unto 935
11:15 have said, G ye far from the LORD: NIH
22:27 to destroy souls, to **g dishonest gain**. 1214+1215
Da 4:14 let the beasts **g away** from under it, and 5111
Joel 3:13 come, g you **down**; for the press is full, 3381
Zep 3:19 I will g them praise and fame in every land 7760
Zec 6: 7 G ye hence, walk to and fro through 1980
Mt 4:10 saith Jesus unto him, G thee **hence**, Satan: 5217
14:22 constrained his disciples to g into a ship, 1684
16:23 said unto Peter, G thee behind me, Satan: 5217
Mk 6:45 constrained his disciples to g into the ship, 1684
8:33 saying, G thee behind me, Satan: 5217
Lk 4: 8 said unto him, G thee behind me, Satan: 5217
9:12 round about, and lodge, and g victuals: 2147
13:31 unto him, G thee **out**, and depart hence: 1831
Ac 7: 3 G thee **out** of thy country, and 1831
10:20 and g thee **down**, and go with them, 2597
22:18 and **g** thee quickly **out** of Jerusalem: 1831
27:43 themselves first into the sea, and g to land: 1826
2Co 2:11 Lest Satan should **g an advantage** of us: 4122
Jas 4:13 there a year, and buy and sell, and **g gain**: 2770

GETHER (2)

Ge 10:23 of Aram; Uz, and Hul, and G, and Mash. 1666
1Ch 1:17 and Uz, and Hul, and G, and Meshech. 1666

GETHSEMANE (2)

Mt 26:36 Jesus with them unto a place called G, 1068
Mk 14:32 they came to a place which was named G: 1068

GETTETH (9) [GET]

2Sa 5: 8 Whosoever **g up** to the gutter, and 5060
Pr 3:13 and the man that g understanding. 6329
9: 7 He that reproveth a scorner g to himself 3947
9: 7 he that rebuketh a wicked man g himself a NIH
15:32 but he that heareth reproof g understanding. 7069
18:15 The heart of the prudent g knowledge; and 7069
19: 8 He that g wisdom loveth his own soul: 7069
Jer 17:11 so he that g riches, and not by right, 6213
48:44 he that **g up** out of the pit shall be taken in 5927

GETTING (3) [GET]

Ge 31:18 which he had gotten, the cattle of his g, 7075
Pr 4: 7 and with all thy g get understanding. 7075
21: 6 The g of treasures by a lying tongue is a 6467

GEUEL (1)

Nu 13:15 Of the tribe of Gad, G the son of Machi. 1345

GEZER (13) [GEZRITES]

Jos 10:33 Horam king of G came up to help Lachish; 1507
12:12 The king of Eglon, one; the king of G, one; 1507
16: 3 coast of Beth-horon the nether, and to G: 1507
16:10 not out the Canaanites that dwelt in G: 1507
21:21 for the slayer; and G with her suburbs, 1507
Jdg 1:29 drive out the Canaanites that dwelt in G; 1507
1:29 but the Canaanites dwelt in G among them. 1507
1Ki 9:15 and Hazor, and Megiddo, and G. 1507
9:16 taken G, and burnt it with fire, and slain 1507

1Ki 9:17 Solomon built **G**, and Beth-horon 1507
1Ch 6:67 *they gave* also **G** with her suburbs, 1507
7:28 and eastward Naaran, and westward **G**, 1507
20: 4 that there arose war at **G** with 1507

GEZRITES (1) [GEZER]
1Sa 27: 8 and the **G**, and the Amalekites: 1511

GHOST (109)
Ge 25: 8 Abraham **gave up the g**, and died in a good 1478
25:17 he **gave up the g** and died; and 1478
35:29 Isaac **gave up the g**, and died, and 1478
49:33 **yielded up the g**, and was gathered unto 1478
Job 3:11 *why* did I *not* **give up the g** when I came 1478
10:18 *Oh that* I had **given up the g**, and no eye 1478
11:20 *shall be as* the **giving up of the g**. 4646+5315
13:19 if I hold my tongue, I shall **give up the g**. 1478
14:10 yea, man **giveth up the g**, and where *is* he? 1478
Jer 15: 9 she hath **given up the g**; her sun is 5301+5315
La 1:19 and mine elders **gave up the g** in the city, 1478
Mt 1:18 she was found with child of the Holy **G**. 4151
1:20 which is conceived in her is of the Holy **G**. 4151
3:11 he shall baptize you with the Holy **G**, and 4151
12:31 the blasphemy against the *Holy* **G** shall not 4151
12:32 whosoever speaketh against the Holy **G**, 4151
27:50 again with a loud voice, yielded up the **g**. 4151
28:19 and of the Son, and of the Holy **G**: 4151
Mk 1: 8 but he shall baptize you with the Holy **G**. 4151
3:29 against the Holy **G** hath never forgiveness, 4151
12:36 For David himself said by the Holy **G**, 4151
13:11 for it is not ye that speak, but the Holy **G**. 4151
15:37 cried with a loud voice, and **gave up the g**. 1606
15:39 so cried out, and **gave up the g**, he said, 1606
Lk 1:15 and he shall be filled with the Holy **G**, 4151
1:35 The Holy **G** shall come upon thee, and 4151
1:41 and Elisabeth was filled with the Holy **G**: 4151
1:67 Zacharias was filled with the Holy **G**, 4151
2:25 of Israel: and the Holy **G** was upon him. 4151
2:26 it was revealed unto him by the Holy **G**, 4151
3:16 he shall baptize you with the Holy **G** and 4151
3:22 And the Holy **G** descended in a bodily 4151
4: 1 And Jesus being full of the Holy **G** 4151
12:10 against the Holy **G** it shall not be forgiven. 4151
12:12 For the Holy **G** shall teach you in the same 4151
23:46 and having said thus, he **gave up the g**. 1606
Jn 1:33 is he which baptizeth with the Holy **G**. 4151
7:39 for the Holy **G** was not yet *given;* because 4151
14:26 But the Comforter, *which is* the Holy **G**, 4151
19:30 and he bowed *his* head, and gave up the **g**. 4151
20:22 saith unto them, Receive ye the Holy **G**. 4151
Ac 1: 2 after that he through the Holy **G** had given 4151
1: 5 ye shall be baptized with the Holy **G** not 4151
1: 8 after that the Holy **G** is come upon you: 4151
1:16 which the Holy **G** by the mouth of David 4151
2: 4 And they were all filled with the Holy **G**, 4151
2:33 of the Father the promise of the Holy **G**, 4151
2:38 and ye shall receive the gift of the Holy **G**. 4151
4: 8 Then Peter, filled with the Holy **G**, 4151
4:31 and they were all filled with the Holy **G**, 4151
5: 3 Satan filled thine heart to lie to the Holy **G**, 4151
5: 5 these words fell down, and **gave up the g**: 1634
5:10 at his feet, and **yielded up the g**: 1634
5:32 and *so is* also the Holy **G**, whom God hath 4151
6: 3 full of the Holy **G** and wisdom, whom we 4151
6: 5 a man full of faith and of the Holy **G**, and 4151
7:51 and ears, ye do always resist the Holy **G**: 4151
7:55 But he, being full of the Holy **G**, looked up 4151
8:15 that they might receive the Holy **G**: 4151
8:17 on them, and they received the Holy **G**. 4151
8:18 the apostles' hands the Holy **G** was given, 4151
8:19 I lay hands, he may receive the Holy **G**. 4151
9:17 thy sight, and be filled with the Holy **G**. 4151
9:31 and in the comfort of the Holy **G**, 4151
10:38 anointed Jesus of Nazareth with the Holy **G** 4151
10:44 the Holy **G** fell on all them which heard 4151
10:45 also was poured out the gift of the Holy **G**. 4151
10:47 which have received the Holy **G** as well as 4151
11:15 I began to speak, the Holy **G** fell on them, 4151
11:16 but ye shall be baptized with the Holy **G**. 4151
11:24 and full of the Holy **G** and of faith: 4151
12:23 he was eaten of worms, and **gave up the g**. 1634
13: 2 and fasted, the Holy **G** said, Separate me 4151
13: 4 So they, being sent forth by the Holy **G**, 4151
13: 9 filled with the Holy **G**, set his eyes on him, 4151
13:52 were filled with joy, and with the Holy **G**. 4151
15: 8 bare them witness, giving them the Holy **G**, 4151
15:28 For it seemed good to the Holy **G**, and 4151
16: 6 were forbidden of the Holy **G** to preach 4151
19: 2 Have ye received the Holy **G** since ye 4151
19: 2 as heard whether there be *any* Holy **G**. 4151
19: 6 upon them, the Holy **G** came on them; 4151
20:23 Save that the Holy **G** witnesseth in every 4151
20:28 over the which the Holy **G** hath made you 4151
21:11 and feet, and said, Thus saith the Holy **G**, 4151
28:25 Well spake the Holy **G** by Esaias 4151
Ro 5: 5 by the Holy **G** which is given unto us. 4151
9: 1 also bearing me witness in the Holy **G**, 4151
14:17 and peace, and joy in the Holy **G**. 4151
15:13 in hope, through the power of the Holy **G**. 4151
15:16 being sanctified by the Holy **G**. 4151
1Co 2:13 but which the Holy **G** teacheth; 4151
6:19 is the temple of the Holy **G** which is in you, 4151
12: 3 that Jesus is the Lord, but by the Holy **G**. 4151
2Co 6: 6 by kindness, by the Holy **G**, 4151
13:14 and the communion of the Holy **G**, *be* with 4151
1Th 1: 5 and in the Holy **G**, and in much assurance; 4151
1: 6 in much affliction, with joy of the Holy **G**: 4151
2Ti 1:14 keep by the Holy **G** which dwelleth in us. 4151
Tit 3: 5 and renewing of the Holy **G**; 4151
Heb 2: 4 divers miracles, and gifts of the Holy **G**, 4151
3: 7 Wherefore, as the Holy **G** saith, To day if 4151
6: 4 and were made partakers of the Holy **G**, 4151
9: 8 The Holy **G** this signifying, that the way 4151
10:15 *Whereof* the Holy **G** also is a witness to us: 4151
1Pe 1:12 with the Holy **G** sent *down* from heaven; 4151
2Pe 1:21 spake *as they were* moved by the Holy **G**. 4151
1Jn 5: 7 the Father, the Word, and the Holy **G**: 4151
Jude 1:20 most holy faith, praying in the Holy **G**, 4151

GIAH (1)
2Sa 2:24 that *lieth* before **G** *by* the way of 1520

GIANT (8) [GIANTS]
2Sa 21:16 which *was* of the sons of the **g**, 7497
21:18 slew Saph, which *was* of the sons of the **g**. 7497
21:20 *in* number; and he also was born to the **g**. 7497
21:22 These four were born to the **g** in Gath, and 7497
1Ch 20: 4 *that was* of the children of the **g**: 7497
20: 6 *each foot:* and he also was the son of the **g**. 7497
20: 8 These were born unto the **g** in Gath; and 7497
Job 16:14 upon breach, he runneth upon me like a **g**. 1368

GIANTS (13) [GIANT]
Ge 6: 4 There were **g** in the earth in those days; 5303
Nu 13:33 there we saw the **g**, the sons of Anak, 5303
13:33 the sons of Anak, *which come* of the **g**: 5303
Dt 2:11 Which also were accounted **g**, as 7497
2:20 (That also was accounted a land of **g**: 7497
2:20 **g** dwelt therein in old time; and 7497
3:11 of Bashan remained of the remnant of **g**; 7497
3:13 all Bashan, which was called the land of **g**. 7497
Jos 12: 4 *which was* of the remnant of the **g**, 7497
13:12 who remained of the remnant of the **g**: 7497
15: 8 which *is* at the end of the valley of the **g** 7497
17:15 in the land of the Perizzites and of the **g**, 7497
18:16 which *is* in the valley of the **g** on the north, 7497

GIBBAR (1)
Ezr 2:20 The children of **G**, ninety and five. 1402

GIBBETHON (6)
Jos 19:44 And Eltekeh, and **G**, and Baalath, 1405
21:23 with her suburbs, **G** with her suburbs, 1405
1Ki 15:27 Baasha smote him at **G**, which *belongeth* to 1405
15:27 for Nadab and all Israel laid siege to **G**. 1405
16:15 the people *were* encamped against **G**, 1405
16:17 Omri went up from **G**, and all Israel with 1405

GIBEA (1)
1Ch 2:49 father of Machbenah, and the father of **G**: 1388

GIBEAH (48) [GIBEATH, GIBEATHITE]
Jos 15:57 Cain, **G**, and Timnah; ten cities with their 1390
Jdg 19:12 children of Israel; we will pass over to **G**. 1390
19:13 places to lodge all night, in **G**, or in Ramah. 1390
19:14 down upon them *when they were* by **G**, 1390
19:15 aside thither, to go in *and* to lodge in **G**: 1390
19:16 of mount Ephraim; and he sojourned in **G**: 1390
20: 4 I came into **G** that *belongeth* to Benjamin, I 1390
20: 5 the men of **G** rose against me, and beset 1390
20: 9 *shall be* the thing which we will do to **G**; 1390
20:10 may do, when they come to **G** of Benjamin, 1387
20:13 the children of Belial, which *are* in **G**, 1390
20:14 together out of the cities unto **G**, 1390
20:15 drew sword, beside the inhabitants of **G**, 1390
20:19 in the morning, and encamped against **G**. 1390
20:20 in array to fight against them at **G**. 1390
20:21 children of Benjamin came forth out of **G**, 1390
20:25 Benjamin went forth against them out of **G** 1390
20:29 And Israel set liers in wait round about **G**. 1390
20:30 put *themselves* in array against **G**, as at 1390
20:31 the other to **G** in the field, about thirty men 1390
20:33 their places, *even* out of the meadows of **G**. 1387
20:34 there came against **G** ten thousand chosen 1390
20:36 liers in wait which they had set beside **G**. 1390
20:37 the liers in wait hasted, and rushed upon **G**; 1390
20:43 trode them down with ease over against **G** 1390
1Sa 10:26 Saul also went home to **G**; and there went 1390
11: 4 came the messengers *to* **G** of Saul, and 1390
13: 2 a thousand were with Jonathan in **G** of 1390
13:15 gat him up from Gilgal *unto* **G** of 1390
13:16 with them, abode in **G** of Benjamin: 1387
14: 2 Saul tarried in the uttermost part of **G** 1390
14: 5 and the other southward over against **G**. 1387
14:16 the watchmen of Saul in **G** of Benjamin 1390
15:34 and Saul went up to his house *to* **G** of Saul. 1390
22: 6 (now Saul abode in **G** under a tree in 1390
23:19 came up the Ziphites to Saul to **G**, saying, 1390
26: 1 the Ziphites came unto Saul to **G**, saying, 1390
2Sa 6: 3 out of the house of Abinadab that *was* in **G**: 1390
6: 4 of the house of Abinadab which *was* at **G**, 1390
21: 6 them up unto the LORD in **G** of Saul, 1390
23:29 Ittai the son of Ribai out of **G** of 1390
1Ch 11:31 Ithai the son of Ribai of **G**, that pertained to 1390
2Ch 13: 2 *was* Michaiah the daughter of Uriel of **G**. 1390
Isa 10:29 at Geba; Ramah is afraid; **G** of Saul is fled. 1390
Hos 5: 8 Blow ye the cornet in **G**, *and* the trumpet in 1390
9: 9 corrupted *themselves*, as *in* the days of **G**: 1390
10: 9 thou hast sinned from the days of **G**: 1390
10: 9 the battle in **G** against the children of 1390

GIBEATH (1) [GIBEAH]
Jos 18:28 which *is* Jerusalem, **G**, *and* Kirjath; 1390

GIBEATHITE (1) [GIBEAH]
1Ch 12: 3 then Joash, the sons of Shemaah the **G**; 1395

GIBEON (37) [GIBEONITE, GIBEONITES]
Jos 9: 3 when the inhabitants of **G** heard what 1391
9:17 Now their cities *were* **G**, and Chephirah, 1391
10: 1 how the inhabitants of **G** had made peace 1391
10: 2 feared greatly, because **G** *was* a great city, 1391
10: 4 and help me, that we may smite **G**: 1391
10: 5 encamped before **G**, and made war against 1391
10: 6 the men of **G** sent unto Joshua to the camp 1391
10:10 slew them *with* a great slaughter at **G**, and 1391
10:12 sight of Israel, Sun, stand thou still upon **G**; 1391
10:41 and all the country of Goshen, even unto **G**. 1391
11:19 save the Hivites the inhabitants of **G**: 1391
Jos 18:25 **G**, and Ramah, and Beeroth, 1391
21:17 **G** with her suburbs, Geba with her suburbs, 1391
2Sa 2:12 son of Saul, went out from Mahanaim to **G**. 1391
2:13 and met together by the pool of **G**: 1391
2:16 called Helkath-hazzurim, which *is* in **G**. 1391
2:24 Giah *by* the way of the wilderness of **G**. 1391
3:30 he had slain their brother Asahel at **G** in 1391
20: 8 they *were* at the great stone which *is* in **G**, 1391
1Ki 3: 4 the king went to **G** to sacrifice there; 1391
3: 5 In **G** the LORD appeared to Solomon in a 1391
9: 2 as he had appeared unto him at **G**. 1391
1Ch 8:29 at **G** dwelt the father of Gibeon; 1391
8:29 at Gibeon dwelt the father of **G**; 1391
9:35 in **G** dwelt the father of Gibeon, Jehiel, 1391
9:35 in Gibeon dwelt the father of **G**, Jehiel, 1391
14:16 of the Philistines from **G** even to Gazer. 1391
16:39 the LORD in the high place that *was* at **G**, 1391
21:29 *were* at that season in the high place at **G**. 1391
2Ch 1: 3 went to the high place that *was* at **G**; 1391
1:13 the high place that *was* at **G** *to* Jerusalem, 1391
Ne 3: 7 the men of **G**, and of Mizpah, 1391
7:25 The children of **G**, ninety and five. 1391
Isa 28:21 he shall be wroth as *in* the valley of **G**, 1391
Jer 28: 1 son of Azur the prophet, which *was* of **G**, 1391
41:12 found him by the great waters that *are* in **G**. 1391
41:16 whom he had brought again from **G**: 1391

GIBEONITE (2) [GIBEON]
1Ch 12: 4 Ismaiah the **G**, a mighty *man* among 1393
Ne 3: 7 next unto them repaired Melatiah the **G**, 1393

GIBEONITES (6) [GIBEON]
2Sa 21: 1 *his* bloody house, because he slew the **G**. 1393
21: 2 the king called the **G**, and said unto them; 1393
21: 2 (now the **G** *were* not of the children of 1393
21: 3 Wherefore David said unto the **G**, 1393
21: 4 the **G** said unto him, We will have no silver 1393
21: 9 he delivered them into the hands of the **G**, 1393

GIBLITES (1) [GEBAL]
Jos 13: 5 the land of the **G**, and all Lebanon, 1382

GIDDALTI (2)
1Ch 25: 4 Hanani, Eliathah, **G**, and Romamti-ezer, 1437
25:29 The two and twentieth to **G**, *he*, his sons, 1437

GIDDEL (4)
Ezr 2:47 The children of **G**, the children of Gahar, 1435
2:56 the children of Darkon, the children of **G**, 1435
Ne 7:49 the children of **G**, the children of Gahar, 1435
7:58 the children of Darkon, the children of **G**, 1435

GIDEON (39) [GEDEON, JERUBBAAL]
Jdg 6:11 his son **G** threshed wheat by the winepress, 1439
6:13 **G** said unto him, O my lord, if the LORD 1439
6:19 **G** went in, and made ready a kid, and 1439
6:22 when **G** perceived that he *was* an angel of 1439
6:22 the LORD, **G** said, Alas, O Lord GOD! 1439
6:24 **G** built an altar there unto the LORD, 1439
6:27 **G** took ten men of his servants, and did as 1439
6:29 **G** the son of Joash hath done this thing. 1439
6:34 the spirit of the LORD came upon **G**, and 1439
6:36 **G** said unto God, If thou wilt save Israel by 1439
6:39 **G** said unto God, Let not thine anger be hot 1439
7: 1 who *is* **G**, and all the people that *were* with 1439
7: 2 the LORD said unto **G**, The people that 1439
7: 4 the LORD said unto **G**, The people *are* yet 1439
7: 5 the LORD said unto **G**, Every one that 1439
7: 7 the LORD said unto **G**, By the three 1439
7:13 when **G** was come, behold, *there was* a 1439
7:14 This *is* nothing else save the sword of **G** 1439
7:15 *so*, when **G** heard the telling of the dream, 1439
7:18 say, *The sword* of the LORD, and of **G**. 1439
7:19 So **G**, and the hundred men that *were* with 1439
7:20 The sword of the LORD, and of **G**. 1439
7:24 **G** sent messengers throughout all mount 1439
7:25 and Zeeb to **G** on the *other* side Jordan. 1439
8: 4 **G** came to Jordan, *and* passed over, he, 1439
8: 7 **G** said, Therefore when the LORD hath 1439
8:11 **G** went up *by* the way of them that dwelt in 1439
8:13 **G** the son of Joash returned from battle 1439
8:21 **G** arose, and slew Zebah and Zalmunna, 1439
8:22 the men of Israel said unto **G**, Rule thou 1439
8:23 **G** said unto them, I will not rule over you, 1439
8:24 **G** said unto them, I would desire a request 1439
8:27 **G** made an ephod thereof, and put it in his 1439
8:27 which *thing* became a snare unto **G**, and 1439
8:28 in quietness forty years in the days of **G**. 1439
8:30 **G** had threescore and ten sons of his body 1439
8:32 **G** the son of Joash died in a good old age, 1439
8:33 it came to pass, as soon as **G** was dead, 1439
8:35 to the house of Jerubbaal, *namely*, **G**, 1439

GIDEONI (5)
Nu 1:11 Of Benjamin; Abidan the son of **G**. 1441
2:22 of Benjamin *shall be* Abidan the son of **G**. 1441
7:60 On the ninth day Abidan the son of **G**, 1441
7:65 *was* the offering of Abidan the son of **G**. 1441
10:24 of Benjamin *was* Abidan the son of **G**. 1441

GIDOM (1)
Jdg 20:45 pursued hard after them unto **G**, and 1440

GIER (2)
Lev 11:18 the swan, and the pelican, and the **g eagle**, 7360
Dt 14:17 and the **g eagle**, and the cormorant, 7360

GIFT (59) [GIVE]
Ge 34:12 Ask me never so much dowry and **g**, and 4976
Ex 23: 8 thou shalt take no **g**: for the gift blindeth 7810
23: 8 for the **g** blindeth the wise, and 7810
Nu 8:19 I have given the Levites *as* a **g** to Aaron 5414
18: 6 to you *they are* given *as* a **g** for the LORD, 4979
18: 7 priest's office *unto you as* a service of **g**: 4979

Nu 18:11 the heave offering of their g, with all 4976
Dt 16:19 shalt not respect persons, neither take a g: 7810
16:19 for a g doth blind the eyes of the wise, and 7810
2Sa 19:42 the king's cost? or hath he given us any g? 5375
Ps 45:12 the daughter of Tyre shall be there with a g; 4503
Pr 17: 8 A g is as a precious stone in the eyes of him 7810
17:23 A wicked man taketh a g out of the bosom 7810
18:16 A man's g maketh room for him, and 4976
21:14 A g in secret pacifieth anger: and a reward 4976
25:14 Whoso boasteth himself of a false g is like 4991
Ecc 3:13 the good of all his labour, it is the g of God. 4991
5:19 to rejoice in his labour; this is the g of God. 4991
7: 7 wise man mad; and a g destroyeth the heart. 4979
Eze 46:16 If the prince give a g unto any of his sons, 4979
46:17 if he give a g of his inheritance to one of 4979
Mt 5:23 Therefore if thou bring thy g to the altar, 1435
5:24 Leave there thy g before the altar, and 1435
5:24 thy brother, and then come and offer thy g. 1435
8: 4 offer the g that Moses commanded for a 1435
15: 5 say to his father or his mother, It is a g, 1435
23:18 whosoever sweareth by the g that is upon it, 1435
23:19 the g, or the altar that sanctifieth the gift? 1435
23:19 the gift, or the altar that sanctifieth the g? 1435
Mk 7:11 or mother, It is Corban, that is to say, a g, 1435
Jn 4:10 If thou knewest the g of God, and who it is 1431
Ac 2:38 ye shall receive the g of the Holy Ghost. 1431
8:20 thou hast thought that the g of God may be 1431
10:45 was poured out the g of the Holy Ghost. 1431
11:17 as God gave them the like g as he did unto 1431
Ro 1:11 that I may impart unto you some spiritual g, 5486
5:15 But not as the offence, so also is the free g. 5486
5:15 and the g by grace, which is by one man, 1431
5:16 not as it was by one that sinned, so is the g: 1434
5:16 the free g is of many offences unto 5486
5:17 of the g of righteousness shall reign in life 1431
5:18 by the righteousness of one the free g came NIG
6:23 the g of God is eternal life through Jesus 5486
1Co 1: 7 So that ye come behind in no g; waiting for 5486
7: 7 But every man hath his proper g of God, 5486
13: 2 And though I have the g of prophecy, and NIG
2Co 1:11 that for the g bestowed upon us by 5486
8: 4 much intreaty that we would receive the g, 5485
9:15 Thanks be unto God for his unspeakable g. 1431
Eph 2: 8 that not of yourselves: it is the g of God: 1435
3: 7 according to the g of the grace of God 1431
4: 7 according to the measure of the g of Christ. 1431
Php 4:17 Not because I desire a g: but I desire fruit 1390
1Ti 4:14 Neglect not the g that is in thee, which was 5486
2Ti 1: 6 remembrance that thou stir up the g of God, 5486
Heb 6: 4 and have tasted of the heavenly g, and 1431
Jas 1:17 Every good g and every perfect gift is from 1394
1:17 good gift and every perfect g is from above, 1434
1Pe 4:10 As every man hath received the g, even so 5486

GIFTS (53) [GIVE]
Ge 25: 6 Abraham gave g, and sent them away from 4979
Ex 28:38 of Israel shall hallow in all their holy g; 4979
Lev 23:38 beside your g, and beside all your vows, 4979
Nu 18:29 Out of all your g ye shall offer every heave 4979
2Sa 8: 2 became David's servants, and brought g. 4503
8: 6 became servants to David, and brought g. 4503
1Ch 18: 2 became David's servants, and brought g. 4503
18: 6 became David's servants, and brought g. 4503
2Ch 19: 7 nor respect of persons, nor taking of g. 7810
21: 3 And their father gave them great g of silver, 4979
26: 8 the Ammonites gave g to Uzziah: and 4503
32:23 many brought g unto the LORD to 4503
Est 2:18 gave g, according to the state of the king. 4864
9:22 portions one to another, and g to the poor. 4979
Ps 68:18 thou hast received g for men; yea, for 4979
72:10 the kings of Sheba and Seba shall offer g. 814
Pr 6:35 he rest content, though thou givest many g. 7810
15:27 own house; but he that hateth g shall live. 4979
19: 6 every man is a friend to him that giveth g. 4976
29: 4 but he that receiveth g overthroweth it. 8641
Isa 1:23 every one loveth g, and followeth after 7810
Eze 16:33 They give g to all whores: but thou givest 5078
16:33 thou givest thy g to all thy lovers, and 5083
20:26 I polluted them in their own g, in that they 4979
20:31 For when ye offer your g, when ye make 4979
20:39 ye my holy name no more with your g, 4979
22:12 In thee have they taken g to shed blood; 7810
Da 2: 6 ye shall receive of me g and rewards and 4978
2:48 gave him many great g, and made him ruler 4978
5:17 Let thy g be to thyself, and give thy 4978
Mt 2:11 their treasures, they presented unto him g; 1435
7:11 know how to give good g unto your 1390
Lk 11:13 know how to give good g unto your 1390
21: 1 saw the rich men casting their g into 1435
21: 5 it was adorned with goodly stones and g, 334
Ro 11:29 For the g and calling of God are without 5486
12: 6 g differing according to the grace that is 5486
1Co 12: 1 Now concerning spiritual g, brethren, NIG
12: 4 Now there are diversities of g, but the same 5486
12: 9 to another the g of healing by the same 5486
12:28 then g of healings, helps, governments, 5486
12:30 Have all the g of healing? do all speak with 5486
12:31 But covet earnestly the best g: and yet shew 5486
14: 1 and desire spiritual g, but rather that ye may NIG
14:12 forasmuch as ye are zealous of spiritual g, NIG
Eph 4: 8 led captivity captive, and gave g unto men. 1390
Heb 2: 4 divers miracles, and g of the Holy Ghost, 3311
5: 1 that he may offer both g and sacrifices for 1435
8: 3 For every high priest is ordained to offer g 1435
8: 4 seeing that there are priests that offer g 1435
9: 9 in which were offered both g and sacrifices, 1435
11: 4 he was righteous, God testifying of his g: 1435
Rev 11:10 and shall send g one to another; 1435

GIHON (6)
Ge 2:13 the name of the second river is G: the same 1521
1Ki 1:33 mine own mule, and bring him down to G: 1521
1:38 king David's mule, and brought him to G. 1521
1:45 the prophet have anointed him king in G: 1521
2Ch 32:30 also stopped the upper watercourse of G, 1521
33:14 on the west side of G, in the valley, even to 1521

GILALAI (1)
Ne 12:36 Shemaiah, and Azarael, Milalai, G, Maai, 1562

GILBOA (8)
1Sa 28: 4 all Israel together, and they pitched in G. 1533
31: 1 and fell down slain in mount G. 1533
31: 8 and his three sons fallen in mount G. 1533
2Sa 1: 6 As I happened by chance upon mount G, 1533
1:21 Ye mountains of G, let there be no dew, 1533
21:12 when the Philistines had slain Saul in G: 1533
1Ch 10: 1 and fell down slain in mount G. 1533
10: 8 found Saul and his sons fallen in mount G. 1533

GILEAD (100) [GILEAD'S, GILEADITE, GILEADITES, JABESH-GILEAD, RAMOTH-GILEAD]
Ge 31:21 and set his face toward the mount G. 1568
31:23 and they overtook him in the mount G. 1568
31:25 his brethren pitched in the mount of G. 1568
37:25 a company of Ishmeelites came from G 1568
Nu 26:29 Machir begat G: of Gilead come the family 1568
26:29 of G come the family of the Gileadites. 1568
26:30 These are the sons of G: of Jeezer, 1568
27: 1 of Hepher, the son of G, the son of Machir, 1568
32: 1 the land of G, that behold, the place was a 1568
32:26 our cattle, shall be there in the cities of G: 1568
32:29 ye shall give them the land of G for a 1568
32:39 of Machir the son of Manasseh went to G, 1568
32:40 Moses gave G unto Machir the son of 1568
36: 1 fathers of the families of the children of G, 1568
Dt 2:36 the city that is by the river, even unto G, 1568
3:10 and all G, and all Bashan, unto Salchah and 1568
3:12 half mount G, and the cities thereof, gave I 1568
3:13 the rest of G, and all Bashan, being 1568
3:15 And I gave G unto Machir. 1568
3:16 unto the Gadites I gave from G even unto 1568
4:43 Ramoth in G, of the Gadites; and Golan in 1568
34: 1 the LORD shewed him all the land of G, 1568
Jos 12: 2 from half G, even unto the river Jabbok, 1568
12: 5 and the Maachathites, and half G, 1568
13:11 G, and the border of the Geshurites and 1568
13:25 all the cities of G, and half the land of 1568
13:31 half G, and Ashtaroth, and Edrei, cities of 1568
17: 1 the firstborn of Manasseh, the father of G: 1568
17: 1 of war, therefore he had G and Bashan. 1568
17: 3 of Hepher, the son of G, the son of Machir, 1568
17: 5 beside the land of G and Bashan, 1568
17: 6 rest of Manasseh's sons had the land of G. 1568
20: 8 Ramoth in G out of the tribe of Gad, and 1568
21:38 of Gad, Ramoth in G with her suburbs, 1568
22: 9 to go unto the country of G, to the land of 1568
22:13 half tribe of Manasseh, into the land of G, 1568
22:15 unto the land of G, and they spake with 1568
22:32 out of the land of G, unto the land of 1568
Jdg 5:17 G abode beyond Jordan: and why did Dan 1568
7: 3 him return and depart early from mount G. 1568
10: 4 unto this day, which are in the land of G. 1568
10: 8 in the land of the Amorites, which is in G. 1568
10:17 gathered together, and encamped in G. 1568
10:18 and princes of G said one to another, 1568
10:18 shall be head over all the inhabitants of G. 1568
11: 1 the son of a harlot: and G begat Jephthah. 1568
11: 5 the elders of G went to fetch Jephthah out 1568
11: 7 Jephthah said unto the elders of G, Did not 1568
11: 8 the elders of G said unto Jephthah, 1568
11: 8 be our head over all the inhabitants of G. 1568
11: 9 Jephthah said unto the elders of G, If ye 1568
11:10 the elders of G said unto Jephthah, 1568
11:11 Jephthah went with the elders of G, and 1568
11:29 he passed over G and Manasseh, and 1568
11:29 passed over Mizpeh of G, and from Mizpeh 1568
11:29 from Mizpeh of G he passed over unto 1568
12: 4 gathered together all the men of G, 1568
12: 4 the men of G smote Ephraim, because 1568
12: 5 that the men of G said unto him, Art thou 1568
12: 7 and was buried in one of the cities of G. 1568
20: 1 with the land of G, unto the LORD in 1568
1Sa 13: 7 went over Jordan to the land of Gad and G. 1568
2Sa 2: 9 he made him king over G, and over 1568
17:26 and Absalom pitched in the land of G. 1568
24: 6 they came to G, and to the land of 1568
1Ki 4:13 Jair the son of Manasseh, which are in G; 1568
4:19 the son of Uri was in the country of G, 1568
17: 1 who was of the inhabitants of G, said unto 1568
22: 3 Know ye that Ramoth in G is ours, and 1568
2Ki 10:33 all the land of G, the Gadites, and 1568
10:33 is by the river Arnon, even G and Bashan. 1568
15:29 and Hazor, and G, and Galilee, 1568
1Ch 2:21 to the daughter of Machir the father of G, 1568
2:22 had three and twenty cities in the land of G. 1568
2:23 to the sons of Machir the father of G. 1568
5: 9 cattle were multiplied in the land of G. 1568
5:10 their tents throughout all the east land of G. 1568
5:14 the son of Jaroah, the son of G, the son of 1568
5:16 they dwelt in G in Bashan, and in her 1568
6:80 Ramoth in G with her suburbs, and 1568
7:14 the Aramitess bare Machir the father of G: 1568
7:17 These were the sons of G, the son of 1568
26:31 them mighty men of valour at Jazer of G. 1568
27:21 Of the half tribe of Manasseh in G, 1568
Ps 60: 7 G is mine, and Manasseh is mine; 1568
108: 8 G is mine; Manasseh is mine; Ephraim also 1568
SS 4: 1 a flock of goats, that appear from mount G. 1568
6: 5 is as a flock of goats that appear from G. 1568
Jer 8:22 Is there no balm in G; is there no physician 1568
22: 6 Thou art G unto me, and the head of 1568
46:11 Go up into G, and take balm, O virgin, 1568
50:19 be satisfied upon mount Ephraim and G. 1568
Eze 47:18 from G, and from the land of Israel by 1568
Hos 6: 8 G is a city of them that work iniquity, and 1568
12:11 Is there iniquity in G? surely they are 1568
Am 1: 3 they have threshed G with threshing 1568
1:13 have ript up the women with child at G, 1568
Ob 1:19 of Samaria: and Benjamin shall possess G. 1568
Mic 7:14 let them feed in Bashan and G, as in 1568
Zec 10:10 and I will bring them into the land of G and 1568

GILEAD'S (1) [GILEAD]
Jdg 11: 2 G wife bare him sons; and his wife's sons 1568

GILEADITE (9) [GILEAD]
Jdg 10: 3 a G, and judged Israel twenty and 1569
11: 1 Now Jephthah the G was a mighty man of 1569
11:40 of Jephthah the G four days in a year. 1569
12: 7 died Jephthah the G, and was buried in one 1569
2Sa 17:27 and Barzillai the G of Rogelim, 1569
19:31 Barzillai the G came down from Rogelim, 1569
1Ki 2: 7 kindness unto the sons of Barzillai the G, 1569
Ezr 2:61 a wife of the daughters of Barzillai the G, 1569
Ne 7:63 of the daughters of Barzillai the G to wife, 1569

GILEADITES (4) [GILEAD]
Nu 26:29 of Gilead come the family of the G. 1569
Jdg 12: 4 Ye G are fugitives of Ephraim among 1568
12: 5 the G took the passages of Jordan before 1568
2Ki 15:25 and with him fifty men of the G: 1121+1569

GILGAL (41)
Dt 11:30 dwell in the champaign over against G, 1537
Jos 4:19 encamped in G, in the east border of 1537
4:20 took out of Jordan, did Joshua pitch in G. 1537
5: 9 the name of the place is called G 1537
5:10 the children of Israel encamped in G, and 1537
9: 6 they went to Joshua unto the camp at G, 1537
10: 6 Gibeon sent unto Joshua to the camp to G, 1537
10: 7 So Joshua ascended from G, he, and all 1537
10: 9 and went up from G all night. 1537
10:15 and all Israel with him, unto the camp to G. 1537
10:43 and all Israel with him, unto the camp to G. 1537
12:23 one; the king of the nations of G, one; 1537
14: 6 children of Judah came unto Joshua in G: 1537
15: 7 so northward, looking toward G, that is 1537
Jdg 2: 1 an angel of the LORD came up from G to 1537
3:19 again from the quarries that were by G, 1537
1Sa 7:16 G, and Mizpeh, and judged Israel in all 1537
10: 8 thou shalt go down before me to G; and 1537
11:14 let us go to G, and renew the kingdom 1537
11:15 all the people went to G; and there they 1537
11:15 made Saul king before the LORD in G; 1537
13: 4 people were called together after Saul to G. 1537
13: 7 he was yet in G, and all the people 1537
13: 8 had appointed: but Samuel came not to G; 1537
13:12 will come down now upon me to G, 1537
13:15 gat him up from G unto Gibeah of 1537
15:12 and passed on, and gone down to G. 1537
15:21 to sacrifice unto the LORD thy God in G. 1537
15:33 Agag in pieces before the LORD in G. 1537
2Sa 19:15 Judah came to G, to go to meet the king, 1537
19:40 the king went on to G, and Chimham went 1537
2Ki 2: 1 that Elijah went with Elisha from G. 1537
4:38 Elisha came again to G: and there was a 1537
Ne 12:29 Also from the house of G, and out of 1537
Hos 4:15 come not ye unto G, neither go ye up to 1537
9:15 All their wickedness is in G, for there I 1537
12:11 they sacrifice bullocks in G; yea, 1537
Am 4: 4 at G multiply transgression; and bring your 1537
5: 5 nor enter into G, and pass not to 1537
5: 5 for G shall surely go into captivity, 1537
Mic 6: 5 Beor answered him; from Shittim unto G; 1537

GILOH (2) [GILONITE]
Jos 15:51 Goshen, and Holon, and G; eleven cities 1542
2Sa 15:12 from his city, even from G, 1542

GILONITE (2) [GILOH]
2Sa 15:12 Absalom sent for Ahithophel the G, 1526
23:34 Eliam the son of Ahithophel the G, 1526

GIMZO (1)
2Ch 28:18 G also and the villages thereof: 1579

GIN (2) [see also GRIN, GRINS]
Isa 8:14 for a g and for a snare to the inhabitants of 6341
Am 3: 5 upon the earth, where no g is for him? 4170

GINATH (2)
1Ki 16:21 of the people followed Tibni the son of G, 1527
16:22 people that followed Tibni the son of G: 1527

GINNETHO (1) [GINNETHON]
Ne 12: 4 Iddo, G, Abijah, 1599

GINNETHON (2) [GINNETHO]
Ne 10: 6 Daniel, G, Baruch, 1599
12:16 Of Iddo, Zechariah; of G, Meshullam; 1599

GIRD (27) [GIRDED, GIRDEDST, GIRDETH, GIRDING, GIRDLE, GIRDLES, GIRT, UNDERGIRDING, UNGIRDED]
Ex 29: 5 g him with the curious girdle of the ephod: 640
29: 9 thou shalt g them with girdles, Aaron and 2296
Jdg 3:16 he did g it under his raiment upon his right 2296
1Sa 25:13 his men, G you on every man his sword. 2296
2Sa 3:31 g you with sackcloth, and mourn before 2296
2Ki 4:29 G up thy loins, and take my staff in thine 2296
9: 1 G up thy loins, and take this box of oil in 2296
Job 38: 3 G up now thy loins like a man; for I will 247
40: 7 G up thy loins now like a man: I will 247
Ps 45: 3 G thy sword upon thy thigh, O most 2296
Isa 8: 9 g yourselves, and ye shall be broken in 247
8: 9 g yourselves, and ye shall be broken in 247
15: 3 In their streets they shall g themselves with 2296
32:11 ye bare, and g sackcloth upon your loins. 2290
Jer 1:17 Thou therefore g up thy loins, and arise, and 247
4: 8 For this g you with sackcloth, lament and 2296
6:26 g thee with sackcloth, and wallow thyself 2296

Jer 49: 3 daughters of Rabbah, **g** ye **with** sackcloth; 2296
Eze 7:18 They shall also **g** *themselves* **with** 2296
27:31 **g** them **with** sackcloth, and they shall weep 2296
44:18 they shall not **g** *themselves* **with** any thing 2296
Joel 1:13 **G** yourselves, and lament, ye priests: howl, 2296
Lk 12:37 that he shall **g** himself, and make them to *4024*
17: 8 and **g** thyself, and serve me, till I have *4024*
Jn 21:18 and another shall **g** thee, and carry *thee* *2224*
Ac 12: 8 **G** thyself, and bind on thy sandals. *4024*
1Pe 1:13 Wherefore **g up** the loins of your mind, *328*

GIRDED (32) [GIRD]
Ex 12:11 *with* your loins **g**, your shoes on your feet, 2296
Lev 8: 7 **g** him with the girdle, and clothed him with 2296
8: 7 he **g** him with the curious girdle of 2296
8:13 **g** them *with* girdles, and put bonnets upon 2296
16: 4 shall be **g** with a linen girdle, and with 2296
Dt 1:41 when ye had **g on** every man his weapons 2296
1Sa 2:18 *being* a child, **g** *with* a linen ephod. 2296
17:39 David **g** his sword upon his armour, and 2296
25:13 they **g on** every man his sword; and 2296
25:13 his sword; and David also **g on** his sword: 2296
2Sa 6:14 and David *was* **g** *with* a linen ephod. 2296
20: 8 Joab's garment that he had put on *was* **g** 2296
21:16 he being **g** *with* a new *sword,* thought to 2296
22:40 For thou hast **g** me with strength to battle: 247
1Ki 18:46 he **g up** his loins, and ran before Ahab to 8151
20:32 So they **g** sackcloth on their loins, and 2296
Ne 4:18 every one had his sword **g** by his side, and *so* 631
Ps 18:39 For thou hast **g** me *with* strength unto 247
30:11 off my sackcloth, and **g** me *with* gladness; 247
65: 6 fast the mountains; *being* **g** with power: 247
93: 1 with strength, *wherewith* he hath **g** himself: 247
109:19 for a girdle where*with* he is **g** continually. 2296
Isa 45: 5 I **g** thee though thou hast not known me: 247
La 2:10 they have **g** themselves **with** sackcloth: 2296
Eze 16:10 and I **g** thee **about** with fine linen, 2280
23:15 **G with** girdles upon their loins, 2289
Da 10: 5 whose loins *were* **g** with fine gold of 2296
Joel 1: 8 Lament like a virgin **g with** sackcloth for 2296
Lk 12:35 Let your loins be **g about**, and *your* lights *4024*
Jn 13: 4 and took a towel, and **g** himself. *1241*
13: 5 *them* with the towel wherewith he was **g**. *1241*
Rev 15: 6 having their breasts **g** with golden girdles. *4024*

GIRDEDST (1) [GIRD]
Jn 21:18 thou **g** thyself, and walkedst whither thou *2224*

GIRDETH (4) [GIRD]
1Ki 20:11 Tell *him,* Let not him that **g on** *his harness* 2296
Job 12:18 bond of kings, and **g** their loins with a girdle. 631
Ps 18:32 *It is* God that **g** me *with* strength, and 247
Pr 31:17 She **g** her loins with strength, and 2296

GIRDING (2) [GIRD]
Isa 3:24 and instead of a stomacher a **g** of sackcloth; 4228
22:12 and to baldness, and to **g with** sackcloth: 2296

GIRDLE (38) [GIRD]
Ex 28: 4 a robe, and a broidered coat, a mitre, and a **g**: 73
28: 8 the **curious g** of the ephod, which *is* upon 2805
28:27 above the **curious g** of the ephod. 2805
28:28 that *it* may be above the **curious g** of 2805
28:39 and thou shalt make the **g** *of* needlework. 73
29: 5 gird him with the **curious g** of the ephod: 2805
39: 5 the **curious g** of his ephod, that *was* upon 2805
39:20 above the **curious g** of the ephod. 2805
39:21 that *it* might be above the **curious g** of 2805
39:29 a **g** *of* fine twined linen, and blue, and purple, 73
Lev 8: 7 girded him with the **g**, and clothed him with 73
8: 7 he girded him with the **curious g** of 2805
16: 4 and shall be girded with a linen **g**, 73
1Sa 18: 4 to his sword, and to his bow, and to his **g**. 2289
2Sa 18:11 given thee ten *shekels of* silver, and a **g**. 2290
20: 8 upon it a **g** with a sword fastened upon his 2289
1Ki 2: 5 put the blood of war upon his **g** that *was* 2290
2Ki 1: 8 girt *with* a **g** of leather about his loins. 232
Job 12:18 of kings, and girdeth their loins with a **g**. 232
Ps 109:19 for a **g** where*with* he is girded continually. 4206
Isa 3:24 instead of a **g** a rent; and instead of well set 2290
5:27 neither shall the **g** of their loins be loosed, 232
11: 5 And righteousness shall be the **g** of his loins, 232
11: 5 his loins, and faithfulness the **g** of his reins. 232
22:21 strengthen him *with* thy **g**, and I will commit 73
Jer 13: 1 Go and get thee a linen **g**, and put it upon thy 232
13: 2 So I got a **g**, according to the word of 232
13: 4 Take the **g** that thou hast got, which *is* upon 232
13: 6 go to Euphrates, and take the **g** from thence, 232
13: 7 took the **g** from the place where I had hid it: 232
13: 7 behold, the **g** was marred, it was profitable 232
13:10 and to worship them, shall even be as this **g**, 232
13:11 For as the **g** cleaveth to the loins of a man, 232
Mt 3: 4 and a leathern **g** about his loins; *2223*
Mk 1: 6 and with a **g** of a skin about his loins; *2223*
Ac 21:11 he took Paul's **g**, and bound his *own* hands *2223*
21:11 at Jerusalem bind the man that oweth this **g**, *2223*
Rev 1:13 and girt about the paps with a golden **g**. *2223*

GIRDLES (6) [GIRD]
Ex 28:40 thou shalt make for them **g**, and bonnets shalt 73
29: 9 thou shalt gird them *with* **g**, Aaron and 73
Lev 8:13 girded them *with* **g**, and put bonnets upon 73
Pr 31:24 and delivereth **g** unto the merchant. 2289
Eze 23:15 Girded with **g** upon their loins, exceeding in 232
Rev 15: 6 having their breasts girded with golden **g**. *2223*

GIRGASHITE (2) [GIRGASHITES]
Ge 10:16 the Jebusite, and the Amorite, and the **G**, 1622
1Ch 1:14 Jebusite also, and the Amorite, and the **G**, 1622

GIRGASHITES (5) [GIRGASHITE]
Ge 15:21 and the **G**, and the Jebusites. 1622
Dt 7: 1 the **G**, and the Amorites, and 1622
Jos 3:10 the **G**, and the Amorites, and the Jebusites. 1622
Jos 24:11 and the **G**, the Hivites, and the Jebusites; 1622
Ne 9: 8 the Perizzites, and the Jebusites, and the **G**, 1622

GIRL (1) [GIRLS]
Joel 3: 3 and sold a **g** for wine, that they might drink. 3207

GIRLS (1) [GIRL]
Zec 8: 5 *of* boys and **g** playing in the streets thereof. 3207

GIRT (5) [GIRD]
1Sa 2: 4 and they that stumbled are **g** with strength. 247
2Ki 1: 8 and **g** *with* a girdle of leather about his loins. 247
Jn 21: 7 he **g** *his* fisher's coat unto him, (for he was *1241*
Eph 6:14 having your loins **g about** with truth, and *4024*
Rev 1:13 and **g** about the paps with a golden girdle. *4024*

GIRZITES See GEZRITES

GISHPA See GISPA

GISPA (1)
Ne 11:21 and Ziha and **G** *were* over the Nethinims. 1658

GITTAH-HEPHER (1) [GATH-HEPHER]
Jos 19:13 thence passeth on along on the east to **G**, 1661

GITTAIM (2)
2Sa 4: 3 the Beerothites fled to **G**, and 1664
Ne 11:33 Hazor, Ramah, **G**, 1664

GITTITE (8) [GATH]
2Sa 6:10 it aside *into* the house of Obed-edom the **G**. 1663
6:11 house of Obed-edom the **G** three months: 1663
15:19 said the king to Ittai the **G**, Wherefore 1663
15:22 Ittai the **G** passed over, and all his men, 1663
18: 2 a third part under the hand of Ittai the **G**. 1663
21:19 slew *the brother of* Goliath the **G**, 1663
1Ch 13:13 it aside into the house of Obed-edom the **G**. 1663
20: 5 slew Lahmi the brother of Goliath the **G**, 1663

GITTITES (2) [GATH]
Jos 13: 3 the Eshkalonites, the **G**, and the Ekronites; 1663
2Sa 15:18 and all the Pelethites, and all the **G**, 1663

GITTITH (3)
Ps 8: T To the chief Musician upon **G**, A Psalm of 1665
81: T To the chief Musician upon **G**, *A Psalm of* 1665
84: T To the chief Musician upon **G**, A Psalm for 1665

GIVE (880) [GAVE, GAVEST, GIFT, GIFTS, GIVEN, GIVER, GIVEST, GIVETH, GIVING, LAWGIVER, THANKSGIVING, THANKSGIVINGS]
Ge 1:15 of the heaven to **g light** upon the earth: 215
1:17 of the heaven to **g light** upon the earth, 215
12: 7 and said, Unto thy seed will I **g** this land: 5414
13:15 to thee will I **g** it, and to thy seed for ever. 5414
13:17 in the breadth of it; for I will **g** it unto thee. 5414
14:21 **G** me the persons, and take the goods to 5414
15: 2 Lord GOD, what wilt thou **g** me, 5414
15: 7 to **g** thee this land to inherit it. 5414
17: 8 I will **g** unto thee, and to thy seed after 5414
17:16 will bless her, and **g** thee a son also of her: 5414
23: 4 **g** me a possession of a buryingplace with 5414
23: 9 That he may **g** me the cave of Machpelah, 5414
23: 9 for as much money as it is worth he shall **g** 5414
23:11 the field **g** I thee, and the cave that *is* 5414
23:11 and the cave that *is* therein, I **g** it thee; 5414
23:11 in the presence of the sons of my people **g** I 5414
23:13 saying, But if thou *wilt* **g** *it,* I pray thee, NIH
23:13 I will **g** *thee* money for the field; take *it* of 5414
24: 7 saying, Unto thy seed will I **g** this land; 5414
24:14 Drink, and I will **g** thy camels **drink** also: 8248
24:41 if they **g** not thee *one,* thou shalt be clear 5414
24:43 **G** me, I pray thee, a little water of thy pitcher **to drink**; 8248
24:46 Drink, and I will **g** thy camels **drink** also: 8248
26: 3 I will **g** all these countries, and I will 5414
26: 4 and will **g** unto thy seed all these countries; 5414
27:28 Therefore God **g** thee of the dew of heaven, 5414
28: 4 **g** thee the blessing of Abraham, to thee, 5414
28:13 to thee will I **g** it, and to thy seed; 5414
28:20 will **g** me bread to eat, and raiment to put 5414
28:22 of all that thou shalt **g** me I will surely give 5414
28:22 I will **surely g the tenth** unto thee. 6237+6237
29:19 Laban said, *It is* better that I **g** her to thee, 5414
29:19 than that I should **g** her to another man: 5414
29:21 **G** *me* my wife, for my days are fulfilled, 3051
29:26 to **g** the younger before the firstborn. 5414
29:27 we will **g** thee this also for the service 5414
30: 1 unto Jacob, **G** me children, or else I die. 3051
30:14 **G** me, I pray thee, of thy son's mandrakes. 5414
30:26 **G** *me* my wives and my children, for whom 5414
30:28 Appoint me thy wages, and I will **g** *it.* 5414
30:31 he said, What shall I **g** thee? And Jacob 5414
30:31 Jacob said, Thou shalt not **g** me any thing: 5414
34: 8 I pray you **g** her him to wife. 5414
34: 9 *and* **g** your daughters unto us, and take our 5414
34:11 and what ye shall say unto me I will **g**. 5414
34:12 I will **g** according as ye shall say unto me: 5414
34:12 say unto me: but **g** me the damsel to wife. 5414
34:14 to **g** our sister to one that is uncircumcised; 5414
34:16 will we **g** our daughters unto you, and we 5414
34:21 for wives, and let us **g** them our daughters. 5414
35:12 to thee I will **g** it, and to thy seed after thee 5414
35:12 and to thy seed after thee will I **g** the land. 5414
38: 9 lest that he should **g** seed to his brother. 5414
38:16 she said, What wilt thou **g** me, that thou 5414
38:17 she said, Wilt thou **g** *me* a pledge, till thou 5414
38:18 he said, What pledge shall I **g** thee? 5414
41:16 God shall **g** Pharaoh **an answer** of peace. 6030
42:25 and to **g** them provision for the way: 5414
42:27 as one *of them* opened his sack to **g** his ass 5414
43:14 God Almighty **g** you mercy before the man, 5414
45:18 I will **g** you the good of the land of Egypt, 5414
Ge 47:15 came unto Joseph, and said, **G** us bread: 3051
47:16 Joseph said, **G** your cattle; and I will give 3051
47:16 I will **g** you for your cattle, if money fail. 5414
47:19 **g** *us* seed, that we may live, and not die, 5414
47:24 that you shall **g** the fifth *part* unto Pharaoh, 5414
48: 4 will **g** this land to thy seed after thee *for* an 5414
Ex 2: 9 nurse it for me, and I will **g** *thee* thy wages. 5414
3:21 I will **g** this people favour in the sight of 5414
5: 7 Ye shall no more **g** the people straw to 5414
5:10 Thus saith Pharaoh, I will not **g** you straw. 5414
6: 4 to **g** them the land of Canaan, the land of 5414
6: 8 *concerning* the which I did swear to **g** it to 5414
6: 8 to Jacob; and I will **g** it you *for* an heritage: 5414
10:25 Thou must **g** us also sacrifices 3027+5414+871.1
12:25 to the land which the LORD will **g** you, 5414
13: 5 which he sware unto thy fathers to **g** thee, 5414
13:11 and to thy fathers, and shall **g** it thee, 5414
13:21 by night in a pillar of fire, to **g** them **light**; 215
15:26 wilt **g ear** to his commandments, and 238
16: 8 *This shall be,* when the LORD shall **g** you 5414
17: 2 and said, **G** us water that we may drink. 5414
18:19 I will **g** thee **counsel**, and God shall be with 3289
21:23 then thou shalt **g** life for life, 5414
21:30 he shall **g** *for* the ransom of his life 5414
21:32 he shall **g** unto their master thirty shekels *of* 5414
21:34 *and* **g** money unto the owner of them; 7725
22:17 If her father utterly refuse to **g** her unto 5414
22:29 the firstborn of thy sons shalt thou **g** unto 5414
22:30 on the eighth day thou shalt **g** it me. 5414
24:12 I will **g** thee tables of stone, and a law, and 5414
25:16 the ark the Testimony which I shall **g** thee. 5414
25:21 shalt put the Testimony that I shall **g** thee. 5414
25:22 **g** thee **in commandment** unto the children 6680
25:37 that they may **g light** over against it. 215
30:12 shall they **g** every man a ransom for his 5414
30:13 This they shall **g**, every one that passeth 5414
30:14 above, shall **g** an offering unto the LORD. 5414
30:15 The rich shall not **g more**, and the poor 7235
30:15 the poor shall not **g less** than half a shekel, 4591
30:15 when *they* **g** an offering unto the LORD, 5414
32:13 all this land that I have spoken of will I **g** 5414
33: 1 to Jacob, saying, Unto thy seed will I **g** it: 5414
33:14 shall go *with thee,* and I will **g** thee **rest**. 5117
Lev 5:16 fifth *part* thereto, and **g** it unto the priest: 5414
6: 5 *and* **g** it unto him to whom it appertaineth, 5414
7:32 the right shoulder shall ye **g** unto the priest 5414
14:34 which I **g** to you for a possession, and I put 5414
15:14 and **g** them unto the priest: 5414
20:24 and I will **g** it unto you to possess it, 5414
22:14 shall **g** *it* unto the priest with the holy 5414
23:10 When ye be come into the land which I **g** 5414
23:38 which ye **g** unto the LORD. 5414
25: 2 When ye come into the land which I **g** you, 5414
25:37 Thou shalt not **g** him thy money upon 5414
25:38 to **g** you the land of Canaan, *and* to be your 5414
25:51 **g again** the price of his redemption out of 7725
25:52 he **g** *him* **again** the price of his redemption. 7725
26: 4 I will **g** you rain in due season, and the land 5414
26: 6 I will **g** peace in the land, and ye shall lie 5414
27:23 he shall **g** thine estimation in that day, *as* a 5414
Nu 3: 9 thou shalt **g** the Levites unto Aaron and 5414
3:48 thou shalt **g** the money, wherewith the odd 5414
5: 7 **g** *it* unto *him* against whom he hath 5414
6:26 countenance upon thee, and **g** thee peace. 7760
7: 5 thou shalt **g** them unto the Levites, to every 5414
8: 2 the seven lamps shall **g light** over against 215
10:29 of which the LORD said, I will **g** it you: 5414
11: 4 and said, Who shall **g** us flesh **to eat**? 398
11:13 Whence should I have flesh to **g** unto all 5414
11:13 saying, **G** us flesh, that we may eat. 5414
11:18 saying, Who shall **g** us flesh **to eat**? 398
11:18 therefore the LORD will **g** you flesh, and 5414
11:21 thou hast said, I will **g** them flesh, that they 5414
13: 2 which I **g** unto the children of Israel: 5414
14: 8 he will bring us into this land, and **g** it us; 5414
15: 2 of your habitations, which I **g** unto you, 5414
15:21 Of the first of your dough ye shall **g** unto 5414
18:28 ye shall **g** thereof the LORD'S heave 5414
19: 3 ye shall **g** her unto Eleazar the priest, 5414
20: 8 it shall **g forth** his water, and thou shalt 5414
20: 8 **g** the congregation and their beasts **drink**. 8248
20:21 Thus Edom refused to **g** Israel passage 5414
21:16 people together, and I will **g** them water. 5414
22:13 for the LORD refuseth to **g** me **leave** to go 5414
22:18 If Balak would **g** me his house full *of* silver 5414
24:13 If Balak would **g** me his house full *of* silver 5414
25:12 Behold, I **g** unto him my covenant of peace: 5414
26:54 To many thou shalt **g** the **more** inheritance, 7235
26:54 to few thou shalt **g** the **less** inheritance: 4591
27: 4 **G** unto us *therefore* a possession among 5414
27: 7 thou shalt **surely g** them a possession 5414+5414
27: 9 ye shall **g** his inheritance unto his brethren. 5414
27:10 ye shall **g** his inheritance unto his father's 5414
27:11 ye shall **g** his inheritance unto his kinsman 5414
27:19 and **g** him **a charge** in their sight. 6680
31:29 their half, and **g** *it* unto Eleazar the priest, 5414
31:30 *of* beasts, and **g** them unto the Levites, 5414
32:29 ye shall **g** them the land of Gilead for a 5414
33:54 to the more ye shall **g** the **more** inheritance, 7235
33:54 to the fewer ye shall **g** the **less** inheritance: 4591
34:13 which the LORD commanded to **g** unto 5414
35: 2 that they **g** unto the Levites of 5414
35: 2 ye shall **g** *also* unto the Levites suburbs for 5414
35: 4 the cities, which ye shall **g** unto the Levites, 5414
35: 6 *among* the cities which ye shall **g** unto 5414
35: 7 *So* all the cities which ye shall **g** to 5414
35: 7 them *shall ye* **g** with their suburbs. NIH
35: 8 the cities which ye shall **g** *shall be* of 5414
35: 8 from *them that have* many ye shall **g many**; 7235
35: 8 but from *them that have* few ye shall **g few**. 4591
35: 8 every one shall **g** of his cities unto 5414
35:13 *of these* cities which ye shall **g** six cities 5414
35:14 Ye shall **g** three cities on *this* side Jordan, 5414
35:14 three cities shall ye **g** in the land of Canaan, 5414
36: 2 The LORD commanded my lord to **g** 5414

G

Nu 36: 2 **g** the inheritance of Zelophehad our brother 5414
Dt 1: 8 to **g** unto them and to their seed after them. 5414
1:20 which the LORD our God doth **g** unto us. 5414
1:25 land which the LORD our God doth **g** us. 5414
1:35 which I sware to **g** unto your fathers, 5414
1:36 to him will I **g** the land that he hath trodden 5414
1:39 unto them will I **g** it, and they shall possess 5414
1:45 hearken to your voice, nor **g ear** unto you. 238
2: 5 for I will not **g** you of their land, no, not so 5414
2: 9 for I will not **g** thee of their land *for* a 5414
2:19 for I will not **g** thee of the land of 5414
2:28 **g** me water for money, that I may drink: 5414
2:31 I have begun to **g** Sihon and his land before 5414
4:38 to **g** thee their land *for* an inheritance, as *it* 5414
5:31 that they may do *them* in the land which I **g** 5414
6:10 to Jacob, to **g** thee great and goodly cities, 5414
6:23 to **g** us the land which he sware unto our 5414
7: 3 thy daughter thou shalt not **g** unto his son, 5414
7:13 which he sware unto thy fathers to **g** thee. 5414
10:11 which I sware unto their fathers to **g** unto 5414
11: 9 sware unto your fathers to **g** unto them 5414
11:14 That I will **g** *you* the rain of your land in his 5414
11:21 LORD sware unto your fathers to **g** them, 5414
14:21 thou shalt **g** it unto the stranger that *is* in 5414
15:10 Thou shalt **surely g** him, and 5414+5414
15:14 hath blessed thee thou shalt **g** unto him. 5414
16:10 which thou shalt **g** *unto the LORD thy* 5414
16:17 Every man *shall* **g** as he is able, according NIH
18: 3 they shall **g** unto the priest the shoulder, 5414
18: 4 of the fleece of thy sheep, shalt thou **g** him. 5414
19: 8 **g** thee all the land which he promised to 5414
19: 8 which he promised to **g** unto thy fathers; 5414
20:16 which the LORD thy God doth **g** thee *for* 5414
22:14 **g** occasions of speech against her, and 7760
22:19 **g** *them* unto the father of the damsel, 5414
22:29 the man that lay with her shall **g** unto 5414
23:14 and to **g up** thine enemies before thee; 5414
24: 1 **g** *it* in her hand, and send her out of his 5414
24:15 At his day thou shalt **g** *him* his hire, 5414
25: 3 Forty **stripes** he may **g** him, *and* 5221
26: 3 LORD sware unto our fathers for to **g** us. 5414
28:11 LORD sware unto thy fathers to **g** thee. 5414
28:12 the heaven to **g** the rain unto thy land in his 5414
28:55 So that *he* will not **g** to any of them of 5414
28:65 the LORD shall **g** thee there a trembling 5414
30:20 to Isaac, and to Jacob, to **g** them. 5414
31: 5 the LORD shall **g** them **up** before your 5414
31: 7 hath sworn unto their fathers to **g** them; 5414
31:14 that I may **g** him **a charge**. 6680
32: 1 **G ear**, O ye heavens, and I will speak; and 238
32:49 which I **g** unto the children of Israel for a 5414
32:52 the land which I **g** the children of Israel. 5414
34: 4 unto Jacob, saying, I will **g** it unto thy seed: 5414
Jos 1: 2 unto the land which I do **g** to them, 5414
1: 6 which I sware unto their fathers to **g** them. 5414
2:12 my father's house, and **g** me a true token: 5414
5: 6 sware unto their fathers that he would **g** us, 5414
7:19 said unto Achan, My son, **g**, I pray thee, 7760
8:18 toward Ai; for I will **g** it into thine hand. 5414
9:24 his servant Moses to **g** you all the land, 5414
14:12 Now therefore **g** me this mountain, 5414
15:16 to him will I **g** Achsah my daughter to wife. 5414
15:19 Who answered, **G** me a blessing; for thou 5414
15:19 a south land; **g** me also springs of water. 5414
17: 4 The LORD commanded Moses to **g** us an 5414
18: 4 **G** out from among you three men for *each* 3051
20: 4 **g** him a place, that he may dwell among 5414
21: 2 the hand of Moses to **g** us cities to dwell in, 5414
21:43 land which he sware to **g** unto their fathers; 5414
Jdg 1:12 to him will I **g** Achsah my daughter to wife. 5414
1:15 she said unto him, **G** me a blessing: 3051
1:15 a south land, **g** me also springs of water. 5414
4:19 **G** me, I pray thee, a little water **to drink**; 8248
5: 3 **g ear**, O ye princes; I, *even* I, will sing unto 238
7: 2 for me to **g** the Midianites into their hands, 5414
8: 5 unto the men of Succoth, **G**, I pray you, 5414
8: 6 that we should **g** bread unto thine army? 5414
8:15 that we should **g** bread unto thy men *that* 5414
8:24 that you would **g** me every man 5414
8:25 We will **willingly g** *them*. And they 5414+5414
14:12 I will **g** you thirty sheets and thirty change 5414
14:13 shall ye **g** me thirty sheets and 5414
16: 5 we will **g** thee every one *of us* eleven 5414
17:10 I will **g** thee ten *shekels* of silver by 5414
20: 7 of Israel; **g** here your advice and counsel. 3051
21: 1 There shall not any of us **g** his daughter 5414
21: 7 will not **g** them of our daughters to wives? 5414
21:18 Howbeit we may not **g** them wives of our 5414
21:22 for ye did not **g** unto them at *this* time, 5414
Ru 4:12 of the seed which the LORD shall **g** thee 5414
1Sa 1:11 wilt **g** unto thine handmaid a man child, 5414
1:11 I will **g** him unto the LORD all the days of 5414
2:10 he shall **g** strength unto his king, and 5414
2:15 **G** flesh to roast for the priest; 5414
2:16 *Nay;* but thou shalt **g** *it me* now: 5414
2:20 The LORD **g** thee seed of this woman for 7760
2:28 did I **g** unto the house of thy father all 5414
2:32 in all *the wealth* which *God* shall **g** Israel: 3190
6: 5 and ye shall **g** glory unto the God of Israel: 5414
8: 6 when they said, **G** us a king to judge us. 5414
8:14 the best *of them,* and **g** *them* to his servants. 5414
8:15 and **g** to his officers, and to his servants. 5414
9: 8 *that* will I **g** to the man of God, to tell us 5414
10: 4 salute thee, and **g** thee two *loaves* of bread; 5414
11: 3 said unto him, **G** us seven days' **respite**, 7503
14:41 **G** a perfect *lot*. And Saul and 3051
17:10 **g** me a man, that we may fight together. 5414
17:25 will **g** him his daughter, and make his 5414
17:44 I will **g** thy flesh unto the fowls of the air, 5414
17:46 I will **g** the carcases of the host of 5414
17:47 and he will **g** you into our hands. 5414
18:17 daughter Merab, her will I **g** thee to wife: 5414
18:21 Saul said, I will **g** him her, that she may be 5414
21: 3 **g** *me* five *loaves of* bread in mine hand, or 5414
21: 9 David said, *There is* none like that; **g** it me. 5414
1Sa 22: 7 will the son of Jesse **g** every one of you 5414
25: 8 **g**, I pray thee, whatsoever cometh to thine 5414
25:11 **g** *it* unto men, whom I know not whence 5414
27: 5 let them **g** me a place in some town in 5414
30:22 we will not **g** them *ought* of the spoil that 5414
2Sa 12:11 **g** *them* unto thy neighbour, and he shall lie 5414
13: 5 **g** me meat, and dress the meat in my sight, 1262
14: 8 and I will **g charge** concerning thee. 6680
16:20 **G** counsel among you what we shall do. 3051
21: 6 And the king said, I will **g** *them.* 5414
22:50 Therefore I will **g thanks** unto thee, 3034
23:15 Oh that one would **g** me **drink** *of* the water 8248
24:23 did Araunah, *as* a king, **g** unto the king. 5414
1Ki 1:12 let me, I pray thee, **g** thee **counsel**, 3289+6098
2:17 that he **g** me Abishag the Shunammite to 5414
3: 5 and God said, Ask what I shall **g** thee. 5414
3: 9 **G** therefore thy servant an understanding 5414
3:21 I rose in the morning to **g** my child **suck**, 3243
3:25 and **g** half to the one, and half to the other. 5414
3:26 **g** her the living child, and in no wise slay it. 5414
3:27 **G** her the living child, and in no wise slay 5414
5: 6 unto thee will I **g** hire for thy servants 5414
8:32 to **g** him according to his righteousness. 5414
8:36 **g** rain upon thy land, which thou hast given 5414
8:39 and **g** to every man according to his ways, 5414
8:50 **g** them compassion before them who 5414
11:11 from thee, and will **g** it to thy servant. 5414
11:13 will **g** one tribe to thy son for David my 5414
11:31 of Solomon, and will **g** ten tribes to thee: 5414
11:35 and will **g** it unto thee, *even* ten tribes. 5414
11:36 unto his son will I **g** one tribe, that David 5414
11:38 built for David, and will **g** Israel unto thee. 5414
12: 9 What **counsel g** ye that we may answer this 3289
13: 7 refresh *thyself,* and I will **g** thee a reward. 5414
13: 8 If thou wilt **g** me half thine house, I will not 5414
14:16 he shall **g** Israel **up** because of the sins of 5414
15: 4 his God **g** him a lamp in Jerusalem, 5414
17:19 he said unto her, **G** me thy son. And he 5414
18:23 Let them therefore **g** us two bullocks; and 5414
21: 2 unto Naboth, saying, **G** me thy vineyard, 5414
21: 2 I will **g** thee for it a better vineyard than it; 5414
21: 2 I will **g** thee the worth of it *in* money. 5414
21: 3 that I should **g** the inheritance of my fathers 5414
21: 4 I will not **g** thee the inheritance of my 5414
21: 6 unto him, **G** me thy vineyard for money; 5414
21: 6 I will **g** thee *another* vineyard for it: 5414
21: 6 he answered, I will not **g** thee my vineyard. 5414
21: 7 I will **g** thee the vineyard of Naboth 5414
21:15 which he refused to **g** thee for money: 5414
2Ki 4:42 he said, **G** unto the people, that they may 5414
4:43 He said again, **G** the people, that they may 5414
5:22 **g** them, I pray thee, a talent of silver, and 5414
6:28 This woman said unto me, **G** thy son, 5414
6:29 next day, **G** thy son, that we may eat him: 5414
8:19 as he promised him to **g** to him alway a 5414
10:15 If it be, **g** *me* thine hand. And he gave *him* 5414
11:10 the captains over hundreds did the priest **g** 5414
14: 9 **G** thy daughter to my son to wife: 5414
15:20 *of* silver, to **g** to the king of Assyria. 5414
18:23 **g pledges** to my lord the king of Assyria, 6148
22: 5 let them **g** it to the doers of the work which 5414
23:35 he taxed the land to **g** the money according 5414
23:35 to his taxation, to **g** *it* unto Pharaoh-nechoh. 5414
1Ch 11:17 Oh that one would **g** me **drink** *of* the water 8248
16: 8 **G thanks** unto the LORD, call upon his 3034
16:18 Unto thee will I **g** the land of Canaan, 5414
16:28 **G** unto the LORD, ye kindreds of 3051
16:28 **g** unto the LORD glory and strength. 3051
16:29 **G** unto the LORD the glory due unto his 3051
16:34 O **g thanks** unto the LORD; for *he is* 3034
16:35 that *we* may **g thanks** to thy holy name, 3034
16:41 to **g thanks** to the LORD, because 3034
21:23 I **g** *thee* the oxen *also* for burnt offerings, 5414
21:23 the wheat for the meat offering; I **g** *it* all. 5414
22: 9 I will **g** him **rest** from all his enemies round 5117
22: 9 I will **g** peace and quietness unto Israel in 5414
22:12 Only the LORD **g** thee wisdom and 5414
22:12 and **g** thee **charge** concerning Israel, 6680
25: 3 to **g thanks** and to praise the LORD. 3034
29:12 *is* to make great, and to **g strength** unto all. 2388
29:19 **g** unto Solomon my son a perfect heart, 5414
2Ch 1: 7 and said unto him, Ask what I shall **g** thee. 5414
1:10 **G** me now wisdom and knowledge, that I 5414
1:12 I will **g** thee riches, and wealth, and honour, 5414
2:10 behold, I will **g** to thy servants, the hewers 5414
10: 6 What **counsel g** ye *me* to return answer to 3289
10: 9 What **advice g** ye that we may return 3289
21: 7 as he promised to **g** a light to him and to his 5414
24:19 against them: but they would not **g ear**. 238
25: 9 The LORD is able to **g** thee much more 5414
25:18 **G** thy daughter to my son to wife: 5414
30:12 Also in Judah the hand of God was to **g** 5414
30:24 For Hezekiah king of Judah did **g** to 7311
31: 2 to **g thanks**, and to praise in the gates of 3034
31: 4 in Jerusalem to **g** the portion of the priests 5414
31:15 set office, to **g** to their brethren by courses, 5414
31:19 to **g** portions to all the males among 5414
32:11 Doth not Hezekiah persuade you to **g over** 5414
35:12 that they might **g** according to the divisions 5414
Ezr 4:21 **G** ye now commandment to cause these 7761
9: 8 and to **g** us a nail in his holy place, 5414
9: 8 and **g** us a little reviving in our bondage. 5414
9: 9 to **g** us a reviving, to set up the house of our 5414
9: 9 to **g** us a wall in Judah and in Jerusalem. 5414
9:12 **g** not your daughters unto their sons, 5414
Ne 2: 8 that he may **g** me timber to make beams for 5414
4: 4 **g** them for a prey in the land of captivity: 5414
9: 8 madest a covenant with him to **g** the land of 5414
9: 8 to **g** *it, I say,* to his seed, and 5414
9:12 to **g** them **light** in the way wherein they 215
9:15 the land which thou hadst sworn to **g** them. 5414
9:30 yet would they not **g ear**: therefore 238
10:30 that we would not **g** our daughters unto 5414
12:24 against them, to praise *and* to **g thanks**, 3034
13:25 *saying,* Ye shall not **g** your daughters unto 5414
Est 1:19 let the king **g** her royal estate unto another 5414
1:20 all the wives shall **g** to their husbands 5414
8: 1 On that day did the king Ahasuerus **g** 5414
Job 2: 4 all that a man hath will he **g** for his life. 5414
3:11 *why* did I not **g up the ghost** when I came 1478
6:22 or, **G a reward** for me of your substance? 7809
13:19 if I hold my tongue, I shall **g up the ghost**. 1478
32:21 neither let me **g flattering titles** unto man. 3655
32:22 For I know not to **g flattering titles**; *in so* 3655
34: 2 ye wise *men;* and **g ear** unto me, 238
Ps 2: 8 I shall **g** *thee* the heathen *for* thine 5414
5: 1 **G ear** to my words, O LORD, consider my 238
6: 5 in the grave who shall **g** thee **thanks**? 3034
17: 1 attend unto my cry, **g ear** unto my prayer, 238
18:49 Therefore will I **g thanks** unto thee, 3034
28: 4 **G** them according to their deeds, and 5414
28: 4 **g** them after the work of their hands; 5414
29: 1 **G** unto the LORD, O ye mighty, give unto 3051
29: 1 **g** unto the LORD glory and strength. 3051
29: 2 **G** unto the LORD the glory due unto his 3051
29:11 The LORD will **g** strength unto his 5414
30: 4 **g thanks** at the remembrance of his 3034
30:12 my God, I will **g thanks** unto thee for ever. 3034
35:18 I will **g** thee **thanks** in the great 3034
37: 4 he shall **g** thee the desires of thine heart. 5414
39:12 O LORD, and **g ear** unto my cry; 238
49: 1 **g ear**, all ye inhabitants of the world: 238
49: 7 *his* brother, nor **g** to God a ransom for him: 5414
51:16 else would I **g** *it:* thou delightest not in 5414
54: 2 O God; **g ear** to the words of my mouth. 238
55: 1 **G ear** to my prayer, O God; and hide not 238
57: 7 my heart is fixed: I will sing and **g praise**. 2167
60:11 **G** us help from trouble: for vain *is* the help 3051
72: 1 **G** the king thy judgments, O God, and 5414
75: 1 Unto thee, O God, do we **g thanks**, 3034
75: 1 we give thanks, *unto thee* do we **g thanks**: 3034
78: 1 **G ear**, O my people, to my law: incline your 238
78:20 streams overflowed; can he **g** bread also? 5414
79:13 sheep of thy pasture will **g** thee **thanks** for 3034
80: 1 **G ear**, O Shepherd of Israel, thou that 238
84: 8 my prayer: **g ear**, O God of Jacob. Selah. 238
84:11 the LORD will **g** grace and glory: no good 5414
85:12 Yea, the LORD shall **g** *that which is* good; 5414
86: 6 **G ear**, O LORD, unto my prayer; and 238
86:16 **g** thy strength unto thy servant, and 5414
91:11 For he shall **g** his angels **charge** over thee, 6680
92: 1 *It is* a good *thing* to **g thanks** unto 3034
94:13 That *thou* mayest **g** him **rest** from the days 8252
96: 7 **G** unto the LORD, O ye kindreds of 3051
96: 7 **g** unto the LORD glory and strength. 3051
96: 8 **G** unto the LORD the glory due unto his 3051
97:12 **g thanks** at the remembrance of his 3034
104:11 They **g drink** to every beast of the field: 8248
104:27 that *thou* mayest **g** *them* their meat in due 5414
105: 1 O **g thanks** unto the LORD; call upon his 3034
105:11 Unto thee will I **g** the land of Canaan, 5414
105:39 a covering; and fire to **g light** in the night. 215
106: 1 O **g thanks** unto the LORD; for *he is* 3034
106:47 to **g thanks** unto thy holy name, *and* 3034
107: 1 O **g thanks** unto the LORD, for *he is* 3034
108: 1 I will sing and **g praise**, even *with* my 2167
108:12 **G** us help from trouble: for vain *is* the help 3051
109: 4 my adversaries: but I **g** *myself unto* prayer. NIH
111: 6 that he may **g** them the heritage of 5414
115: 1 not unto us, but unto thy name **g** glory, 5414
118: 1 O **g thanks** unto the LORD; for *he is* 3034
118:29 O **g thanks** unto the LORD; for *he is* 3034
119:34 **G** me **understanding**, and I shall keep thy 995
119:62 At midnight I will rise to **g thanks** unto 3034
119:73 **g** me **understanding**, that I may learn thy 995
119:125 **g** me **understanding**, that I may know thy 995
119:144 **g** me **understanding**, and I shall live. 995
119:169 **g** me **understanding** according to thy word. 995
122: 4 to **g thanks** unto the name of the LORD. 3034
132: 4 I will not **g** sleep to mine eyes, *or* 5414
136: 1 O **g thanks** unto the LORD; for *he is* 3034
136: 2 O **g thanks** unto the God of gods: for his 3034
136: 3 O **g thanks** to the Lord of lords: for his 3034
136:26 O **g thanks** unto the God of heaven: for his 3034
140:13 Surely the righteous shall **g thanks** unto 3034
141: 1 **g ear** unto my voice, when I cry unto thee. 238
143: 1 O LORD, **g ear** to my supplications: 238
Pr 1: 4 To **g** subtilty to the simple, to the young 5414
3:28 and come again, and to morrow I will **g**; 5414
4: 2 For I **g** you good doctrine, forsake you not 5414
4: 9 She shall **g** to thine head an ornament of 5414
5: 9 Lest thou **g** thine honour unto others, and 5414
6: 4 **G** not sleep to thine eyes, nor slumber to 5414
6:31 he shall **g** all the substance of his house. 5414
9: 9 **G** *instruction* to a wise *man,* and he will be 5414
23:26 **g** me thine heart, and let thine eyes observe 5414
25:21 thine enemy *be* hungry, **g** him bread **to eat**; 398
25:21 and if he *be* thirsty, **g** him water **to drink**: 8248
29:15 The rod and reproof **g** wisdom: but a child 5414
29:17 Correct thy son, and he shall **g** thee **rest**; 5117
29:17 yea, he shall **g** delight unto thy soul. 5414
30: 8 **g** me neither poverty nor riches; feed me 5414
30:15 hath two daughters, *crying,* **G**, give. 3051
30:15 hath two daughters, *crying,* Give, **g**. 3051
31: 3 **G** not thy strength unto women, nor thy 5414
31: 6 **G** strong drink unto him that is ready to 5414
31:31 **G** her of the fruit of her hands; and let her 5414
Ecc 2: 3 I sought in mine heart to **g** myself unto 4900
2:26 that *he* may **g** to *him that is* good before 5414
5: 1 to hear, than to **g** the sacrifice of fools: 5414
11: 2 **G** a portion to seven, and also to eight; 5414
SS 2:13 the vines *with* the tender grape **g** a *good* 5414
7:12 bud forth: there will I **g** thee my loves. 5414
7:13 The mandrakes **g** a smell, and at our gates 5414
8: 7 if a man would **g** all the substance of his 5414
Isa 1: 2 Hear, O heavens, and **g ear**, O earth: for 238
1:10 **g ear** unto the law of our God, ye people of 238
3: 4 I will **g** children *to be* their princes, and 5414
7:14 Therefore the Lord himself shall **g** you a 5414
7:22 for the abundance of milk *that they* shall **g** 6213

Isa 8: 9 in pieces; and g ear, all ye of far countries: 238
10: 6 people of my wrath will I g him a charge, 6680
13:10 the constellations thereof shall not g their 1984
14: 3 LORD shall g thee rest from thy sorrow, 5117
19: 4 the Egyptians will I g over into the hand of 5534
28:23 G ye ear, and hear my voice; hearken, and 238
30:20 though the Lord g you the bread of 5414
30:23 shall he g the rain of thy seed, that thou 5414
32: 9 ye careless daughters, g ear unto my speech. 238
36: 8 Now therefore g pledges, I pray thee, to my 6148
36: 8 and I will g thee two thousand horses, 5414
41:27 I will g to Jerusalem one that bringeth good 5414
42: 6 and g thee for a covenant of the people, 5414
42: 8 my glory will I not g to another, neither my 5414
42:12 Let them g glory unto the LORD, and 7760
42:23 Who among you will g ear to this? who will 238
43: 4 therefore will I g men for thee, and 5414
43: 6 G up; and to the south, Keep not back: 5414
43:20 because I g waters in the wilderness, and 5414
43:20 to g drink to my people, my chosen. 8248
45: 3 I will g thee the treasures of darkness, and 5414
48:11 and I will not g my glory unto another. 5414
49: 6 I will also g thee for a light to the Gentiles, 5414
49: 8 and g thee for a covenant of the people, 5414
49:20 for me: g place to me that I may dwell. 5066
51: 4 my people; and g ear unto me, O my nation: 238
55:10 that it may g seed to the sower, and 5414
56: 5 Even unto them will I g in mine house and 5414
56: 5 I will g them an everlasting name, that shall 5414
60:19 neither for brightness shall the moon g light 215
61: 3 to g unto them beauty for ashes, the oil of 5414
62: 7 g him no rest, till he establish, and till he 5414
62: 8 Surely I will no more g thy corn to be meat 5414
Jer 3:15 I will g you pastors according to mine 5414
3:19 the children, and g thee a pleasant land, 5414
4:12 now also will I g sentence against them. 1696
4:16 g out their voice against the cities of Judah. 5414
6:10 and g warning, that they may hear? 5749
8:10 Therefore will I g their wives unto others, 5414
9:15 and g them water of gall to drink. 8248
11: 5 to g them a land flowing with milk and 5414
13:15 Hear ye, and g ear; be not proud: for 238
13:16 G glory to the LORD your God, before he 5414
14:13 but I will g you assured peace in this place. 5414
14:22 or can the heavens g showers? art not thou 5414
15:13 thy treasures will I g to the spoil without 5414
16: 7 g them the cup of consolation to drink for 8248
17: 3 I will g thy substance and all thy treasures 5414
17:10 even to g every man according to his ways, 5414
18:18 and let us not g heed to any of his words. 7181
18:19 G heed to me, O LORD, and hearken to 7181
19: 7 their carcases will I g to be meat for 5414
20: 4 I will g all Judah into the hand of the king 5414
20: 5 will I g into the hand of their enemies, 5414
22:25 I will g thee into the hand of them that seek 5414
24: 7 I will g them a heart to know me, that I am 5414
24: 8 So will I g Zedekiah the king of Judah, and 5414
25:30 he shall g a shout, as they that tread 1959+6030
25:31 he will g them that are wicked to the sword, 5414
26:24 that they should not g him into the hand of 5414
29: 6 g your daughters to husbands, that they 5414
29:11 and not of evil, to g you an expected end. 5414
30:16 all that prey upon thee will I g for a prey. 5414
32: 3 I will g this city into the hand of the king of 5414
32:19 to g every one according to his ways, and 5414
32:22 which thou didst swear to their fathers to g 5414
32:28 I will g this city into the hand of 5414
32:39 I will g them one heart, and one way, 5414
34: 2 I will g this city into the hand of the king of 5414
34:18 I will g the men that have transgressed my 5414
34:20 I will even g them into the hand of their 5414
34:21 his princes will I g into the hand of their 5414
35: 2 of the chambers, and g them wine to drink. 8248
37:21 that they should g him daily a piece of 5414
38:15 if I g thee counsel, wilt thou not hearken 3289
38:16 neither will I g thee into the hand of these 5414
44:30 I will g Pharaoh-hophra king of Egypt into 5414
45: 5 thy life will I g unto thee for a prey in all 5414
48: 9 G wings unto Moab, that it may flee and 5414
50:34 that he may g rest to the land, and 7280
La 2:18 g thyself no rest; let not the apple of thine 5414
3:65 G them sorrow of heart, thy curse unto 5414
4: 3 the breast, they g suck to their young ones: 3243
Eze 2: 8 open thy mouth, and eat that I g thee. 5414
3: 3 fill thy bowels with this roll that I g thee. 5414
3:17 my mouth, and g them warning from me. 2094
7:21 I will g it into the hands of the strangers for 5414
11: 2 and g wicked counsel in this city: 3289+6098
11:17 and I will g you the land of Israel. 5414
11:19 I will g them one heart, and I will put a new 5414
11:19 their flesh, and will g them a heart of flesh: 5414
15: 6 so will I g the inhabitants of Jerusalem. 5414
16:33 They g gifts to all whores: but thou givest 5414
16:36 thy children, which thou didst g unto them; 5414
16:38 and I will g thee blood in fury and jealousy. 5414
16:39 I will also g thee into their hand, and 5414
16:41 and thou also shalt g no hire any more. 5414
16:61 I will g them unto thee for daughters, but 5414
17:15 that they might g him horses and 5414
20:28 for the which I lifted up mine hand to g it to 5414
20:42 I lifted up mine hand to g it to your fathers. 5414
21:11 to g it into the hand of the slayer. 5414
21:27 come whose right it is; and I will g it him. 5414
23:31 therefore will I g her cup into thine hand. 5414
23:46 and will g them to be removed and spoiled. 5414
25:10 and will g them in possession, 5414
29:19 I will g the land of Egypt unto 5414
29:21 I will g thee the opening of the mouth in 5414
32: 7 and the moon shall not g her light. 215+216
33:15 g again that he had robbed, walk in 7999
33:27 him that is in the open field will I g to 5414
36:26 A new heart also will I g you, and a new 5414
36:26 your flesh, and I will g you a heart of flesh. 5414
39: 4 I will g thee unto the ravenous birds of 5414
39:11 that I will g unto Gog a place there of 5414
Eze 43:19 thou shalt g to the priests the Levites that 5414
44:28 ye shall g them no possession in Israel: 5414
44:30 ye shall also g unto the priest the first of 5414
45: 8 the rest of the land shall they g to the house 5414
45:13 ye shall g the sixth part of an ephah of a 8341
45:16 All the people of the land shall g this 413+1961
45:17 it shall be the prince's part to g burnt NIH
46: 5 for the lambs as he shall be able to g, 4991
46:11 to the lambs as he is able to g, and a hin of 4991
46:16 If the prince g a gift unto any of his sons, 5414
46:17 if he g a gift of his inheritance to one of his 5414
46:18 he shall g his sons inheritance out of his 5157
47:14 up mine hand to g it unto your fathers: 5414
47:23 there shall ye g him his inheritance, 5414
Da 1:12 let them g us pulse to eat, and water to 5414
2:16 desired of the king that he would g him 5415
5:17 be to thyself, and g thy rewards to another; 3052
6: 2 that the princes might g accounts unto 3052
8:13 to g both the sanctuary and the host to be 5414
9:22 I am now come forth to g thee skill and 7919
11:17 he shall g him the daughter of women, 5414
11:21 to whom they shall not g the honour of 5414
Hos 2: 5 that g me my bread and my water, my wool 5414
2:15 I will g her her vineyards from thence, and 5414
4:18 her rulers with shame do love, G ye. 3051
5: 1 of Israel; and g ye ear, O house of the king; 238
9:14 G them, O LORD: what wilt thou give? 5414
9:14 what wilt thou g? give them a miscarrying 5414
9:14 g them a miscarrying womb and 5414
11: 8 How shall I g thee up, Ephraim? how shall 5414
13:10 thou saidst, G me a king and princes? 5414
Joel 1: 2 Hear this, ye old men, and g ear, all ye 238
2:17 and g not thine heritage to reproach, 5414
Mic 1:14 Therefore shalt thou g presents to 5414
5: 3 Therefore will he g them up, until the time 5414
6: 7 shall I g my firstborn for my transgression, 5414
6:14 that which thou deliverest will I g up to 5414
Hag 2: 9 in this place will I g peace, saith 5414
Zec 3: 7 I will g thee places to walk among these 5414
8:12 the vine shall g her fruit, and the ground 5414
8:12 the ground shall g her increase, and 5414
8:12 and the heavens shall g their dew; 5414
10: 1 g them showers of rain, to every one grass 5414
11:12 unto them, If ye think good, g me my price; 3051
Mal 2: 2 to g glory unto my name, saith the LORD 5414
Mt 4: 6 He shall g his angels charge concerning 1781
4: 9 unto him, All these things will I g thee, 1325
5:31 let him g her a writing of divorcement: 1325
5:42 G to him that asketh thee, and from him 1325
6:11 G us this day our daily bread. 1325
7: 6 G not that which is holy unto the dogs, 1325
7: 9 if his son ask bread, will he g him a stone? 1929
7:10 Or if he ask a fish, will he g him a serpent? 1929
7:11 know how to g good gifts unto your 1325
7:11 heaven g good things to them that ask him? 1325
9:24 He said unto them, G place: for the maid is 402
10: 8 out devils: freely ye have received, freely g. 1325
10:42 And whosoever shall g to drink unto one 4222
11:28 and are heavy laden, and I will g you rest. 373
12:36 they shall g account thereof in the day of 591
14: 7 Whereupon he promised with an oath to g 1325
14: 8 G me here John Baptist's head in a charger. 1325
14:16 They need not depart; g ye them to eat. 1325
16:19 And I will g unto thee the keys of 1325
16:26 what shall a man g in exchange for his 1325
17:27 that take, and g unto them for me and thee. 1325
19: 7 command to g a writing of divorcement, 1325
19:21 and g to the poor, and thou shalt have 1325
20: 4 and whatsoever is right I will g you. 1325
20: 8 Call the labourers, and g them their hire, 591
20:14 I will g unto this last, even as unto thee. 1325
20:23 is not mine to g, but it shall be given to 1325
20:28 and to g his life a ransom for many. 1325
22:17 Is it lawful to g tribute unto Cesar, or not? 1325
24:19 and to them that g suck in those days. 2337
24:29 and the moon shall not g her light, and 1325
24:45 to g them meat in due season? 1325
25: 8 foolish said unto the wise, G us of your oil; 1325
25:28 and g it unto him which hath ten talents. 1325
26:15 And said unto them, What will ye g me, 1325
26:53 he shall presently g me more than twelve 3936
Mk 6:22 whatsoever thou wilt, and I will g it thee. 1325
6:23 I will g it thee, unto the half of my 1325
6:25 I will that thou g me by and by in a charger 1325
6:37 and said unto them, G ye them to eat. 1325
6:37 pennyworth of bread, and g them to eat? 1325
8:37 Or what shall a man g in exchange for his 1325
9:41 g you a cup of water to drink in my name, 4222
10:21 and g to the poor, and thou shalt have 1325
10:40 and on my left hand is not mine to g; 1325
10:45 and to g his life a ransom for many. 1325
12: 9 and will g the vineyard unto others. 1325
12:14 Is it lawful to g tribute to Cesar, or not? 1325
12:15 Shall we g, or shall we not give? But he, 1325
12:15 Shall we give, or shall we not g? But he, 1325
13:17 and to them that g suck in those days. 2337
13:24 and the moon shall not g her light, 1325
14:11 were glad, and promised to g him money. 1325
Lk 1:32 the Lord God shall g unto him the throne of 1325
1:77 To g knowledge of salvation unto his 1325
1:79 To g light to them that sit in darkness and 2014
4: 6 All this power will I g thee, and the glory 1325
4: 6 unto me; and to whomsoever I will I g it. 1325
4:10 He shall g his angels charge over thee, to 1781
6:30 G to every man that asketh of thee; and 1325
6:38 G, and it shall be given unto you; 1325
6:38 running over, shall men g into your bosom. 1325
8:55 and he commanded to g her meat. 1325
9:13 But he said unto them, G ye them to eat. 1325
10: 7 and drinking such things as they g: 3588+3844
10:19 I g unto you power to tread on serpents and 1325
11: 3 G us day by day our daily bread. 1325
11: 7 with me in bed; I cannot rise and g thee? 1325
11: 8 Though he will not rise and g him, because 1325
11: 8 will rise and g him as many as he needeth. 1325
Lk 11:11 you that is a father, will he g him a stone? 1929
11:11 a fish, will he for a fish g him a serpent? 1929
11:13 know how to g good gifts unto your 1325
11:13 g the Holy Spirit to them that ask him? 1325
11:36 bright shining of a candle doth g thee light. 5461
11:41 But rather g alms of such things as you 1325
12:32 for it is your Father's good pleasure to g 1325
12:33 Sell that ye have, and g alms; 1325
12:42 to g them their portion of meat in due 1325
12:51 Suppose ye that I am come to g peace on 1325
12:58 g diligence that thou mayest be delivered 1325
14: 9 and say to thee, G this man place; 1325
15:12 g me the portion of goods that falleth to 1325
16: 2 g an account of thy stewardship; for thou 591
16:12 who shall g you that which is your own? 1325
17:18 There are not found that returned to g glory 1325
18:12 in the week, I g tithes of all that I possess. 586
19: 8 Lord, the half of my goods I g to the poor; 1325
19:24 and g it to him that hath ten pounds. 1325
20:10 that they should g him of the fruit of 1325
20:16 and shall g the vineyard to others. 1325
20:22 Is it lawful for us to g tribute unto Cesar, or 1325
21:15 For I will g you a mouth and wisdom, 1325
21:23 and to them that g suck, in those days, 2337
22: 5 were glad, and covenanted to g him money. 1325
23: 2 and forbidding to g tribute to Cesar, saying 1325
Jn 1:22 that we may g an answer to them that sent 1325
4: 7 Jesus saith unto her, G me to drink. 1325
4:10 who it is that saith to thee, G me to drink; 1325
4:14 water that I shall g him shall never thirst; 1325
4:14 the water that I shall g him shall be in him a 1325
4:15 Sir, g me this water, that I thirst not, 1325
6:27 which the Son of man shall g unto you: 1325
6:34 unto him, Lord, evermore g us this bread. 1325
6:51 and the bread that I will g is my flesh, 1325
6:51 which I will g for the life of the world. 1325
6:52 How can this man g us his flesh to eat? 1325
7:19 Did not Moses g you the law, and yet none 1325
9:24 and said unto him, G God the praise: 1325
10:28 And I g unto them eternal life; and 1325
11:22 thou wilt ask of God, God will g it thee. 1325
13:26 He it is, to whom I shall g a sop, 1929
13:29 or that he should g something to the poor. 1325
13:34 A new commandment I g unto you, That ye 1325
14:16 and he shall g you another Comforter, 1325
14:27 I leave with you, my peace I g unto you: 1325
14:27 not as the world giveth, g I unto you. 1325
15:16 of the Father in my name, he may g it you. 1325
16:23 ask the Father in my name, he will g it you. 1325
17: 2 that he should g eternal life to as many as 1325
Ac 3: 6 have I none; but such as I have g I thee: 1325
5:31 for to g repentance to Israel, and 1325
6: 4 But we will g ourselves continually to 4342
7: 5 yet he promised that he would g it to him 1325
7:38 who received the lively oracles to g unto 1325
8:19 Saying, G me also this power, that on 1325
10:43 To him g all the prophets witness, 3140
13:16 of Israel, and ye that fear God, g audience. 191
13:34 I will g you the sure mercies of David. 1325
19:40 there being no cause whereby we may g an 591
20:32 to g you an inheritance among all them 1325
20:35 It is more blessed to g than to receive. 1325
Ro 8:32 how shall he not with him also freely g us 5483
12:19 but rather g place unto wrath: 1325
12:20 feed him; if he thirst, g him drink: 4222
14:12 every one of us shall g account of himself 1325
16: 4 unto whom not only I g thanks, but also all 2168
1Co 7: 5 that ye may g yourselves to fasting and 4980
7:25 yet I g my judgment, as one that hath 1325
10:30 spoken of for that for which I g thanks? 2168
10:32 G none offence, neither to the Jews, nor to 1096
12: 3 Wherefore I g you to understand, that no 1107
13: 3 and though I g my body to be burned, 3860
14: 7 except they g a distinction in the sounds, 1325
14: 8 For if the trumpet g an uncertain sound, 1325
2Co 4: 6 to g the light of the knowledge of the glory NIG
5:12 but g you occasion to glory on our behalf, 1325
8:10 And herein I g my advice: for this is 1325
9: 7 in his heart, so let him g; not grudgingly, NIG
Eph 1:16 Cease not to g thanks for you, 2168
1:17 may g unto you the spirit of wisdom and 1325
4:27 Neither g place to the devil. 1325
4:28 that he may have to g to him that needeth. 3330
5:14 from the dead, and Christ shall g thee light. 2017
Col 1: 3 We g thanks to God and the Father of our 2168
4: 1 g unto your servants that which is just and 3930
1Th 1: 2 We g thanks to God always for you all, 2168
5:18 In every thing g thanks: for this is the will 2168
2Th 2:13 But we are bound to g thanks alway to 2168
3:16 Now the Lord of peace himself g you peace 1325
1Ti 1: 4 Neither g heed to fables and 4337
4:13 Till I come, g attendance to reading, 4337
4:15 Meditate upon these things; g thyself 1510
5: 7 And these things g in charge, that they 3853
5:14 g none occasion to the adversary to speak 1325
6:13 I g thee charge in the sight of God, 3853
2Ti 1:16 The Lord g mercy unto the house of 1325
2: 7 the Lord g thee understanding in all things. 1325
2:25 if God peradventure will g them repentance 1325
4: 8 the righteous judge, shall g me at that day: 591
Heb 2: 1 g the more earnest heed to the things which 4337
13:17 as they that must g account, that they may do 591
Jas 2:16 notwithstanding ye g them not those things 1325
1Pe 3:15 be ready always to g an answer to every NIG
4: 5 Who shall g account to him that is ready to 591
2Pe 1:10 g diligence to make your calling and 4704
1Jn 5:16 he shall g him life for them that sin not 1325
Rev 2: 7 To him that overcometh will I g to eat of 1325
2:10 unto death, and I will g thee a crown of life, 1325
2:17 To him that overcometh will I g to eat of 1325
2:17 and will g him a white stone, and in 1325
2:23 I will g unto every one of you according to 1325
2:26 to him will I g power over the nations: 1325
2:28 And I will g him the morning star. 1325
4: 9 And when those beasts g glory and honour 1325

G

Rev 10: 9 and said unto him, **G** me the little book. *1325*
11: 3 And I will **g** *power* unto my two witnesses, *1325*
11:17 Saying, We **g** thee **thanks**, O Lord God *2168*
11:18 that *thou* shouldest **g** reward unto thy *1325*
13:15 And he had power to **g** life unto the image *1325*
14: 7 a loud voice, Fear God, and **g** glory to him; *1325*
16: 9 and they repented not to **g** him glory. *1325*
16:19 to **g** unto her the cup of the wine of *1325*
17:13 and shall **g** their power and strength unto *1239*
17:17 and **g** their kingdom unto the beast, *1325*
18: 7 so much torment and sorrow **g** her: *1325*
19: 7 be glad and rejoice, and **g** honour to him: *1325*
21: 6 I will **g** unto him that is athirst of *1325*
22:12 to **g** every man according as his work shall *591*

GIVE LIFE See QUICKEN

GIVE TO NEEDY See ALMS

GIVEN (498) [GIVE]

Ge 1:29 I have **g** you every herb bearing seed, 5414
1:30 *is* life, *I have* **g** every green herb for meat: NIH
9: 3 *even* as the green herb have I **g** you all 5414
15: 3 Behold, to me thou hast **g** no seed: 5414
15:18 saying, Unto thy seed have I **g** this land, 5414
16: 5 I have **g** my maid into thy bosom; and 5414
20:16 I have **g** thy brother a thousand *pieces* of 5414
21: 7 that Sarah should have **g** children **suck**? 3243
24:35 he hath **g** him flocks, and herds, and silver, 5414
24:36 and unto him hath he **g** all that he hath. 5414
27:37 all his brethren have I **g** to him for servants; 5414
29:33 he hath therefore **g** me this *son* also: 5414
30: 6 also heard my voice, and hath **g** me a son: 5414
30:18 God hath **g** *me* my hire, because I have 5414
30:18 I have **g** my maiden to my husband: 5414
31: 9 the cattle of your father, and **g** *them* to me. 5414
33: 5 The children which God hath **graciously g** 2603
38:14 and she was not **g** unto him to wife. 5414
43:23 hath **g** you treasure in your sacks: 5414
48: 9 whom God hath **g** me in this *place.* And he 5414
48:22 Moreover I have **g** to thee one portion 5414
Ex 5:16 *There is* no straw **g** unto thy servants, and 5414
5:18 for there shall no straw be **g** you, yet shall 5414
16:15 This *is* the bread which the LORD hath **g** 5414
16:29 for that the LORD hath **g** you the sabbath, 5414
21: 4 If his master have **g** him a wife, and 5414
31: 6 I, behold, I have **g** with him Aholiab, 5414
Lev 6:17 I have **g** it *unto them for* their portion of my 5414
7:34 have **g** them unto Aaron the priest and 5414
7:36 Which the LORD commanded to be **g** 5414
10:14 *which are* **g** out of the sacrifices of peace 5414
10:17 *God* hath **g** it you to bear the iniquity of 5414
17:11 I have **g** it to you upon the altar to make an 5414
19:20 and not at all redeemed, nor freedom **g** her; 5414
20: 3 because he hath **g** of his seed unto Molech, 5414
Nu 3: 9 they *are* **wholly g** unto him out of 5414+5414
8:16 For they *are* **wholly g** unto me from 5414+5414
8:19 I have **g** the Levites *as* a gift to Aaron and 5414
16:14 or **g** us inheritance of fields and vineyards: 5414
18: 6 to you *they are* **g** *as* a gift for the LORD, 5414
18: 7 I have **g** your priest's office *unto you as* a 5414
18: 8 I also have **g** thee the charge of mine heave 5414
18: 8 unto thee have I **g** them by reason of 5414
18:11 I have **g** them unto thee, and to thy sons 5414
18:12 offer unto the LORD, them have I **g** thee. 5414
18:19 have I **g** thee, and thy sons and thy 5414
18:21 I have **g** the children of Levi all the tenth in 5414
18:24 I have **g** to the Levites to inherit: 5414
18:26 have **g** you from them for your inheritance, 5414
20:12 into the land which I have **g** them. 5414
20:24 which I have **g** unto the children of Israel, 5414
21:29 he hath **g** his sons that escaped, and 5414
26:54 *to* every one shall his inheritance be **g** 5414
26:62 there was no inheritance **g** them among 5414
27:12 see the land which I have **g** unto 5414
32: 5 let this land be **g** unto thy servants for a 5414
32: 7 the land which the LORD hath **g** them? 5414
32: 9 into the land which the LORD had **g** them. 5414
33:53 for I have **g** you the land to possess it. 5414
Dt 1: 3 had **g** him **in commandment** unto them; 6680
2: 5 I have **g** mount Seir unto Esau *for* a 5414
2: 9 I have **g** Ar unto the children of Lot *for* a 5414
2:19 I have **g** it unto the children of Lot *for* a 5414
2:24 I have **g** into thy hand Sihon the Amorite, 5414
3:18 The LORD your God hath **g** you this land 5414
3:19 shall abide in your cities which I have **g** 5414
3:20 Until the LORD have **g rest** unto your 5117
3:20 your God hath **g** them beyond Jordan: 5414
3:20 unto his possession, which I have **g** you. 5414
8:10 for the good land which he hath **g** thee. 5414
9:23 and possess the land which I have **g** you; 5414
12:15 the LORD thy God which he hath **g** thee: 5414
12:21 of thy flock, which the LORD hath **g** thee, 5414
13:12 which the LORD thy God hath **g** thee to 5414
16:17 the LORD thy God which he hath **g** thee. 5414
20:14 which the LORD thy God hath **g** thee. 5414
22:17 he hath **g** occasions of speech *against her,* 7760
25:19 when the LORD thy God hath **g** thee **rest** 5117
26: 9 hath **g** us this land, *even* a land that floweth 5414
26:10 the land, which thou, O LORD, hast **g** me. 5414
26:11 the LORD thy God hath **g** unto thee, 5414
26:12 hast **g** *it* unto the Levite, the stranger, 5414
26:13 also have **g** them unto the Levite, and 5414
26:14 *use,* nor **g** *ought* thereof for the dead: 5414
26:15 and the land which thou hast **g** us, 5414
28:31 thy sheep *shall be* **g** unto thine enemies, 5414
28:32 thy daughters *shall be* **g** unto another 5414
28:52 which the LORD thy God hath **g** thee. 5414
28:53 which the LORD thy God hath **g** thee, 5414
29: 4 Yet the LORD hath not **g** you a heart to 5414
29:26 and *whom* he had not **g** unto them: 2505
Jos 1: 3 that have I **g** unto you, as I said unto 5414
1:13 The LORD your God hath **g** you **rest**, and 5117
1:13 given you rest, and hath **g** you this land. 5414
1:15 the LORD have **g** your brethren **rest**, 5117
Jos 1:15 as *he hath* **g** you, and they also have NIH
2: 9 I know that the LORD hath **g** you 5414
2:14 when the LORD hath **g** us the land, 5414
6: 2 I have **g** into thine hand Jericho, and 5414
6:16 Shout; for the LORD hath **g** you the city. 5414
8: 1 I have **g** into thy hand the king of Ai, and 5414
14: 3 For Moses had **g** the inheritance of two 5414
15:19 a blessing; for thou hast **g** me a south land; 5414
17:14 Why hast thou **g** me *but* one lot and 5414
18: 3 LORD God of your fathers hath **g** you? 5414
22: 4 now the LORD your God hath **g rest** unto 5117
22: 7 Moses had **g** *possession* in Bashan: 5414
23: 1 **g rest** unto Israel from all their enemies 5117
23:13 which the LORD your God hath **g** you. 5414
23:15 which the LORD your God hath **g** you. 5414
23:16 off the good land which he hath **g** unto you. 5414
24:13 I have **g** you a land for which ye did not 5414
24:33 which was **g** him in mount Ephraim. 5414
Jdg 1:15 for thou hast **g** me a south land; give me 5414
14:20 But Samson's wife was *g* to his companion, NIH
15: 6 taken his wife, and **g** her to his companion. 5414
15:18 Thou hast **g** this great deliverance into 5414
18:10 for God hath **g** it into your hands; a place 5414
Ru 2:12 a full reward be **g** thee **of** the LORD 4480+5973
1Sa 1:27 the LORD hath **g** me my petition which I 5414
15:28 hath **g** it to a neighbour of thine, *that is* 5414
18:19 daughter should have been **g** to David, 5414
18:19 that she was **g** unto Adriel the Meholathite 5414
22:13 in that thou hast **g** him bread and a sword, 5414
25:27 let it even be **g** unto the young men that 5414
25:44 Saul had **g** Michal his daughter, 5414
28:17 and **g** it to thy neighbour, *even* to David: 5414
30:23 with *that* which the LORD hath **g** us, 5414
2Sa 4:10 who *thought* that I would have **g** him a 5414
7: 1 the LORD had **g** him **rest** round about 5117
9: 9 I have **g** unto thy master's son all that 5414
12: 8 I would **moreover** have **g** unto thee such 3254
12:14 **g great occasion** to the enemies of the
LORD **to blaspheme**, 5006+5006
17: 7 The **counsel** that Ahithophel hath **g** 3289+6098
18:11 I would have **g** thee ten *shekels of* silver, 5414
19:42 of the king's *cost?* or hath he **g** us *any* gift? 5375
22:36 Thou hast also **g** me the shield of thy 5414
22:41 Thou hast also **g** me the necks of mine 5414
1Ki 1:48 which hath **g** *one* to sit on my throne *this* 5414
2:21 Let Abishag the Shunammite be **g** to 5414
3: 6 that thou hast **g** him a son to sit on his 5414
3:12 I have **g** thee a wise and an understanding 5414
3:13 I have also **g** thee *that* which thou hast not 5414
5: 4 now the LORD my God hath **g** me **rest** on 5117
5: 7 which hath **g** unto David a wise son over 5414
8:36 which thou hast **g** to thy people for an 5414
8:56 that hath **g** rest unto his people Israel, 5414
9: 7 Israel out of the land which I have **g** them; 5414
9:12 to see the cities which Solomon had **g** him; 5414
9:13 What cities *are* these which thou hast **g** me, 5414
9:16 **g** it *for* a present unto his daughter, 5414
12: 8 **counsel** of the old men, which they
had **g** 3289+6098
13: 5 of God had **g** by the word of the LORD. 5414
18:26 they took the bullock which was **g** them, 5414
2Ki 5: 1 by him the LORD had **g** deliverance unto 5414
5:17 be **g** to thy servant two mules' burden of 5414
8:29 which the Syrians had **g** him at Ramah, 5221
9:15 of the wounds which the Syrians had **g** him, 5221
23:11 that the kings of Judah had **g** to the sun, 5414
25:30 his allowance was a continual allowance **g** 5414
1Ch 5: 1 his birthright was **g** unto the sons of Joseph 5414
6:61 *were cities* **g** out of the half tribe, NIH
6:63 Unto the sons of Merari *were* **g** by lot, NIH
6:71 Unto the sons of Gershom *were* **g** out of NIH
6:77 Merari *were* **g** out of the tribe of Zebulun, NIH
6:78 *were* **g** *them* out of the tribe of Reuben, NIH
22:18 hath he *not* **g** you **rest** on every side? for he 5117
22:18 for he hath **g** the inhabitants of the land into 5414
23:25 The LORD God of Israel hath **g rest** unto 5117
28: 5 (for the LORD hath **g** me many sons,) 5414
29: 3 *which* I have **g** to the house of my God, 5414
29:14 of thee, and of thine own have we **g** thee. 5414
2Ch 2:12 who hath **g** to David the king a wise son, 5414
6:27 which thou hast **g** unto thy people for an 5414
7:20 roots out of my land which I have **g** them; 5414
14: 6 because the LORD had **g** him **rest**. 5117
14: 7 and he hath **g** us **rest** on every side. 5117
20:11 which thou hast **g** us **to inherit**. 3423
22: 6 of the wounds which were **g** him at Ramah, 5221
25: 9 talents which I have **g** to the army of Israel? 5414
32:29 for God had **g** him substance very much. 5414
34:14 book of the law of the LORD **g** by Moses. NIH
34:18 Hilkiah the priest hath **g** me a book. 5414
36:23 earth hath the LORD God of heaven **g** me; 5414
Ezr 1: 2 The LORD God of heaven hath **g** me all 5414
4:21 until *another* commandment shall be **g** from 7761
6: 4 let the expences be **g** out of the king's 3052
6: 8 forthwith expences be **g** unto these men, 3052
6: 9 let *it* be **g** them day by day without fail: 3052
7: 6 which the LORD God of Israel had **g**: 5414
7:19 The vessels also that *are* **g** thee for 3052
9:13 and hast **g** us *such* deliverance as this; 5414
Ne 2: 7 let letters be **g** me to the governors beyond 5414
10:29 which was **g** by Moses the servant of God, 5414
13: 5 which was commanded *to be* **g** to NIH
13:10 had not been **g** *them:* for the Levites 5414
Est 2: 3 let their things for purification be **g** *them:* 5414
2: 9 *which were* meet to be **g** her, 5414
2:13 whatsoever she desired was **g** her to go 5414
3:11 The silver *is* **g** to thee, the people also, 5414
3:14 **g** in every province *was* published unto all 5414
3:15 and the decree was **g** in Shushan the palace. 5414
4: 8 that was **g** at Shushan to destroy them, 5414
5: 3 it shall be even **g** thee to the half of 5414
7: 3 let my life be **g** me at my petition, and 5414
8: 7 I have **g** Esther the house of Haman, and 5414
8:13 **g** in every province *was* published unto all 5414
8:14 and the decree was **g** at Shushan the palace. 5414
Est 9:14 the decree was **g** at Shushan; and they 5414
Job 3:20 Wherefore is light **g** to him that is in 5414
3:23 *Why is light* **g** to a man whose way is hid, NIH
9:24 The earth is **g** into the hand of the wicked: 5414
10:18 *Oh that* I had **g up the ghost**, and no eye 1478
15:19 Unto whom alone the earth was **g**, and 5414
22: 7 hast not **g** water to the weary **to drink**, 8248
24:23 *Though* it be **g** him *to be* in safety, 5414
33: 4 the breath of the Almighty hath **g** me **life**. 2421
34:13 Who hath **g** him **a charge** over the earth? 6485
37:10 By the breath of God frost is **g**: and 5414
38:36 or who hath **g** understanding to the heart? 5414
39:19 Hast thou **g** the horse strength? hast thou 5414
Ps 16: 7 bless the LORD, who hath **g** me **counsel**: 3289
18:35 Thou hast also **g** me the shield of thy 5414
18:40 Thou hast also **g** me the necks of mine 5414
21: 2 Thou hast **g** him his heart's desire, and 5414
44:11 Thou hast **g** us like sheep appointed for 5414
60: 4 Thou hast **g** a banner to them that fear thee, 5414
61: 5 thou hast **g** *me* the heritage of those that 5414
71: 3 thou hast **g commandment** to save me; 6680
72:15 and to him shall be **g** of the gold of Sheba: 5414
78:24 and had **g** them *of* the corn of heaven. 5414
78:63 and their maidens were not **g to marriage**. 1984
79: 2 The dead bodies of thy servants have they **g** 5414
111: 5 He hath **g** meat unto them that fear him: 5414
112: 9 He hath dispersed, he hath **g** to the poor; 5414
115:16 the earth hath he **g** to the children of men. 5414
118:18 but he hath not **g** me **over** unto death. 5414
120: 3 What shall be **g** unto thee? or what shall be 5414
124: 6 who hath not **g** us *as* a prey to their teeth. 5414
Pr 19:17 that which he hath **g** will he pay him again. 1576
23: 2 thy throat, if thou *be* a man **g to appetite**. 5315
24:21 meddle not with them that are **g to change**: 8138
Ecc 1:13 this sore travail hath God **g** to the sons of 5414
3:10 which God hath **g** to the sons of men to be 5414
5:19 Every man also to whom God hath **g** riches 5414
5:19 hath **g** him **power** to eat thereof, and 7980
6: 2 A man to whom God hath **g** riches, wealth, 5414
8: 8 wickedness deliver **those that are g to** it. 1167
9: 9 which he hath **g** thee under the sun, all 5414
12:11 *which* are **g** from one shepherd. 5414
Isa 3:11 for the reward of his hands shall be **g** him. 6213
8:18 the children whom the LORD hath **g** me 5414
9: 6 unto us a child is born, unto us a Son is **g**: 5414
23:11 the LORD hath **g a commandment** 6680
33:16 bread *shall be* **g** him; his waters *shall be* 5414
35: 2 the glory of Lebanon shall be **g** unto it, 5414
37:10 Jerusalem shall not be **g** into the hand of 5414
43:28 have **g** Jacob to the curse, and Israel to 5414
47: 6 and **g** them into thine hand: 5414
47: 8 *thou that art* **g to pleasures**, that dwellest 5719
50: 4 The Lord GOD hath **g** me the tongue of 5414
55: 4 I have **g** him *for* a witness to the people, 5414
Jer 3: 8 put her away, and **g** her a bill of divorce; 5414
3:18 **g for an inheritance** unto your fathers. 5157
6:13 them every one *is* **g to covetousness**; 1214+1215
8:10 even unto the greatest is **g** to covetousness, 1214
8:13 *the things that* I have **g** them shall pass 5414
8:14 **g** us water of gall **to drink**, because 8248
11:18 the LORD hath **g** me **knowledge** *of it,* 3045
12: 7 I have **g** the dearly beloved of my soul into 5414
13:20 where *is* the flock *that* was **g** thee, 5414
15: 9 she hath **g up the ghost**; her sun is 5301+5315
21:10 it shall be **g** into the hand of the king of 5414
25: 5 dwell in the land that the LORD hath **g** 5414
27: 5 have **g** it unto whom it seemed meet unto 5414
27: 6 now have I **g** all these lands into the hand 5414
27: 6 the beasts of the field have I **g** him also to 5414
28:14 I have **g** him the beasts of the field also. 5414
32:22 hast **g** them this land, which thou didst 5414
32:24 the city is **g** into the hand of the Chaldeans, 5414
32:25 for the city is **g** into the hand of 5414
32:43 beast; it is **g** into the hand of the Chaldeans. 5414
35:15 ye shall dwell in the land which I have **g** to 5414
38: 3 This city shall **surely** be **g** into 5414+5414
38:18 shall this city be **g** into the hand of 5414
39:17 thou shalt not be **g** into the hand of the men 5414
44:20 the people which had **g** him *that* **answer**, 6030
47: 7 seeing the LORD hath **g** it **a charge** 6680
50:15 she hath **g** her hand: her foundations are 5414
52:34 there was a continual diet **g** him of the king 5414
La 1:11 they have **g** their pleasant things for meat to 5414
2: 7 he hath **g up** into the hand of the enemy 5462
5: 6 We have **g** the hand *to* the Egyptians, *and* 5414
Eze 3:20 because thou hast not **g** him **warning**, 2094
4:15 I have **g** thee cow's dung for man's dung, 5414
11:15 unto us is this land **g** in possession. 5414
15: 6 which I have **g** to the fire for fuel, so will I 5414
16:17 which I had **g** thee, and madest to thyself 5414
16:34 no reward is **g** unto thee, therefore thou art 5414
17:18 he had **g** his hand, and hath done all these 5414
18: 7 hath **g** his bread to the hungry, and 5414
18: 8 He *that* hath not **g forth** upon usury, 5414
18:13 Hath **g forth** upon usury, and hath taken 5414
18:16 *but* hath **g** his bread to the hungry, and 5414
20:15 land which I had **g** *them,* flowing with milk 5414
21:11 he hath **g** it to be furbished, that *it* may be 5414
28:25 shall they dwell in their land that I have **g** 5414
29: 5 I have **g** thee for meat to the beasts of 5414
29:20 I have **g** him the land of Egypt *for* his 5414
33:24 *are* many; the land is **g** us for inheritance. 5414
35:12 are laid desolate, they are **g** us to consume. 5414
37:25 they shall dwell in the land that I have **g** 5414
47:11 shall not be healed; they shall be **g** to salt. 5414
Da 2:23 who hast **g** me wisdom and might, and 3052
2:37 for the God of heaven hath **g** thee a 3052
2:38 the fowls of the heaven hath he **g** into thine 3052
4:16 let a beast's heart be **g** unto him; 3052
5:28 is divided, and **g** to the Medes and Persians. 3052
7: 4 feet as a man, and a man's heart was **g** to it. 3052
7: 6 also four heads; and dominion *was* **g** to it. 3052
7:11 body destroyed, and **g** to the burning flame. 3052
7:14 there *was* **g** him dominion, and glory, and 3052
7:22 judgment *was* **g** to the saints of the most 3052

Da 7:25 they shall be g into his hand until a time 3052
7:27 shall be g to the people of the saints of 3052
8:12 a host was g him against the daily sacrifice 5414
11: 6 she shall be g up, and they that brought her, 5414
11:11 but the multitude shall be g into his hand. 5414
Hos 2: 9 and my flax g to cover her nakedness. NIH
2:12 are my rewards that my lovers have g 5414
Joel 2:23 for he hath g you the former rain 5414
3: 3 have g a boy for a harlot, and sold a girl for 5414
Am 4: 6 I also have g you cleanness of teeth in all 5414
9:15 up out of their land which I have g them, 5414
Na 1:14 the LORD hath g a commandment 6680
Mt 7: 7 Ask, and it shall be g you; seek, and 1325
9: 8 which had g such power unto men. 1325
10:19 for it shall be g you in that same hour what 1325
12:39 and there shall no sign be g to it, but 1325
13:11 Because it is g unto you to know 1325
13:11 kingdom of heaven, but to them it is not g. 1325
13:12 to him shall be g, and he shall have more 1325
14: 9 him at meat, he commanded it to be g her. 1325
14:11 brought in a charger, and g to the damsel: 1325
16: 4 and there shall no sign be g unto it, but 1325
19:11 this saying, save they to whom it is g. 1325
20:23 it shall be g to them for whom it is prepared NIG
21:43 g to a nation bringing forth the fruits 1325
22:30 they neither marry, nor are g in marriage, 1547
25:29 For unto every one that hath shall be g, and 1325
26: 9 have been sold for much, and g to the poor. 1325
28:18 All power is g unto me in heaven and 1325
Mk 4:11 Unto you it is g to know the mystery of 1325
4:24 and unto you that hear shall more be g. 4369
4:25 For he that hath, to him shall be g: and 1325
5:43 commanded that something should be g her 1325
6: 2 what wisdom is this which is g unto him, 1325
8:12 There shall no sign be g unto this 1325
10:40 it shall be g to them for whom it is prepared. NIG
12:25 they neither marry, nor are g in marriage; 1061
13:11 but whatsoever shall be g you in that hour, 1325
14: 5 and have been g to the poor. 1325
14:23 and when he had g thanks, he gave it to 2168
14:44 And he that betrayed him had g them a 1325
Lk 6:38 Give, and it shall be g unto you; 1325
8:10 Unto you it is g to know the mysteries of 1325
8:18 for whosoever hath, to him shall be g; and 1325
11: 9 I say unto you, Ask, and it shall be g you; 1325
11:29 and there shall no sign be g it, but the sign 1325
12:48 stripes. For unto whomsoever much is g, 1325
17:27 married wives, they were g in marriage, 1547
19:15 unto him, to whom he had g the money, 1325
19:26 That unto every one which hath shall be g; 1325
20:34 of this world marry, and are g in marriage: 1548
20:35 neither marry, nor are g in marriage: 1548
22:19 saying, This is my body which is g for you: 1325
Jn 1:17 For the law was g by Moses, but grace and 1325
3:27 except it be g him from heaven. 1325
3:35 the Son, and hath g all things into his hand. 1325
4:10 and he would have g thee living water. 1325
5:26 hath he g to the Son to have life in himself; 1325
5:27 And hath g him authority to execute 1325
5:36 for the works which the Father hath g me to 1325
6:11 and when he had g thanks, he distributed 2168
6:23 eat bread, after that the Lord had g thanks:) 2168
6:39 that of all which he hath g me I should lose 1325
6:65 except it were g unto him of my Father. 1325
7:39 for the Holy Ghost was not yet g; because NIG
11:57 and the Pharisees had g a commandment, 1325
12: 5 for three hundred pence, and g to the poor? 1325
13: 3 Jesus knowing that the Father had g all 1325
13:15 For I have g you an example, that ye should 1325
17: 2 As thou hast g him power over all flesh, 1325
17: 2 eternal life to as many as thou hast g him. 1325
17: 7 whatsoever thou hast g me are of thee. 1325
17: 8 For I have g unto them the words which 1325
17: 9 but for them which thou hast g me; 1325
17:11 own name those whom thou hast g me, 1325
17:14 I have g them thy word; and the world hath 1325
17:22 glory which thou gavest me I have g them; 1325
17:24 I will that they also, whom thou hast g me, 1325
17:24 behold my glory, which thou hast g me: 1325
18:11 the cup which my Father hath g me, shall I 1325
19:11 except it were g thee from above: 1325
Ac 1: 2 g commandments unto the Apostles whom 1781
3:16 the faith which is by him hath g him this 1325
4:12 other name under heaven g among men, 1325
5:32 whom God hath g to them that obey him. 1325
8:18 the apostles' hands the Holy Ghost was g, 1325
17:16 he saw the city wholly g to idolatry. 1510+2712
17:31 whereof he hath g assurance unto all men, 3930
20: 2 and had g them much exhortation, 3056+3870
21:40 And when he had g him licence, Paul stood 2010
24:26 that money should have been g him of Paul, 1325
27:24 God hath g thee all them that sail with thee. 5483
Ro 5: 5 by the Holy Ghost which is g unto us. 1325
11: 8 God hath g them the spirit of slumber, 1325
11:35 Or who hath first g to him, and it shall be 4272
12: 3 For I say, through the grace g unto me, 1325
12: 6 according to the grace that is g to us, 1325
12:13 to the necessity of saints; g to hospitality. 1377
15:15 because of the grace that is g to me of God, 1325
1Co 1: 4 for the grace of God which is g you by 1325
2:12 the things that are freely g to us of God. 5483
3:10 According to the grace of God which is g 1325
11:15 to her: for her hair is g her for a covering. 1325
11:24 And when he had g thanks, he brake it, and 2168
12: 7 But the manifestation of the Spirit is g to 1325
12: 8 For to one is g by the Spirit the word of 1325
12:24 having g more abundant honour to that part 1325
16: 1 as I have g order to the churches of 1299
2Co 1:11 thanks may be g by many on our behalf. 2168
1:22 and g the earnest of the Spirit in our hearts. 1325
5: 5 who also hath g unto us the earnest of 1325
5:18 hath g to us the ministry of reconciliation; 1325
9: 9 dispersed abroad; he hath g to the poor: 1325
10: 8 which the Lord hath g us for edification, 1325
12: 7 there was g to me a thorn in the flesh, 1325
2Co 13:10 which the Lord hath g me to edification, 1325
Gal 2: 9 perceived the grace that was g unto me, 1325
3:21 for if there had been a law g which could 1325
3:21 a law given which could have g life, 2227
3:22 Christ might be g to them that believe. 1325
4:15 out your own eyes, and have g them to me. 1325
Eph 3: 2 grace of God which is g me to you-ward: 1325
3: 7 according to the gift of the grace of God g 1325
3: 8 than the least of all saints, is this grace g, 1325
4: 7 But unto every one of us is g grace 1325
4:19 g themselves over unto lasciviousness, 3860
5: 2 and hath g himself for us an offering and 3860
6:19 for me, that utterance may be g unto me, 1325
Php 1:29 For unto you it is g in the behalf of Christ, 5483
2: 9 g him a name which is above every name: 5483
Col 1:25 of God which is g to me for you, 1325
1Th 4: 8 who hath also g unto us his holy Spirit. 1325
2Th 2:16 and hath g us everlasting consolation and 1325
1Ti 3: 2 g to hospitality, apt to teach; 5382
3: 3 Not g to wine, no striker, not greedy of 3943
3: 8 not doubletongued, not g to much wine, 4337
4:14 is in thee, which was g thee by prophecy, 1325
2Ti 1: 7 For God hath not g us the spirit of fear; but 1325
1: 9 which was g us in Christ Jesus before 1325
3:16 All scripture is g by inspiration of God, 2315
Tit 1: 7 not soon angry, not g to wine, no striker, 3943
1: 7 to wine, no striker, not g to filthy lucre; 146
2: 3 not false accusers, not g to much wine, 1402
Phm 1:22 through your prayers I shall be g unto you. 5483
Heb 2:13 I, and the children which God hath g me. 1325
4: 8 For if Jesus had g them rest, then would he 2664
Jas 1: 5 and upbraideth not; and it shall be g him. 1325
2Pe 1: 3 According as his divine power hath g unto 1433
1: 4 Whereby are g unto us exceeding great and 1433
3:15 wisdom g unto him hath written unto you; 1325
1Jn 3:24 in us, by the Spirit which he hath g us. 1325
4:13 he in us, because he hath g us of his Spirit. 1325
5:11 that God hath g to us eternal life, and 1325
5:20 and hath g us an understanding, that we 1325
Rev 6: 2 had a bow; and a crown was g unto him: 1325
6: 4 power was g to him that sat thereon to take 1325
6: 4 and there was g unto him a great sword. 1325
6: 8 And power was g unto them over the fourth 1325
6:11 And white robes were g unto every one of 1325
7: 2 to whom it was g to hurt the earth and 1325
8: 2 and to them were g seven trumpets. 1325
8: 3 and there was g unto him much incense, 1325
9: 1 to him was g the key of the bottomless pit. 1325
9: 3 and unto them was g power, as 1325
9: 5 And to them it was g that they should not 1325
11: 1 And there was g me a reed like unto a rod: 1325
11: 2 measure it not; for it is g unto the Gentiles: 1325
12:14 And to the woman were g two wings of a 1325
13: 5 And there was g unto him a mouth 1325
13: 5 power was g unto him to continue forty and 1325
13: 7 And it was g unto him to make war with 1325
13: 7 and power was g him over all kindreds, and 1325
16: 6 and thou hast g them blood to drink; 1325
16: 8 power was g unto him to scorch men with 1325
20: 4 upon them, and judgment was g unto them: 1325

GIVER (2) [GIVE]

Isa 24: 2 of usury, so with the g of usury to him. 5383
2Co 9: 7 of necessity: for God loveth a cheerful g. 1395

GIVEST (12) [GIVE]

Dt 15: 9 thy poor brother, and thou g him nought; 5414
15:10 thine heart shall not be grieved when thou g 5414
Job 35: 7 If thou be righteous, what g thou him? or 5414
Ps 50:19 Thou g thy mouth to evil, and thy tongue 7971
80: 5 and g them tears to drink in great measure. 8248
104:28 That thou g them they gather: thou openest 5414
145:15 and thou g them their meat in due season. 5414
Pr 6:35 he rest content, though thou g many gifts. 7235
Eze 3:18 thou g him not warning, nor speakest to 2094
16:33 thou g thy gifts to all thy lovers, and 5414
16:34 in that thou g a reward, and no reward is 5414
1Co 14:17 For thou verily g thanks well, but the other 2168

GIVETH (126) [GIVE]

Ge 49:21 is a hind let loose: he g goodly words. 5414
Ex 16:29 he g you on the sixth day the bread of two 5414
20:12 the land which the LORD thy God g thee. 5414
25: 2 of every man that g it willingly with his 5068
Lev 20: 2 that g any of his seed unto Molech; 5414
20: 4 when he g of his seed unto Molech, and 5414
27: 9 all that any man g of such unto the LORD 5414
Nu 5:10 whatsoever any man g the priest, it shall be 5414
Dt 2:29 the land which the LORD our God g us. 5414
4: 1 the LORD God of your fathers g you. 5414
4:21 which the LORD thy God g thee for an 5414
4:40 which the LORD thy God g thee, for ever. 5414
5:16 in the land which the LORD thy God g 5414
8:18 for it is he that g thee power to get wealth, 5414
9: 6 that the LORD thy God g thee not this 5414
11:17 off the good land which the LORD g you. 5414
11:31 land which the LORD your God g you, 5414
12: 1 which the LORD God of thy fathers g 5414
12: 9 which the LORD your God g you. 5414
12:10 the LORD your God g you to inherit, 5157
12:10 when he g you rest from all your enemies 5117
13: 1 of dreams, and g thee a sign or a wonder, 5414
15: 4 God g thee for an inheritance to possess it: 5414
15: 7 thy land which the LORD thy God g thee, 5414
16: 5 which the LORD thy God g thee: 5414
16:18 which the LORD thy God g thee, 5414
16:20 the land which the LORD thy God g thee. 5414
17: 2 gates which the LORD thy God g thee, 5414
17:14 the land which the LORD thy God g thee, 5414
18: 9 the land which the LORD thy God g thee, 5414
19: 1 whose land the LORD thy God g thee, and 5414
19: 2 which the LORD thy God g thee to 5414
19: 3 the LORD thy God g thee to inherit, 5157
19:10 which the LORD thy God g thee for an 5414
Dt 19:14 the LORD thy God g thee to possess it. 5414
21: 1 the LORD thy God g thee to possess it, 5414
21:23 which the LORD thy God g thee for an 5414
24: 3 g it in her hand, and sendeth her out of his 5414
24: 4 which the LORD thy God g thee for an 5414
25:15 the land which the LORD thy God g thee. 5414
25:19 in the land which the LORD thy God g 5414
26: 1 LORD thy God g thee for an inheritance, 5414
26: 2 of thy land that the LORD thy God g thee, 5414
27: 2 the land which the LORD thy God g thee, 5414
27: 3 the land which the LORD thy God g thee, 5414
28: 8 the land which the LORD thy God g thee. 5414
Jos 1:11 which the LORD your God g you to 5414
1:15 land which the LORD your God g them: 5414
Jdg 11:24 which Chemosh thy god g thee to possess? 3423
21:18 Cursed be he that g a wife to Benjamin. 5414
Job 5:10 Who g rain upon the earth, and 5414
14:10 yea, man g up the ghost, and where is he? 1478
32: 8 of the Almighty g them understanding. 995
33:13 for he g not account of any of his matters. 6030
34:29 When he g quietness, who then can make 8252
35:10 God my Maker, who g songs in the night; 5414
35:12 none g answer, because of the pride of evil 6030
36: 6 life of the wicked: but g right to the poor. 5414
36:31 he the people; he g meat in abundance. 5414
Ps 18:50 Great deliverance g he to his king; and 1431
37:21 but the righteous sheweth mercy, and g. 5414
68:35 the God of Israel is he that g strength and 5414
119:130 The entrance of thy words g light; it giveth 215
119:130 it g understanding unto the simple. 995
127: 2 of sorrows: for so he g his beloved sleep. 5414
136:25 Who g food to all flesh: for his mercy 5414
144:10 It is he that g salvation unto kings: 5414
146: 7 which g food to the hungry. The LORD 5414
147: 9 He g to the beast his food, and to the young 5414
147:16 He g snow like wool: he scattereth 5414
Pr 2: 6 For the LORD g wisdom: out of his 5414
3:34 the scorners: but he g grace unto the lowly. 5414
13:15 Good understanding g favour: but the way 5414
17: 4 A wicked doer g heed to false lips; and 7181
17: 4 and a liar g ear to a naughty tongue. 238
19: 6 every man is a friend to him that g gifts. 4976
21:26 but the righteous g and spareth not. 5414
22: 9 be blessed; for he g of his bread to the poor. 5414
22:16 increase his riches, and he that g to the rich, 5414
23:31 when it g his colour in the cup, when it 5414
24:26 Every man shall kiss his lips that g a right 7725
26: 8 in a sling, so is he that g honour to a fool. 5414
28:27 He that g unto the poor shall not lack: but 5414
31:15 g meat to her household, and a portion to 5414
Ecc 2:26 For God g to a man that is good in his sight 5414
2:26 to the sinner he g travail, to gather and 5414
5:18 all the days of his life, which God g him: 5414
6: 2 yet God g him not power to eat thereof, but 7980
7:12 is, that wisdom g life to them that have it. 2421
8:15 of his life, which God g him under the sun. 5414
Isa 40:29 He g power to the faint; and to them that 5414
42: 5 he that g breath unto the people upon it, 5414
Jer 5:24 that g rain, both the former and the latter, 5414
22:13 without wages, and g him not for his work; 5414
31:35 which g the sun for a light by day, and 5414
La 3:30 He g his cheek to him that smiteth him: 5414
Da 2:21 he g wisdom unto the wise, and 3052
4:17 g it to whomsoever he will, and setteth up 5415
4:25 of men, and g it to whomsoever he will. 5415
4:32 of men, and g it to whomsoever he will. 5415
Hab 2:15 Woe unto him that g his neighbour drink, 8248
Mt 5:15 and it g light unto all that are in the house. 2989
Jn 3:34 for God g not the Spirit by measure unto 1325
6:32 my Father g you the true bread from 1325
6:33 from heaven, and g life unto the world. 1325
6:37 All that the Father g me shall come to me; 1325
10:11 the good shepherd g his life for the sheep. 5087
14:27 not as the world g, give I unto you. Let not 1325
21:13 taketh bread, and g them, and fish likewise. 1325
Ac 17:25 as though he needed any thing, seeing he g 1325
Ro 12: 8 he that g, let him do it with simplicity; 3330
14: 6 eateth to the Lord, for he g God thanks; 2168
14: 6 the Lord he eateth not, and g God thanks. 2168
1Co 3: 7 that watereth; but God that g the increase. 837
7:38 then he that g her in marriage doeth well; 1547
7:38 he that g her not in marriage doeth better. 1547
15:38 But God g it a body as it hath pleased him, 1325
15:57 which g us the victory through our Lord 1325
2Co 3: 6 for the letter killeth, but the spirit g life. 2227
1Ti 6:17 who g us richly all things to enjoy; 3930
Jas 1: 5 that g to all men liberally, and 1325
4: 6 But he g more grace. Wherefore he saith, 1325
4: 6 the proud, but g grace unto the humble. 1325
1Pe 4:11 let him do it as of the ability which God g: 5524
5: 5 the proud, and g grace to the humble. 1325
Rev 22: 5 of the sun; for the Lord God g them light: 5461

GIVING (29) [GIVE]

Ge 24:19 when she had done g him drink, she said, 8240
Dt 10:18 the stranger, in g him food and raiment. 5414
21:17 by g him a double portion of all that he 5414
Ru 1: 6 had visited his people in g them bread. 5414
1Ki 5: 9 my desire, in g food for my household. 5414
2Ch 6:23 by g him according to his righteousness. 5414
Ezr 3:11 in praising and g thanks unto the LORD; 3034
Job 11:20 shall be as the g up of the ghost. 4646+5315
Mt 24:38 and drinking, marrying and g in marriage, 1547
Lk 17:16 down on his face at his feet, g him thanks: 2168
Ac 8: 9 g out that himself was some great one: 3004
15: 8 bare them witness, g them the Holy Ghost, 1325
Ro 4:20 but was strong in faith, g glory to God; 1325
9: 4 and the g of the law, and the service of 3548
1Co 14: 7 And even things without life g sound, 1325
14:16 the unlearned say Amen at thy g of thanks, 2169
2Co 6: 3 G no offence in any thing, that the ministry 1325
Eph 5: 4 are not convenient: but rather g of thanks. 2169
5:20 G thanks always for all things unto God 2168
Php 4:15 communicated with me as concerning g 1394
Col 1:12 G thanks unto the Father, which hath made 2168

G

Col 3:17 g thanks to God and the Father by him. 2168
1Ti 2: 1 prayers, intercessions, and g of thanks, 2169
4: 1 g heed to seducing spirits, and doctrines of 4337
Tit 1:14 Not g heed to Jewish fables, and 4337
Heb 13:15 the fruit of our lips g thanks to his name. 3670
1Pe 3: 7 g honour unto the wife, as unto the weaker 632
2Pe 1: 5 And beside this, g all diligence, add to your 3923
Jude 1: 7 manner g themselves over to fornication, 1608

GIZONITE (1)

1Ch 11:34 The sons of Hashem the G, Jonathan 1493

GLAD (89) [GLADLY, GLADNESS]

Ex 4:14 he seeth thee, he will be g in his heart. 8055
Jdg 18:20 the priest's heart was g, and he took 3190
1Sa 11: 9 it to the men of Jabesh; and they were g. 8055
1Ki 8:66 g of heart for all the goodness that 2896
1Ch 16:31 Let the heavens be g, and let the earth 8055
2Ch 7:10 g and merry in heart for the goodness that 8056
Est 5: 9 forth that day joyful and with a g heart: 2896
8:15 and the city of Shushan rejoiced and was g. 8056
Job 3:22 Which rejoice exceedingly, and are g, 7797
22:19 The righteous see it, and are g: and 8055
Ps 9: 2 I will be g and rejoice in thee: I will sing 8055
14: 7 Jacob shall rejoice, and Israel shall be g. 8055
16: 9 Therefore my heart is g, and my glory 8055
21: 6 thou hast made him exceeding g with thy 8057
31: 7 I will be g and rejoice in thy mercy: 1523
32:11 Be g in the LORD, and rejoice, 8055
34: 2 the humble shall hear thereof, and be g. 8055
35:27 Let them shout for joy, and be g, 8055
40:16 that seek thee rejoice and be g in thee: 8055
45: 8 whereby they have made thee g. 8055
46: 4 the streams whereof shall make g the city 8055
48:11 let the daughters of Judah be g, because 1523
53: 6 Jacob shall rejoice, and Israel shall be g. 8055
64:10 The righteous shall be g in the LORD, and 8055
67: 4 O let the nations be g and sing for joy: 8055
68: 3 let the righteous be g; let them rejoice 8055
69:32 The humble shall see this, and be g: and 8055
70: 4 that seek thee rejoice and be g in thee: 8055
90:14 that we may rejoice and be g all our days. 8055
90:15 Make us g according to the days wherein 8055
92: 4 hast made me g through thy work: 8055
96:11 the heavens rejoice, and let the earth be g; 1523
97: 1 let the multitude of isles be g thereof. 8055
97: 8 was g, and the daughters of Judah rejoiced, 8055
104:15 wine that maketh g the heart of man, 8055
104:34 shall be sweet: I will be g in the LORD. 8055
105:38 Egypt was g when they departed: for 8055
107:30 are they g because they be quiet; so 8055
118:24 hath made; we will rejoice and be g in it. 8055
119:74 They that fear thee will be g when they see 8055
122: 1 I was g when they said unto me, Let us go 8055
126: 3 done great things for us; whereof we are g. 8056
Pr 10: 1 A wise son maketh a g father: but a foolish 8055
12:25 it stoop: but a good word maketh it g. 8055
15:20 A wise son maketh a g father: but a foolish 8055
17: 5 he that is g at calamities shall not be 8056
23:25 Thy father and thy mother shall be g, and 8055
24:17 let not thine heart be g when he stumbleth: 1523
27:11 My son, be wise, and make my heart g, 8055
SS 1: 4 we will be g and rejoice in thee, we will 1523
Isa 25: 9 we will be g and rejoice in his salvation. 1523
35: 1 and the solitary place shall be g for them; 7797
39: 2 Hezekiah was g of them, and shewed them 8055
65:18 be you g and rejoice for ever in that which I 7797
66:10 and be g with her, all ye that love her: 1523
Jer 20:15 born unto thee; making him very g. 8055+8055
41:13 that were with him, then they were g. 8055
50:11 Because ye were g, because ye rejoiced, 8055
La 1:21 they are g that thou hast done it: thou wilt 7797
4:21 Rejoice and be g, O daughter of Edom, 8055
Da 6:23 Then was the king exceeding g for him, and 2868
Hos 7: 3 They make the king g with their 8055
Joel 2:21 Fear not, O land; be g and rejoice: for 1523
2:23 Be g then, ye children of Zion, and 1523
Jnh 4: 6 was exceeding g of the gourd. 1419+8055+8057
Hab 1:15 their drag: therefore they rejoice and are g. 1523
Zep 3:14 be g and rejoice with all the heart, 8055
Zec 10: 7 yea, their children shall see it, and be g; 8055
Mt 5:12 Rejoice, and be exceeding g: for great is your 21
Mk 14:11 And when they heard it, they were g, and 5463
Lk 1:19 unto thee, and to shew thee these g tidings. 2097
8: 1 shewing the g tidings of the kingdom of 2097
15:32 meet that we should make merry, and be g: 5463
22: 5 And they were g, and covenanted to give 5463
23: 8 Herod saw Jesus, he was exceeding g: 5463
Jn 8:56 to see my day: and he saw it, and was g. 5463
11:15 And I am g for your sakes that I was not 5463
20:20 Then were the disciples g, when they saw 5463
Ac 2:26 did my heart rejoice, and my tongue was g; 21
11:23 grace of God, was g, and exhorted them all, 5463
13:32 And we declare unto you g tidings, 2097
13:48 when the Gentiles heard this, they were g, 5463
Ro 10:15 and bring g tidings of good things! 2097
16:19 is come abroad unto all men. I am g 5463
1Co 16:17 I am g of the coming of Stephanas and 5463
2Co 2: 2 who is he then that maketh me g, but 2165
13: 9 For we are g, when we are weak, and ye are 5463
1Pe 4:13 ye may be g also with exceeding joy. 5463
Rev 19: 7 Let us be g and rejoice, and give honour to 5463

GLADLY (8) [GLAD]

Mk 6:20 he did many things, and heard him g. 2234
12:37 And the common people heard him g. 2234
Lk 8:40 was returned, the people g received him: 588
Ac 2:41 Then they that g received his word were 780
21:17 to Jerusalem, the brethren received us g. 780
2Co 11:19 For ye suffer fools g, seeing ye yourselves 2234
12: 9 Most g therefore will I rather glory in my 2236
12:15 And I will very g spend and be spent for 2236

GLADNESS (47) [GLAD]

Nu 10:10 Also in the day of your g, and in your 8057
Dt 28:47 with g of heart, for the abundance of all 2898
2Sa 6:12 Obed-edom into the city of David with g. 8057
1Ch 16:27 strength and g are in his place. 2304
29:22 before the LORD on that day with great g. 8057
2Ch 29:30 they sang praises with g, and they bowed 8057
30:21 unleavened bread seven days with great g: 8057
30:23 and they kept other seven days with g. 8057
Ne 8:17 Israel done so. And there was very great g. 8057
12:27 to keep the dedication with g, both with 8057
Est 8:16 Jews had light, and g, and joy, and honour. 8057
8:17 the Jews had joy and g, a feast and a good 8342
9:17 and made it a day of feasting and g. 8057
9:18 and made it a day of feasting and g. 8057
9:19 day of the month Adar a day of g 8057
Ps 4: 7 Thou hast put g in my heart, more than in 8057
30:11 put off my sackcloth, and girded me with g; 8057
45: 7 hath anointed thee with the oil of g above 8342
45:15 With g and rejoicing shall they be brought: 8057
51: 8 Make me to hear joy and g; that the bones 8057
97:11 the righteous, and g for the upright in heart. 8057
100: 2 Serve the LORD with g: come before his 8057
105:43 his people with joy, and his chosen with g: 7440
106: 5 that I may rejoice in the g of thy nation, 8057
Pr 10:28 The hope of the righteous shall be g: but 8057
SS 3:11 and in the day of the g of his heart. 8057
Isa 16:10 g is taken away, and joy out of the plentiful 8057
22:13 behold joy and g, slaying oxen, and 8057
30:29 g of heart, as when one goeth with a pipe to 8057
35:10 they shall obtain joy and g, and sorrow and 8057
51: 3 joy and g shall be found therein, 8057
51:11 they shall obtain g and joy; and sorrow and 8342
Jer 7:34 the voice of mirth, and the voice of g, 8057
16: 9 the voice of mirth, and the voice of g, 8057
25:10 the voice of g, the voice of the bridegroom, 8057
31: 7 Sing with g for Jacob, and shout among 8057
33:11 The voice of joy, and the voice of g, 8057
48:33 and g is taken from the plentiful field, 1524
Joel 1:16 yea, joy and g from the house of our God? 1524
Zec 8:19 shall be to the house of Judah joy and g, 8057
Mk 4:16 the word, immediately receive it with g; 5479
Lk 1:14 And thou shalt have joy and g; and many shall 20
Ac 2:46 did eat their meat with g and singleness of 20
12:14 she opened not the gate for g, but ran in, 5479
14:17 filling our hearts with food and g. 2167
Php 2:29 therefore in the Lord with all g; 5479
Heb 1: 9 hath anointed thee with the oil of g above thy 20

GLASS (9) [GLASSES, LOOKING-GLASSES]

Job 37:18 which is strong, and as a molten looking g? 7209
1Co 13:12 For now we see through a g, darkly; 2072
2Co 3:18 with open face beholding as in a g 2734
Jas 1:23 a man beholding his natural face in a g: 2072
Rev 4: 6 And before the throne there was a sea of g 5193
15: 2 And I saw as it were a sea of g mingled 5193
15: 2 stand on the sea of g, having the harps of 5193
21:18 the city was pure gold, like unto clear g. 5194
21:21 city was pure gold, as it were transparent g. 5194

GLASSES (1) [GLASS]

Isa 3:23 The g, and the fine linen, and the hoods, 1549

GLEAN (10) [GLEANED, GLEANING, GLEANINGS, GRAPEGLEANINGS]

Lev 19:10 thou shalt not g thy vineyard, neither shalt 5953
Dt 24:21 thy vineyard, thou shalt not g it afterward: 5953
Ru 2: 2 g ears of corn after him in whose sight I 3950
2: 7 let me g and gather after the reapers 3950
2: 8 Go not to g in another field, neither go 3950
2:15 when she was risen up to g, Boaz 3950
2:15 Let her g even among the sheaves, and 3950
2:16 leave them, that she may g them, and 3950
2:23 she kept fast by the maidens of Boaz to g 3950
Jer 6: 9 They shall throughly g the remnant 5953+5953

GLEANED (6) [GLEAN]

Jdg 20:45 they g of them in the highways five 5953
Ru 2: 3 came, and g in the field after the reapers: 3950
2:17 So she g in the field until even, and beat out 3950
2:17 field until even, and beat out that she had g: 3950
2:18 her mother in law saw what she had g: and 3950
2:19 said unto her, Where hast thou g to day? 3950

GLEANING (5) [GLEAN]

Lev 23:22 neither shalt thou gather any g of thy 3951
Jdg 8: 2 Is not the g of the grapes of Ephraim better 5955
Isa 17: 6 Yet g grapes shall be left in it, as 5955
24:13 as the g grapes when the vintage is done. 5955
Jer 49: 9 would they not leave some g grapes? 5955

GLEANINGS (1) [GLEAN]

Lev 19: 9 neither shalt thou gather the g of thy 3951

GLEDE (1)

Dt 14:13 the g, and the kite, and the vulture after his 7201

GLISTERING (3)

1Ch 29: 2 g stones, and of divers colours, and 6320
Job 20:25 yea, the g sword cometh out of his gall: 1300
Lk 9:29 and his raiment was white and g. 1823

GLITTER (1) [GLITTERING]

Eze 21:10 sore slaughter; it is furbished that it may g: 1300

GLITTERING (5) [GLITTER]

Dt 32:41 If I whet my g sword, and mine hand take 1300
Job 39:23 against him, the g spear and the shield. 3851
Eze 21:28 it is furbished, to consume because of the g: 1300
Na 3: 3 up both the bright sword and the g spear: 1300
Hab 3:11 they went, and at the shining of thy g spear. 1300

GLOOMINESS (2)

Joel 2: 2 A day of darkness and of g, a day of clouds 653
Zep 1:15 and desolation, a day of darkness and g, 653

GLORIEST (1) [GLORY]

Jer 49: 4 Wherefore g thou in the valleys, 1984

GLORIETH (3) [GLORY]

Jer 9:24 let him that g glory in this, that he 1984
1Co 1:31 That, according as it is written, He that g, 2744
2Co 10:17 But he that g, let him glory in the Lord. 2744

GLORIFIED (50) [GLORY]

Lev 10: 3 and before all the people I will be g. 3513
Isa 26:15 thou art g: thou hadst removed it far unto 3513
44:23 redeemed Jacob, and g himself in Israel. 6286
49: 3 my servant, O Israel, in whom I will be g. 6286
55: 5 the Holy One of Israel; for he hath g thee. 6286
60: 9 Holy One of Israel, because he hath g thee. 6286
60:21 the work of my hands, that I may be g. 6286
61: 3 planting of the LORD, that he might be g. 6286
66: 5 my name's sake, said, Let the LORD be g: 3513
Eze 28:22 and I will be g in the midst of thee: 3513
39:13 to them a renown the day that I shall be g, 3513
Da 5:23 and whose are all thy ways, hast thou not g: 1922
Hag 1: 8 in it, and I will be g, saith the LORD. 3513
Mt 9: 8 and g God, which had given such power 1392
15:31 blind to see: and they g the God of Israel. 1392
Mk 2:12 and g God, saying, We never saw it on this 1392
Lk 4:15 taught in their synagogues, being g of all. 1392
5:26 and they g God, and were filled with fear, 1392
7:16 and they g God, saying, That a great 1392
13:13 she was made straight, and g God. 1392
17:15 turned back, and with a loud voice g God, 1392
23:47 he g God, saying, Certainly this was a 1392
Jn 7:39 given; because that Jesus was not yet g.) 1392
11: 4 that the Son of God might be g thereby. 1392
12:16 but when Jesus was g, then 1392
12:23 is come, that the Son of man should be g. 1392
12:28 saying, I have both g it, and will glorify it 1392
13:31 Now is the Son of man g, and God is 1392
13:31 Son of man glorified, and God is g in him. 1392
13:32 If God be g in him, God shall also glorify 1392
14:13 I do, that the Father may be g in the Son. 1392
15: 8 Herein is my Father g, that ye bear much 1392
17: 4 I have g thee on the earth: I have finished 1392
17:10 and thine are mine; and I am g in them. 1392
Ac 3:13 God of our fathers, hath g his Son Jesus; 1392
4:21 for all men g God for that which was done. 1392
11:18 they held their peace, and g God, saying, 1392
13:48 they were glad, and g the word of the Lord: 1392
21:20 And when they heard it, they g the Lord, 1392
Ro 1:21 they knew God, they g him not as God, 1392
8:17 with him, that we may be also g together. 4888
8:30 and whom he justified, them he also g. 1392
Gal 1:24 And they g God in me. 1392
2Th 1:10 When he shall come to be g in his saints, 1740
1:12 of our Lord Jesus Christ may be g in you, 1740
3: 1 free course, and be g, even as it is with you: 1392
Heb 5: 5 So also Christ g not himself to be made a 1392
1Pe 4:11 that God in all things may be g through 1392
4:14 is evil spoken of, but on your part he is g. 1392
Rev 18: 7 How much she hath g herself, and 1392

GLORIFIETH (1) [GLORY]

Ps 50:23 Whoso offereth praise g me: and to him 3513

GLORIFY (25) [GLORY]

Ps 22:23 all ye the seed of Jacob, g him; and 3513
50:15 I will deliver thee, and thou shalt g me. 3513
86: 9 before thee, O Lord; and shall g thy name. 3513
86:12 and I will g thy name for evermore. 3513
Isa 24:15 Wherefore g ye the LORD in the fires, 3513
25: 3 Therefore shall the strong people g thee, 3513
60: 7 and I will g the house of my glory. 6286
Jer 30:19 I will also g them, and they shall not be 3513
Mt 5:16 and g your Father which is in heaven. 1392
Jn 12:28 Father, g thy name. Then came there a 1392
12:28 I have both glorified it, and will g it again. 1392
13:32 in him, God shall also g him in himself, 1392
13:32 in himself, and shall straightway g him. 1392
16:14 He shall g me: for he shall receive of mine, 1392
17: 1 g thy Son, that thy Son also may glorify 1392
17: 1 thy Son, that thy Son also may g thee: 1392
17: 5 g thou me with thine own self with 1392
21:19 signifying by what death he should g God. 1392
Ro 15: 6 may with one mind and one mouth g God, 1392
15: 9 And that the Gentiles might g God for his 1392
1Co 6:20 therefore g God in your body, and in your 1392
2Co 9:13 g God for your professed subjection unto 1392
1Pe 2:12 shall behold, g God in the day of visitation. 1392
4:16 but let him g God on this behalf. 1392
Rev 15: 4 not fear thee, O Lord, and g thy name? 1392

GLORIFYING (3) [GLORY]

Lk 2:20 g and praising God for all the things that 1392
5:25 and departed to his own house, g God. 1392
18:43 his sight, and followed him, g God: 1392

GLORIOUS (45) [GLORY]

Ex 15: 6 O LORD, is become g in power: 142
15:11 who is like thee, g in holiness, fearful in 142
Dt 28:58 that thou mayest fear this g and fearful 3513
2Sa 6:20 said, How g was the king of Israel to day, 3513
1Ch 29:13 we thank thee, and praise thy g name. 8597
Ne 9: 5 blessed be thy g name, which is exalted 3519
Est 1: 4 When he shewed the riches of his g 3519
Ps 45:13 The king's daughter is all g within: 3520
66: 2 the honour of his name: make his praise g. 3519
72:19 blessed be his g name for ever: and let 3519
76: 4 Thou art more g and excellent than 215
87: 3 G things are spoken of thee, O city of God. 3513
111: 3 His work is honourable and g: and 1926
145: 5 I will speak of the g honour of thy majesty, 3519

Ps 145:12 and the **g** majesty of his kingdom. 3519
Isa 4: 2 branch of the LORD be beautiful and **g**, 3519
11:10 the Gentiles seek: and his rest shall be **g**. 3519
22:23 he shall be for a **g** throne to his father's 3519
28: 1 whose **g** beauty *is* a fading flower, 6643
28: 4 the **g** beauty, which *is* on the head of the fat 6643
30:30 the LORD shall cause his **g** voice to be 1935
33:21 there the **g** LORD *will be* unto us a place of 117
49: 5 yet shall I be **g** in the eyes of the LORD, 3513
60:13 and I will **make** the place of my feet **g**. 3513
63: 1 this *that is* **g** in his apparel, travelling in 1921
63:12 by the right hand of Moses *with* his **g** arm, 8597
63:14 lead thy people, to make thyself a **g** name. 8597
Jer 17:12 A **g** high throne from the beginning *is* 3519
Eze 27:25 and **made** very **g** in the midst of the seas. 3513
Da 11:16 he shall stand in the **g** land, which by his 6643
11:41 He shall enter also into the **g** land, and 6643
11:45 between the seas in the **g** holy mountain; 6643
Lk 13:17 all the people rejoiced for all the **g** *things* *1741*
Ro 8:21 into the **g** liberty of the children of God. *1391*
2Co 3: 7 *and* engraven in stones, was **g**, *1391+1722*
3: 8 ministration of the spirit be rather **g**? *1391+1722*
3:10 For even that which was **made** **g** had no *1392*
3:11 For if that which is done away *was* **g**, *1223+1391*
3:11 more that which remaineth *is* **g**. *1391+1722*
4: 4 lest the light of the **g** gospel of Christ, *1391*
Eph 5:27 That he might present it to himself a **g** *1741*
Php 3:21 that it may be fashioned like unto his **g** *1391*
Col 1:11 according to his **g** power, unto all patience *1391*
1Ti 1:11 According to the **g** gospel of the blessed *1391*
Tit 2:13 and the **g** appearing of the great God and *1391*

GLORIOUSLY (3) [GLORY]

Ex 15: 1 for he hath **triumphed** **g**; 1342+1342
15:21 for he hath **triumphed** **g**; 1342+1342
Isa 24:23 and in Jerusalem, and before his ancients **g**. 3519

GLORY (402) [GLORIEST, GLORIETH, GLORIFIED, GLORIFIETH, GLORIFY, GLORIFYING, GLORIOUS, GLORIOUSLY, GLORYING, VAINGLORY]

Ge 31: 1 *was* of our father's hath he gotten all this **g**. 3519
45:13 you shall tell my father of all my **g** in 3519
Ex 8: 9 Moses said unto Pharaoh, **G** over me: when 6286
16: 7 then ye shall see the **g** of the LORD; 3519
16:10 the **g** of the LORD appeared in the cloud. 3519
24:16 the **g** of the LORD abode upon mount 3519
24:17 the sight of the **g** of the LORD *was* like 3519
28: 2 for Aaron thy brother, for **g** and for beauty. 3519
28:40 thou make for them, for **g** and for beauty. 3519
29:43 *the tabernacle* shall be sanctified by my **g**. 3519
33:18 And he said, I beseech thee, shew me thy **g**. 3519
33:22 shall come to pass, while my **g** passeth by, 3519
40:34 the **g** of the LORD filled the tabernacle. 3519
40:35 the **g** of the LORD filled the tabernacle. 3519
Lev 9: 6 the **g** of the LORD shall appear unto you. 3519
9:23 the **g** of the LORD appeared unto all 3519
Nu 14:10 the **g** of the LORD appeared in 3519
14:21 all the earth shall be filled *with* the **g** of 3519
14:22 all *those* men which have seen my **g**, 3519
16:19 the **g** of the LORD appeared unto all 3519
16:42 and the **g** of the LORD appeared. 3519
20: 6 the **g** of the LORD appeared unto them. 3519
Dt 5:24 the LORD our God hath shewed us his **g** 3519
33:17 His **g** *is like* the firstling of his bullock, and 1926
Jos 7:19 **g** to the LORD God of Israel, and 3519
1Sa 2: 8 and to make them inherit the throne of **g**: 3519
4:21 The **g** is departed from Israel: 3519
4:22 And she said, The **g** is departed from Israel: 3519
6: 5 and ye shall give **g** unto the God of Israel: 3519
1Ki 8:11 for the **g** of the LORD had filled the house 3519
2Ki 14:10 **g** *of this,* and tarry at home: for why 3513
1Ch 16:10 **G** ye in his holy name: let the heart of them 1984
16:24 Declare his **g** among the heathen; 3519
16:27 **G** and honour *are* in his presence; strength 1935
16:28 give unto the LORD **g** and strength. 3519
16:29 Give unto the LORD the **g** due unto his 3519
16:35 to thy holy name, *and* **g** in thy praise. 7623
22: 5 of fame and of **g** throughout all countries: 8597
29:11 and the **g**, and the victory, and the majesty: 8597
2Ch 5:14 for the **g** of the LORD had filled the house 3519
7: 1 and the **g** of the LORD filled the house. 3519
7: 2 the **g** of the LORD had filled 3519
7: 3 and the **g** of the LORD upon the house, 3519
Est 5:11 Haman told them of the **g** of his riches, 3519
Job 19: 9 He hath stript me of my **g**, and taken 3519
29:20 My **g** *was* fresh in me, and my bow was 3519
39:20 the **g** of his nostrils *is* terrible. 1935
40:10 and array thyself with **g** and beauty. 1935
Ps 3: 3 my **g**, and the lifter up of mine head. 3519
4: 2 how long *will ye turn* my **g** into shame? 3519
8: 1 who hast set thy **g** above the heavens. 1935
8: 5 and hast crowned him *with* **g** and honour. 3519
16: 9 my heart is glad, and my **g** rejoiceth: 3519
19: 1 The heavens declare the **g** of God; and 3519
21: 5 His **g** *is* great in thy salvation: honour and 3519
24: 7 and the King of **g** shall come in. 3519
24: 8 Who *is* this King of **g**? the LORD strong 3519
24: 9 and the King of **g** shall come in. 3519
24:10 Who is this King of **g**? The LORD of 3519
24:10 The LORD of hosts, he *is* the King of **g**. 3519
29: 1 give unto the LORD **g** and strength. 3519
29: 2 Give unto the LORD the **g** due unto his 3519
29: 3 the God of **g** thundereth: the LORD *is* 3519
29: 9 in his temple doth every one speak of *his* **g**. 3519
30:12 To the end that *my* **g** may sing *praise* to 3519
45: 3 O *most* mighty, *with* thy **g** and thy majesty. 1935
49:16 when the **g** of his house is increased; 3519
49:17 his **g** shall not descend after him. 3519
57: 5 the heavens; *let* thy **g** *be* above all the earth. 3519
57: 8 Awake up, my **g**; awake, psaltery and harp: 3519
57:11 the heavens: *let* thy **g** *be* above all the earth. 3519
62: 7 In God *is* my salvation and my **g**: the rock 3519
63: 2 To see thy power and thy **g**, so *as* I have 3519
Ps 63:11 every one that sweareth by him shall **g**: 1984
64:10 in him; and all the upright in heart shall **g**. 1984
72:19 let the whole earth be filled *with* his **g**; 3519
73:24 thy counsel, and afterward receive me *to* **g**. 3519
78:61 and his **g** into the enemy's hand. 8597
79: 9 God of our salvation, for the **g** of thy name: 3519
84:11 the LORD will give grace and **g**: no good 3519
85: 9 that fear him; that **g** may dwell in our land. 3519
89:17 For thou *art* the **g** of their strength: and 8597
89:44 Thou hast made his **g** to cease, and cast his 2892
90:16 thy servants, and thy **g** unto their children. 1926
96: 3 Declare his **g** among the heathen, 3519
96: 7 give unto the LORD **g** and strength. 3519
96: 8 Give unto the LORD the **g** due unto his 3519
97: 6 and all the people see his **g**. 3519
102:15 and all the kings of the earth thy **g**. 3519
102:16 shall build up Zion, he shall appear in his **g**. 3519
104:31 The **g** of the LORD shall endure for ever: 3519
105: 3 **G** ye in his holy name: let the heart of them 1984
106: 5 that *I* may **g** with thine inheritance. 1984
106:20 Thus they changed their **g** into 3519
108: 1 I will sing and give praise, even *with* my **g**. 3519
108: 5 the heavens: and thy **g** above all the earth. 3519
113: 4 all nations, *and* his **g** above the heavens. 3519
115: 1 not unto us, but unto thy name give **g**, 3519
138: 5 for great *is* the **g** of the LORD. 3519
145:11 They shall speak of the **g** of thy kingdom, 3519
148:13 his **g** *is* above the earth and heaven. 1935
149: 5 Let the saints be joyful in **g**: let them sing 3519
Pr 3:35 The wise shall inherit **g**: but shame shall be 3519
4: 9 a crown of **g** shall she deliver *to* thee. 8597
16:31 The hoary head *is* a crown of **g**, *if* it be 8597
17: 6 and the **g** of children *are* their fathers. 8597
19:11 and *it is* his **g** to pass over a transgression. 8597
20:29 The **g** of young men *is* their strength: and 8597
25: 2 *It is* the **g** of God to conceal a thing: but 3519
25:27 *for men* to search their own **g** *is not* glory. 3519
25:27 *for men* to search their own glory *is not* **g**. 3519
28:12 righteous *men* do rejoice, *there is* great **g**: 8597
Isa 2:10 of the LORD, and for the **g** of his majesty. 1926
2:19 of the LORD, and for the **g** of his majesty, 1926
2:21 of the LORD, and for the **g** of his majesty, 1926
3: 8 the LORD, to provoke the eyes of his **g**. 3519
4: 5 for upon all the **g** *shall be* a defence. 3519
5:14 their **g**, and their multitude, and their pomp, 1926
6: 3 of hosts: the whole earth *is* full of his **g**. 3519
8: 7 *even* the king of Assyria, and all his **g**: 3519
10: 3 for help? and where will ye leave your **g**? 3519
10:12 king of Assyria, and the **g** of his high looks. 8597
10:16 under his **g** he shall kindle a burning like 3519
10:18 shall consume the **g** of his forest, and of his 3519
13:19 Babylon, the **g** of kingdoms, the beauty of 6643
14:18 of the nations, *even* all of them, lie in **g**, 3519
16:14 and the **g** of Moab shall be contemned, 3519
17: 3 they shall be as the **g** of the children of 3519
17: 4 *that* the **g** of Jacob shall be made thin, and 3519
20: 5 their expectation, and of Egypt their **g**. 8597
21:16 a hireling, and all the **g** of Kedar shall fail: 3519
22:18 there the chariots of thy **g** *shall be* 3519
22:24 they shall hang upon him all the **g** of his 3519
23: 9 to stain the pride of all **g**, *and* to bring into 6643
24:16 we heard songs, *even* **g** to the righteous. 6643
28: 5 the LORD of hosts be for a crown of **g**, 6643
35: 2 the **g** of Lebanon shall be given unto it, 3519
35: 2 they shall see the **g** of the LORD, *and* 3519
40: 5 the **g** of the LORD shall be revealed, and 3519
41:16 *and* shalt **g** in the Holy One of Israel. 1984
42: 8 my **g** will I not give to another, neither my 3519
42:12 Let them give **g** unto the LORD, and 3519
43: 7 for I have created him for my **g**, I have 3519
45:25 the seed of Israel be justified, and shall **g**. 1984
46:13 will place salvation in Zion for Israel my **g**. 8597
48:11 and I will not give my **g** unto another. 3519
58: 8 the **g** of the LORD shall be thy rereward. 3519
59:19 and his **g** from the rising of the sun. 3519
60: 1 and the **g** of the LORD is risen upon thee. 3519
60: 2 and his **g** shall be seen upon thee. 3519
60: 7 and I will glorify the house of my **g**. 8597
60:13 The **g** of Lebanon shall come unto thee, 3519
60:19 thee an everlasting light, and thy God thy **g**. 8597
61: 6 and in their **g** shall you boast yourselves. 3519
62: 2 see thy righteousness, and all kings thy **g**: 3519
62: 3 Thou shalt also be a crown of **g** in the hand 8597
63:15 the habitation of thy holiness and of thy **g**: 8597
66:11 be delighted with the abundance of her **g**. 3519
66:12 the **g** of the Gentiles like a flowing stream: 3519
66:18 and they shall come, and see my **g**. 3519
66:19 not heard my fame, neither have seen my **g**; 3519
66:19 they shall declare my **g** among the Gentiles. 3519
Jer 2:11 my people have changed their **g** for *that* 3519
4: 2 themselves in him, and in him shall they **g**. 1984
9:23 Let not the wise *man* **g** in his wisdom, 1984
9:23 neither let the mighty *man* **g** in his might, 1984
9:23 let not the rich *man* **g** in his riches: 1984
9:24 let him that glorieth **g** in this, that *he* 1984
13:11 for a name, and for a praise, and for a **g**: 8597
13:16 Give **g** to the LORD your God, before he 3519
13:18 shall come down, *even* the crown of your **g**. 8597
14:21 do not disgrace the throne of thy **g**: 3519
22:18 for him, *saying,* Ah lord! or, Ah his **g**. 1935
48:18 come down from *thy* **g**, and sit in thirst; 3519
Eze 1:28 of the likeness of the **g** of the LORD. 3519
3:12 *saying,* Blessed *be* the **g** of the LORD 3519
3:23 behold, the **g** of the LORD stood there, 3519
3:23 as the **g** which I saw by the river of Chebar: 3519
8: 4 the **g** of the God of Israel *was* there, 3519
9: 3 the **g** of the God of Israel was gone up from 3519
10: 4 the **g** of the LORD went up from 3519
10: 4 full of the brightness of the LORD'S **g**. 3519
10:18 the **g** of the LORD departed from off 3519
10:19 the **g** of the God of Israel *was* over them 3519
11:22 the **g** of the God of Israel *was* over them 3519
11:23 the **g** of the LORD went up from the midst 3519
20: 6 and honey, which *is* the **g** of all lands: 6643
20:15 and honey, which *is* the **g** of all lands; 6643
Eze 24:25 the joy of their **g**, the desire of their eyes, 8597
25: 9 the **g** of the country, Beth-jeshimoth, 6643
26:20 and I shall set **g** in the land of the living; 6643
31:18 To whom art thou thus like in **g** and 3519
39:21 And I will set my **g** among the heathen, and 3519
43: 2 the **g** of the God of Israel came from 3519
43: 2 and the earth shined with his **g**. 3519
43: 4 the **g** of the LORD came into the house by 3519
43: 5 the **g** of the LORD filled the house. 3519
44: 4 the **g** of the LORD filled the house of 3519
Da 2:37 thee a kingdom, power, and strength, and **g**. 3367
4:36 for the **g** of my kingdom, mine honour and 3367
5:18 a kingdom, and majesty, and **g**, and honour: 3367
5:20 and they took *his* **g** from him: 3367
7:14 **g**, and a kingdom, that all people, nations, 3367
11:20 a raiser of taxes *in* the **g** of the kingdom: 1925
11:39 he shall acknowledge *and* increase *with* **g**: 3519
Hos 4: 7 *therefore* will I change their **g** into shame. 3519
9:11 their **g** shall fly away like a bird, from 3519
10: 5 for the **g** thereof, because it is departed 3519
Mic 1:15 he shall come unto Adullam the **g** of Israel. 3519
2: 9 children have ye taken *away* my **g** for ever. 1926
Na 2: 9 *and* **g** out of all the pleasant furniture. 3519
Hab 2:14 with the knowledge of the **g** of the LORD, 3519
2:16 Thou art filled *with* shame for **g**: drink thou 3519
2:16 and shameful spuing *shall be* on thy **g**. 3519
3: 3 His **g** covered the heavens, and the earth 1935
Hag 2: 3 you that saw this house in her first **g**? 3519
2: 7 I will fill this house *with* **g**, saith 3519
2: 9 The **g** of this latter house shall be greater 3519
Zec 2: 5 and will be the **g** in the midst of her. 3519
2: 8 After the **g** hath he sent me unto the nations 3519
6:13 he shall bear the **g**, and shall sit and 1935
11: 3 of the shepherds; for their **g** is spoiled: 155
12: 7 that the **g** of the house of David and 8597
12: 7 the **g** of the inhabitants of Jerusalem do not 8597
Mal 2: 2 to give **g** unto my name, saith the LORD 3519
Mt 4: 8 kingdoms of the world, and the **g** of them; *1391*
6: 2 in the streets, that they may **have** **g** of men. *1392*
6:13 and the power, and the **g**, for ever. *1391*
6:29 That even Solomon in all his **g** was not *1391*
16:27 For the Son of man shall come in the **g** of *1391*
19:28 Son of man shall sit in the throne of his **g**, *1391*
24:30 clouds of heaven with power and great **g**. *1391*
25:31 When the Son of man shall come in his **g**, *1391*
25:31 then shall he sit upon the throne of his **g**: *1391*
Mk 8:38 when he cometh in the **g** of his Father with *1391*
10:37 and the other on thy left hand, in thy **g**. *1391*
13:26 in *the* clouds with great power and **g**. *1391*
Lk 2: 9 the **g** of the Lord shone round about them: *1391*
2:14 **G** to God in the highest, and on earth *1391*
2:32 the Gentiles, and the **g** of thy people Israel. *1391*
4: 6 power will I give thee, and the **g** of them: *1391*
9:26 when he shall come in his own **g**, and *in his* *1391*
9:31 Who appeared in **g**, and spake of his *1391*
9:32 they saw his **g**, and the two men that stood *1391*
12:27 *that* Solomon in all his **g** was not arrayed *1391*
17:18 There are not found that returned to give **g** *1391*
19:38 peace in heaven, and **g** in the highest. *1391*
21:27 coming in a cloud with power and great **g**. *1391*
24:26 these *things,* and to enter into his **g**? *1391*
Jn 1:14 and dwelt among us, (and we beheld his **g**, *1391*
1:14 the **g** as of the only begotten of the Father,) *1391*
2:11 Cana of Galilee, and manifested forth his **g**; *1391*
7:18 that speaketh of himself seeketh his own **g**: *1391*
7:18 but he that seeketh his **g** that sent him, *1391*
8:50 And I seek not mine own **g**: there is *one* *1391*
11: 4 is not unto death, but for the **g** of God, *1391*
11:40 thou shouldest see the **g** of God? *1391*
12:41 when he saw his **g**, and spake of him. *1391*
17: 5 **g** which I had with thee before the world *1391*
17:22 And the **g** which thou gavest me I have *1391*
17:24 that they may behold my **g**, which thou hast *1391*
Ac 7: 2 The God of **g** appeared unto our father *1391*
7:55 and saw the **g** of God, and Jesus standing *1391*
12:23 smote him, because he gave not God the **g**: *1391*
22:11 And when I could not see for the **g** of that *1391*
Ro 1:23 And changed the **g** of the uncorruptible *1391*
2: 7 patient continuance in well doing seek for **g** *1391*
2:10 But **g**, honour, and peace, to every *man* that *1391*
3: 7 *more* abounded through my lie unto his **g**; *1391*
3:23 and come short of the **g** of God; *1391*
4: 2 justified by works, he hath whereof to **g**; *2745*
4:20 but was strong in faith, giving **g** to God; *1391*
5: 2 and rejoice in hope of the **g** of God. *1391*
5: 3 not only *so,* but we **g** in tribulations also: *2744*
6: 4 up from the dead by the **g** of the Father, *1391*
8:18 with the **g** which shall be revealed in us. *1391*
9: 4 and the **g**, and the covenants, and the giving *1391*
9:23 the riches of his **g** on the vessels of mercy, *1391*
9:23 which he had afore prepared unto **g**, *1391*
11:36 *are* all *things:* to whom *be* **g** for ever. *1391*
15: 7 as Christ also received us, to the **g** of God. *1391*
15:17 whereof *I* may **g** through Jesus Christ *in* *2746*
16:27 *be* **g** through Jesus Christ for ever. *1391*
1Co 1:29 That no flesh should **g** in his presence. *2744*
1:31 He that glorieth, let him **g** in the Lord. *2744*
2: 7 God ordained before the world unto our **g**: *1391*
2: 8 would not have crucified the Lord of **g**. *1391*
3:21 Therefore let no *man* **g** in men. For all *2744*
4: 7 if thou didst receive *it,* why dost thou **g**, *2744*
9:16 I preach the gospel, I have nothing to **g** of: *2745*
10:31 or whatsoever ye do, do all to the **g** of God. *1391*
11: 7 forasmuch as he is the image and **g** of God: *1391*
11: 7 of God: but the woman is the **g** of the man. *1391*
11:15 if a woman have long hair, it is a **g** to her: *1391*
15:40 but the **g** of the celestial *is* one, and *1391*
15:40 *is* one, and the **g** of the terrestrial *is* another. NIG
15:41 *There is* one **g** of the sun, and another glory *1391*
15:41 and another **g** of the moon, and *1391*
15:41 of the moon, and another **g** of the stars: *1391*
15:41 for *one* star differeth from *another* star in **g**. *1391*
15:43 It is sown in dishonour; it is raised in **g**: *1391*
2Co 1:20 and in him Amen, unto the **g** of God by us. *1391*
3: 7 face of Moses for the **g** of his countenance; *1391*

2Co 3: 7 which g was to be done away: NIG
3: 9 if the ministration of condemnation *be* g, 1391
3: 9 ministration of righteousness exceed in g. 1391
3:10 was made glorious had no g in this respect, 1392
3:10 by reason of the g that excelleth. 1391
3:18 with open face beholding as in a glass the g 1391
3:18 are changed *into* the same image from g to 1391
3:18 *into* the same image from glory to g, 1391
4: 6 to give the light of the knowledge of the g 1391
4:15 of many redound to the g of God. 1391
4:17 far more exceeding *and* eternal weight of g; 1391
5:12 but give you occasion to g on our behalf, 2745
5:12 to *answer* them which g in appearance, 2744
8:19 which is administered by us to the g of 1391
8:23 of the churches, *and* the g of Christ. 1391
10:17 But he that glorieth, let him g in the Lord. 2744
11:12 that wherein they g, they may be found 2744
11:18 Seeing that many g after the flesh, I will 2744
11:18 that many glory after the flesh, I will g also. 2744
11:30 If I must needs g, I will glory of the *things* 2744
11:30 I will g of the *things* which concern mine 2744
12: 1 It is not expedient for me doubtless to g. I 2744
12: 5 Of such a one will I g: yet of myself I will 2744
12: 5 yet of myself I will not g, but in mine 2744
12: 6 For though I would desire to g, I shall not 2744
12: 9 therefore will I rather g in my infirmities, 2744
Gal 1: 5 To whom *be* g for ever and ever. Amen. 1391
5:26 Let us not be desirous of vain g, 2755
6:13 that they may g in your flesh. 2744
6:14 But God forbid that I should g, save in 2744
Eph 1: 6 To the praise of the g of his grace, 1391
1:12 That we should be to the praise of his g, 1391
1:14 unto the praise of his g. 1391
1:17 of our Lord Jesus Christ, the Father of g, 1391
1:18 what the riches of the g of his inheritance in 1391
3:13 at my tribulations for you, which is your g. 1391
3:16 grant you, according to the riches of his g, 1391
3:21 Unto him *be* g in the church by Christ Jesus 1391
Php 1:11 which are by Jesus Christ unto the g and 1391
2:11 Christ *is* Lord, to the g of God the Father. 1391
3:19 *is their* belly, and *whose* g *is* in their shame, 1391
4:19 according to his riches in g by Christ Jesus. 1391
4:20 and our Father *be* g for ever and ever. 1391
Col 1:27 the g of this mystery among the Gentiles; 1391
1:27 which is Christ in you, the hope of g: 1391
3: 4 then shall ye also appear with him in g. 1391
1Th 2: 6 Nor of men sought we g, neither of you, 1391
2:12 hath called you unto his kingdom and g. 1391
2:20 For ye are our g and joy. 1391
2Th 1: 4 So that we ourselves g in you in 2744
1: 9 of the Lord, and from the g of his power; 1391
2:14 to the obtaining of the g of our Lord Jesus 1391
1Ti 1:17 *be* honour and g for ever and ever. 1391
3:16 on in the world, received up into g. 1391
2Ti 2:10 which is in Christ Jesus with eternal g. 1391
4:18 to whom *be* g for ever and ever. Amen. 1391
Heb 1: 3 Who being the brightness of *his* g, and 1391
2: 7 thou crownedst him with g and honour, and 1391
2: 9 of death, crowned with g and honour; 1391
2:10 all *things*, in bringing many sons unto g, 1391
3: 3 For this *man* was counted worthy of more g 1391
9: 5 And over it the cherubims of g shadowing 1391
13:21 to whom *be* g for ever and ever. 1391
Jas 2: 1 *the Lord* of g, with respect of persons. 1391
3:14 g not, and lie *not* against the truth. 2620
1Pe 1: 7 and g at the appearing of Jesus Christ: 1391
1: 8 rejoice with joy unspeakable and full of g: 1392
1:11 of Christ, and the g that should follow. 1391
1:21 him up from the dead, and gave him g; 1391
1:24 and all the g of man as the flower of grass. 1391
2:20 For what g *is it*, if, when ye be buffeted for 2811
4:13 that, when his g shall be revealed, ye may 1391
4:14 happy *are ye*; for the spirit of g and of God 1391
5: 1 also a partaker of the g that shall be 1391
5: 4 ye shall receive a crown of g that fadeth not 1391
5:10 who hath called us unto his eternal g by 1391
5:11 To him *be* g and dominion for ever and 1391
2Pe 1: 3 knowledge of him that hath called us to g 1391
1:17 from God the Father honour and g, 1391
1:17 such a voice to him from the excellent g, 1391
3:18 To him *be* g both now and for ever. Amen. 1391
Jude 1:24 the presence of his g with exceeding joy, 1391
1:25 *be* g and majesty, dominion and power, 1391
Rev 1: 6 to him *be* g and dominion for ever and 1391
4: 9 And when *those* beasts give g and honour 1391
4:11 to receive g and honour and power: 1391
5:12 strength, and honour, and g, and blessing. 1391
5:13 Blessing, and honour, and g, and power, 1391
7:12 and g, and wisdom, and thanksgiving, and 1391
11:13 and gave g to the God of heaven. 1391
14: 7 a loud voice, Fear God, and give g to him; 1391
15: 8 was filled with smoke from the g of God, 1391
16: 9 and they repented not to give him g. 1391
18: 1 and the earth was lightened with his g. 1391
19: 1 Alleluia; Salvation, and g, and honour, 1391
21:11 Having the g of God: and her light *was* like 1391
21:23 for the g of God did lighten it, and 1391
21:24 the kings of the earth do bring their g and 1391
21:26 And they shall bring the g and honour of 1391

GLORYING (4) [GLORY]

1Co 5: 6 Your g *is* not good. Know ye not that a 2745
9:15 than that any *man* should make my g void. 2745
2Co 7: 4 of speech toward you, great *is* my g of you: 2746
12:11 I am become a fool in g; ye have compelled 2744

GLOWING METAL See AMBER

GLUTTON (2) [GLUTTONOUS]

Dt 21:20 obey our voice; *he is* a g, and a drunkard. 2151
Pr 23:21 and the g shall come to poverty: 2151

GLUTTONOUS (2) [GLUTTON]

Mt 11:19 Behold a man g, and a winebibber, 5314
Lk 7:34 ye say, Behold a g man, and a winebibber, 5314

GNASH (2) [GNASHED, GNASHETH, GNASHING]

Ps 112:10 he shall g *with* his teeth, and melt away: 2786
La 2:16 they hiss and g the teeth: they say, We have 2786

GNASHED (2) [GNASH]

Ps 35:16 in feasts, *they* g upon me *with* their teeth. 2786
Ac 7:54 and they g on him *with their* teeth. 1031

GNASHETH (3) [GNASH]

Job 16: 9 he g upon me with his teeth; mine enemy 2786
Ps 37:12 the just, and g upon him *with* his teeth. 2786
Mk 9:18 and g with his teeth, and pineth away: 5149

GNASHING (7) [GNASH]

Mt 8:12 there shall be weeping and g of teeth. 1030
13:42 of fire: there shall be wailing and g of teeth. 1030
13:50 of fire: there shall be wailing and g of teeth. 1030
22:13 there shall be weeping and g of teeth. 1030
24:51 there shall be weeping and g of teeth. 1030
25:30 there shall be weeping and g of teeth. 1030
Lk 13:28 There shall be weeping and g of teeth, 1030

GNAT (1)

Mt 23:24 which strain out a g, and swallow a camel. 2971

GNAW (1) [GNAWED]

Zep 3: 3 they g not the bones till the morrow. 1633

GNAWED (1) [GNAW]

Rev 16:10 and they g their tongues for pain, 3145

GO (1492) [GOEST, GOETH, GOING, GOINGS, GONE, OUTGOINGS, OUTWENT, WENT, WENTEST]

Ge 3:14 upon thy belly shalt thou g, and dust shalt 1980
8:16 G forth of the ark, thou, and thy wife, and 3318
9:10 from all that g out of the ark, to every beast 3318
11: 3 G to, let us make brick, and burn *them* 3051
11: 4 they said, G to, let us build us a city and 3051
11: 7 G to, let us go down, and there confound 3051
11: 7 let us g down, and there confound their 3381
11:31 the Chaldees, to g into the land of Canaan; 1980
12: 5 they went forth to g into the land of 1980
12:19 behold thy wife, take *her*, and g thy way. 1980
13: 9 *take* the left hand, then I will g to the right; 3231
13: 9 *to* the right hand, then I will g to the left. 8041
15: 2 seeing I g childless, and the steward of my 1980
15:15 thou shalt g to thy fathers in peace; 935
16: 2 I pray thee, g in unto my maid; it may be 935
16: 8 whither wilt thou g? And she said, I flee 1980
18:21 I will g down now, and see whether they 3381
19: 2 ye shall rise up early, and g on your ways. 1980
19:34 g thou in, *and* lie with him, that we may 935
22: 5 I and the lad will g yonder and worship, 1980
24: 4 thou shalt g unto my country, and to my 1980
24:11 *even* the time that *women* g out to draw 3318
24:38 thou shalt g unto my father's house, and 1980
24:42 if now thou do prosper my way which I g: 1980
24:51 take *her*, and g, and let her be thy master's 1980
24:55 at the least ten; after *that* she shall g. 1980
24:56 send me away that I may g to my master. 1980
24:58 unto her, Wilt thou g with this man? 1980
24:58 go with this man? And she said, I will g. 1980
26: 2 unto him, and said, G not down into Egypt; 3381
26:16 Abimelech said unto Isaac, G from us; 1980
27: 3 g out to the field, and take me *some* 3318
27: 9 G now to the flock, and fetch me from 1980
27:13 only obey my voice, and g fetch me *them*. 1980
28: 2 Arise, g to Padan-aram, to the house of 1980
28:20 will keep me in this way that I g, and 1980
29: 7 water ye the sheep, and g *and* feed *them*. 1980
29:21 days are fulfilled, that I may g in unto her. 935
30: 3 Behold my maid Bilhah, g in unto her; 935
30:25 that I may g unto mine own place, and 1980
30:26 for whom I have served thee, and let me g: 1980
31:18 for to g to Isaac his father in the land of 935
32:26 he said, Let me g, for the day breaketh. 7971
32:26 he said, I will not let thee g, except thou 7971
33:12 and let us g, and I will go before thee. 1980
33:12 and let us go, and I will g before thee. 1980
35: 1 Arise, g up to Beth-el, and dwell there: 5927
35: 3 let us arise, and g up to Beth-el; and I will 5927
37:14 he said to him, G, I pray thee, see whether 1980
37:17 for I heard *them* say, Let us g to Dothan. 1980
37:30 The child *is* not; and I, whither shall I g? 935
37:35 For I will g down into the grave unto my 3381
38: 8 G in unto thy brother's wife, and marry her, 935
38:16 said, G to, I pray thee, let me come in unto 3051
41:55 said unto all the Egyptians, G unto Joseph; 1980
42:15 By the life of Pharaoh ye shall not g forth 3318
42:19 g ye, carry corn *for* the famine of your 1980
42:38 he said, My son shall not g down with you; 3381
42:38 befall him by the way in the which ye g, 1980
43: 2 unto them, G again, buy us a little food. 7725
43: 4 with us, we will g down and buy thee food: 3381
43: 5 wilt not send *him*, we will not g down: 3381
43: 8 the lad with me, and we will arise and g; 1980
43:13 and arise, g again unto the man: 7725
44:25 G again, *and* buy us a little food. 7725
44:26 we said, We cannot g down: if our 3381
44:26 brother be with us, then will we g down: 3381
44:33 and let the lad g up with his brethren. 5927
44:34 For how shall I g up to my father, and 5927
45: 1 Cause every man to g out from me. 3318
45: 9 and g up to my father, and say unto him, 5927
45:17 lade your beasts, and g, get you unto 1980
45:28 yet alive: I will g and see him before I die. 1980
46: 3 fear not to g down into Egypt; for I will 3381
46: 4 I will g down with thee into Egypt; and 3381
46:31 I will g up, and shew Pharaoh, and say unto 5927
50: 5 Now therefore let me g up, I pray thee, and 5927
50: 6 Pharaoh said, G up, and bury thy father, 5927
Ex 2: 7 Shall I g and call to thee a nurse of 1980
2: 8 Pharaoh's daughter said to her, G. And 1980
3:11 that I should g unto Pharaoh, and that I 1980
3:16 G, and gather the elders of Israel together, 1980
3:18 now let us g, we beseech thee, three days' 1980
3:19 that the king of Egypt will not let you g, 1980
3:20 and after that he will let you g. 7971
3:21 it shall come to pass, that, when ye g, 1980
3:21 that, when ye go, ye shall not g empty: 1980
4:12 Now therefore g, and I will be with thy 1980
4:18 Let me g, I pray thee, and return unto my 1980
4:18 And Jethro said to Moses, G in peace. 1980
4:19 Moses in Midian, G, return *into* Egypt: 1980
4:21 his heart, that he shall not let the people g. 7971
4:23 I say unto thee, Let my son g, that he may 7971
4:23 *if* thou refuse to let him g, behold, I will 7971
4:26 So he let him g: then she said, A bloody 7503
4:27 G into the wilderness to meet Moses. 1980
5: 1 LORD God of Israel, Let my people g, 7971
5: 2 that I should obey his voice to let Israel g? 7971
5: 2 not the LORD, neither will I let Israel g. 7971
5: 3 let us g, we pray thee, three days' journey 1980
5: 7 let them g and gather straw for themselves. 1980
5: 8 Let us g *and* sacrifice to our God. 1980
5:11 G ye, get you straw where you can find *it*: 1980
5:17 Let us g *and* do sacrifice to the LORD. 1980
5:18 G therefore now, *and* work; for there shall 1980
6: 1 for with a strong hand shall he let them g, 7971
6:11 G in, speak unto Pharaoh king of Egypt, 935
6:11 that he let the children of Israel g out of his 7971
7:14 *is* hardened, he refuseth to let the people g. 7971
7:16 saying, Let my people g, that they may 7971
8: 1 G unto Pharaoh, and say unto him, 935
8: 1 Thus saith the LORD, Let my people g, 7971
8: 2 if thou refuse to let *them* g, behold, I will 7971
8: 3 which shall g up and come into thine 5927
8: 8 I will let the people g, that they may do 7971
8:20 Thus saith the LORD, Let my people g, 7971
8:21 Else, if thou wilt not let my people g, 7971
8:25 for Moses and for Aaron, and said, G ye, 1980
8:27 We will g three days' journey into 1980
8:28 Pharaoh said, I will let you g, that ye may 7971
8:28 only you shall not g very far away: 1980
8:29 I g out from thee, and I will intreat 3318
8:29 letting the people g to sacrifice to 7971
8:32 time also, neither would he let the people g. 7971
9: 1 unto Moses, G in unto Pharaoh, and tell him, 935
9: 1 Let my people g, that they may serve me. 7971
9: 2 For if thou refuse to let *them* g, and wilt 7971
9: 7 and he did not let the people g. 7971
9:13 Let my people g, that they may serve me. 7971
9:17 my people, that *thou* wilt not let them g? 7971
9:28 I will let you g, and ye shall stay no longer. 7971
9:35 would he let the children of Israel g; 7971
10: 1 said unto Moses, G in unto Pharaoh: 935
10: 3 let my people g, that they may serve me. 7971
10: 4 Else, if thou refuse to let my people g, 7971
10: 7 let the men g, that they may serve 7971
10: 8 he said unto them, G, serve the LORD 1980
10: 8 your God: *but* who *are they* that shall g? 1980
10: 9 We will g with our young and with our old, 1980
10: 9 our flocks and with our herds will we g; 1980
10:10 as I will let you g, and your little ones: 7971
10:11 g now ye *that are* men, and serve 1980
10:20 he would not let the children of Israel g. 7971
10:24 and said, G ye, serve the LORD; 1980
10:24 let your little ones also g with you. 1980
10:26 Our cattle also shall g with us; there shall 1980
10:27 and he would not let them g. 7971
11: 1 afterwards he will let you g hence: 7971
11: 1 when he shall let *you* g, he shall surely 7971
11: 4 About midnight will I g out into the midst 3318
11: 8 after that I will g out. And he went out 3318
11:10 that he would not let the children of Israel g 7971
12:22 none of you shall g out at the door of his 3318
12:31 and g, serve the LORD, as ye have said. 1980
13:15 when Pharaoh would hardly let us g, 7971
13:17 to pass, when Pharaoh had let the people g, 7971
13:21 to give them light; to g by day and night: 1980
14: 5 that we have let Israel g from serving us? 7971
14:15 the children of Israel, that they g forward: 5265
14:16 the children of Israel shall g on dry *ground* 935
14:21 the LORD caused the sea to g *back* by a 1980
16: 4 the people shall g out and gather a certain 3318
16:29 let no man g out of his place on the seventh 3318
17: 5 G on before the people, and take with thee 5674
17: 5 smotest the river, take in thine hand, and g. 1980
17: 9 us out men, and g out, fight with Amalek: 3318
18:23 all this people shall also g to their place in 935
19:10 G unto the people, and sanctify them to day 1980
19:12 *that ye* g *not* up into the mount, or 5927
19:21 unto Moses, G down, charge the people, 3381
20:26 Neither shalt thou g up by steps unto mine 5927
21: 2 in the seventh he shall g out free for 3318
21: 3 in by himself, he shall g out by himself: 3318
21: 3 then his wife shall g out with him. 3318
21: 4 her master's, and he shall g out by himself. 3318
21: 5 and my children; I will not g out free: 3318
21: 7 she shall not g out as the menservants do. 3318
21:11 then shall she g out free without money. 3318
21:26 he shall let him g free for his eye's sake. 7971
21:27 he shall let him g free for his tooth's sake. 7971
23:23 For mine Angel shall g before thee, and 1980
24: 2 neither shall the people g up with him. 5927
30:20 When they g into the tabernacle of 935
32: 1 Up, make us gods, which shall g before us; 1980
32: 7 said unto Moses, G, get thee down; 1980
32:23 Make us gods, which shall g before us: 1980
32:27 *and* g in and out from gate to gate 5674
32:30 now I will g up unto the LORD; 5927
32:34 Therefore now g, lead the people unto 1980
32:34 behold, mine Angel shall g before thee: 1980
33: 1 *and* g up hence, thou and the people which 5927
33: 3 for I will not g up in the midst of thee; 5927
33:14 My presence shall g *with thee*, and I will 1980

Ex 33:15 If thy presence **g** not *with me,* carry us not 1980
34: 9 let my Lord, I pray thee, **g** amongst us; 1980
34:15 they **g a whoring** after their gods, and 2181
34:16 their daughters **g a whoring** after their 2181
34:16 **make** thy sons **g a whoring** after their 2181
34:24 when thou shalt **g up** to appear before 5927
Lev 6:13 burning upon the altar; it shall never **g out**. 3518
8:33 ye shall not **g out** of the door of 3318
9: 7 **G** unto the altar, and offer thy sin offering, 7126
10: 7 ye shall not **g out** from the door of 3318
10: 9 when ye **g** into the tabernacle of 935
11:27 among all *manner of* beasts that **g** on *all* 1980
14: 3 the priest shall **g forth** out of the camp; 3318
14:36 before the priest **g** *into it* to see the plague, 935
14:36 afterward the priest shall **g in** to see 935
14:38 the priest shall **g out** of the house to 3318
14:53 he shall **let g** the living bird out of the city 7971
15:16 if any man's seed of copulation **g out** from 3318
16:10 to **let** him **g** for a scapegoat into 7971
16:18 he shall **g out** unto the altar that *is* before 3318
16:22 and he shall **let g** the goat in the wilderness. 7971
16:26 he that **let g** the goat for the scapegoat shall 7971
19:16 Thou shalt not **g up and down** *as* a 1980
20: 5 him off, and all that **g a whoring** after him, 2181
20: 6 after wizards, to **g a whoring** after them, 2181
21:11 Neither shall he **g in** to any dead body, 935
21:12 Neither shall he **g out** of the sanctuary, 3318
21:23 Only he shall not **g in** unto the vail, 935
25:28 in the jubile it shall **g out**, and he shall 3318
25:30 it shall not **g out** in the jubile. 3318
25:31 they shall **g out** in the jubile. 3318
25:33 shall **g out** in the *year of* jubile: 3318
25:54 then he shall **g out** in the year of jubile, 3318
26: 6 neither shall the sword **g** through your land. 5674
26:13 of your yoke, and **made** you **g** upright. 1980
Nu 1: 3 all that *are able to* **g forth** *to* war in Israel: 3318
1:20 all that *were able to* **g forth** *to* war; 3318
1:22 all that *were able to* **g forth** *to* war; 3318
1:24 all that *were able to* **g forth** *to* war; 3318
1:26 all that *were able to* **g forth** *to* war; 3318
1:28 all that *were able to* **g forth** *to* war; 3318
1:30 all that *were able to* **g forth** *to* war; 3318
1:32 all that *were able to* **g forth** *to* war; 3318
1:34 all that *were able to* **g forth** *to* war; 3318
1:36 all that *were able to* **g forth** *to* war; 3318
1:38 all that *were able to* **g forth** *to* war; 3318
1:40 all that *were able to* **g forth** *to* war; 3318
1:42 all that *were able to* **g forth** *to* war; 3318
1:45 all that *were able to* **g forth** *to* war in 3318
2:24 And they shall **g forward** in the third rank. 5265
2:31 They shall **g** hindmost with their standards. 5265
4:19 holy *things:* Aaron and his sons shall **g in**, 935
4:20 they shall not **g in** to see when the holy 935
5:12 If any man's wife **g aside**, and commit a 7847
5:22 this water that causeth the curse shall **g** into 935
8:15 after that shall the Levites **g in** to do 935
8:24 upward they shall **g in** to wait upon 935
10: 5 that lie on the east parts shall **g forward**. 5265
10: 9 if ye **g** *to* war in your land against the enemy 935
10:30 he said unto him, I will not **g**; but I will 1980
10:32 it shall be, if thou **g** with us, yea, it shall be, 1980
13:17 and **g up** into the mountain: 5927
13:30 Let us **g up at once**, and possess it; 5927+5927
13:31 We be not able to **g up** against the people; 5927
14:40 will **g up** unto the place which the LORD 5927
14:42 **G** not **up**, for the LORD *is* not among 5927
14:44 they presumed to **g up** unto the hill top: 5927
15:39 after which ye use to **g a whoring**: 2181
16:30 and they **g down** quick into the pit; 3381
16:46 **g** quickly unto the congregation, and 1980
20:17 we will **g** *by* the king's *high* way, we will 1980
20:19 said unto him, We will **g** by the high way: 5927
20:19 without *doing any* thing *else,* **g through** on 5674
20:20 he said, Thou shalt not **g through**. 5674
21:22 *but* we will **g along** by the king's *high* way, 1980
22:12 unto Balaam, Thou shalt not **g** with them; 1980
22:13 refuseth to give me leave to **g** with you. 1980
22:18 I cannot **g beyond** the word of the LORD 5674
22:20 come to call thee, rise up, *and* **g** with them; 1980
22:35 LORD said unto Balaam, **G** with the men: 1980
23: 3 Stand by thy burnt offering, and I will **g**: 1980
23:16 and said, **G again** unto Balak, and say thus. 7725
24:13 I cannot **g beyond** the commandment of 5674
24:14 now behold, I **g** unto my people: come 1980
26: 2 all that *are able to* **g** *to* war in Israel. 3318
27:17 Which may **g out** before them, and 3318
27:17 which may **g in** before them, and which may 935
27:21 at his word shall they **g out**, and at his word 3318
31: 3 let them **g** against the Midianites, and 1961
31:23 ye shall **make** *it* **g** the fire, and it shall be 5674
31:23 all that abideth not the fire ye shall **make g** 5674
32: 6 Shall your brethren **g** to war, and shall ye sit 935
32: 9 that *they* should not **g** into the land which 935
32:17 we ourselves will **g** ready **armed** before 2502
32:20 if ye will **g armed** before the LORD to 2502
32:21 will **g** all of you armed **over** Jordan before 5674
34: 4 shall **g on** *to* Hazar-addar, and pass on to 3318
34: 9 the border shall **g on** to Ziphron, and 3318
34:11 the coast shall **g down** from Shepham *to* 3381
34:12 the border shall **g down** to Jordan, and 3381
Dt 1: 7 **g** *to* the mount of the Amorites, and unto all 935
1: 8 **g in** and possess the land which the LORD 935
1:21 **g up** *and* possess *it,* as the LORD God of 5927
1:22 us word again by what way we must **g up**, 5927
1:26 Notwithstanding ye would not **g up**, but 5927
1:28 Whither shall we **g up**? our brethren have 5927
1:33 to shew you by what way ye should **g**, 1980
1:37 Thou also shalt not **g in** thither. 935
1:38 standeth before thee, he shall **g in** thither: 935
1:39 they shall **g in** thither, and unto them will I 935
1:41 against the LORD, we will **g up** and fight, 5927
1:41 of war, ye were ready to **g up** into the hill. 5927
1:42 Say unto them, **G** not **up**, neither fight; 5927
2:27 I will **g along** by the high way, I will 1980
3:25 let me **g over**, and see the good land that *is* 5674
Dt 3:27 for thou shalt not **g over** this Jordan. 5674
3:28 for he shall **g over** before this people, and 5674
4: 1 **g in** and possess the land which the LORD 935
4: 5 so in the land whither ye **g** to possess it. 935
4:14 in the land whither ye **g over** to possess it. 5674
4:21 sware that I should not **g over** Jordan, and 5674
4:21 that *I* should not **g in** unto *that* good land, 935
4:22 die in this land, I *must* not **g over** Jordan: 5674
4:22 ye *shall* **g over**, and possess that good land. 5674
4:26 whereunto you **g over** Jordan to possess it; 5674
4:34 Or hath God assayed to **g** *and* take him a 935
4:40 that it may **g well** with thee, and with thy 3190
5:16 and that it may **g well** with thee, 3190
5:27 **G** thou **near**, and hear all that the LORD 7126
5:30 **G** say to them, Get you into your tents 1980
6: 1 *them* in the land whither ye **g** to possess it: 5674
6:14 Ye shall not **g** after other gods, of the gods 1980
6:18 *that* thou mayest **g in** and possess the good 935
8: 1 **g in** and possess the land which the LORD 935
9: 1 to **g in** to possess nations greater and 935
9: 5 thine heart, dost thou **g** to possess their land: 935
9:23 **G up** and possess the land which I have 5927
10:11 that they may **g in** and possess the land, 935
11: 8 may be strong, and **g in** and possess the land, 935
11: 8 possess the land, whither ye **g** to possess it; 5674
11:11 the land, whither ye **g** to possess it, *is* a 5674
11:28 to **g** after other gods, which ye have not 1980
11:31 For ye shall pass over Jordan to **g in** to 935
12:10 *when* ye **g over** Jordan and dwell in 5674
12:25 that it may **g well** with thee, and with thy 3190
12:26 **g** unto the place which the LORD shall 935
12:28 that it may **g well** with thee, and with thy 3190
13: 2 saying, Let us **g** after other gods, 1980
13: 6 Let us **g** and serve other gods, 1980
13:13 saying, Let us **g** and serve other gods, 1980
14:25 shalt **g** unto the place which the LORD 1980
15:12 in the seventh year thou shalt **let** him **g** free 7971
15:13 thou shalt not **let** him **g away** empty: 7971
15:16 say unto thee, I will not **g away** from thee; 3318
16: 7 turn in the morning, and **g** unto thy tents. 1980
19:13 from Israel, that *it may* **g** well with thee. NIH
19:21 *but* life *shall* **g** for life, eye for eye, tooth for NIH
20: 5 let him **g** and return to his house, lest he die 1980
20: 6 let him *also* **g** and return unto his house, 1980
20: 7 let him **g** and return unto his house, lest he 1980
20: 8 let him **g** and return unto his house, lest his 1980
21:13 after that thou shalt **g in** unto her, and be her 935
21:14 then thou shalt **let** her **g** whither she will; 7971
22: 1 see thy brother's ox or his sheep **g astray**, 5080
22: 7 thou shalt **in any wise let** the dam **g**, 7971+7971
22:13 take a wife, and **g in** unto her, and hate her, 935
23:10 shall he **g** abroad **out** of the camp, he shall 3318
23:12 whither thou shalt **g forth** abroad: 3318
24: 2 she may **g** and be another man's *wife.* 1980
24: 5 taken a new wife, he shall not **g out** to war, 3318
24:10 thou shalt not **g** into his house to fetch his 935
24:15 neither shall the sun **g down** upon it; 935
24:19 the field, thou shalt not **g again** to fetch it: 7725
24:20 thou shalt not **g over the boughs** again: 6286
25: 5 her husband's brother shall **g in** unto her, 935
25: 7 let his brother's wife **g up** to the gate unto 5927
26: 2 shalt **g** unto the place which the LORD 1980
26: 3 thou shalt **g** unto the priest that shall be in 935
27: 3 that thou mayest **g in** unto the land which 935
28:14 thou shalt not **g aside** from any of 5493
28:14 the left, to **g** after other gods to serve them. 1980
28:25 thou shalt **g out** one way against them, and 3318
28:41 enjoy them; for they shall **g** into captivity. 1980
29:18 to **g** *and* serve the gods of these nations; 1980
30:12 Who shall **g up** for us to heaven, and 5927
30:13 Who shall **g** over the sea for us, and bring it 5674
30:18 whither thou passest over Jordan to **g** to 935
31: 2 *this* day; I can no more **g out** and come in: 3318
31: 2 unto me, Thou shalt not **g over** this Jordan. 5674
31: 3 he will **g over** before thee, *and* he will 5674
31: 3 *and* Joshua, he shall **g over** before thee, 5674
31: 6 thy God, he *it is* that doth **g** with thee; 1980
31: 7 for thou must **g** with this people unto 935
31: 8 the LORD, he *it is* that doth **g** before thee; 1980
31:13 land whither ye **g over** Jordan to possess it. 5674
31:16 **g a whoring** after the gods of the strangers 2181
31:16 whither they **g** *to be* amongst them, and 935
31:21 their imagination which they **g about**, 6213
32:47 whither ye **g over** Jordan to possess it. 5674
32:52 thou shalt not **g** thither unto the land which I 935
34: 4 thine eyes, but thou shalt not **g over** thither. 5674
Jos 1: 2 **g over** this Jordan, thou, and all this people, 5674
1:11 over this Jordan, to **g in** to possess the land, 935
1:16 whithersoever thou sendest us, we will **g**. 1980
2: 1 **G** view the land, even Jericho. 1980
2:16 and afterward may ye **g** your way. 1980
2:19 *that* whosoever shall **g out** of the doors of 3318
3: 3 remove from your place, and **g** after it. 1980
3: 4 ye may know the way by which ye must **g**: 1980
6: 3 of war, *and* **g round about** the city once. 5362
6:22 **G** *into* the harlot's house, and bring out 935
7: 2 saying, **G up** and view the country. 5927
7: 3 said unto him, Let not all the people **g up**; 5927
7: 3 or three thousand men **g up** and smite Ai; 5927
8: 1 of war with thee, and arise, **g up** *to* Ai: 5927
8: 3 all the people of war, to **g up** *against* Ai: 5927
8: 4 **g** not very **far** from the city, but be ye all 7368
9:11 **g** to meet them, and say unto them, We *are* 1980
9:12 on the day we came forth to **g** unto you; 1980
10:13 and hasted not to **g down** about a whole day. 935
14:11 for war, both to **g out**, and to come in. 3318
18: 3 How long *are* you slack to **g** to possess 935
18: 4 **g** through the land, and describe it 1980
18: 8 **G** and walk through the land, and 1980
22: 9 to **g** unto the country of Gilead, to the land 1980
22:12 *at* Shiloh, to **g up** to war against them. 5927
22:33 did not intend to **g up** against them in 5927
23:12 Else if ye do **in any wise g back**, 7725+7725
23:12 and **g in** unto them, and they to you: 935
Jdg 1: 1 Who shall **g up** for us against 5927
Jdg 1: 2 the LORD said, Judah shall **g up**: behold, 5927
1: 3 and I likewise will **g** with thee into thy lot. 1980
1:25 but they **let g** the man and all his family. 7971
2: 1 I **made** you **to g up** out of Egypt, and 5927
2: 6 when Joshua had **let** the people **g**, 7971
4: 6 *saying,* **G** and draw toward mount Tabor, 1980
4: 8 If thou wilt **g** with me, then I will go: 1980
4: 8 If thou wilt go with me, then I will **g**: 1980
4: 8 if thou wilt not **g** with me, *then* I will not 1980
4: 8 thou wilt not go with me, *then* I will not **g**. 1980
4: 9 she said, I will **surely g** with thee: 1980+1980
5:11 shall the people of the LORD **g down** to 3381
6:14 **G** in this thy might, and thou shalt save 1980
7: 3 Now therefore **g to**, proclaim in the ears of 4994
7: 4 This shall **g** with thee, the same shall go 1980
7: 4 go with thee, the same shall **g** with thee; 1980
7: 4 This shall not **g** with thee, the same shall 1980
7: 4 shall not go with thee, the same shall not **g**. 1980
7: 7 let all the *other* people **g** every man unto his 1980
7:10 if thou fear to **g down**, go thou with Phurah 3381
7:10 **g** thou with Phurah thy servant **down** to 3381
7:11 be strengthened to **g down** unto the host. 3381
9: 9 man, and **g** to be promoted over the trees? 1980
9:11 and **g** to be promoted over the trees? 1980
9:13 man, and **g** to be promoted over the trees? 1980
9:38 **g out**, I pray now, and fight with them. 3318
10:14 **G** and cry unto the gods which ye have 1980
11: 8 that thou mayest **g** with us, and 1980
11:35 unto the LORD, and I cannot **g back**. 7725
11:37 that I may **g up** and down upon 1980
11:38 he said, **G**. And he sent her away *for* two 1980
12: 1 and didst not call us to **g** with thee? 1980
12: 5 which were escaped said, Let me **g over**; 5674
15: 1 I will **g in to** my wife into the chamber. 935
15: 1 But her father would not suffer him to **g in**. 935
15: 5 he **let** *them* **g** into the standing corn of 7971
16:17 my strength will **g** from me, and I shall 5493
16:20 I will **g out** as at other times *before,* and 3318
17: 9 I **g** to sojourn where I may find *a place.* 1980
18: 2 they said unto them, **G**, search the land: 1980
18: 5 our way which we **g** shall be prosperous. 1980
18: 6 the priest said unto them, **G** in peace: 1980
18: 6 the LORD *is* your way wherein ye **g**. 1980
18: 9 Arise, that we may **g up** against them: 5927
18: 9 be not slothful to **g**, *and* to enter to possess 1980
18:10 When ye **g**, ye shall come unto a people 935
18:19 **g** with us, and be to us a father and a priest: 1980
19: 5 morsel of bread, and afterward **g** your way. 1980
19: 9 on your way, that thou mayest **g** home. 1980
19:15 aside thither, to **g in** *and* to lodge in Gibeah: 935
19:25 the day began to spring, they **let** her **g**. 7971
19:27 of the house, and went out to **g** his way: 1980
20: 8 We will not any *of us* **g** to his tent, 1980
20: 9 do to Gibeah; *we will* **g** *up* by lot against it; NIH
20:14 to **g out** to battle against the children of 3318
20:18 Which of us shall **g up** first to the battle 5927
20:18 And the LORD said, Judah *shall* **g** *up* first. NIH
20:23 Shall I **g** *up* again to battle against 5066
20:23 And the LORD said, **G up** against him.) 5927
20:28 Shall I yet again **g out** to battle against 3318
20:28 the LORD said, **G up**; for to morrow I 5927
21:10 **G** and smite the inhabitants of 1980
21:20 **G** and lie in wait in the vineyards; 1980
21:21 of Shiloh, and **g** *to* the land of Benjamin. 1980
Ru 1: 8 **G**, return each to her mother's house: 1980
1:11 why will you **g** with me? *are there* yet *any* 1980
1:12 **g** *your way;* for I am too old to have a 1980
1:16 for whither thou goest, I will **g**; and 1980
1:18 she *was* stedfastly minded to **g** with her, 1980
2: 2 Let me now **g** *to* the field, and glean ears of 1980
2: 2 And she said unto her, **G**, my daughter. 1980
2: 8 **G** not to glean in another field, neither go 1980
2: 8 neither **g** from hence, but abide here fast by 5674
2: 9 that they do reap, and **g** thou after them: 1980
2: 9 **g** unto the vessels, and drink of *that* which 1980
2:22 that thou **g out** with his maidens, 3318
3: 4 and thou shalt **g in**, and uncover his feet, and 935
3:17 to me, **G** not empty unto thy mother in law. 935
1Sa 1:17 Eli answered and said, **G** in peace: and 1980
1:22 *I will not* **g** *up* until the child be weaned, NIH
3: 9 Eli said unto Samuel, **G**, lie down: 1980
5:11 let it **g again** to his own place, that it slay 7725
6: 6 did they not **let** the people **g**, and 7971
6: 8 and send it away, that it may **g**. 1980
6:20 and to whom shall he **g up** from us? 5927
8:20 and **g out** before us, and fight our battles. 3318
8:22 of Israel, **G** ye every man unto his city. 1980
9: 3 with thee, and arise, **g** seek the asses. 1980
9: 6 now let us **g** thither; peradventure he can 1980
9: 6 he can shew us our way that we should **g**. 1980
9: 7 behold, *if* we **g**, what shall we bring 1980
9: 9 he spake, Come, and let us **g** to the seer: 1980
9:10 to his servant, Well said; come, let us **g**. 1980
9:13 before he **g up** to the high place to eat: 5927
9:14 against them, for to **g up** *to* the high place. 5927
9:19 **g up** before me unto the high place; for ye 5927
9:19 to morrow I will **let** thee **g**, and will tell 7971
10: 3 shalt thou **g on** forward from thence, and 2498
10: 8 And thou shalt **g down** before me *to* Gilgal; 3381
10: 9 that when he had turned his back to **g** from 1980
11:14 let us **g** *to* Gilgal, and renew the kingdom 1980
12:21 *should ye* **g** after vain *things,* which cannot NIH
14: 1 let us **g over** to the Philistines' garrison, 5674
14: 4 *by* which Jonathan sought to **g over** unto 5674
14: 6 let us **g over** unto the garrison of these 5674
14: 9 in our place, and will not **g up** unto them. 5927
14:10 Come up unto us; then we will **g up**: 5927
14:36 Let us **g down** after the Philistines by night, 3381
14:37 Shall I **g down** after the Philistines? 3381
15: 3 Now **g** and smite Amalek, and 1980
15: 6 Saul said unto the Kenites, **G**, depart, 1980
15:18 **G** and utterly destroy the sinners 1980
15:27 as Samuel turned about to **g away**, he laid 1980
16: 1 fill thine horn *with* oil, and **g**, I will send 1980
16: 2 Samuel said, How can I **g**? if Saul hear *it,* 1980

Book	Ref	Context	Strong's
1Sa	17:32	thy servant will **g** and fight with this	1980
	17:33	Thou art not able to **g** against this Philistine	1980
	17:37	**G**, and the LORD be with thee.	1980
	17:39	upon his armour, and he assayed to **g**;	1980
	17:39	David said unto Saul, I cannot **g** with these;	1980
	17:55	when Saul saw David **g forth** against	3318
	18: 2	would let him **g** no more **home** *to* his	7725
	19: 3	I will **g out** and stand beside my father in	3318
	19:17	answered Saul, He said unto me, **Let** me **g**;	7971
	20: 5	**let** me **g**, that I may hide myself in	7971
	20:11	Come, and let us **g out** *into* the field.	3318
	20:13	thee away, that thou mayest **g** in peace:	1980
	20:19	*then* thou shalt **g down** quickly, and	3381
	20:21	behold, I will send a lad, *saying*, **G**,	1980
	20:22	**g** *thy way:* for the LORD hath sent thee	1980
	20:28	David earnestly asked *leave* of me *to* **g** to	NIH
	20:29	he said, **Let** me **g**, I pray thee; for our	7971
	20:40	said unto him, **G**, carry *them to* the city.	1980
	20:42	Jonathan said to David, **G** in peace,	1980
	23: 2	Shall I **g** and smite these Philistines?	1980
	23: 2	**G**, and smite the Philistines, and	1980
	23: 4	and said, Arise, **g down** *to* Keilah;	3381
	23: 8	to **g down** *to* Keilah, to besiege David and	3381
	23:13	and went whithersoever they could **g**.	1980
	23:13	from Keilah; and he forbare to **g forth**.	3318
	23:22	**G**, I pray you, prepare yet, and know and	1980
	23:23	with the certainty, and I will **g** with you:	1980
	24:19	his enemy, will he **let** him **g** well away?	7971
	25: 5	**g** to Nabal, and greet him in my name:	935
	25:19	she said unto her servants, **G on** before me;	5674
	25:35	said unto her, **G up** in peace to thine house;	5927
	26: 6	Who will **g down** with me to Saul to	3381
	26: 6	And Abishai said, I will **g down** with thee.	3381
	26:11	and the cruse of water, and let us **g**.	1980
	26:19	of the LORD, saying, **G**, serve other gods.	1980
	28: 1	that thou shalt **g out** with me to battle, thou	3318
	28: 7	that I may **g** to her, and inquire of her.	1980
	29: 4	that he may **g again** to his place,	7725
	29: 4	let him not **g down** with us to battle,	3381
	29: 7	Wherefore now return, and **g** in peace,	1980
	29: 8	that I may not **g** fight against the enemies of	935
	29: 9	He shall not **g up** with us to the battle.	5927
	30:10	faint that they could not **g over** the brook	5674
2Sa	1:15	and said, **G near**, *and* fall upon him.	5066
	2: 1	Shall I **g up** into any of the cities of Judah?	5927
	2: 1	the LORD said unto him, **G up**.	5927
	2: 1	David said, Whither shall I **g up**? And he	5927
	3:16	said Abner unto him, **G**, return. And he	1980
	3:21	I will arise and **g**, and will gather all Israel	1980
	5:19	Shall I **g up** to the Philistines?	5927
	5:19	the LORD said unto David, **G up**: for I	5927
	5:23	the LORD, he said, Thou shalt not **g up**;	5927
	5:24	for then shall the LORD **g out** before thee,	3318
	7: 3	to the king, **G**, do all that *is* in thine heart;	1980
	7: 5	**G** and tell my servant David, Thus saith	1980
	11: 1	at the time when kings **g forth** *to battle*,	3318
	11: 8	**G down** to thy house, and wash thy feet.	3381
	11:10	didst thou not **g down** unto thine house?	3381
	11:11	shall I then **g** into mine house, to eat and	935
	12:23	I shall **g** to him, but he shall not return to	1980
	13: 7	**G** now *to* thy brother Amnon's house, and	1980
	13:13	whither shall I **cause** my shame **to g**?	1980
	13:24	and his servants **g** with thy servant.	1980
	13:25	Nay, my son, let us not all now **g**,	1980
	13:25	howbeit he would not **g**, but blessed him.	1980
	13:26	pray thee, let my brother Amnon **g** with us.	1980
	13:26	said unto him, Why should he **g** with thee?	1980
	13:27	that he **let** Amnon and all the king's sons **g**	7971
	13:39	*the soul of* king David longed to **g forth**	3318
	14: 8	**G** to thine house, and I will give charge	1980
	14:21	**g** therefore, bring the young man Absalom	1980
	14:30	he hath barley there; **g** and set it on fire.	1980
	15: 7	I pray thee, let me **g** and pay my vow,	1980
	15: 9	the king said unto him, **G** in peace. So he	1980
	15:20	should I *this* day make thee **g up and down**	1980
	15:20	seeing I **g** whither I may, return thou, and	1980
	15:22	David said to Ittai, **G** and pass over.	1980
	16: 9	let me **g over**, I pray thee, and take off his	5674
	16:21	**G in** unto thy father's concubines,	935
	17:11	*that* thou **g** to battle in thine own person.	1980
	18: 2	**surely g forth** with you myself also.	3318+3318
	18: 3	people answered, Thou shalt not **g forth**:	3318
	18:21	**G** tell the king what thou hast seen.	1980
	19: 7	**g forth**, and speak comfortably unto thy	3318
	19: 7	I swear by the LORD, if thou **g** not **forth**,	3318
	19:15	Judah came to Gilgal, to **g** to meet the king,	1980
	19:20	Joseph to **g down** to meet my lord the king.	3381
	19:26	that I may ride thereon, and **g** to the king;	1980
	19:34	that I should **g up** with the king *unto*	5927
	19:36	Thy servant will **g** a little *way* **over** Jordan	5674
	19:37	let him **g over** with my lord the king; and	5674
	19:38	Chimham shall **g over** with me, and I will	5674
	20:11	he that *is* for David, *let him* **g** after Joab.	NIH
	21:17	Thou shalt **g** no more **out** with us to battle,	3318
	24: 1	them to say, **G**, number Israel and Judah.	1980
	24: 2	**G** now through all the tribes of Israel,	7751
	24:12	**G** and say unto David, Thus saith	1980
	24:18	that day to David, and said unto him, **G up**,	5927
1Ki	1:13	**G** and get thee in unto king David, and	1980
	1:53	Solomon said unto him, **G** to thine house.	1980
	2: 2	I **g** the way of all the earth: be thou strong	1980
	2: 6	let not his hoar head **g down** *to* the grave in	3381
	2:29	son of Jehoiada, saying, **G**, fall upon him.	1980
	2:36	and **g** not **forth** thence any whither.	3318
	3: 7	I know not *how* to **g out** or come in.	3318
	8:44	If thy people **g out** to battle against their	3318
	9: 6	**g** and serve other gods, and worship them:	1980
	11: 2	Ye shall not **g in** to them, neither shall they	935
	11:10	that *he* should not **g** after other gods:	1980
	11:17	father's servants with him, to **g** *into* Egypt;	935
	11:21	that I may **g** to mine own country.	1980
	11:22	thou seekest to **g** to thine own country?	1980
	11:22	howbeit **let** me **g in any wise**.	7971+7971
	12:24	Thus saith the LORD, Ye shall not **g up**,	5927
	12:27	If this people **g up** to do sacrifice in	5927
1Ki	12:27	and **g again** to Rehoboam king of Judah.	7725
	12:28	*It is* too much for you to **g up** *to* Jerusalem:	5927
	13: 8	me half thine house, I will not **g in** with thee,	935
	13:16	may not return with thee, nor **g in** with thee:	935
	13:17	nor turn again to **g** by the way that thou	1980
	14: 3	and a cruse of honey, and **g** to him:	935
	14: 7	**G**, tell Jeroboam, Thus saith the LORD	1980
	15:17	that *he* might not suffer *any* to **g out** or	3318
	17:12	that I may **g in** and dress it for me and my	935
	17:13	Fear not; **g** *and* do as thou hast said:	935
	18: 1	saying, **G**, shew thyself unto Ahab;	1980
	18: 5	**G** into the land, unto all fountains of water,	1980
	18: 8	I *am*: **g**, tell thy lord, Behold, Elijah *is*	1980
	18:11	**G**, tell thy lord, Behold, Elijah *is here*.	1980
	18:14	**G**, tell thy lord, Behold, Elijah *is here*: and	1980
	18:43	his servant, **G up** now, look toward the sea.	5927
	18:43	And he said, **G again** seven times.	7725
	18:44	he said, **G up**, say unto Ahab, Prepare *thy*	5927
	19:11	**G forth**, and stand upon the mount before	3318
	19:15	the LORD said unto him, **G**, return on thy	1980
	19:20	he said unto him, **G** back again: for what	1980
	20:22	said unto him, **G**, strengthen thyself, and	1980
	20:31	our heads, and **g out** to the king of Israel:	3318
	20:33	he said, **G** ye, bring him. Then Ben-hadad	935
	20:42	Because thou hast **let g** out of *thy* hand a	7971
	20:42	therefore thy life shall **g** for his life, and	1961
	21:16	that Ahab rose up to **g down** to	3381
	21:18	Arise, **g down** to meet Ahab king of Israel,	3381
	22: 4	Wilt thou **g** with me to battle *to*	1980
	22: 6	Shall I **g** against Ramoth-gilead to battle, or	1980
	22: 6	they said, **G up**; for the Lord shall deliver *it*	5927
	22:12	**G up** *to* Ramoth-gilead, and prosper:	5927
	22:15	shall we **g** against Ramoth-gilead to battle,	1980
	22:15	he answered him, **G**, and prosper: for	5927
	22:20	that he may **g up** and fall at	5927
	22:22	I will **g forth**, and I will be a lying spirit in	3318
	22:22	and prevail also: **g forth**, and do so.	3318
	22:25	when thou shalt **g into** an inner chamber to	935
	22:48	Jehoshaphat made ships of Tharshish to **g**	1980
	22:49	Let my servants **g** with thy servants in	1980
2Ki	1: 2	he sent messengers, and said unto them, **G**,	1980
	1: 3	**g up** to meet the messengers of the king of	5927
	1: 3	*that* ye **g** to inquire of Baal-zebub the god	1980
	1: 6	a man up to meet us, and said unto us, **G**,	1980
	1:15	said unto Elijah, **G down** with him:	3381
	2:16	let them **g**, we pray thee, and seek thy	1980
	2:18	unto them, Did I not say unto you, **G** not?	1980
	2:23	mocked him, and said unto him, **G up**,	5927
	2:23	thou bald head; **g up**, thou bald head.	5927
	3: 7	wilt thou **g** with me against Moab to battle?	1980
	3: 7	he said, I will **g up**: I *am* as thou *art*, my	5927
	3: 8	he said, Which way shall we **g up**? And he	5927
	4: 3	he said, **G**, borrow thee vessels abroad of	1980
	4: 7	**G**, sell the oil, and pay thy debt, and	1980
	4:23	Wherefore wilt thou **g** to him to day?	1980
	4:24	and **g** *forward;* slack not *thy* riding for me,	1980
	4:29	**g** *thy way:* if thou meet any man,	1980
	5: 5	**G to**, go, and I will send a letter unto	1980
	5: 5	**g**, and I will send a letter unto the king of	935
	5:10	**G** and wash in Jordan seven times, and	1980
	5:19	he said unto him, **G** in peace. So he	1980
	5:24	and he **let** the men **g**, and they departed.	7971
	6: 2	Let us **g**, we pray thee, unto Jordan, and	1980
	6: 2	we may dwell. And he answered, **G** ye.	1980
	6: 3	I pray thee, and **g** with thy servants.	1980
	6: 3	thy servants. And he answered, I will **g**.	1980
	6:13	**G** and spy where he *is*, that I may send and	1980
	6:22	may eat and drink, and **g** to their master.	1980
	7: 5	to **g** unto the camp of the Syrians:	935
	7: 9	that we may **g** and tell the king's household.	935
	7:14	the host of the Syrians, saying, **G** and see.	1980
	8: 1	**g** thou and thine household, and	1980
	8: 8	**g**, meet the man of God, and inquire of	1980
	8:10	Elisha said unto him, **G**, say unto him,	1980
	9: 1	oil in thine hand, and **g** *to* Ramoth-gilead:	1980
	9: 2	**g in**, and make him arise up from among his	935
	9:15	let none **g forth** *nor* escape out of the city	3318
	9:15	out of the city to **g** to tell *it* in Jezreel.	1980
	9:34	**G, see** now this cursed *woman*, and	6485
	10:13	we **g down** to salute the children of	3381
	10:24	*he that letteth him* **g**, his life *shall be* for	NIH
	10:25	and to the captains, **G in**, *and* slay them;	935
	11: 7	two parts of all you that **g forth** on	3318
	11: 9	with them that should **g out** on the sabbath,	3318
	12:17	Hazael set his face to **g up** to Jerusalem.	5927
	17:27	let them **g** and dwell there, and let him	1980
	18:21	it will **g** into his hand, and pierce it:	935
	18:25	**G up** against this land, and destroy it.	5927
	19:31	For out of Jerusalem shall **g forth** a	3318
	20: 5	on the third day thou shalt **g up** *unto*	5927
	20: 8	*that* I shall **g up** *into* the house of	5927
	20: 9	shall the shadow **g forward** ten degrees, or	1980
	20: 9	forward ten degrees, or **g back** ten degrees?	7725
	20:10	It is a light thing for the shadow to **g down**	5186
	22: 4	**G up** to Hilkiah the high priest, that he may	5927
	22:13	**G** ye, inquire of the LORD for me, and	1980
1Ch	7:11	two hundred *soldiers, fit to* **g out** *for* war	3318
	14:10	Shall I **g up** against the Philistines?	5927
	14:10	the LORD said unto him, **G up**; for I will	5927
	14:14	God said unto him, **G** not **up** after them;	5927
	14:15	*that* then thou shalt **g out** to battle:	3318
	17: 4	**G** and tell David my servant, Thus saith	1980
	17:11	when thy days be expired that *thou* must **g**	1980
	20: 1	at the time that kings **g out** *to battle*, Joab	3318
	21: 2	to Joab and to the rulers of the people, **G**,	1980
	21:10	**G** and tell David, saying, Thus saith	1980
	21:18	that David should **g up**, and set up an altar	5927
	21:30	David could not **g** before it to inquire of	1980
2Ch	1:10	that I may **g out** and come in before this	3318
	6:34	If thy people **g out** to war against their	3318
	7:19	shall **g** and serve other gods, and	1980
	11: 4	Thus saith the LORD, Ye shall not **g up**,	5927
	14:11	and in thy name we **g** against this multitude.	935
	16: 1	to the intent that *he* might let none **g out** or	3318
	16: 3	**g**, break thy league with Baasha king of	1980
2Ch	18: 2	persuaded him to **g up** *with him* to	5927
	18: 3	Wilt thou **g** with me *to* Ramoth-gilead?	1980
	18: 5	Shall we **g** to Ramoth-gilead to battle, or	1980
	18: 5	they said, **G up**; for God will deliver *it* into	5927
	18:11	**G up** *to* Ramoth-gilead, and prosper:	5927
	18:14	shall we **g** to Ramoth-gilead to battle, or	1980
	18:14	**G** ye **up**, and prosper, and they shall be	5927
	18:19	that he may **g up** and fall at	5927
	18:21	I will **g out**, and be a lying spirit in	3318
	18:21	shalt also prevail: **g out**, and do *even* so.	3318
	18:24	shalt **g into** an inner chamber to hide thyself.	935
	18:29	will disguise myself, and will **g** to the battle;	935
	20:16	To morrow **g** ye **down** against them:	3381
	20:17	to morrow **g out** against them:	3318
	20:27	of them, to **g again** to Jerusalem with joy;	7725
	20:36	with him to make ships to **g** *to* Tarshish:	1980
	20:37	that they were not able to **g** to Tarshish.	1980
	21:13	**made** Judah and the inhabitants of Jerusalem **to g a whoring**,	2181
	23: 6	the Levites; they shall **g in**, for they *are* holy:	935
	23: 8	with them that were to **g out** on	3318
	24: 5	**G out** unto the cities of Judah, and	3318
	25: 5	choice *men, able to* **g forth** *to* war,	3318
	25: 7	O king, let not the army of Israel **g** with thee;	935
	25: 8	if thou *wilt* **g**, do *it*, be strong for the battle:	935
	25:10	to **g** home *again:* wherefore their anger was	1980
	25:13	that *they* should not **g** with him to battle,	1980
	26:18	**g out** of the sanctuary; for thou hast	3318
	26:20	yea, himself hasted also to **g out**, because	3318
	34:21	**G**, inquire of the LORD for me, and	1980
	36:23	his God *be* with him, and let him **g up**.	5927
Ezr	1: 3	let him **g up** to Jerusalem, which *is* in	5927
	1: 5	to **g up** to build the house of the LORD	5927
	5:15	said unto him, Take these vessels, **g**,	236
	7: 9	first month began he to **g up** from Babylon,	4609
	7:13	*which are* minded of their own freewill to **g**	1946
	7:13	freewill to go *up* to Jerusalem, **g** with thee.	1946
	7:28	out of Israel chief *men* to **g up** with me.	5927
	8:31	*day* of the first month, to **g** *unto* Jerusalem:	1980
	9:11	The land, *unto* which ye **g** to possess it,	935
Ne	3:15	unto the stairs that **g down** from the city of	3381
	4: 3	Even *that* which they build, if a fox **g up**,	5927
	6:11	*being* as I *am*, would **g** into the temple to	935
	6:11	the temple to save his life? I will not **g in**.	935
	8:10	**G** *your way*, eat the fat, and drink	1980
	8:15	**G forth** *unto* the mount, and fetch olive	3318
	9:12	light in the way wherein they should **g**.	1980
	9:15	promisedst them that *they* should **g in** to	935
	9:19	and the way wherein they should **g**.	1980
	9:23	that *they* should **g in** to possess *it*.	935
Est	1:19	let there **g** a royal commandment from him,	3318
	2:12	turn was come to **g in** to king Ahasuerus,	935
	2:13	whatsoever she desired was given her to **g**	935
	2:15	was come to **g in** unto the king, she required	935
	4: 8	to charge her that *she* should **g in** unto	935
	4:16	**G**, gather together all the Jews that are	1980
	4:16	so will I **g in** unto the king, which *is* not	935
	5:14	**g** thou **in** merrily with the king unto	935
Job	4:21	their excellency *which is* in them **g away**?	5265
	6:18	turned aside; they **g** to nothing, and perish.	5927
	10:21	Before I **g** whence I shall not return,	1980
	15:13	and lettest *such* words **g out** of thy mouth?	3318
	15:30	by the breath of his mouth shall he **g away**.	5493
	16:22	I shall **g** the way *whence* I shall not return.	1980
	17:16	They shall **g down** *to* the bars of the pit,	3381
	20:26	it shall **g ill** with him that is left in his	3415
	21:13	and in a moment **g down** *to* the grave.	2865
	21:29	Have ye not asked them that **g by** the way?	5674
	23: 8	I **g** forward, but he *is* not *there;* and	1980
	24: 5	in the desert, **g** they **forth** to their work;	3318
	24:10	They **cause** *him* **to g** naked without	1980
	27: 6	I hold fast, and will not **let** it **g**:	7503
	31:37	as a prince would I **g near** unto him.	7126
	37: 8	the beasts **g** into dens, and remain in their	935
	38:35	that they may **g**, and say unto thee,	1980
	39: 4	they **g forth**, and return not unto them.	3318
	41:19	Out of his mouth **g** burning lamps, *and*	1980
	42: 8	**g** to my servant Job, and offer up for	1980
Ps	22:29	all they that **g down** to the dust shall bow	3381
	26: 4	neither will I **g in** with dissemblers.	935
	28: 1	I become like them that **g down** into	3381
	30: 3	that I should not **g down** *to* the pit.	3381
	30: 9	in my blood, when I **g down** to the pit?	3381
	32: 8	teach thee in the way which thou shalt **g**:	1980
	38: 6	I **g** mourning all the day long.	1980
	39:13	before I **g** hence, and be no more.	1980
	42: 9	why **g** I mourning because of	1980
	43: 2	why **g** I mourning because of	1980
	43: 4	will I **g** unto the altar of God, unto God my	935
	48:12	Walk about Zion, and **g round about** her:	5362
	49:19	He shall **g** to the generation of his fathers;	935
	55:10	night they **g about** it upon the walls	5437
	55:15	*and* let them **g down** quick *into* hell:	3381
	58: 3	they **g astray** as soon as they be born,	8582
	59: 6	like a dog, and **g round about** the city.	5437
	59:14	like a dog, and **g round about** the city.	5437
	60:10	*which* didst not **g out** with our armies?	3318
	63: 9	to destroy *it*, shall **g** into the lower parts of	935
	66:13	I will **g** *into* thy house with burnt offerings:	935
	71:16	I will **g** in the strength of the Lord GOD:	935
	73:27	all them that **g a whoring** from thee.	2181
	78:52	**made** his own people **to g forth** like sheep,	5265
	80:18	So will not we **g** *back* from thee:	5472
	84: 7	They **g** from strength to strength, *every one*	1980
	85:13	Righteousness shall **g** before him; and	1980
	88: 4	I am counted with them that **g down** into	3381
	89:14	mercy and truth shall **g before** thy face.	6923
	104: 8	They **g up** *by* the mountains; they go down	5927
	104: 8	they **g down** *by* the valleys unto the place	3381
	104:26	There **g** the ships: *there is* that leviathan,	1980
	105:20	the ruler of the people, and let him **g free**.	6605
	107: 7	that *they* might **g** to a city of habitation.	1980
	107:23	They that **g down** to the sea in ships,	3381
	107:26	they **g down** *again* to the depths:	3381
	108:11	not thou, O God, **g forth** with our hosts?	3318

G

Ps 115:17 neither any that **g down** into silence. 3381
118:19 I will **g into** them, *and* I will praise 935
119:35 **Make** me **to g** in the path of thy 1869
122: 1 Let us **g** *into* the house of the LORD. 1980
122: 4 Whither the tribes **g up**, the tribes of 5927
129: 8 Neither do they which **g by** say, 5674
132: 3 of my house, nor **g up** into my bed; 5927
132: 7 We will **g into** his tabernacles: we will 935
139: 7 Whither shall I **g** from thy spirit? or 1980
143: 7 lest I be like unto them that **g down** into 3381
Pr 1:12 whole, as those that **g down** into the pit: 3381
2:19 None that **g** *unto* her return *again*, neither 935
3:28 **G**, and come again, and to morrow I will 1980
4:13 Take fast hold of instruction; let *her* not **g**: 7503
4:14 and **g** not in the way of evil *men*. 833
5: 5 Her feet **g down** *to* death; her steps take 3381
5:23 the greatness of his folly he shall **g astray**. 7686
6: 3 **g**, humble thyself, and make sure thy 1980
6: 6 **G** to the ant, thou sluggard; consider her 1980
6:28 Can one **g** upon hot coals, and his feet not 1980
7:25 to her ways, **g** not **astray** in her paths. 8582
9: 6 and live; and **g** in the way of understanding. 833
9:15 To call passengers who **g right** *on* their 3474
14: 7 **G** from the presence of a foolish man, 1980
15:12 neither will he **g** unto the wise. 1980
18: 8 they **g down** *into* the innermost parts of 3381
19: 7 how much more do his friends **g far** from 7368
22: 6 child **in the way** he should **g**: 1870+5921+6310
22:10 out the scorner, and contention shall **g out**; 3318
22:24 and with a furious man thou shalt not **g**: 935
23:30 at the wine; they that **g** to seek mixt wine. 935
25: 8 **G** not **forth** hastily to strive, lest *thou know* 3318
26:22 they **g down** *into* the innermost parts of 3381
27:10 neither **g** *into* thy brother's house in the day 935
28:10 Whoso **causeth** the righteous **to g astray** in 7686
30:27 yet **g** they **forth** all of them by bands; 3318
30:29 There be three *things* which **g** well, yea, 6806
Ecc 2: 1 I said in mine heart, **G to** now, I will prove 1980
3:20 All **g** unto one place; all are of the dust, and 1980
5:15 naked shall he return to **g** as he came, and 1980
5:16 *that* in all points as he came, so shall he **g**: 1980
6: 6 he seen no good: do not all **g** to one place? 1980
7: 2 *It is* better to **g** to the house of mourning, 1980
7: 2 than to **g** to the house of feasting: 1980
8: 3 Be not hasty to **g** out of his sight: stand not 1980
9: 3 they live, and after that *they* **g** to the dead. NIH
9: 7 **G** *thy way*, eat thy bread with joy, and 1980
10:15 he knoweth not how to **g** to the city. 1980
12: 5 and the mourners **g about** the streets: 5437
SS 1: 8 **g** thy **way forth** by the footsteps of 3318
3: 2 **g about** the city in the streets and in 5437
3: 3 The watchmen that **g about** the city found 5437
3: 4 I held him, and would not **let** him **g**, until I 7503
3:11 **G forth**, O ye daughters of Zion, and 3318
6: 6 of sheep which **g up** from the washing, 5927
7: 8 I said, I will **g up** to the palm tree, I will 5927
7:11 my beloved, let us **g forth** *into* the field; 3318
Isa 2: 3 many people shall **g** and say, Come ye, 1980
2: 3 let us **g up** to the mountain of the LORD, 5927
2: 3 for out of Zion shall **g forth** the law, and 3318
2:19 they shall **g** into the holes of the rocks, and 935
2:21 To **g** into the clifts of the rocks, and into 935
3:16 walking and mincing *as* they **g**, and 1980
5: 5 now **g to**, I will tell you what I *will* do to 4994
5:24 and their blossom shall **g up** as dust: 5927
6: 8 Whom shall I send, and who will **g** for us? 1980
6: 9 he said, **G**, and tell this people, Hear ye 1980
7: 3 **G forth** now to meet Ahaz, thou, and 3318
7: 6 Let us **g up** against Judah, and vex it, and 5927
8: 6 refuseth the waters of Shiloah that **g** softly, 1980
8: 7 all his channels, and **g** over all his banks: 1980
8: 8 he shall overflow and **g over**, he shall reach 5674
11:15 and **make** *men* **g over** dryshod. 1869
13: 2 that they may **g** *into* the gates of the nobles. 935
14:19 that **g down** to the stones of the pit; 3381
15: 5 of Luhith with weeping shall they **g** it **up**; 5927
18: 2 *saying*, **G**, ye swift messengers, to a nation 1980
20: 2 **G** and loose the sackcloth from off thy 1980
21: 2 **G up**, O Elam: besiege, O Media; all 5927
21: 6 **G**, set a watchman, let him declare what he 1980
22:15 **G**, get thee unto this treasurer, *even* unto 1980
23:16 Take a harp, **g about** the city, thou harlot 5437
27: 4 I would **g** through them, I would burn them 6585
28:13 that they might **g**, and fall backward, and 1980
30: 2 That walk to **g down** *into* Egypt, and 3381
30: 8 Now **g**, write it before them in a table, and 935
31: 1 Woe to them that **g down** *to* Egypt for help; 3381
33:21 wherein shall **g** no galley with oars, 1980
34:10 the smoke thereof shall **g up** for ever: 5927
35: 9 nor *any* ravenous beast shall **g up** thereon, 5927
36: 6 it will **g** into his hand, and pierce it: 935
36:10 **G up** against this land, and destroy it. 5927
37:32 For out of Jerusalem shall **g forth** a 3318
38: 5 **G** and say to Hezekiah, Thus saith 1980
38:10 my days, I shall **g** to the gates of the grave: 1980
38:15 himself hath done *it*: I shall **g softly** all my 1718
38:18 they that **g down** into the pit cannot hope 3381
38:22 What *is* the sign that I shall **g up** *to* 5927
42:10 ye that **g down** to the sea, and all that is 3381
42:13 The LORD shall **g forth** as a mighty *man*, 3318
45: 2 I will **g** before thee, and make the crooked 1980
45:13 my city, and he shall **let g** my captives, 7971
45:16 they shall **g** to confusion together *that are* 1980
48:17 thee by the way *that* thou shouldest **g**. 1980
48:20 **G** ye **forth** of Babylon, flee ye from 3318
49: 9 *thou* mayest say to the prisoners, **G forth**; 3318
49:17 they that made thee waste shall **g forth** of 3318
51:23 thy soul, Bow down, that we may **g over**: 5674
52:11 Depart ye, depart ye, **g** ye **out** from thence, 3318
52:11 touch no unclean *thing*; **g** ye **out** of 3318
52:12 For ye shall not **g out** with haste, nor go by 3318
52:12 shall not go out with haste, nor **g** by flight: 1980
52:12 for the LORD will **g** before you; and 1980
54: 9 of Noah should no more **g** over the earth; 5674
55:12 For ye shall **g out** with joy, and be led forth 3318
Isa 58: 6 to **let** the oppressed **g** free, and *that* ye 7971
58: 8 thy righteousness shall **g** before thee; 1980
60:20 Thy sun shall no more **g down**; neither shall 935
62: 1 until the righteousness thereof **g forth** as 3318
62:10 **G through**, go through the gates; 5674
62:10 Go through, **g through** the gates; 5674
66:24 they shall **g forth**, and look upon 3318
Jer 1: 7 for thou shalt **g** to all that I shall send thee, 1980
2: 2 **G** and cry in the ears of Jerusalem, saying, 1980
2:25 loved strangers, and after them will I **g**. 1980
2:37 thou shalt **g forth** from him, and 3318
3: 1 she **g** from him, and become another man's, 1980
3:12 **G** and proclaim these words toward 1980
4: 5 and let us **g** into the defenced cities. 935
4:29 they shall **g** into thickets, and climb up upon 935
5:10 **G** ye **up** upon her walls, and destroy; but 5927
6: 4 against her; arise, and let us **g up** at noon. 5927
6: 5 let us **g** by night, and let us destroy her 5927
6:25 **G** not **forth** *into* the field, nor walk by 3318
7:12 **g** ye now unto my place which *was* in 1980
9: 2 I might leave my people, and **g** from them! 1980
10: 5 needs be borne, because they cannot **g**. 6805
11:12 of Judah and inhabitants of Jerusalem **g**, 1980
13: 1 **G** and get thee a linen girdle, and put it 1980
13: 4 **g** to Euphrates, and hide it there in a hole of 1980
13: 6 **g** to Euphrates, and take the girdle from 1980
14:18 If I **g forth** *into* the field, then behold 3318
14:18 the priest **g about** into a land that they 5503
15: 1 *them* out of my sight, and let them **g forth**. 3318
15: 2 say unto thee, Whither shall we **g forth**? 3318
15: 5 or who shall **g aside** to ask how thou doest? 5493
16: 5 neither **g** to lament nor bemoan them: 1980
16: 8 Thou shalt not also **g** *into* the house of 935
17:19 **G** and stand in the gate of the children of 1980
17:19 by the which they **g out**, and in all the gates 3318
18: 2 **g down** *to* the potter's house, and there I 3381
18:11 Now therefore **g to**, speak to the men of 4994
19: 1 **G** and get a potter's earthen bottle, and 1980
19: 2 **g forth** unto the valley of the son of 3318
19:10 in the sight of the men that **g** with thee. 1980
20: 6 all that dwell in thine house shall **g** into 1980
21: 2 wondrous works, that he may **g up** from us. 5927
21:12 lest my fury **g out** like fire, and burn that 3318
22: 1 **G down** *to* the house of the king of Judah, 3381
22:20 **G up** *to* Lebanon, and cry; and lift up thy 5927
22:22 and thy lovers shall **g** into captivity: 1980
25: 6 **g** not after other gods to serve them, and 1980
25:32 evil *shall* **g forth** from nation to nation, and 3318
27:18 of Judah, and at Jerusalem, **g** not to Babylon. 935
28:13 **G** and tell Hananiah, saying, Thus saith 1980
29:12 ye shall **g** and pray unto me, and I will 1980
30:16 every one of them, shall **g** into captivity; 1980
31: 4 shalt **g forth** in the dances of them that 3318
31: 6 let us **g up** *to* Zion unto the LORD our 5927
31:22 How long wilt thou **g about**, O thou 2559
31:24 and they *that* **g forth** with flocks. 5265
31:39 the measuring line shall yet **g forth** over 3318
34: 2 **G** and speak to Zedekiah king of Judah, 1980
34: 3 to mouth, and thou shalt **g** to Babylon. 935
34: 9 *being* a Hebrew or a Hebrewess, **g** free; 7971
34:10 and every one his maidservant, **g** free, 7971
34:10 any more, then they obeyed, and **let** *them* **g**. 7971
34:11 whom they had **let g** free, to return, and 7971
34:14 At the end of seven years **let** ye **g** every 7971
34:14 thou shalt **let** him **g** free from thee: 7971
35: 2 **G** unto the house of the Rechabites, and 1980
35:11 let us **g** *to* Jerusalem for fear of the army of 935
35:13 **G** and tell the men of Judah and 1980
35:15 **g** not after other gods to serve them, and 1980
36: 5 I cannot **g** *into* the house of the LORD: 935
36: 6 Therefore **g** thou, and read in the roll, 935
36:19 **G**, hide thee, thou and Jeremiah; 1980
37:12 Jeremiah went forth out of Jerusalem to **g** 1980
38:17 If thou wilt **assuredly g forth** unto 3318+3318
38:18 if thou wilt not **g forth** to the king of 3318
38:21 if thou refuse to **g forth**, this *is* the word 3318
39:16 **G** and speak to Ebed-melech the Ethiopian, 1980
40: 1 of the guard had **let** him **g** from Ramah, 7971
40: 4 seemeth good and convenient for thee to **g**, 1980
40: 4 and convenient for thee to go, thither **g**. 1980
40: 5 *he said*, **G back** also to Gedaliah the son of 7725
40: 5 **g** wheresoever it seemeth convenient unto 1980
40: 5 it seemeth convenient unto thee to **g**. 1980
40: 5 him victuals and a reward, and **let** him **g**. 7971
40:15 saying, Let me **g**, I pray thee, and I will 1980
41:10 and departed to **g over** to the Ammonites. 5674
41:17 *is* by Beth-lehem, to **g** to enter *into* Egypt, 1980
42:14 we will **g** *into* the land of Egypt, where we 935
42:15 to enter *into* Egypt, and **g** to sojourn there; 935
42:17 their faces to **g** *into* Egypt to sojourn there; 935
42:19 O ye remnant of Judah; **G** ye not *into* Egypt: 935
42:22 in the place whither ye desire to **g** *and* 935
43: 2 to say, **G** not *into* Egypt to sojourn there: 935
43:12 and he shall **g forth** from thence in peace. 3318
44:12 that have set their faces to **g** *into* the land of 935
46: 8 I will **g up**, *and* will cover the earth; 5927
46:11 **G up** *into* Gilead, and take balm, O virgin, 5927
46:16 let us **g again** to our own people, and to 7725
46:19 furnish thyself to **g into captivity**: 1473
46:22 The voice thereof shall **g** like a serpent; 1980
48: 5 up of Luhith continual weeping shall **g up**; 5927
48: 7 Chemosh shall **g forth** into captivity *with* 3318
49: 3 for their king shall **g** into captivity, *and* 1980
49:12 *that* shall **altogether g unpunished**? 5352+5352
49:12 thou shalt not **g unpunished**, but 5352
49:28 **g up** to Kedar, and spoil the men of 5927
50: 4 they shall **g**, and seek the LORD their 1980
50: 6 shepherds have **caused** them **to g astray**, 8582
50: 8 **g forth** out of the land of the Chaldeans, 3318
50:21 **G up** against the land of Merathaim, 5927
50:27 let them **g down** to the slaughter: 3381
50:33 held them fast; they refused to **let** them **g**. 7971
51: 9 and let us **g** every one into his own country: 1980
51:45 **g** ye **out** of the midst of her, and deliver ye 3318
51:50 escaped the sword, **g** *away*, stand not still: 1980
La 4:18 our steps, that *we* cannot **g** in our streets: 1980
Eze 1:12 whither the spirit was to **g**, they went; *and* 1980
1:20 Whithersoever the spirit was to **g**, 1980
1:20 they went, thither *was their* spirit to **g**; 1980
3: 1 and **g** speak unto the house of Israel. 1980
3: 4 he said unto me, Son of man, **g**, get thee 1980
3:11 **g**, get thee to them of the captivity, unto 1980
3:22 **g forth** into the plain, and I will there talk 3318
3:24 and spake with me, and said unto me, **G**, 935
3:25 and thou shalt not **g out** among them: 3318
6: 9 which **g a whoring** after their idols: 2181
8: 6 that *I* should **g far off** from my sanctuary? 7368
8: 9 **G in**, and behold the wicked abominations 935
9: 4 **G through** the midst of the city through 5674
9: 5 **G** ye after him through the city, and smite: 5674
9: 7 **g** ye **forth**. And they went forth, and 3318
10: 2 said, **G** in between the wheels, *even* under 935
12: 4 thou shalt **g forth** at even in their sight, 3318
12: 4 as they that **g forth** into captivity. 4161
12:11 they shall remove *and* **g** into captivity. 1980
12:12 shoulder in the twilight, and shall **g forth**: 3318
13:20 from your arms, and will let the souls **g**, 7971
14:11 of Israel may **g** no more **astray** from me, 8582
14:17 and say, Sword, **g** through the land; 5674
15: 7 they shall **g out** from *one* fire, and *another* 3318
20:10 Wherefore I **caused** them **to g forth** out of 3318
20:29 What *is* the high place whereunto ye **g**? 935
20:39 **G** ye, serve ye every one his idols, and 1980
21: 4 shall my sword **g forth** out of his sheath 3318
21:16 **G** thee **one way or other**, *either* on the right 258
23:44 as *they* **g in** unto a woman that playeth 935
24:14 I will do *it*; I will not **g back**, neither will I 6544
26:11 thy strong garrisons shall **g down** to 3381
26:20 of old, with them that **g down** to the pit, 3381
30: 9 In that day shall messengers **g forth** from 3318
30:17 and these *cities* shall **g** into captivity. 1980
30:18 and her daughters shall **g** into captivity. 1980
31:14 of men, with them that **g down** to the pit. 3381
32:18 with them that **g down** into the pit. 3381
32:19 **g down**, and be thou laid with 3381
32:24 shame with them that **g down** to the pit. 3381
32:25 shame with them that **g down** to the pit: 3381
32:29 and with them that **g down** to the pit. 3381
32:30 bear their shame with them that **g down** to 3381
38:11 I will **g up** to the land of unwalled villages; 5927
38:11 I will **g** *to* them that are at rest, that dwell 935
39: 9 dwell in the cities of Israel shall **g forth**, 3318
40:26 *there were* seven steps to **g up** to it, and 5930
42:14 shall they not **g out** of the holy *place* into 3318
44: 3 and shall **g out** by the way of the same. 3318
44:19 when they **g forth** into the utter court, 3318
46: 2 he shall **g forth**; but the gate shall not be 3318
46: 8 he shall **g in** *by* the way of the porch of *that* 935
46: 8 and he shall **g forth** by the way thereof. 3318
46: 9 shall **g out** *by* the way of the south gate; 3318
46: 9 shall **g forth** *by* the way of the north gate: 3318
46: 9 he came in, but shall **g forth** over against it. 3318
46:10 midst of them, when they **g in**, shall go in; 935
46:10 midst of them, when they go in, shall **g in**; 935
46:10 and when they **g forth**, shall go forth. 3318
46:10 and when they go forth, shall **g forth**. 3318
46:12 he shall **g forth**; and after his going forth 3318
47: 8 **g down** into the desert, and go into the sea: 3381
47: 8 go down into the desert, and **g** into the sea: 935
47:15 the way of Hethlon, as *men* **g** to Zedad; 935
Da 11:44 he shall **g forth** with great fury to destroy, 3318
12: 9 he said, **G** thy way, Daniel: for the words 1980
12:13 **g** thou thy way till the end *be*: for thou shalt 1980
Hos 1: 2 the LORD said to Hosea, **G**, take unto 1980
2: 5 for she said, I will **g** after my lovers, 1980
2: 7 I will **g** and return to my first husband; 1980
3: 1 said the LORD unto me, **G** yet, love a 1980
4:15 neither **g** ye **up** *to* Beth-aven, nor swear, 5927
5: 6 They shall **g** with their flocks and with their 1980
5:14 I, *even* I, will tear and **g away**; I will take 1980
5:15 I will **g** *and* return to my place, till they 1980
7:11 they call to Egypt, they **g** to Assyria. 1980
7:12 When they shall **g**, I will spread my net 1980
11: 3 I **taught** Ephraim also **to g**, taking them by 7270
Joel 2:16 let the bridegroom **g forth** of his chamber, 3318
Am 1: 5 the people of Syria shall **g into captivity** 1540
1:15 their king shall **g** into captivity, he and 1980
2: 7 and his father will **g in** unto the *same* maid, 1980
4: 3 ye shall **g out** *at* the breaches, every *cow at* 3318
5: 5 Gilgal shall **surely g into captivity**, 1540+1540
5:27 **cause** you **to g into captivity** beyond 1540
6: 2 and from thence **g** ye *to* Hamath the great: 1980
6: 2 **g down** *to* Gath of the Philistines: *be they* 3381
6: 7 Therefore now shall they **g captive** with 1540
6: 7 they go captive with the first that **g captive**, 1540
7:12 Amaziah said unto Amos, O thou seer, **g**, 1980
7:15 the LORD said unto me, **G**, prophesy unto 1980
7:17 Israel shall **surely g into captivity** 1540+1540
8: 9 that I will **cause** the sun **to g down** at noon, 935
9: 4 though they **g** into captivity before their 1980
Jnh 1: 2 Arise, **g** to Nineveh, *that* great city, and 1980
1: 3 to **g** with them unto Tarshish from 935
3: 2 Arise, **g** unto Nineveh, *that* great city, and 1980
Mic 1: 8 and howl, I will **g** stript and naked: 1980
2: 3 your necks; neither shall ye **g** haughtily: 1980
3: 6 the sun shall **g down** over the prophets, and 935
4: 2 let us **g up** to the mountain of the LORD, 5927
4: 2 for the law shall **g forth** of Zion, and 3318
4:10 for now shalt thou **g forth** out of the city, 3318
4:10 the field, and thou shalt **g** *even* to Babylon; 935
5: 8 who, if he **g through**, both treadeth down, 5674
Na 3:14 **g** into clay, and tread the morter, 935
Hab 1: 4 and judgment doth never **g forth**: 3318
Hag 1: 8 **G up** *to* the mountain, and bring wood, and 5927
Zec 6: 5 *which* **g forth** from standing before 3318
6: 6 The black horses which *are* therein **g forth** 3318
6: 6 the white **g forth** after them; and 3318
6: 6 the grisled **g forth** toward the south 3318
6: 7 sought to **g** that *they* might walk to and 1980
6: 8 these that **g** toward the north country have 3318

Zec 6:10 g into the house of Josiah the son of 935
8:21 the inhabitants of one city shall g to 1980
8:21 Let us g speedily to pray before 1980+1980
8:21 to seek the LORD of hosts: I will g also. 1980
8:23 that is a Jew, saying, We will g with you: 1980
9:14 and his arrow shall g forth as the lightning: 3318
9:14 and shall g with whirlwinds of the south. 1980
14: 2 half of the city shall g forth into captivity, 3318
14: 3 shall the LORD g forth, and fight against 3318
14: 8 that living waters shall g out from 3318
14:16 g up from year to year to worship the King, 5927
14:18 if the family of Egypt g not up, and 5927
Mal 4: 2 ye shall g forth, and grow up as calves of 3318
Mt 2: 8 G and search diligently for the young child; 4198
2:20 his mother, and g into the land of Israel: 4198
2:22 his father Herod, he was afraid to g thither: 565
5:24 thy gift before the altar, and g thy way; 5217
5:41 And whosoever shall compel thee to g a mile, 29
5:41 compel thee to go a mile, g with him twain. 5217
7:13 and many there be which g in thereat: 1525
8: 4 See thou tell no man; but g thy way, 5217
8: 9 and I say to this man, G, and he goeth; and 4198
8:13 Jesus said unto the centurion, G thy way; 5217
8:21 Lord, suffer me first to g and bury my father. 565
8:31 suffer us to g away into the herd of swine. 565
8:32 And he said unto them, G. And when they 5217
9: 6 take up thy bed, and g unto thine house. 5217
9:13 But g ye and learn what that meaneth, I will 4198
10: 5 G not into the way of the Gentiles, and 565
10: 6 But g rather to the lost sheep of the house 4198
10: 7 And as ye g, preach, saying, The kingdom 4198
10:11 is worthy; and there abide till ye g thence. 1831
11: 4 G and shew John again those things which 4198
13:28 Wilt thou then that we g and gather them up? 565
14:15 that they may g into the villages, and 565
14:22 and to g before him unto the other side, 4254
14:29 he walked on the water, to g to Jesus. 2064
16:21 how that he must g unto Jerusalem, and 565
17:27 g thou to the sea, and cast a hook, and 4198
18:15 g and tell him his fault between thee and 5217
19:21 g and sell that thou hast, and give to 5217
19:24 It is easier for a camel to g through 1330
20: 4 G ye also into the vineyard, and 5217
20: 7 unto them, G ye also into the vineyard; 5217
20:14 Take that thine is, and g thy way: I will 5217
20:18 Behold, we g up to Jerusalem; and the Son 305
21: 2 G into the village over against you, and 4198
21:28 said, Son, g work to day in my vineyard. 5217
21:30 And he answered and said, I g, sir: and NIG
21:31 g into the kingdom of God before you. 4254
22: 9 G ye therefore into the highways, 4198
23:13 for ye neither g in yourselves, 1525
23:13 suffer ye them that are entering to g in. 1525
24:26 Behold, he is in the desert; g not forth: 1831
25: 6 bridegroom cometh; g ye out to meet him. 1831
25: 9 but g ye rather to them that sell, and buy for 4198
25:46 And these shall g away into everlasting 565
26:18 G into the city to such a man, and say unto 5217
26:32 But after I am risen again, I will g before 4254
26:36 Sit ye here, while I g and pray yonder. 565
27:65 g your way, make it as sure as you can. 5217
28: 7 And g quickly, and tell his disciples that he 4198
28:10 g tell my brethren that they go into Galilee, 5217
28:10 go tell my brethren that they g into Galilee, 565
28:19 G ye therefore, and teach all nations, 4198
Mk 1:38 said unto them, Let us g into the next towns, 71
1:44 say nothing to any man: but g thy way, 5217
2:11 up thy bed, and g thy way into thine house. 5217
5:19 G home to thy friends, and tell them how 5217
5:34 g in peace, and be whole of thy plague. 5217
6:36 that they may g into the country round about, 565
6:37 Shall we g and buy two hundred pennyworth 565
6:38 g and see. And when they knew, they say, 5217
6:45 to g to the other side before unto 4254
7:29 he said unto her, For this saying g thy way; 5217
8:26 saying, Neither g into the town, nor tell it 1525
9:43 than having two hands to g into hell, into 565
10:21 g thy way, sell whatsoever thou hast, and 5217
10:25 It is easier for a camel to g through the eye 1330
10:33 Saying, Behold, we g up to Jerusalem; and 305
10:52 And Jesus said unto him, G thy way; 5217
11: 2 G your way into the village over against 5217
11: 6 Jesus had commanded: and they let them g. 863
12:38 which love to g in long clothing, and 4043
13:15 on the housetop not g down into the house, 2597
14:12 Where wilt thou that we g and prepare that 565
14:13 G ye into the city, and there shall meet you 5217
14:14 And wheresoever he shall g in, say ye to 1525
14:28 I am risen, I will g before you into Galilee. 4254
14:42 Rise up, let us g; lo, he that betrayeth me is at 71
16: 7 But g your way, tell his disciples and Peter 5217
16:15 G ye into all the world, and preach 4198
Lk 1:17 And he shall g before him in the spirit and 4281
1:76 for thou shalt g before the face of the Lord 4313
2:15 Let us now g even unto Bethlehem, and 1330
5:14 And he charged him to tell no man: but g, 565
5:24 take up thy couch, and g into thine house. 4198
7: 8 and I say unto one, G, and he goeth; 4198
7:22 G your way, and tell John what things ye 4198
7:50 Thy faith hath saved thee; g in peace. 4198
8:14 g forth, and are choked with cares and 4198
8:22 Let us g over unto the other side of 1330
8:31 not command them to g out into the deep. 565
8:48 thy faith hath made thee whole; g in peace.) 4198
8:51 he suffered no man to g in, save Peter, 1525
9: 5 not receive you, when ye g out of that city, 1831
9:12 that they may g into the towns and 565
9:13 except we should g and buy meat for all 4198
9:51 he stedfastly set his face to g to Jerusalem, 4198
9:53 his face was as though he would g to 4198
9:59 Lord, suffer me first to g and bury my father. 565
9:60 but g thou and preach the kingdom of God. 565
9:61 but let me first g bid them farewell, NIG
10: 3 G your ways: behold, I send you forth as 5217
10: 7 of his hire. G not from house to house. 3327
Lk 10:10 g your ways out into the streets of 1831
10:37 Jesus unto him, G, and do thou likewise. 4198
11: 5 and shall g unto him at midnight, and 4198
13:32 G ye, and tell that fox, Behold, I cast out 4198
14: 4 he took him, and healed him, and let him g; 630
14:10 g and sit down in the lowest room; 4198
14:10 he may say unto thee, Friend, g up higher: 4320
14:18 of ground, and I must needs g and see it: 1831
14:19 five yoke of oxen, and I g to prove them: 4198
14:21 G out quickly into the streets and lanes of 1831
14:23 G out into the highways and hedges, and 1831
15: 4 and g after that which is lost, until he find 4198
15:18 I will arise and g to my father, and will say 4198
15:28 And he was angry, and would not g in: 1525
17: 7 from the field, G and sit down to meat? 3928
17:14 G shew yourselves unto the priests. 4198
17:19 g thy way: thy faith hath made thee whole. 4198
17:23 see there: g not after them, nor follow them. 565
18:25 For it is easier for a camel to g through a 1525
18:31 we g up to Jerusalem, and all things that are 305
19:30 G ye into the village over against you; in 5217
21: 8 draweth near: g ye not therefore after them. 4198
22: 8 saying, G and prepare us the passover, 4198
22:33 Lord, I am ready to g with thee, both into 4198
22:68 you, you will not answer me, nor let me g. 630
23:22 I will therefore chastise him, and let him g. 630
Jn 1:43 The day following Jesus would g forth into 1831
4: 4 And he must needs g through 1330
4:16 G, call thy husband, and come hither. 5217
4:50 saith unto him, G thy way; thy son liveth. 4198
6:67 Jesus unto the twelve, Will ye also g away? 5217
6:68 answered him, Lord, to whom shall we g? 565
7: 3 unto him, Depart hence, and g into Judea, 5217
7: 8 G ye up unto this feast: I go not up yet unto 305
7: 8 I g not up yet unto this feast; for my time is 305
7:19 the law? Why g ye about to kill me? 2212
7:33 and then I g unto him that sent me. 5217
7:35 Whither will he g, that we shall not find 4198
7:35 will he g unto the dispersed among 4198
8:11 unto her, Neither do I condemn thee: g, 4198
8:14 for I know whence I came, and whither I g; 5217
8:14 cannot tell whence I come, and whither I g. 5217
8:21 I g my way, and ye shall seek me, and 5217
8:21 in your sins: whither I g, ye cannot come. 5217
8:22 because he saith, Whither I g, ye cannot 5217
9: 7 And said unto him, G, wash in the pool of 5217
9:11 G to the pool of Siloam, and wash: 5217
10: 9 and shall g in and out, and find pasture. 1525
11: 7 he to his disciples, Let us g into Judea again. 71
11:11 but I g, that I may awake him out of sleep. 4198
11:15 may believe; nevertheless let us g unto him. 71
11:16 unto his fellow-disciples, Let us also g, 71
11:44 saith unto them, Loose him, and let him g. 5217
13:33 the Jews, Whither I g, ye cannot come; 5217
13:36 Jesus answered him, Whither I g, 5217
14: 2 told you. I g to prepare a place for you. 4198
14: 3 And if I g and prepare a place for you, 4198
14: 4 And whither I g ye know, and the way ye 5217
14:12 shall he do; because I g unto my Father. 4198
14:28 I g away, and come again unto you. 5217
14:28 because I said, I g unto the Father: 4198
14:31 even so I do. Arise, let us g hence. 71
15:16 that you should g and bring forth fruit, and 5217
16: 5 But now I g my way to him that sent me; 5217
16: 7 It is expedient for you that I g away: 565
16: 7 for if I g not away, the Comforter will not 565
16:10 because I g to my Father, and ye see me no 5217
16:16 ye shall see me, because I g to the Father. 5217
16:17 see me: and, Because I g to the Father? 5217
16:28 I leave the world, and g to the Father. 4198
18: 8 therefore ye seek me, let these g their way: 5217
19:12 Jews cried out, saying, If thou let this man g, 630
20:17 but g to my brethren, and say unto them, 4198
21: 3 Simon Peter saith unto them, I g a fishing. 5217
21: 3 They say unto him, We also g with thee. 2064
Ac 1:11 come in like manner as ye have seen him g 4198
1:25 that he might g to his own place. 4198
3: 3 and John about to g into the temple, 1524
3:13 when he was determined to let him g. 630
4:15 them to g aside out of the council, 565
4:21 had further threatened them, they let them g, 630
4:23 And being let g, they went to their own 630
5:20 G, stand and speak in the temple to 4198
5:40 speak in the name of Jesus, and let them g. 630
7:40 unto Aaron, Make us gods to g before us: 4313
8:26 g toward the south unto the way that goeth 4198
8:29 G near, and join thyself to this chariot. 4334
9: 6 and g into the city, and it shall be 1525
9:11 g into the street which is called Straight, 4198
9:15 G thy way: for he is a chosen vessel unto 4198
10:20 and get thee down, and g with them, 4198
11:12 And the Spirit bade me g with them, 4905
11:22 that he should g as far as Antioch. 1330
12:17 G shew these things unto James, and to NIG
15: 2 should g up to Jerusalem unto the apostles 305
15:33 they were let g in peace from the brethren 630
15:36 Let us g again and visit our brethren in 1994
16: 3 Him would Paul have to g forth with him; 1831
16: 7 to Mysia, they assayed to g into Bithynia: 4198
16:10 immediately we endeavoured to g into 1831
16:35 sent the sergeants, saying, Let those men g. 630
16:36 The magistrates have sent to let you g: 630
16:36 now therefore depart, and g in peace. 4198
17: 9 of Jason, and of the other, they let them g. 630
17:14 sent away Paul to g as it were to the sea: 4198
18: 6 from henceforth I will g unto the Gentiles. 4198
19:21 and Achaia, to g to Jerusalem, saying, 4198
20: 1 and departed for to g into Macedonia. 4198
20:13 he appointed, minding himself to g afoot. 3978
20:22 I g bound in the spirit unto Jerusalem, 4198
21: 4 that he should not g up to Jerusalem. 305
21:12 besought him not to g up to Jerusalem. 305
22:10 said unto me, Arise, and g into Damascus; 4198
23:10 commanded the soldiers to g down, and 2597
23:23 Make ready two hundred soldiers to g to 4198
Ac 23:32 On the morrow they left the horsemen to g 4198
24:25 and answered, G thy way for this time; 4198
25: 5 g down with me, and accuse this man, 4782
25: 9 Wilt thou g up to Jerusalem, and there be 305
25:12 unto Cesar? unto Cesar shalt thou g. 4198
25:20 I asked him whether he would g to 4198
27: 3 gave him liberty to g unto his friends to 4198
28:18 would have let me g, because there was no 630
28:26 Saying, G unto this people, and say, 4198
Ro 15:25 But now I g unto Jerusalem to minister 4198
1Co 5:10 for then must ye needs g out of the world. 1831
6: 1 g to law before the unjust, and not before 2919
6: 7 ye g to law one with another. 2192+2917
10:27 bid you to a feast, and ye be disposed to g; 4198
16: 4 And if it be meet that I g also, they shall g 4198
16: 4 be meet that I go also, they shall g with me. 4198
16: 6 bring me on my journey whithersoever I g. 4198
2Co 9: 5 that they would g before unto you, and 4281
Gal 2: 9 that we should g unto the heathen, and NIG
Eph 4:26 let not the sun g down upon your wrath: 1931
Php 2:23 as I shall see how it will g with me. 3588+4012
1Th 4: 6 That no man g beyond and defraud his 5233
Heb 6: 1 of Christ, let us g on unto perfection; 5342
11: 8 when he was called to g out into a place 1831
13:13 Let us g forth therefore unto him without 1831
Jas 4:13 G to now, ye that say, To day or to morrow 71
4:13 or to morrow we will g into such a city, 4198
5: 1 G to now, ye rich men, weep and howl for 71
Rev 3:12 of my God, and he shall g no more out: 1831
10: 8 G and take the little book which is open in 5217
13:10 He that leadeth into captivity shall g into 5217
16: 1 G your ways, and pour out the vials of 5217
16:14 which g forth unto the kings of the earth 1607
17: 8 of the bottomless pit, and g into perdition: 5217
20: 8 And shall g out to deceive the nations 1831

GOAD (1) [GOADS]

Jdg 3:31 Philistines six hundred men with an ox g: 4451

GOADS (2) [GOAD]

1Sa 13:21 for the axes, and to sharpen the g. 1861
Ecc 12:11 The words of the wise are as g, and as nails 1861

GOAH See GOATH

GOAT (35) [GOATS, GOATS', GOATSKINS, SCAPEGOAT]

Ge 15: 9 a she g of three years old, and a ram of 5795
Lev 3:12 if his offering be a g, then he shall offer it 5795
4:24 he shall lay his hand upon the head of the g, 8163
7:23 no manner fat, of ox, or of sheep, or of g. 5795
9:15 the people's offering, and took the g, 8163
10:16 Moses diligently sought the g of the sin 8163
16: 9 Aaron shall bring the g upon which 8163
16:10 the g, on which the lot fell to be 8163
16:15 shall he kill the g of the sin offering, that is 8163
16:18 of the blood of the g, and put it upon 8163
16:20 and the altar, he shall bring the live g: 8163
16:21 both his hands upon the head of the live g, 8163
16:21 putting them upon the head of the g, and 8163
16:22 the g shall bear upon him all their iniquities 8163
16:22 and he shall let go the g in the wilderness. 8163
16:26 he that let go the g for the scapegoat shall 8163
16:27 sin offering, and the g for the sin offering, 8163
17: 3 or lamb, or g, in the camp, or that killeth it 5795
22:27 or a sheep, or a g, is brought forth, then 5795
Nu 15:27 he shall bring a she g of the first year for a 5795
18:17 or the firstling of a g, thou shalt not 5795
28:22 one g for a sin offering, to make an 8163
29:22 one g for a sin offering; beside 8163
29:28 one g for a sin offering; beside 8163
29:31 one g for a sin offering; beside 8163
29:34 one g for a sin offering; beside 8163
29:38 one g for a sin offering; beside 8163
Dt 14: 4 shall eat: the ox, the sheep, and the g, 5795+7716
14: 5 the wild g, and the pygarg, and the wild ox, 689
Pr 30:31 a he g also; and a king, against whom there 8495
Eze 43:25 Seven days shalt thou prepare every day a g 8163
Da 8: 5 a he g came from the west on 5795+6842
8: 5 the g had a notable horn between his eyes. 6842
8: 8 Therefore the he g waxed very great: 5795+6842
8:21 the rough g is the king of Grecia: and 6842

GOAT IDOLS See DEVILS

GOATH (1)

Jer 31:39 hill Gareb, and shall compass about to G. 1601

GOATS (87) [GOAT]

Ge 27: 9 me from thence two good kids of the g; 5795
27:16 she put the skins of the kids of the g upon 5795
30:32 and the spotted and speckled among the g: 5795
30:33 is not speckled and spotted amongst the g, 5795
30:35 he removed that day the he g that were 8495
30:35 all the she g that were speckled and 5795
31:38 and thy she g have not cast their young, 5795
32:14 Two hundred she g, and twenty he goats, 5795
32:14 twenty he g, two hundred ewes, and 8495
37:31 killed a kid of the g, and dipped the coat in 5795
Ex 12: 5 take it out from the sheep, or from the g: 5795
Lev 1:10 the sheep, or of the g, for a burnt sacrifice; 5795
4:23 a kid of the g, a male without blemish; 5795
4:28 a kid of the g, a female without blemish, 5795
5: 6 a lamb or a kid of the g, for a sin offering; 5795
9: 3 Take ye a kid of the g for a sin offering; 5795
16: 5 of Israel two kids of the g for a sin offering, 5795
16: 7 he shall take the two g, and present them 8163
16: 8 Aaron shall cast lots upon the two g; 8163
22:19 of the beeves, of the sheep, or of the g. 5795
23:19 ye shall sacrifice one kid of the g for a sin 5795
Nu 7:16 One kid of the g for a sin offering: 5795
7:17 two oxen, five rams, five he g, five lambs 6260
7:22 One kid of the g for a sin offering: 5795
7:23 two oxen, five rams, five he g, five lambs 6260

Nu 7:28 One kid of the **g** for a sin offering: 5795
7:29 two oxen, five rams, five **he g**, five lambs 6260
7:34 One kid of the **g** for a sin offering: 5795
7:35 two oxen, five rams, five he **g**, five lambs 6260
7:40 One kid of the **g** for a sin offering: 5795
7:41 two oxen, five rams, five **he g**, five lambs 6260
7:46 One kid of the **g** for a sin offering: 5795
7:47 two oxen, five rams, five **he g**, five lambs 6260
7:52 One kid of the **g** for a sin offering: 5795
7:53 two oxen, five rams, five **he g**, five lambs 6260
7:58 One kid of the **g** for a sin offering: 5795
7:59 two oxen, five rams, five **he g**, five lambs 6260
7:64 One kid of the **g** for a sin offering: 5795
7:65 two oxen, five rams, five **he g**, five lambs 6260
7:70 One kid of the **g** for a sin offering: 5795
7:71 two oxen, five rams, five **he g**, five lambs 6260
7:76 One kid of the **g** for a sin offering: 5795
7:77 two oxen, five rams, five **he g**, five lambs 6260
7:82 One kid of the **g** for a sin offering: 5795
7:83 two oxen, five rams, five **he g**, five lambs 6260
7:87 the kids of the **g** for sin offering twelve. 5795
7:88 four bullocks, the rams sixty, the **he g** sixty, 6260
15:24 and one kid of the **g** for a sin offering. 5795
28:15 one kid of the **g** for a sin offering unto 5795
28:30 *And* one kid of the **g**, to make an atonement 5795
29: 5 one kid of the **g** for a sin offering, to make 5795
29:11 One kid of the **g** *for* a sin offering; beside 5795
29:16 one kid of the **g** *for* a sin offering; beside 5795
29:19 one kid of the **g** *for* a sin offering; beside 5795
29:25 one kid of the **g** *for* a sin offering; beside 5795
Dt 32:14 and rams of the breed of Bashan, and **g**, 6260
1Sa 24: 2 and his men upon the rocks of the **wild g**. 3277
25: 2 three thousand sheep, and a thousand **g**: 5795
2Ch 17:11 seven thousand and seven hundred **he g**. 8495
29:21 seven lambs, and seven **he g**, 5795+6842
29:23 they brought forth the **he g** for the sin 8163
Ezr 6:17 offering for all Israel, twelve **he g**, 5796+6841
8:35 seven lambs, twelve **he g** *for* a sin offering: 6842
Job 39: 1 Knowest thou the time when the **wild g** of 3277
Ps 50: 9 out of thy house, *nor* **he g** out of thy folds. 6260
50:13 the flesh of bulls, or drink the blood of **g**? 6260
66:15 of rams; I will offer bullocks with **g**. 6260
104:18 The high hills *are* a refuge for the **wild g**; 3277
Pr 27:26 and the **g** *are* the price of the field. 6260
SS 4: 1 thy hair *is* as a flock of **g**, that appear from 5795
6: 5 thy hair *is* as a flock of **g** that appear from 5795
Isa 1:11 blood of bullocks, or of lambs, or of **he g**. 6260
34: 6 *and* with the blood of lambs and **g**, 6260
Jer 50: 8 and be as the he **g** before the flocks. 6260
51:40 lambs to the slaughter, like rams with **he g**. 6260
Eze 27:21 with thee in lambs, and rams, and **g**: 6260
34:17 and cattle, between the rams and the **he g**. 6260
39:18 of rams, of lambs, and of **g**, of bullocks, 6260
43:22 of the **g** without blemish for a sin offering; 5795
45:23 and a kid of the **g** daily *for* a sin offering. 5795
Zec 10: 3 against the shepherds, and I punished the **g**: 6260
Mt 25:32 as a shepherd divideth *his* sheep from the **g**: *2056*
25:33 on his right hand, but the **g** on the left. *2055*
Heb 9:12 Neither by the blood of **g** and calves, *5131*
9:13 For if the blood of bulls and of **g**, and *5131*
9:19 he took the blood of calves and of **g**, *5131*
10: 4 of bulls and of **g** should take away sins. *5131*

GOATS' (10) [GOAT]

Ex 25: 4 and scarlet, and fine linen, and **g** *hair*, 5795
26: 7 thou shalt make curtains *of* **g** *hair* to be a 5795
35: 6 and scarlet, and fine linen, and **g** *hair*, 5795
35:23 **g** *hair*, and red skins of rams, and 5795
35:26 stirred them up in wisdom spun **g** *hair*. 5795
36:14 he made curtains *of* **g** *hair* for the tent over 5795
Nu 31:20 all work of **g** *hair*, and all things made of 5795
1Sa 19:13 put a pillow of **g** *hair for* his bolster, and 5795
19:16 with a pillow of **g** *hair for* his bolster. 5795
Pr 27:27 *thou shalt have* **g** milk enough for thy food, 5795

GOATSKINS (1) [GOAT, SKIN]

Heb 11:37 wandered about in sheepskins and **g**, *122+1192*

GOB (2)

2Sa 21:18 was again a battle with the Philistines at **G**: 1359
21:19 there was again a battle in **G** with 1359

GOBLET (1)

SS 7: 2 Thy navel *is like* a round **g**, *which* wanteth 101

GOD (4135) [BETH-EL, GOD'S, GOD-WARD, GODDESS, GODHEAD, GODLINESS, GODLY, GODS, UNGODLINESS; See also GOD*]

Ge 1: 1 In the beginning **G** created the heaven and 430
1: 2 the Spirit of **G** moved upon the face of 430
1: 3 **G** said, Let there be light: and there was 430
1: 4 **G** saw the light, that *it was* good: and 430
1: 4 and **G** divided the light from the darkness. 430
1: 5 **G** called the light Day, and the darkness he 430
1: 6 **G** said, Let there be a firmament in the midst 430
1: 7 **G** made the firmament, and divided 430
1: 8 **G** called the firmament Heaven. And 430
1: 9 **G** said, Let the waters under the heaven be 430
1:10 **G** called the dry *land* Earth; and 430
1:10 called he Seas: and **G** saw that *it was* good. 430
1:11 **G** said, Let the earth bring forth grass, 430
1:12 after his kind: and **G** saw that *it was* good. 430
1:14 **G** said, Let there be lights in the firmament 430
1:16 **G** made two great lights; the greater light to 430
1:17 **G** set them in the firmament of the heaven to 430
1:18 the darkness: and **G** saw that *it was* good. 430
1:20 **G** said, Let the waters bring forth abundantly 430
1:21 **G** created great whales, and every living 430
1:21 after his kind: and **G** saw that *it was* good. 430
1:22 And **G** blessed them, saying, Be fruitful, and 430
1:24 **G** said, Let the earth bring forth the living 430
1:25 **G** made the beast of the earth after his kind, 430
1:25 after his kind: and **G** saw that *it was* good. 430
1:26 And **G** said, Let us make man in our image, 430
Ge 1:27 So **G** created man in his own image, in 430
1:27 in the image of **G** created he him; 430
1:28 **G** blessed them, and God said unto them, 430
1:28 **G** said unto them, Be fruitful, and multiply, 430
1:29 **G** said, Behold, I have given you every herb 430
1:31 **G** saw every thing that he had made, and 430
2: 2 on the seventh day **G** ended his work which 430
2: 3 **G** blessed the seventh day, and sanctified it: 430
2: 3 rested from all his work which **G** created 430
2: 4 in the day that the LORD **G** made the earth 430
2: 5 for the LORD **G** had not caused it to rain 430
2: 7 the LORD **G** formed man *of* the dust of 430
2: 8 the LORD **G** planted a garden eastward in 430
2: 9 out of the ground made the LORD **G** to 430
2:15 the LORD **G** took the man, and put him 430
2:16 the LORD **G** commanded the man, saying, 430
2:18 the LORD **G** said, *It is* not good that 430
2:19 out of the ground the LORD **G** formed 430
2:21 the LORD **G** caused a deep sleep to fall 430
2:22 which the LORD **G** had taken from man, 430
3: 1 of the field which the LORD **G** had made. 430
3: 1 he said unto the woman, Yea, hath **G** said, 430
3: 3 **G** hath said, Ye shall not eat of it, 430
3: 5 For **G** doth know that in the day ye eat 430
3: 8 they heard the voice of the LORD **G** 430
3: 8 LORD **G** amongst the trees of the garden. 430
3: 9 the LORD **G** called unto Adam, and 430
3:13 the LORD **G** said unto the woman, What *is* 430
3:14 the LORD **G** said unto the serpent, 430
3:21 to his wife did the LORD **G** make coats of 430
3:22 the LORD **G** said, Behold, the man is 430
3:23 Therefore the LORD **G** sent him forth from 430
4:25 For **G**, *said she*, hath appointed me another 430
5: 1 In the day that **G** created man, in 430
5: 1 in the likeness of **G** made he him; 430
5:22 Enoch walked with **G** after he begat 430
5:24 And Enoch walked with **G**: and he *was* not; 430
5:24 with God: and he *was* not; for **G** took him. 430
6: 2 That the sons of **G** saw the daughters of men 430
6: 4 when the sons of **G** came in unto 430
6: 9 in his generations, *and* Noah walked with **G**. 430
6:11 The earth also was corrupt before **G**, and 430
6:12 **G** looked upon the earth, and behold, it was 430
6:13 **G** said unto Noah, The end of all flesh is 430
6:22 according to all that **G** commanded him, so 430
7: 9 and the female, as **G** had commanded Noah. 430
7:16 of all flesh, as **G** had commanded him: 430
8: 1 **G** remembered Noah, and every living thing, 430
8: 1 **G** made a wind to pass over the earth, and 430
8:15 And **G** spake unto Noah, saying, 430
9: 1 **G** blessed Noah and his sons, and said unto 430
9: 6 be shed: for in the image of **G** made he man. 430
9: 8 **G** spake unto Noah, and to his sons with 430
9:12 **G** said, This *is* the token of the covenant 430
9:16 the everlasting covenant between **G** 430
9:17 **G** said unto Noah, This *is* the token of 430
9:26 he said, Blessed *be* the LORD **G** of Shem; 430
9:27 **G** shall enlarge Japheth, and he shall dwell 430
14:18 and he *was* the priest of the most high **G**. 410
14:19 said, Blessed *be* Abram of the most high **G**, 410
14:20 blessed *be* the most high **G**, which hath 410
14:22 the most high **G**, the possessor of heaven 410
16:13 that spake unto her, Thou **G** seest me: 410
17: 1 and said unto him, I *am* the Almighty **G**; 410
17: 3 on his face: and **G** talked with him, saying, 430
17: 7 to be a **G** unto thee, and to thy seed after 430
17: 8 everlasting possession; and I will be their **G**. 430
17: 9 **G** said unto Abraham, Thou shalt keep my 430
17:15 **G** said unto Abraham, *As for* Sarai thy wife, 430
17:18 Abraham said unto **G**, O that Ishmael might 430
17:19 **G** said, Sarah thy wife shall bear thee a son 430
17:22 with him, and **G** went up from Abraham. 430
17:23 in the selfsame day, as **G** had said unto him. 430
19:29 when **G** destroyed the cities of the plain, 430
19:29 that **G** remembered Abraham, and sent Lot 430
20: 3 **G** came to Abimelech in a dream by night, 430
20: 6 **G** said unto him in a dream, Yea, I know 430
20:11 Surely the fear of **G** *is* not in this place; 430
20:13 when **G** caused me to wander from my 430
20:17 So Abraham prayed unto **G**: and God healed 430
20:17 **G** healed Abimelech, and his wife, and 430
21: 2 at the set time of which **G** had spoken to 430
21: 4 eight days old, as **G** had commanded him. 430
21: 6 **G** hath made me to laugh, *so that* all that 430
21:12 **G** said unto Abraham, Let it not be grievous 430
21:17 **G** heard the voice of the lad; and the angel 430
21:17 the angel of **G** called to Hagar out of heaven, 430
21:17 for **G** hath heard the voice of the lad where 430
21:19 **G** opened her eyes, and she saw a well of 430
21:20 **G** was with the lad; and he grew, and 430
21:22 **G** *is* with thee in all that thou doest: 430
21:23 swear unto me here by **G** that thou wilt not 430
21:33 the name of the LORD, the everlasting **G**. 410
22: 1 that **G** did tempt Abraham, and said unto 430
22: 3 went unto the place of which **G** had told 430
22: 8 **G** will provide himself a lamb for a burnt 430
22: 9 they came to the place which **G** had told him 430
22:12 for now I know that thou fearest **G**, 430
24: 3 the **G** of heaven, and the God of the earth, 430
24: 3 the God of heaven, and the **G** of the earth, 430
24: 7 The LORD **G** of heaven, which took me 430
24:12 O LORD **G** of my master Abraham, I pray 430
24:27 Blessed *be* the LORD **G** of my master 430
24:42 said, O LORD **G** of my master Abraham, 430
24:48 blessed the LORD **G** of my master 430
25:11 of Abraham, that **G** blessed his son Isaac; 430
26:24 and said, I *am* the **G** of Abraham thy father: 430
27:20 Because the LORD thy **G** brought *it* to me. 430
27:28 Therefore **G** give thee of the dew of heaven, 430
28: 3 **G** Almighty bless thee, and make thee 410
28: 4 art a stranger, which **G** gave unto Abraham. 430
28:12 behold the angels of **G** ascending and 430
28:13 I *am* the LORD **G** of Abraham thy father, 430
28:13 of Abraham thy father, and the **G** of Isaac: 430
28:17 this *is* none other but the house of **G**, and 430
Ge 28:20 If **G** will be with me, and will keep me in 430
28:21 in peace; then shall the LORD be my **G**: 430
30: 6 **G** hath judged me, and hath also heard my 430
30:17 **G** hearkened unto Leah, and she conceived, 430
30:18 **G** hath given *me* my hire, because I have 430
30:20 **G** hath endued me with a good dowry; 430
30:22 **G** remembered Rachel, and God hearkened 430
30:22 **G** hearkened to her, and opened her womb. 430
30:23 and said, **G** hath taken away my reproach: 430
31: 5 the **G** of my father hath been with me. 430
31: 7 ten times; but **G** suffered him not to hurt me. 430
31: 9 Thus **G** hath taken away the cattle of your 430
31:11 the angel of **G** spake unto me in a dream, 430
31:13 I *am* the **G** of Beth-el, where thou anointedst 410
31:16 For all the riches which **G** hath taken from 430
31:16 whatsoever **G** hath said unto thee, do. 430
31:24 **G** came to Laban the Syrian in a dream by 430
31:29 the **G** of your father spake unto me 430
31:42 Except the **G** of my father, the God of 430
31:42 the **G** of Abraham, and the fear of Isaac, 430
31:42 **G** hath seen mine affliction and the labour of 430
31:50 see, **G** *is* witness betwixt me and thee. 430
31:53 The **G** of Abraham, and the God of Nahor, 430
31:53 The God of Abraham, and the **G** of Nahor, 430
31:53 the **G** of their father, judge betwixt us. 430
32: 1 on his way, and the angels of **G** met him. 430
32: 9 O **G** of my father Abraham, and God of my 430
32: 9 father Abraham, and **G** of my father Isaac, 430
32:28 for as a prince hast thou power with **G** and 430
32:30 for I have seen **G** face to face, and my life is 430
33: 5 The children which **G** hath graciously given 430
33:10 as though I had seen the face of **G**, and 430
33:11 because **G** hath dealt graciously with me, 430
35: 1 **G** said unto Jacob, Arise, go up to Beth-el, 430
35: 1 make there an altar unto **G**, that appeared 410
35: 3 I will make there an altar unto **G**, 410
35: 5 the terror of **G** was upon the cities that *were* 430
35: 7 because there **G** appeared unto him, when he 430
35: 9 **G** appeared unto Jacob again, when he came 430
35:10 **G** said unto him, Thy name *is* Jacob: 430
35:11 **G** said unto him, I *am* God Almighty: 430
35:11 God said unto him, I *am* **G** Almighty: 410
35:13 **G** went up from him in the place where he 430
35:15 Jacob called the name of the place where **G** 430
39: 9 do this great wickedness, and sin against **G**? 430
40: 8 *Do* not interpretations *belong* to **G**? 430
41:16 **G** shall give Pharaoh an answer of peace. 430
41:25 **G** hath shewed Pharaoh what he *is* about to 430
41:28 What **G** *is* about to do he sheweth unto 430
41:32 *it is* because the thing *is* established by **G**, 430
41:32 by God, and **G** will shortly bring it to pass. 430
41:38 as this *is*, a man in whom the spirit of **G** *is*? 430
41:39 Forasmuch as **G** hath shewed thee all this, 430
41:51 For **G**, *said he*, hath made me forget all my 430
41:52 For **G** hath caused me to be fruitful in 430
42:18 the third day, This do, and live; *for* I fear **G**: 430
42:28 What *is* this *that* **G** hath done unto us? 430
43:14 **G** Almighty give you mercy before the man, 410
43:23 your **G**, and the God of your father, 430
43:23 your God, and the **G** of your father, 430
43:29 he said, **G** be gracious unto thee, my son. 430
44: 7 **G forbid** that thy servants should do 2486
44:16 **G** hath found out the iniquity of thy 430
44:17 he said, **G forbid** that I should do so: *but* 2486
45: 5 for **G** did send me before you to preserve 430
45: 7 **G** sent me before you to preserve you a 430
45: 8 *it was* not you *that* sent me hither, but **G**: 430
45: 9 **G** hath made me lord of all Egypt: 430
46: 1 offered sacrifices unto the **G** of his father 430
46: 2 **G** spake unto Israel in the visions of 430
46: 3 he said, I *am* **G**, the God of thy father: 410
46: 3 he said, I *am* God, the **G** of thy father: 430
48: 3 **G** Almighty appeared unto me at Luz in 410
48: 9 whom **G** hath given me in this *place*. And he 430
48:11 and lo, **G** hath shewed me also thy seed. 430
48:15 he blessed Joseph, and said, **G**, before whom 430
48:15 the **G** which fed me all my life long unto this 430
48:20 **G** make thee as Ephraim and as Manasseh: 430
48:21 **G** shall be with you, and bring you again 430
49:24 by the hands of the mighty **G** of Jacob; NIH
49:25 *Even* by the **G** of thy father, who shall help 410
50:17 forgive the trespass of the servants of the **G** 430
50:19 Fear not: for *am* I in the place of **G**? 430
50:20 *but* **G** meant it unto good, to bring to pass, 430
50:24 **G** will surely visit you, and bring you out of 430
50:25 **G** will surely visit you, and ye shall carry up 430
Ex 1:17 the midwives feared **G**, and did not as 430
1:20 Therefore **G** dealt well with the midwives: 430
1:21 to pass, because the midwives feared **G**, 430
2:23 their cry came up unto **G** by reason of 430
2:24 **G** heard their groaning, and 430
2:24 **G** remembered his covenant with Abraham, 430
2:25 **G** looked upon the children of Israel, and 430
2:25 of Israel, and **G** had respect unto *them*. 430
3: 1 came to the mountain of **G**, *even* to Horeb. 430
3: 4 **G** called unto him out of the midst of 430
3: 6 Moreover he said, I *am* the **G** of thy father, 430
3: 6 the **G** of Abraham, the God of Isaac, and 430
3: 6 the **G** of Isaac, and the God of Jacob. 430
3: 6 the God of Isaac, and the **G** of Jacob. 430
3: 6 his face; for he was afraid to look upon **G**. 430
3:11 Moses said unto **G**, Who *am* I, that I should 430
3:12 ye shall serve **G** upon this mountain. 430
3:13 Moses said unto **G**, Behold, *when* I come 430
3:13 The **G** of your fathers hath sent me unto you; 430
3:14 And **G** said unto Moses, I AM THAT I AM: 430
3:15 **G** said moreover unto Moses, Thus shalt 430
3:15 The LORD **G** of your fathers, the God of 430
3:15 the **G** of Abraham, the God of Isaac, and 430
3:15 the **G** of Isaac, and the God of Jacob, 430
3:15 the God of Isaac, and the **G** of Jacob, 430
3:16 unto them, The LORD **G** of your fathers, 430
3:16 the **G** of Abraham, of Isaac, and of Jacob, 430
3:18 The LORD **G** of the Hebrews hath met 430
3:18 that we may sacrifice to the LORD our **G**. 430

G

Ex 4: 5 That they may believe that the LORD **G** of 430
4: 5 the **G** of Abraham, the God of Isaac, and 430
4: 5 the **G** of Isaac, and the God of Jacob, 430
4: 5 the God of Isaac, and the **G** of Jacob, 430
4:16 and thou shalt be to him instead of **G**. 430
4:20 and Moses took the rod of **G** in his hand. 430
4:27 met him in the mount of **G**, and kissed him. 430
5: 1 Thus saith the LORD **G** of Israel, 430
5: 3 The **G** of the Hebrews hath met with us: 430
5: 3 and sacrifice unto the LORD our **G**; 430
5: 8 saying, Let us go *and* sacrifice to our **G**. 430
6: 2 And **G** spake unto Moses, and said unto him, 430
6: 3 by *the name of* **G** Almighty, but *by* my name 410
6: 7 to me for a people, and I will be to you a **G**: 430
6: 7 ye shall know that I *am* the LORD your **G**, 430
7: 1 See, I have made thee a **g** to Pharaoh: 430
7:16 The LORD **G** of the Hebrews hath sent me 430
8:10 *there is* none like unto the LORD our **G**. 430
8:19 said unto Pharaoh, This *is* the finger of **G**: 430
8:25 said, Go ye, sacrifice to your **G** in the land. 430
8:26 of the Egyptians to the LORD our **G**: 430
8:27 sacrifice to the LORD our **G**, as he shall 430
8:28 that ye may sacrifice to the LORD your **G** 430
9: 1 Thus saith the LORD **G** of the Hebrews, 430
9:13 Thus saith the LORD **G** of the Hebrews, 430
9:30 know that ye will not yet fear the LORD **G**. 430
10: 3 Thus saith the LORD **G** of the Hebrews, 430
10: 7 that they may serve the LORD their **G**: 430
10: 8 unto them, Go, serve the LORD your **G**: 430
10:16 I have sinned against the LORD your **G**, 430
10:17 *this* once, and intreat the LORD your **G**, 430
10:25 we may sacrifice unto the LORD our **G**. 430
10:26 must we take to serve the LORD our **G**; 430
13:17 that **G** led them not *through* the way of 430
13:17 for **G** said, Lest peradventure the people 430
13:18 **G** led the people about, *through* the way of 430
13:19 of Israel, saying, **G** will surely visit you; 430
14:19 the angel of **G**, which went before the camp 430
15: 2 he *is* my **G**, and I will prepare him a 410
15: 2 my father's **G**, and I will exalt him. 430
15:26 hearken to the voice of the LORD thy **G**, 430
16: 3 **Would to G** we had died by the hand 4310+5414
16:12 ye shall know that I *am* the LORD your **G**. 430
17: 9 of the hill with the rod of **G** in mine hand. 430
18: 1 heard of all that **G** had done for Moses, and 430
18: 4 for the **G** of my father, *said he, was* mine 430
18: 5 where he encamped *at* the mount of **G**: 430
18:12 took a burnt offering and sacrifices for **G**: 430
18:12 bread with Moses' father in law before **G**. 430
18:15 the people come unto me to inquire of **G**: 430
18:16 and I do make *them* know the statutes of **G**, 430
18:19 give thee counsel, and **G** shall be with thee: 430
18:19 that thou mayest bring the causes unto **G**: 430
18:21 such as fear **G**, men of truth, 430
18:23 **G** command thee *so*, then thou shalt be able 430
19: 3 Moses went up unto **G**, and the LORD 430
19:17 the people out of the camp to meet with **G**; 430
19:19 and **G** answered him by a voice. 430
20: 1 And **G** spake all these words, saying, 430
20: 2 I *am* the LORD thy **G**, which have brought 430
20: 5 for I the LORD thy **G** *am* a jealous **G**, 430
20: 5 for I the LORD thy God *am* a jealous **G**, 410
20: 7 take the name of the LORD thy **G** in vain; 430
20:10 day *is* the sabbath of the LORD thy **G**: 430
20:12 land which the LORD thy **G** giveth thee. 430
20:19 but let not **G** speak with us, lest we die. 430
20:20 for **G** is come to prove you, and that his fear 430
20:21 near unto the thick darkness where **G** *was*. 430
21:13 not in wait, but **G** deliver *him* into his hand; 430
22:20 He that sacrificeth unto *any* **g**, save unto 430
23:19 bring *into* the house of the LORD thy **G**. 430
23:25 ye shall serve the LORD your **G**, and 430
24:10 they saw the **G** of Israel: and *there was* 430
24:11 also they saw **G**, and did eat and drink. 430
24:13 and Moses went up into the mount of **G**. 430
29:45 the children of Israel, and will be their **G**. 430
29:46 shall know that I *am* the LORD their **G**, 430
29:46 amongst them: I *am* the LORD their **G**. 430
31: 3 I have filled him *with* the spirit of **G**, 430
31:18 tables of stone, written with the finger of **G**. 430
32:11 And Moses besought the LORD his **G**, and 430
32:16 the tables *were* the work of **G**, and 430
32:16 the writing *was* the writing of **G**, graven 430
32:27 Thus saith the LORD **G** of Israel, 430
34: 6 The LORD **G**, merciful and gracious, 410
34:14 For thou shalt worship no other **g**: for 410
34:14 whose name *is* Jealous, *is* a jealous **G**: 410
34:23 before the Lord GOD, the **G** of Israel. 430
34:24 before the LORD thy **G** thrice in the year. 430
34:26 bring *unto* the house of the LORD thy **G**. 430
35:31 he hath filled him *with* the spirit of **G**, 430
Lev 2:13 thy **G** to be lacking from thy meat offering: 430
4:22 **G** *concerning things* which should not be 430
10:17 **G** hath given it you to bear the iniquity of NIH
11:44 For I *am* the LORD your **G**: ye shall 430
11:45 up out of the land of Egypt, to be your **G**: 430
18: 2 and say unto them, I *am* the LORD your **G**. 430
18: 4 to walk therein: I *am* the LORD your **G**. 430
18:21 neither shalt thou profane the name of thy **G**: 430
18:30 yourselves therein: I *am* the LORD your **G**. 430
19: 2 be holy: for I the LORD your **G** *am* holy. 430
19: 3 keep my sabbaths: I *am* the LORD your **G**. 430
19: 4 molten gods: I *am* the LORD your **G**. 430
19:10 and stranger: I *am* the LORD your **G**. 430
19:12 neither shalt thou profane the name of thy **G**: 430
19:14 before the blind, but shalt fear thy **G**: 430
19:25 increase thereof: I *am* the LORD your **G**. 430
19:31 defiled by them: I *am* the LORD your **G**. 430
19:32 the face of the old man, and fear thy **G**: 430
19:34 the land of Egypt: I *am* the LORD your **G**. 430
19:36 I *am* the LORD your **G**, which brought you 430
20: 7 and be ye holy: for I *am* the LORD your **G**. 430
20:24 I *am* the LORD your **G**, which have 430
21: 6 They shall be holy unto their **G**, and 430
21: 6 and not profane the name of their **G**: 430
Lev 21: 6 *and* the bread of their **G**, they do offer: 430
21: 7 from her husband: for he *is* holy unto his **G**. 430
21: 8 for he offereth the bread of thy **G**: 430
21:12 nor profane the sanctuary of his **G**; 430
21:12 for the crown of the anointing oil of his **G** *is* 430
21:17 him not approach to offer the bread of his **G**. 430
21:21 not come nigh to offer the bread of his **G**. 430
21:22 He shall eat the bread of his **G**, *both* of 430
22:25 ye offer the bread of your **G** of any of these; 430
22:33 you out of the land of Egypt, to be your **G**: 430
23:14 ye have brought an offering unto your **G**: 430
23:22 and to the stranger: I *am* the LORD your **G**. 430
23:28 for you before the LORD your **G**. 430
23:40 ye shall rejoice before the LORD your **G** 430
23:43 the land of Egypt: I *am* the LORD your **G**. 430
24:15 Whosoever curseth his **G** shall bear his sin. 430
24:22 own country: for I *am* the LORD your **G**. 430
25:17 one another; but thou shalt fear thy **G**: 430
25:17 fear thy God: for I *am* the LORD your **G**. 430
25:36 fear thy **G**; that thy brother may live with 430
25:38 I *am* the LORD your **G**, which brought you 430
25:38 you the land of Canaan, *and* to be your **G**. 430
25:43 over him with rigour; but shalt fear thy **G**. 430
25:55 the land of Egypt: I *am* the LORD your **G**. 430
26: 1 down unto it: for I *am* the LORD your **G**. 430
26:12 will be your **G**, and ye shall be my people. 430
26:13 I *am* the LORD your **G**, which brought you 430
26:44 with them: for I *am* the LORD their **G**. 430
26:45 sight of the heathen, that *I* might be their **G**: 430
Nu 6: 7 the consecration of his **G** *is* upon his head. 430
10: 9 be remembered before the LORD your **G**, 430
10:10 may be to you for a memorial before your **G**: 430
10:10 before your God: I *am* the LORD your **G**. 430
11:29 **would G that** all the LORD'S 4310+5414
12:13 Heal her now, O **G**, I beseech thee. 410
14: 2 **Would G that** we had died in the land of 3863
14: 2 or **would G** we had died in this wilderness! 3863
15:40 and be holy unto your **G**. 430
15:41 I *am* the LORD your **G**, which brought you 430
15:41 you out of the land of Egypt, to be your **G**: 430
15:41 to be your God: I *am* the LORD your **G**. 430
16: 9 that the **G** of Israel hath separated you from 430
16:22 they fell upon their faces, and said, O **G**, 410
16:22 said, O God, the **G** of the spirits of all flesh, 430
20: 3 **Would G** that we had died when our 3863
21: 5 the people spake against **G**, and 430
22: 9 **G** came unto Balaam, and said, What men 430
22:10 Balaam said unto **G**, Balak the son of 430
22:12 **G** said unto Balaam, Thou shalt not go with 430
22:18 go beyond the word of the LORD my **G**, 430
22:20 **G** came unto Balaam at night, and said unto 430
22:38 the word that **G** putteth in my mouth, that 430
23: 4 **G** met Balaam: and he said unto him, I have 430
23: 8 How shall I curse, whom **G** hath not cursed? 410
23:19 **G** *is* not a man, that he should lie; neither 410
23:21 the LORD his **G** *is* with him, and the shout 430
23:22 **G** brought them out of Egypt; he hath as it 410
23:23 and of Israel, What hath **G** wrought! 410
23:27 peradventure it will please **G** that thou 430
24: 2 and the spirit of **G** came upon him. 430
24: 4 He hath said, which heard the words of **G**, 410
24: 8 **G** brought him forth out of Egypt; he hath as 410
24:16 which heard the words of **G**, and knew 410
24:23 said, Alas, who shall live when **G** doeth this! 410
25:13 because he was zealous for his **G**, and 430
27:16 the LORD, the **G** of the spirits of all flesh, 430
Dt 1: 6 The LORD our **G** spake unto us in Horeb, 430
1:10 The LORD your **G** hath multiplied you, 430
1:11 (The LORD **G** of your fathers make you a 430
1:19 as the LORD our **G** commanded us; 430
1:20 which the LORD our **G** doth give unto us. 430
1:21 the LORD thy **G** hath set the land before 430
1:21 possess *it*, as the LORD **G** of thy fathers 430
1:25 *It is* a good land which the LORD our **G** 430
1:26 the commandment of the LORD your **G**: 430
1:30 The LORD your **G** which goeth before 430
1:31 seen how that the LORD thy **G** bare thee, 430
1:32 thing ye did not believe the LORD your **G**, 430
1:41 according to all that the LORD our **G** 430
2: 7 For the LORD thy **G** hath blessed thee in 430
2: 7 these forty years the LORD thy **G** *hath* 430
2:29 the land which the LORD our **G** giveth us. 430
2:30 for the LORD thy **G** hardened his spirit, 430
2:33 the LORD our **G** delivered him before us; 430
2:36 the LORD our **G** delivered all unto us: 430
2:37 nor *unto* whatsoever the LORD our **G** 430
3: 3 So the LORD our **G** delivered into our 430
3:18 The LORD your **G** hath given you this land 430
3:20 your **G** hath given them beyond Jordan: 430
3:21 your **G** hath done unto these two kings: 430
3:22 for the LORD your **G** he shall fight for 430
3:24 for what **G** *is there* in heaven or in earth, 410
4: 1 possess the land which the LORD **G** of 430
4: 2 the LORD your **G** which I command you. 430
4: 3 the LORD thy **G** hath destroyed them from 430
4: 4 ye that did cleave unto the LORD your **G** 430
4: 5 even as the LORD my **G** commanded me, 430
4: 7 *so* great, who hath **G** *so* nigh unto them, 430
4: 7 as the LORD our **G** *is* in all *things that* we 430
4:10 stoodest before the LORD thy **G** in Horeb, 430
4:19 which the LORD thy **G** hath divided unto 430
4:21 which the LORD thy **G** giveth thee *for* an 430
4:23 forget the covenant of the LORD your **G**, 430
4:23 the LORD thy **G** hath forbidden thee. 430
4:24 For the LORD thy **G** *is* a consuming fire, 430
4:24 God *is* a consuming fire, *even* a jealous **G**. 410
4:25 do evil in the sight of the LORD thy **G**, 430
4:29 thence thou shalt seek the LORD thy **G**, 430
4:30 if thou turn to the LORD thy **G**, and 430
4:31 (For the LORD thy **G** *is* a merciful God;) 430
4:31 (For the LORD thy God *is* a merciful **G**;) 410
4:32 since the day that **G** created man upon 430
4:33 Did *ever* people hear the voice of **G** 430
4:34 Or hath **G** assayed to go *and* take him a 430
4:34 according to all that the LORD your **G** did 430
Dt 4:35 thou mightest know that the LORD he *is* **G**; 430
4:39 that the LORD he *is* **G** in heaven above, 430
4:40 which the LORD thy **G** giveth thee, 430
5: 2 The LORD our **G** made a covenant with us 430
5: 6 I *am* the LORD thy **G**, which brought thee 430
5: 9 for I the LORD thy **G** *am* a jealous God, 430
5: 9 for I the LORD thy God *am* a jealous **G**, 410
5:11 take the name of the LORD thy **G** in vain: 430
5:12 as the LORD thy **G** hath commanded thee. 430
5:14 day *is* the sabbath of the LORD thy **G**: 430
5:15 *that* the LORD thy **G** brought thee out 430
5:15 the LORD thy **G** commanded thee to keep 430
5:16 as the LORD thy **G** hath commanded thee; 430
5:16 in the land which the LORD thy **G** giveth 430
5:24 the LORD our **G** hath shewed us his glory 430
5:24 we have seen this day that **G** doth talk with 430
5:25 if we hear the voice of the LORD our **G** 430
5:26 that hath heard the voice of the living **G** 430
5:27 and hear all that the LORD our **G** shall say: 430
5:27 speak thou unto us all that the LORD our **G** 430
5:32 as the LORD your **G** hath commanded you: 430
5:33 the LORD your **G** hath commanded you, 430
6: 1 which the LORD your **G** commanded to 430
6: 2 That thou mightest fear the LORD thy **G**, 430
6: 3 as the LORD **G** of thy fathers hath 430
6: 4 O Israel: The LORD our **G** *is* one LORD: 430
6: 5 thou shalt love the LORD thy **G** with all 430
6:10 when the LORD thy **G** shall have brought 430
6:13 Thou shalt fear the LORD thy **G**, and 430
6:15 (For the LORD thy **G** *is* a jealous God 430
6:15 (For the LORD thy God *is* a jealous **G** 410
6:15 lest the anger of the LORD thy **G** be 430
6:16 Ye shall not tempt the LORD your **G**, as ye 430
6:17 the commandments of the LORD your **G**, 430
6:20 which the LORD our **G** hath commanded 430
6:24 to fear the LORD our **G**, for our good 430
6:25 commandments before the LORD our **G**, 430
7: 1 When the LORD thy **G** shall bring thee 430
7: 2 when the LORD thy **G** shall deliver them 430
7: 6 *art* a holy people unto the LORD thy **G**: 430
7: 6 the LORD thy **G** hath chosen thee to be a 430
7: 9 Know therefore that the LORD thy **G**, he *is* 430
7: 9 he *is* **G**, the faithful God, which keepeth 430
7: 9 he *is* God, the faithful **G**, which keepeth 410
7:12 that the LORD thy **G** shall keep unto thee 430
7:16 which the LORD thy **G** shall deliver thee; 430
7:18 shalt well remember what the LORD thy **G** 430
7:19 where*by* the LORD thy **G** brought thee out: 430
7:19 shall the LORD thy **G** do unto all 430
7:20 Moreover the LORD thy **G** will send 430
7:21 for the LORD thy **G** *is* among you, 430
7:21 God *is* among you, a mighty **G** and terrible. 410
7:22 the LORD thy **G** will put out those nations 430
7:23 the LORD thy **G** shall deliver them unto 430
7:25 it *is* an abomination to the LORD thy **G**. 430
8: 2 **G** led thee these forty years in 430
8: 5 *so* the LORD thy **G** chasteneth thee. 430
8: 6 the commandments of the LORD thy **G**, 430
8: 7 For the LORD thy **G** bringeth thee into a 430
8:10 thou shalt bless the LORD thy **G** for 430
8:11 that thou forget not the LORD thy **G**, 430
8:14 lifted up, and thou forget the LORD thy **G**, 430
8:18 But thou shalt remember the LORD thy **G**: 430
8:19 if thou do at all forget the LORD thy **G**, 430
8:20 unto the voice of the LORD your **G**. 430
9: 3 that the LORD thy **G** *is* he which goeth 430
9: 4 after that the LORD thy **G** hath cast them 430
9: 5 thy **G** doth drive them out from before thee, 430
9: 6 that the LORD thy **G** giveth thee not this 430
9: 7 how thou provokedst the LORD thy **G** to 430
9:10 tables of stone written with the finger of **G**; 430
9:16 ye had sinned against the LORD your **G**, 430
9:23 the commandment of the LORD your **G**, 430
10: 9 according as the LORD thy **G** promised 430
10:12 what doth the LORD thy **G** require of thee, 430
10:12 to fear the LORD thy **G**, to walk in all his 430
10:12 to serve the LORD thy **G** with all thy heart 430
10:14 heaven of heavens *is* the LORD'S thy **G**, 430
10:17 For the LORD your **G** *is* God of gods, and 430
10:17 For the LORD your God *is* **G** of gods, and 430
10:17 of lords, a great **G**, a mighty, and a terrible, 410
10:20 Thou shalt fear the LORD thy **G**; him shalt 430
10:21 He *is* thy praise, and he *is* thy **G**, that hath 430
10:22 now the LORD thy **G** hath made thee as 430
11: 1 Therefore thou shalt love the LORD thy **G**, 430
11: 2 seen the chastisement of the LORD your **G**, 430
11:12 A land which the LORD thy **G** careth for: 430
11:12 the eyes of the LORD thy **G** *are* always 430
11:13 to love the LORD your **G**, and to serve him 430
11:22 to do them, to love the LORD your **G**, 430
11:25 *for* the LORD your **G** shall lay the fear of 430
11:27 the commandments of the LORD your **G**, 430
11:28 the commandments of the LORD your **G**, 430
11:29 when the LORD thy **G** hath brought thee in 430
11:31 land which the LORD your **G** giveth you, 430
12: 1 which the LORD **G** of thy fathers giveth 430
12: 4 Ye shall not do so unto the LORD your **G**. 430
12: 5 unto the place which the LORD your **G** 430
12: 7 there ye shall eat before the LORD your **G**, 430
12: 7 where*in* the LORD thy **G** hath blessed thee. 430
12: 9 which the LORD your **G** giveth you. 430
12:10 dwell in the land which the LORD your **G** 430
12:11 **G** shall choose to cause his name to dwell 430
12:12 ye shall rejoice before the LORD your **G**, 430
12:15 the LORD thy **G** which he hath given thee: 430
12:18 thou must eat them before the LORD thy **G** 430
12:18 place which the LORD thy **G** shall choose, 430
12:18 thou shalt rejoice before the LORD thy **G** 430
12:20 When the LORD thy **G** shall enlarge thy 430
12:21 If the place which the LORD thy **G** hath 430
12:27 upon the altar of the LORD thy **G**: 430
12:27 out upon the altar of the LORD thy **G**, 430
12:28 and right in the sight of the LORD thy **G**. 430
12:29 When the LORD thy **G** shall cut off 430
12:31 Thou shalt not do so unto the LORD thy **G**: 430

Dt 13: 3 for the LORD your **G** proveth you, to know 430
13: 3 love the LORD your **G** with all your heart 430
13: 4 Ye shall walk after the LORD your **G**, and 430
13: 5 to turn *you* away from the LORD your **G**, 430
13: 5 LORD thy **G** commanded thee to walk in. 430
13:10 to thrust thee away from the LORD thy **G**, 430
13:12 which the LORD thy **G** hath given thee to 430
13:16 thereof every whit, for the LORD thy **G**: 430
13:18 hearken to the voice of the LORD thy **G**, 430
13:18 *is* right in the eyes of the LORD thy **G**. 430
14: 1 Ye *are* the children of the LORD your **G**: 430
14: 2 *art* a holy people unto the LORD thy **G**, 430
14:21 *art* a holy people unto the LORD thy **G**. 430
14:23 And thou shalt eat before the LORD thy **G**, 430
14:23 learn to fear the LORD thy **G** always. 430
14:24 which the LORD thy **G** shall choose to set 430
14:24 when the LORD thy **G** hath blessed thee: 430
14:25 place which the LORD thy **G** shall choose: 430
14:26 shalt eat there before the LORD thy **G**, 430
14:29 that the LORD thy **G** may bless thee in all 430
15: 4 **G** giveth thee *for* an inheritance to possess 430
15: 5 hearken unto the voice of the LORD thy **G**, 430
15: 6 For the LORD thy **G** blesseth thee, as he 430
15: 7 land which the LORD thy **G** giveth thee, 430
15:10 that for this thing the LORD thy **G** shall 430
15:14 *of that* where*with* the LORD thy **G** hath 430
15:15 and the LORD thy **G** redeemed thee: 430
15:18 the LORD thy **G** shall bless thee in all that 430
15:19 thou shalt sanctify unto the LORD thy **G**: 430
15:20 Thou shalt eat it before the LORD thy **G** 430
15:21 shalt not sacrifice it unto the LORD thy **G**. 430
16: 1 keep the passover unto the LORD thy **G**: 430
16: 1 for in the month of Abib the LORD thy **G** 430
16: 2 the passover unto the LORD thy **G**, 430
16: 5 which the LORD thy **G** giveth thee: 430
16: 6 at the place which the LORD thy **G** shall 430
16: 7 eat *it* in the place which the LORD thy **G** 430
16: 8 *be* a solemn assembly to the LORD thy **G**: 430
16:10 **G** *with* a tribute of a freewill offering of 430
16:10 *G*, according as the LORD thy God hath NIH
16:10 as the LORD thy **G** hath blessed thee: 430
16:11 thou shalt rejoice before the LORD thy **G**, 430
16:11 in the place which the LORD thy **G** hath 430
16:15 **G** in the place which the LORD shall 430
16:15 the LORD thy **G** shall bless thee in all thy 430
16:16 thy **G** in the place which he shall choose; 430
16:17 the LORD thy **G** which he hath given thee. 430
16:18 which the LORD thy **G** giveth thee, 430
16:20 inherit the land which the LORD thy **G** 430
16:21 near unto the altar of the LORD thy **G**, 430
16:22 *any* image; which the LORD thy **G** hateth. 430
17: 1 unto the LORD thy **G** *any* bullock, 430
17: 1 *is* an abomination unto the LORD thy **G**. 430
17: 2 gates which the LORD thy **G** giveth thee, 430
17: 2 in the sight of the LORD thy **G**, 430
17: 8 place which the LORD thy **G** shall choose; 430
17:12 to minister there before the LORD thy **G**, 430
17:14 land which the LORD thy **G** giveth thee, 430
17:15 whom the LORD thy **G** shall choose: 430
17:19 that he may learn to fear the LORD his **G**, 430
18: 5 For the LORD thy **G** hath chosen him out 430
18: 7 minister in the name of the LORD his **G**, 430
18: 9 land which the LORD thy **G** giveth thee, 430
18:12 of these abominations the LORD thy **G** 430
18:13 shalt be perfect with the LORD thy **G**. 430
18:14 the LORD thy **G** hath not suffered thee so 430
18:15 The LORD thy **G** will raise up unto thee a 430
18:16 thy **G** in Horeb in the day of the assembly, 430
18:16 hear again the voice of the LORD my **G**, 430
19: 1 When the LORD thy **G** hath cut off 430
19: 1 whose land the LORD thy **G** giveth thee, 430
19: 2 which the LORD thy **G** giveth thee to 430
19: 3 which the LORD thy **G** giveth thee to 430
19: 8 if the LORD thy **G** enlarge thy coast, as he 430
19: 9 to love the LORD thy **G**, and to walk ever 430
19:10 which the LORD thy **G** giveth thee *for* an 430
19:14 the LORD thy **G** giveth thee to possess it. 430
20: 1 for the LORD thy **G** *is* with thee, 430
20: 4 For the LORD your **G** *is* he that goeth with 430
20:13 when the LORD thy **G** hath delivered it 430
20:14 which the LORD thy **G** hath given thee. 430
20:16 which the LORD thy **G** doth give thee *for* 430
20:17 as the LORD thy **G** hath commanded thee: 430
20:18 so should ye sin against the LORD your **G**. 430
21: 1 the LORD thy **G** giveth thee to possess it, 430
21: 5 for them the LORD thy **G** hath chosen to 430
21:10 the LORD thy **G** hath delivered them into 430
21:23 (for he that is hanged *is* accursed of **G**;) 430
21:23 which the LORD thy **G** giveth thee *for* an 430
22: 5 so *are* abomination unto the LORD thy **G**. 430
23: 5 Nevertheless the LORD thy **G** would not 430
23: 5 the LORD thy **G** turned the curse into a 430
23: 5 because the LORD thy **G** loved thee. 430
23:14 For the LORD thy **G** walketh in the midst 430
23:18 *into* the house of the LORD thy **G** for any 430
23:18 *are* abomination unto the LORD thy **G**. 430
23:20 that the LORD thy **G** may bless thee in all 430
23:21 shalt vow a vow unto the LORD thy **G**, 430
23:21 for the LORD thy **G** will surely require it 430
23:23 as thou hast vowed unto the LORD thy **G**, 430
24: 4 which the LORD thy **G** giveth thee *for* an 430
24: 9 Remember what the LORD thy **G** did unto 430
24:13 unto thee before the LORD thy **G**. 430
24:18 the LORD thy **G** redeemed thee thence: 430
24:19 that the LORD thy **G** may bless thee in all 430
25:15 land which the LORD thy **G** giveth thee. 430
25:16 *are* an abomination unto the LORD thy **G**. 430
25:18 *wast* faint and weary; and he feared not **G**. 430
25:19 when the LORD thy **G** hath given thee rest 430
25:19 in the land which the LORD thy **G** giveth 430
26: 1 LORD thy **G** giveth thee *for* an inheritance, 430
26: 2 thy land that the LORD thy **G** giveth thee, 430
26: 2 thy **G** shall choose to place his name there. 430
26: 3 I profess *this* day unto the LORD thy **G**, 430
26: 4 down before the altar of the LORD thy **G**. 430

Dt 26: 5 and say before the LORD thy **G**, 430
26: 7 when we cried unto the LORD **G** of our 430
26:10 thou shalt set it before the LORD thy **G**, 430
26:10 and worship before the LORD thy **G**: 430
26:11 the LORD thy **G** hath given unto thee, 430
26:13 thou shalt say before the LORD thy **G**, 430
26:14 hearkened to the voice of the LORD my **G**, 430
26:16 This day the LORD thy **G** hath commanded 430
26:17 avouched the LORD *this* day to be thy **G**, 430
26:19 be a holy people unto the LORD thy **G**, 430
27: 2 land which the LORD thy **G** giveth thee, 430
27: 3 land which the LORD thy **G** giveth thee, 430
27: 3 as the LORD **G** of thy fathers hath 430
27: 5 thou build an altar unto the LORD thy **G**, 430
27: 6 altar of the LORD thy **G** *of* whole stones: 430
27: 6 offerings thereon unto the LORD thy **G**: 430
27: 7 and rejoice before the LORD thy **G**. 430
27: 9 art become the people of the LORD thy **G**. 430
27:10 obey the voice of the LORD thy **G**, 430
28: 1 unto the voice of the LORD thy **G**, 430
28: 1 that the LORD thy **G** will set thee on high 430
28: 2 hearken unto the voice of the LORD thy **G**. 430
28: 8 land which the LORD thy **G** giveth thee. 430
28: 9 the commandments of the LORD thy **G**, 430
28:13 the commandments of the LORD thy **G**, 430
28:15 hearken unto the voice of the LORD thy **G**, 430
28:45 not unto the voice of the LORD thy **G**, 430
28:47 Because thou servedst not the LORD thy **G** 430
28:52 which the LORD thy **G** hath given thee. 430
28:53 which the LORD thy **G** hath given thee, 430
28:58 and fearful name, THE LORD THY **G**; 430
28:62 not obey the voice of the LORD thy **G**. 430
28:67 shalt say, **Would G** it were even! 4310+5414
28:67 shalt say, **Would G** it were morning! 4310+5414
29: 6 might know that I *am* the LORD your **G**. 430
29:10 day all of you before the LORD your **G**; 430
29:12 enter into covenant with the LORD thy **G**, 430
29:12 which the LORD thy **G** maketh with thee 430
29:13 *that* he may be unto thee a **G**, as he hath said 430
29:15 with us *this* day before the LORD our **G**, 430
29:18 away *this* day from the LORD our **G**, 430
29:25 covenant of the LORD **G** of their fathers, 430
29:29 secret *things belong* unto the LORD our **G**: 430
30: 1 whither the LORD thy **G** hath driven thee, 430
30: 2 And shalt return unto the LORD thy **G**, and 430
30: 3 the LORD thy **G** will turn thy captivity, 430
30: 3 whither the LORD thy **G** hath scattered 430
30: 4 from thence will the LORD thy **G** gather 430
30: 5 the LORD thy **G** will bring thee into 430
30: 6 the LORD thy **G** will circumcise thine 430
30: 6 to love the LORD thy **G** with all thine 430
30: 7 the LORD thy **G** will put all these curses 430
30: 9 the LORD thy **G** will make thee plenteous 430
30:10 hearken unto the voice of the LORD thy **G**, 430
30:10 if thou turn unto the LORD thy **G** with all 430
30:16 thee *this* day to love the LORD thy **G**, 430
30:16 the LORD thy **G** shall bless thee in the land 430
30:20 That thou mayest love the LORD thy **G**, 430
31: 3 The LORD thy **G**, he will go over before 430
31: 6 for the LORD thy **G**, he *it is* that doth go 430
31:11 thy **G** in the place which he shall choose, 430
31:12 fear the LORD your **G**, and observe to do 430
31:13 and learn to fear the LORD your **G**, 430
31:17 upon us, because our **G** *is* not amongst us? 430
31:26 ark of the covenant of the LORD your **G**, 430
32: 3 ascribe ye greatness unto our **G**. 430
32: 4 a **G** of truth and without iniquity, just and 410
32:12 and *there was* no strange **g** with him. 410
32:15 then he forsook **G** *which* made him, 433
32:17 They sacrificed unto devils, not *to* **G**; 433
32:18 and hast forgotten **G** that formed thee. 410
32:21 me to jealousy with *that which is* not **G**; 410
32:39 *even* I, *am* he, and *there is* no **g** with me: 430
33: 1 wherewith Moses the man of **G** blessed 430
33:26 *There is* none like unto the **G** of Jeshurun, 410
33:27 The eternal **G** *is thy* refuge, and underneath 430
Jos 1: 9 for the LORD thy **G** *is* with thee 430
1:11 which the LORD your **G** giveth you to 430
1:13 The LORD your **G** hath given you rest, and 430
1:15 land which the LORD your **G** giveth them: 430
1:17 only the LORD thy **G** be with thee, as he 430
2:11 for the LORD your **G**, he *is* God in heaven 430
2:11 he *is* **G** in heaven above, and in earth 430
3: 3 ark of the covenant of the LORD your **G**, 430
3: 9 and hear the words of the LORD your **G**. 430
3:10 Hereby ye shall know that the living **G** *is* 410
4: 5 the LORD your **G** into the midst of Jordan, 430
4:23 For the LORD your **G** dried up the waters 430
4:23 as the LORD your **G** did to the Red sea, 430
4:24 that ye might fear the LORD your **G** for 430
7: 7 **would to G** we had been content, 3863+2050.1
7:13 for thus saith the LORD **G** of Israel, 430
7:19 glory to the LORD **G** of Israel, and 430
7:20 Indeed I have sinned against the LORD **G** 430
8: 7 for the LORD your **G** will deliver it into 430
8:30 Joshua built an altar unto the LORD **G** of 430
9: 9 because of the name of the LORD thy **G**: 430
9:18 sworn unto them by the LORD **G** of Israel. 430
9:19 We have sworn unto them by the LORD **G** 430
9:23 and drawers of water for the house of my **G**. 430
9:24 how that the LORD thy **G** commanded his 430
10:19 for the LORD your **G** hath delivered them 430
10:40 as the LORD **G** of Israel commanded. 430
10:42 the LORD **G** of Israel fought for Israel. 430
13:14 the sacrifices of the LORD **G** of Israel 430
13:33 the LORD **G** of Israel *was* their 430
14: 6 unto Moses the man of **G** concerning me 430
14: 8 I wholly followed the LORD my **G**. 430
14: 9 hast wholly followed the LORD my **G**. 430
14:14 that he wholly followed the LORD **G** of 430
18: 3 which the LORD **G** of your fathers hath 430
18: 6 lots for you here before the LORD our **G**. 430
22: 3 of the commandment of the LORD your **G**. 430
22: 4 now the LORD your **G** hath given rest unto 430
22: 5 to love the LORD your **G**, and to walk in 430

Jos 22:16 ye have committed against the **G** of Israel, 430
22:19 altar beside the altar of the LORD our **G**. 430
22:22 The LORD **G** of gods, the LORD God of 410
22:22 the LORD **G** of gods, he knoweth, and 410
22:24 What have you to do with the LORD **G** of 430
22:29 **G forbid** that we should rebel against 2486
22:29 besides the altar of the LORD our **G** that *is* 430
22:33 the children of Israel blessed **G**, and did not 430
22:34 a witness between us that the LORD *is* **G**. 430
23: 3 ye have seen all that the LORD your **G** 430
23: 3 for the LORD your **G** *is* he that hath fought 430
23: 5 the LORD your **G**, he shall expel them 430
23: 5 as the LORD your **G** hath promised unto 430
23: 8 cleave unto the LORD your **G**, as ye have 430
23:10 for the LORD your **G**, he *it is* that fighteth 430
23:11 that ye love the LORD your **G**. 430
23:13 for a certainty that the LORD your **G** 430
23:13 which the LORD your **G** hath given you. 430
23:14 the LORD your **G** spake concerning you; 430
23:15 which the LORD your **G** promised you; 430
23:15 which the LORD your **G** hath given you. 430
23:16 the covenant of the LORD your **G**, 430
24: 1 and they presented themselves before **G**. 430
24: 2 Thus saith the LORD **G** of Israel, 430
24:16 **G forbid** that we should forsake 2486
24:17 For the LORD our **G**, he *it is* that brought 430
24:18 we also serve the LORD; for he *is* our **G**. 430
24:19 for he *is* a holy **G**; he *is* a jealous God; 430
24:19 for he *is* a holy God; he *is* a jealous **G**; 410
24:23 incline your heart unto the LORD **G** of 430
24:24 The LORD our **G** will we serve, and his 430
24:26 these words in the book of the law of **G**, 430
24:27 a witness unto you, lest ye deny your **G**. 430
Jdg 1: 7 as I have done, so **G** hath requited me. 430
2:12 they forsook the LORD **G** of their fathers, 430
3: 7 forgat the LORD their **G**, and 430
3:20 I have a message from **G** unto thee. 430
4: 6 Hath not the LORD **G** of Israel 430
4:23 So **G** subdued on that day Jabin the king of 430
5: 3 I will sing *praise* to the LORD **G** of Israel. 430
5: 5 *even* that Sinai from before the LORD **G** of 430
6: 8 Thus saith the LORD **G** of Israel, 430
6:10 I said unto you, I *am* the LORD your **G**; 430
6:20 the angel of **G** said unto him, Take the flesh 430
6:26 build an altar unto the LORD thy **G** upon 430
6:31 if he *be* a **g**, let him plead for himself, 430
6:36 Gideon said unto **G**, If thou wilt save Israel 430
6:39 Gideon said unto **G**, Let not thine anger be 430
6:40 **G** did so that night: for it was dry upon 430
7:14 *for* into his hand hath **G** delivered Midian, 430
8: 3 **G** hath delivered into your hands the princes 430
8:33 after Baalim, and made Baal-berith their **g**. 430
8:34 Israel remembered not the LORD their **G**, 430
9: 7 of Shechem, that **G** may hearken unto you. 430
9: 9 wherewith by me they honour **G** and man, 430
9:13 which cheereth **G** and man, and go to be 430
9:23 **G** sent an evil spirit between Abimelech 430
9:27 went *into* the house of their **g**, and did eat 430
9:29 **would to G** this people were under 4310+5414
9:46 into a hold of the house of the **g** Berith. 410
9:56 Thus **G** rendered the wickedness of 430
9:57 all the evil of the men of Shechem did **G** 430
10:10 both because we have forsaken our **G**, and 430
11:21 And the LORD **G** of Israel delivered Sihon 430
11:23 So now the LORD **G** of Israel hath 430
11:24 Chemosh thy **g** giveth thee to possess? 430
11:24 So whomsoever the LORD our **G** shall 430
13: 5 for the child shall be a Nazarite unto **G** from 430
13: 6 A man of **G** came unto me, and 430
13: 6 *was* like the countenance of an angel of **G**, 430
13: 7 to **G** from the womb to the day of his death. 430
13: 8 let the man of **G** which thou didst send come 430
13: 9 **G** hearkened to the voice of Manoah; and 430
13: 9 the angel of **G** came again unto the woman 430
13:22 shall surely die, because we have seen **G**. 430
15:19 **G** clave a hollow place that *was* in the jaw, 430
16:17 for I *have been* a Nazarite unto **G** from my 430
16:23 to offer a great sacrifice unto Dagon their **g**, 430
16:23 Our **g** hath delivered Samson our enemy into 430
16:24 the people saw him, they praised their **g**: 430
16:24 Our **g** hath delivered into our hands our 430
16:28 I pray thee, only this once, O **G**, 430
18: 5 unto him, Ask *counsel*, we pray thee, of **G**, 430
18:10 for **G** hath given it into your hands; a place 430
18:31 all the time that the house of **G** was in 430
20: 2 in the assembly of the people of **G**, 430
20:18 went up *to* the house of **G**, and 410
20:18 of God, and asked *counsel* of **G**, and said, 430
20:26 and came *unto* the house of **G**, and wept, and 410
20:27 (for the ark of the covenant of **G** *was* there 430
20:31 *of* which one goeth up *to* the house of **G**, and 410
21: 2 And the people came *to* the house of **G**, and 410
21: 2 abode there till even before **G**, and lift up 430
21: 3 said, O LORD **G** of Israel, why is this 430
Ru 1:16 *shall be* my people, and thy **G** my God: 430
1:16 *shall be* my people, and thy God my **G**: 430
2:12 a full reward be given thee of the LORD **G** 430
1Sa 1:17 the **G** of Israel grant *thee* thy petition that 430
2: 2 neither *is there* any rock like our **G**. 430
2: 3 for the LORD *is* a **G** of knowledge, and 410
2:27 there came a man of **G** unto Eli, and 430
2:30 Wherefore the LORD **G** of Israel saith, 430
2:32 in all *the wealth* which *G* shall give Israel: NIH
3: 3 ere the lamp of **G** went out in the temple of 430
3: 3 where the ark of **G** *was*, and Samuel was 430
3:17 **G** do so to thee, and more also, if thou hide 430
4: 4 *were* there with the ark of the covenant of **G**. 430
4: 7 for they said, **G** is come into the camp. 430
4:11 the ark of **G** was taken; and the two sons of 430
4:13 for his heart trembled for the ark of **G**. 430
4:17 are dead, and the ark of **G** is taken. 430
4:18 when he made mention of the ark of **G**, 430
4:19 when she heard the tidings that the ark of **G** 430
4:21 because the ark of **G** was taken, and because 430
4:22 from Israel: for the ark of **G** is taken. 430

1Sa 5: 1 the Philistines took the ark of **G**, and 430
5: 2 When the Philistines took the ark of **G**, they 430
5: 7 The ark of the **G** of Israel shall not abide 430
5: 7 hand is sore upon us, and upon Dagon our **g**. 430
5: 8 What shall we do with the ark of the **G** of 430
5: 8 Let the ark of the **G** of Israel be carried 430
5: 8 they carried the ark of the **G** of Israel about 430
5:10 Therefore they sent the ark of **G** *to* Ekron. 430
5:10 came to pass, as the ark of **G** came *to* Ekron, 430
5:10 They have brought about the ark of the **G** of 430
5:11 Send away the ark of the **G** of Israel, and 430
5:11 the city; the hand of **G** was very heavy there. 430
6: 3 If ye send away the ark of the **G** of Israel, 430
6: 5 and ye shall give glory unto the **G** of Israel: 430
6:20 is able to stand before this holy LORD **G**? 430
7: 8 Cease not to cry unto the LORD our **G** for 430
9: 6 *there is* in this city a man of **G**, and *he is* an 430
9: 7 *is* not a present to bring to the man of **G**: 430
9: 8 *that* will I give to the man of **G**, to tell us our 430
9: 9 when a man went to inquire of **G**, thus he 430
9:10 went unto the city where the man of **G** *was*. 430
9:27 a while, that I may shew thee the word of **G**. 430
10: 3 thee three men going up to **G** *to* Beth-el, 430
10: 5 After that thou shalt come to the hill of **G**, 430
10: 7 do as occasion serve thee; for **G** *is* with thee. 430
10: 9 go from Samuel, **G** gave him another heart: 430
10:10 the spirit of **G** came upon him, and 430
10:18 Thus saith the LORD **G** of Israel, I brought 430
10:19 ye have *this* day rejected your **G**, 430
10:24 people shouted, and said, **G save** the king. 2421
10:26 a band of men, whose hearts **G** had touched. 430
11: 6 the spirit of **G** came upon Saul when he 430
12: 9 when they forgat the LORD their **G**, he 430
12:12 when the LORD your **G** *was* your king. 430
12:14 you continue following the LORD your **G**: 430
12:19 Pray for thy servants unto the LORD thy **G**, 430
12:23 **G forbid** that I should sin against 2486
13:13 the commandment of the LORD thy **G**, 430
14:18 said unto Ahiah, Bring hither the ark of **G**. 430
14:18 For the ark of **G** was at that time with 430
14:36 the priest, Let us draw near hither unto **G**. 430
14:37 Saul asked *counsel* of **G**, Shall I go down 430
14:41 Therefore Saul said unto the LORD **G** of 430
14:44 And Saul answered, **G** do so and more also: 430
14:45 **G forbid**: *as* the LORD liveth, there shall 2486
14:45 for he hath wrought with **G** this day. 430
15:15 to sacrifice unto the LORD thy **G**; 430
15:21 to sacrifice unto the LORD thy **G** in Gilgal. 430
15:30 that I may worship the LORD thy **G**. 430
16:15 an evil spirit from **G** troubleth thee. 430
16:16 when the evil spirit from **G** is upon thee, 430
16:23 when the *evil* spirit from **G** was upon Saul, 430
17:26 he should defy the armies of the living **G**? 430
17:36 he hath defied the armies of the living **G**. 430
17:45 the **G** of the armies of Israel, whom thou 430
17:46 that all the earth may know that there is a **G** 430
18:10 that the evil spirit from **G** came upon Saul, 430
19:20 the spirit of **G** was upon the messengers of 430
19:23 the spirit of **G** was upon him also, and 430
20: 2 he said unto him, **G forbid**; thou shalt not 2486
20:12 said unto David, O LORD **G** of Israel, 430
22: 3 with you, till I know what **G** will do for me. 430
22:13 and a sword, and hast inquired of **G** for him, 430
22:15 Did I then begin to inquire of **G** for him? 430
23: 7 **G** hath delivered him into mine hand; 430
23:10 said David, O LORD **G** of Israel, 430
23:11 O LORD **G** of Israel, I beseech thee, 430
23:14 but **G** delivered him not into his hand. 430
23:16 the wood, and strengthened his hand in **G**. 430
25:22 more also do **G** unto the enemies of David, 430
25:29 in the bundle of life with the LORD thy **G**; 430
25:32 Blessed *be* the LORD **G** of Israel, 430
25:34 very deed, *as* the LORD **G** of Israel liveth, 430
26: 8 **G** hath delivered thine enemy into thine 430
28:15 **G** is departed from me, and answereth me no 430
29: 9 thou *art* good in my sight, as an angel of **G**: 430
30: 6 encouraged himself in the LORD his **G**. 430
30:15 he said, Swear unto me by **G**, that thou wilt 430
2Sa 2:27 Joab said, *As* **G** liveth, unless thou hadst 430
3: 9 So do **G** to Abner, and more also, except, 430
3:35 So do **G** to me, and more also, 430
5:10 and the LORD **G** of hosts *was* with him. 430
6: 2 to bring up from thence the ark of **G**, 430
6: 3 they set the ark of **G** upon a new cart, and 430
6: 4 *was* at Gibeah, accompanying the ark of **G**: 430
6: 6 Uzzah put forth *his hand* to the ark of **G**, and 430
6: 7 **G** smote him there for *his* error; and there he 430
6: 7 *his* error; and there he died by the ark of **G**. 430
6:12 *pertaineth* unto him, because of the ark of **G**. 430
6:12 brought up the ark of **G** from the house of 430
7: 2 but the ark of **G** dwelleth within curtains. 430
7:22 Wherefore thou art great, O LORD **G**: 136
7:22 like thee, neither *is there any* **G** beside thee, 430
7:23 whom **G** went to redeem for a people to 430
7:24 and thou, LORD, art become their **G**. 430
7:25 now, O LORD **G**, the word that thou hast 430
7:26 The LORD of hosts *is* the **G** over Israel: 430
7:27 For thou, O LORD of hosts, **G** of Israel, 430
7:28 thou *art* that **G**, and thy words be true, and 430
9: 3 that I may shew the kindness of **G** unto him? 430
10:12 for our people, and for the cities of our **G**: 430
12: 7 Thus saith the LORD **G** of Israel, 430
12:16 David therefore besought **G** for the child; 430
14:11 let the king remember the LORD thy **G**, 430
14:13 such a thing against the people of **G**? 430
14:14 up *again;* neither doth **G** respect *any* person: 430
14:16 my son together out of the inheritance of **G**. 430
14:17 for as an angel of **G**, so *is* my lord the king 430
14:17 the LORD thy **G** will be with thee. 430
14:20 according to the wisdom of an angel of **G**, 430
15:24 bearing the ark of the covenant of **G**: 430
15:24 they set down the ark of **G**; and 430
15:25 Carry back the ark of **G** *into* the city: 430
15:29 Abiathar carried the ark of **G** again *to* 430
15:32 top *of the mount*, where he worshipped **G**, 430

2Sa 16:16 **G save** the king, God save the king. 2421
16:16 God save the king, **G save** the king. 2421
16:23 as if a man had inquired at the oracle of **G**: 430
18:28 and said, Blessed *be* the LORD thy **G**, 430
18:33 would **G** I had died for thee, O Absalom, 5414
19:13 **G** do so to me, and more also, if thou be not 430
19:27 but my lord the king *is* as an angel of **G**: 430
21:14 And after that **G** was intreated for the land. 430
22: 3 The **G** of my rock; in him will I trust: *he is* 430
22: 7 called upon the LORD, and cried to my **G**: 430
22:22 and have not wickedly departed from my **G**. 430
22:30 a troop: by my **G** have I leaped over a wall. 430
22:31 *As for* **G**, his way *is* perfect; the word of 410
22:32 For who *is* **G**, save the LORD? and who *is* 410
22:32 the LORD? and who *is* a rock, save our **G**? 430
22:33 **G** *is* my strength *and* power: and he maketh 410
22:47 exalted be the **G** of the rock of my salvation. 430
22:48 *It is* **G** that avengeth me, and that bringeth 410
23: 1 the anointed of the **G** of Jacob, and the sweet 430
23: 3 The **G** of Israel said, the Rock of Israel 430
23: 3 men *must be* just, ruling *in* the fear of **G**. 430
23: 5 Although my house *be* not so with **G**; yet he 410
24: 3 Now the LORD thy **G** add unto the people, 430
24:23 the king, The LORD thy **G** accept thee. 430
24:24 my **G** of that which doth cost me nothing. 430
1Ki 1:17 thou swarest by the LORD thy **G** unto thine 430
1:25 before him, and say, **G save** king Adonijah. 2421
1:30 Even as I sware unto thee by the LORD **G** 430
1:34 and say, **G save** king Solomon. 2421
1:36 the LORD **G** of my lord the king say so 430
1:39 all the people said, **G save** king Solomon. 2421
1:47 **G** make the name of Solomon better than thy 430
1:48 the king, Blessed *be* the LORD **G** of Israel, 430
2: 3 keep the charge of the LORD thy **G**, 430
2:23 **G** do so to me, and more also, 430
3: 5 and **G** said, Ask what I shall give thee. 430
3: 7 now, O LORD my **G**, thou hast made thy 430
3:11 **G** said unto him, Because thou hast asked 430
3:28 for they saw that the wisdom of **G** *was* in 430
4:29 **G** gave Solomon wisdom and 430
5: 3 **G** for the wars which were about him on 430
5: 4 now the LORD my **G** hath given me rest on 430
5: 5 a house unto the name of the LORD my **G**, 430
8:15 he said, Blessed *be* the LORD **G** of Israel, 430
8:17 for the name of the LORD **G** of Israel. 430
8:20 for the name of the LORD **G** of Israel. 430
8:23 he said, LORD **G** of Israel, *there is* no God 430
8:23 *there is* no **G** like thee, in heaven above, or 430
8:25 Therefore now, LORD **G** of Israel, 430
8:26 now, O **G** of Israel, let thy word, I pray thee, 430
8:27 will **G** indeed dwell on the earth? behold, 430
8:28 to his supplication, O LORD my **G**, 430
8:57 The LORD our **G** be with us, as he was 430
8:59 be nigh unto the LORD our **G** day and 430
8:60 of the earth may know that the LORD *is* **G**, 430
8:61 therefore be perfect with the LORD our **G**, 430
8:65 before the LORD our **G**, seven days and 430
9: 9 Because they forsook the LORD their **G**, 430
10: 9 Blessed be the LORD thy **G**, 430
10:24 his wisdom, which **G** had put in his heart. 430
11: 4 heart was not perfect with the LORD his **G**, 430
11: 9 his heart was turned from the LORD **G** of 430
11:23 **G** stirred him up *another* adversary, Rezon 430
11:31 saith the LORD, the **G** of Israel, Behold, 430
11:33 Chemosh the **g** of the Moabites, and Milcom 430
11:33 and Milcom the **g** of the children of Ammon, 430
12:22 the word of **G** came unto Shemaiah the man 430
12:22 of God came unto Shemaiah the man of **G**, 430
13: 1 there came a man of **G** out of Judah by 430
13: 4 Jeroboam heard the saying of the man of **G**, 430
13: 5 according to the sign which the man of **G** 430
13: 6 king answered and said unto the man of **G**, 430
13: 6 Intreat now the face of the LORD thy **G**, 430
13: 6 And the man of **G** besought the LORD, and 430
13: 7 the king said unto the man of **G**, Come home 430
13: 8 the man of **G** said unto the king, If thou wilt 430
13:11 told him all the works that the man of **G** had 430
13:12 sons had seen what way the man of **G** went, 430
13:14 went after the man of **G**, and found him 430
13:14 *Art* thou the man of **G** that camest from 430
13:21 he cried unto the man of **G** that came from 430
13:21 which the LORD thy **G** commanded thee, 430
13:26 It *is* the man of **G**, who was disobedient unto 430
13:29 prophet took up the carcase of the man of **G**, 430
13:31 sepulchre wherein the man of **G** *is* buried; 430
14: 7 Thus saith the LORD **G** of Israel, 430
14:13 **G** of Israel in the house of Jeroboam. 430
15: 3 heart was not perfect with the LORD his **G**, 430
15: 4 LORD his **G** give him a lamp in Jerusalem, 430
15:30 provoked the LORD **G** of Israel to anger. 430
16:13 in provoking the LORD **G** of Israel to 430
16:26 to provoke the LORD **G** of Israel to anger 430
16:33 Ahab did more to provoke the LORD **G** of 430
17: 1 *As* the LORD **G** of Israel liveth, 430
17:12 she said, *As* the LORD thy **G** liveth, I have 430
17:14 For thus saith the LORD **G** of Israel, 430
17:18 have I to do with thee, O thou man of **G**? 430
17:20 unto the LORD, and said, O LORD my **G**, 430
17:21 and said, O LORD my **G**, I pray thee, 430
17:24 Now *by* this I know that thou *art* a man of **G**, 430
18:10 *As* the LORD thy **G** liveth, there is no 430
18:21 if the LORD *be* **G**, follow him: but if Baal, 430
18:24 the **G** that answereth by fire, let him be God. 430
18:24 the God that answereth by fire, let him be **G**. 430
18:27 for he *is* a **g**; either he is talking, or he is 430
18:36 and said, LORD **G** of Abraham, Isaac, and 430
18:36 let it be known this day that thou *art* **G** in 430
18:37 may know that thou *art* the LORD **G**, 430
18:39 they said, The LORD, he *is* the **G**; 430
18:39 he *is* the God; the LORD, he *is* the **G**. 430
19: 8 and forty nights unto Horeb the mount of **G**. 430
19:10 I have been very jealous for the LORD **G** 430
19:14 I have been very jealous for the LORD **G** 430
20:28 there came a man of **G**, and spake unto 430
20:28 The LORD *is* **G** of the hills, but he *is* not 430

1Ki 20:28 he *is* not **G** of the valleys, therefore will I 430
21:10 Thou didst blaspheme **G** and the king. 430
21:13 Naboth did blaspheme **G** and the king. 430
22:53 provoked to anger the LORD **G** of Israel, 430
2Ki 1: 2 inquire of Baal-zebub the **g** of Ekron 430
1: 3 *Is it* not because *there is* not a **G** in Israel, 430
1: 3 *that* ye go to inquire of Baal-zebub the **g** of 430
1: 6 *Is it* not because *there is* not a **G** in Israel, 430
1: 6 to inquire of Baal-zebub the **g** of Ekron? 430
1: 9 Thou man of **G**, the king hath said, 430
1:10 If I *be* a man of **G**, then let fire come down 430
1:11 he answered and said unto him, O man of **G**, 430
1:12 and said unto them, If I *be* a man of **G**, 430
1:12 the fire of **G** came down from heaven, and 430
1:13 O man of **G**, I pray thee, let my life, and 430
1:16 to inquire of Baal-zebub the **g** of Ekron, 430
1:16 *there is* no **G** in Israel to inquire of his word? 430
2:14 and said, Where *is* the LORD **G** of Elijah? 430
4: 7 she came and told the man of **G**. And he 430
4: 9 I perceive that this *is* a holy man of **G**, 430
4:16 And she said, Nay, my lord, thou man of **G**, 430
4:21 and laid him on the bed of the man of **G**, and 430
4:22 that I may run to the man of **G**, and 430
4:25 came unto the man of **G** to mount Carmel. 430
4:25 to pass, when the man of **G** saw her afar off, 430
4:27 when she came to the man of **G** to the hill, 430
4:27 the man of **G** said, Let her alone; for her soul 430
4:40 they cried out, and said, O thou man of **G**, 430
4:42 brought the man of **G** bread of the firstfruits, 430
5: 3 **Would G** my lord *were* with the prophet that 305
5: 7 and said, *Am* I **G**, to kill and to make alive, 430
5: 8 when Elisha the man of **G** had heard that 430
5:11 call on the name of the LORD his **G**, and 430
5:14 according to the saying of the man of **G**: 430
5:15 he returned to the man of **G**, he and all his 430
5:15 now I know that *there is* no **G** in all 430
5:20 the servant of Elisha the man of **G**, said, 430
6: 6 the man of **G** said, Where fell it? And he 430
6: 9 the man of **G** sent unto the king of Israel, 430
6:10 to the place which the man of **G** told him 430
6:15 when the servant of the man of **G** was risen 430
6:31 he said, **G** do so and more also to me, if 430
7: 2 the king leaned answered the man of **G**, 430
7:17 and he died, as the man of **G** had said, 430
7:18 it came to pass as the man of **G** had spoken 430
7:19 *that* lord answered the man of **G**, and said, 430
8: 2 and did after the saying of the man of **G**: 430
8: 4 with Gehazi the servant of the man of **G**, 430
8: 7 saying, The man of **G** is come hither. 430
8: 8 go, meet the man of **G**, and inquire of 430
8:11 *he* was ashamed: and the man of **G** wept. 430
9: 6 unto him, Thus saith the LORD **G** of Israel, 430
10:31 of the LORD **G** of Israel with all his heart: 430
11:12 clapt their hands, and said, **G save** the king. 2421
13:19 the man of **G** was wroth with him, and said, 430
14:25 according to the word of the LORD **G** of 430
16: 2 *was* right in the sight of the LORD his **G**, 430
17: 7 had sinned against the LORD their **G**, 430
17: 9 *were* not right against the LORD their **G**, 430
17:14 that did not believe in the LORD their **G**. 430
17:16 the commandments of the LORD their **G**, 430
17:19 the commandments of the LORD their **G**, 430
17:26 know not the manner of the **G** of the land: 430
17:26 they know not the manner of the **G** of 430
17:27 let him teach them the manner of the **G** of 430
17:39 the LORD your **G** ye shall fear; and 430
18: 5 He trusted in the LORD **G** of Israel; so 430
18:12 obeyed not the voice of the LORD their **G**, 430
18:22 say unto me, We trust in the LORD our **G**: 430
19: 4 It may be the LORD thy **G** will hear all 430
19: 4 his master hath sent to reproach the living **G**; 430
19: 4 words which the LORD thy **G** hath heard: 430
19:10 Let not thy **G** in whom thou trustest deceive 430
19:15 said, O LORD **G** of Israel, which dwellest 430
19:15 thou *art* the **G**, *even* thou alone, of all 430
19:16 hath sent him to reproach the living **G**. 430
19:19 O LORD our **G**, I beseech thee, 430
19:19 earth may know that thou *art* the LORD **G**, 430
19:20 Thus saith the LORD **G** of Israel, 430
19:37 worshipping *in* the house of Nisroch his **g**, 430
20: 5 saith the LORD, the **G** of David thy father, 430
21:12 Therefore thus saith the LORD **G** of Israel, 430
21:22 And he forsook the LORD **G** of his fathers, 430
22:15 Thus saith the LORD **G** of Israel, 430
22:18 to him, Thus saith the LORD **G** of Israel, 430
23:16 the LORD which the man of **G** proclaimed, 430
23:17 *It is* the sepulchre of the man of **G**, 430
23:21 Keep the passover unto the LORD your **G**, 430
1Ch 4:10 And Jabez called on the **G** of Israel, saying, 430
4:10 And **G** granted *him that* which he requested. 430
5:20 for they cried to **G** in the battle, and he was 430
5:22 down many slain, because the war *was* of **G**. 430
5:25 they transgressed against the **G** of their 430
5:25 of the land, whom **G** destroyed before them. 430
5:26 the **G** of Israel stirred up the spirit of Pul 430
6:48 service of the tabernacle of the house of **G**. 430
6:49 according to all that Moses the servant of **G** 430
9:11 son of Ahitub, the ruler of the house of **G**; 430
9:13 *for* the work of the service of the house of **G**. 430
9:26 and treasuries of the house of **G**. 430
9:27 they lodged round about the house of **G**, 430
11: 2 the LORD thy **G** said unto thee, Thou shalt 430
11:19 said, My **G** forbid it me, that *I* should do this 430
12:17 the **G** of our fathers look *thereon*, and 430
12:18 *be* to thine helpers; for thy **G** helpeth thee. 430
12:22 until it was a great host, like the host of **G**. 430
13: 2 And *that it be* of the LORD our **G**, 430
13: 3 And let us bring again the ark of our **G** to us: 430
13: 5 to bring the ark of **G** from Kirjath-jearim. 430
13: 6 to bring up thence the ark of **G** the LORD, 430
13: 7 they carried the ark of **G** in a new cart out of 430
13: 8 all Israel played before **G** with all *their* 430
13:10 hand to the ark: and there he died before **G**. 430
13:12 And David was afraid of **G** that day, saying, 430
13:12 How shall I bring the ark of **G** *home* to me? 430

1Ch 13:14 the ark of **G** remained with the family of 430
14:10 David inquired of **G**, saying, Shall I go up 430
14:11 **G** hath broken in upon mine enemies by 430
14:14 Therefore David inquired again of **G**; and 430
14:14 **G** said unto him, Go not up after them; 430
14:15 for **G** is gone forth before thee to smite 430
14:16 David therefore did as **G** commanded him: 430
15: 1 prepared a place for the ark of **G**, and 430
15: 2 None ought to carry the ark of **G** but 430
15: 2 the LORD chosen to carry the ark of **G**, 430
15:12 **G** of Israel unto *the place that* I have 430
15:13 the LORD our **G** made a breach upon us, 430
15:14 bring up the ark of the LORD **G** of Israel. 430
15:15 the children of the Levites bare the ark of **G** 430
15:24 blow with the trumpets before the ark of **G**: 430
15:26 when **G** helped the Levites that bare the ark 430
16: 1 So they brought the ark of **G**, and set it in 430
16: 1 and peace offerings before **G**. 430
16: 4 to thank and praise the LORD **G** of Israel: 430
16: 6 before the ark of the covenant of **G**. 430
16:14 He *is* the LORD our **G**; his judgments *are* 430
16:35 O **G** of our salvation, and gather us together, 430
16:36 Blessed *be* the LORD **G** of Israel for ever 430
16:42 a sound, and with musical instruments of **G**. 430
17: 2 all that *is* in thine heart; for **G** *is* with thee. 430
17: 3 that the word of **G** came to Nathan, saying, 430
17:16 *am* I, O LORD **G**, and what *is* mine house, 430
17:17 *yet* this was a small thing in thine eyes, O **G**; 430
17:17 estate of a man of high degree, O LORD **G**. 430
17:20 like thee, neither *is there any* **G** besides thee, 430
17:21 whom **G** went to redeem *to be* his own 430
17:22 and thou, LORD, becamest their **G**. 430
17:24 The LORD of hosts *is* the **G** of Israel, 430
17:24 hosts *is* the God of Israel, *even* a **G** to Israel: 430
17:25 For thou, O my **G**, hast told thy servant that 430
17:26 thou *art* **G**, and hast promised this goodness 430
19:13 for our people, and for the cities of our **G**: 430
21: 7 **G** was displeased with this thing; therefore 430
21: 8 David said unto **G**, I have sinned greatly, 430
21:15 **G** sent an angel unto Jerusalem to destroy it: 430
21:17 David said unto **G**, *Is it* not I *that* 430
21:17 O LORD my **G**, be on me, and on my 430
21:30 David could not go before it to inquire of **G**: 430
22: 1 This *is* the house of the LORD **G**, and 430
22: 2 hew wrought stones to build the house of **G**. 430
22: 6 to build a house for the LORD **G** of Israel. 430
22: 7 a house unto the name of the LORD my **G**: 430
22:11 and build the house of the LORD thy **G**, 430
22:12 mayest keep the law of the LORD thy **G**. 430
22:18 *Is* not the LORD your **G** with you? and 430
22:19 and your soul to seek the LORD your **G**; 430
22:19 and build ye the sanctuary of the LORD **G**, 430
22:19 of the LORD, and the holy vessels of **G**, 430
23:14 Now *concerning* Moses the man of **G**, 430
23:25 The LORD **G** of Israel hath given rest unto 430
23:28 the work of the service of the house of **G**; 430
24: 5 governors *of the house* of **G**, were of 430
24:19 as the LORD **G** of Israel had commanded 430
25: 5 of Heman the king's seer in the words of **G**, 430
25: 5 **G** gave to Heman fourteen sons and 430
25: 6 and harps, for the service of the house of **G**, 430
26: 5 Peulthai the eighth: for **G** blessed him. 430
26:20 *was* over the treasures of the house of **G**, 430
26:32 for every matter pertaining to **G**, and 430
28: 2 for the footstool of our **G**, and had made 430
28: 3 **G** said unto me, Thou shalt not build a house 430
28: 4 Howbeit the LORD **G** of Israel chose me 430
28: 8 in the audience of our **G**, keep and seek for 430
28: 8 the commandments of the LORD your **G**: 430
28: 9 know thou the **G** of thy father, and serve him 430
28:12 of the treasuries of the house of **G**, and 430
28:20 for the LORD **G**, *even* my God, *will be* 430
28:20 LORD God, *even* my **G**, *will be* with thee; 430
28:21 *thee* for all the service of the house of **G**: 430
29: 1 whom alone **G** hath chosen, *is yet* young and 430
29: 1 palace *is* not for man, but for the LORD **G**. 430
29: 2 my **G** the gold for *things to be made of* gold, 430
29: 3 have set my affection to the house of my **G**, 430
29: 3 *which* I have given to the house of my **G**, 430
29: 7 gave for the service of the house of **G** *of* 430
29:10 LORD **G** of Israel our father, for ever and 430
29:13 our **G**, we thank thee, and praise thy glorious 430
29:16 O LORD our **G**, all this store that we have 430
29:17 I know also, my **G**, that thou triest the heart, 430
29:18 O LORD **G** of Abraham, Isaac, and 430
29:20 Now bless the LORD your **G**. 430
29:20 all the congregation blessed the LORD **G** 430
2Ch 1: 1 the LORD his **G** *was* with him, and 430
1: 3 was the tabernacle of the congregation of **G**, 430
1: 4 the ark of **G** had David brought up from 430
1: 7 In that night did **G** appear unto Solomon, 430
1: 8 Solomon said unto **G**, Thou hast shewed 430
1: 9 Now, O LORD **G**, let thy promise unto 430
1:11 **G** said to Solomon, Because this was in 430
2: 4 a house to the name of the LORD my **G**, 430
2: 4 on the solemn feasts of the LORD our **G**. 430
2: 5 *is* great: for great *is* our **G** above all gods. 430
2:12 Blessed *be* the LORD **G** of Israel, 430
3: 3 instructed for the building of the house of **G**. 430
4:11 make for king Solomon for the house of **G**; 430
4:19 all the vessels that *were for* the house of **G**, 430
5: 1 he among the treasures of the house of **G**. 430
5:14 of the LORD had filled the house of **G**. 430
6: 4 he said, Blessed *be* the LORD **G** of Israel, 430
6: 7 for the name of the LORD **G** of Israel. 430
6:10 for the name of the LORD **G** of Israel. 430
6:14 said, O LORD **G** of Israel, *there is* no God 430
6:14 *there is* no **G** like thee in the heaven, nor in 430
6:16 Now therefore, O LORD **G** of Israel, 430
6:17 Now then, O LORD **G** of Israel, let thy 430
6:18 will **G** in very deed dwell with men on 430
6:19 to his supplication, O LORD my **G**, 430
6:40 Now, my **G**, let, I beseech thee, thine eyes 430
6:41 Now therefore arise, O LORD **G**, into thy 430
6:41 let thy priests, O LORD **G**, be clothed *with* 430

2Ch 6:42 O LORD **G**, turn not away the face of thine 430
7: 5 and all the people dedicated the house of **G**. 430
7:22 Because they forsook the LORD **G** of their 430
8:14 for so had David the man of **G** commanded. 430
9: 8 Blessed be the LORD thy **G**, 430
9: 8 his throne, to be king for the LORD thy **G**: 430
9: 8 because thy **G** loved Israel, to establish them 430
9:23 hear his wisdom, that **G** had put in his heart. 430
10:15 for the cause was of **G**, that the LORD 430
11: 2 the LORD came to Shemaiah the man of **G**, 430
11:16 the LORD **G** of Israel came *to* Jerusalem, 430
11:16 to sacrifice unto the LORD **G** of their 430
13: 5 Ought you not to know that the LORD **G** of 430
13:10 the LORD *is* our **G**, and we have not 430
13:11 for we keep the charge of the LORD our **G**; 430
13:12 **G** *himself is* with us for *our* captain, and 430
13:12 fight ye not against the LORD **G** of your 430
13:15 that **G** smote Jeroboam and all Israel before 430
13:16 and **G** delivered them into their hand. 430
13:18 they relied upon the LORD **G** of their 430
14: 2 and right in the eyes of the LORD his **G**: 430
14: 4 commanded Judah to seek the LORD **G** of 430
14: 7 because we have sought the LORD our **G**, 430
14:11 Asa cried unto the LORD his **G**, and said, 430
14:11 help us, O LORD our **G**; for we rest on 430
14:11 O LORD, thou *art* our **G**; let not man 430
15: 1 the spirit of **G** came upon Azariah the son of 430
15: 3 season Israel *hath been* without the true **G**, 430
15: 4 trouble did turn unto the LORD **G** of Israel, 430
15: 6 for **G** did vex them with all adversity. 430
15: 9 when they saw that the LORD his **G** *was* 430
15:12 LORD **G** of their fathers with all their heart 430
15:13 LORD **G** of Israel should be put to death, 430
15:18 he brought *into* the house of **G** *the things* 430
16: 7 not relied on the LORD thy **G**, therefore 430
17: 4 sought to the *LORD* **G** of his father, and 430
18: 5 for **G** will deliver *it* into the king's hand. 430
18:13 even what my **G** saith, that will I speak. 430
18:31 and **G** moved them *to depart* from him. 430
19: 3 and hast prepared thine heart to seek **G**. 430
19: 4 brought them back unto the LORD **G** of 430
19: 7 *there is* no iniquity with the LORD our **G**, 430
20: 6 said, O LORD **G** of our fathers, *art* not thou 430
20: 6 God of our fathers, *art* not thou **G** in heaven? 430
20: 7 *Art* not thou our **G**, who didst drive out 430
20:12 O our **G**, wilt thou not judge them? for we 430
20:19 stood up to praise the LORD **G** of Israel 430
20:20 Believe in the LORD your **G**, so shall you 430
20:29 the fear of **G** was on all the kingdoms of 430
20:30 for his **G** gave him rest round about. 430
20:33 their hearts unto the **G** of their fathers. 430
21:10 he had forsaken the LORD **G** of his fathers. 430
21:12 Thus saith the LORD **G** of David thy 430
22: 7 the destruction of Ahaziah was of **G** by 430
22:12 he was with them hid in the house of **G** six 430
23: 3 a covenant with the king in the house of **G**. 430
23: 9 king David's, which *were in* the house of **G**. 430
23:11 anointed him, and said, **G save** the king. 2421
24: 5 repair the house of your **G** from year to year, 430
24: 7 had broken up the house of **G**; 430
24: 9 of **G** laid upon Israel in the wilderness. 430
24:13 they set the house of **G** in his state, and 430
24:16 both towards **G**, and *towards* his house. 430
24:18 they left the house of the LORD **G** of their 430
24:20 the spirit of **G** came upon Zechariah the son 430
24:20 and said unto them, Thus saith **G**, 430
24:24 they had forsaken the LORD **G** of their 430
24:27 and the repairing of the house of **G**, 430
25: 7 there came a man of **G** to him, saying, 430
25: 8 **G** shall make thee fall before the enemy: 430
25: 8 for **G** hath power to help, and to cast down. 430
25: 9 Amaziah said to the man of **G**, But what 430
25: 9 the man of **G** answered, The LORD is able 430
25:16 I know that **G** hath determined to destroy 430
25:20 for it *came* of **G**, that *he* might deliver them 430
25:24 found in the house of **G** with Obed-edom, 430
26: 5 he sought **G** in the days of Zechariah, 430
26: 5 who had understanding in the visions of **G**: 430
26: 5 sought the LORD, **G** made him to prosper. 430
26: 7 **G** helped him against the Philistines, and 430
26:16 he transgressed against the LORD his **G**, 430
26:18 *it be* for thine honour from the LORD **G**. 430
27: 6 prepared his ways before the LORD his **G**. 430
28: 5 Wherefore the LORD his **G** delivered him 430
28: 6 they had forsaken the LORD **G** of their 430
28: 9 the LORD **G** of your fathers was wroth 430
28:10 with you, sins against the LORD your **G**? 430
28:24 together the vessels of the house of **G**, 430
28:24 cut in pieces the vessels of the house of **G**, 430
28:25 provoked to anger the LORD **G** of his 430
29: 5 sanctify the house of the LORD **G** of your 430
29: 6 *was* evil in the eyes of the LORD our **G**, 430
29: 7 in the holy *place* unto the **G** of Israel. 430
29:10 a covenant with the LORD **G** of Israel, 430
29:36 the people, that **G** had prepared the people: 430
30: 1 to keep the passover unto the LORD **G** of 430
30: 5 unto the LORD **G** of Israel at Jerusalem: 430
30: 6 turn again unto the LORD **G** of Abraham, 430
30: 7 which trespassed against the LORD **G** of 430
30: 8 serve the LORD your **G**, that the fierceness 430
30: 9 for the LORD your **G** *is* gracious and 430
30:12 Also in Judah the hand of **G** was to give 430
30:16 according to the law of Moses the man of **G**: 430
30:19 *That* prepareth his heart to seek **G**, 430
30:19 to seek God, the LORD **G** of his fathers, 430
30:22 making confession to the LORD **G** of their 430
31: 6 were consecrated unto the LORD their **G**, 430
31:13 and Azariah the ruler of the house of **G**. 430
31:14 *was* over the freewill offerings of **G**, 430
31:20 and right and truth before the LORD his **G**. 430
31:21 he began in the service of the house of **G**, 430
31:21 and in the commandments, to seek his **G**, 430
32: 8 with us *is* the LORD our **G** to help us, and 430
32:11 The LORD our **G** shall deliver us out of 430
32:14 that your **G** should be able to deliver you out 430

2Ch 32:15 for no **g** of any nation or kingdom was able 433
32:15 how much less shall your **G** deliver you out 430
32:16 spake yet *more* against the LORD **G**, 430
32:17 He wrote also letters to rail on the LORD **G** 430
32:17 shall not the **G** of Hezekiah deliver his 430
32:19 they spake against the **G** of Jerusalem, 430
32:21 when he was come *into* the house of his **g**, 430
32:29 for **G** had given him substance very much. 430
32:31 **G** left him, to try him, that *he* might know 430
33: 7 idol which he had made, in the house of **G**, 430
33: 7 of which **G** had said to David and 430
33:12 he besought the LORD his **G**, and 430
33:12 humbled himself greatly before the **G** of his 430
33:13 Manasseh knew that the LORD he *was* **G**. 430
33:16 commanded Judah to serve the LORD **G** of 430
33:17 *yet* unto the LORD their **G** only. 430
33:18 his prayer unto his **G**, and the words of 430
33:18 him in the name of the LORD **G** of Israel, 430
33:19 *how* **G** was intreated of him, and all his sin, NIH
34: 3 he began to seek after the **G** of David his 430
34: 8 to repair the house of the LORD his **G**. 430
34: 9 money that was brought *into* the house of **G**, 430
34:23 Thus saith the LORD **G** of Israel, 430
34:26 Thus saith the LORD **G** of Israel 430
34:27 and thou didst humble thyself before **G**, 430
34:32 did according to the covenant of **G**, 430
34:32 the covenant of God, the **G** of their fathers. 430
34:33 to serve, *even* to serve the LORD their **G**. 430
34:33 following the LORD, the **G** of their fathers. 430
35: 3 serve now the LORD your **G**, and his 430
35: 8 and Jehiel, rulers of the house of **G**, 430
35:21 for **G** commanded me to make haste: 430
35:21 forbear thee from meddling with **G**, who *is* 430
35:22 the words of Necho from the mouth of **G**, 430
36: 5 *was* evil in the sight of the LORD his **G**. 430
36:12 *was* evil in the sight of the LORD his **G**, 430
36:13 who had made him swear by **G**: 430
36:13 from turning unto the LORD **G** of Israel. 430
36:15 the LORD **G** of their fathers sent to them 430
36:16 they mocked the messengers of **G**, and 430
36:18 all the vessels of the house of **G**, great and 430
36:19 they burnt the house of **G**, and brake down 430
36:23 hath the LORD **G** of heaven given me; 430
36:23 The LORD his **G** *be* with him, and let him 430
Ezr 1: 2 The LORD **G** of heaven hath given me all 430
1: 3 his **G** be with him, and let him go up to 430
1: 3 build the house of the LORD **G** of Israel, 430
1: 3 of the LORD God of Israel, (he *is* the **G**,) 430
1: 4 for the house of **G** that *is* in Jerusalem. 430
1: 5 with all *them* whose spirit **G** had raised, 430
2:68 offered freely for the house of **G** to set it up 430
3: 2 and builded the altar of the **G** of Israel, 430
3: 2 is written in the law of Moses the man of **G**. 430
3: 8 coming unto the house of **G** at Jerusalem, 430
3: 9 set forward the workmen in the house of **G**: 430
4: 1 the temple unto the LORD **G** of Israel; 430
4: 2 for we seek your **G**, as ye *do*; and we do 430
4: 3 to do with us to build a house unto our **G**; 430
4: 3 will build unto the LORD **G** of Israel, 430
4:24 ceased the work of the house of the **G** which 426
5: 1 and Jerusalem in the name of the **G** of Israel, 426
5: 2 began to build the house of **G** which *is* at 426
5: 2 with them *were* the prophets of **G** helping 426
5: 5 the eye of their **G** was upon the elders of 426
5: 8 to the house of the great **G**, which *is* builded 426
5:11 We are the servants of the **G** of heaven and 426
5:12 after that our fathers had provoked the **G** of 426
5:13 made a decree to build this house of **G**. 426
5:14 also of gold and silver of the house of **G**, 426
5:15 let the house of **G** be builded in his place. 426
5:16 laid the foundation of the house of **G** which 426
5:17 king to build this house of **G** at Jerusalem, 426
6: 3 *concerning* the house of **G** at Jerusalem, 426
6: 5 and silver vessels of the house of **G**, 426
6: 5 his place, and place *them* in the house of **G**. 426
6: 7 Let the work of this house of **G** alone; let 426
6: 7 the elders of the Jews build this house of **G** 426
6: 8 Jews for the building of this house of **G**: 426
6: 9 for the burnt offerings of the **G** of heaven, 426
6:10 of sweet savours unto the **G** of heaven, 426
6:12 the **G** that hath caused his name to dwell 426
6:12 to destroy this house of **G** which *is* at 426
6:14 to the commandment of the **G** of Israel, 426
6:16 kept the dedication of this house of **G** with 426
6:17 offered at the dedication of this house of **G** 426
6:18 for the service of **G**, which *is* at Jerusalem; 426
6:21 to seek the LORD **G** of Israel, did eat, 430
6:22 their hands in the work of the house of **G**, 430
6:22 work of the house of God, the **G** of Israel. 430
7: 6 which the LORD **G** of Israel had given: 430
7: 6 according to the hand of the LORD his **G** 430
7: 9 according to the good hand of his **G** upon 430
7:12 a scribe of the law of the **G** of heaven, 426
7:14 according to the law of thy **G** which *is* in 426
7:15 have freely offered unto the **G** of Israel, 426
7:16 offering willingly for the house of their **G** 426
7:17 the house of your **G** which *is* in Jerusalem. 426
7:18 and gold, *that* do after the will of your **G**. 426
7:19 thee for the service of the house of thy **G**, 426
7:19 *those* deliver thou before the **G** of Jerusalem. 426
7:20 more *shall be* needful for the house of thy **G**, 426
7:21 the scribe of the law of the **G** of heaven, 426
7:23 Whatsoever *is* commanded by the **G** of 426
7:23 it be diligently done for the house of the **G** 426
7:24 or ministers of this house of **G**, 426
7:25 thou, Ezra, after the wisdom of thy **G**, that *is* 426
7:25 the river, all such as know the laws of thy **G**; 426
7:26 And whosoever will not do the law of thy **G**, 426
7:27 Blessed *be* the LORD **G** of our fathers, 430
7:28 the hand of the LORD my **G** *was* upon me, 430
8:17 unto us ministers for the house of our **G**. 430
8:18 by the good hand of our **G** upon us they 430
8:21 that *we* might afflict ourselves before our **G**, 430
8:22 The hand of our **G** *is* upon all them for good 430
8:23 So we fasted and besought our **G** for this: 430

G

Ezr 8:25 *even* the offering of the house of our **G**, 430
8:28 offering unto the LORD **G** of your fathers. 430
8:30 *them* to Jerusalem unto the house of our **G**. 430
8:31 the hand of our **G** was upon us, and 430
8:33 the vessels weighed in the house of our **G** by 430
8:35 offered burnt offerings unto the **G** of Israel, 430
8:36 furthered the people, and the house of **G**. 430
9: 4 that trembled at the words of the **G** of Israel, 430
9: 5 spread out my hands unto the LORD my **G**, 430
9: 6 said, O my **G**, I am ashamed and blush to lift 430
9: 6 and blush to lift up my face to thee, my **G**: 430
9: 8 hath been *shewed* from the LORD our **G**, 430
9: 8 that our **G** may lighten our eyes, and give us 430
9: 9 yet our **G** hath not forsaken us in our 430
9: 9 to set up the house of our **G**, and to repair 430
9:10 now, O our **G**, what shall we say after this? 430
9:13 seeing that thou our **G** hast punished us less 430
9:15 O LORD **G** of Israel, thou *art* righteous: 430
10: 1 casting himself down before the house of **G**, 430
10: 2 We have trespassed against our **G**, and 430
10: 3 let us make a covenant with our **G** to put 430
10: 3 that tremble at the commandment of our **G**; 430
10: 6 Ezra rose up from before the house of **G**, 430
10: 9 the people sat in the street of the house of **G**, 430
10:11 make confession unto the LORD **G** of your 430
10:14 until the fierce wrath of our **G** for this matter 430
Ne 1: 4 and prayed before the **G** of heaven, 430
1: 5 O LORD **G** of heaven, the great and 430
1: 5 the great and terrible **G**, that keepeth 410
2: 4 So I prayed to the **G** of heaven. 430
2: 8 according to the good hand of my **G** upon 430
2:12 neither told I *any* man what my **G** had put in 430
2:18 I told them of the hand of my **G** which was 430
2:20 said unto them, The **G** of heaven, he will 430
4: 4 Hear, O our **G**; for we are despised: and 430
4: 9 we made our prayer unto our **G**, 430
4:15 **G** had brought their counsel to nought, 430
4:20 ye thither unto us: our **G** shall fight for us. 430
5: 9 ought ye not to walk in the fear of our **G** 430
5:13 So **G** shake out every man from his house, 430
5:15 but so did not I, because of the fear of **G**. 430
5:19 Think upon me, my **G**, for good, 430
6: 9 Now therefore, *O G*, strengthen my hands. NIH
6:10 Let us meet together in the house of **G**, 430
6:12 And lo, I perceived that **G** had not sent him; 430
6:14 My **G**, think thou upon Tobiah and Sanballat 430
6:16 that this work was wrought of our **G**. 430
7: 2 a faithful man, and feared **G** above many. 430
7: 5 my **G** put into mine heart to gather together 430
8: 6 Ezra blessed the LORD, the great **G**. 430
8: 8 So they read in the book in the law of **G** 430
8: 9 *This* day *is* holy unto the LORD your **G**; 430
8:16 in the courts of the house of **G**, and in 430
8:18 last day, he read in the book of the law of **G**. 430
9: 3 LORD their **G** *one* fourth *part* of the day; 430
9: 3 and worshipped the LORD their **G**. 430
9: 4 with a loud voice unto the LORD their **G**. 430
9: 5 *and* bless the LORD your **G** for ever and 430
9: 7 Thou *art* the LORD the **G**, who didst 430
9:17 thou *art* a **G** ready to pardon, gracious and 433
9:18 This *is* thy **G** that brought thee up out of 430
9:31 for thou *art* a gracious and merciful **G**. 410
9:32 our **G**, the great, the mighty, and the terrible 430
9:32 the great, the mighty, and the terrible **G**, 410
10:28 the people of the lands unto the law of **G**, 430
10:29 which was given by Moses the servant of **G**, 430
10:32 shekel for the service of the house of our **G**; 430
10:33 and *for* all the work of the house of our **G**. 430
10:34 to bring *it* into the house of our **G**, 430
10:34 to burn upon the altar of the LORD our **G**, 430
10:36 of our flocks, to bring to the house of our **G**, 430
10:36 priests that minister in the house of our **G**: 430
10:37 to the chambers of the house of our **G**; 430
10:38 tithe of the tithes unto the house of our **G**, 430
10:39 and we will not forsake the house of our **G**. 430
11:11 of Ahitub, *was* the ruler of the house of **G**. 430
11:16 of the outward business of the house of **G**. 430
11:22 *were* over the business of the house of **G**. 430
12:24 to the commandment of David the man of **G**, 430
12:36 musical instruments of David the man of **G**, 430
12:40 *of them that gave* thanks in the house of **G**, 430
12:43 for **G** had made them rejoice *with* great joy: 430
12:45 and the porters kept the ward of their **G**, 430
12:46 songs of praise and thanksgiving unto **G**. 430
13: 1 come into the congregation of **G** for ever; 430
13: 2 howbeit our **G** turned the curse into a 430
13: 4 of the chamber of the house of our **G**, 430
13: 7 a chamber in the courts of the house of **G**. 430
13: 9 I again the vessels of the house of **G**, 430
13:11 and said, Why is the house of **G** forsaken? 430
13:14 Remember me, O my **G**, concerning this, 430
13:14 that I have done for the house of my **G**, 430
13:18 and *did not* our **G** bring all this evil upon us, 430
13:22 Remember me, O my **G**, *concerning* this 430
13:25 off their hair, and made them swear by **G**, 430
13:26 who was beloved of his **G**, and God made 430
13:26 and **G** made him king over all Israel: 430
13:27 to transgress against our **G** in marrying 430
13:29 O my **G**, because they have defiled 430
13:31 Remember me, O my **G**, for good. 430
Job 1: 1 and one that feared **G**, and eschewed evil. 430
1: 5 have sinned, and cursed **G** in their hearts. 430
1: 6 Now there was a day when the sons of **G** 430
1: 8 one that feareth **G**, and escheweth evil? 430
1: 9 and said, Doth Job fear **G** for nought? 430
1:16 The fire of **G** is fallen from heaven, and 430
1:22 this Job sinned not, nor charged **G** foolishly. 430
2: 1 Again there was a day when the sons of **G** 430
2: 3 one that feareth **G**, and escheweth evil? 430
2: 9 still retain thine integrity? curse **G**, and die. 430
2:10 shall we receive good at the hand of **G**, and 430
3: 4 let not **G** regard it from above, neither let 433
3:23 way is hid, and whom **G** hath hedged in? 433
4: 9 By the blast of **G** they perish, and by 433
4:17 Shall mortal man be more just than **G**? 433

Job 5: 8 I would seek unto **G**, and unto God would I 410
5: 8 and unto **G** would I commit my cause: 430
5:17 happy *is* the man whom **G** correcteth: 433
6: 4 the terrors of **G** do set *themselves* in array 433
6: 8 *that* **G** would grant *me* the thing that I long 433
6: 9 Even *that* it would please **G** to destroy me: 433
8: 3 Doth **G** pervert judgment? or doth 410
8: 5 If thou wouldest seek unto **G** betimes, and 410
8:13 So *are* the paths of all that forget **G**; and 410
8:20 **G** will not cast away a perfect *man*, neither 410
9: 2 a truth: but how should man be just with **G**? 410
9:13 *If* **G** will not withdraw his anger, the proud 433
10: 2 I will say unto **G**, Do not condemn me; 433
11: 5 O that **G** would speak, and open his lips 433
11: 6 that **G** exacteth of thee *less* than thine 433
11: 7 Canst thou *by* searching find out **G**? 433
12: 4 who calleth upon **G**, and he answereth him: 433
12: 6 and they that provoke **G** are secure; 410
12: 6 into whose hand **G** bringeth *abundantly*. 433
13: 3 the Almighty, and I desire to reason with **G**. 410
13: 7 Will you speak wickedly for **G**? and 410
13: 8 ye accept his person? will ye contend for **G**? 410
15: 4 off fear, and restrainest prayer before **G**. 410
15: 8 Hast thou heard the secret of **G**? and 433
15:11 *Are* the consolations of **G** small with thee? 410
15:13 That thou turnest thy spirit against **G**, and 410
15:25 For he stretcheth out his hand against **G**, and 410
16:11 **G** hath delivered me to the ungodly, and 410
16:20 *but* mine eye poureth out *tears* unto **G**. 433
16:21 O that *one* might plead for a man with **G**, 433
18:21 this *is* the place *of him that* knoweth not **G**. 410
19: 6 Know now that **G** hath overthrown me, and 433
19:21 for the hand of **G** hath touched me. 433
19:22 Why do ye persecute me as **G**, and are not 410
19:26 this *body*, yet in my flesh shall I see **G**: 433
20:15 up again: **G** shall cast them out of his belly. 410
20:23 *G* shall cast the fury of his wrath upon him, NIH
20:29 This *is* the portion of a wicked man from **G**, 430
20:29 and the heritage appointed unto him by **G**. 410
21: 9 from fear, neither *is* the rod of **G** upon them. 433
21:14 Therefore they say unto **G**, Depart from us; 410
21:17 *G* distributeth sorrows in his anger. NIH
21:19 **G** layeth up his iniquity for his children: 433
21:22 Shall *any* teach **G** knowledge? seeing he 410
22: 2 Can a man be profitable unto **G**, as he that is 410
22:12 *Is* not **G** *in* the height of heaven? and 433
22:13 thou sayest, How doth **G** know? can he 410
22:17 Which said unto **G**, Depart from us: and 410
22:26 and shalt lift up thy face unto **G**. 433
23:16 For **G** maketh my heart soft, and 410
24:12 crieth out: yet **G** layeth not folly *to them*. 433
25: 4 How then can man be justified with **G**? or 410
27: 2 *As* **G** liveth, *who* hath taken away my 410
27: 3 *is* in me, and the spirit of **G** *is* in my nostrils; 433
27: 5 **G forbid** that I should justify you: till I die 2486
27: 8 hath gained, when **G** taketh away his soul? 433
27: 9 Will **G** hear his cry when trouble cometh 410
27:10 the Almighty? will he always call upon **G**? 433
27:11 I will teach you by the hand of **G**: *that* which 410
27:13 This *is* the portion of a wicked man with **G**, 410
27:22 For *G* shall cast upon him, and not spare: NIH
28:23 **G** understandeth the way thereof, and 430
29: 2 as *in* the days *when* **G** preserved me; 433
29: 4 when the secret of **G** *was* upon my 433
31: 2 For what portion of **G** *is there* from above? 433
31: 6 that **G** may know mine integrity. 433
31:14 What then shall I do when **G** riseth up? and 410
31:23 For destruction from **G** *was* a terror to me, 410
31:28 for I should have denied the **G** *that is* above. 410
32: 2 because he justified himself rather than **G**. 430
32:13 out wisdom: **G** thrusteth him down, not man. 410
33: 4 The Spirit of **G** hath made me, and 410
33:12 will answer thee, that **G** is greater than man. 433
33:14 For **G** speaketh once, yea twice, *yet man* 410
33:26 He shall pray unto **G**, and he will be 433
33:29 all these *things* worketh **G** oftentimes with 410
34: 5 and **G** hath taken away my judgment. 410
34: 9 that he should delight himself with **G**. 430
34:10 far be it from **G**, *that he should do* 410
34:12 Yea, surely **G** will not do wickedly, 410
34:23 that *he* should enter into judgment with **G**. 410
34:31 Surely it is *meet to be* said unto **G**, I have 410
34:37 and multiplieth his words against **G**. 410
35:10 none saith, Where *is* **G** my Maker, 433
35:13 Surely **G** will not hear vanity, neither will 410
36: 5 **G** *is* mighty, and despiseth not *any: he is* 410
36:22 Behold, **G** exalteth by his power: 410
36:26 Behold, **G** *is* great, and we know *him* not, 410
37: 5 **G** thundereth marvellously with his voice; 410
37:10 By the breath of **G** frost is given: and 410
37:14 and consider the wondrous works of **G**. 410
37:15 Dost thou know when **G** disposed them, and 433
37:22 out of the north: with **G** *is* terrible majesty. 433
38: 7 and all the sons of **G** shouted for joy? 430
38:41 when his young ones cry unto **G**, 410
39:17 Because **G** hath deprived her of wisdom, 433
40: 2 Almighty instruct *him?* he that reproveth **G**, 433
40: 9 Hast thou an arm like **G**? or, canst thou 410
40:19 He *is* the chief of the ways of **G**: he that 410
Ps 3: 2 of my soul, *There is* no help for him in **G**. 430
3: 7 Arise, O LORD; save me, O my **G**: 430
4: 1 me when I call, O **G** of my righteousness: 430
5: 2 the voice of my cry, my King, and my **G**: 430
5: 4 For thou *art* not a **G** that hath pleasure in 410
5:10 Destroy thou them, O **G**; let them fall by 430
7: 1 O LORD my **G**, in thee do I put my trust: 430
7: 3 O LORD my **G**, if I have done this; if there 430
7: 9 for the righteous **G** trieth the hearts and 430
7:10 My defence *is* of **G**, which saveth 430
7:11 **G** judgeth the righteous, and God is angry 430
7:11 and **G** is angry *with the wicked* every day. 410
9:17 into hell, *and* all the nations that forget **G**. 430
10: 4 will not seek *after G*: God *is* not *in* all his NIH
10: 4 will not seek *after* God: **G** *is* not *in* all his 430
10:11 He hath said in his heart, **G** hath forgotten: 410

Ps 10:12 Arise, O LORD; O **G**, lift up thine hand: 410
10:13 Wherefore doth the wicked contemn **G**? 430
13: 3 Consider *and* hear me, O LORD my **G**: 430
14: 1 fool hath said in his heart, *There is* no **G**. 430
14: 2 were *any* that did understand, *and* seek **G**. 430
14: 5 for **G** *is* in the generation of the righteous. 430
16: 1 Preserve me, O **G**: for in thee do I put my 410
16: 4 *g*: their drink offerings of blood will I not NIH
17: 6 called upon thee, for thou wilt hear me, O **G**: 410
18: 2 my **G**, my strength, in whom I will trust; 410
18: 6 upon the LORD, and cried unto my **G**: 430
18:21 and have not wickedly departed from my **G**. 430
18:28 the LORD my **G** will enlighten my 430
18:29 and by my **G** have I leaped over a wall. 430
18:30 *As for* **G**, his way *is* perfect: the word of 410
18:31 For who *is* **G** save the LORD? or who *is* a 433
18:31 the LORD? or who *is* a rock save our **G**? 430
18:32 *It is* **G** that girdeth me *with* strength, and 410
18:46 and let the **G** of my salvation be exalted. 430
18:47 *It is* **G** that avengeth me, and subdueth 410
19: 1 The heavens declare the glory of **G**; and 410
20: 1 the name of the **G** of Jacob defend thee; 430
20: 5 in the name of our **G** we will set up *our* 430
20: 7 remember the name of the LORD our **G**. 430
22: 1 My **G**, my God, why hast thou forsaken me? 410
22: 1 My God, my **G**, why hast thou forsaken me? 410
22: 2 O my **G**, I cry in the daytime, but 430
22:10 thou *art* my **G** from my mother's belly. 410
24: 5 righteousness from the **G** of his salvation. 430
25: 2 O my **G**, I trust in thee: let me not be 430
25: 5 for thou *art* the **G** of my salvation; on thee 430
25:22 Redeem Israel, O **G**, out of all his troubles. 430
27: 9 neither forsake me, O **G** of my salvation. 430
29: 3 the **G** of glory thundereth: the LORD *is* 410
30: 2 O LORD my **G**, I cried unto thee, and 430
30:12 O LORD my **G**, I will give thanks unto 430
31: 5 hast redeemed me, O LORD **G** of truth. 410
31:14 in thee, O LORD: I said, Thou *art* my **G**. 430
33:12 Blessed *is* the nation whose **G** *is* 430
35:23 *even* unto my cause, my **G** and my Lord. 430
35:24 Judge me, O LORD my **G**, according to thy 430
36: 1 *that there is* no fear of **G** before his eyes. 430
36: 7 How excellent *is* thy lovingkindness, O **G**! 430
37:31 The law of his **G** *is* in his heart; none of his 430
38:15 do I hope: thou wilt hear, O Lord my **G**. 430
38:21 O LORD: O my **G**, be not far from me. 430
40: 3 song in my mouth, *even* praise unto our **G**: 430
40: 5 Many, O LORD my **G**, *are* thy wonderful 430
40: 8 I delight to do thy will, O my **G**: yea, 430
40:17 my deliverer; make no tarrying, O my **G**. 430
41:13 Blessed *be* the LORD **G** of Israel from 430
42: 1 so panteth my soul after thee, O **G**. 430
42: 2 My soul thirsteth for **G**, for the living God: 430
42: 2 My soul thirsteth for God, for the living **G**: 410
42: 2 when shall I come and appear before **G**? 430
42: 3 continually say unto me, Where *is* thy **G**? 430
42: 4 I went with them to the house of **G**, with 430
42: 5 hope thou in **G**: for I shall yet praise him *for* 430
42: 6 O my **G**, my soul is cast down within me: 430
42: 8 *and my* prayer unto the **G** of my life. 410
42: 9 I will say unto **G** my rock, Why hast thou 410
42:10 they say daily unto me, Where *is* thy **G**? 430
42:11 hope thou in **G**: for I shall yet praise him, 430
42:11 *is* the health of my countenance, and my **G**. 430
43: 1 O **G**, and plead my cause against an ungodly 430
43: 2 For thou *art* the **G** of my strength: why dost 430
43: 4 will I go unto the altar of **G**, unto God my 430
43: 4 the altar of God, unto **G** my exceeding joy: 410
43: 4 the harp will I praise thee, O **G** my God. 430
43: 4 the harp will I praise thee, O God my **G**. 430
43: 5 hope in **G**: for I shall yet praise him, *who is* 430
43: 5 *is* the health of my countenance, and my **G**. 430
44: 1 with our ears, O **G**, our fathers have told us, 430
44: 4 Thou *art* my King, O **G**: 430
44: 8 In **G** we boast all the day long, and 430
44:20 If we have forgotten the name of our **G**, or 430
44:20 or stretched out our hands to a strange **g**; 410
44:21 Shall not **G** search this out? for he knoweth 430
45: 2 therefore **G** hath blessed thee for ever. 430
45: 6 Thy throne, O **G**, *is* for ever and ever: 430
45: 7 therefore **G**, thy God, hath anointed thee 430
45: 7 therefore God, thy **G**, hath anointed thee 430
46: 1 **G** *is* our refuge and strength, a very present 430
46: 4 whereof shall make glad the city of **G**, 430
46: 5 **G** *is* in the midst of her; she shall not be 430
46: 5 **G** shall help her, *and that* right early. 430
46: 7 hosts *is* with us; the **G** of Jacob *is* our refuge. 430
46:10 Be still, and know that I *am* **G**: I will be 430
46:11 hosts *is* with us; the **G** of Jacob *is* our refuge. 430
47: 1 shout unto **G** with the voice of triumph. 430
47: 5 **G** is gone up with a shout, the LORD with 430
47: 6 Sing *praises* to **G**, sing *praises*: sing *praises* 430
47: 7 For **G** *is* the King of all the earth: sing ye 430
47: 8 **G** reigneth over the heathen: God sitteth 430
47: 8 **G** sitteth upon the throne of his holiness. 430
47: 9 *even* the people of the **G** of Abraham: 430
47: 9 for the shields of the earth *belong* unto **G**: 430
48: 1 and greatly to be praised in the city of our **G**, 430
48: 3 **G** is known in her palaces for a refuge. 430
48: 8 of the LORD of hosts, in the city of our **G**: 430
48: 8 our God: **G** will establish it for ever. Selah. 430
48: 9 O **G**, in the midst of thy temple. 430
48:10 O **G**, so *is* thy praise unto the ends of 430
48:14 For this **G** *is* our God for ever and ever: 430
48:14 For this God *is* our **G** for ever and ever: 430
49: 7 *his* brother, nor give to **G** a ransom for him: 430
49:15 **G** will redeem my soul from the power of 430
50: 1 The mighty **G**, *even* the LORD, 430
50: 2 the perfection of beauty, **G** hath shined. 430
50: 3 Our **G** shall come, and shall not keep 430
50: 6 for **G** *is* judge himself. Selah. 430
50: 7 testify against thee: I *am* **G**, *even* thy God. 430
50: 7 testify against thee: I *am* God, *even* thy **G**. 430
50:14 Offer unto **G** thanksgiving; and pay thy 430
50:16 unto the wicked **G** saith, What hast thou to 430

Ps 50:22 Now consider this, ye that forget G, lest I 433
50:23 *aright* will I shew the salvation of G. 430
51: 1 Have mercy upon me, O G, according to thy 430
51:10 Create in me a clean heart, O G; and renew a 430
51:14 O G, thou God of my salvation: 430
51:14 O God, thou G of my salvation: 430
51:17 The sacrifices of G *are* a broken spirit: 430
51:17 a broken and a contrite heart, O G, thou wilt 430
52: 1 O mighty *man?* the goodness of G *endureth* 410
52: 5 G shall likewise destroy thee for ever, 410
52: 7 *this is* the man *that* made not G his strength; 430
52: 8 *am* like a green olive tree in the house of G: 430
52: 8 I trust in the mercy of G for ever and ever. 430
53: 1 fool hath said in his heart, *There is* no G. 430
53: 2 G looked down from heaven upon 430
53: 2 *any* that did understand, that did seek G. 430
53: 4 they eat bread: they have not called upon G. 430
53: 5 for G hath scattered the bones of him that 430
53: 5 to shame, because G hath despised them. 430
53: 6 When G bringeth back the captivity of his 430
54: 1 Save me, O G, by thy name, and judge me 430
54: 2 Hear my prayer, O G; give ear to the words 430
54: 3 they have not set G before them. Selah. 430
54: 4 Behold, G *is* mine helper: the Lord *is* with 430
55: 1 Give ear to my prayer, O G; and hide not 430
55:14 *and* walked unto the house of G in company. 430
55:16 *As for* me, I will call upon G; and 430
55:19 G shall hear, and afflict them, even he that 410
55:19 have no changes, therefore they fear not G. 430
55:23 thou, O G, shalt bring them down into the pit 430
56: 1 Be merciful unto me, O G: for man would 430
56: 4 In G I will praise his word, in God I have 430
56: 4 praise his word, in G I have put my trust; 430
56: 7 in *thine* anger cast down the people, O G. 430
56: 9 turn back: this I know; for G *is* for me. 430
56:10 In G will I praise *his* word: in the LORD 430
56:11 In G have I put my trust: I will not be afraid 430
56:12 Thy vows *are* upon me, O G: I will render 430
56:13 that *I* may walk before G in the light of 430
57: 1 merciful unto me, O G, be merciful unto me: 430
57: 2 I will cry unto G most High; unto God that 430
57: 2 unto G that performeth *all things* for me. 410
57: 3 G shall send forth his mercy and his truth. 430
57: 5 Be thou exalted, O G, above the heavens; 430
57: 7 My heart is fixed, O G, my heart is fixed: 430
57:11 Be thou exalted, O G, above the heavens: 430
58: 6 Break their teeth, O G, in their mouth: 430
58:11 verily he is a G that judgeth in the earth. 430
59: 1 Deliver me from mine enemies, O my G: 430
59: 5 Thou therefore, O LORD G *of* hosts, 430
59: 5 O LORD God *of* hosts, the G of Israel, 430
59: 9 will I wait upon thee: for G *is* my defence. 430
59:10 The G of my mercy shall prevent me: 430
59:10 G shall let me see *my desire* upon mine 430
59:13 let them know that G ruleth in Jacob unto 430
59:17 for G *is* my defence, *and* the God of my 430
59:17 God *is* my defence, *and* the G of my mercy. 430
60: 1 O G, thou hast cast us off, thou hast 430
60: 6 G hath spoken in his holiness; I will rejoice, 430
60:10 *Wilt* not thou, O G, *which* hadst cast us off? 430
60:10 *thou,* O G, *which* didst not go out with our 430
60:12 Through G we shall do valiantly: for he *it is* 430
61: 1 Hear my cry, O G; attend unto my prayer. 430
61: 5 For thou, O G, hast heard my vows: 430
61: 7 He shall abide before G for ever: O prepare 430
62: 1 Truly my soul waiteth upon G: from him 430
62: 5 My soul, wait thou only upon G; for my 430
62: 7 In G *is* my salvation and my glory: the rock 430
62: 7 rock of my strength, *and* my refuge, *is* in G. 430
62: 8 heart before him: G *is* a refuge for us. Selah. 430
62:11 G hath spoken once; twice have I heard this; 430
62:11 I heard this; that power *belongeth* unto G. 430
63: 1 O G, thou *art* my God; early will I seek thee: 430
63: 1 O God, thou *art* my G; early will I seek thee: 410
63:11 the king shall rejoice in G; every one that 430
64: 1 Hear my voice, O G, in my prayer: 430
64: 7 G shall shoot at them *with* an arrow; 430
64: 9 shall fear, and shall declare the work of G; 430
65: 1 Praise waiteth for thee, O G, in Zion: and 430
65: 5 wilt thou answer us, O G of our salvation; 430
65: 9 thou greatly enrichest it *with* the river of G, 430
66: 1 Make a joyful noise unto G, all ye lands: 430
66: 3 Say unto G, How terrible *art thou in* thy 430
66: 5 Come and see the works of G: *he is* terrible 430
66: 8 O bless our G, ye people, and make 430
66:10 For thou, O G, hast proved us: thou hast 430
66:16 all ye that fear G, and I will declare what he 430
66:19 *But* verily G hath heard *me;* he hath attended 430
66:20 Blessed *be* G, which hath not turned away 430
67: 1 G be merciful unto us, and bless us; *and* 430
67: 3 Let the people praise thee, O G; let all 430
67: 5 Let the people praise thee, O G; let all 430
67: 6 *and* G, *even* our own God, shall bless us. 430
67: 6 *and* God, *even* our own G, shall bless us. 430
67: 7 G shall bless us; and all the ends of the earth 430
68: 1 Let G arise, let his enemies be scattered: 430
68: 2 *so* let the wicked perish at the presence of G. 430
68: 3 righteous be glad; let them rejoice before G: 430
68: 4 Sing unto G, sing *praises to* his name: 430
68: 5 of the widows, *is* G in his holy habitation. 430
68: 6 G setteth the solitary in families: he bringeth 430
68: 7 O G, when thou wentest forth before thy 430
68: 8 heavens also dropped at the presence of G: 430
68: 8 Sinai itself *was moved* at the presence of G, 430
68: 8 at the presence of God, the G of Israel. 430
68: 9 Thou, O G, didst send a plentiful rain, 430
68:10 thou, O G, hast prepared of thy goodness for 430
68:15 The hill of G *is as* the hill of Bashan; a high 430
68:16 *this is* the hill *which* G desireth to dwell in; 430
68:17 The chariots of G *are* twenty thousand, 430
68:18 that the LORD G might dwell *among* 430
68:19 us *with benefits, even* the G of our salvation. 410
68:20 *He that is* our G *is* the God of salvation; and 410
68:20 *He that is* our God *is* the G of salvation; and 410
68:21 G shall wound the head of his enemies, *and* 430

Ps 68:24 They have seen thy goings, O G; *even* 430
68:24 *even* the goings of my G, my King, in 410
68:26 Bless ye G in the congregations, *even* 430
68:28 Thy G hath commanded thy strength: 430
68:28 strengthen, O G, that which thou hast 430
68:31 shall soon stretch out her hands unto G. 430
68:32 Sing unto G, ye kingdoms of the earth; 430
68:34 Ascribe ye strength unto G: his excellency *is* 430
68:35 O G, *thou art* terrible out of thy holy places: 430
68:35 the G of Israel *is* he that giveth strength and 410
68:35 and power unto *his* people. Blessed *be* G. 430
69: 1 Save me, O G; for the waters are come in 430
69: 3 mine eyes fail while *I* wait for my G. 430
69: 5 O G, thou knowest my foolishness; and 430
69: 6 be confounded for my sake, O G of Israel. 430
69:13 O G, in the multitude of thy mercy hear me, 430
69:29 let thy salvation, O G, set me up on high. 430
69:30 I will praise the name of G with a song; and 430
69:32 and your heart shall live that seek G. 430
69:35 For G will save Zion, and will build 430
70: 1 *Make haste,* O G, to deliver me; make haste 430
70: 4 say continually, Let G be magnified. 430
70: 5 make haste unto me, O G: thou *art* my help 430
71: 4 Deliver me, O my G, out of the hand of 430
71:11 Saying, G hath forsaken him: persecute and 430
71:12 O G, be not far from me: O my God, 430
71:12 from me: O my G, make haste for my help. 430
71:17 O G, thou hast taught me from my youth: 430
71:18 also when I am old and grayheaded, O G, 430
71:19 Thy righteousness also, O G, *is* very high, 430
71:19 very high, who hast done great *things:* O G, 430
71:22 with the psaltery, *even* thy truth, O my G: 430
72: 1 O G, and thy righteousness unto the king's 430
72:18 Blessed *be* the LORD G, the God of Israel, 430
72:18 Blessed *be* the LORD God, the G of Israel, 430
73: 1 Truly G *is* good to Israel, *even* to such as are 430
73:11 they say, How doth G know? and is there 410
73:17 Until I went into the sanctuary of G; *then* 410
73:26 *but* G *is* the strength of my heart, and 430
73:28 *it is* good for me to draw near to G: I have 430
74: 1 O G, why hast thou cast *us* off for ever? 430
74: 8 they have burnt up all the synagogues of G 410
74:10 O G, how long shall the adversary reproach? 430
74:12 For G *is* my King of old, working salvation 430
74:22 Arise, O G, plead thine own cause: 430
75: 1 Unto thee, O G, do we give thanks, 430
75: 7 But G *is* the judge: he putteth down one, and 430
75: 9 I will sing *praises* to the G of Jacob. 430
76: 1 In Judah *is* G known: his name *is* great in 430
76: 6 At thy rebuke, O G of Jacob, both 430
76: 9 When G arose to judgment, to save all 430
76:11 Vow, and pay unto the LORD your G: 430
77: 1 I cried unto G *with* my voice, *even* unto God 430
77: 1 *with* my voice, *even* unto G *with* my voice; 430
77: 3 I remembered G, and was troubled: 430
77: 9 Hath G forgotten to be gracious? hath he in 410
77:13 Thy way, O G, *is* in the sanctuary: who *is so* 430
77:13 who *is so* great a G as *our* God? 410
77:13 who *is so* great a God as *our* G? 430
77:14 Thou *art* the G that doest wonders: thou hast 410
77:16 waters saw thee, O G, the waters saw thee; 430
78: 7 That they might set their hope in G, and 430
78: 7 not forget the works of G, but keep his 410
78: 8 and whose spirit was not stedfast with G. 410
78:10 They kept not the covenant of G, and 430
78:18 they tempted G in their heart by asking meat 410
78:19 Yea, they spake against G; they said, Can 430
78:19 Can G furnish a table in the wilderness? 410
78:22 Because they believed not in G, and 430
78:31 The wrath of G came upon them, and 430
78:34 and they returned and inquired early after G. 410
78:35 And they remembered that G *was* their rock, 430
78:35 their rock, and the high G their redeemer. 410
78:41 they turned *back* and tempted G, and 410
78:56 they tempted and provoked the most high G, 430
78:59 When G heard *this,* he was wroth, and 430
79: 1 O G, the heathen are come into thine 430
79: 9 Help us, O G of our salvation, for the glory 430
79:10 should the heathen say, Where *is* their G? 430
80: 3 us again, O G, and cause thy face to shine; 430
80: 4 O LORD G *of* hosts, how long wilt thou be 430
80: 7 O G *of* hosts, and cause thy face to shine; 430
80:14 Return, we beseech thee, O G *of* hosts: 430
80:19 Turn us again, O LORD G *of* hosts, 430
81: 1 Sing aloud unto G our strength: make a 430
81: 1 make a joyful noise unto the G of Jacob. 430
81: 4 for Israel, *and* a law of the G of Jacob. 430
81: 9 There shall no strange g be in thee; 410
81: 9 neither shalt thou worship *any* strange g. 410
81:10 I *am* the LORD thy G, which brought thee 430
82: 1 G standeth in the congregation of 430
82: 8 Arise, O G, judge the earth: for thou shalt 430
83: 1 Keep not thou silence, O G: hold not thy 430
83: 1 hold not thy peace, and be not still, O G. 410
83:12 Let us take to ourselves the houses of G in 430
83:13 O my G, make them like a wheel; as 430
84: 2 and my flesh crieth out for the living G. 410
84: 3 O LORD of hosts, my King, and my G. 430
84: 7 *one of them* in Zion appeareth before G. 430
84: 8 O LORD G *of* hosts, hear my prayer: 430
84: 8 my prayer: give ear, O G of Jacob. Selah. 430
84: 9 O G our shield, and look upon the face of 430
84:10 rather be a doorkeeper in the house of my G, 430
84:11 For the LORD G *is* a sun and shield: 430
85: 4 O G of our salvation, and cause thine anger 430
85: 8 I will hear what G the LORD will speak: 410
86: 2 O thou my G, save thy servant that trusteth 430
86:10 and doest wondrous *things:* thou *art* G alone. 430
86:12 I will praise thee, O Lord my G, with all my 430
86:14 O G, the proud are risen against me, and 430
86:15 *art* a G full of compassion, and gracious, 410
87: 3 *things* are spoken of thee, O city of G. 430
88: 1 O LORD G of my salvation, I have cried 430
89: 7 G *is* greatly to be feared in the assembly of 410
89: 8 O LORD G of hosts, who *is* a strong 430

Ps 89:26 my G, and the rock of my salvation. 410
90: T A Prayer of Moses the man of G. 430
90: 2 from everlasting to everlasting, thou *art* G. 410
90:17 let the beauty of the LORD our G be upon 430
91: 2 and my fortress: my G; in him will I trust. 430
92:13 LORD shall flourish in the courts of our G. 430
94: 1 O LORD G, to whom vengeance 410
94: 1 O G, to whom vengeance belongeth, 410
94: 7 neither shall the G of Jacob regard *it.* 430
94:22 and my G *is* the rock of my refuge. 430
94:23 *yea,* the LORD our G shall cut them off. 430
95: 3 For the LORD *is* a great G, and a great 410
95: 7 For he *is* our G; and we *are* the people of his 430
98: 3 of the earth have seen the salvation of our G. 430
99: 5 Exalt ye the LORD our G, and worship at 430
99: 8 Thou answeredst them, O LORD our G: 430
99: 8 thou wast a G that forgavest them, 410
99: 9 Exalt the LORD our G, and worship at his 430
99: 9 his holy hill; for the LORD our G *is* holy. 430
100: 3 Know ye that the LORD he *is* G: *it is* he 430
102:24 I said, O my G, take me not away in 410
104: 1 O LORD my G, thou art very great; 430
104:21 after *their* prey, and seek their meat from G. 410
104:33 I will sing *praise* to my G while I have my 430
105: 7 He *is* the LORD our G: his judgments *are* 430
106:14 the wilderness, and tempted G in the desert. 410
106:21 They forgat G their saviour, which had done 410
106:47 O LORD our G, and gather us from among 430
106:48 Blessed *be* the LORD G of Israel from 430
107:11 they rebelled against the words of G, 410
108: 1 O G, my heart is fixed; I will sing and 430
108: 5 Be thou exalted, O G, above the heavens: 430
108: 7 G hath spoken in his holiness; I will rejoice, 430
108:11 *Wilt* not *thou,* O G, *who* hast cast us off? 430
108:11 wilt not thou, O G, go forth with our hosts? 430
108:13 Through G we shall do valiantly: for he *it is* 430
109: 1 Hold not thy peace, O G of my praise; 430
109:26 Help me, O LORD my G: O save me 430
113: 5 Who *is* like unto the LORD our G, who 430
114: 7 the Lord, at the presence of the G of Jacob; 433
115: 2 the heathen say, Where *is* now their G? 430
115: 3 our G *is* in the heavens: he hath done 430
116: 5 and righteous; yea, our G *is* merciful. 430
118:27 G *is* the LORD, which hath shewed us 410
118:28 Thou *art* my G, and I will praise thee: 410
118:28 praise thee: *thou art* my G, I will exalt thee. 430
119:115 for I will keep the commandments of my G. 430
122: 9 Because of the house of the LORD our G I 430
123: 2 so our eyes *wait* upon the LORD our G, 430
132: 2 *and* vowed unto the mighty G of Jacob; NIH
132: 5 a habitation for the mighty G of Jacob. NIH
135: 2 in the courts of the house of our G, 430
136: 2 O give thanks unto the G of gods: for his 430
136:26 O give thanks unto the G of heaven: for his 410
139:17 precious also are thy thoughts unto me, O G: 410
139:19 Surely thou wilt slay the wicked, O G: 433
139:23 Search me, O G, and know my heart: try me, 410
140: 6 I said unto the LORD, Thou *art* my G: 410
143:10 Teach me to do thy will; for thou *art* my G: 430
144: 9 I will sing a new song unto thee, O G: 430
144:15 *is that* people, whose G *is* the LORD. 430
145: 1 I will extol thee, my G, O king; and I will 430
146: 2 I will sing *praises* unto my G while I have 430
146: 5 Happy *is he* that *hath* the G of Jacob for his 410
146: 5 his help, whose hope *is* in the LORD his G: 430
146:10 *even* thy G, O Zion, unto all generations. 430
147: 1 for *it is* good to sing *praises* unto our G; 430
147: 7 sing *praise* upon the harp unto our G: 430
147:12 O Jerusalem; praise thy G, O Zion. 430
149: 6 *Let* the high *praises* of G *be* in their mouth, 410
150: 1 Praise G in his sanctuary: praise him in 410
Pr 2: 5 of the LORD, and find the knowledge of G. 430
2:17 and forgetteth the covenant of her G. 430
3: 4 good understanding in the sight of G and 430
21:12 G overthroweth the wicked for *their* NIH
25: 2 *It is* the glory of G to conceal a thing: but 430
26:10 The great G that formed all *things* both NIH
30: 5 Every word of G *is* pure: he *is* a shield unto 433
30: 9 steal, and take the name of my G *in vain.* 430
Ecc 1:13 this sore travail hath G given to the sons of 430
2:24 also I saw, that it *was* from the hand of G. 430
2:26 For G giveth to a man that *is* good in his NIH
2:26 *he* may give to *him that is* good before G. 430
3:10 which G hath given to the sons of men to be 430
3:11 that no man can find out the work that G 430
3:13 the good of all his labour, it *is* the gift of G. 430
3:14 I know that, whatsoever G doeth, it shall be 430
3:14 G doeth *it,* that *men* should fear before him. 430
3:15 and G requireth that which is past. 430
3:17 G shall judge the righteous and the wicked: 430
3:18 that G might manifest them, and that *they* 430
5: 1 thy foot when thou goest to the house of G, 430
5: 2 heart be hasty to utter *any* thing before G: 430
5: 2 for G *is* in heaven, and thou upon earth: 430
5: 4 When thou vowest a vow unto G, defer not 430
5: 6 wherefore should G be angry at thy voice, 430
5: 7 *are* also *divers* vanities: but fear thou G. 430
5:18 all the days of his life, which G giveth him: 430
5:19 Every man also to whom G hath given 430
5:19 to rejoice in his labour; this *is* the gift of G. 430
5:20 G answereth *him* in the joy of his heart. 430
6: 2 A man to whom G hath given riches, wealth, 430
6: 2 yet G giveth him not power to eat thereof, 430
7:13 Consider the work of G: for who can make 430
7:14 G also hath set the one over against 430
7:18 for he that feareth G shall come forth of 430
7:26 whoso pleaseth G shall escape from her; but 430
7:29 have I found, that G hath made man upright; 430
8: 2 and *that* in regard of the oath of G. 430
8:12 that it shall be well with them that fear G, 430
8:13 a shadow; because he feareth not before G. 430
8:15 his life, which G giveth him under the sun. 430
8:17 I beheld all the work of G, that a man cannot 430
9: 1 and their works, *are* in the hand of G: 430
9: 7 merry heart; for G now accepteth thy works. 430

Ecc	11: 5	thou knowest not the works of **G** who	430
	11: 9	that for all these *things* **G** will bring thee into	430
	12: 7	the spirit shall return unto **G** who gave it.	430
	12:13	Fear **G**, and keep his commandments:	430
	12:14	For **G** shall bring every work into judgment,	430
Isa	1:10	give ear unto the law of our **G**, ye people of	430
	2: 3	the LORD, to the house of the **G** of Jacob;	430
	5:16	**G** that is holy shall be sanctified in	410
	7:11	Ask thee a sign of the LORD thy **G**; ask it	430
	7:13	to weary men, but will ye weary my **G** also?	430
	8:10	and it shall not stand: for **G** *is* with us.	410
	8:19	should not a people seek unto their **G**?	430
	8:21	curse their king and their **G**, and	430
	9: 6	Counseller, The mighty **G**, The everlasting	410
	10:21	the remnant of Jacob, unto the mighty **G**.	410
	12: 2	Behold, **G** *is* my salvation; I will trust, and	410
	13:19	shall be as when **G** overthrew Sodom and	430
	14:13	I will exalt my throne above the stars of **G**:	410
	17: 6	saith the LORD **G** of Israel.	430
	17:10	Because thou hast forgotten the **G** of thy	430
	17:13	***G*** shall rebuke them, and they shall flee far	NIH
	21:10	the **G** of Israel, have I declared unto you.	430
	21:17	for the LORD **G** of Israel hath spoken *it*.	430
	24:15	*even* the name of the LORD **G** of Israel in	430
	25: 1	O LORD, thou *art* my **G**; I will exalt thee,	430
	25: 9	it shall be said in that day, Lo, this *is* our **G**;	430
	26: 1	salvation will ***G*** appoint *for* walls and	NIH
	26:13	O LORD our **G**, *other* lords besides thee	430
	28:26	For his **G** doth instruct him to discretion, *and*	430
	29:23	One of Jacob, and shall fear the **G** of Israel.	430
	30:18	for the LORD *is* a **G** of judgment:	430
	31: 3	Now the Egyptians *are* men, and not **G**; and	410
	35: 2	of the LORD, *and* the excellency of our **G**.	430
	35: 4	behold, your **G** will come *with* vengeance,	430
	35: 4	*with* vengeance, *even* **G** *with* a recompence;	430
	36: 7	say to me, We trust in the LORD our **G**:	430
	37: 4	It may be the LORD thy **G** will hear	430
	37: 4	his master hath sent to reproach the living **G**,	430
	37: 4	words which the LORD thy **G** hath heard:	430
	37:10	saying, Let not thy **G**, in whom thou trustest,	430
	37:16	O LORD of hosts, **G** of Israel, that dwellest	430
	37:16	thou *art* the **G**, *even* thou alone, of all	430
	37:17	which hath sent to reproach the living **G**.	430
	37:20	Now therefore, O LORD our **G**, save us	430
	37:21	Thus saith the LORD **G** of Israel,	430
	37:38	worshipping *in* the house of Nisroch his **g**,	430
	38: 5	saith the LORD, the **G** of David thy father,	430
	40: 1	comfort ye my people, saith your **G**.	430
	40: 3	straight in the desert a highway for our **G**.	430
	40: 8	but the word of our **G** shall stand for ever.	430
	40: 9	say unto the cities of Judah, Behold your **G**.	430
	40:18	To whom then will ye liken **G**? or	410
	40:27	and my judgment is passed over from my **G**?	430
	40:28	*that* the everlasting **G**, the LORD,	430
	41:10	be not dismayed; for I *am* thy **G**: I will	430
	41:13	For I the LORD thy **G** will hold thy right	430
	41:17	*I* the **G** of Israel will not forsake them.	430
	42: 5	Thus saith **G** the LORD, he that created	410
	43: 3	For I *am* the LORD thy **G**, the Holy One of	430
	43:10	before me there was no **G** formed,	410
	43:12	when *there was* no strange ***g*** among you:	NIH
	43:12	my witnesses, saith the LORD, that I *am* **G**.	410
	44: 6	I *am* the last; and besides me *there is* no **G**.	430
	44: 8	Is there a **G** besides me? yea, *there is* no	433
	44: 8	yea, *there is* no **G**; I know not *any*.	6697
	44:10	Who hath formed a **g**, or molten a graven	410
	44:15	he maketh a **g**, and worshippeth *it*; he	410
	44:17	the residue thereof he maketh a **g**, *even* his	410
	44:17	and saith, Deliver me; for thou *art* my **g**.	410
	45: 3	call *thee* by thy name, *am* the **G** of Israel.	430
	45: 5	*there is* none else, *there is* no **G** besides me:	430
	45:14	unto thee, *saying*, Surely **G** *is* in thee;	410
	45:14	in thee; and *there is* none else, *there is* no **G**.	430
	45:15	Verily thou *art* a **G** that hidest thyself,	410
	45:15	that hidest thyself, O **G** of Israel, the saviour.	430
	45:18	**G** himself that formed the earth and made it;	430
	45:20	and pray unto a **g** *that* cannot save.	410
	45:21	and *there is* no **G** else beside me; a just God	430
	45:21	a just **G** and a saviour; *there is* none beside	410
	45:22	the earth: for I *am* **G**, and *there is* none else.	410
	46: 6	and hire a goldsmith; and he maketh it a **g**:	410
	46: 9	for I *am* **G**, and *there is* none else; *I am* God,	410
	46: 9	none else; *I am* **G**, and *there is* none like me,	430
	48: 1	make mention of the **G** of Israel, *but* not in	430
	48: 2	and stay themselves upon the **G** of Israel;	430
	48:17	I *am* the LORD thy **G** which teacheth thee	430
	49: 4	with the LORD, and my work with my **G**.	430
	49: 5	the LORD, and my **G** shall be my strength.	430
	50:10	name of the LORD, and stay upon his **G**.	430
	51:15	I *am* the LORD thy **G**, that divided the sea,	430
	51:20	the fury of the LORD, the rebuke of thy **G**.	430
	51:22	thy **G** *that* pleadeth the cause of his people,	430
	52: 7	that saith unto Zion, Thy **G** reigneth!	430
	52:10	of the earth shall see the salvation of our **G**.	430
	52:12	and the **G** of Israel *will be* your rereward.	430
	53: 4	him stricken, smitten of **G**, and afflicted.	430
	54: 5	The **G** of the whole earth shall he be called.	430
	54: 6	when thou wast refused, saith thy **G**.	430
	55: 5	run unto thee because of the LORD thy **G**,	430
	55: 7	and to our **G**, for he will abundantly pardon.	430
	57:21	*is* no peace, saith my **G**, to the wicked.	430
	58: 2	and forsook not the ordinance of their **G**:	430
	58: 2	they take delight in approaching to **G**.	430
	59: 2	have separated between you and your **G**,	430
	59:13	departing away from our **G**,	430
	60: 9	unto the name of the LORD thy **G**, and	430
	60:19	an everlasting light, and thy **G** thy glory.	430
	61: 2	and the day of vengeance of our **G**;	430
	61: 6	*men* shall call you the Ministers of our **G**:	430
	61:10	my soul shall be joyful in my **G**;	430
	62: 3	and a royal diadem in the hand of thy **G**.	430
	62: 5	the bride, *so* shall thy **G** rejoice over thee.	430
	64: 4	neither hath the eye seen, O **G**, besides thee,	430
	65:16	earth shall bless himself in the **G** of truth;	430
	65:16	in the earth shall swear by the **G** of truth;	430
Isa	66: 9	bring forth, and shut *the womb?* saith thy **G**.	430
Jer	2:17	in that thou hast forsaken the LORD thy **G**,	430
	2:19	that thou hast forsaken the LORD thy **G**,	430
	3:13	hast transgressed against the LORD thy **G**,	430
	3:21	*and* they have forgotten the LORD their **G**.	430
	3:22	unto thee; for thou *art* the LORD our **G**.	430
	3:23	truly in the LORD our **G** *is* the salvation of	430
	3:25	we have sinned against the LORD our **G**,	430
	3:25	not obeyed the voice of the LORD our **G**.	430
	5: 4	of the LORD, *nor* the judgment of their **G**.	430
	5: 5	of the LORD, *and* the judgment of their **G**:	430
	5:14	Wherefore thus saith the LORD **G** of hosts,	430
	5:19	Wherefore doth the LORD our **G** all these	430
	5:24	Let us now fear the LORD our **G**,	430
	7: 3	the **G** of Israel, Amend your ways and	430
	7:21	saith the LORD of hosts, the **G** of Israel;	430
	7:23	I will be your **G**, and ye shall be my people:	430
	7:28	obeyeth not the voice of the LORD their **G**,	430
	8:14	for the LORD our **G** hath put us to silence,	430
	9:15	saith the LORD of hosts, the **G** of Israel;	430
	10:10	the LORD *is* the true **G**, he *is* the living	430
	10:10	he *is* the living **G**, and an everlasting king:	430
	11: 3	Thus saith the LORD **G** of Israel;	430
	11: 4	shall ye be my people, and I will be your **G**:	430
	13:12	Thus saith the LORD **G** of Israel,	430
	13:16	Give glory to the LORD your **G**, before he	430
	14:22	*art* not thou he, O LORD our **G**? therefore	430
	15:16	called by thy name, O LORD **G** of hosts.	430
	16: 9	saith the LORD of hosts, the **G** of Israel;	430
	16:10	have committed against the LORD our **G**?	430
	19: 3	saith the LORD of hosts, the **G** of Israel;	430
	19:15	saith the LORD of hosts, the **G** of Israel;	430
	21: 4	Thus saith the LORD **G** of Israel; Behold,	430
	22: 9	the covenant of the LORD their **G**,	430
	23: 2	Therefore thus saith the LORD **G** of Israel	430
	23:23	*Am* I a **G** at hand, saith the LORD, and	430
	23:23	saith the LORD, and not a **G** afar off?	430
	23:36	ye have perverted the words of the living **G**,	430
	23:36	living God, of the LORD of hosts our **G**.	430
	24: 5	Thus saith the LORD, the **G** of Israel;	430
	24: 7	shall be my people, and I will be their **G**:	430
	25:15	For thus saith the LORD **G** of Israel unto	430
	25:27	saith the LORD of hosts, the **G** of Israel;	430
	26:13	and obey the voice of the LORD your **G**;	430
	26:16	to us in the name of the LORD our **G**.	430
	27: 4	saith the LORD of hosts, the **G** of Israel;	430
	27:21	saith the LORD of hosts, the **G** of Israel,	430
	28: 2	the LORD of hosts, the **G** of Israel, saying,	430
	28:14	saith the LORD of hosts, the **G** of Israel;	430
	29: 4	saith the LORD of hosts, the **G** of Israel,	430
	29: 8	saith the LORD of hosts, the **G** of Israel;	430
	29:21	the **G** of Israel, of Ahab the son of Kolaiah,	430
	29:25	the LORD of hosts, the **G** of Israel, saying,	430
	30: 2	Thus speaketh the LORD **G** of Israel,	430
	30: 9	But they shall serve the LORD their **G**, and	430
	30:22	ye shall be my people, and I will be your **G**.	430
	31: 1	will I be the **G** of all the families of Israel,	430
	31: 6	let us go up *to* Zion unto the LORD our **G**.	430
	31:18	be turned; for thou *art* the LORD my **G**.	430
	31:23	saith the LORD of hosts, the **G** of Israel;	430
	31:33	will be their **G**, and they shall be my people.	430
	32:14	saith the LORD of hosts, the **G** of Israel;	430
	32:15	saith the LORD of hosts, the **G** of Israel;	430
	32:18	the Great, the Mighty **G**, the LORD of	410
	32:27	Behold, I *am* the LORD, the **G** of all flesh:	430
	32:36	the **G** of Israel, concerning this city,	430
	32:38	shall be my people, and I will be their **G**:	430
	33: 4	For thus saith the LORD, the **G** of Israel,	430
	34: 2	Thus saith the LORD, the **G** of Israel; Go	430
	34:13	Thus saith the LORD, the **G** of Israel;	430
	35: 4	of Hanan, the son of Igdaliah, a man of **G**,	430
	35:13	saith the LORD of hosts, the **G** of Israel;	430
	35:17	Therefore thus saith the LORD **G** of hosts,	430
	35:17	the LORD God of hosts, the **G** of Israel;	430
	35:18	saith the LORD of hosts, the **G** of Israel;	430
	35:19	saith the LORD of hosts, the **G** of Israel;	430
	37: 3	Pray now unto the LORD our **G** for us.	430
	37: 7	Thus saith the LORD, the **G** of Israel;	430
	38:17	the **G** of hosts, the God of Israel;	430
	38:17	the God of hosts, the **G** of Israel;	430
	39:16	saith the LORD of hosts, the **G** of Israel;	430
	40: 2	The LORD thy **G** hath pronounced this evil	430
	42: 2	pray for us unto the LORD thy **G**, *even* for	430
	42: 3	That the LORD thy **G** may shew us	430
	42: 4	I *will* pray unto the LORD your **G**	430
	42: 5	the LORD thy **G** shall send thee to us.	430
	42: 6	we will obey the voice of the LORD our **G**,	430
	42: 6	we obey the voice of the LORD our **G**.	430
	42: 9	Thus saith the LORD, the **G** of Israel,	430
	42:13	obey the voice of the LORD your **G**,	430
	42:15	saith the LORD of hosts, the **G** of Israel;	430
	42:18	saith the LORD of hosts, the **G** of Israel;	430
	42:20	when ye sent me unto the LORD your **G**,	430
	42:20	Pray for us unto the LORD our **G**;	430
	42:20	according unto all that the LORD our **G**	430
	42:21	not obeyed the voice of the LORD your **G**,	430
	43: 1	people all the words of the LORD their **G**,	430
	43: 1	*for* which the LORD their **G** had sent him	430
	43: 2	the LORD our **G** hath not sent thee to say,	430
	43:10	saith the LORD of hosts, the **G** of Israel;	430
	44: 2	saith the LORD of hosts, the **G** of Israel;	430
	44: 7	the **G** of hosts, the God of Israel;	430
	44: 7	the God of hosts, the **G** of Israel;	430
	44:11	saith the LORD of hosts, the **G** of Israel;	430
	44:25	the LORD of hosts, the **G** of Israel, saying;	430
	45: 2	the **G** of Israel, unto thee, O Baruch;	430
	46:25	The LORD of hosts, the **G** of Israel, saith;	430
	48: 1	saith the LORD of hosts, the **G** of Israel;	430
	50: 4	they shall go, and seek the LORD their **G**.	430
	50:18	saith the LORD of hosts, the **G** of Israel;	430
	50:28	in Zion the vengeance of the LORD our **G**,	430
	50:40	As **G** overthrew Sodom and Gomorrah and	430
	51: 5	nor Judah of his **G**, of the LORD of hosts;	430
	51:10	in Zion the work of the LORD our **G**.	430
	51:33	saith the LORD of hosts, the **G** of Israel;	430
Jer	51:56	for the LORD **G** of recompences shall	410
La	3:41	heart with *our* hands unto **G** in the heavens.	410
Eze	1: 1	were opened, and I saw visions of **G**.	430
	8: 3	brought me in the visions of **G** to Jerusalem,	430
	8: 4	the glory of the **G** of Israel *was* there,	430
	9: 3	the glory of the **G** of Israel was gone up	430
	10: 5	as the voice of the Almighty **G** when he	410
	10:19	the glory of the **G** of Israel *was* over them	430
	10:20	under the **G** of Israel by the river of Chebar;	430
	11:20	shall be my people, and I will be their **G**.	430
	11:22	the glory of the **G** of Israel *was* over them	430
	11:24	brought me in vision by the Spirit of **G** into	430
	14:11	and I may be their **G**, saith the Lord GOD.	430
	20: 5	unto them, saying, I *am* the LORD your **G**;	430
	20: 7	the idols of Egypt: I *am* the LORD your **G**.	430
	20:19	I *am* the LORD your **G**; walk in my	430
	20:20	*ye* may know that I *am* the LORD your **G**.	430
	28: 2	thou hast said, I *am* a **G**, I sit *in* the seat of	410
	28: 2	hast said, I *am* a God, I sit *in* the seat of **G**,	430
	28: 2	yet thou *art* a man, and not **G**, though thou	410
	28: 2	though thou set thine heart as the heart of **G**:	430
	28: 6	thou hast set thine heart as the heart of **G**;	430
	28: 9	yet say before him that slayeth thee, I *am* **G**?	430
	28: 9	thou *shalt be* a man, and no **G**, in the hand of	410
	28:13	Thou hast been in Eden the garden of **G**;	430
	28:14	*so:* thou wast upon the holy mountain of **G**;	430
	28:16	thee as profane out of the mountain of **G**:	430
	28:26	shall know that I *am* the LORD their **G**.	430
	31: 8	The cedars in the garden of **G** could not hide	430
	31: 8	nor any tree in the garden of **G** was like unto	430
	31: 9	that *were* in the garden of **G**, envied him.	430
	34:24	I the LORD will be their **G**, and my servant	430
	34:30	that I the LORD their **G** *am* with them,	430
	34:31	*are* men, *and* I *am* your **G**, saith the Lord	430
	36:28	ye shall be my people, and I will be your **G**.	430
	37:23	they be my people, and I will be their **G**.	430
	37:27	I will be their **G**, and they shall be my	430
	39:22	that I *am* the LORD their **G** from that day	430
	39:28	they know that I *am* the LORD their **G**,	430
	40: 2	In the visions of **G** brought he me into	430
	43: 2	the glory of the **G** of Israel came from	430
	44: 2	because the LORD, the **G** of Israel,	430
Da	1: 2	with part of the vessels of the house of **G**:	430
	1: 2	*into* the land of Shinar *to* the house of his **g**;	430
	1: 2	the vessels *into* the treasure house of his **g**.	430
	1: 9	Now **G** had brought Daniel into favour and	430
	1:17	**G** gave them knowledge and skill in all	430
	2:18	That *they* would desire mercies of the **G** of	426
	2:19	Then Daniel blessed the **G** of heaven.	426
	2:20	Blessed be the name of **G** for ever and ever:	426
	2:23	and praise thee, O thou **G** of my fathers,	426
	2:28	there is a **G** in heaven that revealeth secrets,	426
	2:37	for the **G** of heaven hath given thee a	426
	2:44	in the days of these kings shall the **G** of	426
	2:45	the great **G** hath made known to the king	426
	2:47	Of a truth *it is*, that your **G** *is* a God of gods,	426
	2:47	Of a truth *it is*, that your God *is* a **G** of gods,	426
	3:15	who *is* that **G** that shall deliver you out of	426
	3:17	our **G** whom we serve *is* able to deliver us	426
	3:25	the form of the fourth *is* like the Son of **G**.	426
	3:26	ye servants of the most high **G**, come forth,	426
	3:28	said, Blessed *be* the **G** of Shadrach,	426
	3:28	that they might not serve nor worship any **g**,	426
	3:28	nor worship any god, except their own **G**.	426
	3:29	which speak any thing amiss against the **G**	426
	3:29	there is no other **G** that can deliver after this	426
	4: 2	wonders that the high **G** hath wrought	426
	4: 8	according to the name of my **g**, and in whom	426
	5: 3	of the house of **G** which *was* at Jerusalem;	426
	5:18	the most high **G** gave Nebuchadnezzar thy	426
	5:21	till he knew that the most high **G** ruled in	426
	5:23	the **G** in whose hand thy breath *is*, and	426
	5:26	**G** hath numbered thy kingdom, and	426
	6: 5	*it* against him concerning the law of his **G**.	426
	6: 7	that whosoever shall ask a petition of any **G**	426
	6:10	prayed, and gave thanks before his **G**, as he	426
	6:11	and making supplication before his **G**.	426
	6:12	every man that shall ask *a petition* of any **G**	426
	6:16	Thy **G** whom thou servest continually,	426
	6:20	O Daniel, servant of the living **G**, is thy	426
	6:20	servant of the living God, is thy **G**,	426
	6:22	My **G** hath sent his angel, and hath shut	426
	6:23	upon him, because he believed in his **G**.	426
	6:26	and fear before the **G** of Daniel:	426
	6:26	for he *is* the living **G**, and stedfast for ever,	426
	9: 3	I set my face unto the Lord **G**, to seek *by*	430
	9: 4	I prayed unto the LORD my **G**, and	430
	9: 4	and said, O Lord, the great and dreadful **G**,	410
	9: 9	To the Lord our **G** *belong* mercies and	430
	9:10	we obeyed the voice of the LORD our **G**,	430
	9:11	written in the law of Moses the servant of **G**,	430
	9:13	we not our prayer before the LORD our **G**,	430
	9:14	for the LORD our **G** *is* righteous in all his	430
	9:15	now, O Lord our **G**, that hast brought thy	430
	9:17	Now therefore, O our **G**, hear the prayer of	430
	9:18	O my **G**, incline thine ear, and hear;	430
	9:19	do; defer not, for thine own sake, O my **G**:	430
	9:20	my **G** for the holy mountain of my God;	430
	9:20	my God for the holy mountain of my **G**;	430
	10:12	to chasten thyself before thy **G**, thy words	430
	11:32	the people that do know their **G** shall be	430
	11:36	magnify himself above every **g**, and	410
	11:36	shall speak marvellous *things* against the **G**	410
	11:37	Neither shall he regard the **G** of his fathers,	430
	11:37	nor the desire of women, nor regard any **g**:	433
	11:38	in his estate shall he honour the **G** of forces:	433
	11:38	a **g** whom his fathers knew not shall he	433
	11:39	do in the most strong holds with a strange **g**,	433
Hos	1: 6	***G*** said unto him, Call her name	NIH
	1: 7	will save them by the LORD their **G**, and	430
	1: 9	said ***G***, Call his name Lo-ammi: for ye *are*	NIH
	1: 9	not my people, and I will not be your ***G***.	NIH
	1:10	unto them, *Ye are* the sons of the living **G**.	410
	2:23	and they shall say, *Thou art* my **G**.	430
	3: 5	seek the LORD their **G**, and David their	430

Hos 4: 1 nor mercy, nor knowledge of **G** in the land. 430
4: 6 seeing thou hast forgotten the law of thy **G**, 430
4:12 have gone a whoring from under their **G**. 430
5: 4 not frame their doings to turn unto their **G**: 430
6: 6 the knowledge of **G** more than burnt 430
7:10 they do not return to the LORD their **G**, 430
8: 2 shall cry unto me, My **G**, we know thee. 430
8: 6 the workman made it; therefore it *is* not **G**: 430
9: 1 for thou hast gone a whoring from thy **G**, 430
9: 8 The watchman of Ephraim *was* with my **G**: 430
9: 8 his ways, *and* hatred in the house of his **G**. 430
9:17 My **G** will cast them away, because they did 430
11: 9 for I *am* **G**, and not man; the Holy One in 410
11:12 Judah yet ruleth with **G**, and is faithful with 410
12: 3 and by his strength he had power with **G**: 430
12: 5 Even the LORD **G** of hosts; the LORD *is* 430
12: 6 Therefore turn thou to thy **G**: keep mercy 430
12: 6 judgment, and wait on thy **G** continually. 430
12: 9 I *that am* the LORD thy **G** from the land of 430
13: 4 Yet I *am* the LORD thy **G** from the land of 430
13: 4 of Egypt, and thou shalt know no **g** but me: 430
13:16 for she hath rebelled against her **G**: 430
14: 1 O Israel, return unto the LORD thy **G**; 430
Joel 1:13 all night in sackcloth, ye ministers of my **G**; 430
1:13 is withholden from the house of your **G**. 430
1:14 land *into* the house of the LORD your **G**, 430
1:16 and gladness from the house of our **G**? 430
2:13 and turn unto the LORD your **G**: 430
2:14 a drink offering unto the LORD your **G**? 430
2:17 say among the people, Where *is* their **G**? 430
2:23 of Zion, and rejoice in the LORD your **G**: 430
2:26 and praise the name of the LORD your **G**, 430
2:27 *that* I *am* the LORD your **G**, and none else: 430
3:17 I *am* the LORD your **G** dwelling in Zion, 430
Am 2: 8 of the condemned *in* the house of their **g**. 430
3:13 saith the Lord GOD, the **G** of hosts, 430
4:11 as **G** overthrew Sodom and Gomorrah, and 430
4:12 unto thee, prepare to meet thy **G**, O Israel. 430
4:13 The LORD, The **G** of hosts, *is* his name. 430
5:14 so the LORD, the **G** of hosts, shall be with 430
5:15 it may be that the LORD **G** of hosts will be 430
5:16 the **G** of hosts, the Lord, saith thus; 430
5:26 and Chiun your images, the star of your **g**, 430
5:27 the LORD, whose name *is* The **G** of hosts. 430
6: 8 saith the LORD the **G** of hosts, I abhor 430
6:14 of Israel, saith the LORD the **G** of hosts; 430
8:14 of Samaria, and say, Thy **g**, O Dan, liveth; 430
9:15 I have given them, saith the LORD thy **G**. 430
Jnh 1: 5 cried every man unto his **g**, and cast forth 430
1: 6 call upon thy **G**, if so be that God will think 430
1: 6 if so be that **G** will think upon us, that we 430
1: 9 I fear the LORD, the **G** of heaven, 430
2: 1 Jonah prayed unto the LORD his **G** out of 430
2: 6 my life from corruption, O LORD my **G**. 430
3: 5 So the people of Nineveh believed **G**, and 430
3: 8 with sackcloth, and cry mightily unto **G**: 430
3: 9 Who can tell *if* **G** will turn and repent, and 430
3:10 **G** saw their works, that they turned from 430
3:10 **G** repented of the evil, that he had said that 430
4: 2 for I knew that thou *art* a gracious **G**, and 410
4: 6 the LORD **G** prepared a gourd, and made *it* 430
4: 7 **G** prepared a worm when the morning rose 430
4: 8 that **G** prepared a vehement east wind; 430
4: 9 **G** said to Jonah, Doest thou well to be angry 430
Mic 3: 7 cover their lips; for *there is* no answer of **G**. 430
4: 2 and to the house of the **G** of Jacob; 430
4: 5 will walk every one in the name of his **g**, 430
4: 5 in the name of the LORD our **G** for ever 430
5: 4 majesty of the name of the LORD his **G**; 430
6: 6 *and* bow myself before the high **G**? 430
6: 8 love mercy, and to walk humbly with thy **G**? 430
7: 7 I will wait for the **G** of my salvation: 430
7: 7 the God of my salvation: my **G** will hear me. 430
7:10 said unto me, Where is the LORD thy **G**? 430
7:17 they shall be afraid of the LORD our **G**, 430
7:18 Who *is* a **G** like unto thee, that pardoneth 410
Na 1: 2 **G** *is* jealous, and the LORD revengeth; 410
Hab 1:11 offend, *imputing* this his power unto his **g**. 433
1:12 O LORD my **G**, mine Holy One? 430
1:12 and, O **mighty** **G**, thou hast established 6697
3: 3 **G** came from Teman, and the Holy One 433
3:18 I will joy in the **G** of my salvation. 430
Zep 2: 7 for the LORD their **G** shall visit them, and 430
2: 9 saith the LORD of hosts, the **G** of Israel, 430
3: 2 in the LORD; she drew not near to her **G**. 430
3:17 The LORD thy **G** in the midst of thee *is* 430
Hag 1:12 obeyed the voice of the LORD their **G**, and 430
1:12 as the LORD their **G** had sent him, and 430
1:14 in the house of the LORD of hosts, their **G**, 430
Zec 6:15 obey the voice of the LORD your **G**. 430
7: 2 When they had sent *unto* the house of **G** 410
8: 8 I will be their **G**, in truth and 430
8:23 for we have heard *that* **G** *is* with you. 430
9: 7 *shall be* for our **G**, and he shall be as a 430
9:16 the LORD their **G** shall save them in that 430
10: 6 for I *am* the LORD their **G**, and will hear 430
11: 4 Thus saith the LORD my **G**; Feed the flock 430
12: 5 my strength in the LORD of hosts their **G**. 430
12: 8 the house of David *shall be* as **G**, as 430
13: 9 and they shall say, The LORD *is* my **G**. 430
14: 5 the LORD my **G** shall come, *and* all 430
Mal 1: 9 beseech **G** that he will be gracious unto us: 410
2:10 hath not one **G** created us? why do we deal 410
2:11 and hath married the daughter of a strange **g**. 410
2:16 *For* the LORD, the **G** of Israel, saith that he 430
2:17 in them; or, Where *is* the **G** of judgment? 430
3: 8 Will a man rob **G**? Yet ye *have* robbed me. 430
3:14 Ye have said, It *is* vain to serve **G**: and 430
3:15 yea, *they that* tempt **G** are even delivered 430
3:18 between him that serveth **G** and *him* that 430
Mt 1:23 which being interpreted is, **G** with us. *2316*
2:12 And being **warned of G** in a dream that *5537*
2:22 being **warned of G** in a dream, *5537*
3: 9 that **G** is able of these stones to raise up *2316*
3:16 he saw the Spirit of **G** descending like a *2316*
Mt 4: 3 to him, he said, If thou be the Son of **G**, *2316*
4: 4 that proceedeth out of the mouth of **G**. *2316*
4: 6 If thou be the Son of **G**, cast thyself down: *2316*
4: 7 Thou shalt not tempt the Lord thy **G**. *2316*
4:10 Thou shalt worship the Lord thy **G**, and *2316*
5: 8 *are* the pure in heart: for they shall see **G**. *2316*
5: 9 for they shall be called the children of **G**. *2316*
6:24 the other. Ye cannot serve **G** and mammon. *2316*
6:30 if **G** so clothe the grass of the field, *2316*
6:33 But seek ye first the kingdom of **G**, and *2316*
8:29 we to do with thee, Jesus, *thou* Son of **G**? *2316*
9: 8 and glorified **G**, which had given such *2316*
12: 4 How he entered into the house of **G**, and *2316*
12:28 But if I cast out devils by the Spirit of **G**, *2316*
12:28 then the kingdom of **G** is come unto you. *2316*
14:33 saying, Of a truth thou art the Son of **G**. *2316*
15: 3 the commandment of **G** by your tradition? *2316*
15: 4 For **G** commanded, saying, Honour thy *2316*
15: 6 of **G** of none effect by your tradition. *2316*
15:31 to see: and they glorified the **G** of Israel. *2316*
16:16 Thou art the Christ, the Son of the living **G**. *2316*
16:23 thou savourest not the *things* that be of **G**, *2316*
19: 6 What therefore **G** hath joined together, *2316*
19:17 *there is* none good but one, *that is*, **G**: but *2316*
19:24 a rich *man* to enter into the kingdom of **G**. *2316*
19:26 but with **G** all *things* are possible. *2316*
21:12 And Jesus went into the temple of **G**, and *2316*
21:31 the harlots go into the kingdom of **G** before *2316*
21:43 The kingdom of **G** shall be taken from you, *2316*
22:16 art true, and teachest the way of **G** in truth, *2316*
22:21 and unto **G** the *things* that are God's. *2316*
22:29 knowing the scriptures, nor the power of **G**. *2316*
22:30 but are as *the* angels of **G** in heaven. *2316*
22:31 read that which was spoken unto you by **G**, *2316*
22:32 I am the **G** of Abraham, and the God of *2316*
22:32 and the **G** of Isaac, and the God of Jacob? *2316*
22:32 and the God of Isaac, and the **G** of Jacob? *2316*
22:32 **G** is not the God of the dead, but of *2316*
22:32 God is not the **G** of the dead, but of *2316*
22:37 Thou shalt love the Lord thy **G** with all thy *2316*
23:22 sweareth by the throne of **G**, and by him *2316*
26:61 I am able to destroy the temple of **G**, and *2316*
26:63 said unto him, I adjure thee by the living **G**, *2316*
26:63 whether thou be the Christ, the Son of **G**. *2316*
27:40 If thou be the Son of **G**, come down from *2316*
27:43 He trusted in **G**; let him deliver him now, *2316*
27:43 have him: for he said, I am the Son of **G**. *2316*
27:46 that is to say, My **G**, my God, why hast *2316*
27:46 that is to say, My God, my **G**, why hast *2316*
27:54 saying, Truly this was the Son of **G**. *2316*
Mk 1: 1 of the gospel of Jesus Christ, the Son of **G**; *2316*
1:14 preaching the gospel of the kingdom of **G**, *2316*
1:15 and the kingdom of **G** is at hand: *2316*
1:24 thee who thou art, the Holy One of **G**. *2316*
2: 7 who can forgive sins but **G** only? *2316*
2:12 and glorified **G**, saying, We never saw *it* on *2316*
2:26 How he went into the house of **G** in *2316*
3:11 and cried, saying, Thou art the Son of **G**. *2316*
3:35 For whosoever shall do the will of **G**, *2316*
4:11 to know the mystery of the kingdom of **G**: *2316*
4:26 And he said, So is the kingdom of **G**, as if a *2316*
4:30 shall we liken the kingdom of **G**? *2316*
5: 7 Jesus, *thou* Son of the most high **G**? *2316*
5: 7 I adjure thee by **G**, that thou torment me *2316*
7: 8 For laying aside the commandment of **G**, *2316*
7: 9 Full well ye reject the commandment of **G**, *2316*
7:13 Making the word of **G** of none effect *2316*
8:33 thou savourest not the *things* that be of **G**, *2316*
9: 1 till they have seen the kingdom of **G** come *2316*
9:47 enter into the kingdom of **G** with one eye, *2316*
10: 6 But from the beginning of the creation **G** *2316*
10: 9 What therefore **G** hath joined together, *2316*
10:14 them not: for of such is the kingdom of **G**. *2316*
10:15 receive the kingdom of **G** as a little child, *2316*
10:18 *there is* none good but one, *that is*, **G**. *2316*
10:23 have riches enter into the kingdom of **G**! *2316*
10:24 in riches to enter into the kingdom of **G**! *2316*
10:25 a rich *man* to enter into the kingdom of **G**. *2316*
10:27 With men *it is* impossible, but not with **G**: *2316*
10:27 for with **G** all *things* are possible. *2316*
11:22 answering saith unto them, Have faith in **G**. *2316*
12:14 of men, but teachest the way of **G** in truth: *2316*
12:17 and to **G** the *things* that are God's. *2316*
12:24 not the scriptures, neither the power of **G**? *2316*
12:26 how in the bush **G** spake unto him, saying, *2316*
12:26 I *am* the **G** of Abraham, and the God of *2316*
12:26 and the **G** of Isaac, and the God of Jacob? *2316*
12:26 and the God of Isaac, and the **G** of Jacob? *2316*
12:27 He is not the **G** of the dead, but the God of *2316*
12:27 the God of the dead, but the **G** of the living: *2316*
12:29 O Israel; The Lord our **G** is one Lord: *2316*
12:30 And thou shalt love the Lord thy **G** with all *2316*
12:32 for there is one **G**; and there is none other *2316*
12:34 Thou art not far from the kingdom of **G**. *2316*
13:19 the creation which **G** created unto this time, *2316*
14:25 day that I drink it new in the kingdom of **G**. *2316*
15:34 which is, being interpreted, My **G**, my God, *2316*
15:34 which is, being interpreted, My God, my **G**, *2316*
15:39 he said, Truly this man was the Son of **G**. *2316*
15:43 which also waited for the kingdom of **G**, *2316*
16:19 into heaven, and sat on the right hand of **G**. *2316*
Lk 1: 6 And they were both righteous before **G**, *2316*
1: 8 office before **G** in the order of his course, *2316*
1:16 of Israel shall he turn to the Lord their **G**. *2316*
1:19 am Gabriel, that stand in the presence of **G**; *2316*
1:26 was sent from **G** unto a city of Galilee, *2316*
1:30 Mary: for thou hast found favour with **G**. *2316*
1:32 the Lord **G** shall give unto him the throne *2316*
1:35 born of thee shall be called the Son of **G**. *2316*
1:37 For with **G** nothing shall be unpossible. *2316*
1:47 And my spirit hath rejoiced in **G** my *2316*
1:64 and he spake, and praised **G**. *2316*
1:68 Blessed *be* the Lord **G** of Israel; for he hath *2316*
1:78 Through the tender mercy of our **G**; *2316*
2:13 multitude of the heavenly host praising **G**, *2316*
Lk 2:14 Glory to **G** in the highest, and on earth *2316*
2:20 praising **G** for all *the things* that they had *2316*
2:28 *up* in his arms, and blessed **G**, and said, *2316*
2:37 but served **G** with fastings and prayers night NIG
2:40 and the grace of **G** was upon him. *2316*
2:52 and stature, and in favour with **G** and man. *2316*
3: 2 the word of **G** came unto John the son of *2316*
3: 6 And all flesh shall see the salvation of **G**. *2316*
3: 8 That **G** is able of these stones to raise up *2316*
3:38 *the son* of Adam, which was *the son* of **G**. *2316*
4: 3 said unto him, If thou be the Son of **G**, *2316*
4: 4 by bread alone, but by every word of **G**. *2316*
4: 8 Thou shalt worship the Lord thy **G**, and *2316*
4: 9 and said unto him, If thou be the Son of **G**, *2316*
4:12 Thou shalt not tempt the Lord thy **G**. *2316*
4:34 thee who thou art, the Holy One of **G**. *2316*
4:41 and saying, Thou art Christ the Son of **G**. *2316*
4:43 I must preach the kingdom of **G** to other *2316*
5: 1 pressed upon him to hear the word of **G**, *2316*
5:21 Who can forgive sins, but **G** alone? *2316*
5:25 departed to his own house, glorifying **G**. *2316*
5:26 and they glorified **G**, and were filled with *2316*
6: 4 How he went into the house of **G**, and *2316*
6:12 and continued all night in prayer to **G**. *2316*
6:20 *be ye* poor: for yours is the kingdom of **G**. *2316*
7:16 and they glorified **G**, saying, That a great *2316*
7:16 and, That **G** hath visited his people. *2316*
7:28 he that is least in the kingdom of **G** is *2316*
7:29 heard *him*, and the publicans, justified **G**, *2316*
7:30 lawyers rejected the counsel of **G** against *2316*
8: 1 the glad tidings of the kingdom of **G**: *2316*
8:10 to know the mysteries of the kingdom of **G**: *2316*
8:11 parable is this: The seed is the word of **G**. *2316*
8:21 are these which hear the word of **G**, *2316*
8:28 with thee, Jesus, *thou* Son of **G** most high? *2316*
8:39 shew how great *things* **G** hath done unto *2316*
9: 2 he sent them to preach the kingdom of **G**, *2316*
9:11 and spake unto them of the kingdom of **G**, *2316*
9:20 Peter answering said, The Christ of **G**. *2316*
9:27 of death, till they see the kingdom of **G**. *2316*
9:43 were all amazed at the mighty power of **G**. *2316*
9:60 but go thou and preach the kingdom of **G**. *2316*
9:62 looking back, is fit for the kingdom of **G**. *2316*
10: 9 The kingdom of **G** is come nigh unto you. *2316*
10:11 that the kingdom of **G** is come nigh unto *2316*
10:27 Thou shalt love the Lord thy **G** with all thy *2316*
11:20 But if I with the finger of **G** cast out devils, *2316*
11:20 no doubt the kingdom of **G** is come upon *2316*
11:28 blessed *are* they that hear the word of **G**, *2316*
11:42 and pass over judgment and the love of **G**: *2316*
11:49 Therefore also said the wisdom of **G**, I will *2316*
12: 6 and not one of them is forgotten before **G**? *2316*
12: 8 of man also confess before the angels of **G**: *2316*
12: 9 men shall be denied before the angels of **G**. *2316*
12:20 But **G** said unto him, *Thou* fool, this night *2316*
12:21 for himself, and is not rich towards **G**. *2316*
12:24 storehouse nor barn; and **G** feedeth them: *2316*
12:28 If then **G** so clothe the grass, which is to *2316*
12:31 But rather seek ye the kingdom of **G**; *2316*
13:13 she was made straight, and glorified **G**. *2316*
13:18 Unto what is the kingdom of **G** like? *2316*
13:20 Whereunto shall I liken the kingdom of **G**? *2316*
13:28 in the kingdom of **G**, and you yourselves *2316*
13:29 and shall sit down in the kingdom of **G**. *2316*
14:15 *he* that shall eat bread in the kingdom of **G**. *2316*
15:10 angels of **G** over one sinner that repenteth. *2316*
16:13 the other. Ye cannot serve **G** and mammon. *2316*
16:15 before men; but **G** knoweth your hearts: *2316*
16:15 men is abomination in the sight of **G**. *2316*
16:16 since that time the kingdom of **G** is *2316*
17:15 and with a loud voice glorified **G**, *2316*
17:18 not found that returned to give glory to **G**, *2316*
17:20 when the kingdom of **G** should come, *2316*
17:20 The kingdom of **G** cometh not with *2316*
17:21 for behold, the kingdom of **G** is within you. *2316*
18: 2 which feared not **G**, neither regarded man: *2316*
18: 4 Though I fear not **G**, nor regard man; *2316*
18: 7 And shall not **G** avenge his own elect, *2316*
18:11 prayed thus with himself, **G**, I thank thee, *2316*
18:13 saying, **G** be merciful to me a sinner. *2316*
18:16 them not: for of such is the kingdom of **G**. *2316*
18:17 **G** as a little child shall in no wise enter *2316*
18:19 none *is* good, save one, *that is*, **G**. *2316*
18:24 have riches enter into the kingdom of **G**! *2316*
18:25 a rich *man* to enter into the kingdom of **G**. *2316*
18:27 unpossible with men are possible with **G**. *2316*
18:43 his sight, and followed him, glorifying **G**: *2316*
18:43 when they saw *it*, gave praise unto **G**. *2316*
19:11 they thought that the kingdom of **G** should *2316*
19:37 praise **G** with a loud voice for all *2316*
20:16 they heard *it*, they said, **G forbid**. *1096+3361*
20:21 *of any*, but teachest the way of **G** truly: *2316*
20:25 and unto **G** the *things* which be God's. *2316*
20:36 and are the children of **G**, being *2316*
20:37 when he calleth the Lord the **G** of *2316*
20:37 and the **G** of Isaac, and the God of Jacob. *2316*
20:37 and the God of Isaac, and the **G** of Jacob. *2316*
20:38 For he is not a **G** of the dead, but of *2316*
21: 4 abundance cast in unto the offerings of **G**: *2316*
21:31 know ye that the kingdom of **G** is nigh at *2316*
22:16 until it be fulfilled in the kingdom of **G**. *2316*
22:18 until the kingdom of **G** shall come. *2316*
22:69 sit on the right hand of the power of **G**. *2316*
22:70 said they all, Art thou then the Son of **G**? *2316*
23:35 if he be Christ, the chosen of **G**. *2316*
23:40 rebuked him, saying, Dost not thou fear **G**, *2316*
23:47 he glorified **G**, saying, Certainly this was a *2316*
23:51 also himself waited for the kingdom of **G**. *2316*
24:19 and word before **G** and all the people: *2316*
24:53 in the temple, praising and blessing **G**. *2316*
Jn 1: 1 and the Word was with **G**, and the Word *2316*
1: 1 Word was with God, and the Word was **G**. *2316*
1: 2 The same was in the beginning with **G**. *2316*
1: 6 There was a man sent from **G**, whose name *2316*
1:12 gave he power to become the sons of **G**, *2316*

Jn 1:13 the flesh, nor of the will of man, but of G. 2316
1:18 No *man* hath seen G at any time; the only 2316
1:29 and saith, Behold the Lamb of G, 2316
1:34 and bare record that this is the Son of G. 2316
1:36 he walked, he saith, Behold the Lamb of G. 2316
1:49 unto him, Rabbi, thou art the Son of G; 2316
1:51 and the angels of G ascending and 2316
3: 2 know that thou art a teacher come from G: 2316
3: 2 that thou doest, except G be with him. 2316
3: 3 he cannot see the kingdom of G. 2316
3: 5 he cannot enter into the kingdom of G. 2316
3:16 For G so loved the world, that he gave his 2316
3:17 For G sent not his Son into the world to 2316
3:18 in the name of the only begotten Son of G. 2316
3:21 made manifest, that they are wrought in G. 2316
3:33 testimony hath set to *his* seal that G is true. 2316
3:34 For he whom G hath sent speaketh 2316
3:34 God hath sent speaketh the words of G: 2316
3:34 for G giveth not the Spirit by measure *unto* 2316
3:36 see life; but the wrath of G abideth on him. 2316
4:10 If thou knewest the gift of G, and who it is 2316
4:24 G *is* a Spirit: and they that worship him 2316
5:18 but said also that G was his Father, 2316
5:18 his Father, making himself equal with G. 2316
5:25 dead shall hear the voice of the Son of G: 2316
5:42 that ye have not the love of G in you. 2316
5:44 seek not the honour that *cometh* from G 2316
6:27 unto you: for him hath G the Father sealed. 2316
6:28 we do, that we might work the works of G? 2316
6:29 and said unto them, This is the work of G, 2316
6:33 For the bread of G is he which cometh 2316
6:45 And they shall be all taught of G. 2316
6:46 save he which is of G, he hath seen 2316
6:69 thou art *that* Christ, the Son of the living G. 2316
7:17 whether it be of G, or *whether* I speak of 2316
8:40 told you the truth, which I have heard of G: 2316
8:41 of fornication; we have one Father, *even* G. 2316
8:42 If G were your Father, ye would love me: 2316
8:42 for I proceeded forth and came from G; 2316
8:47 He that is of G heareth God's words: ye 2316
8:47 hear *them* not, because ye are not of G. 2316
8:54 of whom ye say, that he is your G: 2316
9: 3 that the works of G should be made 2316
9:16 This man is not of G, because he keepeth 2316
9:24 and said unto him, Give G the praise: 2316
9:29 We know that G spake unto Moses: *as for* 2316
9:31 Now we know that G heareth not sinners: 2316
9:31 but if any *man* be a **worshipper of G**, and 2318
9:33 If this *man* were not of G, he could do 2316
9:35 Dost thou believe on the Son of G? 2316
10:33 that thou, being a man, makest thyself G. 2316
10:35 unto whom the word of G came, and 2316
10:36 because I said, I am the Son of G? 2316
11: 4 is not unto death, but for the glory of G, 2316
11: 4 that the Son of G might be glorified 2316
11:22 even now, whatsoever thou wilt ask of G, 2316
11:22 thou wilt ask of God, G will give *it* thee. 2316
11:27 that thou art the Christ, the Son of G, 2316
11:40 thou shouldest see the glory of G? 2316
11:52 children of G that were scattered abroad. 2316
12:43 praise of men more than the praise of G. 2316
13: 3 and that he was come from G, and went to 2316
13: 3 that he was come from God, and went to G; 2316
13:31 of man glorified, and G is glorified in him. 2316
13:32 If G be glorified in him, God shall also 2316
13:32 in him, G shall also glorify him in himself, 2316
14: 1 ye believe in G, believe also in me. 2316
16: 2 you will think that he doeth G service. 2316
16:27 and have believed that I came out from G. 2316
16:30 we believe that thou camest forth from G. 2316
17: 3 that they might know thee the only true G, 2316
19: 7 because he made himself the Son of G. 2316
20:17 your Father; and *to* my G, and your God. 2316
20:17 your Father; and *to* my God, and your G. 2316
20:28 and said unto him, My Lord and my G. 2316
20:31 that Jesus is the Christ, the Son of G; 2316
21:19 by what death he should glorify G. 2316
Ac 1: 3 the *things* pertaining to the kingdom of G: 2316
2:11 in our tongues the wonderful works of G. 2316
2:17 shall come to pass in the last days, saith G, 2316
2:22 a man approved of G among you by 2316
2:22 which G did by him in the midst of you, 2316
2:23 and foreknowledge of G, 2316
2:24 Whom G hath raised up, having loosed 2316
2:30 knowing that G had sworn with an oath to 2316
2:32 This Jesus hath G raised up, whereof we all 2316
2:33 Therefore being by the right hand of G 2316
2:36 that G hath made that same Jesus, whom ye 2316
2:39 *even* as many as the Lord our G shall call. 2316
2:47 Praising G, and having favour with all 2316
3: 8 walking, and leaping, and praising G. 2316
3: 9 people saw him walking and praising G: 2316
3:13 The G of Abraham, and of Isaac, and 2316
3:13 of Isaac, and of Jacob, the G of our fathers, 2316
3:15 of life, whom G hath raised from the dead; 2316
3:18 But *those things*, which G before had 2316
3:21 G hath spoken by the mouth of all his holy 2316
3:22 A prophet shall the Lord your G raise up 2316
3:25 of the covenant which G made with our 2316
3:26 Unto you first G, having raised up his Son 2316
4:10 ye crucified, whom G raised from the dead, 2316
4:19 Whether it be right in the sight of G to 2316
4:19 God to hearken unto you more than unto G, 2316
4:21 for all *men* glorified G for that which was 2316
4:24 lift up their voice to G with one accord, 2316
4:24 and said, Lord, thou *art* G, which hast made 2316
4:31 they spake the word of G with boldness. 2316
5: 4 thou hast not lied unto men, but unto G. 2316
5:29 said, We ought to obey G rather than men. 2316
5:30 The G of our fathers raised up Jesus, 2316
5:31 Him hath G exalted with his right hand *to* 2316
5:32 whom G hath given to them that obey him. 2316
5:39 But if it be of G, ye cannot overthrow it; 2316
5:39 haply ye be found even to **fight against G**. 2314
6: 2 reason that we should leave the word of G, 2316
Ac 6: 7 And the word of G increased; and 2316
6:11 words against Moses, and *against* G. 2316
7: 2 The G of glory appeared unto our father 2316
7: 6 And G spake on this wise, That his seed 2316
7: 7 shall be in bondage will I judge, said G: 2316
7: 9 Joseph into Egypt: but G was with him, 2316
7:17 which G had sworn to Abraham, the people 2316
7:25 that G by his hand would deliver them: 2316
7:32 *Saying*, I *am* the G of thy fathers, the God 2316
7:32 the G of Abraham, and the God of Isaac, 2316
7:32 and the G of Isaac, and the God of Jacob. 2316
7:32 and the God of Isaac, and the G of Jacob. 2316
7:35 the same did G send *to be* a ruler and 2316
7:37 A prophet shall the Lord your G raise up 2316
7:42 Then G turned, and gave them up to 2316
7:43 of Moloch, and the star of your g Remphan, 2316
7:45 whom G drave out before the face of our 2316
7:46 Who found favour before G, and desired to 2316
7:46 desired to find a tabernacle for the G of 2316
7:55 and saw the glory of G, and Jesus standing 2316
7:55 and Jesus standing on the right hand of G, 2316
7:56 of man standing on the right hand of G. 2316
7:59 calling upon *G*, and saying, Lord Jesus, NIG
8:10 saying, This *man* is the great power of G. 2316
8:12 the *things* concerning the kingdom of G, 2316
8:14 that Samaria had received the word of G, 2316
8:20 thou hast thought that the gift of G may be 2316
8:21 for thy heart is not right in the sight of G. 2316
8:22 of this thy wickedness, and pray G, 2316
8:37 I believe that Jesus Christ is the Son of G. 2316
9:20 in the synagogues, that he is the Son of G. 2316
10: 2 and one that feared G with all his house, 2316
10: 2 alms to the people, and prayed to G alway. 2316
10: 3 an angel of G coming in to him, and 2316
10: 4 alms are come up for a memorial before G. 2316
10:15 What G hath cleansed, *that* call not thou 2316
10:22 and one that feareth G, and of good report 2316
10:22 was **warned from G** by a holy angel to 5537
10:28 G hath shewed me that *I* should not call 2316
10:31 are had in remembrance in the sight of G. 2316
10:33 therefore are we all here present before G, 2316
10:33 all *things* that are commanded thee of G. 2316
10:34 Of a truth I perceive that G is no respecter 2316
10:36 The word which *G* sent unto the children of NIG
10:38 How G anointed Jesus of Nazareth with 2316
10:38 oppressed of the devil; for G was with him. 2316
10:40 Him G raised up the third day, and 2316
10:41 but unto witnesses chosen before of G, 2316
10:42 was ordained of G *to be* the Judge of quick 2316
10:46 them speak with tongues, and magnify G. 2316
11: 1 Gentiles had also received the word of G. 2316
11: 9 What G hath cleansed, *that* call not thou 2316
11:17 as G gave them the like gift as *he did* unto 2316
11:17 what was I, that I could withstand G? 2316
11:18 held their peace, and glorified G, saying, 2316
11:18 Then hath G also to the Gentiles granted 2316
11:23 and had seen the grace of G, was glad, and 2316
12: 5 ceasing of the church unto G for him. 2316
12:22 *saying, It is* the voice of a g, and not of a 2316
12:23 because he gave not G the glory: 2316
12:24 But the word of G grew and multiplied. 2316
13: 5 they preached the word of G in 2316
13: 7 Saul, and desired to hear the word of G. 2316
13:16 Men of Israel, and *ye* that fear G, 2316
13:17 The G of this people of Israel chose our 2316
13:21 and G gave unto them Saul the son of Cis, 2316
13:23 Of this *man's* seed hath G according to *his* 2316
13:26 and whosoever among you feareth G, 2316
13:30 But G raised him from the dead: 2316
13:33 G hath fulfilled the same unto us their 2316
13:36 served his own generation by the will of G, 2316
13:37 whom G raised *again*, saw no corruption. 2316
13:43 them to continue in the grace of G. 2316
13:44 whole city together to hear the word of G. 2316
13:46 It was necessary that the word of G should 2316
14:15 turn from these vanities unto the living G, 2316
14:22 tribulation enter into the kingdom of G. 2316
14:26 of G for the work which they fulfilled. 2316
14:27 they rehearsed all that G had done with 2316
15: 4 they declared all *things* that G had done 2316
15: 7 ye know how that a good while ago G 2316
15: 8 And G, which knoweth the hearts, 2316
15:10 Now therefore why tempt ye G, to put a 2316
15:12 wonders G had wrought among 2316
15:14 Simeon hath declared how G at the first did 2316
15:18 Known unto G are all his works from 2316
15:19 from among the Gentiles are turned to G: 2316
15:40 by the brethren unto the grace of G. 2316
16:14 the city of Thyatira, which worshipped G, 2316
16:17 men are the servants of the most high G, 2316
16:25 and Silas prayed, and sang praises unto G: 2316
16:34 rejoiced, believing in G with all his house. 2316
17:13 word of G was preached of Paul at Berea, 2316
17:23 this inscription, TO *THE* UNKNOWN G. 2316
17:24 G that made the world and all *things* 2316
17:29 then as we are the offspring of G, 2316
17:30 And the times of *this* ignorance G winked 2316
18: 7 named Justus, one that worshipped G, 2316
18:11 teaching the word of G among them. 2316
18:13 This *fellow* persuadeth men to worship G 2316
18:21 but I will return again unto you, if G will. 2316
18:26 expounded unto him the way of G more 2316
19: 8 the *things* concerning the kingdom of G. 2316
19:11 And G wrought special miracles by 2316
19:20 So mightily grew the word of G and 2962
20:21 repentance toward G, and faith toward our 2316
20:24 to testify the gospel of the grace of G. 2316
20:25 I have gone preaching the kingdom of G, 2316
20:27 to declare unto you all the counsel of G. 2316
20:28 to feed the church of G, which he hath 2316
20:32 I commend you to G, and to the word of his 2316
21:19 he declared particularly what *things* G had 2316
22: 3 and was zealous towards G, as ye all are 2316
22:14 The G of our fathers hath chosen thee, 2316
23: 1 have lived in all good conscience before G 2316
Ac 23: 3 G shall smite thee, *thou* whited wall: 2316
23: 9 spoken to him, let us not **fight against G**. 2313
24:14 so worship I the G of my fathers, 2316
24:15 And have hope towards G, which they 2316
24:16 a conscience void of offence toward G, 2316
26: 6 of the promise made of G unto *our* fathers: 2316
26: 7 instantly serving *G* day and night, hope to NIG
26: 8 with you, that G should raise the dead? 2316
26:18 and *from* the power of Satan unto G, 2316
26:20 that *they* should repent and turn to G, and 2316
26:22 Having therefore obtained help of G, 2316
26:29 And Paul said, I would to G, that not only 2316
27:23 there stood by me this night *the* angel of G, 2316
27:24 G hath given thee all them that sail with 2316
27:25 for I believe G, that it shall be even as it 2316
27:35 gave thanks to G in presence of *them* all: 2316
28: 6 *their minds*, and said that he was a g. 2316
28:15 Paul saw, he thanked G, and took courage. 2316
28:23 and testified the kingdom of G, 2316
28:28 that the salvation of G is sent unto 2316
28:31 Preaching the kingdom of G, and 2316
Ro 1: 1 an apostle, separated unto the gospel of G, 2316
1: 4 *And* declared *to be* the Son of G with 2316
1: 7 in Rome, beloved of G, called *to be* saints: 2316
1: 7 Grace to you and peace from G our Father, 2316
1: 8 I thank my G through Jesus Christ for you 2316
1: 9 For G is my witness, whom I serve with 2316
1:10 journey by the will of G to come unto you. 2316
1:16 for it is the power of G unto salvation to 2316
1:17 For therein is the righteousness of G 2316
1:18 For the wrath of G is revealed from heaven 2316
1:19 Because that which may be known of G is 2316
1:19 in them; for G hath shewed *it* unto them. 2316
1:21 Because that, when they knew G, 2316
1:21 knew God, they glorified *him* not as G, 2316
1:23 G into an image made like to corruptible 2316
1:24 Wherefore G also gave them up to 2316
1:25 Who changed the truth of G into a lie, and 2316
1:26 For this cause G gave them up unto vile 2316
1:28 And even as they did not like to retain G in 2316
1:28 G gave them over to a reprobate mind, 2316
1:30 **haters of G**, despiteful, proud, boasters, 2319
1:32 Who knowing the judgment of G, that they 2316
2: 2 But we are sure that the judgment of G is 2316
2: 3 that thou shalt escape the judgment of G? 2316
2: 4 not knowing that the goodness of G leadeth 2316
2: 5 revelation of the righteous judgment of G; 2316
2:11 For there is no respect of persons with G. 2316
2:13 not the hearers of the law *are* just before G, 2316
2:16 In the day when G shall judge the secrets of 2316
2:17 in the law, and makest thy boast of G, 2316
2:23 breaking the law dishonourest thou G? 2316
2:24 For the name of G is blasphemed among 2316
2:29 whose praise *is* not of men, but of G. 2316
3: 2 them were committed the oracles of G. 2316
3: 3 shall their unbelief make the faith of G 2316
3: 4 **G forbid**: yea, let G be true, but 1096+3361
3: 4 yea, let G be true, but every man a liar; as it 2316
3: 5 commend the righteousness of G, 2316
3: 5 *Is* G unrighteous who taketh vengeance? 2316
3: 6 **G forbid**: for then how shall God 1096+3361
3: 6 then how shall G judge the world? 2316
3: 7 For if the truth of G hath *more* abounded 2316
3:11 there is none that seeketh after G. 2316
3:18 There is no fear of G before their eyes. 2316
3:19 all the world may become guilty before G. 2316
3:21 But now the righteousness of G without 2316
3:22 Even the righteousness of G *which is* by 2316
3:23 and come short of the glory of G; 2316
3:25 Whom G hath set forth *to be* a propitiation 2316
3:25 that are past, through the forbearance of G; 2316
3:29 *Is he* the G of the Jews only? *is he* not also 2316
3:30 Seeing *it is* one G, which shall justify 2316
3:31 **G forbid**: yea, we establish the law. 1096+3361
4: 2 he hath whereof to glory; but not before G. 2316
4: 3 Abraham believed G, and it was counted 2316
4: 6 unto whom G imputeth righteousness 2316
4:17 *even* G, who quickeneth the dead, and 2316
4:20 He staggered not at the promise of G 2316
4:20 but was strong in faith, giving glory to G; 2316
5: 1 we have peace with G through our Lord 2316
5: 2 and rejoice in hope of the glory of G. 2316
5: 5 the love of G is shed abroad in our hearts 2316
5: 8 But G commendeth his love toward us, 2316
5:10 we were reconciled to G by the death of his 2316
5:11 we also joy in G through our Lord Jesus 2316
5:15 much more the grace of G, and the gift by 2316
6: 2 **G forbid**. How shall we, that are 1096+3361
6:10 but in that he liveth, he liveth unto G. 2316
6:11 alive unto G through Jesus Christ our Lord. 2316
6:13 but yield yourselves unto G, as *those that* 2316
6:13 *as* instruments of righteousness unto G. 2316
6:15 the law, but under grace? **G forbid**. 1096+3361
6:17 But G be thanked, that ye were the servants 2316
6:22 and become servants to G, ye have your 2316
6:23 the gift of G *is* eternal life through Jesus 2316
7: 4 that we should bring forth fruit unto G. 2316
7: 7 **G forbid**. Nay, I had not known sin, 1096+3361
7:13 **G forbid**. But sin, that it might 1096+3361
7:22 For I delight in the law of G after 2316
7:25 I thank G through Jesus Christ our Lord. So 2316
7:25 with the mind I myself serve the law of G; 2316
8: 3 G sending his own Son in the likeness of 2316
8: 7 the carnal mind *is* enmity against G: 2316
8: 7 for it is not subject to the law of G, 2316
8: 8 they that are in the flesh cannot please G. 2316
8: 9 if so be that the Spirit of G dwell in you. 2316
8:14 For as many as are led by the Spirit of G, 2316
8:14 by the Spirit of God, they are the sons of G. 2316
8:16 our spirit, that we are the children of G: 2316
8:17 heirs of G, and joint-heirs with Christ; if so 2316
8:19 for the manifestation of the sons of G. 2316
8:21 the glorious liberty of the children of G. 2316
8:27 for the saints according to *the will of* G. 2316
8:28 work together for good to them that love G, 2316

Ro 8:31 then say to these *things?* If G *be* for us, 2316
8:33 of God's elect? *It is* G that justifieth. 2316
8:34 *again,* who is even at the right hand of G, 2316
8:39 be able to separate us from the love of G, 2316
9: 4 and the service *of* G, and the promises; NIG
9: 5 *came,* who is over all, G blessed for ever. 2316
9: 6 Not as though the word of G hath taken 2316
9: 8 of the flesh, these *are* not the children of G: 2316
9:11 that the purpose of G according to election 2316
9:14 *Is there* unrighteousness with G? 2316
9:14 with God? G **forbid**. 1096+3361
9:16 that runneth, but of G that sheweth mercy. 2316
9:20 who art thou that repliest against G? 2316
9:22 What if G, willing to shew *his* wrath, and 2316
9:26 they be called the children of the living G. 2316
10: 1 heart's desire and prayer to G for Israel is, 2316
10: 2 bear them record that they have a zeal of G, 2316
10: 3 themselves unto the righteousness of G. 2316
10: 9 shalt believe in thine heart that G hath 2316
10:17 by hearing, and hearing by the word of G. 2316
11: 1 I say then, Hath G cast away his people? 2316
11: 1 G **forbid**. For I also am an Israelite, 1096+3361
11: 2 G hath not cast away his people which he 2316
11: 2 how he maketh intercession to G against 2316
11: 4 But what saith the **answer of** G unto him? 5538
11: 8 G hath given them the spirit of slumber, 2316
11:11 that they should fall? G **forbid**: 1096+3361
11:21 For if G spared not the natural branches, 2316
11:22 therefore the goodness and severity of G: 2316
11:23 for G is able to graff them in again. 2316
11:29 and calling of G *are* without repentance. 2316
11:30 For as ye in times past have not believed G, 2316
11:32 For G hath concluded *them* all in unbelief, 2316
11:33 both of the wisdom and knowledge of G! 2316
12: 1 brethren, by the mercies of G, 2316
12: 1 holy, acceptable unto G, *which is* your 2316
12: 2 and acceptable, and perfect, will of G. 2316
12: 3 according as G hath dealt to every man 2316
13: 1 For there is no power but of G: the powers 2316
13: 1 the powers that be are ordained of G. 2316
13: 2 the power, resisteth the ordinance of G: 2316
13: 4 For he is the minister of G to thee for good. 2316
13: 4 for he is the minister of G, a revenger to 2316
14: 3 him that eateth: for G hath received him. 2316
14: 4 holden up: for G is able to make him stand. 2316
14: 6 eateth to the Lord, for he giveth G thanks; 2316
14: 6 Lord he eateth not, and giveth G thanks. 2316
14:11 to me, and every tongue shall confess to G. 2316
14:12 of us shall give account of himself to G. 2316
14:17 For the kingdom of G is not meat and 2316
14:18 *things* serveth Christ *is* acceptable to G, 2316
14:20 For meat destroy not the work of G. 2316
14:22 have *it* to thyself before G. Happy *is* he that 2316
15: 5 Now the G of patience and consolation 2316
15: 6 with one mind *and* one mouth glorify G, 2316
15: 7 Christ also received us, to the glory of G. 2316
15: 8 of the circumcision for the truth of G, 2316
15: 9 And that the Gentiles might glorify G for 2316
15:13 Now the G of hope fill you with all joy and 2316
15:15 of the grace that is given to me of G, 2316
15:16 ministering the gospel of G, that 2316
15:17 Christ *in those things* which pertain to G. 2316
15:19 wonders, by the power of the Spirit of G; 2316
15:30 with me in *your* prayers to G for me; 2316
15:32 come unto you with joy by the will of G, 2316
15:33 Now the G of peace *be* with you all. Amen. 2316
16:20 And the G of peace shall bruise Satan 2316
16:26 to the commandment of the everlasting G, 2316
16:27 To G only wise, *be* glory through Jesus 2316
1Co 1: 1 of Jesus Christ through the will of G, 2316
1: 2 Unto the church of G which is at Corinth, 2316
1: 3 from G our Father, and *from* the Lord Jesus 2316
1: 4 I thank my G always on your behalf, 2316
1: 4 for the grace of G which is given you by 2316
1: 9 G *is* faithful, by whom ye were called unto 2316
1:14 I thank G that I baptized none of you, but 2316
1:18 us which are saved it is the power of G. 2316
1:20 hath not G made foolish the wisdom of this 2316
1:21 For after that in the wisdom of G the world 2316
1:21 of God the world by wisdom knew not G, 2316
1:21 it pleased G by the foolishness of preaching 2316
1:24 Christ the power of G, and the wisdom of 2316
1:24 the power of God, and the wisdom of G. 2316
1:25 Because the foolishness of G is wiser than 2316
1:25 the weakness of G is stronger than men. 2316
1:27 But G hath chosen the foolish *things* of 2316
1:27 G hath chosen the weak *things* of the world 2316
1:28 hath G chosen, *yea,* and *things* which are 2316
1:30 who of G is made unto us wisdom, and 2316
2: 1 declaring unto you the testimony of G. 2316
2: 5 the wisdom of men, but in the power of G. 2316
2: 7 But we speak the wisdom of G in a 2316
2: 7 *even* the hidden *wisdom,* which G ordained 2316
2: 9 *the things* which G hath prepared for them 2316
2:10 But G hath revealed *them* unto us by his 2316
2:10 all *things,* yea, the deep things of G. 2316
2:11 so the *things* of G knoweth no *man,* but 2316
2:11 God knoweth no *man,* but the Spirit of G. 2316
2:12 of the world, but the Spirit which is of G; 2316
2:12 the *things* that are freely given to us of G. 2316
2:14 receiveth not the *things* of the Spirit of G: 2316
3: 6 Apollos watered; but G gave the increase. 2316
3: 7 but G that giveth the increase. 2316
3: 9 For we are labourers together with G: 2316
3:10 According to the grace of G which is given 2316
3:16 Know ye not that ye are the temple of G, 2316
3:16 and *that* the Spirit of G dwelleth in you? 2316
3:17 If any *man* defile the temple of G, 2316
3:17 the temple of God, him shall G destroy; 2316
3:17 for the temple of G is holy, which *temple* 2316
3:19 wisdom of this world is foolishness with G. 2316
4: 1 and stewards of the mysteries of G. 2316
4: 5 and then shall every man have praise of G. 2316
4: 8 and I would *to* G ye did reign, that we also NIG
4: 9 For I think that G hath set forth us 2316
1Co 4:20 For the kingdom of G *is* not in word, but 2316
5:13 But them that are without G judgeth. 2316
6: 9 shall not inherit the kingdom of G? 2316
6:10 shall inherit the kingdom of G. 2316
6:11 the Lord Jesus, and by the Spirit of our G. 2316
6:13 but G shall destroy both it and them. 2316
6:14 And G hath both raised up the Lord, and 2316
6:15 the members of a harlot? G **forbid**. 1096+3361
6:19 which ye have of G, and ye are not your 2316
6:20 therefore glorify G in your body, and 2316
7: 7 But every man hath his proper gift of G, 2316
7:15 such *cases:* but G hath called us to peace. 2316
7:17 But as G hath distributed to every man, 2316
7:19 the keeping of the commandments of G. 2316
7:24 wherein he is called, therein abide with G. 2316
7:40 and I think also that *I* have the Spirit of G. 2316
8: 3 But if any *man* love G, the same is known 2316
8: 4 and that *there is* none other G but one. 2316
8: 6 But to us *there is but* one G, the Father, 2316
8: 8 But meat commendeth us not to G: 2316
9: 9 out the corn. Doth G take care for oxen? 2316
9:21 (being not without law to G, but under 2316
10: 5 But with many of them G was not well 2316
10:13 but G *is* faithful, who will not suffer you to 2316
10:20 they sacrifice to devils, and not to G: 2316
10:31 whatsoever ye do, do all to the glory of G. 2316
10:32 nor to the Gentiles, nor to the church of G: 2316
11: 3 *is* the man; and the head of Christ *is* G. 2316
11: 7 as he is the image and glory of G: 2316
11:12 also by the woman; but all *things* of G. 2316
11:13 is it comely that a woman pray unto G 2316
11:16 no such custom, neither the churches of G. 2316
11:22 to drink *in?* or despise ye the church of G, 2316
12: 3 that no *man* speaking by the Spirit of G 2316
12: 6 it is the same G which worketh all in all. 2316
12:18 But now hath G set the members every one 2316
12:24 but G hath tempered the body together, 2316
12:28 And G hath set some in the church, 2316
14: 2 tongue speaketh not unto men, but unto G: 2316
14:18 I thank my G, I speak with tongues more 2316
14:25 falling down on *his* face he will worship G, 2316
14:25 and report that G is in you of a truth. 2316
14:28 and let him speak to himself, and to G. 2316
14:33 For G is not *the author* of confusion, but 2316
14:36 came the word of G out from you? or 2316
15: 9 because I persecuted the church of G. 2316
15:10 But by the grace of G I am what I am: and 2316
15:10 but the grace of G which was with me. 2316
15:15 and we are found false witnesses of G; 2316
15:15 we have testified of G that he raised up 2316
15:24 shall have delivered up the kingdom to G, 2316
15:28 *things* under him, that G may be all in all. 2316
15:34 for some have not the knowledge of G: 2316
15:38 But G giveth it a body as it hath pleased 2316
15:50 and blood cannot inherit the kingdom of G; 2316
15:57 But thanks *be* to G, which giveth us 2316
16: 2 as *G* hath prospered him, that there be no NIG
2Co 1: 1 an apostle of Jesus Christ by the will of G, 2316
1: 1 unto the church of G which is at Corinth, 2316
1: 2 *be* to you and peace from G our Father, 2316
1: 3 Blessed *be* G, even the Father of our Lord 2316
1: 3 Father of mercies, and the G of all comfort; 2316
1: 4 we ourselves are comforted of G. 2316
1: 9 but in G which raiseth the dead: 2316
1:12 with fleshly wisdom, but by the grace of G, 2316
1:18 But *as* G *is* true, our word toward you was 2316
1:19 For the Son of G, Jesus Christ, who was 2316
1:20 For all the promises of G in him *are* yea, 2316
1:20 in him Amen, unto the glory of G by us. 2316
1:21 you in Christ, and hath anointed us, *is* G; 2316
1:23 Moreover I call G for a record upon my 2316
2:14 Now thanks *be* unto G, which always 2316
2:15 For we are unto G a sweet savour of Christ, 2316
2:17 not as many, which corrupt the word of G: 2316
2:17 but as of sincerity, but as of G, in the sight 2316
2:17 in the sight of G speak we in Christ. 2316
3: 3 with ink, but with the Spirit of the living G; 2316
3: 5 as of ourselves; but our sufficiency *is* of G; 2316
4: 2 nor handling the word of G deceitfully; 2316
4: 2 every man's conscience in the sight of G. 2316
4: 4 In whom the **g** of this world hath blinded 2316
4: 4 who is the image of G, should shine unto 2316
4: 6 For G, who commanded the light to shine 2316
4: 6 of the glory of G in the face of Jesus Christ. 2316
4: 7 the excellency of the power may be of G, 2316
4:15 of many redound to the glory of G. 2316
5: 1 we have a building of G, a house not made 2316
5: 5 hath wrought us for the selfsame *thing is* G, 2316
5:11 but we are made manifest unto G; and 2316
5:13 whether we be besides ourselves, *it is* to G: 2316
5:18 And all *things are* of G, who hath 2316
5:19 that G was in Christ reconciling the world 2316
5:20 as though G did beseech *you* by us: 2316
5:20 in Christ's stead, be ye reconciled to G. 2316
5:21 be made the righteousness of G in him. 2316
6: 1 that ye receive not the grace of G in vain. 2316
6: 4 approving ourselves as the ministers of G, 2316
6: 7 By the word of truth, by the power of G, 2316
6:16 And what agreement hath the temple of G 2316
6:16 for ye are the temple of the living G; 2316
6:16 as G hath said, I will dwell in them, and 2316
6:16 and walk in *them;* and I will be their G, and 2316
7: 1 spirit, perfecting holiness in the fear of G. 2316
7: 6 Nevertheless G, that comforteth *those that* 2316
7:12 that our care for you in the sight of G might 2316
8: 1 we do you to wit of the grace of G 2316
8: 5 to the Lord, and unto us by the will of G. 2316
8:16 But thanks *be* to G, which put the same 2316
9: 7 of necessity: for G loveth a cheerful giver. 2316
9: 8 And G *is* able to make all grace abound 2316
9:11 causeth through us thanksgiving to G. 2316
9:12 also by many thanksgivings unto G; 2316
9:13 G for your professed subjection unto 2316
9:14 you for the exceeding grace of G in you. 2316
9:15 Thanks *be* unto G for his unspeakable gift. 2316
2Co 10: 4 mighty through G to the pulling down of 2316
10: 5 exalteth itself against the knowledge of G, 2316
10:13 of the rule which G hath distributed to us, 2316
11: 1 Would *to* G you could bear with me a little NIG
11: 7 I have preached to you the gospel of G 2316
11:11 because I love you not? G knoweth. 2316
11:31 The G and Father of our Lord Jesus Christ, 2316
12: 2 G knoweth;) such a one caught up to 2316
12: 3 out of the body, I cannot tell: G knoweth;) 2316
12:19 we speak before G in Christ: but *we do* all 2316
12:21 my G will humble *me* among you, and 2316
13: 4 yet he liveth by the power of G. 2316
13: 4 we shall live with him by the power of G 2316
13: 7 Now I pray to G that ye do no evil; not that 2316
13:11 and the G of love and peace shall be with 2316
13:14 and the love of G, and the communion of 2316
Gal 1: 1 but by Jesus Christ, and G the Father, 2316
1: 3 *be* to you and peace from G the Father, 2316
1: 4 according to the will of G and our Father: 2316
1:10 For do I now persuade men, or G? or do I 2316
1:13 measure I persecuted the church of G, 2316
1:15 But when it pleased G, who separated me 2316
1:20 I write unto you, behold, before G, I lie not. 2316
1:24 And they glorified G in me. 2316
2: 6 G accepteth no man's person:) for they 2316
2:17 Christ the minister of sin? G **forbid**. 1096+3361
2:19 dead to the law, that I might live unto G. 2316
2:20 the flesh I live by the faith of the Son of G, 2316
2:21 I do not frustrate the grace of G: for if 2316
3: 6 Even as Abraham believed G, and it was 2316
3: 8 foreseeing that G would justify the heathen 2316
3:11 is justified by the law in the sight of G, 2316
3:17 that was confirmed before of G in Christ, 2316
3:18 but G gave *it* to Abraham by promise. 2316
3:20 is not *a mediator* of one, but G is one. 2316
3:21 *Is* the law then against the promises of G? 2316
3:21 G **forbid**: for if there had been a law 1096+3361
3:26 For ye are all the children of G by faith in 2316
4: 4 G sent forth his Son, made of a woman, 2316
4: 6 G hath sent forth the Spirit of his Son into 2316
4: 7 if a son, then an heir of G through Christ. 2316
4: 8 Howbeit then, when ye knew not G, ye did 2316
4: 9 after that ye have known G, or rather are 2316
4: 9 or rather are known of G, how turn ye 2316
4:14 but received me as an angel of G, *even* as 2316
5:21 *things* shall not inherit the kingdom of G. 2316
6: 7 Be not deceived; G is not mocked: 2316
6:14 But G **forbid** that I should glory, 1096+3361
6:16 and mercy, and upon the Israel of G. 2316
Eph 1: 1 an apostle of Jesus Christ by the will of G, 2316
1: 2 from G our Father, and *from* the Lord Jesus 2316
1: 3 Blessed *be* the G and Father of our Lord 2316
1:17 That the G of our Lord Jesus Christ, 2316
2: 4 But G, who is rich in mercy, for his great 2316
2: 8 that not of yourselves: *it is* the gift of G: 2316
2:10 which G hath before ordained that we 2316
2:12 having no hope, and **without** G in the world: 112
2:16 And *that* he might reconcile both unto G in 2316
2:19 with the saints, and of the household of G; 2316
2:22 for a habitation of G through the Spirit. 2316
3: 2 grace of G which is given me to you-ward: 2316
3: 7 according to the gift of the grace of G 2316
3: 9 beginning of the world hath been hid in G, 2316
3:10 by the church the manifold wisdom of G, 2316
3:19 ye might be filled with all the fulness of G. 2316
4: 6 One G and Father of all, who *is* above all, 2316
4:13 and of the knowledge of the Son of G, 2316
4:18 being alienated from the life of G through 2316
4:24 which after G is created in righteousness 2316
4:30 And grieve not the holy Spirit of G, 2316
4:32 even as G for Christ's sake hath forgiven 2316
5: 1 Be ye therefore followers of G, as dear 2316
5: 2 a sacrifice to G for a sweetsmelling savour. 2316
5: 5 in the kingdom of Christ and of G. 2316
5: 6 of these *things* cometh the wrath of G upon 2316
5:20 Giving thanks always for all *things* unto G 2316
5:21 yourselves one to another in the fear of G. 2316
6: 6 doing the will of G from the heart; 2316
6:11 Put on the whole armour of G, that ye may 2316
6:13 take unto *you* the whole armour of G, 2316
6:17 sword of the Spirit, which is the word of G: 2316
6:23 from G the Father and the Lord Jesus 2316
Php 1: 2 from G our Father, and *from* the Lord Jesus 2316
1: 3 I thank my G upon every remembrance of 2316
1: 8 For G is my record, how *greatly* I long 2316
1:11 Jesus Christ unto the glory and praise of G. 2316
1:28 but to you of salvation, and that of G. 2316
2: 6 Who, being in the form of G, thought it not 2316
2: 6 thought it not robbery to be equal with G: 2316
2: 9 Wherefore G also hath highly exalted him, 2316
2:11 Christ *is* Lord, to the glory of G the Father. 2316
2:13 For it is G which worketh in you both to 2316
2:15 harmless, the sons of G without rebuke, 2316
2:27 but G had mercy on him; and not on him 2316
3: 3 which worship G in the spirit, and 2316
3: 9 the righteousness which is of G by faith: 2316
3:14 of the high calling of G in Christ Jesus. 2316
3:15 G shall reveal even this unto you. 2316
3:19 whose G *is their* belly, and *whose* glory *is* 2316
4: 6 let your requests be made known unto G. 2316
4: 7 And the peace of G, which passeth all 2316
4: 9 do: and the G of peace shall be with you. 2316
4:18 a sacrifice acceptable, well pleasing to G. 2316
4:19 But my G shall supply all your need 2316
4:20 Now unto G and our Father *be* glory for 2316
Col 1: 1 an apostle of Jesus Christ by the will of G, 2316
1: 2 from G our Father and the Lord Jesus 2316
1: 3 We give thanks to G and the Father of our 2316
1: 6 of it, and knew the grace of G in truth. 2316
1:10 and increasing in the knowledge of G; 2316
1:15 Who is the image of the invisible G, 2316
1:25 according to the dispensation of G which is 2316
1:25 given to me for you, to fulfil the word of G; 2316
1:27 To whom G would make known what *is* 2316
2: 2 the acknowledgement of the mystery of G 2316

G

Col 2:12 *him* through the faith of the operation of G, 2316
2:19 increaseth *with* the increase of G. 2316
3: 1 where Christ sitteth on the right hand of G. 2316
3: 3 and your life is hid with Christ in G. 2316
3: 6 For which *things'* sake the wrath of G 2316
3:12 as the elect of G, holy and beloved, 2316
3:15 And let the peace of G rule in your hearts, 2316
3:17 giving thanks to G and the Father by him. 2316
3:22 but in singleness of heart, fearing G: 2316
4: 3 that G would open unto us a door of 2316
4:11 *my* fellowworkers unto the kingdom of G, 2316
4:12 and complete in all the will of G. 2316
1Th 1: 1 the Thessalonians *which is* in G the Father 2316
1: 1 from G our Father, and the Lord Jesus 2316
1: 2 We give thanks to G always for you all, 2316
1: 3 in the sight of G and our Father; 2316
1: 4 brethren beloved, your election of G. 2316
1: 9 how ye turned to G from idols to serve 2316
1: 9 from idols to serve the living and true G, 2316
2: 2 we were bold in our G to speak unto you 2316
2: 2 you the gospel of G with much contention. 2316
2: 4 But as we were allowed of G to be put in 2316
2: 4 not as pleasing men, but G, which trieth 2316
2: 5 nor a cloke of covetousness; G *is* witness: 2316
2: 8 not the gospel of G only, but also our own 2316
2: 9 we preached unto you the gospel of G. 2316
2:10 and G *also,* how holily and justly and 2316
2:12 That ye would walk worthy of G, who hath 2316
2:13 For this cause also thank we G without 2316
2:13 when ye received the word of G which *ye* 2316
2:13 of men, but as it is in truth, the word of G, 2316
2:14 became followers of the churches of G 2316
2:15 and they please not G, and are contrary to 2316
3: 2 and minister of G, and our fellowlabourer 2316
3: 9 For what thanks can we render to G again 2316
3: 9 we joy for your sakes before our G; 2316
3:11 Now G himself and our Father, and 2316
3:13 hearts unblameable in holiness before G, 2316
4: 1 us how ye ought to walk and to please G, 2316
4: 3 For this is the will of G, *even* your 2316
4: 5 even as the Gentiles which know not G: 2316
4: 7 For G hath not called us unto uncleanness, 2316
4: 8 that despiseth, despiseth not man, but G, 2316
4: 9 for ye yourselves are **taught of G** to love 2312
4:14 them also which sleep in Jesus will G bring 2316
4:16 of the archangel, and with the trump of G: 2316
5: 9 For G hath not appointed us to wrath, but 2316
5:18 for this *is* the will of G in Christ Jesus 2316
5:23 And the very G of peace sanctify you 2316
5:23 and *I pray* G your whole spirit and soul and NIG
2Th 1: 1 unto the church of the Thessalonians in G 2316
1: 2 from G our Father and the Lord Jesus 2316
1: 3 We are bound to thank G always for you, 2316
1: 4 you in the churches of G for your patience 2316
1: 5 token of the righteous judgment of G, 2316
1: 5 be counted worthy of the kingdom of G, 2316
1: 6 Seeing *it is* a righteous *thing* with G to 2316
1: 8 taking vengeance on them that know not G, 2316
1:11 that our G would count you worthy of *this* 2316
1:12 according to the grace of our G and 2316
2: 4 exalteth himself above all that is called G, 2316
2: 4 so that he as G sitteth in the temple of God, NIG
2: 4 so that he as God sitteth in the temple of G, 2316
2: 4 of God, shewing himself that he is G. 2316
2:11 And for this cause G shall send them strong 2316
2:13 bound to give thanks alway to G for you, 2316
2:13 G hath from the beginning chosen you to 2316
2:16 and G, even our Father, which hath loved 2316
3: 5 Lord direct your hearts into the love of G, 2316
1Ti 1: 1 by the commandment of G our Saviour, 2316
1: 2 from G our Father and Jesus Christ our 2316
1:11 to the glorious gospel of the blessed G, 2316
1:17 immortal, invisible, the only wise G, 2316
2: 3 acceptable in the sight of G our Saviour; 2316
2: 5 For *there is* one G, and one mediator 2316
2: 5 and one mediator between G and men, 2316
3: 5 how shall he take care of the church of G?) 2316
3:15 to behave thyself in the house of G, 2316
3:15 which is the church of the living G, 2316
3:16 G was manifest in the flesh, justified in 2316
4: 3 which G hath created to be received with 2316
4: 4 For every creature of G *is* good, and 2316
4: 5 For it is sanctified by the word of G and 2316
4:10 because we trust in the living G, 2316
5: 4 for that is good and acceptable before G. 2316
5: 5 trusteth in G, and continueth in 2316
5:21 I charge *thee* before G, and the Lord Jesus 2316
6: 1 that the name of G and *his* doctrine be not 2316
6:11 But thou, O man of G, flee these *things;* 2316
6:13 I give thee charge in the sight of G, 2316
6:17 trust in uncertain riches, but in the living G, 2316
2Ti 1: 1 an apostle of Jesus Christ by the will of G, 2316
1: 2 from G the Father and Christ Jesus our 2316
1: 3 I thank G, whom I serve from *my* 2316
1: 6 remembrance that *thou* stir up the gift of G, 2316
1: 7 For G hath not given us the spirit of fear; 2316
1: 8 of the gospel according to the power of G; 2316
2: 9 unto bonds; but the word of G is not bound. 2316
2:15 Study to shew thyself approved unto G, 2316
2:19 Nevertheless the foundation of G standeth 2316
2:25 if G peradventure will give them 2316
3: 4 lovers of pleasures more than **lovers of G;** 5377
3:16 All scripture *is* **given by inspiration of G,** 2315
3:17 That the man of G may be perfect, 2316
4: 1 I charge *thee* therefore before G, and 2316
4:16 *I pray* G that it may not be laid to their NIG
Tit 1: 1 a servant of G, and an apostle of Jesus 2316
1: 2 of eternal life, which G, that cannot lie, 2316
1: 3 to the commandment of G our Saviour; 2316
1: 4 from G the Father and the Lord Jesus 2316
1: 7 must be blameless, as the steward of G; 2316
1:16 They profess that *they* know G; but 2316
2: 5 that the word of G be not blasphemed. 2316
2:10 that they may adorn the doctrine of G our 2316
2:11 For the grace of G that bringeth salvation 2316

Tit 2:13 the glorious appearing of the great G and 2316
3: 4 love of G our Saviour toward man 2316
3: 8 that they which have believed in G might 2316
Phm 1: 3 from G our Father and the Lord Jesus 2316
1: 4 I thank my G, making mention of thee 2316
Heb 1: 1 G, who at sundry times and in divers 2316
1: 6 And let all the angels of G worship him. 2316
1: 8 *saith,* Thy throne, O G, *is* for ever and ever: 2316
1: 9 therefore G, *even* thy God, hath anointed 2316
1: 9 therefore God, *even* thy G, hath anointed 2316
2: 4 G also bearing *them* witness, both with 2316
2: 9 that he by the grace of G should taste 2316
2:13 I, and the children which G hath given me. 2316
2:17 high priest *in things* pertaining to G, 2316
3: 4 some *man;* but he that built all *things is* G. 2316
3:12 of unbelief, in departing from the living G. 2316
4: 4 And G did rest the seventh day from all his 2316
4: 9 therefore a rest to the people of G. 2316
4:10 from his own works, as G *did* from his. 2316
4:12 For the word of G *is* quick, and powerful, 2316
4:14 Jesus the Son of G, let us hold fast *our* 2316
5: 1 ordained for men *in things* pertaining to G, 2316
5: 4 but he that is called of G, as *was* Aaron. 2316
5:10 Called of G a high priest after the order of 2316
5:12 *be* the first principles of the oracles of G; 2316
6: 1 from dead works, and of faith towards G, 2316
6: 3 And this will we do, if G permit. 2316
6: 5 And have tasted the good word of G, and 2316
6: 6 crucify to themselves the Son of G afresh, 2316
6: 7 it is dressed, receiveth blessing from G: 2316
6:10 For G *is* not unrighteous to forget your 2316
6:13 For when G made promise to Abraham, 2316
6:17 Wherein G, willing more abundantly to 2316
6:18 in which *it was* impossible for G to lie, 2316
7: 1 king of Salem, priest of the most high G, 2316
7: 3 of life; but made like unto the Son of G; 2316
7:19 *did;* by the which we draw nigh unto G. 2316
7:25 to the uttermost that come unto G by him, 2316
8: 5 **admonished of G** when he was about to 5537
8:10 and I will be to them a G, and they shall be 2316
9: 6 accomplishing the service *of* G. NIG
9:14 Spirit offered himself without spot to G, 2316
9:14 from dead works to serve the living G? 2316
9:20 This *is* the blood of the testament which G 2316
9:24 now to appear in the presence of G for us: 2316
10: 7 it is written of me,) to do thy will, O G. 2316
10: 9 said he, Lo, I come to do thy will, O G. 2316
10:12 for ever, sat down on the right hand of G; 2316
10:21 *having* a high priest over the house of G; 2316
10:29 who hath trodden under foot the Son of G, 2316
10:31 *thing* to fall into the hands of the living G. 2316
10:36 that, after ye have done the will of G, 2316
11: 3 the worlds were framed by the word of G, 2316
11: 4 By faith Abel offered unto G a more 2316
11: 4 he was righteous, G testifying of his gifts: 2316
11: 5 not found, because G had translated him: 2316
11: 5 he had this testimony, that *he* pleased G. 2316
11: 6 he that cometh to G must believe that he is, 2316
11: 7 being **warned of** G of *things* not seen as 5537
11:10 whose builder and maker *is* G. 2316
11:16 wherefore G is not ashamed to be called 2316
11:16 God is not ashamed to be called their G: 2316
11:19 Accounting that G *was* able to raise *him* 2316
11:25 to suffer affliction with the people of G, 2316
11:40 G having provided some better *thing* for us, 2316
12: 2 down at the right hand of the throne of G. 2316
12: 7 G dealeth with you as with sons; 2316
12:15 lest any *man* fail of the grace of G; 2316
12:22 and unto the city of the living G, 2316
12:23 and to G the Judge of all, and to the spirits 2316
12:28 whereby we may serve G acceptably with 2316
12:29 For our G *is* a consuming fire. 2316
13: 4 and adulterers G will judge. 2316
13: 7 who have spoken unto you the word of G: 2316
13:15 let us offer the sacrifice of praise to G 2316
13:16 for with such sacrifices G is well pleased. 2316
13:20 Now the G of peace, that brought again 2316
Jas 1: 1 a servant of G and of the Lord Jesus Christ, 2316
1: 5 any of you lack wisdom, let him ask of G, 2316
1:13 say when he is tempted, I am tempted of G: 2316
1:13 for G cannot be tempted with evil, 2316
1:20 of man worketh not the righteousness of G. 2316
1:27 Pure religion and undefiled before G and 2316
2: 5 Hath not G chosen the poor of this world 2316
2:19 Thou believest that there is one G; 2316
2:23 Abraham believed G, and it was imputed 2316
2:23 and he was called the Friend of G. 2316
3: 9 Therewith bless we G, even the Father; and 2316
3: 9 which are made after the similitude of G. 2316
4: 4 friendship of the world is enmity with G? 2316
4: 4 be a friend of the world is the enemy of G. 2316
4: 6 G resisteth the proud, but giveth grace unto 2316
4: 7 Submit yourselves therefore to G. Resist 2316
4: 8 Draw nigh to G, and he will draw nigh to 2316
1Pe 1: 2 Elect according to the foreknowledge of G 2316
1: 3 Blessed *be* the G and Father of our Lord 2316
1: 5 Who are kept by the power of G through 2316
1:21 Who by him do believe in G, that raised 2316
1:21 that your faith and hope might be in G. 2316
1:23 by the word of G, which liveth and 2316
2: 4 of men, but chosen of G, *and* precious, 2316
2: 5 acceptable to G by Jesus Christ. 2316
2:10 not a people, but *are* now the people of G: 2316
2:12 glorify G in the day of visitation. 2316
2:15 For so is the will of G, that with well doing 2316
2:16 of maliciousness, but as the servants of G. 2316
2:17 the brotherhood. Fear G. Honour the king. 2316
2:19 if a man for conscience toward G endure 2316
2:20 take it patiently, this *is* acceptable with G. 2316
3: 4 which is in the sight of G of great price. 2316
3: 5 who trusted in G, adorned themselves, 2316
3:15 But sanctify the Lord G in your hearts: and 2316
3:17 For *it is* better, if the will of G be so, 2316
3:18 for the unjust, that he might bring us to G, 2316
3:20 when once the longsuffering of G waited in 2316

1Pe 3:21 answer of a good conscience toward G,) 2316
3:22 into heaven, and is on the right hand of G; 2316
4: 2 to the lusts of men, but to the will of G. 2316
4: 6 but live according to G in the spirit. 2316
4:10 good stewards of the manifold grace of G. 2316
4:11 *let him speak* as the oracles of G; 2316
4:11 *let him do it* as of the ability which G 2316
4:11 that G in all *things* may be glorified 2316
4:14 spirit of glory and of G resteth upon you: 2316
4:16 but let him glorify G on this behalf. 2316
4:17 judgment must begin at the house of G: 2316
4:17 *be* of them that obey not the gospel of G? 2316
4:19 G commit the keeping of their souls *to him* 2316
5: 2 Feed the flock of G which is among you, 2316
5: 5 for G resisteth the proud, and giveth grace 2316
5: 6 therefore under the mighty hand of G, 2316
5:10 But the G of all grace, who hath called us 2316
5:12 testifying that this is the true grace of G 2316
2Pe 1: 1 with us through the righteousness of G 2316
1: 2 unto you through the knowledge of G, 2316
1:17 For he received from G the Father honour 2316
1:21 holy men of G spake *as they were* moved 2316
2: 4 For if G spared not the angels that sinned, 2316
3: 5 that by the word of G the heavens were of 2316
3:12 hasting *unto* the coming of the day of G, 2316
1Jn 1: 5 that G is light, and in him is no darkness at 2316
2: 5 in him verily is the love of G perfected: 2316
2:14 and the word of G abideth in you, and 2316
2:17 he that doeth the will of G abideth for ever. 2316
3: 1 that we should be called the sons of G: 2316
3: 2 now are we the sons of G, and it doth not 2316
3: 8 For this purpose the Son of G was 2316
3: 9 Whosoever is born of G doth not commit 2316
3: 9 and he cannot sin, because he is born of G. 2316
3:10 In this the children of G are manifest, and 2316
3:10 doeth not righteousness is not of G, 2316
3:16 Hereby perceive we the love *of* G, because NIG
3:17 how dwelleth the love of G in him? 2316
3:20 G is greater than our heart, and 2316
3:21 us not, *then* have we confidence towards G. 2316
4: 1 but try the spirits whether they are of G: 2316
4: 2 Hereby know ye the Spirit of G: 2316
4: 2 Jesus Christ is come in the flesh is of G: 2316
4: 3 Christ is come in the flesh is not of G: 2316
4: 4 Ye are of G, little children, and 2316
4: 6 We are of G: he that knoweth God heareth 2316
4: 6 he that knoweth G heareth us; *he* that is not 2316
4: 6 *he* that is not of G heareth not us. 2316
4: 7 for love is of G; and every one that loveth 2316
4: 7 and every one that loveth is born of G, and 2316
4: 7 that loveth is born of God, and knoweth G. 2316
4: 8 He that loveth not, knoweth not G; for God 2316
4: 8 loveth not, knoweth not God; for G is love. 2316
4: 9 In this was manifested the love of G 2316
4: 9 that G sent his only begotten Son into 2316
4:10 not that we loved G, but that he loved us, 2316
4:11 Beloved, if G so loved us, we ought also to 2316
4:12 No *man* hath seen G at any time. If we love 2316
4:12 G dwelleth in us, and his love is perfected 2316
4:15 shall confess that Jesus is the Son of G, 2316
4:15 of God, G dwelleth in him, and he in God. 2316
4:15 of God, God dwelleth in him, and he in G. 2316
4:16 and believed the love that G hath to us. 2316
4:16 G is love; and he that dwelleth in love 2316
4:16 and he that dwelleth in love dwelleth in G, 2316
4:16 in love dwelleth in God, and G in him. 2316
4:20 I love G, and hateth his brother, he is a liar: 2316
4:20 how can he love G whom he hath not seen? 2316
4:21 That he who loveth G love his brother also. 2316
5: 1 that Jesus is the Christ is born of G: 2316
5: 2 we know that we love the children of G, 2316
5: 2 when we love G, and keep his 2316
5: 3 For this is the love of G, that we keep his 2316
5: 4 For whatsoever is born of G overcometh 2316
5: 5 he that believeth that Jesus is the Son of G? 2316
5: 9 witness of men, the witness of G is greater: 2316
5: 9 for this is the witness of G which he hath 2316
5:10 He that believeth on the Son of G hath 2316
5:10 he that believeth not G hath made him a 2316
5:10 he believeth not the record that G gave of 2316
5:11 that G hath given to us eternal life, and 2316
5:12 he that hath not the Son of G hath not life. 2316
5:13 that believe on the name of the Son of G; 2316
5:13 may believe on the name of the Son of G. 2316
5:18 We know that whosoever is born of G 2316
5:18 he that is begotten of G keepeth himself, 2316
5:19 *And* we know that we are of G, and 2316
5:20 And we know that the Son of G is come, 2316
5:20 This is the true G, and eternal life. 2316
2Jn 1: 3 from G the Father, and from the Lord Jesus 2316
1: 9 not in the doctrine of Christ, hath not G. 2316
1:10 into *your* house, neither bid him **G speed:** 5463
1:11 For he that biddeth him **G speed** is partaker 5463
3Jn 1:11 He that doeth good is of G: but he that 2316
1:11 but he that doeth evil hath not seen G. 2316
Jude 1: 1 to them that are sanctified by G the Father, 2316
1: 4 ungodly *men,* turning the grace of our G 2316
1: 4 and denying the only Lord G, and our Lord 2316
1:21 Keep yourselves in the love of G, 2316
1:25 To the only wise G our Saviour, *be* glory 2316
Rev 1: 1 of Jesus Christ, which G gave unto him, 2316
1: 2 Who bare record of the word of G, and 2316
1: 6 us kings and priests unto G and his Father; 2316
1: 9 for the word of G, and for the testimony of 2316
2: 7 which is in the midst of the paradise of G. 2316
2:18 These *things* saith the Son of G, who hath 2316
3: 1 saith he that hath the seven spirits of G, 2316
3: 2 have not found thy works perfect before G. 2316
3:12 will I make a pillar in the temple of my G, 2316
3:12 I will write upon him the name of my G, 2316
3:12 and the name of the city of my G, *which is* 2316
3:12 cometh down out of heaven from my G: 2316
3:14 the beginning of the creation of G; 2316
4: 5 the throne, which are the seven spirits of G. 2316
4: 8 saying, Holy, holy, holy, Lord G Almighty, 2316

Rev 5: 6 which are the seven spirits of **G** sent forth *2316*
5: 9 hast redeemed us to **G** by thy blood out of *2316*
5:10 And hast made us unto our **G** kings and *2316*
6: 9 of them that were slain for the word of **G**, *2316*
7: 2 the east, having the seal of the living **G**: *2316*
7: 3 till we have sealed the servants of our **G** in *2316*
7:10 Salvation to our **G** which sitteth upon *2316*
7:11 throne on their faces, and worshipped **G**, *2316*
7:12 and might, *be* unto our **G** for ever and ever. *2316*
7:15 Therefore are they before the throne of **G**, *2316*
7:17 **G** shall wipe away all tears from their eyes. *2316*
8: 2 saw the seven angels which stood before **G**; *2316*
8: 4 ascended up before **G** out of the angel's *2316*
9: 4 have not the seal of **G** in their foreheads. *2316*
9:13 horns of the golden altar which is before **G**, *2316*
10: 7 the mystery of **G** should be finished, *2316*
11: 1 and measure the temple of **G**, and the altar, *2316*
11: 4 the two candlesticks standing before the **G** *2316*
11:11 a half the spirit of life from **G** entered into *2316*
11:13 and gave glory to the **G** of heaven. *2316*
11:16 which sat before **G** on their seats, *2316*
11:16 fell upon their faces, and worshipped **G**, *2316*
11:17 O Lord **G** Almighty, which art, and wast, *2316*
11:19 And the temple of **G** was opened in heaven, *2316*
12: 5 and her child was caught up unto **G**, and *2316*
12: 6 where she hath a place prepared of **G**, *2316*
12:10 and the kingdom of our **G**, and the power *2316*
12:10 which accused them before our **G** day and *2316*
12:17 which keep the commandments of **G**, and *2316*
13: 6 opened his mouth in blasphemy against **G**, *2316*
14: 4 *being* the firstfruits unto **G** and to *2316*
14: 5 are without fault before the throne of **G**. *2316*
14: 7 a loud voice, Fear **G**, and give glory to him; *2316*
14:10 shall drink of the wine of the wrath of **G**, *2316*
14:12 *are* they that keep the commandments of **G**, *2316*
14:19 into the great winepress of the wrath of **G**. *2316*
15: 1 for in them is filled up the wrath of **G**. *2316*
15: 2 on the sea of glass, having *the* harps of **G**. *2316*
15: 3 sing the song of Moses the servant of **G**, *2316*
15: 3 *are* thy works, Lord **G** Almighty; *2316*
15: 7 seven golden vials full of the wrath of **G**, *2316*
15: 8 was filled with smoke from the glory of **G**, *2316*
16: 1 pour out the vials of the wrath of **G** upon *2316*
16: 7 Lord **G** Almighty, true and righteous *are* *2316*
16: 9 and blasphemed the name of **G**, which hath *2316*
16:11 And blasphemed the **G** of heaven because *2316*
16:14 the battle of that great day of **G** Almighty. *2316*
16:19 Babylon came in remembrance before **G**, *2316*
16:21 and men blasphemed **G** because of *2316*
17:17 For **G** hath put in their hearts to fulfil his *2316*
17:17 until the words of **G** shall be fulfilled. *2316*
18: 5 and **G** hath remembered her iniquities. *2316*
18: 8 for strong *is* the Lord **G** who judgeth her. *2316*
18:20 for **G** hath avenged you on her. *2316*
19: 1 honour, and power, unto the Lord our **G**: *2316*
19: 4 and worshipped **G** that sat on the throne, *2316*
19: 5 saying, Praise our **G**, all ye his servants, *2316*
19: 6 for the Lord **G** Omnipotent reigneth. *2316*
19: 9 unto me, These are the true sayings of **G**. *2316*
19:10 worship **G**: for the testimony of Jesus is *2316*
19:13 and his name is called The Word of **G**. *2316*
19:15 of the fierceness and wrath of Almighty **G**. *2316*
19:17 together unto the supper of the great **G**; *2316*
20: 4 and for the word of **G**, and which had not *2316*
20: 6 but they shall be priests of **G** and of Christ, *2316*
20: 9 and fire came down from **G** out of heaven, *2316*
20:12 the dead, small and great, stand before **G**; *2316*
21: 2 coming down from **G** out of heaven, *2316*
21: 3 the tabernacle of **G** *is* with men, and he will *2316*
21: 3 and **G** himself shall be with them, *and* *2316*
21: 3 himself shall be with them, *and be* their **G**. *2316*
21: 4 And **G** shall wipe away all tears from their *2316*
21: 7 shall inherit all *things*; and I will be his **G**, *2316*
21:10 descending out of heaven from **G**, *2316*
21:11 Having the glory of **G**: and her light *was* *2316*
21:22 for the Lord **G** Almighty and the Lamb are *2316*
21:23 for the glory of **G** did lighten it, and *2316*
22: 1 proceeding out of the throne of **G** and *2316*
22: 3 but the throne of **G** and of the Lamb shall *2316*
22: 5 the sun; for the Lord **G** giveth them light: *2316*
22: 6 the Lord **G** of the holy prophets sent his *2316*
22: 9 keep the sayings of this book: worship **G**. *2316*
22:18 If any *man* shall add unto these *things*, **G** *2316*
22:19 **G** shall take away his part out of the book *2316*

GOD* (309) [LORD*; this is the proper name of God, *Yahweh* or *Jehovah*, used in the phrase Lord GOD]

Ge 6: 5 **G** saw that the wickedness of man *was* 3068
15: 2 Abram said, Lord **G**, what wilt thou give 3068
15: 8 he said, Lord **G**, whereby shall I know that 3068
Ex 23:17 thy males shall appear before the Lord **G**. 3068
34:23 men children appear before the Lord **G**, 3068
Dt 3:24 O Lord **G**, thou hast begun to shew thy 3068
9:26 unto the LORD, and said, O Lord **G**, 3068
Jos 7: 7 Joshua said, Alas, O Lord **G**, 3068
Jdg 6:22 the LORD, Gideon said, Alas, O Lord **G**! 3068
16:28 said, O Lord **G**, remember me, I pray thee, 3068
2Sa 7:18 and he said, Who *am* I, O Lord **G**? 3068
7:19 yet a small thing in thy sight, O Lord **G**; 3068
7:19 And *is* this the manner of man, O Lord **G**? 3068
7:20 for thou, Lord **G**, knowest thy servant. 3068
7:28 now, O Lord **G**, thou *art* that God, and 3068
7:29 for thou, O Lord **G**, hast spoken *it*: and 3068
12:22 Who can tell *whether* **G** will be gracious to 3068
1Ki 2:26 thou barest the ark of the Lord **G** before 3068
8:53 our fathers out of Egypt, O Lord **G**. 3068
Ps 68:20 unto **G** the Lord *belong* the issues from 3068
69: 6 O Lord **G** of hosts, be ashamed for my 3068
71: 5 For thou *art* my hope, O Lord **G**: *thou art* 3068
71:16 I will go in the strength of the Lord **G**: 3068
73:28 I have put my trust in the Lord **G**, that *I* 3068
109:21 do thou for me, O **G** the Lord, for thy 3068
140: 7 O **G** the Lord, the strength of my salvation, 3068
Ps 141: 8 mine eyes *are* unto thee, O **G** the Lord: 3068
Isa 3:15 of the poor? saith the Lord **G** of hosts. 3068
7: 7 Thus saith the Lord **G**, It shall not stand, 3068
10:23 For the Lord **G** of hosts shall make a 3068
10:24 Therefore thus saith the Lord **G** of hosts, 3068
22: 5 of perplexity by the Lord **G** of hosts in 3068
22:12 in that day did the Lord **G** of hosts call to 3068
22:14 you till ye die, saith the Lord **G** of hosts. 3068
22:15 Thus saith the Lord **G** of hosts, Go, get thee 3068
25: 8 the Lord **G** will wipe away tears from off 3068
28:16 Therefore thus saith the Lord **G**, Behold, 3068
28:22 for I have heard from the Lord **G** of hosts a 3068
30:15 For thus saith the Lord **G**, the Holy One of 3068
40:10 the Lord **G** will come with strong *hand*, and 3068
48:16 now the Lord **G**, and his Spirit, hath sent 3068
49:22 Thus saith the Lord **G**, Behold, I will lift up 3068
50: 4 The Lord **G** hath given me the tongue of 3068
50: 5 The Lord **G** hath opened mine ear, and 3068
50: 7 For the Lord **G** will help me; therefore 3068
50: 9 Behold, the Lord **G** will help me; who *is* he 3068
52: 4 For thus saith the Lord **G**, My people went 3068
56: 8 The Lord **G** which gathereth the outcasts of 3068
61: 1 The Spirit of the Lord **G** *is* upon me; 3068
61:11 so the Lord **G** will cause righteousness and 3068
65:13 Therefore thus saith the Lord **G**, Behold, 3068
65:15 for the Lord **G** shall slay thee, and call his 3068
Jer 1: 6 said I, Ah, Lord **G**, behold, I cannot speak: 3068
2:19 *is* not in thee, saith the Lord **G** of hosts. 3068
2:22 *is* marked before me, saith the Lord **G**. 3068
4:10 (Then said I, Ah, Lord **G**! surely thou hast 3068
7:20 Therefore thus saith the Lord **G**; Behold, 3068
14:13 said I, Ah Lord **G**! behold, the prophets say 3068
32:17 Ah Lord **G**! behold, thou hast made 3068
32:25 thou hast said unto me, O Lord **G**, Buy thee 3068
44:26 land of Egypt, saying, The Lord **G** liveth. 3068
46:10 For this *is* the day of the Lord **G** of hosts, 3068
46:10 for the Lord **G** of hosts hath a sacrifice in 3068
49: 5 a fear upon thee, saith the Lord **G** of hosts, 3068
50:25 for this *is* the work of the Lord **G** of hosts 3068
50:31 *thou* most proud, saith the Lord **G** of hosts: 3068
Eze 2: 4 shalt say unto them, Thus saith the Lord **G**. 3068
3:11 and tell them, Thus saith the Lord **G**; 3068
3:27 shalt say unto them, Thus saith the Lord **G**; 3068
4:14 said I, Ah Lord **G**, behold, my soul *hath* not 3068
5: 5 Thus saith the Lord **G**; This *is* Jerusalem: 3068
5: 7 Therefore thus saith the Lord **G**; 3068
5: 8 Therefore thus saith the Lord **G**; Behold, I, 3068
5:11 Wherefore, *as* I live, saith the Lord **G**; 3068
6: 3 of Israel, hear the word of the Lord **G**; 3068
6: 3 Thus saith the Lord **G** to the mountains, 3068
6:11 Thus saith the Lord **G**; Smite with thine 3068
7: 2 thus saith the Lord **G** unto the land of 3068
7: 5 Thus saith the Lord **G**; An evil, an only 3068
8: 1 that the hand of the Lord **G** fell there upon 3068
9: 8 my face, and cried, and said, Ah Lord **G**! 3068
11: 7 Therefore thus saith the Lord **G**; Your slain 3068
11: 8 bring a sword upon you, saith the Lord **G**. 3068
11:13 *with* a loud voice, and said, Ah Lord **G**, 3068
11:16 Therefore say, Thus saith the Lord **G**; 3068
11:17 Therefore say, Thus saith the Lord **G**; I will 3068
11:21 upon their own heads, saith the Lord **G**. 3068
12:10 Say thou unto them, Thus saith the Lord **G**; 3068
12:19 Thus saith the Lord **G**, of the inhabitants of 3068
12:23 Tell them therefore, Thus saith the Lord **G**; 3068
12:25 and will perform it, saith the Lord **G**. 3068
12:28 say unto them, Thus saith the Lord **G**; 3068
12:28 spoken shall be done, saith the Lord **G**. 3068
13: 3 Thus saith the Lord **G**; Woe unto 3068
13: 8 Therefore thus saith the Lord **G**; 3068
13: 8 I *am* against you, saith the Lord **G**. 3068
13: 9 and ye shall know that I *am* the Lord **G**. 3068
13:13 Therefore thus saith the Lord **G**; I will even 3068
13:16 and *there is* no peace, saith the Lord **G**. 3068
13:18 say, Thus saith the Lord **G**; Woe to 3068
13:20 Wherefore thus saith the Lord **G**; Behold, 3068
14: 4 and say unto them, Thus saith the Lord **G**; 3068
14: 6 the house of Israel, Thus saith the Lord **G**; 3068
14:11 and I may be their God, saith the Lord **G**. 3068
14:14 by their righteousness, saith the Lord **G**. 3068
14:16 men *were* in it, *as* I live, saith the Lord **G**, 3068
14:18 men *were* in it, *as* I live, saith the Lord **G**, 3068
14:20 Job, *were* in it, *as* I live, saith the Lord **G**, 3068
14:21 For thus saith the Lord **G**; How much more 3068
14:23 all that I have done in it, saith the Lord **G**. 3068
15: 6 Therefore thus saith the Lord **G**; As 3068
15: 8 committed a trespass, saith the Lord **G**. 3068
16: 3 Thus saith the Lord **G** unto Jerusalem; 3068
16: 8 saith the Lord **G**, and thou becamest mine. 3068
16:14 I had put upon thee, saith the Lord **G**. 3068
16:19 and *thus* it was, saith the Lord **G**. 3068
16:23 (woe, woe unto thee! saith the Lord **G**;) 3068
16:30 How weak is thine heart, saith the Lord **G**, 3068
16:36 Thus saith the Lord **G**; Because thy 3068
16:43 thy way upon *thine* head, saith the Lord **G**: 3068
16:48 *As* I live, saith the Lord **G**, Sodom thy 3068
16:59 For thus saith the Lord **G**; I will even deal 3068
16:63 for all that thou hast done, saith the Lord **G**. 3068
17: 3 say, Thus saith the Lord **G**; A great eagle 3068
17: 9 Say thou, Thus saith the Lord **G**; Shall it 3068
17:16 *As* I live, saith the Lord **G**, surely in 3068
17:19 Therefore thus saith the Lord **G**; *As* I live, 3068
17:22 Thus saith the Lord **G**; I will also take of 3068
18: 3 *As* I live, saith the Lord **G**, ye shall not 3068
18: 9 he shall surely live, saith the Lord **G**. 3068
18:23 saith the Lord **G**: *and* not that he should 3068
18:30 according to his ways, saith the Lord **G**. 3068
18:32 death of him that dieth, saith the Lord **G**: 3068
20: 3 and say unto them, Thus saith the Lord **G**; 3068
20: 3 *As* I live, saith the Lord **G**, I will not be 3068
20: 5 say unto them, Thus saith the Lord **G**; 3068
20:27 and say unto them, Thus saith the Lord **G**; 3068
20:30 the house of Israel, Thus saith the Lord **G**; 3068
20:31 *As* I live, saith the Lord **G**, I will not be 3068
20:33 *As* I live, saith the Lord **G**, surely with a 3068
20:36 so will I plead with you, saith the Lord **G**. 3068
Eze 20:39 O house of Israel, thus saith the Lord **G**; 3068
20:40 saith the Lord **G**, there shall all the house 3068
20:44 O ye house of Israel, saith the Lord **G**. 3068
20:47 Thus saith the Lord **G**; Behold, I *will* 3068
20:49 said I, Ah Lord **G**, they say of me, Doth he 3068
21: 7 shall be brought to pass, saith the Lord **G**. 3068
21:13 it shall be no *more*, saith the Lord **G**. 3068
21:24 Therefore thus saith the Lord **G**; 3068
21:26 Thus saith the Lord **G**; Remove 3068
21:28 Thus saith the Lord **G** concerning 3068
22: 3 say thou, Thus saith the Lord **G**, The city 3068
22:12 and hast forgotten me, saith the Lord **G**. 3068
22:19 Therefore thus saith the Lord **G**; 3068
22:28 unto them, saying, Thus saith the Lord **G**, 3068
22:31 upon their heads, saith the Lord **G**. 3068
23:22 O Aholibah, thus saith the Lord **G**; 3068
23:28 For thus saith the Lord **G**; Behold, I *will* 3068
23:32 Thus saith the Lord **G**; Thou shalt drink *of* 3068
23:34 for I have spoken *it*, saith the Lord **G**. 3068
23:35 Therefore thus saith the Lord **G**; 3068
23:46 For thus saith the Lord **G**; *I will* bring up a 3068
23:49 and ye shall know that I *am* the Lord **G**. 3068
24: 3 and say unto them, Thus saith the Lord **G**; 3068
24: 6 Wherefore thus saith the Lord **G**; Woe to 3068
24: 9 Therefore thus saith the Lord **G**; Woe to 3068
24:14 shall they judge thee, saith the Lord **G**. 3068
24:21 the house of Israel, Thus saith the Lord **G**; 3068
24:24 ye shall know that I *am* the Lord **G**. 3068
25: 3 Hear the word of the Lord **G**; 3068
25: 3 Thus saith the Lord **G**; Because thou saidst, 3068
25: 6 For thus saith the Lord **G**; Because thou 3068
25: 8 Thus saith the Lord **G**; Because that Moab 3068
25:12 Thus saith the Lord **G**; Because that Edom 3068
25:13 Therefore thus saith the Lord **G**; I will also 3068
25:14 know my vengeance, saith the Lord **G**. 3068
25:15 Thus saith the Lord **G**; Because 3068
25:16 Therefore thus saith the Lord **G**; Behold, 3068
26: 3 Therefore thus saith the Lord **G**; Behold, 3068
26: 5 for I have spoken *it*, saith the Lord **G**: and 3068
26: 7 For thus saith the Lord **G**; Behold, I *will* 3068
26:14 LORD have spoken *it*, saith the Lord **G**. 3068
26:15 Thus saith the Lord **G** to Tyrus; Shall not 3068
26:19 For thus saith the Lord **G**; When I shall 3068
26:21 never be found again, saith the Lord **G**. 3068
27: 3 for many isles, Thus saith the Lord **G**; 3068
28: 2 the prince of Tyrus, Thus saith the Lord **G**; 3068
28: 6 Therefore thus saith the Lord **G**; 3068
28:10 for I have spoken *it*, saith the Lord **G**. 3068
28:12 and say unto him, Thus saith the Lord **G**; 3068
28:22 say, Thus saith the Lord **G**; Behold, I *am* 3068
28:24 and they shall know that I *am* the Lord **G**. 3068
28:25 Thus saith the Lord **G**; When I shall have 3068
29: 3 Speak, and say, Thus saith the Lord **G**; 3068
29: 8 Therefore thus saith the Lord **G**; Behold, 3068
29:13 Yet thus saith the Lord **G**; At the end of 3068
29:16 but they shall know that I *am* the Lord **G**. 3068
29:19 Therefore thus saith the Lord **G**; Behold, 3068
29:20 they wrought for me, saith the Lord **G**. 3068
30: 2 prophesy and say, Thus saith the Lord **G**; 3068
30: 6 fall in it by the sword, saith the Lord **G**. 3068
30:10 Thus saith the Lord **G**; I will also make 3068
30:13 Thus saith the Lord **G**; I will also destroy 3068
30:22 Therefore thus saith the Lord **G**; Behold, 3068
31:10 Therefore thus saith the Lord **G**; 3068
31:15 Thus saith the Lord **G**; In the day when he 3068
31:18 and all his multitude, saith the Lord **G**. 3068
32: 3 Thus saith the Lord **G**; I will therefore 3068
32: 8 darkness upon thy land, saith the Lord **G**. 3068
32:11 For thus saith the Lord **G**; The sword of 3068
32:14 their rivers to run like oil, saith the Lord **G**. 3068
32:16 and for all her multitude, saith the Lord **G**. 3068
32:31 army slain by the sword, saith the Lord **G**. 3068
32:32 and all his multitude, saith the Lord **G**. 3068
33:11 Say unto them, *As* I live, saith the Lord **G**, 3068
33:25 say unto them, Thus saith the Lord **G**; 3068
33:27 thou thus unto them, Thus saith the Lord **G**; 3068
34: 2 Thus saith the Lord **G** unto the shepherds; 3068
34: 8 saith the Lord **G**, surely because my flock 3068
34:10 Thus saith the Lord **G**; Behold, I *am* 3068
34:11 For thus saith the Lord **G**; Behold, I, 3068
34:15 cause them to lie down, saith the Lord **G**. 3068
34:17 *for* you, O my flock, thus saith the Lord **G**; 3068
34:20 Therefore thus saith the Lord **G** unto them; 3068
34:30 of Israel, *are* my people, saith the Lord **G**. 3068
34:31 *and* I *am* your God, saith the Lord **G**. 3068
35: 3 say unto it, Thus saith the Lord **G**; Behold, 3068
35: 6 Therefore, *as* I live, saith the Lord **G**, I will 3068
35:11 Therefore, *as* I live, saith the Lord **G**, I will 3068
35:14 Thus saith the Lord **G**; When the whole 3068
36: 2 Thus saith the Lord **G**; Because the enemy 3068
36: 3 and say, Thus saith the Lord **G**; 3068
36: 4 of Israel, hear the word of the Lord **G**; 3068
36: 4 Thus saith the Lord **G** to the mountains, 3068
36: 5 Therefore thus saith the Lord **G**; Surely in 3068
36: 6 and to the valleys, Thus saith the Lord **G**; 3068
36: 7 Therefore thus saith the Lord **G**; I have 3068
36:13 Thus saith the Lord **G**; Because they say 3068
36:14 thy nations any more, saith the Lord **G**. 3068
36:15 nations to fall any more, saith the Lord **G**. 3068
36:22 the house of Israel, Thus saith the Lord **G**; 3068
36:23 that I *am* the LORD, saith the Lord **G**, 3068
36:32 for your sakes do I *this*, saith the Lord **G**, 3068
36:33 Thus saith the Lord **G**; In the day that I 3068
36:37 Thus saith the Lord **G**; I will yet *for* this be 3068
37: 3 And I answered, O Lord **G**, thou knowest. 3068
37: 5 Thus saith the Lord **G** unto these bones; 3068
37: 9 and say to the wind, Thus saith the Lord **G**; 3068
37:12 and say unto them, Thus saith the Lord **G**; 3068
37:19 Say unto them, Thus saith the Lord **G**; 3068
37:21 say unto them, Thus saith the Lord **G**; 3068
38: 3 say, Thus saith the Lord **G**; Behold, I *am* 3068
38:10 Thus saith the Lord **G**; It shall also come to 3068
38:14 and say unto Gog, Thus saith the Lord **G**; 3068
38:17 Thus saith the Lord **G**; *Art* thou he of 3068
38:18 saith the Lord **G**, *that* my fury shall come 3068

Eze 38:21 all my mountains, saith the Lord **G**: 3068
39: 1 and say, Thus saith the Lord **G**; 3068
39: 5 for I have spoken *it*, saith the Lord **G**. 3068
39: 8 it is come, and it is done, saith the Lord **G**; 3068
39:10 those that robbed them, saith the Lord **G**. 3068
39:13 that I shall be glorified, saith the Lord **G**. 3068
39:17 thou son of man, thus saith the Lord **G**; 3068
39:20 and *with* all men of war, saith the Lord **G**. 3068
39:25 Therefore thus saith the Lord **G**; Now will I 3068
39:29 upon the house of Israel, saith the Lord **G**. 3068
43:18 Son of man, thus saith the Lord **G**; 3068
43:19 to minister unto me, saith the Lord **G**, 3068
43:27 and I will accept you, saith the Lord **G**. 3068
44: 6 the house of Israel, Thus saith the Lord **G**; 3068
44: 9 Thus saith the Lord **G**; No stranger, 3068
44:12 saith the Lord **G**, and they shall bear their 3068
44:15 me the fat and the blood, saith the Lord **G**: 3068
44:27 offer his sin offering, saith the Lord **G**. 3068
45: 9 Thus saith the Lord **G**; Let it suffice you, 3068
45: 9 from my people, saith the Lord **G**. 3068
45:15 reconciliation for them, saith the Lord **G**. 3068
45:18 Thus saith the Lord **G**; In the first *month*, 3068
46: 1 Thus saith the Lord **G**; The gate of 3068
46:16 Thus saith the Lord **G**; If the prince give a 3068
47:13 Thus saith the Lord **G**; This *shall be* 3068
47:23 give *him* his inheritance, saith the Lord **G**. 3068
48:29 these *are* their portions, saith the Lord **G**. 3068
Am 1: 8 Philistines shall perish, saith the Lord **G**. 3068
3: 7 Surely the Lord **G** will do nothing, but he 3068
3: 8 the Lord **G** hath spoken, who can but 3068
3:11 Therefore thus saith the Lord **G**; 3068
3:13 saith the Lord **G**, the God of hosts, 3068
4: 2 The Lord **G** hath sworn by his holiness, 3068
4: 5 O ye children of Israel, saith the Lord **G**. 3068
5: 3 For thus saith the Lord **G**; The city that 3068
6: 8 The Lord **G** hath sworn by himself, saith 3068
7: 1 Thus hath the Lord **G** shewed unto me; and 3068
7: 2 I said, O Lord **G**, forgive, I beseech thee: 3068
7: 4 Thus hath the Lord **G** shewed unto me: and 3068
7: 4 the Lord **G** called to contend by fire, and 3068
7: 5 said I, O Lord **G**, cease, I beseech thee: 3068
7: 6 This also shall not be, saith the Lord **G**. 3068
8: 1 Thus hath the Lord **G** shewed unto me: and 3068
8: 3 be howlings in that day, saith the Lord **G**: 3068
8: 9 come to pass in that day, saith the Lord **G**, 3068
8:11 Behold, the days come, saith the Lord **G**, 3068
9: 5 the Lord **G** of hosts *is* he that toucheth 3068
9: 8 the eyes of the Lord **G** *are* upon the sinful 3068
Ob 1: 1 Thus saith the Lord **G** concerning Edom; 3068
Mic 1: 2 let the Lord **G** be witness against you, 3068
Hab 3:19 The Lord **G** *is* my strength, and he will 3068
Zep 1: 7 thy peace at the presence of the Lord **G**: 3068
Zec 9:14 the Lord **G** shall blow the trumpet, and 3068

GOD'S (26) [GOD]

Ge 28:22 I have set *for* a pillar, shall be **G** house: 430
30: 2 he said, *Am* I in **G** stead, who hath withheld 430
32: 2 Jacob saw them, he said, This *is* **G** host: 430
Nu 22:22 **G** anger was kindled because he went: and 430
Dt 1:17 of the face of man; for the judgment *is* **G**: 430
2Ch 20:15 for the battle *is* not yours, but **G**. 430+3807.1
Ne 10:29 a curse, and into an oath, to walk in **G** law, 430
Job 33: 6 I *am* according to thy wish in **G** stead: 410
35: 2 My righteousness *is* more than **G**? 410
36: 2 thee that *I have* yet to speak on **G** behalf. 433
Mt 5:34 at all; neither by heaven; for it is **G** throne: 2316
22:21 and unto God the *things* that are **G**. 2316
Mk 12:17 and to God the *things* that are **G**. 2316
Lk 18:29 or children, for the kingdom of **G** sake, 2316
20:25 and unto God the *things* which be **G**. 2316
Jn 8:47 He that is of God heareth **G** words: ye 2316
Ac 23: 4 stood by said, Revilest thou **G** high priest? 2316
Ro 8:33 Who shall lay any thing to the charge of **G** 2316
10: 3 For they being ignorant of **G** righteousness, 2316
13: 6 for they are **G** ministers, 2316
1Co 3: 9 ye are **G** husbandry, *ye are* God's building. 2316
3: 9 ye are God's husbandry, *ye are* **G** building. 2316
3:23 And ye *are* Christ's; and Christ *is* **G**. 2316
6:20 your body, and in your spirit, which are **G**. 2316
Tit 1: 1 according to the faith of **G** elect, and 2316
1Pe 5: 3 Neither as being lords over **G** heritage, but NIG

GODDESS (5) [GOD]

1Ki 11: 5 For Solomon went after Ashtoreth the **g** of 430
11:33 have worshipped Ashtoreth the **g** of 430
Ac 19:27 also that the temple of the great **g** Diana 2299
19:35 is a worshipper of the great **g** Diana, 2299
19:37 of churches, nor yet blasphemers of your **g**. 2299

GODHEAD (3) [GOD]

Ac 17:29 we ought not to think that the **G** is like unto 2304
Ro 1:20 are made, *even* his eternal power and **G**; 2305
Col 2: 9 For in him dwelleth all the fulness of the **G** 2320

GODLINESS (15) [GOD]

1Ti 2: 2 and peaceable life in all **g** and honesty. 2150
2:10 But (which becometh women professing **g**) 2317
3:16 controversy great is the mystery of **g**: 2150
4: 7 and exercise thyself *rather* unto **g**. 2150
4: 8 **g** is profitable unto all *things*, having 2150
6: 3 and to the doctrine which is according to **g**; 2150
6: 5 of the truth, supposing that gain is **g**: 2150
6: 6 But **g** with contentment is great gain. 2150
6:11 **g**, faith, love, patience, meekness. 2150
2Ti 3: 5 Having a form of **g**, but denying the power 2150
Tit 1: 1 acknowledging of the truth which is after **g**, 2150
2Pe 1: 3 us all *things* that *pertain* unto life and **g**, 2150
1: 6 to temperance patience; and to patience **g**; 2150
1: 7 And to **g** brotherly kindness; and 2150
3:11 ye to be in all holy conversation and **g**, 2150

GODLY (15) [GOD]

Ps 4: 3 hath set apart *him that is* **g** for himself: 2623
12: 1 Help, LORD; for the **g** *man* ceaseth; 2623
32: 6 For this shall every one *that is* **g** pray unto 2623
Mal 2:15 That he might seek a **g** seed. Therefore take 430
2Co 1:12 that in simplicity and **g** sincerity, not with 2316
7: 9 for ye were made sorry after a **g** manner, 2316
7:10 For **g** sorrow worketh repentance to 2316+2596
7:11 *thing*, that ye sorrowed after a **g** sort, 2316
11: 2 For I am jealous over you with **g** jealousy: 2316
1Ti 1: 4 rather than **g** edifying which is in faith: 2316
2Ti 3:12 all that will live **g** in Christ Jesus shall 2153
Tit 2:12 and **g**, in *this* present world; 2153
Heb 12:28 God acceptably with reverence and **g fear**: 2124
2Pe 2: 9 The Lord knoweth *how* to deliver the **g** out 2152
3Jn 1: 6 forward on their journey after a **g** sort, 2316

GODS (244) [GOD]

Ge 3: 5 and ye shall be as **g**, knowing good and evil. 430
31:30 *yet* wherefore hast thou stolen my **g**? 430
31:32 With whomsoever thou findest thy **g**, let him 430
35: 2 Put away the strange **g** that *are* among you, 430
35: 4 they gave unto Jacob all the strange **g** which 430
Ex 12:12 against all the **g** of Egypt I will execute 430
15:11 *is* like unto thee, O LORD, among the **g**? 410
18:11 I know that the LORD *is* greater than all **g**: 430
20: 3 Thou shalt have no other **g** before me. 430
20:23 Ye shall not make with me **g** of silver, 430
20:23 neither shall ye make unto you **g** of gold. 430
22:28 Thou shalt not revile the **g**, nor curse 430
23:13 and make no mention of the name of other **g**, 430
23:24 Thou shalt not bow down to their **g**, 430
23:32 no covenant with them, nor with their **g**. 430
23:33 for if thou serve their **g**, it will surely be a 430
32: 1 said unto him, Up, make us **g**, which shall go 430
32: 4 they said, These *be* thy **g**, O Israel, 430
32: 8 and said, These *be* thy **g**, O Israel, 430
32:23 For they said unto me, Make us **g**, 430
32:31 a great sin, and have made them **g** of gold. 430
34:15 they go a whoring after their **g**, and 430
34:15 do sacrifice unto their **g**, and *one* call thee, 430
34:16 their daughters go a whoring after their **g**, 430
34:16 make thy sons go a whoring after their **g**. 430
34:17 Thou shalt make thee no molten **g**. 430
Lev 19: 4 unto idols, nor make to yourselves molten **g**: 430
Nu 25: 2 the people unto the sacrifices of their **g**: 430
25: 2 people did eat, and bowed down to their **g**. 430
33: 4 upon their **g** also the LORD executed 430
Dt 4:28 there ye shall serve **g**, the work of men's 430
5: 7 Thou shalt have none other **g** before me. 430
6:14 Ye shall not go after other **g**, of the gods of 430
6:14 of the **g** of the people which *are* round about 430
7: 4 following me, that they may serve other **g**: 430
7:16 neither shalt thou serve their **g**; for that *will* 430
7:25 The graven images of their **g** shall ye burn 430
8:19 walk after other **g**, and serve them, and 430
10:17 For the LORD your God *is* God of **g**, and 430
11:16 and serve other **g**, and worship them; 430
11:28 to go after other **g**, which ye have not 430
12: 2 which ye shall possess served their **g**, 430
12: 3 shall hew down the graven images of their **g**, 430
12:30 that thou inquire not after their **g**, saying, 430
12:30 saying, How did these nations serve their **g**? 430
12:31 which he hateth, have they done unto their **g**; 430
12:31 they have burnt in the fire to their **g**. 430
13: 2 saying, Let us go after other **g**, which thou 430
13: 6 saying, Let us go and serve other **g**, 430
13: 7 *Namely,* of the **g** of the people which *are* 430
13:13 saying, Let us go and serve other **g**, which ye 430
17: 3 hath gone and served other **g**, and 430
18:20 or that shall speak in the name of other **g**, 430
20:18 which they have done unto their **g**; 430
28:14 *to* the left, to go after other **g** to serve them. 430
28:36 and there shalt thou serve other **g**, wood and 430
28:64 there thou shalt serve other **g**, which neither 430
29:18 to go *and* serve the **g** of these nations; 430
29:26 For they went and served other **g**, and 430
29:26 **g** whom they knew not, and *whom* he had 430
30:17 and worship other **g**, and serve them; 430
31:16 go a whoring after the **g** of the strangers of 430
31:18 in that they are turned unto other **g**. 430
31:20 will they turn unto other **g**, and serve them, 430
32:16 **g**, with abominations provoked they him to NIH
32:17 *to* **g** whom they knew not, *to* new *gods that* 430
32:17 knew not, *to* new **g** *that* came newly up, NIH
32:37 he shall say, Where *are* their **g**, *their* rock in 430
Jos 22:22 The LORD God of **g**, the LORD God of 430
22:22 the LORD God of **g**, he knoweth, and 430
23: 7 neither make mention of the name of their **g**, 430
23:16 have gone and served other **g**, and 430
24: 2 father of Nachor: and they served other **g**. 430
24:14 put away the **g** which your fathers served on 430
24:15 whether the **g** which your fathers served that 430
24:15 or the **g** of the Amorites, in whose land ye 430
24:16 should forsake the LORD, to serve other **g**; 430
24:20 serve strange **g**, then he will turn and do you 430
24:23 *said he,* the strange **g** which *are* among you, 430
Jdg 2: 3 and their **g** shall be a snare unto you. 430
2:12 of the land of Egypt, and followed other **g**, 430
2:12 of the **g** of the people that *were* round about 430
2:17 they went a whoring after other **g**, and 430
2:19 in following other **g** to serve them, and 430
3: 6 daughters to their sons, and served their **g**. 430
5: 8 They chose new **g**; then *was* war in 430
6:10 fear not the **g** of the Amorites, in whose land 430
10: 6 the **g** of Syria, and the gods of Zidon, and 430
10: 6 the **g** of Zidon, and the gods of Moab, and 430
10: 6 the **g** of Moab, and the gods of the children 430
10: 6 the **g** of the children of Ammon, and 430
10: 6 the **g** of the Philistines, and forsook 430
10:13 Yet ye have forsaken me, and served other **g**: 430
10:14 Go and cry unto the **g** which ye have chosen; 430
10:16 they put away the strange **g** from among 430
17: 5 the man Micah had a house of **g**, and 430
18:24 Ye have taken away my **g** which I made, and 430
Ru 1:15 is gone back unto her people, and unto her **g**: 430
1Sa 4: 8 us out of the hand of these mighty **G**? 430
4: 8 these *are* the **G** that smote the Egyptians 430
6: 5 and from off your **g**, and from off your land. 430
7: 3 *then* put away the strange **g** and Ashtaroth 430
8: 8 and served other **g**, so do they also unto thee. 430
17:43 And the Philistine cursed David by his **g**. 430
26:19 of the LORD, saying, Go, serve other **g**. 430
28:13 unto Saul, I saw **g** ascending out of the earth. 430
2Sa 7:23 from Egypt, *from* the nations and their **g**? 430
1Ki 9: 6 but go and serve other **g**, and worship them: 430
9: 9 have taken hold upon other **g**, and 430
11: 2 they will turn away your heart after their **g**: 430
11: 4 his wives turned away his heart after other **g**: 430
11: 8 burnt incense and sacrificed unto their **g**. 430
11:10 this thing, that *he* should not go after other **g**: 430
12:28 behold thy **g**, O Israel, which brought thee 430
14: 9 for thou hast gone and made thee other **g**, 430
18:24 call ye on the name of your **g**, and I will call 430
18:25 call on the name of your **g**, but put no fire 430
19: 2 saying, So let the **g** do *to me*, and more also, 430
20:10 said, The **g** do so unto me, and more also, 430
20:23 said unto him, Their **g** *are* gods of the hills; 430
20:23 said unto him, Their gods *are* **g** of the hills; 430
2Ki 5:17 burnt offering nor sacrifice unto other **g**, 430
17: 7 king of Egypt, and had feared other **g**, 430
17:29 Howbeit every nation made **g** of their own, 430
17:31 and Anammelech, the **g** of Sepharvaim. 430
17:33 feared the LORD, and served their own **g**, 430
17:35 saying, Ye shall not fear other **g**, 430
17:37 for evermore; and ye shall not fear other **g**. 430
17:38 shall not forget; neither shall ye fear other **g**. 430
18:33 Hath any of the **g** of the nations delivered at 430
18:34 Where *are* the **g** of Hamath, and of Arpad? 430
18:34 where *are* the **g** of Sepharvaim, Hena, and 430
18:35 Who *are they* among all the **g** of 430
19:12 Have the **g** of the nations delivered them 430
19:18 have cast their **g** into the fire: for they *were* 430
19:18 for they *were* no **g**, but the work of men's 430
22:17 and have burnt incense unto other **g**, 430
1Ch 5:25 went a whoring after the **g** of the people of 430
10:10 they put his armour *in* the house of their **g**, 430
14:12 when they had left their **g** there, David gave 430
16:25 he also *is* to be feared above all **g**. 430
16:26 For all the **g** of the people *are* idols: but 430
2Ch 2: 5 *is* great: for great *is* our God above all **g**. 430
7:19 shall go and serve other **g**, and 430
7:22 laid hold on other **g**, and worshipped them, 430
13: 8 which Jeroboam made you for **g**. 430
13: 9 *same* may be a priest of *them that are* no **g**. 430
14: 3 For he took away the altars of the strange **g**, NIH
25:14 that he brought the **g** of the children of Seir, 430
25:14 set them up to be his **g**, and bowed down 430
25:15 Why hast thou sought after the **g** of 430
25:20 because they sought after the **g** of Edom. 430
28:23 For he sacrificed unto the **g** of Damascus, 430
28:23 Because the **g** of the kings of Syria help 430
28:25 high places to burn incense unto other **g**, 430
32:13 were the **g** of the nations of *those* lands any 430
32:14 Who *was there* among all the **g** of those 430
32:17 As the **g** of the nations of *other* lands have 430
32:19 as against the **g** of the people of the earth, 430
33:15 he took away the strange **g**, and the idol out 430
34:25 and have burned incense unto other **g**, 430
Ezr 1: 7 and had put them in the house of his **g**; 430
Ps 82: 1 of the mighty; he judgeth among the **g**. 430
82: 6 I have said, Ye *are* **g**; and all of you *are* 430
86: 8 Among the **g** *there is* none like unto thee, 430
95: 3 *is* a great God, and a great King above all **g**. 430
96: 4 to be praised: he *is* to be feared above all **g**. 430
96: 5 For all the **g** of the nations *are* idols: but 430
97: 7 themselves of idols: worship him, all ye **g**. 430
97: 9 all the earth: thou art exalted far above all **g**. 430
135: 5 *is* great, and *that* our Lord *is* above all **g**. 430
136: 2 O give thanks unto the God of **g**: for his 430
138: 1 before the **g** will I sing *praise* unto thee. 430
Isa 21: 9 all the graven images of her **g** he hath broken 430
36:18 Hath any of the **g** of the nations delivered his 430
36:19 Where *are* the **g** of Hamath and Arphad? 430
36:19 where *are* the **g** of Sepharvaim? and have 430
36:20 Who *are they* amongst all the **g** of these 430
37:12 Have the **g** of the nations delivered them 430
37:19 have cast their **g** into the fire: for they *were* 430
37:19 for they *were* no **g**, but the work of men's 430
41:23 that we may know that ye *are* **g**: 430
42:17 that say to the molten images, Ye *are* our **g**. 430
Jer 1:16 have burnt incense unto other **g**, and 430
2:11 Hath a nation changed *their* **g**, which *are* yet 430
2:11 changed *their* gods, which *are* yet no **g**? 430
2:28 where *are* thy **g** that thou hast made thee? 430
2:28 to the number of thy cities are thy **g**, 430
5: 7 and sworn by *them that are* no **g**: 430
5:19 served strange **g** in your land, so shall ye 430
7: 6 neither walk after other **g** to your hurt: 430
7: 9 and walk after other **g** whom ye know not; 430
7:18 and to pour out drink offerings unto other **g**, 430
10:11 The **g** that have not made the heavens and 426
11:10 and they went after other **g** to serve them: 430
11:12 cry unto the **g** unto whom they offer incense: 430
11:13 *to* the number of thy cities were thy **g**, 430
13:10 walk after other **g**, to serve them, and 430
16:11 have walked after other **g**, and have served 430
16:13 there shall ye serve other **g** day and night; 430
16:20 Shall a man make **g** unto himself, and 430
16:20 make gods unto himself, and they *are* no **g**? 430
19: 4 and have burnt incense in it unto other **g**, 430
19:13 have poured out drink offerings unto other **g**. 430
22: 9 and worshipped other **g**, and served them. 430
25: 6 go not after other **g** to serve them, and 430
32:29 and poured out drink offerings unto other **g**, 430
35:15 go not after other **g** to serve them, and 430
43:12 I will kindle a fire in the houses of the **g** of 430
43:13 the houses of the **g** of the Egyptians shall he 430
44: 3 *and* to serve other **g**, whom they knew not, 430
44: 5 to burn no incense unto other **g**. 430
44: 8 burning incense unto other **g** in the land of 430
44:15 their wives had burnt incense unto other **g**, 430
46:25 and Egypt, with their **g**, and their kings; 430

Jer 48:35 and him that burneth incense to his **g**. 430
Da 2:11 except the **g**, whose dwelling is not with 426
2:47 Of a truth *it is,* that your God *is* a God of **g**, 426
3:12 they serve not thy **g**, nor worship the golden 426
3:14 and Abed-nego, do not ye serve my **g**, 426
3:18 O king, that we will not serve thy **g**, 426
4: 8 and in whom *is* the spirit of the holy **g**: 426
4: 9 I know that the spirit of the holy **g** *is* in thee, 426
4:18 *art* able; for the spirit of the holy **g** *is* in thee. 426
5: 4 praised the **g** of gold, and of silver, of brass, 426
5:11 in whom *is* the spirit of the holy **g**; 426
5:11 and wisdom, like the wisdom of the **g**, 426
5:14 that the spirit of the **g** *is* in thee, and 426
5:23 thou hast praised the **g** of silver, and gold, 426
11: 8 shall also carry captives *into* Egypt their **g**, 430
11:36 marvellous *things* against the God of **g**, 410
Hos 3: 1 who look to other **g**, and love flagons of 430
14: 3 more to the work of our hands, *Ye are* our **g**: 430
Na 1:14 out of the house of thy **g** will I cut off 430
Zep 2:11 for he will famish all the **g** of the earth; and 430
Jn 10:34 it not written in your law, I said, Ye are **g**? *2316*
10:35 If he called them **g**, unto whom the word of *2316*
Ac 7:40 unto Aaron, Make us **g** to go before us: *2316*
14:11 The **g** are come down to us in the likeness *2316*
17:18 He seemeth to be a setter forth of strange **g**: *1140*
19:26 much people, saying that they be no **g**, *2316*
1Co 8: 5 For though there be that are called **g**, *2316*
8: 5 (as there be **g** many, and lords many,) *2316*
Gal 4: 8 service unto them which by nature are no **g**. *2316*

GOD-WARD (3) [GOD]

Ex 18:19 be thou for the people **to G**, 430+4136+1886.1
2Co 3: 4 such trust have we through Christ to **G**: *2316*
1Th 1: 8 also in every place your faith to **G** is spread *2316*

GOEST (46) [GO]

Ge 10:19 as thou **g** unto Sodom, and Gomorrah, and 935
10:30 as thou **g** unto Sephar, a mount of the east. 935
25:18 *is* before Egypt, as thou **g** towards Assyria: 935
28:15 will keep thee in all *places* whither thou **g**, 1980
32:17 whither **g** thou? and whose *are* these before 1980
Ex 4:21 When thou **g** to return into Egypt, 1980
33:16 *is it* not in that thou **g** with us? so shall we 1980
34:12 the inhabitants of the land whither thou **g**, 935
Nu 14:14 *that* thou **g** before them, by day time in a 1980
Dt 7: 1 into the land whither thou **g** to possess it, 935
11:10 For the land, whither thou **g in** to possess it, 935
11:29 in unto the land whither thou **g** to possess it, 935
12:29 whither thou **g** to possess them, and 935
20: 1 When thou **g out** to battle against thine 3318
21:10 When thou **g forth** to war against thine 3318
23:20 to in the land whither thou **g** to possess it. 935
28: 6 and blessed *shalt* thou *be* when thou **g out**. 3318
28:19 and cursed *shalt* thou *be* when thou **g out**. 3318
28:21 off the land, whither thou **g** to possess it. 935
28:63 off the land whither thou **g** to possess it. 935
30:16 thee in the land whither thou **g** to possess it. 935
32:50 die in the mount whither thou **g up**, and 5927
Jos 1: 7 thou mayest prosper whithersoever thou **g**. 1980
1: 9 thy God *is* with thee whithersoever thou **g**. 1980
Jdg 14: 3 that thou **g** to take a wife of 1980
19:17 the old man said, Whither **g** thou? and 1980
Ru 1:16 for whither thou **g**, I will go; and 1980
1Sa 27: 8 the inhabitants of the land as thou **g** to Shur, 935
28:22 have strength, when thou **g** on *thy* way. 1980
2Sa 15:19 the Gittite, Wherefore **g** thou also with us? 1980
1Ki 2:37 *that* on the day thou **g out**, and passest over 3318
2:42 on the day thou **g out**, and walkest *abroad* 3318
Ps 44: 9 to shame; and **g** not **forth** with our armies. 3318
Pr 4:12 When thou **g** thy steps shall not be 1980
6:22 When thou **g**, it shall lead thee; when thou 1980
Ecc 5: 1 Keep thy foot when thou **g** to the house of 1980
9:10 nor wisdom, in the grave, whither thou **g**. 1980
Jer 45: 5 thee for a prey in all places whither thou **g**. 1980
Zec 2: 2 said I, Whither **g** thou? And he said unto 1980
Mt 8:19 I will follow thee whithersoever thou **g**. *565*
Lk 9:57 I will follow thee whithersoever thou **g**. *565*
12:58 When thou **g** with thine adversary to *5217*
Jn 11: 8 to stone thee; and **g** thou thither again? *5217*
13:36 Peter said unto him, Lord, whither **g** thou? *5217*
14: 5 Lord, we know not whither thou **g**; *5217*
16: 5 none of you asketh me, Whither **g** thou? *5217*

GOETH (135) [GO]

Ge 2:14 that *is it* which **g** toward the east of 1980
32:20 I will appease him with the present that **g** 1980
33:14 according as the cattle that **g** before me and 7272
38:13 Behold thy father in law **g up** to Timnath to 5927
Ex 7:15 lo, he **g out** unto the water; and thou shalt 3318
22:26 deliver it unto him by that the sun **g down**: 935
28:29 when he **g in** unto the holy *place,* for a 935
28:30 when he **g in** before the LORD: 935
28:35 his sound shall be heard when he **g in** unto 935
Lev 11:21 flying creeping thing that **g** upon *all* four, 1980
11:27 whatsoever **g** upon his paws, among all 1980
11:42 Whatsoever **g** upon the belly, and 1980
11:42 whatsoever **g** upon *all* four, or 1980
14:46 Moreover he that **g** into the house all 935
15:32 *of him* whose seed **g** from him, and is 3318
16:17 **g in** to make an atonement in the holy *place,* 935
22: 3 that **g** unto the holy *things* which 7126
22: 4 the dead, or a man whose seed **g** from him; 3318
27:21 the field, when it **g out** in the jubile, 3318
Nu 5:29 when a wife **g aside** *to another* instead of 7847
21:15 *at* the stream of the brooks that **g down** to 5186
Dt 1:30 The LORD your God which **g** before you, 1980
9: 3 the LORD thy God *is* he which **g over** 5674
11:30 by the way where the sun **g down**, in 3996
19: 5 As when *a man* **g** into the wood with his 935
20: 4 For the LORD your God *is* he that **g** with 1980
23: 9 When the host **g forth** against thine 3318
24:13 him the pledge again when the sun **g down**, 935
Jos 10:10 chased them *along* the way that **g up** to 4608
11:17 from the mount Halak, that **g up** *to* Seir, 5927
Jos 12: 7 unto the mount Halak, that **g up** to Seir; 5927
16: 1 *to* the wilderness that **g up** from Jericho 5927
16: 2 **g out** from Beth-el to Luz, and 3318
16: 3 **g down** westward to the coast of Japhleti, 3381
19:12 *then* **g out** to Daberath, and goeth up *to* 3318
19:12 goeth out to Daberath, and **g up** *to* Japhia, 5927
19:13 and **g out** *to* Remmon-methoar *to* Neah; 3318
19:27 Neiel, and **g out** to Cabul on the left hand, 3318
19:34 **g out** from thence to Hukkok, and 3318
Jdg 5:31 *be* as the sun when he **g forth** in his might. 3318
20:31 *of* which one **g up** *to* the house of God, and 5927
21:19 on the east side of the highway that **g up** 5927
1Sa 6: 9 if it **g up** *by* the way of his own coast *to* 5927
22:14 **g** at thy bidding, and *is* honourable in thine 5493
30:24 as his part *is* that **g down** to the battle, so 3381
2Ki 5:18 *that* when my master **g** *into* the house of 935
11: 8 be ye with the king as he **g out** and as he 3318
12:20 the house of Millo, which **g down** *to* Silla. 3381
2Ch 23: 7 when he cometh in, and when he **g out**. 3318
Ezr 5: 8 this work **g** fast **on**, and prospereth in their 5648
Job 7: 9 he that **g down** *to* the grave shall come up 3381
9:11 Lo, he **g** by me, and I see *him* not: 5674
34: 8 Which **g** in company with the workers of 732
37: 2 and the sound *that* **g out** of his mouth. 3318
39:21 He **g on** to meet the armed men. 3318
41:20 Out of his nostrils **g** smoke, as *out of* a 3318
41:21 and a flame **g out** of his mouth. 3318
Ps 17: 1 my prayer, *that* **g** not out of feigned lips. NIH
41: 6 to itself; *when* he **g** abroad, he telleth *it.* 3318
68:21 the hairy scalp of such a one as **g on still** in 1980
88:16 Thy fierce wrath **g** over me; thy terrors 5674
97: 3 A fire **g** before him, and burneth up his 1980
104:23 Man **g forth** unto his work and to his 3318
126: 6 He that **g forth** and weepeth, 1980+1980
146: 4 His breath **g forth**, he returneth to his earth; 3318
Pr 6:29 So he that **g in** to his neighbour's wife; 935
7:22 He **g** after her straightway, as an ox goeth 1980
7:22 as an ox **g** to the slaughter, or as a fool to 935
11:10 When it **g well** with the righteous, the city 2898
16:18 Pride **g** before destruction, and a haughty NIH
20:19 He that **g about** *as* a talebearer revealeth 1980
26: 9 *As* a thorn **g up** into the hand of a 5927
26:20 Where no wood is, *there* the fire **g out**: so 3518
31:18 *is* good: her candle **g** not **out** by night. 3518
Ecc 1: 5 the sun **g down**, and hasteth to his place 935
1: 6 The wind **g** toward the south, and 1980
3:21 Who knoweth the spirit of man that **g** 5927
3:21 the spirit of the beast that **g** downward to 3381
12: 5 because man **g** to his long home, and 1980
SS 7: 9 for my beloved, that **g** *down* sweetly, 1980
Isa 28:19 From the time that it **g forth** it shall take 5674
30:29 as when one **g** with a pipe to come into 1980
55:11 So shall my word be that **g forth** out of my 3318
59: 8 whosoever **g** therein shall not know peace. 1869
63:14 As a beast **g down** into the valley, 3381
Jer 5: 6 every one that **g out** thence shall be torn in 3318
6: 4 for the day **g away**, for the shadows of 6437
21: 9 he that **g out**, and falleth to the Chaldeans 3318
22:10 *but* weep sore for him that **g away**: for he 1980
30:23 the whirlwind of the LORD **g forth** *with* 3318
38: 2 he that **g forth** to the Chaldeans shall live; 3318
44:17 thing **g forth** out of our own mouth, 3318
49:17 every one that **g** by it shall be astonished, 5674
50:13 every one that **g** by Babylon shall be 5674
Eze 7:14 to make all ready; but none **g** to the battle: 1980
33:31 *but* their heart **g** after their covetousness. 1980
40:40 as one **g up** to the entry of the north gate, 5927
42: 9 as one **g** into them from the utter court. 935
44:27 in the day that he **g** into the sanctuary, 935
48: 1 as *one* **g** to Hamath, Hazar-enan, the border 935
Hos 6: 4 and as the early dew *it* **g away**. 1980
6: 5 thy judgments *are as* the light *that* **g forth**. 3318
Zec 5: 3 This *is* the curse that **g forth** over the face 3318
5: 5 thine eyes, and see what *is* this that **g forth**. 3318
5: 6 he said, This *is* an ephah that **g forth**. 3318
Mt 8: 9 and I say to this *man,* Go, and he **g**; and *4198*
12:45 Then **g** he, and taketh with himself seven *4198*
13:44 and for joy thereof **g** and selleth all that he *5217*
15:11 Not that which **g into** the mouth *1525*
15:17 that whatsoever entereth in at the mouth **g** *5562*
17:21 Howbeit this kind **g** not **out** but by prayer *1607*
18:12 and **g** into the mountains, and seeketh that *4198*
26:24 The Son of man **g** as it is written of him: *5217*
28: 7 and behold, he **g before** you into Galilee; *4254*
Mk 3:13 And he **g up** into a mountain, and *305*
7:19 into the belly, and **g out** into the draught, *1607*
14:21 The Son of man indeed **g**, as it is written of *5217*
14:45 he **g** straightway to him, and saith, Master, *4334*
16: 7 and Peter that he **g before** you into Galilee: *4254*
Lk 7: 8 and I say unto one, Go, and he **g**; *4198*
11:26 Then **g** he, and taketh to *him* seven other *4198*
22:22 And truly the Son of man **g**, as it was *4198*
Jn 3: 8 not tell whence it cometh, and whither it **g**: *5217*
7:20 Thou hast a devil: who **g about** to kill thee? *2212*
10: 4 he **g** before them, and the sheep follow *4198*
11:31 saying, She **g** unto the grave to weep there. *5217*
12:35 in darkness knoweth not whither he **g**. *5217*
Ac 8:26 that **g down** from Jerusalem unto Gaza, *2597*
1Co 6: 6 But brother **g to law** with brother, and *2919*
9: 7 Who **g a warfare** any time at his own *4754*
Jas 1:24 and **g** his **way**, and straightway forgetteth *565*
1Jn 2:11 and knoweth not whither he **g**, because *5217*
Rev 14: 4 which follow the Lamb whithersoever he **g**. *5217*
17:11 and is of the seven, and **g** into perdition. *5217*
19:15 And **out** of his mouth **g** a sharp sword, *1607*

GOG (11) [HAMON-GOG]

1Ch 5: 4 his son, **G** his son, Shimei his son, 1463
Eze 38: 2 Son of man, set thy face against **G**, the land 1463
38: 3 Behold, I *am* against thee, O **G**, the chief 1463
38:14 son of man, prophesy and say unto **G**, 1463
38:16 sanctified in thee, O **G**, before their eyes. 1463
38:18 **G** shall come against the land of Israel, 1463
39: 1 son of man, prophesy against **G**, and say, 1463
39: 1 Behold, I *am* against thee, O **G**, the chief 1463
Eze 39:11 *that* I will give unto **G** a place there of 1463
39:11 there shall they bury **G** and all his 1463
Rev 20: 8 **G** and Magog, to gather them together to *1136*

GOING (92) [GO]

Ge 12: 9 **g on** still toward the south. 1980
15:12 when the sun was **g down**, a deep sleep fell 935
37:25 and myrrh, **g** to carry *it* down to Egypt. 1980
Ex 17:12 his hands were steady until the **g down** of 935
23: 4 meet thine enemy's ox or his ass **g astray**, 8582
37:18 And six branches **g out** of the sides thereof; 3318
37:19 throughout the six branches **g out** of 3318
37:21 according to the six branches **g out** of it. 3318
Lev 11:20 All fowls that creep, **g** upon *all* four, 1980
Nu 32: 7 **g over** into the land which the LORD hath 5674
34: 4 the **g forth** thereof shall be from the south 8444
Dt 16: 6 at the **g down** of the sun, *at* the season that 935
33:18 he said, Rejoice, Zebulun, in thy **g out**; 3318
Jos 1: 4 unto the great sea *toward* the **g down** of 3996
6: 9 *the priests* **g on**, and blowing with 1980
6:11 compassed the city, **g about** *it* once: 5362
6:13 *the priests* **g on**, and blowing with 1980
7: 5 and smote them in the **g down**: 4174
10:11 *and* were in the **g down** to Beth-horon, 4174
10:27 it came to pass at the time of the **g down** of 935
15: 7 that *is* before the **g up** to Adummim, 4608
18:17 which *is* over against the **g up** of 4608
23:14 *this* day I am **g** the way of all the earth: 1980
Jdg 1:36 Amorites *was* from the **g up** to Akrabbim, 4608
19:18 I am *now* **g** *to* the house of the LORD; 1980
19:28 he said unto her, Up, and let us be **g**. 1980
1Sa 9:11 they found young maidens **g out** to draw 3318
9:27 *And* as they were **g down** to the end of 3381
10: 3 there shall meet thee three men **g up** to God 5927
17:20 as the host was **g forth** to the fight, and 3318
29: 6 thy **g out** and thy coming in with me in 3318
2Sa 2:19 in **g** he turned not to the right hand nor to 1980
3:25 to know thy **g out** and thy coming in, and 4161
5:24 when thou hearest the sound of a **g** in 6807
1Ki 17:11 as she was **g** to fetch *it,* he called to her, 1980
22:36 the host about the **g down** of the sun, 935
2Ki 2:23 as he was **g up** by the way, there came 5927
9:27 *And they did so* at the **g up** to Gur, 4608
19:27 thy **g out**, and thy coming in, and thy rage 3318
1Ch 14:15 when thou shalt hear a sound of **g** in 6807
26:16 by the causeway of the **g up**, ward against 5927
2Ch 11: 4 and returned from **g** against Jeroboam. 1980
18:34 about the time of the sun **g down** he died. 935
Ne 3:19 another piece over against the **g up** to 5927
3:31 and to the **g up** of the corner. 5944
3:32 between the **g up** of the corner unto 5944
12:37 at the **g up** of the wall, above the house of 4608
Job 1: 7 From **g to and fro** in the earth, and 7751
2: 2 From **g to and fro** in the earth, and 7751
33:24 saith, Deliver him from **g down** *to* the pit: 3381
33:28 He will deliver his soul from **g** into the pit, 5674
Ps 19: 6 His **g forth** *is* from the end of the heaven, 4161
50: 1 rising of the sun unto the **g down** thereof. 3996
104:19 for seasons: the sun knoweth his **g down**. 3996
113: 3 From the rising of the sun unto the **g down** 3996
121: 8 The LORD shall preserve thy **g out** and 3318
144:14 *that there be* no breaking in, nor **g out**; 3318
Pr 7:27 to hell, **g down** to the chambers of death. 3381
14:15 but the prudent *man* looketh well to his **g**. 838
30:29 which go well, yea, four are comely in **g**: 1980
Isa 13:10 the sun shall be darkened in his **g forth**, 3318
37:28 thy **g out**, and thy coming in, and thy rage 3318
Jer 48: 5 For *in* the **g up** of Luhith continual 4608
48: 5 for in the **g down** of Horonaim the enemies 4174
50: 4 children of Judah together, **g** and weeping: 1980
Eze 27:19 **g to and fro** occupied in thy fairs: 235+4480
40:31 and the **g up** to it *had* eight steps. 4608
40:34 that side: and the **g up** to it *had* eight steps. 4608
40:37 that side: and the **g up** to it *had* eight steps. 4608
44: 5 with every **g forth** of the sanctuary. 4161
46:12 and after his **g forth** *one* shall shut the gate. 3318
Da 6:14 he laboured till the **g down** of the sun to 4606
9:25 *that* from the **g forth** of the commandment 4161
Hos 6: 3 his **g forth** *is* prepared as the morning; and 4161
Jnh 1: 3 *to* Joppa; and he found a ship **g** to Tarshish: 935
Mal 1:11 **g down** of the same my name *shall be* great 3996
Mt 4:21 And **g on** from thence, he saw other two *4260*
20:17 And Jesus **g up** to Jerusalem took the twelve *305*
26:46 Rise, let us be **g**: behold, he is at hand that *71*
28:11 Now when they were **g**, behold, some of *4198*
Mk 6:31 for there were many coming and **g**, and *5217*
10:32 And they were in the way **g up** to Jerusalem; *305*
Lk 14:31 **g** to make war against another king, *4198*
Jn 4:51 And as he was now **g down**, his servants *2597*
8:59 **g** through the midst of them, and so *1330*
Ac 9:28 them coming in and **g out** at Jerusalem. *1607*
20: 5 These **g before** tarried for us at Troas. *4281*
Ro 10: 3 **g about** to establish their own *2212*
1Ti 5:24 are open beforehand, **g before** to judgment; *4254*
Heb 7:18 commandment **g before** for the weakness *4254*
1Pe 2:25 For ye were as sheep **g astray**; but are now *4105*
Jude 1: 7 and **g** after strange flesh, are set forth for an *565*

GOINGS (26) [GO]

Nu 33: 2 Moses wrote their **g out** according to their 4161
33: 2 *are* their journeys according to their **g out**. 4161
34: 5 and the **g out** of it shall be at the sea. 8444
34: 8 the **g forth** of the border shall be to Zedad: 8444
34: 9 and the **g out** of it shall be at Hazar-enan: 8444
34:12 and the **g out** of it shall be *at* the salt sea: 8444
Jos 15: 4 and the **g out** of that coast were at the sea: 8444
15: 7 and the **g out** thereof were at En-rogel: 8444
15:11 and the **g out** of the border were at the sea. 8444
16: 3 and the **g out** thereof are at the sea. 8444
16: 8 and the **g out** thereof were at the sea. 8444
18:12 the **g out** thereof were at the wilderness of 8444
18:14 the **g out** thereof were at Kirjath-baal, 8444
Job 34:21 the ways of man, and he seeth all his **g**. 6806
Ps 17: 5 Hold up my **g** in thy paths, *that* my footsteps 838
40: 2 my feet upon a rock, *and* established my **g**. 838

Ps 68:24 They have seen thy **g**, O God; *even* 1979
68:24 *even* the **g** of my God, my King, in 1979
140: 4 who have purposed to overthrow my **g**. 6471
Pr 5:21 of the LORD, and he pondereth all his **g**. 4570
20:24 Man's **g** *are* of the LORD; how can a man 4703
Isa 59: 8 and *there is* no judgment in their **g**: 4570
Eze 42:11 all their **g out** *were* both according to their 4161
43:11 the **g out** thereof, and the comings in 4161
48:30 these *are* the **g out** of the city: on the north 8444
Mic 5: 2 whose **g forth** *have been* from of old, 4163

GOLAN (4)

Dt 4:43 and **G** in Bashan, of the Manassites. 1474
Jos 20: 8 **G** in Bashan out of the tribe of Manasseh. 1474
21:27 *they gave* **G** in Bashan with her suburbs, 1474
1Ch 6:71 **G** in Bashan with her suburbs, and 1474

GOLD (417) [GOLDEN, GOLDSMITH, GOLDSMITH'S, GOLDSMITHS]

Ge 2:11 the whole land of Havilah, where *there is* **g**; 2091
2:12 the **g** of that land *is* good: there *is* bdellium 2091
13: 2 *was* very rich in cattle, in silver, and in **g**. 2091
24:22 for her hands of ten *shekels* weight of **g**; 2091
24:35 **g**, and menservants, and maidservants, and 2091
24:53 jewels of **g**, and raiment, and gave *them* to 2091
41:42 fine linen, and put a **g** chain about his neck; 2091
44: 8 we steal out of thy lord's house silver or **g**? 2091
Ex 3:22 of silver, and jewels of **g**, and raiment: 2091
11: 2 jewels of silver, and jewels of **g**. 2091
12:35 of silver, and jewels of **g**, and raiment: 2091
20:23 neither shall ye make unto you gods of **g**. 2091
25: 3 shall take of them; **g**, and silver, and brass, 2091
25:11 thou shalt overlay it with pure **g**, within 2091
25:11 shalt make upon it a crown *of* **g** round 2091
25:12 thou shalt cast four rings of **g** for it, and 2091
25:13 of shittim wood, and overlay them with **g**. 2091
25:17 thou shalt make a mercy seat *of* pure **g**: 2091
25:18 thou shalt make two cherubims *of* **g**, 2091
25:24 thou shalt overlay it with pure **g**, and 2091
25:24 and make thereto a crown *of* **g** round about. 2091
25:26 thou shalt make for it four rings of **g**, and 2091
25:28 overlay them with **g**, that the table may be 2091
25:29 *of* pure **g** shalt thou make them. 2091
25:31 thou shalt make a candlestick of pure **g**: 2091
25:36 all it *shall be* one beaten work *of* pure **g**. 2091
25:38 the snuffdishes thereof, *shall be of* pure **g**. 2091
25:39 *Of* a talent of pure **g** shall he make it, 2091
26: 6 thou shalt make fifty taches of **g**, and 2091
26:29 thou shalt overlay the boards with **g**, and 2091
26:29 make their rings *of* **g** *for* places for the bars: 2091
26:29 and thou shalt overlay the bars with **g**. 2091
26:32 four pillars of shittim *wood* overlaid with **g**: 2091
26:32 their hooks *shall be of* **g**, upon the four 2091
26:37 of shittim *wood*, and overlay them with **g**, 2091
26:37 with gold, *and* their hooks *shall be of* **g**: 2091
28: 5 they shall take **g**, and blue, and purple, and 2091
28: 6 they shall make the ephod *of* **g**, *of* blue, 2091
28: 8 *even of* **g**, *of* blue, and purple, and scarlet, 2091
28:11 shalt make them to be set *in* ouches *of* **g**. 2091
28:13 And thou shalt make ouches *of* **g**; 2091
28:14 two chains *of* pure **g** at the ends; 2091
28:15 *of* **g**, *of* blue, and *of* purple, and *of* scarlet, 2091
28:20 they shall be set in **g** in their inclosings. 2091
28:22 at the ends *of* wreathen work *of* pure **g**. 2091
28:23 make upon the breastplate two rings of **g**, 2091
28:24 thou shalt put the two wreathen *chains of* **g** 2091
28:26 thou shalt make two rings of **g**, and 2091
28:27 two *other* rings of **g** thou shalt make, and 2091
28:33 and bells of **g** between them round about: 2091
28:36 thou shalt make a plate *of* pure **g**, and 2091
30: 3 thou shalt overlay it with pure **g**, the top 2091
30: 3 thou shalt make unto it a crown *of* **g** round 2091
30: 5 *of* shittim wood, and overlay them with **g**. 2091
31: 4 to work in **g**, and in silver, and in brass, 2091
32:24 Whosoever hath *any* **g**, let them break *it* 2091
32:31 a great sin, and have made them gods of **g**. 2091
35: 5 of the LORD; **g**, and silver, and brass, 2091
35:22 and rings, and tablets, all jewels of **g**: 2091
35:22 *offered* an offering of **g** unto the LORD. 2091
35:32 to work in **g**, and in silver, and in brass, 2091
36:13 he made fifty taches of **g**, and coupled 2091
36:34 he overlaid the boards with **g**, and made 2091
36:34 made their rings *of* **g** *to be* places for 2091
36:34 for the bars, and overlaid the bars with **g**. 2091
36:36 of shittim *wood*, and overlaid them with **g**: 2091
36:36 their hooks *were of* **g**; and he cast for them 2091
36:38 their chapiters and their fillets with **g**: 2091
37: 2 he overlaid it with pure **g** within 2091
37: 2 and made a crown *of* **g** to it round about. 2091
37: 3 he cast for it four rings of **g**, *to be set* by 2091
37: 4 of shittim wood, and overlaid them with **g**. 2091
37: 6 he made the mercy seat *of* pure **g**: 2091
37: 7 he made two cherubims *of* **g**, beaten out of 2091
37:11 he overlaid it with pure **g**, and 2091
37:11 made thereunto a crown *of* **g** round about. 2091
37:12 made a crown of **g** for the border thereof 2091
37:13 he cast for it four rings of **g**, and put 2091
37:15 and overlaid them with **g**, to bear the table. 2091
37:16 and *his* covers to cover withal, *of* pure **g**. 2091
37:17 he made the candlestick *of* pure **g**: 2091
37:22 all of it *was* one beaten work *of* pure **g**. 2091
37:23 his snuffers, and his snuffdishes, *of* pure **g**. 2091
37:24 *Of* a talent *of* pure **g** made he it, and all 2091
37:26 he overlaid it with pure **g**, *both* the top of it, 2091
37:26 also he made unto it a crown *of* **g** round 2091
37:27 he made two rings of **g** for it under 2091
37:28 *of* shittim wood, and overlaid them with **g**. 2091
38:24 All the **g** that was occupied for the work in 2091
38:24 of the holy *place*, even the **g** of the offering, 2091
39: 2 he made the ephod *of* **g**, blue, and purple, 2091
39: 3 And they did beat the **g** into thin plates, and 2091
39: 5 *of* **g**, blue, and purple, and scarlet, and 2091
39: 6 onyx stones inclosed *in* ouches *of* **g**, 2091
39: 8 *of* **g**, blue, and purple, and scarlet, and 2091
Ex 39:13 *they were* inclosed *in* ouches *of* **g** in their 2091
39:15 at the ends, *of* wreathen work *of* pure **g**. 2091
39:16 they made two ouches *of* **g**, and two gold 2091
39:16 made two ouches *of* gold, and two **g** rings; 2091
39:17 they put the two wreathen *chains of* **g** in 2091
39:19 they made two rings of **g**, and put *them* on 2091
39:25 they made bells of pure **g**, and put the bells 2091
39:30 made the plate of the holy crown *of* pure **g**, 2091
40: 5 thou shalt set the altar of **g** for the incense 2091
Nu 7:14 One spoon of ten *shekels* of **g**, full *of* 2091
7:20 One spoon of **g** of ten *shekels*, full *of* 2091
7:84 twelve silver bowls, twelve spoons of **g**: 2091
7:86 all the **g** of the spoons *was* an hundred and 2091
8: 4 work of the candlestick *was of* beaten **g**, 2091
22:18 give me his house full *of* silver and **g**, 2091
24:13 give me his house full *of* silver and **g**, 2091
31:22 Only the **g**, and the silver, the brass, 2091
31:50 *of* jewels of **g**, chains, and bracelets, rings, 2091
31:51 and Eleazar the priest took the **g** of them, 2091
31:52 all the **g** of the offering that they offered up 2091
31:54 Eleazar the priest took the **g** of the captains 2091
Dt 7:25 not desire the silver or **g** *that is* on them, 2091
8:13 thy silver and thy **g** is multiplied, and 2091
17:17 he greatly multiply to himself silver and **g**. 2091
29:17 their idols, wood and stone, silver and **g**, 2091
Jos 6:19 and **g**, and vessels of brass and iron, 2091
6:24 the **g**, and the vessels of brass and of iron, 2091
7:21 a wedge of **g** of fifty shekels weight, then 2091
7:24 the wedge of **g**, and his sons, and his 2091
22: 8 with **g**, and with brass, and with iron, and 2091
Jdg 8:26 a thousand and seven hundred *shekels* of **g**; 2091
1Sa 6: 8 put the jewels of **g**, which ye return him *for* 2091
6:11 the coffer with the mice of **g** and 2091
6:15 wherein the jewels of **g** *were*, and put *them* 2091
2Sa 1:24 who put on ornaments of **g** upon your 2091
8: 7 David took the shields of **g** that were on 2091
8:10 and vessels of **g**, and vessels of brass: 2091
8:11 **g** that he had dedicated of all nations which 2091
12:30 the weight whereof *was* a talent of **g** with 2091
21: 4 We will have no silver nor **g** of Saul, nor of 2091
1Ki 6:20 he overlaid it with pure **g**; and *so* 2091
6:21 overlaid the house within with pure **g**: 2091
6:21 he made a partition by the chains of **g** 2091
6:21 before the oracle; and he overlaid it with **g**. 2091
6:22 the whole house he overlaid with **g**, until *he* 2091
6:22 that *was* by the oracle he overlaid with **g**. 2091
6:28 And he overlaid the cherubims with **g**. 2091
6:30 the floor of the house he overlaid with **g**, 2091
6:32 overlaid *them* with **g**, and spread gold upon 2091
6:32 spread **g** upon the cherubims, and upon 2091
6:35 covered *them* with **g** fitted upon the carved 2091
7:48 the altar of **g**, and the table *of* gold, 2091
7:48 the altar of gold, and the table *of* **g**, 2091
7:49 the candlesticks *of* pure **g**, five on the right 2091
7:49 and the lamps, and the tongs *of* **g**, 2091
7:50 and the spoons, and the censers *of* pure **g**; 2091
7:50 the hinges *of* **g**, *both* for the doors of 2091
7:51 *even* the silver, and the **g**, and the vessels, 2091
9:11 with cedar trees and fir trees, and with **g**, 2091
9:14 Hiram sent to the king sixscore talents of **g**. 2091
9:28 fet from thence **g**, four hundred and 2091
10: 2 and very much **g**, and precious stones: 2091
10:10 the king an hundred and twenty talents of **g**, 2091
10:11 also of Hiram, that brought **g** from Ophir, 2091
10:14 Now the weight of **g** that came to Solomon 2091
10:14 six hundred threescore and six talents of **g**, 2091
10:16 made two hundred targets *of* beaten **g**: 2091
10:16 six hundred *shekels* of **g** went to one target. 2091
10:17 *he made* three hundred shields *of* beaten **g**; 2091
10:17 three pound *of* **g** went to one shield: 2091
10:18 of ivory, and overlaid it with the best **g**. 2091
10:21 king Solomon's drinking vessels *were of* **g**, 2091
10:21 of the forest of Lebanon *were of* pure **g**: 2091
10:22 bringing **g**, and silver, ivory, and apes, and 2091
10:25 and vessels of **g**, and garments, and armour, 2091
12:28 made two calves of **g**, and said unto them, 2091
14:26 he took away all the shields of **g** which 2091
15:15 of the LORD, silver, and **g**, and vessels. 2091
15:18 the **g** that were left in the treasures of 2091
15:19 sent unto thee a present of silver and **g**; 2091
20: 3 Thy silver and thy **g** *is* mine; thy wives also 2091
20: 5 and thy **g**, and thy wives, and thy children; 2091
20: 7 and for my silver, and for my **g**; 2091
22:48 ships of Tharshish to go to Ophir for **g**: 2091
2Ki 5: 5 six thousand *pieces* of **g**, and ten changes of 2091
7: 8 and **g**, and raiment, and went and hid *it*; and 2091
12:13 any vessels of **g**, or vessels of silver, 2091
12:18 all the **g** that was found in the treasures of 2091
14:14 he took all the **g** and silver, and all 2091
16: 8 **g** that was found *in* the house of 2091
18:14 talents of silver and thirty talents of **g**. 2091
18:16 At that time did Hezekiah cut off *the* **g** *from* NIH
20:13 the **g**, and the spices, and the precious 2091
23:33 hundred talents of silver, and a talent of **g**. 2091
23:35 gave the silver and the **g** to Pharaoh; 2091
23:35 and the **g** of the people of the land, 2091
24:13 cut in pieces all the vessels of **g** which 2091
25:15 *and* such *things* as *were of* **g**, *in* gold, and 2091
25:15 *were of* gold, *in* **g**, and *of* silver, *in* silver, 2091
1Ch 18: 7 David took the shields of **g** that were on 2091
18:10 *with him* all *manner of* vessels of **g** and 2091
18:11 the **g** that he brought from all *these* nations; 2091
20: 2 found it to weigh a talent of **g**, and 2091
21:25 place six hundred shekels of **g** *by* weight. 2091
22:14 LORD an hundred thousand talents *of* **g**, 2091
22:16 Of the **g**, the silver, and the brass, and 2091
28:14 *He gave* of **g** by weight for *things of* gold, 2091
28:14 *He gave* of gold by weight for *things of* **g**, 2091
28:15 Even the weight for the candlesticks of **g**, 2091
28:15 *for* their lamps of **g**, by weight for every 2091
28:16 *by* weight *he gave* **g** for the tables of 2091
28:17 Also pure **g** *for* the fleshhooks, and NIH
28:17 for the golden basons *he gave* **g** by weight NIH
28:18 for the altar of incense refined **g** by weight; 2091
28:18 **g** for the pattern of the chariot of 2091
1Ch 29: 2 my God the **g** for *things to be made of* gold, 2091
29: 2 my God the gold for *things to be made of* **g**, 2091
29: 3 of mine own proper good, *of* **g** and silver, 2091
29: 4 *Even* three thousand talents of **g**, of 2091
29: 4 of the **g** of Ophir, and seven thousand 2091
29: 5 The **g** for *things of* gold, and the silver for 2091
29: 5 The gold for *things of* **g**, and the silver for 2091
29: 7 the house of God *of* **g** five thousand talents 2091
2Ch 1:15 and **g** at Jerusalem *as plenteous* as stones, 2091
2: 7 therefore a man cunning to work in **g**, 2091
2:14 skilful to work in **g**, and in silver, in brass, 2091
3: 4 and he overlaid it within with pure **g**. 2091
3: 5 which he overlaid with fine **g**, and 2091
3: 6 for beauty: and the **g** *was* gold of Parvaim. 2091
3: 6 for beauty: and the gold *was* **g** of Parvaim. 2091
3: 7 walls thereof, and the doors thereof, with **g**; 2091
3: 8 he overlaid it with fine **g**, *amounting* to six 2091
3: 9 weight of the nails *was* fifty shekels of **g**. 2091
3: 9 And he overlaid the upper chambers with **g**. 2091
3:10 of image work, and overlaid them with **g**. 2091
4: 7 he made ten candlesticks of **g** according to 2091
4: 8 And he made an hundred basons of **g**. 2091
4:20 the manner before the oracle, *of* pure **g**; 2091
4:21 *made he of* **g**, *and* that perfect gold; 2091
4:21 *made he of* gold, *and* that perfect **g**; 2091
4:22 and the spoons, and the censers, of pure **g**: 2091
4:22 doors of the house of the temple, *were of* **g**. 2091
5: 1 and the **g**, and all the instruments, 2091
8:18 thence four hundred and fifty talents of **g**, 2091
9: 1 and **g** in abundance, and precious stones: 2091
9: 9 the king an hundred and twenty talents of **g**, 2091
9:10 which brought **g** from Ophir, 2091
9:13 Now the weight of **g** that came to Solomon 2091
9:13 and threescore and six talents of **g**; 2091
9:14 governors of the country brought **g** and 2091
9:15 made two hundred targets *of* beaten **g**: 2091
9:15 six hundred *shekels* of beaten **g** went to one 2091
9:16 three hundred shields *made he of* beaten **g**: 2091
9:16 three hundred *shekels* of **g** went to one 2091
9:17 throne of ivory, and overlaid it with pure **g**. 2091
9:18 with a footstool of **g**, *which were* fastened 2091
9:20 vessels of king Solomon *were of* **g**, 2091
9:20 of the forest of Lebanon *were of* pure **g**: 2091
9:21 once came the ships of Tarshish bringing **g**, 2091
9:24 vessels of **g**, and raiment, harness, and 2091
12: 9 he carried away also the shields of **g** which 2091
13:11 the candlestick of **g** with the lamps thereof, 2091
15:18 had dedicated, silver, and **g**, and vessels. 2091
16: 2 **g** out of the treasures of the house of 2091
16: 3 behold, I have sent thee silver and **g**; go, 2091
21: 3 of **g**, and of precious things, with fenced 2091
24:14 and spoons, and vessels of **g** and silver. 2091
25:24 *he took* all the **g** and the silver, and all 2091
32:27 for **g**, and for precious stones, and 2091
36: 3 hundred talents of silver and a talent of **g**. 2091
Ezr 1: 4 with **g**, and with goods, and with beasts, 2091
1: 6 with **g**, with goods, and with beasts, and 2091
1: 9 thirty chargers of **g**, a thousand chargers of 2091
1:10 Thirty basons of **g**, silver basons of a 2091
1:11 All the vessels of **g** and of silver *were* five 2091
2:69 and one thousand drams *of* **g**, 2091
5:14 the vessels also of **g** and silver of the house 1722
7:15 to carry the silver and **g**, which the king 1722
7:16 **g** that thou canst find in all the province of 1722
7:18 to do with the rest of the silver and **g**, 1722
8:25 them the silver, and the **g**, and the vessels, 2091
8:26 *and of* **g** an hundred talents; 2091
8:27 Also twenty basons of **g**, of a thousand 2091
8:27 two vessels of fine copper, precious as **g**. 2091
8:28 the **g** *are* a freewill offering unto 2091
8:30 of the silver, and the **g**, and the vessels, 2091
8:33 the fourth day was the silver and the **g** and 2091
Ne 7:70 gave to the treasure a thousand drams *of* **g**, 2091
7:71 of the work twenty thousand drams *of* **g**, 2091
7:72 gave *was* twenty thousand drams *of* **g**, 2091
Est 1: 6 the beds *were of* **g** and silver, upon a 2091
1: 7 *they* gave *them* drink in vessels of **g**, 2091
8:15 *with* a great crown of **g**, and *with* a garment 2091
Job 3:15 Or with princes that had **g**, who filled their 2091
22:24 shalt thou lay up **g** as dust, and *the gold of* 1220
22:24 *the* **g** *of* Ophir as the stones of the brooks. NIH
23:10 he hath tried me, I shall come forth as **g**. 2091
28: 1 and a place for **g** *where* they fine *it*. 2091
28: 6 the place of sapphires: and it hath dust of **g**. 2091
28:15 It cannot be gotten for **g**, neither shall silver 5458
28:16 It cannot be valued with the **g** of Ophir, 3800
28:17 The **g** and the crystal cannot equal it: and 2091
28:17 of it *shall not be for* jewels of **fine g**. 6337
28:19 neither shall it be valued with pure **g**. 3800
31:24 If I have made **g** my hope, or have said to 2091
31:24 or have said to the **fine g**, *Thou art* my 3800
36:19 *no*, not **g**, nor all the forces of strength. 1222
42:11 of money, and every one an earring of **g**. 2091
Ps 19:10 More to be desired *are they* than **g**, yea, 2091
19:10 *are they* than gold, yea, than much **fine g**: 6337
21: 3 thou settest a crown of **pure g** on his head. 6337
45: 9 hand did stand the queen in **g** of Ophir. 3800
45:13 her clothing *is* of wrought **g**. 2091
68:13 with silver, and her feathers with yellow **g**. 2742
72:15 and to him shall be given of the **g** of Sheba: 2091
105:37 brought them forth also with silver and **g**: 2091
115: 4 Their idols *are* silver and **g**, the work of 2091
119:72 mouth *is* better unto me than thousands of **g** 2091
119:127 I love thy commandments above **g**; 2091
119:127 above gold; yea, above **fine g**. 6337
135:15 The idols of the heathen *are* silver and **g**, 2091
Pr 3:14 of silver, and the gain thereof than **fine g**. 2742
8:10 and knowledge rather than choice **g**. 2742
8:19 My fruit *is* better than **g**, yea, than fine 2742
8:19 fruit *is* better than gold, yea, than **fine g**; 6337
11:22 *As* a jewel of **g** in a swine's snout, *so is* a 2091
16:16 much better *is it* to get wisdom than **g**! 2742
17: 3 pot *is* for silver, and the furnace for **g**: 2091
20:15 There is **g**, and a multitude of rubies: but 2091
22: 1 *and* loving favour rather than silver and **g**. 2091

Pr 25:11 A word fitly spoken *is like* apples of **g** in 2091
25:12 *As* an earring of **g**, and an ornament of fine 2091
25:12 an ornament of **fine g**, *so is* a wise reprover 3800
27:21 fining pot for silver, and the furnace for **g**; 2091
Ecc 2: 8 I gathered me also silver and **g**, and 2091
SS 1:10 rows *of jewels*, thy neck with chains *of* **g**. NIH
1:11 We will make thee borders of **g** with studs 2091
3:10 the bottom thereof *of* **g**, the covering of it 2091
5:11 His head *is as* the most **fine g**, his locks *are* 6337
5:14 His hands *are as* **g** rings set with the beryl: 2091
5:15 of marble, set upon sockets of **fine g**: 6337
Isa 2: 7 Their land also is full *of* silver and **g**, 2091
2:20 cast his idols of silver, and his idols of **g**, 2091
13:12 will make a man more precious than **fine g**; 6337
13:17 and *as for* **g**, they shall not delight in it. 2091
30:22 the ornament of thy molten images of **g**: 2091
31: 7 his idols of **g**, which your own hands have 2091
39: 2 the **g**, and the spices, and the precious 2091
40:19 the goldsmith spreadeth it over with **g**, and 2091
46: 6 They lavish **g** out of the bag, and 2091
60: 6 they shall bring **g** and incense; and 2091
60: 9 from far, their silver and their **g** with them, 2091
60:17 For brass I will bring **g**, and for iron I will 2091
Jer 4:30 thou deckest thee with ornaments of **g**, 2091
10: 4 They deck it with silver and with **g**; 2091
10: 9 **g** from Uphaz, the work of the workman, 2091
52:19 *that* which *was of* **g** *in* gold, and *that* which 2091
52:19 *that* which *was of* gold *in* **g**, and *that* which 2091
La 4: 1 How is the **g** become dim! *how* is the most 2091
4: 1 *how* is the most **fine g** changed! the stones 3800
4: 2 sons of Zion, comparable to **fine g**, 6337
Eze 7:19 in the streets, and their **g** shall be removed: 2091
7:19 their **g** shall not be able to deliver them in 2091
16:13 Thus wast thou decked *with* **g** and silver; 2091
16:17 Thou hast also taken thy fair jewels of my **g** 2091
27:22 and with all precious stones, and **g**. 2091
28: 4 hast gotten **g** and silver into thy treasures: 2091
28:13 the emerald, and the carbuncle, and **g**: 2091
38:13 to carry away silver and **g**, to take *away* 2091
Da 2:32 This image's head *was* of fine **g**, his breast 1722
2:35 the clay, the brass, the silver, and the **g**, 1722
2:38 ruler over them all. Thou *art* this head of **g**. 1722
2:45 the brass, the clay, the silver, and the **g**; 1722
3: 1 the king made an image of **g**, 1722
5: 4 praised the gods of **g**, and of silver, of 1722
5: 7 *have* a chain of **g** about his neck, and 1722
5:16 *have* a chain of **g** about thy neck, and 1722
5:23 **g**, of brass, iron, wood, and stone, which 1722
5:29 *put* a chain of **g** about his neck, and made a 1722
10: 5 whose loins *were* girded with **fine g** of 3800
11: 8 their precious vessels *of* silver and *of* **g**; 2091
11:38 his fathers knew not shall he honour with **g**, 2091
11:43 he shall have power over the treasures of **g** 2091
Hos 2: 8 and oil, and multiplied her silver and **g**, 2091
8: 4 and their **g** have they made them idols, 2091
Joel 3: 5 Because ye have taken my silver and my **g**, 2091
Na 2: 9 ye the spoil of silver, take the spoil of **g**: 2091
Hab 2:19 it *is* laid over *with* **g** and silver, and *there is* 2091
Zep 1:18 Neither their silver nor their **g** shall be able 2091
Hag 2: 8 The silver *is* mine, and the **g** *is* mine, 2091
Zec 4: 2 and behold, a candlestick all of **g**, 2091
6:11 take silver and **g**, and make crowns, and 2091
9: 3 and **fine g** as the mire of the streets. 2742
13: 9 is refined, and will try them as **g** is tried: 2091
14:14 **g**, and silver, and apparel, in great 2091
Mal 3: 3 of Levi, and purge them as **g** and silver, 2091
Mt 2:11 him gifts; **g**, and frankincense, and myrrh. *5557*
10: 9 Provide neither **g**, nor silver, nor brass in *5557*
23:16 whosoever shall swear by the **g** of *5557*
23:17 the **g**, or the temple that sanctifieth *5557*
23:17 or the temple that sanctifieth the **g**? *5557*
Ac 3: 6 Then Peter said, Silver and **g** have I none; *5553*
17:29 not to think that the Godhead is like unto **g**, *5557*
20:33 coveted no *man's* silver, or **g**, or apparel. *5553*
1Co 3:12 if any *man* build upon this foundation **g**, *5557*
1Ti 2: 9 or **g**, or pearls, or costly array; *5557*
2Ti 2:20 a great house there are not only vessels **of g** *5552*
Heb 9: 4 the covenant overlaid round about with **g**, *5553*
Jas 2: 2 unto your assembly a man **with a g ring**, *5554*
5: 3 Your **g** and silver is cankered; and the rust *5557*
1Pe 1: 7 *being* much more precious than of **g** that *5553*
1:18 with corruptible *things*, *as* silver and **g**, *5553*
3: 3 and of wearing of **g**, or of putting on of *5553*
Rev 3:18 I counsel thee to buy of me **g** tried in *5553*
4: 4 and they had on their heads crowns of **g**. *5552*
9: 7 their heads *were* as *it were* crowns like **g**, *5557*
9:20 should not worship devils, and idols of **g**, *5552*
17: 4 and **decked with g** and *5557+5558*
18:12 The merchandise of **g**, and silver, and *5557*
18:16 and decked with **g**, and precious stones, and *5557*
21:18 and the city *was* pure **g**, like unto clear *5553*
21:21 and the street of the city *was* pure **g**, as *it* *5553*

GOLDEN (66) [GOLD]

Ge 24:22 that the man took a **g** earring of half a 2091
Ex 25:25 thou shalt make a **g** crown to the border 2091
28:34 A **g** bell and a pomegranate, a golden bell 2091
28:34 a pomegranate, a **g** bell and a pomegranate, 2091
30: 4 two **g** rings shalt thou make to it under 2091
32: 2 said unto them, Break off the **g** earrings, 2091
32: 3 all the people brake off the **g** earrings 2091
39:20 they made two *other* **g** rings, and put them 2091
39:38 the **g** altar, and the anointing oil, and 2091
40:26 he put the **g** altar in the tent of 2091
Lev 8: 9 did he put the **g** plate, the holy crown; 2091
Nu 4:11 upon the **g** altar they shall spread a cloth of 2091
7:26 One **g** spoon of ten *shekels*, full *of* incense: 2091
7:32 One **g** spoon *of* ten *shekels*, full *of* incense: 2091
7:38 One **g** spoon of ten *shekels*, full *of* incense: 2091
7:44 One **g** spoon of ten *shekels*, full *of* incense: 2091
7:50 One **g** spoon of ten *shekels*, full *of* incense: 2091
7:56 One **g** spoon of ten *shekels*, full *of* incense: 2091
7:62 One **g** spoon of ten *shekels*, full *of* incense: 2091
7:68 One **g** spoon of ten *shekels*, full *of* incense: 2091
7:74 One **g** spoon of ten *shekels*, full *of* incense: 2091
7:80 One **g** spoon of ten *shekels*, full *of* incense: 2091
7:86 The **g** spoons *were* twelve, full *of* incense, 2091
Jdg 8:24 (For they had **g** earrings, because they *were* 2091
8:26 the weight of the **g** earrings that he 2091
1Sa 6: 4 Five **g** emerods, and five golden mice, 2091
6: 4 Five golden emerods, and five **g** mice, 2091
6:17 these *are* the **g** emerods which 2091
6:18 the **g** mice, *according to* the number of all 2091
2Ki 10:29 *to wit*, the **g** calves that *were in* Beth-el, 2091
1Ch 28:17 for the **g** basons *he gave gold* by weight for 2091
2Ch 4:19 the **g** altar also, and the tables whereon 2091
13: 8 and *there are* with you **g** calves, 2091
Ezr 6: 5 also let the **g** and silver vessels of the house 1722
Est 4:11 whom the king shall hold out the **g** sceptre, 2091
5: 2 the king held out to Esther the **g** sceptre 2091
8: 4 the king held out the **g** sceptre toward 2091
Ecc 12: 6 or the **g** bowl be broken, or the pitcher be 2091
Isa 13:12 even a man than the **g wedge** of Ophir. 3800
14: 4 the oppressor ceased! the **g city** ceased! 4062
Jer 51: 7 Babylon *hath been* a **g** cup in the LORD'S 2091
Da 3: 5 worship the **g** image that Nebuchadnezzar 1722
3: 7 worshipped the **g** image that 1722
3:10 shall fall down and worship the **g** image: 1722
3:12 nor worship the **g** image which thou hast 1722
3:14 nor worship the **g** image which I have set 1722
3:18 nor worship the **g** image which thou hast 1722
5: 2 commanded to bring the **g** and 1722
5: 3 they brought the **g** vessels that were taken 1722
Zec 4:12 **g** pipes empty the golden *oil* out of 2091
4:12 pipes empty the **g** *oil* out of themselves? 2091
Heb 9: 4 Which had the **g** censer, and the ark of *5552*
9: 4 wherein *was* the **g** pot that had manna, and *5552*
Rev 1:12 being turned, I saw seven **g** candlesticks; *5552*
1:13 and girt about the paps with a **g** girdle. *5552*
1:20 right hand, and the seven **g** candlesticks. *5552*
2: 1 who walketh in the midst of the seven **g** *5552*
5: 8 and **g** vials full of odours, which are *5552*
8: 3 and stood at the altar, having a **g** censer; *5552*
8: 3 the **g** altar which was before the throne. *5552*
9:13 I heard a voice from the four horns of the **g** *5552*
14:14 having on his head a **g** crown, and in his *5552*
15: 6 having their breasts girded with **g** girdles. *5552*
15: 7 seven **g** vials full of the wrath of God, *5552*
17: 4 having a **g** cup in her hand full of *5552*
21:15 And he that talked with me had a **g** reed to *5552*

GOLDSMITH (3) [GOLD]

Isa 40:19 the **g** spreadeth it over with gold, and 6884
41: 7 So the carpenter encouraged the **g**, *and* 6884
46: 6 weigh silver in the balance, *and* hire a **g**; 6884

GOLDSMITH'S (1) [GOLD]

Ne 3:31 After him repaired Malchiah the **g** son unto 6885

GOLDSMITHS (2) [GOLD]

Ne 3: 8 Uzziel the son of Harhaiah, *of* the **g**. 6884
3:32 corner unto the sheep gate repaired the **g** 6884

GOLGOTHA (3) [CALVARY]

Mt 27:33 they were come unto a place called **G**, *1115*
Mk 15:22 And they bring him unto the place **G**, *1115*
Jn 19:17 of a skull, which is called in the Hebrew **G**: *1115*

GOLIATH (6)

1Sa 17: 4 named **G**, of Gath, whose height *was* six 1555
17:23 the Philistine of Gath, **G** by name, 1555
21: 9 priest said, The sword of **G** the Philistine, 1555
22:10 and gave him the sword of **G** the Philistine. 1555
2Sa 21:19 slew *the brother of* **G** the Gittite, 1555
1Ch 20: 5 slew Lahmi the brother of **G** the Gittite, 1555

GOMER (6)

Ge 10: 2 **G**, and Magog, and Madai, and Javan, and 1586
10: 3 the sons of **G**; Ashkenaz, and Riphath, and 1586
1Ch 1: 5 **G**, and Magog, and Madai, and Javan, and 1586
1: 6 the sons of **G**; Ashchenaz, and Riphath, 1586
Eze 38: 6 **G**, and all his bands; the house of 1586
Hos 1: 3 and took **G** the daughter of Diblaim; 1586

GOMORRAH (19) [GOMORRHA]

Ge 10:19 **G**, and Admah, and Zeboim, even unto 6017
13:10 the LORD destroyed Sodom and **G**, 6017
14: 2 with Birsha king of **G**, Shinab king of 6017
14: 8 the king of **G**, and the king of Admah, and 6017
14:10 the kings of Sodom and **G** fled, and 6017
14:11 they took all the goods of Sodom and **G**, 6017
18:20 Because the cry of Sodom and **G** is great, 6017
19:24 upon **G** brimstone and fire from 6017
19:28 he looked toward Sodom and **G**, and 6017
Dt 29:23 of Sodom, and **G**, Admah, and Zeboim, 6017
32:32 the vine of Sodom, and of the fields of **G**: 6017
Isa 1: 9 *and* we should have been like unto **G**. 6017
1:10 unto the law of our God, ye people of **G**. 6017
13:19 be as when God overthrew Sodom and **G**. 6017
Jer 23:14 as Sodom, and the inhabitants thereof as **G**. 6017
49:18 and **G** and the neighbour *cities* thereof, 6017
50:40 As God overthrew Sodom and **G** and 6017
Am 4:11 as God overthrew Sodom and **G**, and 6017
Zep 2: 9 the children of Ammon as **G**, *even* 6017

GOMORRHA (5) [GOMORRAH]

Mt 10:15 of Sodom and **G** in the day of judgment, *1116*
Mk 6:11 for Sodom and **G** in the day of judgment, *1116*
Ro 9:29 as Sodoma, and been made like unto **G**. *1116*
2Pe 2: 6 **G** into ashes condemned *them* with an *1116*
Jude 1: 7 *Even* as Sodom and **G**, and the cities about *1116*

GONE (214) [GO]

Ge 27:30 Jacob was yet **scarce g out** from 3318+3318
28: 7 and his mother, and was **g** to Padan-aram; 1980
31:30 *though* thou wouldest **needs be g**, 1980+1980
34:17 will we take our daughter, and we will be **g**. 1980
42:33 the famine of your households, and be **g**: 1980
44: 4 *And* when they were **g out** of the city, *and* 3318
49: 9 from the prey, my son, thou art **g up**: 5927
Ex 9:29 unto him, As soon as I am **g out** of the city, 3318
12:32 and your herds, as ye have said, and be **g**; 1980
16:14 when the dew that lay was **g up**, behold, 5927
19: 1 when the children of Israel were **g forth** 3318
33: 8 until he was **g** into the tabernacle. 935
Lev 17: 7 after whom they have **g a whoring**. 2181
Nu 5:19 if thou hast not **g aside** *to* uncleanness *with* 7847
5:20 if thou hast **g aside** *to another* instead of 7847
7:89 when Moses was **g** into the tabernacle of 935
13:32 through which we have **g** to search it, 5674
16:46 for there is wrath **g out** from the LORD; 3318
21:28 For there is a fire **g out** of Heshbon, 3318
Dt 9: 9 When I was **g up** into the mount to receive 5927
13:13 are **g out** from among you, and 3318
17: 3 hath **g** and served other gods, and 1980
23:23 **That which is g out** of thy lips thou shalt 4161
27: 4 Therefore it shall be when ye be **g over** 5674
32:36 when he seeth that *their* power is **g**, and 235
Jos 2: 7 they which pursued after them were **g out**, 3318
4:23 up from before us, until we were **g over**: 5674
23:16 have **g** and served other gods, and 1980
Jdg 3:24 When he was **g out**, his servants came; and 3318
4:12 son of Abinoam was **g up** *to* mount Tabor. 5927
4:14 is not the LORD **g out** before thee? 3318
18:24 I made, and the priest, and ye are **g away**: 1980
20: 3 the children of Israel were **g up** *to* Mizpeh.) 5927
Ru 1:13 the hand of the LORD is **g out** against me. 3318
1:15 thy sister in law is **g back** unto her people, 7725
1Sa 14: 3 the people knew not that Jonathan was **g**. 1980
14:17 Number now, and see who is **g** from us. 1980
15:12 is **g about**, and passed on, and gone down 5437
15:12 and passed on, and **g down** *to* Gilgal. 3381
15:20 have **g** the way which the LORD sent me, 1980
20:41 *And* as soon as the lad was **g**, David arose 935
25:37 when the wine was **g out** of Nabal, and 3318
2Sa 2:27 in the morning the people had **g up** every 5927
3: 7 Wherefore hast thou **g in** unto my father's 935
3:22 had sent him away, and he was **g** in peace. 1980
3:23 he hath sent him away, and he is **g** in peace. 1980
3:24 sent him away, and he is **quite g**? 1980+1980
6:13 ark of the LORD had **g** six **paces**, 6805+6806
13:15 And Amnon said unto her, Arise, be **g**. 1980
17:20 They be **g over** the brook of water. 5674
17:22 not one *of them* that was not **g over** Jordan. 5674
23: 9 and the men of Israel were **g away**: 5927
24: 8 So when they had **g** through all the land, 7751
1Ki 1:25 For he is **g down** *this* day, and hath slain 3381
2:41 it was told Solomon that Shimei had **g** from 1980
9:16 *For* Pharaoh king of Egypt had **g up**, and 5927
11:15 Joab the captain of the host was **g up** to 5927
13:24 when he was **g**, a lion met him by the way, 1980
14: 9 for thou hast **g** and made thee other gods, 1980
14:10 as *a man* taketh away dung, till it be **all g**. 8552
18:12 come to pass, *as soon as* I am **g** from thee, 1980
20:40 servant was busy here and there, he was **g**. 369
21:18 whither he is **g down** to possess it. 3381
22:13 the messenger that was **g** to call Micaiah 1980
2Ki 1: 4 down from *that* bed on which thou art **g up**, 5927
1: 6 down from *that* bed on which thou art **g up**, 5927
1:16 down off *that* bed on which thou art **g up**, 5927
2: 9 it came to pass, when they were **g over**, 5674
5: 2 the Syrians had **g out** *by* companies, and 3318
6:15 **g forth**, behold, a host compassed the city 3318
7:12 are they **g out** of the camp to hide 3318
20: 4 afore Isaiah was **g out** *into* the middle 3318
20:11 by which it had **g down** in the dial of Ahaz. 3381
1Ch 14:15 for God is **g forth** before thee to smite 3318
17: 5 have **g** from tent to tent, and from *one* 1961
Job 1: 5 the days of *their* feasting were **g about**, 5362
7: 4 When shall I arise, and the night be **g**? 4059
19:10 destroyed me on every side, and I am **g**: 1980
23:12 Neither have I **g back from** 4185
24:24 for a little while, but are **g** and brought low, 369
28: 4 are dried up, they are **g away** from men. 5128
Ps 14: 3 They are all **g aside**, they are *all* together 5493
19: 4 Their line is **g out** through all the earth, and 3318
38: 4 For mine iniquities are **g** *over* mine head: 5674
38:10 the light of mine eyes, it also is **g** from me. 369
42: 4 for I had **g** with the multitude, I went with 5674
42: 7 thy waves and thy billows are **g** over me. 5674
47: 5 God is **g up** with a shout, the LORD with 5927
51: T unto him, after he had **g in** to Bath-sheba. 935
53: 3 Every one of them is **g back**, they are 5472
73: 2 *as for* me, my feet were almost **g**; my steps 5186
77: 8 Is his mercy **clean g** for ever? doth *his* 656
89:34 nor alter the **thing that is g out** of my lips. 4161
103:16 For the wind passeth over it, and it is **g**; and 369
109:23 I am **g** like the shadow when it declineth: 1980
119:176 I have **g astray** like a lost sheep; seek thy 8582
124: 4 the stream had **g over** our soul: 5674
124: 5 Then the proud waters had **g over** our soul. 5674
Pr 7:19 *is* not at home, he is **g** a long journey: 1980
20:14 but when he is **g** his **way**, then he boasteth. 235
Ecc 8:10 had come and **g** from the place of the holy, 1980
SS 2:11 the winter is past, the rain is over *and* **g**; 1980
5: 6 beloved had withdrawn himself, *and* was **g**: 5674
6: 1 Whither is thy beloved **g**, O thou fairest 1980
6: 2 My beloved is **g down** into his garden, 3381
Isa 1: 4 unto anger, they are **g away** backward. 2114
5:13 Therefore my people are **g into captivity**, 1540
10:29 They are **g over** the passage: they have 5674
15: 2 He is **g up** *to* Bajith, and *to* Dibon, the high 5927
15: 8 For the cry is **g round about** the borders of 5362
16: 8 are stretched out, they are **g over** the sea. 5674
22: 1 that thou art wholly **g up** to the housetops? 5927
24:11 joy is darkened, the mirth of the land is **g**. 1540
38: 8 which is **g down** in the sun dial of Ahaz, 3381
38: 8 by which degrees it was **g down**. 3381
41: 3 *even by* the way *that* he had not **g** with his 935
45:23 the word is **g out** of my mouth *in* 3318
46: 2 but themselves are **g** into captivity. 1980
51: 5 my salvation is **g forth**, and mine arms 3318
53: 6 All we like sheep have **g astray**; we have 8582
57: 8 *thyself to another* than me, and art **g up**; 5927

Jer 2: 5 that they are **g far** from me, and 7368
2:23 am not polluted, I have not g after Baalim? 1980
3: 6 she is **g up** upon every high mountain and 1980
4: 7 he is **g forth** from his place to make thy 3318
5:23 a rebellious heart; they are revolted and **g**. 1980
9:10 and the beast are fled; they are **g**. 1980
10:20 my children are **g forth** *of* me, and they *are* 3318
14: 2 and the cry of Jerusalem is **g up**. 5927
15: 6 saith the LORD, thou art **g** backward: 1980
15: 9 her sun is **g down** while *it was* yet day: 935
23:15 is profaneness **g forth** into all the land. 3318
23:19 a whirlwind of the LORD is **g forth** *in* 3318
29:16 *of* your brethren that are not **g forth** with 3318
34:21 Babylon's army, which are **g up** from you. 5927
40: 5 Now while he was not yet **g back**, *he said,* 7725
44: 8 whither ye be **g** to dwell, that ye might cut 935
44:14 which are **g** into the land of Egypt to sojourn 935
44:28 that are **g** into the land of Egypt to sojourn 935
48:11 to vessel, neither hath he **g** into captivity: 1980
48:15 **g up** *out of* her cities, and his chosen young 5927
48:15 his chosen young men are **g down** to 3381
48:32 thy plants are **g over** the sea, they reach 5674
50: 6 they have **g** from mountain to hill, 1980
La 1: 3 Judah is **g into captivity** because 1540
1: 5 her children are **g** *into* captivity before 1980
1: 6 they are **g** without strength before 1980
1:18 and my young men are **g** into captivity. 1980
Eze 7:10 the morning is **g forth**; the rod hath 3318
9: 3 the glory of the God of Israel was **g up** 5927
13: 5 Ye have not **g up** into the gaps, 5927
19:14 fire is **g out** of a rod of her branches, 3318
23:30 thou hast **g a whoring** after the heathen, 2181
24: 6 and whose scum is not **g out** of it! 3318
31:12 all the people of the earth are **g down** from 3381
32:21 they are **g down**, they lie uncircumcised, 3381
32:24 which are **g down** uncircumcised into 3381
32:27 which are **g down** *to* hell with their 3381
32:30 which are **g down** with the slain; 3381
36:20 the LORD, and are **g forth** out of his land. 3318
37:21 whither they be **g**, and will gather them on 1980
44:10 the Levites that are **g away far** from me, 7368
Da 2: 5 to the Chaldeans, The thing is **g** from me: 230
2: 8 because ye see the thing is **g** from me. 230
2:14 which was **g forth** to slay the wise *men* of 5312
10:20 when I am **g forth**, lo, the prince of Grecia 3318
Hos 4:12 they have **g a whoring** from under their 2181
8: 9 For they are **g up** *to* Assyria, a wild ass 5927
9: 1 for thou hast **g a whoring** from thy God, 2181
9: 6 For lo, they are **g** because of destruction: 1980
Am 8: 5 Saying, When will the new moon be **g**, 5674
Jnh 1: 5 Jonah was **g down** into the sides of 3381
Mic 1:16 for they are **g into captivity** from thee. 1540
2:13 passed through the gate, and are **g out** by it: 3318
Mal 3: 7 ye are **g away** from mine ordinances, 5493
Mt 10:23 Ye shall not have **g over** the cities of Israel, *5055*
12:43 When the unclean spirit is **g out** of a man, *1831*
14:34 And when they were **g over**, they came into *1276*
18:12 and one of them be **g astray**, doth he not *4105*
18:12 and seeketh that which is **g astray**? *4105*
25: 8 Give us of your oil; for our lamps are **g out**. *4570*
26:71 And when he was **g out** into the porch, *1831*
Mk 1:19 And when he had **g** a little **further** thence, *4260*
5:30 in himself that virtue had **g out** of him, *1831*
7:29 thy way; the devil is **g out** of thy daughter. *1831*
7:30 she found the devil **g out**, and *her* daughter *1831*
10:17 And when he was **g forth** into the way, *1607*
Lk 2:15 as the angels were **g away** from them into *565*
5: 2 but the fishermen were **g out** of them, and *576*
8:46 for I perceive that virtue is **g out** of me. *1831*
11:14 when the devil was **g out**, the dumb spake; *1831*
11:24 When the unclean spirit is **g out** of a man, *1831*
19: 7 That he was **g** to be guest with a man *that is* *1525*
24:28 he made as though *he* would have **g** further. *4198*
Jn 4: 8 (For his disciples were **g away** unto the city *565*
6:22 but *that* his disciples were **g away** alone; *565*
7:10 But when his brethren were **g up**, then *305*
12:19 behold, the world is **g** after him. *565*
13:31 Therefore, when he was **g out**, Jesus said, *1831*
Ac 13: 6 And when they had **g through** the isle unto *1330*
13:42 And when the Jews were **g out** of *1826*
16: 6 Now when they had **g throughout** Phrygia *1330*
16:19 saw that the hope of their gains was **g**, *1831*
18:22 and **g up**, and saluted the church, he went *305*
20: 2 And when he had **g over** those parts, and *1330*
20:25 among whom I have **g** preaching *1330*
24: 6 Who also hath **g about** to profane *3985*
26:31 And when they were **g aside**, they talked *402*
27:28 and when they had **g** a little **further**, *1339*
Ro 3:12 They are all **g out of the way**, they are *1578*
1Pe 3:22 Who is **g** into heaven, and is on the right *4198*
2Pe 2:15 forsaken the right way, and are **g astray**, *4105*
1Jn 4: 1 many false prophets are **g out** into *1831*
Jude 1:11 for they have **g** in the way of Cain, and *4198*

GOOD (720) [BEST, BETTER, BETTERED, GOODLIER, GOODLIEST, GOODLINESS, GOODLY, GOODMAN, GOODNESS, GOODNESS', GOODS]

Ge 1: 4 God saw the light, that *it was* **g**: and 2896
1:10 called he Seas: and God saw that *it was* **g**. 2896
1:12 after his kind: and God saw that *it was* **g**. 2896
1:18 the darkness: and God saw that *it was* **g**. 2896
1:21 after his kind: and God saw that *it was* **g**. 2896
1:25 after his kind: and God saw that *it was* **g**. 2896
1:31 he had made, and, behold, *it was* very **g**. 2896
2: 9 that is pleasant to the sight, and **g** for food; 2896
2: 9 and the tree of knowledge of **g** and evil. 2896
2:12 the gold of that land *is* **g**: there *is* bdellium 2896
2:17 of the tree of the knowledge of **g** and evil, 2896
2:18 *It is* not **g** that the man should be alone; 2896
3: 5 ye shall be as gods, knowing **g** and evil. 2896
3: 6 when the woman saw that the tree *was* **g** for 2896
3:22 is become as one of us, to know **g** and evil: 2896
15:15 thou shalt be buried in a **g** old age. 2896
Ge 18: 7 fetcht a calf tender and **g**, and gave *it* unto a 2896
19: 8 and do ye to them as *is* **g** in your eyes: 2896
21:16 sat her down over against *him* **a g way off**, 7368
24:12 **send** me **g speed** *this* day, 6440+7136+3807.1
24:50 we cannot speak unto thee bad or **g**. 2896
25: 8 died in a **g** old age, an old man, and full *of* 2896
26:29 as we have done unto thee nothing but **g**, 2896
27: 9 fetch me from thence two **g** kids of 2896
27:46 the daughters of the land, **what g** 4100+3807.1
30:20 God hath endued me with a **g** dowry; 2896
31:24 heed that thou speak not to Jacob either **g** 2896
31:29 heed that thou speak not to Jacob either **g** 2896
32:12 I will **surely do** thee **g**, and make thy 3190+3190
40:16 baker saw that the interpretation was **g**, 2896
41: 5 of corn came up upon one stalk, rank and **g**. 2896
41:22 seven ears came up in one stalk, full and **g**: 2896
41:24 the thin ears devoured the seven **g** ears: 2896
41:26 The seven **g** kine *are* seven years; and 2896
41:26 and the seven **g** ears *are* seven years: 2896
41:35 let them gather all the food of those **g** years 2896
41:37 the thing was **g** in the eyes of Pharaoh, and 3190
43:28 Thy servant our father *is* **in g health**, he *is* 7965
44: 4 Wherefore have ye rewarded evil for **g**? 2896
45:18 I will give you the **g** of the land of Egypt, 2898
45:20 for the **g** of all the land of Egypt *is* yours. 2898
45:23 ten asses laden with the **g things** of Egypt, 2898
46:29 his neck, and wept on his neck **a g while**. 5750
49:15 he saw that rest *was* **g**, and the land that *it* 2896
50:20 *but* God meant it unto **g**, to bring to pass, 2896
Ex 3: 8 to bring them up out of that land unto a **g** 2896
18:17 unto him, The thing that thou doest *is* not **g**. 2896
21:34 The owner of the pit shall **make** *it* **g**, *and* 7999
22:11 accept *thereof,* and he shall not **make** *it* **g**. 7999
22:13 he shall not **make g** that which was torn. 7999
22:14 not with it, he shall **surely make** *it* **g**. 7999+7999
22:15 thereof *be* with it, he shall not **make** *it* **g**: 7999
Lev 5: 4 with *his* lips to do evil, or to **do g**, 3190
24:18 he that killeth a beast shall **make** it **g**; 7999
27:10 change it, a **g** for a bad, or a bad for a good: 2896
27:10 change it, a good for a bad, or a bad for a **g**: 2896
27:12 priest shall value it, whether it be **g** or bad: 2896
27:14 shall estimate it, whether it be **g** or bad: 2896
27:33 He shall not search whether it be **g** or bad, 2896
Nu 10:29 come thou with us, and we will **do** thee **g**: 2895
10:29 for the LORD hath spoken **g** concerning 2896
13:19 *is* that they dwell in, whether it *be* **g** or bad; 2896
13:20 be ye **of g courage**, and bring of the fruit of 2388
14: 7 through to search it, *is* an exceeding **g** land. 2896
23:19 hath he spoken, and shall he not **make** it **g**? 6965
24:13 to do *either* **g** or bad of mine own mind; 2896
Dt 1:14 The thing which thou hast spoken *is* **g** *for* 2896
1:25 *It is* a **g** land which the LORD our God 2896
1:35 men of this evil generation see that **g** land, 2896
1:39 *in that* day had no knowledge between **g** 2896
2: 4 take ye **g** heed unto yourselves therefore: 3966
3:25 and see the **g** land that *is* beyond Jordan, 2896
4:15 Take ye therefore **g** heed unto yourselves; 3966
4:21 and that *I* should not go in unto *that* **g** land, 2896
4:22 ye *shall* go over, and possess that **g** land. 2896
6:11 houses full *of* all **g** *things,* which thou 2898
6:18 *is* right and **g** in the sight of the LORD: 2896
6:18 possess the **g** land which the LORD sware 2896
6:24 fear the LORD our God, for our **g** always, 2896
8: 7 thy God bringeth thee into a **g** land, 2896
8:10 for the **g** land which he hath given thee. 2896
8:16 prove thee, to **do** thee **g** at thy latter end; 3190
9: 6 **g** land to possess it for thy righteousness; 2896
10:13 which I command thee *this* day for thy **g**? 2896
11:17 *lest* ye perish quickly from off the **g** land 2896
12:28 when thou doest *that which is* **g** and right in 2896
26:11 thou shalt rejoice in every **g** *thing* which 2896
28:12 The LORD shall open unto thee his **g** 2896
28:63 the LORD rejoiced over you to **do** you **g**, 3190
30: 5 he will **do** thee **g**, and multiply thee above 3190
30: 9 thy cattle, and in the fruit of thy land, for **g**: 2896
30: 9 LORD will again rejoice over thee for **g**, 2896
30:15 I have set before thee *this* day life and **g**, 2896
31: 6 Be strong and **of a g courage**, fear not, 553
31: 7 of all Israel, Be strong and **of a g courage**: 553
31:23 said, Be strong and **of a g courage**: 553
33:16 *for* the **g will** of him that dwelt in the bush: 7522
Jos 1: 6 Be strong and **of a g courage**: for unto this 553
1: 8 and then thou shalt **have g success**. 7919
1: 9 Be strong and **of a g courage**; be not afraid, 553
1:18 to death: only be strong and **of a g courage**. 553
9:25 as it seemeth **g** and right unto thee to do 2896
10:25 be dismayed, be strong and **of g courage**: 553
21:45 There failed not ought of any **g** thing which 2896
23:11 Take **g** heed therefore unto yourselves, that 3966
23:13 until ye perish from off this **g** land which 2896
23:14 that not one thing hath failed of all the **g** 2896
23:15 *that* as all **g** things are come upon you, 2896
23:15 until he have destroyed you from off this **g** 2896
23:16 ye shall perish quickly from off the **g** land 2896
24:20 after that he hath **done** you **g**. 3190
Jdg 8:32 Gideon the son of Joash died in a **g** old age, 2896
9:11 my **g** fruit, and go to be promoted over 2896
10:15 do thou unto us whatsoever seemeth **g** unto 2896
17:13 Now know I that the LORD will **do** me **g**, 3190
18: 9 have seen the land, and behold, it *is* very **g**: 2896
18:22 *And* when they were a **g way** from 7368
19:24 and do with them what seemeth **g** unto you: 2896
Ru 2:22 *It is* **g**, my daughter, that thou go out with 2896
1Sa 1:23 said unto her, Do what seemeth thee **g**; 2896
2:24 my sons; for *it is* no **g** report that I hear: 2896
3:18 let him do what seemeth him **g**. 2896
11:10 ye shall do with us all that seemeth **g** unto 2896
12:23 but I will teach you the **g** and the right way: 2896
14:36 Do whatsoever seemeth **g** unto thee. 2896
14:40 unto Saul, Do what seemeth **g** unto thee. 2896
15: 9 all *that was* **g**, and would not utterly destroy 2896
19: 4 Jonathan spake **g** of David unto Saul his 2896
19: 4 his works *have been* to thee-ward very **g**: 2896
20:12 *if there be* **g** toward David, and I then 2895
24: 4 do to him as it shall seem **g** unto thee. 3190
1Sa 24:17 for thou hast rewarded me **g**, whereas I 2896
24:19 wherefore the LORD reward thee **g** for 2896
25: 3 *she was* a woman of **g** understanding, and 2896
25: 8 for we come in a **g** day: give, I pray thee, 2896
25:15 the men *were* very **g** unto us, and we were 2896
25:21 and he hath requited me evil for **g**. 2896
25:30 the **g** that he hath spoken concerning thee, 2896
26:16 This thing *is* not **g** that thou hast done. 2896
29: 6 thy coming in with me in the host *is* **g** in 2896
29: 9 I know that thou *art* **g** in my sight, 2896
2Sa 3:19 David in Hebron all that seemed **g** to Israel, 2896
3:19 that seemed **g** to the whole house of NIH
4:10 thinking to have **brought g tidings**, 1319
6:19 a **g piece** *of flesh,* and a flagon *of wine.* So 829
10:12 Be **of g courage**, and let us play the men 2388
10:12 the LORD do that which seemeth him **g**. 2896
13:22 unto his brother Amnon neither **g** nor bad: 2896
14:17 so *is* my lord the king to discern **g** and bad: 2896
14:32 *it had been* **g** for me *to have been* there 2896
15: 3 unto him, See, thy matters *are* **g** and right; 2896
15:26 let him do to me as seemeth **g** unto him. 2896
16:12 that the LORD will requite me **g** for his 2896
17: 7 Ahithophel hath given *is* not **g** at this time. 2896
17:14 to defeat the **g** counsel of Ahithophel, 2896
18:27 He *is* a **g** man, and cometh with good 2896
18:27 *is* a good man, and cometh with **g** tidings. 2896
19:18 and to do what he thought **g**. 2896
19:27 do therefore what *is* **g** in thine eyes. 2896
19:35 *and* can I discern between **g** and evil? can 2896
19:37 and do to him what shall seem **g** unto thee. 2896
19:38 I will do to him *that* which shall seem **g** 2896
24:22 and offer up what seemeth **g** unto him: 2896
1Ki 1:42 *art* a valiant man, and bringest **g** tidings. 2896
2:38 Shimei said unto the king, The saying *is* **g**: 2896
2:42 unto me, The word *that* I have heard *is* **g**. 2896
3: 9 that *I* may discern between **g** and bad: 2896
8:36 that thou teach them the **g** way wherein 2896
8:56 there hath not failed one word of all his **g** 2896
12: 7 speak **g** words to them, then they will be 2896
14:13 in him there is found *some* **g** thing toward 2896
14:15 he shall root up Israel out of this **g** land, 2896
21: 2 *or,* if it seem **g** to thee, I will give thee 2896
22: 8 for he doth not prophesy **g** concerning me, 2896
22:13 the words of the prophets *declare* **g** unto 2896
22:13 of one of them, and speak *that which is* **g**. 2896
22:18 he would prophesy no **g** concerning me, 2896
2Ki 3:19 shall fell every **g** tree, and stop all wells of 2896
3:19 and mar every **g** piece of land with stones. 2896
3:25 *on* every **g** piece of land cast every man his 2896
3:25 the wells of water, and felled all the **g** trees: 2896
7: 9 this day *is* a day of **g tidings**, and we hold 1309
8: 9 even *of* every **g thing** of Damascus, 2898
10: 5 do thou *that* which *is* **g** in thine eyes. 2896
20: 3 and have done *that* which *is* **g** in thy sight. 2896
20:19 **G** *is* the word of the LORD which thou 2896
20:19 *Is it* not **g**, if peace and truth be in my days? NIH
1Ch 4:40 they found fat pasture and **g**, and the land 2896
13: 2 If *it seem* **g** unto you, and *that it be* of 2895
16: 3 and a **g piece** *of flesh,* and a flagon *of wine.* 829
16:34 for *he is* **g**; for his mercy *endureth* for ever. 2896
19:13 Be **of g courage**, and let us behave 2388
19:13 let the LORD do *that* which *is* **g** in his 2896
21:23 let my lord the king do *that* which *is* **g** in 2896
22:13 be strong, and **of g courage**; dread not, 553
28: 8 that ye may possess *this* **g** land, and leave *it* 2896
28:20 Be strong and **of g courage**, and do *it:* fear 553
29: 3 I have of mine own **proper g**, *of* gold and 5459
29:28 he died in a **g** old age, full of days, riches, 2896
2Ch 5:13 praised the LORD, *saying,* For *he is* **g**; 2896
6:27 when thou hast taught them the **g** way, 2896
7: 3 praised the LORD, *saying,* For *he is* **g**; 2896
10: 7 please them, and speak **g** words to them, 2896
14: 2 Asa did *that* which *was* **g** and right in 2896
18: 7 for he never prophesied **g** unto me, 2896
18:12 the words of the prophets *declare* **g** to 2896
18:12 be like one of theirs, and speak thou **g**. 2896
18:17 thee *that* he would not prophesy **g** unto me, 2896
19: 3 Nevertheless there are **g** things found in 2896
19:11 and the LORD shall be with the **g**. 2896
24:16 because he had done **g** in Israel, 2896
30:18 The **g** LORD pardon every one 2896
30:22 that taught the **g** knowledge of the LORD: 2896
31:20 and wrought *that* which *was* **g** and right and 2896
Ezr 3:11 because *he is* **g**, for his mercy *endureth* for 2896
5:17 Now therefore, if *it seem* **g** to the king, 2869
7: 9 according to the **g** hand of his God upon 2896
7:18 whatsoever shall **seem g** to thee, and to thy 3191
8:18 by the **g** hand of our God upon us they 2896
8:22 The hand of our God *is* upon all them for **g** 2896
9:12 eat the **g** of the land, and leave *it* for an 2898
10: 4 *be* with thee: be **of g courage**, and do *it.* 2388
Ne 2: 8 according to the **g** hand of my God upon 2896
2:18 the hand of my God which was **g** upon me; 2896
2:18 So they strengthened their hands for *this* **g** 2896
5: 9 Also I said, It *is* not **g** that ye do: ought ye 2896
5:19 Think upon me, my God, for **g**, 2896
6:19 Also they reported his **g deeds** before me, 2896
9:13 true laws, **g** statutes and commandments: 2896
9:20 Thou gavest also thy **g** spirit to instruct 2896
9:36 to eat the fruit thereof and the **g** thereof, 2898
13:14 wipe not out my **g deeds** that I have done 2617
13:31 Remember me, O my God, for **g**. 2896
Est 3:11 to do with them as it seemeth **g** to thee. 2896
5: 4 If *it seem* **g** unto the king, let the king and 2895
7: 9 who had spoken **g** for the king, standeth in 2896
8:17 had joy and gladness, a feast and a **g** day. 2896
9:19 a **g** day, and *of* sending portions one to 2896
9:22 to joy, and from mourning into a **g** day: 2896
Job 2:10 shall we receive **g** at the hand of God, and 2896
5:27 it *is;* hear it, and know thou *it* **for** thy **g**. 3807.1
7: 7 life *is* wind: mine eye shall no more see **g**. 2896
9:25 than a post: they flee away, they see no **g**. 2896
10: 3 *Is it* **g** unto thee that thou shouldest oppress, 2895
13: 9 *Is it* **g** that he should search you out? or 2895
15: 3 *with* speeches wherewith he can **do** no **g**? 3276

Job 21:16 Lo, their **g** *is* not in their hand: the counsel 2898
22:18 Yet he filled their houses *with* **g** *things:* but 2896
22:21 be at peace: thereby **g** shall come *unto* thee. 2896
24:21 beareth not: and **doeth** not **g** to the widow. 3190
30:26 When I looked for **g**, then evil came *unto* 2896
34: 4 let us know among ourselves what *is* **g**. 2896
39: 4 Their young ones are **in g liking**, they grow 2492
Ps 4: 6 *be* many that say, Who will shew us *any* **g**? 2896
14: 1 *there is* none that doeth **g**. 2896
14: 3 *there is* none that doeth **g**, no, not one. 2896
25: 8 **G** and upright *is* the LORD: therefore 2896
27:14 be **of g courage**, and he shall strengthen 2388
31:24 Be **of g courage**, and he shall strengthen 2388
34: 8 O taste and see that the LORD *is* **g**: 2896
34:10 the LORD shall not want any **g** *thing.* 2896
34:12 *and* loveth *many* days, that *he* may see **g**? 2896
34:14 Depart from evil, and do **g**; seek peace, and 2896
35:12 They rewarded me evil for **g** *to* the spoiling 2896
36: 3 he hath left off to be wise, *and* to **do g**. 3190
36: 4 he setteth himself in a way *that is* not **g**; 2896
37: 3 Trust in the LORD, and do **g**; *so* 2896
37:23 The steps of a **g** man are ordered by NIH
37:27 Depart from evil, and do **g**; and dwell for 2896
38:20 They also that render evil for **g** are mine 2896
38:20 because I follow *the thing that* **g** *is.* 2896
39: 2 *with* silence, I held my peace, *even* from **g**; 2896
45: 1 My heart is inditing a **g** matter: I speak of 2896
51:18 **Do g** in thy good pleasure unto Zion: 3190
51:18 Do good in thy **g pleasure** unto Zion: 7522
52: 3 Thou lovest evil more than **g**; *and* 2896
52: 9 on thy name; for *it is* **g** before thy saints. 2896
53: 1 *there is* none that doeth **g**. 2896
53: 3 *there is* none that doeth **g**, no, not one. 2896
54: 6 will praise thy name, O LORD; for *it is* **g**. 2896
69:16 O LORD; for thy lovingkindness *is* **g**: 2896
73: 1 Truly God *is* **g** to Israel, *even* to such as are 2896
73:28 *it is* **g** for me to draw near to God: I have 2896
84:11 no **g** *thing* will he withhold from them that 2896
85:12 Yea, the LORD shall give *that which is* **g**; 2896
86: 5 For thou, Lord, *art* **g**, and ready to forgive; 2896
86:17 Shew me a token for **g**; that they which 2896
92: 1 *It is a* **g** *thing* to give thanks unto 2896
100: 5 For the LORD *is* **g**; his mercy *is* 2896
103: 5 Who satisfieth thy mouth with **g** *things; so* 2896
104:28 openest thine hand, they are filled *with* **g**. 2896
106: 1 O give thanks unto the LORD; for *he is* **g**: 2896
106: 5 That *I* may see the **g** of thy chosen, that *I* 2896
107: 1 O give thanks unto the LORD, for *he is* **g**: 2896
109: 5 they have rewarded me evil for **g**, and 2896
109:21 because thy mercy *is* **g**, deliver thou me. 2896
111:10 a **g** understanding have all they that do *his* 2896
112: 5 A **g** man sheweth favour, and lendeth: 2896
118: 1 O give thanks unto the LORD; for *he is* **g**: 2896
118:29 O give thanks unto the LORD; for *he is* **g**: 2896
119:39 which I fear: for thy judgments *are* **g**. 2896
119:66 Teach me **g** judgment and knowledge: for I 2898
119:68 Thou *art* **g**, and doest good; teach me thy 2896
119:68 Thou *art* good, and **doest g**; teach me thy 2895
119:71 *It is* **g** for me that I have been afflicted; that 2896
119:122 Be surety for thy servant for **g**: let not 2896
122: 9 of the LORD our God I will seek thy **g**. 2896
125: 4 **Do g**, O LORD, unto *those that be* good, 2895
125: 4 unto *those that be* **g**, and to *them that are* 2896
128: 5 thou shalt see the **g** of Jerusalem all 2898
133: 1 how **g** and how pleasant *it is* for brethren to 2896
135: 3 Praise the LORD; for the LORD *is* **g**: 2896
136: 1 O give thanks unto the LORD; for *he is* **g**: 2896
143:10 thy spirit *is* **g**; lead me into the land of 2896
145: 9 The LORD *is* **g** to all: and his tender 2896
147: 1 for *it is* **g** to sing *praises* unto our God; 2896
Pr 2: 9 judgment, and equity; *yea,* every **g** path. 2896
2:20 That thou mayest walk in the way of **g** 2896
3: 4 and **g** understanding in the sight of God and 2896
3:27 Withhold not **g** from them to whom it is 2896
4: 2 For I give you **g** doctrine, forsake you not 2896
11:17 The merciful man **doeth g** to his own soul: 1580
11:23 The desire of the righteous *is* only **g**: *but* 2896
11:27 He that diligently seeketh **g** procureth 2896
12: 2 A **g** *man* obtaineth favour of the LORD: 2896
12:14 A man shall be satisfied *with* **g** by the fruit 2896
12:25 it stoop: but a **g** word maketh it glad. 2896
13: 2 A man shall eat **g** by the fruit of *his* mouth: 2896
13:15 **G** understanding giveth favour: but the way 2896
13:21 but to the righteous **g** shall be repayed. 2896
13:22 A **g** *man* leaveth an inheritance to *his* 2896
14:14 and a **g** man *shall be satisfied* from himself. 2896
14:19 The evil bow before the **g**; and the wicked 2896
14:22 and truth *shall be to* them that devise **g**. 2896
15: 3 in every place, beholding the evil and the **g**. 2896
15:23 a word *spoken* in due season, how **g** *is it!* 2896
15:30 *and* a **g** report maketh the bones fat. 2896
16:20 that handleth a matter wisely shall find **g**: 2896
16:29 and leadeth him into the way *that is* not **g**. 2896
17:13 Whoso rewardeth evil for **g**, evil shall not 2896
17:20 He that hath a froward heart findeth no **g**: 2896
17:22 A merry heart **doeth g** *like* a medicine: but 3190
17:26 Also to punish the just *is* not **g**, *nor* to strike 2896
18: 5 *It is* not **g** to accept the person of 2896
18:22 *Whoso* findeth a wife findeth a **g** *thing,* and 2896
19: 2 the soul *be* without knowledge, *it is* not **g**; 2896
19: 8 he that keepeth understanding shall find **g**. 2896
20:18 by counsel: and with **g advice** make war. 8458
20:23 the LORD; and a false balance *is* not **g**. 2896
22: 1 A **g** name *is* rather to be chosen than great NIH
24:13 My son, eat thou honey, because *it is* **g**; and 2896
24:23 *It is* not **g** to have respect of persons in 2896
24:25 and a **g** blessing shall come upon them. 2896
25:25 so *is* **g** news from a far country. 2896
25:27 *It is* not **g** to eat much honey: so *for men* to 2896
28:10 the upright shall have **g** *things* in 2896
28:21 To have respect of persons *is* not **g**: for for 2896
31:12 She will do him **g** and not evil all the days 2896
31:18 She perceiveth that her merchandise *is* **g**: 2896
Ecc 2: 3 till I might see what *was* that **g** for the sons 2896
2:24 *that* he should make his soul enjoy **g** in his 2896

Ecc 2:26 For *God* giveth to a man that *is* **g** in his 2896
2:26 that *he* may give to *him that is* **g** before 2896
3:12 I know that *there is* no **g** in them, but for *a* 2896
3:12 for *a man* to rejoice, and to do **g** in his life. 2896
3:13 and drink, and enjoy the **g** of all his labour, 2896
4: 8 do I labour, and bereave my soul of **g**? 2896
4: 9 they have a **g** reward for their labour. 2896
5:11 what **g** *is there* to the owners thereof, 3788
5:18 *it is* **g** and comely *for one* to eat and 2896
5:18 to enjoy the **g** of all his labour that he 2896
6: 3 his soul be not filled with **g**, and also *that* 2896
6: 6 years twice *told,* yet hath he seen no **g**: 2896
6:12 For who knoweth what *is* **g** for man in *this* 2896
7: 1 A **g** name *is* better than precious ointment; NIH
7:11 Wisdom *is* **g** with an inheritance: and *by it* 2896
7:18 *It is* **g** that thou shouldest take hold of this; 2896
7:20 upon earth, that doeth **g**, and sinneth not. 2896
9: 2 to the **g** and to the clean, and to 2896
9: 2 as *is* the **g**, so *is* the sinner; *and* he that 2896
9:18 of war: but one sinner destroyeth much **g**. 2896
11: 6 that, or whether they both *shall be* alike **g**. 2896
12: 9 he **gave g heed**, and sought out, *and* set in 239
12:14 with every secret *thing,* whether *it be* **g**, or 2896
SS 1: 3 Because of the savour of thy **g** ointments 2896
2:13 the vines *with* the tender grape give a **g** NIH
Isa 1:19 and obedient, ye shall eat the **g** of the land: 2898
5:20 Woe unto them that call evil **g**, and good 2896
5:20 unto them that call evil good, and **g** evil; 2896
7:15 know to refuse the evil, and choose the **g**. 2896
7:16 know to refuse the evil, and choose the **g**, 2896
38: 3 and have done *that* which *is* **g** in thy sight. 2896
39: 8 **G** *is* the word of the LORD which thou 2896
40: 9 O Zion, that **bringest g tidings**, get thee up 1319
40: 9 O Jerusalem, that **bringest g tidings**, lift up 1319
41: 6 *one* said to his brother, Be of **g courage**. 2388
41:23 yea, **do g**, or do evil, that we may be 3190
41:27 to Jerusalem one that **bringeth g tidings**. 1319
52: 7 are the feet of him that **bringeth g tidings**, 1319
52: 7 that **bringeth g tidings** of good, 1319
52: 7 that bringeth good tidings of **g**, 2896
55: 2 eat ye *that which is* **g**, and let your soul 2896
61: 1 me to **preach g tidings unto** the meek; 1319
65: 2 which walketh *in* a way *that was* not **g**, 2896
Jer 4:22 but to **do g** they have no knowledge. 3190
5:25 your sins have withholden **g** *things* from 2896
6:16 where *is* the **g** way, and walk therein, 2896
8:15 no **g** *came; and* for a time of health, and 2896
10: 5 do evil, neither also *is it* in them to **do g**. 3190
13:10 be as this girdle, which is **g** for nothing. 6743
13:23 *then* may ye also **do g**, that are accustomed 3190
14:11 Pray not for this people for *their* **g**. 2896
14:19 *we* looked for peace, and *there is* no **g**; and 2896
17: 6 and shall not see when **g** cometh; 2896
18: 4 as seemed **g** to the potter to make *it.* 3474
18:10 not my voice, then I will repent of the **g**, 2896
18:11 and **make** your ways and your doings **g**. 3190
18:20 Shall evil be recompensed for **g**? for they 2896
18:20 that I stood before thee to speak **g** for them, 2896
21:10 for evil, and not for **g**, saith the LORD: 2896
24: 2 One basket *had* very **g** figs, *even* like 2896
24: 3 the **g** figs, very good; and the evil, 2896
24: 3 the good figs, very **g**; and the evil, 2896
24: 5 Like these **g** figs, so will I acknowledge 2896
24: 5 *into* the land of the Chaldeans for *their* **g**. 2896
24: 6 For I will set mine eyes upon them for **g**, 2896
26:14 do with me as seemeth **g** and meet unto 2896
29:10 perform my **g** word towards you, in causing 2896
29:32 neither shall he behold the **g** that I will do 2896
32:39 for the **g** of them, and of their children after 2896
32:40 not turn away from them, to **do** them **g**; 3190
32:41 I will rejoice over them to **do** them **g**, and 2895
32:42 will I bring upon them all the **g** that I have 2896
33: 9 which shall hear all the **g** that I do unto 2896
33:11 for the LORD *is* **g**; for his mercy *endureth* 2896
33:14 that I will perform *that* **g** thing which I have 2896
39:16 words upon this city for evil, and not for **g**; 2896
40: 4 If it seem **g** unto thee to come with me *into* 2896
40: 4 whither it seemeth **g** and convenient for 2896
42: 6 Whether *it be* **g**, or whether *it be* evil, 2896
44:27 *will* watch over them for evil, and not for **g**: 2896
La 3:25 The LORD *is* **g** unto them that wait for 2896
3:26 *It is* **g** that *a man should* both hope and 2896
3:27 *It is* **g** for a man that he bear the yoke in his 2896
3:38 of the most High proceedeth not evil and **g**. 2896
Eze 16:50 therefore I took them away as I saw **g**. NIH
17: 8 It *was* planted in a **g** soil by great waters, 2896
18:18 did *that* which *is* not **g** among his people, 2896
20:25 I gave them also statutes *that were* not **g**, 2896
24: 4 *even* every **g** piece, the thigh, and 2896
34:14 I will feed them in a **g** pasture, and 2896
34:14 there shall they lie in a **g** fold, and *in* a fat 2896
34:18 unto you to have eaten up the **g** pasture, 2896
36:31 your doings that *were* not **g**, and shall lothe 2896
Da 4: 2 I thought it **g** to shew the signs and 8232
Hos 4:13 and elms, because the shadow thereof *is* **g**: 2896
8: 3 Israel hath cast off *the thing that is* **g**: 2896
Am 5:14 Seek **g**, and not evil, that ye may live: and 2896
5:15 love the **g**, and establish judgment in 2896
9: 4 mine eyes upon them for evil, and not for **g**. 2896
Mic 1:12 inhabitant of Maroth waited carefully for **g**: 2896
2: 7 do not my words **do g** to him that walketh 3190
3: 2 Who hate the **g**, and love the evil; 2896
6: 8 He hath shewed thee, O man, what *is* **g**; and 2896
7: 2 The **g** *man* is perished out of the earth: and 2623
Na 1: 7 The LORD *is* **g**, a strong hold in the day 2896
1:15 the feet of him that **bringeth g tidings**, 1319
Zep 1:12 in their heart, The LORD will not **do g**, 3190
Zec 1:13 the angel that talked with me *with* **g** words 2896
11:12 unto them, If ye think **g**, give *me* my price, 2896
Mal 2:13 or receiveth *it with* **g will** at your hand. 7522
2:17 Every one that doeth evil *is* **g** in the sight of 2896
Mt 3:10 every tree which bringeth not forth **g** fruit *2570*
5:13 it is thenceforth **g** for nothing, but to be cast *2480*
5:16 that they may see your **g** works, and *2570*
5:44 do **g** to them that hate you, and pray for *2573*

Mt 5:45 his sun to rise on the evil and *on* the **g**, *18*
7:11 know how to give **g** gifts unto your children, *18*
7:11 in heaven give **g** *things* to them that ask him? *18*
7:17 *Even* so every **g** tree bringeth forth good fruit; *18*
7:17 so every good tree bringeth forth **g** fruit; *2570*
7:18 A **g** tree cannot bring forth evil fruit, *18*
7:18 neither *can* a corrupt tree bring forth **g** fruit. *2570*
7:19 Every tree that bringeth not forth **g** fruit is *2570*
8:30 And there was a **g way off** from them a *3112*
9: 2 Son, **be of g cheer**; thy sins be forgiven *2293*
9:22 he said, Daughter, **be of g comfort**; *2293*
11:26 Father: for so it seemed **g** in thy sight. *2107*
12:33 Either make the tree **g**, and his fruit good; *2570*
12:33 Either make the tree good, and his fruit **g**; *2570*
12:34 speak **g** *things?* for out of the abundance of *18*
12:35 A **g** man out of the good treasure of the heart *18*
12:35 A good man out of the **g** treasure of the heart *18*
12:35 treasure of the heart bringeth forth **g** *things:* *18*
13: 8 But other fell into **g** ground, and *2570*
13:23 But he that received seed into the **g** ground *2570*
13:24 unto a man which sowed **g** seed in his field: *2570*
13:27 Sir, didst not thou sow **g** seed in thy field? *2570*
13:37 He that soweth the **g** seed is the Son of *2570*
13:38 the **g** seed are the children of the kingdom; *2570*
13:48 and gathered the **g** into vessels, but cast *2570*
14:27 spake unto them, saying, **Be of g cheer**; *2293*
17: 4 unto Jesus, Lord, it is **g** for us to be here: *2570*
19:10 so with *his* wife, it is not **g** to marry. *4851*
19:16 one came and said unto him, **G** Master, *18*
19:16 Good Master, what **g** *thing* shall I do, *18*
19:17 And he said unto him, Why callest thou me **g**? *18*
19:17 *there is* none **g** but one, *that is,* God: but *18*
20:15 mine own? Is thine eye evil, because I am **g**? *18*
22:10 all as many as they found, both bad and **g**: *18*
25:21 Well *done, thou* **g** and faithful servant: *18*
25:23 unto him, Well *done,* **g** and faithful servant; *18*
26:10 for she hath wrought a **g** work upon me. *2570*
26:24 it had been **g** for that man if he had not *2570*
Mk 3: 4 Is it lawful to **do g** on the sabbath days, or *15*
4: 8 And other fell on **g** ground, and did yield *2570*
4:20 And these are they which are sown on **g** *2570*
6:50 and saith unto them, **Be of g cheer**: *2293*
9: 5 to Jesus, Master, it is **g** for us to be here: *2570*
9:50 Salt *is* **g**: but if the salt have lost his *2570*
10:17 and kneeled to him, and asked him, **G** Master, *18*
10:18 Jesus said unto him, Why callest thou me **g**? *18*
10:18 *there is* none **g** but one, *that is,* God. *18*
10:49 saying unto him, **Be of g comfort**, rise; *2293*
14: 6 you her? she hath wrought a **g** work on me. *2570*
14: 7 and whensoever ye will ye may do them **g**: *2095*
14:21 **g** were it for that man if he had never been *2570*
Lk 1: 3 It **seemed g** to me also, having had perfect *1380*
1:53 He hath filled the hungry with **g** *things;* and *18*
2:10 I **bring** you **g tidings** of great joy, *2097*
2:14 and on earth peace, **g will** towards men. *2107*
3: 9 which bringeth not forth **g** fruit is hewn *2570*
6: 9 *thing;* Is it lawful on the sabbath days to **do g**, *15*
6:27 your enemies, do **g** to them which hate you, *2573*
6:33 And if ye **do g** to them which do good to you, *15*
6:33 And if ye do good to them which **do g** to you, *15*
6:35 and **do g**, and lend, hoping for nothing again; *15*
6:38 **g** measure, pressed down, and *2570*
6:43 For a **g** tree bringeth not forth corrupt fruit; *2570*
6:43 neither doth a corrupt tree bring forth **g** *2570*
6:45 A **g** man out of the good treasure of his heart *18*
6:45 A good man out of the **g** treasure of his heart *18*
6:45 of his heart bringeth forth that which is **g**; *18*
8: 8 And other fell on **g** ground, and sprang up, *18*
8:15 But that on the **g** ground are they, which in *2570*
8:15 which in an honest and **g** heart, having heard *18*
8:48 said unto her, Daughter, **be of g comfort**: *2293*
9:33 unto Jesus, Master, it is **g** for us to be here: *2570*
10:21 Father; for so it seemed **g** in thy sight. *2107*
10:42 and Mary hath chosen *that* **g** part, which shall *18*
11:13 know how to give **g** gifts unto your children: *18*
12:32 for it is your Father's **g pleasure** to give *2106*
14:34 Salt *is* **g**: but if the salt have lost his savour, *2570*
16:25 thou in thy lifetime receivedst thy **g** *things,* *18*
18:18 a certain ruler asked him, saying, **G** Master, *18*
18:19 Jesus said unto him, Why callest thou me **g**? *18*
18:19 me good? none *is* **g**, save one, *that is,* God. *18*
19:17 And he said unto him, Well, *thou* **g** servant: *18*
23:50 a counseller; *and he was* a **g** man, and a just: *18*
Jn 1:46 Can there any **g** *thing* come out of Nazareth? *18*
2:10 Every man at the beginning doth set forth **g** *2570*
2:10 *but* thou hast kept the **g** wine until now. *2570*
5:29 they that have done **g**, unto the resurrection of *18*
7:12 some said, He is a **g** *man:* others said, Nay; *18*
10:11 I am the **g** shepherd: the good shepherd *2570*
10:11 the **g** shepherd giveth his life for the sheep. *2570*
10:14 I am the **g** shepherd, and know my *sheep,* *2570*
10:32 Many **g** works have I shewed you from my *2570*
10:33 saying, For a **g** work we stone thee not; *2570*
16:33 but **be of g cheer**; I have overcome *2293*
Ac 4: 9 If we this day be examined of the **g deed** *2108*
9:36 this *woman* was full of **g** works and *18*
10:22 of **g report** among all the nation of *3140*
10:38 who went about **doing g**, and healing all *2109*
11:24 For he was a **g** man, and full of the Holy *18*
14:17 not himself without witness, in that he **did g**, *15*
15: 7 ye know how that a **g while ago** *575+744+2250*
15:25 It **seemed g** unto us, being assembled with *1380*
15:28 For it **seemed g** to the Holy Ghost, and *1380*
15:38 But Paul **thought** not **g** to take him with *515*
18:18 *after this* tarried *there* yet a **g while**, *2250+2425*
22:12 **having a g report** of all the Jews which *3140*
23: 1 I have lived in all **g** conscience before God *18*
23:11 by him, and said, **Be of g cheer**, Paul: *2293*
27:22 And now I exhort you to **be of g cheer**: *2114*
27:25 Wherefore, sirs, **be of g cheer**: for I believe *2114*
27:36 Then were they all **of g cheer**, and *2115*
Ro 2:10 and peace, to every *man* that worketh **g**, *18*
3: 8 that we say,) Let us do evil, that **g** may come? *18*
3:12 there is none that doeth **g**, no, not one. *5544*
5: 7 yet peradventure for a **g** *man* some would *18*

Ro 7:12 and the commandment holy, and just, and **g**. 18
7:13 then that which is **g** made death unto me? 18
7:13 working death in me by that which is **g**; 18
7:16 I consent unto the law that *it is* **g**. 2570
7:18 dwelleth no **g** *thing:* for to will is present with 18
7:18 *how* to perform that which is **g** I find not. 2570
7:19 For the **g** that I would I do not: but the evil 18
7:21 I find then a law, that, when I would do **g**, 2570
8:28 work together for **g** to them that love God, 18
9:11 yet born, neither having done any **g** or evil, 18
10:15 of peace, and bring glad tidings of **g** *things!* 18
11:24 contrary to nature into a **g olive tree**: 2565
12: 2 that ye may prove what *is that* **g**, and 18
12: 9 *that which is* evil; cleave to *that which is* **g**. 18
12:21 overcome of evil, but overcome evil with **g**. 18
13: 3 For rulers are not a terror to **g** works, but 18
13: 3 do *that which is* **g**, and thou shalt have praise 18
13: 4 For he is the minister of God to thee for **g**. 18
14:16 Let not then your **g** be evil spoken of: 18
14:21 *It is* **g** neither to eat flesh, nor to drink 2570
15: 2 please *his* neighbour for *his* **g** to edification. 18
16:18 and by **g words** and fair speeches deceive 5542
16:19 I would have you wise unto *that which is* **g**, 18
1Co 5: 6 Your glorying *is* not **g**. Know ye not that a 2570
7: 1 *It is* **g** for a man not to touch a woman. 2570
7: 8 It is **g** for them if they abide even as I. 2570
7:26 that this is **g** for the present distress, 2570
7:26 *I say,* that *it is* **g** for a man so to be. 2570
15:33 evil communications corrupt **g** manners. 5543
2Co 5:10 to that he hath done, whether *it be* **g** or bad. 18
6: 8 and dishonour, by evil report and **g report**: 2162
9: 8 in all *things,* may abound to every **g** work: 18
13:11 Be perfect, be **of g comfort**, be of one 3870
Gal 4:18 But *it is* **g** to be zealously affected always 2570
4:18 to be zealously affected always in a **g** *thing,* 2570
6: 6 unto him that teacheth in all **g** *things.* 18
6:10 let us do **g** unto all *men,* especially unto them 18
Eph 1: 5 according to the **g pleasure** of his will, 2107
1: 9 according to his **g pleasure** which he had 2107
2:10 created in Christ Jesus unto **g** works, 18
4:28 working with *his* hands the *thing which is* **g**, 18
4:29 but that which *is* **g** to the use of edifying, 18
6: 7 With **g will** doing service, as to the Lord, 2133
6: 8 Knowing that whatsoever **g** *thing* any man 18
Php 1: 6 **g** work in you will perform *it* until the day of 18
1:15 of envy and strife; and some also of **g will**: 2107
2:13 both to will and to do of *his* **g pleasure**. 2107
2:19 that I also may be **of g comfort**, when I 2174
4: 8 whatsoever *things are* of **g report**; 2163
Col 1:10 being fruitful in every **g** work, and 18
1Th 3: 1 we **thought** it **g** to be left at Athens alone; 2106
3: 6 and **brought** us **g tidings** of your faith and 2097
3: 6 and that ye have **g** remembrance of us always, 18
5:15 unto any *man;* but ever follow *that which is* **g**, 18
5:21 Prove all *things;* hold fast *that which is* **g**. 2570
2Th 1:11 fulfil all the **g pleasure** of *his* goodness, 2107
2:16 and **g** hope through grace, 18
2:17 and stablish you in every **g** word and work. 18
1Ti 1: 5 and *of* a **g** conscience, and *of* faith unfeigned: 18
1: 8 But we know that the law *is* **g**, if a man use 2570
1:18 that thou by them mightest war a **g** warfare; 2570
1:19 Holding faith, and a **g** conscience; 18
2: 3 For this *is* **g** and acceptable in the sight of 2570
2:10 women professing godliness) with **g** works. 18
3: 1 the office of a bishop, he desireth a **g** work. 2570
3: 2 vigilant, sober, of **g behaviour**, given to 2887
3: 7 Moreover he must have a **g** report of them 2570
3:13 well purchase to themselves a **g** degree, 2570
4: 4 For every creature of God *is* **g**, and 2570
4: 6 thou shalt be a **g** minister of Jesus Christ, 2570
4: 6 up in the words of faith and of **g** doctrine, 2570
5: 4 for that is **g** and acceptable before God. 2570
5:10 Well reported of for **g** works; if she have 2570
5:10 if she have diligently followed every **g** work. 18
5:25 Likewise also the **g** works *of some* are 2570
6:12 Fight the **g** fight of faith, lay hold on 2570
6:12 hast professed a **g** profession before many 2570
6:13 who before Pontius Pilate witnessed a **g** 2570
6:18 That *they* **do g**, that *they* be rich in good 14
6:18 that *they* be rich in **g** works, ready to 2570
6:19 Laying up in store for themselves a **g** 2570
2Ti 1:14 *That* **g thing** which was committed unto 2570
2: 3 as a **g** soldier of Jesus Christ. 2570
2:21 master's use, *and* prepared unto every **g** work. 18
3: 3 fierce, **despisers of** *those that are* **g**, 865
3:17 throughly furnished unto all **g** works. 18
4: 7 I have fought a **g** fight, I have finished *my* 2570
Tit 1: 8 **a lover of g** *men,* sober, just, holy, 5358
1:16 disobedient, and unto every **g** work reprobate. 18
2: 3 given to much wine, **teachers of g things**; 2567
2: 5 *To be* discreet, chaste, keepers at home, **g**, 18
2: 7 In all *things* shewing thyself a pattern of **g** 2570
2:10 Not purloining, but shewing all **g** fidelity; 18
2:14 a peculiar people, zealous of **g** works. 2570
3: 1 obey magistrates, to be ready to every **g** work, 18
3: 8 God might be careful to maintain **g** works. 2570
3: 8 These *things* are **g** and profitable unto men. 2570
3:14 And let ours also learn to maintain **g** works 2570
Phm 1: 6 every **g** *thing* which is in you in Christ Jesus. 18
Heb 5:14 their senses exercised to discern both **g** 2570
6: 5 And have tasted the **g** word of God, and 2570
9:11 But Christ being come a high priest of **g** 18
10: 1 For the law having a shadow of **g** *things* to 18
10:24 to provoke unto love and to **g** works: 2570
11: 2 For by it the elders **obtained a g report**. 3140
11:12 and him **as g as dead**, *so many* as the stars 3499
11:39 having **obtained a g report** through faith, 3140
13: 9 For *it is* a **g** *thing* that the heart be 2570
13:16 But to **do g** and to communicate forget not: 2140
13:18 for we trust we have a **g** conscience, in all 2570
13:21 Make you perfect in every **g** work to do his 18
Jas 1:17 Every **g** gift and every perfect gift is from 18
2: 3 and say unto him, Sit thou here in a **g** place; 2573
3:13 let him shew out of a **g** conversation his 2570
3:17 full of mercy and **g** fruits, without partiality, 18
Jas 4:17 Therefore to him that knoweth to do **g**, and 2570
1Pe 2:12 they may by *your* **g** works, *which* they shall 2570
2:18 not only to the **g** and gentle, but also to 18
3:10 For he that will love life, and see **g** days, 18
3:11 Let him eschew evil, and do **g**; let him seek 18
3:13 if ye be followers of *that which is* **g**? 18
3:16 Having a **g** conscience; that, whereas they 18
3:16 falsely accuse your **g** conversation in Christ. 18
3:21 but the answer of a **g** conscience toward God,) 18
4:10 as **g** stewards of the manifold grace of God. 2570
1Jn 3:17 But whoso hath *this* world's **g**, and seeth his 979
3Jn 1:11 not *that which is* evil, but *that which is* **g**. 18
1:11 He that **doeth g** is of God: but he that doeth 15
1:12 Demetrius **hath g report** of all *men,* and 3140

GOODLIER (1) [GOOD]

1Sa 9: 2 the children of Israel a **g** person than he: 2896

GOODLIEST (2) [GOOD]

1Sa 8:16 your **g** young men, and your asses, and put 2896
1Ki 20: 3 and thy children, *even* the **g**, *are* mine. 2896

GOODLINESS (1) [GOOD]

Isa 40: 6 all the **g** thereof *is* as the flower of the field: 2617

GOODLY (33) [GOOD]

Ge 27:15 Rebekah took **g** raiment of her eldest son 2532
39: 6 Joseph was a **g** *person,* and 3303+8389
49:21 *is* a hind let loose: he giveth **g** words. 8233
Ex 2: 2 when she saw him that he *was* a **g** *child,* 2896
39:28 **g** bonnets *of* fine linen, and linen breeches 6287
Lev 23:40 you on the first day the boughs of **g** trees, 1926
Nu 24: 5 How **g** are thy tents, O Jacob, *and* 2895
31:10 they dwelt, and all their **g castles**, with fire. 2918
Dt 3:25 that **g** mountain, and Lebanon. 2896
6:10 and to Jacob, to give thee great and **g** cities, 2896
8:12 and hast built **g** houses, and dwelt *therein;* 2896
Jos 7:21 When I saw among the spoils a **g** 2896
1Sa 9: 2 *was* Saul, a choice *young man,* and a **g**: 2896
16:12 a beautiful countenance, and **g** to look to. 2896
2Sa 23:21 he slew an Egyptian, a **g** man: and 4758
1Ki 1: 6 he also *was* a very **g** *man;* and 2896+8389
2Ch 36:10 with the **g** vessels of the house of 2532
36:19 and destroyed all the **g** vessels thereof. 4261
Job 39:13 *Gavest thou* the **g** wings unto the peacocks? 7443
Ps 16: 6 in pleasant *places;* yea, I have a **g** heritage. 8231
80:10 the boughs thereof *were like* the **g** cedars. 410
Jer 3:19 a **g** heritage of the hosts of nations? 6643
11:16 A green olive tree, fair, *and* of **g** fruit: 8389
Eze 17: 8 *it* might bear fruit, that *it* might be a **g** vine. 155
17:23 and bear fruit, and be a **g** cedar: 117
Hos 10: 1 of his land they have **made g** images. 2895
Joel 3: 5 have carried into your temples my **g** 2896
Zec 10: 3 hath made them as his **g** horse in the battle. 1935
11:13 a **g** price that I was prised at of them. And I 145
Mt 13:45 like unto a merchant man, seeking **g** pearls: 2570
Lk 21: 5 how it was adorned with **g** stones and gifts, 2570
Jas 2: 2 in **g** apparel, and there come in also a poor 2986
Rev 18:14 *were* dainty and **g** are departed from thee, 2986

GOODMAN (6) [GOOD, MAN]

Pr 7:19 For the **g** *is* not at home, he is gone a long 376
Mt 20:11 they murmured against the **g of the house**, 3617
24:43 that if the **g of the house** had known in 3617
Mk 14:14 say ye to the **g of the house**, The Master 3617
Lk 12:39 that if the **g of the house** had known what 3617
22:11 And ye shall say unto the **g** of the house, 3617

GOODNESS (50) [GOOD]

Ex 18: 9 Jethro rejoiced for all the **g** which 2896
33:19 I will make all my **g** pass before thee, and 2898
34: 6 longsuffering, and abundant in **g** and truth, 2617
Nu 10:32 *that* what **g** the LORD shall do unto us, 2896
Jdg 8:35 according to all the **g** which he had shewed 2896
2Sa 7:28 thou hast promised this **g** unto thy servant: 2896
1Ki 8:66 glad of heart for all the **g** that the LORD 2896
1Ch 17:26 and hast promised this **g** unto thy servant: 2896
2Ch 6:41 and let thy saints rejoice in **g**. 2896
7:10 merry in heart for the **g** that the LORD 2896
32:32 of the acts of Hezekiah, and his **g**, behold, 2617
35:26 the rest of the acts of Josiah, and his **g**, 2617
Ne 9:25 and delighted themselves in thy great **g**. 2898
9:35 in thy great **g** that thou gavest them, and 2898
Ps 16: 2 *art* my Lord: my **g** *extendeth* not to thee; 2896
21: 3 thou preventest him *with* the blessings of **g**: 2896
23: 6 Surely **g** and mercy shall follow me all 2896
27:13 **g** of the LORD in the land of the living. 2898
31:19 O how great *is* thy **g**, which thou hast laid 2898
33: 5 the earth is full *of* the **g** of the LORD. 2617
52: 1 O mighty *man?* the **g** of God *endureth* 2617
65: 4 we shall be satisfied with the **g** of thy 2898
65:11 Thou crownest the year with thy **g**; and 2898
68:10 O God, hast prepared of thy **g** for the poor. 2896
107: 8 *men* would praise the LORD *for* his **g**, 2617
107: 9 and filleth the hungry soul *with* **g**. 2896
107:15 *men* would praise the LORD *for* his **g**, 2617
107:21 *men* would praise the LORD *for* his **g**, 2617
107:31 *men* would praise the LORD *for* his **g**, 2617
144: 2 My **g**, and my fortress; my high tower, and 2617
145: 7 abundantly utter the memory of thy great **g**, 2898
Pr 20: 6 men will proclaim every one his own **g**: 2617
Isa 63: 7 and the great **g** towards the house of Israel, 2898
Jer 2: 7 to eat the fruit thereof and the **g** thereof; 2898
31:12 shall flow *together* to the **g** of the LORD, 2898
31:14 my people shall be satisfied with my **g**, 2898
33: 9 they shall fear and tremble for all the **g** and 2896
Hos 3: 5 fear the LORD and his **g** in the latter days. 2898
6: 4 for your **g** *is* as a morning cloud, and as 2617
10: 1 according to the **g** of his land they have 2896
Zec 9:17 For how great *is* his **g**, and how great *is* his 2898
Ro 2: 4 Or despisest thou the riches of his **g** and 5544
2: 4 not knowing that the **g** of God leadeth thee 5543
11:22 Behold therefore the **g** and severity of God: 5544
11:22 but toward thee, **g**, if thou continue in *his* 5544
Ro 11:22 goodness, if thou continue in *his* **g**: 5544
15:14 my brethren, that ye also are full of **g**, 19
Gal 5:22 joy, peace, longsuffering, gentleness, **g**, faith, 19
Eph 5: 9 (For the fruit of the Spirit *is* in all **g** and 19
2Th 1:11 and fulfil all the good pleasure of *his* **g**, and 19

GOODNESS' (1) [GOOD]

Ps 25: 7 mercy remember thou me for thy **g** sake, 2898

GOODS (42) [GOOD]

Ge 14:11 they took all the **g** of Sodom and 7399
14:12 dwelt in Sodom, and his **g**, and departed. 7399
14:16 he brought back all the **g**, and also brought 7399
14:16 his **g**, and the women also, and the people. 7399
14:21 me the persons, and take the **g** to thyself. 7399
24:10 for all the **g** of his master *were* in his hand: 2898
31:18 all his **g** which he had gotten, the cattle of 7399
46: 6 they took their cattle, and their **g**, 7399
Ex 22: 8 have put his hand unto his neighbour's **g**. 4399
22:11 not put his hand unto his neighbour's **g**; 4399
Nu 16:32 that *appertained* unto Korah, and all *their* **g**. 7399
31: 9 and all their flocks, and all their **g**. 2428
35: 3 and for their **g**, and for all their beasts. 7399
Dt 28:11 the LORD shall make thee plenteous in **g**, 2896
2Ch 21:14 thy children, and thy wives, and all thy **g**: 7399
Ezr 1: 4 and with gold, and with **g**, and with beasts, 7399
1: 6 with **g**, and with beasts, and with precious 7399
6: 8 that of the king's **g**, *even* of the tribute 5232
7:26 or to confiscation of **g**, or to imprisonment. 5232
Ne 9:25 fat land, and possessed houses full *of* all **g**, 2898
Job 20:10 the poor, and his hands shall restore their **g**. 202
20:21 therefore shall no *man* look for his **g**. 2898
20:28 *his* **g** *shall* flow away in the day of his NIH
Ecc 5:11 When **g** increase, they are increased that eat 2896
Eze 38:12 which have gotten cattle and **g**, that dwell 7075
38:13 and gold, to take *away* cattle and **g**, 7075
Zep 1:13 Therefore their **g** shall become a booty, and 2428
Mt 12:29 and spoil his **g**, except he first bind 4632
24:47 That he shall make him ruler over all his **g**. 5225
25:14 and delivered unto them his **g**. 5225
Mk 3:27 and spoil his **g**, except he will first bind 4632
Lk 6:30 of him that taketh away thy **g** ask *them* not NIG
11:21 keepeth his palace, his **g** are in peace: 5225
12:18 there will I bestow all my fruits and my **g**. 18
12:19 thou hast much **g** laid up for many years; 18
15:12 give me the portion of **g** that falleth to *me.* 3776
16: 1 accused unto him that he had wasted his **g**. 5225
19: 8 Lord, the half of my **g** I give to the poor; 5225
Ac 2:45 And sold their possessions and **g**, and 5223
1Co 13: 3 And though I bestow all my **g** to feed 5225
Heb 10:34 and took joyfully the spoiling of your **g**, 5225
Rev 3:17 and **increased with g**, and have need of 4147

GOPHER (1)

Ge 6:14 Make thee an ark of **g** wood; rooms shalt 1613

GORE (1) [GORED]

Ex 21:28 If an ox **g** a man or a woman, that they die: 5055

GORED (2) [GORE]

Ex 21:31 Whether he have **g** a son, or have gored a 5055
21:31 he have gored a son, or have **g** a daughter, 5055

GORGEOUS (1) [GORGEOUSLY]

Lk 23:11 mocked *him,* and arrayed him in a **g** robe, 2986

GORGEOUSLY (2) [GORGEOUS]

Eze 23:12 captains and rulers clothed **most g**, 4358
Lk 7:25 they which are **g** apparelled, and 1722+1741

GOSHEN (15)

Ge 45:10 thou shalt dwell in the land of **G**, and 1657
46:28 him unto Joseph, to direct his face unto **G**; 1657
46:28 and they came into the land of **G**. 1657
46:29 to **G**, and presented himself unto him; 1657
46:34 that ye may dwell in the land of **G**; 1657
47: 1 and behold, they *are* in the land of **G**. 1657
47: 4 let thy servants dwell in the land of **G**. 1657
47: 6 to dwell; in the land of **G** let them dwell: 1657
47:27 in the land of Egypt, in the country of **G**; 1657
50: 8 and their herds, they left in the land of **G**. 1657
Ex 8:22 I will sever in that day the land of **G**, 1657
9:26 Only in the land of **G**, where the children 1657
Jos 10:41 and all the country of **G**, even unto Gibeon. 1657
11:16 all the south *country,* and all the land of **G**, 1657
15:51 **G**, and Holon, and Giloh; eleven cities with 1657

GOSPEL (101) [GOSPEL'S]

Mt 4:23 and preaching the **g** of the kingdom, 2098
9:35 and preaching the **g** of the kingdom, and 2098
11: 5 and the poor have **the g preached** to them. 2097
24:14 And this **g** of the kingdom shall be 2098
26:13 Wheresoever this **g** shall be preached in 2098
Mk 1: 1 The beginning of the **g** of Jesus Christ, 2098
1:14 preaching the **g** of the kingdom of God, 2098
1:15 God is at hand: repent ye, and believe the **g**. 2098
13:10 And the **g** must first be published among all 2098
14: 9 Wheresoever this **g** shall be preached 2098
16:15 and preach the **g** to every creature. 2098
Lk 4:18 he hath anointed me to **preach the g** to 2097
7:22 are raised, to the poor the **g** is **preached**. 2097
9: 6 **preaching the g**, and healing every where. 2097
20: 1 and **preached the g**, the chief priests and 2097
Ac 8:25 **preached the g** in many villages of 2097
14: 7 And there they **preached the g**. 2097
14:21 And when they had **preached the g** to that 2097
15: 7 by my mouth should hear the word of the **g**, 2098
16:10 called us for to **preach the g** unto them. 2097
20:24 to testify the **g** of the grace of God. 2098
Ro 1: 1 *be* an apostle, separated unto the **g** of God, 2098
1: 9 whom I serve with my spirit in the **g** of his 2098
1:15 I am ready to **preach the g** to you that are 2097
1:16 For I am not ashamed of the **g** of Christ: 2098
2:16 of men by Jesus Christ according to my **g**. 2098

Ro 10:15 the feet of them that **preach the g** of peace, 2097
10:16 But they have not all obeyed the **g**. 2098
11:28 As concerning the **g**, *they are* enemies for 2098
15:16 ministering the **g** of God, that the offering 2098
15:19 I have fully preached the **g** of Christ. 2098
15:20 Yea, so have I strived to **preach the g**, 2097
15:29 fulness of the blessing of the **g** of Christ. 2098
16:25 of power to stablish you according to my **g**, 2098
1Co 1:17 sent me not to baptize, but to **preach the g**: 2097
4:15 Jesus I have begotten you through the **g**. 2098
9:12 suffer all *things*, lest we should hinder the **g** 2098
9:14 preach the **g** should live of the gospel. 2098
9:14 preach the gospel should live of the **g**. 2098
9:16 For though I **preach the g**, I have nothing 2097
9:16 yea, woe is unto me, if I **preach** not the **g**! 2097
9:17 a dispensation *of the* **g** is committed unto NIG
9:18 *Verily* that, when I **preach the g**, I may 2097
9:18 I may make the **g** of Christ without charge, 2098
9:18 that *I* abuse not my power in the **g**. 2098
15: 1 I declare unto you the **g** which I preached 2098
2Co 2:12 when I came to Troas to *preach* Christ's **g**, 2098
4: 3 But if our **g** be hid, it is hid to them that are 2098
4: 4 lest the light of the glorious **g** of Christ, 2098
8:18 whose praise *is* in the **g** throughout all 2098
9:13 professed subjection unto the **g** of Christ, 2098
10:14 as to you also in *preaching* the **g** of Christ: 2098
10:16 To **preach the g** in the *regions* beyond you, 2097
11: 4 which ye have not received, or another **g**, 2098
11: 7 I have preached to you the **g** of God freely? 2098
Gal 1: 6 you into the grace of Christ unto another **g**: 2098
1: 7 and would pervert the **g** of Christ. 2098
1: 8 **preach** any other **g** unto you than *that* 2097
1: 9 If any *man* **preach** any other **g** unto you 2097
1:11 that the **g** which was preached of me is not 2098
2: 2 communicated unto them *that* **g** which I 2098
2: 5 that the truth of the **g** might continue with 2098
2: 7 when they saw that the **g** of 2098
2: 7 as *the* **g** of the circumcision *was* unto Peter; NIG
2:14 not uprightly according to the truth of the **g**, 2098
3: 8 **preached before the g** unto Abraham, 4283
4:13 flesh I **preached the g** unto you at the first. 2097
Eph 1:13 the word of truth, the **g** of your salvation: 2098
3: 6 partakers of his promise in Christ by the **g**: 2098
6:15 shod with the preparation of the **g** of peace; 2098
6:19 to make known the mystery of the **g**, 2098
Php 1: 5 For your fellowship in the **g** from the first 2098
1: 7 *in* the defence and confirmation of the **g**, 2098
1:12 out rather unto the furtherance of the **g**; 2098
1:17 that I am set for the defence of the **g**. 2098
1:27 be as it becometh the **g** of Christ: 2098
1:27 mind striving together for the faith of the **g**; 2098
2:22 *the* father, he hath served with me in the **g**. 2098
4: 3 *women* which laboured with me in the **g**, 2098
4:15 know also, that in the beginning of the **g**, 2098
Col 1: 5 before in the word of the truth of the **g**; 2098
1:23 *be* not moved away from the hope of the **g**, 2098
1Th 1: 5 For our **g** came not unto you in word only, 2098
2: 2 you the **g** of God with much contention. 2098
2: 4 allowed of God to be put in trust with the **g**, 2098
2: 8 not the **g** of God only, but also our own 2098
2: 9 of you, we preached unto you the **g** of God. 2098
3: 2 and our fellowlabourer in the **g** of Christ, 2098
2Th 1: 8 that obey not the **g** of our Lord Jesus 2098
2:14 Whereunto he called you by our **g**, to 2098
1Ti 1:11 According to the glorious **g** of the blessed 2098
2Ti 1: 8 be thou partaker of the afflictions of the **g** 2098
1:10 and immortality to light through the **g**: 2098
2: 8 raised from the dead according to my **g**: 2098
Phm 1:13 ministered unto me in the bonds of the **g**: 2098
Heb 4: 2 For unto us was **the g preached**, as well as 2097
1Pe 1:12 **preached the g** unto you with the Holy 2097
1:25 word which by the **g** is **preached** unto you. 2097
4: 6 For for this cause was the **g preached** also 2097
4:17 end *be* of them that obey not the **g** of God? 2098
Rev 14: 6 having the everlasting **g** to preach unto 2098

GOSPEL'S (3) [GOSPEL]
Mk 8:35 shall lose his life for my sake and the **g**, 2098
10:29 children, or lands, for my sake, and the **g**, 2098
1Co 9:23 And this I do for the **g** sake, that I might be 2098

GOSSIP See TALEBEARER

GOSSIPS See TATTLERS

GOT (7) [GET]
Ge 36: 6 which he had **g** in the land of Canaan; 7408
39:12 in her hand, and fled, and **g** him out. 3318
39:15 garment with me, and fled, and **g** him out. 3318
Ps 44: 3 For they **g** not the land **in possession** by 3423
Ecc 2: 7 I **g** *me* servants and maidens, and 7069
Jer 13: 2 So I **g** a girdle, according to the word of 7069
13: 4 Take the girdle that thou hast **g**, which *is* 7069

GOTTEN (25) [GET]
Ge 4: 1 and said, I have **g** a man from the LORD. 7069
12: 5 and the souls that they had **g** in Haran; 6213
31: 1 of *that* which *was* of our father's hath he **g** 6213
31:18 all his goods which he had **g**, the cattle of 7408
31:18 his getting, which he had **g** in Padan-aram, 7408
46: 6 which they had **g** in the land of Canaan, 7408
Ex 14:18 when I have **g** me **honour** upon Pharaoh, 3513
Lev 6: 4 thing which he hath **deceitfully g**, 6231+6233
Nu 31:50 what every man hath **g**, *of* jewels of gold, 4672
Dt 8:17 the might of mine hand hath **g** me this 6213
2Sa 17:13 if he be **g** into a city, then shall all Israel 622
Job 28:15 It cannot be **g** for gold, neither shall silver 5414
31:25 and because mine hand had **g** much; 4672
Ps 98: 1 and his holy arm, hath **g** him the **victory**. 3467
Pr 13:11 Wealth *g* by vanity shall be diminished: but NIH
20:21 An inheritance *may be* **g hastily** at 926
Ecc 1:16 have **g more** wisdom than all *they* that 3254
Isa 15: 7 Therefore the abundance they have **g**, and 6213
Jer 48:36 the riches *that* he hath **g** are perished. 6213
Eze 28: 4 with thine understanding thou hast **g** thee 6213
28: 4 hast **g** gold and silver into thy treasures: 6213
38:12 which have **g** cattle and goods, that dwell in 6213
Da 9:15 and hast **g** thee renown, as *at* this day; 6213
Ac 21: 1 that after we were **g from** them, and 645
Rev 15: 2 them that had **g the victory** over the beast, 3528

GOURD (5) [GOURDS]
Jnh 4: 6 the LORD God prepared a **g**, and made *it* 7021
4: 6 So Jonah was exceeding glad of the **g**. 7021
4: 7 and it smote the **g**, that it withered. 7021
4: 9 Doest thou well to be angry for the **g**? 7021
4:10 the LORD, Thou hast had pity on the **g**, 7021

GOURDS (1) [GOURD]
2Ki 4:39 gathered thereof wild **g** his lap full, and 6498

GOVERN (3) [GOVERNMENT, GOVERNMENTS, GOVERNOR, GOVERNOR'S, GOVERNORS]
1Ki 21: 7 Dost thou now **g** the kingdom of Israel? 6213
Job 34:17 Shall even he that hateth right **g**? and wilt 2280
Ps 67: 4 and **g** the nations upon earth. 5148

GOVERNMENT (4) [GOVERN]
Isa 9: 6 the **g** shall be upon his shoulder: and 4951
9: 7 Of the increase of *his* **g** and peace *there* 4951
22:21 and I will commit thy **g** into his hand: 4475
2Pe 2:10 in the lust of uncleanness, and despise **g**. 2963

GOVERNMENTS (1) [GOVERN]
1Co 12:28 then gifts of healings, helps, **g**, 2941

GOVERNOR (59) [GOVERN]
Ge 42: 6 Joseph *was* the **g** over the land, *and* he *it* 7989
45:26 and he *is* **g** over all the land of Egypt. 4910
1Ki 18: 3 which *was* the **g**[S] **of** *his* house. 5921
22:26 carry him back unto Amon the **g** of the city, 8269
2Ki 23: 8 in of the gate of Joshua the **g** of the city, 8269
25:23 the king of Babylon had **made** Gedaliah **g**, 6485
1Ch 29:22 *him* unto the LORD to be the **chief g**, 5057
2Ch 1: 2 to the judges, and to every **g** in all Israel, 5387
18:25 carry him back to Amon the **g** of the city, 8269
28: 7 Azrikam the **g** of the house, and Elkanah 5057
34: 8 Maaseiah the **g** of the city, and Joah the son 8269
Ezr 5: 3 **g** on *this* side the river, and Shethar-boznai, 6347
5: 6 **g** on *this* side the river, and Shethar-boznai, 6347
5:14 *was* Sheshbazzar, whom he had made **g**; 6347
6: 6 Now *therefore*, Tatnai, **g** beyond the river, 6347
6: 7 let the **g** of the Jews and the elders of 6347
6:13 Tatnai, **g** on *this* side the river, 6347
Ne 3: 7 unto the throne of the **g** on *this* side 6346
5:14 appointed to be their **g** in the land of Judah, 6346
5:14 brethren have not eaten the bread of the **g**. 6346
5:18 for *all* this required not I the bread of the **g**, 6346
12:26 in the days of Nehemiah the **g**, and of Ezra 6346
Ps 22:28 and *he is* the **g** among the nations. 4910
Jer 20: 1 who *was* also chief **g** in the house of 6496
30:21 their **g** shall proceed from the midst of 4910
40: 5 whom the king of Babylon hath **made g** 6485
40: 7 **made** Gedaliah the son of Ahikam **g** in 6485
41: 2 whom the king of Babylon had **made g** 6485
41:18 whom the king of Babylon **made g** in 6485
Hag 1: 1 **g** of Judah, and to Joshua the son of 6346
1:14 **g** of Judah, and the spirit of Joshua the son 6346
2: 2 **g** of Judah, and to Joshua the son of 6346
2:21 Speak to Zerubbabel, **g** of Judah, saying, 6346
Zec 9: 7 he shall be as a **g** in Judah, and Ekron as a 441
Mal 1: 8 offer it now unto thy **g**; will he be pleased 6346
Mt 2: 6 for out of thee shall come a **G**, that shall 2233
27: 2 and delivered him to Pontius Pilate the **g**. 2232
27:11 And Jesus stood before the **g**: and 2232
27:11 and the **g** asked him, saying, Art thou 2232
27:14 insomuch that the **g** marvelled greatly. 2232
27:15 Now at *that* feast the **g** was wont to release 2232
27:21 The **g** answered and said unto them, 2232
27:23 And the **g** said, Why, what evil hath he 2232
27:27 Then the soldiers of the **g** took Jesus into 2232
Lk 2: 2 first made when Cyrenius was **g** of Syria.) 2230
3: 1 Pontius Pilate being **g** of Judea, and 2230
20:20 him unto the power and authority of the **g**. 2232
Jn 2: 8 out now, and bear unto the **g of the feast**. 755
2: 9 the **g of the feast** called the bridegroom, 755
Ac 7:10 and he made him **g** over Egypt and all his 2233
23:24 and bring *him* safe unto Felix the **g**. 2232
23:26 Claudius Lysias unto the most excellent **g** 2232
23:33 and delivered the epistle to the **g**, 2232
23:34 And when the **g** had read *the letter*, he 2232
24: 1 who informed the **g** against Paul. 2232
24:10 after that the **g** had beckoned unto him to 2232
26:30 thus spoken, the king rose up, and the **g**, 2232
2Co 11:32 In Damascus the **g** under Aretas the king 1481
Jas 3: 4 small helm, whithersoever the **g** listeth. 3730

GOVERNOR'S (1) [GOVERN]
Mt 28:14 And if this come to the **g** ears, we will 2232

GOVERNORS (22) [GOVERN]
Jdg 5: 9 My heart *is* toward the **g** of Israel, 2710
5:14 out of Machir came down **g**, and out of 2710
1Ki 10:15 kings of Arabia, and *of* the **g** of the country. 6346
1Ch 24: 5 for the **g** of the sanctuary, and governors *of* 8269
24: 5 **g** *of* the house of God, were of the sons of 8269
2Ch 9:14 **g** of the country brought gold and silver to 6346
23:20 the **g** of the people, and all the people of 4910
Ezr 8:36 and *to* the **g** on *this* side the river: 6346
Ne 2: 7 let letters be given me to the **g** beyond 6346
2: 9 I came to the **g** beyond the river, and 6346
5:15 the former **g** that *had been* before me were 6346
Est 3:12 to the **g** that *were* over every province, 6346
Da 2:48 chief of the **g** over all the wise *men* of 5460
3: 2 the **g**, and the captains, the judges, 5460
3: 3 the **g** and captains, the judges, 5460
3:27 **g**, and captains, and the king's counsellers, 5460
6: 7 the **g**, and the princes, the counsellers and 5460
Zec 12: 5 the **g** of Judah shall say in their heart, 441
12: 6 In that day will I make the **g** of Judah like a 441
Mt 10:18 And ye shall be brought before **g** and kings 2232
Gal 4: 2 and **g** until the time appointed of the father. 3623
1Pe 2:14 Or unto **g**, as unto them that are sent by him 2232

GOZAN (5)
2Ki 17: 6 in Halah and in Habor *by* the river of **G**, 1470
18:11 in Halah and in Habor *by* the river of **G**, 1470
19:12 *as* **G**, and Haran, and Rezeph, and 1470
1Ch 5:26 Habor, and Hara, and to the river **G**, 1470
Isa 37:12 *as* **G**, and Haran, and Rezeph, and 1470

GRACE (170) [GRACIOUS, GRACIOUSLY]
Ge 6: 8 Noah found **g** in the eyes of the LORD. 2580
19:19 thy servant hath found **g** in thy sight, and 2580
32: 5 tell my lord, that I may find **g** in thy sight. 2580
33: 8 *These are* to find **g** in the sight of my lord. 2580
33:10 if now I have found **g** in thy sight, then 2580
33:15 let me find **g** in the sight of my lord. 2580
34:11 Let me find **g** in your eyes, and what ye 2580
39: 4 Joseph found **g** in his sight, and he served 2580
47:25 let us find **g** in the sight of my lord, and 2580
47:29 If now I have found **g** in thy sight, put, 2580
50: 4 If now I have found **g** in your eyes, speak, 2580
Ex 33:12 and thou hast also found **g** in my sight. 2580
33:13 I pray thee, if I have found **g** in thy sight, 2580
33:13 know thee, that I may find **g** in thy sight: 2580
33:16 and thy people have found **g** in thy sight? 2580
33:17 for thou hast found **g** in my sight, and 2580
34: 9 If now I have found **g** in thy sight, O Lord, 2580
Nu 32: 5 said they, if we have found **g** in thy sight, 2580
Jdg 6:17 If now I have found **g** in thy sight, then 2580
Ru 2: 2 corn after *him* in whose sight I shall find **g**. 2580
2:10 Why have I found **g** in thine eyes, 2580
1Sa 1:18 Let thine handmaid find **g** in thy sight. 2580
20: 3 knoweth that I have found **g** in thine eyes; 2580
27: 5 If I have now found **g** in thine eyes, 2580
2Sa 14:22 knoweth that I have found **g** in thy sight, 2580
16: 4 I humbly beseech thee *that* I may find **g** in 2580
Ezr 9: 8 now for a little space **g** hath been *shewed* 8467
Est 2:17 she obtained **g** and favour in his sight more 2580
Ps 45: 2 **g** is poured into thy lips: therefore God hath 2580
84:11 the LORD will give **g** and glory: no good 2580
Pr 1: 9 For they *shall be* an ornament of **g** unto thy 2580
3:22 be life unto thy soul, and **g** to thy neck. 2580
3:34 the scorners: but he giveth **g** unto the lowly. 2580
4: 9 shall give to thine head an ornament of **g**: 2580
22:11 *for* the **g** of his lips the king *shall be* his 2580
Jer 31: 2 left of the sword found **g** in the wilderness, 2580
Zec 4: 7 *with* shoutings, *crying*, **G**, grace unto it. 2580
4: 7 *with* shoutings, *crying*, Grace, **g** unto it. 2580
12:10 the spirit of **g** and of supplications: 2580
Lk 2:40 and the **g** of God was upon him. 5485
Jn 1:14 begotten of the Father,) full of **g** and truth. 5485
1:16 have all we received, and **g** for grace. 5485
1:16 have all we received, and grace for **g**. 5485
1:17 *but* **g** and truth came by Jesus Christ. 5485
Ac 4:33 Lord Jesus: and great **g** was upon them all. 5485
11:23 and had seen the **g** of God, was glad, and 5485
13:43 persuaded them to continue in the **g** of God. 5485
14: 3 gave testimony unto the word of his **g**, 5485
14:26 **g** of God for the work which they fulfilled. 5485
15:11 But we believe that through the **g** of 5485
15:40 by the brethren unto the **g** of God. 5485
18:27 them much which had believed through **g**: 5485
20:24 to testify the gospel of the **g** of God. 5485
20:32 you to God, and to the word of his **g**, 5485
Ro 1: 5 By whom we have received **g** and 5485
1: 7 **G** to you and peace from God our Father, 5485
3:24 Being justified freely by his **g** through 5485
4: 4 worketh is the reward not reckoned of **g**, 5485
4:16 *it is* of faith, that *it might be* by **g**; 5485
5: 2 by faith into this **g** wherein we stand, 5485
5:15 much more the **g** of God, and the gift by 5485
5:15 and the gift by **g**, which is by one man, 5485
5:17 more they which receive abundance of **g** 5485
5:20 sin abounded, **g** did much more abound: 5485
5:21 might **g** reign through righteousness unto 5485
6: 1 we continue in sin, that **g** may abound? 5485
6:14 for ye are not under the law, but under **g**. 5485
6:15 we are not under the law, but under **g**? 5485
11: 5 is a remnant according to the election of **g**. 5485
11: 6 And if by **g**, *then is it* no more of works: 5485
11: 6 otherwise **g** is no more grace. But if *it be* of 5485
11: 6 otherwise grace is no more **g**. But if *it be* of 5485
11: 6 But if *it be* of works, *then* is it no more **g**: 5485
12: 3 For I say, through the **g** given unto me, 5485
12: 6 gifts differing according to the **g** that is 5485
15:15 because of the **g** that is given to me of God, 5485
16:20 The **g** of our Lord Jesus Christ *be* with you. 5485
16:24 The **g** of our Lord Jesus Christ *be* with you 5485
1Co 1: 3 **G** *be* unto you, and peace, from God our 5485
1: 4 for the **g** of God which is given you by 5485
3:10 According to the **g** of God which is given 5485
10:30 For if I by **g** be a partaker, why am I evil 5485
15:10 But by the **g** of God I am what I am: and 5485
15:10 his **g** which was *bestowed* upon me was not 5485
15:10 not I, but the **g** of God which was with me. 5485
16:23 The **g** of *our* Lord Jesus Christ *be* with you. 5485
2Co 1: 2 **G** *be* to you and peace from God our 5485
1:12 with fleshly wisdom, but by the **g** of God, 5485
4:15 that the abundant **g** might through 5485
6: 1 that ye receive not the **g** of God in vain. 5485
8: 1 we do you to wit of the **g** of God bestowed 5485
8: 6 he would also finish in you the same **g** also. 5485
8: 7 love to us, *see* that ye abound in this **g** also. 5485
8: 9 For ye know the **g** of our Lord Jesus Christ, 5485
8:19 of the churches to travel with us with this **g**, 5485
9: 8 And God *is* able to make all **g** abound 5485
9:14 which long after you for the exceeding **g** of 5485
12: 9 he said unto me, My **g** is sufficient for thee: 5485
13:14 The **g** of the Lord Jesus Christ, and the love 5485
Gal 1: 3 **G** *be* to you and peace from God 5485
1: 6 into the **g** of Christ unto another gospel: 5485
1:15 my mother's womb, and called *me* by his **g**, 5485

G

Gal 2: 9 perceived the **g** that was given unto me, *5485*
2:21 I do not frustrate the **g** of God: for if *5485*
5: 4 justified by the law; ye are fallen from **g**. *5485*
6:18 the **g** of our Lord Jesus Christ *be* with your *5485*
Eph 1: 2 **G** *be* to you, and peace, from God our *5485*
1: 6 To the praise of the glory of his **g**, *5485*
1: 7 of sins, according to the riches of his **g**; *5485*
2: 5 *us* together with Christ, (by **g** ye are saved;) *5485*
2: 7 **g** in *his* kindness towards us through Christ *5485*
2: 8 For by **g** are ye saved through faith; and *5485*
3: 2 If ye have heard of the dispensation of the **g** *5485*
3: 7 according to the gift of the **g** of God given *5485*
3: 8 than the least of all saints, is this **g** given, *5485*
4: 7 But unto every one of us is given **g** *5485*
4:29 that it may minister **g** unto the hearers. *5485*
6:24 **G** *be* with all them that love our Lord Jesus *5485*
Php 1: 2 **G** *be* unto you, and peace, from God our *5485*
1: 7 of the gospel, ye all are partakers of my **g**. *5485*
4:23 The **g** of our Lord Jesus Christ *be* with you *5485*
Col 1: 2 **G** *be* unto you, and peace, from God our *5485*
1: 6 heard of *it*, and knew the **g** of God in truth: *5485*
3:16 singing with **g** in your hearts to the Lord. *5485*
4: 6 Let your speech *be* alway with **g**, *5485*
4:18 my bonds. **G** *be* with you. Amen. *5485*
1Th 1: 1 **G** *be* unto you, and peace, from God our *5485*
5:28 The **g** of our Lord Jesus Christ *be* with you. *5485*
2Th 1: 2 **G** unto you, and peace, from God our *5485*
1:12 according to the **g** of our God and the Lord *5485*
2:16 and good hope through **g**, *5485*
3:18 The **g** of our Lord Jesus Christ *be* with you *5485*
1Ti 1: 2 **G**, mercy, *and* peace, from God our Father *5485*
1:14 And the **g** of our Lord was exceeding *5485*
6:21 the faith. **G** *be* with thee. Amen. *5485*
2Ti 1: 2 **G**, mercy, *and* peace, from God the Father *5485*
1: 9 but according to his own purpose and **g**, *5485*
2: 1 be strong in the **g** that is in Christ Jesus. *5485*
4:22 *be* with thy spirit. **G** *be* with you. Amen. *5485*
Tit 1: 4 **G**, mercy, *and* peace, from God the Father *5485*
2:11 For the **g** of God that bringeth salvation *5485*
3: 7 That being justified by his **g**, we should be *5485*
3:15 us in the faith. **G** *be* with you all. Amen. *5485*
Phm 1: 3 **G** to you, and peace, from God our Father *5485*
1:25 The **g** of our Lord Jesus Christ *be* with your *5485*
Heb 2: 9 that he by the **g** of God should taste death *5485*
4:16 therefore come boldly unto the throne of **g**, *5485*
4:16 and find **g** to help in time of need. *5485*
10:29 and hath done despite unto the Spirit of **g**? *5485*
12:15 diligently lest any *man* fail of the **g** *5485*
12:28 let us have **g**, whereby we may serve God *5485*
13: 9 *thing* that the heart be established with **g**; *5485*
13:25 **G** *be* with you all. Amen. *5485*
Jas 1:11 and the **g** of the fashion of it perisheth: *2143*
4: 6 But he giveth more **g**. Wherefore *he* saith, *5485*
4: 6 the proud, but giveth **g** unto the humble. *5485*
1Pe 1: 2 **G** unto you, and peace, be multiplied. *5485*
1:10 who prophesied of the **g** *that should come* *5485*
1:13 hope to the end for the **g** that is *to be* *5485*
3: 7 and as *being* heirs together of the **g** of life; *5485*
4:10 as good stewards of the manifold **g** of God. *5485*
5: 5 the proud, and giveth **g** to the humble. *5485*
5:10 But the God of all **g**, who hath called us *5485*
5:12 testifying that this is the true **g** of God *5485*
2Pe 1: 2 **G** and peace be multiplied unto you *5485*
3:18 But grow in **g**, and *in* the knowledge of our *5485*
2Jn 1: 3 **G** be with you, mercy, *and* peace, *5485*
Jude 1: 4 ungodly *men*, turning the **g** of our God into *5485*
Rev 1: 4 **G** *be* unto you, and peace, from him which *5485*
22:21 The **g** of our Lord Jesus Christ *be* with you *5485*

GRACIOUS (31) [GRACE]

Ge 43:29 And he said, God be **g** unto thee, my son. 2603
Ex 22:27 crieth unto me, that I will hear; for I *am* **g**. 2587
33:19 will be **g** to whom I will be gracious, and 2603
33:19 will be gracious to whom I will be **g**, and 2603
34: 6 merciful and **g**, longsuffering, and 2587
Nu 6:25 face shine upon thee, and be **g** unto thee: 2603
2Sa 12:22 Who can tell *whether* GOD will be **g** to 2603
2Ki 13:23 the LORD was **g** unto them, and 2603
2Ch 30: 9 for the LORD your God *is* **g** and merciful, 2587
Ne 9:17 **g** and merciful, slow to anger, and of great 2587
9:31 for thou *art* a **g** and merciful God. 2587
Job 33:24 he is **g** unto him, and saith, Deliver him 2603
Ps 77: 9 Hath God forgotten to be **g**? hath he in 2589
86:15 **g**, longsuffering, and plenteous in mercy 2587
103: 8 The LORD *is* merciful and **g**, slow to 2587
111: 4 the LORD *is* **g** and full of compassion. 2587
112: 4 *he is* **g**, and full of compassion, and 2587
116: 5 **G** *is* the LORD, and righteous; yea, 2587
145: 8 The LORD *is* **g**, and full of compassion; 2587
Pr 11:16 A **g** woman retaineth honour: and 2580
Ecc 10:12 The words of a wise *man's* mouth *are* **g**; 2580
Isa 30:18 that *he* may be **g** unto you, and therefore 2603
30:19 he will be **very g** unto thee at 2603+2603
33: 2 O LORD, be **g** unto us; we have waited 2603
Jer 22:23 how **g** shalt thou be when pangs come upon 2603
Joel 2:13 for he *is* **g** and merciful, slow to anger, and 2587
Am 5:15 hosts will be **g** unto the remnant of Joseph. 2603
Jnh 4: 2 for I knew that thou *art* a **g** God, and 2587
Mal 1: 9 beseech God that he will be **g** unto us: 2603
Lk 4:22 wondered at the **g** words which proceeded *5485*
1Pe 2: 3 If so be ye have tasted that the Lord *is* **g**. *5543*

GRACIOUSLY (4) [GRACE]

Ge 33: 5 The children which God hath **g given** thy 2603
33:11 because God hath **dealt g** with me, and 2603
Ps 119:29 the way of lying: and **grant** me thy law **g**. 2603
Hos 14: 2 Take away all iniquity, and receive *us* **g**: 2896

GRAFF (1) [GRAFFED]

Ro 11:23 for God is able to **g** them **in** again. *1461*

GRAFFED (5) [GRAFF]

Ro 11:17 wert **g in** amongst them, and with *them* *1461*
11:19 were broken off, that I might be **g in**. *1461*
11:23 they bide not still in unbelief, shall be **g in**: *1461*
11:24 wert **g** contrary to nature into a good olive *1461*
11:24 which be the natural *branches*, be **g into** *1461*

GRAFT; GRAFTED See GRAFF; GRAFFED

GRAIN (8)

Am 9: 9 yet shall not the **least g** fall *upon* the earth. 6872
Mt 13:31 of heaven is like unto a **g of** mustard **seed**, *2848*
17:20 If ye have faith as a **g of** mustard **seed**, *2848*
Mk 4:31 *It is* like a **g of** mustard **seed**, which, *2848*
Lk 13:19 It is like a **g of** mustard **seed**, which a man *2848*
17: 6 If ye had faith as a **g of** mustard **seed**, *2848*
1Co 15:37 but bare **g**, it may chance of wheat, or *2848*
15:37 it may chance of wheat, or of some other *g*. NIG

GRANDMOTHER (1) [MOTHER]

2Ti 1: 5 which dwelt first in thy **g** Lois, and *3125*

GRANT (22) [GRANTED]

Lev 25:24 in all the land of your possession ye shall **g** 5414
Ru 1: 9 The LORD **g** you that you may find rest, 5414
1Sa 1:17 the God of Israel **g** *thee* thy petition that 5414
1Ch 21:22 **G** me the place of *this* threshingfloor, 5414
21:22 thou shalt **g** it me for the full price: that 5414
2Ch 12: 7 but I will **g** them some deliverance; 5414
Ezr 3: 7 according to the **g** that they had of Cyrus 7558
Ne 1:11 and **g** him mercy in the sight of this man. 5414
Est 5: 8 if it please the king to **g** my petition, and 5414
Job 6: 8 *that* God would **g** *me* the thing that I long 5414
Ps 20: 4 **G** thee according to thine own heart, and 5414
85: 7 O LORD, and **g** us thy salvation. 5414
119:29 way of lying: and **g** me thy law **graciously**. 2603
140: 8 **G** not, O LORD, the desires of 5414
Mt 20:21 **G** that these my two sons may sit, *3004*
Mk 10:37 said unto him, **G** unto us that we may sit, *1325*
Lk 1:74 That *he* would **g** unto us, that *we* being *1325*
Ac 4:29 and **g** unto thy servants, that with all *1325*
Ro 15: 5 consolation **g** you to be likeminded one *1325*
Eph 3:16 That he would **g** you, according to *1325*
2Ti 1:18 The Lord **g** unto him that *he* may find *1325*
Rev 3:21 To him that overcometh will I **g** to sit with *1325*

GRANTED (15) [GRANT]

1Ch 4:10 And God **g** *him that* which he requested. 935
2Ch 1:12 Wisdom and knowledge *is* **g** unto thee; and 5414
Ezr 7: 6 the king **g** him all his request, according to 5414
Ne 2: 8 the king **g** me, according to the good hand 5414
Est 5: 6 it shall be **g** thee: and what *is* thy request? 5414
7: 2 it shall be **g** thee: and what *is* thy request? 5414
8:11 Where*in* the king **g** the Jews which *were* in 5414
9:12 it shall be **g** thee: or what *is* thy request 5414
9:13 let it be **g** to the Jews which *are* in Shushan 5414
Job 10:12 Thou hast **g** me life and favour, and 6213
Pr 10:24 but the desire of the righteous shall be **g**. 5414
Ac 3:14 and desired a murderer to be **g** unto you; *5483*
11:18 Then hath God also to the Gentiles **g** *1325*
14: 3 and **g** signs and wonders to be done by their *1325*
Rev 19: 8 And to her was **g** that she should be arrayed *1325*

GRAPE (8) [GRAPEGATHERER, GRAPEGATHERERS, GRAPE-GATHERERS, GRAPEGLEANINGS, GRAPES]

Lev 19:10 neither shalt thou gather *every* **g** of thy 6528
Dt 32:14 thou didst drink the pure blood of the **g**. 6025
Job 15:33 He shall shake off his **unripe g** as the vine, 1154
SS 2:13 the vines *with* the **tender g** give a *good* 5563
7:12 *whether* the **tender g** appear, *and* 5563
Isa 18: 5 and the **sour g** is ripening in the flower, 1155
Jer 31:29 The fathers have eaten a **sour g**, and 1155
31:30 every man that eateth the **sour g**, his teeth 1155

GRAPEGATHERER (1) [GRAPE, GATHER]

Jer 6: 9 turn back thine hand as a **g** into the baskets. 1219

GRAPEGATHERERS, GRAPE-GATHERERS (2) [GRAPE, GATHER]

Jer 49: 9 If **g** come to thee, would they not leave 1219
Ob 1: 5 if the **g** came to thee, would they not leave 1219

GRAPEGLEANINGS (1) [GRAPE, GLEAN]

Mic 7: 1 the summer fruits, as the **g** of the vintage: 5955

GRAPES (37) [GRAPE]

Ge 40:10 the clusters thereof brought forth ripe **g**: 6025
40:11 I took the **g**, and pressed them into 6025
49:11 in wine, and his clothes in the blood of **g**: 6025
Lev 25: 5 neither gather the **g** of thy vine undressed: 6025
25:11 nor gather *the* **g** in it of thy vine undressed. NIH
Nu 6: 3 neither shall he drink any liquor of **g**, 6025
6: 3 liquor of grapes, nor eat moist **g**, or dried. 6025
13:20 the time *was* the time of the first ripe **g**. 6025
13:23 from thence a branch with one cluster of **g**, 6025
13:24 of the **cluster of g** which the children of 811
Dt 23:24 thou mayest eat **g** thy fill at thine own 6025
24:21 When thou **gatherest** the **g** of thy vineyard, 1219
28:30 and shalt not **gather the g** thereof. 2490
28:39 nor gather *the* **g**; for the worms shall eat NIH
32:32 their **g** *are* grapes of gall, their clusters *are* 6025
32:32 their grapes *are* **g** of gall, their clusters *are* 6025
Jdg 8: 2 *Is* not the **gleaning of** the **g** of Ephraim 5955
9:27 trode *the* **g**, and made merry, and went *into* NIH
Ne 13:15 **g**, and figs, and all *manner of* burdens, 6025
SS 2:15 spoil the vines: for our vines *have* **tender g**. 5563
7: 7 a palm tree, and thy breasts to clusters *of* **g**. NIH
Isa 5: 2 he looked that *it* should bring forth **g**, and 6025
5: 2 forth grapes, and it brought forth **wild g**. 891
5: 4 when I looked that *it* should bring forth **g**, 6025
5: 4 bring forth grapes, brought it forth **wild g**? 891
17: 6 Yet **gleaning g** shall be left in it, as 5955
24:13 as the **gleaning g** when the vintage is done. 5955
Jer 8:13 *there shall be* no **g** on the vine, nor figs on 6025
25:30 as they that tread *the* **g**, against all NIH
49: 9 would they not leave *some* **gleaning g**? 5955
Eze 18: 2 The fathers have eaten **sour g**, and 1155
Hos 9:10 I found Israel like **g** in the wilderness; I saw 6025
Am 9:13 and the treader of **g** him that soweth seed; 6025
Ob 1: 5 came to thee, would they not leave *some* **g**? 5955
Mt 7:16 Do *men* gather **g** of thorns, or figs of *4718*
Lk 6:44 nor of a bramble bush gather they **g**. *4718*
Rev 14:18 vine of the earth; for her **g** are fully ripe. *4718*

GRASS (62)

Ge 1:11 God said, Let the earth bring forth **g**, 1877
1:12 the earth brought forth **g**, *and* herb yielding 1877
Nu 22: 4 as the ox licketh up the **g** of the field. 3418
Dt 11:15 And I will send **g** in thy fields for thy cattle, 6212
29:23 nor beareth, nor any **g** groweth therein, 6212
32: 2 tender herb, and as the showers upon the **g**: 6212
2Sa 23: 4 *as* the **tender g** *springing* out of the earth 1877
1Ki 18: 5 peradventure we may find **g** to save 2682
2Ki 19:26 they were *as* the **g** of the field, and *as* 6212
19:26 *as* the **g** on the housetops, and *as* corn 2682
Job 5:25 and thine offspring as the **g** of the earth. 6212
6: 5 Doth the wild ass bray when he hath **g**? or 1877
40:15 I made with thee; he eateth **g** as an ox. 2682
Ps 37: 2 For they shall soon be cut down like the **g**, 2682
72: 6 come down like rain upon the **mown g**: 1488
72:16 *they* of the city shall flourish like **g** of 6212
90: 5 in the morning *they are* like **g** *which* 2682
92: 7 When the wicked spring as the **g**, and 6212
102: 4 My heart is smitten, and withered like **g**; so 6212
102:11 that declineth; and I am withered like **g**. 6212
103:15 *As for* man, his days *are* as **g**: as a flower of 2682
104:14 He causeth the **g** to grow for the cattle, and 2682
106:20 into the similitude of an ox that eateth **g**. 6212
129: 6 Let them be as the **g** upon the housetops, 2682
147: 8 who maketh **g** to grow *upon* the mountains. 2682
Pr 19:12 a lion; but his favour *is* as dew upon the **g**. 6212
27:25 the **tender g** sheweth itself, and herbs of 1877
Isa 15: 6 the **g** faileth, there is no green thing. 1877
35: 7 each lay, *shall be* **g** with reeds and rushes. 2682
37:27 they were *as* the **g** of the field, and *as* 6212
37:27 *as* the **g** on the housetops, and *as* corn 2682
40: 6 All flesh *is* **g**, and all the goodliness thereof 2682
40: 7 The **g** withereth, the flower fadeth: because 2682
40: 7 bloweth upon it: surely the people *is* **g**. 2682
40: 8 The **g** withereth, the flower fadeth: but 2682
44: 4 they shall spring up *as* among the **g**, 2682
51:12 of the son of man *which* shall be made *as* **g**; 2682
Jer 14: 5 and forsook *it*, because there was no **g**. 1877
14: 6 their eyes did fail, because *there was* no **g**. 6212
50:11 because ye are grown fat as the heifer at **g**, 1877
Da 4:15 and brass, in the **tender g** of the field; 1883
4:15 *let* his portion *be* with the beasts in the **g** of 6211'
4:23 and brass, in the **tender g** of the field; 1883
4:25 they shall make thee to eat **g** as oxen, 6211'
4:32 they shall make thee to eat **g** as oxen, and 6211'
4:33 did eat **g** as oxen, and his body was wet 6211'
5:21 they fed him with **g** like oxen, and his body 6211'
Am 7: 2 had made an end of eating the **g** of the land, 6212
Mic 5: 7 as the showers upon the **g**, that tarrieth not 6212
Zec 10: 1 showers of rain, to every one **g** in the field. 6212
Mt 6:30 if God so clothe the **g** of the field, *5528*
14:19 the multitude to sit down on the **g**, *5528*
Mk 6:39 sit down by companies upon the green **g**. *5528*
Lk 12:28 If then God so clothe the **g**, which is to day *5528*
Jn 6:10 Now there was much **g** in the place. So *5528*
Jas 1:10 as the flower of the **g** he shall pass away. *5528*
1:11 but it withereth the **g**, and the flower *5528*
1Pe 1:24 For all flesh *is* as **g**, and all the glory of *5528*
1:24 and all the glory of man as the flower of **g**. *5528*
1:24 The **g** withereth, and the flower thereof *5528*
Rev 8: 7 was burnt up, and all green **g** was burnt up. *5528*
9: 4 that they should not hurt the **g** of the earth, *5528*

GRASSHOPPER (3) [GRASSHOPPERS]

Lev 11:22 after his kind, and the **g** after his kind. 2284
Job 39:20 Canst thou make him afraid as a **g**? the glory 697
Ecc 12: 5 the **g** shall be a burden, and desire shall 2284

GRASSHOPPERS (7) [GRASSHOPPER]

Nu 13:33 we were in our own sight as **g**, and so 2284
Jdg 6: 5 their tents, and they came as **g** for multitude; 697
7:12 lay along in the valley like **g** for multitude; 697
Isa 40:22 and the inhabitants thereof *are* as **g**; 2284
Jer 46:23 because they are more than the **g**, and 697
Am 7: 1 he formed **g** in the beginning of 1462
Na 3:17 and thy captains as the **great g**, 1462+1462

GRATE (6) [GRAVE, GRAVE'S, GRAVECLOTHES, GRAVED, GRAVEN, GRAVES, GRAVETH, GRAVING, GRAVINGS]

Ex 27: 4 thou shalt make for it a **g** of network *of* 4345
35:16 altar of burnt offering with his brasen **g**, 4345
38: 4 he made for the altar a brasen **g** of network 4345
38: 5 he cast four rings for the four ends of the **g** 4345
38:30 the brasen **g** for it, and all the vessels of 4345
39:39 his **g** of brass, his staves, and all his 4345

GRATING See NETWORKS

GRAVE (67) [GRATE]

Ge 35:20 Jacob set a pillar upon her **g**: that *is* 6900
35:20 that *is* the pillar of Rachel's **g** unto *this* day. 6900
37:35 For I will go down into the **g** unto my son 7585
42:38 down my gray hairs with sorrow to the **g**. 7585
44:29 down my gray hairs with sorrow to the **g**. 7585
44:31 thy servant our father with sorrow to the **g**. 7585
50: 5 in my **g** which I have digged for me in 6913
Ex 28: 9 **g** on them the names of the children of 6605
28:36 **g** upon it, *like* the engravings of a signet, 6605
Nu 19:16 or a dead *body*, or a bone of a man, or a **g**, 6913
19:18 a bone, or one slain, or one dead, or a **g**: 6913
1Sa 2: 6 he bringeth down *to* the **g**, and bringeth up. 7585
2Sa 3:32 up his voice, and wept at the **g** of Abner; 6913
19:37 *and be buried* by the **g** of my father and 6913

1Ki 2: 6 let not his hoar head go down *to* the **g** in 7585
2: 9 his hoar head bring thou down *to* the **g** with 7585
13:30 he laid his carcase in his own **g**; and 6913
14:13 he only of Jeroboam shall come to the **g**, 6913
2Ki 22:20 thou shalt be gathered into thy **g** in peace; 6913
2Ch 2: 7 that can skill to **g** with the cunning 6603+3807.1
2:14 also to **g** any *manner of* graving, and to find 6605
34:28 thou shalt be gathered to thy **g** in peace, 6913
Job 3:22 are glad, when they can find the **g**? 6913
5:26 Thou shalt come to *thy* **g** in a full age, 6913
7: 9 he that goeth down *to* the **g** shall come up 7585
10:19 have been carried from the womb to the **g**. 6913
14:13 O that thou wouldest hide me in the **g**, 7585
17:13 If I wait, the **g** *is* mine house: I have made 7585
21:13 and in a moment go down *to* the **g**. 7585
21:32 Yet shall he be brought to the **g**, and 6913
24:19 *so doth* the **g** *those which* have sinned. 7585
30:24 *he* will not stretch out *his* hand to the **g**, 5856
33:22 his soul draweth near unto the **g**, and 7845
Ps 6: 5 of thee: in the **g** who shall give thee thanks? 7585
30: 3 thou hast brought up my soul from the **g**: 7585
31:17 be ashamed, *and* let them be silent in the **g**. 7585
49:14 Like sheep they are laid in the **g**; 7585
49:14 their beauty shall consume *in* the **g** from 7585
49:15 redeem my soul from the power of the **g**: 7585
88: 3 and my life draweth nigh unto the **g**. 7585
88: 5 the dead, like the slain that lie in the **g**, 6913
88:11 thy lovingkindness be declared in the **g**? 6913
89:48 he deliver his soul from the hand of the **g**? 7585
Pr 1:12 Let us swallow them up alive as the **g**; and 7585
30:16 The **g**; and the barren womb; the earth *that* 7585
Ecc 9:10 nor knowledge, nor wisdom, in the **g**, 7585
SS 8: 6 *is* strong as death; jealousy *is* cruel as the **g**: 7585
Isa 14:11 Thy pomp is brought down *to* the **g**, *and* 7585
14:19 thou art cast out of thy **g** like an 6913
38:10 of my days, I shall go to the gates of the **g**: 7585
38:18 For the **g** cannot praise thee, death can *not* 7585
53: 9 he made his **g** with the wicked, and 6913
Jer 20:17 or that my mother might have been my **g**, 6913
Eze 31:15 In the day when he went down to the **g** I 7585
32:23 and her company is round about her **g**: 6900
32:24 and all her multitude round about her **g**, 6900
Hos 13:14 I will ransom them from the power of the **g**; 7585
13:14 thy plagues; O **g**, I will be thy destruction: 7585
Na 1:14 I will make thy **g**; for thou art vile. 6913
Jn 11:17 he found that he had *lien* in the **g** four days *3419*
11:31 saying, She goeth unto the **g** to weep there. *3419*
11:38 again groaning in himself cometh to the **g**. *3419*
12:17 him when he called Lazarus out of *his* **g**, *3419*
1Co 15:55 where *is* thy sting? O **g**, where *is* thy victory? *86*
1Ti 3: 8 Likewise *must* the deacons *be* **g**, *4586*
3:11 Even so *must their* wives *be* **g**, *4586*
Tit 2: 2 **g**, temperate, sound in faith, in charity, *4586*

GRAVE'S (1) [GRATE]

Ps 141: 7 Our bones are scattered at the **g** mouth, 7585

GRAVECLOTHES (1) [CLOTHE, GRATE]

Jn 11:44 came forth, bound hand and foot with **g**: *2750*

GRAVED (2) [GRATE]

1Ki 7:36 he **g** cherubims, lions, and palm trees, 6605
2Ch 3: 7 with gold; and **g** cherubims on the walls. 6605

GRAVEL (3)

Pr 20:17 afterwards his mouth shall be filled *with* **g**. 2687
Isa 48:19 the offspring of thy bowels like the **g** 4579
La 3:16 hath also broken my teeth with **g stones**, 2687

GRAVEN (55) [GRATE]

Ex 20: 4 shalt not make unto thee *any* **g image**, 6459
32:16 *was* the writing of God, **g** upon the tables. 2801
39: 6 **g** *as* signets are graven, with the names of 6603
39: 6 graven *as* signets are **g**, with the names of 6605
Lev 26: 1 Ye shall make you no idols nor **g image**, 6459
Dt 4:16 and make you a **g image**, 6459
4:23 make you a **g image**, *or* the likeness of any 6459
4:25 corrupt *yourselves*, and make a **g image**, 6459
5: 8 Thou shalt not make thee *any* **g image**, *or* 6459
7: 5 and burn their **g images** with fire. 6456
7:25 The **g images** of their gods shall ye burn 6456
12: 3 you shall hew down the **g images** of their 6456
27:15 Cursed *be* the man that maketh *any* **g** or 6459
Jdg 17: 3 to make a **g image** and a molten image: 6459
17: 4 who made thereof a **g image** and a molten 6459
18:14 and a **g image**, and a molten image? 6459
18:17 *and* took the **g image**, and the ephod, and 6459
18:20 the **g image**, and went in the midst of 6459
18:30 the children of Dan set up the **g image**: 6459
18:31 they set them up Micah's **g image**, 6459
2Ki 17:41 served their **g images**, both their children, 6456
21: 7 he set a **g image** of the grove that he had 6459
2Ch 33:19 set up groves and **g images**, before he was 6456
34: 7 had beaten the **g images** into powder, and 6456
Job 19:24 That they were **g**[illegible]h an iron pen and 2672
Ps 78:58 moved him to jealousy with their **g images**. 6456
97: 7 be all they that serve **g images**, 6459
Isa 10:10 whose **g images** did excel *them of* 6456
21: 9 all the **g images** of her gods he hath broken 6456
30:22 also the covering of thy **g images** of silver, 6456
40:19 The workman melteth a **g image**, and 6459
40:20 a cunning workman to prepare a **g image**, 6459
42: 8 to another, neither my praise to **g images**. 6456
42:17 that trust in **g images**, that say to 6459
44: 9 They that make a **g image** *are* all of them 6459
44:10 molten a **g image** *that* is profitable for 6459
44:15 worshippeth *it*; he maketh it a **g image**, and 6459
44:17 thereof he maketh a god, *even* his **g image**: 6459
45:20 that set up the wood of their **g image**, 6459
48: 5 my **g image**, and my molten image, 6459
49:16 I have **g** thee upon the palms of *my* hands; 2710
Jer 8:19 provoked me to anger with their **g images**, 6456
10:14 founder is confounded by the **g image**: 6459
17: 1 *it is* **g** upon the table of their heart, and 2790
50:38 for it *is* the land of **g images**, and they are 6456
51:17 founder is confounded by the **g image**: 6459
51:47 that I will do judgment upon the **g images** 6456
51:52 that I will do judgment upon her **g images**: 6456
Hos 11: 2 and burned incense to **g images**. 6456
Mic 1: 7 all the **g images** thereof shall be beaten to 6456
5:13 Thy **g images** also will I cut off, and 6456
Na 1:14 house of thy gods will I cut off the **g image** 6459
Hab 2:18 What profiteth the **g image** that the maker 6459
2:18 image that the maker thereof hath **g** it; 6458
Ac 17:29 silver, or stone, **g** by art and man's device. *5480*

GRAVES (21) [GRATE]

Ex 14:11 Because *there were* no **g** in Egypt, 6913
2Ki 23: 6 cast the powder thereof upon the **g** of 6913
2Ch 34: 4 strowed *it* upon the **g** of them that had 6913
Job 17: 1 my days are extinct, the **g** *are ready* for me. 6913
Isa 65: 4 Which remain among the **g**, and lodge in 6913
Jer 8: 1 the inhabitants of Jerusalem, out of their **g**: 6913
26:23 cast his dead body into the **g** of 6913
Eze 32:22 his **g** *are* about him: all of them slain, fallen 6913
32:23 Whose **g** are set in the sides of the pit, and 6913
32:25 her **g** *are* round about him: all of them 6913
32:26 her **g** *are* round about him: all of them 6913
37:12 I *will* open your **g**, and cause you to come 6913
37:12 cause you to come up out of your **g**, and 6913
37:13 when I have opened your **g**, O my people, 6913
37:13 and brought you up out of your **g**, 6913
39:11 *that* I will give unto Gog a place there of **g** 6913
Mt 27:52 And the **g** were opened; and many bodies *3419*
27:53 And came out of the **g** after his *3419*
Lk 11:44 for ye are as **g** which appear not, and *3419*
Jn 5:28 in the which all that are in the **g** shall hear *3419*
Rev 11: 9 not suffer their dead bodies to be put in **g**. *3418*

GRAVETH (1) [GRATE]

Isa 22:16 that **g** a habitation for himself in a rock? 2710

GRAVING (3) [GRATE]

Ex 32: 4 fashioned it with a **g tool**, after he had 2747
2Ch 2:14 also to grave any *manner of* **g**, and to find 6603
Zec 3: 9 behold, I *will* engrave the **g** thereof, 6603

GRAVINGS (1) [GRATE]

1Ki 7:31 also upon the mouth of it *were* **g** with their 4734

GRAVITY (2)

1Ti 3: 4 having *his* children in subjection with all **g**; *4587*
Tit 2: 7 *shewing* uncorruptness, **g**, sincerity, *4587*

GRAY (6) [GRAYHEADED]

Ge 42:38 shall ye bring down my **g hairs** with 7872
44:29 ye shall bring down my **g hairs** with 7872
44:31 thy servants shall bring down the **g hairs** of 7872
Dt 32:25 the suckling *also* with the man of **g hairs**. 7872
Pr 20:29 and the beauty of old men *is* the **g head**. 7872
Hos 7: 9 yea, **g hairs** are here and there upon him, 7872

GRAYHEADED (3) [GRAY, HEAD]

1Sa 12: 2 I am old and **g**; and behold, my sons *are* 7867
Job 15:10 With us *are* both the **g** and very aged men, 7867
Ps 71:18 Now also when I am old and **g**, O God, 7872

GREASE (1)

Ps 119:70 Their heart is as fat as **g**; *but* I delight *in* thy 2459

GREAT (962) [GREATER, GREATEST, GREATLY, GREATNESS]

Ge 1:16 God made two **g** lights; the greater light to 1419
1:21 God created **g** whales, and every living 1419
6: 5 the wickedness of man *was* **g** in the earth, 7227
7:11 the same day were all the fountains of the **g** 7227
10:12 and Calah: the same *is* a **g** city. 1419
12: 2 I will make of thee a **g** nation, and I will 1419
12: 2 and I will bless thee, and **make** thy name **g**; 1431
12:17 his house with **g** plagues because of Sarai 1419
13: 6 for their substance was **g**, so that they could 7227
15: 1 *am* thy shield, *and* thy exceeding **g** reward. 7235
15:12 lo, a horror of **g** darkness fell upon him. 1419
15:14 afterward shall they come out with **g** 1419
15:18 from the river of Egypt unto the **g** river, 1419
17:20 he beget, and I will make him a **g** nation. 1419
18:18 that Abraham shall surely become a **g** 1419
18:20 the cry of Sodom and Gomorrah is **g**, 7227
19:11 the house with blindness, both small and **g**; 1419
19:13 the cry of them is **waxen g** before the face 1431
20: 9 brought on me and on my kingdom a **g** sin? 1419
21: 8 Abraham made a **g** feast the *same* day that 1419
21:18 thine hand; for I will make him a **g** nation. 1419
24:35 my master greatly; and he is become **g**: 1431
26:13 the man **waxed g**, and went forward, 1431
26:13 and grew until he **became** very **g**: 1431
26:14 of herds, and **g store** of servants: 7227
27:34 he cried with a **g** and exceeding bitter cry, 1419
29: 2 and a **g** stone *was* upon the well's mouth. 1419
30: 8 With **g wrestlings** have I wrestled with my 430
39: 9 how then can I do this **g** wickedness, and 1419
41:29 there come seven years of **g** plenty 1419
45: 7 and to save your lives by a **g** deliverance. 1419
46: 3 for I will there make of thee a **g** nation. 1419
48:19 become a people, and he also shall be **g**: 1431
50: 9 horsemen: and it was a very **g** company. 3515
50:10 there they mourned with a **g** and very sore 1419
Ex 3: 3 I will now turn aside, and see this **g** sight, 1419
6: 6 a stretched out arm, and with **g** judgments: 1419
7: 4 out of the land of Egypt by **g** judgments. 1419
11: 3 Moreover the man Moses *was* very **g** in 1419
11: 6 there shall be a **g** cry throughout all 1419
11: 8 And he went out from Pharaoh in a **g** anger. 2750
12:30 and there was a **g** cry in Egypt; 1419
14:31 Israel saw *that* **g** work which the LORD 1419
18:22 *that* every **g** matter they shall bring unto 1419
29:20 upon the **g toe** of their right foot, and 931
32:10 and I will make of thee a **g** nation. 1419
Ex 32:11 forth out of the land of Egypt with **g** power, 1419
32:21 thou hast brought *so* **g** a sin upon them? 1419
32:30 unto the people, Ye have sinned a **g** sin: 1419
32:31 this people have sinned a **g** sin, and 1419
Lev 8:23 and upon the **g toe** of his right foot. 931
8:24 and upon the **g toes** of their right feet: 931
11:17 little owl, and the cormorant, and the **g owl**, 3244
14:14 and upon the **g toe** of his right foot: 931
14:17 and upon the **g toe** of his right foot, 931
14:25 and upon the **g toe** of his right foot: 931
14:28 and upon the **g toe** of his right foot, 931
Nu 11:33 the LORD smote the people *with* a very **g** 7227
13:28 and the cities *are* walled, *and* very **g**: 1419
13:32 that we saw in it *are* men of a **g stature**. 4060
14:17 let the power of my Lord be **g**, 1431
14:18 of **g** mercy, forgiving iniquity and 7227
22:17 For I will promote thee unto **very g** honour, 3966
23:24 the people shall rise up as a **g lion**, and 3833
24: 9 he lay down as a lion, and as a **g lion**: 3833
24:11 to **promote** thee **unto g honour**; 3513+3513
32: 1 the children of Gad had a very **g** multitude 6099
34: 6 you shall even have the **g** sea for a border: 1419
34: 7 from the **g** sea you shall point out for you 1419
Dt 1: 7 *unto* Lebanon, unto the **g** river, the river 1419
1:17 you shall hear the small as well as the **g**; 1419
1:19 we went *through* all that **g** and terrible 1419
1:28 the cities *are* **g** and walled up to heaven; 1419
2: 7 he knoweth thy walking *through* this **g** 1419
2:10 a people **g**, and many, and tall, as 1419
2:21 A people **g**, and many, and tall, as 1419
3: 5 and bars; beside unwalled towns a **g** many. 3966
4: 6 Surely this **g** nation *is* a wise and 1419
4: 7 For what nation *is there so* **g**, who hath God 1419
4: 8 what nation *is there so* **g**, that hath statutes 1419
4:32 hath been *any such thing* as this **g** thing *is*, 1419
4:34 by a stretched out arm, and by **g** terrors, 1419
4:36 upon earth he shewed thee his **g** fire; and 1419
5:22 and of the thick darkness, *with* a **g** voice: 1419
5:25 for this **g** fire will consume us: if we hear 1419
6:10 to Jacob, to give thee **g** and goodly cities, 1419
6:22 shewed signs and wonders, **g** and sore, 1419
7:19 The **g** temptations which thine eyes saw, 1419
8:15 Who led thee through *that* **g** and terrible 1419
9: 1 cities **g** and fenced up to heaven, 1419
9: 2 A people **g** and tall, the children of 1419
10:17 of lords, a **g** God, a mighty, and a terrible, 1419
10:21 that hath done for thee these **g** and terrible 1419
11: 7 your eyes have seen all the **g** acts of 1419
14:16 The little owl, and the **g owl**, and the swan, 3244
18:16 neither let me see this **g** fire any more, 1419
25:13 in thy bag divers weights, a **g** and a small. 1419
25:14 house divers measures, a **g** and a small. 1419
26: 5 there a nation, **g**, mighty, and populous: 1419
26: 8 with **g** terribleness, and with signs, and 1419
27: 2 that thou shalt set thee up **g** stones, and 1419
28:59 *even* **g** plagues, and of long continuance, 1419
29: 3 The **g** temptations which thine eyes have 1419
29: 3 have seen, the signs, and those **g** miracles: 1419
29:24 what *meaneth* the heat of this **g** anger? 1419
29:28 in **g** indignation, and cast them into another 1419
34:12 in all the **g** terror which Moses shewed in 1419
Jos 1: 4 and this Lebanon even unto the **g** river, 1419
1: 4 unto the **g** sea *toward* the going down of 1419
6: 5 all the people shall shout *with* a **g** shout; 1419
6:20 the people shouted *with* a **g** shout, that 1419
7: 9 and what wilt thou do unto thy **g** name? 1419
7:26 they raised over him a **g** heap of stones 1419
8:29 raise thereon a **g** heap of stones, 1419
9: 1 in all the coasts of the **g** sea over against 1419
10: 2 because Gibeon *was* a **g** city, 1419
10:10 and slew them *with* a **g** slaughter at Gibeon, 1419
10:11 that the LORD cast down **g** stones from 1419
10:18 Roll **g** stones upon the mouth of the cave, 1419
10:20 end of slaying them *with* a very **g** slaughter, 1419
10:27 laid **g** stones in the cave's mouth, 1419
11: 8 chased them unto **g** Zidon, and 7227
14:12 and *that* the cities *were* **g** *and* fenced: 1419
14:15 which *Arba was* a **g** man among 1419
15:12 the west border *was* to the **g** sea, and 1419
15:47 and the **g** sea, and the border *thereof*. 1419
17:14 portion to inherit, seeing I *am* a **g** people, 7227
17:15 If thou *be* a **g** people, *then* get thee up to 7227
17:17 Thou *art* a **g** people, and hast great power: 7227
17:17 Thou *art* a great people, and hast **g** power: 1419
19:28 Hammon, and Kanah, *even* unto **g** Zidon; 7227
22:10 there an altar by Jordan, a **g** altar to see to. 1419
23: 4 have cut off, even *unto* the **g** sea westward. 1419
23: 9 hath driven out from before you **g** nations 1419
24:17 which did those **g** signs in our sight, and 1419
24:26 took a **g** stone, and set it up there under an 1419
Jdg 1: 6 and cut off his thumbs and his **g toes**. 7272
1: 7 having their thumbs and their **g toes** cut off, 7272
2: 7 who had seen all the **g** works of 1419
5:15 For the divisions of Reuben *there were* **g** 1419
5:16 For the divisions of Reuben *there were* **g** 1419
11:33 of the vineyards, *with* a very **g** slaughter. 1419
12: 2 my people were at **g** strife with the children 3966
15: 8 them hip and thigh *with* a **g** slaughter: 1419
15:18 Thou hast given this **g** deliverance into 1419
16: 5 see wherein his **g** strength *lieth*, and 1419
16: 6 wherein thy **g** strength *lieth*, and 1419
16:15 hast not told me wherein thy **g** strength 1419
16:23 to offer a **g** sacrifice unto Dagon their god, 1419
20:38 that they should make a **g** flame with 7235
21: 5 For *they* had made a **g** oath concerning *him* 1419
1Sa 2:17 young men was very **g** before the LORD: 1419
4: 5 all Israel shouted *with* a **g** shout, so that 1419
4: 6 What *meaneth* the noise of this **g** shout in 1419
4:10 there was a very **g** slaughter; for there fell 1419
4:17 there hath been also a **g** slaughter among 1419
5: 9 against the city *with* a very **g** destruction: 1419
5: 9 both small and **g**, and they had emerods in 1419
6: 9 *then* he hath done us this **g** evil: 1419
6:14 stood there, where *there was* a **g** stone: 1419
6:15 of gold *were*, and put *them* on the **g** stone: 1419

G

G

1Sa 6:18 even unto the g stone of Abel, 1419
6:19 many of the people with a g slaughter. 1419
7:10 the LORD thundered with a g thunder on 1419
12:16 Now therefore stand and see this g thing, 1419
12:17 and see that your wickedness is g, 7227
12:22 forsake his people for his g name's sake: 1419
12:24 for consider how g things he hath done for 1431
14:15 earth quaked: so it was a very g trembling. 430
14:20 and there was a very g discomfiture. 1419
14:33 roll a g stone unto me this day. 1419
14:45 who hath wrought this g salvation in Israel? 1419
15:22 Hath the LORD as g delight in burnt NIH
17:25 the king will enrich him with g riches, and 1419
19:5 the LORD wrought a g salvation for all 1419
19:8 and slew them with a g slaughter; 1419
19:22 and came to a g well that is in Sechu: 1419
20:2 my father will do nothing either g or small, 1419
23:5 and smote them with a g slaughter. 1419
25:2 the man was very g, and he had three 1419
26:13 hill afar off; a g space being between them: 7227
26:25 thou shalt both do g things, and 6213+6213
30:2 either g or small, but carried them away, 1419
30:16 of all the g spoil that they had taken out of 1419
30:19 neither small nor g, neither sons nor 1419
2Sa 3:22 a troop, and brought in a g spoil with them: 7227
3:38 and a g man fallen this day in Israel? 1419
5:10 grew g, and the LORD God of hosts was 1419
7:9 of thy sight, and have made thee a g name, 1419
7:9 like unto the name of the g men that are in 1419
7:19 house for a g while to come. 4480+7350
7:21 hast thou done all these g things, 1420
7:22 Wherefore thou art g, O LORD God: 1431
7:23 to do for you g things and terrible, for thy 1420
12:14 given g occasion to the enemies of the
LORD to blaspheme, 5006+5006
12:30 he brought forth the spoil of the city in g 3966
18:7 there was there a g slaughter that day of 1419
18:9 the mule went under the thick boughs of a g 1419
18:17 cast him into a g pit in the wood, and laid a 1419
18:17 and laid a very g heap of stones upon him: 1419
18:29 I saw a g tumult, but I knew not what it 1419
19:32 lay at Mahanaim; for he was a very g man. 1419
20:8 When they were at the g stone which is in 1419
21:20 where was a man of g stature, that had on NIH
22:36 and thy gentleness hath made me g. 7235
23:10 the LORD wrought a g victory that day; 1419
23:12 and the LORD wrought a g victory. 1419
24:14 And David said unto Gad, I am in a g strait: 3966
24:14 hand of the LORD; for his mercies are g: 7227
1Ki 1:40 rejoiced with g joy, so that the earth rent 1419
3:4 for that was the g high place: 1419
3:6 unto thy servant David my father g mercy, 1419
3:6 thou hast kept for him this g kindness, that 1419
3:8 a g people, that cannot be numbered nor 7227
3:9 who is able to judge this thy so g a people? 3515
4:13 threescore g cities with walls and 1419
5:7 unto David a wise son over this g people. 7227
5:17 they brought g stones, costly stones, and 1419
7:9 and so on the outside toward the g court. 1419
7:10 even g stones, stones of ten cubits, and 1419
7:12 the g court round about was with three 1419
8:42 (For they shall hear of thy g name, and of 1419
8:65 and all Israel with him, a g congregation, 1419
10:2 she came to Jerusalem with a very g train, 3515
10:10 of spices very g store, and precious stones: 7235
10:11 brought in from Ophir g plenty of almug 3966
10:18 Moreover the king made a g throne of 1419
11:19 Hadad found g favour in the sight of 3966
18:32 as g as would contain two measures of 3509.1
18:45 and wind, and there was a g rain. 1419
19:7 eat; because the journey is too g for thee. 7227
19:11 and a g and strong wind rent the mountains, 1419
20:13 Hast thou seen all this g multitude? 1419
20:21 and slew the Syrians with a g slaughter. 1419
20:28 will I deliver all this g multitude into thine 1419
22:31 saying, Fight neither with small nor g, 1419
2Ki 3:27 there was g indignation against Israel: and 1419
4:8 passed to Shunem, where was a g woman; 1419
4:38 Set on the g pot, and seethe pottage for 1419
5:1 was a g man with his master, and 1419
5:13 if the prophet had bid thee do some g thing, 1419
6:14 he thither horses, and chariots, and a g host: 3515
6:23 he prepared g provision for them: and 1419
6:25 there was a g famine in Samaria: and 1419
7:6 noise of horses, even the noise of a g host: 1419
8:4 all the g things that Elisha hath done. 1419
8:13 a dog, that he should do this g thing? 1419
10:6 were with the g men of the city, 1419
10:11 all his g men, and his kinsfolks, and 1419
10:19 for I have a g sacrifice to do to Baal; 1419
16:15 Upon the g altar burn the morning burnt 1419
17:21 the LORD, and made them sin a g sin. 1419
17:36 up out of the land of Egypt with g power 1419
18:17 Hezekiah with a g host against Jerusalem. 3515
18:19 Thus saith the g king, the king of Assyria, 1419
18:28 spake, saying, Hear the word of the g king, 1419
22:13 for g is the wrath of the LORD that is 1419
23:2 and all the people, both small and g: 1419
23:26 not from the fierceness of his g wrath, 1419
25:9 and every g man's house burnt he with fire. 1419
25:26 both small and g, and the captains of 1419
1Ch 11:14 the LORD saved them by a g deliverance. 1419
11:23 a man of g stature, five cubits high; and NIH
12:22 until it was a g host, like the host of God. 1419
16:25 For g is the LORD, and greatly to be 1419
17:8 the name of the g men that are in the earth. 1419
17:17 house for a g while to come, 4480+7350
17:19 in making known all these g things. 1420
20:6 where was a man of g stature, whose fingers NIH
21:13 And David said unto Gad, I am in a g strait: 3966
21:13 of the LORD; for very g are his mercies: 7227
22:8 blood abundantly, and hast made g wars: 1419
25:8 against ward, as well the small as the g, 1419
26:13 they cast lots, as well the small as the g, 1419
29:1 is yet young and tender, and the work is g: 1419
1Ch 29:9 and David the king also rejoiced with g joy. 1419
29:12 in thine hand it is to make g, and to give 1431
29:22 drink before the LORD on that day with g 1419
2Ch 1:8 Thou hast shewed g mercy unto David my 1419
1:10 who can judge this thy people, that is so g? 1419
2:5 the house which I build is g: for great is our 1419
2:5 is great: for g is our God above all gods. 1419
2:9 I am about to build shall be wonderful g. 1419
4:9 and the g court, and doors for the court, and 1419
4:18 Thus Solomon made all these vessels in g 3966
6:32 is come from a far country for thy g name's 1419
7:8 all Israel with him, a very g congregation, 1419
9:1 with a very g company, and camels that 3515
9:9 of spices g abundance, and precious stones: 3966
9:17 Moreover the king made a g throne of 1419
13:8 ye be a g multitude, and there are with you 7227
13:17 his people slew them with a g slaughter: 7227
15:5 g vexations were upon all the inhabitants of 7227
15:13 whether small or g, whether man or 1419
16:12 until his disease was exceeding g: yet in his NIH
16:14 and they made a very g burning for him. 1419
17:12 And Jehoshaphat waxed g exceedingly; and 1432
18:30 saying, Fight ye not with small or g, 1419
20:2 There cometh a g multitude against thee 7227
20:12 for we have no might against this g 7227
20:15 nor dismayed by reason of this g multitude; 7227
21:3 their father gave them g gifts of silver, and 7227
21:14 with a g plague will the LORD smite thy 1419
21:15 thou shalt have g sickness by disease of thy 7227
24:24 the LORD delivered a very g host into 7230
24:25 from him, (for they left him in g diseases,) 7227
25:10 and they returned home in g anger. 2750
26:15 to shoot arrows and g stones withal. 1419
28:5 carried away a g multitude of them 1419
28:5 who smote him with a g slaughter. 1419
28:13 for our trespass is g, and there is fierce 7227
30:13 in the second month, a very g congregation. 7230
30:21 bread seven days with g gladness: 1419
30:24 a g number of priests sanctified 7230+3807.1
30:26 So there was g joy in Jerusalem: for since 1419
31:10 and that which is left is this g store. 1995
31:15 by courses, as well to the g as to the small: 1419
33:14 raised it up a very g height, and 1361
34:21 for g is the wrath of the LORD that is 1419
34:30 the Levites, and all the people, g and small: 1419
36:18 g and small, and the treasures of the house 1419
Ezr 3:11 all the people shouted with a g shout, 1419
4:10 the rest of the nations whom the g and 7229
5:8 to the house of the g God, which is builded 7229
5:8 which is builded with g stones, and 1560
5:11 which a g king of Israel builded and set up. 7229
6:4 With three rows of g stones, and a row of 1560
9:7 have we been in a g trespass unto this day; 1419
9:13 us for our evil deeds, and for our g trespass, 1419
10:1 out of Israel a very g congregation of men 7227
10:9 because of this matter, and for the g rain. 1653
Ne 1:3 there in the province are in g affliction 1419
1:5 the g and terrible God, that keepeth 1419
1:10 whom thou hast redeemed by thy g power, 1419
3:27 over against the g tower that lieth out, 1419
4:1 took g indignation, and mocked the Jews. 7235
4:14 which is g and terrible, and fight for your 1419
4:19 The work is g and large, and we are 7235
5:1 there was a g cry of the people and of their 1419
5:7 And I set a g assembly against them. 1419
6:3 I am doing a g work, so that I cannot come 1419
7:4 Now the city was large and g: but 1419
8:6 Ezra blessed the LORD, the g God. 1419
8:12 to make g mirth, because they had 1419
8:17 done so. And there was very g gladness. 1419
9:17 and of g kindness, and forsookest them not. 7227
9:18 of Egypt, and had wrought g provocations; 1419
9:25 delighted themselves in thy g goodness. 1419
9:26 to thee, and they wrought g provocations. 1419
9:31 Nevertheless for thy g mercies' sake thou 7227
9:32 our God, the g, the mighty, and the terrible 1419
9:35 in thy g goodness that thou gavest them, 7227
9:37 at their pleasure, and we are in g distress. 1419
11:14 was Zabdiel, the son of one of the g men. 1419
12:31 appointed two g companies of them that 1419
12:43 Also that day they offered g sacrifices, and 1419
12:43 for God had made them rejoice with g joy: 1419
13:5 he had prepared for him a g chamber, 1419
13:27 then hearken unto you to do all this g evil, 1419
Est 1:5 both unto g and small, seven days, in 1419
1:20 throughout all his empire, (for it is g,) 7227
1:20 their husbands honour, both to g and small. 1419
2:18 the king made a g feast unto all his princes 1419
4:3 there was g mourning among the Jews, and 1419
8:15 with a g crown of gold, and with a garment 1419
9:4 For Mordecai was g in the king's house, 1419
10:3 g among the Jews, and accepted of 1419
Job 1:3 hundred she asses, and a very g household; 7227
1:19 there came a g wind from the wilderness, 1419
2:13 for they saw that his grief was very g. 1431
3:19 The small and g are there; and the servant 1419
5:9 Which doeth g things and unsearchable; 1419
5:25 shalt know also that thy seed shall be g, 7227
9:10 Which doeth g things past finding out; yea, 1419
22:5 Is not thy wickedness g? and 7227
23:6 Will he plead against me with his g power? 7230
30:18 By the g force of my disease is my garment 7230
31:25 If I rejoiced because my wealth was g, and 7227
31:34 Did I fear a g multitude, or did 7227
32:9 G men are not always wise: neither do 7227
35:15 yet he knoweth it not in g extremity: 3966
36:18 then a g ransom cannot deliver thee. 7230
36:26 Behold, God is g, and we know him not, 7689
37:5 g things doeth he, which we cannot 1419
37:6 small rain, and to the g rain of his strength. 4306
38:21 or because the number of thy days is g? 7227
39:11 thou trust him, because his strength is g? 7227
Ps 14:5 There were they in g fear: for God is 6342+6343
18:35 me up, and thy gentleness hath made me g. 7235
18:50 G deliverance giveth he to his king; and 1431
Ps 19:11 and in keeping of them there is g reward. 7227
19:13 I shall be innocent from the g transgression. 7227
21:5 His glory is g in thy salvation: honour and 1419
22:25 My praise shall be of thee in the g 7227
25:11 O LORD, pardon mine iniquity; for it is g. 7227
31:19 O how g is thy goodness, which thou hast 7227
32:6 surely in the floods of g waters they shall 7227
33:17 neither shall he deliver any by his g 7230
35:18 I will give thee thanks in the g 7227
36:6 Thy righteousness is like the g mountains; 410
36:6 thy judgments are a g deep: 7227
37:35 I have seen the wicked in g power, and 6184
40:9 I have preached righteousness in the g 7227
40:10 and thy truth from the g congregation. 7227
47:2 is terrible; he is a g King over all the earth. 1419
48:1 G is the LORD, and greatly to be praised 1419
48:2 sides of the north, the city of the g King. 7227
53:5 There were they in g fear, where no 6342+6343
57:10 For thy mercy is g unto the heavens, and 1419
58:6 break out the g teeth of the young lions, 4459
68:11 g was the company of those that published 7227
71:19 very high, who hast done g things: O God, 1419
71:20 Thou, which hast shewed me g and 7227
76:1 is God known: his name is g in Israel. 1419
77:13 who is so g a God as our God? 1419
77:19 thy path in the g waters, and thy footsteps 7227
78:15 and gave them drink as out of the g depths. 7227
78:71 From following the ewes g with young he 5763
80:5 and givest them tears to drink in g measure. NIH
86:10 For thou art g, and doest wondrous things: 1419
86:13 For g is thy mercy toward me: and 1419
92:5 O LORD, how g are thy works! and 1431
95:3 For the LORD is a g God, and a great 1419
95:3 is a great God, and a g King above all gods. 1419
96:4 For the LORD is g, and greatly to be 1419
99:2 The LORD is g in Zion; and he is high 1419
99:3 Let them praise thy g and terrible name; 1419
103:11 g is his mercy toward them that fear him. 1396
104:1 O LORD my God, thou art very g; 1431
104:25 So is this g and wide sea, wherein are 1419
104:25 both small and g beasts. 1419
106:21 which had done g things in Egypt; 1419
107:23 sea in ships, that do business in g waters; 7227
108:4 For thy mercy is g above the heavens: and 1419
111:2 The works of the LORD are g, sought out 1419
115:13 that fear the LORD, both small and g. 1419
117:2 For his merciful kindness is g toward us: 1396
119:156 G are thy tender mercies, O LORD: 7227
119:162 at thy word, as one that findeth g spoil. 7227
119:165 G peace have they which love thy law: and 7227
126:2 The LORD hath done g things for them. 1431
126:3 The LORD hath done g things for us; 1431
131:1 neither do I exercise myself in g matters, or 1419
135:5 For I know that the LORD is g, and 1419
135:10 Who smote g nations, and slew mighty 7227
136:4 To him who alone doeth g wonders: for his 1419
136:7 To him that made g lights: for his mercy 1419
136:17 To him which smote g kings: for his mercy 1419
138:5 for g is the glory of the LORD. 1419
139:17 unto me, O God: how g is the sum of them! 6105
144:7 rid me, and deliver me out of g waters, 7227
145:3 G is the LORD, and greatly to be praised; 1419
145:7 utter the memory of thy g goodness, 7227
145:8 slow to anger, and of g mercy. 1419
147:5 G is our Lord, and of great power: 1419
147:5 Great is our Lord, and of g power: 7227
Pr 13:7 that maketh himself poor, yet hath g riches. 7227
14:29 He that is slow to wrath is of g 7227
15:16 with the fear of the LORD than g treasure 7227
16:8 Better is a little with righteousness than g 7230
18:9 work is brother to him that is a g waster. 1167
18:16 for him, and bringeth him before g men. 1419
19:19 A man of g wrath shall suffer punishment: 1419
22:1 A good name is rather to be chosen than g 7227
25:6 and stand not in the place of g men: 1419
26:10 The g God that formed all things both 7227
28:12 righteous men do rejoice, there is g glory: 7227
28:16 understanding is also a g oppressor: 7227
Ecc 1:16 Lo, I am come to g estate, and have gotten 1431
1:16 my heart had g experience of wisdom and 7235
2:4 I made me g works; I builded me houses; 1431
2:7 also I had g possessions of great and 7235
2:7 had great possessions of g and small cattle 1241
2:9 So I was g, and increased more than all that 1431
2:21 his portion. This also is vanity and a g evil. 7227
8:6 therefore the misery of man is g upon him. 7227
9:13 under the sun, and it seemed g unto me: 1419
9:14 there came a g king against it, and 1419
9:14 besieged it, and built g bulwarks against it: 1419
10:4 thy place; for yielding pacifieth g offences. 1419
10:6 Folly is set in g dignity, and the rich sit in 7227
SS 2:3 sat down under his shadow with g delight, 2530
Isa 2:9 and the g man humbleth himself; NIH
5:9 even g and fair, without inhabitant. 1419
6:12 there be a g forsaking in the midst of 7227
8:1 Take thee a g roll, and write in it with a 1419
9:2 that walked in darkness have seen a g light: 1419
12:6 for g is the Holy One of Israel in the midst 1419
13:4 in the mountains, like as of a g people; 7227
16:14 be contemned, with all that g multitude; 7227
19:20 and a g one, and he shall deliver them. 7227
23:3 by g waters the seed of Sihor, the harvest of 7227
27:1 day the LORD with his sore and g and 1419
27:13 that the g trumpet shall be blown, and 1419
29:6 g noise, with storm and tempest, and 1419
30:25 streams of waters in the day of the g 7227
32:2 as the shadow of a g rock in a weary land. 3515
33:23 is the prey of a g spoil divided; the lame 4766
34:6 and a g slaughter in the land of Idumea. 7227
34:15 There shall the g owl make her nest, and 7091
36:2 unto king Hezekiah with a g army. 3515
36:4 Thus saith the g king, the king of Assyria, 1419
36:13 said, Hear ye the words of the g king, 1419
38:17 Behold, for peace I had g bitterness: 4751+4843
47:9 for the g abundance of thine enchantments. 3966

Isa 51:10 hath dried the sea, the waters of the **g** deep; 7227
53:12 will I divide him *a portion* with the **g**, 7227
54: 7 but with **g** mercies will I gather thee. 1419
54:13 and **g** *shall be* the peace of thy children. 7227
63: 7 the **g** goodness towards the house of Israel, 7227
Jer 4: 6 evil from the north, and a **g** destruction. 1419
5: 5 I will get me unto the **g men**, and 1419
5:27 therefore they are become **g**, and 1431
6: 1 out of the north, and **g** destruction. 1419
6:22 a **g** nation shall be raised from the sides of 1419
10: 6 thou *art* **g**, and thy name *is* great in might. 1419
10: 6 thou *art* great, and thy name *is* **g** in might. 1419
10:22 a **g** commotion out of the north country, 1419
11:16 with the noise of a **g** tumult he hath kindled 1419
13: 9 of Judah, and the **g** pride of Jerusalem. 7227
14:17 of my people is broken *with* a **g** breach, 1419
16: 6 Both the **g** and the small shall die in this 1419
16:10 pronounced all this **g** evil against us? 1419
20:17 and her womb *to be* always **g** *with me.* 2030
21: 5 even in anger, and in fury, and in **g** wrath. 1419
21: 6 and beast: they shall die of a **g** pestilence. 1419
22: 8 hath the LORD done thus unto this **g** city? 1419
25:14 **g** kings shall serve themselves of them also: 1419
25:32 a **g** whirlwind shall be raised up from 1419
26:19 Thus *might* we procure **g** evil against our 1419
27: 5 by my **g** power and by my outstretched 1419
27: 7 and **g** kings shall serve themselves of him. 1419
28: 8 and against **g** kingdoms, of war, and of evil, 1419
30: 7 for that day *is* **g**, so that none *is* like it: it *is* 1419
31: 8 a **g** company shall return thither. 1419
32:17 the earth by thy **g** power and stretched out 1419
32:18 the **G**, the Mighty God, the LORD of 1419
32:19 **G** in counsel, and mighty in work: for thine 1419
32:21 with a stretched out arm, and with **g** terror; 1419
32:37 mine anger, and in my fury, and in **g** wrath; 1419
32:42 Like as I have brought all this **g** evil upon 1419
33: 3 shew thee **g** and mighty *things,* which thou 1419
36: 7 for **g** *is* the anger and the fury that 1419
41:12 found him by the **g** waters that *are* in 7227
43: 9 Take **g** stones in thine hand, and hide them 1419
44: 7 Wherefore commit ye *this* **g** evil against 1419
44:15 all the women that stood *by,* a **g** multitude, 1419
44:26 Behold, I have sworn by my **g** name, 1419
45: 5 seekest thou **g** *things* for thyself? seek *them* 1419
48: 3 from Horonaim, spoiling and **g** destruction. 1419
50: 9 of **g** nations from the north country: 1419
50:22 of battle *is* in the land, and of **g** destruction. 1419
50:41 a **g** nation, and many kings shall be raised 1419
51:54 **g** destruction from the land of 1419
51:55 and destroyed out of her the **g** voice; 1419
51:55 when her waves do roar like **g** waters, 7227
52:13 all the houses of the **g** *men,* burnt he with 1419
La 1: 1 she *that was* **g** among the nations, *and* 7227
1: 3 of affliction, and because of **g** servitude: 7230
2:13 for thy breach *is* **g** like the sea: who can 1419
3:23 new every morning: **g** *is* thy faithfulness. 7227
Eze 1: 4 a **g** cloud, and a fire infolding itself, and 1419
1:24 like the noise of **g** waters, as the voice of 7227
3:12 I heard behind me a voice of a **g** rushing, 1419
3:13 against them, and a noise of a **g** rushing. 1419
8: 6 *even* the **g** abominations that the house of 1419
9: 9 house of Israel and Judah *is* exceeding **g**, 1419
13:11 ye, O **g hailstones**, shall fall; and 68+417
13:13 **g hailstones** in *my* fury to consume *it.* 68+417
16: 7 thou hast increased and **waxen g**, and 1431
16:26 the Egyptians thy neighbours, **g** of flesh; 1432
17: 3 A **g** eagle with great wings, longwinged, 1419
17: 3 A great eagle with **g** wings, longwinged, 1419
17: 5 he placed *it* by **g** waters, *and* set it *as* a 7227
17: 7 There was also another **g** eagle with great 1419
17: 7 There was also another great eagle with **g** 1419
17: 8 It *was* planted in a good soil by **g** waters, 7227
17: 9 even without **g** power or many people to 1419
17:17 and **g** company make for him in the war, 7227
21:14 it *is* the sword of the **g** *men that are* slain, 1419
23:23 captains and rulers, **g lords** and renowned, 7991
24: 9 I will even **make** the pile for fire **g**. 1431
24:12 and her **g** scum went not forth out of her: 7227
25:17 I will execute **g** vengeance upon them with 1419
26:19 upon thee, and **g** waters shall cover thee; 7227
27:26 Thy rowers have brought thee into **g** 7227
28: 5 By thy **g** wisdom *and* by thy traffick hast 7230
29: 3 the **g** dragon that lieth in the midst of his 1419
29:18 his army to serve a **g** service against Tyrus: 1419
30: 4 **g pain** shall be in Ethiopia, when the slain 2479
30: 9 **g pain** shall come upon them, as *in* the day 2479
30:16 Sin shall **have g pain**, and No shall 2342+2342
31: 4 The waters **made** him **g**, the deep set him 1431
31: 6 and under his shadow dwelt all **g** nations. 7227
31: 7 his branches: for his root was by **g** waters. 7227
31:15 and the **g** waters were stayed: 7227
32:13 beasts thereof from besides the **g** waters; 7227
36:23 I will sanctify my **g** name, which was 1419
37:10 up upon their feet, an exceeding **g** army. 1419
38: 4 *of armour, even* a **g** company *with* bucklers 7227
38:13 *away* cattle and goods, to take a **g** spoil? 1419
38:15 a **g** company, and a mighty army: 1419
38:19 Surely in that day there shall be a **g** shaking 1419
38:22 and **g hailstones**, fire, and brimstone. 68+417
39:17 *even* a **g** sacrifice upon the mountains of 1419
41: 8 chambers *were* a full reed of six **g** cubits. 679
47: 9 there shall be a very **g multitude** of fish, 7227
47:10 as the fish of the **g** sea, exceeding many. 1419
47:15 from the **g** sea, the way of Hethlon, as *men* 1419
47:19 of strife *in* Kadesh, *the* river to the **g** sea. 1419
47:20 The west side also *shall be* the **g** sea from 1419
48:28 *and to the* river toward the **g** sea. 1419
Da 2: 6 of me gifts and rewards and **g** honour: 7690
2:31 O king, sawest, and behold a **g** image. 7690
2:31 This **g** image, whose brightness *was* 7229
2:35 the stone that smote the image became a **g** 7229
2:45 the **g** God hath made known to the king 7229
2:48 the king **made** Daniel a **g** man, and 7236
2:48 gave him many **g** gifts, and made him ruler 7260
4: 3 How **g** *are* his signs! and how mighty *are* 7260

Da 4:10 of the earth, and the height thereof *was* **g**. 7690
4:30 king spake, and said, *Is* not this **g** Babylon, 7229
5: 1 Belshazzar the king made a **g** feast to a 7229
7: 2 winds of the heaven strove upon the **g** sea. 7229
7: 3 four **g** beasts came up from the sea, 7260
7: 7 strong exceedingly; and it had **g** iron teeth: 7260
7: 8 of man, and a mouth speaking **g** *things.* 7260
7:11 of the voice of the **g** words which the horn 7260
7:17 These **g** beasts, which *are* four, *are* four 7260
7:20 a mouth that spake **very g** *things,* whose 7229
7:25 he shall speak **g** words against the most NIH
8: 4 he did according to his will, and became **g**. 1431
8: 8 Therefore the he goat **waxed** very **g**: and 1431
8: 8 when he was strong, the **g** horn was broken; 1419
8: 9 which waxed exceeding **g**, toward 1431
8:10 And it **waxed g**, *even* to the host of heaven; 1431
8:21 the **g** horn that *is* between his eyes *is* 1419
9: 4 and said, O Lord, the **g** and dreadful God, 1419
9:12 judged us, by bringing upon us a **g** evil: 1419
9:18 our righteousnesses, but for thy **g** mercies. 7227
10: 4 as I was by the side of the **g** river, which *is* 1419
10: 7 a **g** quaking fell upon them, so that they 1419
10: 8 saw this **g** vision, and there remained no 1419
11: 3 that shall rule *with* **g** dominion, and 7227
11: 5 his dominion *shall be* a **g** dominion. 7227
11:10 and shall assemble a multitude of **g** forces: 7227
11:11 he shall set forth a **g** multitude; but 7227
11:13 come after certain years with a **g** army 1419
11:25 against the king of the south with a **g** army; 1419
11:25 shall be stirred up to battle with a very **g** 1419
11:28 shall he return *into* his land with **g** riches; 1419
11:44 he shall go forth with **g** fury to destroy, 1419
12: 1 the **g** prince which standeth for the children 1419
Hos 1: 2 land hath **committed g whoredom**, 2181+2181
1:11 of the land: for **g** *shall be* the day of Jezreel. 1419
8:12 I have written to him the **g things** of my 7230
9: 7 of thine iniquity, and the **g** hatred. 7227
10:15 because of your **g wickedness**; 7451+7465
13: 5 in the wilderness, in the land of **g drought**. 8514
Joel 1: 6 and he hath the cheek-teeth of a **g lion**. 3833
2: 2 a **g** people and a strong; there hath not been 7227
2:11 for his camp *is* very **g**: for *he is* strong that 7227
2:11 for the day of the LORD *is* **g** and 1419
2:13 of **g** kindness, and repenteth him of 7227
2:20 come up, because he hath done **g things**. 1431
2:21 rejoice: for the LORD will do **g things**. 1431
2:25 my **g** army which I sent among you. 1419
2:31 before the **g** and the terrible day of 1419
3:13 the fats overflow; for their wickedness *is* **g**. 7227
Am 3: 9 behold the **g** tumults in the midst thereof, 7227
3:15 the **g** houses shall have an end, saith 7227
6: 2 and from thence go ye *to* Hamath the **g**: 7227
6:11 he will smite the **g** house *with* breaches, 1419
7: 4 it devoured the **g** deep, and did eat up a 7227
8: 5 the shekel **g**, and falsifying the balances by 1431
Jnh 1: 2 to Nineveh, *that* **g** city, and cry against it; 1419
1: 4 the LORD sent out a **g** wind into the sea, 1419
1:12 for I know that for my sake this **g** tempest 1419
1:17 Now the LORD had prepared a **g** fish to 1419
3: 2 *that* **g** city, and preach unto it the preaching 1419
3: 3 Now Nineveh was an exceeding **g** city of 1419
4: 2 of **g** kindness, and repentest thee of 7227
4:11 And should not I spare Nineveh, *that* **g** city, 1419
Mic 2:12 they shall **make g noise** by reason of 1949
5: 4 for now shall he be **g** unto the ends of 1431
7: 3 the **g** *man,* he uttereth his mischievous 1419
Na 1: 3 **g** in power, and will not at all acquit 1419
3: 3 of slain, and a **g number** of carcases; 3514
3:10 and all her **g** *men* were bound in chains. 1419
3:17 thy captains as the **g grasshoppers**, 1462+1462
Hab 3:15 thine horses, *through* the heap of **g** waters. 7227
Zep 1:10 the second, and a **g** crashing from the hills. 1419
1:14 The **g** day of the LORD *is* near, *it is* near, 1419
Zec 1:14 and for Zion *with* a **g** jealousy. 1419
4: 7 Who *art* thou, O **g** mountain? 1419
7:12 came a **g** wrath from the LORD of hosts. 1419
8: 2 I was jealous for Zion *with* **g** jealousy, and 1419
8: 2 and I was jealous for her *with* **g** fury. 1419
9:17 For **how g** *is* his goodness, and how great *is* 4100
9:17 *is* his goodness, and **how g** *is* his beauty! 4100
12:11 In that day shall there be a **g** mourning in 1431
14: 4 the west, *and there shall be* a very **g** valley; 1419
14:13 *that* a **g** tumult from the LORD shall be 7227
14:14 and silver, and apparel, in **g** abundance. 3966
Mal 1:11 my name *shall be* **g** among the Gentiles; 1419
1:11 for my name *shall be* **g** among the heathen, 1419
1:14 the Lord a corrupt *thing:* for I *am* a **g** King, 1419
4: 5 the prophet before the coming of the **g** 1419
Mt 2:10 the star, they rejoiced *with* exceeding **g** joy. *3173*
2:18 lamentation, and weeping, and **g** mourning, *4183*
4:16 The people which sat in darkness saw **g** *3173*
4:25 And there followed him **g** multitudes *of* *4183*
5:12 for **g** *is* your reward in heaven: for so *4183*
5:19 teach *them,* the same shall be called **g** in *3173*
5:35 for it is the city of the **g** King. *3173*
6:23 in thee be darkness, **how g** *is* that darkness? *4214*
7:27 and it fell: and **g** was the fall of it. *3173*
8: 1 the mountain, **g** multitudes followed him. *4183*
8:10 I have not found **so g** faith, no not in Israel. *5118*
8:18 Now when Jesus saw **g** multitudes about *4183*
8:24 there arose a **g** tempest in the sea, *3173*
8:26 and the sea; and there was a **g** calm. *3173*
12:15 and **g** multitudes followed him, and *4183*
13: 2 And **g** multitudes were gathered together *4183*
13:46 when he had found one pearl of **g price**, *4186*
14:14 and saw a **g** multitude, and was moved with *4183*
15:28 and said unto her, O woman, **g** *is* thy faith: *3173*
15:30 And **g** multitudes came unto him, *4183*
15:33 the wilderness, as to fill **so g** a multitude? *5118*
19: 2 And **g** multitudes followed him; and *4183*
19:22 away sorrowful: for he had **g** possessions. *4183*
20:25 they *that are* **g** exercise authority upon *3173*
20:26 but whosoever will be **g** among you, *3173*
20:29 from Jericho, a **g** multitude followed him. *4183*
21: 8 And a **very g** multitude spread their *4183*

Mt 22:36 which *is* the **g** commandment in the law? *3173*
22:38 This is the first and **g** commandment. *3173*
24:21 For then shall be **g** tribulation, such as was *3173*
24:24 and shall shew **g** signs and wonders; *3173*
24:30 clouds of heaven with power and **g** glory. *4183*
24:31 And he shall send his angels with a **g** sound *3173*
26:47 with him a **g** multitude with swords and *4183*
27:60 he rolled a **g** stone to the door of *3173*
28: 2 And behold, there was a **g** earthquake: *3173*
28: 8 from the sepulchre with fear and **g** joy; *3173*
Mk 1:35 rising up a **g while** before day, he went out, *3029*
3: 7 a **g** multitude from Galilee followed him, *4183*
3: 8 they about Tyre and Sidon, a **g** multitude, *4183*
3: 8 when they had heard **what g** *things* he did, *3745*
4: 1 there was gathered unto him a **g** multitude, *4183*
4:32 than all herbs, and shooteth out **g** branches; *3173*
4:37 And there arose a **g** storm of wind, and *3173*
4:39 the wind ceased, and there was a **g** calm. *3173*
5:11 the mountains a **g** herd of swine feeding. *3173*
5:19 tell them **how g** *things* the Lord hath done *3745*
5:20 began to publish in Decapolis **how g** *things* *3745*
5:42 And they were astonished with a **g** *3173*
7:36 much the more a **g deal** they published *it;* *4054*
8: 1 In those days the multitude being **very g**, *3827*
9:14 he saw a **g** multitude about them, and *4183*
10:22 away grieved: for he had **g** possessions. *4183*
10:42 their **g ones** exercise authority upon them. *3173*
10:43 but whosoever will be **g** among you, *3173*
10:46 his disciples and a **g number** of people, *2425*
10:48 but he cried the more a **g deal**, *Thou* Son of *4183*
13: 2 said unto him, Seest thou these **g** buildings? *3173*
13:26 of man coming in *the* clouds with **g** power *4183*
14:43 with him a **g** multitude with swords and *4183*
16: 4 stone was rolled away: for it was very **g**. *3173*
Lk 1:15 For he shall be **g** in the sight of the Lord, *3173*
1:32 He shall be **g**, and shall be called the Son of *3173*
1:49 he *that is* mighty hath done to me **g things**; *3167*
1:58 the Lord had **shewed g** mercy upon her; *3170*
2: 5 his espoused wife, being **g with child**. *1471*
2:10 I bring you good tidings of **g** joy, *3173*
2:36 of the tribe of Aser: she was of a **g** age, *4183*
4:25 when **g** famine was throughout all the land; *3173*
4:38 wife's mother was taken with a **g** fever; *3173*
5: 6 they inclosed a **g** multitude of fishes: *4183*
5:15 and **g** multitudes came together to hear, and *4183*
5:29 And Levi made him a **g** feast in his own *3173*
5:29 there was a **g** company of publicans and *4183*
6:17 a **g** multitude of people out of all Judea and *4183*
6:23 *joy:* for behold, your reward *is* **g** in heaven: *4183*
6:35 and your reward shall be **g**, and ye shall be *4183*
6:49 it fell; and the ruin of that house was **g**. *3173*
7: 9 I have not found **so g** faith, no, not in Israel. *5118*
7:16 That a **g** prophet is risen up among us; *3173*
8:37 from them; for they were taken with **g** fear: *3173*
8:39 shew **how g** *things* God hath done unto *3745*
8:39 published throughout the whole city **how g** *3745*
9:48 is least among you all, the same shall be **g**. *3173*
10: 2 The harvest truly *is* **g**, but the labourers *are* *4183*
10:13 they had a **g while ago** repented, sitting in *3819*
13:19 and it grew, and waxed a **g** tree; and *3173*
14:16 A certain man made a **g** supper, and *3173*
14:25 And there went **g** multitudes with him: and *4183*
14:32 Or else, while the other is yet a **g way off**, *4206*
15:20 But when he was yet a **g way** off, his father *3112*
16:26 between us and you there is a **g** gulf fixed: *3173*
21:11 And **g** earthquakes shall be in divers places, *3173*
21:11 and **g** signs shall there be from heaven. *3173*
21:23 for there shall be **g** distress in the land, and *3173*
21:27 coming in a cloud with power and **g** glory. *4183*
22:44 his sweat was as it were **g** drops of blood NIG
23:27 And there followed him a **g** company of *4183*
24:52 and returned to Jerusalem with **g** joy: *3173*
Jn 5: 3 In these lay a **g** multitude of impotent *folk,* *4183*
6: 2 And a **g** multitude followed him, because *4183*
6: 5 and saw a **g** company come unto him, *4183*
6:18 And the sea arose by reason of a **g** wind *3173*
7:37 *that* **g** *day* of the feast, Jesus stood and *3173*
21:11 and drew the net to land full of **g** fishes, *3173*
Ac 2:20 before *that* **g** and notable day of the Lord *3173*
4:33 And with **g** power gave the apostles witness *3173*
4:33 Lord Jesus: and **g** grace was upon them all. *3173*
5: 5 **g** fear came on all them that heard these *3173*
5:11 And **g** fear came upon all the church, and *3173*
6: 7 a **g** company of the priests were obedient to *4183*
6: 8 did **g** wonders and miracles among *3173*
7:11 land of Egypt and Canaan, and **g** affliction: *3173*
8: 1 And at that time there was a **g** persecution *3173*
8: 2 and made **g** lamentation over him. *3173*
8: 8 And there was **g** joy in that city. *3173*
8: 9 giving out that himself was some **g one**: *3173*
8:10 saying, This *man* is the **g** power of God. *3173*
8:27 an eunuch **of g authority** under Candace *1413*
9:16 For I will shew him **how g** *things* he must *3745*
10:11 as *it had been* a **g** sheet knit at the four *3173*
11: 5 vessel descend, as *it had been* a **g** sheet, *3173*
11:21 and a **g** number believed, and turned unto *4183*
11:28 signified by the Spirit that there should be **g** *3173*
14: 1 that a **g** multitude both of the Jews and *4183*
15: 3 and they caused **g** joy unto all the brethren. *3173*
16:26 And suddenly there was a **g** earthquake, so *3173*
17: 4 and of the devout Greeks a **g** multitude, and *4183*
19:27 also that the temple of the **g** goddess Diana *3173*
19:28 saying, **G** *is* Diana of the Ephesians. *3173*
19:34 cried out, **G** *is* Diana of the Ephesians. *3173*
19:35 is a worshipper of the **g** goddess Diana, *3173*
21:40 And when there was made a **g** silence, *4183*
22: 6 suddenly there shone from heaven a **g** light *2425*
22:28 With a **g** sum obtained I this freedom. *4183*
23: 9 And there arose a **g** cry: and the scribes *that* *3173*
23:10 And when there arose a **g** dissension, *4183*
23:14 have **bound** ourselves **under a g curse**, *331+332*
24: 2 Seeing that by thee we enjoy **g** quietness, *4183*
24: 7 with **g** violence took *him* away out of our *4183*
25:23 with **g** pomp, and were entered into *4183*
26:22 this day, witnessing both to small and **g**, *3173*

G

Ac 28: 6 but after they had looked a g **while**, 1909+4183
28:29 and had g reasoning among themselves. 4183
Ro 9: 2 That I have g heaviness and 3173
15:23 having a g **desire** these many years to come 1974
1Co 9:11 g *thing* if we shall reap your carnal *things?* 3173
16: 9 For a g door and effectual is opened unto 3173
2Co 1:10 Who delivered us from **so** g a death, and 5082
3:12 such hope, we use g plainness of speech: 4183
7: 4 G *is* my boldness of speech toward you, 4183
7: 4 toward you, g *is* my glorying of you: 4183
8: 2 How that in a g trial of affliction 4183
8:22 upon the g confidence which *I have* in you. 4183
11:15 Therefore *it is* no g *thing* if his ministers 3173
Eph 2: 4 for his g love wherewith he loved us, 4183
5:32 This is a g mystery: but I speak concerning 3173
Col 2: 1 For I would that ye knew **what** g conflict I 2245
4:13 that he hath a g zeal for you, and them that 4183
1Th 2:17 abundantly to see your face with g desire. 4183
1Ti 3:13 g boldness in the faith which is in Christ 4183
3:16 And without controversy g is the mystery 3173
6: 6 But godliness with contentment is g gain. 3173
2Ti 2:20 But in a g house there are not only vessels 3173
Tit 2:13 the glorious appearing of the g God and 3173
Phm 1: 7 For we have g joy and consolation in thy 4183
Heb 2: 3 we escape, if we neglect so g salvation; 5082
4:14 Seeing then that we have a g high priest, 3173
7: 4 Now consider **how** g this *man was,* unto 4080
10:32 ye endured a g fight of afflictions; 4183
10:35 which hath g recompence of reward. 3173
12: 1 about with **so** g a cloud of witnesses, 5118
13:20 *that* g shepherd of the sheep, through 3173
Jas 3: 4 which though they be **so** g, and are driven 5082
3: 5 is a little member, and boasteth g **things**. 3173
3: 5 **how** g a matter a little fire kindleth. 2245
1Pe 3: 4 which is in the sight of God of g **price**. 4185
2Pe 1: 4 Whereby are given unto us **exceeding** g 3176
2:18 For when they speak g **swelling** *words* of 5246
3:10 the heavens shall pass away with a g **noise**, 4500
Jude 1: 6 darkness unto the judgment of the g day. 3173
1:16 their mouth speaketh g **swelling** *words,* 5246
Rev 1:10 and heard behind me a g voice, as of a 3173
2:22 them that commit adultery with her into g 3173
6: 4 and there was given unto him a g sword. 3173
6:12 sixth seal, and lo, there was a g earthquake; 3173
6:15 and the g **men**, and the rich *men,* and 3175
6:17 For the g day of his wrath is come; and 3173
7: 9 After this I beheld, and lo, a g multitude, 4183
7:14 These are they which came out of g 3173
8: 8 as *it were* a g mountain burning with fire 3173
8:10 and there fell a g star from heaven, 3173
9: 2 out of the pit, as the smoke of a g furnace; 3173
9:14 which are bound in the g river Euphrates. 3173
11: 8 bodies *shall lie* in the street of the g city, 3173
11:11 and g fear fell upon them which saw them. 3173
11:12 And they heard a g voice from heaven 3173
11:13 And the same hour was there a g 3173
11:15 and there were g voices in heaven, saying, 3173
11:17 thou hast taken *to thee* thy g power, 3173
11:18 and them that fear thy name, small and g; 3173
11:19 thunderings, and an earthquake, and g hail. 3173
12: 1 And there appeared a g wonder in heaven; 3173
12: 3 and behold a g red dragon, having seven 3173
12: 9 And the g dragon was cast *out, that* old 3173
12:12 having g wrath, because he knoweth that he 3173
12:14 woman were given two wings of a g eagle, 3173
13: 2 his power, and his seat, and g authority. 3173
13: 5 given unto him a mouth speaking g *things* 3173
13:13 And he doeth g wonders, so that he maketh 3173
13:16 *both* small and g, rich and poor, free and 3173
14: 2 and as the voice of a g thunder: 3173
14: 8 Babylon is fallen, is fallen, *that* g city, 3173
14:19 cast *it* into the g winepress of the wrath of 3173
15: 1 another sign in heaven, g and marvellous, 3173
15: 3 saying, G and marvellous *are* thy works, 3173
16: 1 And I heard a g voice out of the temple 3173
16: 9 And men were scorched *with* g heat, and 3173
16:12 out his vial upon the g river Euphrates; 3173
16:14 to gather them to the battle of that g day of 3173
16:17 there came a g voice out of the temple of 3173
16:18 and there was a g earthquake, such as was 3173
16:18 so mighty an earthquake, *and* so g. 3173
16:19 And the g city was *divided* into three parts, 3173
16:19 g Babylon came in remembrance before 3173
16:21 And there fell upon men a g hail out of 3173
16:21 for the plague thereof was exceeding g. 3173
17: 1 I will shew unto thee the judgment of the g 3173
17: 5 MYSTERY, BABYLON THE G, 3173
17: 6 I saw her, I wondered *with* g admiration. 3173
17:18 And the woman which thou sawest is *that* g 3173
18: 1 come down from heaven, having g power; 3173
18: 2 saying, Babylon the g is fallen, is fallen, 3173
18:10 saying, Alas, alas, *that* g city Babylon, 3173
18:16 And saying, Alas, alas, *that* g city, that was 3173
18:17 in one hour **so** g riches is come to nought. 5118
18:18 saying, What *city is* like unto *this* g city? 3173
18:19 and wailing, saying, Alas, alas, *that* g city, 3173
18:21 And a mighty angel took up a stone like a g 3173
18:21 Thus with violence shall *that* g city 3173
18:23 for thy merchants were the g **men** of 3175
19: 1 And after these *things* I heard a g voice of 3173
19: 2 for he hath judged the g whore, which did 3173
19: 5 and ye that fear him, both small and g. 3173
19: 6 And I heard as *it were* the voice of a g 4183
19:17 together unto the supper of the g God; 3173
19:18 *men,* both free and bond, both small and g. 3173
20: 1 the bottomless *pit* and a g chain in his hand. 3173
20:11 And I saw a g white throne, and him that 3173
20:12 the dead, small and g, stand before God; 3173
21: 3 And I heard a g voice out of heaven saying, 3173
21:10 And he carried me away in the spirit to a g 3173
21:10 high mountain, and shewed me *that* g city, 3173
21:12 And had a wall g and high, and had twelve 3173

GREATER (77) [GREAT]

Ge 1:16 the g light to rule the day, and the lesser 1419
4:13 My punishment *is* g than *I* can bear. 1419
39: 9 *There is* none g in this house than I; neither 1419
41:40 only *in* the throne will I be g than thou. 1431
48:19 truly his younger brother shall be g than he, 1431
Ex 18:11 Now I know that the LORD *is* g than all 1419
Nu 14:12 will make of thee a g nation and 1419
Dt 1:28 The people *is* g and taller than we; 1419
4:38 To drive out nations from before thee g and 1419
7: 1 seven nations g and mightier than thou; 7227
9: 1 to go in to possess nations g and 1419
9:14 of thee a nation mightier and g than they. 7227
11:23 ye shall possess g nations and mightier than 1419
Jos 10: 2 because it *was* g than Ai, and all the men 1419
1Sa 14:30 for had there not been now a **much** g 7235
2Sa 13:15 g than the love wherewith he had loved her. 1419
13:16 this evil in sending me away *is* g than 1419
1Ki 1:37 **make** his throne g than the throne of my 1431
1:47 and **make** his throne g than thy throne. 1431
1Ch 11: 9 So David **waxed** g and greater: 1980+1980
11: 9 So David waxed greater and g: for 1419
2Ch 3: 5 the g house he cieled with fir tree, which he 1419
Est 9: 4 for *this* man Mordecai **waxed** g and 1980
9: 4 for *this* man Mordecai waxed greater and g. 1419
Job 33:12 I will answer thee, that God is g than man. 7235
La 4: 6 g than the punishment of the sin of Sodom, 1431
Eze 8: 6 *and* thou shalt see g abominations. 1419
8:13 thou shalt see g abominations that they 1419
8:15 thou shalt see g abominations than these. 1419
43:14 from the lesser settle *even* to the g settle 1419
Da 11:13 shall set forth a multitude g than 7227
Am 6: 2 or their border g than your border? 7227
Hag 2: 9 The glory of this latter house shall be g 1419
Mt 11:11 hath not risen a g **than** John the Baptist: 3187
11:11 in the kingdom of heaven is g **than** he. 3187
12: 6 That in this place is *one* g **than** the temple. 3187
12:41 and behold, a g **than** Jonas *is* here. 4183
12:42 and behold, a g **than** Solomon *is* here. 4183
23:14 therefore ye shall receive the g damnation. 4053
23:17 for whether is g, the gold, or the temple that 3187
23:19 for whether *is* g, the gift, or the altar that 3187
Mk 4:32 and becometh g **than** all herbs, and 3187
12:31 There is none other commandment g **than** 3187
12:40 these shall receive g damnation. 4053
Lk 7:28 is not a g prophet **than** John the Baptist: 3187
7:28 is least in the kingdom of God is g **than** he. 3187
11:31 and behold, a g **than** Solomon *is* here. 4183
11:32 and behold, a g **than** Jonas *is* here. 4183
12:18 I will pull down my barns, and build g; and 3187
20:47 the same shall receive g damnation. 4054
22:27 For whether *is* g, he that sitteth at meat, or 3187
Jn 1:50 thou shalt see g *things* **than** these. 3187
4:12 Art thou g **than** our father Jacob, 3187
5:20 and he will shew him g works **than** these, 3187
5:36 But I have g witness **than** *that of* John: 3187
8:53 Art thou g **than** our father Abraham, 3187
10:29 which gave *them* me, is g **than** all; 3187
13:16 The servant is not g **than** his lord; 3187
13:16 neither he that is sent g **than** he that sent 3187
14:12 and g *works* **than** these shall he do; 3187
14:28 unto the Father: for my Father is g **than** I. 3187
15:13 G love hath no *man* **than** this, that a man 3187
15:20 The servant is not g **than** his lord. 3187
19:11 he that delivered me unto thee hath the g 3187
Ac 15:28 to lay upon you no g burden than these 4183
1Co 14: 5 for g *is* he that prophesieth than he that 3187
15: 6 of whom the g **part** remain unto this 4183
Heb 6:13 because he could swear by no g, he sware 3187
6:16 For men verily swear by the g: and an oath 3187
9:11 by a g and more perfect tabernacle, 3187
11:26 Christ g riches **than** the treasures in Egypt: 3187
Jas 3: 1 knowing that we shall receive the g 3187
2Pe 2:11 which are g in power and might, 3187
1Jn 3:20 God is g **than** our heart, and knoweth all 3187
4: 4 because g is he that is in you, than he that is 3187
5: 9 the witness of men, the witness of God is g: 3187
3Jn 1: 4 I have no g joy **than** to hear that my 3186

GREATEST (21) [GREAT]

1Ch 12:14 over an hundred, and the g over a thousand. 1419
12:29 for hitherto the g **part** of them had kept 4768
Job 1: 3 that this man was the g of all the men of 1419
Jer 6:13 For from the least of them even unto the g 1419
8:10 even unto the g is given to covetousness, 1419
31:34 from the least of them unto the g of them, 1419
42: 1 the people from the least even unto the g, 1419
42: 8 all the people from the least even to the g, 1419
44:12 from the least even unto the g, by the sword 1419
Jnh 3: 5 from the g of them even to the least of 1419
Mt 13:32 it is the g among herbs, and becometh a 3187
18: 1 Who is the g in the kingdom of heaven? 3187
18: 4 the same is g in the kingdom of heaven. 3187
23:11 But he that is g among you shall be your 3187
Mk 9:34 among themselves, who *should be* the g. 3187
Lk 9:46 among them, which of them should be g. 3187
22:24 which of them should be accounted the g. 3187
22:26 but he that is g among you, let him be as 3187
Ac 8:10 gave heed, from the least to the g, saying, 3173
1Co 13:13 these three; but the g of these *is* charity. 3187
Heb 8:11 all shall know me, from the least to the g. 3173

GREATLY (87) [GREAT]

Ge 3:16 I will g **multiply** thy sorrow and 7235+7235
7:18 and were increased g upon the earth; 3966
19: 3 he pressed upon them g; and they turned in 3966
24:35 the LORD hath blessed my master g; and 3966
32: 7 Then Jacob was g afraid and distressed: and 3966
Ex 19:18 a furnace, and the whole mount quaked g. 3966
Nu 11:10 and the anger of the LORD was kindled g; 3966
14:39 of Israel: and the people mourned g. 3966
Dt 15: 4 for the LORD shall g **bless** thee in 1288+1288
17:17 neither shall he g multiply to himself silver 3966
Jos 10: 2 That they feared g, because Gibeon *was* a 3966
Jdg 2:15 unto them: and they were g distressed. 3966
6: 6 Israel was g impoverished because of 3966
1Sa 11: 6 those tidings, and his anger was kindled g. 3966
11:15 and all the men of Israel rejoiced g. 3966
12:18 all the people g feared the LORD and 3966
16:21 he loved him g; and he became his 3966
17:11 they were dismayed, and g afraid. 3966
28: 5 he was afraid, and his heart g trembled. 3966
30: 6 David was g distressed; for the people 3966
2Sa 10: 5 because the men were g ashamed: 3966
12: 5 David's anger was g kindled against 3966
24:10 I have sinned g *in* that I have done: 3966
1Ki 2:12 and his kingdom was established g. 3966
5: 7 that he rejoiced g, and said, Blessed *be* 3966
18: 3 (Now Obadiah feared the LORD g: 3966
1Ch 4:38 house of their fathers increased g. 7230+3807.1
16:25 great *is* the LORD, and g to be praised: 3966
19: 5 for the men were g ashamed. And the king 3966
21: 8 I have sinned g, because I have done this 3966
2Ch 25:10 their anger was g kindled against Judah, 3966
33:12 humbled himself g before the God of his 3966
Job 3:25 For the thing which I g **feared** is come 6343
8: 7 yet thy latter end should g increase. 3966
Ps 21: 1 and in thy salvation how g shall he rejoice! 3966
28: 7 therefore my heart g **rejoiceth**; and 5937
38: 6 I am troubled; I am bowed down g; 3966+5704
45:11 So shall the king g **desire** thy beauty: for he 183
47: 9 the earth *belong* unto God: he is g exalted. 3966
48: 1 and g to be praised in the city of our God, 3966
62: 2 *he is* my defence; I shall not be g moved. 7227
65: 9 thou g enrichest it *with* the river of God, 7227
71:23 My lips shall g **rejoice** when I sing unto 7442
78:59 *this,* he was wroth, and g abhorred Israel: 3966
89: 7 God *is* g to be feared in the assembly of 7227
96: 4 the LORD *is* great, and g to be praised: 3966
105:24 he increased his people g; and made them 3966
107:38 them also, so that they are multiplied g; 3966
109:30 I will g praise the LORD with my mouth; 3966
112: 1 *that* delighteth g in his commandments. 3966
116:10 therefore have I spoken: I was g afflicted: 3966
119:51 The proud have had me g in derision: 3966+5704
145: 3 Great *is* the LORD, and g to be praised; 3966
Pr 23:24 of the righteous shall g **rejoice**: 1523+1524
Isa 42:17 turned back, they shall be g **ashamed**, 954+1322
61:10 I will g **rejoice** in the LORD, 7797+7797
Jer 3: 1 shall not that land be g **polluted**? 2610+2610
4:10 surely thou hast g **deceived** this 5377+5377
9:19 we are g confounded, because we have 3966
20:11 they shall be g ashamed: for they shall not 3966
Eze 20:13 in them; and my sabbaths they g polluted: 3966
25:12 hath g **offended**, and revenged himself 816+816
Da 5: 9 *was* king Belshazzar g troubled, and 7690
9:23 come to shew *thee;* for thou *art* g **beloved**: 2532
10:11 said unto me, O Daniel, a man g **beloved**, 2532
10:19 said, O man g **beloved**, fear not: peace *be* 2532
Ob 1: 2 among the heathen: thou *art* g despised. 3966
Zep 1:14 the LORD *is* near, *it is* near, and hasteth g, 3966
Zec 9: 9 Rejoice g, O daughter of Zion; shout, 3966
Mt 27:14 insomuch that the governor marvelled g. 3029
27:54 that were done, they feared g, saying, 4970
Mk 5:23 And besought him g, saying, My little 4183
5:38 and them that wept and wailed g. 4183
9:15 were g **amazed**, and running to *him* saluted 1568
12:27 the God of the living: ye therefore do g err. 4183
Jn 3:29 **rejoiceth** g because of 5463+5479
Ac 3:11 that is called Solomon's, g **wondering**. 1569
6: 7 of the disciples multiplied in Jerusalem g; 4970
1Co 16:12 I g desired him to come unto you with 4183
Php 1: 8 how g I long after you all in the bowels of NIG
4:10 But I rejoiced in the Lord g, that now at 3171
1Th 3: 6 **desiring** g to see us, as we also *to see* you: 1971
2Ti 1: 4 G **desiring** to see thee, being mindful of 1971
4:15 for he hath g withstood our words. 3029
1Pe 1: 6 Wherein ye g **rejoice**, though now for a 21
2Jn 1: 4 I rejoiced g that I found of thy children 3029
3Jn 1: 3 For I rejoiced g, when *the* brethren came 3029

GREATNESS (32) [GREAT]

Ex 15: 7 in the g of thine excellency thou hast 7230
15:16 by the g of thine arm they shall be *as* still as 1419
Nu 14:19 people according unto the g of thy mercy, 1433
Dt 3:24 thou hast begun to shew thy servant thy g, 1433
5:24 our God hath shewed us his glory and his g, 1433
9:26 which thou hast redeemed through thy g, 1433
11: 2 his g, his mighty hand, and his stretched 1433
32: 3 of the LORD: ascribe ye g unto our God. 1433
1Ch 17:19 to thine own heart, hast thou done all this g, 1420
17:21 to make thee a name of g and terribleness, 1420
29:11 *is* the g, and the power, and the glory, and 1420
2Ch 9: 6 *the one* half of the g of thy wisdom was not 4768
24:27 the g of the burdens *laid* upon him, and 7230
Ne 13:22 spare me according to the g of thy mercy. 7230
Est 10: 2 and the declaration of the g of Mordecai, 1420
Ps 66: 3 through the g of thy power shall thine 7230
71:21 Thou shalt increase my g, and comfort me 1420
79:11 according to the g of thy power: 1433
145: 3 to be praised; and his g *is* unsearchable. 1420
145: 6 of thy terrible acts: and I will declare thy g. 1420
150: 2 praise him according to his excellent g. 1433
Pr 5:23 and in the g of his folly he shall go astray. 7230
Isa 40:26 he calleth them all by names by the g of *his* 7230
57:10 Thou art wearied in the g of thy way; 7230
63: 1 travelling in the g of his strength? 7230
Jer 13:22 For the g of thine iniquity are thy skirts 7230
Eze 31: 2 his multitude; Whom art thou like in thy g? 1433
31: 7 Thus was he fair in his g, in the length of 1433
31:18 in glory and in g among the trees of Eden? 1433
Da 4:22 for thy g is grown, and reacheth unto 7238
7:27 the g of the kingdom under the whole 7238
Eph 1:19 And what *is* the exceeding g of his power 3174

GREAVES (1)

1Sa 17: 6 *he had* g of brass upon his legs, and a target 4697

GRECIA (3) [GREECE]

Da 8:21 the rough goat *is* the king of G: and 3120
10:20 gone forth, lo, the prince of G shall come. 3120

Da 11: 2 he shall stir up all against the realm of G. 3120

GRECIANS (4) [GREECE]
Joel 3: 6 Jerusalem have ye sold unto the G, 1121+3125
Ac 6: 1 there arose a murmuring of the G against *1675*
9:29 the Lord Jesus, and disputed against the G: *1675*
11:20 spake unto the G, preaching the Lord Jesus. *1675*

GREECE (2) [GRECIA, GRECIANS, GREEK, GREEKS]
Zec 9:13 O G, and made thee as the sword of a 3120
Ac 20: 2 them much exhortation, he came into G, *1671*

GREEDILY (3) [GREEDINESS]
Pr 21:26 He coveteth g all the day long: but 183+8378
Eze 22:12 thou hast g gained of thy neighbours by 1214
Jude 1:11 ran g after the error of Balaam for reward, *1632*

GREEDINESS (1) [GREEDILY, GREEDY]
Eph 4:19 to work all uncleanness with g. *4124*

GREEDY (6) [GREEDINESS]
Ps 17:12 Like as a lion *that* is g of his prey, and as it 3700
Pr 1:19 ways of every one that is g of gain; 1214+1215
15:27 He that is g of gain troubleth his own 1214+1215
Isa 56:11 *they are* g dogs *which* can never 5315+5794
1Ti 3: 3 to wine, no striker, not g of filthy lucre; *146*
3: 8 given to much wine, not g of filthy lucre; *146*

GREEK (12) [GREECE]
Mk 7:26 The woman was a G, a Syrophenician by *1674*
Lk 23:38 also was written over him in letters of G, *1673*
Jn 19:20 it was written in Hebrew, *and* G, *and* Latin. *1676*
Ac 16: 1 and believed; but his father *was* a G: *1672*
16: 3 for they knew all that his father was a G. *1672*
21:37 unto thee? Who said, Canst thou speak G? *1676*
Ro 1:16 to the Jew first, and *also* to the G. *1672*
10:12 is no difference between the Jew and the G: *1672*
Gal 2: 3 neither Titus, who was with me, being a G, *1672*
3:28 There is neither Jew nor G, there is neither *1672*
Col 3:11 Where there is neither G nor Jew, *1672*
Rev 9:11 in the G *tongue* hath *his* name Apollyon. *1673*

GREEKS (14) [GREECE]
Jn 12:20 And there were certain G among them that *1672*
Ac 14: 1 both of the Jews and *also* of the G believed. *1672*
17: 4 and of the devout G a great multitude, and *1672*
17:12 also of honourable women which were G, *1674*
18: 4 and persuaded *the* Jews and *the* G. *1672*
18:17 Then all the G took Sosthenes, the *chief* *1672*
19:10 word of the Lord Jesus, both Jews and G. *1672*
19:17 the Jews and G also dwelling at Ephesus; *1672*
20:21 and *also* to the G, repentance toward God, *1672*
21:28 and further brought G also into the temple, *1672*
Ro 1:14 I am debtor both to the G, and to *1672*
1Co 1:22 a sign, and the G seek after wisdom: *1672*
1:23 and unto the G foolishness; *1672*
1:24 both Jews and G, Christ the power of God, *1672*

GREEN (41) [GREENISH, GREENNESS]
Ge 1:30 *is* life, *I have given* every g herb for meat: 3418
9: 3 *even* as the g herb have I given you all 3418
30:37 Jacob took him rods of g poplar, and of 3892
Ex 10:15 there remained not any g thing in the trees, 3418
Lev 2:14 thy firstfruits g ears of corn dried by the fire, 24
23:14 neither bread, nor parched *corn*, nor g ears, 3759
Dt 12: 2 and upon the hills, and under every g tree: 7488
Jdg 16: 7 If they bind me with seven g withs that 3892
16: 8 her seven g withs which had not been dried, 3892
1Ki 14:23 on every high hill, and under every g tree. 7488
2Ki 16: 4 and on the hills, and under every g tree. 7488
17:10 in every high hill, and under every g tree: 7488
19:26 *as* the g herb, *as* the grass on the housetops, 3419
2Ch 28: 4 and on the hills, and under every g tree. 7488
Est 1: 6 g, and blue *hangings*, fastened with cords 3768
Job 8:16 He *is* g before the sun, and his branch 7373
15:32 his time, and his branch shall not be g. 7488
39: 8 and he searcheth after every g thing. 3387
Ps 23: 2 He maketh me to lie down in g pastures: 1877
37: 2 like the grass, and wither as the g herb. 3418
37:35 and spreading himself like a g bay tree. 7488
52: 8 I *am* like a g olive tree in the house of God: 7488
SS 1:16 yea, pleasant: also our bed *is* g. 7488
2:13 The fig tree putteth forth her g figs, and 6291
Isa 15: 6 the grass faileth, there is no g thing. 3418
37:27 *as* the g herb, *as* the grass on the housetops, 3419
57: 5 yourselves with idols under every g tree, 7488
Jer 2:20 and under every g tree thou wanderest, 7488
3: 6 high mountain and under every g tree, 7488
3:13 ways to the strangers under every g tree, 7488
11:16 A g olive tree, fair, *and* of goodly fruit: 7488
17: 2 their groves by the g trees upon the high 7488
17: 8 when heat cometh, but her leaf shall be g; 7488
Eze 6:13 under every g tree, and under every thick 7488
17:24 have dried up the g tree, and have made 3892
20:47 it shall devour every g tree in thee, and 3892
Hos 14: 8 I *am* like a g fir tree. From me is thy fruit 7488
Mk 6:39 all sit down by companies upon the g grass. *5515*
Lk 23:31 For if they do these *things* in a g tree, *5200*
Rev 8: 7 was burnt up, and all g grass was burnt up. *5515*
9: 4 neither any g *thing*, neither any tree; *5515*

GREENISH (2) [GREEN]
Lev 13:49 *if* the plague be g or reddish in the garment, 3422
14:37 g or reddish, which in sight *are* lower than 3422

GREENNESS (1) [GREEN]
Job 8:12 Whilst it *is* yet in his g, *and* not cut down, it 3

GREET (16) [GREETETH, GREETING, GREETINGS]
1Sa 25: 5 and g him in my name: 7592+7965+3807.1
Ro 16: 3 G Priscilla and Aquila my helpers in Christ *782*
16: 5 Likewise *g* the church that is in their house. NIG
16: 6 G Mary, who bestowed much labour on us. *782*
16: 8 G Amplias my beloved in the Lord. *782*
16:11 G them that be of the *household* of *782*
1Co 16:20 All the brethren g you. Greet ye one another *782*
16:20 greet you. G ye one another with a holy kiss. *782*
2Co 13:12 G one another with a holy kiss. *782*
Php 4:21 The brethren which are with me g you. *782*
Col 4:14 the beloved physician, and Demas, g you. *782*
1Th 5:26 G all the brethren with a holy kiss. *782*
Tit 3:15 G them that love us in the faith. Grace *be* *782*
1Pe 5:14 G ye one another with a kiss of charity. *782*
2Jn 1:13 The children of thy elect sister g thee. Amen. *782*
3Jn 1:14 friends salute thee. G the friends by name. *782*

GREETETH (1) [GREET]
2Ti 4:21 Eubulus g thee, and Pudens, and Linus, and *782*

GREETING (3) [GREET]
Ac 15:23 brethren *send* g unto the brethren which are *5463*
23:26 most excellent governor Felix *sendeth* g. *5463*
Jas 1: 1 twelve tribes which are scattered abroad, g. *5463*

GREETINGS (3) [GREET]
Mt 23: 7 And g in the markets, and to be called of *783*
Lk 11:43 in the synagogues, and g in the markets. *783*
20:46 and love g in the markets, and the highest *783*

GREW (28) [GROW]
Ge 2: 5 and every herb of the field before it g: 6779
19:25 and that which g upon the ground. 6780
21: 8 the child g, and was weaned: and 1431
21:20 he g, and dwelt in the wilderness, and 1431
25:27 the boys g: and Esau was a cunning hunter, 1431
26:13 and g until he became very great: 1432
47:27 and g, and multiplied exceedingly. 6509
Ex 1:12 the more they multiplied and g. 6555
2:10 the child g, and she brought him unto 1431
Jdg 11: 2 *his* wife's sons g up, and they thrust out 1431
13:24 the child g, and the LORD blessed him. 1431
1Sa 2:21 And the child Samuel g before the LORD. 1431
2:26 the child Samuel g on, and was in favour 1432
3:19 Samuel g, and the LORD was with him, 1431
2Sa 5:10 g great, and the LORD God of hosts *was* 1419
12: 3 it g up together with him, and with his 1431
Eze 17: 6 it g, and became a spreading vine of low 6779
17:10 it shall wither in the furrows where it g. 6780
Da 4:11 The tree g, and was strong, and the height 7236
4:20 that thou sawest, which g, and was strong, 7236
Mk 4: 7 and the thorns g up, and choked it, and *305*
5:26 nothing bettered, but rather g worse, *1519+2064*
Lk 1:80 And the child g, and waxed strong in spirit, *837*
2:40 And the child g, and waxed strong in spirit, *837*
13:19 and it g, and waxed a great tree; and *837*
Ac 7:17 the people g and multiplied in Egypt, *837*
12:24 But the word of God g and multiplied. *837*
19:20 So mightily g the word of God and *837*

GREYHOUND (1)
Pr 30:31 A g; a he goat also; and a king, 2223+4975

GRIEF (26) [GRIEFS, GRIEVANCE, GRIEVE, GRIEVED, GRIEVETH, GRIEVING, GRIEVOUS, GRIEVOUSLY, GRIEVOUSNESS]
Ge 26:35 Which were a g of mind unto Isaac and 4786
1Sa 1:16 my complaint and g have I spoken hitherto. 3708
25:31 That this shall be no g unto thee, 6330
2Ch 6:29 one shall know his own sore and his own g, 4341
Job 2:13 for they saw that *his* g was very great. 3511
6: 2 Oh that my g were throughly weighed, 3708
16: 5 moving of my lips should asswage *your* g. NIH
16: 6 Though I speak, my g is not asswaged: and 3511
Ps 6: 7 Mine eye is consumed because of g; 3708
31: 9 mine eye is consumed with g, *yea*, my soul 3708
31:10 For my life is spent with g, and my years 3015
69:26 they talk to the g of those whom thou hast 4341
Pr 17:25 A foolish son *is* a g to his father, and 3708
Ecc 1:18 For in much wisdom *is* much g: and he that 3708
2:23 all his days *are* sorrows, and his travail g; 3708
Isa 17:11 the harvest *shall be* a heap in the day of g 2470
53: 3 a man of sorrows, and acquainted with g: 2483
53:10 to bruise him; he hath put *him* to g: 2470
Jer 6: 7 before me continually *is* g and wounds. 2483
10:19 I said, Truly this *is* a g, and I must bear it. 2483
45: 3 for the LORD hath added g to my sorrow; 3015
La 3:32 though he cause g, yet will he have 3013
Jnh 4: 6 over his head, to deliver him from his g. 7451
2Co 2: 5 But if any have caused g, he hath not *3076*
Heb 13:17 that they may do it with joy, and not with g: *4727*
1Pe 2:19 a man for conscience toward God endure g, *3077*

GRIEFS (1) [GRIEF]
Isa 53: 4 Surely he hath borne our g, and carried our 2483

GRIEVANCE (1) [GRIEF]
Hab 1: 3 me iniquity, and cause *me* to behold g? 5999

GRIEVE (5) [GRIEF]
1Sa 2:33 to consume thine eyes, and to g thine heart: 109
1Ch 4:10 keep *me* from evil, that it may not g me. 6087
Ps 78:40 in the wilderness, *and* g him in the desert! 6087
La 3:33 For he doth not afflict willingly nor g 3013
Eph 4:30 And g not the holy Spirit of God, *3076*

GRIEVED (40) [GRIEF]
Ge 6: 6 man on the earth, and it g him at his heart. 6087
34: 7 when they heard *it*: and the men were g, 6087
45: 5 Now therefore be not g, nor angry with 6087
49:23 The archers have sorely g him, and shot *at* 4843
Ex 1:12 they were g because of the children of 6973
Dt 15:10 thine heart shall not be g when thou givest 3415
Jdg 10:16 and his soul was g for the misery of Israel. 7114
1Sa 1: 8 why is thy heart g? *am* not I better to thee 3415
15:11 it g Samuel; and he cried unto the LORD 2734
20: 3 Let not Jonathan know this, lest he be g: 6087
20:34 for he was g for David, because his father 6087
30: 6 because the soul of all the people was g, 4843
2Sa 19: 2 say that day *how* the king was g for his son. 6087
Ne 2:10 g them exceedingly that there 1419+7451+7489
8:11 for the day *is* holy; neither be ye g. 6087
13: 8 it g me sore: therefore I cast forth all 3415
Est 4: 4 was the queen exceedingly g; and she sent 2342
Job 4: 2 to commune with thee, wilt thou be g? 3811
30:25 in trouble? was *not* my soul g for the poor? 5701
Ps 73:21 Thus my heart was g, and I was pricked *in* 2556
95:10 Forty years long was I g with *this* 6962
112:10 The wicked shall see *it*, and be g; he shall 3707
119:158 I beheld the transgressors, and was g; 6962
139:21 am not I g with those that rise up against 6962
Isa 54: 6 thee as a woman forsaken and g in spirit, 6087
57:10 of thine hand; therefore thou wast not g. 2470
Jer 5: 3 hast stricken them, but they have not g; 2342
Da 7:15 I Daniel was g in my spirit in the midst of 3735
11:30 therefore he shall be g, and return, and 3512
Am 6: 6 they are not g for the affliction of Joseph. 2470
Mk 3: 5 being g for the hardness of their hearts, *4818*
10:22 he was sad at *that* saying, and went away g: *3076*
Jn 21:17 Peter was g because he said unto him *3076*
Ac 4: 2 Being g that they taught the people, and *1278*
16:18 being g, turned and said to the spirit, *1278*
Ro 14:15 But if thy brother be g with *thy* meat, *3076*
2Co 2: 4 not that you should be g, but that ye might *3076*
2: 5 caused grief, he hath not g me, but in part: *3076*
Heb 3:10 Wherefore I was g with that generation, *4360*
3:17 But with whom was he g forty years? *was it* *4360*

GRIEVETH (2) [GRIEF]
Ru 1:13 for it g me much for your sakes that 4843
Pr 26:15 it g him to bring it again to his mouth. 3811

GRIEVING (1) [GRIEF]
Eze 28:24 nor *any* g thorn of all *that are* round about 3510

GRIEVOUS (38) [GRIEF]
Ge 12:10 for the famine *was* g in the land. 3515
18:20 is great, and because their sin is very g; 3513
21:11 the thing was very g in Abraham's sight 3415
21:12 Let it not be g in thy sight because of 3415
41:31 that famine following; for it *shall be* very g. 3515
50:11 This *is* a g mourning to the Egyptians: 3515
Ex 8:24 there came a g swarm *of flies* into 3515
9: 3 the sheep: *there shall be* a very g murrain. 3515
9:18 *this* time I will cause it to rain a very g hail, 3515
9:24 and fire mingled with the hail, very g, 3515
10:14 very g *were they*; before them there were 3515
1Ki 2: 8 which cursed me *with* a g curse in the day 4834
12: 4 Thy father made our yoke g: now therefore 7185
12: 4 make thou the g service of thy father, 7186
2Ch 10: 4 Thy father made our yoke g: now therefore 7185
10: 4 ease thou somewhat the g servitude of thy 7186
Ps 10: 5 His ways are always g; thy judgments *are* 2342
31:18 which speak g things proudly and 6277
Pr 15: 1 away wrath: but g words stir up anger. 6089
15:10 Correction *is* g unto him that forsaketh 7451
Ecc 2:17 the work that is wrought under the sun *is* g 7451
Isa 15: 4 shall cry out; his life shall be g unto him. 3415
21: 2 A g vision is declared unto me; 7186
Jer 6:28 They *are* all g revolters, walking with 5493
10:19 my wound *is* g: but I said, Truly this *is* a 2470
14:17 *with* a great breach, *with* a very g blow. 2470
16: 4 They shall die of g deaths; they shall not be 8463
23:19 is gone forth *in* fury, even a g whirlwind: 2342
30:12 Thy bruise *is* incurable, *and* thy wound *is* g. 2470
Na 3:19 *is* no healing of thy bruise; thy wound *is* g: 2470
Mt 23: 4 they bind heavy burdens and g to be borne, *1419*
Lk 11:46 ye lade men *with* burdens g to be borne, *1419*
Ac 20:29 that after my departing shall g wolves enter *926*
25: 7 laid many and g complaints against Paul, *926*
Php 3: 1 to me indeed *is* not g, but for you *it is* safe. *3636*
Heb 12:11 for the present seemeth to be joyous, but g: *3077*
1Jn 5: 3 and his commandments are not g. *926*
Rev 16: 2 g sore upon the men which had the mark of *4190*

GRIEVOUSLY (7) [GRIEF]
Isa 9: 1 afterward did more g afflict *her by* the way 3513
Jer 23:19 it shall fall g upon the head of the wicked. 2342
La 1: 8 Jerusalem hath g sinned; therefore 2398+2399
1:20 within me; for I have g rebelled: 4784+4784
Eze 14:13 sinneth against me by trespassing g, 4603+4604
Mt 8: 6 lieth at home sick of the palsy, g tormented. *1171*
15:22 my daughter is g vexed with a devil. *2560*

GRIEVOUSNESS (2) [GRIEF]
Isa 10: 1 that write g *which* they have prescribed; 5999
21:15 from the bent bow, and from the g of war. 3514

GRIN (1) [GRINS; see also GIN]
Job 18: 9 The g shall take *him* by the heel, *and* 6341

GRIND (7) [GRINDERS, GRINDING]
Jdg 16:21 of brass; and he did g in the prison house. 2912
Job 31:10 *Then* let my wife g unto another, and 2912
Isa 3:15 to pieces, and g the faces of the poor? 2912
47: 2 Take the millstones, and g meal: 2912
La 5:13 They took the young men to g, and 2911
Mt 21:44 it shall fall, it will g him to powder. *3039*
Lk 20:18 it shall fall, it will g him to powder. *3039*

GRINDERS (1) [GRIND]
Ecc 12: 3 the g cease because they are few, and 2912

GRINDING (3) [GRIND]
Ecc 12: 4 when the sound of the g is low, and he shall 2913
Mt 24:41 Two *women shall be* g at the mill; *the* one *229*
Lk 17:35 Two *women* shall be g together; the one *229*

GRINS (2) [GRIN; see also GIN]
Ps 140: 5 net by the way side; they have set g for me. 4170
141: 9 for me, and the g of the workers of iniquity. 4170

GRISLED (4)

Ge 31:10 the cattle *were* ringstraked, speckled, and **g**. 1261
31:12 the cattle *are* ringstraked, speckled, and **g**. 1261
Zec 6: 3 and in the fourth chariot **g** *and* bay horses. 1261
6: 6 and the **g** go forth toward the south country. 1261

GROAN (7) [GROANED, GROANETH, GROANING, GROANINGS]

Job 24:12 Men **g** from out of the city, and the soul of 5008
Jer 51:52 and through all her land the wounded shall **g**. 602
Eze 30:24 he shall **g** before him *with* the groanings of 5008
Joel 1:18 How do the beasts **g**! the herds of cattle are 584
Ro 8:23 even we ourselves **g** within ourselves, *4727*
2Co 5: 2 For in this we **g**, earnestly desiring to be *4727*
5: 4 For we that are in *this* tabernacle do **g**, *4727*

GROANED (1) [GROAN]

Jn 11:33 he **g** in the spirit, and was troubled, *1690*

GROANETH (1) [GROAN]

Ro 8:22 For we know that the whole creation **g** and *4959*

GROANING (9) [GROAN]

Ex 2:24 God heard their **g**, and God remembered 5009
6: 5 I have also heard the **g** of the children of 5009
Job 23: 2 my stroke is heavier than my **g**. 585
Ps 6: 6 I am weary with my **g**; all the night make I 585
38: 9 *is* before thee; and my **g** is not hid from thee. 585
102: 5 By reason of the voice of my **g** my bones 585
102:20 To hear the **g** of the prisoner; to loose those 603
Jn 11:38 again **g** in himself cometh to the grave. *1690*
Ac 7:34 and I have heard their **g**, and am come *4726*

GROANINGS (3) [GROAN]

Jdg 2:18 of their **g** by reason of them that oppressed 5009
Eze 30:24 he shall groan before him *with* the **g** of a 5009
Ro 8:26 for us with **g** which cannot be uttered. *4726*

GROPE (5) [GROPETH]

Dt 28:29 thou shalt **g** at noondays, as the blind 4959
Job 5:14 and **g** in the noonday as in the night. 4959
12:25 They **g** *in* the dark without light, and 4959
Isa 59:10 We **g** for the wall like the blind, and 1659
59:10 the blind, and we **g** as if *we had* no eyes: 1659

GROPETH (1) [GROPE]

Dt 28:29 as the blind **g** in darkness, and thou shalt 4959

GROSS (4)

Isa 60: 2 cover the earth, and **g darkness** the people: 6205
Jer 13:16 shadow of death, *and* make *it* **g darkness**. 6205
Mt 13:15 For this people's heart is **waxed g**, and *3975*
Ac 28:27 For the heart of this people is **waxed g**, and *3975*

GROUND (192) [AGROUND, GROUNDED]

Ge 2: 5 and *there was* not a man to till the **g**. 127
2: 6 and watered the whole face of the **g**. 127
2: 7 God formed man *of* the dust of the **g**, 127
2: 9 out of the **g** made the LORD God to grow 127
2:19 out of the **g** the LORD God formed every 127
3:17 cursed *is* the **g** for thy sake; in sorrow shalt 127
3:19 thou eat bread, till thou return unto the **g**; 127
3:23 to till the **g** from whence he was taken. 127
4: 2 of sheep, but Cain was a tiller of the **g**. 127
4: 3 that Cain brought of the fruit of the **g** an 127
4:10 brother's blood crieth unto me from the **g**. 127
4:12 When thou tillest the **g**, it shall not 127
5:29 of the **g** which the LORD hath cursed. 127
7:23 destroyed which *was* upon the face of the **g**, 127
8: 8 were abated from off the face of the **g**; 127
8:13 and behold, the face of the **g** was dry. 127
8:21 I will not again curse the **g** any more for 127
18: 2 tent door, and bowed himself toward the **g**, 776
19: 1 he bowed himself with his face toward the **g**; 776
19:25 of the cities, and that which grew upon the **g**. 127
33: 3 and bowed himself to the **g** seven times, 776
38: 9 his brother's wife, that he spilled *it* on the **g**, 776
44:11 took down every man his sack to the **g**, 776
44:14 yet there: and they fell before him on the **g**. 776
Ex 3: 5 the place whereon thou standest *is* holy **g**. 127
4: 3 he said, Cast it on the **g**. And he cast it on 776
4: 3 he cast it on the **g**, and it became a serpent; 776
8:21 *of flies*, and also the **g** whereon they *are*. 127
9:23 and hail, and the fire ran along upon the **g**; 776
14:16 the children of Israel shall go on dry **g** NIH
14:22 into the midst of the sea upon the dry **g**: NIH
16:14 *as* small as the hoar frost on the **g**. 776
32:20 **g** *it* to powder, and strawed *it* upon 2912
Lev 20:25 *manner of living thing* that creepeth *on* the **g**, 127
Nu 11: 8 gathered *it*, and **g** *it* in mills, or beat *it* in a 2912
16:31 that the **g** clave asunder that *was* under them: 127
Dt 4:18 likeness of any *thing* that creepeth on the **g**, 127
9:21 and stamped it, *and* **g** *it* **very small**, 2912
15:23 thou shalt pour it upon the **g** as water. 776
22: 6 or on the **g**, *whether they be* young ones, or 776
28: 4 the fruit of thy **g**, and the fruit of thy cattle, 127
28:11 fruit of thy cattle, and in the fruit of thy **g**, 127
28:56 sole of her foot upon the **g** for delicateness 776
Jos 3:17 stood firm on dry **g** in the midst of Jordan, NIH
3:17 all the Israelites passed over on dry **g**, until NIH
24:32 in a parcel of **g** which Jacob bought of 7704
Jdg 4:21 into his temples, and fastened *it* into the **g**: 776
6:39 and upon all the **g** let there be dew. 776
6:40 fleece only, and there was dew on all the **g**. 776
13:20 looked on *it*, and fell on their faces to the **g**. 776
20:21 destroyed *down* to the **g** of the Israelites that 776
20:25 destroyed *down* to the **g** of the children of 776
Ru 2:10 bowed herself to the **g**, and said unto him, 776
1Sa 3:19 and did let none of his words fall to the **g**. 776
5: 4 Dagon *was* fallen upon his face to the **g** 776
8:12 *will set them* to ear his **g**, and to reap his 2758
14:25 to a wood; and there was honey upon the **g**. 7704
14:32 oxen, and calves, and slew *them* on the **g**: 776
1Sa 14:45 shall not one hair of his head fall to the **g**; 776
20:31 as long as the son of Jesse liveth upon the **g**, 127
20:41 fell on his face to the **g**, and bowed himself 776
25:23 on her face, and bowed herself *to* the **g**, 776
26: 7 and his spear stuck in the **g** *at* his bolster: 776
28:14 he stooped *with his* face to the **g**, and 776
2Sa 2:22 wherefore should I smite thee to the **g**? how 776
8: 2 them with a line, casting them down to the **g**; 776
14: 4 she fell on her face to the **g**, and 776
14:14 needs die, and *are* as water spilt on the **g**, 776
14:22 Joab fell to the **g** on his face, and 776
14:33 bowed himself on his face to the **g** before 776
17:12 *light* upon him as the dew falleth on the **g**: 127
17:19 well's mouth, and spread **g corn** thereon; 7383
18:11 why didst thou not smite him there to the **g**? 776
20:10 fifth *rib*, and shed out his bowels to the **g**, 776
23:11 where was a piece of **g** full *of* lentiles: 7704
23:12 he stood in the midst of the **g**, and 2513
24:20 before the king *on* his face upon the **g**. 776
1Ki 1:23 before the king with his face to the **g**. 776
7:46 in the clay **g** between Succoth and Zarthan. 127
2Ki 2: 8 thither, so that they two went over on dry **g**. NIH
2:15 and bowed themselves to the **g** before him. 776
2:19 but the water *is* naught, and the **g** barren. 776
4:37 bowed herself to the **g**, and took up her son, 776
9:26 cast him into the plat *of* **g**, according to NIH
13:18 unto the king of Israel, Smite upon the **g**. 776
1Ch 11:13 where was a parcel of **g** full *of* barley; 7704
21:21 himself to David *with his* face to the **g**. 776
27:26 tillage of the **g** *was* Ezri the son of Chelub: 127
2Ch 4:17 in the clay **g** between Succoth and 127
7: 3 *with their* faces to the **g** upon the pavement, 776
20:18 bowed his head *with his* face to the **g**: 776
Ne 8: 6 the LORD *with their* faces to the **g**. 776
10:35 to bring the firstfruits of our **g**, and 127
10:37 the tithes of our **g** unto the Levites, that 127
Job 1:20 and fell down upon the **g**, and worshipped, 776
2:13 So they sat down with him upon the **g** seven 776
5: 6 neither doth trouble spring out of the **g**; 127
14: 8 the earth, and the stock thereof die in the **g**; 6083
16:13 not spare; he poureth out my gall upon the **g**. 776
18:10 The snare *is* laid for him in the **g**, and a trap 776
38:27 To satisfy the desolate and waste **g**; and NIH
39:24 He swalloweth the **g** with fierceness and 776
Ps 74: 7 the dwelling place of thy name to the **g**. 776
89:39 profaned his crown *by casting it* to the **g**. 776
89:44 to cease, and cast his throne down to the **g**. 776
105:35 their land, and devoured the fruit of their **g**. 127
107:33 and the watersprings into **dry g**; 6774
107:35 standing water, and dry **g** into watersprings; 776
143: 3 he hath smitten my life down to the **g**; 776
147: 6 he casteth the wicked down to the **g**. 776
Isa 3:26 and she *being* desolate shall sit upon the **g**. 776
14:12 *how* art thou cut down to the **g**, which didst 776
21: 9 of her gods he hath broken unto the **g**. 776
25:12 lay low, *and* bring to the **g**, *even* to the dust. 776
26: 5 layeth it low; he layeth it low, *even* to the **g**; 776
28:24 doth he open and break the clods of his **g**? 127
29: 4 *and* shalt speak out of the **g**, and thy speech 776
29: 4 out of the **g**, and thy speech shall whisper 776
30:23 of thy seed, that thou shalt sow the **g** withal; 127
30:24 the young asses that ear the **g** shall eat clean 127
35: 7 the **parched g** shall become a pool, and 8273
44: 3 floods upon the dry **g**: I will pour my spirit NIH
47: 1 O virgin daughter of Babylon, sit on the **g**: 776
51:23 thou hast laid thy body as the **g**, and as 776
53: 2 as a tender plant, and as a root out of a dry **g**: 776
Jer 4: 3 Break up your **fallow g**, and sow not 5215
7:20 trees of the field, and upon the fruit of the **g**; 127
14: 2 they are black unto the **g**; and the cry of 776
14: 4 Because the **g** is chapt, for there was no rain 127
25:33 nor buried; they shall be dung upon the **g**. 127
27: 5 the man and the beast that *are* upon the **g**, 776
La 2: 2 he hath brought *them* down to the **g**: 776
2: 9 Her gates are sunk into the **g**; he hath 776
2:10 elders of the daughter of Zion sit upon the **g**, 776
2:10 of Jerusalem hang down their heads to the **g**. 776
2:21 and the old lie on the **g** in the streets: 776
Eze 12: 6 shalt cover thy face, that thou see not the **g**: 776
12:12 his face, that he see not the **g** with *his* eyes. 776
13:14 and bring it down to the **g**, 776
19:12 she was cast down to the **g**, and the east 776
19:13 in the wilderness, in a dry and thirsty **g**. 776
24: 7 she poured it not upon the **g**, to cover it with 776
26:11 thy strong garrisons shall go down to the **g**. 776
26:16 they shall sit upon the **g**, and shall tremble at 776
28:17 I will cast thee to the **g**, I will lay thee before 776
38:20 shall fall, and every wall shall fall to the **g**. 776
41:16 *from* the **g** up to the windows, and 776
41:20 From the **g** unto above the door *were* 776
42: 6 the lowest and the middlemost from the **g**. 776
43:14 from the bottom *upon* the **g** *even* to 776
Da 8: 5 of the whole earth, and touched not the **g**: 776
8: 7 he cast him down to the **g**, and stamped upon 776
8:10 *some* of the host and of the stars to the **g**, 776
8:12 and it cast down the truth to the **g**; 776
8:18 was in a deep sleep on my face toward the **g**: 776
10: 9 sleep on my face, and my face toward the **g**. 776
10:15 I set my face toward the **g**, and I became 776
Hos 2:18 and *with* the creeping things of the **g**: 127
10:12 reap in mercy; break up your **fallow g**: 5215
Am 3:14 of the altar shall be cut off, and fall to the **g**. 776
Ob 1: 3 his heart, Who shall bring me down *to* the **g**? 776
Hag 1:11 and upon *that* which the **g** bringeth forth, and 127
Zec 8:12 the **g** shall give her increase, and the heavens 776
Mal 3:11 and he shall not destroy the fruits of your **g**; 127
Mt 10:29 one of them shall not fall on the **g** without *1093*
13: 8 But other fell into good **g**, and *1093*
13:23 But he that received seed into the good **g** is *1093*
15:35 the multitude to sit down on the **g**. *1093*
Mk 4: 5 And some fell on **stony g**, where it had not *4075*
4: 8 And other fell on good **g**, and did yield fruit *1093*
4:16 they likewise which are sown on **stony g**; *4075*
4:20 these are they which are sown on good **g**; *1093*
4:26 as if a man should cast seed into the **g**, *1093*
Mk 8: 6 the people to sit down on the **g**: *1093*
9:20 and he fell on the **g**, and *1093*
14:35 and fell on the **g**, and prayed that, if it were *1093*
Lk 8: 8 And other fell on good **g**, and sprang up, *1093*
8:15 But that on the good **g** are they, which in an *1093*
12:16 The **g** of a certain rich man brought forth *5561*
13: 7 cut it down; why cumbereth it the **g**? *1093*
14:18 I have bought a **piece of g**, and I must needs *68*
19:44 And shall **lay** thee **even with the g**, and thy *1474*
22:44 great drops of blood falling down to the **g**. *1093*
Jn 4: 5 near to the **parcel of g** that Jacob gave to *5564*
8: 6 and with *his* finger wrote on the **g**, *1093*
8: 8 again he stooped down, and wrote on the **g**. *1093*
9: 6 he spat **on the g**, and made clay of *5476*
12:24 Except a corn of wheat fall into the **g** and *1093*
18: 6 *he*, they went backward, and fell **to the g**. *5476*
Ac 7:33 for the place where thou standest is holy **g**. *1093*
22: 7 And I fell unto the **g**, and heard a voice *1475*
1Ti 3:15 the living God, the pillar and **g** of the truth. *1477*

GROUNDED (3) [GROUND]

Isa 30:32 *in* every *place* where the **g** staff shall pass, 4145
Eph 3:17 by faith; that ye, being rooted and **g** in love, *2311*
Col 1:23 If ye continue in the faith **g** and settled, and *2311*

GROVE (17) [GROVES]

Ge 21:33 And *Abraham* planted a **g** in Beer-sheba, and 815
Dt 16:21 Thou shalt not plant thee a **g** *of* any trees 842
Jdg 6:25 father hath, and cut down the **g** that *is* by it: 842
6:26 offer a burnt sacrifice with the wood of the **g** 842
6:28 the **g** was cut down that *was* by it, and 842
6:30 he hath cut down the **g** that *was* by it. 842
1Ki 15:13 because she had made an idol in a **g**; 842
16:33 Ahab made a **g**; and Ahab did more to 842
2Ki 13: 6 there remained the **g** also in Samaria.) 842
17:16 made a **g**, and worshipped all the host of 842
21: 3 and made a **g**, as did Ahab king of Israel; 842
21: 7 he set a graven image of the **g** that he had 842
23: 4 and for the **g**, and for all the host of heaven: 842
23: 6 he brought out the **g** from the house of 842
23: 7 where the women wove hangings for the **g**. 842
23:15 stampt *it* small to powder, and burnt the **g**. 842
2Ch 15:16 because she had made an idol in a **g**: 842

GROVES (24) [GROVE]

Ex 34:13 break their images, and cut down their **g**: 842
Dt 7: 5 cut down their **g**, and burn their graven 842
12: 3 break their pillars, and burn their **g** with fire; 842
Jdg 3: 7 their God, and served Baalim and the **g**. 842
1Ki 14:15 because they have made their **g**, 842
14:23 images, and **g**, on every high hill, and 842
18:19 fifty, and the prophets of the **g** four hundred, 842
2Ki 17:10 set them up images and **g** in every high hill, 842
18: 4 cut down the **g**, and brake in pieces 842
23:14 cut down the **g**, and filled their places *with* 842
2Ch 14: 3 brake down the images, and cut down the **g**: 842
17: 6 away the high places and **g** out of Judah. 842
19: 3 in that thou hast taken away the **g** out of 842
24:18 God of their fathers, and served **g** and idols: 842
31: 1 the images *in pieces*, and cut down the **g**, 842
33: 3 made **g**, and worshipped all the host of 842
33:19 set up **g** and graven images, before he was 842
34: 3 the **g**, and the carved images, and the molten 842
34: 4 the **g**, and the carved images, and the molten 842
34: 7 he had broken down the altars and the **g**, 842
Isa 17: 8 have made, either the **g**, or the images. 842
27: 9 the **g** and images shall not stand up. 842
Jer 17: 2 their **g** by the green trees upon the high hills. 842
Mic 5:14 I will pluck up thy **g** out of the midst of thee: 842

GROW (38) [GREW, GROWETH, GROWN, GROWTH]

Ge 2: 9 **made** the LORD God **to g** every tree that 6779
48:16 let them **g** into a multitude in the midst of 1711
Nu 6: 5 shall let the locks of the hair of his head **g**. 1431
Jdg 16:22 Howbeit the hair of his head began to **g** 6779
2Sa 23: 5 all *my* desire, although he **make** *it* not **to g**. 6779
2Ki 19:29 *this* year **such things as g of themselves**, 5599
Ezr 4:22 why should damage **g** to the hurt of 7680
Job 8:11 Can the rush **g up** without mire? can 1342
8:11 without mire? can the flag **g** without water? 7685
8:19 his way, and out of the earth shall others **g**. 6779
14:19 thou washest away the **things which g** out 5599
31:40 Let thistles **g** instead of wheat, and 3318
39: 4 are in good liking, they **g up** with corn; 7235
Ps 92:12 he shall **g** like a cedar in Lebanon. 7685
104:14 He **causeth** the grass **to g** for the cattle, and 6779
147: 8 who **maketh** grass **to g** *upon* 6779
Ecc 11: 5 *nor* how the bones *do* **g** in the womb of her NIH
Isa 11: 1 and a Branch shall **g** out of his roots: 6509
17:11 In the day shalt thou **make** thy plant **to g**, 7735
53: 2 For he shall **g up** before him as a tender 5927
Jer 12: 2 they **g**, yea, they bring forth fruit: thou *art* 1980
33:15 **cause** the Branch of righteousness **to g up** 6779
Eze 44:20 their heads, nor **suffer** *their* locks **to g long**; 7971
47:12 and on that side, shall **g** all trees for meat, 5927
Hos 14: 5 he shall **g** as the lily, and cast forth his roots 6524
14: 7 shall revive *as* the corn, and **g** as the vine: 6524
Jnh 4:10 thou hast not laboured, neither **madest** it **g**; 1431
Zec 6:12 he shall **g up** out of his place, and he shall 6779
Mal 4: 2 go forth, and **g up** as calves of the stall. 6335
Mt 6:28 Consider the lilies of the field, how they **g**; *837*
13:30 Let both **g together** until the harvest: and *4885*
21:19 Let no fruit **g** on thee henceforward for *1096*
Mk 4:27 day, and the seed should spring and **g up**, *3373*
Lk 12:27 Consider the lilies how they **g**: they toil not, *837*
Ac 5:24 doubted of them whereunto this would **g**. *1096*
Eph 4:15 may **g** *up* into him in all *things*, which is *837*
1Pe 2: 2 milk of the word, that ye may **g** thereby: *837*
2Pe 3:18 But **g** in grace, and *in* the knowledge of our *837*

GROWETH (14) [GROW]

Ex 10: 5 shall eat every tree which **g** for you out of 6779
Lev 13:39 it *is* a freckled spot *that* **g** in the skin: 6524

Lev 25: 5 **That which g of it own accord** of thy 5599
25:11 neither reap **that which g of itself** in it, 5599
Dt 29:23 nor beareth, nor any grass **g** therein, 5927
Jdg 19: 9 behold, the day **g to an end**, lodge here, 2583
Job 38:38 When the dust **g** into hardness, and 3332
Ps 90: 5 the morning *they are* like grass *which* **g up**. 2498
90: 6 In the morning it flourisheth, and **g up**; 2498
129: 6 which withereth afore it **g up**: 8025
Isa 37:30 Ye shall eat *this* year **such as g of itself**; 5599
Mk 4:32 it **g up**, and becometh greater than all herbs, *305*
Eph 2:21 together **g** unto a holy temple in the Lord: *837*
2Th 1: 3 because that your faith **g exceedingly**, and *5232*

GROWN (23) [GROW]

Ge 38:11 thy father's house, till Shelah my son be **g**: 1431
38:14 for she saw that Shelah was **g**, and she was 1431
Ex 2:11 to pass in those days, when Moses was **g**, 1431
9:32 rye were not smitten: for they *were* **not g up**. 648
Lev 13:37 and *that* there is black hair **g up** therein; 6779
Dt 32:15 thou art waxed fat, thou art **g thick**, thou art 5666
Ru 1:13 Would ye tarry for them till they were **g**? 1431
2Sa 10: 5 Tarry at Jericho until your beards be **g**, and 6779
1Ki 12: 8 the young men that were **g up** with him, 1431
12:10 the young men that were **g up** with him 1431
2Ki 4:18 when the child was **g**, it fell on a day, 1431
19:26 and *as* corn blasted before it be **g up**. 7054
1Ch 19: 5 Tarry at Jericho until your beards be **g**, and 6779
Ezr 9: 6 and our trespass is **g up** unto the heavens. 1431
Ps 144:12 That our sons *may be* as plants **g up** in their 1431
Pr 24:31 it was all **g over** *with* thorns, *and* 5927
Isa 37:27 and *as* corn blasted before it be **g up**. 7054
Jer 50:11 because ye are **g fat** as the heifer at grass, 6335
Eze 16: 7 thine hair is **g**, whereas thou *wast* naked 6779
Da 4:22 O king, that art **g** and become strong: 7236
4:22 for thy greatness is **g**, and reacheth unto 7236
4:33 till his hairs were **g** like eagles' *feathers*, 7236
Mt 13:32 but when it is **g**, it is the greatest among *837*

GROWTH (2) [GROW]

Am 7: 1 of the shooting up of the **latter g**; 3954
7: 1 *it was* the **latter g** after the king's 3954

GRUDGE (3) [GRUDGING, GRUDGINGLY]

Lev 19:18 nor **bear any g against** the children of thy 5201
Ps 59:15 for meat, and **g** if they be not satisfied. 3885
Jas 5: 9 **G** not one against another, brethren, lest ye *4727*

GRUDGING (1) [GRUDGE]

1Pe 4: 9 Use hospitality one to another without **g**. *1112*

GRUDGINGLY (1) [GRUDGE]

2Co 9: 7 in *his* heart, *so let him give;* not **g**, *1537+3077*

GRUMBLE; GRUMBLED; GRUMBLERS; GRUMBLING See MURMUR; MURMURED; MURMURERS; MURMURING; MURMURINGS

GUARANTEE; GUARANTEED See SURETY

GUARD (50) [GUARD'S, SAFEGUARD]

Ge 37:36 officer of Pharaoh's, *and* captain of the **g**. 2876
39: 1 of Pharaoh, captain of the **g**, an Egyptian, 2876
40: 3 in ward *in* the house of the captain of the **g**, 2876
40: 4 The captain of the **g** charged Joseph with 2876
41:12 a Hebrew, servant to the captain of the **g**; 2876
2Sa 23:23 *first* three. And David set him over his **g**. 4928
1Ki 14:27 *them* unto the hands of the chief of the **g**, 7323
14:28 *that* the **g** bare them, and brought them 7323
14:28 and brought them back into the **g** chamber. 7323
2Ki 10:25 that Jehu said to the **g** and to the captains, 7323
10:25 the **g** and the captains cast *them* out, and 7323
11: 4 with the captains and the **g**, and 7323
11: 6 and a third *part* at the gate behind the **g**: 7323
11:11 the **g** stood, every man with his weapons in 7323
11:13 when Athaliah heard the noise of the **g** *and* 7323
11:19 and the **g**, and all the people of the land; 7323
11:19 came *by* the way of the gate of the **g** *to* 7323
25: 8 came Nebuzar-adan, captain of the **g**, 2876
25:10 that *were with* the captain of the **g**, 2876
25:11 did Nebuzar-adan the captain of the **g** carry 2876
25:12 the captain of the **g** left of the poor of 2876
25:15 *in* silver, the captain of the **g** took *away*. 2876
25:18 the captain of the **g** took Seraiah the chief 2876
25:20 Nebuzar-adan captain of the **g** took these, 2876
1Ch 11:25 *first* three: and David set him over his **g**. 4928
2Ch 12:10 *them* to the hands of the chief of the **g**, 7323
12:11 the **g** came and fet them, and brought them 7323
12:11 and brought them again into the **g** chamber. 7323
Ne 4:22 that in the night they may be a **g** to us, and 4929
4:23 nor the men of the **g** which followed me, 4929
Jer 39: 9 Nebuzar-adan the captain of the **g** carried 2876
39:10 Nebuzar-adan the captain of the **g** left of 2876
39:11 to Nebuzar-adan the captain of the **g**, 2876
39:13 So Nebuzar-adan the captain of the **g** sent, 2876
40: 1 after that Nebuzar-adan the captain of the **g** 2876
40: 2 the captain of the **g** took Jeremiah, and 2876
40: 5 So the captain of the **g** gave him victuals 2876
41:10 whom Nebuzar-adan the captain of the **g** 2876
43: 6 **g** had left with Gedaliah the son of Ahikam 2876
52:12 came Nebuzar-adan, captain of the **g**, 2876
52:14 that *were* with the captain of the **g**, 2876
52:15 Nebuzar-adan the captain of the **g** carried 2876
52:16 Nebuzar-adan the captain of the **g** left 2876
52:19 *in* silver, took the captain of the **g** *away*. 2876
52:24 the captain of the **g** took Seraiah the chief 2876
52:26 So Nebuzar-adan the captain of the **g** took 2876
52:30 **g** carried away captive *of* the Jews seven 2876
Eze 38: 7 unto thee, and be thou a **g** unto them. 4929
Da 2:14 to Arioch the captain of the king's **g**, 2877
Ac 28:16 the prisoners to the **captain of the g**: *4759*

GUARD'S (1) [GUARD]

Ge 41:10 put me in ward *in* the captain of the **g** 2876

GUARDIANS See TUTORS

GUDGODAH (2)

Dt 10: 7 From thence they journeyed *unto* **G**; and 1412
10: 7 from **G** to Jotbath, a land of rivers of 1412

GUEST (1) [GUESTCHAMBER, GUESTS]

Lk 19: 7 That he was gone to be **g** with a man *that is* *2647*

GUEST ROOM See GUESTCHAMBER

GUESTCHAMBER (2) [CHAMBER, GUEST]

Mk 14:14 the house, The Master saith, Where is the **g**, *2646*
Lk 22:11 The Master saith unto thee, Where is the **g**, *2646*

GUESTS (6) [GUEST]

1Ki 1:41 all the **g** that *were* with him heard *it* as they 7121
1:49 all the **g** that *were* with Adonijah were 7121
Pr 9:18 *and that* her **g** *are* in the depths of hell. 7121
Zep 1: 7 hath prepared a sacrifice, he hath bid his **g**. 7121
Mt 22:10 good: and the wedding was furnished with **g**. *345*
22:11 And when the king came in to see the **g**, *345*

GUIDE (23) [GUIDED, GUIDES, GUIDING]

Job 38:32 or canst thou **g** Arcturus with his sons? 5148
Ps 25: 9 The meek will he **g** in judgment: and 1869
31: 3 for thy name's sake lead me, and **g** me. 5095
32: 8 thou shalt go: I will **g** thee with mine eye. 3289
48:14 and ever: he will be our **g** *even* unto death. 5090
55:13 mine equal, my **g**, and mine acquaintance. 441
73:24 Thou shalt **g** me with thy counsel, and 5148
112: 5 he will **g** his affairs with discretion. 3557
Pr 2:17 Which forsaketh the **g** of her youth, and 441
6: 7 Which having no **g**, overseer, or ruler, 7101
11: 3 The integrity of the upright shall **g** them: 5148
23:19 and be wise, and **g** thine heart in the way. 833
Isa 49:10 even by the springs of water shall he **g** 5095
51:18 *There is* none to **g** her among all the sons 5095
58:11 the LORD shall **g** thee continually, and 5148
Jer 3: 4 My father, thou *art* the **g** of my youth? 441
Mic 7: 5 not in a friend, put ye not confidence in a **g**: 441
Lk 1:79 to **g** our feet into the way of peace. *2720*
Jn 16:13 is come, he will **g** you into all truth: *3594*
Ac 1:16 which was **g** to them that took Jesus. *3595*
8:31 How can I, except some *man* should **g** me? *3594*
Ro 2:19 And art confident that thou thyself art a **g** *3595*
1Ti 5:14 *women* marry, bear children, **g the house**, *3616*

GUIDED (5) [GUIDE]

Ex 15:13 thou hast **g** *them* in thy strength unto thy 5095
2Ch 32:22 hand of all *other*, and **g** them on every side. 5095
Job 31:18 and I have **g** her from my mother's womb;) 5148
Ps 78:52 and **g** them in the wilderness like a flock. 5090
78:72 and **g** them by the skilfulness of his hands. 5148

GUIDES (2) [GUIDE]

Mt 23:16 Woe unto you, *ye* blind **g**, which say, *3595*
23:24 *Ye* blind **g**, which strain out a gnat, and *3595*

GUIDING (1) [GUIDE]

Ge 48:14 Manasseh's head, **g** his hands **wittingly**; 7919

GUILE (11)

Ex 21:14 upon his neighbour, to slay him with **g**; 6195
Ps 32: 2 and in whose spirit *there is* no **g**. 7423
34:13 from evil, and thy lips from speaking **g**. 4820
55:11 and **g** depart not from her streets. 4820
Jn 1:47 an Israelite indeed, in whom is no **g**. *1388*
2Co 12:16 being crafty, I caught you with **g**. *1388*
1Th 2: 3 not of deceit, nor of uncleanness, nor in **g**: *1388*
1Pe 2: 1 and all **g**, and hypocrisies, and envies, and *1388*
2:22 no sin, neither was **g** found in his mouth. *1388*
3:10 from evil, and his lips that *they* speak no **g**: *1388*
Rev 14: 5 And in their mouth was found no **g**: *1388*

GUILT (2) [BLOODGUILTINESS, GUILTINESS, GUILTLESS, GUILTY]

Dt 19:13 thou shalt put away *the* **g** *of* innocent blood NIH
21: 9 So shalt thou put away the **g** *of* innocent NIH

GUILTINESS (1) [GUILT]

Ge 26:10 and thou shouldest have brought **g** upon us. 817

GUILTLESS (10) [GUILT]

Ex 20: 7 for the LORD will not **hold** him **g** that 5352
Nu 5:31 shall the man be **g** from iniquity, and this 5352
32:22 be **g** before the LORD, and before Israel; 5355
Dt 5:11 for the LORD will not **hold** *him* **g** that 5352
Jos 2:19 *shall be* upon his head, and we *will be* **g**: 5355
1Sa 26: 9 against the LORD'S anointed, and be **g**? 5352
2Sa 3:28 my kingdom *are* **g** before the LORD for 5355
14: 9 and the king and his throne *be* **g**. 5355
1Ki 2: 9 Now therefore **hold** him not **g**: for thou *art* 5352
Mt 12: 7 ye would not have condemned the **g**. *338*

GUILTY (26) [GUILT]

Ge 42:21 We *are* verily **g** concerning our brother, 818
Ex 34: 7 *that* will by no means clear *the* **g**; visiting NIH
Lev 4:13 *things* which should not be done, and are **g**; 816
4:22 *things* which should not be done, and is **g**; 816
4:27 *things* which ought not to be done, and be **g**; 816
5: 2 from him; he also shall be unclean, and **g**. 816
5: 3 when he knoweth *of it*, then he shall be **g**. 816
5: 4 *of it*, then he shall be **g** in one of these. 816
5: 5 when he shall be **g** in one of these *things*, 816
5:17 *it* not, yet is he **g**, and shall bear his iniquity. 816
6: 4 it shall be, because he hath sinned, and is **g**, 816
Nu 5: 6 against the LORD, and that person be **g**; 816
14:18 by no means clearing *the* **g**, visiting NIH
35:27 kill the slayer; he shall not be **g** of blood: 3807.1
35:31 the life of a murderer, which *is* **g** of death: 7563
Jdg 21:22 unto them at *this* time, *that* you should be **g**. 816
Ezr 10:19 *being* **g**, *they offered* a ram of the flock for 818
Pr 30:10 lest he curse thee, and thou be **found g**. 816
Eze 22: 4 Thou art become **g** in thy blood that thou 816
Zec 11: 5 slay them, and **hold** themselves not **g**: 816
Mt 23:18 sweareth by the gift that is upon it, he is **g**. *3784*
26:66 They answered and said, He is **g** of death. *1777*
Mk 14:64 And they all condemned him to be **g** of *1777*
Ro 3:19 all the world may become **g before** God. *5267*
1Co 11:27 shall be **g** of the body and blood of *1777*
Jas 2:10 and *yet* offend in one *point*, he is **g** of all. *1777*

GULF (1)

Lk 16:26 between us and you there is a great **g** fixed: *5490*

GULL See CUCKOW

GUM RESIN See STACTE

GUNI (4) [GUNITES]

Ge 46:24 Jahzeel, and **G**, and Jezer, and Shillem. 1476
Nu 26:48 of **G**, the family of the Gunites: 1476
1Ch 5:15 Ahi the son of Abdiel, the son of **G**, 1476
7:13 Jahziel, and **G**, and Jezer, and Shallum, 1476

GUNITES (1) [GUNI]

Nu 26:48 of Guni, the family of the **G**: 1477

GUR (1)

2Ki 9:27 *And they did so* at the going up to **G**, 1483

GUR-BAAL (1) [BAAL]

2Ch 26: 7 against the Arabians that dwelt in **G**, and 1485

GUSH (1) [GUSHED]

Jer 9:18 and our eyelids **g out** with waters. 5140

GUSHED (5) [GUSH]

1Ki 18:28 and lancets, till the blood **g out** upon them. 8210
Ps 78:20 that the waters **g out**, and the streams 2100
105:41 He opened the rock, and the waters **g out**; 2100
Isa 48:21 he clave the rock also, and the waters **g out**. 2100
Ac 1:18 in the midst, and all his bowels **g out**. *1632*

GUTTER (1) [GUTTERS]

2Sa 5: 8 Whosoever getteth up to the **g**, and 6794

GUTTERS (2) [GUTTER]

Ge 30:38 **g** in the watering troughs when the flocks 7298
30:41 rods before the eyes of the cattle in the **g**, 7298

H

H

HA (2) [AHA]

Job 39:25 He saith among the trumpets, **H**, ha; and 1889
39:25 He saith among the trumpets, Ha, **h**; and NIH

HAAHASHTARI (1)

1Ch 4: 6 and Hepher, and Temeni, and **H**. 326

HABAIAH (2)

Ezr 2:61 the children of **H**, the children of Koz, 2252
Ne 7:63 the children of **H**, the children of Koz, 2252

HABAKKUK (2)

Hab 1: 1 The burden which **H** the prophet did see. 2265
3: 1 A prayer of **H** the prophet upon Shigionoth. 2265

HABAZINIAH (1)

Jer 35: 3 the son of **H**, and his brethren, and all his 2262

HABAZZINIAH See HABAZINIAH

HABERGEON (3) [HABERGEONS]

Ex 28:32 as it were the hole of an **h**, *that* it be not 8473
39:23 as the hole of an **h**, *with* a band round about 8473
Job 41:26 cannot hold: the spear, the dart, nor the **h**. 8302

HABERGEONS (2) [HABERGEON]

2Ch 26:14 and **h**, and bows, and slings to cast stones. 8302
Ne 4:16 the shields, and the bows, and the **h**; 8302

HABIT See WONT

HABITABLE (1) [INHABIT]

Pr 8:31 Rejoicing in the **h part** of his earth; and 8398

HABITATION (58) [INHABIT]

Ex 15: 2 he *is* my God, and I will **prepare** him **a h**; 5115
15:13 *them* in thy strength unto thy holy **h**. 5116
Lev 13:46 without the camp *shall* his **h** *be*. 4186
Dt 12: 5 *even* unto his **h** shall ye seek, and 7931
26:15 Look down from thy holy **h**, from heaven, 4583
1Sa 2:29 which I have commanded *in my* **h**; 4583
2:32 thou shalt see an enemy *in my* **h**, in all 4583
2Sa 15:25 me again, and shew me *both* it, and his **h**: 5116
2Ch 6: 2 I have built a house of **h** for thee, and 2073
29: 6 have turned away their faces from the **h** of 4908
Ezr 7:15 the God of Israel, whose **h** *is* in Jerusalem, 4907
Job 5: 3 taking root: but suddenly I cursed his **h**. 5116
5:24 and thou shalt visit thy **h**, and shalt not sin. 5116

Job 8: 6 make the **h** of thy righteousness 5116
18:15 brimstone shall be scattered upon his **h**. 5116
Ps 26: 8 I have loved the **h** of thy house, and 4583
33:14 From the place of his **h** he looketh upon all 3427
68: 5 a judge of the widows, *is* God in his holy **h**. 4583
69:25 Let their **h** be desolate; *and* let none dwell 2918
71: 3 Be thou my strong **h**, whereunto *I* may 4583
89:14 and judgment *are* the **h** of thy throne: 4349
91: 9 *is* my refuge, *even* the most High, thy **h**; 4583
97: 2 and judgment *are* the **h** of his throne. 4349
104:12 shall the fowls of the heaven have their **h**, 7931
107: 7 right way, that *they* might go to a city of **h**. 4186
107:36 to dwell, that they may prepare a city for **h**; 4186
132: 5 a **h** for the mighty *God* of Jacob. 4908
132:13 chosen Zion; he hath desired *it* for his **h**. 4186
Pr 3:33 but he blesseth the **h** of the just. 5116
Isa 22:16 *and that* graveth a **h** for himself in a rock? 4908
27:10 *and* the **h** forsaken, and left like a 5116
32:18 my people shall dwell in a peaceable **h**, 5116
33:20 thine eyes shall see Jerusalem a quiet **h**, 5116
34:13 it shall be a **h** of dragons, *and* a court for 5116
35: 7 in the **h** of dragons, where each lay, 5116
63:15 behold from the **h** of thy holiness and 2073
Jer 9: 6 Thine **h** *is* in the midst of deceit; 3427
10:25 and have made his **h** desolate. 5116
25:30 and utter his voice from his holy **h**; 4583
25:30 he shall mightily roar upon his **h**; he shall 5116
31:23 O **h** of justice, *and* mountain of holiness. 5116
33:12 shall be a **h** of shepherds causing *their* 5116
41:17 and dwelt in the **h** of Chimham, 1628
49:19 of Jordan against the **h** of the strong: 5116
50: 7 the **h** of justice, even the LORD, the hope 5116
50:19 I will bring Israel again to his **h**, and 5116
50:44 swelling of Jordan unto the **h** of the strong: 5116
50:45 surely he shall make *their* **h** desolate with 5116
Eze 29:14 the land of Pathros, into the land of their **h**; 4351
Da 4:21 the fowls of the heaven had their **h**: 7932
Ob 1: 3 in the clefts of the rock, whose **h** *is* high; 7675
Hab 3:11 The sun *and* moon stood still in *their* **h**: 2073
Zec 2:13 for he is raised up out of his holy **h**. 4583
Ac 1:20 Let his **h** be desolate, and let no man dwell *1886*
17:26 before appointed, and the bounds of their **h**; *2733*
Eph 2:22 together for a **h** of God through the Spirit. *2732*
Jude 1: 6 not their first estate, but left their own **h**, *3613*
Rev 18: 2 is fallen, and is become the **h** of devils, *2732*

HABITATIONS (20) [INHABIT]

Ge 36:43 according to their **h** in the land of their 4186
49: 5 instruments of cruelty *are in* their **h**. 4380
Ex 12:20 in all your **h** shall ye eat unleavened bread. 4186
35: 3 Ye shall kindle no fire throughout your **h** 4186
Lev 23:17 Ye shall bring out of your **h** two wave 4186
Nu 15: 2 When ye be come into the land of your **h**, 4186
1Ch 4:33 These *were* their **h**, and their genealogy. 4186
4:41 the **h** that were found there, and 4583
7:28 and **h** *were*, Beth-el and the towns thereof, 4186
Ps 74:20 of the earth are full *of the* **h** of cruelty. 4999
78:28 midst of their camp, round about their **h**. 4908
Isa 54: 2 them stretch forth the curtains of thine **h**: 4908
Jer 9:10 for the **h** of the wilderness a lamentation, 4999
21:13 against us? or who shall enter into our **h**? 4585
25:37 the peaceable **h** are cut down because of 4999
49:20 surely he shall make their **h** desolate with 5116
La 2: 2 The Lord hath swallowed up all the **h** of 4999
Eze 6:14 wilderness toward Diblath, in all their **h**: 4186
Am 1: 2 the **h** of the shepherds shall mourn, and 4999
Lk 16: 9 they may receive you into everlasting **h**. *4633*

HABOR (3)

2Ki 17: 6 in Halah and in **H** *by* the river of Gozan, 2249
18:11 in Halah and in **H** *by* the river of Gozan, 2249
1Ch 5:26 **H**, and Hara, and to the river Gozan, 2249

HACALIAH See HACHALIAH

HACHALIAH (2)

Ne 1: 1 The words of Nehemiah the son of **H**. 2446
10: 1 the Tirshatha, the son of **H**, and Zidkijah, 2446

HACHILAH (3)

1Sa 23:19 in the hill of **H**, which *is* on the south of 2444
26: 1 not David hide himself in the hill of **H**, 2444
26: 3 Saul pitched in the hill of **H**, which *is* 2444

HACHMONI (1) [HACHMONITE]

1Ch 27:32 Jehiel the son of **H** *was* with the king's 2453

HACHMONITE (1) [HACHMONI]

1Ch 11:11 a **H**, the chief of the captains: 1121+2453

HACMONI See HACHMONI

HACMONITE See HACHMONITE

HAD (2030) [HAVE]

Ge 1:31 God saw every thing that he **h** made, and NIH
2: 2 day God ended his work which he **h** made; NIH
2: 2 day from all his work which he **h** made. NIH
2: 3 that in it he **h** rested from all his work NIH
2: 5 for the LORD God **h** not caused it to rain NIH
2: 8 there he put the man whom he **h** formed. NIH
2:22 which the LORD God **h** taken from man, NIH
3: 1 of the field which the LORD God **h** made. NIH
4: 4 the LORD **h** respect unto Abel and to his NIH
4: 5 and to his offering he **h** not respect. NIH
5: 4 the days of Adam after he **h** begotten Seth NIH
6: 6 it repented the LORD that he **h** made man NIH
6:12 for all flesh **h** corrupted his way upon NIH
7: 9 and the female, as God **h** commanded Noah. NIH
7:16 of all flesh, as God **h** commanded him: NIH
8: 6 the window of the ark which he **h** made: NIH
9:24 knew what his younger son **h** done unto NIH
11: 3 they **h** brick for stone, and slime 1961+3807.1
11: 3 and slime **h** they for morter. 1961+3807.1
11:30 But Sarai was barren; she **h** no child. 3807.1
12: 1 Now the LORD **h** said unto Abram, NIH
12: 4 as the LORD **h** spoken unto him; NIH
12: 5 all their substance that they **h** gathered, and NIH
12: 5 and the souls that they **h** gotten in Haran; NIH
12:16 he **h** sheep, and oxen, and he asses, 1961+3807.1
12:20 him away, and his wife, and all that he **h**. 3807.1
13: 1 and all that he **h**, and Lot with him, 3807.1
13: 3 unto the place where his tent **h** been at NIH
13: 4 the altar, which he **h** made there at the first: NIH
13: 5 **h** flocks, and herds, and tents. 1961+3807.1
14:13 there came one that **h** escaped, and NIH
16: 1 him no *children:* and she **h** a handmaid, 3807.1
16: 3 after Abram **h** dwelt ten years in the land 3807.1
16: 4 when she saw that she **h** conceived, her NIH
16: 5 when she saw that she **h** conceived, I was NIH
17:23 in the selfsame day, as God **h** said unto him. NIH
18: 8 the calf which he **h** dressed, and set *it* NIH
18:33 as soon as he **h** left communing with NIH
19:17 when they **h** brought them forth abroad, that NIH
20: 4 Abimelech **h** not come near her: and NIH
20:18 For the LORD **h** fast closed up all NIH
21: 1 the LORD visited Sarah as he **h** said, and NIH
21: 1 the LORD did unto Sarah as he **h** spoken. NIH
21: 2 at the set time of which God **h** spoken to NIH
21: 4 eight days old, as God **h** commanded him. NIH
21: 9 which she **h** born unto Abraham, mocking. NIH
21:25 which Abimelech's servants **h** violently NIH
22: 3 went unto the place of which God **h** told NIH
22: 9 they came to the place which God **h** told NIH
23:16 which he **h** named in the audience of NIH
24: 1 the LORD **h** blessed Abraham in all NIH
24: 2 of his house that ruled over all that he **h**, 3807.1
24:15 before he **h** done speaking, that behold, NIH
24:16 a virgin, neither **h** any man known her: NIH
24:19 when she **h** done giving him drink, she said, NIH
24:21 to wit whether the LORD **h** made his NIH
24:22 to pass, as the camels **h** done drinking, NIH
24:29 Rebekah **h** a brother, and his name *was* 3807.1
24:45 And before I **h** done speaking in mine heart, NIH
24:48 which **h** led me in the right way to take my NIH
24:65 For she **h** said unto the servant, What man NIH
24:65 the servant **h** said, It *is* my master: therefore NIH
24:66 the servant told Isaac all things that he **h** NIH
25: 5 Abraham gave all that he **h** unto Isaac. 3807.1
25: 6 which Abraham **h**, Abraham gave gifts, 3807.1
26: 8 to pass, when he **h** been there a long time, NIH
26:14 For he **h** possession of flocks, and 1961+3807.1
26:15 **h** digged in the days of Abraham his father, NIH
26:15 the Philistims **h** stopped them, and NIH
26:18 which they **h** digged in the days of NIH
26:18 for the Philistims **h** stopped them after NIH
26:18 names by which his father **h** called them. NIH
26:32 told him concerning the well which they **h** NIH
27:17 and the bread, which she **h** prepared, NIH
27:30 as soon as Isaac **h** made an end of blessing NIH
27:31 he also **h** made savoury meat, and brought *it* NIH
28: 6 When Esau saw that Isaac **h** blessed Jacob, NIH
28: 9 took unto the wives which he **h** Mahalath 3807.1
28:18 took the stone that he **h** put *for* his pillows, NIH
29:16 Laban **h** two daughters: the name of 3807.1
29:20 *but* a few days, for the love he **h** to her. NIH
30: 9 When Leah saw that she **h** left bearing, she NIH
30:25 it came to pass, when Rachel **h** born Joseph, NIH
30:35 *and* every one that **h** *some* white in it, and NIH
30:38 he set the rods which he **h** pilled before NIH
30:43 **h** much cattle, and maidservants, 1961+3807.1
31:18 all his goods which he **h** gotten, the cattle of NIH
31:18 which he **h** gotten in Padan-aram, NIH
31:19 Rachel **h** stolen the images that *were* her NIH
31:21 So he fled with all that he **h**; and he rose 3807.1
31:25 Now Jacob **h** pitched his tent in the mount: NIH
31:32 For Jacob knew not that Rachel **h** stolen NIH
31:34 Now Rachel **h** taken the images, and NIH
31:42 and the fear of Isaac, **h** been with me, NIH
32:23 over the brook, and sent over that he **h**. 3807.1
33:10 as though I **h** seen the face of God, and NIH
33:19 parcel of a field, where he **h** spread his tent, NIH
34: 5 Jacob heard that he **h** defiled Dinah his NIH
34: 7 he **h** wrought folly in Israel in lying with NIH
34:13 said, because he **h** defiled Dinah their sister: NIH
34:19 because he **h** delight in Jacob's daughter: NIH
34:27 the city, because they **h** defiled their sister. NIH
35:16 and Rachel travailed, and she **h** hard labour. NIH
36: 6 which he **h** got in the land of Canaan; NIH
38:15 be a harlot; because she **h** covered her face. NIH
38:30 that **h** the scarlet thread upon his hand: NIH
39: 1 which **h** brought him down thither. NIH
39: 4 all *that* he **h** he put into his hand. 3426+3807.1
39: 5 it came to pass from the time *that* he **h** made NIH
39: 5 over all that he **h**, that the LORD 3426+3807.1
39: 5 was upon all that he **h** in the house, 3426+3807.1
39: 6 he left all that he **h** in Joseph's hand; and 3807.1
39: 6 he knew not ought he **h**, save the bread 854
39:13 when she saw that he **h** left his garment in NIH
40: 1 *his* baker **h** offended their lord the king of NIH
40:16 behold, *I* **h** three white baskets on my head: NIH
40:22 chief baker: as Joseph **h** interpreted to them. NIH
41:21 when they **h** eaten them up, it could not be NIH
41:21 it could not be known that they **h** eaten NIH
41:43 to ride in the second chariot which he **h**; 3807.1
41:54 began to come, according as Joseph **h** said: NIH
43: 2 when they **h** eaten up the corn which they NIH
43: 2 the corn which they **h** brought out of Egypt, NIH
43: 6 *as* to tell the man whether ye **h** yet a 3807.1
43:10 For except we **h** lingered, surely now we NIH
43:10 surely now we **h** returned this second time. NIH
43:23 I **h** your money. And he brought 413+935
44: 2 he did according to the word that Joseph **h** NIH
45:27 of Joseph, which he **h** said unto them: NIH
45:27 when he saw the wagons which Joseph **h** NIH
46: 1 his journey with all that he **h**, 2050.2+3807.1
46: 5 in the wagons which Pharaoh **h** sent to carry NIH
46: 6 which they **h** gotten in the land of Canaan, NIH
47:11 land of Rameses, as Pharaoh **h** commanded. NIH
Ge 47:18 is spent; my lord also **h** our herds of cattle; 413
47:22 for the priests **h** a portion assigned them of NIH
47:27 and they **h** **possession** therein, and grew, and 270
48:11 unto Joseph, I **h** not thought to see thy face: NIH
49:33 when Jacob **h** made an end of commanding NIH
50:14 bury his father, after he **h** buried his father. NIH
Ex 2: 6 when she **h** opened *it*, she saw the child: NIH
2: 6 she **h** **compassion** on him, and said, This *is* 2550
2:16 Now the priest of Midian **h** seven 3807.1
2:25 of Israel, and God **h** **respect unto** *them*. 3045
4:28 the words of the LORD who **h** sent him, NIH
4:28 all the signs which he **h** commanded him. NIH
4:30 which the LORD **h** spoken unto Moses, NIH
4:31 when they heard that the LORD **h** visited NIH
4:31 that he **h** looked upon their affliction, then NIH
5:14 which Pharaoh's taskmasters **h** set over NIH
7:10 they did so as the LORD **h** commanded: NIH
7:13 not unto them; as the LORD **h** said. NIH
7:22 hearken unto them; as the LORD **h** said. NIH
7:25 after *that* the LORD **h** smitten the river. NIH
8:12 of the frogs which he **h** brought against NIH
8:15 not unto them; as the LORD **h** said. NIH
8:19 not unto them; as the LORD **h** said. NIH
9:12 as the LORD **h** spoken unto Moses. NIH
9:35 as the LORD **h** spoken by Moses. NIH
10:15 all the fruit of the trees which the hail **h** left: NIH
10:23 all the children of Israel **h** light in 1961+3807.1
12:28 did as the LORD **h** commanded Moses and NIH
12:39 neither **h** they prepared for themselves *any* NIH
13:17 to pass, when Pharaoh **h** let the people go, NIH
13:19 for he **h** straitly sworn the children of Israel, NIH
14:12 For *it* **h** *been* better for us to serve NIH
15:25 *which* when he **h** cast into the waters, NIH
16: 3 Would to God we **h** died by the hand of NIH
16:18 he that gathered much **h** nothing **over**, and 5736
16:18 and he that gathered little **h** no **lack**; 2637
17:10 So Joshua did as Moses **h** said to him, and NIH
18: 1 heard of all that God **h** done for Moses, and NIH
18: 1 that the LORD **h** brought Israel out of NIH
18: 2 Moses' wife, after he **h** sent her *back*, NIH
18: 8 all that the LORD **h** done unto Pharaoh NIH
18: 8 all the travail that **h** come upon them by NIH
18: 9 which the LORD **h** done to Israel, NIH
18: 9 whom he **h** delivered out of the hand of NIH
18:24 his father in law, and did all that he **h** said. NIH
19: 2 of Sinai, and **h** pitched in the wilderness; NIH
31:18 when he **h** made an end of communing with NIH
32: 4 after he **h** made it a molten calf: NIH
32:20 he took the calf which they **h** made, and NIH
32:25 (for Aaron **h** made them naked unto *their* NIH
32:29 For Moses **h** said, Consecrate yourselves to NIH
33: 5 For the LORD **h** said unto Moses, NIH
34: 4 as the LORD **h** commanded him, and NIH
34:32 LORD **h** spoken with him in mount Sinai. NIH
34:33 *till* Moses **h** done speaking with them, he NIH
35:25 brought that which they **h** spun, *both* of NIH
35:29 which the LORD **h** commanded to be NIH
36: 1 according to all that the LORD **h** NIH
36: 2 in whose heart the LORD **h** put wisdom, NIH
36: 3 which the children of Israel **h** brought for NIH
36: 7 For the stuff *they* **h** was sufficient for all NIH
36:22 One board **h** two tenons, equally distant 3807.1
39:43 they **h** done it as the LORD had NIH
39:43 they had done it as the LORD **h** NIH
39:43 had commanded, *even* so **h** they done it: NIH
40:23 as the LORD **h** commanded Moses. NIH
Lev 5:10 for him for his sin which he **h** sinned, NIH
10: 5 their coats out of the camp; as Moses **h** said. NIH
10:19 *if* I **h** eaten the sin offering to day, should it NIH
21: 3 which hath **h** no husband; 1961+3807.1
24:23 that they should bring forth him that **h** NIH
Nu 1:48 For the LORD **h** spoken unto Moses, NIH
3: 4 of Sinai, and they **h** no children: 1961+3807.1
7: 1 it came to pass on the day that Moses **h** 3807.1
7: 1 **h** anointed it, and sanctified it, and all NIH
7: 1 and **h** anointed them, and sanctified them; NIH
8: 4 pattern which the LORD **h** shewed Moses, NIH
8:22 as the LORD **h** commanded Moses NIH
12: 1 of the Ethiopian woman whom he **h** NIH
12: 1 for he **h** married an Ethiopian woman. NIH
12:14 If her father **h** but spit in her face, NIH
13:32 they **h** searched unto the children of Israel, NIH
14: 2 Would God that we **h** died in the land of NIH
14: 2 or would God we **h** died in this wilderness! NIH
14:24 because he **h** another spirit with him, and 1961
16:31 as he **h** made an end of speaking all these NIH
16:39 wherewith they that were burnt **h** offered; NIH
20: 3 Would God that we **h** died when our NIH
21: 9 to pass, that if a serpent **h** bitten *any* man, NIH
21:26 who **h** fought against the former king of NIH
22: 2 Balak the son of Zippor saw all that Israel **h** NIH
22:33 unless she **h** turned from me, surely now NIH
22:33 surely now also I **h** slain thee, and saved her NIH
23: 2 Balak did as Balaam **h** spoken; and Balak NIH
23:30 Balak did as Balaam **h** said, and offered a NIH
26:33 Zelophehad the son of Hepher **h** no 1961+3807.1
26:65 For the LORD **h** said of them, They shall NIH
27: 3 died in his own sin, and **h** no sons. 1961+3807.1
30: 6 if she **h** **at all** a husband, 1961+1961+3807.1
31:32 of the prey which the men of war **h** caught, NIH
31:35 of women that **h** not known man by lying NIH
31:53 (*For* the men of war **h** taken spoil, NIH
32: 1 the children of Gad **h** a very great 1961+3807.1
32: 9 the land which the LORD **h** given them. NIH
32:13 that **h** done evil in the sight of the LORD, NIH
33: 4 which the LORD **h** smitten among them: NIH
Dt 1: 3 according unto all that the LORD **h** given NIH
1: 4 After he **h** slain Sihon the king of NIH
1:39 which *in that* day **h** no **knowledge** between 3045
1:41 when ye **h** girded on every man his NIH
2:12 when they **h** destroyed them from before NIH
7: 8 he would keep the oath which he **h** sworn NIH
9:16 ye **h** sinned against the LORD your God, NIH
9:16 your God, *and* **h** made you a molten calf: NIH
9:16 ye **h** turned aside quickly out of the way NIH

Dt 9:16 way which the LORD **h** commanded you. NIH
9:21 the calf which ye **h** made, and burnt it with NIH
9:25 the LORD **h** said he would destroy you. NIH
10: 5 put the tables in the ark which I **h** made; NIH
10:15 Only the LORD **h** a **delight** in thy fathers 2836
19:19 as he **h** thought to have done unto his NIH
29:26 and *whom* he **h** not given unto them: NIH
31:24 when Moses **h** made an end of writing NIH
32:30 except their Rock **h** sold them, and NIH
32:30 sold them, and the LORD **h** shut them up? NIH
34: 9 for Moses **h** laid his hands upon him: NIH
Jos 2: 6 she **h** brought them up to the roof of NIH
2: 6 which she **h** laid in order upon the roof. NIH
2:11 as soon as we **h** heard *these things,* our NIH
4: 4 whom he **h** prepared of the children of NIH
5: 1 heard that the LORD **h** dried up the waters NIH
5: 5 out of Egypt, *them* they **h** not circumcised. NIH
5: 7 they **h** not circumcised them by the way. NIH
5: 8 when they **h** done circumcising all NIH
5:12 they **h** eaten of the old corn of the land; NIH
5:12 neither **h** the children of Israel manna any 1961
6: 8 when Joshua **h** spoken unto the people, NIH
6:10 Joshua **h** commanded the people, saying, NIH
6:22 Joshua **h** said unto the two men that had NIH
6:22 Joshua had said unto the two men that **h** NIH
6:23 and her brethren, and all that she **h**; 3807.1
6:25 her father's household, and all that she **h**; 3807.1
7: 7 would to God we **h** been content, and NIH
7:24 his sheep, and his tent, and all that he **h**: 3807.1
7:25 after they **h** stoned them with stones. NIH
8:13 when they **h** set the people, *even* all the host NIH
8:18 Joshua stretched out the spear that *he* **h** in NIH
8:19 they ran as soon as *he* **h** stretched out his NIH
8:20 they **h** no power to flee this way or 1961
8:21 all Israel saw that the ambush **h** taken NIH
8:24 when Israel **h** made an end of slaying all NIH
8:26 until *he* **h** utterly destroyed all NIH
8:33 as Moses the servant of the LORD **h** NIH
9: 3 heard what Joshua **h** done unto Jericho NIH
9: 4 and made as if they **h** been ambassadors, NIH
9:16 days after they **h** made a league with them, NIH
9:18 the princes of the congregation **h** sworn NIH
9:21 as the princes **h** promised them. NIH
10: 1 when Adoni-zedek king of Jerusalem **h** NIH
10: 1 had heard how Joshua **h** taken Ai, NIH
10: 1 had taken Ai, and **h** utterly destroyed it; NIH
10: 1 as he **h** done to Jericho and her king, so NIH
10: 1 her king, so he **h** done to Ai and her king; NIH
10: 1 how the inhabitants of Gibeon **h** made NIH
10:13 until the people **h** avenged themselves upon NIH
10:20 the children of Israel **h** made an end of NIH
10:27 cast them into the cave wherein they **h** been NIH
10:32 according to all that he **h** done to Libnah. NIH
10:33 until *he* **h** left him none remaining. NIH
10:35 according to all that he **h** done to Lachish. NIH
10:37 according to all that he **h** done to Eglon; NIH
10:39 as he **h** done to Hebron, so he did to Debir, NIH
10:39 as he **h** done also to Libnah, and to her king. NIH
11: 1 when Jabin king of Hazor **h** heard *those* NIH
11:14 until they **h** destroyed them, neither left NIH
14: 3 For Moses **h** given the inheritance of two NIH
14:15 And the land **h** **rest** from war. 8252
17: 1 therefore he **h** Gilead and Bashan. 1961+3807.1
17: 3 **h** no sons, but daughters: 1961+3807.1
17: 6 Because the daughters of Manasseh **h** an 5157
17: 6 the rest of Manasseh's sons **h** 1961+3807.1
17: 8 *Now* Manasseh **h** the land of 1961+3807.1
17:11 Manasseh **h** in Issachar and 1961+3807.1
18: 2 which **h** not *yet* received their inheritance. NIH
19: 2 they **h** in their inheritance 1961+3807.1
19: 9 the children of Simeon **h** **their inheritance** NIH
19:49 When they **h** made an end of dividing NIH
21: 4 **h** by lot out of the tribe of Judah, 1961+3807.1
21: 5 the rest of the children of Kohath **h** by lot NIH
21: 6 the children of Gershon *h* by lot out of NIH
21: 7 The children of Merari by their families *h* NIH
21:10 *were* of the children of Levi, **h**: 1961+3807.1
21:20 even they **h** the cities of their lot out of 1961
21:45 LORD **h** spoken unto the house of Israel; NIH
22: 7 Moses **h** given *possession* in Bashan: NIH
23: 1 **h** given rest unto Israel from all their NIH
24:31 which **h** known all the works of NIH
24:31 of the LORD, that he **h** done for Israel. NIH
Jdg 1: 8 Now the children of Judah **h** fought against NIH
1: 8 **h** taken it, and smitten it with the edge of NIH
1:19 because they **h** chariots of iron. 3807.1
2: 6 when Joshua **h** let the people go, NIH
2: 7 who **h** seen all the great works of NIH
2:10 nor yet the works which he **h** done for NIH
2:15 as the LORD **h** said, and as the LORD NIH
2:15 and as the LORD **h** sworn unto them: NIH
3: 1 *even* as many *of Israel* as **h** not known all NIH
3:11 the land **h** **rest** forty years. And Othniel 8252
3:12 they **h** done evil in the sight of the LORD. NIH
3:16 Ehud made him a dagger which **h** two 3807.1
3:18 when he **h** made an end to offer the present, NIH
3:20 which he **h** for himself alone. NIH
3:30 And the land **h** **rest** fourscore years. 8252
4: 3 for he **h** nine hundred chariots of iron; 3807.1
4:11 **h** severed himself from the Kenites, and NIH
4:18 when he **h** turned in unto her into the tent, NIH
4:24 until they **h** destroyed Jabin king of Canaan. NIH
5:26 when she **h** pierced and stricken through his NIH
5:31 his might. And the land **h** **rest** forty years. 8252
6: 3 *so* it was, when Israel **h** sown, that NIH
6:27 and did as the LORD **h** said unto him: NIH
7:19 *and* they **h** but newly set the watch: NIH
8: 3 was abated toward him, when he **h** said that. NIH
8: 8 him as the men of Succoth **h** answered *him.* NIH
8:19 if ye **h** saved them alive, I would not slay NIH
8:24 (For they **h** golden earrings, because 3807.1
8:30 Gideon **h** threescore and ten sons 1961+3807.1
8:30 for he **h** many wives. 1961+3807.1
8:34 who **h** delivered them out of the hands of all NIH
8:35 according to all the goodness which he **h** NIH
Jdg 9:22 When Abimelech **h** reigned three years over NIH
10: 4 he **h** thirty sons that rode on thirty 1961+3807.1
10: 4 they **h** thirty cities, which are called 3807.1
11:34 beside her he **h** neither son nor daughter. 3807.1
11:39 her *according to* his vow which he **h** vowed: NIH
12: 9 he **h** thirty sons, and 1961+3807.1
12:14 he **h** forty sons and thirty nephews, 1961+3807.1
14: 4 for at that time the Philistines **h** **dominion** 4910
14: 6 rent a kid, and *he* **h** nothing in his hand: NIH
14: 6 not his father or his mother what he **h** done. NIH
14: 9 he told not them that he **h** taken the honey NIH
14:18 If ye **h** not plowed with my heifer, NIH
14:18 my heifer, ye **h** not found out my riddle. NIH
14:20 whom he **h** used as his friend. NIH
15: 5 when he **h** set the brands on fire, he let *them* NIH
15: 6 because he **h** taken his wife, and given her NIH
15:17 when he **h** made an end of speaking, NIH
15:19 when he **h** drunk, his spirit came again, and NIH
16: 8 seven green withs which **h** not been dried, NIH
16:18 when Delilah saw that he **h** told her all his NIH
17: 3 when he **h** restored the eleven hundred NIH
17: 3 I **h** wholly dedicated the silver unto NIH
17: 5 the man Micah **h** a house of gods, and 3807.1
18: 1 **h** not fallen unto them among the tribes of NIH
18: 7 and **h** no business with *any* man. 3807.1
18:27 they took *the things* which Micah **h** made, NIH
18:27 the priest which he **h**, and 1961+3807.1
18:28 and they **h** no business with *any* man; 3807.1
19: 6 for the damsel's father **h** said unto the man, NIH
19:17 when he **h** lift up his eyes, he saw a NIH
20:36 liers in wait which they **h** set beside Gibeah. NIH
21: 1 Now the men of Israel **h** sworn in Mizpeh, NIH
21: 5 For *they* **h** made a great oath concerning NIH
21:12 that **h** known no man by lying with *any* NIH
21:14 they gave them wives which they **h** saved NIH
21:15 that the LORD **h** made a breach in NIH
Ru 1: 6 for she **h** heard in the country of Moab how NIH
1: 6 **h** visited his people in giving them bread. NIH
2: 1 Naomi **h** a kinsman of her husband's, 3807.1
2:17 until even, and beat out that she **h** gleaned: NIH
2:18 her mother in law saw what she **h** gleaned: NIH
2:18 gave to her that she **h** **reserved** after she 3498
2:19 mother in law with whom she **h** wrought, NIH
3: 7 when Boaz **h** eaten and drunk, and his heart NIH
3:16 she told her all that the man **h** done to her. NIH
1Sa 1: 2 he **h** two wives; the name of the one *was* 3807.1
1: 2 Peninnah **h** children, but 1961+3807.1
1: 2 had children, but Hannah **h** no children. 3807.1
1: 5 but the LORD **h** shut up her womb. NIH
1: 6 because the LORD **h** shut up her womb. NIH
1: 9 So Hannah rose up after *they* **h** eaten in NIH
1: 9 had eaten in Shiloh, and after *they* **h** drunk. NIH
1:13 therefore Eli thought she **h** been drunken. NIH
1:20 was come about after Hannah **h** conceived, NIH
1:24 when she **h** weaned him, she took him up NIH
3: 8 Eli perceived that the LORD **h** called NIH
4:18 heavy. And he **h** judged Israel forty years. NIH
5: 9 it was *so,* that after they **h** carried it about, NIH
5: 9 and they **h** emerods in their secret parts. NIH
6: 6 when he **h** wrought wonderfully among NIH
6:16 when the five lords of the Philistines **h** seen NIH
6:19 they **h** looked into the ark of the LORD, NIH
6:19 the LORD **h** smitten *many* of the people NIH
7:14 the cities which the Philistines **h** taken from NIH
9: 2 he **h** a son, whose name *was* Saul, 1961+3807.1
9:15 Now the LORD **h** told Samuel in his ear a NIH
10: 9 that when he **h** turned his back to go from NIH
10:13 when he **h** made an end of prophesying, NIH
10:20 when Samuel **h** caused all the tribes of NIH
10:21 When he **h** caused the tribe of Benjamin to NIH
10:26 band of men, whose hearts God **h** touched. NIH
13: 1 when he **h** reigned two years over Israel, NIH
13: 4 all Israel heard say *that* Saul **h** smitten a NIH
13: 4 *that* Israel also was **h** **in abomination** with 887
13: 8 according to the set time that Samuel *h* NIH
13:10 that as soon as he **h** made an end of 3807.1
13:21 Yet they **h** a file for the mattocks, and 1961
14:11 of the holes where they **h** hid themselves. NIH
14:17 when they **h** numbered, behold Jonathan NIH
14:22 Likewise all the men of Israel which **h** hid NIH
14:24 for Saul **h** adjured the people, saying, NIH
14:30 if haply the people **h** eaten freely to day of NIH
14:30 for **h** there not been now a much greater NIH
15:35 the LORD repented that he **h** made Saul NIH
17: 5 *he* **h** a helmet of brass upon his head, and NIH
17: 6 *he* **h** greaves of brass upon his legs, and NIH
17:12 name *was* Jesse; and he **h** eight sons: 3807.1
17:20 took, and went, as Jesse **h** commanded him; NIH
17:21 and the Philistines **h** put *the battle* in array, NIH
17:39 for he **h** not proved *it.* And David said unto NIH
17:40 put them in a shepherd's bag which he **h**, 3807.1
19:18 and told him all that Saul **h** done to him. NIH
20:34 because his father **h** done him shame. NIH
20:37 place of the arrow which Jonathan **h** shot, NIH
22:21 Abiathar shewed David that Saul **h** slain NIH
24: 5 smote him, because he **h** cut off Saul's skirt. NIH
24:10 **h** delivered thee to day into mine hand in NIH
24:16 when David **h** made an end of speaking NIH
24:18 forasmuch as when the LORD **h** delivered NIH
25: 2 he **h** three thousand sheep, and 3807.1
25:21 Now David **h** said, Surely in vain have I NIH
25:34 surely there **h** not been left unto Nabal by NIH
25:35 of her hand *that* which she **h** brought him, NIH
25:37 his wife **h** told him these things, that his NIH
25:44 Saul **h** given Michal his daughter, NIH
26: 5 and came to the place where Saul **h** pitched: NIH
28: 3 all Israel **h** lamented him, and buried him in NIH
28: 3 Saul **h** put away those that had familiar NIH
28: 3 Saul had put away those that **h** familiar NIH
28:20 for he **h** eaten no bread all the day, nor all NIH
28:24 the woman **h** a fat calf in the house; and 3807.1
30: 1 that the Amalekites **h** invaded the south, NIH
30: 2 **h** taken the women captives, that *were* NIH
30: 4 wept, until they **h** no more power to weep. 871.1
30:12 when he **h** eaten, his spirit came again to NIH
1Sa 30:12 for he **h** eaten no bread, nor drunk *any* NIH
30:16 when he **h** brought him down, behold *they* NIH
30:16 of all the great spoil that they **h** taken out of NIH
30:18 David recovered all that the Amalekites **h** NIH
30:19 nor any *thing* that they **h** taken to them: NIH
30:21 whom they **h** made also to abide at NIH
31:11 of that which the Philistines **h** done to Saul, NIH
2Sa 1: 1 and David **h** abode two days in Ziklag; NIH
1:21 *as though he* **h** not *been* anointed with oil. NIH
2:27 in the morning the people **h** gone up every NIH
2:30 when he **h** gathered all the people together, NIH
2:31 the servants of David **h** smitten of NIH
3: 7 Saul **h** a concubine, whose name *was* 3807.1
3:17 Abner **h** communication with the elders of 1961
3:22 for he **h** sent him away, and he was gone in NIH
3:30 he **h** slain their brother Asahel at Gibeon in NIH
4: 2 Saul's son **h** two men *that were* captains of 1961
4: 4 **h** a son *that was* lame of *his* feet, *and* 3807.1
5:12 David perceived that the LORD **h** NIH
5:12 that he **h** exalted his kingdom for his people NIH
5:17 when the Philistines heard that they **h** NIH
5:25 did so, as the LORD **h** commanded him; NIH
6: 8 the LORD **h** made a breach upon Uzzah: NIH
6:13 the ark of the LORD **h** gone six paces, NIH
6:17 in the midst of the tabernacle that David **h** NIH
6:18 as soon as David **h** made an end of offering NIH
6:22 spoken of, of them shall I be **h** **in honour**. 3513
6:23 **h** no child unto the day of her 1961+3807.1
7: 1 the LORD **h** given him rest round about NIH
8: 9 David **h** smitten all the host of Hadadezer, NIH
8:10 because he **h** fought against Hadadezer, and NIH
8:10 for Hadadezer **h** **wars with** Toi. 376+1961+4421
8:11 gold that he **h** dedicated of all nations which NIH
9: 2 when they **h** called him unto David, NIH
9:10 Now Ziba **h** fifteen sons and 3807.1
9:12 Mephibosheth **h** a young son, 3807.1
11:10 when they **h** told David, saying, Uriah went NIH
11:13 when David **h** called him, he did eat and NIH
11:22 shewed David all that Joab **h** sent him for. NIH
11:27 the thing that David **h** done displeased NIH
12: 2 The rich *man* **h** exceeding many 1961+3807.1
12: 3 the poor *man* **h** nothing, save one little 3807.1
12: 3 which he **h** bought and nourished up: NIH
12: 6 he did this thing, and because he **h** no **pity**. 2550
12: 8 if *that* **h** *been too* little, I would moreover NIH
13: 1 that Absalom the son of David **h** a fair 3807.1
13: 3 Amnon **h** a friend, whose name *was* 3807.1
13:10 Tamar took the cakes which she **h** made, NIH
13:11 when she **h** brought *them* unto him to eat, NIH
13:15 than the love wherewith he **h** loved her. NIH
13:18 *she* **h** a garment of divers colours upon her: NIH
13:22 because he **h** forced his sister Tamar. NIH
13:23 that Absalom **h** sheepshearers in 1961
13:28 Now Absalom **h** commanded his servants, NIH
13:29 did unto Amnon as Absalom **h** commanded. NIH
13:36 as soon as he **h** made an end of speaking, 3807.1
14: 2 be as a woman *that* **h** a long time mourned NIH
14: 6 thy handmaid **h** two sons, and they two 3807.1
14:32 *it* **h** been good for me *to have been* there NIH
14:33 when he **h** called for Absalom, he came to NIH
15: 2 *that when* any man that **h** a 1961+3807.1
15:24 until all the people **h** done passing out of NIH
15:30 **h** his head covered, and he went barefoot: 3807.1
16:23 *was* as if a man **h** inquired at the oracle of NIH
17:14 For the LORD **h** appointed to defeat NIH
17:18 in Bahurim, which **h** a well in his court; 3807.1
17:20 when they **h** sought and could not find NIH
18:18 Now Absalom in his lifetime **h** taken and NIH
18:33 would God I **h** died for thee, O Absalom, NIH
19: 6 that if Absalom **h** lived, and all we had died NIH
19: 6 all we **h** died *this* day, then it had pleased NIH
19: 6 died *this* day, then it **h** pleased thee well. NIH
19: 8 for Israel **h** fled every man to his tent. NIH
19:24 **h** neither dressed his feet, nor trimmed his NIH
19:32 he **h** provided the king of sustenance while NIH
19:43 that our advice should not be first **h** in 3807.1
20: 3 whom he **h** left to keep the house, and NIH
20: 5 than the set time which he **h** appointed him. NIH
20: 8 Joab's garment that he **h** put on *was* girded NIH
21: 2 the children of Israel **h** sworn unto them: NIH
21:11 of Aiah, the concubine of Saul, **h** done. NIH
21:12 which **h** stolen them from the street of NIH
21:12 where the Philistines **h** hanged them, NIH
21:12 when the Philistines **h** slain Saul in Gilboa: NIH
21:15 Moreover the Philistines **h** yet war 1961+3807.1
21:20 that **h** on every hand six fingers, and NIH
22: 1 **h** delivered him out of the hand of all his NIH
22:38 turned not again until I **h** consumed them. NIH
23: 8 names of the mighty *men* whom David **h**: 3807.1
23:18 slew them, and **h** the name among three. 3807.1
23:20 of Kabzeel, who **h** done many acts, NIH
23:21 the Egyptian **h** a spear in his hand; but NIH
23:22 **h** the name among three mighty *men.* 3807.1
24: 8 So when they **h** gone through all the land, NIH
24:10 David's heart smote him after that he **h** NIH
1Ki 1: 6 his father **h** not displeased him at any time NIH
1:41 heard *it* as they **h** made an end of eating. NIH
2:28 for Joab **h** turned after Adonijah, though he NIH
2:41 it was told Solomon that Shimei **h** gone NIH
3: 1 until he **h** made an end of building his own NIH
3:10 the Lord, that Solomon **h** asked this thing. NIH
3:21 when I **h** considered it in the morning, NIH
3:28 of the judgment which the king **h** judged; NIH
4: 2 these *were* the princes which he **h**; 3807.1
4: 7 Solomon **h** twelve officers over all Israel, 3807.1
4:11 which **h** Taphath the daughter of 1961+3807.1
4:14 Ahinadab the son of Iddo *h* Mahanaim: NIH
4:24 For he **h** dominion over all *the region* on NIH
4:24 **h** peace on all sides round about 1961+3807.1
4:26 Solomon **h** forty thousand stalls of 1961+3807.1
4:34 of the earth, which **h** heard of his wisdom. NIH
5: 1 for he **h** heard that they had anointed him NIH
5: 1 for he had heard that they **h** anointed him NIH
5:15 Solomon **h** threescore and 1961+3807.1
6:22 with gold, until *he* **h** finished all the house: NIH

1Ki 7: 8 his house where he dwelt ***h*** another court NIH
7: 8 whom he **h** taken *to wife,* like unto this NIH
7:20 the chapiters upon the two pillars ***h*** NIH
7:28 bases *was on* this *manner:* they **h** borders, 3807.1
7:30 every base **h** four brasen wheels, and 3807.1
7:30 the four corners thereof **h** undersetters: 3807.1
7:37 all of them **h** one casting, one measure, 3807.1
7:51 *things* which David his father **h** dedicated; NIH
8:11 for the glory of the LORD **h** filled NIH
8:54 *that* when Solomon **h** made an end of NIH
8:66 the LORD **h** done for David his servant, NIH
9: 1 when Solomon **h** finished the building of NIH
9: 2 as he **h** appeared unto him at Gibeon. NIH
9:10 when Solomon **h** built the two houses, NIH
9:11 (*Now* Hiram the king of Tyre **h** furnished NIH
9:12 see the cities which Solomon **h** given him; NIH
9:16 *For* Pharaoh king of Egypt **h** gone up, and NIH
9:19 the cities of store that Solomon **h**, 1961+3807.1
9:24 her house which *Solomon* **h** built for her: NIH
9:27 shipmen that **h** knowledge of the sea, NIH
10: 4 when the queen of Sheba **h** seen all NIH
10: 4 and the house that he **h** built, NIH
10: 7 I came, and mine eyes **h** seen *it:* and behold, NIH
10:15 Besides *that he **h*** of the merchantmen, NIH
10:19 The throne **h** six steps, and the top of 3807.1
10:22 For the king **h** at sea a navy of Tharshish 3807.1
10:24 his wisdom, which God **h** put in his heart. NIH
10:26 he **h** a thousand and four hundred 1961+3807.1
10:28 Solomon **h** horses brought out of Egypt, 3807.1
11: 3 he **h** seven hundred wives, 1961+3807.1
11: 9 of Israel, which **h** appeared unto him twice, NIH
11:10 **h** commanded him concerning this thing, NIH
11:15 after he **h** smitten every male in Edom; NIH
11:16 until he **h** cut off every male in Edom:) NIH
11:29 he **h** clad himself with a new garment; and NIH
12: 8 which they **h** given him, and consulted with NIH
12:12 as the king **h** appointed, saying, Come to NIH
12:32 sacrificing unto the calves that he **h** made: NIH
12:32 priests of the high places which he **h** made. NIH
12:33 So he offered upon the altar which he **h** NIH
12:33 *even* in the month which he **h** devised of his NIH
13: 4 which **h** cried against the altar in Beth-el, NIH
13: 5 of God **h** given by the word of the LORD. NIH
13:11 him all the works that the man of God **h** NIH
13:11 the words which he **h** spoken unto the king, NIH
13:12 For his sons **h** seen what way the man of NIH
13:23 after he **h** eaten bread, and after he had NIH
13:23 he had eaten bread, and after he **h** drunk, NIH
13:23 *to wit,* for the prophet whom he **h** brought NIH
13:28 the lion **h** not eaten the carcase, nor torn NIH
13:31 it came to pass, after he **h** buried him, that NIH
14:22 with their sins which they **h** committed, NIH
14:22 above all that their fathers **h** done. NIH
14:26 the shields of gold which Solomon **h** made. NIH
15: 3 of his father, which he **h** done before him: NIH
15:12 removed all the idols that his fathers **h** NIH
15:13 because she **h** made an idol in a grove; NIH
15:15 he brought in *the things* which his father **h** NIH
15:15 *the things* which himself **h** dedicated, NIH
15:20 sent the captains of the hosts which he **h** 3807.1
15:22 where*with* Baasha **h** builded; NIH
15:29 until *he* **h** destroyed him, according unto NIH
16:31 as if it **h** been a light thing for him to walk NIH
16:32 house of Baal, which he **h** built in Samaria. NIH
17: 7 because there **h** been no rain in the land. NIH
19: 1 Ahab told Jezebel all that Elijah **h** done, NIH
19: 1 withal how he **h** slain all the prophets with NIH
21: 1 *that* Naboth the Jezreelite **h** a 1961+3807.1
21: 4 of the word which Naboth the Jezreelite **h** NIH
21: 4 for he **h** said, I will not give thee NIH
21:11 did as Jezebel **h** sent unto them, *and* as *it* NIH
21:11 as *it was* written in the letters which she **h** NIH
22:31 two captains that **h** rule over *his* chariots, NIH
22:53 according unto all that his father **h** done. NIH
2Ki 1:17 word of the LORD which Elijah **h** spoken. NIH
1:17 of Judah; because he **h** no son. 1961+3807.1
2:14 when he also **h** smitten the waters, they NIH
3: 2 the image of Baal that his father **h** made. NIH
4:12 when he **h** called her, she stood before him. NIH
4:15 when he **h** called her, she stood in the door. NIH
4:17 bare a son at that season that Elisha **h** said NIH
4:20 when he **h** taken him, and brought him to NIH
5: 1 by him the LORD **h** given deliverance NIH
5: 2 the Syrians **h** gone out *by* companies, and NIH
5: 2 **h** brought away captive out of the land of NIH
5: 7 when the king of Israel **h** read the letter, NIH
5: 8 when Elisha the man of God **h** heard that NIH
5: 8 that the king of Israel **h** rent his clothes, NIH
5:13 *if* the prophet **h** bid thee *do some* great NIH
6:23 when they **h** eaten and drunk, he sent them NIH
6:30 *he* **h** sackcloth within upon his flesh. NIH
7: 6 For the Lord **h** made the host of the Syrians NIH
7:15 which the Syrians **h** cast away in their haste. NIH
7:17 and he died, as the man of God **h** said, NIH
7:18 it came to pass as the man of God **h** spoken NIH
8: 1 whose son he **h** restored to life, saying, NIH
8: 5 *as* he was telling the king how he **h** restored NIH
8: 5 the woman, whose son he **h** restored to life, NIH
8:29 which the Syrians **h** given him at Ramah, NIH
9:14 (Now Joram **h** kept Ramoth-gilead, he and 1961
9:15 the wounds which the Syrians **h** given him, NIH
9:31 she said, ***H*** Zimri peace, who slew his NIH
10: 1 Ahab **h** seventy sons in Samaria. 3807.1
10:17 till *he* **h** destroyed him, according to NIH
10:25 as soon as he **h** made an end of offering NIH
11:15 For the priest **h** said, Let her not be slain *in* NIH
12: 6 twentieth year of king Jehoash the priests **h** NIH
12:11 that **h** the **oversight** *of* the house of 6485
12:18 **h** dedicate, and his own hallowed *things,* NIH
13: 7 for the king of Syria **h** destroyed them, and NIH
13: 7 and **h** made them like the dust by threshing. NIH
13:23 **h compassion** on them, and had respect 7355
13:23 **h** respect unto them, because of his NIH
13:25 which he **h** taken out of the hand of NIH
14: 5 that he slew his servants which **h** slain NIH

2Ki 15: 3 according to all that his father Amaziah **h** NIH
15: 9 sight of the LORD, as his fathers **h** done: NIH
15:34 to all that his father Uzziah **h** done. NIH
16:11 to all that king Ahaz **h** sent from Damascus: NIH
16:18 the covert for the sabbath that they **h** built in NIH
17: 4 for he **h** sent messengers to So king of NIH
17: 4 king of Assyria, as *he **h** done* year by year: NIH
17: 7 that the children of Israel **h** sinned against NIH
17: 7 which **h** brought them up out of the land of NIH
17: 7 king of Egypt, and **h** feared other gods, NIH
17: 8 of the kings of Israel, which they **h** made. NIH
17:12 whereof the LORD **h** said unto them, NIH
17:15 *concerning* whom the LORD **h** charged NIH
17:20 until *he* **h** cast them out of his sight. NIH
17:23 as he **h** said by all his servants the prophets. NIH
17:28 one of the priests whom they **h** carried away NIH
17:29 high places which the Samaritans **h** made, NIH
17:35 With whom the LORD **h** made a covenant, NIH
18: 4 the brasen serpent that Moses **h** made: NIH
18:16 which Hezekiah king of Judah **h** overlaid, NIH
18:18 when they **h** called to the king, there came NIH
19: 8 for he **h** heard that he was departed from NIH
20:11 by which it **h** gone down in the dial of NIH
20:12 for he **h** heard that Hezekiah had been sick. NIH
20:12 for he had heard that Hezekiah **h** been sick. NIH
21: 3 which Hezekiah his father **h** destroyed; NIH
21: 7 he set a graven image of the grove that he **h** NIH
21:16 till he **h** filled Jerusalem from one end to NIH
21:24 the people of the land slew all them that **h** NIH
22:11 when the king **h** heard the words of NIH
23: 5 whom the kings of Judah **h** ordained to burn NIH
23: 8 defiled the high places where the priests **h** NIH
23:11 that the kings of Judah **h** given to the sun, NIH
23:12 which the kings of Judah **h** made, and NIH
23:12 the altars which Manasseh **h** made in NIH
23:13 which Solomon the king of Israel **h** builded NIH
23:15 **h** made, both that altar and the high place he NIH
23:19 which the kings of Israel **h** made to provoke NIH
23:19 to all the acts that he **h** done in Beth-el. NIH
23:26 of all the provocations that Manasseh **h** NIH
23:29 slew him at Megiddo, when he **h** seen him. NIH
23:32 according to all that his fathers **h** done. NIH
23:37 according to all that his fathers **h** done. NIH
24: 7 for the king of Babylon **h** taken from NIH
24: 9 according to all that his father **h** done. NIH
24:13 Israel **h** made in the temple of the LORD, NIH
24:13 of the LORD, as the LORD **h** said. NIH
24:19 according to all that Jehoiakim **h** done. NIH
24:20 until he **h** cast them out from his presence, NIH
25:16 the bases which Solomon **h** made for NIH
25:17 like unto these **h** the second pillar with 3807.1
25:22 whom Nebuchadnezzar king of Babylon **h** NIH
25:23 heard that the king of Babylon **h** made NIH
1Ch 2:22 who **h** three and twenty cities in 1961+3807.1
2:26 Jerahmeel **h** also another wife, 1961+3807.1
2:34 Now Sheshan **h** no sons, but 1961+3807.1
2:34 Sheshan **h** a servant, an Egyptian, whose 3807.1
2:52 the father of Kirjath-jearim **h** sons; 1961+3807.1
4: 5 Ashur the father of Tekoa **h** two 1961+3807.1
4:22 who **h** the dominion in Moab, and NIH
4:27 Shimei **h** sixteen sons and six daughters; 3807.1
4:27 his brethren **h** not many children, NIH
4:40 for *they* of Ham **h** dwelt there of old. NIH
6:31 of the LORD, after that the ark **h** rest. NIH
6:32 until Solomon **h** built the house of NIH
6:49 Moses the servant of God **h** commanded. NIH
6:66 **h** cities of their coasts out of the tribe of 1961
7: 4 thirty thousand *men:* for they **h** many wives NIH
7:15 and Zelophehad **h** daughters. 1961+3807.1
8: 8 country of Moab, after he **h** sent them away; NIH
8:38 Azel **h** six sons, whose names *are* these, 3807.1
8:40 archers, and **h many** sons, and sons' sons, 7235
9:23 their children **h** the oversight of the gates of NIH
9:28 *certain* of them **h** the charge of NIH
9:31 **h** the set office over the things that were 871.1
9:44 Azel **h** six sons, whose names *are* these, 3807.1
10: 9 when they **h** stripped him, they took his NIH
10:11 heard all that the Philistines **h** done to Saul, NIH
10:13 also for asking *counsel* of *one that **h*** a NIH
11:10 chief of the mighty *men* whom David **h**, 3807.1
11:11 of the mighty *men* whom David **h**; 3807.1
11:20 and **h** a name among the three. 3807.1
11:22 man of Kabzeel, who **h** done many acts; NIH
11:24 and **h** the name among the three mighties. 3807.1
12:15 when it **h** overflown all his banks; NIH
12:29 for hitherto the greatest part of them **h** kept NIH
12:32 that **h understanding** of the times, 998+3045
12:39 for their brethren **h** prepared for them. NIH
13:11 the LORD **h** made a breach upon Uzza: NIH
13:14 house of Obed-edom, and all that he **h**. 3807.1
14: 2 David perceived that the LORD **h** NIH
14: 4 children which he **h** in Jerusalem; 1961+3807.1
14:12 when they **h** left their gods there, David NIH
15: 3 unto his place, which he **h** prepared for it. NIH
15:27 David also ***h*** upon him an ephod of linen. NIH
16: 1 set it in the midst of the tent that David **h** NIH
16: 2 when David **h** made an end of offering NIH
18: 9 **h** smitten all the host of Hadarezer king of NIH
18:10 because he **h** fought against Hadarezer, and NIH
18:10 (for Hadarezer **h with** Tou;) 376+1961+4421
19: 6 they **h** made themselves odious to David, NIH
19:17 So when David **h** put the battle in array NIH
21:28 **h** answered him in the threshingfloor of NIH
23:11 Jeush and Beriah **h** not many sons; therefore NIH
23:17 Eliezer **h** none other sons; but 1961+3807.1
23:22 and **h** no sons, but daughters: 1961+3807.1
24: 2 their father, and **h** no children: 1961+3807.1
24:19 as the LORD God of Israel **h** commanded NIH
24:28 *came* Eleazar, who **h** no sons. 1961+3807.1
26: 9 Meshelemiah **h** sons and brethren, 3807.1
26:10 of the children of Merari, **h** sons; 3807.1
26:26 and the captains of the host, **h** dedicated. NIH
26:28 and Joab the son of Zeruiah, **h** dedicated; NIH
26:28 whosoever **h** dedicated *anything, it was* NIH
27:23 the LORD **h** said *he* would increase Israel NIH

1Ch 28: 2 *As for me,* I ***h*** in mine heart to build a house NIH
28: 2 our God, and **h** made ready for the building: NIH
28:12 the pattern of all that he **h** by 1961+5973
29:25 bestowed upon him *such* royal majesty as **h** NIH
2Ch 1: 3 which Moses the servant of the LORD **h** NIH
1: 4 the ark of God **h** David brought up from NIH
1: 4 to *the place which* David **h** prepared for it: NIH
1: 4 for he **h** pitched a tent for it at Jerusalem. NIH
1: 5 the son of Uri, the son of Hur, **h** made, NIH
1:12 such as none of the kings have **h** that *have* 1961
1:14 he **h** a thousand and four hundred 1961+3807.1
1:16 Solomon **h** horses brought out of Egypt, 3807.1
2:17 David his father **h** numbered them; NIH
3: 1 in the place that David **h** prepared in NIH
5: 1 *the things* that David his father **h** dedicated; NIH
5:14 for the glory of the LORD **h** filled NIH
6:13 For Solomon **h** made a brasen scaffold, NIH
6:13 and **h** set it in the midst of the court: NIH
7: 1 Now when Solomon **h** made an end of NIH
7: 2 the glory of the LORD **h** filled NIH
7: 6 which David the king **h** made to praise NIH
7: 7 the brasen altar which Solomon **h** made was NIH
7:10 that the LORD **h** shewed unto David, NIH
8: 1 wherein Solomon **h** built the house of NIH
8: 2 That the cities which Huram **h** restored to NIH
8: 6 all the store cities that Solomon **h**, 1961+3807.1
8:11 David unto the house that he **h** built for her: NIH
8:12 which he **h** built before the porch, NIH
8:14 for so **h** David the man of God commanded. NIH
8:18 and servants that **h** knowledge of the sea; NIH
9: 3 when the queen of Sheba **h** seen the wisdom NIH
9: 3 of Solomon, and the house that he **h** built, NIH
9: 6 I came, and mine eyes **h** seen *it:* and behold, NIH
9:12 besides *that* which she **h** brought unto NIH
9:23 hear his wisdom, that God **h** put in his heart. NIH
9:25 Solomon **h** four thousand stalls for 1961+3807.1
10: 2 whither he **h** fled from the presence of NIH
10: 6 **h** stood before Solomon his father while he 1961
11:14 his sons **h** cast them off from executing NIH
11:15 and for the calves which he **h** made. NIH
12: 1 when Rehoboam **h** established the kingdom, NIH
12: 1 **h** strengthened himself, he forsook the law NIH
12: 2 they **h** transgressed against the LORD, NIH
12: 9 the shields of gold which Solomon **h** made. NIH
12:13 the city which the LORD **h** chosen out of NIH
14: 6 for the land **h** rest, and he had no war in NIH
14: 6 had rest, and he **h** no war in those years; 5973
14: 6 because the LORD **h** given him rest. NIH
14: 8 Asa **h** an army *of men* that bare 1961+3807.1
15: 8 out of the cities which he **h** taken from NIH
15:11 of the spoil *which* they **h** brought, NIH
15:15 for they **h** sworn with all their heart, and NIH
15:16 because she **h** made an idol in a grove: NIH
15:18 God *the things* that his father **h** dedicated, NIH
15:18 that he himself **h** dedicated, silver, and gold, NIH
16:14 which he **h** made for himself in the city of NIH
17: 2 of Ephraim, which Asa his father **h** taken. NIH
17: 5 **h** riches and honour in abundance. 1961+3807.1
17: 9 ***h*** the book of the law of the LORD with NIH
17:13 he **h** much business in the cities of 1961+3807.1
18: 1 Now Jehoshaphat **h** riches and 1961+3807.1
18: 2 for the people that *he **h*** with him, and NIH
18:10 Zedekiah the son of Chenaanah **h** made him NIH
18:30 Now the king of Syria **h** commanded NIH
20:21 when he **h** consulted with the people, he NIH
20:23 when they **h** made an end of the inhabitants NIH
20:27 for the LORD **h** made them to rejoice over NIH
20:29 when they **h** heard that the LORD fought NIH
20:33 for as yet the people **h** not prepared their NIH
21: 2 he **h** brethren the sons of Jehoshaphat, 3807.1
21: 6 for he **h** the daughter of Ahab to 1961+3807.1
21: 7 of the covenant that he **h** made with David, NIH
21:10 he **h** forsaken the LORD God of his NIH
22: 1 Arabians to the camp **h** slain all the eldest. NIH
22: 7 whom the LORD **h** anointed to cut off NIH
22: 9 and when they **h** slain him, they buried him: NIH
22: 9 So the house of Ahaziah **h** no power to keep NIH
23: 8 that Jehoiada the priest **h** commanded, NIH
23: 9 and shields, that ***h** been* king David's, NIH
23:18 whom David **h** distributed in the house of NIH
23:21 after that they **h** slain Athaliah with NIH
24: 7 **h** broken up the house of God; NIH
24:10 cast into the chest, until *they* **h** made an end. NIH
24:14 when they **h** finished *it,* they brought NIH
24:16 because he **h** done good in Israel, NIH
24:22 which Jehoiada his father **h** done to him, NIH
24:24 they **h** forsaken the LORD God of their NIH
25: 3 that he slew his servants that **h** killed NIH
26: 5 who **h understanding** in the visions of God: 995
26:10 for he **h** much cattle, both in 1961+3807.1
26:11 Moreover Uzziah **h** a host of 1961+3807.1
26:19 and ***h*** a censer in his hand to burn incense: NIH
26:20 go out, because the LORD **h** smitten him. NIH
28: 3 **h** cast out before the children of Israel. NIH
28: 6 they **h** forsaken the LORD God of their NIH
28:17 For again the Edomites **h** come and NIH
28:18 The Philistines also **h** invaded the cities of NIH
28:18 **h** taken Beth-shemesh, and Ajalon, and NIH
29: 2 according to all that David his father **h** NIH
29:22 likewise, when they **h** killed the rams, they NIH
29:29 when *they* **h** made an end of offering, NIH
29:34 until the *other* priests **h** sanctified NIH
29:36 the people, that God **h** prepared the people: NIH
30: 2 For the king **h** taken counsel, and NIH
30: 3 the priests **h** not sanctified themselves NIH
30: 3 neither **h** the people gathered themselves NIH
30: 5 for they **h** not done *it* of a long *time in such* NIH
30:17 the Levites **h the charge of** the killing of 5921
30:18 and Zebulun, **h** not cleansed themselves, NIH
31: 1 until *they* **h** utterly destroyed *them all.* Then NIH
31:10 *we* have **h enough** to eat, and have left 7646
32:27 Hezekiah **h** exceeding much riches 1961+3807.1
32:29 for God **h** given him substance very much. NIH
33: 2 whom the LORD **h** cast out before NIH
33: 3 which Hezekiah his father **h** broken down, NIH

2Ch 33: 4 whereof the LORD **h** said, In Jerusalem NIH
33: 7 the idol which he **h** made, in the house of NIH
33: 7 of which God **h** said to David and NIH
33: 9 whom the LORD **h** destroyed before NIH
33:15 all the altars that he **h** built in the mount of NIH
33:22 images which Manasseh his father **h** made, NIH
33:23 as Manasseh his father **h** humbled himself; NIH
33:25 the people of the land slew all them that **h** NIH
34: 4 strowed *it* upon the graves of them that **h** NIH
34: 7 when he **h** broken down the altars and NIH
34: 7 **h** beaten the graven images into powder, NIH
34: 8 when he **h** purged the land, and the house, NIH
34: 9 which the Levites that kept the doors **h** NIH
34:10 **h** the oversight of the house of the LORD, NIH
34:11 which the kings of Judah **h** destroyed. NIH
34:19 when the king **h** heard the words of the law, NIH
34:22 *they* that the king ***h** appointed,* went to NIH
35:20 all this, when Josiah **h** prepared the temple, NIH
35:24 put him in the second chariot that he **h**; 3807.1
36:13 who **h** made him swear by God: NIH
36:14 LORD which he **h** hallowed in Jerusalem. NIH
36:15 because he **h compassion** on his people, 2550
36:17 **h** no **compassion** upon young man or 2550
36:20 them that **h** escaped from the sword carried NIH
36:21 until the land **h** enjoyed her sabbaths: NIH
Ezr 1: 5 with all *them* whose spirit God **h** raised, NIH
1: 7 which Nebuchadnezzar **h** brought forth out NIH
1: 7 and **h** put them in the house of his gods; NIH
2: 1 *of* those which **h** been carried away, NIH
2: 1 of Babylon **h** carried away unto Babylon, NIH
3: 7 according to the grant that they **h** of Cyrus 5921
3:12 *who were* ancient men that **h** seen the first NIH
5:12 after that our fathers **h** provoked the God of NIH
5:14 whom he **h** made governor; NIH
6:13 according to that which Darius the king **h** NIH
6:21 all such as **h** separated themselves unto NIH
6:22 for the LORD **h** made them joyful, and NIH
7: 6 which the LORD God of Israel **h** given: NIH
7:10 For Ezra **h** prepared his heart to seek NIH
8:20 the princes **h** appointed for the service of 3807.1
8:22 because we **h** spoken unto the king, saying, NIH
8:25 and all Israel *there* present, **h** offered: NIH
8:35 *Also* the children of those that **h** been NIH
9: 4 of the transgression of those that **h** been NIH
10: 1 Now when Ezra **h** prayed, and when he had NIH
10: 1 when he **h** confessed, weeping and NIH
10: 6 of the transgression of them that **h** been NIH
10: 8 of those that **h** been carried away. NIH
10:17 they made an end with all the men that **h** NIH
10:18 there were found that **h** taken strange wives: NIH
10:44 All these **h** taken strange wives: and NIH
10:44 *some* of them **h** wives by *whom* they had 3426
10:44 *some* of them had wives by *whom* they **h** 7760
Ne 1: 2 I asked them concerning the Jews that **h** NIH
2: 1 Now I **h** not been *beforetime* sad in his NIH
2: 9 Now the king **h** sent captains of the army NIH
2:12 neither told I *any* man what my God **h** put NIH
2:16 neither **h** I as yet told *it* to the Jews, nor to NIH
2:18 as also the king's words that he **h** spoken NIH
4: 6 for the people **h** a mind to work. 1961+3807.1
4:15 God **h** brought their counsel to nought, NIH
4:18 every one **h** his sword girded by his side, NIH
5:15 the former governors that *h been* before me NIH
5:15 **h** taken of them bread and wine, NIH
6: 1 heard that I **h** builded the wall, and NIH
6: 1 (though at that time I **h** not set up the doors NIH
6:12 And lo, I perceived that God **h** not sent him; NIH
6:12 for Tobiah and Sanballat **h** hired him. NIH
6:18 his son Johanan **h** taken the daughter of NIH
7: 1 and I **h** set up the doors, and the porters and NIH
7: 6 *of* those that **h** been carried away, NIH
7: 6 the king of Babylon **h** carried away, NIH
7:67 they **h** two hundred forty and five singing 3807.1
8: 1 which the LORD **h** commanded to Israel. NIH
8: 4 which they **h** made for the purpose; NIH
8:12 they **h** understood the words that were NIH
8:14 which the LORD **h** commanded by Moses, NIH
8:17 that day **h** not the children of Israel done so. NIH
9:18 when they **h** made them a molten calf, and NIH
9:18 of Egypt, and **h** wrought great provocations; NIH
9:28 after they **h** rest, they did evil again 3807.1
9:28 so that they **h** the dominion over them: NIH
10:28 all they that **h** separated themselves from NIH
11:16 **h the oversight** of the outward business of 5921
12:29 for the singers **h** builded them villages NIH
12:43 for God **h** made them rejoice *with* great joy: NIH
13: 3 it came to pass, when they **h** heard the law, NIH
13: 5 And he **h** prepared for him a great chamber, NIH
13:10 I perceived that the portions of the Levites **h** NIH
13:23 In those days also saw I Jews *that* **h** married NIH
Est 1: 8 the king **h** appointed to all the officers of his NIH
2: 1 what she **h** done, and what was decreed NIH
2: 6 Who **h** been carried away from Jerusalem NIH
2: 6 **h** been carried away with Jeconiah king of NIH
2: 6 the king of Babylon **h** carried away. NIH
2: 7 for she **h** neither father nor mother, and 3807.1
2:10 Esther **h** not shewed her people nor her NIH
2:10 for Mordecai **h** charged her that she should NIH
2:12 after that she **h** been twelve months, NIH
2:15 who **h** taken *her* for his daughter, was come NIH
2:20 Esther **h** not *yet* shewed her kindred nor her NIH
2:20 nor her people; as Mordecai **h** charged her: NIH
3: 2 for the king **h** so commanded concerning NIH
3: 4 for he **h** told them that he *was* a Jew. NIH
3: 6 for they **h** shewed him the people of NIH
3:12 **h** commanded unto the king's lieutenants, NIH
4: 5 whom he **h** appointed to attend upon her, NIH
4: 7 Mordecai told him of all that **h** happened NIH
4: 7 of the sum of the money that Haman **h** NIH
4:17 did according to all that Esther **h** NIH
5: 5 Haman came to the banquet that Esther **h** NIH
5:11 all *the things* where*in* the king **h** promoted NIH
5:11 how he **h** advanced him above the princes NIH
5:12 king unto the banquet that she **h** prepared NIH
6: 2 that Mordecai **h** told of Bigthana and NIH
Est 6: 4 on the gallows that he **h** prepared for him. NIH
6:13 all his friends every *thing* that **h** befallen NIH
6:14 unto the banquet that Esther **h** prepared. NIH
7: 4 if we **h** been sold for bondmen and NIH
7: 4 and bondwomen, I **h** held my tongue, NIH
7: 9 which Haman **h** made for Mordecai, NIH
7: 9 who **h** spoken good for the king, standeth in NIH
7:10 gallows that he **h** prepared for Mordecai. NIH
8: 1 for Esther **h** told what he *was* unto her. NIH
8: 2 which he **h** taken from Haman, and gave it NIH
8: 3 his device that he **h** devised against NIH
8:16 The Jews **h** light, and gladness, and 1961+3807.1
8:17 the Jews **h** joy and gladness, a feast and 3807.1
9: 1 the Jews **h** rule over them that hated them;) NIH
9:16 **h** rest from their enemies, and slew of their NIH
9:23 the Jews undertook to do as they **h** begun, NIH
9:23 and as Mordecai **h** written unto them; NIH
9:24 **h** devised against the Jews to destroy them, NIH
9:24 **h** cast Pur, that *is,* the lot, to consume them, NIH
9:26 *of that* which they **h** seen concerning this NIH
9:26 this *matter,* and which **h** come unto them, NIH
9:31 and Esther the queen **h** enjoined them, NIH
9:31 as they **h** decreed for themselves and NIH
Job 2:11 for they **h** made an appointment together to NIH
3:13 I should have slept: then **h** I been at rest, 3807.1
3:15 Or with princes that **h** gold, who filled 3807.1
3:16 Or as a hidden untimely birth I **h** not been; NIH
3:26 I was not in safety, neither **h** I rest, NIH
6:20 were confounded because they **h** hoped; NIH
9:16 If I **h** called, and he had answered me; NIH
9:16 If I had called, and he **h** answered me; NIH
9:16 *yet* would I not believe that he **h** hearkened NIH
10:18 *Oh that* I **h** given up the ghost, and no eye NIH
10:18 given up the ghost, and no eye **h** seen me! NIH
10:19 I should have been as though I **h** not been; I NIH
22: 8 *as for* the mighty man, he **h** the earth; and 3807.1
24:16 *which* they **h** marked for themselves in NIH
29:12 and *him that* **h** none to help him. NIH
31:25 and because mine hand **h** gotten much; NIH
31:31 tabernacle said not, O that we **h** of his flesh! NIH
31:35 and *that* mine adversary **h** written a book. NIH
32: 3 because they **h** found no answer, and NIH
32: 3 found no answer, and *yet* **h** condemned Job. NIH
32: 4 Now Elihu **h** waited till Job had spoken, NIH
32: 4 Now Elihu had waited till Job **h** spoken, NIH
32:16 When I **h** waited, (for they spake not, but NIH
38: 8 *as if* it **h** issued out of the womb? NIH
42: 7 that after the LORD **h** spoken these words NIH
42:10 gave Job twice as much as he **h** before. 3807.1
42:11 all *they that* **h** *been of* his acquaintance NIH
42:11 evil that the LORD **h** brought upon him: NIH
42:12 for he **h** fourteen thousand sheep, 1961+3807.1
42:13 He **h** also seven sons and 1961+3807.1
Ps 27:13 *I* ***h** fainted,* unless I had believed to see NIH
27:13 *I had fainted,* unless I **h** believed to see NIH
35:14 I behaved myself as though *he* ***h** been* my NIH
42: 4 for I **h** gone with the multitude, I went with NIH
51: T unto him, after he **h** gone in to Bath-sheba. NIH
55: 6 O that I **h** wings like a dove, *for then* 3807.1
73: 2 almost gone; my steps **h** well nigh slipt. NIH
74: 5 *A man* was famous according as he **h** lifted NIH
78:11 and his wonders that he **h** shewed them. NIH
78:23 Though he **h** commanded the clouds from NIH
78:24 **h** rained down manna upon them to eat, NIH
78:24 and **h** given them *of* the corn of heaven. NIH
78:43 How he **h** wrought his signs in Egypt, and NIH
78:44 **h** turned their rivers into blood; and NIH
78:54 *which* his right hand **h** purchased. NIH
81:13 O that my people **h** hearkened unto me, *and* NIH
81:13 unto me, *and* Israel **h** walked in my ways! NIH
84:10 I **h** rather be a doorkeeper in the house of NIH
89: 7 to be **h in reverence** of all them that are 3372
94:17 Unless the LORD ***h** been* my help, my soul NIH
94:17 my help, my soul **h** almost dwelt in silence. NIH
105:26 his servant; *and* Aaron whom he **h** chosen. NIH
106:21 which **h** done great *things* in Egypt; NIH
106:23 **h** not Moses his chosen stood before him in NIH
119:51 The proud have **h** me greatly **in derision**: 3887
119:56 This I **h**, because I kept thy 1961+3807.1
119:87 They **h** almost consumed me upon earth; NIH
119:92 Unless thy law ***h** been* my delights, I should NIH
124: 1 If *it* **h** not *been* the LORD who was on our NIH
124: 2 If *it* **h** not *been* the LORD who was on our NIH
124: 3 they **h** swallowed us up quick, when their NIH
124: 4 the waters **h** overwhelmed us, the stream NIH
124: 4 the stream **h** gone over our soul: NIH
124: 5 Then the proud waters **h** gone over our soul. NIH
Pr 8:26 While as yet he **h** not made the earth, NIH
24:31 *and* nettles **h** covered the face thereof, and NIH
Ecc 1:16 my heart **h** great **experience** of wisdom and 7200
2: 7 maidens, and **h** servants born in *my* house; 1961
2: 7 also I **h** great possessions of great and 1961
2:11 I looked on all the works that my hands **h** NIH
2:11 and on the labour that I **h** laboured to do: NIH
2:18 I hated all my labour which I **h** taken under NIH
4: 1 were oppressed, and they **h** no comforter; 3807.1
4: 1 *there was* power; but they **h** no comforter. 3807.1
8:10 who **h** come and gone from the place of NIH
8:10 they were forgotten in the city where they **h** NIH
SS 3: 4 until I **h** brought him into my mother's NIH
5: 6 my beloved **h** withdrawn himself, *and* NIH
8:11 Solomon **h** a vineyard at 1961+3807.1
Isa 1: 9 Except the LORD of hosts **h** left unto us a NIH
6: 2 each one **h** six wings; with twain he 3807.1
6: 6 *which* he **h** taken with the tongs from off NIH
22:11 neither **h** respect unto him that fashioned it NIH
26:13 besides thee have **h dominion over** us: 1166
29:16 him that framed it, He **h** no understanding? NIH
37: 8 for he **h** heard that he was departed from NIH
38: 9 when he **h** been sick, and was recovered of NIH
38:17 Behold, for peace I **h** great bitterness: 3807.1
38:21 For Isaiah **h** said, Let them take a lump of NIH
38:22 Hezekiah also **h** said, What *is* the sign that I NIH
39: 1 for he **h** heard that he had been sick, and NIH
39: 1 for he had heard that he **h** been sick, and NIH
Isa 41: 3 *even by* the way *that* he **h** not gone with his NIH
48:18 **h** thy peace been as a river, and NIH
48:19 Thy seed also **h** been as the sand, and NIH
49:21 I was left alone; these, where ***h** they been?* NIH
52:15 for *that* which **h** not been told them shall NIH
52:15 *that* which they **h** not heard shall they NIH
53: 9 because he **h** done no violence, neither *was* NIH
59:10 the blind, and we grope as if *we* ***h*** no eyes: NIH
60:10 but in my favour have I **h mercy** on thee. 7355
Jer 2:21 Yet I **h** planted thee a noble vine, wholly a NIH
3: 7 I said after she **h** done all these *things,* Turn NIH
3: 8 Israel committed adultery I **h** put her away, NIH
4:23 void; and the heavens, and they ***h*** no light. NIH
5: 7 when I **h** fed them to the full, they then NIH
6:15 Were they ashamed when they **h** committed NIH
8:12 Were they ashamed when they **h** committed NIH
9: 2 O that I **h** in the wilderness a lodging place NIH
11:19 I knew not that they **h** devised devices NIH
13: 7 took the girdle from the place where I **h** hid NIH
16:15 from all the lands whither he **h** driven them: NIH
19:14 whither the LORD **h** sent him to prophesy; NIH
23: 8 from all countries whither I **h** driven them; NIH
23:22 if they **h** stood in my counsel, and NIH
23:22 **h** caused my people to hear my words, then NIH
24: 1 **h** carried away captive Jeconiah the son of NIH
24: 1 and **h** brought them *to* Babylon. NIH
24: 2 One basket ***h*** very good figs, *even* like NIH
24: 2 the other basket ***h*** very naughty figs, NIH
25:17 to drink, unto whom the LORD **h** sent me: NIH
26: 8 when Jeremiah **h** made an end of speaking NIH
26: 8 **h** commanded *him* to speak unto all NIH
26:19 evil which he **h** pronounced against them? NIH
28:12 **h** broken the yoke from off the neck of NIH
29: 1 to all the people whom Nebuchadnezzar **h** NIH
32: 3 For Zedekiah king of Judah **h** shut him up, NIH
32:16 Now when I **h** delivered the evidence of NIH
34: 8 after that the king Zedekiah **h** made a NIH
34:10 which **h** entered into the covenant, NIH
34:11 whom they **h** let go free, to return, and NIH
34:15 now turned, and **h** done right in my sight, NIH
34:15 ye **h** made a covenant before me in NIH
34:16 whom ye **h** set at liberty at their pleasure, NIH
34:18 the covenant which they **h** made before me, NIH
36: 4 which he **h** spoken unto him, upon a roll of NIH
36:11 **h** heard out of the book all the words of NIH
36:13 unto them all the words that he **h** heard, NIH
36:16 Now it came to pass when they **h** heard all NIH
36:23 *that* when Jehudi **h** read three or four leaves, NIH
36:25 Gemariah **h** made intercession to the king NIH
36:27 after that the king **h** burnt the roll, and NIH
36:32 Jehoiakim king of Judah **h** burnt in the fire: NIH
37: 4 for they **h** not put him *into* prison. NIH
37:10 For though ye **h** smitten the whole army of NIH
37:15 the scribe: for they **h** made that the prison. NIH
37:16 and Jeremiah **h** remained there many days; NIH
38: 1 heard the words that Jeremiah **h** spoken NIH
38: 7 heard that they **h** put Jeremiah in NIH
38:27 all these words that the king **h** commanded. NIH
39: 5 when they **h** taken him, they brought him up NIH
39:10 which **h** nothing, in the land of Judah, 3807.1
40: 1 of the guard **h** let him go from Ramah, NIH
40: 1 when he **h** taken him being bound in chains NIH
40: 7 heard that the king of Babylon **h** made NIH
40: 7 **h** committed unto him men, and women, NIH
40:11 heard that the king of Babylon **h** left a NIH
40:11 that he **h** set over them Gedaliah the son of NIH
41: 2 whom the king of Babylon **h** made governor NIH
41: 4 it came to pass the second day after *he* **h** NIH
41: 9 Now the pit wherein Ishmael **h** cast all NIH
41: 9 whom he **h** slain because of Gedaliah, NIH
41: 9 *was* it which Asa the king **h** made for fear NIH
41:10 **h** committed to Gedaliah the son of NIH
41:11 that Ishmael the son of Nethaniah **h** done, NIH
41:14 So all the people that Ishmael **h** carried NIH
41:16 all the remnant of the people whom he **h** NIH
41:16 after *that* he **h** slain Gedaliah the son of NIH
41:16 whom he **h** brought again from Gibeon: NIH
41:18 Ishmael the son of Nethaniah **h** slain NIH
43: 1 *that* when Jeremiah **h** made an end of NIH
43: 1 *for* which the LORD their God **h** sent him NIH
43: 5 whither they **h** been driven, to dwell in NIH
43: 6 **h** left with Gedaliah the son of Ahikam NIH
44:15 all the men which knew that their wives **h** NIH
44:17 for *then* **h** we **plenty** of victuals, and 7646
44:20 to all the people which **h** given him *that* NIH
45: 1 when he **h** written these words in a book at NIH
52: 2 according to all that Jehoiakim **h** done. NIH
52: 3 till he **h** cast them out from his presence, NIH
52:20 which king Solomon **h** made in the house of NIH
52:25 which **h** the charge of the men of war; 1961
La 1: 7 pleasant things that she **h** in the days of old, 1961
1: 9 she **h** no comforter. O LORD, behold 3807.1
2:17 The LORD hath done *that* which he **h** NIH
2:17 he hath fulfilled his word that he **h** NIH
Eze 1: 5 they **h** the likeness of a man. NIH
1: 6 *every* one **h** four faces, and every one had 3807.1
1: 6 four faces, and every one **h** four wings. 3807.1
1: 8 *they* ***h*** the hands of a man under their wings NIH
1: 8 they four **h** their faces and their wings. 3807.1
1:10 they four **h** the face of a man, and 3807.1
1:10 they four **h** the face of an ox on the left 3807.1
1:10 they four also **h** the face of an eagle. 3807.1
1:16 they four **h** one likeness: and 3807.1
1:23 every one **h** two, which covered on this 3807.1
1:23 on this *side,* and every one **h** two, 3807.1
1:25 they stood, *and* **h** let down their wings. NIH
1:27 of fire, and it **h** brightness round about. 3807.1
3: 6 Surely, **h** I sent thee to them, they would NIH
8: 8 when I **h** digged in the wall, behold a door. NIH
9: 3 which ***h*** the writer's inkhorn by his side; NIH
9:11 which ***h*** the inkhorn by his side, NIH
10: 6 *that* when he **h** commanded the man clothed NIH
10:10 their appearances, they four **h** one likeness, NIH
10:10 as if a wheel **h** been in the midst of a wheel. NIH
10:12 *even* the wheels that they four **h**. 3807.1

Eze 10:14 *every* one **h** four faces: the first face *was* 3807.1
10:21 Every one **h** four faces apiece, and every 3807.1
11:24 So the vision that I **h** seen went up from me. NIH
11:25 all the things that the LORD **h** shewed me. NIH
16:14 which I **h** put upon thee, saith the Lord NIH
16:17 which I **h** given thee, and madest to thyself NIH
17: 3 full *of* feathers, which **h** divers colours, 3807.1
17:18 he **h** given his hand, and hath done all these NIH
19: 5 Now when she saw that she **h** waited, *and* NIH
19:11 she **h** strong rods for the sceptres of them 1961
20: 6 of Egypt into a land that I **h** espied for them, NIH
20:15 which I **h** given *them,* flowing with milk NIH
20:24 Because they **h** not executed my judgments, NIH
20:24 **h** despised my statutes, and had polluted my NIH
20:24 **h** polluted my sabbaths, and their eyes were NIH
20:28 *For* when I **h** brought them into the land, NIH
23:10 for they **h** executed judgment upon her. NIH
23:19 wherein she **h** played the harlot in the land NIH
23:32 be laughed to scorn and **h** in derision; 3807.1
23:39 For when they **h** slain their children to their NIH
29:18 yet **h** he no wages, nor his army, 1961+3807.1
29:18 for the service that he **h** served against it: NIH
33:15 give again that he **h** robbed, walk in NIH
33:21 *that* one that **h** escaped out of Jerusalem NIH
33:22 **h** opened my mouth, until *he* came to me in NIH
35: 5 Because thou hast **h** a perpetual 1961+3807.1
35: 5 in the time *that their* iniquity *h* an end: NIH
36:18 for the blood that they **h** shed upon the land, NIH
36:18 for their idols *wherewith* they **h** polluted it: NIH
36:21 I **h pity** for mine holy name, which 2550
36:21 which the house of Israel **h** profaned among NIH
40:10 the posts **h** one measure on this side and 3807.1
40:26 it **h** palm trees, one on this side, and 3807.1
40:31 and the going up to it *h* eight steps. NIH
40:34 and the going up to it *h* eight steps. NIH
40:37 and the going up to it *h* eight steps. NIH
41: 6 but they **h** not hold in the wall of the house. 1961
41:18 a cherub; and *every* cherub **h** two faces; 3807.1
41:23 the temple and the sanctuary **h** two doors. 3807.1
41:24 the doors **h** two leaves *apiece,* two 3807.1
42: 6 **h** not pillars as the pillars of the courts: 3807.1
42:15 Now when he **h** made an end of measuring NIH
42:20 it **h** a wall round about, five hundred 3807.1
44:22 or a widow that **h** a priest **before.** 1961+4480
44:25 or for sister that hath **h** no husband, 1961+3807.1
47: 3 when the man that **h** the line in his hand NIH
47: 7 Now when I **h** returned, behold, at the bank NIH
Da 1: 4 such as *h* ability in them to stand in NIH
1: 9 Now God **h** brought Daniel into favour and NIH
1:11 whom the prince of the eunuchs **h** set over NIH
1:17 Daniel **h** understanding in all visions and NIH
1:18 Now at the end of the days that the king **h** 3807.1
2:24 whom the king **h** ordained to destroy NIH
3: 2 which Nebuchadnezzar the king **h** set up. NIH
3: 3 that Nebuchadnezzar the king **h** set up; NIH
3: 3 the image that Nebuchadnezzar **h** set up. NIH
3: 7 that Nebuchadnezzar the king **h** set up. NIH
3:27 upon whose bodies the fire **h** no power, NIH
3:27 nor the smell of fire **h** passed on them. NIH
4:12 the beasts of the field **h** shadow under it, NIH
4:21 the fowls of the heaven **h** their habitation: NIH
5: 2 **h** taken out of the temple which *was* in NIH
6:24 they brought those men which **h** accused NIH
6:24 the lions **h** the mastery of them, and NIH
7: 1 king of Babylon Daniel **h**[S] a dream 2370
7: 4 first *was* like a lion, and **h** eagle's wings: 3807.2
7: 5 *it* **h** three ribs in the mouth of it between NIH
7: 6 which **h** upon the back of it four wings of 3807.2
7: 6 the beast **h** also four heads; and 3807.2
7: 7 and it **h** great iron teeth: 3807.2
7: 7 that *were* before it; and it **h** ten horns. 3807.2
7:12 they **h** their dominion taken away: NIH
7:20 even *of* that horn that **h** eyes, and a mouth 3807.2
8: 3 there stood before the river a ram which **h** 3807.1
8: 5 the goat *h* a notable horn between his eyes. NIH
8: 6 he came to the ram that **h** two horns, 1167
8: 6 which I **h** seen standing before the river, NIH
8:15 **h** seen the vision, and sought for NIH
9:21 whom I **h** seen in the vision at NIH
10: 1 and **h** understanding of the vision. 3807.1
10:11 when he **h** spoken this word unto me, I NIH
10:15 And when he **h** spoken such words unto me, NIH
10:19 when he **h** spoken unto me, I was NIH
Hos 1: 8 Now when she **h** weaned Lo-ruhamah, NIH
2:23 I will have mercy upon her that **h** not NIH
12: 3 and by his strength he **h power** with God: 8280
12: 4 he **h power** over *the* angel, and prevailed: 7786
Am 7: 2 *that* when they **h** made an end of eating NIH
Ob 1: 5 would they not have stolen till they **h** NIH
1:16 and they shall be as though they **h** not been. NIH
Jnh 1:10 of the LORD, because he **h** told them. NIH
1:17 Now the LORD **h** prepared a great fish to NIH
3:10 that he **h** said that he would do unto them; NIH
4:10 the LORD, Thou hast **h pity** on the gourd, 2347
Na 3: 8 *that h* the waters round about it, NIH
Hab 3: 4 the light; he **h** horns *coming* out of his hand: NIH
Hag 1:12 as the LORD their God **h** sent him, and NIH
Zec 1:12 *against* which thou hast **h** indignation these NIH
5: 9 for they **h** wings like the wings of a stork: 3807.1
7: 2 When they **h** sent *unto* the house of God NIH
10: 6 they shall be as though I **h** not cast them NIH
11:10 that *I* might break my covenant which I **h** NIH
Mal 2:15 Yet **h** he the residue of the spirit. And NIH
Mt 1: 6 David the king begat Solomon of *her that* **h** NIG
1:24 did as the angel of the Lord **h** bidden him, NIG
1:25 And knew her not till she **h** brought forth NIG
2: 3 When Herod the king **h** heard *these things,* NIG
2: 4 And when he **h** gathered all the chief priests NIG
2: 7 when he **h** privily called the wise men, NIG
2: 9 When they **h** heard the king, they departed; NIG
2:11 and when they **h** opened their treasures, NIG
2:16 according to the time which he **h** diligently NIG
3: 4 And the same John **h** his raiment of *2192*
4: 2 And when he **h** fasted forty days and NIG
4:12 Now when Jesus **h** heard that John was cast NIG
Mt 4:24 were lunatick, and those that **h the palsy;** *3885*
7:28 to pass, when Jesus **h** ended these sayings, NIG
9: 8 which **h** given such power unto men. NIG
10: 1 And when he **h** called unto *him* his twelve NIG
11: 1 when Jesus **h** made an end of commanding NIG
11: 2 Now when John **h** heard in the prison NIG
11:21 **h** been done in Tyre and Sidon they would NIG
11:23 been done in thee, **h** been done in Sodom, NIG
12: 7 But if ye **h** known what *this* meaneth, I will NIG
12:10 there was a man which **h** *his* hand withered. *2192*
13: 5 Some fell upon stony *places,* where they **h** *2192*
13: 5 because *they* **h** no deepness of earth: *2192*
13: 6 and because *they* **h** not root, they withered *2192*
13:46 when he **h** found one pearl of great price, NIG
13:46 went and sold all that he **h**, and bought it. *2192*
13:53 *that* when Jesus **h** finished these parables, NIG
14: 3 For Herod **h** laid hold on John, and NIG
14:13 when the people **h** heard *thereof,* they NIG
14:21 And they that **h** eaten were about five NIG
14:23 And when he **h** sent the multitudes away, NIG
14:35 the men of that place **h knowledge** of him, *1921*
16: 5 other side, they **h** forgotten to take bread. NIG
17: 8 And when they **h** lift up their eyes, they saw NIG
18:24 And when he **h** begun to reckon, one was NIG
18:25 But forasmuch as he **h** not to pay, his lord *2192*
18:25 and all that he **h**, and payment to be made. *2192*
18:32 Then his lord, after that he **h** called him, NIG
18:33 Shouldest not thou also have **h compassion** *1653*
18:33 thy fellowservant, even as I **h pity** on thee? *1653*
19: 1 *that* when Jesus **h** finished these sayings, NIG
19:22 away sorrowful: for he **h** great possessions. *2192*
20: 2 And when he **h** agreed with the labourers NIG
20:11 And when they **h** received *it,* they NIG
20:34 So Jesus **h compassion** *on them,* and *4697*
21:28 A *certain* man **h** two sons; and he came to *2192*
21:32 when ye **h** seen *it,* repented not afterward, NIG
21:45 and Pharisees **h** heard his parables, NIG
22:11 he saw there a man which **h** not **on a** *1746*
22:22 When they **h** heard *these words,* they NIG
22:25 when he **h** married *a wife,* deceased, and, NIG
22:28 shall she be of the seven? for they all **h** her. *2192*
22:34 But when the Pharisees **h** heard that he had NIG
22:34 But when the Pharisees had heard that he **h** NIG
23:30 If we **h** been in the days of our fathers, NIG
24:43 that if the goodman of the house **h** known in NIG
25:16 Then he that **h** received the five talents NIG
25:17 And likewise he that *h received* two, he also NIG
25:18 But he that **h** received one went and NIG
25:20 *so* he that **h** received five talents came and NIG
25:22 He also that **h** received two talents came NIG
25:24 Then he which **h** received the one talent NIG
26: 1 when Jesus **h** finished all these sayings, NIG
26: 8 when his disciples saw *it,* they **h indignation,** *23*
26:19 And the disciples did as Jesus **h** appointed NIG
26:24 it **h** been good for that man if he had not NIG
26:24 it had been good for that man if he **h** not NIG
26:30 And when they **h** sung a hymn, they went NIG
26:57 And they that **h** laid hold on Jesus led *him* NIG
27: 2 And when they **h** bound him, they led *him* NIG
27: 3 Then Judas, which **h** betrayed him, when he NIG
27:16 And they **h** then a notable prisoner, *2192*
27:18 For he knew that for envy they **h** delivered NIG
27:26 and when he **h** scourged Jesus, he delivered NIG
27:29 And when they **h** platted a crown of thorns, NIG
27:31 And after that they **h** mocked him, they took NIG
27:34 when he **h** tasted *thereof,* he would not NIG
27:50 when he **h** cried again with a loud voice, NIG
27:59 And when Joseph **h** taken the body, NIG
27:60 new tomb, which he **h** hewn out in the rock: NIG
28:12 and **h** taken counsel, they gave large money NIG
28:16 into a mountain where Jesus **h** appointed NIG
Mk 1:19 And when he **h** gone a little further thence, NIG
1:22 for he taught them as *one* that **h** authority, *2192*
1:26 And when the unclean spirit **h** torn him, and NIG
1:37 And when they **h** found him, they said unto NIG
1:42 And as soon as he **h** spoken, NIG
2: 4 and when they **h** broken *it* up, they let down NIG
2:25 when he **h** need, and was a hungred, he, *2192*
3: 1 there was a man there which **h** a withered *2192*
3: 3 And he saith unto the man which **h** *2192*
3: 5 And when he **h** looked round about on them NIG
3: 8 when they **h** heard what great *things* he did, NIG
3:10 For he **h** healed many; insomuch that *they* NIG
3:10 him for to touch him, as many as **h** plagues. *2192*
4: 5 on stony ground, where it **h** not much earth; *2192*
4: 5 it sprang up, because *it* **h** no depth of earth: *2192*
4: 6 and because *it* **h** no root, it withered away. *2192*
4:36 And when they **h** sent away the multitude, NIG
5: 3 Who **h** *his* dwelling among the tombs; *2192*
5: 4 Because that he **h** been often bound with NIG
5: 4 the chains **h** been plucked asunder by him, NIG
5:15 and **h** the legion, sitting, and clothed, and *2192*
5:18 he that **h** been possessed with the devil NIG
5:19 for thee, and hath **h compassion** on thee. *1653*
5:20 how great *things* Jesus **h** done for him: NIG
5:25 which **h** an issue of blood twelve years, *1510*
5:26 And **h** suffered many *things* of many NIG
5:26 and **h** spent all that she had, NIG
5:26 and had spent all that she **h**, *3588+3844*
5:27 When she **h** heard of Jesus, came in NIG
5:30 in himself that virtue **h** gone out of him, NIG
5:32 about to see her that **h** done this *thing.* NIG
5:40 But when he **h** put *them* all out, he taketh NIG
6:17 For Herod himself **h** sent forth and laid hold NIG
6:17 brother Philip's wife: for he **h** married her. NIG
6:18 For John **h** said unto Herod, It is not lawful NIG
6:19 Therefore Herodias **h a quarrel against** *1758*
6:30 told him all *things,* both what they **h** done, NIG
6:30 what they had done, and what they **h** taught. NIG
6:31 and they **h** no **leisure** so much as to eat. *2119*
6:41 And when he **h** taken the five loaves and NIG
6:46 And when he **h** sent them away, he departed NIG
6:49 they supposed *it* **h** been a spirit, and NIG
6:53 And when they **h** passed over, they came NIG
7:14 And when he **h** called all the people unto NIG
Mk 7:25 whose young daughter **h** an unclean spirit, *2192*
7:32 and **h** an impediment in his speech; NIG
8: 7 And they **h** a few small fishes: and *2192*
8: 9 And they that **h** eaten were about four NIG
8:14 Now *the disciples* **h** forgotten to take bread, NIG
8:14 neither **h** they in the ship with them more *2192*
8:23 and when he **h** spit on his eyes, and put *his* NIG
8:33 But when he **h** turned about and looked on NIG
8:34 And when he **h** called the people unto *him* NIG
9: 8 when they **h** looked round about, NIG
9: 9 should tell no *man* what *things* they **h** seen, NIG
9:34 for by the way they **h** disputed among NIG
9:36 and when he **h** taken him in his arms, NIG
10:22 away grieved: for he **h** great possessions. *2192*
11: 6 And they said unto them even as Jesus **h** NIG
11:11 when he **h** looked round about upon all NIG
12:12 for they knew that he **h** spoken the parable NIG
12:22 And the seven **h** her, and left no seed: *2983*
12:23 she be of them? for the seven **h** her to wife. *2192*
12:28 perceiving that he **h** answered them well, NIG
12:44 she of her want did cast in all that she **h**, *2192*
13:20 And except that the Lord **h** shortened *those* NIG
14: 4 And there were some that **h indignation** *23*
14:16 the city, and found as he **h** said unto them: NIG
14:21 good were it for that man if he **h** never been NIG
14:23 and when he **h** given thanks, he gave *it* to NIG
14:26 And when they **h** sung a hymn, they went NIG
14:44 And he that betrayed him **h** given them a NIG
15: 7 *which lay* bound with them that **h** made NIG
15: 7 **h** committed murder in the insurrection. NIG
15: 8 *him to do* as he **h** ever done unto them. NIG
15:10 For he knew that the chief priests **h** NIG
15:15 when he **h** scourged *him,* to be crucified. NIG
15:20 And when they **h** mocked him, they took off NIG
15:24 And when they **h** crucified him, they parted NIG
15:44 he asked him whether he **h** been any while NIG
16: 1 and Salome, **h** bought *sweet* spices, NIG
16: 9 out of whom he **h** cast seven devils. NIG
16:10 and told them that **h** been with him, NIG
16:11 when they **h** heard that he was alive, and NIG
16:11 and **h** been seen of her, believed not. NIG
16:14 they believed not them which **h** seen him NIG
16:19 So then after the Lord **h** spoken unto them, NIG
Lk 1: 3 having **h** perfect understanding of all *things* NIG
1: 7 And they **h** no child, because that Elisabeth *1510*
1:22 they perceived that he **h** seen a vision in NIG
1:58 her cousins heard how the Lord **h** shewed NIG
2:17 And when they **h** seen *it,* they made known NIG
2:20 praising God for all *the things* that they **h** NIG
2:26 before he **h** seen the Lord's Christ. NIG
2:36 **h** lived with a husband seven years from her NIG
2:39 And when they **h** performed all *things* NIG
2:43 And when they **h** fulfilled the days, as they NIG
3:19 and for all the evils which Herod **h** done, NIG
4:13 And when the devil **h** ended all NIG
4:16 to Nazareth, where he **h** been brought up: NIG
4:17 And when he **h** opened the book, he found NIG
4:33 which **h** a spirit of an unclean devil, and *2192*
4:35 And when the devil **h** thrown him in NIG
4:40 all they that **h** *any* sick with divers diseases *2192*
5: 4 Now when he **h** left speaking, he said unto NIG
5: 6 And when they **h** this done, they inclosed a NIG
5: 9 at the draught of the fishes which they **h** NIG
5:11 And when they **h** brought *their* ships to NIG
6: 8 said to the man which **h** the withered hand, *2192*
7: 1 Now when he **h** ended all his sayings in NIG
7:10 found the servant whole that **h** been sick. NIG
7:13 he **h compassion** on her, and said unto her, *4697*
7:39 Now when the Pharisee which **h** bidden him NIG
7:41 There was a certain creditor which **h** two *1510*
7:42 And when they **h** nothing to pay, he frankly *2192*
8: 2 which **h** been healed of evil spirits and NIG
8:27 which **h** devils long time, and ware no *2192*
8:29 (For he **h** commanded the unclean spirit to NIG
8:29 For oftentimes it **h** caught him: and he was NIG
8:39 how great *things* Jesus **h** done unto him. NIG
8:42 For he **h** one only daughter, about twelve *1510*
8:43 which **h** spent all *her* living upon NIG
8:47 people for what cause she **h** touched him, NIG
9: 8 And of some, that Elias **h** appeared; and NIG
9:10 were returned, told him all that they **h** done. NIG
9:11 and healed them that **h** need of healing. *2192*
9:36 days any of *those things* which they **h** seen. NIG
10:13 for if the mighty works **h** been done in Tyre NIG
10:13 they **h** a great while ago repented, sitting in *302*
10:33 he saw him, he **h compassion** *on him,* *4697*
10:39 And she **h** a sister called Mary, which also *1510*
11:38 that he **h** not first washed before dinner. NIG
12:39 that if the goodman of the house **h** known NIG
13: 1 whose blood Pilate **h** mingled with their NIG
13: 6 A certain *man* **h** a fig tree planted in his *2192*
13:11 there was a woman which **h** a spirit of *2192*
13:14 that Jesus **h** healed on the sabbath day, NIG
13:17 And when he **h** said these *things,* all his NIG
14: 2 man before him, which **h the dropsy.** *5203*
15: 9 for I have found the piece which I **h** lost. NIG
15:11 And he said, A certain man **h** two sons: *2192*
15:14 And when he **h** spent all, there arose a NIG
15:20 and **h compassion,** and ran, and fell on his *4697*
16: 1 was a certain rich man, which **h** a steward; *2192*
16: 1 the same was accused unto him that he **h** NIG
16: 8 unjust steward, because he **h** done wisely: NIG
17: 6 If ye **h** faith as a grain of mustard seed, *2192*
19:15 unto him, to whom he **h** given the money, NIG
19:15 that he might know how much every *man* **h** NIG
19:28 And when he **h** thus spoken, he went NIG
19:32 and found even as he **h** said unto them. NIG
19:37 for all the mighty works that they **h** seen; NIG
20:19 for they perceived that he **h** spoken this NIG
20:33 of them is she? for seven **h** her to wife. *2192*
21: 4 penury hath cast in all the living that she **h**. *2192*
22:13 and found as he **h** said unto them: NIG
22:55 And when they **h** kindled a fire in the midst NIG
22:61 how he **h** said unto him, Before *the* cock NIG
22:64 And when they **h** blindfolded him, NIG

Lk 23: 8 because *he* **h** heard many *things* of him; NIG
23:13 when he **h** called together the chief priests NIG
23:25 was cast into prison, whom they **h** desired; NIG
23:46 And when Jesus **h** cried with a loud voice, NIG
23:51 (The same **h** not consented to the counsel *1510*
24: 1 bringing the spices which they **h** prepared, NIG
24:14 of all these *things* which **h** happened. NIG
24:21 But we trusted that it **h** been he which NIG
24:23 that *they* **h** also seen a vision of angels, NIG
24:24 and found *it* even so as the women **h** said: NIG
24:37 and supposed that *they* **h** seen a spirit. NIG
24:40 And when he **h** thus spoken, he shewed NIG
Jn 2: 9 When the ruler of the feast **h** tasted NIG
2:15 And when he **h** made a scourge of small NIG
2:22 his disciples remembered that he **h** said this NIG
2:22 and the word which Jesus **h** said. NIG
4: 1 the Lord knew how the Pharisees **h** heard NIG
4:18 For thou hast **h** five husbands; and *2192*
4:50 And the man believed the word that Jesus **h** NIG
5: 4 made whole of whatsoever disease he **h**. *2722*
5: 5 which **h** an infirmity thirty *and* eight years. *2192*
5: 6 knew that he **h** been now a long time *in that* NIG
5:13 for Jesus **h** conveyed himself away, NIG
5:15 that it was Jesus, which **h** made him whole. NIG
5:16 he **h** done these *things* on the sabbath day. NIG
5:18 because he not only **h** broken the sabbath, NIG
5:46 For **h** ye believed Moses, ye would have NIG
6:11 and when he **h** given thanks, he distributed NIG
6:13 and above unto them that **h** eaten. NIG
6:14 when they **h** seen the miracle that Jesus did, NIG
6:19 So when they **h** rowed about five and NIG
6:23 after that the Lord **h** given thanks:) NIG
6:25 And when they **h** found him on the other NIG
6:60 his disciples, when they **h** heard *this*, said, NIG
7: 9 When he **h** said these *words* unto them, NIG
8: 3 and when they **h** set her in the midst, NIG
8:10 When Jesus **h** lift up *himself*, and saw none NIG
8:19 if ye **h** known me, ye should have known NIG
9: 6 When he **h** thus spoken, he spat on NIG
9: 8 they which before **h** seen him that he was NIG
9:15 also asked him how he **h** received his sight. NIG
9:18 that he **h** been blind, and received his sight, NIG
9:18 until they called the parents of him that **h** NIG
9:22 for the Jews **h** agreed already, that if any NIG
9:35 Jesus heard that they **h** cast him out; NIG
9:35 and when he **h** found him, he said unto NIG
11: 6 When he **h** heard therefore that he was sick, NIG
11:13 they thought that he **h** spoken of taking of NIG
11:17 he found that he **h** *lien* in the grave four *2192*
11:21 thou hadst been here, my brother **h** not died. *302*
11:28 And when she **h** so said, she went her way, NIG
11:32 thou hadst been here, my brother **h** not died. *302*
11:43 And when he thus **h** spoken, he cried with a NIG
11:45 and **h** seen *the things* which Jesus did, NIG
11:46 and told them what *things* Jesus **h** done. NIG
11:57 and the Pharisees **h** given a commandment, NIG
12: 1 where Lazarus was which **h** been dead, NIG
12: 6 and **h** the bag, and bare what was put *2192*
12: 9 whom he **h** raised from the dead. NIG
12:14 And Jesus, when he **h** found a young ass, NIG
12:16 and *that* they **h** done these *things* unto him. NIG
12:18 for that they heard that he **h** done this NIG
12:37 But though he **h** done so many miracles NIG
13: 3 Jesus knowing that the Father **h** given all NIG
13:12 So after he **h** washed their feet, and NIG
13:12 and **h** taken his garments, and was set down NIG
13:21 When Jesus **h** thus said, he was troubled in NIG
13:26 when I have dipped *it*. And when he **h** NIG
13:29 *of them* thought, because Judas **h** the bag, *2192*
13:29 had the bag, that Jesus **h** said unto him, NIG
14: 7 If ye **h** known me, ye should have known NIG
15:22 If I **h** not come and spoken unto them, NIG
15:22 and spoken unto them, they **h** not had sin: *2192*
15:22 and spoken unto them, they had not **h** sin: NIG
15:24 If I **h** not done among them the works NIG
15:24 none other *man* did, they **h** not had sin: *2192*
15:24 none other *man* did, they had not **h** sin: NIG
17: 5 which I **h** with thee before the world was. *2192*
18: 1 When Jesus **h** spoken these *words*, he went NIG
18: 6 As soon then as he **h** said unto them, I am NIG
18:18 officers stood *there*, who **h** made a fire of NIG
18:22 And when he **h** thus spoken, one of NIG
18:24 Now Annas **h** sent him bound unto NIG
18:38 And when he **h** said this, he went out again NIG
19:23 the soldiers, when they **h** crucified Jesus, NIG
19:30 therefore **h** received the vinegar, NIG
20:12 at the feet, where the body of Jesus **h** lain. NIG
20:14 And when she **h** thus said, she turned NIG
20:18 told the disciples that she **h** seen the Lord, NIG
20:18 and *that* he **h** spoken these *things* unto her. NIG
20:20 And when he **h** so said, he shewed unto NIG
20:22 And when he **h** said this, he breathed on NIG
21:15 So when they **h** dined, Jesus saith to Simon NIG
21:19 And when he **h** spoken this, he saith unto NIG
Ac 1: 2 after that he through the Holy Ghost **h** given NIG
1: 2 unto the Apostles whom he **h** chosen: NIG
1: 9 And when he **h** spoken these *things*, while NIG
1:17 with us, and **h** obtained part of this ministry. NIG
2:30 knowing that God **h** sworn with an oath to NIG
2:44 were together, and **h** all *things* common; *2192*
2:45 parted them to all *men*, as every *man* **h** *2192*
3:10 amazement at that which **h** happened unto NIG
3:12 or holiness we **h** made this *man* to walk? NIG
3:18 But *those things*, which God before **h** NIG
4: 7 And when they **h** set them in the midst, NIG
4:13 of them, that they **h** been with Jesus. NIG
4:15 But when they **h** commanded them to go NIG
4:21 So when they **h** further threatened *them*, NIG
4:23 chief priests and elders **h** said unto them. NIG
4:31 And when they **h** prayed, the place was NIG
4:32 was his own; but they **h** all *things* common. *1510*
4:35 unto every man according as he **h** need. *2192*
5:23 but when we **h** opened, we found no *man* NIG
5:27 And when they **h** brought them, they set NIG
5:34 **h** in reputation among all the people, and NIG

Ac 5:40 and when they **h** called the apostles, and NIG
6: 6 and when they **h** prayed, they laid *their* NIG
6:15 saw his face as it **h** been the face of an NIG
7: 5 seed after him, when *as yet* he **h** no child. *1510*
7:17 which God **h** sworn to Abraham, the people NIG
7:36 after that he **h** shewed wonders and signs in NIG
7:44 Our fathers **h** the tabernacle of Witness in *1510*
7:44 as he **h** appointed, speaking unto Moses, NIG
7:44 it according to the fashion that he **h** seen. NIG
7:60 And when he **h** said this, he fell asleep. NIG
8:11 And to him they **h** **regard**, because that of *4337*
8:11 that of long time *he* **h** bewitched them with NIG
8:14 that Samaria **h** received the word of God, NIG
8:25 when they **h** testified and preached the word NIG
8:27 who **h** the charge of all her treasure, and *1510*
8:27 and **h** come to Jerusalem for to worship, NIG
9:18 there fell from his eyes **as it h been** scales: *5616*
9:19 And when he **h** received meat, he was NIG
9:27 declared unto them how he **h** seen the Lord NIG
9:27 and that he **h** spoken to him, and how he NIG
9:27 how he **h** preached boldly at Damascus in NIG
9:31 Then **h** the churches rest throughout all *2192*
9:33 which **h** kept his bed eight years, and was NIG
9:37 whom when they **h** washed, they laid *her* in NIG
9:38 the disciples **h** heard that Peter was there, NIG
9:41 and when he **h** called the saints and widows, NIG
10: 8 And when he **h** declared all *these things* NIG
10:11 as *it h been* a great sheet knit at the four NIG
10:17 *this* vision which he **h** seen should mean, NIG
10:17 the men which were sent from Cornelius **h** NIG
10:24 and **h** called together his kinsmen and near NIG
10:31 thine alms are **h** in remembrance in NIG
11: 1 Gentiles **h** also received the word of God. NIG
11: 5 vessel descend, as *it h been* a great sheet, NIG
11: 6 Upon the which when I **h** fastened mine NIG
11:13 And he shewed us how he **h** seen an angel NIG
11:23 and **h** seen the grace of God, was glad, and NIG
11:26 And when he **h** found him, he brought him NIG
12: 4 And when he **h** apprehended him, he put NIG
12:12 And when he **h** considered *the thing*, he NIG
12:16 and when they **h** opened *the door*, and NIG
12:17 declared unto them how the Lord **h** brought NIG
12:19 And when Herod **h** sought for him, and NIG
12:25 when they **h** fulfilled *their* ministry, and NIG
13: 1 which **h** been brought up with Herod NIG
13: 3 And when they **h** fasted and prayed, and NIG
13: 5 and they **h** also John to *their* minister. *2192*
13: 6 And when they **h** gone through the isle unto NIG
13:19 And when he **h** destroyed seven nations in NIG
13:22 And when he **h** removed him, he raised up NIG
13:24 When John **h** first preached before his NIG
13:29 And when they **h** fulfilled all that was NIG
13:36 after he **h** served his own generation by NIG
14: 8 his mother's womb, who never **h** walked: NIG
14: 9 and perceiving that he **h** faith to be healed, *2192*
14:11 And when the people saw what Paul **h** done, NIG
14:18 that *they* **h** not done sacrifice unto them. NIG
14:19 out of the city, supposing he **h** been dead. NIG
14:21 And when they **h** preached the gospel to NIG
14:21 and **h** taught many, they returned *again* to NIG
14:23 And when they **h** ordained them elders in NIG
14:23 and **h** prayed with fasting, NIG
14:24 And after they **h** passed throughout Pisidia, NIG
14:25 And when they **h** preached the word in NIG
14:26 from whence they **h** been recommended to NIG
14:27 and **h** gathered the church together, NIG
14:27 they rehearsed all that God **h** done with NIG
14:27 how he **h** opened *the* door of faith unto NIG
15: 2 and Barnabas **h** no small dissension and *1096*
15: 4 they declared all *things* that God **h** done NIG
15: 7 And when there **h** been much disputing, NIG
15:12 wonders God **h** wrought among the Gentiles NIG
15:13 And after they **h** held their peace, NIG
15:30 when they **h** gathered the multitude NIG
15:31 *Which* when they **h** read, they rejoiced for NIG
15:33 And after they **h** tarried *there* a space, NIG
16: 6 Now when they **h** gone throughout Phrygia NIG
16:10 And after he **h** seen the vision, NIG
16:10 assuredly gathering that the Lord **h** called us NIG
16:23 And when they **h** laid many stripes upon NIG
16:27 supposing that the prisoners **h** been fled. NIG
16:34 And when he **h** brought them into his house, NIG
16:40 and when they **h** seen the brethren, NIG
17: 1 Now when they **h** passed through NIG
17: 9 And when they **h** taken security of Jason, NIG
17:13 But when the Jews of Thessalonica **h** NIG
18: 2 that Claudius **h** commanded all Jews to NIG
18:18 shorn *his* head in Cenchrea: for he **h** a vow. *2192*
18:22 And when he **h** landed at Cesarea, and NIG
18:23 And after he **h** spent some time *there*, he NIG
18:26 whom when Aquila and Priscilla **h** heard, NIG
18:27 helped them much which **h** believed NIG
19: 6 And when Paul **h** laid *his* hands upon them, NIG
19:13 took upon them to call over them which **h** *2192*
19:21 when he **h** passed through Macedonia and NIG
19:35 And when the townclerk **h** appeased NIG
19:41 And when he **h** thus spoken, he dismissed NIG
20: 2 And when he **h** gone over those parts, and NIG
20: 2 and **h** given them much exhortation, NIG
20:11 was come up *again*, and **h** broken bread, NIG
20:13 for so he **h** appointed, minding himself to *1510*
20:16 For Paul **h** determined to sail by Ephesus, NIG
20:36 And when he **h** thus spoken, he kneeled NIG
21: 1 we were gotten from them, and **h** launched, NIG
21: 3 Now when we **h** discovered Cyprus, we left NIG
21: 5 And when we **h** accomplished *those* days, *1096*
21: 6 And when we **h** taken our leave one of NIG
21: 7 And when we **h** finished *our* course from NIG
21: 9 And the same *man* **h** four daughters, *1510*
21:19 And when he **h** saluted them, he declared NIG
21:19 he declared particularly what *things* God **h** NIG
21:29 (For they **h** seen before with him in the city *1510*
21:29 whom they supposed that Paul **h** brought NIG
21:33 who he was, and what he **h** done. *1510*
21:40 And when he **h** given *him* licence, NIG

Ac 22:29 was a Roman, and because he **h** bound him. *1510*
23: 7 And when he **h** so said, there arose a NIG
23:12 neither eat nor drink till they **h** killed Paul. NIG
23:13 And they were more *than* forty which **h** NIG
23:30 to say before thee what *they* **h** against him. NIG
23:34 And when the governor **h** read *the letter*, he NIG
24:10 after that the governor **h** beckoned unto him NIG
24:19 and object, if they **h** ought against me. *2192*
25: 6 And when he **h** tarried among them more NIG
25:12 when he **h** conferred with the council, NIG
25:14 And when they **h** been there many days, NIG
25:19 But **h** certain questions against him of their *2192*
25:21 But when Paul **h** appealed to be reserved NIG
25:25 But when I found that he **h** committed NIG
25:26 O king Agrippa, that, after examination **h**, *1096*
26:30 And when he **h** thus spoken, the king rose NIG
26:32 at liberty, if he **h** not appealed unto Cesar. NIG
27: 4 And when we **h** launched from thence, NIG
27: 5 And when we **h** sailed over the sea of NIG
27: 7 And when we **h** sailed slowly many days, NIG
27:13 supposing that *they* **h** obtained *their* NIG
27:16 **h much work** to come by the boat: *2480+3433*
27:17 Which when they **h** taken up, they used NIG
27:28 and when they **h** gone a little further, NIG
27:30 when they **h** let down the boat into the sea, NIG
27:35 And when he **h** thus spoken, he took bread, NIG
27:35 and when he **h** broken *it*, he began to eat. NIG
27:38 And when they **h** eaten enough, NIG
27:40 And when they **h** taken up the anchors, NIG
28: 3 And when Paul **h** gathered a bundle of NIG
28: 6 but after they **h** looked a great while, and NIG
28: 9 which **h** diseases in the island, came, and *2192*
28:11 which **h** wintered in the isle, *whose* sign NIG
28:18 Who, when they **h** examined me, NIG
28:19 not that I **h** ought to accuse my nation of. *2192*
28:23 And when they **h** appointed him a day, NIG
28:25 after that Paul **h** spoken one word, NIG
28:29 And when he **h** said these *words*, the Jews NIG
28:29 and **h** great reasoning among themselves. *2192*
Ro 1: 2 (Which he **h** promised afore by his prophets NIG
4:11 faith which he **h** *yet* being uncircumcised: NIG
4:12 which he **h** being *yet* uncircumcised. NIG
4:21 what he **h** promised, he was able also to NIG
5:14 even over them that **h** not sinned after NIG
6:21 What fruit **h** ye then *in those things* *2192*
7: 7 Nay, I **h** not known sin, but by the law: for I NIG
7: 7 for I **h** not known lust, except the law had NIG
7: 7 except the law **h** said, Thou shalt not covet. NIG
9:10 but when Rebecca also **h** conceived by one, *2192*
9:23 which he **h** afore prepared unto glory, NIG
9:29 Except the Lord of sabaoth **h** left us a seed, NIG
9:29 we **h** been as Sodoma, and been made like *302*
1Co 1:15 Lest any should say that I **h** baptized in NIG
2: 8 for **h** they known *it*, they would not have *1487*
7:29 that have wives be as though they **h** none; *2192*
11:24 And when he **h** given thanks, he brake *it*, NIG
11:25 when *he* **h** supped, saying, This cup is NIG
14:19 Yet in the church I **h rather** speak five *2309*
2Co 1: 9 But we **h** the sentence of death in *2192*
1:12 we have **h** our **conversation** in the world, *390*
2:13 I **h** no rest in my spirit, because I found not *2192*
3:10 made glorious **h** no **glory** in this respect, *1392*
7: 5 our flesh **h** no rest, but *we were* troubled on *2192*
7:12 *I did it* not for his cause that **h** done NIG
8: 6 that as he **h** begun, so he would also finish NIG
8:15 He that *h gathered* much had nothing over; NIG
8:15 He that *had gathered* much **h** nothing **over**; *4121*
8:15 and he that **h** *gathered* little had no lack. NIG
8:15 and he that *had gathered* little **h** no **lack**. *1641*
9: 5 whereof *ye* **h notice before**, that the same *4293*
11:21 as though we **h** been weak. NIG
Gal 1:23 But they **h** heard only, That he which *1510*
2: 2 by any means I should run, or **h** run, in vain. NIG
3:21 for if there **h** been a law given which could NIG
4:15 I bear you record, that if *it* **h** *been* possible, NIG
4:22 For it is written, that Abraham **h** two sons, *2192*
Eph 1: 9 according to his good pleasure which he **h** NIG
2: 3 **h** our **conversation** in times past in the lusts *390*
Php 2:26 that ye **h** heard that he had been sick. NIG
2:26 that ye had heard that he **h** been sick. NIG
2:27 but God **h mercy** on him; and not on him *1653*
3:12 Not as though I **h** already attained, NIG
1Th 1: 9 what manner of entering in we **h** unto you, *2192*
2: 2 But even after that we **h** suffered before, NIG
2Th 2:12 the truth, but **h** pleasure in unrighteousness. NIG
Tit 1: 5 elders in every city, as I **h** appointed thee: NIG
Heb 1: 3 when he **h** by himself purged our sins, NIG
2:14 destroy him that **h** the power of death, *2192*
3:16 For some, when they **h** heard, did provoke: NIG
3:17 *was it* not with them that **h** sinned, NIG
4: 8 For if Jesus **h** given them rest, *then* NIG
5: 7 when he **h** offered up prayers and NIG
6:15 And so, after he **h** patiently endured, NIG
7: 6 and blessed him that **h** the promises. *2192*
8: 7 For if that first *covenant* **h** been faultless, NIG
9: 1 Then verily the first *covenant* **h** also *2192*
9: 4 Which **h** the golden censer, and the ark of *2192*
9: 4 wherein *was* the golden pot that **h** manna, *2192*
9:19 For when Moses **h** spoken every precept to NIG
10: 2 should have **h** no more conscience of sins. *2192*
10: 6 *sacrifices* for sin thou hast **h** no **pleasure**. *2106*
10:12 But this *man*, after he **h** offered one NIG
10:15 witness to us: for after that *he* **h** said before, NIG
10:34 For ye **h compassion** *of me* in my bonds, *4834*
11: 5 not found, because God **h** translated him: NIG
11: 5 for before his translation he **h** this NIG
11:11 she judged him faithful who **h** promised. NIG
11:15 if they **h** been mindful of that *country* from NIG
11:15 they might have **h** opportunity to have *2192*
11:17 he that **h** received the promises offered up NIG
11:26 for he **h** respect unto the recompence of NIG
11:31 when she **h** received the spies with peace. NIG
11:36 And others **h** trial of *cruel* mockings and *2983*
12: 9 Furthermore we have **h** fathers of our flesh *2192*
Jas 2:21 when he **h** offered Isaac his son upon NIG

Jas 2:25 when she **h** received the messengers, and NIG
2:25 and **h** sent *them* out another way? NIG
1Pe 2:10 which **h** not obtained mercy, but now have NIG
2Pe 2:21 For it **h** been better for them not to have NIG
1Jn 2: 7 an old commandment which ye **h** from *2192*
2:19 for if they **h** been of us, they would *no* NIG
2Jn 1: 5 but *that* which we **h** from the beginning, *2192*
3Jn 1:13 I **h** many *things* to write, *2192*
Rev 1:16 And he **h** in his right hand seven stars: and *2192*
4: 4 and they **h** on their heads crowns of gold. *2192*
4: 7 and the third beast **h** a face as a man, and *2192*
4: 8 And the four beasts **h** each of them six *2192*
5: 6 stood a Lamb as *it* **h** *been* slain, NIG
5: 8 And when he **h** taken the book, the four NIG
6: 2 and he that sat on him **h** a bow; and *2192*
6: 3 And when he **h** opened the second seal, NIG
6: 5 And when he **h** opened the third seal, NIG
6: 5 he that sat on him **h** a pair of balances in *2192*
6: 7 And when he **h** opened the fourth seal, NIG
6: 9 And when he **h** opened the fifth seal, I saw NIG
6:12 And I beheld when he **h** opened the sixth NIG
8: 1 And when he **h** opened the seventh seal, NIG
8: 6 And the seven angels which **h** the seven *2192*
8: 9 which were in the sea, and **h** life, died; *2192*
9: 8 And they **h** hair as the hair of women, and *2192*
9: 9 And they **h** breastplates, as *it were* *2192*
9:10 And they **h** tails like unto scorpions, and *2192*
9:11 And they **h** a king over them, *which is* *2192*
9:14 Saying to the sixth angel which **h** *2192*
9:19 and **h** heads, and with them they do hurt. *2192*
10: 2 And he **h** in his hand a little book open: and *2192*
10: 3 and when he **h** cried, seven thunders uttered NIG
10: 4 And when the seven thunders **h** uttered their NIG
10:10 and as soon as I **h** eaten it, my belly was NIG
13:11 and he **h** two horns like a lamb, and *2192*
13:14 he **h power** to do in the sight of the beast; *1325*
13:14 which **h** the wound by a sword, and *2192*
13:15 And he **h power** to give life unto the image *1325*
13:17 save he that **h** the mark, or the name of *2192*
14:18 out from the altar, which **h** power over fire; *2192*
14:18 cried with a loud cry to him that **h** the sharp *2192*
15: 2 them that **h** gotten the victory over NIG
16: 2 grievous sore upon the men which **h** *2192*
17: 1 of the seven angels which **h** the seven vials, *2192*
18:19 wherein were made rich all that **h** ships in *2192*
19:12 and he **h** a name written, that no *man* knew, *2192*
19:20 with which he deceived them that **h** NIG
20: 4 and which **h** not worshipped the beast, NIG
20: 4 neither **h** received *his* mark upon their NIG
21: 9 **h** the seven vials full of the seven last *2192*
21:12 And **h** a wall great and high, and *2192*
21:12 and **h** twelve gates, and at the gates twelve *2192*
21:14 And the wall of the city **h** twelve *2192*
21:15 And he that talked with me **h** a golden reed *2192*
21:23 And the city **h** no need of the sun, *2192*
22: 8 and heard *them*. And when I **h** heard and NIG

HADAD (14) [HADADEZER, HADADRIMMON]
Ge 36:35 And Husham died, and **H** the son of Bedad, 1908
36:36 **H** died, and Samlah of Masrekah reigned in 1908
1Ki 11:14 adversary unto Solomon, **H** the Edomite: 1908
11:17 That **H** fled, he and certain Edomites of his 111
11:17 to go *into* Egypt; **H** *being yet* a little child. 1908
11:19 **H** found great favour in the sight of 1908
11:21 when **H** heard in Egypt that David slept 1908
11:21 **H** said to Pharaoh, Let me depart, that I 1908
11:25 beside the mischief that **H** *did:* and 1908
1Ch 1:30 Mishma, and Dumah, Massa, **H**, and Tema, 2301
1:46 Husham was dead, **H** the son of Bedad, 1908
1:47 when **H** was dead, Samlah of Masrekah 1908
1:50 was dead, **H** reigned in his stead: 1908
1:51 **H** died also. And the dukes of Edom were; 1908

HADADEZER (9) [HADAD, HADAREZER]
2Sa 8: 3 David smote also **H**, the son of Rehob, 1909
8: 5 came to succour **H** king of Zobah, 1909
8: 7 of gold that were on the servants of **H**, 1909
8: 8 from Betah, and from Berothai, cities of **H**, 1909
8: 9 that David had smitten all the host of **H**, 1909
8:10 because he had fought against **H**, and 1909
8:10 for **H** had wars with Toi. And *Joram* 1909
8:12 of Amalek, and of the spoil of **H**, son of 1909
1Ki 11:23 which fled from his lord **H** king of Zobah: 1909

HADADRIMMON (1) [HADAD, RIMMON]
Zec 12:11 as the mourning of **H** in the valley of 1910

HADAR (2) [HADAREZER]
Ge 25:15 **H**, and Tema, Jetur, Naphish, and 2316
36:39 of Achbor died, and **H** reigned in his stead: 1924

HADAREZER (12) [HADADEZER, HADAR]
2Sa 10:16 **H** sent, and brought out the Syrians that 1928
10:16 Shobach the captain of the host of **H** *went* 1928
10:19 when all the kings *that were* servants to **H** 1928
1Ch 18: 3 David smote **H** king of Zobah unto 1928
18: 5 Damascus came to help **H** king of Zobah, 1928
18: 7 of gold that were on the servants of **H**, 1928
18: 8 from Tibhath, and from Chun, cities of **H**, 1928
18: 9 had smitten all the host of **H** king of Zobah; 1928
18:10 because he had fought against **H**, and 1928
18:10 (for **H** had war with Tou;) and *with him* all 1928
19:16 Shophach the captain of the host of **H** *went* 1928
19:19 when the servants of **H** saw that they were 1928

HADASHAH (1)
Jos 15:37 Zenan, and **H**, and Migdal-gad, 2322

HADASSAH (1) [ESTHER]
Est 2: 7 he brought up **H**, that *is*, Esther, his uncle's 1919

HADATTAH See HAZOR HADATTAH

HADID (3)
Ezr 2:33 The children of Lod, **H**, and Ono, 2307
Ne 7:37 The children of Lod, **H**, and Ono, 2307
11:34 **H**, Zeboim, Neballat, 2307

HADLAI (1)
2Ch 28:12 son of Shallum, and Amasa the son of **H**, 2311

HADORAM (4)
Ge 10:27 And **H**, and Uzal, and Diklah, 1913
1Ch 1:21 **H** also, and Uzal, and Diklah, 1913
18:10 He sent **H** his son to king David, to inquire 1913
2Ch 10:18 king Rehoboam sent **H** that *was* over 1913

HADRACH (1)
Zec 9: 1 of the word of the LORD in the land of **H**, 2317

HADST (22) [HAVE]
Ge 30:30 For *it was* little which thou **h** 1961+3807.1
31:42 surely thou **h** sent me away now empty. NIH
Jdg 15: 2 I verily thought that thou **h** utterly hated NIH
1Sa 25:34 except thou **h** hasted and come to meet me, NIH
2Sa 2:27 unless thou **h** spoken, surely then in NIH
2Ki 13:19 **h** thou smitten Syria till *thou* hadst NIH
13:19 hadst thou smitten Syria till *thou* **h** NIH
Ezr 9:14 be angry with us till *thou* **h** consumed *us*, NIH
Ne 9:15 the land which thou **h** sworn to give them. 5375
9:23 *concerning* which thou **h** promised to their NIH
Ps 44: 3 because thou **h a favour** unto them. 7521
60:10 *Wilt* not thou, O God, *which* **h** cast us off? NIH
90: 2 or ever thou **h** formed the earth and NIH
Isa 26:15 thou **h** removed *it* far *unto* all the ends of NIH
48:18 O that thou **h** hearkened to my NIH
Jer 3: 3 thou **h** a whore's forehead, 1961+3807.1
Jnh 2: 3 For thou **h** cast me *into* the deep, in NIH
Lk 19:42 Saying, If thou **h** known, even thou, at least NIG
Jn 11:21 Lord, if thou **h** been here, my brother had NIG
11:32 saying unto him, Lord, if thou **h** been here, NIG
1Co 4: 7 dost thou glory, as if thou **h** not received *it?* NIG
Heb 10: 8 neither **h** pleasure *therein:* which are offered NIG

HAELEPH See ELEPH

HAFT (1)
Jdg 3:22 the **h** also went in after the blade; and 5325

HAGAB (1) [HAGABA, HAGABAH]
Ezr 2:46 The children of **H**, the children of Shalmai, 2285

HAGABA (1) [HAGAB]
Ne 7:48 The children of Lebana, the children of **H**, 2286

HAGABAH (1) [HAGAB]
Ezr 2:45 the children of **H**, the children of Akkub, 2286

HAGAR (12) [AGAR]
Ge 16: 1 an Egyptian, whose name *was* **H**. 1904
16: 3 Sarai Abram's wife took **H** her maid 1904
16: 4 he went in unto **H**, and she conceived: and 1904
16: 8 he said, **H**, Sarai's maid, whence camest 1904
16:15 **H** bare Abram a son: and Abram called his 1904
16:15 his son's name, which **H** bare, Ishmael. 1904
16:16 years old, when **H** bare Ishmael to Abram. 1904
21: 9 Sarah saw the son of **H** the Egyptian, 1904
21:14 and a bottle of water, and gave *it* unto **H**, 1904
21:17 the angel of God called to **H** out of heaven, 1904
21:17 and said unto her, What aileth thee, **H**? 1904
25:12 Abraham's son, whom **H** the Egyptian, 1904

HAGARENES (1) [HAGARITES]
Ps 83: 6 and the Ishmaelites; of Moab, and the **H**; 1905

HAGARITES (3) [HAGARENES, HAGERITE]
1Ch 5:10 the days of Saul they made war with the **H**, 1905
5:19 they made war with the **H**, with Jetur, and 1905
5:20 the **H** were delivered into their hand, and 1905

HAGERITE (1) [HAGARITES]
1Ch 27:31 over the flocks *was* Jaziz the **H**. All these 1905

HAGGAI (11)
Ezr 5: 1 **H** the prophet, and Zechariah the son of 2292
6:14 through the prophesying of **H** the prophet 2292
Hag 1: 1 came the word of the LORD by **H** 2292
1: 3 came the word of the LORD by **H** 2292
1:12 the words of **H** the prophet, as the LORD 2292
1:13 spake **H** the LORD'S messenger in 2292
2: 1 the word of the LORD by the prophet **H**, 2292
2:10 came the word of the LORD by **H** 2292
2:13 said **H**, If *one that is* unclean *by* a dead 2292
2:14 answered **H**, and said, So *is* this people, 2292
2:20 again the word of the LORD came unto **H** 2292

HAGGERI (1)
1Ch 11:38 the brother of Nathan, Mibhar the son of **H**, 1905

HAGGI (2) [HAGGITES]
Ge 46:16 **H**, Shuni, and Ezbon, Eri, and Arodi, and 2291
Nu 26:15 of **H**, the family of the Haggites: of Shuni, 2291

HAGGIAH (1)
1Ch 6:30 Shimea his son, **H** his son, Asaiah his son. 2293

HAGGITES (1) [HAGGI]
Nu 26:15 of Haggi, the family of the **H**: of Shuni, 2291

HAGGITH (5)
2Sa 3: 4 the fourth, Adonijah the son of **H**; and 2294
1Ki 1: 5 Adonijah the son of **H** exalted himself, 2294
1:11 that Adonijah the son of **H** doth reign, 2294
2:13 Adonijah the son of **H** came to Bath-sheba 2294
1Ch 3: 2 the fourth, Adonijah the son of **H**: 2294

HAGRI See HAGGERI

HAGRITE See HAGARITES; HAGERITE

HAI (2) [AI]
Ge 12: 8 Beth-el on the west, and **H** on the east: 5857
13: 3 at the beginning, between Beth-el and **H**; 5857

HAIL (36) [HAILSTONES, HAIL-STONES]
Ex 9:18 I will cause it to rain a very grievous **h**, 1259
9:19 the **h** shall come down upon them, and 1259
9:22 that there may be **h** in all the land of Egypt, 1259
9:23 the LORD sent thunder and **h**, and the fire 1259
9:23 the LORD rained **h** upon the land of 1259
9:24 So there was **h**, and fire mingled with 1259
9:24 and fire mingled with the **h**, very grievous, 1259
9:25 the **h** smote throughout all the land of 1259
9:25 the **h** smote every herb of the field, and 1259
9:26 the children of Israel *were*, was there no **h**. 1259
9:28 there be no *more* mighty thunderings and **h**; 1259
9:29 neither shall there be any more **h**; 1259
9:33 the thunders and **h** ceased, and the rain was 1259
9:34 and the **h** and the thunders were ceased, 1259
10: 5 which remaineth unto you from the **h**, 1259
10:12 of the land, *even* all that the **h** hath left. 1259
10:15 all the fruit of the trees which the **h** had 1259
Job 38:22 or hast thou seen the treasures of the **h**, 1259
Ps 78:47 He destroyed their vines with **h**, and 1259
78:48 He gave up their cattle also to the **h**, and 1259
105:32 He gave them **h** *for* rain, *and* flaming fire in 1259
148: 8 Fire, and **h**; snow, and vapour; stormy wind 1259
Isa 28: 2 *which* as a tempest of **h** *and* a destroying 1259
28:17 the **h** shall sweep away the refuge of lies, 1259
32:19 When it shall **h**, coming down *on* 1258
Hag 2:17 and with **h** in all the labours of your hands; 1259
Mt 26:49 he came to Jesus, and said, **H**, master; *5463*
27:29 and mocked him, saying, **H**, King of *5463*
28: 9 behold, Jesus met them, saying, *All* **h**. *5463*
Mk 15:18 began to salute him, **H**, King of the Jews. *5463*
Lk 1:28 and said, **H**, *thou that art* highly favoured, *5463*
Jn 19: 3 And said, **H**, King of the Jews: and *5463*
Rev 8: 7 and there followed **h** and fire mingled with *5464*
11:19 and an earthquake, and great **h**. *5464*
16:21 And there fell upon men a great **h** out of *5464*
16:21 because of the plague of the **h**; *5464*

HAILSTONES, HAIL-STONES (7) [HAIL, STONE]
Jos 10:11 **h** than *they* whom the children 68+1259+1886.1
Ps 18:12 clouds passed, **h** and coals of fire. 1259
18:13 gave his voice; **h** and coals of fire. 1259
Isa 30:30 *with* scattering, and tempest, and **h**. 68+1259
Eze 13:11 ye, O **great h**, shall fall; and a stormy 68+417
13:13 and **great h** in *my* fury to consume *it*. 68+417
38:22 and **great h**, fire, and brimstone. 68+417

HAIR (64) [HAIRS, HAIRY]
Ex 25: 4 and scarlet, and fine linen, and goats' *h*, NIH
26: 7 thou shalt make curtains *of* goats' *h* to be a NIH
35: 6 and scarlet, and fine linen, and goats' *h*, NIH
35:23 goats' *h*, and red skins of rams, and NIH
35:26 stirred them up in wisdom spun goats' *h*. NIH
36:14 he made curtains *of* goats' *h* for the tent NIH
Lev 13: 3 *when* the **h** in the plague is turned white, 8181
13: 4 and the **h** thereof be not turned white; 8181
13:10 it have turned the **h** white, and *there be* 8181
13:20 the skin, and the **h** thereof be turned white; 8181
13:25 *if* the **h** in the bright spot be turned white, 8181
13:26 *there be* no white **h** in the bright spot, and 8181
13:30 *there be* in it a yellow thin **h**; then the priest 8181
13:31 the skin, and *that there is* no black **h** in it; 8181
13:32 there be in it no yellow **h**, and the scall *be* 8181
13:36 the priest shall not seek for yellow **h**; 8181
13:37 and *that* there is black **h** grown up therein; 8181
13:40 And the man whose **h** is **fallen off** his head, 4803
13:41 he that hath his **h fallen off** from the part of 4803
14: 8 shave off all his **h**, and wash *himself* in 8181
14: 9 *that* he shall shave all his **h** off his head and 8181
14: 9 even all his **h** he shall shave off: 8181
Nu 6: 5 shall let the locks of the **h** of his head grow. 8181
6:18 shall take the **h** of the head of his 8181
6:19 after *the* **h** *of* his separation is shaven: NIH
31:20 all work of goats' *h*, and all things made of NIH
Jdg 16:22 Howbeit the **h** of his head began to grow 8181
20:16 every one could sling stones at a **h** *breadth*, 8185
1Sa 14:45 there shall not one **h** of his head fall to 8185
19:13 put a pillow of goats' **h** *for* his bolster, and NIH
19:16 with a pillow of goats' **h** *for* his bolster. NIH
2Sa 14:11 there shall not one **h** of thy son fall to 8185
14:26 polled *it:* because the **h** was heavy on him, NIH
14:26 he weighed the **h** of his head *at* two 8181
1Ki 1:52 there shall not a **h** of him fall to the earth: 8185
Ezr 9: 3 pluckt off the **h** of my head and of my 8181
Ne 13:25 **pluckt off** their **h**, and made them swear by 4803
Job 4:15 before my face; the **h** of my flesh stood up: 8185
SS 4: 1 thy **h** *is* as a flock of goats, that appear 8181
6: 5 thy **h** *is* as a flock of goats that appear from 8181
7: 5 and the **h** of thine head like purple; 1803
Isa 3:24 instead of **well set h** baldness; and 4639+4748
7:20 of Assyria, the head, and the **h** of the feet: 8181
50: 6 my cheeks to them that **plucked off** the **h**: 4803
Jer 7:29 Cut off thine **h**, *O Jerusalem*, and cast *it* 5145
Eze 5: 1 thee balances to weigh, and divide *the* **h**. NIH
16: 7 thine **h** is grown, whereas thou *wast* naked 8181
Da 3:27 nor was a **h** of their head singed, 8177
7: 9 and the **h** of his head like the pure wool: 8177
Mt 3: 4 the same John had his raiment of camel's **h**, *2359*
5:36 thou canst not make one **h** white or black. *2359*
Mk 1: 6 And John was clothed with camel's **h**, and *2359*
Lk 21:18 But there shall not a **h** of your head perish. *2359*
Jn 11: 2 and wiped his feet with her **h**, *2359*
12: 3 feet of Jesus, and wiped his feet with her **h**: *2359*
Ac 27:34 for there shall not a **h** fall from the head of *2359*
1Co 11:14 that, if a man **have long h**, it is a shame *2863*
11:15 But if a woman **have long h**, it is a glory to *2863*

1Co 11:15 to her: for *her* **h** is given her for a covering. *2864*
1Ti 2: 9 and sobriety; not with **broided h**, *4117*
1Pe 3: 3 be that outward *adorning* of plaiting the **h**, *2359*
Rev 6:12 and the sun became black as sackcloth of **h**, *5155*
9: 8 And they had **h** as the hair of women, and *2359*
9: 8 And they had hair as the **h** of women, and *2359*

HAIRS (15) [HAIR]
Ge 42:38 shall ye bring down my **gray h** with sorrow 7872
44:29 ye shall bring down my **gray h** with sorrow 7872
44:31 thy servants shall bring down the **gray h** of 7872
Lev 13:21 *there be* no white **h** therein, and *if* it *be* not 8181
Dt 32:25 the suckling *also* with the man of **gray h**. 7872
Ps 40:12 *up;* they are moe than the **h** of mine head: 8185
69: 4 a cause are moe than the **h** of mine head: 8185
Isa 46: 4 *even* to **hoar h** will I carry *you:* I have 7872
Da 4:33 till his **h** were grown like eagles' *feathers,* 8177
Hos 7: 9 yea, **gray h** are here and there upon him, 7872
Mt 10:30 But the very **h** of your head are all *2359*
Lk 7:38 and did wipe *them* with the **h** of her head, *2359*
7:44 and wiped *them* with the **h** of her head. *2359*
12: 7 But even the *very* **h** of your head are all *2359*
Rev 1:14 His head and *his* **h** *were* white like wool, *2359*

HAIRY (5) [HAIR]
Ge 25:25 came out red, all over like a **h** garment; 8181
27:11 Esau my brother *is* a **h** man, and I *am* a 8163
27:23 him not, because his hands were **h**, 8163
2Ki 1: 8 *He was* a **h** man, and girt *with* a girdle of 8181
Ps 68:21 the **h** scalp of such a one as goeth on still in 8181

HAKILAH See HACHILAH

HAKKATAN (1)
Ezr 8:12 Johanan the son of **H**, and with him an 6997

HAKKOZ (1)
1Ch 24:10 The seventh to **H**, the eighth to Abijah, 6976

HAKUPHA (2)
Ezr 2:51 the children of **H**, the children of Harhur, 2709
Ne 7:53 the children of **H**, the children of Harhur, 2709

HALAH (3)
2Ki 17: 6 placed them in **H** and in Habor *by* the river 2477
18:11 put them in **H** and in Habor *by* the river of 2477
1Ch 5:26 brought them unto **H**, and Habor, and Hara, 2477

HALAK (2)
Jos 11:17 *Even* from the mount **H**, that goeth up *to* 2510
12: 7 valley of Lebanon even unto the mount **H**, 2510

HALE (1) [HALING]
Lk 12:58 lest he **h** thee to the judge, and the judge *2694*

HALF (136)
Ge 24:22 took a golden earring of **h a shekel** weight, 1235
Ex 24: 6 Moses took **h** of the blood, and put *it* in 2677
24: 6 and **h** of the blood he sprinkled on the altar. 2677
25:10 and a **h** *shall be* the length thereof, 2677
25:10 a cubit and a **h** the breadth thereof, and 2677
25:10 and a cubit and a **h** the height thereof. 2677
25:17 and a **h** *shall be* the length thereof, 2677
25:17 and a cubit and a **h** the breadth thereof. 2677
25:23 and a cubit and a **h** the height thereof. 2677
26:12 the **h** curtain that remaineth, shall hang 2677
26:16 and a **h** *shall be* the breadth of one board. 2677
30:13 **h** a shekel after the shekel of the sanctuary: 4276
30:13 a **h** shekel *shall be* the offering of 4276
30:15 the poor shall not give less than **h** a shekel, 4276
30:23 and of sweet cinnamon **h so much**, 4276
36:21 the breadth of a board one cubit and a **h**. 2677
37: 1 two cubits and a **h** *was* the length of it, and 2677
37: 1 a cubit and a **h** the breadth of it, and a cubit 2677
37: 1 of it, and a cubit and a **h** the height of it: 2677
37: 6 two cubits and a **h** *was* the length thereof, 2677
37: 6 and one cubit and a **h** the breadth thereof. 2677
37:10 and a cubit and a **h** the height thereof: 2677
38:26 A bekah for every man, *that is,* **h** a shekel, 4276
Lev 6:20 **h** of it in the morning, and half thereof at 4276
6:20 of it in the morning, and **h** thereof at night. 4276
Nu 12:12 of whom the flesh is **h** consumed when he 2677
15: 9 deals *of* flour mingled with **h** a hin of oil. 2677
15:10 thou shalt bring for a drink offering **h** a hin 2677
28:14 their drink offerings shall be **h** a hin of 2677
31:29 Take *it* of their **h**, and give *it* unto Eleazar 4276
31:30 of the children of Israel's **h**, thou shalt take 4276
31:36 the **h**, *which was* the portion of them that 4275
31:42 of the children of Israel's **h**, which Moses 4276
31:43 (Now the **h** that pertained unto 4275
31:47 Even of the children of Israel's **h**, 4276
32:33 unto **h** the tribe of Manasseh the son of 2677
34:13 give unto the nine tribes, and *to* the **h** tribe: 2677
34:14 **h** the tribe of Manasseh have received their 2677
34:15 The **h** tribe have received their inheritance 2677
Dt 3:12 **h** mount Gilead, and the cities thereof, 2677
3:13 of Og, gave I unto the **h** tribe of Manasseh; 2677
3:16 **h** the valley, and the border, even unto 8432
29: 8 the Gadites, and to the **h** tribe of Manasseh. 2677
Jos 1:12 to **h** the tribe of Manasseh, spake Joshua, 2677
4:12 of Gad, and **h** the tribe of Manasseh, 2677
8:33 **h** of them over against mount Gerizim, and 2677
8:33 and **h** of them over against mount Ebal; 2677
12: 2 *from* **h** Gilead, even unto the river Jabbok, 2677
12: 5 and the Maachathites, and **h** Gilead, 2677
12: 6 the Gadites, and the **h** tribe of Manasseh. 2677
13: 7 the nine tribes, and the **h** tribe of Manasseh, 2677
13:25 and **h** the land of the children of Ammon, 2677
13:29 Moses gave *inheritance* unto the **h** tribe of 2677
13:29 *this* was *the possession* of the **h** tribe of 2677
13:31 **h** Gilead, and Ashtaroth, and Edrei, 2677
13:31 *even* to the **one h** of the children of Machir 2677
14: 2 for the nine tribes, and *for* the **h** tribe. 2677
14: 3 and a **h** tribe on the *other* side Jordan: 2677
Jos 18: 7 and Reuben, and **h** the tribe of Manasseh, 2677
21: 5 out of the **h** tribe of Manasseh, ten cities. 2677
21: 6 out of the **h** tribe of Manasseh in Bashan, 2677
21:25 out of the **h** tribe of Manasseh, Tanach with 4276
21:27 out of the *other* **h** tribe of Manasseh *they* 2677
22: 1 the Gadites, and the **h** tribe of Manasseh, 2677
22: 7 Now to the *one* **h** of the tribe of Manasseh 2677
22: 7 unto the *other* **h** thereof gave Joshua among 2677
22: 9 and the **h** tribe of Manasseh returned, 2677
22:10 the **h** tribe of Manasseh built there an altar 2677
22:11 the **h** tribe of Manasseh have built an altar 2677
22:13 of Gad, and to the **h** tribe of Manasseh, 2677
22:15 of Gad, and to the **h** tribe of Manasseh, 2677
22:21 and the **h** tribe of Manasseh answered, 2677
1Sa 14:14 within as it were a **h** acre of land, 2677
2Sa 10: 4 shaved off the *one* **h** of their beards, and 2677
18: 3 neither if **h** of us die, will they care for us: 2677
19:40 the king, and also **h** the people of Israel. 2677
1Ki 3:25 and give **h** to the one, and half to the other. 2677
3:25 and give half to the one, and **h** to the other. 2677
7:31 *after* the work of the base, a cubit and a **h**: 2677
7:32 height of a wheel *was* a cubit and **h** a cubit. 2677
7:35 *there* a round compass of **h** a cubit high: 2677
10: 7 seen *it:* and behold, the **h** was not told me: 2677
13: 8 If thou wilt give me **h** thine house, I will 2677
16: 9 captain of **h** *his* chariots, conspired against 4276
16:21 **h** of the people followed Tibni the son of 2677
16:21 to make him king; and **h** followed Omri. 2677
1Ch 2:52 Haroeh, *and* **h** of the Manahethites. 2677
2:54 and **h** of the Manahethites, the Zorites. 2677
5:18 the Gadites, and **h** the tribe of Manasseh, 2677
5:23 the children of the **h** tribe of Manasseh 2677
5:26 the **h** tribe of Manasseh, and brought them 2677
6:61 *were cities given* out of the **h** tribe, 2677
6:61 *namely, out of* the **h** *tribe* of Manasseh, 4276
6:70 out of the **h** tribe of Manasseh; Aner with 4276
6:71 of the family of the **h** tribe of Manasseh, 2677
12:31 of the **h** tribe of Manasseh eighteen 2677
12:37 the Gadites, and of the **h** tribe of Manasseh, 2677
26:32 the Gadites, and the **h** tribe of Manasseh, 2677
27:20 of the **h** tribe of Manasseh, Joel the son of 2677
27:21 Of the **h** *tribe* of Manasseh in Gilead, 2677
2Ch 9: 6 *the one* **h** of the greatness of thy wisdom 2677
Ne 3: 9 of Hur, the ruler of the **h** part of Jerusalem. 2677
3:12 the ruler of the **h** part of Jerusalem, he and 2677
3:16 the ruler of the **h** part of Beth-zur, 2677
3:17 the ruler of the **h** part of Keilah, in his part. 2677
3:18 the ruler of the **h** part of Keilah. 2677
4: 6 all the wall was joined together unto the **h** 2677
4:16 *that* the **h** of my servants wrought in 2677
4:16 the *other* **h** of them held both the spears, 2677
4:21 **h** of them held the spears from the rising of 2677
12:32 and **h** of the princes of Judah, 2677
12:38 and the **h** of the people upon the wall, 2677
12:40 and I, and the **h** of the rulers with me: 2677
13:24 their children spake **h** in the speech of 2677
Est 5: 3 it shall be even given thee to the **h** of 2677
5: 6 even to the **h** of the kingdom it shall be 2677
7: 2 *even* to the **h** of the kingdom. 2677
Ps 55:23 deceitful men shall not **live out h** their 2673
Eze 16:51 Neither hath Samaria committed **h** of thy 2677
40:42 of a cubit and a **h** long, and a cubit and 2677
40:42 a cubit and a **h** broad, and one cubit high: 2677
43:17 the border about it *shall be* **h** a cubit; and 2677
Da 12: 7 that *it shall be* for a time, times, and a **h**; 2677
Hos 3: 2 homer of barley, and a **h homer** of barley: 3963
Zec 14: 2 **h** of the city shall go forth into captivity, 2677
14: 4 **h** of the mountain shall remove toward 2677
14: 4 the north, and **h** of it toward the south. 2677
14: 8 **h** of them toward the former sea, and 2677
14: 8 and **h** of them toward the hinder sea: 2677
Mk 6:23 will give *it* thee, unto the **h** of my kingdom. *2255*
Lk 10:30 and departed, leaving *him* **h dead**. *2253*
19: 8 Lord, the **h** of my goods I give to the poor; *2255*
Rev 8: 1 in heaven about the space of **h an hour**. *2256*
11: 9 see their dead bodies three days and a **h**, *2255*
11:11 a **h** the spirit of life from God entered into *2255*
12:14 and times, and **h** a time, from the face of *2255*

HALHUL (1)
Jos 15:58 **H**, Beth-zur, and Gedor, 2478

HALI (1)
Jos 19:25 and **H**, and Beten, and Achshaph, 2482

HALING (1) [HALE]
Ac 8: 3 and **h** men and women committed *them* to *4951*

HALL (8)
Mt 27:27 governor took Jesus into the **common h**, *4232*
Mk 15:16 And the soldiers led him away into the **h**, *833*
Lk 22:55 they had kindled a fire in the midst of the **h**, *833*
Jn 18:28 from Caiaphas unto the **h of judgment**: *4232*
18:28 themselves went not into the **judgment h**, *4232*
18:33 Then Pilate entered into the **judgment h** *4232*
19: 9 And went again into the **judgment h**, and *4232*
Ac 23:35 him to be kept in Herod's **judgment h**. *4232*

HALLELUIA See ALLELUIA

HALLOHESH (2)
Ne 3:12 unto him repaired Shallum the son of **H**, 3873
10:24 **H**, Pileha, Shobek, 3873

HALLOW (15) [HALLOWED]
Ex 28:38 of Israel shall **h** in all their holy gifts; 6942
29: 1 that thou shalt do unto them to **h** them, 6942
40: 9 shalt **h** it, and all the vessels thereof: 6942
Lev 16:19 **h** it from the uncleanness of the children of 6942
22: 2 name *in those things* which they **h** unto me: 6942
22: 3 the children of Israel **h** unto the LORD, 6942
22:32 of Israel: I *am* the LORD which **h** you, 6942
25:10 ye shall **h** the fiftieth year, and 6942
Nu 6:11 and shall **h** his head that *same* day. 6942
1Ki 8:64 The same day did the king **h** the middle of 6942
Jer 17:22 do ye any work, but **h** ye the sabbath day, 6942
17:24 **h** the sabbath day, to do no work therein; 6942
17:27 if you will not hearken unto me to **h** 6942
Eze 20:20 **h** my sabbaths; and they shall be a sign 6942
44:24 and they shall **h** my sabbaths. 6942

HALLOWED (22) [HALLOW]
Ex 20:11 LORD blessed the sabbath day, and **h** it. 6942
29:21 he shall be **h**, and his garments, and 6942
Lev 12: 4 she shall touch no **h** *thing,* nor come into 6944
19: 8 he hath profaned the **h** *thing* of 6944
22:32 but I will be **h** among the children of Israel: 6942
Nu 3:13 Egypt I **h** unto me all the firstborn in Israel, 6942
5:10 every man's **h** *things* shall be his: 6944
16:37 scatter thou the fire yonder; for they are **h**. 6942
16:38 before the LORD, therefore they are **h**: 6942
18: 8 of all the **h** *things* of the children of Israel; 6944
18:29 *even* the **h** *part* thereof out of it. 4720
Dt 26:13 I have brought away the **h** *things* out of 6944
1Sa 21: 4 under mine hand, but there is **h** bread; 6944
21: 6 So the priest gave him **h** *bread:* for there 6944
1Ki 9: 3 I have **h** this house, which thou hast built, 6942
9: 7 *this* house, which I have **h** for my name, 6942
2Ki 12:18 Jehoash king of Judah took all the **h** *things* 6944
12:18 his own **h** *things,* and all the gold that was 6944
2Ch 7: 7 Moreover Solomon **h** the middle of 6942
36:14 the LORD which he had **h** in Jerusalem. 6942
Mt 6: 9 Father which art in heaven, **H** be thy name. *37*
Lk 11: 2 Father which art in heaven, **H** be thy name. *37*

HALT (6) [HALTED, HALTETH, HALTING]
1Ki 18:21 said, How long **h** ye between two opinions? 6452
Ps 38:17 For I *am* ready to **h**, and my sorrow *is* 6761
Mt 18: 8 it is better for thee to enter into life **h** or *5560*
Mk 9:45 it is better for thee to enter **h** into life, *5560*
Lk 14:21 and the maimed, and the **h**, and the blind. *5560*
Jn 5: 3 **h**, withered, waiting for the moving of *5560*

HALTED (2) [HALT]
Ge 32:31 sun rose upon him, and he **h** upon his thigh. 6760
Mic 4: 7 I will make her that **h** a remnant, and 6760

HALTETH (2) [HALT]
Mic 4: 6 will I assemble her that **h**, and I will gather 6760
Zep 3:19 I will save her that **h**, and gather her that 6760

HALTING (1) [HALT]
Jer 20:10 All my familiars watched for my **h**, 6763

HAM (17)
Ge 5:32 and Noah begat Shem, **H**, and Japheth. 2526
6:10 begat three sons, Shem, **H**, and Japheth. 2526
7:13 Shem, and **H**, and Japheth, the sons of 2526
9:18 of the ark, were Shem, and **H**, and Japheth: 2526
9:18 and Japheth: and **H** *is* the father of Canaan. 2526
9:22 **H**, the father of Canaan, saw the nakedness 2526
10: 1 of the sons of Noah, Shem, **H**, and Japheth: 2526
10: 6 And the sons of **H**; Cush, and Mizraim, and 2526
10:20 These *are* the sons of **H**, after their 2526
14: 5 the Zuzims in **H**, and the Emims in Shaveh 1990
1Ch 1: 4 Noah, Shem, **H**, and Japheth. 2526
1: 8 The sons of **H**; Cush, and Mizraim, Put, 2526
4:40 for *they* of **H** had dwelt there of old. 2526
Ps 78:51 of *their* strength in the tabernacles of **H**: 2526
105:23 and Jacob sojourned in the land of **H**. 2526
105:27 among them, and wonders in the land of **H**. 2526
106:22 Wondrous works in the land of **H**, *and* 2526

HAMAN (50) [HAMAN'S]
Est 3: 1 **H** the son of Hammedatha the Agagite, 2001
3: 2 the king's gate, bowed, and reverenced **H**: 2001
3: 4 hearkened not unto them, that they told **H**, 2001
3: 5 And when **H** saw that Mordecai bowed not, 2001
3: 5 him reverence, *then* was **H** full *of* wrath. 2001
3: 6 wherefore **H** sought to destroy all the Jews 2001
3: 7 before **H** from day to day, and from month 2001
3: 8 **H** said unto king Ahasuerus, There is a 2001
3:10 gave it unto **H** the son of Hammedatha 2001
3:11 the king said unto **H**, The silver *is* given to 2001
3:12 there was written according to all that **H** 2001
3:15 the king and **H** sat down to drink; but 2001
4: 7 of the sum of the money that **H** had 2001
5: 4 **H** come *this* day unto the banquet that I 2001
5: 5 the king said, Cause **H** to make haste, that 2001
5: 5 **H** came to the banquet that Esther had 2001
5: 8 **H** come to the banquet that I shall prepare 2001
5: 9 went **H** forth that day joyful and with a 2001
5: 9 when **H** saw Mordecai in the king's gate, 2001
5:10 Nevertheless **H** refrained himself: and 2001
5:11 **H** told them of the glory of his riches, and 2001
5:12 **H** said moreover, Yea, Esther the queen did 2001
5:14 the thing pleased **H**; and he caused 2001
6: 4 Now **H** was come into the outward court of 2001
6: 5 unto him, Behold, **H** standeth in the court. 2001
6: 6 So **H** came in. And the king said unto him, 2001
6: 6 Now **H** thought in his heart, To whom 2001
6: 7 **H** answered the king, *For* the man whom 2001
6:10 the king said to **H**, Make haste, *and* take 2001
6:11 took **H** the apparel and the horse, and 2001
6:12 **H** hasted to his house mourning, and 2001
6:13 **H** told Zeresh his wife and all his friends 2001
6:14 hasted to bring **H** unto the banquet that 2001
7: 1 **H** came to banquet with Esther the queen. 2001
7: 6 The adversary and enemy *is* this wicked **H**. 2001
7: 6 **H** was afraid before the king and the queen. 2001
7: 7 **H** stood *up* to make request for his life to 2001
7: 8 **H** was fallen upon the bed whereon Esther 2001
7: 9 which **H** had made for Mordecai, 2001
7: 9 for the king, standeth in the house of **H**. 2001
7:10 So they hanged **H** on the gallows that he 2001
8: 1 **H** the Jews' enemy unto Esther the queen. 2001
8: 2 which he had taken from **H**, and gave it 2001
8: 2 Esther set Mordecai over the house of **H**. 2001

Est 8: 3 to put away the mischief of **H** the Agagite, 2001
8: 5 by **H** the son of Hammedatha the Agagite, 2001
8: 7 I have given Esther the house of **H**, and 2001
9:10 The ten sons of **H** the son of Hammedatha, 2001
9:12 Shushan the palace, and the ten sons of **H**; 2001
9:24 Because **H** the son of Hammedatha, 2001

HAMAN'S (3) [HAMAN]
Est 7: 8 of the king's mouth, they covered **H** face. 2001
9:13 let **H** ten sons be hanged upon the gallows. 2001
9:14 at Shushan; and they hanged **H** ten sons. 2001

HAMATH (34) [HAMATH-ZOBAH, HAMATHITE]
Nu 13:21 of Zin unto Rehob, as *men* come to **H**. 2574
34: 8 out *your border* unto the entrance of **H**; 2574
Jos 13: 5 mount Hermon unto the entering into **H**. 2574
Jdg 3: 3 Baal-hermon unto the entering in of **H**. 2574
2Sa 8: 9 When Toi king of **H** heard that David had 2574
1Ki 8:65 from the entering in of **H** unto the river of 2574
2Ki 14:25 the entering of **H** unto the sea of the plain, 2574
14:28 and **H**, *which belonged* to Judah, for Israel, 2574
17:24 from **H**, and from Sepharvaim, and 2574
17:30 and the men of **H** made Ashima, 2574
18:34 Where *are* the gods of **H**, and of Arpad? 2574
19:13 Where *is* the king of **H**, and the king of 2574
23:33 put him in bands at Riblah in the land of **H**, 2574
25:21 and slew them at Riblah in the land of **H**. 2574
1Ch 18: 3 smote Hadarezer king of Zobah unto **H**, 2574
18: 9 Now when Tou king of **H** heard how David 2574
2Ch 7: 8 from the entering in of **H** unto the river of 2574
8: 4 and all the store cities, which he built in **H**. 2574
Isa 10: 9 *is* not **H** as Arpad? *is* not Samaria as 2574
11:11 from **H**, and from the islands of the sea. 2574
36:19 Where *are* the gods of **H** and Arphad? 2574
37:13 Where *is* the king of **H**, and the king of 2574
Jer 39: 5 king of Babylon to Riblah in the land of **H**, 2574
49:23 **H** is confounded, and Arpad: for they have 2574
52: 9 king of Babylon to Riblah in the land of **H**; 2574
52:27 them to death in Riblah in the land of **H**. 2574
Eze 47:16 **H**, Berothah, Sibraim, which *is* between 2574
47:16 border of Damascus and the border of **H**; 2574
47:17 the north northward, and the border of **H**. 2574
47:20 the border, till *a man* come over against **H**. 2574
48: 1 as *one* goeth to **H**, Hazar-enan, the border 2574
48: 1 of Damascus northward, to the coast of **H**; 2574
Am 6: 2 see; and from thence go ye *to* **H** the great: 2574
Zec 9: 2 **H** also shall border thereby; Tyrus, and 2574

HAMATHITE (2) [HAMATH]
Ge 10:18 the Arvadite, and the Zemarite, and the **H**: 2577
1Ch 1:16 the Arvadite, and the Zemarite, and the **H**. 2577

HAMATH-ZOBAH (1) [HAMATH, ZOBAH]
2Ch 8: 3 Solomon went *to* **H**, and prevailed against 2574

HAMMATH (1)
Jos 19:35 Zer, and **H**, Rakkath, and Chinnereth, 2575

HAMMEDATHA (5)
Est 3: 1 promote Haman the son of **H** the Agagite, 4099
3:10 gave it unto Haman the son of **H** 4099
8: 5 by Haman the son of **H** the Agagite, 4099
9:10 The ten sons of Haman the son of **H**, 4099
9:24 Because Haman the son of **H**, the Agagite, 4099

HAMMELECH (2)
Jer 36:26 king commanded Jerahmeel the son of **H**, 4429
38: 6 into the dungeon of Malchiah the son of **H**, 4429

HAMMER (7) [HAMMERS]
Jdg 4:21 took a **h** in her hand, and went softly unto 4717
5:26 and her right hand to the workmen's **h**; 1989
5:26 with the **h** she smote Sisera, she smote off NIH
1Ki 6: 7 that there was neither **h** nor axe *nor* any 4717
Isa 41: 7 he that smootheth *with* the **h** him that 6360
Jer 23:29 like a **h** *that* breaketh the rock in pieces? 6360
50:23 How is the **h** of the whole earth cut asunder 6360

HAMMERS (3) [HAMMER]
Ps 74: 6 work thereof at once with axes and **h**. 3597
Isa 44:12 fashioneth it with **h**, and worketh it with 4717
Jer 10: 4 they fasten it with nails and with **h**, that it 4717

HAMMOLEKETH (1)
1Ch 7:18 his sister **H** bare Ishod, and Abiezer, and 4447

HAMMON (2)
Jos 19:28 and Rehob, and **H**, and Kanah, 2540
1Ch 6:76 **H** with her suburbs, and Kirjathaim with 2540

HAMMOTH-DOR (1) [DOR]
Jos 21:32 **H** with her suburbs, and Kartan with her 2576

HAMMUEL See HAMUEL

HAMONAH (1)
Eze 39:16 also the name of the city *shall be* **H**. 1997

HAMON-GOG (2) [GOG]
Eze 39:11 and they shall call *it* The valley of **H**. 1995
39:15 the buriers have buried it in the valley of **H**. 1995

HAMOR (12) [EMMOR, HAMOR'S]
Ge 33:19 at the hand of the children of **H**, 2544
34: 2 when Shechem the son of **H** the Hivite, 2544
34: 4 Shechem spake unto his father **H**, saying, 2544
34: 6 **H** the father of Shechem went out unto 2544
34: 8 **H** communed with them, saying, The soul 2544
34:13 and **H** his father deceitfully, 2544
34:18 their words pleased **H**, and Shechem 2544
34:20 **H** and Shechem his son came unto the gate 2544
34:24 unto **H** and unto Shechem his son 2544
34:26 they slew **H** and Shechem his son with 2544
Jos 24:32 **H** the father of Shechem for an hundred 2544
Jdg 9:28 serve the men of **H** the father of Shechem: 2544

HAMOR'S (1) [HAMOR]
Ge 34:18 words pleased Hamor, and Shechem **H** son. 2544

HAMSTRING See HOUGH

HAMUEL (1)
1Ch 4:26 **H** his son, Zacchur his son, Shimei his son. 2536

HAMUL (3) [HAMULITES]
Ge 46:12 the sons of Pharez were Hezron and **H**. 2538
Nu 26:21 of **H**, the family of the Hamulites. 2538
1Ch 2: 5 The sons of Pharez; Hezron, and **H**. 2538

HAMULITES (1) [HAMUL]
Nu 26:21 of Hamul, the family of the **H**. 2539

HAMUTAL (3)
2Ki 23:31 his mother's name *was* **H**, the daughter of 2537
24:18 his mother's name *was* **H**, the daughter of 2537
Jer 52: 1 his mother's name *was* **H** the daughter of 2537

HANAMEEL (4)
Jer 32: 7 **H** the son of Shallum thine uncle *shall* 2601
32: 8 So **H** mine uncle's son came to me in 2601
32: 9 And I bought the field of **H** my uncle's son, 2601
32:12 in the sight of **H** mine uncle's *son,* and 2601

HANAMEL See HANAMEEL

HANAN (12) [BAAL-HANAN, ELON-BETH-HANAN]
1Ch 8:23 And Abdon, and Zichri, and **H**, 2605
8:38 and Sheariah, and Obadiah, and **H**. 2605
9:44 and Sheariah, and Obadiah, and **H**: 2605
11:43 **H** the son of Maachah, and Joshaphat 2605
Ezr 2:46 the children of Shalmai, the children of **H**, 2605
Ne 7:49 The children of **H**, the children of Giddel, 2605
8: 7 Jozabad, **H**, Pelaiah, and the Levites, 2605
10:10 Shebaniah, **H**, Hodijah, Kelita, Pelaiah, **H**, 2605
10:22 Pelatiah, **H**, Anaiah, 2605
10:26 And Ahijah, **H**, Anan, 2605
13:13 next to them *was* **H** the son of Zaccur, 2605
Jer 35: 4 into the chamber of the sons of **H**, the son 2605

HANANEEL (4)
Ne 3: 1 they sanctified it, unto the tower of **H**. 2606
12:39 and the tower of **H**, and the tower of Meah, 2606
Jer 31:38 the tower of **H** unto the gate of the corner. 2606
Zec 14:10 *from* the tower of **H** unto the king's 2606

HANANEL See HANANEEL

HANANI (11)
1Ki 16: 1 came to Jehu the son of **H** against Baasha, 2607
16: 7 **H** came the word of the LORD against 2607
1Ch 25: 4 **H**, Eliathah, Giddalti, and Romamti-ezer, 2607
25:25 The eighteenth to **H**, *he,* his sons, and 2607
2Ch 16: 7 at that time **H** the seer came to Asa king of 2607
19: 2 Jehu the son of **H** the seer went out to meet 2607
20:34 written in the book of Jehu the son of **H**, 2607
Ezr 10:20 of the sons of Immer; **H**, and Zebadiah. 2607
Ne 1: 2 That **H**, one of my brethren, came, he and 2607
7: 2 That I gave my brother **H**, and Hananiah 2607
12:36 Gilalai, Maai, Nethaneel, and Judah, **H**, 2607

HANANIAH (29)
1Ch 3:19 and **H**, and Shelomith their sister: 2608
3:21 the sons of **H**; Pelatiah, and Jesaiah: 2608
8:24 And **H**, and Elam, and Antothijah, 2608
25: 4 **H**, Hanani, Eliathah, Giddalti, and 2608
25:23 The sixteenth to **H**, *he,* his sons, and 2608
2Ch 26:11 Maaseiah the ruler, under the hand of **H**, 2608
Ezr 10:28 Jehohanan, **H**, Zabbai, *and* Athlai. 2608
Ne 3: 8 Next unto him also repaired **H** the son of 2608
3:30 After him repaired **H** the son of Shelemiah, 2608
7: 2 **H** the ruler of the palace, charge over 2608
10:23 Hoshea, **H**, Hashub, 2608
12:12 of Seraiah, Meraiah; of Jeremiah, **H**; 2608
12:41 Michaiah, Elioenai, Zechariah, *and* **H**, 2608
Jer 28: 1 *that* **H** the son of Azur the prophet, 2608
28: 5 the prophet **H** in the presence of the priests, 2608
28:10 **H** the prophet took the yoke from off 2608
28:11 **H** spake in the presence of all the people, 2608
28:12 **H** the prophet had broken the yoke from off 2608
28:13 Go and tell **H**, saying, Thus saith 2608
28:15 said the prophet Jeremiah unto **H** 2608
28:15 unto Hananiah the prophet, Hear now, **H**; 2608
28:17 So **H** the prophet died the same year in 2608
36:12 Zedekiah the son of **H**, and all the princes. 2608
37:13 the son of Shelemiah, the son of **H**; 2608
Da 1: 6 of Judah, Daniel, **H**, Mishael, and Azariah: 2608
1: 7 to **H**, of Shadrach; and to Mishael, 2608
1:11 set over Daniel, **H**, Mishael, and Azariah, 2608
1:19 none like Daniel, **H**, Mishael, and Azariah: 2608
2:17 made the thing known to **H**, Mishael, and 2608

HAND (1470) [BROKENHANDED, HANDBREADTH, HANDED, HANDFUL, HANDFULS, HANDS, HANDSTAVES, HANDWRITING, HANDYWORK, LEFTHANDED]
Ge 3:22 lest he put forth his **h**, and take also of 3027
4:11 to receive thy brother's blood from thy **h**. 3027
8: 9 he put forth his **h**, and took her, and 3027
9: 2 of the sea; into your **h** are they delivered. 3027
9: 5 at the **h** of every beast will I require it, and 3027
9: 5 beast will I require it, and at the **h** of man; 3027
9: 5 at the **h** of every man's brother will I 3027
13: 9 if *thou wilt take* the **left h**, then I will go to 8040
13: 9 or if *thou depart to* the **right h**, then I will 3225
14:15 which *is* on the **left h** of Damascus. 8040
14:20 hath delivered thine enemies into thy **h**. 3027
14:22 I have lift up mine **h** unto the LORD, 3027
16: 6 unto Sarai, Behold, thy maid *is* in thy **h**; 3027
16:12 his **h** *will be* against every man, and 3027
16:12 every man, and every man's **h** against him; 3027
19:10 the men put forth their **h**, and pulled Lot 3027
19:16 the men laid hold upon his **h**, and upon 3027
19:16 upon the **h** of his wife, and upon the hand 3027
19:16 and upon the **h** of his two daughters; 3027
21:18 lift up the lad, and hold him in thine **h**; 3027
21:30 seven ewe lambs shalt thou take of my **h**, 3027
22: 6 he took the fire in his **h**, and a knife; and 3027
22:10 Abraham stretched forth his **h**, and took 3027
22:12 he said, Lay not thine **h** upon the lad, 3027
24: 2 Put, I pray thee, thy **h** under my thigh: 3027
24: 9 the servant put his **h** under the thigh of 3027
24:10 all the goods of his master *were* in his **h**: 3027
24:18 let down her pitcher upon her **h**, and 3027
24:49 that I may turn to the **right h**, or to the left. 3225
25:26 and his **h** took hold on Esau's heel; 3027
27:17 had prepared, into the **h** of her son Jacob. 3027
27:41 days of mourning for my father are **at h**; 7126
30:35 and gave *them* into the **h** of his sons. 3027
31:29 It is in the power of my **h** to do you hurt: 3027
31:39 of my **h** didst thou require it, 3027
32:11 I pray thee, from the **h** of my brother, 3027
32:11 the hand of my brother, from the **h** of Esau: 3027
32:13 took of that which came to his **h** a present 3027
32:16 he delivered *them* into the **h** of his servants, 3027
33:10 thy sight, then receive my present at my **h**: 3027
33:19 at the **h** of the children of Hamor, 3027
35: 4 all the strange gods which *were* in their **h**, 3027
37:22 lay no **h** upon him, that he might rid him 3027
37:27 and let not our **h** be upon him; 3027
38:18 thy bracelets, and thy staff that *is* in thine **h**. 3027
38:20 Judah sent the kid by the **h** of his friend 3027
38:20 to receive *his* pledge from the woman's **h**: 3027
38:28 she travailed, that *the one* put out *his* **h**: 3027
38:28 and bound upon his **h** a scarlet thread, 3027
38:29 to pass, as he drew back his **h**, that, behold, 3027
38:30 that had the scarlet thread upon his **h**: 3027
39: 1 bought him of the **h** of the Ishmeelites, 3027
39: 3 made all that he did to prosper in his **h**. 3027
39: 4 and all *that* he had he put into his **h**. 3027
39: 6 he left all that he had in Joseph's **h**; and 3027
39: 8 he hath committed all that he hath to my **h**; 3027
39:12 he left his garment in her **h**, and fled, and 3027
39:13 saw that he had left his garment in her **h**, 3027
39:22 **h** all the prisoners that *were* in the prison; 3027
39:23 not to any thing *that was* under his **h**; 3027
40:11 Pharaoh's cup *was* in my **h**: and I took 3027
40:11 and I gave the cup into Pharaoh's **h**. 3709
40:13 thou shalt deliver Pharaoh's cup into his **h**, 3027
40:21 and he gave the cup into Pharaoh's **h**: 3709
41:35 and lay up corn under the **h** of Pharaoh, and 3027
41:42 Pharaoh took off his ring from his **h**, and 3027
41:42 put it upon Joseph's **h**, and arrayed him in 3027
41:44 without thee shall no man lift up his **h** or 3027
42:37 deliver him into my **h**, and I will bring him 3027
43: 9 for him; of my **h** shalt thou require him: 3027
43:12 take double money in your **h**; and 3027
43:12 of your sacks, carry *it* again in your **h**; 3027
43:15 they took double money in their **h**, and 3027
43:21 we have brought it again in our **h**. 3027
43:26 present which *was* in their **h** into the house, 3027
44:17 *but* the man in whose **h** the cup is found, 3027
46: 4 and Joseph shall put his **h** upon thine eyes. 3027
47:29 thy **h** under my thigh, and deal kindly and 3027
48:13 Ephraim in his **right h** toward Israel's left 3225
48:13 in his right hand toward Israel's **left h**, 8040
48:13 Manasseh in his **left h** towards Israel's 8040
48:13 in his left hand towards Israel's **right h**, 3225
48:14 Israel stretched out his **right h**, and laid *it* 3225
48:14 and his **left h** upon Manasseh's head, 8040
48:17 laid his right **h** upon the head of Ephraim, 3027
48:17 he held up his father's **h**, to remove it from 3027
48:18 the firstborn; put thy **right h** upon his head. 3225
48:22 which I took out of the **h** of the Amorite 3027
49: 8 thy **h** *shall be* in the neck of thine enemies; 3027
Ex 2:19 An Egyptian delivered us out of the **h** of 3027
3: 8 deliver them out of the **h** of the Egyptians, 3027
3:19 will not let you go, no, not by a mighty **h**. 3027
3:20 I will stretch out my **h**, and smite Egypt 3027
4: 2 said unto him, What *is* that in thine **h**? 3027
4: 4 Put forth thine **h**, and take it by the tail. 3027
4: 4 he put forth his **h**, and caught it, and 3027
4: 4 and caught it, and it became a rod in his **h**: 3709
4: 6 unto him, Put now thine **h** into thy bosom. 3027
4: 6 he put his **h** into his bosom: and when he 3027
4: 6 it out, behold, his **h** *was* leprous as snow. 3027
4: 7 he said, Put thine **h** into thy bosom again. 3027
4: 7 he put his **h** into his bosom again; and 3027
4:13 by the **h** *of him whom* thou wilt send. 3027
4:17 thou shalt take this rod in thine **h**, 3027
4:20 and Moses took the rod of God in his **h**. 3027
4:21 which I have put in thine **h**: 3027
5:21 to put a sword in their **h** to slay us. 3027
6: 1 for with a strong **h** shall he let them go, and 3027
6: 1 with a strong **h** shall he drive them out of 3027
7: 4 that I may lay my **h** upon Egypt, and 3027
7: 5 when I stretch forth mine **h** upon Egypt, 3027
7:15 to a serpent shalt thou take in thine **h**. 3027
7:17 I will smite with the rod that *is* in mine **h** 3027
7:19 stretch out thine **h** upon the waters of 3027
8: 5 Stretch forth thine **h** with thy rod over 3027
8: 6 Aaron stretched out his **h** over the waters of 3027
8:17 for Aaron stretched out his **h** with his rod, 3027
9: 3 the **h** of the LORD is upon thy cattle 3027
9:15 For now I will stretch out my **h**, that I may 3027
9:22 Stretch forth thine **h** toward heaven, 3027
10:12 Stretch out thine **h** over the land of Egypt 3027
10:21 Stretch out thine **h** toward heaven, 3027
10:22 Moses stretched forth his **h** toward heaven; 3027
12:11 shoes on your feet, and your staff in your **h**; 3027
13: 3 for by strength of **h** the LORD brought 3027
13: 9 it shall be for a sign unto thee upon thine **h**, 3027

Ex 13: 9 for with a strong **h** hath the LORD 3027
13:14 By strength of **h** the LORD brought us out 3027
13:16 it shall be for a token upon thine **h**, and 3027
13:16 for by strength of **h** the LORD brought us 3027
14: 8 children of Israel went out with a high **h**. 3027
14:16 stretch out thine **h** over the sea, and 3027
14:21 And Moses stretched out his **h** over the sea; 3027
14:22 *were* a wall unto them on their **right h**, 3225
14:26 Stretch out thine **h** over the sea, 3027
14:27 Moses stretched forth his **h** over the sea, 3027
14:29 *were* a wall unto them on their **right h**, 3225
14:30 that day out of the **h** of the Egyptians; 3027
15: 6 Thy **right h**, O LORD, is become glorious 3225
15: 6 thy **right h**, O LORD, hath dashed in 3225
15: 9 draw my sword, my **h** shall destroy them. 3027
15:12 Thou stretchedst out thy **right h**, the earth 3225
15:20 the sister of Aaron, took a timbrel in her **h**; 3027
16: 3 Would to God we had died by the **h** of 3027
17: 5 smotest the river, take in thine **h**, and go. 3027
17: 9 of the hill with the rod of God in mine **h**. 3027
17:11 it came to pass, when Moses held up his **h**, 3027
17:11 when he let down his **h**, Amalek prevailed. 3027
18: 9 whom he had delivered out of the **h** of 3027
18:10 who hath delivered you out of the **h** of 3027
18:10 the Egyptians, and out of the **h** of Pharaoh, 3027
18:10 people from under the **h** of the Egyptians. 3027
19:13 There shall not a **h** touch it, but he shall 3027
21:13 not in wait, but God deliver *him* into his **h**; 3027
21:16 and selleth him, or if he be found in his **h**, 3027
21:20 with a rod, and he die under his **h**; 3027
21:24 tooth for tooth, **h** for hand, foot for foot, 3027
21:24 tooth for tooth, hand for **h**, foot for foot, 3027
22: 4 If the theft be certainly found in his **h** alive, 3027
22: 8 *to see* whether he have put his **h** unto his 3027
22:11 that he hath not put his **h** unto his 3027
23: 1 put not thine **h** with the wicked to be an 3027
23:31 the inhabitants of the land into your **h**; 3027
24:11 of the children of Israel he laid not his **h**: 3027
29:20 upon the thumb of their right **h**, and 3027
32: 4 he received *them* at their **h**, and fashioned it 3027
32:11 with great power, and with a mighty **h**? 3027
32:15 two tables of the Testimony were in his **h**: 3027
33:22 will cover thee with my **h** while I pass by: 3709
33:23 I will take away mine **h**, and thou shalt see 3709
34: 4 and took in his **h** the two tables of stone. 3027
34:29 the two tables of Testimony in Moses' **h**, 3027
35:29 commanded to be made by the **h** of Moses. 3027
38:15 on **this h** and that hand, *were* hangings of 2088
38:15 on this hand and **that h**, *were* hangings of 2088
38:21 by the **h** of Ithamar, son to Aaron the priest. 3027
Lev 1: 4 he shall put his **h** upon the head of 3027
3: 2 he shall lay his **h** upon the head of his 3027
3: 8 he shall lay his **h** upon the head of his 3027
3:13 he shall lay his **h** upon the head of it, and 3027
4: 4 shall lay his **h** upon the bullock's head, and 3027
4:24 he shall lay his **h** upon the head of the goat, 3027
4:29 he shall lay his **h** upon the head of the sin 3027
4:33 he shall lay his **h** upon the head of the sin 3027
8:23 upon the thumb of his right **h**, and upon 3027
8:36 the LORD commanded by the **h** of Moses. 3027
9:22 Aaron lift up his **h** towards the people, and 3027
10:11 hath spoken unto them by the **h** of Moses. 3027
14:14 upon the thumb of his right **h**, and upon 3027
14:15 and pour *it* into the **palm of** his own left **h**: 3709
14:16 his right finger in the oil that *is* in his left **h**, 3709
14:17 of the rest of the oil that *is* in his **h** shall 3709
14:17 upon the thumb of his right **h**, and upon 3027
14:18 **h** he shall pour upon the head of him that is 3709
14:25 upon the thumb of his right **h**, and upon 3027
14:26 of the oil into the **palm of** his own left **h**: 3709
14:27 in his left **h** seven times before the LORD: 3709
14:28 the priest shall put of the oil that *is* in his **h** 3709
14:28 upon the thumb of his right **h**, and upon 3027
14:29 the rest of the oil that *is* in the priest's **h** he 3709
14:32 whose **h is** not **able to get** *that which* 3027+5381
16:21 shall send *him* away by the **h** of a fit man 3027
22:25 Neither from a stranger's **h** shall ye offer 3027
25:14 or buyest *ought* of thy neighbour's **h**, 3027
25:28 that which is sold shall remain in the **h** of 3027
26:25 ye shall be delivered into the **h** of 3027
26:46 of Israel in mount Sinai by the **h** of Moses. 3027
Nu 4:28 their charge *shall be* under the **h** of Ithamar 3027
4:33 under the **h** of Ithamar the son of Aaron 3027
4:37 of the LORD by the **h** of Moses. 3027
4:45 the word of the LORD by the **h** of Moses. 3027
4:49 they were numbered by the **h** of Moses, 3027
5:18 the priest shall have in his **h** the bitter water 3027
5:25 the jealousy offering out of the woman's **h**, 3027
6:21 besides *that* that his **h** shall get: 3027
7: 8 under the **h** of Ithamar the son of Aaron 3027
9:23 of the LORD by the **h** of Moses. 3027
10:13 of the LORD by the **h** of Moses. 3027
11:15 **kill** me, I pray thee, **out of h**, 2026+2026
11:23 Is the LORD'S **h** waxed short? 3027
15:23 hath commanded you by the **h** of Moses, 3027
16:40 as the LORD said to him by the **h** of 3027
20:11 Moses lift up his **h**, and with his rod he 3027
20:17 we will not turn *to* the **right h** nor *to* 3225
20:20 him with much people, and with a strong **h**. 3027
21: 2 wilt indeed deliver this people into my **h**, 3027
21:26 taken all his land out of his **h**, *even* unto 3027
21:34 for I have delivered him into thy **h**, and all 3027
22: 7 with the rewards of divination in their **h**; 3027
22:23 in the way, and his sword drawn in his **h**: 3027
22:26 *was* no way to turn *either to* the **right h** 3225
22:29 I would there were a sword in mine **h**, 3027
22:31 in the way, and his sword drawn in his **h**: 3027
25: 7 and took a javelin in his **h**; 3027
27:18 *is* the spirit, and lay thine **h** upon him; 3027
27:23 as the LORD commanded by the **h** of 3027
31: 6 and the trumpets to blow in his **h**. 3027
33: 1 with their armies under the **h** of Moses 3027
33: 3 a high **h** in the sight of all the Egyptians. 3027
35:18 Or *if* he smite him with a **h** weapon of 3027
35:21 Or in enmity smite him with his **h**, that he 3027
Nu 35:25 slayer out of the **h** of the revenger of blood, 3027
36:13 which the LORD commanded by the **h** of 3027
Dt 1:27 to deliver us into the **h** of the Amorites, 3027
2: 7 hath blessed thee in all the works of thy **h**: 3027
2:15 For indeed the **h** of the LORD was against 3027
2:24 I have given into thy **h** Sihon the Amorite, 3027
2:27 I will neither turn *unto* the **right h** nor *to* 3225
2:30 that he might deliver him into thy **h**, 3027
3: 2 and all his people, and his land, into thy **h**; 3027
3: 8 we took at that time out of the **h** of the two 3027
3:24 thy servant thy greatness, and thy mighty **h**: 3027
4:34 by a mighty **h**, and by a stretched out arm, 3027
5:15 brought thee out thence through a mighty **h** 3027
5:32 ye shall not turn aside *to* the **right h** or 3225
6: 8 shalt bind them for a sign upon thine **h**, 3027
6:21 brought us out of Egypt with a mighty **h**: 3027
7: 8 LORD brought you out with a mighty **h**, 3027
7: 8 from the **h** of Pharaoh king of Egypt. 3027
7:19 the mighty **h**, and the stretched out arm, 3027
7:24 he shall deliver their kings into thine **h**, 3027
8:17 the might of mine **h** hath gotten me this 3027
9:26 brought forth out of Egypt with a mighty **h**. 3027
10: 3 the mount, having the two tables in mine **h**. 3027
11: 2 his mighty **h**, and his stretched out arm, 3027
11:18 and bind them for a sign upon your **h**, 3027
12: 6 heave offerings of your **h**, and your vows, 3027
12: 7 ye shall rejoice in all that you put your **h** 3027
12:11 the heave offering of your **h**, and all your 3027
12:17 or heave offering of thine **h**: 3027
13: 9 thine **h** shall be first upon him to put him to 3027
13: 9 and afterwards the **h** of all the people. 3027
13:17 nought of the cursed thing to thine **h**: 3027
14:25 bind up the money in thine **h**, and shalt go 3027
14:29 in all the work of thine **h** which thou doest. 3027
15: 3 *that* which is thine with thy brother thine **h** 3027
15: 7 nor shut thine **h** from thy poor brother: 3027
15: 8 thou shalt open thine **h** wide unto him, and 3027
15: 9 seventh year, the year of release, is **at h**; 7126
15:10 and in all that thou puttest thine **h** unto. 3027
15:11 Thou shalt open thine **h** wide unto thy 3027
16:10 a tribute of a freewill offering of thine **h**, 3027
17:11 shew thee, *to* the **right h**, nor *to* the left. 3225
17:20 *to* the **right h**, or *to* the left: 3225
19: 5 his **h** fetcheth a stroke with the axe to cut 3027
19:12 deliver him into the **h** of the avenger of 3027
19:21 tooth for tooth, **h** for hand, foot for foot. 3027
19:21 tooth for tooth, hand for **h**, foot for foot. 3027
23:20 **h** to in the land whither thou goest to 3027
23:25 thou mayest pluck the ears with thine **h**; 3027
24: 1 give *it* in her **h**, and send her out of his 3027
24: 3 giveth *it* in her **h**, and sendeth her out of his 3027
25:11 out of the **h** of him that smiteth him, 3027
25:11 putteth forth her **h**, and taketh him by 3027
25:12 thou shalt cut off her **h**, thine eye shall not 3709
26: 4 priest shall take the basket out of thine **h**, 3027
26: 8 us forth out of Egypt with a mighty **h**, 3027
28: 8 and in all that thou settest thine **h** unto; 3027
28:12 and to bless all the work of thine **h**: 3027
28:14 *to* the **right h**, or *to* the left, to go after 3225
28:20 in all that thou settest thine **h** unto for to do, 3027
28:32 and *there shall be* no might in thine **h**. 3027
30: 9 thee plenteous in every work of thine **h**, 3027
32:27 Our **h** is high, and the LORD hath not 3027
32:35 for the day of their calamity *is* **at h**, and 7138
32:39 *is there any* that can deliver out of my **h**. 3027
32:40 For I lift up my **h** to heaven, and say, I live 3027
32:41 and mine **h** take hold on judgment; 3027
33: 2 from his **right h** *went* a fiery law for them. 3225
33: 3 loved the people; all his saints *are* in thy **h**: 3027
34:12 in all *that* mighty **h**, and in all the great 3027
Jos 1: 7 turn not from it *to* the **right h** or *to* the left, 3225
2:19 *shall be* on our head, if *any* **h** be upon him. 3027
4:24 the earth might know the **h** of the LORD, 3027
5:13 against him with his sword drawn in his **h**: 3027
6: 2 I have given into thine **h** Jericho, and 3027
7: 7 to deliver us into the **h** of the Amorites, 3027
8: 1 I have given into thy **h** the king of Ai, and 3027
8: 7 your God will deliver it into your **h**. 3027
8:18 Stretch out the spear that *is* in thy **h** toward 3027
8:18 toward Ai; for I will give it into thine **h**. 3027
8:18 spear that *he had* in his **h** toward the city. 3027
8:19 ran as soon as *he* had stretched out his **h**: 3027
8:26 For Joshua drew not his **h** back, 3027
9:25 now, behold, we *are* in thine **h**: as it 3027
9:26 delivered them out of the **h** of the children 3027
10: 6 Slack not thy **h** from thy servants; 3027
10: 8 for I have delivered them into thine **h**; 3027
10:19 your God hath delivered them into your **h**. 3027
10:30 the king thereof, into the **h** of Israel; 3027
10:32 the LORD delivered Lachish into the **h** of 3027
11: 8 the LORD delivered them into the **h** of 3027
14: 2 as the LORD commanded by the **h** of 3027
17: 7 the border went *along* on the **right h** unto 3225
19:27 Neiel, and goeth out to Cabul on the **left h**, 8040
20: 2 whereof I spake unto you by the **h** of 3027
20: 5 shall not deliver the slayer up into his **h**; 3027
20: 9 not die by the **h** of the avenger of blood, 3027
21: 2 The LORD commanded by the **h** of 3027
21: 8 as the LORD commanded by the **h** of 3027
21:44 delivered all their enemies into their **h**. 3027
22: 9 the word of the LORD by the **h** of Moses. 3027
22:31 of Israel out of the **h** of the LORD. 3027
23: 6 *ye* turn not aside therefrom *to* the **right h** 3225
24: 8 I gave them into your **h**, that ye might 3027
24:10 you still: so I delivered you out of his **h**. 3027
24:11 and I delivered them into your **h**. 3027
Jdg 1: 2 behold, I have delivered the land into his **h**. 3027
1: 4 and the Perizzites into their **h**: 3027
1:35 yet the **h** of the house of Joseph prevailed, 3027
2:15 the **h** of the LORD was against them for 3027
2:16 which delivered them out of the **h** of those 3027
2:18 delivered them out of the **h** of their enemies 3027
2:23 neither delivered he them into the **h** of 3027
3: 4 which he commanded their fathers by the **h** 3027
3: 8 he sold them into the **h** of 3027
Jdg 3:10 king of Mesopotamia into his **h**; 3027
3:10 his **h** prevailed against Chushan rishathaim. 3027
3:21 Ehud put forth his left **h**, and took 3027
3:28 your enemies the Moabites into your **h**. 3027
3:30 So Moab was subdued that day under the **h** 3027
4: 2 the LORD sold them into the **h** of Jabin 3027
4: 7 and I will deliver him into thine **h**. 3027
4: 9 for the LORD shall sell Sisera into the **h** 3027
4:14 LORD hath delivered Sisera into thine **h**: 3027
4:21 took a hammer in her **h**, and went softly 3027
4:24 the **h** of the children of Israel prospered, 3027
5:26 She put her **h** to the nail, and her right hand 3027
5:26 and her **right h** to the workmen's hammer; 3225
6: 1 the LORD delivered them into the **h** of 3027
6: 2 the **h** of Midian prevailed against Israel: 3027
6: 9 I delivered you out of the **h** of 3027
6: 9 out of the **h** of all that oppressed you, and 3027
6:14 thou shalt save Israel from the **h** of 3709
6:21 forth the end of the staff that *was* in his **h**, 3027
6:36 If thou wilt save Israel by mine **h**, as thou 3027
6:37 I know that thou wilt save Israel by mine **h**, 3027
7: 2 saying, Mine own **h** hath saved me. 3027
7: 6 putting their **h** to their mouth, were three 3027
7: 7 and deliver the Midianites into thine **h**: 3027
7: 8 So the people took victuals in their **h**, and 3027
7: 9 the host; for I have delivered it into thine **h**. 3027
7:14 *for* into his **h** hath God delivered Midian, 3027
7:15 for the LORD hath delivered into your **h** 3027
7:16 he put a trumpet in every man's **h**, 3027
8: 6 of Zebah and Zalmunna now in thine **h**, 3027
8: 7 delivered Zebah and Zalmunna into mine **h**, 3027
8:15 of Zebah and Zalmunna now in thine **h**, 3027
8:22 for thou hast delivered us from the **h** of 3027
9:17 and delivered you out of the **h** of Midian: 3027
9:29 would to God this people were under my **h**; 3027
9:48 Abimelech took an axe in his **h**, and 3027
10:12 to me, and I delivered you out of their **h**. 3027
11:21 and all his people into the **h** of Israel, 3027
12: 3 and the LORD delivered them into my **h**: 3027
13: 1 the LORD delivered them into the **h** of 3027
13: 5 he shall begin to deliver Israel out of the **h** 3027
14: 6 have rent a kid, and *he had* nothing in his **h**: 3027
15:12 that we may deliver thee into the **h** of 3027
15:13 bind thee fast, and deliver thee into their **h**: 3027
15:15 put forth his **h**, and took it, and slew a 3027
15:17 that he cast away the jawbone out of his **h**, 3027
15:18 great deliverance into the **h** of thy servant: 3027
15:18 and fall into the **h** of the uncircumcised? 3027
16:18 up unto her, and brought money in their **h**. 3027
16:23 delivered Samson our enemy into our **h**. 3027
16:26 said unto the lad that held him by the **h**, 3027
16:29 of the one with his **right h**, and of the other 3225
17: 3 unto the LORD from my **h** for my son, 3027
18:19 lay thine **h** upon thy mouth, and go with us, 3027
20:28 to morrow I will deliver them into thine **h**. 3027
20:48 as the beast, and all that **came to h**: 4672
Ru 1:13 the **h** of the LORD is gone out against me. 3027
4: 5 What day thou buyest the field of the **h** of 3027
4: 9 and Mahlon's, of the **h** of Naomi. 3027
1Sa 2:13 with a fleshhook of three teeth in his **h**; 3027
4: 3 it may save us out of the **h** of our enemies. 3709
4: 8 who shall deliver us out of the **h** of these 3027
5: 6 the **h** of the LORD was heavy upon them 3027
5: 7 for his **h** is sore upon us, and upon Dagon 3027
5: 9 the **h** of the LORD was against the city 3027
5:11 the city; the **h** of God was very heavy there. 3027
6: 3 it shall be known to you why his **h** is not 3027
6: 5 peradventure he will lighten his **h** from off 3027
6: 9 we shall know that *it is* not his **h** *that* smote 3027
6:12 turned not aside *to* the **right h** or *to* the left; 3225
7: 3 he will deliver you out of the **h** of 3027
7: 8 that he will save us out of the **h** of 3027
7:13 the **h** of the LORD was against 3027
9: 8 I have here at **h** the fourth part of a shekel 3027
9:16 that *he* may save my people out of the **h** of 3027
10:18 delivered you out of the **h** of the Egyptians, 3027
10:18 out of the **h** of all kingdoms, *and* of them 3027
12: 3 of whose **h** have I received *any* bribe to 3027
12: 4 hast thou taken ought of any man's **h**. 3027
12: 5 that ye have not found ought in my **h**. 3027
12: 9 he sold them into the **h** of Sisera, captain of 3027
12: 9 into the **h** of the Philistines, and into 3027
12: 9 into the **h** of the king of Moab, and 3027
12:10 now deliver us out of the **h** of our enemies, 3027
12:11 delivered you out of the **h** of your enemies 3027
12:15 shall the **h** of the LORD be against you, 3027
13:22 **h** of any of the people that *were* with Saul 3027
14:10 the LORD hath delivered them into our **h**: 3027
14:12 hath delivered them into the **h** of Israel. 3027
14:19 Saul said unto the priest, Withdraw thine **h**. 3027
14:26 but no man put his **h** to his mouth: 3027
14:27 forth the end of the rod that *was* in his **h**, 3027
14:27 a honeycomb, and put his **h** to his mouth; 3027
14:37 wilt thou deliver them into the **h** of Israel? 3027
14:43 with the end of the rod that *was* in mine **h**, 3027
16:16 that he shall play with his **h**, and thou shalt 3027
16:23 David took a harp, and played with his **h**: 3027
17:22 David left his carriage in the **h** of 3027
17:37 he will deliver me out of the **h** of this 3027
17:40 he took his staff in his **h**, and chose him 3027
17:40 even in a scrip; and his sling *was* in his **h**: 3027
17:46 will the LORD deliver thee into mine **h**; 3027
17:49 David put his **h** in *his* bag, and took thence 3027
17:50 but *there was* no sword in the **h** of David. 3027
17:57 Saul with the head of the Philistine in his **h**. 3027
18:10 David played with his **h**, as at other times: 3027
18:10 and *there was* a javelin in Saul's **h**. 3027
18:17 Let not mine **h** be upon him, but let 3027
18:17 but let the **h** of the Philistines be upon him. 3027
18:21 that the **h** of the Philistines may be against 3027
18:25 Saul thought to make David fall by the **h** of 3027
19: 5 For he did put his life in his **h**, and slew 3709
19: 9 he sat in his house with his javelin in his **h**: 3027
19: 9 in his hand: and David played with *his* **h**. 3027
20:16 even require *it* at the **h** of David's enemies. 3027

1Sa 20:19 hide thyself when the business was *in* **h**, NIH
21: 3 Now therefore what is under thine **h**? 3027
21: 3 give *me* five *loaves of* bread in mine **h**, or 3027
21: 4 *There is* no common bread under mine **h**, 3027
21: 8 is there not here under thine **h** spear or 3027
22: 6 having his spear in his **h**, and all his 3027
22:17 because their **h** also *is* with David, and 3027
22:17 **h** to fall upon the priests of the LORD. 3027
23: 4 for I will deliver the Philistines into thine **h**. 3027
23: 6 *that* he came down *with* an ephod in his **h**. 3027
23: 7 God hath delivered him into mine **h**; 3027
23:11 the men of Keilah deliver me up into his **h**? 3027
23:12 deliver me and my men into the **h** of Saul? 3027
23:14 but God delivered him not into his **h**. 3027
23:16 the wood, and strengthened his **h** in God. 3027
23:17 for the **h** of Saul my father shall not find 3027
23:20 *shall be* to deliver him into the king's **h**. 3027
24: 4 I will deliver thine enemy into thine **h**, 3027
24: 6 to stretch forth mine **h** against him, 3027
24:10 thee to day into mine **h** in the cave: 3027
24:10 I will not put forth mine **h** against my lord; 3027
24:11 see, yea see the skirt of thy robe in my **h**: 3027
24:11 *is* neither evil nor transgression in mine **h**, 3027
24:12 of thee: but mine **h** shall not be upon thee. 3027
24:13 but mine **h** shall not be upon thee. 3027
24:15 my cause, and deliver me out of thine **h**. 3027
24:18 the LORD had delivered me into thine **h**, 3027
24:20 of Israel shall be established in thine **h**. 3027
25: 8 whatsoever cometh to thine **h** unto thy 3027
25:26 *from* avenging thyself with thine own **h**, 3027
25:33 *from* avenging myself with mine own **h**. 3027
25:35 So David received of her **h** *that* which she 3027
25:39 cause of my reproach from the **h** of Nabal, 3027
26: 8 hath delivered thine enemy into thine **h** 3027
26: 9 for who can stretch forth his **h** against 3027
26:11 mine **h** against the LORD'S anointed: 3027
26:18 have I done? or what evil *is* in mine **h**? 3027
26:23 for the LORD delivered thee into *my* **h** to 3027
26:23 I would not stretch forth mine **h** against 3027
27: 1 I shall now perish one day by the **h** of Saul: 3027
27: 1 of Israel: so shall I escape out of his **h**. 3027
28:17 hath rent the kingdom out of thine **h**, 3027
28:19 Israel with thee into the **h** of the Philistines: 3027
28:19 host of Israel into the **h** of the Philistines. 3027
28:21 I have put my life in my **h**, and 3709
30:23 company that came against us into our **h**. 3027
2Sa 1:14 thine **h** to destroy the LORD'S anointed? 3027
2:19 in going he turned not to the **right h** nor to 3225
2:21 Turn thee aside to thy **right h** or to thy left, 3225
3: 8 have not delivered thee into the **h** of David, 3027
3:12 behold, my **h** *shall be* with thee, to bring 3027
3:18 By the **h** of my servant David I will save 3027
3:18 people Israel out of the **h** of the Philistines, 3027
3:18 and out of the **h** of all their enemies. 3027
4:11 therefore now require his blood of your **h**, 3027
5:19 wilt thou deliver them into mine **h**? 3027
5:19 deliver the Philistines into thine **h**. 3027
6: 6 Uzzah put forth *his* **h** to the ark of God, and NIH
8: 1 David took Metheg-ammah out of the **h** of 3027
10: 2 David sent to comfort him by the **h** of his 3027
10:10 delivered into the **h** of Abishai his brother, 3027
11:14 letter to Joab, and sent *it* by the **h** of Uriah. 3027
12: 7 and I delivered thee out of the **h** of Saul; 3027
12:25 And he sent by the **h** of Nathan the prophet; 3027
13: 5 that I may see *it*, and eat *it* at her **h**. 3027
13: 6 of cakes in my sight, that I may eat at her **h**. 3027
13:10 *into* the chamber, that I may eat of thine **h**. 3027
13:19 laid her **h** on her head, and went on crying. 3027
14:16 to deliver his handmaid out of the **h** of 3709
14:19 *Is not* the **h** of Joab with thee in all this? 3027
14:19 none can **turn to the right h** or to the left 3231
15: 5 he put forth his **h**, and took him, and 3027
16: 6 all the mighty *men were* on his **right h** and 3225
16: 8 the kingdom into the **h** of Absalom thy son: 3027
18: 2 third part of the people under the **h** of Joab, 3027
18: 2 a third part under the **h** of Abishai the son 3027
18: 2 a third part under the **h** of Ittai the Gittite. 3027
18:12 a thousand *shekels of* silver in mine **h**, 3709
18:12 *yet* would I not put forth mine **h** against 3027
18:14 he took three darts in his **h**, and thrust them 3709
18:28 that lift up their **h** against my lord the king. 3027
19: 9 The king saved us out of the **h** of our 3709
19: 9 he delivered us out of the **h** of 3709
20: 9 by the beard with the right **h** to kiss him. 3027
20:10 no heed to the sword that *was* in Joab's **h**: 3027
20:21 hath lift up his **h** against the king, 3027
21:20 that had on every **h** six fingers, and 3027
21:22 fell by the **h** of David, and by the hand of 3027
21:22 hand of David, and by the **h** of his servants. 3027
22: 1 him out of the **h** of all his enemies, 3709
22: 1 of all his enemies, and out of the **h** of Saul: 3709
23:10 smote the Philistines until his **h** was weary, 3027
23:10 was weary, and his **h** clave unto the sword: 3027
23:21 the Egyptian had a spear in his **h**; but 3027
23:21 plucked the spear out of the Egyptian's **h**, 3027
24:14 let us fall now into the **h** of the LORD; 3027
24:14 and let me not fall into the **h** of man. 3027
24:16 when the angel stretched out his **h** *upon* 3027
24:16 stay now thine **h**. And the angel of 3027
24:17 let thine **h**, I pray thee, be against me, and 3027
1Ki 2:19 king's mother; and she sat on his **right h**. 3225
2:25 king Solomon sent by the **h** of Benaiah 3027
2:46 the kingdom was established in the **h** of 3027
8:15 and hath with his **h** fulfilled *it*, saying, 3027
8:24 hast fulfilled *it* with thine **h**, as *it is* this 3027
8:42 of thy strong **h**, and of thy stretched out 3027
8:53 as thou spakest by the **h** of Moses thy 3027
8:56 which he promised by the **h** of Moses his 3027
11:12 *but* I will rend it out of the **h** of thy son. 3027
11:26 even he lift up *his* **h** against the king. 3027
11:27 this *was* the cause that he lift up *his* **h** 3027
11:31 I will rent the kingdom out of the **h** of 3027
11:34 not take the whole kingdom out of his **h**: 3027
11:35 I will take the kingdom out of his son's **h**, 3027
13: 4 that he put forth his **h** from the altar, 3027

1Ki 13: 4 his **h**, which he put forth against him, 3027
13: 6 that my **h** may be restored me again. 3027
13: 6 the king's **h** was restored him again, and 3027
14:18 which he spake by the **h** of his servant 3027
15:18 delivered them into the **h** of his servants: 3027
16: 7 also by the **h** of the prophet Jehu the son of 3027
17:11 I pray thee, a morsel of bread in thine **h**. 3027
18: 9 deliver thy servant into the **h** of Ahab, 3027
18:44 a little cloud out of the sea, like a man's **h**. 3709
18:46 the **h** of the LORD was on Elijah; and 3027
20: 6 they shall put *it* in their **h**, and take *it* away. 3027
20:13 I will deliver it into thine **h** *this* day; 3027
20:28 deliver all this great multitude into thine **h**, 3027
20:42 Because thou hast let go out of *thy* **h** a man 3027
22: 3 take it not out of the **h** of the king of Syria? 3027
22: 6 for the Lord shall deliver *it* into the **h** of 3027
22:12 LORD shall deliver *it* into the king's **h**. 3027
22:15 for the LORD shall deliver *it* into the **h** of 3027
22:19 of heaven standing by him on his **right h** 3225
22:34 Turn thine **h**, and carry me out of the host; 3027
2Ki 3:10 to deliver them into the **h** of Moab. 3027
3:13 to deliver them into the **h** of Moab. 3027
3:15 that the **h** of the LORD came upon him. 3027
3:18 will deliver the Moabites also into your **h**. 3027
4:29 take my staff in thine **h**, and go *thy way*: if 3027
5:11 strike his **h** over the place, and recover 3027
5:18 he leaneth on my **h**, and I bow myself *in* 3027
5:24 he took *them* from their **h**, and 3027
6: 7 to thee. And he put out his **h**, and took it. 3027
7: 2 a lord on whose **h** the king leaned answered 3027
7:17 the king appointed the lord on whose **h** he 3027
8: 8 Take a present in thine **h**, and go, meet 3027
8:20 In his days Edom revolted from under the **h** 3027
8:22 Yet Edom revolted from under the **h** of 3027
9: 1 take this box of oil in thine **h**, and go *to* 3027
9: 7 servants of the LORD, at the **h** of Jezebel. 3027
10:15 If it be, give *me* thine **h**. And he gave *him* 3027
10:15 he gave *him* his **h**; and he took him up to 3027
11: 8 every man with his weapons in his **h**: 3027
11:11 every man with his weapons in his **h**, 3027
12:15 into whose **h** they delivered the money to 3027
13: 3 he delivered them into the **h** of Hazael king 3027
13: 3 into the **h** of Ben-hadad the son of Hazael, 3027
13: 5 that they went out from under the **h** of 3027
13:16 king of Israel, Put thine **h** upon the bow. 3027
13:16 he put his **h** *upon it*: and Elisha put his 3027
13:25 **h** of Ben-hadad the son of Hazael the cities, 3027
13:25 which he had taken out of the **h** of 3027
14: 5 as the kingdom was confirmed in his **h**, 3027
14:25 which he spake by the **h** of his servant 3027
14:27 he saved them by the **h** of Jeroboam the son 3027
15:19 that his **h** might be with him to confirm 3027
15:19 with him to confirm the kingdom in his **h**. 3027
16: 7 save me out of the **h** of the king of Syria, 3709
16: 7 out of the **h** of the king of Israel, which rise 3709
17: 7 from under the **h** of Pharaoh king of Egypt, 3027
17:20 and delivered them into the **h** of spoilers, 3027
17:39 he shall deliver you out of the **h** of all your 3027
18:21 man lean, it will go into his **h**, and pierce it: 3709
18:29 shall not be able to deliver you out of his **h**: 3027
18:30 this city shall not be delivered into the **h** of 3027
18:33 his land out of the **h** of the king of Assyria? 3027
18:34 have they delivered Samaria out of mine **h**? 3027
18:35 have delivered their country out of mine **h**, 3027
18:35 should deliver Jerusalem out of mine **h**? 3027
19:10 Jerusalem shall not be delivered into the **h** 3027
19:14 Hezekiah received the letter of the **h** of 3027
19:19 I beseech thee, save *thou* us out of his **h**, 3027
20: 6 this city out of the **h** of the king of Assyria; 3709
21:14 deliver them into the **h** of their enemies; 3027
22: 2 turned not aside *to* the **right h** or *to* the left. 3225
22: 5 let them deliver it into the **h** of the doers of 3027
22: 7 the money that was delivered into their **h**, 3027
22: 9 have delivered it into the **h** of them that do 3027
23: 8 which *were* on a man's **left h** at the gate of 8040
23:13 which *were* on the **right h** of the mount of 3225
1Ch 4:10 that thine **h** might be with me, and that thou 3027
5:10 war with the Hagarites, who fell by their **h**: 3027
5:20 the Hagarites were delivered into their **h**, 3027
6:15 and Jerusalem by the **h** of Nebuchadnezzar. 3027
6:39 brother Asaph, who stood on his **right h**, 3225
6:44 the sons of Merari *stood* on the **left h**: 8040
11:23 in the Egyptian's **h** *was* a spear like a 3027
11:23 pluckt the spear out of the Egyptian's **h**, 3027
12: 2 could **use** both **the right h** and the left in 3231
13: 9 Uzza put forth his **h** to hold the ark; 3027
13:10 smote him, because he put his **h** to the ark: 3027
14:10 wilt thou deliver them into mine **h**? 3027
14:10 Go up; for I will deliver them into thine **h**. 3027
14:11 by mine **h** like the breaking forth of waters: 3027
16: 7 to thank the LORD into the **h** of Asaph 3027
18: 1 her towns out of the **h** of the Philistines. 3027
19:11 delivered unto the **h** of Abishai his brother, 3027
20: 6 six *on each* **h**, and six *on each foot*: and NIH
20: 8 they fell by the **h** of David, and by the hand 3027
20: 8 hand of David, and by the **h** of his servants. 3027
21:13 let me fall now into the **h** of the LORD; 3027
21:13 but let me not fall into the **h** of man. 3027
21:15 *It is* enough, stay now thine **h**. 3027
21:16 having a drawn sword in his **h** stretched out 3027
21:17 let thine **h**, I pray thee, O LORD my God, 3027
22:18 the inhabitants of the land into mine **h**; 3027
26:28 *anything, it was* under the **h** of Shelomith, 3027
28:19 me understand in writing by *his* **h** upon me, 3027
29: 8 by the **h** of Jehiel the Gershonite. 3027
29:12 in thine **h** *is* power and might; and in thine 3027
29:12 in thine **h** *it is* to make great, and to give 3027
29:16 for thine holy name *cometh* of thine **h**, 3027
2Ch 3:17 one on the **right h**, and the other on 3225
3:17 called the name of *that on* the **right h** 3233
4: 6 put five on the **right h**, and five on the left, 3225
4: 7 five on the **right h**, and five on the left. 3225
6:15 hast fulfilled *it* with thine **h**, as *it is* this 3027
6:32 thy mighty **h**, and thy stretched out arm; 3027
10:15 which he spake by the **h** of Ahijah 3027

2Ch 12: 5 have I also left you in the **h** of Shishak. 3027
12: 7 out upon Jerusalem by the **h** of Shishak. 3027
13: 8 the LORD in the **h** of the sons of David; 3027
13:16 and God delivered them into their **h**. 3027
16: 7 of the king of Syria escaped out of thine **h**. 3027
16: 8 the LORD, he delivered them into thine **h**. 3027
17: 5 LORD stablished the kingdom in his **h**; 3027
18: 5 for God will deliver *it* into the king's **h**. 3027
18:11 for the LORD shall deliver *it* into the **h** of 3027
18:14 and they shall be delivered into your **h**. 3027
18:18 the host of heaven standing on his **right h** 3225
18:33 he said to *his* chariot man, Turn thine **h**, 3027
20: 6 and in thine **h** *is there not* power and might, 3027
21:10 So the Edomites revolted from under the **h** 3027
21:10 also did Libnah revolt from under his **h**; 3027
23: 7 every man with his weapons in his **h**; 3027
23:10 every man having his weapon in his **h**, 3027
23:18 LORD by the **h** of the priests the Levites, 3027
24:11 the king's office by the **h** of the Levites, 3027
24:24 delivered a very great host into their **h**, 3027
25:15 not deliver their own people out of thine **h**? 3027
25:20 that *he* might deliver them into the **h** *of* 3027
26:11 of their account by the **h** of Jeiel the scribe 3027
26:11 the ruler, under the **h** of Hananiah, 3027
26:13 under their **h** *was* an army, three hundred 3027
26:19 and *had* a censer in his **h** to burn incense: 3027
28: 5 him into the **h** of the king of Syria; 3027
28: 5 he was also delivered into the **h** of the king 3027
28: 9 he hath delivered them into your **h**, and 3027
30: 6 that are escaped out of the **h** of the kings of 3709
30:12 Also in Judah the **h** of God was to give 3027
30:16 *which they received* of the **h** of the Levites. 3027
31:13 *were* overseers under the **h** of Cononiah 3027
32:11 us out of the **h** of the king of Assyria? 3709
32:13 able to deliver their lands out of mine **h**? 3027
32:14 that could deliver his people out of mine **h**, 3027
32:14 be able to deliver you out of mine **h**? 3027
32:15 able to deliver his people out of mine **h**, 3027
32:15 mine hand, and out of the **h** of my fathers: 3027
32:15 shall your God deliver you out of mine **h**? 3027
32:17 not delivered their people out of mine **h**, 3027
32:17 Hezekiah deliver his people out of mine **h**. 3027
32:22 the inhabitants of Jerusalem from the **h** of 3027
32:22 from the **h** of all *other*, and guided them on 3027
33: 8 and the ordinances by the **h** of Moses. 3027
34: 2 declined neither *to* the **right h**, nor *to* 3225
34: 9 doors had gathered of the **h** of Manasseh 3027
34:10 they put *it* in the **h** of the workmen that had 3027
34:17 have delivered it into the **h** of the overseers, 3027
34:17 the overseers, and to the **h** of the workmen. 3027
35: 6 the word of the LORD by the **h** of Moses. 3027
36:17 stooped for age: he gave *them* all into his **h**. 3027
Ezr 1: 8 forth by the **h** of Mithredath the treasurer, 3027
5:12 he gave them into the **h** of Nebuchadnezzar 3028
6:12 that shall put to their **h** to alter *and* 3028
7: 6 according to the **h** of the LORD his God 3027
7: 9 according to the good **h** of his God upon 3027
7:14 to the law of thy God which *is* in thine **h**; 3028
7:25 that *is* in thine **h**, set magistrates and 3028
7:28 I was strengthened as the **h** of the LORD 3027
8:18 by the good **h** of our God upon us they 3027
8:22 The **h** of our God *is* upon all them for good 3027
8:26 I even weighed unto their **h** six hundred 3027
8:31 the **h** of our God was upon us, and 3027
8:31 he delivered us from the **h** of the enemy, 3709
8:33 **h** of Meremoth the son of Uriah the priest; 3027
9: 2 the **h** of the princes and rulers hath been 3027
9: 7 been delivered into the **h** of the kings of 3027
Ne 1:10 by thy great power, and by thy strong **h**. 3027
2: 8 according to the good **h** of my God upon 3027
2:18 I told them of the **h** of my God which was 3027
4:17 and with the other *h* held a weapon. NIH
6: 5 the fifth time with an open letter in his **h**; 3027
8: 4 and Hilkiah, and Maaseiah, on his **right h**; 3225
8: 4 and on his **left h**, Pedaiah, and Mishael, and 8040
9:14 and laws, by the **h** of Moses thy servant: 3027
9:27 Therefore thou deliveredst them into the **h** 3027
9:27 who saved them out of the **h** of their 3027
9:28 leftest thou them in the **h** of their enemies, 3027
9:30 gavest thou them into the **h** of the people of 3027
11:24 *was* at the king's **h** in all matters 3027
12:31 whereof *one* went on the **right h** upon 3225
Est 2:21 and sought to lay **h** on the king Ahasuerus. 3027
3:10 the king took his ring from his **h**, and 3027
5: 2 Esther the golden sceptre that *was* in his **h**. 3027
6: 2 who sought to lay **h** on the king Ahasuerus. 3027
6: 9 horse be delivered to the **h** of one of 3027
8: 7 because he laid his **h** upon the Jews. 3027
9: 2 to lay **h** on such as sought their hurt: 3027
9:10 but on the spoil laid they not their **h**. 3027
9:15 but on the prey they laid not their **h**. 3027
Job 1:11 put forth thine **h** now, and touch all that he 3027
1:12 only upon himself put not forth thine **h**. 3027
2: 5 put forth thine **h** now, and touch his bone 3027
2: 6 said unto Satan, Behold, he *is* in thine **h**; 3027
2:10 shall we receive good **at the h of** God, 854+4480
5:15 their mouth, and from the **h** of the mighty. 3027
6: 9 *that* he would let loose his **h**, and cut me 3027
6:23 Or, Deliver me from the enemy's **h**? or, 3027
6:23 or, Redeem me from the **h** of the mighty? 3027
9:24 The earth is given into the **h** of the wicked: 3027
9:33 *that* might lay his **h** upon us both. 3027
10: 7 *there is* none that can deliver out of thine **h**. 3027
11:14 If iniquity *be* in thine **h**, put it far away, and 3027
12: 6 into whose **h** God bringeth *abundantly*. 3027
12: 9 Who knoweth not in all these that the **h** of 3027
12:10 In whose **h** *is* the soul of every living *thing*, 3027
13:14 in my teeth, and put my life in mine **h**? 3709
13:21 Withdraw thine **h** far from me: and let not 3709
15:23 that the day of darkness is ready at his **h**. 3027
15:25 For he stretcheth out his **h** against God, and 3027
19:21 for the **h** of God hath touched me. 3027
20:22 every **h** of the wicked shall come *upon* him. 3027
21: 5 and lay *your* **h** upon *your* mouth. 3027
21:16 Lo, their good *is* not in their **h**: the counsel 3027

Job 23: 9 *On* the **left h**, where he doth work, but 8040
23: 9 *him:* he hideth *himself on* the **right h**, 3225
26:13 his **h** hath formed the crooked serpent. 3027
27:11 I will teach you by the **h** of God: *that* which 3027
27:22 not spare: he would fain flee out of his **h**. 3027
28: 9 He putteth forth his **h** upon the rock; 3027
29: 9 and laid *their* **h** on their mouth. 3709
29:20 in me, and my bow was renewed in my **h**. 3027
30:12 Upon *my* **right h** rise the youth; they push 3225
30:21 with thy strong **h** thou opposest thyself 3027
30:24 Howbeit *he* will not stretch out *his* **h** to 3027
31:21 If I have lift up my **h** against the fatherless, 3027
31:25 and because mine **h** had gotten much; 3027
31:27 or my mouth hath kissed my **h**: 3027
33: 7 neither shall my **h** be heavy upon thee. 405
34:20 the mighty shall be taken away without **h**. 3027
35: 7 thou him? or what receiveth he of thine **h**? 3027
37: 7 He sealeth up the **h** of every man; that all 3027
40: 4 I will lay my **h** upon my mouth. 3027
40:14 thee that thine own **right h** can save thee. 3225
41: 8 Lay thine **h** upon him, remember the battle, 3709
Ps 10:12 Arise, O LORD; O God, lift up thine **h**: 3027
10:14 and spite, to requite *it* with thy **h**: 3027
16: 8 because *he is* at my **right h**, I shall not be 3225
16:11 at thy **right h** *there are* pleasures for 3225
17: 7 O thou that savest by thy **right h** them 3225
17:14 From men *which are* thy **h**, O LORD, 3027
18: T delivered him from the **h** of all his enemies, 3709
18: T of all his enemies, and from the **h** of Saul: 3027
18:35 thy **right h** hath holden me up, and 3225
20: 6 with the saving strength of his **right h**. 3225
21: 8 Thine **h** shall find out all thine enemies: 3027
21: 8 thy **right h** shall find out those that hate 3225
26:10 and their **right h** is full *of* bribes. 3225
31: 5 Into thine **h** I commit my spirit: thou hast 3027
31: 8 hast not shut me up into the **h** of 3027
31:15 My times *are* in thy **h**: deliver me from 3027
31:15 deliver me from the **h** of mine enemies, and 3027
32: 4 and night thy **h** was heavy upon me: 3027
36:11 and let not the **h** of the wicked remove me. 3027
37:24 for the LORD upholdeth *him with* his **h**. 3027
37:33 The LORD will not leave him in his **h**, 3027
38: 2 stick fast in me, and thy **h** presseth me sore. 3027
39:10 I am consumed by the blow of thine **h**. 3027
44: 2 thou didst drive out the heathen *with* thy **h**, 3027
44: 3 thy **right h**, and thine arm, and the light of 3225
45: 4 thy **right h** shall teach thee terrible *things.* 3225
45: 9 **right h** did stand the queen in gold of 3225
48:10 thy **right h** is full *of* righteousness. 3225
60: 5 save *with* thy **right h**, and hear me. 3225
63: 8 hard after thee: thy **right h** upholdeth me. 3225
71: 4 O my God, out of the **h** of the wicked, 3027
71: 4 out of the **h** of the unrighteous and 3709
73:23 thou hast holden *me* by my right **h**. 3027
74:11 Why withdrawest thou thy **h**, even thy right 3027
74:11 thou thy hand, even thy **right h**? 3225
75: 8 For in the **h** of the LORD *there is* a cup, 3027
77:10 *I will remember* the years of the **right h** of 3225
77:20 thy people like a flock by the **h** of Moses 3027
78:42 They remembered not his **h**: *nor* the day 3027
78:54 *which* his **right h** had purchased. 3225
78:61 and his glory into the enemy's **h**. 3027
80:15 the vineyard which thy **right h** hath 3225
80:17 Let thy **h** be upon the man of thy right 3027
80:17 thy hand be upon the man of thy **right h**, 3225
81:14 and turned my **h** against their adversaries. 3027
82: 4 needy: rid *them* out of the **h** of the wicked. 3027
88: 5 no more: and they are cut off from thy **h**. 3027
89:13 strong is thy **h**, *and* high is thy right hand. 3027
89:13 strong is thy hand, *and* high is thy **right h**. 3225
89:21 With whom my **h** shall be established: 3027
89:25 I will set his **h** also in the sea, and his right 3027
89:25 also in the sea, and his **right h** in the rivers. 3225
89:42 Thou hast set up the **right h** of his 3225
89:48 shall he deliver his soul from the **h** of 3027
91: 7 at thy side, and ten thousand at thy **right h**; 3225
95: 4 In his **h** *are* the deep places of the earth: 3027
95: 7 of his pasture, and the sheep of his **h**. 3027
97:10 he delivereth them out of the **h** of 3027
98: 1 hath done marvellous *things:* his **right h**, 3225
104:28 thou openest thine **h**, they are filled *with* 3027
106:10 he saved them from the **h** of him that hated 3027
106:10 redeemed them from the **h** of the enemy. 3027
106:26 Therefore he lifted up his **h** against them, 3027
106:41 And he gave them into the **h** of the heathen; 3027
106:42 were brought into subjection under their **h**. 3027
107: 2 whom he hath redeemed from the **h** of 3027
108: 6 save *with* thy **right h**, and answer me. 3225
109: 6 over him: and let Satan stand at his **right h**. 3225
109:27 That they may know that this *is* thy **h**; 3027
109:31 For he shall stand at the **right h** of the poor, 3225
110: 1 said unto my Lord, Sit thou at my **right h**, 3225
110: 5 The Lord at thy **right h** shall strike through 3225
118:15 the **right h** of the LORD doeth valiantly. 3225
118:16 The **right h** of the LORD is exalted: 3225
118:16 the **right h** of the LORD doeth valiantly. 3225
119:109 My soul *is* continually in my **h**: yet do I not 3709
119:173 Let thine **h** help me; for I have chosen thy 3027
121: 5 the LORD *is* thy shade upon thy right **h**. 3225
123: 2 as the eyes of servants *look* unto the **h** of 3027
123: 2 as the eyes of a maiden unto the **h** of her 3027
127: 4 As arrows *are* in the **h** of a mighty *man;* so 3027
129: 7 Where*with* the mower filleth not his **h**; 3709
136:12 With a strong **h**, and with a stretched out 3027
137: 5 let my **right h** forget *her cunning.* 3225
138: 7 thou shalt stretch forth thine **h** against 3027
138: 7 and thy **right h** shall save me. 3225
139: 5 and before, and laid thine **h** upon me. 3709
139:10 Even there shall thy **h** lead me, and 3027
139:10 lead me, and thy **right h** shall hold me. 3225
142: 4 I looked *on my* **right h**, and beheld, but 3225
144: 7 Send thine **h** from above; rid me, and 3027
144: 7 from the **h** of strange children; 3027
144: 8 their **right h** *is* a right hand of falsehood. 3225
144: 8 their right hand *is* a **right h** of falsehood. 3225
Ps 144:11 deliver me from the **h** of strange children, 3027
144:11 their **right h** *is* a right hand of falsehood: 3225
144:11 their right hand *is* a **right h** of falsehood: 3225
145:16 Thou openest thine **h**, and satisfiest 3027
149: 6 and a twoedged sword in their **h**; 3027
Pr 1:24 I have stretched out my **h**, and no man 3027
3:16 Length of days *is* in her **right h**; and in her 3225
3:16 and in her **left h** riches and honour. 8040
3:27 when it is in the power of thine **h** to do *it.* 3027
4:27 Turn not *to* the **right h** nor *to* the left: 3225
6: 1 *if* thou hast stricken thy **h** with a stranger, 3709
6: 3 when thou art come into the **h** of thy friend; 3709
6: 5 Deliver thyself as a roe from the **h** *of* 3027
6: 5 and as a bird from the **h** of the fowler. 3027
10: 4 *becometh* poor that dealeth *with* a slack **h**: 3709
10: 4 but the **h** of the diligent maketh rich. 3027
11:21 *Though* **h** *join* in hand, the wicked shall not 3027
11:21 *Though* hand *join* in **h**, the wicked shall not 3027
12:24 The **h** of the diligent shall bear rule: but 3027
16: 5 *though* **h** *join* in hand, he shall not be 3027
16: 5 *though* hand *join* in **h**, he shall not be 3027
17:16 Wherefore *is there* a price in the **h** of a fool 3027
19:24 A slothful *man* hideth his **h** in *his* bosom, 3027
21: 1 The king's heart *is* in the **h** of the LORD, 3027
26: 6 He that sendeth a message by the **h** of a 3027
26: 9 *As* a thorn goeth up into the **h** of a 3027
26:15 The slothful hideth his **h** in *his* bosom; 3027
27:16 the wind, and the ointment of his **right h**, 3225
30:32 thought evil, *lay thine* **h** upon thy mouth. 3027
31:20 She stretcheth out her **h** to the poor; yea, 3709
Ecc 2:24 also I saw, that it *was* from the **h** of God. 3027
5:14 a son, and *there is* nothing in his **h**. 3027
5:15 which he may carry away in his **h**. 3027
7:18 yea, also from this withdraw not thine **h**: 3027
9: 1 and their works, *are* in the **h** of God: 3027
9:10 Whatsoever thy **h** findeth to do, do *it* with 3027
10: 2 A wise *man's* heart *is* at his **right h**; but 3225
11: 6 and in the evening withhold not thine **h**: 3027
SS 2: 6 His **left h** *is* under my head, and his right 8040
2: 6 my head, and his **right h** doth embrace me. 3225
5: 4 My beloved put in his **h** by the hole *of* 3027
8: 3 His **left h** *should be* under my head, and 8040
8: 3 and his **right h** should embrace me. 3225
Isa 1:12 who hath required this at your **h**, to tread 3027
1:25 I will turn my **h** upon thee, and purely 3027
3: 6 our ruler, and *let* this ruin *be* under thy **h**: 3027
5:25 he hath stretched forth his **h** against them, 3027
5:25 turned away, but his **h** *is* stretched out still. 3027
6: 6 unto me, having a live coal in his **h**, 3027
8:11 LORD spake thus to me with a strong **h**, 3027
9:12 turned away, but his **h** *is* stretched out still. 3027
9:17 turned away, but his **h** *is* stretched out still. 3027
9:20 he shall snatch on the **right h**, and 3225
9:20 he shall eat on the **left h**, and they shall not 8040
9:21 turned away, but his **h** *is* stretched out still. 3027
10: 4 turned away, but his **h** *is* stretched out still. 3027
10: 5 and the staff in their **h** *is* mine indignation. 3027
10:10 As my **h** hath found the kingdoms of 3027
10:13 By the strength of my **h** I have done *it,* and 3027
10:14 my **h** hath found as a nest the riches of 3027
10:32 he shall shake his **h** *against* the mount of 3027
11: 8 the weaned child shall put his **h** on 3027
11:11 *that* the Lord shall set his **h** again 3027
11:14 they shall lay their **h** upon Edom and 3027
11:15 with his mighty wind shall he shake his **h** 3027
13: 2 exalt the voice unto them, shake the **h**, 3027
13: 6 Howl ye; for the day of the LORD *is* **at h**; 7138
14:26 this *is* the **h** that is stretched out upon all 3027
14:27 shall disannul *it?* and his **h** *is* stretched out, 3027
19: 4 the Egyptians will I give over into the **h** of 3027
19:16 of the shaking of the **h** of the LORD of 3027
22:21 I will commit thy government into his **h**: 3027
23:11 He stretched out his **h** over the sea, 3027
25:10 For in this mountain shall the **h** of 3027
26:11 LORD, *when* thy **h** is lifted up, they will 3027
28: 2 shall cast down to the earth with the **h**. 3027
28: 4 while it is yet in his **h** he eateth it up. 3709
30:21 when ye **turn to the right h**, and when ye 541
31: 3 When the LORD shall stretch out his **h**, 3027
34:17 and his **h** hath divided it unto them by line: 3027
36: 6 man lean, it will go into his **h**, and pierce it: 3709
36:15 this city shall not be delivered into the **h** of 3027
36:18 his land out of the **h** of the king of Assyria? 3027
36:19 have they delivered Samaria out of my **h**? 3027
36:20 that have delivered their land out of my **h**, 3027
36:20 should deliver Jerusalem out of my **h**? 3027
37:10 Jerusalem shall not be given into the **h** of 3027
37:14 Hezekiah received the letter from the **h** of 3027
37:20 O LORD our God, save us from his **h**, 3027
38: 6 this city out of the **h** of the king of Assyria: 3709
40: 2 for she hath received of the LORD'S **h** 3027
40:10 the Lord GOD will come with strong *h*, NIH
40:12 measured the waters in the **hollow of** his **h**, 8168
41:10 I will uphold thee with the **right h** of my 3225
41:13 I the LORD thy God will hold thy **right h**, 3225
41:20 that the **h** of the LORD hath done this, 3027
42: 6 will hold thine **h**, and will keep thee, and 3027
43:13 *there is* none that can deliver out of my **h**: 3027
44: 5 another shall subscribe *with* his **h** unto 3027
44:20 nor say, *Is there* not a lie in my **right h**? 3225
45: 1 to Cyrus, whose **right h** I have holden, to 3225
47: 6 and given them into thine **h**: 3027
48:13 Mine **h** also hath laid the foundation of 3027
48:13 and my **right h** hath spanned the heavens: 3225
49: 2 in the shadow of his **h** hath he hid me, and 3027
49:22 I will lift up mine **h** to the Gentiles, and 3027
50: 2 Is my **h** shortened at all, that *it* cannot 3027
50:11 This shall ye have of mine **h**, ye shall lie 3027
51:16 have covered thee in the shadow of mine **h**, 3027
51:17 which hast drunk at the **h** of the LORD 3027
51:18 neither *is there any* that taketh her by the **h** 3027
51:22 I have taken out of thine **h** the cup of 3027
51:23 I will put it into the **h** of them that afflict 3027
53:10 of the LORD shall prosper in his **h**. 3027
54: 3 For thou shalt break forth *on* the **right h** 3225
Isa 56: 2 and keepeth his **h** from doing any evil. 3027
57:10 thou hast found the life of thine **h**; therefore 3027
59: 1 Behold, the LORD'S **h** is not shortened, 3027
62: 3 Thou shalt also be a crown of glory in the **h** 3027
62: 3 and a royal diadem in the **h** of thy God. 3709
62: 8 The LORD hath sworn by his **right h**, and 3225
63:12 That led *them* by the **right h** of Moses *with* 3225
64: 8 and we all *are* the work of thine **h**. 3027
66: 2 For all those *things* hath mine **h** made, and 3027
66:14 the **h** of the LORD shall be known 3027
Jer 1: 9 the LORD put forth his **h**, and touched my 3027
6: 9 turn back thine **h** as a grapegatherer into 3027
6:12 for I will stretch out my **h** upon 3027
11:21 of the LORD, that thou die not by our **h**: 3027
12: 7 of my soul into the **h** of her enemies. 3709
15: 6 will I stretch out my **h** against thee, 3027
15:17 nor rejoiced; I sat alone because of thy **h**: 3027
15:21 I will deliver thee out of the **h** of 3027
15:21 I will redeem thee out of the **h** of 3709
16:21 I will cause them to know mine **h** and my 3027
18: 4 of clay was marred in the **h** of the potter: 3027
18: 6 as the clay *is* in the potter's **h**, so *are* ye in 3027
18: 6 so *are* ye in mine **h**, O house of Israel. 3027
20: 4 I will give all Judah into the **h** of the king 3027
20: 5 will I give into the **h** of their enemies, 3027
20:13 the soul of the poor from the **h** of evildoers. 3027
21: 5 fight against you with an outstretched **h** 3027
21: 7 into the **h** of Nebuchadrezzar king of 3027
21: 7 into the **h** of their enemies, and into 3027
21: 7 and into the **h** of those that seek their life: 3027
21:10 it shall be given into the **h** of the king of 3027
21:12 deliver *him that is* spoiled out of the **h** of 3027
22: 3 deliver the spoiled out of the **h** of 3027
22:24 of Judah were the signet upon my right **h**, 3027
22:25 I will give thee into the **h** of them that seek 3027
22:25 into the **h** *of them* whose face thou fearest, 3027
22:25 even into the **h** of Nebuchadrezzar king of 3027
22:25 and into the **h** of the Chaldeans. 3027
23:23 *Am* I a God at **h**, saith the LORD, and 7138
25:15 Take the wine cup of this fury at mine **h**, 3027
25:17 took I the cup at the LORD'S **h**, and 3027
25:28 if they refuse to take the cup at thine **h** to 3027
26:14 As for me, behold, I *am* in your **h**: do with 3027
26:24 Nevertheless the **h** of Ahikam the son of 3027
26:24 that *they* should not give him into the **h** of 3027
27: 3 by the **h** of the messengers which come *to* 3027
27: 6 now have I given all these lands into the **h** 3027
27: 8 until I have consumed them by his **h**. 3027
29: 3 By the **h** of Elasah the son of Shaphan, and 3027
29:21 I will deliver them into the **h** of 3027
31:11 ransomed him from the **h** of *him that was* 3027
31:32 fathers in the day *that* I took them by the **h**, 3027
32: 3 I *will* give this city into the **h** of the king of 3027
32: 4 not escape out of the **h** of the Chaldeans, 3027
32: 4 shall surely be delivered into the **h** of 3027
32:21 with a strong **h**, and with a stretched out 3027
32:24 the city is given into the **h** of 3027
32:25 for the city is given into the **h** of 3027
32:28 I *will* give this city into the **h** of 3027
32:28 into the **h** of Nebuchadrezzar king of 3027
32:36 It shall be delivered into the **h** of the king 3027
32:43 it is given into the **h** of the Chaldeans. 3027
34: 2 I *will* give this city into the **h** of the king of 3027
34: 3 thou shalt not escape out of his **h**, but 3027
34: 3 surely be taken, and delivered into his **h**; 3027
34:20 I will even give them into the **h** of their 3027
34:20 and into the **h** of them that seek their life: 3027
34:21 his princes will I give into the **h** of their 3027
34:21 into the **h** of them that seek their life, and 3027
34:21 into the **h** of the king of Babylon's army, 3027
36:14 Take in thine **h** the roll wherein thou hast 3027
36:14 the son of Neriah took the roll in his **h**, 3027
37:17 thou shalt be delivered into the **h** of 3027
38: 3 This city shall surely be given into the **h** of 3027
38: 5 the king said, Behold, he *is* in your **h**: 3027
38:16 neither will I give thee into the **h** of these 3027
38:18 shall this city be given into the **h** of 3027
38:18 and thou shalt not escape out of their **h**. 3027
38:19 lest they deliver me into their **h**, and 3027
38:23 thou shalt not escape out of their **h**, but 3027
38:23 shalt be taken by the **h** of the king of 3027
39:17 thou shalt not be given into the **h** of 3027
40: 4 from the chains which *were* upon thine **h**. 3027
41: 5 with offerings and incense in their **h**, 3027
42:11 to save you, and to deliver you from his **h**. 3027
43: 3 for to deliver us into the **h** of 3027
43: 9 Take great stones in thine **h**, and hide them 3027
44:25 and fulfilled with your **h**, saying, 3027
44:30 king of Egypt into the **h** of his enemies, 3027
44:30 and into the **h** of them that seek his life; 3027
44:30 as I gave Zedekiah king of Judah into the **h** 3027
46:24 she shall be delivered into the **h** of 3027
46:26 I will deliver them into the **h** of those that 3027
46:26 into the **h** of Nebuchadrezzar king of 3027
46:26 of Babylon, and into the **h** of his servants: 3027
50:15 she hath given her **h**: her foundations are 3027
51: 7 *hath been* a golden cup in the LORD'S **h**, 3027
51:25 I will stretch out mine **h** upon thee, and 3027
La 1: 7 when her people fell into the **h** of the 3027
1:10 The adversary hath spread out his **h** upon 3027
1:14 of my transgressions is bound by his **h**: 3027
2: 3 he hath drawn back his **right h** from before 3225
2: 4 *he* stood *with* his **right h** as an adversary, 3225
2: 7 he hath given up into the **h** of the enemy 3027
2: 8 he hath not withdrawn his **h** from 3027
3: 3 he turneth his **h** *against* me all the day. 3027
5: 6 We have given the **h** *to* the Egyptians, *and* 3027
5: 8 *is* none that doth deliver *us* out of their **h**. 3027
5:12 Princes are hanged up by their **h**: the faces 3027
Eze 1: 3 the **h** of the LORD was there upon him. 3027
2: 9 I looked, behold, a **h** *was* sent unto me; 3027
3:14 the **h** of the LORD was strong upon me. 3027
3:18 but his blood will I require at thine **h**. 3027
3:20 but his blood will I require at thine **h**. 3027
3:22 the **h** of the LORD was there upon me; 3027

Eze 6:11 Smite with thine **h**, and stamp with thy 3709
6:14 So will I stretch out mine **h** upon them, and 3027
8: 1 that the **h** of the Lord GOD fell there upon 3027
8: 3 he put forth the form of a **h**, and took me 3027
8:11 with every man his censer in his **h**; 3027
9: 1 man *with* his destroying weapon in his **h**. 3027
9: 2 and every man a slaughter weapon in his **h**; 3027
10: 2 fill thine **h** *with* coals of fire from between 2651
10: 7 *one* cherub stretched forth his **h** from 3027
10: 8 the form of a man's **h** under their wings. 3027
12: 7 I digged through the wall with mine **h**; 3027
12:23 The days are **at h**, and the effect of every 7126
13: 9 mine **h** shall be upon the prophets that see 3027
13:21 deliver my people out of your **h**, and 3027
13:21 they shall be no more in your **h** to be 3027
13:23 for I will deliver my people out of your **h**: 3027
14: 9 I will stretch out my **h** upon him, and 3027
14:13 will I stretch out mine **h** upon it, and 3027
16:27 I have stretched out my **h** over thee, and 3027
16:39 I will also give thee into their **h**, and 3027
16:46 and her daughters that dwell at thy **left h**: 8040
16:46 that dwelleth at thy **right h**, *is* Sodom and 3225
16:49 neither did she strengthen the **h** of the poor 3027
17:18 he had given his **h**, and hath done all these 3027
18: 8 *that* hath withdrawn his **h** from iniquity, 3027
18:17 *That* hath taken off his **h** from the poor, 3027
20: 5 lifted up mine **h** unto the seed of the house 3027
20: 5 when I lifted up mine **h** unto them, saying, 3027
20: 6 In the day *that* I lifted up mine **h** unto them, 3027
20:15 Yet also I lifted up my **h** unto them in 3027
20:22 Nevertheless I withdrew mine **h**, and 3027
20:23 I lifted up mine **h** unto them also in 3027
20:28 *for* the which I lifted up mine **h** to give it to 3027
20:33 surely with a mighty **h**, and with a stretched 3027
20:34 with a mighty **h**, and with a stretched out 3027
20:42 I lifted up mine **h** to give it to your fathers. 3027
21:11 to give it into the **h** of the slayer. 3027
21:16 other, *either* **on the right h**, *or* on the left, 3231
21:22 At his **right h** was the divination for 3225
21:24 ye shall be taken with the **h**. 3709
21:31 deliver thee into the **h** of brutish men, *and* 3027
22:13 I have smitten mine **h** at thy dishonest gain 3709
23: 9 Wherefore I have delivered her into the **h** 3027
23: 9 into the **h** of the Assyrians, upon whom she 3027
23:28 I *will* deliver thee into the **h** *of them* whom 3027
23:28 into the **h** *of them* from whom thy mind is 3027
23:31 therefore will I give her cup into thine **h**. 3027
25: 7 I will stretch out mine **h** upon thee, and 3027
25:13 I will also stretch out mine **h** upon Edom, 3027
25:14 upon Edom by the **h** of my people Israel: 3027
25:16 I *will* stretch out mine **h** upon 3027
27:15 isles *were* the merchandise of thine **h**: 3027
28: 9 no God, in the **h** of him that slayeth thee. 3027
28:10 of the uncircumcised by the **h** of strangers: 3027
29: 7 When they took hold of thee by thy **h**, 3709
30:10 the **h** of Nebuchadrezzar king of Babylon. 3027
30:12 and sell the land into the **h** of the wicked: 3027
30:12 and all that is therein, by the **h** of strangers: 3027
30:22 I will cause the sword to fall out of his **h**. 3027
30:24 of Babylon, and put my sword in his **h**: 3027
30:25 when I shall put my sword into the **h** of 3027
31:11 delivered him into the **h** of the mighty one 3027
33: 6 blood will I require at the watchman's **h**. 3027
33: 8 but his blood will I require at thine **h**. 3027
33:22 Now the **h** of the LORD was upon me in 3027
34:10 I will require my flock at their **h**, and 3027
34:27 delivered them out of the **h** of those that 3027
35: 3 I will stretch out mine **h** against thee, and 3027
36: 7 I have lifted up mine **h**, Surely the heathen 3027
36: 8 people of Israel; for they are **at h** to come. 7126
37: 1 The **h** of the LORD was upon me, and 3027
37:17 and they shall become one in thine **h**. 3027
37:19 which *is* in the **h** of Ephraim, and the tribes 3027
37:19 one stick, and they shall be one in mine **h**. 3027
37:20 writest shall be in thine **h** before their eyes. 3027
38:12 to turn thine **h** upon the desolate places *that* 3027
39: 3 I will smite thy bow out of thy left **h**, and 3027
39: 3 cause thine arrows to fall out of thy right **h**. 3027
39:21 and my **h** that I have laid upon them. 3027
39:23 and gave them into the **h** of their enemies: 3027
40: 1 in the selfsame day the **h** of the LORD 3027
40: 3 with a line of flax in his **h**, and a measuring 3027
40: 5 in the man's **h** a measuring reed of six 3027
40: 5 cubits *long* by the cubit and a **h breadth**: 2948
40:43 **a h broad**, fastened round about: 2948
43:13 The cubit *is* a cubit and a **h breadth**; 2948
44:12 have I lift up mine **h** against them, 3027
46: 7 for the lambs according as his **h** shall attain 3027
47: 3 when the man that had the line in his **h** 3027
47:14 *concerning* the which I lifted up mine **h** to 3027
Da 1: 2 gave Jehoiakim king of Judah into his **h**, 3027
2:38 of the heaven hath he given into thine **h**, 3028
3:17 he will deliver *us* out of thine **h**, O king. 3028
4:35 none can stay his **h**, or say unto him, 3028
5: 5 same hour came forth fingers of a man's **h**, 3028
5: 5 the king saw the part of the **h** that wrote. 3028
5:23 the God in whose **h** thy breath *is*, and 3028
5:24 *was* the part of the **h** sent from him; and 3028
7:25 they shall be given into his **h** until a time 3028
8: 4 *there any* that could deliver out of his **h**; 3027
8: 7 none that could deliver the ram out of his **h**. 3027
8:25 also he shall cause craft to prosper in his **h**; 3027
8:25 but he shall be broken without **h**. 3027
9:15 out of the land of Egypt with a mighty **h**, 3027
10:10 behold, a **h** touched me, which set me upon 3027
11:11 but the multitude shall be given into his **h**. 3027
11:16 which by his **h** shall be consumed. 3027
11:41 these shall escape out of his **h**, *even* Edom, 3027
11:42 He shall stretch forth his **h** also upon 3027
12: 7 when he held up his **right h** and his left 3225
12: 7 his right hand and his **left h** unto heaven, 8040
Hos 2:10 and none shall deliver her out of mine **h**, 3027
7: 5 he stretched out his **h** with scorners. 3027
12: 7 the balances of deceit *are* in his **h**: 3027
Joel 1:15 for the day of the LORD *is* **at h**, and as a 7138

Joel 2: 1 of the LORD cometh, for *it is* **nigh at h**; 7138
3: 8 your daughters into the **h** of the children of 3027
Am 1: 8 and I will turn mine **h** against Ekron: 3027
5:19 leaned his **h** on the wall, and a serpent bit 3027
7: 7 by a plumbline, with a plumbline in his **h**. 3027
9: 2 dig into hell, thence shall mine **h** take them; 3027
Jnh 4:11 that cannot discern between their **right h** 3225
4:11 between their right hand and their **left h**; 8040
Mic 2: 1 because it is in the power of their **h**. 3027
4:10 redeem thee from the **h** of thine enemies. 3709
5: 9 Thine **h** shall be lift up upon thine 3027
5:12 I will cut off witchcrafts out of thine **h**; 3027
7:16 they shall lay *their* **h** upon *their* mouth, 3027
Hab 2:16 the cup of the LORD'S **right h** shall be 3225
3: 4 the light; he had horns *coming* out of his **h**: 3027
Zep 1: 4 I will also stretch out mine **h** upon Judah, 3027
1: 7 for the day of the LORD *is* **at h**: for 7138
2:13 he will stretch out his **h** against the north, 3027
2:15 passeth by her shall hiss, *and* wag his **h**. 3027
Zec 2: 1 a man with a measuring line in his **h**. 3027
2: 9 I *will* shake mine **h** upon them, and 3027
3: 1 Satan standing at his **right h** to resist him. 3225
4:10 shall see the plummet in the **h** of 3027
8: 4 every man with his staff in his **h** for very 3027
11: 6 the men every one into his neighbour's **h**, 3027
11: 6 and into the **h** of his king: 3027
11: 6 and out of their **h** I will not deliver *them*. 3027
12: 6 round about, on the **right h** and on the left: 3225
13: 7 and I will turn mine **h** upon the little ones. 3027
14:13 they shall lay hold every one on the **h** of his 3027
14:13 his **h** shall rise up against the hand of his 3027
14:13 his hand shall rise up against the **h** of his 3027
Mal 1:10 neither will I accept an offering at your **h**. 3027
1:13 should I accept this of your **h**? saith 3027
2:13 or receiveth *it with* good will at your **h**. 3027
Mt 3: 2 for the kingdom of heaven is **at h**. *1448*
3:12 Whose fan *is* in his **h**, and he will throughly *5495*
4:17 Repent: for the kingdom of heaven is **at h**. *1448*
5:30 And if thy **right h** offend thee, cut it off, *5495*
6: 3 let not thy **left h** know what thy right hand *710*
6: 3 let not thy left hand know what thy **right h** *1188*
8: 3 And Jesus put forth *his* **h**, and touched him, *5495*
8:15 And he touched her **h**, and the fever left *5495*
9:18 but come and lay thy **h** upon her, and *5495*
9:25 and took her by the **h**, and the maid arose. *5495*
10: 7 saying, The kingdom of heaven is **at h**. *1448*
12:10 there was a man which had *his* **h** withered. *5495*
12:13 saith he to the man, Stretch forth thine **h**. *5495*
12:49 And he stretched forth his **h** toward his *5495*
14:31 immediately Jesus stretched forth *his* **h**, *5495*
18: 8 Wherefore if thy **h** or thy foot offend thee, *5495*
20:21 the one on thy **right h**, and the other on *1188*
20:23 am baptized *with*: but to sit on my **right h**, *1188*
22:13 Bind him **h** and foot, and take him away, *5495*
22:44 said unto my Lord, Sit thou on my **right h**, *1188*
25:33 And he shall set the sheep on his **right h**, *1188*
25:34 shall the King say unto them on his **right h**, *1188*
25:41 shall he say also unto them on the **left h**, *2176*
26:18 The Master saith, My time is **at h**; *1451*
26:23 He that dippeth *his* **h** with me in the dish, *5495*
26:45 the hour is **at h**, and the Son of man is *1448*
26:46 behold, he is **at h** that doth betray me. *1448*
26:51 which were with Jesus stretched out *his* **h**, *5495*
26:64 Son of man sitting on the **right h** of power, *1188*
27:29 *it* upon his head, and a reed in his **right h**: *1188*
27:38 one on the **right h**, and another on the left. *1188*
Mk 1:15 and the kingdom of God is **at h**: *1448*
1:31 And he came and took her by the **h**, and *5495*
1:41 put forth *his* **h**, and touched him, and *5495*
3: 1 was a man there which had a withered **h**. *5495*
3: 3 unto the man which had the withered **h**, *5495*
3: 5 he saith unto the man, Stretch forth thine **h**. *5495*
3: 5 and his **h** was restored whole as the other. *5495*
5:41 And he took the damsel by the **h**, and *5495*
7:32 they beseech him to put *his* **h** upon him. *5495*
8:23 And he took the blind man by the **h**, and *5495*
9:27 But Jesus took him by the **h**, and lifted him *5495*
9:43 And if thy **h** offend thee, cut it off: it is *5495*
10:37 one on thy **right h**, and the other on thy left *1188*
10:37 and the other on thy **left h**, in thy glory. *2176*
10:40 But to sit on my **right h** and on my left *1188*
10:40 and on my **left h** is not mine to give; *2176*
12:36 said to my Lord, Sit thou on my **right h**, *1188*
14:42 let us go; lo, he that betrayeth me is **at h**. *1448*
14:62 Son of man sitting on the **right h** of power, *1188*
15:27 the one on *his* **right h**, and the other on his *1188*
16:19 into heaven, and sat on the **right h** of God. *1188*
Lk 1: 1 Forasmuch as many have **taken in h** to set *2021*
1:66 And the **h** of the Lord was with him. *5495*
1:71 and from the **h** of all that hate us; *5495*
1:74 that *we* being delivered out of the **h** of our *5495*
3:17 Whose fan *is* in his **h**, and he will throughly *5495*
5:13 And he put forth *his* **h**, and touched him, *5495*
6: 6 there was a man whose right **h** was *5495*
6: 8 said to the man which had the withered **h**, *5495*
6:10 he said unto the man, Stretch forth thy **h**. *5495*
6:10 and his **h** was restored whole as the other. *5495*
8:54 and took her by the **h**, and called, saying, *5495*
9:62 No *man* having put his **h** to the plough, and *5495*
15:22 and put *it* on him; and put a ring on his **h**, *5495*
20:42 said to my Lord, Sit thou on my **right h**, *1188*
21:30 own selves that summer is now **nigh at h**. *1451*
21:31 ye that the kingdom of God is **nigh at h**. *1451*
22:21 the **h** of him that betrayeth me *is* with me *5495*
22:69 man sit on the **right h** of the power of God. *1188*
23:33 one on the **right h**, and the other on *1188*
Jn 2:13 And the Jews' passover was **at h**, and *1451*
3:35 and hath given all *things* into his **h**. *5495*
7: 2 the Jews' feast of tabernacles was **at h**. *1451*
10:28 shall any *man* pluck them out of my **h**. *5495*
10:29 is able to pluck *them* out of my Father's **h**. *5495*
10:39 to take him: but he escaped out of their **h**, *5495*
11:44 bound **h** and foot with graveclothes: *5495*
11:55 And the Jews' passover was **nigh at h**: and *1451*
18:22 **stroke** Jesus **with the palm of** his **h**, *1325+4475*

Jn 19:42 *day;* for the sepulchre was **nigh at h**. *1451*
20:25 and thrust my **h** into his side, I will not *5495*
20:27 and reach *hither* thy **h**, and thrust *it* into my *5495*
Ac 2:25 for he is on my **right h**, that I should not be *1188*
2:33 Therefore being by the **right h** of God *1188*
2:34 said unto my Lord, Sit thou on my **right h**, *1188*
3: 7 And he took him by the **right h**, and lift *him* *5495*
4:28 For to do whatsoever thy **h** and thy counsel *5495*
4:30 By stretching forth thine **h** to heal; and *5495*
5:31 Him hath God exalted with his **right h** *to* *1188*
7:25 how that God by his **h** would deliver them: *5495*
7:35 a deliverer by the **h** of the angel which *5495*
7:50 Hath not my **h** made all these *things?* *5495*
7:55 and Jesus standing on the **right h** of God, *1188*
7:56 the Son of man standing on the **right h** of *1188*
9: 8 he saw no *man:* but they **led** him **by the h**, *5496*
9:12 and putting *his* **h** on him, that he might *5495*
9:41 And he gave her *his* **h**, and lift her up, and *5495*
11:21 And the **h** of the Lord was with them: and *5495*
12:11 hath delivered me out of the **h** of Herod, *5495*
12:17 beckoning unto them with the **h** to hold *5495*
13:11 the **h** of the Lord *is* upon thee, and *5495*
13:11 about seeking *some* to **lead** him **by the h**. *5497*
13:16 and beckoning with *his* **h** said, Men of *5495*
19:33 And Alexander beckoned with the **h**, and *5495*
21: 3 we left it on the **left h**, and sailed into *2176*
21:40 and beckoned with the **h** unto the people. *5495*
22:11 being **led by the h** of them that were with *5496*
23:19 Then the chief captain took him by the **h**, *5495*
26: 1 Then Paul stretched forth the **h**, and *5495*
28: 3 viper out of the heat, and fastened on his **h**. *5495*
28: 4 saw the *venomous* beast hang on his **h**, *5495*
Ro 8:34 *again,* who is even at the **right h** of God, *1188*
13:12 The night is far spent, the day is **at h**: let us *1448*
1Co 12:15 the foot shall say, Because I am not the **h**, *5495*
12:21 And the eye cannot say unto the **h**, I have *5495*
16:21 The salutation of *me* Paul with mine own **h**. *5495*
2Co 5: 1 a house **not made with h**, eternal in *886*
6: 7 the armour of righteousness on the **right h** *1188*
10:16 line of *things* **made ready to** our **h**. *1519+2092*
Gal 3:19 *it was* ordained by angels in the **h** of a *5495*
6:11 I have written unto you with mine own **h**. *5495*
Eph 1:20 set *him* at his own **right h** in the heavenly *1188*
Php 4: 5 be known unto all men. The Lord *is* **at h**. *1451*
Col 3: 1 where Christ sitteth on the **right h** of God. *1188*
4:18 The salutation by the **h** of me Paul. *5495*
2Th 2: 2 as from us, as that the day of Christ is **at h**. *1764*
3:17 The salutation of Paul with mine own **h**, *5495*
2Ti 4: 6 and the time of my departure is **at h**. *2186*
Phm 1:19 I Paul have written *it* with mine own **h**, *5495*
Heb 1: 3 sat down on the **right h** of the Majesty on *1188*
1:13 Sit on my **right h**, until I make thine *1188*
8: 1 who is set on the **right h** of the throne of *1188*
8: 9 the **h** to lead them out of the land of Egypt; *5495*
10:12 for ever, sat down on the **right h** of God; *1188*
12: 2 is set down at the **right h** of the throne of *1188*
1Pe 3:22 into heaven, and is on the **right h** of God; *1188*
4: 7 But the end of all *things* is **at h**: be ye *1448*
5: 6 therefore under the mighty **h** of God, *5495*
Rev 1: 3 are written therein: for the time *is* **at h**. *1451*
1:16 And he had in his right **h** seven stars: and *5495*
1:17 And he laid his right **h** upon me, *5495*
1:20 stars which thou sawest in my **right h**, *1188*
2: 1 that holdeth the seven stars in his **right h**, *1188*
5: 1 And I saw in the **right h** of him that sat on *1188*
5: 7 took the book out of the **right h** of him that *1188*
6: 5 sat on him had a pair of balances in his **h**. *5495*
8: 4 up before God out of the angel's **h**. *5495*
10: 2 And he had in his **h** a little book open: and *5495*
10: 5 upon the earth lifted up his **h** to heaven, *5495*
10: 8 take the little book which is open in the **h** *5495*
10:10 I took the little book out of the angel's **h**, *5495*
13:16 to receive a mark in their right **h**, or in their *5495*
14: 9 *his* mark in his forehead, or in his **h**, *5495*
14:14 a golden crown, and in his **h** a sharp sickle. *5495*
17: 4 having a golden cup in her **h** full of *5495*
19: 2 avenged the blood of his servants at her **h**. *5495*
20: 1 bottomless *pit* and a great chain in his **h**. *5495*
22:10 prophecy of this book: for the time is **at h**. *1451*

HANDBREADTH (5) [BREADTH, HAND]

Ex 25:25 thou shalt make unto it a border of a **h** 2948
37:12 Also he made thereunto a border of a **h** 2948
1Ki 7:26 it *was* a **h** thick, and the brim thereof was 2947
2Ch 4: 5 the thickness of it *was* a **h**, and the brim of 2947
Ps 39: 5 Behold, thou hast made my days *as* a **h**; 2947

HANDED (1) [HAND]

2Sa 17: 2 upon him while he *is* weary and weak **h**, 3027

HANDFUL (9) [HAND]

Lev 2: 2 he shall **take** thereout his **h** of 4393+7061+7062
5:12 the priest shall **take** his **h** of it, 4393+7061+7062
6:15 he shall take of it his **h**, of the flour of 7062
9:17 **took a h** thereof, and burnt *it* upon 3709+4390
Nu 5:26 the priest shall **take a h** of the offering, 7061
1Ki 17:12 a **h** of meal in a barrel, and a little oil 3709+4393
Ps 72:16 There shall be a **h** of corn in the earth upon 6451
Ecc 4: 6 Better *is* a **h** *with* quietness, 3709+4393
Jer 9:22 as the **h** after the harvestman, and 5995

HANDFULS (5) [HAND]

Ge 41:47 years the earth brought forth by **h**. 7062
Ex 9: 8 Take to you **h** of ashes of 2651+4393
Ru 2:16 let fall also *some* of the **h** of purpose for 6653
1Ki 20:10 if the dust of Samaria shall suffice for **h** for 8168
Eze 13:19 will ye pollute me among my people for **h** 8168

HANDKERCHIEFS (1) [KERCHIEFS]

Ac 19:12 from his body were brought unto the sick **h** *4676*

HANDLE (11) [HANDLED, HANDLES, HANDLETH, HANDLING]

Ge 4:21 he was the father of all such as **h** the harp 8610

Jdg 5:14 out of Zebulun they that h the pen of 4900
1Ch 12:8 the battle, that could h shield and buckler, 6186
2Ch 25:5 forth *to* war, that could h spear and shield. 270
Ps 115:7 They *have* hands, but they h not: feet *have* 4184
Jer 2:8 they that h the law knew me not: 8610
46:9 and the Libyans, that h the shield; 8610
46:9 and the Lydians, that h *and* bend the bow. 8610
Eze 27:29 all that h the oar, the mariners, *and* all 8610
Lk 24:39 h me, and see; for a spirit hath not flesh and *5584*
Col 2:21 (Touch not; taste not; h not; *2345*

HANDLED (3) [HANDLE]
Eze 21:11 that *it* may be h: 3709+8610+871.1+1886.1
Mk 12:4 the head, and sent *him* away **shamefully** h. *821*
1Jn 1:1 and our hands have h, of the Word of life; *5584*

HANDLES (1) [HANDLE]
SS 5:5 smelling myrrh, upon the h of the lock. 3709

HANDLETH (3) [HANDLE]
Pr 16:20 He that h a matter **wisely** shall find good: 7919
Jer 50:16 him that h the sickle in the time of harvest; 8610
Am 2:15 Neither shall he stand that h the bow; and 8610

HANDLING (2) [HANDLE]
Eze 38:4 and shields, all of them h swords: 8610
2Co 4:2 nor h the word of God **deceitfully**; *1389*

HANDMAID (45) [MAID]
Ge 16:1 wife bare him no *children:* and she had a h, 8198
25:12 Sarah's h, bare unto Abraham: 8198
29:24 his daughter Leah Zilpah his maid *for* a h. 8198
29:29 his daughter Bilhah his h to be her maid. 8198
30:4 And she gave him Bilhah her h to wife: and 8198
35:25 the sons of Bilhah, Rachel's h; Dan, and 8198
35:26 the sons of Zilpah, Leah's h; Gad, and 8198
Ex 23:12 the son of thy h, and the stranger, may be 519
Jdg 19:19 for thy h, and for the young man *which is* 519
Ru 2:13 that thou hast spoken friendly unto thine h, 8198
3:9 And she answered, I *am* Ruth thine h: spread 519
3:9 spread therefore thy skirt over thine h, 519
1Sa 1:11 wilt indeed look on the affliction of thine h, 519
1:11 not forget thine h, but wilt give unto thine 519
1:11 wilt give unto thine h a man child, then 519
1:16 Count not thine h for a daughter of Belial: 519
1:18 she said, Let thine h find grace in thy sight. 8198
25:24 *upon* me *let this* iniquity *be:* and let thine h, 519
25:24 and hear the words of thine h. 519
25:25 I thine h saw not the young men of my lord, 519
25:27 now this blessing which thine h hath 8198
25:28 I pray thee, forgive the trespass of thine h: 519
25:31 well with my lord, then remember thine h. 519
25:41 *let* thine h *be* a servant to wash the feet of 519
28:21 thine h hath obeyed thy voice, and I have 8198
28:22 hearken thou also unto the voice of thine h, 8198
2Sa 14:6 thy h had two sons, and they two strove 8198
14:7 the whole family is risen against thine h, 8198
14:12 the woman said, Let thine h, I pray thee, 8198
14:15 thy h said, I will now speak unto the king; 8198
14:15 the king will perform the request of his h. 519
14:16 to deliver his h out of the hand of the man 519
14:17 thine h said, The word of my lord the king 8198
14:19 put all these words in the mouth of thine h: 8198
20:17 she said unto him, Hear the words of thine h. 519
1Ki 1:13 my lord O king, swear unto thine h, saying, 519
1:17 swarest by the LORD thy God unto thine h, 519
3:20 while thine h slept, and laid it in her bosom, 519
2Ki 4:2 Thine h hath not any thing in the house, 8198
4:16 thou man of God, do not lie unto thine h. 8198
Ps 86:16 unto thy servant, and save the son of thine h. 519
116:16 I *am* thy servant, *and* the son of thy h: 519
Pr 30:23 and a h that is heir to her mistress. 8198
Jer 34:16 man his servant, and every man his h, 8198
Lk 1:38 And Mary said, Behold the h of the Lord; *1399*

HANDMAIDEN (1) [MAID]
Lk 1:48 he hath regarded the low estate of his h: *1399*

HANDMAIDENS (3) [MAID]
Ge 33:6 the h came near, they and their children, 8198
Ru 2:13 though I be not like unto one of thy h. 8198
Ac 2:18 on my h I will pour out in those days of my *1399*

HANDMAIDS (8) [MAID]
Ge 33:1 and unto Rachel, and unto the two h. 8198
33:2 he put the h and their children foremost, 8198
2Sa 6:20 to day in the eyes of the h of his servants, 519
Isa 14:2 the land of the LORD for servants and h: 8198
Jer 34:11 caused the servants and the h, whom they 8198
34:11 them into subjection for servants and for h. 8198
34:16 to be unto you for servants and for h. 8198
Joel 2:29 upon the h in those days will I pour out my 8198

HANDS (459) [HAND]
Ge 5:29 us concerning our work and toil of our h, 3027
16:9 and submit thyself under her h. 3027
20:5 and innocency of my h have I done this. 3709
24:22 two bracelets for her h of ten *shekels* 3027
24:30 and bracelets upon his sister's h, 3027
24:47 upon her face, and the bracelets upon her h. 3027
27:16 skins of the kids of the goats upon his h, 3027
27:22 but the h *are* the hands of Esau. 3027
27:22 but the hands *are* the h of Esau. 3027
27:23 him not, because his h were hairy, 3027
27:23 hands were hairy, as his brother Esau's h: 3027
31:42 seen mine affliction and the labour of my h, 3709
37:21 and he delivered him out of their h; 3027
37:22 that he might rid him out of their h, 3027
43:22 we brought down in our h to buy food: 3027
48:14 Manasseh's head, guiding his h wittingly; 3027
49:24 the arms of his h were made strong by 3027
49:24 strong by the h of the mighty *God* of Jacob; 3027
Ex 9:29 I will spread abroad my h unto the LORD; 3709
9:33 spread abroad his h unto the LORD: 3709
Ex 15:17 O Lord, *which* thy h have established. 3027
17:12 Moses' h *were* heavy; and they took a 3027
17:12 Aaron and Hur stayed up his h, the one on 3027
17:12 his h were steady until the going down of 3027
29:10 his sons shall put their h upon the head of 3027
29:15 his sons shall put their h upon the head of 3027
29:19 his sons shall put their h upon the head of 3027
29:24 thou shalt put all in the h of Aaron, and 3709
29:24 hands of Aaron, and in the h of his sons; 3709
29:25 thou shalt receive them of their h, and 3027
30:19 and his sons shall wash their h and 3027
30:21 So they shall wash their h and their feet, 3027
32:19 he cast the tables out of his h, and 3027
35:25 that were wise hearted did spin with their h, 3027
40:31 and Aaron and his sons washed their h and 3027
Lev 4:15 h upon the head of the bullock before 3027
7:30 His own h shall bring the offerings of 3027
8:14 his sons laid their h upon the head of 3027
8:18 his sons laid their h upon the head of 3027
8:22 his sons laid their h upon the head of 3027
8:24 upon the thumbs of their right h, and 3027
8:27 he put all upon Aaron's h, and upon his 3709
8:27 upon his sons' h, and waved them *for* a 3709
8:28 Moses took them from off their h, and 3709
15:11 hath not rinsed his h in water, he shall wash 3027
16:12 his h full of sweet incense beaten small, 2651
16:21 Aaron shall lay both his h upon the head of 3027
24:14 let all that heard *him* lay their h upon his 3027
Nu 5:18 and put the offering of memorial in her h, 3709
6:19 shall put *them* upon the h of the Nazarite, 3709
8:10 the children of Israel shall put their h upon 3027
8:12 the Levites shall lay their h upon the heads 3027
24:10 and he smote his h together: 3709
27:23 he laid his h upon him, and gave him a 3027
Dt 1:25 they took of the fruit of the land in their h, 3027
3:3 our God delivered into our h Og also, 3027
4:28 the work of men's h, wood and stone, 3027
9:15 tables of the covenant *were* in my two h. 3027
9:17 cast them out of my two h, and brake them 3027
12:18 thy God in all that thou puttest thine h unto. 3027
16:15 in all the works of thine h, therefore 3027
17:7 The h of the witnesses shall be first upon 3027
17:7 and afterward the h of all the people. 3027
20:13 thy God hath delivered it into thine h, 3027
21:6 h over the heifer that is beheaded in 3027
21:7 and say, Our h have not shed this blood, 3027
21:10 thy God hath delivered them into thine h, 3027
24:19 may bless thee in all the work of thine h. 3027
27:15 the work of the h of the craftsman, and 3027
31:29 him to anger through the work of your h. 3027
33:7 let his h *be* sufficient for him; and be thou a 3027
33:11 his substance, and accept the work of his h: 3027
34:9 for Moses had laid his h upon him: 3027
Jos 2:24 Truly the LORD hath delivered into our h 3027
Jdg 2:14 he delivered them into the h of spoilers that 3027
2:14 he sold them into the h of their enemies 3027
6:13 delivered us into the h of the Midianites. 3709
7:2 for me to give the Midianites into their h, 3027
7:11 afterward shall thine h be strengthened to 3027
7:19 and brake the pitchers that *were* in their h. 3027
7:20 held the lamps in their left h, and 3027
7:20 the trumpets in their right h to blow *withal:* 3027
8:3 God hath delivered into your h the princes 3027
8:6 *Are* the h of Zebah and Zalmunna now in 3709
8:15 *Are* the h of Zebah and Zalmunna now in 3709
8:34 who had delivered them out of the h of all 3027
9:16 him according to the deserving of his h; 3027
10:7 he sold them into the h of the Philistines, 3027
10:7 and into the h of the children of Ammon. 3027
11:30 deliver the children of Ammon into mine h, 3027
11:32 and the LORD delivered them into his h. 3027
12:2 ye delivered me not out of their h. 3027
12:3 I put my life in my h, and passed over 3709
13:23 burnt offering and a meat offering at our h, 3027
14:9 he took thereof in his h, and went on 3709
15:14 and his bands loosed from off his h. 3027
16:24 Our god hath delivered into our h our 3027
18:10 for God hath given it into your h; a place 3027
19:27 and her h *were* upon the threshold. 3027
1Sa 5:4 both the palms of his h *were* cut off upon 3027
7:14 Israel deliver out of the h of the Philistines. 3027
10:4 which thou shalt receive of their h. 3027
11:7 the coasts of Israel by the h of messengers, 3027
14:13 Jonathan climbed up upon his h and 3027
14:48 delivered Israel out of the h of them that 3027
17:47 and he will give you into our h. 3027
21:13 feigned himself mad in their h, and 3027
30:15 nor deliver me into the h of my master, and 3027
2Sa 2:7 Therefore now let your h be strengthened, 3027
3:34 Thy h *were* not bound, nor thy feet put into 3027
4:1 his h were feeble, and all the Israelites were 3027
4:12 cut off their h and their feet, and 3027
16:21 shall the h of all that *are* with thee be 3027
21:9 he delivered them into the h of 3027
22:21 according to the cleanness of my h hath he 3027
22:35 He teacheth my h to war; so that a bow of 3027
23:6 because they cannot be taken with h: 3027
1Ki 8:22 and spread forth his h *toward* heaven: 3709
8:38 and spread forth his h towards this house: 3709
8:54 from kneeling on his knees with his h 3709
14:27 committed *them* unto the h of the chief of 3027
16:7 him to anger with the work of his h, 3027
2Ki 3:11 which poured water on the h of Elijah. 3027
4:34 upon his eyes, and his h upon his hands: 3709
4:34 upon his eyes, and his hands upon his h: 3709
5:20 in not receiving at his h *that* which he 3027
9:23 Joram turned his h, and fled, and said to 3027
9:35 and the feet, and the palms of *her* h. 3027
10:24 whom I *have* brought into your h escape, 3027
11:12 they clapt their h, and said, God save 3709
11:16 they laid h on her; and she went *by* the way 3027
12:11 into the h of *them* that did the work, 3027
13:16 and Elisha put his h upon the king's hands. 3027
13:16 and Elisha put his hands upon the king's h. 3027
19:18 but the work of men's h, wood and stone: 3027
2Ki 22:17 me to anger with all the works of their h; 3027
1Ch 12:17 seeing *there is* no wrong in mine h, the God 3709
25:2 the sons of Asaph under the h of Asaph, 3027
25:3 six, under the h of their father Jeduthun, 3027
25:6 All these *were* under the h of their father 3027
29:5 for all *manner of* work *to be made* by the h 3027
2Ch 6:4 who hath with his h fulfilled *that* which he 3027
6:12 of Israel, and spread forth his h: 3709
6:13 and spread forth his h towards heaven, 3709
6:29 and shall spread forth his h in this house: 3709
8:18 Huram sent him by the h of his servants 3027
12:10 committed *them* to the h of the chief of 3027
15:7 and let not your h be weak: 3027
23:15 So they laid h on her; and when she was 3027
29:23 and laid their h upon them: 3027
32:19 *which were* the work of the h of man. 3027
34:25 me to anger with all the works of their h; 3027
35:11 the priests sprinkled *the blood* from their h, 3027
Ezr 1:6 strengthened their h with vessels of silver, 3027
4:4 the people of the land weakened the h of 3027
5:8 goeth fast on, and prospereth in their h. 3028
6:22 to strengthen their h in the work of 3027
9:5 spread out my h unto the LORD my God, 3709
10:19 they gave their h that *they* would put away 3027
Ne 2:18 So they strengthened their h for *this* good 3027
4:17 *every one* with one of his h wrought in 3027
6:9 Their h shall be weakened from the work, 3027
6:9 Now therefore, *O God,* strengthen my h. 3027
8:6 Amen, Amen, with lifting up their h: 3027
9:24 and gavest them into their h, 3027
13:21 if ye do *so* again, I will lay h on you. 3027
Est 3:6 he thought scorn to lay h on Mordecai 3027
3:9 h of those that have the charge of 3027
9:16 but they laid not their h on the prey, 3027
Job 1:10 thou hast blessed the work of his h, and 3027
4:3 and thou hast strengthened the weak h. 3027
5:12 that their h cannot perform *their* enterprise. 3027
5:18 he woundeth, and his h make whole. 3027
9:30 snow water, and make my h never so clean; 3709
10:3 thou shouldest despise the work of thine h, 3709
10:8 Thine h have made me and fashioned me 3027
11:13 and stretch out thine h toward him; 3709
14:15 wilt have a desire to the work of thine h. 3027
16:11 turned me over into the h of the wicked. 3027
16:17 Not for *any* injustice in mine h: also my 3709
17:3 who *is* he *that* will strike h with me? 3027
17:9 he that hath clean h shall be stronger and 3027
20:10 the poor, and his h shall restore their goods. 3027
22:30 it is delivered by the pureness of thine h. 3709
27:23 *Men* shall clap their h at him, and shall hiss 3709
30:2 whereto *might* the strength of their h profit 3027
31:7 and *if any* blot hath cleaved to my h; 3709
34:19 the poor? for they all *are* the work of his h. 3027
34:37 he clappeth *his h* amongst us, and NIH
Ps 7:3 have done this; if there be iniquity in my h; 3709
8:6 to have dominion over the works of thy h; 3027
9:16 wicked is snared in the work of his own h. 3709
18:20 according to the cleanness of my h hath he 3027
18:24 according to the cleanness of my h in his 3027
18:34 He teacheth my h to war, so that a bow of 3027
22:16 they pierced my h and my feet. 3027
24:4 He that hath clean h, and a pure heart; 3709
26:6 I will wash mine h in innocency: so will I 3709
26:10 In whose h *is* mischief, and their right hand 3027
28:2 when I lift up my h toward thy holy oracle. 3027
28:4 give them after the work of their h; 3027
28:5 nor the operation of his h, he shall destroy 3027
44:20 or stretched out our h to a strange god; 3709
47:1 O clap *your* h, all ye people; shout unto 3709
55:20 He hath put forth his h against such as be at 3027
58:2 you weigh the violence of your h in 3027
63:4 while I live: I will lift up my h in thy name. 3709
68:31 Ethiopia shall soon stretch out her h unto 3027
73:13 *in* vain, and washed my h in innocency. 3709
76:5 of the men of might have found their h. 3027
78:72 and guided them by the skilfulness of his h. 3709
81:6 his h were delivered from the pots. 3709
88:9 I have stretched out my h unto thee. 3709
90:17 establish thou the work of our h upon us; 3027
90:17 yea, the work of our h establish thou it. 3027
91:12 They shall bear thee up in *their* h, lest thou 3709
92:4 I will triumph in the works of thy h. 3027
95:5 he made it: and his h formed the dry *land.* 3027
98:8 Let the floods clap *their* h: let the hills be 3709
102:25 and the heavens *are* the work of thy h. 3027
111:7 The works of his h *are* verity and 3027
115:4 *are* silver and gold, the work of men's h. 3027
115:7 They *have* h, but they handle not: feet *have* 3027
119:48 My h also will I lift up unto thy 3709
119:73 Thy h have made me and fashioned me: 3027
125:3 lest the righteous put forth their h unto 3027
128:2 For thou shalt eat the labour of thine h: 3709
134:2 Lift up your h *in* the sanctuary, and 3027
135:15 *are* silver and gold, the work of men's h. 3027
138:8 forsake not the works of thine own h. 3027
140:4 O LORD, from the h of the wicked; 3027
141:2 the lifting up of my h *as* the evening 3709
143:5 all thy works; I muse on the work of thy h. 3027
143:6 I stretch forth my h unto thee: my soul 3027
144:1 which teacheth my h to war, *and* 3027
Pr 6:10 a little folding of the h to sleep: 3027
6:17 and h that shed innocent blood, 3027
12:14 the recompence of a man's h shall be 3027
14:1 but the foolish plucketh it down with her h. 3027
17:18 A man void of understanding striketh h, 3709
21:25 killeth him; for his h refuse to labour. 3027
22:26 Be not thou *one* of them that strike h, *or* 3709
24:33 a little folding of the h to sleep: 3027
30:28 The spider taketh hold with her h, and *is* in 3027
31:13 and flax, and worketh willingly with her h. 3709
31:16 with the fruit of her h she planteth a 3709
31:19 She layeth her h to the spindle, and 3027
31:19 to the spindle, and her h hold the distaff. 3709
31:20 yea, she reacheth forth her h to the needy. 3027
31:31 Give her of the fruit of her h; and let her 3027

Ecc 2:11 I looked on all the works that my **h** had 3027
4: 5 The fool foldeth his **h** together, and 3027
4: 6 than **both** the **h** full *with* travail and 2651
5: 6 thy voice, and destroy the work of thine **h**? 3027
7:26 heart *is* snares and nets, *and* her **h** *as* bands: 3027
10:18 through idleness of the **h** the house 3027
SS 5: 5 my **h** dropped *with* myrrh, and my fingers 3027
5:14 His **h** *are as* gold rings set with the beryl: 3027
7: 1 the work of the **h** of a cunning workman. 3027
Isa 1:15 when ye spread forth your **h**, I will hide 3709
1:15 I will not hear: your **h** are full *of* blood. 3027
2: 8 they worship the work of their own **h**, 3027
3:11 for the reward of his **h** shall be given him. 3027
5:12 neither consider the operation of his **h**. 3027
13: 7 Therefore shall all **h** be faint, and 3027
17: 8 not look to the altars, the work of his **h**, 3027
19:25 Assyria the work of my **h**, and Israel mine 3027
25:11 he shall spread forth his **h** in the midst of 3027
25:11 as he that swimmeth spreadeth forth *his* **h** to NIH
25:11 pride together with the spoils of their **h**. 3027
29:23 the work of mine **h**, in the midst of him, 3027
31: 7 which your own **h** have made unto you *for* 3027
33:15 that shaketh his **h** from holding of bribes, 3709
35: 3 Strengthen ye the weak **h**, and confirm 3027
37:19 but the work of men's **h**, wood and stone: 3027
45: 9 makest thou? or thy work, He hath no **h**? 3027
45:11 concerning the work of my **h** command ye 3027
45:12 I, *even* my **h**, have stretched out 3027
49:16 I have graven thee upon the **palms of** *my* **h**; 3709
55:12 all the trees of the field shall clap *their* **h**. 3709
59: 3 For your **h** are defiled with blood, and 3709
59: 6 and the act of violence *is* in their **h**. 3709
60:21 the work of my **h**, that *I* may be glorified. 3027
65: 2 I have spread out mine **h** all the day unto a 3027
65:22 elect shall long enjoy the work of their **h**. 3027
Jer 1:16 and worshipped the works of their own **h**. 3027
2:37 from him, and thine **h** upon thine head: 3027
4:31 *that* bewaileth herself, *that* spreadeth her **h**, 3709
6:24 our **h** wax feeble: anguish hath taken hold 3027
10: 3 the work of the **h** of the workman, with 3027
10: 9 the workman, and of the **h** of the founder: 3027
19: 7 and by the **h** of them that seek their lives: 3027
21: 4 back the weapons of war that *are* in your **h**, 3027
23:14 they strengthen also the **h** of evildoers, 3027
25: 6 me not to anger with the works of your **h**; 3027
25: 7 with the works of your **h** to your own hurt. 3027
25:14 and according to the works of their own **h**. 3027
30: 6 wherefore do I see every man *with* his **h** on 3027
32:30 me to anger with the work of their **h**, 3027
33:13 shall the flocks pass again under the **h** of 3027
38: 4 for thus he weakeneth the **h** of the men of 3027
38: 4 the **h** of all the people, in speaking such 3027
44: 8 me unto wrath with the works of your **h**, 3027
47: 3 back to *their* children for feebleness of **h**; 3027
48:37 upon all the **h** *shall be* cuttings, and 3027
50:43 the report of them, and his **h** waxed feeble: 3027
La 1:14 the Lord hath delivered me into *their* **h**, 3027
1:17 Zion spreadeth forth her **h**, *and there is* 3027
2:15 All that pass by clap *their* **h** at thee; 3709
2:19 lift up thy **h** toward him for the life of thy 3709
3:41 Let us lift up our heart with *our* **h** unto God 3709
3:64 according to the work of their **h**. 3027
4: 2 the work of the **h** of the potter! 3027
4: 6 as in a moment, and no **h** stayed on her. 3027
4:10 The **h** of the pitiful women have sodden 3027
Eze 1: 8 *they had* the **h** of a man under their wings 3027
7:17 All **h** shall be feeble, and all knees shall be 3027
7:21 I will give it into the **h** of the strangers for a 3027
7:27 the **h** of the people of the land shall be 3027
10: 7 put *it* into the **h** of *him that was* clothed 2651
10:12 their **h**, and their wings, and the wheels, 3027
10:21 the likeness of the **h** of a man *was* under 3027
11: 9 deliver you into the **h** of strangers, and 3027
13:22 strengthened the **h** of the wicked, that *he* 3027
16:11 I put bracelets upon thine **h**, and a chain on 3027
21: 7 all **h** shall be feeble, and every spirit shall 3027
21:14 smite *thine* **h together**, and 413+3709+3709
21:17 will also smite mine **h together**, 413+3709+3709
22:14 thine heart endure, or can thine **h** be strong, 3027
23:37 blood *is* in their **h**, and with their idols have 3027
23:42 which put bracelets upon their **h**, and 3027
23:45 *are* adulteresses, and blood *is* in their **h**. 3027
25: 6 Because thou hast clapped *thine* **h**, and 3027
Da 2:34 till that a stone was cut out without **h**, 3028
2:45 was cut out of the mountain without **h**, 3028
3:15 that God that shall deliver you out of my **h**? 3028
10:10 my knees and *upon* the palms of my **h**. 3027
Hos 14: 3 will we say any more to the work of our **h**: 3027
Ob 1:13 nor have laid *h* on their substance in the day NIH
Jnh 3: 8 and from the violence that *is* in their **h**. 3709
Mic 5:13 shalt no more worship the work of thine **h**. 3027
7: 3 That *they* may do evil with both **h** 3709
Na 3:19 the bruit of thee shall clap the **h** over thee: 3709
Hab 3:10 uttered his voice, *and* lift up his **h** on high. 3027
Zep 3:16 *and to* Zion, Let not thine **h** be slack. 3027
Hag 1:11 and upon all the labour of the **h**. 3709
2:14 so *is* every work of their **h**; and *that* which 3027
2:17 and with hail *in* all the labours of your **h**; 3027
Zec 4: 9 The **h** of Zerubbabel have laid 3027
4: 9 his **h** shall also finish *it;* and thou shalt 3027
8: 9 Let your **h** be strong, ye that hear in these 3027
8:13 fear not, *but* let your **h** be strong. 3027
13: 6 What *are* these wounds in thine **h**? 3027
Mt 4: 6 and in *their* **h** they shall bear thee up, lest at *5495*
15: 2 for they wash not their **h** when they eat *5495*
15:20 to eat with unwashen **h** defileth not a man. *5495*
17:22 The Son of man shall be betrayed into the **h** *5495*
18: 8 rather than having two **h** or two feet to be *5495*
18:28 and he **laid h on** him, and took *him* by *2902*
19:13 that he should put *his* **h** on them, and pray: *5495*
19:15 And he laid *his* **h** on them, and *5495*
21:46 But when they sought to **lay h on** him, *2902*
26:45 the Son of man is betrayed into the **h** of *5495*
26:50 and laid **h** on Jesus, and took him. *5495*
26:67 **smote** *him* **with the palms of** their **h**, *4474*
Mt 27:24 and washed *his* **h** before the multitude, *5495*
Mk 5:23 *I pray thee,* come and lay *thy* **h** on her, *5495*
6: 2 such mighty works are wrought by his **h**? *5495*
6: 5 save that he laid *his* **h** upon a few sick *folk,* *5495*
7: 2 that is to say, with unwashen, **h**, they found *5495*
7: 3 except they wash *their* **h** oft, eat not, *5495*
7: 5 the elders, but eat bread with unwashen **h**? *5495*
8:23 spit on his eyes, and put *his* **h** upon him, *5495*
8:25 After that he put *his* **h** again upon his eyes, *5495*
9:31 The Son of man is delivered into the **h** of *5495*
9:43 than having two **h** to go into hell, into *5495*
10:16 put *his* **h** upon them, and blessed them. *5495*
14:41 the Son of man is betrayed into the **h** of *5495*
14:46 And they laid their **h** on him, and took him. *5495*
14:58 destroy this temple that is **made with h**, *5499*
14:58 days I will build another **made without h**. *886*
14:65 **strike** him **with the palms of** their **h**. *906+4475*
16:18 they shall lay **h** on the sick, and they shall *5495*
Lk 4:11 And in *their* **h** they shall bear thee up, *5495*
4:40 and he laid *his* **h** on every one of them, and *5495*
6: 1 and did eat, rubbing *them* in *their* **h**. *5495*
9:44 of man shall be delivered into the **h** of men. *5495*
13:13 And he laid *his* **h** on her: and *5495*
20:19 the scribes the same hour sought to lay **h** on *5495*
21:12 they shall lay their **h** on you, and *5495*
22:53 ye stretched forth no **h** against me: *5495*
23:46 Father, into thy **h** I commend my spirit: *5495*
24: 7 must be delivered into the **h** of sinful men, *5495*
24:39 Behold my **h** and my feet, that it is I *5495*
24:40 he shewed them *his* **h** and *his* feet. *5495*
24:50 and he lift up his **h**, and blessed them. *5495*
Jn 7:30 but no *man* laid **h** on him, because his hour *5495*
7:44 have taken him; but no *man* laid **h** on him. *5495*
8:20 and no *man* **laid h on** him; for his hour was *4084*
13: 3 the Father had given all *things* into his **h**, *5495*
13: 9 my feet only, but also *my* **h** and *my* head. *5495*
19: 3 and they **smote** him **with** their **h**. *1325+4475*
20:20 he shewed unto them *his* **h** and his side. *5495*
20:25 Except I shall see in his **h** the print of *5495*
20:27 Reach hither thy finger, and behold my **h**; *5495*
21:18 thou shalt stretch forth thy **h**, and *5495*
Ac 2:23 and by wicked **h** have crucified and slain: *5495*
4: 3 And they laid **h** on them, and put *them* in *5495*
5:12 And by the **h** of the apostles were many *5495*
5:18 And laid their **h** on the apostles, and *5495*
6: 6 they had prayed, they laid *their* **h** on them. *5495*
7:41 and rejoiced in the works of their own **h**. *5495*
7:48 High dwelleth not in temples **made with h**; *5499*
8:17 Then laid they *their* **h** on them, and *5495*
8:18 the apostles' **h** the Holy Ghost was given, *5495*
8:19 this power, that on whomsoever I lay **h**, *5495*
9:17 and putting his **h** on him said, Brother Saul, *5495*
11:30 sent it to the elders by the **h** of Barnabas *5495*
12: 1 forth *his* **h** to vex certain of the church. *5495*
12: 7 And his chains fell off from *his* **h**. *5495*
13: 3 and prayed, and laid *their* **h** on them, *5495*
14: 3 and wonders to be done by their **h**. *5495*
17:24 dwelleth not in temples **made with h**; *5499*
17:25 Neither is worshipped with men's **h**, *5495*
19: 6 And when Paul had laid *his* **h** upon them, *5495*
19:11 And God wrought special miracles by the **h** *5495*
19:26 they be no gods, which are made with **h**: *5495*
20:34 that these **h** have ministered unto my *5495*
21:11 and bound his *own* **h** and feet, and said, *5495*
21:11 shall deliver *him* into the **h** of the Gentiles. *5495*
21:27 stirred up all the people, and laid **h** on him, *5495*
24: 7 great violence took *him* away out of our **h**, *5495*
27:19 *out* **with** our **own h** the tackling of the ship. *849*
28: 8 and laid *his* **h** on him, and healed him. *5495*
28:17 from Jerusalem into the **h** of the Romans. *5495*
Ro 10:21 All day long have I stretched forth my **h** *5495*
1Co 4:12 And labour, working with our own **h**: *5495*
2Co 11:33 I let down by the wall, and escaped his **h**. *5495*
Gal 2: 9 and Barnabas the **right h** of fellowship; *1188*
Eph 2:11 the Circumcision in the flesh **made by h**; *5499*
4:28 working with *his* **h** the *thing which is* good, *5495*
Col 2:11 with the circumcision **made without h**, *886*
1Th 4:11 and to work with your own **h**, *5495*
1Ti 2: 8 lifting up holy **h**, without wrath and *5495*
4:14 with the laying on of the **h** of *5495*
5:22 Lay **h** suddenly on no *man,* neither be *5495*
2Ti 1: 6 which is in thee by the putting on of my **h**. *5495*
Heb 1:10 and the heavens are the works of thine **h**: *5495*
2: 7 and didst set him over the works of thy **h**: *5495*
6: 2 and of laying on of **h**, and of resurrection of *5495*
9:11 not **made with h**, that is to say, not of this *5499*
9:24 entered into the holy *places* **made with h**, *5499*
10:31 *It is* a fearful *thing* to fall into the **h** of *5495*
12:12 Wherefore lift up the **h** which hang down, *5495*
Jas 4: 8 Cleanse *your* **h**, *ye* sinners; and purify *your* *5495*
1Jn 1: 1 and our **h** have handled, of the Word of *5495*
Rev 7: 9 with white robes, and palms in their **h**; *5495*
9:20 *yet* repented not of the works of their **h**, *5495*
20: 4 *his* mark upon their foreheads, or in their **h**; *5495*

HANDSOME See GOODLIER; GOODLIEST; GOODLY

HANDSTAVES (1) [HAND, STAFF]
Eze 39: 9 the **h**, and the spears, and they shall 3027+4731

HANDWRITING (1) [HAND, WRITE]
Col 2:14 Blotting out the **h** of ordinances that was *5498*

HANDYWORK (1) [HAND, WORK]
Ps 19: 1 and the firmament sheweth his **h**. 3027+4639

HANES (1)
Isa 30: 4 at Zoan, and his ambassadors came to **H**. 2609

HANG (19) [HANGED, HANGETH, HANGING, HANGINGS]
Ge 40:19 from off thee, and shall **h** thee on a tree; 8518
Ex 26:12 shall **h** over the backside of the tabernacle. 5628
Ex 26:13 it shall **h** over the sides of the tabernacle on 5628
26:32 thou shalt **h** it upon four pillars of shittim 5414
26:33 thou shalt **h up** the vail under the taches, 5414
40: 8 and **h up** the hanging at the court gate. 5414
Nu 25: 4 **h** them **up** before the LORD against 3363
Dt 21:22 *to be* put to death, and thou **h** him on a tree: 8518
28:66 thy life shall **h in doubt** before thee; and 8511
2Sa 21: 6 we will **h** them **up** unto the LORD in 3363
Est 6: 4 to speak unto the king to **h** Mordecai on 8518
7: 9 Then the king said, **H** him thereon. 8518
SS 4: 4 whereon there **h** a thousand bucklers, 8518
Isa 22:24 they shall **h** upon him all the glory of his 8518
La 2:10 the virgins of Jerusalem **h down** their heads 3381
Eze 15: 3 will *men* take a pin of it to **h** any vessel 8518
Mt 22:40 On these two commandments **h** all the law *2910*
Ac 28: 4 saw the *venomous* beast **h** on his hand, *2910*
Heb 12:12 Wherefore lift up the hands which **h down**, *3935*

HANGED (30) [HANG]
Ge 40:22 he **h** the chief baker: as Joseph had 8518
41:13 he restored unto mine office, and him he **h**. 8518
Dt 21:23 (for he that is **h** *is* accursed of God;) 8518
Jos 8:29 the king of Ai he **h** on a tree until eventide: 8518
10:26 and slew them, and **h** them on five trees: 8518
2Sa 4:12 and **h** *them* **up** over the pool in Hebron. 8518
17:23 **h** himself, and died, and was buried in 2614
18:10 said, Behold, I saw Absalom **h** in an oak. 8518
21: 9 they **h** them in the hill before the LORD: 3363
21:12 where the Philistines had **h** them, when 8511
21:13 gathered the bones of them that were **h**. 3363
Ezr 6:11 and being set up, let him be **h** thereon; 4223
Est 2:23 therefore they were both **h** on a tree: 8518
5:14 the king that Mordecai may be **h** thereon: 8518
7:10 So they **h** Haman on the gallows that he 8518
8: 7 him they have **h** upon the gallows, because 8518
9:13 let Haman's ten sons be **h** upon 8518
9:14 at Shushan; and they **h** Haman's ten sons. 8518
9:25 and his sons should be **h** on the gallows. 8518
Ps 137: 2 We **h** our harps upon the willows in 8518
La 5:12 Princes are **h up** by their hand: the faces of 8518
Eze 27:10 they **h** the shield and helmet in thee; 8518
27:11 they **h** their shields upon thy walls round 8518
Mt 18: 6 were better for him that a millstone were **h** *2910*
27: 5 and departed, and went and **h** himself. *519*
Mk 9:42 it is better for him that a millstone were **h** *4029*
Lk 17: 2 a millstone were **h about** his neck, *4029*
23:39 And one of the malefactors which were **h** *2910*
Ac 5:30 up Jesus, whom ye slew and **h** on a tree. *2910*
10:39 whom they slew and **h** on a tree: *2910*

HANGETH (2) [HANG]
Job 26: 7 empty place, *and* **h** the earth upon nothing. 8518
Gal 3:13 Cursed *is* every one that **h** on a tree: *2910*

HANGING (18) [HANG]
Ex 26:36 thou shalt make a **h** for the door of the tent, 4539
26:37 thou shalt make for the **h** five pillars of 4539
27:16 for the gate of the court *shall be* a **h** of 4539
35:15 the **h** for the door at the entering in of 4539
35:17 and the **h** for the door of the court, 4539
36:37 he made a **h** for the tabernacle door *of* blue, 4539
38:18 the **h** for the gate of the court *was* 4539
39:38 and the **h** for the tabernacle door, 4539
39:40 the **h** for the court gate, his cords, and 4539
40: 5 and put the **h** of the door to the tabernacle. 4539
40: 8 and hang up the **h** at the court gate. 4539
40:28 he set up the **h** at the door of the tabernacle. 4539
40:33 the altar, and set up the **h** of the court gate. 4539
Nu 3:25 the **h** for the door of the tabernacle of 4539
3:31 and the **h**, and all the service thereof. 4539
4:25 the **h** for the door of the tabernacle of 4539
4:26 the **h** for the door of the gate of the court, 4539
Jos 10:26 they were **h** upon the trees until 8518

HANGINGS (18) [HANG]
Ex 27: 9 the south side southward *there shall be* **h** 7050
27:11 *there shall be* **h** of an hundred *cubits* long, 7050
27:12 on the west side *shall be* **h** of fifty cubits: 7050
27:14 The **h** of *one* side *of the gate shall be* 7050
27:15 on the other side *shall be* **h**, fifteen *cubits:* 7050
35:17 The **h** of the court, his pillars, and 7050
38: 9 on the south side southward the **h** of 7050
38:11 for the north side *the* **h** *were* an hundred NIH
38:12 And for the west side *were* **h** of fifty cubits, 7050
38:14 The **h** of the *one* side *of the gate were* 7050
38:15 and that hand, *were* **h** of fifteen cubits; 7050
38:16 All the **h** of the court round about *were of* 7050
38:18 answerable to the **h** of the court. 7050
39:40 The **h** of the court, his pillars, and his 7050
Nu 3:26 the **h** of the court, and the curtain for 7050
4:26 the **h** of the court, and the hanging for 7050
2Ki 23: 7 where the women wove **h** for the grove. 1004
Est 1: 6 blue *h*, fastened with cords of fine linen and NIH

HANIEL (1)
1Ch 7:39 the sons of Ulla; Arah, and **H**, and Rezia. 2592

HANNAH (13)
1Sa 1: 2 the name of the one *was* **H**, and the name 2584
1: 2 had children, but **H** had no children. 2584
1: 5 unto **H** he gave a worthy portion; for he 2584
1: 5 he gave a worthy portion; for he loved **H**: 2584
1: 8 her husband to her, **H**, why weepest thou? 2584
1: 9 So **H** rose up after *they* had eaten in Shiloh, 2584
1:13 Now **H**, she spake in her heart; only her 2584
1:15 **H** answered and said, No, my lord, I *am* a 2584
1:19 Elkanah knew **H** his wife; and the LORD 2584
1:20 when the time was come about after **H** had 2584
1:22 **H** went not up; for she said unto her 2584
2: 1 **H** prayed, and said, My heart rejoiceth in 2584
2:21 the LORD visited **H**, so that she 2584

HANNATHON (1)
Jos 19:14 compasseth it on the north side *to* **H**: 2615

HANNIEL (1)
Nu 34:23 children of Manasseh, **H** the son of Ephod. 2592

HANOCH (5) [HANOCHITES]
Ge 25: 4 and Epher, and **H**, and Abidah, and Eldaah. 2585
46: 9 **H**, and Phallu, and Hezron, and Carmi. 2585
Ex 6:14 of Israel; **H**, and Pallu, Hezron, and Carmi: 2585
Nu 26: 5 **H**, *of whom cometh* the family of 2585
1Ch 5: 3 of Reuben the firstborn of Israel *were*, **H**, 2585

HANOCHITES (1) [HANOCH]
Nu 26: 5 *of whom cometh* the family of the **H**: 2599

HANUN (11)
2Sa 10: 1 and **H** his son reigned in his stead. 2586
10: 2 I will shew kindness unto **H** the son of 2586
10: 3 children of Ammon said unto **H** their lord, 2586
10: 4 Wherefore **H** took David's servants, and 2586
1Ch 19: 2 I will shew kindness unto **H** the son of 2586
19: 2 the land of the children of Ammon to **H**, 2586
19: 3 of the children of Ammon said to **H**, 2586
19: 4 Wherefore **H** took David's servants, and 2586
19: 6 **H** and the children of Ammon sent a 2586
Ne 3:13 The valley gate repaired **H**, and 2586
3:30 **H** the sixth son of Zalaph, another piece. 2586

HAP (1) [HAPPEN]
Ru 2: 3 her **h** was to light on a part of the field 4745

HAPHARAIM (1)
Jos 19:19 And **H**, and Shion, and Anaharath, 2663

HAPLY (6) [HAPPEN]
1Sa 14:30 **if h** the people had eaten freely to day of 3863
Mk 11:13 if **h** he might find any *thing* thereon: *686*
Lk 14:29 **Lest h**, after he hath laid the foundation, *3379*
Ac 5:39 **lest h** ye be found even to fight against *3379*
17:27 if **h** they might feel after him, and *686+1065*
2Co 9: 4 **Lest h** if they of Macedonia come with me, *3381*

HAPPEN (4) [HAP, HAPLY, HAPPENED, HAPPENETH]
1Sa 28:10 there shall no punishment **h** to thee for this 7136
Pr 12:21 There shall no evil **h** to the just: but 579
Isa 41:22 bring *them* forth, and shew us what shall **h**: 7136
Mk 10:32 began to tell them what *things* should **h** *4819*

HAPPENED (12) [HAPPEN]
1Sa 6: 9 *that* smote us; it *was* a chance *that* **h** to us. 1961
2Sa 1: 6 As I **h by chance** upon mount Gilboa, 7122
20: 1 there **h to be** there a man of Belial, whose 7122
Est 4: 7 Mordecai told him of all that had **h** unto 7136
Jer 44:23 therefore this evil is **h unto** you, as *at* this 7122
Lk 24:14 together of all these *things* which had **h**. *4819*
Ac 3:10 amazement at that which had **h** unto him. *4819*
Ro 11:25 that blindness in part is **h** to Israel, until *1096*
1Co 10:11 Now all these *things* **h** unto them for *4819*
Php 1:12 that the *things which* **h** unto me have fallen NIG
1Pe 4:12 as though *some* strange *thing* **h** unto you: *4819*
2Pe 2:22 But it is **h** unto them according to the true *4819*

HAPPENETH (6) [HAPPEN]
Ecc 2:14 I myself perceived also that one event **h** to 7136
2:15 As it **h** to the fool, so it happeneth even to 4745
2:15 it happeneth to the fool, so it **h** even to me; 7136
8:14 that there be just *men*, unto whom it **h** 5060
8:14 there be wicked *men*, to whom it **h** 5060
9:11 of skill; but time and chance **h** to them all. 7136

HAPPIER (1) [HAPPY]
1Co 7:40 But she is **h** if she so abide, after my *3107*

HAPPIZZEZ See APHSES

HAPPY (28) [HAPPIER]
Ge 30:13 Leah said, **H** am I, for the daughters will call 837
Dt 33:29 **H** *art* thou, O Israel: who *is* like unto thee, 835
1Ki 10: 8 **H** *are* thy men, happy *are* these thy servants, 835
10: 8 Happy *are* thy men, **h** *are* these thy servants, 835
2Ch 9: 7 **H** *are* thy men, and happy *are* these thy 835
9: 7 *are* thy men, and **h** *are* these thy servants, 835
Job 5:17 Behold, **h** *is* the man whom God correcteth: 835
Ps 127: 5 **H** *is* the man that hath his quiver full of 835
128: 2 **h** *shalt* thou *be*, and *it shall be* well with 835
137: 8 **h** *shall he be*, that rewardeth thee as thou 835
137: 9 **H** *shall he be* that taketh and dasheth thy 835
144:15 **H** *is that* people, that is in such a case: *yea*, 835
144:15 *yea*, **h** *is that* people, whose God *is* 835
146: 5 **H** *is he* that *hath* the God of Jacob for his 835
Pr 3:13 **H** *is* the man *that* findeth wisdom, and 835
3:18 and **h** *is* every one that retaineth her. 833
14:21 but he that hath mercy on the poor, **h** *is* he. 835
16:20 and whoso trusteth in the LORD, **h** *is* he. 835
28:14 **H** *is* the man that feareth alway: but he that 835
29:18 but he that keepeth the law, **h** *is* he. 835
Jer 12: 1 *wherefore* are all they **h** that deal very 7951
Mal 3:15 now we **call** the proud **h**; yea, they that work 833
Jn 13:17 If ye know these *things*, **h** are ye if ye do *3107*
Ac 26: 2 I think myself **h**, king Agrippa, because *3107*
Ro 14:22 **H** *is* he that condemneth not himself in *that* *3107*
Jas 5:11 Behold, we **count** them **h** which endure. *3106*
1Pe 3:14 **h** *are ye*: and be not afraid of their terror, *3107*
4:14 **h** *are ye*; for the spirit of glory and of God *3107*

HARA (1)
1Ch 5:26 Habor, and **H**, and to the river Gozan, 2024

HARADAH (2)
Nu 33:24 from mount Shapher, and encamped in **H**. 2732
33:25 they removed from **H**, and pitched in 2732

HARAN (19) [BETH-HARAN, CHARRAN]
Ge 11:26 and begat Abram, Nahor, and **H**. 2039
11:27 Terah begat Abram, Nahor, and **H**; and 2039
11:27 and Haran; and **H** begat Lot. 2039
11:28 **H** died before his father Terah in the land 2039
11:29 Milcah, the daughter of **H**, the father of 2039
11:31 Lot the son of **H** his son's son, and Sarai 2039
11:31 and they came unto **H**, and dwelt there. 2771
11:32 five years: and Terah died in **H**. 2771
12: 4 five years old when he departed out of **H**. 2771
12: 5 and the souls that they had gotten in **H**; 2771
27:43 arise, flee thou to Laban my brother to **H**; 2771
28:10 out from Beer-sheba, and went toward **H**. 2771
29: 4 whence *be* ye? And they said, Of **H** *are* we. 2771
2Ki 19:12 **H**, and Rezeph, and the children of Eden 2771
1Ch 2:46 bare **H**, and Moza, and Gazez: 2771
2:46 and Moza, and Gazez: and **H** begat Gazez. 2771
23: 9 Shelomith, and Haziel, and **H**, three. 2039
Isa 37:12 **H**, and Rezeph, and the children of Eden 2771
Eze 27:23 **H**, and Canneh, and Eden, the merchants of 2771

HARARITE (5)
2Sa 23:11 him *was* Shammah the son of Agee the **H**. 2043
23:33 Shammah the **H**, Ahiam the son of Sharar 2043
23:33 Ahiam the son of Sharar the **H**, 2043
1Ch 11:34 Jonathan the son of Shage the **H**, 2043
11:35 Ahiam the son of Sacar the **H**, Eliphal 2043

HARBONA (1) [HARBONAH]
Est 1:10 Biztha, **H**, Bigtha, and Abagtha, Zethar, 2726

HARBONAH (1) [HARBONA]
Est 7: 9 **H**, one of the chamberlains, said before 2726

HARD (45) [HARDEN, HARDENED, HARDENETH, HARDER, HARDHEARTED, HARDLY, HARDNESS]
Ge 18:14 Is any thing too **h** for the LORD? At 6381
35:16 and Rachel travailed, and she had **h** labour. 7185
35:17 it came to pass, when she was in **h** labour, 7185
Ex 1:14 they made their lives bitter with **h** bondage, 7186
18:26 the **h** causes they brought unto Moses, but 7186
Lev 3: 9 he take off **h by** the back bone; 5980+3807.1
Dt 1:17 the cause that is too **h** for you, bring *it* unto 7185
15:18 It shall not seem **h** unto thee, when thou 7185
17: 8 If there arise a matter too **h** for thee in 6381
26: 6 afflicted us, and laid upon us **h** bondage: 7186
Jdg 9:52 **went h** unto the door of the tower to burn it 5066
20:45 **pursued h** after them unto Gidom, and 1692
1Sa 14:22 even they also **followed h** after them in 1692
31: 2 the Philistines **followed h** upon Saul and 1692
2Sa 1: 6 and horsemen **followed h after** him. 1692
3:39 these men the sons of Zeruiah *be* too **h** for 7186
13: 2 Amnon thought it **h** for him to do any thing 6381
1Ki 10: 1 she came to prove him with **h questions**. 2420
21: 1 **h by** the palace of Ahab king of Samaria. 681
2Ki 2:10 he said, Thou hast asked a **h thing**: 7185
1Ch 10: 2 the Philistines **followed h** after Saul, and 1692
19: 4 cut off their garments in the midst **h by** 5704
2Ch 9: 1 Solomon with **h questions** at Jerusalem, 2420
Job 41:24 yea, as **h** as a piece of the nether *millstone*. 3332
Ps 60: 3 Thou hast shewed thy people **h** *things:* thou 7186
63: 8 My soul **followeth h** after thee: thy right 1692
88: 7 Thy wrath **lieth h** upon me, and thou hast 5564
94: 4 shall they utter *and* speak **h** *things? and* 6277
Pr 13:15 but the way of transgressors *is* **h**. 386
Isa 14: 3 from the **h** bondage wherein thou wast 7186
Jer 32:17 out arm, *and* there is nothing too **h** for thee: 6381
32:27 of all flesh: is there any thing too **h** for me? 6381
Eze 3: 5 of a strange speech and of a **h** language, 3515
3: 6 of a strange speech and of a **h** language, 3515
Da 5:12 shewing of **h sentences**, and dissolving of 280
Jnh 1:13 Nevertheless the men **rowed h** to bring *it* to 2864
Mt 25:24 Lord, I knew thee that thou art a **h** man, *4642*
Mk 10:24 how **h** is it for them that trust in riches to *1422*
Jn 6:60 they had heard *this*, said, This is a **h** saying; *4642*
Ac 9: 5 *it is* **h** for thee to kick against the pricks. *4642*
18: 7 whose house **joined h** to the synagogue. *4927*
26:14 *it is* **h** for thee to kick against the pricks. *4642*
Heb 5:11 and **h** to be uttered, seeing ye are dull of *1421*
2Pe 3:16 which are some *things* **h to be understood**, *1425*
Jude 1:15 of all *their* **h** *speeches* which ungodly *4642*

HARDEN (12) [HARD]
Ex 4:21 I will **h** his heart, that he shall not let 2388
7: 3 I will **h** Pharaoh's heart, and multiply my 7185
14: 4 I will **h** Pharaoh's heart, that he shall 2388
14:17 I will **h** the hearts of the Egyptians, and 2388
Dt 15: 7 thou shalt not **h** thy heart, nor shut thine 553
Jos 11:20 For it was of the LORD to **h** their hearts, 2388
1Sa 6: 6 Wherefore then do ye **h** your hearts, as 3513
Job 6:10 yea, I would **h** myself in sorrow; let him 5539
Ps 95: 8 **H** not your heart, as *in* the provocation, *and* 7185
Heb 3: 8 **H** not your hearts, as in the provocation, *4645*
3:15 **h** not your hearts, as in the provocation. *4645*
4: 7 if ye will hear his voice, **h** not your hearts. *4645*

HARDENED (33) [HARD]
Ex 7:13 he **h** Pharaoh's heart, that he hearkened not 2388
7:14 Pharaoh's heart *is* **h**, he refuseth to let 3515
7:22 Pharaoh's heart was **h**, neither did he 2388
8:15 he **h** his heart, and hearkened not unto 3513
8:19 Pharaoh's heart was **h**, and he hearkened 2388
8:32 Pharaoh **h** his heart at this time also, 3513
9: 7 the heart of Pharaoh was **h**, and he did not 3513
9:12 the LORD **h** the heart of Pharaoh, and 2388
9:34 and **h** his heart, he and his servants. 3513
9:35 the heart of Pharaoh was **h**, neither would 2388
10: 1 for I have **h** his heart, and the heart of his 3513
10:20 the LORD **h** Pharaoh's heart, so that he 2388
10:27 the LORD **h** Pharaoh's heart, and 2388
11:10 the LORD **h** Pharaoh's heart, so that he 2388
14: 8 the LORD **h** the heart of Pharaoh king of 2388
Dt 2:30 for the LORD thy God **h** his spirit, and 7185
1Sa 6: 6 the Egyptians and Pharaoh **h** their hearts? 3513
2Ki 17:14 **h** their necks, like to the neck of their 7185
2Ch 36:13 **h** his heart from turning unto the LORD 553
Ne 9:16 **h** their necks, and hearkened not to thy 7185
9:17 **h** their necks, and in their rebellion 7185
9:29 and **h** their neck, and would not hear. 7185
Job 9: 4 who hath **h** *himself* against him, and 7185
39:16 She is **h against** her young ones, as though 7188
Isa 63:17 thy ways, *and* **h** our heart from thy fear? 7188
Jer 7:26 nor inclined their ear, but **h** their neck: 7185
19:15 because they have **h** their necks, that *they* 7185
Da 5:20 heart was lifted up, and his mind **h** in pride, 8631
Mk 6:52 *miracle* of the loaves: for their heart was **h**. *4456*
8:17 have ye your heart yet **h**? *4456*
Jn 12:40 hath blinded their eyes, and **h** their heart; *4456*
Ac 19: 9 But when divers were **h**, and believed not, *4645*
Heb 3:13 lest any of you be **h** through *4645*

HARDENETH (4) [HARD]
Pr 21:29 A wicked man **h** his face: but *as for* 5810
28:14 he that **h** his heart shall fall into mischief. 7185
29: 1 He, that being often reproved **h** *his* neck, 7185
Ro 9:18 he will *have mercy*, and whom he will he **h**. *4645*

HARDER (3) [HARD]
Pr 18:19 A brother offended *is* **h** *to be won* than a NIH
Jer 5: 3 they have **made** their faces **h** than a rock; 2388
Eze 3: 9 As an adamant **h** than flint have I made thy 2389

HARDHEARTED (1) [HARD, HEART]
Eze 3: 7 house of Israel *are* impudent and **h**. 3820+7186

HARDLY (8) [HARD]
Ge 16: 6 when Sarai **dealt h with** her, she fled from 6031
Ex 13:15 to pass, when Pharaoh would **h** let us go, 7185
Isa 8:21 pass through it, **h bestead** and hungry: 7185
Mt 19:23 That a rich *man* shall **h** enter into *1423*
Mk 10:23 How **h** shall they that have riches enter into *1423*
Lk 9:39 and bruising him **h** departeth from him. *3425*
18:24 How **h** shall they that have riches enter into *1423*
Ac 27: 8 And **h** passing it, came unto a place *which* *3433*

HARDNESS (7) [HARD]
Job 38:38 When the dust groweth into **h**, and 4165
Mt 19: 8 of the **h** of your **hearts** suffered you to put *4641*
Mk 3: 5 being grieved for the **h** of their hearts, *4457*
10: 5 For the **h of** your **heart** he wrote you this *4641*
16:14 them with their unbelief and **h of heart**, *4641*
Ro 2: 5 But after thy **h** and impenitent heart *4643*
2Ti 2: 3 Thou therefore **endure h**, as a good soldier *2553*

HARDSHIP; HARDSHIPS See TRAVAIL; TRAVAILED; TRAVAILEST; TRAVAILETH

HARE (2)
Lev 11: 6 the **h**, because he cheweth the cud, but 768
Dt 14: 7 *as* the camel, and the **h**, and the coney: 768

HAREPH (1)
1Ch 2:51 of Beth-lehem, **H** the father of Beth-gader. 2780

HARETH (1)
1Sa 22: 5 and came *into* the forest of **H**. 2802

HARHAIAH (1)
Ne 3: 8 unto him repaired Uzziel the son of **H**, 2736

HARHAS (1)
2Ki 22:14 the son of **H**, keeper of the wardrobe; 2745

HARHUR (2)
Ezr 2:51 the children of Hakupha, the children of **H**, 2744
Ne 7:53 the children of Hakupha, the children of **H**, 2744

HARIM (11)
1Ch 24: 8 The third to **H**, the fourth to Seorim, 2766
Ezr 2:32 The children of **H**, three hundred and 2766
2:39 The children of **H**, a thousand and 2766
10:21 of the sons of **H**; Maaseiah, and Elijah, 2766
10:31 *of* the sons of **H**; Eliezer, Ishijah, Malchiah, 2766
Ne 3:11 Malchijah the son of **H**, and Hashub 2766
7:35 The children of **H**, three hundred and 2766
7:42 The children of **H**, a thousand *and* 2766
10: 5 **H**, Meremoth, Obadiah, 2766
10:27 Malluch, **H**, Baanah. 2766
12:15 Of **H**, Adna; of Meraioth, Helkai; 2766

HARIPH (2)
Ne 7:24 The children of **H**, an hundred *and* twelve. 2756
10:19 **H**, Anathoth, Nebai, 2756

HARLOT (40) [HARLOT'S, HARLOTS, HARLOTS']
Ge 34:31 Should he deal with our sister as with a **h**? 2181
38:15 Judah saw her, he thought her to be a **h**; 2181
38:21 saying, Where *is* the **h**, that *was* openly by 6948
38:21 they said, There was no **h** in this *place*. 6948
38:22 *that* there was no **h** in this *place*. 6948
38:24 thy daughter in law hath **played the h**; 2181
Lev 21:14 or a divorced *woman*, or profane, *or* a **h**, 2181
Jos 6:17 only Rahab the **h** shall live, she and all that 2181
6:25 Joshua saved Rahab the **h** alive, and her 2181
Jdg 11: 1 *man* of valour, and he *was* the son of a **h**: 2181
16: 1 and saw there a **h**, and went in unto her. 2181
Pr 7:10 met him a woman *with* the attire of a **h**, 2181
Isa 1:21 How is the faithful city become a **h**! *it was* 2181
23:15 end of seventy years shall Tyre sing as a **h**. 2181
23:16 the city, thou **h** that hast been forgotten; 2181
Jer 2:20 green tree thou wanderest, **playing the h**. 2181
3: 1 thou hast **played the h** with many lovers; 2181
3: 6 green tree, and there hath **played the h**. 2181
3: 8 feared not, but went and **played the h** also. 2181
Eze 16:15 **playedst the h** because of thy renown, and 2181
16:16 and **playedst the h** thereupon: 2181
16:28 thou hast **played the h** with them, and 2181
16:31 hast not been as a **h**, in that *thou* scornest 2181
16:35 Wherefore, O **h**, hear the word of 2181

H

Eze 16:41 cause thee to cease from **playing the h**, 2181
23: 5 Aholah **played the h** when she was mine; 2181
23:19 wherein she had **played the h** in the land of 2181
23:44 go in unto a woman that **playeth the h**: 2181
Hos 2: 5 For their mother hath **played the h**: 2181
3: 3 thou shalt not **play the h**, and thou shalt not 2181
4:15 Though thou, Israel, **play the h**, *yet* let not 2181
Joel 3: 3 have given a boy for a **h**, and sold a girl for 2181
Am 7:17 Thy wife shall be a **h** in the city, and 2181
Mic 1: 7 for she gathered *it* of the hire of a **h**, and 2181
1: 7 and they shall return to the hire of a **h**. 2181
Na 3: 4 of the whoredoms of the wellfavoured **h**, 2181
1Co 6:15 and make *them* the members of a **h**? *4204*
6:16 know ye not that he which is joined to a **h** *4204*
Heb 11:31 By faith the **h** Rahab perished not with *4204*
Jas 2:25 Likewise also was not Rahab the **h** justified *4204*

HARLOT'S (2) [HARLOT]
Jos 2: 1 came *into* a **h** house, named Rahab, and 2181
6:22 Go *into* the **h** house, and bring out thence 2181

HARLOTS (7) [HARLOT]
1Ki 3:16 *that were* **h**, unto the king, and stood before 2181
Pr 29: 3 he that keepeth company with **h** spendeth 2181
Hos 4:14 with whores, and they sacrifice with **h**: 6948
Mt 21:31 the **h** go into the kingdom of God before *4204*
21:32 but the publicans and the **h** believed him: *4204*
Lk 15:30 which hath devoured thy living with **h**, *4204*
Rev 17: 5 THE MOTHER OF **H** AND *4204*

HARLOTS' (1) [HARLOT]
Jer 5: 7 assembled themselves by troops *in* the **h** 2181

HARM (16) [HARMLESS]
Ge 31:52 over this heap and this pillar unto me, for **h**. 7451
Lev 5:16 the **h** that he hath **done** in the holy *thing*, 2398
Nu 35:23 *was* not his enemy, neither sought his **h**: 7451
1Sa 26:21 for I will no more **do** thee **h**, because my 7489
2Sa 20: 6 of Bichri **do** us more **h** than *did* Absalom: 3415
2Ki 4:41 may eat. And there was no **h** in the pot. 7451
1Ch 16:22 mine anointed, and **do** my prophets no **h**. 7489
Ps 105:15 mine anointed, and **do** my prophets no **h**. 7489
Pr 3:30 without cause, if he have done thee no **h**. 7451
Jer 39:12 and look well to him, and do him no **h**; 7451
Ac 16:28 with a loud voice, saying, Do thyself no **h**: *2556*
27:21 and to have gained this **h** and loss. *5196*
28: 5 off the beast into the fire, and felt no **h**. *2556*
28: 6 and saw no **h** come to him, they changed *824*
28:21 that came shewed or spake any **h** of thee. *4190*
1Pe 3:13 And who *is* he that will **h** you, if ye be *2559*

HARMLESS (3) [HARM]
Mt 10:16 therefore wise as serpents, and **h** as doves. *185*
Php 2:15 That ye may be blameless and **h**, the sons of *185*
Heb 7:26 *who is* holy, **h**, undefiled, separate from *172*

HARMONY See CONCORD

HARNEPHER (1)
1Ch 7:36 and **H**, and Shual, and Beri, and Imrah, 2774

HARNESS (5) [HARNESSED]
1Ki 20:11 Tell *him*, Let not him that girdeth on *his* **h** NIH
22:34 king of Israel between the joints of the **h**: 8302
2Ch 9:24 raiment, **h**, and spices, horses, and mules, 5402
18:33 king of Israel between the joints of the **h**: 8302
Jer 46: 4 **H** the horses; and get up, ye horsemen, and 631

HARNESSED (1) [HARNESS]
Ex 13:18 the children of Israel went up **h** out of 2571

HAROD (1) [HARODITE]
Jdg 7: 1 up early, and pitched beside the well of **H**: 5878

HARODITE (2) [HAROD]
2Sa 23:25 Shammah the **H**, Elika the Harodite, 2733
23:25 Shammah the Harodite, Elika the **H**, 2733

HAROEH (1)
1Ch 2:52 had sons; **H**, *and* half of the Manahethites. 7204

HARORITE (1)
1Ch 11:27 Shammoth the **H**, Helez the Pelonite, 2033

HAROSHETH (3)
Jdg 4: 2 which dwelt in **H** of the Gentiles. 2800
4:13 from **H** of the Gentiles unto the river of 2800
4:16 and after the host, unto **H** of the Gentiles: 2800

HARP (30) [HARPED, HARPERS, HARPING, HARPS]
Ge 4:21 he was the father of all such as handle the **h** 3658
31:27 and with songs, with tabret, and with **h**? 3658
1Sa 10: 5 a tabret, and a pipe, and a **h**, before them; 3658
16:16 out a man, *who is* a cunning player on a **h**: 3658
16:23 that David took a **h**, and played with his 3658
1Ch 25: 3 who prophesied with a **h**, to give thanks 3658
Job 21:12 They take the timbrel and **h**, and rejoice at 3658
30:31 My **h** also is *turned* to mourning, and 3658
Ps 33: 2 Praise the LORD with **h**: sing unto him 3658
43: 4 yea, upon the **h** will I praise thee, O God 3658
49: 4 I will open my dark saying upon the **h**. 3658
57: 8 my glory; awake, psaltery and **h**: 3658
71:22 unto thee will I sing with the **h**, O thou 3658
81: 2 the timbrel, the pleasant **h** with the psaltery. 3658
92: 3 upon the **h** with a solemn sound. 3658
98: 5 Sing unto the LORD with the **h**; with 3658
98: 5 with the **h**, and the voice of a psalm. 3658
108: 2 Awake, psaltery and **h**: I *myself* will awake 3658
147: 7 sing *praise* upon the **h** unto our God: 3658
149: 3 *praises* unto him with the timbrel and **h**. 3658
150: 3 praise him with the psaltery and **h**. 3658
Isa 5:12 the **h**, and the viol, the tabret, and pipe, 3658
16:11 Wherefore my bowels shall sound like a **h** 3658
Isa 23:16 Take a **h**, go about the city, thou harlot that 3658
24: 8 that rejoice endeth, the joy of the **h** ceaseth. 3658
Da 3: 5 flute, **h**, sackbut, psaltery, dulcimer, and 7030
3: 7 flute, **h**, sackbut, psaltery, and all kinds of 7030
3:10 flute, **h**, sackbut, psaltery, and dulcimer, 7030
3:15 flute, **h**, sackbut, psaltery, and dulcimer, 7030
1Co 14: 7 life giving sound, whether pipe or **h**, *2788*

HARPED (1) [HARP]
1Co 14: 7 how shall it be known what is piped or **h**? *2789*

HARPERS (2) [HARP]
Rev 14: 2 I heard the voice of **h** harping with their *2790*
18:22 And the voice of **h**, and musicians, and *2790*

HARPING (1) [HARP]
Rev 14: 2 I heard the voice of harpers **h** with their *2789*

HARPIST See MINSTREL

HARPS (20) [HARP]
2Sa 6: 5 even on **h**, and on psalteries, and 3658
1Ki 10:12 **h** also and psalteries for singers: 3658
1Ch 13: 8 with **h**, and with psalteries, and 3658
15:16 psalteries and **h** and cymbals, sounding, 3658
15:21 Azaziah, with **h** on the Sheminith to excel. 3658
15:28 making a noise with psalteries and **h**. 3658
16: 5 Jeiel with psalteries and with **h**; but 3658
25: 1 of Jeduthun, who should prophesy with **h**, 3658
25: 6 with cymbals, psalteries, and **h**, for 3658
2Ch 5:12 having cymbals and psalteries and **h**, 3658
9:11 and **h** and psalteries for singers: 3658
20:28 **h** and trumpets unto the house of 3658
29:25 with psalteries, and with **h**, according to 3658
Ne 12:27 *with* cymbals, psalteries, and with **h**. 3658
Ps 137: 2 We hanged our **h** upon the willows in 3658
Isa 30:32 lay upon him, *it* shall be with tabrets and **h**: 3658
Eze 26:13 the sound of thy **h** shall be no more heard. 3658
Rev 5: 8 having every one *of them* **h**, and *2788*
14: 2 the voice of harpers harping with their **h**: *2788*
15: 2 on the sea of glass, having *the* **h** of God. *2788*

HARROW (1) [HARROWS]
Job 39:10 or will he **h** the valleys after thee? 7702

HARROWS (2) [HARROW]
2Sa 12:31 under **h** of iron, and under axes of iron, and 2757
1Ch 20: 3 and with **h** of iron, and with axes. 2757

HARSH See FROWARD; SHARPNESS; STOUT

HARSHA (2)
Ezr 2:52 the children of Mehida, the children of **H**, 2797
Ne 7:54 the children of Mehida, the children of **H**, 2797

HART (9) [HARTS]
Dt 12:15 as of the roebuck, and as of the **h**. 354
12:22 Even as the roebuck and the **h** is eaten, so 354
14: 5 The **h**, and the roebuck, and the fallow deer, 354
15:22 *eat it* alike, as the roebuck, and as the **h**. 354
Ps 42: 1 As the **h** panteth after the water brooks, so 354
SS 2: 9 My beloved *is* like a roe or a young **h**: 354
2:17 or a young **h** upon the mountains of Bether. 354
8:14 to a young **h** upon the mountains of spices. 354
Isa 35: 6 shall the lame *man* leap as a **h**, and 354

HARTS (2) [HART]
1Ki 4:23 beside **h**, and roebucks, and fallowdeer, and 354
La 1: 6 her princes are become like **h** *that* find no 354

HARUM (1)
1Ch 4: 8 and the families of Aharhel the son of **H**. 2037

HARUMAPH (1)
Ne 3:10 unto them repaired Jedaiah the son of **H**, 2739

HARUPHITE (1)
1Ch 12: 5 and Shemariah, and Shephatiah the **H**, 2741

HARUZ (1)
2Ki 21:19 the daughter of **H** of Jotbah. 2743

HARVEST (61) [HARVESTMAN]
Ge 8:22 seedtime and **h**, and cold and heat, and 7105
30:14 Reuben went in the days of wheat **h**, and 7105
45: 6 which *there shall* neither *be* earing nor **h**. 7105
Ex 23:16 the feast of **h**, the firstfruits of thy labours, 7105
34:21 in earing time and in **h** thou shalt rest. 7105
34:22 of the firstfruits of wheat **h**, and the feast of 7105
Lev 19: 9 when ye reap the **h** of your land, thou shalt 7105
19: 9 shalt thou gather the gleanings of thy **h**. 7105
23:10 shall reap the **h** thereof, then ye shall bring 7105
23:10 of the firstfruits of your **h** unto the priest: 7105
23:22 when ye reap the **h** of your land, thou shalt 7105
23:22 shalt thou gather *any* gleaning of thy **h**: 7105
25: 5 it own accord of thy **h** thou shalt not reap, 7105
Dt 24:19 When thou **cuttest down** thine **h** in 7105+7114
Jos 3:15 overfloweth all his banks all the time of **h**,) 7105
Jdg 15: 1 in the time of wheat **h**, that Samson visited 7105
Ru 1:22 *to* Beth-lehem in the beginning of barley **h**. 7105
2:21 young men, until they have ended all my **h**. 7105
2:23 of Boaz to glean unto the end of barley **h** 7105
2:23 the end of barley harvest and of wheat **h**; 7105
1Sa 6:13 *were* reaping *their* wheat **h** in the valley: 7105
8:12 to reap his **h**, and to make his instruments 7105
12:17 *Is it* not wheat **h** to day? I will call unto 7105
2Sa 21: 9 and were put to death in the days of **h**, 7105
21: 9 the first *days*, in the beginning of barley **h**. 7105
21:10 from the beginning of **h** until water 7105
23:13 came to David in the **h time** unto the cave 7105
Job 5: 5 Whose **h** the hungry eateth up, and taketh it 7105
Pr 6: 8 *and* gathereth her food in the **h**. 7105
10: 5 he that sleepeth in **h** *is* a son that causeth 7105
Pr 20: 4 therefore shall he beg in **h**, and 7105
25:13 As the cold of snow in the time of **h**, *so is* a 7105
26: 1 as rain in **h**, so honour *is* not seemly for a 7105
Isa 9: 3 joy before thee according to the joy in **h**, 7105
16: 9 thy summer fruits and for thy **h** is fallen. 7105
17:11 *but* the **h** *shall be* a heap in the day of grief 7105
18: 4 *and* like a cloud of dew in the heat of **h**. 7105
18: 5 For afore the **h**, when the bud is perfect, 7105
23: 3 of Sihor, the **h** of the river, *is* her revenue; 7105
Jer 5:17 they shall eat up thine **h**, and thy bread, 7105
5:24 unto us the appointed weeks of the **h**. 7105
8:20 The **h** is past, the summer is ended, and 7105
50:16 that handleth the sickle in the time of **h**; 7105
51:33 and the time of her **h** shall come. 7105
Hos 6:11 Also, O Judah, he hath set a **h** for thee, 7105
Joel 1:11 because the **h** of the field is perished. 7105
3:13 Put ye in the sickle, for the **h** is ripe: come, 7105
Am 4: 7 when *there were* yet three months to the **h**: 7105
Mt 9:37 The **h** truly is plenteous, but the labourers *2326*
9:38 Pray ye therefore the Lord of the **h**, that he *2326*
9:38 that he will send forth labourers into his **h**. *2326*
13:30 Let both grow together until the **h**: and *2326*
13:30 in the time of **h** I will say to the reapers, *2326*
13:39 the **h** is the end of the world; and *2326*
Mk 4:29 putteth in the sickle, because the **h** is come. *2326*
Lk 10: 2 The **h** truly *is* great, but the labourers *are* *2326*
10: 2 pray ye therefore the Lord of the **h**, that he *2326*
10: 2 he would send forth labourers into his **h**. *2326*
Jn 4:35 are yet four months, and *then* cometh **h**? *2326*
4:35 the fields; for they are white already to **h**. *2326*
Rev 14:15 thee to reap; for the **h** of the earth is ripe. *2326*

HARVESTMAN (2) [HARVEST, MAN]
Isa 17: 5 it shall be as when the **h** gathereth the corn, 7105
Jer 9:22 as the handful after the **h**, and none shall 7114

HASADIAH (1)
1Ch 3:20 Ohel, and Berechiah, and **H**, Jushabhesed, 2619

HASENUAH (1)
1Ch 9: 7 the son of Hodaviah, the son of **H**, 5574

HASHABIAH (15)
1Ch 6:45 The son of **H**, the son of Amaziah, the son 2811
9:14 the son of Azrikam, the son of **H**, of 2811
25: 3 Zeri, and Jeshaiah, **H**, and Mattithiah, six, 2811
25:19 The twelfth to **H**, *he*, his sons, and 2811
26:30 **H** and his brethren, men of valour, 2811
27:17 Of the Levites, **H** the son of Kemuel: of 2811
2Ch 35: 9 his brethren, and **H** and Jeiel and Jozabad, 2811
Ezr 8:19 **H**, and with him Jeshaiah of the sons of 2811
8:24 **H**, and ten of their brethren with them, 2811
Ne 3:17 Next unto him repaired **H**, the ruler of 2811
10:11 Micha, Rehob, **H**, 2811
11:15 of Azrikam, the son of **H**, the son of Bunni; 2811
11:22 the son of **H**, the son of Mattaniah, the son 2811
12:21 Of Hilkiah, **H**; of Jedaiah, Nethaneel. 2811
12:24 **H**, Sherebiah, and Jeshua the son of 2811

HASHABNAH (1)
Ne 10:25 Rehum, **H**, Maaseiah, 2812

HASHABNEIAH See HASHABNIAH

HASHABNIAH (2)
Ne 3:10 unto him repaired Hattush the son of **H**. 2813
9: 5 Jeshua and Kadmiel, Bani, **H**, Sherebiah, 2813

HASHBADANA (1)
Ne 8: 4 and Malchiah, and Hashum, and **H**, 2806

HASHBADDANA See HASHBADANA

HASHEM (1)
1Ch 11:34 The sons of **H** the Gizonite, Jonathan 2044

HASHMONAH (2)
Nu 33:29 they went from Mithcah, and pitched in **H**. 2832
33:30 they departed from **H**, and encamped at 2832

HASHUB (4)
Ne 3:11 **H** the son of Pahath-moab, repaired 2815
3:23 and **H** over against their house. 2815
10:23 Hoshea, Hananiah, **H**, 2815
11:15 Shemaiah the son of **H**, the son of 2815

HASHUBAH (1)
1Ch 3:20 **H**, and Ohel, and Berechiah, and Hasadiah, 2807

HASHUM (5)
Ezr 2:19 The children of **H**, two hundred twenty and 2828
10:33 Of the sons of **H**; Mattenai, Mattathah, 2828
Ne 7:22 The children of **H**, three hundred twenty 2828
8: 4 and Malchiah, and **H**, and Hashbadana, 2828
10:18 Hodijah, **H**, Bezai, 2828

HASHUPHA (1) [HASUPHA]
Ne 7:46 the children of Ziha, the children of **H**, 2817

HASRAH (1)
2Ch 34:22 the son of **H**, keeper of the wardrobe; 2641

HASSENAAH (1)
Ne 3: 3 the fish gate did the sons of **H** build, 5570

HASSENUAH See HASENUAH; SENUAH

HASSHUB (1)
1Ch 9:14 Shemaiah the son of **H**, the son of 2815

HAST (1071) [HAVE]
Ge 3:11 **H** thou eaten of the tree, whereof I NIH
3:13 the woman, What *is* this *that* thou **h** done? NIH

Ge 3:14 Because thou **h** done this, thou *art* cursed NIH
3:17 Because thou **h** hearkened unto the voice of NIH
3:17 **h** eaten of the tree, of which I commanded NIH
4:10 he said, What **h** thou done? the voice of thy NIH
4:14 thou **h** driven me out *this* day from the face NIH
12:18 said, What *is* this *that* thou **h** done unto me? NIH
15: 3 Behold, to me thou **h** given no seed: NIH
18: 5 And they said, So do, as thou **h** said. NIH
19:12 said unto Lot, **H** thou here any besides? 3807.1
19:12 and whatsoever thou **h** in the city, 3807.1
19:19 thy sight, and thou **h** magnified thy mercy, NIH
19:19 which thou **h** shewed unto me in saving my NIH
19:21 *this* city, for the which thou **h** spoken. NIH
20: 3 for the woman which thou **h** taken; NIH
20: 9 said unto him, What **h** thou done unto us? NIH
20: 9 that thou **h** brought on me and on my NIH
20: 9 thou **h** done deeds unto me that ought not to NIH
20:10 sawest thou, that thou **h** done this thing? NIH
21:23 and to the land wherein thou **h** sojourned. NIH
21:29 ewe lambs which thou **h** set by themselves? NIH
22:12 seeing thou **h** not withheld thy son, thine NIH
22:16 for because thou **h** done this thing, and NIH
22:16 **h** not withheld thy son, thine only *son:* NIH
22:18 because thou **h** obeyed my voice. NIH
24:14 *let the same be* she *that* thou **h** appointed for NIH
24:14 thereby shall I know that thou **h** shewed NIH
26:10 What *is* this thou **h** done unto us? NIH
27:20 How *is it that* thou **h** found *it so* quickly, my NIH
27:36 **H** thou not reserved a blessing for me? NIH
27:38 **H** thou but one blessing, my father? 3807.1
27:45 he forget *that* which thou **h** done to him: NIH
29:25 to Laban, What *is* this thou **h** done unto me? NIH
29:25 then **h** thou beguiled me? NIH
30:15 *Is it* a small matter that thou **h** taken my NIH
31:26 Laban said to Jacob, What **h** thou done, NIH
31:26 that thou **h** stolen away unawares to me, and NIH
31:28 **h** not suffered me to kiss my sons and my NIH
31:28 thou **h** now done foolishly in *so* doing. NIH
31:30 *yet* wherefore **h** thou stolen my gods? NIH
31:36 that thou **h** *so* hotly pursued after me? NIH
31:37 Whereas thou **h** searched all my stuff, NIH
31:37 what **h** thou found of all thy household NIH
31:41 and thou **h** changed my wages ten times. NIH
32:10 which thou **h** shewed unto thy servant; NIH
32:28 for **as a prince h** thou **power** with God and 8280
32:28 with God and with men, and **h** prevailed. NIH
33: 9 my brother; keep that thou **h** unto thyself. 3807.1
37:10 What *is* this dream that thou **h** dreamed? NIH
38:23 I sent this kid, and thou **h** not found her. NIH
38:29 she said, How **h** thou broken forth? NIH
39:17 which thou **h** brought unto us, NIH
45:10 and thy herds, and all that thou **h**: 3807.1
45:11 and thy household, and all that thou **h**, 3807.1
47:25 they said, Thou **h** saved our lives: let us find NIH
47:30 And he said, I will do as thou **h** said. NIH
Ex 3:12 When thou **h** brought forth the people out of NIH
4:10 nor since thou **h** spoken unto thy servant: NIH
5:22 wherefore **h** thou *so* evil entreated this NIH
5:22 this people? why *is* it *that* thou **h** sent me? NIH
5:23 neither **h** thou delivered thy people at all. NIH
9:19 thy cattle, and all that thou **h** in the field; 3807.1
10:29 Moses said, Thou **h** spoken well, I will see NIH
12:44 when thou **h** circumcised him, then shall he NIH
13:12 cometh of a beast which thou **h**; 1961+3807.1
14:11 **h** thou taken us away to die in NIH
14:11 wherefore **h** thou dealt thus with us, to carry NIH
15: 7 in the greatness of thine excellency thou **h** NIH
15:13 Thou in thy mercy **h** led forth the people NIH
15:13 led forth the people *which* thou **h** redeemed: NIH
15:13 thou **h** guided *them* in thy strength unto thy NIH
15:16 people pass over, *which* thou **h** purchased. NIH
15:17 *which* thou **h** made for thee to dwell in, NIH
17: 3 Wherefore *is* this *that* thou **h** brought us up NIH
20:25 lift up thy tool upon it, thou **h** polluted it. NIH
23:16 thy labours, which thou **h** sown in the field: NIH
23:16 when thou **h** gathered in thy labours out of NIH
29:36 when thou **h** made an atonement for it, and NIH
32:11 which thou **h** brought forth out of the land NIH
32:21 that thou **h** brought *so* great a sin upon NIH
32:32 out of thy book which thou **h** written. NIH
33: 1 the people which thou **h** brought up out of NIH
33:12 thou **h** not let me know whom thou wilt NIH
33:12 Yet thou **h** said, I know thee by name, and NIH
33:12 and thou **h** also found grace in my sight. NIH
33:17 I will do this thing also that thou **h** spoken: NIH
33:17 for thou **h** found grace in my sight, and NIH
Nu 5:19 if thou **h** not gone aside *to* uncleanness *with* NIH
5:20 if thou **h** gone aside *to another* instead of NIH
11:11 Wherefore **h** thou afflicted thy servant? NIH
11:21 thou **h** said, I will give them flesh, that they NIH
14:17 according as thou **h** spoken, saying, NIH
14:19 as thou **h** forgiven this people, from Egypt NIH
16:13 *Is it* a small thing that thou **h** brought us up NIH
16:14 Moreover thou **h** not brought us into a land NIH
22:28 that thou **h** smitten me these three times? NIH
22:29 unto the ass, Because thou **h** mocked me. NIH
22:30 upon which thou **h** ridden ever since *I was* NIH
22:32 Wherefore **h** thou smitten thine ass these NIH
23:11 unto Balaam, What **h** thou done unto me? NIH
23:11 and behold, thou **h** blessed *them* altogether. NIH
24:10 thou **h** altogether blessed *them* these three NIH
27:13 when thou **h** seen it, thou also shalt be NIH
Dt 1:14 The thing which thou **h** spoken *is* good *for* NIH
1:31 where thou **h** seen how that the LORD thy NIH
2: 7 *hath been* with thee; thou **h** lacked nothing. NIH
3:24 thou **h** begun to shew thy servant thy NIH
4:33 midst of the fire, as thou **h** heard, and live? NIH
8:10 When thou **h** eaten and art full, then NIH
8:12 Lest *when* thou **h** eaten and art full, and NIH
8:12 **h** built goodly houses, and dwelt *therein;* NIH
8:13 and all that thou **h** is multiplied; 3807.1
9: 2 *of whom* thou **h** heard *say,* Who can stand NIH
9:12 for thy people which thou **h** brought forth NIH
9:26 which thou **h** redeemed through thy NIH
9:26 which thou **h** brought forth out of Egypt NIH
Dt 12:26 Only thy holy *things* which thou **h**, 1961+3807.1
13: 2 which thou **h** not known, and let us serve NIH
13: 6 which thou **h** not known, thou, nor thy NIH
16:13 after that thou **h** gathered in thy corn and NIH
17: 4 thou **h** heard *of it,* and inquired diligently, NIH
21: 8 whom thou **h** redeemed, and lay not NIH
21:10 thine hands, and thou **h** taken them captive, NIH
21:11 **h a desire** unto her, that thou wouldest 2836
21:14 of her, because thou **h** humbled her. NIH
22: 3 which he hath lost, and thou **h** found, shalt NIH
22: 9 lest the fruit of *thy* seed which thou **h** sown, NIH
23:23 according as thou **h** vowed unto the LORD NIH
23:23 which thou **h** promised with thy mouth. NIH
24:19 **h** forgot a sheaf in the field, thou shalt not NIH
26:10 which thou, O LORD, **h** given me. NIH
26:12 When thou **h** made an end of tithing all NIH
26:12 **h** given *it* unto the Levite, the stranger, NIH
26:13 which thou **h** commanded me: NIH
26:14 have done according to all that thou **h** NIH
26:15 and the land which thou **h** given us, NIH
26:17 Thou **h** avouched the LORD *this* day to be NIH
28:20 of thy doings, where*by* thou **h** forsaken me. NIH
32:18 and **h** forgotten God that formed thee. NIH
Jos 2:17 this thine oath which thou **h** made us swear. NIH
2:20 we will be quit of thine oath which thou **h** NIH
7: 7 wherefore **h** thou at all brought this people NIH
7:19 tell me now what thou **h** done; hide *it* not NIH
7:25 Joshua said, Why **h** thou troubled us? NIH
14: 9 thou **h** wholly followed the LORD my NIH
15:19 a blessing; for thou **h** given me a south land; NIH
17:14 Why **h** thou given me *but* one lot and NIH
17:17 Thou *art* a great people, and **h** great power: NIH
Jdg 1:15 for thou **h** given me a south land; give me NIH
5:21 O my soul, thou **h** trodden down strength. NIH
6:36 save Israel by mine hand, as thou **h** said, NIH
6:37 save Israel by mine hand, as thou **h** said. NIH
8: 1 Why **h** thou served us thus, that *thou* NIH
8:22 for thou **h** delivered us from the hand of NIH
9:38 *is* not this the people that thou **h** despised? NIH
11:12 saying, What **h** thou to do with me, 3807.1
11:35 thou **h** brought me very low, and thou art NIH
11:36 *if* thou **h** opened thy mouth unto NIH
14:16 thou **h** put forth a riddle unto the children of NIH
14:16 of my people, and **h** not told *it* me. 3807.1
15:11 what *is* this *that* thou **h** done unto us? NIH
15:18 Thou **h** given this great deliverance into NIH
16:10 thou **h** mocked me, and told me lies: NIH
16:13 Hitherto thou **h** mocked me, and told me NIH
16:15 thou **h** mocked me these three times, and NIH
16:15 **h** not told me wherein thy great strength NIH
18: 3 thou in this *place?* and what **h** thou here? 3807.1
Ru 2:11 all that thou **h** done unto thy mother in law NIH
2:11 *how* thou **h** left thy father and thy mother, NIH
2:13 for that thou **h** comforted me, and for that NIH
2:13 for that thou **h** spoken friendly unto thine NIH
2:19 said unto her, Where **h** thou gleaned to day? NIH
3:10 *for* thou **h** shewed more kindness in NIH
3:15 Bring the vail that *thou **h*** upon thee, and NIH
1Sa 1:17 *thee* thy petition that thou **h** asked of him. NIH
4:20 *unto her,* Fear not; for thou **h** born a son. NIH
12: 4 they said, Thou **h** not defrauded us, NIH
12: 4 neither **h** thou taken ought of any man's NIH
13:11 Samuel said, What **h** thou done? And Saul NIH
13:13 Samuel said to Saul, Thou **h** done foolishly: NIH
13:13 thou **h** not kept the commandment of NIH
13:14 thou **h** not kept *that* which the LORD NIH
14:43 said to Jonathan, Tell me what thou **h** done. NIH
15:23 Because thou **h** rejected the word of NIH
15:26 for thou **h** rejected the word of the LORD, NIH
17:28 with whom **h** thou left those few sheep in NIH
17:45 of the armies of Israel, whom thou **h** defied. NIH
19:17 Why **h** thou deceived me so, and sent away NIH
20: 8 for thou **h** brought thy servant into a NIH
20:19 *when* thou **h** stayed three days, *then* NIH
20:30 **h** chosen the son of Jesse to thine own NIH
22:13 in that thou **h** given him bread and a sword, NIH
22:13 and a sword, and **h** inquired of God for him, NIH
24:17 for thou **h** rewarded me good, whereas I NIH
24:18 thou **h** shewed *this* day how that thou hast NIH
24:18 thou hast shewed *this* day how that thou **h** NIH
24:19 good for that thou **h** done unto me this day. NIH
25: 6 and peace *be unto* all that thou **h**. 3807.1
25: 7 now I have heard that thou **h** shearers: 3807.1
25:31 either that thou **h** shed blood causeless, or NIH
25:33 which **h** kept me this day from coming to NIH
26:15 then **h** thou not kept thy lord the king? NIH
26:16 This thing *is* not good that thou **h** done. NIH
28:12 to Saul, saying, Why **h** thou deceived me? NIH
28:15 Why **h** thou disquieted me, to bring me up? NIH
29: 4 which thou **h** appointed him, and let him not NIH
29: 6 thou ***h** been* upright, and thy going out and NIH
29: 8 what **h** thou found in thy servant so long as NIH
2Sa 1:26 very pleasant **h** thou been unto me: thy love NIH
3: 7 Wherefore **h** thou gone in unto my father's NIH
3:24 to the king, and said, What **h** thou done? NIH
3:24 why *is* it *that* thou **h** sent him away, and NIH
6:22 of the maidservants which thou **h** spoken of, NIH
7:18 my house, that thou **h** brought me hitherto? NIH
7:19 thou **h** spoken also of thy servant's house NIH
7:21 **h** thou done all these great things, NIH
7:24 For thou **h** confirmed to thyself thy people NIH
7:25 the word that thou **h** spoken concerning thy NIH
7:25 establish *it* for ever, and do as thou **h** said. NIH
7:27 of Israel, **h** revealed to thy servant, saying, NIH
7:28 thou **h** promised this goodness unto thy NIH
7:29 **h** spoken *it:* and with thy blessing let NIH
11:19 When thou **h** made an end of telling NIH
12: 9 Wherefore **h** thou despised NIH
12: 9 thou **h** killed Uriah the Hittite with NIH
12: 9 **h** taken his wife to be thy wife, and hast NIH
12: 9 **h** slain him with the sword of the children NIH
12:10 because thou **h** despised me, and hast taken NIH
12:10 **h** taken the wife of Uriah the Hittite to be NIH
12:14 by this deed thou **h** given great occasion to NIH
12:21 What thing *is* this that thou **h** done? NIH
2Sa 14:13 **h** thou thought such a thing against NIH
15:35 ***h** thou* not there with thee Zadok and NIH
16: 8 of Saul, in whose stead thou **h** reigned; NIH
16:10 then say, Wherefore **h** thou done so? NIH
18:21 to Cushi, Go tell the king what thou **h** seen. NIH
18:22 my son, seeing that thou **h** no tidings ready? NIH
19: 5 Thou **h** shamed *this* day the faces of all thy NIH
19: 6 for thou **h** declared *this* day, that thou NIH
22:36 Thou **h** also given me the shield of thy NIH
22:37 Thou **h** enlarged my steps under me; so NIH
22:40 For thou **h** girded me with strength to battle: NIH
22:40 them that rose up against me **h** thou NIH
22:41 Thou **h** also given me the necks of mine NIH
22:44 Thou also **h** delivered me from the strivings NIH
22:44 thou **h** kept me to be head of the heathen: NIH
22:49 thou also **h** lifted me up on high above them NIH
22:49 thou **h** delivered me from the violent man. NIH
1Ki 1: 6 at any time in saying, Why **h** thou done so? NIH
1:11 **H** thou not heard that Adonijah the son of NIH
1:24 Nathan said, My lord O king, **h** thou said, NIH
1:27 and thou **h** not shewed *it* unto thy servant, NIH
2: 8 *thou **h*** with thee Shimei the son of Gera, NIH
2:26 thou **h** been afflicted in all where*in* my NIH
2:43 then **h** thou not kept the oath of the LORD, NIH
3: 6 Thou **h** shewed unto thy servant David my NIH
3: 6 thou **h** kept for him this great kindness, that NIH
3: 6 that thou **h** given him a son to sit on his NIH
3: 7 thou **h** made thy servant king instead of NIH
3: 8 midst of thy people which thou **h** chosen, NIH
3:11 Because thou **h** asked this thing, and NIH
3:11 and **h** not asked for thyself long life; NIH
3:11 neither **h** asked riches for thyself, nor hast NIH
3:11 nor **h** asked the life of thine enemies; NIH
3:11 **h** asked for thyself understanding to discern NIH
3:13 I have also given thee *that* which thou **h** not NIH
8:24 Who **h** kept with thy servant David my NIH
8:24 **h** fulfilled *it* with thine hand, as *it is* this NIH
8:25 that they walk before me as thou **h** walked NIH
8:29 *even* toward the place of which thou **h** said, NIH
8:36 which thou **h** given to thy people for an NIH
8:44 toward the city which thou **h** chosen, NIH
8:48 the city which thou **h** chosen, and the house NIH
9: 3 that thou **h** made before me: NIH
9: 3 hallowed this house, which thou **h** built, NIH
9:13 What cities *are* these which thou **h** given NIH
11:11 thou **h** not kept my covenant and NIH
11:22 what ***h*** thou lacked with me, that behold, NIH
13:21 Forasmuch as thou **h** disobeyed the mouth NIH
13:21 **h** not kept the commandment which NIH
13:22 **h** eaten bread and drunk water in the place, NIH
14: 8 *yet* thou **h** not been as my servant David, NIH
14: 9 **h** done evil above all that were before thee: NIH
14: 9 for thou **h** gone and made thee other gods, NIH
14: 9 me to anger, and **h** cast me behind thy back: NIH
16: 2 thou **h** walked in the way of Jeroboam, and NIH
16: 2 **h** made my people Israel to sin, to provoke NIH
17:13 unto her, Fear not; go *and* do as thou **h** said: NIH
17:20 **h** thou also brought evil upon the widow NIH
18:18 of the LORD, and thou **h** followed Baalim. NIH
18:37 *that* thou **h** turned their heart back again. NIH
20:13 **H** thou seen all this great multitude? NIH
20:25 like the army that thou **h** lost, horse for NIH
20:36 Because thou **h** not obeyed the voice of NIH
20:40 So *shall* thy judgment *be;* thyself **h** decided NIH
20:42 Because thou **h** let go out of *thy* hand a man NIH
21:19 **H** thou killed, and also taken possession? NIH
21:20 to Elijah, **H** thou found me, O mine enemy? NIH
21:20 thou **h** sold thyself to work evil in the sight NIH
21:22 for the provocation wherewith thou **h** NIH
2Ki 1:16 Forasmuch as thou **h** sent messengers to NIH
2:10 he said, Thou **h** asked a hard thing: NIH
4: 2 tell me, what **h** thou in the house? 3426+3807.1
4:13 thou **h** been careful for us with all this care; NIH
5: 8 Wherefore **h** thou rent thy clothes? NIH
6:22 whom thou **h** taken captive with thy sword NIH
9:18 Jehu said, What **h** thou to do with peace? 3807.1
9:19 What **h** thou to do with peace? 3807.1
10:30 Because thou **h** done well in executing *that* NIH
10:30 **h** done unto the house of Ahab according to NIH
14:10 Thou **h** indeed smitten Edom, and NIH
17:26 The nations which thou **h** removed, and NIH
19: 6 Be not afraid of the words which thou **h** NIH
19:11 thou **h** heard what the kings of Assyria have NIH
19:15 of the earth; thou **h** made heaven and earth. NIH
19:20 *That* which thou **h** prayed to me against NIH
19:22 Whom **h** thou reproached and blasphemed? NIH
19:22 against whom **h** thou exalted *thy* voice, and NIH
19:23 By thy messengers thou **h** reproached NIH
19:23 thou hast reproached the Lord, and **h** said, NIH
19:25 **H** thou not heard long ago *how* I have done NIH
20:19 word of the LORD which thou **h** spoken. NIH
22:18 *As touching* the words which thou **h** heard; NIH
22:19 thou **h** humbled thyself before the LORD, NIH
22:19 and **h** rent thy clothes, and wept before me; NIH
23:17 proclaimed these things that thou **h** done NIH
1Ch 17: 8 I have been with thee whithersoever thou **h** NIH
17:16 that thou **h** brought me hitherto? NIH
17:17 for thou **h** *also* spoken of thy servant's NIH
17:17 **h** regarded me according to the estate of a NIH
17:19 own heart, **h** thou done all this greatness, NIH
17:21 whom thou **h** redeemed out of Egypt? NIH
17:23 let the thing that thou **h** spoken concerning NIH
17:23 established for ever, and do as thou **h** said. NIH
17:25 **h** told thy servant that *thou* wilt build him a NIH
17:26 **h** promised this goodness unto thy servant: NIH
22: 8 Thou **h** shed blood abundantly, and NIH
22: 8 blood abundantly, and **h** made great wars: NIH
22: 8 thou **h** shed much blood upon the earth in NIH
28: 3 because thou ***h** been* a man of war, and NIH
28: 3 *hast been* a man of war, and **h** shed blood. NIH
28:20 until *thou* **h** finished all the work for NIH
29:17 the heart, and **h pleasure** in uprightness. 7521
2Ch 1: 8 Thou **h** shewed great mercy unto David my NIH
1: 8 and **h** made me to reign in his stead. NIH
1: 9 for thou **h** made me king over a people like NIH

2Ch 1:11 thou **h** not asked riches, wealth, or honour, NIH
1:11 thine enemies, neither yet **h** asked long life; NIH
1:11 **h** asked wisdom and knowledge for thyself, NIH
6:15 Thou which **h** kept with thy servant David NIH
6:15 my father *that* which thou **h** promised him; NIH
6:15 **h** fulfilled *it* with thine hand, as *it is* this NIH
6:16 my father *that* which thou **h** promised him, NIH
6:16 in my law, as thou **h** walked before me. NIH
6:17 which thou **h** spoken unto thy servant NIH
6:20 upon the place whereof thou **h** said that NIH
6:27 when thou **h** taught them the good way, NIH
6:27 which thou **h** given unto thy people for an NIH
6:34 thee toward this city which thou **h** chosen, NIH
6:38 *toward* the city which thou **h** chosen, and NIH
16:7 Because thou **h** relied on the king of Syria, NIH
16:9 Herein thou **h** done foolishly: therefore NIH
19:3 in that thou **h** taken away the groves out of NIH
19:3 and **h** prepared thine heart to seek God. NIH
20:11 which thou **h** given us to inherit. NIH
20:37 Because thou **h** joined thyself with Ahaziah, NIH
21:12 Because thou **h** not walked in the ways of NIH
21:13 **h** walked in the way of the kings of Israel, NIH
21:13 **h** made Judah and the inhabitants of NIH
21:13 also **h** slain thy brethren of thy father's NIH
24:6 Why **h** thou not required of the Levites to NIH
25:15 Why **h** thou sought after the gods of NIH
25:16 because thou **h** done this, and hast not NIH
25:16 and **h** not hearkened unto my counsel. NIH
25:19 Lo, thou **h** smitten the Edomites; NIH
26:18 out of the sanctuary; for thou **h** trespassed; NIH
34:26 *concerning* the words which thou **h** heard; NIH
Ezr 9:11 Which thou **h** commanded by thy servants NIH
9:13 seeing that thou our God **h** punished us less NIH
9:13 and **h** given us *such* deliverance as this; NIH
10:12 a loud voice, As thou **h** said, so must we do. NIH
Ne 1:10 whom thou **h** redeemed by thy great power, NIH
6:7 thou **h** also appointed prophets to preach of NIH
9:6 thou **h** made heaven, the heaven of heavens, NIH
9:8 *say,* to his seed, and **h** performed thy words; NIH
9:33 for thou **h** done right, but we have done NIH
9:37 unto the kings whom thou **h** set over us NIH
Est 6:10 as thou **h** said, and do *even* so to Mordecai NIH
6:10 let nothing fail of all that thou **h** spoken. NIH
6:13 before whom thou **h** begun to fall, NIH
Job 1:8 **H** thou considered my servant Job, NIH
1:10 **H** not thou made a hedge about him, and NIH
1:10 thou **h** blessed the work of his hands, and NIH
2:3 **H** thou considered my servant Job, NIH
4:3 thou **h** instructed many, and thou hast NIH
4:3 and thou **h** strengthened the weak hands. NIH
4:4 and thou **h** strengthened the feeble knees. NIH
7:20 why **h** thou set me as a mark against thee, NIH
10:4 **H** thou eyes of flesh? or seest thou as 3807.1
10:9 that thou **h** made me as the clay; NIH
10:10 **H** thou not poured me out as milk, and NIH
10:11 Thou **h** clothed me with skin and flesh, and NIH
10:11 and **h** fenced me with bones and sinews. NIH
10:12 Thou **h** granted me life and favour, and NIH
10:13 these *things* **h** thou hid in thine heart: NIH
10:18 **h** thou brought me forth out of the womb? NIH
11:4 For thou **h** said, My doctrine *is* pure, and NIH
14:5 thou **h** appointed his bounds that he cannot NIH
15:8 **H** thou heard the secret of God? and NIH
16:7 thou **h** made desolate all my company. NIH
16:8 thou **h** filled me with wrinkles, *which* is a 3807.1
17:4 For thou **h** hid their heart from NIH
22:6 For thou **h** taken a pledge from thy brother NIH
22:7 Thou **h** not given water to the weary to NIH
22:7 thou **h** withholden bread from the hungry. NIH
22:9 Thou **h** sent widows away empty, and NIH
22:15 **H** thou marked the old way which wicked NIH
26:2 How **h** thou helped *him that is* without NIH
26:3 How **h** thou counselled *him that hath* no NIH
26:3 *how* **h** thou plentifully declared the thing as NIH
26:4 To whom **h** thou uttered words? and NIH
33:8 Surely thou **h** spoken in mine hearing, and NIH
33:32 If *thou* **h** any thing to say, answer me: 3426
34:16 If now *thou* **h** understanding, hear this: NIH
36:17 thou **h** fulfilled the judgment of the wicked: NIH
36:21 for this **h** thou chosen rather than affliction. NIH
36:23 or who can say, Thou **h** wrought iniquity? NIH
37:18 **H** thou with him spread out the sky, NIH
38:4 the earth? declare, if thou **h** understanding. 3045
38:12 **H** thou commanded the morning since thy NIH
38:16 **H** thou entered into the springs of the sea? NIH
38:16 or **h** thou walked in the search of the depth? NIH
38:17 **h** thou seen the doors of the shadow of NIH
38:18 **H** thou perceived the breadth of the earth? NIH
38:22 **H** thou entered into the treasures of NIH
38:22 or **h** thou seen the treasures of the hail, NIH
39:19 **H** thou given the horse strength? hast thou NIH
39:19 **h** thou clothed his neck with thunder? NIH
40:9 **H** thou an arm like God? or, canst thou NIH
Ps 3:7 for thou **h** smitten all mine enemies *upon* NIH
3:7 thou **h** broken the teeth of the ungodly. NIH
4:1 thou **h** enlarged me *when I was* in distress; NIH
4:7 Thou **h** put gladness in my heart, more than NIH
7:6 awake for me *to* the judgment *that* thou **h** NIH
8:1 who **h** set thy glory above the heavens. NIH
8:2 sucklings **h** thou ordained strength because NIH
8:3 and the stars, which thou **h** ordained; NIH
8:5 For thou **h** made him a little lower than NIH
8:5 and **h** crowned him *with* glory and honour. NIH
8:6 thou **h** put all *things* under his feet: NIH
9:4 For thou **h** maintained my right and NIH
9:5 Thou **h** rebuked the heathen, thou hast NIH
9:5 the heathen, thou **h** destroyed the wicked, NIH
9:5 thou **h** put out their name for ever and ever. NIH
9:6 thou **h** destroyed cities; their memorial is NIH
9:10 LORD, **h** not forsaken them that seek thee. NIH
10:14 Thou **h** seen *it;* for thou beholdest mischief NIH
10:17 thou **h** heard the desire of the humble: NIH
16:2 *O my soul,* thou **h** said unto the LORD, NIH
17:3 Thou **h** proved mine heart; thou hast visited NIH
17:3 thou **h** visited *me* in the night; thou hast NIH

Ps 17:3 thou **h** tried me, *and* shalt find nothing; NIH
18:35 Thou **h** also given me the shield of thy NIH
18:36 Thou **h** enlarged my steps under me, NIH
18:39 For thou **h** girded me *with* strength unto NIH
18:39 thou **h** subdued under me those that rose up NIH
18:40 Thou **h** also given me the necks of mine NIH
18:43 Thou **h** delivered me from the strivings of NIH
18:43 thou **h** made me the head of the heathen: NIH
18:48 thou **h** delivered me from the violent man. NIH
21:2 Thou **h** given him his heart's desire, and NIH
21:2 and **h** not withholden the request of his lips. NIH
21:5 honour and majesty **h** thou laid upon him. NIH
21:6 For thou **h** made him most blessed for ever: NIH
21:6 thou **h** made him exceeding glad with thy NIH
22:1 My God, my God, why **h** thou forsaken me? NIH
22:15 thou **h** brought me into the dust of death. NIH
22:21 for thou **h** heard me from the horns of NIH
27:9 thou **h** been my help; leave me not, NIH
30:1 for thou **h** lifted me up, and hast not made NIH
30:1 and **h** not made my foes to rejoice over me. NIH
30:2 I cried unto thee, and thou **h** healed me. NIH
30:3 thou **h** brought up my soul from the grave: NIH
30:3 thou **h** kept me alive, that I should not go NIH
30:7 by thy favour thou **h** made my mountain to NIH
30:11 Thou **h** turned for me my mourning into NIH
30:11 thou **h** put off my sackcloth, and girded me NIH
31:5 thou **h** redeemed me, O LORD God of NIH
31:7 for thou **h** considered my trouble; thou hast NIH
31:7 thou **h** known my soul in adversities; NIH
31:8 **h** not shut me up into the hand of NIH
31:8 thou **h** set my feet in a large room. NIH
31:19 which thou **h** laid up for them that fear thee; NIH
31:19 *which* thou **h** wrought for them that trust in NIH
35:22 *This* thou **h** seen, O LORD: keep not NIH
39:5 thou **h** made my days *as* a handbreadth; NIH
40:5 *are* thy wonderful works *which* thou **h** done, NIH
40:6 didst not desire; mine ears **h** thou opened: NIH
40:6 and sin offering **h** thou not required. NIH
42:9 God my rock, Why **h** thou forgotten me? NIH
44:7 thou **h** saved us from our enemies, and NIH
44:7 and **h** put them to shame that hated us. NIH
44:9 thou **h** cast off, and put us to shame; and NIH
44:11 Thou **h** given us like sheep appointed for NIH
44:11 and **h** scattered us among the heathen. NIH
44:19 Though thou **h** sore broken us in the place NIH
50:16 What **h** thou to do to declare my statutes, or NIH
50:18 and **h** been partaker with adulterers. NIH
50:21 These *things* **h** thou done, and I kept NIH
51:8 *that* the bones *which* thou **h** broken may NIH
52:9 because thou **h** done *it:* and I will wait on NIH
53:5 thou **h** put *them* to shame, because God hath NIH
56:13 For thou **h** delivered my soul from death: NIH
59:16 for thou **h** been my defence and refuge in NIH
60:1 O God, thou **h** cast us off, thou hast NIH
60:1 thou hast cast us off, thou **h** scattered us, NIH
60:1 hast scattered us, thou **h** been displeased; NIH
60:2 Thou **h** made the earth to tremble; thou hast NIH
60:2 made the earth to tremble; thou **h** broken it: NIH
60:3 Thou **h** shewed thy people hard *things:* thou NIH
60:3 **h** made us to drink the wine *of* NIH
60:4 Thou **h** given a banner to them that fear NIH
61:3 For thou **h** been a shelter for me, *and* NIH
61:5 For thou, O God, **h** heard my vows: NIH
61:5 thou **h** given *me* the heritage of those that NIH
63:7 Because thou **h** been my help, therefore NIH
65:9 them corn, when thou **h** so provided for it. NIH
66:10 For thou, O God, **h** proved us: thou hast NIH
66:10 proved us: thou **h** tried us, as silver is tried. NIH
66:12 Thou **h** caused men to ride over our heads; NIH
68:10 **h** prepared of thy goodness for the poor. NIH
68:18 Thou **h** ascended on high, thou hast led NIH
68:18 on high, thou **h** led captivity captive: NIH
68:18 thou **h** received gifts for men; yea, *for* NIH
68:28 O God, that which thou **h** wrought for us. NIH
69:19 Thou **h** known my reproach, and my shame, NIH
69:26 For they persecute *him* whom thou **h** NIH
69:26 they talk to the grief of those whom thou **h** NIH
71:3 thou **h** given commandment to save me; NIH
71:17 O God, thou **h** taught me from my youth: NIH
71:19 very high, who **h** done great *things:* O God, NIH
71:20 *Thou,* which **h** shewed me great and NIH
71:23 and my soul, which thou **h** redeemed. NIH
73:23 thou **h** holden *me* by my right hand. NIH
73:27 thou **h** destroyed all them that go a whoring NIH
74:1 O God, why **h** thou cast *us* off for ever? NIH
74:2 *which* thou **h** purchased of old; NIH
74:2 thine inheritance, *which* thou **h** redeemed; NIH
74:2 this mount Zion, wherein thou **h** dwelt. NIH
74:16 thou **h** prepared the light and the sun. NIH
74:17 Thou **h** set all the borders of the earth: NIH
74:17 the earth: thou **h** made summer and winter. NIH
77:14 thou **h** declared thy strength among NIH
77:15 Thou **h** with *thine* arm redeemed thy NIH
80:8 Thou **h** brought a vine out of Egypt: NIH
80:8 thou **h** cast out the heathen, and planted it. NIH
80:12 Why **h** thou *then* broken down her hedges, NIH
85:1 thou **h** been favourable unto thy land: NIH
85:1 thou **h** brought back the captivity of Jacob. NIH
85:2 Thou **h** forgiven the iniquity of thy people, NIH
85:2 of thy people, thou **h** covered all their sin. NIH
85:3 Thou **h** taken away all thy wrath: thou hast NIH
85:3 thou **h** turned *thyself* from the fierceness of NIH
86:9 All nations whom thou **h** made shall come NIH
86:13 thou **h** delivered my soul from the lowest NIH
86:17 LORD, **h** holpen me, and comforted me. NIH
88:6 Thou **h** laid me in the lowest pit, NIH
88:7 and thou **h** afflicted *me* with all thy waves. NIH
88:8 Thou **h** put away mine acquaintance far NIH
88:8 thou **h** made me an abomination unto them: NIH
88:18 Lover and friend **h** thou put far from me, NIH
89:10 Thou **h** broken Rahab in pieces, as one that NIH
89:10 thou **h** scattered thine enemies with thy NIH
89:11 the fulness thereof, thou **h** founded them. NIH
89:12 and the south thou **h** created them: NIH
89:13 Thou **h** a mighty arm: strong is thy hand, 3807.1

Ps 89:38 thou **h** cast off and abhorred, thou hast been NIH
89:38 thou **h** been wroth with thine anointed. NIH
89:39 Thou **h** made void the covenant of thy NIH
89:39 thou **h** profaned his crown *by casting it* to NIH
89:40 Thou **h** broken down all his hedges; NIH
89:40 thou **h** brought his strong holds to ruin. NIH
89:42 Thou **h** set up the right hand of his NIH
89:42 thou **h** made all his enemies to rejoice. NIH
89:43 Thou **h** also turned the edge of his sword, NIH
89:43 and **h** not made him to stand in the battle. NIH
89:44 Thou **h** made his glory to cease, and cast his NIH
89:45 The days of his youth **h** thou shortened: NIH
89:45 thou **h** covered him with shame. Selah. NIH
89:47 wherefore **h** thou made all men in vain? NIH
90:1 thou **h** been our dwelling place in all NIH
90:8 Thou **h** set our iniquities before thee, NIH
90:15 to the days *wherein* thou **h** afflicted us, NIH
91:9 Because thou **h** made the LORD, *which is* NIH
92:4 LORD, **h** made me glad through thy work: NIH
102:10 for thou **h** lifted me up, and cast me down. NIH
102:25 Of old **h** thou laid the foundation of NIH
104:8 the place which thou **h** founded for them. NIH
104:9 Thou **h** set a bound *that* they may not pass NIH
104:24 in wisdom **h** thou made them all: the earth NIH
104:26 *whom* thou **h** made to play therein. NIH
108:11 *Wilt* not *thou,* O God, *who* **h** cast us off? NIH
109:27 *is* thy hand; *that* thou, LORD, **h** done it. NIH
110:3 the morning: thou **h** the dew of thy youth. 3807.1
116:8 For thou **h** delivered my soul from death, NIH
116:16 of thy handmaid: thou **h** loosed my bonds. NIH
118:13 Thou **h** thrust sore at me that *I* might fall: NIH
118:21 for thou **h** heard me, and art become my NIH
119:4 Thou **h** commanded *us* to keep thy precepts NIH
119:21 Thou **h** rebuked the proud *that are* cursed, NIH
119:49 upon which thou **h** caused me to hope. NIH
119:65 Thou **h** dealt well with thy servant, NIH
119:75 and *that* thou *in* faithfulness **h** afflicted me. NIH
119:90 thou **h** established the earth, and it abideth. NIH
119:93 for with them thou **h** quickened me. NIH
119:98 Thou *through* thy commandments **h** made NIH
119:102 from thy judgments: for thou **h** taught me. NIH
119:118 Thou **h** trodden down all them that err from NIH
119:138 Thy testimonies *that* thou **h** commanded *are* NIH
119:152 I have known of old that thou **h** founded NIH
119:171 when thou **h** taught me thy statutes. NIH
137:8 *be,* that rewardeth thee as thou **h** served us. NIH
138:2 for thou **h** magnified thy word above all thy NIH
139:1 thou **h** searched me, and known *me.* NIH
139:5 Thou **h** beset me behind and before, and NIH
139:13 For thou **h** possessed my reins: thou hast NIH
139:13 thou **h** covered me in my mother's womb. NIH
140:7 thou **h** covered my head in the day of battle. NIH
Pr 3:28 morrow I will give; when thou **h** it by thee. 3426
6:1 *if* thou **h** stricken thy hand with a stranger, NIH
22:27 If thou **h** nothing to pay, why should he 3807.1
23:8 The morsel *which* thou **h** eaten shalt thou NIH
24:14 when thou **h** found *it,* then there shall be a NIH
25:16 **H** thou found honey? eat so much as is NIH
30:32 If thou **h** done foolishly in lifting up thyself, NIH
30:32 or if thou **h** thought evil, *lay thine* hand NIH
Ecc 5:4 in fools: pay that which thou **h** vowed. NIH
7:22 that thou thyself likewise **h** cursed others. NIH
SS 1:15 behold, thou *art* fair; thou **h** doves' eyes. NIH
4:1 *art* fair; thou **h** doves' eyes within thy locks: NIH
4:9 Thou **h** ravished my heart, my sister, NIH
4:9 thou **h** ravished my heart with one of thine NIH
Isa 2:6 Therefore thou **h** forsaken thy people NIH
3:6 *saying,* Thou **h** clothing, be thou our 3807.1
9:3 Thou **h** multiplied the nation, *and* NIH
9:4 For thou **h** broken the yoke of his burden, NIH
14:13 For thou **h** said in thine heart, I will ascend NIH
14:20 because thou **h** destroyed thy land, *and* NIH
17:10 Because thou **h** forgotten the God of thy NIH
17:10 **h** not been mindful of the rock of thy NIH
22:16 What **h** thou here? and whom hast thou 3807.1
22:16 whom **h** thou here, that thou hast hewed 3807.1
22:16 that thou **h** hewed thee out a sepulchre here, NIH
23:16 the city, thou harlot that **h** been forgotten; NIH
25:1 thy name; for thou **h** done wonderful things; NIH
25:2 For thou **h** made of a city a heap; *of* a NIH
25:4 For thou **h** been a strength to the poor, NIH
26:12 for thou also **h** wrought all our works in us. NIH
26:14 therefore **h** thou visited and destroyed them, NIH
26:15 Thou **h** increased the nation, O LORD, NIH
26:15 O LORD, thou **h** increased the nation: NIH
37:6 Be not afraid of the words that thou **h** heard, NIH
37:11 thou **h** heard what the kings of Assyria have NIH
37:16 of the earth: thou **h** made heaven and earth. NIH
37:21 Whereas thou **h** prayed to me against NIH
37:23 Whom **h** thou reproached and blasphemed? NIH
37:23 against whom **h** thou exalted *thy* voice, and NIH
37:24 By thy servants **h** thou reproached the Lord, NIH
37:24 hast thou reproached the Lord, and **h** said, NIH
37:26 **H** thou not heard long ago, *how* I have done NIH
38:17 thou **h** in love to my soul *delivered it* from NIH
38:17 for thou **h** cast all my sins behind thy back. NIH
39:8 word of the LORD which thou **h** spoken. NIH
40:28 **H** thou not known? hast thou not heard, NIH
40:28 **h** thou not heard, *that* the everlasting God, NIH
43:4 thou **h** been honourable, and I have loved NIH
43:22 But thou **h** not called upon me, O Jacob; but NIH
43:22 but thou **h** been weary of me, O Israel. NIH
43:23 Thou **h** not brought me the small cattle of NIH
43:23 neither **h** thou honoured me *with* thy NIH
43:24 Thou **h** bought me no sweet cane with NIH
43:24 neither **h** thou filled me *with* the fat of thy NIH
43:24 thou **h** made me to serve with thy sins, NIH
43:24 thou **h** wearied me with thine iniquities. NIH
45:4 though thou **h** not known me. NIH
45:5 I girded thee though thou **h** not known me: NIH
45:10 to the woman, What **h** thou brought forth? NIH
47:6 upon the ancient **h** thou very heavily laid NIH
47:10 For thou **h** trusted in thy wickedness: NIH
47:10 thou **h** said, None seeth me. Thy wisdom NIH
47:10 thou **h** said in thine heart, I *am,* and NIH

Isa 47:12 wherein thou **h** laboured from thy youth; NIH
47:15 be unto thee *with* whom thou **h** laboured, NIH
48: 6 Thou **h** heard, see all this; and will not ye NIH
49:20 after thou **h** lost the other, shall say again in NIH
51:13 **h** feared continually every day because of NIH
51:17 which **h** drunk at the hand of the LORD NIH
51:17 thou **h** drunken the dregs of the cup of NIH
51:23 thou **h** laid thy body as the ground, and NIH
57: 6 even to them **h** thou poured a drink offering, NIH
57: 6 thou **h** offered a meat offering. NIH
57: 7 and high mountain **h** thou set thy bed: NIH
57: 8 the posts **h** thou set up thy remembrance: NIH
57: 8 for thou **h** discovered *thyself to another* than NIH
57: 8 thou **h** enlarged thy bed, and made thee *a* NIH
57:10 thou **h** found the life of thine hand; NIH
57:11 of whom **h** thou been afraid or feared, NIH
57:11 that thou **h** lied, and hast not remembered NIH
57:11 thou hast lied, and **h** not remembered me, NIH
60:15 Whereas thou **h** been forsaken and hated, so NIH
62: 8 thy wine, for the which thou **h** laboured: NIH
63:17 why **h** thou made us to err from thy ways, NIH
64: 7 for thou **h** hid thy face from us, and NIH
64: 7 **h** consumed us, because of our iniquities. NIH
Jer 1:12 said the LORD unto me, Thou **h** well seen: NIH
2:17 **H** thou not procured this unto thyself, NIH
2:17 in that thou **h** forsaken the LORD thy God, NIH
2:18 now what **h** thou to do in the way of 3807.1
2:18 or what **h** thou to do in the way of 3807.1
2:19 that thou **h** forsaken the LORD thy God, NIH
2:23 way in the valley, know what thou **h** done: NIH
2:27 and to a stone, Thou **h** brought me forth: NIH
2:28 where *are* thy gods that thou **h** made thee? NIH
2:33 **h** thou also taught the wicked ones thy NIH
3: 1 thou **h** played the harlot with many lovers; NIH
3: 2 and see where thou **h** not been lien with. NIH
3: 2 In the ways **h** thou sat for them, as NIH
3: 2 thou **h** polluted the land with thy NIH
3: 5 thou **h** spoken and done evil *things* as thou NIH
3: 6 **H** thou seen *that* which backsliding Israel NIH
3:13 that thou **h** transgressed against the LORD NIH
3:13 **h** scattered thy ways to the strangers under NIH
4:10 surely thou **h** greatly deceived this people NIH
4:19 my peace, because thou **h** heard, O my soul, NIH
5: 3 thou **h** stricken them, but they have not NIH
5: 3 thou **h** consumed them, *but* they have NIH
12: 2 Thou **h** planted them, yea, they have taken NIH
12: 3 thou **h** seen me, and tried mine heart NIH
12: 5 If thou **h** run with the footmen, and NIH
13: 4 Take the girdle that thou **h** got, which *is* NIH
13:21 for thou **h** taught them *to be* captains, *and* NIH
13:25 because thou **h** forgotten me, and trusted in NIH
14:19 **H** thou utterly rejected Judah? hath thy soul NIH
14:19 why **h** thou smitten us, and *there is* no NIH
14:22 upon thee: for thou **h** made all these *things.* NIH
15: 6 Thou **h** forsaken me, saith the LORD, NIH
15:10 that thou **h** borne me a man of strife and NIH
15:17 for thou **h** filled me *with* indignation. NIH
20: 6 thy friends, to whom thou **h** prophesied lies. NIH
20: 7 thou **h** deceived me, and I was deceived: NIH
20: 7 thou art stronger than I, and **h** prevailed: NIH
26: 9 Why **h** thou prophesied in the name of NIH
28: 6 thy words which thou **h** prophesied, NIH
28:13 Thou **h** broken the yokes of wood; but NIH
28:16 thou **h** taught rebellion against the LORD. NIH
29:25 Because thou **h** sent letters in thy name unto NIH
29:27 why **h** thou not reproved Jeremiah of NIH
30:13 bound up: thou **h** no healing medicines. 3807.1
31:18 himself *thus;* Thou **h** chastised me, NIH
32:17 thou **h** made the heaven and the earth by thy NIH
32:20 Which **h** set signs and wonders in the land NIH
32:20 and **h** made thee a name, as *at* this day; NIH
32:21 **h** brought forth thy people Israel out of NIH
32:22 **h** given them this land, which thou didst NIH
32:23 thou **h** caused all this evil to come upon NIH
32:24 what thou **h** spoken is come to pass; and NIH
32:25 thou **h** said unto me, O Lord GOD, NIH
36: 6 which thou **h** written from my mouth, NIH
36:14 Take in thine hand the roll wherein thou **h** NIH
36:29 Thou **h** burnt this roll, saying, Why hast NIH
36:29 Why **h** thou written therein, saying, NIH
38:25 Declare unto us now what thou **h** said unto NIH
39:18 because thou **h** put thy trust in me, saith NIH
44:16 *As for* the word that thou **h** spoken unto us NIH
48: 7 For because thou **h** trusted in thy works and NIH
50:24 because thou **h** striven against the LORD. NIH
51:62 O LORD, thou **h** spoken against this place, NIH
51:63 when thou **h** made an end of reading this NIH
La 1:21 they are glad that thou **h** done *it:* thou wilt NIH
1:21 *it:* thou wilt bring the day *that* thou **h** called, NIH
1:22 as thou **h** done unto me for all my NIH
2:20 and consider to whom thou **h** done this. NIH
2:21 thou **h** slain *them* in the day of thine anger; NIH
2:21 of thine anger; thou **h** killed, *and* not pitied. NIH
2:22 Thou **h** called as *in* a solemn day my terrors NIH
3:17 thou **h** removed my soul far off from peace: NIH
3:42 and have rebelled: thou **h** not pardoned. NIH
3:43 Thou **h** covered with anger, and NIH
3:43 thou **h** slain, thou hast not pitied. NIH
3:43 thou hast slain, thou **h** not pitied. NIH
3:44 Thou **h** covered thyself with a cloud, NIH
3:45 Thou **h** made us *as* the offscouring and NIH
3:56 Thou **h** heard my voice: hide not thine ear at NIH
3:58 thou **h** pleaded the causes of my soul; NIH
3:58 causes of my soul; thou **h** redeemed my life. NIH
3:59 O LORD, thou **h** seen my wrong: NIH
3:60 Thou **h** seen all their vengeance *and* all their NIH
3:61 Thou **h** heard their reproach, O LORD, NIH
5:22 thou **h** utterly rejected us; thou art very NIH
Eze 3:19 his iniquity; but thou **h** delivered thy soul. NIH
3:20 because thou **h** not given him warning, NIH
3:21 he is warned; also thou **h** delivered thy soul. NIH
4: 6 when thou **h** accomplished them, lie again NIH
4: 8 till thou **h** ended the days of thy siege. NIH
5:11 thou **h** defiled my sanctuary with all thy NIH
8:12 **h** thou seen what the ancients of the house NIH
Eze 8:15 unto me, **H** thou seen *this,* O son of man? NIH
8:17 unto me, **H** thou seen *this,* O son of man? NIH
9:11 I have done as thou **h** commanded me. NIH
16: 7 thou **h** increased and waxen great, and NIH
16:17 Thou **h** also taken thy fair jewels of my gold NIH
16:18 thou **h** set mine oil and mine incense before NIH
16:19 thou **h** even set it before them for a sweet NIH
16:20 Moreover thou **h** taken thy sons and thy NIH
16:20 whom thou **h** borne unto me, and these hast NIH
16:20 these **h** thou sacrificed unto them to be NIH
16:21 That thou **h** slain my children, and NIH
16:22 thy whoredoms thou **h** not remembered NIH
16:24 *That* thou **h** also built unto thee an eminent NIH
16:24 **h** made thee a high place in every street. NIH
16:25 Thou **h** built thy high place at every head of NIH
16:25 **h** made thy beauty to be abhorred, and NIH
16:25 **h** opened thy feet to every one that passed NIH
16:26 Thou **h** also committed fornication with NIH
16:26 **h** increased thy whoredoms, to provoke me NIH
16:28 Thou **h** played the whore also with NIH
16:28 thou **h** played the harlot with them, and NIH
16:29 Thou **h** moreover multiplied thy fornication NIH
16:31 **h** not been as a harlot, in that *thou* scornest NIH
16:37 with whom thou **h** taken pleasure, and all NIH
16:37 all *them* that thou **h** loved, with all *them* NIH
16:37 hast loved, with all *them* that thou **h** hated; NIH
16:43 Because thou **h** not remembered the days of NIH
16:43 **h** fretted me in all these *things;* behold NIH
16:47 Yet **h** thou not walked after their ways, NIH
16:48 as thou **h** done, thou and thy daughters. NIH
16:51 thou **h** multiplied thine abominations more NIH
16:51 **h** justified thy sisters in all thine NIH
16:51 all thine abominations which thou **h** done. NIH
16:52 Thou also, which **h** judged thy sisters, NIH
16:52 **h** committed more abominable than they: NIH
16:52 in that thou **h** justified thy sisters. NIH
16:54 mayest be confounded in all that thou **h** NIH
16:58 Thou **h** borne thy lewdness and thine NIH
16:59 I will even deal with thee as thou **h** done, NIH
16:59 which **h** despised the oath in breaking NIH
16:63 toward thee for all that thou **h** done, NIH
22: 4 become guilty in thy blood that thou **h** shed; NIH
22: 4 **h** defiled *thyself* in thine idols which thou NIH
22: 4 *thyself* in thine idols which thou **h** made; NIH
22: 4 thou **h** caused thy days to draw near, and NIH
22: 8 Thou **h** despised mine holy *things,* and hast NIH
22: 8 holy *things,* and **h** profaned my sabbaths. NIH
22:12 thou **h** taken usury and increase, and NIH
22:12 thou **h** greedily gained of thy neighbours by NIH
22:12 and **h** forgotten me, saith the Lord GOD. NIH
22:13 at thy dishonest gain which thou **h** made, NIH
23:30 thou **h** gone a whoring after the heathen, NIH
23:31 Thou **h** walked in the way of thy sister; NIH
23:35 Because thou **h** forgotten me, and cast me NIH
23:41 whereupon thou **h** set mine incense and NIH
25: 6 Because thou **h** clapped *thine* hands, and NIH
27: 3 O Tyrus, thou **h** said, I *am* of perfect NIH
28: 2 thou **h** said, I *am* a God, I sit *in* the seat of NIH
28: 4 with thine understanding thou **h** gotten thee NIH
28: 4 **h** gotten gold and silver into thy treasures: NIH
28: 5 by thy traffick **h** thou increased thy riches, NIH
28: 6 Because thou **h** set thine heart as the heart NIH
28:13 Thou **h** been in Eden the garden of God; NIH
28:14 thou **h** walked up and down in the midst of NIH
28:16 of thee *with* violence, and thou **h** sinned: NIH
28:17 thou **h** corrupted thy wisdom by reason of NIH
28:18 Thou **h** defiled thy sanctuaries by NIH
31:10 Because thou **h** lifted up thyself in height, NIH
32: 9 into the countries which thou **h** not known. NIH
33: 9 his iniquity; but thou **h** delivered thy soul. NIH
35: 5 Because thou **h** had a perpetual hatred, and NIH
35: 5 **h** shed *the blood of* the children of Israel by NIH
35: 6 sith thou **h** not hated blood, even blood shall NIH
35:10 Because thou **h** said, These two nations and NIH
35:11 according to thine envy which thou **h** used NIH
35:12 **h** spoken against the mountains of Israel, NIH
36:13 up men, and **h** bereaved thy nations; 1961
38:13 **h** thou gathered thy company to take a NIH
43:23 When thou **h** made an end of cleansing *it,* NIH
47: 6 **h** thou seen *this?* Then he brought me, and NIH
Da 2:23 who **h** given me wisdom and might, NIH
2:23 **h** made known unto me now what we NIH
2:23 for thou **h** *now* made known unto us NIH
3:10 Thou, O king, **h** made a decree, that every NIH
3:12 There are certain Jews whom thou **h** set NIH
3:12 nor worship the golden image which thou **h** NIH
3:18 nor worship the golden image which thou **h** NIH
5:22 O Belshazzar, **h** not humbled thine heart, NIH
5:23 **h** lifted up thyself against the Lord of NIH
5:23 thou **h** praised the gods of silver, and gold, NIH
5:23 *are* all thy ways, **h** thou not glorified: 3807.2
6:12 **H** thou not signed a decree, that every man NIH
6:13 nor the decree that thou **h** signed, but NIH
9: 7 through all the countries whither thou **h** NIH
9:15 that **h** brought thy people forth out of NIH
9:15 and **h** gotten thee renown, as *at* this day; NIH
10:19 my lord speak; for thou **h** strengthened me. NIH
Hos 4: 6 because thou **h** rejected knowledge, I will NIH
4: 6 seeing thou **h** forgotten the law of thy God, NIH
9: 1 for thou **h** gone a whoring from thy God, NIH
9: 1 thou **h** loved a reward upon every cornfloor. NIH
10: 9 thou **h** sinned from the days of Gibeah: NIH
13: 9 O Israel, *thou* **h** destroyed thyself; but in me NIH
14: 1 thy God; for thou **h** fallen by thine iniquity. NIH
Ob 1:15 as thou **h** done, it shall be done unto thee; NIH
Jnh 1:10 said unto him, Why **h** thou done this? NIH
1:14 O LORD, **h** done as it pleased thee. NIH
2: 6 yet **h** thou brought up my life from NIH
4:10 the LORD, Thou **h** had pity on the gourd, NIH
4:10 for the which thou **h** not laboured, neither NIH
Mic 7:20 which thou **h** sworn unto our fathers from NIH
Na 3:16 Thou **h** multiplied thy merchants above NIH
Hab 1:12 thou **h** ordained them for judgment; NIH
1:12 thou **h** established them for correction. NIH
2: 8 Because thou **h** spoiled many nations, NIH
Hab 2:10 Thou **h** consulted shame to thy house by NIH
2:10 many people, and **h** sinned *against* thy soul. NIH
Zep 3:11 wherein thou **h** transgressed against me: NIH
Zec 1:12 *against* which thou **h** had indignation these NIH
Mal 1: 2 Yet ye say, Wherein **h** thou loved us? *was* NIH
2:14 against whom thou **h** dealt treacherously: NIH
Mt 5:26 till thou **h** paid the uttermost farthing. NIG
6: 6 thy closet, and when thou **h** shut thy door, NIG
8:13 and as thou **h** believed, *so* be it done unto NIG
11:25 thou **h** hid these *things* from the wise and NIG
11:25 prudent, and **h** revealed them unto babes. NIG
17:27 and when thou **h** opened his mouth, NIG
18:15 shall hear thee, thou **h** gained thy brother. NIG
19:21 go *and* sell that thou **h**, and give to *5225*
20:12 and thou **h** made them equal unto us, NIG
21:16 and sucklings thou **h** perfected praise? NIG
25:21 thou **h** been faithful over a few *things,* I will NIG
25:23 thou **h** been faithful over a few *things,* I will NIG
25:24 reaping where thou **h** not sown, and NIG
25:24 and gathering where thou **h** not strawed: NIG
25:25 in the earth: lo, *there* thou **h** *that is* thine. *2192*
26:25 is it I? He said unto him, Thou **h** said. NIG
26:64 Jesus saith unto him, Thou **h** said: NIG
27:46 My God, my God, why **h** thou forsaken me? NIG
Mk 10:21 sell whatsoever thou **h**, and give to *2192*
12:32 Well, Master, thou **h** said the truth: NIG
15:34 My God, my God, why **h** thou forsaken me? NIG
Lk 1: 4 wherein thou **h** been instructed. NIG
1:30 Mary: for thou **h** found favour with God. NIG
2:31 Which thou **h** prepared before the face of all NIG
2:48 Son, why **h** thou thus dealt with us? NIG
7:43 he said unto him, Thou **h** rightly judged. NIG
10:21 that thou **h** hid these *things* from the wise NIG
10:21 prudent, and **h** revealed them unto babes: NIG
10:28 he said unto him, Thou **h** answered right: NIG
11:27 and the paps which thou **h** sucked. NIG
12:19 thou **h** much goods laid up for many years; *2192*
12:20 *those things* be, which thou **h** provided? NIG
12:59 till thou **h** paid the very last mite. NIG
13:26 and thou **h** taught in our streets. NIG
14:22 it is done as thou **h** commanded, and NIG
15:30 thou **h** killed for him the fatted calf. NIG
18:22 lackest thou one *thing:* sell all that thou **h**, *2192*
19:17 because thou **h** been faithful in a very little, NIG
20:39 answering said, Master, thou **h** well said. NIG
24:18 **h** not known the *things* which are come to NIG
Jn 2:10 *but* thou **h** kept the good wine until now. NIG
4:11 Sir, thou **h** nothing to draw with, and *2192*
4:11 from whence then **h** thou *that* living water? *2192*
4:17 Thou **h** well said, I have no husband: NIG
4:18 For thou **h** had five husbands; and he whom NIG
4:18 he whom thou now **h** is not thy husband: *2192*
6:68 we go? thou **h** the words of eternal life. *2192*
7:20 people answered and said, Thou **h** a devil: *2192*
8:48 that thou art a Samaritan, and **h** a devil? *2192*
8:52 Now we know that thou **h** a devil. *2192*
8:57 fifty years old, and **h** thou seen Abraham? NIG
9:37 Thou **h** both seen him, and it is he that NIG
11:41 Father, I thank thee that thou **h** heard me. NIG
11:42 *it,* that they may believe that thou **h** sent me. NIG
13: 8 If I wash thee not, thou **h** no part with me. *2192*
13:38 shall not crow, till thou **h** denied me thrice. NIG
14: 9 and *yet* **h** thou not known me, Philip? NIG
17: 2 As thou **h** given him power over all flesh, NIG
17: 2 eternal life to as many as thou **h** given him. NIG
17: 3 and Jesus Christ, whom thou **h** sent. NIG
17: 7 whatsoever thou **h** given me are of thee. NIG
17: 9 but for *them* which thou **h** given me; NIG
17:11 own name those whom thou **h** given me, NIG
17:18 As thou **h** sent me into the world, even *so* NIG
17:21 that the world may believe that thou **h** sent NIG
17:23 that the world may know that thou **h** sent NIG
17:23 and **h** loved them, as thou hast loved me. NIG
17:23 and hast loved them, as thou **h** loved me. NIG
17:24 I will that they also, whom thou **h** given me, NIG
17:24 behold my glory, which thou **h** given me: NIG
17:25 and these have known that thou **h** sent me. NIG
17:26 where*with* thou **h** loved me may be in them, NIG
18:35 delivered thee unto me: what **h** thou done? NIG
20:15 him *hence,* tell me where thou **h** laid him, NIG
20:29 Thomas, because thou **h** seen me, thou hast NIG
20:29 because thou hast seen me, thou **h** believed: NIG
Ac 1:24 shew whether of these two thou **h** chosen, NIG
2:28 Thou **h** made known to me the ways of life; NIG
4:24 which **h** made heaven, and earth, and NIG
4:25 Who by the mouth of thy servant David **h** NIG
4:27 whom thou **h** anointed, both Herod, and NIG
5: 4 why **h** thou conceived this thing in thine NIG
5: 4 thou **h** not lied unto men, but unto God. NIG
8:20 thou **h** thought that the gift of God may be NIG
8:21 Thou **h** neither part nor lot in this matter: *1510*
10:33 and thou **h** well done that thou art come. NIG
22:15 his witness unto all men of what thou **h** seen NIG
23:11 for as thou **h** testified of me in Jerusalem, so NIG
23:19 asked *him,* What is that thou **h** to tell me? *2192*
23:22 *man* that thou **h** shewed these *things* to me. NIG
24:10 Forasmuch as I know that thou **h** been of NIG
25:12 answered, **H** thou appealed unto Cesar? NIG
26:16 a witness both of *these things* which thou **h** NIG
Ro 2:20 which **h** the form of knowledge and of *2192*
9:20 that formed *it,* Why **h** thou made me thus? NIG
14:22 **H** thou faith? have *it* to thyself before God. *2192*
1Co 4: 7 and what **h** thou that thou didst not receive? *2192*
7:28 But and if thou marry, thou **h** not sinned; NIG
8:10 For if any *man* see thee which **h** knowledge *2192*
Col 4:17 Take heed to the ministry which thou **h** NIG
1Ti 4: 6 good doctrine, whereunto thou **h** attained. NIG
6:12 **h** professed a good profession before many NIG
2Ti 1:13 which thou **h** heard of me, in faith and NIG
2: 2 And *the things* that thou **h** heard of me NIG
3:10 But thou **h** fully known my doctrine, NIG
3:14 thou in *the things* which thou **h** learned NIG
3:14 thou hast learned and **h** been assured of, NIG
3:14 knowing of whom thou **h** learned *them;* NIG
3:15 And that from a child thou **h** known NIG

H

Phm 1: 5 which thou **h** toward the Lord Jesus, and *2192*
Heb 1: 9 Thou **h** loved righteousness, and NIG
1:10 in the beginning **h** laid the foundation of NIG
2: 8 Thou **h** put all *things* in subjection under his NIG
10: 5 but a body **h** thou prepared me: NIG
10: 6 *sacrifices* for sin thou **h** had no pleasure. NIG
Jas 2:18 may say, Thou **h** faith, and I have works: *2192*
Rev 1:19 Write *the things* which thou **h** seen, and NIG
2: 2 thou **h** tried them which say *they* are NIG
2: 2 and are not, and **h** found them liars: NIG
2: 3 And **h** borne, and hast patience, and for my NIG
2: 3 and **h** patience, and for my name's sake *2192*
2: 3 and for my name's sake **h** laboured, and NIG
2: 3 sake hast laboured, and **h** not fainted. NIG
2: 4 because thou **h** left thy first love. NIG
2: 6 But this thou **h**, that thou hatest the deeds *2192*
2:13 fast my name, and **h** not denied my faith, NIG
2:14 thou **h** there them that hold the doctrine of *2192*
2:15 So **h** thou also them that hold the doctrine *2192*
3: 1 that thou **h** a name that thou livest, and *2192*
3: 3 therefore how thou **h** received and heard, NIG
3: 4 Thou **h** a few names even in Sardis, *2192*
3: 8 for thou **h** a little strength, and hast kept my *2192*
3: 8 and **h** kept my word, and hast not denied NIG
3: 8 kept my word, and **h** not denied my name. NIG
3:10 Because thou **h** kept the word of my NIG
3:11 hold *that* fast which thou **h**, that no *man* *2192*
4:11 for thou **h** created all *things*, and for thy NIG
5: 9 **h** redeemed us to God by thy blood out of NIG
5:10 And **h** made us unto our God kings and NIG
11:17 thou **h** taken *to thee* thy great power, NIG
11:17 *to thee* thy great power, and **h** reigned. NIG
16: 5 and shalt be, because thou **h** judged thus. NIG
16: 6 and thou **h** given them blood to drink; NIG

HASTE (56) [HASTED, HASTEN, HASTENED, HASTENETH, HASTETH, HASTILY, HASTING, HASTY]

Ge 19:22 **H** thee, escape thither; for I cannot do any 4116
24:46 she **made h**, and let down her pitcher from 4116
43:30 Joseph **made h**; for his bowels did yern 4116
45: 9 **H** you, and go up to my father, and 4116
45:13 ye shall **h** and bring down my father hither. 4116
Ex 10:16 Pharaoh called for Moses and Aaron **in h**; 4116
12:11 staff in your hand; and ye shall eat it in **h**: 2649
12:33 they might send them out of the land **in h**; 4116
34: 8 Moses **made h**, and bowed his head toward 4116
Dt 16: 3 camest forth out of the land of Egypt in **h**: 2649
32:35 things that shall come upon them **make h**. 2363
Jdg 9:48 me do, **make h**, *and* do as I *have done*. 4116
13:10 the woman **made h**, and ran, and 4116
1Sa 9:12 **make h** now, for he came to day to the city; 4116
20:38 cried after the lad, Make speed, **h**, stay not. 2363
21: 8 because the king's business required **h**. 5169
23:26 David **made h** to get away for fear of Saul; 2648
23:27 unto Saul, saying, **H** thee, and come; 4116
25:18 Abigail **made h**, and took two hundred 4116
2Sa 4: 4 as she **made h** to flee, that he fell, and 2648
2Ki 7:15 which the Syrians had cast away in their **h**. 2648
2Ch 24: 5 year to year, and *see that* ye **h** the matter. 4116
35:21 for God commanded me to **make h**: 926
Ezr 4:23 they went up in **h** to Jerusalem unto 924
Est 5: 5 the king said, **Cause** Haman **to make h**, 4116
6:10 **Make h**, *and* take the apparel and 4116
Job 20: 2 cause me to answer, and for *this* I **make h**. 2363
Ps 22:19 O my strength, **h** thee to help me. 2363
31:22 For I said in my **h**, I am cut off from before 2648
38:22 **Make h** to help me, O Lord my salvation. 2363
40:13 deliver me: O LORD, **make h** to help me. 2363
70: 1 *Make* **h**, O God, to deliver me; make haste NIH
70: 1 deliver me; **make h** to help me, O LORD. 2363
70: 5 **make h** unto me, O God: thou *art* my help 2363
71:12 from me: O my God, **make h** for my help. 2363
116:11 I said in my **h**, All men *are* liars. 2648
119:60 I **made h**, and delayed not to keep thy 2363
141: 1 **make h** unto me; give ear unto my voice, 2363
Pr 1:16 feet run to evil, and **make h** to shed blood. 4116
28:20 he that **maketh h** to be rich shall not be 213
SS 8:14 **Make h**, my beloved, and be thou like to a 1272
Isa 28:16 he that believeth shall not **make h**. 2363
49:17 Thy children shall **make h**; thy destroyers 4116
52:12 For ye shall not go out with **h**, nor go by 2649
59: 7 and they **make h** to shed innocent blood: 4116
Jer 9:18 let them **make h**, and take up a wailing for 4116
Da 2:25 brought in Daniel before the king in **h**, 927
3:24 rose up in **h**, *and* spake, and said unto his 927
6:19 and went in **h** unto the den of lions. 927
Na 2: 5 they shall **make h** *to* the wall thereof, and 4116
Mk 6:25 And she came in straightway with **h** unto *4710*
Lk 1:39 and went into the hill country with **h**, into a *4710*
2:16 And they came **with h**, and found Mary, *4692*
19: 5 Zaccheus, **make h**, and come down; *4692*
19: 6 And he **made h**, and came down, and *4692*
Ac 22:18 **Make h**, and get *thee* quickly out of *4692*

HASTED (24) [HASTE]

Ge 18: 7 *it* unto a young man; and he **h** to dress it. 4116
24:18 she **h**, and let down her pitcher upon her 4116
24:20 she **h**, and emptied her pitcher into 4116
Ex 5:13 the taskmasters **h** *them*, saying, Fulfil your 213
Jos 4:10 and the people **h** and passed over. 4116
8:14 when the king of Ai saw *it*, that they **h** and 4116
8:19 and took it, and **h** and set the city on fire. 4116
10:13 and **h** not to go down about a whole day. 213
Jdg 20:37 the liers in wait **h**, and rushed upon Gibeah; 2363
1Sa 17:48 that David **h**, and ran *toward* the army to 4116
25:23 she **h**, and lighted off the ass, and 4116
25:34 except thou hadst **h** and come to meet me, 4116
25:42 Abigail **h**, and rode upon an ass, 4116
28:24 she **h**, and killed it, and took flour, and 4116
2Sa 19:16 **h** and came down with the men of Judah to 4116
1Ki 20:41 he **h**, and took the ashes away from his 4116
2Ki 9:13 they **h**, and took every man his garment, 4116
2Ch 26:20 yea, himself **h** also to go out, because 1765
Est 6:12 Haman **h** to his house mourning, and 1765
6:14 **h** to bring Haman unto the banquet that 926
Job 31: 5 with vanity, or *if* my foot hath **h** to deceit; 2363
Ps 48: 5 they were troubled, *and* **h away**. 2648
104: 7 at the voice of thy thunder they **h away**. 2648
Ac 20:16 for he **h**, if it were possible for him, to be at *4692*

HASTEN (7) [HASTE]

1Ki 22: 9 said, **H** *hither* Micaiah the son of Imlah. 4116
Ps 16: 4 Their sorrows shall be multiplied *that* **h** 4116
55: 8 I would **h** my escape from the windy storm 2363
Ecc 2:25 or who else can **h** *hereunto*, more than I? 2363
Isa 5:19 *and* **h** his work, that we may see *it*: and 2363
60:22 I the LORD will **h** it in his time. 2363
Jer 1:12 for I will **h** my word to perform it. 8245

HASTENED (6) [HASTE]

Ge 18: 6 Abraham **h** into the tent unto Sarah, and 4116
19:15 the angels **h** Lot, saying, Arise, take thy 213
2Ch 24: 5 the matter. Howbeit the Levites **h** *it* not. 4116
Est 3:15 being **h** by the king's commandment, and 1765
8:14 being **h** and pressed on by the king's 926
Jer 17:16 I have not **h** from *being* a pastor to follow 213

HASTENETH (1) [HASTE]

Isa 51:14 The captive exile **h** that *he* may be loosed, 4116

HASTETH (9) [HASTE]

Job 9:26 swift ships: as the eagle *that* **h** to the prey. 2907
40:23 Behold, he drinketh up a river, *and* **h** not: 2648
Pr 7:23 as a bird **h** to the snare, and knoweth not 4116
19: 2 not good; and he that **h** with *his* feet, sinneth. 213
28:22 He that **h** to be rich *hath* an evil eye, and 926
Ecc 1: 5 and **h** to his place where he arose. 7602
Jer 48:16 *is* near to come, and his affliction **h** fast. 4116
Hab 1: 8 they shall fly as the eagle *that* **h** to eat. 2363
Zep 1:14 the LORD *is* near, *it is* near, and **h** greatly, 4118

HASTILY (8) [HASTE]

Ge 41:14 they **brought** him **h** out of the dungeon: 7323
Jdg 2:23 those nations, without driving them out **h**; 4118
9:54 he called **h** unto the young man his 4120
1Sa 4:14 And the man came in **h**, and told Eli. 4116
1Ki 20:33 did **h** catch *it*: and they said, Thy brother 4116
Pr 20:21 An inheritance *may be* **gotten h** at 926
25: 8 Go not forth **h** to strive, lest *thou know not* 4118
Jn 11:31 that she rose up **h** and went out, *5030*

HASTING (2) [HASTE]

Isa 16: 5 and seeking judgment, and **h** righteousness. 4106
2Pe 3:12 and **h** *unto* the coming of the day of God, *4692*

HASTY (9) [HASTE]

Pr 14:29 but *he that is* **h** of spirit exalteth folly. 7116
21: 5 but *of* every one that is **h** only to want. 213
29:20 Seest thou a man that is **h** in his words? 213
Ecc 5: 2 let not thine heart be **h** to utter *any* thing 4116
7: 9 Be not **h** in thy spirit to be angry: for anger 926
8: 3 Be not **h** to go out of his sight: stand not in 926
Isa 28: 4 *and* as the **h fruit** before the summer; 1061
Da 2:15 Why *is* the decree *so* **h** from the king? 2685
Hab 1: 6 up the Chaldeans, *that* bitter and **h** nation, 4116

HASUPHA (1) [HASHUPHA]

Ezr 2:43 the children of Ziha, the children of **H**, 2817

HATACH (4)

Est 4: 5 called Esther for **H**, *one* of the king's 2047
4: 6 So **H** went forth to Mordecai unto the street 2047
4: 9 **H** came and told Esther the words of 2047
4:10 Again Esther spake unto **H**, and gave him 2047

HATCH (2) [HATCHETH]

Isa 34:15 lay, and **h**, and gather under her shadow: 1234
59: 5 They **h** cockatrice' eggs, and weave 1234

HATCHETH (1) [HATCH]

Jer 17:11 partridge sitteth *on eggs*, and **h** *them* not; 3205

HATE (87) [HATED, HATEFUL, HATEFULLY, HATERS, HATEST, HATETH, HATING, HATRED]

Ge 24:60 possess the gate of those which **h** them. 8130
26:27 seeing ye **h** me, and have sent me away 8130
50:15 Joseph will peradventure **h** us, and 7852
Ex 20: 5 and fourth *generation* of them that **h** me; 8130
Lev 19:17 Thou shalt not **h** thy brother in thine heart: 8130
26:17 they that **h** you shall reign over you; and 8130
Nu 10:35 and let them that **h** thee flee before thee. 8130
Dt 5: 9 and fourth *generation* of them that **h** me, 8130
7:10 repayeth them that **h** him to their face, 8130
7:15 but will lay them upon all *them* that **h** thee. 8130
19:11 if any man **h** his neighbour, and lie in wait 8130
22:13 take a wife, and go in unto her, and **h** her, 8130
24: 3 *if* the latter husband **h** her, and write her a 8130
30: 7 on them that **h** thee, which persecuted thee. 8130
32:41 and will reward them that **h** me. 8130
33:11 of them that **h** him, that they rise not again. 8130
Jdg 11: 7 Did not ye **h** me, and expel me out of my 8130
14:16 Thou dost but **h** me, and lovest me not: 8130
2Sa 22:41 that I might destroy them that **h** me. 8130
1Ki 22: 8 I **h** him; for he doth not prophesy good 8130
2Ch 18: 7 I **h** him; for he never prophesied good unto 8130
19: 2 and love them that **h** the LORD? 8130
Job 8:22 They that **h** thee shall be clothed with 8130
Ps 9:13 trouble *which I suffer* of them that **h** me, 8130
18:40 that I might destroy them that **h** me. 8130
21: 8 thy right hand shall find out those that **h** 8130
25:19 are many; and they **h** me *with* cruel hatred. 8130
34:21 they that **h** the righteous shall be desolate. 8130
35:19 *neither* let them wink *with* the eye that **h** 8130
38:19 they that **h** me wrongfully are multiplied. 8130
41: 7 All that **h** me whisper together against me: 8130
44:10 and they which **h** us spoil for themselves. 8130
Ps 55: 3 iniquity upon me, and in wrath they **h** me. 7852
68: 1 let them also that **h** him flee before him. 8130
69: 4 They that **h** me without a cause are moe 8130
69:14 let me be delivered from them that **h** me, 8130
83: 2 and they that **h** thee have lift up the head. 8130
86:17 that they which **h** me may see *it*, and 8130
89:23 his face, and plague them that **h** him. 8130
97:10 Ye that love the LORD, **h** evil: 8130
101: 3 I **h** the work of them that turn aside; *it* shall 8130
105:25 He turned their heart to **h** his people, 8130
118: 7 shall I see *my desire* upon them that **h** me. 8130
119:104 I **h** every false way. 8130
119:113 I **h** *vain* thoughts: but thy law do I love. 8130
119:128 *things* to be right; *and* I **h** every false way. 8130
119:163 I **h** and abhor lying: *but* thy law do I love. 8130
129: 5 be confounded and turned back that **h** Zion. 8130
139:21 Do not I **h** them, O LORD, that hate thee? 8130
139:21 Do not I hate them, O LORD, that **h** thee? 8130
139:22 I **h** them *with* perfect hatred: I count them 8130
Pr 1:22 in their scorning, and fools **h** knowledge? 8130
6:16 These six *things* doth the LORD **h**: yea, 8130
8:13 The fear of the LORD *is* to **h** evil: pride, 8130
8:13 evil way, and the froward mouth, do I **h**. 8130
8:36 his own soul: all they that **h** me love death. 8130
9: 8 Reprove not a scorner, lest he **h** thee: 8130
19: 7 All the brethren of the poor do **h** him: 8130
25:17 lest he be weary *of* thee, and *so* **h** thee. 8130
29:10 The bloodthirsty **h** the upright: but the just 8130
Ecc 3: 8 A time to love, and a time to **h**; a time of 8130
Isa 61: 8 I **h** robbery for burnt offering; 8130
Jer 44: 4 Oh, do not this abominable thing that I **h**. 8130
Eze 16:27 delivered thee unto the will of them that **h** 8130
Da 4:19 the dream *be* to them that **h** thee, and 8131
Am 5:10 They **h** him that rebuketh in the gate, and 8130
5:15 **H** the evil, and love the good, and 8130
5:21 I **h**, I despise your feast *days*, and I will not 8130
6: 8 the excellency of Jacob, and **h** his palaces: 8130
Mic 3: 2 Who **h** the good, and love the evil; 8130
Zec 8:17 for all these *are things* that I **h**, saith 8130
Mt 5:43 love thy neighbour, and **h** thine enemy. *3404*
5:44 do good to them that **h** you, and pray for *3404*
6:24 for either he will **h** the one, and love *3404*
24:10 betray one another, and shall **h** one another. *3404*
Lk 1:71 and from the hand of all that **h** us; *3404*
6:22 when men shall **h** you, and when they shall *3404*
6:27 do good to them which **h** you, *3404*
14:26 and **h** not his father, and mother, and wife, *3404*
16:13 for either he will **h** the one, and love *3404*
Jn 7: 7 The world cannot **h** you; but me it hateth, *3404*
15:18 If the world **h** you, ye know that it hated *3404*
Ro 7:15 that do I not; but what I **h**, that do I. *3404*
1Jn 3:13 my brethren, if the world **h** you. *3404*
Rev 2: 6 the deeds of the Nicolaitans, which I also **h**. *3404*
2:15 doctrine of the Nicolaitans, which *thing* I **h**. *3404*
17:16 these shall **h** the whore, and shall make her *3404*

HATED (60) [HATE]

Ge 27:41 Esau **h** Jacob because of the blessing 7852
29:31 when the LORD saw that Leah *was* **h**, 8130
29:33 the LORD hath heard that I *was* **h**, 8130
37: 4 they **h** him, and could not speak peaceably 8130
37: 5 his brethren: and they **h** him yet the more. 8130
37: 8 they **h** him yet the more for his dreams, 8130
49:23 grieved him, and shot *at him*, and **h** him: 7852
Dt 1:27 and said, Because the LORD **h** us, 8135
4:42 and **h** him not in times past; 8130
9:28 because he **h** them, he hath brought them 8135
19: 4 whom he **h** not in time past; 8130
19: 6 inasmuch as he **h** him not in time past. 8130
21:15 another **h**, and they have born him children, 8130
21:15 him children, *both* the beloved and the **h**; 8130
21:15 and *if* the firstborn son be hers that was **h**: 8146
21:16 beloved firstborn before the son of the **h**, 8130
21:17 he shall acknowledge the son of the **h** *for* 8130
Jos 20: 5 and **h** him not beforetime. 8130
Jdg 15: 2 thought that thou hadst **utterly h** her; 8130+8130
2Sa 5: 8 and the blind, *that are* **h** of David's soul, 8130
13:15 **h** her **exceedingly**; 1419+3966+8130+8135
13:15 that the hatred wherewith he **h** her *was* 8130
13:22 for Absalom **h** Amnon, because he had 8130
22:18 strong enemy, *and* from them that **h** me: 8130
Est 9: 1 the Jews had rule over them that **h** them;) 8130
9: 5 did what they would unto those that **h** 8130
Job 31:29 If I rejoiced at the destruction of him that **h** 8130
Ps 18:17 strong enemy, and from them which **h** me: 8130
26: 5 I have **h** the congregation of evildoers; and 8130
31: 6 I have **h** them that regard lying vanities: but 8130
44: 7 and hast put them to shame that **h** us. 8130
55:12 **h** me *that* did magnify *himself* against me; 8130
106:10 he saved them from the hand of him that **h** 8130
106:41 and they that **h** them ruled over them. 8130
Pr 1:29 For that they **h** knowledge, and did not 8130
5:12 How have I **h** instruction, and my heart 8130
14:17 and a man of wicked devices is **h**. 8130
14:20 The poor is **h** even of his own neighbour: 8130
Ecc 2:17 Therefore I **h** life; because the work that is 8130
2:18 I **h** all my labour which I *had* taken under 8130
Isa 60:15 Whereas thou hast been forsaken and **h**, so 8130
66: 5 Your brethren that **h** you, that cast you out 8130
Jer 12: 8 crieth out against me: therefore have I **h** it. 8130
Eze 16:37 hast loved, with all *them* that thou hast **h**; 8130
35: 6 sith thou hast not **h** blood, even blood shall 8130
Hos 9:15 wickedness *is* in Gilgal, for there I **h** them: 8130
Mal 1: 3 I **h** Esau, and laid his mountains and his 8130
Mt 10:22 And ye shall be **h** of all *men* for my name's *3404*
24: 9 ye shall be **h** of all nations for my name's *3404*
Mk 13:13 And ye shall be **h** of all *men* for my name's *3404*
Lk 19:14 But his citizens **h** him, and sent a message *3404*
21:17 And ye shall be **h** of all *men* for my name's *3404*
Jn 15:18 ye know that it **h** me before *it hated* you. *3404*
15:18 ye know that it hated me before *it* **h** you. NIG
15:24 both seen and **h** both me and my Father. *3404*
15:25 in their law, They **h** me without a cause. *3404*
17:14 and the world hath **h** them, because *3404*
Ro 9:13 Jacob have I loved, but Esau have I **h**. *3404*

Eph 5:29 For no *man* ever yet **h** his own flesh; but *3404*
Heb 1: 9 hast loved righteousness, and **h** iniquity; *3404*

HATEFUL (3) [HATE]
Ps 36: 2 until his iniquity be found to be **h**. 8130
Tit 3: 3 and envy, **h**, *and* hating one another. *4767*
Rev 18: 2 and a cage of every unclean and **h** bird. *3404*

HATEFULLY (1) [HATE]
Eze 23:29 they shall deal with thee **h**, and 8135+871.1

HATERS (2) [HATE]
Ps 81:15 The **h** of the LORD should have 8130
Ro 1:30 **h of God**, despiteful, proud, boasters, *2319*

HATEST (6) [HATE]
2Sa 19: 6 lovest thine enemies, and **h** thy friends: 8130
Ps 5: 5 in thy sight: thou **h** all workers of iniquity. 8130
45: 7 lovest righteousness, and **h** wickedness: 8130
50:17 Seeing thou **h** instruction, and castest my 8130
Eze 23:28 thee into the hand *of them* whom thou **h**, 8130
Rev 2: 6 that thou **h** the deeds of the Nicolaitans, *3404*

HATETH (31) [HATE]
Ex 23: 5 If thou see the ass of him that **h** thee lying 8130
Dt 7:10 he will not be slack to him that **h** him, 8130
12:31 which he **h**, have they done unto their gods; 8130
16:22 *any* image; which the LORD thy God **h**. 8130
22:16 unto this man to wife, and he **h** her; 8130
Job 16: 9 He teareth *me* in his wrath, who **h** me: 7852
34:17 Shall even he that **h** right govern? and wilt 8130
Ps 11: 5 and him that loveth violence his soul **h**. 8130
120: 6 My soul hath long dwelt with him that **h** 8130
Pr 11:15 smart *for it:* and he that **h** suretiship *is* sure. 8130
12: 1 but he that **h** reproof *is* brutish. 8130
13: 5 A righteous *man* **h** lying: but a wicked *man* 8130
13:24 He that spareth his rod **h** his son: but 8130
15:10 the way: *and* he that **h** reproof shall die. 8130
15:27 his own house; but he that **h** gifts shall live. 8130
26:24 He that **h** dissembleth with his lips, and 8130
26:28 A lying tongue **h** *those that are* afflicted by 8130
28:16 he that **h** covetousness shall prolong *his* 8130
29:24 Whoso is partner with a thief **h** his own 8130
Isa 1:14 and your appointed feasts my soul **h**: 8130
Mal 2:16 God of Israel, saith that he **h** putting away: 8130
Jn 3:20 For every one that doeth evil **h** the light, *3404*
7: 7 but me it **h**, because I testify of it, that *3404*
12:25 he that **h** his life in this world shall keep it *3404*
15:19 out of the world, therefore the world **h** you. *3404*
15:23 He that **h** me hateth my Father also. *3404*
15:23 He that hateth me **h** my Father also. *3404*
1Jn 2: 9 and **h** his brother, is in darkness *even* until *3404*
2:11 But he that **h** his brother is in darkness, and *3404*
3:15 Whosoever **h** his brother is a murderer: and *3404*
4:20 I love God, and **h** his brother, he is a liar: *3404*

HATH (2262) [HAVE]
Ge 1:20 abundantly the moving creature that **h** life, NIH
3: 1 he said unto the woman, Yea, **h** God said, NIH
3: 3 God **h** said, Ye shall not eat of it, NIH
4:11 which **h** opened her mouth to receive thy NIH
4:25 *said she,* **h** appointed me another seed NIH
5:29 of the ground which the LORD **h** cursed. NIH
14:20 which **h** delivered thine enemies into thy NIH
16: 2 the LORD **h** restrained me from bearing: NIH
16:11 because the LORD **h** heard thy affliction. NIH
17:14 from his people; he **h** broken my covenant. NIH
18:19 Abraham that which he **h** spoken of him. NIH
19:13 and the LORD **h** sent us to destroy it. NIH
19:19 thy servant **h** found grace in thy sight, and NIH
21: 6 God **h** made me to laugh, *so that* all that NIH
21:12 in all that Sarah **h** said unto thee, NIH
21:17 for God **h** heard the voice of the lad where NIH
21:26 I wot not who **h** done this thing: NIH
22:20 she **h** also born children unto thy brother NIH
23: 9 he **h**, which *is* in the end of his field; 3807.1
24:27 who **h** not left destitute my master of his NIH
24:35 the LORD **h** blessed my master greatly; NIH
24:35 he **h** given him flocks, and herds, and silver, NIH
24:36 and unto him **h** he given all that he hath. NIH
24:36 and unto him hath he given all that he **h**. 3807.1
24:44 **h** appointed out for my master's son. NIH
24:51 son's wife, as the LORD **h** spoken. NIH
24:56 seeing the LORD **h** prospered my way; NIH
26:22 For now the LORD **h** made room for us, NIH
27:27 of a field which the LORD **h** blessed: NIH
27:33 where *is* he that **h** taken venison, and NIH
27:35 and **h** taken away thy blessing. NIH
27:36 for he **h** supplanted me these two times: he NIH
27:36 behold, now he **h** taken away my blessing. NIH
29:32 Surely the LORD **h** looked upon my NIH
29:33 Because the LORD **h** heard that I *was* NIH
29:33 he **h** therefore given me this *son* also: NIH
30: 2 who **h** withheld from thee the fruit of NIH
30: 6 God **h** judged me, and hath also heard my NIH
30: 6 **h** also heard my voice, and hath given me a NIH
30: 6 also heard my voice, and **h** given me a son: NIH
30:18 God **h** given *me* my hire, because I have NIH
30:20 God **h** endued me with a good dowry; NIH
30:23 and said, God **h** taken away my reproach: NIH
30:27 that the LORD **h** blessed me for thy sake. NIH
30:30 the LORD **h** blessed thee since my NIH
31: 1 Jacob **h** taken away all that *was* our NIH
31: 1 of *that* which *was* of our father's **h** he gotten NIH
31: 5 the God of my father **h** been with me. NIH
31: 7 your father **h** deceived me, and changed my NIH
31: 9 Thus God **h** taken away the cattle of your NIH
31:15 for he **h** sold us, and hath quite devoured NIH
31:15 and **h** quite devoured also our money. NIH
31:16 For all the riches which God **h** taken from NIH
31:16 whatsoever God **h** said unto thee, do. NIH
31:42 God **h** seen mine affliction and the labour of NIH
33: 5 The children which God **h** graciously given NIH
33:11 because God **h** dealt graciously with me, NIH

Ge 37:20 will say, *Some* evil beast **h** devoured him: NIH
37:33 son's coat; an evil beast **h** devoured him; NIH
38:24 Tamar thy daughter in law **h** played NIH
38:26 and said, She **h** been more righteous than I; NIH
39: 8 he **h** committed all that he hath to my hand; NIH
39: 8 all that he **h** to my hand; 3426+3807.1
39: 9 neither **h** he kept back any thing from me NIH
39:14 he **h** brought in a Hebrew unto us to mock NIH
41:25 God **h** shewed Pharaoh what he *is* about to NIH
41:39 Forasmuch as God **h** shewed thee all this, NIH
41:51 *said he,* **h** made me forget all my toil, and NIH
41:52 For God **h** caused me to be fruitful in NIH
42:28 What *is* this *that* God **h** done unto us? NIH
43:23 **h** given you treasure in your sacks: NIH
44:16 God **h** found out the iniquity of thy NIH
45: 6 For these two years ***h*** the famine *been* in NIH
45: 8 he **h** made me a father to Pharaoh, and lord NIH
45: 9 God **h** made me lord of all Egypt: NIH
46:32 for their trade **h** been to feed cattle; NIH
46:34 Thy servants' trade **h** been about cattle from NIH
48: 9 whom God **h** given me in this *place.* And he NIH
48:11 and lo, God **h** shewed me also thy seed. NIH
Ex 3:13 The God of your fathers **h** sent me unto NIH
3:14 children of Israel, I AM **h** sent me unto you. NIH
3:15 and the God of Jacob, **h** sent me unto you: NIH
3:18 The LORD God of the Hebrews **h** met NIH
4: 1 The LORD **h** not appeared unto thee. NIH
4: 5 and the God of Jacob, **h** appeared unto thee. NIH
4:11 said unto him, Who **h** made man's mouth? NIH
5: 3 The God of the Hebrews **h** met with us: NIH
5:23 in thy name, he **h** done evil to this people; NIH
7:16 The LORD God of the Hebrews **h** sent me NIH
9:18 such as **h** not been in Egypt since NIH
10:12 herb of the land, *even* all that the hail **h** left. NIH
12:25 according as he **h** promised, that ye shall NIH
13: 9 for with a strong hand **h** the LORD NIH
14: 3 in the land, the wilderness **h** shut them in. NIH
15: 1 the LORD, for he **h** triumphed gloriously: NIH
15: 1 and his rider **h** he thrown into the sea. NIH
15: 4 and his host **h** he cast into the sea: NIH
15: 6 O LORD, **h** dashed in pieces the enemy. NIH
15:21 the LORD, for he **h** triumphed gloriously; NIH
15:21 and his rider **h** he thrown into the sea. NIH
16: 6 ye shall know that the LORD **h** brought NIH
16: 9 for he **h** heard your murmurings. NIH
16:15 This *is* the bread which the LORD **h** given NIH
16:16 This *is* the thing which the LORD **h** NIH
16:23 This *is that* which the LORD **h** said, NIH
16:29 for that the LORD **h** given you NIH
17:16 Because the LORD **h** sworn *that* NIH
18:10 who **h** delivered you out of the hand of NIH
18:10 who **h** delivered the people from under NIH
19: 8 All that the LORD **h** spoken we will do. NIH
21: 8 who **h** betrothed her to himself, then 3807.1
21: 8 seeing he **h** dealt deceitfully with her. NIH
21:29 it **h** been testified to his owner, and he hath NIH
21:29 he **h** not kept him in, but that he hath killed NIH
21:29 but that he **h** killed a man or a woman; NIH
21:36 Or *if* it be known that the ox ***h*** used to push NIH
21:36 time past, and his owner **h** not kept him in; NIH
22:11 that he **h** not put his hand unto his NIH
24: 3 All the words which the LORD **h** said will NIH
24: 7 All that the LORD **h** said will we do, and NIH
24: 8 which the LORD **h** made with you NIH
32:24 Whosoever **h** *any* gold, let them break *it* 3807.1
32:33 Whosoever **h** sinned against me, him will I NIH
35: 1 These *are* the words which the LORD **h** NIH
35:10 make all that the LORD **h** commanded; NIH
35:30 the LORD **h** called by name Bezaleel NIH
35:31 he **h** filled him *with* the spirit of God, NIH
35:34 he **h** put in his heart that *he* may teach, 3807.1
35:35 Them **h** he filled *with* wisdom of heart, NIH
Lev 4: 3 let him bring for his sin, which he **h** sinned, NIH
4:22 When a ruler **h** sinned, and done somewhat NIH
4:23 Or if his sin, wherein he **h** sinned, come to NIH
4:28 Or if his sin, which he **h** sinned, come to his NIH
4:28 for his sin which he **h** sinned. NIH
4:35 atonement for his sin that he **h** committed, NIH
5: 1 whether he **h** seen or known *of it;* if he do NIH
5: 5 shall confess that he **h** sinned in that *thing:* NIH
5: 6 the LORD for his sin which he **h** sinned, NIH
5: 7 which he **h** committed, two turtledoves, or NIH
5:13 his sin that he **h** sinned in one of these, NIH
5:16 he shall make amends for the harm that he **h** NIH
5:19 he **h** certainly trespassed against NIH
6: 2 by violence, or **h** deceived his neighbour; NIH
6: 4 shall be, because he **h** sinned, and is guilty, NIH
6: 4 or the thing which he **h** deceitfully gotten, NIH
6: 5 Or all *that* about which he **h** sworn falsely; NIH
6: 7 of all that he **h** done in trespassing therein. NIH
6:10 take up the ashes which the fire **h** consumed NIH
7: 8 of the burnt offering which he **h** offered. NIH
8:34 As he **h** done this day, *so* the LORD hath NIH
8:34 *so* the LORD **h** commanded to do, NIH
10: 6 bewail the burning which the LORD **h** NIH
10:11 **h** spoken unto them by the hand of Moses. NIH
10:15 for ever; as the LORD **h** commanded. NIH
10:17 *God* **h** given it you to bear the iniquity of NIH
11: 9 whatsoever **h** fins and scales in 3807.1
11:12 Whatsoever **h** no fins nor scales in 3807.1
11:42 whatsoever **h** more feet among all creeping NIH
12: 7 This *is* the law for her that **h** born a male or NIH
13: 4 the priest shall shut up *him that* **h** the plague NIH
13: 7 after that he **h** been seen of the priest for his NIH
13:12 the leprosy cover all the skin of *him that* **h** NIH
13:13 he shall pronounce *him* clean *that* **h** NIH
13:17 the priest shall pronounce *him* clean *that* **h** NIH
13:29 woman **h** a plague upon the head or 1961+871.1
13:31 the priest shall shut up *him that* **h** the plague NIH
13:33 the priest shall shut up *him that* **h** the scall NIH
13:41 he that **h** his hair fallen off from the part of NIH
13:50 and shut up *it that* **h** the plague seven days: NIH
14:43 after *that* he **h** taken away the stones, and NIH
14:43 after he **h** scraped the house, and after it is NIH
14:48 the plague **h** not spread in the house, NIH

Lev 15: 2 When any man **h** a running issue out of his 1961
15: 4 whereon he lieth that **h** the issue, is unclean: NIH
15: 6 he sat that **h** the issue shall wash his clothes, NIH
15: 7 he that toucheth the flesh of him that **h** NIH
15: 8 if he that **h** the issue spit upon him that is NIH
15: 9 what saddle soever he rideth upon that **h** NIH
15:11 whomsoever he toucheth that **h** the issue, NIH
15:11 **h** not rinsed his hands in water, he shall NIH
15:12 that he toucheth which **h** the issue, shall be NIH
15:13 when he that **h** an issue is cleansed of his NIH
15:32 This *is* the law of him that **h** an issue, and NIH
15:33 of him that **h** an issue, of the man, and 2100
16:20 when he **h** made an end of reconciling NIH
17: 2 This *is* the thing which the LORD **h** 3807.1
17: 4 he **h** shed blood; and that man shall be cut NIH
19: 8 he **h** profaned the hallowed *thing* of NIH
19:22 the LORD for his sin which he **h** done: NIH
19:22 the sin which he **h** done shall be forgiven NIH
20: 3 because he **h** given of his seed unto Molech, NIH
20: 9 he **h** cursed his father or his mother; NIH
20:11 the man that lieth with his father's wife **h** NIH
20:17 he **h** uncovered his sister's nakedness; NIH
20:18 he **h** discovered her fountain, and she hath NIH
20:18 she **h** uncovered the fountain of her blood: NIH
20:20 he **h** uncovered his uncle's nakedness: NIH
20:21 he **h** uncovered his brother's nakedness; NIH
20:27 or woman that **h** a familiar spirit, 1961+871.1
21: 3 is nigh unto him, which **h** had no husband; NIH
21:17 their generations that **h** *any* blemish, 1961+871.1
21:18 For whatsoever man *he be* that **h** a 871.1
21:18 or he that **h** a flat nose, or any thing NIH
21:20 or that **h** a blemish in his eye, or be scurvy, NIH
21:20 or scabbed, or **h** his stones broken; NIH
21:21 No man that **h** a blemish, of the seed of 871.1
21:21 he **h** a blemish; he shall not come nigh to 871.1
21:23 unto the altar, because he **h** a blemish; 871.1
22: 4 of Aaron *is* a leper, or **h** a running issue; NIH
22: 5 whatsoever uncleanness he **h**; 3807.1
22: 6 The soul which **h** touched *any* such shall be NIH
22:20 *But* whatsoever **h** a blemish, *that* shall ye 871.1
22:23 or a lamb that **h any thing superfluous** or 8311
24:14 Bring forth him that **h** cursed without NIH
24:19 as he **h** done, so shall it be done to him; NIH
24:20 as he **h** caused a blemish in a man, so NIH
25:25 **h** sold away *some* of his possession, and NIH
25:28 him that **h** bought it until the year of jubile: NIH
27:22 unto the LORD a field which he **h** bought, NIH
27:28 devote unto the LORD of all that he **h**, 3807.1
Nu 5: 2 every one that **h** an issue, and whosoever is NIH
5: 7 *it* unto *him* against whom he **h trespassed**. 816
5:20 *some* man **h** lain with thee beside thine 5414
5:27 And when he **h** made her to drink the water, NIH
6: 9 he **h** defiled the head of his consecration; NIH
6:21 This *is* the law of the Nazarite who **h** NIH
10:29 for the LORD **h** spoken good concerning NIH
12: 2 **H** the LORD indeed spoken only by NIH
12: 2 **h** he not spoken also by us? And NIH
14: 3 wherefore ***h*** the LORD brought us unto NIH
14:16 therefore he **h** slain them in the wilderness. NIH
14:24 spirit with him, and **h** followed me fully, NIH
14:40 the place which the LORD **h** promised: NIH
15:22 which the LORD **h** spoken unto Moses, NIH
15:23 *Even* all that the LORD **h** commanded you NIH
15:31 Because he **h** despised the word of NIH
15:31 **h** broken his commandment, that soul shall NIH
16: 5 even *him* whom he **h** chosen will he cause NIH
16: 9 that the God of Israel **h** separated you from NIH
16:10 he **h** brought thee near *to him,* and all thy NIH
16:28 Hereby ye shall know that the LORD **h** NIH
16:29 of all men; *then* the LORD **h** not sent me. NIH
19: 2 the law which the LORD **h** commanded, NIH
19:15 which **h** no covering bound upon it, NIH
19:20 he **h** defiled the sanctuary of the LORD: NIH
19:20 the water of separation **h** not been sprinkled NIH
20:14 Thou knowest all the travail that **h** befallen NIH
20:16 and **h** brought us forth out of Egypt: NIH
21:28 it **h** consumed Ar of Moab, *and* the lords of NIH
21:29 he **h** given his sons that escaped, and NIH
22:10 king of Moab, **h** sent unto me, *saying,* NIH
23: 7 Balak the king of Moab **h** brought me from NIH
23: 8 How shall I curse, whom God **h** not cursed? NIH
23: 8 I defy, *whom* the LORD **h** not defied? NIH
23:12 that which the LORD **h** put in my mouth? NIH
23:17 said unto him, What **h** the LORD spoken? NIH
23:19 **h** he said, and shall he not do *it?* or hath he NIH
23:19 shall he not do *it?* or **h** he spoken, and NIH
23:20 and he **h** blessed; and I cannot reverse it. NIH
23:21 He **h** not beheld iniquity in Jacob, NIH
23:21 neither **h** he seen perverseness in Israel: NIH
23:22 he **h** as it were the strength of an unicorn. NIH
23:23 and of Israel, What **h** God wrought! NIH
24: 3 Balaam the son of Beor **h** said, and the man NIH
24: 3 and the man whose eyes are open **h** said: NIH
24: 4 He **h** said, which heard the words of God, NIH
24: 6 of lign aloes *which* the LORD **h** planted, NIH
24: 8 he **h** as it were the strength of an unicorn: NIH
24:11 the LORD **h** kept thee back from honour. NIH
24:15 Balaam the son of Beor **h** said, and the man NIH
24:15 and the man whose eyes are open **h** said: NIH
24:16 He **h** said, which heard the words of God, NIH
25:11 **h** turned my wrath away from the children NIH
27: 4 among his family, because he **h** no son? NIH
30: 1 This *is* the thing which the LORD **h** NIH
30: 4 her bond wherewith she **h** bound her soul, NIH
30: 4 every bond wherewith she **h** bound her soul NIH
30: 5 of her bonds wherewith she **h** bound her NIH
30:12 if her husband **h** utterly made them void on NIH
30:12 her husband **h** made them void; and NIH
30:15 make them void after *that* he **h** heard *them;* NIH
31:17 kill every woman that **h** known man by NIH
31:19 whosoever **h** killed *any* person, and NIH
31:19 whosoever **h** touched *any* slain, purify *both* NIH
31:50 what every man **h** gotten, *of* jewels of gold, NIH
32: 7 the land which the LORD **h** given them? NIH
32:21 until he **h** driven out his enemies from NIH

H

Nu 32:24 do that which **h** proceeded out of your NIH
32:31 As the LORD **h** said unto thy servants, so NIH
36: 5 The tribe of the sons of Joseph **h** said well. NIH
Dt 1:10 The LORD your God **h** multiplied you, NIH
1:11 and bless you, as he **h** promised you!) NIH
1:21 the LORD thy God **h** set the land before NIH
1:21 LORD God of thy fathers **h** said unto thee; NIH
1:27 he **h** brought us forth out of the land of NIH
1:36 to him will I give the land that he **h** trodden NIH
1:36 because he **h** wholly followed the LORD. NIH
2: 7 For the LORD thy God **h** blessed thee in NIH
2: 7 these forty years the LORD thy God ***h*** NIH
3:18 The LORD your God **h** given you this land NIH
3:20 your God **h** given them beyond Jordan: NIH
3:21 your God **h** done unto these two kings: NIH
4: 3 the LORD thy God **h** destroyed them from NIH
4: 7 *so* great, who **h** God *so* nigh unto them, NIH
4: 8 that **h** statutes and judgments *so* 3807.1
4:19 which the LORD thy God **h** divided unto NIH
4:20 the LORD **h** taken you, and brought you NIH
4:23 the LORD thy God **h** forbidden thee. NIH
4:32 whether there **h** been *any such thing* as this NIH
4:32 as this great thing *is,* or **h** been heard like it? NIH
4:34 Or **h** God assayed to go *and* take him a NIH
5:12 as the LORD thy God **h** commanded thee. NIH
5:16 as the LORD thy God **h** commanded thee; NIH
5:24 the LORD our God **h** shewed us his glory NIH
5:26 that **h** heard the voice of the living God NIH
5:32 as the LORD your God **h** commanded you: NIH
5:33 the LORD your God **h** commanded you, NIH
6: 3 as the LORD God of thy fathers **h** 3807.1
6:17 his statutes, which he **h** commanded thee. NIH
6:19 from before thee, as the LORD **h** spoken. NIH
6:20 which the LORD our God **h** commanded NIH
6:25 LORD our God, as he **h** commanded us. NIH
7: 1 **h** cast out many nations before thee, NIH
7: 6 the LORD thy God **h** chosen thee to be a NIH
7: 8 **h** the LORD brought you out with a NIH
8:10 for the good land which he **h** given thee. NIH
8:17 the might of mine hand **h** gotten me this NIH
9: 3 as the LORD **h** said unto thee. NIH
9: 4 after that the LORD thy God **h** cast them NIH
9: 4 For my righteousness the LORD **h** brought NIH
9:28 he **h** brought them out to slay them in NIH
10: 9 Wherefore Levi **h** no part nor 1961+3807.1
10:21 that **h** done for thee these great and terrible NIH
10:22 now the LORD thy God **h** made thee as NIH
11: 4 *how* the LORD **h** destroyed them unto this NIH
11:25 ye shall tread upon, as he **h** said unto you. NIH
11:29 when the LORD thy God **h** brought thee in NIH
12: 7 where*in* the LORD thy God **h** blessed NIH
12:12 forasmuch as he **h** no part nor inheritance 3807.1
12:15 the LORD thy God which he **h** given thee: NIH
12:20 as he **h** promised thee, and thou shalt say, NIH
12:21 If the place which the LORD thy God **h** NIH
12:21 thy flock, which the LORD **h** given thee, NIH
13: 5 he **h** spoken to turn *you* away from NIH
13:10 he **h** sought to thrust thee away from NIH
13:12 which the LORD thy God **h** given thee to NIH
13:17 as he **h** sworn unto thy fathers; NIH
14: 2 the LORD **h** chosen thee to be a peculiar NIH
14:10 whatsoever **h** not fins and scales ye may 3807.1
14:24 when the LORD thy God **h** blessed thee: NIH
14:27 for he **h** no part nor inheritance with thee. 3807.1
14:29 he **h** no part nor inheritance with thee,) 3807.1
15:14 *of that* where*with* the LORD thy God **h** NIH
15:18 for he **h** been worth a double hired servant NIH
16:10 as the LORD thy God **h** blessed thee: NIH
16:11 in the place which the LORD thy God **h** NIH
16:17 the LORD thy God which he **h** given thee. NIH
17: 2 that **h** wrought wickedness in the sight of NIH
17: 3 **h** gone and served other gods, and NIH
17:16 forasmuch as the LORD **h** said unto you, NIH
18: 2 *is* their inheritance, as he **h** said unto them. NIH
18: 5 For the LORD thy God **h** chosen him out NIH
18:14 the LORD thy God **h** not suffered thee so NIH
18:21 the word which the LORD **h** not spoken? NIH
18:22 that *is* the thing which the LORD **h** not NIH
18:22 *but* the prophet **h** spoken it presumptuously: NIH
19: 1 When the LORD thy God **h** cut off NIH
19: 8 as he **h** sworn unto thy fathers, and NIH
19:18 *and* **h** testified falsely against his brother; NIH
20: 5 What man *is there* that **h** built a new house, NIH
20: 5 built a new house, and **h** not dedicated it? NIH
20: 6 what man *is he* that **h** planted a vineyard, NIH
20: 6 a vineyard, and **h** not *yet* eaten of it? NIH
20: 7 what man *is there* that **h** betrothed a wife, NIH
20: 7 hath betrothed a wife, and **h** not taken her? NIH
20:13 when the LORD thy God **h** delivered it NIH
20:14 which the LORD thy God **h** given thee. 3807.1
20:17 as the LORD thy God **h** commanded thee: NIH
21: 1 *and* it be not known who **h** slain him: NIH
21: 3 which **h** not been wrought with, *and* NIH
21: 3 *and* which **h** not drawn in the yoke; NIH
21: 5 for them the LORD thy God **h** chosen to NIH
21:10 the LORD thy God **h** delivered them into NIH
21:16 his sons to inherit *that* which he **h**, 1961+3807.1
21:17 a double portion of all that he **h**: 4672+3807.1
22: 3 which he **h** lost, and thou hast found, shalt NIH
22:17 he **h** given occasions of speech *against her,* NIH
22:19 he **h** brought up an evil name upon a virgin NIH
22:21 because she **h** wrought folly in Israel, NIH
22:24 because he **h** humbled his neighbour's wife: NIH
22:29 because he **h** humbled her, he may not put NIH
23: 1 in the stones, or **h** *his* privy member cut off, NIH
24: 1 When a man **h** taken a wife, and NIH
24: 1 he **h** found some uncleanness in her: NIH
24: 5 When a man **h** taken a new wife, he shall NIH
24: 5 shall cheer up his wife which he **h** taken. NIH
25:10 The house of him that **h** his shoe loosed. NIH
25:19 when the LORD thy God **h** given thee 3807.1
26: 9 he **h** brought us into this place, and NIH
26: 9 **h** given us this land, *even* a land that NIH
26:11 the LORD thy God **h** given unto thee, NIH
26:16 This day the LORD thy God **h** NIH
Dt 26:18 the LORD **h** avouched thee *this* day to be NIH
26:18 as he **h** promised thee, and that *thou* NIH
26:19 high above all nations which he **h** made, NIH
26:19 unto the LORD thy God, as he **h** spoken. NIH
27: 3 as the LORD God of thy fathers **h** NIH
28: 9 unto himself, as he **h** sworn unto thee, NIH
28:52 which the LORD thy God **h** given thee. NIH
28:53 which the LORD thy God **h** given thee, NIH
28:55 because he **h** nothing left him in the siege, NIH
29: 4 Yet the LORD **h** not given you a heart to NIH
29:13 as he **h** said unto thee, and as he hath sworn NIH
29:13 as he **h** sworn unto thy fathers, to Abraham, NIH
29:22 the sicknesses which the LORD **h** laid NIH
29:24 Wherefore **h** the LORD done thus unto NIH
30: 1 whither the LORD thy God **h** driven thee, NIH
30: 3 whither the LORD thy God **h** scattered NIH
31: 2 also the LORD **h** said unto me, Thou shalt NIH
31: 3 go over before thee, as the LORD **h** said. NIH
31: 7 **h** sworn unto their fathers to give them; NIH
32: 6 *is* not he thy father *that* **h** bought thee? NIH
32: 6 **h** he *not* made thee, and established thee? NIH
32:27 is high, and the LORD **h** not done all this. NIH
Jos 1:13 The LORD your God **h** given you rest, 3807.1
1:13 given you rest, and **h** given you this land. 3807.1
1:15 as *he **h** given* you, and they also have NIH
2: 9 I know that the LORD **h** given you NIH
2:14 when the LORD **h** given us the land, NIH
2:24 Truly the LORD **h** delivered into our NIH
6:16 Shout; for the LORD **h** given you the city. NIH
6:22 and all that she **h**, as ye sware unto her. 3807.1
7:11 Israel **h** sinned, and they have also NIH
7:15 shall be burnt with fire, he and all that he **h**: NIH
7:15 he **h** transgressed the covenant of NIH
7:15 and because he **h** wrought folly in Israel. NIH
8:31 over which no *man* **h** lift up *any* iron: NIH
10: 4 for it **h** made peace with Joshua and NIH
10:19 for the LORD your God **h** delivered them NIH
14:10 the LORD **h** kept me alive, as he said, NIH
17:14 forasmuch as the LORD **h** blessed me NIH
18: 3 which the LORD God of your fathers **h** NIH
22: 4 now the LORD your God **h** given rest unto NIH
22:25 For the LORD **h** made Jordan a border NIH
23: 3 have seen all that the LORD your God **h** NIH
23: 3 for the LORD your God *is* he that **h** fought NIH
23: 5 as the LORD your God **h** promised unto NIH
23: 9 For the LORD **h** driven out from before NIH
23: 9 no man **h** *been able to* stand before you unto NIH
23:10 that fighteth for you, as he **h** promised you. NIH
23:13 which the LORD your God **h** given you. NIH
23:14 that not one thing **h** failed of all the good NIH
23:14 unto you, *and* not one thing **h** failed thereof. NIH
23:15 which the LORD your God **h** given you. NIH
23:16 the good land which he **h** given unto you. NIH
24:20 after that he **h** done you good. NIH
24:27 for it **h** heard all the words of the LORD NIH
Jdg 1: 7 as I have done, so God **h** requited me. NIH
2:20 Because that this people **h** transgressed my NIH
3:28 for the LORD **h** delivered your enemies NIH
4: 6 **H** not the LORD God of Israel NIH
4:14 for this *is* the day in which the LORD **h** NIH
6:13 now the LORD **h** forsaken us, and NIH
6:25 down the altar of Baal that thy father **h**, NIH
6:29 said one to another, Who **h** done this thing? NIH
6:29 Gideon the son of Joash **h** done this thing. NIH
6:30 because he **h** cast down the altar of Baal, NIH
6:30 he **h** cut down the grove that *was* by it. NIH
6:31 because *one* **h** cast down his altar. NIH
6:32 because he **h** thrown down his altar. NIH
7: 2 saying, Mine own hand **h** saved me. NIH
7:14 *for* into his hand **h** God delivered Midian, NIH
7:15 for the LORD **h** delivered into your hand NIH
8: 3 God **h** delivered into your hands the princes NIH
8: 7 Therefore when the LORD **h** delivered NIH
11:23 So now the LORD God of Israel **h** NIH
11:36 do to me according to that which **h** NIH
11:36 forasmuch as the LORD **h** taken NIH
13:10 Behold, the man **h** appeared unto me, NIH
15: 6 the Philistines said, Who **h** done this? NIH
15:10 come up, to do to him as he **h** done to us. NIH
16:17 There **h** not come a razor upon mine head; NIH
16:18 *this* once, for he **h** shewed me all his heart. NIH
16:23 Our god **h** delivered Samson our enemy into NIH
16:24 Our god **h** delivered into our hands our NIH
18: 4 and **h** hired me, and I am his priest. NIH
18:10 for God **h** given it into your hands; a place NIH
21:11 and every woman that **h** lien by man. 3045
Ru 1:20 for the Almighty **h** dealt very bitterly with NIH
1:21 the LORD **h** brought me *home* again NIH
1:21 seeing the LORD **h** testified against me, NIH
1:21 and the Almighty **h** afflicted me? NIH
2: 7 **h** continued even from the morning until NIH
2:11 said unto her, It **h** fully been shewed me, NIH
2:20 who **h** not left off his kindness to the living NIH
4:14 which **h** not left thee *this* day without a NIH
4:15 better to thee than seven sons, **h** born him. NIH
1Sa 1:27 the LORD **h** given me my petition which I NIH
2: 5 so that the barren **h** born seven; and she that NIH
2: 5 she that **h** many children is waxed feeble. NIH
2: 8 and he **h** set the world upon them. NIH
3:17 What *is* the thing that *the LORD* **h** said NIH
4: 3 Wherefore **h** the LORD smitten us to day NIH
4: 7 for there **h** not been such *a thing* heretofore. NIH
4:17 there **h** been also a great slaughter among NIH
6: 7 on which there **h** come no yoke, and tie NIH
6: 9 *then* he **h** done us this great evil: NIH
7:12 Hitherto **h** the LORD helped us. NIH
9:24 for unto *this* time **h** *it* been kept for thee NIH
10: 1 the LORD **h** anointed thee to be captain NIH
10: 2 and lo, thy father **h** left the care of the asses, NIH
10:22 Behold, he **h** hid himself among the stuff. NIH
10:24 See ye him whom the LORD **h** chosen, NIH
11:13 for to day the LORD **h** wrought salvation NIH
12:13 behold, the LORD **h** set a king over you. NIH
12:22 it **h** pleased the LORD to make you his NIH
12:24 for consider how great things he **h** done for NIH
1Sa 13:14 the LORD **h** sought him a man after his NIH
13:14 the LORD **h** commanded him to be captain NIH
14:10 for the LORD **h** delivered them into our NIH
14:12 for the LORD **h** delivered them into NIH
14:29 My father **h** troubled the land: NIH
14:38 and see wherein this sin **h** been *this* day. NIH
14:45 who **h** wrought this great salvation in NIH
14:45 for he **h** wrought with God this day. NIH
15:11 and **h** not performed my commandments. NIH
15:16 I will tell thee what the LORD **h** said to NIH
15:22 **H** the LORD *as great* delight in burnt 3807.1
15:23 he **h** also rejected thee from *being* king. NIH
15:26 the LORD **h** rejected thee from being king NIH
15:28 The LORD **h** rent the kingdom of Israel NIH
15:28 **h** given it to a neighbour of thine, *that is* NIH
15:33 As thy sword **h** made women childless, so NIH
16: 8 he said, Neither **h** the LORD chosen this. NIH
16: 9 he said, Neither **h** the LORD chosen this. NIH
16:10 unto Jesse, The LORD **h** not chosen these. NIH
16:22 for he **h** found favour in my sight. NIH
17:36 seeing he **h** defied the armies of the living NIH
18: 7 Saul **h** slain his thousands, and David his NIH
18:22 the king **h** delight in thee, and all his NIH
19: 4 because he **h** not sinned against thee, and NIH
20:13 be with thee, as he **h** been with my father. NIH
20:15 not when the LORD **h** cut off the enemies NIH
20:22 go *thy way:* for the LORD **h** sent thee NIH
20:26 for he thought, Something **h** befallen him, NIH
20:29 for our family **h** a sacrifice in the city; and NIH
20:29 he **h** commanded me *to be there:* and now, NIH
20:32 shall he be slain? what **h** he done? NIH
21: 2 The king **h** commanded me a business, and NIH
21: 2 me a business, and **h** said unto me, NIH
21:11 Saul **h** slain his thousands, and David his NIH
22: 8 *there is* none that sheweth me that my son **h** NIH
22: 8 sheweth unto me that my son **h** stirred up NIH
23: 7 God **h** delivered him into mine hand; NIH
23: 7 by entering into a town that **h** gates and NIH
23:10 thy servant **h** certainly heard that Saul NIH
23:11 Saul come down, as thy servant **h** heard? NIH
23:22 his haunt is, *and* who **h** seen him there: NIH
25:21 all that this *fellow* **h** in the wilderness, 3807.1
25:21 and he **h** requited me evil for good. NIH
25:26 seeing the LORD **h** withholden thee from NIH
25:27 now this blessing which thine handmaid **h** NIH
25:28 evil **h** not been found in thee *all* thy days. NIH
25:30 the good that he **h** spoken concerning thee, NIH
25:31 or that my lord **h** avenged himself: NIH
25:34 which **h** kept me back from hurting thee, NIH
25:39 that **h** pleaded the cause of my reproach NIH
25:39 of Nabal, and **h** kept his servant from evil: NIH
25:39 for the LORD **h** returned the wickedness NIH
26: 8 God **h** delivered thine enemy into thine NIH
27:12 He **h** made his people Israel utterly to 871.1
28: 7 Seek me a woman that **h** a familiar spirit, 1172
28: 7 *there is* a woman that **h** a familiar spirit at 1172
28: 9 Behold, thou knowest what Saul **h** done, NIH
28: 9 how he **h** cut off those that have familiar NIH
28:17 the LORD **h** done to him, as he spake by NIH
28:17 for the LORD **h** rent the kingdom out of NIH
28:18 **h** the LORD done this thing unto thee this NIH
28:21 thine handmaid **h** obeyed thy voice, and NIH
29: 3 which **h** been with me these days, or NIH
30:23 with *that* which the LORD **h** given us, NIH
30:23 who **h** preserved us, and delivered NIH
2Sa 1:16 for thy mouth **h** testified against thee, NIH
3: 9 as the LORD **h** sworn to David, even so NIH
3:18 do *it:* for the LORD **h** spoken of David, NIH
3:23 he **h** sent him away, and he is gone in NIH
3:29 from the house of Joab one that **h an issue,** 2100
4: 8 the LORD **h** avenged my lord the king this NIH
4: 9 who **h** redeemed my soul out of all NIH
5:20 The LORD **h** broken forth upon mine NIH
6:12 The LORD **h** blessed the house of NIH
7:27 **h** thy servant found in his heart to pray this NIH
9: 3 Jonathan **h** yet a son, *which is* lame on 3807.1
9:11 According to all that my lord the king **h** NIH
10: 3 that he **h** sent comforters unto thee? NIH
10: 3 **h** not David *rather* sent his servants unto NIH
12: 5 the man that **h** done this *thing* shall surely NIH
12:13 The LORD also **h** put away thy sin; NIH
13:20 **H** Amnon thy brother been with thee? NIH
13:24 Behold now, thy servant **h** sheepshearers; NIH
13:30 Absalom **h** slain all the king's sons, and NIH
13:32 for by the appointment of Absalom *this* **h** NIH
14:19 from ought that my lord the king **h** spoken: NIH
14:20 To fetch about *this* form of speech **h** thy NIH
14:22 in that the king **h** fulfilled the request of his NIH
14:30 field is near mine, and he **h** barley there; 3807.1
15: 4 that every man which **h** *any* suit or 1961+3807.1
16: 8 The LORD **h** returned upon thee all NIH
16: 8 the LORD **h** delivered the kingdom into NIH
16:10 because the LORD **h** said unto him, NIH
16:11 let him curse; for the LORD **h** bidden him. NIH
16:21 which he **h** left to keep the house; NIH
17: 6 Ahithophel **h** spoken after this manner: NIH
17: 7 The counsel that Ahithophel **h** given *is* not NIH
17:21 for thus **h** Ahithophel counselled against NIH
18:19 how that the LORD **h** avenged him of his NIH
18:28 which **h** delivered up the men that lift up NIH
18:31 for the LORD **h** avenged thee *this* day of NIH
19:27 he **h** slandered thy servant unto my lord NIH
19:42 the king's *cost?* or **h** he given us *any* gift? 3807.1
20:21 **h** lift up his hand against the king, NIH
22:21 according to the cleanness of my hands **h** he NIH
22:25 Therefore the LORD **h** recompensed me NIH
22:36 and thy gentleness **h** made me great. NIH
23: 5 yet he **h** made with me an everlasting NIH
1Ki 1:19 he **h** slain oxen and fat cattle and sheep in NIH
1:19 **h** called all the sons of the king, and NIH
1:19 but Solomon thy servant **h** he not called. NIH
1:25 **h** slain oxen and fat cattle and sheep in NIH
1:25 **h** called all the king's sons, and the captains NIH
1:26 and thy servant Solomon, **h** he not called. NIH
1:29 that **h** redeemed my soul out of all distress, NIH

1Ki 1:37 As the LORD **h** been with my lord NIH
1:43 Verily our lord king David **h** made Solomon NIH
1:44 the king **h** sent with him Zadok the priest, NIH
1:48 which **h** given *one* to sit on my throne *this* NIH
1:51 he **h** caught hold on the horns of the altar, NIH
2:24 which **h** established me, and set me on NIH
2:24 who **h** made me a house, as he promised, NIH
2:31 Do as he **h** said, and fall upon him, and NIH
2:38 as my lord the king **h** said, so will thy NIH
5: 4 now the LORD my God **h** given me rest 3807.1
5: 7 which **h** given unto David a wise son over NIH
8:15 and **h** with his hand fulfilled *it,* saying, NIH
8:20 the LORD **h** performed his word that he NIH
8:56 that **h** given rest unto his people Israel, NIH
8:56 there **h** not failed one word of all his good NIH
9: 8 Why **h** the LORD done thus unto this land, NIH
9: 9 **h** the LORD brought upon them all this NIH
12:11 my father **h** chastised you with whips, but NIH
13: 3 This *is* the sign which the LORD **h** NIH
13:26 the LORD **h** delivered him unto the lion, NIH
13:26 which **h** torn him, and slain him, NIH
14:11 of the air eat: for the LORD **h** spoken *it.* NIH
16:16 Zimri **h** conspired, and hath also slain NIH
16:16 hath conspired, and **h** also slain the king: NIH
18:10 whither my lord **h** not sent to seek thee: NIH
19:18 and every mouth which **h** not kissed him. NIH
22:23 the LORD **h** put a lying spirit in the mouth NIH
22:23 the LORD **h** spoken evil concerning thee. NIH
22:28 in peace, the LORD **h** not spoken by me. NIH
2Ki 1: 9 man of God, the king **h** said, Come down. NIH
1:11 O man of God, thus **h** the king said, NIH
2: 2 for the LORD **h** sent me to Beth-el. NIH
2: 4 for the LORD **h** sent me *to* Jericho. NIH
2: 6 here; for the LORD **h** sent me to Jordan. NIH
2:16 lest peradventure the spirit of the LORD **h** NIH
3: 7 The king of Moab **h** rebelled against me: NIH
3:10 that the LORD **h** called these three kings NIH
3:13 for the LORD **h** called these three kings NIH
4: 2 Thine handmaid **h** not any thing in 3807.1
4:14 Verily she **h** no child, and her husband is 3807.1
4:27 the LORD **h** hid *it* from me, and hath not NIH
4:27 hath hid *it* from me, and **h** not told me. NIH
5:20 my master **h** spared Naaman this Syrian, NIH
5:22 My master **h** sent me, saying, Behold, NIH
6:29 that we may eat him: and she **h** hid her son. NIH
6:32 See ye how this son of a murderer **h** sent to NIH
7: 6 the king of Israel **h** hired against us NIH
8: 1 for the LORD **h** called for a famine; and NIH
8: 4 all the great *things* that Elisha **h** done. NIH
8: 9 Thy son Ben-hadad king of Syria **h** sent me NIH
8:10 howbeit the LORD **h** shewed me that he NIH
8:13 The LORD **h** shewed me *that* thou *shalt be* NIH
10:10 for the LORD **h** done *that* which he spake NIH
14:10 and thine heart **h** lifted thee up: NIH
17:26 therefore he **h** sent lions among them, NIH
18:22 and whose altars Hezekiah **h** taken away, NIH
18:22 and **h** said to Judah and Jerusalem, NIH
18:27 **H** my master sent me to thy master, and NIH
18:27 *h he* not *sent me* to the men which sit on NIH
18:33 **H** any of the gods of the nations delivered at NIH
19: 4 whom the king of Assyria his master **h** sent NIH
19: 4 words which the LORD thy God **h** heard: NIH
19:16 which **h** sent him to reproach the living NIH
19:21 This *is* the word that the LORD **h** spoken NIH
19:21 The virgin the daughter of Zion **h** despised NIH
19:21 the daughter of Jerusalem **h** shaken her head NIH
20: 9 that the LORD will do the thing that he **h** NIH
21:11 Because Manasseh king of Judah **h** done NIH
21:11 **h** done wickedly above all that the Amorites NIH
21:11 and **h** made Judah also to sin with his idols: NIH
22:10 Hilkiah the priest **h** delivered me a book. NIH
22:16 of the book which the king of Judah **h** read: NIH
1Ch 14:11 God **h** broken in upon mine enemies by NIH
15: 2 for them **h** the LORD chosen to carry NIH
16:12 Remember his marvellous works that he **h** NIH
16:17 **h** confirmed the same to Jacob for a law, NIH
17:25 thy servant **h** found *in his heart* to pray NIH
19: 3 that he **h** sent comforters unto thee? NIH
22:11 of the LORD thy God, as he **h** said of thee. NIH
22:18 **h** he *not* given you rest on every side? NIH
22:18 for he **h** given the inhabitants of the land NIH
23:25 The LORD God of Israel **h** given rest unto NIH
28: 4 for he **h** chosen Judah to be the ruler; and NIH
28: 5 (for the LORD **h** given me many sons,) NIH
28: 5 he **h** chosen Solomon my son to sit upon NIH
28:10 for the LORD **h** chosen thee to build a NIH
29: 1 whom alone God **h** chosen, *is yet* young and NIH
2Ch 2:11 Because the LORD **h** loved his people, NIH
2:11 his people, he **h** made thee king over them. NIH
2:12 who **h** given to David the king a wise son, NIH
2:15 and the wine, which my lord **h** spoken of, NIH
6: 1 The LORD **h** said that *he* would dwell in NIH
6: 4 who **h** with his hands fulfilled *that* which he NIH
6:10 **h** performed his word that he hath spoken: NIH
6:10 hath performed his word that he **h** spoken: NIH
7:21 Why **h** the LORD done thus unto this land, NIH
7:22 **h** he brought all this evil upon them. NIH
8:11 whereunto the ark of the LORD **h** come. NIH
13: 6 is risen up, and **h** rebelled against his lord. NIH
14: 7 and he **h** given us rest on every side. NIH
15: 3 Now for a long season Israel *h been* without NIH
18:22 the LORD **h** put a lying spirit in the mouth NIH
18:22 and the LORD **h** spoken evil against thee. NIH
18:27 *then* **h** not the LORD spoken by me. NIH
20:37 the LORD **h** broken thy works. NIH
23: 3 as the LORD **h** said of the sons of David. NIH
24:20 the LORD, he **h** also forsaken you. NIH
25: 8 **h** power to help, and to cast down. 3426+871.1
25:16 I know that God **h** determined to destroy NIH
28: 9 he **h** delivered them into your hand, and NIH
29: 8 and he **h** delivered them to trouble, NIH
29:11 for the LORD **h** chosen you to stand NIH
30: 8 which he **h** sanctified for ever: NIH
31:10 for the LORD **h** blessed his people; and NIH
32:12 **H** not the same Hezekiah taken away his NIH
2Ch 34:18 Hilkiah the priest **h** given me a book. NIH
36:23 All the kingdoms of the earth **h** the LORD NIH
36:23 he **h** charged me to build him a house in NIH
Ezr 1: 2 The LORD God of heaven **h** given me all NIH
1: 2 he **h** charged me to build him a house at NIH
4: 3 as king Cyrus the king of Persia **h** NIH
4:18 The letter which ye sent unto us *h been* NIH
4:19 search **h** been made, and it is found that this NIH
4:19 it is found that this city of old time *h* made NIH
5: 3 Who **h** commanded you to build this house, NIH
5:16 since that time even until now *h it been* in NIH
6:12 the God that **h** caused his name to dwell NIH
7:27 which **h** put *such a thing* as this in NIH
7:28 **h** extended mercy unto me before the king, NIH
9: 2 and rulers **h** been chief in this trespass. NIH
9: 8 now for a little space grace **h** been *shewed* NIH
9: 9 yet our God **h** not forsaken us in our NIH
9: 9 **h** extended mercy unto us in the sight of NIH
Ne 9:32 that **h** come upon us, on our kings, on our NIH
Est 1:15 she **h** not performed the commandment of NIH
1:16 Vashti the queen **h** not done wrong to NIH
5: 5 make haste, that *he* may do as Esther **h** said. NIH
5: 8 and I will do to morrow as the king **h** said. NIH
6: 3 dignity **h** been done to Mordecai for this? 3807.1
Job 1:10 and about all that he **h** on every side? 3807.1
1:11 touch all that he **h,** and he will curse thee 3807.1
1:12 Behold, all that he **h** *is* in thy power; 3807.1
1:16 **h** burnt up the sheep, and the servants, and NIH
1:21 the LORD **h** taken *away;* blessed be NIH
2: 4 yea, all that a man **h** will he give for his life. NIH
3:23 way is hid, and whom God **h** hedged in? NIH
5:16 So the poor **h** hope, and 1961+3807.1
6: 5 Doth the wild ass bray when he **h** grass? or NIH
7: 8 The eye of him that **h** seen me shall see me NIH
9: 4 who **h** hardened *himself* against him, and NIH
9: 4 *himself* against him, and **h** prospered? NIH
10:12 and thy visitation **h** preserved my spirit. NIH
12: 9 that the hand of the LORD **h** wrought this? NIH
12:13 strength, he **h** counsel and understanding. 3807.1
13: 1 mine eye **h** seen all *this,* mine ear hath NIH
13: 1 mine eye hath seen all *this,* mine ear **h** NIH
16: 7 now he **h** made me weary: thou hast made NIH
16:11 God **h** delivered me to the ungodly, and NIH
16:12 I was at ease, but he **h** broken me asunder: NIH
16:12 he **h** also taken *me* by my neck, and NIH
17: 6 He **h** made me also a byword of the people; NIH
17: 9 he that **h** clean hands shall be stronger and NIH
19: 6 Know now that God **h** overthrown me, and NIH
19: 6 and **h** compassed me with his net. NIH
19: 8 He **h** fenced up my way that I cannot pass, NIH
19: 8 and he **h** set darkness in my paths. NIH
19: 9 He **h** stript me of my glory, and taken NIH
19:10 He **h** destroyed me on every side, and I am NIH
19:10 and mine hope **h** he removed like a tree. NIH
19:11 He **h** also kindled his wrath against me, and NIH
19:13 He **h** put my brethren far from me, and NIH
19:21 for the hand of God **h** touched me. NIH
20:15 He **h** swallowed down riches, and he shall NIH
20:19 Because he **h** oppressed *and* hath forsaken NIH
20:19 he hath oppressed *and* **h** forsaken the poor; NIH
20:19 he **h** violently taken away a house which he NIH
21:21 For what pleasure **h** he in his house after NIH
21:31 and who shall repay him *what* he **h** done? NIH
23:10 *when* he **h** tried me, I shall come forth as NIH
23:11 My foot **h** held his steps, his way have I NIH
23:17 *neither* **h** he covered the darkness from my NIH
26: 2 *how* savest thou the arm *that* **h** no strength? NIH
26: 3 How hast thou counselled *him that* **h** no NIH
26: 6 before him, and destruction **h** no covering. NIH
26:10 He **h** compassed the waters with bounds, NIH
26:13 By his spirit he **h** garnished the heavens; NIH
26:13 his hand **h** formed the crooked serpent. NIH
27: 2 *who* **h** taken away my judgment; NIH
27: 2 and the Almighty, *who* **h** vexed my soul; NIH
27: 8 though he **h** gained, when God taketh away NIH
28: 6 place of sapphires: and it **h** dust of gold. 3807.1
28: 7 and which the vulture's eye **h** not seen: NIH
30:11 Because he **h** loosed my cord, and NIH
30:19 He **h** cast me into the mire, and I am NIH
31: 5 with vanity, or *if* my foot **h** hasted to deceit; NIH
31: 7 If my step **h** turned out of the way, and NIH
31: 7 and *if any* blot **h** cleaved to my hands; NIH
31:17 and the fatherless **h** not eaten thereof; NIH
31:27 my heart **h** been secretly enticed, or NIH
31:27 or my mouth **h** kissed my hand: NIH
32:14 Now he **h** not directed *his* words against NIH
32:19 my belly *is* as wine *which* **h** no vent; NIH
33: 2 my tongue **h** spoken in my mouth. NIH
33: 4 The Spirit of God **h** made me, and NIH
33: 4 the breath of the Almighty **h** given me life. NIH
34: 5 For Job **h** said, I am righteous: and NIH
34: 5 and God **h** taken away my judgment. NIH
34: 9 For he **h** said, It profiteth a man nothing that NIH
34:13 Who **h** given him a charge over the earth? NIH
34:13 or who **h** disposed the whole world? NIH
34:35 Job **h** spoken without knowledge, and NIH
35:15 *it is* not *so,* he **h** visited *in* his anger; NIH
36:23 Who **h** enjoined him his way? or who can NIH
38: 5 Who **h** laid the measures thereof, if thou NIH
38: 5 or who **h** stretched the line upon it? NIH
38:25 Who **h** divided a watercourse for NIH
38:28 **H** the rain a father? or who hath 3426+3807.1
38:28 or who **h** begotten the drops of dew? NIH
38:29 hoary frost of heaven, who **h** gendered it? NIH
38:36 Who **h** put wisdom in the inward parts? or NIH
38:36 or who **h** given understanding to the heart? NIH
39: 5 Who **h** sent out the wild ass free? or NIH
39: 5 or who **h** loosed the bands of the wild ass? NIH
39:17 Because God **h** deprived her of wisdom, NIH
39:17 neither **h** he imparted to her understanding. NIH
41:11 Who **h** prevented me, that I should repay NIH
42: 7 *the thing that is* right, as my servant Job **h.** NIH
Ps 2: 7 the LORD **h** said unto me, Thou *art* my NIH
4: 3 know that the LORD **h** set apart *him that is* NIH
5: 4 For thou *art* not a God that **h** pleasure in NIH
Ps 6: 8 for the LORD **h** heard the voice of my NIH
6: 9 The LORD **h** heard my supplication; NIH
7:12 he **h** bent his bow, and made it ready. NIH
7:13 He **h** also prepared for him the instruments NIH
7:14 **h** conceived mischief, and brought forth NIH
9: 7 he **h** prepared his throne for judgment. NIH
10: 6 He **h** said in his heart, I shall not be moved: NIH
10:11 He **h** said in his heart, God hath forgotten: NIH
10:11 He hath said in his heart, God **h** forgotten: NIH
10:13 he **h** said in his heart, Thou wilt not require NIH
13: 6 because he **h** dealt bountifully with me. NIH
14: 1 The fool **h** said in his heart, *There is* no NIH
16: 7 bless the LORD, who **h** given me counsel: NIH
18:20 according to the cleanness of my hands **h** he NIH
18:24 Therefore **h** the LORD recompensed me NIH
18:35 thy right hand **h** holden me up, and NIH
18:35 me up, and thy gentleness **h** made me great. NIH
19: 4 In them **h** he set a tabernacle for the sun, NIH
22:24 For he **h** not despised nor abhorred NIH
22:24 neither **h** he hid his face from him; but NIH
22:31 that *shall be* born, that he **h** done *this.* NIH
24: 2 For he **h** founded it upon the seas, and NIH
24: 4 He that **h** clean hands, and a pure heart; NIH
24: 4 who **h** not lift up his soul unto vanity, NIH
28: 6 he **h** heard the voice of my supplications. NIH
31:21 for he **h** shewed me his marvellous kindness NIH
33:12 the people *whom* he **h** chosen for his own NIH
35: 8 and let his net that he **h** hid catch himself: NIH
35:21 *and* said, Aha, aha, our eye **h** seen *it.* NIH
35:27 which **h** pleasure in the prosperity of his NIH
36: 3 he **h** left off to be wise, *and* to do good. NIH
37:16 A little that a righteous *man* **h** *is* better than NIH
40: 3 he **h** put a new song in my mouth, NIH
41: 9 *of* my bread, **h** lift up *his* heel against me. NIH
44:15 and the shame of my face **h** covered me, NIH
45: 2 therefore God **h** blessed thee for ever. NIH
45: 7 **h** anointed thee *with* the oil of gladness NIH
46: 8 what desolations he **h** made in the earth. NIH
50: 1 **h** spoken, and called the earth from NIH
50: 2 the perfection of beauty, God **h** shined. NIH
53: 1 The fool **h** said in his heart, *There is* no NIH
53: 5 for God **h** scattered the bones of him that NIH
53: 5 to shame, because God **h** despised them. NIH
54: 7 For he **h** delivered me out of all trouble: and NIH
54: 7 mine eye **h** seen *his desire* upon mine NIH
55: 5 upon me, and horror **h** overwhelmed me. NIH
55:18 He **h** delivered my soul in peace from NIH
55:20 He **h** put forth his hands against such as be NIH
55:20 peace with him: he **h** broken his covenant. NIH
60: 6 God **h** spoken in his holiness; I will rejoice, NIH
62:11 God **h** spoken once; twice have I heard this; NIH
66:14 my mouth **h** spoken, when I was in trouble. NIH
66:16 I will declare what he **h** done for my soul. NIH
66:19 *But* verily God **h** heard *me;* he hath NIH
66:19 *But* verily God hath heard *me;* he **h** NIH
66:20 which **h** not turned away my prayer, NIH
68:10 Thy congregation **h** dwelt therein: thou, NIH
68:28 Thy God **h** commanded thy strength: NIH
69: 7 borne reproach; shame **h** covered my face. NIH
69: 9 For the zeal of thine house **h** eaten me up; NIH
69:20 Reproach **h** broken my heart; and I am full NIH
69:31 an ox *or* bullock that **h** horns *and* hoofs. NIH
71:11 Saying, God **h** forsaken him: persecute and NIH
72:12 the poor also, and *him* that **h** no helper. 3807.1
74: 3 *even* all *that* the enemy **h** done wickedly in NIH
74:18 *that* the enemy **h** reproached, O LORD, NIH
77: 9 **H** God forgotten to be gracious? hath he in NIH
77: 9 **h** he in anger shut up his tender mercies? NIH
78: 4 and his wonderful works that he **h** done. NIH
78:69 the earth which he **h** established for ever. NIH
80:15 the vineyard which thy right hand **h** planted, NIH
84: 3 the sparrow **h** found a house, and NIH
88: 4 the pit: I am as a man *that* **h** no strength: NIH
91:14 Because he **h** set his love upon me, NIH
91:14 him on high, because he **h** known my name. NIH
93: 1 *wherewith* he **h** girded himself: NIH
98: 1 for he **h** done marvellous *things:* his right NIH
98: 1 and his holy arm, **h** gotten him the victory. NIH
98: 2 The LORD **h** made known his salvation: NIH
98: 2 his righteousness **h** he openly shewed in NIH
98: 3 He **h** remembered his mercy and his truth NIH
100: 3 *it is* he *that* **h** made us, and not we NIH
101: 5 him that **h** a high look and a proud heart NIH
102:19 For he **h** looked down from the height of his NIH
103:10 He **h** not dealt with us after our sins; NIH
103:12 far **h** he removed our transgressions from NIH
103:19 The LORD **h** prepared his throne in NIH
104:16 the cedars of Lebanon, which he **h** planted; NIH
105: 5 Remember his marvellous works that he **h** NIH
105: 8 He **h** remembered his covenant for ever, NIH
107: 2 whom he **h** redeemed from the hand of NIH
107:16 For he **h** broken the gates of brass, and NIH
108: 7 God **h** spoken in his holiness; I will rejoice, NIH
109:11 Let the extortioner catch all that he **h;** and 3807.1
110: 4 The LORD **h** sworn, and will not repent, NIH
111: 4 He **h** made his wonderful works to be NIH
111: 5 He **h** given meat unto them that fear him: NIH
111: 6 He **h** shewed his people the power of his NIH
111: 9 he **h** commanded his covenant for ever: NIH
112: 9 He **h** dispersed, he hath given to the poor; NIH
112: 9 He hath dispersed, he **h** given to the poor; NIH
115: 3 he **h** done whatsoever he pleased. NIH
115:12 The LORD **h** been mindful of us: he will NIH
115:16 the earth **h** he given to the children of men. NIH
116: 1 because he **h** heard my voice *and* NIH
116: 2 Because he **h** inclined his ear unto me, NIH
116: 7 for the LORD **h** dealt bountifully with NIH
118:18 The LORD **h** chastened me sore: but NIH
118:18 but he **h** not given me over unto death. NIH
118:24 This *is* the day *which* the LORD **h** made; NIH
118:27 *is* the LORD, which **h** shewed us light: NIH
119:20 My soul breaketh for the longing *that it* **h** NIH
119:50 my affliction: for thy word **h** quickened me. NIH
119:53 Horror **h** taken hold upon me because of NIH
119:139 My zeal **h** consumed me, because NIH

Ps 119:167 My soul **h** kept thy testimonies; and *I* love NIH
120: 6 My soul **h** long dwelt with him that hateth NIH
124: 6 who **h** not given us *as* a prey to their teeth. NIH
126: 2 LORD **h** done great things for them. 3807.1
126: 3 The LORD **h** done great things for us; 3807.1
127: 5 Happy *is* the man that **h** his quiver full of NIH
129: 4 he **h** cut asunder the cords of the wicked. NIH
132:11 The LORD **h** sworn *in* truth unto David; NIH
132:13 For the LORD **h** chosen Zion; he hath NIH
132:13 he **h** desired *it* for his habitation. NIH
135: 4 For the LORD **h** chosen Jacob unto NIH
136:24 **h** redeemed us from our enemies: for his NIH
138: 6 *be* high, yet **h** he **respect** unto the lowly: 7200
143: 3 For the enemy **h** persecuted my soul; NIH
143: 3 he **h** smitten my life down to the ground; NIH
143: 3 he **h** made me to dwell in darkness, as those NIH
146: 5 Happy *is he* that *h* the God of Jacob for his NIH
147:13 For he **h** strengthened the bars of thy gates; NIH
147:13 he **h** blessed thy children within thee. NIH
147:20 He **h** not dealt so with any nation: and *as for* NIH
148: 6 He **h** also stablished them for ever and ever: NIH
148: 6 he **h** made a decree which shall not pass. NIH
150: 6 Let every *thing that* **h** breath praise NIH
Pr 3:19 The LORD by wisdom **h** founded NIH
3:19 by understanding **h** he established NIH
7:20 He **h** taken a bag of money with him, NIH
7:26 For she **h** cast down many wounded: yea, NIH
9: 1 Wisdom **h** builded her house, she hath hewn NIH
9: 1 her house, she **h** hewn out her seven pillars: NIH
9: 2 She **h** killed her beasts; she hath mingled NIH
9: 2 killed her beasts; she **h** mingled her wine; NIH
9: 2 her wine; she **h** also furnished her table. NIH
9: 3 She **h** sent forth her maidens: she crieth NIH
10:13 In the lips of him that **h understanding** 995
10:23 but a man of understanding **h** wisdom. NIH
12: 9 *He that is* despised, and **h** a servant, *is* better NIH
13: 4 soul of the sluggard desireth, and *h* nothing: NIH
13: 7 is that maketh himself rich, yet *h* nothing: NIH
13: 7 that maketh himself poor, yet *h* great riches. NIH
14:20 own neighbour: but the rich *h* many friends. NIH
14:21 he that **h mercy** on the poor, happy *is* he. 2603
14:31 he that honoureth him **h mercy** on the poor. 2603
14:32 but the righteous **h** hope in his death. NIH
14:33 in the heart of him that **h understanding**: 995
15:14 The heart of him that **h understanding** 995
15:15 *he that is* of a merry heart *h* a continual NIH
15:23 A man **h** joy by the answer of his mouth: 3807.1
16: 4 The LORD **h** made all *things* for himself: NIH
16:22 *is* a wellspring of life unto **him that h** it: 1167
17: 8 precious stone in the eyes of **him that h** it: 1167
17:16 to get wisdom, seeing *he* **h** no heart *to it?* NIH
17:20 He that **h** a froward heart findeth no good: NIH
17:20 he that **h** a perverse tongue falleth into NIH
17:21 and the father of a fool **h** no **joy**. 8055
17:24 *is* before him that **h understanding**; 995
17:27 He that **h knowledge** spareth his 1847+3045
18: 2 A fool **h** no delight in understanding, but NIH
18:24 A man that **h** friends must shew himself NIH
19:17 He that **h pity** upon the poor lendeth unto 2603
19:17 that which he **h** given will he pay him NIH
19:23 *he that h it* shall abide satisfied; he shall not NIH
19:25 reprove one that **h understanding**, *and* 995
20:12 the LORD **h** made even both of them. NIH
22: 9 He that **h** a bountiful eye shall be blessed; NIH
23: 6 Eat thou not the bread of *him that* **h** an evil NIH
23:29 Who **h** woe? who hath sorrow? who hath 3807.1
23:29 who **h** sorrow? who hath contentions? 3807.1
23:29 who **h** contentions? who hath babbling? 3807.1
23:29 who **h** babbling? who hath wounds 3807.1
23:29 who **h** wounds without cause? who hath 3807.1
23:29 without cause? who **h** redness of eyes? 3807.1
24:29 I will do so to him as he **h** done to me: NIH
25: 8 when thy neighbour **h** put thee to shame. NIH
25:28 He that *h* no rule over his own spirit *is like* NIH
28:11 the poor that **h** understanding searcheth him NIH
28:22 He that hasteth to be rich *h* an evil eye, and NIH
30: 4 Who **h** ascended up *into* heaven, or NIH
30: 4 who **h** gathered the wind in his fists? NIH
30: 4 who **h** bound the waters in a garment? NIH
30: 4 who **h** established all the ends of the earth? NIH
30:15 The horseleach **h** two daughters, 3807.1
Ecc 1: 3 What profit **h** a man of all his labour which NIH
1: 9 The thing that **h** been, *it is* that which shall NIH
1:10 it **h** been already of old time, which was NIH
1:13 this sore travail **h** God given to the sons of NIH
2:12 *even* that which **h** been already done. NIH
2:21 yet to a man that **h** not laboured therein NIH
2:22 For what **h** man of all his labour, 1933+3807.1
2:22 wherein he *h* laboured under the sun? NIH
3: 9 What profit *h* he that worketh in *that* NIH
3:10 which God **h** given to the sons of men to be NIH
3:11 He **h** made every *thing* beautiful in his time: NIH
3:11 also he **h** set the world in their heart, so that NIH
3:15 That which **h** been, *is* now; and *that* which NIH
3:15 *that* which *is* to be **h** already been; and God NIH
3:19 that a man **h** no **preeminence** above a 4195
4: 3 *is he* than both they, which **h** not yet been, NIH
4: 3 who **h** not seen the evil work that is done NIH
4: 8 yea, he **h** neither child nor brother: 3807.1
4:10 for *he* **h** not another to help him up. NIH
5: 4 not to pay it; for *he h* no pleasure in fools: NIH
5:16 what profit **h** he that hath laboured for 3807.1
5:16 what profit hath he that **h** laboured for NIH
5:17 *he h* much sorrow and wrath with his NIH
5:19 Every man also to whom God **h** given NIH
5:19 **h** given him power to eat thereof, and NIH
6: 2 A man to whom God **h** given riches, wealth, NIH
6: 5 Moreover he **h** not seen the sun, nor known NIH
6: 5 nor known *any thing:* this **h** more rest 3807.1
6: 6 years twice *told,* yet **h** he seen no good: NIH
6: 8 For what **h** the wise more than the fool? 3807.1
6: 8 what **h** the poor, that knoweth to walk 3807.1
6:10 That which **h** been is named already, and NIH
7:13 *that* straight, which he **h** made crooked? NIH
7:14 God also **h** set the one over against NIH

Ecc 7:29 have I found, that God **h** made man upright; NIH
8: 8 *There is* no man that **h** power over the spirit NIH
8: 8 neither *h he* power in the day of death: NIH
8:15 a man **h** no better *thing* under the sun, NIH
9: 9 which he **h** given thee under the sun, all NIH
10:20 **that which h** wings shall tell the matter. 1167
SS 1: 4 the king **h** brought me *into* his chambers: NIH
1: 6 because the sun **h** looked upon me: NIH
3: 8 every man *h* his sword upon his thigh NIH
8: 6 of fire, *which h* a most vehement flame. NIH
8: 8 have a little sister, and she **h** no breasts: 3807.1
Isa 1: 2 for the LORD **h** spoken, I have nourished NIH
1:12 who **h** required this at your hand, to tread NIH
1:20 for the mouth of the LORD **h** spoken *it.* NIH
1:30 leaf fadeth, and as a garden that **h** no water. NIH
5: 1 My wellbeloved **h** a vineyard in a 1961+3807.1
5:14 Therefore hell **h** enlarged herself, NIH
5:25 he **h** stretched forth his hand against them, NIH
5:25 his hand against them, and **h** smitten them: NIH
6: 7 and said, Lo, this **h** touched thy lips; NIH
8:18 the children whom the LORD **h** given me NIH
9: 2 of death, upon them **h** the light shined. NIH
9: 8 into Jacob, and it **h** lighted upon Israel. NIH
10:10 As my hand **h** found the kingdoms of NIH
10:12 *that* when the Lord **h** performed his whole NIH
10:14 my hand **h** found as a nest the riches of NIH
10:28 at Michmash he **h** laid up his carriages: NIH
12: 5 the LORD; for he **h** done excellent things: NIH
14: 4 and say, How **h** the oppressor ceased! NIH
14: 5 The LORD **h** broken the staff of NIH
14: 9 it **h** raised up from their thrones all NIH
14:24 The LORD of hosts **h** sworn, saying, NIH
14:27 For the LORD of hosts **h** purposed, and NIH
14:32 That the LORD **h** founded Zion, and NIH
16:13 This *is* the word that the LORD **h** spoken NIH
16:14 now the LORD **h** spoken, saying, NIH
19:12 let them know what the LORD of hosts **h** NIH
19:14 The LORD **h** mingled a perverse spirit in NIH
19:17 of hosts, which he **h** determined against it. NIH
20: 3 Like as my servant Isaiah **h** walked naked NIH
21: 4 the night of my pleasure **h** he turned into NIH
21: 6 For thus **h** the Lord said unto me, Go, set a NIH
21: 9 all the graven images of her gods he **h** NIH
21:16 For thus **h** the Lord said unto me, Within a NIH
21:17 for the LORD God of Israel **h** spoken *it.* NIH
22:25 shall be cut off: for the LORD **h** spoken *it.* NIH
23: 4 for the sea **h** spoken, *even* the strength of NIH
23: 8 Who **h** taken this counsel against Tyre, NIH
23: 9 The LORD of hosts **h** purposed it, to stain NIH
23:11 the LORD **h** given a commandment NIH
24: 3 for the LORD **h** spoken this word. NIH
24: 6 Therefore **h** the curse devoured the earth, NIH
25: 8 all the earth: for the LORD **h** spoken *it.* NIH
27: 7 **H** he smitten him, as he smote those that NIH
28: 2 the LORD **h** a mighty and strong one, 3807.1
28:25 When he **h** made plain the face thereof, NIH
29: 4 as of one that **h** a familiar spirit, out of NIH
29: 8 behold, *he is* faint, and his soul **h** appetite: NIH
29:10 For the LORD **h** poured out upon you NIH
29:10 spirit of deep sleep, and **h** closed your eyes: NIH
29:10 and your rulers, the seers **h** he covered. NIH
30:24 which **h** been winnowed with the shovel NIH
30:33 it is prepared; he **h** made *it* deep *and* large: NIH
31: 4 For thus **h** the LORD spoken unto me, NIH
33: 5 he **h** filled Zion *with* judgment and NIH
33: 8 he **h** broken the covenant, he hath despised NIH
33: 8 he **h** despised the cities, he regardeth no NIH
33:14 fearfulness **h** surprised the hypocrites. NIH
34: 2 he **h** utterly destroyed them, he hath NIH
34: 2 he **h** delivered them to the slaughter. NIH
34: 6 for the LORD **h** a sacrifice in Bozrah, 3807.1
34:16 for my mouth it **h** commanded, and NIH
34:16 and his spirit it **h** gathered them. NIH
34:17 he **h** cast the lot for them, and his hand hath NIH
34:17 and his hand **h** divided it unto them by line: NIH
36: 7 and whose altars Hezekiah **h** taken away, NIH
36:12 **H** my master sent me to thy master and NIH
36:12 *h he* not *sent me* to the men that sit upon NIH
36:18 **H** any of the gods of the nations delivered NIH
37: 4 whom the king of Assyria his master **h** sent NIH
37: 4 words which the LORD thy God **h** heard: NIH
37:17 which **h** sent to reproach the living God. NIH
37:22 This *is* the word which the LORD **h** NIH
37:22 **h** despised thee, *and* laughed thee to scorn; NIH
37:22 the daughter of Jerusalem **h** shaken her head NIH
38: 7 that the LORD will do this thing that he **h** NIH
38:15 he **h** both spoken unto me, and himself hath NIH
38:15 himself **h** done *it:* I shall go softly all my NIH
40: 2 for she **h** received of the LORD'S hand NIH
40: 5 for the mouth of the LORD **h** spoken *it.* NIH
40:12 Who **h** measured the waters in the hollow of NIH
40:13 Who **h** directed the spirit of the LORD, or NIH
40:13 or *being* his counseller **h** taught him? NIH
40:20 impoverished that he **h** no oblation chooseth NIH
40:21 **h** it not been told you from the beginning? NIH
40:26 behold who **h** created these *things,* that NIH
41: 4 Who **h** wrought and done *it,* calling NIH
41:20 that the hand of the LORD **h** done this, NIH
41:20 and the Holy One of Israel **h** created it. NIH
41:26 Who **h** declared from the beginning, that we NIH
42:25 Therefore he **h** poured upon him the fury of NIH
42:25 it **h** set him on fire round about, yet he knew NIH
43:27 Thy first father **h** sinned, and thy teachers NIH
44:10 Who **h** formed a god, or molten a graven NIH
44:18 for he **h** shut their eyes, that *they* cannot NIH
44:20 a deceived heart **h** turned him aside, that he NIH
44:23 for the LORD **h** done *it:* shout, ye lower NIH
44:23 for the LORD **h** redeemed Jacob, and NIH
45: 9 or thy work, He **h** no hands? 3807.1
45:18 he **h** established it, he created it not in vain, NIH
45:21 who **h** declared this from ancient time? NIH
45:21 *who* **h** told it from that time? *have* not I NIH
47:10 and thy knowledge, it **h** perverted thee; NIH
48: 5 Mine idol **h** done them, and my graven NIH
48: 5 and my molten image, **h** commanded them. NIH

Isa 48:13 Mine hand also **h** laid the foundation of NIH
48:13 and my right hand **h** spanned the heavens: NIH
48:14 which among them **h** declared these *things?* NIH
48:14 these *things?* The LORD **h** loved him: NIH
48:16 the Lord GOD, and his Spirit, **h** sent me. NIH
48:20 The LORD **h** redeemed his servant Jacob. NIH
49: 1 The LORD **h** called me from the womb; NIH
49: 1 from the bowels of my mother **h** he made NIH
49: 2 he **h** made my mouth like a sharp sword; NIH
49: 2 in the shadow of his hand **h** he hid me, and NIH
49: 2 a polished shaft; in his quiver **h** he hid me; NIH
49:10 for he that **h mercy** on them shall lead 7355
49:13 for the LORD **h** comforted his people, and NIH
49:14 The LORD **h** forsaken me, and my Lord NIH
49:14 forsaken me, and my Lord **h** forgotten me. NIH
49:21 Who **h** begotten me these, seeing I have lost NIH
49:21 who **h** brought up these? Behold, I was left NIH
50: 4 The Lord GOD **h** given me the tongue of NIH
50: 5 The Lord GOD **h** opened mine ear, and NIH
50:10 that walketh *in* darkness, and **h** no light? NIH
51: 9 *Art* thou not it that **h** cut Rahab, *and* NIH
51:10 *Art* thou not it which **h** dried the sea, NIH
51:10 that **h** made the depths of the sea a way for NIH
51:13 that **h** stretched forth the heavens, and NIH
51:18 all the sons *whom* she **h** brought forth; NIH
51:18 hand of all the sons *that* she **h** brought up. NIH
52: 9 for the LORD **h** comforted his people, NIH
52: 9 his people, he **h** redeemed Jerusalem. NIH
52:10 The LORD **h** made bare his holy arm in NIH
53: 1 Who **h** believed our report? and to whom is NIH
53: 2 he **h** no form nor comeliness; and when we NIH
53: 4 Surely he **h** borne our griefs, and carried our NIH
53: 6 the LORD **h** laid on him the iniquity of us NIH
53:10 LORD to bruise him; he **h** put *him* to grief: NIH
53:12 because he **h** poured out his soul unto death: NIH
54: 6 For the LORD **h** called thee as a woman NIH
54:10 saith the LORD that **h mercy** on thee. 7355
55: 1 ye to the waters, and he that **h** no money; NIH
55: 5 Holy One of Israel; for he **h** glorified thee. NIH
56: 3 that **h** joined himself to the LORD, speak, NIH
56: 3 The LORD **h** utterly separated me from his NIH
58:14 for the mouth of the LORD **h** spoken *it.* NIH
59: 3 your tongue **h** muttered perverseness. NIH
60: 9 One of Israel, because he **h** glorified thee. NIH
61: 1 the LORD **h** anointed me to preach good NIH
61: 1 he **h** sent me to bind up the broken-hearted, NIH
61: 9 that they *are* the seed *which* the LORD **h** NIH
61:10 for he **h** clothed me with the garments of NIH
61:10 he **h** covered me with the robe of NIH
62: 8 The LORD **h** sworn by his right hand, and NIH
62:11 the LORD **h** proclaimed unto the end of NIH
63: 7 according to all that the LORD **h** bestowed NIH
63: 7 which he **h** bestowed on them according to NIH
64: 4 neither **h** the eye seen, O God, besides thee, NIH
64: 4 *what* he **h** prepared for him that waiteth for NIH
65:20 nor an old man that **h** not filled his days: NIH
66: 2 For all those *things* **h** mine hand made, and NIH
66: 8 Who **h** heard such *a thing?* who hath seen NIH
66: 8 Who hath heard such *a thing?* who **h** seen NIH
Jer 2:11 **H** a nation changed *their* gods, which *are* NIH
2:30 your own sword **h** devoured your prophets, NIH
2:37 for the LORD **h** rejected thy confidences, NIH
3: 3 and there **h** been no latter rain; NIH
3: 6 seen *that* which backsliding Israel **h** done? NIH
3: 6 green tree, and there **h** played the harlot. NIH
3:10 yet for all this her treacherous sister Judah **h** NIH
3:11 The backsliding Israel **h** justified herself NIH
3:24 For shame **h** devoured the labour of our NIH
4:17 because she **h** been rebellious against me, NIH
4:27 For thus **h** the LORD said, The whole land NIH
5:23 this people **h** a revolting and 1961+3807.1
6: 6 For thus **h** the LORD of hosts said, NIH
6:24 anguish **h** taken hold of us, *and* pain, as of a NIH
6:30 because the LORD **h** rejected them. NIH
7:29 for the LORD **h** rejected and forsaken NIH
8:14 for the LORD our God **h** put us to silence, NIH
8:21 am black; astonishment **h** taken hold on me. NIH
9:12 whom the mouth of the LORD **h** spoken, NIH
10:12 He **h** made the earth by his power, he hath NIH
10:12 he **h** established the world by his wisdom, NIH
10:12 **h** stretched out the heavens by his NIH
11:15 What **h** my beloved **to do** in mine house, 3807.1
11:15 *seeing* she **h** wrought lewdness *with* many, NIH
11:16 with the noise of a great tumult he **h** kindled NIH
11:17 **h** pronounced evil against thee, NIH
11:18 the LORD **h** given me knowledge *of it,* NIH
13:15 be not proud: for the LORD **h** spoken. NIH
14:19 **h** thy soul lothed Zion? why hast thou NIH
15: 9 She that **h** borne seven languisheth: she hath NIH
15: 9 she **h** given up the ghost; her sun is gone NIH
15: 9 she **h** been ashamed and confounded: and NIH
16:10 Wherefore **h** the LORD pronounced all NIH
18:13 who **h** heard such *things:* the virgin of Israel NIH
18:13 virgin of Israel **h** done a very horrible thing. NIH
18:15 Because my people **h** forgotten me, NIH
20: 3 The LORD **h** not called thy name Pashur, NIH
20:13 for he **h** delivered the soul of the poor from NIH
22: 8 Wherefore **h** the LORD done thus unto NIH
22:21 This *h been* thy manner from thy youth, NIH
23: 9 like a man whom wine **h** overcome, because NIH
23:17 The LORD **h** said, Ye shall have peace; NIH
23:18 For who **h** stood in the counsel of NIH
23:18 and **h** perceived and heard his word? NIH
23:18 who **h** marked his word, and heard *it?* NIH
23:28 The prophet that **h** a dream, let him tell a 854
23:28 he that **h** my word, let him speak my word 854
23:35 his brother, What **h** the LORD answered? NIH
23:35 and, What **h** the LORD spoken? NIH
23:37 What **h** the LORD answered thee? NIH
23:37 and, What **h** the LORD spoken? NIH
25: 3 the word of the LORD **h** come unto me, NIH
25: 4 the LORD **h** sent unto you all his servants NIH
25: 5 dwell in the land that the LORD **h** given NIH
25:13 which Jeremiah **h** prophesied against all NIH
25:31 for the LORD **h** a controversy with NIH

Jer 25:36 *shall be heard:* for the LORD **h** spoiled NIH
25:38 He **h** forsaken his covert, as the lion: NIH
26:11 for he **h** prophesied against this city, as ye NIH
26:13 the evil that he **h** pronounced against you. NIH
26:15 for of a truth the LORD **h** sent me unto NIH
26:16 for he **h** spoken to us in the name of NIH
27:13 as the LORD **h** spoken against the nation NIH
28: 9 be known, that the LORD **h** truly sent him. NIH
28:15 The LORD **h** not sent thee; but NIH
29:15 The LORD **h** raised us up prophets in NIH
29:26 The LORD **h** made thee priest in the stead NIH
29:31 Because that Shemaiah **h** prophesied unto NIH
29:32 he **h** taught rebellion against the LORD. NIH
31: 3 The LORD **h** appeared of old unto me, NIH
31:11 For the LORD **h** redeemed Jacob, and NIH
31:22 for the LORD **h** created a new *thing* in NIH
32:31 For this city **h** been to me *as* a provocation NIH
33:24 The two families which the LORD **h** NIH
33:24 hath chosen, he **h** even cast them off? NIH
34:14 a Hebrew, which **h** been sold unto thee; NIH
34:14 when he **h** served thee six years, thou shalt NIH
35: 8 our father in all that he **h** charged us, NIH
35:16 but this people **h** not hearkened unto me: NIH
35:18 done according unto all that he **h** NIH
36: 7 the fury that the LORD **h** pronounced NIH
36:28 which Jehoiakim the king of Judah **h** burnt. NIH
38:21 this *is* the word that the LORD **h** shewed NIH
40: 2 The LORD thy God **h** pronounced this evil NIH
40: 3 Now the LORD **h** brought *it,* and NIH
40: 3 brought *it,* and done according as he **h** said: NIH
40: 5 whom the king of Babylon **h** made governor NIH
40:14 **h** sent Ishmael the son of Nethaniah to slay NIH
42:18 my fury **h** been poured forth upon NIH
42:19 The LORD **h** said concerning you, O ye NIH
42:21 nor any *thing* for the which he **h** sent me NIH
43: 2 the LORD our God **h** not sent thee to say, NIH
45: 3 for the LORD **h** added grief to my sorrow; NIH
46:10 for the Lord GOD of hosts **h** a sacrifice in NIH
46:12 *of* thy shame, and thy cry **h** filled the land: NIH
46:12 for the mighty *man* **h** stumbled against NIH
46:17 *but* a noise; he **h** passed the time appointed NIH
47: 7 seeing the LORD **h** given it a charge NIH
47: 7 the sea shore? there **h** he appointed it. NIH
48: 8 shall be destroyed, as the LORD **h** spoken. NIH
48:11 Moab **h** been at ease from his youth, and NIH
48:11 he **h** settled on his lees, and hath not been NIH
48:11 **h** not been emptied from vessel to vessel, NIH
48:11 to vessel, neither **h** he gone into captivity: NIH
48:36 the riches *that* he **h** gotten are perished. NIH
48:39 how **h** Moab turned the back with shame! NIH
48:42 he **h** magnified *himself* against the LORD. NIH
49: 1 thus saith the LORD; **H** Israel no sons? 3807.1
49: 1 **H** he no heir? why *then* doth their king 3807.1
49:16 Thy terribleness **h** deceived thee, *and* NIH
49:20 the LORD, that he **h** taken against Edom; NIH
49:20 that he **h** purposed against the inhabitants of NIH
49:24 fear **h** seized on *her:* anguish and NIH
49:30 for Nebuchadrezzar king of Babylon **h** NIH
49:30 and **h** conceived a purpose against you. NIH
50: 6 My people **h** been lost sheep: NIH
50:14 for she **h** sinned against the LORD. NIH
50:15 she **h** given her hand: her foundations are NIH
50:15 upon her; as she **h** done, do unto her. NIH
50:17 first the king of Assyria **h** devoured him; NIH
50:17 last this Nebuchadrezzar king of Babylon **h** NIH
50:25 The LORD **h** opened his armoury, and NIH
50:25 **h** brought forth the weapons of his NIH
50:29 according to all that she **h** done, do unto NIH
50:29 for she **h** been proud against the LORD, NIH
50:43 The king of Babylon **h** heard the report of NIH
50:45 that he **h** taken against Babylon; NIH
50:45 that he **h** purposed against the land of NIH
51: 5 For Israel *h* not *been* forsaken, nor Judah of NIH
51: 7 Babylon **h** *been* a golden cup in NIH
51:10 The LORD **h** brought forth our NIH
51:11 the LORD **h** raised up the spirit of NIH
51:12 for the LORD **h** both devised and NIH
51:14 The LORD of hosts **h** sworn by himself, NIH
51:15 He **h** made the earth by his power, he hath NIH
51:15 he **h** established the world by his wisdom, NIH
51:15 **h** stretched out the heaven by his NIH
51:30 their might **h** failed; they became as NIH
51:34 Nebuchadrezzar the king of Babylon **h** NIH
51:34 he **h** crushed me, he hath made me an NIH
51:34 crushed me, he **h** made me an empty vessel, NIH
51:34 he **h** swallowed me up like a dragon, NIH
51:34 he **h** filled his belly with my delicates, NIH
51:34 belly with my delicates, he **h** cast me out. NIH
51:44 of his mouth that which he **h** swallowed up: NIH
51:49 As Babylon *h caused* the slain of Israel to NIH
51:51 shame **h** covered our faces: for strangers are NIH
51:55 Because the LORD *h* spoiled Babylon, and NIH
La 1: 2 among all her lovers she **h** none to 3807.1
1: 5 for the LORD **h** afflicted her for NIH
1: 8 Jerusalem **h** grievously sinned; therefore NIH
1: 9 for the enemy **h** magnified *himself* NIH
1:10 The adversary **h** spread out his hand upon NIH
1:10 for she **h** seen *that* the heathen entered into NIH
1:12 wherewith the LORD **h** afflicted *me* in NIH
1:13 From above **h** he sent fire into my bones, NIH
1:13 he **h** spread a net for my feet, he hath turned NIH
1:13 a net for my feet, he **h** turned me back; NIH
1:13 he **h** made me desolate *and* faint all the day. NIH
1:14 he **h** made my strength to fall, the Lord hath NIH
1:14 the Lord **h** delivered me into *their* hands, NIH
1:15 The Lord **h** trodden under foot all my NIH
1:15 he **h** called an assembly against me to crush NIH
1:15 the Lord **h** trodden the virgin, the daughter NIH
1:17 the LORD **h** commanded concerning NIH
2: 1 How **h** the Lord covered the daughter of NIH
2: 2 The Lord **h** swallowed up all the habitations NIH
2: 2 all the habitations of Jacob, and **h** not pitied: NIH
2: 2 he **h** thrown down in his wrath the strong NIH
2: 2 he **h** brought *them* down to the ground: NIH
2: 2 he **h** polluted the kingdom and the princes NIH
La 2: 3 He **h** cut off in *his* fierce anger all the horn NIH
2: 3 he **h** drawn back his right hand from before NIH
2: 4 He **h** bent his bow like an enemy: *he* stood NIH
2: 5 he **h** swallowed up Israel, he hath NIH
2: 5 up Israel, he **h** swallowed up all her palaces: NIH
2: 5 he **h** destroyed his strong holds, and NIH
2: 5 **h** increased in the daughter of Judah NIH
2: 6 he **h** violently taken away his tabernacle, NIH
2: 6 he **h** destroyed his places of the assembly: NIH
2: 6 the LORD **h** caused the solemn feasts and NIH
2: 6 **h** despised in the indignation of his anger NIH
2: 7 The Lord **h** cast off his altar, he hath NIH
2: 7 off his altar, he **h** abhorred his sanctuary, NIH
2: 7 he **h** given up into the hand of the enemy NIH
2: 8 The LORD **h** purposed to destroy the wall NIH
2: 8 he **h** stretched out a line, he hath not NIH
2: 8 he **h** not withdrawn his hand from NIH
2: 9 he **h** destroyed and broken her bars: NIH
2:17 The LORD **h** done *that* which he had NIH
2:17 he **h** fulfilled his word that he had NIH
2:17 he **h** thrown down, and hath not pitied: and NIH
2:17 he hath thrown down, and **h** not pitied: and NIH
2:17 he **h** caused *thine* enemy to rejoice over NIH
2:17 he **h** set up the horn of thine adversaries. NIH
2:22 and brought up **h** mine enemy consumed. NIH
3: 1 I *am* the man *that* **h** seen affliction by NIH
3: 2 He **h** led me, and brought *me into* darkness, NIH
3: 4 My flesh and my skin **h** he made old; NIH
3: 4 hath he made old; he **h** broken my bones. NIH
3: 5 He **h** builded against me, and NIH
3: 6 He **h** set me in dark places, as they that be NIH
3: 7 He **h** hedged me about, that I cannot get NIH
3: 7 I cannot get out: he **h** made my chain heavy. NIH
3: 9 He **h** inclosed my ways with hewn stone, NIH
3: 9 hewn stone, he **h** made my paths crooked. NIH
3:11 He **h** turned aside my ways, and pulled me NIH
3:11 pulled me in pieces: he **h** made me desolate. NIH
3:12 He **h** bent his bow, and set me as a mark for NIH
3:13 He **h** caused the arrows of his quiver to NIH
3:15 He **h** filled me with bitterness, he hath made NIH
3:15 he **h** made me drunken *with* wormwood. NIH
3:16 He **h** also broken my teeth with gravel NIH
3:16 gravel stones, he **h** covered me with ashes. NIH
3:20 My soul **h** *them* still in remembrance, and NIH
3:28 because he **h** borne *it* upon him. NIH
4:11 The LORD **h** accomplished his fury; NIH
4:11 he **h** poured out his fierce anger, and NIH
4:11 **h** kindled a fire in Zion, and it hath NIH
4:11 and it **h** devoured the foundations thereof. NIH
4:16 The anger of the LORD **h** divided them; NIH
Eze 2: 3 to a rebellious nation that **h** rebelled against NIH
2: 5 yet shall know that there **h** been a prophet NIH
3:20 his righteousness which he **h** done shall not NIH
4:14 behold, my soul *h* not *been* polluted: NIH
5: 6 she **h** changed my judgments into NIH
6: 9 which **h** departed from me, and with their NIH
7:10 the rod **h** blossomed, pride hath budded. NIH
7:10 the rod hath blossomed, pride **h** budded. NIH
8:12 us not; the LORD **h** forsaken the earth. NIH
9: 9 The LORD **h** forsaken the earth, and NIH
12: 9 Son of man, **h** not the house of Israel, NIH
13: 6 the LORD **h** not sent them: and they have NIH
14: 9 if the prophet be deceived when he **h** NIH
15: 5 when the fire **h** devoured it, and it is NIH
16:48 Lord GOD, Sodom thy sister **h** not done, NIH
16:51 Neither **h** Samaria committed half of thy NIH
17:12 **h** taken the king thereof, and the princes NIH
17:13 **h** taken of the king's seed, and made a NIH
17:13 with him, and **h** taken an oath of him: NIH
17:13 he **h** also taken the mighty of the land: NIH
17:18 **h** done all these *things,* he shall not escape. NIH
17:19 surely mine oath that he **h** despised, and NIH
17:19 and my covenant that he **h** broken, NIH
17:20 his trespass that he **h** trespassed against me. NIH
18: 6 *And* **h** not eaten upon the mountains, NIH
18: 6 neither **h** lift up his eyes to the idols of NIH
18: 6 neither **h** defiled his neighbour's wife, NIH
18: 6 neither **h** come near to a menstruous NIH
18: 7 **h** not oppressed any, *but* hath restored *to* NIH
18: 7 *but* **h** restored *to* the debtor his pledge, NIH
18: 7 **h** spoiled none by violence, hath given his NIH
18: 7 **h** given his bread to the hungry, and NIH
18: 7 and **h** covered the naked with a garment; NIH
18: 8 He *that* **h** not given forth upon usury, NIH
18: 8 upon usury, neither **h** taken any increase, NIH
18: 8 *that* **h** withdrawn his hand from iniquity, NIH
18: 8 **h** executed true judgment between man and NIH
18: 9 **H** walked in my statutes, and hath kept my NIH
18: 9 and **h** kept my judgments, to deal truly; NIH
18:11 but even **h** eaten upon the mountains, NIH
18:12 **H** oppressed the poor and needy, NIH
18:12 the poor and needy, **h** spoiled by violence, NIH
18:12 **h** not restored the pledge, and hath lift up NIH
18:12 and **h** lift up his eyes to the idols, NIH
18:12 eyes to the idols, **h** committed abomination, NIH
18:13 **H** given forth upon usury, and hath taken NIH
18:13 forth upon usury, and **h** taken increase: NIH
18:13 he **h** done all these abominations; he shall NIH
18:14 that seeth all his father's sins which he **h** NIH
18:15 *That* **h** not eaten upon the mountains, NIH
18:15 neither **h** lift up his eyes to the idols of NIH
18:15 of Israel, **h** not defiled his neighbour's wife, NIH
18:16 Neither **h** oppressed any, hath not NIH
18:16 oppressed any, **h** not withholden the pledge, NIH
18:16 neither **h** spoiled by violence, *but* NIH
18:16 *but* **h** given his bread to the hungry, and NIH
18:16 and **h** covered the naked with a garment, NIH
18:17 *That* **h** taken off his hand from the poor, NIH
18:17 *that* **h** not received usury nor increase, NIH
18:17 **h** executed my judgments, hath walked in NIH
18:17 my judgments, **h** walked in my statutes; NIH
18:19 When the son **h** done that which is lawful NIH
18:19 *and* **h** kept all my statutes, and hath done NIH
18:19 and **h** done them, he shall surely live. NIH
18:21 turn from all his sins that he **h** committed, NIH
Eze 18:22 All his transgressions that he **h** committed, NIH
18:22 in his righteousness that he **h** done he shall NIH
18:24 All his righteousness that he **h** done shall NIH
18:24 in his trespass that he **h** trespassed, and NIH
18:24 in his sin that he **h** sinned, in them shall he NIH
18:26 for his iniquity that he **h** done shall he die. NIH
18:27 from his wickedness that he **h** committed, NIH
18:28 all his transgressions that he **h** committed, NIH
19:14 *which* **h** devoured her fruit, so that she hath NIH
19:14 that she **h** no strong rod *to be* a 1961+871.1
21:11 he **h** given it to be furbished, that *it* may be NIH
22:11 one **h** committed abomination with his NIH
22:11 another **h** lewdly defiled his daughter in NIH
22:11 another in thee **h** humbled his sister, NIH
22:13 at thy blood which **h** been in the midst of NIH
22:28 when the LORD **h** not spoken. NIH
24:12 She **h** wearied *herself with* lies, and NIH
24:24 according to all that he **h** done shall ye do: NIH
25:12 Because that Edom **h** dealt against NIH
25:12 **h** greatly offended, and revenged himself NIH
26: 2 because that Tyrus **h** said against Jerusalem, NIH
27:26 the east wind **h** broken thee in the midst of NIH
29: 3 which **h** said, My river *is* mine own, and NIH
29: 9 because he **h** said, The river *is* mine, and NIH
31:10 he **h** shot up his top among the thick NIH
33:13 for his iniquity that he **h** committed, he shall NIH
33:16 None of his sins that he **h** committed shall NIH
33:16 he **h** done that which is lawful and right; NIH
33:32 lovely song *of* one that **h** a pleasant voice, NIH
33:33 shall they know that a prophet **h** been NIH
36: 2 Because the enemy **h** said against you, Aha, NIH
44: 2 **h** entered in by it, therefore it shall be shut. NIH
44:25 or for sister that **h** had no husband, NIH
Da 1:10 who **h** appointed your meat and your drink: NIH
2:27 The secret which the king **h** demanded NIH
2:37 for the God of heaven **h** given thee a NIH
2:38 the fowls of the heaven **h** he given into NIH
2:38 and **h** made thee ruler over them all. NIH
2:45 the great God **h** made known to the king NIH
3: 5 that Nebuchadnezzar the king **h** set up: NIH
3:28 who **h** sent his angel, and delivered his NIH
4: 2 wonders that the high God **h** wrought NIH
5:26 God **h** numbered thy kingdom, and NIH
6:22 My God **h** sent his angel, and hath shut NIH
6:22 **h** shut the lions' mouths, that they have not NIH
6:27 who **h** delivered Daniel from the power of NIH
9:12 he **h** confirmed his words, which he spake NIH
9:12 for under the whole heaven **h** not been done NIH
9:12 been done as **h** been done upon Jerusalem. NIH
9:14 Therefore **h** the LORD watched upon NIH
11:12 *And* when he **h** taken away the multitude, NIH
Hos 1: 2 for the land **h** committed great whoredom, NIH
2: 5 For their mother **h** played the harlot: NIH
2: 5 she that conceived them **h** done shamefully: NIH
2:12 and her fig trees, whereof she **h** said, NIH
4: 1 for the LORD **h** a controversy with 3807.1
4:12 for the spirit of whoredoms **h** caused *them* NIH
4:19 The wind **h** bound her up in her wings, and NIH
5: 6 they shall not find *him;* he **h** withdrawn NIH
6: 1 for he **h** torn, and he will heal us; he hath NIH
6: 1 he **h** smitten, and he will bind us up. NIH
6:11 Also, O Judah, he **h** set a harvest for thee, NIH
7: 4 *who* ceaseth from raising after *he* **h** kneaded NIH
7: 8 he **h** mixed himself among the people; NIH
7:12 as their congregation **h** heard. NIH
8: 3 Israel **h** cast off *the thing that is* good: NIH
8: 5 Thy calf, O Samaria, **h** cast *thee* off; NIH
8: 7 it **h** no stalk: the bud shall yield no meal: 3807.1
8: 9 alone by himself: Ephraim **h** hired lovers. NIH
8:11 Because Ephraim **h** made many altars to NIH
8:14 For Israel **h** forgotten his Maker, and NIH
8:14 and Judah **h** multiplied fenced cities: NIH
10: 1 according to the multitude of his fruit he **h** NIH
12: 2 The LORD **h** also a controversy with 3807.1
13:16 for she **h** rebelled against her God. NIH
Joel 1: 2 **H** this been in your days, or even in NIH
1: 4 That which the palmerworm **h** left hath NIH
1: 4 That which the palmerworm hath left **h** NIH
1: 4 that which the locust **h** left hath NIH
1: 4 that which the locust hath left **h** NIH
1: 4 that which the cankerworm **h** left hath NIH
1: 4 that which the cankerworm hath left **h** NIH
1: 6 and he **h** the cheek-teeth of a great lion. NIH
1: 7 He **h** laid my vine waste, and barked my fig NIH
1: 7 he **h** made it clean bare, and cast *it* away; NIH
1:19 for the fire **h** devoured the pastures of NIH
1:19 the flame **h** burnt all the trees of the field. NIH
1:20 the fire **h** devoured the pastures of NIH
2: 2 there **h** not been ever the like, neither shall NIH
2:20 come up, because he **h** done great things. NIH
2:23 for he **h** given you the former rain NIH
2:25 to you the years that the locust **h** eaten, NIH
2:26 that **h** dealt wondrously with you: NIH
2:32 as the LORD **h** said, and in the remnant NIH
3: 8 people far off: for the LORD **h** spoken *it.* NIH
Am 3: 1 Hear this word that the LORD **h** spoken NIH
3: 4 lion roar in the forest, when he **h** no prey? 3807.1
3: 6 in a city, and the LORD **h** not done *it?* NIH
3: 8 The lion **h** roared, who will not fear? NIH
3: 8 the Lord GOD **h** spoken, who can but NIH
4: 2 The Lord GOD **h** sworn by his holiness, NIH
6: 8 The Lord GOD **h** sworn by himself, saith NIH
7: 1 Thus **h** the Lord GOD shewed unto me; NIH
7: 4 Thus **h** the Lord GOD shewed unto me: NIH
7:10 Amos **h** conspired against thee in the midst NIH
8: 1 Thus **h** the Lord GOD shewed unto me: NIH
8: 7 The LORD **h** sworn by the excellency of NIH
9: 6 and **h** founded his troop in the earth; NIH
Ob 1: 3 The pride of thine heart **h** deceived thee, NIH
1:18 house of Esau; for the LORD **h** spoken *it.* NIH
Jnh 1: 9 which **h** made the sea and the dry *land.* NIH
Mic 2: 4 he **h** changed the portion of my people: NIH
2: 4 how **h** he removed *it* from me! turning away NIH
2: 4 turning away he **h** divided our fields. NIH
4: 4 for the mouth of the LORD of hosts **h** NIH

Mic 5: 1 he **h** laid siege against us: they shall smite NIH
5: 3 until the time *that* she which travaileth **h** NIH
6: 2 for the LORD **h** a controversy with his 3807.1
6: 8 He **h** shewed thee, O man, what *is* good; NIH
6: 9 hear ye the rod, and who **h** appointed it. NIH
Na 1: 3 the LORD ***h*** his way in the whirlwind NIH
1:14 the LORD **h** given a commandment NIH
2: 2 For the LORD **h** turned *away* NIH
3:19 for upon whom **h** not thy wickedness passed NIH
Hab 2:18 image that the maker thereof **h** graven it; NIH
Zep 1: 7 for the LORD **h** prepared a sacrifice, NIH
1: 7 prepared a sacrifice, he **h** bid his guests. NIH
3:15 The LORD **h** taken away thy judgments, NIH
3:15 thy judgments, he **h** cast out thine enemy: NIH
Hag 2:19 and the olive tree, **h** not brought forth: NIH
Zec 1: 2 The LORD **h** been sore displeased with NIH
1: 6 to our doings, so **h** he dealt with us. NIH
1:10 These *are they* whom the LORD **h** sent to NIH
2: 8 After the glory **h** he sent me unto NIH
2: 9 ye shall know that the LORD of hosts **h** NIH
2:11 thou shalt know that the LORD of hosts **h** NIH
3: 2 even the LORD that **h** chosen Jerusalem NIH
4: 9 thou shalt know that the LORD of hosts **h** NIH
4:10 For who **h** despised the day of small *things?* NIH
6:15 ye shall know that the LORD of hosts **h** NIH
7: 7 the LORD **h** cried by the former prophets, NIH
7:12 the words which the LORD of hosts **h** sent NIH
10: 3 for the LORD of hosts **h** visited his flock NIH
10: 3 **h** made them as his goodly horse in NIH
13: 4 one of his vision, when he **h** prophesied; NIH
Mal 1: 4 The people *against* whom the LORD **h** NIH
1: 9 this **h** been by your means: will he regard NIH
1:14 which **h** in his flock a male, and voweth, 3426
2:10 **h** not one God created us? why do we deal NIH
2:11 Judah **h** dealt treacherously, and NIH
2:11 for Judah **h** profaned the holiness of NIH
2:11 and **h** married the daughter of a strange god. NIH
2:14 Because the LORD **h** been witness NIH
Mt 3: 7 who **h** warned you to flee from the wrath to NIG
5:23 there rememberest that thy brother **h** ought 2192
5:28 **h** committed adultery with her already in his NIG
5:31 It **h** been said, Whosoever shall put away NIG
5:33 ye have heard that it **h** been said by them of NIG
5:38 Ye have heard that it **h** been said, An eye NIG
5:43 Ye have heard that it **h** been said, NIG
8:20 the Son of man **h** not where to lay *his* head. 2192
9: 6 that ye may know that the Son of man **h** 2192
9:22 good comfort; thy faith **h** made thee whole. NIG
11:11 **h** not risen a greater than John the Baptist: NIG
11:15 He that **h** ears to hear, let him hear. 2192
11:18 nor drinking, and they say, He **h** a devil. 2192
13: 9 Who **h** ears to hear, let him hear. 2192
13:12 For whosoever **h**, to him shall be given, 2192
13:12 but whosoever **h** not, from him shall be 2192
13:12 him shall be taken away even that he **h**. 2192
13:21 Yet **h** he not root in himself, but dureth for 2192
13:27 in thy field? from whence then **h** it tares? 2192
13:28 He said unto them, An enemy **h** done this. NIG
13:43 Who **h** ears to hear, let him hear. 2192
13:44 the which when a man **h** found, he hideth, NIG
13:44 joy thereof goeth and selleth all that he **h**, 2192
13:54 Whence **h** this *man* this wisdom, and NIG
13:56 Whence then **h** this *man* all these *things?* NIG
15:13 which my heavenly Father **h** not planted, NIG
16:17 and blood **h** not revealed *it* unto thee, NIG
19: 6 What therefore God **h** joined together, NIG
19:29 And every one that **h** forsaken houses, or NIG
20: 7 say unto him, Because no *man* **h** hired us. NIG
21: 3 ye shall say, The Lord **h** need of them; 2192
24:45 whom his lord **h** made ruler over his NIG
25:28 and give *it* unto him which **h** ten talents. 2192
25:29 For unto every one that **h** shall be given, 2192
25:29 from him that **h** not shall be taken away 2192
25:29 shall be taken away even *that* which he **h**. 2192
26:10 for she **h** wrought a good work upon me. NIG
26:12 For in that she **h** poured this ointment on NIG
26:13 *there* shall also *this,* that this *woman* **h** NIG
26:65 his clothes, saying, He **h** spoken blasphemy; NIG
27:23 governor said, Why, what evil **h** he done? NIG
Mk 2:10 that ye may know that the Son of man **h** 2192
3:22 He **h** Beelzebub, and by the prince of 2192
3:26 be divided, he cannot stand, but **h** an end. 2192
3:29 against the Holy Ghost **h** never forgiveness, 2192
3:30 Because they said, He **h** an unclean spirit. 2192
4: 9 He that **h** ears to hear, let him hear. 2192
4:25 For he that **h**, to him shall be given: and 2192
4:25 and he that **h** not, from him shall be taken 2192
4:25 him shall be taken even *that* which he **h**. 2192
5:19 tell them how great *things* the Lord **h** done NIG
5:19 for thee, and **h** had compassion on thee. NIG
5:34 Daughter, thy faith **h** made thee whole; NIG
6: 2 From whence **h** this *man* these *things?* and NIG
7: 6 Well **h** Esaias prophesied of you hypocrites, NIG
7:37 saying, He **h** done all *things* well: NIG
9:17 unto thee my son, which **h** a dumb spirit: 2192
9:22 And ofttimes it **h** cast him into the fire, and NIG
10: 9 What therefore God **h** joined together, NIG
10:29 There is no *man* that **h** left house, or NIG
10:52 Go thy way; thy faith **h** made thee whole. NIG
11: 3 say ye that the Lord **h** need of him; and 2192
12:43 That this poor widow **h** cast more in, NIG
13:20 but for the elect's sake, whom he **h** chosen, NIG
13:20 he hath chosen, he **h** shortened the days. NIG
14: 6 you her? she **h** wrought a good work on me. NIG
14: 8 She **h** done what she could: she is come 2192
14: 9 *this* also that she **h** done shall be spoken of NIG
15:14 said unto them, Why, what evil **h** he done? NIG
Lk 1:25 Thus **h** the Lord dealt with me in the days NIG
1:36 she **h** also conceived a son in her old age: NIG
1:47 And my spirit **h** rejoiced in God my NIG
1:48 For he **h** regarded the low estate of his NIG
1:49 For he *that is* mighty **h** done to me great NIG
1:51 He **h** shewed strength with his arm; he hath NIG
1:51 he **h** scattered the proud in the imagination NIG
1:52 He **h** put down the mighty from *their* seats, NIG
Lk 1:53 He **h** filled the hungry with good *things;* NIG
1:53 and the rich he **h** sent empty away. NIG
1:54 He **h** holpen his servant Israel, NIG
1:68 for he **h** visited and redeemed his people, NIG
1:69 And **h** raised up a horn of salvation for us in NIG
1:78 whereby the dayspring from on high **h** NIG
2:15 which the Lord **h** made known unto us. NIG
3: 7 who **h** warned you to flee from the wrath to NIG
3:11 and saith unto them, He that **h** two coats, 2192
3:11 let him impart to him that **h** none; 2192
3:11 and he that **h** meat, let him do likewise. 2192
4:18 he **h** anointed me to preach the gospel to NIG
4:18 he **h** sent me to heal the broken-hearted, NIG
5:24 that ye may know that the Son of man **h** 2192
7: 5 our nation, and he **h** built us a synagogue. NIG
7:16 and, That God **h** visited his people. NIG
7:20 John Baptist **h** sent us unto thee, saying, NIG
7:33 nor drinking wine; and ye say, He **h** a devil. 2192
7:44 but she **h** washed my feet with tears, and NIG
7:45 this *woman* since the time I came in **h** not NIG
7:46 this *woman* **h** anointed my feet with NIG
7:50 said to the woman, Thy faith **h** saved thee; NIG
8: 8 He that **h** ears to hear, let him hear. 2192
8:16 No *man,* when he **h** lighted a candle, NIG
8:18 for whosoever **h**, to him shall be given; and 2192
8:18 and whosoever **h** not, from him shall be 2192
8:39 shew how great *things* God **h** done unto NIG
8:46 And Jesus said, Somebody **h** touched me: NIG
8:48 thy faith **h** made thee whole; go in peace.) NIG
9:58 the Son of man **h** not where to lay *his* head. 2192
10:40 dost thou not care that my sister **h** left me to NIG
10:42 and Mary **h** chosen *that* good part, NIG
11:33 No *man,* when he **h** lighted a candle, NIG
12: 5 which after *he* **h** killed hath power to cast NIG
12: 5 which after *he* hath killed **h** power to cast 2192
12:44 he will make him ruler over all that he **h**. 5225
13:16 whom Satan **h** bound, lo *these* eighteen NIG
13:25 and **h** shut to the door, and ye begin to stand NIG
14:29 after he **h** laid the foundation, and is not NIG
14:33 *he be* of you that forsaketh not all that he **h**, 5225
14:35 it out. He that **h** ears to hear, let him hear. 2192
15: 5 And when he **h** found *it,* he layeth *it* on his NIG
15: 9 And when she **h** found *it,* she calleth *her* NIG
15:27 and thy father **h** killed the fatted calf, NIG
15:27 because he **h** received him *safe and* sound. NIG
15:30 which **h** devoured thy living with harlots, NIG
17:19 go *thy way:* thy faith **h** made thee whole. NIG
18:29 There is no *man* that **h** left house, or NIG
18:42 Receive thy sight: thy faith **h** saved thee. NIG
19:16 Lord, thy pound **h** gained ten pounds. NIG
19:18 Lord, thy pound **h** gained five pounds. NIG
19:24 and give *it* to him that **h** ten pounds. 2192
19:25 they said unto him, Lord, he **h** ten pounds.) 2192
19:26 That unto every one which **h** shall be 2192
19:26 and from him that **h** not, even that he hath 2192
19:26 even that he **h** shall be taken away from 2192
19:31 unto him, Because the Lord **h** need of him. 2192
19:34 And they said, The Lord **h** need of him. 2192
20:24 Whose image and superscription **h** it? 2192
21: 3 that this poor widow **h** cast in more than NIG
21: 4 she of her penury **h** cast in all the living that NIG
22:29 as my Father **h** appointed unto me; NIG
22:31 Simon, behold, Satan **h** desired *to have* you, NIG
22:36 But now, he that **h** a purse, let him take *it,* 2192
22:36 and he that **h** no sword, let him sell his 2192
23:22 the third time, Why, what evil **h** he done? NIG
23:41 but this *man* **h** done nothing amiss. NIG
24:34 is risen indeed, and **h** appeared to Simon. NIG
24:39 for a spirit **h** not flesh and bones, as ye see 2192
Jn 1:18 No *man* **h** seen God at any time; the only NIG
1:18 the bosom of the Father, he **h** declared *him.* NIG
2:17 The zeal of thine house **h** eaten me up. NIG
3:13 And no *man* **h** ascended up to heaven, but NIG
3:18 he **h** not believed in the name of the only NIG
3:29 He that **h** the bride is the bridegroom: but 2192
3:32 And what he **h** seen and heard, that he NIG
3:33 He that **h** received his testimony hath set to NIG
3:33 He that hath received his testimony **h** set to NIG
3:34 For he whom God **h** sent speaketh NIG
3:35 and **h** given all *things* into his hand. NIG
3:36 He that believeth on the Son **h** everlasting 2192
4:33 **H** any *man* brought him *ought* to eat? NIG
4:44 that a prophet **h** no honour in his own 2192
5:22 but **h** committed all judgment unto the Son: NIG
5:23 honoureth not the Father which **h** sent him. NIG
5:24 **h** everlasting life, and shall not come into 2192
5:26 For as the Father **h** life in himself; so 2192
5:26 **h** he given to the Son to have life in NIG
5:27 And **h** given him authority to execute NIG
5:30 but the will of the Father which **h** sent me. NIG
5:36 for the works which the Father **h** given me NIG
5:36 witness of me, that the Father **h** sent me. NIG
5:37 And the Father himself, which **h** sent me, NIG
5:37 which hath sent me, **h** borne witness of me. NIG
5:38 for whom he **h** sent, him ye believe not. NIG
6: 9 which **h** five barley loaves, and two small 2192
6:27 unto you: for him **h** God the Father sealed. NIG
6:29 that ye believe on *him* whom he **h** sent. NIG
6:39 And this is the Father's will which **h** sent NIG
6:39 that of all which he **h** given me I should NIG
6:44 except the Father which **h** sent me draw NIG
6:45 Every *man* therefore that **h** heard, and NIG
6:45 that hath heard, and **h** learned of the Father, NIG
6:46 Not that any *man* **h** seen the Father, save he NIG
6:46 he which is of God, he **h** seen the Father. NIG
6:47 He that believeth on me **h** everlasting life. 2192
6:54 and drinketh my blood, **h** eternal life; 2192
6:57 As the living Father **h** sent me, and I live by NIG
7:29 for I am from him, and he **h** sent me. NIG
7:31 miracles than these which this *man* **h** done? NIG
7:38 that believeth on me, as the scripture **h** said, NIG
7:42 **H** not the scripture said, That Christ cometh NIG
8:10 thine accusers? **h** no *man* condemned thee? NIG
8:28 but as my Father **h** taught me, I speak these NIG
8:29 the Father **h** not left me alone; for I do NIG
Jn 8:37 because my word **h** no **place** in you. 5562
8:40 a man that **h** told you the truth, which I have NIG
9: 3 Neither **h** this *man* sinned, nor his parents: NIG
9:17 thou of him, that he **h** opened thine eyes? NIG
9:21 or who **h** opened his eyes, we know not: NIG
9:30 he is, and *yet* he **h** opened mine eyes. NIG
10:20 of them said, He **h** a devil, and is mad; 2192
10:21 are not the words of him that **h a devil.** 1139
10:36 Say ye *of him,* whom the Father **h** NIG
11:39 he stinketh: for he **h** been *dead* four days. NIG
12: 7 against the day of my burying **h** she kept NIG
12:38 he spake, Lord, who **h** believed our report? NIG
12:38 to whom **h** the arm of the Lord been NIG
12:40 He **h** blinded their eyes, and hardened their NIG
12:48 not my words, **h** *one* that judgeth him: 2192
13:18 He that eateth bread with me **h** lift up his NIG
14: 9 he that **h** seen me hath seen the Father; and NIG
14: 9 he that hath seen me **h** seen the Father; and NIG
14:21 He that **h** my commandments, and 2192
14:30 of this world cometh, and **h** nothing in me. 2192
15: 9 As the Father **h** loved me, so have I loved NIG
15:13 Greater love **h** no *man* than this, that a man 2192
16: 6 *things* unto you, sorrow **h** filled your heart. NIG
16:15 All *things* that the Father **h** are mine: 2192
16:21 A woman when she is in travail **h** sorrow, 2192
17:14 and the world **h** hated them, because NIG
17:25 the world **h** not known thee: NIG
18:11 the cup which my Father **h** given me, shall I NIG
19:11 he that delivered me unto thee **h** the greater 2192
20:21 as *my* Father **h** sent me, even *so* send I you. NIG
Ac 1: 7 which the Father **h** put in his own power. NIG
2:24 Whom God **h** raised up, having loosed NIG
2:32 This Jesus **h** God raised up, whereof we all NIG
2:33 he **h** shed forth this, which ye now see and NIG
2:36 that God **h** made that same Jesus, whom ye NIG
3:13 of our fathers, **h** glorified his Son Jesus; NIG
3:15 of life, whom God **h** raised from the dead; NIG
3:16 And his name through faith in his name **h** NIG
3:16 the faith which is by him **h** given him this NIG
3:18 that Christ should suffer, he **h** so fulfilled. NIG
3:21 **h** spoken by the mouth of all his holy NIG
4:16 for that indeed a notable miracle **h** been NIG
5: 3 why **h** Satan filled thine heart to lie to NIG
5:31 Him **h** God exalted with his right hand *to be* NIG
5:32 whom God **h** given to them that obey him. NIG
7:50 **H** not my hand made all these *things?* NIG
9:12 And **h** seen in a vision a man named NIG
9:13 how much evil he **h** done to thy saints at NIG
9:14 And here he **h** authority from the chief 2192
9:17 **h** sent me, that thou mightest receive thy NIG
10:15 What God **h** cleansed, *that* call not thou NIG
10:28 God **h** shewed me that *I* should not call any NIG
11: 8 unclean **h** at any time entered into my NIG
11: 9 What God **h** cleansed, *that* call not thou NIG
11:18 Then **h** God also to the Gentiles granted NIG
12:11 that the Lord **h** sent his angel, and NIG
12:11 **h** delivered me out of the hand of Herod, NIG
13:23 Of this *man's* seed **h** God according to *his* NIG
13:33 God **h** fulfilled the same unto us their NIG
13:33 in that he **h** raised up Jesus again; NIG
13:47 For so **h** the Lord commanded us, *saying,* I NIG
15:14 Simeon **h** declared how God at the first did NIG
15:21 For Moses of old time **h** in every city them 2192
17: 7 Whom Jason **h** received: and these all do NIG
17:26 And **h** made of one blood all nations of men NIG
17:26 **h** determined the times before appointed, NIG
17:31 Because he **h** appointed a day, in the which NIG
17:31 by *that* man whom he **h** ordained; NIG
17:31 *whereof* he **h** given assurance unto all *men,* NIG
17:31 *men,* in that he **h** raised him from the dead. NIG
19:26 this Paul **h** persuaded and turned away NIG
20:28 over the which the Holy Ghost **h** made you NIG
20:28 which he **h** purchased with his own blood. NIG
21:28 the temple, and **h** polluted this holy place. NIG
22:14 The God of our fathers **h** chosen thee, NIG
23: 9 but if a spirit or an angel **h** spoken to him, NIG
23:17 for he **h** a certain *thing* to tell him. 2192
23:18 who **h** something to say unto thee. 2192
24: 6 Who also **h** gone about to profane NIG
25:25 and *that* he himself **h** appealed to Augustus, NIG
27:24 God **h** given thee all them that sail with NIG
28: 4 whom, though he **h** escaped the sea, NIG
Ro 1:19 in them; for God **h** shewed *it* unto them. NIG
3: 1 What advantage then **h** the Jew? or NIG
3: 7 For if the truth of God **h** *more* abounded NIG
3:25 Whom God **h** set forth *to be* a propitiation NIG
4: 1 as pertaining to the flesh, **h** found? NIG
4: 2 justified by works, he **h** whereof to glory; 2192
5:15 Jesus Christ, **h** abounded unto many. NIG
5:21 That as sin **h** reigned unto death, even so NIG
6: 9 death **h** no more dominion over him. NIG
7: 1 how that the law **h dominion over** a man, 2961
7: 2 For the woman which **h** a husband is bound NIG
8: 2 Jesus **h** made me free from the law of sin NIG
8:20 by reason of him who **h** subjected *the same,* NIG
9: 6 Not as though the word of God **h** taken NIG
9:18 Therefore **h** he **mercy** on whom he will 1653
9:19 yet find fault? For who **h** resisted his will? NIG
9:21 **H** not the potter power over the clay, of 2192
9:24 Even us, whom he **h** called, not of the Jews NIG
9:31 **h** not attained to the law of righteousness. NIG
10: 9 shalt believe in thine heart that God **h** raised NIG
10:16 Lord, who **h** believed our report? NIG
11: 1 I say then, **H** God cast away his people? NIG
11: 2 God **h** not cast away his people which he NIG
11: 7 Israel **h** not obtained that which he seeketh NIG
11: 7 but the election **h** obtained *it,* and the rest NIG
11: 8 God **h** given them the spirit of slumber, NIG
11:32 For God **h** concluded *them* all in unbelief, NIG
11:34 For who **h** known the mind of the Lord? or NIG
11:34 of the Lord? or who **h** been his counseller? NIG
11:35 Or who **h** first given to him, and it shall be NIG
12: 3 according as God **h** dealt to every man NIG
13: 8 for he that loveth another **h** fulfilled the law. NIG
14: 3 him that eateth: for God **h** received him. NIG

Ro 15:18 *things* which Christ **h** not wrought by me, NIG
15:26 For it **h** pleased *them of* Macedonia and NIG
15:27 It **h** pleased them verily; and their debtors NIG
16: 2 in whatsoever business she **h** need of you: NIG
16: 2 for she **h** been a succourer of many, and NIG
1Co 1:11 For it **h** been declared unto me of you, NIG
1:20 **h** not God made foolish the wisdom of this NIG
1:27 But God **h** chosen the foolish *things* of NIG
1:27 God **h** chosen the weak *things* of the world NIG
1:28 **h** God chosen, *yea,* and *things* which are NIG
2: 9 it is written, Eye **h** not seen, nor ear heard, NIG
2: 9 *the things* which God **h** prepared for them NIG
2:10 But God **h** revealed *them* unto us by his NIG
2:16 For who **h** known the mind of the Lord, NIG
3:14 If any *man's* work abide which he **h** built NIG
4: 9 For I think that God **h** set forth us NIG
5: 2 that he that **h** done this deed might be taken NIG
5: 3 *concerning* him that **h** so done this *deed,* NIG
6:14 And God **h** both raised up the Lord, and NIG
7: 4 The wife **h** not **power** of her own body, but 1850
7: 4 likewise also the husband **h** not **power** of 1850
7: 7 But every man **h** his proper gift of God, 2192
7:12 If any brother **h** a wife that believeth not, 2192
7:13 And the woman which **h** a husband that 2192
7:15 in such *cases:* but God **h** called us to peace. NIG
7:17 But as God **h** distributed to every man, NIG
7:17 as the Lord **h** called every one, so let him NIG
7:25 as one that **h** obtained mercy of the Lord to NIG
7:28 and if a virgin marry, she **h** not sinned. NIG
7:37 but **h** power over his own will, and hath so 2192
7:37 and **h** so decreed in his heart that *he* will NIG
9:14 **h** the Lord ordained that they which preach NIG
10:13 There **h** no temptation taken you but such as NIG
12:12 and **h** many members, and all the members 2192
12:18 But now **h** God set the members every one NIG
12:18 of them in the body, as **it h pleased** him. 2309
12:24 but God **h** tempered the body together, NIG
12:28 And God **h** set some in the church, NIG
14:26 every one of you **h** a psalm, hath a doctrine, 2192
14:26 **h** a doctrine, hath a tongue, hath a 2192
14:26 hath a doctrine, **h** a tongue, hath a 2192
14:26 a doctrine, hath a tongue, **h** a revelation, 2192
14:26 hath a revelation, **h** an interpretation. 2192
15:25 till he **h** put all enemies under his feet. NIG
15:27 For he **h** put all *things* under his feet. NIG
15:38 But God giveth it a body as it **h** pleased NIG
16: 2 as *God* **h** prospered him, that there be no NIG
2Co 1:21 you in Christ, and **h** anointed us, *is* God; NIG
1:22 Who **h** also sealed us, and given the earnest NIG
2: 5 he **h** not grieved me, but in part: NIG
3: 6 Who also **h** made us able ministers of NIG
4: 4 In whom the god of this world **h** blinded NIG
4: 6 out of darkness, **h** shined in our hearts, NIG
5: 5 Now he that **h** wrought us for the selfsame NIG
5: 5 who also **h** given unto us the earnest of NIG
5:10 according to that he **h** done, whether *it be* NIG
5:18 who **h** reconciled us to himself by Jesus NIG
5:18 **h** given to us the ministry of reconciliation; NIG
5:19 **h** committed unto us the word of NIG
5:21 For he **h** made him *to be* sin for us, NIG
6:14 for what fellowship **h** righteousness with NIG
6:14 and what communion **h** light with darkness? NIG
6:15 And what concord **h** Christ with Belial? or NIG
6:15 what part **h** he that believeth with an NIG
6:16 And what agreement **h** the temple of God NIG
6:16 as God **h** said, I will dwell in them, and NIG
7: 8 for I perceive that the same epistle **h** made NIG
8:12 *it is* accepted according to that a man **h**, 2192
8:12 *and* not according to that he **h** not. 2192
9: 2 and your zeal **h** provoked very many. NIG
9: 9 (As it is written, He **h** dispersed abroad; NIG
9: 9 dispersed abroad; he **h** given to the poor: NIG
10: 8 which the Lord **h** given us for edification, NIG
10:13 of the rule which God **h** distributed to us, NIG
13:10 according to the power which the Lord **h** NIG
Gal 3: 1 O foolish Galatians, who **h** bewitched you, NIG
3: 1 before whose eyes Jesus Christ **h** been NIG
3:13 Christ **h** redeemed us from the curse of NIG
3:22 But the scripture **h** concluded all under sin, NIG
4: 6 God **h** sent forth the Spirit of his Son into NIG
4:27 for the desolate **h** many moe children than NIG
4:27 moe children than she which **h** a husband. 2192
5: 1 in the liberty wherewith Christ **h** made us NIG
Eph 1: 3 who **h** blessed us with all spiritual blessings NIG
1: 4 According as he **h** chosen us in him before NIG
1: 6 wherein he **h** made us accepted in NIG
1: 8 Wherein he **h** abounded toward us in all NIG
1:22 And **h** put all *things* under his feet, and NIG
2: 1 And you ***h** he quickened,* who were dead in NIG
2: 5 **h** quickened *us* together with Christ, (by NIG
2: 6 And **h** raised *us* up together, and made *us* sit NIG
2:10 which God **h** before ordained that we NIG
2:14 who **h** made both one, and hath broken NIG
2:14 **h** broken down the middle wall of partition NIG
3: 9 which from the beginning of the world **h** NIG
4:32 even as God for Christ's sake **h** forgiven NIG
5: 2 as Christ also **h** loved us, and hath given NIG
5: 2 and **h** given himself for us an offering and NIG
5: 5 **h** *any* inheritance in the kingdom of Christ 2192
Php 1: 6 **h** begun a good work in you will perform *it* NIG
2: 9 Wherefore God also **h** highly exalted him, NIG
2:22 he **h** served with me in the gospel. NIG
3: 4 If any other *man* thinketh that *he* **h** *whereof* NIG
4:10 that now at the last your care of me **h** NIG
Col 1:12 which **h** made us meet to be partakers of NIG
1:13 Who **h** delivered us from the power of NIG
1:13 **h** translated *us* into the kingdom of his dear NIG
1:21 by wicked works, yet now **h** he reconciled NIG
1:26 *Even* the mystery which **h** been hid from NIG
2:12 of God, who **h** raised him from the dead. NIG
2:13 **h** he quickened together with him, NIG
2:18 intruding into *those things* which he **h** not NIG
3:25 receive *for* the wrong which he **h** done: NIG
4:13 that he **h** a great zeal for you, and them that 2192
1Th 2:12 who **h** called you unto his kingdom and NIG
4: 7 For God **h** not called us unto uncleanness, NIG
4: 8 who **h** also given unto us his holy Spirit. NIG
5: 9 For God **h** not appointed us to wrath, but NIG
2Th 2:13 God **h** from the beginning chosen you to NIG
2:16 which **h** loved us, and hath given *us* NIG
2:16 and **h** given *us* everlasting consolation and NIG
1Ti 1:12 who **h** enabled me, for that he counted me NIG
4: 3 which God **h** created to be received with NIG
5: 8 he **h** denied the faith, and is worse than an NIG
6:16 Who only **h** immortality, dwelling in 2192
6:16 whom no man **h** seen, nor can see: NIG
2Ti 1: 7 For God **h** not given us the spirit of fear; but NIG
1: 9 Who **h** saved us, and called *us* with a holy NIG
1:10 who **h** abolished death, and hath brought NIG
1:10 and **h** brought life and immortality to light NIG
2: 4 that he may please him who **h** chosen *him* NIG
4:10 For Demas **h** forsaken me, having loved *this* NIG
4:15 for he **h** greatly withstood our words. NIG
Tit 1: 3 But **h** in due times manifested his word NIG
1: 9 Holding fast the faithful word as *he* **h** been NIG
2:11 bringeth salvation **h** appeared to all men, NIG
Phm 1:18 If he **h** wronged thee, or oweth *thee* ought, NIG
Heb 1: 2 **H** in these last days spoken unto us by *his* NIG
1: 2 whom he **h** appointed heir of all *things,* by NIG
1: 4 as he **h** by inheritance obtained a more NIG
1: 9 **h** anointed thee *with* the oil of gladness NIG
2: 5 For unto *the* angels **h** he not put in NIG
2:13 I, and the children which God **h** given me. NIG
2:18 For in that he himself **h** suffered being NIG
3: 3 inasmuch as he who **h** builded the house NIG
3: 3 the house **h** more honour than the house. 2192
4:10 he also **h** ceased from his own works, NIG
7:24 **h** an unchangeable priesthood. 2192
8: 6 But now **h** he obtained a more excellent NIG
8:13 A new *covenant,* he **h** made the first old. NIG
9:20 testament which God **h** enjoined unto you. NIG
9:26 now once in the end of the world **h** he NIG
10:14 For by one offering he **h** perfected for ever NIG
10:20 living way, which he **h** consecrated for us, NIG
10:29 who **h** trodden under foot the Son of God, NIG
10:29 and **h** counted the blood of the covenant, NIG
10:29 and **h** done despite unto the Spirit of grace? NIG
10:30 For we know him that **h** said, NIG
10:35 which **h** great recompence of reward. 2192
11:10 For he looked for a city which **h** 2192
11:16 their God: for he **h** prepared for them a city. NIG
12:26 but now he **h** promised, saying, Yet once NIG
13: 5 for he **h** said, I will never leave thee, NIG
Jas 1:12 which the Lord **h** promised to them that NIG
1:15 Then when lust **h** conceived, it bringeth NIG
2: 5 **H** not God chosen the poor of this world NIG
2: 5 heirs of the kingdom which he **h** promised NIG
2:13 without mercy, that **h** shewed no mercy; NIG
2:14 though a man say *he* **h** faith, and have not 2192
2:17 Even so faith, if it **h** not works, is dead, 2192
3: 7 is tamed, and **h** been tamed of mankind: NIG
5: 7 and **h long patience** for it, until he receive 3114
1Pe 1: 3 which according to his abundant mercy **h** NIG
1:15 But as he which **h** called you is holy, so NIG
2: 9 **h** called you out of darkness into his NIG
3:18 For Christ also **h** once suffered for sins, NIG
4: 1 then as Christ **h** suffered for us in the flesh, NIG
4: 1 for he that **h** suffered in the flesh hath NIG
4: 1 for he that hath suffered in the flesh **h** NIG
4:10 As every man **h** received *the* gift, *even so* NIG
5:10 who **h** called us into his eternal glory by NIG
2Pe 1: 3 According as his divine power **h** given unto NIG
1: 3 through the knowledge of him that **h** called NIG
1: 9 **h** forgotten that *he* was purged from his old NIG
1:14 even as our Lord Jesus Christ **h** shewed me. NIG
3:15 wisdom given unto him **h** written unto you; NIG
1Jn 2:11 because that darkness **h** blinded his eyes. NIG
2:23 denieth the Son, the same **h** not the Father: 2192
2:23 *he that acknowledgeth the Son* **h** *the Father* NIG
2:25 And this is the promise that he **h** promised NIG
2:27 and is no lie, and even as it **h** taught you, NIG
3: 1 what manner of love the Father **h** bestowed NIG
3: 3 And every *man* that **h** this hope in him 2192
3: 6 whosoever sinneth **h** not seen him, NIG
3:15 ye know that no murderer **h** eternal life 2192
3:17 But whoso **h** *this* world's good, and 2192
3:17 and seeth his brother **h** need, and 2192
3:24 in us, by the Spirit which he **h** given us. NIG
4:12 No *man* **h** seen God at any time. If we love NIG
4:13 he in us, because he **h** given us of his Spirit. NIG
4:16 and believed the love that God **h** to us. 2192
4:18 because fear **h** torment. He that feareth is 2192
4:20 for he that loveth not his brother whom he **h** NIG
4:20 how can he love God whom he **h** not seen? NIG
5: 9 for this is the witness of God which he **h** NIG
5:10 He that believeth on the Son of God **h** 2192
5:10 he that believeth not God **h** made him a liar; NIG
5:11 that God **h** given to us eternal life, and NIG
5:12 He that **h** the Son hath life; *and* he that hath 2192
5:12 He that hath the Son **h** life; *and* he that hath 2192
5:12 he that **h** not the Son of God hath not life. 2192
5:12 he that hath not the Son of God **h** not life. 2192
5:20 and **h** given us an understanding, that we NIG
2Jn 1: 9 not in the doctrine of Christ, **h** not God. 2192
1: 9 of Christ, he **h** both the Father and the Son. 2192
3Jn 1:11 but he that doeth evil **h** not seen God. NIG
1:12 Demetrius **h good report** of all *men,* and 3140
Jude 1: 6 he **h** reserved in everlasting chains under NIG
Rev 1: 6 And **h** made us kings and priests unto God NIG
2: 7 He that **h** an ear, let him hear what 2192
2:11 He that **h** an ear, let him hear what 2192
2:12 These *things* saith he which **h** the sharp 2192
2:17 He that **h** an ear, let him hear what 2192
2:18 who **h** his eyes like unto a flame of fire, 2192
2:29 He that **h** an ear, let him hear what 2192
3: 1 These *things* saith he that **h** the seven 2192
3: 6 He that **h** an ear, let him hear what 2192
3: 7 he *that is* true, he that **h** the key of David, 2192
3:13 He that **h** an ear, let him hear what 2192
3:22 He that **h** an ear, let him hear what 2192
Rev 5: 5 **h** prevailed to open the book, and to loose NIG
9:11 in the Greek *tongue* **h** *his* name Apollyon. 2192
10: 7 as he **h** declared to his servants NIG
12: 6 where she **h** a place prepared of God, 2192
12:12 because he knoweth that he **h** *but* a short 2192
13:18 Let him that **h** understanding count 2192
16: 9 of God, which **h** power over these plagues: 2192
17: 7 which **h** the seven heads and ten horns. 2192
17: 9 *And* here *is* the mind which **h** wisdom. 2192
17:17 For God **h** put in their hearts to fulfil his NIG
18: 5 and God **h** remembered her iniquities. NIG
18: 6 in the cup which she **h** filled fill to her NIG
18: 7 How much she **h** glorified herself, and NIG
18:20 for God **h** avenged you on her. NIG
19: 2 for he **h** judged the great whore, which did NIG
19: 2 **h** avenged the blood of his servants at her NIG
19: 7 is come, and his wife **h** made herself ready. NIG
19:16 And he **h** on *his* vesture and on his thigh a 2192
20: 6 holy *is* he that **h** part in the first 2192
20: 6 on such the second death **h** no power, but 2192

HATHACH See HATACH

HATHATH (1)
1Ch 4:13 and Seraiah: and the sons of Othniel; **H.** 2867

HATING (3) [HATE]
Ex 18:21 as fear God, men of truth, **h** covetousness; 8130
Tit 3: 3 and envy, hateful, *and* **h** one another. 3404
Jude 1:23 **h** even the garment spotted by the flesh. 3404

HATIPHA (2)
Ezr 2:54 The children of Neziah, the children of **H.** 2412
Ne 7:56 The children of Neziah, the children of **H.** 2412

HATITA (2)
Ezr 2:42 the children of Akkub, the children of **H,** 2410
Ne 7:45 the children of Akkub, the children of **H,** 2410

HATRED (18) [HATE]
Nu 35:20 if he thrust him of **h**, or hurl at him by 8135
2Sa 13:15 that the **h** wherewith he hated her *was* 8135
Ps 25:19 and they hate me *with* **cruel h.** 2555+8135
109: 3 compassed me about also *with* words of **h**; 8135
109: 5 me evil for good, and **h** for my love. 8135
139:22 I hate them *with* perfect **h**: I count them 8135
Pr 10:12 **H** stirreth up strifes: but love covereth all 8135
10:18 He that hideth **h** *with* lying lips, and he that 8135
15:17 love is, than a stalled ox and **h** therewith. 8135
26:26 *Whose* **h** is covered by deceit, 8135
Ecc 9: 1 either love or **h** *by* all *that is* before them. 8135
9: 6 Also their love, and their **h**, and their envy, 8135
Eze 25:15 a despiteful heart, to destroy *it for* the old **h**; 342
35: 5 Because thou hast had a perpetual **h**, and 342
35:11 thou hast used out of thy **h** against them; 8135
Hos 9: 7 multitude of thine iniquity, and the great **h**. 4895
9: 8 all his ways, *and* **h** in the house of his God. 4895
Gal 5:20 Idolatry, witchcraft, **h**, variance, 2189

HATS (1)
Da 3:21 their **h**, and their *other* garments, and 3737

HATTIL (2)
Ezr 2:57 children of Shephatiah, the children of **H,** 2411
Ne 7:59 children of Shephatiah, the children of **H,** 2411

HATTUSH (5)
1Ch 3:22 **H**, and Igeal, and Bariah, and Neariah, and 2407
Ezr 8: 2 of Ithamar; Daniel: of the sons of David; **H.** 2407
Ne 3:10 next unto him repaired **H** the son of 2407
10: 4 **H**, Shebaniah, Malluch, 2407
12: 2 Amariah, Malluch, **H**, 2407

HAUGHTILY (1) [HAUGHTY]
Mic 2: 3 remove your necks; neither shall ye go **h**: 7317

HAUGHTINESS (5) [HAUGHTY]
Isa 2:11 the **h** of men shall be bowed down, and 7312
2:17 and the **h** of men shall be made low: 7312
13:11 and will lay low the **h** of the terrible. 1346
16: 6 *even* of his **h**, and his pride, and his wrath: 1346
Jer 48:29 and his pride, and the **h** of his heart. 7312

HAUGHTY (10) [HAUGHTINESS]
2Sa 22:28 thine eyes *are* upon the **h**, *that* thou mayest 7311
Ps 131: 1 LORD, my heart is not **h**, nor mine eyes 1361
Pr 16:18 and a **h** spirit before a fall. 1363
18:12 Before destruction the heart of man is **h**, 1361
21:24 Proud *and* **h** scorner *is* his name, 3093
Isa 3:16 Because the daughters of Zion are **h**, and 1361
10:33 *be* hewn down, and the **h** shall be humbled. 1364
24: 4 the **h** people of the earth do languish. 4791
Eze 16:50 they were **h**, and committed abomination 1361
Zep 3:11 thou shalt no more be **h** because of my holy 1361

HAUNT (3)
1Sa 23:22 know and see his place where his **h** is, *and* 7272
30:31 David himself and his men were **wont to h.** 1980
Eze 26:17 which cause their terror *to be* on all that **h** 3427

HAURAN (2)
Eze 47:16 Hazar-hatticon, which *is* by the coast of **H.** 2362
47:18 the east side ye shall measure from **H**, and 2362

HAVE (3902) [HAD, HADST, HAST, HATH, HAVING]
Ge 1:26 let them **h dominion** over the fish of 7287
1:28 **h dominion** over the fish of the sea, and 7287
1:29 I **h** given you every herb bearing seed, NIH
1:30 *is* life, *I* **h** *given* every green herb for meat: NIH
4: 1 and said, I **h** gotten a man from the LORD. NIH
4:20 as dwell in tents, and *of such as* **h** cattle. NIH
4:23 for I **h** slain a man to my wounding, and NIH

Ge 6: 7 I will destroy man whom I **h** created from NIH
6: 7 for it repenteth me that I **h** made them. NIH
7: 1 for thee **h** I seen righteous before me in this NIH
7: 4 every living substance that I **h** made will I NIH
8:21 any more every *thing* living, as I **h** done. NIH
9: 3 *even* as the green herb **h** I given you all NIH
9:17 which I **h** established between me and all NIH
11: 6 *is* one, and they **h** all one language; 3807.1
11: 6 from them, which they **h** imagined to do. NIH
12:19 so I might **h** taken her to me to wife: now NIH
14:22 I **h** lift up mine hand unto the LORD, NIH
14:23 thou shouldest say, I **h** made Abram rich: NIH
14:24 Save only that which the young men **h** NIH
15:18 saying, Unto thy seed **h** I given this land, NIH
16: 5 I **h** given my maid into thy bosom; and NIH
16:13 **H** I also here looked after him that seeth NIH
17: 5 for a father of many nations **h** I made thee. NIH
17:20 as for Ishmael, I **h** heard thee: Behold, NIH
17:20 I **h** blessed him, and will make him fruitful, NIH
18: 3 if now I **h** found favour in thy sight, NIH
18:10 and lo, Sarah thy wife shall **h** a son. 3807.1
18:12 I am waxed old shall I **h** pleasure, 1961+3807.1
18:14 the time of life, and Sarah shall **h** a son. 3807.1
18:21 see whether they **h** done altogether NIH
18:27 I **h** taken upon me to speak unto the Lord, NIH
18:31 I **h** taken upon me to speak unto the Lord: NIH
19: 8 I **h** two daughters which have not known 3807.1
19: 8 I have two daughters which **h** not known NIH
19:21 See, I **h** accepted thee concerning this thing, NIH
20: 5 and innocency of my hands **h** I done this. NIH
20: 9 what **h** I offended thee, that thou hast NIH
20:16 I **h** given thy brother a thousand *pieces* of NIH
21: 7 she said, Who would **h** said unto Abraham, NIH
21: 7 that Sarah should **h** given children suck? NIH
21: 7 for I **h** born *him* a son in his old age. NIH
21:23 according to the kindness that I **h** done unto NIH
21:30 a witness unto me, that I **h** digged this well. NIH
22:16 said, By myself **h** I sworn, saith NIH
24:19 thy camels also, until they **h** done drinking. NIH
24:25 We **h** both straw and provender enough, 5973
24:31 for I **h** prepared the house, and room for NIH
24:33 I will not eat, until I **h** told mine errand. NIH
26:10 one of the people might lightly **h** lien with NIH
26:10 thou shouldest **h** brought guiltiness upon us. NIH
26:27 ye hate me, and **h** sent me away from you? NIH
26:29 as we **h** not touched thee, and as we have NIH
26:29 as we **h** done unto thee nothing but good, NIH
26:29 but good, and **h** sent thee away in peace: NIH
26:32 and said unto him, We **h** found water. NIH
27:19 I **h** done according as thou badest me: NIH
27:33 I **h** eaten of all before thou camest, and NIH
27:33 all before thou camest, and **h** blessed him? NIH
27:37 I **h** made him thy lord, and all his brethren NIH
27:37 all his brethren **h** I given to him for NIH
27:37 and with corn and wine **h** I sustained him: NIH
27:40 it shall come to pass when thou shalt **h** NIH
28:15 until I **h** done *that* which I have spoken to NIH
28:15 until I have done *that* which I **h** spoken to NIH
28:22 this stone, which I **h** set *for* a pillar, shall be NIH
29:34 unto me, because I **h** born him three sons: NIH
30: 3 that I may also **h children** by her. 1129
30: 8 With great wrestlings **h** I wrestled with my NIH
30: 8 I wrestled with my sister, and I **h** prevailed: NIH
30:16 for surely I **h** hired thee with my son's NIH
30:18 I **h** given my maiden to my husband: NIH
30:20 with me, because I **h** born him six sons: NIH
30:26 for whom I **h** served thee, and let me go: NIH
30:26 for thou knowest my service which I **h** done NIH
30:27 I pray thee, if I **h** found favour in thine eyes, NIH
30:27 *tarry: for* I **h** learned by experience that NIH
30:29 Thou knowest how I **h** served thee, and how NIH
31: 6 ye know that with all my power I **h** served NIH
31:12 for I **h** seen all that Laban doeth unto thee. NIH
31:27 that I might **h** sent thee away with mirth, NIH
31:38 This twenty years ***h*** I *been* with thee; NIH
31:38 and thy she goats **h** not cast their young, NIH
31:38 and the rams of thy flock **h** I not eaten. NIH
31:41 Thus **h** I been twenty years in thy house; 3807.1
31:43 or unto their children which they **h** born? NIH
31:51 which I **h** cast betwixt me and thee; NIH
32: 4 I **h** sojourned with Laban, and stayed *there* NIH
32: 5 I **h** oxen, and asses, flocks, and 1961+3807.1
32: 5 I **h** sent to tell my lord, that I may find grace NIH
32:30 for I **h** seen God face to face, and my life is NIH
33: 9 Esau said, I **h** enough, my brother; 3426+3807.1
33:10 if now I **h** found grace in thy sight, then NIH
33:10 for therefore I **h** seen thy face, as though I NIH
33:11 with me, and because I **h** enough. 3426+3807.1
34:30 Ye **h** troubled me to make me to stink NIH
35:17 Fear not; thou shalt **h** this son also. 3807.1
37: 6 I pray you, this dream which I **h** dreamed: NIH
37: 8 or shalt thou **indeed h dominion** 4910+4910
37: 9 said, Behold, I **h** dreamed a dream more; NIH
37:32 *it* to their father; and said, This **h** we found: NIH
40: 8 We **h** dreamed a dream, and *there is* no NIH
40:15 here also **h** I done nothing that they should NIH
41:15 I **h** dreamed a dream, and *there is* none that NIH
41:15 I **h** heard say of thee, *that* thou canst NIH
41:28 This *is* the thing which I **h** spoken unto NIH
41:41 See, I **h** set thee over all the land of Egypt. NIH
42: 2 I **h** heard that there is corn in Egypt: NIH
42:36 Me **h** ye bereaved of my children: NIH
43: 7 **h** ye *another* brother? and we told 3426+3807.1
43:21 we **h** brought it again in our hand. NIH
43:22 other money **h** we brought down in our NIH
44: 4 Wherefore **h** ye rewarded evil for good? NIH
44: 5 he divineth? ye **h** done evil in *so* doing. NIH
44:15 What deed *is* this that ye **h** done? NIH
44:19 **H** ye a father, or a brother? 3426+3807.1
44:20 We **h** a father, an old man, and 3426+3807.1
45:13 glory in Egypt, and of all that you **h** seen; NIH
46:30 since I **h** seen thy face, because thou *art* yet NIH
46:32 they **h** brought their flocks, and their herds, NIH
46:32 and their herds, and all that they **h**. 3807.1
47: 1 and their herds, and all that they **h**, 3807.1

Ge 47: 4 for thy servants **h** no pasture for their 3807.1
47: 9 evil **h** the days of the years of my life been, 1961
47: 9 **h** not attained unto the days of the years of NIH
47:23 I **h** bought you *this* day and your land for NIH
47:26 *that* Pharaoh should **h** the fifth *part;* 3807.1
47:29 If now I **h** found grace in thy sight, put, NIH
48:22 Moreover I **h** given to thee one portion NIH
49:18 I **h** waited for thy salvation, O LORD. NIH
49:23 The archers **h** sorely grieved him, and NIH
49:26 The blessings of thy father **h** prevailed NIH
50: 4 If now I **h** found grace in your eyes, speak, NIH
50: 5 in my grave which I **h** digged for me in NIH
Ex 1:18 Why **h** ye done this thing, and have saved NIH
1:18 and **h** saved the men children alive? NIH
2:20 why *is* it *that* ye **h** left the man? call him, NIH
2:22 I **h** been a stranger in a strange land. NIH
3: 7 I **h** surely seen the affliction of my people NIH
3: 7 **h** heard their cry by reason of their NIH
3: 9 I **h** also seen the oppression wherewith NIH
3:12 *shall be* a token unto thee, that I **h** sent thee: NIH
3:16 I **h** surely visited you, and *seen* that which NIH
3:17 I **h** said, I will bring you up out of NIH
4:11 or the blind? **h** not I the LORD? NIH
4:21 before Pharaoh, which I **h** put in thine hand: NIH
5:14 Wherefore **h** ye not fulfilled your task in NIH
5:21 you **h** made our savour to be abhorred in NIH
6: 4 I **h** also established my covenant with them, NIH
6: 5 I **h** also heard the groaning of the children NIH
6: 5 and I **h** remembered my covenant. NIH
6:12 the children of Israel **h** not hearkened unto NIH
7: 1 See, I **h** made thee a god to Pharaoh: NIH
9:16 in very deed for this cause **h** I raised thee NIH
9:27 and said unto them, I **h** sinned *this* time: NIH
10: 1 for I **h** hardened his heart, and the heart of NIH
10: 2 what things I **h** wrought in Egypt, and my NIH
10: 2 and my signs which I **h** done amongst them; NIH
10: 6 thy fathers, nor thy fathers' fathers **h** seen, NIH
10:16 I **h** sinned against the LORD your God, NIH
12:17 for in this selfsame day **h** I brought your NIH
12:31 and go, serve the LORD, as ye **h** said. NIH
12:32 and your herds, as ye **h** said, and be gone; NIH
14: 5 they said, Why **h** we done this, that we have NIH
14: 5 that we **h** let Israel go from serving us? NIH
14:13 for the Egyptians whom ye **h** seen to day, NIH
14:18 when I **h** gotten me honour upon Pharaoh, NIH
15: 5 The depths **h** covered them: they sank into NIH
15:17 O Lord, *which* thy hands **h** established. NIH
15:26 which I **h** brought upon the Egyptians: NIH
16: 3 for ye **h** brought us forth into this NIH
16:12 I **h** heard the murmurings of the children of NIH
16:32 that they may see the bread wherewith I **h** NIH
17:16 ***h*** war with Amalek from generation *to* NIH
18: 3 he said, I **h** been an alien in a strange land: NIH
18:16 When they **h** a matter, they come 1961+3807.1
19: 4 Ye **h** seen what I did unto the Egyptians, NIH
20: 2 which **h** brought thee out of the land of NIH
20: 3 Thou shalt **h** no other gods before 1961+3807.1
20:22 Ye **h** seen that I have talked with you from NIH
20:22 Ye have seen that I **h** talked with you from NIH
21: 4 If his master **h** given him a wife, and NIH
21: 4 and she **h** born him sons or daughters; NIH
21: 8 unto a strange nation he shall **h** no **power**, 4910
21: 9 if he **h** betrothed her unto his son, he shall NIH
21:31 Whether he **h** gored a son, or have gored a NIH
21:31 he have gored a son, or **h** gored a daughter, NIH
22: 3 if he **h** nothing, then he shall be sold for 3807.1
22: 8 *to see* whether he **h** put his hand unto his NIH
23:13 in all *things* that I **h** said unto you be NIH
23:20 to bring thee into the place which I **h** NIH
24:12 and commandments which I **h** written; NIH
24:14 if any man **h** any matters to do, let him NIH
26: 2 every one of the curtains shall **h** one NIH
28: 3 whom I **h** filled with the spirit of wisdom, NIH
28: 7 It shall **h** the two shoulderpieces 1961+3807.1
28:32 it shall **h** a binding of woven work 1961+3807.1
29:35 according to all *things* which I **h** NIH
31: 2 I **h** called by name Bezaleel the son of Uri, NIH
31: 3 I **h** filled him *with* the spirit of God, NIH
31: 6 I, behold, I **h** given with him Aholiab, NIH
31: 6 in the hearts of all that are wise hearted I **h** NIH
31: 6 that they may make all that I **h** commanded NIH
31:11 all that I **h** commanded thee shall they do. NIH
32: 7 the land of Egypt, **h** corrupted *themselves:* NIH
32: 8 They **h** turned aside quickly out of the way NIH
32: 8 they **h** made them a molten calf, and NIH
32: 8 **h** worshipped it, and have sacrificed NIH
32: 8 **h** sacrificed thereunto, and said, These *be* NIH
32: 8 which **h** brought thee up out of the land of NIH
32: 9 I **h** seen this people, and behold, it *is* a NIH
32:13 all this land that I **h** spoken of will I give NIH
32:30 unto the people, Ye **h** sinned a great sin: NIH
32:31 this people **h** sinned a great sin, and NIH
32:31 a great sin, and **h** made them gods of gold. NIH
32:34 lead the people unto *the place* of which I **h** NIH
33:13 I pray thee, if I **h** found grace in thy sight, NIH
33:16 and thy people **h** found grace in thy sight? NIH
34: 9 If now I **h** found grace in thy sight, O Lord, NIH
34:10 such as **h** not been done in all the earth, NIH
34:27 for after the tenor of these words I **h** made a NIH
Lev 4:13 they **h** done somewhat against any of NIH
4:14 which they **h** sinned against it, is known, NIH
6: 3 Or **h** found that which was lost, and NIH
6:17 I **h** given it *unto them for* their portion of NIH
7: 7 atonement therewith shall **h** *it.* 1961+3807.1
7: 8 *even* the priest shall **h** to himself the skin of 1961
7:10 dry, shall all the sons of Aaron **h**, 1961+3807.1
7:33 **h** the right shoulder for *his* part. 1961+3807.1
7:34 the heave shoulder **h** I taken of the children NIH
7:34 **h** given them unto Aaron the priest and NIH
10:17 Wherefore **h** ye not eaten the sin offering in NIH
10:18 **h** eaten it in the holy *place,* as I NIH
10:19 *this* day **h** they offered their sin offering and NIH
10:19 the LORD; and such things **h** befallen me: NIH
10:19 should it **h** been accepted in the sight of NIH
11:10 all that **h** not fins nor scales in the seas, 3807.1

Lev 11:11 you shall **h** their carcases in abomination. NIH
11:13 these *are they which* ye shall **h** in NIH
11:21 which **h** legs above their feet, to leap 3807.1
11:23 which **h** four feet, *shall be* an 3807.1
12: 2 If a woman **h** conceived seed, and born a NIH
13: 2 When a man shall **h** in the skin of his flesh 1961
13:10 it **h** turned the hair white, and *there be* quick NIH
13:13 *if* the leprosy **h** covered all his flesh, NIH
13:24 the quick *flesh* that burneth **h** a white bright 1961
13:38 a woman **h** in the skin of their flesh bright 1961
13:55 *if* the plague **h** not changed his colour, and NIH
15:19 if a woman **h** an issue, *and* her issue in her 1961
15:25 if a woman **h an issue** of her blood 2100+2101
16: 4 he shall **h** the linen breeches upon his flesh, 1961
16:17 **h** made an atonement for himself, and NIH
17: 7 after whom they **h** gone a whoring. NIH
17:11 I **h** given it to you upon the altar to make an NIH
18:27 (For all these abominations **h** the men of NIH
19:23 shall **h** planted all *manner of* trees for food, NIH
19:31 Regard not them that **h** familiar spirits, NIH
19:36 and a just hin, shall ye **h**: 1961+3807.1
20: 6 the soul that turneth after such as **h** familiar NIH
20:12 they **h** wrought confusion; their blood *shall* NIH
20:13 both of them **h** committed an abomination: NIH
20:24 I **h** said unto you, Ye shall inherit their land, NIH
20:24 which **h** separated you from *other* people. NIH
20:25 which I **h** separated from you as unclean. NIH
20:26 **h** severed you from *other* people, that *ye* NIH
22:13 **h** no child, and is returned unto her 3807.1
23: 7 In the first day ye shall **h** a holy 1961+3807.1
23:14 until the selfsame day that ye **h** brought an NIH
23:24 of the month, shall ye **h** a sabbath, 1961+3807.1
23:39 when ye **h** gathered in the fruit of the land, NIH
24:22 Ye shall **h** one manner of law, 1961+3807.1
25:26 if the man **h** none to redeem *it,* and 1961+3807.1
25:31 the houses of the villages which **h** no wall NIH
25:44 thy bondmaids, which thou shalt **h**, 1961+3807.1
26: 9 For I will **h** respect unto you, and make you NIH
26:13 I **h** broken the bands of your yoke, and NIH
26:26 *And* when I **h** broken the staff of your NIH
26:37 ye shall **h** no power to stand before 1961+3807.1
26:40 that also they **h** walked contrary unto me; NIH
26:41 *And that* I also **h** walked contrary unto NIH
26:41 **h** brought them into the land of their NIH
27:20 or if he **h** sold the field to another man, NIH
Nu 3:12 I **h** taken the Levites from among NIH
3:32 ***h*** the oversight of them that keep the charge NIH
4:15 his sons **h** made an end of covering NIH
5: 7 they shall confess their sin which they **h** NIH
5: 8 if the man **h** no kinsman to recompense 3807.1
5:18 the priest shall **h** in his hand the bitter water 1961
5:19 If no man **h** lain with thee, and if thou hast NIH
5:27 and **h** done trespass against her husband, NIH
8:16 children of Israel, **h** I taken them unto me. NIH
8:18 I **h** taken the Levites for all the firstborn of NIH
8:19 I **h** given the Levites *as* a gift to Aaron and NIH
9:14 ye shall **h** one ordinance, both for 1961+3807.1
11:11 wherefore **h** I not found favour in thy sight, NIH
11:12 **H** I conceived all this people? have I NIH
11:12 **h** I begotten them, that thou shouldest say NIH
11:13 Whence should I **h** flesh to give unto all 3807.1
11:15 out of hand, if I **h** found favour in thy sight; NIH
11:18 for you **h** wept in the ears of the LORD, NIH
11:20 that ye **h** despised the LORD which *is* NIH
11:20 **h** wept before him, saying, Why came we NIH
12:11 wherein we **h** done foolishly, and NIH
12:11 done foolishly, and wherein we **h** sinned. NIH
13:32 through which we **h** gone to search it, NIH
14:11 for all the signs which I **h** shewed among NIH
14:14 *for* they **h** heard that thou LORD *art* NIH
14:15 the nations which **h** heard the fame of thee NIH
14:20 I **h** pardoned according to thy word: NIH
14:22 Because all *those* men which **h** seen my NIH
14:22 **h** tempted me *now* these ten times, and NIH
14:22 ten times, and **h** not hearkened to my voice; NIH
14:27 I **h** heard the murmurings of the children of NIH
14:28 as ye **h** spoken in mine ears, so will I do to NIH
14:29 and upward, which **h** murmured against me, NIH
14:31 they shall know the land which ye **h** NIH
14:35 I the LORD **h** said, I will surely do it unto NIH
14:40 the LORD hath promised: for we **h** sinned. NIH
15:22 if ye **h** erred, and not observed all these NIH
15:29 You shall **h** one law for him that 1961+3807.1
16:15 I **h** not taken one ass from them, NIH
16:15 ass from them, neither **h** I hurt one of them. NIH
16:28 for *I **h** not done them* of mine own mind. NIH
16:30 ye shall understand that these men **h** NIH
16:41 Ye **h** killed the people of the LORD. NIH
18: 6 I **h** taken your brethren the Levites from NIH
18: 7 I **h** given your priest's office *unto you as* a NIH
18: 8 I also **h** given thee the charge of mine heave NIH
18: 8 unto thee **h** I given them by reason of NIH
18:11 I **h** given them unto thee, and to thy sons NIH
18:12 offer unto the LORD, them **h** I given thee. NIH
18:19 **h** I given thee, and thy sons and thy NIH
18:20 Thou shalt **h** no **inheritance** in their land, 5157
18:20 shalt thou **h** any part among them: 1961+3807.1
18:21 I **h** given the children of Levi all the tenth in NIH
18:23 of Israel they **h** no **inheritance**. 5157+5159
18:24 I **h** given to the Levites to inherit: NIH
18:24 therefore I **h** said unto them, Among NIH
18:24 of Israel they shall **h** no **inheritance**. 5157+5159
18:26 **h** given you from them for your inheritance, NIH
18:30 When ye **h** heaved the best thereof from it, NIH
18:32 when ye **h** heaved from it the best of it: NIH
20: 4 why **h** ye brought up the congregation of NIH
20: 5 wherefore **h** ye made us to come up out of NIH
20:12 into the land which I **h** given them. NIH
20:15 and we **h** dwelt in Egypt a long time; NIH
20:17 *to* the left, until we **h** passed thy borders. NIH
20:24 for he shall not enter into the land which I **h** NIH
21: 5 Wherefore **h** ye brought us up out of Egypt NIH
21: 7 came to Moses, and said, We **h** sinned, NIH
21: 7 for we **h** spoken against the LORD, and NIH
21:30 We **h** shot at them; Heshbon is perished NIH

Nu 21:30 we **h** laid *them* waste even unto Nophah, NIH
21:34 for I **h** delivered him into thy hand, and all NIH
22:28 said unto Balaam, What **h** I done unto thee, NIH
22:34 unto the angel of the LORD, I **h** sinned; NIH
22:38 **h** I now any power at all to say any thing? NIH
23: 4 I **h** prepared seven altars, and I have offered NIH
23: 4 I **h** offered upon *every* altar a bullock and NIH
23:20 I **h** received *commandment* to bless: NIH
24:19 Out of Jacob shall come *he* that shall **h** NIH
25:13 he shall **h** it, and his seed after him, 1961+3807.1
25:18 wherewith they **h** beguiled you in the matter NIH
27: 8 **h** no son, then ye shall cause his 3807.1
27: 9 if he **h** no daughter, then ye shall give his 3807.1
27:10 if he **h** no brethren, then ye shall give his 3807.1
27:11 if his father **h** no brethren, then ye shall 3807.1
27:12 see the land which I **h** given unto NIH
27:17 be not as sheep which **h** no shepherd. 3807.1
28:25 on the seventh day ye shall **h** a 1961+3807.1
28:26 after your weeks *be out,* ye shall **h** 1961+3807.1
29: 1 ye shall **h** a holy convocation; 1961+3807.1
29: 7 ye shall **h** on the tenth *day* of this 1961+3807.1
29:12 ye shall **h** a holy convocation; 1961+3807.1
29:35 On the eighth day ye shall **h** a 1961+3807.1
30: 9 wherewith they **h** bound their souls, NIH
31:15 unto them, **H** ye saved all the women alive? NIH
31:18 that **h** not known a man by lying with him, NIH
31:49 Thy servants **h** taken the sum of the men of NIH
31:50 We **h** therefore brought an oblation for NIH
32: 4 a land for cattle, and thy servants **h** cattle: 3807.1
32: 5 said they, if we **h** found grace in thy sight, NIH
32:11 because they **h** not wholly followed me: NIH
32:12 for they **h** wholly followed the LORD. NIH
32:17 until we **h** brought them unto their place: NIH
32:18 until the children of Israel **h** inherited every NIH
32:23 behold, ye **h** sinned against the LORD: NIH
32:30 they shall **h possessions** among you in 270
33:53 for I **h** given you the land to possess it. NIH
34: 6 you shall even **h** the great sea for a border: 1961
34:14 **h** received *their inheritance;* and half NIH
34:14 half the tribe of Manasseh **h** received their NIH
34:15 the half tribe **h** received their inheritance on NIH
35: 3 the cities shall they **h** to dwell in; 1961+3807.1
35: 8 from *them that* **h** many ye shall give many; NIH
35: 8 but from *them that* **h** few ye shall give few: NIH
35:13 ye shall give six cities shall ye **h** for refuge. 1961
35:22 **h** cast upon him any thing without laying of NIH
35:28 Because he should **h** remained in the city of NIH
Dt 1: 6 Ye **h** dwelt long enough in this mount: NIH
1: 8 Behold, I **h** set the land before you: go in NIH
1:28 our brethren **h** discouraged our heart, NIH
1:28 moreover we **h** seen the sons of NIH
1:41 unto me, We **h** sinned against the LORD, NIH
2: 3 Ye **h** compassed this mountain long 3807.1
2: 5 I **h** given mount Seir unto Esau *for* a NIH
2: 9 I **h** given Ar unto the children of Lot *for* a NIH
2:19 I **h** given it unto the children of Lot *for* a NIH
2:24 I **h** given into thy hand Sihon the Amorite, NIH
2:31 I **h** begun to give Sihon and his land before NIH
3:19 (*for* I know that ye **h** much cattle,) 3807.1
3:19 shall abide in your cities which I **h** given NIH
3:20 Until the LORD **h** given rest unto your 3807.1
3:20 unto his possession, which I **h** given you. NIH
3:21 Thine eyes **h** seen all that the LORD your NIH
4: 3 Your eyes **h** seen what the LORD did NIH
4: 5 I **h** taught you statutes and judgments, NIH
4: 9 forget the things which thine eyes **h** seen, NIH
4:25 ye shall **h** remained long in the land, and NIH
5: 7 Thou shalt **h** none other gods 1961+3807.1
5:24 we **h** heard his voice out of the midst of NIH
5:24 we **h** seen this day that God doth talk with NIH
5:26 of the midst of the fire, as we *h,* and lived? NIH
5:28 I **h** heard the voice of the words of this NIH
5:28 this people, which they **h** spoken unto thee: NIH
5:28 they **h** well *said* all that they have spoken. NIH
5:28 they have well *said* all that they **h** spoken. NIH
6:10 when the LORD thy God shall **h** brought NIH
6:11 when thou shalt **h** eaten and be full; NIH
7:16 thine eye shall **h** no pity upon them: NIH
7:24 before thee, until thou **h** destroyed them. NIH
9: 7 ye **h** been rebellious against the LORD. NIH
9: 8 that the LORD was angry with you to **h** NIH
9:12 **h** corrupted *themselves;* they are quickly NIH
9:12 they **h** made them a molten image. NIH
9:13 saying, I **h** seen this people, and behold, it *is* NIH
9:20 the LORD was very angry with Aaron to **h** NIH
9:23 and possess the land which I **h** given you; NIH
9:24 You **h** been rebellious against the LORD NIH
10:21 and terrible *things,* which thine eyes **h** seen. NIH
11: 2 for *I speak* not with your children which **h** NIH
11: 2 which **h** not seen the chastisement of NIH
11: 7 your eyes **h** seen all the great acts of NIH
11:28 go after other gods, which ye **h** not known. NIH
12:21 as I **h** commanded thee, and thou shalt eat NIH
12:31 he hateth, **h** they done unto their gods; NIH
12:31 their daughters they **h** burnt in the fire to NIH
13:13 **h** withdrawn the inhabitants of their city, NIH
13:13 serve other gods, which ye **h** not known; NIH
13:17 **h compassion** upon thee, and 7355
14: 9 all that **h** fins and scales shall ye eat: 3807.1
15:21 *if it be* lame, or blind, *or* **h** any ill blemish, NIH
17: 3 host of heaven, which I **h** not commanded; NIH
17: 5 which **h** committed that wicked thing, NIH
18: 1 **h** no part nor inheritance with 1961+3807.1
18: 2 Therefore shall they **h** no 1961+3807.1
18: 8 They shall **h** like portions to eat, beside that NIH
18:17 They **h** well *spoken that* which they have NIH
18:17 They have well *spoken that* which they **h** NIH
18:20 which I **h** not commanded him to speak, or NIH
19:14 which they of old time **h** set in thine NIH
19:19 as he had thought to **h** done unto his NIH
20: 9 when the officers **h** made an end of NIH
20:18 which they **h** done unto their gods; NIH
21: 7 and say, Our hands **h** not shed this blood, NIH
21: 7 shed this blood, neither **h** our eyes seen *it.* NIH
21:11 that thou wouldest **h** *her* to thy wife; 3947

Dt 21:14 if thou **h** no delight in her, then thou shalt NIH
21:15 If a man **h** two wives, one beloved, 1961+3807.1
21:15 another hated, and they **h** born him children, NIH
21:18 If a man **h** a stubborn and 1961+3807.1
21:18 and *that,* when they **h** chastened him, NIH
21:22 if a man **h** committed a sin worthy of death, NIH
23:12 Thou shalt **h** a place also without 1961+3807.1
23:13 thou shalt **h** a paddle upon thy 1961+3807.1
25: 5 and one of them die, and **h** no child, 3807.1
25:13 Thou shalt not **h** in thy bag divers 1961+3807.1
25:14 Thou shalt not **h** in thine house 1961+3807.1
25:15 *But* thou shalt **h** a perfect and 1961+3807.1
25:15 and just measure shalt thou **h**: 1961+3807.1
26:10 I **h** brought the firstfruits of the land, NIH
26:13 I **h** brought away the hallowed *things* out of NIH
26:13 also **h** given them unto the Levite, and NIH
26:13 I **h** not transgressed thy commandments, NIH
26:13 neither **h** I forgotten *them:* NIH
26:14 I **h** not eaten thereof in my mourning, NIH
26:14 neither **h** I taken away *ought* thereof for *any* NIH
26:14 I **h** hearkened to the voice of the LORD NIH
26:14 **h** done according to all that thou hast NIH
28:21 until he **h** consumed thee from off the land, NIH
28:31 and thou shalt **h** none to rescue *them.* 3807.1
28:36 which neither thou nor thy fathers **h** known; NIH
28:40 Thou shalt **h** olive trees throughout 1961+3807.1
28:48 upon thy neck, until he **h** destroyed thee. NIH
28:51 of thy sheep, until he **h** destroyed thee. NIH
28:64 which neither thou nor thy fathers **h** known, NIH
28:65 shall the sole of thy foot **h** rest: 1961+3807.1
28:66 night, and shalt **h** none assurance of thy life: NIH
29: 2 Ye **h** seen all that the LORD did before NIH
29: 3 The great temptations which thine eyes **h** NIH
29: 5 I **h** led you forty years in the wilderness: NIH
29: 6 Ye **h** not eaten bread, neither have you NIH
29: 6 neither **h** you drunk wine or strong drink: NIH
29:16 (For ye know how we **h** dwelt in the land of NIH
29:17 ye **h** seen their abominations, and their NIH
29:19 in his heart, saying, I shall **h** peace, 1961+3807.1
29:25 Because they **h** forsaken the covenant of NIH
30: 1 which I **h** set before thee, and thou shalt call NIH
30: 3 **h compassion** upon thee, and will return 7355
30:15 I **h** set before thee *this* day life and good, NIH
30:19 *that* I **h** set before you life and death, NIH
31: 5 commandments which I **h** commanded you. NIH
31:13 which **h** not known *any thing,* may hear, NIH
31:16 break my covenant which I **h** made with NIH
31:18 for all the evils which they shall **h** wrought, NIH
31:20 *For* when I shall **h** brought them into NIH
31:20 and they shall **h** eaten and filled *themselves,* NIH
31:21 before I **h** brought them into the land which NIH
31:27 ye **h** been rebellious against the LORD; NIH
31:29 turn aside from the way which I **h** NIH
32: 5 They **h** corrupted themselves, their spot *is* NIH
32:21 They **h** moved me to jealousy with *that* NIH
32:21 they **h** provoked me to anger with their NIH
33: 9 and to his mother, I **h** not seen him; NIH
33: 9 for they **h** observed thy word, and kept thy NIH
34: 4 I **h** caused thee to see *it* with thine eyes, but NIH
Jos 1: 3 that **h** I given unto you, as I said unto NIH
1: 8 and then thou shalt **h good success.** 7919
1: 9 **H** not I commanded thee? Be strong and NIH
1:15 Until the LORD **h** given your brethren NIH
1:15 they also **h** possessed the land which NIH
2:10 For we **h** heard how the LORD dried up NIH
2:12 the LORD, since I **h** shewed you kindness, NIH
2:13 all that they **h,** and deliver our lives from 3807.1
3: 4 for ye **h** not passed *this* way heretofore. NIH
5: 9 *This* day **h** I rolled away the reproach of NIH
6: 2 I **h** given into thine hand Jericho, and NIH
7:11 they **h** also transgressed my covenant which NIH
7:11 for they **h** even taken of the accursed thing, NIH
7:11 **h** also stolen, and dissembled also, and NIH
7:11 they **h** put *it* even amongst their own stuff. NIH
7:20 Indeed I **h** sinned against the LORD God NIH
7:20 of Israel, and thus and thus **h** I done: NIH
8: 1 I **h** given into thy hand the king of Ai, and NIH
8: 6 till we **h** drawn them from the city; for they NIH
8: 8 it shall be, when ye **h** taken the city, *that* ye NIH
8: 8 shall ye do. See, I **h** commanded you. NIH
9: 9 for we **h** heard the fame of him, and all that NIH
9:19 We **h** sworn unto them by the LORD God NIH
9:22 saying, Wherefore **h** ye beguiled us, saying, NIH
9:24 because of you, and **h** done this thing. NIH
10: 8 for I **h** delivered them into thine hand; NIH
11:20 *and* that they might **h** no favour, but that *he* 1961
13: 6 for an inheritance, as I **h** commanded thee. NIH
13: 8 and the Gadites **h** received their inheritance, NIH
14: 9 Surely the land whereon thy feet **h** trodden NIH
17:16 in the land of the valley **h** chariots of iron, NIH
17:17 thou shalt not **h** one lot *only:* 1961+3807.1
17:18 though they **h** iron chariots, *and* though they NIH
18: 7 the Levites **h** no part among you; for 3807.1
18: 7 **h** received their inheritance beyond Jordan NIH
22: 2 Ye **h** kept all that Moses the servant of NIH
22: 2 **h** obeyed my voice in all that I commanded NIH
22: 3 Ye **h** not left your brethren these many days NIH
22: 3 **h** kept the charge of the commandment of NIH
22:11 the half tribe of Manasseh **h** built an altar NIH
22:16 What trespass *is* this that ye **h** committed NIH
22:16 in that ye **h** builded you an altar, that ye NIH
22:23 That we **h** built us an altar to turn from NIH
22:24 if we **h** not *rather* done it for fear of *this* NIH
22:24 What **h** you **to do with** the LORD God 3807.1
22:25 of Gad; ye **h** no part in the LORD: 3807.1
22:27 to come, Ye **h** no part in the LORD. 3807.1
22:31 ye **h** not committed this trespass against NIH
22:31 now ye **h** delivered the children of Israel out NIH
23: 3 ye **h** seen all that the LORD your God hath NIH
23: 4 I **h** divided unto you *by lot* these nations NIH
23: 4 with all the nations that I **h** cut off, NIH
23: 8 your God, as ye **h** done unto this day. NIH
23:15 until he **h** destroyed you from off this good NIH
23:16 When ye **h** transgressed the covenant of NIH
23:16 **h** gone and served other gods, and NIH

Jos 24: 7 your eyes **h** seen what I have done in Egypt: NIH
24: 7 your eyes have seen what I **h** done in Egypt: NIH
24:13 I **h** given you a land for which ye did not NIH
24:22 *are* witnesses against yourselves that ye **h** NIH
Jdg 1: 2 behold, I **h** delivered the land into his hand. NIH
1: 7 as I **h** done, so God hath requited me. NIH
2: 1 **h** brought you unto the land which I sware NIH
2: 2 ye **h** not obeyed my voice: why have ye NIH
2: 2 not obeyed my voice: why **h** ye done this? NIH
2:20 and **h** not hearkened unto my voice; NIH
3:19 said, I **h** a secret errand unto thee, O king: 3807.1
3:20 I **h** a message from God unto thee. 3807.1
5:13 **made** him that remaineth **h dominion over** 7287
5:13 the LORD **made** me **h dominion over** 7287
5:30 **H** they not sped? have they *not* divided NIH
5:30 **h** they *not* divided the prey; to every man a NIH
6:10 ye dwell: but ye **h** not obeyed my voice. NIH
6:14 hand of the Midianites: **h** not I sent thee? NIH
6:17 If now I **h** found grace in thy sight, then NIH
6:22 I **h** seen an angel of the LORD face to NIH
7: 9 the host; for I **h** delivered it into thine hand. NIH
8: 2 What **h** I done now in comparison of you? NIH
9:16 if ye **h** done truly and sincerely, NIH
9:16 in that ye **h** made Abimelech king, and if ye NIH
9:16 if ye **h** dealt well with Jerubbaal and his NIH
9:16 **h** done unto him according to the deserving NIH
9:18 **h** slain his sons, threescore and ten persons, NIH
9:18 upon one stone, and **h** made Abimelech, NIH
9:19 If ye then **h** dealt truly and sincerely with NIH
9:48 What ye **h** seen me do, make haste, *and* NIH
9:48 me do, make haste, *and* do as I *h done.* NIH
10:10 We **h** sinned against thee, both because NIH
10:10 both because we **h** forsaken our God, and NIH
10:13 Yet ye **h** forsaken me, and served other NIH
10:14 and cry unto the gods which ye **h** chosen; NIH
10:15 Israel said unto the LORD, We **h** sinned: NIH
11:27 Wherefore I **h** not sinned against thee, but NIH
11:35 for I **h** opened my mouth unto the LORD, NIH
13:15 until we shall **h** made ready a kid for thee. NIH
13:22 shall surely die, because we **h** seen God. NIH
13:23 he would not **h** received a burnt offering NIH
13:23 neither would he **h** shewed us all these NIH
13:23 as *at this* time **h** told us *such things* as these. NIH
14: 2 I **h** seen a woman in Timnath of NIH
14: 6 he rent him as *he* would **h** rent a kid, and NIH
14:15 **h** ye called us to take that we have? *is it* not NIH
14:15 have ye called us to **take that** we **h**? *is it* 3423
14:16 I **h** not told *it* my father nor my mother, and NIH
15: 7 Though ye **h** done this, yet will I be NIH
15:11 As they did unto me, so **h** I done unto them. NIH
15:16 with the jaw of an ass **h** I slain a thousand NIH
16:17 for I *h been* a Nazarite unto God from my NIH
17:13 me good, seeing I **h** a Levite to *my* priest. 1961
18: 9 for we **h** seen the land, and behold, it *is* very NIH
18:14 now therefore consider what ye **h** to do. NIH
18:24 Ye **h** taken away my gods which I made, NIH
18:24 what **h** I more? and what *is* this *that* ye 3807.1
20: 5 me by night, *and* thought to **h** slain me: NIH
20: 5 my concubine **h** they forced, that she is NIH
20: 6 for they **h** committed lewdness and folly in NIH
20:10 according to all the folly that they **h** NIH
21: 7 seeing we **h** sworn by the LORD that *we* NIH
21:18 for the children of Israel **h** sworn, saying, NIH
Ru 1: 8 as ye **h** dealt with the dead, and with me. NIH
1:12 go *your way;* for I am too old to **h** 1961+3807.1
1:12 If I should say, I **h** hope, *if* I should have a 3426
1:12 *if* I should **h** a husband also to 1961+3807.1
2: 9 **h** I not charged the young men that *they* NIH
2: 9 drink of *that* which the young men **h** drawn. NIH
2:10 Why **h** I found grace in thine eyes, NIH
2:21 until they **h** ended all my harvest. NIH
3: 3 until he shall **h** done eating and drinking. NIH
3:18 in rest, until he **h** finished the thing *this* day. NIH
4: 9 that I **h** bought all that *was* Elimelech's, and NIH
4:10 of Mahlon, **h** I purchased to be my wife, NIH
1Sa 1:15 I **h** drunk neither wine nor strong drink, but NIH
1:15 **h** poured out my soul before the LORD. NIH
1:16 my complaint and grief **h** I spoken hitherto. NIH
1:20 *saying,* Because I **h** asked him of NIH
1:23 thee good; tarry until thou **h** weaned him; NIH
1:28 Therefore also I **h** lent him to the LORD; NIH
2: 5 *They that were* full **h** hired out themselves NIH
2:15 for he will not **h** sodden flesh of thee, but 3947
2:29 which I **h** commanded *in my* habitation; NIH
3:12 which I **h** spoken concerning his house: NIH
3:13 For I **h** told him that I will judge his house NIH
3:14 I **h** sworn unto the house of Eli, NIH
4: 9 unto the Hebrews, as they **h** been to you: NIH
5:10 They **h** brought about the ark of the God of NIH
6:21 The Philistines **h** brought again the ark of NIH
7: 6 said there, We **h** sinned against the LORD. NIH
8: 7 for they **h** not rejected thee, but they have NIH
8: 7 not rejected thee, but they **h** rejected me, NIH
8: 8 According to all the works which they **h** NIH
8: 8 wherewith they **h** forsaken me, and NIH
8:18 of your king which ye shall **h** chosen you; NIH
8:19 Nay, but we will **h** a king over us; 1961
9: 7 to bring to the man of God: what **h** we? 854
9: 8 I **h** here at hand the fourth part of a shekel NIH
9:16 for I **h** looked upon my people, because NIH
9:24 for thee since *I* said, I **h** invited the people. NIH
10:19 ye **h** *this* day rejected your God, NIH
10:19 ye **h** said unto him, *Nay,* but set a king over NIH
11: 9 *time* the sun be hot, ye shall **h** help. 1961+3807.1
12: 1 I **h** hearkened unto your voice in all that ye NIH
12: 1 said unto me, and **h** made a king over you. NIH
12: 2 I **h** walked before you from my childhood NIH
12: 3 whose ox **h** I taken? or whose ass have I NIH
12: 3 or whose ass **h** I taken? or whom have I NIH
12: 3 or whom **h** I defrauded? whom have I NIH
12: 3 whom **h** I oppressed? or of whose hand NIH
12: 3 of whose hand **h** I received *any* bribe to NIH
12: 5 that ye **h** not found ought in my hand. NIH
12:10 said, We **h** sinned, because we have NIH
12:10 because we **h** forsaken the LORD, and NIH

H

1Sa 12:10 and **h** served Baalim and Ashtaroth: NIH
12:13 behold the king whom ye **h** chosen, NIH
12:13 ye have chosen, *and* whom ye **h** desired: NIH
12:17 which ye **h** done in the sight of the LORD, NIH
12:19 for we **h** added unto all our sins *this* evil, NIH
12:20 ye **h** done all this wickedness: yet turn not NIH
13:12 I **h** not made supplication unto the LORD: NIH
13:13 for now would the LORD **h** established NIH
14:29 how mine eyes **h** been enlightened, because NIH
14:33 he said, Ye **h** transgressed: roll a great stone NIH
15: 3 utterly destroy all that they **h**, and 3807.1
15:11 It repenteth me that I **h** set up Saul to be NIH
15:13 I **h** performed the commandment of NIH
15:15 They **h** brought them from the Amalekites: NIH
15:15 and the rest we **h** utterly destroyed. NIH
15:20 I **h** obeyed the voice of the LORD, and NIH
15:20 **h** gone the way which the LORD sent me, NIH
15:20 **h** brought Agag the king of Amalek, and NIH
15:20 and **h** utterly destroyed the Amalekites. NIH
15:21 the chief of the things which should **h** been NIH
15:24 Saul said unto Samuel, I **h** sinned: for I NIH
15:24 for I **h** transgressed the commandment of NIH
15:30 he said, I **h** sinned: *yet* honour me now, NIH
16: 1 seeing I **h** rejected him from reigning over NIH
16: 1 for I **h** provided me a king among his sons. NIH
16: 7 of his stature; because I **h** refused him: NIH
16:18 I **h** seen a son of Jesse the Beth-lehemite, NIH
17:25 **H** ye seen this man that is come up? NIH
17:29 David said, What **h** I now done? *Is there* not NIH
17:39 for I **h** not proved *them.* And David put NIH
18: 8 They **h** ascribed unto David ten thousands, NIH
18: 8 and to me they **h** ascribed *but* thousands: NIH
18: 8 and *what* can he **h** more but the kingdom? 3807.1
18:19 daughter should **h** been given to David, NIH
19: 4 his works **h** *been* to thee-ward very good: NIH
20: 1 and said before Jonathan, What **h** I done? NIH
20: 3 Thy father certainly knoweth that I **h** found NIH
20: 7 *It is* well; thy servant shall **h** peace: NIH
20:12 when I **h** sounded my father about to NIH
20:23 the matter which thou and I **h** spoken of, NIH
20:29 and now, if I **h** found favour in thine eyes, NIH
20:42 forasmuch as we **h** sworn both of us in NIH
21: 2 I send thee, and what I **h** commanded thee: NIH
21: 2 I **h** appointed *my* servants to such and NIH
21: 4 if the young men **h** kept themselves at least NIH
21: 5 Of a truth women ***h*** *been* kept from us about NIH
21: 8 for I **h** neither brought my sword nor my NIH
21:14 *then* **h** ye brought him to me? NIH
21:15 ***H*** I need of mad men, that ye have brought NIH
21:15 that ye **h** brought this *fellow* to play the mad NIH
22: 8 That all of you **h** conspired against me, and NIH
22:13 Why **h** ye conspired against me, thou and NIH
22:22 I **h** occasioned *the death* of all the persons NIH
23:21 the LORD; for ye **h compassion** on me. 2550
23:27 come; for the Philistines **h** invaded the land. NIH
24:10 this day thine eyes **h** seen how that NIH
24:11 mine hand, and I **h** not sinned against thee; NIH
24:17 me good, whereas I **h** rewarded thee evil. NIH
25: 7 now I **h** heard that thou hast shearers: NIH
25:11 and my flesh that I **h** killed for my shearers, NIH
25:21 Surely in vain **h** I kept all that this *fellow* NIH
25:30 when the LORD shall **h** done to my lord NIH
25:30 and shall **h** appointed thee ruler over Israel; NIH
25:31 when the LORD shall **h** dealt well with my NIH
25:35 I **h** hearkened to thy voice, and NIH
25:35 to thy voice, and **h** accepted thy person. NIH
26:16 to die, because ye **h** not kept your master, NIH
26:18 for what **h** I done? or what evil *is* in mine NIH
26:19 If the LORD **h** stirred thee up against me, NIH
26:19 for they **h** driven me out *this* day from NIH
26:21 said Saul, I **h** sinned: return, my son David: NIH
26:21 I **h** played the fool, and have erred NIH
26:21 played the fool, and **h** erred exceedingly. NIH
27: 5 If I **h** now found grace in thine eyes, NIH
27:10 Whither **h** ye made a road to day? NIH
28: 9 how he hath cut off those that **h** familiar NIH
28:15 therefore I **h** called thee, that *thou* mayest NIH
28:21 I **h** put my life in thy hand, and NIH
28:21 **h** hearkened unto thy words which thou NIH
28:22 eat, that thou mayest **h** strength, 1961+871.1
29: 3 I **h** found no *fault* in him since he fell *unto* NIH
29: 6 for I **h** not found evil in thee since the day NIH
29: 8 David said unto Achish, But what **h** I done? NIH
29: 8 so long as I **h** been with thee unto this day, NIH
29: 9 the princes of the Philistines **h** said, NIH
29:10 up early in the morning, and **h light**, depart. 215
30:22 them *ought* of the spoil that we **h** recovered, NIH
2Sa 1:10 and **h** brought them hither unto my lord. NIH
1:16 I **h** slain the LORD'S anointed. NIH
2: 5 that ye **h** shewed this kindness unto your NIH
2: 5 your lord, *even* unto Saul, and **h** buried him. NIH
2: 6 this kindness, because ye **h** done this thing. NIH
2: 7 also the house of Judah **h** anointed me king NIH
3: 8 **h** not delivered thee into the hand of David, NIH
4: 6 *as though* they would **h** fetched wheat; NIH
4:10 is dead, thinking to **h** brought good tidings, NIH
4:10 who *thought* that I would **h** given him a NIH
4:11 when wicked men **h** slain a righteous person NIH
7: 6 Whereas I **h** not dwelt in *any* house since NIH
7: 6 but **h** walked in a tent and in a tabernacle. NIH
7: 7 In all *the places* wherein I **h** walked with all NIH
7: 9 **h** cut off all thine enemies out of thy sight, NIH
7: 9 of thy sight, and **h** made thee a great name, NIH
7:11 **h** caused thee to rest from all thine enemies. NIH
7:22 according to all that we **h** heard with our NIH
9: 9 I **h** given unto thy master's son all that NIH
9:10 thy master's son may **h** food to eat: 1961+3807.1
12: 8 I would moreover **h** given unto thee such NIH
12:13 unto Nathan, I **h** sinned against the LORD. NIH
12:27 I **h** fought against Rabbah, and have taken NIH
12:27 and **h** taken the city of waters. NIH
13: 9 Amnon said, **H out** all men from me. 3318
13:28 **h** not I commanded you? be courageous, NIH
13:32 Let not my lord suppose *that* they **h** slain all NIH
14:15 *it is* because the people **h** made me afraid: NIH

2Sa 14:21 unto Joab, Behold now, I **h** done this thing: NIH
14:22 To day thy servant knoweth that I **h** found NIH
14:29 sent for Joab, to **h** sent him to the king; NIH
14:31 Wherefore **h** thy servants set my field on NIH
14:32 *it had been* good for me *to* **h** *been* there still: NIH
15: 7 which I **h** vowed unto the LORD, NIH
15:26 if he thus say, I **h** no delight in thee; behold, NIH
15:34 as I ***h*** *been* thy father's servant hitherto, so NIH
15:36 *they* **h** there with them their two sons, NIH
16:10 the king said, What **h** I to do with you, 3807.1
16:19 as I **h** served in thy father's presence, so NIH
17:15 of Israel; and thus and thus **h** I counselled. NIH
18:11 I would **h** given thee ten *shekels of* silver, NIH
18:13 Otherwise I should **h** wrought falsehood NIH
18:13 thou thyself wouldest **h** set thyself against NIH
18:18 I **h** no son to keep my name in 3807.1
19: 5 which *this* day **h** saved thy life, and NIH
19:20 For thy servant doth know that I **h** sinned: NIH
19:22 David said, What **h** I to do with you, 3807.1
19:28 **h** I yet to cry any more unto the king? 3426
19:29 I **h** said, Thou and Ziba divide the land. NIH
19:34 said unto the king, How long **h** I to live, NIH
19:41 Why **h** our brethren the men of Judah stolen NIH
19:41 **h** brought the king, and his household, and NIH
19:42 **h** we eaten at all of the king's *cost?* or NIH
19:43 We **h** ten parts in the king, and we have 3807.1
19:43 and we **h** also more *right* in David than ye: NIH
20: 1 and said, We **h** no part in David, 3807.1
20: 1 neither **h** we inheritance in the son of 3807.1
21: 4 We will **h** no silver nor gold of Saul, 3807.1
21:16 *with* a new *sword,* thought to **h** slain David. NIH
22:22 For I **h** kept the ways of the LORD, and NIH
22:22 and **h** not wickedly departed from my God. NIH
22:24 and **h** kept myself from mine iniquity. NIH
22:30 For by thee I **h** run *through* a troop: by my NIH
22:30 a troop: by my God **h** I leaped over a wall. NIH
22:38 I **h** pursued mine enemies, and NIH
22:39 I **h** consumed them, and wounded them, NIH
24:10 I **h** sinned greatly *in* that I have done: NIH
24:10 I have sinned greatly *in* that I **h** done: NIH
24:10 of thy servant; for I **h** done very foolishly. NIH
24:17 Lo, I **h** sinned, and I have done wickedly: NIH
24:17 Lo, I have sinned, and I **h** done wickedly: NIH
24:17 these sheep, what **h** they done? let thine NIH
1Ki 1:35 I **h** appointed him to be ruler over Israel and NIH
1:44 they **h** caused him to ride upon the king's NIH
1:45 Nathan the prophet **h** anointed him king in NIH
1:45 rang again. This *is* the noise that ye **h** heard. NIH
2:14 I **h** somewhat to say unto thee. 3807.1
2:23 if Adonijah **h** not spoken this word against NIH
2:42 unto me, The word *that* I **h** heard *is* good. NIH
2:43 the commandment that I **h** charged thee NIH
3:12 Behold, I **h** done according to thy word: lo, NIH
3:12 I **h** given thee a wise and an understanding NIH
3:13 I **h** also given thee *that* which thou hast not NIH
5: 8 I **h** considered *the things* which thou sentest NIH
8:13 I **h** surely built thee a house to dwell in, NIH
8:20 **h** built a house for the name of the LORD NIH
8:21 I **h** set there a place for the ark, wherein *is* NIH
8:27 how much less this house that I **h** builded? NIH
8:28 Yet **h** thou **respect** unto the prayer of thy 6437
8:33 because they **h** sinned against thee, and NIH
8:35 no rain, because they **h** sinned against thee; NIH
8:43 which I **h** builded, is called by thy name. NIH
8:44 *toward* the house that I **h** built for thy name: NIH
8:47 We **h** sinned, and have done perversely, NIH
8:47 We have sinned, and **h** done perversely, NIH
8:47 we **h** committed wickedness; NIH
8:48 and the house which I **h** built for thy name: NIH
8:50 forgive thy people that **h** sinned against NIH
8:50 all their transgressions wherein they **h** NIH
8:50 that they may **h compassion** on them: 7355
8:59 wherewith I **h** made supplication before NIH
9: 3 I **h** heard thy prayer and thy supplication, NIH
9: 3 I **h** hallowed this house, which thou hast NIH
9: 4 to do according to all that I **h** commanded NIH
9: 6 *and* my statutes which I **h** set before you, NIH
9: 7 will I cut off Israel out of the land which I **h** NIH
9: 7 which I **h** hallowed for my name, NIH
9: 9 **h** taken hold upon other gods, and NIH
9: 9 and **h** worshipped them, and served them: NIH
11:11 my statutes, which I **h** commanded thee, NIH
11:13 and for Jerusalem's sake, which I **h** chosen. NIH
11:32 (But he shall **h** one tribe for my 1961+3807.1
11:32 the city which I **h** chosen out of all NIH
11:33 Because that they **h** forsaken me, and NIH
11:33 **h** worshipped Ashtoreth the goddess of NIH
11:33 **h** not walked in my ways, to do *that* which NIH
11:36 that David my servant may **h** a 1961+3807.1
11:36 the city which I **h** chosen me to put my NIH
12: 9 this people, who **h** spoken to me, saying, NIH
12:16 What portion **h** we in David? 3807.1
12:16 neither ***h*** *we* inheritance in the son of Jesse: NIH
14:15 because they **h** made their groves, NIH
15:19 I **h** sent unto thee a present of silver and NIH
17: 4 I **h** commanded the ravens to feed thee NIH
17: 9 I **h** commanded a widow woman there to NIH
17:12 I **h** not a cake, but a handful of 3426+3807.1
17:18 What **h** I to do with thee, O thou man of 3807.1
18: 9 he said, What **h** I sinned, that thou wouldest NIH
18:18 he answered, I **h** not troubled Israel; but NIH
18:18 in that ye **h** forsaken the commandments of NIH
18:36 *that* I **h** done all these things at thy word. NIH
19:10 I **h** been very jealous for the LORD God of NIH
19:10 for the children of Israel **h** forsaken thy NIH
19:14 I **h** been very jealous for the LORD God of NIH
19:14 the children of Israel **h** forsaken thy NIH
19:18 Yet I **h** left *me* seven thousand in Israel, NIH
19:18 all the knees which **h** not bowed unto Baal, NIH
19:20 Go back again: for what **h** I done to thee? NIH
20: 4 to thy saying, I *am* thine, and all that I **h**. 3807.1
20: 5 Although I **h** sent unto thee, saying, NIH
20:28 the LORD, Because the Syrians **h** said, NIH
20:31 we **h** heard that the kings of the house of NIH
21: 2 that I may **h** it for a garden of 1961+3807.1

1Ki 21:20 I **h** found *thee:* because thou hast sold NIH
22:11 the Syrians, until *thou* **h** consumed them. NIH
22:17 the hills, as sheep that **h** not a shepherd: 3807.1
22:17 the LORD said, These **h** no master: 3807.1
2Ki 2:21 saith the LORD, I **h** healed these waters; NIH
3:13 king of Israel, What **h** I to do with thee? 3807.1
3:23 surely slain, and they **h** smitten one another: NIH
3:27 he took his eldest son that should **h** reigned NIH
5: 6 I **h** *therewith* sent Naaman my servant to NIH
5:13 wouldest thou not **h** done *it?* how much NIH
7:12 I will now shew you what the Syrians **h** NIH
7:17 hand he leaned to **h the charge of** the gate: 5921
9: 3 I **h** anointed thee king over Israel. NIH
9: 5 he said, I **h** an errand to thee, O captain. 3807.1
9: 6 I **h** anointed thee king over the people of NIH
9:12 I **h** anointed thee king over Israel. NIH
9:26 Surely I **h** seen yesterday the blood of NIH
10: 8 They **h** brought the heads of the king's sons. NIH
10:19 for I **h** a great sacrifice *to do* to Baal; 3807.1
10:24 *If* any of the men whom I **h** brought into NIH
11:15 unto them, **H** her **forth** without the ranges: 3318
13:17 in Aphek, till *thou* **h** consumed *them.* NIH
13:19 *Thou* shouldest **h** smitten five or six times; NIH
17:38 the covenant that I **h** made with you ye shall NIH
18:14 of Assyria to Lachish, saying, I **h** offended; NIH
18:20 *I* **h** counsel and strength for the war. NIH
18:34 **h** they delivered Samaria out of mine hand? NIH
18:35 that **h** delivered their country out of mine NIH
19: 6 of the king of Assyria **h** blasphemed me. NIH
19:11 thou hast heard what the kings of Assyria **h** NIH
19:12 **H** the gods of the nations delivered them NIH
19:12 them which my fathers **h** destroyed; NIH
19:17 the kings of Assyria **h** destroyed the nations NIH
19:18 **h** cast their gods into the fire: for they *were* NIH
19:18 and stone: therefore they **h** destroyed them. NIH
19:20 Sennacherib king of Assyria I **h** heard. NIH
19:24 I **h** digged and drunk strange waters, and NIH
19:24 with the sole of my feet **h** I dried up all NIH
19:25 Hast thou not heard long ago *how* I **h** done NIH
19:25 *and* of ancient times that I **h** formed it? NIH
19:25 now **h** I brought it to pass, that thou NIH
20: 3 remember now how I **h** walked before thee NIH
20: 3 and **h** done *that* which *is* good in thy sight. NIH
20: 5 I **h** heard thy prayer, I have seen thy tears: NIH
20: 5 I have heard thy prayer, I **h** seen thy tears: NIH
20: 9 This sign shalt thou **h** of the LORD, 3807.1
20:15 he said, What **h** they seen in thine house? NIH
20:15 All *the things* that *are* in mine house **h** they NIH
20:15 there is nothing among my treasures that I **h** NIH
20:17 *that* which thy fathers **h** laid up in store unto NIH
21: 7 which I **h** chosen out of all tribes of Israel, NIH
21: 8 according to all that I **h** commanded them, NIH
21:15 Because they **h** done *that* which *was* evil in NIH
21:15 **h** provoked me to anger, since the day their 1961
22: 4 which the keepers of the door **h** gathered of NIH
22: 5 that **h** the oversight of the house of NIH
22: 8 I **h** found the book of the law in the house NIH
22: 9 Thy servants **h** gathered the money that was NIH
22: 9 **h** delivered it into the hand of them that do NIH
22: 9 that **h** the **oversight** *of* the house of 6485
22:13 our fathers **h** not hearkened unto the words NIH
22:17 Because they **h** forsaken me, and have burnt NIH
22:17 and **h** burnt incense unto other gods, NIH
22:19 I also **h** heard *thee,* saith the LORD. NIH
23:27 as I **h** removed Israel, and will cast off this NIH
23:27 will cast off this city Jerusalem which I **h** NIH
1Ch 11:19 men that **h put** their lives **in jeopardy**? 871.1
15:12 Israel unto *the place that* I **h** prepared for it. NIH
17: 5 For I **h** not dwelt in a house since the day NIH
17: 5 **h** gone from tent to tent, and from *one* NIH
17: 6 Wheresoever I **h** walked with all Israel, NIH
17: 6 Why **h** ye not built me a house of cedars? NIH
17: 8 I **h** been with thee whithersoever thou hast NIH
17: 8 **h** cut off all thine enemies from before thee, NIH
17: 8 **h** made thee a name like the name of NIH
17:20 according to all that we **h** heard with our NIH
21: 8 I **h** sinned greatly, because I have done this NIH
21: 8 sinned greatly, because I **h** done this thing: NIH
21: 8 of thy servant; for I **h** done very foolishly. NIH
21:17 even I *it is* that **h** sinned and done evil NIH
21:17 *as for* these sheep, what **h** they done? NIH
22:14 in my trouble I **h** prepared for the house of NIH
22:14 timber also and stone **h** I prepared; and NIH
28: 6 for I **h** chosen him to be my son, and I will NIH
29: 2 Now I **h** prepared with all my might for NIH
29: 3 I **h** set my affection to the house of my God, NIH
29: 3 I **h** of mine own proper good, *of* gold and 3426
29: 3 *which* I **h** given to the house of my God, NIH
29: 3 above all *that* I **h** prepared for the holy NIH
29:14 of thee, and of thine own **h** we given thee. NIH
29:16 all this store that we **h** prepared to build NIH
29:17 in the uprightness of mine heart I **h** NIH
29:17 and now **h** I seen with joy thy people, NIH
29:19 *for* the which I **h** made provision. NIH
2Ch 1:11 my people, over whom I **h** made thee king: NIH
1:12 such as none of the kings **h** had that *have* NIH
1:12 such as none of the kings have had that **h** NIH
1:12 neither shall there any after thee **h** the like. 1961
2:13 now I **h** sent a cunning man, endued with NIH
6: 2 I **h** built a house of habitation for thee, and NIH
6: 6 I **h** chosen Jerusalem, that my name might NIH
6: 6 **h** chosen David to be over my people Israel. NIH
6:10 **h** built the house for the name of NIH
6:11 in it **h** I put the ark, wherein *is* the covenant NIH
6:18 how much less this house which I **h** built? NIH
6:19 **H respect** therefore to the prayer of thy 6437
6:24 because they **h** sinned against thee; NIH
6:26 no rain, because they **h** sinned against thee; NIH
6:33 may know that this house which I **h** built is NIH
6:34 the house which I **h** built for thy name; NIH
6:37 saying, We **h** sinned, we have done amiss, NIH
6:37 we **h** done amiss, and have dealt wickedly; NIH
6:37 we have done amiss, and **h** dealt wickedly; NIH
6:38 whither they **h** carried them captives, and NIH
6:38 toward the house which I **h** built for thy NIH

2Ch 6:39 forgive thy people which **h** sinned against NIH
7:12 I **h** heard thy prayer, and have chosen this NIH
7:12 **h** chosen this place to myself for a house of NIH
7:16 For now **h** I chosen and sanctified this NIH
7:17 do according to all that I **h** commanded NIH
7:18 according as I **h** covenanted with David thy NIH
7:19 which I **h** set before you, and shall go and NIH
7:20 roots out of my land which I **h** given them; NIH
7:20 which I **h** sanctified for my name, NIH
10: 9 which **h** spoken to me, saying, NIH
10:16 What portion **h** we in David? 3807.1
10:16 *we* **h** none inheritance in the son of Jesse: NIH
12: 5 Ye **h** forsaken me, and *therefore* have I also NIH
12: 5 **h** I also left you in the hand of Shishak. NIH
12: 7 They **h** humbled themselves; NIH
13: 7 **h** strengthened themselves against NIH
13: 9 **H** ye not cast out the priests of the LORD, NIH
13: 9 **h** made you priests after the manner of NIH
13:10 *is* our God, and we **h** not forsaken him; NIH
13:11 the LORD our God; but ye **h** forsaken him. NIH
14: 7 because we **h** sought the LORD our God, NIH
14: 7 we **h** sought *him,* and he hath given us rest NIH
14:11 with many, *or* with *them that* **h** no power: NIH
16: 3 behold, I **h** sent thee silver and gold; go, NIH
16: 9 from henceforth thou shalt **h** wars. 3426+5973
18:16 as sheep that **h** no shepherd: 3807.1
18:16 the LORD said, These **h** no master; 3807.1
20: 8 **h** built thee a sanctuary therein for thy NIH
20:12 for we **h** no might against this great 871.1
21:15 thou *shalt* **h** great sickness by disease of thy NIH
23:14 said unto them, **H** her **forth** of the ranges: 3318
24:20 because ye **h** forsaken the LORD, he hath NIH
25: 9 which I **h** given to the army of Israel? NIH
28: 9 ye **h** slain them in a rage *that* reacheth up NIH
28:11 which ye **h** taken captive of your brethren: NIH
28:13 for whereas we **h** offended against NIH
29: 6 For our fathers **h** trespassed, and done *that* NIH
29: 6 **h** forsaken him, and have turned away their NIH
29: 6 **h** turned away their faces from NIH
29: 7 Also they **h** shut up the doors of the porch, NIH
29: 7 **h** not burnt incense nor offered burnt NIH
29: 9 our fathers **h** fallen by the sword, and NIH
29:18 We **h** cleansed all the house of the LORD, NIH
29:19 **h** we prepared and sanctified, and behold, NIH
29:31 Now ye **h** consecrated yourselves unto NIH
31:10 *we* **h** had enough to eat, and have left NIH
31:10 have had enough to eat, and **h** left plenty: NIH
32:13 my fathers **h** done unto all the people of NIH
32:17 As the gods of the nations of *other* lands **h** NIH
33: 7 which I **h** chosen before all the tribes of NIH
33: 8 land which I **h** appointed for your fathers; NIH
33: 8 that they will take heed to do all that I **h** NIH
34:15 I **h** found the book of the law in the house NIH
34:17 they **h** gathered together the money that was NIH
34:17 **h** delivered it into the hand of the overseers, NIH
34:21 our fathers **h** not kept the word of NIH
34:24 which they **h** read before the king of Judah: NIH
34:25 Because they **h** forsaken me, and NIH
34:25 and **h** burned incense unto other gods, NIH
34:27 I **h** even heard *thee* also, saith the LORD. NIH
35:21 saying, What **h** I to do with thee, 3807.1
35:21 but against the house wherewith I **h** war: NIH
35:23 the king said to his servants, **H** me **away**; 5674
Ezr 4: 3 You **h** nothing to do with us to build a 3807.1
4:12 **h** set up the walls *thereof,* and joined NIH
4:14 **h maintenance** from *the king's* 4415+4416
4:14 therefore **h** we sent and certified the king; NIH
4:15 that they **h** moved sedition within the same NIH
4:16 by this means thou shalt **h** no 383+3807.2
4:19 and sedition ***h*** *been* made therein. NIH
4:20 There **h** been mighty kings also over NIH
4:20 which **h** ruled over all *countries* beyond NIH
6: 9 that which *they* **h need of,** both young 2818
6:11 Also I **h** made a decree, that whosoever NIH
6:12 I Darius **h** made a decree; let it be done with NIH
7:15 his counsellers **h** freely offered unto NIH
7:20 which thou shalt **h occasion** to bestow, 5308
9: 1 **h** not separated themselves from the people NIH
9: 2 For they **h** taken of their daughters for NIH
9: 2 that the holy seed **h** mingled themselves NIH
9: 7 Since the days of our fathers ***h*** *we been* in a NIH
9: 7 for our iniquities **h** we, our kings, *and* NIH
9:10 for we **h** forsaken thy commandments, NIH
9:11 which **h** filled it from one end to another NIH
10: 2 We **h** trespassed against our God, and NIH
10: 2 **h** taken strange wives of the people of NIH
10:10 Ye **h** transgressed, and have taken strange NIH
10:10 and **h** taken strange wives, NIH
10:13 for we are many that **h** transgressed in 3807.1
10:14 let all *them* which **h** taken strange wives in NIH
Ne 1: 6 of Israel, which we **h** sinned against thee: NIH
1: 6 both I and my father's house **h** sinned. NIH
1: 7 We **h** dealt very corruptly against thee, and NIH
1: 7 **h** not kept the commandments, nor NIH
1: 9 will bring them unto the place that I **h** NIH
2: 5 if thy servant **h** found favour in thy sight, NIH
2:20 you **h** no portion, nor right, nor memorial, NIH
4: 5 for they **h** provoked *thee* to anger before NIH
5: 3 We **h** mortgaged our lands, vineyards, and NIH
5: 4 We **h** borrowed money for the king's NIH
5: 5 *to redeem them;* for other men **h** our lands NIH
5: 8 We after our ability **h** redeemed our NIH
5:14 my brethren **h** not eaten the bread of NIH
5:19 *according to* all that I **h** done for this NIH
6:13 might **h** *matter* for an evil report, 1961+3807.1
6:14 the prophets, that would **h** put me in fear. 1961
9:33 hast done right, but we **h** done wickedly: NIH
9:34 Neither **h** our kings, our princes, our priests, NIH
9:35 For they **h** not served thee in their kingdom, NIH
9:37 also they **h dominion** over our bodies, and 4910
10:37 that the same Levites *might* **h** the tithes in NIH
13:14 wipe not out my good deeds that I **h** done NIH
13:29 because they **h** defiled the priesthood, and NIH
Est 1:18 which **h** heard of the deed of the queen. NIH
3: 9 of those that **h** the charge of the business, NIH

Est 4:11 I **h** not been called to come in unto the king NIH
5: 4 unto the banquet that I **h** prepared for him. NIH
5: 8 If I **h** found favour in the sight of the king, NIH
7: 3 and said, If I **h** found favour in thy sight, NIH
8: 5 if I **h** found favour in his sight, and the thing NIH
8: 7 I **h** given Esther the house of Haman, and NIH
8: 7 him they **h** hanged upon the gallows, NIH
9: 1 of the Jews hoped to **h power** over them, 7980
9:12 The Jews **h** slain and destroyed five NIH
9:12 what **h** they done in the rest of the king's NIH
Job 1: 5 It may be that my sons **h** sinned, and NIH
1:15 they **h** slain the servants with the edge of NIH
1:17 **h** carried them away, yea, and slain NIH
3: 9 let it look for light, but ***h*** none; neither let it NIH
3:13 For now should I **h** lien *still* and been quiet, NIH
3:13 lien *still* and been quiet, I should **h** slept: NIH
4: 4 Thy words **h** upholden him that was falling, NIH
4: 8 Even as I **h** seen, they that plow iniquity, NIH
5: 3 I **h** seen the foolish taking root: but NIH
5:27 we **h** searched it, so it *is;* hear it, and NIH
6: 8 O that I might **h** my request; and *that* God 935
6:10 should I yet **h** comfort; yea, I would harden 1961
6:10 for I **h** not concealed the words of the Holy NIH
6:15 My brethren **h** dealt deceitfully as a brook, NIH
6:24 cause me to understand wherein I **h** erred. NIH
7:20 I **h** sinned; what shall I do unto thee, O thou NIH
8: 4 If thy children **h** sinned against him, and NIH
8: 4 he **h** cast them away for their transgression; NIH
8:18 *it* shall deny him, *saying,* I **h** not seen thee. NIH
10: 8 Thine hands **h** made me and fashioned me NIH
10:19 I should **h** been as though I had not been; I NIH
10:19 I should **h** been carried from the womb to NIH
12: 3 I **h** understanding as well as you; I *am* not 3807.1
13:18 Behold now, I **h** ordered *my* cause; I know NIH
14:15 thou wilt **h** a **desire** to the work of thine 3700
14:22 his flesh upon him shall **h pain**, and 3510
15:17 and that which I **h** seen I will declare; NIH
15:18 Which wise *men* **h** told from their fathers, NIH
15:18 told from their fathers, and **h** not hid *it:* NIH
16: 2 I **h** heard many such *things:* miserable NIH
16: 3 Shall vain words **h an end**? or 7093
16:10 They **h** gaped upon me with their mouth; NIH
16:10 they **h** smitten me upon the cheek NIH
16:10 they **h** gathered themselves together against NIH
16:15 I **h** sewed sackcloth upon my skin, and NIH
16:18 and let my cry **h** no place. 1961+3807.1
17:13 I **h** made my bed in the darkness. NIH
17:14 I **h** said to corruption, Thou *art* my father: NIH
18:17 and he shall **h** no name in the street. 3807.1
18:19 He shall neither **h** son nor nephew among 3807.1
19: 3 These ten times **h** ye reproached me: NIH
19: 4 be it indeed *that* I **h** erred, mine error NIH
19:14 My kinsfolk **h** failed, and my familiar NIH
19:14 and my familiar friends **h** forgotten me. NIH
19:21 **H pity** upon me, have pity upon me, O ye 2603
19:21 upon me, **h pity** upon me, O ye my friends; 2603
20: 3 I **h** heard the check of my reproach, and NIH
20: 7 they which **h** seen him shall say, Where *is* NIH
21: 3 and after that I **h** spoken, mock on. NIH
21:15 what profit should we **h**, if we pray unto NIH
21:29 **H** ye not asked them that go by the way? NIH
22: 9 the arms of the fatherless **h** been broken. NIH
22:15 the old way which wicked men **h** trodden? NIH
22:25 and thou shalt **h** plenty of silver. 3807.1
22:26 shalt thou **h** thy **delight** in the Almighty, 6026
23:11 his steps, his way **h** I kept, and not declined. NIH
23:12 Neither **h** I gone back from NIH
23:12 I **h** esteemed the words of his mouth more NIH
24: 7 that *they* **h** no covering in the cold. NIH
24:19 *so doth* the grave *those which* **h** sinned. NIH
27:12 all ye yourselves **h** seen *it;* why then are ye NIH
28: 8 The lion's whelps **h** not trodden it, nor NIH
28:22 We **h** heard the fame thereof with our ears. NIH
30: 1 now *they that are* younger than I **h** me in 3807.1
30: 1 whose fathers I would **h** disdained to have NIH
30: 1 to **h** set with the dogs of my flock. 3807.1
30:11 they **h** also let loose the bridle before me. NIH
30:13 forward my calamity, they **h** no helper. 3807.1
30:16 the days of affliction **h** taken hold upon me. NIH
31: 5 If I **h** walked with vanity, or *if* my foot hath NIH
31: 9 If mine heart **h** been deceived by a woman, NIH
31: 9 or *if* I **h** laid wait at my neighbour's door; NIH
31:16 If I **h** withheld the poor from *their* desire, or NIH
31:16 or **h** caused the eyes of the widow to fail; NIH
31:17 Or **h** eaten my morsel myself alone, and NIH
31:18 I **h** guided her from my mother's womb;) NIH
31:19 If I **h** seen *any* perish for want of clothing, NIH
31:20 If his loins **h** not blessed me, and *if* he were NIH
31:21 If I **h** lift up my hand against the fatherless, NIH
31:24 If I **h** made gold my hope, or have said to NIH
31:24 or **h** said to the fine gold, *Thou art* my NIH
31:28 for I should **h** denied the God *that is* above. NIH
31:30 (Neither **h** I suffered my mouth to sin by NIH
31:39 If I **h** eaten the fruits thereof without NIH
31:39 **h** caused the owners thereof to lose their NIH
32:13 ye should say, We **h** found out wisdom: NIH
33: 2 Behold now I **h** opened my mouth, NIH
33: 8 I **h** heard the voice of *thy* words, NIH
33:24 going down *to* the pit: I **h** found a ransom. NIH
33:27 I **h** sinned, and perverted *that which was* NIH
34: 2 and give ear unto me, ye that **h knowledge**. 3045
34:31 I **h** borne *chastisement,* I will not offend NIH
34:32 if I **h** done iniquity, I will do no more. NIH
35: 3 *and,* What profit shall I **h**, *if I be cleansed* NIH
36: 2 I will shew thee that *I* ***h*** yet to speak on NIH
36: 9 their transgressions that they **h** exceeded. NIH
36:16 would he **h** removed thee out of the strait NIH
38:17 **H** the gates of death been opened unto thee? NIH
38:23 Which I **h** reserved against the time of NIH
39: 6 Whose house I **h** made the wilderness, and NIH
40: 5 Once **h** I spoken; but I will not answer: yea, NIH
42: 3 therefore **h** I uttered that I understood not; NIH
42: 5 I **h** heard of thee by the hearing of the ear: NIH
42: 7 for ye **h** not spoken of me *the thing that is* NIH
42: 8 in that ye **h** not spoken of me *the thing* NIH

Ps 2: 4 the LORD shall **h** them in derision. 3807.1
2: 6 Yet **h** I set my king upon my holy hill of NIH
2: 7 Thou *art* my Son; *this* day **h** I begotten thee. NIH
3: 6 that **h** set *themselves* against me round NIH
4: 1 **h mercy** upon me, and hear my prayer. 2603
5:10 for they **h** rebelled against thee. NIH
6: 2 **H mercy** upon me, O LORD; for I *am* 2603
7: 3 O LORD my God, if I **h** done this; if there NIH
7: 4 If I **h** rewarded evil *unto* him that was at NIH
7: 4 I **h** delivered him that without cause is mine NIH
8: 6 Thou **madest** him **to h dominion** over 4910
9:13 **H mercy** upon me, O LORD; consider my 2603
10: 2 let them be taken in the devices that they **h** NIH
12: 4 Who **h** said, With our tongue will we NIH
13: 4 mine enemy say, I **h** prevailed against him; NIH
13: 5 I **h** trusted in thy mercy; my heart shall NIH
14: 1 are corrupt, they **h** done abominable works, NIH
14: 4 **H** all the workers of iniquity no knowledge? NIH
14: 6 You **h** shamed the counsel of the poor, NIH
16: 6 pleasant *places;* yea, I **h** a goodly heritage. 5921
16: 8 I **h** set the LORD always before me: NIH
17: 4 by the word of thy lips I **h** kept *me from* NIH
17: 6 I **h** called upon thee, for thou wilt hear me, NIH
17:11 They **h** now compassed us *in* our steps: NIH
17:11 they **h** set their eyes bowing down to NIH
17:14 *which* **h** their portion in *this* life, and NIH
18:21 For I **h** kept the ways of the LORD, and NIH
18:21 and **h** not wickedly departed from my God. NIH
18:29 For by thee I **h** run *through* a troop; and NIH
18:29 and by my God **h** I leaped over a wall. NIH
18:37 I **h** pursued mine enemies, and NIH
18:38 I **h** wounded them that they were not able to NIH
18:43 a people *whom* I **h** not known shall serve NIH
19:13 *sins;* let them not **h dominion** over me: 4910
22:12 Many bulls **h** compassed me: strong *bulls* of NIH
22:12 strong *bulls* of Bashan **h** beset me round. NIH
22:16 For dogs **h** compassed me: the assembly of NIH
22:16 the assembly of the wicked **h** inclosed me: NIH
25: 6 for they ***h*** *been* ever of old. NIH
25:16 Turn thee unto me, and **h mercy** upon me; 2603
26: 1 O LORD; for I **h** walked in mine integrity: NIH
26: 1 I **h** trusted also in the LORD; *therefore* NIH
26: 3 mine eyes: and I **h** walked in thy truth. NIH
26: 4 I **h** not sat with vain persons, neither will I NIH
26: 5 I **h** hated the congregation of evildoers; and NIH
26: 8 I **h** loved the habitation of thy house, and NIH
27: 4 One *thing* **h** I desired of the LORD, that NIH
27: 7 **h mercy** also upon me, and answer me. 2603
30:10 Hear, O LORD, and **h mercy** upon me: 2603
31: 4 Pull me out of the net that they **h** laid NIH
31: 6 I **h** hated them that regard lying vanities: NIH
31: 9 **H mercy** upon me, O LORD, for I am in 2603
31:13 For I **h** heard the slander of many: fear *was* NIH
31:17 O LORD; for I **h** called upon thee: NIH
32: 5 sin unto thee, and mine iniquity **h** I not hid. NIH
32: 9 *or* as the mule, *which* **h** no understanding: NIH
33:21 because we **h** trusted in his holy name. NIH
35: 7 For without cause **h** they hid for me their NIH
35: 7 *which* without cause they **h** digged for my NIH
35:25 not say in their hearts, Ah, so would we **h** it: NIH
35:25 let them not say, We **h** swallowed him up. NIH
37:14 The wicked **h** drawn out the sword, and NIH
37:14 **h** bent their bow, to cast down the poor and NIH
37:25 I **h** been young, and *now* am old; yet have I NIH
37:25 yet **h** I not seen the righteous forsaken, NIH
37:35 I **h** seen the wicked in great power, and NIH
38: 8 I **h** roared by reason of the disquietness of NIH
40: 9 I **h** preached righteousness in the great NIH
40: 9 lo, I **h** not refrained my lips, O LORD, NIH
40:10 I **h** not hid thy righteousness within my NIH
40:10 I **h** declared thy faithfulness and NIH
40:10 I **h** not concealed thy lovingkindness and NIH
40:12 For innumerable evils **h** compassed me NIH
40:12 mine iniquities **h** taken hold upon me, so NIH
41: 4 heal my soul; for I **h** sinned against thee. NIH
42: 3 My tears **h** been my meat day and night, NIH
44: 1 We **h** heard with our ears, O God, NIH
44: 1 with our ears, O God, our fathers **h** told us, NIH
44:17 yet **h** we not forgotten thee, neither have we NIH
44:17 neither **h** we dealt falsely in thy covenant. NIH
44:18 neither **h** our steps declined from thy way; NIH
44:20 If we **h** forgotten the name of our God, or NIH
45: 1 I speak of the things which I **h** made NIH
45: 8 *where*by they **h** made thee glad. NIH
48: 8 As we **h** heard, so have we seen in the city NIH
48: 8 **h** we seen in the city of the LORD of NIH
48: 9 We **h** thought of thy lovingkindness, NIH
49:14 the upright shall **h** dominion over them in NIH
50: 5 those that **h** made a covenant with me by NIH
50: 8 *to* ***h*** *been* continually before me. NIH
51: 1 **H mercy** upon me, O God, according to 2603
51: 4 **h** I sinned, and done *this* evil in thy sight: NIH
53: 1 are they, and **h** done abominable iniquity: NIH
53: 4 **H** the workers of iniquity no knowledge? NIH
53: 4 they eat bread: they **h** not called upon God. NIH
54: 3 they **h** not set God before them. Selah. NIH
55: 9 for I **h** seen violence and strife in the city. NIH
55:12 I could **h** borne *it:* neither *was it* he that NIH
55:12 then I would **h** hid myself from him: NIH
55:19 Because they **h** no changes, therefore 3807.1
56: 4 praise his word, in God I **h** put my trust; NIH
56:11 In God **h** I put my trust: I will not be afraid NIH
57: 6 They **h** prepared a net for my steps; my soul NIH
57: 6 they **h** digged a pit before me, into the midst NIH
59: 8 thou shalt **h** all the heathen **in derision**. 3932
62:11 God hath spoken once; twice **h** I heard this; NIH
63: 2 so *as* I **h** seen thee in the sanctuary. NIH
66:14 Which my lips **h** uttered, and my mouth NIH
68:13 Though ye **h** lien among the pots, *yet shall* NIH
68:24 They **h** seen thy goings, O God; even NIH
69: 7 Because for thy sake I **h** borne reproach; NIH
69:22 *that which should* ***h*** *been* for *their* welfare, NIH
69:35 may dwell there, and **h** it **in possession**. 3423
71: 6 By thee **h** I been holden up from the womb: NIH
71:17 hitherto **h** I declared thy wondrous works. NIH

H

Ps 71:18 until I **h** shewed thy strength unto *this* NIH
72: 8 He shall **h** dominion also from sea to sea, NIH
73: 7 they **h more than** heart could wish. 5674
73:13 Verily I **h** cleansed my heart *in* vain, and NIH
73:14 For all the day long **h** I been plagued, and NIH
73:25 Whom **h** I in heaven *but thee?* and 3807.1
73:28 I **h** put my trust in the Lord GOD, that *I* NIH
74: 7 They **h** cast fire into thy sanctuary, NIH
74: 7 they **h** defiled *by casting down* the dwelling NIH
74: 8 they **h** burnt up all the synagogues of God NIH
74:18 *that* the foolish people **h** blasphemed thy NIH
74:20 **H respect** unto the covenant: for the dark 5027
76: 5 are spoiled, they **h** slept their sleep: NIH
76: 5 none of the men of might **h** found their NIH
77: 5 I **h** considered the days of old, the years of NIH
78: 3 Which we **h** heard and known, and NIH
78: 3 and known, and our fathers **h** told us. NIH
79: 1 thy holy temple **h** they defiled; they have NIH
79: 1 they **h** laid Jerusalem on heaps. NIH
79: 2 The dead bodies of thy servants **h** they NIH
79: 3 Their blood **h** they shed like water round NIH
79: 6 Pour out thy wrath upon the heathen that **h** NIH
79: 6 upon the kingdoms that **h** not called upon NIH
79: 7 For they **h** devoured Jacob, and laid waste NIH
79:12 wherewith they **h** reproached thee, O Lord. NIH
81:14 I should soon **h** subdued their enemies, and NIH
81:15 The haters of the LORD should **h** NIH
81:15 but their time should **h** endured for ever. NIH
81:16 He should **h** fed them also with the finest of NIH
81:16 *with* honey out of the rock should I **h** NIH
82: 6 I **h** said, Ye *are* gods; and all of you *are* NIH
83: 2 and they that hate thee **h** lift up the head. NIH
83: 3 They **h** taken crafty counsel against thy NIH
83: 4 They **h** said, Come, and let us cut them off NIH
83: 5 For they **h** consulted together *with one* NIH
83: 8 they **h** holpen the children of Lot. Selah. 1961
85:10 and peace **h** kissed *each other.* NIH
86:14 the assemblies of violent *men* **h** sought after NIH
86:14 my soul; and **h** not set thee before them. NIH
86:16 O turn unto me, and **h mercy** upon me; 2603
88: 1 I **h** cried day *and* night before thee: NIH
88: 9 LORD, I **h** called daily upon thee, I have NIH
88: 9 I **h** stretched out my hands unto thee. NIH
88:13 unto thee **h** I cried, O LORD; and in NIH
88:16 goeth over me; thy terrors **h** cut me off. NIH
89: 2 For I **h** said, Mercy shall be built up for NIH
89: 3 I **h** made a covenant with my chosen, I have NIH
89: 3 I **h** sworn unto David my servant, NIH
89:19 saidst, I **h** laid help upon *one that is* mighty; NIH
89:19 I **h** exalted *one* chosen out of the people. NIH
89:20 I **h** found David my servant; with my holy NIH
89:20 with my holy oil **h** I anointed him: NIH
89:35 Once **h** I sworn by my holiness that I will NIH
89:51 Wherewith thine enemies **h** reproached, NIH
89:51 wherewith they **h** reproached the footsteps NIH
90:15 *and* the years *wherein* we **h** seen evil. NIH
93: 3 The floods **h** lifted up, O LORD, NIH
93: 3 the floods **h** lifted up their voice; NIH
94:20 Shall the throne of iniquity **h** fellowship NIH
95:10 *their* heart, and they **h** not known my ways: NIH
98: 3 all the ends of the earth **h** seen the salvation NIH
102: 9 For I **h** eaten ashes like bread, and NIH
102:13 Thou shalt arise, *and* **h mercy** upon Zion: 7355
102:27 *art* the same, and thy years shall **h** no end. NIH
104:12 By them shall the fowls of the heaven **h** NIH
104:33 to my God **while** I **h** my **being.** 5750+871.1
106: 6 We **h** sinned with our fathers, we have NIH
106: 6 we **h** committed iniquity, we have done NIH
106: 6 committed iniquity, we **h** done wickedly. NIH
109: 2 they **h** spoken against me *with* a lying NIH
109: 5 they **h** rewarded me evil for good, and NIH
111: 2 sought out of all them that **h** pleasure NIH
111:10 a good understanding **h** all they that do 3807.1
115: 5 They **h** mouths, but they speak not: 3807.1
115: 5 speak not: eyes **h** they, but they see not: 3807.1
115: 6 They **h** ears, but they hear not: 3807.1
115: 6 hear not: noses **h** they, but they smell not: 3807.1
115: 7 They *h* hands, but they handle not: feet *have* NIH
115: 7 feet *h* they, but they walk not: neither speak NIH
116:10 I believed, therefore **h** I spoken: I was NIH
118:26 we **h** blessed you out of the house of NIH
119: 6 when I **h** respect unto all thy NIH
119: 7 when I shall **h** learned thy righteous NIH
119:10 With my whole heart **h** I sought thee: O let NIH
119:11 Thy word **h** I hid in mine heart, that I might NIH
119:13 With my lips **h** I declared all the judgments NIH
119:14 I **h** rejoiced in the way of thy testimonies, NIH
119:15 thy precepts, and **h respect** unto thy ways. 5027
119:22 and contempt; for I **h** kept thy testimonies. NIH
119:26 I **h** declared my ways, and thou heardest NIH
119:30 I **h** chosen the way of truth: thy judgments NIH
119:30 of truth: thy judgments **h** I laid *before me.* NIH
119:31 I **h** stuck unto thy testimonies: O LORD, NIH
119:40 Behold, I **h** longed after thy precepts: NIH
119:42 So shall I **h** wherewith to answer him that NIH
119:43 my mouth; for I **h** hoped in thy judgments. NIH
119:47 in thy commandments, which I **h** loved. NIH
119:48 unto thy commandments, which I **h** loved; NIH
119:51 The proud **h** had me greatly in derision: NIH
119:51 *yet* **h** I not declined from thy law. NIH
119:52 of old, O LORD; and **h** comforted myself. NIH
119:54 Thy statutes **h** been my songs in the house NIH
119:55 I **h** remembered thy name, O LORD, in NIH
119:55 O LORD, in the night, and **h** kept thy law. NIH
119:57 I **h** said that *I* would keep thy words. NIH
119:61 The bands of the wicked **h** robbed me: *but* NIH
119:61 robbed me: *but* I **h** not forgotten thy law. NIH
119:66 for I **h** believed thy commandments. NIH
119:67 I went astray: but now **h** I kept thy word. NIH
119:69 The proud **h** forged a lie against me: *but* NIH
119:71 *It is* good for me that I **h** been afflicted; that NIH
119:73 Thy hands **h** made me and fashioned me: NIH
119:74 they see me; because I **h** hoped in thy word. NIH
119:79 and those that **h** known thy testimonies. NIH
119:85 The proud **h** digged pits for me, which *are* NIH

Ps 119:92 I should then **h** perished in mine affliction. NIH
119:94 save me; for I **h** sought thy precepts. NIH
119:95 The wicked **h** waited for me to destroy me: NIH
119:96 I **h** seen an end of all perfection: *but* NIH
119:99 I **h** more **understanding** than all my 7919
119:101 I **h** refrained my feet from every evil way, NIH
119:102 I **h** not departed from thy judgments: NIH
119:106 I **h** sworn, and I will perform *it,* that *I* will NIH
119:110 The wicked **h** laid a snare for me: yet I NIH
119:111 Thy testimonies **h** I taken as an heritage for NIH
119:112 I **h** inclined mine heart to perform thy NIH
119:117 I will **h respect** unto thy statutes 8159
119:121 I **h** done judgment and justice: leave me not NIH
119:126 to work: *for* they **h** made void thy law. NIH
119:133 let not any iniquity **h dominion** over me. 7980
119:139 mine enemies **h** forgotten thy words. NIH
119:143 Trouble and anguish **h** taken hold on me: NIH
119:152 I **h** known of old that thou hast founded NIH
119:161 Princes **h** persecuted me without a cause: NIH
119:165 Great peace **h** they which love thy law: 3807.1
119:166 I **h** hoped for thy salvation, and done thy NIH
119:168 I **h** kept thy precepts and thy testimonies: NIH
119:173 hand help me; for I **h** chosen thy precepts. NIH
119:174 I **h** longed for thy salvation, O LORD; and NIH
119:176 I **h** gone astray like a lost sheep; seek thy NIH
123: 2 our God, until that he **h mercy** upon us. 2603
123: 3 **H mercy** upon us, O LORD, have mercy 2603
123: 3 upon us, O LORD, **h mercy** upon us: 2603
129: 1 Many a time **h** they afflicted me from my NIH
129: 2 Many a time **h** they afflicted me from my NIH
129: 2 yet they **h** not prevailed against me. NIH
130: 1 Out of the depths **h** I cried unto thee, NIH
131: 2 Surely I **h** behaved and quieted myself, as a NIH
132:14 for ever: here will I dwell; for I **h** desired it. NIH
132:17 I **h** ordained a lamp for mine anointed. NIH
135:16 They **h** mouths, but they speak not; 3807.1
135:16 speak not; eyes **h** they, but they see not; 3807.1
135:17 They **h** ears, but they hear not; neither is 3807.1
140: 3 They **h** sharpened their tongues like a NIH
140: 4 who **h** purposed to overthrow my goings. NIH
140: 5 The proud **h** hid a snare for me, and cords; NIH
140: 5 cords; they **h** spread a net by the way side; NIH
140: 5 net by the way side; they **h** set grins for me. NIH
141: 9 Keep me from the snare *which* they **h** laid NIH
142: 3 In the way wherein I walked **h** they privily NIH
143: 3 in darkness, as those that **h** been long dead. NIH
146: 2 unto my God **while** I **h** *any* **being.** 5750+871.1
147:20 *for his* judgments, they **h** not known them. NIH
149: 9 this honour **h** all his saints. Praise ye 3807.1
Pr 1:14 among us; let us all **h** one purse: 1961+3807.1
1:24 Because I **h** called, and ye refused; I have NIH
1:24 I **h** stretched out my hand, and no man NIH
1:25 ye **h** set at nought all my counsel, and NIH
3:30 without cause, if he **h** done thee no harm. NIH
4:11 I **h** taught thee in the way of wisdom; I have NIH
4:11 way of wisdom; I **h** led thee in right paths. NIH
4:16 they sleep not, except they **h** done mischief; NIH
5:12 How **h** I hated instruction, and my heart NIH
5:13 **h** not obeyed the voice of my teachers, NIH
7:14 *I h* peace offerings with me; *this* day have I NIH
7:14 with me; *this* day **h** I payed my vows. NIH
7:15 to seek thy face, and I **h** found thee. NIH
7:16 I **h** deckt my bed *with* coverings of tapestry, NIH
7:17 I **h** perfumed my bed *with* myrrh, aloes, and NIH
7:26 yea, many strong *men* **h** *been* slain by her. NIH
8:14 I *am* understanding; I **h** strength. 3807.1
9: 5 and drink of the wine *which* I **h** mingled. NIH
13: 3 he that openeth wide his lips shall **h** NIH
14:26 and his children shall **h** a place of refuge. 1961
17: 2 A wise servant shall **h rule** over a son that 4910
17: 2 shall **h part** of the inheritance among 2505
19:10 much less for a servant to **h rule** over 4910
20: 4 shall he beg in harvest, and *h* nothing. NIH
20: 9 Who can say, I **h** made my heart clean, I am NIH
22:19 I **h** made known to thee *this* day, even *to* NIH
22:20 **H** not I written to thee excellent things in NIH
22:28 ancient landmark, which thy fathers **h** set. NIH
23:24 he that begetteth a wise *child* shall **h joy** of 8055
23:35 They **h** stricken me, *shalt thou say, and* NIH
23:35 not sick; they **h** beaten me, *and* I felt *it* not: NIH
24:23 *It is* not good to **h** respect of persons in NIH
25: 7 of the prince whom thine eyes **h** seen. NIH
27:27 *thou shalt h* goats' milk enough for thy NIH
28:10 the upright shall **h** good *things* in NIH
28:13 and forsaketh *them* shall **h mercy.** 7355
28:19 He that tilleth his land shall **h plenty** *of* 7646
28:19 after vain *persons* shall **h** poverty **enough.** 7646
28:21 To **h** respect of persons *is* not good: for for NIH
28:27 he that hideth his eyes shall **h** many a curse. NIH
29:21 shall **h** him become *his* son at the length. NIH
30: 2 and **h** not the understanding of a man. 3807.1
30: 3 nor **h** the **knowledge** of the holy. 1847+3045
30: 7 Two *things* **h** I required of thee; deny me NIH
30:20 and saith, I **h** done no wickedness. NIH
30:27 The locusts **h** no king, yet go they forth 3807.1
31:11 in her, so that he shall **h** no **need** of spoil. 2637
31:29 Many daughters **h** done virtuously, but NIH
Ecc 1:14 I **h** seen all the works that are done under NIH
1:16 **h** gotten more wisdom than all *they* that NIH
1:16 all *they* that **h** been before me in Jerusalem: NIH
2:19 yet shall he **h rule** over all my labour 7980
2:19 over all my labour where*in* I **h** laboured, NIH
2:19 where*in* I **h** shewed myself wise under NIH
3:10 I **h** seen the travail, which God hath given NIH
3:19 yea, they **h** all one breath; so that a man 3426+3807.1
4: 9 **h** a good reward for their labour. 3426+3807.1
4:11 Again, if two lie together, then they **h heat:** 2552
4:16 *even* of all that **h** been before them: NIH
5:13 There is a sore evil *which* I **h** seen under NIH
5:18 Behold *that* which I **h** seen: *it is* good and NIH
6: 1 There is an evil which I **h** seen under NIH
6: 3 and also *that* he **h** no burial; 1961+3807.1
7:12 *that* wisdom giveth life to **them that h** it. 1167
7:15 All *things* **h** I seen in the days of my vanity: NIH
7:23 All this **h** I proved by wisdom: I said, I will NIH

Ecc 7:27 Behold, this **h** I found, saith the Preacher, NIH
7:28 one man among a thousand **h** I found; but NIH
7:28 but a woman among all those **h** I not found. NIH
7:29 Lo, this only **h** I found, that God hath made NIH
7:29 but they **h** sought out many inventions. NIH
8: 9 All this **h** I seen, and applied my heart unto NIH
9: 5 neither **h** they any more a reward; 3807.1
9: 6 neither **h** they any more a portion for ever 3807.1
9:13 This wisdom **h** I seen also under the sun, NIH
10: 5 There is an evil *which* I **h** seen under NIH
10: 7 I **h** seen servants upon horses, and NIH
12: 1 thou shalt say, I **h** no pleasure in them; 3807.1
SS 1: 6 *but* mine own vineyard **h** I not kept. 3807.1
1: 9 I **h** compared thee, O my love, to a NIH
2:15 the vines: for our vines *h* tender grapes. NIH
5: 1 I **h** gathered my myrrh with my spice; NIH
5: 1 I **h** eaten my honeycomb with my honey; NIH
5: 1 I **h** drunk my wine with my milk: NIH
5: 3 I **h** put off my coat; how shall I put it on? NIH
5: 3 I **h** washed my feet; how shall I defile NIH
6: 5 eyes from me, for they **h** overcome me: NIH
7:13 and old, *which* I **h** laid up for thee, NIH
8: 8 We **h** a little sister, and she hath no 3807.1
8:12 *must h* a thousand, and those that keep NIH
Isa 1: 2 I **h** nourished and brought up children, and NIH
1: 2 up children, and they **h** rebelled against me. NIH
1: 4 they **h** forsaken the LORD, they have NIH
1: 4 they **h** provoked the Holy One of Israel unto NIH
1: 6 they **h** not been closed, neither bound up, NIH
1: 9 we should **h** been as Sodom, *and* we should NIH
1: 9 *and* we should **h** been like unto Gomorrah. NIH
1:29 be ashamed of the oaks which ye **h** desired, NIH
1:29 for the gardens that ye **h** chosen. NIH
2: 8 *that* which their own fingers **h** made: NIH
3: 9 for they **h** rewarded evil unto themselves. NIH
3:14 for ye **h** eaten up the vineyard; the spoil of NIH
4: 4 When the Lord shall **h** washed away NIH
4: 4 shall **h** purged the blood of Jerusalem from NIH
5: 4 What could **h** been done more to my NIH
5: 4 more to my vineyard, that I **h** not done in it? NIH
5:13 because *they h* no knowledge: NIH
5:24 they **h** cast away the law of the LORD of NIH
6: 5 for mine eyes **h** seen the King, the LORD NIH
6:12 the LORD **h** removed men far away, and NIH
7: 5 **h** taken evil counsel against thee, saying, NIH
7:17 thy father's house, days that **h** not come, NIH
8: 4 For before the child shall **h** knowledge to NIH
8:19 Seek unto them that **h** familiar spirits, and NIH
9: 2 The people that walked in darkness **h** seen a NIH
9:17 Therefore the Lord shall **h** no joy in their NIH
9:17 neither shall **h mercy** on their fatherless 7355
10: 1 that write grievousness *which* they **h** NIH
10:11 as I **h** done unto Samaria and her idols, so NIH
10:13 By the strength of my hand I **h** done *it,* and NIH
10:13 I **h** removed the bounds of the people, and NIH
10:13 **h** robbed their treasures, and I have put NIH
10:13 I **h** put down the inhabitants like a valiant NIH
10:14 eggs *that are* left, **h** I gathered all the earth; NIH
10:29 they **h** taken up their lodging at Geba; NIH
13: 3 I **h** commanded my sanctified ones, I have NIH
13: 3 I **h** also called my mighty ones for mine NIH
13:18 they shall **h** no **pity** on the fruit of 7355
14: 1 For the LORD will **h mercy** on Jacob, and 7355
14:24 Surely as I **h** thought, so shall it come to NIH
14:24 and as I **h** purposed, *so* shall it stand: NIH
15: 7 Therefore the abundance they **h** gotten, and NIH
15: 7 have gotten, and that which they **h** laid up, NIH
16: 6 We **h** heard of the pride of Moab; *he is* very NIH
16: 8 the lords of the heathen **h** broken down NIH
16:10 I **h** made *their vintage* shouting to cease. NIH
17: 7 his eyes shall **h** respect to the Holy One of NIH
17: 8 neither shall respect *that* which his fingers **h** NIH
18: 2 whose land the rivers **h** spoiled. NIH
18: 7 under foot, whose land the rivers **h** spoiled, NIH
19: 3 to them that **h** familiar spirits, and to NIH
19:13 they **h** also seduced Egypt, *even they that* NIH
19:14 they **h** caused Egypt to err in every work NIH
21: 2 all the sighing thereof **h** I made to cease. NIH
21: 3 pangs **h** taken hold upon me, as the pangs of NIH
21:10 that which I **h** heard of the LORD of hosts, NIH
21:10 the God of Israel, **h** I declared unto you. NIH
22: 3 are bound together, *which* **h** fled from far. NIH
22: 9 Ye **h** seen also the breaches of the city of NIH
22:10 ye **h** numbered the houses of Jerusalem, NIH
22:10 the houses **h** ye broken down to fortify NIH
22:11 ye **h** not looked unto the Maker thereof, NIH
23: 2 that pass over the sea, **h** replenished. NIH
23:12 *to* Chittim; there also shalt thou **h** no rest. 3807.1
24: 5 because they **h** transgressed the laws, NIH
24:16 From the uttermost part of the earth **h** we NIH
24:16 the treacherous dealers **h** dealt NIH
24:16 the treacherous dealers **h** dealt very NIH
25: 9 we **h** waited for him, and he will save us: NIH
25: 9 we **h** waited for him, we will be glad and NIH
26: 1 We **h** a strong city; salvation will *God* 3807.1
26: 8 O LORD, **h** we waited for thee; NIH
26: 9 *With* my soul **h** I desired thee in the night; NIH
26:13 *other* lords besides thee **h** had dominion NIH
26:16 LORD, in trouble **h** they visited thee, NIH
26:17 so **h** we been in thy sight, O LORD. NIH
26:18 We **h** been with child, we have been in pain, NIH
26:18 We have been with child, we **h** been in pain, NIH
26:18 in pain, we **h** as it were brought forth wind; NIH
26:18 we **h** not wrought any deliverance *in* NIH
26:18 neither **h** the inhabitants of the world fallen. NIH
27:11 he that made them will not **h mercy** on 7355
28: 7 they also **h** erred through wine, and NIH
28: 7 the prophet **h** erred through strong drink, NIH
28:15 Because ye **h** said, We have made a NIH
28:15 We **h** made a covenant with death, and NIH
28:15 for we **h** made lies our refuge, and NIH
28:15 and under falsehood **h** we hid ourselves: NIH
28:22 for I **h** heard from the Lord GOD of hosts NIH
29:13 **h** removed their heart far from me, and NIH
30: 2 *into* Egypt, and **h** not asked *at* my mouth; NIH

Isa 30: 7 therefore **h** I cried concerning this, NIH
30:18 be exalted, that *he* may **h mercy** upon you: 7355
30:29 Ye shall **h** a song, as *in* the night 1961+3807.1
31: 6 the children of Israel **h** deeply revolted. NIH
31: 7 which your own hands **h** made unto you *for* NIH
33: 2 be gracious unto us; we **h** waited for thee: NIH
33:13 Hear, ye *that are* far off, what I **h** done; and NIH
36: 5 *I* **h** counsel and strength for war: NIH
36:19 **h** they delivered Samaria out of my hand? NIH
36:20 that **h** delivered their land out of my hand, NIH
37: 6 of the king of Assyria **h** blasphemed me. NIH
37:11 thou hast heard what the kings of Assyria **h** NIH
37:12 **H** the gods of the nations delivered them NIH
37:12 them which my fathers **h** destroyed, NIH
37:18 the kings of Assyria **h** laid waste all NIH
37:19 **h** cast their gods into the fire: for they *were* NIH
37:19 and stone: therefore they **h** destroyed them. NIH
37:25 I **h** digged, and drunk water; and with NIH
37:25 with the sole of my feet **h** I dried up all NIH
37:26 thou not heard long ago, *how* I **h** done it; NIH
37:26 *and* of ancient times, that I **h** formed it? NIH
37:26 now **h** I brought it to pass, that thou NIH
38: 3 how I **h** walked before thee in truth and NIH
38: 3 and **h** done *that which is* good in thy sight. NIH
38: 5 I **h** heard thy prayer, I have seen thy tears: NIH
38: 5 I have heard thy prayer, I **h** seen thy tears: NIH
38:12 I **h** cut off like a weaver my life: he will cut NIH
39: 4 said he, What **h** they seen in thine house? NIH
39: 4 All that *is* in mine house **h** they seen: NIH
39: 4 there is nothing among my treasures that I **h** NIH
39: 6 *that* which thy fathers **h** laid up in store until NIH
40:21 **H** ye not known? have ye not heard? hath it NIH
40:21 **h** ye not heard? hath it not been told you NIH
40:21 **h** ye not understood *from* the foundations of NIH
40:29 to *them that* **h** no might he increaseth NIH
41: 8 *art* my servant, Jacob whom I **h** chosen, NIH
41: 9 *Thou* whom I **h** taken from the ends of NIH
41: 9 I **h** chosen thee, and not cast thee away. NIH
41:25 I **h** raised up *one* from the north, and NIH
42: 1 soul delighteth; I **h** put my spirit upon him: NIH
42: 4 till he **h** set judgment in the earth: NIH
42: 6 I the LORD **h** called thee in righteousness, NIH
42:14 I **h** long time holden my peace; I have been NIH
42:14 I **h** been still, *and* refrained myself: NIH
42:16 I will lead them in paths *that* they **h** not NIH
42:24 the LORD, he against whom we **h** sinned? NIH
43: 1 for I **h** redeemed thee, I have called *thee* by NIH
43: 1 redeemed thee, I **h** called *thee* by thy name; NIH
43: 4 hast been honourable, and I **h** loved thee: NIH
43: 7 for I **h** created him for my glory, I have NIH
43: 7 created him for my glory, I **h** formed him; NIH
43: 7 I have formed him; yea, I **h** made him. NIH
43: 8 Bring forth the blind people that **h** eyes, 3426
43: 8 that have eyes, and the deaf that **h** ears. 3807.1
43:10 and my servant whom I **h** chosen: NIH
43:12 I **h** declared, and have saved, and I have NIH
43:12 and **h** saved, and I have shewed, NIH
43:12 and have saved, and I **h** shewed, NIH
43:14 For your sake I **h** sent to Babylon, and NIH
43:14 **h** brought down all their nobles, and NIH
43:21 This people **h** I formed for myself; NIH
43:23 I **h** not caused thee to serve with an NIH
43:27 and thy teachers **h** transgressed against me. NIH
43:28 Therefore I **h** profaned the princes of NIH
43:28 **h** given Jacob to the curse, and Israel to NIH
44: 1 my servant; and Israel, whom I **h** chosen: NIH
44: 2 and *thou,* Jeshurun, whom I **h** chosen. NIH
44: 8 **h** not I told thee from that time, and NIH
44: 8 and **h** declared *it?* ye *are* even my witnesses. NIH
44:16 and saith, Aha, I am warm, I **h** seen the fire: NIH
44:18 They **h** not known nor understood: for he NIH
44:19 to say, I **h** burnt part of it in the fire; NIH
44:19 also I **h** baked bread upon the coals thereof; NIH
44:19 I **h** roasted flesh, and eaten *it:* and shall I NIH
44:21 I **h** formed thee; thou *art* my servant: NIH
44:22 I **h** blotted out, as a thick cloud, NIH
44:22 return unto me; for I **h** redeemed thee. NIH
45: 1 to Cyrus, whose right hand I **h** holden, to NIH
45: 4 I **h** even called thee by thy name: NIH
45: 4 I **h** surnamed thee, though thou hast not NIH
45: 8 up together; I the LORD **h** created it. NIH
45:12 I **h** made the earth, and created man upon it: NIH
45:12 **h** stretched out the heavens, and all their NIH
45:12 and all their host **h** I commanded. NIH
45:13 I **h** raised him up in righteousness, and NIH
45:19 I **h** not spoken in secret, in a dark place of NIH
45:20 they **h** no knowledge that set up the wood of NIH
45:21 ***h*** not I the LORD? and *there is* no God NIH
45:23 I **h** sworn by myself, the word is gone out of NIH
45:24 in the LORD **h** I righteousness and 3807.1
46: 4 *even* to hoar hairs will I carry *you:* I **h** NIH
46:11 I **h** spoken *it,* I will also bring it to pass; NIH
46:11 it to pass; I **h** purposed *it,* I will also do it. NIH
47: 6 I **h** polluted mine inheritance, and NIH
48: 3 I **h** declared the former *things* from NIH
48: 5 I **h** even from the beginning declared *it* to NIH
48: 6 will not ye declare *it?* I **h** shewed thee new NIH
48:10 Behold, I **h** refined thee, but not with silver; NIH
48:10 I **h** chosen thee in the furnace of affliction. NIH
48:15 I, *even* I, **h** spoken; yea, I have called him: NIH
48:15 I, *even* I, have spoken; yea, I **h** called him: NIH
48:15 I **h** brought him, and he shall make his way NIH
48:16 I **h** not spoken in secret from the beginning; NIH
48:19 his name should not **h** been cut off nor NIH
49: 4 I said, I **h** laboured in vain, I have spent my NIH
49: 4 I **h** spent my strength for nought, and NIH
49: 8 In an acceptable time **h** I heard thee, and NIH
49: 8 and in a day of salvation **h** I helped thee: NIH
49:13 and will **h mercy** upon his afflicted. 7355
49:15 that *she* should not **h compassion** on 7355
49:16 I **h** graven thee upon the palms of *my* NIH
49:20 The children which thou shalt **h**, after thou NIH
49:21 seeing I **h** lost my children, and NIH
50: 1 mother's divorcement, whom I **h** put away? NIH
50: 1 which of my creditors *is it* to whom I **h** sold NIH

Isa 50: 1 for your iniquities **h** you sold yourselves, NIH
50: 2 or **h** I no power to deliver? behold, at my 871.1
50: 7 therefore **h** I set my face like a flint, and NIH
50:11 and in the sparks *that* ye **h** kindled. NIH
50:11 This shall ye **h** of mine hand; 1961+3807.1
51:16 I **h** put my words in thy mouth, and NIH
51:16 **h** covered thee in the shadow of mine hand, NIH
51:20 Thy sons **h** fainted, they lie at the head of NIH
51:22 I **h** taken out of thine hand the cup of NIH
51:23 which **h** said to thy soul, Bow down, NIH
52: 3 Ye **h** sold yourselves for nought; NIH
52: 5 Now therefore, what **h** I here, saith 3807.1
53: 6 All we like sheep **h** gone astray; we have NIH
53: 6 we **h** turned every one to his own way; and NIH
54: 7 For a small moment **h** I forsaken thee; but NIH
54: 8 with everlasting kindness will I **h mercy** on 7355
54: 9 for *as* I **h** sworn that the waters of Noah NIH
54: 9 **h** I sworn that *I* would not be wroth with NIH
54:16 I **h** created the smith that bloweth the coals NIH
54:16 and I **h** created the waster to destroy. NIH
55: 4 I **h** given him *for* a witness to the people, NIH
55: 7 and he will **h mercy** upon him; 7355
56:11 *they are* greedy dogs *which* can never **h** 3045
57:11 **h** not I held my peace even of old, and thou NIH
57:16 before me, and the souls *which* I **h** made. NIH
57:18 I **h** seen his ways, and will heal him: I will NIH
58: 3 Wherefore **h** we fasted, *say they,* and NIH
58: 3 *wherefore* **h** we afflicted our soul, and NIH
58: 5 Is it such a fast that I **h** chosen? a day for a NIH
58: 6 *Is* not this the fast that I **h** chosen? to loose NIH
59: 2 your iniquities **h** separated between you 1961
59: 2 and your sins **h** hid *his* face from you, NIH
59: 3 your lips **h** spoken lies, your tongue hath NIH
59: 8 they **h** made them crooked paths: NIH
59:21 and my words which I **h** put in thy mouth, NIH
60:10 but in my favour **h** I had mercy on thee. NIH
61: 7 For your shame *you shall* **h** double; and NIH
62: 6 I **h** set watchmen upon thy walls, NIH
62: 9 they that **h** gathered it shall eat it, and NIH
62: 9 they that **h** brought it together shall drink it NIH
63: 3 I **h** trodden the winepress alone; and of NIH
63:18 The people of thy holiness **h** possessed *it* NIH
63:18 our adversaries **h** trodden down thy NIH
64: 4 For since the beginning of the world *men* **h** NIH
64: 5 behold, thou art wroth; for we **h** sinned: NIH
64: 6 like the wind, **h** taken us away. NIH
65: 2 I **h** spread out mine hands all the day unto a NIH
65: 7 which **h** burnt incense upon the mountains, NIH
65:10 lie down in, for my people that **h** sought me. NIH
66: 2 all those *things* **h** been, saith the LORD: NIH
66: 3 they **h** chosen their own ways, and their NIH
66:19 the isles afar off, that **h** not heard my fame, NIH
66:19 not heard my fame, neither **h** seen my glory; NIH
66:24 look upon the carcases of the men that **h** NIH
Jer 1: 9 Behold, I **h** put my words in thy mouth. NIH
1:10 I **h** this day set thee over the nations and NIH
1:16 who **h** forsaken me, and have burnt incense NIH
1:16 **h** burnt incense unto other gods, and NIH
1:18 I **h** made thee *this* day a defenced city, and NIH
2: 5 What iniquity **h** your fathers found in me, NIH
2: 5 **h** walked after vanity, and are become vain? NIH
2:11 my people **h** changed their glory for *that* NIH
2:13 For my people **h** committed two evils; NIH
2:13 they **h** forsaken me the fountain of living NIH
2:16 Tahapanes **h** broken the crown of thy head. NIH
2:20 For of old time I **h** broken thy yoke, *and* NIH
2:23 am not polluted, I **h** not gone after Baalim? NIH
2:25 for I **h** loved strangers, and after them will I NIH
2:27 for they **h** turned *their* back unto me, and NIH
2:29 ye all **h** transgressed against me, saith NIH
2:30 In vain **h** I smitten your children; NIH
2:31 **H** I been a wilderness unto Israel? a land of NIH
2:32 yet my people **h** forgotten me days without NIH
2:34 I **h** not found it by secret search, but NIH
2:35 because thou sayest, I **h** not sinned. NIH
3: 3 Therefore the showers **h** been withholden, NIH
3:13 ye **h** not obeyed my voice, saith NIH
3:18 **h** given for an inheritance unto your fathers. NIH
3:20 so **h** you dealt treacherously with me, NIH
3:21 for they **h** perverted their way, *and* NIH
3:21 *and* they **h** forgotten the LORD their God. NIH
3:25 for we **h** sinned against the LORD our NIH
3:25 **h** not obeyed the voice of the LORD our NIH
4:10 Jerusalem, saying, Ye shall **h** peace; 1961
4:18 thy doings **h** procured these *things* unto NIH
4:22 my people *is* foolish, they **h** not known me; NIH
4:22 and they **h** none **understanding**: 995
4:22 but to do good they **h** no knowledge. NIH
4:28 I **h** spoken *it,* I have purposed *it,* and NIH
4:28 I have spoken *it,* I **h** purposed *it,* and NIH
4:31 For I **h** heard a voice as of a woman in NIH
5: 3 hast stricken them, but they **h** not grieved; NIH
5: 3 *but* they **h** refused to receive correction: NIH
5: 3 they **h** made their faces harder than a rock; NIH
5: 3 harder than a rock; they **h** refused to return. NIH
5: 5 for they **h** known the way of the LORD, NIH
5: 5 these **h** altogether broken the yoke, *and* NIH
5: 7 thy children **h** forsaken me, and sworn by NIH
5:11 the house of Judah **h** dealt very NIH
5:12 They **h** belied the LORD, and said, *It is* NIH
5:19 Like as ye **h** forsaken me, and NIH
5:21 which **h** eyes, and see not; which have 3807.1
5:21 and see not; which **h** ears, and hear not: 3807.1
5:22 which **h** placed the sand *for* the bound of NIH
5:25 Your iniquities **h** turned away these *things,* NIH
5:25 your sins **h** withholden good *things* from NIH
5:31 their means; and my people love *to* **h** *it* so: NIH
6: 2 I **h** likened the daughter of Zion *to* a comely NIH
6:10 them a reproach; they **h** no delight in it. NIH
6:14 They **h** healed also the hurt of *the daughter* NIH
6:19 they **h** not hearkened unto my words, NIH
6:23 and spear; they *are* cruel, and **h** no **mercy**; 7355
6:24 We **h** heard the fame thereof: our hands NIH
6:27 I **h** set thee *for* a tower *and* a fortress among NIH
7:11 Behold, even I **h** seen *it,* saith the LORD. NIH

Jer 7:13 because ye **h** done all these works, NIH
7:14 and to your fathers, as I **h** done to Shiloh. NIH
7:15 as I **h** cast out all your brethren, *even* NIH
7:23 walk ye in all the ways that I **h** commanded NIH
7:25 I **h** even sent unto you all my servants NIH
7:30 For the children of Judah **h** done evil in my NIH
7:30 they **h** set their abominations in the house NIH
7:31 they **h** built the high places of Tophet, NIH
8: 2 whom they **h** loved, and whom they have NIH
8: 2 whom they **h** served, and after whom they NIH
8: 2 after whom they **h** walked, and whom they NIH
8: 2 whom they **h** sought, and whom they have NIH
8: 2 have sought, and whom they **h** worshipped: NIH
8: 3 which remain in all the places whither I **h** NIH
8: 6 of his wickedness, saying, What **h** I done? NIH
8: 9 lo, they **h** rejected the word of the LORD; NIH
8:11 For they **h** healed the hurt of the daughter of NIH
8:13 *the things that* I **h** given them shall pass NIH
8:14 because we **h** sinned against the LORD. NIH
8:16 and **h** devoured the land, and all that is in it; NIH
8:19 Why **h** they provoked me to anger with NIH
9: 5 they **h** taught their tongue to speak lies, *and* NIH
9:13 Because they **h** forsaken my law which I set NIH
9:13 **h** not obeyed my voice, neither walked NIH
9:14 **h** walked after the imagination of their own NIH
9:16 whom neither they nor their fathers **h** NIH
9:16 a sword after them, till I **h** consumed them. NIH
9:19 because we **h** forsaken the land, because NIH
9:19 because our dwellings **h** cast *us* out. NIH
10:11 The gods that **h** not made the heavens and NIH
10:21 and **h** not sought the LORD: NIH
10:25 for they **h** eaten up Jacob, and NIH
10:25 and **h** made his habitation desolate. NIH
11: 5 That *I* may perform the oath which I **h** NIH
11:10 the house of Judah **h** broken my covenant NIH
11:13 **h** ye set up altars to *that* shameful thing, NIH
11:17 which they **h** done against themselves to NIH
11:20 for unto thee **h** I revealed my cause. NIH
12: 2 hast planted them, yea, they **h** taken root: NIH
12: 5 they **h** wearied thee, then how canst thou NIH
12: 6 even they **h** dealt treacherously with thee; NIH
12: 6 yea, they **h** called a multitude after thee: NIH
12: 7 I **h** forsaken mine house, I have left mine NIH
12: 7 forsaken mine house, I **h** left mine heritage; NIH
12: 7 I **h** given the dearly beloved of my soul into NIH
12: 8 crieth out against me: therefore **h** I hated it. NIH
12:10 Many pastors **h** destroyed my vineyard, NIH
12:10 they **h** trodden my portion under foot, NIH
12:10 they **h** made my pleasant portion a desolate NIH
12:11 They **h** made it desolate, *and being* desolate NIH
12:12 *other* end of the land: no flesh *shall* **h** peace. NIH
12:13 They **h** sown wheat, but shall reap thorns: NIH
12:13 they **h** put themselves to pain, *but* shall not NIH
12:14 that touch the inheritance which I **h** caused NIH
12:15 after that I **h** plucked them out, I will return, NIH
12:15 **h compassion** on them, and will bring 7355
13:11 **h** I caused to cleave unto me the whole NIH
13:14 nor spare, nor **h mercy**, but destroy them. 7355
13:27 I **h** seen thine adulteries, and thy neighings, NIH
14: 3 their nobles **h** sent their little ones to NIH
14: 7 are many; we **h** sinned against thee. NIH
14:10 Thus **h** they loved to wander, they have not NIH
14:10 they **h** not refrained their feet, therefore NIH
14:13 neither shall ye **h** famine; 1961+3807.1
14:14 sent them not, neither **h** I commanded them, NIH
14:16 they *shall* **h** none to bury them, them, 3807.1
14:20 of our fathers: for we **h** sinned against thee. NIH
15: 5 For who shall **h pity** upon thee, 2550
15: 8 I **h** brought upon them against the mother of NIH
15: 8 I **h** caused *him* to fall upon it suddenly, and NIH
15:10 I **h** neither lent on usury, nor *men* have lent NIH
15:10 on usury, nor *men* **h** lent to me on usury; NIH
15:15 know that for thy sake I **h** suffered rebuke. NIH
16: 2 neither shalt thou **h** sons nor 1961+3807.1
16: 5 for I **h** taken away my peace from this NIH
16:10 what *is* our sin that we **h** committed against NIH
16:11 Because your fathers **h** forsaken me, NIH
16:11 **h** walked after other gods, and have served NIH
16:11 **h** served them, and have worshipped them, NIH
16:11 **h** worshipped them, and have forsaken me, NIH
16:11 **h** forsaken me, and have not kept my law; NIH
16:11 have forsaken me, and **h** not kept my law; NIH
16:12 ye **h** done worse than your fathers; NIH
16:18 because they **h** defiled my land, they have NIH
16:18 they **h** filled mine inheritance with NIH
16:19 Surely our fathers **h** inherited lies, vanity, NIH
17: 4 for ye **h** kindled a fire in mine anger, NIH
17:13 because they **h** forsaken the LORD, NIH
17:16 I **h** not hastened from *being* a pastor to NIH
17:16 neither **h** I desired the woeful day; NIH
18: 8 that nation, against whom I **h** pronounced, NIH
18:15 they **h** burnt incense to vanity, and NIH
18:15 they **h** caused them to stumble in their ways NIH
18:20 for they **h** digged a pit for my soul. NIH
18:22 for they **h** digged a pit to take me, and NIH
19: 4 Because they **h** forsaken me, and NIH
19: 4 **h** estranged this place, and have burnt NIH
19: 4 and **h** burnt incense in it unto other gods, NIH
19: 4 whom neither they nor their fathers **h** NIH
19: 4 **h** filled this place *with* the blood of NIH
19: 5 They **h** built also the high places of Baal, NIH
19:13 of all the houses upon whose roofs they **h** NIH
19:13 **h** poured out drink offerings unto other NIH
19:15 upon all her towns all the evil that I **h** NIH
19:15 because they **h** hardened their necks, NIH
20:12 on them: for unto thee **h** I opened my cause. NIH
20:17 or that my mother might **h** been my grave, NIH
21: 7 spare them, neither **h pity**, nor have mercy. 2550
21: 7 spare them, neither have pity, nor **h mercy**. 7355
21:10 For I **h** set my face against this city for evil, NIH
22: 9 Because they **h** forsaken the covenant of NIH
22:12 he shall die in the place whither they **h** led NIH
23: 2 Ye **h** scattered my flock, and driven them NIH
23: 2 driven them away, and **h** not visited them: NIH
23: 3 out of all countries whither I **h** driven them, NIH

Jer 23:11 in my house **h** I found their wickedness, NIH
23:13 I **h** seen folly in the prophets of Samaria; NIH
23:14 I **h** seen also in the prophets of Jerusalem a NIH
23:17 hath said, Ye shall **h** peace; 1961+3807.1
23:20 until he **h** executed, and till he have NIH
23:20 till he **h** performed the thoughts of his heart: NIH
23:21 I **h** not sent *these* prophets, yet they ran: NIH
23:21 I **h** not spoken to them, yet they prophesied. NIH
23:22 they should **h** turned them from their evil NIH
23:25 I **h** heard what the prophets said, NIH
23:25 saying, I **h** dreamed, I have dreamed. NIH
23:25 saying, I have dreamed, I **h** dreamed. NIH
23:27 as their fathers **h** forgotten my name for NIH
23:36 for ye **h** perverted the words of the living NIH
23:38 I **h** sent unto you, saying, Ye shall not say, NIH
24: 5 whom I **h** sent out of this place *into* the land NIH
25: 3 I **h** spoken unto you, rising early and NIH
25: 3 and speaking; but ye **h** not hearkened. NIH
25: 4 and sending *them;* but ye **h** not hearkened, NIH
25: 7 Yet ye **h** not hearkened unto me, saith NIH
25: 8 of hosts; Because ye **h** not heard my words, NIH
25:13 my words which I **h** pronounced against it, NIH
25:35 the shepherds shall **h no** way to flee, 6+4480
26: 4 to walk in my law, which I **h** set before you, NIH
26: 5 and sending *them,* but ye **h** not hearkened; NIH
26:11 this city, as ye **h** heard with your ears. NIH
26:12 against this city all the words that ye **h** NIH
27: 5 I **h** made the earth, the man and the beast NIH
27: 5 **h** given it unto whom it seemed meet unto NIH
27: 6 now **h** I given all these lands into the hand NIH
27: 6 the beasts of the field **h** I given him also to NIH
27: 8 until I **h** consumed them by his hand. NIH
27:15 For I **h** not sent them, saith the LORD, NIH
28: 2 I **h** broken the yoke of the king of Babylon. NIH
28: 8 The prophets that **h** been before me and NIH
28:14 I **h** put a yoke of iron upon the neck of all NIH
28:14 I **h** given him the beasts of the field also. NIH
29: 4 whom I **h** caused to be carried away from NIH
29: 7 seek the peace of the city whither I **h** caused NIH
29: 7 the peace thereof shall ye **h** peace. 1961+3807.1
29: 9 I **h** not sent them, saith the LORD. NIH
29:14 from all the places whither I **h** driven you, NIH
29:15 Because ye **h** said, The LORD hath raised NIH
29:18 among all the nations whither I **h** driven NIH
29:19 Because they **h** not hearkened to my words, NIH
29:20 whom I **h** sent from Jerusalem to Babylon: NIH
29:23 Because they **h** committed villany in Israel, NIH
29:23 **h** committed adultery with their neighbours' NIH
29:23 **h** spoken lying words in my name, which I NIH
29:23 my name, which I **h** not commanded them; NIH
29:32 he shall not **h** a man to dwell 1961+3807.1
30: 2 Write thee all the words that I **h** spoken NIH
30: 5 We **h** heard a voice of trembling, of fear, NIH
30:11 end of all nations whither I **h** scattered thee, NIH
30:14 All thy lovers **h** forgotten thee; they seek NIH
30:14 for I **h** wounded thee *with* the wound of an NIH
30:15 I **h** done these things unto thee. NIH
30:18 and **h mercy** on his dwelling places; 7355
30:24 until he **h** done *it,* and until he have NIH
30:24 until he **h** performed the intents of his heart: NIH
31: 3 I **h** loved thee *with* an everlasting love; NIH
31: 3 *with* lovingkindness **h** I drawn thee. NIH
31:18 I **h** surely heard Ephraim bemoaning NIH
31:20 I will **surely h mercy** upon him, 7355+7355
31:25 For I **h** satiated the weary soul, and I have NIH
31:25 and I **h** replenished every sorrowful soul. NIH
31:28 *that* like as I **h** watched over them, to pluck NIH
31:29 The fathers **h** eaten a sour grape, and NIH
31:37 all the seed of Israel for all that they **h** done, NIH
32:23 they **h** done nothing of all that thou NIH
32:29 upon whose roofs they **h** offered incense NIH
32:30 the children of Judah **h** only done evil 1961
32:30 for the children of Israel **h** only provoked NIH
32:32 which they **h** done to provoke me to anger, NIH
32:33 they **h** turned unto me the back, and not NIH
32:33 teaching *them,* yet they **h** not hearkened to NIH
32:37 whither I **h** driven them in mine anger, and NIH
32:42 Like as I **h** brought all this great evil upon NIH
32:42 will I bring upon them all the good that I **h** NIH
33: 5 whom I **h** slain in mine anger and in my NIH
33: 5 for all whose wickedness I **h** hid my face NIH
33: 8 whereby they **h** sinned against me, and NIH
33: 8 whereby they **h** sinned, and whereby they NIH
33: 8 whereby they **h** transgressed against me. NIH
33:14 that I will perform *that* good thing which I **h** NIH
33:21 that he should not **h** a son to reign 1961+3807.1
33:24 Considerest thou not what this people **h** NIH
33:24 thus they **h** despised my people, that *they* NIH
33:25 *if* I **h** not appointed the ordinances of NIH
33:26 captivity to return, and **h mercy** on them. 7355
34: 5 for I **h** pronounced the word, saith NIH
34:17 Ye **h** not hearkened unto me, in proclaiming NIH
34:18 I will give the men that **h** transgressed my NIH
34:18 which **h** not performed the words of NIH
35: 7 nor **h** *any:* but all your days ye 1961+3807.1
35: 8 Thus **h** we obeyed the voice of Jonadab NIH
35: 9 **h** we vineyard, nor field, nor seed: 1961+3807.1
35:10 we **h** dwelt in tents, and have obeyed, and NIH
35:10 **h** obeyed, and done according to all that NIH
35:14 notwithstanding I **h** spoken unto you, NIH
35:15 I **h** sent also unto you all my servants NIH
35:15 ye shall dwell in the land which I **h** given to NIH
35:15 ye **h** not inclined your ear, nor hearkened NIH
35:16 **h** performed the commandment of their NIH
35:17 the evil that I **h** pronounced against them: NIH
35:17 because I **h** spoken unto them, but they have NIH
35:17 spoken unto them, but they **h** not heard; NIH
35:17 I **h** called unto them, but they have not NIH
35:17 called unto them, but they **h** not answered. NIH
35:18 Because ye **h** obeyed the commandment of NIH
36: 2 write therein all the words that I **h** spoken NIH
36:30 He shall **h** none to sit upon 1961+3807.1
36:31 all the evil that I **h** pronounced against NIH
37:18 What **h** I offended against thee, or NIH
37:18 this people, that ye **h** put me in prison? NIH

Jer 38: 2 for he shall **h** his life for a prey, and 1961
38: 9 these men **h** done evil in all that they have NIH
38: 9 these men have done evil in all that they **h** NIH
38: 9 whom they **h** cast into the dungeon; NIH
38:22 Thy friends **h** set thee on, and NIH
38:22 set thee on, and **h** prevailed against thee: NIH
38:25 if the princes hear that I **h** talked with thee, NIH
40: 3 because ye **h** sinned against the LORD, NIH
40: 3 **h** not obeyed his voice, therefore this thing NIH
40:10 and dwell in your cities that ye **h** taken. NIH
41: 8 for we **h** treasures in the field, 3426+3807.1
42: 4 said unto them, I **h** heard *you;* behold, NIH
42:10 for I repent me of the evil that I **h** done unto NIH
42:12 that he may **h mercy** upon you, and 7355
42:14 sound of the trumpet, nor **h** hunger of bread; NIH
42:19 know certainly that I **h** admonished you *this* NIH
42:21 And *now* I **h** *this* day declared *it* to you; but NIH
42:21 ye **h** not obeyed the voice of the LORD NIH
43:10 will set his throne upon these stones that I **h** NIH
44: 2 Ye **h** seen all the evil that I have brought NIH
44: 2 Ye have seen all the evil that I **h** brought NIH
44: 3 Because of their wickedness which they **h** NIH
44: 9 **H** ye forgotten the wickedness of your NIH
44: 9 which they **h** committed in the land of NIH
44:10 neither **h** they feared, nor walked in my law, NIH
44:12 that **h** set their faces to go *into* the land of NIH
44:13 as I **h** punished Jerusalem, by the sword, NIH
44:14 to the which they **h a desire** to return 5315+5375
44:17 as we **h** done, we, and our fathers, NIH
44:18 we **h** wanted all *things,* and have been NIH
44:18 **h** been consumed by the sword and by NIH
44:22 of the abominations which ye **h** committed; NIH
44:23 Because you **h** burnt incense, and because NIH
44:23 because ye **h** sinned against the LORD, NIH
44:23 **h** not obeyed the voice of the LORD, NIH
44:25 your wives **h** both spoken with your NIH
44:25 We will surely perform our vows that we **h** NIH
44:26 Behold, I **h** sworn by my great name, NIH
45: 4 *that* which I **h** built *will* I break down, and NIH
45: 4 *that* which I **h** planted I *will* pluck up, NIH
46: 5 Wherefore **h** I seen them dismayed *and* NIH
46:12 The nations **h** heard *of* thy shame, and NIH
46:28 of all the nations whither I **h** driven thee: NIH
48: 2 in Heshbon they **h** devised evil against it; NIH
48: 4 her little ones **h** caused a cry to be heard. NIH
48: 5 the enemies **h** heard a cry of destruction. NIH
48:29 We **h** heard the pride of Moab; *he is* NIH
48:33 I **h** caused wine to fail from the wine NIH
48:34 *even* unto Jahaz, **h** they uttered their voice, NIH
48:38 for I **h** broken Moab like a vessel wherein *is* NIH
49: 9 they will destroy till they **h** enough. NIH
49:10 I **h** made Esau bare, I have uncovered his NIH
49:10 I **h** uncovered his secret places, and he shall NIH
49:12 not to drink of the cup **h** assuredly drunken; NIH
49:13 For I **h** sworn by myself, saith the LORD, NIH
49:14 I **h** heard a rumour from the LORD, and NIH
49:23 for they **h** heard evil tidings: they are NIH
49:24 sorrows **h** taken her as a woman in travail. NIH
49:31 which **h** neither gates nor bars, 3807.1
49:37 sword after them, till I **h** consumed them: NIH
50: 6 their shepherds **h** caused them to go astray, NIH
50: 6 they **h** turned them away *on* the mountains: NIH
50: 6 they **h** gone from mountain to hill, NIH
50: 6 to hill, they **h** forgotten their resting place. NIH
50: 7 All that found them **h** devoured them: and NIH
50: 7 because they **h** sinned against the LORD, NIH
50:17 the lions **h** driven *him* away: NIH
50:18 as I **h** punished the king of Assyria. NIH
50:21 do according to all that I **h** commanded NIH
50:24 I **h** laid a snare for thee, and thou art also NIH
51: 7 the nations **h** drunken of her wine; therefore NIH
51: 9 We would **h** healed Babylon, but she is not NIH
51:24 evil that they **h** done in Zion in your sight, NIH
51:30 The mighty *men* of Babylon **h** forborn to NIH
51:30 to fight, they **h** remained in *their* holds: NIH
51:30 they **h** burnt her dwelling places; her bars NIH
51:32 the reeds they **h** burnt with fire, and the men NIH
51:50 Ye that **h** escaped the sword, go *away,* stand NIH
51:51 because we **h** heard reproach: NIH
La 1: 2 her friends **h** dealt treacherously with her, NIH
1: 8 because they **h** seen her nakedness: NIH
1:11 they **h** given their pleasant things for meat NIH
1:18 for I **h** rebelled against his commandment: NIH
1:20 within me; for I **h** grievously rebelled: NIH
1:21 They **h** heard that I sigh; *there is* none to NIH
1:21 all mine enemies **h** heard of my trouble; NIH
2: 7 they **h** made a noise in the house of NIH
2:10 they **h** cast up dust upon their heads; NIH
2:10 they **h** girded themselves with sackcloth: NIH
2:14 Thy prophets **h** seen vain and foolish things NIH
2:14 they **h** not discovered thine iniquity, to turn NIH
2:14 **h** seen for thee false burdens and causes of NIH
2:16 All thine enemies **h** opened their mouth NIH
2:16 they say, We **h** swallowed *her* up: NIH
2:16 we looked for; we **h** found, we have seen it. NIH
2:16 we looked for; we have found, we **h** seen it. NIH
2:22 those that I **h** swaddled and brought up hath NIH
3:21 This I recall to my mind, therefore **h** I hope. NIH
3:32 yet will he **h compassion** according to 7355
3:42 We **h** transgressed and have rebelled: NIH
3:42 We have transgressed and **h** rebelled: NIH
3:46 All our enemies **h** opened their mouths NIH
3:53 They **h** cut off my life in the dungeon, and NIH
4:10 The hands of the pitiful women **h** sodden NIH
4:12 would not **h** believed that the adversary and NIH
4:12 the enemy should **h** entered into the gates of NIH
4:13 that **h** shed the blood of the just in the midst NIH
4:14 They **h** wandered *as* blind *men* in NIH
4:14 they **h** polluted themselves with blood, so NIH
4:17 in our watching we **h** watched for a nation NIH
5: 4 We **h** drunken our water for money; NIH
5: 5 we labour, *and* **h** no rest. 3807.1
5: 6 We **h** given the hand *to* the Egyptians, *and* NIH
5: 7 Our fathers **h** sinned, *and are* not; *and* NIH
5: 7 *and are* not; *and* we **h** borne their iniquities. NIH

La 5: 8 Servants **h** ruled over us: *there is* none that NIH
5:14 The elders **h** ceased from the gate, NIH
5:16 our head: woe unto us, that we **h** sinned! NIH
Eze 2: 3 and their fathers **h** transgressed against me, NIH
3: 6 to them, they would **h** hearkened unto thee. NIH
3: 8 I **h** made thy face strong against their faces, NIH
3: 9 As an adamant harder than flint **h** I made NIH
3:17 I **h** made thee a watchman unto the house of NIH
4: 5 For I **h** laid upon thee the years of their NIH
4: 6 I **h** appointed thee each day for a year. NIH
4:14 for from my youth up even till now **h** I not NIH
4:15 I **h** given thee cow's dung for man's dung, NIH
5: 5 I **h** set it in the midst of the nations and NIH
5: 6 for they **h** refused my judgments, and NIH
5: 6 and my statutes, they **h** not walked in them. NIH
5: 7 *and* **h** not walked in my statutes, NIH
5: 7 in my statutes, neither **h** kept my judgments, NIH
5: 7 neither **h** done according to the judgments NIH
5: 9 I will do in thee that which I **h** not done, NIH
5:11 mine eye spare, neither will I **h** any **pity**. 2550
5:13 they shall know that I the LORD **h** spoken NIH
5:13 when I **h** accomplished my fury in them. NIH
5:15 furious rebukes. I the LORD **h** spoken *it.* NIH
5:17 sword upon thee. I the LORD **h** spoken *it.* NIH
6: 8 that ye may **h** *some* that shall 1961+3807.1
6: 9 they **h** committed in all their abominations. NIH
6:10 *that* I **h** not said in vain that *I* would do this NIH
7: 4 shall not spare thee, neither will I **h pity**: 2550
7: 9 eye shall not spare, neither will I **h pity**: 2550
7:14 They **h** blown the trumpet, even to make all NIH
7:20 therefore **h** I set it far from them. NIH
8:17 for they **h** filled the land *with* violence, and NIH
8:17 and **h** returned to provoke me to anger: NIH
8:18 eye shall not spare, neither will I **h pity**: 2550
9: 1 Cause them **that h charge over** the city to 6486
9: 5 let not your eye spare, neither **h** ye **pity**: 2550
9:10 neither will I **h pity,** *but* I will recompense 2550
9:11 I **h** done as thou hast commanded me. NIH
11: 5 Thus **h** ye said, O house of Israel: NIH
11: 6 Ye **h** multiplied your slain in this city, NIH
11: 6 ye **h** filled the streets thereof *with* the slain. NIH
11: 7 Your slain whom ye **h** laid in the midst of it, NIH
11: 8 Ye **h** feared the sword; and I will bring a NIH
11:12 for ye **h** not walked in my statutes, NIH
11:12 **h** done after the manners of the heathen that NIH
11:15 whom the inhabitants of Jerusalem **h** said, NIH
11:16 Although I **h** cast them far off among NIH
11:16 although I **h** scattered them among NIH
11:17 of the countries where ye **h** been scattered, NIH
12: 2 which **h** eyes to see, and see not; 3807.1
12: 2 see not; they **h** ears to hear, and hear not: 3807.1
12: 6 for I **h** set thee *for* a sign unto the house of NIH
12:11 like as I **h** done, so shall it be done unto NIH
12:22 what *is* that proverb *that* ye **h** in the land 3807.1
12:28 the word which I **h** spoken shall be done, NIH
13: 3 their own spirit, and **h** seen nothing! 3807.1
13: 5 Ye **h** not gone up into the gaps, NIH
13: 6 They **h** seen vanity and lying divination, NIH
13: 6 they **h** made *others* to hope that *they* would NIH
13: 7 **H** ye not seen a vain vision, and have ye not NIH
13: 7 **h** ye not spoken a lying divination, NIH
13: 7 The LORD saith *it;* albeit I **h** not spoken? NIH
13: 8 Because ye **h** spoken vanity, and seen lies, NIH
13:10 even because they **h** seduced my people, NIH
13:12 Where *is* the daubing where*with* ye **h** NIH
13:14 So will I break down the wall that ye **h** NIH
13:15 upon them that **h** daubed it *with* untempered NIH
13:22 Because *with* lies *ye* **h** made the heart of NIH
13:22 the righteous sad, whom I **h** not made sad; NIH
14: 3 these men **h** set up their idols in their heart, NIH
14: 9 I the LORD **h** deceived that prophet, and NIH
14:22 the evil that I **h** brought upon Jerusalem, NIH
14:22 *even* concerning all that I **h** brought upon it. NIH
14:23 ye shall know that I **h** not done without NIH
14:23 done without cause all that I **h** done in it, NIH
15: 6 which I **h** given to the fire for fuel, so will I NIH
15: 8 because they **h** committed a trespass, saith NIH
16: 5 unto thee, to **h compassion** upon thee; 2550
16: 7 I **h** caused thee to multiply as the bud of NIH
16:27 I **h** stretched out my hand over thee, and NIH
16:27 **h** diminished thine ordinary *food,* and NIH
17:21 ye shall know that I the LORD **h** spoken NIH
17:24 I the LORD **h** brought down the high tree, NIH
17:24 **h** exalted the low tree, have dried up NIH
17:24 **h** dried up the green tree, and have made NIH
17:24 and **h** made the dry tree to flourish: NIH
17:24 I the LORD **h** spoken and have done *it.* NIH
17:24 I the LORD have spoken and **h** done *it.* NIH
18: 2 The fathers **h** eaten sour grapes, and NIH
18: 3 ye shall not **h** *occasion* any more to 1961+3807.1
18:23 **H** I any pleasure at all that the wicked NIH
18:31 whereby ye **h** transgressed; NIH
18:32 For I **h** no pleasure in the death of him that NIH
20:27 Yet *in* this your fathers **h** blasphemed me, NIH
20:27 in that they **h** committed a trespass against NIH
20:41 gather you out of the countries wherein ye **h** NIH
20:43 all your doings, wherein ye **h** been defiled; NIH
20:43 sight for all your evils that ye **h** committed. NIH
20:44 when I **h** wrought with you for my name's NIH
20:48 all flesh shall see that I the LORD **h** NIH
21: 5 That all flesh may know that I the LORD **h** NIH
21:15 I **h** set the point of the sword against all NIH
21:17 my fury to rest: I the LORD **h** said *it.* NIH
21:23 in their sight, to them that **h** sworn oaths: NIH
21:24 Because ye **h** made your iniquity to be NIH
21:25 day is come, when iniquity *shall* **h** an end, NIH
21:29 is come, when *their* iniquity *shall* **h** an end. NIH
21:32 for I the LORD **h** spoken *it.* NIH
22: 4 **h** I made thee a reproach unto the heathen, NIH
22: 7 In thee **h** they set light by father and NIH
22: 7 in the midst of thee **h** they dealt by NIH
22: 7 in thee **h** they vexed the fatherless and NIH
22:10 In thee **h** they discovered their father's NIH
22:10 in thee **h** they humbled her that was set NIH
22:12 In thee **h** they taken gifts to shed blood; NIH

Eze 22:13 I **h** smitten mine hand at thy dishonest gain NIH
22:14 I the LORD **h** spoken *it,* and will do *it.* NIH
22:22 ye shall know that I the LORD **h** poured NIH
22:25 they **h** devoured souls; they have taken NIH
22:25 they **h** taken the treasure and NIH
22:25 they **h** made her many widows in the midst NIH
22:26 Her priests **h** violated my law, and NIH
22:26 **h** profaned mine holy *things:* they have put NIH
22:26 have profaned mine holy *things:* they **h** put NIH
22:26 neither **h** they shewed *difference* between NIH
22:26 **h** hid their eyes from my sabbaths, and I am NIH
22:28 her prophets **h** daubed them *with* NIH
22:29 The people of the land **h** used oppression, NIH
22:29 and **h** vexed the poor and needy: NIH
22:29 they **h** oppressed the stranger wrongfully. NIH
22:31 Therefore **h** I poured out mine indignation NIH
22:31 I **h** consumed them with the fire of my NIH
22:31 their own way **h** I recompensed upon their NIH
23: 9 Wherefore I **h** delivered her into the hand of NIH
23:34 for I **h** spoken *it,* saith the Lord GOD. NIH
23:37 That they **h** committed adultery, and NIH
23:37 with their idols **h** they committed adultery, NIH
23:37 **h** also caused their sons, whom they bare NIH
23:38 Moreover this they **h** done unto me: NIH
23:38 they **h** defiled my sanctuary in the same NIH
23:38 the same day, and **h** profaned my sabbaths. NIH
23:39 thus **h** they done in the midst of mine house. NIH
23:40 that ye **h** sent for men to come from far, NIH
24: 8 I **h** set her blood upon the top of a rock, NIH
24:13 because I **h** purged thee, and thou wast not NIH
24:13 till I **h** caused my fury to rest upon thee. NIH
24:14 I the LORD **h** spoken *it:* it shall come to NIH
24:21 your daughters whom ye **h** left shall fall by NIH
24:22 ye shall do as I **h** done: ye shall not cover NIH
25:15 Because the Philistines **h** dealt by revenge, NIH
25:15 **h** taken vengeance with a despiteful heart, NIH
26: 5 for I **h** spoken *it,* saith the Lord GOD: and NIH
26:14 for I the LORD **h** spoken *it,* saith the Lord NIH
27: 4 thy builders **h** perfected thy beauty. NIH
27: 5 They **h** made all thy *ship* boards of fir trees NIH
27: 5 they **h** taken cedars from Lebanon to make NIH
27: 6 *Of* the oaks of Bashan **h** they made thine NIH
27: 6 the company of the Ashurites **h** made thy NIH
27:11 they **h** made thy beauty perfect. NIH
27:26 Thy rowers **h** brought thee into great NIH
28:10 for I **h** spoken *it,* saith the Lord GOD. NIH
28:14 I **h** set thee *so:* thou wast upon the holy NIH
28:16 By the multitude of thy merchandise they **h** NIH
28:22 when I shall **h** executed judgments in her, NIH
28:25 When I shall **h** gathered the house of Israel NIH
28:25 shall they dwell in their land that I **h** given NIH
28:26 when I **h** executed judgments upon all those NIH
29: 3 *is* mine own, and I **h** made *it* for myself. NIH
29: 5 I **h** given thee for meat to the beasts of NIH
29: 6 they **h** been a staff of reed to the house of NIH
29: 9 The river *is* mine, and I **h** made *it.* NIH
29:20 I **h** given him the land of Egypt *for* his NIH
30: 8 when I **h** set a fire in Egypt, and *when* all NIH
30:12 of strangers: I the LORD **h** spoken *it.* NIH
30:16 Sin shall **h great pain,** and No shall 2342+2342
30:16 and Noph *shall* **h** distresses daily. NIH
30:21 I **h** broken the arm of Pharaoh king of NIH
31: 9 I **h** made him fair by the multitude of his NIH
31:11 I **h** therefore delivered him into the hand of NIH
31:11 I **h** driven him out for his wickedness. NIH
31:12 **h** cut him off, and have left him: NIH
31:12 have cut him off, and **h** left him: NIH
31:12 gone down from his shadow, and **h** left him. NIH
32:24 yet **h** they borne their shame with them that NIH
32:25 They **h** set her a bed in the midst of the slain NIH
32:25 yet **h** they borne their shame with them that NIH
32:27 they **h** laid their swords under their heads, NIH
32:32 For I **h** caused my terror in the land of NIH
33: 7 I **h** set thee a watchman unto the house of NIH
33:11 I **h** no pleasure in the death of the wicked; NIH
33:29 when I **h** laid the land most desolate NIH
33:29 of all their abominations which they **h** NIH
34: 4 The diseased **h** ye not strengthened, NIH
34: 4 neither **h** ye healed that which was sick, NIH
34: 4 neither **h** ye bound up that which was NIH
34: 4 neither **h** ye brought again that which was NIH
34: 4 neither **h** ye sought that which was lost; NIH
34: 4 with force and with cruelty **h** ye ruled them. NIH
34:12 where they **h** been scattered in the cloudy NIH
34:18 *Seemeth it* a small thing unto you to **h** eaten NIH
34:18 to **h** drunk of the deep waters, but ye must NIH
34:19 they eat that which ye **h** trodden with your NIH
34:19 they drink that which ye **h** fouled with your NIH
34:21 Because ye **h** thrust with side and NIH
34:21 your horns, till ye **h** scattered them abroad; NIH
34:24 among them; I the LORD **h** spoken *it.* NIH
34:27 when I **h** broken the bands of their yoke, NIH
35:11 known amongst them, when I **h** judged thee. NIH
35:12 *that* I **h** heard all thy blasphemies which NIH
35:13 Thus with your mouth ye **h** boasted against NIH
35:13 and **h** multiplied your words against me: NIH
35:13 your words against me: I **h** heard *them.* NIH
36: 3 Because *they* **h** made *you* desolate, and NIH
36: 5 Surely in the fire of my jealousy **h** I spoken NIH
36: 5 which **h** appointed my land into their NIH
36: 6 I **h** spoken in my jealousy and in my fury, NIH
36: 6 ye **h** borne the shame of the heathen: NIH
36: 7 I **h** lifted up mine hand, Surely the heathen NIH
36:22 which ye **h** profaned among the heathen, NIH
36:23 which ye **h** profaned in the midst of them; NIH
36:33 In the day that I shall **h** cleansed you from NIH
36:36 I the LORD **h** spoken *it,* and I will do *it.* NIH
37:13 when I **h** opened your graves, O my people, NIH
37:14 shall ye know that I the LORD **h** spoken *it,* NIH
37:23 wherein they **h** sinned, and will cleanse NIH
37:24 and they all shall **h** one shepherd: 1961+3807.1
37:25 they shall dwell in the land that I **h** given NIH
37:25 my servant, wherein your fathers **h** dwelt; NIH
38: 8 of Israel, which **h** been always waste: NIH
38:12 which **h** gotten cattle and goods, that dwell NIH

Eze 38:17 *Art* thou he of whom I **h** spoken in old time NIH
38:19 *and* in the fire of my wrath **h** I spoken, NIH
39: 5 for I **h** spoken *it,* saith the Lord GOD. NIH
39: 8 this *is* the day whereof I **h** spoken. NIH
39:15 till the buriers **h** buried it in the valley of NIH
39:19 of my sacrifice which I **h** sacrificed for you. NIH
39:21 shall see my judgment that I **h** executed, NIH
39:21 and my hand that I **h** laid upon them. NIH
39:24 according to their transgressions **h** I done NIH
39:25 **h mercy** upon the whole house of Israel, 7355
39:26 After that they **h** borne their shame, and all NIH
39:26 all their trespasses whereby they **h** NIH
39:27 When I **h** brought them again from NIH
39:28 I **h** gathered them unto their own land, and NIH
39:28 and **h** left none of them any more there. NIH
39:29 for I **h** poured out my spirit upon the house NIH
41: 6 that *they* might **h** hold, but they had not 1961
43: 8 they **h** even defiled my holy name by their NIH
43: 8 their abominations that they **h** committed: NIH
43: 8 wherefore I **h** consumed them in mine NIH
43:11 if they be ashamed of all that they **h** done, NIH
44: 7 In that ye **h** brought *into my sanctuary* NIH
44: 7 they **h** broken my covenant because of all NIH
44: 8 ye **h** not kept the charge of mine holy NIH
44: 8 ye **h** set keepers of my charge in my NIH
44:12 therefore **h** I lift up mine hand against them, NIH
44:13 their abominations which they **h** committed. NIH
44:18 They shall **h** linen bonnets upon their 1961
44:18 and shall **h** linen breeches upon their loins; 1961
45: 5 of the house, **h** for themselves, 1961+3807.1
45:10 Ye shall **h** just balances, and a just 1961+3807.1
45:21 ye shall **h** the passover, a feast of 1961+3807.1
47:13 tribes of Israel: Joseph *shall* **h** *two* portions. NIH
47:22 they shall **h inheritance** with you 5159+5307
48:11 which **h** kept my charge, which went not NIH
48:13 the Levites *shall* **h** five and twenty thousand NIH
48:23 the west side, Benjamin *shall* **h** *a portion.* NIH
48:24 the west side, Simeon *shall* **h** *a portion.* NIH
Da 2: 3 I **h** dreamed a dream, and my spirit was NIH
2: 9 for ye **h** prepared lying and corrupt words to NIH
2:25 I **h** found a man of the captives of Judah, NIH
2:26 known unto me the dream which I **h** seen, NIH
2:30 *any* wisdom that I **h** more than any living, 383
3:12 these men, O king, **h** not regarded thee: NIH
3:14 nor worship the golden image which I **h** set NIH
3:15 and worship the image which I **h** made; NIH
3:25 in the midst of the fire, and they **h** no hurt; 383
3:28 **h** changed the king's word, and NIH
4: 9 tell *me* the visions of my dream that I **h** NIH
4:18 This dream I king Nebuchadnezzar **h** seen. NIH
4:26 after that thou shalt **h** known that NIH
4:30 that I **h** built for the house of the kingdom NIH
5: 7 *h* a chain of gold about his neck, and NIH
5:14 I **h** even heard of thee, that the spirit of NIH
5:15 **h** been brought in before me, that they NIH
5:16 I **h** heard of thee, that thou canst make NIH
5:16 *h* a chain of gold about thy neck, and NIH
5:23 they **h** brought the vessels of his house NIH
5:23 and thy concubines, *h* drunk wine in them; NIH
6: 2 and the king should **h** no damage. 1934
6: 7 **h** consulted together to establish a royal NIH
6:22 the lions' mouths, that they **h** not hurt me: NIH
6:22 also before thee, O king, **h** I done no hurt. NIH
9: 5 We **h** sinned, and have committed iniquity, NIH
9: 5 **h** committed iniquity, and have done NIH
9: 5 and **h** done wickedly, and have rebelled, NIH
9: 5 and have done wickedly, and **h** rebelled, NIH
9: 6 Neither **h** we hearkened unto thy servants NIH
9: 7 of their trespass that they **h** trespassed NIH
9: 8 because we **h** sinned against thee. NIH
9: 9 though we **h** rebelled against him; NIH
9:10 Neither **h** we obeyed the voice of NIH
9:11 Yea, all Israel **h** transgressed thy law, NIH
9:11 of God, because we **h** sinned against him. NIH
9:15 we **h** sinned, we have done wickedly. NIH
9:15 we have sinned, we **h** done wickedly. NIH
10:16 upon me, and I **h** retained no strength. NIH
11: 5 be strong above him, and **h dominion;** 4910
11:24 he shall do *that* which his fathers **h** not NIH
11:30 and **h** indignation against the holy covenant: NIH
11:30 **h** intelligence with them that forsake NIH
11:43 he shall **h power** over the treasures of gold 4910
12: 7 when *he* shall **h** accomplished to scatter NIH
Hos 1: 6 for I will no more **h mercy** upon the house 7355
1: 7 I will **h mercy** upon the house of Judah, 7355
2: 4 I will not **h mercy** upon her children; 7355
2:12 These *are* my rewards that my lovers **h** NIH
2:23 I will **h mercy** upon her that had not 7355
4:10 For they shall eat, and not **h enough:** 7646
4:10 they **h** left off to take heed to the LORD. NIH
4:12 they **h** gone a whoring from under their NIH
4:18 they **h** committed whoredom continually: NIH
5: 1 because ye **h** been a snare on Mizpah, and NIH
5: 2 though I **h** *been* a rebuker of them all. NIH
5: 4 of them, and they **h** not known the LORD. NIH
5: 7 They **h** dealt treacherously against NIH
5: 7 for they **h** begotten strange children: NIH
5: 9 among the tribes of Israel **h** I made known NIH
6: 5 Therefore **h** I hewed *them* by the prophets; NIH
6: 5 I **h** slain them by the words of my mouth: NIH
6: 7 they like men **h** transgressed the covenant: NIH
6: 7 there **h** they dealt treacherously against me. NIH
6:10 I **h** seen a horrible thing in the house of NIH
7: 1 When I *would* **h** healed Israel, then NIH
7: 2 now their own doings **h** beset them about; NIH
7: 5 *In* the day of our king the princes **h** made NIH
7: 6 For they **h** made ready their heart like an NIH
7: 7 hot as an oven, and **h** devoured their judges; NIH
7: 9 Strangers **h** devoured his strength, and NIH
7:13 for they **h** fled from me: destruction unto NIH
7:13 because they **h** transgressed against me: NIH
7:13 though I **h** redeemed them, yet they have NIH
7:13 yet they **h** spoken lies against me. NIH
7:14 they **h** not cried unto me with their heart, NIH
7:15 Though I **h** bound *and* strengthened their NIH

Hos 8: 1 because they **h** transgressed my covenant, NIH
8: 4 They **h** set up kings, but not by me: NIH
8: 4 they **h** made princes, and I knew *it* not: NIH
8: 4 and their gold **h** they made them idols, NIH
8: 7 For they **h** sown the wind, and they shall NIH
8:10 Yea, though they **h** hired among the nations, NIH
8:12 I **h** written to him the great things of my NIH
9: 9 They **h** deeply corrupted *themselves,* as *in* NIH
10: 1 according to the goodness of his land they **h** NIH
10: 3 We **h** no king, because we feared not 3807.1
10: 4 They **h** spoken words, swearing falsely in NIH
10:13 Ye **h** plowed wickedness, ye have reaped NIH
10:13 plowed wickedness, ye **h** reaped iniquity; NIH
10:13 reaped iniquity; ye **h** eaten the fruit of lies: NIH
12: 8 become rich, I **h** found me out substance: NIH
12:10 I **h** also spoken by the prophets, and I have NIH
12:10 I **h** multiplied visions, and used similitudes NIH
13: 2 **h** made them molten images of their silver, NIH
13: 6 was exalted; therefore **h** they forgotten me. NIH
14: 8 *say,* What **h** I **to do** any more **with** idols? 3807.1
14: 8 I **h** heard *him,* and observed him: I *am* like a NIH
Joel 1:18 are perplexed, because they **h** no pasture; 3807.1
3: 2 whom they **h** scattered among the nations, NIH
3: 3 they **h** cast lots for my people; and NIH
3: 3 **h** given a boy for a harlot, and sold a girl for NIH
3: 4 Yea, and what **h** ye to do with me, O Tyre, NIH
3: 5 Because ye **h** taken my silver and my gold, NIH
3: 5 **h** carried into your temples my goodly NIH
3: 6 the children of Jerusalem **h** ye sold unto NIH
3: 7 out of the place whither ye **h** sold them, NIH
3:19 they **h** shed innocent blood in their land. NIH
3:21 For I will cleanse their blood *that* I **h** not NIH
Am 1: 3 they **h** threshed Gilead with threshing NIH
1:13 they **h** ript up the women with child at NIH
2: 4 they **h** despised the law of the LORD, NIH
2: 4 **h** not kept his commandments, and their lies NIH
2: 4 after the which their fathers **h** walked: NIH
3: 2 You only **h** I known of all the families of NIH
3: 4 cry out of his den, if he **h** taken nothing? NIH
3: 5 from the earth, and **h** taken nothing at all? NIH
3:15 the great houses shall **h an end,** saith 5486
4: 6 I also **h** given you cleanness of teeth in all NIH
4: 6 yet **h** ye not returned unto me, saith NIH
4: 7 also I **h** withholden the rain from you, when NIH
4: 8 yet **h** ye not returned unto me, saith NIH
4: 9 I **h** smitten you with blasting and mildew: NIH
4: 9 the palmerworm devoured *them:* yet **h** ye NIH
4:10 I **h** sent among you the pestilence after NIH
4:10 your young men **h** I slain with the sword, NIH
4:10 the sword, and **h** taken away your horses; NIH
4:10 I **h** made the stink of your camps to come NIH
4:10 yet **h** ye not returned unto me, saith NIH
4:11 I **h** overthrown *some* of you, as God NIH
4:11 yet **h** ye not returned unto me, saith NIH
5:11 ye **h** built houses of hewn stone, but ye shall NIH
5:11 ye **h** planted pleasant vineyards, but ye shall NIH
5:14 of hosts, shall be with you, as ye **h** spoken. NIH
5:25 **H** ye offered unto me sacrifices and NIH
5:26 ye **h** borne the tabernacle of your Moloch NIH
6:12 for ye **h** turned judgment into gall, and NIH
6:13 **H** we not taken to us horns by our own NIH
9: 7 **H** not I brought up Israel out of the land of NIH
9:15 up out of their land which I **h** given them, NIH
Ob 1: 1 We **h** heard a rumour from the LORD, and NIH
1: 2 I **h** made thee small among the heathen: NIH
1: 5 would they not **h** stolen till they had NIH
1: 7 All the men of thy confederacy **h** brought NIH
1: 7 the men that were at peace with thee **h** NIH
1: 7 *they that eat* thy bread **h** laid a wound under NIH
1:12 thou shouldest not **h** looked on the day of NIH
1:12 neither shouldest thou **h** rejoiced over NIH
1:12 neither shouldest thou **h** spoken proudly in NIH
1:13 Thou shouldest not **h** entered into the gate NIH
1:13 thou shouldest not **h** looked on their NIH
1:13 nor **h** laid *hands* on their substance in NIH
1:14 Neither shouldest thou **h** stood in NIH
1:14 neither shouldest thou **h** delivered up those NIH
1:16 For as ye **h** drunk upon my holy mountain, NIH
Jnh 2: 9 I will pay *that* that I **h** vowed. NIH
Mic 2: 5 Therefore thou shalt **h** none that 1961+3807.1
2: 9 The women of my people **h** ye cast out from NIH
2: 9 from their children **h** ye taken *away* my NIH
2:13 they **h** broken up, and have passed through NIH
2:13 **h** passed through the gate, and are gone out NIH
3: 4 as they **h** behaved themselves ill in their NIH
3: 6 *be* unto you, that *ye* shall not **h** a vision; NIH
4: 6 that is driven out, and *her* that I **h** afflicted; NIH
4: 9 for pangs **h** taken thee as a woman in NIH
5: 2 whose goings forth **h** *been* from of old, NIH
5:12 thou shalt **h** no *more* soothsayers: 1961+3807.1
5:15 upon the heathen, such as they **h** not heard. NIH
6: 3 O my people, what **h** I done unto thee? and NIH
6: 3 wherein **h** I wearied thee? testify against NIH
6:12 the inhabitants thereof **h** spoken lies, and NIH
7: 1 for I am as when they **h** gathered NIH
7: 9 because I **h** sinned against him, until he NIH
7:19 turn again, he will **h compassion** upon us; 7355
Na 1:12 Though I **h** afflicted thee, I will afflict thee NIH
2: 2 for the emptiers **h** emptied them out, and NIH
Hab 1:14 creeping things, *that h* no ruler over them? NIH
3: 2 I **h** heard thy speech, *and* was afraid: NIH
Zep 1: 6 *those* that **h** not sought the LORD, nor NIH
1:17 because they **h** sinned against the LORD: NIH
2: 3 of the earth, which **h** wrought his judgment; NIH
2: 8 I **h** heard the reproach of Moab, and NIH
2: 8 whereby they **h** reproached my people, and NIH
2:10 This shall they **h** for their pride, because 3807.1
2:10 because they **h** reproached and NIH
3: 4 her priests **h** polluted the sanctuary, NIH
3: 4 they **h** done violence to the law. NIH
3: 6 I **h** cut off *the* nations: their towers are NIH
3:19 fame in every land where they **h** been put to NIH
Hag 1: 6 Ye **h** sown much, and bring in little; *ye* eat, NIH
1: 6 *ye* eat, but ye **h** not enough; *ye* drink, but 3807.1
2:23 for I **h** chosen thee, saith the LORD of NIH

H

Zec 1: 4 unto whom the former prophets **h** cried, NIH
1:11 We **h** walked to and fro through the earth, NIH
1:12 how long wilt thou not **h mercy** on 7355
1:19 These *are* the horns which **h** scattered NIH
1:21 These *are* the horns which **h** scattered NIH
2: 6 for I **h** spread you abroad as the four winds NIH
3: 4 I **h** caused thine iniquity to pass from thee, NIH
3: 9 For behold the stone that I **h** laid before NIH
4: 2 I said, I **h** looked, and behold, a candlestick NIH
4: 9 The hands of Zerubbabel **h** laid NIH
6: 8 these that go toward the north country **h** NIH
7: 3 as I **h** done these so many years? NIH
8:15 So again **h** I thought in these days to do NIH
8:23 for we **h** heard *that* God *is* with you. NIH
9: 8 any more: for now **h** I seen with mine eyes. NIH
9:11 by the blood of thy covenant I **h** sent forth NIH
9:13 When I **h** bent Judah for me, filled the bow NIH
10: 2 For the idols **h** spoken vanity, and NIH
10: 2 the diviners **h** seen a lie, and have told false NIH
10: 2 have seen a lie, and **h** told false dreams; NIH
10: 6 to place them; for I **h mercy** upon them: 7355
10: 8 and gather them; for I **h** redeemed them: NIH
10: 8 and they shall increase as they **h** increased. NIH
12:10 they shall look upon me whom they **h** NIH
14:12 the people that **h** fought against Jerusalem; NIH
14:18 that ***h*** no *rain;* there shall be the plague, NIH
Mal 1: 2 I **h** loved you, saith the LORD. Yet ye say, NIH
1: 6 ye say, Wherein **h** we despised thy name? NIH
1: 7 and ye say, Wherein **h** we polluted thee? NIH
1:10 I **h** no pleasure in you, saith the LORD 3807.1
1:12 ye ***h*** profaned it, in that ye say, The table of NIH
1:13 a weariness *is it!* and ye **h** snuffed at it, NIH
2: 2 yea, I **h** cursed them already, because ye do NIH
2: 4 ye shall know that I **h** sent this NIH
2: 8 ye **h** caused many to stumble at the law; NIH
2: 8 ye **h** corrupted the covenant of Levi, NIH
2: 9 Therefore **h** I also made you contemptible NIH
2: 9 according as ye **h** not kept my ways, but NIH
2: 9 kept my ways, but **h** been partial in the law. NIH
2:10 **H** we not all one father? hath not one 3807.1
2:13 this **h** ye done again, covering the altar of NIH
2:17 Ye **h** wearied the LORD with your words. NIH
2:17 Wherein **h** we wearied *him?* When ye say, NIH
3: 7 **h** not kept *them.* Return unto me, and I will NIH
3: 8 Yet ye ***h*** robbed me. But ye say, Wherein NIH
3: 8 ye say, Wherein **h** we robbed thee? *In* tithes NIH
3: 9 for ye ***h*** robbed me, *even* this whole nation. NIH
3:13 Your words **h** been stout against me, NIH
3:13 What **h** we spoken so much against thee? NIH
3:14 Ye **h** said, It *is* vain to serve God: and NIH
3:14 what profit *is it* that we **h** kept his NIH
3:14 that we **h** walked mournfully before NIH
Mt 2: 2 for we **h** seen his star in the east, and NIG
2: 8 when ye **h** found *him,* bring me word again, NIG
2:15 saying, Out of Egypt **h** I called my son. NIG
3: 9 We **h** Abraham to *our* father: *2192*
3:14 I **h** need to be baptized of thee, and *2192*
5:13 but if the salt **h** lost his savour, NIG
5:21 Ye **h** heard that it was said by them of old NIG
5:27 Ye **h** heard that it was said by them of old NIG
5:33 ye **h** heard that it hath been said by them of NIG
5:38 Ye **h** heard that it hath been said, An eye for NIG
5:40 take *away* thy coat, **let** him **h** *thy* cloke also. *863*
5:43 Ye **h** heard that it hath been said, Thou shalt NIG
5:46 them which love you, what reward **h** ye? *2192*
6: 1 otherwise ye **h** no reward of your Father *2192*
6: 2 in the streets, that they may **h glory** of men. *1392*
6: 2 Verily I say unto you, They **h** their reward. *568*
6: 5 Verily I say unto you, They **h** their reward. *568*
6: 8 for your Father knoweth what *things* ye **h** *2192*
6:16 Verily I say unto you, They **h** their reward. *568*
6:32 knoweth that ye **h need** of all these *things.* *5535*
7:22 Lord, **h** we not prophesied in thy name? NIG
7:22 and in thy name **h** cast out devils? NIG
8:10 I **h** not found so great faith, no not in Israel. NIG
8:20 The foxes **h** holes, and the birds of the air *2192*
8:20 have holes, and the birds of the air ***h*** nests; NIG
8:29 saying, What **h** we to do with thee, Jesus, NIG
9:13 I will **h** mercy, and not sacrifice: *2309*
9:27 saying, *Thou* Son of David, **h mercy** on us. *1653*
10: 8 out devils: freely ye **h** received, freely give. NIG
10:23 Ye shall not **h** gone over the cities of Israel, NIG
10:25 If they **h** called the master of the house NIG
11: 5 and the poor **h** the gospel preached to them. NIG
11:17 We **h** piped unto you, and ye have not NIG
11:17 have piped unto you, and ye **h** not danced; NIG
11:17 we **h** mourned unto you, and ye have not NIG
11:17 mourned unto you, and ye **h** not lamented. NIG
11:21 Sidon they **would h** repented long ago in *302*
11:23 mighty works, which **h** been done in thee, NIG
11:23 it **would h** remained until this day. *302*
12: 3 unto them, **H** ye not read what David did, NIG
12: 5 Or **h** ye not read in the law, how that on NIG
12: 7 I will **h** mercy, and not sacrifice, *2309*
12: 7 ye **would** not **h** condemned the guiltless. *302*
12:11 that shall **h** one sheep, and if it fall into a *2192*
12:18 Behold my servant, whom I **h** chosen; my NIG
13:12 be given, and he shall **h** *more* **abundance**: *4052*
13:15 dull of hearing, and their eyes they **h** closed; NIG
13:17 righteous *men* **h** desired to see *those things* NIG
13:17 and **h** not seen *them;* and to hear *those* NIG
13:17 *things* which ye hear, and **h** not heard *them.* NIG
13:35 I will utter *things which* **h** *been* kept secret NIG
13:51 **H** ye understood all these *things?* They say NIG
14: 4 unto him, It is not lawful for thee to **h** her. *2192*
14: 5 And when he would **h** put him to death, NIG
14:17 We **h** here but five loaves, and two fishes. *2192*
15: 6 *he shall be free.* Thus **h** ye made NIG
15:22 unto him, saying, **H mercy** on me, O Lord, *1653*
15:32 and said, I **h compassion** on the multitude, *4697*
15:32 me now three days, and **h** nothing to eat: *2192*
15:33 Whence should we **h** so much bread in NIG
15:34 saith unto them, How many loaves **h** ye? *2192*
16: 7 saying, *It is* because we **h** taken no bread. NIG
16: 8 because ye **h** brought no bread? NIG

Mt 17:12 but **h** done unto him whatsoever they listed. NIG
17:15 Lord, **h mercy** on my son: for he is *1653*
17:20 If ye **h** faith as a grain of mustard seed, *2192*
18:12 if a man **h** an hundred sheep, and one of *1096*
18:26 **h patience** with me, and I will pay thee all. *3114*
18:29 **H patience** with me, and I will pay thee all. *3114*
18:33 **Shouldest** not thou also **h** had compassion *1163*
19: 4 and said unto them, **H** ye not read, NIG
19:12 which **h** made themselves eunuchs for NIG
19:16 *thing* shall I do, that I may **h** eternal life? *2192*
19:20 All these *things* **h** I kept from my youth up: NIG
19:21 and thou shalt **h** treasure in heaven: *2192*
19:27 we **h** forsaken all, and followed thee; NIG
19:27 followed thee; what shall we **h** therefore? *1510*
19:28 That ye which **h** followed me, in NIG
20:10 they supposed that they should **h** received NIG
20:12 These last **h** wrought *but* one hour, and NIG
20:12 which **h** borne the burden and heat of NIG
20:30 cried out, saying, **H mercy** on us, O Lord, *1653*
20:31 saying, **H mercy** on us, O Lord, *thou* Son *1653*
21:13 of prayer; but ye **h** made it a den of thieves. NIG
21:16 **h** ye never read, Out of the mouth of babes NIG
21:21 I say unto you, If ye **h** faith, and doubt not, *2192*
22: 4 are bidden, Behold, I **h** prepared my dinner: NIG
22:31 **h** ye not read that which was spoken unto NIG
23:23 **h** omitted the weightier *matters* of the law, NIG
23:23 these **ought** *ye* **to h** done, and not to leave *1163*
23:30 we **would** not **h** been partakers with them in *302*
23:37 how often would I **h** gathered thy children NIG
24:25 Behold, I **h** told you before. NIG
24:43 he **would h** watched, and would not have *302*
24:43 **would** not **h** suffered his house to be broken *302*
25:20 I **h** gained besides them five talents moe. NIG
25:22 I **h** gained two other talents besides them. NIG
25:26 and gather where I **h** not strawed: NIG
25:27 Thou **oughtest** therefore **to h** put my *1163*
25:27 at my coming I **should h** received mine own *302*
25:29 shall be given, and he shall **h abundance**: *4052*
25:40 Inasmuch as ye **h** done *it* unto one of NIG
25:40 of these my brethren, ye **h** done *it* unto me. NIG
26: 9 For this ointment **might h** been sold for *1410*
26:11 For ye **h** the poor always with you; but *2192*
26:11 always with you; but me ye **h** not always. *2192*
26:65 what further need **h** we of witnesses? *2192*
26:65 behold, now ye **h** heard his blasphemy. NIG
27: 4 I **h** sinned in that I have betrayed NIG
27: 4 I have sinned in that I **h** betrayed NIG
27:19 **H** thou nothing to do with that just *man:* for NIG
27:19 I **h** suffered many *things* this day in a dream NIG
27:43 let him deliver him now, if he will **h** him: NIG
27:65 Pilate said unto them, Ye **h** a watch: *2192*
28: 7 there shall ye see him: lo, I **h** told you. NIG
28:20 all *things* whatsoever I **h** commanded you: NIG
Mk 1: 8 I indeed **h** baptized you with water: but NIG
1:24 what **h** we to do with thee, *thou* Jesus of NIG
2:17 They that are whole **h** no need of *2192*
2:19 as long as they **h** the bridegroom with *2192*
2:25 **H** ye never read what David did, when he NIG
3:15 And to **h** power to heal sicknesses, and to *2192*
4:15 but when they **h** heard, Satan cometh NIG
4:16 who, when they **h** heard the word, NIG
4:17 And **h** no root in themselves, and so endure *2192*
4:23 If any *man* **h** ears to hear, let him hear. *2192*
4:40 ye so fearful? how *is it that* you **h** no faith? *2192*
5: 7 and said, What **h** I to do with thee, Jesus, NIG
6:18 It is not lawful for thee to **h** thy brother's *2192*
6:19 against him, and would **h** killed him; NIG
6:36 themselves bread: for they **h** nothing to eat. *2192*
6:38 saith unto them, How many loaves **h** ye? *2192*
6:48 upon the sea, and would **h** passed by them. NIG
7: 4 which they **h** received to hold, *as* NIG
7:13 your tradition, which ye **h** delivered: NIG
7:16 If any *man* **h** ears to hear, let him hear. *2192*
7:24 and **would h** no *man* know *it:* but he could *2309*
8: 2 I **h compassion** on the multitude, because *4697*
8: 2 they **h** now been with me three days, NIG
8: 2 with me three days, and **h** nothing to eat: *2192*
8: 5 he asked them, How many loaves **h** ye? *2192*
8:16 saying, *It is* because we **h** no bread. *2192*
8:17 Why reason ye, because ye **h** no bread? *2192*
8:17 **h** ye your heart yet hardened? *2192*
9: 1 till they **h** seen the kingdom of God come NIG
9:13 they **h** done unto him whatsoever they NIG
9:17 Master, I **h** brought unto thee my son, NIG
9:22 if thou canst do any *thing,* **h compassion** *4697*
9:50 but if the salt **h** lost his saltness, *1096*
9:50 **H** salt in yourselves, and have peace one *2192*
9:50 and **h peace** one with another. *1514*
10:20 all these **h** I observed from my youth. NIG
10:21 and thou shalt **h** treasure in heaven: *2192*
10:23 How hardly shall they that **h** riches enter *2192*
10:28 Lo, we **h** left all, and have followed thee. NIG
10:28 Lo, we have left all, and **h** followed thee. NIG
10:47 Jesus, *thou* Son of David, **h mercy** on me. *1653*
10:48 *Thou* Son of David, **h mercy** on me. *1653*
11:17 of prayer? but ye **h** made it a den of thieves. NIG
11:22 answering saith unto them, **H** faith in God. *2192*
11:23 to pass; he shall **h** whatsoever he saith. *1510*
11:24 that ye receive *them,* and ye shall **h** *them.* *1510*
11:25 forgive, if ye **h** ought against any: *2192*
12:10 And **h** ye not read this scripture; The stone NIG
12:26 **h** ye not read in the book of Moses, how in NIG
12:43 than all they which **h** cast into the treasury: NIG
13:23 ye heed: behold, I **h** foretold you all *things.* NIG
14: 5 For it might **h** been sold for more than three NIG
14: 5 and **h** been given to the poor. NIG
14: 7 For ye **h** the poor with you always, and *2192*
14: 7 may do them good: but me ye **h** not always. *2192*
14:64 Ye **h** heard the blasphemy: what think ye? NIG
Lk 1: 1 Forasmuch as many **h** taken in hand to set NIG
1:14 And thou shalt **h** joy and gladness; and *1510*
1:62 to his father, how he would **h** him called. *2309*
1:70 which **h** been since the world began:) NIG
2:30 For mine eyes **h** seen thy salvation, NIG
2:44 supposing him to **h** been in the company, NIG

Lk 2:48 thy father and I **h** sought thee sorrowing. NIG
3: 8 We **h** Abraham to *our* father: *2192*
4:23 whatsoever we **h** heard done in Capernaum, NIG
4:34 what **h** we to do with thee, *thou* Jesus of NIG
5: 5 we **h** toiled all the night, and have taken NIG
5: 5 toiled all the night, and **h** taken nothing: NIG
5:26 saying, We **h** seen strange *things* to day. NIG
6: 3 **H** ye not read so much as this, what David NIG
6:24 are rich: for ye **h** received your consolation. NIG
6:32 them which love you, what thank **h** ye? *1510*
6:33 which do good to you, what thank **h** ye? *1510*
6:34 whom ye hope to receive, what thank **h** ye? *1510*
7: 9 I **h** not found so great faith, no, not in Israel. NIG
7:22 and tell John what *things* ye **h** seen and NIG
7:32 We **h** piped unto you, and ye have not NIG
7:32 have piped unto you, and ye **h** not danced; NIG
7:32 we **h** mourned to you, and ye have not wept. NIG
7:32 we have mourned to you, and ye **h** not wept. NIG
7:39 **would h** known who and what manner of *302*
7:40 Simon, I **h** somewhat to say unto thee. *2192*
8:13 and these **h** no root, which for a while *2192*
8:14 which, when they **h** heard, go *forth,* and NIG
8:18 be taken even *that* which he seemeth to **h**. *2192*
8:28 voice said, What **h** I to do with thee, Jesus, NIG
9: 3 neither money; neither **h** two coats apiece. *2192*
9: 9 And Herod said, John **h** I beheaded: but NIG
9:13 We **h** no more but five loaves and *1510*
9:58 Foxes **h** holes, and birds of the air *have* *2192*
9:58 have holes, and birds of the air **h** nests; NIG
10:13 and Sidon, which **h** been done in you, NIG
10:24 kings **h** desired to see *those things* which ye NIG
10:24 and **h** not seen *them;* and to hear *those* NIG
10:24 *things* which ye hear, and **h** not heard *them.* NIG
11: 5 Which of you shall **h** a friend, and shall go *2192*
11: 6 to me, and I **h** nothing to set before him: *2192*
11:41 rather give alms *of* such *things* as *you* **h**; *1751*
11:42 these ought *ye* to **h** done, and not to leave NIG
11:52 for ye **h** taken away the key of knowledge: NIG
12: 3 Therefore whatsoever ye **h** spoken in NIG
12: 3 *that* which ye **h** spoken in the ear in closets NIG
12: 4 and after that **h** no more that *they* can do. *2192*
12:17 I **h** no room where to bestow my fruits? *2192*
12:24 which neither **h** storehouse nor barn; and *1510*
12:30 your Father knoweth that ye **h need** of *5535*
12:33 Sell that ye **h**, and give alms; *5225*
12:39 he **would h** watched, and not have suffered *302*
12:39 not **h** suffered his house to be broken NIG
12:48 and to whom *men* **h** committed much, NIG
12:50 But I **h** a baptism to be baptized *with;* and *2192*
13:26 We **h** eaten and drunk in thy presence, and NIG
13:34 how often would I **h** gathered thy children NIG
14: 5 Which of you shall **h** an ass or an ox fallen NIG
14:10 shalt thou **h** worship in the presence of *1510*
14:18 I **h** bought a piece of ground, and I must NIG
14:18 and see it: I pray thee **h** me excused. *2192*
14:19 I **h** bought five yoke of oxen, and I go to NIG
14:19 to prove them: I pray thee **h** me excused. *2192*
14:20 I **h** married a wife, and therefore I cannot NIG
14:28 whether he **h** sufficient to finish it? *2192*
14:34 but if the salt **h** lost his savour, NIG
15: 6 for I **h** found my sheep which was lost. NIG
15: 9 for I **h** found the piece which I had lost. NIG
15:16 And he would fain **h** filled his belly with NIG
15:17 my father's **h** bread **enough and to spare**, *4052*
15:18 I **h** sinned against heaven, and before thee, NIG
15:21 I **h** sinned against heaven, and in thy sight, NIG
15:31 art ever with me, and all that I **h** is thine. *1699*
16:11 ye **h** not been faithful in the unrighteous NIG
16:12 And if ye **h** not been faithful in that which NIG
16:24 **h mercy** on me, and send Lazarus, *1653*
16:28 For I **h** five brethren; that he may testify *2192*
16:29 unto him, They **h** Moses and the prophets; *2192*
17: 8 and serve me, till I **h** eaten and drunken; NIG
17:10 when ye shall **h** done all those *things* which NIG
17:10 we **h** done *that* which was our duty to do. NIG
17:13 and said, Jesus, Master, **h mercy** on us. *1653*
18:21 All these **h** I kept from my youth up. NIG
18:22 and thou shalt **h** treasure in heaven: *2192*
18:24 How hardly shall they that **h** riches enter *2192*
18:28 Then Peter said, Lo, we **h** left all, NIG
18:38 Jesus, *thou* Son of David, **h mercy** on me. *1653*
18:39 *Thou* Son of David, **h mercy** on me. *1653*
19: 8 if I **h** taken any *thing* from any *man* by false NIG
19:14 We will not **h** this *man* to reign over us. NIG
19:17 very little, **h** thou authority over ten cities. *2192*
19:20 which I **h** kept laid up in a napkin: NIG
19:23 that at my coming I **might h** required *mine* *302*
19:46 of prayer: but ye **h** made it a den of thieves. NIG
21: 4 For all these **h** of their abundance cast in NIG
22:15 With desire I **h** desired to eat this passover NIG
22:28 Ye are they which **h** continued with me in NIG
22:31 Simon, behold, Satan hath desired ***to h*** you, NIG
22:32 But I **h** prayed for thee, that thy faith fail NIG
22:37 for the *things* concerning me **h** an end. *2192*
22:71 for we ourselves **h** heard of his own mouth. NIG
23: 8 he hoped to **h** seen some miracle done by NIG
23:14 unto them, Ye **h** brought this man unto me, NIG
23:14 **h** found no fault in this man *touching those* NIG
23:22 I **h** found no cause of death in him: I will NIG
24:17 *are* these that ye **h** one to another, *474*
24:20 condemned to death, and **h** crucified him. NIG
24:21 been he which should **h** redeemed Israel: NIG
24:25 to believe all that the prophets **h** spoken: NIG
24:26 Ought not Christ to **h** suffered these *things,* NIG
24:28 he made as though *he* would **h** gone further. NIG
24:39 hath not flesh and bones, as ye see me **h**. *2192*
24:41 he said unto them, **H** ye here any meat? *2192*
Jn 1:16 And of his fulness **h** all we received, and NIG
1:41 We **h** found the Messias, which is, NIG
1:45 and saith unto him, We **h** found him, NIG
2: 3 of Jesus saith unto him, They **h** no wine. *2192*
2: 4 unto her, Woman, what **h** I to do with thee? NIG
2:10 and when men **h** well drunk, then NIG
3:11 that we do know, and testify that we **h** seen; NIG
3:12 If I **h** told you earthly *things,* and ye believe NIG

Jn 3:15 in him should not perish, but **h** eternal life. 2192
3:16 should not perish, but **h** everlasting life. 2192
4: 9 For the Jews **h** no **dealings with** 4798
4:10 thou **wouldest h** asked of him, and he would 302
4:10 and he **would h** given thee living water. 302
4:17 woman answered and said, I **h** no husband. 2192
4:17 Thou hast well said, I **h** no husband: 2192
4:32 I **h** meat to eat that ye know not of. 2192
4:42 for we **h** heard *him* ourselves, and NIG
5: 7 Sir, I **h** no man, when the water is troubled, 2192
5:26 hath he given to the Son to **h** life in 2192
5:29 they that **h** done good, unto the resurrection NIG
5:29 and they that **h** done evil, unto NIG
5:36 But I **h** greater witness than *that of* John: 2192
5:37 Ye **h** neither heard his voice at any time, NIG
5:38 And ye **h** not his word abiding in you: 2192
5:39 for in them ye think ye **h** eternal life: 2192
5:40 will not come to me, that ye might **h** life. 2192
5:42 that ye **h** not the love of God in you. 2192
5:46 ye believed Moses, ye **would h** believed me: 302
6:36 That ye also **h** seen me, and believe not. NIG
6:40 believeth on him, may **h** everlasting life: 2192
6:53 and drink his blood, ye **h** no life in you. 2192
6:70 **H** not I chosen you twelve, and one of you NIG
7:21 I **h** done one work, and ye all marvel. NIG
7:23 I **h** made a man every whit whole on NIG
7:44 And some of them would **h** taken him; but NIG
7:45 said unto them, Why **h** ye not brought him? NIG
7:48 **H** any of the rulers or of the Pharisees NIG
8: 6 that they might **h** to accuse him. 2192
8:12 in darkness, but shall **h** the light of life. 2192
8:19 ye should **h** known my Father also. NIG
8:26 I **h** many *things* to say and to judge of you: 2192
8:26 I speak to the world those *things* which I **h** NIG
8:28 When ye **h** lift up the Son of man, then NIG
8:38 I speak *that* which I **h** seen with my Father: NIG
8:38 ye do *that* which ye **h** seen with your father. NIG
8:40 told you the truth, which I **h** heard of God: NIG
8:41 of fornication; we **h** one Father, *even* God. 2192
8:49 Jesus answered, I **h** not a devil; but 2192
8:55 Yet ye **h** not known him; but I know him: NIG
9:27 I **h** told you already, and ye did not hear: NIG
9:41 If ye were blind, ye should **h** no sin: 2192
10:10 I am come that they might **h** life, and 2192
10:10 and that they might **h** *it more* abundantly. 2192
10:16 And other sheep I **h**, which are not of this 2192
10:18 I **h** power to lay it down, and I have power 2192
10:18 lay it down, and I **h** power to take it again. 2192
10:18 This commandment **h** I received of my NIG
10:32 Many good works **h** I shewed you from my NIG
11:34 And said, Where **h** ye laid him? They say NIG
11:37 **h** caused that even this *man* should not have NIG
11:37 have caused that even this *man* should not **h** NIG
12: 8 For the poor always ye **h** with you; but 2192
12: 8 ye have with you; but me ye **h** not always. 2192
12:28 *saying,* I **h** both glorified *it,* and will glorify NIG
12:34 We **h** heard out of the law that Christ NIG
12:35 Walk while ye **h** the light, lest darkness 2192
12:36 While ye **h** light, believe in the light, 2192
12:48 the word that I **h** spoken, the same shall NIG
12:49 For I **h** not spoken of myself; but the Father NIG
13:12 unto them, Know ye what I **h** done to you? NIG
13:14 *your* Lord and Master, **h** washed your feet; NIG
13:15 For I **h** given you an example, that ye NIG
13:15 that ye should do as I **h** done to you. NIG
13:18 I know whom I **h** chosen: but that NIG
13:26 when I **h** dipped *it.* And when he had NIG
13:29 Buy *those things* that we **h** need of against 2192
13:34 as I **h** loved you, that ye also love one NIG
13:35 my disciples, if ye **h** love one to another. 2192
14: 2 if *it were* not *so,* I **would h** told you. I go to 302
14: 7 ye **should h** known my Father also: 302
14: 7 henceforth ye know him, and **h** seen him. NIG
14: 9 **H** I been so long time with you, and *yet* hast NIG
14:25 These *things* **h** I spoken unto you, being *yet* NIG
14:26 what*soever* I **h** said unto you. NIG
14:28 Ye **h** heard how I said unto you, I go away, NIG
14:29 And now I **h** told you before it come to NIG
15: 3 the word which I **h** spoken unto you. NIG
15: 9 the Father hath loved me, so **h** I loved you: NIG
15:10 even as I **h** kept my Father's NIG
15:11 These *things* **h** I spoken unto you, that my NIG
15:12 That ye love one another, as I **h** loved you. NIG
15:15 but I **h** called you friends; for all *things* that NIG
15:15 for all *things* that I **h** heard of my Father I NIG
15:15 of my Father I **h** made known unto you. NIG
15:16 Ye **h** not chosen me, but I have chosen you, NIG
15:16 but I **h** chosen you, and ordained you, NIG
15:19 but I **h** chosen you out of the world, NIG
15:20 If they **h** persecuted me, they will also NIG
15:20 if they **h** kept my saying, they will keep NIG
15:22 but now they **h** no cloke for their sin. 2192
15:24 but now **h** they both seen and hated both me NIG
15:27 ye **h** been with me from the beginning. NIG
16: 1 These *things* **h** I spoken unto you, that ye NIG
16: 3 because they **h** not known the Father, NIG
16: 4 But these *things* **h** I told you, that when NIG
16: 6 But because I **h** said these *things* unto you, NIG
16:12 I **h** yet many *things* to say unto you, but 2192
16:22 And ye now therefore **h** sorrow: but I will 2192
16:24 Hitherto **h** ye asked nothing in my name: NIG
16:25 These *things* **h** I spoken unto you in NIG
16:27 because ye **h** loved me, and have believed NIG
16:27 and **h** believed that I came out from God. NIG
16:33 These *things* I **h** spoken unto you, that in NIG
16:33 unto you, that in me ye might **h** peace. 2192
16:33 In the world ye shall **h** tribulation: but be of 2192
16:33 be of good cheer; I **h** overcome the world. NIG
17: 4 I **h** glorified thee on the earth: I have NIG
17: 4 I **h** finished the work which thou gavest me NIG
17: 6 I **h** manifested thy name unto the men NIG
17: 6 gavest them me; and they **h** kept thy word. NIG
17: 7 Now they **h** known that all *things* NIG
17: 8 For I **h** given unto them the words which NIG
17: 8 and they **h** received *them,* and have known NIG

Jn 17: 8 **h** known surely that I came out from thee, NIG
17: 8 and they **h** believed that thou didst send me. NIG
17:12 *those* that thou gavest me I **h** kept, and NIG
17:13 that they might **h** my joy fulfilled in 2192
17:14 I **h** given them thy word; and the world hath NIG
17:18 even *so* **h** I also sent them into the world. NIG
17:22 And the glory which thou gavest me I **h** NIG
17:25 but I **h** known thee, and these have known NIG
17:25 and these **h** known that thou hast sent me. NIG
17:26 And I **h** declared unto them thy name, and NIG
18: 8 I **h** told you that I am *he:* if therefore NIG
18: 9 Of them which thou gavest me **h** I lost NIG
18:20 always resort; and in secret **h** I said nothing. NIG
18:21 ask them which heard *me,* what I **h** said NIG
18:23 Jesus answered him, If I **h** spoken evil, NIG
18:30 we **would** not **h** delivered him up unto thee. 302
18:35 the chief priests **h** delivered thee unto me: NIG
18:39 But ye **h** a custom, that I should release 1510
19: 7 We **h** a law, and by our law he ought to die, 2192
19:10 knowest thou not that I **h** power to crucify 2192
19:10 crucify thee, and **h** power to release thee? 2192
19:11 Thou couldest **h** no power *at all* against me, 2192
19:15 priests answered, We **h** no king but Cesar. 2192
19:22 What I **h** written I have written. NIG
19:22 What I have written I **h** written. NIG
20: 2 They **h** taken away the Lord out of NIG
20: 2 and we know not where they **h** laid him. NIG
20:13 Because they **h** taken away my Lord, and NIG
20:13 and I know not where they **h** laid him. NIG
20:15 if thou **h** borne him *hence,* tell me where NIG
20:25 said unto him, We **h** seen the Lord. NIG
20:29 blessed *are* they that **h** not seen, and NIG
20:29 they that have not seen, and *yet* **h** believed. NIG
20:31 that believing ye might **h** life through his 2192
21: 5 saith unto them, Children, **h** ye any meat? 2192
21:10 Bring of the fish which ye **h** now caught. NIG
Ac 1: 1 The former treatise **h** I made, O Theophilus, NIG
1: 4 which, *saith he,* ye **h** heard of me. NIG
1:11 come *in* like manner as ye **h** seen him go NIG
1:16 this scripture must needs **h** been fulfilled, NIG
1:21 Wherefore of these men which **h** companied NIG
2:23 ye **h** taken, and by wicked hands have NIG
2:23 and by wicked hands **h** crucified and slain: NIG
2:36 whom ye **h** crucified, both Lord and Christ. NIG
3: 6 Then Peter said, Silver and gold **h** I none; 5225
3: 6 have I none; but such as I **h** give I thee: 2192
3:24 that follow after, as many as **h** spoken, NIG
3:24 **h** likewise foretold of these days. NIG
4: 7 or by what name, **h** ye done this? NIG
4:20 but speak the *things* which we **h** seen and NIG
5: 9 How *is it* that ye **h** agreed together to tempt NIG
5: 9 the feet of them which **h** buried thy husband NIG
5:21 and sent to the prison to **h** them brought. NIG
5:26 the people, lest they should **h** been stoned. NIG
5:28 ye **h** filled Jerusalem with your doctrine, NIG
6:11 We **h** heard him speak blasphemous words NIG
6:14 For we **h** heard him say, that this Jesus of NIG
7:25 For he supposed his brethren would **h** NIG
7:26 and would **h** set them at one *again,* saying, NIG
7:34 I **h** seen, I have seen the affliction of my NIG
7:34 I **h** seen the affliction of my people which is NIG
7:34 and I **h** heard their groaning, and am come NIG
7:42 **h** ye offered to me slain beasts and NIG
7:52 Which of the prophets **h** not your fathers NIG
7:52 they **h** slain them which shewed before of NIG
7:52 of whom ye **h** been now the betrayers and NIG
7:53 Who **h** received the law by the disposition NIG
7:53 the disposition of angels, and **h** not kept *it.* NIG
8:24 that none of *these things* which ye **h** spoken NIG
9: 6 Lord, what wilt thou **h** me to do? 2309
9:13 Lord, I **h** heard by many of this man, NIG
10:10 he became very hungry, and would **h** eaten: NIG
10:14 for I **h** never eaten any *thing that is* common NIG
10:20 doubting nothing: for I **h** sent them. NIG
10:29 therefore for what intent ye **h** sent for me? NIG
10:47 which **h** received the Holy Ghost as well as NIG
12: 6 And when Herod would **h** brought him NIG
13: 2 Saul for the work whereunto I **h** called NIG
13:15 if ye **h** *any* word of exhortation for 1510
13:22 and said, I **h** found David the *son* of Jesse, NIG
13:27 they **h** fulfilled *them* in condemning *him.* NIG
13:33 Thou art my Son, this day **h** I begotten thee. NIG
13:46 of God should first **h** been spoken to you: NIG
13:47 *saying,* I **h** set thee to be a light of NIG
14:13 and would **h** done sacrifice with the people. NIG
15:24 Forasmuch as we **h** heard, that certain NIG
15:24 that certain which went out from us **h** NIG
15:26 Men that **h** hazarded their lives for the name NIG
15:27 We **h** sent therefore Judas and Silas, NIG
15:36 visit our brethren in every city where we **h** NIG
16: 3 Him would Paul **h** to go forth with him; and NIG
16:15 If ye **h** judged me to be faithful to the Lord, NIG
16:27 out his sword, and **would h** killed himself, 3195
16:36 The magistrates **h** sent to let you go: NIG
16:37 They **h** beaten us openly uncondemned, NIG
16:37 being Romans, and **h** cast *us* into prison; NIG
17: 3 that Christ must needs **h** suffered, and NIG
17: 6 These that **h** turned the world upside down NIG
17:28 in him we live, and move, and **h** our **being;** 1510
17:28 as certain also of your own poets **h** said, NIG
18:10 hurt thee: for I **h** much people in this city. 1510
19: 2 **H** ye received the Holy Ghost since ye NIG
19: 2 We **h** not so much as heard whether there NIG
19:21 to Jerusalem, saying, After I **h** been there, NIG
19:25 ye know that by this craft we **h** our wealth. 1510
19:30 And when Paul would **h** entered in unto NIG
19:33 would **h** made *his* defence unto the people. NIG
19:37 For ye **h** brought *hither* these men, NIG
19:38 **h** a matter against any *man,* the law is open, 2192
20:18 after what manner I **h** been with you at all NIG
20:20 was profitable *unto you,* but **h** shewed you, NIG
20:20 and **h** taught you publickly, and from house NIG
20:24 which I **h** received of the Lord Jesus, NIG
20:25 among whom I **h** gone preaching NIG
20:27 For I **h** not shunned to declare unto you all NIG

Ac 20:33 I **h** coveted no *man's* silver, or gold, or NIG
20:34 that these hands **h** ministered unto my NIG
20:35 I **h** shewed you all *things,* how that so NIG
21:23 We **h** four men which have a vow on them; 1510
21:23 We have four men which **h** a vow on them; 2192
21:25 we **h** written and concluded that they NIG
22:29 from him which should **h** examined him: NIG
22:30 he would **h** known the certainty wherefore NIG
23: 1 I **h** lived in all good conscience before God NIG
23:10 fearing lest Paul should **h** been pulled in NIG
23:14 We **h** bound ourselves under a great curse, NIG
23:14 that *we* will eat nothing until we **h** slain NIG
23:20 The Jews **h** agreed to desire thee that thou NIG
23:21 which **h** bound themselves with an oath, NIG
23:21 that *they* will neither eat nor drink till they **h** NIG
23:27 the Jews, and should **h** been killed of them: NIG
23:28 And when I would **h** known the cause NIG
23:29 to **h** nothing laid to his charge worthy of 2192
24: 5 For we **h** found this man a pestilent *fellow,* NIG
24: 6 and would **h** judged according to our law. NIG
24:15 And **h** hope towards God, which they 2192
24:16 to **h** always a conscience void of offence 2192
24:19 Who ought to **h** been here before thee, and NIG
24:20 if they **h** found any evil doing in me, NIG
24:23 and to let *him* **h** liberty, and that *he* should 2192
24:25 when I **h** a convenient season, I will call for 3335
24:26 He hoped also that money should **h** been NIG
25: 8 against Cesar, **h** I offended any *thing at all.* NIG
25:10 to the Jews **h** I done no wrong, as thou very NIG
25:11 or **h** committed any *thing* worthy of death, NIG
25:15 *me,* desiring to **h** judgment against him. NIG
25:16 before that he which is accused **h** 2192
25:16 **h** licence to answer for himself concerning 2983
25:24 the multitude of the Jews **h** dealt with me, NIG
25:25 to Augustus, I **h** determined to send him. NIG
25:26 Of whom I **h** no certain *thing* to write unto 2192
25:26 Wherefore I **h** brought him forth before NIG
25:26 I might **h** somewhat to write. 2192
26:16 for I **h** appeared unto thee for this *purpose,* NIG
26:32 This man **might h** been set at liberty, 1410
27:21 *ye* **should h** hearkened unto me, and 1163
27:21 and not **h** loosed from Crete, and to have NIG
27:21 and to **h** gained this harm and loss. NIG
27:29 Then fearing lest we should **h** fallen upon NIG
27:30 under colour as though they **would h** cast 3195
27:33 This day is the fourteenth day that ye **h** NIG
28: 6 Howbeit they looked when he should **h** NIG
28:17 though I **h** committed nothing against NIG
28:18 **would h** let *me* go, because there was no 1014
28:20 For this cause therefore **h** I called for you, NIG
28:27 dull of hearing, and their eyes **h** they closed; NIG
Ro 1: 5 By whom we **h** received grace and NIG
1:10 **h a prosperous journey** by the will of God 2137
1:13 Now I would not **h** you ignorant, brethren, NIG
1:13 that I might **h** some fruit among you also, 2192
1:32 but **h** pleasure in them that do *them.* NIG
2:12 For as many as **h** sinned without law shall NIG
2:12 as many as **h** sinned in the law shall be NIG
2:14 For when *the* Gentiles, which **h** not the law, 2192
3: 9 for we **h** before proved both Jews and NIG
3:13 with their tongues they **h** used deceit; NIG
3:17 And the way of peace **h** they not known: NIG
3:23 For all **h** sinned, and come short of NIG
4:17 I **h** made thee a father of many nations,) NIG
5: 1 we **h** peace with God through our Lord 2192
5: 2 By whom also we **h** access by faith into 2192
5:11 by whom we **h** now received the atonement. NIG
5:12 passed upon all men, for that all **h** sinned: NIG
6: 5 For if we **h** been planted together in NIG
6:14 For sin shall not **h** dominion over you: NIG
6:17 ye **h** obeyed from the heart *that* form of NIG
6:19 for as ye **h** yielded your members servants NIG
6:22 ye **h** your fruit unto holiness, and the end 2192
8: 9 Now if any *man* **h** not the Spirit of Christ, 2192
8:15 For ye **h** not received the spirit of bondage NIG
8:15 but ye **h** received the Spirit of adoption, NIG
8:23 which **h** the firstfruits of the Spirit, 2192
9: 2 That I **h** great heaviness and 1510
9: 9 time will I come, and Sara shall **h** a son. 1510
9:13 As it is written, Jacob **h** I loved, NIG
9:13 Jacob have I loved, but Esau **h** I hated. NIG
9:15 I will **h mercy** on whom I will have mercy, 1653
9:15 I will have mercy on whom I will **h mercy,** 1653
9:15 I will **h compassion** on whom I will have 3627
9:15 compassion on whom I will **h compassion.** 3627
9:17 Even for this same *purpose* **h** I raised thee NIG
9:18 Therefore hath he mercy on whom he will ***h*** NIG
9:30 **h** attained to righteousness, NIG
10: 2 For I bear them record that they **h** a zeal of 2192
10: 3 **h** not submitted themselves unto NIG
10:14 shall they call on *him* in whom they **h** not NIG
10:14 believe *in him* of whom they **h** not heard? NIG
10:16 But they **h** not all obeyed the gospel. NIG
10:18 But I say, **H** they not heard? Yes verily, NIG
10:21 All day long **h** I stretched forth my hands NIG
11: 3 they **h** killed thy prophets, and digged down NIG
11: 4 I **h** reserved to myself seven thousand men, NIG
11: 4 who **h** not bowed the knee to *the image of* NIG
11:11 **H** they stumbled that they should fall? NIG
11:30 For as ye in times past **h** not believed God, NIG
11:30 yet **h** now obtained mercy through their NIG
11:31 *Even* so **h** these also now not believed, NIG
11:32 in unbelief, that he might **h mercy** upon all. 1653
12: 4 For as we **h** many members in one body, 2192
12: 4 and all members **h** not the same office: 2192
13: 3 and thou shalt **h** praise of the same: 2192
14:22 **h** *it* to thyself before God. Happy *is* he that 2192
15: 4 and comfort of the scriptures might **h** hope. 2192
15:15 I **h** written the more boldly unto you in NIG
15:17 I **h** therefore whereof I may glory through 2192
15:19 I **h** fully preached the gospel of Christ. NIG
15:20 Yea, so **h** I strived to preach the gospel, NIG
15:21 and they that **h** not heard shall understand. NIG
15:22 For which cause also I **h** been much NIG
15:27 For if the Gentiles **h** been made partakers NIG

Ro 15:28 When therefore I **h** performed this, and NIG
15:28 and **h** sealed to them this fruit, NIG
15:31 that my service which I **h** for Jerusalem NIG
16:4 Who **h** for my life laid down their own NIG
16:17 offences contrary to the doctrine which ye **h** NIG
16:19 yet I would **h** you wise unto that which is 1510
1Co 2:8 for had they known it, they **would** not **h** 302
2:9 neither **h** entered into the heart of man, NIG
2:12 Now we **h** received, not the spirit of NIG
2:16 instruct him? But we **h** the mind of Christ. 2192
3:2 I **h** fed you with milk, and not with meat: NIG
3:6 I **h** planted, Apollos watered; but God gave NIG
3:10 I **h** laid the foundation, and another buildeth NIG
4:5 and then shall every man **h** praise of God. 1096
4:6 I **h** in a figure transferred to myself and NIG
4:8 are rich, ye **h** reigned as kings without us: NIG
4:11 and **h no certain dwelling place**; 790
4:15 For though you **h** ten thousand instructors 2192
4:15 in Christ, yet **h** ye not many fathers: NIG
4:15 for in Christ Jesus I **h** begotten you through NIG
4:17 For this cause **h** I sent unto you Timotheus, NIG
5:1 that one should **h** his father's wife. 2192
5:2 ye are puffed up, and **h** not rather mourned, NIG
5:3 but present in spirit, **h** judged already, NIG
5:11 But now I **h** written unto you not to keep NIG
5:12 For **what h I to do** to judge them 1473+5101
6:4 ye **h** judgments of things pertaining to this 2192
6:19 which ye **h** of God, and ye are not your 2192
7:2 let every man **h** his own wife, and let every 2192
7:2 and let every woman **h** her own husband. 2192
7:25 Now concerning virgins I **h** no 2192
7:28 Nevertheless such shall **h** trouble in 2192
7:29 that both they that **h** wives be as though 2192
7:32 But I would **h** you without carefulness. 1510
7:40 and I think also that I **h** the Spirit of God. 2192
8:1 we know that we all **h** knowledge. 2192
9:1 **h** I not seen Jesus Christ our Lord? are not NIG
9:4 **H** we not power to eat and to drink? 2192
9:5 **H** we not power to lead about a sister, 2192
9:6 **h** not we power to forbear working? 2192
9:11 If we **h** sown unto you spiritual things, is it NIG
9:12 Nevertheless we **h** not used this power; but NIG
9:15 But I **h** used none of these things: neither NIG
9:15 **h** I written these things, that it should be NIG
9:16 I preach the gospel, I **h** nothing to glory of: 1510
9:17 For if I do this thing willingly, I **h** a reward: 2192
9:19 For though I be free from all men, yet **h** I NIG
9:27 by any means, when I **h** preached to others, NIG
10:20 I would not that ye should **h** fellowship 1096
11:3 But I would **h** you know, that the head of NIG
11:10 For this cause ought the woman to **h** power 2192
11:14 that, if a man **h long hair**, it is a shame 2863
11:15 But if a woman **h long hair**, it is a glory to 2863
11:16 we **h** no such custom, neither the churches 2192
11:22 **h** ye not houses to eat and to drink in? or 2192
11:22 church of God, and shame them that **h** not? 2192
11:23 For I **h** received of the Lord that which also NIG
12:1 gifts, brethren, I would not **h** you ignorant. NIG
12:13 and **h** been all made to drink into one Spirit. NIG
12:21 say unto the hand, I **h** no need of thee: 2192
12:21 the head to the feet, I **h** no need of you. 2192
12:23 our uncomely parts **h** more abundant 2192
12:24 For our comely parts **h** no need: 2192
12:25 that the members should **h** the same **care** 3309
12:30 **H** all the gifts of healing? do all speak with 2192
13:1 of men and of angels, and **h** not charity, 2192
13:2 And though I **h** the gift of prophecy, and 2192
13:2 and though I **h** all faith, so that I could 2192
13:2 and **h** no charity, I am nothing. 2192
13:3 and **h** not charity, it profiteth me nothing. 2192
15:1 which also you **h** received, and wherein ye NIG
15:2 unto you, unless ye **h** believed in vain. NIG
15:15 we **h** testified of God that he raised up NIG
15:19 If in this life only we **h** hope in Christ, 1510
15:24 when he shall **h** delivered up the kingdom NIG
15:24 when he shall **h** put down all rule and NIG
15:31 I protest by your rejoicing which I **h** in 2192
15:32 If after the manner of men I **h** fought with NIG
15:34 for some **h** not the knowledge of God: 2192
15:49 And as we **h** borne the image of the earthy, NIG
15:54 So when this corruptible shall **h** put on NIG
15:54 and this mortal shall **h** put on immortality, NIG
16:1 as I **h** given order to the churches of NIG
16:12 come when he shall **h convenient time**. 2119
16:15 that they **h** addicted themselves to NIG
16:17 was lacking on your part they **h** supplied. NIG
16:18 For they **h** refreshed my spirit and yours: NIG
2Co 1:8 **h** you **ignorant** of our trouble which came to 50
1:12 we **h** had our conversation in the world, and NIG
1:14 As also you **h** acknowledged us in part, NIG
1:15 that you might **h** a second benefit; 2192
1:24 Not for that we **h dominion over** your 2961
2:3 I should **h** sorrow from them of whom I 2192
2:4 that ye might know the love which I **h** more 2192
2:5 But if any **h** caused grief, he hath not NIG
3:4 And such trust **h** we through Christ to 2192
3:12 Seeing then that we **h** such hope, we use 2192
4:1 Therefore seeing we **h** this ministry, as we 2192
4:1 as we **h** received mercy, we faint not; NIG
4:2 But **h** renounced the hidden things of NIG
4:7 But we **h** this treasure in earthen vessels, 2192
4:13 I believed, and therefore **h** I spoken; NIG
5:1 we **h** a building of God, a house not made 2192
5:12 that you may **h** somewhat to answer them 2192
5:16 though we **h** known Christ after the flesh, NIG
6:2 I **h** heard thee in a time accepted, and in NIG
6:2 in the day of salvation **h** I succoured thee: NIG
7:2 we **h** wronged no man, we have corrupted NIG
7:2 we have wronged no man, we **h** corrupted NIG
7:2 corrupted no man, we **h** defrauded no man. NIG
7:3 I speak not this to condemn you: for I **h** said NIG
7:11 In all things ye **h** approved yourselves to be NIG
7:14 For if I **h** boasted any thing to him of you, NIG
7:16 that I **h confidence** in you in all things. 2292
8:10 who **h** begun before, not only to do, but NIG
2Co 8:11 a performance also out of that which you **h**. 2192
8:18 And we **h** sent with him the brother, NIG
8:22 And we **h** sent with them our brother, NIG
8:22 whom we **h** oftentimes proved diligent in NIG
8:22 upon the great confidence which I **h** in you. NIG
9:3 Yet **h** I sent the brethren, lest our boasting NIG
11:2 for I **h** espoused you to one husband, that I NIG
11:4 whom we **h** not preached, or if ye receive NIG
11:4 which ye **h** not received, or another gospel, NIG
11:4 or another gospel, which ye **h** not accepted, NIG
11:6 we **h** been throughly made manifest among NIG
11:7 **H** I committed an offence in abasing myself NIG
11:7 I **h** preached to you the gospel of God NIG
11:9 in all things I **h** kept myself from being NIG
11:25 a night and a day I **h** been in the deep; NIG
12:11 a fool in glorying; ye **h** compelled me: NIG
12:11 for I ought to **h** been commended of you: NIG
12:21 that I shall bewail many which **h** sinned NIG
12:21 and **h** not repented of the uncleanness and NIG
12:21 and lasciviousness which they **h** committed. NIG
13:2 I write to them which heretofore **h** sinned, NIG
Gal 1:8 than that which we **h** preached unto you, NIG
1:9 gospel unto you than that ye **h** received, NIG
1:13 For ye **h** heard of my conversation in time NIG
2:4 out our liberty which we **h** in Christ Jesus, 2192
2:16 even we **h** believed in Jesus Christ, NIG
3:4 **H** ye suffered so many things in vain? if it NIG
3:21 been a law given which could **h** given life, NIG
3:21 verily righteousness **should h** been by 302
3:27 For as many of you as **h** been baptized into NIG
3:27 been baptized into Christ **h** put on Christ. NIG
4:9 after that ye **h** known God, or rather are NIG
4:11 lest I **h** bestowed upon you labour in vain. NIG
4:12 be as I am; for I am as ye are: ye **h** not NIG
4:15 ye would **h** plucked out your own eyes, and NIG
4:15 out your own eyes, and **h** given them to me. NIG
5:10 I **h** confidence in you through the Lord, NIG
5:13 For, brethren, ye **h** been called unto liberty; NIG
5:21 you before, as I **h** also told you in time past, NIG
5:24 And they that are Christ's **h** crucified NIG
6:4 then shall he **h** rejoicing in himself alone, 2192
6:10 As we **h** therefore opportunity, let us do 2192
6:11 Ye see how large a letter I **h** written unto NIG
6:13 but desire to **h** you circumcised, that they NIG
Eph 1:7 In whom we **h** redemption through his 2192
1:11 In whom also we **h** obtained an inheritance, NIG
2:18 For through him we both **h** access by one 2192
3:2 If ye **h** heard of the dispensation of NIG
3:12 In whom we **h** boldness and access with 2192
4:19 Who being past feeling **h** given themselves NIG
4:20 But ye **h** not so learned Christ; NIG
4:21 If so be that ye **h** heard him, and have been NIG
4:21 and **h** been taught by him, as the truth is in NIG
4:28 that he may **h** to give to him that needeth. 2192
5:11 And **h** no **fellowship with** the unfruitful 4790
6:22 Whom I **h** sent unto you for the same NIG
Php 1:7 this of you all, because I **h** you in my heart; 2192
1:12 that the things which happened unto me **h** NIG
2:12 my beloved, as ye **h** always obeyed, NIG
2:16 that I **h** not run in vain, neither laboured in NIG
2:20 For I **h** no man likeminded, who will 2192
2:27 lest I should **h** sorrow upon sorrow. 2192
3:3 and **h** no **confidence** in the flesh. 3982
3:4 Though I might also **h** confidence in 2192
3:8 for whom I **h** suffered the loss of all things, NIG
3:13 I count not myself to **h** apprehended: NIG
3:16 whereto we **h** already attained, NIG
3:17 which walk so as ye **h** us for an ensample. 2192
3:18 of whom I **h** told you often, and now tell NIG
4:9 Those things, which ye **h** both learned, and NIG
4:11 for I **h** learned, in whatsoever state I am, NIG
4:14 Notwithstanding ye **h** well done, that ye did NIG
4:18 But I **h** all, and abound: I am full, 568
Col 1:4 and of the love which ye **h** to all the saints, NIG
1:14 In whom we **h** redemption through his 2192
1:18 that in all things he might **h** 1096
1:23 which ye **h** heard, and which was preached NIG
2:1 ye knew what great conflict I **h** for you, 2192
2:1 for as many as **h** not seen my face in NIG
2:6 As ye **h** therefore received Christ Jesus NIG
2:7 stablished in the faith, as ye **h** been taught, NIG
2:23 Which things **h** indeed a shew of wisdom 2192
3:9 seeing that ye **h** put off the old man with his NIG
3:10 And **h** put on the new man, which is NIG
3:13 if any man **h** a quarrel against any: 2192
4:1 knowing that ye also **h** a Master in heaven. 2192
4:8 Whom I **h** sent unto you for the same NIG
4:11 of God, which **h** been a comfort unto me. NIG
1Th 2:6 when we might **h** been burdensome, NIG
2:8 we were willing to **h** imparted unto you, NIG
2:14 for ye also **h** suffered like things of your NIG
2:14 even as they **h** of the Jews: NIG
2:15 their own prophets, and **h** persecuted us; NIG
2:18 Wherefore we would **h** come unto you, NIG
3:5 lest by some means the tempter **h** tempted NIG
3:6 that ye **h** good remembrance of us always, 2192
4:1 that as ye **h** received of us how ye ought to NIG
4:6 as we also **h** forewarned you and testified. NIG
4:12 and that ye may **h** lack of nothing. 2192
4:13 But I would not **h** you to be ignorant, 2309
4:13 even as others which **h** no hope. 2192
5:1 ye **h** no need that I write unto you. 2192
2Th 2:15 hold the traditions which ye **h** been taught, NIG
3:1 that the word of the Lord may **h** free course, NIG
3:2 and wicked men: for all men **h** not faith. NIG
3:4 And we **h** confidence in the Lord touching NIG
3:9 Not because we **h** not power, but to make 2192
3:14 that man, and **h** no **company with** him, 4874
1Ti 1:6 From which some having swerved **h** turned NIG
1:19 concerning faith **h** made shipwrack: NIG
1:20 whom I **h** delivered unto Satan, that they NIG
2:4 Who **will h** all men to be saved, and 2309
3:7 Moreover he must **h** a good report of them 2192
3:13 For they that **h** used the office of a deacon NIG
5:4 But if any widow **h** children or nephews, 2192
1Ti 5:10 if she **h** brought up children, if she have NIG
5:10 up children, if she **h** lodged strangers, NIG
5:10 if she **h** washed the saints' feet, NIG
5:10 saints' feet, if she **h** relieved the afflicted, NIG
5:10 if she **h** diligently followed every good NIG
5:11 for when they **h** begun to wax wanton NIG
5:12 because they **h** cast off their first faith. NIG
5:16 or woman that believeth **h** widows, 2192
6:2 And they that **h** believing masters, let them 2192
6:10 they **h** erred from the faith, and NIG
6:21 Which some professing **h** erred concerning NIG
2Ti 1:3 that without ceasing I **h** remembrance of 2192
1:12 for I know whom I **h** believed, and I am NIG
1:12 I **h** committed unto him against that day. NIG
2:18 Who concerning the truth **h** erred, NIG
4:7 I **h** fought a good fight, I have finished my NIG
4:7 I **h** finished my course, I have kept the faith: NIG
4:7 I have finished my course, I **h** kept the faith: NIG
4:12 And Tychicus **h** I sent to Ephesus. NIG
4:20 but Trophimus **h** I left at Miletum sick. NIG
Tit 3:5 Not by works of righteousness which we **h** NIG
3:8 that they which **h** believed in God might be NIG
3:12 for I **h** determined there to winter. NIG
Phm 1:7 For we **h** great joy and consolation in thy 2192
1:10 whom I **h** begotten in my bonds: NIG
1:12 Whom I **h** sent again: thou therefore NIG
1:13 Whom I would **h** retained with me, that in NIG
1:13 that in thy stead he might **h** ministered unto NIG
1:19 I Paul **h** written it with mine own hand, NIG
1:20 brother, let me **h** joy of thee in the Lord: NIG
Heb 1:5 art my Son, this day **h** I begotten thee? NIG
2:1 earnest heed to the things which we **h** heard, NIG
3:10 their heart; and they **h** not known my ways. NIG
4:3 For we which **h** believed do enter into rest, NIG
4:3 as he said, As I **h** sworn in my wrath, if they NIG
4:8 would he not afterward **h** spoken of another NIG
4:13 the eyes of him with whom we **h to do**. 3056
4:14 Seeing then that we **h** a great high priest, 2192
4:15 For we **h** not a high priest which cannot be 2192
5:2 Who can **h compassion** on the ignorant, 3356
5:5 Thou art my Son, to day **h** I begotten thee. NIG
5:11 Of whom we **h** many things to say, and NIG
5:12 ye **h** need that one teach you again which 2192
5:12 and are become such as **h** need of milk, and 2192
5:14 even those who by reason of use **h** their 2192
6:4 and **h** tasted of the heavenly gift, and NIG
6:5 And **h** tasted the good word of God, and NIG
6:10 which ye **h** shewed toward his name, NIG
6:10 in that ye **h** ministered to the saints, and NIG
6:18 to lie, we might **h** a strong consolation, 2192
6:18 who **h** fled for refuge to lay hold upon NIG
6:19 Which hope we **h** as an anchor of the soul, 2192
7:5 **h** a commandment to take tithes of 2192
7:28 maketh men high priests which **h** infirmity; 2192
8:1 Now of the things which we **h** spoken this is NIG
8:1 We **h** such a high priest, who is set on 2192
8:3 wherefore it is of necessity that this man **h** 2192
8:7 **should** no place **h** been sought for 302
9:26 must he often **h** suffered since NIG
10:2 then **would** they not **h** ceased to be offered? 302
10:2 that the worshippers once purged should **h** NIG
10:26 For if we sin wilfully after that we **h** NIG
10:34 knowing in yourselves that ye **h** in heaven 2192
10:36 For ye **h** need of patience, that, after ye 2192
10:36 that, after ye **h** done the will of God, NIG
10:38 my soul shall **h** no **pleasure** in him. 2106
11:15 they might **h** had opportunity to have NIG
11:15 they might have had opportunity to **h** NIG
12:4 Ye **h** not yet resisted unto blood, NIG
12:5 And ye **h** forgotten the exhortation which NIG
12:9 Furthermore we **h** had fathers of our flesh NIG
12:17 when he would **h** inherited the blessing, NIG
12:28 let us **h** grace, whereby we may serve God 2192
13:2 for thereby some **h** entertained angels NIG
13:5 and be content with such things as ye **h**: 3918
13:7 Remember them which **h the rule over** 2233
13:7 who **h** spoken unto you the word of God: NIG
13:9 which **h** not profited them that have been NIG
13:9 which have not profited them that **h** been NIG
13:10 We **h** an altar, whereof they have no right 2192
13:10 whereof they **h** no right to eat which serve 2192
13:14 For here **h** we no continuing city, but 2192
13:17 Obey them that **h the rule over** you, and 2233
13:18 for we trust we **h** a good conscience, in all 2192
13:22 for I **h** written a letter unto you in few NIG
13:24 Salute all them that **h the rule over** you, 2233
Jas 1:4 But let patience **h** her perfect work, that ye 2192
2:1 **h** not the faith of our Lord Jesus Christ, 2192
2:3 And ye **h** respect to him that weareth NIG
2:6 But ye **h** despised the poor. Do not rich men NIG
2:9 But if ye **h respect to persons**, ye commit 4380
2:13 For he shall **h** judgment without mercy, NIG
2:14 a man say he hath faith, and **h** not works? 2192
2:18 may say, Thou hast faith, and I **h** works: 2192
3:14 But if ye **h** bitter envying and strife in your 2192
4:2 Ye lust, and **h** not: ye kill, and desire to 2192
4:2 ye kill, and desire to **h**, and cannot obtain: NIG
4:2 ye fight and war, yet ye **h** not, because ye 2192
5:3 ye **h** heaped treasure together for the last NIG
5:4 the hire of the labourers which **h** reaped NIG
5:4 the cries of them which **h** reaped are entered NIG
5:5 Ye **h** lived in pleasure on the earth, and NIG
5:5 ye **h** nourished your hearts, as in a day of NIG
5:6 Ye **h** condemned and killed the just; and NIG
5:10 who **h** spoken in the name of the Lord, NIG
5:11 Ye **h** heard of the patience of Job, and NIG
5:11 of Job, and **h** seen the end of the Lord; NIG
5:15 and if he **h** committed sins, they shall be 1510
1Pe 1:10 Of which salvation the prophets **h** inquired NIG
1:12 **h** preached the gospel unto you with NIG
1:22 Seeing ye **h** purified your souls in obeying NIG
2:3 If so be ye **h** tasted that the Lord is gracious. NIG
2:10 obtained mercy, but now **h** obtained mercy. NIG
4:3 us to **h** wrought the will of the Gentiles, NIG
4:8 And above all things **h** fervent charity 2192

1Pe 5:10 after that ye **h** suffered a while, make you NIG
5:12 I **h** written briefly, exhorting, and NIG
2Pe 1: 1 to them that **h** obtained like precious faith NIG
1:15 to **h** these *things* always in remembrance. *2192*
1:16 For we **h** not followed cunningly devised NIG
1:19 We **h** also a more sure word of prophecy; *2192*
2:14 a heart they **h** exercised with covetous *2192*
2:15 Which **h** forsaken the right way, and NIG
2:20 For if after they **h** escaped the pollutions of NIG
2:21 For it had been better for them not to **h** NIG
2:21 after they **h** known *it,* to turn from the holy NIG
1Jn 1: 1 which we **h** heard, which we have seen with NIG
1: 1 have heard, which we **h** seen with our eyes, NIG
1: 1 which we **h** looked upon, and our hands NIG
1: 1 and our hands **h** handled, of the Word of NIG
1: 2 and we **h** seen *it,* and bear witness, and NIG
1: 3 *That* which we **h** seen and heard declare we NIG
1: 3 that ye also may **h** fellowship with us: *2192*
1: 5 is the message which we **h** heard of him, NIG
1: 6 If we say that we **h** fellowship with him, *2192*
1: 7 we **h** fellowship one with another, and *2192*
1: 8 If we say that we **h** no sin, we deceive *2192*
1:10 If we say that we **h** not sinned, we make NIG
2: 1 *man* sin, we **h** an advocate with the Father, *2192*
2: 7 word which ye **h** heard from the beginning. NIG
2:13 ye **h** known him that is from the beginning. NIG
2:13 because you **h** overcome the wicked one. NIG
2:13 because ye **h** known the Father. NIG
2:14 I **h** written unto you, fathers, because NIG
2:14 ye **h** known him that is from the beginning. NIG
2:14 I **h** written unto you, young men, because NIG
2:14 in you, and ye **h** overcome the wicked one. NIG
2:18 and as ye **h** heard that antichrist shall come, NIG
2:19 they **would** *no doubt* **h** continued with us: *302*
2:20 But ye **h** an unction from the Holy One, *2192*
2:21 I **h** not written unto you because ye know NIG
2:24 which ye **h** heard from the beginning. NIG
2:24 If *that* which ye **h** heard from the beginning NIG
2:26 These *things* **h** I written unto you NIG
2:27 But the anointing which ye **h** received of NIG
2:28 we may **h** confidence, and not be ashamed *2192*
3:14 We know that we **h** passed from death unto NIG
3:21 us not, *then* **h** we confidence towards God. *2192*
4: 3 whereof you **h** heard that it should come; NIG
4: 4 little children, and **h** overcome them: NIG
4:14 And we **h** seen and do testify that the Father NIG
4:16 And we **h** known and believed the love that NIG
4:17 that we may **h** boldness in the day of *2192*
4:21 And this commandment **h** we from him, *2192*
5:13 These *things* **h** I written unto you that NIG
5:13 that ye may know that ye **h** eternal life, and *2192*
5:14 And this is the confidence that we **h** in him, *2192*
5:15 we know that we **h** the petitions that we *2192*
2Jn 1: 1 but also all they that **h** known the truth; NIG
1: 4 as we **h** received a commandment from NIG
1: 6 That, as ye **h** heard from the beginning, NIG
1: 8 that we lose not *those things* which we **h** NIG
3Jn 1: 4 I **h** no greater joy than to hear that my *2192*
1: 6 Which **h** borne witness of thy charity before NIG
1: 9 who **loveth to h** the **preeminence among** *5383*
Jude 1:11 for they **h** gone in the way of Cain, and NIG
1:15 deeds which they **h** ungodly committed, NIG
1:15 ungodly sinners **h** spoken against him. NIG
1:22 And of some **h compassion**, making a *1653*
Rev 1:18 and **h** the keys of hell and of death. *2192*
2: 4 Nevertheless I **h** *somewhat* against thee, *2192*
2:10 be tried; and ye shall **h** tribulation ten days: *2192*
2:14 But I **h** a few *things* against thee, because *2192*
2:20 Notwithstanding I **h** a few *things* against *2192*
2:24 as many as **h** not this doctrine, and *2192*
2:24 and which **h** not known the depths of Satan, NIG
2:25 But *that* which ye **h** *already* hold fast till I *2192*
3: 2 for I **h** not found thy works perfect before NIG
3: 4 which **h** not defiled their garments; NIG
3: 8 I **h** set before thee an open door, and no NIG
3: 9 thy feet, and to know that I **h** loved thee. NIG
3:17 with goods, and **h** need of nothing; *2192*
7: 3 till we **h** sealed the servants of our God in NIG
7:14 and **h** washed their robes, and made them NIG
9: 3 as the scorpions of the earth **h** power. *2192*
9: 4 only *those* men which **h** not the seal of God *2192*
11: 6 These **h** power to shut heaven, that it rain *2192*
11: 6 **h** power over waters to turn them to blood, *2192*
11: 7 And when they shall **h** finished their NIG
12:17 and **h** the testimony of Jesus Christ. *2192*
13: 9 If any *man* **h** an ear, let him hear. *2192*
14:11 and they **h** no rest day nor night, *2192*
16: 6 For they **h** shed the blood of saints and NIG
17: 2 With whom the kings of the earth **h** NIG
17: 2 the inhabiters of the earth **h** been made NIG
17:12 which **h** received no kingdom as yet; NIG
17:13 These **h** one mind, and shall give their *2192*
18: 3 For all nations **h** drunk of the wine of NIG
18: 3 the kings of the earth **h** committed NIG
18: 5 For her sins **h** reached unto heaven, and NIG
18: 9 who **h** committed fornication and NIG
19:10 of thy brethren that **h** the testimony of *2192*
21: 8 shall **h** their part in the lake which burneth NIG
22:14 that they may **h** right to the tree of life, and *1510*
22:16 I Jesus **h** sent mine angel to testify unto you NIG

HAVEN (5) [HAVENS]

Ge 49:13 Zebulun shall dwell at the **h** of the sea; and 2348
49:13 he *shall be* for a **h** of ships; and his border 2348
Ps 107:30 so he bringeth them unto their desired **h**. 4231
Ac 27:12 the **h** was not commodious to winter in, *3040*
27:12 *which is* a **h** of Crete, and lieth toward *3040*

HAVENS (1) [HAVEN]

Ac 27: 8 unto a place *which is* called The **fair h**; *2568*

HAVILAH (7)

Ge 2:11 *is it* which compasseth the whole land of **H**, 2341
10: 7 **H**, and Sabtah, and Raamah, and Sabtecha: 2341
Ge 10:29 Ophir, and **H**, and Jobab: all these *were* 2341
25:18 they dwelt from **H** unto Shur, that *is* before 2341
1Sa 15: 7 Saul smote the Amalekites from **H** *until* 2341
1Ch 1: 9 **H**, and Sabta, and Raamah, and Sabtecha. 2341
1:23 Ophir, and **H**, and Jobab. All these *were* 2341

HAVING (193) [HAVE]

Ge 12: 8 **h** Beth-el on the west, and Hai on the east: NIH
Lev 7:20 the LORD, **h** his uncleanness upon him, NIH
20:18 man shall lie with a woman **h** her **sickness**, 1739
22: 3 **h** his uncleanness upon him, that soul shall NIH
22:22 maimed, or **h a wen**, or scurvy, or scabbed, 2990
Nu 24: 4 falling *into a trance,* but **h** his eyes open: NIH
24:16 falling *into a trance,* but **h** his eyes open: NIH
Dt 10: 3 the mount, **h** the two tables in mine hand. NIH
Jdg 1: 7 **h** their thumbs and their great toes cut off, 1961
19: 3 **h** his servant with him, and a couple of NIH
Ru 1:13 would ye stay for them from **h** 1961+3807.1
1Sa 22: 6 **h** his spear in his hand, and all his servants NIH
26: 2 **h** three thousand chosen men of Israel 2050.1
1Ki 22:10 sat each on his throne, **h** put on *their* robes, NIH
1Ch 4:42 **h** for their captains Pelatiah, and Neariah, NIH
21:16 **h** a drawn sword in his hand stretched out NIH
26:12 the chief men, **h** wards one against another, NIH
2Ch 5:12 **h** cymbals and psalteries and harps, 871.1
11:12 **h** Judah and Benjamin on his side. 1961
23:10 every man **h** his weapon in his hand, NIH
Ezr 9: 5 **h** rent my garment and my mantle, I fell NIH
Ne 10:28 every one **h knowledge**, *and* 3045
10:28 having knowledge, *and* **h understanding**; 995
13: 4 **h the oversight** of the chamber of 5414+871.1
Est 6:12 house mourning, and **h** his head covered. NIH
Ps 13: 2 in my soul, **h** sorrow in my heart daily? NIH
Pr 6: 7 Which **h** no guide, overseer, or ruler, 3807.1
18: 1 **h** separated himself, seeketh *and* NIH
Isa 6: 6 unto me, **h** a live coal in his hand, NIH
41:15 a new sharp threshing instrument **h** teeth: 1167
Jer 41: 5 **h** their beards shaven, and their clothes rent, NIH
41: 5 **h** cut themselves, with offerings and NIH
Eze 38:11 and **h** neither bars nor gates, 3807.1
40:44 one at the side of the east gate **h** NIH
44:11 **h** charge at the gates of the house, and NIH
Da 8:20 The ram which thou sawest **h** two horns *are* 1167
Mic 1:11 inhabitant of Saphir, **h** *thy* shame naked: NIH
Zec 9: 9 he *is* just, and **h salvation**; lowly, and 3467
Mt 7:29 For he taught them as *one* **h** authority, and *2192*
8: 9 a man under authority, **h** soldiers under me: *2192*
9:36 scattered abroad, as sheep **h** no shepherd. *2192*
15:30 **h** with them *those that were* lame, blind, *2192*
18: 8 rather than **h** two hands or two feet to be *2192*
18: 9 rather than **h** two eyes to be cast into hell *2192*
22:12 how camest thou in hither not **h** a wedding *2192*
22:24 Moses said, If a man die, **h** no children, *2192*
22:25 and, **h** no issue, left his wife unto his *2192*
26: 7 There came unto him a woman **h** an *2192*
Mk 6:34 they were as sheep not **h** a shepherd: *2192*
8: 1 and **h** nothing to eat, Jesus called his *2192*
8:18 **H** eyes, see ye not? and having ears, *2192*
8:18 and **h** ears, hear ye not? and do ye not *2192*
9:43 than **h** two hands to go into hell, into *2192*
9:45 into life, than **h** two feet to be cast into hell, *2192*
9:47 than **h** two eyes to be cast into hell fire: *2192*
11:13 And seeing a fig tree afar off **h** leaves, *2192*
12: 6 **H** yet therefore one son, his wellbeloved, *2192*
12:28 and **h** heard them reasoning together, and NIG
14: 3 there came a woman **h** an alabaster box of *2192*
14:51 **h** a linen cloth cast about *his* naked *body;* NIG
Lk 1: 3 **h** had perfect understanding of all *things* NIG
5:39 No *man* also **h** drunk old *wine* straightway NIG
7: 8 **h** under me soldiers, and I say unto one, *2192*
8:15 **h** heard the word, keep *it,* and bring forth NIG
8:43 And a woman **h** an issue of blood twelve *1510*
9:62 No *man* **h** put his hand to the plough, and NIG
11:36 therefore *be* full of light, **h** no part dark, *2192*
15: 4 What man of you, **h** an hundred sheep, if he *2192*
15: 8 Either what woman **h** ten pieces of silver, *2192*
17: 7 **h** a servant plowing or feeding cattle, *2192*
19:15 **h** received the kingdom, then NIG
20:28 **h** a wife, and he die without children, *2192*
23:14 and behold, I, **h** examined *him* before you, NIG
23:46 and **h** said thus, he gave up the ghost. NIG
Jn 4:45 **h** seen all *the things* that he did at Jerusalem NIG
5: 2 Hebrew tongue Bethesda, **h** five porches. *2192*
7:15 knoweth this *man* letters, **h** never learned? NIG
13: 1 **h** loved his own which were in the world, NIG
13: 2 the devil **h** now put into the heart of Judas NIG
13:30 **h** received the sop went immediately out: NIG
18: 3 **h** received a band *of men,* and officers from NIG
18:10 Then Simon Peter **h** a sword drew it, and *2192*
Ac 2:24 hath raised up, **h** loosed the pains of death: NIG
2:33 **h** received of the Father the promise of NIG
2:47 and **h** favour with all the people. *2192*
3:26 you first God, **h** raised up his Son Jesus, NIG
4:37 **H** land, sold *it,* and brought the money, and NIG
12:20 **h** made Blastus the king's chamberlain their NIG
14:19 and, **h** stoned Paul, drew *him* out of the city, NIG
16:24 Who, **h** received such a charge, thrust them NIG
18:18 **h** shorn *his* head in Cenchrea: for he had a NIG
19: 1 Paul **h** passed through the upper coasts NIG
19:29 and **h** caught Gaius and Aristarchus, men of NIG
22:12 **h a good report** of all the Jews which *3140*
23:27 **h** understood that he was a Roman. NIG
24:22 And when Felix heard these *things,* **h** more NIG
26:10 **h** received authority from the chief priests; NIG
26:22 **H** therefore obtained help of God, NIG
27:33 and continued fasting, **h** taken nothing. NIG
Ro 2:14 these, **h** not the law, are a law unto *2192*
9:11 yet born, neither **h** done any good or evil, NIG
12: 6 **H** then gifts differing according to *2192*
15:23 But now **h** no more place in these parts, *2192*
15:23 **h** a great desire these many years to come *2192*
1Co 6: 1 any of you, **h** a matter against another, *2192*
7:37 **h** no necessity, but hath power over his *2192*
11: 4 or prophesying, **h** *his* head covered, *2192*
12:24 **h** given more abundant honour to that *part* NIG
2Co 2: 3 **h** confidence in you all, that my joy is NIG
4:13 We **h** the same spirit of faith, according as *2192*
6:10 as **h** nothing, and *yet* possessing all *things.* *2192*
7: 1 **H** therefore these promises, dearly beloved, *2192*
9: 8 always **h** all sufficiency in all *things,* may *2192*
10: 6 And **h** in a readiness to revenge all *2192*
10:15 but **h** hope, when your faith is increased, *2192*
Gal 3: 3 **h** begun in the Spirit, are ye now made NIG
Eph 1: 5 **H** predestinated us unto the adoption of NIG
1: 9 **H** made known unto us the mystery of his NIG
2:12 **h** no hope, and without God in the world: *2192*
2:15 **H** abolished in his flesh the enmity, NIG
2:16 by the cross, **h** slain the enmity thereby: NIG
4:18 **H** the understanding darkened, NIG
5:27 not **h** spot, or wrinkle, or any such *thing;* *2192*
6:13 in the evil day, and **h** done all, to stand. NIG
6:14 **h** your loins girt about with truth, and NIG
6:14 and **h on** the breastplate of righteousness; *1746*
Php 1:23 **h** a desire to depart, and to be with Christ; *2192*
1:25 And **h** this **confidence**, I know that I shall *3982*
1:30 **H** the same conflict which ye saw in me, *2192*
2: 2 **h** the same love, *being* of one accord, *2192*
3: 9 not **h** mine own righteousness, which is of *2192*
4:18 **h** received of Epaphroditus the *things which* NIG
Col 1:20 **h** made peace through the blood of his NIG
2:13 with him, **h** forgiven you all trespasses; NIG
2:15 *And* **h** spoiled principalities and powers, NIG
2:19 and bands **h** nourishment ministered, NIG
1Th 1: 6 **h** received the word in much affliction, NIG
1Ti 1: 6 From which some **h** swerved have turned NIG
1:19 which some **h** put away, concerning faith NIG
3: 4 **h** *his* children in subjection with all gravity; *2192*
4: 2 **h** their conscience seared with a hot iron; NIG
4: 8 godliness is profitable unto all *things,* **h** *2192*
5: 9 years old, **h** been the wife of one man, NIG
5:12 **H** damnation, because they have cast off *2192*
6: 8 And **h** food and raiment let us be therewith *2192*
2Ti 2:19 **h** this seal, The Lord knoweth them that are *2192*
3: 5 **H** a form of godliness, but denying *2192*
4: 3 heap to themselves teachers, **h** itching ears; NIG
4:10 **h** loved *this* present world, and is departed NIG
Tit 1: 6 **h** faithful children not accused of riot or *2192*
2: 8 be ashamed, **h** no evil *thing* to say of you. *2192*
Phm 1:21 **H confidence** in thy obedience I wrote unto *3982*
Heb 7: 3 **h** neither beginning of days, nor end of life; *2192*
9:12 *place,* **h** obtained eternal redemption *for us.* NIG
10: 1 For the law **h** a shadow of good *things* to *2192*
10:19 **H** therefore, brethren, boldness to enter into *2192*
10:21 And **h** a high priest over the house of God; NIG
10:22 **h** *our* hearts sprinkled from an evil NIG
11:13 not **h** received the promises, but NIG
11:13 but **h** seen them afar off, and NIG
11:39 **h** obtained a good report through faith, NIG
11:40 God **h** provided some better *thing* for us, NIG
1Pe 1: 8 Whom **h** not seen, ye love; in whom, NIG
2:12 **H** your conversation honest among *2192*
3: 8 **h** compassion one of another, love as NIG
3:16 **H** a good conscience; that, whereas they *2192*
2Pe 1: 4 **h** escaped the corruption that is in the world NIG
2:14 **H** eyes full of adultery and that cannot *2192*
2Jn 1:12 **H** many *things* to write unto you, I would *2192*
Jude 1: 5 **h** saved the people out of the land of Egypt, NIG
1:16 **h** *men's* persons **in admiration** 2296+4383
1:19 sensual, **h** not the Spirit. *2192*
Rev 5: 6 *been* slain, **h** seven horns and seven eyes, *2192*
5: 8 **h** every one *of them* harps, and golden vials *2192*
7: 2 from the east, **h** the seal of the living God: *2192*
8: 3 and stood at the altar, **h** a golden censer; *2192*
9:17 **h** breastplates of fire, and of jacinth, and *2192*
12: 3 **h** seven heads and ten horns, and *2192*
12:12 **h** great wrath, because he knoweth that he *2192*
13: 1 **h** seven heads and ten horns, and upon his *2192*
14: 1 **h** his Father's name written in their *2192*
14: 6 **h** the everlasting gospel to preach unto *2192*
14:14 **h** on his head a golden crown, and in his *2192*
14:17 which is in heaven, he also **h** a sharp sickle. *2192*
15: 1 seven angels **h** the seven last plagues; *2192*
15: 2 on the sea of glass, **h** *the* harps of God. *2192*
15: 6 **h** the seven plagues, clothed in pure and *2192*
15: 6 **h** their breasts girded with golden girdles. NIG
17: 3 of blasphemy, **h** seven heads and ten horns. *2192*
17: 4 **h** a golden cup in her hand full of *2192*
18: 1 come down from heaven, **h** great power; *2192*
20: 1 **h** the key of the bottomless *pit* and a great *2192*
21:11 **H** the glory of God: and her light *was* like *2192*

HAVOCK (1)

Ac 8: 3 As for Saul, he **made h** of the church, *3075*

HAVOTH-JAIR (2) [BASHAN-HAVOTH-JAIR]

Nu 32:41 the small towns thereof, and called them **H**. 2334
Jdg 10: 4 which are called **H** unto this day, 2334

HAVVOTH JAIR See BASHAN-HAVOTH-JAIR; HAVOTH-JAIR

HAWK (5)

Lev 11:16 the **night h**, and the cuckow, and the hawk 8464
11:16 and the cuckow, and the **h** after his kind, 5322
Dt 14:15 the **night h**, and the cuckow, and the hawk 8464
14:15 and the cuckow, and the **h** after his kind, 5322
Job 39:26 Doth the **h** fly by thy wisdom, *and* 5322

HAY (3)

Pr 27:25 The **h** appeareth, and the tender grass 2682
Isa 15: 6 for the **h** is withered away, the grass faileth, 2682
1Co 3:12 silver, precious stones, wood, **h**, stubble; *5528*

HAZAEL (23)

1Ki 19:15 anoint **H** to be king over Syria: 2371
19:17 *that* him that escapeth the sword of **H** shall 2371
2Ki 8: 8 the king said unto **H**, Take a present in 2371
8: 9 So **H** went to meet him, and took a present 2371
8:12 **H** said, Why weepeth my lord? And he 2371

H

2Ki 8:13 **H** said, But what, *is* thy servant a dog, 2371
8:15 so that he died: and **H** reigned in his stead. 2371
8:28 against **H** king of Syria in Ramoth-gilead; 2371
8:29 when he fought against **H** king of Syria. 2371
9:14 and all Israel, because of **H** king of Syria. 2371
9:15 when he fought with **H** king of Syria.) 2371
10:32 **H** smote them in all the coasts of Israel; 2371
12:17 **H** king of Syria went up, and fought against 2371
12:17 and **H** set his face to go up to Jerusalem. 2371
12:18 king's house, and sent *it* to **H** king of Syria: 2371
13: 3 he delivered them into the hand of **H** king 2371
13: 3 into the hand of Ben-hadad the son of **H**, 2371
13:22 **H** king of Syria oppressed Israel all 2371
13:24 So **H** king of Syria died; and Ben-hadad his 2371
13:25 hand of Ben-hadad the son of **H** the cities, 2371
2Ch 22: 5 against **H** king of Syria at Ramoth-gilead: 2371
22: 6 when he fought with **H** king of Syria. 2371
Am 1: 4 I will send a fire into the house of **H**, 2371

HAZAIAH (1)
Ne 11: 5 the son of **H**, the son of Adaiah, the son of 2382

HAZAR-ADDAR (1) [ADDAR]
Nu 34: 4 shall go on *to* **H**, and pass on to Azmon: 2692

HAZARDED (1)
Ac 15:26 Men that have **h** their lives for the name of *3860*

HAZAR-ENAN (4) [ENAN]
Nu 34: 9 and the goings out of it shall be at **H**: 2704
34:10 ye shall point out your east border from **H** 2704
Eze 47:17 the border from the sea shall be **H**, 2703
48: 1 as *one* goeth to Hamath, **H**, the border of 2704

H

HAZAR-GADDAH (1)
Jos 15:27 And **H**, and Heshmon, and Beth-palet, 2693

HAZAR-HATTICON (1)
Eze 47:16 **H**, which *is* by the coast of Hauran. 2691

HAZARMAVETH (2)
Ge 10:26 and Sheleph, and **H**, and Jerah, 2700
1Ch 1:20 and Sheleph, and **H**, and Jerah, 2700

HAZAR-SHUAL (4) [SHUAL]
Jos 15:28 And **H**, and Beer-sheba, and Bizjothjah, 2705
19: 3 And **H**, and Balah, and Azem, 2705
1Ch 4:28 dwelt at Beer-sheba, and Moladah, and **H**, 2705
Ne 11:27 at **H**, and at Beer-sheba, and *in* the villages 2705

HAZAR-SUSAH (1) [HAZAR-SUSIM]
Jos 19: 5 And Ziklag, and Beth-marcaboth, and **H**, 2701

HAZAR-SUSIM (1) [HAZAR-SUSAH]
1Ch 4:31 and **H**, and at Beth-birei, and at Shaaraim. 2702

HAZAZON-TAMAR (1) [HAZEZON-TAMAR, TAMAR]
2Ch 20: 2 and behold, they *be* in **H**, which *is* En-gedi. 2688

HAZEL (1)
Ge 30:37 green poplar, and of the **h** and chesnut tree; 3869

HAZELELPONI (1)
1Ch 4: 3 Idbash: and the name of their sister *was* **H**: 6753

HAZER HATTICON See HAZAR-HATTICON

HAZERIM (1)
Dt 2:23 the Avims which dwelt in **H**, *even* unto 2699

HAZEROTH (6)
Nu 11:35 journeyed from Kibroth-hattaavah *unto* **H**; 2698
11:35 *unto* Hazeroth; and abode at **H**. 2698
12:16 afterward the people removed from **H**, and 2698
33:17 and encamped at **H**. 2698
33:18 they departed from **H**, and pitched in 2698
Dt 1: 1 and Laban, and **H**, and Dizahab. 2698

HAZEZON-TAMAR (1) [HAZAZON-TAMAR, TAMAR]
Ge 14: 7 and also the Amorites, that dwelt in **H**. 2688

HAZIEL (1)
1Ch 23: 9 Shelomith, and **H**, and Haran, three. 2381

HAZO (1)
Ge 22:22 **H**, and Pildash, and Jidlaph, and Bethuel. 2375

HAZOR (18) [BAAL-HAZOR, HAZOR HADATTAH]
Jos 11: 1 when Jabin king of **H** had heard *those* 2674
11:10 took **H**, and smote the king thereof with 2674
11:10 for **H** beforetime *was* the head of all those 2674
11:11 left to breathe: and he burnt **H** with fire. 2674
11:13 Israel burned none of them, save **H** only; 2674
12:19 king of Madon, one; the king of **H**, one; 2674
15:23 And Kedesh, and **H**, and Ithnan, 2674
15:25 and Kerioth, *and* Hezron, which *is* **H**, 2674
19:36 And Adamah, and Ramah, and **H**, 2674
Jdg 4: 2 of Jabin king of Canaan, that reigned in **H**; 2674
4:17 *was* peace between Jabin the king of **H** 2674
1Sa 12: 9 captain of the host of **H**, and into the hand 2674
1Ki 9:15 and **H**, and Megiddo, and Gezer. 2674
2Ki 15:29 and **H**, and Gilead, and Galilee, 2674
Ne 11:33 **H**, Ramah, Gittaim, 2674
Jer 49:28 and concerning the kingdoms of **H**, 2674
49:30 far off, dwell deep, O ye inhabitants of **H**, 2674
49:33 **H** shall be a dwelling for dragons, *and* 2674

HAZOR HADATTAH (1) [HAZOR]
Jos 15:25 **H**, and Kerioth, *and* Hezron, 2675

HAZZELELPONI See HAZELELPONI

HAZZOBEBAH See ZOBEBAH

HE (10430) [HIM, HIMSELF, HIS] See Index of Articles, Etc.

HEAD (364) [FOREHEAD, FOREHEADS, GRAYHEADED, HEADBANDS, HEADLONG, HEADS, HEADSTONE, HEADY]
Ge 3:15 it shall bruise thy **h**, and thou shalt bruise 7218
24:26 the man **bowed down** his **h**, and 6915
24:48 I **bowed down** my **h**, and worshipped 6915
40:13 three days shall Pharaoh lift up thine **h**, 7218
40:16 behold, *I had* three white baskets on my **h**: 7218
40:17 did eat them out of the basket upon my **h**. 7218
40:19 shall Pharaoh lift up thy **h** from off thee, 7218
40:20 he lifted up the **h** of the chief butler and 7218
47:31 And Israel bowed himself upon the bed's **h**. 7218
48:14 laid *it* upon Ephraim's **h**, who *was* 7218
48:14 and his left hand upon Manasseh's **h**, 7218
48:17 laid his right hand upon the **h** of Ephraim, 7218
48:17 to remove it from Ephraim's **h** unto 7218
48:17 it from Ephraim's head unto Manasseh's **h**. 7218
48:18 the firstborn; put thy right hand upon his **h**. 7218
49:26 they shall be on the **h** of Joseph, and on 7218
49:26 on the **crown of the h** of him *that was* 6936
Ex 12: 9 his **h** with his legs, and with the purtenance 7218
12:27 the people **bowed the h** and worshipped. 6915
26:24 they shall be coupled together above the **h** 7218
29: 6 thou shalt put the mitre upon his **h**, and 7218
29: 7 and pour *it* upon his **h**, and anoint him. 7218
29:10 his sons shall put their hands upon the **h** of 7218
29:15 his sons shall put their hands upon the **h** of 7218
29:17 put *them* unto his pieces, and unto his **h**. 7218
29:19 his sons shall put their hands upon the **h** of 7218
34: 8 **bowed** his **h** toward the earth, and 6915
36:29 coupled together at the **h** thereof, to one 7218
Lev 1: 4 he shall put his hand upon the **h** of 7218
1: 8 shall lay the parts, the **h**, and the fat, 7218
1:12 cut it into his pieces, with his **h** and his fat: 7218
1:15 and wring off his **h**, and burn *it* on the altar; 7218
3: 2 he shall lay his hand upon the **h** of his 7218
3: 8 he shall lay his hand upon the **h** of his 7218
3:13 he shall lay his hand upon the **h** of it, and 7218
4: 4 shall lay his hand upon the bullock's **h**, and 7218
4:11 with his **h**, and with his legs, and 7218
4:15 the **h** of the bullock before the LORD: 7218
4:24 he shall lay his hand upon the **h** of the goat, 7218
4:29 he shall lay his hand upon the **h** of the sin 7218
4:33 he shall lay his hand upon the **h** of the sin 7218
5: 8 wring off his **h** from his neck, but shall not 7218
8: 9 he put the mitre upon his **h**; also upon 7218
8:12 poured of the anointing oil upon Aaron's **h**, 7218
8:14 his sons laid their hands upon the **h** of 7218
8:18 his sons laid their hands upon the **h** of 7218
8:20 Moses burnt the **h**, and the pieces, and 7218
8:22 his sons laid their hands upon the **h** of 7218
9:13 with the pieces thereof, and the **h**: 7218
13:12 *hath* the plague from his **h** even to his foot, 7218
13:29 or woman hath a plague upon the **h** or 7218
13:30 *even* a leprosy upon the **h** or beard. 7218
13:40 the man whose hair is fallen off his **h**, he *is* 7218
13:41 off from the part of *his h toward* his face, NIH
13:42 if there be in the **bald h**, or bald forehead, 7146
13:42 it *is* a leprosy sprung up in his **bald h**, or 7146
13:43 of the sore *be* white reddish in his **bald h**, 7146
13:44 him utterly unclean, his plague *is* in his **h**. 7218
13:45 his **h** bare, and he shall put a covering upon 7218
14: 9 *that* he shall shave all his hair off his **h** and 7218
14:18 upon the **h** of him that is to be cleansed: 7218
14:29 put upon the **h** of him that is to be cleansed, 7218
16:21 Aaron shall lay both his hands upon the **h** 7218
16:21 putting them upon the **h** of the goat, and 7218
19:32 Thou shalt rise up before the **hoary h**, and 7872
21: 5 They shall not make baldness upon their **h**, 7218
21:10 upon whose **h** the anointing oil was poured, 7218
21:10 shall not uncover his **h**, nor rend his 7218
24:14 that heard *him* lay their hands upon his **h**, 7218
Nu 1: 4 every one **h** of the house of his fathers. 7218
5:18 uncover the woman's **h**, and put 7218
6: 5 there shall no rasor come upon his **h**: 7218
6: 5 shall let the locks of the hair of his **h** grow. 7218
6: 7 the consecration of his God *is* upon his **h**. 7218
6: 9 he hath defiled the **h** of his consecration; 7218
6: 9 he shall shave his **h** in the day of his 7218
6:11 and shall hallow his **h** that *same* day. 7218
6:18 the Nazarite shall shave the **h** of his 7218
6:18 shall take the hair of the **h** of his separation, 7218
17: 3 for one rod *shall be* for the **h** of the house 7218
22:31 he **bowed down** his **h**, and fell flat on his 6915
25:15 he *was* **h** over a people, *and* of a chief 7218
Dt 19: 5 the **h** slippeth from the helve, and 1270
21:12 she shall shave her **h**, and pare her nails; 7218
28:13 the LORD shall make thee the **h**, and 7218
28:23 thy heaven that *is* over thy **h** shall be brass, 7218
28:35 the sole of thy foot unto the **top of** thy **h**. 6936
28:44 he shall be the **h**, and thou shalt be the tail. 7218
33:16 let *the blessing* come upon the **h** of Joseph, 7218
33:16 upon the **top of the h** of him *that was* 6936
33:20 teareth the arm with the **crown of the h**. 6936
Jos 2:19 his blood *shall be* upon his **h**, and we *will* 7218
2:19 his blood *shall be* on our **h**, if *any* hand be 7218
11:10 for Hazor beforetime *was* the **h** of all those 7218
22:14 each one *was* a **h** of the house of their 7218
Jdg 5:26 she smote off his **h**, when she had pierced 7218
9:53 a piece of a millstone upon Abimelech's **h**, 7218
10:18 he shall be **h** over all the inhabitants of 7218
11: 8 be our **h** over all the inhabitants of Gilead. 7218
11: 9 deliver them before me, shall I be your **h**? 7218
11:11 the people made him **h** and captain over 7218
13: 5 a son; and no rasor shall come on his **h**: 7218
16:13 If thou weavest the seven locks of my **h** 7218
16:17 There hath not come a rasor upon mine **h**; 7218
16:19 *him* to shave off the seven locks of his **h**; 7218
16:22 Howbeit the hair of his **h** began to grow 7218
1Sa 1:11 and there shall no rasor come upon his **h**. 7218
4:12 his clothes rent, and *with* earth upon his **h**. 7218
5: 4 the **h** of Dagon and both the palms of his 7218
10: 1 poured *it* upon his **h**, and kissed him, and 7218
14:45 there shall not one hair of his **h** fall to 7218
15:17 *wast* thou not *made* the **h** of the tribes of 7218
17: 5 *he had* a helmet of brass upon his **h**, and 7218
17: 7 his spear's **h** *weighed* six hundred shekels 3852
17:38 and he put a helmet of brass upon his **h**; 7218
17:46 will smite thee, and take thine **h** from thee; 7218
17:51 and slew him, and cut off his **h** therewith. 7218
17:54 David took the **h** of the Philistine, and 7218
17:57 brought him before Saul with the **h** of 7218
25:39 the wickedness of Nabal upon his own **h**. 7218
28: 2 will I make thee keeper of mine **h** for ever. 7218
31: 9 they cut off his **h**, and stripped off his 7218
2Sa 1: 2 with his clothes rent, and earth upon his **h**: 7218
1:10 I took the crown that *was* upon his **h**, and 7218
1:16 said unto him, Thy blood *be* upon thy **h**; 7218
2:16 they caught every one his fellow by the **h**, 7218
3: 8 of Ish-bosheth, and said, *Am* I a dog's **h**, 7218
3:29 Let it rest on the **h** of Joab, and on all his 7218
4: 7 took his **h**, and gat them away through 7218
4: 8 they brought the **h** of Ish-bosheth unto 7218
4: 8 Behold the **h** of Ish-bosheth the son of Saul 7218
4:12 they took the **h** of Ish-bosheth, and buried *it* 7218
12:30 he took their king's crown from off his **h**, 7218
12:30 it was *set* on David's **h**. And he brought 7218
13:19 Tamar put ashes on her **h**, and rent her 7218
13:19 laid her hand on her **h**, and went on crying. 7218
14:25 **crown of** his **h** there was no blemish in 6936
14:26 when he polled his **h**, (for it was at every 7218
14:26 he weighed the hair of his **h** *at* two hundred 7218
15:30 had his **h** covered, and he went barefoot: 7218
15:30 that *was* with him covered every man his **h**, 7218
15:32 with his coat rent, and earth upon his **h**: 7218
16: 9 me go over, I pray thee, and take off his **h**. 7218
18: 9 his **h** caught hold of the oak, and he was 7218
20:21 his **h** *shall be* thrown to thee over the wall. 7218
20:22 they cut off the **h** of Sheba the son of 7218
22:44 thou hast kept me to be **h** of the heathen: 7218
1Ki 2: 6 let not his **hoar h** go down *to* the grave in 7872
2: 9 his **hoar h** bring thou down *to* the grave 7872
2:32 shall return his blood upon his own **h**, 7218
2:33 therefore return upon the **h** of Joab, 7218
2:33 of Joab, and upon the **h** of his seed for ever: 7218
2:37 thy blood shall be upon thine own **h**. 7218
2:44 return thy wickedness upon thine own **h**; 7218
8:32 the wicked, to bring his way upon his **h**; 7218
19: 6 on the coals, and a cruse of water *at* his **h**. 4763
2Ki 2: 3 take away thy master from thy **h** to day? 7218
2: 5 take away thy master from thy **h** to day? 7218
2:23 and said unto him, Go up, thou **bald h**; 7142
2:23 Go up, thou bald head; go up, thou **bald h**. 7142
4:19 he said unto his father, My **h**, my head. 7218
4:19 he said unto his father, My head, my **h**. 7218
6: 5 felling a beam, the **axe h** fell into the water: 1270
6:25 until an ass's **h** was *sold* for fourscore 7218
6:31 if the **h** of Elisha the son of Shaphat shall 7218
6:32 a murderer hath sent to take away mine **h**? 7218
9: 3 pour *it* on his **h**, and say, Thus saith 7218
9: 6 he poured the oil on his **h**, and said unto 7218
9:30 tired her **h**, and looked out at a window. 7218
19:21 of Jerusalem hath shaken her **h** at thee. 7218
25:27 did lift up the **h** of Jehoiachin king of Judah 7218
1Ch 10: 9 they took his **h**, and his armour, and 7218
10:10 and fastened his **h** *in* the temple of Dagon. 1538
20: 2 took the crown of their king from off his **h**, 7218
20: 2 stones in it; and it was *set* upon David's **h**: 7218
29:11 and *thou* art exalted as **h** above all. 7218
2Ch 6:23 by recompensing his way upon his own **h**; 7218
20:18 Jehoshaphat **bowed** his **h** *with his* face to 6915
Ezr 9: 3 pluckt off the hair of my **h** and of my 7218
9: 6 for our iniquities are increased over *our* **h**, 7218
Ne 4: 4 turn their reproach upon their own **h**, and 7218
Est 2:17 so that he set the royal crown upon her **h**, 7218
6: 8 the crown royal which is set upon his **h**: 7218
6:12 house mourning, and having his **h** covered. 7218
9:25 should return upon his own **h**, and that he 7218
Job 1:20 shaved his **h**, and fell down upon 7218
10:15 *if* I be righteous, *yet* will I not lift up my **h**. 7218
16: 4 against you, and shake mine **h** at you. 7218
19: 9 my glory, and taken the crown *from* my **h**. 7218
20: 6 and his **h** reach unto the clouds; 7218
29: 3 When his candle shined upon my **h**, *and* 7218
41: 7 barbed irons? or his **h** with fish spears? 7218
Ps 3: 3 my glory, and the lifter up of mine **h**. 7218
7:16 His mischief shall return upon his own **h**, 7218
18:43 thou hast made me the **h** of the heathen: 7218
21: 3 thou settest a crown of pure gold on his **h**. 7218
22: 7 shoot out the lip, they shake the **h**, *saying*, 7218
23: 5 thou anointest my **h** with oil; my cup 7218
27: 6 now shall mine **h** be lifted up above mine 7218
38: 4 For mine iniquities are gone *over* mine **h**: 7218
40:12 *up*; they are moe than the hairs of mine **h**: 7218
44:14 a shaking of the **h** among the people. 7218
60: 7 Ephraim also *is* the strength of mine **h**; 7218
68:21 God shall wound the **h** of his enemies, *and* 7218
69: 4 a cause are moe than the hairs of mine **h**: 7218
83: 2 and they that hate thee have lift up the **h**. 7218
108: 8 Ephraim also *is* the strength of mine **h**; 7218
110: 7 in the way: therefore shall he lift up the **h**. 7218
118:22 refused is become the **h** *stone* of the corner. 7218
133: 2 *It is* like the precious ointment upon the **h**, 7218
140: 7 thou hast covered my **h** in the day of battle. 7218
140: 9 *As for* the **h** of those that compass me 7218
141: 5 excellent oil, *which* shall not break my **h**: 7218
Pr 1: 9 *shall be* an ornament of grace unto thy **h**, 7218
4: 9 She shall give to thine **h** an ornament of 7218
10: 6 Blessings *are* upon the **h** of the just: but 7218
11:26 blessing *shall be* upon the **h** of him that 7218
16:31 The **hoary h** *is* a crown of glory, *if* it be 7872
20:29 and the beauty of old men *is* the **gray h**. 7872

Pr 25:22 For thou shalt heap coals of fire upon his **h**, 7218
Ecc 2:14 The wise *man's* eyes *are* in his **h**; but 7218
9: 8 and let thy **h** lack no ointment. 7218
SS 2: 6 His left hand *is* under my **h**, and his right 7218
5: 2 for my **h** is filled *with* dew, *and* my locks 7218
5:11 His **h** *is as* the most fine gold, his locks *are* 7218
7: 5 Thine **h** upon thee *is* like Carmel, and 7218
7: 5 and the hair of thine **h** like purple; 7218
8: 3 His left hand *should be* under my **h**, and 7218
Isa 1: 5 the whole **h** *is* sick, and the whole heart 7218
1: 6 From the sole of the foot even unto the **h** 7218
3:17 **crown of the h** of the daughters of Zion, 6936
7: 8 For the **h** of Syria *is* Damascus, and 7218
7: 8 and the **h** of Damascus *is* Rezin; 7218
7: 9 the **h** of Ephraim *is* Samaria, and the head 7218
7: 9 and the **h** of Samaria *is* Remaliah's son. 7218
7:20 of Assyria, the **h**, and the hair of the feet: 7218
9:14 the LORD will cut off from Israel **h** 7218
9:15 The ancient and honourable, he *is* the **h**; 7218
19:15 which the **h** or tail, branch or rush, may do. 7218
28: 1 which *are* on the **h** of the fat valleys of 7218
28: 4 which *is* on the **h** of the fat valley, shall be 7218
37:22 of Jerusalem hath shaken her **h** at thee. 7218
51:11 and everlasting joy *shall be* upon their **h**: 7218
51:20 they lie at the **h** of all the streets, as a wild 7218
58: 5 *is it* to bow down his **h** as a bulrush, and 7218
59:17 and a helmet of salvation upon his **h**; 7218
Jer 2:16 Tahapanes have broken the **crown of** thy **h**. 6936
2:37 from him, and thine hands upon thine **h**: 7218
9: 1 O that my **h** were waters, and mine eyes a 7218
18:16 thereby shall be astonished, and wag his **h**. 7218
22: 6 *art* Gilead unto me, *and* the **h** of Lebanon: 7218
23:19 it shall fall grievously upon the **h** of 7218
30:23 it shall fall with pain upon the **h** of 7218
48:37 For every **h** *shall be* bald, and every beard 7218
48:45 the **crown of the h** of the tumultuous ones. 6936
52:31 lifted up the **h** of Jehoiachin king of Judah, 7218
La 2:15 wag their **h** at the daughter of Jerusalem, 7218
3:54 Waters flowed over mine **h**; *then* I said, 7218
5:16 The crown is fallen *from* our **h**: woe unto 7218
Eze 5: 1 cause *it* to pass upon thine **h** and upon thy 7218
8: 3 of a hand, and took me by a lock of mine **h**; 7218
9:10 I will recompense their way upon their **h**. 7218
10: 1 in the firmament that *was* above the **h** of 7218
10:11 *to* the place whither the **h** looked they 7218
13:18 make kerchiefs upon the **h** of every stature 7218
16:12 and a beautiful crown upon thine **h**. 7218
16:25 Thou hast built thy high place at every **h** of 7218
16:31 thine eminent place in the **h** of every way, 7218
16:43 also will recompense thy way upon *thine* **h**, 7218
17:19 even it will I recompense upon his own **h**. 7218
21:19 choose *it*, at the **h** of the way to the city. 7218
21:21 at the **h** of the two ways, to use divination: 7218
24:17 bind the **tire of** thine **h** upon thee, and 6287
29:18 every **h** *was* made bald, and every shoulder 7218
33: 4 his blood shall be upon his own **h**. 7218
42:12 the south *was* a door in the **h** of the way, 7218
Da 1:10 shall ye make *me* endanger my **h** to 7218
2:28 the visions of thy **h** upon thy bed, *are* these; 7217
2:32 This image's **h** *was* of fine gold, his breast 7217
2:38 ruler over them all. Thou *art* this **h** of gold. 7217
3:27 nor was a hair of their **h** singed, 7217
4: 5 and the visions of my **h** troubled me. 7217
4:10 Thus *were* the visions of mine **h** in my bed; 7217
4:13 I saw in the visions of my **h** upon my bed, 7217
7: 1 a dream and visions of his **h** upon his bed: 7217
7: 9 and the hair of his **h** like the pure wool: 7217
7:15 and the visions of my **h** troubled me. 7217
7:20 of the ten horns that *were* in his **h**, and 7217
Hos 1:11 appoint themselves one **h**, and they shall 7218
Joel 3: 4 I return your recompence upon your own **h**; 7218
3: 7 return your recompence upon your own **h**: 7218
Am 2: 7 the dust of the earth on the **h** of the poor, 7218
8:10 upon all loins, and baldness upon every **h**; 7218
9: 1 cut them in the **h**, all of them; and I will 7218
Ob 1:15 thy reward shall return upon thine own **h**. 7218
Jnh 2: 5 the weeds *were* wrapt about my **h**. 7218
4: 6 that *it* might be a shadow over his **h**, 7218
4: 8 the sun beat upon the **h** of Jonah, that he 7218
Mic 2:13 and the LORD on the **h** of them. 7218
Hab 3:13 thou woundedst the **h** out of the house of 7218
3:14 with his staves the **h** of his villages: 7218
Zec 1:21 so that no man did lift up his **h**: 7218
3: 5 I said, Let them set a fair mitre upon his **h**. 7218
3: 5 So they set a fair mitre upon his **h**, and 7218
6:11 set *them* upon the **h** of Joshua the son of 7218
Mt 5:36 Neither shalt thou swear by thy **h**, because *2776*
6:17 anoint thine **h**, and wash thy face; *2776*
8:20 the Son of man hath not where to lay *his* **h**. *2776*
10:30 But the very hairs of your **h** are all *2776*
14: 8 Give me here John Baptist's **h** in a charger. *2776*
14:11 And his **h** was brought in a charger, and *2776*
21:42 the same is become the **h** of the corner: *2776*
26: 7 and poured *it* on his **h**, as he sat at meat. *2776*
27:29 they put *it* upon his **h**, and a reed in his *2776*
27:30 and took the reed, and smote him on the **h**. *2776*
27:37 And set up over his **h** his accusation *2776*
Mk 6:24 And she said, The **h** of John the Baptist. *2776*
6:25 by in a charger the **h** of John the Baptist. *2776*
6:27 and commanded his **h** to be brought: *2776*
6:28 And brought his **h** in a charger, and gave it *2776*
12: 4 and **wounded** *him* **in the h**, and sent *him* *2775*
12:10 rejected is become the **h** of the corner: *2776*
14: 3 she brake the box, and poured *it* on his **h**. *2776*
15:17 a crown of thorns, and put *it* about his **h**, NIG
15:19 And they smote him on the **h** with a reed, *2776*
Lk 7:38 and did wipe *them* with the hairs of her **h**, *2776*
7:44 and wiped *them* with the hairs of her **h**. *2776*
7:46 Mine **h** with oil thou didst not anoint: but *2776*
9:58 the Son of man hath not where to lay *his* **h**. *2776*
12: 7 But even the *very* hairs of your **h** are all *2776*
20:17 the same is become the **h** of the corner? *2776*
21:18 But there shall not a hair of your **h** perish. *2776*
Jn 13: 9 my feet only, but also *my* hands and *my* **h**. *2776*
19: 2 and put *it* on his **h**, and they put on him a *2776*
Jn 19:30 and he bowed *his* **h**, and gave up the ghost. *2776*
20: 7 And the napkin, that was about his **h**, *2776*
20:12 the one at the **h**, and the other at the feet, *2776*
Ac 4:11 which is become the **h** of the corner. *2776*
18:18 having shorn *his* **h** in Cenchrea: for he had *2776*
27:34 for there shall not a hair fall from the **h** of *2776*
Ro 12:20 doing thou shalt heap coals of fire on his **h**. *2776*
1Co 11: 3 that the **h** of every man is Christ; *2776*
11: 3 and the **h** of the woman *is* the man; and *2776*
11: 3 *is* the man; and the **h** of Christ *is* God. *2776*
11: 4 or prophesying, having *his* **h** covered, *2776*
11: 4 *his* head covered, dishonoureth his **h**. *2776*
11: 5 prophesieth with *her* **h** uncovered *2776*
11: 5 *her* head uncovered dishonoureth her **h**: *2776*
11: 7 For a man indeed ought not to cover *his* **h**, *2776*
11:10 ought the woman to have power on *her* **h** *2776*
12:21 nor again the **h** to the feet, I have no need *2776*
Eph 1:22 gave him *to be* the **h** over all *things* to *2776*
4:15 *up* into him *in* all *things*, which is the **h**, *2776*
5:23 For the husband is the **h** of the wife, *2776*
5:23 even as Christ *is* the **h** of the church: *2776*
Col 1:18 And he is the **h** of the body, the church: *2776*
2:10 which is the **h** of all principality and power: *2776*
2:19 And not holding the **h**, from which all *2776*
1Pe 2: 7 the same is made the **h** of the corner, *2776*
Rev 1:14 His **h** and *his* hairs *were* white like wool, *2776*
10: 1 and a rainbow *was* upon *his* **h**, and his face *2776*
12: 1 and upon her **h** a crown of twelve stars: *2776*
14:14 having on his **h** a golden crown, and in his *2776*
19:12 of fire, and on his **h** *were* many crowns; *2776*

HEADBANDS (1) [BAND, HEAD]

Isa 3:20 and the **h**, and the tablets, and the earrings, 7196

HEADDRESSES See BONNETS

HEADLONG (3) [HEAD]

Job 5:13 and the counsel of the froward is **carried h**. 4116
Lk 4:29 was built, that *they* might **cast** him **down h**. *2630*
Ac 1:18 and **falling h**, he burst asunder in *1096+4248*

HEADS (110) [HEAD]

Ge 2:10 it was parted, and became into four **h**. 7218
43:28 they **bowed down** their **h**, and 6915
Ex 4:31 then they **bowed** their **h** and worshipped. 6915
6:14 These *be* the **h** of their fathers' houses: 7218
6:25 these *are* the **h** of the fathers of the Levites 7218
18:25 made them **h** over the people, rulers of 7218
Lev 10: 6 unto Ithamar his sons, Uncover not your **h**, 7218
19:27 Ye shall not round the corners of your **h**, 7218
Nu 1:16 of their fathers, **h** of thousands in Israel. 7218
7: 2 of Israel, **h** of the house of their fathers, 7218
8:12 the Levites shall lay their hands upon the **h** 7218
10: 4 *which are* **h** of the thousands of Israel, 7218
13: 3 all those men *were* **h** of the children of 7218
25: 4 Take all the **h** of the people, and hang them 7218
30: 1 Moses spake unto the **h** of the tribes 7218
Dt 1:15 and known, and made them **h** over you, 7218
5:23 *even* all the **h** of your tribes, and 7218
33: 5 when the **h** of the people *and* the tribes of 7218
33:21 he came *with* the **h** of the people, 7218
Jos 7: 6 elders of Israel, and put dust upon their **h**. 7218
14: 1 the **h** of the fathers of the tribes of 7218
19:51 the **h** of the fathers of the tribes of 7218
21: 1 came near the **h** of the fathers of 7218
21: 1 unto the **h** of the fathers of the tribes of 7218
22:21 said unto the **h** of the thousands of Israel, 7218
22:30 **h** of the thousands of Israel which *were* 7218
23: 2 for their **h**, and for their judges, and 7218
24: 1 for their **h**, and for their judges, and 7218
Jdg 7:25 brought the **h** of Oreb and Zeeb to Gideon 7218
8:28 so that they lifted up their **h** no more. 7218
9:57 of Shechem did God render upon their **h**: 7218
1Sa 29: 4 *should it* not *be* with the **h** of these men? 7218
1Ki 8: 1 elders of Israel, and all the **h** of the tribes, 7218
20:31 ropes upon our **h**, and go out to the king of 7218
20:32 *put* ropes on their **h**, and came to the king 7218
2Ki 10: 6 take ye the **h** of the men your master's 7218
10: 7 put their **h** in baskets, and sent him *them* to 7218
10: 8 They have brought the **h** of the king's sons. 7218
1Ch 5:24 these *were* the **h** of the house of their 7218
5:24 *and* **h** of the house of their fathers. 7218
7: 2 and Shemuel, **h** of their fathers' house, 7218
7: 7 **h** of the house of *their* fathers, mighty *men* 7218
7: 9 **h** of the house of their fathers, mighty *men* 7218
7:11 by the **h** of *their* fathers, mighty *men* of 7218
7:40 **h** of *their* fathers' house, choice *and* 7218
8: 6 these *are* the **h** of the fathers of 7218
8:10 These *were* his sons, **h** of the fathers. 7218
8:13 who *were* **h** of the fathers of the inhabitants 7218
8:28 These *were* **h** of the fathers, by their 7218
9:13 **h** of the house of their fathers, a thousand 7218
12:19 to his master Saul to *the jeopardy of* our **h**. 7218
12:32 the **h** of them *were* two hundred; and 7218
29:20 **bowed down** their **h**, and worshipped 6915
2Ch 3:16 and put *them* on the **h** of the pillars; 7218
5: 2 elders of Israel, and all the **h** of the tribes, 7218
28:12 certain of the **h** of the children of Ephraim, 7218
29:30 and they **bowed** their **h** and worshipped. 6915
Ne 8: 6 they **bowed** their **h**, and worshipped 6915
Job 2:12 sprinkled dust upon their **h** toward heaven. 7218
Ps 24: 7 Lift up your **h**, O ye gates; and be ye lift 7218
24: 9 Lift up your **h**, O ye gates; even lift *them* 7218
66:12 Thou hast caused men to ride over our **h**; 7218
74:13 thou brakest the **h** of the dragons in 7218
74:14 Thou brakest the **h** of leviathan in pieces, 7218
109:25 they looked upon me they shaked their **h**. 7218
110: 6 he shall wound the **h** over many countries. 7218
Isa 15: 2 on all their **h** *shall be* baldness, *and* 7218
35:10 with songs and everlasting joy upon their **h**: 7218
Jer 14: 3 and confounded, and covered their **h**. 7218
14: 4 were ashamed, they covered their **h**. 7218
La 2:10 they have cast up dust upon their **h**; 7218
2:10 the virgins of Jerusalem hang down their **h** 7218
Eze 1:22 the likeness of the firmament upon the **h** of 7218
1:22 stretched forth over their **h** above. 7218
1:25 from the firmament that *was* over their **h**, 7218
1:26 above the firmament that *was* over their **h** 7218
7:18 all faces, and baldness upon all their **h**. 7218
11:21 recompense their way upon their own **h**, 7218
22:31 own way have I recompensed upon their **h**, 7218
23:15 exceeding in dyed attire upon their **h**, all of 7218
23:42 and beautiful crowns upon their **h**. 7218
24:23 your tires *shall be* upon your **h**, and 7218
27:30 and shall cast up dust upon their **h**, 7218
32:27 they have laid their swords under their **h**, 7218
44:18 They shall have linen bonnets upon their **h**, 7218
44:20 Neither shall they shave their **h**, nor suffer 7218
44:20 to grow long; they shall only poll their **h**. 7218
Da 7: 6 the beast had also four **h**; and 7217
Mic 3: 1 O **h** of Jacob, and ye princes of the house 7218
3: 9 ye **h** of the house of Jacob, and princes of 7218
3:11 The **h** thereof judge for reward, and 7218
Mt 27:39 passed by, reviled him, wagging their **h**, *2776*
Mk 15:29 wagging their **h**, and saying, Ah, *thou* that *2776*
Lk 21:28 to pass, *then* look up, and lift up your **h**; *2776*
Ac 18: 6 Your blood *be* upon your own **h**; *2776*
21:24 with them, that they may shave *their* **h**: *2776*
Rev 4: 4 and they had on their **h** crowns of gold. *2776*
9: 7 on their **h** *were* as *it were* crowns like gold, *2776*
9:17 the **h** of the horses *were* as the heads of *2776*
9:17 the heads of the horses *were* as the **h** of *2776*
9:19 and had **h**, and with them they do hurt. *2776*
12: 3 having seven **h** and ten horns, and *2776*
12: 3 ten horns, and seven crowns upon his **h**. *2776*
13: 1 having seven **h** and ten horns, and upon his *2776*
13: 1 and upon his **h** the name of blasphemy. *2776*
13: 3 And I saw one of his **h** as *it were* wounded *2776*
17: 3 having seven **h** and ten horns. *2776*
17: 7 which hath the seven **h** and ten horns. *2776*
17: 9 The seven **h** are seven mountains, on which *2776*
18:19 And they cast dust on their **h**, and cried, *2776*

HEADSTONE (1) [HEAD, STONE]

Zec 4: 7 he shall bring forth the **h** *thereof with* 68+7222

HEADY (1) [HEAD]

2Ti 3: 4 Traitors, **h**, highminded, lovers of pleasures *4312*

HEAL (40) [HEALED, HEALER, HEALETH, HEALING, HEALINGS, HEALTH]

Nu 12:13 **H** her now, O God, I beseech thee. 7495
Dt 32:39 I kill, and I make alive; I wound, and I **h**: 7495
2Ki 20: 5 behold, I will **h** thee: on the third day thou 7495
20: 8 *shall be* the sign that the LORD will **h** me, 7495
2Ch 7:14 will forgive their sin, and will **h** their land. 7495
Ps 6: 2 O LORD, **h** me; for my bones are vexed. 7495
41: 4 **h** my soul; for I have sinned against thee. 7495
60: 2 **h** the breaches thereof; for it shaketh. 7495
Ecc 3: 3 A time to kill, and a time to **h**; a time to 7495
Isa 19:22 *he* shall smite and **h** *it*: and they shall return 7495
19:22 shall be intreated of them, and shall **h** them. 7495
57:18 I have seen his ways, and will **h** him: I will 7495
57:19 *is* near, saith the LORD; and I will **h** him. 7495
Jer 3:22 *and* I will **h** your backslidings. 7495
17:14 **H** me, O LORD, and I shall be healed; 7495
30:17 I will **h** thee of thy wounds, saith 7495
La 2:13 *is* great like the sea: who can **h** thee? 7495
Hos 5:13 yet could he not **h** you nor cure you of your 7495
6: 1 for he hath torn, and he will **h** us; he hath 7495
14: 4 I will **h** their backsliding, I will love them 7495
Zec 11:16 nor **h** that that is broken, nor feed that that 7495
Mt 8: 7 saith unto him, I will come and **h** him. *2323*
10: 1 and to **h** all *manner of* sickness and *2323*
10: 8 **H** the sick, cleanse the lepers, raise *2323*
12:10 Is it lawful to **h** on the sabbath days? *2323*
13:15 should be converted, and I should **h** them. *2390*
Mk 3: 2 whether he would **h** him on the sabbath *2323*
3:15 And to have power to **h** sicknesses, and to *2323*
Lk 4:18 he hath sent me to **h** the broken-hearted, *2390*
4:23 unto me this proverb, Physician, **h** thyself: *2323*
5:17 the power of the Lord was *present* to **h** *2390*
6: 7 whether he would **h** on the sabbath day; *2323*
7: 3 him that he would come and **h** his servant. *1295*
9: 2 the kingdom of God, and to **h** the sick. *2390*
10: 9 And **h** the sick that are therein, *2323*
14: 3 saying, Is it lawful to **h** on the sabbath day? *2323*
Jn 4:47 that he would come down, and **h** his son: *2390*
12:40 and be converted, and I should **h** them. *2390*
Ac 4:30 By stretching forth thine hand to **h**; and *2392*
28:27 should be converted, and I should **h** them. *2390*

HEALED (79) [HEAL]

Ge 20:17 God **h** Abimelech, and his wife, and 7495
Ex 21:19 shall **cause** *him* **to be thoroughly h**. 7495+7495
Lev 13:18 in the skin thereof, was a boil, and is **h**, 7495
13:37 grown up therein; the scall is **h**, he *is* clean: 7495
14: 3 *if* the plague of leprosy be **h** in the leper; 7495
14:48 the house clean, because the plague is **h**. 7495
Dt 28:27 with the itch, where*of* thou canst not be **h**. 7495
28:35 the legs, with a sore botch that cannot be **h**, 7495
1Sa 6: 3 ye shall be **h**, and it shall be known to you 7495
2Ki 2:21 saith the LORD, I have **h** these waters; 7495
2:22 So the waters were **h** unto this day, 7495
8:29 king Joram went back to be **h** in Jezreel of 7495
9:15 king Joram was returned to be **h** in Jezreel 7495
2Ch 22: 6 he returned to be **h** in Jezreel because of 7495
30:20 hearkened to Hezekiah, and **h** the people. 7495
Ps 30: 2 I cried unto thee, and thou hast **h** me. 7495
107:20 **h** them, and delivered *them* from their 7495
Isa 6:10 *with* their heart, and convert, and be **h**. 7495
53: 5 upon him; and with his stripes we are **h**. 7495
Jer 6:14 They have **h** also the hurt of *the daughter of* 7495
8:11 For they have **h** the hurt of the daughter of 7495
15:18 wound incurable, *which* refuseth to be **h**? 7495
17:14 Heal me, O LORD, and I shall be **h**; 7495
51: 8 balm for her pain, if so be she may be **h**. 7495
51: 9 We would have **h** Babylon, but she is not 7495

Jer 51: 9 have healed Babylon, but she is not **h**: 7495
Eze 30:21 lo, it shall not be bound up to be **h**, to put a 7499
34: 4 neither have ye **h** that which was sick, 7495
47: 8 forth into the sea, the waters shall be **h**. 7495
47: 9 for they shall be **h**; and every *thing* shall 7495
47:11 and the marishes thereof shall not be **h**; 7495
Hos 7: 1 When I *would have* **h** Israel, then 7495
11: 3 their arms; but they knew not that I **h** them. 7495
Mt 4:24 and those that had the palsy; and he **h** them. 2323
8: 8 the word only, and my servant shall be **h**. 2390
8:13 And his servant was **h** in the selfsame hour. 2390
8:16 with *his* word, and **h** all that were sick: 2323
12:15 multitudes followed him, and he **h** them all, 2323
12:22 and he **h** him, insomuch that the blind and 2323
14:14 toward them, and he **h** their sick. 2323
15:30 them *down* at Jesus' feet; and he **h** them: 2323
19: 2 followed him; and he **h** them there. 2323
21:14 came to him in the temple; and he **h** them. 2323
Mk 1:34 And he **h** many *that were* sick of divers 2323
3:10 For he had **h** many; insomuch that *they* 2323
5:23 lay *thy* hands on her, that she may be **h**; 4982
5:29 she felt in *her* body that she was **h** of *that* 2390
6: 5 hands upon a few sick *folk,* and **h** *them.* 2323
6:13 with oil many *that were* sick, and **h** *them.* 2323
Lk 4:40 hands on every one of them, and **h** them. 2323
5:15 and to be **h** by him of their infirmities. 2323
6:17 to hear him, and to be **h** of their diseases; 2390
6:18 with unclean spirits: and they were **h**. 2323
6:19 went virtue out of him, and **h** *them* all. 2390
7: 7 say in a word, and my servant shall be **h**. 2390
8: 2 which had been **h** of evil spirits and 2323
8:36 he that was possessed of the devils was **h**. 4982
8:43 upon physicians, neither could be **h** of any, 2323
8:47 and how she was **h** immediately. 2390
9:11* and **h** them that had need of healing. 2390
9:42 and **h** the child, and delivered him again to 2390
13:14 that Jesus had **h** on the sabbath day, 2323
13:14 in them therefore come and be **h**, and 2323
14: 4 And he took *him,* and **h** him, and let *him* 2390
17:15 when he saw that he was **h**, turned back, 2390
22:51 thus far. And he touched his ear, and **h** him. 2390
Jn 5:13 And he that was **h** wist not who it was: 2390
Ac 3:11 And as the lame *man* which was **h** held 2390
4:14 And beholding the man which was **h** 2323
5:16 unclean spirits: and they were **h** every one. 2323
8: 7 with palsies, and *that were* lame, were **h**. 2323
14: 9 and perceiving that he had faith to be **h**, 4982
28: 8 and laid *his* hands on him, and **h** him. 2390
28: 9 diseases in the island, came, and were **h**: 2323
Heb 12:13 turned out of the way; but let it rather be **h**. 2390
Jas 5:16 and pray one for another, that ye may be **h**. 2390
1Pe 2:24 by whose stripes ye were **h**. 2390
Rev 13: 3 to death; and his deadly wound was **h**: 2323
13:12 the first beast, whose deadly wound was **h**. 2323

HEALER (1) [HEAL]

Isa 3: 7 shall he swear, saying, I will not be a **h**; 2280

HEALETH (4) [HEAL]

Ex 15:26 for I *am* the LORD that **h** thee. 7495
Ps 103: 3 all thine iniquities; who **h** all thy diseases; 7495
147: 3 He **h** the broken in heart, and bindeth up 7495
Isa 30:26 his people, and **h** the stroke of their wound. 7495

HEALING (14) [HEAL]

Jer 14:19 thou smitten us, and *there is* no **h** for us? 4832
14:19 and for the time of **h**, and behold trouble. 4832
30:13 be bound up: thou hast no **h** medicines. 8585
Na 3:19 *There is* no **h** of thy bruise; thy wound *is* 3545
Mal 4: 2 of righteousness arise with **h** in his wings; 4832
Mt 4:23 and **h** all *manner of* sickness and 2323
9:35 and **h** every sickness and every disease 2323
Lk 9: 6 preaching the gospel, and **h** every where. 2323
9:11 of God, and healed them that had need of **h**. 2322
Ac 4:22 on whom this miracle of **h** was shewed. 2392
10:38 and **h** all that were oppressed of the devil; 2390
1Co 12: 9 to another the gifts of **h** by the same Spirit; 2386
12:30 Have all the gifts of **h**? do all speak with 2386
Rev 22: 2 the leaves of the tree *were* for the **h** of 2322

HEALINGS (1) [HEAL]

1Co 12:28 then gifts of **h**, helps, governments, 2386

HEALTH (17) [HEAL]

Ge 43:28 Thy servant our father *is* **in good h**, he *is* 7965
2Sa 20: 9 said to Amasa, *Art* thou **in h**, my brother? 7965
Ps 42:11 *who is* the **h** of my countenance, and 3444
43: 5 *who is* the **h** of my countenance, and 3444
67: 2 upon earth, thy **saving h** among all nations. 3444
Pr 3: 8 It shall be **h** to thy navel, and marrow to thy 7500
4:22 those that find them, and **h** to all their flesh. 4832
12:18 of a sword: but the tongue of the wise *is* **h**. 4832
13:17 but a faithful ambassador *is* **h**. 4832
16:24 sweet to the soul, and **h** to the bones. 4832
Isa 58: 8 and thine **h** shall spring forth speedily: 724
Jer 8:15 no good *came; and* for a time of **h**, and 4832
8:22 is not the **h** of the daughter of my people 724
30:17 For I will restore **h** unto thee, and I will heal 724
33: 6 I *will* bring it **h** and cure, and I will cure 724
Ac 27:34 for this is for your **h**: for there shall not a 4991
3Jn 1: 2 *things* that thou mayest prosper and be in **h**, 5198

HEAP (38) [HEAPED, HEAPETH, HEAPS]

Ge 31:46 and they took stones, and made a **h**: 1530
31:46 a heap: and they did eat there upon the **h**. 1530
31:48 This **h** *is* a witness between me and thee 1530
31:51 Behold this **h**, and behold *this* pillar, 1530
31:52 This **h** *be* witness, and *this* pillar *be* 1530
31:52 that I will not pass over this **h** to thee, and 1530
31:52 that thou shalt not pass over this **h** and 1530
Ex 15: 8 the floods stood upright as a **h**, *and* 5067
Dt 13:16 it shall be a **h** for ever; it shall not be built 8510
32:23 I will **h** mischiefs upon them; I will spend 5595
Jos 3:13 from above; and they shall stand *upon* a **h**. 5067
3:16 above stood *and* rose up *upon* a **h** very far, 5067
7:26 they raised over him a great **h** of stones 1530
8:28 Joshua burnt Ai, and made it a **h** for ever, 8510
8:29 raise thereon a great **h** of stones, 1530
Ru 3: 7 he went to lie down at the end of the **h** *of* 6194
2Sa 18:17 and laid a very great **h** of stones upon him: 1530
Job 8:17 His roots are wrapped about the **h**, *and* 1530
16: 4 I could **h up** words against you, and 2266
27:16 Though he **h up** silver as the dust, and 6651
36:13 the hypocrites in heart **h up** wrath: they cry 7760
Ps 33: 7 the waters of the sea together as a **h**: 5067
78:13 and he made the waters to stand as a **h**. 5067
Pr 25:22 For thou shalt **h** coals of fire upon his head, 2846
Ecc 2:26 he giveth travail, to gather and to **h up**, 3664
SS 7: 2 thy belly *is like* a **h** of wheat set about with 6194
Isa 17: 1 *being* a city, and it shall be a ruinous **h**. 4596
17:11 the harvest *shall be* a **h** in the day of grief 5067
25: 2 For thou hast made of a city a **h**; *of* a 1530
Jer 30:18 the city shall be builded upon her own **h**, 8510
49: 2 it shall be a desolate **h**, and her daughters 8510
Eze 24:10 **H** on wood, kindle the fire, consume 7235
Mic 1: 6 Therefore I will make Samaria as a **h** of 5856
Hab 1:10 for they shall **h** dust, and take it. 6651
3:15 thine horses, *through* the **h** of great waters. 2563
Hag 2:16 when *one* came to a **h** of twenty *measures,* 6194
Ro 12:20 doing thou shalt **h** coals of fire on his head. 4987
2Ti 4: 3 after their own lusts shall they **h** to 2002

HEAPED (2) [HEAP]

Zec 9: 3 **h up** silver as the dust, and fine gold as 6651
Jas 5: 3 ye have **h treasure together** for the last 2343

HEAPETH (2) [HEAP]

Ps 39: 6 he **h up** *riches,* and knoweth not who shall 6651
Hab 2: 5 him all nations, and **h** unto him all people: 6908

HEAPS (20) [HEAP]

Ex 8:14 they gathered them together **upon h**: 2563+2563
Jdg 15:16 With the jawbone of an ass, **h** upon heaps, 2565
15:16 With the jawbone of an ass, heaps upon **h**, 2565
2Ki 10: 8 Lay ye them *in* two **h** *at* the entering in of 6652
19:25 be to lay waste fenced cities *into* ruinous **h**. 1530
2Ch 31: 6 their God, and laid *them* **by h**. 6194+6194
31: 7 they began to lay the foundation of the **h**, 6194
31: 8 and the princes came and saw the **h**, 6194
31: 9 and the Levites concerning the **h**. 6194
Ne 4: 2 will they revive the stones out of the **h** of 6194
Job 15:28 which are ready to become **h**. 1530
Ps 79: 1 they defiled; they have laid Jerusalem on **h**. 5856
Isa 37:26 to lay waste defenced cities *into* ruinous **h**. 1530
Jer 9:11 I will make Jerusalem **h**, *and* a den of 1530
26:18 Jerusalem shall become **h**, and 5856
31:21 Set thee up waymarks, make thee **high h**: 8564
50:26 cast her up as **h**, and destroy her utterly: 6194
51:37 Babylon shall become **h**, a dwelling place 1530
Hos 12:11 their altars *are* as **h** in the furrows of 1530
Mic 3:12 Jerusalem shall become **h**, and 5856

HEAR (550) [HEARD, HEARDEST, HEARER, HEARERS, HEAREST, HEARETH, HEARING]

Ge 4:23 his wives, Adah and Zillah, **H** my voice; 8085
21: 6 *so that* all that **h** will laugh with me. 8085
23: 6 **H** us, my lord: thou *art* a mighty prince 8085
23: 8 **h** me, and intreat for me to Ephron the son 8085
23:11 Nay, my lord, **h** me: the field give I thee, 8085
23:13 But if thou *wilt give it,* I pray thee, **h** me: 8085
37: 6 he said unto them, **H**, I pray you, this 8085
42:21 when he besought us, and we would not **h**; 8085
42:22 sin against the child; and ye would not **h**? 8085
49: 2 and **h**, ye sons of Jacob; 8085
Ex 6:12 how then shall Pharaoh **h** me, who *am* of 8085
7:16 and behold, hitherto thou wouldest not **h**. 8085
15:14 The people shall **h**, *and* be afraid: 8085
19: 9 that the people may **h** when I speak with 8085
20:19 Speak thou with us, and we will **h**: 8085
22:23 all unto me, I will **surely h** their cry; 8085+8085
22:27 when he crieth unto me, that I will **h**; 8085
32:18 *but* the noise of *them that* sing do I **h**. 8085
Lev 5: 1 **h** the voice of swearing, and *is* a witness, 8085
Nu 9: 8 I will **h** what the LORD will command 8085
12: 6 he said, **H** now my words: If there be a 8085
14:13 the Egyptians shall **h** *it,* (for thou 8085
16: 8 unto Korah, **H**, I pray you, ye sons of Levi: 8085
20:10 and he said unto them, **H** now, ye rebels; 8085
23:18 his parable, and said, Rise up, Balak, and **h**; 8085
30: 4 her father **h** her vow, and her bond 8085
Dt 1:16 **H** *the causes* between your brethren, and 8085
1:17 you shall **h** the small as well as the great; 8085
1:17 for you, bring *it* unto me, and I will **h** it. 8085
1:43 you would not **h**, but rebelled against 8085
2:25 who shall **h** report of thee, and 8085
3:26 me for your sakes, and would not **h** me: 8085
4: 6 which shall **h** all these statutes, and say, 8085
4:10 and I will **make** them **h** my words, 8085
4:28 which neither see, nor **h**, nor eat, nor smell. 8085
4:33 Did *ever* people **h** the voice of God 8085
4:36 Out of heaven he **made** thee **to h** his voice, 8085
5: 1 **H**, O Israel, the statutes and judgments 8085
5:25 if we **h** the voice of the LORD our God 8085
5:27 **h** all that the LORD our God shall say: 8085
5:27 speak unto thee; and we will **h** *it,* and do *it.* 8085
6: 3 **H** therefore, O Israel, and observe to do *it;* 8085
6: 4 **H**, O Israel: The LORD our God *is* one 8085
9: 1 **H**, O Israel: Thou art to pass over Jordan 8085
12:28 **h** all these words which I command thee, 8085
13:11 all Israel shall **h**, and fear, and shall do no 8085
13:12 If thou shalt **h** *say* in one of thy cities, 8085
17:13 all the people shall **h**, and fear, and do no 8085
18:16 Let me not **h** again the voice of the LORD 8085
19:20 those which remain shall **h**, and fear, and 8085
20: 3 shall say unto them, **H**, O Israel, 8085
21:21 among you; and all Israel shall **h**, and fear. 8085
29: 4 and eyes to see, and ears to **h**, unto this day. 8085
30:12 bring it unto us, that we may **h** it, and do it? 8085
30:13 bring it unto us, that we may **h** it, and do it? 8085
30:17 so that thou wilt not **h**, but shalt be drawn 8085
31:12 that they may **h**, and that they may learn, 8085
31:13 which have not known *any thing,* may **h**, 8085
32: 1 and **h**, O earth, the words of my mouth. 8085
33: 7 and he said, **H**, LORD, the voice of Judah, 8085
Jos 3: 9 and **h** the words of the LORD your God. 8085
6: 5 *and when* ye **h** the sound of the trumpet, 8085
7: 9 all the inhabitants of the land shall **h** *of it,* 8085
Jdg 5: 3 **H**, O ye kings; give ear, O ye princes; I, 8085
5:16 to **h** the bleatings of the flocks? 8085
7:11 thou shalt **h** what they say; and 8085
14:13 Put forth thy riddle, that we may **h** it. 8085
1Sa 2:23 for I **h** of your evil dealings by all this 8085
2:24 my sons; for *it is* no good report that I **h**: 8085
8:18 and the LORD will not **h** you in that day. 6030
13: 3 all the land, saying, Let the Hebrews **h**. 8085
15:14 and the lowing of the oxen which I **h**? 8085
16: 2 if Saul **h** *it,* he will kill me. And 8085
22: 7 stood about him, **H** now, ye Benjamites; 8085
22:12 Saul said, **H** now, thou son of Ahitub. 8085
25:24 and **h** the words of thine handmaid. 8085
26:19 let my lord the king **h** the words of his 8085
2Sa 14:16 For the king will **h**, to deliver his handmaid 8085
15: 3 *there is* no man *deputed* of the king to **h** 8085
15:10 As soon as ye **h** the sound of the trumpet, 8085
15:35 *that* what thing soever thou shalt **h** out of 8085
15:36 send unto me every thing that ye can **h**. 8085
16:21 all Israel shall **h** that thou art abhorred of 8085
17: 5 and let us **h** likewise what he saith. 8085
19:35 can I **h** any more the voice of singing *men* 8085
20:16 cried a wise woman out of the city, **H**, hear; 8085
20:16 cried a wise woman out of the city, Hear, **h**; 8085
20:17 unto him, **H** the words of thine handmaid. 8085
20:17 thine handmaid. And he answered, I do **h**. 8085
22: 7 he did **h** my voice out of his temple, and 8085
22:45 as soon as they **h**, they shall be 241+8085
1Ki 4:34 there came of all people to **h** the wisdom of 8085
8:30 **h** thou in heaven thy dwelling place: and 8085
8:32 **h** thou *in* heaven, and do, and judge thy 8085
8:34 **h** thou *in* heaven, and forgive the sin of thy 8085
8:36 **h** thou *in* heaven, and forgive the sin of thy 8085
8:39 **h** thou *in* heaven thy dwelling place, and 8085
8:42 (For they shall **h** of thy great name, and of 8085
8:43 **H** thou *in* heaven thy dwelling place, and 8085
8:45 **h** thou *in* heaven their prayer and their 8085
8:49 **h** thou their prayer and their supplication *in* 8085
10: 8 before thee, *and* that **h** thy wisdom. 8085
10:24 to **h** his wisdom, which God had put in his 8085
18:26 even until noon, saying, O Baal, **h** us. 6030
18:37 **H** me, O LORD, hear me, that this people 6030
18:37 Hear me, O LORD, **h** me, that this people 6030
22:19 **H** thou therefore the word of the LORD: 8085
2Ki 7: 1 Elisha said, **H** ye the word of the LORD; 8085
7: 6 **made** the host of the Syrians **to h** a noise of 8085
14:11 Amaziah would not **h**. Therefore Jehoash 8085
17:14 Notwithstanding they would not **h**, but 8085
18:12 and would not **h** *them,* nor do *them.* 8085
18:28 spake, saying, **H** the word of the great king, 8085
19: 4 It may be the LORD thy God will **h** all 8085
19: 7 he shall **h** a rumour, and shall return to his 8085
19:16 LORD, bow down thine ear, and **h**: open, 8085
19:16 **h** the words of Sennacherib, which hath 8085
20:16 unto Hezekiah, **H** the word of the LORD. 8085
1Ch 14:15 when thou shalt **h** a sound of going in 8085
28: 2 said, **H** me, my brethren, and my people: 8085
2Ch 6:21 **h** thou from thy dwelling place, *even* from 8085
6:23 **h** thou from heaven, and do, and judge thy 8085
6:25 **h** thou from the heavens, and forgive 8085
6:27 **h** thou *from* heaven, and forgive the sin of 8085
6:30 **h** thou from heaven thy dwelling place, 8085
6:33 **h** thou from the heavens, *even* from thy 8085
6:35 **h** thou from the heavens their prayer and 8085
6:39 **h** thou from the heavens, *even* from thy 8085
7:14 will I **h** from heaven, and will forgive their 8085
9: 7 continually before thee, and **h** thy wisdom. 8085
9:23 to **h** his wisdom, that God had put in his 8085
13: 4 said, **H** me, *thou* Jeroboam, and all Israel; 8085
15: 2 **H** ye me, Asa, and all Judah and Benjamin; 8085
18:18 Therefore **h** the word of the LORD; 8085
20: 9 in our affliction, then thou wilt **h** and help. 8085
20:20 Jehoshaphat stood and said, **H** me, 8085
25:20 Amaziah would not **h**; for it *came* of God, 8085
28:11 Now **h** me therefore, and deliver 8085
29: 5 said unto them, **H** me, ye Levites, 8085
Ne 1: 6 that *thou* mayest **h** the prayer of thy 8085
4: 4 **H**, O our God; for we are despised: and 8085
4:20 *therefore* ye **h** the sound of the trumpet, 8085
8: 2 and all that could **h** with understanding, 8085
9:29 and hardened their neck, and would not **h**. 8085
Job 3:18 they **h** not the voice of the oppressor. 8085
5:27 so it *is;* **h** it, and know thou *it* for thy good. 8085
13: 6 **H** now my reasoning, and hearken to 8085
13:17 **H diligently** my speech, and 8085+8085
15:17 I will shew thee, **h** me; and that which I 8085
21: 2 **H diligently** my speech, and let this 8085+8085
22:27 he shall **h** thee, and thou shalt pay thy 8085
27: 9 Will God **h** his cry when trouble cometh 8085
30:20 I cry unto thee, and thou dost not **h** me: 6030
31:35 O that one would **h** me! behold, my desire 8085
33: 1 **h** my speeches, and hearken to all my 8085
34: 2 **H** my words, O ye wise *men;* and give ear 8085
34:16 If now *thou hast* understanding, **h** this: 8085
35:13 Surely God will not **h** vanity, neither will 8085
37: 2 **H attentively** the noise of his voice, and 8085
42: 4 **H**, I beseech thee, and I will speak: I will 8085
Ps 4: 1 **H** me when I call, O God of my 6030
4: 1 have mercy upon me, and **h** my prayer. 8085
4: 3 the LORD will **h** when I call unto him. 8085
5: 3 My voice shalt thou **h** *in* the morning, 8085
10:17 their heart, thou wilt **cause** thine ear **to h**: 7181
13: 3 Consider *and* **h** me, O LORD my God: 6030
17: 1 **H** the right, O LORD, attend unto my cry, 8085
17: 6 upon thee, for thou wilt **h** me, O God: 6030
17: 6 incline thine ear unto me, *and* **h** my speech. 8085

Ps 18:44 As soon as they **h** *of me,* they shall obey 8088
20: 1 The LORD **h** thee in the day of trouble; 6030
20: 6 he will **h** him from his holy heaven with 6030
20: 9 LORD: let the king **h** us when we call. 6030
27: 7 **H**, O LORD, *when* I cry *with* my voice: 8085
28: 2 **H** the voice of my supplications, when I cry 8085
30:10 **H**, O LORD, and have mercy upon me: 8085
34: 2 the humble shall **h** *thereof,* and be glad. 8085
38:15 do I hope: thou wilt **h**, O Lord my God. 6030
38:16 *H me,* lest *otherwise* they should rejoice NIH
39:12 **H** my prayer, O LORD, and give ear unto 8085
49: 1 **H** this, all ye people; give ear, all ye 8085
50: 7 **H**, O my people, and I will speak; O Israel, 8085
51: 8 **Make** me **to h** joy and gladness; *that* 8085
54: 2 **H** my prayer, O God; give ear to the words 8085
55: 2 Attend unto me, and **h** me: I mourn in my 6030
55:17 and cry aloud: and he shall **h** my voice. 8085
55:19 God shall **h**, and afflict them, even he that 8085
59: 7 *are* in their lips: for who, *say they,* doth **h**? 8085
60: 5 save *with* thy right hand, and **h** me. 6030
61: 1 **H** my cry, O God; attend unto my prayer. 8085
64: 1 **H** my voice, O God, in my prayer: 8085
66:16 Come *and* **h**, all ye that fear God, and I will 8085
66:18 in my heart, the Lord will not **h** *me:* 8085
69:13 O God, in the multitude of thy mercy **h** me, 6030
69:16 **H** me, O LORD; for thy lovingkindness *is* 6030
69:17 for I am in trouble: **h** me speedily. 6030
81: 8 **H**, O my people, and I will testify unto 8085
84: 8 O LORD God *of* hosts, **h** my prayer: 8085
85: 8 I will **h** what God the LORD will speak: 8085
86: 1 Bow down thine ear, O LORD, **h** me: for I 6030
92:11 mine ears shall **h** *my desire* of the wicked 8085
94: 9 He that planted the ear, shall he not **h**? he 8085
95: 7 of his hand. To day if ye will **h** his voice, 8085
102: 1 **H** my prayer, O LORD, and let my cry 8085
102:20 To **h** the groaning of the prisoner; to loose 8085
115: 6 They have ears, but they **h** not: noses have 8085
119:145 with *my* whole heart; **h** me, O LORD: 6030
119:149 **H** my voice according unto thy 8085
130: 2 Lord, **h** my voice: let thine ears be attentive 8085
135:17 They have ears, but they **h** not; neither is 238
138: 4 when they **h** the words of thy mouth. 8085
140: 6 **h** the voice of my supplications, O LORD. 238
141: 6 in stony places, they shall **h** my words; 8085
143: 1 **H** my prayer, O LORD, give ear to my 8085
143: 7 **H** me speedily, O LORD: my spirit 6030
143: 8 **Cause** me **to h** thy lovingkindness in 8085
145:19 he also will **h** their cry, and will save them. 8085
Pr 1: 5 A wise *man* will **h**, and will increase 8085
1: 8 **h** the instruction of thy father, and 8085
4: 1 **H**, ye children, the instruction of a father, 8085
4:10 **H**, O my son, and receive my sayings; and 8085
5: 7 **H** me now therefore, O ye children, and 8085
8: 6 **H**, for I will speak of excellent things; and 8085
8:33 **H** instruction, and be wise, and refuse *it* 8085
19:20 **H** counsel, and receive instruction, 8085
19:27 to **h** the instruction *that causeth* to err from 8085
22:17 **h** the words of the wise, and apply thine 8085
23:19 **H** thou, my son, and be wise, and 8085
Ecc 5: 1 *be* more ready to **h**, than to give 8085
7: 5 *It is* better to **h** the rebuke of the wise, 8085
7: 5 than for a man to **h** the song of fools. 8085
7:21 lest thou **h** thy servant curse thee: 8085
12:13 Let us **h** the conclusion of the whole 8085
SS 2:14 me see thy countenance, let me **h** thy voice; 8085
8:13 hearken to thy voice: **cause** me **to h** *it.* 8085
Isa 1: 2 **H**, O heavens, and give ear, O earth: for 8085
1:10 **H** the word of the LORD, ye rulers of 8085
1:15 when ye make many prayers, I will not **h**: 8085
6: 9 **H** ye **indeed**, but understand not; 8085+8085
6:10 **h** with their ears, and understand *with* their 8085
7:13 he said, **H** ye now, O house of David; *Is it* a 8085
18: 3 and when *he* bloweth a trumpet, **h** ye. 8085
28:12 this *is* the refreshing: yet they would not **h**. 8085
28:14 Wherefore **h** the word of the LORD, 8085
28:23 Give ye ear, and **h** my voice; hearken, and 8085
28:23 hear my voice; hearken, and **h** my speech. 8085
29:18 in that day shall the deaf **h** the words of 8085
30: 9 children *that* will not **h** the law of 8085
30:19 when *he* shall **h** it, he will answer thee. 8085
30:21 thine ears shall **h** a word behind thee, 8085
32: 3 and the ears of them that **h** shall hearken. 8085
32: 9 ye women that are at ease, **h** my voice; 8085
33:13 **H**, ye *that are* far off, what I have done; and 8085
34: 1 Come near, ye nations, to **h**; and hearken, 8085
34: 1 let the earth **h**, and all that is therein; 8085
36:13 said, **H** ye the words of the great king, 8085
37: 4 It may be the LORD thy God will **h** 8085
37: 7 he shall **h** a rumour, and return to his own 8085
37:17 Incline thine ear, O LORD, and **h**; 8085
37:17 **h** all the words of Sennacherib, which hath 8085
39: 5 **H** the word of the LORD of hosts: 8085
41:17 faileth for thirst, I the LORD will **h** them, 6030
42:18 **H**, ye deaf; and look, ye blind, that *ye* may 8085
42:23 will hearken and **h** for the time to come? 8085
43: 9 or let them **h**, and say, *It is* truth. 8085
44: 1 Yet now **h**, O Jacob my servant; and Israel, 8085
47: 8 Therefore **h** now this, *thou that art* given to 8085
48: 1 **H** ye this, O house of Jacob, which are 8085
48:14 All ye, assemble yourselves, and **h**; 8085
48:16 Come ye near unto me, **h** ye this; I have not 8085
50: 4 he wakeneth mine ear to **h** as the learned. 8085
51:21 Therefore **h** now this, thou afflicted, and 8085
55: 3 **h**, and your soul shall live; and I will make 8085
59: 1 neither his ear heavy, that *it* cannot **h**: 8085
59: 2 hid *his* face from you, that *he* will not **h**. 8085
65:12 when I spake, ye did not **h**; but did evil 8085
65:24 and whiles they are yet speaking, I will **h**. 8085
66: 4 did answer; when I spake, they did not **h**: 8085
66: 5 **H** the word of the LORD, ye that tremble 8085
Jer 2: 4 **H** ye the word of the LORD, O house of 8085
4:21 *and* **h** the sound of the trumpet? 8085
5:21 **H** now this, O foolish people, and 8085
5:21 and see not; which have ears, and **h** not: 8085
6:10 I speak, and give warning, that they may **h**? 8085

Jer 6:18 Therefore **h**, ye nations, and know, 8085
6:19 **H**, O earth: behold, I will bring evil upon 8085
7: 2 say, **H** the word of the LORD, all *ye of* 8085
7:16 intercession to me: for I *will* not **h** thee. 8085
9:10 neither can *men* **h** the voice of the cattle; 8085
9:20 Yet **h** the word of the LORD, O ye 8085
10: 1 **H** ye the word which the LORD speaketh 8085
11: 2 **H** ye the words of this covenant, and 8085
11: 6 **H** ye the words of this covenant, and 8085
11:10 which refused to **h** my words; 8085
11:14 for I will not **h** *them* in the time that they 8085
13:10 evil people, which refuse to **h** my words, 8085
13:11 and for a glory: but they would not **h**. 8085
13:15 **H** ye, and give ear; be not proud: for 8085
13:17 if ye will not **h** it, my soul shall weep in 8085
14:12 When they fast, I will not **h** their cry; and 8085
17:20 **H** ye the word of the LORD, ye kings of 8085
17:23 made their neck stiff, that *they* might not **h**, 8085
18: 2 and there I will **cause** thee **to h** my words. 8085
19: 3 say, **H** ye the word of the LORD, O kings 8085
19:15 that *they* might not **h** my words. 8085
20:16 let him **h** the cry in the morning, and 8085
21:11 *say,* **H** ye the word of the LORD. 8085
22: 2 say, **H** the word of the LORD, O king of 8085
22: 5 if ye will not **h** these words, I swear by 8085
22:21 thy prosperity; *but* thou saidst, I will not **h**. 8085
22:29 earth, earth, **h** the word of the LORD. 8085
23:22 had **caused** my people **to h** my words, then 8085
25: 4 not hearkened, nor inclined your ear to **h**. 8085
28: 7 Nevertheless **h** thou now this word that I 8085
28:15 Hananiah the prophet, **H** now, Hananiah; 8085
29:19 and sending *them;* but ye would not **h**, 8085
29:20 **H** ye therefore the word of the LORD, 8085
31:10 **H** the word of the LORD, O ye nations, 8085
33: 9 which shall **h** all the good that I do unto 8085
34: 4 Yet **h** the word of the LORD, O Zedekiah 8085
36: 3 It may be that the house of Judah will **h** all 8085
36:25 not burn the roll: but he would not **h** them. 8085
37:20 Therefore **h** now, I pray thee, O my lord 8085
38:25 if the princes **h** that I have talked with thee, 8085
42:14 nor **h** the sound of the trumpet, nor have 8085
42:15 therefore **h** the word of the LORD, 8085
44:24 all the women, **H** the word of the LORD, 8085
44:26 Therefore **h** ye the word of the LORD, 8085
49:20 Therefore **h** the counsel of the LORD, 8085
50:45 Therefore **h** ye the counsel of the LORD, 8085
La 1:18 **h**, I pray you, all people, and behold my 8085
Eze 2: 5 whether they will **h**, or whether they will 8085
2: 7 whether they will **h**, or whether they will 8085
2: 8 son of man, **h** what I say unto thee; 8085
3:10 receive in thine heart, and **h** with thine ears. 8085
3:11 whether they will **h**, or whether they will 8085
3:17 therefore **h** the word at my mouth, and 8085
3:27 He that heareth, let him **h**; and he that 8085
6: 3 of Israel, **h** the word of the Lord GOD; 8085
8:18 *with* a loud voice, *yet* will I not **h** them. 8085
12: 2 see not; they have ears to **h**, and hear not: 8085
12: 2 see not; they have ears to hear, and **h** not: 8085
13: 2 own hearts, **H** ye the word of the LORD; 8085
13:19 by your lying to my people that **h** *your* lies? 8085
16:35 O harlot, **h** the word of the LORD: 8085
18:25 **H** now, O house of Israel; Is not my way 8085
20:47 of the south, **H** the word of the LORD; 8085
24:26 to **cause** *thee* **to h** *it* with *thine* ears? 2045
25: 3 **H** the word of the Lord GOD; 8085
33: 7 thou shalt **h** the word at my mouth, 8085
33:30 **h** what *is* the word that cometh forth from 8085
33:31 they **h** thy words, but they will not do 8085
33:32 for they **h** thy words, but they do them not. 8085
34: 7 ye shepherds, **h** the word of the LORD; 8085
34: 9 O ye shepherds, **h** the word of the LORD; 8085
36: 1 of Israel, **h** the word of the LORD: 8085
36: 4 of Israel, **h** the word of the Lord GOD; 8085
36:15 Neither will I **cause** *men* **to h** in thee 8085
37: 4 O ye dry bones, **h** the word of the LORD. 8085
40: 4 **h** with thine ears, and set thine heart upon 8085
44: 5 **h** with thine ears all that I say unto thee 8085
Da 3: 5 *That* at what time ye **h** the sound of 8086
3:10 that every man that shall **h** the sound of 8086
3:15 Now if ye be ready that at what time ye **h** 8086
5:23 stone, which see not, nor **h**, nor know: 8086
9:17 **h** the prayer of thy servant, and 8085
9:18 O my God, incline thine ear, and **h**; 8085
9:19 O Lord, **h**; O Lord, forgive; O Lord, 8085
Hos 2:21 I will **h**, saith the LORD, I will hear 6030
2:21 I will **h** the heavens, and they shall hear 6030
2:21 hear the heavens, and they shall **h** the earth; 6030
2:22 the earth shall **h** the corn, and the wine, 6030
2:22 and the oil; and they shall **h** Jezreel. 6030
4: 1 **H** the word of the LORD, ye children of 8085
5: 1 **H** ye this, O priests; and hearken, ye house 8085
Joel 1: 2 **H** this, ye old men, and give ear, all ye 8085
Am 3: 1 **H** this word that the LORD hath spoken 8085
3:13 **H** ye, and testify in the house of Jacob, 8085
4: 1 **H** this word, ye kine of Bashan, that *are* in 8085
5: 1 **H** ye this word which I take up against you, 8085
5:23 for I will not **h** the melody of thy viols. 8085
7:16 therefore **h** thou the word of the LORD: 8085
8: 4 **H** this, O ye that swallow up the needy, 8085
Mic 1: 2 **H**, all ye people; hearken, O earth, and 8085
3: 1 I said, **H**, I pray you, O heads of Jacob, 8085
3: 4 unto the LORD, but he will not **h** them: 6030
3: 9 **H** this, I pray you, ye heads of the house of 8085
6: 1 **H** ye now what the LORD saith; Arise, 8085
6: 1 the mountains, and let the hills **h** thy voice. 8085
6: 2 **H** ye, O mountains, the LORD'S 8085
6: 9 **h** ye the rod, and who hath appointed it. 8085
7: 7 God of my salvation: my God will **h** me. 8085
Na 3:19 all that **h** the bruit of thee shall clap 8085
Hab 1: 2 how long shall I cry, and thou wilt not **h**? 8085
Zec 1: 4 they did not **h**, nor hearken unto me, 8085
3: 8 **H** now, O Joshua the high priest, thou, and 8085
7: 7 *Should ye* not **h** the words which NIH
7:11 stopped their ears, that *they* should not **h**. 8085
7:12 lest *they* should **h** the law, and the words 8085

Zec 7:13 *that* as he cried, and they would not **h**; 8085
7:13 so they cried, and I would not **h**, saith 8085
8: 9 ye that **h** in these days these words by 8085
10: 6 *am* the LORD their God, and will **h** them. 6030
13: 9 shall call on my name, and I will **h** them: 6030
Mal 2: 2 If ye will not **h**, and if ye will not lay *it* to 8085
Mt 10:14 nor **h** your words, when ye depart out of that *191*
10:27 and what ye **h** in the ear, *that* preach ye upon *191*
11: 4 shew John again *those things* which ye do **h** *191*
11: 5 and the deaf **h**, the dead are raised up, and *191*
11:15 He that hath ears to **h**, let him hear. *191*
11:15 He that hath ears to hear, let him **h**. *191*
12:19 neither shall any *man* **h** his voice in *191*
12:42 of the earth to **h** the wisdom of Solomon; *191*
13: 9 Who hath ears to **h**, let him hear. *191*
13: 9 Who hath ears to hear, let him **h**. *191*
13:13 and hearing they **h** not, neither do they *191*
13:14 By hearing ye shall **h**, and shall not *191*
13:15 see with *their* eyes, and **h** with *their* ears, *191*
13:16 for they see: and your ears, for they **h**. *191*
13:17 and to **h** *those things* which ye hear, *191*
13:17 and to hear *those things* which ye **h**, *191*
13:18 **H** ye therefore the parable of the sower. *191*
13:43 Who hath ears to **h**, let him hear. *191*
13:43 Who hath ears to hear, let him **h**. *191*
15:10 and said unto them, **H**, and understand: *191*
17: 5 in whom I am well pleased; **h** ye him. *191*
18:15 if he shall **h** thee, thou hast gained thy *191*
18:16 But if he will not **h** *thee, then* take with thee *191*
18:17 And if he shall **neglect to h** them, tell *it* *3878*
18:17 but if he **neglect to h** the church, let him be *3878*
21:33 **H** another parable: There was a certain *191*
24: 6 And ye shall **h** of wars and rumours of wars: *191*
Mk 4: 9 He that hath ears to **h**, let him hear. *191*
4: 9 He that hath ears to hear, let him **h**. *191*
4:12 and hearing they may **h**, and not understand; *191*
4:18 are sown among thorns; such as **h** the word, *191*
4:20 such as **h** the word, and receive *it,* and *191*
4:23 If any *man* have ears to **h**, let him hear. *191*
4:23 If any *man* have ears to hear, let him **h**. *191*
4:24 he said unto them, Take heed what you **h**: *191*
4:24 and unto you that **h** shall more be given. *191*
4:33 word unto them, as they were able to **h** *it.* *191*
6:11 nor **h** you, when ye depart thence, *191*
7:16 If any *man* have ears to **h**, let him hear. *191*
7:16 If any *man* have ears to hear, let him **h**. *191*
7:37 he maketh both the deaf to **h**, and the dumb *191*
8:18 and having ears, **h** ye not? and do ye not *191*
9: 7 saying, This is my beloved Son: **h** him. *191*
12:29 The first of all the commandments *is,* **H**, *191*
13: 7 And when ye shall **h** of wars and rumours of *191*
Lk 5: 1 as the people pressed upon him to **h** *191*
5:15 and great multitudes came together to **h**, and *191*
6:17 which came to **h** him, and to be healed of *191*
6:27 But I say unto you which **h**, Love your *191*
7:22 are cleansed, the deaf **h**, the dead are raised, *191*
8: 8 he cried, He that hath ears to **h**, let him hear. *191*
8: 8 he cried, He that hath ears to hear, let him **h**. *191*
8:12 Those by the way side are they that **h**; then *191*
8:13 when they **h**, receive the word with joy; *191*
8:18 Take heed therefore how ye **h**: *191*
8:21 my brethren are these which **h** the word of *191*
9: 9 of whom I **h** such *things?* And he desired to *191*
9:35 saying, This is my beloved Son: **h** him. *191*
10:24 and to **h** *those things* which ye hear, *191*
10:24 and to hear *those things* which ye **h**, *191*
11:28 blessed *are* they that **h** the word of God, and *191*
11:31 of the earth to **h** the wisdom of Solomon; *191*
14:35 it out. He that hath ears to **h**, let him hear. *191*
14:35 it out. He that hath ears to hear, let him **h**. *191*
15: 1 all the publicans and sinners for to **h** him. *191*
16: 2 said unto him, How *is* it *that* I **h** this of thee? *191*
16:29 and the prophets; let them **h** them. *191*
16:31 If they **h** not Moses and the prophets, *191*
18: 6 the Lord said, **H** what the unjust judge saith. *191*
19:48 for all the people were very attentive to **h** *191*
21: 9 But when ye shall **h** of wars and *191*
21:38 morning to him in the temple, for to **h** him. *191*
Jn 5:25 when the dead shall **h** the voice of the Son of *191*
5:25 of the Son of God: and they that **h** shall live. *191*
5:28 in the which all that are in the graves shall **h** *191*
5:30 as I **h**, I judge: and my judgment is just; *191*
6:60 This is a hard saying; who can **h** it? *191*
7:51 before it **h** him, and know what he doeth? *191*
8:43 *even* because ye cannot **h** my word. *191*
8:47 ye therefore **h** *them* not, because ye are not *191*
9:27 I have told you already, and ye did not **h**: *191*
9:27 wherefore would you **h** *it* again? will ye also *191*
10: 3 porter openeth; and the sheep **h** his voice: *191*
10: 8 and robbers: but the sheep did not **h** them. *191*
10:16 also I must bring, and they shall **h** my voice; *191*
10:20 He hath a devil, and is mad; why **h** ye him? *191*
10:27 My sheep **h** my voice, and I know them, and *191*
12:47 And if any *man* **h** my words, and *191*
14:24 and the word which you **h** is not mine, but *191*
16:13 but whatsoever he shall **h**, *that* shall he *191*
Ac 2: 8 And how **h** we every man in our own *191*
2:11 we do **h** them speak in our tongues *191*
2:22 Ye men of Israel, **h** these words; Jesus of *191*
2:33 hath shed forth this, which ye now see and **h**. *191*
3:22 him shall ye **h** in all *things* whatsoever he *191*
3:23 every soul, which will not **h** that prophet, *191*
7:37 your brethren, like unto me; him shall ye **h**. *191*
10:22 thee into his house, and to **h** words of thee. *191*
10:33 to **h** all *things* that are commanded thee of *191*
13: 7 and Saul, and desired to **h** the word of God. *191*
13:44 whole city together to **h** the word of God. *191*
15: 7 that the Gentiles by my mouth should **h** *191*
17:21 but either to tell, or to **h** some new *thing.)* *191*
17:32 We will **h** thee again of this *matter.* *191*
19:26 Moreover ye see and **h**, that not alone at *191*
21:22 for they will **h** that thou art come. *191*
22: 1 **h** ye my defence *which I make* now unto *191*
22:14 and shouldest **h** the voice of his mouth. *191*
23:35 I will **h** thee, said he, when thine accusers *1251*

H

Ac 24: 4 I pray *thee* that thou wouldest **h** us of thy *191*
25:22 unto Festus, I would also **h** the man myself. *191*
25:22 To morrow, said he, thou shalt **h** him. *191*
26: 3 wherefore I beseech thee to **h** me patiently. *191*
26:29 but also all that **h** me this day, were both *191*
28:22 But we desire to **h** of thee what thou *191*
28:26 Hearing ye shall **h**, and shall not understand; *191*
28:27 and **h** with *their* ears, and understand with *191*
28:28 sent unto the Gentiles, and *that* they will **h** it. *191*
Ro 10:14 and how shall they **h** without a preacher? *191*
11: 8 not see, and ears that *they* should not **h**;) *191*
1Co 11:18 I **h** that there be divisions among you; *191*
14:21 and yet for all that will they not **h** me, *1522*
Gal 4:21 to be under the law, do ye not **h** the law? *191*
Php 1:27 or *else* be absent, I may **h** of your affairs, *191*
1:30 which ye saw in me, and now **h** *to be* in me. *191*
2Th 3:11 For we **h** that *there are* some which walk *191*
1Ti 4:16 shalt both save thyself, and them that **h** thee. *191*
2Ti 4:17 and *that* all the Gentiles might **h**: *191*
Heb 3: 7 Ghost saith, To day if ye will **h** his voice, *191*
3:15 it is said, To day if ye will **h** his voice, *191*
4: 7 as it is said, To day if ye will **h** his voice, *191*
Jas 1:19 let every man be swift to **h**, slow to speak, *191*
1Jn 5:15 And if we know that he **h** us, whatsoever we *191*
3Jn 1: 4 I have no greater joy than to **h** that my *191*
Rev 1: 3 and they that **h** the words of *this* prophecy, *191*
2: 7 let him **h** what the Spirit saith unto *191*
2:11 let him **h** what the Spirit saith unto *191*
2:17 let him **h** what the Spirit saith unto *191*
2:29 let him **h** what the Spirit saith unto *191*
3: 6 let him **h** what the Spirit saith unto *191*
3:13 let him **h** what the Spirit saith unto *191*
3:20 if any *man* **h** my voice, and open the door, I *191*
3:22 let him **h** what the Spirit saith unto *191*
9:20 which neither can see, nor **h**, nor walk: *191*
13: 9 If any *man* have an ear, let him **h**. *191*

HEARD (641) [HEAR]

Ge 3: 8 they **h** the voice of the LORD God 8085
3:10 I **h** thy voice in the garden, and I was 8085
14:14 when Abram **h** that his brother was taken 8085
16:11 because the LORD hath **h** thy affliction. 8085
17:20 as for Ishmael, I have **h** thee: Behold, 8085
18:10 Sarah **h** *it in* the tent door, which *was* 8085
21:17 God **h** the voice of the lad; and the angel of 8085
21:17 for God hath **h** the voice of the lad where 8085
21:26 thou tell me, neither yet **h** I *of it*, but to day. 8085
24:30 when he **h** the words of Rebekah his sister, 8085
24:52 when Abraham's servant **h** their words, 8085
27: 5 Rebekah **h** when Isaac spake to Esau his 8085
27: 6 I **h** thy father speak unto Esau thy brother, 8085
27:34 when Esau **h** the words of his father, he 8085
29:13 when Laban **h** the tidings of Jacob his 8085
29:33 Because the LORD hath **h** that I *was* 8085
30: 6 hath also **h** my voice, and hath given me a 8085
31: 1 he **h** the words of Laban's sons, saying, 8085
34: 5 Jacob **h** that he had defiled Dinah his 8085
34: 7 Jacob came out of the field when they **h** *it*: 8085
35:22 Israel **h** *it*. Now the sons of Jacob were 8085
37:17 for I **h** *them* say, Let us go to Dothan. 8085
37:21 Reuben **h** *it*, and he delivered him out of 8085
39:15 when he **h** that I lifted up my voice and 8085
39:19 when his master **h** the words of his wife, 8085
41:15 I have **h** say of thee, *that* thou canst 8085
42: 2 Behold, I have **h** that there is corn in Egypt: 8085
43:25 for they **h** that they should eat bread there. 8085
45: 2 the Egyptians and the house of Pharaoh **h**. 8085
45:16 the fame *thereof* was **h** *in* Pharaoh's house, 8085
Ex 2:15 Now when Pharaoh **h** this thing, he sought 8085
2:24 God **h** their groaning, and God remembered 8085
3: 7 have **h** their cry by reason of their 8085
4:31 when they **h** that the LORD had visited 8085
6: 5 I have also **h** the groaning of the children of 8085
16: 9 for he hath **h** your murmurings. 8085
16:12 I have **h** the murmurings of the children of 8085
18: 1 **h** of all that God had done for Moses, and 8085
23:13 neither let it be **h** out of thy mouth. 8085
28:35 his sound shall be **h** when he goeth in unto 8085
32:17 when Joshua **h** the noise of the people as 8085
33: 4 when the people **h** these evil tidings, they 8085
Lev 10:20 And when Moses **h** *that*, he was content. 8085
24:14 let all that **h** *him* lay their hands upon his 8085
Nu 7:89 he **h** the voice of one speaking unto him 8085
11: 1 the LORD **h** *it*; and his anger was kindled; 8085
11:10 Moses **h** the people weep throughout their 8085
12: 2 spoken also by us? And the LORD **h** *it*. 8085
14:14 *for* they have **h** that thou LORD *art* 8085
14:15 the nations which have **h** the fame of thee 8085
14:27 I have **h** the murmurings of the children of 8085
16: 4 And when Moses **h** *it*, he fell upon his face: 8085
20:16 he **h** our voice, and sent an angel, and 8085
21: 1 **h** *tell* that Israel came *by* the way of 8085
22:36 when Balak **h** that Balaam was come, he 8085
24: 4 He hath said, which **h** the words of God, 8085
24:16 which **h** the words of God, and knew 8085
30: 7 her husband **h** *it*, and held his peace at her 8085
30: 7 held his peace at her in the day that he **h** *it*: 8085
30: 8 disallow her on the day that he **h** *it*; 8085
30:11 her husband **h** *it*, and held his peace at her, 8085
30:12 made them void on the day he **h** *them*; 8085
30:14 he held his peace at her in the day that he **h** 8085
30:15 make them void after *that* he hath **h** *them*; 8085
33:40 **h** of the coming of the children of Israel. 8085
Dt 1:34 the LORD **h** the voice of your words, and 8085
4:12 ye **h** the voice of the words, but saw no 8085
4:12 but saw no similitude; only *ye* **h** a voice. NIH
4:32 as this great thing *is*, or hath been **h** like it? 8085
4:33 midst of the fire, as thou hast **h**, and live? 8085
5:23 when ye **h** the voice out of the midst of 8085
5:24 we have **h** his voice out of the midst of 8085
5:26 that hath **h** the voice of the living God 8085
5:28 the LORD **h** the voice of your words, 8085
5:28 I have **h** the voice of the words of this 8085
9: 2 *of whom* thou hast **h** *say*, Who can stand 8085
17: 4 thou hast **h** *of it*, and inquired diligently, 8085
Dt 26: 7 the LORD **h** our voice, and looked on our 8085
Jos 2:10 For we have **h** how the LORD dried up 8085
2:11 as soon as we had **h** *these things*, our hearts 8085
5: 1 **h** that the LORD had dried up the waters 8085
6:20 when the people **h** the sound of 8085
9: 1 the Hivite, and the Jebusite, **h** *thereof*; 8085
9: 3 when the inhabitants of Gibeon **h** what 8085
9: 9 for we have **h** the fame of him, and all that 8085
9:16 that they **h** that they *were* their neighbours, 8085
10: 1 when Adoni-zedek king of Jerusalem had **h** 8085
11: 1 when Jabin king of Hazor had **h** *those* 8085
22:11 the children of Israel **h** say, Behold, 8085
22:12 when the children of Israel **h** *of it*, 8085
22:30 **h** the words that the children of Reuben and 8085
24:27 for it hath **h** all the words of the LORD 8085
Jdg 7:15 *so*, when Gideon **h** the telling of the dream, 8085
9:30 when Zebul the ruler of the city **h** 8085
9:46 **h** *that*, they entered into a hold of the house 8085
18:25 Let not thy voice be **h** among us, lest angry 8085
20: 3 (Now the children of Benjamin **h** that 8085
Ru 1: 6 for she had **h** in the country of Moab how 8085
1Sa 1:13 her lips moved, but her voice was not **h**: 8085
2:22 and **h** all that his sons did unto all Israel; 8085
4: 6 when the Philistines **h** the noise of 8085
4:14 when Eli **h** the noise of the crying, he said, 8085
4:19 when she **h** the tidings that the ark of God 8085
7: 7 when the Philistines **h** that the children of 8085
7: 7 when the children of Israel **h** *it*, they were 8085
7: 9 LORD for Israel; and the LORD **h** him. 6030
8:21 Samuel **h** all the words of the people, and 8085
11: 6 spirit of God came upon Saul when he **h** 8085
13: 3 the Philistines **h** *of it*. And Saul blew 8085
13: 4 all Israel **h** say *that* Saul had smitten a 8085
14:22 *when* they **h** that the Philistines fled, 8085
14:27 Jonathan **h** not when his father charged 8085
17:11 all Israel **h** those words of the Philistine, 8085
17:23 to the same words: and David **h** *them*. 8085
17:28 Eliab his eldest brother **h** when he spake 8085
17:31 when the words were **h** which David spake, 8085
22: 1 all his father's house **h** *it*, they went down 8085
22: 6 When Saul **h** that David was discovered, 8085
23:10 thy servant hath **certainly h** that Saul 8085+8085
23:11 Saul come down, as thy servant hath **h**? 8085
23:25 when Saul **h** *that*, he pursued after David *in* 8085
25: 4 David **h** in the wilderness that Nabal did 8085
25: 7 now I have **h** that thou hast shearers: 8085
25:39 when David **h** that Nabal was dead, he said, 8085
31:11 when the inhabitants of Jabesh-gilead **h** of 8085
2Sa 3:28 afterward when David **h** *it*, he said, I and 8085
4: 1 when Saul's son **h** that Abner was dead in 8085
5:17 when the Philistines **h** that they had 8085
5:17 David **h** *of it*, and went down to the hold. 8085
7:22 according to all that we have **h** with our 8085
8: 9 When Toi king of Hamath **h** that David had 8085
10: 7 when David **h** *of it*, he sent Joab, and all 8085
11:26 when the wife of Uriah **h** that Uriah her 8085
13:21 when king David **h** of all these things, he 8085
18: 5 all the people **h** when the king gave all 8085
19: 2 for the people **h** say that day *how* the king 8085
1Ki 1:11 Hast thou not **h** that Adonijah the son of 8085
1:41 all the guests that *were* with him **h** *it* as 8085
1:41 when Joab **h** the sound of the trumpet, he 8085
1:45 rang again. This *is* the noise that ye have **h**. 8085
2:42 unto me, The word *that* I have **h** *is* good. 8085
3:28 all Israel **h** of the judgment which the king 8085
4:34 of the earth, which had **h** of his wisdom. 8085
5: 1 for he had **h** that they had anointed him 8085
5: 7 when Hiram **h** the words of Solomon, 8085
6: 7 nor axe *nor* any tool of iron **h** in the house, 8085
9: 3 I have **h** thy prayer and thy supplication, 8085
10: 1 when the queen of Sheba **h** of the fame of 8085
10: 6 It was a true report that I **h** in mine own 8085
10: 7 prosperity exceedeth the fame which I **h**. 8085
11:21 when Hadad **h** in Egypt that David slept 8085
12: 2 **h** *of it*, (for he was fled from the presence 8085
12:20 when all Israel **h** that Jeroboam was come 8085
13: 4 when king Jeroboam **h** the saying of 8085
13:26 him back from the way **h** *thereof*, he said, 8085
14: 6 *so*, when Ahijah **h** the sound of her feet, 8085
15:21 when Baasha **h** *thereof*, that he left off 8085
16:16 the people that *were* encamped **h** say, 8085
17:22 the LORD **h** the voice of Elijah; and 8085
19:13 when Elijah **h** *it*, that he wrapped his face 8085
20:12 when *Ben-hadad* **h** this message, as he *was* 8085
20:31 we have **h** that the kings of the house of 8085
21:15 when Jezebel **h** that Naboth was stoned, 8085
21:16 when Ahab **h** that Naboth was dead, 8085
21:27 it came to pass, when Ahab **h** those words, 8085
2Ki 3:21 when all the Moabites **h** that the kings were 8085
5: 8 when Elisha the man of God had **h** that 8085
6:30 when the king **h** the words of the woman, 8085
9:30 Jezebel **h** *of it*; and she painted her face, 8085
11:13 And when Athaliah **h** the noise of the guard 8085
19: 1 when king Hezekiah **h** *it*, that he rent his 8085
19: 4 words which the LORD thy God hath **h**: 8085
19: 6 not afraid of the words which thou hast **h**, 8085
19: 8 for he had **h** that he was departed from 8085
19: 9 when he **h** say of Tirhakah king of 8085
19:11 thou hast **h** what the kings of Assyria have 8085
19:20 Sennacherib king of Assyria I have **h**. 8085
19:25 Hast thou not **h** long ago *how* I have done 8085
20: 5 I have **h** thy prayer, I have seen thy tears: 8085
20:12 for he had **h** that Hezekiah had been sick. 8085
22:11 when the king had **h** the words of the book 8085
22:18 *As touching* the words which thou hast **h**; 8085
22:19 I also have **h** *thee*, saith the LORD. 8085
25:23 **h** that the king of Babylon had made 8085
1Ch 10:11 when all Jabesh-gilead **h** all that 8085
14: 8 when the Philistines **h** that David was 8085
14: 8 David **h** *of it*, and went out against them. 8085
17:20 according to all that we have **h** with our 8085
18: 9 Now when Tou king of Hamath **h** how 8085
19: 8 when David **h** *of it*, he sent Joab, and all 8085
2Ch 5:13 to **make** one sound **to be h** in praising and 8085
7:12 I have **h** thy prayer, and have chosen this 8085
2Ch 9: 1 when the queen of Sheba **h** of the fame of 8085
9: 5 *It was* a true report which I **h** in mine own 8085
9: 6 *for* thou exceedest the fame that I **h**. 8085
10: 2 **h** *it*, that Jeroboam returned out of Egypt. 8085
15: 8 when Asa **h** these words, and the prophecy 8085
16: 5 when Baasha **h** *it*, that he left off building 8085
20:29 when they had **h** that the LORD fought 8085
23:12 Now when Athaliah **h** the noise of 8085
30:27 their voice was **h**, and their prayer came *up* 8085
33:13 **h** his supplication, and brought him again 8085
34:19 when the king had **h** the words of the law, 8085
34:26 *concerning* the words which thou hast **h**; 8085
34:27 I have even **h** *thee* also, saith the LORD. 8085
Ezr 3:13 a loud shout, and the noise was **h** afar off. 8085
4: 1 Benjamin **h** that the children of 8085
9: 3 when I **h** this thing, I rent my garment and 8085
Ne 1: 4 when I **h** these words, *that* I sat down and 8085
2:10 **h** *of it*, it grieved them exceedingly that 8085
2:19 **h** *it*, they laughed us to scorn, and 8085
4: 1 that when Sanballat **h** that we builded 8085
4: 7 **h** that the walls of Jerusalem were made up, 8085
4:15 when our enemies **h** that it was known unto 8085
5: 6 I was very angry when I **h** their cry and 8085
6: 1 **h** that I had builded the wall, and *that* there 8085
6:16 that when all our enemies **h** *thereof*, and 8085
8: 9 when they **h** the words of the law. 8085
12:43 that the joy of Jerusalem was **h** even afar 8085
13: 3 it came to pass, when they had **h** the law, 8085
Est 1:18 which have **h** of the deed of the queen. 8085
2: 8 king's commandment and his decree was **h**, 8085
Job 2:11 Now when Job's three friends **h** of all this 8085
4:16 *there was* silence, and I **h** a voice, *saying*, 8085
13: 1 mine eye hath seen all *this*, mine ear hath **h** 8085
15: 8 Hast thou **h** the secret of God? and 8085
16: 2 I have **h** many such *things*: miserable 8085
19: 7 Behold, I cry out *of* wrong, but I am not **h**: 6030
20: 3 I have **h** the check of my reproach, and 8085
26:14 how little a portion is **h** of him? but 8085
28:22 We have **h** the fame thereof with our ears. 8085
29:11 When the ear **h** *me*, then it blessed me; and 8085
33: 8 I have **h** the voice of *thy* words, 8085
37: 4 he will not stay them when his voice is **h**. 8085
42: 5 I have **h** of thee by the hearing of the ear: 8085
Ps 3: 4 my voice, and he **h** me out of his holy hill. 6030
6: 8 for the LORD hath **h** the voice of my 8085
6: 9 The LORD hath **h** my supplication; 8085
10:17 thou hast **h** the desire of the humble: 8085
18: 6 he **h** my voice out of his temple, and 8085
19: 3 nor language, *where* their voice is not **h**. 8085
22:21 for thou hast **h** me from the horns of 6030
22:24 but when he cried unto him, he **h**. 8085
28: 6 he hath **h** the voice of my supplications. 8085
31:13 For I have **h** the slander of many: fear *was* 8085
34: 4 he **h** me, and delivered me from all my 6030
34: 6 the LORD **h** *him*, and saved him out of all 8085
38:13 I, as a deaf *man*, **h** not; and *I was* as a dumb 8085
40: 1 and he inclined unto me, and **h** my cry. 8085
44: 1 We have **h** with our ears, O God, 8085
48: 8 As we have **h**, so have we seen in the city 8085
61: 5 For thou, O God, hast **h** my vows: thou hast 8085
62:11 God hath spoken once; twice have I **h** this; 8085
66: 8 and **make** the voice of his praise **to be h**: 8085
66:19 *But* verily God hath **h** *me*; he hath attended 8085
76: 8 Thou didst **cause** judgment **to be h** from 8085
78: 3 Which we have **h** and known, and 8085
78:21 Therefore the LORD **h** *this*, and 8085
78:59 When God **h** *this*, he was wroth, and 8085
81: 5 *where* I **h** a language *that* I understood not. 8085
97: 8 Zion **h**, and was glad, and the daughters of 8085
106:44 their affliction, when he **h** their cry: 8085
116: 1 because he hath **h** my voice *and* 8085
118:21 for thou hast **h** me, and art become my 6030
120: 1 I cried unto the LORD, and he **h** me. 6030
132: 6 Lo, we **h** *of* it at Ephratah: we found it in 8085
Pr 21:13 he also shall cry himself, but shall not be **h**. 6030
Ecc 9:16 *is* despised, and his words *are* not **h**. 8085
9:17 The words of wise *men are* **h** in quiet, 8085
SS 2:12 and the voice of the turtle is **h** in our land; 8085
Isa 6: 8 Also I **h** the voice of the Lord, saying, 8085
10:30 **cause** *it* **to be h** unto Laish, O poor 7181
15: 4 their voice shall be **h** *even* unto Jahaz: 8085
16: 6 We have **h** of the pride of Moab; *he is* very 8085
21:10 that which I have **h** of the LORD of hosts, 8085
24:16 uttermost part of the earth have we **h** songs, 8085
28:22 for I have **h** from the Lord GOD of hosts a 8085
30:30 shall **cause** his glorious voice **to be h**, 8085
37: 1 when king Hezekiah **h** *it*, that he rent his 8085
37: 4 words which the LORD thy God hath **h**: 8085
37: 6 Be not afraid of the words that thou hast **h**, 8085
37: 8 for he had **h** that he was departed from 8085
37: 9 he **h** say concerning Tirhakah king of 8085
37: 9 when he **h** *it*, he sent messengers to 8085
37:11 thou hast **h** what the kings of Assyria have 8085
37:26 Hast thou not **h** long ago, *how* I have done 8085
38: 5 I have **h** thy prayer, I have seen thy tears: 8085
39: 1 for he had **h** that he had been sick, and 8085
40:21 have ye not **h**? hath it not been told you 8085
40:28 hast thou not **h**, *that* the everlasting God, 8085
42: 2 nor **cause** his voice **to be h** in the street. 8085
48: 6 Thou hast **h**, see all this; and will not ye 8085
49: 8 In an acceptable time have I **h** thee, and 6030
52:15 *that* which they had not **h** shall they 8085
58: 4 to **make** your voice **to be h** on high. 8085
60:18 Violence shall no more be **h** in thy land, 8085
64: 4 the beginning of the world *men* have not **h**, 8085
65:19 the voice of weeping shall be no more **h** in 8085
66: 8 Who hath **h** such *a thing*? who hath seen 8085
66:19 the isles afar off, that have not **h** my fame, 8085
Jer 3:21 A voice was **h** upon the high places, 8085
4:19 my peace, because thou hast **h**, O my soul, 8085
4:31 For I have **h** a voice as of a woman in 8085
6: 7 violence and spoil is **h** in her; before me 8085
6:24 We have **h** the fame thereof: our hands wax 8085
7:13 rising up early and speaking, but ye **h** not; 8085
8: 6 I hearkened and **h**, *but* they spake not 8085

Jer 8:16 The snorting of his horses was **h** from Dan: 8085
9:19 For a voice of wailing is **h** out of Zion, 8085
18:13 who hath **h** such *things:* the virgin of Israel 8085
18:22 Let a cry be **h** from their houses, when thou 8085
20: 1 **h** *that* Jeremiah prophesied these things. 8085
20:10 For I **h** the defaming of many, fear on 8085
23:18 and hath perceived and **h** his word? 8085
23:18 who hath marked his word, and **h** *it?* 8085
23:25 I have **h** what the prophets said, 8085
25: 8 of hosts; Because ye have not **h** my words, 8085
25:36 *shall be* **h:** for the LORD *hath* spoiled their NIH
26: 7 all the people **h** Jeremiah speaking these 8085
26:10 When the princes of Judah **h** these things, 8085
26:11 this city, as ye have **h** with your ears. 8085
26:12 this city all the words that ye have **h**. 8085
26:21 and all the princes, **h** his words, 8085
26:21 when Urijah **h** *it,* he was afraid, and fled, 8085
30: 5 We have **h** a voice of trembling, of fear, 8085
31:15 A voice was **h** in Ramah, lamentation, *and* 8085
31:18 I have **surely h** Ephraim bemoaning 8085+8085
33:10 Again there shall be **h** in this place, which 8085
34:10 **h** that every one should let his manservant, 8085
35:17 spoken unto them, but they have not **h**; 8085
36:11 had **h** out of the book all the words of 8085
36:13 unto them all the words that he had **h**, 8085
36:16 Now it came to pass when they had **h** all 8085
36:24 nor any of his servants that **h** all these 8085
37: 5 that besieged Jerusalem **h** tidings of them, 8085
38: 1 **h** the words that Jeremiah had spoken unto 8085
38: 7 **h** that they had put Jeremiah in 8085
40: 7 **h** that the king of Babylon had made 8085
40:11 **h** that the king of Babylon had left a 8085
41:11 **h** of all the evil that Ishmael the son of 8085
42: 4 said unto them, I have **h** *you;* behold, 8085
46:12 The nations have **h** *of* thy shame, and 8085
48: 4 her little ones have **caused** a cry **to be h**. 8085
48: 5 the enemies have **h** a cry of destruction. 8085
48:29 We have **h** the pride of Moab; *he is* 8085
49: 2 that I will **cause** an alarm of war **to be h** in 8085
49:14 I have **h** a rumour from the LORD, and 8085
49:21 the noise thereof was **h** in the Red sea. 8085
49:23 for they have **h** evil tidings: they are 8085
50:43 The king of Babylon hath **h** the report of 8085
50:46 and the cry is **h** among the nations. 8085
51:46 ye fear for the rumour that shall be **h** in 8085
51:51 because we have **h** reproach: 8085
La 1:21 They have **h** that I sigh; *there is* none to 8085
1:21 all mine enemies have **h** of my trouble; 8085
3:56 Thou hast **h** my voice: hide not thine ear at 8085
3:61 Thou hast **h** their reproach, O LORD, *and* 8085
Eze 1:24 they went, I **h** the noise of their wings, 8085
1:28 my face, and I **h** a voice of one that spake. 8085
2: 2 my feet, that I **h** him that spake unto me. 8085
3:12 I **h** behind me a voice of a great rushing, 8085
3:13 *I h* also the noise of the wings of the living NIH
10: 5 the sound of the cherubims' wings was **h** 8085
19: 4 The nations also **h** of him; he was taken in 8085
19: 9 that his voice should no more be **h** upon 8085
26:13 the sound of thy harps shall be no more **h**. 8085
27:30 shall **cause** their voice **to be h** against thee, 8085
33: 5 He **h** the sound of the trumpet, and took not 8085
35:12 *that* I have **h** all thy blasphemies which 8085
35:13 your words against me: I have **h** *them.* 8085
43: 6 I **h** *him* speaking unto me out of the house; 8085
Da 3: 7 when all the people **h** the sound of 8086
5:14 I have even **h** of thee, that the spirit of 8086
5:16 I have **h** of thee, that thou canst make 8086
6:14 the king, when he **h** *these* words, was sore 8086
8:13 I **h** one saint speaking, and another saint 8085
8:16 I **h** a man's voice between *the banks of* 8085
10: 9 Yet **h** I the voice of his words: and when I 8085
10: 9 when I **h** the voice of his words, then was I 8085
10:12 thy words were **h**, and I am come for thy 8085
12: 7 I **h** the man clothed in linen, which *was* 8085
12: 8 I **h**, but I understood not: then said I, O my 8085
Hos 7:12 chastise them, as their congregation hath **h**. 8088
14: 8 I have **h** *him,* and observed him: I *am* like a 6030
Ob 1: 1 We have **h** a rumour from the LORD, and 8085
Jnh 2: 2 affliction unto the LORD, and he **h** me; 6030
Mic 5:15 upon the heathen, such as they have not **h**. 8085
Na 2:13 voice of thy messengers shall no more be **h**. 8085
Hab 3: 2 I have **h** thy speech, *and* was afraid: 8085
3:16 When I **h**, my belly trembled; my lips 8085
Zep 2: 8 I have **h** the reproach of Moab, and 8085
Zec 8:23 for we have **h** *that* God *is* with you. 8085
Mal 3:16 **h** *it,* and a book of remembrance was 8085
Mt 2: 3 When Herod the king had **h** *these things,* he *191*
2: 9 When they had **h** the king, they departed; *191*
2:18 In Rama was there a voice **h**, lamentation, *191*
2:22 But when he **h** that Archelaus did reign in *191*
4:12 Now when Jesus had **h** that John was cast *191*
5:21 Ye have **h** that it was said by them of old *191*
5:27 Ye have **h** that it was said by them of old *191*
5:33 ye have **h** that it hath been said by them of *191*
5:38 Ye have **h** that it hath been said, An eye for *191*
5:43 Ye have **h** that it hath been said, Thou shalt *191*
6: 7 they shall be **h** for their much speaking. *1522*
8:10 When Jesus **h** *it,* he marvelled, and said to *191*
9:12 But when Jesus **h** *that,* he said unto them, *191*
11: 2 Now when John had **h** in the prison *191*
12:24 But when the Pharisees **h** *it,* they said, *191*
13:17 *things* which ye hear, and have not **h** *them.* *191*
14: 1 At that time Herod the tetrarch **h** of the fame *191*
14:13 When Jesus **h** *of it,* he departed thence by *191*
14:13 when the people had **h** *thereof,* they *191*
15:12 were offended, after they **h** *this* saying? *191*
17: 6 And when the disciples **h** *it,* they fell on *191*
19:22 But when the young man **h** *that* saying, *191*
19:25 When his disciples **h** *it,* they were *191*
20:24 And when the ten **h** *it,* they were moved *191*
20:30 when they **h** that Jesus passed by, cried out, *191*
21:45 and Pharisees had **h** his parables, *191*
22: 7 But when the king **h** *thereof,* he was wroth: *191*
22:22 When they had **h** *these words,* they *191*
22:33 And when the multitude **h** *this,* they were *191*
22:34 But when the Pharisees had **h** that he had put *191*
26:65 behold, now ye have **h** his blasphemy. *191*
27:47 when they **h** *that,* said, This *man* calleth for *191*
Mk 2:17 When Jesus **h** *it,* he saith unto them, They *191*
3: 8 when they had **h** what great things he did, *191*
3:21 And when his friends **h** *of it,* they went out *191*
4:15 but when they have **h**, Satan cometh *191*
4:16 who, when they have **h** the word, *191*
5:27 When she had **h** of Jesus, came in the press *191*
5:36 As soon as Jesus **h** the word *that was* *191*
6:14 And king Herod **h** *of him;* (for his name was *191*
6:16 But when Herod **h** *thereof,* he said, It is *191*
6:20 and when he **h** him, he did many *things,* and *191*
6:20 he did many *things,* and **h** him gladly. *191*
6:29 And when his disciples **h** *of it,* they came *191*
6:55 those that were sick, where they **h** he was. *191*
7:25 daughter had an unclean spirit, **h** of him, *191*
10:41 And when the ten **h** *it,* they began to be *191*
10:47 And when he **h** that it was Jesus of Nazareth, *191*
11:14 hereafter for ever. And his disciples **h** *it.* *191*
11:18 And the scribes and chief priests **h** *it,* and *191*
12:28 and having **h** them reasoning together, and *191*
12:37 And the common people **h** him gladly. *191*
14:11 And when they **h** *it,* they were glad, and *191*
14:58 We **h** him say, I will destroy this temple that *191*
14:64 Ye have **h** the blasphemy: what think ye? *191*
15:35 when they **h** *it,* said, Behold, he calleth *191*
16:11 when they had **h** that he was alive, and *191*
Lk 1:13 for thy prayer is **h**; and thy wife Elisabeth *1522*
1:41 And it came to pass *that,* when Elisabeth **h** *191*
1:58 her cousins **h** how the Lord had shewed *191*
1:66 And all they that **h** *them* laid *them* up in *191*
2:18 And all they that **h** *it* wondered at those *191*
2:20 God for all *the things* that they had **h** *191*
2:47 And all that **h** him were astonished at his *191*
4:23 whatsoever we have **h** done in Capernaum, *191*
4:28 when they **h** these *things,* were filled with *191*
7: 3 And when he **h** of Jesus, he sent unto him *191*
7: 9 When Jesus **h** these *things,* he marvelled at *191*
7:22 tell John what *things* ye have seen and **h**; *191*
7:29 And all the people that **h** *him,* and *191*
8:14 which, when they have **h**, go *forth,* and *191*
8:15 having **h** the word, keep *it,* and bring forth *191*
8:50 But when Jesus **h** *it,* he answered him, *191*
9: 7 Now Herod the tetrarch **h** of all that was *191*
10:24 *things* which ye hear, and have not **h** *them.* *191*
10:39 which also sat at Jesus' feet, and **h** his word. *191*
12: 3 spoken in darkness shall be **h** in the light; *191*
14:15 with *him* **h** these *things,* he said unto him, *191*
15:25 nigh to the house, he **h** musick and dancing. *191*
16:14 **h** all these *things:* and they derided him. *191*
18:22 Now when Jesus **h** these *things,* he said unto *191*
18:23 And when he **h** this, he was very sorrowful: *191*
18:26 And they that **h** *it* said, Who then can be *191*
19:11 And as they **h** these *things,* he added and *191*
20:16 And when they **h** *it,* they said, God forbid. *191*
22:71 for we ourselves have **h** of his own mouth. *191*
23: 6 When Pilate **h** of Galilee, he asked whether *191*
23: 8 because he had **h** many *things* of him; *191*
Jn 1:37 And the two disciples **h** him speak, and *191*
1:40 One of the two which **h** John speak, and *191*
3:32 And what he hath seen and **h**, that he *191*
4: 1 the Lord knew how the Pharisees had **h** that *191*
4:42 for we have **h** *him* ourselves, and know that *191*
4:47 When he **h** that Jesus was come out of Judea *191*
5:37 Ye have neither **h** his voice at any time, *191*
6:45 Every *man* therefore that hath **h**, and *191*
6:60 of his disciples, when they had **h** *this,* said, *191*
7:32 The Pharisees **h** that the people murmured *191*
7:40 when they **h** *this* saying, said, Of a truth this *191*
8: 6 on the ground, *as though he h them not.* NIG
8: 9 And they which **h** *it,* being convicted by *191*
8:26 world those *things* which I have **h** of him. *191*
8:40 told you the truth, which I have **h** of God: *191*
9:32 Since the world began was it not **h** that any *191*
9:35 Jesus **h** that they had cast him out; *191*
9:40 which were with him **h** these *words,* *191*
11: 4 When Jesus **h** *that,* he said, This sickness is *191*
11: 6 When he had **h** therefore that he was sick, he *191*
11:20 as soon as she **h** that Jesus was coming, went *191*
11:29 As soon as she **h** *that,* she arose quickly, and *191*
11:41 said, Father, I thank thee that thou hast **h** me. *191*
12:12 when they **h** that Jesus was coming to *191*
12:18 for that they **h** that he had done this miracle. *191*
12:29 that stood *by,* and **h** *it,* said that it thundered: *191*
12:34 We have **h** out of the law that Christ abideth *191*
14:28 Ye have **h** how I said unto you, I go away, *191*
15:15 for all *things* that I have **h** of my Father I *191*
18:21 ask them which **h** *me,* what I have said unto *191*
19: 8 When Pilate therefore **h** that saying, he was *191*
19:13 When Pilate therefore **h** that saying, *191*
21: 7 Now when Simon Peter **h** that it was *191*
Ac 1: 4 the Father, which, *saith he,* ye have **h** of me. *191*
2: 6 that every man **h** them speak in his own *191*
2:37 Now when they **h** *this,* they were pricked in *191*
4: 4 Howbeit many of them which **h** the word *191*
4:20 speak *the things* which we have seen and **h**. *191*
4:24 And when they **h** *that,* they lift up their voice *191*
5: 5 great fear came on all them that **h** these *191*
5:11 and upon as many as **h** these *things.* *191*
5:21 And when they **h** *that,* they entered into *191*
5:24 and the chief priests **h** these things, *191*
5:33 When they **h** *that,* they were cut *to the heart,* *191*
6:11 We have **h** him speak blasphemous words *191*
6:14 For we have **h** him say, that this Jesus of *191*
7:12 But when Jacob **h** that there was corn in *191*
7:34 and I have **h** their groaning, and am come *191*
7:54 When they **h** these *things,* they were cut to *191*
8:14 **h** that Samaria had received the word of *191*
8:30 to *him,* and **h** him read the prophet Esaias, *191*
9: 4 and **h** a voice saying unto him, Saul, Saul, *191*
9:13 Lord, I have **h** by many of this man, *191*
9:21 But all that **h** *him* were amazed, and said; *191*
9:38 and the disciples had **h** that Peter was there, *191*
10:31 thy prayer is **h**, and thine alms are had in *1522*
10:44 the Holy Ghost fell on all them which **h** *191*
10:46 For they **h** them speak with tongues, and *191*
11: 1 brethren that were in Judea **h** that *191*
11: 7 And I **h** a voice saying unto me, Arise, Peter; *191*
11:18 When they **h** these *things,* they held their *191*
13:48 And when the Gentiles **h** *this,* they were *191*
14: 9 The same **h** Paul speak: who stedfastly *191*
14:14 **h** *of,* they rent their clothes, and ran in *191*
15:24 Forasmuch as we have **h**, that certain which *191*
16:14 **h** *us:* whose heart the Lord opened, *191*
16:25 praises unto God: and the prisoners **h** them. *1874*
16:38 when they **h** that they were Romans, *191*
17: 8 rulers of the city, when they **h** these *things.* *191*
17:32 And when they **h** of the resurrection of *191*
18:26 whom when Aquila and Priscilla had **h**, *191*
19: 2 much as **h** whether there be *any* Holy Ghost. *191*
19: 5 When they **h** *this,* they were baptized in *191*
19:10 that all they which dwelt in Asia **h** the word *191*
19:28 And when they **h** *these sayings,* they were *191*
21:12 And when we **h** these *things,* both we, and *191*
21:20 And when they **h** *it,* they glorified the Lord, *191*
22: 2 (And when they **h** that he spake in *191*
22: 7 and **h** a voice saying unto me, Saul, Saul, *191*
22: 9 they **h** not the voice of him that spake to me. *191*
22:15 unto all men of what thou hast seen and **h**. *191*
22:26 When the centurion **h** *that,* he went and *191*
23:16 And when Paul's sister's son **h** of *their* lying *191*
24:22 And when Felix **h** these *things,* having more *191*
24:24 and **h** him concerning the faith in Christ. *191*
26:14 I **h** a voice speaking unto me, and saying in *191*
28:15 And from thence, when the brethren **h** of us, *191*
Ro 10:14 believe *in him* of whom they have not **h**? *191*
10:18 But I say, Have they not **h**? Yes verily, *191*
15:21 and they that have not **h** shall understand. *191*
1Co 2: 9 as it is written, Eye hath not seen, nor ear **h**, *191*
2Co 6: 2 I have **h** thee in a time accepted, and in *1873*
12: 4 and **h** unspeakable words, which *it is* not *191*
Gal 1:13 For ye have **h** of my conversation in time *191*
1:23 But they had **h** only, That he which *191*
Eph 1:13 In whom ye also *trusted,* after that ye **h** *191*
1:15 after I **h** of your faith in the Lord Jesus, and *191*
3: 2 If ye have **h** of the dispensation of the grace *191*
4:21 If so be that ye have **h** him, and have been *191*
Php 2:26 because that ye had **h** that he had been sick. *191*
4: 9 and received, and **h**, and seen in me, do: *191*
Col 1: 4 Since we **h** of your faith in Christ Jesus, and *191*
1: 5 whereof ye **h before** in the word of *4257*
1: 6 since the day ye **h** of *it,* and knew the grace *191*
1: 9 since the day we **h** *it,* do not cease to pray *191*
1:23 which ye have **h**, *and* which was preached to *191*
1Th 2:13 received the word of God which *ye* **h** of us, *189*
2Ti 1:13 which thou hast **h** of me, in faith and *191*
2: 2 And *the things* that thou hast **h** of me among *191*
Heb 2: 1 earnest heed to the *things* which we have **h**, *191*
2: 3 was confirmed unto us by them that **h** *him;* *191*
3:16 For some, when they had **h**, did provoke: *191*
4: 2 not being mixed with faith in them that **h** *it.* *191*
5: 7 from death, and was **h** in that *he* feared; *1522*
12:19 which *voice* they that **h** intreated that *191*
Jas 5:11 Ye have **h** of the patience of Job, and *191*
2Pe 1:18 this voice which came from heaven we **h**, *191*
1Jn 1: 1 which we have **h**, which we have seen with *191*
1: 3 we have seen and **h** declare we unto you, *191*
1: 5 then is the message which we have **h** of him, *191*
2: 7 word which ye have **h** from the beginning. *191*
2:18 and as ye have **h** that antichrist shall come, *191*
2:24 in you, which ye have **h** from the beginning. *191*
2:24 If *that* which ye have **h** from the beginning *191*
3:11 For this is the message that ye **h** from *191*
4: 3 whereof you have **h** that it should come; *191*
2Jn 1: 6 That, as ye have **h** from the beginning, *191*
Rev 1:10 and **h** behind me a great voice, as of a *191*
3: 3 therefore how thou hast received and **h**, *191*
4: 1 the first voice which I **h** *was* as *it were* of a *191*
5:11 I **h** the voice of many angels round about *191*
5:13 **h** I saying, Blessing, and honour, and glory, *191*
6: 1 and I **h**, as *it were* the noise of thunder, *191*
6: 3 I **h** the second beast say, Come and see. *191*
6: 5 I **h** the third beast say, Come and see. *191*
6: 6 And I **h** a voice in the midst of the four *191*
6: 7 I **h** the voice of the fourth beast say, Come *191*
7: 4 And I **h** the number of them which were *191*
8:13 **h** an angel flying through the midst of *191*
9:13 I **h** a voice from the four horns of the golden *191*
9:16 and I **h** the number of them. *191*
10: 4 and I **h** a voice from heaven saying unto me, *191*
10: 8 And the voice which I **h** from heaven spake *191*
11:12 And they **h** a great voice from heaven saying *191*
12:10 And I **h** a loud voice saying in heaven, *191*
14: 2 And I **h** a voice from heaven, as the voice of *191*
14: 2 and I **h** the voice of harpers harping with their *191*
14:13 And I **h** a voice from heaven saying unto *191*
16: 1 And I **h** a great voice out of the temple *191*
16: 5 And I **h** the angel of the waters say, Thou art *191*
16: 7 And I **h** another out of the altar say, Even so, *191*
18: 4 And I **h** another voice from heaven, saying, *191*
18:22 trumpeters, shall be **h** no more at all in thee; *191*
18:22 the sound of a millstone shall be **h** no more *191*
18:23 of the bride shall be **h** no more at all in thee: *191*
19: 1 And after these *things* I **h** a great voice of *191*
19: 6 And I **h** as *it were* the voice of a great *191*
21: 3 And I **h** a great voice out of heaven saying, *191*
22: 8 and **h** *them.* And when I had heard and seen, *191*
22: 8 and heard *them.* And when I had **h** and seen, *191*

HEARDEST (12) [HEAR]

Dt 4:36 thou **h** his words out of the midst of 8085
Jos 14:12 for thou **h** in that day how the Anakims 8085
2Ki 22:19 when thou **h** what I spake against this 8085
2Ch 34:27 when thou **h** his words against this place, 8085
Ne 9: 9 in Egypt, and **h** their cry by the Red sea; 8085
9:27 cried unto thee, thou **h** *them* from heaven; 8085
9:28 cried unto thee, thou **h** *them* from heaven; 8085
Ps 31:22 nevertheless thou **h** the voice of my 8085
119:26 I have declared my ways, and thou **h** me: 6030

Isa 48: 7 even before the day when thou **h** them not; 8085
48: 8 Yea, thou **h** not; yea, thou knewest not; 8085
Jnh 2: 2 belly of hell cried I, *and* thou **h** my voice. 8085

HEARER (2) [HEAR]
Jas 1:23 For if any be a **h** of the word, and not a doer, *202*
1:25 *therein,* he being not a forgetful **h**, *202*

HEARERS (4) [HEAR]
Ro 2:13 (For not the **h** of the law *are* just before God, *202*
Eph 4:29 that it may minister grace unto the **h**. *191*
2Ti 2:14 to no profit, *but* to the subverting of the **h**. *191*
Jas 1:22 and not **h** only, deceiving your own selves. *202*

HEAREST (11) [HEAR]
Ru 2: 8 Boaz unto Ruth, **H** thou not, my daughter? 8085
1Sa 24: 9 Wherefore **h** thou men's words, saying, 8085
2Sa 5:24 when thou **h** the sound of a going in 8085
1Ki 8:30 dwelling place: and when thou **h**, forgive. 8085
2Ch 6:21 from heaven; and when thou **h**, forgive. 8085
Ps 22: 2 I cry in the daytime, but thou **h** not; 6030
65: 2 O thou that **h** prayer, unto thee shall all 8085
Mt 21:16 And said unto him, **H** thou what these say? *191*
27:13 **H** thou not how many *things* they witness *191*
Jn 3: 8 and thou **h** the sound thereof, but canst not *191*
11:42 And I knew that thou **h** me always: but *191*

HEARETH (52) [HEAR]
Ex 16: 7 for that he **h** your murmurings against 8085
16: 8 for that the LORD **h** your murmurings 8085
Nu 30: 5 her father disallow her in the day that he **h**; 8085
Dt 29:19 to pass, when he **h** the words of this curse, 8085
1Sa 3: 9 shalt say, Speak, LORD; for thy servant **h**. 8085
3:10 Samuel answered, Speak; for thy servant **h**. 8085
3:11 *at* which both the ears of every one that **h** it 8085
2Sa 17: 9 the first, that whosoever **h** *it* will say, 8085+8085
2Ki 21:12 and Judah, that whosoever **h** of it, 8085
Job 34:28 unto him, and he **h** the cry of the afflicted. 8085
Ps 34:17 the LORD **h**, and delivereth them out of 8085
38:14 Thus I was as a man that **h** not, and 8085
69:33 For the LORD **h** the poor, and despiseth 8085
Pr 8:34 Blessed *is* the man that **h** me, watching 8085
13: 1 A wise son ***h*** *his* father's instruction: but NIH
13: 1 but a scorner **h** not rebuke. 8085
13: 8 *are* his riches: but the poor **h** not rebuke. 8085
15:29 but he **h** the prayer of the righteous. 8085
15:31 The ear that **h** the reproof of life abideth 8085
15:32 but he that **h** reproof getteth understanding. 8085
18:13 He that answereth a matter before he **h** *it,* it 8085
21:28 but the man that **h**, speaketh constantly. 8085
25:10 Lest he that **h** *it* put thee to shame, and 8085
29:24 he **h** cursing, and bewrayeth *it* not. 8085
Isa 41:26 yea, *there is* none that **h** your words. 8085
42:20 opening the ears, but he **h** not. 8085
Jer 19: 3 the which whosoever **h**, his ears shall 8085
Eze 3:27 He that **h**, let him hear; and he that 8085
33: 4 whosoever **h** the sound of 8085+8085
Mt 7:24 Therefore whosoever **h** these sayings of *191*
7:26 And every one that **h** these sayings of mine, *191*
13:19 When any one **h** the word of the kingdom, *191*
13:20 stony *places,* the same is he that **h** the word, *191*
13:22 seed among the thorns is he that **h** the word; *191*
13:23 into the good ground is he that **h** the word, *191*
Lk 6:47 to me, and **h** my sayings, and doeth them, *191*
6:49 But he that **h**, and doeth not, is like a man *191*
10:16 He that **h** you heareth me; and he that *191*
10:16 He that heareth you **h** me; and he that *191*
Jn 3:29 which standeth and **h** him, rejoiceth greatly *191*
5:24 He that **h** my word, and believeth on him *191*
8:47 He that is of God **h** God's words: ye *191*
9:31 Now we know that God **h** not sinners: but *191*
9:31 of God, and doeth his will, him he **h**. *191*
18:37 Every one that is of the truth **h** my voice. *191*
2Co 12: 6 which he seeth me *to be,* or that he **h** of me. *191*
1Jn 4: 5 they of the world, and the world **h** them. *191*
4: 6 he that knoweth God **h** us; *he* that is not of *191*
4: 6 heareth us; *he* that is not of God **h** not us. *191*
5:14 ask any *thing* according to his will, he **h** us: *191*
Rev 22:17 And let him that **h** say, Come. And let him *191*
22:18 For I testify unto every *man* that **h** the words *191*

HEARING (39) [HEAR]
Dt 31:11 shalt read this law before all Israel in their **h**. 241
2Sa 18:12 for in our **h** the king charged thee and 241
2Ki 4:31 but *there was* neither voice, nor **h**. 7182
Job 33: 8 Surely thou hast spoken in mine **h**, and 241
42: 5 I have heard of thee by the **h** of the ear: but 8088
Pr 20:12 The **h** ear, and the seeing eye, the LORD 8085
28: 9 He that turneth away his ear from **h** 8085
Ecc 1: 8 with seeing, nor the ear filled with **h**. 8085
Isa 11: 3 neither reprove after the **h** of his ears: 4926
21: 3 I was bowed down at the **h** *of it;* I was 8085
33:15 that stoppeth his ears from **h** of blood, and 8085
Eze 9: 5 to the others he said in mine **h**, Go ye after 241
10:13 it was cried unto them in my **h**, O wheel. 241
Am 8:11 but of **h** the words of the LORD: 8085
Mt 13:13 and **h** they hear not, neither do they *191*
13:14 By **h** ye shall hear, and shall not understand; *189*
13:15 and *their* ears are dull of **h**, and their eyes *191*
Mk 4:12 and **h** they may hear, and not understand; *191*
6: 2 and many **h** *him* were astonished, saying, *191*
Lk 2:46 both **h** them, and asking them *questions.* *191*
8:10 not see, and **h** they might not understand. *191*
18:36 And **h** the multitude pass by, he asked what *191*
Ac 5: 5 And Ananias **h** these words fell down, and *191*
8: 6 **h** and seeing the miracles which he did. *191*
9: 7 **h** a voice, but seeing no *man.* *191*
18: 8 and many of the Corinthians **h** believed, and *191*
25:21 to be reserved unto the **h** of Augustus, *1233*
25:23 and were entered into the **place of h**, *201*
28:26 **H** ye shall hear, and shall not understand; *189*
28:27 and *their* ears are dull of **h**, and their eyes *191*
Ro 10:17 So then faith *cometh* by **h**, *189*
10:17 by hearing, and **h** by the word of God. *189*
1Co 12:17 whole body *were* an eye, where *were* the **h**? *189*
12:17 If the whole *were* **h**, where *were* *189*
Gal 3: 2 by the works of the law, or by the **h** of faith? *189*
3: 5 by the works of the law, or by the **h** of faith? *189*
Phm 1: 5 **H** of thy love and faith, which thou hast *191*
Heb 5:11 hard to be uttered, seeing ye are dull of **h**. *189*
2Pe 2: 8 *man* dwelling among them, in seeing and **h**, *189*

HEARKEN (153) [HEARKENED, HEARKENEDST, HEARKENETH, HEARKENING]
Ge 4:23 ye wives of Lamech, **h** unto my speech: 238
21:12 Sarah hath said unto thee, **h** unto her voice; 8085
23:15 My lord, **h** unto me: the land *is worth* four 8085
34:17 if ye will not **h** unto us, to be circumcised; 8085
49: 2 sons of Jacob; and **h** unto Israel your father. 8085
Ex 3:18 they shall **h** to thy voice: and thou shalt 8085
4: 1 will not believe me, nor **h** unto my voice: 8085
4: 8 neither **h** to the voice of the first sign, 8085
4: 9 these two signs, neither **h** unto thy voice, 8085
6:30 and how shall Pharaoh **h** unto me? 8085
7: 4 Pharaoh shall not **h** unto you, that I may lay 8085
7:22 was hardened, neither did he **h** unto them; 8085
11: 9 unto Moses, Pharaoh shall not **h** unto you; 8085
15:26 If thou wilt **diligently h** to the voice 8085+8085
18:19 **H** now unto my voice, I will give thee 8085
Lev 26:14 if ye will not **h** unto me, and will not do all 8085
26:18 And if ye will not yet for *all* this **h** unto me, 8085
26:21 contrary unto me, and will not **h** unto me; 8085
26:27 And if ye will not for *all* this **h** unto me, but 8085
Nu 23:18 and hear; **h** unto me, thou son of Zippor: 238
Dt 1:45 the LORD would not **h** to your voice, 8085
4: 1 Now therefore **h**, O Israel, unto the statutes 8085
7:12 if ye **h** to these judgments, and keep, and 8085
11:13 if you shall **h diligently** unto my 8085+8085
13: 3 Thou shalt not **h** unto the words of that 8085
13: 8 shalt not consent unto him, nor **h** unto him; 8085
13:18 When thou shalt **h** to the voice of 8085
15: 5 Only if thou **carefully h** unto 8085+8085
17:12 will not **h** unto the priest that standeth to 8085
18:15 like unto me; unto him ye shall **h**; 8085
18:19 *that* whosoever will not **h** unto my words 8085
21:18 have chastened him, will not **h** unto them: 8085
23: 5 LORD thy God would not **h** unto Balaam; 8085
26:17 and his judgments, and to **h** unto his voice: 8085
27: 9 saying, Take heed, and **h**, O Israel; 8085
28: 1 if thou shalt **h diligently** unto 8085+8085
28: 2 if thou shalt **h** unto the voice of the LORD 8085
28:13 if that thou **h** unto the commandments of 8085
28:15 if thou wilt not **h** unto the voice of 8085
30:10 If thou shalt **h** unto the voice of the LORD 8085
Jos 1:17 Moses in all *things,* so will we **h** unto thee: 8085
1:18 will not **h** unto thy words in all that thou 8085
24:10 I would not **h** unto Balaam; therefore 8085
Jdg 2:17 yet they would not **h** unto their judges, but 8085
3: 4 to know whether they would **h unto** 8085
9: 7 and cried, and said unto them, **H** unto me, 8085
9: 7 men of Shechem, that God may **h** unto you. 8085
11:17 the king of Edom would not **h** *thereto.* And 8085
19:25 the men would not **h** to him: so the man 8085
20:13 the children of Benjamin would not **h** to 8085
1Sa 8: 7 **H** unto the voice of the people in all that 8085
8: 9 Now therefore **h** unto their voice: 8085
8:22 **H** unto their voice, and make them a king. 8085
15: 1 **h** thou unto the voice of the words of 8085
15:22 than sacrifice, *and* to **h** than the fat of rams. 7181
28:22 **h** thou also unto the voice of thine 8085
30:24 For who will **h** unto you in this matter? but 8085
2Sa 12:18 and he would not **h** unto our voice: 8085
13:14 Howbeit he would not **h** unto her voice: 8085
13:16 didst unto me. But he would not **h** unto her. 8085
1Ki 8:28 to **h** unto the cry and to the prayer, 8085
8:29 that *thou* mayest **h** unto the prayer which 8085
8:30 **h** thou to the supplication of thy servant, 8085
8:52 to **h** unto them in all that they call for unto 8085
11:38 if thou wilt **h** unto all that I command thee, 8085
20: 8 said unto him, **H** not *unto him,* nor consent. 8085
22:28 he said, **H**, O people, every one of you. 8085
2Ki 10: 6 ye *be* mine, and *if* ye will **h** unto my voice, 8085
17:40 Howbeit they did not **h**, but they did after 8085
18:31 **H** not to Hezekiah: for thus saith the king 8085
18:32 **h** not unto Hezekiah, when he persuadeth 8085
2Ch 6:19 to **h** unto the cry and the prayer which thy 8085
6:20 to **h** unto the prayer which thy servant 8085
6:21 **H** therefore unto the supplications of thy 8085
10:16 saw that the king would not **h** unto them, 8085
18:27 by me. And he said, **H**, all ye people. 8085
20:15 **H** ye, all Judah, and ye inhabitants of 7181
33:10 and to his people: but they would not **h**. 7181
Ne 13:27 then **h** unto you to do all this great evil, 8085
Job 13: 6 and **h** to the pleadings of my lips. 7181
32:10 Therefore I said, **H** to me; I also will shew 8085
33: 1 hear my speeches, and **h** to all my words. 238
33:31 Mark well, O Job, **h** unto me: hold thy 8085
33:33 If not, **h** unto me: hold thy peace, and 8085
34:10 Therefore **h** unto me, ye men of 8085
34:16 hear this: **h** to the voice of my words. 238
34:34 tell me, and let a wise man **h** unto me. 8085
37:14 **H** unto this, O Job: stand still, and 238
Ps 5: 2 **H** unto the voice of my cry, my King, and 7181
34:11 Come, ye children, **h** unto me: I will teach 8085
45:10 **H**, O daughter, and consider, and 8085
58: 5 Which will not **h** to the voice of charmers, 8085
81: 8 unto thee: O Israel, if thou wilt **h** unto me; 8085
81:11 my people would not **h** to my voice; and 8085
Pr 7:24 **H** unto me now therefore, O ye children, 8085
8:32 Now therefore **h** unto me, O ye children: 8085
23:22 **H** unto thy father that begat thee, and 8085
29:12 If a ruler **h** to lies, all his servants *are* 7181
SS 8:13 the gardens, the companions **h** to thy voice: 7181
Isa 28:23 and hear my voice; **h**, and hear my speech. 7181
32: 3 and the ears of them that hear shall **h**. 7181
34: 1 ye nations, to hear; and **h**, ye people: 7181
36:16 **H** not to Hezekiah: for thus saith the king 8085
42:23 *who* will **h** and hear for the time to come? 7181
46: 3 **H** unto me, O house of Jacob, and all 8085
46:12 **H** unto me, ye stouthearted, that *are* far 8085
48:12 **H** unto me, O Jacob, and Israel my called; 8085
49: 1 unto me; and **h**, ye people, from afar; 7181
51: 1 **H** to me, ye that follow after righteousness, 8085
51: 4 **H** unto me, my people; and give ear unto 7181
51: 7 **H** unto me, ye that know righteousness, 8085
55: 2 **h diligently** unto me, and eat ye *that which* 8085
Jer 6:10 ear *is* uncircumcised, and they cannot **h**: 7181
6:17 *saying,* **H** to the sound of the trumpet. 7181
6:17 the trumpet. But they said, We will not **h**. 7181
7:27 unto them; but they will not **h** to thee: 8085
11:11 shall cry unto me, I will not **h** unto them. 8085
16:12 his evil heart, that *they* may not **h** unto me: 8085
17:24 if ye **diligently h** unto me, saith 8085+8085
17:27 if you will not **h** unto me to hallow 8085
18:19 **h** to the voice of them that contend with 8085
23:16 **H** not unto the words of the prophets that 8085
26: 3 If so be they will **h**, and turn every man 8085
26: 4 If ye will not **h** to me, to walk in my law, 8085
26: 5 To **h** to the words of my servants 8085
27: 9 Therefore **h** not ye to your prophets, nor to 8085
27:14 Therefore **h** not unto the words of 8085
27:16 **H** not to the words of your prophets that 8085
27:17 **H** not unto them; serve the king of 8085
29: 8 neither **h** to your dreams which ye cause to 8085
29:12 and pray unto me, and I will **h** unto you. 8085
35:13 Will ye not receive instruction to **h** to my 8085
37: 2 did **h** unto the words of the LORD, 8085
38:15 give thee counsel, wilt thou not **h** unto me? 8085
44:16 of the LORD, we will not **h** unto thee. 8085
Eze 3: 7 the house of Israel will not **h** unto thee; 8085
3: 7 unto thee; for they will not **h** unto me: 8085
20: 8 against me, and would not **h** unto me: 8085
20:39 and hereafter *also,* if ye will not **h** unto me: 8085
Da 9:19 hear; O Lord, forgive; O Lord, **h** and do; 7181
Hos 5: 1 **h**, ye house of Israel; and give ye ear, 7181
9:17 because they did not **h** unto him: 8085
Mic 1: 2 ye people; **h**, O earth, and all that therein is: 7181
Zec 1: 4 they did not hear, nor **h** unto me, saith 7181
7:11 they refused to **h**, and pulled away 7181
Mk 4: 3 **H**; Behold, there went out a sower to sow: *191*
7:14 **H** unto me every one of you, and *191*
Ac 2:14 this known unto you, and **h** to my words: *1801*
4:19 Whether it be right in the sight of God to **h** *191*
7: 2 And he said, Men, brethren, and fathers, **h**; *191*
12:13 a damsel came to **h**, named Rhoda. *5219*
15:13 saying, Men *and* brethren, **h** unto me: *191*
Jas 2: 5 **H**, my beloved brethren, Hath not God *191*

HEARKENED (81) [HEARKEN]
Ge 3:17 Because thou hast **h** unto the voice of thy 8085
16: 2 by her. And Abram **h** to the voice of Sarai. 8085
23:16 Abraham **h** unto Ephron; and 8085
30:17 God **h** unto Leah, and she conceived, and 8085
30:22 and God **h** to her, and opened her womb. 8085
34:24 unto Shechem his son **h** all that went out of 8085
39:10 that he **h** not unto her, to lie by her, *or* to be 8085
Ex 6: 9 they **h** not unto Moses for anguish of spirit, 8085
6:12 the children of Israel have not **h** unto me; 8085
7:13 Pharaoh's heart, that he **h** not unto them; 8085
8:15 he hardened his heart, and **h** not unto them; 8085
8:19 was hardened, and he **h** not unto them; 8085
9:12 heart of Pharaoh, and he **h** not unto them; 8085
16:20 Notwithstanding they **h** not unto Moses; 8085
18:24 So Moses **h** to the voice of his father in 8085
Nu 14:22 ten times, and have not **h** to my voice; 8085
21: 3 the LORD **h** to the voice of Israel, and 8085
Dt 9:19 But the LORD **h** unto me at that time also. 8085
9:23 and ye believed him not, nor **h** to his voice. 8085
10:10 and the LORD **h** unto me at that time also, 8085
18:14 **h** unto observers of times, and 8085
26:14 I have **h** to the voice of the LORD my 8085
34: 9 the children of Israel **h** unto him, and did as 8085
Jos 1:17 According as we **h** unto Moses in all 8085
10:14 that the LORD **h** unto the voice of a man: 8085
Jdg 2:20 their fathers, and have not **h** unto my voice; 8085
11:28 **h** not unto the words of Jephthah which he 8085
13: 9 God **h** to the voice of Manoah; and 8085
1Sa 2:25 Notwithstanding they **h** not unto the voice 8085
12: 1 I have **h** unto your voice in all that ye said 8085
19: 6 Saul **h** unto the voice of Jonathan: and 8085
25:35 I have **h** to thy voice, and have accepted 8085
28:21 have **h** unto thy words which thou spakest 8085
28:23 compelled him; and he **h** unto their voice. 8085
1Ki 12:15 Wherefore the king **h** not unto the people; 8085
12:16 So when all Israel saw that the king **h** not 8085
12:24 They **h** therefore to the word of 8085
15:20 So Ben-hadad **h** unto king Asa, and sent 8085
20:25 And he **h** unto their voice, and did so. 8085
2Ki 13: 4 the LORD, and the LORD **h** unto him: 8085
16: 9 the king of Assyria **h** unto him: for the king 8085
20:13 Hezekiah **h** unto them, and shewed them all 8085
21: 9 they **h** not: and Manasseh seduced them to 8085
22:13 our fathers have not **h** unto the words of 8085
2Ch 10:15 So the king **h** not unto the people: for 8085
16: 4 Ben-hadad **h** unto king Asa, and sent 8085
24:17 to the king. Then the king **h** unto them. 8085
25:16 done this, and hast not **h** unto my counsel. 8085
30:20 the LORD **h** to Hezekiah, and healed 8085
35:22 **h** not unto the words of Necho from 8085
Ne 9:16 and **h** not to thy commandments, 8085
9:29 **h** not unto thy commandments, but 8085
9:34 nor **h** unto thy commandments and thy 7181
Est 3: 4 he **h** not unto them, that they told Haman, 8085
Job 9:16 *yet* would I not believe that he had **h** unto 238
Ps 81:13 O that my people had **h** unto me, *and* 8085
106:25 *and* **h** not unto the voice of the LORD. 8085
Isa 21: 7 and he **h diligently** *with* much heed: 7181+7182
48:18 O that thou hadst **h** to my commandments! 7181
Jer 6:19 because they have not **h** unto my words, 7181
7:24 they **h** not, nor inclined their ear, but 8085
7:26 Yet they **h** not unto me, nor inclined their 8085
8: 6 I **h** and heard, *but* they spake not aright: 7181
25: 3 and speaking; but ye have not **h**. 8085
25: 4 and sending *them;* but ye have not **h**, 8085

Jer 25: 7 Yet ye have not **h** unto me, saith 8085
26: 5 and sending *them,* but ye have not **h**; 8085
29:19 Because they have not **h** to my words, 8085
32:33 teaching *them,* yet they have not **h** to 8085
34:14 your fathers **h** not unto me, neither inclined 8085
34:17 Ye have not **h** unto me, in proclaiming 8085
35:14 and speaking; but ye **h** not unto me. 8085
35:15 have not inclined your ear, nor **h** unto me. 8085
35:16 but this people hath not **h** unto me: 8085
36:31 pronounced against them; but they **h** not. 8085
37:14 he **h** not to him: so Irijah took Jeremiah, 8085
44: 5 they **h** not, nor inclined their ear to turn 8085
Eze 3: 6 thee to them, they would have **h** unto thee. 8085
Da 9: 6 Neither have we **h** unto thy servants 8085
Mal 3:16 the LORD **h**, and heard *it,* and a book of 7181
Ac 27:21 *ye* should have **h** unto me, and not have *3980*

HEARKENEDST (1) [HEARKEN]
Dt 28:45 thou **h** not unto the voice of the LORD thy 8085

HEARKENETH (2) [HEARKEN]
Pr 1:33 whoso **h** unto me shall dwell safely, and 8085
12:15 but he that **h** unto counsel *is* wise. 8085

HEARKENING (1) [HEARKEN]
Ps 103:20 **h** unto the voice of his word. 8085

HEART (830) [BROKEN-HEARTED, FAINTHEARTED, HARDHEARTED, HEART'S, HEARTED, HEARTS, MERRYHEARTED, STOUTHEARTED, TENDERHEARTED]
Ge 6: 5 thoughts of his **h** *was* only evil continually. 3820
6: 6 on the earth, and it grieved him at his **h**. 3820
8:21 the LORD said in his **h**, I will not again 3820
8:21 for the imagination of man's **h** *is* evil from 3820
17:17 his face, and laughed, and said in his **h**, 3820
20: 5 in the integrity of my **h** and innocency of 3824
20: 6 that thou didst this in the integrity of thy **h**; 3824
24:45 before I had done speaking in mine **h**, 3820
27:41 Esau said in his **h**, The days of mourning 3820
42:28 their **h** failed *them,* and they were afraid, 3820
45:26 *Jacob's* **h** fainted, for he believed them not. 3820
Ex 4:14 when he seeth thee, he will be glad in his **h**. 3820
4:21 I will harden his **h**, that he shall not let 3820
7: 3 I will harden Pharaoh's **h**, and multiply my 3820
7:13 he hardened Pharaoh's **h**, that he hearkened 3820
7:14 Pharaoh's **h** *is* hardened, he refuseth to let 3820
7:22 Pharaoh's **h** was hardened, neither did he 3820
7:23 neither did he set his **h** to this also. 3820
8:15 he hardened his **h**, and hearkened not unto 3820
8:19 Pharaoh's **h** was hardened, and 3820
8:32 Pharaoh hardened his **h** at this time also, 3820
9: 7 the **h** of Pharaoh was hardened, and he did 3820
9:12 the LORD hardened the **h** of Pharaoh, 3820
9:14 this time send all my plagues upon thine **h**, 3820
9:34 and hardened his **h**, he and his servants. 3820
9:35 the **h** of Pharaoh was hardened, 3820
10: 1 for I have hardened his **h**, and the heart of 3820
10: 1 his heart, and the **h** of his servants, 3820
10:20 the LORD hardened Pharaoh's **h**, so 3820
10:27 the LORD hardened Pharaoh's **h**, and 3820
11:10 the LORD hardened Pharaoh's **h**, so 3820
14: 4 I will harden Pharaoh's **h**, that he shall 3820
14: 5 the **h** of Pharaoh and of his servants was 3824
14: 8 the LORD hardened the **h** of Pharaoh king 3820
15: 8 the depths were congealed in the **h** of 3820
23: 9 for ye know the **h** of a stranger, seeing ye 5315
25: 2 with his **h** ye shall take my offering. 3820
28:29 in the breastplate of judgment upon his **h**, 3820
28:30 they shall be upon Aaron's **h**, when he 3820
28:30 upon his **h** before the LORD continually. 3820
35: 5 whosoever *is* of a willing **h**, let him bring 3820
35:21 every one whose **h** stirred him up, and 3820
35:26 all the women whose **h** stirred them up in 3820
35:29 whose **h** made them willing to bring for all 3820
35:34 he hath put in his **h** that *he* may teach, 3820
35:35 Them hath he filled *with* wisdom of **h**, 3820
36: 2 in whose **h** the LORD had put wisdom, 3820
36: 2 *even* every one whose **h** stirred him up to 3820
Lev 19:17 Thou shalt not hate thy brother in thine **h**: 3824
26:16 consume the eyes, and cause sorrow of **h**: 5315
Nu 15:39 that ye seek not after your own **h** and 3824
32: 7 wherefore discourage ye the **h** of 3820
32: 9 they discouraged the **h** of the children of 3820
Dt 1:28 our brethren have discouraged our **h**, 3824
2:30 made his **h** obstinate, that he might deliver 3824
4: 9 lest they depart from thy **h** all the days of 3824
4:29 find *him,* if thou seek him with all thy **h** 3824
4:39 *this* day, and consider *it* in thine **h**, 3824
5:29 O that there were such a **h** in them, 3824
6: 5 love the LORD thy God with all thine **h**, 3824
6: 6 command thee *this* day, shall be in thine **h**: 3824
7:17 If thou shalt say in thine **h**, These nations 3824
8: 2 to prove thee, to know what *was* in thine **h**, 3824
8: 5 Thou shalt also consider in thine **h**, that, 3824
8:14 thine **h** be lifted up, and thou forget 3824
8:17 thou say in thine **h**, My power and 3824
9: 4 Speak not thou in thine **h**, after that 3824
9: 5 or for the uprightness of thine **h**, 3824
10:12 to serve the LORD thy God with all thy **h** 3824
10:16 therefore the foreskin of your **h**, 3824
11:13 to serve him with all your **h** and with all 3824
11:16 that your **h** be not deceived, and ye turn 3824
11:18 shall ye lay up these my words in your **h** 3824
13: 3 love the LORD your God with all your **h** 3824
15: 7 thou shalt not harden thy **h**, nor shut thine 3824
15: 9 that there be not a thought in thy wicked **h**, 3824
15:10 thine **h** shall not be grieved when thou 3824
17:17 wives to himself, that his **h** turn not away: 3824
17:20 That his **h** be not lifted up above his 3824
18:21 if thou say in thine **h**, How shall we know 3824
19: 6 while his **h** is hot, and overtake him, 3824
20: 8 lest his brethren's **h** faint as well as his 3824
20: 8 his brethren's heart faint as well as his **h**. 3824

Dt 24:15 for he *is* poor, and setteth his **h** upon it: 5315
26:16 therefore keep and do them with all thine **h**, 3824
28:28 and blindness, and astonishment of **h**: 3824
28:47 with gladness of **h**, for the abundance of 3824
28:65 LORD shall give thee there a trembling **h**, 3820
28:67 for the fear of thine **h** where*with* thou shalt 3824
29: 4 Yet the LORD hath not given you a **h** to 3820
29:18 whose **h** turneth away *this* day from 3824
29:19 that he bless himself in his **h**, saying, I shall 3824
29:19 though I walk in the imagination of mine **h**, 3820
30: 2 with all thine **h**, and with all thy soul; 3824
30: 6 LORD thy God will circumcise thine **h**, 3824
30: 6 the **h** of thy seed, to love the LORD thy 3824
30: 6 love the LORD thy God with all thine **h**, 3824
30:10 unto the LORD thy God with all thine **h**, 3824
30:14 in thy mouth, and in thy **h**, that *thou* mayest 3824
30:17 if thine **h** turn away, so that thou wilt not 3824
Jos 5: 1 we were passed over, that their **h** melted, 3824
14: 7 him word again as *it was* in mine **h**. 3824
14: 8 up with me made the **h** of the people melt: 3820
22: 5 to serve him with all your **h** and with all 3824
24:23 incline your **h** unto the LORD God of 3824
Jdg 5: 9 My **h** *is* toward the governors of Israel, 3820
5:15 of Reuben *there were* great thoughts of **h**. 3820
5:16 of Reuben *there were* great searchings of **h**. 3820
16:15 I love thee, when thine **h** *is* not with me? 3820
16:17 That he told her all his **h**, and said unto her, 3820
16:18 Delilah saw that he had told her all his **h**, 3820
16:18 *this* once, for he hath shewed me all his **h**. 3820
18:20 the priest's **h** was glad, and he took 3820
19: 5 Comfort thine **h** *with* a morsel of bread, 3820
19: 6 and tarry all night, and let thine **h** be merry. 3820
19: 8 father said, Comfort thine **h**, I pray thee. 3824
19: 9 lodge here, that thine **h** may be merry; 3824
Ru 3: 7 had eaten and drunk, and his **h** was merry, 3820
1Sa 1: 8 why is thy **h** grieved? *am* not I better to 3824
1:13 Now Hannah, she spake in her **h**; only her 3820
2: 1 and said, My **h** rejoiceth in the LORD, 3820
2:33 consume thine eyes, and to grieve thine **h**: 5315
2:35 shall do according to *that which is* in my **h** 3824
4:13 for his **h** trembled for the ark of God. 3820
9:19 and will tell thee all that *is* in thine **h**. 3824
10: 9 go from Samuel, God gave him another **h**: 3820
12:20 but serve the LORD with all your **h**; 3824
12:24 and serve him in truth with all your **h**: 3824
13:14 hath sought him a man after his own **h**, 3824
14: 7 said unto him, Do all that *is* in thine **h**: 3824
14: 7 behold, I *am* with thee according to thy **h**. 3824
16: 7 but the LORD looketh on the **h**. 3824
17:28 thy pride, and the naughtiness of thine **h**; 3824
17:32 to Saul, Let no man's **h** fail because of him; 3820
21:12 David laid up these words in his **h**, and 3824
24: 5 that David's **h** smote him, because he had 3820
25:31 unto thee, nor offence of **h** unto my lord, 3820
25:36 Nabal's **h** *was* merry within him, for he 3820
25:37 that his **h** died within him, and he became 3820
27: 1 David said in his **h**, I shall now perish one 3820
28: 5 he was afraid, and his **h** greatly trembled. 3820
2Sa 3:21 that thou mayest reign over all that thine **h** 5315
6:16 the LORD; and she despised him in her **h**. 3820
7: 3 to the king, Go, do all that *is* in thine **h**; 3824
7:21 word's sake, and according to thine own **h**, 3820
7:27 hath thy servant found in his **h** to pray this 3820
13:28 Mark ye now when Amnon's **h** is merry 3820
13:33 not my lord the king take the thing to his **h**, 3820
14: 1 that the king's **h** *was* toward Absalom. 3820
17:10 whose **h** *is* as the heart of a lion, 3820
17:10 whose heart *is* as the **h** of a lion, 3820
18:14 and thrust them through the **h** of Absalom, 3820
19:14 he bowed the **h** of all the men of Judah, 3824
19:14 the men of Judah, *even* as *the **h** of* one man; NIH
19:19 that the king should take *it* to his **h**. 3820
24:10 David's **h** smote him after that he had 3820
1Ki 2: 4 to walk before me in truth with all their **h** 3824
2:44 the wickedness which thine **h** is privy to, 3824
3: 6 and in uprightness of **h** with thee; 3824
3: 9 thy servant an understanding **h** to judge thy 3820
3:12 given thee a wise and an understanding **h**; 3820
4:29 exceeding much, and largeness of **h**, 3820
8:17 it was in the **h** of David my father to build a 3824
8:18 Whereas it was in thine **h** to build a house 3824
8:18 thou didst well that it was in thine **h**. 3824
8:23 that walk before thee with all their **h**: 3820
8:38 know every man the plague of his own **h**, 3824
8:39 to his ways, whose **h** thou knowest; 3824
8:48 And *so* return unto thee with all their **h**, and 3824
8:61 Let your **h** therefore be perfect with 3824
8:66 glad of **h** for all the goodness that 3820
9: 3 and mine **h** shall be there perpetually. 3820
9: 4 in integrity of **h**, and in uprightness, 3824
10: 2 with him of all that was in her **h**. 3824
10:24 his wisdom, which God had put in his **h**. 3820
11: 2 *for* surely they will turn away your **h** after 3824
11: 3 and his wives turned away his **h**. 3820
11: 4 *that* his wives turned away his **h** after other 3824
11: 4 his **h** was not perfect with the LORD his 3824
11: 4 his God, as *was* the **h** of David his father. 3824
11: 9 his **h** was turned from the LORD God of 3824
12:26 Jeroboam said in his **h**, Now shall 3820
12:27 shall the **h** of this people turn again unto 3820
12:33 month which he had devised of his own **h**; 3820
14: 8 and who followed me with all his **h**, 3824
15: 3 his **h** was not perfect with the LORD his 3824
15: 3 his God, as the **h** of David his father. 3824
15:14 nevertheless Asa's **h** was perfect with 3824
18:37 and *that* thou hast turned their **h** back again. 3820
21: 7 *and* eat bread, and let thine **h** be merry: 3820
2Ki 5:26 Went not mine **h** *with thee,* when the man 3820
6:11 Therefore the **h** of the king of Syria was 3820
9:24 the arrow went out at his **h**, and he sunk 3820
10:15 and said to him, Is thine **h** right, 3824
10:15 thine heart right, as my **h** *is* with thy heart? 3824
10:15 thine heart right, as my heart *is* with thy **h**? 3824
10:30 Ahab according to all that *was* in mine **h**, 3824
10:31 of the LORD God of Israel with all his **h**: 3824

2Ki 12: 4 all the money that cometh into any man's **h** 3820
14:10 and thine **h** hath lifted thee up: 3820
20: 3 before thee in truth and with a perfect **h**, 3824
22:19 Because thine **h** was tender, and thou hast 3824
23: 3 his statutes with all *their* **h** and all *their* 3820
23:25 that turned to the LORD with all his **h**, 3824
1Ch 12:17 to help me, mine **h** shall be knit unto you: 3824
12:33 *they were* not of **double h**. 3820+3820+2050.1
12:38 came with a perfect **h** to Hebron, 3824
12:38 all the rest also of Israel *were of* one **h** to 3820
15:29 and playing: and she despised him in her **h**. 3820
16:10 let the **h** of them rejoice that seek 3820
17: 2 said unto David, Do all that *is* in thine **h**; 3824
17:19 and according to thine own **h**, 3820
17:25 thy servant hath found *in his* **h** to pray NIH
22:19 Now set your **h** and your soul to seek 3824
28: 2 *As for me,* I *had* in mine **h** to build a house 3824
28: 9 serve him with a perfect **h** and with a 3820
29: 9 with perfect **h** they offered willingly to 3820
29:17 that thou triest the **h**, and hast pleasure in 3824
29:17 in the uprightness of mine **h** I have 3824
29:18 of the thoughts of the **h** of thy people, 3824
29:18 of thy people, and prepare their **h** unto thee: 3824
29:19 And give unto Solomon my son a perfect **h**, 3824
2Ch 1:11 Because this was in thine **h**, and thou hast 3824
6: 7 Now it was in the **h** of David my father to 3824
6: 8 Forasmuch as it was in thine **h** to build a 3824
6: 8 thou didst well *in* that it was in thine **h**: 3824
6:30 unto all his ways, whose **h** thou knowest; 3824
6:38 If they return to thee with all their **h** and 3820
7:10 merry in **h** for the goodness that 3820
7:11 all that came into Solomon's **h** to make in 3820
7:16 and mine **h** shall be there perpetually. 3820
9: 1 with him of all that was in her **h**. 3824
9:23 hear his wisdom, that God had put in his **h**. 3820
12:14 he prepared not his **h** to seek the LORD. 3820
15:12 LORD God of their fathers with all their **h** 3824
15:15 for they had sworn with all their **h**, and 3824
15:17 nevertheless the **h** of Asa was perfect all 3824
16: 9 of *them* whose **h** *is* perfect towards him. 3824
17: 6 his **h** was lift up in the ways of the LORD: 3820
19: 3 and hast prepared thine **h** to seek God. 3824
19: 9 faithfully, and with a perfect **h**. 3824
22: 9 who sought the LORD with all his **h**. 3824
25: 2 of the LORD, but not with a perfect **h**. 3824
25:19 and thine **h** lifteth thee up to boast: 3820
26:16 his **h** was lifted up to *his* destruction: 3820
29:10 Now *it is* in mine **h** to make a covenant 3824
29:31 as many as were of a free **h** burnt offerings. 3820
29:34 for the Levites *were* more upright in **h** to 3824
30:12 one **h** to do the commandment of the king 3820
30:19 *That* prepareth his **h** to seek God, 3824
31:21 he did *it* with all his **h**, and prospered. 3824
32:25 *done* unto him; for his **h** was lifted up: 3820
32:26 humbled himself for the pride of his **h**, 3820
32:31 that *he* might know all *that was* in his **h**. 3824
34:27 Because thine **h** was tender, and thou didst 3824
34:31 with all his **h**, and with all his soul, 3824
36:13 hardened his **h** from turning unto 3824
Ezr 6:22 turned the **h** of the king of Assyria unto 3820
7:10 For Ezra had prepared his **h** to seek the law 3824
7:27 hath put *such a thing* as this in the king's **h**, 3820
Ne 2: 2 this *is* nothing *else* but sorrow of **h**. Then I 3820
2:12 God had put in my **h** to do at Jerusalem: 3820
6: 8 but thou feignest them out of thine own **h**. 3820
7: 5 my God put into mine **h** to gather together 3820
9: 8 And foundest his **h** faithful before thee, and 3824
Est 1:10 when the **h** of the king was merry with 3820
5: 9 forth that day joyful and with a glad **h**: 3820
6: 6 Now Haman thought in his **h**, To whom 3820
7: 5 *is* he, that durst presume in his **h** to do so? 3820
Job 7:17 that thou shouldest set thine **h** upon him? 3820
8:10 *and* tell thee, and utter words out of their **h**? 3820
9: 4 *He is* wise in **h**, and mighty in strength: 3824
10:13 these *things* hast thou hid in thine **h**: I know 3824
11:13 If thou prepare thine **h**, and stretch out 3820
12:24 He taketh away the **h** of the chief of 3820
15:12 Why doth thine **h** carry thee away? and 3820
17: 4 For thou hast hid their **h** from 3820
17:11 are broken off, *even* the thoughts of my **h**. 3824
22:22 his mouth, and lay up his words in thine **h**. 3824
23:16 For God maketh my **h** soft, and 3820
27: 6 my **h** shall not reproach *me* so long as I 3824
29:13 and I caused the widow's **h** to sing for joy. 3820
31: 7 mine **h** walked after mine eyes, and *if any* 3820
31: 9 If mine **h** have been deceived by a woman, 3820
31:27 my **h** hath been secretly enticed, or 3820
33: 3 words *shall be of* the uprightness of my **h**: 3820
34:14 If he set his **h** upon *man, if* he gather unto 3820
36:13 the hypocrites in **h** heap up wrath: they cry 3820
37: 1 At this also my **h** trembleth, and is moved 3820
37:24 he respecteth not any *that are* wise of **h**. 3820
38:36 or who hath given understanding to the **h**? 7907
41:24 His **h** is as firm as a stone; yea, as hard as 3820
Ps 4: 4 commune with your own **h** upon your bed, 3824
4: 7 Thou hast put gladness in my **h**, more than 3820
7:10 *is* of God, which saveth the upright in **h**. 3820
9: 1 praise *thee,* O LORD, with my whole **h**; 3820
10: 6 He hath said in his **h**, I shall not be moved: 3820
10:11 He hath said in his **h**, God hath forgotten: 3820
10:13 he hath said in his **h**, Thou wilt not require 3820
10:17 thou wilt prepare their **h**, thou wilt cause 3820
11: 2 *they* may privily shoot at the upright in **h**. 3820
12: 2 a **double h** do they speak. 3820+3820+2050.1
13: 2 in my soul, *having* sorrow in my **h** daily? 3824
13: 5 my **h** shall rejoice in thy salvation. 3820
14: 1 The fool hath said in his **h**, *There is* no 3820
15: 2 and speaketh the truth in his **h**. 3824
16: 9 Therefore my **h** is glad, and my glory 3820
17: 3 Thou hast proved mine **h**; thou hast visited 3820
19: 8 of the LORD *are* right, rejoicing the **h**: 3820
19:14 the meditation of my **h**, be acceptable in 3820
20: 4 Grant thee according to thine own **h**, and 3824
22:14 my **h** is like wax; it is melted in the midst 3820
22:26 that seek him: your **h** shall live for ever. 3824

H

Ps 24: 4 He that hath clean hands, and a pure **h**; 3824
25:17 The troubles of my **h** are enlarged: O bring 3824
26: 2 and prove me; try my reins and my **h**. 3820
27: 3 encamp against me, my **h** shall not fear: 3820
27: 8 my **h** said unto thee, Thy face, LORD, 3820
27:14 and he shall strengthen thine **h**: 3820
28: 7 my **h** trusted in him, and I am helped: 3820
28: 7 therefore my **h** greatly rejoiceth; and 3820
31:24 and he shall strengthen your **h**, 3824
32:11 shout for joy, all *ye that are* upright in **h**. 3820
33:11 the thoughts of his **h** to all generations. 3820
33:21 For our **h** shall rejoice in him, because 3820
34:18 *is* nigh unto them that are of a broken **h**; 3820
36: 1 of the wicked saith within my **h**, 3820
36:10 and thy righteousness to the upright in **h**. 3820
37: 4 and he shall give thee the desires of thine **h**. 3820
37:15 Their sword shall enter into their own **h**, 3820
37:31 The law of his God *is* in his **h**; none of his 3820
38: 8 by reason of the disquietness of my **h**. 3820
38:10 My **h** panteth, my strength faileth me: 3820
39: 3 My **h** was hot within me, while I was 3820
40: 8 O my God: yea, thy law *is* within my **h**. 4578
40:10 have not hid thy righteousness within my **h**; 3820
40:12 of mine head: therefore my **h** faileth me. 3820
41: 6 his **h** gathereth iniquity to itself; *when* he 3820
44:18 Our **h** is not turned back, neither have our 3820
44:21 for he knoweth the secrets of the **h**. 3820
45: 1 My **h** is inditing a good matter: I speak of 3820
45: 5 Thine arrows *are* sharp in the **h** of 3820
49: 3 the meditation of my **h** *shall be of* 3820
51:10 Create in me a clean **h**, O God; and renew a 3820
51:17 a broken and a contrite **h**, O God, thou wilt 3820
53: 1 The fool hath said in his **h**, *There is* no 3820
55: 4 My **h** is sore pained within me: and 3820
55:21 smoother than butter, but war *was* in his **h**: 3820
57: 7 My **h** is fixed, O God, my heart is fixed: 3820
57: 7 My heart is fixed, O God, my **h** is fixed: 3820
58: 2 Yea, in **h** you work wickedness; you weigh 3820
61: 2 cry unto thee, when my **h** is overwhelmed: 3820
62: 8 ye people, pour out your **h** before him: 3824
62:10 riches increase, set not *your* **h** *upon them.* 3820
64: 6 *thought* of every one *of them,* and the **h**, 3820
64:10 in him; and all the upright in **h** shall glory. 3820
66:18 If I regard iniquity in my **h**, the Lord will 3820
69:20 Reproach hath broken my **h**; and I am full 3820
69:32 and your **h** shall live that seek God. 3824
73: 1 to Israel, *even* to such as are of a clean **h**. 3824
73: 7 they have more than **h** could wish. 3824
73:13 Verily I have cleansed my **h** *in* vain, and 3824
73:21 Thus my **h** was grieved, and I was pricked 3824
73:26 My flesh and my **h** faileth: *but* God *is* 3824
73:26 *but* God *is* the strength of my **h**, and 3824
77: 6 I commune with mine own **h**: and my spirit 3824
78: 8 a generation *that* set not their **h** aright, and 3820
78:18 they tempted God in their **h** by asking meat 3824
78:37 For their **h** was not right with him, 3820
78:72 fed them according to the integrity of his **h**; 3824
84: 2 my **h** and my flesh crieth out for the living 3820
84: 5 in thee; in whose **h** *are* the ways *of them.* 3824
86:11 in thy truth: unite my **h** to fear thy name. 3824
86:12 praise thee, O Lord my God, with all my **h**: 3824
94:15 and all the upright in **h** shall follow it. 3820
95: 8 Harden not your **h**, as *in* the provocation, 3824
95:10 It *is* a people that do err in *their* **h**, and 3824
97:11 and gladness for the upright in **h**. 3820
101: 2 will walk within my house with a perfect **h**. 3824
101: 4 A froward **h** shall depart from me: I will 3824
101: 5 a high look and a proud **h** will not I suffer. 3824
102: 4 My **h** is smitten, and withered like grass; so 3820
104:15 wine *that* maketh glad the **h** of man, 3824
104:15 and bread *which* strengtheneth man's **h**. 3824
105: 3 let the **h** of them rejoice that seek 3820
105:25 He turned their **h** to hate his people, to deal 3820
107:12 Therefore he brought down their **h** with 3820
108: 1 O God, my **h** is fixed; I will sing and 3820
109:16 that *he* might even slay the broken in **h**. 3824
109:22 needy, and my **h** is wounded within me. 3820
111: 1 I will praise the LORD with *my* whole **h**, 3824
112: 7 his **h** is fixed, trusting in the LORD. 3820
112: 8 His **h** *is* established, he shall not be afraid, 3820
119: 2 *and that* seek him with the whole **h**. 3820
119: 7 I will praise thee with uprightness of **h**, 3824
119:10 With my whole **h** have I sought thee: O let 3820
119:11 Thy word have I hid in mine **h**, that I might 3820
119:32 when thou shalt enlarge my **h**. 3820
119:34 yea, I shall observe it with *my* whole **h**. 3820
119:36 Incline my **h** unto thy testimonies, and 3820
119:58 I intreated thy favour with *my* whole **h**: 3820
119:69 I will keep thy precepts with *my* whole **h**. 3820
119:70 Their **h** is as fat as grease; *but* I delight *in* 3820
119:80 Let my **h** be sound in thy statutes; that I be 3820
119:111 for ever: for they *are* the rejoicing of my **h**. 3820
119:112 I have inclined mine **h** to perform thy 3820
119:145 I cried with *my* whole **h**; hear me, 3820
119:161 but my **h** standeth in awe of thy word. 3820
131: 1 LORD, my **h** is not haughty, nor mine 3820
138: 1 I will praise thee with my whole **h**: 3820
139:23 Search me, O God, and know my **h**: try me, 3824
140: 2 Which imagine mischiefs in *their* **h**; 3820
141: 4 Incline not my **h** to *any* evil thing, 3820
143: 4 within me; my **h** within me is desolate. 3820
147: 3 He healeth the broken in **h**, and bindeth up 3820
Pr 2: 2 *and* apply thine **h** to understanding; 3820
2:10 When wisdom entereth into thine **h**, and 3820
3: 1 but let thine **h** keep my commandments: 3820
3: 3 write them upon the table of thine **h**: 3820
3: 5 Trust in the LORD with all thine **h**; and 3820
4: 4 said unto me, Let thine **h** retain my words: 3820
4:21 keep them in the midst of thine **h**. 3824
4:23 Keep thy **h** with all diligence; for out of it 3820
5:12 and my **h** despised reproof; 3820
6:14 Frowardness *is* in his **h**, he deviseth 3820
6:18 A **h** that deviseth wicked imaginations, 3820
6:21 Bind them continually upon thine **h**, *and* 3820
6:25 Lust not after her beauty in thine **h**; 3824

Pr 7: 3 write them upon the table of thine **h**. 3820
7:10 *with* the attire of a harlot, and subtil of **h**. 3820
7:25 Let not thine **h** decline to her ways, go not 3820
8: 5 and, ye fools, be ye of an understanding **h**. 3820
10: 8 The wise in **h** will receive commandments: 3820
10:20 the **h** of the wicked *is* little worth. 3820
11:20 *They that are* of a froward **h** *are* 3820
11:29 the fool *shall be* servant to the wise of **h**. 3820
12: 8 he that is of a perverse **h** shall be despised. 3820
12:20 Deceit *is* in the **h** of them that imagine evil: 3820
12:23 but the **h** of fools proclaimeth foolishness. 3820
12:25 Heaviness in the **h** of man maketh it stoop: 3820
13:12 Hope deferred maketh the **h** sick: but 3820
14:10 The **h** knoweth his own bitterness; and 3820
14:13 Even in laughter the **h** is sorrowful; and 3820
14:14 The backslider in **h** shall be filled with his 3820
14:30 A sound **h** *is* the life of the flesh: but 3820
14:33 Wisdom resteth in the **h** of him that hath 3820
15: 7 but the **h** of the foolish *doeth* not so. 3820
15:13 A merry **h** maketh a cheerful countenance: 3820
15:13 but by sorrow of the **h** the spirit *is* broken. 3820
15:14 The **h** of him that hath understanding 3820
15:15 *he that is* of a merry **h** *hath* a continual 3820
15:28 The **h** of the righteous studieth to answer: 3820
15:30 The light of the eyes rejoiceth the **h**: *and* 3820
16: 1 The preparations of the **h** in man, and 3820
16: 5 Every one *that is* proud in **h** *is* an 3820
16: 9 A man's **h** deviseth his way: but 3820
16:21 The wise in **h** shall be called prudent: and 3820
16:23 The **h** of the wise teacheth his mouth, and 3820
17:16 to get wisdom, seeing *he hath* no **h** *to it?* 3820
17:20 He that hath a froward **h** findeth no good: 3820
17:22 A merry **h** doeth good *like* a medicine: but 3820
18: 2 but that his **h** may discover itself. 3820
18:12 Before destruction the **h** of man is haughty, 3820
18:15 The **h** of the prudent getteth knowledge; 3820
19: 3 and his **h** fretteth against the LORD. 3820
19:21 *There are* many devices in a man's **h**; 3820
20: 5 Counsel in the **h** of man *is like* deep water; 3820
20: 9 Who can say, I have made my **h** clean, I am 3820
21: 1 The king's **h** *is* in the hand of the LORD, 3820
21: 4 a proud **h**, *and* the plowing of the wicked, 3820
22:11 He that loveth pureness of **h**, *for* the grace 3820
22:15 Foolishness *is* bound in the **h** of a child; *but* 3820
22:17 and apply thine **h** unto my knowledge. 3820
23: 7 For as he thinketh in his **h**, so *is* he: Eat and 5315
23: 7 saith he to thee; but his **h** *is* not with thee. 3820
23:12 Apply thine **h** unto instruction, and 3820
23:15 My son, if thine **h** be wise, my heart shall 3820
23:15 be wise, my **h** shall rejoice, even mine. 3820
23:17 Let not thine **h** envy sinners: but *be thou* in 3820
23:19 and be wise, and guide thine **h** in the way. 3820
23:26 give me thine **h**, and let thine eyes observe 3820
23:33 and thine **h** shall utter perverse things. 3820
24: 2 For their **h** studieth destruction, and 3820
24:12 doth not he that pondereth the **h** consider 3826
24:17 let not thine **h** be glad when he stumbleth: 3820
25: 3 and the **h** of kings *is* unsearchable. 3820
25:20 so *is* he that singeth songs to a heavy **h**. 3820
26:23 a wicked **h** *are like* a potsherd covered with 3820
26:25 for *there are* seven abominations in his **h**. 3820
27: 9 Ointment and perfume rejoice the **h**: so 3820
27:11 My son, be wise, and make my **h** glad, 3820
27:19 *answereth* to face, so the **h** of man to man. 3820
28:14 he that hardeneth his **h** shall fall into 3820
28:25 He that is of a proud **h** stirreth up strife: but 5315
28:26 He that trusteth in his own **h** *is* a fool: but 3820
31:11 The **h** of her husband doth *safely* trust in 3820
Ecc 1:13 I gave my **h** to seek and search out by 3820
1:16 I communed with mine own **h**, saying, Lo, 3820
1:16 my **h** had great experience of wisdom and 3820
1:17 I gave my **h** to know wisdom, and to know 3820
2: 1 I said in mine **h**, Go to now, I will prove 3820
2: 3 I sought in mine **h** to give myself unto 3820
2: 3 (yet acquainting mine **h** with wisdom) 3820
2:10 I withheld not my **h** from any joy; 3820
2:10 any joy; for my **h** rejoiced in all my labour: 3820
2:15 said I in my **h**, As it happeneth to the fool, 3820
2:15 Then I said in my **h**, that this also *is* vanity. 3820
2:20 Therefore I went about to cause my **h** to 3820
2:22 all his labour, and of the vexation of his **h**, 3820
2:23 yea, his **h** taketh not rest in the night. 3820
3:11 also he hath set the world in their **h**, so that 3820
3:17 I said in mine **h**, God shall judge 3820
3:18 I said in my **h** concerning the estate of 3820
5: 2 let not thine **h** be hasty to utter *any* thing 3820
5:20 God answereth *him* in the joy of his **h**. 3820
7: 2 all men; and the living will lay *it* to his **h**. 3820
7: 3 for by the sadness of the countenance the **h** 3820
7: 4 The **h** of the wise *is* in the house of 3820
7: 4 but the **h** of fools *is* in the house of mirth. 3820
7: 7 wise *man* mad; and a gift destroyeth the **h**. 3820
7:22 For oftentimes also thine own **h** knoweth 3820
7:25 I applied mine **h** to know, and to search, 3820
7:26 whose **h** *is* snares and nets, *and* her hands 3820
8: 5 a wise *man's* **h** discerneth *both* time and 3820
8: 9 applied my **h** unto every work that is done 3820
8:11 the **h** of the sons of men is fully set in them 3820
8:16 When I applied mine **h** to know wisdom, 3820
9: 1 For all this I considered in my **h** even to 3820
9: 3 also the **h** of the sons of men is full *of* evil, 3820
9: 3 madness *is* in their **h** while they live, and 3824
9: 7 and drink thy wine with a merry **h**; 3820
10: 2 A wise *man's* **h** *is* at his right hand; but 3820
10: 2 *is* at his right hand; but a fool's **h** at his left. 3820
11: 9 let thy **h** cheer thee in the days of thy 3820
11: 9 walk in the ways of thine **h**, and in the sight 3820
11:10 Therefore remove sorrow from thy **h**, and 3820
SS 3:11 and in the day of the gladness of his **h**. 3820
4: 9 Thou hast **ravished** my **h**, my sister, 3823
4: 9 thou hast **ravished** my **h** with one of thine 3823
5: 2 I sleep, but my **h** waketh: *it is* the voice of 3820
8: 6 Set me as a seal upon thine **h**, as a seal 3820
Isa 1: 5 whole head *is* sick, and the whole **h** faint. 3824
6:10 Make the **h** of this people fat, and 3820

Isa 6:10 understand *with* their **h**, and convert, and 3824
7: 2 his **h** was moved, and the heart of his 3824
7: 2 heart was moved, and the **h** of his people, 3824
9: 9 that say in the pride and stoutness of **h**, 3824
10: 7 meaneth not so, neither doth his **h** think so; 3824
10: 7 *it is* in his **h** to destroy and cut off nations 3824
10:12 I will punish the fruit of the stout **h** of 3824
13: 7 be faint, and every man's **h** shall melt: 3824
14:13 For thou hast said in thine **h**, I will ascend 3824
15: 5 My **h** shall cry out for Moab; his fugitives 3820
19: 1 the **h** of Egypt shall melt in the midst of it. 3824
21: 4 My **h** panted, fearfulness affrighted me: 3824
29:13 have removed their **h** far from me, and 3820
30:29 gladness of **h**, as when one goeth with a 3824
32: 4 The **h** also of the rash shall understand 3824
32: 6 his **h** will work iniquity, to practise 3820
33:18 Thine **h** shall meditate terror. Where *is* 3820
35: 4 Say to them that are of a fearful **h**, 3820
38: 3 before thee in truth and with a perfect **h**, 3820
42:25 and it burned him, yet he laid *it* not to **h**. 3820
44:19 none considereth in his **h**, neither *is there* 3820
44:20 a deceived **h** hath turned him aside, that he 3820
47: 7 that thou didst not lay these *things* to thy **h**, 3820
47: 8 that sayest in thine **h**, I *am*, and none else 3824
47:10 thou hast said in thine **h**, I *am*, and 3820
49:21 shalt thou say in thine **h**, Who hath 3824
51: 7 the people in whose **h** *is* my law; 3820
57: 1 and no man layeth *it* to **h**: 3820
57:11 not remembered me, nor laid *it* to thy **h**? 3820
57:15 and to revive the **h** of the contrite ones. 3820
57:17 he went on frowardly in the way of his **h**. 3820
59:13 and uttering from the **h** words of falsehood. 3820
60: 5 flow *together*, and thine **h** shall fear, and 3824
63: 4 For the day of vengeance *is* in mine **h**, and 3820
63:17 *and* hardened our **h** from thy fear? 3820
65:14 my servants shall sing for joy of **h**, but 3820
65:14 ye shall cry for sorrow of **h**, and shall howl 3820
66:14 when ye see *this*, your **h** shall rejoice, and 3820
Jer 3:10 hath not turned unto me with her whole **h**, 3820
3:15 I will give you pastors according to mine **h**, 3820
3:17 more after the imagination of their evil **h**. 3820
4: 4 take away the foreskins of your **h**, ye men 3824
4: 9 *that* the **h** of the king shall perish, and 3820
4: 9 king shall perish, and the **h** of the princes; 3820
4:14 wash thine **h** from wickedness, 3820
4:18 *it is* bitter, because it reacheth unto thine **h**. 3820
4:19 I am pained *at* my **very h**; I am pained *at my* heart 3820+7023
4:19 my **h** maketh a noise in me; I cannot hold 3820
5:23 people hath a revolting and a rebellious **h**; 3820
5:24 Neither say they in their **h**, Let us now fear 3824
7:24 *and* in the imagination of their evil **h**, 3820
7:31 *them* not, neither came it into my **h**. 3820
8:18 myself against sorrow, my **h** *is* faint in me. 3820
9: 8 with his mouth, but in **h** he layeth his wait. 7130
9:14 after the imagination of their own **h**, 3820
9:26 house of Israel *are* uncircumcised in the **h**. 3820
11: 8 every one in the imagination of their evil **h**: 3820
11:20 that triest the reins and the **h**, 3820
12: 3 seen me, and tried mine **h** towards thee: 3820
12:11 because no man layeth *it* to **h**. 3820
13:10 which walk in the imagination of their **h**, 3820
13:22 if thou say in thine **h**, Wherefore come 3824
14:14 a thing of nought, and the deceit of their **h**. 3820
15:16 unto me the joy and rejoicing of mine **h**: 3824
16:12 one after the imagination of his evil **h**, 3820
17: 1 *it is* graven upon the table of their **h**, and 3820
17: 5 and whose **h** departeth from the LORD. 3820
17: 9 The **h** *is* deceitful above all *things*, and 3820
17:10 I the LORD search the **h**, *I* try the reins, 3820
18:12 every one do the imagination of his evil **h**. 3820
20: 9 *his word* was in mine **h** as a burning fire 3820
20:12 the righteous, *and* seest the reins and the **h**, 3820
22:17 thine eyes and thine **h** *are* not but for thy 3820
23: 9 Mine **h** within me is broken because of 3820
23:16 they speak a vision of their own **h**, *and* 3820
23:17 walketh after the imagination of his own **h**, 3820
23:20 he have performed the thoughts of his **h**: 3820
23:26 How long shall *this* be in the **h** of 3820
23:26 *are* prophets of the deceit of their own **h**; 3820
24: 7 I will give them a **h** to know me, that I *am* 3820
24: 7 shall return unto me with their whole **h**. 3820
29:13 ye shall search for me with all your **h**. 3824
30:21 for who *is* this that engaged his **h** to 3820
30:24 until he have performed the intents of his **h**: 3820
31:21 set thine **h** toward the highway, *even* 3820
32:39 I will give them one **h**, and one way, 3820
32:41 in this land assuredly with my whole **h** 3820
48:29 and his pride, and the haughtiness of his **h**. 3820
48:31 *mine* **h** shall mourn for the men of NIH
48:36 Therefore mine **h** shall sound for Moab like 3820
48:36 mine **h** shall sound like pipes for the men 3820
48:41 shall be as the **h** of a woman in her pangs. 3820
49:16 hath deceived thee, *and* the pride of thine **h**, 3820
49:22 at that day shall the **h** of the mighty *men* of 3820
49:22 Edom be as the **h** of a woman in her pangs. 3820
51:46 lest your **h** faint, and ye fear for the rumour 3824
La 1:20 are troubled; mine **h** is turned within me; 3820
1:22 for my sighs *are* many, and my **h** *is* faint. 3820
2:18 Their **h** cried unto the Lord, O wall of 3820
2:19 pour out thine **h** like water before the face 3820
3:41 Let us lift up our **h** with *our* hands unto 3824
3:51 Mine eye affecteth mine **h** because of all 5315
3:65 Give them sorrow of **h**, thy curse unto 3820
5:15 The joy of our **h** is ceased; our dance is 3820
5:17 For this our **h** is faint; for these *things* our 3820
Eze 3:10 I shall speak unto thee receive in thine **h**, 3824
6: 9 because I am broken with their whorish **h**, 3820
11:19 I will give them one **h**, and I will put a new 3820
11:19 and I will take the stony **h** out of their flesh, 3820
11:19 their flesh, and will give them a **h** of flesh: 3820
11:21 *as for them* whose **h** walketh after the heart 3820
11:21 *as for them* whose heart walketh after the **h** 3820
13:17 which prophesy out of their own **h**; 3820
13:22 Because *with* lies *ye* have made the **h** of 3820
14: 3 these men have set up their idols in their **h**, 3820

Eze 14: 4 of Israel that setteth up his idols in his **h**, 3820
14: 5 may take the house of Israel in their own **h**, 3820
14: 7 setteth up his idols in his **h**, and putteth 3820
16:30 How weak is thine **h**, saith the Lord GOD, 3826
18:31 and make you a new **h** and a new spirit: 3820
20:16 for their **h** went after their idols. 3820
21: 7 every **h** shall melt, and all hands shall be 3820
21:15 that *their* **h** may faint, and *their* ruins be 3820
22:14 Can thine **h** endure, or can thine hands be 3820
25: 6 rejoiced in **h** with all thy despite against 5315
25:15 have taken vengeance with a despiteful **h**, 5315
27:31 they shall weep for thee with bitterness of **h** 5315
28: 2 Because thine **h** *is* lifted up, and thou hast 3820
28: 2 though thou set thine **h** as the heart of God: 3820
28: 2 though thou set thine heart as the **h** of God: 3820
28: 5 thine **h** is lifted up because of thy riches: 3824
28: 6 Because thou hast set thine **h** as the heart of 3824
28: 6 Because thou hast set thine heart as the **h** of 3820
28:17 Thine **h** was lifted up because of thy 3820
31:10 and his **h** is lifted up in his height; 3824
33:31 *but* their **h** goeth after their covetousness. 3820
36: 5 their possession with the joy of all *their* **h**, 3824
36:26 A new **h** also will I give you, and a new 3820
36:26 I will take away the stony **h** out of your 3820
36:26 your flesh, and I will give you a **h** of flesh. 3820
40: 4 set thine **h** upon all that I shall shew thee; 3820
44: 7 uncircumcised in **h**, and uncircumcised in 3820
44: 9 No stranger, uncircumcised in **h**, 3820
Da 1: 8 Daniel purposed in his **h** that he would not 3820
2:30 thou mightest know the thoughts of thy **h**. 3825
4:16 Let his **h** be changed from man's, and let a 3825
4:16 let a beast's **h** be given unto him; 3825
5:20 when his **h** was lifted up, and his mind 3825
5:21 his **h** was made like the beasts, and 3825
5:22 O Belshazzar, hast not humbled thine **h**, 3825
6:14 and set *his* **h** on Daniel to deliver him: 1079
7: 4 as a man, and a man's **h** was given to it. 3825
7:28 in me: but I kept the matter in my **h**. 3821
8:25 he shall magnify *himself* in his **h**, and 3824
10:12 that thou didst set thine **h** to understand, 3820
11:12 away the multitude, his **h** shall be lifted up; 3824
11:28 his **h** *shall be* against the holy covenant; 3824
Hos 4: 8 and they set their **h** on their iniquity. 5315
4:11 and wine and new wine take *away* the **h**. 3820
7: 6 For they have made ready their **h** like an 3820
7:11 Ephraim also is like a silly dove, without **h**: 3820
7:14 they have not cried unto me with their **h**, 3820
10: 2 Their **h** is divided; now shall they be found 3820
11: 8 mine **h** is turned within me, my repentings 3820
13: 6 they were filled, and their **h** was exalted; 3820
13: 8 will rent the caul of their **h**, and there will I 3820
Joel 2:12 turn ye *even* to me with all your **h**, and 3824
2:13 rent your **h**, and not your garments, and 3824
Ob 1: 3 The pride of thine **h** hath deceived thee, 3820
1: 3 that saith in his **h**, Who shall bring me 3820
Na 2:10 the **h** melteth, and the knees smite together, 3820
Zep 1:12 that say in their **h**, The LORD will not do 3824
2:15 that said in her **h**, I *am*, and *there is* none 3824
3:14 be glad and rejoice with all the **h**, 3820
Zec 7:10 imagine evil against his brother in your **h**. 3824
10: 7 and their **h** shall rejoice as *through* wine: 3820
10: 7 be glad; their **h** shall rejoice in the LORD. 3820
12: 5 the governors of Judah shall say in their **h**, 3820
Mal 2: 2 will not hear, and if ye will not lay *it* to **h**, 3820
2: 2 them already, because ye do not lay *it* to **h**. 3820
4: 6 he shall turn the **h** of the fathers to 3820
4: 6 the **h** of the children to their fathers, lest I 3820
Mt 5: 8 Blessed *are* the pure in **h**: for they shall see 2588
5:28 adultery with her already in his **h**. 2588
6:21 your treasure is, there will your **h** be also. 2588
11:29 learn of me; for I am meek and lowly in **h**: 2588
12:34 the abundance of the **h** the mouth speaketh. 2588
12:35 treasure of the **h** bringeth forth good *things:* 2588
12:40 and three nights in the **h** of the earth. 2588
13:15 For this people's **h** is waxed gross, and 2588
13:15 and should understand with *their* **h**, and 2588
13:19 away that which was sown in his **h**. 2588
15: 8 with *their* lips; but their **h** is far from me. 2588
15:18 out of the mouth come forth from the **h**; 2588
15:19 For out of the **h** proceed evil thoughts, 2588
22:37 shalt love the Lord thy God with all thy **h**, 2588
24:48 *and* if that evil servant shall say in his **h**, 2588
Mk 6:52 of the loaves: for their **h** was hardened. 2588
7: 6 with *their* lips, but their **h** is far from me. 2588
7:19 Because it entereth not into his **h**, but 2588
7:21 For from within, out of the **h** of men, 2588
8:17 have ye your **h** yet hardened? 2588
10: 5 For the **hardness of** your **h** he wrote you 4641
11:23 and shall not doubt in his **h**, but 2588
12:30 shalt love the Lord thy God with all thy **h**, 2588
12:33 And to love him with all the **h**, and with all 2588
16:14 them with their unbelief and **hardness of h**, 4641
Lk 2:19 these things, and pondered *them* in her **h**. 2588
2:51 his mother kept all these sayings in her **h**. 2588
6:45 of his **h** bringeth forth that which is good; 2588
6:45 an evil man out of the evil treasure of his **h** 2588
6:45 for of the abundance of the **h** his mouth 2588
8:15 which in an honest and good **h**, 2588
9:47 perceiving the thought of their **h**, 2588
10:27 shalt love the Lord thy God with all thy **h**, 2588
12:34 your treasure is, there will your **h** be also. 2588
12:45 But and if that servant say in his **h**, My lord 2588
24:25 slow of **h** to believe all that the prophets 2588
24:32 to another, Did not our **h** burn within us, 2588
Jn 12:40 blinded their eyes, and hardened their **h**; 2588
12:40 nor understand with *their* **h**, and 2588
13: 2 the devil having now put into the **h** of Judas 2588
14: 1 Let not your **h** be troubled: ye believe in 2588
14:27 Let not your **h** be troubled, neither let it be 2588
16: 6 *things* unto you, sorrow hath filled your **h**. 2588
16:22 and your **h** shall rejoice, and your joy no 2588
Ac 2:26 Therefore did my **h** rejoice, and my tongue 2588
2:37 heard *this,* they were pricked in *their* **h**, 2588
2:46 meat with gladness and singleness of **h**, 2588
4:32 of them that believed were of one **h** 2588

Ac 5: 3 why hath Satan filled thine **h** to lie to 2588
5: 4 hast thou conceived this thing in thine **h**? 2588
5:33 they heard *that,* they were cut *to the h,* NIG
7:23 it came into his **h** to visit his brethren 2588
7:51 and uncircumcised in **h** and ears, 2588
7:54 heard these *things,* they were cut to the **h**, 2588
8:21 for thy **h** is not right in the sight of God. 2588
8:22 if perhaps the thought of thine **h** may be 2588
8:37 If thou believest with all *thine* **h**, 2588
11:23 that with purpose of **h** *they* would cleave 2588
13:22 a man after mine own **h**, which shall fulfil 2588
16:14 heard *us:* whose **h** the Lord opened, 2588
21:13 mean ye to weep and to break mine **h**? 2588
28:27 For the **h** of this people is waxed gross, and 2588
28:27 and understand with *their* **h**, and should be 2588
Ro 1:21 and their foolish **h** was darkened. 2588
2: 5 impenitent **h** treasurest up unto thyself 2588
2:29 and circumcision *is that* of the **h**, in 2588
6:17 ye have obeyed from the **h** *that* form of 2588
9: 2 and continual sorrow in my **h**. 2588
10: 6 Say not in thine **h**, Who shall ascend into 2588
10: 8 nigh thee, *even* in thy mouth, and in thy **h**: 2588
10: 9 shalt believe in thine **h** that God hath raised 2588
10:10 For with the **h** *man* believeth unto 2588
1Co 2: 9 neither have entered into the **h** of man, 2588
7:37 he that standeth stedfast in *his* **h**, 2588
7:37 decreed in his **h** that *he* will keep his virgin, 2588
14:25 And thus are the secrets of his **h** made 2588
2Co 2: 4 anguish of **h** I wrote unto you with many 2588
3: 3 tables of stone, but in fleshy tables of the **h**. 2588
3:15 Moses is read, the vail is upon their **h**. 2588
5:12 which glory in appearance, and not in **h**. 2588
6:11 mouth is open unto you, our **h** is enlarged. 2588
8:16 which put the same earnest care into the **h** 2588
9: 7 man according as he purposeth in *his* **h**, 2588
Eph 4:18 in them, because of the blindness of their **h**: 2588
5:19 and making melody in your **h** to the Lord; 2588
6: 5 and trembling, in singleness of your **h**, 2588
6: 6 of Christ, doing the will of God from the **h**; 5590
Php 1: 7 this of you all, because I have you in *my* **h**; 2588
Col 3:22 but in singleness of **h**, fearing God: 2588
1Th 2:17 you for a short time in presence, not in **h**, 2588
1Ti 1: 5 commandment is charity out of a pure **h**, 2588
2Ti 2:22 them that call on the Lord out of a pure **h**. 2588
Heb 3:10 and said, They do alway err in *their* **h**; 2588
3:12 lest there be in any of you an evil **h** of 2588
4:12 of the thoughts and intents of the **h**. 2588
10:22 Let us draw near with a true **h** in full 2588
13: 9 For *it is* a good *thing* that the **h** be 2588
Jas 1:26 not his tongue, but deceiveth his own **h**, 2588
1Pe 1:22 *see that ye* love one another with a pure **h** 2588
3: 4 But *let it be* the hidden man of the **h**, in *that* 2588
2Pe 2:14 a **h** they have exercised with covetous 2588
1Jn 3:20 For if *our* **h** condemn us, God is greater 2588
3:20 God is greater than our **h**, and knoweth all 2588
3:21 if our **h** condemn us not, *then* have we 2588
Rev 18: 7 for she saith in her **h**, I sit a queen, and 2588

HEART'S (4) [HEART]

Ps 10: 3 For the wicked boasteth of his **h** desire, and 5315
21: 2 Thou hast given him his **h** desire, and 3820
81:12 So I gave them up unto their own **h** lust: 3820
Ro 10: 1 my **h** desire and prayer to God for Israel is, 2588

HEARTED (10) [HEART]

Ex 28: 3 thou shalt speak unto all *that are* wise **h**, 3820
31: 6 in the hearts of all that are wise **h** I have put 3820
35:10 every wise **h** among you shall come, and 3820
35:22 as many as were willing **h**, *and* 3820
35:25 all the women that were wise **h** did spin 3820
36: 1 and Aholiab, and every wise **h** man, 3820
36: 2 and Aholiab, and every wise **h** man, 3820
36: 8 every wise **h** *man* among them that 3820
2Ch 13: 7 when Rehoboam was young and tender **h**, 3824
Eze 2: 4 For *they are* impudent children and stiff **h**. 3820

HEARTH (7)

Ge 18: 6 knead *it,* and make cakes upon the **h**. NIH
Ps 102: 3 like smoke, and my bones are burnt as a **h**. 4168
Isa 30:14 of it a sheard to take fire from the **h**, 3344
Jer 36:22 *there was a fire on* the **h** burning before him. 254
36:23 cast *it* into the fire that *was* on the **h**, 254
36:23 was consumed in the fire that *was* on the **h**. 254
Zec 12: 6 of Judah like a **h** of fire among the wood, 3595

HEARTILY (1) [HEARTY]

Col 3:23 **h**, as to the Lord, and not unto men; 1537+5590

HEARTS (112) [HEART]

Ge 18: 5 a morsel of bread, and comfort ye your **h**; 3820
Ex 14:17 I will harden the **h** of the Egyptians, and 3820
31: 6 in the **h** of all that are wise hearted I have 3820
Lev 26:36 into their **h** in the lands of their enemies; 3824
26:41 if then their uncircumcised **h** be humbled, 3824
Dt 20: 3 let not your **h** faint, fear not, and do not 3824
32:46 Set your **h** unto all the words which I 3824
Jos 2:11 as soon as we had heard *these things,* our **h** 3824
7: 5 wherefore the **h** of the people melted, and 3824
11:20 For it was of the LORD to harden their **h**, 3820
23:14 ye know in all your **h** and in all your souls, 3824
Jdg 9: 3 their **h** inclined to follow Abimelech; 3820
16:25 when their **h** were merry, that they said, 3820
19:22 *Now* as they were making their **h** merry, 3820
1Sa 6: 6 Wherefore then do ye harden your **h**, as 3824
6: 6 and Pharaoh hardened their **h**? 3820
7: 3 do return unto the LORD with all your **h**, 3824
7: 3 prepare your **h** unto the LORD, and 3824
10:26 a band of men, whose **h** God had touched, 3820
2Sa 15: 6 so Absalom stole the **h** of the men of Israel. 3820
15:13 The **h** of the men of Israel are after 3820
1Ki 8:39 knowest the **h** of all the children of men;) 3824
8:58 That *he* may incline our **h** unto him, 3824
1Ch 28: 9 for the LORD searcheth all **h**, and 3824
2Ch 6:14 that walk before thee with all their **h**: 3820

2Ch 6:30 (for thou only knowest the **h** of the children 3824
11:16 **h** to seek the LORD God of Israel came *to* 3824
20:33 their **h** unto the God of their fathers. 3824
Job 1: 5 have sinned, and cursed God in their **h**. 3824
Ps 7: 9 for the righteous God trieth the **h** and reins. 3826
28: 3 their neighbours, but mischief *is* in their **h**. 3824
33:15 He fashioneth their **h** alike; he considereth 3820
35:25 Let them not say in their **h**, Ah, so 3820
74: 8 They said in their **h**, Let us destroy them 3820
90:12 that we may apply *our* **h** *unto* wisdom. 3824
125: 4 and to *them that are* upright in their **h**. 3826
Pr 15:11 then the **h** of the children of men? 3826
17: 3 for gold: but the LORD trieth the **h**. 3826
21: 2 own eyes: but the LORD pondereth the **h**. 3826
31: 6 and wine unto those that be of heavy **h**. 5315
Isa 44:18 *and* their **h**, that *they* cannot understand. 3826
Jer 31:33 in their inward parts, and write it in their **h**; 3820
32:40 I will put my fear in their **h**, that *they* shall 3824
42:20 For ye dissembled in your **h**, when ye sent 5315
48:41 the mighty *men's* **h** in Moab at that day 3820
Eze 13: 2 unto them that prophesy out of their own **h**, 3820
32: 9 I will also vex the **h** of many people, 3820
Da 11:27 both these kings' **h** *shall be* to do mischief, 3824
Hos 7: 2 they consider not in their **h** *that* I remember 3824
Zec 7:12 they made their **h** *as* an adamant stone, 3820
8:17 let none of you imagine evil in your **h** 3824
Mt 9: 4 Wherefore think ye evil in your **h**? 2588
18:35 if ye from your **h** forgive not every one his 2588
19: 8 of the **hardness of** your **h** suffered you to 4641
Mk 2: 6 sitting there, and reasoning in their **h**, 2588
2: 8 Why reason ye these *things* in your **h**? 2588
3: 5 being grieved for the hardness of their **h**, 2588
4:15 away the word that was sown in their **h**. 2588
Lk 1:17 to turn the **h** of the fathers to the children, 2588
1:51 the proud in the imagination of their **h**. 2588
1:66 that heard *them* laid *them* up in their **h**, 2588
2:35 that the thoughts of many **h** may be 2588
3:15 and all *men* mused in their **h** of John, 2588
5:22 said unto them, What reason ye in your **h**? 2588
8:12 and taketh away the word out of their **h**, 2588
16:15 before men; but God knoweth your **h**. 2588
21:14 Settle *it* therefore in your **h**, not to meditate 2588
21:26 Men's **h failing** them for fear, and 674
21:34 lest at any time your **h** be overcharged with 2588
24:38 and why do thoughts arise in your **h**? 2588
Ac 1:24 which **knowest** the **h** of all *men,* shew 2589
7:39 and in their **h** turned *back again* into Egypt, 2588
14:17 filling our **h** with food and gladness. 2588
15: 8 And God, which **knoweth** the **h**, bare them 2589
15: 9 and them, purifying their **h** by faith. 2588
Ro 1:24 through the lusts of their own **h**, 2588
2:15 shew the work of the law written in their **h**, 2588
5: 5 the love of God is shed abroad in our **h** by 2588
8:27 And he that searcheth the **h** knoweth what 2588
16:18 fair speeches deceive the **h** of the simple. 2588
1Co 4: 5 will make manifest the counsels of the **h**: 2588
2Co 1:22 and given the earnest of the Spirit in our **h**. 2588
3: 2 Ye are our epistle written in our **h**, known 2588
4: 6 shine out of darkness, hath shined in our **h**, 2588
7: 3 that you are in our **h** to die and live with 2588
Gal 4: 6 sent forth the Spirit of his Son into your **h**, 2588
Eph 3:17 That Christ may dwell in your **h** by faith; 2588
6:22 and *that* he might comfort your **h**. 2588
Php 4: 7 shall keep your **h** and minds through Christ 2588
Col 2: 2 That their **h** might be comforted, being knit 2588
3:15 And let the peace of God rule in your **h**, 2588
3:16 singing with grace in your **h** to the Lord. 2588
4: 8 know your estate, and comfort your **h**; 2588
1Th 2: 4 pleasing men, but God, which trieth our **h**. 2588
3:13 To the end *he* may stablish your **h** 2588
2Th 2:17 Comfort your **h**, and stablish you in every 2588
3: 5 And the Lord direct your **h** into the love of 2588
Heb 3: 8 Harden not your **h**, as in the provocation, 2588
3:15 harden not your **h**, as in the provocation. 2588
4: 7 if ye will hear his voice, harden not your **h**. 2588
8:10 into their mind, and write them in their **h**: 2588
10:16 I will put my laws into their **h**, and in their 2588
10:22 having *our* **h** sprinkled from an evil 2588
Jas 3:14 ye have bitter envying and strife in your **h**, 2588
4: 8 and purify *your* **h**, *ye* double minded. 2588
5: 5 ye have nourished your **h**, as in a day of 2588
5: 8 Be ye also patient; stablish your **h**: for 2588
1Pe 3:15 But sanctify the Lord God in your **h**: and 2588
2Pe 1:19 day dawn, and the day star arise in your **h**: 2588
1Jn 3:19 the truth, and shall assure our **h** before him. 2588
Rev 2:23 I am he which searcheth the reins and **h**: 2588
17:17 For God hath put in their **h** to fulfil his will, 2588

HEARTY (1) [HEARTILY]

Pr 27: 9 *doth* the sweetness of a man's friend by **h** 5315

HEAT (33) [HEATED]

Ge 8:22 cold and **h**, and summer and winter, and 2527
18: 1 he sat *in* the tent door in the **h** of the day; 2527
Dt 29:24 what *meaneth* the **h** of this great anger? 2750
32:24 devoured with **burning h**, and with bitter 7565
1Sa 11:11 slew the Ammonites until the **h** of the day: 2527
2Sa 4: 5 came about the **h** of the day to the house of 2527
1Ki 1: 1 covered him with clothes, but he **gat** no **h**. 3179
1: 2 that my lord the king may **get h**. 2552
Job 24:19 Drought and **h** consume the snow waters: 2527
30:30 upon me, and my bones are burnt with **h**. 2721
Ps 19: 6 and there is nothing hid from the **h** thereof. 2535
Ecc 4:11 if two lie together, then they **have h**: 2552
Isa 4: 6 for a shadow in the daytime from the **h**, 2721
18: 4 dwelling place like a clear **h** upon herbs, 2527
18: 4 *and* like a cloud of dew in the **h** of harvest. 2527
25: 4 from the storm, a shadow from the **h**, 2721
25: 5 noise of strangers, as the **h** in a dry place; 2721
25: 5 *even* the **h** with the shadow of a cloud: 2721
49:10 neither shall the **h** nor sun smite them: 8273
Jer 17: 8 shall not see when **h** cometh, but her leaf 2527
36:30 body shall be cast out in the day to the **h**, 2721
51:39 In their **h** I will make their feasts, and I will 2527
Eze 3:14 I went in bitterness, in the **h** of my spirit; 2534

H

Da 3:19 commanded that *they* should **h** the furnace 228
3:19 seven *times* more than *it was* wont to be **h**. 228
Mt 20:12 have borne the burden and **h** of the day. 2742
Lk 12:55 south wind blow, ye say, There will be **h**; 2742
Ac 28: 3 there came a viper out of the **h**, and 2329
Jas 1:11 sun is no sooner risen with a **burning h**, 2742
2Pe 3:10 and the elements shall melt with **fervent h**, 2741
3:12 and the elements shall melt with **fervent h**? 2741
Rev 7:16 shall the sun light on them, nor any **h**. 2738
16: 9 And men were scorched *with* great **h**, and 2738

HEATED (1) [HEAT]

Hos 7: 4 all adulterers, as an oven **h** by the baker, 1197

HEATH (2)

Jer 17: 6 For he shall be like the **h** in the desert, and 6199
48: 6 and be like the **h** in the wilderness. 6176

HEATHEN (150)

Lev 25:44 *shall be* of the **h** that *are* round about you; 1471
26:33 I will scatter you among the **h**, and 1471
26:38 ye shall perish among the **h**, and the land of 1471
26:45 of the land of Egypt in the sight of the **h**, 1471
Dt 4:27 ye shall be left few in number among the **h**, 1471
2Sa 22:44 thou hast kept me to be head of the **h**: 1471
22:50 among the **h**, and I will sing praises unto 1471
2Ki 16: 3 according to the abominations of the **h**, 1471
17: 8 walked in the statutes of the **h**, whom 1471
17:11 as *did* the **h** whom the LORD carried 1471
17:15 *went* after the **h** that *were* round about 1471
21: 2 after the abominations of the **h**, whom 1471
1Ch 16:24 Declare his glory among the **h**; 1471
16:35 us together, and deliver us from the **h**, 1471
2Ch 20: 6 *not* thou over all the kingdoms of the **h**? 1471
28: 3 **h** whom the LORD had cast out before 1471
33: 2 like unto the abominations of the **h**, 1471
33: 9 to err, *and* to do worse than the **h**, 1471
36:14 much after all the abominations of the **h**; 1471
Ezr 6:21 from the filthiness of the **h** of the land, 1471
Ne 5: 8 the Jews, which were sold unto the **h**; 1471
5: 9 of the reproach of the **h** our enemies? 1471
5:17 unto us from among the **h** that *are* about us. 1471
6: 6 *It is* reported among the **h**, and 1471
6:16 all the **h** that *were* about us saw *these* 1471
Ps 2: 1 Why do the **h** rage, and the people imagine 1471
2: 8 I shall give *thee* the **h** *for* thine inheritance, 1471
9: 5 Thou hast rebuked the **h**, thou hast 1471
9:15 The **h** are sunk down in the pit *that* they 1471
9:19 let the **h** be judged in thy sight. 1471
10:16 and ever: the **h** are perished out of his land. 1471
18:43 *and* thou hast made me the head of the **h**: 1471
18:49 among the **h**, and sing *praises* unto thy 1471
33:10 The LORD bringeth the counsel of the **h** 1471
44: 2 *How* thou didst drive out the **h** *with* thy 1471
44:11 and hast scattered us among the **h**. 1471
44:14 Thou makest us a byword among the **h**, 1471
46: 6 The **h** raged, the kingdoms were moved: 1471
46:10 I will be exalted among the **h**, I will be 1471
47: 8 God reigneth over the **h**: God sitteth upon 1471
59: 5 the God of Israel, awake to visit all the **h**: 1471
59: 8 thou shalt have all the **h** in derision. 1471
78:55 He cast out the **h** also before them, and 1471
79: 1 the **h** are come into thine inheritance; 1471
79: 6 Pour out thy wrath upon the **h** that have not 1471
79:10 Wherefore should the **h** say, Where *is* their 1471
79:10 let him be known among the **h** in our sight 1471
80: 8 thou hast cast out the **h**, and planted it. 1471
94:10 He that chastiseth the **h**, shall not he 1471
96: 3 Declare his glory among the **h**, his wonders 1471
96:10 Say among the **h** *that* the LORD reigneth: 1471
98: 2 hath he openly shewed in the sight of the **h**. 1471
102:15 So the **h** shall fear the name of the LORD, 1471
105:44 gave them the lands of the **h**: and 1471
106:35 were mingled among the **h**, and 1471
106:41 he gave them into the hand of the **h**; and 1471
106:47 our God, and gather us from among the **h**, 1471
110: 6 He shall judge among the **h**, he shall fill 1471
111: 6 that *he* may give them the heritage of the **h**. 1471
115: 2 Wherefore should the **h** say, Where *is* now 1471
126: 2 said they among the **h**, The LORD hath 1471
135:15 The idols of the **h** *are* silver and gold, 1471
149: 7 To execute vengeance upon the **h**, *and* 1471
Isa 16: 8 the lords of the **h** have broken down 1471
Jer 9:16 I will scatter them also among the **h**, 1471
10: 2 Learn not the way of the **h**, and be not 1471
10: 2 of heaven; for the **h** are dismayed at them. 1471
10:25 Pour out thy fury upon the **h** that know thee 1471
18:13 Ask ye now among the **h**, who hath heard 1471
49:14 an ambassador *is* sent unto the **h**, 1471
49:15 I will make thee small among the **h**, *and* 1471
La 1: 3 she dwelleth among the **h**, she findeth no 1471
1:10 for she hath seen *that* the **h** entered into her 1471
4:15 they said among the **h**, They shall no more 1471
4:20 his shadow we shall live among the **h**. 1471
Eze 7:24 Wherefore I will bring the worst of the **h**, 1471
11:12 have done after the manners of the **h** that 1471
11:16 I have cast them far off among the **h**, 1471
12:16 among the **h** whither they come; 1471
16:14 thy renown went forth among the **h** for thy 1471
20: 9 that *it* should not be polluted before the **h**, 1471
20:14 that *it* should not be polluted before the **h**, 1471
20:22 should not be polluted in the sight of the **h**, 1471
20:23 that *I* would scatter them among the **h**, and 1471
20:32 that ye say, We will be as the **h**, as 1471
20:41 and I will be sanctified in you before the **h**. 1471
22: 4 have I made thee a reproach unto the **h**, 1471
22:15 I will scatter thee among the **h**, and 1471
22:16 inheritance in thyself in the sight of the **h**, 1471
23:30 thou hast gone a whoring after the **h**, 1471
25: 7 and will deliver thee for a spoil to the **h**; 1471
25: 8 the house of Judah *is* like unto all the **h**; 1471
28:25 be sanctified in them in the sight of the **h**, 1471
30: 3 a cloudy day; it shall be the time of the **h**. 1471
31:11 into the hand of the mighty one of the **h**; 1471
Eze 31:17 under his shadow in the midst of the **h**. 1471
34:28 they shall no more be a prey to the **h**, 1471
34:29 neither bear the shame of the **h** any more. 1471
36: 3 be a possession unto the residue of the **h**, 1471
36: 4 derision to the residue of the **h** that *are* 1471
36: 5 have I spoken against the residue of the **h**, 1471
36: 6 because ye have borne the shame of the **h**: 1471
36: 7 mine hand, Surely the **h** that *are* about you, 1471
36:15 to hear in thee the shame of the **h** any more, 1471
36:19 I scattered them among the **h**, and 1471
36:20 when they entered unto the **h**, whither they 1471
36:21 house of Israel had profaned among the **h**, 1471
36:22 which ye have profaned among the **h**, 1471
36:23 which was profaned among the **h**, 1471
36:23 the **h** shall know that I *am* the LORD, 1471
36:24 For I will take you from among the **h**, and 1471
36:30 no more reproach of famine among the **h**. 1471
36:36 the **h** that are left round about you shall 1471
37:21 the children of Israel from among the **h**, 1471
37:28 the **h** shall know that I the LORD do 1471
38:16 against my land, that the **h** may know me, 1471
39: 7 the **h** shall know that I *am* the LORD, 1471
39:21 I will set my glory among the **h**, and all 1471
39:21 all the **h** shall see my judgment that I have 1471
39:23 the **h** shall know that the house of Israel 1471
39:28 them to be led into captivity among the **h**: 1471
Joel 2:17 that the **h** should rule over them: 1471
2:19 no more make you a reproach among the **h**: 1471
3:11 all ye **h**, and gather yourselves together 1471
3:12 Let the **h** be wakened, and come up to 1471
3:12 for there will I sit to judge all the **h** round 1471
Am 9:12 of all the **h**, which are called by my name, 1471
Ob 1: 1 an ambassador is sent among the **h**, 1471
1: 2 I have made thee small among the **h**: 1471
1:15 day of the LORD *is* near upon all the **h**: 1471
1:16 *so* shall all the **h** drink continually, yea, 1471
Mic 5:15 vengeance in anger and fury upon the **h**, 1471
Hab 1: 5 Behold ye among the **h**, and regard, and 1471
3:12 thou didst thresh the **h** in anger. 1471
Zep 2:11 from his place, *even* all the isles of the **h**. 1471
Hag 2:22 the strength of the kingdoms of the **h**; 1471
Zec 1:15 I am very sore displeased with the **h** *that* 1471
8:13 *that* as ye were a curse among the **h**, 1471
9:10 he shall speak peace unto the **h**: and 1471
14:14 the wealth of all the **h** round about shall be 1471
14:18 where*with* the LORD will smite the **h** that 1471
Mal 1:11 for my name *shall be* great among the **h**, 1471
1:14 and my name *is* dreadful among the **h**. 1471
Mt 6: 7 as the **h** *do*: for they think that they shall be 1482
18:17 let him be unto thee as a **h** *man* and 1482
Ac 4:25 Why did the **h** rage, and the people 1484
2Co 11:26 *in* perils by the **h**, *in* perils in the city, 1484
Gal 1:16 that I might preach him among the **h**; 1484
2: 9 that we *should go* unto the **h**, and they unto 1484
3: 8 foreseeing that God would justify the **h** 1484

HEAVE (29) [HEAVED]

Ex 29:27 the shoulder of the **h offering**, which is 8641
29:28 for it *is* a **h offering**: and it shall be a heave 8641
29:28 it shall be a **h offering** from the children of 8641
29:28 *even* their **h offering** unto the LORD. 8641
Lev 7:14 oblation *for* a **h offering** unto the LORD, 8641
7:32 **h offering** of the sacrifices of your peace 8641
7:34 the **h** shoulder have I taken of the children 8641
10:14 and **h** shoulder shall ye eat in a clean place; 8641
10:15 The **h** shoulder and the wave breast shall 8641
Nu 6:20 with the wave breast and **h** shoulder: 8641
15:19 ye shall offer up a **h offering** unto 8641
15:20 *of* the first of your dough *for* a **h offering**: 8641
15:20 as *ye do* the **h offering** of 8641
15:20 of the threshingfloor, so shall ye **h** it. 7311
15:21 LORD a **h offering** in your generations. 8641
18: 8 **h offerings** of all the hallowed *things* of 8641
18:11 the **h offering** of their gift, with all 8641
18:19 All the **h offerings** of the holy *things*, 8641
18:24 which they offer *as* a **h offering** unto 8641
18:26 ye shall offer up a **h offering** of it for 8641
18:27 *this* your **h offering** shall be reckoned unto 8641
18:28 Thus you also shall offer a **h offering** unto 8641
18:28 LORD'S **h offering** to Aaron the priest. 8641
18:29 shall offer every **h offering** of the LORD, 8641
31:29 the priest, *for* a **h offering** of the LORD. 8641
31:41 *which was* the LORD'S **h offering**, 8641
Dt 12: 6 **h offerings** of your hand, and your vows, 8641
12:11 the **h offering** of your hand, and all your 8641
12:17 or **h offering** of thine hand: 8641

HEAVED (3) [HEAVE]

Ex 29:27 which is waved, and which is **h up**, of 7311
Nu 18:30 When ye have **h** the best thereof from it, 7311
18:32 of it, when ye have **h** from it the best of it: 7311

HEAVEN (582) [HEAVEN'S, HEAVENLY, HEAVENS]

Ge 1: 1 In the beginning God created the **h** and 8064
1: 8 God called the firmament **H**. And 8064
1: 9 Let the waters under the **h** be gathered 8064
1:14 Let there be lights in the firmament of the **h** 8064
1:15 of the **h** to give light upon the earth: 8064
1:17 God set them in the firmament of the **h** to 8064
1:20 above the earth in the open firmament of **h**. 8064
6:17 wherein *is* the breath of life, from under **h**; 8064
7:11 and the windows of **h** were opened. 8064
7:19 that *were* under the whole **h**, were covered. 8064
7:23 the creeping things, and the fowl of the **h**; 8064
8: 2 and the windows of **h** were stopped, 8064
8: 2 and the rain from **h** was restrained; 8064
11: 4 and a tower, whose top *may reach* unto **h**; 8064
14:19 most high God, possessor of **h** and earth: 8064
14:22 high God, the possessor of **h** and earth, 8064
15: 5 Look now towards **h**, and tell the stars, 8064
19:24 and fire from the LORD out of **h**; 8064
21:17 the angel of God called to Hagar out of **h**, 8064
22:11 of the LORD called unto him out of **h**, 8064
22:15 unto Abraham out of **h** the second time, 8064
Ge 22:17 I will multiply thy seed as the stars of the **h**, 8064
24: 3 the God of **h**, and the God of the earth, 8064
24: 7 The LORD God of **h**, which took me from 8064
26: 4 make thy seed to multiply as the stars of **h**, 8064
27:28 Therefore God give thee of the dew of **h**, 8064
27:39 the earth, and of the dew of **h** from above; 8064
28:12 on the earth, and the top of it reached to **h**: 8064
28:17 the house of God, and this *is* the gate of **h**. 8064
49:25 who shall bless thee *with* blessings of **h** 8064
Ex 9: 8 let Moses sprinkle it towards the **h** in 8064
9:10 Moses sprinkled it *up* toward **h**; and 8064
9:22 Stretch forth thine hand toward **h**, 8064
9:23 Moses stretched forth his rod toward **h**: 8064
10:21 Stretch out thine hand toward **h**, 8064
10:22 Moses stretched forth his hand toward **h**; 8064
16: 4 Behold, I will rain bread from **h** for you; 8064
17:14 the remembrance of Amalek from under **h**. 8064
20: 4 any likeness *of any thing* that *is* in **h** above, 8064
20:11 For *in* six days the LORD made **h** and 8064
20:22 seen that I have talked with you from **h**. 8064
24:10 as it were the body of **h** in *his* clearness. 8064
31:17 for *in* six days the LORD made **h** and 8064
32:13 I will multiply your seed as the stars of **h**, 8064
Lev 26:19 I will make your **h** as iron, and your earth 8064
Dt 1:10 you *are this* day as the stars of **h** for 8064
1:28 the cities *are* great and walled up to **h**; and 8064
2:25 upon the nations *that are* under the whole **h**, 8064
3:24 for what God *is there* in **h** or in earth, 8064
4:11 burnt with fire unto the midst of **h**, 8064
4:19 lest thou lift up thine eyes unto **h**, and 8064
4:19 and the stars, *even* all the host of **h**, 8064
4:19 divided unto all nations under the whole **h**. 8064
4:26 I call **h** and earth to witness against you *this* 8064
4:32 *ask* from the one side of **h** unto the other, 8064
4:36 Out of **h** he made thee to hear his voice, 8064
4:39 that the LORD he *is* God in **h** above, and 8064
5: 8 any likeness *of any thing* that *is* in **h** above, 8064
7:24 thou shalt destroy their name from under **h**: 8064
9: 1 than thyself, cities great and fenced up to **h**, 8064
9:14 and blot out their name from under **h**: 8064
10:14 the **h** and the heaven of heavens *is* 8064
10:14 the **h** of heavens *is* the LORD'S thy God, 8064
10:22 made thee as the stars of **h** for multitude. 8064
11:11 valleys, *and* drinketh water of the rain of **h**: 8064
11:17 he shut up the **h**, that there be no rain, and 8064
11:21 give them, as the days of **h** upon the earth. 8064
17: 3 the sun, or moon, or any of the host of **h**, 8064
25:19 the remembrance of Amalek from under **h**; 8064
26:15 from **h**, and bless thy people Israel, and 8064
28:12 the **h** to give the rain unto thy land in his 8064
28:23 thy **h** that *is* over thy head shall be brass, 8064
28:24 from **h** shall it come down upon thee, 8064
28:62 whereas ye were as the stars of **h** for 8064
29:20 shall blot out his name from under **h**. 8064
30: 4 be driven out unto the outmost parts of **h**, 8064
30:12 It *is* not in **h**, that *thou* shouldest say, 8064
30:12 Who shall go up for us to **h**, and bring it 8064
30:19 I call **h** and earth to record *this* day against 8064
31:28 call **h** and earth to record against them. 8064
32:40 For I lift up my hand to **h**, and say, I live 8064
33:13 for the precious things of **h**, for the dew, 8064
33:26 *who* rideth *upon* the **h** in thy help, and 8064
Jos 2:11 he *is* God in **h** above, and in earth beneath. 8064
8:20 the smoke of the city ascended up to **h**, and 8064
10:11 stones from **h** upon them unto Azekah, 8064
10:13 So the sun stood still in the midst of **h**, and 8064
Jdg 5:20 They fought from **h**; the stars in their 8064
13:20 when the flame went up toward **h** from off 8064
20:40 the flame of the city ascended up to **h**. 8064
1Sa 2:10 out of **h** shall he thunder upon them: 8064
5:12 and the cry of the city went up *to* **h**. 8064
2Sa 18: 9 he was taken up between the **h** and 8064
21:10 until water dropped upon them out of **h**, 8064
22: 8 the foundations of **h** moved and shook, 8064
22:14 The LORD thundered from **h**, and 8064
1Ki 8:22 and spread forth his hands *toward* **h**: 8064
8:23 in **h** above, or on earth beneath, 8064
8:27 the **h** and heaven of heavens cannot contain 8064
8:27 and **h** of heavens cannot contain thee; 8064
8:30 hear thou in **h** thy dwelling place: and 8064
8:32 hear thou *in* **h**, and do, and judge thy 8064
8:34 hear thou *in* **h**, and forgive the sin of thy 8064
8:35 When **h** is shut up, and there is no rain, 8064
8:36 hear thou in **h**, and forgive the sin of thy 8064
8:39 hear thou *in* **h** thy dwelling place, and 8064
8:43 Hear thou *in* **h** thy dwelling place, and 8064
8:45 hear thou *in* **h** their prayer and their 8064
8:49 their supplication *in* **h** thy dwelling place, 8064
8:54 on his knees with his hands spread *up* to **h**. 8064
18:45 that the **h** was black *with* clouds and wind, 8064
22:19 all the host of **h** standing by him on his 8064
2Ki 1:10 let fire come down from **h**, and 8064
1:10 there came down fire from **h**, and 8064
1:12 let fire come down from **h**, and 8064
1:12 the fire of God came down from **h**, and 8064
1:14 there came fire down from **h**, and burnt up 8064
2: 1 would take up Elijah *into* **h** by a whirlwind, 8064
2:11 and Elijah went up by a whirlwind *into* **h**. 8064
7: 2 *if* the LORD would make windows in **h**, 8064
7:19 *if* the LORD should make windows in **h**, 8064
14:27 blot out the name of Israel from under **h**: 8064
17:16 worshipped all the host of **h**, and 8064
19:15 of the earth; thou hast made **h** and earth. 8064
21: 3 worshipped all the host of **h**, and 8064
21: 5 he built altars for all the host of **h** in 8064
23: 4 and for the grove, and for all the host of **h**: 8064
23: 5 and to the planets, and to all the host of **h**. 8064
1Ch 21:16 LORD stand between the earth and the **h**, 8064
21:26 he answered him from **h** by fire upon 8064
29:11 for all *that is* in the **h** and in the earth *is* 8064
2Ch 2: 6 seeing the **h** and heaven of heavens cannot 8064
2: 6 and **h** of heavens cannot contain him? 8064
2:12 God of Israel, that made **h** and earth, 8064
6:13 and spread forth his hands towards **h**, 8064
6:14 *there is* no God like thee in the **h**, nor in 8064

2Ch 6:18 **h** and the heaven of heavens cannot contain 8064
6:18 and the **h** of heavens cannot contain thee; 8064
6:21 thou from thy dwelling place, *even* from **h**; 8064
6:23 hear thou from **h**, and do, and judge thy 8064
6:26 When the **h** is shut up, and there is no rain, 8064
6:27 hear thou *from* **h**, and forgive the sin of thy 8064
6:30 hear thou from **h** thy dwelling place, and 8064
7: 1 the fire came down from **h**, and 8064
7:13 If I shut up **h** that there be no rain, or if I 8064
7:14 will I hear from **h**, and will forgive their 8064
18:18 all the host of **h** standing on his right hand 8064
20: 6 God of our fathers, *art* not thou God in **h**? 8064
28: 9 slain them in a rage *that* reacheth up unto **h**. 8064
30:27 *up* to his holy dwelling place, *even* unto **h**. 8064
32:20 the son of Amoz, prayed and cried *to* **h**. 8064
33: 3 worshipped all the host of **h**, and 8064
33: 5 he built altars for all the host of **h** in 8064
36:23 earth hath the LORD God of **h** given me; 8064
Ezr 1: 2 The LORD God of **h** hath given me all 8064
5:11 We are the servants of the God of **h** and 8065
5:12 had provoked the God of **h** unto wrath, 8065
6: 9 for the burnt offerings of the God of **h**, 8065
6:10 of sweet savours unto the God of **h**, 8065
7:12 a scribe of the law of the God of **h**, 8065
7:21 the scribe of the law of the God of **h**, 8065
7:23 *is* commanded by the God of **h**, 8065
7:23 done for the house of the God of **h**: 8065
Ne 1: 4 and fasted, and prayed before the God of **h**, 8064
1: 5 O LORD God of **h**, the great and terrible 8064
1: 9 cast out unto the uttermost part of the **h**, 8064
2: 4 make request? So I prayed to the God of **h**. 8064
2:20 said unto them, The God of **h**, he will 8064
9: 6 thou hast made **h**, the heaven of heavens, 8064
9: 6 the **h** of heavens, with all their host, 8064
9: 6 and the host of **h** worshippeth thee. 8064
9:13 spakest with them from **h**, and gavest them 8064
9:15 gavest them bread from **h** for their hunger, 8064
9:23 also multipliedst thou as the stars of **h**, 8064
9:27 cried unto thee, thou heardest *them* from **h**; 8064
9:28 cried unto thee, thou heardest *them* from **h**; 8064
Job 1:16 The fire of God is fallen from **h**, and 8064
2:12 sprinkled dust upon their heads toward **h**. 8064
11: 8 *It is* as high as **h**; what canst thou do? 8064
16:19 behold my witness *is* in **h**, and my record *is* 8064
20:27 The **h** shall reveal his iniquity; and 8064
22:12 *Is* not God *in* the height of **h**? and 8064
22:14 and he walketh *in* the circuit of **h**. 8064
26:11 The pillars of **h** tremble and are astonished 8064
28:24 of the earth, *and* seeth under the whole **h**; 8064
35:11 and maketh us wiser than the fowls of **h**? 8064
37: 3 He directeth it under the whole **h**, and 8064
38:29 the hoary frost of **h**, who hath gendered it? 8064
38:33 Knowest thou the ordinances of **h**? canst 8064
38:37 or who can stay the bottles of **h**, 8064
41:11 *whatsoever is* under the whole **h** *is* mine. 8064
Ps 11: 4 holy temple, the LORD'S throne *is* in **h**: 8064
14: 2 The LORD looked down from **h** upon 8064
19: 6 His going forth *is* from the end of the **h**, 8064
20: 6 he will hear him from his holy **h** with 8064
33:13 The LORD looketh from **h**; he beholdeth 8064
53: 2 God looked down from **h** upon the children 8064
57: 3 He shall send from **h**, and save me *from* 8064
69:34 Let the **h** and earth praise him, the seas, and 8064
73:25 Whom have I in **h** *but thee?* and *there is* 8064
76: 8 didst cause judgment to be heard from **h**; 8064
77:18 The voice of thy thunder *was* in the **h**: 1534
78:23 from above, and opened the doors of **h**, 8064
78:24 to eat, and had given them *of* the corn of **h**. 8064
78:26 He caused an east wind to blow in the **h**: 8064
79: 2 given *to be* meat unto the fowls of the **h**, 8064
80:14 look down from **h**, and behold, and 8064
85:11 and righteousness shall look down from **h**. 8064
89: 6 For who in the **h** can be compared unto 7834
89:29 for ever, and his throne as the days of **h**. 8064
89:37 as the moon, and *as* a faithful witness in **h**. 7834
102:19 from **h** did the LORD behold the earth; 8064
103:11 For as the **h** is high above the earth, *so* 8064
104:12 By them shall the fowls of the **h** have their 8064
105:40 and satisfied them *with* the bread of **h**. 8064
107:26 They mount up *to* the **h**, they go down 8064
113: 6 *himself* to behold *the things that are* in **h**, 8064
115:15 *are* blessed of the LORD which made **h** 8064
115:16 The **h**, *even* the heavens, *are* the LORD'S: 8064
119:89 O LORD, thy word *is* settled in **h**. 8064
121: 2 from the LORD, which made **h** and earth. 8064
124: 8 of the LORD, who made **h** and earth. 8064
134: 3 The LORD that made **h** and earth bless 8064
135: 6 *that* did he in **h**, and in earth, in the seas, 8064
136:26 O give thanks unto the God of **h**: for his 8064
139: 8 If I ascend up *into* **h**, thou *art* there: if I 8064
146: 6 Which made **h**, and earth, the sea, and all 8064
147: 8 Who covereth the **h** with clouds, 8064
148:13 his glory *is* above the earth and **h**. 8064
Pr 23: 5 they fly away as an eagle *toward* **h**. 8064
25: 3 The **h** for height, and the earth for depth, 8064
30: 4 Who hath ascended up *into* **h**, or 8064
Ecc 1:13 concerning all *things* that are done under **h**: 8064
2: 3 which they should do under the **h** all 8064
3: 1 and a time to every purpose under the **h**: 8064
5: 2 for God *is* in **h**, and thou upon earth: 8064
Isa 13: 5 from the end of the **h**, *even* the LORD, 8064
13:10 For the stars of **h** and the constellations 8064
14:12 How art thou fallen from **h**, O Lucifer, 8064
14:13 hast said in thine heart, I will ascend *into* **h**, 8064
34: 4 And all the host of **h** shall be dissolved, and 8064
34: 5 For my sword shall be bathed in **h**: behold, 8064
37:16 of the earth: thou hast made **h** and earth. 8064
40:12 meted out **h** with the span, and 8064
55:10 the snow from **h**, and returneth not thither, 8064
63:15 Look down from **h**, and behold from 8064
66: 1 The **h** *is* my throne, and the earth *is* my 8064
Jer 7:18 to make cakes to the queen of **h**, and 8064
7:33 people shall be meat for the fowls of the **h**, 8064
8: 2 the moon, and all the host of **h**, whom they 8064
8: 7 the stork in the **h** knoweth her appointed 8064
Jer 10: 2 and be not dismayed at the signs of **h**; 8064
15: 3 the fowls of the **h**, and the beasts of 8064
16: 4 carcases shall be meat for the fowls of **h**, 8064
19: 7 will I give to be meat for the fowls of the **h**, 8064
19:13 have burnt incense unto all the host of **h**, 8064
23:24 Do not I fill **h** and earth? saith the LORD. 8064
31:37 If **h** above can be measured, and 8064
32:17 thou hast made the **h** and the earth by thy 8064
33:22 As the host of **h** cannot be numbered, 8064
33:25 *If* I have not appointed the ordinances of **h** 8064
34:20 shall be for meat unto the fowls of the **h**, 8064
44:17 to burn incense unto the queen of **h**, and 8064
44:18 left off to burn incense to the queen of **h**, 8064
44:19 when we burnt incense to the queen of **h**, 8064
44:25 to burn incense to the queen of **h**, and 8064
49:36 the four winds from the four quarters of **h**, 8064
51: 9 for her judgment reacheth unto **h**, and 8064
51:15 hath stretched out the **h** by his 8064
51:48 the **h** and the earth, and all that *is* therein, 8064
51:53 Though Babylon should mount up *to* **h**, and 8064
La 2: 1 cast down from **h** *unto* the earth the beauty 8064
3:50 the LORD look down, and behold from **h**. 8064
4:19 are swifter than the eagles of the **h**: 8064
Eze 8: 3 lift me up between the earth and the **h**, 8064
29: 5 beasts of the field and to the fowls of the **h**. 8064
31: 6 All the fowls of **h** made their nests in his 8064
31:13 Upon his ruin shall all the fowls of the **h** 8064
32: 4 will cause all the fowls of the **h** to remain 8064
32: 7 I will cover the **h**, and make the stars 8064
32: 8 All the bright lights of **h** will I make dark 8064
38:20 the fowls of the **h**, and the beasts of 8064
Da 2:18 of the God of **h** concerning this secret; 8065
2:19 Then Daniel blessed the God of **h**. 8065
2:28 there is a God in **h** that revealeth secrets, 8065
2:37 for the God of **h** hath given thee a 8065
2:38 the fowls of the **h** hath he given into thine 8065
2:44 the days of these kings shall the God of **h** 8065
4:11 the height thereof reached unto **h**, and 8065
4:12 the fowls of the **h** dwelt in the boughs 8065
4:13 and a holy one came down from **h**; 8065
4:15 let it be wet with the dew of **h**, and *let* his 8065
4:20 whose height reached unto the **h**, and 8065
4:21 upon whose branches the fowls of the **h** 8065
4:22 reacheth unto **h**, and thy dominion to 8065
4:23 and a holy one coming down from **h**, 8065
4:23 let it be wet with the dew of **h**, and *let* his 8065
4:25 they *shall* wet thee with the dew of **h**, 8065
4:31 there fell a voice from **h**, *saying*, O king 8065
4:33 and his body was wet with the dew of **h**, 8065
4:34 I Nebuchadnezzar lift up mine eyes unto **h**, 8065
4:35 according to his will in the army of **h**, 8065
4:37 and extol and honour the King of **h**, 8065
5:21 and his body was wet with the dew of **h**; 8065
5:23 hast lifted up thyself against the Lord of **h**; 8065
6:27 and wonders in **h** and in earth, 8065
7: 2 the four winds of the **h** strove upon 8065
7:13 the Son of man came with the clouds of **h**, 8065
7:27 of the kingdom under the whole **h**, 8065
8: 8 notable ones toward the four winds of **h**. 8064
8:10 it waxed great, *even* to the host of **h**; and 8064
9:12 for under the whole **h** hath not been done as 8064
11: 4 shall be divided toward the four winds of **h**; 8064
12: 7 up his right hand and his left hand unto **h**, 8064
Hos 2:18 with the fowls of **h**, and *with* the creeping 8064
4: 3 beasts of the field, and with the fowls of **h**; 8064
7:12 will bring them down as the fowls of the **h**; 8064
Am 9: 2 though they climb up *to* **h**, thence will I 8064
9: 6 *It is* he that buildeth his stories in the **h**, and 8064
Jnh 1: 9 I fear the LORD, the God of **h**, which hath 8064
Na 3:16 thy merchants above the stars of **h**: 8064
Zep 1: 3 I will consume the fowls of the **h**, and 8064
1: 5 them that worship the host of **h** upon 8064
Hag 1:10 Therefore the **h** over you is stayed from 8064
Zec 2: 6 you abroad as the four winds of the **h**, 8064
5: 9 up the ephah between the earth and the **h**. 8064
Mal 3:10 if I will not open you the windows of **h**, 8064
Mt 3: 2 Repent ye: for the kingdom of **h** is at hand. *3772*
3:17 And lo a voice from **h**, saying, This is my *3772*
4:17 Repent: for the kingdom of **h** is at hand. *3772*
5: 3 in spirit: for theirs is the kingdom of **h**. *3772*
5:10 for theirs is the kingdom of **h**. *3772*
5:12 for great *is* your reward in **h**: for so *3772*
5:16 and glorify your Father which is in **h**. *3772*
5:18 Till **h** and earth pass, one jot or one tittle *3772*
5:19 be called the least in the kingdom of **h**: *3772*
5:19 shall be called great in the kingdom of **h**. *3772*
5:20 in no case enter into the kingdom of **h**. *3772*
5:34 say unto you, Swear not at all; neither by **h**; *3772*
5:45 the children of your Father which is in **h**: *3772*
5:48 even as your Father which is in **h** is perfect. *3772*
6: 1 no reward of your Father which is in **h**. *3772*
6: 9 Our Father which art in **h**, Hallowed be thy *3772*
6:10 Thy will be done in earth, as *it is* in **h**. *3772*
6:20 But lay up for yourselves treasures in **h**, *3772*
7:11 in **h** give good *things* to them that ask him? *3772*
7:21 Lord, shall enter into the kingdom of **h**; *3772*
7:21 doeth the will of my Father which is in **h**. *3772*
8:11 and Isaac, and Jacob, in the kingdom of **h**. *3772*
10: 7 saying, The kingdom of **h** is at hand. *3772*
10:32 also before my Father which is in **h**. *3772*
10:33 I also deny before my Father which is in **h**. *3772*
11:11 least in the kingdom of **h** is greater than he. *3772*
11:12 now the kingdom of **h** suffereth violence, *3772*
11:23 Capernaum, which art exalted unto **h**, *3772*
11:25 Lord of **h** and earth, because thou hast hid *3772*
12:50 shall do the will of my Father which is in **h**, *3772*
13:11 to know the mysteries of the kingdom of **h**, *3772*
13:24 The kingdom of **h** is likened unto a man *3772*
13:31 The kingdom of **h** is like unto a grain of *3772*
13:33 The kingdom of **h** is like unto leaven, *3772*
13:44 the kingdom of **h** is like unto treasure hid in *3772*
13:45 the kingdom of **h** is like unto a merchant *3772*
13:47 Again, the kingdom of **h** is like unto a net, *3772*
13:52 **h** is like unto a man *that is* a householder, *3772*
14:19 and looking up to **h**, he blessed, and brake, *3772*
Mt 16: 1 that *he* would shew them a sign from **h**. *3772*
16:17 *it* unto thee, but my Father which is in **h**. *3772*
16:19 unto thee the keys of the kingdom of **h**: *3772*
16:19 shalt bind on earth shall be bound in **h**: *3772*
16:19 shalt loose on earth shall be loosed in **h**. *3772*
18: 1 Who is the greatest in the kingdom of **h**? *3772*
18: 3 ye shall not enter into the kingdom of **h**. *3772*
18: 4 the same is greatest in the kingdom of **h**. *3772*
18:10 That in **h** their angels do always behold *3772*
18:10 behold the face of my Father which is in **h**. *3772*
18:14 is not the will of your Father which is in **h**, *3772*
18:18 ye shall bind on earth shall be bound in **h**: *3772*
18:18 ye shall loose on earth shall be loosed in **h**. *3772*
18:19 done for them of my Father which is in **h**. *3772*
18:23 Therefore is the kingdom of **h** likened unto *3772*
19:14 unto me: for of such is the kingdom of **h**. *3772*
19:21 the poor, and thou shalt have treasure in **h**: *3772*
19:23 shall hardly enter into the kingdom of **h**. *3772*
20: 1 For the kingdom of **h** is like unto a man *3772*
21:25 from **h**, or of men? And they reasoned with *3772*
21:25 saying, If we shall say, From **h**; *3772*
22: 2 The kingdom of **h** is like unto a certain *3772*
22:30 but are as *the* angels of God in **h**. *3772*
23: 9 for one is your Father, which is in **h**. *3772*
23:13 for ye shut up the kingdom of **h** against *3772*
23:22 And he that shall swear by **h**, sweareth by *3772*
24:29 and the stars shall fall from **h**, and *3772*
24:30 appear the sign of the Son of man in **h**: *3772*
24:30 man coming in the clouds of **h** with power *3772*
24:31 four winds, from one end of **h** to the other. *3772*
24:35 **H** and earth shall pass away, but my words *3772*
24:36 not the angels of **h**, but my Father only. *3772*
25: 1 Then shall the kingdom of **h** be likened *3772*
25:14 For *the kingdom of h is* as a man travelling NIG
26:64 of power, and coming in the clouds of **h**. *3772*
28: 2 for *the* angel of the Lord descended from **h**, *3772*
28:18 All power is given unto me in **h** and *3772*
Mk 1:11 And there came a voice from **h**, *3772*
6:41 he looked up to **h**, and blessed, and *3772*
7:34 And looking up to **h**, he sighed, and *3772*
8:11 seeking of him a sign from **h**, *3772*
10:21 the poor, and thou shalt have treasure in **h**: *3772*
11:25 that your Father also which is in **h** may *3772*
11:26 neither will your Father which is in **h** *3772*
11:30 baptism of John, was *it* from **h**, or of men? *3772*
11:31 saying, If we shall say, From **h**; *3772*
12:25 but are as *the* angels which are in **h**. *3772*
13:25 And the stars of **h** shall fall, *3772*
13:25 the powers that are in **h** shall be shaken. *3772*
13:27 part of the earth to the uttermost part of **h**. *3772*
13:31 **H** and earth shall pass away: but my words *3772*
13:32 not the angels which are in **h**, neither *3772*
14:62 of power, and coming in the clouds of **h**. *3772*
16:19 he was received up into **h**, and sat on *3772*
Lk 2:15 angels were gone away from them into **h**, *3772*
3:21 and praying, the **h** was opened, *3772*
3:22 and a voice came from **h**, which said, *3772*
4:25 when the **h** was shut up three years and *3772*
6:23 *joy*: for behold, your reward *is* great in **h**: *3772*
9:16 and the two fishes, and looking up to **h**, *3772*
9:54 we command fire to come down from **h**, *3772*
10:15 Capernaum, which art exalted to **h**, *3772*
10:18 I beheld Satan as lightning fall from **h**. *3772*
10:20 because your names are written in **h**. *3772*
10:21 I thank thee, O Father, Lord of **h** and earth, *3772*
11: 2 ye pray, say, Our Father which art in **h**, *3772*
11: 2 Thy will be done, as in **h**, so in earth. *3772*
11:16 tempting *him*, sought of him a sign from **h**. *3772*
15: 7 that likewise joy shall be in **h** over one *3772*
15:18 I have sinned against **h**, and before thee, *3772*
15:21 I have sinned against **h**, and in thy sight, *3772*
16:17 And it is easier for **h** and earth to pass, *3772*
17:24 that lighteneth out of the one *part* under **h**, *3772*
17:24 shineth unto the other *part* under **h**; *3772*
17:29 Sodom it rained fire and brimstone from **h**, *3772*
18:13 not lift up so much as *his* eyes unto **h**, *3772*
18:22 the poor, and thou shalt have treasure in **h**: *3772*
19:38 peace in **h**, and glory in the highest. *3772*
20: 4 baptism of John, was it from **h**, or of men? *3772*
20: 5 saying, If we shall say, From **h**; *3772*
21:11 and great signs shall there be from **h**. *3772*
21:26 for the powers of **h** shall be shaken. *3772*
21:33 **H** and earth shall pass away: but my words *3772*
22:43 there appeared an angel unto him from **h**, *3772*
24:51 parted from them, and carried up into **h**. *3772*
Jn 1:32 I saw the Spirit descending from **h** like a *3772*
1:51 Hereafter ye shall see **h** open, and *3772*
3:13 And no *man* hath ascended up to **h**, but he *3772*
3:13 but he that came down from **h**, *even* *3772*
3:13 *even* the Son of man which is in **h**. *3772*
3:27 except it be given him from **h**. *3772*
3:31 he that cometh from **h** is above all. *3772*
6:31 He gave them bread from **h** to eat. *3772*
6:32 Moses gave you not *that* bread from **h**; *3772*
6:32 my Father giveth you the true bread from **h**. *3772*
6:33 of God is he which cometh down from **h**, *3772*
6:38 For I came down from **h**, not to do mine *3772*
6:41 I am the bread which came down from **h**. *3772*
6:42 then *that* he saith, I came down from **h**? *3772*
6:50 is the bread which cometh down from **h**, *3772*
6:51 the living bread which came down from **h**: *3772*
6:58 is *that* bread which came down from **h**: *3772*
12:28 Then came there a voice from **h**, *saying*, I *3772*
17: 1 and lift up his eyes to **h**, and said, Father, *3772*
Ac 1:10 And while they looked stedfastly toward **h** *3772*
1:11 of Galilee, why stand ye gazing up into **h**? *3772*
1:11 which is taken up from you into **h**, shall so *3772*
1:11 like manner as ye have seen him go into **h**. *3772*
2: 2 And suddenly there came a sound from **h** *3772*
2: 5 devout men, out of every nation under **h**. *3772*
2:19 And I will shew wonders in **h** above, and *3772*
3:21 Whom the **h** must receive until the times of *3772*
4:12 for there is none other name under **h** given *3772*
4:24 which hast made **h**, and earth, and the sea, *3772*
7:42 and gave them up to worship the host of **h**; *3772*

H

Ac 7:49 H *is* my throne, and earth *is* my footstool: 3772
7:55 looked up stedfastly into h, and saw 3772
9: 3 shined round about him a light from h: 3772
10:11 And saw h opened, and a certain vessel 3772
10:16 and the vessel was received up again into h. 3772
11: 5 let down from h by four corners; 3772
11: 9 But *the* voice answered me again from h, 3772
11:10 and all were drawn up again into h. 3772
14:15 which made h, and earth, and the sea, and 3772
14:17 and gave us rain **from** h, and 3771
17:24 seeing that he is Lord of h and earth, 3772
22: 6 suddenly there shone from h a great light 3772
26:13 O king, I saw in the way a light **from** h, 3771
Ro 1:18 For the wrath of God is revealed from h 3772
10: 6 not in thine heart, Who shall ascend into h? 3772
1Co 8: 5 whether in h or in earth, (as there be gods 3772
15:47 earthy: the second man *is* the Lord from h. 3772
2Co 5: 2 upon with our house which is from h: 3772
12: 2 such a one caught up to the third h. 3772
Gal 1: 8 But though we, or an angel from h, 3772
Eph 1:10 both which are in h, and which are on 3772
3:15 Of whom the whole family in h and earth is 3772
6: 9 knowing that your Master also is in h; 3772
Php 2:10 of *things* **in** h, and *things* in earth, and 2032
3:20 For our conversation is in h; from whence 3772
Col 1: 5 For the hope which is laid up for you in h, 3772
1:16 that are in h, and that are in earth, visible 3772
1:20 *they be things* in earth, or *things* in h. 3772
1:23 to every creature which is under h; 3772
4: 1 knowing that ye also have a Master in h. 3772
1Th 1:10 And to wait for his Son from h, whom he 3772
4:16 For the Lord himself shall descend from h 3772
2Th 1: 7 be revealed from h with his mighty angels, 3772
Heb 9:24 but into h itself, now to appear in 3772
10:34 knowing in yourselves that *ye* have in h a 3772
12:23 which are written in h, and to God 3772
12:25 turn away from him that *speaketh* from h: 3772
12:26 *more* I shake not the earth only, but also h. 3772
Jas 5:12 swear not, neither by h, neither by 3772
5:18 and the h gave rain, and the earth brought 3772
1Pe 1: 4 that fadeth not away, reserved in h for you, 3772
1:12 you with the Holy Ghost sent *down* from h; 3772
3:22 Who is gone into h, and is on the right hand 3772
2Pe 1:18 And this voice which came from h we 3772
1Jn 5: 7 For there are three that bear record in h, 3772
Rev 3:12 which cometh down out of h from my God: 3772
4: 1 and behold, a door *was* opened in h: 3772
4: 2 a throne was set in h, and one sat on 3772
5: 3 And no *man* in h, nor in earth, 3772
5:13 And every creature which is in h, and 3772
6:13 And the stars of h fell unto the earth, 3772
6:14 And the h departed as a scrole when it is 3772
8: 1 there was silence in h about the space of 3772
8:10 and there fell a great star from h, 3772
8:13 an angel flying through the **midst of h**, 3321
9: 1 and I saw a star fall from h unto the earth: 3772
10: 1 another mighty angel come down from h, 3772
10: 4 and I heard a voice from h saying unto me, 3772
10: 5 and upon the earth lifted up his hand to h, 3772
10: 6 who created h, and the *things* that therein 3772
10: 8 And the voice which I heard from h spake 3772
11: 6 These have power to shut h, that it rain not 3772
11:12 And they heard a great voice from h saying 3772
11:12 And they ascended up to h in a cloud; and 3772
11:13 and gave glory to the God of h. 3772
11:15 and there were great voices in h, saying, 3772
11:19 And the temple of God was opened in h, 3772
12: 1 And there appeared a great wonder in h; 3772
12: 3 And there appeared another wonder in h; 3772
12: 4 his tail drew the third *part* of the stars of h, 3772
12: 7 And there was war in h: Michael and 3772
12: 8 was their place found any more in h. 3772
12:10 And I heard a loud voice saying in h, 3772
13: 6 his tabernacle, and them that dwell in h. 3772
13:13 that he maketh fire come down from h on 3772
14: 2 And I heard a voice from h, as the voice of 3772
14: 6 I saw another angel fly in the **midst of h**, 3321
14: 7 and worship him that made h, and earth, 3772
14:13 And I heard a voice from h saying unto me, 3772
14:17 angel came out of the temple which is in h, 3772
15: 1 And I saw another sign in h, great and 3772
15: 5 of the testimony in h was opened: 3772
16:11 And blasphemed the God of h because 3772
16:17 came a great voice out of the temple of h, 3772
16:21 there fell upon men a great hail out of h, 3772
18: 1 I saw another angel come down from h, 3772
18: 4 And I heard another voice from h, saying, 3772
18: 5 For her sins have reached unto h, and God 3772
18:20 *thou* h, and ye holy apostles and prophets; 3772
19: 1 I heard a great voice of much people in h, 3772
19:11 And I saw h opened, and behold a white 3772
19:14 And the armies which were in h followed 3772
19:17 to all the fowls that fly in the **midst of h**, 3321
20: 1 And I saw an angel come down from h, 3772
20: 9 and fire came down from God out of h, 3772
20:11 face the earth and the h fled *away*; and 3772
21: 1 And I saw a new h and a new earth: for 3772
21: 1 for the first h and the first earth were 3772
21: 2 coming down from God out of h, 3772
21: 3 And I heard a great voice out of h saying, 3772
21:10 descending out of h from God, 3772

HEAVEN'S (1) [HEAVEN]

Mt 19:12 eunuchs for the kingdom of h sake. 3772

HEAVENLY (23) [HEAVEN]

Mt 6:14 your h Father will also forgive you: 3770
6:26 into barns; yet your h Father feedeth them. 3770
6:32 for your h Father knoweth that ye have 3770
15:13 which my h Father hath not planted, 3770
18:35 So likewise shall my h Father do *also* unto 2032
Lk 2:13 a multitude of the h host praising God, 3770
11:13 how much more shall *your* h Father 1537+3772
Jn 3:12 shall ye believe, if I tell you *of* h *things*? 2032
Ac 26:19 I was not disobedient unto the h vision: 3770
1Co 15:48 and as *is* the h, such *are they* also *that are* 2032
15:48 the heavenly, such *are they* also *that are* h. 2032
15:49 we shall also bear the image of the h. 2032
Eph 1: 3 all spiritual blessings in h *places* in Christ: 2032
1:20 set *him* at his own right hand in the h 2032
2: 6 made *us* sit together in h *places* in Christ 2032
3:10 powers in h *places* might be known by 2032
2Ti 4:18 and will preserve *me* unto his h kingdom: 2032
Heb 3: 1 holy brethren, partakers of the h calling, 2032
6: 4 and have tasted of the h gift, and 2032
8: 5 shadow of h *things*, as Moses was 2032
9:23 the h *things* themselves with better 2032
11:16 they desire a better *country*, that is, a h: 2032
12:22 the h Jerusalem, and to an innumerable 2032

HEAVENS (133) [HEAVEN]

Ge 2: 1 Thus the h and the earth were finished, and 8064
2: 4 These *are* the generations of the h and 8064
2: 4 the LORD God made the earth and the h, 8064
Dt 10:14 the heaven of h *is* the LORD'S thy God, 8064
32: 1 Give ear, O ye h, and I will speak; and 8064
33:28 and wine; also his h shall drop down dew. 8064
Jdg 5: 4 the earth trembled, and the h dropped, 8064
2Sa 22:10 He bowed the h also, and came down; and 8064
1Ki 8:27 and heaven of h cannot contain thee; 8064
1Ch 16:26 *are* idols: but the LORD made the h. 8064
16:31 Let the h be glad, and let the earth rejoice: 8064
27:23 increase Israel like to the stars of the h. 8064
2Ch 2: 6 and heaven of h cannot contain him? 8064
6:18 and the heaven of h cannot contain thee; 8064
6:25 hear thou from the h, and forgive the sin of 8064
6:33 hear thou from the h, *even* from thy 8064
6:35 hear thou from the h their prayer and their 8064
6:39 hear thou from the h, *even* from thy 8064
Ezr 9: 6 and our trespass is grown up unto the h. 8064
Ne 9: 6 the heaven of h, with all their host, 8064
Job 9: 8 Which alone spreadeth out the h, and 8064
14:12 till the h *be* no more, they shall not awake, 8064
15:15 yea, the h are not clean in his sight. 8064
20: 6 Though his excellency mount up to the h, 8064
26:13 By his spirit he hath garnished the h; 8064
35: 5 Look unto the h, and see; and behold 8064
Ps 2: 4 He that sitteth in the h shall laugh: 8064
8: 1 who hast set thy glory above the h. 8064
8: 3 When I consider thy h, the work of thy 8064
18: 9 He bowed the h also, and came down: and 8064
18:13 The LORD also thundered in the h, and 8064
19: 1 The h declare the glory of God; and 8064
33: 6 By the word of the LORD were the h 8064
36: 5 Thy mercy, O LORD, *is* in the h; *and* 8064
50: 4 He shall call to the h from above, and to 8064
50: 6 the h shall declare his righteousness: 8064
57: 5 Be thou exalted, O God, above the h; 8064
57:10 For thy mercy *is* great unto the h, and 8064
57:11 Be thou exalted, O God, above the h: 8064
68: 4 extol him that rideth upon the h by his 6160
68: 8 the h also dropped at the presence of God: 8064
68:33 To him that rideth upon the h of heavens, 8064
68:33 To him that rideth upon the heavens of h, 8064
73: 9 They set their mouth against the h, and 8064
89: 2 shalt thou establish in the very h. 8064
89: 5 the h shall praise thy wonders, O LORD: 8064
89:11 The h *are* thine, the earth also *is* thine: 8064
96: 5 *are* idols: but the LORD made the h. 8064
96:11 Let the h rejoice, and let the earth be glad; 8064
97: 6 The h declare his righteousness, and all 8064
102:25 and the h *are* the work of thy hands. 8064
103:19 LORD hath prepared his throne in the h; 8064
104: 2 who stretchest out the h like a curtain: 8064
108: 4 For thy mercy *is* great above the h: and 8064
108: 5 Be thou exalted, O God, above the h: and 8064
113: 4 all nations, *and* his glory above the h. 8064
115: 3 our God *is* in the h: he hath done 8064
115:16 The heaven, *even* the h, *are* the LORD'S: 8064
123: 1 up mine eyes, O thou that dwellest in the h. 8064
136: 5 To him that by wisdom made the h: for his 8064
144: 5 Bow thy h, O LORD, and come down: 8064
148: 1 Praise ye the LORD from the h: 8064
148: 4 ye h of heavens, and ye waters that *be* 8064
148: 4 ye heavens of h, and ye waters that *be* 8064
148: 4 and ye waters that *be* above the h. 8064
Pr 3:19 by understanding hath he established the h. 8064
8:27 When he prepared the h, I *was* there: 8064
Isa 1: 2 Hear, O h, and give ear, O earth: for 8064
5:30 and the light is darkened in the h thereof. 6183
13:13 Therefore I will shake the h, and the earth 8064
34: 4 the h shall be rolled together as a scrole: 8064
40:22 that stretcheth out the h as a curtain, and 8064
42: 5 he that created the h, and stretched them 8064
44:23 Sing, O ye h; for the LORD hath done *it*: 8064
44:24 all *things*; that stretcheth forth the h alone; 8064
45: 8 Drop down, ye h, from above, and let 8064
45:12 have stretched out the h, and all their host 8064
45:18 thus saith the LORD that created the h; 8064
48:13 and my right hand hath spanned the h: 8064
49:13 Sing, O h; and be joyful, O earth; and 8064
50: 3 I clothe the h with blackness, and I make 8064
51: 6 Lift up your eyes to the h, and look upon 8064
51: 6 for the h shall vanish away like smoke, and 8064
51:13 that hath stretched forth the h, and laid 8064
51:16 that I may plant the h, and lay 8064
55: 9 For *as* the h are higher than the earth, so 8064
64: 1 O that thou wouldest rend the h, that thou 8064
65:17 behold, I create new h and a new earth: 8064
66:22 For as the new h and the new earth, which I 8064
Jer 2:12 O ye h, at this, and be horribly afraid, 8064
4:23 and void; and the h, and they *had* no light. 8064
4:25 no man, and all the birds of the h were fled. 8064
4:28 the earth mourn, and the h above be black: 8064
9:10 both the fowl of the h and the beast are 8064
10:11 The gods that have not made the h and 8065
10:11 from the earth, and from under these h. 8065
10:12 hath stretched out the h by his discretion. 8064
10:13 *there is* a multitude of waters in the h, and 8064
14:22 or can the h give showers? *art* not thou he, 8064
Jer 51:16 *there is* a multitude of waters in the h; 8064
La 3:41 our heart with *our* hands unto God in the h. 8064
3:66 destroy them in anger from under the h of 8064
Eze 1: 1 *that* the h were opened, and I saw visions 8064
Da 4:26 after that thou shalt have known that the h 8065
Hos 2:21 I will hear the h, and they shall hear 8064
Joel 2:10 quake before them; the h shall tremble: 8064
2:30 I will shew wonders in the h and in 8064
3:16 and the h and the earth shall shake: 8064
Hab 3: 3 His glory covered the h, and the earth was 8064
Hag 2: 6 I *will* shake the h, and the earth, and 8064
2:21 I *will* shake the h and the earth; 8064
Zec 6: 5 unto me, These *are* the four spirits of the h, 8064
8:12 her increase, and the h shall give their dew; 8064
12: 1 which stretcheth forth the h, and layeth 8064
Mt 3:16 and lo, the h were opened unto him, and 3772
24:29 and the powers of the h shall be shaken: 3772
Mk 1:10 he saw the h opened, and the Spirit like a 3772
Lk 12:33 a treasure in the h that faileth not, where no 3772
Ac 2:34 For David is not ascended into the h: but 3772
7:56 And said, Behold, I see the h opened, 3772
2Co 5: 1 house not made with hand, eternal in the h. 3772
Eph 4:10 same also that ascended up far above all h, 3772
Heb 1:10 and the h are the works of thine hands: 3772
4:14 that is passed into the h, Jesus the Son of 3772
7:26 from sinners, and made higher than the h; 3772
8: 1 hand of the throne of the Majesty in the h; 3772
9:23 in the h should be purified with these; 3772
2Pe 3: 5 that by the word of God the h were of old, 3772
3: 7 But the h and the earth, which are now, 3772
3:10 in the which the h shall pass away with a 3772
3:12 wherein the h being on fire shall be 3772
3:13 look for new h and a new earth, 3772
Rev 12:12 ye h, and ye that dwell in them. 3772

HEAVIER (3) [HEAVY]

Job 6: 3 For now it would be h than the sand of 3513
23: 2 my stroke is h than my groaning. 3513
Pr 27: 3 but a fool's wrath *is* h than them both. 3515

HEAVILY (3) [HEAVY]

Ex 14:25 that they drave them h: 3517+871.1
Ps 35:14 I bowed down h, as one that mourneth for 6937
Isa 47: 6 upon the ancient hast thou very h **laid** thy 3513

HEAVINESS (14) [HEAVY]

Ezr 9: 5 the evening sacrifice I arose up from my h; 8589
Job 9:27 I will leave off my h, and comfort myself: 6440
Ps 69:20 hath broken my heart; and I am **full of** h: 5136
119:28 My soul melteth for h: strengthen thou me 8424
Pr 10: 1 but a foolish son *is* the h of his mother. 8424
12:25 H in the heart of man maketh it stoop: but 1674
14:13 is sorrowful; and the end of that mirth *is* h. 8424
Isa 29: 2 and there shall be h and sorrow: 8386
61: 3 the garment of praise for the spirit of h; 3544
Ro 9: 2 That I have great h and continual sorrow in 3077
2Co 2: 1 that *I* would not come again to you in h. 3077
Php 2:26 and *was* **full of** h, because that ye had heard 85
Jas 4: 9 be turned to mourning, and *your* joy to h. 2726
1Pe 1: 6 ye are in h through manifold temptations: 3076

HEAVY (40) [HEAVIER, HEAVILY, HEAVINESS]

Ex 17:12 Moses' hands *were* h; and they took a 3515
18:18 for *this* thing *is* too h for thee; thou art not 3515
Nu 11:14 people alone, because *it is* too h for me. 3515
1Sa 4:18 for he was an old man, and h. And he had 3515
5: 6 the hand of the LORD was h upon them 3513
5:11 the city; the hand of God was very h there. 3513
2Sa 14:26 he polled *it*: because *the hair* was h on him, 3513
1Ki 12: 4 his h yoke which he put upon us, lighter, 3515
12:10 Thy father **made** our yoke h, but make thou 3513
12:11 my father did lade you with a h yoke, 3515
12:14 My father **made** your yoke h, and I will 3513
14: 6 for I *am* sent to thee *with* h *tidings*. 7186
20:43 the king of Israel went to his house h and 5620
21: 4 Ahab came into his house h and displeased 5620
2Ch 10: 4 his h yoke that he put upon us, and we will 3515
10:10 Thy father **made** our yoke h, but make thou 3513
10:11 For whereas my father put a h yoke upon 3515
10:14 My father **made** your yoke h, but I will add 3513
Ne 5:18 the bondage was h upon this people. 3513
Job 33: 7 neither shall my hand be h upon thee. 3513
Ps 32: 4 For day and night thy hand was h upon me: 3513
38: 4 as a h burden they are too heavy for me. 3515
38: 4 as a heavy burden they are too h for me. 3513
Pr 25:20 so *is* he that singeth songs to a h heart. 7451
27: 3 A stone *is* h, and the sand weighty; but 3514
31: 6 and wine unto those that be of h hearts. 4751
Isa 6:10 and **make** their ears h, and shut their eyes; 3513
24:20 the transgression thereof shall be h upon it; 3513
30:27 *with* his anger, and the burden *thereof is* h: 3514
46: 1 your carriages *were* h **loaden**; *they are* a 6006
58: 6 to undo the h burdens, and to let 4133
59: 1 neither his ear h, that *it* cannot hear: 3513
La 3: 7 I cannot get out: he hath **made** my chain h. 3513
Mt 11:28 all *ye* that labour and are h **laden**, and I 5412
23: 4 For they bind h burdens and grievous to be 926
26:37 and began to be sorrowful and **very** h. 85
26:43 them asleep again: for their eyes were h. 916
Mk 14:33 began to be sore amazed, and to be **very** h; 85
14:40 them asleep again, (for their eyes were h,) 916
Lk 9:32 they that were with him were h with sleep: 916

HEBER (13) [EBER, HEBER'S, HEBERITES]

Ge 46:17 and the sons of Beriah; H, and Malchiel. 2268
Nu 26:45 of H, the family of the Heberites: 2268
Jdg 4:11 Now H the Kenite, *which was* of 2268
4:17 to the tent of Jael the wife of H the Kenite: 2268
4:17 of Hazor and the house of H the Kenite. 2268
5:24 shall Jael the wife of H the Kenite be, 2268
1Ch 4:18 H the father of Socho, and Jekuthiel 2268
5:13 Jorai, and Jachan, and Zia, and H, seven. 5677
7:31 H, and Malchiel, who *is* the father of 2268
7:32 H begat Japhlet, and Shomer, and Hotham, 2268

1Ch 8:17 and Meshullam, and Hezeki, and **H**, 2268
8:22 And Ishpan, and Heber, and Eliel, 5677
Lk 3:35 which was *the son* of **H**, which was *the son* *1443*

HEBER'S (1) [HEBER]
Jdg 4:21 Jael **H** wife took a nail of the tent, and 2268

HEBERITES (1) [HEBER]
Nu 26:45 of Heber, the family of the **H**: of Malchiel, 2277

HEBREW (26) [HEBREWESS, HEBREWS, HEBREWS']
Ge 14:13 that had escaped, and told Abram the **H**; 5680
39:14 he hath brought in a **H** unto us to mock us; 5680
39:17 saying, The **H** servant, which thou hast 5680
41:12 a **H**, servant to the captain of the guard; 5680
Ex 1:15 the king of Egypt spake to the **H** midwives, 5680
1:16 do the office of a midwife to the **H women**, 5680
1:19 Because the **H women** *are* not as 5680
2:7 and call to thee a nurse of the **H** women, 5680
2:11 he spied an Egyptian smiting a **H**, *one* of 5680
21:2 If thou buy a **H** servant, six years he shall 5680
Dt 15:12 a **H man**, or a Hebrew woman, be sold 5680
15:12 a Hebrew man, or a **H woman**, be sold 5680
Jer 34:9 *being* a **H** or a Hebrewess, go free; 5680
34:14 years let ye go every man his brother a **H**, 5680
Jnh 1:9 he said unto them, I *am* a **H**; and I fear 5680
Lk 23:38 and Latin, and **H**, THIS IS THE KING OF *1444*
Jn 5:2 which is called **in the H tongue** Bethesda, *1447*
19:13 the Pavement, but **in the H**, Gabbatha. *1447*
19:17 a skull, which is called **in the H** Golgotha: *1447*
19:20 and it was written **in H**, *and* Greek, *and* *1447*
Ac 21:40 he spake unto *them* **in the H** tongue, *1446*
22:2 that he spake **in the H** tongue to them, *1446*
26:14 and saying **in the H** tongue, Saul, Saul, *1446*
Php 3:5 the tribe of Benjamin, a **H** of the Hebrews; *1445*
Rev 9:11 whose name **in the H tongue** *is* Abaddon, *1447*
16:16 place called **in the H tongue** Armageddon. *1447*

HEBREWESS (1) [HEBREW]
Jer 34:9 *being* a Hebrew or a **H**, go free; 5680

HEBREWS (21) [HEBREW]
Ge 40:15 I was stolen away out of the land of the **H**: 5680
43:32 Egyptians might not eat bread with the **H**; 5680
Ex 2:13 two men of the **H** strove together: 5680
3:18 The LORD God of the **H** hath met with 5680
5:3 The God of the **H** hath met with us: 5680
7:16 The LORD God of the **H** hath sent me 5680
9:1 Thus saith the LORD God of the **H**, 5680
9:13 Thus saith the LORD God of the **H**, 5680
10:3 Thus saith the LORD God of the **H**, 5680
1Sa 4:6 of this great shout in the camp of the **H**? 5680
4:9 that ye be not servants unto the **H**, 5680
13:3 all the land, saying, Let the **H** hear. 5680
13:7 *some of the* **H** went over Jordan *to* the land 5680
13:19 Lest the **H** make *them* swords or spears: 5680
14:11 the **H** come forth out of the holes where 5680
14:21 Moreover the **H** *that* were with 5680
29:3 What *do* these **H** *here*? And Achish said 5680
Ac 6:1 a murmuring of the Grecians against the **H**, *1445*
2Co 11:22 Are they **H**? so *am* I. Are they Israelites? so *1445*
Php 3:5 the tribe of Benjamin, a Hebrew of the **H**; *1445*
Heb 13:S Written to the **H** from Italy by Timothy. *1445*

HEBREWS' (1) [HEBREW]
Ex 2:6 and said, This *is one* of the **H** children. 5680

HEBRON (73) [HEBRONITES]
Ge 13:18 which *is* in **H**, and built there an altar unto 2275
23:2 the same *is* **H** in the land of Canaan: 2275
23:19 the same *is* **H** in the land of Canaan. 2275
35:27 which *is* **H**, where Abraham and 2275
37:14 So he sent him out of the vale of **H**, and 2275
Ex 6:18 Amram, and Izhar, and **H**, and Uzziel: 2275
Nu 3:19 Amram, and Izehar, **H**, and Uzziel. 2275
13:22 ascended by the south, and came unto **H**; 2275
13:22 *were*. (Now **H** was built seven years before 2275
Jos 10:3 of Jerusalem sent unto Hoham king of **H**, 2275
10:5 the king of **H**, the king of Jarmuth, the king 2275
10:23 the king of **H**, the king of Jarmuth, the king 2275
10:36 and all Israel with him, unto **H**; 2275
10:39 as he had done to **H**, so he did to Debir, and 2275
11:21 from **H**, from Debir, from Anab, and 2275
12:10 king of Jerusalem, one; the king of **H**, one; 2275
14:13 gave unto Caleb the son of Jephunneh **H** 2275
14:14 **H** therefore became the inheritance of 2275
14:15 the name of **H** before *was* Kirjath-arba; 2275
15:13 of Arba the father of Anak, which *city is* **H**. 2275
15:54 and Kirjath-arba, which *is* **H**, and Zior; 2275
19:28 **H**, and Rehob, and Hammon, and Kanah, 5683
20:7 Kirjath-arba, which *is* **H**, in the mountain 2275
21:11 which *city is* **H**, in the hill *country* of 2275
21:13 of Aaron the priest **H** with her suburbs, 2275
Jdg 1:10 against the Canaanites that dwelt in **H**: 2275
1:10 (now the name of **H** before *was* 2275
1:20 they gave **H** unto Caleb, as Moses said: 2275
16:3 them up to the top of a hill that *is* before **H**. 2275
1Sa 30:31 to *them* which *were* in **H**, and to all 2275
2Sa 2:1 shall I go up? And he said, Unto **H**. 2275
2:3 and they dwelt in the cities of **H**. 2275
2:11 the time that David was king in **H** over 2275
2:32 and they came to **H** at break of day. 2275
3:2 unto David were sons born in **H**: and 2275
3:5 These were born to David in **H**. 2275
3:19 David in **H** all that seemed good to Israel, 2275
3:20 So Abner came to David to **H**, and 2275
3:22 Abner *was* not with David in **H**; for he had 2275
3:27 when Abner was returned *to* **H**, Joab took 2275
3:32 they buried Abner in **H**: and the king lift up 2275
4:1 Saul's son heard that Abner was dead in **H**, 2275
4:8 the head of Ish-bosheth unto David *to* **H**, 2275
4:12 and hanged *them* up over the pool in **H**. 2275
4:12 buried *it* in the sepulchre of Abner in **H**. 2275
5:1 all the tribes of Israel to David unto **H**, 2275
2Sa 5:3 the elders of Israel came to the king to **H**; 2275
5:3 king David made a league with them in **H** 2275
5:5 In **H** he reigned over Judah seven years and 2275
5:13 of Jerusalem, after he was come from **H**: 2275
15:7 I have vowed unto the LORD, in **H**. 2275
15:9 Go in peace. So he arose, and went to **H**. 2275
15:10 then ye shall say, Absalom reigneth in **H**. 2275
1Ki 2:11 seven years reigned he in **H**, and thirty and 2275
1Ch 2:42 and the sons of Mareshah the father of **H**. 2275
2:43 the sons of **H**; Korah, and Tappuah, and 2275
3:1 of David, which were born unto him in **H**; 2275
3:4 *These* six were born unto him in **H**; and 2275
6:2 Amram, Izhar, and **H**, and Uzziel. 2275
6:18 and Izhar, and **H**, and Uzziel. 2275
6:55 And they gave them **H** in the land of Judah, 2275
6:57 *namely*, **H**, *the city* of refuge, and Libnah 2275
11:1 gathered themselves to David unto **H**, 2275
11:3 all the elders of Israel to the king to **H**; 2275
11:3 David made a covenant with them in **H** 2275
12:23 *and* came to David to **H**, to turn 2275
12:38 keep rank, came with a perfect heart to **H**, 2275
15:9 Of the sons of **H**; Eliel the chief, and 2275
23:12 Amram, Izhar, **H**, and Uzziel, four. 2275
23:19 *Of* the sons of **H**; Jeriah the first, 2275
24:23 the sons *of* **H**; Jeriah *the first*, Amariah NIH
29:27 seven years reigned he in **H**, and thirty and 2275
2Ch 11:10 Zorah, and Aijalon, and **H**, which *are* in 2275

HEBRONITES (6) [HEBRON]
Nu 3:27 the family of the **H**, and the family of 2276
26:58 family of the Libnites, the family of the **H**, 2276
1Ch 26:23 the Izharites, the **H**, *and the* Uzzielites: 2276
26:30 *And* of the **H**, Hashabiah and his brethren, 2276
26:31 Among the **H** *was* Jerijah the chief, 2276
26:31 *even* among the **H**, according to 2276

HEDGE (9) [HEDGED, HEDGES]
Job 1:10 Hast not thou **made a h** about him, and 7753
Pr 15:19 The way of the slothful *man is* as a **h** of 4881
Ecc 10:8 whoso breaketh a **h**, a serpent shall bite 1447
Isa 5:5 I *will* take away the **h** thereof, and it shall 4881
Eze 13:5 neither **made up** the **h** for the house 1443+1447
22:30 that *should* **make up** the **h**, 1443+1447
Hos 2:6 I will **h up** thy way with thorns, and make a 7753
Mic 7:4 the *most* upright *is sharper* than a **thorn h**: 4534
Mk 12:1 and set a **h** about *it*, and digged *a place for* *5418*

HEDGED (3) [HEDGE]
Job 3:23 way is hid, and whom God hath **h in**? 5526
La 3:7 He hath **h** me about, that I cannot get out: 1443
Mt 21:33 and **h** it round about, and digged a *5418*

HEDGES (6) [HEDGE]
1Ch 4:23 and those that dwelt amongst plants and **h**: 1448
Ps 80:12 Why hast thou *then* broken down her **h**, so 1447
89:40 Thou hast broken down all his **h**; thou hast 1448
Jer 49:3 lament, and run to and fro by the **h**; 1448
Na 3:17 which camp in the **h** in the cold day, *but* 1448
Lk 14:23 Go out into the *high*ways and **h**, and *5418*

HEED (80)
Ge 31:24 **Take h** that thou speak not to Jacob either 8104
31:29 **Take** thou **h** that thou speak not to Jacob 8104
Ex 10:28 Get thee from me, **take h** to thyself, see my 8104
19:12 saying, **Take h** to yourselves, *that* ye go 8104
34:12 **Take h** to thyself, lest thou make a 8104
Nu 23:12 Must I not **take h** to speak that which 8104
Dt 2:4 **take** ye good **h** unto yourselves therefore: 8104
4:9 Only **take h** to thyself, and keep thy soul 8104
4:15 **Take** ye therefore good **h** unto yourselves; 8104
4:23 **Take h** unto yourselves, lest ye forget 8104
11:16 **Take h** to yourselves, that your heart be not 8104
12:13 **Take h** to thyself that thou offer not thy 8104
12:19 **Take h** to thyself that thou forsake not 8104
12:30 **Take h** to thyself that thou be not snared by 8104
24:8 **Take h** in the plague of leprosy, that *thou* 8104
27:9 **Take h**, and hearken, O Israel; 5535
Jos 22:5 But **take** diligent **h** to do the commandment 8104
23:11 **Take** good **h** therefore unto yourselves, 8104
1Sa 19:2 **take h** to thyself until the morning, and 8104
2Sa 20:10 Amasa **took** no **h** to the sword that *was* in 8104
1Ki 2:4 saying, If thy children **take h** to their way, 8104
8:25 so that thy children **take h** to their way, 8104
2Ki 10:31 Jehu **took** no **h** to walk in the law of 8104
1Ch 22:13 if thou **takest h** to fulfil the statutes and 8104
28:10 **Take h** now; for the LORD hath chosen 7200
2Ch 6:16 that thy children **take h** to their way to 8104
19:6 said to the judges, **Take h** what ye do: 7200
19:7 **take h** and do *it*: for *there is* no iniquity 8104
33:8 that they will **take h** to do all that I have 8104
Ezr 4:22 **Take h** now that ye fail not to do this: why 2095
Job 36:21 **Take h**, regard not iniquity: for this hast 8104
Ps 39:1 I said, I will **take h** to my ways, that I sin 8104
119:9 by **taking h** *thereto* according to thy word. 8104
Pr 17:4 A wicked doer **giveth h** to false lips; *and* 7181
Ecc 7:21 Also **take** no **h** unto all words that 3820+5414
12:9 he **gave good h**, and sought out, *and* set in 239
Isa 7:4 say unto him, **Take h**, and be quiet; 8104
21:7 and he hearkened diligently *with* much **h**: 7182
Jer 9:4 **Take** ye **h** every one of his neighbour, and 8104
17:21 **Take h** to yourselves, and bear no burden 8104
18:18 and let us not **give h** to any of his words. 7181
18:19 **Give h** to me, O LORD, and hearken to 7181
Hos 4:10 they have left off to **take h** to the LORD. 8104
Mal 2:15 Therefore **take h** to your spirit, and 8104
2:16 therefore **take h** to your spirit, that ye deal 8104
Mt 6:1 **Take h** that *ye* do not your alms before *4337*
16:6 **Take h** and beware of the leaven of *3708*
18:10 **Take h** that ye despise not one of these *3708*
24:4 unto them, **Take h** that no *man* deceive you. *991*
Mk 4:24 he said unto them, **Take h** what you hear: *991*
8:15 And he charged them, saying, **Take h**, *3708*
13:5 to say, **Take h** lest any *man* deceive you: *991*
13:9 But **take h** to yourselves: for they shall *991*
Mk 13:23 But **take** ye **h**: behold, I have foretold you *991*
13:33 **Take** ye **h**, watch and pray: for ye know not *991*
Lk 8:18 **Take h** therefore how ye hear: *991*
11:35 **Take h** therefore that the light which is in *4648*
12:15 **Take h**, and beware of covetousness: *3708*
17:3 **Take h** to yourselves: If thy brother *4337*
21:8 And he said, **Take h** that ye be not deceived: *991*
21:34 And **take h** to yourselves, lest at any time *4337*
Ac 3:5 And he gave **h** unto them, expecting to *1907*
5:35 **take h** to yourselves what ye intend to do *4337*
8:6 And the people with one accord **gave h** *4337*
8:10 To whom they all **gave h**, from the least to *4337*
20:28 **Take h** therefore unto yourselves, and *4337*
22:26 saying, **Take h** what thou doest: *3708*
Ro 11:21 *take* **h** lest he also spare not thee. NIG
1Co 3:10 But let every man **take h** how he buildeth *991*
8:9 But **take h** lest by any means this liberty of *991*
10:12 that thinketh he standeth **take h** lest he fall. *991*
Gal 5:15 **take h** ye be not consumed one of another. *991*
Col 4:17 **Take h** to the ministry which thou hast *991*
1Ti 1:4 Neither **give h** to fables and *4337*
4:1 **giving h** to seducing spirits, and *4337*
4:16 **Take h** unto thyself, and unto the doctrine; *1907*
Tit 1:14 Not **giving h** to Jewish fables, and *4337*
Heb 2:1 **give** the more earnest **h to** the *things* which *4337*
3:12 **Take h**, brethren, lest there be in any of you *991*
2Pe 1:19 whereunto ye do well that ye **take h**, *4337*

HEEL (6) [HEELS]
Ge 3:15 bruise thy head, and thou shalt bruise his **h**. 6119
25:26 and his hand took hold on Esau's **h**; 6119
Job 18:9 The grin shall take *him* by the **h**, *and* 6119
Ps 41:9 *of* my bread, hath lift up *his* **h** against me. 6119
Hos 12:3 He **took** his brother **by the h** in the womb, 6117
Jn 13:18 bread with me hath lift up his **h** against me. *4418*

HEELS (4) [HEEL]
Ge 49:17 that biteth the horse **h**, so that his rider shall 6119
Job 13:27 thou settest a print upon the **h** of my feet. 8328
Ps 49:5 *when* the iniquity of my **h** shall compass 6120
Jer 13:22 thy skirts discovered, *and* thy **h** made bare. 6119

HEGAI (3) [HEGE]
Est 2:8 to the custody of **H**, that Esther was 1896
2:8 to the custody of **H**, keeper of the women. 1896
2:15 but what **H** the king's chamberlain, 1896

HEGE (1) [HEGAI]
Est 2:3 unto the custody of **H** the king's 1896

HEIFER (19) [HEIFER'S]
Ge 15:9 Take me a **h** of three years old, and a she 5697
Nu 19:2 that they bring thee a red **h** without spot, 6510
19:5 *one* shall burn the **h** in his sight; her skin, 6510
19:6 *it* into the midst of the burning of the **h**. 6510
19:9 *is* clean shall gather up the ashes of the **h**, 6510
19:10 he that gathereth the ashes of the **h** shall 6510
19:17 ashes of the burnt **h** of purification for sin, NIH
Dt 21:3 the elders of that city shall take a **h**, 1241+5697
21:4 shall bring down the **h** unto a rough valley, 5697
21:6 over the **h** that is beheaded in the valley: 5697
Jdg 14:18 unto them, If ye had not plowed with my **h**, 5697
1Sa 16:2 Take a **h** with thee, and say, 1241+5697
Isa 15:5 *shall flee* unto Zoar, a **h** of three years old: 5697
Jer 46:20 Egypt *is like* a very fair **h**, *but* 5697
48:34 unto Horonaim, *as* a **h** of three years old: 5697
50:11 because ye are grown fat as the **h** at grass, 5697
Hos 4:16 For Israel slideth back as a backsliding **h**: 6510
10:11 Ephraim *is as* a **h** *that is* taught, *and* 5697
Heb 9:13 and the ashes of a **h** sprinkling the unclean, *1151*

HEIFER'S (1) [HEIFER]
Dt 21:4 shall strike off the **h** neck there in 5697

HEIGHT (62) [HIGH]
Ge 6:15 it fifty cubits, and the **h** of it thirty cubits. 6967
Ex 25:10 and a cubit and a half the **h** thereof. 6967
25:23 and a cubit and a half the **h** thereof. 6967
27:1 and the **h** thereof *shall be* three cubits. 6967
27:18 the **h** five cubits *of* fine twined linen, and 6967
30:2 two cubits *shall be* the **h** thereof: the horns 6967
37:1 of it, and a cubit and a half the **h** of it: 6967
37:10 and a cubit and a half the **h** thereof: 6967
37:25 and two cubits *was* the **h** of it; 6967
38:1 and three cubits the **h** thereof. 6967
38:18 and the **h** in the breadth *was* five cubits, 6967
1Sa 16:7 his countenance, or on the **h** of his stature; 1364
17:4 of Gath, whose **h** *was* six cubits and a span. 1363
1Ki 6:2 and the **h** thereof thirty cubits. 6967
6:20 and twenty cubits in the **h** thereof: 6967
6:26 The **h** of the one cherub *was* ten cubits, and 6967
7:2 fifty cubits, and the **h** thereof thirty cubits, 6967
7:16 the **h** of the one chapiter *was* five cubits, 6967
7:16 the **h** of the other chapiter *was* five cubits: 6967
7:23 round all about, and his **h** *was* five cubits: 6967
7:27 breadth thereof, and three cubits the **h** of it. 6967
7:32 the **h** of a wheel *was* a cubit and half a 6967
2Ki 19:23 I am come up to the **h** of the mountains, 4791
25:17 The **h** of the one pillar *was* eighteen cubits, 6967
25:17 the **h** of the chapiter three cubits; and 6967
2Ch 3:4 and the **h** *was* an hundred and twenty: 1363
4:1 and ten cubits the **h** thereof. 6967
4:2 in compass, and five cubits the **h** thereof; 6967
33:14 **raised** it **up** a very **great h**, and 1361
Ezr 6:3 the **h** thereof threescore cubits, *and* 7314
Job 22:12 *Is* not God in the **h** of heaven? and 1363
22:12 behold the **h** of the stars, how high they are. 7218
Ps 102:19 For he hath looked down from the **h** of his 4791
Pr 25:3 The heaven for **h**, and the earth for depth, 7312
Isa 7:11 ask it either in the depth, or in the **h** above. 1361
37:24 am I come up *to* the **h** of the mountains, 4791
37:24 I will enter into the **h** of his border, *and* 4791
Jer 31:12 they shall come and sing in the **h** of Zion, 4791
49:16 of the rock, that holdest the **h** of the hill: 4791

H

Jer 51:53 though she should fortify the **h** of her 4791
52:21 the **h** of one pillar *was* eighteen cubits; 6967
52:22 the **h** of one chapiter *was* five cubits, 6967
Eze 17:23 In the mountain of the **h** of Israel will I 4791
19:11 she appeared in her **h** with the multitude of 1363
20:40 in the mountain of the **h** of Israel, saith 4791
31: 5 Therefore his **h** was exalted above all 6967
31:10 Because thou hast lifted up thyself in **h**, and 6967
31:10 and his heart is lifted up in his **h**; 1363
31:14 by the waters exalt themselves for their **h**, 6967
31:14 neither their trees stand up in their **h**, 1363
32: 5 and fill the valleys *with* thy **h**. 7419
40: 5 the building, one reed; and the **h**, one reed. 6967
41: 8 I saw also the **h** of the house round about: 1363
Da 3: 1 whose **h** *was* threescore cubits, *and* 7314
4:10 of the earth, and the **h** thereof *was* great. 7314
4:11 the **h** thereof reached unto heaven, and 7314
4:20 whose **h** reached unto the heaven, and 7314
Am 2: 9 whose **h** *was* like the height of the cedars, 1363
2: 9 whose height *was* like the **h** of the cedars, 1363
Ro 8:39 Nor **h**, nor depth, nor any other creature, *5313*
Eph 3:18 *is* the breadth, and length, and depth, and **h**; *5311*
Rev 21:16 and the breadth and the **h** of it are equal. *5311*

HEIGHTS (2) [HIGH]

Ps 148: 1 from the heavens: praise him in the **h**. 4791
Isa 14:14 I will ascend above the **h** of the clouds; 1116

HEINOUS (1)

Job 31:11 For this *is* a **h crime**; yea, it *is* an iniquity 2154

HEIR (18) [FELLOWHEIRS, HEIRS, JOINT-HEIRS]

Ge 15: 3 and lo, one born in my house is mine **h**. 3423
15: 4 unto him, saying, This shall not be thine **h**; 3423
15: 4 out of thine own bowels shall be thine **h**. 3423
21:10 bondwoman shall not be **h** with my son, 3423
2Sa 14: 7 he slew; and we will destroy the **h** also: 3423
Pr 30:23 and a handmaid that is **h** to her mistress. 3423
Jer 49: 1 Hath he no **h**? why *then* doth their king 3423
49: 2 shall Israel be **h** unto them that were his 3423
Mic 1:15 Yet will I bring an **h** unto thee, 3423
Mt 21:38 they said among themselves, This is the **h**; *2818*
Mk 12: 7 said amongst themselves, This is the **h**; *2818*
Lk 20:14 among themselves, saying, This is the **h**: *2818*
Ro 4:13 that he should be the **h** of the world, *2818*
Gal 4: 1 Now I say, *That* the **h**, as long as he is a *2818*
4: 7 if a son, then an **h** of God through Christ. *2818*
4:30 not be **h** with the son of the freewoman. *2816*
Heb 1: 2 whom he hath appointed **h** of all *things*, by *2818*
11: 7 became **h** of the righteousness which is by *2818*

HEIRS (11) [HEIR]

Jer 49: 2 Israel be heir unto them that were his **h**, 3423
Ro 4:14 For if they which are of the law *be* **h**, faith *2818*
8:17 And if children, then **h**; heirs of God, and *2818*
8:17 **h** of God, and joint-heirs with Christ; if so *2818*
Gal 3:29 and **h** according to the promise. *2818*
Tit 3: 7 we should be made **h** according to the hope *2818*
Heb 1:14 for them who shall be **h** of salvation? *2816*
6:17 willing more abundantly to shew unto the **h** *2818*
11: 9 Jacob, the **h with** *him* of the same promise: *4789*
Jas 2: 5 **h** of the kingdom which he hath promised *2818*
1Pe 3: 7 and as *being* **h together** of the grace of life; *4789*

HELAH (2)

1Ch 4: 5 of Tekoa had two wives, **H** and Naarah. 2458
4: 7 the sons of **H** *were*, Zereth, and Jezoar, 2458

HELAM (2)

2Sa 10:16 they came *to* **H**; and Shobach the captain of 2431
10:17 and passed over Jordan, and came to **H**. 2431

HELBAH (1)

Jdg 1:31 nor of **H**, nor of Aphik, nor of Rehob: 2462

HELBON (1)

Eze 27:18 in the wine of **H**, and white wool. 2463

HELD (52) [HOLD]

Ge 24:21 the man wondering at her **h** his **peace**, 2790
34: 5 Jacob **h** his **peace** until they were come. 2790
48:17 he **h up** his father's hand, to remove it from 8551
Ex 17:11 it came to pass, when Moses **h up** his hand, 7311
36:12 the loops **h** one *curtain* to another. 6901
Lev 10: 3 I will be glorified. And Aaron **h** his **peace**. 1826
Nu 30: 7 **h** his **peace** at her in the day that he heard 2790
30:11 husband heard *it*, and **h** his **peace** at her, 2790
30:14 he **h** his **peace** at her in the day that he 2790
Jdg 7:20 **h** the lamps in their left hands, and 2388
16:26 Samson said unto the lad that **h** him by 2388
Ru 3:15 when she **h** it, he measured six *measures* of 270
1Sa 10:27 no presents. But he **h** his **peace**. 2790+3509.1
25:36 behold, he **h** a feast in his house, like 3807.1
2Sa 18:16 after Israel: for Joab **h back** the people. 2820
1Ki 8:65 at that time Solomon **h** a feast, and 6213
2Ki 18:36 the people **h** their **peace**, and answered him 2790
2Ch 4: 5 *and* it received and **h** three thousand baths. 3557
Ne 4:16 the *other* half of them **h** both the spears, 2388
4:17 and with the other *hand* **h** a weapon. 2388
4:21 half of them **h** the spears from the rising of 2388
5: 8 **h** they their **peace**, and found nothing *to* 2790
Est 5: 2 the king **h out** to Esther the golden sceptre 3447
7: 4 and bondwomen, I had **h** my **tongue**, 2790
8: 4 the king **h out** the golden sceptre toward 3447
Job 23:11 My foot hath **h** his steps, his way have I 270
29:10 The nobles **h** their **peace**, and 2244+6963
Ps 32: 9 whose mouth must be **h in** with bit and 1102
39: 2 I **h** my **peace**, *even* from good; 2814
94:18 thy mercy, O LORD, **h** me **up**. 5582
SS 3: 4 I **h** him, and would not let him go, until I had 270
7: 5 like purple; the king *is* **h** in the galleries. 631
Isa 36:21 they **h** their **peace**, and answered him not a 2790
57:11 have not I **h** my **peace** even of old, and 2814
Jer 50:33 all that took them captives **h** them **fast**; 2388
Da 12: 7 when he **h up** his right hand and his left 7311
Mt 12:14 went out, and **h** a council against him, *2983*
26:63 But Jesus **h** his **peace**. And the high priest *4623*
28: 9 And they came and **h** him by the feet, and *2902*
Mk 3: 4 save life, or to kill? But they **h** their **peace**. *4623*
9:34 But they **h** their **peace**: for by the way they *4623*
14:61 But he **h** his **peace**, and answered nothing. *4623*
15: 1 priests **h** a consultation with the elders *4160*
Lk 14: 4 And they **h** their **peace**. And he took *him*, *2270*
20:26 marvelled at his answer, and **h** their **peace**. *4601*
22:63 And the men that **h** Jesus mocked him, and *4912*
Ac 3:11 And as the lame *man* which was healed **h** *2902*
11:18 they heard these *things*, they **h** their **peace**, *2270*
14: 4 and part **h** with the Jews, and part with *1510*
15:13 And after they had **h** their **peace**, *4601*
Ro 7: 6 *that* being dead wherein we were **h**; *2722*
Rev 6: 9 of God, and for the testimony which they **h**: *2192*

HELD FAST See CLEAVE; CLEAVED; CLEAVETH

HELDAI (2)

1Ch 27:15 the twelfth month *was* **H** the Netophathite, 2469
Zec 6:10 *even* of **H**, of Tobijah, and of Jedaiah, 2469

HELEB (1)

2Sa 23:29 **H** the son of Baanah, a Netophathite, 2460

HELED (1)

1Ch 11:30 **H** the son of Baanah the Netophathite, 2466

HELEK (2) [HELEKITES]

Nu 26:30 of **H**, the family of the Helekites: 2507
Jos 17: 2 for the children of **H**, and for the children 2507

HELEKITES (1) [HELEK]

Nu 26:30 of Helek, the family of the **H**: 2516

HELEM (2)

1Ch 7:35 the son of his brother **H**; Zophah, and 1987
Zec 6:14 the crowns shall be to **H**, and to Tobijah, 2494

HELEPH (1)

Jos 19:33 their coast was from **H**, from Allon to 2501

HELEZ (5)

2Sa 23:26 **H** the Paltite, Ira the son of Ikkesh 2503
1Ch 2:39 Azariah begat **H**, and Helez begat Eleasah, 2503
2:39 Azariah begat Helez, and **H** begat Eleasah, 2503
11:27 Shammoth the Harorite, **H** the Pelonite, 2503
27:10 for the seventh month *was* **H** the Pelonite, 2503

HELI (1)

Lk 3:23 the son of Joseph, which was *the son* of **H**, *2242*

HELKAI (1)

Ne 12:15 Of Harim, Adna; of Meraioth, **H**; 2517

HELKATH (2) [HELKATH-HAZZURIM]

Jos 19:25 their border was **H**, and Hali, and Beten, 2520
21:31 **H** with her suburbs, and Rehob with her 2520

HELKATH-HAZZURIM (1) [HELKATH]

2Sa 2:16 wherefore that place was called **H**, which *is* 2521

HELL (54)

Dt 32:22 shall burn unto the lowest **h**, and 7585
2Sa 22: 6 The sorrows of **h** compassed me about; 7585
Job 11: 8 deeper than **h**; what canst thou know? 7585
26: 6 **H** *is* naked before him, and destruction hath 7585
Ps 9:17 The wicked shall be turned into **h**, *and* 7585
16:10 For thou wilt not leave my soul in **h**; 7585
18: 5 The sorrows of **h** compassed me about: 7585
55:15 *and* let them go down quick *into* **h**: 7585
86:13 hast delivered my soul from the lowest **h**. 7585
116: 3 and the pains of **h** gat hold upon me: 7585
139: 8 if I make my bed in **h**, behold, thou *art* 7585
Pr 5: 5 go down *to* death; her steps take hold on **h**. 7585
7:27 Her house *is* the way to **h**, going down to 7585
9:18 *and that* her guests *are* in the depths of **h**. 7585
15:11 **H** and destruction *are* before the LORD: 7585
15:24 that *he* may depart from **h** beneath. 7585
23:14 the rod, and shalt deliver his soul from **h**. 7585
27:20 **H** and destruction are never full; so 7585
Isa 5:14 Therefore **h** hath enlarged herself, 7585
14: 9 **H** from beneath is moved for thee to meet 7585
14:15 Yet thou shalt be brought down to **h**, to 7585
28:15 with death, and with **h** are we at agreement; 7585
28:18 and your agreement with **h** shall not stand; 7585
57: 9 and didst debase *thyself even* unto **h**. 7585
Eze 31:16 when I cast him down to **h** with them that 7585
31:17 They also went down into **h** with him unto 7585
32:21 of the midst of **h** with them that help him: 7585
32:27 which are gone down *to* **h** with their 7585
Am 9: 2 Though they dig into **h**, thence shall mine 7585
Jnh 2: 2 out of the belly of **h** cried I, *and* 7585
Hab 2: 5 who enlargeth his desire as **h**, and *is* as 7585
Mt 5:22 *Thou* fool, shall be in danger of **h** fire. *1067*
5:29 *that* thy whole body should be cast into **h**. *1067*
5:30 *that* thy whole body should be cast into **h**. *1067*
10:28 is able to destroy both soul and body in **h**. *1067*
11:23 unto heaven, shalt be brought down to **h**: *86*
16:18 and the gates of **h** shall not prevail against it. *86*
18: 9 than having two eyes to be cast into **h** *1067*
23:15 ye make him twofold more *the* child of **h** *1067*
23:33 how can ye escape the damnation of **h**? *1067*
Mk 9:43 than having two hands to go into **h**, into *1067*
9:45 than having two feet to be cast into **h**, *1067*
9:47 than having two eyes to be cast into **h** fire: *1067*
Lk 10:15 exalted to heaven, shalt be thrust down to **h**. *86*
12: 5 *he* hath killed hath power to cast into **h**; *1067*
16:23 And in **h** he lift up his eyes, being in *86*
Ac 2:27 Because thou wilt not leave my soul in **h**, *86*
2:31 of Christ, that his soul was not left in **h**, *86*
Jas 3: 6 course of nature; and it is set on fire of **h**. *1067*
2Pe 2: 4 but **cast** *them* **down to h**, and *5020*
Rev 1:18 Amen; and have the keys of **h** and of death. *86*
6: 8 on him *was* Death, and **H** followed with him. *86*
20:13 **h** delivered up the dead which were in them: *86*
20:14 and **h** were cast into the lake of fire. *86*

HELM (1)

Jas 3: 4 are they turned about with a very small **h**, *4079*

HELMET (8) [HELMETS]

1Sa 17: 5 *he had* a **h** of brass upon his head, and 3553
17:38 and he put a **h** of brass upon his head; 6959
Isa 59:17 and a **h** of salvation upon his head; 3553
Eze 23:24 thee buckler and shield and **h** round about: 6959
27:10 they hanged the shield and **h** in thee; 3553
38: 5 with them; all of them *with* shield and **h**: 3553
Eph 6:17 And take the **h** of salvation, and the sword *4030*
1Th 5: 8 and love; and for a **h**, the hope of salvation. *4030*

HELMETS (2) [HELMET]

2Ch 26:14 **h**, and habergeons, and bows, and slings to 3553
Jer 46: 4 ye horsemen, and stand forth with *your* **h**; 3553

HELON (5)

Nu 1: 9 Of Zebulun; Eliab the son of **H**. 2497
2: 7 Eliab the son of **H** *shall be* captain of 2497
7:24 On the third day Eliab the son of **H**, 2497
7:29 this *was* the offering of Eliab the son of **H**. 2497
10:16 children of Zebulun *was* Eliab the son of **H**. 2497

HELP (126) [FELLOWHELPER, FELLOWHELPERS, HELPED, HELPER, HELPERS, HELPETH, HELPING, HELPS, HOLPEN]

Ge 2:18 be alone; I will make him a **h** meet for him. 5828
2:20 for Adam there was not found a **h** meet for 5828
49:25 by the God of thy father, who shall **h** thee; 5826
Ex 18: 4 *said he, was* mine **h**, and delivered me from 5828
23: 5 wouldest forbear to **h** him, thou shalt surely 5800
23: 5 thou shalt **surely h** with him. 5800+5800
Dt 22: 4 thou shalt surely **h** him to lift *them* up 5973
32:38 let them rise up and **h** you, *and* be your 5826
33: 7 and be thou a **h** *to him* from his enemies. 5828
33:26 *who* rideth *upon* the heaven in thy **h**, and 5828
33:29 the shield of thy **h**, and who *is* the sword of 5828
Jos 1:14 all the mighty *men* of valour, and **h** them; 5826
10: 4 Come up unto me, and **h** me, that we may 5826
10: 6 up to us quickly, and save us, and **h** us: 5826
10:33 Horam king of Gezer came up to **h** 5826
Jdg 5:23 they came not to the **h** of the LORD, 5833
5:23 to the **h** of the LORD against the mighty. 5833
1Sa 11: 9 by *that time* the sun be hot, ye shall have **h**. 8668
2Sa 10:11 strong for me, then thou shalt **h** me: 1961+3444
10:11 strong for thee, then I will come and **h** thee. 3467
10:19 So the Syrians feared to **h** the children of 3467
14: 4 and did obeisance, and said, **H**, O king. 3467
2Ki 6:26 unto him, saying, **H**, my lord, O king. 3467
6:27 he said, *If* the LORD do not **h** thee, 3467
6:27 do not help thee, whence shall I **h** thee? 3467
1Ch 12:17 If ye be come peaceably unto me to **h** me, 5826
12:22 day by day there came to David to **h** him, 5826
18: 5 when the Syrians of Damascus came to **h** 5826
19:12 strong for me, then thou shalt **h** me: 1961+8668
19:12 be too strong for thee, then I will **h** thee. 3467
19:19 neither would the Syrians **h** the children of 3467
22:17 the princes of Israel to **h** Solomon his son, 5826
2Ch 14:11 said, LORD, *it is* nothing with thee to **h**, 5826
14:11 **h** us, O LORD our God; for we rest on 5826
19: 2 Shouldest thou **h** the ungodly, and 5826
20: 4 to ask ***h*** of the LORD: NIH
20: 9 in our affliction, then thou wilt hear and **h**. 3467
25: 8 for God hath power to **h**, and to cast down. 5826
26:13 to **h** the king against the enemy. 5826
28:16 send unto the kings of Assyria to **h** him. 5826
28:23 Because the gods of the kings of Syria **h** 5826
28:23 will I sacrifice to them, that they may **h** me. 5826
29:34 wherefore their brethren the Levites did **h** 2388
32: 3 *were* without the city: and they did **h** him. 5826
32: 8 with us *is* the LORD our God to **h** us, and 5826
Ezr 1: 4 let the men of his place **h** him with silver, 5375
8:22 horsemen to **h** us against the enemy in 5826
Job 6:13 *Is* not my **h** in me? and is wisdom driven 5833
8:20 will he **h** the evil doers: 2388+3027+871.1
29:12 and *him that had* none to **h** him. 5826
31:21 the fatherless, when I saw my **h** in the gate: 5833
Ps 3: 2 of my soul, *There is* no **h** for him in God. 3444
12: 1 **H**, LORD; for the godly *man* ceaseth; 3467
20: 2 Send thee **h** from the sanctuary, and 5828
22:11 for trouble *is* near; for *there is* none to **h**. 5826
22:19 O my strength, haste thee to **h** me. 5833
27: 9 thou hast been my **h**; leave me not, 5833
33:20 for the LORD: he *is* our **h** and our shield. 5828
35: 2 and buckler, and stand up for mine **h**. 5833
37:40 the LORD shall **h** them, and deliver them: 5826
38:22 Make haste to **h** me, O Lord my salvation. 5833
40:13 deliver me: O LORD, make haste to **h** me. 5833
40:17 thou *art* my **h** and my deliverer; make no 5833
42: 5 for I shall yet praise him *for* the **h** of his 3444
44:26 Arise for our **h**, and redeem us for thy 5833
46: 1 and strength, a very present **h** in trouble. 5833
46: 5 God shall **h** her, *and that* right early. 5826
59: 4 *my* fault: awake to **h** me, and behold. 7125
60:11 Give us **h** from trouble: for vain *is* the help 5833
60:11 help from trouble: for vain *is* the **h** of man. 8668
63: 7 Because thou hast been my **h**, therefore 5833
70: 1 deliver me; make haste to **h** me, O LORD. 5833
70: 5 thou *art* my **h** and my deliverer; O LORD, 5828
71:12 from me: O my God, make haste for my **h**. 5833
79: 9 **H** us, O God of our salvation, for the glory 5826
89:19 I have laid **h** upon *one that is* mighty; 5828
94:17 Unless the LORD *had been* my **h**, my soul 5833
107:12 they fell down, and *there was* none to **h**. 5826
108:12 Give us **h** from trouble: for vain *is* the help 5833

Ps 108:12 help from trouble: for vain *is* the **h** of man. 8668
109:26 **H** me, O LORD my God: O save me 5826
115: 9 the LORD: he *is* their **h** and their shield. 5828
115:10 the LORD: he *is* their **h** and their shield. 5828
115:11 the LORD: he *is* their **h** and their shield. 5828
118: 7 taketh my part with them that **h** me: 5826
119:86 they persecute me wrongfully; **h** thou me. 5826
119:173 Let thine hand **h** me; for I have chosen thy 5826
119:175 praise thee; and let thy judgments **h** me. 5826
121: 1 unto the hills, from whence cometh my **h**. 5828
121: 2 My **h** *cometh* from the LORD, 5828
124: 8 Our **h** *is* in the name of the LORD, 5828
146: 3 in the son of man, in whom *there is* no **h**. 8668
146: 5 *is he* that *hath* the God of Jacob for his **h**, 5828
Ecc 4:10 for *he hath* not another to **h** him **up**. 6965
Isa 10: 3 to whom will ye flee for **h**? and where will 5833
20: 6 whither we flee for **h** to be delivered from 5833
30: 5 nor be a **h** nor profit, but a shame, and 5828
30: 7 For the Egyptians shall **h** in vain, and to no 5826
31: 1 Woe to them that go down *to* Egypt for **h**; 5833
31: 2 against the **h** of them that work iniquity. 5833
41:10 yea, I will **h** thee; yea, I will uphold thee 5826
41:13 saying unto thee, Fear not; I will **h** thee. 5826
41:14 I will **h** thee, saith the LORD, and 5826
44: 2 thee from the womb, *which* will **h** thee; 5826
50: 7 For the Lord GOD will **h** me; therefore 5826
50: 9 Behold, the Lord GOD will **h** me; who *is* 5826
63: 5 I looked, and *there was* none to **h**; and 5826
Jer 37: 7 which is come forth to **h** you, 5833
La 1: 7 the hand of the enemy, and none did **h** her: 5826
4:17 for us, our eyes as yet failed for our vain **h**: 5833
Eze 12:14 every wind all that *are* about him to **h** him, 5828
32:21 of the midst of hell with them that **h** him: 5826
Da 10:13 one of the chief princes, came to **h** me; 5826
11:34 they shall be holpen *with* a little **h**: 5828
11:45 shall come to his end, and none shall **h** him. 5826
Hos 13: 9 hast destroyed thyself; but in me *is* thine **h**. 5828
Mt 15:25 and worshipped him, saying, Lord, **h** me. *997*
Mk 9:22 any *thing*, have compassion on us, and **h** us. *997*
9:24 Lord, I believe; **h** thou mine unbelief. *997*
Lk 5: 7 that *they* should come and **h** them. *4815*
10:40 bid her therefore that she **h** me. *4878*
Ac 16: 9 Come over into Macedonia, and **h** us. *997*
21:28 Crying out, Men of Israel, **h**: This is *997*
26:22 Having therefore obtained **h** of God, *1947*
Php 4: 3 **h** those *women* which laboured with me in *4815*
Heb 4:16 and find grace to **h** in time of need. *996*

HELPED (24) [HELP]
Ex 2:17 Moses stood up and **h** them, and 3467
1Sa 7:12 Hitherto hath the LORD **h** us. 5826
1Ki 1: 7 and they following Adonijah **h** *him*. 5826
20:16 the thirty and two kings that **h** him. 5826
1Ch 5:20 they were **h** against them, and the Hagarites 5826
12:19 they **h** them not: for the lords of 5826
12:21 they **h** David against the band *of the rovers:* 5826
15:26 when God **h** the Levites that bare the ark of 5826
2Ch 18:31 cried out, and the LORD **h** him; 5826
20:23 of Seir, every one **h** to destroy another. 5826
26: 7 God **h** him against the Philistines, and 5826
26:15 for he was marvellously **h**, till he was 5826
28:21 unto the king of Assyria: but he **h** him not. 5833
Ezr 10:15 and Shabbethai the Levite **h** them. 5826
Est 9: 3 and officers of the king, **h** the Jews; 5375
Job 26: 2 How hast thou **h** *him that is* without 5826
Ps 28: 7 my heart trusted in him, and I am **h**: 5826
116: 6 the simple: I was brought low, and he **h** me. 3467
118:13 me that *I* might fall: but the LORD **h** me. 5826
Isa 41: 6 They **h** every one his neighbour; and 5826
49: 8 and in a day of salvation have I **h** thee: 5826
Zec 1:15 and they **h** **forward** the affliction. 5826
Ac 18:27 **h** them much which had believed through *4820*
Rev 12:16 And the earth **h** the woman, and the earth *997*

HELPER (9) [HELP]
2Ki 14:26 shut up, nor any left, nor any **h** for Israel. 5826
Job 30:13 set forward my calamity, they have no **h**. 5826
Ps 10:14 unto thee; thou art the **h** of the fatherless. 5826
30:10 mercy upon me: LORD, be thou my **h**. 5826
54: 4 Behold, God *is* mine **h**: the Lord *is* with 5826
72:12 the poor also, and *him* that hath no **h**. 5826
Jer 47: 4 and Zidon every **h** that remaineth: 5826
Ro 16: 9 Salute Urban our **h** in Christ, and *4904*
Heb 13: 6 The Lord *is* my **h**, and I will not fear what *998*

HELPERS (7) [HELP]
1Ch 12: 1 they *were* among the mighty *men*, **h** of 5826
12:18 peace *be* unto thee, and peace *be* to thine **h**; 5826
Job 9:13 his anger, the proud **h** do stoop under him. 5826
Eze 30: 8 and *when* all her **h** shall be destroyed. 5826
Na 3: 9 *it was* infinite; Put and Lubim were thy **h**. 5833
Ro 16: 3 and Aquila my **h** in Christ Jesus: *4904*
2Co 1:24 over your faith, but are **h** of your joy: *4904*

HELPETH (4) [HELP]
1Ch 12:18 *be* to thine helpers; for thy God **h** thee. 5826
Isa 31: 3 both he that **h** shall fall, and he that is 5826
Ro 8:26 Likewise the Spirit also **h** our infirmities: *4878*
1Co 16:16 and to every one that **h** **with** *us*, and *4903*

HELPING (3) [HELP]
Ezr 5: 2 with them *were* the prophets of God **h** 5583
Ps 22: 1 *why art thou so* far from **h** me, and 3444
2Co 1:11 You also **h** **together** by prayer for us, *4943*

HELPING THE POOR See ALMSDEEDS

HELPS (2) [HELP]
Ac 27:17 taken up, they used **h**, undergirding the ship; *996*
1Co 12:28 then gifts of healings, **h**, governments, *484*

HELVE (1)
Dt 19: 5 the head slippeth from the **h**, and 6086

HEM (7) [HEMS]
Ex 28:33 *beneath* upon the **h** of it thou shalt make 7757
28:33 and of scarlet, round about the **h** thereof; 7757
28:34 upon the **h** of the robe round about. 7757
39:25 the pomegranates upon the **h** of the robe, 7757
39:26 round about the **h** of the robe to minister *in;* 7757
Mt 9:20 and touched the **h** of his garment: *2899*
14:36 they might only touch the **h** of his garment: *2899*

HEMAM (1)
Ge 36:22 the children of Lotan were Hori and **H**; 1967

HEMAN (17)
1Ki 4:31 **H**, and Chalcol, and Darda, the sons of 1968
1Ch 2: 6 and Ethan, and **H**, and Calcol, and Dara: 1968
6:33 **H** a singer, the son of Joel, the son of 1968
15:17 So the Levites appointed **H** the son of Joel; 1968
15:19 So the singers, **H**, Asaph, and Ethan, 1968
16:41 with them **H** and Jeduthun, and the rest that 1968
16:42 with them **H** and Jeduthun *with* trumpets 1968
25: 1 of **H**, and of Jeduthun, who should 1968
25: 4 Of **H**: the sons of Heman; Bukkiah, 1968
25: 4 the sons of **H**; Bukkiah, Mattaniah, Uzziel, 1968
25: 5 All these *were* the sons of **H** the king's seer 1968
25: 5 God gave to **H** fourteen sons and 1968
25: 6 the king's order *to* Asaph, Jeduthun, and **H**. 1968
2Ch 5:12 of **H**, of Jeduthun, with their sons and 1968
29:14 of the sons of **H**; Jehiel, and Shimei: and 1968
35:15 and **H**, and Jeduthun the king's seer; 1968
Ps 88: T Maschil of **H** the Ezrahite. 1968

HEMATH (3)
1Ch 2:55 These *are* the Kenites that came of **H**, 2575
13: 5 of Egypt even unto the entering of **H**, 2574
Am 6:14 in of **H** unto the river of the wilderness. 2574

HEMDAN (1)
Ge 36:26 **H**, and Eshban, and Ithran, and Cheran. 2533

HEMLOCK (2)
Hos 10: 4 thus judgment springeth up as **h** in 7219
Am 6:12 and the fruit of righteousness into **h**: 3939

HEMS (1) [HEM]
Ex 39:24 they made upon the **h** of the robe 7757

HEN (3)
Zec 6:14 to Jedaiah, and to **H** the son of Zephaniah, 2581
Mt 23:37 even as a **h** gathereth her chickens under *3733*
Lk 13:34 as a **h** *doth gather* her brood under *her* *3733*

HENA (3)
2Ki 18:34 *are* the gods of Sepharvaim, **H**, and Ivah? 2012
19:13 of the city of Sepharvaim, *of* **H**, and Ivah? 2012
Isa 37:13 of the city of Sepharvaim, **H**, and Ivah? 2012

HENADAD (4)
Ezr 3: 9 the sons of **H**, *with* their sons and 2582
Ne 3:18 repaired their brethren, Bavai the son of **H**, 2582
3:24 After him repaired Binnui the son of **H** 2582
10: 9 Binnui of the sons of **H**, Kadmiel; 2582

HENCE (30) [HENCEFORTH, HENCEFORWARD]
Ge 37:17 the man said, They are departed **h**; 2088+4480
42:15 of Pharaoh ye shall not go forth **h**, 2088+4480
50:25 and ye shall carry up my bones from **h**. 2088
Ex 11: 1 afterwards he will let you go **h**: 2088+4480
11: 1 surely thrust you out **h** altogether. 2088+4480
13:19 ye shall carry up my bones away **h** with 2088
33: 1 *and* go up **h**, thou and the people which 2088
33:15 go not *with me*, carry us not up **h**. 2088+4480
Dt 9:12 Arise, get thee down quickly from **h**; 2088
Jos 4: 3 Take you **h** out of the midst of Jordan, NIH
Jdg 6:18 Depart not **h**, I pray thee, until I 2088+4480
Ru 2: 8 neither go from **h**, but abide here fast by 2088
1Ki 17: 3 Get thee **h**, and turn thee eastward, 2088+4480
Ps 39:13 before I go **h**, and be no more. NIH
Isa 30:22 thou shalt say unto it, **Get** thee **h**. 3318
Jer 38:10 Take from **h** thirty men with thee, and 2088
Zec 6: 7 Get ye *h*, walk to and fro through the earth. NIH
Mt 4:10 saith Jesus unto him, **Get** thee **h**, Satan: *5217*
17:20 this mountain, Remove **h** to yonder place; *1782*
Lk 4: 9 the Son of God, cast thyself down **from** **h**: *1782*
13:31 unto him, Get *thee* out, and depart **h**: *1782*
16:26 that they which would pass **from** **h** to you *1782*
Jn 2:16 them that sold doves, Take these *things* **h**; *1782*
7: 3 said unto him, Depart **h**, and go into Judea, *1782*
14:31 *even* so I do. Arise, let us go **h**. *1782*
18:36 but now is my kingdom not **from** **h**. *1782*
20:15 if thou have borne him *h*, tell me where NIG
Ac 1: 5 the Holy Ghost not many days **h**. *3326+3778*
22:21 for I will send thee **far** **h** unto the Gentiles. *3112*
Jas 4: 1 *come they* not **h**, *even* of your lusts that *1782*

HENCEFORTH (33) [FORTH, HENCE]
Ge 4:12 it shall not **h** yield unto thee her strength; 3254
Nu 18:22 Neither must the children of Israel **h** come 5750
Dt 17:16 Ye shall **h** return no more that way. 3254
19:20 shall **h** commit no more any such evil 3254
Jdg 2:21 I also will not **h** drive out any from before 3254
2Ki 5:17 for thy servant will **h** offer neither burnt 5750
2Ch 16: 9 therefore from **h** thou shalt have wars. 6258
Ps 125: 2 about his people from **h** even for ever. 6258
131: 3 Let Israel hope in the LORD from **h** and 6258
Isa 9: 7 and with justice from **h** even for ever. 6258
52: 1 for **h** there shall no more come into thee 3254
59:21 saith the LORD, from **h** and for ever. 6258
Eze 36:12 thou shalt no more **h** bereave them of men. 3254
Mic 4: 7 reign over them in mount Zion from **h**, 6258
Mt 23:39 Ye shall not see me **h**, till ye shall say, *575+737*
26:29 will not drink **h** of this fruit of the vine, *575+737*
Lk 1:48 from **h** all generations shall call me *3568+3588*
5:10 from **h** thou shalt catch men. *3568+3588*
Lk 12:52 For from **h** there shall be five in one *3568+3588*
Jn 14: 7 and from **h** ye know him, and have seen him. *737*
15:15 **H** I call you **not** servants; for the servant *3765*
Ac 4:17 that *they* speak **h** to no man in this name. *3371*
18: 6 from **h** I will go unto the Gentiles. *3568*
Ro 6: 6 that **h** we should **not** serve sin. *3371*
2Co 5:15 that they which live should **not** **h** live unto *3371*
5:16 Wherefore **h** know we no *man* *575+3568+3588*
5:16 the flesh, yet **now** **h** know we *him* no more. *3568*
Gal 6:17 **From** **h** let no *man* trouble me: for I *3062+3588*
Eph 4:14 That we *h* be no more children, tossed to NIG
4:17 that ye **h** walk **not** as other Gentiles walk, *3371*
2Ti 4: 8 **H** there is laid up for me a crown of *3062*
Heb 10:13 From **h** expecting till his enemies be *3062+3588*
Rev 14:13 *are* the dead which die in the Lord from **h**: *534*

HENCEFORWARD (2) [FORWARD, HENCE]
Nu 15:23 and **h** among your generations; 1973
Mt 21:19 Let **no** fruit grow on thee **h** for ever. *3371*

HENNA See CAMPHIRE

HENOCH (2) [ENOCH]
1Ch 1: 3 **H**, Methuselah, Lamech, 2585
1:33 and Epher, and **H**, and Abida, and Eldaah. 2585

HEPHER (9) [GATH-HEPHER, HEPHERITES]
Nu 26:32 and *of* **H**, the family of the Hepherites. 2660
26:33 Zelophehad the son of **H** had no sons, but 2660
27: 1 the son of **H**, the son of Gilead, the son of 2660
Jos 12:17 king of Tappuah, one; the king of **H**, one; 2660
17: 2 for the children of **H**, and for the children 2660
17: 3 Zelophehad, the son of **H**, the son of 2660
1Ki 4:10 *pertained* Sochoh, and all the land of **H**: 2660
1Ch 4: 6 and **H**, and Temeni, and Haahashtari. 2660
11:36 **H** the Mecherathite, Ahijah the Pelonite, 2660

HEPHERITES (1) [HEPHER]
Nu 26:32 and *of* Hepher, the family of the **H**. 2662

HEPHZI-BAH (2)
2Ki 21: 1 And his mother's name *was* **H**. 2657
Isa 62: 4 thou shalt be called **H**, and thy land Beulah: 2657

HER (1993) [SHE] See Index of Articles, Etc.

HERALD (1)
Da 3: 4 a **h** cried aloud, To you it is commanded, 3744

HERB (19) [HERBS]
Ge 1:11 the **h** yielding seed, *and* the fruit tree 6212
1:12 *and* **h** yielding seed after his kind, and 6212
1:29 I have given you every **h** bearing seed, 6212
1:30 *is* life, *I have given* every green **h** for meat: 6212
2: 5 and every **h** of the field before it grew: 6212
3:18 to thee; and thou shalt eat the **h** of the field; 6212
9: 3 *even* as the green **h** have I given you all 6212
Ex 9:22 upon beast, and upon every **h** of the field, 6212
9:25 the hail smote every **h** of the field, and 6212
10:12 eat every **h** of the land, *even* all that the hail 6212
10:15 they did eat every **h** of the land, and all 6212
Dt 32: 2 as the small rain upon the **tender** **h**, and 1877
2Ki 19:26 *as* the green **h**, *as* the grass on 1877
Job 8:12 cut down, it withereth before any *other* **h**. 2682
38:27 to cause the bud of the **tender** **h** to spring 1877
Ps 37: 2 like the grass, and wither as the green **h**. 1877
104:14 for the cattle, and **h** for the service of man: 6212
Isa 37:27 *as* the green **h**, *as* the grass on 1877
66:14 and your bones shall flourish like an **h**: 1877

HERBS (10) [HERB]
Ex 10:15 or in the **h** of the field, through all the land 6212
12: 8 *and* with bitter **h** they shall eat it. NIH
Nu 9:11 eat it with unleavened bread and bitter *h*. NIH
Dt 11:10 wateredst *it* with thy foot, as a garden of **h**: 3419
1Ki 21: 2 that I may have it for a garden of **h**, 3419
2Ki 4:39 one went out into the field to gather **h**, and 219
Ps 105:35 did eat up all the **h** in their land, and 6212
Pr 15:17 Better *is* a dinner of **h** where love is, than a 3419
27:25 and **h** of the mountains are gathered. 6212
Isa 18: 4 my dwelling place like a clear heat upon **h**, 216
26:19 for thy dew *is as* the dew of **h**, and the earth 219
42:15 and hills, and dry up all their **h**; 6212
Jer 12: 4 land mourn, and the **h** of every field wither, 6212
Mt 13:32 it is the greatest among **h**, and becometh a *3001*
Mk 4:32 and becometh greater than all **h**, and *3001*
Lk 11:42 ye tithe mint and rue and all *manner of* **h**, *3001*
Ro 14: 2 all *things:* another, who is weak, eateth **h**. *3001*
Heb 6: 7 bringeth forth **h** meet for them by whom it *1008*

HERD (22) [HERDMAN, HERDMEN, HERDS, SHEPHERD, SHEPHERD'S, SHEPHERDS, SHEPHERDS']
Ge 18: 7 Abraham ran unto the **h**, and fetcht a calf 1241
Lev 1: 2 of the cattle, *even* of the **h**, and of the flock. 1241
1: 3 If his offering *be* a burnt sacrifice of the **h**, 1241
3: 1 of peace offering, if he offer *it* of the **h**; 1241
27:32 *concerning* the tithe of the **h**, or of 1241
Nu 15: 3 unto the LORD, of the **h**, or of the flock: 1241
Dt 12:21 thou shalt kill of thy **h** and of thy flock, 1241
15:19 All the firstling males that come of thy **h** 1241
16: 2 the LORD thy God, *of* the flock and the **h**, 1241
1Sa 11: 5 Saul came after the **h** out of the field; 1241
2Sa 12: 4 to take of his own flock and of his own **h**, 1241
Jer 31:12 and for the young of the flock and of the **h**: 1241
Jnh 3: 7 man nor beast, **h** nor flock, taste any thing: 1241
Hab 3:17 and *there shall be* no **h** in the stalls: 1241
Mt 8:30 And there was a good way off from them a **h** *34*
8:31 suffer us to go away into the **h** of swine. *34*
8:32 were come out, they went into the **h** of swine: *34*
8:32 the whole **h** of swine ran violently down a *34*
Mk 5:11 unto the mountains a great **h** of swine feeding. *34*
5:13 the **h** ran violently down a steep place into *34*
Lk 8:32 And there was there a **h** of many swine *34*

Lk 8:33 the h ran violently down a steep place into 34

HERDMAN (1) [HERD, MAN]
Am 7:14 I *was* a h, and a gatherer of sycomore fruit: 951

HERDMEN (8) [HERD, MAN]
Ge 13: 7 there was a strife between the h of Abram's 7462
13: 7 of Abram's cattle and the h of Lot's cattle: 7462
13: 8 and between my h and thy herdmen; 7462
13: 8 and between my herdmen and thy h; 7462
26:20 the h of Gerar did strive with Isaac's 7462
26:20 herdmen of Gerar did strive with Isaac's h, 7462
1Sa 21: 7 the chiefest of the h that *belonged* to Saul. 7462
Am 1: 1 of Amos, who was among the h of Tekoa, 5349

HERDS (33) [HERD]
Ge 13: 5 with Abram, had flocks, and h, and tents. 1241
24:35 h, and silver, and gold, and menservants, 1241
26:14 possession of h, and great store of servants: 1241
32: 7 the flocks, and h, and the camels, into two 1241
33:13 the flocks and h with young *are* with me: 1241
45:10 thy flocks, and thy h, and all that thou hast: 1241
46:32 and their h, and all that they have. 1241
47: 1 and their h, and all that they have, 1241
47:17 and for the cattle of the h, and for the asses: 1241
47:18 is spent; my lord also had our h of cattle; 4735
50: 8 little ones, and their flocks, and their h, 1241
Ex 10: 9 with our flocks and with our h will we go; 1241
10:24 only let your flocks and your h be stayed: 1241
12:32 Also take your flocks and your h, as ye 1241
12:38 and flocks, and h, *even* very much cattle. 1241
34: 3 neither let the flocks nor h feed before that 1241
Nu 11:22 Shall the flocks and the h be slain for them, 1241
Dt 8:13 *when* thy h and thy flocks multiply, and 1241
12: 6 the firstlings of your h and of your flocks: 1241
12:17 or the firstlings of thy h or of thy flock, 1241
14:23 and the firstlings of thy h and of thy flocks; 1241
1Sa 30:20 David took all the flocks and the h, 1241
2Sa 12: 2 rich *man* had exceeding many flocks and h: 1241
1Ch 27:29 over the h that fed in Sharon *was* Shitrai 1241
27:29 over the h *that were* in the valleys *was* 1241
2Ch 32:29 possessions of flocks and h in abundance: 1241
Ne 10:36 and the firstlings of our h and of our flocks, 1241
Pr 27:23 state of thy flocks, *and* look well to thy h. 5739
Isa 65:10 the valley of Achor a place for the h to lie 1241
Jer 3:24 their flocks and their h, their sons and their 1241
5:17 they shall eat up thy flocks and thine h: 1241
Hos 5: 6 and with their h to seek the LORD; 1241
Joel 1:18 the h of cattle are perplexed, because 5739

HERE (162) [HEREAFTER, HEREBY, HEREIN, HEREOF, HERETOFORE, HEREUNTO, HEREWITH]
Ge 16:13 Have I also h looked after him that seeth 1988
19:12 said unto Lot, Hast thou h any besides? 6311
19:15 and thy two daughters, which are h; 4672
21:23 swear unto me h by God that thou wilt not 2008
22: 1 Abraham: and he said, Behold, *h* I *am.* NIH
22: 5 his young men, Abide you h with the ass; 6311
22: 7 he said, H *am* I, my son. And he said, 2009
22:11 Abraham, Abraham: and he said, H *am* I. 2009
24:13 Behold, I stand *h* by the well of water; and NIH
27: 1 and he said unto him, Behold, *h am* I. NIH
27:18 and he said, H *am* I; who *art* thou, my son? 2009
31:11 a dream, *saying,* Jacob: And I said, H *am* I. 2009
31:37 set *it* h before my brethren and 3541
37:13 unto them. And he said to him, H *am* I. 2009
40:15 h also have I done nothing that they should 6311
42:33 *men;* leave one of your brethren *h* with me, NIH
46: 2 said, Jacob, Jacob. And he said, H *am* I. 2009
47:23 lo, *h is* seed for you, and ye shall sow NIH
Ex 3: 4 said, Moses, Moses. And he said, H *am* I. 2009
24:14 unto the elders, Tarry ye h for us, 2088+871.1
33:16 For wherein shall it be known h that I and 645
Nu 14:40 we *be h,* and will go up unto the place NIH
22: 8 Lodge h *this* night, and I will bring you 6311
22:19 I pray you, tarry ye also h *this* night, 2088+871.1
23: 1 Build me h seven altars, and 2088+871.1
23: 1 prepare me h seven oxen and 2088+871.1
23:15 unto Balak, Stand h by thy burnt offering, 3541
23:29 Build me h seven altars, and 2088+871.1
23:29 prepare me h seven bullocks and 2088+871.1
32: 6 your brethren go to war, and shall ye sit h? 6311
32:16 We will build sheepfolds h for our cattle, 6311
Dt 5: 3 *even* us, who *are* all of us h alive *this* day. 6311
5:31 stand thou h by me, and I will speak unto 6311
12: 8 do after all *the things* that we do h *this* day, 6311
29:15 with *him* that standeth h with us *this* day 6311
29:15 also with *him* that *is* not h with us *this* day: 6311
Jos 18: 6 that I may cast lots for you h before 6311
18: 8 that I may h cast lots for you before 6311
21: 9 these cities which are *h* mentioned by name, NIH
Jdg 4:20 of thee, and say, Is there any man h? 6311
18: 3 thou in this *place?* and what hast thou h? 6311
19: 9 behold, the day groweth to an end, lodge h, 6311
19:24 *h is* my daughter a maiden, and NIH
20: 7 of Israel; give h your advice and counsel. 1988
Ru 2: 8 but abide h fast by my maidens: 3541
4: 1 *Ho,* such a one, turn aside, sit down h. 6311
4: 2 elders of the city, and said, Sit ye down h. 6311
1Sa 1:26 *am* the woman that stood by thee h, 2088+871.1
3: 4 called Samuel: and he answered, H *am* I. 2009
3: 5 he ran unto Eli, and said, H *am* I; for thou 2009
3: 6 and went to Eli, and said, H *am* I; 2009
3: 8 he arose and went to Eli, and said, H *am* I; 2009
3:16 Samuel, my son. And he answered, H *am* I. 2009
9: 8 I have h at hand the fourth part of a shekel 4672
9:11 and said unto them, Is the seer h? 2088
12: 3 **Behold,** h I *am:* witness against me before 2009
14:34 his sheep, and slay *them* h, and eat; 2088+871.1
16:11 said unto Jesse, Are h all *thy* children? NIH
21: 8 is there not h under thine hand spear or 6311
21: 9 it *is h* wrapt in a cloth behind the ephod: NIH
21: 9 *it:* for *there is* no other save that h. 2088+871.1
1Sa 22:12 And he answered, H I *am,* my lord. 2009
23: 3 unto him, Behold, we *be* afraid h in Judah: 6311
29: 3 What *do* these Hebrews *h?* And Achish said NIH
2Sa 1: 7 called unto me. And I answered, H *am* I. 2009
11:12 Tarry h to day also, and to morrow I 2088+871.1
15:26 behold, *h am* I, let him do to me as seemeth NIH
18:30 king said *unto him,* Turn aside, *and* stand h. 3541
20: 4 *within* three days, and be thou h present. 6311
24:22 *h be* oxen for burnt sacrifice, and threshing NIH
1Ki 2:30 he said, Nay; but I will die h. And Benaiah 6311
18: 8 I *am:* go, tell thy lord, Behold, Elijah *is h.* NIH
18:11 Go, tell thy lord, Behold, Elijah *is h.* NIH
18:14 Behold, Elijah *is h:* and he shall slay me. NIH
19: 9 said unto him, What doest thou h, Elijah? 6311
19:13 and said, What doest thou h, Elijah? 6311
20:40 as thy servant was busy h and there, he was 2008
22: 7 *Is there* not h a prophet of the LORD 6311
2Ki 2: 2 said unto Elisha, Tarry h, I pray thee; 6311
2: 4 said unto him, Elisha, tarry h, I pray thee; 6311
2: 6 Elijah said unto him, Tarry, I pray thee, h; 6311
3:11 *Is there* not h a prophet of the LORD, 6311
3:11 and said, H *is* Elisha the son of Shaphat, 6311
7: 3 one to another, Why sit we h until we die? 6311
7: 4 if we sit still h, we die also. Now therefore 6311
10:23 look that there be h with you none of 6311
1Ch 29:17 which are present h, to offer willingly unto 6311
2Ch 18: 6 *Is there* not h a prophet of the LORD 6311
Job 38:11 and h shall thy proud waves be stayed? 6311
38:35 they may go, and say unto thee, H we *are?* 2009
Ps 132:14 h will I dwell; for I have desired it. 6311
Isa 6: 8 go for us? Then I said, H *am* I; send me. 2009
21: 9 behold, h cometh a chariot of men, *with* a 2088
22:16 What hast thou h? and whom hast thou 6311
22:16 whom hast thou h, that thou hast hewed 6311
22:16 that thou hast hewed thee out a sepulchre h, 6311
28:10 line upon line; h a little, *and* there a little: 8033
28:13 line upon line; h a little, *and* there a little; 8033
52: 5 Now therefore, what have I h, saith 6311
58: 9 H I *am.* If thou take away from the midst of 2009
Eze 8: 6 that the house of Israel committeth h, 6311
8: 9 the wicked abominations that they do h. 6311
8:17 the abominations which they commit h? 6311
Hos 7: 9 yea, gray hairs are h **and there** upon him, 2236
Mt 12:41 and behold, a greater than Jonas *is* h. 5602
12:42 and behold, a greater than Solomon *is* h. 5602
14: 8 Give me h John Baptist's head in a charger. 5602
14:17 We have h but five loaves, and two fishes. 5602
16:28 I say unto you, There be some standing h, 5602
17: 4 unto Jesus, Lord, it is good for us to be h: 5602
17: 4 if thou wilt, let us make h three tabernacles: 5602
20: 6 unto them, Why stand ye h all the day idle? 5602
24: 2 There shall not be left h one stone upon 5602
24:23 shall say unto you, Lo, h *is* Christ, or there; 5602
26:36 Sit ye h, while I go and pray yonder. 846
26:38 unto death: tarry ye h, and watch with me. 5602
28: 6 He is not h: for he is risen, as he said. 5602
Mk 6: 3 and are not his sisters h with us? And they 5602
8: 4 these *men* with bread h in the wilderness? 5602
9: 1 That there be some of them that stand h, 5602
9: 5 to Jesus, Master, it is good for us to be h: 5602
13: 1 manner of stones and what buildings *are h.* NIG
13:21 if any *man* shall say to you, Lo, h *is* Christ; 5602
14:32 to his disciples, Sit ye h, while I shall pray. 5602
14:34 sorrowful unto death: tarry ye h, and watch. 5602
16: 6 he is risen; he is not h: behold the place 5602
Lk 4:23 in Capernaum, do also h in thy country. 5602
9:12 get victuals: for we are h in a desert place. 5602
9:27 you of a truth, there be some standing h, 5602
9:33 unto Jesus, Master, it is good for us to be h: 5602
11:31 and behold, a greater than Solomon *is* h. 5602
11:32 and behold, a greater than Jonas *is* h. 5602
17:21 Neither shall they say, Lo h: or, lo there: 5602
17:23 And they shall say to you, See h; or, 5602
19:20 saying, Lord, behold, *h is* thy pound, NIG
22:38 they said, Lord, behold, h *are* two swords. 5602
24: 6 He is not h, but is risen: remember how he 5602
24:41 he said unto them, Have ye h any meat? 1759
Jn 6: 9 There is a lad h, which hath five barley 5602
11:21 Lord, if thou hadst been h, my brother had 5602
11:32 saying unto him, Lord, if thou hadst been h, 5602
Ac 4:10 *even* by him doth this *man* stand h **before** 1799
8:36 and the eunuch said, See, *h is* water; NIG
9:10 Ananias. And he said, Behold, I *am h,* Lord. NIG
9:14 And h he hath authority from the chief 5602
10:33 therefore are we all h **present** before God, 3918
16:28 Do thyself no harm: for we are all h. 1759
24:19 Who ought to have been h before thee, and 3918
24:20 Or else let these same *h* say, if they have NIG
25:24 and all men which are h **present with** us, 4840
25:24 both at Jerusalem, and *also* h, crying that 1759
Col 4: 9 unto you all *things* which *are done* h. 5602
Heb 7: 8 And h men that die receive tithes; but 5602
13:14 For h have we no continuing city, but 5602
Jas 2: 3 say unto him, Sit thou h **in a good place;** 5602
2: 3 thou there, or sit h under my footstool: 5602
1Pe 1:17 pass the time of your sojourning *h* in fear: NIG
Rev 13:10 H is the patience and the faith of the saints. 5602
13:18 H is wisdom. Let him that hath 5602
14:12 H is the patience of the saints: here *are* they 5602
14:12 h *are* they that keep the commandments of 5602
17: 9 *And* h *is* the mind which hath wisdom. 5602

HEREAFTER (14) [AFTER, HERE]
Isa 41:23 Shew the *things* that are to come h, that we 268
Eze 20:39 and h *also,* if ye will not hearken unto me: 310
Da 2:29 thy bed, what should come to pass h: 311+1836
2:45 to the king what shall come to pass h: 311+1836
Mt 26:64 H shall ye see the Son of man sitting on *575+737*
Mk 11:14 unto it, No *man* eat fruit of thee h for ever. *3371*
Lk 22:69 H shall the Son of man sit on *575+3568+3588*
Jn 1:51 H ye shall see heaven open, and *575+737*
13: 7 not now; but thou shalt know h. *3326+3778*
14:30 H I will **not** talk much with you: for *3765*
1Ti 1:16 for a pattern to them which should h *3195*
Rev 1:19 and *the things* which shall be h; *3326+3778*
Rev 4: 1 shew thee *things* which must be h. *3326+3778*
9:12 there come two woes more h. *3326+3778*

HEREBY (13) [BY, HERE]
Ge 42:15 H ye shall be proved: By the life of 2063+871.1
42:33 said unto us, H shall I know that ye 2088+871.1
Nu 16:28 Moses said, H ye shall know that 2088+871.1
Jos 3:10 H ye shall know that the living God 2088+871.1
1Co 4: 4 by myself; yet am I not h justified: *1722+3778*
1Jn 2: 3 And h we do know that we know *1722+3778*
2: 5 h know we that we are in him. *1722+3778*
3:16 H perceive we the love *of God,* *1722+3778*
3:19 And h we know that we are of *1722+3778*
3:24 And h we know that he abideth in us, *1722+3778*
4: 2 H know ye the Spirit of God: *1722+3778*
4: 6 H know we the spirit of truth, and *1537+3778*
4:13 H know we that we dwell in him, *1722+3778*

HEREIN (9) [HERE, IN]
Ge 34:22 Only h will the men consent unto us 2063+871.1
2Ch 16: 9 H thou hast done foolishly: therefore 2088+5921
Jn 4:37 And h is *that* saying true, One *1722+3778*
9:30 Why h is a marvellous *thing,* that ye *1722+3778*
15: 8 H is my Father glorified, that ye bear *1722+3778*
Ac 24:16 And h do I exercise myself, to have *1722+3778*
2Co 8:10 And h I give *my* advice: for this is *1722+3778*
1Jn 4:10 H is love, not that we loved God, but *1722+3778*
4:17 H is our love made perfect, that we *1722+3778*

HEREOF (2) [HERE, OF]
Mt 9:26 And the fame h went abroad into all that *3778*
Heb 5: 3 And **by reason** h he ought, as for *1223+3778*

HERES (1)
Jdg 1:35 the Amorites would dwell in mount H in 2776

HERESH (1)
1Ch 9:15 H, and Galal, and Mattaniah the son of 2792

HERESIES (3) [HERESY]
1Co 11:19 For there must be also h among you, *139*
Gal 5:20 emulations, wrath, strife, seditions, h, *139*
2Pe 2: 1 who privily shall bring in damnable h, *139*

HERESY (1) [HERESIES, HERETICK]
Ac 24:14 that after the way which they call h, so *139*

HERETICK (1) [HERESY]
Tit 3:10 A man *that is* a h after the first and *141*

HERETOFORE (8) [HERE, TO]
Ex 4:10 neither h, 1571+4480+4480+8032+8543
5: 7 the people straw to make brick, as h: 8032+8543
5: 8 which they did make h, you shall lay 8032+8543
5:14 both yesterday and to day, as h? 8032+8543
Jos 3: 4 ye have not passed *this* way h. 4480+8032+8543
Ru 2:11 a people which thou knewest not h. 8032+8543
1Sa 4: 7 for there hath not been such a *thing* h. 865+8032
2Co 13: 2 now I write to them which h have **sinned,** *4258*

HEREUNTO (2) [HERE, UNTO]
Ecc 2:25 or who else can hasten *h,* more than I? NIH
1Pe 2:21 For *even* h were ye called: because *1519+3778*

HEREWITH (2) [HERE, WITH]
Eze 16:29 and yet thou wast not satisfied h. 2063+871.1
Mal 3:10 prove me now h, saith the LORD 2063+871.1

HERITAGE (30) [HERITAGES]
Ex 6: 8 and to Jacob; and I will give it you *for* an h: 4181
Job 20:29 and the h appointed unto him by God. 5159
27:13 the h of oppressors, *which* they shall 5159
Ps 16: 6 in pleasant *places;* yea, I have a goodly h. 5159
61: 5 thou hast given *me* the h of those that fear 3425
94: 5 thy people, O LORD, and afflict thine h. 5159
111: 6 that *he* may give them the h of the heathen. 5159
119:111 Thy testimonies have I **taken as an** h for 5157
127: 3 Lo, children *are* an h of the LORD: *and* 5159
135:12 gave their land *for* an h, an heritage unto 5159
135:12 *for* an heritage, an h unto Israel his people. 5159
136:21 gave their land for an h: for his mercy 5159
136:22 *Even* an h unto Israel his servant: for his 5159
Isa 54:17 This *is* the h of the servants of the LORD, 5159
58:14 feed thee with the h of Jacob thy father: 5159
Jer 2: 7 my land, and made mine h an abomination. 5159
3:19 a goodly h of the hosts of nations? 5159
12: 7 forsaken mine house, I have left mine h; 5159
12: 8 Mine h is unto me as a lion in the forest; 5159
12: 9 Mine h *is* unto me *as* a speckled bird, 5159
12:15 every man to his h, and every man to his 5159
17: 4 shalt discontinue from thine h that I gave 5159
50:11 O ye destroyers of mine h, because ye are 5159
Joel 2:17 and give not thine h to reproach, 5159
3: 2 there for my people and *for* my h Israel, 5159
Mic 2: 2 a man and his house, even a man and his h. 5159
7:14 people with thy rod, the flock of thine h, 5159
7:18 the transgression of the remnant of his h? 5159
Mal 1: 3 his h waste for the dragons of 5159
1Pe 5: 3 Neither as being lords over *God's* h, but *2819*

HERITAGES (1) [HERITAGE]
Isa 49: 8 the earth, to cause to inherit the desolate h; 5159

HERMAS (1)
Ro 16:14 Phlegon, H, Patrobas, Hermes, and *2057*

HERMES (1)
Ro 16:14 H, and the brethren which are with them. *2060*

HERMOGENES (1)
2Ti 1:15 from me; of whom are Phygellus and H. *2061*

HERMON (13) [BAAL-HERMON, HERMONITES]
Dt 3: 8 from the river of Arnon unto mount **H**; 2768
3: 9 (*Which* **H** the Sidonians call Sirion; and 2768
4:48 even unto mount Sion, which *is* **H**, 2768
Jos 11: 3 *to* the Hivite under **H** in the land of 2768
11:17 in the valley of Lebanon under mount **H**: 2768
12: 1 from the river Arnon unto mount **H**, and 2768
12: 5 reigned in mount **H**, and in Salcah, and 2768
13: 5 from Baal-gad under mount **H** unto 2768
13:11 all mount **H**, and all Bashan unto Salcah; 2768
1Ch 5:23 and Senir, and *unto* mount **H**. 2768
Ps 89:12 Tabor and **H** shall rejoice in thy name. 2768
133: 3 As the dew of **H**, *and as the dew* that 2768
SS 4: 8 from the top of Shenir and **H**, from 2768

HERMONITES (1) [HERMON]
Ps 42: 6 and of the **H**, from the hill Mizar. 2769

HEROD (40) [HEROD'S, HERODIANS]
Mt 2: 1 of Judea in the days of **H** the king, *2264*
2: 3 When **H** the king had heard *these things*, he *2264*
2: 7 Then **H**, when he had privily called *2264*
2:12 in a dream that *they* should not return to **H**, *2264*
2:13 for **H** will seek the young child to destroy *2264*
2:15 And was there until the death of **H**: that it *2264*
2:16 Then **H**, when he saw that he was mocked *2264*
2:19 But when **H** was dead, behold, an angel of *2264*
2:22 reign in Judea in the room of his father **H**, *2264*
14: 1 At that time **H** the tetrarch heard of *2264*
14: 3 For **H** had laid hold on John, and *2264*
14: 6 danced before them, and pleased **H**. *2264*
Mk 6:14 And king **H** heard *of him*; (for his name *2264*
6:16 But when **H** heard *thereof*, he said, It is *2264*
6:17 For **H** himself had sent forth and laid hold *2264*
6:18 For John had said unto **H**, It is not lawful *2264*
6:20 For **H** feared John, knowing that he *was* a *2264*
6:21 that **H** on his birthday made a supper to his *2264*
6:22 and pleased **H** and them that sat with *him*, *2264*
8:15 of the Pharisees, and *of* the leaven of **H**. *2264*
Lk 1: 5 There was in the days of **H**, the king of *2264*
3: 1 and **H** being tetrarch of Galilee, and *2264*
3:19 But **H** the tetrarch, being reproved by him *2264*
3:19 and for all the evils which **H** had done, *2264*
9: 7 Now **H** the tetrarch heard of all that was *2264*
9: 9 And **H** said, John have I beheaded: but *2264*
13:31 and depart hence: for **H** will kill thee. *2264*
23: 7 he sent him to **H**, who himself also was at *2264*
23: 8 And when **H** saw Jesus, he was exceeding *2264*
23:11 And **H** with his men of war set him at *2264*
23:12 Pilate and **H** were made friends together: *2264*
23:15 No, nor yet **H**: for I sent you to him; *2264*
Ac 4:27 both **H**, and Pontius Pilate, with *2264*
12: 1 Now about that time **H** the king stretched *2264*
12: 6 And when **H** would have brought him *2264*
12:11 and hath delivered me out of the hand of **H**, *2264*
12:19 And when **H** had sought for him, and *2264*
12:20 And **H** was highly displeased with them of *2264*
12:21 And upon a set day **H**, arrayed in royal *2264*
13: 1 which had been brought up with **H** *2264*

HEROD'S (4) [HEROD]
Mt 14: 6 But when **H** birthday was kept, *2264*
Lk 8: 3 And Joanna the wife of Chuza **H** steward, *2264*
23: 7 knew that he belonged unto **H** jurisdiction, *2264*
Ac 23:35 And he commanded him to be kept in **H** *2264*

HERODIANS (3) [HEROD]
Mt 22:16 sent out unto him their disciples with the **H**, *2265*
Mk 3: 6 straightway took counsel with the **H** *2265*
12:13 him certain of the Pharisees and of the **H**, *2265*

HERODIAS (4) [HERODIAS']
Mt 14: 6 the daughter of **H** danced before them, and *2266*
Mk 6:19 Therefore **H** had a quarrel against him, and *2266*
6:22 And when the daughter of the said **H** came *2266*
Lk 3:19 being reproved by him for **H** his brother *2266*

HERODIAS' (2) [HERODIAS]
Mt 14: 3 and put *him* in prison for **H** sake, *2266*
Mk 6:17 and bound him in prison for **H** sake, *2266*

HERODION (1)
Ro 16:11 Salute **H** my kinsman. Greet them that be *2267*

HERON (2)
Lev 11:19 the **h** after her kind, and the lapwing, and 601
Dt 14:18 the **h** after her kind, and the lapwing, and 601

HERS (4) [SHE]
Dt 21:15 and *if* the firstborn son be **h** that was hated: NIH
1Sa 25:42 with five damsels of **h** that went after her, 1886.3
2Ki 8: 6 Restore all that *was* **h**, and all 1886.3+3807.1
Job 39:16 as though *they were* not **h**: 1886.3+3807.1

HERSELF (42) [SELF, SHE]
Ge 18:12 Therefore Sarah laughed within **h**, 1886.3
20: 5 she, even **she h** said, He *is* my brother: 1931
24:65 therefore she took a vail, and covered **h**. NIH
38:14 and wrapped **h**, and sat in an open place, NIH
Ex 2: 5 Pharaoh came down to wash **h** at the river; NIH
Lev 15:28 she shall number to **h** seven days, and 1886.3
21: 9 if she profane **h** by playing the whore, she NIH
Nu 22:25 she thrust **h** unto the wall, and NIH
30: 3 bind **h** *by* a bond, *being* in her father's NIH
Jdg 5:29 *her*, yea, she returned answer to **h**, 1886.3
Ru 2:10 bowed **h** to the ground, and said unto him, NIH
1Sa 4:19 were dead, she bowed **h** and travailed; NIH
25:23 on her face, and bowed **h** *to* the ground, NIH
25:41 bowed **h** *on her* face to the earth, and said, NIH
2Sa 11: 2 from the roof he saw a woman washing **h**; NIH
1Ki 14: 5 that she shall feign **h** to be another *woman*. NIH
2Ki 4:37 bowed **h** to the ground, and took up her son, NIH
Job 39:18 What time she lifteth up **h** on high, NIH
Ps 84: 3 the swallow a nest for **h**, where she may 1886.3
Pr 31:22 She maketh **h** coverings of tapestry; 1886.3
Isa 5:14 Therefore hell hath enlarged **h**, 5315+1886.3
34:14 rest there, and find for **h** a place of rest. 1886.3
61:10 and as a bride adorneth **h** *with* her jewels. NIH
Jer 3:11 **h** more than treacherous Judah. 5315+1886.3
4:31 *that* bewaileth **h**, *that* spreadeth her hands, NIH
49:24 *and* turneth **h** to flee, and fear hath seized 1886.3
Eze 22: 3 maketh idols against **h** to defile *herself*. 1886.3
22: 3 and maketh idols against herself to defile **h**. NIH
23: 7 she doted: with all their idols she defiled **h**. NIH
24:12 She hath wearied **h** *with* lies, and her great NIH
Hos 2:13 she decked **h** with her earrings and NIH
Zec 9: 3 Tyrus did build **h** a strong hold, and 1886.3
Mt 9:21 For she said within **h**, If I may but touch his *1438*
Mk 4:28 For the earth bringeth forth fruit **of h**; *844*
Lk 1:24 and hid **h** five months, saying, *1438*
13:11 and could in no wise lift up **h**. NIG
Jn 20:14 when she had thus said, she turned **h** back, NIG
20:16 She turned **h**, and saith unto him, Rabboni; NIG
Heb 11:11 Through faith also Sara **h** received strength *846*
Rev 2:20 which calleth **h** a prophetess, to teach and *1438*
18: 7 How much she hath glorified **h**, and *1438*
19: 7 is come, and his wife hath made **h** ready. *1438*

HESED (1)
1Ki 4:10 The son of **H**, in Aruboth; to him *pertained* 2618

HESHBON (38)
Nu 21:25 in **H**, and in all the villages thereof. 2809
21:26 For **H** *was* the city of Sihon the king of 2809
21:27 Come *into* **H**, let the city of Sihon be built 2809
21:28 For there is a fire gone out of **H**, a flame 2809
21:30 **H** is perished even unto Dibon, and 2809
21:34 king of the Amorites, which dwelt at **H**. 2809
32: 3 **H**, and Elealeh, and Shebam, and Nebo, 2809
32:37 the children of Reuben built **H**, and 2809
Dt 1: 4 which dwelt in **H**, and Og the king of 2809
2:24 Sihon the Amorite, king of **H**, and his land: 2809
2:26 unto Sihon king of **H** *with* words of peace, 2809
2:30 Sihon king of **H** would not let us pass by 2809
3: 2 king of the Amorites, which dwelt at **H**. 2809
3: 6 as we did unto Sihon king of **H**, 2809
4:46 who dwelt at **H**, whom Moses and 2809
29: 7 Sihon the king of **H**, and Og the king of 2809
Jos 9:10 to Sihon king of **H**, and to Og king of 2809
12: 2 who dwelt in **H**, *and* ruled from Aroer, 2809
12: 5 half Gilead, the border of Sihon king of **H**. 2809
13:10 which reigned in **H**, unto the border of 2809
13:17 **H**, and all her cities that *are* in the plain; 2809
13:21 king of the Amorites, which reigned in **H**, 2809
13:26 from **H** unto Ramath-mizpeh, and Betonim; 2809
13:27 the rest of the kingdom of Sihon king of **H**, 2809
21:39 **H** with her suburbs, Jazer with her suburbs; 2809
Jdg 11:19 Sihon king of the Amorites, the king of **H**; 2809
11:26 While Israel dwelt in **H** and her towns, and 2809
1Ch 6:81 **H** with her suburbs, and Jazer with her 2809
Ne 9:22 the land of the king of **H**, and the land of 2809
SS 7: 4 thine eyes *like* the *fish*pools in **H**, by 2809
Isa 15: 4 **H** shall cry, and Elealeh: their voice shall 2809
16: 8 For the fields of **H** languish, *and* the vine of 2809
16: 9 water thee *with* my tears, O **H**, and Elealeh: 2809
Jer 48: 2 in **H** they have devised evil against it; 2809
48:34 From the cry of **H** *even* unto Elealeh, *and* 2809
48:45 They that fled stood under the shadow of **H** 2809
48:45 a fire shall come forth out of **H**, and 2809
49: 3 Howl, O **H**, for Ai is spoiled: cry, 2809

HESHMON (1)
Jos 15:27 And Hazar-gaddah, and **H**, and Beth-palet, 2829

HETH (14)
Ge 10:15 Canaan begat Sidon his firstborn, and **H**, 2845
23: 3 and spake unto the sons of **H**, saying, 2845
23: 5 the children of **H** answered Abraham, 2845
23: 7 of the land, *even* to the children of **H**. 2845
23:10 Ephron dwelt amongst the children of **H**: 2845
23:10 in the audience of the children of **H**, 2845
23:16 named in the audience of the sons of **H**, 2845
23:18 in the presence of the children of **H**, 2845
23:20 of a buryingplace by the sons of **H**. 2845
25:10 Abraham purchased of the sons of **H**: 2845
27:46 of my life because of the daughters of **H**: 2845
27:46 if Jacob take a wife of the daughters of **H**, 2845
49:32 that *is* therein *was* from the children of **H**. 2845
1Ch 1:13 Canaan begat Zidon his firstborn, and **H**, 2845

HETHLON (2)
Eze 47:15 from the great sea, the way of **H**, as *men* go 2855
48: 1 the north end to the coast of the way of **H**, 2855

HEW (12) [HEWED, HEWER, HEWERS, HEWETH, HEWN]
Ex 34: 1 **H** thee two tables of stone like unto 6458
Dt 10: 1 **H** thee two tables of stone like unto 6458
12: 3 you shall **h down** the graven images of 1438
19: 5 the wood with his neighbour to **h** wood, 2404
1Ki 5: 6 command thou that they **h** me cedar trees 3772
5: 6 skill to **h** timber like unto the Sidonians. 3772
5:18 Hiram's builders did **h** *them*, and 6458
1Ch 22: 2 he set masons to **h** wrought stones to build 2672
2Ch 2: 2 fourscore thousand to **h** in the mountain, 2672
Jer 6: 6 **H** ye **down** trees, and cast a mount against 3772
Da 4:14 **H down** the tree, and cut off his branches, 1414
4:23 saying, **H** the tree **down**, and destroy it; 1414

HEWED (13) [HEW]
Ex 34: 4 he **h** two tables of stone like unto the first, 6458
Dt 10: 3 **h** two tables of stone like unto the first, and 6458
1Sa 11: 7 **h** them **in pieces**, and sent *them* throughout 5408
15:33 Samuel **h** Agag **in pieces** before 8158
1Ki 5:17 great stones, costly stones, *and* **h** stones, 1496
6:36 the inner court *with* three rows of **h stone**, 1496
7: 9 according to the measures of **h stones**, 1496
7:11 after the measures of **h stones**, and cedars. 1496
7:12 about *was with* three rows *of* **h stones**, 1496
2Ki 12:12 **h** stone to repair the breaches of the house 4274
Isa 22:16 that thou hast **h** thee **out** a sepulchre here, 2672
Jer 2:13 **h** them **out** cisterns, broken cisterns, 2672
Hos 6: 5 Therefore have I **h** *them* by the prophets; 2672

HEWER (1) [HEW]
Dt 29:11 from the **h** of thy wood unto the drawer of 2404

HEWERS (9) [HEW]
Jos 9:21 let them be **h** of wood and drawers of water 2404
9:23 **h** of wood and drawers of water for 2404
9:27 Joshua made them that day **h** of wood and 2404
1Ki 5:15 and fourscore thousand **h** in the mountains; 2672
2Ki 12:12 **h** of stone, and to buy timber and 2672
1Ch 22:15 **h** and workers of stone and timber, and 2672
2Ch 2:10 give to thy servants, the **h** that cut timber, 2404
2:18 fourscore thousand *to be* **h** in the mountain, 2672
Jer 46:22 come against her with axes, as **h** of wood. 2404

HEWETH (3) [HEW]
Isa 10:15 Shall the axe boast itself against him that **h** 2672
22:16 *as he* that **h** him **out** a sepulchre on high, 2672
44:14 *He* **h** him **down** cedars, and taketh 3772

HEWN (17) [HEW]
Ex 20:25 of stone, thou shalt not build it *of* **h stone**: 1496
2Ki 22: 6 buy timber and **h** stone to repair the house. 4274
2Ch 34:11 and builders gave they *it*, to buy **h** stone, 4274
Pr 9: 1 her house, she hath **h out** her seven pillars: 2672
Isa 9:10 but we will build *with* **h stones**: 1496
10:33 the high ones of stature *shall be* **h down**, 1438
33: 9 Lebanon is ashamed *and* **h down**: Sharon is 7060
51: 1 look unto the rock *whence* ye are **h**, and 2672
La 3: 9 He hath inclosed my ways with **h stone**, 1496
Eze 40:42 the four tables *were of* **h** stone for the burnt 1496
Am 5:11 ye have built houses of **h stone**, but 1496
Mt 3:10 bringeth not forth good fruit is **h down**, *1581*
7:19 that bringeth not forth good fruit is **h down**, *1581*
27:60 new tomb, which he had **h out** in the rock: *2998*
Mk 15:46 laid him in a sepulchre which was **h** out of *2998*
Lk 3: 9 bringeth not forth good fruit is **h down**, *1581*
23:53 laid it in a sepulchre *that was* **h in stone**, *2991*

HEZEKI (1)
1Ch 8:17 and Meshullam, and **H**, and Heber, 2395

HEZEKIAH (128) [EZEKIAS]
2Ki 16:20 and **H** his son reigned in his stead. 2396
18: 1 *that* **H** the son of Ahaz king of Judah *began* 2396
18: 9 it came to pass in the fourth year of king **H**, 2396
18:10 *even* in the sixth year of **H**, that *is* the ninth 2396
18:13 Now in the fourteenth year of king **H** did 2396
18:14 **H** king of Judah sent to the king of Assyria 2396
18:14 the king of Assyria appointed unto **H** king 2396
18:15 **H** gave *him* all the silver that was found *in* 2396
18:16 At that time did **H** cut off *the gold from* 2396
18:16 *from* the pillars which **H** king of Judah had 2396
18:17 Rab-shakeh from Lachish to king **H** with a 2396
18:19 Speak ye now to **H**, Thus saith the great 2396
18:22 and whose altars **H** hath taken away, 2396
18:29 Thus saith the king, Let not **H** deceive you: 2396
18:30 Neither let **H** make you trust in 2396
18:31 Hearken not to **H**: for thus saith the king of 2396
18:32 hearken not unto **H**, when he persuadeth 2396
18:37 to **H** with *their* clothes rent, and told him 2396
19: 1 when king **H** heard *it*, that he rent his 2396
19: 3 they said unto him, Thus saith **H**, This day 2396
19: 5 So the servants of king **H** came to Isaiah. 2396
19: 9 he sent messengers again unto **H**, saying, 2396
19:10 Thus shall ye speak to **H** king of Judah, 2396
19:14 **H** received the letter of the hand of 2396
19:14 **H** went up *into* the house of the LORD, 2396
19:15 And **H** prayed before the LORD, and said, 2396
19:20 Isaiah the son of Amoz sent to **H**, saying, 2396
20: 1 In those days was **H** sick unto death. 2396
20: 3 *is* good in thy sight. And **H** wept sore. 2396
20: 5 and tell **H** the captain of my people, 2396
20: 8 **H** said unto Isaiah, What *shall be* the sign 2396
20:10 **H** answered, It is a light thing for 3169
20:12 sent letters and a present unto **H**: 2396
20:12 for he had heard that **H** had been sick. 2396
20:13 **H** hearkened unto them, and shewed them 2396
20:13 all his dominion, that **H** shewed them not. 2396
20:14 came Isaiah the prophet unto king **H**, and 2396
20:14 **H** said, They are come from a far country, 2396
20:15 **H** answered, All *the things* that *are* in mine 2396
20:16 Isaiah said unto **H**, Hear the word of 2396
20:19 said **H** unto Isaiah, Good *is* the word of 2396
20:20 the rest of the acts of **H**, and all his might, 2396
20:21 **H** slept with his fathers: and Manasseh his 2396
21: 3 places which **H** his father had destroyed; 2396
1Ch 3:13 Ahaz his son, **H** his son, Manasseh his son, 2396
3:23 Elioenai, and **H**, and Azrikam, three. 2396
4:41 name came in the days of **H** king of Judah, 3169
2Ch 28:27 and **H** his son reigned in his stead. 3169
29: 1 **H** *began* to reign *when he was* five and 3169
29:18 they went in to **H** the king, and said, 3169
29:20 **H** the king rose early, and gathered 3169
29:27 **H** commanded to offer the burnt offering 2396
29:30 Moreover **H** the king and the princes 3169
29:31 **H** answered and said, Now ye have 3169
29:36 **H** rejoiced, and all the people, that God had 3169
30: 1 **H** sent to all Israel and Judah, and 3169
30:18 **H** prayed for them, saying, The good 3169
30:20 the LORD hearkened to **H**, and healed 3169
30:22 **H** spake comfortably unto all the Levites 3169
30:24 For **H** king of Judah did give to 2396
31: 2 **H** appointed the courses of the priests and 3169
31: 8 when **H** and the princes came and saw 3169
31: 9 **H** questioned with the priests and 3169
31:11 **H** commanded to prepare chambers in 3169
31:13 at the commandment of **H** the king, and 3169

2Ch 31:20 thus did H throughout all Judah, and 3169
32: 2 when H saw that Sennacherib was come, 3169
32: 8 upon the words of H king of Judah. 3169
32: 9 unto H king of Judah, and unto all Judah 3169
32:11 Doth not H persuade you to give over 3169
32:12 Hath not the same H taken away his high 3169
32:15 Now therefore let not H deceive you, 2396
32:16 the LORD God, and against his servant H. 3169
32:17 shall not the God of H deliver his people 3169
32:20 for this cause H the king, and the prophet 3169
32:22 Thus the LORD saved H and 3169
32:23 and presents to H king of Judah: 3169
32:24 In those days H was sick to the death, and 3169
32:25 H rendered not again according to 3169
32:26 Notwithstanding H humbled himself for 3169
32:26 came not upon them in the days of H. 3169
32:27 H had exceeding much riches and honour: 3169
32:30 This same H also stopped the upper 3169
32:30 And H prospered in all his works. 3169
32:32 Now the rest of the acts of H, and 3169
32:33 H slept with his fathers, and they buried 3169
33: 3 For he built again the high places which H 3169
Ezr 2:16 The children of Ater of H, ninety and eight. 3169
Ne 7:21 The children of Ater of H, ninety and eight. 2396
Pr 25: 1 which the men of H king of Judah copied 2396
Isa 1: 1 Jotham, Ahaz, and H, kings of Judah. 3169
36: 1 to pass in the fourteenth year of king H, 2396
36: 2 Jerusalem unto king H with a great army. 2396
36: 4 Say ye now to H, Thus saith the great king, 2396
36: 7 and whose altars H hath taken away, 2396
36:14 Thus saith the king, Let not H deceive you: 2396
36:15 Neither let H make you trust in 2396
36:16 Hearken not to H: for thus saith the king of 2396
36:18 Beware lest H persuade you, saying, 2396
36:22 to H with their clothes rent, and told him 2396
37: 1 when king H heard it, that he rent his 2396
37: 3 they said unto him, Thus saith H, This day 2396
37: 5 So the servants of king H came to Isaiah. 2396
37: 9 when he heard it, he sent messengers to H, 2396
37:10 Thus shall ye speak to H king of Judah, 2396
37:14 H received the letter from the hand of 2396
37:14 H went up unto the house of the LORD, 2396
37:15 And H prayed unto the LORD, saying, 2396
37:21 Isaiah the son of Amoz sent unto H, saying, 2396
38: 1 In those days was H sick unto death. 2396
38: 2 H turned his face toward the wall, and 2396
38: 3 is good in thy sight. And H wept sore. 2396
38: 5 Go and say to H, Thus saith the LORD, 2396
38: 9 The writing of H, king of Judah, when he 2396
38:22 H also had said, What is the sign that I 2396
39: 1 of Babylon, sent letters and a present to H: 2396
39: 2 H was glad of them, and shewed them 2396
39: 2 all his dominion, that H shewed them not. 2396
39: 3 came Isaiah the prophet unto king H, and 2396
39: 3 H said, They are come from a far country 2396
39: 4 H answered, All that is in mine house have 2396
39: 5 said Isaiah to H, Hear the word of 2396
39: 8 said H to Isaiah, Good is the word of 2396
Jer 15: 4 of Manasseh the son of H king of Judah, 3169
26:18 prophesied in the days of H king of Judah, 2396
26:19 Did H king of Judah and all Judah put him 2396
Hos 1: 1 Jotham, Ahaz, and H, kings of Judah, and 3169
Mic 1: 1 Ahaz, and H, kings of Judah, which he saw 3169

HEZION (1)

1Ki 15:18 of Tabrimon, the son of H, king of Syria, 2383

HEZIR (2)

1Ch 24:15 The seventeenth to H, the eighteenth to 2387
Ne 10:20 Magpiash, Meshullam, H, 2387

HEZRAI (1)

2Sa 23:35 H the Carmelite, Paarai the Arbite, 2695

HEZRO (1)

1Ch 11:37 H the Carmelite, Naarai the son of Ezbai, 2695

HEZRON (17) [ESROM, HEZRON'S, HEZRONITES]

Ge 46: 9 Hanoch, and Phallu, and H, and Carmi. 2696
46:12 And the sons of Pharez were H and Hamul. 2696
Ex 6:14 of Israel; Hanoch, and Pallu, H, and Carmi: 2696
Nu 26: 6 Of H, the family of the Hezronites: 2696
26:21 of H, the family of the Hezronites: 2696
Jos 15: 3 passed along to H, and went up to Adar, 2696
15:25 Hazor, Hadattah, and Kerioth, and H, 2696
Ru 4:18 the generations of Pharez: Pharez begat H, 2696
4:19 H begat Ram, and Ram begat Amminadab, 2696
1Ch 2: 5 The sons of Pharez; H, and Hamul. 2696
2: 9 The sons also of H, that were born unto 2696
2:18 Caleb the son of H begat children of 2696
2:21 afterward H went in to the daughter of 2696
2:24 after that H was dead in Caleb-ephratah, 2696
2:25 the sons of Jerahmeel the firstborn of H 2696
4: 1 H, and Carmi, and Hur, and Shobal. 2696
5: 3 were, Hanoch, and Pallu, H, and Carmi. 2696

HEZRON'S (1) [HEZRON]

1Ch 2:24 Abiah H wife bare him Ashur the father of 2696

HEZRONITES (2) [HEZRON]

Nu 26: 6 Of Hezron, the family of the H: of Carmi, 2697
26:21 of Hezron, the family of the H: 2697

HID (130) [HIDE]

Ge 3: 8 his wife h themselves from the presence of 2244
3:10 because I was naked; and I h myself. 2244
4:14 from thy face shall I be h; and I shall be a 5641
35: 4 Jacob h them under the oak which was by 2934
Ex 2: 2 a goodly child, she h him three months. 6845
2:12 slew the Egyptian, and h him in the sand. 2934
3: 6 Moses h his face; for he was afraid to look 5641
Lev 4:13 the thing be h from the eyes of 5956
5: 3 be defiled withal, and it be h from him; 5956
5: 4 with an oath, and it be h from him; 5956
Nu 5:13 it be h from the eyes of her husband, and 5956
Dt 33:19 of the seas, and of treasures h in the sand. 2934
Jos 2: 4 h them, and said thus, There came men 6845
2: 6 h them with the stalks of flax, which she 2934
6:17 because she h the messengers that we sent. 2244
6:25 because she h the messengers, 2244
7:21 they are h in the earth in the midst of my 2934
7:22 it was h in his tent, and the silver under it. 2934
10:16 and h themselves in a cave at Makkedah. 2244
10:17 The five kings are found h in a cave at 2244
10:27 into the cave wherein they had been h, 2244
Jdg 9: 5 son of Jerubbaal was left; for he h himself. 2244
1Sa 3:18 him every whit, and h nothing from him. 3582
10:22 Behold, he hath h himself among the stuff. 2244
14:11 of the holes where they had h themselves. 2244
14:22 Likewise all the men of Israel which had h 2244
20:24 So David h himself in the field: and 5641
2Sa 17: 9 he is h now in some pit, or in some other 2244
18:13 for there is no matter h from the king, and 3582
1Ki 10: 3 there was not any thing h from the king, 5956
18: 4 h them by fifty in a cave, and fed them with 2244
18:13 how I h an hundred men of the LORD'S 2244
2Ki 4:27 the LORD hath h it from me, and hath not 5956
6:29 we may eat him: and she hath h her son. 2244
7: 8 went and h it; and came again, and 2934
7: 8 and carried thence also, and went and h it. 2934
11: 2 they h him, even him and his nurse, in 5641
11: 3 he was with her h in the house of 2244
1Ch 21:20 and his four sons with him h themselves. 2244
2Ch 9: 2 there was nothing h from Solomon which 5956
22: 9 they caught him, (for he was h in Samaria,) 2244
22:11 h him from Athaliah, so that she slew him 5641
22:12 he was with them h in the house of God six 2244
Job 3:10 nor h sorrow from mine eyes. 5641
3:21 and dig for it more than for h treasures; 4301
3:23 is light given to a man whose way is h, 5641
5:21 Thou shalt be h from the scourge of 2244
6:16 of the ice, and wherein the snow is h: 5956
10:13 these things hast thou h in thine heart: 6845
15:18 told from their fathers, and have not h it: 3582
17: 4 For thou hast h their heart from 6845
20:26 All darkness shall be h in his secret places: 2934
28:11 the thing that is h bringeth he forth to 8587
28:21 Seeing it is h from the eyes of all living, 5956
29: 8 The young men saw me, and h themselves: 2244
38:30 The waters are h as with a stone, and 2244
Ps 9:15 in the net which they h is their own foot 2934
17:14 whose belly thou fillest with thy h treasure: 6845
19: 6 there is nothing h from the heat thereof. 5641
22:24 neither hath he h his face from him; but 5641
32: 5 unto thee, and mine iniquity have I not h. 3680
35: 7 For without cause have they h for me their 2934
35: 8 and let his net that he hath h catch himself: 2934
38: 9 and my groaning is not h from thee. 5641
40:10 I have not h thy righteousness within my 3680
55:12 then I would have h myself from him: 5641
69: 5 and my sins are not h from thee. 3582
119:11 Thy word have I h in mine heart, that I 6845
139:15 My substance was not h from thee, when I 3582
140: 5 The proud have h a snare for me, and 2934
Pr 2: 4 and searchest for her as for h treasures; 4301
Isa 28:15 and under falsehood have we h ourselves: 5641
29:14 of their prudent men shall be h. 5641
40:27 My way is h from the LORD, and 5641
42:22 in holes, and they are h in prison houses: 2244
49: 2 in the shadow of his hand hath he h me, 2244
49: 2 a polished shaft; in his quiver hath he h me; 5641
50: 6 I h not my face from shame and spitting. 5641
53: 3 we h as it were our faces from him; he was 4564
54: 8 In a little wrath I h my face from thee for a 5641
57:17 I h me, and was wroth, and he went on 5641
59: 2 and your sins have h his face from you, 5641
64: 7 for thou hast h thy face from us, and 5641
65:16 and because they are h from mine eyes. 5641
Jer 13: 5 So I went, and h it by Euphrates, as 2934
13: 7 the girdle from the place where I had h it: 2934
16:17 they are not h from my face, neither is their 5641
16:17 neither is their iniquity h from mine eyes. 6845
18:22 a pit to take me, and h snares for my feet. 2934
33: 5 for all whose wickedness I have h my face 5641
36:26 the prophet: but the LORD h them. 5641
43:10 his throne upon these stones that I have h; 2934
Eze 22:26 have h their eyes from my sabbaths, and 5956
39:23 therefore h I my face from them, and 5641
39:24 done unto them, and h my face from them. 5641
Hos 5: 3 know Ephraim, and Israel is not h from me: 3582
13:12 of Ephraim is bound up; his sin is h. 6845
13:14 repentance shall be h from mine eyes. 5641
Am 9: 3 though they be h from my sight in 5641
Ob 1: 6 how are his h things sought up! 4710
Na 3:11 thou shalt be h, thou also shalt seek 5956
Zep 2: 3 it may be ye shall be h in the day of 5641
Mt 5:14 A city that is set on a hill cannot be h. 2928
10:26 be revealed; and h, that shall not be known. 2927
11:25 thou hast h these things from the wise and 613
13:33 and h in three measures of meal, 1470
13:44 of heaven is like unto treasure h in a field; 2928
25:18 digged in the earth, and h his lord's money. 613
25:25 and went and h thy talent in the earth: 2928
Mk 4:22 For there is nothing h, which shall not be 2927
7:24 no man know it: but he could not be h. 2990
Lk 1:24 and h herself five months, saying, 4032
8:17 neither any thing h, that shall not be known 614
8:47 when the woman saw that she was not h, 2990
9:45 and it was h from them, that they perceived 3871
10:21 that thou hast h these things from 613
12: 2 neither h, that shall not be known. 2927
13:21 and h in three measures of meal, 1470
18:34 and this saying was h from them, 2928
19:42 but now they are h from thine eyes. 2928
Jn 8:59 but Jesus h himself, and went out of 2928
2Co 4: 3 But if our gospel be h, it is hid to them that 2572
4: 3 gospel be hid, it is h to them that are lost: 2572
Eph 3: 9 beginning of the world hath been h in God, 613
Col 1:26 mystery which hath been h from ages 613
Col 2: 3 In whom are h all the treasures of wisdom 614
3: 3 and your life is h with Christ in God. 2928
1Ti 5:25 and they that are otherwise cannot be h. 2928
Heb 11:23 was h three months of his parents, because 2928
Rev 6:15 every free man, h themselves in the dens 2928

HIDDAI (1)

2Sa 23:30 the Pirathonite, H of the brooks of Gaash, 1914

HIDDEKEL (2)

Ge 2:14 the name of the third river is H: that is it 2313
Da 10: 4 by the side of the great river, which is H; 2313

HIDDEN (16) [HIDE]

Lev 5: 2 creeping things, and if it be h from him; 5956
Dt 30:11 it is not h from thee, neither is it far off. 6381
Job 3:16 Or as a h untimely birth I had not been; 2934
15:20 the number of years is h to the oppressor. 6845
24: 1 seeing times are not h from the Almighty, 6845
Ps 51: 6 in the h part thou shalt make me to know 5640
83: 3 and consulted against thy h ones. 6845
Pr 28:12 but when the wicked rise, a man is h. 2664
Isa 45: 3 h riches of secret places, that thou mayest 4301
48: 6 even h things, and thou didst not know 5341
Ac 26:26 that none of these things are h from him; 2990
1Co 2: 7 even the h wisdom, which God ordained 613
4: 5 who both will bring to light the h things of 2927
2Co 4: 2 But have renounced the h things of 2927
1Pe 3: 4 But let it be the h man of the heart, in that 2927
Rev 2:17 will I give to eat of the h manna, 2928

HIDE (83) [HID, HIDDEN, HIDEST, HIDETH, HIDING]

Ge 18:17 Shall I h from Abraham that thing which I 3680
47:18 unto him, We will not h it from my lord, 3582
Ex 2: 3 when she could not longer h him, she took 6845
Lev 8:17 and his h, his flesh, and his dung, 5785
9:11 the h he burnt with fire without the camp. 5785
20: 4 any ways h their eyes from the man, 5956+5956
Dt 7:20 and h themselves from thee, be destroyed. 5641
22: 1 sheep go astray, and h thyself from them: 5956
22: 3 thou do likewise: thou mayest not h thyself. 5956
22: 4 down by the way, and h thyself from them: 5956
31:17 I will h my face from them, and they shall 5641
31:18 I will surely h my face in that day 5641+5641
32:20 he said, I will h my face from them, I will 5641
Jos 2:16 h yourselves there three days, until 2244
7:19 now what thou hast done; h it not from me. 3582
Jdg 6:11 the winepress, to h it from the Midianites. 5127
1Sa 3:17 I pray thee h it not from me: God do so 3582
3:17 if thou h any thing from me of all 3582
13: 6 the people did h themselves in caves, and 2244
19: 2 and abide in a secret place, and h thyself: 2244
20: 2 why should my father h this thing from 5641
20: 5 that I may h myself in the fields unto 5641
20:19 come to the place where thou didst h 5641
23:19 Doth not David h himself with us in strong 5641
26: 1 Doth not David h himself in the hill of 5641
2Sa 14:18 the woman, H not from me, I pray thee, 3582
1Ki 17: 3 h thyself by the brook Cherith, 5641
22:25 shalt go into an inner chamber to h thyself. 2247
2Ki 7:12 are they gone out of the camp to h 2247
2Ch 18:24 shalt go into an inner chamber to h thyself. 2244
Job 13:20 unto me: then will I not h myself from thee. 5641
14:13 O that thou wouldest h me in the grave, 6845
20:12 his mouth, though he h it under his tongue; 3582
24: 4 the poor of the earth h themselves together. 2244
33:17 from his purpose, and h pride from man. 3680
34:22 where the workers of iniquity may h 5641
40:13 H them in the dust together; and bind their 2934
Ps 13: 1 how long wilt thou h thy face from me? 5641
17: 8 h me under the shadow of thy wings, 5641
27: 5 For in the time of trouble he shall h me in 6845
27: 5 in the secret of his tabernacle shall he h me; 5641
27: 9 H not thy face far from me; put not thy 5641
30: 7 thou didst h thy face, and I was troubled. 5641
31:20 Thou shalt h them in the secret of thy 5641
51: 9 H thy face from my sins, and blot out all 5641
54: T to Saul, Doth not David h himself with us? 5641
55: 1 and h not thyself from my supplication. 5956
56: 6 they h themselves, they mark my steps, 6845
64: 2 H me from the secret counsel of 5641
69:17 h not thy face from thy servant; for I am in 5641
78: 4 We will not h them from their children, 3582
89:46 wilt thou h thyself, for ever? shall thy 5641
102: 2 H not thy face from me in the day when I 5641
119:19 h not thy commandments from me. 5641
143: 7 h not thy face from me, lest I be like unto 5641
143: 9 mine enemies: I flee unto thee to h me. 3680
Pr 2: 1 and h my commandments with thee; 6845
28:28 When the wicked rise, men h themselves: 5641
Isa 1:15 your hands, I will h mine eyes from you: 5956
2:10 Enter into the rock, and h thee in the dust, 2934
3: 9 declare their sin as Sodom, they h it not. 3582
16: 3 h the outcasts; bewray not him that 5641
26:20 h thyself as it were for a little moment, 2247
29:15 Woe unto them that seek deep to h their 5641
58: 7 that thou h not thyself from thine own 5956
Jer 13: 4 and h it there in a hole of the rock. 2934
13: 6 which I commanded thee to h there. 2934
23:24 Can any h himself in secret places that I 5641
36:19 Go, h thee, thou and Jeremiah; 5641
38:14 I will ask thee a thing; h nothing from me. 3582
38:25 h it not from us, and we will not put thee to 3582
43: 9 and h them in the clay in the brickkiln, 2934
49:10 and he shall not be able to h himself: 2247
La 3:56 h not thine ear at my breathing, at my cry. 5956
Eze 28: 3 there is no secret that they can h from thee: 6004
31: 8 in the garden of God could not h him: 6004
39:29 Neither will I h my face any more from 5641
Da 10: 7 so that they fled to h themselves. 2244
Am 9: 3 though they h themselves in the top of 2244
Mic 3: 4 he will even h his face from them at that 5641
Jn 12:36 and departed, and did h himself from them. 2928

Jas 5:20 from death, and shall **h** a multitude of sins. *2572*
Rev 6:16 **h** us from the face of him that sitteth on *2928*

HIDEST (6) [HIDE]

Job 13:24 Wherefore **h** thou thy face, and holdest me 5641
Ps 10: 1 *why* **h** thou *thyself* in times of trouble? 5956
44:24 Wherefore **h** thou thy face, *and* 5641
88:14 off my soul? *why* **h** thou thy face from me? 5641
104:29 Thou **h** thy face, they are troubled: 5641
Isa 45:15 Verily thou *art* a God that **h** thyself, O God 5641

HIDETH (16) [HIDE]

1Sa 23:23 all the lurking places where he **h** himself, 2244
Job 23: 9 I cannot behold *him:* he **h** *himself on* 5848
34:29 when he **h** *his* face, who then can behold 5641
42: 3 Who *is* he that **h** counsel without 5956
Ps 10:11 he **h** his face; he will never see *it.* 5641
139:12 Yea, the darkness **h** not from thee; but 2821
Pr 10:18 He that **h** hatred *with* lying lips, and he that 3680
19:24 A slothful *man* **h** his hand in *his* bosom, 2934
22: 3 *man* foreseeth the evil, and **h** himself: 5641
26:15 The slothful **h** his hand in *his* bosom; 2934
27:12 *man* foreseeth the evil, *and* **h** himself; 5641
27:16 Whosoever **h** her, hideth the wind, and 6845
27:16 **h** the wind, and the ointment of his right 6845
28:27 he that **h** his eyes shall have many a curse. 5956
Isa 8:17 that **h** his face from the house of Jacob, and 5641
Mt 13:44 he **h**, and for joy thereof goeth and *2928*

HIDING (6) [HIDE]

Job 31:33 as Adam, by **h** mine iniquity in my bosom: 2934
Ps 32: 7 Thou *art* my **h place**; thou shalt preserve 5643
119:114 Thou *art* my **h place** and my shield: I hope 5643
Isa 28:17 and the waters shall overflow the **h place.** 5643
32: 2 a man shall be as a **h place** from the wind, 4224
Hab 3: 4 his hand: and there *was* the **h** of his power. 2253

HIEL (1)

1Ki 16:34 In his days did **H** the Bethelite build 2419

HIERAPOLIS (1)

Col 4:13 them that are in Laodicea, and them in **H.** *2404*

HIGGAION (1)

Ps 9:16 in the work of his own hands. **H.** Selah. 1902

HIGH (416) [HEIGHT, HEIGHTS, HIGHER, HIGHEST, HIGHLY, HIGHMINDED, HIGH-MINDED, HIGHNESS, HIGHWAY, HIGHWAYS]

Ge 7:19 all the **h** hills, that *were* under the whole 1364
14:18 and he *was* the priest of the **most H** God. 5945
14:19 said, Blessed *be* Abram of the **most h** God, 5945
14:20 blessed *be* the **most h** God, which hath 5945
14:22 the **most h** God, the possessor of heaven 5945
29: 7 he said, Lo, *it is* yet **h** day, neither *is it* time 1419
Ex 14: 8 the children of Israel went out with a **h** 7311
25:20 forth *their* wings **on h,** 4605+1886.5+3807.1
37: 9 out *their* wings **on h,** 4605+1886.5+3807.1
39:31 **on h** upon the mitre; 4480+4605+1886.5+3807.1
Lev 21:10 *he that is* the **h** priest among his brethren, 1419
26:22 and your ***h*** ways shall be desolate. NIH
26:30 I will destroy your **h places,** and cut down 1116
Nu 11:31 as it were two cubits ***h*** upon the face of NIH
20:17 we will go *by* the king's ***h*** way, we will not NIH
20:19 said unto him, We will go by the **h way:** 4546
21:22 *but* we will go along by the king's ***h*** way, NIH
21:28 *and* the lords of the **h places** of Arnon. 1116
22:41 brought him up *into* the **h places** of Baal, 1116
23: 3 I will tell thee. And he went to a **h place.** 8205
24:16 and knew the knowledge of the **most H,** 5945
33: 3 a **h** hand in the sight of all the Egyptians. 7311
33:52 and quite pluck down all their **h places:** 1116
35:25 he shall abide in it unto the death of the **h** 1419
35:28 of his refuge until the death of the **h** priest: 1419
35:28 after the death of the **h** priest the slayer 1419
Dt 2:27 I will go along by the **h way,** I will neither 1870
3: 5 All these cities *were* fenced *with* **h** walls, 1364
12: 2 upon the **h** mountains, and upon the hills, 7311
26:19 to make thee **h** above all nations which he 5945
28: 1 that the LORD thy God will set thee **on h** 5945
28:43 above thee **very h;** 4605+4605+1886.5+1886.5
28:52 until thy **h** and fenced walls come down, 1364
32: 8 When the **most H** divided to the nations 5945
32:13 He made him ride on the **h places** of 1116
32:27 Our hand is **h,** and the LORD hath not 7311
33:29 and thou shalt tread upon their **h places.** 1116
Jos 20: 6 until the death of the **h** priest that shall be 1419
Jdg 5:18 unto the death in the **h places** of the field. 4791
1Sa 9:12 of the people to day in the **h place:** 1116
9:13 before he go up to the **h place** to eat: 1116
9:14 against them, for to go up *to* the **h place.** 1116
9:19 go up before me *unto* the **h place;** for ye 1116
9:25 come down from the **h place** *into* the city, 1116
10: 5 down from the **h place** with a psaltery, 1116
10:13 end of prophesying, he came *to* the **h place.** 1116
13: 6 and in rocks, and in **h places,** and in pits. 6877
2Sa 1:19 beauty of Israel *is* slain upon thy **h places:** 1116
1:25 *thou wast* slain in thine **h places.** 1116
22: 3 my **h tower,** and my refuge, my saviour; 4869
22:14 and the **most H** uttered his voice. 5945
22:34 and setteth me upon my **h places.** 1116
22:49 thou also hast **lifted** me **up on h** above 7311
23: 1 and the man *who* was raised up **on h,** 5920
1Ki 3: 2 Only the people sacrificed in **h places,** 1116
3: 3 he sacrificed and burnt incense in **h places.** 1116
3: 4 for that *was* the great **h place:** 1116
6:10 against all the house, five cubits **h.** 6967
6:23 cherubims *of* olive tree, each ten cubits **h.** 6967
7:15 pillars *of* brass, of eighteen cubits **h** apiece: 6967
7:35 *there* a round compass of half a cubit **h:** 6967
9: 8 *at* this house, *which* is **h,** every one that 5945
11: 7 did Solomon build a **h place** for Chemosh, 1116
12:31 he made a house of **h places,** and 1116
1Ki 12:32 priests of the **h places** which he had made. 1116
13: 2 of the **h places** that burn incense upon thee, 1116
13:32 against all the houses of the **h places** which 1116
13:33 lowest of the people priests of the **h places:** 1116
13:33 became *one of* the priests of the **h places.** 1116
14:23 For they also built them **h places,** and 1116
14:23 on every **h** hill, and under every green tree. 1364
15:14 the **h places** were not removed: 1116
21: 9 and set Naboth on **h** among the people: 7218
21:12 and set Naboth on **h** among the people. 7218
22:43 the **h places** were not taken away; 1116
22:43 and burnt incense yet in the **h places.** 1116
2Ki 12: 3 the **h places** were not taken away: 1116
12: 3 and burnt incense in the **h places.** 1116
12:10 the king's scribe and the **h** priest came up, 1419
14: 4 Howbeit the **h places** were not taken away: 1116
14: 4 and burnt incense on the **h places.** 1116
15: 4 Save that the **h places** were not removed: 1116
15: 4 and burnt incense still on the **h places.** 1116
15:35 Howbeit the **h places** were not removed: 1116
15:35 and burnt incense still in the **h places.** 1116
16: 4 and burnt incense in the **h places,** 1116
17: 9 they built them **h places** in all their cities, 1116
17:10 them up images and groves in every **h** hill, 1364
17:11 there they burnt incense in all the **h places,** 1116
17:29 put *them* in the houses of the **h places** 1116
17:32 the lowest of them priests of the **h places,** 1116
17:32 for them in the houses of the **h places.** 1116
18: 4 He removed the **h places,** and brake 1116
18:22 whose **h places** and whose altars Hezekiah 1116
19:22 *thy* voice, and lift up thine eyes **on h?** 4791
21: 3 For he built *up* again the **h places** which 1116
22: 4 Go up to Hilkiah the **h** priest, that he may 1419
22: 8 Hilkiah the **h** priest said unto Shaphan 1419
23: 4 the king commanded Hilkiah the **h** priest, 1419
23: 5 in the **h places** in the cities of Judah, 1116
23: 8 defiled the **h places** where the priests had 1116
23: 8 brake down the **h places** of the gates that 1116
23: 9 Nevertheless the priests of the **h places** 1116
23:13 the **h places** that *were* before Jerusalem, 1116
23:15 the **h place** which Jeroboam the son of 1116
23:15 that altar and the **h place** he brake down, 1116
23:15 burnt the **h place,** *and* stamp*ed it* small to 1116
23:19 all the houses also of the **h places** that *were* 1116
23:20 he slew all the priests of the **h places** that 1116
1Ch 11:23 five cubits ***h;*** and in the Egyptian's hand NIH
14: 2 kingdom *was* lift up **on h,** 4605+1886.5+3807.1
16:39 LORD in the **h place** that *was* at Gibeon, 1116
17:17 to the estate of a man of **h degree,** 4609
21:29 *were* at that season in the **h place** at 1116
2Ch 1: 3 went to the **h place** that *was* at Gibeon; 1116
1:13 **h place** that *was* at Gibeon *to* Jerusalem, 1116
3:15 house two pillars of thirty and five cubits **h,** 753
6:13 three cubits **h,** and had set it in the midst of 6967
7:21 this house, which is **h,** shall be an 5945
11:15 he ordained him priests for the **h places,** 1116
14: 3 altars of the strange *gods,* and the **h places,** 1116
14: 5 out of all the cities of Judah the **h places** 1116
15:17 the **h places** were not taken away out of 1116
17: 6 moreover he took away the **h places** and 1116
20:19 with a loud voice **on h.** 4605+1886.5+3807.1
20:33 Howbeit the **h places** were not taken away: 1116
21:11 Moreover he made **h places** in 1116
23:20 they came through the **h** gate *into* 5945
24:11 and the **h** priest's officer came and 7218
27: 3 He built the **h** gate of the house of 5945
28: 4 and burnt incense in the **h places,** 1116
28:25 **h places** to burn incense unto other gods, 1116
31: 1 threw down the **h places** and the altars out 1116
32:12 the same Hezekiah taken away his **h places** 1116
33: 3 For he built again the **h places** which 1116
33:17 the people did sacrifice still in the **h places,** 1116
33:19 the places wherein he built **h places,** and 1116
34: 3 and Jerusalem from the **h places,** 1116
34: 4 the images, that *were* **on h** 4605+1886.5+3807.1
34: 9 when they came to Hilkiah the **h** priest, 1419
Ne 3: 1 Eliashib the **h** priest rose up with his 1419
3:20 door of the house of Eliashib the **h** priest. 1419
3:25 the tower which lieth out from the king's **h** 5945
13:28 of Joiada, the son of Eliashib the **h** priest, 1419
Est 5:14 Let a gallows be made of fifty cubits **h,** and 1364
7: 9 Behold also, the gallows fifty cubits **h,** 1364
Job 5:11 To set up on **h** those that be low; that those 4791
11: 8 *It is* as **h** as heaven; what canst thou do? 1363
16:19 witness *is* in heaven, and my record *is* on **h.** 4791
21:22 seeing he judgeth those that are **h.** 7311
22:12 the height of the stars, how **h** they are. 7311
25: 2 with him, he maketh peace in his **h places.** 4791
31: 2 inheritance of the Almighty from **on h?** 4791
38:15 and the **h** arm shall be broken. 7311
39:18 What time she lifteth up herself on **h,** 4791
39:27 at thy command, and **make** her nest **on h?** 7311
41:34 He beholdeth all **h** *things:* he *is* a king over 1364
Ps 7: 7 for their sakes therefore return thou on **h.** 4791
7:17 *praise* to the name of the LORD **most H** 5945
9: 2 sing *praise* to thy name, O thou **most H.** 5945
18: 2 the horn of my salvation, *and* my **h tower.** 4869
18:27 but wilt bring down **h** looks. 7311
18:33 and setteth me upon my **h places.** 1116
21: 7 through the mercy of the **most H** he shall 5945
46: 4 holy *place* of the tabernacles of the **most H.** 5945
47: 2 For the LORD **most H** *is* terrible; *he is* a 5945
49: 2 Both low and **h**[S], rich and poor, 376+1121
50:14 and pay thy vows unto the **most H:** 5945
56: 2 many that fight against me, O thou *most* **H.** 4791
57: 2 I will cry unto God **most H;** unto God that 5945
62: 9 *and* **men of h degree** *are* a lie: 376+1121
68:15 of Bashan; a **h** hill *as* the hill of Bashan. 1386
68:16 Why leap ye, ye **h** hills? *this is* the hill 1386
68:18 Thou hast ascended on **h,** thou hast led 4791
69:29 let thy salvation, O God, **set** me **up on h.** 7682
71:19 righteousness also, O God, *is* **very h,** 4791+5704
73:11 and is there knowledge in the **most H?** 5945
75: 5 Lift not up your horn on **h:** speak *not* with a 4791
77:10 the years of the right hand of the **most H.** 5945
Ps 78:17 by provoking the **most H** in the wilderness. 5945
78:35 their rock, and the **h** God their redeemer. 5945
78:56 and provoked the **most h** God, 5945
78:58 provoked him to anger with their **h places,** 1116
78:69 he built his sanctuary like **h** *palaces,* like 7311
82: 6 and all of you *are* children of the **most H.** 5945
83:18 *art* the **most H** over all the earth. 5945
89:13 strong is thy hand, *and* **h** is thy right hand. 7311
91: 1 **most H** shall abide under the shadow of 5945
91: 9 my refuge, *even* the **most H,** thy habitation; 5945
91:14 I will **set** him **on h,** because he hath known 7682
92: 1 to sing *praises* unto thy name, O **most H:** 5945
92: 8 But thou, LORD, *art most* **h** for evermore. 4791
93: 4 The LORD **on h** *is* 4791+871.1+1886.1
97: 9 LORD, *art* **H** above all the earth: 5945
99: 2 in Zion; and he *is* **h** above all the people. 7311
101: 5 him that hath a **h** look and a proud heart 1362
103:11 For as the heaven is **h** above the earth, *so* 1361
104:18 The **h** hills *are* a refuge for the wild goats; 1364
107:11 and contemned the counsel of the **most H:** 5945
107:41 Yet **setteth** he the poor **on h** from 7682
113: 4 The LORD *is* **h** above all nations, *and* 7311
113: 5 the LORD our God, who dwelleth on **h,** 1361
131: 1 in great *matters,* or in *things* too **h** for me. 6381
138: 6 Though the LORD *be* **h,** yet hath he 7311
139: 6 for me; it is **h,** I cannot attain unto it. 7682
144: 2 my **h tower,** and my deliverer; my shield, 4869
149: 6 *Let* the **h** *praises* of God *be* in their mouth, 7319
150: 5 praise him upon the **h sounding** cymbals. 8643
Pr 8: 2 She standeth in the top of **h places** by 4791
9:14 on a seat in the **h places** of the city, 4791
18:11 and as a **h** wall in his own conceit. 7682
21: 4 A **h** look, and a proud heart, *and* 7312
24: 7 Wisdom *is too* **h** for a fool: he openeth not 7311
Ecc 12: 5 *when* they shall be afraid of *that which is* **h,** 1364
Isa 2:13 that are **h** and lifted up, and upon all 7311
2:14 upon all the **h** mountains, and upon all 7311
2:15 upon every **h** tower, and upon every fenced 1364
6: 1 **h** and lifted up, and his train filled 7311
10:12 of Assyria, and the glory of his **h** looks. 7312
10:33 the **h ones** of stature *shall be* hewn down, 7311
13: 2 Lift ye up a banner upon the **h** mountain, 8192
14:14 of the clouds; I will be like the **most H.** 5945
15: 2 and *to* Dibon, the **h places,** to weep: 1116
16:12 is seen that Moab is weary on the **h place,** 1116
22:16 *as* he that heweth him out a sepulchre **on h,** 4791
24:18 for the windows from **on h** are open, and 4791
24:21 the host of the **h ones** *that are* on high, 4791
24:21 the host of the high ones *that are* on **h,** 4791
25:12 the fortress of the **h fort** of thy walls shall 4869
26: 5 For he bringeth down them that dwell **on h;** 4791
30:13 swelling out in a **h** wall, whose breaking 7682
30:25 there shall be upon every **h** mountain, and 1364
30:25 upon every **h** hill, rivers *and* streams of 5375
32:15 the spirit be poured upon us from **on h,** 4791
33: 5 LORD *is* exalted; for he dwelleth **on h:** 4791
33:16 He shall dwell **on h:** his place of defence 4791
36: 7 whose **h places** and whose altars Hezekiah 1116
37:23 *thy* voice, and lifted up thine eyes **on h?** 4791
40: 9 get thee up into the **h** mountain; 1364
40:26 Lift up your eyes **on h,** and behold who 4791
41:18 I will open rivers in **h places,** and 8205
49: 9 and their pastures *shall be* in all **h places.** 8205
52:13 be exalted and extolled, and be very **h.** 1361
57: 7 and **h** mountain hast thou set thy bed: 5375
57:15 For thus saith the **h** and lofty One that 7311
57:15 I dwell *in* the **h** and holy *place,* with him 4791
58: 4 to make your voice to be heard on **h.** 4791
58:14 I will cause thee to ride upon the **h places** 1116
Jer 2:20 when upon every **h** hill and under every 1364
3: 2 Lift up thine eyes unto the **h places,** and 8205
3: 6 she is gone up upon every **h** mountain and 1364
3:21 A voice was heard upon the **h places,** 8205
4:11 A dry wind of the **h places** in 8205
7:29 and take up a lamentation on **h places;** 8205
7:31 they have built the **h places** of Tophet, 1116
12:12 The spoilers are come upon all **h places** 8205
14: 6 the wild asses did stand in the **h places,** 8205
17: 2 their groves by the green trees upon the **h** 1364
17: 3 *and* thy **h places** for sin, throughout all thy 1116
17:12 A glorious **h** throne from the beginning *is* 4791
19: 5 They have built also the **h places** of Baal, 1116
20: 2 put him in the stocks that *were* in the **h** gate 5945
25:30 The LORD shall roar from **on h,** and 4791
26:18 the mountain of the house as the **h places** 1116
31:21 Set thee up waymarks, make thee **h heaps:** 8564
32:35 they built the **h places** of Baal, which *are* in 1116
48:35 him that offereth *in* the **h places,** and 1116
49:16 though thou shouldest **make** thy nest as **h** 1361
51:58 her **h** gates shall be burnt with fire; 1364
La 3:35 of a man before the face of the **most H,** 5945
3:38 Out of the mouth of the **most H** proceedeth 5945
Eze 1:18 they were so **h** that they were dreadful; 1363
6: 3 upon you, and I will destroy your **h places.** 1116
6: 6 and the **h places** shall be desolate; 1116
6:13 upon every **h** hill, in all the tops of 7311
16:16 deckedst thy **h places** with divers colours, 1116
16:24 hast made thee a **h place** in every street. 7413
16:25 Thou hast built thy **h place** at every head of 7413
16:31 and makest thine **h place** in every street; 7413
16:39 and shall break down thy **h places:** 7413
17:22 take of the highest branch of the **h** cedar, 7311
17:22 will plant *it* upon a **h** mountain and 1364
17:24 I the LORD have brought down the **h** tree, 1364
20:28 they saw every **h** hill, and all the thick 7311
20:29 What *is* the **h place** whereunto ye go? 1116
21:26 *him that is* low, and abase *him that is* **h.** 1364
31: 3 a shadowing shrowd, and of a **h** stature; 1362
31: 4 the deep **set** him **up on h** with her rivers 7311
34: 6 all the mountains, and upon every **h** hill: 7311
34:14 upon the **h** mountains of Israel shall their 4791
36: 2 even the ancient **h places** are ours in 1116
40: 2 set me upon a very **h** mountain, by which 1364
40:42 a cubit and a half broad, and one cubit **h:** 1363
41:22 The altar *of* wood *was* three cubits **h,** and 1364

H

Eze 43: 7 the carcases of their kings *in* their **h places**. 1116
Da 3:26 ye servants of the **most h** God, come forth, 5943
4: 2 wonders that the **h** God hath wrought 5943
4:17 the **most H** ruleth in the kingdom of men, 5943
4:24 and this *is* the decree of the **most H**, 5943
4:25 till thou know that the **most H** ruleth in 5943
4:32 until thou know that the **most H** ruleth in 5943
4:34 I blessed the **most H**, and I praised and 5943
5:18 the **most h** God gave Nebuchadnezzar thy 5943
5:21 till he knew that the **most h** God ruled in 5943
7:18 the saints of the **most H** shall take 5946
7:22 *was* given to the saints of the **most H**; 5946
7:25 shall speak *great* words against the **most H**, 5943
7:25 shall wear out the saints of the **most H**, and 5946
7:27 to the people of the saints of the **most H**, 5946
8: 3 the two horns *were* **h**; but one *was* higher 1364
Hos 7:16 They return, *but* not *to* the **most H**: they are 5920
10: 8 The **h places** also of Aven, the sin of Israel, 1116
11: 7 though they called them to the **most H**, 5920
Am 4:13 treadeth upon the **h places** of the earth, 1116
7: 9 the **h places** of Isaac shall be desolate, and 1116
Ob 1: 3 the clefts of the rock, whose habitation *is* **h**; 4791
Mic 1: 3 and tread upon the **h places** of the earth. 1116
1: 5 what *are* the **h places** of Judah? *are they* 1116
3:12 the mountain of the house as the **h places** 1116
6: 6 *and* bow myself before the **h** God? 4791
Hab 2: 9 that *he* may set his nest on **h**, that *he* may 4791
3:10 uttered his voice, *and* lift up his hands on **h**. 7315
3:19 will make me to walk upon mine **h places**. 1116
Zep 1:16 the fenced cities, and against the **h** towers. 1364
Hag 1: 1 to Joshua the son of Josedech the **h** priest, 1419
1:12 Joshua the son of Josedech the **h** priest, 1419
1:14 of Joshua the son of Josedech the **h** priest, 1419
2: 2 to Joshua the son of Josedech the **h** priest 1419
2: 4 O Joshua, son of Josedech, the **h** priest; 1419
Zec 3: 1 he shewed me Joshua the **h** priest standing 1419
3: 8 O Joshua the **h** priest, thou, and thy fellows 1419
6:11 of Joshua the son of Josedech the **h** priest; 1419
Mt 4: 8 the devil taketh him *up* into an exceeding **h** 5308
17: 1 bringeth them up into a **h** mountain apart, 5308
26: 3 of the people, unto the palace of the **h priest**, 749
26:51 and stroke a servant of the **h priest's**, and 749
26:57 Jesus led *him* away to Caiaphas the **h priest**, 749
26:58 him afar off unto the **h priest's** palace, 749
26:62 And the **h priest** arose, and said unto him, 749
26:63 And the **h priest** answered and said unto 749
26:65 Then the **h priest** rent his clothes, saying, 749
Mk 2:26 of God in the days of Abiathar the **h priest**, 749
5: 7 Jesus, *thou* Son of the **most h** God? 5310
6:21 **h captains**, and chief *estates* of Galilee; 5506
9: 2 leadeth them up into a **h** mountain apart by 5308
14:47 and smote a servant of the **h priest**, and 749
14:53 And they led Jesus away to the **h priest**: and 749
14:54 afar off, even into the palace of the **h priest**: 749
14:60 And the **h priest** stood up in the midst, and 749
14:61 Again the **h priest** asked him, and said unto 749
14:63 Then the **h priest** rent his clothes, and saith, 749
14:66 cometh one of the maids of the **h priest**: 749
Lk 1:78 whereby the dayspring from **on h** hath 5311
3: 2 Annas and Caiaphas being the **h priests**, 749
4: 5 the devil, taking him up into a **h** mountain, 5308
8:28 with thee, Jesus, *thou* Son of God **most h**? 5310
22:50 of them smote the servant of the **h priest**, 749
22:54 and brought him into the **h priest's** house. 749
24:49 until ye be endued with power from **on h**. 5311
Jn 11:49 being the **h priest** that *same* year, said unto 749
11:51 but being **h priest** that year, he prophesied 749
18:10 and smote the **h priest's** servant, and cut off 749
18:13 which was the **h priest** that *same* year. 749
18:15 that disciple was known unto the **h priest**, 749
18:15 in with Jesus into the palace of the **h priest**. 749
18:16 which was known unto the **h priest**, and 749
18:19 The **h priest** then asked Jesus of his 749
18:22 saying, Answerest thou the **h priest** so? 749
18:24 sent him bound unto Caiaphas the **h priest**. 749
18:26 One of the servants of the **h priest**, being *his* 749
19:31 (for that sabbath day was a **h** day,) 3173
Ac 4: 6 And Annas the **h priest**, and Caiaphas, and 749
4: 6 many as were of the kindred of the **h priest**, 748
5:17 Then the **h priest** rose up, and all they that 749
5:21 But the **h priest** came, and they that were 749
5:24 Now when the *h* priest and the captain of NIG
5:27 the council: and the **h priest** asked them, 749
7: 1 Then said the **h priest**, Are these *things* so? 749
7:48 Howbeit the **most H** dwelleth not in 5310
9: 1 disciples of the Lord, went unto the **h priest**, 749
13:17 and with a **h** arm brought he them out of it. 5308
16:17 These men are the servants of the **most h** 5310
22: 5 As also the **h priest** doth bear me witness, 749
23: 2 And the **h priest** Ananias commanded them 749
23: 4 stood by said, Revilest thou God's **h priest**? 749
23: 5 I wist not, brethren, that he was the **h priest**: 749
24: 1 And after five days Ananias the **h priest** 749
25: 2 Then the **h priest** and the chief of the Jews 749
Ro 12:16 Mind not **h** *things*, but condescend to *men* 5308
13:11 **now** *it is* **h time** to awake out of 2235+5610
2Co 10: 5 every **h** thing that exalteth itself against 5313
Eph 4: 8 *he* saith, When he ascended up on **h**, 5311
6:12 against spiritual wickedness in **h** *places*. 2032
Php 3:14 I press toward the mark for the prize of the **h** 507
Heb 1: 3 on the right hand of the Majesty on **h**; 5308
2:17 faithful **h priest** *in things* pertaining to God, 749
3: 1 the Apostle and **H Priest** of our profession, 749
4:14 Seeing then that we have a great **h priest**, 749
4:15 For we have not a **h priest** which cannot be 749
5: 1 For every **h priest** taken from among men is 749
5: 5 glorified not himself to be made a **h priest**; 749
5:10 Called of God a **h priest** after the order of 749
6:20 made a **h priest** for ever after the order of 749
7: 1 king of Salem, priest of the **most h** God, 5310
7:26 For such a **h priest** became us, *who is* holy, 749
7:27 as *those* **h priests**, to offer up sacrifice, 749
7:28 For the law maketh men **h priests** which 749
8: 1 We have such a **h priest**, who is set on 749
8: 3 For every **h priest** is ordained to offer gifts 749
Heb 9: 7 But into the second *went* the **h priest** alone 749
9:11 But Christ being come a **h priest** of good 749
9:25 as the **h priest** entereth into the holy *place* 749
10:21 And *having* a **h** priest over the house of 3173
13:11 into the sanctuary by the **h priest** for sin, 749
Rev 21:10 in the spirit to a great and **h** mountain, 5308
21:12 And had a wall great and **h**, and had twelve 5308

HIGHER (21) [HIGH]

Nu 24: 7 his king shall be **h** than Agag, and 7311
1Sa 9: 2 upward *he was* **h** than any of the people. 1364
10:23 he was **h** than any of the people from his 1361
2Ki 15:35 He built the **h** gate of the house of 5945
Ne 4:13 places behind the wall, *and* on the **h places**, 6706
Job 35: 5 behold the clouds *which* are **h** than thou. 1361
Ps 61: 2 lead me to the rock *that* is **h** than I. 7311
89:27 *my* firstborn, **h** than the kings of the earth. 5945
Ecc 5: 8 for *he that is* **h** than the highest regardeth; 1364
5: 8 highest regardeth; and *there be* **h** than they. 1364
Isa 55: 9 For *as* the heavens are **h** than the earth, so 1361
55: 9 so are my ways **h** than your ways, and 1361
Jer 36:10 in the **h** court *at* the entry of the new gate of 5945
Eze 9: 2 six men came from the way of the **h** gate, 5945
42: 5 for the galleries were **h** than these, than 398
43:13 and this *shall be* the **h place** of the altar. 1354
Da 8: 3 one *was* **h** than the other, and the higher 1364
8: 3 than the other, and the **h** came up last. 1364
Lk 14:10 he may say unto thee, Friend, go up **h**: 511
Ro 13: 1 Let every soul be subject unto the **h** 5242
Heb 7:26 and made **h than** the heavens; 5308

HIGHEST (18) [HIGH]

Ps 18:13 in the heavens, and the **H** gave his voice; 5945
87: 5 and the **H** himself shall establish her. 5945
Pr 8:26 nor the **h part** of the dust of the world. 7218
9: 3 crieth upon the **h places** of the city, 1610+4791
Ecc 5: 8 for *he that is* higher than the **h** regardeth; 1364
Eze 17: 3 and took the **h branch** of the cedar: 6788
17:22 I will also take of the **h branch** of the high 6788
41: 7 increased *from* the lowest *chamber* to the **h** 5945
Mt 21: 9 in the name of the Lord; Hosanna in the **h**. 5310
Mk 11:10 in the name of the Lord: Hosanna in the **h**. 5310
Lk 1:32 and shall be called the Son of the **H**: 5310
1:35 the power of the **H** shall overshadow thee: 5310
1:76 child, shalt be called the prophet of the **H**: 5310
2:14 Glory to God in the **h**, and on earth peace, 5310
6:35 and ye shall be the children of the **H**: 5310
14: 8 to a wedding, sit not down in the **h room**; 4411
19:38 peace in heaven, and glory in the **h**. 5310
20:46 and the **h seats** in the synagogues, and 4410

HIGHLY (6) [HIGH]

Lk 1:28 and said, Hail, *thou that art* **h favoured**, 5487
16:15 for that which is **h esteemed** amongst men 5308
Ac 12:20 And Herod was **h displeased** with them of 2371
Ro 12: 3 not to **think** *of himself* more **h** than he 5252
Php 2: 9 Wherefore God also hath **h exalted** him, 5251
1Th 5:13 And to esteem them very **h** in love 1537+4053

HIGHMINDED, HIGH-MINDED (3) [HIGH, MIND]

Ro 11:20 thou standest by faith. Be not **h**, but fear: 5309
1Ti 6:17 that *they* be not **h**, nor trust in uncertain 5309
2Ti 3: 4 Traitors, heady, **h**, lovers of pleasures more 5187

HIGHNESS (2) [HIGH]

Job 31:23 and by reason of his **h** I could not endure. 7613
Isa 13: 3 mine anger, *even* them that rejoice in my **h**. 1346

HIGHWAY (16) [HIGH, WAY]

Jdg 21:19 on the east side of the **h** that goeth up from 4546
1Sa 6:12 *and* went along the **h**, lowing as they went, 4546
2Sa 20:12 wallowed in blood in the midst of the **h**. 4546
20:12 he removed Amasa out of the **h** *into* 4546
20:13 When he was removed out of the **h**, all 4546
2Ki 18:17 which *is* in the **h** of the fuller's field. 4546
Pr 16:17 The **h** of the upright *is* to depart from evil: 4546
Isa 7: 3 the upper pool in the **h** of the fuller's field; 4546
11:16 there shall be a **h** for the remnant of his 4546
19:23 In that day shall there be a **h** out of Egypt 4546
35: 8 a **h** shall be there, and a way, and it shall be 4547
36: 2 the upper pool in the **h** of the fuller's field. 4546
40: 3 make straight in the desert a **h** for our God. 4546
62:10 cast up, cast up the **h**; gather out the stones; 4546
Jer 31:21 set thine heart toward the **h**, *even* the way 4546
Mk 10:46 of Timeus, sat by the *h*way **side** begging. 3598

HIGHWAYS (10) [HIGH, WAY]

Jdg 5: 6 the **h** were unoccupied, and the travellers 734
20:31 *and* kill, as at other times, in the **h**, 4546
20:32 and draw them from the city unto the **h**. 4546
20:45 they gleaned of them in the **h** five thousand 4546
Isa 33: 8 The **h** lie waste, the wayfaring man 4546
49:11 a way, and my **h** shall be exalted. 4546
Am 5:16 and they shall say in all the **h**, Alas! 2351
Mt 22: 9 Go ye therefore into the **h**, 1327+3588+3598
22:10 So those servants went out into the *h*ways, 3598
Lk 14:23 Go out into the *h*ways and hedges, and 3598

HILEN (1)

1Ch 6:58 **H** with her suburbs, Debir with her 2432

HILKIAH (33) [HILKIAH'S]

2Ki 18:18 came out to them Eliakim the son of **H**, 2518
18:26 said Eliakim the son of **H**, and Shebna, 2518
18:37 came Eliakim the son of **H**, which *was* over 2518
22: 4 Go up to **H** the high priest, that he may sum 2518
22: 8 **H** the high priest said unto Shaphan 2518
22: 8 **H** gave the book to Shaphan, and he read it. 2518
22:10 **H** the priest hath delivered me a book. 2518
22:12 the king commanded **H** the priest, and 2518
22:14 So **H** the priest, and Ahikam, and Achbor, 2518
23: 4 the king commanded **H** the high priest, 2518
23:24 **H** the priest found *in* the house of 2518
1Ch 6:13 Shallum begat **H**, and Hilkiah begat 2518
6:13 begat Hilkiah, and **H** begat Azariah, 2518
6:45 the son of Amaziah, the son of **H**, 2518
9:11 Azariah the son of **H**, the son of 2518
26:11 **H** the second, Tebaliah the third, 2518
2Ch 34: 9 when they came to **H** the high priest, 2518
34:14 **H** the priest found a book of the law of 2518
34:15 **H** answered and said to Shaphan the scribe, 2518
34:15 And **H** delivered the book to Shaphan. 2518
34:18 **H** the priest hath given me a book. 2518
34:20 the king commanded **H**, and Ahikam 2518
34:22 **H**, and *they* that the king *had appointed*, 2518
35: 8 **H** and Zechariah and Jehiel, rulers of 2518
Ezr 7: 1 the son of Azariah, the son of **H**, 2518
Ne 8: 4 Anaiah, and Urijah, and **H**, and Maaseiah, 2518
11:11 Seraiah the son of **H**, the son of 2518
12: 7 Sallu, Amok, **H**, Jedaiah. These *were* 2518
12:21 Of **H**, Hashabiah; of Jedaiah, Nethaneel. 2518
Isa 22:20 I will call my servant Eliakim the son of **H**: 2518
36:22 came Eliakim, the son of **H**, that *was* over 2518
Jer 1: 1 The words of Jeremiah the son of **H**, of 2518
29: 3 of Shaphan, and Gemariah the son of **H**, 2518

HILKIAH'S (1) [HILKIAH]

Isa 36: 3 **H** son, which *was* over the house, and 2518

HILL (75) [AREOPAGUS, DUNGHILL, DUNGHILLS, HILL'S, HILLS, MARS' HILL]

Ex 17: 9 to morrow I will stand on the top of the **h** 1389
17:10 Aaron, and Hur went up *to* the top of the **h**. 1389
24: 4 builded an altar under the **h**, and 2022
Nu 14:44 they presumed to go up unto the **h** top: 2022
14:45 the Canaanites which dwelt in that **h**, 2022
Dt 1:41 of war, ye were ready to go up into the **h**. 2022
1:43 and went presumptuously up into the **h**. 2022
Jos 5: 3 circumcised the children of Israel at the **h** 1389
13: 6 All the inhabitants of the **h country** from 2022
15: 9 the border was drawn from the top of the **h** 2022
17:16 of Joseph said, The **h** is not enough for us: 2022
18:13 near the **h** that *lieth* on the south side of 2022
18:14 from the **h** that *lieth* before Beth-horon 2022
21:11 *city is* Hebron, in the **h** *country* of Judah, 2022
24:30 on the north side of the **h** of Gaash. 2022
24:33 they buried him in a **h** that pertained to 1389
Jdg 2: 9 on the north side of the **h** Gaash. 2022
7: 1 of them, by the **h** of Moreh, in the valley. 1389
16: 3 carried them up to the top of a **h** that *is* 2022
1Sa 7: 1 it into the house of Abinadab in the **h**, 1389
9:11 *And* as they went up the **h** to the city, they 4608
10: 5 After that thou shalt come to the **h** of God, 1389
10:10 when they came thither to the **h**, behold, 1389
23:19 in the **h** of Hachilah, which *is* on the south 1389
25:20 that she came down by the covert of the **h**, 2022
26: 1 Doth not David hide himself in the **h** of 1389
26: 3 Saul pitched in the **h** of Hachilah, which *is* 1389
26:13 and stood on the top of a **h** afar off; 2022
2Sa 2:24 when they were come to the **h** of Ammah, 1389
2:25 one troop, and stood on the top of a **h**. 1389
13:34 people by the way of the **h** side behind him. 2022
16: 1 was a little past the top *of the* **h**, behold, NIH
21: 9 they hanged them in the **h** before 2022
1Ki 11: 7 in the **h** that *is* before Jerusalem, and 2022
14:23 on every high **h**, and under every green 1389
16:24 he bought the **h** Samaria of Shemer for two 2022
16:24 built *on* the **h**, and called the name of 2022
16:24 name of Shemer, owner of the **h**, Samaria. 2022
2Ki 1: 9 behold, he sat on the top of a **h**. And he 2022
4:27 when she came to the man of God to the **h**, 2022
17:10 them up images and groves in every high **h**, 1389
Ps 2: 6 Yet have I set my king upon my holy **h** of 2022
3: 4 and he heard me out of his holy **h**. 2022
15: 1 who shall dwell in thy holy **h**? 2022
24: 3 Who shall ascend into the **h** of 2022
42: 6 and of the Hermonites, from the **h** Mizar. 2022
43: 3 let them bring me unto thy holy **h**, and 2022
68:15 The **h** of God *is as* the hill of Bashan; 2022
68:15 The hill of God *is as* the **h** of Bashan; 2022
68:15 of Bashan; a high **h** *as* the hill of Bashan. 2022
68:15 of Bashan; a high hill *as* the **h** of Bashan. 2022
68:16 *this is* the **h** *which* God desireth to dwell in; 2022
99: 9 our God, and worship at his holy **h**; 2022
SS 4: 6 of myrrh, and to the **h** of frankincense. 1389
Isa 5: 1 hath a vineyard in a very fruitful **h**: 7161
10:32 of the daughter of Zion, the **h** of Jerusalem. 1389
30:17 top of a mountain, and as an ensign on a **h**. 1389
30:25 upon every high **h**, rivers *and* streams of 1389
31: 4 fight for mount Zion, and for the **h** thereof. 1389
40: 4 every mountain and **h** shall be made low: 1389
Jer 2:20 when upon every high **h** and under every 1389
16:16 from every **h**, and out of the holes of 1389
31:39 go forth over against it upon the **h** Gareb, 1389
49:16 of the rock, that holdest the height of the **h**: 1389
50: 6 they have gone from mountain to **h**, 1389
Eze 6:13 upon every high **h**, in all the tops of 1389
20:28 they saw every high **h**, and all the thick 1389
34: 6 all the mountains, and upon every high **h**: 1389
34:26 and the places round about my **h** a blessing; 1389
Mt 5:14 A city that is set on a **h** cannot be hid. 3735
Lk 1:39 and went into the **h country** with haste, 3714
1:65 throughout all the **h country** of Judea. 3714
3: 5 every mountain and **h** shall be brought low; 1015
4:29 led him unto the brow of the **h** whereon 3735
9:37 when they were come down from the **h**, 3735

HILL'S (1) [HILL]

2Sa 16:13 Shimei went along on the **h** side over 2022

HILLEL (2)

Jdg 12:13 after him Abdon the son of **H**, 1985
12:15 Abdon the son of **H** the Pirathonite died, 1985

HILLS (65) [HILL]

Ge 7:19 all the high **h**, that *were* under the whole 2022
49:26 unto the utmost bound of the everlasting **h**: 1389

Nu 23: 9 I see him, and from the **h** I behold him: 1389
Dt 1: 7 in the **h**, and in the vale, and in the south, 2022
8: 7 depths that spring out of the valleys and **h**; 2022
8: 9 and out of whose **h** thou mayest dig brass. 2042
11:11 *is* a land of **h** and valleys, *and* 2022
12: 2 and upon the **h**, and under every green tree: 1389
33:15 and for the precious things of the lasting **h**, 1389
Jos 9: 1 in the **h**, and in the valleys, and in all 2022
10:40 So Joshua smote all the country of the **h**, 2022
11:16 the **h**, and all the south *country*, and all 2022
1Ki 20:23 said unto him, Their gods *are* gods of the **h**; 2022
20:28 The LORD *is* God of the **h**, but he *is* not 2022
22:17 I saw all Israel scattered upon the **h**, 2022
2Ki 16: 4 and on the **h**, and under every green tree. 1389
2Ch 28: 4 and on the **h**, and under every green tree. 1389
Job 15: 7 was born? or wast thou made before the **h**? 1389
Ps 18: 7 the foundations also of the **h** moved and 2022
50:10 *is* mine, *and* the cattle upon a thousand **h**. 2042
65:12 and the **little h** rejoice on every side. 1389
68:16 Why leap ye, ye high **h**? *this is* the hill 2022
72: 3 and the **little h**, by righteousness. 1389
80:10 The **h** were covered *with* the shadow of it, 2022
95: 4 of the earth: the strength of the **h** *is* his also. 2022
97: 5 The **h** melted like wax at the presence of 2022
98: 8 *their* hands: let the **h** be joyful together 2022
104:10 into the valleys, *which* run among the **h**. 2022
104:13 He watereth the **h** from his chambers: 2022
104:18 The high **h** *are* a refuge for the wild goats; 2022
104:32 he toucheth the **h**, and they smoke. 2022
114: 4 like rams, *and* the **little h** like lambs. 1389
114: 6 like rams; *and* ye **little h**, like lambs? 1389
121: 1 I will lift up mine eyes unto the **h**, 2022
148: 9 Mountains, and all **h**; fruitful trees, and 1389
Pr 8:25 before the **h** was I brought forth: 1389
SS 2: 8 upon the mountains, skipping upon the **h**. 1389
Isa 2: 2 and *shall be* exalted above the **h**; 1389
2:14 upon all the **h** that are lifted up, 1389
5:25 the **h** did tremble, and their carcases were 2022
7:25 *on* all **h** that shall be digged with 2022
40:12 mountains in scales, and the **h** in a balance? 1389
41:15 *them* small, and shalt make the **h** as chaff. 1389
42:15 I will make waste mountains and **h**, and 1389
54:10 shall depart, and the **h** be removed; 1389
55:12 the **h** shall break forth before you *into* 1389
65: 7 and blasphemed me upon the **h**: 1389
Jer 3:23 in vain *is salvation hoped for* from the **h**, 1389
4:24 they trembled, and all the **h** moved lightly. 1389
13:27 thine abominations on the **h** in the fields. 1389
17: 2 groves by the green trees upon the high **h**. 1389
Eze 6: 3 to the **h**, to the rivers, and to the valleys; 1389
35: 8 his mountains *with* his slain *men*: in thy **h**, 1389
36: 4 to the **h**, to the rivers, and to the valleys, 1389
36: 6 to the **h**, to the rivers, and to the valleys, 1389
Hos 4:13 burn incense upon the **h**, under oaks and 1389
10: 8 Cover us; and to the **h**, Fall on us. 1389
Joel 3:18 the **h** shall flow *with* milk, and all the rivers 1389
Am 9:13 drop sweet wine, and all the **h** shall melt. 1389
Mic 4: 1 and *it shall be* exalted above the **h**; 1389
6: 1 the mountains, and let the **h** hear thy voice. 1389
Na 1: 5 the **h** melt, and the earth is burnt at his 1389
Hab 3: 6 were scattered, the perpetual **h** did bow: 1389
Zep 1:10 the second, and a great crashing from the **h**. 1389
Lk 23:30 Fall on us; and to the **h**, Cover us. *1015*

HIM (6667) [HE] See Index of Articles, Etc.

HIMSELF (528) [HE, SELF]

Ge 14:15 he divided **h** against them, he and NIH
18: 2 tent door, and bowed **h** toward the ground, NIH
19: 1 he bowed **h** with his face toward NIH
22: 8 God will provide **h** a lamb for a burnt 2050.2
23: 7 and bowed **h** to the people of the land, NIH
23:12 Abraham bowed down **h** before the people NIH
24:52 the LORD, *bowing* **h** to the earth. NIH
27:42 as touching thee, doth comfort **h**, NIH
30:36 he set three days' journey betwixt **h** and 2050.2
32:21 and **h** lodged that night in the company. 1931
33: 3 and bowed **h** to the ground seven times, NIH
41:14 he shaved ***h***, and changed his raiment, and NIH
42: 7 made **h** strange unto them, and NIH
42:24 he turned **h** about from them, and wept; NIH
43:31 went out, and refrained **h**, and said, Set on NIH
43:32 they set on for him **by h**, 905+2050.2+3807.1
45: 1 Joseph could not refrain **h** before all them NIH
45: 1 while Joseph made **h** known unto his NIH
46:29 to Goshen, and presented **h** unto him; NIH
47:31 And Israel bowed **h** upon the bed's head. NIH
48: 2 Israel strengthened **h**, and sat upon the bed. NIH
48:12 and he bowed **h** with his face to the earth. NIH
Ex 10: 6 he turned **h**, and went out from Pharaoh. NIH
21: 3 If he came in by **h**, he shall go out 1610+2050.2
21: 3 in by himself, he shall go out by **h**: 1610+2050.2
21: 4 and he shall go out by **h**. 1610+2050.2
21: 8 who hath betrothed her to **h**, then shall he 2050.2
Lev 7: 8 *even* the priest shall have to **h** the skin of 2050.2
9: 8 calf of the sin offering, which *was* for **h**. 2050.2
14: 8 shave off all his hair, and wash ***h*** in water, NIH
15: 5 bathe ***h*** in water, and be unclean until NIH
15: 6 bathe ***h*** in water, and be unclean until NIH
15: 7 bathe ***h*** in water, and be unclean until NIH
15: 8 bathe ***h*** in water, and be unclean until NIH
15:10 bathe ***h*** in water, and be unclean until NIH
15:11 bathe ***h*** in water, and be unclean until NIH
15:13 he shall number to **h** seven days for his 2050.2
15:21 bathe ***h*** in water, and be unclean until NIH
15:22 bathe **h** in water, and be unclean until NIH
15:27 bathe ***h*** in water, and be unclean until NIH
16: 6 which *is* for **h**, and make an atonement 2050.2
16: 6 make an atonement for **h**, and for his 2050.2
16:11 which *is* for **h**, and shall make an 2050.2
16:11 shall make an atonement for **h**, and 2050.2
16:11 bullock of the sin offering which *is* for **h**: 2050.2
16:17 have made an atonement for **h**, and 2050.2
16:24 make an atonement for **h**, and for 2050.2
17:15 bathe ***h*** in water, and be unclean until NIH
Lev 21: 4 *But* he shall not defile **h**, *being* a chief man NIH
21: 4 man among his people, to profane **h**. 2050.2
21:11 nor defile **h** for his father, or for his mother; NIH
22: 8 *beasts*, he shall not eat to defile ***h*** therewith: NIH
25:26 to redeem *it*, and **h** be able to redeem it; 2050.2
25:47 sell **h** unto the stranger *or* sojourner by thee, NIH
25:49 or if he be able, he may redeem **h**. NIH
27: 8 he shall present **h** before the priest, and 2050.2
Nu 6: 3 He shall separate ***h*** from wine and NIH
6: 5 *in* the which he separateth **h** unto NIH
6: 6 All the days that he separateth ***h*** unto NIH
6: 7 He shall not make **h** unclean for his father, NIH
16: 9 to bring you near to **h** to do the service of 2050.2
19:12 He shall purify **h** with it on the third day, NIH
19:12 if he purify not **h** the third day, then NIH
19:13 purifieth not **h**, defileth the tabernacle of NIH
19:19 on the seventh day he shall purify **h**, 2050.2
19:19 bathe ***h*** in water, and shall be clean at even. NIH
19:20 that shall be unclean, and shall not purify **h**, NIH
23:24 as a great lion, and lift up **h** as a young lion: NIH
25: 3 Israel joined **h** unto Baal-peor: and NIH
31:53 of war had taken spoil, every man for **h**.) 2050.2
35:19 The revenger of blood **h** shall slay 1931
36: 7 **h** to the inheritance of the tribe of his NIH
36: 9 of Israel shall keep **h** to his own inheritance. NIH
Dt 7: 6 chosen thee to be a special people unto **h**, 2050.2
14: 2 thee to be a peculiar people unto **h**, 2050.2
17:16 he shall not multiply horses to **h**, 2050.2
17:17 Neither shall he multiply wives to **h**, 2050.2
17:17 neither shall he greatly multiply to **h** 2050.2
23:11 cometh on, he shall wash ***h*** with water: NIH
28: 9 shall establish thee a holy people unto **h**, 2050.2
29:13 establish thee to day for a people unto **h**, 2050.2
29:19 that he bless **h** in his heart, saying, I shall NIH
32:36 his people, and repent **h** for his servants, NIH
33:21 he provided the first *part* for **h**, because 2050.2
Jos 22:23 let the LORD **h** require *it*; 1931
Jdg 3:19 he **h** turned again from the quarries that 1931
3:20 which he had for **h** alone. 2050.2
4:11 had severed **h** from the Kenites, and NIH
6:31 let him plead for **h**, because *one* hath cast 2050.2
7: 5 dog lappeth, him shalt thou set **by h**; 905+3807.1
9: 5 son of Jerubbaal was left; for he hid **h**. NIH
16:30 he bowed ***h*** with *all his* might; and NIH
Ru 3: 8 that the man was afraid, and turned **h**: NIH
1Sa 2:14 brought up the priest took for **h**. 2050.2
3:21 for the LORD revealed **h** to Samuel in NIH
8:11 appoint *them* for **h**, for his chariots, and 2050.2
10:19 who **h** saved you out of all your adversities 1931
10:22 Behold, he hath hid **h** among the stuff. NIH
14:47 whithersoever he turned **h**, he vexed *them*. NIH
17:16 and evening, and presented **h** forty days. NIH
18: 4 Jonathan stript **h** of the robe that *was* upon NIH
18: 5 Saul sent him, *and* behaved **h** wisely: 1930.2
18:14 David behaved **h** wisely in all his ways; NIH
18:15 Saul saw that he behaved **h** very wisely, NIH
18:30 *that* David behaved **h** more wisely than all NIH
20:24 So David hid **h** in the field: and when NIH
20:41 to the ground, and bowed **h** three times: NIH
21:13 feigned **h** mad in their hands, and NIH
23:19 Doth not David hide **h** with us in strong NIH
23:23 of all the lurking places where he hideth **h**, NIH
24: 8 *with his* face to the earth, and bowed **h**. NIH
25:31 or that my lord hath avenged **h**: 2050.2
26: 1 Doth not David hide **h** in the hill of NIH
28: 8 Saul disguised **h**, and put on other raiment, NIH
28:14 *with his* face to the ground, and bowed **h**. NIH
29: 4 for wherewith should he reconcile **h** unto NIH
30: 6 David encouraged **h** in the LORD his God. NIH
30:31 to all the places where David **h** and his men 1931
2Sa 3: 6 that Abner made **h** strong for the house of NIH
3:31 And king David ***h*** followed the bier NIH
6:20 who uncovered **h** to day in the eyes of NIH
6:20 the vain *fellows* shamelessly uncovereth **h**! NIH
7:23 God went to redeem for a people to **h**, 2050.2
9: 8 he bowed **h**, and said, What *is* thy servant, NIH
12:18 how will he then vex **h**, if we tell him *that* NIH
12:20 anointed ***h***, and changed his apparel, and NIH
13: 6 So Amnon lay down, and made **h** sick: and NIH
14:22 and bowed **h**, and thanked the king: NIH
14:33 bowed **h** on his face to the ground before 2050.2
15:23 the king also ***h*** passed over the brook NIH
17:23 hanged **h**, and died, and was buried in NIH
18:18 had taken and reared up for **h** a pillar, 2050.2
18:21 And Cushi bowed **h** unto Joab, and ran. NIH
24:20 bowed **h** before the king *on* his face upon NIH
1Ki 1: 5 Adonijah the son of Haggith exalted **h**, NIH
1:23 he bowed **h** before the king with his face to NIH
1:47 And the king bowed **h** upon the bed. NIH
1:52 If he will shew **h** a worthy man, NIH
1:53 he came and bowed **h** to king Solomon: NIH
2:19 bowed **h** unto her, and sat down on his NIH
11:29 he had clad **h** with a new garment; and NIH
15:15 *the things* which **h** had dedicated, *into* 2050.2
16: 9 drinking **h** drunk *in* the house of Arza NIH
17:21 he stretched **h** upon the child three times, NIH
18: 2 Elijah went to shew **h** unto Ahab. And *there* NIH
18: 6 Ahab went one way **by h**, 905+2050.2+3807.1
18: 6 went another way **by h**. 905+2050.2+3807.1
18:42 he cast **h** down upon the earth, and put his NIH
19: 4 he **h** went a day's journey into 1931
19: 4 he requested for **h** that he might 5315+2050.2
20:11 *his harness* boast **h** as he that putteth *it* off. NIH
20:16 Ben-hadad *was* drinking ***h*** drunk in NIH
20:38 and disguised **h** with ashes upon his face. NIH
21:25 which did sell **h** to work wickedness in NIH
21:29 Seest thou how Ahab humbleth **h** before NIH
21:29 because he humbleth **h** before me, I will not NIH
22:30 the king of Israel disguised **h**, and went into NIH
2Ki 4:34 he stretched **h** upon the child; and the flesh NIH
4:35 fro; and went up, and stretched **h** upon him: NIH
5:14 and dipped ***h*** seven times in Jordan, NIH
6:10 and warned him of, and saved **h** there, NIH
19: 1 covered **h** with sackcloth, and went *into* NIH
23:16 as Josiah turned **h**, he spied the sepulchres NIH
1Ch 12: 1 while he yet kept **h** close because of Saul NIH
13:13 So David brought not the ark *home* to **h** 2050.2
21:21 bowed **h** to David *with his* face to NIH
2Ch 12: 1 had strengthened **h**, he forsook the law of 2050.2
12:12 when he humbled **h**, the wrath of NIH
12:13 So king Rehoboam strengthened **h** in NIH
13: 9 that whosoever cometh to consecrate **h** 2050.2
13:12 God ***h*** *is* with us for *our* captain, and NIH
15:18 that he **h** had dedicated, silver, and gold, NIH
16: 9 to shew **h** strong in the behalf of *them* NIH
16:14 which he had made for **h** in the city of 2050.2
17: 1 his stead, and strengthened **h** against Israel. NIH
17:16 who willingly offered **h** unto the LORD; NIH
18:29 So the king of Israel disguised **h**; and NIH
18:34 howbeit the king of Israel stayed ***h*** up in *his* NIH
20: 3 set **h** to seek the LORD, and 6440+2050.2
20:35 of Judah join **h** with Ahaziah king of Israel, NIH
20:36 he joined **h** with him to make ships to go 1930.2
21: 4 he strengthened **h**, and slew all his brethren NIH
23: 1 in the seventh year Jehoiada strengthened **h**, NIH
25:11 Amaziah strengthened **h**, and led forth his NIH
25:14 bowed down **h** before them, and NIH
26: 8 for he strengthened ***h*** exceedingly. NIH
26:20 yea, **h** hasted also to go out, because 1931
32: 1 and thought to win them for **h**. 2050.2
32: 5 Also he strengthened **h**, and built up all NIH
32: 9 (but he **h** *laid siege* against Lachish, and NIH
32:26 Notwithstanding Hezekiah humbled **h** for NIH
32:27 he made **h** treasuries for silver, and 2050.2
33:12 humbled **h** greatly before the God of his NIH
33:23 humbled not **h** before the LORD, NIH
33:23 as Manasseh his father had humbled **h**; NIH
35:22 disguised **h**, that *he* might fight with him, NIH
36:12 humbled not **h** before Jeremiah the prophet NIH
Ezr 10: 1 casting **h** down before the house of God, NIH
10: 8 **h** separated from the congregation of those 1931
Est 5:10 Nevertheless Haman refrained **h**: and NIH
Job 1:12 only upon **h** put not forth thine hand. 2050.2
2: 1 Satan came also among them to present **h** NIH
2: 8 he took him a potsherd to scrape **h** withal; NIH
4: 2 but who can withhold **h** from speaking? NIH
9: 4 who hath hardened ***h*** against him, and NIH
15:25 and strengtheneth **h** against the Almighty. NIH
17: 8 the innocent shall stir up **h** against NIH
18: 4 He teareth **h** in his anger: shall 5315+2050.2
22: 2 he that is wise may be profitable unto **h**? 4123.1
23: 9 I cannot behold *him*: he hideth ***h*** *on* NIH
27:10 Will he delight **h** in the Almighty? will he NIH
32: 2 he justified **h** rather than God. 5315+2050.2
34: 9 that he should delight **h** with God. 2050.2
34:14 upon *man*, *if* he gather unto **h** his spirit 2050.2
41:25 When he raiseth up ***h***, the mighty are afraid: NIH
Ps 4: 3 hath set apart *him that is* godly for **h**: 2050.2
10:10 He croucheth, *and* humbleth **h**, that NIH
10:14 the poor committeth ***h*** unto thee; thou art NIH
35: 8 and let his net that he hath hid catch **h**: 2050.2
36: 2 For he flattereth **h** in his own eyes, 2050.2
36: 4 he setteth **h** in a way *that is* not good; NIH
37:35 and spreading **h** like a green bay tree. NIH
50: 6 for God *is* judge **h**. Selah. 1931
52: 7 *and* strengthened **h** in his wickedness. NIH
54: T said to Saul, Doth not David hide **h** with us? NIH
55:12 hated me *that* did magnify ***h*** against me; NIH
68:30 *till every one* submit **h** with pieces of silver: NIH
87: 5 in her: and the Highest **h** shall establish her. 1931
93: 1 with strength, *wherewith* he hath girded **h**: NIH
109:18 As he clothed **h** with cursing like as with his NIH
113: 6 Who humbleth ***h*** to behold *the things that* NIH
132:18 but upon **h** shall his crown flourish. 2050.2
135: 4 the LORD hath chosen Jacob unto **h**, 2050.2
135:14 he will repent **h** concerning his servants. NIH
Pr 5:22 own iniquities shall take the wicked **h**, 2050.2
9: 7 He that reproveth a scorner getteth to **h** 2050.2
9: 7 he that rebuketh a wicked *man getteth* **h** a 2050.2
11:25 he that watereth shall be watered also **h**. 1931
12: 9 *is* better than he that honoureth **h**, and NIH
13: 7 There is that maketh **h** rich, yet *hath* NIH
13: 7 *there is* that maketh **h** poor, yet *hath* great NIH
14:14 and a good man *shall be satisfied* from **h**. 2050.2
16: 4 LORD hath made all *things* for **h**: 4617+1930.2
16:26 He that laboureth laboureth for **h**; for his 2050.2
18: 1 having separated **h**, seeketh *and* NIH
18:24 A man that hath friends must shew **h** NIH
21:13 he also shall cry **h**, but shall not be heard. NIH
22: 3 *man* foreseeth the evil, and hideth **h**: NIH
25: 9 Debate thy cause with thy neighbour ***h***; and NIH
25:14 Whoso boasteth **h** of a false gift *is like* NIH
27:12 *man* foreseeth the evil, *and* hideth **h**; NIH
28:10 an evil way, he shall fall **h** into his own pit: 1931
29:15 a child left *to* ***h*** bringeth his mother to NIH
Ecc 5: 9 *is* for all: the king ***h*** is served by the field. NIH
10:12 but the lips of a fool will swallow up **h**. 5105.2
SS 2: 9 the windows, shewing **h** through the lattice. NIH
3: 9 King Solomon made **h** a chariot of 2050.2
5: 6 my beloved had withdrawn **h**, *and* NIH
Isa 2: 9 and the great man humbleth **h**; NIH
2:20 which they made *each one* for **h** to 2050.2
3: 5 the child shall behave **h** proudly against NIH
7:14 Therefore the Lord **h** shall give you a sign; 1931
8:13 Sanctify the LORD of hosts **h**; and 2050.2
19:17 mention thereof shall be afraid in **h**, 2050.2
22:16 that graveth a habitation for **h** in a rock? 2050.2
28:20 is shorter than that *a man* can stretch **h** *on it*: NIH
28:20 narrower than that *he* can wrap **h** *in it*. NIH
31: 4 nor abase **h** for the noise of them: NIH
37: 1 covered **h** with sackcloth, and went *into* NIH
38:15 **h** hath done *it*: I shall go softly all my years 1931
44: 5 another shall call ***h*** by the name of Jacob; NIH
44: 5 and surname ***h*** by the name of Israel. NIH
44:14 which he strengtheneth for **h** among 2050.2
44:15 for he will take thereof, and warm **h**; yea, NIH
44:16 yea, he warmeth **h**, and saith, Aha, I am NIH
44:23 redeemed Jacob, and glorified **h** in Israel. NIH
45:18 God **h** that formed the earth and made it; 1931
56: 3 that hath joined **h** to the LORD, speak, NIH

Isa 59:15 he *that* departeth from evil maketh **h** a prey: NIH
61:10 as a bridegroom decketh ***h*** with ornaments, NIH
63:12 to make **h** an everlasting name? 2050.2
64: 7 that stirreth up **h** to take hold of thee: NIH
65:16 That he who blesseth **h** in the earth shall NIH
65:16 in the earth shall bless **h** in the God of truth; NIH
Jer 10:23 I know that the way of man *is* not in **h**: 2050.2
16:20 Shall a man make gods unto **h**, and 2050.2
23:24 Can any hide **h** in secret places that I shall NIH
29:26 man *that is* mad, and maketh **h** a prophet, NIH
29:27 which maketh **h** a prophet to you? NIH
31:18 I have surely heard Ephraim bemoaning **h** NIH
34: 9 that none should serve **h** of them, *to wit,* of NIH
37:12 to separate **h** thence in the midst of NIH
43:12 he shall array **h** with the land of Egypt, as a NIH
48:26 for he magnified ***h*** against the LORD: NIH
48:42 he hath magnified ***h*** against the LORD. NIH
49:10 and he shall not be able to hide **h**: NIH
51: 3 against *him that* lifteth **h** up in his NIH
51:14 LORD of hosts hath sworn by **h**, 5315+2050.2
La 1: 9 for the enemy hath magnified ***h***. NIH
Eze 7:13 neither shall any strengthen **h** in the iniquity NIH
14: 7 which separateth **h** from me, and setteth up NIH
24: 2 the king of Babylon set **h** against Jerusalem NIH
25:12 and revenged **h** upon them; NIH
45:22 that day shall the prince prepare for **h** 2050.2
Da 1: 8 defile **h** with the portion of the king's meat, NIH
1: 8 of the eunuchs that he might not defile **h**. NIH
6:14 was sore displeased with **h**, and set *his* 1958.2
8:11 he magnified ***h*** *even* to the prince of NIH
8:25 he shall magnify ***h*** in his heart, and NIH
9:26 shall Messiah be cut off, but not for **h**: 2050.2
11:36 he shall exalt **h**, and magnify himself above NIH
11:36 magnify **h** above every god, and shall speak NIH
11:37 any god: for he shall magnify **h** above all. NIH
Hos 5: 6 find *him;* he hath withdrawn **h** from them. NIH
7: 8 he hath mixed **h** among the people; NIH
8: 9 gone up *to* Assyria, a wild ass alone by **h**: 2050.2
10: 1 empty vine, he bringeth forth fruit unto **h**: 2050.2
13: 1 spake trembling, he exalted **h** in Israel; NIH
Am 2:14 neither shall the mighty deliver **h**: 5315+2050.2
2:15 *he that is* swift of foot shall not deliver ***h***: NIH
2:15 he that rideth the horse deliver **h**. 5315+2050.2
6: 8 The Lord GOD hath sworn by **h**, 5315+2050.2
Jnh 4: 8 and wished in **h** to die, and said, 5315+2050.2
Hab 2: 6 and to him that ladeth **h** with thick clay! NIH
Mt 6: 4 thy Father which seeth in secret **h** shall *846*
8:17 saying **H** took our infirmities, and bare our *846*
12:15 But when Jesus knew *it,* he withdrew **h** NIG
12:26 cast out Satan, he is divided against **h**; *1438*
12:45 taketh with **h** seven other spirits more *1438*
12:45 seven other spirits more wicked than **h**, *1438*
13:21 Yet hath he not root in **h**, but dureth for a *1438*
16:24 let him deny **h**, and take up his cross, and *1438*
18: 4 therefore shall humble **h** as this little child, *1438*
23:12 And whosoever shall exalt **h** shall be *1438*
23:12 and he that shall humble **h** shall be exalted. *1438*
27: 3 repented **h**, and brought again the thirty NIG
27: 5 and departed, and went and hanged **h**. NIG
27:42 He saved others; **h** he cannot save. If he be *1438*
27:57 who also **h** was Jesus' disciple: *846*
Mk 3: 7 But Jesus withdrew **h** with his disciples to NIG
3:21 hold on him: for they said, He is **beside h**. *1839*
3:26 And if Satan rise up against **h**, and *1438*
5: 5 crying, and cutting **h** with stones. *1438*
5:30 And Jesus immediately knowing in **h** that *1438*
6:17 For Herod **h** had sent forth and laid hold *846*
8:34 let him deny **h**, and take up his cross, and *1438*
12:33 the strength, and to love *his* neighbour as **h**, *1438*
12:36 For David **h** said by the Holy Ghost, *846*
12:37 David therefore **h** calleth him Lord; and *846*
14:54 with the servants, and warmed **h** at the fire. NIG
14:67 And when she saw Peter warming **h**, NIG
15:31 He saved others; **h** he cannot save. *1438*
Lk 3:23 And Jesus **h** began *to be* about thirty years of *846*
5:16 And he withdrew **h** into the wilderness, and NIG
6: 3 when **h** was a hungred, and they which were *846*
7:39 had bidden him saw *it,* he spake within **h**, *1438*
9:23 let him deny **h**, and take up his cross daily, *1438*
9:25 whole world, and lose **h**, or be cast away? *1438*
10: 1 and place, whither he **h** would come. *846*
10:29 But he, willing to justify **h**, said unto Jesus, *1438*
11:18 If Satan also be divided against **h**, *1438*
11:26 *him* seven other spirits more wicked than **h**; *1438*
12:17 And he thought within **h**, saying, *1438*
12:21 So *is* he that layeth up treasure for **h**, and *1438*
12:37 that he shall gird **h**, and make them to sit NIG
12:47 prepared not ***h***, neither did according to his NIG
14:11 For whosoever exalteth **h** shall be abased; *1438*
14:11 and he that humbleth **h** shall be exalted. *1438*
15:15 and joined **h** to a citizen of that country; NIG
15:17 And when he came to **h**, he said, How *1438*
16: 3 Then the steward said within **h**, What shall *1438*
18: 4 but afterward he said within **h**, Though I *1438*
18:11 The Pharisee stood and prayed thus with **h**, *1438*
18:14 for every one that exalteth **h** shall be *1438*
18:14 and he that humbleth **h** shall be exalted. *1438*
19:12 a far country to receive for **h** a kingdom, *1438*
20:42 And David **h** saith in the book of Psalms, *846*
23: 2 to Cesar, saying that **he h** is Christ a King. *1438*
23: 7 who **h** also was at Jerusalem at that time. *846*
23:35 let him save **h**, if he be Christ, the chosen *1438*
23:51 who also **h** waited for the kingdom of God. *846*
24:12 wondering in **h** at that which was come to *1438*
24:15 Jesus **h** drew near, and went with them. *846*
24:27 in all the scriptures the *things* concerning **h**. *1438*
24:36 Jesus **h** stood in the midst of them, and *846*
Jn 2:24 But Jesus did not commit **h** unto them, *1438*
4: 2 (Though Jesus **h** baptized not, but *846*
4:12 and drank thereof **h**, and his children, and *846*
4:44 For Jesus **h** testified, that a prophet hath no *846*
4:53 and **h** believed, and his whole house. *846*
5:13 for Jesus had conveyed **h** away, a multitude NIG
5:18 was his Father, making **h** equal with God. *1438*
5:19 The Son can do nothing of **h**, but what he *1438*
Jn 5:20 and sheweth him all *things* that **h** doeth: *846*
5:26 For as the Father hath life in **h**; so hath he *1438*
5:26 hath he given to the Son to have life in **h**; *1438*
5:37 And the Father **h**, which hath sent me, *846*
6: 6 prove him: for he **h** knew what he would do. *846*
6:15 he departed again into a mountain **h** alone. *846*
6:61 When Jesus knew in **h** that his disciples *1438*
7: 4 and he **h** seeketh to be known openly. *846*
7:18 He that speaketh of **h** seeketh his own *1438*
8: 7 he lift up ***h***, and said unto them, He that is NIG
8:10 When Jesus had lift up ***h***, and saw none but NIG
8:22 Then said the Jews, Will he kill **h**? because *1438*
8:59 but Jesus hid **h**, and went out of the temple, NIG
9:21 he is of age; ask him: he shall speak for **h**. *846*
11:38 again groaning in **h** cometh to the grave. *1438*
11:51 And this spake he not of **h**: but being high *1438*
12:36 and departed, and did hide **h** from them. NIG
13: 4 and took a towel, and girded **h**. *1438*
13:32 in him, God shall also glorify him in **h**, *1438*
16:13 for he shall not speak of **h**; but *1438*
16:27 For the Father **h** loveth you, because ye have *846*
18:18 and Peter stood with them, and warmed **h**. NIG
18:25 And Simon Peter stood and warmed **h**. NIG
19: 7 to die, because he made **h** the Son of God. *1438*
19:12 whosoever maketh **h** a king speaketh against *846*
21: 1 After these *things* Jesus shewed **h** again to *1438*
21: 1 of Tiberias; and on this wise shewed he ***h***. NIG
21: 7 he was naked,) and did cast **h** into the sea. *1438*
21:14 time *that* Jesus shewed **h** to his disciples, NIG
Ac 1: 3 To whom also he shewed **h** alive after his *1438*
2:34 but he saith **h**, The LORD said unto my *846*
5:13 And of the rest durst no *man* join **h** to them: NIG
5:36 up Theudas, boasting **h** to be somebody; *1438*
7:26 And the next day he shewed **h** unto them as NIG
8: 9 giving out that **h** was some great one: *1438*
8:13 Then Simon **h** believed also: and when he *846*
8:34 prophet this? of **h**, or of some other *man?* *1438*
9:26 he assayed to join **h** to the disciples: NIG
10:17 Now while Peter doubted in **h** what *this* *1438*
12:11 And when Peter was come to **h**, he said, *1438*
14:17 Nevertheless he left not **h** without witness, *1438*
16:27 out his sword, and would have killed **h**, *1438*
18:19 but he **h** entered into the synagogue, and *846*
19:22 Erastus; but he **h** stayed in Asia for a season. *846*
19:31 desiring *him* that *he* would not adventure **h** *1438*
20:13 so had he appointed, minding **h** to go afoot. *846*
21:26 the next day purifying **h** with them entered NIG
25: 4 and that he **h** would depart shortly *thither.* *1438*
25: 8 While he **answered for h**, Neither against *626*
25:16 have licence to answer for **h** concerning NIG
25:25 and *that* he **h** hath appealed to Augustus, *846*
26: 1 forth the hand, and answered for **h**: NIG
26:24 And as he thus spake for **h**, Festus said with NIG
27: 3 liberty to go unto *his* friends to refresh **h**. NIG
28:16 Paul was suffered to dwell by **h** with a *1438*
Ro 12: 3 not to think *of **h*** more highly than he ought NIG
14: 7 For none of us liveth to **h**, and no *man* dieth *1438*
14: 7 us liveth to himself, and no *man* dieth to **h**. *1438*
14:12 every one of us shall give account of **h** to *1438*
14:22 Happy *is* he that condemneth not **h** in *that* *1438*
15: 3 For even Christ pleased not **h**; but, as it is *1438*
1Co 2:15 all *things,* yet **he h** is judged of no *man.* *846*
3:15 but **he h** shall be saved; yet so as by fire. *846*
3:18 Let no *man* deceive **h**. If any *man* among *1438*
7:36 But if any *man* think that *he* behaveth **h** NIG
11:28 But let a man examine **h**, and so let him eat *1438*
11:29 eateth and drinketh damnation to **h**, *1438*
14: 4 speaketh in an *unknown* tongue edifieth **h**; *1438*
14: 8 who shall prepare **h** to the battle? NIG
14:28 and let him speak to **h**, and to God. *1438*
14:37 If any *man* think **h** to be a prophet, or NIG
15:28 shall the Son also **h** be subject unto him that *846*
2Co 5:18 who hath reconciled us to **h** by Jesus *1438*
5:19 was in Christ reconciling the world unto **h**, *1438*
10: 7 If any *man* trust to **h** that *he* is Christ's, *1438*
10: 7 let him of **h** think this again, that, as he *is* *1438*
10:18 For not he that commendeth **h** is approved, *1438*
11:14 for Satan **h** is transformed into an angel of *846*
11:20 *you,* if a man take *of you,* if a man exalt **h**, NIG
Gal 1: 4 Who gave **h** for our sins, that he might *1438*
2:12 were come, he withdrew and separated **h**, *1438*
2:20 of God, who loved me, and gave **h** for me. *1438*
6: 3 For if a man think **h** to be something, NIG
6: 3 when he is nothing, he deceiveth **h**. *1438*
6: 4 and then shall he have rejoicing in **h** alone, *1438*
Eph 1: 5 the adoption of children by Jesus Christ to **h**, *846*
1: 9 good pleasure which he had purposed in **h**: *846*
2:15 for to make in **h** of twain one new man, *so* *1438*
2:20 Jesus Christ **h** being the chief corner *stone;* *846*
5: 2 and hath given **h** for us an offering and *1438*
5:25 also loved the church, and gave **h** for it; *1438*
5:27 That he might present it to **h** a glorious *1438*
5:28 He that loveth his wife loveth **h**. *1438*
5:33 you in particular so love his wife even as **h**; *1438*
Php 2: 7 But made **h** of no reputation, and took *upon* *1438*
2: 8 he humbled **h**, and became obedient unto *1438*
3:21 he is able even to subdue all *things* unto **h**. *1438*
Col 1:20 by him to reconcile all *things* unto **h**; *846*
1Th 3:11 Now God **h** and our Father, and our Lord *846*
4:16 For the Lord **h** shall descend from heaven *846*
2Th 2: 4 and exalteth **h** above all that is called God, NIG
2: 4 temple of God, shewing **h** that he is God. *1438*
2:16 Now our Lord Jesus Christ **h**, and God, *846*
3:16 Now the Lord of peace **h** give you peace *846*
1Ti 2: 6 Who gave **h** a ransom for all, to be testified *1438*
2Ti 2: 4 No *man* that warreth entangleth **h** with NIG
2:13 *yet* he abideth faithful: he cannot deny **h**. *1438*
2:21 If a man therefore purge **h** from these, *1438*
Tit 2:14 Who gave **h** for us, that he might redeem us *1438*
2:14 and purify unto **h** a peculiar people, *1438*
3:11 and sinneth, being **condemned of h**. *843*
Heb 1: 3 when he had by **h** purged our sins, *1438*
2:14 he also **h** likewise took part of the same; *846*
2:18 For in that he **h** hath suffered being tempted, *846*
5: 2 for that he **h** also is compassed with *846*
Heb 5: 3 the people, so also for **h**, to offer for sins. *1438*
5: 4 And no *man* taketh *this* honour unto **h**, but *1438*
5: 5 So also Christ glorified not **h** to be made a *1438*
6:13 could swear by no greater, he sware by **h**, *1438*
7:27 for this he did once, when he offered up **h**. *1438*
9: 7 which he offered for **h**, and *for* the errors of *1438*
9:14 who through the eternal Spirit offered **h** *1438*
9:25 Nor yet that he should offer **h** often, as *1438*
9:26 to put away sin by the sacrifice of **h**. *846*
12: 3 such contradiction of sinners against **h**, *846*
Jas 1:24 For he beholdeth **h**, and goeth his way, and *1438*
1:27 *and* to keep **h** unspotted from the world. *1438*
1Pe 2:23 committed ***h*** to him that judgeth NIG
1Jn 2: 6 He that saith *he* abideth in him ought **h** also *846*
3: 3 *man* that hath this hope in him purifieth **h**, *1438*
5:10 on the Son of God hath the witness in **h**: *1438*
5:18 but he that is begotten of God keepeth **h**, *1438*
3Jn 1:10 neither doth he **h** receive the brethren, and *846*
Rev 19:12 a name written, that no *man* knew, but he **h**. *846*
21: 3 and God **h** shall be with them, *and be* their *846*

HIN (22)

Ex 29:40 with the fourth part of a **h** of beaten oil; 1969
29:40 the fourth *part* of a **h** of wine *for* a drink 1969
30:24 shekel of the sanctuary, and of oil olive a **h**: 1969
Lev 19:36 just weights, a just ephah, and a just **h**, 1969
23:13 *shall be of* wine, the fourth *part* of a **h**. 1969
Nu 15: 4 mingled with the fourth *part* of a **h** of oil. 1969
15: 5 the fourth *part* of a **h** *of* wine for a drink 1969
15: 6 mingled with the third *part* of a **h** of oil. 1969
15: 7 shalt offer the third *part* of a **h** *of* wine, 1969
15: 9 deals *of* flour mingled with half a **h** of oil. 1969
15:10 thou shalt bring for a drink offering half a **h** 1969
28: 5 mingled with the fourth *part* of a **h** of 1969
28: 7 *be* the fourth *part* of a **h** for the one lamb: 1969
28:14 their drink offerings shall be half a **h** of 1969
28:14 the third *part* of a **h** unto a ram, and 1969
28:14 a ram, and a fourth *part* of a **h** unto a lamb: 1969
Eze 4:11 also water by measure, the sixth *part* of a **h**: 1969
45:24 for a ram, and a **h** of oil for an ephah. 1969
46: 5 be able to give, and a **h** of oil to an ephah. 1969
46: 7 shall attain unto, and a **h** of oil to an ephah. 1969
46:11 is able to give, and a **h** of oil to an ephah. 1969
46:14 of an ephah, and the third *part* of a **h** of oil, 1969

HIND (3) [HINDS, HINDS']

Ge 49:21 Naphtali *is* a **h** let loose: he giveth goodly 355
Pr 5:19 *Let her be as* the loving **h** and pleasant roe; 365
Jer 14: 5 the **h** also calved in the field, and forsook *it,* 365

HINDER (16) [HINDERED, HINDERETH, HINDERMOST, HINDMOST]

Ge 24:56 he said unto them, **H** me not, seeing 309
Nu 22:16 I pray thee, **h** thee from coming unto me: 4513
2Sa 2:23 wherefore Abner with the **h end** of the spear 310
1Ki 7:25 and all their **h parts** *were* inward. 268
2Ch 4: 4 and all their **h parts** *were* inward. 268
Ne 4: 8 fight against Jerusalem, and to **h** it. 6213+8442
Job 9:12 Behold, he taketh away, who can **h** him? 7725
11:10 or gather together, then who can **h** him? 7725
Ps 78:66 he smote his enemies in the **h parts**: he put 268
Joel 2:20 his **h part** towards the utmost sea, and 5490
Zec 14: 8 and half of them toward the **h** sea: 314
Mk 4:38 And he was in the **h part of the ship**, *4403*
Ac 8:36 *is* water; what doth **h** me to be baptized? *2967*
27:41 the **h part** was broken with the violence of *4403*
1Co 9:12 suffer all *things,* lest we should **h** *1325+1464*
Gal 5: 7 who did **h** you that *ye* should not obey *348*

HINDERED (5) [HINDER]

Ezr 6: 8 be given unto these men, that *they* be not **h**. 989
Lk 11:52 and them that were entering in ye **h**. *2967*
Ro 15:22 I have been much **h from** coming to you. *1465*
1Th 2:18 even I Paul, once and again; but Satan **h** us. *1465*
1Pe 3: 7 the grace of life; that your prayers be not **h**. *1581*

HINDERETH (1) [HINDER]

Isa 14: 6 nations in anger, *is* persecuted, *and* none **h**. 2820

HINDERMOST (2) [HINDER]

Ge 33: 2 her children after, and Rachel and Joseph **h**. 314
Jer 50:12 the **h** of the nations *shall be* a wilderness, 319

HINDMOST (3) [HINDER]

Nu 2:31 They shall go **h** with their standards. 314
Dt 25:18 thee by the way, and **smote the h** of thee, 2179
Jos 10:19 your enemies, and **smite the h** of them; 2179

HINDS (4) [HIND]

Job 39: 1 *or* canst thou mark when the **h** do calve? 355
Ps 29: 9 The voice of the LORD maketh the **h** to 355
SS 2: 7 by the roes, and by the **h** of the field, that ye 355
3: 5 by the roes, and by the **h** of the field, that ye 355

HINDS' (3) [HIND]

2Sa 22:34 He maketh my feet like **h** *feet:* and 355
Ps 18:33 He maketh my feet like **h** *feet,* and 355
Hab 3:19 he will make my feet like **h** *feet,* and he will 355

HINGES (2)

1Ki 7:50 the **h** *of* gold, *both* for the doors of 6596
Pr 26:14 *As* the door turneth upon his **h**, so *doth* 6735

HINNOM (13)

Jos 15: 8 son of **H** unto the south side of the Jebusite; 2011
15: 8 that *lieth* before the valley of **H** westward, 2011
18:16 that *lieth* before the valley of the son of **H**, 2011
18:16 descended *to* the valley of **H**, to the side of 2011
2Ki 23:10 which *is* in the valley of the children of **H**, 2011
2Ch 28: 3 burnt incense in the valley of the son of **H**, 2011
33: 6 the fire in the valley of the son of **H**: 2011
Ne 11:30 from Beer-sheba unto the valley of **H**. 2011
Jer 7:31 which *is* in the valley of the son of **H**, 2011

Jer 7:32 nor the valley of the son of H, but 2011
19: 2 go forth unto the valley of the son of H, 2011
19: 6 nor The valley of the son of H, but The 2011
32:35 which *are* in the valley of the son of H, 2011

HIP (1)
Jdg 15: 8 he smote them h and thigh *with* a great 7785

HIRAH (2)
Ge 38: 1 a certain Adullamite, whose name *was* H. 2437
38:12 he and his friend H the Adullamite. 2437

HIRAM (22) [HIRAM'S]
2Sa 5:11 H king of Tyre sent messengers to David, 2438
1Ki 5: 1 H king of Tyre sent his servants unto 2438
5: 1 his father: for H was ever a lover of David. 2438
5: 2 And Solomon sent to H, saying, 2438
5: 7 when H heard the words of Solomon, 2438
5: 8 H sent to Solomon, saying, I have 2438
5:10 So H gave Solomon cedar trees and 2438
5:11 Solomon gave H twenty thousand measures 2438
5:11 thus gave Solomon to H year by year. 2438
5:12 there was peace between H and Solomon; 2438
7:13 king Solomon sent and fet H out of Tyre. 2438
7:40 H made the lavers, and the shovels, and 2438
7:40 So H made an end of doing all the work 2438
7:45 which H made to king Solomon *for* 2438
9:11 (*Now* H the king of Tyre had furnished 2438
9:11 king Solomon gave H twenty cities in 2438
9:12 H came out from Tyre to see the cities 2438
9:14 H sent to the king sixscore talents of gold. 2438
9:27 H sent in the navy his servants, 2438
10:11 the navy also of H, that brought gold from 2438
10:22 sea a navy of Tharshish with the navy of H: 2438
1Ch 14: 1 Now H king of Tyre sent messengers to 2438

HIRAM'S (1) [HIRAM]
1Ki 5:18 H builders did hew *them*, and 2438

HIRE (23) [HIRED, HIRELING, HIRES, HIREST]
Ge 30:18 God hath given *me* my h, because I have 7939
30:32 the goats: and *of such* shall be my h. 7939
30:33 when it shall come for my h before thy 7939
31: 8 he said thus, The ringstraked shall be thy h; 7939
Ex 22:15 if it *be* a hired *thing*, it came for his h. 7939
Dt 23:18 Thou shalt not bring the h of a whore, or 868
24:15 At his day thou shalt give *him* his h, 7939
1Ki 5: 6 unto thee will I give h for thy servants 7939
1Ch 19: 6 thousand talents of silver to h them chariots 7936
Isa 23:17 she shall turn to her h, and shall commit 868
23:18 and her h shall be holiness to the LORD: 868
46: 6 silver in the balance, *and* h a goldsmith; 7936
Eze 16:31 not been as a harlot, in that *thou* scornest h; 868
16:41 and thou also shalt give no h any more. 868
Mic 1: 7 for she gathered *it* of the h of a harlot, and 868
1: 7 and they shall return to the h of a harlot. 868
3:11 the priests thereof teach for h, and 4242
Zec 8:10 For before these days there was no h for 7939
8:10 was no hire for man, nor any h for beast; 7939
Mt 20: 1 which went out early in the morning to h *3409*
20: 8 Call the labourers, and give them *their* h, *3408*
Lk 10: 7 for the labourer is worthy of his h. Go not *3408*
Jas 5: 4 the h of the labourers which have reaped *3408*

HIRED (34) [HIRE]
Ge 30:16 for **surely** I have h thee with my 7936+7936
Ex 12:45 and a h **servant** shall not eat thereof. 7916
22:15 if it *be* a h *thing*, it came for his hire. 7916
Lev 19:13 neither rob *him:* the wages of **him that is h** 7916
22:10 or a h **servant**, shall not eat *of* the holy 7916
25: 6 for thy h **servant**, and for thy stranger that 7916
25:40 *But* as a h **servant**, *and* as a sojourner, 7916
25:50 according to the time of a h **servant** shall it 7916
25:53 *And* as a yearly h **servant** shall he be with 7916
Dt 15:18 for he hath been worth a double h **servant** 7916
23: 4 they h against thee Balaam the son of Beor 7936
24:14 Thou shalt not oppress a h **servant** *that is* 7916
Jdg 9: 4 wherewith Abimelech h vain and 7936
18: 4 with me, and hath h me, and I am his priest. 7936
1Sa 2: 5 *They that were* full have h **out** themselves 7936
2Sa 10: 6 and h the Syrians of Beth-rehob, 7936
2Ki 7: 6 the king of Israel hath h against us 7936
1Ch 19: 7 So they h thirty and two thousand chariots, 7936
2Ch 24:12 h masons and carpenters to repair the house 7936
25: 6 He h also an hundred thousand mighty *men* 7936
Ezr 4: 5 h counsellers against them, to frustrate their 7936
Ne 6:12 for Tobiah and Sanballat had h him. 7936
6:13 Therefore *was* he h, that I should be afraid, 7936
13: 2 and with water, but h Balaam against them, 7936
Isa 7:20 shall the Lord shave with a rasor that is h, 7917
Jer 46:21 Also her h **men** *are* in the midst of her like 7916
Hos 8: 9 alone by himself: Ephraim hath h lovers. 8566
8:10 though they have h among the nations, 8566
Mt 20: 7 say unto him, Because no *man* hath h us. *3409*
20: 9 And when they came that *were* h about NIG
Mk 1:20 Zebedee in the ship with the h **servants**, *3411*
Lk 15:17 How many h *servants* of my father's have *3407*
15:19 thy son: make me as one of thy h *servants*. *3407*
Ac 28:30 dwelt two whole years in his own h **house**, *3410*

HIRED HAND; HIRED MAN See HIRELING

HIRELING (9) [HIRE]
Job 7: 1 *are not* his days also like the days of a h? 7916
7: 2 as a h looketh for the reward of his work: 7916
14: 6 till he shall accomplish, as a h, his day. 7916
Isa 16:14 as the years of a h, and the glory of Moab 7916
21:16 according to the years of a h, and all 7916
Mal 3: 5 against those that oppress the h in *his* 7916
Jn 10:12 But *he that is* a h, and not the shepherd, *3411*
10:13 The h fleeth, because he is a hireling, and *3411*
10:13 because he is a h, and careth not for *3411*

HIRES (1) [HIRE]
Mic 1: 7 all the h thereof shall be burnt with the fire, 868

HIREST (1) [HIRE]
Eze 16:33 thy gifts to all thy lovers, and h them, 7809

HIS (8478) [HE] See Index of Articles, Etc.

HISS (12) [HISSING]
1Ki 9: 8 by it shall be astonished, and shall h; 8319
Job 27:23 at him, and shall h him out of his place. 8319
Isa 5:26 will h unto them from the end of the earth: 8319
7:18 *that* the LORD shall h for the fly that *is* in 8319
Jer 19: 8 and h because of all the plagues thereof. 8319
49:17 and shall h at all the plagues thereof. 8319
50:13 be astonished, and h at all her plagues. 8319
La 2:15 they h and wag their head at the daughter 8319
2:16 they h and gnash the teeth: they say, 8319
Eze 27:36 The merchants among the people shall h at 8319
Zep 2:15 every one that passeth by her shall h, *and* 8319
Zec 10: 8 I will h for them, and gather them; for I 8319

HISSING (8) [HISS]
2Ch 29: 8 to astonishment, and to h, as ye see with 8322
Jer 18:16 make their land desolate, *and* a perpetual h; 8292
19: 8 I will make this city desolate, and a h; 8322
25: 9 and a h, and perpetual desolations. 8322
25:18 an astonishment, a h, and a curse; 8322
29:18 an astonishment, and a h, and a reproach, 8322
51:37 an astonishment, and a h, without an 8322
Mic 6:16 and the inhabitants thereof a h: 8322

HIT (2)
1Sa 31: 3 sore against Saul, and the archers h him; 4672
1Ch 10: 3 the archers h him, and he was wounded of 4672

HITHER (67) [HITHERTO]
Ge 15:16 generation they shall come h again: 2008+1886.5
42:15 except your youngest brother come h. 2008
45: 5 angry with yourselves, that ye sold me h: 2008
45: 8 So now *it was* not you *that* sent me h, but 2008
45:13 ye shall haste and bring down my father h. 2008
Ex 3: 5 he said, Draw not nigh h: put off thy shoes 1988
Jos 2: 2 there came men **in** h to night of 2008
3: 9 Come h, and hear the words of the LORD 2008
18: 6 and bring *the description* h to me, 2008
Jdg 16: 2 *told* the Gazites, saying, Samson is come h. 2008
18: 3 and said unto him, Who brought thee h? 1988
19:12 We will not turn aside h into the city of a NIH
Ru 2:14 At mealtime come thou h, and eat of 1988
1Sa 13: 9 **Bring** h a burnt offering to me, and peace 5066
14:18 said unto Ahiah, **Bring** h the ark of God. 5066
14:34 **Bring** me h every man his ox, and 5066
14:36 the priest, Let us draw near h unto God. 1988
14:38 Saul said, Draw ye near h, all the chief of 1988
15:32 **Bring** you h to me Agag the king of 5066
16:11 for we will not sit down till he come h. 6311
17:28 and he said, Why camest thou down h? 2088
23: 9 to Abiathar the priest, **Bring** h the ephod. 5066
30: 7 I pray thee, **bring** me h the ephod. 5066
2Sa 1:10 and have brought them h unto my lord. 2008
5: 6 and the lame, thou shalt not come in h: 2008
5: 6 in hither: thinking, David cannot come in h. 2008
14:32 Behold, I sent unto thee, saying, Come h, 2008
20:16 I pray you, unto Joab, Come near h, 2008+5704
1Ki 22: 9 said, Hasten *h* Micaiah the son of Imlah. NIH
2Ki 2: 8 they were divided h and thither, so 2008
2:14 the waters, they parted h and thither: 2008
8: 7 The man of God is come h. 2008+5704
1Ch 11: 5 Jebus said to David, Thou shalt not come h. 2008
2Ch 28:13 Ye shall not bring in the captives h. 2008
Ezr 4: 2 king of Assur, which brought us up h. 6311
Ps 73:10 Therefore his people return h: and 1988
81: 2 Take a psalm, and bring h the timbrel, NIH
Pr 9: 4 Whoso *is* simple, let him turn in h: *as for* 2008
9:16 Whoso *is* simple, let him turn in h: and 2008
25: 7 *it is* that it be said unto thee, Come up h; 2008
Isa 57: 3 draw near h, ye sons of the sorceress, 2008
Eze 40: 4 shew *them* unto thee art thou brought h: 2008
Da 3:26 come *h*. Then Shadrach, Meshach, and NIH
Mt 8:29 art thou come h to torment us before *5602*
14:18 He said, Bring them h to me. *5602*
17:17 long shall I suffer you? bring him h to me. *5602*
22:12 how camest thou in h not having a wedding *5602*
Mk 11: 3 of him; and straightway he will send him h. *5602*
Lk 9:41 with you, and suffer you? Bring thy son h. *5602*
14:21 and bring in h the poor, and the maimed, *5602*
15:23 And **bring** h the fatted calf, and kill *it;* and *5342*
19:27 bring h, and slay *them* before me. *5602*
19:30 never man sat: loose him, and bring *him h*. NIG
Jn 4:15 that I thirst not, neither come h to draw. *1759*
4:16 unto her, Go, call thy husband, and come h. *1759*
6:25 said unto him, Rabbi, when camest thou h? *5602*
20:27 Reach h thy finger, and behold my hands; *5602*
20:27 and reach *h* thy hand, and thrust *it* into my NIG
Ac 9:21 came h for that *intent*, that he might bring *5602*
10:32 Send therefore to Joppa, and call h Simon, *3333*
17: 6 the world upside down are come h also; *1759*
19:37 For ye have brought h these men, *which are* NIG
25:17 Therefore, when they were come h, *1759*
Rev 4: 1 Come up h, and I will shew thee *things* *5602*
11:12 from heaven saying unto them, Come up h. *5602*
17: 1 talked with me, saying unto me, *Come* h; *1204*
21: 9 and talked with me, saying, *Come* h, I will *1204*

HITHERTO (19) [HITHER, TO]
Ex 7:16 behold, h thou wouldest not hear. 3541+5704
Jos 17:14 as the LORD hath blessed me h? 3541+5704
Jdg 16:13 H thou hast mocked me, and told me 2008+5704
1Sa 1:16 and grief have I spoken h. 2008+5704
7:12 H hath the LORD helped us. 2008+5704
2Sa 7:18 that thou hast brought me h? 1988+5704
15:34 as I *have been* thy father's servant h, 227+4480
1Ch 9:18 Who h *waited* in the king's 2008+5704+2050.1
12:29 for h the greatest part of them had 2008+5704
17:16 that thou hast brought me h? 1988+5704
Job 38:11 H shalt thou come, but no further: 5704+6311
Ps 71:17 h have I declared thy wondrous 2008+5704
Isa 18: 2 to a people terrible from their beginning h; 1973
18: 7 a people terrible from their beginning h; 1973
Da 7:28 H *is* the end of the matter. *As for* me 3542+5705
Jn 5:17 answered them, My Father worketh h, *737+2193*
16:24 H have ye asked nothing in my name: *737+2193*
Ro 1:13 come unto you, (but was let h,) *891+1204+3588*
1Co 3: 2 for h ye were **not** able *to bear it*, neither yet *3768*

HITTITE (26) [HITTITES]
Ge 23:10 Ephron the H answered Abraham in 2850
25: 9 the field of Ephron the son of Zohar the H, 2850
26:34 to wife Judith the daughter of Beeri the H, 2850
26:34 and Bashemath the daughter of Elon the H: 2850
36: 2 Adah the daughter of Elon the H, and 2850
49:29 the cave that *is* in the field of Ephron the H, 2850
49:30 the H for a possession of a buryingplace. 2850
50:13 of a buryingplace of Ephron the H, 2850
Ex 23:28 the Canaanite, and the H, from before thee. 2850
33: 2 and the H, and the Perizzite, the Hivite, and 2850
34:11 and the H, and the Perizzite, and the Hivite, 2850
Jos 9: 1 the H, and the Amorite, the Canaanite, 2850
11: 3 the H, and the Perizzite, and the Jebusite in 2850
1Sa 26: 6 and said to Ahimelech the H, 2850
2Sa 11: 3 daughter of Eliam, the wife of Uriah the H? 2850
11: 6 sent to Joab, *saying*, Send me Uriah the H. 2850
11:17 of David; and Uriah the H died also. 2850
11:21 Thy servant Uriah the H is dead also. 2850
11:24 and thy servant Uriah the H is dead also. 2850
12: 9 thou hast killed Uriah the H with 2850
12:10 hast taken the wife of Uriah the H to be thy 2850
23:39 Uriah the H: thirty and seven *in* all. 2850
1Ki 15: 5 save only in the matter of Uriah the H. 2850
1Ch 11:41 Uriah the H, Zabad the son of Ahlai, 2850
Eze 16: 3 father *was* an Amorite, and thy mother a H. 2850
16:45 your mother *was* a H, and your father an 2850

HITTITES (22) [HITTITE]
Ge 15:20 the H, and the Perizzites, and 2850
Ex 3: 8 the H, and the Amorites, and the Perizzites, 2850
3:17 the H, and the Amorites, and the Perizzites, 2850
13: 5 the H, and the Amorites, and the Hivites, 2850
23:23 the H, and the Perizzites, and 2850
Nu 13:29 the H, and the Jebusites, and the Amorites, 2850
Dt 7: 1 the H, and the Girgashites, and 2850
20:17 *namely*, the H, and the Amorites, 2850
Jos 1: 4 all the land of the H, and unto the great sea 2850
3:10 the H, and the Hivites, and the Perizzites, 2850
12: 8 in the south *country;* the H, the Amorites, 2850
24:11 the H, and the Girgashites, the Hivites, and 2850
Jdg 1:26 the man went *into* the land of the H, and 2850
3: 5 H, and Amorites, and Perizzites, 2850
1Ki 9:20 H, Perizzites, Hivites, and Jebusites, 2850
10:29 so for all the kings of the H, and for 2850
11: 1 Ammonites, Edomites, Zidonians, *and* H; 2850
2Ki 7: 6 hath hired against us the kings of the H, 2850
2Ch 1:17 they out *horses* for all the kings of the H, 2850
8: 7 *As for* all the people that were left of the H, 2850
Ezr 9: 1 the H, the Perizzites, the Jebusites, 2850
Ne 9: 8 the H, the Amorites, and the Perizzites, and 2850

HIVITE (9) [HIVITES]
Ge 10:17 And the H, and the Arkite, and the Sinite, 2340
34: 2 when Shechem the son of Hamor the H, 2340
36: 2 of Anah the daughter of Zibeon the H; 2340
Ex 23:28 which shall drive out the H, the Canaanite, 2340
33: 2 and the Perizzite, the H, and the Jebusite: 2340
34:11 the Perizzite, and the H, and the Jebusite. 2340
Jos 9: 1 the Perizzite, the H, and the Jebusite, 2340
11: 3 *to* the H under Hermon in the land of 2340
1Ch 1:15 And the H, and the Arkite, and the Sinite, 2340

HIVITES (16) [HIVITE]
Ex 3: 8 the Perizzites, and the H, and the Jebusites. 2340
3:17 the Perizzites, and the H, and the Jebusites, 2340
13: 5 the Amorites, and the H, and the Jebusites, 2340
23:23 the Canaanites, the H, and the Jebusites: 2340
Dt 7: 1 the Perizzites, and the H, and the Jebusites, 2340
20:17 and the Perizzites, the H, and the Jebusites; 2340
Jos 3:10 the H, and the Perizzites, and 2340
9: 7 the men of Israel said unto the H, 2340
11:19 save the H the inhabitants of Gibeon: 2340
12: 8 the Perizzites, the H, and the Jebusites: 2340
24:11 the Girgashites, the H, and the Jebusites; 2340
Jdg 3: 3 and the H that dwelt in mount Lebanon, 2340
3: 5 and Perizzites, and H, and Jebusites: 2340
2Sa 24: 7 *to* all the cities of the H, and of 2340
1Ki 9:20 Hittites, Perizzites, H, and Jebusites, 2340
2Ch 8: 7 the Perizzites, and the H, and the Jebusites, 2340

HIZKI See HEZEKI

HIZKIAH (1)
Zep 1: 1 the son of Amariah, the son of H, 2396

HIZKIJAH (1)
Ne 10:17 Ater, H, Azzur, 2396

HO (4)
Ru 4: 1 *H*, such a one, turn aside, sit down here. NIH
Isa 55: 1 H, every one that thirsteth, come ye to 1945
Zec 2: 6 H, ho, *come forth*, and flee from the land of 1945
2: 6 Ho, h, *come forth*, and flee from the land of 1945

HOAR (4) [HOARFROST, HOARY]
Ex 16:14 *as* small as the **h frost** on the ground. 3713
1Ki 2: 6 let not his **h head** go down *to* the grave in 7872
2: 9 his **h head** bring thou down *to* the grave 7872
Isa 46: 4 *even* to **h hairs** will I carry *you:* I have 7872

H

HOARFROST (1) [FROST, HOAR]
Ps 147:16 like wool: he scattereth the h like ashes. 3713

HOARY (4) [HOAR]
Lev 19:32 Thou shalt rise up before the h head, and 7872
Job 38:29 the h frost of heaven, who hath gendered 3713
41:32 after him; *one* would think the deep to be h. 7872
Pr 16:31 The h head *is* a crown of glory, *if* it be 7872

HOBAB (2)
Nu 10:29 Moses said unto H, the son of Raguel 2246
Jdg 4:11 *which was* of the children of H the father in 2246

HOBAH (1)
Ge 14:15 and smote them, and pursued them unto H, 2327

HOBAIAH See HABAIAH

HOD (1)
1Ch 7:37 H, and Shamma, and Shilshah, and Ithran, 1936

HODAIAH (1)
1Ch 3:24 the sons of Elioenai *were*, H, and Eliashib, 1939

HODAVIAH (3)
1Ch 5:24 Azriel, and Jeremiah, and H, and Jahdiel, 1938
9: 7 the son of H, the son of Hasenuah, 1938
Ezr 2:40 of the children of H, seventy and four. 1938

HODESH (1)
1Ch 8: 9 he begat of H his wife, Jobab, and Zibia, 2321

HODEVAH (1)
Ne 7:43 *and* of the children of H, seventy and four. 1937

HODIAH (1)
1Ch 4:19 the sons of *his* wife H the sister of Naham, 1940

HODIJAH (5)
Ne 8: 7 H, Maaseiah, Kelita, Azariah, Jozabad, 1941
9: 5 Sherebiah, H, Shebaniah, *and* Pethahiah, 1941
10:10 Shebaniah, H, Kelita, Pelaiah, Hanan, 1941
10:13 H, Bani, Beninu. 1941
10:18 H, Hashum, Bezai, 1941

HOGLAH (4)
Nu 26:33 and Noah, H, Milcah, and Tirzah. 2295
27: 1 Noah, and H, and Milcah, and Tirzah. 2295
36:11 Tirzah, and H, and Milcah, and Noah, 2295
Jos 17: 3 Mahlah, and Noah, H, Milcah, and Tirzah. 2295

HOHAM (1)
Jos 10: 3 of Jerusalem sent unto H king of Hebron, 1944

HOISED (1)
Ac 27:40 and h up the mainsail to the wind, and *1869*

HOLD (185) [HELD, HOLDEN, HOLDEST, HOLDETH, HOLDING, HOLDS]
Ge 19:16 the men laid h upon his hand, and upon 2388
21:18 lift up the lad, and h him in thine hand; 2388
25:26 and his hand took h on Esau's heel; 270
Ex 5: 1 that they may h a feast unto me in 2287
9: 2 refuse to let *them* go, and wilt h them still, 2388
10: 9 for we *must* h a feast unto the LORD. NIH
14:14 fight for you, and ye shall h your peace. 2790
15:14 sorrow shall take h on the inhabitants of 270
15:15 of Moab, trembling shall take h upon them; 270
20: 7 for the LORD will not h him guiltless that 5352
26: 5 that the loops may take h one of another. 6901
Nu 30: 4 and her father shall h his peace at her: 2790
30:14 altogether h his peace at her from 2790+2790
Dt 5:11 for the LORD will not h *him* guiltless that 5352
21:19 his father and his mother lay h on him, 8610
22:28 lay h on her, and lie with her, and they be 8610
32:41 and mine hand take h on judgment; 270
Jdg 9:46 into a h of the house of the god Berith. 6877
9:49 put *them* to the h, and set the hold on fire 6877
9:49 to the hold, and set the h on fire upon them; 6877
16:29 Samson took h of the two middle pillars 3943
18:19 they said unto him, H thy peace, lay thine 2790
19:29 laid h on his concubine, and divided her, 2388
Ru 3:15 the vail that *thou hast* upon thee, and h it. 270
1Sa 15:27 he laid h upon the skirt of his mantle, and 2388
22: 4 him all the while that David was in the h. 4686
22: 5 Gad said unto David, Abide not in the h; 4686
24:22 David and his men gat them up unto the h. 4686
2Sa 1:11 David took h on his clothes, and rent them; 2388
2:21 and lay thee h on one of the young men, and 270
2:22 should I h up my face to Joab thy brother? 5375
4:10 I took h of him, and slew him in Ziklag, 270
5: 7 Nevertheless David took the strong h of 4686
5:17 David heard *of it*, and went down to the h. 4686
6: 6 *his hand* to the ark of God, and took h of it; 270
13:11 he took h of her, and said unto her, 2388
13:20 h now thy peace, my sister: he *is* thy 2790
18: 9 his head caught h of the oak, and he was 2388
23:14 David *was* then in a h, and the garrison of 4686
24: 7 came *to* the strong h of Tyre, and *to* all 4013
1Ki 1:50 and caught h on the horns of the altar. 2388
1:51 he hath caught h on the horns of the altar, 270
2: 9 Now therefore h him not guiltless: for thou 5352
2:28 and caught h on the horns of the altar. 2388
9: 9 have taken h upon other gods, and 2388
13: 4 hand from the altar, saying, Lay h on him. 8610
2Ki 2: 3 he said, Yea, I know *it*; h you your peace. 2814
2: 5 Yea, I know *it*; h you your peace. 2814
2:12 he took h of his own clothes, and rent them 2388
6:32 shut the door, and h him fast at the door: 3905
7: 9 a day of good tidings, and we h our peace: 2814
1Ch 11:16 David *was* then in the h, and 4686
12: 8 into the h to the wilderness men of might, 4679
12:16 of Benjamin and Judah to the h unto David. 4679
1Ch 13: 9 Uzza put forth his hand to h the ark; 270
2Ch 7:22 laid h on other gods, and worshipped them, 2388
Ne 8:11 H your peace, for the day *is* holy; 2013
Est 4:11 except such to whom the king shall h out 3447
Job 6:24 Teach me, and I will h my tongue: and 2790
8:15 he shall h it fast, but it shall not endure. 2388
9:28 I know that thou wilt not h me innocent. 5352
11: 3 Should thy lies make men h their peace? 2790
13: 5 you would altogether h your peace, 2790+2790
13:13 H your peace, let me alone, that I may 2790
13:19 for now, if I h my tongue, I shall give up 2790
17: 9 The righteous also shall h on his way, and 270
21: 6 and trembling taketh h on my flesh. 270
27: 6 My righteousness I h fast, and will not let 2388
27:20 Terrors take h on him as waters, a tempest 5381
30:16 the days of affliction have taken h upon me. 270
33:31 unto me: h thy peace, and I will speak. 2790
33:33 h thy peace, and I shall teach thee wisdom. 2790
36:17 judgment and justice take h on *thee*. 8551
38:13 That *it* might take h of the ends of the earth, 270
41:26 sword of him that layeth at him cannot h: 6965
Ps 17: 5 H up my goings in thy paths, *that* my 8551
35: 2 Take h of shield and buckler, and stand up 2388
39:12 unto my cry; h not thy peace at my tears: 2790
40:12 mine iniquities have taken h upon me, so 5381
48: 6 Fear took h upon them there, *and* pain, as of 270
69:24 and let thy wrathful anger take h of them. 5381
83: 1 h not thy peace, and be not still, O God. 2790
109: 1 H not thy peace, O God of my praise; 2790
116: 3 and the pains of hell gat h upon me: 4672
119:53 Horror hath taken h upon me because of 270
119:117 H thou me up, and I shall be safe: and 5582
119:143 Trouble and anguish have taken h on me: 4672
139:10 hand lead me, and thy right hand shall h me. 270
Pr 2:19 neither take they h of the paths of life. 5381
3:18 She *is* a tree of life to them that lay h upon 2388
4:13 Take fast h of instruction; let *her* not go: 2388
5: 5 go down *to* death; her steps take h on hell. 8551
30:28 The spider taketh h with her hands, and 8610
31:19 to the spindle, and her hands h the distaff. 8551
Ecc 2: 3 to lay h on folly, till I might see what *was* 270
7:18 *It is* good that thou shouldest take h of this; 270
SS 3: 8 They all h swords, *being* expert in war: 270
7: 8 I will take h of the boughs thereof: 270
Isa 3: 6 When a man shall take h of his brother *of* 8610
4: 1 in that day seven women shall take h of 2388
5:29 lay h of the prey, and shall carry *it* away 270
13: 8 sorrows shall take h of *them;* they shall be 270
21: 3 pangs have taken h upon me, as the pangs 270
27: 5 Or let him take h of my strength, *that* he 2388
31: 9 he shall pass over *to* his strong h for fear, 5553
41:13 For I the LORD thy God will h thy right 2388
42: 6 will h thine hand, and will keep thee, and 2388
56: 2 and the son of man *that* layeth h on it; 2388
56: 4 that please me, and take h of my covenant; 2388
56: 6 polluting it, and taketh h of my covenant; 2388
62: 1 For Zion's sake will I not h my peace, and 2814
62: 6 *which* shall never h their peace day nor 2814
64: 7 that stirreth up himself to take h of thee: 2388
64:12 wilt thou h thy peace, and afflict us very 2814
Jer 2:13 broken cisterns, that can h no water. 3557
4:19 I cannot h my peace, because thou hast 2790
6:23 They shall lay h on bow and spear; they *are* 2388
6:24 anguish hath taken h of us, *and* pain, as of 2388
8: 5 they h fast deceit, they refuse to return. 2388
8:21 astonishment hath taken h on me. 2388
50:42 They shall h the bow and the lance: 2388
50:43 anguish took h of him, *and* pangs as of a 2388
Eze 29: 7 When they took h of thee by thy hand, 8610
30:21 to bind it, to make it strong to h the sword. 8610
41: 6 that *they* might have h, but they had not hold 270
41: 6 but they had not h in the wall of the house. 270
Am 6:10 shall he say, H thy tongue: for *we may* not 2013
Mic 4: 8 the strong h of the daughter of Zion, 6077
6:14 thou shalt take h, but shalt not deliver; and 5253
Na 1: 7 *is* good, a strong h in the day of trouble; 4581
Hab 1:10 they shall deride every strong h; for they 4013
Zep 1: 7 H thy peace at the presence of the Lord 2013
Zec 1: 6 did they not take h of your fathers? 5381
8:23 take h out of all languages of the nations, 2388
8:23 even shall take h of the skirt of him that is 2388
9: 3 And Tyrus did build herself a strong h, and 4692
9:12 Turn ye to the strong h, ye prisoners of 1225
11: 5 slay them, and h themselves not guilty: 816
14:13 they shall lay h every one on the hand of 2388
Mt 6:24 or else he will h to the one, and despise *472*
12:11 will he not lay h on it, and lift *it* out? *2902*
14: 3 For Herod had laid h on John, and *2902*
20:31 because they should h their peace: *4623*
21:26 fear the people; for all h John as a prophet. *2192*
26:48 I shall kiss, that *same* is he: h him fast. *2902*
26:55 in the temple, and ye laid no h on me. *2902*
26:57 And they that had laid h on Jesus led *him* *2902*
Mk 1:25 saying, H thy peace, and come out of him. *5392*
3:21 heard *of it*, they went out to lay h on him: *2902*
6:17 had sent forth and laid h upon John, *2902*
7: 4 which they have received to h, *as* *2902*
7: 8 ye h the tradition of men, *as* the washing of *2902*
10:48 charged him that he should h his peace: *4623*
12:12 And they sought to lay h on him, but *2902*
14:51 and the young men laid h on him: *2902*
Lk 4:35 saying, H thy peace, and come out of him. *5392*
16:13 or else he will h to the one, and despise *472*
18:39 rebuked him, that he should h his peace: *4623*
19:40 I tell you that, if these should h their peace, *4623*
20:20 *men,* that they might take h of his words, *1949*
20:26 And they could not take h of his words *1949*
23:26 they laid h upon one Simon, a Cyrenian, *1949*
Ac 4: 3 and put *them* in h unto the next day: *5084*
12:17 unto them with the hand to h their peace, *4601*
18: 9 not afraid, but speak, and h not thy peace: *4623*
Ro 1:18 of men, who h the truth in unrighteousness; *2722*
1Co 14:30 that sitteth *by*, let the first h his peace. *4601*
Php 2:29 with all gladness; and h such in reputation: *2192*
1Th 5:21 Prove all *things;* h fast *that which* is good. *2722*
2Th 2:15 h the traditions which ye have been taught, *2902*
1Ti 6:12 the good fight of faith, lay h on eternal life, *1949*
6:19 to come, that they may lay h on eternal life. *1949*
2Ti 1:13 H fast the form of sound words, *2192*
Heb 3: 6 if we h fast the confidence and *2722*
3:14 if we h the beginning of *our* confidence *2722*
4:14 the Son of God, let us h fast *our* profession. *2902*
6:18 who have fled for refuge to lay h upon *2902*
10:23 Let us h fast the profession of *our* hope *2722*
Rev 2:14 thou hast there them that h the doctrine of *2902*
2:15 So hast thou also them that h the doctrine *2902*
2:25 But *that* which ye have *already* h fast till I NIG
3: 3 and heard, and h fast, and repent. *5083*
3:11 h *that* fast which thou hast, that no *man* *2902*
18: 2 and the h of every foul spirit, and a cage of *5438*
20: 2 And he laid h on the dragon, *that* old *2902*

HOLD FAST See CLEAVE; CLEAVED; CLEAVETH

HOLD GUILTY See IMPUTE; IMPUTED; IMPUTETH; IMPUTING

HOLDEN (12) [HOLD]
2Ki 23:22 Surely there was not h such a passover 6213
23:23 *wherein* this passover was h to the LORD 6213
Job 36: 8 in fetters, *and* be h in cords of affliction; 3920
Ps 18:35 thy right hand hath h me up, and 5582
71: 6 By thee have I been h up from the womb: 5564
73:23 with thee: thou hast h *me* by my right hand. 270
Pr 5:22 he shall be h with the cords of his sins. 8551
Isa 42:14 I have long time h my peace; I have been 2814
45: 1 to Cyrus, whose right hand I have h, to 2388
Lk 24:16 But their eyes were h that *they* should not *2902*
Ac 2:24 it was not possible that he should be h of it. *2902*
Ro 14: 4 Yea, he shall be h up: for God is able to *2476*

HOLDEST (6) [HOLD]
Est 4:14 For if thou altogether h thy peace at 2790+2790
Job 13:24 thou thy face, and h me for thine enemy? 2803
Ps 77: 4 Thou h mine eyes waking: I am *so* 270
Jer 49:16 of the rock, that h the height of the hill: 8610
Hab 1:13 h thy tongue when the wicked devoureth 2790
Rev 2:13 Satan's seat *is:* and thou h fast my name, *2902*

HOLDETH (9) [HOLD]
Job 2: 3 still he h fast his integrity, although thou 2388
26: 9 He h back the face of *his* throne, *and* 270
Ps 66: 9 Which h our soul in life, and suffereth not 7760
Pr 11:12 but a man of understanding h his peace. 2790
17:28 Even a fool, when he h his peace, 2790
Da 10:21 *there is* none that h with me in these *things*, 2388
Am 1: 5 him that h the sceptre from the house of 8551
1: 8 him that h the sceptre from Ashkelon, and 8551
Rev 2: 1 These *things* saith he that h the seven stars *2902*

HOLDING (9) [HOLD]
Isa 33:15 that shaketh his hands from h of bribes, 8551
Jer 6:11 fury of the LORD; I am weary with h in: 3557
Mk 7: 3 eat not, h the tradition of the elders. *2902*
Php 2:16 H forth the word of life; that I may rejoice *1907*
Col 2:19 And not h the head, from which all *2902*
1Ti 1:19 H faith, and a good conscience; *2192*
3: 9 H the mystery of the faith in a pure *2192*
Tit 1: 9 H fast the faithful word as *he* hath been *472*
Rev 7: 1 h the four winds of the earth, that the wind *2902*

HOLDS (21) [HOLD]
Nu 13:19 dwell in, whether in tents, or in strong h; 4013
Jdg 6: 2 in the mountains, and caves, and strong h. 4679
1Sa 23:14 David abode in the wilderness in strong h, 4679
23:19 himself with us in strong h in the wood, 4679
23:29 and dwelt in strong h at En-gedi. 4679
2Ki 8:12 their strong h wilt thou set on fire, and 4013
2Ch 11:11 he fortified the strong h, and put captains 4694
Ps 89:40 thou hast brought his strong h to ruin. 4013
Isa 23:11 *city,* to destroy the strong h thereof. 4581
Jer 48:18 *and* he shall destroy thy strong h. 4013
48:41 the strong h are surprised, and the mighty 4679
51:30 to fight, they have remained in *their* h: 4679
La 2: 2 the strong h of the daughter of Judah; 4013
2: 5 he hath destroyed his strong h, and 4013
Eze 19: 9 they brought him into h, that his voice 4685
Da 11:24 forecast his devices against the strong h, 4013
11:39 Thus shall he do in the most strong h with a 4013
Mic 5:11 thy land, and throw down all thy strong h: 4013
Na 3:12 All thy strong h *shall be like* fig trees with 4013
3:14 waters for the siege, fortify thy strong h: 4013
2Co 10: 4 God to the pulling down of strong h;) *3794*

HOLE (12) [ARMHOLES, HOLE'S, HOLES]
Ex 28:32 there shall be a h in the top of it, in 6310
28:32 of woven work round about the h of it, 6310
28:32 as it were the h of an habergeon, *that* it be 6310
39:23 *there was* a h in the midst of the robe, 6310
39:23 as the h of an habergeon, *with* a band round 6310
39:23 *with* a band round about the h, *that* it 6310
2Ki 12: 9 bored a h in the lid of it, and set it beside 2356
SS 5: 4 My beloved put in his hand by the h *of* 2356
Isa 11: 8 the sucking child shall play on the h of 2352
51: 1 to the h of the pit *whence* ye are digged. 4718
Jer 13: 4 and hide it there in a h of the rock. 5357
Eze 8: 7 and when I looked, behold a h in the wall. 2356

HOLE'S (1) [HOLE]
Jer 48:28 maketh her nest in the sides of the h mouth. 6354

HOLES (11) [HOLE]
1Sa 14:11 the Hebrews come forth out of the h where 2356
Isa 2:19 they shall go into the h of the rocks, and 4631
7:19 in the h of the rocks, and upon all thorns, 5357
42:22 *they are* all of them snared in h, and 2352
Jer 16:16 every hill, and out of the h of the rocks. 5357

Mic 7:17 they shall move out of their **h** like worms 4526
Na 2:12 filled his **h** *with* prey, and his dens *with* 2356
Hag 1: 6 earneth wages *to put it* into a bag with **h**. 5344
Zec 14:12 their eyes shall consume away in their **h**, 2356
Mt 8:20 The foxes have **h**, and the birds of the air *5454*
Lk 9:58 Foxes have **h**, and birds of the air *have* *5454*

HOLIER (1) [HOLY]
Isa 65: 5 come not near to me; for I am **h** than thou. 6942

HOLIEST (3) [HOLY]
Heb 9: 3 the tabernacle which is called the **h of all**; *40+40*
9: 8 that the way into the **h** *of all* was not yet made *40*
10:19 boldness to enter into the **h** by the blood of *40*

HOLILY (1) [HOLY]
1Th 2:10 and God *also*, how **h** and justly and *3743*

HOLINESS (43) [HOLY]
Ex 15:11 who *is* like thee, glorious in **h**, fearful *in* 6944
28:36 engravings of a signet, **H** TO THE LORD. 6944
39:30 engravings of a signet, **H** TO THE LORD. 6944
1Ch 16:29 worship the LORD in the beauty of **h**. 6944
2Ch 20:21 that should praise the beauty of **h**, as *they* 6944
31:18 set office they sanctified themselves *in* **h**: 6944
Ps 29: 2 worship the LORD in the beauty of **h**. 6944
30: 4 give thanks at the remembrance of his **h**. 6944
47: 8 God sitteth upon the throne of his **h**. 6944
48: 1 city of our God, *in* the mountain of his **h**. 6944
60: 6 God hath spoken in his **h**; I will rejoice, 6944
89:35 Once have I sworn by my **h** that I will not 6944
93: 5 **h** becometh thine house, O LORD, 6944
96: 9 O worship the LORD in the beauty of **h**: 6944
97:12 give thanks at the remembrance of his **h**. 6944
108: 7 God hath spoken in his **h**; I will rejoice, 6944
110: 3 in the beauties of **h** from the womb of 6944
Isa 23:18 and her hire shall be **h** to the LORD: 6944
35: 8 a way, and it shall be called The way of **h**; 6944
62: 9 together shall drink it in the courts of my **h**. 6944
63:15 behold from the habitation of thy **h** and 6944
63:18 The people of thy **h** have possessed *it* but 6944
Jer 2: 3 Israel *was* **h** unto the LORD, *and* 6944
23: 9 and because of the words of his **h**. 6944
31:23 O habitation of justice, *and* mountain of **h**. 6944
Am 4: 2 The Lord GOD hath sworn by his **h**, 6944
Ob 1:17 shall be deliverance, and there shall be **h**; 6944
Zec 14:20 bells of the horses, **H** UNTO THE LORD; 6944
14:21 in Judah shall be **h** unto the LORD of 6944
Mal 2:11 for Judah hath profaned the **h** of 6944
Lk 1:75 In **h** and righteousness before him, all *3742*
Ac 3:12 or **h** we had made this *man* to walk? *2150*
Ro 1: 4 according to the Spirit of **h**, by *42*
6:19 members servants to righteousness unto **h**. *38*
6:22 ye have your fruit unto **h**, and the end *38*
2Co 7: 1 and spirit, perfecting **h** in the fear of God. *42*
Eph 4:24 God is created in righteousness and true **h**. *3742*
1Th 3:13 your hearts unblameable in **h** before God, *42*
4: 7 not called us unto uncleanness, but unto **h**. *38*
1Ti 2:15 in faith and charity and **h** with sobriety. *38*
Tit 2: 3 *that they be* in behaviour **as becometh h**, *2412*
Heb 12:10 *our* profit, that *we* might be partakers of his **h**. *41*
12:14 Follow peace with all *men*, and **h**, *38*

HOLLOW (10)
Ge 32:25 against him, he touched the **h** of his thigh; 3709
32:25 the **h** of Jacob's thigh was out of joint, 3709
32:32 which *is* upon the **h** of the thigh, unto this 3709
32:32 he touched the **h** of Jacob's thigh in 3709
Ex 27: 8 **H** with boards shalt thou make it: as it was 5014
38: 7 it withal; he made *the altar* **h** with boards. 5014
Lev 14:37 *be* in the walls of the house with **h strakes**, 8258
Jdg 15:19 God clave a **h place** that *was* in the jaw, 4388
Isa 40:12 measured the waters in the **h** of his **hand**, 8168
Jer 52:21 thickness thereof *was* four fingers: *it was* **h**. 5014

HOLON (3)
Jos 15:51 Goshen, and **H**, and Giloh; eleven cities 2473
21:15 **H** with her suburbs, and Debir with her 2473
Jer 48:21 upon **H**, and upon Jahazah, and 2473

HOLPEN (5) [HELP]
Ps 83: 8 they have **h** the children of Lot. Selah. 2220
86:17 LORD, hast **h** me, and comforted me. 5826
Isa 31: 3 he that is **h** shall fall down, and they all 5826
Da 11:34 shall fall, they shall be **h** *with* a little help: 5826
Lk 1:54 He hath **h** his servant Israel, in remembrance *482*

HOLY (611) [HOLIER, HOLIEST, HOLILY, HOLINESS, HOLYDAY, UNHOLY]
Ex 3: 5 for the place whereon thou standest *is* **h** 6944
12:16 in the first day *there shall be* a **h** 6944
12:16 in the seventh day there shall be a **h** 6944
15:13 *them* in thy strength unto thy **h** habitation. 6944
16:23 To morrow *is* the rest of the **h** sabbath unto 6944
19: 6 me a kingdom of priests, and a **h** nation. 6918
20: 8 Remember the sabbath day, to **keep** it **h**. 6942
22:31 ye shall be **h** men unto me: neither shall ye 6944
26:33 the vail shall divide unto you between the **h** 6944
26:33 the holy *place* and the **most h**. 6944+6944
26:34 the Testimony in the **most h** *place*. 6944+6944
28: 2 thou shalt make **h** garments for Aaron thy 6944
28: 4 they shall make **h** garments for Aaron thy 6944
28:29 when he goeth in unto the **h** *place*, for a 6944
28:35 in unto the **h** *place* before the LORD, 6944
28:38 that Aaron may bear the iniquity of the **h** 6944
28:38 of Israel shall hallow in all their **h** gifts; 6944
28:43 in the **h** *place;* that they bear not iniquity, 6944
29: 6 and put the **h** crown upon the mitre. 6944
29:29 the **h** garments of Aaron shall be his sons' 6944
29:30 the congregation to minister in the **h** *place*. 6944
29:31 and seethe his flesh in the **h** place. 6918
29:33 shall not eat *thereof*, because they *are* **h**. 6944
29:34 it shall not be eaten, because it *is* **h**. 6944
29:37 and it shall be an altar **most h**: 6944+6944

Ex 29:37 whatsoever toucheth the altar shall be **h**. 6942
30:10 it *is* **most h** unto the LORD. 6944+6944
30:25 And thou shalt make it an oil of **h** ointment, 6944
30:25 the apothecary: it shall be a **h** anointing oil. 6944
30:29 that they may be **most h**: 6944+6944
30:29 whatsoever toucheth them shall be **h**. 6942
30:31 This shall be a **h** anointing oil unto me 6944
30:32 of it: it *is* **h**, *and* it shall be holy unto you. 6944
30:32 of it: it *is* holy, *and* it shall be **h** unto you. 6944
30:35 tempered together, pure *and* **h**: 6944
30:36 it shall be unto you **most h**. 6944+6944
30:37 it shall be unto thee **h** for the LORD. 6944
31:10 the **h** garments for Aaron the priest, and 6944
31:11 sweet incense for the **h** *place:* according to 6944
31:14 the sabbath therefore; for it *is* **h** unto you: 6944
31:15 *is* the sabbath of rest, **h** to the LORD: 6944
35: 2 on the seventh day there shall be to you a **h** 6944
35:19 to do service in the **h** *place*, the holy 6944
35:19 to do service in the holy *place*, the **h** 6944
35:21 for all his service, and for the **h** garments. 6944
37:29 he made the **h** anointing oil, and the pure 6944
38:24 the **h** *place*, even the gold of the offering, 6944
39: 1 to do service in the **h** *place*, and made 6944
39: 1 and made the **h** garments for Aaron; 6944
39:30 they made the plate of the **h** crown *of* pure 6944
39:41 The clothes of service to do service in the **h** 6944
39:41 and the **h** garments for Aaron the priest, 6944
40: 9 and all the vessels thereof: and it shall be **h**. 6944
40:10 and it shall be an altar **most h**. 6944+6944
40:13 thou shalt put upon Aaron the **h** garments, 6944
Lev 2: 3 *it is a thing* **most h** of the offerings 6944+6944
2:10 *it is* a **thing most h** of the offerings 6944+6944
5:15 in the **h** *things* of the LORD; 6944
5:16 the harm that he hath done in the **h** *thing*, 6944
6:16 bread shall it be eaten in the **h** place; 6918
6:17 it *is* **most h**, as *is* the sin offering, 6944+6944
6:18 every one that toucheth them shall be **h**. 6942
6:25 before the LORD: it *is* **most h**. 6944+6944
6:26 in the **h** place shall it be eaten, in the court 6918
6:27 shall touch the flesh thereof shall be **h**: 6942
6:27 whereon it was sprinkled in the **h** place. 6918
6:29 priests shall eat thereof: it *is* **most h**. 6944+6944
6:30 *withal* in the **h** *place*, shall be eaten: 6944
7: 1 of the trespass offering: it *is* **most h**. 6944+6944
7: 6 it shall be eaten in the **h** place: it *is* most 6918
7: 6 eaten in the holy place: it *is* **most h**. 6944+6944
8: 9 did he put the golden plate, the **h** crown; 6944
10:10 that *ye* may put difference between **h** and 6944
10:12 beside the altar: for it *is* **most h**: 6944+6944
10:13 ye shall eat it in the **h** place, because it *is* 6918
10:17 ye not eaten the sin offering in the **h** place, 6944
10:17 seeing it *is* **most h**, and *God* hath 6944+6944
10:18 **h** *place:* ye should indeed have eaten it in 6944
10:18 eaten it in the **h** *place*, as I commanded. 6944
11:44 sanctify yourselves, and ye shall be **h**; 6918
11:44 and ye shall be holy; for I *am* **h**: 6918
11:45 ye shall therefore be **h**, for I *am* holy. 6918
11:45 ye shall therefore be holy, for I *am* **h**. 6918
14:13 and the burnt offering, in the **h** place: 6944
14:13 *is* the trespass offering: it *is* **most h**: 6944+6944
16: 2 that he come not at all times into the **h** 6944
16: 3 Thus shall Aaron come into the **h** *place:* 6944
16: 4 He shall put on the **h** linen coat, and 6944
16: 4 these *are* **h** garments; therefore shall he 6944
16:16 he shall make an atonement for the **h** *place*, 6944
16:17 atonement in the **h** *place*, until he come out, 6944
16:20 made an end of reconciling the **h** *place*, 6944
16:23 which he put on when he went into the **h** 6944
16:24 he shall wash his flesh with water in the **h** 6918
16:27 **h** *place*, shall *one* carry forth without 6944
16:32 on the linen clothes, *even* the **h** garments: 6944
16:33 he shall make an atonement for the **h** 6944
19: 2 of Israel, and say unto them, Ye shall be **h**: 6918
19: 2 be holy: for I the LORD your God *am* **h**. 6918
19:24 shall be **h** to praise the LORD *withal*. 6944
20: 3 my sanctuary, and to profane my **h** name. 6944
20: 7 Sanctify yourselves therefore, and be ye **h**: 6918
20:26 ye shall be **h** unto me: for I the LORD *am* 6918
20:26 for I the LORD *am* **h**, and have severed 6918
21: 6 They shall be **h** unto their God, and 6918
21: 6 they do offer: therefore they shall be **h**. 6944
21: 7 from her husband: for he *is* **h** unto his God. 6918
21: 8 he shall be **h** unto thee: for I the LORD, 6918
21: 8 for I the LORD, which sanctify you, *am* **h**. 6918
21:22 *both* of the **most h**, and of the holy. 6944+6944
21:22 *both* of the most holy, and of the **h**. 6944
22: 2 that they separate themselves from the **h** 6944
22: 2 that they profane not my **h** name *in those* 6944
22: 3 that goeth unto the **h** *things* which 6944
22: 4 he shall not eat of the **h** *things*, until he be 6944
22: 6 shall not eat of the **h** *things*, unless he wash 6944
22: 7 shall afterward eat of the **h** *things;* because 6944
22:10 There shall no stranger eat *of* the **h** *thing:* a 6944
22:10 a hired servant, shall not eat *of* the **h** *thing*. 6944
22:12 she may not eat of an offering of the **h** 6944
22:14 if a man eat *of* the **h** *thing* unwittingly, then 6944
22:14 shall give *it* unto the priest with the **h** 6944
22:15 they shall not profane the **h** *things* of 6944
22:16 when they eat their **h** *things:* for I 6944
22:32 Neither shall ye profane my **h** name; but 6944
23: 2 which ye shall proclaim *to be* **h** 6944
23: 3 day *is* the sabbath of rest, a **h** convocation; 6944
23: 4 feasts of the LORD, *even* **h** convocations, 6944
23: 7 In the first day ye shall have a **h** 6944
23: 8 in the seventh day *is* a **h** convocation: 6944
23:20 they shall be **h** to the LORD for the priest. 6944
23:21 *that* it may be a **h** convocation unto you: 6944
23:24 of blowing of trumpets, a **h** convocation. 6944
23:27 it shall be a **h** convocation unto you; and 6944
23:35 On the first day *shall be* a **h** convocation: 6944
23:36 on the eighth day shall be a **h** convocation 6944
23:37 which ye shall proclaim *to be* **h** 6944
24: 9 and they shall eat it in the **h** place: 6918
24: 9 for it *is* **most h** unto him of 6944+6944
25:12 For it *is* the jubile; it shall be **h** unto you: 6944

Lev 27: 9 giveth of such unto the LORD shall be **h**. 6944
27:10 then it and the exchange thereof shall be **h**. 6944
27:14 when a man shall sanctify his house *to be* **h** 6944
27:21 shall be **h** unto the LORD, as a field 6944
27:23 in that day, *as* a **h** *thing* unto the LORD. 6944
27:28 every devoted thing *is* **most h** unto 6944+6944
27:30 *is* the LORD'S: *it is* **h** unto the LORD. 6944
27:32 the tenth shall be **h** unto the LORD. 6944
27:33 both it and the change thereof shall be **h**; 6944
Nu 4: 4 *about* the **most h** *things:* 6944+6944
4:15 they shall not touch *any* **h** *thing*, lest they 6944
4:19 unto the **most h** *things:* Aaron 6944+6944
4:20 they shall not go in to see when the **h** 6944
5: 9 every offering of all the **h** *things* of 6944
5:17 the priest shall take **h** water in an earthen 6918
6: 5 he shall be **h**, *and* shall let the locks of 6918
6: 8 All the days of his separation he *is* **h** unto 6918
6:20 this *is* **h** for the priest, with the wave breast 6944
15:40 and be **h** unto your God. 6918
16: 3 seeing all the congregation *are* **h**, every one 6918
16: 5 will shew who *are* his, and *who is* **h**; 6918
16: 7 the LORD doth choose, he *shall be* **h**: 6918
18: 9 This shall be thine of the **most h** 6944+6944
18: 9 *be* **most h** for thee and for thy sons. 6944+6944
18:10 In the **most h** *place* shalt thou eat it; 6944+6944
18:10 male shall eat it: it shall be **h** unto thee. 6944
18:17 of a goat, thou shalt not redeem; they *are* **h**: 6944
18:19 All the heave offerings of the **h** *things*, 6944
18:32 neither shall ye pollute the **h** *things* of 6944
28: 7 in the **h** *place* shalt thou cause the strong 6944
28:18 In the first day *shall be* a **h** convocation; 6944
28:25 on the seventh day ye shall have a **h** 6944
28:26 after your weeks *be out*, ye shall have a **h** 6944
29: 1 the month, ye shall have a **h** convocation; 6944
29: 7 *day* of this seventh month a **h** convocation; 6944
29:12 month ye shall have a **h** convocation; 6944
31: 6 with the **h** instruments, and the trumpets to 6944
35:25 which was anointed with the **h** oil. 6944
Dt 7: 6 For thou *art* a **h** people unto the LORD 6918
12:26 Only thy **h** *things* which thou hast, and 6944
14: 2 For thou *art* a **h** people unto the LORD 6918
14:21 for thou *art* a **h** people unto the LORD thy 6918
23:14 before thee; therefore shall thy camp be **h**: 6918
26:15 Look down from thy **h** habitation, 6944
26:19 that thou mayest be a **h** people unto 6918
28: 9 The LORD shall establish thee a **h** people 6918
33: 8 and thy Urim *be* with thy **h** one, 2623
Jos 5:15 for the place whereon thou standest *is* **h**. 6944
24:19 for he *is* a **h** God; he *is* a jealous God; 6918
1Sa 2: 2 *There is* none **h** as the LORD: for *there is* 6918
6:20 Who is able to stand before this **h** LORD 6918
21: 5 and the vessels of the young men are **h**, and 6944
1Ki 6:16 *even* for the **most h** *place*. 6944+6944
7:50 the **most h** *place, and* for the doors 6944+6944
8: 4 all the **h** vessels that *were* in the tabernacle, 6944
8: 6 to the **most h** *place*, even under 6944+6944
8: 8 seen out in the **h** *place* before the oracle, 6944
8:10 when the priests were come out of the **h** 6944
2Ki 4: 9 I perceive that this *is* a **h** man of God, 6918
19:22 on high? *even* against the **H One** of Israel. 6918
1Ch 6:49 for all the work of the *place* **most h**, 6944+6944
16:10 Glory ye in his **h** name: let the heart of 6944
16:35 that *we* may give thanks to thy **h** name, 6944
22:19 of the LORD, and the **h** vessels of God, 6944
23:13 should sanctify the **most h** *things*, he 6944+6944
23:28 in the purifying of all **h** *things*, and 6944
23:32 the charge of the **h** *place*, and the charge of 6944
29: 3 above all *that* I have prepared for the **h** 6944
29:16 for thine **h** name *cometh* of thine hand, 6944
2Ch 3: 8 he made the **most h** house, the length 6944+6944
3:10 in the **most h** house he made two 6944+6944
4:22 doors thereof for the **most h** *place*, 6944+6944
5: 5 all the **h** vessels that *were* in the tabernacle, 6944
5: 7 into the **most h** *place*, even under 6944+6944
5:11 when the priests were come out of the **h** 6944
8:11 because *the places are* **h**, whereunto the ark 6944
23: 6 the Levites; they shall go in, for they *are* **h**: 6944
29: 5 carry forth the filthiness out of the **h** *place*. 6944
29: 7 in the **h** *place* unto the God of Israel. 6944
30:27 their prayer came *up* to his **h dwelling** 6944
31: 6 the tithe of **h** *things* which were 6944
31:14 the LORD, and the **most h** *things*. 6944+6944
35: 3 all Israel, which were **h** unto the LORD, 6918
35: 3 Put the **h** ark in the house which Solomon 6944
35: 5 stand in the **h** *place* according to 6944
35:13 the *other* **h** *offerings* sod they in pots, and 6944
Ezr 2:63 **most h** *things* till there stood *up* a 6944+6944
8:28 said unto them, Ye *are* **h** unto the LORD; 6944
8:28 the vessels *are* **h** also; and the silver and 6944
9: 2 that the **h** seed have mingled themselves 6944
9: 8 and to give us a nail in his **h** place, 6944
Ne 7:65 **most h** *things*, till there stood *up* a 6944+6944
8: 9 *This* day *is* **h** unto the LORD your God; 6918
8:10 for *this* day *is* **h** unto our Lord: neither be 6918
8:11 Hold your peace, for the day *is* **h**; 6918
9:14 madest known unto them thy **h** sabbath, 6944
10:31 *it* of them on the sabbath, or on the **h** day: 6944
10:33 for the **h** *things*, and for the sin offerings to 6944
11: 1 one of ten to dwell in Jerusalem the **h** city, 6944
11:18 All the Levites in the **h** city *were* two 6944
12:47 they sanctified ***h*** *things* unto the Levites; NIH
Job 6:10 not concealed the words of the **H One**. 6918
Ps 2: 6 Yet have I set my king upon my **h** hill of 6944
3: 4 my voice, and he heard me out of his **h** hill. 6944
5: 7 in thy fear will I worship toward thy **h** 6944
11: 4 The LORD *is* in his **h** temple, 6944
15: 1 who shall dwell in thy **h** hill? 6944
16:10 neither wilt thou suffer thine **H One** to see 2623
20: 6 he will hear him from his **h** heaven with 6944
22: 3 thou *art* **h**, O thou that inhabitest the praises 6918
24: 3 and who shall stand in his **h** place? 6944
28: 2 when I lift up my hands toward thy **h** 6944
33:21 because we have trusted in his **h** name. 6944
43: 3 let them bring me unto thy **h** hill, and to thy 6944
46: 4 the **h** *place* of the tabernacles of the most 6918

Ps 51:11 and take not thy **h** Spirit from me. 6944
65: 4 of thy house, *even* of thy **h** temple. 6918
68: 5 of the widows, *is* God in his **h** habitation. 6944
68:17 *is* among them, *as in* Sinai, in the **h** *place*. 6944
68:35 O God, *thou art* terrible out of thy **h places**: 4720
71:22 sing with the harp, O thou **H One** of Israel. 6918
78:41 and limited the **H One** of Israel. 6918
79: 1 thy **h** temple have they defiled; they have 6944
86: 2 Preserve my soul; for I *am* **h**: O thou my 2623
87: 1 His foundation *is* in the **h** mountains. 6944
89:18 and the **H One** of Israel *is* our king. 6918
89:19 thou spakest in vision to thy **h one**, and 2623
89:20 with my **h** oil have I anointed him: 6944
98: 1 and his **h** arm, hath gotten him the victory. 6944
99: 3 thy great and terrible name; *for* it *is* **h**. 6918
99: 5 and worship at his footstool; *for* he *is* **h**. 6918
99: 9 LORD our God, and worship at his **h** hill; 6944
99: 9 his holy hill; for the LORD our God *is* **h**. 6918
103: 1 and all that is within me, *bless* his **h** name. 6944
105: 3 Glory ye in his **h** name: let the heart of 6944
105:42 For he remembered his **h** promise, 6944
106:47 to give thanks unto thy **h** name, *and* 6944
111: 9 for ever: **h** and reverend *is* his name. 6918
138: 2 I will worship toward thy **h** temple, and 6944
145:17 in all his ways, and **h** in all his works. 2623
145:21 let all flesh bless his **h** name for ever and 6944
Pr 9:10 the knowledge of the **h** *is* understanding. 6918
20:25 to the man *who* devoureth *that which is* **h**, 6944
30: 3 nor have the knowledge of the **h**. 6918
Ecc 8:10 had come and gone from the place of the **h**, 6918
Isa 1: 4 they have provoked the **H One** of Israel 6918
4: 3 remaineth in Jerusalem, shall be called **h**, 6918
5:16 God that is **h** shall be sanctified in 6918
5:19 let the counsel of the **H One** of Israel draw 6918
5:24 despised the word of the **H One** of Israel. 6918
6: 3 said, **H**, holy, holy, *is* the LORD of hosts: 6918
6: 3 said, Holy, **h**, holy, *is* the LORD of hosts: 6918
6: 3 said, Holy, holy, **h**, *is* the LORD of hosts: 6918
6:13 *so* the **h** seed *shall be* the substance thereof. 6944
10:17 be for a fire, and his **H One** for a flame: 6918
10:20 the LORD, the **H One** of Israel, in truth. 6918
11: 9 They shall not hurt nor destroy in all my **h** 6944
12: 6 for great *is* the **H One** of Israel in the midst 6918
17: 7 his eyes shall have respect to the **H One** of 6918
27:13 shall worship the LORD in the **h** mount at 6944
29:19 men shall rejoice in the **H One** of Israel. 6918
29:23 sanctify the **H One** of Jacob, and shall fear 6918
30:11 cause the **H One** of Israel to cease from 6918
30:12 Wherefore thus saith the **H One** of Israel, 6918
30:15 saith the Lord GOD, the **H One** of Israel; 6918
30:29 as *in* the night when a **h** solemnity is **kept**; 6942
31: 1 they look not unto the **H One** of Israel, 6918
37:23 on high? *even* against the **H One** of Israel. 6918
40:25 or shall I be equal? saith the **H One**. 6918
41:14 and thy redeemer, the **H One** of Israel. 6918
41:16 *and* shalt glory in the **H One** of Israel. 6918
41:20 and the **H One** of Israel hath created it. 6918
43: 3 thy God, the **H One** of Israel, thy Saviour: 6918
43:14 your redeemer, the **H One** of Israel; 6918
43:15 I *am* the LORD, your **H One**, the creator 6918
45:11 the **H One** of Israel, and his maker, 6918
47: 4 of hosts *is* his name, the **H One** of Israel. 6918
48: 2 For they call themselves of the **h** city, and 6944
48:17 thy redeemer, the **H One** of Israel; 6918
49: 7 the redeemer of Israel, *and* his **H One**, 6918
49: 7 *and* the **H One** of Israel, and he shall 6918
52: 1 beautiful garments, O Jerusalem, the **h** city: 6944
52:10 The LORD hath made bare his **h** arm in 6944
54: 5 and thy redeemer the **H One** of Israel; 6918
55: 5 thy God, and for the **H One** of Israel; 6918
56: 7 Even them will I bring to my **h** mountain, 6944
57:13 the land, and shall inherit my **h** mountain; 6944
57:15 that inhabiteth eternity, whose name *is* **H**; 6918
57:15 **h** *place*, with him also *that is* of a contrite 6918
58:13 *from* doing thy pleasure on my **h** day; 6944
58:13 a delight, the **h** of the LORD, honourable; 6918
60: 9 to the **H One** of Israel, because he hath 6918
60:14 The Zion of the **H One** of Israel. 6918
62:12 they shall call them, The **h** people, 6944
63:10 they rebelled, and vexed his **h** Spirit: 6944
63:11 where *is* he that put his **h** Spirit within him? 6944
64:10 Thy **h** cities are a wilderness, Zion is a 6944
64:11 Our **h** and our beautiful house, where our 6944
65:11 that forget my **h** mountain, that prepare a 6944
65:25 They shall not hurt nor destroy in all my **h** 6944
66:20 to my **h** mountain Jerusalem, saith 6944
Jer 11:15 and the **h** flesh is passed from thee? 6944
25:30 and utter his voice from his **h** habitation; 6944
31:40 the east, *shall be* **h** unto the LORD; 6944
50:29 the LORD, against the **H One** of Israel. 6918
51: 5 filled *with* sin against the **H One** of Israel. 6918
Eze 7:24 to cease; and their **h places** shall be defiled. 6942
20:39 pollute ye my **h** name no more with your 6944
20:40 For in mine **h** mountain, in the mountain of 6944
20:40 of your oblations, with all your **h** *things*. 6944
21: 2 drop *thy word* toward the **h places**, and 4720
22: 8 Thou hast despised mine **h** *things*, and hast 6944
22:26 have profaned mine **h** *things*: they have put 6944
22:26 they have put no difference between the **h** 6944
28:14 *so*: thou wast upon the **h** mountain of God; 6944
36:20 they went, they profaned my **h** name, 6944
36:21 I had pity for mine **h** name, which 6944
36:22 house of Israel, but for mine **h** name's sake, 6944
36:38 As the **h** flock, as the flock of Jerusalem in 6944
39: 7 So will I make my **h** name known in 6944
39: 7 I will not let *them* pollute my **h** name any 6944
39: 7 that I *am* the LORD, the **H One** in Israel. 6918
39:25 and will be jealous for my **h** name; 6944
41: 4 unto me, This *is* the **most h** *place*. 6944+6944
42:13 the separate place, they *be* **h** chambers, 6944
42:13 **most h** *things*: there shall they lay 6944+6944
42:13 shall they lay the **most h** *things*, 6944+6944
42:13 and the trespass offering; for the place *is* **h**. 6918
42:14 shall they not go out of the **h** *place* into 6944
42:14 for they *are* **h**; and shall put on other 6944
Eze 43: 7 my **h** name, shall the house of Israel no 6944
43: 8 they have even defiled my **h** name by their 6944
43:12 thereof round about *shall be* **most h**. 6944+6944
44: 8 ye have not kept the charge of mine **h** 6944
44:13 nor to come near to any of my **h** *things*, in 6944
44:13 my holy *things*, in the **most h** *place*: 6944+6944
44:19 lay them in the **h** chambers, and they shall 6944
44:23 my people *the difference* between the **h** 6944
45: 1 unto the LORD, a **h** *portion* of the land: 6944
45: 1 This *shall be* **h** in all the borders thereof 6944
45: 3 the sanctuary *and* the **most h** *place*. 6944+6944
45: 4 The **h** *portion* of the land shall be for 6944
45: 4 and a **h place** for the sanctuary. 4720
45: 6 over against the oblation of the **h** *portion*: it 6944
45: 7 on the other side of the oblation of the **h** 6944
45: 7 before the oblation of the **h** *portion*, and 6944
46:19 into the **h** chambers of the priests, 6944
48:10 *even* for the priests, shall be *this* **h** oblation; 6944
48:12 **most h** by the border of the Levites. 6944+6944
48:14 of the land: for *it is* **h** unto the LORD. 6944
48:18 **h** *portion shall be* ten thousand eastward, 6944
48:18 it shall be over against the oblation of the **h** 6944
48:20 ye shall offer the **h** oblation foursquare, 6944
48:21 one side and on the other of the **h** oblation, 6944
48:21 it shall be the **h** oblation; and the sanctuary 6944
Da 4: 8 and in whom *is* the spirit of the **h** gods: 6922
4: 9 I know that the spirit of the **h** gods *is* in 6922
4:13 and a **h one** came down from heaven; 6922
4:17 and the demand *by* the word of the **h ones**: 6922
4:18 for the spirit of the **h** gods *is* in thee. 6922
4:23 and a **h one** coming down from heaven, 6922
5:11 in whom *is* the spirit of the **h** gods; 6922
8:24 shall destroy the mighty and the **h** people. 6918
9:16 from thy city Jerusalem, thy **h** mountain: 6944
9:20 my God for the **h** mountain of my God; 6944
9:24 upon thy people and upon thy **h** city, 6944
9:24 prophecy, and to anoint the **most H**. 6944+6944
11:28 his heart *shall be* against the **h** covenant; 6944
11:30 have indignation against the **h** covenant: 6944
11:30 with them that forsake the **h** covenant. 6944
11:45 the seas in the glorious **h** mountain; 6944
12: 7 to scatter the power of the **h** people, 6944
Hos 11: 9 not man; the **H One** in the midst of thee: 6918
Joel 2: 1 and sound an alarm in my **h** mountain: 6944
3:17 God dwelling in Zion, my **h** mountain: 6944
3:17 shall Jerusalem be **h**, and there shall no 6944
Am 2: 7 unto the *same* maid, to profane my **h** name: 6944
Ob 1:16 For as ye have drunk upon my **h** mountain, 6944
Jnh 2: 4 yet I will look again toward thy **h** temple. 6944
2: 7 came in unto thee, into thine **h** temple. 6944
Mic 1: 2 against you, the Lord from his **h** temple. 6944
Hab 1:12 O LORD my God, mine **H One**? 6918
2:20 the LORD *is* in his **h** temple: let all 6944
3: 3 and the **H One** from mount Paran. 6918
Zep 3:11 be haughty because of my **h** mountain. 6944
Hag 2:12 If one bear **h** flesh in the skirt of his 6944
2:12 or wine, or oil, or any meat, shall it be **h**? 6942
Zec 2:12 shall inherit Judah his portion in the **h** land, 6944
2:13 for he is raised up out of his **h** habitation. 6944
8: 3 the mountain of the LORD of hosts the **h** 6944
Mt 1:18 she was found with child of the **H** Ghost. *40*
1:20 for that which is conceived in her is of the **H** *40*
3:11 he shall baptize you with the **H** Ghost, and *40*
4: 5 Then the devil taketh him *up* into the **h** city, *40*
7: 6 Give not that which is **h** unto the dogs, *40*
12:31 the blasphemy against the ***H*** Ghost shall not NIG
12:32 but whosoever speaketh against the **H** Ghost, *40*
24:15 stand in the **h** place, (whoso readeth, let him *40*
25:31 and all the **h** angels with him, then shall he sit *40*
27:53 and went into the **h** city, and appeared unto *40*
28:19 and of the Son, and of the **H** Ghost: *40*
Mk 1: 8 but he shall baptize you with the **H** Ghost. *40*
1:24 I know thee who thou art, the **H One** of God. *40*
3:29 But he that shall blaspheme against the **H** *40*
6:20 knowing that he *was* a just man and a **h**, and *40*
8:38 in the glory of his Father with the **h** angels. *40*
12:36 For David himself said by the **H** Ghost, *40*
13:11 for it is not ye that speak, but the **H** Ghost. *40*
Lk 1:15 and he shall be filled with the **H** Ghost, *40*
1:35 The **H** Ghost shall come upon thee, and *40*
1:35 also *that* **h thing** which shall be born of thee *40*
1:41 and Elisabeth was filled with the **H** Ghost: *40*
1:49 done to me great things; and **h** *is* his name. *40*
1:67 And his father Zacharias was filled with the **H** *40*
1:70 (As he spake by the mouth of his **h** prophets, *40*
1:72 our fathers, and to remember his **h** covenant; *40*
2:23 the womb shall be called **h** to the Lord;) *40*
2:25 of Israel: and the **H** Ghost was upon him. *40*
2:26 And it was revealed unto him by the **H** Ghost, *40*
3:16 he shall baptize you with the **H** Ghost and *40*
3:22 And the **H** Ghost descended in a bodily shape *40*
4: 1 And Jesus being full of the **H** Ghost returned *40*
4:34 I know thee who thou art, the **H One** of God. *40*
9:26 and *in his* Father's, and of the **h** angels. *40*
11:13 Father give the **H** Spirit to them that ask him? *40*
12:10 unto him that blasphemeth against the **H** *40*
12:12 For the **H** Ghost shall teach you in the same *40*
Jn 1:33 the same is he which baptizeth with the **H** *40*
7:39 for the **H** Ghost was not yet *given*; because *40*
14:26 But the Comforter, *which is* the **H** Ghost, *40*
17:11 **H** Father, keep through thine own name those *40*
20:22 and saith unto them, Receive ye the **H** Ghost: *40*
Ac 1: 2 after that he through the **H** Ghost had given *40*
1: 5 ye shall be baptized with the **H** Ghost not *40*
1: 8 after that the **H** Ghost is come upon you: *40*
1:16 which the **H** Ghost by the mouth of David *40*
2: 4 And they were all filled with the **H** Ghost, *40*
2:27 neither wilt thou suffer thine **H One** to see *3741*
2:33 of the Father the promise of the **H** Ghost, *40*
2:38 and ye shall receive the gift of the **H** Ghost. *40*
3:14 But ye denied the **H One** and the Just, and *40*
3:21 of all his **h** prophets since the world began. *40*
4: 8 Then Peter, filled with the **H** Ghost, said unto *40*
4:27 For of a truth against thy **h** child Jesus, *40*
4:30 wonders may be done by the name of thy **h** *40*
Ac 4:31 and they were all filled with the **H** Ghost, and *40*
5: 3 hath Satan filled thine heart to lie to the **H** *40*
5:32 and *so is* also the **H** Ghost, whom God hath *40*
6: 3 full of the **H** Ghost and wisdom, whom we *40*
6: 5 a man full of faith and of the **H** Ghost, and *40*
6:13 blasphemous words against this **h** place, *40*
7:33 for the place where thou standest is **h** ground. *40*
7:51 and ears, ye do always resist the **H** Ghost: *40*
7:55 But he, being full of the **H** Ghost, looked up *40*
8:15 for them, that they might receive the **H** Ghost: *40*
8:17 on them, and they received the **H** Ghost. *40*
8:18 of the apostles' hands the **H** Ghost was given, *40*
8:19 I lay hands, he may receive the **H** Ghost. *40*
9:17 thy sight, and be filled with the **H** Ghost. *40*
9:31 and in the comfort of the **H** Ghost, *40*
10:22 was warned from God by a **h** angel to send *40*
10:38 anointed Jesus of Nazareth with the **H** Ghost *40*
10:44 the **H** Ghost fell on all them which heard *40*
10:45 also was poured out the gift of the **H** Ghost. *40*
10:47 which have received the **H** Ghost as well as *40*
11:15 as I began to speak, the **H** Ghost fell on them, *40*
11:16 but ye shall be baptized with the **H** Ghost. *40*
11:24 and full of the **H** Ghost and of faith: *40*
13: 2 and fasted, the **H** Ghost said, Separate me *40*
13: 4 So they, being sent forth by the **H** Ghost, *40*
13: 9 filled with the **H** Ghost, set his eyes on him, *40*
13:35 not suffer thine **H One** to see corruption. *3741*
13:52 were filled with joy, and with the **H** Ghost. *40*
15: 8 bare them witness, giving them the **H** Ghost, *40*
15:28 For it seemed good to the **H** Ghost, and to us, *40*
16: 6 were forbidden of the **H** Ghost to preach *40*
19: 2 Have ye received the **H** Ghost since ye *40*
19: 2 much as heard whether there be *any* **H** Ghost. *40*
19: 6 hands upon them, the **H** Ghost came on them; *40*
20:23 Save that the **H** Ghost witnesseth in every *40*
20:28 over the which the **H** Ghost hath made you *40*
21:11 and feet, and said, Thus saith the **H** Ghost, *40*
21:28 into the temple, and hath polluted this **h** place. *40*
28:25 Well spake the **H** Ghost by Esaias the prophet *40*
Ro 1: 2 afore by his prophets in the **h** scriptures,) *40*
5: 5 hearts by the **H** Ghost which is given unto us. *40*
7:12 Wherefore the law *is* **h**, and *40*
7:12 and the commandment **h**, and just, and good. *40*
9: 1 also bearing me witness in the **H** Ghost, *40*
11:16 For if the firstfruit *be* **h**, the lump *is* also *holy*: *40*
11:16 the lump *is* also ***h***: and if the root *be* holy, NIG
11:16 the lump *is* also *holy*: and if the root *be* **h**, so *40*
12: 1 **h**, acceptable unto God, *which is* your *40*
14:17 and peace, and joy in the **H** Ghost. *40*
15:13 in hope, through the power of the **H** Ghost. *40*
15:16 being sanctified by the **H** Ghost. *40*
16:16 Salute one another with a **h** kiss. The *40*
1Co 2:13 but which the **H** Ghost teacheth; *40*
3:17 for the temple of God is **h**, which *temple* ye *40*
6:19 is the temple of the **H** Ghost which is in you, *40*
7:14 your children unclean; but now are they **h**. *40*
7:34 that she may be **h** both in body and in spirit: *40*
9:13 **h** *things* live of *the things of* the temple? *2413*
12: 3 say that Jesus is the Lord, but by the **H** Ghost. *40*
16:20 greet you. Greet ye one another with a **h** kiss. *40*
2Co 6: 6 by kindness, by the **H** Ghost, *40*
13:12 Greet one another with a **h** kiss. *40*
13:14 and the communion of the **H** Ghost, *be* with *40*
Eph 1: 4 that we should be **h** and without blame before *40*
1:13 ye were sealed with *that* **h** Spirit of promise, *40*
2:21 together groweth unto a **h** temple in the Lord: *40*
3: 5 as it is now revealed unto his **h** apostles and *40*
4:30 And grieve not the **h** Spirit of God, *40*
5:27 or any such *thing*; but that it should be **h** and *40*
Col 1:22 to present you **h** and unblameable and *40*
3:12 **h** and beloved, bowels of mercies, kindness, *40*
1Th 1: 5 and in the **H** Ghost, and in much assurance; *40*
1: 6 in much affliction, with joy of the **H** Ghost: *40*
4: 8 God, who hath also given unto us his **h** Spirit. *40*
5:26 Greet all the brethren with a **h** kiss. *40*
5:27 *this* epistle be read unto all the **h** brethren. *40*
1Ti 2: 8 lifting up **h** hands, without wrath and *3741*
2Ti 1: 9 hath saved us, and called *us* with a **h** calling, *40*
1:14 keep by the **H** Ghost which dwelleth in us. *40*
3:15 a child thou hast known the **h** scriptures, *2413*
Tit 1: 8 of good *men*, sober, just, **h**, temperate; *3741*
3: 5 of regeneration, and renewing of the **H** Ghost; *40*
Heb 2: 4 with divers miracles, and gifts of the **H** Ghost, *40*
3: 1 Wherefore, **h** brethren, partakers of *40*
3: 7 Wherefore, as the **H** Ghost saith, To day if ye *40*
6: 4 and were made partakers of the **H** Ghost, *40*
7:26 *who is* **h**, harmless, undefiled, *3741*
9: 8 The **H** Ghost this signifying, that the way into *40*
9:12 **h** *place*, having obtained eternal redemption *40*
9:24 For Christ is not entered into the **h** *places* *40*
9:25 as the high priest entereth into the **h** *place* *40*
10:15 *Whereof* the **H** Ghost also is a witness to us: *40*
1Pe 1:12 you with the **H** Ghost sent *down* from heaven; *40*
1:15 But as he which hath called you is **h**, so be ye *40*
1:15 so be ye **h** in all *manner of* conversation; *40*
1:16 Because it is written, Be ye **h**; for I am holy. *40*
1:16 Because it is written, Be ye holy; for I am **h**. *40*
2: 5 are built *up* a spiritual house, a **h** priesthood, *40*
2: 9 a **h** nation, a peculiar people; *40*
3: 5 For after this manner in the old time the **h** *40*
2Pe 1:18 when we were with him in the **h** mount. *40*
1:21 **h** men of God spake *as they were* moved by NIG
1:21 spake *as they were* moved by the **H** Ghost. *40*
2:21 after they have known *it*, to turn from the **h** *40*
3: 2 which were spoken before by the **h** prophets, *40*
3:11 *of persons* ought ye to be in all **h** conversation *40*
1Jn 2:20 But ye have an unction from the **H One**, and *40*
5: 7 the Father, the Word, and the **H** Ghost: *40*
Jude 1:20 building up yourselves on your **most h** faith, *40*
1:20 your most holy faith, praying in the **H** Ghost, *40*
Rev 3: 7 These *things* saith he *that is* **h**, he *that is* true, *40*
4: 8 rest not day and night, saying, **H**, holy, holy, *40*
4: 8 rest not day and night, saying, Holy, **h**, holy, *40*
4: 8 rest not day and night, saying, Holy, holy, **h**, *40*
6:10 saying, How long, O Lord, **h** and true, *40*

Rev 11: 2 the **h** city shall they tread under foot forty *and* 40
14:10 and brimstone in the presence of the **h** angels, 40
15: 4 for *thou* only *art* **h**: for all nations shall 3741
18:20 *thou* heaven, and ye **h** apostles and prophets; 40
20: 6 **h** *is* he that hath part in the first resurrection: 40
21: 2 And I John saw the **h** city, new Jerusalem, 40
21:10 shewed me *that* great city, the **h** Jerusalem, 40
22: 6 the Lord God of the **h** prophets sent his angel 40
22:11 and *he that is* **h**, let him be holy still. 40
22:11 and *he that is* holy, let him be **h** still. 37
22:19 and out of the **h** city, and *from* the *things* 40

HOLY SPIRIT See also HOLY GHOST

HOLYDAY (2) [DAY, HOLY]
Ps 42: 4 and praise, *with* a multitude that **kept h**. 2287
Col 2:16 or in respect of a **h**, or of the new moon, or 1859

HOMAM (1)
1Ch 1:39 the sons of Lotan; Hori, and **H**: and 1950

HOME (51) [HOMEBORN]
Ge 39:16 his garment by her, until his lord came **h**. 1004
43:16 Bring *these* men **h**, and slay, and 1004
43:26 when Joseph came **h**, they brought him 1004
Ex 9:19 shall not be brought **h**, the hail shall come 1004
Lev 18: 9 *whether she be* born at **h**, or born abroad, 1004
Dt 21:12 thou shalt bring her **h** to thine house; and NIH
24: 5 *but* he shall be free at **h** one year, and 1004
Jos 2:18 and all thy father's household, **h** unto thee. 1004
Jdg 11: 9 If ye bring me ***h*** again to fight against NIH
19: 9 early on your way, that thou mayest go **h**. 168
Ru 1:21 the LORD hath brought me ***h*** again empty: NIH
1Sa 2:20 And they went unto their own **h**. 4725
6: 7 and bring their calves **h** from them: 1004
6:10 to the cart, and shut up their calves at **h**: 1004
10:26 Saul also went **h** to Gibeah; and there went 1004
18: 2 would let him **go** no more **h** *to* his father's 7725
24:22 Saul went **h**; but David and his men gat 1004
2Sa 13: 7 David sent **h** to Tamar, saying, Go now *to* 1004
14:13 in that the king doth not fetch **h** again his NIH
17:23 arose, and gat him ***h*** to his house, to his NIH
1Ki 5:14 were in Lebanon, *and* two months at **h**: 1004
13: 7 Come **h** with me, and refresh *thyself*, and 1004
13:15 unto him, Come **h** with me, and eat bread. 1004
2Ki 14:10 glory *of this*, and tarry at **h**: for why 1004
1Ch 13:12 How shall I bring the ark of God ***h*** to me? NIH
13:13 So David brought not the ark ***h*** to himself to NIH
2Ch 25:10 to go **h** *again:* wherefore their anger was 4725
25:10 and they returned **h** in great anger. 4725
25:19 abide now at **h**; why shouldest thou meddle 1004
Est 5:10 when he came **h**, he sent and called for his 1004
Job 39:12 that he will **bring h** thy seed, and gather *it* 7725
Ps 68:12 she that tarried at **h** divided the spoil. 1004
Pr 7:19 For the goodman *is* not at **h**, he is gone a 1004
7:20 *and* will come **h** at the day appointed. 1004
Ecc 12: 5 because man goeth to his long **h**, and 1004
Jer 39:14 son of Shaphan, that *he* should carry him **h**: 1004
La 1:20 the sword bereaveth, at **h** *there is* as death. 1004
Hab 2: 5 *he is* a proud man, neither **keepeth at h**, 5115
Hag 1: 9 when ye brought *it* **h**, I did blow upon it. 1004
Mt 8: 6 my servant lieth at **h** sick of the palsy, 3614
Mk 5:19 Go **h** to thy *friends,* and tell them how great 3624
Lk 9:61 them farewell, which are *at* **h** in my house. NIG
15: 6 And when he cometh **h**, he calleth together 3624
Jn 19:27 hour *that* disciple took her unto his own ***h***. NIG
20:10 went away again unto **their own h**. 1438
Ac 21: 6 and they returned **h** *again*. 1519+2398+3588
1Co 11:34 And if any *man* hunger, let him eat at **h**; 3624
14:35 any *thing,* let them ask their husbands at **h**: 3624
2Co 5: 6 whilst we are **at h** in the body, 1736
1Ti 5: 4 let them learn first to shew piety at **h**, and 3614
Tit 2: 5 *To be* discreet, chaste, **keepers at h**, good, 3626

HOMEBORN (2) [BEAR, HOME]
Ex 12:49 One law shall be to him that is **h**, and 249
Jer 2:14 *is* he a **h** *slave?* why is he spoiled? 1004+3211

HOMELAND See HABITATION; NATIVITY

HOMER (11) [HOMERS]
Lev 27:16 a **h** of barley seed *shall be valued* at fifty 2563
Isa 5:10 and the seed of a **h** shall yield an ephah. 2563
Eze 45:11 the bath may contain the tenth part of a **h**, 2563
45:11 and the ephah the tenth *part* of a **h**: 2563
45:11 the measure thereof shall be after the **h**. 2563
45:13 the sixth *part* of an ephah of a **h** of wheat, 2563
45:13 the sixth part of an ephah of a **h** of barley: 2563
45:14 out of the cor, *which is* a **h** of ten baths; 2563
45:14 a homer of ten baths; for ten baths *are* a **h**: 2563
Hos 3: 2 *for* a **h** of barley, and a half homer of 2563
3: 2 a homer of barley, and a **half h** of barley. 3963

HOMERS (1) [HOMER]
Nu 11:32 he that gathered least gathered ten **h**: and 2563

HONEST (7) [HONESTLY, HONESTY]
Lk 8:15 which in an **h** and good heart, having heard 2570
Ac 6: 3 ye out among you seven men **of h report**, 3140
Ro 12:17 Provide *things* **h** in the sight of all men. 2570
2Co 8:21 Providing *for* **h** *things,* not only in the sight 2570
13: 7 but that ye should do *that which is* **h**, 2570
Php 4: 8 whatsoever *things are* **h**, whatsoever *things* 4586
1Pe 2:12 Having your conversation **h** among 2570

HONESTLY (3) [HONEST]
Ro 13:13 Let us walk **h**, as in the day; not in rioting 2156
1Th 4:12 That ye may walk **h** toward them that are 2156
Heb 13:18 in all *things* willing to live **h**. 2573

HONESTY (1) [HONEST]
1Ti 2: 2 and peaceable life in all godliness and **h**. 4587

HONEY (56) [HONEYCOMB]
Ge 43:11 a little **h**, spices, and myrrh, nuts, and 1706
Ex 3: 8 unto a land flowing with milk and **h**; 1706
3:17 unto a land flowing with milk and **h**. 1706
13: 5 give thee, a land flowing with milk and **h**, 1706
16:31 the taste of it *was* like wafers *made* with **h**. 1706
33: 3 Unto a land flowing with milk and **h**: for I 1706
Lev 2:11 for ye shall burn no leaven, nor any **h**, 1706
20:24 a land that floweth with milk and **h**: 1706
Nu 13:27 and surely it floweth with milk and **h**; 1706
14: 8 it us; a land which floweth with milk and **h**. 1706
16:13 out of a land that floweth with milk and **h**, 1706
16:14 us into a land that floweth with milk and **h**, 1706
Dt 6: 3 *in* the land that floweth with milk and **h**. 1706
8: 8 pomegranates; a land of oil olive, and **h**; 1706
11: 9 a land that floweth with milk and **h**. 1706
26: 9 *even* a land that floweth with milk and **h**. 1706
26:15 a land that floweth with milk and **h**. 1706
27: 3 a land that floweth with milk and **h**; 1706
31:20 their fathers, that floweth with milk and **h**; 1706
32:13 he made him to suck **h** out of the rock, and 1706
Jos 5: 6 a land that floweth with milk and **h**. 1706
Jdg 14: 8 of bees and **h** in the carcase of the lion. 1706
14: 9 he told not them that he had taken the **h** out 1706
14:18 sun went down, What *is* sweeter than **h**? 1706
1Sa 14:25 a wood; and there was **h** upon the ground. 1706
14:26 come into the wood, behold the **h** dropped; 1706
14:29 because I tasted a little of this **h**. 1706
14:43 taste a little **h** with the end of the rod that 1706
2Sa 17:29 **h**, and butter, and sheep, and cheese of 1706
1Ki 14: 3 cracknels, and a cruse of **h**, and go to him: 1706
2Ki 18:32 and vineyards, a land of oil olive and of **h**, 1706
2Ch 31: 5 oil, and **h**, and of all the increase of 1706
Job 20:17 the floods, the brooks of **h** and butter. 1706
Ps 19:10 sweeter also than **h** and the honeycomb. 1706
81:16 *with* **h** out of the rock should I have 1706
119:103 my taste! *yea, sweeter* than **h** to my mouth! 1706
Pr 24:13 My son, eat thou **h**, because *it is* good; and 1706
25:16 Hast thou found **h**? eat so much as is 1706
25:27 *It is* not good to eat much **h**: so *for men* to 1706
SS 4:11 **h** and milk *are* under thy tongue; and 1706
5: 1 I have eaten my honeycomb with my **h**; 1706
Isa 7:15 Butter and **h** shall he eat, that he may know 1706
7:22 **h** shall every one eat that is left in the land. 1706
Jer 11: 5 give them a land flowing with milk and **h**, 1706
32:22 give them, a land flowing with milk and **h**; 1706
41: 8 and *of* barley, and *of* oil, and *of* **h**. 1706
Eze 3: 3 and it was in my mouth as **h** for sweetness. 1706
16:13 thou didst eat fine flour, and **h**, and oil: 1706
16:19 fine flour, and oil, and **h**, *wherewith* I fed 1706
20: 6 flowing with milk and **h**, which *is* the glory 1706
20:15 I had given *them,* flowing with milk and **h**, 1706
27:17 and Pannag, and **h**, and oil, and balm. 1706
Mt 3: 4 and his meat was locusts and wild **h**. 3192
Mk 1: 6 his loins; and he did eat locusts and wild **h**; 3192
Rev 10: 9 but it shall be in thy mouth sweet as **h**. 3192
10:10 it up; and it was in my mouth sweet as **h**: 3192

HONEYCOMB (9) [HONEY]
1Sa 14:27 dipt it in a **h**, and put his 1706+3295+1886.1
Ps 19:10 sweeter also than honey and the **h**. 5317+6688
Pr 5: 3 For the lips of a strange *woman* drop *as* a **h**, 5317
16:24 Pleasant words *are as* a **h**, sweet to 1706+6688
24:13 and the **h**, *which is* sweet to thy taste: 5317
27: 7 The full soul loatheth a **h**; but *to* the hungry 5317
SS 4:11 Thy lips, O *my* spouse, drop *as* the **h**: 5317
5: 1 I have eaten my **h** with my honey; I have 3293
Lk 24:42 him a piece of a broiled fish, and of a **h**. 3193

HONOR See UPPERMOST

HONOUR (146) [HONOURABLE, HONOURED, HONOUREST, HONOURETH, HONOURS]
Ge 49: 6 their assembly, mine **h**, be not thou united: 3519
Ex 14:17 I will **get** me **h** upon Pharaoh, and upon all 3513
14:18 when I have **gotten** me **h** upon Pharaoh, 3513
20:12 **H** thy father and thy mother: that thy days 3513
Lev 19:15 of the poor, nor **h** the person of the mighty: 1921
19:32 **h** the face of the old man, and fear thy God: 1921
Nu 22:17 will **promote** thee **unto** very great **h**, 3513+3513
22:37 am I not able indeed to **promote** thee to **h**? 3513
24:11 to **promote** thee **unto great h**; 3513+3513
24:11 lo, the LORD hath kept thee back from **h**. 3519
27:20 thou shalt put *some* of thine **h** upon him, 1935
Dt 5:16 **H** thy father and thy mother, as the LORD 3513
26:19 hath made, in praise, and in name, and in **h**; 8597
Jdg 4: 9 that thou takest shall not be for thine **h**; 8597
9: 9 wherewith by me they **h** God and man, and 3513
13:17 sayings come to pass we may **do** thee **h**? 3513
1Sa 2:30 for them that **h** me I will honour, and 3513
2:30 for them that honour me I will **h**, and 3513
15:30 *yet* **h** me now, I pray thee, before the elders 3513
2Sa 6:22 hast spoken of, of them shall I be **had in h**. 3513
10: 3 Thinkest thou that David doth **h** thy father, 3513
1Ki 3:13 thou hast not asked, both riches, and **h**. 3519
1Ch 16:27 Glory and **h** *are* in his presence; strength 1926
17:18 *speak* more to thee for the **h** of thy servant? 3519
19: 3 Thinkest thou that David doth **h** thy father, 3513
29:12 Both riches and **h** *come* of thee, and 3519
29:28 a good old age, full of days, riches, and **h**: 3519
2Ch 1:11 and thou hast not asked riches, wealth, or **h**, 3519
1:12 I will give thee riches, and wealth, and **h**, 3519
17: 5 and he had riches and **h** in abundance. 3519
18: 1 Jehoshaphat had riches and **h** in abundance, 3519
26:18 neither *shall it be* for thine **h** from 3519
32:27 had exceeding much riches and **h**: 3519
32:33 the inhabitants of Jerusalem did him **h** at 3519
Est 1: 4 the **h** of his excellent majesty many days, 3366
1:20 all the wives shall give to their husbands **h**, 3366
6: 3 What **h** and dignity hath been done to 3366
6: 6 the man whom the king delighteth to **h**? 3366
6: 6 To whom would the king delight to do **h** 3366
6: 7 *For* the man whom the king delighteth to **h**, 3366
6: 9 man *withal* whom the king delighteth to **h**, 3366
Est 6: 9 to the man whom the king delighteth to **h**. 3366
6:11 the man whom the king delighteth to **h**. 3366
8:16 had light, and gladness, and joy, and **h**. 3366
Job 14:21 His sons **come to h**, and he knoweth *it* not; 3513
Ps 7: 5 upon the earth, and lay mine **h** in the dust. 3519
8: 5 and hast crowned him *with* glory and **h**. 1926
21: 5 **h** and majesty hast thou laid upon him. 1935
26: 8 and the place where thine **h** dwelleth. 3519
49:12 Nevertheless man *being* in **h** abideth not: 3366
49:20 Man *that is* in **h**, and understandeth not, 3366
66: 2 Sing forth the **h** of his name: make his 3519
71: 8 *with* thy praise *and with* thy **h** all the day. 8597
91:15 in trouble; I will deliver him, and **h** him. 3513
96: 6 **H** and majesty *are* before him: strength and 1935
104: 1 thou art clothed with **h** and majesty. 1935
112: 9 for ever; his horn shall be exalted with **h**. 3519
145: 5 I will speak of the glorious **h** of thy 1926
149: 9 this **h** have all his saints. Praise ye 1926
Pr 3: 9 **H** the LORD with thy substance, and 3513
3:16 and in her left hand riches and **h**. 3519
4: 8 she shall **bring** thee **to h**, when thou dost 3513
5: 9 Lest thou give thine **h** unto others, and 1935
8:18 Riches and **h** *are* with me; *yea,* durable 3519
11:16 A gracious woman retaineth **h**: and 3519
14:28 In the multitude of people *is* the king's **h**: 1927
15:33 of wisdom; and before **h** *is* humility. 3519
18:12 of man is haughty, and before **h** *is* humility. 3519
20: 3 *It is* an **h** for a man to cease from strife: but 3519
21:21 mercy findeth life, righteousness, and **h**. 3519
22: 4 of the LORD *are* riches, and **h**, and life. 3519
25: 2 but the **h** of kings *is* to search out a matter. 3519
26: 1 in harvest, so **h** *is* not seemly for a fool. 3519
26: 8 in a sling, so *is* he that giveth **h** to a fool. 3519
29:23 but **h** shall uphold the humble in spirit. 3519
31:25 Strength and **h** *are* her clothing; and 1926
Ecc 6: 2 **h**, so that he wanteth nothing for his soul of 3519
10: 1 *him that is* in reputation for wisdom *and* **h**. 3519
Isa 29:13 with their lips do **h** me, but have removed 3513
43:20 The beast of the field shall **h** me, 3513
58:13 shalt **h** him, not doing thine own ways, 3513
Jer 33: 9 and an **h** before all the nations of the earth, 8597
Da 2: 6 of me gifts and rewards and great **h**: 3367
4:30 of my power, and for the **h** of my majesty? 3367
4:36 mine **h** and brightness returned unto me; 1923
4:37 and extol and **h** the King of heaven, 1922
5:18 a kingdom, and majesty, and glory, and **h**: 1923
11:21 to whom they shall not give the **h** of 1935
11:38 in his estate shall he **h** the God of forces: 3513
11:38 a god whom his fathers knew not shall he **h** 3513
Mal 1: 6 if then I *be* a father, where *is* mine **h**? and 3519
Mt 13:57 A prophet is not **without h**, save in his own 820
15: 4 saying, **H** thy father and mother: 5091
15: 6 And **h** not his father or his mother, *he shall* 5091
19:19 **H** thy father and *thy* mother: and, 5091
Mk 6: 4 A prophet is not **without h**, but in his own 820
7:10 Moses said, **H** thy father and thy mother; 5091
10:19 Defraud not, **H** thy father and mother. 5091
Lk 18:20 false witness, **H** thy father and thy mother. 5091
Jn 4:44 that a prophet hath no **h** in his own country. 5092
5:23 That all *men* should **h** the Son, even as they 5091
5:23 honour the Son, even as they **h** the Father. 5091
5:41 I receive not **h** from men. 1391
5:44 which receive **h** one of another, and 1391
5:44 seek not the **h** that *cometh* from God only? 1391
8:49 but I **h** my Father, and ye do dishonour me. 5091
8:54 Jesus answered, If I **h** myself, my honour is 1392
8:54 If I honour myself, my **h** is nothing: 1391
12:26 if any *man* serve me, him will *my* Father **h**. 5091
Ro 2: 7 doing seek for glory and **h** and immortality, 5092
2:10 But glory, **h**, and peace, to every *man* that 5092
9:21 the same lump to make one vessel unto **h**, 5092
12:10 brotherly love; in **h** preferring one another; 5092
13: 7 fear to whom fear, **h** to whom honour. 5092
13: 7 fear to whom fear; honour to whom **h**. 5092
1Co 12:23 upon these we bestow more abundant **h**; 5092
12:24 having given more abundant **h** to that *part* 5092
2Co 6: 8 By **h** and dishonour, by evil report and 1391
Eph 6: 2 **H** thy father and mother; (which is the first 5091
Col 2:23 not in any **h** to the satisfying of the flesh. 5092
1Th 4: 4 to possess his vessel in sanctification and **h**; 5092
1Ti 1:17 wise God, *be* **h** and glory for ever and ever. 5092
5: 3 **H** widows that are widows indeed. 5091
5:17 rule well be counted worthy of double **h**, 5092
6: 1 count their own masters worthy of all **h**, 5092
6:16 to whom *be* **h** and power everlasting. 5092
2Ti 2:20 and some to **h**, and some to dishonour. 5092
2:21 he shall be a vessel unto **h**, sanctified, and 5092
Heb 2: 7 thou crownedst him with glory and **h**, and 5092
2: 9 of death, crowned with glory and **h**; 5092
3: 3 the house hath more **h** than the house. 5092
5: 4 And no *man* taketh *this* **h** unto himself, but 5092
1Pe 1: 7 might be found unto praise and **h** and 5092
2:17 **H** all *men.* Love the brotherhood. 5091
2:17 the brotherhood. Fear God. **H** the king. 5091
3: 7 giving **h** unto the wife, as unto the weaker 5092
2Pe 1:17 For he received from God the Father **h** and 5092
Rev 4: 9 when *those* beasts give glory and **h** and 5092
4:11 O Lord, to receive glory and **h** and power: 5092
5:12 strength, and **h**, and glory, and blessing. 5092
5:13 Blessing, and **h**, and glory, and power, 5092
7:12 and **h**, and power, and might, 5092
19: 1 Alleluia; Salvation, and glory, and **h**, 5092
19: 7 us be glad and rejoice, and give **h** to him: 1391
21:24 the earth do bring their glory and **h** into it. 5092
21:26 bring the glory and **h** of the nations into it. 5092

HONOURABLE (30) [HONOUR]
Ge 34:19 he *was* more **h** than all the house of his 3513
Nu 22:15 again princes, more, and more **h** than they. 3513
1Sa 9: 6 this city a man of God, and *he is* an **h** man; 3513
22:14 at thy bidding, and *is* **h** in thine house? 3513
2Sa 23:19 Was he not most **h** of three? therefore 3513
23:23 He was more **h** than the thirty, but 3513
2Ki 5: 1 **h**, because by him the LORD had 5375+6440
1Ch 4: 9 Jabez was more **h** than his brethren: and 3513

H

1Ch 11:21 Of the three, he was more **h** than the two; 3513
11:25 he was **h** among the thirty, but attained not 3513
Job 22: 8 the earth; and the **h** *man* dwelt in it. 5375+6440
Ps 45: 9 Kings' daughters *were* among thy **h** 3368
111: 3 His work *is* **h** and glorious: and 1935
Isa 3: 3 the **h** *man,* and the counseller, and 5375+6440
3: 5 the ancient, and the base against the **h**. 3513
5:13 their **h** men *are* famished, and 3519
9:15 The ancient and **h**, he *is* the head; 5375+6440
23: 8 whose traffickers *are* the **h** of the earth? 3513
23: 9 to bring into contempt all the **h** of the earth. 3513
42:21 he will magnify the law, and **make** *it* **h**. 142
43: 4 thou hast been **h**, and I have loved thee: 3513
58:13 a delight, the holy of the LORD, **h**; 3513
Na 3:10 they cast lots for her **h** *men,* and all her 3513
Mk 15:43 Joseph of Arimathea, an **h** counseller, *2158*
Lk 14: 8 lest a **more h** *man* **than** thou be bidden of *1784*
Ac 13:50 Jews stirred up the devout and **h** women, *2158*
17:12 also of **h** women which were Greeks, and *2158*
1Co 4:10 ye *are* strong; ye *are* **h**, but we *are* despised. *1741*
12:23 of the body, which we think to be **less h**, *820*
Heb 13: 4 Marriage *is* **h** in all, and the bed undefiled: *5093*

HONOURED (9) [HONOUR]

Ex 14: 4 I will be **h** upon Pharaoh, and upon all his 3513
Pr 13:18 but he that regardeth reproof shall be **h**. 3513
27:18 so he that waiteth on his master shall be **h**. 3513
Isa 43:23 neither hast thou **h** me *with* thy sacrifices. 3513
La 1: 8 all that **h** her despise her, because they have 3513
5:12 their hand: the faces of elders were not **h**. 1921
Da 4:34 and I praised and **h** him that liveth for ever, 1922
Ac 28:10 Who also **h** us with many honours; and *5091*
1Co 12:26 suffer with *it;* or one member be **h**, *1392*

HONOUREST (1) [HONOUR]

1Sa 2:29 **h** thy sons above me, to make yourselves 3513

HONOURETH (9) [HONOUR]

Ps 15: 4 but he **h** them that fear the LORD. 3513
Pr 12: 9 *is* better than he that **h** himself, and 3513
14:31 but he that **h** him hath mercy on the poor. 3513
Mal 1: 6 A son **h** *his* father, and a servant his master: 3513
Mt 15: 8 with their mouth, and **h** me with *their* lips; *5091*
Mk 7: 6 This people **h** me with *their* lips, but *5091*
Jn 5:23 He that **h** not the Son honoureth not *5091*
5:23 He that honoureth not the Son **h** not *5091*
8:54 it is my Father that **h** me; of whom ye say, *1392*

HONOURS (1) [HONOUR]

Ac 28:10 Who also honoured us with many **h**; and *5092*

HOODS (1)

Isa 3:23 and the fine linen, and the **h**, and the vails. 6797

HOOF (12) [HOOFS, HORSEHOOFS]

Ex 10:26 with us; there shall not a **h** be left behind; 6541
Lev 11: 3 Whatsoever parteth the **h**, and 6541
11: 4 chew the cud, or of them that divide the **h**: 6541
11: 4 he cheweth the cud, but divideth not the **h**; 6541
11: 5 he cheweth the cud, but divideth not the **h**; 6541
11: 6 he cheweth the cud, but divideth not the **h**; 6541
11: 7 though he divide the **h**, and 6541
11:26 of every beast which divideth the **h**, 6541
Dt 14: 6 every beast that parteth the **h**, and 6541
14: 7 the cud, or of them that divide the cloven **h**; 6541
14: 7 for they chew the cud, but divide not the **h**; 6541
14: 8 the swine, because it divideth the **h**, 6541

HOOFS (6) [HOOF]

Ps 69:31 than an ox *or* bullock that hath horns *and* **h**. 6536
Isa 5:28 their horses' **h** shall be counted like flint, 6541
Jer 47: 3 At the noise of the stamping of the **h** of his 6541
Eze 26:11 With the **h** of his horses shall he tread 6541
32:13 any more, nor the **h** of beasts trouble them. 6541
Mic 4:13 horn iron, and I will make thy **h** brass: 6541

HOOK (5) [FISHHOOKS, FLESHHOOK, FLESHHOOKS, HOOKS, PRUNINGHOOKS]

2Ki 19:28 therefore I will put my **h** in thy nose, and 2397
Job 41: 1 Canst thou draw out leviathan with a **h**? or 2443
41: 2 Canst thou put a **h** into his nose? or bore his 100
Isa 37:29 therefore will I put my **h** in thy nose, and 2397
Mt 17:27 and cast a **h**, and take up the fish that first *44*

HOOKS (18) [HOOK]

Ex 26:32 their **h** *shall be of* gold, upon the four 2053
26:37 with gold, *and* their **h** *shall be of* gold: 2053
27:10 the **h** of the pillars and their fillets *shall be* 2053
27:11 the **h** of the pillars and their fillets *of* silver. 2053
27:17 their **h** *shall be of* silver, and their sockets 2053
36:36 their **h** *were of* gold; and he cast for them 2053
36:38 the five pillars of it with their **h**: and 2053
38:10 the **h** of the pillars and their fillets *were of* 2053
38:11 the **h** of the pillars and their fillets *of* silver. 2053
38:12 the **h** of the pillars and their fillets *of* silver. 2053
38:17 the **h** of the pillars and their fillets *of* silver; 2053
38:19 their **h** *of* silver, and the overlaying of their 2053
38:28 and five *shekels* he made **h** for the pillars, 2053
Isa 18: 5 both cut off the sprigs with **pruning h**, 4211
Eze 29: 4 I will put **h** in thy jaws, and I will cause 2397
38: 4 put **h** into thy jaws, and I will bring thee 2397
40:43 within *were* **h**, a hand broad, 8240
Am 4: 2 that he will take you away with **h**, and 6793

HOOPOE See LAPWING

HOPE (130) [HOPE'S, HOPED, HOPETH, HOPING]

Ru 1:12 If I should say, I have **h**, *if* I should have a 8615
Ezr 10: 2 yet now there is **h** in Israel concerning this 4723
Job 4: 6 *Is not this* thy fear, thy confidence, thy **h**; 8615
5:16 So the poor hath **h**, and iniquity stoppeth 8615
6:11 What *is* my strength, that I should **h**? and 3176
7: 6 a weaver's shuttle, and are spent without **h**. 8615
8:13 and the hypocrite's **h** shall perish: 8615
Job 8:14 Whose **h** shall be cut off, and whose trust 3689
11:18 thou shalt be secure, because there is **h**; 8615
11:20 their **h** *shall be as* the giving up of 8615
14: 7 For there is **h** of a tree, if it be cut down, 8615
14:19 the earth; and thou destroyest the **h** of man. 8615
17:15 where *is* now my **h**? as for my hope, 8615
17:15 my hope? as for my **h**, who shall see it? 8615
19:10 and mine **h** hath he removed like a tree. 8615
27: 8 For what *is* the **h** of the hypocrite, 8615
31:24 If I have made gold my **h**, or have said to 3689
41: 9 Behold, the **h** of him is in vain: shall not 8431
Ps 16: 9 glory rejoiceth: my flesh also shall rest in **h**. 983
22: 9 thou didst **make** me **h** *when I was* upon my 982
31:24 your heart, all ye that **h** in the LORD. 3176
33:18 fear him, upon them that **h** in his mercy; 3176
33:22 be upon us, according as we **h** in thee. 3176
38:15 For in thee, O LORD, do I **h**: thou wilt 3176
39: 7 Lord, what wait I for? my **h** *is* in thee. 8431
42: 5 **h** thou in God: for I shall yet praise him *for* 3176
42:11 **h** thou in God: for I shall yet praise him, 3176
43: 5 **h** in God: for I shall yet praise him, *who is* 3176
71: 5 For thou *art* my **h**, O Lord GOD: *thou art* 8615
71:14 I will **h** continually, and will yet praise thee 3176
78: 7 That they might set their **h** in God, and 3689
119:49 upon which thou hast **caused** me **to h**. 3176
119:81 for thy salvation: *but* I **h** in thy word. 3176
119:114 hiding place and my shield: I **h** in thy word. 3176
119:116 and let me not be ashamed of my **h**. 7664
130: 5 my soul doth wait, and in his word do I **h**. 3176
130: 7 Let Israel **h** in the LORD: for with 3176
131: 3 Let Israel **h** in the LORD from henceforth 3176
146: 5 his help, whose **h** *is* in the LORD his God: 7664
147:11 that fear him, in those that **h** in his mercy. 3176
Pr 10:28 The **h** of the righteous *shall be* gladness: 8431
11: 7 and the **h** of unjust *men* perisheth. 8431
13:12 **H** deferred maketh the heart sick: but 8431
14:32 but the righteous hath **h** in his death. 2620
19:18 Chasten thy son while there is **h**, and let not 8615
26:12 *there is* more **h** of a fool than of him. 8615
29:20 *there is* more **h** of a fool than of him. 8615
Ecc 9: 4 him that is joined to all the living there is **h**: 986
Isa 38:18 they that go down into the pit cannot **h** for 7663
57:10 thy way; *yet* saidst thou not, There is **no h**: 2976
Jer 2:25 thou saidst, There is **no h**: no; for I have 2976
14: 8 O the **h** of Israel, the saviour thereof in 4723
17: 7 in the LORD, and whose **h** the LORD is. 4009
17:13 O LORD, the **h** of Israel, all that forsake 4723
17:17 unto me: thou *art* my **h** in the day of evil. 4268
18:12 they said, There is **no h**: but we will walk 2976
31:17 there is **h** in thine end, saith the LORD, 8615
50: 7 even the LORD, the **h** of their fathers. 4723
La 3:18 and my **h** is perished from the LORD: 8431
3:21 This I recall to my mind, therefore have I **h**. 3176
3:24 saith my soul; therefore will I **h** in him. 3176
3:26 *It is* good *that a man should* both **h** and 3175
3:29 mouth in the dust; if so be there may be **h**. 8615
Eze 13: 6 they have **made** *others* **to h** that *they* would 3176
19: 5 *and* her **h** was lost, then she took another of 8615
37:11 Our bones are dried, and our **h** is lost: 8615
Hos 2:15 and the valley of Achor for a door of **h**: 8615
Joel 3:16 the LORD *will be* the **h** of his people, and 4268
Zec 9:12 ye to the strong hold, ye prisoners of **h**: 8615
Lk 6:34 And if ye lend *to them* of whom ye **h** to *1679*
Ac 2:26 moreover also my flesh shall rest in **h**: *1680*
16:19 And when her masters saw that the **h** of *1680*
23: 6 of the **h** and resurrection of the dead I am *1680*
24:15 And have **h** towards God, which they *1680*
26: 6 am judged for the **h** of the promise made of *1680*
26: 7 serving *God* day and night, **h** to come. *1679*
27:20 no small tempest lay on *us,* all **h** that we *1680*
28:20 that for the **h** of Israel I am bound with this *1680*
Ro 4:18 Who against **h** believed in hope, that he *1680*
4:18 Who against hope believed in **h**, that he *1680*
5: 2 and rejoice in **h** of the glory of God. *1680*
5: 4 experience; and experience, **h**: *1680*
5: 5 And **h** maketh not ashamed; because *1680*
8:20 of him who hath subjected *the same,* in **h**, *1680*
8:24 For we are saved by **h**: but hope that is seen *1680*
8:24 but **h** that is seen is not hope: for what a *1680*
8:24 but hope that is seen is not **h**: for what a *1680*
8:24 what a man seeth, why doth he yet **h for**? *1679*
8:25 But if we **h for** that we see not, *then* do we *1679*
12:12 Rejoicing in **h**; patient in tribulation; *1680*
15: 4 and comfort of the scriptures might have **h**. *1680*
15:13 Now the God of **h** fill you with all joy and *1680*
15:13 in believing, that ye may abound in **h**, *1680*
1Co 9:10 that he that ploweth should plow in **h**; and *1680*
9:10 that he that thresheth in **h** should be *1680*
9:10 in hope should be partaker of his **h**. *1680*
13:13 now abideth faith, **h**, charity, these three; *1680*
15:19 If in this life only we have **h** in Christ, *1679*
2Co 1: 7 And our **h** of you *is* stedfast, knowing, *1680*
3:12 Seeing then that we have such **h**, we use *1680*
10:15 but having **h**, when your faith is increased, *1680*
Gal 5: 5 For we through the Spirit wait for the **h** of *1680*
Eph 1:18 that ye may know what is the **h** of his *1680*
2:12 having no **h**, and without God in the world: *1680*
4: 4 even as ye are called in one **h** of your *1680*
Php 1:20 to my earnest expectation and *my* **h**, *1680*
2:23 Him therefore I **h** to send presently, so *1679*
Col 1: 5 For the **h** which is laid up for you in *1680*
1:23 *be* not moved away from the **h** of *1680*
1:27 which is Christ in you, the **h** of glory: *1680*
1Th 1: 3 and patience of **h** in our Lord Jesus Christ, *1680*
2:19 For what *is* our **h**, or joy, or crown of *1680*
4:13 even as others which have no **h**. *1680*
5: 8 love; and for a helmet, the **h** of salvation. *1680*
2Th 2:16 and good **h** through grace, *1680*
1Ti 1: 1 and Lord Jesus Christ, *which is* our **h**; *1680*
Tit 1: 2 In **h** of eternal life, which God, that cannot *1680*
2:13 Looking for *that* blessed **h**, and the glorious *1680*
3: 7 we should be made heirs according to the **h** *1680*
Heb 3: 6 and the rejoicing of the **h** firm unto the end. *1680*
6:11 to the full assurance of **h** unto the end: *1680*
6:18 refuge to lay hold upon the **h** set before *us:* *1680*
Heb 6:19 Which *h* we have as an anchor of the soul, NIG
7:19 the bringing in of a better **h** *did;* by *1680*
10:23 Let us hold fast the profession of *our* **h** *1680*
1Pe 1: 3 **h** by the resurrection of Jesus Christ from *1680*
1:13 **h** to the end for the grace that is *to be* *1679*
1:21 that your faith and **h** might be in God. *1680*
3:15 reason of the **h** that is in you with meekness *1680*
1Jn 3: 3 And every *man* that hath this **h** in him *1680*

HOPE'S (1) [HOPE]

Ac 26: 7 For which **h** sake, king Agrippa, I am *1680*

HOPED (11) [HOPE]

Est 9: 1 in the day that the enemies of the Jews **h** to 7663
Job 6:20 They were confounded because they had **h**; 982
Ps 119:43 my mouth; for I have **h** in thy judgments. 3176
119:74 they see me; because I have **h** in thy word. 3176
119:147 of the morning, and cried: I **h** in thy word. 3176
119:166 I have **h** for thy salvation, and done thy 7663
Jer 3:23 Truly in vain *is salvation* **h** *for* from NIH
Lk 23: 8 he **h** to have seen some miracle done by *1679*
Ac 24:26 He **h** also that money should have been *1679*
2Co 8: 5 And *this they did,* not as we **h**, but *1679*
Heb 11: 1 Now faith is the substance of *things* **h for**, *1679*

HOPETH (1) [HOPE]

1Co 13: 7 Beareth all *things,* believeth all *things,* **h** *1679*

HOPHNI (5)

1Sa 1: 3 the two sons of Eli, **H** and Phinehas, 2652
2:34 upon thy two sons, on **H** and Phinehas; 2652
4: 4 the two sons of Eli, **H** and Phinehas, 2652
4:11 sons of Eli, **H** and Phinehas, were slain. 2652
4:17 **H** and Phinehas, are dead, and the ark of 2652

HOPING (2) [HOPE]

Lk 6:35 and do good, and lend, **h for** nothing **again**; *560*
1Ti 3:14 I unto thee, **h** to come unto thee shortly: *1679*

HOR (12)

Nu 20:22 from Kadesh, and came *unto* mount **H**. 2023
20:23 spake unto Moses and Aaron in mount **H**, 2023
20:25 his son, and bring them up *unto* mount **H**: 2023
20:27 they went up into mount **H** in the sight of 2023
21: 4 they journeyed from mount **H** *by* the way 2023
33:37 pitched in mount **H**, in the edge of the land 2023
33:38 Aaron the priest went up into mount **H** at 2023
33:39 three years old when he died in mount **H**. 2023
33:41 they departed from mount **H**, and 2023
34: 7 sea you shall point out for you mount **H**: 2023
34: 8 From mount **H** ye shall point out *your* 2023
Dt 32:50 as Aaron thy brother died in mount **H**, 2023

HOR HAGGIDGAD See HOR-HAGIDGAD

HORAM (1)

Jos 10:33 **H** king of Gezer came up to help Lachish; 2036

HOREB (17) [SINAI]

Ex 3: 1 came to the mountain of God, *even* to **H**. 2722
17: 6 stand before thee there upon the rock in **H**; 2722
33: 6 of their ornaments by the mount **H**. 2722
Dt 1: 2 (*There are* eleven days' *journey* from **H** *by* 2722
1: 6 The LORD our God spake unto us in **H**, 2722
1:19 when we departed from **H**, we went 2722
4:10 stoodest before the LORD thy God in **H**, 2722
4:15 unto you in **H** out of the midst of the fire: 2722
5: 2 our God made a covenant with us in **H**. 2722
9: 8 Also in **H** ye provoked the LORD to 2722
18:16 thy God in **H** in the day of the assembly, 2722
29: 1 covenant which he made with them in **H**. 2722
1Ki 8: 9 of stone, which Moses put there at **H**, 2722
19: 8 and forty nights unto **H** the mount of God. 2722
2Ch 5:10 two tables which Moses put *therein* at **H**, 2722
Ps 106:19 They made a calf in **H**, and worshipped 2722
Mal 4: 4 which I commanded unto him in **H** for all 2722

HOREM (1)

Jos 19:38 **H**, and Beth-anath, and Beth-shemesh; 2765

HOR-HAGIDGAD (2)

Nu 33:32 from Bene-jaakan, and encamped at **H**. 2735
33:33 they went from **H**, and pitched in 2735

HORI (4) [HORIMS, HORITE, HORITES]

Ge 36:22 the children of Lotan were **H** and Hemam; 2753
36:30 these *are* the dukes *that came* of **H**, 2753
Nu 13: 5 the tribe of Simeon, Shaphat the son of **H**. 2753
1Ch 1:39 And the sons of Lotan; **H**, and Homam: and 2753

HORIMS (2) [HORI]

Dt 2:12 The **H** also dwelt in Seir beforetime; but 2752
2:22 when he destroyed the **H** from before them; 2752

HORITE (1) [HORI]

Ge 36:20 These *are* the sons of Seir the **H**, 2752

HORITES (3) [HORI]

Ge 14: 6 the **H** in their mount Seir, unto El-paran, 2752
36:21 these *are* the dukes of the **H**, the children of 2752
36:29 These *are* the dukes *that came* of the **H**; 2752

HORMAH (9)

Nu 14:45 and discomfited them, *even* unto **H**. 2767
21: 3 and he called the name of the place **H**. 2767
Dt 1:44 and destroyed you in Seir, *even* unto **H**. 2767
Jos 12:14 The king of **H**, one; the king of Arad, one; 2767
15:30 And Eltolad, and Chesil, and **H**, 2767
19: 4 And Eltolad, and Bethul, and **H**, 2767
Jdg 1:17 and the name of the city was called **H**. 2767
1Sa 30:30 to *them* which *were* in **H**, and to *them* 2767
1Ch 4:30 And at Bethuel, and at **H**, and at Ziklag, 2767

H

HORN (36) [HORNS, INKHORN]

Ex 21:29 if the ox *were* **wont to push with his h** in 5056
Jos 6: 5 *they* make a long blast with the ram's **h**, 7161
1Sa 2: 1 mine **h** is exalted in the LORD: 7161
2:10 his king, and exalt the **h** of his anointed. 7161
16: 1 fill thine **h** *with* oil, and go, I will send thee 7161
16:13 Samuel took the **h** of oil, and anointed him 7161
2Sa 22: 3 the **h** of my salvation, my high tower, and 7161
1Ki 1:39 Zadok the priest took a **h** of oil out of 7161
1Ch 25: 5 seer in the words of God, to lift up the **h**. 7161
Job 16:15 upon my skin, and defiled my **h** in the dust. 7161
Ps 18: 2 the **h** of my salvation, *and* my high tower. 7161
75: 4 and to the wicked, Lift not up the **h**: 7161
75: 5 Lift not up your **h** on high: speak *not* with a 7161
89:17 and in thy favour our **h** shall be exalted. 7161
89:24 and in my name shall his **h** be exalted. 7161
92:10 my **h** shalt thou exalt like *the horn of* an 7161
92:10 my horn shalt thou exalt like *the* **h** *of* an NIH
112: 9 for ever; his **h** shall be exalted with honour. 7161
132:17 There will I make the **h** of David to bud: 7161
148:14 He also exalteth the **h** of his people, 7161
Jer 48:25 The **h** of Moab is cut off, and his arm is 7161
La 2: 3 He hath cut off in *his* fierce anger all the **h** 7161
2:17 he hath set up the **h** of thine adversaries. 7161
Eze 29:21 In that day will I cause the **h** of the house 7161
Da 7: 8 there came up among them another little **h**, 7162
7: 8 in this **h** *were* eyes like the eyes of man, 7162
7:11 of the voice of the great words which the **h** 7162
7:20 even *of* that **h** that had eyes, and a mouth 7162
7:21 the same **h** made war with the saints, and 7162
8: 5 the goat *had* a notable **h** between his eyes. 7161
8: 8 he was strong, the great **h** was broken; 7161
8: 9 out of one of them came forth a little **h**, 7161
8:21 the great **h** that *is* between his eyes *is* 7161
Mic 4:13 for I will make thine **h** iron, and I will 7161
Zec 1:21 which lift up *their* **h** over the land of Judah 7161
Lk 1:69 And hath raised up a **h** of salvation for us *2768*

HORNET (2) [HORNETS]

Dt 7:20 thy God will send the **h** among them, 6880
Jos 24:12 I sent the **h** before you, which drave them 6880

HORNETS (1) [HORNET]

Ex 23:28 I will send **h** before thee, which shall drive 6880

HORNS (67) [HORN]

Ge 22:13 *him* a ram caught in a thicket by his **h**: 7161
Ex 27: 2 thou shalt make the **h** of it upon the four 7161
27: 2 his **h** shall be of the same: and thou shalt 7161
29:12 put *it* upon the **h** of the altar with thy 7161
30: 2 the **h** thereof *shall be* of the same. 7161
30: 3 thereof round about, and the **h** thereof; 7161
30:10 Aaron shall make an atonement upon the **h** 7161
37:25 height of it; the **h** thereof were of the same. 7161
37:26 sides thereof round about, and the **h** of it: 7161
38: 2 he made the **h** thereof on the four corners 7161
38: 2 of it; the **h** thereof were of the same: 7161
Lev 4: 7 **h** of the altar of sweet incense before 7161
4:18 he shall put *some* of the blood upon the **h** 7161
4:25 put *it* upon the **h** of the altar of burnt 7161
4:30 put *it* upon the **h** of the altar of burnt 7161
4:34 put *it* upon the **h** of the altar of burnt 7161
8:15 put *it* upon the **h** of the altar round about 7161
9: 9 put *it* upon the **h** of the altar, and poured 7161
16:18 put *it* upon the **h** of the altar round about. 7161
Dt 33:17 and his **h** *are like* the horns of unicorns: 7161
33:17 and his horns *are like* the **h** of unicorns: 7161
Jos 6: 4 before the ark seven trumpets of **rams' h**: 3104
6: 6 of **rams' h** before the ark of the LORD. 3104
6: 8 of **rams' h** passed on before the LORD, 3104
6:13 **rams' h** before the ark of the LORD went 3104
1Ki 1:50 went, and caught hold on the **h** of the altar. 7161
1:51 he hath caught hold on the **h** of the altar, 7161
2:28 and caught hold on the **h** of the altar. 7161
22:11 the son of Chenaanah made him **h** of iron: 7161
2Ch 18:10 son of Chenaanah had made him **h** of iron, 7161
Ps 22:21 for thou hast heard me from the **h** of 7161
69:31 than an ox *or* bullock that hath **h** *and* hoofs. 7160
75:10 All the **h** of the wicked also will I cut off; 7161
75:10 *but* the **h** of the righteous shall be exalted. 7161
118:27 with cords, *even* unto the **h** of the altar. 7161
Jer 17: 1 of their heart, and upon the **h** of your altars; 7161
Eze 27:15 they brought thee *for* a present **h** of ivory 7161
34:21 and pusht all the diseased with your **h**, 7161
43:15 from the altar and upward *shall be* four **h**. 7161
43:20 put *it* on the four **h** of it, and on the four 7161
Da 7: 7 beasts that *were* before it; and it had ten **h**. 7162
7: 8 I considered the **h**, and, behold, there came 7162
7: 8 before whom there were three of the first **h** 7162
7:20 of the ten **h** that *were* in his head, and 7162
7:24 the ten **h** out of this kingdom *are* ten kings 7162
8: 3 before the river a ram which had **two h**: 7161
8: 3 the **two h** *were* high; but one *was* higher 7161
8: 6 he came to the ram that had **two h**, which I 7161
8: 7 and smote the ram, and brake his two **h**: 7161
8:20 The ram which thou sawest having **two h** 7161
Am 3:14 the **h** of the altar shall be cut off, and fall to 7161
6:13 Have we not taken to us **h** by our own 7161
Hab 3: 4 the light; he had **h** *coming* out of his hand: 7161
Zec 1:18 I up mine eyes, and saw, and behold four **h**. 7161
1:19 These *are* the **h** which have scattered 7161
1:21 These *are* the **h** which have scattered 7161
1:21 fray them, to cast out the **h** of the Gentiles, 7161
Rev 5: 6 *been* slain, having seven **h** and seven eyes, *2768*
9:13 I heard a voice from the four **h** of *2768*
12: 3 having seven heads and ten **h**, and *2768*
13: 1 having seven heads and ten **h**, and upon his *2768*
13: 1 and upon his **h** ten crowns, and upon his *2768*
13:11 and he had two **h** like a lamb, and he spake *2768*
17: 3 having seven heads and ten **h**. *2768*
17: 7 which hath the seven heads and ten **h**. *2768*
17:12 And the ten **h** which thou sawest are ten *2768*
17:16 And the ten **h** which thou sawest upon *2768*

HORONAIM (4)

Isa 15: 5 for *in* the way of **H** they shall raise up a cry 2773
Jer 48: 3 A voice of crying *shall be* from **H**, spoiling 2773
48: 5 for in the going down of **H** the enemies 2773
48:34 from Zoar *even* unto **H**, *as* a heifer of three 2773

HORONITE (3)

Ne 2:10 When Sanballat the **H**, and Tobiah 2772
2:19 when Sanballat the **H**, and Tobiah 2772
13:28 *was* son in law to Sanballat the **H**: 2772

HORRIBLE (6) [HORROR]

Ps 11: 6 fire and brimstone, and a **h** tempest: 2152
40: 2 He brought me up also out of a **h** pit, out of 7588
Jer 5:30 and **h thing** is committed in the land; 8186
18:13 virgin of Israel hath done a very **h thing**. 8186
23:14 also in the prophets of Jerusalem a **h thing**: 8186
Hos 6:10 I have seen a **h thing** in the house of Israel: 8186

HORRIBLY (2) [HORROR]

Jer 2:12 O ye heavens, at this, and be **h afraid**, 8175
Eze 32:10 and their kings shall be **h** afraid for thee, 8178

HORROR (4) [HORRIBLE, HORRIBLY]

Ge 15:12 and, lo, a **h** of great darkness fell upon him. 367
Ps 55: 5 upon me, and **h** hath overwhelmed me. 6427
119:53 **H** hath taken hold upon me because of 2152
Eze 7:18 with sackcloth, and **h** shall cover them; 6427

HORSE (43) [HORSEBACK, HORSEHOOFS, HORSELEACH, HORSEMAN, HORSEMEN, HORSES, HORSES']

Ge 49:17 that biteth the **h** heels, so that his rider shall 5483
Ex 15: 1 the **h** and his rider hath he thrown into 5483
15:19 For the **h** of Pharaoh went in with his 5483
15:21 the **h** and his rider hath he thrown into 5483
1Ki 10:29 of silver, and a **h** for an hundred and fifty: 5483
20:20 Ben-hadad the king of Syria escaped on a **h** 5483
20:25 **h** for horse, and chariot for chariot: 5483
20:25 horse for **h**, and chariot for chariot: 5483
2Ch 1:17 of silver, and a **h** for an hundred and fifty: 5483
23:15 when she was come to the entering of the **h** 5483
Ne 3:28 From above the **h** gate repaired the priests, 5483
Est 6: 8 the **h** that the king rideth upon, and 5483
6: 9 **h** be delivered to the hand of one of 5483
6:10 Make haste, *and* take the apparel and the **h**, 5483
6:11 took Haman the apparel and the **h**, and 5483
Job 39:18 on high, she scorneth the **h** and his rider. 5483
39:19 Hast thou given the **h** strength? hast thou 5483
Ps 32: 9 Be ye not as the **h**, *or* as the mule, 5483
33:17 A **h** *is* a vain thing for safety: neither shall 5483
76: 6 the chariot and **h** *are* cast into a dead sleep. 5483
147:10 He delighteth not in the strength of the **h**: 5483
Pr 21:31 The **h** *is* prepared against the day of battle: 5483
26: 3 A whip for the **h**, a bridle for the ass, and 5483
Isa 43:17 Which bringeth forth the chariot and **h**, 5483
63:13 as a **h** in the wilderness, *that* they should 5483
Jer 8: 6 his course, as the **h** rusheth into the battle. 5483
31:40 unto the corner of the **h** gate towards 5483
51:21 with thee will I break in pieces the **h** and 5483
Am 2:15 shall he that rideth the **h** deliver himself. 5483
Zec 1: 8 behold a man riding upon a red **h**, and 5483
9:10 the **h** from Jerusalem, and the battle bow 5483
10: 3 hath made them as his goodly **h** in 5483
12: 4 I will smite every **h** with astonishment, and 5483
12: 4 will smite every **h** of the people with 5483
14:15 so shall be the plague of the **h**, of the mule, 5483
Rev 6: 2 And I saw, and behold a white **h**: and *2462*
6: 4 And there went out another **h** *that was* red: *2462*
6: 5 And I beheld, and lo a black **h**; and he that *2462*
6: 8 And I looked, and behold a pale **h**: and *2462*
14:20 *even* unto the **h** bridles, by the space of a *2462*
19:11 I saw heaven opened, and behold a white **h**; *2462*
19:19 to make war against him that sat on the **h**, *2462*
19:21 with the sword of him that sat upon the **h**, *2462*

HORSEBACK (5) [BACK, HORSE]

2Ki 9:18 So there went one **on h** to meet him, 5483+7392
9:19 he sent *out* a second **on h**, which 5483+7392
Est 6: 9 bring him on **h** through the street of 5483
6:11 **brought** him **on h** through the street of 7392
8:10 sent letters by posts on **h**, *and* riders on 5483

HORSEHOOFS (1) [HOOF, HORSE]

Jdg 5:22 were the **h** broken by the means of 5483+6119

HORSELEACH (1) [HORSE]

Pr 30:15 The **h** hath two daughters, *crying*, Give, 5936

HORSEMAN (2) [HORSE, MAN]

2Ki 9:17 Take a **h**, and send to meet them, and 7395
Na 3: 3 The **h** lifteth up both the bright sword and 6571

HORSEMEN (59) [HORSE, MAN]

Ge 50: 9 there went up with him both chariots and **h**: 6571
Ex 14: 9 of Pharaoh, and his **h**, and his army) 6571
14:17 his host, upon his chariots, and upon his **h**. 6571
14:18 upon his chariots, and upon his **h**. 6571
14:23 all Pharaoh's horses, his chariots, and his **h**. 6571
14:26 upon their chariots, and upon their **h**. 6571
14:28 the **h**, and all the host of Pharaoh that came 6571
15:19 his chariots and with his **h** into the sea, 6571
Jos 24: 6 with chariots and **h** *unto* the Red sea. 6571
1Sa 8:11 for himself, for his chariots, and to be his **h**; 6571
13: 5 six thousand **h**, and people as the sand 6571
2Sa 1: 6 and **h** followed hard after him. 1167+6571
8: 4 a thousand *chariots*, and seven hundred **h**, 6571
10:18 forty thousand **h**, and smote Shobach 6571
1Ki 1: 5 he prepared him chariots and **h**, and 6571
4:26 for his chariots, and twelve thousand **h**. 6571
9:19 cities for his **h**, and that which Solomon 6571
9:22 and rulers of his chariots, and his **h**. 6571
10:26 Solomon gathered together chariots and **h**: 6571
10:26 hundred chariots, and twelve thousand **h**, 6571
20:20 king of Syria escaped on a horse with the **h**. 6571
2Ki 2:12 the chariot of Israel, and the **h** thereof. 6571
13: 7 leave *of* the people to Jehoahaz but fifty **h**, 6571
13:14 the chariot of Israel, and the **h** thereof. 6571
18:24 thy trust on Egypt for chariots and for **h**? 6571
1Ch 18: 4 seven thousand **h**, and twenty thousand 6571
19: 6 them chariots and **h** out of Mesopotamia, 6571
2Ch 1:14 Solomon gathered chariots and **h**: and 6571
1:14 hundred chariots, and twelve thousand **h**, 6571
8: 6 the cities of the **h**, and all that Solomon 6571
8: 9 and captains of his chariots and **h**. 6571
9:25 and chariots, and twelve thousand **h**; 6571
12: 3 and threescore thousand **h**: 6571
16: 8 huge host, with very many chariots and **h**? 6571
Ezr 8:22 **h** to help us against the enemy in the way: 6571
Ne 2: 9 sent captains of the army and **h** with me. 6571
Isa 21: 7 he saw a chariot *with* a couple of **h**, 6571
21: 9 a chariot of men, *with* a couple of **h**. 6571
22: 6 bare the quiver with chariots of men *and* **h**, 6571
22: 7 the **h** shall set themselves in array at 6571
28:28 wheel of his cart, nor bruise it *with* his **h**. 6571
31: 1 in **h**, because they are very strong; but 6571
36: 9 thy trust on Egypt for chariots and for **h**? 6571
Jer 4:29 whole city shall flee for the noise of the **h** 6571
46: 4 ye **h**, and stand forth with *your* helmets; 6571
Eze 23: 6 desirable young men, **h** riding upon horses. 6571
23:12 most gorgeously, **h** riding upon horses, 6571
26: 7 with **h**, and companies, and much people. 6571
26:10 thy walls shall shake at the noise of the **h**, 6571
27:14 in thy fairs with horses and **h** and mules. 6571
38: 4 thee forth, and all thine army, horses and **h**, 6571
Da 11:40 and with **h**, and with many ships; 6571
Hos 1: 7 nor by battle, by horses, nor by **h**. 6571
Joel 2: 4 of horses; and as **h**, so shall they run. 6571
Hab 1: 8 their **h** shall spread themselves, and 6571
1: 8 and their **h** shall come from far; 6571
Ac 23:23 and **h** threescore *and* ten, and spearmen two *2460*
23:32 On the morrow they left the **h** to go with *2460*
Rev 9:16 And the number of the army of the **h** *were* *2461*

HORSES (109) [HORSE]

Ge 47:17 Joseph gave them bread *in exchange* for **h**, 5483
Ex 9: 3 upon the **h**, upon the asses, upon 5483
14: 9 the Egyptians pursued after them (all the **h** 5483
14:23 *even* all Pharaoh's **h**, his chariots, and 5483
Dt 11: 4 of Egypt, unto their **h**, and to their chariots; 5483
17:16 he shall not multiply **h** to himself, 5483
17:16 to the end that he should multiply **h**: 5483
20: 1 seest **h**, and chariots, *and* a people more 5483
Jos 11: 4 with **h** and chariots very many. 5483
11: 6 thou shalt hough their **h**, and burn their 5483
11: 9 he houghed their **h**, and burnt their chariots 5483
2Sa 8: 4 David houghed all the chariot *h*, but NIH
15: 1 that Absalom prepared him chariots and **h**, 5483
1Ki 4:26 Solomon had forty thousand stalls of **h** for 5483
4:28 Barley also and straw for the **h** and 5483
10:25 and armour, and spices, **h**, and mules, 5483
10:28 Solomon had **h** brought out of Egypt, and 5483
18: 5 we may find grass to save the **h** 5483
20: 1 two kings with him, and **h**, and chariots: 5483
20:21 smote the **h** and chariots, and slew 5483
22: 4 people as thy people, my **h** as thy horses. 5483
22: 4 people as thy people, my horses as thy **h**. 5483
2Ki 2:11 and **h** of fire, and parted them both asunder; 5483
3: 7 as thy people, *and* my **h** as thy horses. 5483
3: 7 as thy people, *and* my horses as thy **h**. 5483
5: 9 So Naaman came with his **h** and with his 5483
6:14 Therefore sent he thither **h**, and chariots, 5483
6:15 a host compassed the city both with **h** and 5483
6:17 the mountain was full *of* **h** and chariots of 5483
7: 6 a noise of **h**, *even* the noise of a great host: 5483
7: 7 left their tents, and their **h**, and their asses, 5483
7:10 **h** tied, and asses tied, and the tents as they 5483
7:13 I pray thee, five of the **h** that remain, 5483
7:14 They took therefore two chariot **h**; and 5483
9:33 was sprinkled on the wall, and on the **h**: 5483
10: 2 *there are* with you chariots and **h**, a fenced 5483
11:16 she went *by* the way by the which the **h** 5483
14:20 they brought him on **h**: and he was buried 5483
18:23 and I will deliver thee two thousand **h**, 5483
23:11 he took away the **h** that the kings of Judah 5483
1Ch 18: 4 David also houghed all the chariot *h*, but NIH
2Ch 1:16 Solomon had **h** brought out of Egypt, and 5483
1:17 brought they out *h* for all the kings of NIH
9:24 raiment, harness, and spices, **h**, and mules, 5483
9:25 And Solomon had four thousand stalls for **h** 5483
9:28 they brought unto Solomon **h** out of Egypt, 5483
25:28 they brought him upon **h**, and buried him 5483
Ezr 2:66 Their **h** *were* seven hundred thirty and six; 5483
Ne 7:68 Their **h**, seven hundred thirty and six: 5483
Ps 20: 7 Some *trust* in chariots, and some in **h**: but 5483
Ecc 10: 7 I have seen servants upon **h**, and 5483
SS 1: 9 to a **company of h** in Pharaoh's chariots. 5484
Isa 2: 7 their land is also full *of* **h**, neither *is there* 5483
30:16 ye said, No; for we will flee upon **h**; 5483
31: 1 stay on **h**, and trust in chariots, because 5483
31: 3 not God; and their **h** flesh, and not spirit. 5483
36: 8 and I will give thee two thousand **h**, 5483
66:20 unto the LORD out of all nations upon **h**, 5483
Jer 4:13 his **h** are swifter than eagles. Woe unto us! 5483
5: 8 They were *as* fed **h** in the morning: 5483
6:23 they ride upon **h**, set in array as men for 5483
8:16 The snorting of his **h** was heard from Dan: 5483
12: 5 then how canst thou contend with **h**? 5483
17:25 riding in chariots and on **h**, they, and 5483
22: 4 riding in chariots and on **h**, he, and 5483
46: 4 Harness the **h**; and get up, ye horsemen, 5483
46: 9 Come up, ye **h**; and rage, ye chariots; and 5483
47: 3 his strong *h*, at the rushing of his chariots, NIH
50:37 A sword *is* upon their **h**, and upon their 5483
50:42 they shall ride upon **h**, *every one* put in 5483
51:27 cause the **h** to come up as the rough 5483
Eze 17:15 that *they* might give him **h** and 5483
23: 6 young men, horsemen riding upon **h**. 5483

Eze 23:12 most gorgeously, horsemen riding upon **h**, 5483
23:20 and whose issue *is like* the issue of **h**. 5483
23:23 and renowned, all of them riding upon **h**. 5483
26: 7 with **h**, and with chariots, and 5483
26:10 By reason of the abundance of his **h** their 5483
26:11 With the hoofs of his **h** shall he tread down 5483
27:14 of Togarmah traded in thy fairs with **h** 5483
38: 4 and all thine army, **h** and horsemen, 5483
38:15 all of them riding upon **h**, a great company, 5483
39:20 Thus ye shall be filled at my table *with* **h** 5483
Hos 1: 7 nor by sword, nor by battle, by **h**, nor by 5483
14: 3 we will not ride upon **h**: neither will we say 5483
Joel 2: 4 of them *is* as the appearance of **h**; 5483
Am 4:10 the sword, and have taken away your **h**; 5483
6:12 Shall **h** run upon the rock? will *one* plow 5483
Mic 5:10 that I will cut off thy **h** out of the midst of 5483
Na 3: 2 of the pransing **h**, and of the jumping 5483
Hab 1: 8 Their **h** also are swifter than the leopards, 5483
3: 8 that thou didst ride upon thine **h** *and* 5483
3:15 didst walk through the sea *with* thine **h**, 5483
Hag 2:22 the **h** and their riders shall come down, 5483
Zec 1: 8 behind him *were there* red **h**, speckled, and 5483
6: 2 In the first chariot *were* red **h**; and in 5483
6: 2 and in the second chariot black **h**; 5483
6: 3 in the third chariot white **h**; and in 5483
6: 3 and in the fourth chariot grisled *and* bay **h**. 5483
6: 6 The black **h** which *are* therein go forth into 5483
10: 5 and the riders on **h** shall be confounded. 5483
14:20 day shall there be upon the bells of the **h**, 5483
Rev 9: 7 *were* like unto **h** prepared unto battle; *2462*
9: 9 of chariots of many **h** running to battle. *2462*
9:17 And thus I saw the **h** in the vision, and *2462*
9:17 the heads of the **h** *were* as the heads of *2462*
18:13 and **h**, and chariots, and slaves, and souls of *2462*
19:14 were in heaven followed him upon white **h**, *2462*
19:18 the flesh of mighty *men*, and the flesh of **h**, *2462*

HORSES' (2) [HORSE]

Isa 5:28 their **h** hoofs shall be counted like flint, and 5483
Jas 3: 3 Behold, we put bits in the **h** mouths, *2462*

HOSAH (5)

Jos 19:29 the coast turneth *to* **H**; and the outgoings 2621
1Ch 16:38 the son of Jeduthun and **H** to be porters: 2621
26:10 Also **H**, of the children of Merari, had sons; 2621
26:11 the sons and brethren of **H** *were* thirteen. 2621
26:16 and **H** *the lot came forth* westward, 2621

HOSANNA (6)

Mt 21: 9 cried, saying, **H** to the Son of David: *5614*
21: 9 in the name of the Lord; **H** in the highest. *5614*
21:15 and saying, **H** to the Son of David; *5614*
Mk 11: 9 and they that followed, cried, saying, **H**; *5614*
11:10 in the name of the Lord: **H** in the highest. *5614*
Jn 12:13 and went forth to meet him, and cried, **H**: *5614*

HOSEA (3) [OSEE]

Hos 1: 1 The word of the LORD that came unto **H**, 1954
1: 2 beginning of the word of the LORD by **H**. 1954
1: 2 the LORD said to **H**, Go, take unto thee a 1954

HOSEN (1)

Da 3:21 their **h**, and their hats, and their *other* 6361

HOSHAIAH (3)

Ne 12:32 after them went **H**, and half of the princes 1955
Jer 42: 1 Jezaniah the son of **H**, and all the people 1955
43: 2 spake Azariah the son of **H**, and 1955

HOSHAMA (1)

1Ch 3:18 and Shenazar, Jecamiah, **H**, and Nedabiah. 1953

HOSHEA (11) [JOSHUA]

Dt 32:44 of the people, he and **H** the son of Nun. 1954
2Ki 15:30 **H** the son of Elah made a conspiracy 1954
17: 1 **H** the son of Elah to reign in Samaria over 1954
17: 3 **H** became his servant, and gave him 1954
17: 4 the king of Assyria found conspiracy in **H**: 1954
17: 6 In the ninth year of **H**, the king of Assyria 1954
18: 1 Now it came to pass in the third year of **H** 1954
18: 9 which *was* the seventh year of **H** son of 1954
18:10 that *is* the ninth year of **H** king of Israel, 1954
1Ch 27:20 children of Ephraim, **H** the son of Azaziah: 1954
Ne 10:23 **H**, Hananiah, Hashub, 1954

HOSPITALITY (4)

Ro 12:13 to the necessity of saints; given to **h**. *5381*
1Ti 3: 2 of good behaviour, **given to h**, apt to teach; *5382*
Tit 1: 8 But a **lover of h**, a lover of good *men*, *5382*
1Pe 4: 9 Use **h** one to another without grudging. *5382*

HOST (192) [HOSTS]

Ge 2: 1 earth were finished, and all the **h** of them. 6635
21:22 Phichol the chief captain of his **h** spake 6635
21:32 Phichol the chief captain of his **h**, and 6635
32: 2 Jacob saw them, he said, This *is* God's **h**: 4264
Ex 14: 4 honoured upon Pharaoh, and upon all his **h**; 2428
14:17 upon all his **h**, upon his chariots, and 2428
14:24 **h** of the Egyptians through the pillar of fire 4264
14:24 and troubled the **h** of the Egyptians, 4264
14:28 all the **h** of Pharaoh that came into the sea 2428
15: 4 and his **h** hath he cast into the sea: 2428
16:13 the morning the dew lay round about the **h**. 4264
Nu 2: 4 his **h**, and those that were numbered of 6635
2: 6 his **h**, and those that were numbered 6635
2: 8 his **h**, and those that were numbered 6635
2:11 his **h**, and those that were numbered 6635
2:13 his **h**, and those that were numbered of 6635
2:15 his **h**, and those that were numbered of 6635
2:19 his **h**, and those that were numbered of 6635
2:21 his **h**, and those that were numbered of 6635
2:23 his **h**, and those that were numbered of 6635
2:26 his **h**, and those that were numbered of 6635
2:28 his **h**, and those that were numbered of 6635
Nu 2:30 his **h**, and those that were numbered of 6635
4: 3 until fifty years old, all that enter into the **h**, 6635
10:14 over his **h** *was* Nahshon the son of 6635
10:15 over the **h** of the tribe of the children of 6635
10:16 over the **h** of the tribe of the children of 6635
10:18 over his **h** *was* Elizur the son of Shedeur. 6635
10:19 over the **h** of the tribe of the children of 6635
10:20 over the **h** of the tribe of the children of 6635
10:22 over his **h** *was* Elishama the son of 6635
10:23 over the **h** of the tribe of the children of 6635
10:24 over the **h** of the tribe of the children of 6635
10:25 over his **h** *was* Ahiezer the son of 6635
10:26 over the **h** of the tribe of the children of 6635
10:27 over the **h** of the tribe of the children of 6635
31:14 Moses was wroth with the officers of the **h**, 2428
31:48 which *were* over thousands of the **h**, 6635
Dt 2:14 of war were wasted out from among the **h**, 4264
2:15 to destroy them from among the **h**, 4264
4:19 and the stars, *even* all the **h** of heaven, 6635
17: 3 the sun, or moon, or any of the **h** of heaven, 6635
23: 9 When the **h** goeth forth against thine 4264
Jos 1:11 Pass through the **h**, and command 4264
3: 2 that the officers went through the **h**; 4264
5:14 *as* captain of the **h** of the LORD am I now 6635
5:15 the captain of the LORD'S **h** said unto 6635
8:13 *even* all the **h** that *was* on the north of 4264
18: 9 came *again* to Joshua to the **h** *at* Shiloh. 4264
Jdg 4: 2 the captain of whose **h** *was* Sisera, which 6635
4:15 and all *his* chariots, and all *his* **h**, 4264
4:16 after the **h**, unto Harosheth of the Gentiles: 4264
4:16 all the **h** of Sisera fell upon the edge of 4264
7: 1 that the **h** of the Midianites were on 4264
7: 8 the **h** of Midian was beneath him in 4264
7: 9 unto him, Arise, get thee down unto the **h**; 4264
7:10 with Phurah thy servant down to the **h**: 4264
7:11 be strengthened to go down unto the **h**. 4264
7:11 of the armed *men* that *were* in the **h**. 4264
7:13 a cake of barley bread tumbled into the **h** of 4264
7:14 hath God delivered Midian, and all the **h**. 4264
7:15 returned into the **h** of Israel, and said, 4264
7:15 delivered into your hand the **h** of Midian. 4264
7:21 and all the **h** ran, and cried, and fled. 4264
7:22 his fellow, even throughout all the **h**: 4264
7:22 the **h** fled to Beth-shittah in Zererath, *and* 4264
8:11 of Nobah and Jogbehah, and smote the **h**: 4264
8:11 and smote the host: for the **h** was secure. 4264
8:12 and Zalmunna, and discomfited all the **h**. 4264
1Sa 11:11 they came into the midst of the **h** in 4264
12: 9 captain of the **h** of Hazor, and into the hand 6635
14:15 there was trembling in the **h**, in the field, 4264
14:19 that the noise that *was* in the **h** of 4264
14:48 he gathered a **h**, and smote the Amalekites, 2428
14:50 the name of the captain of his **h** *was* Abner, 6635
17:20 as the **h** was going forth to the fight, and 2428
17:46 I will give the carcases of the **h** of 4264
17:55 unto Abner, the captain of the **h**, Abner, 6635
26: 5 Abner the son of Ner, the captain of his **h**: 6635
28: 5 when Saul saw the **h** of the Philistines, he 4264
28:19 the LORD also shall deliver the **h** of Israel 4264
29: 6 thy coming in with me in the **h** *is* good in 4264
2Sa 2: 8 Abner the son of Ner, captain of Saul's **h**, 6635
3:23 and all the **h** that *was* with him were come, 6635
5:24 to smite the **h** of the Philistines. 4264
8: 9 David had smitten all the **h** of Hadadezer, 2428
8:16 Joab the son of Zeruiah *was* over the **h**; 6635
10: 7 sent Joab, and all the **h** *of* the mighty *men*. 6635
10:16 Shobach the captain of the **h** of Hadarezer 6635
10:18 smote Shobach the captain of their **h**, 6635
17:25 Absalom made Amasa captain of the **h** 6635
19:13 if thou be not captain of the **h** before me 6635
20:23 Now Joab *was* over all the **h** of Israel: and 6635
23:16 the three mighty *men* brake through the **h** 4264
24: 2 the king said to Joab the captain of the **h**, 2428
24: 4 and against the captains of the **h**. 2428
24: 4 the captains of the **h** went out from 2428
1Ki 1:19 the priest, and Joab the captain of the **h**: 6635
1:25 the captains of the **h**, and Abiathar 6635
2:32 captain of the **h** of Israel, and Amasa 6635
2:32 the son of Jether, captain of the **h** of Judah. 6635
2:35 the son of Jehoiada in his room over the **h**: 6635
4: 4 the son of Jehoiada *was* over the **h**: 6635
11:15 Joab the captain of the **h** was gone up to 6635
11:21 that Joab the captain of the **h** was dead, 6635
16:16 all Israel made Omri, the captain of the **h**, 6635
20: 1 king of Syria gathered all his **h** together: 2428
22:19 all the **h** of heaven standing by him on his 6635
22:34 Turn thine hand, and carry me out of the **h**; 4264
22:36 there went a proclamation throughout the **h** 4264
2Ki 3: 9 there was no water for the **h**, and for 4264
4:13 for to the king, or to the captain of the **h**? 6635
5: 1 captain of the **h** of the king of Syria, 6635
6:14 thither horses, and chariots, and a great **h**: 2428
6:15 a **h** compassed the city both with horses 2428
6:24 Ben-hadad king of Syria gathered all his **h**, 4264
7: 4 and let us fall unto the **h** of the Syrians: 4264
7: 6 For the Lord had made the **h** of the Syrians 4264
7: 6 noise of horses, *even* the noise of a great **h**: 2428
7:14 the king sent after the **h** of the Syrians, 4264
9: 5 the captains of the **h** *were* sitting; 2428
11:15 the officers of the **h**, and said unto them, 2428
17:16 worshipped all the **h** of heaven, and 6635
18:17 Hezekiah with a great **h** *against* Jerusalem. 2426
21: 3 worshipped all the **h** of heaven, and 6635
21: 5 he built altars for all the **h** of heaven in 6635
23: 4 for the grove, and for all the **h** of heaven: 6635
23: 5 to the planets, and to all the **h** of heaven. 6635
25: 1 he, and all his **h**, against Jerusalem, and 2428
25:19 in the city, and the principal scribe of the **h**, 6635
1Ch 9:19 *being* over the **h** of the LORD, 4264
11:15 the **h** of the Philistines encamped in 4264
11:18 the three brake through the **h** of 4264
12:14 *were* of the sons of Gad, captains of the **h**: 6635
12:21 *men* of valour, and were captains in the **h**. 6635
12:22 until it was a great **h**, like the host of God. 4264
12:22 until it was a great host, like the **h** of God. 4264
1Ch 14:15 before thee to smite the **h** of the Philistines. 4264
14:16 they smote the **h** of the Philistines from 4264
18: 9 all the **h** of Hadarezer king of Zobah; 2428
18:15 Joab the son of Zeruiah *was* over the **h**; 6635
19: 8 sent Joab, and all the **h** *of* the mighty *men*. 6635
19:16 Shophach the captain of the **h** of Hadarezer 6635
19:18 killed Shophach the captain of the **h**. 6635
25: 1 the captains of the **h** separated to 6635
26:26 and hundreds, and the captains of the **h**, 6635
27: 3 all the captains of the **h** for the first month. 6635
27: 5 The third captain of the **h** for the third 6635
2Ch 14: 9 Ethiopian with a **h** of a thousand thousand, 2428
14:13 before the LORD, and before his **h**; 4264
16: 7 is the **h** of the king of Syria escaped out of 2428
16: 8 the Ethiopians and the Lubims a huge **h**, 2428
18:18 all the **h** of heaven standing on his right 6635
18:33 that thou mayest carry me out of the **h**; 4264
23:14 of hundreds that were set over the **h**, 2428
24:23 *that* the **h** of Syria came up against him: 2428
24:24 the LORD delivered a very great **h** into 2428
26:11 Moreover Uzziah had a **h** of fighting *men*, 2428
26:14 for them throughout all the **h** shields, 6635
28: 9 he went out before the **h** that came to 6635
33: 3 worshipped all the **h** of heaven, and 6635
33: 5 he built altars for all the **h** of heaven in 6635
33:11 the captains of the **h** of the king of Assyria, 6635
Ne 9: 6 with all their **h**, the earth, and all *things* that 6635
9: 6 and the **h** of heaven worshippeth thee. 6635
Ps 27: 3 Though a **h** should encamp against me, 4264
33: 6 all the **h** of them by the breath of his 6635
33:16 is no king saved by the multitude of a **h**: 2428
136:15 and his **h** in the Red sea: 2428
Isa 13: 4 the LORD of hosts mustereth the **h** of 6635
24:21 *that* the LORD shall punish the **h** of 6635
34: 4 all the **h** of heaven shall be dissolved, and 6635
34: 4 all their **h** shall fall down, as the leaf falleth 6635
40:26 *things*, that bringeth out their **h** by number: 6635
45:12 and all their **h** have I commanded. 6635
Jer 8: 2 the moon, and all the **h** of heaven, 6635
19:13 have burnt incense unto all the **h** of heaven, 6635
33:22 As the **h** of heaven cannot be numbered, 6635
51: 3 her young men; destroy ye utterly all her **h**. 6635
52:25 the principal scribe of the **h**, who mustered 6635
Eze 1:24 the voice of speech, as the noise of a **h**: 4264
Da 8:10 it waxed great, *even* to the **h** of heaven; 6635
8:10 it cast down *some* of the **h** and of the stars 6635
8:11 *himself even* to the prince of the **h**, 6635
8:12 a **h** was given *him* against the daily 6635
8:13 and the **h** to be trodden under foot? 6635
Ob 1:20 the captivity of this **h** of the children of 2426
Zep 1: 5 them that worship the **h** of heaven upon 6635
Lk 2:13 a multitude of the heavenly **h** praising God, *4756*
10:35 and gave *them* to the **h**, and said unto him, *3830*
Ac 7:42 gave them up to worship the **h** of heaven; *4756*
Ro 16:23 Gaius mine **h**, and of the whole church, *3581*

HOSTAGES (2)

2Ki 14:14 and **h**, and returned to Samaria. 1121+8594
2Ch 25:24 the **h** also, and returned *to* Samaria. 1121+8594

HOSTILE See VEX; VEXATION; VEXED

HOSTS (299) [HOST]

Ex 12:41 *that* all the **h** of the LORD went out from 6635
Nu 1:52 by his own standard, throughout their **h**. 6635
2:32 their **h** *were* six hundred thousand 6635
10:25 of all the camps throughout their **h**: 6635
Jos 10: 5 they and all their **h**, and encamped before 4264
11: 4 they and all their **h** with them, 4264
Jdg 8:10 *were* in Karkor, and their **h** with them, 4264
8:10 left of all the **h** of the children of the east: 4264
1Sa 1: 3 to sacrifice unto the LORD of **h** in Shiloh. 6635
1:11 she vowed a vow, and said, O LORD of **h**, 6635
4: 4 the ark of the covenant of the LORD of **h**, 6635
15: 2 Thus saith the LORD of **h**, I remember 6635
17:45 to thee in the name of the LORD of **h**, 6635
2Sa 5:10 and the LORD God of **h** *was* with him. 6635
6: 2 of **h** that dwelleth *between* the cherubims. 6635
6:18 the people in the name of the LORD of **h**. 6635
7: 8 Thus saith the LORD of **h**, I took thee 6635
7:26 The LORD of **h** *is* the God over Israel: 6635
7:27 For thou, O LORD of **h**, God of Israel, 6635
1Ki 2: 5 what he did to the two captains of the **h** of 6635
15:20 sent the captains of the **h** which he had 2428
18:15 Elijah said, *As* the LORD of **h** liveth, 6635
19:10 been very jealous for the LORD God of **h**: 6635
19:14 been very jealous for the LORD God of **h**: 6635
2Ki 3:14 And Elisha said, *As* the LORD of **h** liveth, 6635
19:31 the zeal of the LORD *of* **h** shall do this. NIH
1Ch 11: 9 greater: for the LORD of **h** *was* with him. 6635
17: 7 Thus saith the LORD of **h**, I took thee 6635
17:24 The LORD of **h** *is* the God of Israel, 6635
Ps 24:10 The LORD of **h**, he *is* the King of glory. 6635
46: 7 The LORD of **h** *is* with us; the God of 6635
46:11 The LORD of **h** *is* with us; the God of 6635
48: 8 we seen in the city of the LORD of **h**, 6635
59: 5 Thou therefore, O LORD God *of* **h**, 6635
69: 6 O Lord GOD of **h**, be ashamed for my 6635
80: 4 O LORD God *of* **h**, how long wilt thou be 6635
80: 7 O God *of* **h**, and cause thy face to shine; 6635
80:14 Return, we beseech thee, O God *of* **h**: 6635
80:19 Turn us again, O LORD God *of* **h**, 6635
84: 1 *are* thy tabernacles, O LORD of **h**! 6635
84: 3 O LORD of **h**, my King, and my God. 6635
84: 8 O LORD God *of* **h**, hear my prayer: 6635
84:12 O LORD of **h**, blessed *is* the man that 6635
89: 8 O LORD God of **h**, who *is* a strong 6635
103:21 Bless ye the LORD, all ye his **h**; 6635
108:11 wilt not thou, O God, go forth with our **h**? 6635
148: 2 all his angels: praise ye him, all his **h**. 6635
Isa 1: 9 Except the LORD of **h** had left unto us a 6635
1:24 Therefore saith the Lord, the LORD of **h**, 6635
2:12 For the day of the LORD of **h** *shall be* 6635
3: 1 For behold, the Lord, the LORD of **h**, 6635
3:15 of the poor? saith the Lord GOD of **h**. 6635

Isa 5: 7 For the vineyard of the LORD of **h** *is* 6635
5: 9 In mine ears *said* the LORD of **h**, Of a 6635
5:16 the LORD of **h** shall be exalted in 6635
5:24 have cast away the law of the LORD of **h**, 6635
6: 3 said, Holy, holy, holy, *is* the LORD of **h**: 6635
6: 5 eyes have seen the King, the LORD of **h**. 6635
8:13 Sanctify the LORD of **h** himself; and 6635
8:18 for wonders in Israel from the LORD of **h**, 6635
9: 7 The zeal of the LORD of **h** will perform 6635
9:13 neither do they seek the LORD of **h**. 6635
9:19 Through the wrath of the LORD of **h** is 6635
10:16 Therefore shall the Lord, the Lord of **h**, 6635
10:23 For the Lord GOD of **h** shall make a 6635
10:24 Therefore thus saith the Lord GOD of **h**, 6635
10:26 the LORD of **h** shall stir up a scourge for 6635
10:33 Behold, the Lord, the LORD of **h**, 6635
13: 4 the LORD of **h** mustereth the host of 6635
13:13 in the wrath of the LORD of **h**, and in 6635
14:22 saith the LORD of **h**, and cut off from 6635
14:23 of destruction, saith the LORD of **h**. 6635
14:24 The LORD of **h** hath sworn, saying, 6635
14:27 For the LORD of **h** hath purposed, and 6635
17: 3 children of Israel, saith the LORD of **h**. 6635
18: 7 unto the LORD of **h** *of* a people scattered 6635
18: 7 the place of the name of the LORD of **h**, 6635
19: 4 over them, saith the Lord, the LORD of **h**. 6635
19:12 let them know what the LORD of **h** hath 6635
19:16 the shaking of the hand of the LORD of **h**, 6635
19:17 because of the counsel of the LORD of **h**, 6635
19:18 of Canaan, and swear to the LORD of **h**: 6635
19:20 for a witness unto the LORD of **h** in 6635
19:25 Whom the LORD of **h** shall bless, saying, 6635
21:10 that which I have heard of the LORD of **h**, 6635
22: 5 of perplexity by the Lord GOD of **h** in 6635
22:12 in that day did the Lord GOD of **h** call to 6635
22:14 revealed in mine ears *by* the LORD of **h**, 6635
22:14 you till ye die, saith the Lord GOD of **h**. 6635
22:15 Thus saith the Lord GOD of **h**, Go, 6635
22:25 In that day, saith the LORD of **h**, shall 6635
23: 9 The LORD of **h** hath purposed it, to stain 6635
24:23 when the LORD of **h** shall reign in mount 6635
25: 6 in this mountain shall the LORD of **h** 6635
28: 5 In that day shall the LORD of **h** be for a 6635
28:22 for I have heard from the Lord GOD of **h** 6635
28:29 also cometh forth from the LORD of **h**, 6635
29: 6 Thou shalt be visited of the LORD of **h** 6635
31: 4 shall the LORD of **h** come down to fight 6635
31: 5 so will the LORD of **h** defend Jerusalem; 6635
37:16 O LORD of **h**, God of Israel, that dwellest 6635
37:32 the zeal of the LORD of **h** shall do this. 6635
39: 5 Hear the word of the LORD of **h**: 6635
44: 6 and his redeemer the LORD of **h**; 6635
45:13 for price nor reward, saith the LORD of **h**. 6635
47: 4 our redeemer, the LORD of **h** *is* his name, 6635
48: 2 of Israel; The LORD of **h** *is* his name. 6635
51:15 The LORD of **h** *is* his name. 6635
54: 5 the LORD of **h** *is* his name; and 6635
Jer 2:19 *is* not in thee, saith the Lord GOD of **h**. 6635
3:19 a goodly heritage of the **h** of nations? 6635
5:14 Wherefore thus saith the LORD God of **h**, 6635
6: 6 For thus hath the LORD of **h** said, Hew ye 6635
6: 9 Thus saith the LORD of **h**, They shall 6635
7: 3 Thus saith the LORD of **h**, the God of 6635
7:21 Thus saith the LORD of **h**, the God of 6635
8: 3 I have driven them, saith the LORD of **h**. 6635
9: 7 Therefore thus saith the LORD of **h**, 6635
9:15 Therefore thus saith the LORD of **h**, 6635
9:17 Thus saith the LORD of **h**, Consider ye, 6635
10:16 The LORD of **h** *is* his name. 6635
11:17 For the LORD of **h**, that planted thee, 6635
11:20 But, O LORD of **h**, that judgest 6635
11:22 Therefore thus saith the LORD of **h**, 6635
15:16 called by thy name, O LORD God of **h**. 6635
16: 9 For thus saith the LORD of **h**, the God of 6635
19: 3 Thus saith the LORD of **h**, the God of 6635
19:11 say unto them, Thus saith the LORD of **h**; 6635
19:15 Thus saith the LORD of **h**, the God of 6635
20:12 But, O LORD of **h**, that triest 6635
23:15 Therefore thus saith the LORD of **h** 6635
23:16 Thus saith the LORD of **h**, Hearken not 6635
23:36 living God, of the LORD of **h** our God. 6635
25: 8 Therefore thus saith the LORD of **h**; 6635
25:27 Thus saith the LORD of **h**, the God of 6635
25:28 say unto them, Thus saith the LORD of **h**; 6635
25:29 of the earth, saith the LORD of **h**. 6635
25:32 Thus saith the LORD of **h**, Behold, 6635
26:18 saying, Thus saith the LORD of **h**; 6635
27: 4 Thus saith the LORD of **h**, the God of 6635
27:18 now make intercession to the LORD of **h**, 6635
27:19 For thus saith the LORD of **h** concerning 6635
27:21 Yea, thus saith the LORD of **h**, the God of 6635
28: 2 Thus speaketh the LORD of **h**, the God of 6635
28:14 For thus saith the LORD of **h**, the God of 6635
29: 4 Thus saith the LORD of **h**, the God of 6635
29: 8 For thus saith the LORD of **h**, the God of 6635
29:17 Thus saith the LORD of **h**; Behold, I will 6635
29:21 Thus saith the LORD of **h**, the God of 6635
29:25 Thus speaketh the LORD of **h**, the God of 6635
30: 8 to pass in that day, saith the LORD of **h**, 6635
31:23 Thus saith the LORD of **h**, the God of 6635
31:35 thereof roar; The LORD of **h** *is* his name: 6635
32:14 Thus saith the LORD of **h**, the God of 6635
32:15 For thus saith the LORD of **h**, the God of 6635
32:18 Mighty God, the LORD of **h**, *is* his name, 6635
33:11 them that shall say, Praise the LORD of **h**: 6635
33:12 Thus saith the LORD of **h**, Again in this 6635
35:13 Thus saith the LORD of **h**, the God of 6635
35:17 Therefore thus saith the LORD God of **h**, 6635
35:18 Thus saith the LORD of **h**, the God of 6635
35:19 Therefore thus saith the LORD of **h**, 6635
38:17 the God of **h**, the God of Israel; 6635
39:16 saying, Thus saith the LORD of **h**, 6635
42:15 Thus saith the LORD of **h**, the God of 6635
42:18 For thus saith the LORD of **h**, the God of 6635
43:10 Thus saith the LORD of **h**, the God of 6635

Jer 44: 2 Thus saith the LORD of **h**, the God of 6635
44: 7 the God of **h**, the God of Israel; 6635
44:11 Therefore thus saith the LORD of **h**, 6635
44:25 Thus saith the LORD of **h**, the God of 6635
46:10 For this *is* the day of the Lord GOD of **h**, 6635
46:10 for the Lord GOD of **h** hath a sacrifice in 6635
46:18 the King, whose name *is* the LORD of **h**, 6635
46:25 The LORD of **h**, the God of Israel, saith; 6635
48: 1 Against Moab thus saith the LORD of **h**, 6635
48:15 the King, whose name *is* the LORD of **h**. 6635
49: 5 a fear upon thee, saith the Lord GOD of **h**, 6635
49: 7 thus saith the LORD of **h**; 6635
49:26 cut off in that day, saith the LORD of **h**. 6635
49:35 Thus saith the LORD of **h**; Behold, I *will* 6635
50:18 Therefore thus saith the LORD of **h**, 6635
50:25 for this *is* the work of the Lord GOD of **h** 6635
50:31 most proud, saith the Lord GOD of **h**: 6635
50:33 Thus saith the LORD of **h**; The children 6635
50:34 *is* strong; the LORD of **h** *is* his name: 6635
51: 5 nor Judah of his God, of the LORD of **h**; 6635
51:14 The LORD of **h** hath sworn by himself, 6635
51:19 the LORD of **h** *is* his name. 6635
51:33 For thus saith the LORD of **h**, the God of 6635
51:57 the King, whose name *is* the LORD of **h**. 6635
51:58 Thus saith the LORD of **h**; The broad 6635
Hos 12: 5 Even the LORD God of **h**; the LORD *is* 6635
Am 3:13 saith the Lord GOD, the God of **h**, 6635
4:13 The LORD, The God of **h**, *is* his name. 6635
5:14 so the LORD, the God of **h**, shall be with 6635
5:15 it may be that the LORD God of **h** will be 6635
5:16 the God of **h**, the Lord, saith thus; 6635
5:27 the LORD, whose name *is* The God of **h**. 6635
6: 8 saith the LORD the God of **h**, I abhor 6635
6:14 of Israel, saith the LORD the God of **h**; 6635
9: 5 the Lord GOD of **h** *is* he that toucheth 6635
Mic 4: 4 for the mouth of the LORD of **h** hath 6635
Na 2:13 saith the LORD of **h**, and I will burn her 6635
3: 5 I *am* against thee, saith the LORD of **h**; 6635
Hab 2:13 *is it* not of the LORD of **h** that the people 6635
Zep 2: 9 saith the LORD of **h**, the God of Israel, 6635
2:10 against the people of the LORD of **h**. 6635
Hag 1: 2 Thus speaketh the LORD of **h**, saying, 6635
1: 5 Now therefore thus saith the LORD of **h**; 6635
1: 7 Thus saith the LORD of **h**; Consider your 6635
1: 9 saith the LORD of **h**. Because of mine 6635
1:14 did work in the house of the LORD of **h**, 6635
2: 4 for I *am* with you, saith the LORD of **h**: 6635
2: 6 For thus saith the LORD of **h**; Yet once, 6635
2: 7 house *with* glory, saith the LORD of **h**. 6635
2: 8 and the gold *is* mine, saith the LORD of **h**. 6635
2: 9 than of the former, saith the LORD of **h**: 6635
2: 9 will I give peace, saith the LORD of **h**. 6635
2:11 Thus saith the LORD of **h**; Ask now 6635
2:23 In that day, saith the LORD of **h**, will I 6635
2:23 I have chosen thee, saith the LORD of **h**. 6635
Zec 1: 3 unto them, Thus saith the LORD of **h**; 6635
1: 3 saith the LORD of **h**, and I will turn unto 6635
1: 3 I will turn unto you, saith the LORD of **h**. 6635
1: 4 saying, Thus saith the LORD of **h**; 6635
1: 6 Like as the LORD of **h** thought to do unto 6635
1:12 and said, O LORD of **h**, 6635
1:14 saying, Thus saith the LORD of **h**; 6635
1:16 saith the LORD of **h**, and a line shall be 6635
1:17 saying, Thus saith the LORD of **h**; 6635
2: 8 For thus saith the LORD of **h**; After 6635
2: 9 ye shall know that the LORD of **h** hath 6635
2:11 thou shalt know that the LORD of **h** hath 6635
3: 7 Thus saith the LORD of **h**; If thou wilt 6635
3: 9 saith the LORD of **h**, and I will remove 6635
3:10 In that day, saith the LORD of **h**, shall ye 6635
4: 6 but by my spirit, saith the LORD of **h**. 6635
4: 9 thou shalt know that the LORD of **h** hath 6635
5: 4 saith the LORD of **h**, and it shall enter 6635
6:12 Thus speaketh the LORD of **h**, saying, 6635
6:15 ye shall know that the LORD of **h** hath 6635
7: 3 *were* in the house of the LORD of **h**, 6635
7: 4 came the word of the LORD of **h** unto me, 6635
7: 9 Thus speaketh the LORD of **h**, saying, 6635
7:12 the words which the LORD of **h** hath sent 6635
7:12 came a great wrath from the LORD of **h**. 6635
7:13 I would not hear, saith the LORD of **h**: 6635
8: 1 Again the word of the LORD of **h** came *to* 6635
8: 2 Thus saith the LORD of **h**; I was jealous 6635
8: 3 the mountain of the LORD of **h** the holy 6635
8: 4 Thus saith the LORD of **h**; There shall yet 6635
8: 6 Thus saith the LORD of **h**; If it be 6635
8: 6 in my eyes? saith the LORD of **h**. 6635
8: 7 Thus saith the LORD of **h**; Behold, I *will* 6635
8: 9 Thus saith the LORD of **h**; Let your hands 6635
8: 9 of the house of the LORD of **h** was laid, 6635
8:11 *in* the former days, saith the LORD of **h**. 6635
8:14 For thus saith the LORD of **h**; As I 6635
8:14 saith the LORD of **h**, and I repented not: 6635
8:18 the word of the LORD of **h** came unto me, 6635
8:19 Thus saith the LORD of **h**; The fast of 6635
8:20 Thus saith the LORD of **h**; *It shall* yet 6635
8:21 the LORD, and to seek the LORD of **h**: 6635
8:22 come to seek the LORD of **h** in Jerusalem, 6635
8:23 Thus saith the LORD of **h**; In those days *it* 6635
9:15 The LORD of **h** shall defend them; and 6635
10: 3 for the LORD of **h** hath visited his flock 6635
12: 5 my strength in the LORD of **h** their God. 6635
13: 2 to pass in that day, saith the LORD of **h**, 6635
13: 7 *that is* my fellow, saith the LORD of **h**: 6635
14:16 the LORD of **h**, and to keep the feast of 6635
14:17 the LORD of **h**, even upon them shall be 6635
14:21 shall be holiness unto the LORD of **h**: 6635
14:21 Canaanite in the house of the LORD of **h**. 6635
Mal 1: 4 thus saith the LORD of **h**, They shall 6635
1: 6 saith the LORD of **h** unto you, O priests, 6635
1: 8 accept thy person? saith the LORD of **h**. 6635
1: 9 your persons? saith the LORD of **h**. 6635
1:10 no pleasure in you, saith the LORD of **h**, 6635
1:11 among the heathen, saith the LORD of **h**. 6635
1:13 have snuffed at it, saith the LORD of **h**; 6635

Mal 1:14 saith the LORD of **h**, and my name *is* 6635
2: 2 glory unto my name, saith the LORD of **h**, 6635
2: 4 might be with Levi, saith the LORD of **h**. 6635
2: 7 for he *is* the messenger of the LORD of **h**. 6635
2: 8 covenant of Levi, saith the LORD of **h**. 6635
2:12 offereth an offering unto the LORD of **h**. 6635
2:16 with his garment, saith the LORD of **h**: 6635
3: 1 he *shall* come, saith the LORD of **h**. 6635
3: 5 and fear not me, saith the LORD of **h**. 6635
3: 7 will return unto you, saith the LORD of **h**. 6635
3:10 me now herewith, saith the LORD of **h**, 6635
3:11 the time in the field, saith the LORD of **h**. 6635
3:12 a delightsome land, saith the LORD of **h**. 6635
3:14 mournfully before the LORD of **h**? 6635
3:17 they shall be mine, saith the LORD of **h**, 6635
4: 1 shall burn them up, saith the LORD of **h**, 6635
4: 3 that I *shall* do *this*, saith the LORD of **h**. 6635

HOT (31) [HOTLY, HOTTEST]

Ex 16:21 and when the sun **waxed h**, it melted. 2552
22:24 my wrath shall **wax h**, and I will kill you 2734
32:10 that my wrath may **wax h** against them, and 2734
32:11 why doth thy wrath **wax h** against thy 2734
32:19 Moses' anger **waxed h**, and he cast 2734
32:22 Let not the anger of my lord **wax h**: 2734
Lev 13:24 in the skin whereof *there is* a **h** burning, and 784
Dt 9:19 I was afraid of the anger and **h displeasure**, 2534
19: 6 while his heart is **h**, and overtake him, 3179
Jos 9:12 This our bread we took **h** for our provision 2525
Jdg 2:14 the anger of the LORD was **h** against 2734
2:20 the anger of the LORD was **h** against 2734
3: 8 Therefore the anger of the LORD was **h** 2734
6:39 Let not thine anger be **h** against me, and 2734
10: 7 the anger of the LORD was **h** against 2734
1Sa 11: 9 To morrow, by *that time* the sun be **h**, 2527
21: 6 to put **h** bread in the day when it was taken 2527
Ne 7: 3 of Jerusalem be opened until the sun be **h**; 2527
Job 6:17 when it is **h**, they are consumed out of their 2527
Ps 6: 1 neither chasten me in thy **h displeasure**. 2534
38: 1 neither chasten me in thy **h displeasure**. 2534
39: 3 My heart was **h** within me, while I was 2552
78:48 the hail, and their flocks to **h thunderbolts**. 7565
Pr 6:28 Can one go upon **h coals**, and his feet not 1513
Eze 24:11 that the brass of it may be **h**, and may burn, 3179
Da 3:22 *was* urgent, and the furnace exceeding **h**, 228
Hos 7: 7 They are all **h** as an oven, and 2552
1Ti 4: 2 their conscience **seared with a h iron**; *2743*
Rev 3:15 thy works, that thou art neither cold nor **h**: *2200*
3:15 cold nor hot: I would thou wert cold or **h**. *2200*
3:16 thou art lukewarm, and neither cold nor **h**, *2200*

HOTHAM (1)

1Ch 7:32 and Shomer, and **H**, and Shua their sister. 2369

HOTHAN (1)

1Ch 11:44 and Jehiel the sons of **H** the Aroerite, 2369

HOTHIR (2)

1Ch 25: 4 Joshbekashah, Mallothi, **H**, *and* Mahazioth: 1956
25:28 The one and twentieth to **H**, *he*, his sons, 1956

HOTLY (1) [HOT]

Ge 31:36 that thou hast *so* **h pursued** after me? 1814

HOTTEST (1) [HOT]

2Sa 11:15 Set ye Uriah in the forefront of the **h** battle, 2389

HOUGH (1) [HOUGHED]

Jos 11: 6 thou shalt **h** their horses, and burn their 6131

HOUGHED (3) [HOUGH]

Jos 11: 9 he **h** their horses, and burnt their chariots 6131
2Sa 8: 4 David **h** all the chariot *horses*, but 6131
1Ch 18: 4 David also **h** all the chariot *horses*, but 6131

HOUR (94) [HOURS]

Da 3: 6 worshippeth shall the same **h** be cast into 8160
3:15 ye shall be cast the same **h** into the midst of 8160
4:19 was astonied for one **h**, and his thoughts 8160
4:33 The same **h** was the thing fulfilled upon 8160
5: 5 In the same **h** came forth fingers of a man's 8160
Mt 8:13 his servant was healed in the selfsame **h**. *5610*
9:22 the woman was made whole from that **h**.) *5610*
10:19 for it shall be given you in that *same* **h** *5610*
15:28 daughter was made whole from that *very* **h**. *5610*
17:18 and the child was cured from that *very* **h**. *5610*
20: 3 And he went out about the third **h**, and *5610*
20: 5 he went out about the sixth and ninth **h**, *5610*
20: 6 And about the eleventh **h** he went out, and *5610*
20: 9 came that *were hired* about the eleventh **h**, *5610*
20:12 These last have wrought *but* one **h**, and *5610*
24:36 But of that day and **h** knoweth no *man*, no, *5610*
24:42 for ye know not what **h** your Lord doth *5610*
24:44 for in such an **h** as ye think not the Son of *5610*
24:50 for *him*, and in an **h** that he is not ware of, *5610*
25:13 for ye know neither the day nor the **h** *5610*
26:40 What, could ye not watch with me one **h**? *5610*
26:45 the **h** is at hand, and the Son of man is *5610*
26:55 In that *same* **h** said Jesus to the multitudes, *5610*
27:45 Now from the sixth **h** there was darkness *5610*
27:45 darkness over all the land unto the ninth **h**. *5610*
27:46 And about the ninth **h** Jesus cried with a *5610*
Mk 13:11 but whatsoever shall be given you in that **h**, *5610*
13:32 of that day and *that* **h** knoweth no *man*, no, *5610*
14:35 were possible, the **h** might pass from him. *5610*
14:37 couldest not thou watch one **h**? *5610*
14:41 it is enough, the **h** is come; behold, the Son *5610*
15:25 And it was the third **h**, and they crucified *5610*
15:33 And when the sixth **h** was come, there was *5610*
15:33 over the whole land until the ninth **h**. *5610*
15:34 And at the ninth **h** Jesus cried with a loud *5610*
Lk 7:21 And in that *same* **h** he cured many of *their* *5610*
10:21 In that **h** Jesus rejoiced in spirit, and said, *5610*
12:12 you in the same **h** what ye ought to say. *5610*

H

Lk 12:39 had known what **h** the thief would come, 5610
12:40 for the Son of man cometh at an **h** when ye 5610
12:46 for *him,* and at an **h** when he is not ware, 5610
20:19 the scribes the same **h** sought to lay hands 5610
22:14 And when the **h** was come, he sat down, 5610
22:53 but this is your **h**, and the power of 5610
22:59 And about the space of one **h** after another 5610
23:44 And it was about the sixth **h**, and there was 5610
23:44 darkness over all the earth until the ninth **h**. 5610
24:33 And they rose up the same **h**, and 5610
Jn 1:39 him that day: for it was about the tenth **h**. 5610
2: 4 I to do with thee? mine **h** is not yet come. 5610
4: 6 on the well: *and* it was about the sixth **h**. 5610
4:21 Woman, believe me, the **h** cometh, 5610
4:23 But the **h** cometh, and now is, when 5610
4:52 Then inquired he of them the **h** when he 5610
4:52 Yesterday at the seventh **h** the fever left 5610
4:53 the father knew that *it was* at the same **h**, 5610
5:25 say unto you, The **h** is coming, and now is, 5610
5:28 for the **h** is coming, in the which all that are 5610
7:30 on him, because his **h** was not yet come. 5610
8:20 hands on him; for his **h** was not yet come. 5610
12:23 answered them, saying, The **h** is come, 5610
12:27 Father, save me from this **h**: but for this 5610
12:27 but for this cause came I unto this **h**. 5610
13: 1 when Jesus knew that his **h** was come that 5610
16:21 travail hath sorrow, because her **h** is come: 5610
16:32 Behold, the **h** cometh, yea, is now come, 5610
17: 1 to heaven, and said, Father, the **h** is come; 5610
19:14 of the passover, and about the sixth **h**: 5610
19:27 And from that **h** *that* disciple took her unto 5610
Ac 2:15 seeing it is *but* the third **h** of the day. 5610
3: 1 together into the temple at the **h** of prayer, 5610
3: 1 at the hour of prayer, *being* the ninth ***h***. NIG
10: 3 about the ninth **h** of the day, 5610
10: 9 up upon the house to pray about the sixth **h**: 5610
10:30 Four days ago I was fasting until this **h**; 5610
10:30 and at the ninth **h** I prayed in my house, 5610
16:18 out of her. And he came out the same **h**. 5610
16:33 And he took them the same **h** of the night, 5610
22:13 And the same **h** I looked up upon him. 5610
23:23 two hundred, at the third **h** of the night; 5610
1Co 4:11 Even unto this present **h** we both hunger, 5610
8: 7 some with conscience of the idol unto **this h**, 737
15:30 And why stand we in jeopardy every **h**? 5610
Gal 2: 5 gave place by subjection, no, not for an **h**; 5610
Rev 3: 3 thou shalt not know what **h** I will come 5610
3:10 I also will keep thee from the **h** of 5610
8: 1 in heaven about the space of **half an h**. 2256
9:15 which were prepared for an **h**, and a day, 5610
11:13 And the same **h** was there a great 5610
14: 7 to him; for the **h** of his judgment is come: 5610
17:12 receive power as kings one **h** with 5610
18:10 for in one **h** is thy judgment come. 5610
18:17 For in one **h** so great riches is come to 5610
18:19 for in one **h** is she made desolate. 5610

HOURS (3) [HOUR]

Jn 11: 9 Are there not twelve **h** in the day? 5610
Ac 5: 7 And it was about the space of three **h** after, 5610
19:34 all with one voice about the space of two **h** 5610

HOUSE (2025) [HOUSE OF APHRAH, HOUSEHOLD, HOUSEHOLDER, HOUSEHOLDS, HOUSES, HOUSETOP, HOUSETOPS, STOREHOUSE, STOREHOUSES, WINTERHOUSE]

Ge 7: 1 Come thou and all thy **h** into the ark; 1004
12: 1 from thy kindred, and from thy father's **h**, 1004
12:15 and the woman was taken into Pharaoh's **h**. 1004
12:17 his **h** with great plagues because of Sarai 1004
14:14 his trained *servants,* born in his own **h**, 1004
15: 2 the steward of my **h** *is* this Eliezer of 1004
15: 3 and lo, one born in my **h** is mine heir. 1004
17:12 he that is born in the **h**, or bought with 1004
17:13 He that is born in thy **h**, and he that is 1004
17:23 all that were born in his **h**, and all that were 1004
17:23 male among the men of Abraham's **h**; 1004
17:27 all the men of his **h**, born in the house, and 1004
17:27 born in the **h**, and bought with money of 1004
19: 2 into your servant's **h**, and tarry all night, 1004
19: 3 turned in unto him, and entered into his **h**; 1004
19: 4 compassed the **h** round, both old and 1004
19:10 pulled Lot into the **h** to them, and shut to 1004
19:11 *were at* the door of the **h** with blindness, 1004
20:13 caused me to wander from my father's **h**, 1004
20:18 up all the wombs of the **h** of Abimelech, 1004
24: 2 of his **h** that ruled over all that he had, 1004
24: 7 which took me from my father's **h**, and 1004
24:23 is there room *in* thy father's **h** for us to 1004
24:27 the LORD led me to the **h** of my master's 1004
24:28 told *them of* her mother's **h** these things. 1004
24:31 for I have prepared the **h**, and room for 1004
24:32 the man came into the **h**: and he ungirded 1004
24:38 thou shalt go unto my father's **h**, and to my 1004
24:40 son of my kindred, and of my father's **h**: 1004
27:15 which *were* with her in the **h**, and put them 1004
28: 2 to the **h** of Bethuel thy mother's father; 1004
28:17 this *is* none other but the **h** of God, and 1004
28:21 So that I come again to my father's **h** in 1004
28:22 I have set *for* a pillar, shall be God's **h**: 1004
29:13 and kissed him, and brought him to his **h**. 1004
30:30 now when shall I provide for mine own **h** 1004
31:14 or inheritance for us in our father's **h**? 1004
31:30 thou sore longedst after thy father's **h**, 1004
31:41 Thus have I been twenty years in thy **h**; 1004
33:17 built him a **h**, and made booths for his 1004
34:19 he *was* more honourable than all the **h** of 1004
34:26 took Dinah out of Shechem's **h**, and 1004
34:29 and spoiled even all that *was* in the **h**. 1004
34:30 and I shall be destroyed, I and my **h**. 1004
36: 6 all the persons of his **h**, and his cattle, and 1004
38:11 Remain a widow *at* thy father's **h**, 1004
38:11 Tamar went and dwelt *in* her father's **h**. 1004
39: 2 he was in the **h** of his master the Egyptian. 1004

Ge 39: 4 he made him overseer over his **h**, and 1004
39: 5 *that* he had made him overseer in his **h**, 1004
39: 5 that the LORD blessed the Egyptian's **h** 1004
39: 5 LORD was upon all that he had in the **h**, 1004
39: 8 wotteth not what *is* with me in the **h**, 1004
39: 9 *There is* none greater in this **h** than I; 1004
39:11 that *Joseph* went into the **h** to do his 1004
39:11 *there was* none of the men of the **h** there 1004
39:14 That she called unto the men of her **h**, and 1004
40: 3 he put them in ward *in* the **h** of the captain 1004
40: 7 *were* with him in the ward of his lord's **h**, 1004
40:14 unto Pharaoh, and bring me out of this **h**: 1004
41:10 me in ward *in* the captain of the guard's **h**, 1004
41:40 Thou shalt be over my **h**, and 1004
41:51 me forget all my toil, and all my father's **h**. 1004
42:19 brethren be bound in the **h** of your prison: 1004
43:16 he said to the ruler of his **h**, Bring *these* 1004
43:17 the man brought the men into Joseph's **h**. 1004
43:18 because they were brought into Joseph's **h**; 1004
43:19 came near to the steward of Joseph's **h**, 1004
43:19 communed with him *at* the door of the **h**, 1004
43:24 the man brought the men into Joseph's **h**, 1004
43:26 present which *was* in their hand into the **h**, 1004
44: 1 he commanded the steward of his **h**, saying, 1004
44: 8 should we steal out of thy lord's **h** silver or 1004
44:14 and his brethren came to Joseph's **h**; 1004
45: 2 the Egyptians and the **h** of Pharaoh heard. 1004
45: 8 lord of all his **h**, and a ruler throughout all 1004
45:16 the fame *thereof* was heard *in* Pharaoh's **h**, 1004
46:27 all the souls of the **h** of Jacob, which came 1004
46:31 unto his father's **h**, I will go up, and 1004
46:31 unto him, My brethren, and my father's **h**, 1004
47:14 brought the money into Pharaoh's **h**. 1004
50: 4 Joseph spake unto the **h** of Pharaoh, saying, 1004
50: 7 the elders of his **h**, and all the elders of 1004
50: 8 all the **h** of Joseph, and his brethren, and 1004
50: 8 and his brethren, and his father's **h**: 1004
50:22 dwelt in Egypt, he, and his father's **h**: 1004
Ex 2: 1 there went a man of the **h** of Levi, and 1004
3:22 of her that sojourneth in her **h**, jewels of 1004
7:23 Pharaoh turned and went into his **h**, 1004
8: 3 which shall go up and come into thine **h**, 1004
8: 3 into the **h** of thy servants, and upon thy 1004
8:24 swarm *of flies* into the **h** of Pharaoh, 1004
12: 3 according to the **h** of *their* fathers, a lamb 1004
12: 3 to the house of *their* fathers, a lamb for a **h**: 1004
12: 4 his neighbour next unto his **h** take *it* 1004
12:22 none of you shall go out at the door of his **h** 1004
12:30 for *there was* not a **h** where *there was* not 1004
12:46 In one **h** shall it be eaten; thou shalt not 1004
12:46 forth *ought* of the flesh abroad out of the **h**; 1004
13: 3 out from Egypt, out of the **h** of bondage; 1004
13:14 us out from Egypt, from the **h** of bondage: 1004
16:31 the **h** of Israel called the name thereof 1004
19: 3 Thus shalt thou say to the **h** of Jacob, and 1004
20: 2 the land of Egypt, out of the **h** of bondage. 1004
20:17 Thou shalt not covet thy neighbour's **h**, 1004
22: 7 to keep, and it be stolen out of the man's **h**; 1004
22: 8 the master of the **h** shall be brought unto 1004
23:19 bring *into* the **h** of the LORD thy God. 1004
34:26 bring *unto* the **h** of the LORD thy God. 1004
40:38 it by night, in the sight of all the **h** of Israel, 1004
Lev 10: 6 let your brethren, the whole **h** of Israel, 1004
14:34 I put the plague of leprosy in a **h** of the land 1004
14:35 he that owneth the **h** shall come and tell 1004
14:35 to me *there is* as it were a plague in the **h**: 1004
14:36 priest shall command that they empty the **h**, 1004
14:36 that all that *is* in the **h** be not *made* unclean: 1004
14:36 afterward the priest shall go in to see the **h**: 1004
14:37 *if* the plague *be* in the walls of the **h** with 1004
14:38 the priest shall go out of the **h** to the door 1004
14:38 go out of the house to the door of the **h**, 1004
14:38 of the house, and shut up the **h** seven days: 1004
14:39 *if* the plague be spread in the walls of the **h**; 1004
14:41 he shall cause the **h** to be scraped within 1004
14:42 take other morter, and shall plaister the **h**. 1004
14:43 plague come again, and break out in the **h**, 1004
14:43 after he hath scraped the **h**, and after it is 1004
14:44 and behold, *if* the plague be spread in the **h**, 1004
14:44 in the house, it *is* a fretting leprosy in the **h**: 1004
14:45 he shall break down the **h**, the stones of it, 1004
14:45 timber thereof, and all the morter of the **h**; 1004
14:46 Moreover he that goeth into the **h** all 1004
14:47 he that lieth in the **h** shall wash his clothes; 1004
14:47 he that eateth in the **h** shall wash his 1004
14:48 behold, the plague hath not spread in the **h**, 1004
14:48 in the house, after the **h** was plaistered: 1004
14:48 the priest shall pronounce the **h** clean, 1004
14:49 he shall take to cleanse the **h** two birds, 1004
14:51 and sprinkle the **h** seven times: 1004
14:52 he shall cleanse the **h** with the blood of 1004
14:53 and make an atonement for the **h**: 1004
14:55 for the leprosy of a garment, and of a **h**, 1004
16: 6 an atonement for himself, and for his **h**. 1004
16:11 for his **h**, and shall kill the bullock of 1004
17: 3 What man soever *there be* of the **h** of 1004
17: 8 Whatsoever man *there be* of the **h** of Israel, 1004
17:10 whatsoever man *there be* of the **h** of Israel, 1004
22:11 shall eat of it, and he that is born in his **h**: 1004
22:13 and is returned unto her father's **h**, 1004
22:18 Whatsoever *he be* of the **h** of Israel, or 1004
25:29 if a man sell a dwelling **h** in a walled city, 1004
25:30 the **h** that *is* in the walled city shall be 1004
25:33 the **h** that was sold, and the city of his 1004
27:14 when a man shall sanctify his **h** *to be* holy 1004
27:15 if he that sanctified *it* will redeem his **h**, 1004
Nu 1: 2 after their families, by the **h** of their fathers, 1004
1: 4 every one head of the **h** of his fathers. 1004
1:18 by the **h** of their fathers, according to 1004
1:20 after their families, by the **h** of their fathers, 1004
1:22 after their families, by the **h** of their fathers, 1004
1:24 after their families, by the **h** of their fathers, 1004
1:26 after their families, by the **h** of their fathers, 1004
1:28 after their families, by the **h** of their fathers, 1004
1:30 after their families, by the **h** of their fathers, 1004

Nu 1:32 after their families, by the **h** of their fathers, 1004
1:34 after their families, by the **h** of their fathers, 1004
1:36 after their families, by the **h** of their fathers, 1004
1:38 after their families, by the **h** of their fathers, 1004
1:40 after their families, by the **h** of their fathers, 1004
1:42 after their families, by the **h** of their fathers, 1004
1:44 each one was for the **h** of his fathers. 1004
1:45 by the **h** of their fathers, from twenty years 1004
2: 2 with the ensign of their father's **h**: 1004
2:32 children of Israel by the **h** of their fathers: 1004
2:34 according to the **h** of their fathers. 1004
3:15 Number the children of Levi after the **h** of 1004
3:20 Levites according to the **h** of their fathers. 1004
3:24 the chief of the **h** of the father of 1004
3:30 the chief of the **h** of the father of 1004
3:35 the chief of the **h** of the father of 1004
4: 2 after their families, by the **h** of their fathers, 1004
4:29 after their families, by the **h** of their fathers; 1004
4:34 and after the **h** of their fathers, 1004
4:38 their families, and by the **h** of their fathers, 1004
4:40 by the **h** of their fathers, were two thousand 1004
4:42 their families, by the **h** of their fathers, 1004
4:46 and after the **h** of their fathers, 1004
7: 2 of Israel, heads of the **h** of their fathers, 1004
12: 7 *is* not so, who *is* faithful in all mine **h**. 1004
17: 2 a rod according to the **h** of *their* fathers, 1004
17: 2 of all their princes according to the **h** of 1004
17: 3 for one rod *shall be* for the head of the **h** of 1004
17: 8 the rod of Aaron for the **h** of Levi was 1004
18: 1 thy father's **h** with thee shall bear 1004
18:11 every one *that is* clean in thy **h** shall eat of 1004
18:13 every one *that is* clean in thine **h** shall eat 1004
20:29 Aaron thirty days, *even* all the **h** of Israel. 1004
22:18 If Balak would give me his **h** full *of* silver 1004
24:13 If Balak would give me his **h** full *of* silver 1004
25:14 a prince of a chief **h** among the Simeonites. 1004
25:15 over a people, *and* of a chief **h** in Midian. 1004
26: 2 and upward, throughout their fathers' **h**, 1004
30: 3 a bond, *being* in her father's **h** in her youth; 1004
30:10 if she vowed *in* her husband's **h**, or 1004
30:16 *being yet* in her youth *in* her father's **h**. 1004
34:14 Reuben according to the **h** of their fathers, 1004
34:14 of Gad according to the **h** of their fathers, 1004
Dt 5: 6 the land of Egypt, from the **h** of bondage. 1004
5:21 neither shalt thou covet thy neighbour's **h**, 1004
6: 7 talk of them when thou sittest in thine **h**, 1004
6: 9 shalt write them upon the posts of thy **h**, 1004
6:12 the land of Egypt, from the **h** of bondage. 1004
7: 8 and redeemed you out of the **h** of bondmen, 1004
7:26 thou bring an abomination into thine **h**, 1004
8:14 the land of Egypt, from the **h** of bondage; 1004
11:19 of them when thou sittest in thine **h**, 1004
11:20 write them upon the door posts of thine **h**, 1004
13: 5 and redeemed you out of the **h** of bondage, 1004
13:10 the land of Egypt, from the **h** of bondage. 1004
15:16 because he loveth thee and thine **h**, because 1004
20: 5 What man *is there* that hath built a new **h**, 1004
20: 5 let him go and return to his **h**, lest he die in 1004
20: 6 let him *also* go and return unto his **h**, lest he 1004
20: 7 let him go and return unto his **h**, lest he die 1004
20: 8 let him go and return unto his **h**, lest his 1004
21:12 thou shalt bring her home to thine **h**; and 1004
21:13 shall remain in thine **h**, and bewail her 1004
22: 2 thou shalt bring it unto thine own **h**, and 1004
22: 8 When thou buildest a new **h**, then 1004
22: 8 that thou bring not blood upon thine **h**, 1004
22:21 out the damsel to the door of her father's **h**, 1004
22:21 to play the whore *in* her father's **h**: 1004
23:18 *into* the **h** of the LORD thy God for any 1004
24: 1 *it* in her hand, and send her out of his **h**. 1004
24: 2 when she is departed out of his **h**, she may 1004
24: 3 *it* in her hand, and sendeth her out of his **h**; 1004
24:10 thou shalt not go into his **h** to fetch his 1004
25: 9 man that will not build up his brother's **h**. 1004
25:10 The **h** of him that hath his shoe loosed. 1004
25:14 Thou shalt not have in thine **h** divers 1004
26:11 unto thine **h**, thou, and the Levite, and 1004
26:13 away the hallowed *things* out of *mine* **h**, 1004
28:30 thou shalt build a **h**, and thou shalt not 1004
Jos 2: 1 came *into* a harlot's **h**, named Rahab, and 1004
2: 3 to thee, which are entered into thine **h**: 1004
2: 6 had brought them up to the **roof of** the **h**, 1406
2:12 will also shew kindness unto my father's **h**, 1004
2:15 for her **h** *was* upon the town wall, and 1004
2:19 go out of the doors of thy **h** into the street, 1004
2:19 whosoever shall be with thee in the **h**, 1004
6:17 she and all that *are* with her in the **h**, 1004
6:22 Go *into* the harlot's **h**, and bring out thence 1004
6:24 they put *into* the treasury of the **h** of 1004
9:23 and drawers of water for the **h** of my God. 1004
17:17 Joshua spake unto the **h** of Joseph, *even* to 1004
18: 5 the **h** of Joseph shall abide in their coasts 1004
20: 6 unto his own city, and unto his own **h**, 1004
21:45 LORD had spoken unto the **h** of Israel; 1004
22:14 of each chief **h** a prince throughout all 1004
22:14 each one *was* a head of the **h** of their 1004
24:15 as for me and my **h**, we will serve 1004
24:17 from the **h** of bondage, and which did those 1004
Jdg 1:22 the **h** of Joseph, they also went up *against* 1004
1:23 the **h** of Joseph sent to descry Beth-el. 1004
1:35 yet the hand of the **h** of Joseph prevailed, 1004
4:17 of Hazor and the **h** of Heber the Kenite. 1004
6: 8 brought you forth out of the **h** of bondage; 1004
6:15 and I *am* the least in my father's **h**. 1004
8:27 became a snare unto Gideon, and to his **h**. 1004
8:29 son of Joash went and dwelt in his own **h**. 1004
8:35 Neither shewed they kindness to the **h** of 1004
9: 1 with all the family of the **h** of his mother's 1004
9: 4 ten *pieces* of silver out of the **h** of 1004
9: 5 he went unto his father's **h** at Ophrah, and 1004
9: 6 all the **h** of Millo, and went, and 1004
9:16 ye have dealt well with Jerubbaal and his **h**, 1004
9:18 ye are risen up against my father's **h** *this* 1004
9:19 with Jerubbaal and with his **h** this day, 1004
9:20 the men of Shechem, and the **h** of Millo; 1004

Jdg 9:20 from the **h** of Millo, and 1004
9:27 and went *into* the **h** of their god, and did eat 1004
9:46 into a hold of the **h** of the god Berith. 1004
10: 9 and against the **h** of Ephraim; 1004
11: 2 Thou shalt not inherit in our father's **h**; 1004
11: 7 and expel me out of my father's **h**? 1004
11:31 forth of the doors of my **h** to meet me, 1004
11:34 Jephthah came *to* Mizpeh unto his **h**, and 1004
12: 1 we will burn thine **h** upon thee with fire. 1004
14:15 we burn thee and thy father's **h** with fire: 1004
14:19 and he went up *to* his father's **h**. 1004
16:21 of brass; and he did grind in the prison **h**. 1004
16:25 they called for Samson out of the prison **h**; 1004
16:26 feel the pillars whereupon the **h** standeth, 1004
16:27 Now the **h** was full *of* men and women; and 1004
16:29 two middle pillars upon which the **h** stood, 1004
16:30 the **h** fell upon the lords, and upon all 1004
16:31 and all the **h** of his father came down, 1004
17: 4 and they were in the **h** of Micah. 1004
17: 5 the man Micah had a **h** of gods, and 1004
17: 8 he came *to* mount Ephraim to the **h** of 1004
17:12 his priest, and was in the **h** of Micah. 1004
18: 2 to the **h** of Micah, they lodged there. 1004
18: 3 When they *were* by the **h** of Micah, they 1004
18:13 and came unto the **h** of Micah. 1004
18:15 came to the **h** of the young man the Levite, 1004
18:15 *even* unto the **h** of Micah, and saluted him. 1004
18:18 these went into Micah's **h**, and fetched 1004
18:19 *is it* better for thee to be a priest unto the **h** 1004
18:22 they were a good way from the **h** of Micah, 1004
18:22 near to Micah's **h** were gathered together, 1004
18:26 he turned and went back unto his **h**. 1004
18:31 all the time that the **h** of God was in Shiloh. 1004
19: 2 went away from him unto her father's **h** to 1004
19: 3 she brought him *into* her father's **h**: and 1004
19:15 man that took them into *his* **h** to lodging. 1004
19:18 I am *now* going *to* the **h** of the LORD; 1004
19:18 and there *is* no man that receiveth me to **h**. 1004
19:21 So he brought him into his **h**, and 1004
19:22 beset the **h** round about, *and* beat at 1004
19:22 spake to the master of the **h**, the old man, 1004
19:22 Bring forth the man that came into thine **h**, 1004
19:23 the man, the master of the **h**, went out unto 1004
19:23 seeing that this man is come into mine **h**, 1004
19:26 fell down *at* the door of the man's **h** where 1004
19:27 opened the doors of the **h**, and went out to 1004
19:27 *was* fallen down *at* the door of the **h**, 1004
19:29 when he was come into his **h**, he took a 1004
20: 5 beset the **h** round about upon me by night, 1004
20: 8 neither will we any *of us* turn into his **h**. 1004
20:18 went up *to* the **h** of God, and asked *counsel* 1004
20:26 came *unto* the **h** of God, and wept, and 1004
20:31 *of* which one goeth up *to* the **h** of God, and 1004
21: 2 the people came *to* the **h** of God, and 1004
Ru 1: 8 in law, Go, return each to her mother's **h**: 1004
1: 9 each *of you* in the **h** of her husband. 1004
2: 7 until now, that she tarried a little in the **h**. 1004
4:11 that is come into thine **h** like Rachel 1004
4:11 which two did build the **h** of Israel: 1004
4:12 let thy **h** be like the house of Pharez, 1004
4:12 let thy house be like the **h** of Pharez, 1004
1Sa 1: 7 when she went up to the **h** of the LORD, 1004
1:19 returned, and came to their **h** to Ramah: 1004
1:21 the man Elkanah, and all his **h**, went up to 1004
1:24 brought him *unto* the **h** of the LORD *in* 1004
2:11 Elkanah went to Ramah to his **h**. And 1004
2:27 Did I plainly appear unto the **h** of thy 1004
2:27 when they were in Egypt in Pharaoh's **h**? 1004
2:28 did I give unto the **h** of thy father all 1004
2:30 I said indeed *that* thy **h**, and the house of 1004
2:30 *that* thy house, and the **h** of thy father, 1004
2:31 off thine arm, and the arm of thy father's **h**, 1004
2:31 there shall not be an old man in thine **h**. 1004
2:32 there shall not be an old man in thine **h** for 1004
2:33 all the increase of thine **h** shall die in 1004
2:35 I will build him a sure **h**; and he shall walk 1004
2:36 *that* every one that is left in thine **h** 1004
3:12 which I have spoken concerning his **h**: 1004
3:13 For I have told him that I will judge his **h** 1004
3:14 I have sworn unto the **h** of Eli, 1004
3:14 that the iniquity of Eli's **h** shall not be 1004
3:15 opened the doors of the **h** of the LORD. 1004
5: 2 they brought it *into* the **h** of Dagon, and 1004
5: 5 nor any that come *into* Dagon's **h**, 1004
7: 1 brought it into the **h** of Abinadab in the hill, 1004
7: 2 all the **h** of Israel lamented after 1004
7: 3 Samuel spake unto all the **h** of Israel, 1004
7:17 for there *was* his **h**; and there he judged 1004
9:18 Tell me, I pray thee, where the seer's **h** *is*. 1004
9:20 *Is it* not on thee, and on all thy father's **h**? 1004
9:25 communed with Saul upon the **top of** the **h**. 1406
9:26 that Samuel called Saul to the **top of** the **h**, 1406
10:25 all the people away, every man to his **h**. 1004
15:34 Saul went up to his **h** *to* Gibeah of Saul. 1004
17:25 and make his father's **h** free in Israel. 1004
18: 2 let him go no more home *to* his father's **h**. 1004
18:10 and he prophesied in the midst of the **h**: 1004
19: 9 as he sat in his **h** with his javelin in his 1004
19:11 Saul also sent messengers unto David's **h**, 1004
20:15 cut off thy kindness from my **h** for ever: 1004
20:16 So Jonathan made *a covenant* with the **h** of 1004
21:15 shall this *fellow* come into my **h**? 1004
22: 1 all his father's **h** heard *it*, they went down 1004
22:11 the son of Ahitub, and all his father's **h**, 1004
22:14 thy bidding, and *is* honourable in thine **h**? 1004
22:15 his servant, *nor* to all the **h** of my father: 1004
22:16 Ahimelech, thou, and all thy father's **h**. 1004
22:22 *death* of all the persons of thy father's **h**. 1004
23:18 in the wood, and Jonathan went to his **h**. 1004
24:21 not destroy my name out of my father's **h**. 1004
25: 1 and buried him in his **h** at Ramah. 1004
25: 3 his doings; and he *was* **of the h of Caleb**. 3614
25: 6 peace *be* to thine **h**, and peace *be unto* all 1004
25:28 will certainly make my lord a sure **h**; 1004
25:35 said unto her, Go up in peace to thine **h**; 1004
1Sa 25:36 behold, he held a feast in his **h**, like 1004
28:24 the woman had a fat calf in the **h**; and 1004
31: 9 to publish *it in* the **h** of their idols, and 1004
31:10 they put his armour *in* the **h** of Ashtaroth: 1004
2Sa 1:12 of the LORD, and for the **h** of Israel; 1004
2: 4 there they anointed David king over the **h** 1004
2: 7 also the **h** of Judah have anointed me king 1004
2:10 But the **h** of Judah followed David. 1004
2:11 over the **h** of Judah was seven years 1004
3: 1 Now there was long war between the **h** of 1004
3: 1 the house of Saul and the **h** of David: 1004
3: 1 the **h** of Saul waxed weaker and weaker. 1004
3: 6 while there was war between the **h** of Saul 1004
3: 6 the house of Saul and the **h** of David, 1004
3: 6 that Abner made himself strong for the **h** of 1004
3: 8 *this* day unto the **h** of Saul thy father, 1004
3:10 To translate the kingdom from the **h** of 1004
3:19 that seemed *good* to the whole **h** of 1004
3:29 the head of Joab, and on all his father's **h**; 1004
3:29 let there not fail from the **h** of Joab one that 1004
4: 5 came about the heat of the day to the **h** of 1004
4: 6 they came thither into the midst of the **h**, 1004
4: 7 For when they came *into* the **h**, he lay on 1004
4:11 person in his own **h** upon his bed? 1004
5: 8 and the lame shall not come into the **h**. 1004
5:11 masons: and they built David a **h**. 1004
6: 3 brought it out of the **h** of Abinadab that *was* 1004
6: 4 they brought it out of the **h** of Abinadab 1004
6: 5 all the **h** of Israel played before the LORD 1004
6:10 David carried it aside *into* the **h** of 1004
6:11 the ark of the LORD continued *in* the **h** of 1004
6:12 The LORD hath blessed the **h** of 1004
6:12 brought up the ark of God from the **h** of 1004
6:15 all the **h** of Israel brought up the ark of 1004
6:19 all the people departed every one to his **h**. 1004
6:21 me before thy father, and before all his **h**, 1004
7: 1 when the king sat in his **h**, and the LORD 1004
7: 2 I dwell in a **h** of cedar, but the ark of God 1004
7: 5 Shalt thou build me a **h** for me to dwell in? 1004
7: 6 Whereas I have not dwelt in *any* **h** since 1004
7: 7 Why build ye not me a **h** of cedar? 1004
7:11 telleth thee that he will make thee a **h**. 1004
7:13 He shall build a **h** for my name, and I will 1004
7:16 thine **h** and thy kingdom shall be stablished 1004
7:18 what *is* my **h**, that thou hast brought me 1004
7:19 thou hast spoken also of thy servant's **h** for 1004
7:25 concerning his **h**, establish *it* for ever, and 1004
7:26 let the **h** of thy servant David be 1004
7:27 to thy servant, saying, I will build thee a **h**: 1004
7:29 it please thee to bless the **h** of thy servant, 1004
7:29 with thy blessing let the **h** of thy servant be 1004
9: 1 Is there yet *any* that is left of the **h** of Saul, 1004
9: 2 *there was* of the **h** of Saul a servant whose 1004
9: 3 *Is there* not yet any of the **h** of Saul, 1004
9: 4 Behold, he *is in* the **h** of Machir, the son of 1004
9: 5 fet him out of the **h** of Machir, the son of 1004
9: 9 all that pertained to Saul and to all his **h**. 1004
9:12 all that dwelt in the **h** of Ziba *were* servants 1004
11: 2 and walked upon the roof of the king's **h**: 1004
11: 4 and she returned unto her **h**. 1004
11: 8 Go down to thy **h**, and wash thy feet. 1004
11: 8 And Uriah departed out of the king's **h**, and 1004
11: 9 Uriah slept *at* the door of the king's **h** with 1004
11: 9 of his lord, and went not down to his **h**. 1004
11:10 saying, Uriah went not down unto his **h**, 1004
11:10 *then* didst thou not go down unto thine **h**? 1004
11:11 shall I then go into mine **h**, to eat and 1004
11:13 of his lord, but went not down to his **h**. 1004
11:27 David sent and fet her to his **h**, and 1004
12: 8 I gave thee thy master's **h**, and thy master's 1004
12: 8 and gave thee the **h** of Israel and of Judah; 1004
12:10 the sword shall never depart from thine **h**, 1004
12:11 up evil against thee out of thine own **h**, 1004
12:15 Nathan departed unto his **h**. And 1004
12:17 the elders of his **h** arose, *and went* to him, 1004
12:20 came *into* the **h** of the LORD, and 1004
12:20 he came to his own **h**; and when he 1004
13: 7 Go now *to* thy brother Amnon's **h**, and 1004
13: 8 So Tamar went *to* her brother Amnon's **h**; 1004
13:20 desolate *in* her brother Absalom's **h**. 1004
14: 8 Go to thine **h**, and I will give charge 1004
14: 9 iniquity *be* on me, and on my father's **h**: 1004
14:24 Let him turn to his own **h**, and let him not 1004
14:24 So Absalom returned to his own **h**, and 1004
14:31 came to Absalom unto *his* **h**, and said unto 1004
15:16 *which were* concubines, to keep the **h**. 1004
15:35 soever thou shalt hear out of the king's **h**, 1004
16: 3 To day shall the **h** of Israel restore me 1004
16: 5 out a man of the family of the **h** of Saul, 1004
16: 8 upon thee all the blood of the **h** of Saul, 1004
16:21 which he hath left to keep the **h**; 1004
16:22 Absalom a tent upon the **top of** the **h**; 1406
17:18 came to a man's **h** in Bahurim, which had a 1004
17:20 servants came to the woman to the **h**, 1004
17:23 arose, and gat him *home* to his **h**, to his 1004
19: 5 Joab came *into* the **h** to the king, and said, 1004
19:11 ye the last to bring the king back to his **h**? 1004
19:11 all Israel is come to the king, *even* to his **h**. 1004
19:17 Ziba the servant of the **h** of Saul, and 1004
19:20 I am come the first *this* day of all the **h** of 1004
19:28 For all *of* my father's **h** were but dead men 1004
19:30 king is come *again* in peace unto his own **h**. 1004
20: 3 David came to his **h** *at* Jerusalem; and 1004
20: 3 whom he had left to keep the **h**, and 1004
21: 1 for *his* bloody **h**, because he slew 1004
21: 4 no silver nor gold of Saul, nor of his **h**; 1004
23: 5 Although my **h** *be* not so with God; yet he 1004
24:17 be against me, and against my father's **h**. 1004
1Ki 1:53 and Solomon said unto him, Go to thine **h**. 1004
2:24 and who hath made me a **h**, as he promised, 1004
2:27 which he spake concerning the **h** of Eli in 1004
2:31 from me, and from the **h** of my father. 1004
2:33 and upon his **h**, and upon his throne, 1004
2:34 he was buried in his own **h** in 1004
2:36 Build thee a **h** in Jerusalem, and 1004
1Ki 3: 1 he had made an end of building his own **h**, 1004
3: 1 the **h** of the LORD, and the wall of 1004
3: 2 there was no **h** built unto the name of 1004
3:17 my lord, I and this woman dwell in one **h**; 1004
3:17 I was delivered of a child with her in the **h**. 1004
3:18 *there was* no stranger with us in the **h**, 1004
3:18 with us in the house, save we two in the **h**. 1004
5: 3 **h** unto the name of the LORD his God for 1004
5: 5 I purpose to build a **h** unto the name of 1004
5: 5 thy room, he shall build a **h** unto my name. 1004
5:17 to lay the foundation of the **h**. 1004
5:18 prepared timber and stones to build the **h**. 1004
6: 1 that he *began* to build the **h** of the LORD. 1004
6: 2 the **h** which king Solomon built for 1004
6: 3 the porch before the temple of the **h**, 1004
6: 3 according to the breadth of the **h**; 1004
6: 3 cubits *was* the breadth thereof before the **h**. 1004
6: 4 for the **h** he made windows of narrow 1004
6: 5 against the wall of the **h** he built chambers 1004
6: 5 *against* the walls of the **h** round about, 1004
6: 6 for without *in the wall* of the **h** he made 1004
6: 6 should not be fastened in the walls of the **h**. 1004
6: 7 the **h**, when it was in building, was built *of* 1004
6: 7 nor axe *nor* any tool of iron heard in the **h**, 1004
6: 8 chamber *was* in the right side of the **h**: 1004
6: 9 So he built the **h**, and finished it; and 1004
6: 9 covered the **h** with beams and boards of 1004
6:10 *then* he built chambers against all the **h**, 1004
6:10 they rested on the **h** with timber of cedar. 1004
6:12 *Concerning* this **h** which thou art in 1004
6:14 So Solomon built the **h**, and finished it. 1004
6:15 he built the walls of the **h** within with 1004
6:15 both the floor of the **h**, and the walls of 1004
6:15 covered the floor of the **h** with planks of 1004
6:16 he built twenty cubits on the sides of the **h**, 1004
6:17 the **h**, that *is*, the temple before it, 1004
6:18 the cedar of the **h** within *was* carved with 1004
6:19 the oracle he prepared in the **h** within, to 1004
6:21 So Solomon overlaid the **h** within with pure 1004
6:22 the whole **h** he overlaid with gold, until *he* 1004
6:22 with gold, until *he* had finished all the **h**: 1004
6:27 he set the cherubims within the inner **h**: 1004
6:27 touched one another in the midst of the **h**. 1004
6:29 he carved all the walls of the **h** round about 1004
6:30 the floor of the **h** he overlaid with gold, 1004
6:37 the foundation of the **h** of the LORD laid, 1004
6:38 was the **h** finished throughout all the parts 1004
7: 1 Solomon was building his own **h** thirteen 1004
7: 1 thirteen years, and he finished all his **h**. 1004
7: 2 He built also the **h** of the forest of Lebanon; 1004
7: 8 his **h** where he dwelt *had* another court 1004
7: 8 Solomon made also a **h** for Pharaoh's 1004
7:12 both for the inner court of the **h** of 1004
7:12 of the LORD, and for the porch of the **h**. 1004
7:39 he put five bases on the right side of the **h**, 1004
7:39 the house, and five on the left side of the **h**: 1004
7:39 he set the sea on the right side of the **h** 1004
7:40 king Solomon *for* the **h** of the LORD: 1004
7:45 to king Solomon *for* the **h** of the LORD, 1004
7:48 that *pertained unto* the **h** of the LORD: 1004
7:50 *of* gold, *both* for the doors of the inner **h**, 1004
7:50 most holy *place, and* for the doors of the **h**, 1004
7:51 Solomon made *for* the **h** of the LORD. 1004
7:51 did he put among the treasures of the **h** of 1004
8: 6 into the oracle of the **h**, to the most holy 1004
8:10 that the cloud filled the **h** of the LORD, 1004
8:11 for the glory of the LORD had filled the **h** 1004
8:13 I have surely built thee a **h** to dwell in, 1004
8:16 out of all the tribes of Israel to build a **h**, 1004
8:17 **h** for the name of the LORD God of 1004
8:18 Whereas it was in thine heart to build a **h** 1004
8:19 Nevertheless thou shalt not build the **h**; but 1004
8:19 he shall build the **h** unto my name. 1004
8:20 have built a **h** for the name of the LORD 1004
8:27 how much less this **h** that I have builded? 1004
8:29 That thine eyes may be open toward this **h** 1004
8:31 the oath come before thine altar in this **h**: 1004
8:33 and make supplication unto thee in this **h**: 1004
8:38 and spread forth his hands towards this **h**: 1004
8:42 he shall come and pray towards this **h**; 1004
8:43 that *they* may know that this **h**, which I 1004
8:44 *toward* the **h** that I have built for thy name: 1004
8:48 and the **h** which I have built for thy name: 1004
8:63 all the children of Israel dedicated the **h** of 1004
8:64 court that *was* before the **h** of the LORD: 1004
9: 1 the building of the **h** of the LORD, 1004
9: 1 the king's **h**, and all Solomon's desire 1004
9: 3 I have hallowed this **h**, which thou hast 1004
9: 7 *this* **h**, which I have hallowed for my name, 1004
9: 8 *at* this **h**, *which* is high, every one that 1004
9: 8 done thus unto this land, and to this **h**? 1004
9:10 the **h** of the LORD, and the king's house, 1004
9:10 the house of the LORD, and the king's **h**, 1004
9:15 for to build the **h** of the LORD, and his 1004
9:15 his own **h**, and Millo, and the wall of 1004
9:24 her **h** which *Solomon* had built for her. 1004
9:25 before the LORD. So he finished the **h**. 1004
10: 4 and the **h** that he had built, 1004
10: 5 his ascent *by* which he went up *unto* the **h** 1004
10:12 almug trees pillars for the **h** of the LORD, 1004
10:12 for the king's **h**, harps also and 1004
10:17 the king put them *in* the **h** of the forest of 1004
10:21 all the vessels of the **h** of the forest of 1004
11:18 which gave him a **h**, and appointed him 1004
11:20 whom Tahpenes weaned in Pharaoh's **h**: 1004
11:28 ruler over all the charge of the **h** of Joseph. 1004
11:38 build thee a sure **h**, as I built for David, and 1004
12:16 now see to thine own **h**, David. So Israel 1004
12:19 So Israel rebelled against the **h** of David 1004
12:20 there was none that followed the **h** of 1004
12:21 he assembled all the **h** of Judah, with 1004
12:21 to fight against the **h** of Israel, 1004
12:23 unto all the **h** of Judah and Benjamin, and 1004
12:24 return every man to his **h**; for this thing is 1004
12:26 Now shall the kingdom return to the **h** of 1004

Ref	Context	Strong's
1Ki 12:27	If this people go up to do sacrifice in the **h**	1004
12:31	he made a **h** of high places, and	1004
13: 2	a child *shall be* born unto the **h** of David,	1004
13: 8	If thou wilt give me half thine **h**, I will not	1004
13:18	Bring him back with thee into thine **h**,	1004
13:19	and did eat bread in his **h**, and drank water.	1004
13:34	this thing became sin unto the **h** of	1004
14: 4	*to* Shiloh, and came *to* the **h** of Ahijah.	1004
14: 8	rent the kingdom away from the **h** of	1004
14:10	I will bring evil upon the **h** of Jeroboam,	1004
14:10	will take away the remnant of the **h** of	1004
14:12	thou therefore, get thee to thine own **h**:	1004
14:13	LORD God of Israel in the **h** of Jeroboam.	1004
14:14	who shall cut off the **h** of Jeroboam that	1004
14:26	he took away the treasures of the **h** of	1004
14:26	and the treasures of the king's **h**;	1004
14:27	which kept the door of the king's **h**.	1004
14:28	when the king went *into* the **h** of	1004
15:15	*into* the **h** of the LORD, silver, and gold,	1004
15:18	left in the treasures of the **h** of the LORD,	1004
15:18	the treasures of the king's **h**, and	1004
15:27	of the **h** of Issachar, conspired against him;	1004
15:29	*that* he smote all the **h** of Jeroboam;	1004
16: 3	of Baasha, and the posterity of his **h**;	1004
16: 3	will make thy **h** like the house of Jeroboam	1004
16: 3	will make thy house like the **h** of Jeroboam	1004
16: 7	against his **h**, even for all the evil that he	1004
16: 7	his hands, in being like the **h** of Jeroboam;	1004
16: 9	drinking *himself* drunk *in* the **h** of Arza	1004
16: 9	house of Arza steward of *his* **h** in Tirzah.	1004
16:11	his throne, *that* he slew all the **h** of Baasha:	1004
16:12	Thus did Zimri destroy all the **h** of Baasha,	1004
16:18	that he went into the palace of the king's **h**,	1004
16:18	burnt the king's **h** over him with fire, and	1004
16:32	he reared up an altar for Baal *in* the **h** of	1004
17:15	she, and he, and her **h**, did eat *many* days.	1004
17:17	the woman, the mistress of the **h**, fell sick;	1004
17:23	him down out of the chamber into the **h**,	1004
18: 3	which *was* the governor of *his* **h**.	1004
18:18	thou, and thy father's **h**, in that ye have	1004
20: 6	they shall search thine **h**, and the houses of	1004
20:31	we have heard that the kings of the **h** of	1004
20:43	the king of Israel went to his **h** heavy and	1004
21: 2	of herbs, because it *is* near unto my **h**:	1004
21: 4	Ahab came into his **h** heavy and displeased	1004
21:22	will make thine **h** like the house of	1004
21:22	will make thine house like the **h** of	1004
21:22	like the **h** of Baasha the son of Ahijah,	1004
21:29	son's days will I bring the evil upon his **h**.	1004
22:17	let them return every man to his **h** in peace.	1004
22:39	the ivory **h** which he made, and all	1004
2Ki 4: 2	tell me, what hast thou in the **h**? And she	1004
4: 2	Thine handmaid hath not any thing in the **h**,	1004
4:32	when Elisha was come into the **h**, behold,	1004
4:35	he returned, and walked in the **h** to and fro;	1004
5: 9	and stood *at* the door of the **h** of Elisha.	1004
5:18	*that* when my master goeth *into* the **h** of	1004
5:18	and I bow myself *in* the **h** of Rimmon:	1004
5:18	when I bow down myself *in* the **h** of	1004
5:24	their hand, and bestowed *them* in the **h**:	1004
6:32	Elisha sat in his **h**, and the elders sat with	1004
7:11	and they told *it to* the king's **h** within.	1004
8: 3	she went forth to cry unto the king for her **h**	1004
8: 5	cried to the king for her **h** and for her land.	1004
8:18	of the kings of Israel, as did the **h** of Ahab:	1004
8:27	And he walked in the way of the **h** of Ahab,	1004
8:27	sight of the LORD, as *did* the **h** of Ahab:	1004
8:27	for he *was* the son in law of the **h** of Ahab.	1004
9: 6	he arose, and went into the **h**; and	1004
9: 7	thou shalt smite the **h** of Ahab thy master,	1004
9: 8	For the whole **h** of Ahab shall perish: and	1004
9: 9	I will make the **h** of Ahab like the house of	1004
9: 9	I will make the house of Ahab like the **h** of	1004
9: 9	and like the **h** of Baasha the son of Ahijah:	1004
9:27	*this,* he fled *by* the way of the garden **h**.	1004
10: 3	and fight for your master's **h**.	1004
10: 5	*he* that *was* over the **h**, and *he* that *was* over	1004
10:10	which the LORD spake concerning the **h**	1004
10:11	So Jehu slew all that remained of the **h** of	1004
10:12	*And* as he *was at* the shearing **h** in the way,	1004
10:14	slew them at the pit of the shearing **h**,	1004
10:21	they came *into* the **h** of Baal; and the house	1004
10:21	the **h** of Baal was full from one end to	1004
10:23	*into* the **h** of Baal, and said unto	1004
10:25	and went to the city of the **h** of Baal.	1004
10:26	they brought forth the images out of the **h**	1004
10:27	brake down the **h** of Baal, and made it a	1004
10:27	and made it a **draught h** unto *this* day.	4280
10:30	hast done unto the **h** of Ahab according to	1004
11: 3	he was with her hid *in* the **h** of the LORD	1004
11: 4	brought them to him *into* the **h** of	1004
11: 4	took an oath of them in the **h** of	1004
11: 5	be keepers of the watch of the king's **h**;	1004
11: 6	so shall ye keep the watch of the **h**, that it	1004
11: 7	even they shall keep the watch of the **h** of	1004
11:15	Let her not be slain *in* the **h** of the LORD.	1004
11:16	which the horses came *into* the king's **h**:	1004
11:18	all the people of the land went *into* the **h** of	1004
11:18	the priest appointed officers over the **h** of	1004
11:19	they brought down the king from the **h** of	1004
11:19	way of the gate of the guard *to* the king's **h**.	1004
11:20	with the sword *beside* the king's **h**.	1004
12: 4	that is brought *into* the **h** of the LORD,	1004
12: 4	heart to bring *into* the **h** of the LORD,	1004
12: 5	let them repair the breaches of the **h**,	1004
12: 6	had not repaired the breaches of the **h**.	1004
12: 7	Why repair ye not the breaches of the **h**?	1004
12: 7	but deliver it for the breaches of the **h**.	1004
12: 8	neither to repair the breaches of the **h**.	1004
12: 9	on the right side as one cometh *into* the **h**	1004
12: 9	that was brought *into* the **h** of the LORD.	1004
12:10	told the money that was found *in* the **h** of	1004
12:11	that had the oversight *of* the **h** of	1004
12:11	that wrought upon the **h** of the LORD,	1004
12:12	hewed stone to repair the breaches of the **h**	1004
2Ki 12:12	for all that was laid out for the **h** to repair	1004
12:13	Howbeit there were not made *for* the **h** of	1004
12:13	of the money that was brought *into* the **h** of	1004
12:14	and repaired therewith the **h** of the LORD.	1004
12:16	sin money was not brought *into* the **h** of	1004
12:18	in the treasures of the **h** of the LORD,	1004
12:18	*in* the king's **h**, and sent *it* to Hazael king of	1004
12:20	slew Joash *in* the **h** of Millo,	1004
13: 6	not from the sins of the **h** of Jeroboam,	1004
14:14	all the vessels that were found *in* the **h** of	1004
14:14	in the treasures of the king's **h**, and	1004
15: 5	day of his death, and dwelt in a several **h**.	1004
15: 5	Jotham the king's son *was* over the **h**,	1004
15:25	in the palace of the king's **h**, with Argob	1004
15:35	He built the higher gate of the **h** of	1004
16: 8	gold that was found *in* the **h** of the LORD,	1004
16: 8	in the treasures of the king's **h**, and sent *it*	1004
16:14	from the forefront of the **h**, from between	1004
16:14	between the altar and the **h** of the LORD,	1004
16:18	for the sabbath that they had built in the **h**,	1004
16:18	turned he *from* the **h** of the LORD for	1004
17:21	For he rent Israel from the **h** of David; and	1004
18:15	that was found *in* the **h** of the LORD,	1004
18:15	and in the treasures of the king's **h**.	1004
19: 1	and went *into* the **h** of the LORD.	1004
19:14	Hezekiah went up *into* the **h** of the LORD,	1004
19:30	the remnant that is escaped of the **h** of	1004
19:37	as he was worshipping *in* the **h** of Nisroch	1004
20: 1	Thus saith the LORD, Set thine **h** in order;	1004
20: 5	on the third day thou shalt go up *unto* the **h**	1004
20: 8	*that* I shall go up *into* the **h** of the LORD	1004
20:13	shewed them all the **h** of his precious	1004
20:13	all the **h** of his armour, and all that was	1004
20:13	there was nothing in his **h**, nor in all his	1004
20:15	he said, What have they seen in thine **h**?	1004
20:15	All *the things* that *are* in mine **h** have they	1004
20:17	that all that *is* in thine **h**, and *that* which thy	1004
21: 4	he built altars in the **h** of the LORD,	1004
21: 5	in the two courts of the **h** of the LORD.	1004
21: 7	of the grove that he had made in the **h**,	1004
21: 7	his son, In this **h**, and in Jerusalem,	1004
21:13	and the plummet of the **h** of Ahab:	1004
21:18	was buried in the garden of his own **h**,	1004
21:23	and slew the king in his own **h**.	1004
22: 3	the scribe, *to* the **h** of the LORD, saying,	1004
22: 4	which is brought *into* the **h** of the LORD,	1004
22: 5	that have the oversight of the **h** of	1004
22: 5	the work which *is* in the **h** of the LORD,	1004
22: 5	the LORD, to repair the breaches of the **h**,	1004
22: 6	buy timber and hewn stone to repair the **h**.	1004
22: 8	I have found the book of the law in the **h** of	1004
22: 9	gathered the money that was found in the **h**,	1004
22: 9	that have the oversight *of* the **h** of	1004
23: 2	the king went up *into* the **h** of the LORD,	1004
23: 2	which was found in the **h** of the LORD.	1004
23: 6	he brought out the grove from the **h** of	1004
23: 7	that *were* by the **h** of the LORD,	1004
23:11	at the entering in of the **h** of the LORD,	1004
23:12	in the two courts of the **h** of the LORD,	1004
23:24	the priest found *in* the **h** of the LORD.	1004
23:27	the **h** of which I said, My name shall be	1004
24:13	all the treasures of the **h** of the LORD,	1004
24:13	the treasures of the king's **h**, and cut in	1004
25: 9	he burnt the **h** of the LORD, and	1004
25: 9	the king's **h**, and all the houses of	1004
25: 9	and every great *man's* **h** burnt he with fire.	1004
25:13	the pillars of brass that *were in* the **h** of	1004
25:13	the brasen sea that *was* in the **h** of	1004
25:16	had made for the **h** of the LORD;	1004
1Ch 2:54	the **h** of Joab, and half of the Manahethites,	1004
2:55	of Hemath, the father of the **h** of Rechab.	1004
4:21	the families of the **h** of them that wrought	1004
4:21	that wrought fine linen, of the **h** of Ashbea,	1004
4:38	and the **h** of their fathers increased greatly.	1004
5:13	their brethren of the **h** of their fathers *were,*	1004
5:15	son of Guni, chief of the **h** of their fathers.	1004
5:24	these *were* the heads of the **h** of their	1004
5:24	*and* heads of the **h** of their fathers.	1004
6:31	the service of song *in* the **h** of the LORD,	1004
6:32	until Solomon had built the **h** of	1004
6:48	*of* service of the tabernacle of the **h** of God.	1004
7: 2	and Shemuel, heads of their fathers' **h**,	1004
7: 4	after the **h** of their fathers,	1004
7: 7	heads of the **h** of *their* fathers, mighty *men*	1004
7: 9	heads of the **h** of their fathers, mighty *men*	1004
7:23	because it went evil with his **h**.	1004
7:40	heads of *their* fathers' **h**, choice *and*	1004
9: 9	chief of the fathers in the **h** of their fathers.	1004
9:11	the son of Ahitub, the ruler of the **h** of God;	1004
9:13	heads of the **h** of their fathers, a thousand	1004
9:13	*for* the work of the service of the **h** of God.	1004
9:19	his brethren, of the **h** of his father,	1004
9:23	of the gates of the **h** of the LORD,	1004
9:23	*namely,* the **h** of the tabernacle, by wards.	1004
9:26	and treasuries of the **h** of God.	1004
9:27	they lodged round about the **h** of God,	1004
10: 6	his three sons, and all his **h** died together.	1004
10:10	they put his armour *in* the **h** of their gods,	1004
12:28	*of* his father's **h** twenty and two captains.	1004
12:29	of them had kept the ward of the **h** of Saul.	1004
12:30	famous throughout the **h** of their fathers.	1004
13: 7	God in a new cart out of the **h** of Abinadab:	1004
13:13	carried it aside into the **h** of Obed-edom	1004
13:14	of Obed-edom in his **h** three months.	1004
13:14	the LORD blessed the **h** of Obed-edom,	1004
14: 1	and carpenters, to build him a **h**.	1004
15:25	out of the **h** of Obed-edom with joy.	1004
16:43	all the people departed every man to his **h**:	1004
16:43	and David returned to bless his **h**.	1004
17: 1	Now it came to pass, as David sat in his **h**,	1004
17: 1	I dwell in a **h** of cedars, but the ark of	1004
17: 4	Thou shalt not build me a **h** to dwell in:	1004
17: 5	For I have not dwelt in a **h** since the day	1004
17: 6	Why have ye not built me a **h** of cedars?	1004
17:10	thee that the LORD will build thee a **h**.	1004
1Ch 17:12	He shall build me a **h**, and I will stablish	1004
17:14	I will settle him in mine **h** and in my	1004
17:16	*am* I, O LORD God, and what *is* mine **h**,	1004
17:17	for thou hast *also* spoken of thy servant's **h**	1004
17:23	concerning his **h** be established for ever,	1004
17:24	*let* the **h** of David thy servant *be*	1004
17:25	thy servant that *thou* wilt build him a **h**:	1004
17:27	let it please thee to bless the **h** of thy	1004
21:17	my God, be on me, and on my father's **h**;	1004
22: 1	This *is* the **h** of the LORD God, and this *is*	1004
22: 2	hew wrought stones to build the **h** of God.	1004
22: 5	the **h** *that is* to be builded for the LORD	1004
22: 6	charged him to build a **h** for the LORD	1004
22: 7	it was in my mind to build a **h** unto	1004
22: 8	thou shalt not build a **h** unto my name,	1004
22:10	He shall build a **h** for my name; and	1004
22:11	and build the **h** of the LORD thy God,	1004
22:14	in my trouble I have prepared for the **h** of	1004
22:19	into the **h** that is *to be* built to the name of	1004
23: 4	forward the work of the **h** of the LORD;	1004
23:11	according to *their* father's **h**.	1004
23:24	These *were* the sons of Levi after the **h** of	1004
23:24	that did the work for the service of the **h** of	1004
23:28	for the service of the **h** of the LORD,	1004
23:28	and the work of the service of the **h** of God;	1004
23:32	in the service of the **h** of the LORD.	1004
24: 4	sixteen chief *men* of the **h** of *their* fathers,	1004
24: 4	Ithamar according to the **h** of their fathers.	1004
24: 5	governors *of the* **h** of God, were of the sons	NIH
24:19	service to come into the **h** of the LORD,	1004
24:30	of the Levites after the **h** of their fathers.	1004
25: 6	their father for song *in* the **h** of the LORD,	1004
25: 6	and harps, for the service of the **h** of God,	1004
26: 6	that ruled throughout the **h** of their father:	1004
26:12	to minister in the **h** of the LORD.	1004
26:13	according to the **h** of their fathers, for every	1004
26:15	to his sons the **h** of Asuppim.	1004
26:20	Ahijah *was* over the treasures of the **h** of	1004
26:22	*which were* over the treasures of the **h** of	1004
26:27	dedicate to maintain the **h** of the LORD.	1004
28: 2	*As for me,* I *had* in mine heart to build a **h**	1004
28: 3	Thou shalt not build a **h** for my name,	1004
28: 4	**h** of my father to be king over Israel for	1004
28: 4	of the **h** of Judah, the house of my father;	1004
28: 4	of the house of Judah, the **h** of my father;	1004
28: 6	thy son, he shall build my **h** and my courts:	1004
28:10	chosen thee to build a **h** for the sanctuary:	1004
28:12	of the courts of the **h** of the LORD, and	1004
28:12	of the treasuries of the **h** of God, and of	1004
28:13	for all the work of the service of the **h** of	1004
28:13	for all the vessels of service in the **h** of	1004
28:20	for the service of the **h** of the LORD.	1004
28:21	*thee* for all the service of the **h** of God:	1004
29: 2	**h** of my God the gold for *things to be made*	1004
29: 3	I have set my affection to the **h** of my God,	1004
29: 3	*which* I have given to the **h** of my God,	1004
29: 3	all *that* I have prepared for the holy **h**,	1004
29: 7	gave for the service of the **h** of God *of* gold	1004
29: 8	*them* to the treasure of the **h** of the LORD,	1004
29:16	**h** for thine holy name *cometh* of thine	1004
2Ch 2: 1	Solomon determined to build a **h** for	1004
2: 1	of the LORD, and a **h** for his kingdom.	1004
2: 3	didst send him cedars to build him a **h** to	1004
2: 4	I build a **h** to the name of the LORD my	1004
2: 5	the **h** which I build *is* great: for great *is* our	1004
2: 6	who is able to build him a **h**, seeing	1004
2: 6	who *am* I then, that I should build him a **h**,	1004
2: 9	for the **h** which I am about to build *shall be*	1004
2:12	that might build a **h** for the LORD, and	1004
2:12	for the LORD, and a **h** for his kingdom.	1004
3: 1	Solomon began to build the **h** of	1004
3: 3	instructed for the building of the **h** of God.	1004
3: 4	the porch that *was* in the front *of the* **h**,	NIH
3: 4	*of it was* according to the breadth of the **h**,	1004
3: 5	the greater **h** he cieled with fir tree,	1004
3: 6	he garnished the **h** with precious stones for	1004
3: 7	He overlaid also the **h**, the beams,	1004
3: 8	he made the most holy **h**, the length	1004
3: 8	*was* according to the breadth of the **h**,	1004
3:10	in the most holy **h** he made two cherubims	1004
3:11	five cubits, reaching to the wall of the **h**:	1004
3:12	five cubits, reaching to the wall of the **h**:	1004
3:15	Also he made before the **h** two pillars of	1004
4:11	to make for king Solomon for the **h** of God;	1004
4:16	for the **h** of the LORD *of* bright brass.	1004
4:19	all the vessels that *were for* the **h** of God,	1004
4:22	the entry of the **h**, the inner doors thereof	1004
4:22	and the doors of the **h** of the temple,	1004
5: 1	made for the **h** of the LORD was finished:	1004
5: 1	put he among the treasures of the **h** of God.	1004
5: 7	to the oracle of the **h**, into the most holy	1004
5:13	that *then* the **h** was filled *with* a cloud,	1004
5:13	*with* a cloud, *even* the **h** of the LORD;	1004
5:14	for the glory of the LORD had filled the **h**	1004
6: 2	I have built a **h** of habitation for thee, and	1004
6: 5	build a **h** *in,* that my name might be there;	1004
6: 7	**h** for the name of the LORD God of	1004
6: 8	was in thine heart to build a **h** for my name,	1004
6: 9	Notwithstanding thou shalt not build the **h**;	1004
6: 9	thy loins, he shall build the **h** for my name.	1004
6:10	have built the **h** for the name of the LORD	1004
6:18	how much less this **h** which I have built?	1004
6:20	That thine eyes may be open upon this **h**	1004
6:22	the oath come before thine altar in this **h**;	1004
6:24	and make supplication before thee in this **h**;	1004
6:29	and shall spread forth his hands in this **h**:	1004
6:32	out arm; if they come and pray in this **h**;	1004
6:33	may know that this **h** which I have built is	1004
6:34	the **h** which I have built for thy name;	1004
6:38	toward the **h** which I have built for thy	1004
7: 1	and the glory of the LORD filled the **h**.	1004
7: 2	the priests could not enter into the **h** of	1004
7: 2	of the LORD had filled the LORD'S **h**.	1004
7: 3	and the glory of the LORD upon the **h**,	1004
7: 5	and all the people dedicated the **h** of God.	1004

2Ch 7: 7 court that *was* before the **h** of the LORD: 1004
7:11 Thus Solomon finished the **h** of 1004
7:11 the house of the LORD, and the king's **h**: 1004
7:11 heart to make in the **h** of the LORD, 1004
7:11 and in his own **h**, he prosperously effected. 1004
7:12 have chosen this place to myself for a **h** of 1004
7:16 now have I chosen and sanctified this **h**, 1004
7:20 this **h**, which I have sanctified for my 1004
7:21 this **h**, which is high, shall be an 1004
7:21 done thus unto this land, and unto this **h**? 1004
8: 1 wherein Solomon had built the **h** of 1004
8: 1 the house of the LORD, and his own **h**, 1004
8:11 David unto the **h** that he had built for her: 1004
8:11 My wife shall not dwell in the **h** of David 1004
8:16 of the foundation of the **h** of the LORD, 1004
8:16 *So* the **h** of the LORD was perfected. 1004
9: 3 of Solomon, and the **h** that he had built, 1004
9: 4 his ascent *by* which he went up *into* the **h** 1004
9:11 algum trees terraces to the **h** of the LORD, 1004
9:16 the king put them in the **h** of the forest of 1004
9:20 all the vessels of the **h** of the forest of 1004
10:16 *and* now, David, see to thine own **h**. So all 1004
10:19 Israel rebelled against the **h** of David unto 1004
11: 1 he gathered *of* the **h** of Judah and 1004
11: 4 return every man to his **h**, for this thing is 1004
12: 9 took away the treasures of the **h** of 1004
12: 9 and the treasures of the king's **h**; 1004
12:10 that kept the entrance of the king's **h**. 1004
12:11 when the king entered *into* the **h** of 1004
15:18 he brought *into* the **h** of God *the things* that 1004
16: 2 gold out of the treasures of the **h** of 1004
16: 2 house of the LORD and of the king's **h**, 1004
16:10 with the seer, and put him *in* a prison **h**; 1004
17:14 of them according to the **h** of their fathers: 1004
18:16 *therefore* every man to his **h** in peace. 1004
19: 1 returned to his **h** in peace to Jerusalem. 1004
19:11 the ruler of the **h** of Judah, for all the king's 1004
20: 5 and Jerusalem, in the **h** of the LORD, 1004
20: 9 we stand before this **h**, and in thy presence, 1004
20: 9 in thy presence, (for thy name *is* in this **h**,) 1004
20:28 and trumpets unto the **h** of the LORD. 1004
21: 6 kings of Israel, like as did the **h** of Ahab: 1004
21: 7 LORD would not destroy the **h** of David, 1004
21:13 like to the whoredoms of the **h** of Ahab, 1004
21:13 hast slain thy brethren of thy father's **h**, 1004
21:17 substance that was found in the king's **h**, 1004
22: 3 He also walked in the ways of the **h** of 1004
22: 4 the sight of the LORD, like the **h** of Ahab: 1004
22: 7 had anointed to cut off the **h** of Ahab. 1004
22: 8 executing judgment upon the **h** of Ahab, 1004
22: 9 So the **h** of Ahaziah had no power to keep 1004
22:10 destroyed all the seed royal of the **h** of 1004
22:12 he was with them hid in the **h** of God six 1004
23: 3 a covenant with the king in the **h** of God. 1004
23: 5 a third *part shall be* at the king's **h**; and 1004
23: 5 all the people *shall be* in the courts of the **h** 1004
23: 6 let none come *into* the **h** of the LORD, 1004
23: 7 whosoever *else* cometh into the **h**, he shall 1004
23: 9 king David's, which *were in* the **h** of God. 1004
23:12 she came to the people *into* the **h** of 1004
23:14 Slay her not *in* the **h** of the LORD. 1004
23:15 entering of the horse gate *by* the king's **h**, 1004
23:17 all the people went *to* the **h** of Baal, and 1004
23:18 **h** of the LORD by the hand of the priests 1004
23:18 whom David had distributed in the **h** of 1004
23:19 he set the porters at the gates of the **h** of 1004
23:20 brought down the king from the **h** of 1004
23:20 through the high gate *into* the king's **h**, 1004
24: 4 *that* Joash was minded to repair the **h** of 1004
24: 5 gather of all Israel money to repair the **h** of 1004
24: 7 had broken up the **h** of God; 1004
24: 7 also all the dedicate *things* of the **h** of 1004
24: 8 set it without at the gate of the **h** of 1004
24:12 work of the service of the **h** of the LORD, 1004
24:12 carpenters to repair the **h** of the LORD, 1004
24:12 and brass to mend the **h** of the LORD. 1004
24:13 they set the **h** of God in his state, and 1004
24:14 whereof were made vessels for the **h** of 1004
24:14 they offered burnt offerings in the **h** of 1004
24:16 both towards God, and *towards* his **h**. 1004
24:18 they left the **h** of the LORD God of their 1004
24:21 king in the court of the **h** of the LORD. 1004
24:27 and the repairing of the **h** of God, 1004
25:24 all the vessels that were found in the **h** of 1004
25:24 the treasures of the king's **h**, the hostages 1004
26:19 before the priests in the **h** of the LORD, 1004
26:21 and dwelt *in* a several **h**, *being* a leper; 1004
26:21 for he was cut off from the **h** of 1004
26:21 Jotham his son *was* over the king's **h**, 1004
27: 3 He built the high gate of the **h** of 1004
28: 7 Azrikam the governor of the **h**, and 1004
28:21 For Ahaz took away a portion *out* of the **h** 1004
28:21 *out* of the **h** of the king, and of the princes, 1004
28:24 Ahaz gathered together the vessels of the **h** 1004
28:24 cut in pieces the vessels of the **h** of God, 1004
28:24 shut up the doors of the **h** of the LORD, 1004
29: 3 opened the doors of the **h** of the LORD, 1004
29: 5 sanctify the **h** of the LORD God of your 1004
29:15 to cleanse the **h** of the LORD. 1004
29:16 the priests went into the inner part *of* the **h** 1004
29:16 into the court of the **h** of the LORD. 1004
29:17 they sanctified the **h** of the LORD in eight 1004
29:18 We have cleansed all the **h** of the LORD, 1004
29:20 and went up *to* the **h** of the LORD. 1004
29:25 he set the Levites *in* the **h** of the LORD 1004
29:31 thank offerings into the **h** of the LORD. 1004
29:35 So the service of the **h** of the LORD was 1004
30: 1 that *they* should come to the **h** of 1004
30:15 brought in the burnt offerings *into* the **h** of 1004
31:10 Azariah the chief priest of the **h** of Zadok 1004
31:10 the offerings *into* the **h** of the LORD, 1004
31:11 prepare chambers in the **h** of the LORD; 1004
31:13 and Azariah the ruler of the **h** of God. 1004
31:16 *even* unto every one that entereth into the **h** 1004
31:17 of the priests by the **h** of their fathers, 1004

2Ch 31:21 that he began in the service of the **h** of God, 1004
32:21 when he was come *into* the **h** of his god, 1004
33: 4 Also he built altars in the **h** of the LORD, 1004
33: 5 in the two courts of the **h** of the LORD. 1004
33: 7 idol which he had made, in the **h** of God, 1004
33: 7 his son, In this **h**, and in Jerusalem, 1004
33:15 and the idol out of the **h** of the LORD, and 1004
33:15 built in the mount of the **h** of the LORD, 1004
33:20 and they buried him *in* his own **h**: 1004
33:24 against him, and slew him in his own **h**. 1004
34: 8 when he had purged the land, and the **h**, 1004
34: 8 to repair the **h** of the LORD his God. 1004
34: 9 money that was brought *into* the **h** of God, 1004
34:10 had the oversight of the **h** of the LORD, 1004
34:10 that wrought in the **h** of the LORD, 1004
34:10 of the LORD, to repair and mend the **h**: 1004
34:14 that was brought *into* the **h** of the LORD, 1004
34:15 I have found the book of the law in the **h** of 1004
34:17 that was found in the **h** of the LORD, 1004
34:30 the king went up *into* the **h** of the LORD, 1004
34:30 that was found *in* the **h** of the LORD. 1004
35: 2 encouraged them to the service of the **h** of 1004
35: 3 Put the holy ark in the **h** which Solomon 1004
35: 8 and Jehiel, rulers of the **h** of God, 1004
35:21 but against the **h** wherewith I have war: 1004
36: 7 vessels of the **h** of the LORD to Babylon, 1004
36:10 with the goodly vessels of the **h** of 1004
36:14 polluted the **h** of the LORD which he had 1004
36:17 with the sword in the **h** of their sanctuary, 1004
36:18 all the vessels of the **h** of God, great and 1004
36:18 the treasures of the **h** of the LORD, and 1004
36:19 they burnt the **h** of God, and brake down 1004
36:23 he hath charged me to build him a **h** in 1004
Ezr 1: 2 he hath charged me to build him a **h** at 1004
1: 3 build the **h** of the LORD God of Israel, 1004
1: 4 besides the freewill offering for the **h** of 1004
1: 5 to go up to build the **h** of the LORD 1004
1: 7 forth the vessels of the **h** of the LORD, 1004
1: 7 and had put them in the **h** of his gods; 1004
2:36 of the **h** of Jeshua, nine hundred seventy 1004
2:59 they could not shew their fathers' **h**, and 1004
2:68 when they came to the **h** of the LORD 1004
2:68 offered freely for the **h** of God to set it up 1004
3: 8 coming unto the **h** of God at Jerusalem, 1004
3: 8 to set forward the work of the **h** of 1004
3: 9 to set forward the workmen in the **h** of 1004
3:11 the foundation of the **h** of the LORD was 1004
3:12 *were* ancient men that had seen the first **h**, 1004
3:12 when the foundation of this **h** was laid 1004
4: 3 You have nothing to do with us to build a **h** 1004
4:24 ceased the work of the **h** of the God which 1005
5: 2 began to build the **h** of God which *is* at 1005
5: 3 Who hath commanded you to build this **h**, 1005
5: 8 to the **h** of the great God, which *is* builded 1005
5: 9 Who commanded you to build this **h**, and 1005
5:11 build the **h** that was builded these many 1005
5:12 who destroyed this **h**, and carried 1005
5:13 Cyrus made a decree to build this **h** of God. 1005
5:14 also of gold and silver of the **h** of God, 1005
5:15 and let the **h** of God be builded in his place. 1005
5:16 laid the foundation of the **h** of God which *is* 1005
5:17 be search made in the king's treasure **h**, 1005
5:17 king to build this **h** of God at Jerusalem, 1005
6: 1 and search was made in the **h** of the rolls, 1005
6: 3 *concerning* the **h** of God at Jerusalem, 1005
6: 3 Let the **h** be builded, the place where they 1005
6: 4 the expences be given out of the king's **h**: 1005
6: 5 and silver vessels of the **h** of God, 1005
6: 5 his place, and place *them* in the **h** of God. 1005
6: 7 Let the work of this **h** of God alone; let 1005
6: 7 the elders of the Jews build this **h** of God in 1005
6: 8 Jews for the building of this **h** of God: 1005
6:11 let timber be pulled down from his **h**, and 1005
6:11 let his **h** be made a dunghill for this. 1005
6:12 to destroy this **h** of God which *is* at 1005
6:15 this **h** was finished on the third day of 1005
6:16 kept the dedication of this **h** of God with 1005
6:17 offered at the dedication of this **h** of God an 1005
6:22 their hands in the work of the **h** of God, 1004
7:16 offering willingly for the **h** of their God 1005
7:17 offer them upon the altar of the **h** of your 1005
7:19 thee for the service of the **h** of thy God, 1005
7:20 whatsoever more *shall be* needful for the **h** 1005
7:20 bestow *it* out of the king's treasure **h**. 1005
7:23 let it be diligently done for the **h** of the God 1005
7:24 or ministers of this **h** of God, 1005
7:27 to beautify the **h** of the LORD which *is* in 1004
8:17 unto us ministers for the **h** of our God. 1004
8:25 *even* the offering of the **h** of our God, 1004
8:29 *in* the chambers of the **h** of the LORD. 1004
8:30 to bring *them* to Jerusalem unto the **h** of 1004
8:33 the vessels weighed in the **h** of our God by 1004
8:36 they furthered the people, and the **h** of God. 1004
9: 9 to set up the **h** of our God, and to repair 1004
10: 1 casting himself down before the **h** of God, 1004
10: 6 Ezra rose up from before the **h** of God, 1004
10: 9 all the people sat in the street of the **h** of 1004
10:16 after the **h** of their fathers, and all of them 1004
Ne 1: 6 both I and my father's **h** have sinned. 1004
2: 8 of the palace which *appertained* to the **h**, 1004
2: 8 the city, and for the **h** that I shall enter into. 1004
3:10 son of Harumaph, even over against his **h**. 1004
3:16 was made, and unto the **h** of the mighty. 1004
3:20 the door of the **h** of Eliashib the high priest. 1004
3:21 from the door of the **h** of Eliashib even to 1004
3:21 even to the end of the **h** of Eliashib. 1004
3:23 and Hashub over against their **h**. 1004
3:23 of Maaseiah the son of Ananiah by his **h**. 1004
3:24 from the **h** of Azariah unto the turning *of* 1004
3:25 which lieth out from the king's high **h**, 1004
3:28 the priests, every one over against his **h**. 1004
3:29 Zadok the son of Immer over against his **h**. 1004
4:16 the rulers *were* behind all the **h** of Judah. 1004
5:13 So God shake out every man from his **h**, 1004
6:10 Afterward I came *unto* the **h** of Shemaiah 1004

Ne 6:10 Let us meet together in the **h** of God, 1004
7: 3 and every one *to be* over against his **h**. 1004
7:39 of the **h** of Jeshua, nine hundred seventy 1004
7:61 they could not shew their fathers' **h**, 1004
8:16 every one upon the **roof of** his **h**, and 1406
8:16 in the courts of the **h** of God, and in 1004
10:32 a shekel for the service of the **h** of our God; 1004
10:33 and *for* all the work of the **h** of our God. 1004
10:34 to bring *it* into the **h** of our God, 1004
10:35 year by year, unto the **h** of the LORD: 1004
10:36 of our flocks, to bring to the **h** of our God, 1004
10:36 unto the priests that minister in the **h** of our 1004
10:37 to the chambers of the **h** of our God; 1004
10:38 the tithe of the tithes unto the **h** of our God, 1004
10:38 to the chambers, into the treasure **h**. 1004
10:39 and we will not forsake the **h** of our God. 1004
11:11 of Ahitub, *was* the ruler of the **h** of God. 1004
11:12 their brethren that did the work of the **h** 1004
11:16 of the outward business of the **h** of God. 1004
11:22 the singers *were* over the business of the **h** 1004
12:29 Also from the **h** of Gilgal, and out of 1004
12:37 going up of the wall, above the **h** of David, 1004
12:40 *of them that gave* thanks in the **h** of God, 1004
13: 4 of the chamber of the **h** of our God, 1004
13: 7 a chamber in the courts of the **h** of God. 1004
13: 9 thither brought I again the vessels of the **h** 1004
13:11 and said, Why is the **h** of God forsaken? 1004
13:14 deeds that I have done for the **h** of my God, 1004
Est 1: 8 had appointed to all the officers of his **h**, 1004
1: 9 royal **h** which *belonged* to king Ahasuerus. 1004
1:22 every man should bear rule in his own **h**, 1004
2: 3 to the **h** of the women, unto the custody of 1004
2: 8 Esther was brought *also* unto the king's **h**, 1004
2: 9 meet to be given her, out of the king's **h**: 1004
2: 9 her maids unto the best *place* of the **h** of 1004
2:11 day before the court of the women's **h**, 1004
2:13 the **h** of the women unto the king's house. 1004
2:13 the house of the women unto the king's **h**. 1004
2:14 returned into the second **h** of the women, 1004
2:16 into his **h** royal in the tenth month, 1004
4:13 that *thou* shalt escape *in* the king's **h**, 1004
4:14 thou and thy father's **h** shall be destroyed: 1004
5: 1 and stood in the inner court of the king's **h**, 1004
5: 1 the king's house, over against the king's **h**: 1004
5: 1 sat upon his royal throne in the royal **h**, 1004
5: 1 royal house, over against the gate of the **h**. 1004
6: 4 into the outward court of the king's **h**, 1004
6:12 Haman hasted to his **h** mourning, and 1004
7: 8 he force the queen also before me in the **h**? 1004
7: 9 for the king, standeth in the **h** of Haman. 1004
8: 1 **h** of Haman the Jews' enemy unto Esther 1004
8: 2 Esther set Mordecai over the **h** of Haman. 1004
8: 7 I have given Esther the **h** of Haman, and 1004
9: 4 For Mordecai *was* great in the king's **h**, and 1004
Job 1:10 about his **h**, and about all that he hath on 1004
1:13 drinking wine in their eldest brother's **h**: 1004
1:18 drinking wine in their eldest brother's **h**: 1004
1:19 smote the four corners of the **h**, and it fell 1004
7:10 He shall return no more to his **h**, 1004
8:15 He shall lean upon his **h**, but it shall not 1004
17:13 If I wait, the grave *is* mine **h**: I have made 1004
19:15 They that dwell in mine **h**, and 1004
20:19 he hath violently taken away a **h** which he 1004
20:28 The increase of his **h** shall depart, *and* 1004
21:21 For what pleasure hath he in his **h** after 1004
21:28 For ye say, Where *is* the **h** of the prince? 1004
27:18 He buildeth his **h** as a moth, and as a booth 1004
30:23 and *to* the **h** appointed for all living. 1004
38:20 that thou shouldest know the paths to the **h** 1004
39: 6 Whose **h** I have made the wilderness, and 1004
42:11 and did eat bread with him in his **h**: 1004
Ps 5: 7 I will come *into* thy **h** in the multitude of 1004
23: 6 I will dwell in the **h** of the LORD for ever. 1004
26: 8 I have loved the habitation of thy **h**, and 1004
27: 4 that I may dwell in the **h** of the LORD all 1004
30: T Song *at* the dedication of the **h** of David. 1004
31: 2 strong rock, for a **h** of defence to save me. 1004
36: 8 satisfied with the fatness of thy **h**; 1004
42: 4 I went with them to the **h** of God, with 1004
45:10 also thine own people, and thy father's **h**; 1004
49:16 when the glory of his **h** is increased; 1004
50: 9 I will take no bullock out of thy **h**, *nor* he 1004
52: T David is come to the **h** of Ahimelech. 1004
52: 8 I *am* like a green olive tree in the **h** of God: 1004
55:14 *and* walked unto the **h** of God in company. 1004
59: T Saul sent, and they watcht the **h** to kill him. 1004
65: 4 be satisfied with the goodness of thy **h**, 1004
66:13 I will go *into* thy **h** with burnt offerings: 1004
69: 9 For the zeal of thine **h** hath eaten me up; 1004
84: 3 the sparrow hath found a **h**, and 1004
84: 4 Blessed *are* they that dwell in thy **h**: 1004
84:10 I had rather be a doorkeeper in the **h** of my 1004
92:13 Those that be planted in the **h** of 1004
93: 5 holiness becometh thine **h**, O LORD, 1004
98: 3 and his truth toward the **h** of Israel: 1004
101: 2 I will walk within my **h** with a perfect 1004
101: 7 worketh deceit shall not dwell within my **h**: 1004
104:17 *as for* the stork, the fir trees *are* her **h**. 1004
105:21 He made him lord of his **h**, and ruler of all 1004
112: 3 Wealth and riches *shall be* in his **h**: and 1004
113: 9 He maketh the barren *woman* to keep **h**, 1004
114: 1 the **h** of Jacob from a people of strange 1004
115:10 O **h** of Aaron, trust in the LORD: he *is* 1004
115:12 he will bless *us*; he will bless the **h** of 1004
115:12 of Israel; he will bless the **h** of Aaron. 1004
116:19 In the courts of the LORD'S **h**, in 1004
118: 3 Let the **h** of Aaron now say, that his mercy 1004
118:26 we have blessed you out of the **h** of 1004
119:54 Thy statutes have been my songs in the **h** of 1004
122: 1 Let us go *into* the **h** of the LORD. 1004
122: 5 of judgment, the thrones of the **h** of David. 1004
122: 9 Because of the **h** of the LORD our God I 1004
127: 1 Except the LORD build the **h**, they labour 1004
128: 3 *be* as a fruitful vine by the sides of thine **h**: 1004
132: 3 I will not come into the tabernacle of my **h**, 1004

H

Ps 134: 1 which by night stand in the **h** of 1004
135: 2 Ye that stand in the **h** of the LORD, in 1004
135: 2 in the courts of the **h** of our God, 1004
135:19 Bless the LORD, O **h** of Israel: bless 1004
135:19 of Israel: bless the LORD, O **h** of Aaron: 1004
135:20 Bless the LORD, O **h** of Levi: ye that fear 1004
Pr 2:18 For her **h** inclineth unto death, and 1004
3:33 The curse of the LORD *is* in the **h** of 1004
5: 8 and come not nigh the door of her **h**: 1004
5:10 and thy labours *be* in the **h** of a stranger; 1004
6:31 he shall give all the substance of his **h**. 1004
7: 6 For at the window of my **h** I looked 1004
7: 8 her corner; and he went the way to her **h**, 1004
7:11 and stubborn; her feet abide not in her **h**: 1004
7:27 Her **h** *is* the way to hell, going down to 1004
9: 1 Wisdom hath builded her **h**, she hath hewn 1004
9:14 For she sitteth at the door of her **h**, on a 1004
11:29 He that troubleth his own **h** shall inherit 1004
12: 7 but the **h** of the righteous shall stand. 1004
14: 1 Every wise woman buildeth her **h**: but 1004
14:11 The **h** of the wicked shall be overthrown: 1004
15: 6 *In* the **h** of the righteous *is* much treasure: 1004
15:25 The LORD will destroy the **h** of 1004
15:27 that is greedy of gain troubleth his own **h**; 1004
17: 1 than a **h** full *of* sacrifices with strife. 1004
17:13 for good, evil shall not depart from his **h**. 1004
19:14 **H** and riches *are* the inheritance of fathers: 1004
21: 9 than with a brawling woman in a wide **h**. 1004
21:12 The righteous *man* wisely considereth the **h** 1004
24: 3 Through wisdom is a **h** builded; and 1004
24:27 in the field; and afterwards build thine **h**. 1004
25:17 Withdraw thy foot from thy neighbour's **h**; 1004
25:24 with a brawling woman and in a wide **h**. 1004
27:10 neither go *into* thy brother's **h** in the day of 1004
Ecc 2: 7 maidens, and had servants born in *my* **h**; 1004
5: 1 Keep thy foot when thou goest to the **h** of 1004
7: 2 *It is* better to go to the **h** of mourning, 1004
7: 2 of mourning, than to go to the **h** of feasting: 1004
7: 4 The heart of the wise *is* in the **h** of 1004
7: 4 but the heart of fools *is* in the **h** of mirth. 1004
10:18 through idleness of the hands the **h** 1004
12: 3 In the day when the keepers of the **h** shall 1004
SS 1:17 The beams of our **h** *are* cedar, *and* 1004
2: 4 He brought me to the banqueting **h**, and 1004
3: 4 until I had brought him into my mother's **h**, 1004
8: 2 *and* bring thee into my mother's **h**, 1004
8: 7 give all the substance of his **h** for love, 1004
Isa 2: 2 *that* the mountain of the LORD'S **h** shall 1004
2: 3 the LORD, to the **h** of the God of Jacob; 1004
2: 5 O **h** of Jacob, come ye, and let us walk in 1004
2: 6 hast forsaken thy people the **h** of Jacob, 1004
3: 6 hold of his brother *of* the **h** of his father, 1004
3: 7 for in my **h** *is* neither bread nor clothing: 1004
5: 7 of the LORD of hosts *is* the **h** of Israel, 1004
5: 8 Woe unto them that join **h** to house, 1004
5: 8 Woe unto them that join house to **h**, 1004
6: 4 that cried, and the **h** was filled *with* smoke. 1004
7: 2 it was told the **h** of David, saying, Syria is 1004
7:13 he said, Hear ye now, O **h** of David; *Is it* a 1004
7:17 upon thy people, and upon thy father's **h**, 1004
8:17 that hideth his face from the **h** of Jacob, 1004
10:20 and such as are escaped of the **h** of Jacob, 1004
14: 1 and they shall cleave to the **h** of Jacob. 1004
14: 2 the **h** of Israel shall possess them in 1004
14:17 *that* opened not the **h** of his prisoners? 1004
14:18 lie in glory, every one in his own **h**. 1004
22: 8 that day to the armour of the **h** of the forest. 1004
22:15 unto Shebna, which *is* over the **h**, *and say,* 1004
22:18 thy glory *shall be* the shame of thy lord's **h**. 1004
22:21 of Jerusalem, and to the **h** of Judah. 1004
22:22 the key of the **h** of David will I lay upon his 1004
22:23 be for a glorious throne to his father's **h**. 1004
22:24 upon him all the glory of his father's **h**, 1004
23: 1 so that *there is* no **h**, no entering in: 1004
24:10 every **h** is shut up, that no *man may* come 1004
29:22 concerning the **h** of Jacob, 1004
31: 2 will arise against the **h** of the evildoers, and 1004
36: 3 which *was* over the **h**, and Shebna 1004
37: 1 and went *into* the **h** of the LORD. 1004
37:14 Hezekiah went up *unto* the **h** of 1004
37:31 the remnant that is escaped of the **h** of 1004
37:38 as he was worshipping *in* the **h** of Nisroch 1004
38: 1 Thus saith the LORD, Set thine **h** in order: 1004
38:20 the days of our life in the **h** of the LORD. 1004
38:22 What *is* the sign that I shall go up *to* the **h** 1004
39: 2 shewed them the **h** of his precious things, 1004
39: 2 all the **h** of his armour, and all that was 1004
39: 2 there was nothing in his **h**, nor in all his 1004
39: 4 said he, What have they seen in thine **h**? 1004
39: 4 All that *is* in mine **h** have they seen: 1004
39: 6 that all that *is* in thine **h**, and *that* which thy 1004
42: 7 that sit in darkness out of the prison **h**. 1004
44:13 of a man; that it may remain *in* the **h**. 1004
46: 3 O **h** of Jacob, and all the remnant of 1004
46: 3 and all the remnant of the **h** of Israel, 1004
48: 1 Hear ye this, O **h** of Jacob, which are called 1004
56: 5 Even unto them will I give in mine **h** and 1004
56: 7 and make them joyful in my **h** of prayer: 1004
56: 7 for mine **h** shall be called a house of prayer 1004
56: 7 for mine house shall be called a **h** of prayer 1004
58: 1 and the **h** of Jacob their sins. 1004
58: 7 bring the poor that are cast out *to thy* **h**? 1004
60: 7 and I will glorify the **h** of my glory. 1004
63: 7 the great goodness towards the **h** of Israel, 1004
64:11 Our holy and our beautiful **h**, where our 1004
66: 1 where *is* the **h** that ye build unto me? 1004
66:20 in a clean vessel *into* the **h** of the LORD. 1004
Jer 2: 4 O **h** of Jacob, and all the families of 1004
2: 4 and all the families of the **h** of Israel: 1004
2:26 he is found, so is the **h** of Israel ashamed; 1004
3:18 In those days the **h** of Judah shall walk with 1004
3:18 of Judah shall walk with the **h** of Israel, 1004
3:20 with me, O **h** of Israel, saith the LORD. 1004
5:11 For the **h** of Israel and the house of Judah 1004
5:11 the **h** of Judah have dealt very 1004

Jer 5:15 from far, O **h** of Israel, saith the LORD: 1004
5:20 Declare this in the **h** of Jacob, and 1004
7: 2 Stand in the gate of the LORD'S **h**, and 1004
7:10 come and stand before me in this **h**, which 1004
7:11 Is this **h**, which is called by my name, 1004
7:14 Therefore will I do unto *this* **h**, which is 1004
7:30 they have set their abominations in the **h** 1004
9:26 all the **h** of Israel *are* uncircumcised in 1004
10: 1 LORD speaketh unto you, O **h** of Israel: 1004
11:10 the **h** of Israel and the house of Judah have 1004
11:10 the **h** of Judah have broken my covenant 1004
11:15 What hath my beloved to do in mine **h**, 1004
11:17 for the evil of the **h** of Israel and of 1004
11:17 of the house of Israel and of the **h** of Judah, 1004
12: 6 even thy brethren, and the **h** of thy father, 1004
12: 7 I have forsaken mine **h**, I have left mine 1004
12:14 pluck out the **h** of Judah from among them. 1004
13:11 to cleave unto me the whole **h** of Israel 1004
13:11 house of Israel and the whole **h** of Judah, 1004
16: 5 Enter not *into* the **h** of mourning, 1004
16: 8 Thou shalt not also go *into* the **h** of 1004
17:26 *of* praise, *unto* the **h** of the LORD. 1004
18: 2 go down *to* the potter's **h**, and there I will 1004
18: 3 I went down *to* the potter's **h**, and behold, 1004
18: 6 O **h** of Israel, cannot I do with you as this 1004
18: 6 so *are* ye in mine hand, O **h** of Israel. 1004
19:14 he stood in the court of the LORD'S **h**; 1004
20: 1 who *was* also chief governor in the **h** of 1004
20: 2 which *was* by the **h** of the LORD. 1004
20: 6 all that dwell in thine **h** shall go into 1004
21:11 touching the **h** of the king of Judah, 1004
21:12 O **h** of David, thus saith the LORD; 1004
22: 1 Go down *to* the **h** of the king of Judah, and 1004
22: 4 shall there enter in by the gates of this **h** 1004
22: 5 that this **h** shall become a desolation. 1004
22: 6 For thus saith the LORD unto the king's **h** 1004
22:13 Woe unto him that buildeth his **h** by 1004
22:14 I will build me a wide **h** and 1004
23: 8 which led the seed of the **h** of Israel out of 1004
23:11 yea, in my **h** have I found their wickedness, 1004
23:34 I will even punish that man and his **h**. 1004
26: 2 Stand in the court of the LORD'S **h**, and 1004
26: 2 which come to worship *in* the LORD'S **h**, 1004
26: 6 will I make this **h** like Shiloh, and will 1004
26: 7 these words in the **h** of the LORD. 1004
26: 9 This **h** shall be like Shiloh, and this city 1004
26: 9 against Jeremiah in the **h** of the LORD. 1004
26:10 they came up from the king's **h** *unto* 1004
26:10 the king's house *unto* the **h** of the LORD, 1004
26:10 entry of the new gate of the LORD'S ***h***. NIH
26:12 LORD sent me to prophesy against this **h** 1004
26:18 the mountain of the **h** as the high places of 1004
27:16 the vessels of the LORD'S **h** *shall* now 1004
27:18 that the vessels which are left in the **h** of 1004
27:18 *in* the **h** of the king of Judah, and 1004
27:21 concerning the vessels that remain *in* the **h** 1004
27:21 *in* the **h** of the king of Judah and 1004
28: 1 spake unto me in the **h** of the LORD, 1004
28: 3 this place all the vessels of the LORD'S **h**, 1004
28: 5 people that stood in the **h** of the LORD, 1004
28: 6 bring again the vessels of the LORD'S **h**, 1004
29:26 that *ye* should be officers in the **h** of 1004
31:27 that I will sow the **h** of Israel and the house 1004
31:27 and the **h** of Judah *with* the seed of man, 1004
31:31 that I will make a new covenant with the **h** 1004
31:31 the house of Israel, and with the **h** of Judah: 1004
31:33 that I will make with the **h** of Israel; 1004
32: 2 which *was in* the king of Judah's **h**. 1004
32:34 they set their abominations in the **h**, 1004
33:11 sacrifice of praise *into* the **h** of the LORD. 1004
33:14 which I have promised unto the **h** of Israel 1004
33:14 the house of Israel and to the **h** of Judah. 1004
33:17 to sit upon the throne of the **h** of Israel; 1004
34:13 of Egypt, out of the **h** of bondmen, saying, 1004
34:15 ye had made a covenant before me in the **h** 1004
35: 2 Go unto the **h** of the Rechabites, and 1004
35: 2 and bring them *into* the **h** of the LORD, 1004
35: 3 his sons, and the whole **h** of the Rechabites; 1004
35: 4 I brought them *into* the **h** of the LORD, 1004
35: 5 I set before the sons of the **h** of 1004
35: 7 Neither shall ye build **h**, nor sow seed, 1004
35:18 Jeremiah said unto the **h** of the Rechabites, 1004
36: 3 It may be that the **h** of Judah will hear all 1004
36: 5 I cannot go *into* the **h** of the LORD: 1004
36: 6 *in* the LORD'S **h** upon the fasting day: 1004
36: 8 words of the LORD *in* the LORD'S **h**. 1004
36:10 words of Jeremiah *in* the **h** of the LORD, 1004
36:10 entry of the new gate of the LORD'S **h**, 1004
36:12 he went down *into* the king's **h**, into 1004
37:15 put him *in* prison *in* the **h** of Jonathan 1004
37:17 and the king asked him secretly in his **h**, 1004
37:20 that thou cause me not to return *to* the **h** of 1004
38: 7 of the eunuchs which *was* in the king's **h**, 1004
38: 8 Ebed-melech went forth out of the king's **h**, 1004
38:11 went *into* the **h** of the king under 1004
38:14 third entry that *is* in the **h** of the LORD: 1004
38:17 with fire; and thou shalt live, and thine **h**: 1004
38:22 **h** *shall be* brought forth to the king of 1004
38:26 not cause me to return *to* Jonathan's **h**, 1004
39: 8 the Chaldeans burnt the king's **h**, and 1004
41: 5 to bring *them to* the **h** of the LORD. 1004
43: 9 which *is* at the entry of Pharaoh's **h** in 1004
48:13 as the **h** of Israel was ashamed of Beth-el 1004
51:51 into the sanctuaries of the LORD'S **h**. 1004
52:13 burnt the **h** of the LORD, and the king's 1004
52:13 the house of the LORD, and the king's **h**; 1004
52:17 Also the pillars of brass that *were* in the **h** 1004
52:17 the brasen sea that *was* in the **h** of 1004
52:20 which king Solomon had made in the **h** of 1004
La 2: 7 they have made a noise in the **h** of 1004
Eze 2: 5 will forbear, (for they *are* a rebellious **h**,) 1004
2: 6 their looks, though they *be* a rebellious **h**. 1004
2: 8 not thou rebellious like *that* rebellious **h**: 1004
3: 1 this roll, and go speak unto the **h** of Israel. 1004
3: 4 go, get thee unto the **h** of Israel, and 1004

Eze 3: 5 of a hard language, *but* to the **h** of Israel; 1004
3: 7 the **h** of Israel will not hearken unto thee; 1004
3: 7 for all the **h** of Israel *are* impudent 1004
3: 9 their looks, though they *be* a rebellious **h**. 1004
3:17 I have made thee a watchman unto the **h** of 1004
3:24 unto me, Go, shut thyself within thine **h**. 1004
3:26 them a reprover: for they *are* a rebellious **h**. 1004
3:27 let him forbear: for they *are* a rebellious **h**. 1004
4: 3 This *shall be* a sign to the **h** of Israel. 1004
4: 4 lay the iniquity of the **h** of Israel upon it: 1004
4: 5 shalt thou bear the iniquity of the **h** of 1004
4: 6 thou shalt bear the iniquity of the **h** of 1004
5: 4 a fire come forth into all the **h** of Israel. 1004
6:11 Alas for all the evil abominations of the **h** 1004
8: 1 as I sat in mine **h**, and the elders of Judah 1004
8: 6 *even* the great abominations that the **h** of 1004
8:10 and all the idols of the **h** of Israel, 1004
8:11 men of the ancients of the **h** of Israel, 1004
8:12 hast thou seen what the ancients of the **h** of 1004
8:14 LORD'S **h** which *was* towards the north; 1004
8:16 me into the inner court of the LORD'S **h**, 1004
8:17 Is it a light thing to the **h** of Judah that *they* 1004
9: 3 he was, to the threshold of the **h**. 1004
9: 6 at the ancient men which *were* before the **h**. 1004
9: 7 Defile the **h**, and fill the courts *with* 1004
9: 9 The iniquity of the **h** of Israel and Judah *is* 1004
10: 3 cherubims stood on the right side of the **h**, 1004
10: 4 *and stood* over the threshold of the **h**; 1004
10: 4 the **h** was filled with the cloud, and 1004
10:18 departed from off the threshold of the **h**, 1004
10:19 the door of the east gate of the LORD'S **h**; 1004
11: 1 me unto the east gate of the LORD'S **h**, 1004
11: 5 Thus have ye said, O **h** of Israel: 1004
11:15 thy kindred, and all the **h** of Israel wholly, 1004
12: 2 thou dwellest in the midst of a rebellious **h**, 1004
12: 2 and hear not: for they *are* a rebellious **h**. 1004
12: 3 will consider, though they *be* a rebellious **h**. 1004
12: 6 for I have set thee *for* a sign unto the **h** of 1004
12: 9 Son of man, hath not the **h** of Israel, 1004
12: 9 the rebellious **h**, said unto thee, What doest 1004
12:10 and all the **h** of Israel that *are* among them. 1004
12:24 flattering divination within the **h** of Israel. 1004
12:25 for in your days, O rebellious **h**, will I say 1004
12:27 of man, behold, *they of* the **h** of Israel say, 1004
13: 5 neither made up the hedge for the **h** of 1004
13: 9 be written in the writing of the **h** of Israel, 1004
14: 4 Every man of the **h** of Israel that setteth up 1004
14: 5 That *I* may take the **h** of Israel in their own 1004
14: 6 Therefore say unto the **h** of Israel, 1004
14: 7 For every one of the **h** of Israel, or of 1004
14:11 That the **h** of Israel may go no more astray 1004
17: 2 speak a parable unto the **h** of Israel; 1004
17:12 Say now to the rebellious **h**, Know ye not 1004
18: 6 up his eyes to the idols of the **h** of Israel, 1004
18:15 up his eyes to the idols of the **h** of Israel, 1004
18:25 Hear now, O **h** of Israel; Is not my way 1004
18:29 Yet saith the **h** of Israel, The way of 1004
18:29 O **h** of Israel, are not my ways equal? 1004
18:30 Therefore I will judge you, O **h** of Israel, 1004
18:31 for why will ye die, O **h** of Israel? 1004
20: 5 lifted up mine hand unto the seed of the **h** 1004
20:13 the **h** of Israel rebelled against me in 1004
20:27 speak unto the **h** of Israel, and say unto 1004
20:30 Wherefore say unto the **h** of Israel, 1004
20:31 shall I be inquired of by you, O **h** of Israel? 1004
20:39 As for you, O **h** of Israel, thus saith 1004
20:40 Lord GOD, there shall all the **h** of Israel, 1004
20:44 O ye **h** of Israel, saith the Lord GOD. 1004
22:18 the **h** of Israel is to me become dross: 1004
23:39 thus have they done in the midst of mine **h**. 1004
24: 3 utter a parable unto the rebellious **h**, and 1004
24:21 Speak unto the **h** of Israel, Thus saith 1004
25: 3 against the **h** of Judah, when they went into 1004
25: 8 the **h** of Judah *is* like unto all the heathen; 1004
25:12 Because that Edom hath dealt against the **h** 1004
27:14 They of the **h** of Togarmah traded in thy 1004
28:24 more a pricking brier unto the **h** of Israel, 1004
28:25 When I shall have gathered the **h** of Israel 1004
29: 6 they have been a staff of reed to the **h** of 1004
29:16 it shall be no more the confidence of the **h** 1004
29:21 In that day will I cause the horn of the **h** of 1004
33: 7 I have set thee a watchman unto the **h** of 1004
33:10 thou son of man, speak unto the **h** of Israel; 1004
33:11 for why will ye die, O **h** of Israel? 1004
33:20 O ye **h** of Israel, I will judge you every one 1004
34:30 *that* they, *even* the **h** of Israel, *are* my 1004
35:15 rejoice at the inheritance of the **h** of Israel, 1004
36:10 upon you, all the **h** of Israel, *even* all of it: 1004
36:17 when the **h** of Israel dwelt in their own 1004
36:21 which the **h** of Israel had profaned among 1004
36:22 Therefore say unto the **h** of Israel, 1004
36:22 O **h** of Israel, but for mine holy name's 1004
36:32 for your own ways, O **h** of Israel. 1004
36:37 I will yet *for* this be inquired of by the **h** of 1004
37:11 these bones *are* the whole **h** of Israel: 1004
37:16 and *for* all the **h** of Israel his companions: 1004
38: 6 the **h** of Togarmah *of* the north quarters, 1004
39:12 seven months shall the **h** of Israel be 1004
39:22 So the **h** of Israel shall know that I *am* 1004
39:23 the heathen shall know that the **h** of Israel 1004
39:25 have mercy upon the whole **h** of Israel, and 1004
39:29 for I have poured out my spirit upon the **h** 1004
40: 4 declare all that thou seest to the **h** of Israel. 1004
40: 5 behold a wall on the outside of the **h** round 1004
40:45 the keepers of the charge of the **h**. 1004
40:47 and the altar *that was* before the **h**. 1004
40:48 he brought me to the porch of the **h**, and 1004
41: 5 After he measured the wall of the **h**, 1004
41: 5 round about the **h** on every side. 1004
41: 6 of the **h** for the side chambers round about, 1004
41: 6 but they had not hold in the wall of the **h**. 1004
41: 7 for the winding about of the **h** *went* still 1004
41: 7 house *went* still upward round about the **h**: 1004
41: 7 the breadth of the **h** *was still* upward, 1004
41: 8 I saw also the height of the **h** round about: 1004

Eze 41:10 cubits round about the **h** on every side. 1004
41:13 So he measured the **h**, an hundred cubits 1004
41:14 Also the breadth of the face of the **h**, and 1004
41:17 even unto the inner **h**, and without, and 1004
41:19 *it was* made through all the **h** round about. 1004
41:26 *upon* the side chambers of the **h**, and thick 1004
42:15 had made an end of measuring the inner **h**, 1004
43: 4 the glory of the LORD came into the **h** by 1004
43: 5 the glory of the LORD filled the **h**. 1004
43: 6 I heard *him* speaking unto me out of the **h**; 1004
43: 7 shall the **h** of Israel no more defile, 1004
43:10 of man, shew the **h** to the house of Israel, 1004
43:10 of man, shew the house to the **h** of Israel, 1004
43:11 shew them the form of the **h**, and 1004
43:12 This *is* the law of the **h**; Upon the top of 1004
43:12 most holy. Behold, this *is* the law of the **h**. 1004
43:21 shall burn it in the appointed place of the **h**, 1004
44: 4 me the way of the north gate before the **h**: 1004
44: 4 the glory of the LORD filled the **h** of 1004
44: 5 all the ordinances of the **h** of the LORD, 1004
44: 5 mark well the entering in of the **h**, 1004
44: 6 *even* to the **h** of Israel, Thus saith the Lord 1004
44: 6 O ye **h** of Israel, let it suffice you of all 1004
44: 7 in my sanctuary, to pollute it, *even* my **h**, 1004
44:11 *having* charge at the gates of the **h**, and 1004
44:11 gates of the house, and ministering to the **h**: 1004
44:12 caused the **h** of Israel to fall into iniquity; 1004
44:14 make them keepers of the charge of the **h**, 1004
44:22 they shall take maidens of the seed of the **h** 1004
44:30 he may cause the blessing to rest in thine **h**. 1004
45: 5 the ministers of the **h**, have for themselves, 1004
45: 6 *portion*: it shall be for the whole **h** of Israel. 1004
45: 8 *the rest of* the land shall they give to the **h** 1004
45:17 in the sabbaths in all solemnities of the **h** of 1004
45:17 to make reconciliation for the **h** of Israel. 1004
45:19 put *it* upon the posts of the **h**, and upon 1004
45:20 *that is* simple: so shall ye reconcile the **h**. 1004
46:24 where the ministers of the **h** shall boil 1004
47: 1 he brought me again unto the door of the **h**; 1004
47: 1 from under the threshold of the **h** eastward: 1004
47: 1 for the forefront of the **h** *stood toward* 1004
47: 1 from under from the right side of the **h**, 1004
48:21 the sanctuary of the **h** *shall be* in the midst 1004
Da 1: 2 with part of the vessels of the **h** of God: 1004
1: 2 *into* the land of Shinar *to* the **h** of his god; 1004
1: 2 he brought the vessels *into* the treasure **h** of 1004
2:17 Daniel went to his **h**, and made the thing 1005
4: 4 I Nebuchadnezzar was at rest in mine **h**, 1005
4:30 that I have built for the **h** of the kingdom 1005
5: 3 of the **h** of God which *was* at Jerusalem; 1005
5:10 and his lords, came into the banquet **h**: 1005
5:23 they have brought the vessels of his **h** 1005
6:10 the writing *was* signed, he went into his **h**; 1005
Hos 1: 4 the blood of Jezreel upon the **h** of Jehu, 1004
1: 4 will cause to cease the kingdom of the **h** of 1004
1: 6 for I will no more have mercy upon the **h** 1004
1: 7 I will have mercy upon the **h** of Judah, and 1004
5: 1 and hearken, ye **h** of Israel; and give ye ear, 1004
5: 1 of Israel; and give ye ear, O **h** of the king; 1004
5:12 a moth, and to the **h** of Judah as rottenness. 1004
5:14 and as a young lion to the **h** of Judah: 1004
6:10 I have seen a horrible thing in the **h** of 1004
8: 1 *He shall come* as an eagle against the **h** of 1004
9: 4 shall not come *into* the **h** of the LORD. 1004
9: 8 all his ways, *and* hatred in the **h** of his God. 1004
9:15 doings I will drive them out of mine **h**, 1004
11:12 with lies, and the **h** of Israel with deceit: 1004
Joel 1: 9 the drink offering is cut off from the **h** of 1004
1:13 the drink offering is withholden from the **h** 1004
1:14 all the inhabitants of the land *into* the **h** of 1004
1:16 and gladness from the **h** of our God? 1004
3:18 a fountain shall come forth of the **h** of 1004
Am 1: 4 I will send a fire into the **h** of Hazael, 1004
1: 5 him that holdeth the sceptre from the **h** of 1004
2: 8 of the condemned *in* the **h** of their god. 1004
3:13 Hear ye, and testify in the **h** of Jacob, 1004
3:15 I will smite the winter **h** with the summer 1004
3:15 smite the winter house with the summer **h**; 1004
5: 1 *even* a lamentation, O **h** of Israel. 1004
5: 3 hundred shall leave ten, to the **h** of Israel. 1004
5: 4 For thus saith the LORD unto the **h** of 1004
5: 6 lest he break out like fire *in* the **h** of Joseph, 1004
5:19 or went *into* the **h**, and leaned his hand on 1004
5:25 in the wilderness forty years, O **h** of Israel? 1004
6: 1 the nations, to whom the **h** of Israel came! 1004
6: 9 if there remain ten men in one **h**, that they 1004
6:10 to bring out the bones out of the **h**, and 1004
6:10 say unto *him* that *is* by the sides of the **h**, 1004
6:11 he will smite the great **h** *with* breaches, and 1004
6:11 *with* breaches, and the little **h** *with* clefts. 1004
6:14 O **h** of Israel, saith the LORD the God of 1004
7: 9 I will rise against the **h** of Jeroboam with 1004
7:10 against thee in the midst of the **h** of Israel: 1004
7:16 drop not *thy word* against the **h** of Isaac. 1004
9: 8 saving that I will not utterly destroy the **h** 1004
9: 9 I will sift the **h** of Israel among all nations, 1004
Ob 1:17 the **h** of Jacob shall possess their 1004
1:18 the **h** of Jacob shall be a fire, and the house 1004
1:18 the **h** of Joseph a flame, and the house of 1004
1:18 the **h** of Esau for stubble, and they shall 1004
1:18 there shall not be *any* remaining of the **h** of 1004
Mic 1: 5 *is* all this, and for the sins of the **h** of Israel. 1004
2: 2 so they oppress a man and his **h**, even a 1004
2: 7 O *thou that art* named the **h** of Jacob, is the 1004
3: 1 of Jacob, and ye princes of the **h** of Israel; 1004
3: 9 ye heads of the **h** of Jacob, and princes of 1004
3: 9 princes of the **h** of Israel, that abhor 1004
3:12 the mountain of the **h** as the high places of 1004
4: 1 *that* the mountain of the **h** of the LORD 1004
4: 2 and to the **h** of the God of Jacob; 1004
6: 4 and redeemed thee out of the **h** of servants; 1004
6:10 of wickedness *in* the **h** of the wicked, 1004
6:16 all the works of the **h** of Ahab, and ye walk 1004
7: 6 a man's enemies *are* the men of his own **h**. 1004
Na 1:14 out of the **h** of thy gods will I cut off 1004

Hab 2: 9 that coveteth an evil covetousness to his **h**, 1004
2:10 Thou hast consulted shame to thy **h** by 1004
3:13 thou woundedst the head out of the **h** of 1004
Zep 2: 7 the coast shall be for the remnant of the **h** 1004
Hag 1: 2 the time that the LORD'S **h** should be 1004
1: 4 in your cieled houses, and this **h** *lie* waste? 1004
1: 8 and bring wood, and build the **h**; 1004
1: 9 Because of mine **h** that *is* waste, and ye run 1004
1: 9 and ye run every man unto his own **h**. 1004
1:14 did work in the **h** of the LORD of hosts, 1004
2: 3 Who *is* left among you that saw this **h** in 1004
2: 7 I will fill this **h** *with* glory, saith 1004
2: 9 The glory of this latter **h** shall be greater 1004
Zec 1:16 my **h** shall be built in it, saith the LORD 1004
3: 7 thou shalt also judge my **h**, and shalt also 1004
4: 9 have laid the foundation of this **h**; 1004
5: 4 it shall enter into the **h** of the thief, and 1004
5: 4 into the **h** of him that sweareth falsely by 1004
5: 4 it shall remain in the midst of his **h**, and 1004
5:11 To build it a **h** in the land of Shinar: 1004
6:10 go *into* the **h** of Josiah the son of 1004
7: 2 When they had sent *unto* the **h** of God 1004
7: 3 *were* in the **h** of the LORD of hosts, 1004
8: 9 of the **h** of the LORD of hosts was laid, 1004
8:13 O **h** of Judah, and house of Israel; 1004
8:13 O house of Judah, and **h** of Israel; 1004
8:15 well unto Jerusalem and to the **h** of Judah: 1004
8:19 shall be to the **h** of Judah joy and gladness, 1004
9: 8 I will encamp about mine **h** because of 1004
10: 3 hosts hath visited his flock the **h** of Judah, 1004
10: 6 I will strengthen the **h** of Judah, and I will 1004
10: 6 I will save the **h** of Joseph, and I will bring 1004
11:13 cast them to the potter *in* the **h** of 1004
12: 4 I will open mine eyes upon the **h** of Judah, 1004
12: 7 that the glory of the **h** of David and 1004
12: 8 the **h** of David *shall be* as God, as the angel 1004
12:10 I will pour upon the **h** of David, and 1004
12:12 the family of the **h** of David apart, and 1004
12:12 the family of the **h** of Nathan apart, 1004
12:13 The family of the **h** of Levi apart, and 1004
13: 1 shall be a fountain opened to the **h** of David 1004
13: 6 *Those with* which I was wounded *in* the **h** 1004
14:20 the pots in the LORD'S **h** shall be like 1004
14:21 Canaanite in the **h** of the LORD of hosts. 1004
Mal 3:10 that there may be meat in mine **h**, and 1004
Mt 2:11 And when they were come into the **h**, *3614*
5:15 and it giveth light unto all that are in the **h**. *3614*
7:24 a wise man, which built his **h** upon a rock: *3614*
7:25 and the winds blew, and beat upon that **h**; *3614*
7:26 which built his **h** upon the sand: *3614*
7:27 and the winds blew, and beat upon that **h**; *3614*
8:14 And when Jesus was come into Peter's **h**, *3614*
9: 6 Arise, take up thy bed, and go unto thine **h**. *3624*
9: 7 And he arose, and departed to his **h**. *3624*
9:10 as Jesus sat at meat in the **h**, behold, *3614*
9:23 And when Jesus came into the ruler's **h**, *3614*
9:28 And when he was come into the **h**, *3614*
10: 6 But go rather to the lost sheep of the **h** of *3624*
10:12 And when ye come into a **h** salute it. *3614*
10:13 And if the **h** be worthy, let your peace *3614*
10:14 when ye depart out of that **h** or city, *3614*
10:25 If they have called the **master of the h** *3617*
12: 4 How he entered into the **h** of God, and *3624*
12:25 or **h** divided against itself shall not stand: *3614*
12:29 how can one enter into a strong *man's* **h**, *3614*
12:29 strong *man?* and then he will spoil his **h**. *3614*
12:44 I will return into my **h** from whence I came *3624*
13: 1 The same day went Jesus out of the **h**, and *3614*
13:36 the multitude away, and went into the **h**: *3614*
13:57 save in his own country, and in his own **h**. *3614*
15:24 but unto the lost sheep of the **h** of Israel. *3624*
17:25 And when he was come into the **h**, *3614*
20:11 murmured against the **goodman of the h**, *3617*
21:13 My **h** shall be called the house of prayer; *3624*
21:13 My house shall be called the **h** of prayer; *3624*
23:38 Behold, your **h** is left unto you desolate. *3624*
24:17 come down to take any *thing* out of his **h**: *3614*
24:43 that if the **goodman of the h** had known in *3617*
24:43 would not have suffered his **h** to be broken *3614*
26: 6 in Bethany, in the **h** of Simon the leper, *3614*
26:18 I will keep the passover at thy **h** with my NIG
Mk 1:29 they entered into the **h** of Simon and *3614*
2: 1 and it was noised that he was in the **h**. *3624*
2:11 up thy bed, and go thy way into thine **h**. *3624*
2:15 that as *Jesus* sat at meat in his **h**, *3614*
2:26 How he went into the **h** of God in the days *3624*
3:19 also betrayed him. And they went into a **h**. *3624*
3:25 And if a **h** be divided against itself, *3614*
3:25 divided against itself, that **h** cannot stand. *3614*
3:27 No *man* can enter into a strong *man's* **h**, *3614*
3:27 the strong *man;* and then he will spoil his **h**. *3614*
5:35 of the synagogue's *h certain* which said, NIG
5:38 And he cometh to the **h** of the ruler of the *3624*
6: 4 and among his own kin, and in his own **h**. *3614*
6:10 In what place soever ye enter into a **h**, *3614*
7:17 And when he was entered into the **h** from *3624*
7:24 and entered into a **h**, and would have no *3614*
7:30 And when she was come to her **h**, *3624*
8:26 And he sent him away to his **h**, saying, *3624*
9:28 And when he was come into *the* **h**, *3624*
9:33 and being in the **h** he asked them, *3614*
10:10 And in the **h** his disciples asked him again *3614*
10:29 There is no *man* that hath left **h**, or *3614*
11:17 My **h** shall be called of all nations *3624*
11:17 be called of all nations the **h** of prayer? *3624*
13:15 is on the housetop not go down into the **h**, *3614*
13:15 enter *therein,* to take any *thing* out of his **h**: *3614*
13:34 who left his **h**, and gave authority to his *3614*
13:35 for ye know not when the master of the **h** *3614*
14: 3 And being in Bethany in the **h** of Simon *3614*
14:14 say ye to the **goodman of the h**, The *3617*
Lk 1:23 he departed to his own **h**. *3624*
1:27 whose name was Joseph, of the **h** of David; *3624*
1:33 And he shall reign over the **h** of Jacob for *3624*
1:40 And entered into the **h** of Zacharias, and *3624*

Lk 1:56 three months, and returned to her own **h**. *3624*
1:69 for us in the **h** of his servant David; *3624*
2: 4 (because he was of the **h** and lineage of *3624*
4:38 the synagogue, and entered into Simon's **h**. *3614*
5:24 and take up thy couch, and go into thine **h**. *3624*
5:25 and departed to his own **h**, glorifying God. *3624*
5:29 Levi made him a great feast in his own **h**: *3614*
6: 4 How he went into the **h** of God, and *3624*
6:48 He is like a man which built a **h**, and *3614*
6:48 the stream beat vehemently upon that **h**, *3614*
6:49 a foundation built a **h** upon the earth; *3614*
6:49 it fell; and the ruin of that **h** was great. *3614*
7: 6 And when he was now not far from the **h**, *3614*
7:10 And they that were sent, returning to the **h**, *3624*
7:36 And he went into the Pharisee's **h**, *3614*
7:37 that *Jesus* sat at meat in the Pharisee's **h**, *3614*
7:44 I entered into thine **h**, thou gavest me no *3614*
8:27 neither abode in *any* **h**, but in the tombs. *3614*
8:39 Return to thine own **h**, and shew how great *3624*
8:41 him that *he* would come into his **h**: *3624*
8:49 ruler of the synagogue's *h*, saying to him, NIG
8:51 And when he came into the **h**, he suffered *3614*
9: 4 And whatsoever **h** ye enter into, *3614*
9:61 them farewell, which are *at home* in my **h**. *3624*
10: 5 And into whatsoever **h** ye enter, first say, *3614*
10: 5 house ye enter, first say, Peace *be* to this **h**. *3624*
10: 7 And in the same **h** remain, eating and *3614*
10: 7 worthy of his hire. Go not from **h** to house. *3614*
10: 7 worthy of his hire. Go not from house to **h**. *3614*
10:38 named Martha received him into her **h**. *3624*
11:17 and a **h** *divided* against a house falleth. *3624*
11:17 and a house *divided* against a **h** falleth. *3624*
11:24 I will return unto my **h** whence I came out. *3624*
12:39 that if the **goodman of the h** had known *3617*
12:39 not have suffered his **h** to be broken *3624*
12:52 there shall be five in one **h** divided, *3624*
13:25 When once the **master of the h** is risen up, *3617*
13:35 Behold, your **h** is left unto you desolate: *3624*
14: 1 as he went into the **h** of one of the chief *3624*
14:21 **master of the h** being angry said to his *3617*
14:23 *them* to come in, that my **h** may be filled. *3624*
15: 8 and sweep the **h**, and seek diligently till *3614*
15:25 and as he came and drew nigh to the **h**, *3614*
16:27 thou wouldest send him to my father's **h**: *3624*
17:31 be upon the housetop, and his stuff in the **h**, *3614*
18:14 this man went down to his **h** justified *rather* *3624*
18:29 There is no *man* that hath left **h**, or parents, *3614*
19: 5 for to day I must abide at thy **h**. *3624*
19: 9 This day is salvation come to this **h**, *3624*
19:46 It is written, My **h** is the house of prayer: *3624*
19:46 It is written, My house is the **h** of prayer: *3624*
22:10 follow him into the **h** where he entereth in. *3614*
22:11 ye shall say unto the goodman of the **h**, *3614*
22:54 and brought him into the high priest's **h**. *3624*
Jn 2:16 make not my Father's **h** a house of *3624*
2:16 make not my Father's house a **h** of *3624*
2:17 The zeal of thine **h** hath eaten me up. *3624*
4:53 and himself believed, and his whole **h**. *3614*
7:53 And every man went unto his own **h**. *3624*
8:35 And the servant abideth not in the **h** for *3614*
11:20 and met him: but Mary sat *still* in the **h**. *3624*
11:31 then which were with her in the **h**, *3614*
12: 3 the **h** was filled with the odour of *3614*
14: 2 In my Father's **h** are many mansions: if *it* *3614*
Ac 2: 2 it filled all the **h** where they were sitting. *3624*
2:36 Therefore let all the **h** of Israel know *3624*
2:46 and breaking bread **from h to house**, *2596+3624*
2:46 and breaking bread **from house to h**, *2596+3624*
5:42 and **in every h**, they ceased not to *2596+3624*
7:10 him governor over Egypt and all his **h**. *3624*
7:20 nourished up in his father's **h** three months: *3624*
7:42 O *ye* **h** of Israel, have ye offered to me *3624*
7:47 But Solomon built him a **h**. *3624*
7:49 what **h** will ye build me? saith the Lord: or *3624*
8: 3 of the church, entering into **every h**, *2596+3624*
9:11 inquire in the **h** of Judas for *one* called *3614*
9:17 went his way, and entered into the **h**; *3614*
10: 2 and one that feared God with all his **h**, *3624*
10: 6 Simon a tanner, whose **h** is by the sea side: *3614*
10: 9 Peter went up upon the **h** to pray about *1430*
10:17 Cornelius had made inquiry for Simon's **h**, *3614*
10:22 by a holy angel to send for thee into his **h**, *3624*
10:30 and at the ninth hour I prayed in my **h**, and *3624*
10:32 he is lodged in the **h** of *one* Simon a tanner *3614*
11:11 men already come unto the **h** where I was, *3614*
11:12 and we entered into the man's **h**: *3624*
11:13 us how he had seen an angel in his **h**, *3624*
11:14 whereby thou and all thy **h** shall be saved. *3624*
12:12 came to the **h** of Mary the mother of John, *3614*
16:15 come into my **h**, and abide *there.* And she *3624*
16:31 and thou shalt be saved, and thy **h**. *3624*
16:32 of the Lord, and to all that were in his **h**. *3614*
16:34 And when he had brought them into his **h**, *3624*
16:34 rejoiced, believing in God with **all his h**. *3832*
16:40 the prison, and entered into *the* **h** *of* Lydia. NIG
17: 5 and assaulted the **h** of Jason, and sought to *3614*
18: 7 and entered into a certain *man's* **h**, *3614*
18: 7 whose **h** joined hard to the synagogue. *3614*
18: 8 believed on the Lord with all his **h**; *3624*
19:16 so that *they* fled out of that **h** naked and *3624*
20:20 you publickly, and **from h to house**, *2596+3624*
20:20 you publickly, and **from house to h**, *2596+3624*
21: 8 we entered into the **h** of Philip *3624*
28:30 dwelt two whole years in his own **hired h**, *3410*
Ro 16: 5 Likewise *greet* the church that is in their **h**. *3624*
1Co 1:11 by them which are of the **h** of Chloe, NIG
16:15 brethren, (ye know the **h** of Stephanas, *3614*
16:19 the Lord, with the church that is in their **h**. *3624*
2Co 5: 1 For we know that if our earthly **h** of *this* *3614*
5: 1 a **h** not made with hand, eternal in *3614*
5: 2 upon with our **h** which is from heaven: *3613*
Col 4:15 Nymphas, and the church which is in his **h**. *3624*
1Ti 3: 4 One that ruleth well his own **h**, having *his* *3624*
3: 5 if a man know not how to rule his own **h**, *3624*
3:15 oughtest to behave thyself in the **h** of God, *3624*

H

1Ti 5: 8 and specially for those of his own **h**, 3609
5:13 wandering about **from h to house**; 3588+3614
5:13 wandering about **from house to h**; 3588+3614
5:14 *women* marry, bear children, **guide the h**, 3616
2Ti 1:16 The Lord give mercy unto the **h** of 3624
2:20 But in a great **h** there are not only vessels 3614
Phm 1: 2 and to the church in thy **h**: 3624
Heb 3: 2 as also Moses *was faithful* in all his **h**. 3624
3: 3 inasmuch as he who hath builded **the h**[S] 846
3: 3 the house hath more honour than the **h**. 3624
3: 4 For every **h** is builded by some *man;* but 3624
3: 5 And Moses verily *was* faithful in all his **h**, 3624
3: 6 But Christ as a Son over his own **h**; 3624
3: 6 whose **h** are we, if we hold fast 3624
8: 8 make a new covenant with the **h** of Israel 3624
8: 8 the house of Israel and with the **h** of Juda: 3624
8:10 make with the **h** of Israel after those days, 3624
10:21 And *having* a high priest over the **h** of God; 3624
11: 7 prepared an ark to the saving of his **h**; 3624
1Pe 2: 5 as lively stones, are built *up* a spiritual **h**, 3624
4:17 that judgment must begin at the **h** of God: 3624
2Jn 1:10 this doctrine, receive him not into *your* **h**, 3614

HOUSE OF APHRAH (1) [HOUSE]

Mic 1:10 in the **h** roll thyself *in* the dust. 1036

HOUSEHOLD (61) [HOUSE]

Ge 18:19 command his children and his **h** after him, 1004
31:37 what hast thou found of all thy **h** stuff? 1004
35: 2 Jacob said unto his **h**, and to all that *were* 1004
45:11 lest thou, and thy **h**, and all that thou hast, 1004
47:12 and all his father's **h**, *with* bread, 1004
Ex 1: 1 every man and his **h** came with Jacob. 1004
12: 4 if the **h** be too little for the lamb, let him 1004
Lev 16:17 for his **h**, and for all the congregation of 1004
Dt 6:22 upon Pharaoh, and upon all his **h**, 1004
14:26 and thou shalt rejoice, thou and thine **h**, 1004
15:20 the LORD shall choose, thou and thy **h**. 1004
Jos 2:18 and thy brethren, and all thy father's **h**, 1004
6:25 and her father's **h**, and all that she had; 1004
7:14 the **h** which the LORD shall take shall 1004
7:18 he brought his **h** man by man; and Achan, 1004
Jdg 6:27 because he feared his father's **h**, and 1004
18:25 thou lose thy life, with the lives of thy **h**. 1004
1Sa 25:17 against our master, and against all his **h**: 1004
27: 3 he and his men, every man with his **h**, 1004
2Sa 2: 3 did David bring up, every man with his **h**: 1004
6:11 LORD blessed Obed-edom, and all his **h**. 1004
6:20 David returned to bless his **h**. And Michal 1004
15:16 the king went forth, and all his **h** after him. 1004
16: 2 The asses *be* for the king's **h** to ride on; 1004
17:23 put his **h** in order, and hanged himself, and 1004
19:18 over a ferry boat to carry over the king's **h**, 1004
19:41 his **h**, and all David's men with him, 1004
1Ki 4: 6 Ahishar *was* over the **h**: and Adoniram 1004
4: 7 provided victuals for the king and his **h**: 1004
5: 9 my desire, in giving food for my **h**. 1004
5:11 measures of wheat *for* food to his **h**, 1004
11:20 Genubath was *in* Pharaoh's **h** among 1004
2Ki 7: 9 come, that we may go and tell the king's **h**. 1004
8: 1 go thou and thine **h**, and 1004
8: 2 she went with her **h**, and sojourned in 1004
18:18 which *was* over the **h**, and Shebna 1004
18:37 which *was* over the **h**, and Shebna 1004
19: 2 which *was* over the **h**, and Shebna 1004
1Ch 24: 6 one principal **h** being taken for Eleazar, and 1004
Ne 13: 8 I cast forth all the **h** stuff of Tobiah out of 1004
Job 1: 3 five hundred she asses, and a very great **h**; 5657
Pr 27:27 for the food of thy **h**, and *for* 1004
31:15 giveth meat to her **h**, and a portion to her 1004
31:21 She is not afraid of the snow for her **h**: 1004
31:21 for all her **h** *are* clothed with scarlet. 1004
31:27 She looketh well to the ways of her **h**, and 1004
Isa 36:22 that *was* over the **h**, and Shebna the scribe, 1004
37: 2 who *was* over the **h**, and Shebna the scribe, 1004
Mt 10:25 much more *shall they call* them **of** his **h**? 3615
10:36 a man's foes *shall be* they **of** his own **h**. 3615
24:45 whom his lord hath made ruler over his **h**, 2322
Lk 12:42 whom *his* lord shall make ruler over his **h**, 2322
Ac 10: 7 he called two of his **h servants**, and 3610
16:15 and her **h**, she besought *us,* saying, 3624
Ro 16:10 Salute them which are of Aristobulus' *h*. NIG
16:11 Greet them that be of the *h* of Narcissus, NIG
1Co 1:16 And I baptized also the **h** of Stephanas: 3624
Gal 6:10 unto them who are of the **h** of faith. 3609
Eph 2:19 with the saints, and **of the h** of God; 3609
Php 4:22 chiefly they that are of Cesar's **h**. 3614
2Ti 4:19 and Aquila, and the **h** of Onesiphorus. 3624

HOUSEHOLDER (4) [HOUSE]

Mt 13:27 So the servants of the **h** came and said unto 3617
13:52 of heaven is like unto a man *that is* a **h**, 3617
20: 1 of heaven is like unto a man *that is* a **h**, 3617
21:33 There was a certain **h**, which planted a 444+3617

HOUSEHOLDS (7) [HOUSE]

Ge 42:33 take *food for* the famine of your **h**, and 1004
45:18 take your father and your **h**, and come unto 1004
47:24 for them of your **h**, and for food for your 1004
Nu 18:31 ye shall eat it in every place, ye and your **h**: 1004
Dt 11: 6 their **h**, and their tents, and all 1004
12: 7 ye and your **h**, wherein the LORD thy 1004
Jos 7:14 the LORD shall take shall come by **h**; 1004

HOUSES (136) [HOUSE]

Ge 42:19 go ye, carry corn *for* the famine of your **h**: 1004
Ex 1:21 midwives feared God, that he made them **h**. 1004
6:14 These *be* the heads of their fathers' **h**: 1004
8: 9 to destroy the frogs from thee and thy **h**, 1004
8:11 from thy **h**, and from thy servants, and 1004
8:13 the frogs died out of the **h**, out of 1004
8:21 and upon thy people, and into thy **h**: 1004
8:21 the **h** of the Egyptians shall be full of 1004
8:24 *into* his servants' **h**, and into all the land of 1004
Ex 9:20 his servants and his cattle flee into the **h**: 1004
10: 6 they shall fill thy **h**, and the houses of all 1004
10: 6 the **h** of all thy servants, and the houses of 1004
10: 6 thy servants, and the **h** of all the Egyptians; 1004
12: 7 and on the upper door post of the **h**, 1004
12:13 you for a token upon the **h** where you *are:* 1004
12:15 day ye shall put away leaven out of your **h**: 1004
12:19 shall there be no leaven found in your **h**: 1004
12:23 to come in unto your **h** to smite *you.* 1004
12:27 who passed over the **h** of the children of 1004
12:27 smote the Egyptians, and delivered our **h**. 1004
Lev 25:31 the **h** of the villages which have no wall 1004
25:32 *and* the **h** of the cities of their possession, 1004
25:33 for the **h** of the cities of the Levites *are* 1004
Nu 4:22 throughout the **h** of their fathers, by their 1004
16:32 their **h**, and all the men that *appertained* 1004
17: 6 according to their fathers' **h**, *even* twelve 1004
32:18 We will not return unto our **h**, until 1004
Dt 6:11 **h** full *of* all good *things,* which thou filledst 1004
8:12 and hast built goodly **h**, and dwelt *therein;* 1004
19: 1 and dwellest in their cities, and in their **h**; 1004
Jos 9:12 **h** on the day we came forth to go unto you; 1004
Jdg 18:14 Do ye know that there is in these **h** an 1004
18:22 the men that *were* in the **h** near to Micah's 1004
1Ki 9:10 when Solomon had built the two **h**, 1004
13:32 against all the **h** of the high places which 1004
20: 6 thine house, and the **h** of thy servants; 1004
2Ki 17:29 put *them* in the **h** of the high places which 1004
17:32 which sacrificed for them in the **h** of 1004
23: 7 he brake down the **h** of the sodomites, 1004
23:19 all the **h** also of the high places that *were* in 1004
25: 9 all the **h** of Jerusalem, and every great 1004
1Ch 15: 1 *David* made him **h** in the city of David, 1004
28:11 of the **h** thereof, and of the treasuries 1004
29: 4 to overlay the walls of the **h** *withal:* 1004
2Ch 25: 5 according to the **h** of *their* fathers, 1004
34:11 to floor the **h** which the kings of Judah had 1004
35: 4 prepare *yourselves* by the **h** of your fathers, 1004
Ne 4:14 your daughters, your wives, and your **h**. 1004
5: 3 vineyards, and **h**, that we might buy corn, 1004
5:11 their oliveyards, and their **h**, 1004
7: 4 few therein, and the **h** *were* not builded, 1004
9:25 a fat land, and possessed **h** full *of* all goods, 1004
10:34 after the **h** of our fathers, at times appointed 1004
Job 1: 4 his sons went and feasted *in their* **h**, 1004
3:15 that had gold, who filled their **h** *with* silver: 1004
4:19 How much less *in* them that dwell in **h** of 1004
15:28 *and* in **h** which no man inhabiteth, 1004
21: 9 Their **h** *are* safe from fear, neither *is* the rod 1004
22:18 Yet he filled their **h** *with* good *things:* but 1004
24:16 In the dark *they* dig *through* **h**, *which* they 1004
Ps 49:11 Their inward *thought is, that* their **h** *shall* 1004
83:12 Let us take to ourselves the **h** of God in 4999
Pr 1:13 we shall fill our **h** *with* spoil: 1004
30:26 yet make they their **h** in the rocks; 1004
Ecc 2: 4 I builded me **h**; I planted me vineyards: 1004
Isa 3:14 the spoil of the poor *is* in your **h**. 1004
5: 9 Of a truth many **h** shall be desolate, 1004
6:11 the **h** without man, and the land be utterly 1004
8:14 for a rock of offence to both the **h** of Israel, 1004
13:16 their **h** shall be spoiled, and their wives 1004
13:21 their **h** shall be full *of* doleful creatures; 1004
13:22 of the islands shall cry in their **desolate h**, 490
15: 3 on the **tops of** their **h**, and in their streets, 1406
22:10 ye have numbered the **h** of Jerusalem, and 1004
22:10 the **h** have ye broken down to fortify 1004
32:13 yea, upon all the **h** of joy *in* the joyous city: 1004
42:22 in holes, and they are hid in prison **h**: 1004
65:21 they shall build **h**, and inhabit *them;* and 1004
Jer 5: 7 themselves by troops *in* the harlots' **h**. 1004
5:27 *is* full *of* birds, so *are* their **h** full *of* deceit: 1004
6:12 their **h** shall be turned unto others, 1004
17:22 Neither carry forth a burden out of your **h** 1004
18:22 Let a cry be heard from their **h**, when thou 1004
19:13 the **h** of Jerusalem, and the houses of 1004
19:13 and the **h** of the kings of Judah, 1004
19:13 of all the **h** upon whose roofs they have 1004
29: 5 Build ye **h**, and dwell *in them;* and 1004
29:28 build ye **h**, and dwell *in them;* and 1004
32:15 **H** and fields and vineyards shall be 1004
32:29 set fire on this city, and burn it with the **h**, 1004
33: 4 concerning the **h** of this city, 1004
33: 4 concerning the **h** of the kings of Judah, 1004
35: 9 Nor to build **h** for us to dwell *in:* 1004
39: 8 the **h** of the people, with fire, and brake 1004
43:12 I will kindle a fire in the **h** of the gods of 1004
43:13 the **h** of the gods of the Egyptians shall he 1004
52:13 all the **h** of Jerusalem, and all the houses of 1004
52:13 all the **h** of the great *men,* burnt he with 1004
La 5: 2 is turned to strangers, our **h** to aliens. 1004
Eze 7:24 the heathen, and they shall possess their **h**: 1004
11: 3 Which say, *It is* not near; *let us* build **h**: 1004
16:41 they shall burn thine **h** with fire, and 1004
23:47 and burn up their **h** with fire. 1004
26:12 down thy walls, and destroy thy pleasant **h**: 1004
28:26 shall build **h**, and plant vineyards; 1004
33:30 thee by the walls and in the doors of the **h**, 1004
45: 4 it shall be a place for their **h**, and a holy 1004
Da 2: 5 and your **h** shall be made a dunghill. 1005
3:29 and their **h** shall be made a dunghill: 1005
Hos 11:11 I will place them in their **h**, saith 1004
Joel 2: 9 the wall, they shall climb up upon the **h**; 1004
Am 3:15 the **h** of ivory shall perish, and the great 1004
3:15 the great **h** shall have an end, saith 1004
5:11 ye have built **h** of hewn stone, but ye shall 1004
Mic 1:14 the **h** of Achzib *shall be* a lie to the kings of 1004
2: 2 by violence; and **h**, and take *them* away: 1004
2: 9 have ye cast out from their pleasant **h**; 1004
Zep 1: 9 which fill their masters' **h** *with* violence 1004
1:13 become a booty, and their **h** a desolation: 1004
1:13 they shall also build **h**, but not inhabit 1004
2: 7 in the **h** of Ashkelon shall they lie down in 1004
Hag 1: 4 to dwell in your cieled **h**, and this house *lie* 1004
Zec 14: 2 and the **h** rifled, and the women ravished; 1004
Mt 11: 8 they that wear soft *clothing* are in kings' **h**. 3624
Mt 19:29 And every one that hath forsaken **h**, or 3614
23:14 for ye devour widows' **h**, and for a pretence 3614
Mk 8: 3 if I send them away fasting to their own **h**, 3624
10:30 **h**, and brethren, and sisters, and mothers, 3614
12:40 Which devour widows' **h**, and for a 3614
Lk 16: 4 they may receive me into their **h**. 3624
20:47 Which devour widows' **h**, and for a shew 3614
Ac 4:34 as were possessors of lands or **h** sold them, 3614
1Co 11:22 have ye not **h** to eat and to drink *in?* or 3614
1Ti 3:12 ruling *their* children and their own **h** well. 3624
2Ti 3: 6 For of this sort are they which creep into **h**, 3614
Tit 1:11 must be stopped, who subvert whole **h**, 3624

HOUSETOP (7) [HOUSE, TOP]

Ps 102: 7 and am as a sparrow alone upon the **h**. 1406
Pr 21: 9 *It is* better to dwell in a corner of the **h**, 1406
25:24 *It is* better to dwell in a corner of the **h**, 1406
Mt 24:17 Let him which is on the **h** not come down 1430
Mk 13:15 And let him that is on the **h** not go down 1430
Lk 5:19 they went upon the **h**, and let him down 1430
17:31 he which shall be upon the **h**, and his stuff 1430

HOUSETOPS (8) [HOUSE, TOP]

2Ki 19:26 *as* the grass on the **h**, and *as* corn blasted 1406
Ps 129: 6 Let them be as the grass upon the **h**, 1406
Isa 22: 1 that thou art wholly gone up to the **h**? 1406
37:27 *as* the grass on the **h**, and *as* corn blasted 1406
Jer 48:38 generally upon all the **h** of Moab, 1406
Zep 1: 5 that worship the host of heaven upon the **h**; 1406
Mt 10:27 hear in the ear, *that* preach ye upon the **h**. 1430
Lk 12: 3 in closets shall be proclaimed upon the **h**. 1430

HOW (543) [HOWBEIT, HOWSOEVER]

Ge 26: 9 **h** saidst thou, She *is* my sister? And Isaac 349
27:20 **H** *is it that* thou hast found *it so* quickly, 4100
28:17 and said, **H** dreadful *is* this place! 4100
30:29 Thou knowest **h** I have served thee, and how 834
30:29 served thee, and **h** thy cattle was with me. 834
38:29 she said, **H** hast thou broken forth? 4100
39: 9 **h** then can I do this great wickedness, and 349
44: 8 **h** then should we steal out of thy lord's 349
44:16 or **h** shall we clear ourselves? God hath 4100
44:34 For **h** shall I go up to my father, and the lad 349
47: 8 Pharaoh said unto Jacob, **H** old *art* 4100+3509.1
47:18 *it* from my lord, **h** that our money is spent; 518
Ex 2:18 **H** *is it that* you are come so soon to day? 4069
6:12 **h** then shall Pharaoh hear me, who *am* of 349
6:30 and **h** shall Pharaoh hearken unto me? 349
9:29 that thou mayest know **h that** the earth *is* 3588
10: 2 that ye may know **h that** I *am* the LORD. 3588
10: 3 LORD God of the Hebrews, **H long** 4970+5704
10: 7 servants said unto him, **H long** 4970+5704
11: 7 that ye may know **h that** the LORD doth 834
16:28 said unto Moses, **H long** 575+5704+1886.5
18: 8 the way, and *h* the LORD delivered them. NIH
19: 4 *h* I bare you on eagles' wings, and NIH
36: 1 understanding to know **h** to work all *manner* NIH
Nu 10:31 forasmuch as thou knowest **h** we are to NIH
14:11 said unto Moses, **H long** 575+5704+1886.5
14:11 **h long** will it be ere they 575+5704+1886.5
14:27 **H long** *shall I bear* with this evil 4970+5704
20:15 **H** our fathers went down into Egypt, and 2050.1
23: 8 **H** shall I curse, whom God hath not 4100
23: 8 or **h** shall I defy, *whom* the LORD hath 4100
24: 5 **H** goodly are thy tents, O Jacob, *and* 4100
Dt 1:12 **H** can I myself alone bear your cumbrance, 349
1:31 where thou hast seen **h that** the LORD thy 834
7:17 *are* moe than I; **h** can I dispossess them? 349
9: 7 **h** thou provokedst the LORD thy God to 834
11: 4 **h** he made the water of the Red sea to 834
11: 4 *h* the LORD hath destroyed them unto this NIH
11: 6 **h** the earth opened her mouth, and 834
12:30 saying, **H** did these nations serve their gods? 349
18:21 **H** shall we know the word which 349
25:18 **H** he met thee by the way, and smote 834
29:16 (For ye know **h** we have dwelt in the land of 834
29:16 **h** we came through the nations which ye 834
31:27 and **h much more** after my death? 637+3588
32:30 **H** should one chase a thousand, and two put 349
Jos 2:10 For we have heard **h** the LORD dried up 834
9: 7 and **h** shall we make a league with you? 349
9:24 **h that** the LORD thy God commanded his 834
10: 1 Jerusalem had heard **h** Joshua had taken Ai, 3588
10: 1 **h** the inhabitants of Gibeon had made peace 3588
14:12 for thou heardest in that day **h** the Anakims 3588
18: 3 the children of Israel, **H long** 575+5704+1886.5
Jdg 13:12 **H** shall we order the child, and *how* shall 4100
13:12 order the child, and *h* shall we do unto him? NIH
16:15 said unto him, **H** canst thou say, I love thee, 349
18: 7 that *were* therein, **h** they dwelt careless, NIH
20: 3 of Israel, Tell *us,* **h** was this wickedness? 349
21: 7 **H** shall we do for wives for them that 4100
21:16 **H** shall we do for wives for them that 4100
Ru 1: 6 **h that** the LORD had visited his people in 3588
2:11 *h* thou hast left thy father and thy mother, NIH
3:18 until thou know **h** the matter will fall: 349
1Sa 1:14 Eli said unto her, **H long** wilt thou be 4970+5704
2:22 **h** they lay with the women that assembled *at* 834
10:27 of Belial said, **H** shall this *man* save us? 4100
12:24 for consider **h** great things he hath done for 834
14:29 **h** mine eyes have been enlightened, 3588
14:30 **H much more**, if haply the people 637+3588
15: 2 **h** he laid *wait* for him in the way, when he 834
16: 1 LORD said unto Samuel, **H long** 4970+5704
16: 2 Samuel said, **H** can I go? if Saul hear *it,* he 349
17:18 look **h** thy brethren fare, and take their 3807.1
23: 3 **h much more** then if we come *to* Keilah 637
24:10 this day thine eyes have seen **h that** 834
24:18 thou hast shewed *this* day **h that** thou hast 834
28: 9 **h** he hath cut off those that have familiar 834
2Sa 1: 4 David said unto him, **H** went the matter? 4100
1: 5 **H** knowest thou that Saul and Jonathan his 349
1:14 **H** wast thou not afraid to stretch forth thine 349
1:19 thy high places: **h** are the mighty fallen! 349

2Sa 1:25 **H** are the mighty fallen in the midst of 349
1:27 **H** are the mighty fallen, and the weapons of 349
2:22 **h** then should I hold up my face to Joab thy 349
2:26 be bitterness in the latter end? **h long** 4970+5704
4:11 **H much more**, when wicked men have slain 637
6: 9 **H** shall the ark of the LORD come to me? 349
6:20 **H** glorious was the king of Israel to day, 4100
11: 7 demanded *of him* **h** Joab **did**, 7965+3807.1
11: 7 **h** the people **did**, and how the war 7965+3807.1
11: 7 and **h** the war **prospered**. 7965+3807.1
12:18 **h** will he then vex himself, if we tell him *that* 349
16:11 **h much more** now *may this* 637+3588
18:19 **h that** the LORD hath avenged him of his 3588
19: 2 for the people heard say that day ***h*** the king NIH
19:34 unto the king, **H long** 3117+4100+8141+3509.1
24: 3 **h** many soever they be, an hundredfold, 3509.1
1Ki 3: 7 I know not ***h*** to go out or come in. NIH
5: 3 Thou knowest **h that** David my father 3588
8:27 **h much less** this house that I have 637+3588
12: 6 **H** do you advise that *I* may answer this 349
14:19 **h** he warred, and how he reigned, 834
14:19 how he warred, and **h** he reigned, 834
18:13 **h** I hid an hundred men of the LORD'S 2050.1
18:21 **H long** halt ye between two 4970+5704
19: 1 withal **h** he had slain all the prophets with 834
20: 7 and see **h** this *man* seeketh mischief: 3588
21:29 Seest thou **h** Ahab humbleth himself before 3588
22:16 king said unto him, **H many** 4100+5704+3509.1
22:45 his might that he shewed, and **h** he warred, 834
2Ki 5: 7 and see **h** he seeketh a quarrel against me. 3588
5:13 thou not have done *it?* **h much rather** then, 637
6:15 unto him, Alas, my master, **h** shall we do? 349
6:32 See ye **h** this son of a murderer hath sent to 3588
8: 5 *as* he was telling the king **h** he had restored a 834
9:25 for remember **h** that, when I and thou rode NIH
10: 4 stood not before him: **h** then shall we stand? 349
14:15 **h** he fought with Amaziah king of Judah, 834
14:28 **h** he warred, and how he recovered 834
14:28 and **h** he recovered Damascus, and Hamath, 834
17:28 taught them **h** they should fear the LORD. 349
18:24 **H** then wilt thou turn away the face of one 349
19:25 Hast thou not heard long ago ***h*** I have done NIH
20: 3 remember now **h** I have walked before thee 834
20:20 **h** he made a pool, and a conduit, and 834
1Ch 13:12 **H** shall I bring the ark of God *home* to me? 1963
18: 9 Now when Tou king of Hamath heard **h** 3588
19: 5 and told David **h** the men were served. 5921
2Ch 6:18 **h much less** this house which I have 637+3588
7: 3 when all the children of Israel saw **h** 871.1
18:15 king said to him, **H many** 4100+5704+3509.1
20:11 Behold, I say, ***h*** they reward us, to come to NIH
32:15 **h much less** shall your God 637+3588+3808
33:19 ***h*** *God* was intreated of him, and all his sin, NIH
Ezr 7:22 *of* oil, and salt without prescribing ***h*** *much.* NIH
Ne 2: 6 **For h long** shall thy journey be? 4970+5704
2:17 **h** Jerusalem *lieth* waste, and the gates 834
Est 2:11 to know **h** Esther did, and what should NIH
5:11 **h** he had advanced him above the princes 834
8: 6 For **h** can I endure to see the evil that shall 349
8: 6 **h** can I endure to see the destruction of my 349
Job 4:19 **H much less** *in* them that dwell in houses of 637
6:25 **H** forcible are right words! but what doth 4100
7:19 **H long** wilt thou not depart from 4100+3509.1
8: 2 **H long** wilt thou speak these *things?* 575+5704
8: 2 ***h long shall*** the words of thy mouth *be like* NIH
9: 2 a truth: but **h** should man be just with God? 4100
9:14 **H much less** shall I answer him, *and* 637+3588
13:23 **H many** *are* mine iniquities and 4100+3509.1
15:16 **H much more** abominable and 637+3588
18: 2 **H long** *will it be ere* you 575+5704+1886.5
19: 2 **H long** will ye vex my soul, 575+5704+1886.5
21:17 **H oft** is the candle of the wicked 4100+3509.1
21:17 ***h oft*** cometh their destruction upon them! NIH
21:34 **H** then comfort ye me in vain, seeing *in* your 349
22:12 the height of the stars, **h** high they are. 3588
22:13 thou sayest, **H** doth God know? can he 4100
25: 4 **H** then can man be justified with God? or 4100
25: 4 **h** can he be clean *that is* born of a woman? 4100
25: 6 **H much less** man, *that is* a worm? and 637+3588
26: 2 **H** hast thou helped *him that is* without 4100
26: 2 ***h*** savest thou the arm *that hath* no strength? NIH
26: 3 **H** hast thou counselled *him that hath* no 4100
26: 3 ***h*** hast thou plentifully declared the thing as NIH
26:14 **h** little a portion is heard of him? but 4100
34:19 ***H*** *much less to him* that accepteth not NIH
37:17 **H** thy garments *are* warm, when he quieteth 834
Ps 3: 1 **h** are they increased that trouble me! 4100
4: 2 **h long** *will ye turn* my glory into 4100+5704
4: 2 ***h long*** will ye love vanity, *and* seek after NIH
6: 3 but thou, O LORD, **h long?** 4970+5704
8: 1 **h** excellent *is* thy name in all the earth! 4100
8: 9 **h** excellent *is* thy name in all the earth! 4100
11: 1 **h** say ye to my soul, Flee *as* a bird *to* your 349
13: 1 **H long** wilt thou forget me, 575+5704+1886.5
13: 1 for ever? **h long** wilt thou 575+5704+1886.5
13: 2 **H long** shall I take counsel in 575+5704+1886.5
13: 2 **h long** shall mine enemy be 575+5704+1886.5
21: 1 in thy salvation **h** greatly shall he rejoice! 4100
31:19 O **h** great *is* thy goodness, which thou hast 4100
35:17 Lord, **h long** wilt thou look on? 4100+3509.1
36: 7 **H** excellent *is* thy lovingkindness, O God! 4100
39: 4 what it *is; that* I may know **h** frail I *am.* 4100
44: 2 ***H*** thou didst drive out the heathen *with* thy NIH
44: 2 ***h*** thou didst afflict the people, and cast them NIH
62: 3 **H long** will ye imagine 575+5704+1886.5
66: 3 unto God, **H** terrible *art thou in* thy works! 4100
73:11 they say, **H** doth God know? and is there 349
73:19 **H** are they *brought* into desolation, as *in* a 349
74: 9 among us any that knoweth **h long.** 4100+5704
74:10 **h long** shall the adversary reproach? 4970+5704
74:22 remember **h** the foolish *man* reproacheth NIH
78:40 **H oft** did they provoke him in 4100+3509.1
78:43 **H** he had wrought his signs in Egypt, and 834
79: 5 **H long,** LORD? wilt thou be angry, 4100+5704
80: 4 O LORD God *of* hosts, **h long** wilt 4970+5704
Ps 82: 2 **H long** will ye judge unjustly, and 4970+5704
84: 1 **H** amiable *are* thy tabernacles, O LORD 4100
89:46 **H long,** LORD? wilt thou hide 4100+5704
89:47 Remember **h** short my time is: 4100
89:50 ***h*** I do bear in my bosom *the reproach of* all NIH
90:13 Return, O LORD, **h long?** and let it 4970+5704
92: 5 O LORD, **h** great are thy works! *and* 4100
94: 3 LORD, **h long** shall the wicked, 4970+5704
94: 3 **h long** shall the wicked triumph? 4970+5704
94: 4 ***H long*** shall they utter *and* speak hard NIH
104:24 O LORD, **h** manifold are thy works! 4100
119:84 **H many** *are* the days of thy 4100+3509.1
119:97 O **h** love I thy law! it *is* my meditation all 4100
119:103 **H** sweet are thy words unto my taste! 4100
119:159 Consider **h** I love thy precepts: quicken me, 3588
132: 2 **H** he sware unto the LORD, *and* NIH
133: 1 **h** good and how pleasant *it is* for brethren 4100
133: 1 **h** pleasant *it is* for brethren to dwell 4100
137: 4 **H** shall we sing the LORD'S song in a 349
139:17 **H** precious also are thy thoughts unto me, 4100
139:17 O God: **h** great is the sum of them! 4100
Pr 1:22 **H long,** ye simple ones, will ye love 4970+5704
5:12 **H** have I hated instruction, and my heart 349
6: 9 **H long** wilt thou sleep, O sluggard? 4970+5704
15:11 **h much more then** the hearts of 637+3588
15:23 a word *spoken* in due season, **h** good *is it!* 4100
16:16 **H much** better *is it* to get wisdom than 4100
19: 7 **h much more** do his friends go far 637+3588
20:24 **h** can a man then understand his own way? 4100
21:27 **h much more,** *when* he bringeth it 637+3588
30:13 *is* a generation, O **h** lofty are their eyes! 4100
Ecc 2:16 And **h** dieth the wise *man?* as the fool. 349
4:11 have heat: but **h can** one be warm *alone?* 349
10:15 because he knoweth not **h** to go to the city. NIH
11: 5 *nor* **h** the bones *do grow* in the womb of 3509.1
SS 4:10 **H** fair is thy love, my sister, *my* spouse! 4100
4:10 **h much** better is thy love than wine! and 4100
5: 3 I have put off my coat; **h** shall I put it on? 349
5: 3 I have washed my feet; **h** shall I defile them? 349
7: 1 **H** beautiful are thy feet with shoes, 4100
7: 6 **H** fair and how pleasant art thou, O love, 4100
7: 6 How fair and **h** pleasant art thou, O love, 4100
Isa 1:21 **H** is the faithful city become a harlot! *it was* 349
6:11 said I, Lord, **h long?** And he 4970+5704
14: 4 and say, **H** hath the oppressor ceased! 349
14:12 **H** art thou fallen from heaven, O Lucifer, 349
14:12 ***h*** art thou cut down to the ground, NIH
19:11 **h** say ye unto Pharaoh, I *am* the son of 349
20: 6 the king of Assyria: and **h** shall we escape? 349
36: 9 **H** then wilt thou turn away the face of one 349
37:26 thou not heard long ago, ***h*** I have done it; NIH
38: 3 **h** I have walked before thee in truth and 834
48:11 will I do *it:* for **h** should *my name* be 349
50: 4 that *I* should know **h** to speak a word in NIH
52: 7 **H** beautiful upon the mountains are the feet 4100
Jer 2:21 **H** then art thou turned *into* the degenerate 349
2:23 **H** canst thou say, I am not polluted, I have 349
3:19 **H** shall I put thee among the children, and 349
4:14 that thou mayest be saved. **H long** 4970+5704
4:21 **H long** shall I see the standard, *and* 4970+5704
5: 7 **H** shall I pardon thee for this? thy children 335
8: 8 **H** do ye say, We *are* wise, and the law of 349
9: 7 for **h** shall I do for the daughter of my 349
9:19 is heard out of Zion, **H** are we spoiled! 349
12: 4 **H long** shall the land mourn, and 4970+5704
12: 5 then **h** canst thou contend with horses? 349
12: 5 **h** wilt thou do in the swelling of Jordan? 349
15: 5 shall go aside to ask **h** thou **doest?** 7965+3807.1
22:23 **h** gracious shalt thou be when pangs come 4100
23:26 **H long** shall *this* be in the heart of 4970+5704
31:22 **H long** wilt thou go about, O thou 4970+5704
36:17 **H** didst thou write all these words at his 349
46:13 **h** Nebuchadrezzar king of Babylon should NIH
47: 5 the remnant of their valley: **h long** 4970+5704
47: 6 sword of the LORD, **h long** 575+5704+1886.5
47: 7 **H** can it be quiet, seeing the LORD hath 349
48:14 **H** say ye, We *are* mighty and strong men for 349
48:17 **H** is the strong staff broken, *and* 349
48:39 shall howl, *saying,* **H** is it broken down! 349
48:39 **h** hath Moab turned the back with shame! so 349
49:25 **H** is the city of praise not left, the city of my 349
50:23 **H** is the hammer of the whole earth cut 349
50:23 **h** is Babylon become a desolation among 349
51:41 **H** is Sheshach taken! and *how* is the praise 349
51:41 ***h*** is the praise of the whole earth surprised! NIH
51:41 **h** is Babylon become an astonishment 349
La 1: 1 **H** doth the city sit solitary, *that was* full of 349
1: 1 ***h*** is she become as a widow! she *that was* NIH
1: 1 the provinces, ***h*** is she become tributary! NIH
2: 1 **H** hath the Lord covered the daughter of 349
4: 1 **H** is the gold become dim! *how* is the most 349
4: 1 ***h*** is the most fine gold changed! the stones NIH
4: 2 **h** are they esteemed as earthen pitchers, 349
Eze 14:21 **H much more** when I send my four 637+3588
15: 5 **h much less** shall it be meet yet for 637+3588
16:30 **H** weak is thine heart, saith the Lord 4100
26:17 say to thee, **H** art thou destroyed, *that wast* 349
33:10 pine away in them, **h** should we then live? 349
Da 4: 3 **H** great *are* his signs! and how 4101+3509.4
4: 3 **h** mighty *are* his wonders! 4101+3509.4
8:13 certain *saint* which spake, **H long** 4970+5704
10:17 For **h** can the servant of this my lord talk 1963
12: 6 upon the waters of the river, **H long** 4970+5704
Hos 8: 5 anger is kindled against them: **h long** 4970+5704
11: 8 **H** shall I give thee up, Ephraim? *how* shall I 349
11: 8 ***h*** shall I deliver thee, Israel? how shall I NIH
11: 8 **h** shall I make thee as Admah? *how* shall I 349
11: 8 ***h*** shall I set thee as Zeboim? mine heart is NIH
Joel 1:18 **H** do the beasts groan! the herds of cattle 4100
Ob 1: 5 if robbers by night, (**h** art thou cut off!) 349
1: 6 **H** are *the things of* Esau searched out! 349
1: 6 searched out! ***h*** are his hid things sought up! NIH
Mic 2: 4 **h** hath he removed *it* from me! turning away 349
Hab 1: 2 O LORD, **h long** shall I cry, 575+5704+1886.5
2: 6 *that which is* not his! **h long?** 4970+5704
Zep 2:15 **h** is she become a desolation, a place for 349
Hag 2: 3 **h** do ye see it now? *is it* not in your eyes in 4100
Zec 1:12 O LORD of hosts, **h long** wilt thou 4970+5704
9:17 For **h great** *is* his goodness, and how great 4100
9:17 *is* his goodness, and **h great** *is* his beauty! 4100
Mt 6:23 thee be darkness, **h great** *is* that darkness? *4214*
6:28 Consider the lilies of the field, **h** they grow; *4459*
7: 4 Or **h** wilt thou say to thy brother, Let me *4459*
7:11 **know h** to give good gifts unto your *1492*
7:11 **h much** more shall your Father which is in *4214*
10:19 take no thought **h** or what ye shall speak: *4459*
10:25 **h much** more *shall they call* them of his *4214*
12: 4 **H** he entered into the house of God, and *4459*
12: 5 **h that** on the sabbath days the priests in *3754*
12:12 **H much** then is a man better than a sheep? *4214*
12:14 against him, **h** they might destroy him. *3704*
12:26 **h** shall then his kingdom stand? *4459*
12:29 Or else **h** can one enter into a strong *man's* *4459*
12:34 O generation of vipers, **h** can ye, being evil, *4459*
15:34 saith unto them, **H many** loaves have ye? *4214*
16: 9 and **h many** baskets ye took up? *4214*
16:10 and **h many** baskets ye took up? *4214*
16:11 **H** *is it that* ye do not understand that I *4459*
16:12 Then understood they **h that** he bade *them* *3754*
16:21 **h that** he must go unto Jerusalem, and *3754*
17:17 **h long** shall I be with you? *2193+4219*
17:17 **h long** shall I suffer you? bring him *2193+4219*
18:12 **H** think ye? if a man have an hundred *5101*
18:21 **h oft** shall my brother sin against me, and I *4212*
21:20 **H** soon is the fig tree withered away! *4459*
22:12 **h** camest thou in hither not having a *4459*
22:15 took counsel **h** they might entangle him in *3704*
22:43 **H** then doth David in spirit call him Lord, *4459*
22:45 then call him Lord, **h** is he his son? *4459*
23:33 **h can** ye escape the damnation of hell? *4459*
23:37 **h often** would I have gathered thy children *4212*
26:54 *But* **h** then shall the scriptures be fulfilled, *4459*
27:13 Hearest thou not **h many** *things* they *4214*
Mk 2:16 **H** *is it* that he eateth and drinketh with *5101*
2:26 **H** he went into the house of God in *4459*
3: 6 against him, **h** they might destroy him. *3704*
3:23 in parables, **H** can Satan cast out Satan? *4459*
4:13 and **h** *then* will ye know all parables? *4459*
4:27 and grow up, he knoweth not **h.** *5613*
4:40 so fearful? **h** *is it that* you have no faith? *4459*
5:16 And they that saw *it* told them **h** it befell to *4459*
5:19 tell them **h great** *things* the Lord hath done *3745*
5:20 began to publish in Decapolis **h great** *3745*
6:38 saith unto them, **H many** loaves have ye? *4214*
8: 5 he asked them, **H many** have ye? *4214*
8:19 **h many** baskets full of fragments took ye *4214*
8:20 **h many** baskets full of fragments took ye *4214*
8:21 **H** *is it that* ye do not understand? *4459*
9:12 and **h** it is written of the Son of man, *4459*
9:19 **h long** shall I be with you? *2193+4219*
9:19 **h long** shall I suffer you? bring him *2193+4219*
9:21 **H** long is it ago since this came unto him? *4214*
10:23 **H** hardly shall they that have riches enter *4459*
10:24 **h** hard is it for them that trust in riches to *4459*
11:18 and sought **h** they might destroy him: *4459*
12:26 **h** in the bush God spake unto him, saying, *5613*
12:35 **H** say the scribes that Christ is the Son of *4459*
12:41 beheld **h** the people cast money into *4459*
14: 1 the scribes sought **h** they might take him by *4459*
14:11 And he sought **h** he might conveniently *4459*
15: 4 behold **h many** *things* they witness against *4214*
Lk 1:34 **H** shall this be, seeing I know not a man? *4459*
1:58 her cousins heard **h** the Lord had shewed *3754*
1:62 to his father, **h** he would have him called. *5101*
2:49 said unto them, **H** *is it* that ye sought me? *5101*
6: 4 **H** he went into the house of God, and *5613*
6:42 Either **h** canst thou say to thy brother, *4459*
7:22 **h that** the blind see, the lame walk, *3754*
8:18 Take heed therefore **h** ye hear: *4459*
8:39 shew **h great** *things* God hath done unto *3745*
8:39 throughout the whole city **h great** *3745*
8:47 and **h** she was healed immediately. *5613*
9:41 **h long** shall I be with you, and *2193+4219*
10:26 What is written in the law? **h** readest thou? *4459*
11:13 **know h** to give good gifts unto your *1492*
11:13 **h much** more shall *your* heavenly Father *4214*
11:18 against himself, **h** shall his kingdom stand? *4459*
12:11 take ye no thought **h** or what *thing* ye shall *4459*
12:24 **h much** more are ye better than the fowls? *4214*
12:27 Consider the lilies **h** they grow: they toil *4459*
12:28 **h much** more *will he clothe* you, O ye of *4214*
12:50 **h** am I straitened till it be accomplished! *4459*
12:56 but **h** *is it that* ye do not discern this time? *4459*
13:34 **h often** would I have gathered thy children *4212*
14: 7 when he marked **h** they chose out the chief *4459*
15:17 **H many** hired *servants* of my father's have *4214*
16: 2 unto him, **H** *is it that* I hear this of thee? *5101*
16: 5 the first, **H much** owest thou unto my lord? *4214*
16: 7 he to another, And **h much** owest thou? *4214*
18:24 **H** hardly shall they that have riches enter *4459*
19:15 that he might know **h much** every *man* had *5101*
20:41 **H** say they that Christ is David's son? *4459*
20:44 calleth him Lord, **h** is he then his son? *4459*
21: 5 **h** it was adorned with goodly stones and *3754*
22: 2 and scribes sought **h** they might kill him; *4459*
22: 4 captains, **h** he might betray him unto them. *4459*
22:61 **h** he had said unto him, Before *the* cock *5613*
23:55 the sepulchre, and **h** his body was laid. *5613*
24: 6 remember **h** he spake unto you when he *5613*
24:20 And **h** the chief priests and our rulers *3704*
24:35 **h** he was known of them in breaking of *5613*
Jn 3: 4 **H** can a man be born when he is old? *4459*
3: 9 and said unto him, **H** can these *things* be? *4459*
3:12 and ye believe not, **h** shall ye believe, *4459*
4: 1 the Lord knew **h** the Pharisees had heard *3754*
4: 9 **H** *is it that* thou, being a Jew, askest drink *4459*
5:44 **H** can ye believe, which receive honour *4459*
5:47 his writings, **h** shall ye believe my words? *4459*
6:42 **h** *is it* then *that* he saith, I came down from *4459*
6:52 **H** can this *man* give us *his* flesh to eat? *4459*

Jn 7:15 saying, **H** knoweth this *man* letters, *4459*
8:33 were never in bondage to any *man:* **h** sayest *4459*
9:10 they unto him, **H** were thine eyes opened? *4459*
9:15 Then again the Pharisees also asked him **h** *4459*
9:16 **H** can a man *that is* a sinner do such *4459*
9:19 was born blind? **h** then doth he now see? *4459*
9:26 did he to thee? **h** opened he thine eyes? *4459*
10:24 **H long** dost thou make us to doubt? *2193+4219*
11:36 said the Jews, Behold, **h** he loved him. *4459*
12:19 Perceive ye **h** ye prevail nothing? *3754*
12:34 and **h** sayest thou, The Son of man must be *4459*
14: 5 thou goest; and **h** can we know the way? *4459*
14: 9 and **h** sayest thou *then,* Shew us the Father? *4459*
14:22 **h** is it that thou wilt manifest thyself unto *5101*
14:28 Ye have heard **h** I said unto you, I go away, *3754*
Ac 2: 8 And **h** hear we every man in our own *4459*
4:21 finding nothing **h** they might punish them, *4459*
5: 9 **H** *is it* that ye have agreed together to tempt *5101*
7:25 **h that** God by his hand would deliver *3754*
8:31 And he said, **H** can I, *302+1063+4459*
9:13 **h much** evil he hath done to thy saints at *3745*
9:16 For I will shew him **h great** *things* he must *3745*
9:27 declared unto them **h** he had seen the Lord *4459*
9:27 **h** he had preached boldly at Damascus in *4459*
10:28 Ye know **h that** it is an unlawful *thing* for a *5613*
10:38 **H** God anointed Jesus of Nazareth with *5613*
11:13 And he shewed us **h** he had seen an angel *4459*
11:16 **h** that he said, John indeed baptized with *5613*
12:14 and **told h** Peter stood before the gate. *518*
12:17 declared unto them **h** the Lord had brought *4459*
13:32 **h that** the promise which was made unto *3754*
14:27 **h** he had opened *the* door of faith unto *3754*
15: 7 ye know **h that** a good while ago God *3754*
15:14 Simeon hath declared **h** God at the first did *2531*
15:36 the word of the Lord, *and see* **h** they do. *4459*
19:35 what man is there that knoweth not **h** that NIG
20:20 *And* **h** I kept back nothing that was *5613*
20:35 I have shewed you all *things,* **h that** so *3754*
20:35 **h** he said, It is more blessed to give than to *3754*
21:20 **h many** thousands of Jews there are which *4214*
23:30 And when it was told me **h** that the Jews NIG
Ro 3: 6 then **h** shall God judge the world? *4459*
4:10 **H** was it then reckoned? when he was in *4459*
6: 2 **H** shall we, that are dead to sin, live any *4459*
7: 1 **h that** the law hath dominion over a man, *3754*
7:18 *h* to perform that which is good I find not. NIG
8:32 **h** shall he not with him also freely give us *4459*
10:14 **H** then shall they call on *him* in whom they *4459*
10:14 **h** shall they believe *in him* of whom they *4459*
10:14 and **h** shall they hear without a preacher? *4459*
10:15 And **h** shall they preach, except they be *4459*
10:15 **H** beautiful *are* the feet of them that preach *5613*
11: 2 **h** he maketh intercession to God against *5613*
11:12 of the Gentiles; **h much** more their fulness? *4214*
11:24 **h much** more shall these, which be *4214*
11:33 **h** unsearchable *are* his judgments, and *5613*
1Co 1:26 **h that** not many wise *men* after the flesh, *3754*
3:10 But let every man take heed **h** he buildeth *4459*
6: 3 **h much more** *things* that pertain to *this* *3386*
7:16 or **h** knowest thou, O man, whether thou *5101*
7:32 to the Lord, **h** he may please the Lord: *4459*
7:33 *are* of the world, **h** he may please *his* wife. *4459*
7:34 the world, **h** she may please *her* husband. *4459*
10: 1 **h that** all our fathers were under the cloud, *3754*
14: 7 **h** shall it be known what is piped or *4459*
14: 9 **h** shall it be known what is spoken? *4459*
14:16 **h** shall he that occupieth the room of *4459*
14:26 **H** is it then, brethren? when ye come *5101*
15: 3 **h** that Christ died for our sins according to NIG
15:12 **h** say some among you that there is no *4459*
15:35 *man* will say, **H** are the dead raised up? *4459*
2Co 3: 8 **H** shall not the ministration of the spirit be *4459*
7:15 **h** with fear and trembling you received *5613*
8: 2 **H that** in a great trial of affliction *3754*
12: 4 **H that** he was caught up into paradise, and *3754*
13: 5 **h that** Jesus Christ is in you, except ye be *3754*
Gal 1:13 **h that** beyond measure I persecuted *3754*
4: 9 **h** turn ye again to the weak and *4459*
4:13 Ye know **h** through infirmity of the flesh I *3754*
6:11 Ye see **h large** a letter I have written unto *4080*
Eph 3: 3 **H that** by revelation he made known unto *3754*
6:21 *and* **h** I do, Tychicus, a beloved brother and *5101*
Php 1: 8 **h** *greatly* I long after you all in the bowels *5613*
2:23 as I shall see **h it will go with** me. *3588+4012*
4:12 I know both **h** to be abased, and I know *how* NIG
4:12 *how* to be abased, and I know *h* to abound: NIG
Col 4: 6 that *you* may know **h** ye ought to answer *4459*
1Th 1: 9 **h** ye turned to God from idols to serve *4459*
2:10 and God *also,* **h** holily and justly and *5613*
2:11 As you know **h** we exhorted and *5613*
4: 1 that as ye have received of us **h** ye ought to *4459*
4: 4 That every one of you should know **h** to NIG
2Th 3: 7 For yourselves know **h** *ye* ought to follow *4459*
1Ti 3: 5 (For if a man know not **h** to rule his own NIG
3: 5 **h** shall he take care of the church of God?) *4459*
3:15 that thou mayest know **h** *thou* oughtest to *4459*
2Ti 1:18 in **h many** *things* he ministered *unto me* at *3745*
Phm 1:16 to me, but **h much** more unto thee, *4214*
1:19 I will repay *it:* albeit I do not say to thee **h** *3754*
Heb 2: 3 **H** shall we escape, if we neglect so *4459*
7: 4 Now consider **h great** this *man was,* unto *4080*
8: 6 by **h much** also he is the mediator of a *3745*
9:14 **H much** more shall the blood of Christ, *4214*
10:29 Of **h much** sorer punishment, suppose ye, *4214*
12:17 For ye know **h that** afterward, when he *3754*
Jas 2:22 Seest thou **h** faith wrought with his works, *3754*
2:24 then **h that** by works a man is justified, *3754*
3: 5 **h great** a matter a little fire kindleth. *2245*
2Pe 2: 9 The Lord knoweth *h* to deliver the godly NIG
1Jn 3:17 **h** dwelleth the love of God in him? *4459*
4:20 **h** can he love God whom he hath not seen? *4459*
Jude 1: 5 though ye once knew this, **h that** the Lord, *3754*
1:18 **H that** they told you there should be *3754*
Rev 2: 2 **h** thou canst not bear *them which are* evil: *3754*
3: 3 therefore **h** thou hast received and heard, *4459*
Rev 6:10 saying, **H long,** O Lord, holy and *2193+4219*
18: 7 **H much** she hath glorified herself, and *3745*

HOWBEIT (64) [BE, HOW, IT]

Jdg 4:17 **H** Sisera fled away on his feet to the tent 2050.1
11:28 **H** the king of the children of Ammon 2050.1
16:22 **H** the hair of his head began to grow 2050.1
18:29 **h** the name of the city *was* Laish at the first. 199
21:18 **H** we may not give them wives of our 2050.1
Ru 3:12 **h** there is a kinsman nearer than I. 1571+2050.1
1Sa 8: 9 **h yet** protest solemnly unto them, and 389+3588
2Sa 2:23 **H** he refused to turn aside: 2050.1
12:14 **H,** because by this deed thou hast given 657
13:14 **H** he would not hearken unto her voice: 2050.1
13:25 **h** he would not go, but blessed him. 2050.1
23:19 **h** he attained not unto the *first* three. 2050.1
1Ki 2:15 **h** the kingdom is turned about, and 2050.1
10: 7 **H** I believed not the words, until I came, 2050.1
11:13 **H** I will not rend away all the kingdom; *but* 7535
11:22 Nothing: **h** let me go in any wise. 3588
11:34 **H** I will not take the whole kingdom out 2050.1
2Ki 3:25 **h** the slingers went about *it,* and smote it. 2050.1
8:10 **h** the LORD hath shewed me that he 2050.1
10:29 **H** *from* the sins of Jeroboam the son of 7535
12:13 **H** there were not made *for* the house of 389
14: 4 **H** the high places were not taken away: 7535
15:35 **H** the high places were not removed: 7535
17:29 **H** every nation made gods of their own, 2050.1
17:40 **H** they did not hearken, but they did after 2050.1
22: 7 **H** there was no reckoning made with them 389
1Ch 11:21 **h** he attained not to the *first* three. 2050.1
28: 4 **H** the LORD God of Israel chose me 2050.1
2Ch 9: 6 **H** I believed not their words, until I came, 2050.1
18:34 **h** the king of Israel stayed *himself* up in 2050.1
20:33 **H** the high places were not taken away: 389
21: 7 **H** the LORD would not destroy 2050.1
21:20 **H** they buried him in the city of David, 2050.1
24: 5 the matter. **H** the Levites hastened *it* not. 2050.1
27: 2 **h** he entered not into the temple of 7535
32:31 **H** in *the business of* 3651+2050.1
Ne 9:33 **H** thou *art* just in all that is brought upon 2050.1
13: 2 **h** our God turned the curse into a 2050.1
Job 30:24 **H** *he* will not stretch out *his* hand to 389
Isa 10: 7 **H** he meaneth not so, neither doth his 2050.1
Jer 44: 4 **H** I sent unto you all my servants 2050.1
Mt 17:21 **H** this kind goeth not out but by prayer and *1161*
Mk 5:19 **H** Jesus suffered him not, but saith unto *1161*
7: 7 **H** in vain do they worship me, teaching for *1161*
Jn 6:23 (**H** there came other boats from Tiberias *235*
7:13 **H** no *man* spake openly of him for fear of *3305*
7:27 **H** we know this *man* whence he is: but *235*
11:13 **H** Jesus spake of his death: but *1161*
16:13 **H** when he, the Spirit of truth, is come, *1161*
Ac 4: 4 **H** many of them which heard the word *1161*
7:48 **H** the most High dwelleth not in temples *235*
14:20 **H,** as the disciples stood round about him, *1161*
17:34 **H** certain men clave unto him, and *1161*
27:26 **H** we must be cast upon a certain island. *1161*
28: 6 **H** they looked when he should have *1161*
1Co 2: 6 **H** we speak wisdom among *them that are* *1161*
8: 7 **H** *there is* not in every *man* that knowledge: *235*
14: 2 for no *man* understandeth *him;* **h** in *1161*
14:20 in understanding: **h** in malice be ye children, *235*
15:46 **H** *that was* not first *which is* spiritual, but *235*
2Co 11:21 **H whereinsoever** any is *302+1161+1722+3739*
Gal 4: 8 **H** then, when ye knew not God, ye did *235+3303*
1Ti 1:16 **H** for this cause I obtained mercy, that in me *235*
Heb 3:16 **h** not all that came out of Egypt by Moses. *235*

HOWL (29) [HOWLED, HOWLING, HOWLINGS]

Isa 13: 6 **H** ye; for the day of the LORD *is* at hand; 3213
14:31 **H,** O gate; cry, O city; thou, 3213
15: 2 Moab shall **h** over Nebo, and over Medeba: 3213
15: 3 in their streets, every one shall **h,** weeping 3213
16: 7 Therefore shall Moab **h** for Moab, 3213
16: 7 Moab howl for Moab, every one shall **h:** 3213
23: 1 **H,** ye ships of Tarshish; for it is laid waste, 3213
23: 6 to Tarshish; **h,** ye inhabitants of the isle. 3213
23:14 **H,** ye ships of Tarshish: for your strength is 3213
52: 5 they that rule over them **make** *them* **to h,** 3213
65:14 of heart, and shall **h** for vexation of spirit. 3213
Jer 4: 8 this gird you with sackcloth, lament and **h:** 3213
25:34 **H,** ye shepherds, and cry; and 3213
47: 2 and all the inhabitants of the land shall **h.** 3213
48:20 **h** and cry; tell ye *it* in Arnon, that Moab is 3213
48:31 Therefore will I **h** for Moab, and I will cry 3213
48:39 They shall **h,** *saying,* How is it broken 3213
49: 3 **H,** O Heshbon, for Ai is spoiled: cry, 3213
51: 8 **h** for her; take balm for her pain, if so 3213
Eze 21:12 Cry and **h,** son of man: for it shall be upon 3213
30: 2 the Lord GOD; **H** ye, Woe worth the day! 3213
Joel 1: 5 **h,** all ye drinkers of wine, because of 3213
1:11 **h,** O ye vinedressers, for the wheat and 3213
1:13 **h,** ye ministers of the altar: come, lie all 3213
Mic 1: 8 Therefore I will wail and **h,** I will go stript 3213
Zep 1:11 **H,** ye inhabitants of Maktesh, for all 3213
Zec 11: 2 **H,** fir tree; for the cedar is fallen; because 3213
11: 2 **H,** O ye oaks of Bashan; for the forest of 3213
Jas 5: 1 **h** for your miseries that shall come upon *3649*

HOWLED (1) [HOWL]

Hos 7:14 their heart, when they **h** upon their beds: 3213

HOWLING (6) [HOWL]

Dt 32:10 desert land, and in the waste **h** wilderness; 3214
Isa 15: 8 the **h** thereof unto Eglaim, and the howling 3215
15: 8 and the **h** thereof *unto* Beer-elim. 3215
Jer 25:36 and a **h** of the principal of the flock, 3215
Zep 1:10 a **h** from the second, and a great crashing 3215
Zec 11: 3 *There is* a voice of the **h** of the shepherds; 3215

HOWLINGS (1) [HOWL]

Am 8: 3 the songs of the temple shall be **h** in that 3213

HOWSOEVER (4) [EVER, HOW, SO]

Jdg 19:20 with thee; **h** *let* all thy wants *lie* upon me; 7535
2Sa 18:22 **h,** let me, I pray thee, also run after Cushi. 4100
18:23 **h,** *said he,* let me run. And he said unto 4100
Zep 3: 7 not be cut off, **h** I punished them: 834+3605

HUB See NAVES

HUGE (1)

2Ch 16: 8 and the Lubims a **h** host, 7230+3807.1

HUGE FISH See WHALE; WHALE'S; WHALES

HUKKOK (1)

Jos 19:34 goeth out from thence to **H,** and reacheth to 2712

HUKOK (1)

1Ch 6:75 **H** with her suburbs, and Rehob with her 2712

HUL (2)

Ge 10:23 Uz, and **H,** and Gether, and Mash. 2343
1Ch 1:17 and Uz, and **H,** and Gether, and Meshech. 2343

HULDAH (2)

2Ki 22:14 and Asahiah, went unto **H** the prophetess, 2468
2Ch 34:22 *they* that the king *had appointed,* went to **H** 2468

HUMBLE (25) [HUMBLED, HUMBLEDST, HUMBLENESS, HUMBLETH, HUMBLY]

Ex 10: 3 How long wilt thou refuse to **h** thyself 6031
Dt 8: 2 to **h** thee, *and* to prove thee, to know what 6031
8:16 that he might **h** thee, and that he might 6031
Jdg 19:24 **h** ye them, and do with them what seemeth 6031
2Ch 7:14 shall **h** themselves, and pray, and seek my 3665
34:27 and thou didst **h** thyself before God, 3665
Job 22:29 and he shall save the **h person.** 5869+7807
Ps 9:12 he forgetteth not the cry of the **h.** 6035
10:12 O God, lift up thine hand: forget not the **h.** 6035
10:17 LORD, thou hast heard the desire of the **h:** 6035
34: 2 the **h** shall hear *thereof,* and be glad. 6035
69:32 The **h** shall see *this, and* be glad: and 6035
Pr 6: 3 go, **h** thyself, and make sure thy friend. 7511
16:19 Better *it is to be* of an **h** spirit with 8217
29:23 but honour shall uphold the **h** in spirit. 8217
Isa 57:15 him also *that is* of a contrite and **h** spirit, 8217
57:15 to revive the spirit of the **h,** and to revive 8217
Jer 13:18 and to the queen, **H** yourselves, sit down: 8213
Mt 18: 4 therefore shall **h** himself as this little child, *5013*
23:12 and he that shall **h** himself shall be exalted. *5013*
2Co 12:21 my God will **h** *me* among you, and *that* I *5013*
Jas 4: 6 the proud, but giveth grace unto the **h.** *5011*
4:10 **H** yourselves in the sight of the Lord, and *5013*
1Pe 5: 5 the proud, and giveth grace to the **h.** *5011*
5: 6 **H** yourselves therefore under the mighty *5013*

HUMBLED (28) [HUMBLE]

Lev 26:41 if then their uncircumcised hearts be **h,** and 3665
Dt 8: 3 he **h** thee, and suffered thee to hunger, and 6031
21:14 of her, because thou hast **h** her. 6031
22:24 because he hath **h** his neighbour's wife: 6031
22:29 because he hath **h** her, he may not put her 6031
2Ki 22:19 and thou hast **h** thyself before the LORD, 3665
2Ch 12: 6 princes of Israel and the king **h** themselves; 3665
12: 7 when the LORD saw that they **h** 3665
12: 7 saying, They have **h** themselves; 3665
12:12 when he **h** himself, the wrath of 3665
30:11 Manasseh and of Zebulun **h** themselves, 3665
32:26 Notwithstanding Hezekiah **h** himself for 3665
33:12 **h** himself greatly before the God of his 3665
33:19 and graven images, before he was **h:** 3665
33:23 **h** not himself before the LORD, 3665
33:23 as Manasseh his father had **h** himself; 3665
36:12 **h** not himself before Jeremiah the prophet 3665
Ps 35:13 I **h** my soul with fasting; and my prayer 6031
Isa 2:11 The lofty looks of man shall be **h,** and 8213
5:15 the mighty man shall be **h,** and the eyes of 8213
5:15 and the eyes of the lofty shall be **h:** 8213
10:33 *be* hewn down, and the haughty shall be **h.** 8213
Jer 44:10 They are not **h** *even* unto this day, 1792
La 3:20 *them* still in remembrance, and is **h** in me. 7743
Eze 22:10 in thee have they **h** her that was set apart 6031
22:11 another in thee hath **h** his sister, his father's 6031
Da 5:22 O Belshazzar, hast not **h** thine heart, 8214
Php 2: 8 he **h** himself, and became obedient unto *5013*

HUMBLEDST (1) [HUMBLE]

2Ch 34:27 **h** thyself before me, and didst rend thy 3665

HUMBLENESS (1) [HUMBLE]

Col 3:12 kindness, **h of mind,** meekness, *5012*

HUMBLETH (7) [HUMBLE]

1Ki 21:29 Seest thou how Ahab **h** himself before me? 3665
21:29 because he **h** himself before me, I will not 3665
Ps 10:10 He croucheth, *and* **h** himself, that the poor 7817
113: 6 Who **h** *himself* to behold *the things that are* 8213
Isa 2: 9 boweth down, and the great man **h** himself; 8213
Lk 14:11 and he that **h** himself shall be exalted. *5013*
18:14 and he that **h** himself shall be exalted. *5013*

HUMBLY (2) [HUMBLE]

2Sa 16: 4 I **h beseech** thee *that* I may find grace in 7812
Mic 6: 8 to love mercy, and to walk **h** with thy God? 6800

HUMILIATION (1) [HUMILITY]

Ac 8:33 In his **h** his judgment was taken away: and *5014*

HUMILITY (7) [HUMILIATION]

Pr 15:33 of wisdom; and before honour *is* **h.** 6038
18:12 of man is haughty, and before honour *is* **h.** 6038
22: 4 By **h** *and* the fear of the LORD *are* riches, 6038
Ac 20:19 Serving the Lord with all **h of mind,** and *5012*
Col 2:18 beguile you of your reward in a voluntary **h** *5012*

Col 2:23 and **h**, and neglecting of the body, not in *5012*
1Pe 5: 5 one to another, and be clothed with **h**: *5012*

HUMTAH (1)

Jos 15:54 **H**, and Kirjath-arba, which *is* Hebron, and 2547

HUNDRED (590) [HUNDREDFOLD, HUNDREDS, HUNDREDTH]

Ge 5: 3 Adam lived an **h** and thirty years, and 3967
5: 4 he had begotten Seth were eight **h** years: 3967
5: 5 all the days that Adam lived were nine **h** 3967
5: 6 Seth lived an **h** and five years, and 3967
5: 7 Seth lived after he begat Enos eight **h** 3967
5: 8 all the days of Seth were nine **h** and 3967
5:10 Enos lived after he begat Cainan eight **h** 3967
5:11 all the days of Enos were nine **h** and 3967
5:13 lived after he begat Mahalaleel eight **h** 3967
5:14 all the days of Cainan were nine **h** and 3967
5:16 lived after he begat Jared eight **h** 3967
5:17 all the days of Mahalaleel were eight **h** 3967
5:18 Jared lived an **h** sixty and two years, and 3967
5:19 Jared lived after he begat Enoch eight **h** 3967
5:20 all the days of Jared were nine **h** sixty and 3967
5:22 after he begat Methuselah three **h** years, 3967
5:23 all the days of Enoch were three **h** sixty 3967
5:25 Methuselah lived an **h** eighty and seven 3967
5:26 lived after he begat Lamech seven **h** eighty 3967
5:27 all the days of Methuselah were nine **h** 3967
5:28 Lamech lived an **h** eighty and two years, 3967
5:30 Lamech lived after he begat Noah five **h** 3967
5:31 all the days of Lamech were seven **h** 3967
5:32 Noah was five **h** years old: and Noah begat 3967
6: 3 yet his days shall be an **h** and twenty years. 3967
6:15 the length of the ark *shall be* three **h** cubits, 3967
7: 6 Noah *was* six **h** years old when the flood of 3967
7:24 the waters prevailed upon the earth an **h** 3967
8: 3 after the end of the **h** and fifty days 3967
9:28 Noah lived after the flood three **h** and 3967
9:29 all the days of Noah were nine **h** and 3967
11:10 Shem *was* an **h** years old, and 3967
11:11 Shem lived after he begat Arphaxad five **h** 3967
11:13 Arphaxad lived after he begat Salah four **h** 3967
11:15 Salah lived after he begat Eber four **h** 3967
11:17 Eber lived after he begat Peleg four **h** 3967
11:19 Peleg lived after he begat Reu **two h** 3967
11:21 Reu lived after he begat Serug **two h** 3967
11:23 Serug lived after he begat Nahor **two h** 3967
11:25 Nahor lived after he begat Terah an **h** 3967
11:32 the days of Terah were **two h** and 3967
14:14 three **h** and eighteen, and pursued *them* 3967
15:13 and they shall afflict them four **h** years; 3967
17:17 Shall *a child* be born unto him that is an **h** 3967
21: 5 Abraham *was* an **h** years old, when his son 3967
23: 1 Sarah was an **h** and seven and twenty years 3967
23:15 the land *is worth* four **h** shekels of silver; 3967
23:16 four **h** shekels of silver, current *money* with 3967
25: 7 he lived, an **h** threescore and fifteen years. 3967
25:17 of Ishmael, an **h** and thirty and seven years: 3967
32: 6 to meet thee, and four **h** men with him. 3967
32:14 **Two h** she goats, and twenty he goats, 3967
32:14 he goats, **two h** ewes, and twenty rams, 3967
33: 1 Esau came, and with him four **h** men. 3967
33:19 for an **h** pieces of money. 3967
35:28 the days of Isaac were an **h** and 3967
45:22 to Benjamin he gave three **h** *pieces* of 3967
47: 9 days of the years of my pilgrimage *are* an **h** 3967
47:28 so the whole age of Jacob was an **h** forty 3967
50:22 and Joseph lived an **h** and ten years. 3967
50:26 Joseph died, *being* an **h** and ten years old: 3967
Ex 6:16 the years of the life of Levi *were* an **h** thirty 3967
6:18 the years of the life of Kohath *were* an **h** 3967
6:20 the years of the life of Amram *were* an **h** 3967
12:37 about six **h** thousand on foot *that were* men, 3967
12:40 dwelt in Egypt, *was* four **h** and thirty years. 3967
12:41 it came to pass at the end of the four **h** and 3967
14: 7 he took six **h** chosen chariots, and all 3967
27: 9 linen of an **h** cubits long for one side: 3967
27:11 *there shall be* hangings of an **h** *cubits* long, 3967
27:18 The length of the court *shall be* an **h** cubits, 3967
30:23 of pure myrrh five **h** *shekels*, and of sweet 3967
30:23 *even* **two h** and fifty *shekels*, and of sweet 3967
30:23 and of sweet calamus **two h** and 3967
30:24 of cassia five **h** *shekels*, after the shekel of 3967
38: 9 court *were of* fine twined linen, an **h** cubits: 3967
38:11 for the north side *the hangings were* an **h** 3967
38:24 nine talents, and seven **h** and thirty shekels, 3967
38:25 of the congregation *was* an **h** talents, 3967
38:25 a thousand seven **h** and threescore and 3967
38:26 for six **h** thousand and three thousand and 3967
38:26 three thousand and five **h** and fifty *men*. 3967
38:27 of the **h** talents of silver were cast 3967
38:27 an **h** sockets of the hundred talents, a talent 3967
38:27 an hundred sockets of the **h** talents, a talent 3967
38:28 of the thousand seven **h** seventy and 3967
38:29 and two thousand and four **h** shekels. 3967
Lev 26: 8 five of you shall chase an **h**, and 3967
26: 8 an **h** of you shall put ten thousand to flight: 3967
Nu 1:21 *were* forty and six thousand and five **h**. 3967
1:23 *were* fifty and nine thousand and three **h**. 3967
1:25 and five thousand six **h** and fifty. 3967
1:27 and fourteen thousand and six **h**. 3967
1:29 *were* fifty and four thousand and four **h**. 3967
1:31 *were* fifty and seven thousand and four **h**. 3967
1:33 of Ephraim, *were* forty thousand and five **h**. 3967
1:35 *were* thirty and two thousand and **two h**. 3967
1:37 *were* thirty and five thousand and four **h**. 3967
1:39 and two thousand and seven **h**. 3967
1:41 *were* forty and one thousand and five **h**. 3967
1:43 *were* fifty and three thousand and four **h**. 3967
1:46 that were numbered were six **h** thousand 3967
1:46 and three thousand and five **h** and fifty. 3967
2: 4 and fourteen thousand and six **h**. 3967
2: 6 *were* fifty and four thousand and four **h**. 3967
2: 8 *were* fifty and seven thousand and four **h**. 3967

Nu 2: 9 in the camp of Judah *were* an **h** thousand 3967
2: 9 and six thousand and four **h**, 3967
2:11 *were* forty and six thousand and five **h**. 3967
2:13 *were* fifty and nine thousand and three **h**. 3967
2:15 and five thousand and six **h** and fifty. 3967
2:16 in the camp of Reuben *were* an **h** thousand 3967
2:16 fifty and one thousand and four **h** and fifty, 3967
2:19 of them, *were* forty thousand and five **h**. 3967
2:21 *were* thirty and two thousand and **two h**. 3967
2:23 *were* thirty and five thousand and four **h**. 3967
2:24 of the camp of Ephraim *were* an **h** thousand 3967
2:24 and eight thousand and an **h**, 3967
2:26 and two thousand and seven **h**. 3967
2:28 *were* forty and one thousand and five **h**. 3967
2:30 *were* fifty and three thousand and four **h**. 3967
2:31 in the camp of Dan *were* an **h** thousand 3967
2:31 and fifty and seven thousand and six **h**. 3967
2:32 throughout their hosts *were* six **h** thousand 3967
2:32 and three thousand and five **h** and fifty. 3967
3:22 of them *were* seven thousand and five **h**. 3967
3:28 and upward, *were* eight thousand and six **h**, 3967
3:34 and upward, *were* six thousand and **two h**. 3967
3:43 two thousand **two h** and threescore and 3967
3:46 those that are *to be* redeemed of the **two h** 3967
3:50 a thousand three **h** and threescore and 3967
4:36 their families were two thousand seven **h** 3967
4:40 were two thousand and six **h** and thirty. 3967
4:44 were three thousand and **two h**. 3967
4:48 eight thousand and five **h** and fourscore. 3967
7:13 the weight thereof *was* an **h** and 3967
7:19 the weight whereof *was* an **h** and 3967
7:25 the weight whereof *was* an **h** and 3967
7:31 *was* one silver charger of the weight of an **h** 3967
7:37 the weight whereof *was* an **h** and 3967
7:43 *was* one silver charger of the weight of an **h** 3967
7:49 the weight whereof *was* an **h** and 3967
7:55 *was* one silver charger of the weight of an **h** 3967
7:61 the weight whereof *was* an **h** and 3967
7:67 the weight whereof *was* an **h** and 3967
7:73 the weight whereof *was* an **h** and 3967
7:79 the weight whereof *was* an **h** and 3967
7:85 Each charger of silver *weighing* an **h** and 3967
7:85 four **h** *shekels*, after the shekel of 3967
7:86 all the gold of the spoons *was* an **h** and 3967
11:21 amongst whom I *am, are* six **h** thousand 3967
16: 2 **two h** and fifty princes of the assembly, 3967
16:17 man his censer, **two h** and fifty censers; 3967
16:35 consumed the **two h** and fifty men that 3967
16:49 plague were fourteen thousand and seven **h**, 3967
26: 7 and three thousand and seven **h** and thirty. 3967
26:10 what time the fire devoured **two h** and 3967
26:14 twenty and two thousand and **two h**. 3967
26:18 of them, forty thousand and five **h**. 3967
26:22 threescore and sixteen thousand and five **h**. 3967
26:25 threescore and four thousand and three **h**. 3967
26:27 of them, threescore thousand and five **h**. 3967
26:34 fifty and two thousand and seven **h**. 3967
26:37 thirty and two thousand and five **h**. 3967
26:41 *were* forty and five thousand and six **h**. 3967
26:43 and four thousand and four **h**. 3967
26:47 *were* fifty and three thousand and four **h**. 3967
26:50 *were* forty and five thousand and four **h**. 3967
26:51 six **h** thousand and a thousand seven 3967
26:51 and a thousand seven **h** and thirty. 3967
31:28 one soul of five **h**, *both* of the persons, and 3967
31:32 was six **h** thousand and seventy thousand 3967
31:36 was *in* number three **h** thousand and seven 3967
31:36 seven and thirty thousand and five **h** sheep: 3967
31:37 the LORD'S tribute of the sheep was six **h** 3967
31:39 the asses *were* thirty thousand and five **h**; 3967
31:43 unto the congregation was three **h** thousand 3967
31:43 *and* seven thousand and five **h** sheep, 3967
31:45 And thirty thousand asses and five **h**, 3967
31:52 was sixteen thousand seven **h** and 3967
33:39 Aaron *was* an **h** and twenty and three years 3967
Dt 22:19 they shall amerce him in an **h** *shekels* of 3967
31: 2 I *am* an **h** and twenty years old *this* day; 3967
34: 7 Moses *was* an **h** and twenty years old when 3967
Jos 7:21 **two h** shekels *of* silver, and a wedge of 3967
24:29 died, *being* an **h** and ten years old. 3967
24:32 father of Shechem for an **h** pieces of silver: 3967
Jdg 2: 8 died, *being* an **h** and ten years old. 3967
3:31 which slew *of* the Philistines six **h** men 3967
4: 3 for he had nine **h** chariots of iron; and 3967
4:13 *even* nine **h** chariots of iron, and all 3967
7: 6 hand to their mouth, were three **h** men: 3967
7: 7 By the three **h** men that lapped will I save 3967
7: 8 his tent, and retained *those* three **h** men: 3967
7:16 he divided the three **h** men *into* three 3967
7:19 and the **h** men that *were* with him, 3967
7:22 the three **h** blew the trumpets, and 3967
8: 4 he, and the three **h** men that *were* with him, 3967
8:10 for there fell an **h** and twenty thousand men 3967
8:26 a thousand and seven **h** *shekels* of gold; 3967
11:26 by the coasts of Arnon, three **h** years? 3967
15: 4 Samson went and caught three **h** foxes, 3967
16: 5 *us* **eleven h** *pieces* of silver. 505+3967+2050.1
17: 2 The **eleven h** *shekels* of silver 505+3967+2050.1
17: 3 **eleven h** *shekels* of silver to 505+3967+2050.1
17: 4 and his mother took **two h** *shekels* of silver, 3967
18:11 six **h** men appointed *with* weapons of war. 3967
18:16 the six **h** men appointed *with* their weapons 3967
18:17 **h** men that were appointed *with* weapons of 3967
20: 2 four **h** thousand footmen that drew sword. 3967
20:10 we will take ten men of an **h** throughout all 3967
20:10 an **h** of a thousand, and a thousand out of 3967
20:15 *which* were numbered seven **h** chosen men. 3967
20:16 Among all this people *there were* seven **h** 3967
20:17 were numbered four **h** thousand men that 3967
20:35 and five thousand and an **h** men: 3967
20:47 six **h** men turned and fled to the wilderness 3967
21:12 of Jabesh-gilead four **h** young virgins, 3967
1Sa 11: 8 the children of Israel were three **h** 3967
13:15 were present with him, about six **h** men. 3967
14: 2 that *were* with him *were* about six **h** men; 3967

1Sa 15: 4 **two h** thousand footmen, and ten thousand 3967
17: 7 his spear's head *weighed* six **h** shekels *of* 3967
18:25 but an **h** foreskins of the Philistines, 3967
18:27 and slew of the Philistines **two h** men; 3967
22: 2 and there were with him about four **h** men. 3967
23:13 *which were* about six **h**, arose and 3967
25:13 there went up after David about four **h** 3967
25:13 hundred men; and **two h** abode by the stuff. 3967
25:18 took **two h** loaves, and two bottles of wine, 3967
25:18 parched *corn*, and an **h** clusters of raisins, 3967
25:18 **two h** cakes *of figs*, and laid *them* on asses. 3967
27: 2 he passed over with the six **h** men that *were* 3967
30: 9 he and the six **h** men that *were* with him, 3967
30:10 David pursued, he and four **h** men: for two 3967
30:10 for **two h** abode *behind*, which were so 3967
30:17 save four **h** young men, which rode upon 3967
30:21 David came to the **two h** men, which were 3967
2Sa 2:31 *so that* three **h** and threescore men died. 3967
3:14 which I espoused to me for an **h** foreskins 3967
8: 4 a thousand *chariots*, and seven **h** horsemen, 3967
8: 4 but reserved of them *for* an **h** chariots. 3967
10:18 David slew *the men of* seven **h** chariots of 3967
14:26 he weighed the hair of his head *at* **two h** 3967
15:11 with Absalom went **two h** men out of 3967
15:18 six **h** men which came after him from Gath, 3967
16: 1 upon them **two h** *loaves of* bread, and 3967
16: 1 an **h** bunches of raisins, and an hundred of 3967
16: 1 an **h** of summer fruits, and a bottle of wine. 3967
21:16 the weight of whose spear *weighed* three **h** 3967
23: 8 *he lift up his spear* against eight **h**, 3967
23:18 he lift up his spear against three **h**, and 3967
24: 9 there were in Israel eight **h** thousand valiant 3967
24: 9 the men of Judah *were* five **h** thousand 3967
1Ki 4:23 an **h** sheep, beside harts, and roebucks, and 3967
5:16 three thousand and three **h**, which ruled 3967
6: 1 it came to pass in the four **h** and 3967
7: 2 the length thereof *was* an **h** cubits, and 3967
7:20 the pomegranates *were* **two h** *in* rows 3967
7:42 four **h** pomegranates for the two networks, 3967
8:63 and an **h** and twenty thousand sheep. 3967
9:23 five **h** and fifty, which bare rule over 3967
9:28 four **h** and twenty talents, and brought *it* to 3967
10:10 she gave the king an **h** and twenty talents of 3967
10:14 Solomon in one year was six **h** threescore 3967
10:16 king Solomon made **two h** targets *of* beaten 3967
10:16 six **h** *shekels* of gold went to one target. 3967
10:17 *he made* three **h** shields *of* beaten gold; 3967
10:26 he had a thousand and four **h** chariots, and 3967
10:29 went out of Egypt for six **h** *shekels* of 3967
10:29 of silver, and a horse for an **h** and fifty: 3967
11: 3 he had seven **h** wives, princesses, and 3967
11: 3 princesses, and three **h** concubines: 3967
12:21 an **h** and fourscore thousand chosen *men*, 3967
18: 4 that Obadiah took an **h** prophets, and 3967
18:13 how I hid an **h** men of the LORD'S 3967
18:19 the prophets of Baal four **h** and fifty, and 3967
18:19 fifty, and the prophets of the groves four **h**, 3967
18:22 Baal's prophets *are* four **h** and fifty men. 3967
20:15 and they were **two h** and thirty two: 3967
20:29 Syrians an **h** thousand footmen in one day. 3967
22: 6 about four **h** men, and said unto them, Shall 3967
2Ki 3: 4 rendered unto the king of Israel an **h** 3967
3: 4 and an **h** thousand rams, *with* the wool. 3967
3:26 he took with him seven **h** men that drew 3967
4:43 What, should I set this before an **h** men? 3967
14:13 Ephraim unto the corner gate, four **h** cubits. 3967
18:14 king of Judah three **h** talents of silver 3967
19:35 smote in the camp of the Assyrians an **h** 3967
23:33 put the land to a tribute of an **h** talents of 3967
1Ch 4:42 of Simeon, five **h** men, went to mount Seir, 3967
5:18 *were* four and forty thousand seven **h** and 3967
5:21 *of* sheep **two h** and fifty thousand, and 3967
5:21 two thousand, and *of* men an **h** thousand. 3967
7: 2 David two and twenty thousand and six **h**. 3967
7: 9 of valour, *was* twenty thousand and **two h**. 3967
7:11 **two h** *soldiers, fit* to go out *for* war 3967
8:40 many sons, and sons' sons, an **h** and fifty. 3967
9: 6 Jeuel, and their brethren, six **h** and ninety. 3967
9: 9 their generations, nine **h** and fifty and six. 3967
9:13 a thousand and seven **h** and threescore; 3967
9:22 to be porters in the gates *were* **two h** 3967
11:11 he lift up his spear against three **h** slain *by* 3967
11:20 for lifting up his spear against three **h**, 3967
12:14 one of the least *was* over an **h**, and 3967
12:24 and spear *were* six thousand and eight **h**, 3967
12:25 for the war, seven thousand and **one h**. 3967
12:26 children of Levi four thousand and six **h**. 3967
12:27 with him *were* three thousand and seven **h**; 3967
12:30 of Ephraim twenty thousand and eight **h**, 3967
12:32 the heads of them *were* **two h**; and all their 3967
12:35 in war twenty and eight thousand and six **h**. 3967
12:37 for the battle, an **h** and twenty thousand. 3967
15: 5 the chief, and his brethren an **h** and twenty: 3967
15: 6 and his brethren **two h** and twenty: 3967
15: 7 the chief, and his brethren an **h** and thirty: 3967
15: 8 Shemaiah the chief, and his brethren **two h**: 3967
15:10 the chief, and his brethren an **h** and twelve. 3967
18: 4 but reserved of them an **h** chariots. 3967
21: 3 The LORD make his people an **h** times so 3967
21: 5 and an **h** thousand men that drew sword: 3967
21: 5 Judah *was* four **h** threescore and 3967
21:25 So David gave to Ornan for the place six **h** 3967
22:14 the LORD an **h** thousand talents *of* gold, 3967
25: 7 was **two h** fourscore and eight. 3967
26:30 men of valour, a thousand and seven **h**, 3967
26:32 two thousand and seven **h** chief fathers, 3967
29: 7 and **one h** thousand talents *of* iron. 3967
2Ch 1:14 he had a thousand and four **h** chariots, and 3967
1:17 Egypt a chariot for six **h** *shekels* of silver, 3967
1:17 of silver, and a horse for an **h** and fifty: 3967
2: 2 three thousand and six **h** to oversee them. 3967
2:17 they were found an **h** and fifty thousand 3967
2:17 fifty thousand and three thousand and six **h**. 3967
2:18 six **h** overseers to set the people a work. 3967
3: 4 and the height *was* an **h** and twenty: 3967

H

2Ch 3: 8 it with fine gold, *amounting* to six **h** talents. 3967
3:16 made an **h** pomegranates, and put *them* on 3967
4: 8 the left. And he made an **h** basons of gold. 3967
4:13 four **h** pomegranates on the two wreaths; 3967
5:12 with them an **h** and twenty priests sounding 3967
7: 5 and an **h** and twenty thousand sheep: 3967
8:10 *even* **two h** and fifty, that bare rule over 3967
8:18 took thence four **h** and fifty talents of gold, 3967
9: 9 she gave the king an **h** and twenty talents of 3967
9:13 that came to Solomon in one year was six **h** 3967
9:15 king Solomon made **two h** targets *of* beaten 3967
9:15 six **h** *shekels* of beaten gold went to one 3967
9:16 three **h** shields *made he of* beaten gold: 3967
9:16 three **h** *shekels* of gold went to one shield. 3967
11: 1 the house of Judah and Benjamin an **h** and 3967
12: 3 With **twelve h** chariots, and 505+3967+2050.1
13: 3 of war, *even* four **h** thousand chosen men: 3967
13: 3 him with eight **h** thousand chosen men, 3967
13:17 there fell down slain of Israel five **h** 3967
14: 8 and spears, out of Judah three **h** thousand; 3967
14: 8 drew bows, **two h** and fourscore thousand: 3967
14: 9 a thousand thousand, and three **h** chariots; 3967
15:11 seven **h** oxen and seven thousand sheep. 3967
17:11 seven thousand and seven **h** rams, and 3967
17:11 and seven thousand and seven **h** he goats. 3967
17:14 with him mighty *men* of valour three **h** 3967
17:15 with him **two h** and fourscore thousand. 3967
17:16 with him **two h** thousand mighty *men* of 3967
17:17 *men* with bow and shield **two h** thousand. 3967
17:18 with him an **h** and fourscore thousand 3967
18: 5 gathered together *of* prophets four **h** men, 3967
24:15 an **h** and thirty years old *was he* when he 3967
25: 5 found them three **h** thousand choice *men*, 3967
25: 6 He hired also an **h** thousand mighty *men* of 3967
25: 6 out of Israel for an **h** talents of silver. 3967
25: 9 what *shall we* do for the **h** talents which I 3967
25:23 Ephraim to the corner gate, four **h** cubits. 3967
26:12 *men* of valour *were* two thousand and six **h**. 3967
26:13 three **h** thousand and seven thousand and 3967
26:13 and seven thousand and five **h**, 3967
27: 5 him the same year an **h** talents of silver, 3967
28: 6 the son of Remaliah slew in Judah an **h** 3967
28: 8 captive of their brethren **two h** thousand, 3967
29:32 an **h** rams, *and* two hundred lambs: 3967
29:32 an hundred rams, *and* **two h** lambs: 3967
29:33 the consecrated *things were* six **h** oxen and 3967
35: 8 six **h** *small cattle*, and three hundred oxen. 3967
35: 8 six hundred *small cattle*, and three **h** oxen. 3967
35: 9 five thousand *small cattle*, and five **h** oxen. 3967
36: 3 condemned the land in an **h** talents of silver 3967
Ezr 1:10 silver basons of a second sort four **h** and 3967
1:11 and of silver *were* five thousand and four **h**. 3967
2: 3 two thousand an **h** seventy and two. 3967
2: 4 of Shephatiah, three **h** seventy and two. 3967
2: 5 children of Arah, seven **h** seventy and five. 3967
2: 6 *and* Joab, two thousand eight **h** and twelve. 3967
2: 7 of Elam, a thousand **two h** fifty and four. 3967
2: 8 The children of Zattu, nine **h** forty and five. 3967
2: 9 children of Zaccai, seven **h** and threescore. 3967
2:10 The children of Bani, six **h** forty and two. 3967
2:11 children of Bebai, six **h** twenty and three. 3967
2:12 a thousand **two h** twenty and two. 3967
2:13 children of Adonikam, six **h** sixty and six. 3967
2:15 The children of Adin, four **h** fifty and four. 3967
2:17 children of Bezai, three **h** twenty and three. 3967
2:18 The children of Jorah, an **h** and twelve. 3967
2:19 of Hashum, **two h** twenty and three. 3967
2:21 of Beth-lehem, an **h** twenty and three. 3967
2:23 men of Anathoth, an **h** twenty and eight. 3967
2:25 and Beeroth, seven **h** and forty and three. 3967
2:26 of Ramah and Gaba, six **h** twenty and one. 3967
2:27 The men of Michmas, an **h** twenty and two. 3967
2:28 of Beth-el and Ai, **two h** twenty and three. 3967
2:30 The children of Magbish, an **h** fifty and six. 3967
2:31 a thousand **two h** fifty and four. 3967
2:32 The children of Harim, three **h** and twenty. 3967
2:33 Hadid, and Ono, seven **h** twenty and five. 3967
2:34 children of Jericho, three **h** forty and five. 3967
2:35 three thousand and six **h** and thirty. 3967
2:36 house of Jeshua, nine **h** seventy and three. 3967
2:38 a thousand **two h** forty and seven. 3967
2:41 children of Asaph, an **h** twenty and eight. 3967
2:42 of Shobai, *in* all an **h** thirty and nine. 3967
2:58 *were* three **h** ninety and two. 3967
2:60 the children of Nekoda, six **h** fifty and two. 3967
2:64 *and* two thousand three **h** *and* threescore, 3967
2:65 of whom *there were* seven thousand three **h** 3967
2:65 *there were* among them **two h** singing *men* 3967
2:66 Their horses *were* seven **h** thirty and six; 3967
2:66 and six; their mules, **two h** forty and five; 3967
2:67 Their camels, four **h** thirty and five; 3967
2:67 six thousand seven **h** and twenty. 3967
2:69 *of* silver, and **one h** priests' garments. 3967
6:17 of this house of God an **h** bullocks, 3969
6:17 **two h** rams, four hundred lambs; 3969
6:17 two hundred rams, four **h** lambs; 3969
7:22 Unto an **h** talents *of* silver, and to an 3969
7:22 to an **h** measures *of* wheat, and to an 3969
7:22 to an **h** baths *of* wine, and to an hundred 3969
7:22 to an **h** baths *of* oil, and salt without 3969
8: 3 reckoned by genealogy of the males an **h** 3967
8: 4 son of Zerahiah, and with him **two h** males. 3967
8: 5 of Jahaziel, and with him three **h** males. 3967
8: 9 and with him **two h** and eighteen males. 3967
8:10 and with him an **h** and threescore males. 3967
8:12 and with him an **h** and ten males. 3967
8:20 the Levites, **two h** and twenty Nethinims: 3967
8:26 I even weighed unto their hand six **h** and 3967
8:26 silver vessels an **h** talents, *and of* gold an 3967
8:26 an hundred talents, *and of* gold an **h** talents; 3967
Ne 5:17 Moreover *there were* at my table an **h** and 3967
7: 8 two thousand an **h** seventy and two. 3967
7: 9 of Shephatiah, three **h** seventy and two. 3967
7:10 The children of Arah, six **h** fifty and two. 3967
7:11 two thousand and eight **h** *and* eighteen. 3967
Ne 7:12 of Elam, a thousand **two h** fifty and four. 3967
7:13 children of Zattu, eight **h** forty and five. 3967
7:14 children of Zaccai, seven **h** and threescore. 3967
7:15 children of Binnui, six **h** forty and eight. 3967
7:16 children of Bebai, six **h** twenty and eight. 3967
7:17 two thousand three **h** twenty and two. 3967
7:18 of Adonikam, six **h** threescore and seven. 3967
7:20 The children of Adin, six **h** fifty and five. 3967
7:22 of Hashum, three **h** twenty and eight. 3967
7:23 children of Bezai, three **h** twenty and four. 3967
7:24 The children of Hariph, an **h** *and* twelve. 3967
7:26 and Netophah, an **h** fourscore and eight. 3967
7:27 men of Anathoth, an **h** twenty and eight. 3967
7:29 and Beeroth, seven **h** forty and three. 3967
7:30 of Ramah and Geba, six **h** twenty and one. 3967
7:31 men of Michmas, an **h** and twenty and two. 3967
7:32 of Beth-el and Ai, an **h** twenty and three. 3967
7:34 a thousand **two h** fifty and four. 3967
7:35 The children of Harim, three **h** and twenty. 3967
7:36 children of Jericho, three **h** forty and five. 3967
7:37 Hadid, and Ono, seven **h** twenty and one. 3967
7:38 of Senaah, three thousand nine **h** and thirty. 3967
7:39 house of Jeshua, nine **h** seventy and three. 3967
7:41 a thousand **two h** forty and seven. 3967
7:44 the children of Asaph, an **h** forty and eight. 3967
7:45 children of Shobai, an **h** thirty and eight. 3967
7:60 *were* three **h** ninety and two. 3967
7:62 the children of Nekoda, six **h** forty and two. 3967
7:66 two thousand three **h** and threescore, 3967
7:67 of whom *there were* seven thousand three **h** 3967
7:67 they had **two h** forty and five singing *men* 3967
7:68 Their horses, seven **h** thirty and six: 3967
7:68 and six: their mules, **two h** forty and five: 3967
7:69 *Their* camels, four **h** thirty and five: 3967
7:69 six thousand seven **h** and twenty asses. 3967
7:70 five **h** and thirty priests' garments. 3967
7:71 two thousand and **two h** pound *of* silver. 3967
11: 6 dwelt at Jerusalem *were* four **h** threescore 3967
11: 8 Sallai, nine **h** twenty and eight. 3967
11:12 the work of the house *were* eight **h** twenty 3967
11:13 chief of the fathers, **two h** forty and two: 3967
11:14 *men* of valour, an **h** twenty and eight: 3967
11:18 All the Levites in the holy city *were* **two h** 3967
11:19 kept the gates, *were* an **h** seventy and two. 3967
Est 1: 1 *over* an **h** and seven and twenty provinces:) 3967
1: 4 many days, *even* an **h** and fourscore days. 3967
8: 9 an **h** twenty and seven provinces, 3967
9: 6 the Jews slew and destroyed five **h** men. 3967
9:12 destroyed five **h** men in Shushan 3967
9:15 and slew three **h** men at Shushan; 3967
9:30 to the **h** twenty and seven provinces of 3967
Job 1: 3 five **h** yoke of oxen, and five hundred she 3967
1: 3 five **h** she asses, and a very great 3967
42:16 After this lived Job an **h** and forty years, 3967
Pr 17:10 a wise *man* than an **h** stripes into a fool. 3967
Ecc 6: 3 If a man beget an **h** *children*, and live many 3967
8:12 Though a sinner do evil an **h** *times*, and his 3967
SS 8:12 and those that keep the fruit thereof **two h**. 3967
Isa 37:36 smote in the camp of the Assyrians an **h** 3967
65:20 for the child shall die an **h** years old; but 3967
65:20 the sinner *being* an **h** years old shall be 3967
Jer 52:23 upon the network *were* an **h** round about. 3967
52:29 away captive from Jerusalem eight **h** thirty 3967
52:30 away captive *of* the Jews seven **h** forty 3967
52:30 the persons *were* four thousand and six **h**. 3967
Eze 4: 5 of the days, three **h** and ninety days: 3967
4: 9 three **h** and ninety days shalt thou eat 3967
40:19 an **h** cubits east*ward* and north*ward*. 3967
40:23 he measured from gate to gate an **h** cubits. 3967
40:27 gate to gate toward the south an **h** cubits. 3967
40:47 an **h** cubits long, and an hundred cubits 3967
40:47 and an **h** cubits broad, foursquare; 3967
41:13 So he measured the house, an **h** cubits long; 3967
41:13 with the walls thereof, an **h** cubits long; 3967
41:14 separate place toward the east, an **h** cubits. 3967
41:15 one side and on the other side, an **h** cubits, 3967
42: 2 Before the length of an **h** cubits *was* 3967
42: 8 and lo, before the temple *were* an **h** cubits. 3967
42:16 five **h** reeds, with the measuring reed round 3967
42:17 He measured the north side, five **h** reeds, 3967
42:18 five **h** reeds, with the measuring reed. 3967
42:19 measured five **h** reeds with the measuring 3967
42:20 five **h** *reeds* long, and five hundred broad, 3967
42:20 five hundred *reeds* long, and five **h** broad, 3967
45: 2 **h** *in length*, with five hundred *in breadth*, 3967
45: 2 with five **h** *in breadth*, square round about; 3967
45:15 one lamb out of the flock, out of **two h**, 3967
48:16 the north side four thousand and five **h**, and 3967
48:16 and the south side four thousand and five **h**, 3967
48:16 on the east side four thousand and five **h**, 3967
48:16 and the west side four thousand and five **h**. 3967
48:17 of the city shall be toward the north **two h** 3967
48:17 toward the south **two h** and fifty, and 3967
48:17 toward the east **two h** and fifty, and 3967
48:17 fifty, and toward the west **two h** and fifty. 3967
48:30 four thousand and five **h** measures. 3967
48:32 at the east side four thousand and five **h**: 3967
48:33 side four thousand and five **h** measures: 3967
48:34 *At* the west side four thousand and five **h**, 3967
Da 6: 1 Darius to set over the kingdom an **h** 3969
8:14 Unto two thousand and three **h** days; 3967
12:11 *there shall be* a thousand **two h** and 3967
12:12 and cometh to the thousand three **h** *and* five 3967
Am 5: 3 went out *by* a thousand shall leave an **h**, 3967
5: 3 that which went forth *by* an **h** shall leave 3967
Mt 18:12 if a man have an **h** sheep, and one of them *1540*
18:28 which ought him an **h** pence: *1540*
Mk 4: 8 some thirty, and some sixty, and some an **h**. *1540*
4:20 some thirty*fold*, some sixty, and some an **h**. *1540*
6:37 we go and buy **two h** pennyworth of bread, *1250*
14: 5 been sold for more than **three h** pence, *5145*
Lk 7:41 the one ought **five h** pence, and the other *4001*
15: 4 What man of you, having an **h** sheep, if he *1540*
16: 6 And he said, An **h** measures of oil. And he *1540*
16: 7 And he said, An **h** measures of wheat. *1540*
Jn 6: 7 **Two h** pennyworth of bread is not *1250*
12: 5 Why was not this ointment sold for **three h** *5145*
19:39 and aloes, about an **h** pound *weight*. *1540*
21: 8 far from land, but as it were **two h** cubits,) *1250*
21:11 full of great fishes, an **h** and fifty *and* three: *1540*
Ac 1:15 number of names together were about an **h** *1540*
5:36 of men, about **four h**, joined themselves: *5071*
7: 6 and entreat *them* evil **four h** years. *5071*
13:20 *unto them* judges about *the space of* **four h** *5071*
23:23 Make ready **two h** soldiers to go to *1250*
23:23 *and* ten, and spearmen **two h**, *1250*
27:37 And we were in all in the ship **two h** *1250*
Ro 4:19 when he was about an **h year old**, *1541*
1Co 15: 6 he was seen of above **five h** brethren at *4001*
Gal 3:17 which was **four h** and thirty years after, *5071*
Rev 7: 4 *and there were* sealed an **h** *and* forty *and* *1540*
9:16 *were* **two h thousand thousand**: *1417+3461*
11: 3 they shall prophesy a thousand **two h** *and* *1250*
12: 6 they should feed her there a thousand **two h** *1250*
13:18 and his number *is* **Six h threescore** *and* **six**. *5516*
14: 1 and with him an **h** forty *and* four thousand, *1540*
14: 3 but the **h** *and* forty *and* four thousand, *1540*
14:20 the space of a thousand *and* **six h** furlongs. *1812*
21:17 wall thereof, an **h** *and* forty *and* four cubits, *1540*

HUNDREDFOLD (7) [HUNDRED]

Ge 26:12 received in the same year an **h**: 3967+8180
2Sa 24: 3 an **h**, and *that* the eyes of my lord 3967+6471
Mt 13: 8 some an **h**, some sixty*fold*, some *1540*
13:23 some an **h**, some sixty, some thirty. *1540*
19:29 shall receive an **h**, and shall inherit *1542*
Mk 10:30 But he shall receive an **h** now in this time, *1542*
Lk 8: 8 and sprang up, and bare fruit an **h**. *1542*

HUNDREDS (28) [HUNDRED]

Ex 18:21 *and* rulers of **h**, rulers of fifties, and 3967
18:25 rulers of **h**, rulers of fifties, and rulers of 3967
Nu 31:14 captains over **h**, which came from 3967
31:48 and captains of **h**, came near unto Moses: 3967
31:52 of thousands, and of the captains of **h**, 3967
31:54 gold of the captains of thousands and of **h**, 3967
Dt 1:15 captains over **h**, and captains over fifties, 3967
1Sa 22: 7 all captains of thousands, and captains of **h**; 3967
29: 2 the lords of the Philistines passed on by **h**, 3967
2Sa 18: 1 of thousands and captains of **h** over them. 3967
18: 4 all the people came out by **h** and 3967
2Ki 11: 4 year Jehoiada sent and fet the rulers over **h**, 3967
11: 9 the captains over the **h** did according to all 3967
11:10 to the captains over **h** did the priest give 3967
11:15 the priest commanded the captains of the **h**, 3967
11:19 he took the rulers over **h**, and the captains, 3967
1Ch 13: 1 with the captains of thousands and **h**, 3967
26:26 the captains over thousands and **h**, and 3967
27: 1 and captains of thousands and **h**, 3967
28: 1 captains over the **h**, and the stewards over 3967
29: 6 and the captains of thousands and of **h**, 3967
2Ch 1: 2 to the captains of thousands and of **h**, and 3967
23: 1 took the captains of **h**, Azariah the son of 3967
23: 9 priest delivered to the captains of **h** spears, 3967
23:14 captains of **h** that were set over the host, 3967
23:20 he took the captains of **h**, and the nobles, 3967
25: 5 over thousands, and captains over **h**, 3967
Mk 6:40 they sat down in ranks, by **h**, and by fifties. *1540*

HUNDREDTH (3) [HUNDRED]

Ge 7:11 In the six **h** year of Noah's life, in 3967
8:13 it came to pass in the six **h** and first year, 3967
Ne 5:11 also the **h** *part* of the money, and *of* 3967

HUNGER (24) [HUNGER-BITTEN, HUNGERED, HUNGRED, HUNGRY]

Ex 16: 3 to kill this whole assembly with **h**. 7458
Dt 8: 3 **suffered** thee **to h**, and fed thee with 7456
28:48 in **h**, and in thirst, and in nakedness, and 7458
32:24 *They shall be* burnt with **h**, and 7458
Ne 9:15 gavest them bread from heaven for their **h**, 7458
Ps 34:10 The young lions do lack, and **suffer h**: but 7456
Pr 19:15 deep sleep; and an idle soul shall **suffer h**. 7456
Isa 49:10 They shall not **h** nor thirst; neither shall 7456
Jer 38: 9 he is like to die for **h** in the place where he 7458
42:14 sound of the trumpet, nor have **h** of bread; 7456
La 2:19 that faint for **h** in the top of every street. 7458
4: 9 are better than *they that be* slain with **h**: 7458
Eze 34:29 they shall be no more consumed with **h** in 7458
Mt 5: 6 Blessed *are* they which do **h** and thirst after *3983*
Lk 6:21 Blessed *are ye* that **h** now: for ye shall be *3983*
6:25 for ye shall **h**. Woe unto you that laugh *3983*
15:17 and to spare, and I perish with **h**? *3042*
Jn 6:35 he that cometh to me shall never **h**; and *3983*
Ro 12:20 Therefore if thine enemy **h**, feed him; if he *3983*
1Co 4:11 Even unto this present hour we both **h**, and *3983*
11:34 And if any *man* **h**, let him eat at home; *3983*
2Co 11:27 in **h** and thirst, in fastings often, in cold and *3042*
Rev 6: 8 and with **h**, and with death, and with *3042*
7:16 They shall **h** no more, neither thirst any *3983*

HUNGER-BITTEN (1) [BITE, HUNGER]

Job 18:12 His strength shall be **h**, and 7457

HUNGERED (2) [HUNGER]

Mt 21:18 morning as he returned into the city, he **h**. *3983*
Lk 4: 2 and when they were ended, he afterward **h**. *3983*

HUNGRED (9) [HUNGER]

Mt 4: 2 and forty nights, he was afterward a **h**. *3983*
12: 1 and his disciples were a **h**, and began to *3983*
12: 3 when he was a **h**, and they that were with *3983*
25:35 For I was a **h**, and ye gave me meat: I was *3983*
25:37 when saw we thee a **h**, and fed *thee*? or *3983*
25:42 For I was a **h**, and ye gave me no meat: *3983*
25:44 when saw we thee a **h**, or athirst, or *3983*
Mk 2:25 and was a **h**, he, and they *that were* with *3983*
Lk 6: 3 when himself was a **h**, and they which were *3983*

HUNGRY (30) [HUNGER]
1Sa 2: 5 for bread; and they that were h ceased: 7457
2Sa 17:29 The people is h, and weary, and thirsty, 7457
2Ki 7:12 They know that we be h; therefore are they 7457
Job 5: 5 Whose harvest the h eateth up, and taketh it 7457
22: 7 and thou hast withholden bread from the h. 7457
24:10 and they take away the sheaf from the h; 7457
Ps 50:12 If I were h, I would not tell thee: for 7456
107: 5 H and thirsty, their soul fainted in them. 7457
107: 9 and filleth the h soul with goodness. 7457
107:36 there he maketh the h to dwell, that they 7457
146: 7 which giveth food to the h. The LORD 7457
Pr 6:30 if he steal to satisfy his soul when he is h; 7456
25:21 If thine enemy be h, give him bread to eat; 7457
27: 7 but to the h soul every bitter thing is sweet. 7457
Isa 8:21 shall pass through it, hardly bestead and h: 7457
8:21 come to pass, that when they shall be h, 7457
9:20 he shall snatch on the right hand, and be h; 7457
29: 8 It shall even be as when a h man dreameth, 7457
32: 6 to make empty the soul of the h, and 7457
44:12 yea, he is h, and his strength faileth: 7457
58: 7 Is it not to deal thy bread to the h, and 7457
58:10 if thou draw out thy soul to the h, and 7457
65:13 my servants shall eat, but ye shall be h: 7456
Eze 18: 7 hath given his bread to the h, and 7457
18:16 but hath given his bread to the h, and 7457
Mk 11:12 they were come from Bethany, he was h: 3983
Lk 1:53 He hath filled the h with good things; and 3983
Ac 10:10 And he became very h, and would have 4361
1Co 11:21 and one is h, and another is drunken. 3983
Php 4:12 I am instructed both to be full and to be h, 3983

HUNT (12) [HUNTED, HUNTER, HUNTERS, HUNTEST, HUNTETH, HUNTING]
Ge 27: 5 And Esau went to the field to h for venison, 6679
1Sa 26:20 as when one doth h a partridge in 7291
Job 38:39 Wilt thou h the prey for the lion? or fill 6679
Ps 140:11 evil shall h the violent man to overthrow 6679
Pr 6:26 the adulteress will h for the precious life. 6679
Jer 16:16 and they shall h them from every mountain, 6679
La 4:18 They h our steps, that we cannot go in our 6679
Eze 13:18 upon the head of every stature to h souls! 6679
13:18 Will ye h the souls of my people, and 6679
13:20 wherewith ye there h the souls to make 6679
13:20 even the souls that ye h to make them fly. 6679
Mic 7: 2 they h every man his brother with a net. 6679

HUNTED (1) [HUNT]
Eze 13:21 they shall be no more in your hand to be h; 4686

HUNTER (4) [HUNT]
Ge 10: 9 He was a mighty h before the LORD: 6718
10: 9 Even as Nimrod the mighty h before 6718
25:27 Esau was a cunning h, a man of 376+6718
Pr 6: 5 thyself as a roe from the hand of the h, NIH

HUNTERS (1) [HUNT]
Jer 16:16 after will I send for many h, and they shall 6719

HUNTEST (2) [HUNT]
1Sa 24:11 against thee; yet thou h my soul to take it. 6658
Job 10:16 Thou h me as a fierce lion: and again thou 6679

HUNTETH (1) [HUNT]
Lev 17:13 which h and catcheth any beast or fowl that 6679

HUNTING (2) [HUNT]
Ge 27:30 that Esau his brother came in from his h. 6718
Pr 12:27 man roasteth not that which he took in h: 6718

HUPHAM (1) [HUPHAMITES]
Nu 26:39 of H, the family of the Huphamites. 2349

HUPHAMITES (1) [HUPHAM]
Nu 26:39 of Hupham, the family of the H. 2350

HUPPAH (1)
1Ch 24:13 The thirteenth to H, the fourteenth to 2647

HUPPIM (3)
Ge 46:21 Ehi, and Rosh, Muppim, and H, and Ard. 2650
1Ch 7:12 Shuppim also, and H, the children of Ir, 2650
7:15 And Machir took to wife the sister of H and 2650

HUR (16)
Ex 17:10 Aaron, and H went up to the top of the hill. 2354
17:12 Aaron and H stayed up his hands, the one 2354
24:14 behold, Aaron and H are with you: if any 2354
31: 2 of Uri, the son of H, of the tribe of Judah: 2354
35:30 of Uri, the son of H, of the tribe of Judah; 2354
38:22 of Uri, the son of H, of the tribe of Judah, 2354
Nu 31: 8 and Rekem, and Zur, and H, and Reba, 2354
Jos 13:21 Evi, and Rekem, and Zur, and H, and Reba, 2354
1Ki 4: 8 The son of H, in mount Ephraim: 2354
1Ch 2:19 took unto him Ephrath, which bare him H. 2354
2:20 And H begat Uri, and Uri begat Bezaleel. 2354
2:50 These were the sons of Caleb the son of H, 2354
4: 1 Hezron, and Carmi, and H, and Shobal. 2354
4: 4 These are the sons of H, the firstborn of 2354
2Ch 1: 5 the son of Uri, the son of H, had made, 2354
Ne 3: 9 unto them repaired Rephaiah the son of H, 2354

HURAI (1)
1Ch 11:32 H of the brooks of Gaash, Abiel 2360

HURAM (12)
1Ch 8: 5 And Gera, and Shephuphan, and H. 2361
2Ch 2: 3 Solomon sent to H the king of Tyre, 2361
2:11 H the king of Tyre answered in writing, 2361
2:12 H said moreover, Blessed be the LORD 2361
2:13 with understanding, of H my father's, 2361
4:11 H made the pots, and the shovels, and 2361
4:11 H finished the work that he was to make 2361
2Ch 4:16 did H his father make to king Solomon for 2361
8: 2 That the cities which H had restored to 2361
8:18 H sent him by the hands of his servants 2361
9:10 the servants also of H, and the servants of 2361
9:21 went to Tarshish with the servants of H: 2361

HURI (1)
1Ch 5:14 are the children of Abihail the son of H, 2359

HURL (1) [HURLETH, HURLING]
Nu 35:20 or h at him by laying of wait, that he die; 7993

HURLETH (1) [HURL]
Job 27:21 and as a storm h him out of his place. 8175

HURLING (1) [HURL]
1Ch 12: 2 the right hand and the left in h stones and NIH

HURRIED See STRAIGHTWAY

HURT (63) [HURTFUL, HURTING]
Ge 4:23 to my wounding, and a young man to my h. 2250
26:29 That thou wilt do us no h, as we have not 7451
31: 7 but God suffered him not to h me. 7489
31:29 It is in the power of my hand to do you h: 7451
Ex 21:22 h a woman with child, so that her fruit 5062
21:35 if one man's ox h another's, that he die; 5062
22:10 it die, or be h, or driven away, no man 7665
22:14 it be h, or die, the owner thereof being not 7665
Nu 16:15 from them, neither have I h one of them. 7489
Jos 24:20 he will turn and do you h, and 7489
1Sa 20:21 for there is peace to thee, and no h; as 1697
24: 9 Behold, David seeketh thy h? 7451
25: 7 which were with us, we h them not, 3637
25:15 we were not h, neither missed we any 3637
2Sa 18:32 all that rise against thee to do thee h, be as 7451
2Ki 14:10 for why shouldest thou meddle to thy h, 7451
2Ch 25:19 why shouldest thou meddle to thine h, 7451
Ezr 4:22 why should damage grow to the h of 5142
Est 9: 2 to lay hand on such as sought their h: 7451
Job 35: 8 Thy wickedness may h a man as thou art; NIH
Ps 15: 4 He that sweareth to his own h, and 7489
35: 4 and brought to confusion that devise my h. 7451
35:26 to confusion together that rejoice at mine h: 7451
38:12 they that seek my h speak mischievous 7451
41: 7 against me do they devise my h. 7451
70: 2 and put to confusion, that desire my h. 7451
71:13 and dishonour that seek my h. 7451
71:24 are brought unto shame, that seek my h. 7451
105:18 Whose feet they h with fetters: he was laid 6031
Ecc 5:13 kept for the owners thereof to their h. 7451
8: 9 one man ruleth over another to his own h. 7451
10: 9 Whoso removeth stones shall be h 6087
Isa 11: 9 They shall not h nor destroy in all my holy 7489
27: 3 lest any h it, I will keep it night and day. 6485
65:25 They shall not h nor destroy in all my holy 7489
Jer 6:14 They have healed also the h of the daughter 7667
7: 6 neither walk after other gods to your h: 7451
8:11 For they have healed the h of the daughter 7667
8:21 For the h of the daughter of my people am I 7667
8:21 hurt of the daughter of my people am I h; 7665
10:19 Woe is me for my h! my wound is 7667
24: 9 all the kingdoms of the earth for their h, 7451
25: 6 of your hands; and I will do you no h. 7489
25: 7 the works of your hands to your own h. 7451
38: 4 not the welfare of this people, but the h. 7451
Da 3:25 in the midst of the fire, and they have no h; 2257
6:22 the lions' mouths, that they have not h me: 2255
6:22 also before thee, O king, have I done no h. 2248
6:23 no manner of h was found upon him, 2257
Mk 16:18 if they drink any deadly thing, it shall not h 984
Lk 4:35 he came out of him, and h him not. 984
10:19 and nothing shall by any means h you. 91
Ac 18:10 and no man shall set on thee to h thee: 2559
27:10 I perceive that this voyage will be with h 5196
Rev 2:11 He that overcometh shall not be h of 91
6: 6 and see thou h not the oil and the wine. 91
7: 2 to whom it was given to h the earth and 91
7: 3 Saying, H not the earth, neither the sea, 91
9: 4 that they should not h the grass of the earth, 91
9:10 and their power was to h men five months. 91
9:19 and had heads, and with them they do h. 91
11: 5 And if any man will h them, fire proceedeth 91
11: 5 and if any man will h them, he must in this 91

HURTFUL (3) [HURT]
Ezr 4:15 h unto kings and provinces, and that they 5142
Ps 144:10 David his servant from the h sword. 7451
1Ti 6: 9 a snare, and into many foolish and h lusts, 983

HURTING (1) [HURT]
1Sa 25:34 which hath kept me back from h thee, 7489

HUSBAND (120) [HUSBAND'S, HUSBANDMAN, HUSBANDMEN, HUSBANDRY, HUSBANDS]
Ge 3: 6 did eat, and gave also unto her h with her; 376
3:16 thy desire shall be to thy h, and he shall rule 376
16: 3 and gave her to her h Abram to be his wife. 376
29:32 now therefore my h will love me. 376
29:34 Now this time will my h be joined unto me, 376
30:15 it a small matter that thou hast taken my h? 376
30:18 because I have given my maiden to my h: 376
30:20 now will my h dwell with me, because 376
Ex 4:25 and said, Surely a bloody h art thou to me. 2860
4:26 A bloody h thou art, because of 2860
21:22 according as the woman's h will lay upon 1167
Lev 19:20 betrothed to a h, and not at all redeemed, nor 376
21: 3 that is nigh unto him, which hath had no h; 376
21: 7 they take a woman put away from her h: 376
Nu 5:13 it be hid from the eyes of her h, and be kept 376
5:19 to uncleanness with another instead of thy h, 376
5:20 hast gone aside to another instead of thy h, 376
5:20 some man hath lain with thee beside thine h: 376
5:27 and have done trespass against her h, 376
Nu 5:29 wife goeth aside to another instead of her h, 376
30: 6 And if she had at all a h, when she vowed, or 376
30: 7 her h heard it, and held his peace at her in 376
30: 8 if her h disallow her on the day that he heard 376
30:11 And her h heard it, and held his peace at her, 376
30:12 if her h hath utterly made them void on 376
30:12 her h hath made them void; and the LORD 376
30:13 her h may establish it, or her husband may 376
30:13 may establish it, or her h may make it void. 376
30:14 if her h altogether hold his peace at her from 376
Dt 21:13 and be her h, and she shall be thy wife. 1166
22:22 found lying with a woman married to a h, 1167
22:23 damsel that is a virgin be betrothed unto a h, 376
24: 3 if the latter h hate her, and write her a bill of 376
24: 3 or if the latter h die, which took her to be his 376
24: 4 Her former h, which sent her away, 1167
25:11 h out of the hand of him that smiteth him, 376
28:56 her eye shall be evil towards the h of her 376
Jdg 13: 6 the woman came and told her h, saying, 376
13: 9 but Manoah her h was not with her. 376
13:10 ran, and shewed her h, and said unto him, 376
14:15 they said unto Samson's wife, Entice thy h, 376
19: 3 her h arose, and went after her, to speak 376
20: 4 the h of the woman that was slain, answered 376
Ru 1: 3 Elimelech Naomi's h died; and she was left, 376
1: 5 woman was left of her two sons and her h. 376
1: 9 find rest, each of you in the house of her h. 376
1:12 go your way; for I am too old to have a h. 376
1:12 if I should have a h also to night, and 376
2:11 thy mother in law since the death of thine h: 376
1Sa 1: 8 said Elkanah her h to her, Hannah, why 376
1:22 for she said unto her h, I will not go up until 376
1:23 Elkanah her h said unto her, Do what 376
2:19 when she came up with her h to offer 376
4:19 that her father in law and her h were dead, 376
4:21 and because of her father in law and her h. 376
25:19 come after you. But she told not her h Nabal. 376
2Sa 3:15 Ish-bosheth sent, and took her from her h, 376
3:16 her h went with her along weeping behind 376
11:26 of Uriah heard that Uriah her h was dead, 376
11:26 husband was dead, she mourned for her h. 1167
14: 5 indeed a widow woman, and mine h is dead. 376
14: 7 shall not leave to my h neither name nor 376
2Ki 4: 1 saying, Thy servant my h is dead; 376
4: 9 she said unto her h, Behold now, I perceive 376
4:14 Verily she hath no child, and her h is old. 376
4:22 she called unto her h, and said, Send me, 376
4:26 is it well with thy h? is it well with 376
Pr 12: 4 A virtuous woman is a crown to her h: but 1167
31:11 The heart of her h doth safely trust in her, 1167
31:23 Her h is known in the gates, when he sitteth 1167
31:28 her blessed; her h also, and he praiseth her. 1167
Isa 54: 5 For thy Maker is thine h; the LORD of 1166
Jer 3:20 a wife treacherously departeth from her h, 7453
6:11 for even the h with the wife shall be taken, 376
31:32 although I was a h unto them, saith 1166
Eze 16:32 which taketh strangers instead of her h. 376
16:45 that lotheth her h and her children; 376
44:25 for brother, or for sister that hath had no h, 376
Hos 2: 2 for she is not my wife, neither am I her h: 376
2: 7 she say, I will go and return to my first h; 376
Joel 1: 8 with sackcloth for the h of her youth. 1167
Mt 1:16 And Jacob begat Joseph the h of Mary, 435
1:19 Then Joseph her h, being a just man, and 435
Mk 10:12 And if a woman shall put away her h, and 435
Lk 2:36 had lived with a h seven years from her 435
16:18 is put away from her h committeth adultery. 435
Jn 4:16 unto her, Go, call thy h, and come hither. 435
4:17 The woman answered and said, I have no h. 435
4:17 unto her, Thou hast well said, I have no h: 435
4:18 and he whom thou now hast is not thy h: 435
Ac 5: 9 the feet of them which have buried thy h are 435
5:10 and, carrying her forth, buried her by her h. 435
Ro 7: 2 For the woman which hath a h is bound by 5220
7: 2 hath a husband is bound by the law to her h 435
7: 2 but if the h be dead, she is loosed from 435
7: 2 be dead, she is loosed from the law of the h. 435
7: 3 So then if, while her h liveth, she be married 435
7: 3 but if her h be dead, she is free from that 435
1Co 7: 2 and let every woman have her own h. 435
7: 3 Let the h render unto the wife due 435
7: 3 and likewise also the wife unto the h. 435
7: 4 hath not power of her own body, but the h: 435
7: 4 likewise also the h hath not power of his 435
7:10 the Lord, Let not the wife depart from her h: 435
7:11 remain unmarried, or be reconciled to her h: 435
7:11 and let not the h put away his wife. 435
7:13 And the woman which hath a h that 435
7:14 For the unbelieving h is sanctified by 435
7:14 the unbelieving wife is sanctified by the h: 435
7:16 O wife, whether thou shalt save thy h? 435
7:34 of the world, how she may please her h. 435
7:39 wife is bound by the law as long as her h 435
7:39 but if her h be dead, she is at liberty to be 435
2Co 11: 2 for I have espoused you to one h, that I may 435
Gal 4:27 many moe children than she which hath a h. 435
Eph 5:23 For the h is the head of the wife, even as 435
5:33 and the wife see that she reverence her h. 435
1Ti 3: 2 the h of one wife, vigilant, sober, of good 435
Tit 1: 6 If any be blameless, the h of one wife, 435
Rev 21: 2 prepared as a bride adorned for her h. 435

HUSBAND'S (6) [HUSBAND]
Nu 30:10 if she vowed in her h house, or bound her 376
Dt 25: 5 her h brother shall go in unto her, and 2993
25: 5 perform the duty of a h brother unto her. 2992
25: 7 My h brother refuseth to raise up unto his 2993
25: 7 not perform the duty of my h brother. 2992
Ru 2: 1 Naomi had a kinsman of her h, a mighty 376

HUSBANDMAN (7) [HUSBAND, MAN]
Ge 9:20 Noah began to be a h, and 127+376+1886.1
Jer 51:23 and with thee will I break in pieces the h and 406
Am 5:16 they shall call the h to mourning, and 406
Zec 13: 5 I am no prophet, I am a h; 120+376+5647

Jn 15: 1 I am the true vine, and my Father is the **h**. *1092*
2Ti 2: 6 The **h** that laboureth must be first partaker *1092*
Jas 5: 7 the **h** waiteth for the precious fruit of *1092*

HUSBANDMEN (21) [HUSBAND, MAN]
2Ki 25:12 poor of the land to be vinedressers and **h**. 3009
2Ch 26:10 **h** *also*, and vinedressers in the mountains, 406
Jer 31:24 **h**, and they *that* go forth with flocks. 406
52:16 poor of the land for vinedressers and for **h**. 3009
Joel 1:11 Be ye ashamed, O ye **h**; howl, O ye 406
Mt 21:33 and let it out to **h**, and went into a far *1092*
21:34 he sent his servants to the **h**, that *they* *1092*
21:35 And the **h** took his servants, and beat one, *1092*
21:38 But when the **h** saw the son, they said *1092*
21:40 what will he do unto those **h**? *1092*
21:41 and will let out *his* vineyard unto other **h**, *1092*
Mk 12: 1 and let it out to **h**, and went into a far *1092*
12: 2 And at the season he sent to the **h** a servant, *1092*
12: 2 that he might receive from the **h** of the fruit *1092*
12: 7 But those **h** said amongst themselves, This *1092*
12: 9 he will come and destroy the **h**, and *1092*
Lk 20: 9 and let it forth to **h**, and went into a far *1092*
20:10 And at the season he sent a servant to the **h**, *1092*
20:10 but the **h** beat him, and sent *him* away *1092*
20:14 But when the **h** saw him, they reasoned *1092*
20:16 He shall come and destroy these **h**, and *1092*

HUSBANDRY (2) [HUSBAND]
2Ch 26:10 and in Carmel: for he loved **h**. 127
1Co 3: 9 ye are God's **h**, *ye are* God's building. *1091*

HUSBANDS (19) [HUSBAND]
Ru 1:11 sons in my womb, that they may be your **h**? 376
1:13 would ye stay for them from having **h**? nay, 376
Est 1:17 that *they* shall despise their **h** in their eyes, 1167
1:20 all the wives shall give to their **h** honour, 1167
Jer 29: 6 give your daughters to **h**, that they may bear 376
Eze 16:45 which lothed their **h** and their children: 376
Jn 4:18 For thou hast had five **h**; and he whom thou *435*
1Co 14:35 learn any *thing*, let them ask their **h** at home: *435*
Eph 5:22 Wives, submit yourselves unto your own **h**, *435*
5:24 *let* the wives *be* to their own **h** in every *435*
5:25 **H**, love your wives, even as Christ also *435*
Col 3:18 Wives, submit yourselves unto your own **h**, *435*
3:19 **H**, love *your* wives, and be not bitter against *435*
1Ti 3:12 Let the deacons be the **h** of one wife, *435*
Tit 2: 4 to **love** their **h**, to love their children, *1510+5362*
2: 5 at home, good, obedient to their own **h**, *435*
1Pe 3: 1 ye wives, *be* in subjection to your own **h**; *435*
3: 5 being in subjection unto their own **h**: *435*
3: 7 Likewise, ye **h**, dwell with *them* according *435*

HUSHAH (1)
1Ch 4: 4 father of Gedor, and Ezer the father of **H**. 2364

HUSHAI (14)
2Sa 15:32 **H** the Archite *came* to meet him with his 2365
15:37 So **H** David's friend came *into* the city, and 2365
16:16 when **H** the Archite, David's friend, 2365
16:16 that **H** said unto Absalom, God save 2365
16:17 Absalom said to **H**, *Is* this thy kindness to 2365
16:18 **H** said unto Absalom, Nay; but whom 2365
17: 5 Call now **H** the Archite also, and let us hear 2365
17: 6 when **H** was come to Absalom, 2365
17: 7 **H** said unto Absalom, The counsel that 2365
17: 8 For, (said **H**,) thou knowest thy father and 2365
17:14 The counsel of **H** the Archite *is* better than 2365
17:15 said **H** unto Zadok and to Abiathar 2365
1Ki 4:16 Baanah the son of **H** *was* in Asher and 2365
1Ch 27:33 **H** the Archite *was* the king's companion: 2365

HUSHAM (4)
Ge 36:34 **H** of the land of Temani reigned in his 2367
36:35 **H** died, and Hadad the son of Bedad, 2367
1Ch 1:45 **H** of the land of the Temanites reigned in 2367
1:46 when **H** was dead, Hadad the son of Bedad, 2367

HUSHATHITE (5)
2Sa 21:18 Sibbechai the **H** slew Saph, which *was* of 2843
23:27 Abiezer the Anethothite, Mebunnai the **H**, 2843
1Ch 11:29 Sibbecai the **H**, Ilai the Ahohite, 2843
20: 4 at which time Sibbechai the **H** slew Sippai, 2843
27:11 for the eighth month *was* Sibbecai the **H**, 2843

HUSHIM (4)
Ge 46:23 And the sons of Dan; **H**. 2366
1Ch 7:12 the children of Ir, *and* **H**, the sons of Aher. 2366
8: 8 them away; **H** and Baara *were* his wives. 2366
8:11 And of **H** he begat Abitub, and Elpaal. 2366

HUSK (2) [HUSKS]
Nu 6: 4 vine tree, from the kernels even to the **h**. 2085
2Ki 4:42 and full ears of corn in the **h** thereof. 6861

HUSKS (1) [HUSK]
Lk 15:16 his belly with the **h** that the swine did eat: *2769*

HUZ (1)
Ge 22:21 **H** his firstborn, and Buz his brother, and 5780

HUZZAB (1)
Na 2: 7 **H** shall be led away captive, she shall be 5324

HYMENEUS (2)
1Ti 1:20 Of whom is **H** and Alexander; whom I *5211*
2Ti 2:17 *doth* a canker: of whom is **H** and Philetus; *5211*

HYMN (2) [HYMNS]
Mt 26:30 And when they had **sung a h**, they went out *5214*
Mk 14:26 And when they had **sung a h**, they went out *5214*

HYMNS (2) [HYMN]
Eph 5:19 in psalms and **h** and spiritual songs, *5215*
Col 3:16 another in psalms and **h** and spiritual songs, *5215*

HYPOCRISIES (1) [HYPOCRISY]
1Pe 2: 1 and **h**, and envies, and all evil speakings, *5272*

HYPOCRISY (6) [HYPOCRISIES, HYPOCRITE, HYPOCRITE'S, HYPOCRITES, HYPOCRITICAL]
Isa 32: 6 to practise **h**, and to utter error against 2612
Mt 23:28 but within ye are full of **h** and iniquity. *5272*
Mk 12:15 But he, knowing their **h**, said unto them, *5272*
Lk 12: 1 of the leaven of the Pharisees, which is **h**. *5272*
1Ti 4: 2 Speaking lies in **h**, having their conscience *5272*
Jas 3:17 without partiality, and **without h**. *505*

HYPOCRITE (10) [HYPOCRISY]
Job 13:16 for a **h** shall not come before him. 2611
17: 8 innocent shall stir up himself against the **h**. 2611
20: 5 and the joy of the **h** *but* for a moment? 2611
27: 8 For what *is* the hope of the **h**, though he 2611
34:30 That the **h** reign not, lest the people be 120+2611
Pr 11: 9 A **h** with *his* mouth destroyeth his 2611
Isa 9:17 for every one *is* a **h** and an evildoer, and 2611
Mt 7: 5 *Thou* **h**, first cast out the beam out of thine *5273*
Lk 6:42 *Thou* **h**, cast out first the beam out of thine *5273*
13:15 then answered him, and said, *Thou* **h**, *5273*

HYPOCRITE'S (1) [HYPOCRISY]
Job 8:13 forget God; and the **h** hope shall perish: 2611

HYPOCRITES (20) [HYPOCRISY]
Job 15:34 For the congregation of **h** *shall be* desolate, 2611
36:13 the **h** in heart heap up wrath: they cry not 2611
Isa 33:14 are afraid; fearfulness hath surprised the **h**. 2611
Mt 6: 2 as the **h** do in the synagogues and in *5273*
6: 5 thou shalt not be as the **h** *are*: for they love *5273*
6:16 be not as the **h**, of a sad countenance: *5273*
15: 7 *Ye* **h**, well did Esaias prophesy of you, *5273*
16: 3 O *ye* **h**, ye can discern the face of the sky; *5273*
22:18 and said, Why tempt ye me, *ye* **h**? *5273*
23:13 But woe unto you, scribes and Pharisees, **h**! *5273*
23:14 Woe unto you, scribes and Pharisees, **h**! *5273*
23:15 Woe unto you, scribes and Pharisees, **h**! *5273*
23:23 Woe unto you, scribes and Pharisees, **h**! *5273*
23:25 Woe unto you, scribes and Pharisees, **h**! *5273*
23:27 Woe unto you, scribes and Pharisees, **h**! *5273*
23:29 Woe unto you, scribes and Pharisees, **h**! *5273*
24:51 and appoint *him* his portion with the **h**: *5273*
Mk 7: 6 Well hath Esaias prophesied of you **h**, as it *5273*
Lk 11:44 Woe unto you, scribes and Pharisees, **h**! *5273*
12:56 *Ye* **h**, ye can discern the face of the sky and *5273*

HYPOCRITICAL (2) [HYPOCRISY]
Ps 35:16 With **h** mockers in feasts, *they* gnashed 2611
Isa 10: 6 I will send him against a **h** nation, and 2611

HYSSOP (12)
Ex 12:22 ye shall take a bunch of **h**, and dip *it* in 231
Lev 14: 4 clean, and cedar wood, and scarlet, and **h**: 231
14: 6 the **h**, and shall dip them and the living bird 231
14:49 and cedar wood, and scarlet, and **h**: 231
14:51 the **h**, and the scarlet, and the living bird, 231
14:52 and with the **h**, and with the scarlet: 231
Nu 19: 6 **h**, and scarlet, and cast *it* into the midst of 231
19:18 a clean person shall take **h**, and dip *it* in 231
1Ki 4:33 unto the **h** that springeth out of the wall: 231
Ps 51: 7 Purge me with **h**, and I shall be clean: 231
Jn 19:29 and put *it* upon **h**, and put *it* to his mouth. *5301*
Heb 9:19 and **h**, and sprinkled both the book, and *5301*

I

I (8851) [ME, MINE, MY, MYSELF] See Index of Articles, Etc.

IBEX See PYGARG

IBHAR (3)
2Sa 5:15 **I** also, and Elishua, and Nepheg, and 2984
1Ch 3: 6 **I** also, and Elishama, and Eliphelet, 2984
14: 5 And **I**, and Elishua, and Elpalet, 2984

IBLEAM (3)
Jos 17:11 **I** and her towns, and the inhabitants of Dor 2991
Jdg 1:27 nor the inhabitants of **I** and her towns, 2991
2Ki 9:27 *so* at the going up to Gur, which *is* by **I**. 2991

IBNEIAH (1)
1Ch 9: 8 **I** the son of Jeroham, and Elah the son of 2997

IBNIJAH (1)
1Ch 9: 8 the son of Reuel, the son of **I**; 2998

IBRI (1)
1Ch 24:27 Beno, and Shoham, and Zaccur, and **I**. 5681

IBSAM See JIBSAM

IBZAN (2)
Jdg 12: 8 And after him **I** of Beth-lehem judged Israel. 78
12:10 Then died **I**, and was buried at Beth-lehem. 78

ICE (3)
Job 6:16 Which are blackish by reason of the **i**, *and* 7140
38:29 Out of whose womb came the **i**? and 7140
Ps 147:17 He casteth forth his **i** like morsels: who can 7140

ICHABOD (1) [ICHABOD'S]
1Sa 4:21 she named the child **I**, saying, The glory is 350

ICHABOD'S (1) [ICHABOD]
1Sa 14: 3 Ahiah, the son of Ahitub, **I** brother, the son 350

ICONIUM (6)
Ac 13:51 of their feet against them, and came unto **I**. *2430*
14: 1 And it came to pass in **I**, that they went *2430*
14:19 thither *certain* Jews from Antioch and **I**, *2430*
14:21 *again* to Lystra, and *to* **I**, and Antioch, *2430*
16: 2 of by the brethren that were at Lystra and **I**. *2430*
2Ti 3:11 came unto me at Antioch, at **I**, at Lystra; *2430*

IDALAH (1)
Jos 19:15 and Shimron, and **I**, and Beth-lehem: 3030

IDBASH (1)
1Ch 4: 3 father of Etam; Jezreel, and Ishma, and **I**: 3031

IDDO (14)
1Ki 4:14 Ahinadab the son of **I** *had* Mahanaim: 5714
1Ch 6:21 Joah his son, **I** his son, Zerah his son, 5714
27:21 Manasseh in Gilead, **I** the son of Zechariah: 3035
2Ch 9:29 in the visions of **I** the seer against 3260
12:15 and of **I** the seer concerning genealogies? 5714
13:22 *are* written in the story of the prophet **I**. 5714
Ezr 5: 1 the prophet, and Zechariah the son of **I**, 5714
6:14 the prophet and Zechariah the son of **I**. 5714
8:17 I sent them with commandment unto **I** 112
8:17 and I told them what they should say unto **I**, 112
Ne 12: 4 **I**, Ginnetho, Abijah, 5714
12:16 Of **I**, Zechariah; of Ginnethon, Meshullam; 5714
Zec 1: 1 the son of **I** the prophet, saying, 5714
1: 7 the son of **I** the prophet, saying, 5714

IDEA See WIST

IDLE (11) [IDLENESS]
Ex 5: 8 for they *be* **i**; therefore they cry, saying, 7503
5:17 he said, Ye *are* **i**, *ye are* idle: therefore 7503
5:17 he said, Ye *are* idle, *ye are* **i**: therefore 7503
Pr 19:15 and an **i** soul shall suffer hunger. 7423
Mt 12:36 That every **i** word that men shall speak, *692*
20: 3 and saw others standing **i** in the marketplace, *692*
20: 6 and found others standing **i**, and saith unto *692*
20: 6 unto them, Why stand ye here all the day **i**? *692*
Lk 24:11 And their words seemed to them as **i tales**, *3026*
1Ti 5:13 And withal they learn *to be* **i**, *692*
5:13 and not only **i**, but tattlers also and *692*

IDLENESS (3) [IDLE]
Pr 31:27 her household, and eateth not the bread of **i**. 6104
Ecc 10:18 through **i** of the hands the house droppeth 8220
Eze 16:49 abundance of **i** was in her and in her 8252

IDOL (15) [IDOL'S, IDOLATER, IDOLATERS, IDOLATRIES, IDOLATROUS, IDOLATRY, IDOLS]
1Ki 15:13 because she had made an **i** in a grove; 4656
15:13 Asa destroyed her **i**, and burnt *it* by 4656
2Ch 15:16 because she had made an **i** in a grove: 4656
15:16 and Asa cut down her **i**, and stamped *it*, and 4656
33: 7 the **i** which he had made, in the house of 5566
33:15 the **i** out of the house of the LORD, and 5566
Isa 48: 5 Mine **i** hath done them, and my graven 6090
66: 3 he that burneth incense, *as if* he blessed an **i**. 205
Jer 22:28 *Is* this man Coniah a despised broken **i**? 6089
Zec 11:17 Woe to the **i** shepherd that leaveth the flock! 457
Ac 7:41 and offered sacrifice unto the **i**, and *1497*
1Co 8: 4 we know that an **i** *is* nothing in the world, *1497*
8: 7 for some with conscience of the **i** unto this *1497*
8: 7 eat *it* as a **thing offered unto an i**; *1494*
10:19 that the **i** is any *thing*, or that which is *1497*

IDOL'S (1) [IDOL]
1Co 8:10 hast knowledge sit at meat in the **i temple**, *1493*

IDOLATER (2) [IDOL]
1Co 5:11 or an **i**, or a railer, or a drunkard, or *1496*
Eph 5: 5 *person*, nor covetous man who is an **i**, *1496*

IDOLATERS (5) [IDOL]
1Co 5:10 with the covetous, or extortioners, or with **i**; *1496*
6: 9 nor **i**, nor adulterers, nor effeminate, *1496*
10: 7 Neither be ye **i**, as *were* some of them; as it *1496*
Rev 21: 8 and whoremongers, and sorcerers, and **i**, *1496*
22:15 and **i**, and whosoever loveth and maketh a *1496*

IDOLATRIES (1) [IDOL]
1Pe 4: 3 revellings, banquetings, and abominable **i**: *1495*

IDOLATROUS (1) [IDOL]
2Ki 23: 5 he put down the **i priests**, whom the kings 3649

IDOLATRY (5) [IDOL]
1Sa 15:23 and stubbornness *is as* iniquity and **i**. 8655
Ac 17:16 he saw the city **wholly given to i**. *1510+2712*
1Co 10:14 Wherefore, my dearly beloved, flee from **i**. *1495*
Gal 5:20 **I**, witchcraft, hatred, variance, emulations, *1495*
Col 3: 5 and covetousness, which is **i**: *1495*

IDOLS (101) [IDOL]
Lev 19: 4 Turn ye not unto **i**, nor make to yourselves 457
26: 1 Ye shall make you no **i** nor graven image, 457
26:30 your carcases upon the carcases of your **i**, 1544
Dt 29:17 and their **i**, wood and stone, silver and gold, 1544
1Sa 31: 9 to publish *it* in the house of their **i**, and 6091

1Ki 15:12 removed all the i that his fathers had made. 1544
21:26 he did very abominably in following i, 1544
2Ki 17:12 For they served i, whereof the LORD had 1544
21:11 and hath made Judah also to sin with his i: 1544
21:21 and served the i that his father served, 1544
23:24 the i, and all the abominations that were 1544
1Ch 10: 9 to carry tidings unto their i, and to 6091
16:26 For all the gods of the people *are* i: but 457
2Ch 15: 8 put away the **abominable** i out of all 8251
24:18 of their fathers, and served groves and i: 6091
34: 7 cut down all the i throughout all the land of 2553
Ps 96: 5 For all the gods of the nations *are* i: but 457
97: 7 graven images, that boast themselves of i: 457
106:36 they served their i: which were a snare unto 6091
106:38 whom they sacrificed unto the i of Canaan: 6091
115: 4 Their i *are* silver and gold, the work of 6091
135:15 The i of the heathen *are* silver and gold, 6091
Isa 2: 8 Their land also is full *of* i; they worship 457
2:18 And the i he shall utterly abolish. 457
2:20 In that day a man shall cast his i of silver, 457
2:20 cast his idols of silver, and his i of gold, 457
10:10 my hand hath found the kingdoms of the i, 457
10:11 as I have done unto Samaria and her i, so 457
10:11 and her idols, so do to Jerusalem and her i? 6091
19: 1 the i of Egypt shall be moved at his 457
19: 3 they shall seek to the i, and to the charmers, 457
31: 7 day every man shall cast away his i of silver, 457
31: 7 his i of gold, which your own hands have 457
45:16 to confusion together *that are* makers of i. 6736
46: 1 their i were upon the beasts, and upon 6091
57: 5 Inflaming yourselves with i under every 410
Jer 50: 2 her i are confounded, her images are 6091
50:38 and they are mad upon *their* i. 367
Eze 6: 4 cast down your slain *men* before your i. 1544
6: 5 of the children of Israel before their i; 1544
6: 6 your i may be broken and cease, and 1544
6: 9 their eyes, which go a whoring after their i: 1544
6:13 when their slain *men* shall be among their i 1544
6:13 they did offer sweet savour to all their i. 1544
8:10 and all the i of the house of Israel, 1544
14: 3 these men have set up their i in their heart, 1544
14: 4 of Israel that setteth up his i in his heart, 1544
14: 4 cometh according to the multitude of his i; 1544
14: 5 are all estranged from me through their i. 1544
14: 6 Repent, and turn *yourselves* from your i; 1544
14: 7 setteth up his i in his heart, and putteth 1544
16:36 with all the i of thy abominations, and 1544
18: 6 neither hath lift up his eyes to the i of 1544
18:12 the pledge, and hath lift up his eyes to the i, 1544
18:15 neither hath lift up his eyes to the i of 1544
20: 7 defile not yourselves with the i of Egypt: 1544
20: 8 neither did they forsake the i of Egypt: 1544
20:16 for their heart went after their i. 1544
20:18 nor defile yourselves with their i: 1544
20:24 and their eyes were after their fathers' i. 1544
20:31 ye pollute yourselves with all your i, 1544
20:39 serve ye every one his i, and hereafter *also,* 1544
20:39 no more with your gifts, and with your i. 1544
22: 3 maketh i against herself to defile *herself.* 1544
22: 4 hast defiled *thyself* in thine i which thou 1544
23: 7 with all their i she defiled herself. 1544
23:30 *and* because thou art polluted with their i. 1544
23:37 with their i have they committed adultery, 1544
23:39 when they had slain their children to their i, 1544
23:49 and ye shall bear the sins of your i: 1544
30:13 I will also destroy the i, and I will cause 1544
33:25 lift up your eyes toward your i, and 1544
36:18 for their i *wherewith* they had polluted it: 1544
36:25 and from all your i, will I cleanse you. 1544
37:23 defile themselves any more with their i, 1544
44:10 went astray away from me after their i; 1544
44:12 they ministered unto them before their i, 1544
Hos 4:17 Ephraim *is* joined to i: let him alone. 6091
8: 4 and their gold have they made them i, 6091
13: 2 *and* i according to their own understanding, 6091
14: 8 *say,* What have I to do any more with i? 6091
Mic 1: 7 and all the i thereof will I lay desolate: 6091
Hab 2:18 of his work trusteth therein, to make dumb i? 457
Zec 10: 2 For the i have spoken vanity, and 8655
13: 2 *that* I will cut off the names of the i out of 6091
Ac 15:20 that *they* abstain from pollutions of i, and *1497*
15:29 That *ye* abstain from **meats offered to i,** *1494*
21:25 keep themselves from **things offered to i,** *1494*
Ro 2:22 thou that abhorrest i, dost thou commit *1497*
1Co 8: 1 Now as touching **things offered unto i,** *1494*
8: 4 **things** that are **offered in sacrifice unto i,** *1494*
8:10 to eat those **things** which are **offered to i;** *1494*
10:19 that which is **offered in sacrifice to i** is *1494*
10:28 This is **offered in sacrifice unto i,** *1494*
12: 2 carried away unto *these* dumb i, *even* as ye *1497*
2Co 6:16 agreement hath the temple of God with i? *1497*
1Th 1: 9 how ye turned to God from i to serve *1497*
1Jn 5:21 Little children, keep yourselves from i. *1497*
Rev 2:14 to eat **things sacrificed unto i,** and *1494*
2:20 and to eat **things sacrificed unto i.** *1494*
9:20 should not worship devils, and i of gold, *1497*

IDUMEA (5)

Isa 34: 5 it shall come down upon I, and upon 123
34: 6 and a great slaughter in the land of I. 123
Eze 35:15 O mount Seir, and all I, *even* all of it: 123
36: 5 the residue of the heathen, and against all I, 123
Mk 3: 8 and from I, and *from* beyond Jordan; *2401*

IEZER See JEEZER

IEZERITE See JEEZERITES

IF (1595)

Ge 4: 7 I thou doest well, *shalt thou* not be accepted? 518
4: 7 i thou doest not well, sin lieth at the door. 518
4:24 I Cain shall be avenged sevenfold, 3588
8: 8 to see i the waters were abated from off 1886.2
13: 9 i *thou wilt take* the left hand, then I will go 518
13: 9 or i *thou depart to* the right hand, then I will 518
13:16 that i a man can number the dust of the earth, 518
15: 5 tell the stars, i thou be able to number them: 518
18: 3 i now I have found favour in thy sight, 518
18:21 is come unto me; and i not, I will know. 518
18:26 I I find in Sodom fifty righteous within 518
18:28 he said, I I find there forty and five, I will 518
18:30 he said, I will not do *it,* i I find thirty there. 518
20: 7 i thou restore *her* not, know thou that thou 518
23: 8 I it be your mind that I should bury my dead 518
23:13 saying, But i thou *wilt give it,* I pray thee, 518
24: 8 i the woman will not be willing to follow 518
24:41 i they give not thee *one,* thou shalt be clear 518
24:42 i now thou do prosper my way which I go: 518
24:49 now i ye will deal kindly and truly with my 518
24:49 i not, tell me; that I may turn to the right 518
25:22 she said, I *it be* so, why *am* I thus? 518+3651
27:46 i Jacob take a wife of the daughters of Heth, 518
28:20 I God will be with me, and will keep me in 518
30:27 i I have found favour in thine eyes, 518
30:31 i thou wilt do this thing for me, I will again 518
31: 8 I he said thus, The speckled shall be thy 518
31: 8 i he said thus, The ringstraked shall be thy 518
31:50 I thou shalt afflict my daughters, or if thou 518
31:50 i thou shalt take *other* wives beside my 518
32: 8 I Esau come to the one company, and 518
33:10 i now I have found grace in thy sight, then 518
33:13 i *men* should overdrive them one day, NIH
34:15 I ye will be as we *be,* that every male of you 518
34:17 i ye will not hearken unto us, to be 518
34:22 i every male among us be circumcised, 871.1
37:26 What profit *is it* i we slay our brother, and 3588
42:19 I ye be true *men,* let one of your brethren be 518
42:37 Slay my two sons, i I bring him not to thee: 518
42:38 i mischief befall him by the way in 2050.1
43: 4 I thou wilt send our brother with us, we will 518
43: 5 i thou wilt not send *him,* we will not go 518
43: 9 i I bring him not unto thee, and set him 518
43:11 said unto them, I *it must be* so now, do this; 518
43:14 I I be bereaved of my children, I am 834+3509.1
44:22 for *i* he should leave his father, *his father* NIH
44:26 i our youngest brother be with us, then 518
44:29 **And** i ye take this also from me, 2050.1
44:32 I I bring him not unto thee, then I shall bear 518
47: 6 i thou knowest *any* man of activity amongst 518
47:16 I will give you for your cattle, i money fail. 518
47:29 I now I have found grace in thy sight, put, 518
50: 4 I now I have found grace in your eyes, 518
Ex 1:16 i it *be* a son, then ye shall kill him: 518
1:16 but i it *be* a daughter, then she shall live. 518
4: 8 come to pass, i they will not believe thee, 518
4: 9 i they will not believe also these two signs, 518
4:23 *i* thou refuse to let him go, behold, I will NIH
8: 2 i thou refuse to let *them* go, behold, I will 518
8:21 Else, i thou wilt not let my people go, 518
9: 2 For i thou refuse to let *them* go, and wilt 518
10: 4 Else, i thou refuse to let my people go, 518
12: 4 i the household be too little for the lamb, 518
13:13 i thou wilt not redeem *it,* then thou shalt 518
15:26 I thou wilt diligently hearken to the voice of 518
18:23 I thou shalt do this thing, and God command 518
19: 5 i ye will obey my voice indeed, and keep my 518
20:25 i thou wilt make me an altar of stone, 518
20:25 for i thou lift up thy tool upon it, thou hast NIH
21: 2 I thou buy a Hebrew servant, six years he 3588
21: 3 I he came in by himself, he shall go out by 518
21: 3 i he *were* married, then his wife shall go out 518
21: 4 I his master have given him a wife, and 518
21: 5 i the servant shall plainly say, I love my 518
21: 7 i a man sell his daughter to be a 3588
21: 8 I she please not her master, who hath 518
21: 9 i he have betrothed her unto his son, he shall 518
21:10 I he take him another *wife;* her food, 518
21:11 i he do not these three unto her, then 518
21:13 i a man lie not in wait, but God deliver *him* NIH
21:14 i a man come presumptuously upon his 3588
21:16 selleth him, or i he be found in his hand, NIH
21:18 i men strive together, and one smite another 3588
21:19 I he rise again, and walk abroad upon his 518
21:20 i a man smite his servant, or his maid, 3588
21:21 Notwithstanding, i he continue a day or two, 518
21:22 I men strive, and hurt a woman with child, 3588
21:23 i *any* mischief follow, then thou shalt give 518
21:26 i a man smite the eye of his servant, or 3588
21:27 And i he smite out his manservant's tooth, or 518
21:28 I an ox gore a man or a woman, that they 3588
21:29 i the ox *were* wont to push with his horn in 518
21:30 I there be laid on him a sum of money, then 518
21:32 I the ox shall push a manservant or 518
21:33 i a man shall open a pit, or if a man shall 3588
21:33 or i a man shall dig a pit, and not cover it, 3588
21:35 i one man's ox hurt another's, that he die; 3588
21:36 Or *i* it be known that the ox *hath* used to NIH
22: 1 I a man shall steal an ox, or a sheep, and 3588
22: 2 I a thief be found breaking up, and 518
22: 3 I the sun be risen upon him, *there shall be* 518
22: 3 i he have nothing, then he shall be sold for 518
22: 4 I the theft be certainly found in his hand 518
22: 5 I a man shall cause a field or vineyard to be 3588
22: 6 I fire break out, and catch in thorns, so 3588
22: 7 I a man shall deliver unto his neighbour 3588
22: 7 i the thief be found, let him pay double. 518
22: 8 I the thief be not found, then the master of 518
22:10 I a man deliver unto his neighbour an ass, 3588
22:12 i it be stolen from him, he shall make 518
22:13 I it be torn in pieces, *then* let him bring it *for* 518
22:14 i a man borrow *ought* of his neighbour, 3588
22:15 *But* i the owner thereof *be* with it, he shall 518
22:15 i it *be* a hired *thing,* it came for his hire. 518
22:16 i a man entice a maid that is not betrothed, 3588
22:17 I her father utterly refuse to give her unto 518
22:23 I thou afflict them in any wise, and they cry 518
22:25 I thou lend money to *any* of my people *that* 518
22:26 I thou at all take thy neighbour's raiment to 518
23: 4 I thou meet thine enemy's ox or his ass 3588
23: 5 I thou see the ass of him that hateth thee 3588
Ex 23:22 i thou shalt indeed obey his voice, and do all 518
23:33 for i thou serve their gods, it will surely be a NIH
24:14 i any man have any matters to do, let him NIH
29:34 And i *ought* of the flesh of the consecrations, 518
32:32 Yet now, i thou wilt forgive their sin; and 518
32:32 i not, blot me, I pray thee, out of thy book 518
33:13 I pray thee, i I have found grace in thy sight, 518
33:15 I thy presence go not *with me,* carry us not 518
34: 9 I now I have found grace in thy sight, 518
34:20 i thou redeem *him* not, then shalt thou break 518
40:37 i the cloud were not taken up, then 518
Lev 1: 2 I *any* man of you bring an offering unto 3588
1: 3 I his offering *be* a burnt sacrifice of the herd, 518
1:10 i his offering *be* of the flocks, *namely,* of 518
1:14 i the burnt sacrifice for his offering to 518
2: 4 i thou bring an oblation of a meat offering 3588
2: 5 i thy oblation *be* a meat offering *baken* in a 518
2: 7 i thy oblation *be* a meat offering *baken* in 518
2:14 i thou offer a meat offering of *thy* firstfruits 518
3: 1 i his oblation *be* a sacrifice of peace offering, 518
3: 1 of peace offering, i he offer *it* of the herd; 518
3: 6 i his offering for a sacrifice of peace offering 518
3: 7 I he offer a lamb for his offering, then 518
3:12 i his offering *be* a goat, then he shall offer it 518
4: 2 I a soul shall sin through ignorance against 3588
4: 3 I the priest that is anointed do sin according 518
4:13 i the whole congregation of Israel sin 518
4:23 **Or** i his sin, wherein he hath sinned, come to 176
4:27 i any one of the common people sin through 518
4:28 **Or** i his sin, which he hath sinned, come to 176
4:32 i he bring a lamb for a sin offering, he shall 518
5: 1 i a soul sin, and hear the voice of swearing, 3588
5: 1 or known *of it;* i he do not utter *it,* then 518
5: 2 Or i a soul touch any unclean thing, 834
5: 2 and *i* it be hidden from him; NIH
5: 3 Or i he touch the uncleanness of man, 3588
5: 4 Or i a soul swear, pronouncing with *his* lips 3588
5: 7 i he be not able to bring a lamb, then he shall 518
5:11 But i he be not able to bring two turtledoves, 518
5:15 I a soul commit a trespass, and sin through 3588
5:17 i a soul sin, and commit any *of these things* 518
6: 2 I a soul sin, and commit a trespass against 3588
6:28 i it be sodden in a brasen pot, it shall be both 518
7:12 I he offer it for a thanksgiving, then he shall 518
7:16 i the sacrifice of his offering *be* a vow, or 518
7:18 i *any* of the flesh of the sacrifice of his peace 518
10:19 *i* I had eaten the sin offering to day, should NIH
11:37 i *any part* of their carcase fall upon any 3588
11:38 i *any* water be put upon the seed, and 3588
11:39 i any beast, of which ye may eat, die; 3588
12: 2 I a woman have conceived seed, and born a 3588
12: 5 i she bear a maid child, then she shall be 518
12: 8 i she be not able to bring a lamb, then 518
13: 4 I the bright spot *be* white in the skin of his 518
13: 5 *i* the plague in his sight be at a stay, *and* NIH
13: 6 *i* the plague *be* somewhat dark, and NIH
13: 7 i the scab spread much abroad in the skin, 518
13: 8 *i* the priest see that behold, the scab NIH
13:10 *i* the rising *be* white in the skin, and it have NIH
13:12 And i a leprosy break out abroad in the skin, 518
13:13 *i* the leprosy have covered all his flesh, NIH
13:16 Or i the raw flesh turn again, and 3588
13:17 behold, *i* the plague be turned into white; NIH
13:20 i, when the priest seeth it, behold, it *be* in NIH
13:21 i the priest look on it, and behold, *there be* 518
13:21 *i* it *be* not lower than the skin, but *be* NIH
13:22 And i it spread much abroad in the skin, then 518
13:23 i the bright spot stay in his place, *and* 518
13:24 Or i there be *any* flesh, in the skin whereof 3588
13:25 *i* the hair in the bright spot be turned white, NIH
13:26 i the priest look on it, and behold, *there be* 518
13:27 *and* i it be spread much abroad in the skin, 518
13:28 i the bright spot stay in his place, *and* 518
13:29 I a man or woman hath a plague upon 3588
13:30 behold, *i* it *be* in sight deeper than the skin; NIH
13:31 i the priest look on the plague of the scall, 3588
13:32 *i* the scall spread not, and there be in it no NIH
13:34 behold, *i* the scall be not spread in the skin, NIH
13:35 i the scall spread much in the skin after his 518
13:36 behold, *i* the scall be spread in the skin, NIH
13:37 i the scall be in his sight at a stay, and 518
13:38 I a man also or a woman have in the skin of 3588
13:39 *i* the bright spots in the skin of their flesh *be* NIH
13:42 i there be in the bald head, or bald 3588
13:43 *i* the rising of the sore *be* white reddish in NIH
13:49 *i* the plague be greenish or reddish in NIH
13:51 i the plague be spread in the garment, 3588
13:53 i the priest shall look, and behold, the plague 518
13:55 *i* the plague have not changed his colour, NIH
13:56 i the priest look, and behold, the plague *be* 518
13:57 i it appear still in the garment, either in 518
13:58 i the plague be departed from them, then NIH
14: 3 *i* the plague of leprosy be healed in NIH
14:21 i he *be* poor, and cannot get *so much;* then 518
14:37 *i* the plague *be* in the walls of the house NIH
14:39 *i* the plague be spread in the walls of NIH
14:43 i the plague come again, and break out in 518
14:44 behold, *i* the plague be spread in the house, NIH
14:48 i the priest shall come in, and look *upon it,* 518
15: 8 i he that hath the issue spit upon him that is 3588
15:16 i any man's seed of copulation go out from 3588
15:19 i a woman have an issue, *and* her issue in 3588
15:23 i it *be* on *her* bed, or on *any* thing whereon 518
15:24 i any man lie with her at all, and her flowers 518
15:25 i a woman have an issue of her blood many 3588
15:25 i it run beyond the time of her separation; 3588
15:28 i she be cleansed of her issue, then she shall 518
17:16 i he wash *them* not, nor bathe his flesh; then 518
18: 5 which i a man do, he shall live in them: 2050.1
19: 5 i ye offer a sacrifice of peace offerings unto 3588
19: 6 i ought remain until the third day, it shall be NIH
19: 7 I it be eaten at all on the third day, it *is* 518
19:33 i a stranger sojourn with thee in your land, 3588
20: 4 i the people of the land do any ways hide 518
20:12 **And** i a man lie with his daughter in law, 2050.1

Lev 20:13 I a man also lie with mankind, as he lieth 2050.1
20:14 And i a man take a wife and her mother, 2050.1
20:15 And i a man lie with a beast, he shall 2050.1
20:16 And i a woman approach unto any beast, 2050.1
20:17 And i a man shall take his sister, 2050.1
20:18 And i a man shall lie with a woman 2050.1
20:20 And i a man shall lie with his uncle's 2050.1
20:21 And i a man shall take his brother's wife, 2050.1
21: 9 i she profane herself by playing the whore, 3588
22: 9 for it, and die therefore, i they profane it: 3588
22:11 i the priest buy any soul with his money, 3588
22:12 I the priest's daughter also be married unto 3588
22:13 i the priest's daughter be a widow, or 3588
22:14 i a man eat of the holy thing unwittingly, 3588
24:19 i a man cause a blemish in his neighbour; 3588
25:14 i thou sell ought unto thy neighbour, or 3588
25:20 i ye shall say, What shall we eat 3588
25:25 I thy brother be waxen poor, and hath sold 3588
25:25 i any of his kin come to redeem it, then NIH
25:26 i the man have none to redeem it, and 3588
25:28 But i he be not able to restore it to him, then 518
25:29 i a man sell a dwelling house in a walled 3588
25:30 i it be not redeemed within the space of a 518
25:33 i a man purchase of the Levites, then 834
25:35 i thy brother be waxen poor, and fallen in 3588
25:39 i thy brother that dwelleth by thee be 3588
25:47 i a sojourner or stranger wax rich by thee, 3588
25:49 or i he be able, he may redeem himself. NIH
25:51 I there be yet many years behind, according 518
25:52 i there remain but few years unto the year of 518
25:54 i he be not redeemed in these years, then 518
26: 3 I ye walk in my statutes, and keep my 518
26:14 i ye will not hearken unto me, and will not 518
26:15 i ye shall despise my statutes, or if your soul 518
26:15 or i your soul abhor my judgments, so 518
26:18 i ye will not yet for all this hearken unto me, 518
26:21 i ye walk contrary unto me, and will not 518
26:23 i ye will not be reformed by me by these 518
26:27 i ye will not for all this hearken unto me, 518
26:40 I they shall confess their iniquity, and NIH
26:41 i then their uncircumcised hearts be 176+227
27: 4 i it be a female, then thy estimation shall be 518
27: 5 i it be from five years old even unto twenty 518
27: 6 i it be from a month old even unto five years 518
27: 7 i it be from sixty years old and above; if it be 518
27: 7 i it be a male, then thy estimation shall be 518
27: 8 i he be poorer than thy estimation, then 518
27: 9 i it be a beast, whereof men bring an offering 518
27:10 i he shall at all change beast for beast, then 518
27:11 i it be any unclean beast, of which they do 518
27:13 i he will at all redeem it, then he shall add a 518
27:15 i he that sanctified it will redeem his house, 518
27:16 i a man shall sanctify unto the LORD some 518
27:17 I he sanctify his field from the year of jubile, 518
27:18 i he sanctify his field after the jubile, then 518
27:19 i he that sanctified the field will in any wise 518
27:20 i he will not redeem the field, or if he have 518
27:20 or i he have sold the field to another man, 518
27:22 i a man sanctify unto the LORD a field 518
27:27 i it be of an unclean beast, then he shall 518
27:27 or i it be not redeemed, then it shall be sold 518
27:31 i a man will at all redeem ought of his tithes, 518
27:33 i he change it at all, then both it and 518
Nu 5: 8 i the man have no kinsman to recompense 518
5:12 I any man's wife go aside, and commit a 3588
5:14 or i the spirit of jealousy come upon him, NIH
5:19 I no man have lain with thee, and if thou 518
5:19 i thou hast not gone aside to uncleanness 518
5:20 i thou hast gone aside to another instead of 3588
5:20 i thou be defiled, and some man hath lain 3588
5:27 that, i she be defiled, and have done trespass 518
5:28 i the woman be not defiled, but be clean; 518
6: 9 i any man die very suddenly by him, and 3588
9:10 I any man of you or of your posterity shall 3588
9:14 i a stranger shall sojourn among you, and 3588
10: 4 i they blow but with one trumpet, then 518
10: 9 i ye go to war in your land against 3588
10:32 shall be, i thou go with us, yea, it shall be, 3588
11:15 i thou deal thus with me, kill me, I pray thee, 518
11:15 of hand, i I have found favour in thy sight; 518
12: 6 I there be a prophet among you, I 518
14:12 I her father had but spit in her face, 2050.1
14: 8 I the LORD delight in us, then he will 518
14:15 Now i thou shalt kill all this people as one NIH
15:14 i a stranger sojourn with you, or 3588
15:22 i ye have erred, and not observed all these 3588
15:24 i ought be committed by ignorance without 518
15:27 i any soul sin through ignorance, then 518
16:29 I these men die the common death of all 518
16:29 i they be visited after the visitation of all NIH
16:30 i the LORD make a new thing, and 518
19:12 but i he purify not himself the third day, then 518
20:19 and i I and my cattle drink of thy water, then 518
21: 2 I thou wilt indeed deliver this people into 518
21: 9 to pass, that i a serpent had bitten any man, 518
22:18 I Balak would give me his house full of 518
22:20 I the men come to call thee, rise up, and 518
22:34 now therefore, i it displease thee, I will get 518
24:13 I Balak would give me his house full of 518
27: 8 I a man die, and have no son, then ye shall 3588
27: 9 i he have no daughter, then ye shall give his 518
27:10 i he have no brethren, then ye shall give his 518
27:11 i his father have no brethren, then ye shall 518
30: 2 I a man vow a vow unto the LORD, or 3588
30: 3 I a woman also vow a vow unto 3588
30: 5 i her father disallow her in the day that he 518
30: 6 i she had at all a husband, when she vowed, 518
30: 8 i her husband disallow her on the day that he 518
30:10 And i she vowed in her husband's house, or 518
30:12 i her husband hath utterly made them void 518
30:14 i her husband altogether hold his peace at 518
30:15 i he shall any ways make them void after 518
32: 5 said they, i we have found grace in thy sight, 518
32:15 For i ye turn away from after him, he will 3588
32:20 said unto them, I ye will do this thing, 518

Nu 32:20 i ye will go armed before the LORD to war, 518
32:23 i ye will not do so, behold, ye have sinned 518
32:29 I the children of Gad and the children of 518
32:30 But i they will not pass over with you armed, 518
33:55 i ye will not drive out the inhabitants of 518
35:16 i he smite him with an instrument of iron, 518
35:17 i he smite him with throwing a stone, 518
35:18 Or i he smite him with a hand weapon of NIH
35:20 i he thrust him of hatred, or hurl at him by 518
35:22 But i he thrust him suddenly without enmity, 518
35:26 i the slayer shall at any time come without 518
36: 3 i they be married to any of the sons of NIH
Dt 4:29 i from thence thou shalt seek the LORD NIH
4:29 thou shalt find him, i thou seek him with all 3588
4:30 i thou turn to the LORD thy God, and NIH
5:25 i we hear the voice of the LORD our God 518
6:25 i we observe to do all these commandments 3588
7:12 i ye hearken to these judgments, and keep, 6118
7:17 I thou shalt say in thine heart, 3588
8:19 i thou do at all forget the LORD thy God, 518
11:13 i you shall hearken diligently unto my 518
11:22 For i ye shall diligently keep all these 518
11:27 i ye obey the commandments of the LORD 834
11:28 i ye will not obey the commandments of 518
12:21 I the place which the LORD thy God hath 3588
13: 1 I there arise among you a prophet, or 3588
13: 6 I thy brother, the son of thy mother, or 3588
13:12 I thou shalt hear say in one of thy cities, 3588
13:14 behold, i it be truth, and the thing certain, NIH
14:24 i the way be too long for thee, so that thou 3588
14:24 or i the place be too far from thee, 3588
15: 5 Only i thou carefully hearken unto the voice 518
15: 7 I there be among you a poor man of one of 3588
15:12 And i thy brother, a Hebrew man, or 3588
15:16 it shall be, i he say unto thee, I will not go 3588
15:21 i there be any blemish therein, as if it be 3588
15:21 as i it be lame, or blind, or have any ill NIH
17: 2 I there be found among you, within any of 3588
17: 8 I there arise a matter too hard for thee in 3588
18: 6 i a Levite come from any of thy gates out 3588
18:21 i thou say in thine heart, How shall we 3588
18:22 i the thing follow not, nor come to pass, 2050.1
19: 8 And i the LORD thy God enlarge thy coast, 518
19: 9 I thou shalt keep all these commandments 3588
19:11 i any man hate his neighbour, and lie in 3588
19:16 I a false witness rise up against any man to 3588
19:18 i the witness be a false witness, and NIH
20:11 i it make thee answer of peace, and 518
20:12 i it will make no peace with thee, but 518
21: 1 I one be found slain in the land which 3588
21:14 i thou have no delight in her, then thou shalt 518
21:15 I a man have two wives, one beloved, and 3588
21:15 i the firstborn son be hers that was hated: NIH
21:18 I a man have a stubborn and rebellious son, 3588
21:22 i a man have committed a sin worthy of 3588
22: 2 i thy brother be not nigh unto thee, or if thou 518
22: 2 or i thou know him not, then thou shalt NIH
22: 6 I a bird's nest chance to be before thee in 3588
22: 8 thine house, i any man fall from thence. 3588
22:13 I any man take a wife, and go in unto her, 3588
22:20 i this thing be true, and the tokens of 518
22:22 I a man be found lying with a woman 3588
22:23 I a damsel that is a virgin be betrothed unto 3588
22:25 i a man find a betrothed damsel in the field, 518
22:28 I a man find a damsel that is a virgin, 3588
23:10 I there be among you any man, that is not 3588
23:22 i thou shalt forbear to vow, it shall be no 3588
24: 3 i the latter husband hate her, and write her a NIH
24: 3 or i the latter husband die, which took her 3588
24: 7 I a man be found stealing any of his 3588
24:12 i the man be poor, thou shalt not sleep with 518
25: 1 I there be a controversy between men, and 3588
25: 2 i the wicked man be worthy to be beaten, 518
25: 3 i he should exceed, and beat him above NIH
25: 5 I brethren dwell together, and one of them 3588
25: 7 i the man like not to take his brother's wife, 518
25: 8 i he stand to it, and say, I like not to take NIH
28: 1 i thou shalt hearken diligently unto the voice 518
28: 2 i thou shalt hearken unto the voice of 3588
28: 9 i thou shalt keep the commandments of 3588
28:13 i that thou hearken unto the commandments 3588
28:15 i thou wilt not hearken unto the voice of 518
28:58 I thou wilt not observe to do all the words of 518
30: 4 I any of thine be driven out unto the outmost 518
30:10 I thou shalt hearken unto the voice of 3588
30:10 i thou turn unto the LORD thy God with 3588
30:17 i thine heart turn away, so that thou wilt not 518
32:41 I I whet my glittering sword, and mine hand 518
Jos 2:14 life for yours, i ye utter not this our business. 518
2:19 be on our head, i any hand be upon him. 518
2:20 i thou utter this our business, then we will be 518
8:15 all Israel made as i they were beaten before NIH
9: 4 and made as i they had been ambassadors, 6737
14:12 i so be the LORD will be with me, then 194
17:15 I thou be a great people, then get thee up to 518
17:15 i mount Ephraim be too narrow for thee. NIH
20: 5 i the avenger of blood pursue after him, 3588
22:19 i the land of your possession be unclean, 518
22:22 i it be in rebellion, or if in transgression 518
22:22 or i in transgression against the LORD, 518
22:23 or i to offer thereon burnt offering or 518
22:23 or i to offer peace offerings thereon, 518
22:24 i we have not rather done it for fear of this 518
23:12 Else i ye do in any wise go back, and 518
24:15 i it seem evil unto you to serve the LORD, 518
24:20 I ye forsake the LORD, and serve strange 3588
Jdg 4: 8 I thou wilt go with me, then I will go: 518
4: 8 i thou wilt not go with me, then I will not go. 518
6:13 i the LORD be with us, why then is all 2050.1
6:17 I now I have found grace in thy sight, then 518
6:31 i he be a god, let him plead for himself, 518
6:36 I thou wilt save Israel by mine hand, as thou 518
6:37 and i the dew be on the fleece only, and it be 518
7:10 i thou fear to go down, go thou with Phurah 518
8:19 i ye had saved them alive, I would not slay 3863

Jdg 9:15 I in truth ye anoint me king over you, then 518
9:15 i not, let fire come out of the bramble, and 518
9:16 i ye have done truly and sincerely, 518
9:16 i ye have dealt well with Jerubbaal and his 518
9:19 I ye then have dealt truly and sincerely with 518
9:20 But i not, let fire come out from Abimelech, 518
9:36 Thou seest the shadow of the mountains as i NIH
11: 9 I ye bring me home again to fight against 518
11:10 i we do not so according to thy words. 518
11:30 I thou shalt without fail deliver the children 518
11:36 i thou hast opened thy mouth unto NIH
12: 5 Art thou an Ephraimite? I he said, Nay; 2050.1
13:16 i thou wilt offer a burnt offering, thou must 518
13:23 I the LORD were pleased to kill us, 3863
14:12 i you can certainly declare it me within 518
14:13 i ye cannot declare it me, then shall ye give 518
14:18 I ye had not plowed with my heifer, 3884
16: 7 I they bind me with seven green withs that 518
16:11 I they bind me fast with new ropes that 518
16:13 I thou weavest the seven locks of my head 518
16:17 i I be shaven, then my strength will go from 518
21:21 i the daughters of Shiloh come out to dance 518
Ru 1:12 I I should say, I have hope, if I should have 3588
1:12 i I should have a husband also to night, and NIH
1:17 i ought but death part thee and me. NIH
3:13 that i he will perform unto thee the part of a 518
3:13 i he will not do the part of a kinsman to thee, 518
4: 4 I thou wilt redeem it, redeem it: but if thou 518
4: 4 but i thou wilt not redeem it, then tell me, 518
1Sa 1:11 i thou wilt indeed look on the affliction of 518
2:16 i any man said unto him, Let them not fail NIH
2:16 it me now: and i not, I will take it by force. 518
2:25 I one man sin against another, the judge 518
2:25 i a man sin against the LORD, who shall 518
3: 9 it shall be, i he call thee, that thou shalt say, 518
3:17 i thou hide any thing from me of all 518
6: 3 I ye send away the ark of the God of Israel, 518
6: 9 i it goeth up by the way of his own coast to 518
6: 9 i not, then we shall know that it is not his 518
7: 3 I ye do return unto the LORD with all your 518
9: 7 behold, i we go, what shall we bring NIH
10:22 i the man should yet come thither. 1886.2
11: 3 then, i there be no man to save us, we will 518
12:14 I ye will fear the LORD, and serve him, 518
12:15 i ye will not obey the voice of the LORD, 518
12:25 i ye shall still do wickedly, ye shall be 518
14: 9 I they say thus unto us, Tarry until we come 518
14:10 i they say thus, Come up unto us; then 518
14:30 i haply the people had eaten freely to day 3863
16: 2 i Saul hear it, he will kill me. And NIH
17: 9 I he be able to fight with me, and to kill me, 518
17: 9 but i I prevail against him, and kill him, then 518
19:11 saying, I thou save not thy life to night, 518
20: 6 I thy father at all miss me, then say, 518
20: 7 I he say thus, It is well; thy servant shall 518
20: 7 i he be very wroth, then be sure that evil is 518
20: 8 i there be in me iniquity, slay me thyself; 518
20: 9 for i I knew certainly that evil were 518
20:10 or what i thy father answer thee roughly? NIH
20:12 i there be good toward David, and I then NIH
20:13 but i it please my father to do thee evil, 3588
20:21 I I expressly say unto the lad, Behold, 518
20:22 But i I say thus unto the young man, Behold, 518
20:29 and now, i I have found favour in thine eyes, 518
21: 4 i the young men have kept themselves at 518
21: 9 i thou wilt take that, take it: for there is no 518
23: 3 i we come to Keilah against the armies of 3588
23:23 and it shall come to pass, i he be in the land, 518
24:19 For i a man find his enemy, will he let him 3588
25:22 i I leave of all that pertain to him by 518
26:19 I the LORD have stirred thee up against 518
26:19 i they be the children of men, cursed be they 518
27: 5 I I have now found grace in thine eyes, 518
2Sa 3:35 and more also, i I taste bread, or ought else, 518
7:14 I he commit iniquity, I will chasten him 871.1
10:11 I the Syrians be too strong for me, then 518
10:11 i the children of Ammon be too strong for 518
11:20 i so be that the king's wrath arise, and 518
12: 8 i that had been too little, I would moreover 518
12:18 i we tell him that the child is dead? NIH
13:26 said Absalom, I not, I pray thee, let my 2050.1
14:32 i there be any iniquity in me, let him kill me. 518
15: 8 I the LORD shall bring me again indeed to 518
15:25 i I shall find favour in the eyes of 518
15:26 i he thus say, I have no delight in thee; 518
15:33 I thou passest on with me, then thou shalt be 518
15:34 i thou return to the city, and say unto 518
16:23 was as i a man had inquired at 834+3509.1
17: 3 the man whom thou seekest is as i all 3509.1
17: 6 we do after his saying? i not; speak thou. 518
17:13 i he be gotten into a city, then shall all Israel 518
18: 3 for i we flee away, they will not care for us; 518
18: 3 neither i half of us die, will they care for us: 518
18:25 the king said, I he be alone, there is tidings 518
19: 6 that i Absalom had lived, and all we had 3863
19: 7 I swear by the LORD, i thou go not forth, 3588
19:13 i thou be not captain of the host before me 518
1Ki 1:52 I he will shew himself a worthy man, 518
1:52 i wickedness shall be found in him, he shall 518
2: 4 saying, I thy children take heed to their way, 518
2:23 i Adonijah have not spoken this word 3588
3:14 i thou wilt walk in my ways, to keep my 518
6:12 i thou wilt walk in my statutes, and execute 518
8:31 I any man trespass against his neighbour, 834
8:35 i they pray towards this place, and NIH
8:37 I there be in the land famine, if there be 3588
8:37 i there be pestilence, blasting, mildew, 3588
8:37 mildew, locust, or i there be caterpillar; 3588
8:37 i their enemy besiege them in the land of 3588
8:44 I thy people go out to battle against their 3588
8:46 I they sin against thee, (for there is no man 3588
8:47 Yet i they shall bethink themselves in 2050.1
9: 4 i thou wilt walk before me, as David thy 518
9: 6 But i you shall at all turn from following me, 518
11:38 i thou wilt hearken unto all that I command 518

1Ki 12: 7 I thou wilt be a servant unto this people this 518
12:27 I this people go up to do sacrifice in 518
13: 8 I thou wilt give me half thine house, I will 518
16:31 as i it had been a light thing for him to 1886.2
18:21 i the LORD be God, follow him: but 518
18:21 i Baal, then follow him. And the people 518
19: 2 i I make not thy life as the life of one of 3588
20:10 i the dust of Samaria shall suffice for 518
20:39 i by any means he be missing, then shall thy 518
21: 2 or, i it seem good to thee, I will give thee 518
21: 6 or else, i it please thee, I will give thee 518
22:28 Micaiah said, I thou return at all in peace, 518
2Ki 1:10 I I be a man of God, then let fire come down 518
1:12 and said unto them, I I be a man of God, 518
2:10 nevertheless, i thou see me when I am taken 518
2:10 so unto thee; but i not, it shall not be so. 518
4:29 go thy way: i thou meet any man, 3588
4:29 and i any salute thee, answer him not again: 3588
5:13 i the prophet had bid thee do some great NIH
6:27 And he said, I the LORD do not help thee, NIH
6:31 i the head of Elisha the son of Shaphat shall 518
7: 2 i the LORD would make windows in NIH
7: 4 I we say, We will enter into the city, then 518
7: 4 i we sit still here, we die also. Now therefore 518
7: 4 i they save us alive, we shall live; and if they 518
7: 4 shall live; and i they kill us, we shall but die. 518
7: 9 i we tarry till the morning light, 2050.1
7:19 i the LORD should make windows in NIH
9:15 I it be your minds, then let none go forth nor 518
10: 6 I ye be mine, and if ye will hearken unto my 518
10: 6 and i ye will hearken unto my voice, NIH
10:15 I it be, give me thine hand. And he gave 2050.1
10:24 I any of the men whom I have brought into NIH
18:21 even upon Egypt, on which i a man lean, it NIH
18:22 i ye say unto me, We trust in the LORD 3588
18:23 i thou be able on thy part to set riders upon 518
20:19 Is it not good, i peace and truth be in my 518
21: 8 only i they will observe to do according to 518
1Ch 12:17 I ye be come peaceably unto me to help me, 518
12:17 i ye be come to betray me to mine enemies, 518
13: 2 I it seem good unto you, and that it be of 518
19:12 I the Syrians be too strong for me, then thou 518
19:12 i the children of Ammon be too strong for 518
22:13 i thou takest heed to fulfil the statutes and 518
28: 7 i he be constant to do my commandments 518
28: 9 i thou seek him, he will be found of thee; but 518
28: 9 i thou forsake him, he will cast thee off for 518
2Ch 6:22 I a man sin against his neighbour, and 518
6:24 i thy people Israel be put to the worse before 518
6:26 yet i they pray towards this place, NIH
6:28 I there be dearth in the land, if there be 3588
6:28 i there be pestilence, if there be blasting, or 3588
6:28 i there be blasting, or mildew, locusts, or NIH
6:28 i their enemies besiege them in the cities of 3588
6:32 out arm; i they come and pray in this house; NIH
6:34 I thy people go out to war against their 3588
6:36 I they sin against thee, (for there is no man 3588
6:37 Yet i they bethink themselves in the land 2050.1
6:38 I they return to thee with all their heart and NIH
7:13 I I shut up heaven that there be no rain, or 2005
7:13 i I command the locusts to devour the land, 2005
7:13 or i I send pestilence among my people; 518
7:14 I my people, which are called by my 2050.1
7:17 as for thee, i thou wilt walk before me, 518
7:19 i ye turn away, and forsake my statutes and 518
10: 7 I thou be kind to this people, and 518
15: 2 i ye seek him, he will be found of you; but 518
15: 2 but i ye forsake him, he will forsake you. 518
18:27 I thou certainly return in peace, then hath not 518
20: 9 I, when evil cometh upon us, as the sword, 518
25: 8 i thou wilt go, do it, be strong for the battle: 518
30: 9 For i ye turn again unto the LORD, 3588
30: 9 away his face from you, i ye return unto him. 518
Ezr 4:13 i this city be builded, and the walls set up 2006
4:16 i this city be builded again, and the walls 2006
5:17 Now therefore, i it seem good to the king, 2006
Ne 1: 8 saying, I ye transgress, I will scatter you NIH
1: 9 i ye turn unto me, and keep my NIH
2: 5 I it please the king, and if thy servant have 518
2: 5 i thy servant have found favour in thy sight, 518
2: 7 I said unto the king, I it please the king, 518
4: 3 Even that which they build, i a fox go up, 518
9:29 (which i a man do, he shall live in them;) 2050.1
10:31 i the people of the land bring ware or NIH
13:21 i ye do so again, I will lay hands on you. 518
Est 1:19 I it please the king, let there go a royal 518
3: 9 I it please the king, let it be written that they 518
4:14 For I thou altogether holdest thy peace at this 518
4:16 to the law: and i I perish, I perish. 834+3509.1
5: 4 I it seem good unto the king, let the king and 518
5: 8 I I have found favour in the sight of the king, 518
5: 8 i it please the king to grant my petition, and 518
6:13 I Mordecai be of the seed of the Jews, 518
7: 3 and said, I I have found favour in thy sight, 518
7: 3 in thy sight, O king, and i it please the king, 518
7: 4 i we had been sold for bondmen and 432
8: 5 I it please the king, and if I have found 518
8: 5 i I have found favour in his sight, and 518
9:13 said Esther, I it please the king, let it be 518
Job 4: 2 I we assay to commune with thee, wilt thou NIH
5: 1 i there be any that will answer thee; 1886.2
6:28 upon me; for it is evident unto you i I lie. 518
8: 4 I thy children have sinned against him, and 518
8: 5 I thou wouldest seek unto God betimes, and 518
8: 6 I thou wert pure and upright; surely now he 518
8:18 I he destroy him from his place, then it shall 518
9: 3 I he will contend with him, he cannot answer 518
9:13 I God will not withdraw his anger, NIH
9:16 I I had called, and he had answered me; 518
9:19 I I speak of strength, lo, he is strong: and 518
9:19 i of judgment, who shall set me a time to 518
9:20 I I justify myself, mine own mouth shall 518
9:20 i I say, I am perfect, it shall also prove me NIH
9:23 I the scourge slay suddenly, he will laugh at 518
9:24 judges thereof; i not, where, and who is he? 518
Job 9:27 I I say, I will forget my complaint, I will 518
9:29 I I be wicked, why then labour I in vain? NIH
9:30 I I wash myself with snow water, and 518
10:14 I I sin, then thou markest me, and thou wilt 518
10:15 I I be wicked, woe unto me; and if I be 518
10:15 i I be righteous, yet will I not lift up my NIH
11:10 I he cut off, and shut up, or gather together, 518
11:13 I thou prepare thine heart, and stretch out 518
11:14 I iniquity be in thine hand, put it far away, 518
13:10 reprove you, i ye do secretly accept persons. 518
13:19 for now, i I hold my tongue, I shall give up NIH
14: 7 i it be cut down, that it will sprout again, and 518
14:14 I a man die, shall he live again? all the days 518
16: 4 I also could speak as ye do: i your soul 3863
17:13 I I wait, the grave is mine house: I have 518
19: 5 I indeed ye will magnify yourselves against 518
21: 4 i it were so, why should not my spirit be 518
21:15 profit should we have, i we pray unto him? 3588
22:23 I thou return to the Almighty, thou shalt be 518
24:17 i one know them, they are in the terrors of 3588
24:25 i it be not so now, who will make me a liar, 518
27:14 I his children be multiplied, it is for 518
29:24 I I laughed on them, they believed it not; NIH
31: 5 I I have walked with vanity, or if my foot 518
31: 5 or i my foot hath hasted to deceit; NIH
31: 7 I my step hath turned out of the way, and 518
31: 7 and i any blot hath cleaved to my hands; NIH
31: 9 I mine heart have been deceived by a 518
31: 9 or i I have laid wait at my neighbour's door; NIH
31:13 I I did despise the cause of my manservant 518
31:16 I I have withheld the poor from their desire, 518
31:19 I I have seen any perish for want of clothing, 518
31:20 I his loins have not blessed me, and if he 518
31:20 i he were not warmed with the fleece of my NIH
31:21 I I have lift up my hand against 518
31:24 I I have made gold my hope, or have said to 518
31:25 I I rejoiced because my wealth was great, 518
31:26 I I beheld the sun when it shined, or 518
31:29 I I rejoiced at the destruction of him that 518
31:31 I the men of my tabernacle said not, O that 518
31:33 I I covered my transgressions as Adam, by 518
31:38 I my land cry against me, or that the furrows 518
31:39 I I have eaten the fruits thereof without 518
33: 5 I thou canst, answer me, set thy words in 518
33:23 I there be a messenger with him, 518
33:27 i any say, I have sinned, and perverted that NIH
33:32 I thou hast any thing to say, answer me: 518
33:33 I not, hearken unto me: hold thy peace, and 518
34:14 I he set his heart upon man, if he gather unto 518
34:14 If he set his heart upon man, i he gather NIH
34:16 I now thou hast understanding, hear this: 518
34:32 i I have done iniquity, I will do no more. 518
35: 3 shall I have, i I be cleansed from my sin? NIH
35: 6 I thou sinnest, what doest thou against him? 518
35: 6 or i thy transgressions be multiplied, NIH
35: 7 I thou be righteous, what givest thou him? or 518
36: 8 i they be bound in fetters, and be holden in 518
36:11 I they obey and serve him, they shall spend 518
36:12 i they obey not, they shall perish by 518
37:20 i a man speak, surely he shall be swallowed 518
38: 4 the earth? declare, i thou hast understanding. 518
38: 5 laid the measures thereof, i thou knowest? 3588
38: 8 as i it had issued out of the womb? NIH
38:18 of the earth? declare i thou knowest it all. 518
Ps 7: 3 O LORD my God, i I have done this; 518
7: 3 done this; i there be iniquity in my hands; 518
7: 4 I I have rewarded evil unto him that was at 518
7:12 I he turn not, he will whet his sword; he hath 518
11: 3 I the foundations be destroyed, what can 3588
14: 2 to see i there were any that did 1886.2
28: 1 lest, i thou be silent to me, I become like NIH
40: 5 i I would declare and speak of them, they NIH
41: 6 i he come to see me, he speaketh vanity: 518
44:20 I we have forgotten the name of our God, or 518
50:12 I I were hungry, I would not tell thee: for 518
53: 2 to see i there were any that did 1886.2
59:15 for meat, and grudge i they be not satisfied. 518
62:10 i riches increase, set not your heart upon 3588
66:18 I I regard iniquity in my heart, the Lord will 518
73:15 I I say, I will speak thus; behold, I should 518
81: 8 O Israel, i thou wilt hearken unto me; 518
89:30 I his children forsake my law, and walk not 518
89:31 I they break my statutes, and keep not my 518
90:10 i by reason of strength they be fourscore 518
95: 7 of his hand. To day i ye will hear his voice, 518
124: 1 I it had not been the LORD who was on 3884
124: 2 I it had not been the LORD who was on 3884
130: 3 I thou, LORD, shouldest mark iniquities, 518
132:12 I thy children will keep my covenant and 518
137: 5 I I forget thee, O Jerusalem, let my right 518
137: 6 I I do not remember thee, let my tongue 518
137: 6 i I prefer not Jerusalem above my chief joy. 518
139: 8 I I ascend up into heaven, thou art there: if I 518
139: 8 i I make my bed in hell, behold, thou art 2050.1
139: 9 I I take the wings of the morning, and NIH
139:11 I I say, Surely the darkness shall cover 2050.1
139:18 I I should count them, they are more in NIH
139:24 see i there be any wicked way in me, and 518
Pr 1:10 My son, i sinners entice thee, consent thou 518
1:11 I they say, Come with us, let us lay wait for 518
2: 1 i thou wilt receive my words, and hide my 518
2: 3 i thou criest after knowledge, and liftest up 518
2: 4 I thou seekest her as silver, and searchest for 518
3:30 without cause, i he have done thee no harm. 518
6: 1 My son, i thou be surety for thy friend, 518
6: 1 i thou hast stricken thy hand with a stranger, NIH
6:30 i he steal to satisfy his soul when he is 3588
6:31 i he be found, he shall restore sevenfold; NIH
9:12 I thou be wise, thou shalt be wise for thyself: 518
9:12 but i thou scornest, thou alone shalt bear it. NIH
16:31 i it be found in the way of righteousness. NIH
19:19 for i thou deliver him, yet thou must do it 518
22:18 For it is a pleasant thing i thou keep them 3588
22:27 I thou hast nothing to pay, why should he 518
23: 2 thy throat, i thou be a man given to appetite. 518
Pr 23:13 for i thou beatest him with the rod, he shall NIH
23:15 My son, i thine heart be wise, my heart shall 518
24:10 I thou faint in the day of adversity, NIH
24:11 I thou forbear to deliver them that are NIH
24:12 I thou sayest, Behold, we knew it not; 3588
25:21 I thine enemy be hungry, give him bread to 518
25:21 and i he be thirsty, give him water to drink: 518
29: 9 I a wise man contendeth with a foolish man, NIH
29:12 I a ruler hearken to lies, all his servants are NIH
30: 4 what is his son's name, i thou canst tell? 3588
30:32 I thou hast done foolishly in lifting up 518
30:32 or i thou hast thought evil, lay thine hand 518
Ecc 4:10 For i they fall, the one will lift up his fellow: 518
4:11 i two lie together, then they have heat: 518
4:12 i one prevail against him, two shall 518
5: 8 I thou seest the oppression of the poor, and 518
6: 3 I a man beget an hundred children, and 518
10: 4 I the spirit of the ruler rise up against thee, 518
10:10 I the iron be blunt, and he do not whet 518
11: 3 I the clouds be full of rain, they empty 518
11: 3 i the tree fall toward the south, or toward 518
11: 8 i a man live many years, and rejoice in them 518
SS 1: 8 I thou know not, O thou fairest among 518
5: 8 i ye find my beloved, that ye tell him, that I 518
7:12 let us see i the vine flourish, whether 518
8: 7 i a man would give all the substance of his 518
8: 9 I she be a wall, we will build upon her a 518
8: 9 i she be a door, we will inclose her with 518
Isa 1:19 I ye be willing and obedient, ye shall eat 518
1:20 i ye refuse and rebel, ye shall be devoured 518
5:30 i one look unto the land, behold darkness NIH
7: 9 I ye will not believe, surely ye shall not be 518
8:20 i they speak not according to this word, it is 518
10:15 as i the rod should shake itself against 3509.1
10:15 as i the staff should lift up itself, as if it NIH
10:15 as if the staff should lift up itself, as i it NIH
21:12 i ye will inquire, inquire ye: return, come. 518
36: 6 whereon i a man lean, it will go into his NIH
36: 7 i thou say to me, We trust in the LORD 3588
36: 8 i thou be able on thy part to set riders upon 518
47:12 i so be thou shalt be able to profit, if so 194
47:12 be able to profit, i so be thou mayest prevail. 194
51:13 as i he were ready to destroy? 834+3509.1
58: 9 Here I am. I thou take away from the midst 518
58:10 i thou draw out thy soul to the hungry, and NIH
58:13 I thou turn away thy foot from the sabbath, 518
59:10 the blind, and we grope as i we had no eyes: NIH
66: 3 He that killeth an ox is as i he slew a man; NIH
66: 3 a lamb, as i he cut off a dog's neck; NIH
66: 3 an oblation, as i he offered swine's blood; NIH
66: 3 that burneth incense, as i he blessed an idol. NIH
Jer 2:10 and see i there be such a thing. 2005
2:28 i they can save thee in the time of thy 518
3: 1 I a man put away his wife, and she go from 2005
4: 1 I thou wilt return, O Israel, saith 518
4: 1 i thou wilt put away thine abominations out 518
5: 1 the broad places thereof, i ye can find a man, 518
5: 1 i there be any that executeth judgment, 518
7: 5 For i you throughly amend your ways and 518
7: 5 i you throughly execute judgment between a 518
7: 6 I ye oppress not the stranger, the fatherless, NIH
12: 5 I thou hast run with the footmen, and 3588
12: 5 i in the land of peace, wherein thou NIH
12:16 i they will diligently learn the ways of my 518
12:17 i they will not obey, I will utterly pluck up 518
13:17 i ye will not hear it, my soul shall weep in 518
13:22 i thou say in thine heart, Wherefore come 3588
14:18 I I go forth into the field, then behold 518
14:18 i I enter into the city, then behold them that 518
15: 2 it shall come to pass, i they say unto thee, 3588
15:19 I thou return, then will I bring thee again, 518
15:19 i thou take forth the precious from the vile, 518
17:24 i ye diligently hearken unto me, saith 518
17:27 i you will not hearken unto me to hallow 518
18: 8 I that nation, against whom I have NIH
18:10 I it do evil in my sight, that it obey not my NIH
21: 2 i so be that the LORD will deal with us 194
22: 4 For i ye do this thing indeed, then shall there 518
22: 5 i ye will not hear these words, I swear by 518
23:22 i they had stood in my counsel, and 518
25:28 i they refuse to take the cup at thine hand to 3588
26: 3 I so be they will hearken, and turn every 194
26: 4 I ye will not hearken to me, to walk in my 518
26:15 ye for certain, that i ye put me to death, 518
27:18 i they be prophets, and if the word of 518
27:18 and i the word of the LORD be with them, 518
31:36 I those ordinances depart from before me, 518
31:37 I heaven above can be measured, and 518
33:20 I you can break my covenant of the day, and 518
33:25 I my covenant be not with day and night, 518
33:25 i I have not appointed the ordinances of NIH
38:15 said unto Zedekiah, I I declare it unto thee, 3588
38:15 i I give thee counsel, wilt thou not hearken 3588
38:17 I thou wilt assuredly go forth unto the king 518
38:18 i thou wilt not go forth to the king of 518
38:21 i thou refuse to go forth, this is the word that 518
38:25 i the princes hear that I have talked with 3588
40: 4 I it seem good unto thee to come with me 518
40: 4 i it seem ill unto thee to come with me into 518
42: 5 i we do not even according to all things for 518
42:10 I ye will still abide in this land, then will I 518
42:13 i ye say, We will not dwell in this land, 518
42:15 I ye wholly set your faces to enter into 518
49: 9 I grapegatherers come to thee, would they 518
49: 9 i thieves by night, they will destroy till they 518
51: 8 balm for her pain, i so be she may be healed. 194
La 1:12 see i there be any sorrow like unto my 518
2: 6 away his tabernacle, as i it were of a garden: NIH
3:29 mouth in the dust; i so be there may be hope. 194
Eze 3:19 Yet i thou warn the wicked, and he turn not 3588
3:21 Nevertheless i thou warn the righteous 3588
10:10 as i a wheel had been in the midst of a NIH
14: 9 i the prophet be deceived when he hath 3588
14:15 I I cause noisome beasts to pass through 3863
14:17 Or i I bring a sword upon that land, and say, NIH

Eze 14:19 Or i I send a pestilence into that land, NIH
16:47 as i that were a very little thing, thou wast NIH
18: 5 i a man be just, and do that which is lawful 3588
18:10 I he beget a son that is a robber, 2050.1
18:14 Now lo, i he beget a son, that seeth all his NIH
18:21 i the wicked will turn from all his sins that 3588
20:11 which i a man do, he shall even live in NIH
20:13 which i a man do, he shall even live in NIH
20:21 which i a man do, he shall even live in NIH
20:39 hereafter also, i ye will not hearken unto me: 518
21:13 and what i the sword contemn even the rod? 518
33: 2 i the people of the land take a man of their NIH
33: 3 I when he seeth the sword come upon NIH
33: 4 i the sword come, and take him away, NIH
33: 6 i the watchman see the sword come, and 3588
33: 6 i the sword come, and take any person from NIH
33: 8 i thou dost not speak to warn the wicked NIH
33: 9 i thou warn the wicked of his way to turn 3588
33: 9 i he do not turn from his way, he shall die in NIH
33:10 I our transgressions and our sins be upon 3588
33:13 i he trust to his own righteousness, and NIH
33:14 i he turn from his sin, and do that which is NIH
33:15 I the wicked restore the pledge, give again NIH
33:19 i the wicked turn from his wickedness, and 871.1
43:11 i they be ashamed of all that they have done, 518
46:16 I the prince give a gift unto any of his sons, 3588
46:17 I he give a gift of his inheritance to one of 3588
Da 2: 5 i ye will not make known unto me 2006
2: 6 i ye shew the dream, and the interpretation 2006
2: 9 i ye will not make known unto me 2006
3:15 Now i ye be ready that at what time ye hear 2006
3:15 well: but i ye worship not, ye shall be cast 2006
3:17 I it be so, our God whom we serve is able 2006
3:18 i not, be it known unto thee, O king, 2006
4:27 i it may be a lengthening of thy tranquillity. 2006
5:16 now i thou canst read the writing, and 2006
Hos 6: 3 i we follow on to know the LORD: NIH
8: 7 **i so be** it yield, the strangers shall swallow it 194
Joel 2:14 Who knoweth i he will return and repent, NIH
3: 4 i ye recompense me, swiftly and 518
Am 3: 4 cry out of his den, i he have taken nothing? 518
5:19 **As i** a man did flee from a lion, and 834+3509.1
6: 9 i there remain ten men in one house, 518
Ob 1: 5 I thieves came to thee, if robbers by night, 518
1: 5 i robbers by night, (how art thou cut off!) 518
1: 5 i the grape-gatherers came to thee, would 518
Jnh 1: 6 **i so be that** God will think upon us, that we 194
3: 9 Who can tell i God will turn and repent, and NIH
Mic 2:11 I a man walking in the spirit and 3863
5: 8 who, i he go through, both treadeth down, 518
Na 3:12 i they be shaken, they shall even fall into 518
Hag 2:12 I one bear holy flesh in the skirt of his 2005
2:13 I one that is unclean by a dead body touch 518
Zec 3: 7 I thou wilt walk in my ways, and if thou wilt 518
3: 7 i thou wilt keep my charge, then thou shalt 518
6:15 i ye will diligently obey the voice of 518
8: 6 I it be marvellous in the eyes of 3588
11:12 I ye think good, give me my price; 518
11:12 give me my price; and i not, forbear. 518
14:18 i the family of Egypt go not up, and 518
Mal 1: 6 i then I be a father, where is mine honour? 518
1: 6 i I be a master, where is my fear? saith 518
1: 8 i ye offer the blind for sacrifice, is it not 3588
1: 8 i ye offer the lame and sick, is it not evil? 3588
2: 2 I ye will not hear, and if ye will not lay it to 518
2: 2 will not hear, and i ye will not lay it to heart, 518
3:10 i I will not open you the windows of heaven, 518
Mt 4: 3 to him, he said, I thou be the Son of God, 1487
4: 6 I thou be the Son of God, cast thyself 1487
4: 9 i thou wilt fall down and worship me. 1437
5:13 but i the salt have lost his savour, 1437
5:23 Therefore i thou bring thy gift to the altar, 1437
5:29 And i thy right eye offend thee, pluck it 1487
5:30 And i thy right hand offend thee, cut it off, 1487
5:40 And i any man will sue thee at the law, and NIG
5:46 For i ye love them which love you, 1437
5:47 And i ye salute your brethren only, what do 1437
6:14 For i ye forgive men their trespasses, 1437
6:15 But i ye forgive not men their trespasses, 1437
6:22 i therefore thine eye be single, thy whole 1437
6:23 But i thine eye be evil, thy whole body 1437
6:23 I therefore the light that is in thee be 1487
6:30 i God so clothe the grass of the field, 1487
7: 9 whom i his son ask bread, will he give him 1437
7:10 Or i he ask a fish, will he give him a 1437
7:11 I ye then, being evil, know how to give 1487
8: 2 worshipped him, saying, Lord, i thou wilt, 1437
8:31 besought him, saying, I thou cast us out, 1487
9:21 I I may but touch his garment, I shall be 1437
10:13 And i the house be worthy, let your peace 1437
10:13 but i it be **not** worthy, let your peace return 3362
10:25 I they have called the master of the house 1487
11:14 And i ye will receive it, this is Elias, 1487
11:21 for i the mighty works which were done in 1487
11:23 for i the mighty works, which have been 1487
12: 7 But i ye had known what this meaneth, 1487
12:11 and i it fall into a pit on the sabbath day, 1437
12:26 And i Satan cast out Satan, he is divided 1487
12:27 And i I by Beelzebub cast out devils, 1487
12:28 But i I cast out devils by the Spirit of God, 1487
14:28 answered him and said, Lord, i it be thou, 1487
15:14 And i the blind lead the blind, both shall 1437
16:24 **I any** man will come after me, let him deny 1536
16:26 i he shall gain the whole world, and lose his 1437
17: 4 i thou wilt, let us make here three 1487
17:20 I ye have faith as a grain of mustard seed, 1437
18: 8 Wherefore i thy hand or thy foot offend 1487
18: 9 And i thine eye offend thee, pluck it out, 1487
18:12 i a man have an hundred sheep, and one of 1437
18:13 And i so be that he find it, verily I say unto 1437
18:15 Moreover i thy brother shall trespass 1437
18:15 i he shall hear thee, thou hast gained thy 1437
18:16 But i he will not hear thee, then take with 1437
18:17 And i he shall neglect to hear them, tell it 1437
18:17 but i he neglect to hear the church, let him 1437
Mt 18:19 That i two of you shall agree on earth as 1437
18:35 i ye from your hearts forgive not every one 1437
19:10 I the case of the man be so with his wife, 1487
19:17 but i thou wilt enter into life, keep 1487
19:21 I thou wilt be perfect, go and sell that thou 1487
21: 3 And i any man say ought unto you, ye shall 1437
21:21 unto you, I ye have faith, and doubt not, 1437
21:21 but **also i** ye shall say unto this mountain, 2579
21:24 will ask you one thing, which i ye tell me, 1437
21:25 saying, I we shall say, From heaven; 1437
21:26 But i we shall say, Of men; we fear 1437
22:24 Saying, Master, Moses said, I a man die, 1437
22:45 I David then call him Lord, how is he his 1487
23:30 I we had been in the days of our fathers, 1487
24:23 Then i any man shall say unto you, Lo, 1437
24:24 insomuch that, i it were possible, they shall 1487
24:26 Wherefore i they shall say unto you, 1437
24:43 that i the goodman of the house had known 1487
24:48 and i that evil servant shall say in his heart, 1437
26:24 it had been good for that man i he had not 1487
26:39 saying, O my Father, i it be possible, 1487
26:42 i this cup may not pass away from me, 1487
27:40 I thou be the Son of God, come down from 1487
27:42 I he be the King of Israel, let him now 1487
27:43 him deliver him now, i he will have him: 1487
28:14 And i this come to the governor's ears, 1437
Mk 1:40 to him, and saying unto him, I thou wilt, 1437
3:24 And i a kingdom be divided against itself, 1437
3:25 And i a house be divided against itself, 1437
3:26 And i Satan rise up against himself, and 1487
4:23 **I any** man have ears to hear, let him hear. 1536
4:26 as i a man should cast seed into the ground, 1437
5:28 For she said, I I may touch **but** his clothes, 2579
6:56 him that they might touch i it were **but** 2579
7:11 I a man shall say to his father or mother, 1437
7:16 **I any** man have ears to hear, let him hear. 1536
8: 3 And i I send them away fasting to their own 1437
8:23 upon him, he asked him i he saw ought. 1487
8:36 i he shall gain the whole world, and lose his 1437
9:22 i thou canst do any thing, have compassion 1487
9:23 Jesus said unto him, I thou canst believe, 1487
9:35 unto them, **I any** man desire to be first, 1536
9:43 And i thy hand offend thee, cut it off: it is 1437
9:45 And i thy foot offend thee, cut it off: it is 1437
9:47 And i thine eye offend thee, pluck it out: 1437
9:50 but i the salt have lost his saltness, 1437
10:12 And i a woman shall put away her husband, 1437
11: 3 And i any man say unto you, Why do ye 1437
11:13 i haply he might find any thing thereon: 1487
11:25 forgive, i ye have ought against any: 1487
11:26 But i ye do not forgive, neither will your 1487
11:31 saying, I we shall say, From heaven; 1437
11:32 But i we shall say, Of men; they feared 1437
12:19 I a man's brother die, and leave his wife 1437
13:21 And then i any man shall say to you, Lo, 1437
13:22 and wonders, to seduce, i it were possible, 1487
14:21 good were it for that man i he had never 1487
14:31 I I should die with thee, I will not deny thee 1437
14:35 and prayed that, i it were possible, 1487
15:44 And Pilate marvelled i he were already 1487
16:18 **and i** they drink any deadly thing, it shall 2579
Lk 4: 3 said unto him, I thou be the Son of God, 1487
4: 7 I thou therefore wilt worship me, all shall 1437
4: 9 said unto him, I thou be the Son of God, 1487
5:12 and besought him, saying, Lord, i thou wilt, 1437
5:36 **i otherwise**, then both the new maketh a 1490
6:32 For i ye love them which love you, 1487
6:33 And i ye do good to them which do good to 1437
6:34 And i ye lend to them of whom ye hope to 1437
7:39 saying, This man, i he were a prophet, 1487
9:23 I any man will come after me, let him deny 1487
9:25 i he gain the whole world, and lose himself, NIG
10: 6 And i the son of peace be there, your peace 1437
10: 6 rest upon it: **i not**, it shall turn to you again. 1490
10:13 for i the mighty works had been done in 1487
11:11 I a son shall ask bread of any of you that is NIG
11:11 or i he ask a fish, will he for a fish give him 1487
11:12 Or i he shall ask an egg, will he offer him a 1437
11:13 I ye then, being evil, know how to give 1487
11:18 I Satan also be divided against himself, 1487
11:19 And i I by Beelzebub cast out devils, 1487
11:20 But i I with the finger of God cast out 1487
11:36 I thy whole body therefore be full of light, 1487
12:26 I ye then be not able to do that thing which 1487
12:28 I then God so clothe the grass, which is to 1487
12:38 And i he shall come in the second watch, or 1437
12:39 that i the goodman of the house had known 1487
12:45 But and i that servant say in his heart, 1437
12:49 and what will I, i it be already kindled? 1487
13: 9 **And i** it bear fruit, well: and if not, then 2579
13: 9 well: **and i not**, then after that thou shalt 1490
14:26 **I any** man come to me, and hate not his 1536
14:34 but i the salt have lost his savour, 1437
15: 4 i he lose one of them, doth not leave 2532
15: 8 i she lose one piece, doth not light a candle, 1437
16:11 I therefore ye have not been faithful in 1487
16:12 And i ye have not been faithful in that 1487
16:30 but i one went unto them from the dead, 1437
16:31 I they hear not Moses and the prophets, 1487
17: 3 I thy brother trespass against thee, 1437
17: 3 rebuke him; and i he repent, forgive him. 1437
17: 4 And i he trespass against thee seven times 1437
17: 6 I ye had faith as a grain of mustard seed, 1487
19: 8 i I have taken any thing from any man by 1487
19:31 And i any man ask you, Why do ye loose 1437
19:40 you that, i these should hold their peace, 1437
19:42 Saying, I thou hadst known, even thou, 1487
20: 5 saying, I we shall say, From heaven; 1437
20: 6 But and i we say, Of men; all the people 1437
20:28 I any man's brother die, having a wife, and 1437
22:42 Saying, Father, i thou be willing, 1487
22:67 unto them, I I tell you, you will not believe: 1437
22:68 And i I also ask you, you will not answer 1437
23:31 For i they do these things in a green tree, 1487
23:35 i he be Christ, the chosen of God. 1487
Lk 23:37 And saying, I thou be the King of the Jews, 1487
23:39 saying, I thou be Christ, save thyself and 1487
Jn 1:25 i thou be not that Christ, nor Elias, 1487
3:12 I I have told you earthly things, and 1487
3:12 ye believe, i I tell you of heavenly things? 1437
4:10 I thou knewest the gift of God, and who it 1487
5:31 I I bear witness of myself, my witness is 1437
5:43 i another shall come in his own name, 1437
5:47 But i ye believe not his writings, how shall 1487
6:51 i any man eat of this bread, he shall live for 1437
6:62 i ye shall see the Son of man ascend up 1437
7: 4 I thou do these things, shew thyself to 1487
7:17 I any man will do his will, he shall know of 1437
7:23 I a man on the sabbath day receive 1487
7:37 and cried, saying, I any man thirst, 1437
8:16 And yet i I judge, my judgment is true: for I 1437
8:19 i ye had known me, ye should have known 1487
8:24 for i ye believe not that I am he, ye shall 1437
8:31 I ye continue in my word, then are ye my 1437
8:36 I the Son therefore shall make you free, 1437
8:39 unto them, I ye were Abraham's children, 1487
8:42 I God were your Father, ye would love me: 1487
8:46 And i I say the truth, why do ye not believe 1487
8:51 I say unto you, I a man keep my saying, 1437
8:52 and thou sayest, I a man keep my saying, 1437
8:54 Jesus answered, I I honour myself, 1437
8:55 **and i** I should say, I know him not, I shall 2579
9:22 that i any man did confess that he was 1437
9:31 but i any man be a worshipper of God, and 1437
9:33 I this man were not of God, he could do 1487
9:41 Jesus said unto them, I ye were blind, 1487
10: 9 by me i any man enter in, he shall be saved, 1437
10:24 I thou be the Christ, tell us plainly. 1487
10:35 I he called them gods, unto whom the word 1487
10:37 I I do not the works of my Father, 1487
10:38 But i I do, though ye believe not me, 1487
11: 9 I any man walk in the day, he stumbleth 1437
11:10 But i a man walk in the night, he stumbleth, 1437
11:12 Lord, i he sleep, he shall do well. 1487
11:21 Lord, i thou hadst been here, my brother 1487
11:32 unto him, Lord, i thou hadst been here, 1487
11:40 not unto thee, that, i thou wouldest believe, 1437
11:48 I we let him thus alone, all men will 1437
11:57 that, i any man knew where he were, 1437
12:24 but i it die, it bringeth forth much fruit. 1437
12:26 I any man serve me, let him follow me; and 1437
12:26 i any man serve me, him will my Father 1437
12:32 And I, i I be lifted up from the earth, 1437
12:47 And i any man hear my words, and 1437
13: 8 Jesus answered him, I I wash thee not, 1437
13:14 I I then, your Lord and Master, 1487
13:17 I ye know these things, happy are ye if ye 1487
13:17 If ye know these things, happy are ye i ye 1437
13:32 I God be glorified in him, God shall also 1487
13:35 my disciples, i ye have love one to another. 1437
14: 2 i it were **not** so, I would have told you. I go 1490
14: 3 And i I go and prepare a place for you, 1437
14: 7 I ye had known me, ye should have known 1487
14:14 I ye shall ask any thing in my name, I will 1437
14:15 I ye love me, keep my commandments. 1437
14:23 and said unto him, I a man love me, 1437
14:28 I ye loved me, ye would rejoice, because 1487
15: 6 I a man abide not in me, he is cast forth as 1437
15: 7 I ye abide in me, and my words abide in 1437
15:10 I ye keep my commandments, ye shall 1437
15:14 i ye do whatsoever I command you. 1437
15:18 I the world hate you, ye know that it hated 1487
15:19 I ye were of the world, the world would 1487
15:20 I they have persecuted me, they will also 1487
15:20 i they have kept my saying, they will keep 1487
15:22 I I had not come and spoken unto them, 1487
15:24 I I had not done among them the works 1487
16: 7 for i I go not away, the Comforter will not 1437
16: 7 but i I depart, I will send him unto you. 1437
18: 8 I have told you that I am he: i therefore 1487
18:23 Jesus answered him, I I have spoken evil, 1487
18:23 the evil: but i well, why smitest thou me? 1487
18:30 said unto him, I he were not a malefactor, 1487
18:36 i my kingdom were of this world, 1487
19:12 cried out, saying, I thou let this man go, 1437
20:15 i thou have borne him hence, tell me where 1487
21:22 I I will that he tarry till I come, what is that 1437
21:23 but, I I will that he tarry till I come, what is 1437
21:25 i they should be written every one, 1437
Ac 4: 9 I we this day be examined of the good deed 1487
5:38 for i this counsel or this work be of men, 1437
5:39 But i it be of God, ye cannot overthrow it; 1487
8:22 i perhaps the thought of thine heart may be 1487
8:37 I thou believest with all thine heart, 1437
9: 2 that i he found any of this way, 1437
13:15 i ye have any word of exhortation for 1487
15:29 from which i ye keep yourselves, ye shall NIG
16:15 I ye have judged me to be faithful to 1487
17:27 i haply they might feel after him, and 1487
18:14 I it were a matter of wrong or 1487
18:15 But i it be a question of words and names, 1487
18:21 but I will return again unto you, i God will. NIG
19:38 Wherefore i Demetrius, and the craftsmen 1487
19:39 But i ye inquire any thing concerning other 1487
20:16 for he hasted, i it were possible for him, 1487
23: 9 but i a spirit or an angel hath spoken to 1487
24:19 and object, i they had **ought** against me. 1536
24:20 i they have found **any** evil doing in me, 1536
25: 5 this man, i there be **any** wickedness in him. 1536
25:11 For i I be an offender, or have committed 1487
25:11 i there be none of these things whereof 1487
26: 5 from the beginning, i they would testify, 1437
26:32 at liberty, i he had not appealed unto Cesar. 1487
27:12 **i by any means** they might attain to 1513
27:39 i it were possible, to thrust in the ship. 1487
Ro 1:10 **i by any means** now at length I might have 1513
2:25 verily profiteth, i thou keep the law: 1437
2:25 but i thou be a breaker of the law, 1437
2:26 Therefore i the uncircumcision keep 1437
2:27 i it fulfil the law, judge thee, who by NIG

Ro 3: 3 For what i some did not believe? shall their 1487
3: 5 But i our unrighteousness commend 1487
3: 7 For i the truth of God hath more abounded 1487
4: 2 For i Abraham were justified by works, 1487
4:14 For i they which are of the law be heirs, 1487
4:24 i we believe on him that raised up Jesus our NIG
5:10 For i, when we were enemies, we were 1487
5:15 For i through the offence of one many be 1487
5:17 For i by one man's offence death reigned 1487
6: 5 For i we have been planted together in 1487
6: 8 Now i we be dead with Christ, we believe 1487
7: 2 but i the husband be dead, she is loosed 1437
7: 3 So then i, while her husband liveth, she be 1437
7: 3 but i her husband be dead, she is free from 1437
7:16 I then I do that which I would not, 1487
7:20 Now i I do that I would not, it is no more I 1487
8: 9 i so be that the Spirit of God dwell in you. 1512
8: 9 Now i any man have not the Spirit of 1536
8:10 And i Christ be in you, the body is dead 1487
8:11 But i the Spirit of him that raised up Jesus 1487
8:13 For i ye live after the flesh, ye shall die: but 1487
8:13 i ye through the Spirit do mortify the deeds 1487
8:17 And i children, then heirs; heirs of God, 1487
8:17 i so be that we suffer with him, that we 1512
8:25 But i we hope for that we see not, then 1487
8:31 then say to these things? I God be for us, 1487
9:22 What i God, willing to shew his wrath, and 1487
10: 9 That i thou shalt confess with thy mouth 1437
11: 6 And i by grace, then is it no more of works: 1487
11: 6 But i it be of works, then is it no more 1487
11:12 Now i the fall of them be the riches of 1487
11:14 I by any means I may provoke to 1513
11:15 For i the casting away of them be 1487
11:16 For i the firstfruit be holy, the lump is also 1487
11:16 lump is also holy: and i the root be holy, 1487
11:17 And i some of the branches be broken off, 1487
11:18 but i thou boast, thou bearest not the root, 1487
11:21 For i God spared not the natural branches, 1487
11:22 goodness, i thou continue in his goodness: 1437
11:23 they also, i they bide not still in unbelief, 1437
11:24 For i thou wert cut out of the olive tree 1487
12:18 I it be possible, as much as lieth in you, 1487
12:20 Therefore i thine enemy hunger, feed him; 1437
12:20 feed him; i he thirst, give him drink: 1437
13: 4 But i thou do that which is evil, be afraid; 1437
13: 9 and i there be any other commandment, 1536
14:15 But i thy brother be grieved with thy meat, 1487
14:23 And he that doubteth is damned i he eat, 1437
15:24 i first I be somewhat filled with your 1437
15:27 For i the Gentiles have been made 1487
1Co 3:12 Now i any man build upon this foundation 1536
3:14 I any man's work abide which he hath built 1536
3:15 I any man's work shall be burnt, he shall 1536
3:17 I any man defile the temple of God, 1536
3:18 I any man among you seemeth to be wise 1536
4: 7 now i thou didst receive it, why dost thou 1487
4: 7 thou glory, as i thou hadst not received it? NIG
4:19 you shortly, i the Lord will, and will know, 1437
5:11 i any man that is called a brother be a 1437
6: 2 and i the world shall be judged by you, 1487
6: 4 I then ye have judgments of things 1437
7: 8 It is good for them i they abide even as I. 1437
7: 9 But i they cannot contain, let them marry: 1487
7:11 But and i she depart, let her remain 1437
7:12 I any brother hath a wife that believeth not, 1536
7:13 and i he be pleased to dwell with her, let her NIG
7:15 But i the unbelieving depart, let him depart. 1487
7:21 but i thou mayest be made free, use it 1487
7:28 But and i thou marry, thou hast not sinned; 1437
7:28 and i a virgin marry, she hath not sinned. 1437
7:36 But i any man think that he behaveth 1487
7:36 his virgin, i she pass the flower of her age, 1437
7:39 but i her husband be dead, she is at liberty 1437
7:40 But she is happier i she so abide, after my 1437
8: 2 And i any man think that he knoweth any 1487
8: 3 But i any man love God, the same is known 1487
8: 8 for neither, i we eat, are we the better; 1437
8: 8 neither, i we eat not, are we the worse. 1437
8:10 For i any man see thee which hast 1437
8:13 i meat make my brother to offend, 1487
9: 2 I I be not an apostle unto others, 1487
9:11 I we have sown unto you spiritual things, 1487
9:11 thing i we shall reap your carnal things? 1487
9:12 I others be partakers of this power over 1487
9:16 woe is unto me, i I preach not the gospel! 1437
9:17 For i I do this thing willingly, I have a 1487
9:17 but i against my will, a dispensation of 1487
10:27 I any of them that believe not bid you to a 1487
10:28 But i any man say unto you, This is offered 1437
10:30 For i I by grace be a partaker, why am I 1487
11: 5 even all one as i she 846+1520+2532+3588
11: 6 For i the woman be not covered, let her 1487
11: 6 i it be a shame for a woman to be shorn or NIG
11:14 that, i a man have long hair, it is a shame 1437
11:15 But i a woman have long hair, it is a glory 1437
11:16 But i any man seem to be contentious, 1487
11:31 For i we would judge ourselves, we should 1487
11:34 And i any man hunger, let him eat at home; 1487
12:15 I the foot shall say, Because I am not 1437
12:16 And i the ear shall say, Because I am not 1437
12:17 I the whole body were an eye, where were 1487
12:17 I the whole were hearing, where were 1487
12:19 And i they were all one member, 1487
14: 6 i I come unto you speaking with tongues, 1437
14: 8 For i the trumpet give an uncertain sound, 1437
14:11 Therefore i I know not the meaning of 1437
14:14 For i I pray in an unknown tongue, 1437
14:23 I therefore the whole church be come 1437
14:24 But i all prophesy, and there come in one 1437
14:27 I any man speak in an unknown tongue, 1535
14:28 But i there be no interpreter, let him keep 1437
14:30 I any thing be revealed to another that 1437
14:35 And i they will learn any thing, let them 1487
14:37 I any man think himself to be a prophet, or 1536
14:38 But i any man be ignorant, let him be 1536

1Co 15: 2 i ye keep in memory what I preached unto 1487
15:12 Now i Christ be preached that he rose from 1487
15:13 But i there be no resurrection of the dead, 1487
15:14 And i Christ be not risen, then is our 1487
15:15 not up, i so be that the dead rise not. 686+1512
15:16 For i the dead rise not, then is not Christ 1487
15:17 And i Christ be not raised, your faith is 1487
15:19 I in this life only we have hope in Christ, 1487
15:29 for the dead, i the dead rise not at all? 1487
15:32 I after the manner of men I have fought 1487
15:32 what advantageth it me, i the dead rise not? 1487
16: 4 And i it be meet that I go also, they shall go 1437
16: 7 to tarry a while with you, i the Lord permit. 1437
16:10 Now i Timotheus come, see that he may be 1437
16:22 I any man love not the Lord Jesus Christ, 1536
2Co 2: 2 For i I make you sorry, who is he then 1487
2: 5 But i any have caused grief, he hath not 1487
2:10 for i I forgave any thing, to whom I 1536
3: 7 But i the ministration of death, written and 1487
3: 9 For i the ministration of condemnation be 1487
3:11 For i that which is done away was glorious, 1487
4: 3 But i our gospel be hid, it is hid to them 1487
5: 1 For we know that i our earthly house of this 1437
5: 3 I so be that being clothed we shall not be 1489
5:14 that i one died for all, then were all dead: 1487
5:17 Therefore i any man be in Christ, he is a 1536
7:14 For i I have boasted any thing to him of 1536
8:12 For i there be first a willing mind, it is 1487
9: 4 Lest haply i they of Macedonia come with 1437
10: 2 which think of us as i we walked according NIG
10: 7 I any man trust to himself that he is 1536
10: 9 That I may not seem as i I would terrify you 302
11: 4 For i he that cometh preacheth another 1487
11: 4 or i ye receive another spirit, which ye have NIG
11:15 i his ministers also be transformed as 1499
11:16 i otherwise, yet as a fool receive me, that I 1490
11:20 ye suffer, i a man bring you into bondage, 1536
11:20 i a man devour you, if a man take of you, if 1536
11:20 if a man devour you, i a man take of you, if 1536
11:20 if a man take of you, i a man exalt himself, 1536
11:20 i a man smite you on the face. 1536
11:30 I I must needs glory, I will glory of 1487
13: 2 foretell you, as i I were present the second 5613
13: 2 and to all other, that, i I come again, I will 1437
Gal 1: 9 I any man preach any other gospel unto 1536
1:10 for i I yet pleased men, I should not be 1487
2:14 Peter before them all, I thou, being a Jew, 1487
2:17 But i, while we seek to be justified by 1487
2:18 For i I build again the things which I 1487
2:21 for i righteousness come by the law, then 1487
3: 4 so many things in vain? i it be yet in vain. 1489
3:15 but a man's covenant, yet i it be confirmed, NIG
3:18 For i the inheritance be of the law, it is no 1487
3:21 for i there had been a law given which 1487
3:29 And i ye be Christ's, then are ye 1487
4: 7 and i a son, then an heir of God through 1487
4:15 bear you record, that i it had been possible, 1487
5: 2 Paul say unto you, that i ye be circumcised, 1437
5:11 And I, brethren, i I yet preach circumcision, 1487
5:15 But i ye bite and devour one another, 1487
5:18 But i ye be led of the Spirit, ye are not 1487
5:25 I we live in the Spirit, let us also walk in 1487
6: 1 Brethren, i a man be overtaken in a fault, 1437
6: 3 For i a man think himself to be something, 1487
6: 9 in due season we shall reap, i we faint not. NIG
Eph 3: 2 I ye have heard of the dispensation of 1489
4:21 I so be that ye have heard him, and 1489
Php 1:22 But i I live in the flesh, this is the fruit of 1487
2: 1 I there be therefore any consolation in 1536
2: 1 in Christ, i any comfort of love, 1536
2: 1 i any fellowship of the Spirit, if any bowels 1536
2: 1 of the Spirit, i any bowels and mercies, 1536
2:17 and i I be offered upon the sacrifice and 1499
3: 4 I any other man thinketh that he hath 1536
3:11 I by any means I might attain unto 1513
3:12 I follow after, i that I may apprehend that 1499
3:15 and i in any thing ye be otherwise minded, 1536
4: 8 i there be any virtue, and if there be any 1536
4: 8 be any virtue, and i there be any praise, 1536
Col 1:23 I ye continue in the faith grounded and 1489
2:20 Wherefore i ye be dead with Christ from 1487
3: 1 I ye then be risen with Christ, seek those 1487
3:13 i any man have a quarrel against any: 1437
4:10 i he come unto you, receive him;) 1437
1Th 3: 8 For now we live, i ye stand fast in the Lord. 1437
4:14 For i we believe that Jesus died and 1487
2Th 3:10 that i any would not work, neither should 1536
3:14 And i any man obey not our word by this 1487
1Ti 1: 8 that the law is good, i a man use it lawfully; 1437
1:10 i there be any other thing that is contrary to 1536
2:15 i they continue in faith and charity and 1437
3: 1 I a man desire the office of a bishop, 1536
3: 5 (For i a man know not how to rule his own 1487
3:15 But i I tarry long, that thou mayest know 1437
4: 4 i it be received with thanksgiving: NIG
4: 6 I thou put the brethren in remembrance of NIG
5: 4 But i any widow have children or nephews, 1487
5: 8 But i any provide not for his own, and 1487
5:10 i she have brought up children, if she have 1487
5:10 up children, i she have lodged strangers, 1487
5:10 i she have washed the saints' feet, 1487
5:10 i she have relieved the afflicted, 1487
5:10 i she have diligently followed every good 1487
5:16 I any man or woman that believeth have 1536
6: 3 I any man teach otherwise, and consent not 1536
2Ti 2: 5 And i a man also strive for masteries, yet is 1437
2:11 For i we be dead with him, we shall also 1487
2:12 I we suffer, we shall also reign with him: if 1487
2:12 we shall also reign with him: i we deny 1487
2:13 I we believe not, yet he abideth faithful: 1487
2:21 I a man therefore purge himself from these, 1437
2:25 i God peradventure will give them 3379
Tit 1: 6 I any be blameless, the husband of one 1487
Phm 1:17 I thou count me therefore a partner, 1487
1:18 I he hath wronged thee, or oweth thee 1487

Heb 2: 2 For i the word spoken by angels was 1487
2: 3 we escape, i we neglect so great salvation; NIG
3: 6 i we hold fast the confidence and 1437+4007
3: 7 Ghost saith, To day i ye will hear his voice, 1437
3:14 i we hold the beginning of our 1437+4007
3:15 it is said, To day i ye will hear his voice, 1437
4: 3 in my wrath, i they shall enter into my rest: 1487
4: 5 place again, I they shall enter into my rest. 1487
4: 7 as it is said, To day i ye will hear his voice, 1437
4: 8 For i Jesus had given them rest, then 1487
6: 3 And this will we do, i God permit. 1437+4007
6: 6 I they shall fall away, to renew them again NIG
7:11 I therefore perfection were by the Levitical 1487
8: 4 For i he were on earth, he should not be a 1487
8: 7 For i that first covenant had been faultless, 1487
9:13 For i the blood of bulls and of goats, and 1487
10:26 For i we sin wilfully after that we have NIG
10:38 but i any man draw back, my soul shall 1437
11:15 i they had been mindful of that country 1487
12: 7 I ye endure chastening, God dealeth with 1487
12: 8 But i ye be without chastisement, 1487
12:20 And i so much as a beast touch 2579
12:25 for i they escaped not who refused him that 1487
12:25 much more shall not we escape, i we turn NIG
13:23 with whom, i he come shortly, I will see 1437
Jas 1: 5 I any of you lack wisdom, let him ask of 1487
1:23 For i any be a hearer of the word, and not a 1536
1:26 I any man among you seem to be religious, 1536
2: 2 For i there come unto your assembly a man 1437
2: 8 I ye fulfil the royal law according to 1487+3305
2: 9 But i ye have respect to persons, ye commit 1487
2:11 Now i thou commit no adultery, yet if thou 1487
2:11 if thou commit no adultery, yet i thou kill, NIG
2:15 I a brother or sister be naked, and 1437
2:17 Even so faith, i it hath not works, is dead, 1437
3: 2 I any man offend not in word, the same is a 1536
3:14 But i ye have bitter envying and strife in 1487
4:11 but i thou judge the law, thou art not a doer 1487
4:15 I the Lord will, we shall live, and do this, 1437
5:15 and i he have committed sins, they shall be 2579
5:19 i any of you do err from the truth, and 1437
1Pe 1: 6 though now for a season, i need be, 1487
1:17 And i ye call on the Father, who without 1487
2: 3 I so be ye have tasted that the Lord is 1512
2:19 i a man for conscience toward God endure 1487
2:20 For what glory is it, i, when ye be buffeted 1487
2:20 but i, when ye do well, and suffer for it, ye 1487
3: 1 that, i any obey not the word, they also 1536
3:13 i ye be followers of that which is good? 1437
3:14 But and i ye suffer for righteousness' sake, 1487
3:17 For it is better, i the will of God be so, 1487
4:11 I any man speak, let him speak as 1536
4:11 i any man minister, let him do it as of 1536
4:14 I ye be reproached for the name of Christ, 1487
4:16 Yet i any man suffer as a Christian, let him 1487
4:17 and i it first begin at us, what shall the end 1487
4:18 And i the righteous scarcely be saved, 1487
2Pe 1: 8 For i these things be in you, and abound, NIG
1:10 for i ye do these things, ye shall never fall: NIG
2: 4 For i God spared not the angels that sinned, 1487
2:20 For i after they have escaped the pollutions 1487
1Jn 1: 6 I we say that we have fellowship with him, 1437
1: 7 But i we walk in the light, as he is in 1437
1: 8 I we say that we have no sin, we deceive 1437
1: 9 I we confess our sins, he is faithful and 1437
1:10 I we say that we have not sinned, we make 1437
2: 1 And i any man sin, we have an advocate 1437
2: 3 know him, i we keep his commandments. 1437
2:15 I any man love the world, the love of 1437
2:19 for i they had been of us, they would no 1487
2:24 I that which ye have heard from 1437
2:29 I ye know that he is righteous, ye know that 1437
3:13 my brethren, i the world hate you. 1487
3:20 For i our heart condemn us, God is greater 1437
3:21 I our heart condemn us not, then have we 1437
4:11 Beloved, i God so loved us, we ought also 1487
4:12 I we love one another, God dwelleth in us, 1437
4:20 I a man say, I love God, and hateth his 1437
5: 9 I we receive the witness of men, 1487
5:14 i we ask any thing according to his will, 1437
5:15 And i we know that he hear us, 1437
5:16 I any man see his brother sin a sin which is 1437
2Jn 1:10 I there come any unto you, and bring not 1437
3Jn 1: 6 whom i thou bring forward on their journey NIG
1:10 Wherefore, i I come, I will remember his 1437
Rev 1:15 fine brass, as i they burned in a furnace; NIG
3: 3 I therefore thou shalt not watch, I will 1437
3:20 i any man hear my voice, and open 1437
11: 5 And i any man will hurt them, 1536
11: 5 and i any man will hurt them, he must in 1536
13: 9 I any man have an ear, let him hear. 1536
14: 9 I any man worship the beast and his image, 1536
22:18 I any man shall add unto these things, God 1437
22:19 And i any man shall take away from 1437

IGAL (2)

Nu 13: 7 Of the tribe of Issachar, I the son of Joseph. 3000
2Sa 23:36 I the son of Nathan of Zobah, Bani 3008

IGDALIAH (1)

Jer 35: 4 sons of Hanan, the son of I, a man of God, 3012

IGEAL (1)

1Ch 3:22 I, and Bariah, and Neariah, and Shaphat, 3008

IGNOMINY (1)

Pr 18: 3 cometh also contempt, and with i reproach. 7036

IGNORANCE (18) [IGNORANT, IGNORANTLY]

Lev 4: 2 If a soul shall sin through i against any of 7684
4:13 whole congregation of Israel sin through i, 7686
4:22 done somewhat through i against any of 7684
4:27 one of the common people sin through i, 7684
5:15 a soul commit a trespass, and sin through i, 7684

Lev 5:18 for him concerning his **i** wherein he erred 7684
Nu 15:24 if *ought* be committed by **i** without 7684
15:25 and it shall be forgiven them; for it *is* **i**: 7684
15:25 sin offering before the LORD, for their **i**: 7684
15:26 seeing all the people were in **i**. 7684
15:27 if any soul sin through **i**, then he shall bring 7684
15:28 when he sinneth by **i** before the LORD, 7684
15:29 him that **sinneth through i**, 6213+7684+871.1
Ac 3:17 I wot that through **i** ye did *it*, as *did* also your *52*
17:30 And the times of *this* **i** God winked at; but *52*
Eph 4:18 the life of God through the **i** that is in them, *52*
1Pe 1:14 according to the former lusts in your **i**: *52*
2:15 with well doing *ye* may put to silence the **i** *56*

IGNORANT (17) [IGNORANCE]

Ps 73:22 So foolish *was* I, and **i**: I was *as* a 3045+3808
Isa 56:10 they are all **i**, they *are* all dumb dogs, 3045+3808
63:16 though Abraham be **i** of us, and 3045+3808
Ac 4:13 that they were unlearned and **i** men, *2399*
Ro 1:13 Now I would not have you **i**, brethren, *50*
10:3 For they being **i** of God's righteousness, and *50*
11:25 brethren, that ye should be **i** of this mystery, *50*
1Co 10:1 I would not that ye should be **i**, *50*
12:1 *gifts*, brethren, I would not have you **i**. *50*
14:38 But if any *man* be **i**, let him be ignorant. *50*
14:38 But if any *man* be ignorant, let him be **i**. *50*
2Co 1:8 **have** you **i** of our trouble which came to us in *50*
2:11 of us: for we are not **i** of his devices. *50*
1Th 4:13 But I would not have you to be **i**, brethren, *50*
Heb 5:2 Who can have compassion on the **i**, and *50*
2Pe 3:5 For this they willingly are **i** of, that by *2990*
3:8 be not **i** of this one *thing*, that one day *is* *2990*

IGNORANTLY (4) [IGNORANCE]

Nu 15:28 an atonement for the soul that **sinneth i**, 7683
Dt 19:4 Whoso **killeth** his neighbour **i**, 1097+1847+871.1
Ac 17:23 Whom therefore ye **i** worship, him declare I *50*
1Ti 1:13 obtained mercy, because I did *it* **i** in unbelief. *50*

IIM (2)

Nu 33:45 they departed from **I**, and pitched in 5864
Jos 15:29 Baalah, and **I**, and Azem, 5864

IJE-ABARIM (2) [ABARIM]

Nu 21:11 journeyed from Oboth, and pitched at **I**, 5863
33:44 and pitched in **I**, in the border of Moab. 5863

IJON (3)

1Ki 15:20 smote **I**, and Dan, and Abel-beth-maachah, 5859
2Ki 15:29 took **I**, and Abel-beth-maachah, and 5859
2Ch 16:4 and they smote **I**, and Dan, and Abel-maim, 5859

IKKESH (3)

2Sa 23:26 the Paltite, Ira the son of **I** the Tekoite, 6142
1Ch 11:28 Ira the son of **I** the Tekoite, Abi-ezer 6142
27:9 month *was* Ira the son of **I** the Tekoite: 6142

ILAI (1)

1Ch 11:29 Sibbecai the Hushathite, **I** the Ahohite, 5866

ILL (15)

Ge 41:3 out of the river, **i** favoured and leanfleshed; 7451
41:4 the **i** favoured and leanfleshed kine did eat 7451
41:19 poor and very **i** favoured and leanfleshed, 7451
41:20 the **i favoured** kine did eat up the first 7451
41:21 they *were still* **i** favoured, as at 7451
41:27 **i favoured** kine that came up after them *are* 7451
43:6 Wherefore **dealt** ye *so* **i** with me, 7489
Dt 15:21 *it be* lame, or blind, *or have* any **i** blemish, 7451
Job 20:26 it shall **go i** with him that is left in his 3415
Ps 106:32 so that it went **i** with Moses for their sakes: 3415
Isa 3:11 *it shall be* **i** *with him:* for the reward of his 7451
Jer 40:4 if it seem **i** unto thee to come with me *into* 7489
Joel 2:20 his **i savour** shall come up, because he hath 6709
Mic 3:4 as they have **behaved** themselves **i** in their 7489
Ro 13:10 Love worketh no **i** to *his* neighbour: *2556*

ILLUMINATED (1)

Heb 10:32 in which, after ye were **i**, ye endured a great *5461*

ILLYRICUM (1)

Ro 15:19 from Jerusalem, and round about unto **I**, *2437*

IMAGE (100) [IMAGE'S, IMAGERY, IMAGES]

Ge 1:26 God said, Let us make man in our **i**, 6754
1:27 So God created man in his own **i**, in 6754
1:27 own image, in the **i** of God created he him; 6754
5:3 begat *a son* in his own likeness, after his **i**; 6754
9:6 be shed: for in the **i** of God made he man. 6754
Ex 20:4 shalt not make unto thee *any* **graven i**, 6459
Lev 26:1 Ye shall make you no idols nor **graven i**, 6459
26:1 neither rear you up a **standing i**, 4676
26:1 neither shall ye set up *any* **i** of stone in your 4906
Dt 4:16 and make you a **graven i**, 6459
4:23 make you a **graven i**, *or* the likeness of any 6459
4:25 corrupt *yourselves*, and make a **graven i**, 6459
5:8 Thou shalt not make thee *any* **graven i**, *or* 6459
9:12 they have made them a **molten i**. 4541
16:22 Neither shalt thou set thee up *any* **i**; 4676
27:15 man that maketh *any* graven or **molten i**, 4541
Jdg 17:3 to make a **graven i** and a molten image: 6459
17:3 to make a graven image and a **molten i**: 4541
17:4 who made thereof a **graven i** and a molten 6459
17:4 thereof a graven image and a **molten i**: 4541
18:14 and a **graven i**, and a molten image? 6459
18:14 and a graven image, and a **molten i**? 4541
18:17 *and* took the **graven i**, and the ephod, and 6459
18:17 and the teraphim, and the **molten i**: 4541
18:18 fetched the **carved i**, the ephod, and 6459
18:18 and the teraphim, and the **molten i**. 4541
18:20 the **graven i**, and went in the midst of 6459
18:30 the children of Dan set up the **graven i**: 6459
18:31 they set them up Micah's **graven i**, 6459
1Sa 19:13 And Michal took an **i**, and laid *it* in the bed, 8655
1Sa 19:16 come in, behold *there was* an **i** in the bed, 8655
2Ki 3:2 for he put away the **i** of Baal that his father 4676
10:27 they brake down the **i** of Baal, and 4676
21:7 he set a **graven i** of the grove that he had 6459
2Ch 3:10 house he made two cherubims of **i** work, 6816
33:7 he set a **carved i**, the idol which he had 6459
Job 4:16 an **i** *was* before mine eyes, *there was* 8544
Ps 73:20 *thou* awakest, thou shalt despise their **i**. 6754
106:19 calf in Horeb, and worshipped the **molten i**. 4541
Isa 40:19 The workman melteth a **graven i**, and 6459
40:20 a cunning workman to prepare a **graven i**, 6459
44:9 They that make a **graven i** *are* all of them 6459
44:10 molten a **graven i** *that* is profitable for 6459
44:15 and worshippeth *it;* he maketh it a **graven i**, 6459
44:17 thereof he maketh a god, *even* his **graven i**: 6459
45:20 that set up the wood of their **graven i**, 6459
48:5 my **graven i**, and my molten image, 6459
48:5 my graven image, and my **molten i**, 5262
Jer 10:14 founder is confounded by the **graven i**: 6459
10:14 for his **molten i** *is* falsehood, and *there is* 5262
51:17 founder is confounded by the **graven i**: 6459
51:17 for his **molten i** *is* falsehood, and *there is* 5262
Eze 8:3 where *was* the seat of the **i** of jealousy, 5566
8:5 northward at the gate of the altar this **i** of 5566
Da 2:31 Thou, O king, sawest, and behold a great **i**. 6755
2:31 This great **i**, whose brightness *was* 6755
2:34 which smote the **i** upon his feet *that were* of 6755
2:35 the stone that smote the **i** became a great 6755
3:1 Nebuchadnezzar the king made an **i** of 6755
3:2 to come to the dedication of the **i** which 6755
3:3 **i** that Nebuchadnezzar the king had set up; 6755
3:3 they stood before the **i** that 6755
3:5 worship the golden **i** that Nebuchadnezzar 6755
3:7 worshipped the golden **i** that 6755
3:10 shall fall down and worship the golden **i**: 6755
3:12 nor worship the golden **i** which thou hast 6755
3:14 nor worship the golden **i** which I have set 6755
3:15 and worship the **i** which I have made; 6755
3:18 nor worship the golden **i** which thou hast 6755
Hos 3:4 and without an **i**, and without an ephod, and 4676
Na 1:14 house of thy gods will I cut off the **graven i** 6459
1:14 I cut off the graven image and the **molten i**: 4541
Hab 2:18 What profiteth the **graven i** that the maker 6459
2:18 the **molten i**, and a teacher of lies, that 4541
Mt 22:20 Whose *is* this **i** and superscription? *1504*
Mk 12:16 Whose *is* this **i** and superscription? *1504*
Lk 20:24 Whose **i** and superscription hath it? *1504*
Ac 19:35 and of the *i* which fell down from Jupiter? NIG
Ro 1:23 God into an **i** made like to corruptible man, *1504*
8:29 *to be* conformed to the **i** of his Son, *1504*
11:4 who have not bowed the knee to *the i of* NIG
1Co 11:7 forasmuch as he is the **i** and glory of God: *1504*
15:49 And as we have borne the **i** of the earthy, *1504*
15:49 we shall also bear the **i** of the heavenly. *1504*
2Co 3:18 are changed *into* the same **i** from glory to *1504*
4:4 who is the **i** of God, should shine unto *1504*
Col 1:15 Who is the **i** of the invisible God, *1504*
3:10 after the **i** of him that created him: *1504*
Heb 1:3 and the **express i** of his person, and *5481*
10:1 to come, *and* not the very **i** of the things, *1504*
Rev 13:14 that *they* should make an **i** to the beast, *1504*
13:15 And he had power to give life unto the **i** of *1504*
13:15 that the **i** of the beast should both speak, *1504*
13:15 worship the **i** of the beast should be killed. *1504*
14:9 If any *man* worship the beast and his **i**, and *1504*
14:11 who worship the beast and his **i**, and *1504*
15:2 the beast, and over his **i**, and over his mark, *1504*
16:2 and *upon* them which worshipped his **i**. *1504*
19:20 the beast, and them that worshipped his **i**. *1504*
20:4 had not worshipped the beast, neither his **i**, *1504*

IMAGE'S (1) [IMAGE]

Da 2:32 This **i** head *was* of fine gold, his breast and 6755

IMAGERY (1) [IMAGE]

Eze 8:12 every man in the chambers of his **i**? 4906

IMAGES (71) [IMAGE]

Ge 31:19 Rachel had stolen the **i** that *were* her 8655
31:34 Now Rachel had taken the **i**, and put them 8655
31:35 And he searched, but found not the **i**. 8655
Ex 23:24 and quite break down their **i**. 4676
34:13 break their **i**, and cut down their groves: 4676
Lev 26:30 cut down your **i**, and cast your carcases 2553
Nu 33:52 destroy all their molten **i**, and quite pluck 6754
Dt 7:5 break down their **i**, and cut down their 4676
7:5 and burn their **graven i** with fire. 6456
7:25 The **graven i** of their gods shall ye burn 6456
12:3 you shall hew down the **graven i** of their 6456
1Sa 6:5 Wherefore ye shall make **i** of your 6754
6:5 and **i** of your mice that mar the land; 6754
6:11 the mice of gold and the **i** of their emerods. 6754
2Sa 5:21 there they left their **i**, and David and 6091
1Ki 14:9 and made thee other gods, and **molten i**, 4541
14:23 **i**, and groves, on every high hill, and 4676
2Ki 10:26 they brought forth the **i** out of the house of 4676
11:18 and his **i** brake they in pieces throughly, 6754
17:10 they set them up **i** and groves in every high 4676
17:16 made them **molten i**, *even* two calves, and 4541
17:41 served their **graven i**, both their children, 6456
18:4 brake the **i**, and cut down the groves, and 4676
23:14 he brake in pieces the **i**, and cut down 4676
23:24 the **i**, and the idols, and all 8655
2Ch 14:3 brake down the **i**, and cut down the groves: 4676
14:5 the cities of Judah the high places and the **i**: 2553
23:17 brake his altars and his **i** in pieces, and slew 6754
28:2 and made also **molten i** for Baalim. 4541
31:1 brake the **i** *in pieces*, and cut down 4676
33:19 set up groves and **graven i**, before he was 6456
33:22 for Amon sacrificed unto all the **carved i** 6456
34:3 and the **carved i**, and the molten images. 6456
34:3 and the carved images, and the **molten i**. 4541
34:4 the **i**, that *were* on high above them, he cut 2553
34:4 and the **carved i**, and the molten images, 6456
2Ch 34:4 the **molten i**, he brake *in pieces*, and 4541
34:7 had beaten the **graven i** into powder, and 6456
Ps 78:58 moved him to jealousy with their **graven i**. 6456
97:7 Confounded be all they that serve **graven i**, 6459
Isa 10:10 whose **graven i** did excel *them of* 6456
17:8 have made, either the groves, or the **i**. 2553
21:9 all the **graven i** of her gods he hath broken 6456
27:9 the groves and **i** shall not stand up. 2553
30:22 also the covering of thy **graven i** of silver, 6456
30:22 and the ornament of thy **molten i** of gold: 4541
41:29 their **molten i** *are* wind and confusion. 5262
42:8 to another, neither my praise to **graven i**. 6456
42:17 that trust in **graven i**, that say to the molten 6459
42:17 that say to the **molten i**, Ye *are* our gods. 4541
Jer 8:19 provoked me to anger with their **graven i**, 6456
43:13 He shall break also the **i** of Beth-shemesh, 4676
50:2 are confounded, her **i** are broken in pieces. 1544
50:38 for it *is* the land of **graven i**, and they are 6456
51:47 that I will do judgment upon the **graven i** 6456
51:52 that I will do judgment upon her **graven i**: 6456
Eze 6:4 be desolate, and your **i** shall be broken: 2553
6:6 your **i** may be cut down, and your works 2553
7:20 they made the **i** of their abominations *and* 6754
16:17 madest to thyself **i** of men, and 6754
21:21 he consulted with **i**, he looked in the liver. 8655
23:14 the **i** of the Chaldeans pourtrayed with 6754
30:13 and I will cause *their* **i** to cease out of Noph; 457
Hos 10:1 of his land they have made goodly **i**. 4676
10:2 down their altars, he shall spoil their **i**. 4676
11:2 and burned incense to **graven i**. 6456
13:2 have made them **molten i** of their silver, 4541
Am 5:26 of your Moloch and Chiun your **i**, 6754
Mic 1:7 all the **graven i** thereof shall be beaten to 6456
5:13 Thy **graven i** also will I cut off, and 6456
5:13 and thy **standing i** out of the midst of thee; 4676

IMAGINATION (14) [IMAGINE]

Ge 6:5 *that* every **i** of the thoughts of his heart *was* 3336
8:21 for the **i** of man's heart *is* evil from his 3336
Dt 29:19 though I walk in the **i** of mine heart, 8307
31:21 for I know their **i** which they go about, 3336
1Ch 29:18 keep this for ever in the **i** of the thoughts of 3336
Jer 3:17 neither shall they walk any more after the **i** 8307
7:24 the counsels *and* in the **i** of their evil heart, 8307
9:14 have walked after the **i** of their own heart, 8307
11:8 walked every one in the **i** of their evil heart: 8307
13:10 which walk in the **i** of their heart, and 8307
16:12 ye walk every one after the **i** of his evil 8307
18:12 we will every one do the **i** of his evil heart. 8307
23:17 that walketh after the **i** of his own heart, 8307
Lk 1:51 he hath scattered the proud in the **i** of their *1271*

IMAGINATIONS (6) [IMAGINE]

1Ch 28:9 and understandeth all the **i** of the thoughts: 3336
Pr 6:18 A heart that deviseth wicked **i**, feet that be 4284
La 3:60 their vengeance *and* all their **i** against me. 4284
3:61 O LORD, *and* all their **i** against me; 4284
Ro 1:21 but became vain in their **i**, and their foolish *1261*
2Co 10:5 Casting down **i**, and every high thing that *3053*

IMAGINE (12) [IMAGINATION, IMAGINATIONS, IMAGINED, IMAGINETH]

Job 6:26 Do ye **i** to reprove words, and the speeches 2803
21:27 the devices *which* ye **wrongfully i** against 2554
Ps 2:1 and the people **i** a vain *thing?* 1897
38:12 and **i** deceits all the day long. 1897
62:3 How long will ye **i mischief** against a man? 2050
140:2 Which **i** mischiefs in *their* heart; 2803
Pr 12:20 Deceit *is* in the heart of them that **i** evil: but 2790
Hos 7:15 yet do they **i** mischief against me. 2803
Na 1:9 What do ye **i** against the LORD? he *will* 2803
Zec 7:10 let none of you **i** evil against his brother in 2803
8:17 let none of you **i** evil in your hearts against 2803
Ac 4:25 heathen rage, and the people **i** vain *things?* *3191*

IMAGINED (3) [IMAGINE]

Ge 11:6 from them, which they have **i** to do. 2161
Ps 10:2 be taken in the devices that they have **i**. 2803
21:11 they **i** a mischievous device, *which* they 2803

IMAGINETH (1) [IMAGINE]

Na 1:11 that **i** evil against the LORD, a wicked 2803

IMLA (2) [IMLAH]

2Ch 18:7 the same *is* Micaiah the son of **I**. 3229
18:8 said, Fetch quickly Micaiah the son of **I**. 3229

IMLAH (2) [IMLA]

1Ki 22:8 *There is* yet one man, Micaiah the son of **I**, 3229
22:9 said, Hasten *hither* Micaiah the son of **I**. 3229

IMMANUEL (2) [EMMANUEL]

Isa 7:14 and bear a Son, and shall call his name **I**. 6005
8:8 wings shall fill the breadth of thy land, O **I**. 6005

IMMEDIATELY (55)

Mt 4:22 And they **i** left the ship and their father, and *2112*
8:3 thou clean. And **i** his leprosy was cleansed. *2112*
14:31 And **i** Jesus stretched forth *his* hand, and *2112*
20:34 and **i** their eyes received sight, and *2112*
24:29 **I** after the tribulation of those days shall *2112*
26:74 I know not the man. And **i** *the* cock crew. *2112*
Mk 1:12 And **i** the Spirit driveth him into *2112*
1:28 And **i** his fame spread abroad throughout *2112*
1:31 and **i** the fever left her, and she ministered *2112*
1:42 **i** the leprosy departed from him, and he was *2112*
2:8 And **i**, when Jesus perceived in his spirit *2112*
2:12 And **i** he arose, took up the bed, and *2112*
4:5 and **i** it sprang up, because *it* had no depth *2112*
4:15 Satan cometh **i**, and taketh away the word *2112*
4:16 heard the word, **i** receive it with gladness; *2112*
4:17 for the word's sake, **i** they are offended. *2112*
4:29 **i** he putteth in the sickle, because *2112*
5:2 **i** there met him out of the tombs a man with *2112*

Mk 5:30 And Jesus **i** knowing in himself that virtue *2112*
6:27 And **i** the king sent an executioner, and *2112*
6:50 And **i** he talked with them, and saith unto *2112*
10:52 And **i** he received his sight, and *2112*
14:43 And **i**, while he yet spake, cometh Judas, *2112*
Lk 1:64 And his mouth was opened **i**, and *3916*
4:39 and **i** she arose and ministered unto them. *3916*
5:13 And **i** the leprosy departed from him. *2112*
5:25 And **i** he rose up before them, and took up *3916*
6:49 stream did beat vehemently, and **i** it fell; *2112*
8:44 and **i** her issue of blood stanched. *3916*
8:47 touched him, and how she was healed **i**. *3916*
12:36 and knocketh, they may open unto him **i**. *2112*
13:13 and **i** she was made straight, and *3916*
18:43 And **i** he received his sight, and *3916*
19:11 that the kingdom of God should **i** appear. *3916*
19:40 hold their peace, the stones would **i** cry out. NIG
22:60 And **i**, while he yet spake, the cock crew. *3916*
Jn 5: 9 And **i** the man was made whole, and *2112*
6:21 **i** the ship was at the land whither they *2112*
13:30 He then having received the sop went **i** out: *2112*
18:27 then denied again: and **i** *the* cock crew. *2112*
21: 3 They went forth, and entered into a ship **i**; *2112*
Ac 3: 7 and **i** his feet and ankle bones received *3916*
9:18 And **i** there fell from his eyes as it had been *2112*
9:34 arise, and make thy bed. And he arose **i**. *2112*
10:33 **I** therefore I sent to thee; and thou hast well *1824*
11:11 **i** there were three men **already** come unto *1824*
12:23 And **i** *the* angel of the Lord smote him, *3916*
13:11 And **i** there fell on him a mist and *3916*
16:10 **i** we endeavoured to go into Macedonia, *2112*
16:26 and **i** all the doors were opened, and *3916*
17:10 And the brethren **i** sent away Paul and Silas *2112*
17:14 **i** the brethren sent away Paul to go as *it* *2112*
21:32 Who **i** took soldiers and centurions, and *1824*
Gal 1:16 **i** I conferred not with flesh and blood: *2112*
Rev 4: 2 And **i** I was in the spirit: and behold, *2112*

IMMER (10)
1Ch 9:12 the son of Meshillemith, the son of **I**; 564
24:14 The fifteenth to Bilgah, the sixteenth to **I**, 564
Ezr 2:37 The children of **I**, a thousand fifty and two. 564
2:59 Tel-harsa, Cherub, Addan, *and* **I**: 564
10:20 And of the sons of **I**; Hanani, and Zebadiah. 564
Ne 3:29 After them repaired Zadok the son of **I** over 564
7:40 The children of **I**, a thousand fifty and two. 564
7:61 Tel-haresha, Cherub, Addon, and **I**: 564
11:13 the son of Meshillemoth, the son of **I**, 564
Jer 20: 1 Now Pashur the son of **I** the priest, who *was* 564

IMMORAL See WHOREMONGER; WHOREMONGERS

IMMORALITY See LASCIVIOUSNESS

IMMORTAL (1) [IMMORTALITY]
1Ti 1:17 **i**, invisible, the only wise God, *be* honour *862*

IMMORTALITY (5) [IMMORTAL]
Ro 2: 7 well doing seek for glory and honour and **i**, *861*
1Co 15:53 and this mortal *must* put on **i**. *110*
15:54 and this mortal shall have put on **i**, then *110*
1Ti 6:16 Who only hath **i**, dwelling in the light which *110*
2Ti 1:10 brought life and **i** to light through the gospel: *861*

IMMUTABILITY (1) [IMMUTABLE]
Heb 6:17 unto the heirs of promise the **i** of his counsel, *276*

IMMUTABLE (1) [IMMUTABILITY]
Heb 6:18 That by two **i** things, in which *it was* *276*

IMNA (1)
1Ch 7:35 Zophah, and **I**, and Shelesh, and Amal. 3234

IMNAH (2)
1Ch 7:30 **I**, and Isuah, and Ishuai, and Beriah, and 3232
2Ch 31:14 Kore the son of **I** the Levite, the porter 3232

IMNITE See JIMNITES

IMPART (2) [IMPARTED]
Lk 3:11 two coats, let him **i** to him that hath none; *3330*
Ro 1:11 that I may **i** unto you some spiritual gift, *3330*

IMPARTED (2) [IMPART]
Job 39:17 neither hath he **i** to her understanding. 2505
1Th 2: 8 we were willing to have **i** unto you, not *3330*

IMPEDIMENT (1)
Mk 7:32 *that was* deaf, and had an **i** in his **speech**; *3424*

IMPENITENT (1)
Ro 2: 5 **i** heart treasurest up unto thyself wrath *279*

IMPERIOUS (1)
Eze 16:30 *things,* the work of an **i** whorish woman; 7986

IMPERISHABLE See INCORRUPTIBLE; INCORRUPTION

IMPLACABLE (1)
Ro 1:31 without natural affection, **i**, unmerciful: *786*

IMPLEAD (1)
Ac 19:38 there are deputies: let them **i** one another. *1458*

IMPORTUNITY (1)
Lk 11: 8 yet because of his **i** he will rise and give him *335*

IMPOSE (1) [IMPOSED]
Ezr 7:24 it *shall* not *be* lawful to **i** toll, tribute, or 7412

IMPOSED (1) [IMPOSE]
Heb 9:10 **i** *on them* until the time of reformation. *1945*

IMPOSING See STOUT

IMPOSSIBLE (5) [UNPOSSIBLE]
Mk 10:27 With men *it is* **i**, but not with God: *102*
Lk 17: 1 It is **i** but that offences will come: *418*
Heb 6: 4 For *it is* **i** for those who were once *102*
6:18 in which *it was* **i** for God to lie, *102*
11: 6 But without faith *it is* **i** to please *him:* for he *102*

IMPOTENT (4)
Jn 5: 3 In these lay a great multitude of **i** *folk,* of *770*
5: 7 The **i** *man* answered him, Sir, I have no man, *770*
Ac 4: 9 of the good deed done to the **i** man, *772*
14: 8 there sat a certain man at Lystra, **i** in *his* feet, *102*

IMPOVERISH (1) [POVERTY]
Jer 5:17 they shall **i** thy fenced cities, wherein thou 7567

IMPOVERISHED (3) [POVERTY]
Jdg 6: 6 Israel was greatly **i** because of 1809
Isa 40:20 **so i** that he hath no oblation chooseth a tree 5533
Mal 1: 4 We are **i**, but we will return and build 7567

IMPRISONED (1) [PRISON]
Ac 22:19 they know that I **i** and beat in every *5439*

IMPRISONMENT (2) [PRISON]
Ezr 7:26 or to confiscation of goods, or to **i**. 613
Heb 11:36 scourgings, yea, moreover of bonds and **i**: *5438*

IMPRISONMENTS (1) [PRISON]
2Co 6: 5 In stripes, in **i**, in tumults, in labours, *5438*

IMPROPERLY See UNCOMELY

IMPUDENT (3)
Pr 7:13 and with an **i** face said unto him, 5010
Eze 2: 4 For *they are* **i** children and 6440+7186
3: 7 for all the house of Israel *are* **i** 2389+4696

IMPUTE (3) [IMPUTED, IMPUTETH, IMPUTING]
1Sa 22:15 let not the king **i** *any*thing unto his servant, 7760
2Sa 19:19 Let not my lord **i** iniquity unto me, 2803
Ro 4: 8 *is* the man to whom the Lord will not **i** sin. *3049*

IMPUTED (8) [IMPUTE]
Lev 7:18 neither shall it be **i** unto him that offereth it: 2803
17: 4 blood shall be **i** unto that man; he hath shed 2803
Ro 4:11 that righteousness might be **i** unto them *3049*
4:22 therefore it was **i** to him for righteousness. *3049*
4:23 for his sake alone, that it was **i** to him; *3049*
4:24 But for us also, to whom it shall be **i**, if we *3049*
5:13 but sin is not **i** when there is no law. *1677*
Jas 2:23 and it was **i** unto him for righteousness: *3049*

IMPUTETH (2) [IMPUTE]
Ps 32: 2 man unto whom the LORD **i** not iniquity, 2803
Ro 4: 6 unto whom God **i** righteousness without *3049*

IMPUTING (2) [IMPUTE]
Hab 1:11 and offend, *i* this his power unto his god. NIH
2Co 5:19 not **i** their trespasses unto them; *3049*

IMRAH (1)
1Ch 7:36 and Harnepher, and Shual, and Beri, and **I**, 3236

IMRI (2)
1Ch 9: 4 son of Omri, the son of **I**, the son of Bani, 566
Ne 3: 2 next to them builded Zaccur the son of **I**. 566

IN (12674) [HEREIN, INASMUCH, INSOMUCH, INTO, THEREIN, WHEREIN, WHEREINSOEVER, WITHIN] See Index of Articles, Etc.

INASMUCH (9) [AS, IN, MUCH]
Dt 19: 6 of death, **i as** he hated him not in time past. 3588
Ru 3:10 **i as** *thou* followedst not young men, 3807.1
Mt 25:40 **I as** ye have done *it* unto one of *1909+3745*
25:45 **I as** ye did *it* not to one of the least *1909+3745*
Ro 11:13 **i as** I am the apostle of *1909+3303+3745+3767*
Php 1: 7 **i as both** in my bonds, and *in* the defence *5037*
Heb 3: 3 **i as** he who hath builded the house *2596+3745*
7:20 And **i as** not without an oath *he was* *2596+3745*
1Pe 4:13 **i as** ye are partakers of Christ's sufferings; *2526*

INCENSE (129) [FRANKINCENSE]
Ex 25: 6 spices for anointing oil, and for sweet **i**, 7004
30: 1 thou shalt make an altar to burn **i** upon: 7004
30: 7 Aaron shall burn thereon sweet **i** every 7004
30: 7 dresseth the lamps, he shall **burn i** upon it. 6999
30: 8 the lamps at even, he shall **burn i** upon it, 6999
30: 8 a perpetual **i** before the LORD throughout 7004
30: 9 Ye shall offer no strange **i** thereon, nor 7004
30:27 and his vessels, and the altar of **i**, 7004
31: 8 with all his furniture, and the altar of **i**, 7004
31:11 sweet **i** for the holy *place:* according to all 7004
35: 8 spices for anointing oil, and for the sweet **i**, 7004
35:15 the **i** altar and his staves, and the anointing 7004
35:15 the sweet **i**, and the hanging for the door at 7004
35:28 for the anointing oil, and for the sweet **i**. 7004
37:25 he made the **i** altar *of* shittim wood: 7004
37:29 and the pure **i** of sweet spices, 7004
39:38 the sweet **i**, and the hanging for 7004
40: 5 thou shalt set the altar of gold for the **i** 7004
40:27 he burnt sweet **i** thereon; as the LORD 7004
Lev 4: 7 of the altar of sweet **i** before the LORD, 7004
10: 1 put **i** thereon, and offered strange fire 7004
16:12 his hands full of sweet **i** beaten small, and 7004
16:13 he shall put the **i** upon the fire before 7004
16:13 that the cloud of the **i** may cover the mercy 7004
Nu 4:16 and the sweet **i**, and the daily meat offering, 7004
7:14 One spoon of ten *shekels* of gold, full *of* **i**: 7004
7:20 One spoon of gold of ten *shekels,* full *of* **i**: 7004
7:26 One golden spoon of ten *shekels,* full *of* **i**: 7004
7:32 One golden spoon *of* ten *shekels,* full *of* **i**: 7004
7:38 One golden spoon of ten *shekels,* full *of* **i**: 7004
7:44 One golden spoon of ten *shekels,* full *of* **i**: 7004
7:50 One golden spoon of ten *shekels,* full *of* **i**: 7004
7:56 One golden spoon of ten *shekels,* full *of* **i**: 7004
7:62 One golden spoon of ten *shekels,* full *of* **i**: 7004
7:68 One golden spoon of ten *shekels,* full *of* **i**: 7004
7:74 One golden spoon of ten *shekels,* full *of* **i**: 7004
7:80 One golden spoon of ten *shekels,* full *of* **i**: 7004
7:86 full *of* **i**, *weighing* ten *shekels* apiece, 7004
16: 7 put **i** in them before the LORD to morrow: 7004
16:17 put **i** in them, and bring ye before 7004
16:18 laid **i** thereon, and stood *in* the door of 7004
16:35 two hundred and fifty men that offered **i**. 7004
16:40 come near to offer **i** before the LORD; 7004
16:46 put on **i**, and go quickly unto 7004
16:47 he put on **i**, and made an atonement for 7004
Dt 33:10 they shall put **i** before thee, and 6988
1Sa 2:28 to offer upon mine altar, to burn **i**, to wear 7004
1Ki 3: 3 he sacrificed and **burnt i** in high places. 6999
9:25 he **burnt i** upon the altar that *was* before 6999
11: 8 which **burnt i** and sacrificed unto their 6999
12:33 and he offered upon the altar, and **burnt i**. 6999
13: 1 and Jeroboam stood by the altar to **burn i**. 6999
13: 2 of the high places that **burn i** upon thee, 6999
22:43 *for* the people offered and **burnt i** 4480
2Ki 12: 3 and **burnt i** in the high places. 6999
14: 4 did sacrifice and **burnt i** on the high places. 6999
15: 4 and **burnt i** still on the high places. 6999
15:35 and **burnt i** still in the high places. 6999
16: 4 he sacrificed and **burnt i** in the high places, 6999
17:11 there they **burnt i** in all the high places, 6999
18: 4 days the children of Israel did **burn i** to it: 6999
22:17 and have **burnt i** unto other gods, 6999
23: 5 **burn i** in the high places in the cities of 6999
23: 5 them also that **burnt i** unto Baal, to the sun, 6999
23: 8 high places where the priests had **burnt i**, 6999
1Ch 6:49 on the altar of **i**, *and were appointed* for all 7004
23:13 sons for ever, to **burn i** before the LORD, 6999
28:18 for the altar of **i** refined gold by weight; 7004
2Ch 2: 4 *and* to burn before him sweet **i**, and *for* 7004
13:11 every evening burnt sacrifices and sweet **i**: 7004
25:14 before them, and **burned i** unto them. 6999
26:16 LORD to **burn i** upon the altar of incense. 6999
26:16 LORD to burn incense upon the altar of **i**. 7004
26:18 to **burn i** unto the LORD, but to 6999
26:18 of Aaron, that are consecrated to **burn i**: 6999
26:19 and *had* a censer in his hand to **burn i**: 6999
26:19 of the LORD, from beside the **i** altar. 7004
28: 3 Moreover he **burnt i** in the valley of 6999
28: 4 and **burnt i** in the high places, 6999
28:25 made high places to **burn i** unto other gods, 6999
29: 7 have not **burnt i** nor offered burnt 6999+7004
29:11 *you* should minister unto him, and **burn i**. 6999
30:14 all the **altars for i** took they away, and 6999
32:12 before one altar, and **burn i** upon it? 6999
34:25 and have **burned i** unto other gods, 6999
Ps 66:15 sacrifices of fatlings, with the **i** of rams; 7004
141: 2 Let my prayer be set forth before thee *as* **i**; 7004
Isa 1:13 **i** *is* an abomination unto me; the new 7004
43:23 with an offering, nor wearied thee with **i**. 3828
60: 6 they shall bring gold and **i**; and they shall 3828
65: 3 and **burneth i** upon altars of brick; 6999
65: 7 which have **burnt i** upon the mountains, 6999
66: 3 he that burneth **i**, *as if* he blessed an idol. 3828
Jer 1:16 have **burnt i** unto other gods, and 6999
6:20 To what purpose cometh there to me **i** from 3828
7: 9 **burn i** unto Baal, and walk after other gods 6999
11:12 cry unto the gods unto whom they **offer i**: 6999
11:13 *even* altars to **burn i** unto Baal. 6999
11:17 me to anger in **offering i** unto Baal. 6999
17:26 and **i**, and bringing *sacrifices of* praise, 3828
18:15 they have **burnt i** to vanity, and they have 6999
19: 4 and have **burnt i** in it unto other gods, 6999
19:13 have **burnt i** unto all the host of heaven, 6999
32:29 upon whose roofs they have **offered i** unto 6999
41: 5 with offerings and **i** in their hand, 3828
44: 3 in that *they* went to **burn i**, *and* to serve 6999
44: 5 to **burn** no **i** unto other gods. 6999
44: 8 **burning i** unto other gods in the land of 6999
44:15 their wives had **burnt i** unto other gods, 6999
44:17 to **burn i** unto the queen of heaven, and 6999
44:18 since we left off to **burn i** to the queen of 6999
44:19 when we **burnt i** to the queen of heaven, 6999
44:21 The **i** that ye burnt in the cities of Judah, 7002
44:23 Because you have **burnt i**, and because 6999
44:25 to **burn i** to the queen of heaven, and 6999
48:35 and him that **burneth i** to his gods. 6999
Eze 8:11 in his hand; and a thick cloud of **i** went up. 7004
16:18 hast set mine oil and mine **i** before them. 7004
23:41 whereupon thou hast set mine **i** and 7004
Hos 2:13 where*in* she **burnt i** to them, and 6999
4:13 **burn i** upon the hills, under oaks and 6999
11: 2 and **burned i** to graven images. 6999
Hab 1:16 unto their net, and **burn i** unto their drag; 6999
Mal 1:11 in every place **i** *shall be* offered unto my 6999
Lk 1: 9 his lot was to **burn i** when he went into *2370*
1:10 were praying without at the time of **i**. *2368*
1:11 standing on the right side of the altar of **i**. *2368*
Rev 8: 3 and there was given unto him much **i**, *2368*
8: 4 And the smoke of the **i**, *which came* with *2368*

INCENSED (2)
Isa 41:11 all they that were **i** against thee shall be 2734
45:24 all that are **i** against him shall be ashamed. 2734

INCLINE (16) [INCLINED, INCLINETH]
Jos 24:23 **i** your heart unto the LORD God of Israel. 5186

1Ki 8:58 That *he* may i our hearts unto him, to walk 5186
Ps 17: 6 i thine ear unto me, *and* hear my speech. 5186
45:10 O daughter, and consider, and i thine ear; 5186
49: 4 I will i mine ear to a parable: I will open 5186
71: 2 to escape: i thine ear unto me, and save me. 5186
78: 1 i your ears to the words of my mouth. 5186
88: 2 come before thee: i thine ear unto my cry; 5186
102: 2 *when* I am in trouble; i thine ear unto me: 5186
119:36 I my heart unto thy testimonies, and not to 5186
141: 4 I not my heart to *any* evil thing, to practise 5186
Pr 2: 2 So that *thou* i thine ear unto wisdom, *and* 7181
4:20 to my words; i thine ear unto my sayings. 5186
Isa 37:17 I thine ear, O LORD, and hear; open thine 5186
55: 3 I your ear, and come unto me: hear, and 5186
Da 9:18 O my God, i thine ear, and hear; open thine 5186

INCLINED (13) [INCLINE]
Jdg 9: 3 their hearts i to follow Abimelech; for they 5186
Ps 40: 1 and he i unto me, and heard my cry. 5186
116: 2 Because he hath i his ear unto me, therefore 5186
119:112 I have i mine heart to perform thy statutes 5186
Pr 5:13 nor i mine ear to them that instructed me! 5186
Jer 7:24 nor i their ear, but walked in the counsels 5186
7:26 nor i their ear, but hardened their neck: 5186
11: 8 nor i their ear, but walked every one in 5186
17:23 neither i their ear, but made their neck stiff, 5186
25: 4 have not hearkened, nor i your ear to hear. 5186
34:14 hearkened not unto me, neither i their ear. 5186
35:15 ye have not i your ear, nor hearkened unto 5186
44: 5 nor i their ear to turn from their 5186

INCLINETH (1) [INCLINE]
Pr 2:18 For her house i unto death, and her paths 7743

INCLOSE (1) [INCLOSED, INCLOSINGS]
SS 8: 9 a door, we will i her with boards of cedar. 6696

INCLOSED (8) [INCLOSE]
Ex 39: 6 they wrought onyx stones i *in* ouches *of* 5437
39:13 *they were* i *in* ouches *of* gold in their 5437
Jdg 20:43 *Thus* they i the Benjamites **round about**, 3803
Ps 17:10 They are i *in* their own fat: *with* their 5462
22:16 the assembly of the wicked have i me: 5362
SS 4:12 A garden i *is* my sister, *my* spouse; a spring 5274
La 3: 9 He hath i my ways with hewn stone, 1443
Lk 5: 6 this done, they i a great multitude of fishes: *4788*

INCLOSINGS (2) [INCLOSE]
Ex 28:20 a jasper: they shall be set in gold in their i. 4396
39:13 *were* inclosed *in* ouches *of* gold in their i. 4396

INCONTINENCY (1) [INCONTINENT]
1Co 7: 5 that Satan tempt you not for your i. *192*

INCONTINENT (1) [INCONTINENCY]
2Ti 3: 3 trucebreakers, false accusers, i, fierce, *193*

INCORRUPTIBLE (4) [INCORRUPTION]
1Co 9:25 *it* to obtain a corruptible crown; but we an i. *862*
15:52 and the dead shall be raised i, and we shall *862*
1Pe 1: 4 To an inheritance i, and undefiled, and *862*
1:23 but *of* i, by the word of God, which liveth *862*

INCORRUPTION (4) [INCORRUPTIBLE]
1Co 15:42 It is sown in corruption; it is raised in i: *861*
15:50 of God; neither doth corruption inherit i. *861*
15:53 For this corruptible must put on i, and *861*
15:54 So when this corruptible shall have put on i, *861*

INCREASE (88) [INCREASED, INCREASEST, INCREASETH, INCREASING]
Ge 47:24 it shall come to pass in the i, that you shall 8393
Lev 19:25 that *it* may yield unto you the i thereof: 8393
25: 7 in thy land, shall all the i thereof be meat. 8393
25:12 ye shall eat the i thereof out of the field. 8393
25:16 of years thou shalt i the price thereof, 7235
25:20 we shall not sow, nor gather in our i: 8393
25:36 Take thou no usury of him, or i: but 8636
25:37 upon usury, nor lend him thy victuals for i. 4768
26: 4 the land shall yield her i, and the trees of 2981
26:20 for your land shall not yield her i, neither 2981
Nu 18:30 it shall be counted unto the Levites as the i 8393
18:30 and as the i of the winepress. 8393
32:14 up in your fathers' stead, an i of sinful men, 8635
Dt 6: 3 well with thee, and that ye may i mightily, 7235
7:13 the i of thy kine, and the flocks of thy 7698
7:22 lest the beasts of the field i upon thee. 7235
14:22 Thou shalt truly tithe all the i of thy seed, 8393
14:28 forth all the tithe of thine i the same year, 8393
16:15 thy God shall bless thee in all thy i, 8393
26:12 tithing all the tithes of thine i the third year, 8393
28: 4 the i of thy kine, and the flocks of thy 7698
28:18 the i of thy kine, and the flocks of thy 7698
28:51 *or* the i of thy kine, or flocks of thy sheep, 7698
32:13 that he might eat the i of the fields; 8570
32:22 shall consume the earth with her i, and 2981
Jdg 6: 4 destroyed the i of the earth, till thou come 2981
9:29 to Abimelech, I thine army, and come out. 7235
1Sa 2:33 all the i of thine house shall die in 4768
1Ch 27:23 the LORD had said *he* would i Israel like 7235
27:27 over the i of the vineyards for the wine 7945
2Ch 31: 5 oil, and honey, and of all the i of the field; 8393
32:28 Storehouses also for the i of corn, and 8393
Ezr 10:10 to i the trespass of Israel. 3254+5921
Ne 9:37 it **yieldeth** much i unto the kings whom 8393
Job 8: 7 yet thy latter end should greatly i. 7685
20:28 The i of his house shall depart, *and* 2981
31:12 and would root out all mine i. 8393
Ps 44:12 and dost not i *thy wealth* by their price. 7235
62:10 if riches i, set not *your* heart *upon them.* 5107
67: 6 *Then* shall the earth yield her i; *and* God, 2981
71:21 Thou shalt i my greatness, and comfort me 7235
73:12 who prosper in the world; they i *in* riches. 7685
78:46 He gave also their i unto the caterpillar, and 2981
85:12 *is* good; and our land shall yield her i. 2981
107:37 plant vineyards, which may yield fruits of i. 8393
115:14 The LORD shall i you **more and more**, 3254
Pr 1: 5 A wise *man* will hear, and will i learning; 3254
3: 9 and with the firstfruits of all thine i: 8393
9: 9 teach a just *man,* and he will i in learning. 3254
13:11 but he that gathereth by labour shall i. 7235
14: 4 but much i *is* by the strength of the ox. 8393
18:20 *and with* the i of his lips shall he be filled. 8393
22:16 He that oppresseth the poor to i his *riches,* 7235
28:28 but when they perish, the righteous i. 7235
Ecc 5:10 nor he that loveth abundance *with* i: 8393
5:11 When goods i, they are increased that eat 7235
6:11 Seeing there be many things that i vanity, 7235
Isa 9: 7 Of the i of *his* government and peace *there* 4766
29:19 The meek also shall i *their* joy in 3254
30:23 bread of the i of the earth, and it shall be fat 8393
57: 9 didst i thy perfumes, and didst send thy 7235
Jer 2: 3 unto the LORD, *and* the firstfruits of his i: 8393
23: 3 their folds; and they shall be fruitful and i. 7235
Eze 5:16 I *will* i the famine upon you, and will break 3254
18: 8 forth upon usury, neither hath taken any i, 8636
18:13 given forth upon usury, and hath taken i: 8636
18:17 *that* hath not received usury nor i, 8636
22:12 thou hast taken usury and i, and thou hast 8636
34:27 the earth shall yield her i, and they shall be 2981
36:11 and beast; and they shall i and bring fruit: 7235
36:29 and will i it, and lay no famine upon you. 7235
36:30 the fruit of the tree, and the i of the field, 8570
36:37 I will i them *with* men like a flock. 7235
48:18 the i thereof shall be for food unto them 8393
Da 11:39 he shall acknowledge *and* i *with* glory: 7235
Hos 4:10 shall commit whoredom, and shall not i: 6555
Zec 8:12 the ground shall give her i, and the heavens 2981
10: 8 and they shall i as they have increased. 7235
Lk 17: 5 the apostles said unto the Lord, I our faith. *4369*
Jn 3:30 He must i, but I *must* decrease. *837*
1Co 3: 6 Apollos watered; but God **gave** the i. *837*
3: 7 he that watereth; but God that **giveth** the i. *837*
2Co 9:10 and i the fruits of your righteousness;) *837*
Eph 4:16 maketh i of the body unto the edifying of *838*
Col 2:19 knit together, increaseth *with* the i of God. *838*
1Th 3:12 And the Lord **make** you **to** i and abound in *4121*
4:10 brethren, that *ye* i more *and more;* *4052*
2Ti 2:16 for they will i unto more ungodliness. *4298*

INCREASED (49) [INCREASE]
Ge 7:17 the waters i, and bare up the ark, and it was 7235
7:18 and were i greatly upon the earth; 7235
30:30 I *came,* and it is *now* i unto a multitude; 6555
30:43 the man i exceedingly, and had much cattle, 6555
Ex 1: 7 **i abundantly**, and multiplied, and 8317
23:30 until thou be i, and inherit the land. 6509
1Sa 14:19 in the host of the Philistines went on and i: 7227
2Sa 15:12 for the people i continually with Absalom. 7227
1Ki 22:35 the battle i that day: and the king was 5927
1Ch 4:38 and the house of their fathers i greatly. 6555
5:23 they i from Bashan unto Baal-hermon and 7235
2Ch 18:34 the battle i that day: howbeit the king of 5927
Ezr 9: 6 for our iniquities are i over *our* head, and 7235
Job 1:10 his hands, and his substance is i in the land. 6555
Ps 3: 1 LORD, how are they i that trouble me! 7231
4: 7 *in* the time *that* their corn and their wine i. 7231
49:16 made rich, when the glory of his house is i; 7235
105:24 he i his people greatly; and made them 6509
Pr 9:11 and the years of thy life shall be i. 3254
Ecc 2: 9 **i more** than all that were before me in 3254
5:11 goods increase, they are i that eat them: 7231
Isa 9: 3 hast multiplied the nation, *and* not i the joy: 1431
26:15 Thou hast i the nation, O LORD, thou hast 3254
26:15 O LORD, thou hast i the nation: 3254
51: 2 him alone, and blessed him, and i him. 7235
Jer 3:16 when ye be multiplied and i in the land, 6509
5: 6 are many, *and* their backslidings are i. 6105
15: 8 Their widows are i to me above the sand of 6105
29: 6 that ye may be i there, and not diminished. 7235
30:14 of thine iniquity; *because* thy sins were i. 6105
30:15 *because* thy sins were i, I have done these 6105
La 2: 5 hath i in the daughter of Judah mourning 7235
Eze 16: 7 thou hast i and waxen great, and thou art 7235
16:26 hast i thy whoredoms, to provoke me to 7235
23:14 *that* she i her whoredoms: for when she saw 3254
28: 5 *and* by thy traffick hast thou i thy riches, 7235
41: 7 i *from* the lowest *chamber* to the highest by 5927
Da 12: 4 run to and fro, and knowledge shall be i. 7235
Hos 4: 7 As they were i, so they sinned against me: 7230
10: 1 multitude of his fruit he hath i the altars; 7235
Am 4: 9 and your fig trees and your olive trees i, 7235
Zec 10: 8 and they shall increase as they have i. 7235
Mk 4: 8 and did yield fruit that sprang up and i; *837*
Lk 2:52 And Jesus i in wisdom and stature, and *4298*
Ac 6: 7 And the word of God i; and the number of *837*
9:22 But Saul i the more **in strength**, and *1743*
16: 5 in the faith, and i in number daily. *4052*
2Co 10:15 but having hope, when your faith is i, *837*
Rev 3:17 and **i with goods**, and have need of *4147*

INCREASEST (1) [INCREASE]
Job 10:17 and i thine indignation upon me; 7235

INCREASETH (15) [INCREASE]
Job 10:16 For it i. Thou huntest me as a fierce lion: 1342
12:23 He i the nations, and destroyeth them: 7679
Ps 74:23 those that rise up against thee i continually. 5927
Pr 11:24 There is that scattereth, and yet i; and 3254
16:21 and the sweetness of the lips i learning. 3254
23:28 a prey, and i the transgressors among men. 3254
24: 5 yea, a man of knowledge i strength. 553
28: 8 by usury and unjust gain i his substance, 7235
29:16 the wicked are multiplied, transgression i: 7235
Ecc 1:18 and he that i knowledge increaseth sorrow. 3254
1:18 and he that increaseth knowledge i sorrow. 3254
Isa 40:29 to *them that have* no might he i strength. 7235
Hos 12: 1 he daily i lies and desolation; and they do 7235
Hab 2: 6 say, Woe to him that i *that which is* not his! 7235
Col 2:19 and knit together, i *with* the increase of God. *837*

INCREASING (1) [INCREASE]
Col 1:10 good work, and i in the knowledge of God; *837*

INCREDIBLE (1)
Ac 26: 8 Why should it be thought *a thing* i with you, *571*

INCURABLE (6)
2Ch 21:18 him in his bowels with an i disease. 369+4832
Job 34: 6 my wound *is* i without transgression. 605
Jer 15:18 Why is my pain perpetual, and my wound i, 605
30:12 Thy bruise *is* i, *and* thy wound *is* grievous. 605
30:15 thy sorrow *is* i for the multitude of thine 605
Mic 1: 9 For her wound *is* i; for it is come unto Judah; 605

INDEBTED (1) [DEBT]
Lk 11: 4 for we also forgive every one *that is* i to us. *3784*

INDECENT See UNSEEMLY

INDECISIVE See TENDERHEARTED

INDEED (70)
Ge 17:19 Sarah thy wife shall bear thee a son i; 61
20:12 yet i *she is* my sister; she *is* the daughter of 546
37: 8 to him, Shalt thou i **reign** over us? 4427+4427
37: 8 or shalt thou i **have dominion** over 4910+4910
37:10 thy brethren i **come** to bow down 935+935
40:15 For i I was **stolen away** out of 1589+1589
43:20 we **came** i **down** at the first time to 3381+3381
44: 5 and whereby i he **divineth**? 5172+5172
Ex 19: 5 if ye will **obey** my voice i, 8085+8085+871.1
23:22 if thou shalt i **obey** his voice, and 8085+8085
Lev 10:18 i have **eaten** it in the holy *place,* as I 398+398
Nu 12: 2 the LORD i spoken **only** by Moses? 389+7535
21: 2 If thou wilt i **deliver** this people into 5414+5414
22:37 am I not able i to promote thee to honour? 552
Dt 2:15 For i the hand of the LORD was against 1571
21:16 the son of the hated, *which is* i the firstborn: NIH
Jos 7:20 I I have sinned against the LORD God of 546
1Sa 1:11 if thou wilt i **look** on the affliction of 7200+7200
2:30 I **said** i *that* thy house, and the house of 559+559
2Sa 14: 5 I *am* i a widow woman, and mine husband is 61
15: 8 If the LORD shall **bring** me **again** i 7725+7725
1Ki 8:27 will God i dwell on the earth? behold, 552
2Ki 14:10 Thou hast i **smitten** Edom, and 5221+5221
1Ch 4:10 Oh that thou wouldest **bless** me i, 1288+1288
21:17 *it is* that have sinned and **done evil** i; 7489+7489
Job 19: 4 be it i *that* I have erred, mine error remaineth 551
19: 5 If i ye will magnify *yourselves* against me, 551
Ps 58: 1 Do ye i speak righteousness, 552
Isa 6: 9 **Hear** ye i, but understand not; 8085+8085
6: 9 and **see** ye i, but perceive not. 7200+7200
Jer 22: 4 For if ye **do** this thing i, then 6213+6213
Mt 3:11 I i baptize you with water unto repentance: *3303*
13:32 Which i is the least of all seeds: but when it *3303*
20:23 Ye shall drink i *of* my cup, and be baptized *3303*
23:27 which i appear beautiful outward, but *3303*
26:41 the spirit i *is* willing, but the flesh *is* weak. *3303*
Mk 1: 8 I i have baptized you with water: but *3303*
9:13 That Elias is i come, and they have done *2532*
10:39 Ye shall i drink *of* the cup that I drink *of;* *3303*
11:32 *men* counted John, that he was a prophet i. *3689*
14:21 The Son of man i goeth, as it is written of *3303*
Lk 3:16 unto *them* all, I i baptize you with water; *3303*
11:48 for they i killed them, and ye build their *3303*
23:41 And we i justly; for we receive the due *3303*
24:34 The Lord is risen i, and hath appeared to *3689*
Jn 1:47 and saith of him, Behold an Israelite i, *230*
4:42 and know that this is i the Christ, the Saviour *230*
6:55 For my flesh is meat i, *230*
6:55 is meat indeed, and my blood is drink i. *230*
7:26 Do the rulers know i that this is the very *230*
8:31 in my word, *then* are ye my disciples i; *230*
8:36 shall make you free, ye shall be free i. *3689*
Ac 4:16 for that i a notable miracle hath been done *3303*
11:16 that he said, John i baptized with water; *3303*
22: 9 And they that were with me saw i the light, *3303*
Ro 6:11 ye also yourselves to be dead i unto sin, *3303*
8: 7 subject to the law of God, neither i can be. *1063*
14:20 All *things* i *are* pure; but *it is* evil for *that* *3303*
1Co 11: 7 For a man i ought not to cover *his* head, *3303*
2Co 8:17 For i he accepted the exhortation; but *3303*
11: 1 me a little in *my* folly: and i bear with me. *2532*
Php 1:15 Some i preach Christ even of envy and *3303*
2:27 For i he was sick nigh unto death: but God *2532*
3: 1 to me i *is* not grievous, but for you *it is* *3303*
Col 2:23 Which *things* have i a shew of wisdom in *3303*
1Th 4:10 And i ye do it towards all the brethren *2532*
1Ti 5: 3 Honour widows that are widows i. *3689*
5: 5 Now she that is a widow i, and desolate, *3689*
5:16 that it may relieve them that are widows i. *3689*
1Pe 2: 4 disallowed i of men, but chosen of God, *3303*

INDESCRIBABLE See UNSPEAKABLE

INDIA (2)
Est 1: 1 from I even unto Ethiopia, *over* an hundred 1912
8: 9 rulers of the provinces which *are* from I 1912

INDIGNATION (41)
Dt 29:28 in great i, and cast them into another land, 7110
2Ki 3:27 there was great i against Israel: and 7110
Ne 4: 1 **took** great i, and mocked the Jews. 3707
Est 5: 9 for him, he was full *of* i against Mordecai. 2534
Job 10:17 against me, and increasest thine i upon me; 3708
Ps 69:24 Pour out thine i upon them, and let thy 2195
78:49 wrath, and i, and trouble, *by* sending evil 2195
102:10 Because of thine i and thy wrath: for thou 2195
Isa 10: 5 and the staff in their hand *is* mine i. 2195
10:25 the i shall cease, and mine anger in their 2195
13: 5 *even* the LORD, and the weapons of his i, 2195

Isa 26:20 for a little moment, until the **i** be overpast. 2195
30:27 his lips are full *of* **i**, and his tongue as a 2195
30:30 with the **i** of *his* anger, and *with* the flame 2197
34: 2 For the **i** of the LORD *is* upon all nations, 7110
66:14 his servants, and *his* **i** towards his enemies. 2194
Jer 10:10 the nations shall not be able to abide his **i**. 2195
15:17 of thy hand: for thou hast filled me *with* **i**. 2195
50:25 and hath brought forth the weapons of his **i**: 2195
La 2: 6 hath despised in the **i** of his anger the king 2195
Eze 21:31 I will pour out mine **i** upon thee, I will blow 2195
22:24 nor rained upon in the day of **i**. 2195
22:31 Therefore have I poured out mine **i** upon 2195
Da 8:19 know what shall be in the last end of the **i**: 2195
11:30 and have **i** against the holy covenant: 2194
11:36 and shall prosper till the **i** be accomplished: 2195
Mic 7: 9 I will bear the **i** of the LORD, because 2197
Na 1: 6 Who can stand before his **i**? and who can 2195
Hab 3:12 Thou didst march through the land in **i**, 2195
Zep 3: 8 to pour upon them mine **i**, *even* all my 2195
Zec 1:12 *against* which thou hast had **i** these 2194
Mal 1: 4 *against* whom the LORD hath **i** for ever. 2194
Mt 20:24 were **moved with i** against the two brethren. *23*
26: 8 But when his disciples saw *it*, they **had i**, *23*
Mk 14: 4 And there were some that **had i** within *23*
Lk 13:14 the ruler of the synagogue answered with **i**, *23*
Ac 5:17 of the Sadducees,) and were filled with **i**, *2205*
Ro 2: 8 but obey unrighteousness, **i** and wrath, *2372*
2Co 7:11 yea, *what* **i**, yea, *what* fear, yea, *24*
Heb 10:27 fearful looking for of judgment and fiery **i**, *2205*
Rev 14:10 out without mixture into the cup of his **i**; *3709*

INDITING (1)
Ps 45: 1 My heart is **i** a good matter: I speak of 7370

INDUSTRIOUS (1)
1Ki 11:28 seeing the young man that he was **i**, 4399+6213

INEXCUSABLE (1)
Ro 2: 1 Therefore thou art **i**, O man, whosoever thou *379*

INEXPRESSIBLE See UNSPEAKABLE

INFALLIBLE (1)
Ac 1: 3 alive after his passion by many **i proofs**, *5039*

INFAMOUS (1) [INFAMY]
Eze 22: 5 *which art* **i** *and* much vexed. 2931+8034+1886.1

INFAMY (2) [INFAMOUS]
Pr 25:10 thee to shame, and thine **i** turn not away. 1681
Eze 36: 3 lips of talkers, and *are* an **i** of the people: 1681

INFANT (2) [INFANTS]
1Sa 15: 3 **i** and suckling, ox and sheep, camel and 5768
Isa 65:20 There shall be no more thence an **i** of days, 5764

INFANTS (3) [INFANT]
Job 3:16 I had not been; as **i** *which* never saw light. 5768
Hos 13:16 their **i** shall be dashed in pieces, and 5768
Lk 18:15 And they brought unto him also **i**, that he *1025*

INFERIOR (4)
Job 12: 3 as well as you; I *am* not **i** to you: 5307
13: 2 *same* do I know also. I *am* not **i** unto you. 5307
Da 2:39 after thee shall arise another kingdom **i** to 772
2Co 12:13 For what is it wherein ye were **i** to other *2274*

INFIDEL (2)
2Co 6:15 or what part hath he that believeth with an **i**? *571*
1Ti 5: 8 hath denied the faith, and is worse than an **i**. *571*

INFINITE (3)
Job 22: 5 and thine iniquities **i**? 369+7093
Ps 147: 5 of great power: his understanding *is* **i**. 369+4557
Na 3: 9 Egypt *were* her strength, and *it was* **i**; 369+7097

INFIRMITIES (12) [INFIRMITY]
Mt 8:17 saying Himself took our **i**, and bare our *769*
Lk 5:15 to hear, and to be healed by him of their **i**. *769*
7:21 in that *same* hour he cured many of *their* **i** *3554*
8: 2 which had been healed of evil spirits and **i**, *769*
Ro 8:26 Likewise the Spirit also helpeth our **i**: for we *769*
15: 1 that are strong ought to bear the **i** of *771*
2Co 11:30 glory of the *things* which concern mine **i**. *769*
12: 5 yet of myself I will not glory, but in mine **i**. *769*
12: 9 therefore will I rather glory in my **i**, *769*
12:10 Therefore I take pleasure in **i**, in reproaches, *769*
1Ti 5:23 for thy stomach's sake and thine often **i**. *769*
Heb 4:15 cannot be touched with the feeling of our **i**; *769*

INFIRMITY (10) [INFIRMITIES]
Lev 12: 2 the separation for her **i** shall she be unclean. 1738
Ps 77:10 I said, This *is* my **i**: *but I will remember* 2470
Pr 18:14 The spirit of a man will sustain his **i**; but 4245
Lk 13:11 there was a woman which had a spirit of **i** *769*
13:12 unto her, Woman, thou art loosed from thy **i**. *769*
Jn 5: 5 which had an **i** thirty *and* eight years. *769*
Ro 6:19 of men because of the **i** of your flesh: *769*
Gal 4:13 Ye know how through **i** of the flesh I *769*
Heb 5: 2 for that he himself also is compassed with **i**. *769*
7:28 law maketh men high priests which have **i**; *769*

INFLAME (1) [INFLAMING, INFLAMMATION]
Isa 5:11 that continue until night, *till* wine **i** them! 1814

INFLAMING (1) [INFLAME]
Isa 57: 5 **I** yourselves with idols under every green 2552

INFLAMMATION (2) [INFLAME]
Lev 13:28 him clean: for it *is* an **i** of the burning. 6867
Dt 28:22 with an **i**, and with an extreme burning, and 1816

INFLICTED (1)
2Co 2: 6 *is* this punishment, which *was* **i** of many. NIG

INFLUENCES (1)
Job 38:31 Canst thou bind the **sweet i** of Pleiades, or 4575

INFOLDING (1)
Eze 1: 4 a fire **i** itself, and a brightness *was* about it, 3947

INFORM (1) [INFORMED]
Dt 17:10 to do according to all that they **i** thee: 3384

INFORMED (6) [INFORM]
Da 9:22 he **i** *me*, and talked with me, and said, 995
Ac 21:21 And they are **i** of thee, that thou teachest all *2727*
21:24 whereof they were **i** concerning thee, *2727*
24: 1 who **i** the governor against Paul. *1718*
25: 2 the chief of the Jews **i** him against Paul, *1718*
25:15 the elders of the Jews **i** *me*, desiring *to have* *1718*

INGATHERING (2) [GATHER]
Ex 23:16 the feast of **i**, *which is* in the end of the year, 614
34:22 and the feast of **i** *at* the year's end. 614

INHABIT (10) [HABITABLE, HABITATION, HABITATIONS, INHABITANT, INHABITANTS, INHABITED, INHABITERS, INHABITEST, INHABITETH, INHABITING]
Nu 35:34 therefore the land which ye shall **i**, 3427
Pr 10:30 but the wicked shall not **i** the earth. 7931
Isa 42:11 *their voice*, the villages *that* Kedar doth **i**: 3427
65:21 **i** *them*; and they shall plant vineyards, and 3427
65:22 They shall not build, and another **i**; 3427
Jer 17: 6 shall **i** the parched places in the wilderness, 7931
48:18 Thou daughter that dost **i** Dibon, 3427
Eze 33:24 they that **i** those wastes of the land of Israel 3427
Am 9:14 **i** *them*; and they shall plant vineyards, and 3427
Zep 1:13 not **i** *them*; and they shall plant vineyards, 3427

INHABITANT (33) [INHABIT]
Job 28: 4 The flood breaketh out from the **i**; *even* 1481
Isa 5: 9 be desolate, *even* great and fair, without **i**. 3427
6:11 Until the cities be wasted without **i**, and 3427
9: 9 *even* Ephraim and the **i** of Samaria, that say 3427
12: 6 Cry out and shout, thou **i** of Zion: for great 3427
20: 6 the **i** of this isle shall say in that day, 3427
24:17 the snare, *are* upon thee, O **i** of the earth. 3427
33:24 the **i** shall not say, I am sick: the people that 7934
Jer 2:15 land waste: his cities are burnt without **i**. 3427
4: 7 thy cities shall be laid waste, without an **i**. 3427
9:11 the cities of Judah desolate, without an **i**. 3427
10:17 wares out of the land, O **i** of the fortress. 3427
21:13 O **i** of the valley, *and* rock of the plain, 3427
22:23 O **i** of Lebanon, that makest thy nest in 3427
26: 9 and this city shall be desolate without an **i**? 3427
33:10 and without **i**, and without beast, 3427
34:22 the cities of Judah a desolation without an **i**. 3427
44:22 and a curse, without an **i**, as *at* this day. 3427
46:19 shall be waste and desolate without an **i**. 3427
48:19 O **i** of Aroer, stand by the way and espy; 3427
48:43 upon thee, O **i** of Moab, saith the LORD. 3427
51:29 land of Babylon a desolation without an **i**. 3427
51:35 *be* upon Babylon, shall the **i** of Zion say; 3427
51:37 and a hissing, without an **i**. 3427
Am 1: 5 cut off the **i** from the plain of Aven, and 3427
1: 8 I will cut off the **i** from Ashdod, and 3427
Mic 1:11 Pass ye away, thou **i** of Saphir, having *thy* 3427
1:11 the **i** of Zaanan came not forth *in* 3427
1:12 For the **i** of Maroth waited carefully for 3427
1:13 O thou **i** of Lachish, bind the chariot to 3427
1:15 I bring an heir unto thee, O **i** of Mareshah: 3427
Zep 2: 5 even destroy thee, that there shall be no **i**. 3427
3: 6 so that there is no man, that there is none **i**. 3427

INHABITANTS (201) [INHABIT]
Ge 19:25 all the **i** of the cities, and that which grew 3427
34:30 make me to stink among the **i** of the land, 3427
50:11 when the **i** of the land, the Canaanites, saw 3427
Ex 15:14 sorrow shall take hold on the **i** of Palestina. 3427
15:15 all the **i** of Canaan shall melt away. 3427
23:31 for I will deliver the **i** of the land into your 3427
34:12 lest thou make a covenant with the **i** of 3427
34:15 Lest thou make a covenant with the **i** of 3427
Lev 18:25 and the land *itself* vomiteth out her **i**. 3427
25:10 *all* the land unto all the **i** thereof: 3427
Nu 13:32 *is* a land that eateth up the **i** thereof; 3427
14:14 they will tell *it* to the **i** of this land: *for* they 3427
32:17 fenced cities because of the **i** of the land. 3427
33:52 ye shall drive out all the **i** of the land from 3427
33:53 ye shall dispossess *the* **i** *of* the land, and NIH
33:55 if ye will not drive out the **i** of the land 3427
Dt 13:13 have withdrawn the **i** of their city, saying, 3427
13:15 Thou shalt surely smite the **i** of that city 3427
Jos 2: 9 that all the **i** of the land faint because of 3427
2:24 for even all the **i** of the country do faint 3427
7: 9 and all the **i** of the land shall hear *of it*, and 3427
8:24 an end of slaying all the **i** of Ai in the field, 3427
8:26 until *he* had utterly destroyed all the **i** of Ai. 3427
9: 3 when the **i** of Gibeon heard what Joshua 3427
9:11 and all the **i** of our country spake to us, 3427
9:24 to destroy all the **i** of the land from before 3427
10: 1 how the **i** of Gibeon had made peace with 3427
11:19 of Israel, save the Hivites the **i** of Gibeon: 3427
13: 6 All the **i** of the hill country from Lebanon 3427
15:15 he went up thence to the **i** of Debir: and 3427
15:63 As for the Jebusites the **i** of Jerusalem, 3427
17: 7 on the right hand unto the **i** of En-tappuah. 3427
17:11 the **i** of Dor and her towns, and 3427
17:11 the **i** of Endor and her towns, and 3427
17:11 the **i** of Taanach and her towns, and 3427
17:11 and the **i** of Megiddo and her towns, 3427
17:12 could not drive out *the* **i** *of* those cities; NIH
Jdg 1:11 from thence he went against the **i** of Debir: 3427
1:19 he drave out *the* **i** *of* the mountain; but NIH
1:19 could not drive out the **i** of the valley, 3427
1:27 Neither did Manasseh drive out *the* **i** *of* NIH
1:27 her towns, nor the **i** of Dor and her towns, 3427
1:27 nor the **i** of Ibleam and her towns, 3427
1:27 nor the **i** of Megiddo and her towns: 3427
1:30 Neither did Zebulun drive out the **i** of 3427
1:30 inhabitants of Kitron, nor the **i** of Nahalol; 3427
1:31 Neither did Asher drive out the **i** of Accho, 3427
1:31 nor the **i** of Zidon, nor of Ahlab, nor of 3427
1:32 among the Canaanites, the **i** of the land: 3427
1:33 Neither did Naphtali drive out the **i** of 3427
1:33 of Beth-shemesh, nor the **i** of Beth-anath; 3427
1:33 among the Canaanites, the **i** of the land: 3427
1:33 nevertheless the **i** of Beth-shemesh and 3427
2: 2 ye shall make no league with the **i** of this 3427
5: 7 *The* **i** *of* the villages ceased, they ceased in NIH
5:11 *even* the righteous acts *towards the* **i** of his NIH
5:23 the LORD, curse ye bitterly the **i** thereof; 3427
10:18 he shall be head over all the **i** of Gilead. 3427
11: 8 and be our head over all the **i** of Gilead. 3427
11:21 land of the Amorites, the **i** of that country. 3427
20:15 that drew sword, beside the **i** of Gibeah, 3427
21: 9 *there were* none of the **i** of Jabesh-gilead 3427
21:10 smite the **i** of Jabesh-gilead with the edge 3427
21:12 they found among the **i** of Jabesh-gilead 3427
Ru 4: 4 Buy *it* before the **i**, and before the elders of 3427
1Sa 6:21 they sent messengers to the **i** of 3427
23: 5 So David saved the **i** of Keilah. 3427
27: 8 for those *nations were* of old the **i** of 3427
31:11 when the **i** of Jabesh-gilead heard of that 3427
2Sa 5: 6 unto the Jebusites, the **i** of the land: 3427
1Ki 17: 1 *who was* of the **i** of Gilead, said unto Ahab, 8453
21:11 and the nobles who *were* the **i** in his city, 3427
2Ki 19:26 Therefore their **i** *were* of small power, 3427
22:16 evil upon this place, and upon the **i** thereof, 3427
22:19 against the **i** thereof, that *they* should 3427
23: 2 and all the **i** of Jerusalem with him, 3427
1Ch 8: 6 these *are* the heads of the fathers of the **i** of 3427
8:13 who *were* heads of the fathers of the **i** of 3427
8:13 of Aijalon, who drove away the **i** of Gath: 3427
9: 2 Now the first **i** that *dwelt* in their 3427
11: 4 where the Jebusites *were*, the **i** of the land. 3427
11: 5 the **i** of Jebus said to David, Thou shalt not 3427
22:18 for he hath given the **i** of the land into mine 3427
2Ch 15: 5 great vexations *were* upon all the **i** of 3427
20: 7 who didst drive out the **i** of this land before 3427
20:15 ye **i** of Jerusalem, and thou king 3427
20:18 the **i** of Jerusalem fell before the LORD, 3427
20:20 Hear me, O Judah, and ye **i** of Jerusalem; 3427
20:23 Moab stood up against the **i** of mount Seir, 3427
20:23 when they had made an end of the **i** of Seir, 3427
21:11 caused the **i** of Jerusalem to commit 3427
21:13 and the **i** of Jerusalem to go a whoring, 3427
22: 1 the **i** of Jerusalem made Ahaziah his 3427
32:22 the **i** of Jerusalem from the hand of 3427
32:26 *both* he and the **i** of Jerusalem, so that 3427
32:33 the **i** of Jerusalem did him honour at his 3427
33: 9 made Judah and the **i** of Jerusalem to err, 3427
34:24 evil upon this place, and upon the **i** thereof, 3427
34:27 against the **i** thereof, and humbledst thyself 3427
34:28 upon this place, and upon the **i** of the same. 3427
34:30 the **i** of Jerusalem, and the priests, and 3427
34:32 Benjamin to stand *to it*. And the **i** of 3427
35:18 that were present, and the **i** of Jerusalem. 3427
Ezr 4: 6 *him* an accusation against the **i** of Judah 3427
Ne 3:13 gate repaired Hanun, and the **i** of Zanoah; 3427
7: 3 and appoint watches of the **i** of Jerusalem, 3427
9:24 thou subduedst before them the **i** of 3427
Job 26: 5 from under the waters, and the **i** thereof. 7931
Ps 33: 8 let all the **i** of the world stand in awe of 3427
33:14 he looketh upon all the **i** of the earth. 3427
49: 1 all ye people; give ear, all ye **i** of the world: 3427
75: 3 and all the **i** thereof *are* dissolved: 3427
83: 7 Amalek; the Philistines with the **i** of Tyre; 3427
Isa 5: 3 O **i** of Jerusalem, and men of Judah, judge, 3427
8:14 a gin and for a snare to the **i** of Jerusalem. 3427
10:13 I have put down the **i** like a valiant *man*: 3427
10:31 the **i** of Gebim gather themselves to flee. 3427
18: 3 All ye **i** of the world, and dwellers on 3427
21:14 The **i** of the land of Tema brought water to 3427
22:21 he shall be a father to the **i** of Jerusalem, 3427
23: 2 Be still, ye **i** of the isle; thou whom 3427
23: 6 ye over to Tarshish; howl, ye **i** of the isle. 3427
24: 1 and scattereth abroad the **i** thereof. 3427
24: 5 The earth also is defiled under the **i** thereof; 3427
24: 6 therefore the **i** of the earth are burned, and 3427
26: 9 the **i** of the world will learn righteousness. 3427
26:18 neither have the **i** of the world fallen. 3427
26:21 punish the **i** of the earth for their iniquity: 3427
37:27 Therefore their **i** *were* of small power, 3427
38:11 I shall behold man no more with the **i** of 3427
40:22 and the **i** thereof *are* as grasshoppers; 3427
42:10 that is therein; the isles, and the **i** thereof. 3427
42:11 let the **i** of the rock sing, let them shout 3427
49:19 even now be too narrow by reason of the **i**, 3427
Jer 1:14 shall break forth upon all the **i** of the land. 3427
4: 4 ye men of Judah and **i** of Jerusalem: 3427
6:12 for I will stretch out my hand upon the **i** of 3427
8: 1 the bones of the **i** of Jerusalem, out of their 3427
10:18 I will sling out the **i** of the land at this once, 3427
11: 2 the men of Judah, and to the **i** of Jerusalem; 3427
11: 9 of Judah, and among the **i** of Jerusalem. 3427
11:12 the cities of Judah and **i** of Jerusalem go, 3427
13:13 Behold, I *will* fill all the **i** of this land, 3427
13:13 and the prophets, and all the **i** of Jerusalem, 3427
17:20 and all Judah, and all the **i** of Jerusalem, 3427
17:25 the men of Judah, and the **i** of Jerusalem: 3427
18:11 to the **i** of Jerusalem, saying, Thus saith 3427
19: 3 O kings of Judah, and **i** of Jerusalem; 3427
19:12 to the **i** thereof, and *even* make this city as 3427
21: 6 I will smite the **i** of this city, both man and 3427
23:14 as Sodom, and the **i** thereof as Gomorrah. 3427
25: 2 and to all the **i** of Jerusalem, saying, 3427
25: 9 against the **i** thereof, and against all these 3427

Jer 25:29 for I will call for a sword upon all the i of 3427
25:30 the grapes, against all the i of the earth. 3427
26:15 and upon this city, and upon the i thereof: 3427
32:32 the men of Judah, and the i of Jerusalem. 3427
35:13 the men of Judah and the i of Jerusalem, 3427
35:17 upon all the i of Jerusalem all the evil that I 3427
36:31 upon the i of Jerusalem, and upon the men 3427
42:18 my fury hath been poured forth upon the i 3427
46: 8 I will destroy the city and the i thereof. 3427
47: 2 and all the i of the land shall howl. 3427
49: 8 turn back, dwell deep, O i of Dedan; 3427
49:20 that he hath purposed against the i of 3427
49:30 get you far off, dwell deep, O ye i of Hazor, 3427
50:21 even against it, and against the i of Pekod: 3427
50:34 to the land, and disquiet the i of Babylon. 3427
50:35 upon the i of Babylon, and upon her 3427
51:12 done that which he spake against the i of 3427
51:24 to all the i of Chaldea all their evil that they 3427
51:35 my blood upon the i of Chaldea, 3427
La 4:12 kings of the earth, and all the i of the world, 3427
Eze 11:15 are they unto whom the i of Jerusalem have 3427
12:19 of the i of Jerusalem, and of the land of 3427
15: 6 for fuel, so will I give the i of Jerusalem. 3427
26:17 which wast strong in the sea, she and her i, 3427
27: 8 The i of Zidon and Arvad were thy 3427
27:35 All the i of the isles shall be astonished at 3427
29: 6 all the i of Egypt shall know that I am 3427
Da 4:35 all the i of the earth are reputed as nothing: 1753
4:35 of heaven, and among the i of the earth: 1753
9: 7 to the i of Jerusalem, and unto all Israel, 3427
Hos 4: 1 hath a controversy with the i of the land, 3427
10: 5 The i of Samaria shall fear because of 7934
Joel 1: 2 old men, and give ear, all ye i of the land. 3427
1:14 all the i of the land into the house of 3427
2: 1 let all the i of the land tremble: for the day 3427
Mic 6:12 the i thereof have spoken lies, and 3427
6:16 a desolation, and the i thereof a hissing: 3427
Zep 1: 4 and upon all the i of Jerusalem; 3427
1:11 Howl, ye i of Maktesh, for all the merchant 3427
2: 5 Woe unto the i of the sea coast, the nation 3427
Zec 8:20 shall come people, and the i of many cities: 3427
8:21 the i of one city shall go to another, saying, 3427
11: 6 For I will no more pity the i of the land, 3427
12: 5 The i of Jerusalem shall be my strength in 3427
12: 7 the glory of the i of Jerusalem do not 3427
12: 8 In that day shall the LORD defend the i of 3427
12:10 upon the i of Jerusalem, the spirit of grace 3427
13: 1 to the i of Jerusalem for sin and 3427

INHABITED (32) [INHABIT]

Ge 36:20 the sons of Seir the Horite, who i the land; 3427
Ex 16:35 forty years, until they came to a land i; 3427
Lev 16:22 him all their iniquities unto a land not i: 1509
Jdg 1:17 they slew the Canaanites that i Zephath, 3427
1:21 not drive out the Jebusites that i Jerusalem; 3427
1Ch 5: 9 eastward he i unto the entering in of 3427
Isa 13:20 It shall never be i, neither shall it be dwelt 3427
44:26 that saith to Jerusalem, Thou shalt be i; and 3427
45:18 created it not in vain, he formed it to be i: 3427
54: 3 and make the desolate cities to be i. 3427
Jer 6: 8 lest I make thee desolate, a land not i. 3427
17: 6 in the wilderness, in a salt land and not i. 3427
22: 6 thee a wilderness and cities which are not i. 3427
46:26 afterwards it shall be i, as in the days of 7931
50:13 of the wrath of the LORD it shall not be i, 3427
50:39 it shall be no more i for ever; neither shall 3427
Eze 12:20 the cities that are i shall be laid waste, and 3427
26:17 that wast i of seafaring men, the renowned 3427
26:19 a desolate city, like the cities that are not i; 3427
26:20 that go down to the pit, that thou be not i; 3427
29:11 through it, neither shall it be i forty years. 3427
34:13 and in all the i places of the country. 4186
36:10 the cities shall be i, and the wastes shall be 3427
36:35 ruined cities are become fenced, and are i. 3427
38:12 upon the desolate places that are now i, 3427
Zec 2: 4 Jerusalem shall be i as towns without walls 3427
7: 7 when Jerusalem was i and in prosperity, 3427
7: 7 when men i the south and the plain? 3427
9: 5 from Gaza, and Ashkelon shall not be i. 3427
12: 6 Jerusalem shall be i again in her own place, 3427
14:10 it shall be lifted up, and i in her place, from 3427
14:11 but Jerusalem shall be safely i. 3427

INHABITERS (3) [INHABIT]

Rev 8:13 to the i of the earth by reason of the other 2730
12:12 Woe to the i of the earth and of the sea! 2730
17: 2 the i of the earth have been made drunk 2730

INHABITEST (1) [INHABIT]

Ps 22: 3 art holy, O thou that i the praises of Israel. 3427

INHABITETH (2) [INHABIT]

Job 15:28 and in houses which no man i, which are 3427
Isa 57:15 saith the high and lofty One that i eternity, 7931

INHABITING (1) [INHABIT]

Ps 74:14 to be meat to the people i the wilderness. 6728

INHERIT (62) [INHERITANCE, INHERITANCES, INHERITED, INHERITETH, INHERITOR]

Ge 15: 7 the Chaldees, to give thee this land to i it. 3423
15: 8 whereby shall I know that I shall i it? 3423
28: 4 that thou mayest i the land wherein thou art 3423
Ex 23:30 until thou be increased, and i the land. 5157
32:13 unto your seed, and they shall i it for ever. 5157
Lev 20:24 Ye shall i their land, and I will give it unto 3423
25:46 after you, to i them for a possession; 3423
Nu 18:24 I have given to the Levites to i: 5159
26:55 of the tribes of their fathers they shall i. 5157
32:19 For we will not i with them on yonder side 5157
33:54 to the tribes of your fathers ye shall i. 5157
34:13 This is the land which ye shall i by lot, 5157
Dt 1:38 for he shall cause Israel to i it. 5157
2:31 to possess, that thou mayest i his land. 3423
Dt 3:28 he shall cause them to i the land which 5157
12:10 the LORD your God giveth you to i, 5157
16:20 i the land which the LORD thy God 3423
19: 3 which the LORD thy God giveth thee to i, 5157
19:14 which thou shalt i in the land that 5157
21:16 when he maketh his sons to i that which he 5157
31: 7 and thou shalt cause them to i it. 5157
Jos 17:14 given me but one lot and one portion to i, 5159
Jdg 11: 2 Thou shalt not i in our father's house; 5157
1Sa 2: 8 and to make them i the throne of glory: 5157
2Ch 20:11 which thou hast given us to i. 3423
Ps 25:13 dwell at ease; and his seed shall i the earth. 3423
37: 9 upon the LORD, they shall i the earth. 3423
37:11 the meek shall i the earth; and shall delight 3423
37:22 For such as be blessed of him shall i 3423
37:29 The righteous shall i the land, and 3423
37:34 and he shall exalt thee to i the land: 3423
69:36 The seed also of his servants shall i it: and 5157
82: 8 judge the earth: for thou shalt i all nations. 5157
Pr 3:35 The wise shall i glory: but shame shall be 5157
8:21 That I may cause those that love me to i 5157
11:29 He that troubleth his own house shall i 5157
14:18 The simple i folly: but the prudent are 5157
Isa 49: 8 to cause to i the desolate heritages; 5157
54: 3 thy seed shall i the Gentiles, and make 3423
57:13 the land, and shall i my holy mountain; 3423
60:21 they shall i the land for ever, the branch of 3423
65: 9 mine elect shall i it, and my servants shall 3423
Jer 8:10 their fields to them that shall i them: for 3423
12:14 which I have caused my people Israel to i; 5157
49: 1 why then doth their king i Gad, and 3423
Eze 47:13 whereby ye shall i the land according to 5157
47:14 ye shall i it, one as well as another: 5157
Zec 2:12 the LORD shall i Judah his portion in 5157
Mt 5: 5 are the meek: for they shall i the earth. 2816
19:29 an hundredfold, and shall i everlasting life. 2816
25:34 i the kingdom prepared for you from 2816
Mk 10:17 what shall I do that I may i eternal life? 2816
Lk 10:25 Master, what shall I do to i eternal life? 2816
18:18 what shall I do to i eternal life? 2816
1Co 6: 9 Know ye not that the unrighteous shall not i 2816
6:10 shall i the kingdom of God. 2816
15:50 and blood cannot i the kingdom of God; 2816
15:50 neither doth corruption i incorruption. 2816
Gal 5:21 that they which do such things shall not i 2816
Heb 6:12 through faith and patience i the promises. 2816
1Pe 3: 9 thereunto called, that ye should i a blessing. 2816
Rev 21: 7 He that overcometh shall i all things; and 2816

INHERITANCE (239) [INHERIT]

Ge 31:14 or i for us in our father's house? 5159
48: 6 after the name of their brethren in their i. 5159
Ex 15:17 plant them in the mountain of thine i, in 5159
34: 9 and our sin, and take us for thine i. 5157
Lev 25:46 ye shall take them as an i for your children 5157
Nu 16:14 honey, or given us i of fields and vineyards: 5159
18:20 Thou shalt have no i in their land, 5157
18:20 and thine i among the children of Israel. 5159
18:21 of Levi all the tenth in Israel for an i, 5159
18:23 the children of Israel they have no i. 5157+5159
18:24 of Israel they shall have no i. 5157+5159
18:26 I have given you from them for your i, 5159
26:53 Unto these the land shall be divided for an i 5159
26:54 To many thou shalt give the more i, and 5159
26:54 to few thou shalt give the less i: 5159
26:54 to every one shall his i be given according 5159
26:62 there was no i given them among 5159
27: 7 of an i among their father's brethren; 5159
27: 7 thou shalt cause the i of their father to pass 5159
27: 8 ye shall cause his i to pass unto his 5159
27: 9 then ye shall give his i unto his brethren. 5159
27:10 ye shall give his i unto his father's brethren. 5159
27:11 ye shall give his i unto his kinsman that is 5159
32:18 of Israel have inherited every man his i. 5159
32:19 our i is fallen to us on this side Jordan 5159
32:32 that the possession of our i on this side 5159
33:54 divide the land by lot for an i among your 5157
33:54 and to the moe ye shall give the more i, and 5159
33:54 and to the fewer ye shall give the less i: 5159
33:54 every man's i shall be in the place where his NIH
34: 2 is the land that shall fall unto you for an i, 5159
34:14 have received their i; and half the tribe of NIH
34:14 the tribe of Manasseh have received their i: 5159
34:15 the half tribe have received their i on this 5159
34:18 of every tribe, to divide the land by i. 5157
34:29 divide the i unto the children of Israel in 5157
35: 2 that they give unto the Levites of the i of 5159
35: 8 according to his i which he inheriteth. 5159
36: 2 land for an i by lot to the children of Israel: 5159
36: 2 i of Zelophehad our brother unto his 5159
36: 3 shall their i be taken from the inheritance of 5159
36: 3 shall their inheritance be taken from the i of 5159
36: 3 shall be put to the i of the tribe whereinto 5159
36: 3 shall it be taken from the lot of our i. 5159
36: 4 shall their i be put unto the inheritance of 5159
36: 4 shall their inheritance be put unto the i of 5159
36: 4 shall their i be taken away from 5159
36: 4 away from the i of the tribe of our fathers. 5159
36: 7 So shall not the i of the children of Israel 5159
36: 7 himself to the i of the tribe of his fathers. 5159
36: 8 that possesseth an i in any tribe of 5159
36: 8 may enjoy every man the i of his fathers. 5159
36: 9 Neither shall the i remove from one tribe to 5159
36: 9 of Israel shall keep himself to his own i. 5159
36:12 their i remained in the tribe of the family of 5159
Dt 4:20 to be unto him a people of i, as ye are this 5159
4:21 the LORD thy God giveth thee for an i: 5159
4:38 to give thee their land for an i, as it is this 5159
9:26 destroy not thy people and thine i, 5159
9:29 Yet they are thy people and thine i, 5159
10: 9 Wherefore Levi hath no part nor i with his 5159
10: 9 the LORD is his i, according as 5159
12: 9 are not as yet come to the rest and to the i, 5159
12:12 forasmuch as he hath no part nor i with 5159
14:27 for he hath no part nor i with thee. 5159
Dt 14:29 (because he hath no part nor i with thee,) 5159
15: 4 thy God giveth thee for an i to possess it: 5159
18: 1 of Levi, shall have no part nor i with Israel: 5159
18: 1 of the LORD made by fire, and his i. 5159
18: 2 Therefore shall they have no i among their 5159
18: 2 the LORD is their i, as he hath said unto 5159
19:10 the LORD thy God giveth thee for an i, 5159
19:14 which they of old time have set in thine i, 5159
20:16 the LORD thy God doth give thee for an i, 5159
21:23 the LORD thy God giveth thee for an i. 5159
24: 4 the LORD thy God giveth thee for an i. 5159
25:19 thy God giveth thee for an i to possess it, 5159
26: 1 the LORD thy God giveth thee for an i, 5159
29: 8 gave it for an i unto the Reubenites, and 5159
32: 8 most High divided to the nations their i, 5157
32: 9 is his people; Jacob is the lot of his i. 5159
33: 4 even the i of the congregation of Jacob. 4181
Jos 1: 6 people shalt thou divide for an i the land, 5157
11:23 Joshua gave it for an i unto Israel according 5159
13: 6 thou it by lot unto the Israelites for an i, 5159
13: 7 divide this land for an i unto the nine tribes, 5159
13: 8 and the Gadites have received their i, 5159
13:14 Only unto the tribe of Levi he gave none i; 5159
13:14 God of Israel made by fire are their i, 5159
13:15 of Reuben i according to their families. NIH
13:23 the border thereof. This was the i of 5159
13:24 Moses gave i unto the tribe of Gad, NIH
13:28 This is the i of the children of Gad after 5159
13:29 Moses gave i unto the half tribe of NIH
13:32 did distribute for i in the plains of Moab, 5157
13:33 unto the tribe of Levi Moses gave not any i: 5159
13:33 the LORD God of Israel was their i, as he 5159
14: 1 of Israel, distributed for i to them. 5157
14: 2 By lot was their i, as the LORD 5159
14: 3 For Moses had given the i of two tribes and 5159
14: 3 unto the Levites he gave none i among 5159
14: 9 thy feet have trodden shall be thine i, 5159
14:13 the son of Jephunneh Hebron for an i. 5159
14:14 became the i of Caleb the son of Jephunneh 5159
15:20 This is the i of the tribe of the children of 5159
16: 4 Manasseh and Ephraim, took their i. 5157
16: 5 their i on the east side was Ataroth-addar, 5159
16: 8 This is the i of the tribe of the children of 5159
16: 9 among the i of the children of Manasseh, 5159
17: 4 Moses to give us an i among our brethren. 5159
17: 4 an i among the brethren of their father. 5159
17: 6 the daughters of Manasseh had an i 5159
18: 2 which had not yet received their i. 5159
18: 4 and describe it according to the i of them; 5159
18: 7 for the priesthood of the LORD is their i: 5159
18: 7 have received their i beyond Jordan on 5159
18:20 This was the i of the children of Benjamin, 5159
18:28 This is the i of the children of Benjamin 5159
19: 1 their i was within the inheritance of 5159
19: 1 their inheritance was within the i of 5159
19: 2 they had in their i Beer-sheba, or Sheba, 5159
19: 8 This is the i of the tribe of the children of 5159
19: 9 Judah was the i of the children of Simeon: 5159
19: 9 the children of Simeon had their i within 5157
19: 9 had their inheritance within the i of them. 5159
19:10 and the border of their i was unto Sarid: 5159
19:16 This is the i of the children of Zebulun 5159
19:23 This is the i of the tribe of the children of 5159
19:31 This is the i of the tribe of the children of 5159
19:39 This is the i of the tribe of the children of 5159
19:41 the coast of their i was Zorah, and Eshtaol, 5159
19:48 This is the i of the tribe of the children of 5159
19:49 of dividing the land for i by their coasts, 5157
19:49 the children of Israel gave an i to Joshua 5159
19:51 divided for an i by lot in Shiloh before 5157
21: 3 Israel gave unto the Levites out of their i, 5159
23: 4 to be an i for your tribes, from Jordan, 5159
24:28 let the people depart, every man unto his i. 5159
24:30 they buried him in the border of his i in 5159
24:32 it became the i of the children of Joseph. 5159
Jdg 2: 6 every man unto his i to possess the land. 5159
2: 9 they buried him in the border of his i in 5159
18: 1 i to dwell in; for unto that day all their 5159
18: 1 i had not fallen unto them among the tribes 5159
20: 6 sent her throughout all the country of the i 5159
21:17 There must be an i for them that be escaped 3425
21:23 they went and returned unto their i, and 5159
21:24 went out from thence every man to his i. 5159
Ru 4: 5 to raise up the name of the dead upon his i. 5159
4: 6 redeem it for myself, lest I mar mine own i: 5159
4:10 to raise up the name of the dead upon his i, 5159
1Sa 10: 1 hath anointed thee to be captain over his i? 5159
26:19 day from abiding in the i of the LORD, 5159
2Sa 14:16 and my son together out of the i of God. 5159
20: 1 neither have we i in the son of Jesse: 5159
20:19 why wilt thou swallow up the i of 5159
21: 3 that ye may bless the i of the LORD? 5159
1Ki 8:36 thou hast given to thy people for an i. 5159
8:51 For they be thy people, and thine i, 5159
8:53 to be thine i, as thou spakest by the hand of 5159
12:16 neither have we i in the son of Jesse: 5159
21: 3 that I should give the i of my fathers unto 5159
21: 4 I will not give thee the i of my fathers. 5159
2Ki 21:14 I will forsake the remnant of mine i, and 5159
1Ch 16:18 I give the land of Canaan, the lot of your i; 5159
28: 8 leave it for an i for your children after you 5157
2Ch 6:27 thou hast given unto thy people for an i. 5159
10:16 we have none i in the son of Jesse: 5159
Ezr 9:12 leave it for an i to your children for ever. 3423
Ne 11:20 in all the cities of Judah, every one in his i. 5159
Job 31: 2 and what i of the Almighty from on high? 5159
42:15 their father gave them i among their 5159
Ps 2: 8 I shall give thee the heathen for thine i, and 5159
16: 5 The LORD is the portion of mine i and 2506
28: 9 Save thy people, and bless thine i: 5159
33:12 people whom he hath chosen for his own i. 5159
37:18 of the upright: and their i shall be for ever. 5159
47: 4 He shall choose our i for us, the excellency 5159
68: 9 whereby thou didst confirm thine i, when it 5159
74: 2 the rod of thine i, which thou hast 5159

Ps 78:55 divided them an **i** by line, and made 5159
78:62 unto the sword; and was wroth with his **i**. 5159
78:71 to feed Jacob his people, and Israel his **i**. 5159
79: 1 O God, the heathen are come into thine **i**; 5159
94:14 off his people, neither will he forsake his **i**. 5159
105:11 I give the land of Canaan, the lot of your **i**: 5159
106: 5 of thy nation, that *I* may glory with thine **i**. 5159
106:40 insomuch that he abhorred his own **i**. 5159
Pr 13:22 A good *man* **leaveth an i** to *his* children's 5157
17: 2 shall have part of the **i** among the brethren. 5159
19:14 House and riches *are* the **i** of fathers: and 5159
20:21 An **i** *may be* gotten hastily at the beginning; 5159
Ecc 7:11 Wisdom *is* good with an **i**: and *by it there is* 5159
Isa 19:25 the work of my hands, and Israel mine **i**. 5159
47: 6 I have polluted mine **i**, and given them into 5159
63:17 for thy servants' sake, the tribes of thine **i**. 5159
Jer 3:18 that I have **given for an i** unto your fathers. 5157
10:16 of all *things;* and Israel *is* the rod of his **i**: 5159
12:14 that touch the **i** which I have caused my 5159
16:18 they have filled mine **i** with the carcases of 5159
32: 8 for the right of **i** *is* thine, and 3425
51:19 of all *things:* and *Israel is* the rod of his **i**: 5159
La 5: 2 Our **i** is turned to strangers, our houses to 5159
Eze 22:16 thou shalt **take** thine **i** in thyself in the sight 2490
33:24 but we *are* many; the land is given us for **i**. 4181
35:15 As thou didst rejoice at the **i** of the house of 5159
36:12 thou shalt be their **i**, and thou shalt no more 5159
44:28 it shall be unto them for an **i**: I *am* their 5159
44:28 I *am* their **i**; and ye shall give them no 5159
45: 1 when ye shall divide *by lot* the land for **i**, 5159
46:16 of his sons, the **i** thereof shall be his sons'; 5159
46:16 his sons'; it *shall be* their possession by **i**. 5159
46:17 if he give a gift of his **i** to one of his 5159
46:17 but his **i** shall be his sons' for them. 5159
46:18 the prince shall not take of the people's **i**, 5159
46:18 he shall **give** his sons **i** out of his own 5157
47:14 and this land shall fall unto you for **i**. 5159
47:22 *that* ye shall divide it *by lot* for an **i** unto 5159
47:22 they shall **have i** with you among 5159+5307
47:23 there shall ye give *him* his **i**, saith the Lord 5159
48:29 divide *by lot* unto the tribes of Israel for **i**, 5159
Mt 21:38 let us kill him, and let us seize on his **i**. *2817*
Mk 12: 7 let us kill him, and the **i** shall be ours. *2817*
Lk 12:13 to my brother, that *he* divide the **i** with me. *2817*
20:14 come, let us kill him, that the **i** may be ours. *2817*
Ac 7: 5 And he gave him none **i** in it, no, not so *2817*
20:32 to give you an **i** among all them which are *2817*
26:18 **i** among them which are sanctified by faith *2819*
Gal 3:18 For if the **i** *be* of the law, *it is* no more of *2817*
Eph 1:11 In whom also we have **obtained an i**, *2820*
1:14 Which is the earnest of our **i**, until *2817*
1:18 what the riches of the glory of his **i** in *2817*
5: 5 hath *any* **i** in the kingdom of Christ and *2817*
Col 1:12 to be partakers of the **i** of the saints in light: *2819*
3:24 Lord ye shall receive the reward of the **i**: *2817*
Heb 1: 4 as he hath by **i obtained** a more excellent *2816*
9:15 might receive the promise of eternal **i**. *2817*
11: 8 place which he should after receive for an **i**, *2817*
1Pe 1: 4 To an **i** incorruptible, and undefiled, and *2817*

INHERITANCES (1) [INHERIT]
Jos 19:51 These *are* the **i**, which Eleazar the priest, 5159

INHERITED (6) [INHERIT]
Nu 32:18 until the children of Israel have **i** every man 5157
Jos 14: 1 children of Israel **i** in the land of Canaan, 5157
Ps 105:44 and they **i** the labour of the people; 3423
Jer 16:19 Surely our fathers have **i** lies, vanity, and 5157
Eze 33:24 Abraham was one, and he **i** the land: 3423
Heb 12:17 when he would have **i** the blessing, he was *2816*

INHERITETH (1) [INHERIT]
Nu 35: 8 according to his inheritance which he **i**. 5157

INHERITOR (1) [INHERIT]
Isa 65: 9 and out of Judah an **i** of my mountains: 3423

INIQUITIES (56) [INIQUITY]
Lev 16:21 confess over him all the **i** of the children of 5771
16:22 the goat shall bear upon him all their **i** unto 5771
26:39 also in the **i** of their fathers shall they pine 5771
Nu 14:34 shall ye bear your **i**, *even* forty years, and 5771
Ezr 9: 6 for our **i** are increased over *our* head, and 5771
9: 7 for our **i** have we, our kings, *and* 5771
9:13 hast punished us less than our **i** *deserve,* 5771
Ne 9: 2 their sins, and the **i** of their fathers. 5771
Job 13:23 How many *are* mine **i** and sins? make me to 5771
13:26 makest me to possess the **i** of my youth. 5771
22: 5 thy wickedness great? and thine **i** infinite? 5771
Ps 38: 4 For mine **i** are gone *over* mine head: as a 5771
40:12 mine **i** have taken hold upon me, so that I 5771
51: 9 face from my sins, and blot out all mine **i**. 5771
64: 6 They search out **i**; they accomplish a 5766
65: 3 **I** prevail against me: *as for* our 1697+5771
79: 8 O remember not against us former **i**: let thy 5771
90: 8 Thou hast set our **i** before thee, our secret 5771
103: 3 Who forgiveth all thine **i**; who healeth all 5771
103:10 nor rewarded us according to our **i**. 5771
107:17 because of their **i**, are afflicted. 5771
130: 3 If thou, LORD, shouldest mark **i**, O Lord, 5771
130: 8 And he shall redeem Israel from all his **i**. 5771
Pr 5:22 His own **i** shall take the wicked himself, 5771
Isa 43:24 thy sins, thou hast wearied me with thine **i**. 5771
50: 1 for your **i** have you sold yourselves, and 5771
53: 5 our transgressions, *he was* bruised for our **i**: 5771
53:11 justify many; for he shall bear their **i**. 5771
59: 2 your **i** have separated between you 5771
59:12 with us; and *as for* our **i**, we know them; 5771
64: 6 our **i**, like the wind, have taken us away. 5771
64: 7 and hast consumed us, because of our **i**. 5771
65: 7 Your **i**, and the iniquities of your fathers 5771
65: 7 and the **i** of your fathers together, 5771
Jer 5:25 Your **i** have turned away these *things,* and 5771
11:10 They are turned back to the **i** of their 5771

Jer 14: 7 O LORD, though our **i** testify against us, 5771
33: 8 I will pardon all their **i**, whereby they have 5771
La 4:13 sins of her prophets, *and* the **i** of her priests, 5771
5: 7 *and are* not; *and* we have borne their **i**. 5771
Eze 24:23 ye shall pine away for your **i**, and 5771
28:18 thy sanctuaries by the multitude of thine **i**, 5771
32:27 but their **i** shall be upon their bones, 5771
36:31 yourselves in your own sight for your **i** 5771
36:33 I shall have cleansed you from all your **i**, 5771
43:10 that they may be ashamed of their **i**: 5771
Da 4:27 and thine **i** by shewing mercy to the poor; 5758
9:13 that *we* might turn from our **i**, and 5771
9:16 for the **i** of our fathers, Jerusalem and 5771
Am 3: 2 I will punish you for all your **i**. 5771
Mic 7:19 he will subdue our **i**; and thou wilt cast all 5771
Ac 3:26 turning away every one of you from *his* **i**. *4189*
Ro 4: 7 *Saying,* Blessed *are they* whose **i** are *458*
Heb 8:12 and their **i** will I remember no more. *458*
10:17 their sins and **i** will I remember no more. *458*
Rev 18: 5 unto heaven, and God hath remembered her **i**. *92*

INIQUITY (278) [INIQUITIES]
Ge 15:16 for the **i** of the Amorites *is* not yet full. 5771
19:15 lest thou be consumed in the **i** of the city. 5771
44:16 God hath found out the **i** of thy servants: 5771
Ex 20: 5 visiting the **i** of the fathers upon 5771
28:38 that Aaron may bear the **i** of the holy 5771
28:43 in the holy *place;* that they bear not **i**, 5771
34: 7 forgiving **i** and transgression and sin, and 5771
34: 7 the **i** of the fathers upon the children, 5771
34: 9 pardon our **i** and our sin, and take us for 5771
Lev 5: 1 if he do not utter *it,* then he shall bear his **i**. 5771
5:17 *it* not, yet is he guilty, and shall bear his **i**. 5771
7:18 and the soul that eateth of it shall bear his **i**. 5771
10:17 *God* hath given it you to bear the **i** of 5771
17:16 nor bathe his flesh; then he shall bear his **i**. 5771
18:25 therefore I do visit the **i** thereof upon it, and 5771
19: 8 *every one* that eateth it shall bear his **i**, 5771
20:17 his sister's nakedness; he shall bear his **i**. 5771
20:19 his near kin: they shall bear their **i**. 5771
22:16 Or suffer them to bear the **i** of trespass, 5771
26:39 pine away in their **i** in your enemies' lands; 5771
26:40 If they shall confess their **i**, and the iniquity 5771
26:40 their iniquity, and the **i** of their fathers, 5771
26:41 then accept of the **punishment of** their **i**: 5771
26:43 shall accept of the **punishment of** their **i**: 5771
Nu 5:15 of memorial, bringing **i** to remembrance. 5771
5:31 shall the man be guiltless from **i**, and this 5771
5:31 and this woman shall bear her **i**. 5771
14:18 forgiving **i** and transgression, and by no 5771
14:18 **i** of the fathers upon the children unto 5771
14:19 the **i** of this people according unto 5771
15:31 utterly be cut off; his **i** *shall be* upon him. 5771
18: 1 thy father's house with thee shall bear the **i** 5771
18: 1 thy sons with thee shall bear the **i** of your 5771
18:23 and they shall bear their **i**: 5771
23:21 He hath not beheld **i** in Jacob, neither hath 205
30:15 he hath heard *them;* then he shall bear her **i**. 5771
Dt 5: 9 visiting the **i** of the fathers upon 5771
19:15 shall not rise up against a man for any **i**, 5771
32: 4 a God of truth and without **i**, just and 5766
Jos 22:17 *Is* the **i** of Peor *too* little for us, from which 5771
22:20 and that man perished not alone in his **i**. 5771
1Sa 3:13 house for ever for the **i** which he knoweth; 5771
3:14 that the **i** of Eli's house shall not be purged 5771
15:23 and stubbornness *is as* **i** and idolatry. 205
20: 1 what *is* mine **i**? and what *is* my sin before 5771
20: 8 if there be in me **i**, slay me thyself; 5771
25:24 *upon* me *let this* **i** *be:* and let thine 5771
2Sa 7:14 If he **commit i**, I will chasten him with 5753
14: 9 the **i** *be* on me, and on my father's house: 5771
14:32 and if there be *any* **i** in me, let him kill me. 5771
19:19 the king, Let not my lord impute **i** unto me, 5771
22:24 and have kept myself from mine **i**. 5771
24:10 O LORD, take away the **i** of thy servant; 5771
1Ch 21: 8 I beseech thee, do away the **i** of thy servant; 5771
2Ch 19: 7 do *it:* for *there is* no **i** with the LORD our 5766
Ne 4: 5 cover not their **i**, and let not their sin be 5771
Job 4: 8 they that plow **i**, and sow wickedness, 205
5:16 poor hath hope, and **i** stoppeth her mouth. 5766
6:29 Return, I pray you, let it not be **i**; yea, 5766
6:30 Is there **i** in my tongue? cannot my taste 5766
7:21 my transgression, and take away mine **i**? 5771
10: 6 That thou inquirest after mine **i**, and 5771
10:14 and thou wilt not acquit me from mine **i**. 5771
11: 6 that God exacteth of thee *less* than thine **i** 5771
11:14 If **i** *be* in thine hand, put it far away, and 205
14:17 up in a bag, and thou sewest up mine **i**. 5771
15: 5 For thy mouth uttereth thine **i**, and 5771
15:16 filthy *is* man, which drinketh **i** like water? 5766
20:27 The heaven shall reveal his **i**; and the earth 5771
21:19 God layeth up his **i** for his children: 205
22:23 thou shalt be built *up,* thou shalt put away **i** 5766
31: 3 a strange punishment to the workers of **i**? 205
31:11 yea, it *is* an **i** *to be punished by* the judges. 5771
31:28 This also *were* an **i** *to be punished by* 5771
31:33 as Adam, by hiding mine **i** in my bosom: 5771
33: 9 I *am* innocent, neither *is there* **i** in me. 5771
34: 8 goeth in company with the workers of **i**, 205
34:10 the Almighty, *that he should commit* **i**. 5766
34:22 where the workers of **i** may hide themselves. 205
34:32 thou me: if I have done **i**, I will do no more. 5766
36:10 and commandeth that they return from **i**. 205
36:21 Take heed, regard not **i**: for this hast thou 205
36:23 or who can say, Thou hast wrought **i**? 5766
Ps 5: 5 in thy sight: thou hatest all workers of **i**. 205
6: 8 Depart from me, all ye workers of **i**; for 205
7: 3 I have done this; if there be **i** in my hands; 5766
7:14 he travaileth with **i**, and hath conceived 205
14: 4 Have all the workers of **i** no knowledge? 205
18:23 before him, and I kept myself from mine **i**. 5771
25:11 thy name's sake, O LORD, pardon mine **i**; 5771
28: 3 with the wicked, and with the workers of **i**, 205
31:10 my strength faileth because of mine **i**, and 5771
32: 2 man unto whom the LORD imputeth not **i**, 5771

Ps 32: 5 my sin unto thee, and mine **i** have I not hid. 5771
32: 5 and thou forgavest the **i** of my sin. 5771
36: 2 own eyes, until his **i** be found to be hateful. 5771
36: 3 The words of his mouth *are* **i** and deceit: 205
36:12 There are the workers of **i** fallen: they are 205
37: 1 be thou envious against the workers of **i**. 5766
38:18 For I will declare mine **i**; I will be sorry for 5771
39:11 thou with rebukes dost correct man for **i**, 5771
41: 6 his heart gathereth **i** to itself; *when* he goeth 205
49: 5 *when* the **i** of my heels shall compass me 5771
51: 2 Wash me throughly from mine **i**, and 5771
51: 5 Behold, I was shapen in **i**; and in sin did my 5771
53: 1 are they, and have done abominable **i**: 5766
53: 4 Have the workers of **i** no knowledge? 205
55: 3 for they cast **i** upon me, and in wrath they 205
56: 7 *Shall* they escape by **i**? in *thine* anger cast 205
59: 2 Deliver me from the workers of **i**, and 205
64: 2 from the insurrection of the workers of **i**: 205
66:18 If I regard **i** in my heart, the Lord will not 205
69:27 Add **i** unto their iniquity: and let them not 5771
69:27 Add iniquity unto their **i**: and let them not 5771
78:38 forgave *their* **i**, and destroyed *them* not: 5771
85: 2 Thou hast forgiven the **i** of thy people, 5771
89:32 with the rod, and their **i** with stripes. 5771
92: 7 and when all the workers of **i** do flourish; 205
92: 9 all the workers of **i** shall be scattered. 205
94: 4 *and* all the workers of **i** boast themselves? 205
94:16 stand up for me against the workers of **i**? 205
94:20 Shall the throne of **i** have fellowship *with* 1942
94:23 he shall bring upon them their own **i**, and 205
106: 6 we have **committed i**, we have done 5753
106:43 and were brought low for their **i**. 5771
107:42 and rejoice: and all **i** shall stop her mouth. 5766
109:14 Let the **i** of his fathers be remembered with 5771
119: 3 They also do no **i**: they walk in his ways. 5766
119:133 and let not any **i** have dominion over me. 205
125: 3 the righteous put forth their hands unto **i**. 5766
125: 5 shall lead them forth with the workers of **i**: 205
141: 4 practise wicked works with men that work **i**: 205
141: 9 laid for me, and the grins of the workers of **i**. 205
Pr 10:29 but destruction *shall be* to the workers of **i**. 205
16: 6 By mercy and truth **i** is purged: and by 5771
19:28 and the mouth of the wicked devoureth **i**. 205
21:15 but destruction *shall be* to the workers of **i**. 205
22: 8 He that soweth **i** shall reap vanity: and 5766
Ecc 3:16 the place of righteousness, *that* **i** *was* there. 7562
Isa 1: 4 Ah sinful nation, a people laden with **i**, 5771
1:13 away with; *it is* **i**, even the solemn meeting. 205
5:18 Woe unto them that draw **i** with cords of 5771
6: 7 thine **i** is taken away, and thy sin purged. 5771
13:11 for *their* evil, and the wicked for their **i**; 5771
14:21 Prepare slaughter for his children for the **i** 5771
22:14 Surely this **i** shall not be purged from you 5771
26:21 the inhabitants of the earth for their **i**: 5771
27: 9 therefore shall the **i** of Jacob be purged; 5771
29:20 and all that watch for **i** are cut off: 205
30:13 Therefore this **i** shall be to you as a breach 5771
31: 2 and against the help of them that work **i**. 205
32: 6 his heart will work **i**, to practise hypocrisy, 205
33:24 that dwell therein *shall be* forgiven *their* **i**. 5771
40: 2 is accomplished, that her **i** is pardoned: 5771
53: 6 the LORD hath laid on him the **i** of us all. 5771
57:17 For the **i** of his covetousness was I wroth, 5771
59: 3 defiled with blood, and your fingers with **i**; 5771
59: 4 *they* conceive mischief, and bring forth **i**. 205
59: 6 their works *are* works of **i**, and the act of 205
59: 7 their thoughts *are* thoughts of **i**; wasting and 205
64: 9 O LORD, neither remember **i** for ever: 5771
Jer 2: 5 What **i** have your fathers found in me, 5766
2:22 much sope, *yet* thine **i** *is* marked before me, 5771
3:13 Only acknowledge thine **i**, that thou hast 5771
9: 5 *and* weary themselves to **commit i**. 5753
13:22 For the greatness of thine **i** are thy skirts 5771
14:10 he will now remember their **i**, and 5771
14:20 our wickedness, *and* the **i** of our fathers: 5771
16:10 or what *is* our **i**? or what *is* our sin that we 5771
16:17 neither is their **i** hid from mine eyes. 5771
16:18 first I will recompense their **i** and their sin 5771
18:23 against me to slay *me:* forgive not their **i**, 5771
25:12 for their **i**, and the land of the Chaldeans, 5771
30:14 of a cruel one, for the multitude of thine **i**; 5771
30:15 *is* incurable for the multitude of thine **i**: 5771
31:30 every one shall die for his own **i**: every man 5771
31:34 for I will forgive their **i**, and I will 5771
32:18 recompensest the **i** of the fathers into 5771
33: 8 I will cleanse them from all their **i**, 5771
36: 3 that I may forgive their **i** and their sin. 5771
36:31 and his seed and his servants for their **i**; 5771
50:20 the **i** of Israel shall be sought for, and 5771
51: 6 be not cut off in her **i**; for this *is* the time of 5771
La 2:14 they have not discovered thine **i**, to turn 5771
4: 6 For the **punishment of** the **i** of the daughter 5771
4:22 The **punishment of** thine **i** is 5771
4:22 he will visit thine **i**, O daughter of Edom; 5771
Eze 3:18 the same wicked *man* shall die in his **i**; 5771
3:19 from his wicked way, he shall die in his **i**; 5771
3:20 commit **i**, and I lay a stumblingblock before 5766
4: 4 lay the **i** of the house of Israel upon it: 5771
4: 4 thou shalt lie upon it thou shalt bear their **i**. 5771
4: 5 I have laid upon thee the years of their **i**, 5771
4: 5 shalt thou bear the **i** of the house of Israel. 5771
4: 6 thou shalt bear the **i** of the house of Judah 5771
4:17 with another, and consume away for their **i**. 5771
7:13 neither shall any strengthen himself in the **i** 5771
7:16 all of them mourning, every one for his **i**. 5771
7:19 because it is the stumblingblock of their **i**. 5771
9: 9 The **i** of the house of Israel and Judah *is* 5771
14: 3 put the stumblingblock of their **i** before 5771
14: 4 putteth the stumblingblock of his **i** before 5771
14: 7 putteth the stumblingblock of his **i** before 5771
14:10 they shall bear the **punishment of** their **i**: 5771
16:49 this was the **i** of thy sister Sodom, pride, 5771
18: 8 *that* hath withdrawn his hand from **i**, 5766
18:17 he shall not die for the **i** of his father, 5771
18:18 his people, lo, even he shall die in his **i**. 5771

Eze 18:19 doth not the son bear the **i** of the father? 5771
18:20 The son shall not bear the **i** of the father, 5771
18:20 neither shall the father bear the **i** of the son: 5771
18:24 committeth **i**, *and* doeth according to all 5766
18:26 and committeth **i**, and dieth in them; 5766
18:26 for his **i** that he hath done shall he die. 5766
18:30 so **i** shall not be your ruin. 5771
21:23 he will call to remembrance the **i**, that *they* 5771
21:24 Because ye have made your **i** to be 5771
21:25 day is come, when **i** *shall have* an end, 5771
21:29 day is come, when *their* **i** *shall have* an end. 5771
28:15 thou wast created, till **i** was found in thee. 5766
28:18 of thine iniquities, by the **i** of thy traffick; 5766
29:16 which bringeth *their* **i** to remembrance, 5771
33: 6 from among them, he is taken *away* in his **i**; 5771
33: 8 his way, that wicked *man* shall die in his **i**; 5771
33: 9 not turn from his way, he shall die in his **i**; 5771
33:13 to his own righteousness, and commit **i**, 5766
33:13 for his **i** that he hath committed, he shall 5766
33:15 in the statutes of life, without committing **i**; 5766
33:18 and committeth **i**, he shall even die thereby. 5766
35: 5 in the time *that their* **i** *had* an end: 5771
39:23 of Israel went into captivity for their **i**: 5771
44:10 after their idols; they shall even bear their **i**. 5771
44:12 and caused the house of Israel to fall into **i**; 5771
44:12 the Lord GOD, and they shall bear their **i**. 5771
Da 9: 5 have **committed i**, and have done 5753
9:24 to make reconciliation for **i**, and to bring in 5771
Hos 4: 8 and they set their heart on their **i**. 5771
5: 5 shall Israel and Ephraim fall in their **i**; 5771
6: 8 Gilead *is* a city of them that work **i**, *and* 205
7: 1 the **i** of Ephraim was discovered, and 5771
8:13 now will he remember their **i**, and 5771
9: 7 for the multitude of thine **i**, and the great 5771
9: 9 *therefore* he will remember their **i**, he will 5771
10: 9 the battle in Gibeah against the children of **i** 5932
10:13 have plowed wickedness, ye have reaped **i**; 5766
12: 8 *in* all my labours they shall find none **i** in 5771
12:11 *Is there* **i** *in* Gilead? surely they are vanity: 205
13:12 The **i** of Ephraim *is* bound up; his sin *is* hid. 5771
14: 1 thy God; for thou hast fallen by thine **i**. 5771
14: 2 Take away all **i**, and receive *us* graciously: 5771
Mic 2: 1 Woe to them that devise **i**, and work evil 205
3:10 up Zion with blood, and Jerusalem with **i**. 5766
7:18 that pardoneth **i**, and passeth by 5771
Hab 1: 3 Why dost thou shew me **i**, and cause *me* to 205
1:13 than to behold evil, and canst not look on **i**: 5999
2:12 town with blood, and stablisheth a city by **i**! 5766
Zep 3: 5 *is* in the midst thereof; he will not do **i**: 5766
3:13 The remnant of Israel shall not do **i**, 5766
Zec 3: 4 I have caused thine **i** to pass from thee, and 5771
3: 9 I will remove the **i** of that land in one day. 5771
Mal 2: 6 his mouth, and **i** was not found in his lips: 5766
2: 6 and equity, and did turn many away from **i**. 5771
Mt 7:23 knew you: depart from me, ye that work **i**. *458*
13:41 all things that offend, and them which do **i**; *458*
23:28 but within ye are full of hypocrisy and **i**. *458*
24:12 And because **i** shall abound, the love of *458*
Lk 13:27 you are; depart from me, all *ye* workers of **i**. *93*
Ac 1:18 *man* purchased a field with the reward of **i**; *93*
8:23 in the gall of bitterness, and *in* the bond of **i**. *93*
Ro 6:19 to uncleanness and to **i** unto iniquity; *458*
6:19 to uncleanness and to iniquity unto **i**; *458*
1Co 13: 6 Rejoiceth not in **i**, but rejoiceth in the truth; *93*
2Th 2: 7 For the mystery of **i** doth already work: *458*
2Ti 2:19 that nameth the name of Christ depart from **i**. *93*
Tit 2:14 that he might redeem us from all **i**, and *458*
Heb 1: 9 Thou hast loved righteousness, and hated **i**; *458*
Jas 3: 6 And the tongue *is* a fire, a world of **i**: so is *93*
2Pe 2:16 But was rebuked for his **i**: the dumb ass *3892*

INJURED (1) [INJURIOUS]

Gal 4:12 be as I *am;* for I *am* as ye *are:* ye have not **i** *91*

INJURIOUS (1) [INJURED]

1Ti 1:13 a blasphemer, and a persecutor, and **i**: *5197*

INJUSTICE (1)

Job 16:17 Not for *any* **i** in mine hands: also my prayer 2555

INK (4) [INKHORN]

Jer 36:18 and I wrote *them* with **i** in the book. 1773
2Co 3: 3 written not with **i**, but with the Spirit of *3188*
2Jn 1:12 I would not *write* with paper and **i**: *3188*
3Jn 1:13 but I will not with **i** and pen write unto *3188*

INKHORN (3) [HORN, INK]

Eze 9: 2 *with* linen, with a writer's **i** by his side: 7083
9: 3 which *had* the writer's **i** by his side; 7083
9:11 which *had* the **i** by his side, reported 7083

INN (5)

Ge 42:27 his sack to give his ass provender in the **i**, 4411
43:21 it came to pass, when we came to the **i**, 4411
Ex 4:24 it came to pass by the way in the **i**, that 4411
Lk 2: 7 there was no room for them in the **i**. *2646*
10:34 and brought him to an **i**, and took care of *3829*

INNER (37) [INNERMOST]

1Ki 6:27 he set the cherubims within the **i** house: 6442
6:36 he built the **i** court *with* three rows of 6442
7:12 both for the **i** court of the house of 6442
7:50 *of* gold, *both* for the doors of the **i** house, 6442
20:30 the city, into an **i chamber**. 2315+2315+871.1
22:25 an **i chamber** to hide thyself. 2315+2315+871.1
2Ki 9: 2 carry him *to* an **i chamber**: 2315+2315+871.1
1Ch 28:11 of the **i** parlours thereof, and of the place of 6442
2Ch 4:22 the **i** doors thereof for the most holy *place,* 6442
18:24 an **i chamber** to hide thyself. 2315+2315+871.1
29:16 the priests went into the **i part** *of* the house 6441
Est 4:11 shall come unto the king into the **i** court, 6442
5: 1 and stood in the **i** court of the king's house, 6442
Eze 8: 3 to the door of the **i** gate that looketh toward 6442
8:16 he brought me into the **i** court of 6442
Eze 10: 3 went in; and the cloud filled the **i** court. 6442
40:15 of the porch of the **i** gate *were* fifty cubits. 6442
40:19 unto the forefront of the **i** court without, 6442
40:23 the gate of the **i** court *was* over against 6442
40:27 *there was* a gate in the **i** court toward 6442
40:28 he brought me to the **i** court by the south 6442
40:32 he brought me into the **i** court toward 6442
40:44 without the **i** gate *were* the chambers of 6442
40:44 the chambers of the singers in the **i** court, 6442
41:15 with the **i** temple, and the porches of 6442
41:17 even unto the **i** house, and without, and 6442
42: 3 twenty *cubits* which *were* for the **i** court, 6442
42:15 had made an end of measuring the **i** house, 6442
43: 5 me up, and brought me into the **i** court; 6442
44:17 *that* when they enter in at the gates of the **i** 6442
44:17 whiles they minister in the gates of the **i** 6442
44:21 drink wine, when they enter into the **i** court. 6442
44:27 unto the **i** court, to minister in 6442
45:19 and upon the posts of the gate of the **i** court. 6442
46: 1 The gate of the **i** court that looketh *toward* 6442
Ac 16:24 thrust them into the **i** prison, and made their *2082*
Eph 3:16 with might by his Spirit in the **i** man; *2080*

INNERMOST (2) [INNER]

Pr 18: 8 they go down *into* the **i parts** of the belly. 2315
26:22 they go down *into* the **i parts** of the belly. 2315

INNOCENCY (5) [INNOCENT, INNOCENTS]

Ge 20: 5 and **i** of my hands have I done this. 5356
Ps 26: 6 I will wash mine hands in **i**: so will I 5356
73:13 heart *in* vain, and washed my hands in **i**. 5356
Da 6:22 forasmuch as before him **i** was found in 2136
Hos 8: 5 how long *will it be* ere they attain to **i**? 5356

INNOCENT (38) [INNOCENCY]

Ex 23: 7 and the **i** and righteous slay thou not: 5355
Dt 19:10 That **i** blood be not shed in thy land, 5355
19:13 thou shalt put away *the guilt of* **i** blood 5355
21: 8 lay not **i** blood unto thy people of Israel's 5355
21: 9 So shalt thou put away the *guilt of* **i** blood 5355
27:25 Cursed *be* he that taketh reward to slay an **i** 5355
1Sa 19: 5 then wilt thou sin against **i** blood, 5355
1Ki 2:31 that thou mayest take away the **i** blood, 2600
2Ki 21:16 Moreover Manasseh shed **i** blood very 5355
24: 4 also *for* the **i** blood that he shed: for he 5355
24: 4 for he filled Jerusalem *with* **i** blood; 5355
Job 4: 7 I pray thee, who *ever* perished, being **i**? 5355
9:23 he will laugh at the trial of the **i**. 5355
9:28 I know that thou wilt not **hold** me **i**. 5352
17: 8 the **i** shall stir up himself against 5355
22:19 and are glad: and the **i** laugh them to scorn. 5355
22:30 He shall deliver the island of the **i**: and it is 5355
27:17 put *it* on, and the **i** shall divide the silver. 5355
33: 9 I am clean without transgression, I *am* **i**; 2643
Ps 10: 8 in the secret places doth he murder the **i**: 5355
15: 5 to usury, nor taketh reward against the **i**. 5355
19:13 and I shall be **i** from the great transgression. 5352
94:21 of the righteous, and condemn the **i** blood. 5355
106:38 shed **i** blood, *even* the blood of their sons 5355
Pr 1:11 let us lurk privily for the **i** without cause: 5355
6:17 a lying tongue, and hands that shed **i** blood, 5355
6:29 whosoever toucheth her shall not be **i**. 5352
28:20 that maketh haste to be rich shall not be **i**. 5352
Isa 59: 7 and they make haste to shed **i** blood: 5355
Jer 2:35 Yet thou sayest, Because I am **i**, surely his 5352
7: 6 and shed not **i** blood in this place, 5355
22: 3 neither shed **i** blood in this place. 5355
22:17 for to shed **i** blood, and for oppression, and 5355
26:15 ye shall surely bring **i** blood upon 5355
Joel 3:19 they have shed **i** blood in their land. 5355
Jnh 1:14 this man's life, and lay not upon us **i** blood: 5355
Mt 27: 4 I have sinned in that I have betrayed *the* **i** *121*
27:24 I am **i** of the blood of this just *person:* see ye *121*

INNOCENTS (2) [INNOCENCY]

Jer 2:34 is found the blood of the souls of the poor **i**: 5355
19: 4 have filled this place *with* the blood of **i**; 5355

INNUMERABLE (7)

Job 21:33 after him, as *there are* **i** before him. 369+4557
Ps 40:12 For **i** evils have compassed me 369+4557+5704
104:25 wherein *are* things creeping **i**, 369+4557
Jer 46:23 more than the grasshoppers, and *are* **i**. 369+4557
Lk 12: 1 gathered together an **i multitude** of people, *3461*
Heb 11:12 and as the sand which is by the sea shore **i**. *382*
12:22 and to an **i company** of angels, *3461*

INORDINATE (2)

Eze 23:11 she was more corrupt in her **i love** than she, 5691
Col 3: 5 fornication, uncleanness, **i affection**, *3806*

INQUIRE (52) [INQUIRED, INQUIREST, INQUIRY]

Ge 24:57 We will call the damsel, and **i** at her mouth. 7592
25:22 I thus? And she went to **i** of the LORD. 1875
Ex 18:15 Because the people come unto me to **i** of 1875
Dt 12:30 that thou **i** not after their gods, saying, 1875
13:14 shalt thou **i**, and make search, and 1875
17: 9 the judge that shall be in those days, and **i**; 1875
Jdg 4:20 when any man doth come and **i** of thee, and 7592
1Sa 9: 9 when a man went to **i** of God, thus he 1875
17:56 king said, **I** thou whose son the stripling *is.* 7592
22:15 Did I then begin to **i** of God for him? be it 7592
28: 7 that I may go to her, and **i** of her. 1875
1Ki 22: 5 **I**, I pray thee, at the word of the LORD to 1875
22: 7 LORD besides, that we might **i** of him? 1875
22: 8 by whom *we* may **i** of the LORD: 1875
2Ki 1: 2 **i** of Baal-zebub the god of Ekron whether I 1875
1: 3 *that* ye go to **i** of Baal-zebub the god of 1875
1: 6 *that* thou sendest to **i** of Baal-zebub the god 1875
1:16 to **i** of Baal-zebub the god of Ekron, 1875
1:16 *there is* no God in Israel to **i** of his word? 1875
3:11 that we may **i** of the LORD by him? 1875
8: 8 and **i** of the LORD by him, saying, 1875
16:15 and the brasen altar shall be for me to **i** *by.* 1239
2Ki 22:13 **i** of the LORD for me, and for the people, 1875
22:18 to the king of Judah which sent you to **i** of 1875
1Ch 10:13 of *one that had* a familiar spirit, to **i** *of it;* 1875
18:10 to **i** of his welfare, and to congratulate him, 7592
21:30 David could not go before it to **i** of God: 1875
2Ch 18: 4 **I**, I pray thee, at the word of the LORD to 1875
18: 6 LORD besides, that we might **i** of him? 1875
18: 7 by whom we may **i** of the LORD: 1875
32:31 who sent unto him to **i** of the wonder that 1875
34:21 **i** of the LORD for me, and for them that 1875
34:26 who sent you to **i** of the LORD, so 1875
Ezr 7:14 to **i** concerning Judah and Jerusalem, 1240
Job 8: 8 For **i**, I pray thee, of the former age, and 7592
Ps 27: 4 of the LORD, and to **i** in his temple. 1239
Ecc 7:10 for thou dost not **i** wisely concerning this. 7592
Isa 21:12 if ye will **i**, inquire ye: return, come. 1158
21:12 if ye will inquire, **i** ye: return, come. 1158
Jer 21: 2 **I**, I pray thee, of the LORD for us; for 1875
37: 7 of Judah, that sent you unto me to **i of** me; 1875
Eze 14: 7 cometh to a prophet to **i** of him concerning 1875
20: 1 elders of Israel came to **i of** the LORD, 1875
20: 3 the Lord GOD; Are ye come to **i of** me? 1875
Mt 10:11 or town ye shall enter, **i** who in it is worthy; *1833*
Lk 22:23 And they began to **i** among themselves, *4802*
Jn 16:19 Do ye **i** among yourselves of that I said, *2212*
Ac 9:11 **i** in the house of Judas for *one* called Saul, *2212*
19:39 But if ye **i** any *thing* concerning other *1934*
23:15 as though ye would **i** something more *1231*
23:20 as though they would **i** somewhat of him *4441*
2Co 8:23 Whether *any do* **i** of Titus, *he is* my partner NIG

INQUIRED (34) [INQUIRE]

Dt 17: 4 thou hast heard *of it,* and **i** diligently, and 1875
Jdg 6:29 when they **i** and asked, they said, 1875
8:14 man of the men of Succoth, and **i** of him: 7592
20:27 the children of Israel **i** of the LORD, 7592
1Sa 10:22 Therefore they **i** of the LORD further, 7592
22:10 he **i** of the LORD for him, and gave him 7592
22:13 and a sword, and hast **i** of God for him, 7592
23: 2 Therefore David **i** of the LORD, saying, 7592
23: 4 David **i** of the LORD yet again. And 7592
28: 6 when Saul **i** of the LORD, the LORD 7592
30: 8 David **i** at the LORD, saying, Shall I 7592
2Sa 2: 1 that David **i** of the LORD, saying, 7592
5:19 David **i** of the LORD, saying, Shall I go 7592
5:23 when David **i** of the LORD, he said, 7592
11: 3 David sent and **i** after the woman. And *one* 1875
16:23 *was* as if a man had **i** at the oracle of God: 7592
21: 1 and David **i** of the LORD. 1245+6440
1Ch 10:14 **i** not of the LORD: therefore he slew him, 1875
13: 3 to us: for we **i** not *at* it in the days of Saul. 1875
14:10 David **i** of God, saying, Shall I go up 7592
14:14 Therefore David **i** again of God; and God 7592
Ps 78:34 and they returned and **i early after** God. 7836
Eze 14: 3 should I be **i of at all** by them? 1875+1875
20: 3 the Lord GOD, I will not be **i of** by you. 1875
20:31 shall I be **i** of by you, O house of Israel? 1875
20:31 the Lord GOD, I will not be **i of** by you. 1875
36:37 I will yet *for* this be **i of** by the house of 1875
Da 1:20 *and* understanding, that the king **i** of them, 1245
Zep 1: 6 have not sought the LORD, nor **i for** him. 1875
Mt 2: 7 **i** of them **diligently** what time the star *198*
2:16 which he had **diligently i** of the wise men. *198*
Jn 4:52 Then **i** he of them the hour when he began *4441*
2Co 8:23 our brethren *be* **i** *of, they are* the messengers NIG
1Pe 1:10 Of which salvation the prophets have **i** and *1567*

INQUIREST (1) [INQUIRE]

Job 10: 6 That thou **i** after mine iniquity, and 1245

INQUIRY (2) [INQUIRE]

Pr 20:25 *which is* holy, and after vows to **make i**. 1239
Ac 10:17 Cornelius had **made i** for Simon's house, *1331*

INQUISITION (3)

Dt 19:18 the judges shall **make** diligent **i**: and 1875
Est 2:23 when **i was made** of the matter, it was 1245
Ps 9:12 When he **maketh i** for blood, he 1875

INSATIABLE See UNSATIABLE

INSCRIBED See GRAVED; GRAVEN

INSCRIPTION (1)

Ac 17:23 your devotions, I found an altar with this **i**, *1924*

INSIDE (1)

1Ki 6:15 *and* he covered *them* on the **i** with wood, 1004

INSOMUCH (20) [IN, MUCH, SO]

Ps 106:40 **i** that he abhorred his own inheritance. 2050.1
Mal 2:13 **i** that *he* regardeth not the offering any 4480
Mt 8:24 **i that** the ship was covered with the waves: *5620*
12:22 **i that** the blind and dumb both spake and *5620*
13:54 **i that** they were astonished, and said, *5620*
15:31 **I that** the multitude wondered, when they *5620*
24:24 **i that**, if *it were* possible, *they shall* deceive *5620*
27:14 **i that** the governor marvelled greatly. *5620*
Mk 1:27 **i that** they questioned among themselves, *5620*
1:45 **i that** *Jesus* could no more openly enter *5620*
2: 2 **i that** there was no room to receive *them,* *5620*
2:12 **i that** *they* were all amazed, and *5620*
3:10 **i that** *they* pressed upon him for to touch *5620*
9:26 as one dead; **i that** many said, He is dead. *5620*
Lk 12: 1 **i that** *they* trode one upon another, *5620*
Ac 1:19 **i as** that field is called in their proper *5620*
5:15 **I that** *they* brought forth the sick into *2532*
2Co 1: 8 **i that** we despaired even of life: *5620*
8: 6 **I that** we desired Titus, that as he *1519+3588*
Gal 2:13 **i that** Barnabas also was carried away with *5620*

INSPECTION GATE See MIPHKAD

INSPIRATION (2)
Job 32: 8 the **i** of the Almighty giveth them 5397
2Ti 3:16 All scripture *is* **given by i of God**, and *2315*

INSTANT (8) [INSTANTLY]
Isa 29: 5 yea, it shall be at an **i** suddenly. 6621
30:13 whose breaking cometh suddenly at an **i**. 6621
Jer 18: 7 *At what* **i** I shall speak concerning a nation 7281
18: 9 *at what* **i** I shall speak concerning a nation, 7281
Lk 2:38 And she coming in that **i** gave thanks *5610*
23:23 And they were **i** with loud voices, *1945*
Ro 12:12 in tribulation; **continuing i** in prayer; *4342*
2Ti 4: 2 be **i** in season, out of season; reprove, *2186*

INSTANTLY (2) [INSTANT]
Lk 7: 4 came to Jesus, they besought him **i**, saying, *4709*
Ac 26: 7 **i** serving *God* day and night, hope to *1616+1722*

INSTEAD (39)
Ge 2:21 of his ribs, and closed up the flesh **i** thereof; 8478
4:25 hath appointed me another seed **i of** Abel, 8478
44:33 let thy servant abide **i of** the lad a bondman 8478
Ex 4:16 *even* he shall be to thee **i of** a mouth, and 3807.1
4:16 and thou shalt be to him **i of** God. 3807.1
5:12 land of Egypt to gather stubble **i of** straw. 3807.1
Nu 3:12 **i of** all the firstborn that openeth the matrix 8478
3:41 **i of** all the firstborn among the children of 8478
3:41 the cattle of the Levites **i of** all the firstlings 8478
3:45 Take the Levites **i of** all the firstborn 8478
3:45 and the cattle of the Levites **i of** their cattle; 8478
5:19 uncleanness *with another* **i of** thy husband, 8478
5:20 if thou hast gone aside *to another* **i of** thy 8478
5:29 when a wife goeth aside *to another* **i of** her 8478
8:16 **i of** such as open every womb, *even instead* 8478
8:16 *even* **i** *of* the firstborn of all the children of NIH
10:31 and thou mayest be to us **i of** eyes. 3807.1
Jdg 15: 2 than she? take her, I pray thee, **i of** her. 8478
2Sa 17:25 made Amasa captain of the host **i of** Joab: 8478
1Ki 3: 7 thou hast made thy servant king **i of** David 8478
2Ki 14:21 and made him king **i of** his father Amaziah. 8478
17:24 placed *them* in the cities of Samaria **i of** 8478
1Ch 29:23 of the LORD as king **i of** David his father, 8478
2Ch 12:10 **I of** which king Rehoboam made shields of 8478
Est 2: 4 pleaseth the king be queen **i of** Vashti. 8478
2:17 her head, and made her queen **i of** Vashti. 8478
Job 31:40 Let thistles grow **i of** wheat, and 8478
31:40 instead of wheat, and cockle **i of** barley. 8478
Ps 45:16 **I of** thy fathers shall be thy children, 8478
Isa 3:24 *that* **i of** sweet smell there shall be stink; 8478
3:24 **i of** a girdle a rent; and instead of well set 8478
3:24 **i of** well set hair baldness; and instead of a 8478
3:24 **i of** a stomacher a girding of sackcloth; *and* 8478
3:24 of sackcloth; *and* burning **i of** beauty. 8478
55:13 **I of** the thorn shall come up the fir tree, and 8478
55:13 **i of** the brier shall come up the myrtle tree: 8478
Jer 22:11 which reigned **i of** Josiah his father, 8478
37: 1 king Zedekiah the son of Josiah reigned **i of** 8478
Eze 16:32 *which* taketh strangers **i of** her husband. 8478

INSTRUCT (9) [INSTRUCTED, INSTRUCTING, INSTRUCTION, INSTRUCTOR, INSTRUCTORS]
Dt 4:36 thee to hear his voice, that he might **i** thee: 3256
Ne 9:20 Thou gavest also thy good spirit to **i** them, 7919
Job 40: 2 the Almighty **i** *him?* he that reproveth God, 3250
Ps 16: 7 my reins also **i** me *in* the night seasons. 3256
32: 8 I will **i** thee and teach thee in the way 7919
SS 8: 2 into my mother's house, *who* would **i** me: 3925
Isa 28:26 For his God doth **i** him to discretion, *and* 3256
Da 11:33 understand among the people shall **i** many: 995
1Co 2:16 the mind of the Lord, that he may **i** him? *4822*

INSTRUCTED (19) [INSTRUCT]
Dt 32:10 he led him about, he **i** him, he kept him as 995
2Ki 12: 2 his days wherein Jehoiada the priest **i** him. 3384
1Ch 15:22 he **i** about the song, because he *was* skilful. 3256
25: 7 with their brethren *that were* **i** in the songs 3925
2Ch 3: 3 was **i** for the building of the house of God. 3245
Job 4: 3 thou hast **i** many, and thou hast 3256
Ps 2:10 O ye kings: be **i**, ye judges of the earth. 3256
Pr 5:13 nor inclined mine ear to them that **i** me! 3925
21:11 when the wise is **i**, he receiveth knowledge. 7919
Isa 8:11 **i** me that *I* should not walk in the way of 3256
40:14 *who* **i** him, and taught him in the path of 995
Jer 6: 8 Be thou **i**, O Jerusalem, lest my soul depart 3256
31:19 after that I was **i**, I smote upon *my* thigh: 3045
Mt 13:52 Therefore every scribe *which is* **i** unto *3100*
14: 8 And she, being **before i** of her mother, said, *4264*
Lk 1: 4 of *those* things, wherein thou hast been **i**. *2727*
Ac 18:25 This *man* was **i in** the way of the Lord; and *2727*
Ro 2:18 are more excellent, being **i** out of the law; *2727*
Php 4:12 and in all *things* I am **i** both to be full and *3453*

INSTRUCTING (1) [INSTRUCT]
2Ti 2:25 In meekness **i** those that oppose *3811*

INSTRUCTION (33) [INSTRUCT]
Job 33:16 openeth the ears of men, and sealeth their **i**. 4561
Ps 50:17 Seeing thou hatest **i**, and castest my words 4148
Pr 1: 2 To know wisdom and **i**; to perceive 4148
1: 3 To receive the **i** of wisdom, justice, and 4148
1: 7 *but* fools despise wisdom and **i**. 4148
1: 8 hear the **i** of thy father, and forsake not 4148
4: 1 the **i** of a father, and attend to know 4148
4:13 Take fast hold of **i**; let *her* not go: keep her; 4148
5:12 How have I hated **i**, and my heart despised 4148
5:23 He shall die without **i**; and in the greatness 4148
6:23 and reproofs of **i** *are* the way of life: 4148
8:10 Receive my **i**, and not silver; and 4148
8:33 Hear **i**, and be wise, and refuse *it* not. 4148
9: 9 Give *i* to a wise *man*, and he will be yet NIH
10:17 He *is in* the way of life that keepeth **i**: but 4148
12: 1 Whoso loveth **i** loveth knowledge: but 4148
13: 1 A wise son *heareth his* father's **i**: but 4148
Pr 13:18 and shame *shall be to* him that refuseth **i**: 4148
15: 5 A fool despiseth his father's **i**: but he that 4148
15:32 He that refuseth **i** despiseth his own soul: 4148
15:33 The fear of the LORD *is* the **i** of wisdom; 4148
16:22 him that hath it: but the **i** of fools *is* folly. 4148
19:20 Hear counsel, and receive **i**, that thou 4148
19:27 to hear the **i** *that causeth* to err from 4148
23:12 Apply thine heart unto **i**, and thine ears to 4148
23:23 *also* wisdom, and **i**, and understanding. 4148
24:32 *it* well: I looked upon *it, and* received **i**. 4148
Jer 17:23 that *they* might not hear, nor receive **i**. 4148
32:33 yet they have not hearkened to receive **i**. 4148
35:13 Will ye not receive **i** to hearken to my 4148
Eze 5:15 an **i** and an astonishment unto the nations 4148
Zep 3: 7 thou wilt fear me, thou wilt receive **i**; 4148
2Ti 3:16 for correction, for **i** in righteousness: *3809*

INSTRUCTOR (2) [INSTRUCT]
Ge 4:22 an **i** of every artificer in brass and iron: 3913
Ro 2:20 An **i** of the foolish, a teacher of babes, *3810*

INSTRUCTORS (1) [INSTRUCT]
1Co 4:15 For though you have ten thousand **i** in *3807*

INSTRUMENT (8) [INSTRUMENTS]
Nu 35:16 if he smite him with an **i** of iron, so that he 3627
Ps 33: 2 with the psaltery *and* an **i of ten strings**. 6218
92: 3 Upon an **i of ten strings**, and upon 6218
144: 9 an **i of ten strings** will I sing *praises* unto 6218
Isa 28:27 *i*, neither is a cart wheel turned about upon NIH
41:15 I will make thee a new sharp **threshing i** 4173
54:16 and that bringeth forth an **i** for his work; 3627
Eze 33:32 a pleasant voice, and can **play** well **on an i**: 5059

INSTRUMENTS (51) [INSTRUMENT]
Ge 49: 5 **i** of cruelty *are in* their habitations. 3627
Ex 25: 9 the pattern of all the **i** thereof, even so 3627
Nu 3: 8 they shall keep all the **i** of the tabernacle of 3627
4:12 they shall take all the **i** of ministry, 3627
4:26 all the **i** of their service, and all that is made 3627
4:32 with all their **i**, and with all their service: 3627
4:32 by name ye shall reckon the **i** of the charge 3627
7: 1 sanctified it, and all the **i** thereof, both 3627
31: 6 with the holy **i**, and the trumpets to blow in 3627
1Sa 8:12 to make his **i** of war, and instruments of his 3627
8:12 his instruments of war, and **i** of his chariots. 3627
18: 6 with joy, and with **i of musick**. 7991
2Sa 6: 5 on all *manner of* **i** *made of* fir wood, NIH
24:22 **threshing i** and *other* instruments of 4173
24:22 and *other* **i** of the oxen for wood. 3627
1Ki 19:21 and boiled their flesh with the **i** of the oxen, 3627
1Ch 9:29 all the **i** of the sanctuary, and the fine flour, 3627
12:33 expert in war, with all **i** of war, 3627
12:37 with all *manner of* **i** of war for the battle, 3627
15:16 brethren *to be* the singers with **i** of musick, 3627
16:42 make a sound, and with musical **i** of God. 3627
21:23 the **threshing i** for wood, and the wheat for 4173
23: 5 the LORD with the **i** which I made, 3627
28:14 *of* gold, for all **i** of all manner of service; 3627
28:14 *silver also* for all **i** of silver by weight, 3627
28:14 by weight, for all **i** of every kind of service: 3627
2Ch 4:16 and the fleshhooks, and all their **i**, 3627
5: 1 the silver, and the gold, and all the **i**, put he 3627
5:13 the trumpets and cymbals and **i** of musick, 3627
7: 6 the Levites also with **i** of musick of 3627
23:13 also the singers with **i** of musick, and 3627
29:26 the Levites stood with the **i** of David, and 3627
29:27 with the **i** ordained by David king of Israel. 3627
30:21 *singing* with loud **i** unto the LORD. 3627
34:12 all that could skill of **i** of musick. 3627
Ne 12:36 with the musical **i** of David the man of 3627
Ps 7:13 He hath also prepared for him the **i** of 3627
68:25 the **players on i** *followed* after; 5059
87: 7 As well the singers as the **players on i** *shall* 2490
150: 4 praise him with **stringed i** and organs. 4482
Ecc 2: 8 *as* **musical i**, and that **of all sorts**. 7705+7705
Isa 32: 7 The **i** also of the churl *are* evil: he deviseth 3627
38:20 we will **sing** my songs *to* **the stringed i** all 5059
Eze 40:42 whereupon also they laid the **i** wherewith 3627
Da 6:18 neither were **i of musick** brought before 1761
Am 1: 3 they have threshed Gilead with threshing *i* NIH
6: 5 *and* invent to themselves **i** of musick, 3627
Hab 3:19 To the chief singer on my **stringed i**. 5058
Zec 11:15 Take unto thee yet the **i** of a foolish 3627
Ro 6:13 Neither yield ye your members *as* **i** of *3696*
6:13 your members *as* **i** of righteousness unto *3696*

INSURRECTION (5)
Ezr 4:19 city of old time *hath* **made i** against kings, 5376
Ps 64: 2 from the **i** of the workers of iniquity: 7285
Mk 15: 7 **made i with** *him*, who had committed *4955*
15: 7 *him*, who had committed murder in the **i**. *4714*
Ac 18:12 the Jews **made i** with one accord **against** *2721*

INTEGRITY (16)
Ge 20: 5 in the **i** of my heart and innocency of my 8537
20: 6 I know that thou didst this in the **i** of thy 8537
1Ki 9: 4 in **i** of heart, and in uprightness, 8537
Job 2: 3 still he holdeth fast his **i**, although thou 8538
2: 9 wife unto him, Dost thou still retain thine **i**? 8538
27: 5 till I die I will not remove my **i** from me. 8538
31: 6 even balance, that God may know mine **i**. 8538
Ps 7: 8 and according to mine **i** *that is* in me. 8537
25:21 Let **i** and uprightness preserve me; for I 8537
26: 1 O LORD; for I have walked in mine **i**: 8537
26:11 *as for* me, I will walk in mine **i**: redeem me, 8537
41:12 thou upholdest me in mine **i**, and settest me 8537
78:72 So he fed them according to the **i** of his 8537
Pr 11: 3 The **i** of the upright shall guide them: but 8538
19: 1 Better *is* the poor that walketh in his **i**, 8537
20: 7 The just *man* walketh in his **i**: his children 8537

INTELLIGENCE (1)
Da 11:30 have **i** with them that forsake the holy 995

INTEND (4) [INTENDED, INTENDEST, INTENDING, INTENT, INTENTS]
Jos 22:33 and did not **i** to go up against them in battle, 559
2Ch 28:13 LORD *already*, ye **i** to add *more* to our sins 559
Ac 5:28 and **i** to bring this man's blood upon us. *1014*
5:35 take heed to yourselves what ye **i** to do as *3195*

INTENDED (1) [INTEND]
Ps 21:11 For they **i** evil against thee: they imagined a 5186

INTENDEST (1) [INTEND]
Ex 2:14 **i** thou to kill me, as thou killedst 559

INTENDING (3) [INTEND]
Lk 14:28 For which of you, **i** to build a tower, *2309*
Ac 12: 4 **i** after Easter to bring him forth to *1014*
20:13 sailed unto Assos, there **i to** take in Paul: *3195*

INTENT (11) [INTEND]
2Sa 17:14 **to the i** that the LORD might bring evil 3807.1
2Ki 10:19 Jehu did *it* in subtilty, **to the i that** 4616+3807.1
2Ch 16: 1 **to the i that** *he* might let none go out or 3807.1
Eze 40: 4 for **to the i that** *I* might shew *them* 4616+3807.1
Da 4:17 to the **i** that the living may know that 1701
Jn 11:15 I was not there, **to the i** ye may believe; *2443*
13:28 Now no *man* at the table knew for what **i** he NIG
Ac 9:21 came hither for that *i*, that he might bring NIG
10:29 therefore for what **i** ye have sent for me? *3056*
1Co 10: 6 **to the i** we should not lust after evil *1519+3588*
Eph 3:10 **To the i that** now unto the principalities *2443*

INTENTS (2) [INTEND]
Jer 30:24 until he have performed the **i** of his heart: 4209
Heb 4:12 discerner of the thoughts and **i** of the heart. *1771*

INTERCEDE; INTERCEDED See INTREAT; INTREATED; INTREATIES; INTREATY

INTERCESSION (9) [INTERCESSIONS, INTERCESSOR]
Isa 53:12 of many, and **made i** for the transgressors. 6293
Jer 7:16 nor prayer for them, neither **make i** to me: 6293
27:18 let them now **make i** to the LORD of 6293
36:25 Gemariah had **made i** to the king that *he* 6293
Ro 8:26 the Spirit itself **maketh i** for us with *5241*
8:27 he **maketh i** for the saints according to *1793*
8:34 hand of God, who also **maketh i** for us. *1793*
11: 2 how he **maketh i** to God against Israel, *1793*
Heb 7:25 seeing he ever liveth to **make i** for them. *1793*

INTERCESSIONS (1) [INTERCESSION]
1Ti 2: 1 prayers, **i**, *and* giving of thanks, *1783*

INTERCESSOR (1) [INTERCESSION]
Isa 59:16 no man, and wondered that *there was* no **i**: 6293

INTERCOURSE See CARNALLY

INTERMARRY See AFFINITY

INTERMEDDLE (1) [INTERMEDDLETH]
Pr 14:10 and a stranger doth not **i** with his joy. 6148

INTERMEDDLETH (1) [INTERMEDDLE]
Pr 18: 1 seeketh *and* **i** with all wisdom. 1566

INTERMISSION (1)
La 3:49 and ceaseth not, without any **i**, 2014

INTERPRET (8) [INTERPRETATION, INTERPRETATIONS, INTERPRETED, INTERPRETER, INTERPRETING]
Ge 41: 8 *there was* none that could **i** them unto 6622
41:12 each man according to his dream he did **i**. 6622
41:15 a dream, and *there is* none that can **i** it: 6622
41:15 *that* thou canst understand a dream to **i** it. 6622
1Co 12:30 do all speak with tongues? do all **i**? *1329*
14: 5 except he **i**, that the church may receive *1329*
14:13 in an *unknown* tongue pray that he may **i**. *1329*
14:27 *by* three, and *that* by course; and let one **i**. *1329*

INTERPRETATION (46) [INTERPRET]
Ge 40: 5 each man according to the **i** of his dream, 6623
40:12 Joseph said unto him, This *is* the **i** of it: 6623
40:16 When the chief baker saw that the **i** was 6622
40:18 and said, This *is* the **i** thereof: 6623
41:11 we dreamed each man according to the **i** of 6623
Jdg 7:15 the **i** thereof, that he worshipped, and 7667
Pr 1: 6 To understand a proverb, and the **i**; 4426
Ecc 8: 1 and who knoweth the **i** of a thing? 6592
Da 2: 4 servants the dream, and we will shew the **i**. 6591
2: 5 with the **i** thereof, ye shall be cut in pieces, 6591
2: 6 if ye shew the dream, and the **i** thereof, 6591
2: 6 shew me the dream, and the **i** thereof. 6591
2: 7 the dream, and we will shew the **i** of it. 6591
2: 9 I shall know that ye can shew me the **i** 6591
2:16 and that *he* would shew the king the **i**. 6591
2:24 and I will shew unto the king the **i**. 6591
2:25 that will make known unto the king the **i**. 6591
2:26 dream which I have seen, and the **i** thereof? 6591
2:30 for *their* sakes that shall make known the **i** 6591
2:36 we will tell the **i** thereof before the king. 6591
2:45 the dream *is* certain, and the **i** thereof sure. 6591
4: 6 that they might make known unto me the **i** 6591
4: 7 they *did* not make known unto me the **i** 6591
4: 9 dream that I have seen, and the **i** thereof. 6591
4:18 O Belteshazzar, declare the **i** thereof, 6591
4:18 are not able to make known unto me the **i**: 6591
4:19 not the dream, or the **i** thereof, trouble thee. 6591
4:19 and the **i** thereof to thine enemies. 6591
4:24 This *is* the **i**, O king, and this *is* the decree 6591
5: 7 shew me the **i** thereof, shall be clothed with 6591

Da 5: 8 nor make known to the king the i thereof. 6591
5:12 let Daniel be called, and he will shew the i. 6591
5:15 make known unto me the i thereof: 6591
5:15 but they could not shew the i of the thing: 6591
5:16 make known to me the i thereof, thou shalt 6591
5:17 the king, and make known to him the i. 6591
5:26 This *is* the i of the thing: MENE; God hath 6591
7:16 and made me know the i of the things. 6591
Jn 1:42 be called Cephas, which is **by i**, A stone. *2059*
9: 7 in the pool of Siloam, (which is **by i**, Sent.) *2059*
Ac 9:36 which by i is called Dorcas: *1329*
13: 8 the sorcerer (for so is his name **by i**) *3177*
1Co 12:10 of tongues; to another the i of tongues: *2058*
14:26 hath a tongue, hath a revelation, hath an i. *2058*
Heb 7: 2 first being **by i** King of righteousness, and *2059*
2Pe 1:20 prophecy of the scripture is of *any* private i. *1955*

INTERPRETATIONS (2) [INTERPRET]

Ge 40: 8 said unto them, *Do* not i *belong* to God? 6623
Da 5:16 that thou canst **make i**, and dissolve 6590+6591

INTERPRETED (11) [INTERPRET]

Ge 40:22 the chief baker: as Joseph had i to them. 6622
41:12 and we told him, and he i to us our dreams; 6622
41:13 it came to pass, as he i to us, so it was; me 6622
Ezr 4: 7 Syrian tongue, and i in the Syrian tongue. 8638
Mt 1:23 which being i is, God with us. *3177*
Mk 5:41 which is, being i, Damsel (I say unto thee) *3177*
15:22 which is, being i, The place of a skull. *3177*
15:34 which is, being i, My God, my God, why *3177*
Jn 1:38 Rabbi, (which is to say, being i, Master,) *2059*
1:41 the Messias, which is, being i, the Christ. *3177*
Ac 4:36 (which is, being i, The son of consolation,) *3177*

INTERPRETER (4) [INTERPRET]

Ge 40: 8 dreamed a dream, and *there is* no i of it. 6622
42:23 *them;* for he spake unto them by an i. 3887
Job 33:23 with him, an i, one among a thousand, 3887
1Co 14:28 But if there be no i, let him keep silence in *1328*

INTERPRETING (1) [INTERPRET]

Da 5:12 i of dreams, and shewing of hard sentences, 6590

INTO (2015) [IN, TO, THEREINTO, WHEREINTO]

Ge 2: 7 breathed i his nostrils the breath of life; 871.1
2:10 it was parted, and became i four heads. 3807.1
2:15 put him i the garden of Eden to dress it and 871.1
6:18 thou shalt come i the ark, thou, and thy sons, 413
6:19 two of every *sort* shalt thou bring i the ark, 413
7: 1 Come thou and all thy house i the ark; 413
7: 7 i the ark, because of the waters of the flood. 413
7: 9 went in two and two unto Noah i the ark, 413
7:13 three wives of his sons with them, i the ark; 413
7:15 they went in unto Noah i the ark, two and 413
8: 9 she returned unto him i the ark, for 413
8: 9 and pulled her in unto him i the ark. 413
9: 2 of the sea; i your hand are they delivered. 871.1
11:31 the Chaldees, to go i the land of Canaan; 1886.5
12: 5 went forth to go i the land of Canaan; 1886.5
12: 5 and i the land of Canaan they came. 1886.5
12:10 went down i Egypt to sojourn there; 1886.5
12:11 when he was come near to enter i Egypt, 1886.5
12:14 that, when Abram was come i Egypt, 1886.5
12:15 the woman was taken i Pharaoh's house. NIH
13: 1 that he had, and Lot with him, i the south. 1886.5
14:20 which hath delivered thine enemies i thy 871.1
16: 5 I have given my maid i thy bosom; and 871.1
18: 6 Abraham hastened i the tent unto Sarah, 1886.5
19: 2 i your servant's house, and tarry all night, 413
19: 3 turned in unto him, and entered i his house; 413
19:10 pulled Lot i the house to them, and shut 1886.5
19:23 upon the earth when Lot entered i Zoar. 1886.5
21:32 they returned i the land of the Philistines. 413
22: 2 and get thee i the land of Moriah; 413
24:20 emptied her pitcher i the trough, and 413
24:32 the man came i the house: and 1886.5
24:67 Isaac brought her i his mother Sarah's 1886.5
26: 2 unto him, and said, Go not down i Egypt; 1886.5
27:17 had prepared, i the hand of her son Jacob. 871.1
28:15 and will bring thee again i this land; 413
29: 1 came i the land of the people of the east. 1886.5
30:35 and gave *them* i the hand of his sons. 871.1
31:33 Laban went i Jacob's tent, and into Leah's 871.1
31:33 i Leah's tent, and into the two 871.1
31:33 and i the two maidservants' tents; 871.1
31:33 of Leah's tent, and entered i Rachel's tent. 871.1
32: 7 and herds, and the camels, i two bands; 3807.1
32:16 he delivered *them* i the hand of his 871.1
36: 6 went i the country from the face of his 413
37:20 and cast him i some pit, and we will say, 871.1
37:22 cast him i this pit that *is* in the wilderness, 413
37:24 they took him, and cast him i a pit: and 1886.5
37:28 and they brought Joseph i Egypt. 1886.5
37:35 For I will go down i the grave unto my 1886.5
37:36 the Medanites sold him i Egypt unto 413
39: 4 and all *that* he had he put i his hand. 871.1
39:11 that *Joseph* went i the house to do his 1886.5
39:20 master took him, and put him i the prison, 413
40: 3 i the prison, the place where Joseph *was* 413
40:11 pressed them i Pharaoh's cup, and I gave 413
40:11 and I gave the cup i Pharaoh's hand. 5921
40:13 thou shalt deliver Pharaoh's cup i his hand, 871.1
40:15 that they should put me i the dungeon. 871.1
40:21 and he gave the cup i Pharaoh's hand: 5921
41:57 all countries came i Egypt to Joseph for 1886.5
42:17 he put them all together i ward three days. 413
42:25 and to restore every man's money i his sack, 413
42:37 deliver him i my hand, and I will bring him 5921
43:17 man brought the men i Joseph's house. 1886.5
43:18 they were **brought i** Joseph's house; 935
43:24 the man brought the men i Joseph's 1886.5
43:26 which *was* in their hand i the house, 1886.5
43:30 he entered i *his* chamber, and wept there. 1886.5
45: 4 your brother, whom ye sold i Egypt. 1886.5
Ge 45:25 came *i* the land of Canaan unto Jacob their NIH
46: 3 fear not to go down i Egypt; for I will 1886.5
46: 4 I will go down with thee i Egypt; and 1886.5
46: 6 came i Egypt, Jacob, and all his seed with 1886.5
46: 7 all his seed brought he with him i Egypt. 1886.5
46: 8 which came i Egypt, Jacob and his sons: 1886.5
46:26 All the souls that came with Jacob i 1886.5
46:27 which came i Egypt, *were* threescore and 1886.5
46:28 and they came i the land of Goshen. 1886.5
47:14 Joseph brought the money i Pharaoh's 1886.5
48: 5 of Egypt before I came unto thee i Egypt, 1886.5
48:16 let them grow i a multitude in the midst 3807.1
49: 6 O my soul, come not thou i their secret; 871.1
49:33 he gathered up his feet i the bed, and 413
50:13 For his sons carried him i the land of 1886.5
50:14 Joseph returned i Egypt, he, and 1886.5
Ex 1: 1 children of Israel, which came i Egypt; 1886.5
1:22 Every son that is born ye shall cast i 1886.5
3:18 three days' journey i the wilderness, 871.1
4: 6 unto him, Put now thine hand i thy bosom. 871.1
4: 6 he put his hand i his bosom: and when he 871.1
4: 7 he said, Put thine hand i thy bosom again. 413
4: 7 he put his hand i his bosom again; and 413
4:19 unto Moses in Midian, Go, return *i* Egypt: NIH
4:21 When thou goest to return i Egypt, 1886.5
4:27 Go i the wilderness to meet Moses. 1886.5
5: 3 three days' journey i the desert, and 871.1
7:23 Pharaoh turned and went i his house, 413
8: 3 which shall go up and come i thine house, 871.1
8: 3 i thy bedchamber, and upon thy bed, and 871.1
8: 3 i the house of thy servants, and upon thy 871.1
8: 3 i thine ovens, and into thy 871.1
8: 3 thine ovens, and i thy kneadingtroughs: 871.1
8:21 and upon thy people, and i thy houses: 871.1
8:24 there came a grievous swarm *of flies* i 1886.5
8:24 *i* his servants' houses, and into all the land NIH
8:24 and i all the land of Egypt: 871.1
8:27 We will go three days' journey i 871.1
9:20 his servants and his cattle flee i the houses: 413
10: 4 to morrow will I bring the locusts i thy 871.1
10:19 the locusts, and cast them i the Red sea; 1886.5
11: 4 About midnight will I go out i the midst of 871.1
13: 5 shall bring thee i the land of the Canaanites, 413
13:11 shall bring thee i the land of the Canaanites, 413
14:22 the children of Israel went i the midst of 871.1
14:28 all the host of Pharaoh that came i the sea 871.1
15: 1 and his rider hath he thrown i the sea. 871.1
15: 4 and his host hath he cast i the sea: 871.1
15: 5 they sank i the bottom as a stone. 871.1
15:19 and with his horsemen i the sea, 871.1
15:21 and his rider hath he thrown i the sea. 871.1
15:22 and they went out i the wilderness of Shur; 413
15:25 *which* when he had cast i the waters, 413
16: 3 for ye have brought us forth i this 413
18: 5 and his wife unto Moses i the wilderness, 413
18: 7 of *their* welfare; and they came i the tent. 1886.5
18:27 and he went his way i his own land. 413
19: 1 the same day came they *i* the wilderness of NIH
19:12 *that ye* go *not* up i the mount, or touch 871.1
21:13 in wait, but God deliver *him* i his hand; 3807.1
23:19 bring *i* the house of the LORD thy God. NIH
23:20 to bring thee i the place which I have 413
23:31 the inhabitants of the land i your hand; 871.1
24:12 Come up to me i the mount, and be there: 1886.5
24:13 and Moses went up i the mount of God. 413
24:15 Moses went up i the mount, and a cloud 413
24:18 Moses went i the midst of the cloud, and 871.1
24:18 of the cloud, and gat him up i the mount: 413
25:14 thou shalt put the staves i the rings by 871.1
25:16 thou shalt put i the ark the Testimony which 413
26:11 put the taches i the loops, and couple 871.1
27: 7 the staves shall be put i the rings, and 871.1
29: 3 thou shalt put them i one basket, and 5921
29:30 when he cometh i the tabernacle of 413
30:20 When they go i the tabernacle of 413
32:24 I cast it i the fire, and there came out this 871.1
33: 5 I will come up i the midst of thee in a 871.1
33: 8 until he was gone i the tabernacle. 1886.5
33: 9 to pass, as Moses entered i the tabernacle, 1886.5
33:11 he turned again i the camp: but his servant 413
37: 5 he put the staves i the rings by the sides of 871.1
38: 7 he put the staves i the rings on the sides of 871.1
39: 3 And they did beat the gold i thin plates, and NIH
39: 3 cut *it i* wires, to work *it* in the blue, and NIH
40:20 And he took and put the Testimony i the ark, 413
40:21 And he brought the ark i the tabernacle, and 413
40:32 When they went i the tent of 413
40:35 Moses was not able to enter i the tent of 413
Lev 1: 6 the burnt offering, and cut it i his pieces. 3807.1
1:12 he shall cut it i his pieces, with his head 3807.1
6:30 whereof *any* of the blood is brought i 413
8:20 he cut the ram i pieces; and Moses burnt 3807.1
9:23 Aaron went i the tabernacle of 413
10: 9 when ye go i the tabernacle of 413
11:32 it must be put i water, and it shall be 871.1
12: 4 no hallowed *thing*, nor come i the sanctuary, 413
13:17 behold, *if* the plague be turned i white; 3807.1
14: 7 shall let the living bird loose i the open 5921
14: 8 after *that* he shall come i the camp, and 413
14:15 and pour *it* i the palm of his own left hand: 5921
14:26 the priest shall pour of the oil i the palm of 5921
14:34 When ye be come i the land of Canaan, 413
14:36 before the priest go *i it* to see the plague, NIH
14:40 they shall cast them i an unclean place 413
14:41 off without the city i an unclean place: 413
14:45 he shall carry *them* forth out of the city i an 413
14:46 Moreover he that goeth i the house all 413
14:53 he shall let go the living bird out of the city i 413
16: 2 that he come not at all times i the holy *place* 413
16: 3 Thus shall Aaron come i the holy *place:* with 413
16:10 to let him go for a scapegoat i 1886.5
16:21 by the hand of a fit man i the wilderness: 1886.5
16:23 Aaron shall come i the tabernacle of 413
16:23 which he put on when he went i the holy 413
16:26 in water, and afterward come i the camp. 413
Lev 16:28 and afterward he shall come i the camp. 413
19:23 when ye shall come i the land, and 413
23:10 When ye be come i the land which I give 413
25: 2 When ye come i the land which I give you, 413
26:25 ye shall be delivered i the hand of 871.1
26:32 I will **bring** the land **i desolation**: and 8074
26:36 i their hearts in the lands of their enemies; 871.1
26:41 have brought them i the land of their 871.1
Nu 4: 3 fifty years old, all that enter i the host, 3807.1
4:30 every one that entereth i the service, to do 3807.1
4:35 every one that entereth i the service, 3807.1
4:39 every one that entereth i the service, 3807.1
4:43 every one that entereth i the service, 3807.1
5:17 the priest shall take, and put *it* i the water: 413
5:22 this water that causeth the curse shall go i 871.1
5:24 that causeth the curse shall enter i her, 871.1
5:27 that causeth the curse shall enter i her, 871.1
7:89 when Moses was gone i the tabernacle of 413
11:30 Moses gat him i the camp, he and the elders 413
13:17 *way* southward, and go up i the mountain: NIH
14: 3 were it not better for us to return i Egypt? 1886.5
14: 4 make a captain, and let us return i Egypt. 1886.5
14: 8 he will bring us i this land, and give it us; 413
14:16 people i the land which he sware unto them, 413
14:24 him will I bring i the land whereinto he 413
14:25 get you *i* the wilderness *by* the way of NIH
14:30 Doubtless ye shall not come i the land, 413
14:40 gat them up i the top of the mountain, 413
15: 2 When ye be come i the land of your 413
15:18 When ye come i the land whither I bring 413
16:14 Moreover thou hast not brought us i a land 413
16:30 and they go down quick i the pit; 1886.5
16:33 went down alive i the pit, and the earth 1886.5
16:47 and ran i the midst of the congregation; 413
17: 8 that on the morrow Moses went i 413
19: 6 cast *it* i the midst of the burning of 413
19: 7 and afterward he shall come i the camp, and 413
19:14 all that come i the tent, and all that *is* in 413
20: 1 *i* the desert of Zin in the first month: NIH
20: 4 of the LORD i this wilderness, 413
20:12 ye shall not bring this congregation i 413
20:15 How our fathers went down i Egypt, and 1886.5
20:24 for he shall not enter i the land which I have 413
20:27 they went up i mount Hor in the sight of all 413
21: 2 If thou wilt indeed deliver this people i my 871.1
21:22 we will not turn i the fields, or into 871.1
21:22 not turn into the fields, or i the vineyards; 871.1
21:23 went out against Israel i the wilderness: 1886.5
21:27 Come *i* Heshbon, let the city of Sihon be NIH
21:29 his daughters i captivity unto Sihon king of 871.1
21:34 for I have delivered him i thy hand, and all 871.1
22:13 the princes of Balak, Get you i your land: 413
22:23 aside out of the way, and went i the field: 871.1
22:23 Balaam smote the ass, to turn her *i* the way. NIH
22:41 brought him up *i* the high places of Baal, NIH
23:14 he brought him *i* the field of Zophim, to NIH
24: 4 falling *i a trance,* but having his eyes open: NIH
24:16 falling *i a trance,* but having his eyes open: NIH
25: 8 he went after the man of Israel i the tent, 413
27:12 Get thee up i this mount Abarim, and see 413
31:24 and afterward ye shall come i the camp. 413
31:27 **divide** the prey **i two parts**; between them 2673
31:54 brought it i the tabernacle of 413
32: 7 i the land which the LORD hath given 413
32: 9 that *they* should not go i the land which 413
32:32 before the LORD *i* the land of Canaan, NIH
33: 8 passed through the midst of the sea i 1886.5
33:38 Aaron the priest went up i mount Hor at 413
33:51 When ye are passed over Jordan i the land of 413
34: 2 When ye come i the land of Canaan; 413
35:10 When ye be come over Jordan i the land 1886.5
35:28 shall return i the land of his possession. 413
36:12 *And* they were married i the families of 4480
Dt 1:22 go up, and i what cities we shall come. 871.1
1:24 they turned and went up i the mountain, 1886.5
1:27 to deliver us i the hand of the Amorites, 871.1
1:31 way that ye went, until ye came i this place. 5704
1:40 take your journey i the wilderness *by* 1886.5
1:41 of war, ye were ready to go up i the hill. 1886.5
1:43 and went presumptuously up i the hill. 1886.5
2: 1 took our journey i the wilderness *by* 1886.5
2:24 I have given i thy hand Sihon the Amorite, 871.1
2:29 until I shall pass over Jordan i the land 413
2:30 that he might deliver him i thy hand, 871.1
3: 2 and all his people, and his land, i thy hand; 871.1
3: 3 So the LORD our God delivered i our 871.1
3:27 Get thee up *i* the top of Pisgah, and lift up NIH
5: 5 of the fire, and went not up i the mount;) 871.1
5:30 say to them, Get you i your tents again. 3807.1
6:10 i the land which he sware unto thy fathers, 413
7: 1 When the LORD thy God shall bring thee i 413
7:24 he shall deliver their kings i thine hand, 871.1
7:26 Neither shalt thou bring an abomination i 413
8: 7 For the LORD thy God bringeth thee i a 413
9: 9 When I was gone up i the mount to 1886.5
9:21 I cast the dust thereof i the brook that 413
9:28 them i the land which he promised them, 413
10: 1 come up unto me i the mount, and 1886.5
10: 3 went up i the mount, having the two 1886.5
10:22 Thy fathers went down i Egypt with 1886.5
11: 5 in the wilderness, until ye came i this place; 5704
13:16 thou shalt gather all the spoil of it i the midst 413
14: 6 cleaveth the cleft *i* two claws, *and* NIH
14:25 shalt thou turn *it* i money, and bind up 871.1
17: 8 get thee up i the place which the LORD thy 413
18: 9 When thou art come i the land which 413
19: 3 **divide** the coasts of thy land, which the LORD
thy God giveth thee to inherit, **i three parts**, 8027
19: 5 As when *a man* goeth i the wood with his 871.1
19:11 that he die, and fleeth i one of these cities: 413
19:12 deliver him i the hand of the avenger of 871.1
20:13 thy God hath delivered it i thine hands, 871.1
21:10 the LORD thy God hath delivered them i 871.1
23: 1 shall not enter i the congregation of 871.1
23: 2 A bastard shall not enter i the congregation 871.1

Dt 23: 2 not enter **i** the congregation of the LORD. 871.1
23: 3 Moabite shall not enter **i** the congregation 871.1
23: 3 **enter i** the congregation of the LORD for 935
23: 5 the LORD thy God turned the curse **i** a 3807.1
23: 8 **i** the congregation of the LORD *in* their 871.1
23:11 he shall come **i** the camp *again.* 413+8432
23:18 *i* the house of the LORD thy God for any NIH
23:24 When thou comest **i** thy neighbour's 871.1
23:25 When thou comest **i** the standing corn of 871.1
24:10 thou shalt not go **i** his house to fetch his 413
26: 5 he went down **i** Egypt, and 1886.5
26: 9 he hath brought us **i** this place, and 413
28:25 shalt be removed **i** all the kingdoms of 3807.1
28:38 Thou shalt carry much seed out *i* the field, NIH
28:41 enjoy them; for they shall go **i** captivity. 871.1
28:68 the LORD shall bring thee *i* Egypt again NIH
29:12 That thou shouldest enter **i** covenant with 871.1
29:12 **i** his oath, which the LORD thy God 871.1
29:28 and cast them **i** another land, as *it is* this day. 413
30: 5 the LORD thy God will bring thee **i** 413
31:20 *For* when I shall have brought them **i** 413
31:21 before I have brought them **i** the land which 413
31:23 for thou shalt bring the children of Israel **i** 413
32:26 I said, I would **scatter** them **i corners,** 6284
32:49 Get thee up **i** this mountain Abarim, 413
Jos 2: 1 came *i* a harlot's house, named Rahab, and NIH
2: 3 to thee, which are entered **i** thine house: 3807.1
2:18 Behold, *when* we come **i** the land, 871.1
2:19 out of the doors of thy house **i** the street, 1886.5
2:24 Truly the LORD hath delivered **i** our 871.1
3:11 the earth passeth over before you **i** Jordan. 871.1
4: 5 the LORD your God **i** the midst of Jordan, 413
6: 2 I have given **i** thine hand Jericho, and 871.1
6:11 they came *i* the camp, and lodged in NIH
6:14 the city once, and returned *i* the camp: NIH
6:19 they shall come *i* the treasury of NIH
6:20 so that the people went up **i** the city, 1886.5
6:22 Go *i* the harlot's house, and bring out thence NIH
6:24 they put *i* the treasury of the house of NIH
7: 7 to deliver us **i** the hand of the Amorites, 871.1
8: 1 I have given **i** thy hand the king of Ai, and 871.1
8: 7 for the LORD your God will deliver it **i** 871.1
8:13 Joshua went that night **i** the midst of 871.1
8:18 toward Ai; for I will give it **i** thine hand. 871.1
8:19 they entered *i* the city, and took it, and NIH
10: 8 for I have delivered them **i** thine hand; 871.1
10:19 suffer them not to enter **i** their cities: 413
10:19 your God hath delivered them **i** your hand. 871.1
10:20 remained of them entered **i** fenced cities. 413
10:27 cast them **i** the cave wherein they had been 413
10:30 the king thereof, **i** the hand of Israel; 871.1
10:32 the LORD delivered Lachish **i** the hand 871.1
11: 8 the LORD delivered them **i** the hand of 871.1
13: 5 mount Hermon unto the entering **i** Hamath. NIH
18: 5 they shall divide it **i** seven parts: 3807.1
18: 6 therefore describe the land *i* seven parts, NIH
18: 9 described it by cities **i** seven parts in a 3807.1
20: 4 they shall take him **i** the city unto them, 1886.5
20: 5 they shall not deliver the slayer up **i** his 871.1
21:44 the LORD delivered all their enemies **i** 871.1
22:13 half tribe of Manasseh, **i** the land of Gilead, 413
24: 4 Jacob and his children went down *i* Egypt. NIH
24: 8 I brought you **i** the land of the Amorites, 413
24: 8 I gave them **i** your hand, that ye might 871.1
24:11 and I delivered them **i** your hand. 871.1
Jdg 1: 2 I have delivered the land **i** his hand. 871.1
1: 3 his brother, Come up with me **i** my lot, 871.1
1: 3 and I likewise will go with thee **i** thy lot. 871.1
1: 4 and the Perizzites **i** their hand: 871.1
1:16 children of Judah *i* the wilderness of Judah, NIH
1:24 the entrance **i** the city, and we will shew NIH
1:25 when he shewed them the entrance **i** NIH
1:26 the man went *i* the land of the Hittites, and NIH
1:34 the Amorites forced the children of Dan **i** 1886.5
2:14 he delivered them **i** the hands of spoilers 871.1
2:14 he sold them **i** the hands of their enemies 871.1
2:23 neither delivered he them **i** the hand of 871.1
3: 8 he sold them **i** the hand of 871.1
3:10 king of Mesopotamia **i** his hand; 871.1
3:21 his right thigh, and thrust it **i** his belly: 871.1
3:28 your enemies the Moabites **i** your hand. 871.1
4: 2 the LORD sold them **i** the hand of Jabin 871.1
4: 7 and I will deliver him **i** thine hand. 871.1
4: 9 for the LORD shall sell Sisera **i** the hand 871.1
4:14 LORD hath delivered Sisera **i** thine hand: 871.1
4:18 when he had turned in unto her **i** the tent, 1886.5
4:21 smote the nail **i** his temples, and fastened *it* 871.1
4:21 his temples, and fastened *it* **i** the ground: 871.1
4:22 when he came **i** her *tent,* behold, Sisera lay 413
5:15 he was sent on foot **i** the valley. For 871.1
6: 1 the LORD delivered them **i** the hand of 871.1
6: 5 and they entered **i** the land to destroy it. 871.1
6:13 delivered us **i** the hands of the Midianites. 871.1
7: 2 for me to give the Midianites **i** their hands, 871.1
7: 7 and deliver the Midianites **i** thine hand: 871.1
7: 9 for I have delivered it **i** thine hand. 871.1
7:13 a cake of barley bread tumbled **i** the host 871.1
7:14 *for* **i** his hand hath God delivered Midian, 871.1
7:15 returned **i** the host of Israel, and said, Arise; 413
7:15 for the LORD hath delivered **i** your hand 871.1
7:16 he divided the three hundred men *i* three NIH
8: 3 God hath delivered **i** your hands 871.1
8: 7 and Zalmunna **i** mine hand, 871.1
9:27 they went out *i* the fields, and gathered their NIH
9:27 went *i* the house of their god, and did eat NIH
9:42 that the people went out *i* the field; NIH
9:43 divided them **i** three companies, and 3807.1
9:46 **i** a hold of the house of the god Berith. 413
10: 7 he sold them **i** the hands of the Philistines, 871.1
10: 7 and **i** the hands of the children of Ammon. 871.1
11:19 we pray thee, through thy land **i** my place. 5704
11:21 and all his people **i** the hand of Israel, 871.1
11:30 the children of Ammon **i** mine hands, 871.1
11:32 the LORD delivered them **i** his hands. 871.1
12: 3 and the LORD delivered them **i** my hand: 871.1

Jdg 13: 1 the LORD delivered them **i** the hand of 871.1
15: 1 I will go in to my wife **i** the chamber. 413
15: 5 he let *them* go **i** the standing corn of 871.1
15:12 that we may deliver thee **i** the hand of 871.1
15:13 thee fast, and deliver thee **i** their hand: 871.1
15:18 Thou hast given this great deliverance **i** NIH
15:18 and fall **i** the hand of the uncircumcised? 871.1
16:23 delivered Samson our enemy **i** our hand. 871.1
16:24 Our god hath delivered **i** our hands our 871.1
18:10 for God hath given it **i** your hands; a place 871.1
18:18 these went *i* Micah's house, and fetched NIH
19: 3 she brought him *i* her father's house: and NIH
19:11 let us turn in **i** this city of the Jebusites, and 413
19:12 We will not turn aside hither **i** the city of a 413
19:15 for *there was* no man that took them **i** *his* 1886.5
19:21 So he brought him **i** his house, and 3807.1
19:22 Bring forth the man that came **i** thine house, 413
19:23 seeing that this man is come **i** mine house, 413
19:29 when he was come **i** his house, he took a 413
19:29 **i** twelve pieces, and sent her into all 3807.1
19:29 and sent her **i** all the coasts of Israel. 871.1
20: 4 I came **i** Gibeah that *belongeth* to 1886.5
20: 8 neither will we any *of us* turn **i** his house. 3807.1
20:28 for to morrow I will deliver them **i** thine 871.1
Ru 1: 2 they came *i* the country of Moab, and NIH
2:18 she took *it* up, and went *i* the city: and NIH
3:14 Let it not be known that a woman came *i* NIH
3:15 and laid *it* on her: and he went *i* the city. NIH
4:11 The LORD make the woman that is come **i** 413
1Sa 2:14 he stroke *it* **i** the pan, or kettle, or caldron, 871.1
2:36 I pray thee, **i** one of the priests' offices, 413
4: 3 And when the people were come **i** the camp, 413
4: 5 covenant of the LORD came **i** the camp, 413
4: 6 the ark of the LORD was come **i** the camp. 413
4: 7 for they said, God is come **i** the camp. 413
4:10 and they fled every man **i** his tent: 3807.1
4:13 when the man came **i** the city, and told *it,* 871.1
5: 2 they brought it *i* the house of Dagon, and NIH
5: 5 nor any that come *i* Dagon's house, NIH
6:14 the cart came **i** the field of Joshua, 413
6:19 they had looked **i** the ark of the LORD, 871.1
7: 1 brought it **i** the house of Abinadab in the hill, 413
7:13 they came no more **i** the coast of Israel: 871.1
9:13 As soon as ye be come *i* the city, ye shall NIH
9:14 they went up *i* the city: *and* when they were NIH
9:14 *and* when they were come **i** the city, 8432+871.1
9:22 brought them **i** the parlour, and 1886.5
9:25 come down from the high place *i* the city, NIH
10: 6 and shalt be turned **i** another man. 3807.1
11:11 they came **i** the midst of the host in 871.1
12: 8 When Jacob was come *i* Egypt, and NIH
12: 9 he sold them **i** the hand of Sisera, 871.1
12: 9 **i** the hand of the Philistines, and into 871.1
12: 9 **i** the hand of the king of Moab, and 871.1
14:10 for the LORD hath delivered them **i** our 871.1
14:12 for the LORD hath delivered them **i** 871.1
14:21 which went up with them **i** the camp *from* 871.1
14:26 And when the people were come **i** the wood, 413
14:37 wilt thou deliver them **i** the hand of Israel? 871.1
17:22 ran *i* the army, and came and saluted his NIH
17:46 This day will the LORD deliver thee **i** 871.1
17:47 and he will give you **i** our hands. 871.1
17:49 that the stone sunk **i** his forehead; 871.1
19:10 and he smote the javelin **i** the wall: 871.1
20: 8 for thou hast brought thy servant **i** a 871.1
20:11 Come, and let us go out *i* the field. NIH
20:11 And they went out both of them *i* the field. NIH
20:35 that Jonathan went out *i* the field at the time NIH
20:42 and departed: and Jonathan went *i* the city. NIH
21:15 shall this *fellow* come **i** my house? 413
22: 5 depart, and get thee *i* the land of Judah. NIH
22: 5 and came *i* the forest of Hareth. NIH
23: 4 for I will deliver the Philistines **i** thine 871.1
23: 7 God hath delivered him **i** mine hand; 871.1
23: 7 by entering **i** a town that hath gates and 871.1
23:11 Will the men of Keilah deliver me up **i** his 871.1
23:12 deliver me and my men **i** the hand of Saul? 871.1
23:14 but God delivered him not **i** his hand. 871.1
23:16 went to David *i* the wood, and NIH
23:20 our part *shall be* to deliver him **i** the king's 871.1
23:25 wherefore he came down *i* a rock, and NIH
24: 4 I will deliver thine enemy **i** thine hand, 871.1
24:10 thee to day **i** mine hand in the cave: 871.1
24:18 the LORD had delivered me **i** thine hand, 871.1
26: 3 he saw that Saul came after him **i** 1886.5
26: 8 God hath delivered thine enemy **i** thine 871.1
26:10 or he shall descend **i** battle, and perish. 871.1
26:23 for the LORD delivered thee **i** *my* hand to 871.1
27: 1 speedily escape **i** the land of the Philistines; 413
28:19 with thee **i** the hand of the Philistines: 871.1
28:19 host of Israel **i** the hand of the Philistines. 871.1
29:11 to return **i** the land of the Philistines. 413
30:15 nor deliver me **i** the hands of my master, 871.1
30:23 company that came against us **i** our hand. 871.1
31: 9 sent **i** the land of the Philistines round 871.1
2Sa 2: 1 Shall I go up **i** any of the cities of Judah? 871.1
3: 8 have not delivered thee **i** the hand of 871.1
3:34 *were* not bound, nor thy feet put **i** fetters: 3807.1
4: 6 they came thither **i** the midst of the house, 5704
4: 7 For when they came *i* the house, he lay on NIH
5: 8 and the lame shall not come **i** the house. 413
5:19 wilt thou deliver them **i** mine hand? 871.1
5:19 for I will doubtless deliver the Philistines **i** 871.1
6:10 of the LORD unto him **i** the city of David: 5921
6:10 David carried it aside *i* the house of NIH
6:12 *i* the city of David with gladness. NIH
6:16 as the ark of the LORD came *i* the city of NIH
10: 2 David's servants came *i* the land of NIH
10:10 the rest of the people he delivered **i** 871.1
10:14 *also* before Abishai, and entered *i* the city. NIH
11:11 shall I then go **i** mine house, to eat and 413
11:23 came out unto us *i* the field, and we were NIH
12: 8 thy master's wives **i** thy bosom, and 871.1
12:20 came *i* the house of the LORD, and NIH
13:10 Bring the meat *i* the chamber, that I may eat NIH

2Sa 13:10 brought *them* **i** the chamber to Amnon 1886.5
15:25 Carry back the ark of God *i* the city: NIH
15:27 return *i* the city in peace, and your two sons NIH
15:31 **turn** the counsel of Ahithophel **i foolishness.** 5528
15:37 So Hushai David's friend came *i* the city, NIH
15:37 the city, and Absalom came *i* Jerusalem. NIH
16: 8 the LORD hath delivered the kingdom **i** 871.1
17:13 if he be gotten **i** a city, then shall all Israel 413
17:13 to that city, and we will draw it **i** the river, 5704
17:17 for they might not be seen to come **i** 1886.5
18: 6 So the people went out *i* the field against NIH
18:17 cast him **i** a great pit in the wood, and laid a 413
19: 2 the victory that day was *turned* **i** 3807.1
19: 3 the people gat them by stealth that day *i* NIH
19: 5 Joab came *i* the house to the king, and said, NIH
20:12 he removed Amasa out of the highway *i* NIH
21: 9 he delivered them **i** the hands of 871.1
22: 7 his temple, and my cry *did enter* **i** his ears. 871.1
22:20 He brought me forth also **i** a large place: 3807.1
23:11 the Philistines were gathered together **i** a 3807.1
24:14 let us fall now **i** the hand of the LORD; 871.1
24:14 and let me not fall **i** the hand of man. 871.1
1Ki 1:15 Bath-sheba went in unto the king **i** 1886.5
1:28 she came **i** the king's presence, and 3807.1
3: 1 and brought her **i** the city of David, 413
6: 8 they went up with winding stairs **i** 5921
6: 8 and out of the middle **i** the third. 413
8: 6 **i** the oracle of the house, to the most holy 413
11:17 his father's servants with him, to go *i* Egypt; NIH
11:40 Jeroboam arose, and fled *i* Egypt, NIH
13:18 Bring him back with thee **i** thine house, 413
14:12 *and* when thy feet enter **i** the city, 1886.5
14:28 when the king went *i* the house of NIH
14:28 and brought them back **i** the guard chamber. 413
15:15 *i* the house of the LORD, silver, and gold, NIH
15:18 delivered them **i** the hand of his servants: 871.1
16:18 that he went **i** the palace of the king's house, 413
16:21 were the people of Israel divided **i** two 3807.1
17:19 carried him up **i** a loft, where he abode, and 413
17:21 let this child's soul come **i** him again. 5921+7130
17:22 the soul of the child came **i** him 5921+7130
17:23 brought him down out of the chamber **i** 1886.5
18: 5 Go **i** the land, unto all fountains of water, 871.1
18: 9 that thou wouldest deliver thy servant **i** 871.1
19: 4 he himself went a day's journey **i** 871.1
20: 2 to Ahab king of Israel **i** the city, 1886.5
20:13 I will deliver it **i** thine hand *this* day; 871.1
20:28 will I deliver all this great multitude **i** thine 871.1
20:30 the rest fled to Aphek, **i** the city; and *there* a 413
20:30 Ben-hadad fled, and came **i** the city, into an 413
20:30 and came into the city, **i** an inner chamber. NIH
20:33 and he caused him to come up **i** the chariot. 5921
20:39 Thy servant went out **i** the midst of 871.1
21: 4 Ahab came **i** his house heavy and displeased 413
22: 6 for the Lord shall deliver *it* **i** the hand of 871.1
22:12 for the LORD shall deliver *it* **i** the king's 871.1
22:15 for the LORD shall deliver *it* **i** the hand 871.1
22:25 when thou shalt **go i** an inner chamber to 935
22:30 will disguise myself, and enter **i** the battle; 871.1
22:30 disguised himself, and went **i** the battle. 871.1
22:35 the blood ran out of the wound **i** the midst of 413
2Ki 2: 1 when the LORD would take up Elijah *i* NIH
2:11 and Elijah went up by a whirlwind *i* heaven. NIH
2:16 upon some mountain, or **i** some valley. 871.1
3:10 to deliver them **i** the hand of Moab. 871.1
3:13 to deliver them **i** the hand of Moab. 871.1
3:18 he will deliver the Moabites also **i** your 871.1
4: 4 shalt pour out **i** all those vessels, and 5921
4:11 he turned **i** the chamber, and lay there. 413
4:32 when Elisha was come **i** the house, 1886.5
4:39 And one went out **i** the field to gather herbs, 413
4:39 came and shred *them* **i** the pot of pottage: 413
4:41 he cast *it* **i** the pot; and he said, Pour out for 413
5:18 *that* when my master goeth *i* the house of NIH
6: 5 felling a beam, the axe head fell **i** the water: 413
6:20 when they were come *i* Samaria, that Elisha NIH
6:23 So the bands of Syria came no more **i** 871.1
7: 4 We will enter *i* the city, then the famine *is* NIH
7: 8 they went **i** one tent, and did eat and drink, 413
7: 8 entered **i** another tent, and carried thence 413
7:12 we shall catch them alive, and get **i** the city. 413
8:21 and the people fled **i** their tents. 3807.1
9: 6 he arose, and went **i** the house; and 1886.5
9:26 cast him **i** the plat *of ground,* according to 871.1
10:15 and he took him up to him **i** the chariot. 413
10:21 they came *i* the house of Baal; and NIH
10:23 *i* the house of Baal, and said unto NIH
10:24 *If* any of the men whom I *have* brought **i** 5921
11: 4 brought them to him *i* the house of NIH
11:13 she came to the people *i* the temple of NIH
11:16 which the horses came *i* the king's house: NIH
11:18 all the people of the land went *i* the house of NIH
12: 4 that is brought *i* the house of the LORD, NIH
12: 4 all the money that cometh **i** any man's heart 5921
12: 4 heart to bring *i* the house of the LORD, NIH
12: 9 on the right side as one cometh *i* the house NIH
12: 9 that was brought *i* the house of the LORD. NIH
12:11 **i** the hands of *them* that did the work, 5921
12:13 of the money that was brought *i* the house NIH
12:15 **i** whose hand they delivered the money to 5921
12:16 sin money was not brought *i* the house of NIH
13: 3 he delivered them **i** the hand of Hazael 871.1
13: 3 **i** the hand of Ben-hadad the son of Hazael, 871.1
13:21 they cast the man **i** the sepulchre of Elisha: 871.1
17: 6 carried Israel away **i** Assyria, and 1886.5
17:20 and delivered them **i** the hand of spoilers, 871.1
18:21 it will go **i** his hand, and pierce it: 871.1
18:30 this city shall not be delivered **i** the hand of 871.1
19: 1 and went *i* the house of the LORD. NIH
19:10 Jerusalem shall not be delivered **i** the hand 871.1
19:14 Hezekiah went up *i* the house of NIH
19:18 have cast their gods **i** the fire: for they 871.1
19:23 and I will enter *i* the lodgings of his borders, NIH
19:23 his borders, *and* *i* the forest of his Carmel. NIH
19:25 be to lay waste fenced cities *i* ruinous heaps. NIH

2Ki 19:28 and thy tumult is come up i mine ears, 871.1
19:32 He shall not come i this city, nor shoot an 413
19:33 shall not come i this city, saith the LORD. 413
19:37 they escaped i the land of Armenia. NIH
20: 4 afore Isaiah was gone out i the middle court, NIH
20: 8 that I shall go up i the house of the LORD NIH
20:20 a conduit, and brought water i the city, 1886.5
21:14 deliver them i the hand of their enemies; 871.1
22: 4 which is brought i the house of the LORD, NIH
22: 5 let them deliver it i the hand of the doers of 5921
22: 7 the money that was delivered i their hand, 5921
22: 9 have delivered it i the hand of them that do 5921
22:20 thou shalt be gathered i thy grave in peace; 413
23: 2 the king went up i the house of the LORD, NIH
23:12 and cast the dust of them i the brook Kidron. 413
24:15 those carried he i captivity from Jerusalem NIH
1Ch 5:20 the Hagarites were delivered i their hand, 871.1
6:15 Jehozadak went i captivity, when NIH
10: 9 sent i the land of the Philistines round 871.1
11:15 to the rock to David, i the cave of Adullam; 413
12: 8 i the hold to the wilderness men of might, 3807.1
13:13 carried it aside i the house of Obed-edom 413
14:10 wilt thou deliver them i mine hand? 871.1
14:10 Go up; for I will deliver them i thine hand. 871.1
14:17 the fame of David went out i all lands; and 871.1
16: 7 to thank the LORD i the hand of Asaph 871.1
19: 2 So the servants of David came i the land of 413
19:15 Abishai his brother, and entered i the city. 1886.5
21:13 let me fall now i the hand of the LORD; 871.1
21:13 but let me not fall i the hand of man. 871.1
21:27 he put up his sword again i the sheath 413
22:18 the inhabitants of the land i mine hand; 871.1
22:19 i the house that is to be built to the name 3807.1
23: 6 David divided them i courses among NIH
24:19 to come i the house of the LORD, 3807.1
2Ch 5: 7 i the most holy place, even under the wings 413
6:41 i thy resting place, thou, and the ark of 3807.1
7: 2 the priests could not enter i the house of 413
7:10 he sent the people away i their tents, 3807.1
7:11 all that came i Solomon's heart to make in 5921
9: 4 his ascent by which he went up i the house NIH
12:11 when the king entered i the house of NIH
12:11 and brought them again i the guard chamber. 413
13:16 and God delivered them i their hand. 871.1
15:12 they entered i a covenant to seek 871.1
15:18 he brought i the house of God the things NIH
16: 8 he delivered them i thine hand. 871.1
18: 5 for God will deliver it i the king's hand. 871.1
18:11 for the LORD shall deliver it i the hand 871.1
18:14 and they shall be delivered i your hand. 871.1
18:24 shalt see on that day when thou shalt **go i** 935
20:20 and went forth i the wilderness of Tekoa: 3807.1
21:17 they came up i Judah, and brake into it, 871.1
21:17 **brake i** it, and carried away all 1234
23: 1 the son of Zichri, i covenant with him. 871.1
23: 6 let none come i the house of the LORD, NIH
23: 7 whosoever else cometh i the house, he shall 413
23:12 she came to the people i the house of NIH
23:20 they came through the high gate i the king's NIH
24:10 and brought in, and cast i the chest, 3807.1
24:24 the LORD delivered a very great host i 871.1
25:20 that he might deliver them i the hand of 871.1
26:16 went i the temple of the LORD to burn 413
27: 2 howbeit he entered not i the temple of 413
28: 5 him i the hand of the king of Syria; 871.1
28: 5 he was also delivered i the hand of 871.1
28: 9 he hath delivered them i your hand, and 871.1
28:27 they brought him not i the sepulchres of 3807.1
29: 4 gathered them together i the east street, 3807.1
29:16 the priests went i the inner part of 3807.1
29:16 i the court of the house of the LORD. 3807.1
29:16 the Levites took it, to carry it out abroad i 3807.1
29:31 offerings i the house of the LORD. 3807.1
30: 8 enter i his sanctuary, which he hath 3807.1
30: 9 so that they shall come again i this land: 3807.1
30:14 and cast them i the brook Kidron. 3807.1
30:15 brought in the burnt offerings i the house of NIH
31: 1 man to his possession, i their own cities. 3807.1
31:10 the offerings i the house of the LORD, NIH
31:16 even unto every one that entereth i 3807.1
32: 1 entered i Judah, and encamped against 871.1
32:21 when he was come i the house of his god, NIH
33:13 brought him again to Jerusalem i his 3807.1
34: 7 had beaten the graven images i powder, 3807.1
34: 9 they delivered the money that was brought i NIH
34:14 that was brought i the house of the LORD, NIH
34:17 have delivered it i the hand of 5921
34:30 the king went up i the house of the LORD, NIH
36:17 for age: he gave them all i his hand. 871.1
Ezr 5: 8 that we went i the province of Judea, 3807.2
5:12 he gave them i the hand of 871.2
5:12 carried the people away i Babylon. 3807.2
5:14 brought them i the temple of Babylon, 3807.2
5:15 them i the temple that is in Jerusalem, 871.2
9: 7 been delivered i the hand of the kings of 871.1
10: 6 went i the chamber of Johanan the son of 413
Ne 2: 7 that they may convey me over till I come i 413
2: 8 the city, and for the house that I shall enter i. 413
5: 5 we **bring i bondage** our sons and our 3533
6:11 being as I am, would go i the temple to save 413
7: 5 my God put i mine heart to gather together 413
8: 1 i the street that was before the water gate; 413
9:11 their persecutors thou threwest i the deeps, 871.1
9:11 the deeps, as a stone i the mighty waters. 871.1
9:22 nations, and didst divide them i corners: 3807.1
9:23 broughtest them i the land, concerning which 413
9:24 and gavest them i their hands, 871.1
9:27 Therefore thou deliveredst them i the hand 871.1
9:30 gavest thou them i the hand of the people 871.1
10:29 and entered i a curse, and into an oath, 871.1
10:29 and entered into a curse, and i an oath, 871.1
10:34 to bring it i the house of our God, 3807.1
10:38 to the chambers, i the treasure house. 3807.1
12:44 to gather i them out of the fields of 871.1
13: 1 the Moabite should not come i 871.1
Ne 13: 2 howbeit our God turned the curse i a 3807.1
13:15 which they brought i Jerusalem on NIH
Est 1:22 For he sent letters i all the king's provinces, 413
1:22 i every province according to the writing 413
2:14 on the morrow she returned i the second 413
2:16 So Esther was taken unto king Ahasuerus i 413
3: 9 to bring it i the king's treasuries. 413
3:13 the letters were sent by posts i all the king's 413
4: 1 went out i the midst of the city, and 871.1
4: 2 for none might enter i the king's gate clothed 413
4:11 shall come unto the king i the inner court, 413
6: 4 Now Haman was come i the outward 3807.1
7: 7 wine in his wrath went i the palace garden: 413
7: 8 the king returned out of the palace garden i 413
9:22 to joy, and from mourning i a good day: 3807.1
Job 3: 6 let it not come i the number of the months. 871.1
9:24 The earth is given i the hand of 871.1
10: 9 the clay; and wilt thou bring me i dust again? 413
12: 6 i whose hand God bringeth abundantly. 871.1
14: 3 and bringest me i judgment with thee? 871.1
16:11 turned me over i the hands of the wicked. 5921
17:12 They change the night i day: the light is 3807.1
18: 8 For he is cast i a net by his own feet, and 871.1
18:18 He shall be driven from light i darkness, and 413
22: 4 will he enter with thee i judgment? 871.1
30: 3 flying i the wilderness in former time NIH
30:19 He hath cast me i the mire, and I am 3807.1
30:31 my organ i the voice of them that weep. 3807.1
33:28 He will deliver his soul from going i 871.1
34:23 that he should enter i judgment with God. 413
36:16 thee out of the strait i a broad place, NIH
37: 8 the beasts go i dens, and remain in their 1119
38:16 Hast thou entered i the springs of the sea? 5704
38:22 Hast thou entered i the treasures of 413
38:38 When the dust groweth i hardness, and 3807.1
39:12 home thy seed, and gather it i thy barn? NIH
40:23 he trusteth that he can draw up Jordan i his 413
41: 2 Canst thou put a hook i his nose? or 871.1
41:22 and sorrow is **turned i joy** before him. 1750
41:28 slingstones are **turned** with him i stubble. 2015
Ps 4: 2 how long will ye turn my glory i shame? 3807.1
5: 7 I will come i thy house in the multitude of NIH
7:15 and is fallen i the ditch which he made. 871.1
9:17 The wicked shall be turned i hell, and 1886.5
10: 9 the poor, when he draweth him i his net. 871.1
16: 4 not offer, nor take up their names i my lips. 5921
18: 6 my cry came before him, even i his ears. 871.1
18:19 He brought me forth also i a large place; 3807.1
22:15 thou hast brought me i the dust of death. 3807.1
24: 3 Who shall ascend i the hill of the LORD? 871.1
28: 1 I become like them that go down i the pit. NIH
30:11 Thou hast turned for me my mourning i 3807.1
31: 5 I thine hand I commit my spirit: thou hast 871.1
31: 8 hast not shut me up i the hand of 871.1
32: 4 my moisture is turned i the drought of 871.1
35: 8 i that very destruction let him fall. 871.1
35:13 and my prayer returned i mine own bosom. 5921
37:15 Their sword shall enter i their own heart, 871.1
37:20 i smoke shall they consume away. 871.1
45: 2 grace is poured i thy lips: therefore 871.1
45:15 they shall enter i the king's palace. 871.1
46: 2 though the mountains be carried i 871.1
55:15 and let them go down quick i hell: NIH
55:23 shalt bring them down i the pit of 3807.1
56: 8 put thou my tears i thy bottle: are they not 871.1
57: 6 i the midst whereof they are fallen 871.1
60: 9 Who will bring me i the strong city? NIH
60: 9 the strong city? who will lead me i Edom? 5704
63: 9 to destroy it, shall go i the lower parts of 871.1
66: 6 He turned the sea i dry land: they went 3807.1
66:11 Thou broughtest us i the net; thou laidst 871.1
66:12 thou broughtest us out i a wealthy place. 3807.1
66:13 I will go i thy house with burnt offerings: NIH
69: 2 I am come i deep waters, where the floods 871.1
69:27 and let them not come i thy righteousness. 871.1
73:17 Until I went i the sanctuary of God; then 413
73:18 thou castedst them down i destruction. 3807.1
73:19 How are they brought i desolation, as in a 3807.1
74: 7 They have cast fire i thy sanctuary, NIH
76: 6 and horse are **cast i a dead sleep**. 7290
78:44 had turned their rivers i blood; and 3807.1
78:61 delivered his strength i captivity, and 3807.1
78:61 and his glory i the enemy's hand. 871.1
79: 1 the heathen are come i thine inheritance; 871.1
79:12 render unto our neighbours sevenfold i their 413
88: 4 I am counted with them that go down i NIH
88:18 from me, and mine acquaintance i darkness. NIH
95:11 wrath that they should not enter i my rest. 413
96: 8 bring an offering, and come i his courts. 3807.1
100: 4 Enter i his gates with thanksgiving, and NIH
100: 4 and i his courts with praise: NIH
104:10 He sendeth the springs i the valleys, 871.1
105:23 Israel also came i Egypt; and NIH
105:29 He turned their waters i blood, and 3807.1
106:15 their request; but sent leanness i their soul. 871.1
106:20 Thus they changed their glory i 871.1
106:41 he gave them i the hand of the heathen; 871.1
106:42 they were **brought i subjection** under their 3665
107:33 He turneth rivers i a wilderness, and 3807.1
107:33 and the watersprings i dry ground; 3807.1
107:34 A fruitful land i barrenness, for 3807.1
107:35 He turneth the wilderness i a standing 3807.1
107:35 and dry ground i watersprings; 3807.1
108:10 Who will bring me i the strong city? NIH
108:10 the strong city? who will lead me i Edom? 5704
109:18 so let it come i his bowels like water, and 871.1
109:18 bowels like water, and like oil i his bones. 871.1
114: 8 Which turned the rock i a standing water, NIH
114: 8 the flint i a fountain of waters. 3807.1
115:17 neither any that go down i silence. NIH
118:19 I will go i them, and I will praise 871.1
118:20 i which the righteous shall enter. 871.1
122: 1 Let us go i the house of the LORD. NIH
132: 3 Surely I will not come i the tabernacle of 871.1
132: 3 of my house, nor go up i my bed; 5921
Ps 132: 7 We will **go i** his tabernacles: we will 935
132: 8 Arise, O LORD, i thy rest; thou, and 3807.1
135: 9 and wonders i the midst of thee, 871.1
136:13 To him which divided the Red sea i parts: 3807.1
139: 8 If I ascend up i heaven, thou art there: if I NIH
140:10 let them be cast i the fire; into deep pits, 871.1
140:10 i deep pits, that they rise not up again. 871.1
141:10 Let the wicked fall i their own nets, 871.1
143: 2 enter not i judgment with thy servant: 871.1
143: 7 lest I be like unto them that go down i NIH
143:10 is good; lead me i the land of uprightness. 871.1
Pr 1:12 and whole, as those that go down i the pit: NIH
2:10 When wisdom entereth i thine heart, and 871.1
4:14 Enter not i the path of the wicked, and 871.1
6: 3 when thou art come i the hand of thy 871.1
13:17 A wicked messenger falleth i mischief: but 871.1
16:29 and leadeth him i the way that is not good. 871.1
16:33 The lot is cast i the lap; but the whole 871.1
17:10 A reproof entereth more i a wise man than 871.1
17:10 a wise man than an hundred stripes i a fool. NIH
17:20 he that hath a perverse tongue falleth i 871.1
18: 6 A fool's lips enter i contention, and 871.1
18: 8 they go down i the innermost parts of NIH
18:10 the righteous runneth i it, and is safe. 871.1
19:15 Slothfulness **casteth** i a deep sleep; and 5307
23:10 and enter not i the fields of the fatherless: 871.1
24:16 but the wicked shall fall i mischief. 871.1
26: 9 As a thorn goeth up i the hand of a 871.1
26:22 they go down i the innermost parts of NIH
27:10 neither go i thy brother's house in the day of NIH
28:10 evil way, he shall fall himself i his own pit: 871.1
28:14 he that hardeneth his heart shall fall i 871.1
29: 8 Scornful men **bring** a city **i a snare**: but 6315
30: 4 Who hath ascended up i heaven, or NIH
Ecc 1: 7 All the rivers run i the sea; yet the sea is not 413
10: 8 He that diggeth a pit shall fall i it; and 871.1
11: 9 things God will bring thee i judgment. 871.1
12:14 For God shall bring every work i 871.1
SS 1: 4 the king hath brought me i his chambers: NIH
3: 4 until I had brought him i my mother's house, 413
3: 4 and i the chamber of her that conceived me. 413
4:16 Let my beloved come i his garden, and 3807.1
5: 1 I am come i my garden, my sister, 3807.1
6: 2 My beloved is gone down i his garden, 3807.1
6:11 I went down i the garden of nuts to see 413
7:11 my beloved, let us go forth i the field; NIH
8: 2 and bring thee i my mother's house, 413
Isa 2: 4 they shall beat their swords i plowshares, 3807.1
2: 4 and their spears i pruninghooks: 3807.1
2:10 Enter i the rock, and hide thee in the dust, 871.1
2:19 they shall go i the holes of the rocks, and 871.1
2:19 i the caves of the earth, for fear of 871.1
2:21 To go i the clifts of the rocks, and into 871.1
2:21 i the tops of the ragged rocks, for fear of 871.1
3:14 The LORD will enter i judgment with 871.1
5:13 Therefore my people are **gone i captivity**, 1540
5:14 and he that rejoiceth, shall descend i it. 871.1
9: 8 The Lord sent a word i Jacob, and it hath 871.1
9:10 cut down, but we will change them i cedars. NIH
13: 2 that they may go i the gates of the nobles. NIH
13:14 and flee every one i his own land. 413
14: 7 and is quiet: they break forth i singing. NIH
14:13 said in thine heart, I will ascend i heaven, NIH
19: 1 upon a swift cloud, and shall come i Egypt: NIH
19: 4 the Egyptians will I give over i the hand of 871.1
19: 8 all they that cast angle i the brooks shall 871.1
19:23 the Assyrian shall come i Egypt, and 871.1
19:23 the Egyptian i Assyria, and the Egyptians 871.1
21: 4 the night of my pleasure hath he turned i 3807.1
22:18 and toss thee like a ball i a large country: 413
22:21 I will commit thy government i his hand: 871.1
23: 9 to **bring i contempt** all the honourable of 7043
24:18 from the noise of the fear shall fall i the pit; 413
26:20 enter thou i thy chambers, and shut thy 871.1
29:17 Lebanon shall be turned i a fruitful field, 3807.1
30: 2 That walk to go down i Egypt, and have not NIH
30: 6 i the land of trouble and anguish, 871.1
30:20 teachers be **removed i a corner** any more, 3670
30:29 as when one goeth with a pipe to come i 871.1
34: 9 the streams thereof shall be turned i pitch, 3807.1
34: 9 the dust thereof i brimstone, and the land 3807.1
36: 6 it will go i his hand, and pierce it: 871.1
36:15 this city shall not be delivered i the hand of 871.1
37: 1 and went i the house of the LORD. NIH
37:10 Jerusalem shall not be given i the hand of 871.1
37:19 have cast their gods i the fire: for they 871.1
37:24 I will enter i the height of his border, and NIH
37:26 to lay waste defenced cities i ruinous heaps. NIH
37:29 is come up i mine ears, therefore will I put 871.1
37:33 He shall not come i this city, nor shoot an 413
37:34 shall not come i this city, saith the LORD. 413
37:38 and they escaped i the land of Armenia: NIH
38:18 they that go down i the pit cannot hope for NIH
40: 9 get thee up i the high mountain; 5921
44:23 break forth i singing, ye mountains, NIH
46: 2 but themselves are gone i captivity. 871.1
47: 5 Sit thou silent, and get thee i darkness, 871.1
47: 6 and given them i thine hand: 871.1
49:13 and break forth i singing, O mountains: NIH
51:23 I will put it i the hand of them that afflict 871.1
52: 1 for henceforth there shall no more come i 871.1
52: 4 My people went down aforetime i Egypt to NIH
52: 9 Break forth **i joy, sing** together, ye waste 7442
54: 1 break forth i singing, and cry aloud, NIH
55:12 the hills shall break forth before you i NIH
57: 2 He shall enter i peace: they shall rest in their NIH
59: 5 that which is crushed breaketh out i a viper. NIH
63:14 As a beast goeth down i the valley, 871.1
65: 6 even recompense i their bosom, 5921
65: 7 will I measure their former work i their 413
65:17 shall not be remembered, nor come i mind. 5921
66:20 in a clean vessel i the house of the LORD. NIH
Jer 2: 7 I brought you i a plentiful country, to eat 413
2:21 art thou turned i the degenerate plant of a NIH
4: 5 and let us go i the defenced cities. 413

Jer 4:29 they shall go **i** thickets, and climb up upon 871.1
6: 9 turn back thine hand as a grapegatherer **i** 5921
6:25 Go not forth *i* the field, nor walk by NIH
7:31 *them* not, neither came it **i** my heart. 5921
8: 6 his course, as the horse rusheth **i** the battle. 871.1
8:14 let us enter **i** the defenced cities, and let us 413
9:21 For death is come up **i** our windows, *and* 871.1
9:21 *and* is entered **i** our palaces, to cut off 871.1
10: 9 Silver **spread i plates** is brought from 7554
12: 7 of my soul **i** the hand of her enemies. 871.1
13:16 he turn it **i** the shadow of death, *and* 3807.1
14:18 If I go forth *i* the field, then behold the slain NIH
14:18 if I enter *i* the city, then behold them that NIH
14:18 the priest go about **i** a land that they know 413
15: 4 I will cause them to be removed **i** all 3807.1
15:14 enemies **i** a land *which* thou knowest not: 871.1
16: 5 Enter not *i* the house of mourning, NIH
16: 8 Thou shalt not also go *i* the house of NIH
16:13 Therefore will I cast you out of this land **i** a 5921
16:15 I will bring them again **i** their land that I 5921
17:25 shall there enter **i** the gates of this city 871.1
19: 5 nor spake *it,* neither came *it* **i** my mind: 5921
20: 4 I will give all Judah **i** the hand of the king 871.1
20: 4 he shall carry them captive **i** Babylon, 1886.5
20: 5 will I give **i** the hand of their enemies, 871.1
20: 6 all that dwell in thine house shall go **i** 871.1
21: 4 I will assemble them **i** the midst of this city. 413
21: 7 **i** the hand of Nebuchadrezzar king of 871.1
21: 7 **i** the hand of their enemies, and into 871.1
21: 7 and **i** the hand of those that seek their life: 871.1
21:10 it shall be given **i** the hand of the king of 871.1
21:13 or who shall enter **i** our habitations? 871.1
22: 7 thy choice cedars, and cast *them* **i** the fire. 5921
22:22 and thy lovers shall go **i** captivity: 871.1
22:25 I will give thee **i** the hand of them that seek 871.1
22:25 **i** the hand *of them* whose face thou fearest, 871.1
22:25 even **i** the hand of Nebuchadrezzar king of 871.1
22:25 and **i** the hand of the Chaldeans. 871.1
22:26 **i** another country, where ye were not born; 5921
22:28 and are cast **i** a land which they know not? 5921
23:15 is profaneness gone forth **i** all the land. 3807.1
24: 5 whom I have sent out of this place *i* the land NIH
24: 9 I will deliver them to be removed **i** all 3807.1
26:21 *it,* he was afraid, and fled, and went *i* Egypt; NIH
26:22 Jehoiakim the king sent men *i* Egypt, NIH
26:22 and *certain* men with him **i** Egypt. 413
26:23 cast his dead body **i** the graves of 413
26:24 that *they* should not give him **i** the hand of 871.1
27: 6 now have I given all these lands **i** the hand 871.1
28: 3 Within two full years *will* I bring again **i** this 413
28: 4 that went **i** Babylon, saith the LORD: 1886.5
28: 6 away captive, from Babylon **i** this place. 413
29:14 I will bring you again **i** the place whence I 413
29:16 that are not gone forth with you **i** captivity; 871.1
29:21 I will deliver them **i** the hand of 871.1
30: 6 and all faces are turned **i** paleness? 3807.1
30:16 every one of them, shall go **i** captivity; 871.1
31:13 for I will turn their mourning **i** joy, and 3807.1
32: 3 I *will* give this city **i** the hand of the king 871.1
32: 4 shall surely be delivered **i** the hand of 871.1
32:18 recompensest the iniquity of the fathers **i** 413
32:24 the city is given **i** the hand of 871.1
32:25 for the city is given **i** the hand of 871.1
32:28 I *will* give this city **i** the hand of 871.1
32:28 **i** the hand of Nebuchadrezzar king of 871.1
32:35 them not, neither came it **i** my mind, 5921
32:36 It shall be delivered **i** the hand of the king 871.1
32:43 it is given **i** the hand of the Chaldeans. 871.1
33:11 of praise *i* the house of the LORD. NIH
34: 2 I *will* give this city **i** the hand of the king 871.1
34: 3 surely be taken, and delivered **i** his hand; 871.1
34:10 which had entered **i** the covenant, 871.1
34:11 **brought** them **i subjection** for servants and 3533
34:16 to return, and **brought** them **i subjection,** 3533
34:17 I will make you to be removed **i** all 3807.1
34:20 I will even give them **i** the hand of their 871.1
34:20 and **i** the hand of them that seek their life: 871.1
34:21 his princes will I give **i** the hand of their 871.1
34:21 **i** the hand of them that seek their life, and 871.1
34:21 **i** the hand of the king of Babylon's army, 871.1
35: 2 and bring them *i* the house of the LORD, NIH
35: 2 **i** one of the chambers, and give them wine to 413
35: 4 I brought them *i* the house of the LORD, NIH
35: 4 **i** the chamber of the sons of Hanan, the son 413
35:11 king of Babylon came up **i** the land, 413
36: 5 I cannot go *i* the house of the LORD: NIH
36:12 he went down *i* the king's house, into NIH
36:12 the king's house, **i** the scribe's chamber: 5921
36:20 they went in to the king **i** the court, but 1886.5
36:23 cast *it* **i** the fire that *was* on the hearth, 413
37: 4 for they had not put him *i* prison. NIH
37: 7 shall return *to* Egypt **i** their own land. 3807.1
37:12 Jeremiah went forth out of Jerusalem to go *i* NIH
37:16 When Jeremiah was entered **i** the dungeon, 413
37:16 **i** the cabins, and Jeremiah had remained 413
37:17 thou shalt be delivered **i** the hand of 871.1
37:21 commit Jeremiah **i** the court of the prison, 871.1
38: 3 This city shall surely be given **i** the hand of 871.1
38: 6 cast him **i** the dungeon of Malchiah the son 413
38: 9 whom they have cast **i** the dungeon; 413
38:11 went *i* the house of the king under NIH
38:11 let them down by cords **i** the dungeon to 413
38:14 took Jeremiah the prophet unto him **i** 413
38:16 neither will I give thee **i** the hand of these 871.1
38:18 shall this city be given **i** the hand of 871.1
38:19 lest they deliver me **i** their hand, and 871.1
39: 9 *i* Babylon the remnant of the people that NIH
39:17 thou shalt not be given **i** the hand of 871.1
40: 4 If it seem good unto thee to come with me *i* NIH
40: 4 if it seem ill unto thee to come with me *i* NIH
41: 7 *so,* when they came **i** the midst of the city, 413
41: 7 *and cast them* **i** the midst of the pit, he, and 413
41:17 *is* by Beth-lehem, to go to enter *i* Egypt, NIH
42:14 we will go *i* the land of Egypt, where we NIH
42:15 If ye wholly set your faces to enter *i* Egypt, NIH

Jer 42:17 set their faces to go *i* Egypt to sojourn there; NIH
42:18 forth upon you, when ye shall enter *i* Egypt: NIH
42:19 O ye remnant of Judah; Go ye not *i* Egypt: NIH
43: 2 thee to say, Go not *i* Egypt to sojourn there: NIH
43: 3 for to deliver us **i** the hand of 871.1
43: 3 and carry us away captives *i* Babylon. NIH
43: 7 So they came *i* the land of Egypt: for they NIH
44:12 that have set their faces to go *i* the land of NIH
44:14 which are gone **i** the land of Egypt to 871.1
44:14 that *they* should return *i* the land of Judah, NIH
44:21 and came it *not* **i** his mind? 5921
44:28 out of the land of Egypt *i* the land of Judah, NIH
44:28 that are gone **i** the land of Egypt to 3807.1
44:30 I *will* give Pharaoh-hophra king of Egypt **i** 871.1
44:30 and **i** the hand of them that seek his life; 871.1
44:30 as I gave Zedekiah king of Judah **i** 871.1
46:11 Go up *i* Gilead, and take balm, O virgin, NIH
46:19 in Egypt, furnish thyself to **go i captivity:** 1473
46:24 she shall be delivered **i** the hand of 871.1
46:26 I will deliver them **i** the hand of those that 871.1
46:26 **i** the hand of Nebuchadrezzar king of 871.1
46:26 of Babylon, and **i** the hand of his servants: 871.1
47: 6 put up thyself **i** thy scabbard, rest, and 413
48: 7 Chemosh shall go forth **i** captivity *with* his 871.1
48:11 to vessel, neither hath he gone **i** captivity: 871.1
48:44 He that fleeth from the fear shall fall **i** 413
49: 3 for their king shall go **i** captivity, *and* 871.1
49:32 I will scatter **i** all winds them *that are* in 3807.1
51: 9 and let us go every one **i** his own country: 3807.1
51:50 and let Jerusalem come **i** your mind. 5921
51:51 for strangers are come **i** the sanctuaries of 5921
51:59 *i* Babylon in the fourth year of his reign. NIH
51:63 to it, and cast it **i** the midst of Euphrates: 413
52:12 served the king of Babylon, **i** Jerusalem, 871.1
La 1: 3 Judah is **gone i captivity** because 1540
1: 5 her children are gone *i* captivity before NIH
1: 7 when her people fell **i** the hand of 871.1
1:10 for she hath seen *that* the heathen **entered i** 935
1:10 they should not enter **i** thy congregation. 871.1
1:13 From above hath he sent fire **i** my bones, NIH
1:14 the Lord hath delivered me **i** *their* hands, 871.1
1:18 and my young men are gone **i** captivity. 871.1
2: 7 he hath given up **i** the hand of the enemy 871.1
2: 9 Her gates are sunk **i** the ground; he hath 871.1
2:12 when their soul was poured out **i** their 413
3: 2 brought *me* *i* darkness, but not *into* light. NIH
3: 2 brought *me into* darkness, but not *i* light. NIH
3:13 the arrows of his quiver to enter **i** my reins. 871.1
4:12 the enemy should have entered **i** the gates 871.1
4:22 will no more **carry** thee **away i captivity:** 1540
5:15 is ceased; our dance is turned **i** mourning. 3807.1
Eze 2: 2 the spirit entered **i** me when he spake unto 871.1
3:22 go forth **i** the plain, and I will there talk with 413
3:23 Then I arose, and went forth **i** the plain: and 413
3:24 the spirit entered **i** me, and set me upon my 871.1
4:14 neither came there abominable flesh **i** my 871.1
5: 4 cast them **i** the midst of the fire, and 413
5: 4 *for* thereof shall a fire come forth **i** all 413
5: 6 she hath changed my judgments **i** 3807.1
5:10 the whole remnant of thee will I scatter **i** 3807.1
5:12 I will scatter a third *part* **i** all the winds, 3807.1
7:11 Violence is risen up **i** a rod of 3807.1
7:21 I will give it **i** the hands of the strangers for 871.1
7:22 secret *place:* for the robbers shall enter **i** it, 871.1
8:16 he brought me **i** the inner court of 413
10: 7 put *it* **i** the hands of *him that was* clothed 413
11: 5 for I know the **things that come i** your 4609
11: 9 deliver you **i** the hands of strangers, and 871.1
11:24 in vision by the Spirit of God **i** Chaldea, 1886.5
12: 4 their sight, as they that go forth **i** captivity. NIH
12:11 they shall remove *and go* **i** captivity. 871.1
13: 5 Ye have not gone up **i** the gaps, 871.1
13: 9 neither shall they enter **i** the land of Israel; 413
14:19 Or *if* I send a pestilence **i** that land, and 413
15: 4 Behold, it is cast **i** the fire for fuel; 3807.1
16: 8 and entered **i** a covenant with thee, 871.1
16:13 and thou didst prosper **i** a kingdom. 3807.1
16:39 I will also give thee **i** their hand, and 871.1
17: 4 and carried it **i** a land of traffick; 413
17:15 him in sending his ambassadors *i* Egypt, NIH
19: 9 they brought him **i** holds, that his voice 871.1
20: 6 to bring them forth of the land of Egypt **i** a 413
20:10 of Egypt, and brought them **i** the wilderness. 413
20:15 that I would not bring them **i** the land which 413
20:28 *For* when I had brought them **i** the land, 413
20:32 that which cometh **i** your mind shall not be 5921
20:35 I will bring you **i** the wilderness of 413
20:37 I will bring you **i** the bond of the covenant: 871.1
20:38 and they shall not enter **i** the land of Israel: 413
20:42 when I shall bring you **i** the land of Israel, 413
20:42 **i** the country *for* the which I lifted up mine 413
21:11 to give it **i** the hand of the slayer. 871.1
21:14 which **entereth i** their **privy chambers.** 2314
21:30 Shall I cause *it* to return **i** his sheath? I will 413
21:31 deliver thee **i** the hand of brutish men, *and* 871.1
22:19 I will gather you **i** the midst of Jerusalem. 413
22:20 and lead, and tin, **i** the midst of the furnace, 413
23: 9 Wherefore I have delivered her **i** the hand 871.1
23: 9 **i** the hand of the Assyrians, upon whom 871.1
23:16 and sent messengers unto them **i** Chaldea. 1886.5
23:17 the Babylonians came to her **i** the bed of 3807.1
23:28 I *will* deliver thee **i** the hand *of them* 871.1
23:28 **i** the hand *of them* from whom thy mind is 871.1
23:31 therefore will I give her cup **i** thine hand. 871.1
23:39 they came the same day **i** my sanctuary to 413
24: 3 on a pot, set *it* on, and also pour water **i** it: 871.1
24: 4 Gather the pieces thereof **i** it, *even* every 413
25: 3 of Judah, when they went **i** captivity; 871.1
26:10 when he shall enter **i** thy gates, 871.1
26:10 as men **enter i** a city wherein is made a 3996
26:20 thee down with them that descend **i** the pit, NIH
27:26 Thy rowers have brought thee **i** great 871.1
27:27 shall fall **i** the midst of the seas in the day 871.1
28: 4 hast gotten gold and silver **i** thy treasures: 871.1
28:23 For I will send **i** her pestilence, and 871.1

Eze 28:23 into her pestilence, and blood **i** her streets; 871.1
29: 5 I will leave thee *thrown* **i** the wilderness, 1886.5
29:14 will cause them to return **i** the land of NIH
29:14 of Pathros, **i** the land of their habitation; 5921
30:12 and sell the land **i** the hand of the wicked: 871.1
30:17 and these *cities* shall go **i** captivity. 871.1
30:18 and her daughters shall go **i** captivity. 871.1
30:25 when I shall put my sword **i** the hand of 871.1
31:11 delivered him **i** the hand of the mighty one 871.1
31:16 to hell with them that descend **i** the pit: NIH
31:17 They also went down **i** hell with him unto 1886.5
32: 9 **i** the countries which thou hast not known. 5921
32:18 the earth, with them that go down **i** the pit. NIH
32:24 which are gone down uncircumcised **i** 413
36: 5 which have appointed my land **i** their 3807.1
36:24 and will bring you **i** your own land. 413
37: 5 I *will* cause breath to enter **i** you, and 871.1
37:10 the breath came **i** them, and they lived, and 871.1
37:12 and bring you **i** the land of Israel. 413
37:17 join them one to another **i** one stick; and 3807.1
37:21 every side, and bring them **i** their own land: 413
37:22 neither shall they be divided **i** two 3807.1
38: 4 put hooks **i** thy jaws, and I will bring thee 871.1
38: 8 in the latter years thou shalt come **i** the land 413
38:10 *that* at the same time shall things come **i** thy 5921
39:23 of Israel **went i captivity** for their iniquity: 1540
39:23 and gave them **i** the hand of their enemies: 871.1
39:28 which **caused** them **to be led i captivity** 1540
40: 2 In the visions of God brought he me **i** 413
40:17 Then brought he me **i** the outward court, and 413
40:32 he brought me **i** the inner court toward 413
41: 6 they entered **i** the wall which *was* of 871.1
42: 1 he brought me forth **i** the utter court, the way 413
42: 1 he brought me **i** the chamber that *was* over 413
42: 9 as one goeth **i** them from the utter court. 3807.1
42:12 wall toward the east, as *one* **entereth i** them. 935
42:14 shall they not go out of the holy *place* **i** 413
43: 4 the glory of the LORD came **i** the house by 413
43: 5 me up, and brought me **i** the inner court; 413
44: 7 In that ye have brought *i my sanctuary* NIH
44: 9 in flesh, shall enter **i** my sanctuary, 413
44:12 caused the house of Israel to fall **i** iniquity; NIH
44:16 They shall enter **i** my sanctuary, and 413
44:19 when they go forth **i** the utter court, 413
44:19 *even* **i** the utter court to the people, 413
44:21 drink wine, when they enter **i** the inner court. 413
44:27 And in the day that he goeth **i** the sanctuary, 413
46:19 **i** the holy chambers of the priests, 413
46:20 that *they* bear *them* not out **i** the utter court, 413
46:21 he brought me forth **i** the utter court, 413
47: 8 go down **i** the desert, and go into the sea: 5921
47: 8 go down into the desert, and go **i** the sea: 1886.5
47: 8 *which* being brought forth **i** the sea, 413
Da 1: 2 the Lord gave Jehoiakim king of Judah **i** 871.1
1: 2 which he carried *i* the land of Shinar *to* NIH
1: 2 he brought the vessels *i* the treasure house NIH
1: 9 Now God had brought Daniel **i** favour 3807.1
2:29 thy thoughts came *i thy mind* upon thy bed, NIH
2:38 the fowls of the heaven hath he given **i** 871.2
3: 6 worshippeth shall the same hour be cast **i** 3807.2
3:11 *that* he should be cast **i** the midst of a 3807.2
3:15 ye shall be cast the same hour **i** the midst 3807.2
3:20 to cast *them* **i** the burning fiery furnace. 3807.2
3:21 were cast **i** the midst of the burning fiery 3807.2
3:23 fell down bound **i** the midst of 3807.2
3:24 Did not we cast three men bound **i** 3807.2
5:10 and his lords, came **i** the banquet house: 3807.2
6: 7 O king, he shall be cast **i** the den of lions. 3807.2
6:10 writing *was* signed, he went **i** his house; 3807.2
6:12 O king, shall be cast **i** the den of lions? 3807.2
6:16 and cast *him* **i** the den of lions. 3807.2
6:24 they cast *them* **i** the den of lions, them, 3807.2
7:25 they shall be given **i** his hand until a time 871.2
10: 8 for my comeliness was turned in me **i** 3807.1
11: 7 shall enter **i** the fortress of the king of 871.1
11: 8 shall also carry captives *i* Egypt their gods, NIH
11: 9 So the king of the south shall come **i** *his* 871.1
11: 9 *his* kingdom, and shall return **i** his own land. 413
11:11 but the multitude shall be given **i** his hand. 871.1
11:28 shall he return *i* his land with great riches; NIH
11:40 he shall enter **i** the countries, and 871.1
11:41 He shall enter also **i** the glorious land, and 871.1
Hos 2:14 bring her *i* the wilderness, and NIH
4: 7 *therefore* will I change their glory **i** shame. 871.1
9: 4 for their bread for their soul shall not come *i* NIH
11: 5 He shall not return **i** the land of Egypt, but 413
11: 9 of thee: and I will not enter **i** the city. 871.1
12: 1 the Assyrians, and oil is carried **i** Egypt. 3807.1
12:12 Jacob fled *i* the country of Syria, and NIH
Joel 1:14 all the inhabitants of the land *i* the house of NIH
2:20 will drive him **i** a land barren and desolate, 413
2:31 The sun shall be turned **i** darkness, and 3807.1
2:31 the moon **i** blood, before the great and 3807.1
3: 2 will bring them down **i** the valley of 413
3: 5 have **carried i** your temples my goodly 935
3: 8 your daughters **i** the hand of the children of 871.1
3:10 Beat your plowshares **i** swords, and 3807.1
3:10 and your pruninghooks **i** spears: 3807.1
Am 1: 4 I will send a fire **i** the house of Hazael, 871.1
1: 5 the people of Syria shall **go i captivity** unto 1540
1:15 their king shall go **i** captivity, he and 871.1
2: 1 he burnt the bones of the king of Edom **i** 3807.1
4: 3 ye shall cast *them* **i** the palace, saith 1886.5
5: 5 nor enter *i* Gilgal, and pass not *to* NIH
5: 5 for Gilgal shall **surely go i captivity,** 1540+1540
5: 8 the shadow of death **i** the morning, 3807.1
5:19 or went *i* the house, and leaned his hand on NIH
5:27 Therefore will I **cause** you **to go i captivity** 1540
6:12 for ye have turned judgment **i** gall, and 3807.1
6:12 and the fruit of righteousness **i** hemlock: 3807.1
7:12 go, flee thee away **i** the land of Judah, and 413
7:17 Israel shall **surely go i captivity** 1540+1540
8:10 I will turn your feasts **i** mourning, and 3807.1
8:10 and all your songs **i** lamentation; 3807.1
9: 2 Though they dig **i** hell, thence shall mine 871.1

Am 9: 4 though they go **i** captivity before their 871.1
Ob 1:11 foreigners entered *i* his gates, and cast lots NIH
1:13 Thou shouldest not have entered **i** the gate 871.1
Jnh 1: 3 paid the fare thereof, and went down **i** it, 871.1
1: 4 the LORD sent out a great wind **i** the sea, 413
1: 5 cast forth the wares that *were* in the ship **i** 413
1: 5 Jonah was gone down **i** the sides of the ship; 413
1:12 Take me up, and cast me forth **i** the sea; 413
1:15 took up Jonah, and cast him forth **i** the sea: 413
2: 3 For thou hadst cast me *i* the deep, in NIH
2: 7 came in unto thee, **i** thine holy temple. 413
3: 4 Jonah began to enter **i** the city a day's 871.1
Mic 1: 6 I will pour down the stones thereof **i** 3807.1
1:16 for they are **gone i captivity** from thee. 1540
3: 5 he that putteth not **i** their mouths, they even 5921
4: 3 they shall beat their swords **i** plowshares, 3807.1
4: 3 and their spears **i** pruninghooks: 3807.1
4:12 for he shall gather them as the sheaves **i** 1886.5
5: 5 when the Assyrian shall come **i** our land: 871.1
5: 6 when he cometh **i** our land, and when he 871.1
7:19 thou wilt cast all their sins **i** the depths of 871.1
Na 3:10 *was* she carried away, she went **i** captivity: 871.1
3:12 they shall even fall **i** the mouth of the eater. 5921
3:14 go **i** clay, and tread the morter, 871.1
Hab 3:16 rottenness entered **i** my bones, and 871.1
Hag 1: 6 earneth wages *to put it* **i** a bag with holes. 413
Zec 5: 4 and it shall enter **i** the house of the thief, and 413
5: 4 **i** the house of him that sweareth falsely by 413
5: 8 he cast it **i** the midst of the ephah; and 413
6: 6 The black horses which *are* therein go forth **i** 413
6:10 go *i* the house of Josiah the son of NIH
10:10 I will bring them **i** the land of Gilead and 413
11: 6 I *will* deliver the men every one **i** his 871.1
11: 6 and **i** the hand of his king: 871.1
14: 2 half of the city shall go forth **i** captivity, 871.1
Mal 3:10 Bring ye all the tithes **i** the storehouse, that 413
Mt 1:17 from David until the carrying away **i** NIG
1:17 from the carrying away **i** Babylon unto NIG
2:11 And when they were come **i** the house, *1519*
2:12 they departed **i** their own country another *1519*
2:13 and flee **i** Egypt, and be thou there until I *1519*
2:14 his mother by night, and departed **i** Egypt: *1519*
2:20 and his mother, and go **i** the land of Israel: *1519*
2:21 his mother, and came **i** the land of Israel. *1519*
2:22 he turned aside **i** the parts of Galilee: *1519*
3:10 good fruit is hewn down, and cast **i** the fire. *1519*
3:12 his floor, and gather his wheat **i** the garner; *1519*
4: 1 Then was Jesus led up of the Spirit **i** *1519*
4: 5 Then the devil taketh him *up* **i** the holy city, *1519*
4: 8 the devil taketh him *up* **i** an exceeding high *1519*
4:12 had heard that John was **cast i prison**, *3860*
4:12 was cast into prison, he departed **i** Galilee; *1519*
4:18 Andrew his brother, casting a net **i** the sea: *1519*
5: 1 the multitudes, he went up **i** a mountain: *1519*
5:20 ye shall in no case enter **i** the kingdom of *1519*
5:25 thee to the officer, and thou be cast **i** prison. *1519*
5:29 not *that* thy whole body should be cast **i** *1519*
5:30 not *that* thy whole body should be cast **i** *1519*
6: 6 enter **i** thy closet, and when thou hast shut *1519*
6:13 And lead us not **i** temptation, but deliver us *1519*
6:26 neither do they reap, nor gather **i** barns; *1519*
6:30 to day is, and to morrow is cast **i** the oven, *1519*
7:19 good fruit is hewn down, and cast **i** the fire. *1519*
7:21 Lord, shall enter **i** the kingdom of heaven; *1519*
8: 5 And when Jesus was entered **i** Capernaum, *1519*
8:12 kingdom shall be cast out **i** outer darkness: *1519*
8:14 And when Jesus was come **i** Peter's house, *1519*
8:23 And when he was entered **i** a ship, *1519*
8:28 And when he was come to the other side **i** *1519*
8:31 suffer us to go away **i** the herd of swine. *1519*
8:32 come out, they went **i** the herd of swine: *1519*
8:32 ran violently down a steep place **i** the sea, *1519*
8:33 and went their ways **i** the city, and *1519*
9: 1 And he entered **i** a ship, and passed over, *1519*
9: 1 and passed over, and came **i** his own city. *1519*
9:17 Neither do *men* put new wine **i** old bottles: *1519*
9:17 but they put new wine **i** new bottles, and *1519*
9:23 And when Jesus came **i** the ruler's house, *1519*
9:26 And the fame hereof went abroad **i** all that *1519*
9:28 And when he was come **i** the house, *1519*
9:38 that he will send forth labourers **i** his *1519*
10: 5 Go not **i** the way of the Gentiles, and *1519*
10: 5 **i** *any* city of the Samaritans enter ye not: *1519*
10:11 And **i** whatsoever city or town ye shall *1519*
10:12 And when ye **come i** a house salute *1525*
10:23 persecute you in this city, flee ye **i** another: *1519*
11: 7 What went ye out **i** the wilderness to see? *1519*
12: 4 How he entered **i** the house of God, and *1519*
12: 9 departed thence, he went **i** their synagogue: *1519*
12:11 and if it fall **i** a pit on the sabbath day, *1519*
12:29 Or else how can one enter **i** a strong *man's* *1519*
12:44 I will return **i** my house from whence I *1519*
13: 2 unto him, so that he went **i** a ship, and sat; *1519*
13: 8 But other fell **i** good ground, and *1909*
13:20 But he that received the seed **i** stony *places,* *1909*
13:23 But he that received seed **i** the good ground *1909*
13:30 burn them: but gather the wheat **i** my barn. *1519*
13:36 the multitude away, and went **i** the house: *1519*
13:42 And shall cast them **i** a furnace of fire: *1519*
13:47 *that was* cast **i** the sea, and gathered of *1519*
13:48 and gathered the good **i** vessels, but cast *1519*
13:50 And shall cast them **i** the furnace of fire: *1519*
13:54 And when he was come **i** his own country, *1519*
14:13 thence by ship **i** a desert place apart: *1519*
14:15 that they may go **i** the villages, and *1519*
14:22 constrained his disciples to get **i** a ship, *1519*
14:23 he went up **i** a mountain apart to pray: *1519*
14:32 And when they were come **i** the ship, *1519*
14:34 they came **i** the land of Gennesaret. *1519*
14:35 they sent out **i** all that country round about, *1519*
15:11 Not that which **goeth i** the mouth *1525*
15:14 lead the blind, both shall fall **i** the ditch. *1519*
15:17 entereth in at the mouth goeth **i** the belly, *1519*
15:17 into the belly, and is cast out **i** the draught? *1519*
15:21 and departed **i** the coasts of Tyre and Sidon. *1519*

Mt 15:29 and went up **i** a mountain, and sat down *1519*
15:39 and came **i** the coasts of Magdala. *1519*
16:13 When Jesus came **i** the coasts of Cesarea *1519*
17: 1 bringeth them up **i** a high mountain apart, *1519*
17:15 for ofttimes he falleth **i** the fire, and oft into *1519*
17:15 he falleth into the fire, and oft **i** the water. *1519*
17:22 The Son of man shall be betrayed **i** *1519*
17:25 And when he was **come i** the house, *1525*
18: 3 ye shall not enter **i** the kingdom of heaven. *1519*
18: 8 it is better for thee to enter **i** life halt or *1519*
18: 8 or two feet to be cast **i** everlasting fire. *1519*
18: 9 it is better for thee to enter **i** life with one *1519*
18: 9 rather than having two eyes to be cast **i** hell *1519*
18:12 and goeth **i** the mountains, and seeketh that *1909*
18:30 but went and cast him **i** prison, till he *1519*
19: 1 came **i** the coasts of Judea beyond Jordan; *1519*
19:17 but if thou wilt enter **i** life, keep *1519*
19:23 That a rich *man* shall hardly enter **i** *1519*
19:24 than for a rich *man* to enter **i** the kingdom *1519*
20: 1 morning to hire labourers **i** his vineyard. *1519*
20: 2 a penny a day, he sent them **i** his vineyard. *1519*
20: 4 Go ye also **i** the vineyard, and *1519*
20: 7 saith unto them, Go ye also **i** the vineyard; *1519*
21: 2 Go **i** the village over against you, and *1519*
21:10 And when he was **come i** Jerusalem, *1525*
21:12 And Jesus **went i** the temple of God, *1525*
21:17 and went out of the city **i** Bethany; *1519*
21:18 Now in the morning as he returned **i** *1519*
21:21 thou removed, and be thou cast **i** the sea; *1519*
21:23 And when he was come **i** the temple, *1519*
21:31 the harlots go **i** the kingdom of God before *1519*
21:33 to husbandmen, and **went i a far country**: *589*
22: 9 Go ye therefore **i** the highways, *1909*
22:10 So those servants went out **i** the *high*ways, *1519*
22:13 him away, and cast *him* **i** outer darkness; *1519*
24:16 Then let them which be in Judea flee **i** *1909*
24:38 until the day that Noe entered **i** the ark, *1519*
25:14 *is* as a man **travelling i a far country**, *589*
25:21 *things:* enter thou **i** the joy of thy lord. *1519*
25:23 *things:* enter thou **i** the joy of thy lord. *1519*
25:30 And cast ye the unprofitable servant **i** outer *1519*
25:41 from me, ye cursed, **i** everlasting fire, *1519*
25:46 And these shall go away **i** everlasting *1519*
25:46 but the righteous **i** life eternal. *1519*
26:18 Go **i** the city to such a man, and say unto *1519*
26:30 they went out **i** the mount of Olives. *1519*
26:32 risen *again,* I will go before you **i** Galilee. *1519*
26:41 and pray, that ye enter not **i** temptation: *1519*
26:45 the Son of man is betrayed **i** the hands of *1519*
26:52 Put up again thy sword **i** his place: *1519*
26:71 And when he was gone out **i** the porch, *1519*
27: 6 It is not lawful for to put them **i** *1519*
27:27 the governor took Jesus **i** the common hall, *1519*
27:53 and **went i** the holy city, and *1525*
28: 7 and behold, he goeth before you **i** Galilee; *1519*
28:10 go tell my brethren that they go **i** Galilee, *1519*
28:11 some of the watch came **i** the city, and *1519*
28:16 Then the eleven disciples went *away* **i** *1519*
28:16 **i** a mountain where Jesus had appointed *1519*
Mk 1:12 And immediately the Spirit driveth him **i** *1519*
1:14 was put in prison, Jesus came **i** Galilee, *1519*
1:16 Andrew his brother casting a net **i** the sea: *1722*
1:21 And they **went i** Capernaum; and *1531*
1:21 straightway on the sabbath day he entered **i** *1519*
1:29 they entered **i** the house of Simon and *1519*
1:35 and departed **i** a solitary place, and *1519*
1:38 said unto them, Let us go **i** the next towns, *1519*
1:45 *Jesus* could no more openly enter **i** the city, *1519*
2: 1 And again he entered **i** Capernaum after *1519*
2:11 up thy bed, and go thy way **i** thine house. *1519*
2:22 And no *man* putteth new wine **i** old bottles: *1519*
2:22 but new wine must be put **i** new bottles. *1519*
2:26 How he **went i** the house of God in *1525*
3: 1 And he entered again **i** the synagogue; and *1519*
3:13 And he goeth up **i** a mountain, and *1519*
3:19 also betrayed him. And they went **i** a house. *1519*
3:27 No *man* can enter **i** a strong *man's* house, *1519*
4: 1 so that he entered **i** a ship, and sat in *1519*
4:26 as if a man should cast seed **i** the ground, *1909*
4:37 and the waves beat **i** the ship, so that it was *1519*
5: 1 of the sea, **i** the country of the Gadarenes. *1519*
5:12 saying, Send us **i** the swine, that we may *1519*
5:12 us into the swine, that we may enter **i** them. *1519*
5:13 spirits went out, and entered **i** the swine: *1519*
5:13 the herd ran violently down a steep place **i** *1519*
5:18 And when he was come **i** the ship, he that *1519*
6: 1 from thence, and came **i** his own country; *1519*
6:10 In what place soever ye enter **i** a house, *1519*
6:31 Come ye yourselves apart **i** a desert place, *1519*
6:32 And they departed **i** a desert place by ship *1519*
6:36 that they may go **i** the country round about, *1519*
6:36 and *i* the villages, and buy themselves NIG
6:45 constrained his disciples to get **i** the ship, *1519*
6:46 he departed **i** a mountain to pray. *1519*
6:51 And he went up unto them **i** the ship; and *1519*
6:53 they came **i** the land of Genesaret, and *1909*
6:56 he entered, **i** villages, or cities, or country, *1519*
7:15 a man, that entering **i** him can defile him: *1519*
7:17 And when he was entered **i** *the* house from *1519*
7:18 *thing* from without entereth **i** the man, *1519*
7:19 Because it entereth not **i** his heart, but *1519*
7:19 it entereth not into his heart, but **i** the belly, *1519*
7:19 into the belly, and goeth out **i** the draught, *1519*
7:24 and went **i** the borders of Tyre and Sidon, *1519*
7:24 and entered **i** a house, and would have no *1519*
7:33 and put his fingers **i** his ears, and he spit, *1519*
8:10 And straightway he entered **i** a ship with *1519*
8:10 and came **i** the parts of Dalmanutha. *1519*
8:13 entering **i** the ship again departed to *1519*
8:26 saying, Neither **go i** the town, nor tell *it* to *1525*
8:27 **i** the towns of Cesarea Philippi: *1519*
9: 2 leadeth them up **i** a high mountain apart by *1519*
9:22 And ofttimes it hath cast him **i** the fire, and *1519*
9:22 the fire, and **i** the waters, to destroy him: *1519*
9:25 come out of him, and enter no more **i** him. *1519*

Mk 9:28 And when he was **come i** *the* house, *1525*
9:31 The Son of man is delivered **i** the hands of *1519*
9:42 about his neck, and he were cast **i** the sea. *1519*
9:43 it is better for thee to enter **i** life maimed, *1519*
9:43 than having two hands to go **i** hell, into *1519*
9:43 **i** the fire that never shall be quenched: *1519*
9:45 it is better for thee to enter halt **i** life, *1519*
9:45 than having two feet to be cast **i** hell, *1519*
9:45 **i** the fire that never shall be quenched: *1519*
9:47 it is better for thee to enter **i** the kingdom of *1519*
9:47 than having two eyes to be cast **i** hell fire: *1519*
10: 1 cometh **i** the coasts of Judea by the farther *1519*
10:17 And when he was gone forth **i** the way, *1519*
10:23 have riches enter **i** the kingdom of God! *1519*
10:24 in riches to enter **i** the kingdom of God! *1519*
10:25 than for a rich *man* to enter **i** the kingdom *1519*
11: 2 Go your way **i** the village over against you: *1519*
11: 2 and as soon as ye be entered **i** it, ye shall *1519*
11:11 And Jesus entered **i** Jerusalem, and into *1519*
11:11 entered into Jerusalem, and **i** the temple: *1519*
11:15 and Jesus **went i** the temple, and began to *1525*
11:23 thou removed, and be thou cast **i** the sea; *1519*
12: 1 to husbandmen, and **went i a far country**. *589*
12:41 beheld how the people cast money **i** *1519*
12:43 than all they which have cast **i** the treasury: *1519*
13:15 is on the housetop not go down **i** the house, *1519*
14:13 Go ye **i** the city, and there shall meet you a *1519*
14:16 and came **i** the city, and found as he had *1519*
14:26 they went out **i** the mount of Olives. *1519*
14:28 I am risen, I will go before you **i** Galilee. *1519*
14:38 and pray, lest ye enter **i** temptation. *1519*
14:41 the Son of man is betrayed **i** the hands of *1519*
14:54 afar off, even **i** the palace of the high priest: *2080*
14:68 And he went out **i** the porch; and *the* cock *1519*
15:16 And the soldiers led him away **i** the hall, *2080*
16: 5 And entering **i** the sepulchre, they saw a *1519*
16: 7 Peter that he goeth before you **i** Galilee: *1519*
16:12 as they walked, and went **i** the country. *1519*
16:15 Go ye **i** all the world, and preach the gospel *1519*
16:19 he was received up **i** heaven, and sat on *1519*
Lk 1: 9 he **went i** the temple of the Lord. *1525*
1:39 and went **i** the hill country with haste, *1519*
1:39 the hill country with haste, **i** a city of Juda; *1519*
1:40 And entered **i** the house of Zacharias, and *1519*
1:79 to guide our feet **i** the way of peace. *1519*
2: 3 went to be taxed, every one **i** his own city. *1519*
2: 4 of Nazareth, **i** Judea, unto the city of David, *1519*
2:15 as the angels were gone away from them **i** *1519*
2:27 And he came by the Spirit **i** the temple: and *1519*
2:39 they returned **i** Galilee, to their own city *1519*
3: 3 And he came **i** all the country about Jordan, *1519*
3: 9 good fruit is hewn down, and cast **i** the fire. *1519*
3:17 and will gather the wheat **i** his garner; *1519*
4: 1 and was led by the Spirit **i** the wilderness, *1519*
4: 5 the devil, taking him up **i** a high mountain, *1519*
4:14 returned in the power of the Spirit **i** Galilee: *1519*
4:16 he **went i** the synagogue on *1525*
4:37 And the fame of him went out **i** every place *1519*
4:38 and entered **i** Simon's house. *1519*
4:42 he departed and went **i** a desert place: *1519*
5: 3 And he entered **i** one of the ships, *1519*
5: 4 Launch out **i** the deep, and let down your *1519*
5:16 And he withdrew himself **i** the wilderness, *1722*
5:19 with *his* couch **i** the midst before Jesus. *1519*
5:24 and take up thy couch, and go **i** thine house. *1519*
5:37 And no *man* putteth new wine **i** old bottles; *1519*
5:38 But new wine must be put **i** new bottles; *1519*
6: 4 How he **went i** the house of God, *1525*
6: 6 that he entered **i** the synagogue and taught: *1519*
6:12 *that* he went out **i** a mountain to pray, and *1519*
6:38 running over, shall *men* give **i** your bosom. *1519*
6:39 shall they not both fall **i** the ditch? *1519*
7: 1 of the people, he entered **i** Capernaum. *1519*
7:11 *day* after, *that* he went **i** a city called Nain; *1519*
7:24 What went ye out **i** the wilderness for to *1519*
7:36 And he **went i** the Pharisee's house, *1525*
7:44 I entered **i** thine house, thou gavest me no *1519*
8:22 that he went **i** a ship with his disciples: *1519*
8:29 was driven of the devil **i** the wilderness.) *1519*
8:30 because many devils were entered **i** him. *1519*
8:31 not command them to go out **i** the deep. *1519*
8:32 that he would suffer them to enter **i** them. *1519*
8:33 out of the man, and entered **i** the swine: *1519*
8:33 the herd ran violently down a steep place **i** *1519*
8:37 and he went *up* **i** the ship, and *1519*
8:41 besought him that *he* would **come i** *1525*
8:51 And when he **came i** the house, *1525*
9: 4 And whatsoever house ye enter **i**, *1519*
9:10 went aside privately **i** a desert place *1519*
9:12 that they may go **i** the towns and *1519*
9:28 James, and went up **i** a mountain to pray. *1519*
9:34 and they feared as they entered **i** the cloud. *1519*
9:44 Let these sayings sink down **i** your ears: *1519*
9:44 for the Son of man shall be delivered **i** *1519*
9:52 and entered **i** a village of the Samaritans, *1519*
10: 1 and two before his face **i** every city and *1519*
10: 2 that he would send forth labourers **i** his *1519*
10: 5 And **i** whatsoever house ye enter, first say, *1519*
10: 8 And **i** whatsoever city ye enter, and *1519*
10:10 But **i** whatsoever city ye enter, and *1519*
10:10 go *your ways* out **i** the streets of the same, *1519*
10:38 that he entered **i** a certain village: *1519*
10:38 named Martha received him **i** her house. *1519*
11: 4 And **lead** us not **i** temptation; but *1533*
12: 5 *he* hath killed hath power to cast **i** hell; *1519*
12:28 the field, and to morrow is cast **i** the oven; *1519*
12:58 and the officer cast thee **i** prison. *1519*
13:19 which a man took, and cast **i** his garden; *1519*
14: 1 as he went **i** the house of one of the chief *1519*
14: 5 you shall have an ass or an ox fallen **i** a pit, *1519*
14:21 Go out quickly **i** the streets and lanes of *1519*
14:23 Go out **i** the *high*ways and hedges, and *1519*
15:13 and took his journey **i** a far country, and *1519*
15:15 and he sent him **i** his fields to feed swine. *1519*
16: 4 they may receive me **i** their houses. *1519*

Lk 16: 9 they may receive you i everlasting 1519
16:16 is preached, and every man presseth i it. 1519
16:22 was carried by the angels i Abraham's 1519
16:28 lest they also come i this place of torment. 1519
17: 2 and he cast i the sea, than that he should 1519
17:12 And as he entered i a certain village, 1519
17:27 until the day that Noe entered i the ark, and 1519
18:10 Two men went up i the temple to pray; 1519
18:24 have riches enter i the kingdom of God! 1519
18:25 than for a rich man to enter i the kingdom 1519
19: 4 climbed up i a sycomore tree to see him: 1909
19:12 A certain nobleman went i a far country to 1519
19:23 then gavest not thou my money i the bank, 1909
19:30 Go ye i the village over against you; in 1519
19:45 And he **went i** the temple, and 1525
20: 9 and **went i a far country** for a long time. 589
21: 1 saw the rich men casting their gifts i 1519
21:12 and i prisons, being brought before kings NIG
21:24 and shall be led away captive i all nations: 1519
22: 3 Then entered Satan i Judas surnamed 1519
22:10 Behold, when ye are entered i the city, 1519
22:10 follow him i the house where he entereth 1519
22:33 to go with thee, both i prison, and to death. 1519
22:40 Pray that ye enter not i temptation. 1519
22:46 rise and pray, lest ye enter i temptation. 1519
22:54 **brought** him i the high priest's 1521
22:66 and led him i their council, saying, 1519
23:19 the city, and for murder, was cast i prison.) 1519
23:25 for sedition and murder was cast i prison, 1519
23:42 remember me when thou comest i thy 1722
23:46 Father, i thy hands I commend my spirit: 1519
24: 7 The Son of man must be delivered i 1519
24:26 these things, and to enter i his glory? 1519
24:51 parted from them, and carried up i heaven. 1519
Jn 1: 9 which lighteth every man that cometh i 1519
1:43 The day following Jesus would go forth i 1519
3: 4 can he enter the second time i his mother's 1519
3: 5 he cannot enter i the kingdom of God. 1519
3:17 For God sent not his Son i the world to 1519
3:19 that light is come i the world, and men 1519
3:22 and his disciples i the land of Judea; 1519
3:24 For John was not yet cast i prison. 1519
3:35 and hath given all things i his hand. 1722
4: 3 He left Judea, and departed again i Galilee. 1519
4:14 well of water springing up i everlasting life. 1519
4:28 and went her way i the city, and saith to 1519
4:38 and ye are entered i their labours. 1519
4:43 he departed thence, and went i Galilee. 1519
4:45 Then when he was come i Galilee, 1519
4:46 So Jesus came again i Cana of Galilee, 1519
4:47 that Jesus was come out of Judea i Galilee, 1519
4:54 when he was come out of Judea i Galilee. 1519
5: 4 went down at a certain season i the pool, 1722
5: 7 the water is troubled, to put me i the pool: 1519
5:24 and shall not come i condemnation; 1519
6: 3 And Jesus went up i a mountain, and 1519
6:14 that prophet that should come i the world. 1519
6:15 he departed again i a mountain himself 1519
6:17 And entered i a ship, and went over the sea 1519
6:21 Then they willingly received him i the ship: 1519
6:22 that Jesus went not with his disciples i 1519
7: 3 unto him, Depart hence, and go i Judea, 1519
7:14 of the feast Jesus went up i the temple, 1519
8: 2 And early in the morning he came again i 1519
9:39 For judgment I am come i this world, 1519
10: 1 He that entereth not by the door i 1519
10:36 and sent i the world, Thou blasphemest; 1519
10:40 And went away again beyond Jordan i 1519
11: 7 he to his disciples, Let us go i Judea again. 1519
11:27 of God, which should come i the world. 1519
11:30 Now Jesus was not yet come i the town, but 1519
11:54 i a city called Ephraim, and there continued 1519
12:24 Except a corn of wheat fall i the ground and 1519
12:46 I am come a light i the world, 1519
13: 2 the devil having now put i the heart of 1519
13: 3 the Father had given all things i his hands, 1519
13: 5 he poureth water i a bason, and began to 1519
13:27 And after the sop Satan entered i him. 1519
15: 6 and cast them i the fire, and they are 1519
16:13 is come, he will guide you i all truth: 1519
16:20 but your sorrow shall be turned i joy. 1519
16:21 for joy that a man is born i the world. 1519
16:28 from the Father, and am come i the world: 1519
17:18 As thou hast sent me i the world, even so 1519
17:18 even so have I also sent them i the world. 1519
18: 1 i the which he entered, and his disciples. 1519
18:11 unto Peter, Put up thy sword i the sheath: 1519
18:15 went in with Jesus i the palace of the high 1519
18:28 they themselves went not i the judgment 1519
18:33 Then Pilate entered i the judgment hall 1519
18:37 and for this cause came I i the world, 1519
19: 9 And **went** again i the judgment hall, and 1525
19:17 And he bearing his cross went forth i a 1519
20: 6 and **went i** the sepulchre, and seeth 1525
20:11 stooped down, and looked i the sepulchre, 1519
20:25 and put my finger i the print of the nails, 1519
20:25 and thrust my hand i his side, I will not 1519
20:27 hither thy hand, and thrust it i my side: 1519
21: 3 and entered i a ship immediately; 1519
21: 7 was naked,) and did cast himself i the sea. 1519
Ac 1:11 why stand ye gazing up i heaven? 1519
1:11 which is taken up from you i heaven, shall 1519
1:11 manner as ye have seen him go i heaven. 1519
1:13 they went up i an upper room, where abode 1519
2:20 The sun shall be turned i darkness, and 1519
2:20 and the moon i blood, before that great and 1519
2:34 For David is not ascended i the heavens: 1519
3: 1 John went up together i the temple at 1519
3: 2 to ask alms of them that entered i 1519
3: 3 and John about to go i the temple, 1519
3: 8 walked, and entered with them i the temple, 1519
5:15 Insomuch that they brought forth the sick i 2596
5:21 And when they heard that, they entered i 1519
7: 3 come i the land which I shall shew thee. 1519
7: 4 he removed him i this land, wherein ye now 1519

Ac 7: 6 and that they should **bring** them **i bondage**, 1402
7: 9 moved with envy, sold Joseph i Egypt: 1519
7:15 So Jacob went down i Egypt, and died, he, 1519
7:16 And were carried over i Sychem, and 1519
7:23 it came i his heart to visit his brethren 1909
7:34 And now come, I will send thee i Egypt. 1519
7:39 in their hearts turned back again i Egypt, 1519
7:45 with Jesus i the possession of the Gentiles, 1722
7:55 looked up stedfastly i heaven, and saw 1519
8: 3 of the church, **entering** i every house, 1531
8:38 and they went down both i the water, 1519
9: 6 and **go i** the city, and it shall be told 1525
9: 8 and **brought** him i Damascus. 1521
9:11 and go i the street which is called Straight, 1909
9:17 went his way, and entered i the house; 1519
9:39 they brought him i the upper chamber: 1519
10:10 while they made ready, he fell i a trance, 1909
10:16 the vessel was received up again i heaven. 1519
10:22 by a holy angel to send for thee i his house, 1519
10:24 And the morrow after they entered i 1519
11: 8 unclean hath at any time entered i my 1519
11:10 and all were drawn up again i heaven. 1519
11:12 and we entered i the man's house: 1519
12:17 And he departed, and went i another place. 1519
13:14 **went i** the synagogue on the sabbath 1525
14: 1 that they **went** both together i 1525
14:20 he rose up, and **came i** the city: 1525
14:22 tribulation enter i the kingdom of God. 1519
14:25 word in Perga, they went down i Attalia: 1519
16: 7 to Mysia, they assayed to go i Bithynia: 2596
16: 9 Come over i Macedonia, and help us. 1519
16:10 immediately we endeavoured to go i 1519
16:15 **come i** my house, and abide there. 1525
16:19 drew them i the market-place unto 1519
16:23 they cast them i prison, charging the jailor 1519
16:24 thrust them i the inner prison, and 1519
16:34 And when he had brought them i his house, 1519
16:37 being Romans, and have cast us i prison; 1519
16:40 and entered i the house of Lydia: 1519
17:10 who coming thither went i the synagogue 1519
18: 7 and entered i a certain man's house, 1519
18:18 and sailed thence i Syria, and with him 1519
18:19 but he himself entered i the synagogue, and 1519
18:27 And when he was disposed to pass i 1519
19: 8 And he **went i** the synagogue, and 1525
19:22 So he sent i Macedonia two of them that 1519
19:29 they rushed with one accord i the theatre. 1519
19:31 would not adventure himself i the theatre. 1519
20: 1 and departed for to go i Macedonia. 1519
20: 2 them much exhortation, he came i Greece, 1519
20: 3 wait for him, as he was about to sail i Syria, 1519
20: 4 And there accompanied him i Asia Sopater 891
20: 9 being **fallen** i a deep sleep: 2702
20:18 from the first day that I came i Asia, 1519
21: 3 and sailed i Syria, and landed at Tyre: 1519
21: 8 we entered i the house of Philip 1519
21:11 shall deliver him i the hands of 1519
21:26 himself with them entered i the temple, 1519
21:28 **brought** Greeks also i the temple, 1521
21:29 that Paul had **brought** i the temple.) 1521
21:34 he commanded him to be carried i 1519
21:37 And as Paul was to be **led i** 1521
21:38 leddest out i the wilderness four thousand 1519
22: 4 and delivering i prisons both men and 1519
22:10 said unto me, Arise, and go i Damascus; 1519
22:11 that were with me, I came i Damascus. 1519
22:23 off their clothes, and threw dust i the air, 1519
22:24 commanded him to be brought i the castle, 1519
23:10 among them, and to bring him i the castle. 1519
23:16 he went and entered i the castle, and 1519
23:20 bring down Paul to morrow i the council, 1519
23:28 I brought him forth i their council: 1519
24:27 Porcius Festus **came i** Felix' **room**. 1240+2983
25: 1 Now when Festus was **come i** the province, 1910
25:23 and were entered i the place of hearing, 1519
27: 1 was determined that we should sail i Italy, 1519
27: 2 And **entering i** a ship of Adramyttium, 1910
27: 6 found a ship of Alexandria sailing i Italy; 1519
27:15 and could not **bear up i** the wind, we let her 503
27:17 fearing lest they should fall i 1519
27:30 when they had let down the boat i the sea, 1519
27:38 the ship, and cast out the wheat i the sea. 1519
27:39 i the which they were minded, if it were 1519
27:41 And falling i a place where two seas met, 1519
27:43 swim should cast themselves first i the sea, NIG
28: 5 And he shook off the beast i the fire, and 1519
28:17 from Jerusalem i the hands of the Romans. 1519
28:23 there came many to him i his lodging; 1519
Ro 1:23 i an image made like to corruptible man, 1722
1:25 Who changed the truth of God i a lie, and 1722
1:26 natural use i that which is against nature: 1519
5: 2 By whom also we have access by faith i 1519
5:12 as by one man sin entered i the world, and 1519
6: 3 many of us as were baptized i Jesus Christ 1519
6: 3 into Jesus Christ were baptized i his death? 1519
6: 4 we are buried with him by baptism i death: 1519
7:23 **bringing** me **i captivity** to the law of sin 163
8:21 i the glorious liberty of the children of God. 1519
10: 6 in thine heart, Who shall ascend i heaven? 1519
10: 7 Or, Who shall descend i the deep? (that is, 1519
10:18 their sound went i all the earth, and 1519
11:24 wert graffed contrary to nature i a good 1519
11:24 which be the natural branches, be **graffed i** 1461
15:24 Whensoever I take my journey i Spain, 1519
15:28 them this fruit, I will come by you i Spain. 1519
1Co 2: 9 neither have entered i the heart of man, 1909
4:17 who shall **bring** you **i remembrance** of my 363
9:27 under my body, and **bring** it **i subjection**: 1396
11:20 therefore **i one place**, 846+1909+3588
12:13 For by one Spirit are we all baptized i one 1519
12:13 have been all made to drink i one Spirit. 1519
14: 9 what is spoken? for ye shall speak i the air. 1519
14:23 be come together **i one place**, 846+1909+3588
2Co 1:16 And to pass by you i Macedonia, and 1519
2:13 of them, I went from thence i Macedonia. 1519

2Co 3:18 are changed i the same image from glory to NIG
7: 5 For, when we were come i Macedonia, 1519
8:16 which put the same earnest care i the heart 1722
10: 5 **bringing i captivity** every thought to 163
11:13 transforming themselves i the apostles of 1519
11:14 for Satan himself is transformed i an angel 1519
11:20 ye suffer, if a man **bring** you **i bondage**, 2615
12: 4 How that he was caught up i paradise, and 1519
Gal 1: 6 soon removed from him that called you i 1722
1:17 but I went i Arabia, and returned again unto 1519
1:21 Afterwards I came i the regions of Syria 1519
2: 4 that they might **bring** us **i bondage**: 2615
3:27 For as many of you as have been baptized i 1519
4: 6 God hath sent forth the Spirit of his Son i 1519
Eph 4: 9 that he also descended first i the lower parts 1519
4:15 may grow up i him in all things, which is 1519
Col 1:13 hath translated us i the kingdom of his dear 1519
2:18 **intruding i** those things which he hath not 1687
2Th 3: 5 And the Lord direct your hearts i the love 1519
3: 5 of God, and i the patient waiting for Christ. 1519
1Ti 1: 3 still at Ephesus, when I went i Macedonia, 1519
1:12 me faithful, putting me i the ministry; 1519
1:15 that Christ Jesus came i the world to save 1519
3: 6 lest being lifted up with pride he fall i 1519
3: 7 lest he fall i reproach and the snare of 1519
3:16 on in the world, received up i glory. 1722
5: 9 Let not a widow be **taken i the number** 2639
6: 7 For we brought nothing i this world, and 1519
6: 9 But they that will be rich fall i temptation 1519
6: 9 a snare, and i many foolish and hurtful lusts, NIG
2Ti 3: 6 For of this sort are they which creep i 1519
Heb 1: 6 when he bringeth in the firstbegotten i 1519
3:11 in my wrath, They shall not enter i my rest. 1519
3:18 he that they should not enter i his rest, 1519
4: 1 a promise being left us of entering i his 1519
4: 3 For we which have believed do enter i rest, 1519
4: 3 in my wrath, if they shall enter i my rest: 1519
4: 5 place again, If they shall enter i my rest. 1519
4:10 For he that is entered i his rest, he also hath 1519
4:11 Let us labour therefore to enter i that rest, 1519
4:14 that is **passed** i the heavens, Jesus the Son 1330
6:19 and which entereth i that within the vail; 1519
8:10 I will put my laws i their mind, and 1519
9: 6 the priests went always i the first 1519
9: 7 But i the second went the high priest alone 1519
9: 8 that the way i the holiest of all was not yet NIG
9:12 by his own blood he entered in once i 1519
9:24 For Christ is not entered i the holy places 1519
9:24 but i heaven itself, now to appear in 1519
9:25 as the high priest entereth i the holy place 1519
10: 5 Wherefore when he **cometh i** 1525
10:16 I will put my laws **i their hearts**, and in their 1909
10:19 boldness to enter i the holiest by the blood 1519
10:31 It is a fearful thing to fall i the hands of 1519
11: 8 when he was called to go out i a place 1519
13:11 whose blood is brought i the sanctuary by 1519
Jas 1: 2 count it all joy when ye **fall i** divers 4045
1:25 But whoso looketh i the perfect law of 1519
4:13 or to morrow we will go i such a city, 1519
5: 4 entered i the ears of the Lord of sabaoth. 1519
5:12 your nay, nay; lest ye fall i condemnation. 5259
1Pe 1:12 which things the angels desire to look i. 1519
2: 9 you out of darkness i his marvellous light: 1519
3:22 Who is gone i heaven, and is on the right 1519
5:10 who hath called us i his eternal glory by 1519
2Pe 1:11 i the everlasting kingdom of our Lord 1519
2: 4 and **delivered** them i chains of darkness, 3860
2: 6 **turning** the cities of Sodom and Gomorrha
i ashes 5077
1Jn 4: 1 many false prophets are gone out i 1519
4: 9 that God sent his only begotten Son i 1519
2Jn 1: 7 For many deceivers are entered i the world, 1519
1:10 this doctrine, receive him not i your house, 1519
Jude 1: 4 the grace of our God i lasciviousness, 1519
Rev 2:10 the devil shall cast some of you i prison, 1519
2:22 I will cast her i a bed, and them that 1519
2:22 them that commit adultery with her i great 1519
5: 6 spirits of God sent forth i all the earth. 1519
8: 5 with fire of the altar, and cast it i the earth: 1519
8: 8 burning with fire was cast i the sea: 1519
11:11 a half the spirit of life from God entered i 1909
12: 6 And the woman fled i the wilderness, 1519
12: 9 he was cast out i the earth, and his angels 1519
12:14 that she might fly i the wilderness, into her 1519
12:14 i her place, where she is nourished for a 1519
13:10 He that leadeth i captivity shall go into 1519
13:10 He that leadeth into captivity shall go i 1519
14:10 which is poured out without mixture i 1722
14:19 And the angel thrust in his sickle i 1519
14:19 cast it i the great winepress of the wrath of 1519
15: 8 and no man was able to enter i the temple, 1519
16:16 And he gathered them together i a place 1519
16:17 And the seventh angel poured out his vial i 1519
16:19 And the great city was divided i three parts, 1519
17: 3 So he carried me away in the spirit i 1519
17: 8 out of the bottomless pit, and go i perdition: 1519
17:11 and is of the seven, and goeth i perdition. 1519
18:21 great millstone, and cast it i the sea, saying, 1519
19:20 These both were cast alive i a lake of fire 1519
20: 3 And cast him i the bottomless pit, and 1519
20:10 And the devil that deceived them was cast i 1519
20:14 and hell were cast i the lake of fire. 1519
20:15 the book of life was cast i the lake of fire. 1519
21:24 earth do bring their glory and honour i it. 1519
21:26 the glory and honour of the nations i it. 1519
21:27 And there shall in no wise enter i it any 1519
22:14 may enter in through the gates i the city. 1519

INTREAT (15) [ENTREAT, INTREATED, INTREATIES INTREATY]

Ge 23: 8 and i for me to Ephron the son of Zohar, 6293
Ex 8: 8 and Aaron, and said, I the LORD, 6279
8: 9 when shall I i for thee, and for thy servants, 6279
8:28 you shall not go very far away: i for me. 6279
8:29 I will i the LORD that the swarms of flies 6279

Ex 9:28 I the LORD (for *it is* enough) that there be 6279
10:17 only *this* once, and i the LORD your God, 6279
Ru 1:16 I me not to leave thee, *or* to return from 6293
1Sa 2:25 against the LORD, who shall i for him? 6419
1Ki 13: 6 I now the face of the LORD thy God, and 2470
Ps 45:12 among the people shall i thy favour. 2470+6440
Pr 19: 6 Many will i the favour of the prince: and 2470
1Co 4:13 Being defamed, we i: we are made as *3870*
Php 4: 3 And I i thee also, true yokefellow, *2065*
1Ti 5: 1 Rebuke not an elder, but i *him* as a father; *3870*

INTREATED (18) [INTREAT]
Ge 25:21 Isaac i the LORD for his wife, because 6279
25:21 the LORD was i of him, and Rebekah his 6279
Ex 8:30 went out from Pharaoh, and i the LORD. 6279
10:18 went out from Pharaoh, and i the LORD. 6279
Jdg 13: 8 Manoah i the LORD, and said, O my 6279
2Sa 21:14 And after that God was i for the land. 6279
24:25 So the LORD was i for the land, and 6279
1Ch 5:20 to God in the battle, and he was i of them; 6279
2Ch 33:13 he was i of him, and heard his supplication, 6279
33:19 *how God* was i of him, and all his sin, and 6279
Ezr 8:23 our God for this: and he was i of us. 6279
Job 19:16 gave *me* no answer; I i him with my mouth. 2603
19:17 though I i for the children's *sake* of mine 2589
Ps 119:58 I i thy favour with *my* whole heart: 2470
Isa 19:22 he shall be i of them, and shall heal them. 6279
Lk 15:28 therefore came his father out and i him. *3870*
Heb 12:19 which *voice* they that heard i that the word *3868*
Jas 3:17 then peaceable, gentle, *and* easy to be i, *2138*

INTREATIES (1) [INTREAT]
Pr 18:23 The poor useth i; but the rich answereth 8469

INTREATY (1) [INTREAT]
2Co 8: 4 Praying us with much i that we would *3874*

INTRUDING (1)
Col 2:18 i into *those things* which he hath not seen, *1687*

INVADE (2) [INVADED, INVASION]
2Ch 20:10 whom thou wouldest not let Israel i, 935+871.1
Hab 3:16 the people, he will i them with his troops. 1464

INVADED (5) [INVADE]
1Sa 23:27 come; for the Philistines have i the land. 6584
27: 8 i the Geshurites, and the Gezrites, and 6584
30: 1 that the Amalekites had i the south, and 6584
2Ki 13:20 the bands of the Moabites i the land 935+871.1
2Ch 28:18 The Philistines also had i the cities of 6584

INVALID See IMPOTENT

INVASION (1) [INVADE]
1Sa 30:14 We made an i *upon* the south of 6584

INVENT (1) [INVENTED, INVENTIONS, INVENTORS]
Am 6: 5 *and* i to themselves instruments of musick, 2803

INVENTED (1) [INVENT]
2Ch 26:15 i by cunning *men*, to be on the towers and 4284

INVENTIONS (5) [INVENT]
Ps 99: 8 though thou tookest vengeance of their i. 5949
106:29 they provoked *him* to anger with their i: 4611
106:39 and went a whoring with their own i. 4611
Pr 8:12 and find out knowledge of witty i. 4209
Ecc 7:29 but they have sought out many i. 2810

INVENTORS (1) [INVENT]
Ro 1:30 i of evil *things*, disobedient to parents, *2182*

INVESTIGATION See INQUISITION

INVISIBLE (5)
Ro 1:20 For the i *things* of him from the creation of *517*
Col 1:15 Who is the image of the i God, the firstborn *517*
1:16 in heaven, and that are in earth, visible and i, *517*
1Ti 1:17 immortal, i, the only wise God, *be* honour *517*
Heb 11:27 for he endured, as seeing *him who is* i. *517*

INVITED (3)
1Sa 9:24 for thee since *I* said, I have i the people. 7121
2Sa 13:23 and Absalom i all the king's sons. 7121
Est 5:12 to morrow *am* I i unto her also with 7121

INWARD (25) [INWARDLY, INWARDS]
Ex 28:26 which *is* in the side of the ephod i. 1004+1886.5
39:19 *was* on the side of the ephod i. 1004+1886.5
Lev 13:55 it *is* fret i, *whether* it *be* bare within or 871.1
2Sa 5: 9 built round about from Millo and i. 1004+1886.5
1Ki 7:25 and all their hinder parts *were* i. 1004+1886.5
2Ch 3:13 stood on their feet, and their faces *were* i. 1004
4: 4 and all their hinder parts *were* i. 1004+1886.5
Job 19:19 All my i friends abhorred me: and 5475
38:36 Who hath put wisdom in the i parts? or 2910
Ps 5: 9 their i *part is* very wickedness; their throat 7130
49:11 Their i *thought is, that* their houses *shall* 7130
51: 6 Behold, thou desirest truth in the i parts: 2910
64: 6 both the i *thought* of every one *of them*, 7130
Pr 20:27 searching all the i parts of the belly. 2315
20:30 so *do* stripes the i parts of the belly. 2315
Isa 16:11 for Moab, and mine i parts for Kir-haresh. 7130
Jer 31:33 I will put my law in their i parts, and 7130
Eze 40: 9 the porch of the gate *was* i. 1004+4480+1886.1
40:16 windows *were* round about i: 6441+3807.1
41: 3 went he i, and measured the post of 6441+3807.1
42: 4 a walk of ten cubits breadth i, 413+6442+1886.1
Lk 11:39 but your i part is full of ravening and *2081*
Ro 7:22 For I delight in the law of God after the i *2080*
2Co 4:16 yet the i *man* is renewed day by day. *2081*
7:15 And his i affection is more abundant *4698*

INWARDLY (3) [INWARD]
Ps 62: 4 with their mouth, but they curse i. 7130+871.1
Mt 7:15 but i they are ravening wolves. *2081*
Ro 2:29 But he *is* a Jew, which is one i; *1722+2927+3588*

INWARDS (20) [INWARD]
Ex 29:13 thou shalt take all the fat that covereth the i, 7130
29:17 wash the i of him, and his legs, and 7130
29:22 the fat that covereth the i, and the caul 7130
Lev 1: 9 his i and his legs shall he wash in water: 7130
1:13 he shall wash the i and the legs with water: 7130
3: 3 the fat that covereth the i, and all the fat 7130
3: 3 and all the fat that *is* upon the i, 7130
3: 9 the fat that covereth the i, and all the fat 7130
3: 9 and all the fat that *is* upon the i, 7130
3:14 the fat that covereth the i, and all the fat 7130
3:14 and all the fat that *is* upon the i, 7130
4: 8 the fat that covereth the i, and all the fat 7130
4: 8 and all the fat that *is* upon the i, 7130
4:11 and with his legs, and his i, and his dung, 7130
7: 3 the rump, and the fat that covereth the i, 7130
8:16 he took all the fat that *was* upon the i, and 7130
8:21 he washed the i and the legs in water; and 7130
8:25 all the fat that *was* upon the i, and the caul 7130
9:14 he did wash the i and the legs, and 7130
9:19 that which covereth *the i*, and the kidneys, NIH

IPHDEIAH See IPHEDEIAH

IPHEDEIAH (1)
1Ch 8:25 And I, and Penuel, the sons of Shashak; 3301

IPHTAH See JIPHTAH

IPHTAH EL See JIPHTHAH-EL

IR (1)
1Ch 7:12 and Huppim, the children of I, *and* Hushim, 5893

IRA (6)
2Sa 20:26 I also the Jairite was a chief ruler about 5896
23:26 the Paltite, I the son of Ikkesh the Tekoite, 5896
23:38 I an Ithrite, Gareb an Ithrite, 5896
1Ch 11:28 I the son of Ikkesh the Tekoite, 5896
11:40 I the Ithrite, Gareb the Ithrite, 5896
27: 9 The sixth *captain* for the sixth month *was* I 5896

IRAD (2)
Ge 4:18 unto Enoch was born I: and Irad begat 5897
4:18 I begat Mehujael: and Mehujael begat 5897

IRAM (2)
Ge 36:43 Duke Magdiel, duke I: these *be* the dukes 5902
1Ch 1:54 Duke Magdiel, duke I. These *are* the dukes 5902

IRI (1)
1Ch 7: 7 Uzzi, and Uzziel, and Jerimoth, and I, five; 5901

IRIJAH (2)
Jer 37:13 whose name *was* I, the son of Shelemiah, 3376
37:14 so I took Jeremiah, and brought him to 3376

IRNAHASH (1)
1Ch 4:12 and Paseah, and Tehinnah the father of I. 5904

IRON (101) [IRONS]
Ge 4:22 instructor of every artificer in brass and i: 1270
Lev 26:19 I will make your heaven as i, and your 1270
Nu 31:22 the brass, the i, the tin, and the lead, 1270
35:16 if he smite him with an instrument of i, 1270
Dt 3:11 behold, his bedstead *was* a bedstead of i; *is* 1270
4:20 brought you forth out of the i furnace, 1270
8: 9 a land whose stones *are* i, and out of whose 1270
27: 5 thou shalt not lift up *any* i *tool* upon them. 1270
28:23 and the earth that *is* under thee *shall be* i. 1270
28:48 and he shall put a yoke of i upon thy neck, 1270
33:25 Thy shoes *shall be* i and brass; and as thy 1270
Jos 6:19 and gold, and vessels of brass and i, 1270
6:24 the gold, and the vessels of brass and of i, 1270
8:31 over which no *man* hath lift up *any* i: 1270
17:16 in the land of the valley have chariots of i, 1270
17:18 though they have i chariots, *and* 1270
19:38 I, and Migdal-el, Horem, and Beth-anath, 3375
22: 8 and with i, and with very much raiment: 1270
Jdg 1:19 the valley, because they had chariots of i. 1270
4: 3 for he had nine hundred chariots of i; and 1270
4:13 *even* nine hundred chariots of i, and all 1270
1Sa 17: 7 head *weighed* six hundred shekels *of* i: 1270
2Sa 12:31 under harrows of i, and under axes of iron, 1270
12:31 under axes of i, and made them pass 1270
23: 7 *that* shall touch them must be fenced *with* i 1270
1Ki 6: 7 nor axe *nor* any tool of i heard in the house, 1270
8:51 of Egypt, from the midst of the furnace of i: 1270
22:11 the son of Chenaanah made him horns of i: 1270
2Ki 6: 6 and cast *it* in thither; and the i did swim. 1270
1Ch 20: 3 and with harrows of i, and with axes. 1270
22: 3 David prepared i in abundance for the nails 1270
22:14 of brass and i without weight; for it is in 1270
22:16 the gold, the silver, and the brass, and the i, 1270
29: 2 the i for *things of* iron, and wood for *things* 1270
29: 2 the iron for *things of* i, and wood for *things* 1270
29: 7 and one hundred thousand talents *of* i. 1270
2Ch 2: 7 in i, and in purple, and crimson, and blue, 1270
2:14 in brass, in i, in stone, and in timber, 1270
18:10 son of Chenaanah had made him horns of i, 1270
24:12 also such as wrought i and brass to mend 1270
Job 19:24 That they were graven with an i pen and 1270
20:24 He shall flee from the i weapon, *and* 1270
28: 2 I is taken out of the earth, and brass *is* 1270
40:18 pieces of brass; his bones *are* like bars of i. 1270
41:27 He esteemeth i as straw, *and* brass as rotten 1270
Ps 2: 9 Thou shalt break them with a rod of i; 1270
105:18 feet they hurt with fetters: he was laid *in* i: 1270
107:10 of death, *being* bound in affliction and i; 1270
107:16 of brass, and cut the bars of i in sunder. 1270
149: 8 and their nobles with fetters of i; 1270
Pr 27:17 I sharpeneth iron; so a man sharpeneth 1270
27:17 Iron sharpeneth i; so a man sharpeneth 1270
Ecc 10:10 If the i be blunt, and he do not whet 1270
Isa 10:34 cut down the thickets of the forest with i, 1270
45: 2 of brass, and cut in sunder the bars of i: 1270
48: 4 thy neck *is* an i sinew, and thy brow brass: 1270
60:17 for i I will bring silver, and for wood brass, 1270
60:17 and for wood brass, and for stones i: 1270
Jer 1:18 an i pillar, and brasen walls against 1270
6:28 *they are* brass and i; they *are* all corrupters. 1270
11: 4 from the i furnace, saying, Obey my voice, 1270
15:12 Shall i break the northern iron and 1270
15:12 Shall iron break the northern i and 1270
17: 1 The sin of Judah *is* written with a pen of i, 1270
28:13 but thou shalt make for them yokes of i. 1270
28:14 I have put a yoke of i upon the neck of all 1270
Eze 4: 3 Moreover take thou unto thee an i pan, and 1270
4: 3 set it *for* a wall of i between thee and 1270
22:18 all they *are* brass, and tin, and i, and lead, 1270
22:20 and brass, and i, and lead, and tin, 1270
27:12 with silver, i, tin, and lead, they traded in 1270
27:19 bright i, cassia, and calamus, were in thy 1270
Da 2:33 His legs of i, his feet part of iron and 6523
2:33 of iron, his feet part of i and part of clay. 6523
2:34 smote the image upon his feet *that were* of i 6523
2:35 was the i, the clay, the brass, the silver, 6523
2:40 the fourth kingdom shall be strong as i: 6523
2:40 forasmuch as i breaketh in pieces and 6523
2:40 all *things:* and as i that breaketh all these, 6523
2:41 and toes, part of potter's clay, and part of i, 6523
2:41 there shall be in it of the strength of the i, 6523
2:41 forasmuch as thou sawest the i mixed with 6523
2:42 *as* the toes of the feet *were* part of i, and 6523
2:43 whereas thou sawest i mixt with miry clay, 6523
2:43 to another, even as i is not mixed with clay. 6523
2:45 *that* it brake in pieces the i, the brass, 6523
4:15 even with a band of i and brass, in 6523
4:23 even with a band of i and brass, in 6523
5: 4 of brass, of i, of wood, and of stone. 6523
5:23 gold, of brass, i, wood, and stone, which 6523
7: 7 strong exceedingly; and it had great i teeth: 6523
7:19 whose teeth *were of* i, and his nails *of* 6523
Am 1: 3 Gilead with threshing *instruments* of i: 1270
Mic 4:13 for I will make thine horn i, and I will make 1270
Ac 12:10 they came unto the i gate that leadeth unto *4603*
1Ti 4: 2 their conscience seared with a hot i; *2743*
Rev 2:27 And he shall rule them with a rod of i; *4603*
9: 9 as *it were* breastplates of i; *4603*
12: 5 who was to rule all nations with a rod of i: *4603*
18:12 and of brass, and i, and marble, *4604*
19:15 and he shall rule them with a rod of i: and *4603*

IRONS (1) [IRON]
Job 41: 7 Canst thou fill his skin with barbed i? or 7905

IRPEEL (1)
Jos 18:27 And Rekem, and I, and Taralah, 3416

IR-SHEMESH (1)
Jos 19:41 inheritance was Zorah, and Eshtaol, and I, 5905

IRU (1)
1Ch 4:15 the son of Jephunneh; I, Elah, and Naam: 5900

IS (6993) [BE] See Index of Articles, Etc.

ISAAC (128) [ISAAC'S]
Ge 17:19 a son indeed; and thou shalt call his name I: 3327
17:21 my covenant will I establish with I, 3327
21: 3 born unto him, whom Sarah bare to him, I. 3327
21: 4 Abraham circumcised his son I being eight 3327
21: 5 when his son I was born unto him. 3327
21: 8 great feast the *same* day that I was weaned. 3327
21:10 shall not be heir with my son, *even* with I. 3327
21:12 her voice; for in I shall thy seed be called. 3327
22: 2 he said, Take now thy son, thine only *son* I, 3327
22: 3 I his son, and clave the wood for the burnt 3327
22: 6 burnt offering, and laid *it* upon I his son; 3327
22: 7 I spake unto Abraham his father, and said, 3327
22: 9 bound I his son, and laid him on the altar 3327
24: 4 my kindred, and take a wife unto my son I. 3327
24:14 *that* thou hast appointed for thy servant I; 3327
24:62 I came from the way of the well Lahai-roi; 3327
24:63 I went out to meditate in the field at 3327
24:64 when she saw I, she lighted off the camel. 3327
24:66 the servant told I all things that he had 3327
24:67 I brought her into his mother Sarah's tent, 3327
24:67 I was comforted after his mother's *death*. 3327
25: 5 And Abraham gave all that he had unto I. 3327
25: 6 sent them away from I his son, while he yet 3327
25: 9 his sons I and Ishmael buried him in 3327
25:11 of Abraham, that God blessed his son I; 3327
25:11 and I dwelt by the well Lahai-roi. 3327
25:19 these *are* the generations of I, 3327
25:19 of Isaac, Abraham's son: Abraham begat I: 3327
25:20 I was forty years old when he took 3327
25:21 I intreated the LORD for his wife, 3327
25:26 I *was* threescore years old when she bare 3327
25:28 I loved Esau, because he did eat of *his* 3327
26: 1 I went unto Abimelech king of 3327
26: 6 And I dwelt in Gerar: 3327
26: 8 I *was* sporting with Rebekah his wife. 3327
26: 9 Abimelech called I, and said, Behold, of a 3327
26: 9 I said unto him, Because I said, Lest I die 3327
26:12 I sowed in that land, and received in 3327
26:16 Abimelech said unto I, Go from us; 3327
26:17 I departed thence, and pitched his tent in 3327
26:18 I digged again the wells of water, 3327
26:27 I said unto them, Wherefore come ye to 3327
26:31 I sent them away, and they departed from 3327
26:35 Which were a grief of mind unto I and 3327

Ge 27: 1 that when **I** was old, and his eyes were dim, 3327
27: 5 Rebekah heard when **I** spake to Esau his 3327
27:20 **I** said unto his son, How *is* it *that* thou hast 3327
27:21 **I** said unto Jacob, Come near, I pray thee, 3327
27:22 Jacob went near unto **I** his father; and 3327
27:26 his father **I** said unto him, Come near now, 3327
27:30 as soon as **I** had made an end of blessing 3327
27:30 gone out from the presence of **I** his father, 3327
27:32 **I** his father said unto him, Who *art* thou? 3327
27:33 **I** trembled very exceedingly, and said, 3327
27:37 **I** answered and said unto Esau, Behold, 3327
27:39 **I** his father answered and said unto him, 3327
27:46 Rebekah said to **I**, I am weary of my life 3327
28: 1 **I** called Jacob, and blessed him, and 3327
28: 5 **I** sent away Jacob: and he went to 3327
28: 6 When Esau saw that **I** had blessed Jacob, 3327
28: 8 of Canaan pleased not **I** his father; 3327
28:13 of Abraham thy father, and the God of **I**: 3327
31:18 for to go to **I** his father in the land of 3327
31:42 and the fear of **I**, had been with me, 3327
31:53 And Jacob sware by the fear of his father **I**. 3327
32: 9 father Abraham, and God of my father **I**, 3327
35:12 the land which I gave Abraham and **I**, 3327
35:27 Jacob came unto **I** his father unto Mamre, 3327
35:27 where Abraham and **I** sojourned. 3327
35:28 the days of **I** were an hundred 3327
35:29 **I** gave up the ghost, and died, and 3327
46: 1 sacrifices unto the God of his father **I**. 3327
48:15 whom my fathers Abraham and **I** did walk, 3327
48:16 and the name of my fathers Abraham and **I**; 3327
49:31 there they buried **I** and Rebekah his wife; 3327
50:24 he sware to Abraham, to **I**, and to Jacob. 3327
Ex 2:24 with Abraham, with **I**, and with Jacob. 3327
3: 6 the God of **I**, and the God of Jacob. 3327
3:15 the God of **I**, and the God of Jacob, 3327
3:16 of **I**, and of Jacob, appeared unto me, 3327
4: 5 the God of **I**, and the God of Jacob, 3327
6: 3 unto **I**, and unto Jacob, by *the name of* God 3327
6: 8 to give it to Abraham, to **I**, and to Jacob; 3327
32:13 **I**, and Israel, thy servants, 3327
33: 1 to **I**, and to Jacob, saying, Unto thy seed 3327
Lev 26:42 also my covenant with **I**, and also my 3327
Nu 32:11 unto Abraham, unto **I**, and unto Jacob; 3327
Dt 1: 8 Abraham, **I**, and Jacob, to give unto them 3327
6:10 to Abraham, to **I**, and to Jacob, to give thee 3327
9: 5 unto thy fathers, Abraham, **I**, and Jacob. 3327
9:27 thy servants, Abraham, **I**, and Jacob; 3327
29:13 thy fathers, to Abraham, to **I**, and to Jacob. 3327
30:20 to Abraham, to **I**, and to Jacob, to give 3327
34: 4 unto **I**, and unto Jacob, saying, I will give it 3327
Jos 24: 3 and multiplied his seed, and gave him **I**. 3327
24: 4 I gave unto **I** Jacob and Esau: and I gave 3327
1Ki 18:36 LORD God of Abraham, **I**, and of Israel, 3327
2Ki 13:23 **I**, and Jacob, and would not destroy them, 3327
1Ch 1:28 The sons of Abraham; **I**, and Ishmael. 3327
1:34 Abraham begat **I**. The sons of Isaac; Esau 3327
1:34 begat Isaac. The sons of **I**; Esau and Israel. 3327
16:16 made with Abraham, and of his oath unto **I**; 3327
29:18 of Abraham, **I**, and of Israel, our fathers, 3327
2Ch 30: 6 **I**, and Israel, and he will return to 3327
Ps 105: 9 made with Abraham, and his oath unto **I**; 3446
Jer 33:26 over the seed of Abraham, **I**, and Jacob: 3446
Am 7: 9 the high places of **I** shall be desolate, and 3446
7:16 drop not *thy word* against the house of **I**. 3446
Mt 1: 2 Abraham begat **I**; and Isaac begat Jacob; *2464*
1: 2 and **I** begat Jacob; and Jacob begat Judas *2464*
8:11 and **I**, and Jacob, in the kingdom of heaven. *2464*
22:32 and the God of **I**, and the God of Jacob? *2464*
Mk 12:26 and the God of **I**, and the God of Jacob? *2464*
Lk 3:34 *the son* of Jacob, which was *the son* of **I**, *2464*
13:28 and **I**, and Jacob, and all the prophets, *2464*
20:37 and the God of **I**, and the God of Jacob. *2464*
Ac 3:13 God of Abraham, and of **I**, and of Jacob, *2464*
7: 8 and so *Abraham* begat **I**, and *2464*
7: 8 and **I** *begat* Jacob; and Jacob *begat* *2464*
7:32 and the God of **I**, and the God of Jacob. *2464*
Ro 9: 7 but, In **I** shall thy seed be called. *2464*
9:10 had conceived by one, *even* by our father **I**; *2464*
Gal 4:28 Now we, brethren, as **I** was, are *2464*
Heb 11: 9 *country*, dwelling in tabernacles with **I** *2464*
11:17 when he was tried, offered up **I**: *2464*
11:18 was said, That in **I** shall thy seed be called: *2464*
11:20 By faith **I** blessed Jacob and Esau *2464*
Jas 2:21 when he had offered **I** his son upon *2464*

ISAAC'S (4) [ISAAC]
Ge 26:19 **I** servants digged in the valley, and 3327
26:20 the herdmen of Gerar did strive with **I** 3327
26:25 and there **I** servants digged a well. 3327
26:32 that **I** servants came, and told him 3327

ISACHAR (1) [ISSACHAR]
Rev 7: 7 Of the tribe of **I** *were* sealed twelve *2466*

ISAIAH (31) [ESAI, ESAIAS]
2Ki 19: 5 So the servants of king Hezekiah came to **I**. 3470
19: 6 **I** said unto them, Thus shall ye say to your 3470
19:20 **I** the son of Amoz sent to Hezekiah, saying, 3470
20: 1 the prophet **I** the son of Amoz came to him, 3470
20: 4 afore **I** was gone out *into* the middle court, 3470
20: 7 **I** said, Take a lump of figs. And they took 3470
20: 8 Hezekiah said unto **I**, What *shall be* 3470
20: 9 **I** said, This sign shalt thou have of 3470
20:11 **I** the prophet cried unto the LORD: and 3470
20:14 came **I** the prophet unto king Hezekiah, 3470
20:16 **I** said unto Hezekiah, Hear the word of 3470
20:19 said Hezekiah unto **I**, Good *is* the word of 3470
2Ch 26:22 first and last, did **I** the prophet, the son of 3470
32:20 the prophet **I** the son of Amoz, prayed and 3470
32:32 they *are* written in the vision of **I** 3470
Isa 1: 1 The vision of **I** the son of Amoz, which he 3470
2: 1 The word that **I** the son of Amoz saw 3470
7: 3 said the LORD unto **I**, Go forth now to 3470
13: 1 which **I** the son of Amoz did see. 3470
20: 2 At the same time spake the LORD by **I** 3470
20: 3 Like as my servant **I** hath walked naked 3470
37: 2 unto **I** the prophet the son of Amoz. 3470
37: 5 So the servants of king Hezekiah came to **I**. 3470
37: 6 **I** said unto them, Thus shall ye say unto 3470
37:21 **I** the son of Amoz sent unto Hezekiah, 3470
38: 1 **I** the prophet the son of Amoz came unto 3470
38: 4 came the word of the LORD to **I**, saying, 3470
38:21 For **I** had said, Let them take a lump of 3470
39: 3 came **I** the prophet unto king Hezekiah, 3470
39: 5 said **I** to Hezekiah, Hear the word of 3470
39: 8 said Hezekiah to **I**, Good *is* the word of 3470

ISCAH (1)
Ge 11:29 the father of Milcah, and the father of **I**. 3252

ISCARIOT (11)
Mt 10: 4 Simon the Canaanite, and Judas **I**, who also *2469*
26:14 Then one of the twelve, called Judas **I**, *2469*
Mk 3:19 And Judas **I**, which also betrayed him. *2469*
14:10 And Judas **I**, one of the twelve, went unto *2469*
Lk 6:16 and Judas **I**, which also was the traitor. *2469*
22: 3 Then entered Satan into Judas surnamed **I**, *2469*
Jn 6:71 He spake of Judas **I** *the son* of Simon: *2469*
12: 4 Then saith one of his disciples, Judas **I**, *2469*
13: 2 having now put into the heart of Judas **I**, *2469*
13:26 he gave *it* to Judas **I**, *the son* of Simon. *2469*
14:22 Judas saith unto him, not **I**, Lord, how is it *2469*

ISHBAH (1)
1Ch 4:17 and **I** the father of Eshtemoa. 3431

ISHBAK (2)
Ge 25: 2 and Medan, and Midian, and **I**, and Shuah. 3435
1Ch 1:32 and Medan, and Midian, and **I**, and Shuah. 3435

ISHBI-BENOB (1)
2Sa 21:16 **I**, which *was* of the sons of the giant, 3430

ISH-BOSHETH (12) [ESHBAAL]
2Sa 2: 8 took **I** the son of Saul, and brought him over 378
2:10 **I** Saul's son *was* forty years old when he 378
2:12 of Ner, and the servants of **I** the son of Saul, 378
2:15 which *pertained* to **I** the son of Saul, and 378
3: 7 *I* said to Abner, Wherefore hast thou gone NIH
3: 8 was Abner very wroth for the words of **I**, 378
3:14 David sent messengers to **I** Saul's son, 378
3:15 **I** sent, and took her from *her* husband, 378
4: 5 about the heat of the day to the house of **I**, 378
4: 8 they brought the head of **I** unto David *to* 378
4: 8 Behold the head of **I** the son of Saul thine 378
4:12 they took the head of **I**, and buried *it* in 378

ISHHOD See ISHOD

ISHI (6)
1Ch 2:31 the sons of Appaim; **I**. And the sons of Ishi; 3469
2:31 the sons of **I**; Sheshan. And the children of 3469
4:20 the sons of **I** *were*, Zoheth, and Ben-zoheth. 3469
4:42 and Rephaiah, and Uzziel, the sons of **I**. 3469
5:24 **I**, and Eliel, and Azriel, and Jeremiah, and 3469
Hos 2:16 saith the LORD, *that* thou shalt call *me* **I**; 376

ISHIAH (1)
1Ch 7: 3 Michael, and Obadiah, and Joel, **I**, five: 3449

ISHIJAH (1)
Ezr 10:31 Eliezer, **I**, Malchiah, Shemaiah, Shimeon, 3449

ISHMA (1)
1Ch 4: 3 father of Etam; Jezreel, and **I**, and Idbash: 3457

ISHMAEL (47) [ISHMAEL'S, ISHMAELITE, ISHMAELITES, ISHMEELITE, ISHMEELITES]
Ge 16:11 shalt bear a son, and shalt call his name **I**; 3458
16:15 called his son's name, which Hagar bare, **I**. 3458
16:16 six years old, when Hagar bare **I** to Abram. 3458
17:18 unto God, O that **I** might live before thee! 3458
17:20 as for **I**, I have heard thee: Behold, I have 3458
17:23 Abraham took **I** his son, and all that were 3458
17:25 **I** his son *was* thirteen years old, when he 3458
17:26 was Abraham circumcised, and **I** his son. 3458
25: 9 and **I** buried him in the cave of Machpelah, 3458
25:12 Now these *are* the generations of **I**, 3458
25:13 these *are* the names of the sons of **I**, 3458
25:13 the firstborn of **I**, Nebajoth; and Kedar, and 3458
25:16 These *are* the sons of **I**, and these *are* their 3458
25:17 these *are* the years of the life of **I**, 3458
28: 9 went Esau unto **I**, and took unto the wives 3458
28: 9 Mahalath the daughter of **I** Abraham's son, 3458
2Ki 25:23 even **I** the son of Nethaniah, and 3458
25:25 *that* **I** the son of Nethaniah, the son of 3458
1Ch 1:28 The sons of Abraham; Isaac, and **I**. 3458
1:29 The firstborn of **I**, Nebajoth; then Kedar, 3458
1:31 and Kedemah. These *are* the sons of **I**. 3458
8:38 **I**, and Sheariah, and Obadiah, and Hanan. 3458
9:44 **I**, and Sheariah, and Obadiah, and Hanan: 3458
2Ch 19:11 Zebadiah the son of **I**, the ruler of the house 3458
23: 1 **I** the son of Jehohanan, and Azariah the son 3458
Ezr 10:22 Elioenai, Maaseiah, **I**, Nethaneel, Jozabad, 3458
Jer 40: 8 even **I** the son of Nethaniah, and Johanan 3458
40:14 sent **I** the son of Nethaniah to slay thee? 3458
40:15 I will slay **I** the son of Nethaniah, and 3458
40:16 do this thing: for thou speakest falsely of **I**. 3458
41: 1 *that* **I** the son of Nethaniah the son of 3458
41: 2 arose **I** the son of Nethaniah, and the ten 3458
41: 3 **I** also slew all the Jews that were with him, 3458
41: 6 **I** the son of Nethaniah went forth from 3458
41: 7 that **I** the son of Nethaniah slew them, *and* 3458
41: 8 were found among them that said unto **I**, 3458
41: 9 Now the pit wherein **I** had cast all the dead 3458
41: 9 **I** the son of Nethaniah filled it *with them* 3458
41:10 **I** carried away captive all the residue of 3458
Jer 41:10 **I** the son of Nethaniah carried them away 3458
41:11 heard of all the evil that **I** the son of 3458
41:12 went to fight with **I** the son of Nethaniah, 3458
41:13 *that* when all the people which *were* with **I** 3458
41:14 So all the people that **I** had carried away 3458
41:15 **I** the son of Nethaniah escaped from 3458
41:16 had recovered from **I** the son of Nethaniah, 3458
41:18 **I** the son of Nethaniah had slain Gedaliah 3458

ISHMAEL'S (1) [ISHMAEL]
Ge 36: 3 Bashemath **I** daughter, sister of Nebajoth. 3458

ISHMAELITE (1) [ISHMAEL]
1Ch 27:30 Over the camels also *was* Obil the **I**: and 3459

ISHMAELITES (2) [ISHMAEL]
Jdg 8:24 had golden earrings, because they *were* **I**.) 3459
Ps 83: 6 The tabernacles of Edom, and the **I**; 3459

ISHMAIAH (1)
1Ch 27:19 Of Zebulun, **I** the son of Obadiah: 3460

ISHMEELITE (1) [ISHMAEL]
1Ch 2:17 and the father of Amasa *was* Jether the **I**. 3459

ISHMEELITES (4) [ISHMAEL]
Ge 37:25 a company of **I** came from Gilead with 3459
37:27 let us sell him to the **I**, and let not our hand 3459
37:28 sold Joseph to the **I** for twenty *pieces* of 3459
39: 1 bought him of the hand of the **I**, 3459

ISHMERAI (1)
1Ch 8:18 **I** also, and Jezliah, and Jobab, the sons of 3461

ISHOD (1)
1Ch 7:18 his sister Hammoleketh bare **I**, and Abiezer, 379

ISHPAH See ISPAH

ISHPAN (1)
1Ch 8:22 And **I**, and Heber, and Eliel, 3473

ISH-TOB (2)
2Sa 10: 6 and of **I** twelve thousand men. 382
10: 8 of Zoba, and of Rehob, and **I**, and Maacah, 382

ISHUAH (1)
Ge 46:17 **I**, and Ishui, and Beriah, and Serah their 3438

ISHUAI (1)
1Ch 7:30 and **I**, and Beriah, and Serah their sister. 3438

ISHUI (2) [JESUI]
Ge 46:17 and **I**, and Beriah, and Serah their sister: 3440
1Sa 14:49 Saul were Jonathan, and **I**, and Melchishua: 3440

ISHVAH See ISHUAH

ISHVI See ISHUAI; ISHUI; JESUI

ISHVITE See JESUITES

ISLAND (9) [ISLANDS, ISLE, ISLES]
Job 22:30 He shall deliver the **i** of the innocent: and 336
Isa 34:14 shall also meet with the **wild beasts of the i**, 338
Ac 27:16 And running under a certain **i** *which is* *3519*
27:26 Howbeit we must be cast upon a certain **i**. *3520*
28: 1 then they knew that the **i** was called Melita. *3520*
28: 7 were possessions of the chief *man* of the **i**, *3520*
28: 9 which had diseases in the **i**, came, and *3520*
Rev 6:14 and **i** were moved out of their places. *3520*
16:20 And every **i** fled *away*, and the mountains *3520*

ISLANDER See BARBARIANS

ISLANDERS See BARBAROUS

ISLANDS (7) [ISLAND]
Isa 11:11 and from Hamath, and from the **i** of the sea. 339
13:22 the **wild beasts of the i** shall cry in their 338
41: 1 Keep silence before me, O **i**; and let 339
42:12 the LORD, and declare his praise in the **i**. 339
42:15 I will make the rivers **i**, and I will dry up 339
59:18 to the **i** he will repay recompence. 339
Jer 50:39 the **wild beasts of the i** shall dwell *there*, 338

ISLE (6) [ISLAND]
Isa 20: 6 the inhabitant of this **i** shall say in that day, 339
23: 2 Be still, ye inhabitants of the **i**; thou whom 339
23: 6 to Tarshish; howl, ye inhabitants of the **i**. 339
Ac 13: 6 And when they had gone through the **i** unto *3520*
28:11 which had wintered in the **i**, *whose* sign *3520*
Rev 1: 9 was in the **i** that is called Patmos, for *3520*

ISLES (27) [ISLAND]
Ge 10: 5 By these were the **i** of the Gentiles divided in 339
Est 10: 1 upon the land, and *upon* the **i** of the sea. 339
Ps 72:10 of Tarshish and *of* the **i** shall bring presents: 339
97: 1 let the multitude of **i** be glad *thereof*. 339
Isa 24:15 the LORD God of Israel in the **i** of the sea. 339
40:15 he taketh up the **i** as a very little thing. 339
41: 5 The **i** saw *it*, and feared; the ends of the earth 339
42: 4 in the earth: and the **i** shall wait for his law. 339
42:10 is therein; the **i**, and the inhabitants thereof. 339
49: 1 Listen, O **i**, unto me; and hearken, ye people, 339
51: 5 the **i** shall wait upon me, and on mine arm 339
60: 9 Surely the **i** shall wait for me, and the ships 339
66:19 to Tubal, and Javan, *to* the **i** afar off, 339
Jer 2:10 For pass over the **i** of Chittim, and see; and 339
25:22 the kings of the **i** which *are* beyond the sea, 339
31:10 and declare *it* in the **i** afar off, and say, 339
Eze 26:15 Shall not the **i** shake at the sound of thy fall, 339
26:18 Now shall the **i** tremble *in* the day of thy fall; 339

Eze 26:18 the **i** that *are* in the sea shall be troubled at 339
27: 3 *art* a merchant of the people for many **i**, 339
27: 6 *of* ivory, *brought* out of the **i** of Chittim. 339
27: 7 purple from the **i** of Elishah was that which 339
27:15 many **i** *were* the merchandise of thine hand: 339
27:35 All the inhabitants of the **i** shall be 339
39: 6 among them that dwell carelessly in the **i**: 339
Da 11:18 After this shall he turn his face unto the **i**, 339
Zep 2:11 from his place, *even* all the **i** of the heathen. 339

ISMACHIAH (1)
2Ch 31:13 and Eliel, and **I**, and Mahath, and Benaiah, 3253

ISMAIAH (1)
1Ch 12: 4 **I** the Gibeonite, a mighty *man* among 3460

ISMAKIAH See ISMACHIAH

ISPAH (1)
1Ch 8:16 Michael, and **I**, and Joha, the sons of 3472

ISRAEL (2565) [EL-ELOHE-ISRAEL, ISRAEL'S, ISRAELITE, ISRAELITES, ISRAELITISH, JACOB]
Ge 32:28 name shall be called no more Jacob, but **I**: 3478
32:32 Therefore the children of **I** eat not *of* 3478
34: 7 he had wrought folly in **I** in lying with 3478
35:10 any more Jacob, but **I** shall be thy name: 3478
35:10 shall be thy name: and he called his name **I**. 3478
35:21 **I** journeyed, and spread his tent beyond 3478
35:22 when **I** dwelt in that land, that Reuben went 3478
35:22 **I** heard *it*. Now the sons of Jacob were 3478
36:31 reigned *any* king over the children of **I**. 3478
37: 3 Now **I** loved Joseph more than all his 3478
37:13 **I** said unto Joseph, Do not thy brethren feed 3478
42: 5 the sons of **I** came to buy *corn* among those 3478
43: 6 **I** said, Wherefore dealt ye *so* ill with me, 3478
43: 8 Judah said unto **I** his father, Send the lad 3478
43:11 their father **I** said unto them, If *it must be* 3478
45:21 the children of **I** did so: and Joseph gave 3478
45:28 **I** said, *It is* enough; Joseph my son *is* yet 3478
46: 1 **I** took his journey with all that he had, and 3478
46: 2 God spake unto **I** in the visions of 3478
46: 5 the sons of **I** carried Jacob their father, and 3478
46: 8 these *are* the names of the children of **I**, 3478
46:29 and went up to meet **I** his father, to Goshen, 3478
46:30 **I** said unto Joseph, Now let me die, since I 3478
47:27 **I** dwelt in the land of Egypt, in the country 3478
47:29 And the time drew nigh that **I** must die: and 3478
47:31 And **I** bowed himself upon the bed's head. 3478
48: 2 **I** strengthened himself, and sat upon 3478
48: 8 **I** beheld Joseph's sons, and said, Who *are* 3478
48:10 Now the eyes of **I** were dim for age, *so* 3478
48:11 **I** said unto Joseph, I had not thought to see 3478
48:14 **I** stretched out his right hand, and laid *it* 3478
48:20 saying, In thee shall **I** bless, saying, 3478
48:21 **I** said unto Joseph, Behold, I die: but 3478
49: 2 of Jacob; and hearken unto **I** your father. 3478
49: 7 divide them in Jacob, and scatter them in **I**. 3478
49:16 judge his people, as one of the tribes of **I**. 3478
49:24 thence *is* the shepherd, the stone of **I**:) 3478
49:28 All these *are* the twelve tribes of **I**: and 3478
50: 2 his father: and the physicians embalmed **I**. 3478
50:25 Joseph took an oath of the children of **I**, 3478
Ex 1: 1 these *are* the names of the children of **I**, 3478
1: 7 the children of **I** were fruitful, and 3478
1: 9 the people of the children of **I** *are* moe and 3478
1:12 were grieved because of the children of **I**. 3478
1:13 the Egyptians made the children of **I** to 3478
2:23 the children of **I** sighed by reason of 3478
2:25 And God looked upon the children of **I**, and 3478
3: 9 the cry of the children of **I** is come unto 3478
3:10 my people the children of **I** out of Egypt. 3478
3:11 that I should bring forth the children of **I** 3478
3:13 *when* I come unto the children of **I**, and 3478
3:14 Thus shalt thou say unto the children of **I**, 3478
3:15 Thus shalt thou say unto the children of **I**, 3478
3:16 gather the elders of **I** together, and say unto 3478
3:18 thou shalt come, thou and the elders of **I**, 3478
4:22 the LORD, **I** *is* my son, *even* my firstborn: 3478
4:29 together all the elders of the children of **I**: 3478
4:31 the LORD had visited the children of **I**, 3478
5: 1 Thus saith the LORD God of **I**, 3478
5: 2 that I should obey his voice to let **I** go? 3478
5: 2 not the LORD, neither will I let **I** go. 3478
5:14 the officers of the children of **I**, 3478
5:15 the officers of the children of **I** came and 3478
5:19 the officers of the children of **I** did see *that* 3478
6: 5 also heard the groaning of the children of **I**, 3478
6: 6 Wherefore say unto the children of **I**, I *am* 3478
6: 9 Moses spake so unto the children of **I**: but 3478
6:11 that he let the children of **I** go out of his 3478
6:12 the children of **I** have not hearkened unto 3478
6:13 gave them a charge unto the children of **I**, 3478
6:13 to bring the children of **I** out of the land of 3478
6:14 The sons of Reuben the firstborn of **I**; 3478
6:26 Bring out the children of **I** from the land of 3478
6:27 to bring out the children of **I** from Egypt: 3478
7: 2 that he send the children of **I** out of his 3478
7: 4 *and* my people the children of **I**, 3478
7: 5 bring out the children of **I** from among 3478
9: 4 LORD shall sever between the cattle of **I** 3478
9: 4 nothing die of all *that is* the children's of **I**. 3478
9: 6 of the cattle of the children of **I** died not 3478
9:26 where the children of **I** *were*, was there no 3478
9:35 neither would he let the children of **I** go; 3478
10:20 so that he would not let the children of **I** go. 3478
10:23 all the children of **I** had light in their 3478
11: 7 against any of the children of **I** shall not a 3478
11: 7 a difference between the Egyptians and **I**. 3478
11:10 that he would not let the children of **I** go 3478
12: 3 Speak ye unto all the congregation of **I**, 3478
12: 6 whole assembly of the congregation of **I** 3478
12:15 that soul shall be cut off from **I**. 3478
12:19 shall be cut off from the congregation of **I**, 3478
Ex 12:21 Moses called for all the elders of **I**, and 3478
12:27 the houses of the children of **I** in Egypt, 3478
12:28 the children of **I** went away, and did as 3478
12:31 my people, both you and the children of **I**; 3478
12:35 the children of **I** did according to the word 3478
12:37 the children of **I** journeyed from Rameses 3478
12:40 Now the sojourning of the children of **I**, 3478
12:42 of all the children of **I** in their generations. 3478
12:47 All the congregation of **I** shall keep it. 3478
12:50 Thus did all the children of **I**; as 3478
12:51 *that* the LORD did bring the children of **I** 3478
13: 2 openeth the womb among the children of **I**, 3478
13:18 the children of **I** went up harnessed out of 3478
13:19 for he had straitly sworn the children of **I**, 3478
14: 2 Speak unto the children of **I**, that they turn 3478
14: 3 For Pharaoh will say of the children of **I**, 3478
14: 5 that we have let **I** go from serving us? 3478
14: 8 and he pursued after the children of **I**: 3478
14: 8 the children of **I** went out with a high hand. 3478
14:10 the children of **I** lift up their eyes, and 3478
14:10 the children of **I** cried out unto the LORD. 3478
14:15 speak unto the children of **I**, that they go 3478
14:16 the children of **I** shall go on dry *ground* 3478
14:19 which went before the camp of **I**, removed 3478
14:20 camp of the Egyptians and the camp of **I**; 3478
14:22 the children of **I** went into the midst of 3478
14:25 Let us flee from the face of **I**; 3478
14:29 the children of **I** walked upon dry *land* in 3478
14:30 Thus the LORD saved **I** that day out of 3478
14:30 **I** saw the Egyptians dead upon the sea 3478
14:31 **I** saw *that* great work which the LORD 3478
15: 1 the children of **I** this song unto the LORD, 3478
15:19 the children of **I** went on dry *land* in 3478
15:22 So Moses brought **I** from the Red sea, and 3478
16: 1 all the congregation of the children of **I** 3478
16: 2 the whole congregation of the children of **I** 3478
16: 3 the children of **I** said unto them, Would to 3478
16: 6 and Aaron said unto all the children of **I**, 3478
16: 9 all the congregation of the children of **I**, 3478
16:10 the whole congregation of the children of **I**, 3478
16:12 heard the murmurings of the children of **I**: 3478
16:15 when the children of **I** saw *it*, they said one 3478
16:17 the children of **I** did so, and gathered, 3478
16:31 the house of **I** called the name thereof 3478
16:35 the children of **I** did eat manna forty years, 3478
17: 1 all the congregation of the children of **I** 3478
17: 5 and take with thee of the elders of **I**; 3478
17: 6 Moses did so in the sight of the elders of **I**. 3478
17: 7 because of the chiding of the children of **I**, 3478
17: 8 and fought with **I** in Rephidim. 3478
17:11 Moses held up his hand, that **I** prevailed: 3478
18: 1 for **I** his people, *and* that the LORD had 3478
18: 1 that the LORD had brought **I** out of 3478
18: 9 goodness which the LORD had done to **I**, 3478
18:12 Aaron came, and all the elders of **I**, to eat 3478
18:25 Moses chose able men out of all **I**, and 3478
19: 1 when the children of **I** were gone forth out 3478
19: 2 and there **I** camped before the mount. 3478
19: 3 house of Jacob, and tell the children of **I**; 3478
19: 6 thou shalt speak unto the children of **I**. 3478
20:22 Thus thou shalt say unto the children of **I**, 3478
24: 1 and Abihu, and seventy of the elders of **I**; 3478
24: 4 according to the twelve tribes of **I**. 3478
24: 5 And he sent young men of the children of **I**, 3478
24: 9 and Abihu, and seventy of the elders of **I**: 3478
24:10 they saw the God of **I**: and *there was* under 3478
24:11 upon the nobles of the children of **I** he laid 3478
24:17 the mount in the eyes of the children of **I**. 3478
25: 2 Speak unto the children of **I**, that they bring 3478
25:22 in commandment unto the children of **I**. 3478
27:20 thou shalt command the children of **I**, 3478
27:21 on the behalf of the children of **I**. 3478
28: 1 with him, from among the children of **I**, 3478
28: 9 on them the names of the children of **I**: 3478
28:11 stones with the names of the children of **I**: 3478
28:12 stones of memorial unto the children of **I**: 3478
28:21 shall be with the names of the children of **I**, 3478
28:29 **I** in the breastplate of judgment upon his 3478
28:30 **I** upon his heart before the LORD 3478
28:38 of **I** shall hallow in all their holy gifts; 3478
29:28 by a statute for ever from the children of **I**: 3478
29:28 of **I** of the sacrifice of their peace offerings, 3478
29:43 And there I will meet with the children of **I**, 3478
29:45 I will dwell amongst the children of **I**, and 3478
30:12 sum of the children of **I** after their number, 3478
30:16 the atonement money of the children of **I**, 3478
30:16 unto the children of **I** before the LORD, 3478
30:31 thou shalt speak unto the children of **I**, 3478
31:13 Speak thou also unto the children of **I**, 3478
31:16 Wherefore the children of **I** shall keep 3478
31:17 between me and the children of **I** for ever: 3478
32: 4 they said, These *be* thy gods, O **I**, 3478
32: 8 and said, These *be* thy gods, O **I**, 3478
32:13 Isaac, and **I**, thy servants, 3478
32:20 and made the children of **I** drink *of it*. 3478
32:27 unto them, Thus saith the LORD God of **I**, 3478
33: 5 Say unto the children of **I**, Ye *are* a 3478
33: 6 the children of **I** stript themselves of their 3478
34:23 before the Lord GOD, the God of **I**. 3478
34:27 have made a covenant with thee and with **I**. 3478
34:30 and all the children of **I** saw Moses, 3478
34:32 afterward all the children of **I** came nigh: 3478
34:34 spake unto the children of **I** *that* which he 3478
34:35 the children of **I** saw the face of Moses, 3478
35: 1 congregation of the children of **I** together, 3478
35: 4 all the congregation of the children of **I**, 3478
35:20 all the congregation of the children of **I** 3478
35:29 The children of **I** brought a willing offering 3478
35:30 Moses said unto the children of **I**, See, 3478
36: 3 which the children of **I** had brought for 3478
39: 6 with the names of the children of **I**. 3478
39: 7 stones for a memorial to the children of **I**; 3478
39:14 according to the names of the children of **I**, 3478
39:32 the children of **I** did according to all that 3478
39:42 so the children of **I** made all the work. 3478
Ex 40:36 the children of **I** went onward in all their 3478
40:38 it by night, in the sight of all the house of **I**, 3478
Lev 1: 2 Speak unto the children of **I**, and say unto 3478
4: 2 Speak unto the children of **I**, saying, If a 3478
4:13 if the whole congregation of **I** sin through 3478
7:23 Speak unto the children of **I**, saying, 3478
7:29 Speak unto the children of **I**, saying, 3478
7:34 **I** from off the sacrifices of their peace 3478
7:34 for ever from among the children of **I**. 3478
7:36 to be given them of the children of **I**, 3478
7:38 **I** to offer their oblations unto the LORD, 3478
9: 1 and his sons, and the elders of **I**; 3478
9: 3 unto the children of **I** thou shalt speak, 3478
10: 6 let your brethren, the whole house of **I**, 3478
10:11 that *ye* may teach the children of **I** all 3478
10:14 of peace offerings of the children of **I**. 3478
11: 2 Speak unto the children of **I**, saying, 3478
12: 2 Speak unto the children of **I**, saying, If a 3478
15: 2 Speak unto the children of **I**, and say unto 3478
15:31 Thus shall ye separate the children of **I** 3478
16: 5 of **I** two kids of the goats for a sin offering, 3478
16:16 of the uncleanness of the children of **I**, 3478
16:17 and for all the congregation of **I**. 3478
16:19 it from the uncleanness of the children of **I**. 3478
16:21 him all the iniquities of the children of **I**, 3478
16:34 to make an atonement for the children of **I** 3478
17: 2 unto all the children of **I**, and say unto 3478
17: 3 What man soever *there be* of the house of **I**, 3478
17: 5 To the end that the children of **I** may bring 3478
17: 8 Whatsoever man *there be* of the house of **I**, 3478
17:10 whatsoever man *there be* of the house of **I**, 3478
17:12 Therefore I said unto the children of **I**, No 3478
17:13 man *there be* of the children of **I**, 3478
17:14 therefore I said unto the children of **I**, 3478
18: 2 Speak unto the children of **I**, and say unto 3478
19: 2 all the congregation of the children of **I**, 3478
20: 2 Again, thou shalt say to the children of **I**, 3478
20: 2 Whosoever *he be* of the children of **I**, 376+3478
20: 2 or of the strangers that sojourn in **I**, 3478
21:24 to his sons, and unto all the children of **I**. 3478
22: 2 from the holy *things* of the children of **I**, 3478
22: 3 the children of **I** hallow unto the LORD, 3478
22:15 profane the holy *things* of the children of **I**, 3478
22:18 unto all the children of **I**, and say unto 3478
22:18 Whatsoever *he be* of the house of **I**, or 376+3478
22:18 the house of Israel, or of the strangers in **I**, 3478
22:32 I will be hallowed among the children of **I**: 3478
23: 2 Speak unto the children of **I**, and say unto 3478
23:10 Speak unto the children of **I**, and say unto 3478
23:24 Speak unto the children of **I**, saying, In 3478
23:34 Speak unto the children of **I**, saying, The 3478
23:43 I made the children of **I** to dwell in booths, 3478
23:44 Moses declared unto the children of **I** 3478
24: 2 Command the children of **I**, that they bring 3478
24: 8 *being taken* from the children of **I** *by* an 3478
24:10 went out among the children of **I**: 3478
24:10 and a man of **I** strove together in the camp; 3481
24:15 thou shalt speak unto the children of **I**, 3478
24:23 Moses spake to the children of **I**, that they 3478
24:23 the children of **I** did as the LORD 3478
25: 2 Speak unto the children of **I**, and say unto 3478
25:33 their possession among the children of **I**. 3478
25:46 over your brethren the children of **I**, 3478
25:55 For unto me the children of **I** *are* servants; 3478
26:46 the children of **I** in mount Sinai by the hand 3478
27: 2 Speak unto the children of **I**, and say unto 3478
27:34 Moses for the children of **I** in mount Sinai. 3478
Nu 1: 2 of all the congregation of the children of **I**, 3478
1: 3 all that *are able to* go forth *to* war in **I**: 3478
1:16 of their fathers, heads of thousands in **I**. 3478
1:44 and Aaron numbered, and the princes of **I**, 3478
1:45 that were numbered of the children of **I**, 3478
1:45 all that *were able to* go forth *to* war in **I**; 3478
1:49 the sum of them among the children of **I**: 3478
1:52 the children of **I** shall pitch their tents, 3478
1:53 upon the congregation of the children of **I**: 3478
1:54 the children of **I** did according to all that 3478
2: 2 Every man of the children of **I** shall pitch 3478
2:32 children of **I** by the house of their fathers: 3478
2:33 not numbered among the children of **I**; 3478
2:34 the children of **I** did according to all that 3478
3: 8 the charge of the children of **I**, to do 3478
3: 9 given unto him out of the children of **I**. 3478
3:12 **I** instead of all the firstborn that openeth 3478
3:12 openeth the matrix among the children of **I**: 3478
3:13 I hallowed unto me all the firstborn in **I**, 3478
3:38 for the charge of the children of **I**; 3478
3:40 males of the children of **I** from a month old 3478
3:41 of all the firstborn among the children of **I**; 3478
3:41 among the cattle of the children of **I**. 3478
3:42 all the firstborn among the children of **I**. 3478
3:45 of all the firstborn among the children of **I**, 3478
3:46 thirteen of the firstborn of the children of **I**, 3478
3:50 Of the firstborn of the children of **I** took he 3478
4:46 and Aaron and the chief of **I** numbered, 3478
5: 2 Command the children of **I**, that they put 3478
5: 4 the children of **I** did so, and put them out 3478
5: 4 spake unto Moses, so did the children of **I**. 3478
5: 6 Speak unto the children of **I**, When a man 3478
5: 9 of all the holy *things* of the children of **I**, 3478
5:12 Speak unto the children of **I**, and say unto 3478
6: 2 Speak unto the children of **I**, and say unto 3478
6:23 On this wise ye shall bless the children of **I**, 3478
6:27 shall put my name upon the children of **I**; 3478
7: 2 That the princes of **I**, heads of the house of 3478
7:84 when it was anointed, by the princes of **I**: 3478
8: 6 the Levites from among the children of **I**, 3478
8: 9 assembly of the children of **I** together: 3478
8:10 the children of **I** shall put their hands upon 3478
8:11 LORD *for* an offering of the children of **I**, 3478
8:14 the Levites from among the children of **I**: 3478
8:16 unto me from among the children of **I**; 3478
8:16 *of* the firstborn of all the children of **I**, 3478
8:17 For all the firstborn of the children of **I** *are* 3478
8:18 for all the firstborn of the children of **I**. 3478

Nu 8:19 to his sons from among the children of I, 3478
8:19 to do the service of the children of I in 3478
8:19 to make an atonement for the children of I: 3478
8:19 there be no plague among the children of I, 3478
8:19 when the children of I come nigh unto 3478
8:20 all the congregation of the children of I, 3478
8:20 so did the children of I unto them. 3478
9: 2 Let the children of I also keep the passover 3478
9: 4 Moses spake unto the children of I, 3478
9: 5 so did the children of I. 3478
9: 7 appointed season among the children of I? 3478
9:10 Speak unto the children of I, saying, If any 3478
9:17 then after that the children of I journeyed: 3478
9:17 there the children of I pitched their tents. 3478
9:18 of the LORD the children of I journeyed, 3478
9:19 the children of I kept the charge of 3478
9:22 the children of I abode in their tents, and 3478
10: 4 *which are* heads of the thousands of I, 3478
10:12 the children of I took their journeys out of 3478
10:28 the children of I according to their armies, 3478
10:29 the LORD hath spoken good concerning I. 3478
10:36 O LORD, *unto* the many thousands of I. 3478
11: 4 the children of I also wept again, and said, 3478
11:16 unto me seventy men of the elders of I, 3478
11:30 him into the camp, he and the elders of I. 3478
13: 2 which I give unto the children of I: 3478
13: 3 those men *were* heads of the children of I. 3478
13:24 the children of I cut down from thence. 3478
13:26 to all the congregation of the children of I, 3478
13:32 they had searched unto the children of I, 3478
14: 2 all the children of I murmured against 3478
14: 5 of the congregation of the children of I. 3478
14: 7 unto all the company of the children of I, 3478
14:10 congregation before all the children of I. 3478
14:27 heard the murmurings of the children of I, 3478
14:39 told these sayings unto all the children of I: 3478
15: 2 Speak unto the children of I, and say unto 3478
15:18 Speak unto the children of I, and say unto 3478
15:25 for all the congregation of the children of I, 3478
15:26 all the congregation of the children of I, 3478
15:29 him that is born amongst the children of I, 3478
15:32 while the children of I were in 3478
15:38 Speak unto the children of I, and bid them 3478
16: 2 with certain of the children of I, 3478
16: 9 that the God of I hath separated you from 3478
16: 9 separated you from the congregation of I, 3478
16:25 Abiram; and the elders of I followed him. 3478
16:34 all I that *were* round about them fled at 3478
16:38 they shall be a sign unto the children of I. 3478
16:40 *To be* a memorial unto the children of I, 3478
16:41 the children of I murmured against Moses 3478
17: 2 Speak unto the children of I, and take of 3478
17: 5 me the murmurings of the children of I, 3478
17: 6 Moses spake unto the children of I, and 3478
17: 9 the LORD unto all the children of I: 3478
17:12 the children of I spake unto Moses, saying, 3478
18: 5 no wrath any more upon the children of I. 3478
18: 6 the Levites from among the children of I: 3478
18: 8 all the hallowed *things* of the children of I; 3478
18:11 all the wave offerings of the children of I: 3478
18:14 Every thing devoted in I shall be thine. 3478
18:19 the children of I offer unto the LORD, 3478
18:20 thine inheritance among the children of I. 3478
18:21 of Levi all the tenth in I for an inheritance, 3478
18:22 Neither must the children of I henceforth 3478
18:23 that among the children of I they have no 3478
18:24 the tithes of the children of I, which they 3478
18:24 Among the children of I they shall have no 3478
18:26 When ye take of the children of I the tithes 3478
18:28 which ye receive of the children of I; 3478
18:32 pollute the holy *things* of the children of I, 3478
19: 2 saying, Speak unto the children of I, 3478
19: 9 the children of I for a water of separation: 3478
19:10 it shall be unto the children of I, and 3478
19:13 and that soul shall be cut off from I: 3478
20: 1 came the children of I, *even* the whole 3478
20:12 sanctify me in the eyes of the children of I, 3478
20:13 the children of I strove with the LORD, 3478
20:14 Thus saith thy brother I, Thou knowest all 3478
20:19 the children of I said unto him, We will go 3478
20:21 Thus Edom refused to give I passage 3478
20:21 wherefore I turned away from him. 3478
20:22 the children of I, *even* the whole 3478
20:24 which I have given unto the children of I, 3478
20:29 Aaron thirty days, *even* all the house of I. 3478
21: 1 heard *tell* that I came *by* the way of 3478
21: 1 he fought against I, and took *some* of them 3478
21: 2 I vowed a vow unto the LORD, and said, 3478
21: 3 the LORD hearkened to the voice of I, 3478
21: 6 bit the people; and much people of I died. 3478
21:10 the children of I set forward, and pitched in 3478
21:17 I sang this song, Spring up, O well; sing ye 3478
21:21 I sent messengers unto Sihon king of 3478
21:23 Sihon would not suffer I to pass through 3478
21:23 and went out against I into the wilderness: 3478
21:23 and he came *to* Jahaz, and fought against I. 3478
21:24 I smote him with the edge of the sword, 3478
21:25 I took all these cities: and Israel dwelt in all 3478
21:25 I dwelt in all the cities of the Amorites, 3478
21:31 Thus I dwelt in the land of the Amorites. 3478
22: 1 the children of I set forward, and pitched in 3478
22: 2 Balak the son of Zippor saw all that I had 3478
22: 3 was distressed because of the children of I. 3478
23: 7 curse me Jacob, and come, defy I. 3478
23:10 and the number *of* the fourth part of I? 3478
23:21 neither hath he seen perverseness in I: 3478
23:23 neither *is there* any divination against I: 3478
23:23 *this* time it shall be said of Jacob and of I, 3478
24: 1 saw that it pleased the LORD to bless I, 3478
24: 2 he saw I abiding *in his tents* according to 3478
24: 5 thy tents, O Jacob, *and* thy tabernacles, O I! 3478
24:17 a Sceptre shall rise out of I, and shall smite 3478
24:18 for his enemies; and I shall do valiantly. 3478
25: 1 I abode in Shittim, and the people begun to 3478
25: 3 I joined himself unto Baal-peor: and 3478

Nu 25: 3 anger of the LORD was kindled against I. 3478
25: 4 of the LORD may be turned away from I. 3478
25: 5 Moses said unto the judges of I, Slay ye 3478
25: 6 one of the children of I came and 3478
25: 6 of all the congregation of the children of I, 3478
25: 8 he went after the man of I into the tent, 3478
25: 8 the man of I, and the woman through her 3478
25: 8 plague was stayed from the children of I. 3478
25:11 my wrath away from the children of I, 3478
25:11 that I consumed not the children of I in my 3478
25:13 made an atonement for the children of I. 3478
26: 2 of all the congregation of the children of I, 3478
26: 2 all that *are able to* go *to* war in I. 3478
26: 4 commanded Moses and the children of I, 3478
26: 5 Reuben, the eldest son of I: the children of 3478
26:51 *were* the numbered of the children of I, 3478
26:62 not numbered among the children of I, 3478
26:62 given them among the children of I. 3478
26:63 who numbered the children of I in 3478
26:64 when they numbered the children of I in 3478
27: 8 thou shalt speak unto the children of I, 3478
27:11 it shall be unto the children of I a statute of 3478
27:12 which I have given unto the children of I. 3478
27:20 that all the congregation of the children of I 3478
27:21 *both* he, and all the children of I with him, 3478
28: 2 Command the children of I, and say unto 3478
29:40 Moses told the children of I according to 3478
30: 1 of the tribes concerning the children of I, 3478
31: 2 Avenge the children of I of the Midianites: 3478
31: 4 throughout all the tribes of I, shall ye send 3478
31: 5 were delivered out of the thousands of I, 3478
31: 9 the children of I took *all* the women of 3478
31:12 unto the congregation of the children of I, 3478
31:16 Behold, these caused the children of I, 3478
31:54 *for* a memorial for the children of I before 3478
32: 4 LORD smote before the congregation of I, 3478
32: 7 I from going over into the land which 3478
32: 9 discouraged the heart of the children of I, 3478
32:13 the LORD'S anger was kindled against I, 3478
32:14 the fierce anger of the LORD toward I, 3478
32:17 go ready armed before the children of I, 3478
32:18 until the children of I have inherited every 3478
32:22 guiltless before the LORD, and before I; 3478
32:28 fathers of the tribes of the children of I: 3478
33: 1 These *are* the journeys of the children of I, 3478
33: 3 I went out with a high hand in the sight of 3478
33: 5 the children of I removed from Rameses, 3478
33:38 in the fortieth year after the children of I 3478
33:40 heard of the coming of the children of I. 3478
33:51 Speak unto the children of I, and say unto 3478
34: 2 Command the children of I, and say unto 3478
34:13 Moses commanded the children of I, 3478
34:29 unto the children of I in the land of Canaan. 3478
35: 2 Command the children of I, that they give 3478
35: 8 *be* of the possession of the children of I: 3478
35:10 Speak unto the children of I, and say unto 3478
35:15 *both* for the children of I, and for 3478
35:34 the LORD dwell among the children of I. 3478
36: 1 the chief fathers of the children of I: 3478
36: 2 an inheritance by lot to the children of I: 3478
36: 3 sons of the *other* tribes of the children of I, 3478
36: 4 when the jubile of the children of I shall be, 3478
36: 5 Moses commanded the children of I 3478
36: 7 the children of I remove from tribe to tribe: 3478
36: 7 for every one of the children of I shall keep 3478
36: 8 inheritance in any tribe of the children of I, 3478
36: 8 that the children of I may enjoy every man 3478
36: 9 every one of the tribes of the children of I 3478
36:13 I in the plains of Moab by Jordan *near* 3478
Dt 1: 1 all I on *this* side Jordan in the wilderness, 3478
1: 3 *that* Moses spake unto the children of I, 3478
1:38 for he shall cause I to inherit it. 3478
2:12 as I did unto the land of his possession, 3478
3:18 before your brethren the children of I, 3478
4: 1 Now therefore hearken, O I, unto 3478
4:44 which Moses set before the children of I: 3478
4:45 which Moses spake unto the children of I, 3478
4:46 whom Moses and the children of I smote, 3478
5: 1 Moses called all I, and said unto them, 3478
5: 1 Hear, O I, the statutes and judgments which 3478
6: 3 O I, and observe to do *it;* that it may be 3478
6: 4 Hear, O I: The LORD our God *is* one 3478
9: 1 Hear, O I: Thou art to pass over Jordan *this* 3478
10: 6 the children of I took their journey from 3478
10:12 now, I, what doth the LORD thy God 3478
11: 6 in their possession, in the midst of all I: 3478
13:11 all I shall hear, and fear, and shall do no 3478
17: 4 *that* such abomination is wrought in I: 3478
17:12 and thou shalt put away the evil from I. 3478
17:20 he, and his children, in the midst of I. 3478
18: 1 shall have no part nor inheritance with I: 3478
18: 6 come from any of thy gates out of all I, 3478
19:13 put away *the guilt of* innocent blood from I, 3478
20: 3 shall say unto them, Hear, O I, 3478
21: 8 Be merciful, O LORD, unto thy people I, 3478
21:21 among you; and all I shall hear, and fear. 3478
22:19 brought up an evil name upon a virgin of I: 3478
22:21 because she hath wrought folly in I, to play 3478
22:22 so shalt thou put away evil from I. 3478
23:17 shall be no whore of the daughters of I, 3478
23:17 of Israel, nor a sodomite of the sons of I. 3478
24: 7 any of his brethren of the children of I, 3478
25: 6 is dead, that his name be not put out of I. 3478
25: 7 to raise up unto his brother a name in I, 3478
25:10 his name shall be called in I, The house of 3478
26:15 bless thy people I, and the land which thou 3478
27: 1 Moses with the elders of I commanded 3478
27: 9 and the priests the Levites spake unto all I, 3478
27: 9 saying, Take heed, and hearken, O I; 3478
27:14 say unto all the men of I *with* a loud voice, 3478
29: 1 with the children of I in the land of Moab, 3478
29: 2 Moses called unto all I, and said unto them, 3478
29:10 and your officers, *with* all the men of I, 3478
29:21 him unto evil out of all the tribes of I, 3478
31: 1 and spake these words unto all I. 3478

Dt 31: 7 said unto him in the sight of all I, Be strong 3478
31: 9 of the LORD, and unto all the elders of I. 3478
31:11 When all I is come to appear before 3478
31:11 thou shalt read this law before all I in their 3478
31:19 song for you, and teach it the children of I: 3478
31:19 a witness for me against the children of I. 3478
31:22 same day, and taught it the children of I. 3478
31:23 for thou shalt bring the children of I into 3478
31:30 congregation of I the words of this song, 3478
32: 8 to the number of the children of I. 3478
32:45 an end of speaking all these words to all I: 3478
32:49 which I give unto the children of I for a 3478
32:51 of I at the waters of Meribah-Kadesh, 3478
32:51 me not in the midst of the children of I. 3478
32:52 unto the land which I give the children of I. 3478
33: 1 blessed the children of I before his death. 3478
33: 5 *and* the tribes of I were gathered together. 3478
33:10 teach Jacob thy judgments, and I thy law: 3478
33:21 of the LORD, and his judgments with I. 3478
33:28 I then shall dwell *in* safety alone: 3478
33:29 Happy *art* thou, O I: who *is* like unto thee, 3478
34: 8 the children of I wept for Moses in 3478
34: 9 the children of I hearkened unto him, and 3478
34:10 there arose not a prophet since in I like 3478
34:12 which Moses shewed in the sight of all I. 3478
Jos 1: 2 I do give to them, *even* to the children of I. 3478
2: 2 the children of I to search out the country. 3478
3: 1 he and all the children of I, and 3478
3: 7 I begin to magnify thee in the sight of all I, 3478
3: 9 Joshua said unto the children of I, 3478
3:12 take ye twelve men out of the tribes of I, 3478
4: 4 whom he had prepared of the children of I, 3478
4: 5 number of the tribes of the children of I: 3478
4: 7 a memorial unto the children of I for ever. 3478
4: 8 the children of I did so as Joshua 3478
4: 8 number of the tribes of the children of I, 3478
4:12 passed over armed before the children of I, 3478
4:14 magnified Joshua in the sight of all I; 3478
4:21 And he spake unto the children of I, saying, 3478
4:22 I came over this Jordan on dry *land.* 3478
5: 1 of Jordan from before the children of I, 3478
5: 1 any more, because of the children of I. 3478
5: 2 circumcise again the children of I 3478
5: 3 circumcised the children of I at the hill of 3478
5: 6 For the children of I walked forty years in 3478
5:10 the children of I encamped in Gilgal, and 3478
5:12 neither had the children of I manna any 3478
6: 1 straitly shut up because of the children of I: 3478
6:18 make the camp of I a curse, and trouble it. 3478
6:23 and left them without the camp of I. 3478
6:25 she dwelleth in I *even* unto this day; 3478
7: 1 the children of I committed a trespass in 3478
7: 1 was kindled against the children of I. 3478
7: 6 he and the elders of I, and put dust upon 3478
7: 8 when I turneth *their* backs before their 3478
7:11 I hath sinned, and they have also 3478
7:12 Therefore the children of I could not stand 3478
7:13 for thus saith the LORD God of I, 3478
7:13 an accursed thing in the midst of thee, O I: 3478
7:15 and because he hath wrought folly in I. 3478
7:16 the morning, and brought I by their tribes; 3478
7:19 glory to the LORD God of I, and 3478
7:20 I have sinned against the LORD God of I, 3478
7:23 unto all the children of I, and laid them out 3478
7:24 Joshua, and all I with him, took Achan 3478
7:25 all I stoned him *with* stones, and 3478
8:10 and went up, he and the elders of I, 3478
8:14 the men of the city went out against I to 3478
8:15 all I *made as if they* were beaten before 3478
8:17 in Ai or Beth-el, that went not out after I: 3478
8:17 they left the city open, and pursued after I. 3478
8:21 all I saw that the ambush had taken 3478
8:22 so they were in the midst of I, some on this 3478
8:24 when I had made an end of slaying all 3478
8:27 the spoil of that city I took for a prey unto 3478
8:30 unto the LORD God of I in mount Ebal, 3478
8:31 the LORD commanded the children of I, 3478
8:32 wrote in the presence of the children of I. 3478
8:33 all I, and their elders, and officers, and 3478
8:33 that they should bless the people of I. 3478
8:35 read not before all the congregation of I, 3478
9: 2 to fight with Joshua and with I, *with* one 3478
9: 6 said unto him, and to the men of I, We be 3478
9: 7 the men of I said unto the Hivites, 3478
9:17 the children of I journeyed, and came unto 3478
9:18 the children of I smote them not, because 3478
9:18 sworn unto them by the LORD God of I. 3478
9:19 sworn unto them by the LORD God of I: 3478
9:26 them out of the hand of the children of I, 3478
10: 1 of Gibeon had made peace with I, 3478
10: 4 with Joshua and with the children of I. 3478
10:10 And the LORD discomfited them before I, 3478
10:11 as they fled from before I, *and* were in 3478
10:11 the children of I slew with the sword. 3478
10:12 up the Amorites before the children of I, 3478
10:12 he said in the sight of I, Sun, stand thou 3478
10:14 of a man: for the LORD fought for I. 3478
10:15 Joshua returned, and all I with him, 3478
10:20 the children of I had made an end of 3478
10:21 his tongue against any of the children of I. 3478
10:24 that Joshua called for all the men of I, and 3478
10:29 all I with him, *unto* Libnah, and 3478
10:30 the king thereof, into the hand of I; 3478
10:31 all I with him, unto Lachish, and 3478
10:32 delivered Lachish into the hand of I, 3478
10:34 passed unto Eglon, and all I with him; 3478
10:36 and all I with him, unto Hebron; 3478
10:38 and all I with him, to Debir; 3478
10:40 as the LORD God of I commanded. 3478
10:42 the LORD God of I fought for Israel. 3478
10:42 the LORD God of Israel fought for I. 3478
10:43 Joshua returned, and all I with him, 3478
11: 5 at the waters of Merom, to fight against I. 3478
11: 6 will I deliver them up all slain before I: 3478
11: 8 LORD delivered them into the hand of I, 3478

Jos 11:13 I burned none of them, save Hazor only; 3478
11:14 the children of I took for a prey unto 3478
11:16 the mountain of I, and the valley of 3478
11:19 city that made peace with the children of I, 3478
11:20 that *they* should come against I *in* battle, 3478
11:21 of Judah, and from all the mountains of I: 3478
11:22 left in the land of the children of I: 3478
11:23 Joshua gave it for an inheritance unto I 3478
12: 1 which the children of I smote, and 3478
12: 6 of the LORD and the children of I smite: 3478
12: 7 the children of I smote on *this* side Jordan 3478
12: 7 which Joshua gave unto the tribes of I *for* a 3478
13: 6 I drive out from before the children of I: 3478
13:13 (Nevertheless the children of I expelled not 3478
13:14 the sacrifices of the LORD God of I made 3478
13:22 did the children of I slay with the sword 3478
13:33 the LORD God of I *was* their inheritance, 3478
14: 1 of I inherited in the land of Canaan, 3478
14: 1 the fathers of the tribes of the children of I, 3478
14: 5 so the children of I did, and they divided 3478
14:10 while *the children of* I wandered in 3478
14:14 he wholly followed the LORD God of I. 3478
17:13 when the children of I were waxen strong, 3478
18: 1 the whole congregation of the children of I 3478
18: 2 there remained among the children of I 3478
18: 3 Joshua said unto the children of I, How 3478
18:10 children of I according to their divisions. 3478
19:49 the children of I gave an inheritance to 3478
19:51 the fathers of the tribes of the children of I, 3478
20: 2 Speak to the children of I, saying, 3478
20: 9 the cities appointed for all the children of I, 3478
21: 1 the fathers of the tribes of the children of I; 3478
21: 3 the children of I gave unto the Levites out 3478
21: 8 the children of I gave by lot unto 3478
21:41 possession of the children of I *were* forty 3478
21:43 the LORD gave unto I all the land which 3478
21:45 the LORD had spoken unto the house of I; 3478
22: 9 departed from the children of I out of 3478
22:11 the children of I heard say, Behold, 3478
22:11 at the passage of the children of I. 3478
22:12 when the children of I heard *of it,* 3478
22:12 of I gathered themselves together *at* Shiloh, 3478
22:13 the children of I sent unto the children of 3478
22:14 a prince throughout all the tribes of I; 3478
22:14 of their fathers among the thousands of I. 3478
22:16 ye have committed against the God of I, 3478
22:18 be wroth with the whole congregation of I. 3478
22:20 and wrath fell on all the congregation of I? 3478
22:21 said unto the heads of the thousands of I, 3478
22:22 of gods, he knoweth, and I he shall know; 3478
22:24 have you to do with the LORD God of I? 3478
22:30 heads of the thousands of I which *were* 3478
22:31 now ye have delivered the children of I out 3478
22:32 to the children of I, and brought them word 3478
22:33 the thing pleased the children of I; and 3478
22:33 the children of I blessed God, and did not 3478
23: 1 unto I from all their enemies round about, 3478
23: 2 Joshua called for all I, *and* for their elders, 3478
24: 1 Joshua gathered all the tribes of I to 3478
24: 1 called for the elders of I, and for their 3478
24: 2 Thus saith the LORD God of I, 3478
24: 9 arose and warred against I, and sent and 3478
24:23 your heart unto the LORD God of I. 3478
24:31 I served the LORD all the days of Joshua, 3478
24:31 of the LORD, that he had done for I. 3478
24:32 which the children of I brought up out of 3478
Jdg 1: 1 that the children of I asked the LORD, 3478
1:28 it came to pass, when I was strong, 3478
2: 4 spake these words unto all the children of I, 3478
2: 6 the children of I went every man unto his 3478
2: 7 works of the LORD, that he did for I. 3478
2:10 nor yet the works which he had done for I. 3478
2:11 the children of I did evil in the sight of 3478
2:14 the anger of the LORD was hot against I, 3478
2:20 the anger of the LORD was hot against I; 3478
2:22 That through them I may prove I, 3478
3: 1 which the LORD left, to prove I by them, 3478
3: 1 *even* as many *of* I as had not known all NIH
3: 2 of the children of I might know, 3478
3: 4 they were to prove I by them, to know 3478
3: 5 the children of I dwelt among 3478
3: 7 the children of I did evil in the sight of 3478
3: 8 the anger of the LORD was hot against I, 3478
3: 8 the children of I served 3478
3: 9 when the children of I cried unto 3478
3: 9 raised up a deliverer to the children of I, 3478
3:10 and he judged I, and went out to war: 3478
3:12 the children of I did evil again in the sight 3478
3:12 Eglon the king of Moab against I, 3478
3:13 went and smote I, and possessed the city of 3478
3:14 So the children of I served Eglon the king 3478
3:15 when the children of I cried unto 3478
3:15 by him the children of I sent a present unto 3478
3:27 the children of I went down with him from 3478
3:30 was subdued that day under the hand of I. 3478
3:31 with an ox goad: and he also delivered I. 3478
4: 1 the children of I again did evil in the sight 3478
4: 3 the children of I cried unto the LORD: 3478
4: 3 he mightily oppressed the children of I. 3478
4: 4 wife of Lapidoth, she judged I at that time. 3478
4: 5 the children of I came up to her for 3478
4: 6 Hath not the LORD God of I commanded, 3478
4:23 the king of Canaan before the children of I. 3478
4:24 the hand of the children of I prospered, 3478
5: 2 Praise ye the LORD for the avenging of I, 3478
5: 3 I will sing *praise* to the LORD God of I. 3478
5: 5 Sinai from before the LORD God of I. 3478
5: 7 they ceased in I, until that I Deborah arose, 3478
5: 7 I Deborah arose, that I arose a mother in I. 3478
5: 8 or spear seen among forty thousand in I? 3478
5: 9 My heart *is* toward the governors of I, 3478
5:11 *towards the inhabitants* of his villages in I: 3478
6: 1 the children of I did evil in the sight of 3478
6: 2 And the hand of Midian prevailed against I: 3478
6: 2 of the Midianites the children of I made 3478

Jdg 6: 3 *so* it was, when I had sown, that 3478
6: 4 left no sustenance for I, neither sheep, 3478
6: 6 I was greatly impoverished because of 3478
6: 6 the children of I cried unto the LORD. 3478
6: 7 when the children of I cried unto 3478
6: 8 sent a prophet unto the children of I, 3478
6: 8 unto them, Thus saith the LORD God of I, 3478
6:14 thou shalt save I from the hand of 3478
6:15 O my Lord, wherewith shall I save I? 3478
6:36 If thou wilt save I by mine hand, as thou 3478
6:37 shall I know that thou wilt save I by mine 3478
7: 2 lest I vaunt themselves against me, saying, 3478
7: 8 he sent all *the rest of* I every man unto his 3478
7:14 of Gideon the son of Joash, a man of I: 3478
7:15 returned into the host of I, and said, Arise; 3478
7:23 the men of I gathered themselves together 3478
8:22 the men of I said unto Gideon, Rule thou 3478
8:27 all I went thither a whoring after it: 3478
8:28 Midian subdued before the children of I, 3478
8:33 that the children of I turned again, and 3478
8:34 the children of I remembered not 3478
8:35 the goodness which he had shewed unto I. 3478
9:22 Abimelech had reigned three years over I, 3478
9:55 when the men of I saw that Abimelech was 3478
10: 1 after Abimelech there arose to defend I 3478
10: 2 he judged I twenty and three years, and 3478
10: 3 and judged I twenty and two years. 3478
10: 6 the children of I did evil again in the sight 3478
10: 7 the anger of the LORD was hot against I, 3478
10: 8 they vexed and oppressed the children of I: 3478
10: 8 all the children of I that *were* on the *other* 3478
10: 9 of Ephraim; so that I was sore distressed. 3478
10:10 the children of I cried unto the LORD, 3478
10:11 And the LORD said unto the children of I, 3478
10:15 And the children of I said unto the LORD, 3478
10:16 his soul was grieved for the misery of I. 3478
10:17 the children of I assembled themselves 3478
11: 4 the children of Ammon made war against I. 3478
11: 5 the children of Ammon made war against I, 3478
11:13 Because I took away my land, when they 3478
11:15 I took not away the land of Moab, 3478
11:16 when I came up from Egypt, and 3478
11:17 I sent messengers unto the king of Edom, 3478
11:17 would not consent: and I abode in Kadesh. 3478
11:19 I sent messengers unto Sihon king of 3478
11:19 I said unto him, Let us pass, we pray thee, 3478
11:20 Sihon trusted not I to pass through his 3478
11:20 and pitched in Jahaz, and fought against I. 3478
11:21 the LORD God of I delivered Sihon and 3478
11:21 and all his people into the hand of I, 3478
11:21 so I possessed all the land of the Amorites, 3478
11:23 So now the LORD God of I hath 3478
11:23 the Amorites from before his people I, 3478
11:25 did he ever strive against I, or did he ever 3478
11:26 While I dwelt in Heshbon and her towns, 3478
11:27 be judge *this* day between the children of I 3478
11:33 were subdued before the children of I. 3478
11:39 she knew no man. And it was a custom in I, 3478
11:40 *That* the daughters of I went yearly to 3478
12: 7 Jephthah judged I six years. Then died 3478
12: 8 after him Ibzan of Beth-lehem judged I. 3478
12: 9 for his sons. And he judged I seven years. 3478
12:11 after him Elon, a Zebulonite, judged I; and 3478
12:11 judged Israel; and he judged I ten years. 3478
12:13 the son of Hillel, a Pirathonite, judged I. 3478
12:14 ten ass colts: and he judged I eight years. 3478
13: 1 the children of I did evil again in the sight 3478
13: 5 he shall begin to deliver I out of the hand 3478
14: 4 time the Philistines had dominion over I. 3478
15:20 he judged I in the days of the Philistines 3478
16:31 his father. And he judged I twenty years. 3478
17: 6 In those days *there was* no king in I, *but* 3478
18: 1 In those days *there was* no king in I: and 3478
18: 1 not fallen unto them among the tribes of I. 3478
18:19 be a priest unto a tribe and a family in I? 3478
18:29 of Dan their father, who was born unto I: 3478
19: 1 in those days, when *there was* no king in I, 3478
19:12 of a stranger, that *is* not of the children of I; 3478
19:29 and sent her into all the coasts of I. 3478
19:30 I came up out of the land of Egypt unto this 3478
20: 1 all the children of I went out, and 3478
20: 2 of all the people, *even* of all the tribes of I, 3478
20: 3 the children of I were gone up *to* Mizpeh.) 3478
20: 3 said the children of I, Tell *us,* how was this 3478
20: 6 all the country of the inheritance of I: 3478
20: 6 have committed lewdness and folly in I. 3478
20: 7 Behold, ye *are* all children of I; give here 3478
20:10 of an hundred throughout all the tribes of I, 3478
20:10 to all the folly that they have wrought in I. 3478
20:11 So all the men of I were gathered against 3478
20:12 the tribes of I sent men through all the tribe 3478
20:13 them to death, and put away evil from I. 3478
20:13 the voice of their brethren the children of I: 3478
20:14 to go out to battle against the children of I. 3478
20:17 the men of I, beside Benjamin, 3478
20:18 the children of I arose, and went up *to* 3478
20:19 the children of I rose up in the morning, 3478
20:20 the men of I went out to battle against 3478
20:20 the men of I put *themselves* in array to 3478
20:22 the people the men of I encouraged 3478
20:23 (And the children of I went up and 3478
20:24 the children of I came near against 3478
20:25 children of I again eighteen thousand men; 3478
20:26 all the children of I, and all the people, 3478
20:27 the children of I inquired of the LORD, 3478
20:29 And I set liers in wait round about Gibeah. 3478
20:30 the children of I went up against 3478
20:31 to Gibeah in the field, about thirty men of I. 3478
20:32 the children of I said, Let us flee, and 3478
20:33 all the men of I rose up out of their place, 3478
20:33 the liers in wait of I came forth out of their 3478
20:34 ten thousand chosen men out of all I, 3478
20:35 the LORD smote Benjamin before I: and 3478
20:35 the children of I destroyed of 3478
20:36 for the men of I gave place to 3478

Jdg 20:38 an appointed sign between the men of I 3478
20:39 when the men of I retired in the battle, 3478
20:39 kill of the men of I about thirty persons: 3478
20:41 when the men of I turned *again,* the men of 3478
20:42 men of I unto the way of the wilderness; 3478
20:48 the men of I turned again upon the children 3478
21: 1 Now the men of I had sworn in Mizpeh, 3478
21: 3 said, O LORD God of I, why is this come 3478
21: 3 God of Israel, why is this come to pass in I, 3478
21: 3 should be to day one tribe lacking in I? 3478
21: 5 the children of I said, Who *is there* among 3478
21: 5 Who *is there* among all the tribes of I that 3478
21: 6 the children of I repented them for 3478
21: 6 There is one tribe cut off from I *this* day. 3478
21: 8 What one *is there* of the tribes of I that 3478
21:15 had made a breach in the tribes of I. 3478
21:17 that a tribe be not destroyed out of I. 3478
21:18 for the children of I have sworn, saying, 3478
21:24 the children of I departed thence at that 3478
21:25 In those days *there was* no king in I: 3478
Ru 2:12 be given thee of the LORD God of I, 3478
4: 7 in former time in I concerning redeeming 3478
4: 7 and this *was* a testimony in I. 3478
4:11 which two did build the house of I: 3478
4:14 that his name may be famous in I. 3478
1Sa 1:17 the God of I grant *thee* thy petition that 3478
2:22 and heard all that his sons did unto all I; 3478
2:28 did I choose him out of all the tribes of I to 3478
2:28 offerings made by fire of the children of I? 3478
2:29 chiefest of all the offerings of I my people? 3478
2:30 Wherefore the LORD God of I saith, 3478
2:32 in all *the wealth* which *God* shall give I: 3478
3:11 to Samuel, Behold, I will do a thing in I, 3478
3:20 all I from Dan even to Beer-sheba knew 3478
4: 1 the word of Samuel came to all I. 3478
4: 1 Now I went out against the Philistines to 3478
4: 2 put *themselves* in array against I: 3478
4: 2 I was smitten before the Philistines: 3478
4: 3 come into the camp, the elders of I said, 3478
4: 5 all I shouted *with* a great shout, so that 3478
4:10 I was smitten, and they fled every man into 3478
4:10 for there fell of I thirty thousand footmen. 3478
4:17 I is fled before the Philistines, and 3478
4:18 heavy. And he had judged I forty years. 3478
4:21 The glory is departed from I: 3478
4:22 she said, The glory is departed from I: 3478
5: 7 The ark of the God of I shall not abide with 3478
5: 8 shall we do with the ark of the God of I? 3478
5: 8 Let the ark of the God of I be carried about 3478
5: 8 they carried the ark of the God of I about 3478
5:10 brought about the ark of the God of I to us, 3478
5:11 Send away the ark of the God of I, and 3478
6: 3 If ye send away the ark of the God of I, 3478
6: 5 and ye shall give glory unto the God of I: 3478
7: 2 all the house of I lamented after 3478
7: 3 Samuel spake unto all the house of I, 3478
7: 4 the children of I did put away Baalim and 3478
7: 5 Gather all I to Mizpeh, and I will pray for 3478
7: 6 Samuel judged the children of I in Mizpeh. 3478
7: 7 of I were gathered together to Mizpeh, 3478
7: 7 lords of the Philistines went up against I. 3478
7: 7 when the children of I heard *it,* they were 3478
7: 8 the children of I said to Samuel, Cease not 3478
7: 9 Samuel cried unto the LORD for I; and 3478
7:10 the Philistines drew near to battle against I: 3478
7:10 and they were smitten before I. 3478
7:11 the men of I went out of Mizpeh, and 3478
7:13 and they came no more into the coast of I: 3478
7:14 had taken from I were restored to Israel, 3478
7:14 had taken from Israel were restored to I, 3478
7:14 the coasts thereof did I deliver out of 3478
7:14 there was peace between I and 3478
7:15 Samuel judged I all the days of his life. 3478
7:16 and judged I in all those places. 3478
7:17 there he judged I; and there he built an altar 3478
8: 1 that he made his sons judges over I. 3478
8: 4 all the elders of I gathered themselves 3478
8:22 Samuel said unto the men of I, Go ye every 3478
9: 2 *there was* not among the children of I a 3478
9: 9 (Beforetime in I, when a man went to 3478
9:16 anoint him to be captain over my people I, 3478
9:20 on whom *is* all the desire of I? *Is it* not on 3478
9:21 of the smallest of the tribes of I? 3478
10:18 said unto the children of I, Thus saith 3478
10:18 Thus saith the LORD God of I, I brought 3478
10:18 I brought up I out of Egypt, and 3478
10:20 when Samuel had caused all the tribes of I 3478
11: 2 and lay it *for* a reproach upon all I. 3478
11: 3 send messengers unto all the coasts of I: 3478
11: 7 sent *them* throughout all the coasts of I by 3478
11: 8 the children of I were three hundred 3478
11:13 the LORD hath wrought salvation in I. 3478
11:15 and all the men of I rejoiced greatly. 3478
12: 1 Samuel said unto all I, Behold, I have 3478
13: 1 and when he had reigned two years over I, 3478
13: 2 Saul chose him three thousand *men* of I; 3478
13: 4 all I heard say *that* Saul had smitten a 3478
13: 4 *that* I also was had in abomination with 3478
13: 5 themselves together to fight with I, 3478
13: 6 When the men of I saw that they were in a 3478
13:13 established thy kingdom upon I for ever. 3478
13:19 no smith found throughout all the land of I: 3478
14:12 hath delivered them into the hand of I. 3478
14:18 God was at that time with the children of I. 3478
14:22 Likewise all the men of I which had hid 3478
14:23 So the LORD saved I that day: and 3478
14:24 the men of I were distressed that day: 3478
14:37 wilt thou deliver them into the hand of I? 3478
14:39 For, *as* the LORD liveth, which saveth I, 3478
14:40 said he unto all I, Be ye on one side, and 3478
14:41 Saul said unto the LORD God of I, 3478
14:45 who hath wrought this great salvation in I? 3478
14:47 So Saul took the kingdom over I, and 3478
14:48 delivered I out of the hands of them that 3478
15: 1 thee to be king over his people, over I: 3478

1Sa 15: 2 I remember *that* which Amalek did to I, 3478
15: 6 ye shewed kindness to all the children of I, 3478
15:17 thou not *made* the head of the tribes of I, 3478
15:17 and the LORD anointed thee king over I? 3478
15:26 hath rejected thee from being king over I. 3478
15:28 The LORD hath rent the kingdom of I 3478
15:29 also the Strength of I will not lie nor 3478
15:30 and before I, and turn again with me, 3478
15:35 repented that he had made Saul king over I. 3478
16: 1 I have rejected him from reigning over I? 3478
17: 2 and the men of I were gathered together, 3478
17: 3 I stood on a mountain on the other side: 3478
17: 8 he stood and cried unto the armies of I, 3478
17:10 I defy the armies of I this day; 3478
17:11 all I heard those words of the Philistine, 3478
17:19 Now Saul, and they, and all the men of I, 3478
17:21 For I and the Philistines had put *the battle* 3478
17:24 all the men of I, when they saw the man, 3478
17:25 the men of I said, Have ye seen this man 3478
17:25 surely to defy I is he come up: and it shall 3478
17:25 and make his father's house free in I. 3478
17:26 and taketh away the reproach from I? 3478
17:45 the God of the armies of I, whom thou hast 3478
17:46 the earth may know that there is a God in I. 3478
17:52 the men of I and of Judah arose, and 3478
17:53 the children of I returned from chasing 3478
18: 6 that the women came out of all cities of I, 3478
18:16 all I and Judah loved David, because 3478
18:18 what *is* my life, *or* my father's family in I, 3478
19: 5 LORD wrought a great salvation for all I: 3478
20:12 said unto David, O LORD God of I, 3478
23:10 said David, O LORD God of I, 3478
23:11 O LORD God of I, I beseech thee, tell thy 3478
23:17 thou shalt be king over I, and I shall be 3478
24: 2 three thousand chosen men out of all I, 3478
24:14 After whom is the king of I come out? 3478
24:20 *that* the kingdom of I shall be established in 3478
25:30 and shall have appointed thee ruler over I; 3478
25:32 Blessed *be* the LORD God of I, 3478
25:34 very deed, *as* the LORD God of I liveth, 3478
26: 2 having three thousand chosen men of I with 3478
26:15 who *is* like to thee in I? wherefore then 3478
26:20 for the king of I is come out to seek a flea, 3478
27: 1 to seek me any more in any coast of I: 3478
27:12 He hath made his people I utterly to abhor 3478
28: 1 armies together for warfare, to fight with I. 3478
28: 3 all I had lamented him, and buried him in 3478
28: 4 Saul gathered all I together, and 3478
28:19 Moreover the LORD will also deliver I 3478
28:19 the LORD also shall deliver the host of I 3478
29: 3 this David, the servant of Saul the king of I, 3478
30:25 and an ordinance for I unto this day. 3478
31: 1 Now the Philistines fought against I: and 3478
31: 1 the men of I fled from before 3478
31: 7 when the men of I that *were* on the *other* 3478
31: 7 saw that the men of I fled, and that Saul 3478
2Sa 1: 3 Out of the camp of I am I escaped. 3478
1:12 of the LORD, and for the house of I; 3478
1:19 The beauty of I *is* slain upon thy high 3478
1:24 Ye daughters of I, weep over Saul, 3478
2: 9 and over Benjamin, and over all I. 3478
2:10 years old when he *began* to reign over I, 3478
2:17 Abner was beaten, and the men of I, before 3478
2:28 stood still, and pursued after I no more, 3478
3:10 and to set up the throne of David over I and 3478
3:12 *be* with thee, to bring about all I unto thee. 3478
3:17 had communication with the elders of I, 3478
3:18 people I out of the hand of the Philistines, 3478
3:19 David in Hebron all that seemed good to I, 3478
3:21 and will gather all I unto my lord the king, 3478
3:37 all I understood that day that it was not of 3478
3:38 and a great *man* fallen this day in I? 3478
5: 1 came all the tribes of I to David unto 3478
5: 2 wast he that leddest out and broughtest in I: 3478
5: 2 Thou shalt feed my people I, and thou shalt 3478
5: 2 and thou shalt be a captain over I. 3478
5: 3 So all the elders of I came to the king to 3478
5: 3 and they anointed David king over I. 3478
5: 5 and three years over all I and Judah. 3478
5:12 LORD had established him king over I, 3478
5:17 that they had anointed David king over I, 3478
6: 1 gathered together all the chosen *men* of I, 3478
6: 5 all the house of I played before the LORD 3478
6:15 all the house of I brought up the ark of 3478
6:19 *even* among the whole multitude of I, 3478
6:20 said, How glorious was the king of I to day, 3478
6:21 ruler over the people of the LORD, over I: 3478
7: 6 I brought up the children of I out of Egypt, 3478
7: 7 I spake I a word with any of the tribes of 3478
7: 7 spake I a word with any of the tribes of I, 3478
7: 7 whom I commanded to feed my people I, 3478
7: 8 to be ruler over my people, over I: 3478
7:10 I will appoint a place for my people I, 3478
7:11 commanded judges *to be* over my people I, 3478
7:23 *even* like I, whom God went to redeem for 3478
7:24 people I to be a people unto thee for ever; 3478
7:26 The LORD of hosts *is* the God over I: 3478
7:27 For thou, O LORD of hosts, God of I, 3478
8:15 David reigned over all I; and David 3478
10: 9 he chose of all the choice *men* of I, and 3478
10:15 saw that they were smitten before I, 3478
10:17 he gathered all I together, and passed over 3478
10:18 the Syrians fled before I; and David slew 3478
10:19 saw that they were smitten before I, 3478
10:19 they made peace with I, and served them. 3478
11: 1 and his servants with him, and all I; 3478
11:11 The ark, and I, and Judah, abide in tents; 3478
12: 7 Thus saith the LORD God of I, I anointed 3478
12: 7 I anointed thee king over I, and I delivered 3478
12: 8 and gave thee the house of I and of Judah; 3478
12:12 I will do this thing before all I, and 3478
13:12 for no such thing ought to be done in I: 3478
13:13 thou shalt be as one of the fools in I. 3478
14:25 in all I there was none to be so 3478
15: 2 Thy servant *is* of one of the tribes of I. 3478
2Sa 15: 6 on this manner did Absalom to all I that 3478
15: 6 so Absalom stole the hearts of the men of I. 3478
15:10 sent spies throughout all the tribes of I, 3478
15:13 The hearts of the men of I are after 3478
16: 3 To day shall the house of I restore me 3478
16:15 and all the people the men of I, 3478
16:18 this people, and all the men of I, choose, 3478
16:21 all I shall hear that thou art abhorred of thy 3478
16:22 his father's concubines in the sight of all I. 3478
17: 4 Absalom well, and all the elders of I. 3478
17:10 for all I knoweth that thy father *is* a mighty 3478
17:11 Therefore I counsel *that* all I be generally 3478
17:13 shall all I bring ropes to that city, and 3478
17:14 Absalom and all the men of I said, 3478
17:15 counsel Absalom and the elders of I; 3478
17:24 he and all the men of I with him. 3478
17:26 So I and Absalom pitched *in* the land of 3478
18: 6 the people went out *into* the field against I: 3478
18: 7 Where the people of I were slain before 3478
18:16 the people returned from pursuing after I: 3478
18:17 and all I fled every one to his tent. 3478
19: 8 for I had fled every man to his tent. 3478
19: 9 were at strife throughout all the tribes of I, 3478
19:11 seeing the speech of all I is come to 3478
19:22 there any man be put to death *this* day in I? 3478
19:22 not I know that I *am this* day king over I? 3478
19:40 the king, and also half the people of I. 3478
19:41 all the men of I came to the king, and 3478
19:42 all the men of Judah answered the men of I, 3478
19:43 the men of I answered the men of Judah, 3478
19:43 were fiercer than the words of the men of I. 3478
20: 1 son of Jesse: every man to his tents, O I. 3478
20: 2 So every man of I went up from after 3478
20:14 he went through all the tribes of I unto 3478
20:19 *of them that are* peaceable *and* faithful in I: 3478
20:19 seekest to destroy a city and a mother in I: 3478
20:23 Now Joab *was* over all the host of I: and 3478
21: 2 the Gibeonites *were* not of the children of I, 3478
21: 2 and the children of I had sworn unto them: 3478
21: 2 to slay them in his zeal to the children of I 3478
21: 4 neither for us *shalt thou* kill any man in I. 3478
21: 5 from remaining in any of the coasts of I, 3478
21:15 the Philistines had yet war again with I; 3478
21:17 to battle, that thou quench not the light of I. 3478
21:21 when he defied I, Jonathan the son of 3478
23: 1 of Jacob, and the sweet psalmist of I, said, 3478
23: 3 The God of I said, the Rock of Israel spake 3478
23: 3 of Israel said, the Rock of I spake to me, 3478
23: 9 to battle, and the men of I were gone away: 3478
24: 1 anger of the LORD was kindled against I, 3478
24: 1 them to say, Go, number I and Judah. 3478
24: 2 Go now through all the tribes of I, 3478
24: 4 of the king, to number the people *of* I. 3478
24: 9 there were in I eight hundred thousand 3478
24:15 So the LORD sent a pestilence upon I 3478
24:25 the land, and the plague was stayed from I. 3478
1Ki 1: 3 a fair damsel throughout all the coasts of I, 3478
1:20 lord O king, the eyes of all I *are* upon thee, 3478
1:30 I sware unto thee by the LORD God of I, 3478
1:34 the prophet anoint him there king over I: 3478
1:35 I have appointed him to be ruler over I and 3478
1:48 the king, Blessed *be* the LORD God of I, 3478
2: 4 fail thee (said he) a man on the throne of I. 3478
2: 5 he did to the two captains of the hosts of I, 3478
2:11 the days that David reigned over I *were* 3478
2:15 *that* all I set their faces on me, that *I* should 3478
2:32 captain of the host of I, and Amasa the son 3478
3:28 all I heard of the judgment which the king 3478
4: 1 So king Solomon was king over all I. 3478
4: 7 Solomon had twelve officers over all I, 3478
4:20 Judah and I *were* many, as the sand which 3478
4:25 Judah and I dwelt safely, every man under 3478
5:13 king Solomon raised a levy out of all I; 3478
6: 1 eightieth year after the children of I were 3478
6: 1 the fourth year of Solomon's reign over I, 3478
6:13 I will dwell among the children of I, and 3478
6:13 of Israel, and will not forsake my people I. 3478
8: 1 Solomon assembled the elders of I, 3478
8: 1 the chief of the fathers of the children of I, 3478
8: 2 all the men of I assembled themselves unto 3478
8: 3 all the elders of I came, and the priests took 3478
8: 5 and all the congregation of I, 3478
8: 9 made *a covenant* with the children of I, 3478
8:14 and blessed all the congregation of I: 3478
8:14 (and all the congregation of I stood;) 3478
8:15 he said, Blessed *be* the LORD God of I, 3478
8:16 I brought forth my people I out of Egypt, 3478
8:16 I chose no city out of all the tribes of I to 3478
8:16 but I chose David to be over my people I. 3478
8:17 for the name of the LORD God of I. 3478
8:20 sit on the throne of I, as the LORD 3478
8:20 for the name of the LORD God of I. 3478
8:22 in the presence of all the congregation of I, 3478
8:23 he said, LORD God of I, *there is* no God 3478
8:25 Therefore now, LORD God of I, 3478
8:25 a man in my sight to sit on the throne of I; 3478
8:26 now, O God of I, let thy word, I pray thee, 3478
8:30 of thy people I, when they shall pray 3478
8:33 When thy people I be smitten down before 3478
8:34 forgive the sin of thy people I, and 3478
8:36 the sin of thy servants, and of thy people I, 3478
8:38 be *made* by any man, *or* by all thy people I, 3478
8:41 that *is* not of thy people I, but cometh out 3478
8:43 thy name, to fear thee, as *do* thy people I; 3478
8:52 unto the supplication of thy people I, 3478
8:55 blessed all the congregation of I *with* a 3478
8:56 that hath given rest unto his people I, 3478
8:59 the cause of his people I at all times, as 3478
8:62 the king, and all I with him, 3478
8:63 all the children of I dedicated the house of 3478
8:65 and all I with him, a great congregation, 3478
8:66 for David his servant, and for I his people. 3478
9: 5 the throne of thy kingdom upon I for ever, 3478
9: 5 not fail thee a man upon the throne of I. 3478
9: 7 will I cut off I out of the land which I have 3478
1Ki 9: 7 I shall be a proverb and a byword among 3478
9:20 which *were* not of the children of I, 3478
9:21 whom the children of I also were not able 3478
9:22 of the children of I did Solomon make no 3478
10: 9 in thee, to set thee on the throne of I: 3478
10: 9 because the LORD loved I for ever, 3478
11: 2 the LORD said unto the children of I, 3478
11: 9 was turned from the LORD God of I, 3478
11:16 six months did Joab remain there with all I, 3478
11:25 he was an adversary to I all the days of 3478
11:25 mischief that Hadad *did:* and he abhorred I, 3478
11:31 saith the LORD, the God of I, Behold, 3478
11:32 I have chosen out of all the tribes of I:) 3478
11:37 thy soul desireth, and shalt be king over I. 3478
11:38 I built for David, and will give I unto thee. 3478
11:42 in Jerusalem over all I *was* forty years. 3478
12: 1 for all I were come *to* Shechem to make 3478
12: 3 and all the congregation of I came, 3478
12:16 So when all I saw that the king hearkened 3478
12:16 to your tents, O I: now see to thine own 3478
12:16 David. So I departed unto their tents. 3478
12:17 *as for* the children of I which dwelt in 3478
12:18 all I stoned him with stones, that he died. 3478
12:19 So I rebelled against the house of David 3478
12:20 when all I heard that Jeroboam was come 3478
12:20 and made him king over all I: 3478
12:21 to fight against the house of I, 3478
12:24 against your brethren the children of I: 3478
12:28 behold thy gods, O I, which brought thee 3478
12:33 and ordained a feast unto the children of I: 3478
14: 7 Thus saith the LORD God of I, 3478
14: 7 and made thee prince over my people I, 3478
14:10 *and him that is* shut up and left in I, and 3478
14:13 all I shall mourn for him, and bury him: 3478
14:13 LORD God of I in the house of Jeroboam. 3478
14:14 LORD shall raise him up a king over I, 3478
14:15 For the LORD shall smite I, as a reed is 3478
14:15 he shall root up I out of this good land, 3478
14:16 he shall give I up because of the sins of 3478
14:16 who did sin, and who made I to sin. 3478
14:18 all I mourned for him, according to 3478
14:19 the book of the chronicles of the kings of I. 3478
14:21 LORD did choose out of all the tribes of I, 3478
14:24 LORD cast out before the children of I. 3478
15: 9 in the twentieth year of Jeroboam king of I 3478
15:16 and Baasha king of I all their days. 3478
15:17 Baasha king of I went up against Judah, 3478
15:19 *and* break thy league with Baasha king of I, 3478
15:20 hosts which he had against the cities of I, 3478
15:25 I in the second year of Asa king of Judah, 3478
15:25 of Judah, and reigned over I two years. 3478
15:26 and in his sin wherewith he made I to sin. 3478
15:27 for Nadab and all I laid siege to Gibbethon. 3478
15:30 which he sinned, and which he made I sin, 3478
15:30 he provoked the LORD God of I to anger. 3478
15:31 the book of the chronicles of the kings of I? 3478
15:32 and Baasha king of I all their days. 3478
15:33 son of Ahijah to reign over all I in Tirzah, 3478
15:34 and in his sin wherewith he made I to sin. 3478
16: 2 and made thee prince over my people I; 3478
16: 2 hast made my people I to sin, to provoke 3478
16: 5 the book of the chronicles of the kings of I? 3478
16: 8 the son of Baasha to reign over I in Tirzah, 3478
16:13 and *by* which they made I to sin, 3478
16:13 in provoking the LORD God of I to anger 3478
16:14 the book of the chronicles of the kings of I? 3478
16:16 wherefore all I made Omri, the captain of 3478
16:16 the host, king over I that day in the camp. 3478
16:17 all I with him, and they besieged Tirzah. 3478
16:19 and in his sin which he did, to make I sin. 3478
16:20 the book of the chronicles of the kings of I? 3478
16:21 were the people of I divided into two parts: 3478
16:23 king of Judah *began* Omri to reign over I, 3478
16:26 and in his sin wherewith he made I to sin, 3478
16:26 to provoke the LORD God of I to anger 3478
16:27 the book of the chronicles of the kings of I? 3478
16:29 Ahab the son of Omri to reign over I: 3478
16:29 Ahab the son of Omri reigned over I in 3478
16:33 I to anger than all the kings of Israel that 3478
16:33 than all the kings of I that were before him. 3478
17: 1 unto Ahab, *As* the LORD God of I liveth, 3478
17:14 For thus saith the LORD God of I, 3478
18:17 said unto him, *Art* thou he that troubleth I? 3478
18:18 he answered, I have not troubled I; but 3478
18:19 *and* gather to me all I unto mount Carmel, 3478
18:20 So Ahab sent unto all the children of I, and 3478
18:31 LORD came, saying, I shall be thy name: 3478
18:36 LORD God of Abraham, Isaac, and of I, 3478
18:36 it be known *this* day that thou *art* God in I, 3478
19:10 for the children of I have forsaken thy 3478
19:14 the children of I have forsaken thy 3478
19:16 Nimshi shalt thou anoint to be king over I: 3478
19:18 Yet I have left *me* seven thousand in I, 3478
20: 2 he sent messengers to Ahab king of I into 3478
20: 4 the king of I answered and said, My lord, 3478
20: 7 the king of I called all the elders of 3478
20:11 the king of I answered and said, Tell *him,* 3478
20:13 there came a prophet unto Ahab king of I, 3478
20:15 *even* all the children of I, *being* seven 3478
20:20 the Syrians fled; and I pursued them: and 3478
20:21 the king of I went out, and smote the horses 3478
20:22 the prophet came to the king of I, and 3478
20:26 and went up to Aphek, to fight against I. 3478
20:27 the children of I were numbered, and 3478
20:27 the children of I pitched before them like 3478
20:28 spake unto the king of I, and said, 3478
20:29 the children of I slew *of* the Syrians an 3478
20:31 kings of the house of I *are* merciful kings: 3478
20:31 upon our heads, and go out to the king of I: 3478
20:32 and came to the king of I, and said, 3478
20:40 the king of I said unto him, So *shall* thy 3478
20:41 the king of I discerned him that he *was* of 3478
20:43 the king of I went to his house heavy and 3478
21: 7 Dost thou now govern the kingdom of I? 3478
21:18 Arise, go down to meet Ahab king of I, 3478

I

1Ki 21:21 and *him that is* shut up and left in I, 3478
21:22 provoked *me* to anger, and made I to sin. 3478
21:26 LORD cast out before the children of I). 3478
22: 1 years without war between Syria and I. 3478
22: 2 king of Judah came down to the king of I. 3478
22: 3 the king of I said unto his servants, Know 3478
22: 4 Jehoshaphat said to the king of I, I *am* as 3478
22: 5 Jehoshaphat said unto the king of I, 3478
22: 6 the king of I gathered the prophets 3478
22: 8 the king of I said unto Jehoshaphat, 3478
22: 9 the king of I called an officer, and said, 3478
22:10 the king of I and Jehoshaphat the king of 3478
22:17 he said, I saw all I scattered upon the hills, 3478
22:18 the king of I said unto Jehoshaphat, Did I 3478
22:26 the king of I said, Take Micaiah, and 3478
22:29 So the king of I and Jehoshaphat the king 3478
22:30 the king of I said unto Jehoshaphat, I will 3478
22:30 the king of I disguised himself, and 3478
22:31 nor great, save only with the king of I. 3478
22:32 that they said, Surely it *is* the king of I. 3478
22:33 perceived that it *was* not the king of I, 3478
22:34 smote the king of I between the joints of 3478
22:39 the book of the chronicles of the kings of I? 3478
22:41 Judah in the fourth year of Ahab king of I. 3478
22:44 Jehoshaphat made peace with the king of I. 3478
22:51 I in Samaria the seventeenth year of 3478
22:51 of Judah, and reigned two years over I. 3478
22:52 the son of Nebat, who made I to sin: 3478
22:53 provoked to anger the LORD God of I, 3478
2Ki 1: 1 Moab rebelled against I after the death of 3478
1: 3 *Is it* not because *there is* not a God in I, 3478
1: 6 *Is it* not because *there is* not a God in I, 3478
1:16 *there is* no God in I to inquire of his word? 3478
1:18 the book of the chronicles of the kings of I? 3478
2:12 the chariot of I, and the horsemen thereof. 3478
3: 1 I in Samaria the eighteenth year of 3478
3: 3 the son of Nebat, which made I to sin; 3478
3: 4 rendered unto the king of I an hundred 3478
3: 5 king of Moab rebelled against the king of I. 3478
3: 6 Samaria the same time, and numbered all I. 3478
3: 9 So the king of I went, and the king of 3478
3:10 the king of I said, Alas, that the LORD 3478
3:12 So the king of I and Jehoshaphat and 3478
3:13 Elisha said unto the king of I, What have I 3478
3:13 the king of I said unto him, Nay: for 3478
3:24 when they came to the camp of I, 3478
3:27 there was great indignation against I: and 3478
5: 2 captive out of the land of I a little maid; 3478
5: 4 thus said the maid that *is* of the land of I. 3478
5: 5 and I will send a letter unto the king of I. 3478
5: 6 he brought the letter to the king of I, 3478
5: 7 when the king of I had read the letter, 3478
5: 8 heard that the king of I had rent his clothes, 3478
5: 8 he shall know that there is a prophet in I. 3478
5:12 better than all the waters of I? 3478
5:15 *there is* no God in all the earth, but in I: 3478
6: 8 the king of Syria warred against I, and 3478
6: 9 And the man of God sent unto the king of I, 3478
6:10 the king of I sent to the place which 3478
6:11 shew me which of us *is* for the king of I? 3478
6:12 Elisha, the prophet that *is* in I, telleth 3478
6:12 telleth the king of I the words that thou 3478
6:21 the king of I said unto Elisha, when he saw 3478
6:23 of Syria came no more into the land of I. 3478
6:26 as the king of I was passing by upon 3478
7: 6 the king of I hath hired against us the kings 3478
7:13 they *are* as all the multitude of I that are 3478
8:12 evil that thou wilt do unto the children of I: 3478
8:16 year of Joram the son of Ahab king of I, 3478
8:18 he walked in the way of the kings of I, 3478
8:25 I did Ahaziah the son of Jehoram king of 3478
8:26 the daughter of Omri king of I. 3478
9: 3 I have anointed thee king over I. 3478
9: 6 unto him, Thus saith the LORD God of I, 3478
9: 6 over the people of the LORD, *even* over I. 3478
9: 8 and *him that is* shut up and left in I: 3478
9:12 I have anointed thee king over I. 3478
9:14 he and all I, because of Hazael king of 3478
9:21 Joram king of I and Ahaziah king of Judah 3478
10:21 Jehu sent through all I: and all 3478
10:28 Thus Jehu destroyed Baal out of I. 3478
10:29 who made I to sin, Jehu departed not from 3478
10:30 *generation* shall sit on the throne of I. 3478
10:31 of the LORD God of I with all his heart: 3478
10:31 the sins of Jeroboam, which made I to sin. 3478
10:32 In those days the LORD began to cut I 3478
10:32 Hazael smote them in all the coasts of I; 3478
10:34 the book of the chronicles of the kings of I? 3478
10:36 the time that Jehu reigned over I in Samaria 3478
13: 1 of Jehu *began* to reign over I in Samaria, 3478
13: 2 the son of Nebat, which made I to sin; 3478
13: 3 anger of the LORD was kindled against I, 3478
13: 4 for he saw the oppression of I, because 3478
13: 5 (And the LORD gave I a saviour, so 3478
13: 5 the children of I dwelt in their tents, 3478
13: 6 who made I sin, *but* walked therein: 3478
13: 8 the book of the chronicles of the kings of I? 3478
13:10 son of Jehoahaz to reign over I in Samaria, 3478
13:11 the son of Nebat, who made I sin: 3478
13:12 the book of the chronicles of the kings of I? 3478
13:13 was buried in Samaria with the kings of I. 3478
13:14 Joash the king of I came down unto him, 3478
13:14 the chariot of I, and the horsemen thereof. 3478
13:16 he said to the king of I, Put thine hand upon 3478
13:18 took *them.* And he said unto the king of I, 3478
13:22 Hazael king of Syria oppressed I all 3478
13:25 beat him, and recovered the cities of I. 3478
14: 1 I reigned Amaziah the son of Joash king of 3478
14: 8 son of Jehu, king of I, saying, Come, 3478
14: 9 Jehoash the king of I sent to Amaziah king 3478
14:11 Therefore Jehoash king of I went up; and 3478
14:12 Judah was put to the worse before I; and 3478
14:13 Jehoash king of I took Amaziah king of 3478
14:15 the book of the chronicles of the kings of I? 3478
14:16 was buried in Samaria with the kings of I; 3478
2Ki 14:17 son of Jehoahaz king of I fifteen years. 3478
14:23 Joash king of I *began* to reign in Samaria, 3478
14:24 the son of Nebat, who made I to sin. 3478
14:25 He restored the coast of I from the entering 3478
14:25 to the word of the LORD God of I, 3478
14:26 For the LORD saw the affliction of I, 3478
14:26 shut up, nor any left, nor any helper for I. 3478
14:27 blot out the name of I from under heaven: 3478
14:28 *which belonged* to Judah, for I, 3478
14:28 the book of the chronicles of the kings of I? 3478
14:29 with his fathers, *even* with the kings of I; 3478
15: 1 seventh year of Jeroboam king of I *began* 3478
15: 8 reign over I in Samaria six months. 3478
15: 9 the son of Nebat, who made I to sin. 3478
15:11 the book of the chronicles of the kings of I. 3478
15:12 Thy sons shall sit on the throne of I unto 3478
15:15 the book of the chronicles of the kings of I. 3478
15:17 Menahem the son of Gadi to reign over I, 3478
15:18 the son of Nebat, who made I to sin. 3478
15:20 Menahem exacted the money of I, *even* of 3478
15:21 the book of the chronicles of the kings of I? 3478
15:23 Menahem *began* to reign over I in Samaria, 3478
15:24 the son of Nebat, who made I to sin. 3478
15:26 the book of the chronicles of the kings of I. 3478
15:27 Remaliah *began* to reign over I in Samaria, 3478
15:28 the son of Nebat, who made I to sin. 3478
15:29 In the days of Pekah king of I came 3478
15:31 the book of the chronicles of the kings of I. 3478
15:32 I *began* Jotham the son of Uzziah king of 3478
16: 3 he walked in the way of the kings of I, yea, 3478
16: 3 cast out from before the children of I. 3478
16: 5 Pekah son of Remaliah king of I came up 3478
16: 7 out of the hand of the king of I, which rise 3478
17: 1 Elah to reign in Samaria over I nine years. 3478
17: 2 not as the kings of I that were before him. 3478
17: 6 carried I away into Assyria, and 3478
17: 7 that the children of I had sinned against 3478
17: 8 cast out from before the children of I, 3478
17: 8 and of the kings of I, which they had made. 3478
17: 9 the children of I did secretly *those* things 3478
17:13 Yet the LORD testified against I, and 3478
17:18 the LORD was very angry with I, 3478
17:19 walked in the statutes of I which they 3478
17:20 the LORD rejected all the seed of I, and 3478
17:21 For he rent I from the house of David; and 3478
17:21 Jeroboam drave I from following 3478
17:22 For the children of I walked in all the sins 3478
17:23 Until the LORD removed I out of his 3478
17:23 So was I carried away out of their own land 3478
17:24 of Samaria instead of the children of I: 3478
17:34 the children of Jacob, whom he named I; 3478
18: 1 third year of Hoshea son of Elah king of I, 3478
18: 4 for unto those days the children of I did 3478
18: 5 He trusted in the LORD God of I; so 3478
18: 9 year of Hoshea son of Elah king of I, 3478
18:10 that *is* the ninth year of Hoshea king of I, 3478
18:11 the king of Assyria did carry away I unto 3478
19:15 said, O LORD God of I, which dwellest 3478
19:20 Thus saith the LORD God of I, 3478
19:22 on high? *even* against the Holy One of I. 3478
21: 2 LORD cast out before the children of I. 3478
21: 3 and made a grove, as did Ahab king of I; 3478
21: 7 which I have chosen out of all tribes of I, 3478
21: 8 Neither will I make the feet of I move any 3478
21: 9 LORD destroyed before the children of I. 3478
21:12 Therefore thus saith the LORD God of I, 3478
22:15 unto them, Thus saith the LORD God of I, 3478
22:18 to him, Thus saith the LORD God of I, 3478
23:13 which Solomon the king of I had builded 3478
23:15 who made I to sin, had made, both that 3478
23:19 which the kings of I had made to provoke 3478
23:22 from the days of the judges that judged I, 3478
23:22 nor *in* all the days of the kings of I, nor of 3478
23:27 as I have removed I, and will cast off this 3478
24:13 of I had made in the temple of the LORD, 3478
1Ch 1:34 begat Isaac. The sons of Isaac; Esau and I. 3478
1:43 *any* king reigned over the children of I; 3478
2: 1 These *are* the sons of I; Reuben, Simeon, 3478
2: 7 Achar, the troubler of I, who transgressed 3478
4:10 Jabez called on the God of I, saying, 3478
5: 1 Now the sons of Reuben the firstborn of I, 3478
5: 1 given unto the sons of Joseph the son of I: 3478
5: 3 *I say,* of Reuben the firstborn of I *were,* 3478
5:17 and in the days of Jeroboam king of I. 3478
5:26 the God of I stirred up the spirit of Pul king 3478
6:38 son of Kohath, the son of Levi, the son of I. 3478
6:49 most holy, and to make an atonement for I, 3478
6:64 the children of I gave to the Levites *these* 3478
7:29 dwelt the children of Joseph the son of I. 3478
9: 1 So all I were reckoned by genealogies; and 3478
9: 1 *were* written in the book of the kings of I 3478
10: 1 Now the Philistines fought against I; and 3478
10: 1 the men of I fled from before 3478
10: 7 when all the men of I that *were* in 3478
11: 1 all I gathered themselves to David unto 3478
11: 2 *wast* he that leddest out and broughtest in I: 3478
11: 2 Thou shalt feed my people I, and thou shalt 3478
11: 2 and thou shalt be ruler over my people I. 3478
11: 3 Therefore came all the elders of I to 3478
11: 3 they anointed David king over I, 3478
11: 4 David and all I went *to* Jerusalem, which *is* 3478
11:10 *and* with all I, to make him king, 3478
11:10 to the word of the LORD concerning I. 3478
12:32 of the times, to know what I ought to do; 3478
12:38 to Hebron, to make David king over all I: 3478
12:38 all the rest also of I *were of* one heart to 3478
12:40 sheep abundantly: for *there was* joy in I. 3478
13: 2 David said unto all the congregation of I, 3478
13: 2 that are left in all the land of I, and 3478
13: 5 So David gathered all I together, 3478
13: 6 David went up, and all I, to Baalah, *that is,* 3478
13: 8 all I played before God with all *their* might, 3478
14: 2 the LORD had confirmed him king over I, 3478
14: 2 *was* lift up on high, because of his people I. 3478
14: 8 that David was anointed king over all I, 3478
1Ch 15: 3 David gathered all I together to Jerusalem, 3478
15:12 I unto *the place that* I have prepared for it. 3478
15:14 to bring up the ark of the LORD God of I. 3478
15:25 the elders of I, and the captains over 3478
15:28 Thus all I brought up the ark of 3478
16: 3 he dealt to every one of I, both man and 3478
16: 4 to thank and praise the LORD God of I: 3478
16:13 O ye seed of I his servant, ye children of 3478
16:17 a law, *and* to I *for* an everlasting covenant, 3478
16:36 Blessed *be* the LORD God of I for ever 3478
16:40 of the LORD, which he commanded I; 3478
17: 5 the day that I brought up I unto this day; 3478
17: 6 Wheresoever I have walked with all I, 3478
17: 6 spake I a word to any of the judges of I, 3478
17: 7 *thou* shouldest be ruler over my people I: 3478
17: 9 Also I will ordain a place for my people I, 3478
17:10 commanded judges *to be* over my people I. 3478
17:21 one nation in the earth *is* like thy people I, 3478
17:22 For thy people I didst thou make thine own 3478
17:24 The LORD of hosts *is* the God of I, 3478
17:24 hosts *is* the God of Israel, *even* a God to I: 3478
18:14 So David reigned over all I, and executed 3478
19:10 he chose out of all the choice of I, and 3478
19:16 that they were put to the worse before I, 3478
19:17 he gathered all I, and passed over Jordan, 3478
19:18 the Syrians fled before I; and David slew of 3478
19:19 that they were put to the worse before I, 3478
20: 7 when he defied I, Jonathan the son of 3478
21: 1 Satan stood *up* against I, and 3478
21: 1 and provoked David to number I. 3478
21: 2 number I from Beer-sheba even to Dan; 3478
21: 3 why will he be a cause of trespass to I? 3478
21: 4 went throughout all I, and came *to* 3478
21: 5 all *they of* I were a thousand thousand and 3478
21: 7 with this thing; therefore he smote I. 3478
21:12 destroying throughout all the coasts of I. 3478
21:14 So the LORD sent pestilence upon I: and 3478
21:14 and there fell of I seventy thousand men. 3478
21:16 the elders *of I, who were* clothed in NIH
22: 1 this *is* the altar of the burnt offering for I. 3478
22: 2 the strangers that *were* in the land of I; 3478
22: 6 to build a house for the LORD God of I. 3478
22: 9 give peace and quietness unto I in his days. 3478
22:10 the throne of his kingdom over I for ever. 3478
22:12 and give thee charge concerning I, 3478
22:13 LORD charged Moses with concerning I: 3478
22:17 David also commanded all the princes of I 3478
23: 1 he made Solomon his son king over I. 3478
23: 2 he gathered together all the princes of I, 3478
23:25 The LORD God of I hath given rest unto 3478
24:19 as the LORD God of I had commanded 3478
26:29 sons *were* for the outward business over I, 3478
26:30 *were* officers among them of I on *this* side 3478
27: 1 Now the children of I after their number, 3478
27:16 Furthermore over the tribes of I: the ruler 3478
27:22 These *were* the princes of the tribes of I. 3478
27:23 the LORD had said *he* would increase I 3478
27:24 because there fell wrath for it against I; 3478
28: 1 David assembled all the princes of I, 3478
28: 4 Howbeit the LORD God of I chose me 3478
28: 4 of my father to be king over I for ever: 3478
28: 4 he liked me to make *me* king over all I: 3478
28: 5 of the kingdom of the LORD over I. 3478
28: 8 in the sight of all I the congregation of 3478
29: 6 of the fathers and princes of the tribes of I, 3478
29:10 LORD God of I our father, for ever and 3478
29:18 of Abraham, Isaac, and of I, our fathers, 3478
29:21 and sacrifices in abundance for all I: 3478
29:23 and prospered; and all I obeyed him. 3478
29:25 Solomon exceedingly in the sight of all I, 3478
29:25 had not been on any king before him in I. 3478
29:26 David the son of Jesse reigned over all I. 3478
29:27 the time that he reigned over I *was* forty 3478
29:30 over I, and over all the kingdoms of 3478
2Ch 1: 2 Solomon spake unto all I, to the captains of 3478
1: 2 to the judges, and to every governor in all I, 3478
1:13 of the congregation, and reigned over I. 3478
2: 4 our God. This *is an ordinance* for ever to I. 3478
2:12 Blessed *be* the LORD God of I, that made 3478
2:17 all the strangers that *were* in the land of I, 3478
5: 2 Solomon assembled the elders of I, and 3478
5: 2 the chief of the fathers of the children of I, 3478
5: 3 Wherefore all the men of I assembled 3478
5: 4 all the elders of I came; and the Levites 3478
5: 6 all the congregation of I that were 3478
5:10 made *a covenant* with the children of I, 3478
6: 3 and blessed the whole congregation of I: 3478
6: 3 and all the congregation of I stood. 3478
6: 4 he said, Blessed *be* the LORD God of I, 3478
6: 5 I to build a house *in,* that my name might 3478
6: 5 I any man to be a ruler over my people I: 3478
6: 6 have chosen David to be over my people I. 3478
6: 7 for the name of the LORD God of I. 3478
6:10 am set on the throne of I, as the LORD 3478
6:10 for the name of the LORD God of I. 3478
6:11 that he made with the children of I. 3478
6:12 in the presence of all the congregation of I, 3478
6:13 his knees before all the congregation of I, 3478
6:14 said, O LORD God of I, *there is* no God 3478
6:16 Now therefore, O LORD God of I, 3478
6:16 man in my sight to sit upon the throne of I; 3478
6:17 Now then, O LORD God of I, let thy 3478
6:21 of thy servant, and of thy people I, 3478
6:24 if thy people I be put to the worse before 3478
6:25 forgive the sin of thy people I, and 3478
6:27 the sin of thy servants, and of thy people I, 3478
6:29 or of all thy people I, when every one shall 3478
6:32 which *is* not of thy people I, but is come 3478
6:33 as *doth* thy people I, and may know that 3478
7: 3 when all the children of I saw how the fire 3478
7: 6 trumpets before them, and all I stood. 3478
7: 8 all I with him, a very great congregation, 3478
7:10 and to Solomon, and to I his people. 3478
7:18 shall not fail thee a man *to be* ruler in I. 3478
8: 2 and caused the children of I to dwell there. 3478

2Ch 8: 7 and the Jebusites, which *were* not of **I**, 3478
8: 8 whom the children of **I** consumed not, 3478
8: 9 of the children of **I** did Solomon make no 3478
8:11 not dwell in the house of David king of **I**, 3478
9: 8 because thy God loved **I**, to establish them 3478
9:30 Solomon reigned in Jerusalem over all **I** 3478
10: 1 for *to* Shechem were all **I** come to make 3478
10: 3 So Jeroboam and all **I** came and spake to 3478
10:16 when all **I** saw that the king would not 3478
10:16 every man to your tents, O **I**: *and* now, 3478
10:16 own house. So all **I** went to their tents. 3478
10:17 *as for* the children of **I** that dwelt in 3478
10:18 the children of **I** stoned him with stones, 3478
10:19 **I** rebelled against the house of David unto 3478
11: 1 to fight against **I**, that *he* might bring 3478
11: 3 and to all **I** in Judah and Benjamin, saying, 3478
11:13 the Levites that *were* in all **I** resorted to him 3478
11:16 after them out of all the tribes of **I** such as 3478
11:16 the LORD God of **I** came *to* Jerusalem, 3478
12: 1 the law of the LORD, and all **I** with him. 3478
12: 6 Whereupon the princes of **I** and the king 3478
12:13 had chosen out of all the tribes of **I**, 3478
13: 4 said, Hear me, *thou* Jeroboam, and all **I**; 3478
13: 5 **I** gave the kingdom over Israel to David for 3478
13: 5 gave the kingdom over **I** to David for ever, 3478
13:12 O children of **I**, fight ye not against 3478
13:15 and all **I** before Abijah and Judah. 3478
13:16 the children of **I** fled before Judah: and 3478
13:17 there fell down slain of **I** five hundred 3478
13:18 Thus the children of **I** were brought under 3478
15: 3 Now for a long season **I** *hath been* without 3478
15: 4 trouble did turn unto the LORD God of **I**, 3478
15: 9 for they fell to him out of **I** in abundance, 3478
15:13 LORD God of **I** should be put to death, 3478
15:17 high places were not taken away out of **I**: 3478
16: 1 Baasha king of **I** came up against Judah, 3478
16: 3 go, break thy league with Baasha king of **I**, 3478
16: 4 of his armies against the cities of **I**; 3478
16:11 in the book of the kings of Judah and **I**. 3478
17: 1 and strengthened himself against **I**. 3478
17: 4 and not after the doings of **I**. 3478
18: 3 Ahab king of **I** said unto Jehoshaphat king 3478
18: 4 Jehoshaphat said unto the king of **I**, 3478
18: 5 Therefore the king of **I** gathered together *of* 3478
18: 7 the king of **I** said unto Jehoshaphat, 3478
18: 8 the king of **I** called for one *of his* officers, 3478
18: 9 the king of **I** and Jehoshaphat king of Judah 3478
18:16 I did see all **I** scattered upon the mountains, 3478
18:17 the king of **I** said to Jehoshaphat, Did I not 3478
18:19 Who shall entice Ahab king of **I**, that he 3478
18:25 the king of **I** said, Take ye Micaiah, and 3478
18:28 So the king of **I** and Jehoshaphat the king 3478
18:29 the king of **I** said unto Jehoshaphat, I will 3478
18:29 So the king of **I** disguised himself; and 3478
18:30 or great, save only with the king of **I**. 3478
18:31 that they said, It *is* the king of **I**. 3478
18:32 perceived that it was not the king of **I**, 3478
18:33 smote the king of **I** between the joints of 3478
18:34 howbeit the king of **I** stayed *himself* up in 3478
19: 8 and of the chief of the fathers of **I**, 3478
20: 7 inhabitants of this land before thy people **I**, 3478
20:10 whom thou wouldest not let **I** invade, 3478
20:19 stood up to praise the LORD God of **I** 3478
20:29 LORD fought against the enemies of **I**. 3478
20:34 is mentioned in the book of the kings of **I**. 3478
20:35 Judah join himself with Ahaziah king of **I**, 3478
21: 2 *were* the sons of Jehoshaphat king of **I**. 3478
21: 4 and *divers* also of the princes of **I**. 3478
21: 6 he walked in the way of the kings of **I**, 3478
21:13 hast walked in the way of the kings of **I**, 3478
22: 5 **I** to war against Hazael king of Syria at 3478
23: 2 the chief of the fathers of **I**, and they came 3478
24: 5 gather of all **I** money to repair the house of 3478
24: 6 of the congregation of **I**, for the tabernacle 3478
24: 9 of God laid upon **I** in the wilderness. 3478
24:16 because he had done good in **I**, 3478
25: 6 out of **I** for an hundred talents of silver. 3478
25: 7 O king, let not the army of **I** go with thee; 3478
25: 7 for the LORD *is* not with **I**, *to wit, with* all 3478
25: 9 talents which I have given to the army of **I**? 3478
25:17 the son of Jehu, king of **I**, saying, Come, 3478
25:18 Joash king of **I** sent to Amaziah king of 3478
25:21 So Joash the king of **I** went up; and 3478
25:22 Judah was put to the worse before **I**, and 3478
25:23 Joash the king of **I** took Amaziah king of 3478
25:25 son of Jehoahaz king of **I** fifteen years. 3478
25:26 in the book of the kings of Judah and **I**? 3478
27: 7 *are* written in the book of the kings of **I** 3478
28: 2 For he walked in the ways of the kings of **I**, 3478
28: 3 had cast out before the children of **I**. 3478
28: 5 delivered into the hand of the king of **I**, 3478
28: 8 the children of **I** carried away captive of 3478
28:13 is great, and *there is* fierce wrath against **I** 3478
28:19 Judah low because of Ahaz king of **I**; 3478
28:23 But they were the ruin of him, and of all **I**. 3478
28:26 in the book of the kings of Judah and **I**. 3478
28:27 not into the sepulchres of the kings of **I**: 3478
29: 7 in the holy *place* unto the God of **I**. 3478
29:10 a covenant with the LORD God of **I**, 3478
29:24 the altar, to make an atonement for all **I**: 3478
29:24 the sin offering *should be made* for all **I**. 3478
29:27 instruments ordained by David king of **I**. 3478
30: 1 Hezekiah sent to all **I** and Judah, and 3478
30: 1 the passover unto the LORD God of **I**. 3478
30: 5 to make proclamation throughout all **I**, 3478
30: 5 unto the LORD God of **I** at Jerusalem: 3478
30: 6 and his princes throughout all **I** and Judah, 3478
30: 6 of the king, saying, Ye children of **I**, 3478
30: 6 **I**, and he will return to the remnant of you, 3478
30:21 the children of **I** that were present at 3478
30:25 all the congregation that came out of **I**, and 3478
30:25 the strangers that came out of the land of **I**, 3478
30:26 of **I** *there was* not the like in Jerusalem. 3478
31: 1 all **I** that were present went out to the cities 3478
31: 1 *all.* Then all the children of **I** returned, 3478
2Ch 31: 5 the children of **I** brought in abundance 3478
31: 6 *concerning* the children of **I** and Judah, 3478
31: 8 they blessed the LORD, and his people **I**. 3478
32:17 also letters to rail on the LORD God of **I**, 3478
32:32 *and* in the book of the kings of Judah and **I**. 3478
33: 2 had cast out before the children of **I**. 3478
33: 7 I have chosen before all the tribes of **I**, 3478
33: 8 will I any more remove the foot of **I** 3478
33: 9 had destroyed before the children of **I**. 3478
33:16 Judah to serve the LORD God of **I**. 3478
33:18 to him in the name of the LORD God of **I**, 3478
33:18 *are written* in the book of the kings of **I**. 3478
34: 7 all the idols throughout all the land of **I**, 3478
34: 9 of all the remnant of **I**, and of all Judah and 3478
34:21 and for them that are left in **I** and in Judah, 3478
34:23 Thus saith the LORD God of **I**, 3478
34:26 Thus saith the LORD God of **I** *concerning* 3478
34:33 countries that *pertained* to the children of **I**, 3478
34:33 and made all that were present in **I** to serve, 3478
35: 3 said unto the Levites that taught all **I**, 3478
35: 3 the son of David king of **I** did build; 3478
35: 3 the LORD your God, and his people **I**, 3478
35: 4 according to the writing of David king of **I**, 3478
35:17 the children of **I** that were present kept 3478
35:18 kept in **I** from the days of Samuel 3478
35:18 neither did all the kings of **I** keep such a 3478
35:18 all Judah and **I** that were present, and 3478
35:25 *this* day, and made them an ordinance in **I**: 3478
35:27 *are* written in the book of the kings of **I** 3478
36: 8 *are* written in the book of the kings of **I** 3478
36:13 from turning unto the LORD God of **I**. 3478
Ezr 1: 3 build the house of the LORD God of **I**, 3478
2: 2 The number of the men of the people of **I**: 3478
2:59 and their seed, whether they *were* of **I**: 3478
2:70 dwelt in their cities, and all **I** in their cities. 3478
3: 1 and the children of **I** *were* in the cities, 3478
3: 2 and builded the altar of the God of **I**, 3478
3:10 after the ordinance of David king of **I**. 3478
3:11 for his mercy *endureth* for ever towards **I**. 3478
4: 1 the temple unto the LORD God of **I**; 3478
4: 3 and the rest of the chief of the fathers of **I**, 3478
4: 3 will build unto the LORD God of **I**, 3478
5: 1 and Jerusalem in the name of the God of **I**, 3479
5:11 which a great king of **I** builded and set up. 3479
6:14 to the commandment of the God of **I**, 3479
6:16 the children of **I**, the priests, and 3479
6:17 for a sin offering for all **I**, twelve he goats, 3479
6:17 according to the number of the tribes of **I**. 3479
6:21 the children of **I**, which were come again 3478
6:21 to seek the LORD God of **I**, did eat, 3478
6:22 the work of the house of God, the God of **I**. 3478
7: 6 which the LORD God of **I** had given: 3478
7: 7 there went up *some* of the children of **I**, 3478
7:10 to do *it,* and to teach in **I** statutes and 3478
7:11 of the LORD, and of his statutes to **I**. 3478
7:13 that all they of the people of **I**, and *of* his 3479
7:15 have freely offered unto the God of **I**, 3479
7:28 I gathered together out of **I** chief *men* to go 3478
8:18 sons of Mahli, the son of Levi, the son of **I**; 3478
8:25 his lords, and all **I** *there* present, had 3478
8:29 the Levites, and chief of the fathers of **I**, 3478
8:35 offered burnt offerings unto the God of **I**, 3478
8:35 twelve bullocks for all **I**, ninety and 3478
9: 1 The people of **I**, and the priests, and 3478
9: 4 that trembled at the words of the God of **I**, 3478
9:15 O LORD God of **I**, thou *art* righteous: 3478
10: 1 there assembled unto him out of **I** a very 3478
10: 2 yet now there is hope in **I** concerning this 3478
10: 5 the chief priests, the Levites, and all **I**, 3478
10:10 strange wives, to increase the trespass of **I**. 3478
10:25 Moreover of **I**: of the sons of Parosh; 3478
Ne 1: 6 for the children of **I** thy servants, and 3478
1: 6 confess the sins of the children of **I**, 3478
2:10 man to seek the welfare of the children of **I**. 3478
7: 7 *I say,* of the men of the people of **I** *was* 3478
7:61 nor their seed, whether they *were* of **I**. 3478
7:73 of the people, and the Nethinims, and all **I**, 3478
7:73 the children of **I** *were* in their cities. 3478
8: 1 which the LORD had commanded to **I**. 3478
8:14 that the children of **I** should dwell in booths 3478
8:17 that day had not the children of **I** done so. 3478
9: 1 fourth day of this month the children of **I** 3478
9: 2 the seed of **I** separated themselves from all 3478
10:33 sin offerings to make an atonement for **I**, 3478
10:39 For the children of **I** and the children of 3478
11: 3 *to wit,* **I**, the priests, and the Levites, and 3478
11:20 the residue of **I**, of the priests, *and* 3478
12:47 all **I** in the days of Zerubbabel, and in 3478
13: 2 Because they met not the children of **I** with 3478
13: 3 that they separated from **I** all the mixed 3478
13:18 yet ye bring more wrath upon **I** by 3478
13:26 Did not Solomon king of **I** sin by these 3478
13:26 his God, and God made him king over all **I**. 3478
Ps 14: 7 O that the salvation of **I** *were come* out of 3478
14: 7 Jacob shall rejoice, *and* **I** *shall be* glad. 3478
22: 3 O thou that inhabitest the praises of **I**. 3478
22:23 and fear him, all ye the seed of **I**. 3478
25:22 Redeem **I**, O God, out of all his troubles. 3478
41:13 Blessed *be* the LORD God of **I** from 3478
50: 7 O **I**, and I will testify against thee: 3478
53: 6 O that the salvation of **I** *were come* out of 3478
53: 6 Jacob shall rejoice, *and* **I** shall be glad. 3478
59: 5 O LORD God *of* hosts, the God of **I**, 3478
68: 8 at the presence of God, the God of **I**. 3478
68:26 *even* the Lord, from the fountain of **I**. 3478
68:34 his excellency *is* over **I**, and his strength *is* 3478
68:35 the God of **I** *is* he that giveth strength and 3478
69: 6 be confounded for my sake, O God of **I**. 3478
71:22 I sing with the harp, O thou Holy One of **I** 3478
72:18 Blessed *be* the LORD God, the God of **I**, 3478
73: 1 Truly God *is* good to **I**, *even* to such as are 3478
76: 1 Judah *is* God known: his name *is* great in **I**. 3478
78: 5 appointed a law in **I**, which he commanded 3478
78:21 and anger also came up against **I**; 3478
78:31 and smote down the chosen *men* of **I**. 3478
Ps 78:41 and limited the Holy One of **I**. 3478
78:55 made the tribes of **I** to dwell in their tents. 3478
78:59 *this,* he was wroth, and greatly abhorred **I**: 3478
78:71 feed Jacob his people, and **I** his inheritance. 3478
80: 1 Give ear, O Shepherd of **I**, thou that leadest 3478
81: 4 For this *was* a statute for **I**, *and* a law of 3478
81: 8 O **I**, if thou wilt hearken unto me; 3478
81:11 to my voice; and **I** would none of me. 3478
81:13 unto me, *and* **I** had walked in my ways! 3478
83: 4 that the name of **I** may be no more in 3478
89:18 and the Holy One of **I** *is* our king. 3478
98: 3 and his truth toward the house of **I**: 3478
103: 7 unto Moses, his acts unto the children of **I**. 3478
105:10 a law, *and* to **I** *for* an everlasting covenant: 3478
105:23 **I** also came *into* Egypt; and 3478
106:48 Blessed *be* the LORD God of **I** from 3478
114: 1 When **I** went out of Egypt, the house of 3478
114: 2 was his sanctuary, *and* **I** his dominion. 3478
115: 9 O **I**, trust thou in the LORD: he *is* their 3478
115:12 will bless *us;* he will bless the house of **I**; 3478
118: 2 Let **I** now say, that his mercy *endureth* for 3478
121: 4 he that keepeth **I** shall neither slumber nor 3478
122: 4 of the LORD, *unto* the testimony of **I**, 3478
124: 1 who was on our side, now may **I** say; 3478
125: 5 of iniquity: *but* peace *shall be* upon **I**. 3478
128: 6 thy children's children, *and* peace upon **I**. 3478
129: 1 me from my youth, may **I** now say: 3478
130: 7 Let **I** hope in the LORD: for with 3478
130: 8 he shall redeem **I** from all his iniquities. 3478
131: 3 Let **I** hope in the LORD from henceforth 3478
135: 4 unto himself, *and* **I** for his peculiar treasure. 3478
135:12 an heritage, an heritage unto **I** his people. 3478
135:19 Bless the LORD, O house of **I**: bless 3478
136:11 brought out **I** from among them: for his 3478
136:14 made **I** to pass through the midst of it: 3478
136:22 *Even* an heritage unto **I** his servant: for his 3478
147: 2 he gathereth together the outcasts of **I**. 3478
147:19 his statutes and his judgments unto **I**. 3478
148:14 *even* of the children of **I**, a people near unto 3478
149: 2 Let **I** rejoice in him that made him: let 3478
Pr 1: 1 of Solomon the son of David, king of **I**. 3478
Ecc 1:12 I the Preacher was king over **I** in Jerusalem. 3478
SS 3: 7 valiant *men are* about it, of the valiant of **I**. 3478
Isa 1: 3 *but* **I** doth not know, my people doth not 3478
1: 4 they have provoked the Holy One of **I** unto 3478
1:24 LORD of hosts, the mighty One of **I**, Ah, 3478
4: 2 and comely for them that are escaped of **I**. 3478
5: 7 of the LORD of hosts *is* the house of **I**, 3478
5:19 let the counsel of the Holy One of **I** draw 3478
5:24 despised the word of the Holy One of **I**. 3478
7: 1 and Pekah the son of Remaliah, king of **I**, 3478
8:14 a rock of offence to both the houses of **I**, 3478
8:18 for wonders in **I** from the LORD of hosts, 3478
9: 8 word into Jacob, and it hath lighted upon **I**. 3478
9:12 they shall devour **I** with open mouth. 3478
9:14 Therefore the LORD will cut off from **I** 3478
10:17 the light of **I** shall be for a fire, and 3478
10:20 *that* the remnant of **I**, and such as are 3478
10:20 the LORD, the Holy One of **I**, in truth. 3478
10:22 For though thy people **I** be as the sand of 3478
11:12 shall assemble the outcasts of **I**, and 3478
11:16 like as it was to **I** in the day that he came 3478
12: 6 for great *is* the Holy One of **I** in the midst 3478
14: 1 will yet choose **I**, and set them in their own 3478
14: 2 the house of **I** shall possess them in 3478
17: 3 shall be as the glory of the children of **I**, 3478
17: 6 saith the LORD God of **I**. 3478
17: 7 shall have respect to the Holy One of **I**. 3478
17: 9 which they left because of the children of **I**: 3478
19:24 In that day shall **I** be the third with Egypt 3478
19:25 work of my hands, and **I** mine inheritance. 3478
21:10 the God of **I**, have I declared unto you. 3478
21:17 for the LORD God of **I** hath spoken *it.* 3478
24:15 *even* the name of the LORD God of **I** in 3478
27: 6 **I** shall blossom and bud, and fill the face of 3478
27:12 be gathered one by one, O ye children of **I**. 3478
29:19 men shall rejoice in the Holy One of **I**. 3478
29:23 One of Jacob, and shall fear the God of **I**. 3478
30:11 cause the Holy One of **I** to cease from 3478
30:12 Wherefore thus saith the Holy One of **I**, 3478
30:15 saith the Lord GOD, the Holy One of **I**; 3478
30:29 of the LORD, to the mighty One of **I**. 3478
31: 1 they look not unto the Holy One of **I**, 3478
31: 6 the children of **I** have deeply revolted. 3478
37:16 O LORD of hosts, God of **I**, that dwellest 3478
37:21 Thus saith the LORD God of **I**, 3478
37:23 on high? *even* against the Holy One of **I**. 3478
40:27 sayest thou, O Jacob, and speakest, O **I**, 3478
41: 8 thou, **I**, *art* my servant, Jacob whom I have 3478
41:14 thou worm Jacob, *and* ye men of **I**; 3478
41:14 and thy redeemer, the Holy One of **I**. 3478
41:16 *and* shalt glory in the Holy One of **I**. 3478
41:17 *I* the God of **I** will not forsake them. 3478
41:20 and the Holy One of **I** hath created it. 3478
42:24 gave Jacob for a spoil, and **I** to the robbers? 3478
43: 1 and he that formed thee, O **I**, Fear not: 3478
43: 3 thy God, the Holy One of **I**, thy Saviour: 3478
43:14 your redeemer, the Holy One of **I**; 3478
43:15 your Holy One, the creator of **I**, your King. 3478
43:22 but thou hast been weary of me, O **I**. 3478
43:28 Jacob to the curse, and **I** to reproaches. 3478
44: 1 my servant; and **I**, whom I have chosen: 3478
44: 5 and surname *himself* by the name of **I**. 3478
44: 6 Thus saith the LORD the King of **I**, and 3478
44:21 Remember these, O Jacob and **I**; for thou 3478
44:21 O **I**, thou shalt not be forgotten of me. 3478
44:23 redeemed Jacob, and glorified himself in **I**. 3478
45: 3 call *thee* by thy name, *am* the God of **I**. 3478
45: 4 Jacob my servant's sake, and **I** mine elect, 3478
45:11 the Holy One of **I**, and his maker, 3478
45:15 that hidest thyself, O God of **I**, the saviour. 3478
45:17 *But* **I** shall be saved in the LORD *with* an 3478
45:25 In the LORD shall all the seed of **I** be 3478
46: 3 and all the remnant of the house of **I**, 3478
46:13 I will place salvation in Zion for **I** my 3478

Isa 47: 4 of hosts *is* his name, the Holy One of I. 3478
48: 1 which are called by the name of I, and 3478
48: 1 make mention of the God of I, *but* not in 3478
48: 2 and stay themselves upon the God of I; 3478
48:12 unto me, O Jacob, and I my called; 3478
48:17 thy redeemer, the Holy One of I; 3478
49: 3 said unto me, Thou *art* my servant, O I, 3478
49: 5 again to him, Though I be not gathered, 3478
49: 6 of Jacob, and to restore the preserved of I: 3478
49: 7 the redeemer of I, *and* his Holy One, 3478
49: 7 *and* the Holy One of I, and he shall choose 3478
52:12 and the God of I *will be* your rereward. 3478
54: 5 and thy redeemer the Holy One of I; 3478
55: 5 thy God, and for the Holy One of I; 3478
56: 8 which gathereth the outcasts of I saith, 3478
60: 9 to the Holy One of I, because he hath 3478
60:14 the LORD, The Zion of the Holy One of I. 3478
63: 7 the great goodness towards the house of I, 3478
63:16 ignorant of us, and I acknowledge us not: 3478
66:20 as the children of I bring an offering in a 3478
Jer 2: 3 I *was* holiness unto the LORD, *and* 3478
2: 4 and all the families of the house of I: 3478
2:14 *Is* I a servant? *is* he a homeborn *slave?* why 3478
2:26 he is found, so is the house of I ashamed; 3478
2:31 Have I been a wilderness unto I? a land of 3478
3: 6 Hast thou seen *that* which backsliding I 3478
3: 8 I committed adultery I had put her away, 3478
3:11 The backsliding I hath justified herself 3478
3:12 say, Return, thou backsliding I, saith 3478
3:18 of Judah shall walk with the house of I, 3478
3:20 with me, O house of I, saith the LORD. 3478
3:21 *and* supplications of the children of I: 3478
3:23 in the LORD our God *is* the salvation of I. 3478
4: 1 O I, saith the LORD, return unto me: 3478
5:11 For the house of I and the house of Judah 3478
5:15 from far, O house of I, saith the LORD: 3478
6: 9 They shall throughly glean the remnant of I 3478
7: 3 the God of I, Amend your ways and 3478
7:12 did to it for the wickedness of my people I. 3478
7:21 saith the LORD of hosts, the God of I; 3478
9:15 saith the LORD of hosts, the God of I; 3478
9:26 all the house of I *are* uncircumcised in 3478
10: 1 LORD speaketh unto you, O house of I: 3478
10:16 and I *is* the rod of his inheritance: 3478
11: 3 unto them, Thus saith the LORD God of I; 3478
11:10 the house of I and the house of Judah have 3478
11:17 for the evil of the house of I and of 3478
12:14 which I have caused my people I to inherit; 3478
13:11 to cleave unto me the whole house of I 3478
13:12 Thus saith the LORD God of I, 3478
14: 8 O the hope of I, the saviour thereof in time 3478
16: 9 saith the LORD of hosts, the God of I; 3478
16:14 that brought up the children of I out of 3478
16:15 that brought up the children of I from 3478
17:13 O LORD, the hope of I, all that forsake 3478
18: 6 O house of I, cannot I do with you as this 3478
18: 6 so *are* ye in mine hand, O house of I. 3478
18:13 who hath heard such *things:* the virgin of I 3478
19: 3 saith the LORD of hosts, the God of I; 3478
19:15 saith the LORD of hosts, the God of I; 3478
21: 4 Thus saith the LORD God of I; Behold, 3478
23: 2 Therefore thus saith the LORD God of I 3478
23: 6 shall be saved, and I shall dwell safely: 3478
23: 7 which brought up the children of I out of 3478
23: 8 which led the seed of the house of I out of 3478
23:13 in Baal, and caused my people I to err. 3478
24: 5 Thus saith the LORD, the God of I; 3478
25:15 For thus saith the LORD God of I unto 3478
25:27 saith the LORD of hosts, the God of I; 3478
27: 4 saith the LORD of hosts, the God of I, 3478
27:21 saith the LORD of hosts, the God of I, 3478
28: 2 the LORD of hosts, the God of I, saying, 3478
28:14 saith the LORD of hosts, the God of I; 3478
29: 4 saith the LORD of hosts, the God of I, 3478
29: 8 saith the LORD of hosts, the God of I; 3478
29:21 the God of I, of Ahab the son of Kolaiah, 3478
29:23 Because they have committed villany in I, 3478
29:25 the LORD of hosts, the God of I, saying, 3478
30: 2 Thus speaketh the LORD God of I, 3478
30: 3 bring again the captivity of my people I 3478
30: 4 words that the LORD spake concerning I 3478
30:10 saith the LORD; neither be dismayed, O I: 3478
31: 1 will I be the God of all the families of I, 3478
31: 2 *even* I when *I* went to cause him to rest. 3478
31: 4 and thou shalt be built, O virgin of I: 3478
31: 7 save thy people, the remnant of I. 3478
31: 9 for I am a father to I, and Ephraim *is* my 3478
31:10 He that scattered I will gather him, and 3478
31:21 turn again, O virgin of I, turn again to these 3478
31:23 saith the LORD of hosts, the God of I; 3478
31:27 that I will sow the house of I and the house 3478
31:31 make a new covenant with the house of I, 3478
31:33 that I will make with the house of I; 3478
31:36 the seed of I also shall cease from being a 3478
31:37 I will also cast off all the seed of I for all 3478
32:14 saith the LORD of hosts, the God of I; 3478
32:15 saith the LORD of hosts, the God of I; 3478
32:20 this day, and in I, and amongst *other* men; 3478
32:21 hast brought forth thy people I out of 3478
32:30 For the children of I and the children of 3478
32:30 for the children of I have only provoked me 3478
32:32 Because of all the evil of the children of I 3478
32:36 the God of I, concerning this city, 3478
33: 4 For thus saith the LORD, the God of I, 3478
33: 7 of Judah and the captivity of I to return, 3478
33:14 which I have promised unto the house of I 3478
33:17 to sit upon the throne of the house of I; 3478
34: 2 Thus saith the LORD, the God of I; Go 3478
34:13 Thus saith the LORD, the God of I; 3478
35:13 saith the LORD of hosts, the God of I; 3478
35:17 the LORD God of hosts, the God of I; 3478
35:18 saith the LORD of hosts, the God of I; 3478
35:19 saith the LORD of hosts, the God of I; 3478
36: 2 that I have spoken unto thee against I, 3478
37: 7 Thus saith the LORD, the God of I; 3478

Jer 38:17 the LORD, the God of hosts, the God of I; 3478
39:16 saith the LORD of hosts, the God of I; 3478
41: 9 king had made for fear of Baasha king of I: 3478
42: 9 Thus saith the LORD, the God of I, 3478
42:15 saith the LORD of hosts, the God of I; 3478
42:18 saith the LORD of hosts, the God of I; 3478
43:10 saith the LORD of hosts, the God of I; 3478
44: 2 saith the LORD of hosts, the God of I; 3478
44: 7 the LORD, the God of hosts, the God of I; 3478
44:11 saith the LORD of hosts, the God of I; 3478
44:25 the LORD of hosts, the God of I, saying; 3478
45: 2 the God of I, unto thee, O Baruch; 3478
46:25 The LORD of hosts, the God of I, saith; 3478
46:27 servant Jacob, and be not dismayed, O I: 3478
48: 1 saith the LORD of hosts, the God of I; 3478
48:13 as the house of I was ashamed of Beth-el 3478
48:27 For was not I a derision unto thee? was he 3478
49: 1 thus saith the LORD; Hath I no sons? 3478
49: 2 shall I be heir unto them that were his 3478
50: 4 the children of I shall come, they and 3478
50:17 I *is* a scattered sheep; the lions have driven 3478
50:18 saith the LORD of hosts, the God of I; 3478
50:19 I will bring I again to his habitation, and 3478
50:20 the iniquity of I shall be sought for, and 3478
50:29 the LORD, against the Holy One of I. 3478
50:33 The children of I and the children of Judah 3478
51: 5 For I *hath* not *been* forsaken, nor Judah of 3478
51: 5 filled *with* sin against the Holy One of I. 3478
51:19 all *things:* and *I is* the rod of his inheritance: NIH
51:33 saith the LORD of hosts, the God of I; 3478
51:49 As Babylon *hath caused* the slain of I to 3478
La 2: 1 from heaven *unto* the earth the beauty of I, 3478
2: 3 cut off in *his* fierce anger all the horn of I: 3478
2: 5 he hath swallowed up I, he hath swallowed 3478
Eze 2: 3 Son of man, I send thee to the children of I, 3478
3: 1 this roll, and go speak unto the house of I. 3478
3: 4 go, get thee unto the house of I, and 3478
3: 5 of a hard language, *but* to the house of I; 3478
3: 7 the house of I will not hearken unto thee; 3478
3: 7 for all the house of I *are* impudent 3478
3:17 made thee a watchman unto the house of I: 3478
4: 3 This *shall be* a sign to the house of I. 3478
4: 4 lay the iniquity of the house of I upon it: 3478
4: 5 thou bear the iniquity of the house of I. 3478
4:13 Even thus shall the children of I eat their 3478
5: 4 a fire come forth into all the house of I. 3478
6: 2 set thy face towards the mountains of I, and 3478
6: 3 say, Ye mountains of I, hear the word of 3478
6: 5 of the children of I before their idols; 3478
6:11 all the evil abominations of the house of I: 3478
7: 2 saith the Lord GOD unto the land of I; 3478
8: 4 the glory of the God of I *was* there, 3478
8: 6 that the house of I committeth here, 3478
8:10 and all the idols of the house of I, 3478
8:11 men of the ancients of the house of I, 3478
8:12 ancients of the house of I do in the dark, 3478
9: 3 the glory of the God of I was gone up from 3478
9: 8 *wilt* thou destroy all the residue of I in thy 3478
9: 9 The iniquity of the house of I and Judah *is* 3478
10:19 the glory of the God of I *was* over them 3478
10:20 under the God of I by the river of Chebar; 3478
11: 5 Thus have ye said, O house of I: 3478
11:10 I will judge you in the border of I; and 3478
11:11 *but* I will judge you in the border of I: 3478
11:13 thou make a full end of the remnant of I? 3478
11:15 thy kindred, and all the house of I wholly, 3478
11:17 and I will give you the land of I. 3478
11:22 the glory of the God of I *was* over them 3478
12: 6 have set thee *for* a sign unto the house of I. 3478
12: 9 Son of man, hath not the house of I, 3478
12:10 and all the house of I that *are* among them. 3478
12:19 of Jerusalem, *and* of the land of I; 3478
12:22 *is* that proverb *that* ye have in the land of I, 3478
12:23 they shall no more use it as a proverb in I; 3478
12:24 flattering divination within the house of I. 3478
12:27 of man, behold, *they of* the house of I say, 3478
13: 2 prophesy against the prophets of I that 3478
13: 4 O I, thy prophets are like the foxes in 3478
13: 5 I to stand in the battle in the day of 3478
13: 9 be written in the writing of the house of I, 3478
13: 9 neither shall they enter into the land of I; 3478
13:16 *To wit,* the prophets of I which prophesy 3478
14: 1 came certain of the elders of I unto me, 3478
14: 4 Every man of the house of I that setteth up 3478
14: 5 That *I* may take the house of I in their own 3478
14: 6 Therefore say unto the house of I, 3478
14: 7 For every one of the house of I, or of 3478
14: 7 or of the stranger that sojourneth in I, 3478
14: 9 destroy him from the midst of my people I. 3478
14:11 That the house of I may go no more astray 3478
17: 2 speak a parable unto the house of I; 3478
17:23 In the mountain of the height of I will I 3478
18: 2 use this proverb concerning the land of I, 3478
18: 3 *occasion* any more to use this proverb in I. 3478
18: 6 up his eyes to the idols of the house of I, 3478
18:15 up his eyes to the idols of the house of I, 3478
18:25 Hear now, O house of I; Is not my way 3478
18:29 Yet saith the house of I, The way of 3478
18:29 O house of I, are not my ways equal? 3478
18:30 Therefore I will judge you, O house of I, 3478
18:31 for why will ye die, O house of I? 3478
19: 1 thou up a lamentation for the princes of I, 3478
19: 9 no more be heard upon the mountains of I. 3478
20: 1 *that* certain of the elders of I came to 3478
20: 3 speak unto the elders of I, and say unto 3478
20: 5 In the day when I chose I, and lifted up 3478
20:13 the house of I rebelled against me in 3478
20:27 speak unto the house of I, and say unto 3478
20:30 Wherefore say unto the house of I, 3478
20:31 shall I be inquired of by you, O house of I? 3478
20:38 and they shall not enter into the land of I: 3478
20:39 As for you, O house of I, thus saith 3478
20:40 in the mountain of the height of I, saith 3478
20:40 Lord GOD, there shall all the house of I, 3478
20:42 when I shall bring you into the land of I, 3478

Eze 20:44 O ye house of I, saith the Lord GOD. 3478
21: 2 and prophesy against the land of I, 3478
21: 3 say to the land of I, Thus saith the LORD; 3478
21:12 it *shall be* upon all the princes of I: 3478
21:25 thou, profane wicked prince of I, 3478
22: 6 Behold, the princes of I, every one were in 3478
22:18 the house of I is to me become dross: 3478
24:21 Speak unto the house of I, Thus saith 3478
25: 3 against the land of I, when it was desolate; 3478
25: 6 with all thy despite against the land of I; 3478
25:14 upon Edom by the hand of my people I: 3478
27:17 Judah, and the land of I, they *were* thy 3478
28:24 more a pricking brier unto the house of I, 3478
28:25 When I shall have gathered the house of I 3478
29: 6 have been a staff of reed to the house of I. 3478
29:16 no more the confidence of the house of I, 3478
29:21 the horn of the house of I to bud forth, 3478
33: 7 set thee a watchman unto the house of I; 3478
33:10 thou son of man, speak unto the house of I; 3478
33:11 for why will ye die, O house of I? 3478
33:20 O ye house of I, I will judge you every one 3478
33:24 inhabit those wastes of the land of I speak, 3478
33:28 the mountains of I shall be desolate, 3478
34: 2 prophesy against the shepherds of I, 3478
34: 2 Woe *be* to the shepherds of I that do feed 3478
34:13 feed them upon the mountains of I by 3478
34:14 upon the high mountains of I shall their 3478
34:14 shall they feed upon the mountains of I. 3478
34:30 *that* they, *even* the house of I, *are* my 3478
35: 5 hast shed *the blood of* the children of I by 3478
35:12 hast spoken against the mountains of I, 3478
35:15 rejoice at the inheritance of the house of I, 3478
36: 1 prophesy unto the mountains of I, and say, 3478
36: 1 say, Ye mountains of I, hear the word of 3478
36: 4 Therefore, ye mountains of I, hear the word 3478
36: 6 therefore concerning the land of I, 3478
36: 8 ye, O mountains of I, ye shall shoot forth 3478
36: 8 and yield your fruit to my people of I; 3478
36:10 upon you, all the house of I, *even* all of it: 3478
36:12 men to walk upon you, *even* my people I; 3478
36:17 when the house of I dwelt in their own 3478
36:21 which the house of I had profaned among 3478
36:22 Therefore say unto the house of I, 3478
36:22 O house of I, but for mine holy name's 3478
36:32 for your own ways, O house of I. 3478
36:37 yet *for* this be inquired of by the house of I, 3478
37:11 these bones *are* the whole house of I: 3478
37:12 and bring you into the land of I. 3478
37:16 and for the children of I his companions: 3478
37:16 and *for* all the house of I his companions: 3478
37:19 the tribes of I his fellows, and will put them 3478
37:21 I *will* take the children of I from among 3478
37:22 nation in the land upon the mountains of I; 3478
37:28 shall know that I the LORD do sanctify I, 3478
38: 8 against the mountains of I, which have 3478
38:14 In that day when my people of I dwelleth 3478
38:16 thou shalt come up against my people of I, 3478
38:17 old time by my servants the prophets of I, 3478
38:18 when Gog shall come against the land of I, 3478
38:19 shall be a great shaking in the land of I; 3478
39: 2 will bring thee upon the mountains of I: 3478
39: 4 Thou shalt fall upon the mountains of I, 3478
39: 7 name known in the midst of my people I; 3478
39: 7 that I *am* the LORD, the Holy One in I. 3478
39: 9 they that dwell in the cities of I shall go 3478
39:11 give unto Gog a place there of graves in I, 3478
39:12 seven months shall the house of I be 3478
39:17 a great sacrifice upon the mountains of I, 3478
39:22 So the house of I shall know that I *am* 3478
39:23 the heathen shall know that the house of I 3478
39:25 have mercy upon the whole house of I, and 3478
39:29 poured out my spirit upon the house of I, 3478
40: 2 of God brought he me into the land of I, 3478
40: 4 declare all that thou seest to the house of I. 3478
43: 2 the glory of the God of I came from 3478
43: 7 in the midst of the children of I for ever, 3478
43: 7 shall the house of I no more defile, 3478
43:10 of man, shew the house to the house of I, 3478
44: 2 because the LORD, the God of I, 3478
44: 6 *even* to the house of I, Thus saith the Lord 3478
44: 6 O ye house of I, let it suffice you of all 3478
44: 9 any stranger that *is* among the children of I. 3478
44:10 away far from me, when I went astray, 3478
44:12 caused the house of I to fall into iniquity; 3478
44:15 the children of I went astray from me, 3478
44:22 take maidens of the seed of the house of I, 3478
44:28 ye shall give them no possession in I: I *am* 3478
44:29 and every dedicate thing in I shall be theirs. 3478
45: 6 *portion:* it shall be for the whole house of I. 3478
45: 8 In the land shall be his possession in I: and 3478
45: 8 to the house of I according to their tribes. 3478
45: 9 Let it suffice you, O princes of I: 3478
45:15 of two hundred, out of the fat pastures of I; 3478
45:16 shall give this oblation for the prince in I. 3478
45:17 in all solemnities of the house of I: 3478
45:17 to make reconciliation for the house of I. 3478
47:13 the land according to the twelve tribes of I: 3478
47:18 and from the land of I *by* Jordan, 3478
47:21 land unto you according to the tribes of I. 3478
47:22 in the country among the children of I; 3478
47:22 inheritance with you among the tribes of I. 3478
48:11 astray when the children of I went astray, 3478
48:19 city shall serve it out of all the tribes of I. 3478
48:29 *by lot* unto the tribes of I for inheritance, 3478
48:31 *shall be* after the names of the tribes of I: 3478
Da 1: 3 *he* should bring *certain* of the children of I, 3478
9: 7 unto all I, *that are* near, and *that are* far off, 3478
9:11 Yea, all I have transgressed thy law, 3478
9:20 my sin and the sin of my people I, 3478
Hos 1: 1 of Jeroboam the son of Joash, king of I. 3478
1: 4 to cease the kingdom of the house of I. 3478
1: 5 that I will break the bow of I in the valley 3478
1: 6 no more have mercy upon the house of I; 3478
1:10 Yet the number of the children of I shall be 3478
1:11 and the children of I be gathered together, 3478

Hos 3: 1 of the LORD toward the children of **I**, 3478
3: 4 For the children of **I** shall abide many days 3478
3: 5 Afterward shall the children of **I** return, and 3478
4: 1 the word of the LORD, ye children of **I**: 3478
4:15 Though thou, **I**, play the harlot, *yet* let not 3478
4:16 For **I** slideth back as a backsliding heifer: 3478
5: 1 hearken, ye house of **I**; and give ye ear, 3478
5: 3 I know Ephraim, and **I** is not hid from me: 3478
5: 3 committest whoredom, *and* **I** is defiled. 3478
5: 5 the pride of **I** doth testify to his face: 3478
5: 5 therefore shall **I** and Ephraim fall in their 3478
5: 9 among the tribes of **I** have I made known 3478
6:10 have seen a horrible thing in the house of **I**: 3478
6:10 *is* the whoredom of Ephraim, **I** is defiled. 3478
7: 1 When I *would have* healed **I**, then 3478
7:10 the pride of **I** testifieth to his face: and 3478
8: 2 **I** shall cry unto me, My God, we know 3478
8: 3 **I** hath cast off *the thing that is* good: 3478
8: 6 For from **I** *was* it also: the workman made 3478
8: 8 **I** is swallowed up: now shall they be 3478
8:14 For **I** hath forgotten his Maker, and 3478
9: 1 Rejoice not, O **I**, for joy, as *other* people: 3478
9: 7 **I** shall know *it:* the prophet *is* a fool, 3478
9:10 I found **I** like grapes in the wilderness; 3478
10: 1 **I** *is* an empty vine, he bringeth forth fruit 3478
10: 6 and **I** shall be ashamed of his own counsel. 3478
10: 8 of Aven, the sin of **I**, shall be destroyed: 3478
10: 9 O **I**, thou hast sinned from the days of 3478
10:15 in a morning shall the king of **I** utterly be 3478
11: 1 When **I** *was* a child, then I loved him, and 3478
11: 8 *how* shall I deliver thee, **I**? how shall I 3478
11:12 with lies, and the house of **I** with deceit: 3478
12:12 **I** served for a wife, and for a wife he kept 3478
12:13 by a prophet the LORD brought **I** out of 3478
13: 1 spake trembling, he exalted *himself* in **I**; 3478
13: 9 O **I**, *thou* hast destroyed thyself; but in me 3478
14: 1 O **I**, return unto the LORD thy God; 3478
14: 5 I will be as the dew unto **I**: he shall grow as 3478
Joel 2:27 ye shall know that I *am* in the midst of **I**, 3478
3: 2 there for my people and *for* my heritage **I**, 3478
3:16 and the strength of the children of **I**. 3478
Am 1: 1 which he saw concerning **I** in the days of 3478
1: 1 of Jeroboam the son of Joash king of **I**, 3478
2: 6 For three transgressions of **I**, and for four, 3478
2:11 *Is it* not even thus, O ye children of **I**? 3478
3: 1 hath spoken against you, O children of **I**, 3478
3:12 shall the children of **I** be taken out that 3478
3:14 **I** upon him I will also visit the altars of 3478
4: 5 for this liketh you, O ye children of **I**, 3478
4:12 Therefore thus will I do unto thee, O **I**: *and* 3478
4:12 unto thee, prepare to meet thy God, O **I**. 3478
5: 1 *even* a lamentation, O house of **I**. 3478
5: 2 The virgin of **I** is fallen; she shall no more 3478
5: 3 hundred shall leave ten, to the house of **I**. 3478
5: 4 thus saith the LORD unto the house of **I**, 3478
5:25 in the wilderness forty years, O house of **I**? 3478
6: 1 the nations, to whom the house of **I** came! 3478
6:14 O house of **I**, saith the LORD the God of 3478
7: 8 set a plumbline in the midst of my people **I**: 3478
7: 9 and the sanctuaries of **I** shall be laid waste; 3478
7:10 priest of Beth-el sent to Jeroboam king of **I**, 3478
7:10 against thee in the midst of the house of **I**: 3478
7:11 **I** shall surely be led away captive out of 3478
7:15 unto me, Go, prophesy unto my people **I**. 3478
7:16 Prophesy not against **I**, and drop not *thy* 3478
7:17 **I** shall surely go into captivity forth of his 3478
8: 2 The end is come upon my people *of* **I**; 3478
9: 7 of the Ethiopians unto me, O children of **I**? 3478
9: 7 Have not I brought up **I** out of the land of 3478
9: 9 I will sift the house of **I** among all nations, 3478
9:14 bring again the captivity of my people of **I**, 3478
Ob 1:20 the captivity of this host of the children of **I** 3478
Mic 1: 5 *is* all this, and for the sins of the house of **I**. 3478
1:13 for the transgressions of **I** were found in 3478
1:14 of Achzib *shall be* a lie to the kings of **I**. 3478
1:15 he shall come unto Adullam the glory of **I**. 3478
2:12 I will surely gather the remnant of **I**; 3478
3: 1 of Jacob, and ye princes of the house of **I**; 3478
3: 8 Jacob his transgression, and to **I** his sin. 3478
3: 9 princes of the house of **I**, that abhor 3478
5: 1 they shall smite the judge of **I** with a rod 3478
5: 2 come forth unto me *that is* to be ruler in **I**; 3478
5: 3 brethren shall return unto the children of **I**. 3478
6: 2 with his people, and he will plead with **I**. 3478
Na 2: 2 excellency of Jacob, as the excellency of **I**: 3478
Zep 2: 9 saith the LORD of hosts, the God of **I**, 3478
3:13 The remnant of **I** shall not do iniquity, 3478
3:14 shout, O **I**; be glad and rejoice with all 3478
3:15 the king of **I**, *even* the LORD, *is* in 3478
Zec 1:19 have scattered Judah, **I**, and Jerusalem. 3478
8:13 O house of Judah, and house of **I**; 3478
9: 1 the eyes of man, as of all the tribes of **I**, 3478
11:14 break the brotherhood between Judah and **I**. 3478
12: 1 burden of the word of the LORD for **I**, 3478
Mal 1: 1 The burden of the word of the LORD to **I** 3478
1: 5 will be magnified from the border of **I**. 3478
2:11 an abomination is committed in **I** and 3478
2:16 *For* the LORD, the God of **I**, saith that he 3478
4: 4 I commanded unto him in Horeb for all **I**, 3478
Mt 2: 6 a Governor, that shall rule my people **I**. *2474*
2:20 and his mother, and go into the land of **I**: *2474*
2:21 and his mother, and came into the land of **I**. *2474*
8:10 I have not found so great faith, no not in **I**. *2474*
9:33 saying, It was never so seen in **I**. *2474*
10: 6 go rather to the lost sheep of the house of **I**. *2474*
10:23 Ye shall not have gone over the cities of **I**, *2474*
15:24 but unto the lost sheep of the house of **I**. *2474*
15:31 to see: and they glorified the God of **I**. *2474*
19:28 judging the twelve tribes of **I**. *2474*
27: 9 whom they of the children of **I** did value; *2474*
27:42 If he be the King of **I**, let him now come *2474*
Mk 12:29 first of all the commandments *is*, Hear, O **I**; *2474*
15:32 Let Christ the King of **I** descend now from *2474*
Lk 1:16 And many of the children of **I** shall he turn *2474*
1:54 He hath holpen his servant **I**, *2474*
Lk 1:68 Blessed *be* the Lord God of **I**; for he hath *2474*
1:80 deserts till the day of his shewing unto **I**. *2474*
2:25 devout, waiting for the consolation of **I**: *2474*
2:32 the Gentiles, and the glory of thy people **I**. *2474*
2:34 for the fall and rising again of many in **I**; *2474*
4:25 many widows were in **I** in the days of *2474*
4:27 And many lepers were in **I** in the time of *2474*
7: 9 I have not found so great faith, no, not in **I**. *2474*
22:30 sit on thrones judging the twelve tribes of **I**. *2474*
24:21 had been he which should have redeemed **I**: *2474*
Jn 1:31 but that he should be made manifest to **I**, *2474*
1:49 art the Son of God; thou art the King of **I**. *2474*
3:10 Art thou a master of **I**, and knowest not *2474*
12:13 Blessed *is* the King of **I** that cometh in *2474*
Ac 1: 6 at this time restore again the kingdom to **I**? *2474*
2:22 Ye men **of I**, hear these words; Jesus of *2475*
2:36 Therefore let all the house of **I** know *2474*
3:12 Ye men **of I**, why marvel ye at this? *2475*
4: 8 Ye rulers of the people, and elders of **I**, *2474*
4:10 unto you all, and to all the people of **I**, *2474*
4:27 with the Gentiles, and the people of **I**, *2474*
5:21 and all the senate of the children of **I**, and *2474*
5:31 for to give repentance to **I**, and *2474*
5:35 And said unto them, Ye men **of I**, take heed *2475*
7:23 heart to visit his brethren the children of **I**. *2474*
7:37 which said unto the children of **I**, *2474*
7:42 O *ye* house of **I**, have ye offered to me slain *2474*
9:15 and kings, and the children of **I**: *2474*
10:36 word which *God* sent unto the children of **I**, *2474*
13:16 Men of **I**, and *ye* that fear God, *2475*
13:17 The God of this people of **I** chose our *2474*
13:23 to *his* promise raised unto **I** a Saviour, *2474*
13:24 baptism of repentance to all the people of **I**. *2474*
21:28 Crying out, Men **of I**, help: This is the man, *2475*
28:20 that for the hope of **I** I am bound with this *2474*
Ro 9: 6 For they *are* not all **I**, which are of Israel: *2474*
9: 6 For they *are* not all Israel, which are of **I**: *2474*
9:27 Esaias also crieth concerning **I**, Though *2474*
9:27 Though the number of the children of **I** be *2474*
9:31 But **I**, which followed *after* the law of *2474*
10: 1 heart's desire and prayer to God for **I** is, *2474*
10:19 But I say, Did not **I** know? First Moses *2474*
10:21 But to **I** he saith, All day long have I *2474*
11: 2 he maketh intercession to God against **I**, *2474*
11: 7 **I** hath not obtained that which he seeketh *2474*
11:25 that blindness in part is happened to **I**, *2474*
11:26 And so all **I** shall be saved: as it is written, *2474*
1Co 10:18 Behold **I** after the flesh: are not they which *2474*
2Co 3: 7 that the children of **I** could not stedfastly *2474*
3:13 that the children of **I** could not stedfastly *2474*
Gal 6:16 and mercy, and upon the **I** of God. *2474*
Eph 2:12 being aliens from the commonwealth of **I**, *2474*
Php 3: 5 of the stock of **I**, of the tribe of Benjamin, *2474*
Heb 8: 8 make a new covenant with the house of **I** *2474*
8:10 make with the house of **I** after those days, *2474*
11:22 of the departing of the children of **I**; *2474*
Rev 2:14 a stumblingblock before the children of **I**, *2474*
7: 4 of all the tribes of the children of **I**. *2474*
21:12 of the twelve tribes of the children of **I**: *2474*

ISRAEL'S (10) [ISRAEL]

Ge 48:13 Ephraim in his right hand toward **I** left 3478
48:13 Manasseh in his left hand towards **I** right 3478
Ex 18: 8 and to the Egyptians for **I** sake, 3478
Nu 1:20 **I** eldest son, *by* their generations, after their 3478
31:30 of the children of **I** half, thou shalt take one 3478
31:42 of the children of **I** half, which Moses 3478
31:47 Even of the children of **I** half, Moses took 3478
Dt 21: 8 lay not innocent blood unto thy people of **I** 3478
2Sa 5:12 exalted his kingdom for his people **I** sake. 3478
2Ki 3:11 one of the king of **I** servants answered and 3478

ISRAELITE (4) [ISRAEL]

Nu 25:14 Now the name of the **I** that was slain, 376+3478
2Sa 17:25 a man's son, whose name *was* Ithra an **I**, 3481
Jn 1:47 and saith of him, Behold an **I** indeed, *2475*
Ro 11: 1 For I also am an **I**, of the seed of Abraham, *2475*

ISRAELITES (18) [ISRAEL]

Ex 9: 7 there was not one of the cattle of the **I** dead. 3478
Lev 23:42 all that are **I** born shall dwell in booths: 3478
Jos 3:17 all the **I** passed over on dry *ground,* until all 3478
8:24 that all the **I** returned *unto* Ai, and smote it 3478
13: 6 only divide thou it *by lot* unto the **I** for an 3478
13:13 the Maachathites dwell among the **I** until 3478
Jdg 20:21 destroyed *down* to the ground of the **I** that 3478
1Sa 2:14 So they did in Shiloh unto all the **I** that 3478
13:20 all the **I** went down *to* the Philistines, 3478
14:21 even they also *turned* to be with the **I** that 3478
25: 1 all the **I** were gathered together, and 3478
29: 1 the **I** pitched by a fountain which *is* in 3478
2Sa 4: 1 were feeble, and all the **I** were troubled. 3478
2Ki 3:24 the **I** rose up and smote the Moabites, so 3478
7:13 the multitude of the **I** that are consumed:) 3478
1Ch 9: 2 their possessions in their cities *were,* the **I**, 3478
Ro 9: 4 Who are **I**; to whom pertaineth *2475*
2Co 11:22 Are they **I**? so *am* I. Are they the seed of *2475*

ISRAELITISH (3) [ISRAEL]

Lev 24:10 the son of an **I** woman, whose father *was* 3482
24:10 *this* son of the **I** *woman* and a man of Israel 3482
24:11 the **I** woman's son blasphemed the name *of* 3482

ISSACHAR (43) [ISACHAR]

Ge 30:18 to my husband: and she called his name **I**. 3485
35:23 and Levi, and Judah, and **I**, and Zebulun: 3485
46:13 the sons of **I**; Tola, and Phuvah, and Job, 3485
49:14 **I** *is* a strong ass couching down between 3485
Ex 1: 3 **I**, Zebulun, and Benjamin, 3485
Nu 1: 8 Of **I**; Nethaneel the son of Zuar. 3485
1:28 Of the children of **I**, *by* their generations, 3485
1:29 *even* of the tribe of **I**, *were* fifty and 3485
2: 5 pitch next unto him *shall be* the tribe of **I**: 3485
2: 5 of Zuar *shall be* captain of the children of **I**. 3485
Nu 7:18 the son of Zuar, prince of **I**, did offer: 3485
10:15 of **I** *was* Nethaneel the son of Zuar. 3485
13: 7 Of the tribe of **I**, Igal the son of Joseph. 3485
26:23 *Of* the sons of **I** after their families: 3485
26:25 These *are* the families of **I** according to 3485
34:26 the prince of the tribe of the children of **I**, 3485
Dt 27:12 Judah, and **I**, and Joseph, and Benjamin: 3485
33:18 in thy going out; and, **I**, in thy tents. 3485
Jos 17:10 in Asher on the north, and in **I** on the east. 3485
17:11 Manasseh had in **I** and in Asher Beth-shean 3485
19:17 *And* the fourth lot came out to **I**, for 3485
19:17 for the children of **I** according to their 3485
19:23 the children of **I** according to their families, 3485
21: 6 by lot out of the families of the tribe of **I**, 3485
21:28 out of the tribe of **I**, Kishon with her 3485
Jdg 5:15 the princes of **I** *were* with Deborah; 3485
5:15 *were* with Deborah; even **I**, *and* also Barak: 3485
10: 1 son of Puah, the son of Dodo, a man of **I**; 3485
1Ki 4:17 Jehoshaphat the son of Paruah, in **I**: 3485
15:27 of the house of **I**, conspired against him; 3485
1Ch 2: 1 Simeon, Levi, and Judah, **I**, and Zebulun, 3485
6:62 their families out of the tribe of **I**, 3485
6:72 out of the tribe of **I**; Kedesh with her 3485
7: 1 Now the sons of **I** *were,* Tola, and Puah, 3485
7: 5 their brethren among all the families of **I** 3485
12:32 of the children of **I**, *which were men* that 3485
12:40 *even* unto **I** and Zebulun and Naphtali, 3485
26: 5 Ammiel the sixth, **I** the seventh, 3485
27:18 of David: of **I**, Omri the son of Michael: 3485
2Ch 30:18 of Ephraim, and Manasseh, **I**, and Zebulun, 3485
Eze 48:25 the east side unto the west side, **I** a *portion.* 3485
48:26 by the border of **I**, from the east side unto 3485
48:33 one gate of Simeon, one gate of **I**, one gate 3485

ISSHIAH (3)

1Ch 24:21 of the sons of Rehabiah, the first *was* **I**. 3449
24:25 The brother of Michah *was* **I**: of the sons of 3449
24:25 *was* Isshiah: of the sons of **I**; Zechariah. 3449

ISSUE (40) [ISSUED, ISSUES]

Ge 48: 6 thy **i**, which thou begettest after them, 4138
Lev 12: 7 she shall be cleansed from the **i** of her 4726
15: 2 When any man hath a **running i** out of his 2100
15: 2 of his flesh, *because of* his **i** he *is* unclean. 2101
15: 3 this shall be his uncleanness in his **i**: 2101
15: 3 *whether* his flesh run with his **i**, or his flesh 2101
15: 3 or his flesh be stopped from his **i**, it *is* his 2101
15: 4 whereon he lieth that hath the **i**, is unclean: 2100
15: 6 he sat that hath the **i** shall wash his clothes, 2100
15: 7 of him that hath the **i** shall wash his clothes, 2100
15: 8 if he that hath the **i** spit upon him that is 2100
15: 9 rideth upon that hath the **i** shall be unclean. 2100
15:11 whomsoever he toucheth that hath the **i**, 2100
15:12 that he toucheth which hath the **i**, shall be 2100
15:13 when he that hath an **i** is cleansed of his 2100
15:13 he that hath an issue is cleansed of his **i**; 2101
15:15 for him before the LORD for his **i**. 2101
15:19 If a woman have an **i**, *and* her issue in her 2100
15:19 an issue, *and* her **i** in her flesh be blood, 2101
15:25 if a woman **have an i** of her blood 2100+2101
15:25 all the days of the **i** of her uncleanness shall 2101
15:26 **i** shall be unto her as the bed of her 2101
15:28 if she be cleansed of her **i**, then she shall 2101
15:30 the LORD for the **i** of her uncleanness. 2101
15:32 This *is* the law of him that hath an **i**, and 2100
15:33 of him that hath an **i**, of the man, and of 2101
22: 4 of Aaron *is* a leper, or hath a **running i**; 2100
Nu 5: 2 every one that hath an **i**, and whosoever is 2100
2Sa 3:29 from the house of Joab one that **hath an i**, 2100
2Ki 20:18 of thy sons that shall **i** from thee, 3318
Isa 22:24 the offspring and the **i**, all vessels of small 6849
39: 7 of thy sons that shall **i** from thee, 3318
Eze 23:20 and whose **i** *is like* the issue of horses. 2231
23:20 and whose issue *is like* the **i** of horses. 2231
47: 8 These waters **i out** toward the east country, 3318
Mt 9:20 which was **diseased with an i of blood** *131*
22:25 and, having no **i**, left his wife unto his *4690*
Mk 5:25 which had an **i** of blood twelve years, *4511*
Lk 8:43 And a woman having an **i** of blood twelve *4511*
8:44 and immediately her **i** of blood stanched. *4511*

ISSUED (7) [ISSUE]

Jos 8:22 And the other **i out** of the city against them; 3318
Job 38: 8 brake forth, *as if* it had **i out** of the womb? 3318
Eze 47: 1 waters **i out** from under the threshold of 3318
47:12 their waters they **i out** of the sanctuary: 3318
Da 7:10 A fiery stream **i** and came forth from before 5047
Rev 9:17 and out of their mouths **i** fire and smoke *1607*
9:18 the brimstone, which **i out** of their mouths. *1607*

ISSUES (2) [ISSUE]

Ps 68:20 unto GOD the Lord *belong* the **i** from 8444
Pr 4:23 all diligence; for out of it *are* the **i** of life. 8444

ISUAH (1)

1Ch 7:30 **I**, and Ishuai, and Beriah, and Serah their 3440

IT (6132) [HOWBEIT, ITSELF] See Index of Articles, Etc.

ITALIAN (1) [ITALY]

Ac 10: 1 a centurion of the band called the **I** *band,* *2483*

ITALY (5) [ITALIAN]

Ac 18: 2 born in Pontus, lately come from **I**, with his *2482*
27: 1 it was determined that we should sail into **I**, *2482*
27: 6 found a ship of Alexandria sailing into **I**; *2482*
Heb 13:24 and all the saints. They of **I** salute you. *2482*
13: S Written to the Hebrews from **I** by Timothy. *2482*

ITCH (1) [ITCHING]

Dt 28:27 and with the scab, and with the **i**, 2775

ITCHING (1) [ITCH]
2Ti 4: 3 heap to themselves teachers, having **i** ears; *2833*

ITHAI (1)
1Ch 11:31 **I** the son of Ribai of Gibeah, that pertained 863

ITHAMAR (21)
Ex 6:23 bare him Nadab, and Abihu, Eleazar, and **I**. 385
28: 1 Nadab and Abihu, Eleazar and **I**, 385
38:21 by the hand of **I**, son to Aaron the priest. 385
Lev 10: 6 unto Eleazar and unto **I** his sons, 385
10:12 and unto **I** his sons that were left, 385
10:16 **I** the sons of Aaron which were left *alive,* 385
Nu 3: 2 the firstborn, and Abihu, Eleazar, and **I**. 385
3: 4 **I** ministered in the priest's office in the sight 385
4:28 their charge *shall be* under the hand of **I** 385
4:33 under the hand of **I** the son of Aaron 385
7: 8 under the hand of **I** the son of Aaron 385
26:60 was born Nadab, and Abihu, Eleazar, and **I**. 385
1Ch 6: 3 of Aaron; Nadab, and Abihu, Eleazar, and **I**. 385
24: 1 of Aaron; Nadab, and Abihu, Eleazar, and **I**. 385
24: 2 Eleazar and **I** executed the priest's office. 385
24: 3 of Eleazar, and Ahimelech of the sons of **I**, 385
24: 4 of the sons of Eleazar than of the sons of **I**; 385
24: 4 eight among the sons of **I** according to 385
24: 5 of the sons of Eleazar, and of the sons of **I**. 385
24: 6 being taken for Eleazar, and *one* taken for **I**. 385
Ezr 8: 2 of the sons of **I**; Daniel: of the sons of 385

ITHIEL (3)
Ne 11: 7 of Maaseiah, the son of **I**, the son of Jesaiah. 384
Pr 30: 1 the man spake unto **I**, even unto Ithiel and 384
30: 1 man spake unto Ithiel, even unto **I** and Ucal. 384

ITHLAH See JETHLAH

ITHMAH (1)
1Ch 11:46 the sons of Elnaam, and **I** the Moabite, 3495

ITHNAN (1)
Jos 15:23 And Kedesh, and Hazor, and **I**, 3497

J

ITHRA (1)
2Sa 17:25 man's son, whose name *was* **I** an Israelite, 3501

ITHRAN (3)
Ge 36:26 Hemdan, and Eshban, and **I**, and Cheran. 3506
1Ch 1:41 Amram, and Eshban, and **I**, and Cheran. 3506
7:37 Shamma, and Shilshah, and **I**, and Beera. 3506

ITHREAM (2)
2Sa 3: 5 the sixth, **I**, by Eglah David's wife. 3507
1Ch 3: 3 of Abital: the sixth, **I** by Eglah his wife. 3507

ITHRITE (4)
2Sa 23:38 Ira an **I**, Gareb an Ithrite, 3505
23:38 Ira an Ithrite, Gareb an **I**, 3505
1Ch 11:40 Ira the **I**, Gareb the Ithrite, 3505
11:40 Ira the Ithrite, Gareb the **I**, 3505

ITHRITES (1)
1Ch 2:53 the **I**, and the Puhites, and the Shumathites, 3505

ITSELF (50) [IT, SELF]
Ge 1:11 whose seed *is* in **i**, upon the earth: 2050.2
1:12 whose seed *was* in **i**, after his kind: 2050.2
Lev 7:24 the fat of the **beast that dieth of i**, and 5038
17:15 every soul that eateth **that which died of i**, 5038
18:25 and the land **i** vomiteth out her inhabitants. NIH
22: 8 **That which dieth of i**, or is torn *with* 5038
25:11 neither reap **that which groweth of i** in it, 5599
Dt 14:21 Ye shall not eat of any thing that **dieth of i**: 5038
1Ki 7:34 *and* the undersetters *were* of the *very* base **i**. NIH
Job 10:22 A land of darkness, as darkness **i**; *and of* NIH
Ps 41: 6 his heart gathereth iniquity to **i**; *when* he 2050.2
68: 8 *even* Sinai **i** *was moved* at the presence of 2088
Pr 18: 2 but that his heart may discover **i**. NIH
23:31 colour in the cup, *when* it moveth **i** aright. NIH
27:16 of his right hand, *which* bewrayeth **i**. NIH
27:25 the tender grass sheweth **i**, and herbs of NIH
Isa 10:15 Shall the axe boast **i** against him that NIH
10:15 shall the saw magnify **i** against him that NIH
10:15 as if the rod should shake **i** *against* them that NIH
10:15 as if the staff should lift up **i**, *as if it were* no NIH
37:30 Ye shall eat *this* year **such as groweth of i**; 5599
55: 2 and let your soul delight **i** in fatness. NIH
60:20 go down; neither shall thy moon withdraw **i**: NIH
Jer 31:24 there shall dwell in Judah **i**, and *in* all 1886.3
Eze 1: 4 a fire infolding **i**, and a brightness *was* about NIH
4:14 have I not eaten *of* that which **dieth of i**, 5038
17:14 that *it* might not lift **i** up, *but* that by keeping NIH
29:15 neither shall it exalt **i** any more above NIH
44:31 shall not eat *of* any thing **that is dead of i**, 5038
Da 7: 5 it raised up **i** on one side, and *it had* three NIH
Mt 6:34 shall take thought for the *things* of **i**. *1438*
12:25 Every kingdom divided against **i** is brought *1438*
12:25 or house divided against **i** shall not stand: *1438*
Mk 3:24 And if a kingdom be divided against **i**, *1438*
3:25 And if a house be divided against **i**, *1438*
Lk 11:17 Every kingdom divided against **i** is brought *1438*
Jn 15: 4 As the branch cannot bear fruit of **i**, *1438*
20: 7 but wrapped together in a place **by i**. *5565*
21:25 I suppose that even the world **i** could not *846*
Ro 8:16 The Spirit **i** beareth witness with our spirit, *846*
8:21 Because the creature **i** also shall be delivered *846*
8:26 the Spirit **i** maketh intercession for us with *846*
14:14 that *there is* nothing unclean of **i**: *1438*
1Co 11:14 Doth not even nature **i** teach you, that, if a *846*
13: 4 charity vaunteth not **i**, is not puffed up, NIG
13: 5 Doth not behave **i** unseemly, seeketh not her NIG
2Co 10: 5 every high thing that exalteth **i** against NIG
Eph 4:16 of the body unto the edifying of **i** in love. *1438*
Heb 9:24 but into heaven **i**, now to appear in *846*
3Jn 1:12 good report of all *men,* and of the truth **i**: *846*

ITTAH-KAZIN (1)
Jos 19:13 to **I**, and goeth out *to* Remmon-methoar *to* 6278

ITTAI (8)
2Sa 15:19 said the king to **I** the Gittite, Wherefore 863
15:21 **I** answered the king, and said, *As* 863
15:22 David said to **I**, Go and pass over. And Ittai 863
15:22 **I** the Gittite passed over, and all his men, 863
18: 2 a third part under the hand of **I** the Gittite. 863
18: 5 king commanded Joab and Abishai and **I**, 863
18:12 the king charged thee and Abishai and **I**, 863
23:29 **I** the son of Ribai out of Gibeah of 863

ITUREA (1)
Lk 3: 1 and his brother Philip tetrarch of **I** and *2484*

IVAH (3)
2Ki 18:34 *are* the gods of Sepharvaim, Hena, and **I**? 5755
19:13 of the city of Sepharvaim, *of* Hena, and **I**? 5755
Isa 37:13 of the city of Sepharvaim, Hena, and **I**? 5755

IVORY (13)
1Ki 10:18 Moreover the king made a great throne of **i**, 8127
10:22 and silver, **i**, and apes, and peacocks. 8143
22:39 the **i** house which he made, and all 8127
2Ch 9:17 Moreover the king made a great throne of **i**, 8127
9:21 and silver, **i**, and apes, and peacocks. 8143
Ps 45: 8 and aloes, *and* cassia, out of the **i** palaces, 8127
SS 5:14 his belly *is as* bright **i** overlaid *with* 8127
7: 4 Thy neck *is* as a tower of **i**; thine eyes *like* 8127
Eze 27: 6 the Ashurites have made thy benches *of* **i**, 8127
27:15 they brought thee *for* a present horns of **i** 8127
Am 3:15 the houses of **i** shall perish, and the great 8127
6: 4 That lie upon beds of **i**, and 8127
Rev 18:12 and all *manner* vessels of **i**, and all *manner* *1661*

IVVAH See IVAH

IYE ABARIM See IJE-ABARIM

IZEHAR (1) [IZEHARITES]
Nu 3:19 Amram, and **I**, Hebron, and Uzziel. 3324

IZEHARITES (1) [IZEHAR]
Nu 3:27 the family of the **I**, and the family of 3325

IZHAR (8) [IZHARITES]
Ex 6:18 Amram, and **I**, and Hebron, and Uzziel: 3324
6:21 the sons of **I**; Korah, and Nepheg, and 3324
Nu 16: 1 Now Korah, the son of **I**, the son of 3324
1Ch 6: 2 Amram, **I**, and Hebron, and Uzziel. 3324
6:18 and **I**, and Hebron, and Uzziel. 3324
6:38 The son of **I**, the son of Kohath, the son of 3324
23:12 Amram, **I**, Hebron, and Uzziel, four. 3324
23:18 *Of* the sons of **I**; Shelomith the chief. 3324

IZHARITES (3) [IZHAR]
1Ch 24:22 Of the **I**; Shelomoth: of the sons of 3325
26:23 *and* the **I**, the Hebronites, *and* 3325
26:29 Of the **I**, Chenaniah and his sons *were* for 3325

IZLIAH See JEZLIAH

IZRAHIAH (2)
1Ch 7: 3 the sons of Uzzi; **I**: and the sons of 3156
7: 3 the sons of **I**; Michael, and Obadiah, and 3156

IZRAHITE (1)
1Ch 27: 8 for the fifth month *was* Shamhuth the **I**: 3155

IZRI (1)
1Ch 25:11 The fourth to **I**, *he,* his sons, and 3339

IZZIAH See JEZIAH

J

JAAKAN (1) [BENE-JAAKAN]
Dt 10: 6 Beeroth of the children of **J** *to* Mosera: 3292

JAAKOBAH (1)
1Ch 4:36 **J**, and Jeshohaiah, and Asaiah, and Adiel, 3291

JAALA (1) [JAALAH]
Ne 7:58 The children of **J**, the children of Darkon, 3279

JAALAH (1) [JAALA]
Ezr 2:56 The children of **J**, the children of Darkon, 3279

JAALAM (4)
Ge 36: 5 Aholibamah bare Jeush, and **J**, and Korah: 3281
36:14 she bare to Esau Jeush, and **J**, and Korah. 3281
36:18 duke Jeush, duke **J**, duke Korah: 3281
1Ch 1:35 Reuel, and Jeush, and **J**, and Korah. 3281

JAANAI (1)
1Ch 5:12 the next, and **J**, and Shaphat in Bashan. 3285

JAARE-OREGIM (1)
2Sa 21:19 where Elhanan the son of **J**, 3296

JAARESHIAH See JARESIAH

JAASAU (1)
Ezr 10:37 Mattaniah, Mattenai, and **J**, 3299

JAASIEL (1)
1Ch 27:21 of Benjamin, **J** the son of Abner: 3300

JAASU See JAASAU

JAAZANIAH (4)
2Ki 25:23 **J** the son of a Maachathite, they and 2970
Jer 35: 3 I took **J** the son of Jeremiah, the son of 2970
Eze 8:11 in the midst of them stood **J** the son of 2970
11: 1 among whom I saw **J** the son of Azur, and 2970

JAAZER (2)
Nu 21:32 Moses sent to spy out **J**, and they took 3270
32:35 And Atroth, Shophan, and **J**, and Jogbehah, 3270

JAAZIAH (2)
1Ch 24:26 *were* Mahli and Mushi: the sons of **J**; Beno. 3269
24:27 The sons of Merari by **J**; Beno, and 3269

JAAZIEL (1)
1Ch 15:18 **J**, and Shemiramoth, and Jehiel, and Unni, 3268

JABAL (1)
Ge 4:20 Adah bare **J**: he was the father of such as 2989

JABBOK (7)
Ge 32:22 his eleven sons, and passed over the ford **J**. 2999
Nu 21:24 possessed his land from Arnon unto **J**, 2999
Dt 2:37 *nor unto* any place of the river **J**, nor *unto* 2999
3:16 and the border, even unto the river **J**, 2999
Jos 12: 2 and *from* half Gilead, even unto the river **J**, 2999
Jdg 11:13 from Arnon even unto **J**, and unto Jordan: 2999
11:22 from Arnon even unto **J**, and from 2999

JABESH (12) [JABESH-GILEAD]
1Sa 11: 1 all the men of **J** said unto Nahash, Make a 3003
11: 3 the elders of **J** said unto him, Give us seven 3003
11: 5 they told him the tidings of the men of **J**. 3003
11: 9 and shewed *it* to the men of **J**; 3003
11:10 Therefore the men of **J** said, To morrow we 3003
31:12 and came to **J**, and burnt them there. 3003
31:13 buried *them* under a tree at **J**, and 3003
2Ki 15:10 Shallum the son of **J** conspired against him, 3003
15:13 Shallum the son of **J** *began* to reign in 3003
15:14 smote Shallum the son of **J** in Samaria, and 3003
1Ch 10:12 brought them to **J**, and buried their bones 3003
10:12 buried their bones under the oak in **J**, and 3003

JABESH-GILEAD (12) [GILEAD, JABESH]
Jdg 21: 8 there came none to the camp from **J** to 3003
21: 9 *there were* none of the inhabitants of **J** 3003
21:10 smite the inhabitants of **J** with the edge of 3003
21:12 they found among the inhabitants of **J** four 3003
21:14 they had saved alive of the women of **J**: 3003
1Sa 11: 1 came up, and encamped against **J**: 3003
11: 9 Thus shall ye say unto the men of **J**, 3003
31:11 when the inhabitants of **J** heard of that 3003
2Sa 2: 4 *That* the men of **J** *were they* that buried 3003
2: 5 David sent messengers unto the men of **J**, 3003
21:12 of Jonathan his son from the men of **J**, 3003
1Ch 10:11 when all **J** heard all that the Philistines had 3003

JABEZ (4)
1Ch 2:55 the families of the scribes which dwelt at **J**; 3258
4: 9 **J** was more honourable than his brethren: 3258
4: 9 his mother called his name **J**, saying, 3258
4:10 **J** called on the God of Israel, saying, 3258

JABIN (7) [JABIN'S]
Jos 11: 1 when **J** king of Hazor had heard *those* 2985
Jdg 4: 2 the LORD sold them into the hand of **J** 2985
4:17 for *there was* peace between **J** the king of 2985
4:23 So God subdued on that day **J** the king of 2985
4:24 prevailed against **J** the king of Canaan, 2985
4:24 until they had destroyed **J** king of Canaan. 2985
Ps 83: 9 as *to* Sisera, as *to* **J**, at the brook of Kison: 2985

JABIN'S (1) [JABIN]
Jdg 4: 7 the captain of **J** army, with his chariots and 2985

JABNEEL (2)
Jos 15:11 *to* mount Baalah, and went out *unto* **J**; 2995
19:33 and Adami, Nekeb, and **J**, unto Lakum; 2995

JABNEH (1)
2Ch 26: 6 the wall of **J**, and the wall of Ashdod, and 2996

JACAN See JACHAN

JACHAN (1)
1Ch 5:13 and Jorai, and **J**, and Zia, and Heber, seven. 3275

JACHIN (8) [JACHINITES]
Ge 46:10 **J**, and Zohar, and Shaul the son of a 3199
Ex 6:15 **J**, and Zohar, and Shaul the son of a 3199
Nu 26:12 of **J**, the family of the Jachinites: 3199
1Ki 7:21 right pillar, and called the name thereof **J**: 3199
1Ch 9:10 of the priests; Jedaiah, and Jehoiarib, and **J**, 3199
24:17 The one and twentieth to **J**, the two and 3199
2Ch 3:17 called the name of *that on* the right hand **J**, 3199
Ne 11:10 Of the priests: Jedaiah the son of Joiarib, **J**, 3199

JACHINITES (1) [JACHIN]
Nu 26:12 the Jaminites: of Jachin, the family of the **J**: 3200

JACINTH (2)
Rev 9:17 breastplates of fire, and of **j**, and brimstone: *5191*

Rev 21:20 the eleventh, a j; the twelfth, an amethyst. *5192*

JACKAL; JACKALS See DRAGON; DRAGONS; FOXES; MONSTERS

JACOB (358) [ISRAEL, JACOB'S]
Ge 25:26 on Esau's heel; and his name was called J: 3290
25:27 and J *was* a plain man, dwelling in tents. 3290
25:28 did eat of *his* venison: but Rebekah loved J. 3290
25:29 J sod pottage: and Esau came from 3290
25:30 Esau said to J, Feed me, I pray thee, 3290
25:31 And J said, Sell me *this* day thy birthright. 3290
25:33 J said, Swear to me *this* day; and he sware 3290
25:33 to him: and he sold his birthright unto J. 3290
25:34 J gave Esau bread and pottage of lentiles; 3290
27: 6 Rebekah spake unto J her son, saying, 3290
27:11 J said to Rebekah his mother, Behold, 3290
27:15 and put them upon J her younger son: 3290
27:17 had prepared, into the hand of her son J. 3290
27:19 J said unto his father, I *am* Esau thy 3290
27:21 Isaac said unto J, Come near, I pray thee, 3290
27:22 J went near unto Isaac his father; and 3290
27:30 as Isaac had made an end of blessing J, 3290
27:30 J was yet scarce gone out from 3290
27:36 he said, Is not he rightly named J? for he 3290
27:41 Esau hated J because of the blessing 3290
27:41 are at hand; then will I slay my brother J. 3290
27:42 she sent and called J her younger son, and 3290
27:46 if J take a wife of the daughters of Heth, 3290
28: 1 Isaac called J, and blessed him, and 3290
28: 5 Isaac sent away J: and he went to 3290
28: 6 When Esau saw that Isaac had blessed J, 3290
28: 7 that J obeyed his father and his mother, 3290
28:10 J went out from Beer-sheba, and 3290
28:16 J awaked out of his sleep, and he said, 3290
28:18 J rose up early in the morning, and took 3290
28:20 J vowed a vow, saying, If God will be with 3290
29: 1 J went on his journey, and came into 3290
29: 4 J said unto them, My brethren, whence *be* 3290
29:10 when J saw Rachel the daughter of Laban 3290
29:10 that J went near, and rolled the stone from 3290
29:11 J kissed Rachel, and lifted up his voice, 3290
29:12 J told Rachel that he *was* her father's 3290
29:13 when Laban heard the tidings of J his 3290
29:15 Laban said unto J, Because thou *art* my 3290
29:18 J loved Rachel; and said, I will serve thee 3290
29:20 J served seven years for Rachel; and 3290
29:21 J said unto Laban, Give *me* my wife, 3290
29:28 J did so, and fulfilled her week: and 3290
30: 1 when Rachel saw that she bare J no 3290
30: 1 said unto J, Give me children, or else I die. 3290
30: 4 handmaid to wife: and J went in unto her. 3290
30: 5 And Bilhah conceived, and bare J a son. 3290
30: 7 conceived again, and bare J a second son. 3290
30: 9 Zilpah her maid, and gave her J to wife. 3290
30:10 And Zilpah Leah's maid bare J a son. 3290
30:12 Zilpah Leah's maid bare J a second son. 3290
30:16 J came out of the field in the evening, and 3290
30:17 and she conceived, and bare J the fifth son. 3290
30:19 conceived again, and bare J the sixth son. 3290
30:25 that J said unto Laban, Send me away, 3290
30:31 J said, Thou shalt not give me any thing: 3290
30:36 three days' journey betwixt himself and J: 3290
30:36 and J fed the rest of Laban's flocks. 3290
30:37 J took him rods of green poplar, and of 3290
30:40 J did separate the lambs, and set the faces 3290
30:41 that J laid the rods before the eyes of 3290
31: 1 J hath taken away all that *was* our father's; 3290
31: 2 J beheld the countenance of Laban, and 3290
31: 3 the LORD said unto J, Return unto 3290
31: 4 J sent and called Rachel and Leah to 3290
31:11 God spake unto me in a dream, *saying,* J: 3290
31:17 J rose up, and set his sons and his wives 3290
31:20 J stale away unawares to Laban the Syrian, 3290
31:22 it was told Laban on the third day that J 3290
31:24 Take heed that thou speak not to J either 3290
31:25 Laban overtook J. Now Jacob had pitched 3290
31:25 Now J had pitched his tent in the mount: 3290
31:26 Laban said to J, What hast thou done, 3290
31:29 Take thou heed that thou speak not to J 3290
31:31 J answered and said to Laban, Because I 3290
31:32 For J knew not that Rachel had stolen 3290
31:36 J was wroth, and chode with Laban: and 3290
31:36 J answered and said to Laban, What *is* my 3290
31:43 Laban answered and said unto J, *These* 3290
31:45 J took a stone, and set it up *for* a pillar. 3290
31:46 J said unto his brethren, Gather stones; 3290
31:47 it Jegar-sahadutha: but J called it Galeed. 3290
31:51 Laban said to J, Behold this heap, 3290
31:53 And J sware by the fear of his father Isaac. 3290
31:54 J offered sacrifice upon the mount, and 3290
32: 1 J went on his way, and the angels of God 3290
32: 2 when J saw them, he said, This *is* God's 3290
32: 3 J sent messengers before him to Esau his 3290
32: 4 Thy servant J saith thus, I have sojourned 3290
32: 6 the messengers returned to J, saying, 3290
32: 7 J was greatly afraid and distressed: and 3290
32: 9 J said, O God of my father Abraham, and 3290
32:20 Behold, thy servant J *is* behind us. 3290
32:24 J was left alone; and there wrestled a man 3290
32:27 What *is* thy name? And he said, J. 3290
32:28 Thy name shall be called no more J, but 3290
32:29 J asked *him,* and said, Tell *me,* I pray thee, 3290
32:30 J called the name of the place Peniel: for I 3290
33: 1 J lifted up his eyes, and looked, and 3290
33:10 J said, Nay, I pray thee, if now I have 3290
33:17 J journeyed to Succoth, and built him a 3290
33:18 J came to Shalem, a city of Shechem, 3290
34: 1 daughter of Leah, which she bare unto J, 3290
34: 3 his soul clave unto Dinah the daughter of J, 3290
34: 5 J heard that he had defiled Dinah his 3290
34: 5 and J held his peace until they were come. 3290
34: 6 went out unto J to commune with him. 3290
34: 7 the sons of J came out of the field when 3290
Ge 34:13 the sons of J answered Shechem and 3290
34:25 that two of the sons of J, Simeon and Levi, 3290
34:27 The sons of J came upon the slain, and 3290
34:30 J said to Simeon and Levi, Ye have 3290
35: 1 God said unto J, Arise, go up to Beth-el, 3290
35: 2 J said unto his household, and to all that 3290
35: 4 they gave unto J all the strange gods which 3290
35: 4 J hid them under the oak which *was* by 3290
35: 5 and they did not pursue after the sons of J. 3290
35: 6 So J came to Luz, which *is* in the land of 3290
35: 9 God appeared unto J again, when he came 3290
35:10 God said unto him, Thy name *is* J: 3290
35:10 thy name shall not be called any more J, 3290
35:14 J set up a pillar in the place where he 3290
35:15 J called the name of the place where God 3290
35:20 J set a pillar upon her grave: that *is* 3290
35:22 Israel heard *it.* Now the sons of J were 3290
35:26 these *are* the sons of J, which were born to 3290
35:27 J came unto Isaac his father unto Mamre, 3290
35:29 and his sons Esau and J buried him. 3290
36: 6 the country from the face of his brother J. 3290
37: 1 J dwelt in the land wherein his father was a 3290
37: 2 These *are* the generations of J. Joseph, 3290
37:34 J rent his clothes, and put sackcloth upon 3290
42: 1 Now when J saw that there was corn in 3290
42: 1 J said unto his sons, Why do ye look one 3290
42: 4 J sent not with his brethren; 3290
42:29 they came unto J their father unto the land 3290
42:36 J their father said unto them, Me have ye 3290
45:25 came *into* the land of Canaan unto J their 3290
45:27 the spirit of J their father revived: 3290
46: 2 the visions of the night, and said, J, Jacob. 3290
46: 2 the visions of the night, and said, Jacob, J. 3290
46: 5 J rose up from Beer-sheba: and the sons of 3290
46: 5 the sons of Israel carried J their father, and 3290
46: 6 into Egypt, J, and all his seed with him: 3290
46: 8 which came into Egypt, J and his sons: 3290
46:15 which she bare unto J in Padan-aram, 3290
46:18 these she bare unto J, *even* sixteen souls. 3290
46:22 the sons of Rachel, which were born to J: 3290
46:25 his daughter, and she bare these unto J: 3290
46:26 All the souls that came with J into Egypt, 3290
46:27 all the souls of the house of J, which came 3290
47: 7 Joseph brought in J his father, and set him 3290
47: 7 him before Pharaoh: and J blessed Pharaoh. 3290
47: 8 Pharaoh said unto J, How old *art* thou? 3290
47: 9 J said unto Pharaoh, The days of the years 3290
47:10 J blessed Pharaoh, and went out from 3290
47:28 J lived in the land of Egypt seventeen 3290
47:28 so the whole age of J was an hundred forty 3290
48: 2 *one* told J, and said, Behold, thy son Joseph 3290
48: 3 J said unto Joseph, God Almighty appeared 3290
49: 1 J called unto his sons, and said, 3290
49: 2 yourselves together, and hear, ye sons of J; 3290
49: 7 I will divide them in J, and scatter them in 3290
49:24 strong by the hands of the mighty *God* of J; 3290
49:33 when J had made an end of commanding 3290
50:24 he sware to Abraham, to Isaac, and to J. 3290
Ex 1: 1 every man and his household came with J. 3290
1: 5 all the souls that came *out of* the loins of J 3290
2:24 with Abraham, with Isaac, and with J. 3290
3: 6 the God of Isaac, and the God of J. 3290
3:15 the God of Isaac, and the God of J, 3290
3:16 of Isaac, and of J, appeared unto me, 3290
4: 5 the God of Isaac, and the God of J, 3290
6: 3 unto Isaac, and unto J, by *the name of* God 3290
6: 8 to give it to Abraham, to Isaac, and to J; 3290
19: 3 Thus shalt thou say to the house of J, and 3290
33: 1 to Isaac, and to J, saying, Unto thy seed 3290
Lev 26:42 will I remember my covenant with J, and 3290
Nu 23: 7 curse me J, and come, defy Israel. 3290
23:10 Who can count the dust of J, and 3290
23:21 He hath not beheld iniquity in J, 3290
23:23 Surely *there is* no enchantment against J, 3290
23:23 according to *this* time it shall be said of J 3290
24: 5 O J, *and* thy tabernacles, O Israel! 3290
24:17 there shall come a Star out of J, and 3290
24:19 Out of J shall come *he* that shall have 3290
32:11 unto Abraham, unto Isaac, and unto J; 3290
Dt 1: 8 Abraham, Isaac, and J, to give unto them 3290
6:10 to Abraham, to Isaac, and to J, to give thee 3290
9: 5 unto thy fathers, Abraham, Isaac, and J. 3290
9:27 thy servants, Abraham, Isaac, and J; 3290
29:13 thy fathers, to Abraham, to Isaac, and to J. 3290
30:20 to Abraham, to Isaac, and to J, to give 3290
32: 9 *is* his people; J *is* the lot of his inheritance. 3290
33: 4 the inheritance of the congregation of J. 3290
33:10 They shall teach J thy judgments, and 3290
33:28 the fountain of J *shall be* upon a land of 3290
34: 4 unto Isaac, and unto J, saying, I will give it 3290
Jos 24: 4 I gave unto Isaac J and Esau: and I gave 3290
24: 4 J and his children went down *into* Egypt. 3290
24:32 in a parcel of ground which J bought of 3290
1Sa 12: 8 When J was come *into* Egypt, and 3290
2Sa 23: 1 the anointed of the God of J, and the sweet 3290
1Ki 18:31 to the number of the tribes of the sons of J, 3290
2Ki 13:23 Isaac, and J, and would not destroy them, 3290
17:34 the LORD commanded the children of J, 3290
1Ch 16:13 ye children of J, his chosen *ones.* 3290
16:17 hath confirmed the same to J for a law, 3290
Ps 14: 7 J shall rejoice, *and* Israel shall be glad. 3290
20: 1 the name of the God of J defend thee; 3290
22:23 all ye the seed of J, glorify him; and 3290
24: 6 them that seek him, that seek thy face, O J. 3290
44: 4 O God: command deliverances for J. 3290
46: 7 hosts *is* with us; the God of J *is* our refuge. 3290
46:11 hosts *is* with us; the God of J *is* our refuge. 3290
47: 4 for us, the excellency of J whom he loved. 3290
53: 6 J shall rejoice, *and* Israel shall be glad. 3290
59:13 let them know that God ruleth in J unto 3290
75: 9 for ever; I will sing *praises* to the God of J. 3290
76: 6 At thy rebuke, O God of J, both the chariot 3290
77:15 thy people, the sons of J and Joseph. 3290
78: 5 For he established a testimony in J, and 3290
78:21 so a fire was kindled against J, and 3290
Ps 78:71 young he brought him to feed J his people, 3290
79: 7 For they have devoured J, and laid waste 3290
81: 1 make a joyful noise unto the God of J. 3290
81: 4 statute for Israel, *and* a law of the God of J. 3290
84: 8 my prayer: give ear, O God of J. Selah. 3290
85: 1 thou hast brought back the captivity of J. 3290
87: 2 of Zion more than all the dwellings of J. 3290
94: 7 neither shall the God of J regard *it.* 3290
99: 4 executest judgment and righteousness in J. 3290
105: 6 his servant, ye children of J, his chosen. 3290
105:10 confirmed the same unto J for a law, *and* 3290
105:23 and J sojourned in the land of Ham. 3290
114: 1 the house of J from a people of strange 3290
114: 7 of the Lord, at the presence of the God of J; 3290
132: 2 *and* vowed unto the mighty *God* of J; 3290
132: 5 a habitation for the mighty *God* of J. 3290
135: 4 For the LORD hath chosen J unto 3290
146: 5 Happy *is he* that *hath* the God of J for his 3290
147:19 He sheweth his word unto J, his statutes 3290
Isa 2: 3 the LORD, to the house of the God of J; 3290
2: 5 O house of J, come ye, and let us walk in 3290
2: 6 hast forsaken thy people the house of J, 3290
8:17 that hideth his face from the house of J, 3290
9: 8 The Lord sent a word into J, and it hath 3290
10:20 and such as are escaped of the house of J, 3290
10:21 *even* the remnant of J, unto the mighty 3290
14: 1 For the LORD will have mercy on J, and 3290
14: 1 and they shall cleave to the house of J. 3290
17: 4 *that* the glory of J shall be made thin, and 3290
27: 6 He shall cause them that come of J to take 3290
27: 9 shall the iniquity of J be purged; 3290
29:22 concerning the house of J, 3290
29:22 of Jacob, J shall not now be ashamed, 3290
29:23 sanctify the Holy One of J, and shall fear 3290
40:27 sayest thou, O J, and speakest, O Israel, 3290
41: 8 *art* my servant, J whom I have chosen, 3290
41:14 thou worm J, *and* ye men of Israel; 3290
41:21 your strong *reasons,* saith the King of J. 3290
42:24 Who gave J for a spoil, and Israel to 3290
43: 1 O J, and he that formed thee, O Israel, 3290
43:22 thou hast not called upon me, O J; but 3290
43:28 have given J to the curse, and Israel to 3290
44: 1 Yet now hear, O J my servant; and Israel, 3290
44: 2 Fear not, O J, my servant; and 3290
44: 5 another shall call *himself* by the name of J; 3290
44:21 Remember these, O J and Israel; for thou 3290
44:23 for the LORD hath redeemed J, and 3290
45: 4 For J my servant's sake, and Israel mine 3290
45:19 I said not unto the seed of J, Seek ye me in 3290
46: 3 O house of J, and all the remnant of 3290
48: 1 Hear ye this, O house of J, which are called 3290
48:12 unto me, O J, and Israel my called; 3290
48:20 The LORD hath redeemed his servant J. 3290
49: 5 to bring J again to him, Though Israel be 3290
49: 6 be my servant to raise up the tribes of J, 3290
49:26 and thy redeemer, the mighty One of J. 3290
58: 1 and the house of J their sins. 3290
58:14 feed thee with the heritage of J thy father: 3290
59:20 unto them that turn from transgression in J, 3290
60:16 and thy redeemer, the mighty One of J. 3290
65: 9 I will bring forth a seed out of J, and out of 3290
Jer 2: 4 O house of J, and all the families of 3290
5:20 Declare this in the house of J, and 3290
10:16 The portion of J *is* not like them: for he *is* 3290
10:25 for they have eaten up J, and 3290
30:10 thou not, O my servant J, saith the LORD; 3290
30:10 J shall return, and shall be in rest, and 3290
31: 7 Sing with gladness for J, and shout among 3290
31:11 For the LORD hath redeemed J, and 3290
33:26 will I cast away the seed of J, and 3290
33:26 over the seed of Abraham, Isaac, and J: 3290
46:27 O my servant J, and be not dismayed, 3290
46:27 J shall return, and be in rest and at ease, 3290
46:28 Fear thou not, O J my servant, saith 3290
51:19 The portion of J *is* not like them; for he *is* 3290
La 1:17 the LORD hath commanded concerning J, 3290
2: 2 hath swallowed up all the habitations of J, 3290
2: 3 he burned against J like a flaming fire, 3290
Eze 20: 5 mine hand unto the seed of the house of J, 3290
28:25 their land that I have given to my servant J. 3290
37:25 land that I have given unto J my servant, 3290
39:25 Now will I bring again the captivity of J, 3290
Hos 10:11 shall plow, *and* J shall break his clods. 3290
12: 2 and *will* punish J according to his ways; 3290
12:12 J fled *into* the country of Syria, and 3290
Am 3:13 Hear ye, and testify in the house of J, 3290
6: 8 I abhor the excellency of J, and hate his 3290
7: 2 *by* whom shall J arise? for he *is* small. 3290
7: 5 *by* whom shall J arise? for he *is* small. 3290
8: 7 LORD hath sworn by the excellency of J, 3290
9: 8 I will not utterly destroy the house of J, 3290
Ob 1:10 For *thy* violence against thy brother J 3290
1:17 the house of J shall possess their 3290
1:18 the house of J shall be a fire, and the house 3290
Mic 1: 5 For the transgression of J *is* all this, and 3290
1: 5 What *is* the transgression of J? *is it* not 3290
2: 7 O *thou that art* named the house of J, is 3290
2:12 I will surely assemble, O J, all of thee; 3290
3: 1 O heads of J, and ye princes of the house of 3290
3: 8 to declare unto J his transgression, and 3290
3: 9 ye heads of the house of J, and princes of 3290
4: 2 and to the house of the God of J; 3290
5: 7 the remnant of J shall be in the midst of 3290
5: 8 the remnant of J shall be among 3290
7:20 Thou wilt perform the truth to J, *and* 3290
Na 2: 2 hath turned *away* the excellency of J, 3290
Mal 1: 2 saith the LORD: yet I loved J, 3290
2:12 out of the tabernacles of J, and him that 3290
3: 6 therefore ye sons of J are not consumed. 3290
Mt 1: 2 and Isaac begat J; and Jacob begat Judas *2384*
1: 2 and J begat Judas and his brethren; *2384*
1:15 begat Matthan; and Matthan begat J; *2384*
1:16 And J begat Joseph the husband of Mary, *2384*
8:11 and Isaac, and J, in the kingdom of heaven. *2384*
22:32 and the God of Isaac, and the God of J? *2384*

J

Mk 12:26 and the God of Isaac, and the God of J? *2384*
Lk 1:33 And he shall reign over the house of J for *2384*
3:34 Which was *the son* of J, which was *the son* *2384*
13:28 and Isaac, and J, and all the prophets, in *2384*
20:37 and the God of Isaac, and the God of J. *2384*
Jn 4: 5 near to the parcel of ground that J gave to *2384*
4:12 Art thou greater than our father J, *2384*
Ac 3:13 God of Abraham, and of Isaac, and of J, *2384*
7: 8 and Isaac *begat* J; and Jacob *begat* *2384*
7: 8 and J *begat* the twelve patriarchs. *2384*
7:12 But when J heard that there was corn in *2384*
7:14 and called his father J to *him*, and all his *2384*
7:15 So J went down into Egypt, and died, he, *2384*
7:32 and the God of Isaac, and the God of J. *2384*
7:46 to find a tabernacle for the God of J. *2384*
Ro 9:13 As it is written, J have I loved, *2384*
11:26 and shall turn away ungodliness from J: *2384*
Heb 11: 9 dwelling in tabernacles with Isaac and J, *2384*
11:20 By faith Isaac blessed J and Esau *2384*
11:21 By faith J, when he was a dying, *2384*

JACOB'S (19) [JACOB]
Ge 27:22 The voice *is* J voice, but the hands *are* 3290
28: 5 brother of Rebekah, J and Esau's mother. 3290
30: 2 J anger was kindled against Rachel: and 3290
30:42 feebler were Laban's, and the stronger J. 3290
31:33 Laban went into J tent, and into Leah's 3290
32:18 thou shalt say, *They be* thy servant J; it *is* a 3290
32:25 the hollow of J thigh was out of joint, as he 3290
32:32 he touched the hollow of J thigh in 3290
34: 7 folly in Israel in lying with J daughter; 3290
34:19 because he had delight in J daughter: 3290
35:23 J firstborn, and Simeon, and Levi, and 3290
45:26 *J* heart fainted, for he believed them not. NIH
46: 8 Jacob and his sons: Reuben, J firstborn. 3290
46:19 The sons of Rachel J wife; Joseph, and 3290
46:26 out of his loins, besides J sons' wives, 3290
Jer 30: 7 it *is* even the time of J trouble; but he shall 3290
30:18 I *will* bring again the captivity of J tents, 3290
Mal 1: 2 *was* not Esau J brother? saith 3290+3807.1
Jn 4: 6 Now J well was there. Jesus therefore, *2384*

JADA (2)
1Ch 2:28 the sons of Onam were, Shammai, and J. 3047
2:32 the sons of J the brother of Shammai; 3047

JADAU (1)
Ezr 10:43 Zabad, Zebina, J, and Joel, Benaiah. 3035

JADDAI See JADAU

JADDUA (3)
Ne 10:21 Meshezabeel, Zadok, J, 3037
12:11 begat Jonathan, and Jonathan begat J. 3037
12:22 Joiada, and Johanan, and J, *were* recorded 3037

JADON (1)
Ne 3: 7 J the Meronothite, the men of Gibeon, and 3036

JAEL (6)
Jdg 4:17 the tent of J the wife of Heber the Kenite: 3278
4:18 J went out to meet Sisera, and said unto 3278
4:21 J Heber's wife took a nail of the tent, and 3278
4:22 J came out to meet him, and said unto him, 3278
5: 6 in the days of J, the highways were 3278
5:24 Blessed above women shall J the wife of 3278

JAGUR (1)
Jos 15:21 southward were Kabzeel, and Eder, and J, 3017

JAH (1) [LORD*]
Ps 68: 4 that rideth upon the heavens by his name J, 3050

JAHATH (8)
1Ch 4: 2 Reaiah the son of Shobal begat J; and 3189
4: 2 and J begat Ahumai, and Lahad. 3189
6:20 Libni his son, J his son, Zimmah his son, 3189
6:43 The son of J, the son of Gershom, the son 3189
23:10 the sons of Shimei *were*, J, Zina, and 3189
23:11 J was the chief, and Zizah the second: but 3189
24:22 Shelomoth: of the sons of Shelomoth; J. 3189
2Ch 34:12 the overseers of them *were* J and Obadiah, 3189

JAHAZ (5)
Nu 21:23 and he came *to* J, and fought against Israel. 3096
Dt 2:32 he and all his people, to fight *at* J. 3096
Jdg 11:20 and pitched in J, and fought against Israel. 3096
Isa 15: 4 their voice shall be heard *even* unto J: 3096
Jer 48:34 *and even* unto J, have they uttered their 3096

JAHAZAH (3)
Jos 13:18 And J, and Kedemoth, and Mephaath, 3096
21:36 with her suburbs, and J with her suburbs, 3096
Jer 48:21 and upon J, and upon Mephaath, 3096

JAHAZIAH (1)
Ezr 10:15 J the son of Tikvah were employed about 3167

JAHAZIEL (6)
1Ch 12: 4 J, and Johanan, and Josabad 3166
16: 6 J the priests with trumpets continually 3166
23:19 J the third, and Jekameam the fourth. 3166
24:23 J the third, Jekameam the fourth. 3166
2Ch 20:14 upon J the son of Zechariah, the son of 3166
Ezr 8: 5 the son of J, and with him three hundred 3166

JAHDAI (1)
1Ch 2:47 the sons of J; Regem, and Jotham, and 3056

JAHDIEL (1)
1Ch 5:24 Azriel, and Jeremiah, and Hodaviah, and J, 3164

JAHDO (1)
1Ch 5:14 of Jeshishai, the son of J, the son of Buz; 3163

JAHLEEL (2) [JAHLEELITES]
Ge 46:14 sons of Zebulun; Sered, and Elon, and J. 3177
Nu 26:26 of J, the family of the Jahleelites. 3177

JAHLEELITES (1) [JAHLEEL]
Nu 26:26 the Elonites: of Jahleel, the family of the J. 3178

JAHMAI (1)
1Ch 7: 2 and Jeriel, and J, and Jibsam, and Shemuel, 3181

JAHZAH (1)
1Ch 6:78 with her suburbs, and J with her suburbs, 3096

JAHZEEL (2) [JAHZEELITES, JAHZIEL]
Ge 46:24 J, and Guni, and Jezer, and Shillem. 3183
Nu 26:48 of J, the family of the Jahzeelites: of Guni, 3183

JAHZEELITES (1) [JAHZEEL]
Nu 26:48 of Jahzeel, the family of the J: of Guni, 3184

JAHZEIAH See JAHAZIAH

JAHZERAH (1)
1Ch 9:12 the son of J, the son of Meshullam, the son 3170

JAHZIEL (1) [JAHZEEL]
1Ch 7:13 J, and Guni, and Jezer, and Shallum, 3185

JAILOR (1)
Ac 16:23 charging the j to keep them safely: *1200*

JAIR (10) [BASHAN-HAVOTH-JAIR]
Nu 32:41 J the son of Manasseh went and took 2971
Dt 3:14 J the son of Manasseh took all the country 2971
Jos 13:30 and all the towns of J, which *are* in Bashan, 2971
Jdg 10: 3 after him arose J, a Gileadite, and 2971
10: 5 And J died, and was buried in Camon. 2971
1Ki 4:13 to him *pertained* the towns of J the son of 2971
1Ch 2:22 Segub begat J, who had three and 2971
2:23 Aram, with the towns of J, from them, 2971
20: 5 Elhanan the son of J slew Lahmi 3265
Est 2: 5 the son of J, the son of Shimei, the son of 2971

JAIRITE (1)
2Sa 20:26 Ira also the J was a chief ruler about David. 2972

JAIRUS (2)
Mk 5:22 of the rulers of the synagogue, J by name; *2383*
Lk 8:41 there came a man named J, and he was a *2383*

JAKAN (1)
1Ch 1:42 The sons of Ezer; Bilhan, and Zavan, *and* J. 3292

JAKEH (1)
Pr 30: 1 The words of Agur the son of J, *even* 3348

JAKIM (2)
1Ch 8:19 And J, and Zichri, and Zabdi, 3356
24:12 The eleventh to Eliashib, the twelfth to J, 3356

JAKIN See JACHIN

JAKINITE See JACHINITES

JALAM See JAALAM

JALON (1)
1Ch 4:17 *were*, Jether, and Mered, and Epher, and J: 3210

JAMBRES (1)
2Ti 3: 8 Now as Jannes and J withstood Moses, so *2387*

JAMES (42)
Mt 4:21 J the *son* of Zebedee, and John his brother, *2385*
10: 2 J, the *son* of Zebedee, and John his brother; *2385*
10: 3 J the *son* of Alpheus, and Lebbeus, *2385*
13:55 called Mary? and his brethren, J, and Joses, *2385*
17: 1 J, and John his brother, and bringeth them *2385*
27:56 and Mary the mother of J and Joses, and *2385*
Mk 1:19 he saw J the *son* of Zebedee, and John his *2385*
1:29 of Simon and Andrew, with J and John. *2385*
3:17 And J the *son* of Zebedee, and John *2385*
3:17 *son* of Zebedee, and John the brother of J; *2385*
3:18 and J the *son* of Alpheus, and Thaddeus, *2385*
5:37 and J, and John the brother of James. *2385*
5:37 and James, and John the brother of J. *2385*
6: 3 the brother of J, and Joses, and of Juda, and *2385*
9: 2 and J, and John, and leadeth them up into a *2385*
10:35 And J and John, the sons of Zebedee, *2385*
10:41 *it*, they began to be much displeased with J *2385*
13: 3 Peter and J and John and Andrew asked *2385*
14:33 he taketh with him Peter and J and John, *2385*
15:40 and Mary the mother of J the less and *2385*
16: 1 and Mary the *mother* of J, and Salome, *2385*
Lk 5:10 And so *was* also J, and John, *the* sons of *2385*
6:14 J and John, Philip and Bartholomew, *2385*
6:15 J the *son* of Alpheus, and Simon called *2385*
6:16 *And* Judas *the brother* of J, and *2385*
8:51 and J, and John, and the father and *2385*
9:28 he took Peter and John and J, and went up *2385*
9:54 And when his disciples J and John saw *2385*
24:10 and Mary *the mother* of J, and other *2385*
Ac 1:13 and J, and John, and Andrew, Philip, and *2385*
1:13 J *the son* of Alpheus, and Simon Zelotes, *2385*
1:13 Simon Zelotes, and Judas *the brother* of J. *2385*
12: 2 And he killed J the brother of John with *2385*
12:17 *Go* shew these *things* unto J, and to *2385*
15:13 J answered, saying, Men *and* brethren, *2385*
21:18 *day* following Paul went in with us unto J; *2385*
1Co 15: 7 After that, he was seen of J; then of all *2385*
Gal 1:19 saw I none, save J the Lord's brother. *2385*
2: 9 And when J, Cephas, and John, *2385*
2:12 For before that certain came from J, he did *2385*
Jas 1: 1 J, a servant of God and of the Lord Jesus *2385*
Jude 1: 1 servant of Jesus Christ, and brother of J, *2385*

JAMIN (6) [JAMINITES]
Ge 46:10 J, and Ohad, and Jachin, and Zohar, and 3226
Ex 6:15 J, and Ohad, and Jachin, and Zohar, and 3226
Nu 26:12 of J, the family of the Jaminites: of Jachin, 3226
1Ch 2:27 of Jerahmeel were, Maaz, and J, and Eker. 3226
4:24 and J, Jarib, Zerah, *and* Shaul: 3226
Ne 8: 7 Bani, and Sherebiah, J, Akkub, Shabbethai, 3226

JAMINITES (1) [JAMIN]
Nu 26:12 of Jamin, the family of the J: of Jachin, 3228

JAMLECH (1)
1Ch 4:34 and J, and Joshah the son of Amaziah, 3230

JANAI See JAANAI

JANGLING (1)
1Ti 1: 6 swerved have turned aside unto **vain j**; *3150*

JANIM See JANUM

JANNA (1)
Lk 3:24 which was *the son* of J, which was *the son* *2388*

JANNAI See JANNA

JANNES (1)
2Ti 3: 8 Now as J and Jambres withstood Moses, so *2389*

JANOAH (1)
2Ki 15:29 J, and Kedesh, and Hazor, and Gilead, and 3239

JANOHAH (2)
Jos 16: 6 and passed by it on the east *to* J; 3239
16: 7 it went down from J *to* Ataroth, and 3239

JANUM (1)
Jos 15:53 And J, and Beth-tappuah, and Aphekah, 3241

JAPHETH (11)
Ge 5:32 and Noah begat Shem, Ham, and J. 3315
6:10 Noah begat three sons, Shem, Ham, and J. 3315
7:13 Shem, and Ham, and J, the sons of Noah, 3315
9:18 of the ark, were Shem, and Ham, and J: 3315
9:23 Shem and J took a garment, and laid *it* 3315
9:27 God shall enlarge J, and he shall dwell in 3315
10: 1 of the sons of Noah, Shem, Ham, and J: 3315
10: 2 The sons of J; Gomer, and Magog, and 3315
10:21 the brother of J the elder, even to him were 3315
1Ch 1: 4 Noah, Shem, Ham, and J. 3315
1: 5 The sons of J; Gomer, and Magog, and 3315

JAPHIA (5)
Jos 10: 3 unto J king of Lachish, and unto Debir king 3309
19:12 goeth out to Daberath, and goeth up *to* J, 3309
2Sa 5:15 Ibhar also, and Elishua, and Nepheg, and J, 3309
1Ch 3: 7 And Nogah, and Nepheg, and J, 3309
14: 6 And Nogah, and Nepheg, and J, 3309

JAPHLET (3)
1Ch 7:32 Heber begat J, and Shomer, and Hotham, 3310
7:33 the sons of J; Pasach, and Bimhal, and 3310
7:33 and Ashvath. These *are* the children of J. 3310

JAPHLETI (1)
Jos 16: 3 goeth down westward to the coast of J, 3311

JAPHLETITES See JAPHLETI

JAPHO (1)
Jos 19:46 and Rakkon, with the border before J. 3305

JAR; JARS See BARREL; BARRELS; CRUSE; WATERPOT; WATERPOTS

JARAH (2)
1Ch 9:42 Ahaz begat J; and Jarah begat Alemeth, 3294
9:42 J begat Alemeth, and Azmaveth, and 3294

JAREB (2)
Hos 5:13 to the Assyrian, and sent to king J: 3377
10: 6 carried unto Assyria *for* a present to king J: 3377

JARED (6)
Ge 5:15 lived sixty and five years, and begat J: 3382
5:16 Mahalaleel lived after he begat J eight 3382
5:18 J lived an hundred sixty and two years, 3382
5:19 J lived after he begat Enoch eight hundred 3382
5:20 all the days of J were nine hundred sixty 3382
Lk 3:37 *the son* of Enoch, which was *the son* of J, *2391*

JARESIAH (1)
1Ch 8:27 J, and Eliah, and Zichri, the sons of 3298

JARHA (2)
1Ch 2:34 a servant, an Egyptian, whose name *was* J. 3398
2:35 Sheshan gave his daughter to J his servant 3398

JARIB (3)
1Ch 4:24 and Jamin, J, Zerah, *and* Shaul: 3402
Ezr 8:16 and for J, and for Elnathan, and for Nathan, 3402
10:18 and Eliezer, and J, and Gedaliah. 3402

JARMUTH (7)
Jos 10: 3 unto Piram king of J, and unto Japhia king 3412
10: 5 the king of Hebron, the king of J, the king 3412

Jos 10:23 the king of Hebron, the king of J, the king 3412
12:11 The king of J, one; the king of Lachish, 3412
15:35 J, and Adullam, Socoh, and Azekah, 3412
21:29 J with her suburbs, En-gannim with her 3412
Ne 11:29 And at En-rimmon, and at Zareah, and at J, 3412

JAROAH (1)
1Ch 5:14 the son of J, the son of Gilead, the son of 3386

JASHAR See JASHER

JASHEN (1)
2Sa 23:32 the Shaalbonite, *of* the sons of J, Jonathan, 3464

JASHER (2)
Jos 10:13 *Is* not this written in the book of J? So 3477
2Sa 1:18 behold, *it is* written in the book of J.) 3477

JASHOBEAM (3)
1Ch 11:11 J, a Hachmonite, the chief of the captains: 3434
12: 6 and Jesiah, and Azareel, and Joezer, and J, 3434
27: 2 the first month *was* J the son of Zabdiel: 3434

JASHUB (3) [JASHUBITES]
Nu 26:24 Of J, the family of the Jashubites: 3437
1Ch 7: 1 *were*, Tola, and Puah, J, and Shimron, four. 3437
Ezr 10:29 and Adaiah, J, and Sheal, and Ramoth. 3437

JASHUBI-LEHEM (1)
1Ch 4:22 who had the dominion in Moab, and J. 3433

JASHUBITES (1) [JASHUB]
Nu 26:24 Of Jashub, the family of the J: of Shimron, 3432

JASIEL (1)
1Ch 11:47 Eliel, and Obed, and J the Mesobaite. 3300

JASON (5)
Ac 17: 5 and assaulted the house of J, and sought to *2394*
17: 6 they drew J and certain brethren unto *2394*
17: 7 Whom J hath received: and these all do *2394*
17: 9 And when they had taken security of J, and *2394*
Ro 16:21 and Lucius, and J, and Sosipater, *2394*

JASPER (7)
Ex 28:20 fourth row a beryl, and an onyx, and a j: 3471
39:13 the fourth row, a beryl, an onyx, and a j: 3471
Eze 28:13 the beryl, the onyx, and the j, the sapphire, 3471
Rev 4: 3 And he that sat was to look upon like a j *2393*
21:11 *even* like a j stone, clear as crystal; *2393*
21:18 And the building of the wall of it was *of* j: *2393*
21:19 The first foundation *was* j; the second, *2393*

JATHNIEL (1)
1Ch 26: 2 the second, Zebadiah the third, J the fourth, 3496

JATTIR (4)
Jos 15:48 the mountains, Shamir, and J, and Socoh, 3492
21:14 J with her suburbs, and Eshtemoa with her 3492
1Sa 30:27 and to *them* which *were* in J, 3492
1Ch 6:57 and J, and Eshtemoa, with their suburbs, 3492

JAVAN (7)
Ge 10: 2 and J, and Tubal, and Meshech, and Tiras. 3120
10: 4 the sons of J; Elishah, and Tarshish, 3120
1Ch 1: 5 and J, and Tubal, and Meshech, and Tiras. 3120
1: 7 the sons of J; Elishah, and Tarshish, 3120
Isa 66:19 Lud, that draw the bow, *to* Tubal, and J, 3120
Eze 27:13 J, Tubal, and Meshech, they *were* thy 3120
27:19 Dan also and J going to and fro occupied in 3120

JAVELIN (7)
Nu 25: 7 the congregation, and took a j in his hand; 7420
1Sa 18:10 and *there was* a j in Saul's hand. 2595
18:11 Saul cast the j; for he said, I will smite 2595
19: 9 as he sat in his house with his j in his hand: 2595
19:10 to smite David even to the wall with the j; 2595
19:10 and he smote the j into the wall: 2595
20:33 Saul cast a j at him to smite him: 2595

JAVELINS See DARTS

JAW (4) [JAWBONE, JAWS]
Jdg 15:16 with the j of an ass have I slain a thousand 3895
15:19 God clave a hollow place that *was* in the j, 3895
Job 41: 2 or bore his j through with a thorn? 3895
Pr 30:14 *are as* swords, and their **j teeth** *as* knives, 4973

JAWBONE (3) [BONE, JAW]
Jdg 15:15 he found a new j of an ass, and put forth his 3895
15:16 Samson said, With the j of an ass, 3895
15:17 that he cast away the j out of his hand, and 3895

JAWS (6) [JAW]
Job 29:17 I brake the j of the wicked, and pluckt 4973
Ps 22:15 my tongue cleaveth *to* my j; and thou hast 4455
Isa 30:28 *there shall be* a bridle in the j of the people, 3895
Eze 29: 4 I will put hooks in thy j, and I will cause 3895
38: 4 put hooks into thy j, and I will bring thee 3895
Hos 11: 4 as they that take off the yoke on their j, 3895

JAZER (11)
Nu 32: 1 when they saw the land of J, and the land 3270
32: 3 J, and Nimrah, and Heshbon, and Elealeh, 3270
Jos 13:25 their coast was J, and all the cities of 3270
21:39 with her suburbs, J with her suburbs; 3270
2Sa 24: 5 the midst of the river of Gad, and toward J: 3270
1Ch 6:81 with her suburbs, and J with her suburbs. 3270
26:31 them mighty *men* of valour at J of Gilead. 3270
Isa 16: 8 they are come *even* unto J, they wandered 3270
16: 9 with the weeping of J the vine of Sibmah: 3270
Jer 48:32 I will weep for thee with the weeping of J: 3270
48:32 the sea, they reach *even* to the sea of J: 3270

JAZIZ (1)
1Ch 27:31 over the flocks *was* J the Hagerite. 3151

JEALOUS (19) [JEALOUSY]
Ex 20: 5 for I the LORD thy God *am* a j God, 7067
34:14 for the LORD, whose name *is* J, *is* a 7067
34:14 whose name *is* Jealous, *is* a j God: 7067
Nu 5:14 and he be j of his wife, and she be defiled: 7065
5:14 he be j of his wife, and she be not defiled: 7065
5:30 he be j over his wife, and shall set 7065
Dt 4:24 thy God *is* a consuming fire, *even* a j God. 7067
5: 9 for I the LORD thy God *am* a j God, 7067
6:15 (For the LORD thy God *is* a j God among 7067
Jos 24:19 for he *is* a holy God; he *is* a j God; he will 7072
1Ki 19:10 I have been **very** j for the LORD 7065+7065
19:14 I have been **very** j for the LORD 7065+7065
Eze 39:25 of Israel, and will be j for my holy name; 7065
Joel 2:18 will the LORD be j for his land, and 7065
Na 1: 2 God *is* j, and the LORD revengeth; 7072
Zec 1:14 I am j for Jerusalem and for Zion *with* a 7065
8: 2 I was j for Zion *with* great jealousy, and 7065
8: 2 and I was j for her *with* great fury. 7065
2Co 11: 2 For I am j over you with godly jealousy: *2206*

JEALOUSIES (1) [JEALOUSY]
Nu 5:29 This *is* the law of j, when a wife goeth 7068

JEALOUSY (34) [JEALOUS, JEALOUSIES]
Nu 5:14 the spirit of j come upon him, and he be 7068
5:14 or if the spirit of j come upon him, and 7068
5:15 for it *is* an offering of j, an offering of 7068
5:18 in her hands, which *is* the j offering: 7068
5:25 the priest shall take the j offering out of 7068
5:30 Or when the spirit of j cometh upon him, 7068
25:11 consumed not the children of Israel in my j. 7068
Dt 29:20 and his j shall smoke against that man, 7068
32:16 They **provoked** him **to** j with strange *gods*, 7065
32:21 They have **moved** me **to** j with *that which* 7065
32:21 I will **move** them **to** j with *those which are* 7065
1Ki 14:22 they **provoked** him **to** j with their sins 7065
Ps 78:58 **moved** him **to** j with their graven images. 7065
79: 5 for ever? shall thy j burn like fire? 7068
Pr 6:34 For j *is* the rage of a man: therefore he will 7068
SS 8: 6 *is* strong as death; j *is* cruel as the grave: 7068
Isa 42:13 *man*, he shall stir up j like a man of war: 7068
Eze 8: 3 where *was* the seat of the image of j, 7068
8: 3 image of jealousy, which **provoketh to** j. 7069
8: 5 gate of the altar this image of j in the entry. 7068
16:38 and I will give thee blood in fury and j. 7068
16:42 my j shall depart from thee, and I will be 7068
23:25 I will set my j against thee, and they shall 7068
36: 5 Surely in the fire of my j have I spoken 7068
36: 6 I have spoken in my j and in my fury, 7068
38:19 For in my j *and* in the fire of my wrath 7068
Zep 1:18 land shall be devoured by the fire of his j: 7068
3: 8 shall be devoured with the fire of my j. 7068
Zec 1:14 for Jerusalem and for Zion *with* a great j. 7068
8: 2 I was jealous for Zion *with* great j, and 7068
Ro 10:19 I will **provoke** you **to** j by *them that are* no *3863*
11:11 unto the Gentiles, for to **provoke** them **to** j. *3863*
1Co 10:22 Do we **provoke** the Lord **to** j? are we *3863*
2Co 11: 2 For I am jealous over you with godly j: *2205*

JEARIM (1) [KIRJATH-JEARIM]
Jos 15:10 passed along unto the side of mount J, 3297

JEATERAI (1)
1Ch 6:21 Iddo his son, Zerah his son, J his son. 2979

JEATHERAI See JEATERAI

JEBERECHIAH (1)
Isa 8: 2 the priest, and Zechariah the son of J. 3000

JEBEREKIAH See JEBERECHIAH

JEBUS (4) [JEBUSI, JEBUSITE, JEBUSITES, JERUSALEM]
Jdg 19:10 and departed, and came over against J, 2982
19:11 *And* when they *were* by J, the day was far 2982
1Ch 11: 4 and all Israel went *to* Jerusalem, which *is* J; 2982
11: 5 the inhabitants of J said to David, 2982

JEBUSI (2) [JEBUS]
Jos 18:16 to the side of J on the south, and 2983
18:28 Zelah, Eleph, and J, which *is* Jerusalem, 2983

JEBUSITE (14) [JEBUS]
Ge 10:16 the J, and the Amorite, and the Girgashite, 2983
Ex 33: 2 and the Perizzite, the Hivite, and the J: 2983
34:11 and the Perizzite, and the Hivite, and the J. 2983
Jos 9: 1 the Perizzite, the Hivite, and the J, 2983
11: 3 the J in the mountains, and *to* the Hivite 2983
15: 8 son of Hinnom unto the south side of the J; 2983
2Sa 24:16 by the threshingplace of Araunah the J. 2983
24:18 in the threshingfloor of Araunah the J. 2983
1Ch 1:14 The J also, and the Amorite, and the 2983
21:15 stood by the threshingfloor of Ornan the J. 2983
21:18 in the threshingfloor of Ornan the J. 2983
21:28 him in the threshingfloor of Ornan the J, 2983
2Ch 3: 1 in the threshingfloor of Ornan the J. 2983
Zec 9: 7 as a governor in Judah, and Ekron as a J. 2983

JEBUSITES (25) [JEBUS]
Ge 15:21 and the Girgashites, and the J. 2983
Ex 3: 8 the Perizzites, and the Hivites, and the J. 2983
3:17 the Perizzites, and the Hivites, and the J, 2983
13: 5 the Amorites, and the Hivites, and the J, 2983
23:23 and the Canaanites, the Hivites, and the J: 2983
Nu 13:29 the Hittites, and the J, and the Amorites, 2983
Dt 7: 1 the Perizzites, and the Hivites, and the J, 2983
20:17 and the Perizzites, the Hivites, and the J; 2983
Jos 3:10 and the Amorites, and the J. 2983
12: 8 the Perizzites, the Hivites, and the J: 2983
15:63 As for the J the inhabitants of Jerusalem, 2983
15:63 the J dwell with the children of Judah at 2983
24:11 and the Girgashites, the Hivites, and the J; 2983
Jdg 1:21 not drive out the J that inhabited Jerusalem; 2983
1:21 the J dwell with the children of Benjamin 2983
3: 5 and Perizzites, and Hivites, and J: 2983
19:11 let us turn in into this city of the J, and 2983
2Sa 5: 6 and his men went *to* Jerusalem unto the J, 2983
5: 8 smiteth the J, and the lame and the blind, 2983
1Ki 9:20 Hittites, Perizzites, Hivites, and J, 2983
1Ch 11: 4 where the J *were*, the inhabitants of 2983
11: 6 Whosoever smiteth the J first shall be chief 2983
2Ch 8: 7 the Perizzites, and the Hivites, and the J, 2983
Ezr 9: 1 the Hittites, the Perizzites, the J, 2983
Ne 9: 8 and the J, and the Girgashites, 2983

JECAMIAH (1)
1Ch 3:18 Pedaiah, and Shenazar, J, Hoshama, and 3359

JECHOLIAH (1) [JECOLIAH]
2Ki 15: 2 And his mother's name *was* J of Jerusalem. 3203

JECHONIAS (2) [JECONIAH]
Mt 1:11 And Josias begat J and his brethren, *2423*
1:12 were brought to Babylon, J begat Salathiel; *2423*

JECOLIAH (1) [JECHOLIAH]
2Ch 26: 3 His mother's name also *was* J of 3203

JECONIAH (7) [JECHONIAS]
1Ch 3:16 of Jehoiakim: J his son, Zedekiah his son. 3204
3:17 And the sons of J; Assir, Salathiel his son, 3204
Est 2: 6 been carried away with J king of Judah, 3204
Jer 24: 1 J the son of Jehoiakim king of Judah, 3204
27:20 when he carried away captive J the son of 3204
28: 4 I *will* bring again to this place J the son of 3204
29: 2 (After that J the king, and the queen, and 3204

JEDAIAH (13)
1Ch 4:37 the son of Allon, the son of J, the son of 3042
9:10 of the priests; J, and Jehoiarib, and Jachin, 3048
24: 7 lot came forth to Jehoiarib, the second to J, 3048
Ezr 2:36 the children of J, of the house of Jeshua, 3048
Ne 3:10 next unto them repaired J the son of 3042
7:39 the children of J, of the house of Jeshua, 3048
11:10 Of the priests: J the son of Joiarib, Jachin, 3048
12: 6 Shemaiah, and Joiarib, J, 3048
12: 7 Sallu, Amok, Hilkiah, J. These *were* 3048
12:19 And of Joiarib, Mattenai; of J, Uzzi; 3048
12:21 Of Hilkiah, Hashabiah; of J, Nethaneel. 3048
Zec 6:10 *even* of Heldai, of Tobijah, and of J, 3048
6:14 and to J, and to Hen the son of Zephaniah, 3048

JEDIAEL (6)
1Ch 7: 6 Bela, and Becher, and J, three. 3043
7:10 The sons also of J; Bilhan: and the sons of 3043
7:11 All these the sons of J, by the heads of *their* 3043
11:45 J the son of Shimri, and Joha his brother, 3043
12:20 J, and Michael, and Jozabad, and Elihu, 3043
26: 2 J the second, Zebadiah the third, 3043

JEDIDAH (1)
2Ki 22: 1 his mother's name *was* J, the daughter of 3040

JEDIDIAH (1) [SOLOMON]
2Sa 12:25 he called his name J, because of 3041

JEDUTHUN (17)
1Ch 9:16 the son of J, and Berechiah the son of Asa, 3038
16:38 Obed-edom also the son of J and Hosah to 3038
16:41 with them Heman and J, and the rest that 3038
16:42 with them Heman and J *with* trumpets and 3038
16:42 of God. And the sons of J *were* porters. 3038
25: 1 of Heman, and of J, who should prophesy 3038
25: 3 Of J: the sons of Jeduthun; Gedaliah, and 3038
25: 3 the sons of J; Gedaliah, and Zeri, and 3038
25: 3 six, under the hands of their father J, 3038
25: 6 to the king's order *to* Asaph, J, and Heman. 3038
2Ch 5:12 of Heman, of J, with their sons and 3038
29:14 and of the sons of J; Shemaiah, and Uzziel. 3038
35:15 Asaph, and Heman, and J the king's seer; 3038
Ne 11:17 of Shammua, the son of Galal, the son of J. 3038
Ps 39: T *even* to J, A Psalm of David. 3038
62: T the chief Musician, to J, A Psalm of David. 3038
77: T the chief Musician, to J, A Psalm of Asaph. 3038

JEEZER (1) [JEEZERITES]
Nu 26:30 *of* J, the family of the Jeezerites: of Helek, 372

JEEZERITES (1) [JEEZER]
Nu 26:30 *of* Jeezer, the family of the J: of Helek, 373

JEGAR-SAHADUTHA (1)
Ge 31:47 Laban called it J: but Jacob called it 3026

JEHALELEEL (1)
1Ch 4:16 the sons of J; Ziph, and Ziphah, Tiria, and 3094

JEHALELEL (1)
2Ch 29:12 the son of Abdi, and Azariah the son of J: 3094

JEHALLELEL See JEHALELEEL; JEHALELEL

JEHDEIAH (2)
1Ch 24:20 Shubael: of the sons of Shubael; J. 3165
27:30 and over the asses *was* J the Meronothite: 3165

JEHEZEKEL (1)
1Ch 24:16 nineteenth to Pethahiah, the twentieth to J, 3168

JEHEZKEL See JEHEZEKEL

J

JEHIAH (1)
1Ch 15:24 and J *were* doorkeepers for the ark. 3174

JEHIEL (16)
1Ch 9:35 J, whose wife's name *was* Maachah: 3273
11:44 and J the sons of Hothan the Aroerite, 3273
15:18 J, and Unni, Eliab, and Benaiah, and 3171
15:20 J, and Unni, and Eliab, and Maaseiah, and 3171
16: 5 J, and Mattithiah, and Eliab, and Benaiah, 3171
23: 8 the chief *was* J, and Zetham, and Joel, 3171
27:32 J the son of Hachmoni *was* with the king's 3171
29: 8 by the hand of J the Gershonite. 3171
2Ch 21: 2 J, and Zechariah, and Azariah, and 3171
29:14 of the sons of Heman; J, and Shimei: and 3171
31:13 J, and Azaziah, and Nahath, and Asahel, 3171
35: 8 Hilkiah and Zechariah and J, rulers of 3171
Ezr 8: 9 Obadiah the son of J, and with him two 3171
10: 2 Shechaniah the son of J, *one* of the sons of 3171
10:21 Elijah, and Shemaiah, and J, and Uzziah. 3171
10:26 and J, and Abdi, and Jeremoth, and Eliah. 3171

JEHIELI (2)
1Ch 26:21 *even* of Laadan the Gershonite, *were* J. 3172
26:22 The sons of J; Zetham, and Joel his 3172

JEHIZKIAH (1)
2Ch 28:12 J the son of Shallum, and Amasa the son of 3169

JEHOADAH (2)
1Ch 8:36 Ahaz begat J; and Jehoadah begat Alemeth, 3085
8:36 J begat Alemeth, and Azmaveth, and 3085

JEHOADDAH See JEHOADAH

JEHOADDAN (2)
2Ki 14: 2 And his mother's name *was* J of Jerusalem. 3086
2Ch 25: 1 And his mother's name *was* J of Jerusalem. 3086

JEHOAHAZ (23)
2Ki 10:35 And J his son reigned in his stead. 3059
13: 1 J the son of Jehu *began* to reign over Israel 3059
13: 4 J besought the LORD, and the LORD 3059
13: 7 Neither did he leave *of* the people to J but 3059
13: 8 Now the rest of the acts of J, and all that he 3059
13: 9 J slept with his fathers; and they buried 3059
13:10 the son of J to reign over Israel in Samaria, 3059
13:22 of Syria oppressed Israel all the days of J. 3059
13:25 Jehoash the son of J took again out of 3059
13:25 which he had taken out of the hand of J his 3059
14: 1 In the second year of Joash son of J king of 3099
14: 8 the son of J son of Jehu, king of Israel, 3059
14:17 son of J king of Israel fifteen years. 3059
23:30 the people of the land took J the son of 3059
23:31 J *was* twenty and three years old when he 3059
23:34 took J *away*: and he came *to* Egypt, and 3059
2Ch 21:17 left him, save J, the youngest of his sons. 3059
25:17 sent to Joash, the son of J, the son of Jehu, 3059
25:23 the son of Joash, the son of J, 3059
25:25 Joash son of J king of Israel fifteen years. 3059
36: 1 the people of the land took J the son of 3059
36: 2 J *was* twenty and three years old when he 3099
36: 4 Necho took J his brother, and carried him 3099

JEHOASH (17)
2Ki 11:21 Seven years old *was* J when he *began* to 3060
12: 1 In the seventh year of Jehu J *began* to 3060
12: 2 J did *that* which *was* right in the sight of 3060
12: 4 J said to the priests, All the money of 3060
12: 6 twentieth year of king J the priests had not 3060
12: 7 king J called for Jehoiada the priest, and 3060
12:18 J king of Judah took all the hallowed *things* 3060
13:10 J the son of Jehoahaz to reign over Israel in 3060
13:25 J the son of Jehoahaz took again out of 3060
14: 8 Amaziah sent messengers to J, the son of 3060
14: 9 J the king of Israel sent to Amaziah king of 3060
14:11 Therefore J king of Israel went up; and he 3060
14:13 J king of Israel took Amaziah king of 3060
14:13 the son of J the son of Ahaziah, 3060
14:15 Now the rest of the acts of J which he did, 3060
14:16 J slept with his fathers, and was buried in 3060
14:17 J son of Jehoahaz king of Israel fifteen 3060

JEHOHANAN (6)
1Ch 26: 3 Elam the fifth, J the sixth, Elioenai 3076
2Ch 17:15 next to him *was* J the captain, and with him 3076
23: 1 Ishmael the son of J, and Azariah the son 3076
Ezr 10:28 of Bebai; J, Hananiah, Zabbai, *and* Athlai. 3076
Ne 12:13 Of Ezra, Meshullam; of Amariah, J; 3076
12:42 and J, and Malchijah, and Elam, and Ezer. 3076

JEHOIACHIN (10) [CONIAH, JEHOIACHIN'S]
2Ki 24: 6 and J his son reigned in his stead. 3078
24: 8 J *was* eighteen years old when he *began* to 3078
24:12 J the king of Judah went out to the king of 3078
24:15 he carried away J to Babylon, and 3078
25:27 thirtieth year of the captivity of J king of 3078
25:27 did lift up the head of J king of Judah out 3078
2Ch 36: 8 Judah: and J his son reigned in his stead. 3078
36: 9 J *was* eight years old when he *began* to 3078
Jer 52:31 thirtieth year of the captivity of J king of 3078
52:31 reign lifted up the head of J king of Judah, 3078

JEHOIACHIN'S (1) [JEHOIACHIN]
Eze 1: 2 which *was* the fifth year of king J captivity, 3112

JEHOIADA (52)
2Sa 8:18 Benaiah the son of J *was over* both 3077
20:23 Benaiah the son of J *was* over 3077
23:20 Benaiah the son of J, the son of a valiant 3077
23:22 These *things* did Benaiah the son of J, and 3077
1Ki 1: 8 Benaiah the son of J, and Nathan 3077
1:26 Benaiah the son of J, and thy servant 3077
1:32 the prophet, and Benaiah the son of J. 3077
1Ki 1:36 Benaiah the son of J answered the king, 3077
1:38 Benaiah the son of J, and the Cherethites, 3077
1:44 Benaiah the son of J, and the Cherethites, 3077
2:25 sent by the hand of Benaiah the son of J; 3077
2:29 Solomon sent Benaiah the son of J, saying, 3077
2:34 So Benaiah the son of J went up, and 3077
2:35 the king put Benaiah the son of J in his 3077
2:46 the king commanded Benaiah the son of J; 3077
4: 4 Benaiah the son of J *was* over the host: 3077
2Ki 11: 4 the seventh year J sent and fet the rulers 3077
11: 9 to all *things* that J the priest commanded: 3077
11: 9 out on the sabbath, and came to J the priest. 3077
11:15 J the priest commanded the captains of 3077
11:17 J made a covenant between the LORD 3077
12: 2 days where*in* J the priest instructed him. 3077
12: 7 king Jehoash called for J the priest, and 3077
12: 9 J the priest took a chest, and bored a hole 3077
1Ch 11:22 Benaiah the son of J, the son of a valiant 3077
11:24 These *things* did Benaiah the son of J, and 3077
12:27 J *was* the leader of the Aaronites, and 3077
18:17 Benaiah the son of J *was* over 3077
27: 5 the third month *was* Benaiah the son of J, 3077
27:34 after Ahithophel *was* J the son of Benaiah, 3077
2Ch 22:11 of king Jehoram, the wife of J the priest, 3077
23: 1 in the seventh year J strengthened himself, 3077
23: 8 all Judah did according to all *things* that J 3077
23: 8 for J the priest dismissed not the courses. 3077
23: 9 Moreover J the priest delivered to 3077
23:11 J and his sons anointed him, and said, 3077
23:14 J the priest brought out the captains of 3077
23:16 J made a covenant between him, and 3077
23:18 Also J appointed the offices of the house of 3077
24: 2 of the LORD all the days of J the priest. 3077
24: 3 J took for him two wives; and he begat 3077
24: 6 the king called for J the chief, and 3077
24:12 J gave it to such as did the work of 3077
24:14 the rest of the money before the king and J, 3077
24:14 of the LORD continually all the days of J. 3077
24:15 J waxed old, and was full *of* days when he 3077
24:17 Now after the death of J came the princes 3077
24:20 upon Zechariah the son of J the priest, 3077
24:22 which J his father had done to him, 3077
24:25 him for the blood of the sons of J the priest, 3077
Ne 3: 6 Moreover the old gate repaired J the son of 3111
Jer 29:26 made thee priest in the stead of J the priest, 3077

JEHOIAKIM (37) [ELIAKIM]
2Ki 23:34 turned his name *to* J, and took Jehoahaz 3079
23:35 J gave the silver and the gold to Pharaoh; 3079
23:36 J *was* twenty and five year old when he 3079
24: 1 and J became his servant three years: 3079
24: 5 Now the rest of the acts of J, and all that he 3079
24: 6 So J slept with his fathers: and 3079
24:19 according to all that J had done. 3079
1Ch 3:15 the second J, the third Zedekiah, the fourth 3079
3:16 the sons of J: Jeconiah his son, 3079
2Ch 36: 4 and Jerusalem, and turned his name *to* J. 3079
36: 5 J *was* twenty and five years old when he 3079
36: 8 Now the rest of the acts of J, and 3079
Jer 1: 3 It came also in the days of J the son of 3079
22:18 J the son of Josiah king of Judah; 3079
22:24 though Coniah the son of J king of Judah 3079
24: 1 captive Jeconiah the son of J king of Judah, 3079
25: 1 year of J the son of Josiah king of Judah, 3079
26: 1 In the beginning of the reign of J the son of 3079
26:21 when J the king, with all his mighty *men*, 3079
26:22 J the king sent men *into* Egypt, *namely*, 3079
26:23 of Egypt, and brought him unto J the king; 3079
27: 1 In the beginning of the reign of J the son of 3079
27:20 J king of Judah from Jerusalem to Babylon, 3079
28: 4 place Jeconiah the son of J king of Judah, 3079
35: 1 days of J the son of Josiah king of Judah, 3079
36: 1 it came to pass in the fourth year of J 3079
36: 9 it came to pass in the fifth year of J the son 3079
36:28 which J the king of Judah hath burnt. 3079
36:29 thou shalt say to J king of Judah, 3079
36:30 Therefore thus saith the LORD of J king 3079
36:32 which J king of Judah had burnt in the fire: 3079
37: 1 reigned instead of Coniah the son of J, 3079
45: 1 in the fourth year of J the son of Josiah 3079
46: 2 year of J the son of Josiah king of Judah. 3079
52: 2 according to all that J had done. 3079
Da 1: 1 In the third year of the reign of J king of 3079
1: 2 the Lord gave J king of Judah into his 3079

JEHOIARIB (2)
1Ch 9:10 of the priests; Jedaiah, and J, and Jachin, 3080
24: 7 Now the first lot came forth to J, 3080

JEHONADAB (3)
2Ki 10:15 he lighted on J the son of Rechab *coming* 3082
10:15 J answered, It is. If it be, give *me* thine 3082
10:23 Jehu went, and J the son of Rechab, 3082

JEHONATHAN (3)
1Ch 27:25 and in the castles, *was* J the son of Uzziah: 3083
2Ch 17: 8 J, and Adonijah, and Tobijah, and 3083
Ne 12:18 Of Bilgah, Shammua; of Shemaiah, J; 3083

JEHORAM (23)
1Ki 22:50 and J his son reigned in his stead. 3088
2Ki 1:17 J reigned in his stead in the second year of 3088
1:17 of J the son of Jehoshaphat king of Judah; 3088
3: 1 Now J the son of Ahab *began* to reign over 3088
3: 6 king J went out of Samaria the same time, 3088
8:16 J the son of Jehoshaphat king of Judah 3088
8:25 the son of J king of Judah *begin* to reign. 3088
8:29 Ahaziah the son of J king of Judah went 3088
9:24 smote J between his arms, and the arrow 3088
12:18 J, and Ahaziah, his fathers, kings of Judah, 3088
2Ch 17: 8 and with them Elishama and J, priests. 3088
21: 1 And J his son reigned in his stead. 3088
21: 3 the kingdom gave he to J; because he *was* 3088
21: 4 Now when J was risen up to the kingdom 3088
2Ch 21: 5 J *was* thirty and two years old when he 3088
21: 9 J went forth with his princes, and all *his* 3088
21:16 Moreover the LORD stirred up against J 3088
22: 1 So Ahaziah the son of J king of Judah 3088
22: 5 went with J the son of Ahab king of Israel 3088
22: 6 Azariah the son of J king of Judah went 3088
22: 6 down to see J the son of Ahab at Jezreel, 3088
22: 7 he went out with J against Jehu the son of 3088
22:11 So Jehoshabeath, the daughter of king J, 3088

JEHOSHABEATH (2)
2Ch 22:11 J, the daughter of the king, took Joash 3090
22:11 So J, the daughter of king Jehoram, 3090

JEHOSHAPHAT (85) [JOSAPHAT]
2Sa 8:16 and J the son of Ahilud *was* recorder; 3092
20:24 and J the son of Ahilud *was* recorder: 3092
1Ki 4: 3 scribes; J the son of Ahilud, the recorder. 3092
4:17 J the son of Paruah, in Issachar: 3092
15:24 and J his son reigned in his stead. 3092
22: 2 that J the king of Judah came down to 3092
22: 4 he said unto J, Wilt thou go with me to 3092
22: 4 J said to the king of Israel, I *am* as thou *art*, 3092
22: 5 J said unto the king of Israel, Inquire, 3092
22: 7 J said, *Is there* not here a prophet of 3092
22: 8 the king of Israel said unto J, *There is* yet 3092
22: 8 And J said, Let not the king say so. 3092
22:10 J the king of Judah sat each on his throne, 3092
22:18 the king of Israel said unto J, Did I not tell 3092
22:29 J the king of Judah went up *to* 3092
22:30 the king of Israel said unto J, I will 3092
22:32 when the captains of the chariots saw J, 3092
22:32 aside to fight against him: and J cried out. 3092
22:41 J the son of Asa *began* to reign over Judah 3092
22:42 J *was* thirty and five years old when he 3092
22:44 And J made peace with the king of Israel. 3092
22:45 Now the rest of the acts of J, and his might 3092
22:48 J made ships of Tharshish to go to Ophir 3092
22:49 said Ahaziah the son of Ahab unto J, 3092
22:49 thy servants in the ships. But J would not. 3092
22:50 J slept with his fathers, and was buried 3092
22:51 the seventeenth year of J king of Judah, 3092
2Ki 1:17 year of Jehoram the son of J king of Judah; 3092
3: 1 the eighteenth year of J king of Judah, 3092
3: 7 he went and sent to J the king of Judah, 3092
3:11 J said, *Is there* not here a prophet of 3092
3:12 J said, The word of the LORD is with 3092
3:12 So the king of Israel and J and the king of 3092
3:14 were it not that I regard the presence of J 3092
8:16 king of Israel, J *being* then king of Judah, 3092
8:16 Jehoram the son of J king of Judah *began* 3092
9: 2 look out there Jehu the son of J the son of 3092
9:14 So Jehu the son of J the son of Nimshi 3092
12:18 of Judah took all the hallowed *things* that J, 3092
1Ch 3:10 Abia his son, Asa his son, J his son, 3092
15:24 J, and Nethaneel, and Amasai, and 3146
18:15 the host; and J the son of Ahilud, recorder. 3092
2Ch 17: 1 J his son reigned in his stead, and 3092
17: 3 the LORD was with J, because he walked 3092
17: 5 all Judah brought to J presents; and he had 3092
17:10 so that they made no war against J. 3092
17:11 Also *some* of the Philistines brought J 3092
17:12 J waxed great exceedingly; and he built in 3092
18: 1 Now J had riches and honour in 3092
18: 3 Ahab king of Israel said unto J king of 3092
18: 4 J said unto the king of Israel, Inquire, 3092
18: 6 J said, *Is there* not here a prophet of 3092
18: 7 the king of Israel said unto J, *There is* yet 3092
18: 7 of Imla. And J said, Let not the king say so. 3092
18: 9 J king of Judah sat either of them on his 3092
18:17 the king of Israel said to J, Did I not tell 3092
18:28 J the king of Judah went up to 3092
18:29 the king of Israel said unto J, I will 3092
18:31 when the captains of the chariots saw J, 3092
18:31 J cried out, and the LORD helped him; 3092
19: 1 J the king of Judah returned to his house in 3092
19: 2 said to king J, Shouldest thou help 3092
19: 4 J dwelt at Jerusalem: and he went out again 3092
19: 8 Moreover in Jerusalem did J set of 3092
20: 1 the Ammonites, came against J to battle. 3092
20: 2 there came *some* that told J, saying, 3092
20: 3 J feared, and set himself to seek 3092
20: 5 J stood in the congregation of Judah and 3092
20:15 inhabitants of Jerusalem, and thou king J, 3092
20:18 J bowed his head *with his* face to 3092
20:20 J stood and said, Hear me, O Judah, and 3092
20:25 when J and his people came to take away 3092
20:27 Jerusalem, and J in the forefront of them, 3092
20:30 So the realm of J was quiet: for his God 3092
20:31 J reigned over Judah: *he was* thirty and 3092
20:34 Now the rest of the acts of J, first and last, 3092
20:35 after this did J king of Judah join himself 3092
20:37 of Mareshah prophesied against J, 3092
21: 1 Now J slept with his fathers, and 3092
21: 2 he had brethren the sons of J, Azariah, and 3092
21: 2 all these *were* the sons of J king of Israel. 3092
21:12 hast not walked in the ways of J thy father, 3092
22: 9 Because, said they, he *is* the son of J, 3092
Joel 3: 2 will bring them down into the valley of J, 3092
3:12 and come up to the valley of J: 3092

JEHOSHEBA (1)
2Ki 11: 2 J, the daughter of king Joram, sister of 3089

JEHOSHUA (2) [JOSHUA]
Nu 13:16 And Moses called Oshea the son of Nun, J. 3091
1Ch 7:27 Non his son, J his son. 3091

JEHOVAH (4) [GOD*, JEHOVAH-JIREH, JEHOVAH-NISSI, JEHOVAH-SHALOM, LORD*]
Ex 6: 3 *by* my name J was I not known to them. 3068
Ps 83:18 know that thou, whose name alone *is* J, 3068
Isa 12: 2 for the LORD J *is* my strength and 3068
26: 4 for in the LORD J *is* everlasting strength: 3068

JEHOVAH-JIREH (1) [JEHOVAH]
Ge 22:14 Abraham called the name of that place J: 3070

JEHOVAH-NISSI (1) [JEHOVAH]
Ex 17:15 built an altar, and called the name of it J: 3071

JEHOVAH-SHALOM (1) [JEHOVAH]
Jdg 6:24 altar there unto the LORD, and called it J: 3073

JEHOZABAD (4)
2Ki 12:21 J the son of Shomer, his servants, 3075
1Ch 26: 4 J the second, Joah the third, and Sacar 3075
2Ch 17:18 next him *was* J, and with him an hundred 3075
24:26 and J the son of Shimrith a Moabitess. 3075

JEHOZADAK (2)
1Ch 6:14 Azariah begat Seraiah, and Seraiah begat J, 3087
6:15 J went *into captivity,* when the LORD 3087

JEHU (59)
1Ki 16: 1 the word of the LORD came to J the son 3058
16: 7 also by the hand of the prophet J the son of 3058
16:12 which he spake against Baasha by J 3058
19:16 J the son of Nimshi shalt thou anoint to be 3058
19:17 escapeth the sword of Hazael shall J slay: 3058
19:17 him that escapeth from the sword of J shall 3058
2Ki 9: 2 look out there J the son of Jehoshaphat 3058
9: 5 J said, Unto which of all us? And he said, 3058
9:11 J came forth to the servants of his lord: 3058
9:13 and blew with trumpets, saying, J is king. 3058
9:14 So J the son of Jehoshaphat the son of 3058
9:15 J said, If it be your minds, *then* let none go 3058
9:16 So J rode *in a chariot,* and went to Jezreel; 3058
9:17 he spied the company of J as he came, and 3058
9:18 J said, What hast thou to do with peace? 3058
9:19 J answered, What hast thou to do with 3058
9:20 the driving *is* like the driving of J the son 3058
9:21 they went out against J, and met him in 3058
9:22 when Joram saw J, that he said, *Is it* peace, 3058
9:22 Joram saw Jehu, that he said, *Is it* peace, J? 3058
9:24 J drew a bow with his full strength, and 3058
9:25 said J to Bidkar his captain, Take up, *and* NIH
9:27 J followed after him, and said, Smite him 3058
9:30 when J was come to Jezreel, Jezebel heard 3058
9:31 as J entered in at the gate, she said, *Had* 3058
10: 1 J wrote letters, and sent *to* Samaria, 3058
10: 5 the bringers up *of the children,* sent to J, 3058
10:11 So J slew all that remained of the house of 3058
10:13 J met with the brethren of Ahaziah king of 3058
10:18 J gathered all the people together, and 3058
10:18 Baal a little; *but* J shall serve him much. 3058
10:19 J did *it* in subtilty, to the intent that *he* 3058
10:20 J said, Proclaim a solemn assembly for 3058
10:21 J sent through all Israel: and all 3058
10:23 J went, and Jehonadab the son of Rechab, 3058
10:24 J appointed fourscore men without, and 3058
10:25 that J said to the guard and to the captains, 3058
10:28 Thus J destroyed Baal out of Israel. 3058
10:29 to sin, J departed not from after them, 3058
10:30 the LORD said unto J, Because thou hast 3058
10:31 J took no heed to walk in the law of 3058
10:34 Now the rest of the acts of J, and all that he 3058
10:35 J slept with his fathers: and they buried 3058
10:36 the time that J reigned over Israel in 3058
12: 1 In the seventh year of J Jehoash *began* to 3058
13: 1 of J *began* to reign over Israel in Samaria, 3058
14: 8 the son of Jehoahaz son of J, king of Israel, 3058
15:12 word of the LORD which he spake unto J, 3058
1Ch 2:38 And Obed begat J, and Jehu begat Azariah, 3058
2:38 And Obed begat Jehu, and J begat Azariah, 3058
4:35 Joel, and J the son of Josibiah, the son of 3058
12: 3 and Berachah, and J the Antothite, 3058
2Ch 19: 2 J the son of Hanani the seer went out to 3058
20:34 behold they *are* written in the book of J 3058
22: 7 he went out with Jehoram against J the son 3058
22: 8 that when J was executing judgment upon 3058
22: 9 *was* hid in Samaria,) and brought him to J: 3058
25:17 the son of J, king of Israel, saying, Come, 3058
Hos 1: 4 the blood of Jezreel upon the house of J, 3058

JEHUBBAH (1)
1Ch 7:34 of Shamer; Ahi, and Rohgah, J, and Aram. 3160

JEHUCAL (1)
Jer 37: 3 Zedekiah the king sent J the son of 3081

JEHUD (1)
Jos 19:45 And J, and Bene-berak, and Gath-rimmon, 3055

JEHUDI (4)
Jer 36:14 Therefore all the princes sent J the son of 3065
36:21 So the king sent J to fet the roll: and 3065
36:21 J read it in the ears of the king, and in 3065
36:23 *that* when J had read three or four leaves, 3065

JEHUDIJAH (1)
1Ch 4:18 his wife J bare Jered the father of Gedor, 3057

JEHUSH (1)
1Ch 8:39 J the second, and Eliphelet the third. 3266

JEIEL (11)
1Ch 5: 7 *were* the chief, J, and Zechariah, 3273
15:18 and Obed-edom, and J, the porters. 3273
15:21 and Obed-edom, and J, and Azaziah, 3273
16: 5 J, and Shemiramoth, and Jehiel, and 3273
16: 5 J with psalteries and with harps; but 3273
2Ch 20:14 the son of Benaiah, the son of J, the son of 3273
26:11 of their account by the hand of J the scribe 3273
29:13 of the sons of Elizaphan; Shimri, and J: 3273
35: 9 and Hashabiah and J and Jozabad, 3273
Ezr 8:13 J, and Shemaiah, and with them threescore 3273
10:43 J, Mattithiah, Zabad, Zebina, Jadau, and 3273

JEKABZEEL (1)
Ne 11:25 and at J, and *in* the villages thereof, 3343

JEKAMEAM (2)
1Ch 23:19 Jahaziel the third, and J the fourth. 3360
24:23 the second, Jahaziel the third, J the fourth. 3360

JEKAMIAH (2)
1Ch 2:41 Shallum begat J, and Jekamiah begat 3359
2:41 begat Jekamiah, and J begat Elishama. 3359

JEKUTHIEL (1)
1Ch 4:18 father of Socho, and J the father of Zanoah. 3354

JEMIMA (1)
Job 42:14 he called the name of the first, J; and 3224

JEMUEL (2)
Ge 46:10 J, and Jamin, and Ohad, and Jachin, and 3223
Ex 6:15 J, and Jamin, and Ohad, and Jachin, and 3223

JEOPARDED (1) [JEOPARDY]
Jdg 5:18 Naphtali *were* a people *that* j their lives 2778

JEOPARDY (6) [JEOPARDED]
2Sa 23:17 of the men that went in *j of* their lives? NIH
1Ch 11:19 of these men that **have put** their lives **in j**? 871.1
11:19 for with *the j of* their lives they brought it. NIH
12:19 He will fall to his master Saul to *the j of* our NIH
Lk 8:23 they were filled *with water,* and were **in j**. *2793*
1Co 15:30 And why **stand** we **in j** every hour? *2793*

JEPHTHAE (1) [JEPHTHAH]
Heb 11:32 and *of* Barak, and *of* Samson, and *of* J; *2422*

JEPHTHAH (29) [JEPHTHAE]
Jdg 11: 1 Now J the Gileadite was a mighty *man* of 3316
11: 1 *was* the son of a harlot: and Gilead begat J. 3316
11: 2 and they thrust out J, and said unto him, 3316
11: 3 J fled from his brethren, and dwelt in 3316
11: 3 there were gathered vain men to J, and 3316
11: 5 the elders of Gilead went to fetch J out of 3316
11: 6 they said unto J, Come, and be our captain, 3316
11: 7 J said unto the elders of Gilead, Did not ye 3316
11: 8 the elders of Gilead said unto J, 3316
11: 9 J said unto the elders of Gilead, If ye bring 3316
11:10 the elders of Gilead said unto J, 3316
11:11 J went with the elders of Gilead, and 3316
11:11 J uttered all his words before the LORD 3316
11:12 J sent messengers unto the king of 3316
11:13 answered unto the messengers of J, 3316
11:14 J sent messengers again unto the king of 3316
11:15 said unto him, Thus saith J, Israel took not 3316
11:28 not unto the words of J which he sent him. 3316
11:29 the spirit of the LORD came upon J, and 3316
11:30 J vowed a vow unto the LORD, and said, 3316
11:32 So J passed over unto the children of 3316
11:34 J came *to* Mizpeh unto his house, and 3316
11:40 of J the Gileadite four days in a year. 3316
12: 1 and went northward, and said unto J, 3316
12: 2 J said unto them, I and my people were at 3316
12: 4 J gathered together all the men of Gilead, 3316
12: 7 J judged Israel six years. Then died 3316
12: 7 died J the Gileadite, and was buried in *one* 3316
1Sa 12:11 J, and Samuel, and delivered you out of 3316

JEPHUNNEH (16)
Nu 13: 6 Of the tribe of Judah, Caleb the son of J. 3312
14: 6 the son of Nun, and Caleb the son of J, 3312
14:30 save Caleb the son of J, and Joshua the son 3312
14:38 the son of Nun, and Caleb the son of J, 3312
26:65 save Caleb the son of J, and Joshua the son 3312
32:12 Save Caleb the son of J the Kenezite, and 3312
34:19 Of the tribe of Judah, Caleb the son of J. 3312
Dt 1:36 Save Caleb the son of J, he shall see it, and 3312
Jos 14: 6 Caleb the son of J the Kenezite said unto 3312
14:13 gave unto Caleb the son of J Hebron for an 3312
14:14 the inheritance of Caleb the son of J 3312
15:13 unto Caleb the son of J he gave a part 3312
21:12 gave they to Caleb the son of J for his 3312
1Ch 4:15 the sons of Caleb the son of J; Iru, Elah, 3312
6:56 they gave to Caleb the son of J. 3312
7:38 the sons of Jether; J, and Pispah, and Ara. 3312

JERAH (2)
Ge 10:26 and Sheleph, and Hazarmaveth, and J, 3392
1Ch 1:20 and Sheleph, and Hazarmaveth, and J, 3392

JERAHMEEL (8) [JERAHMEELITES]
1Ch 2: 9 born unto him; J, and Ram, and Chelubai. 3396
2:25 the sons of J the firstborn of Hezron were, 3396
2:26 J had also another wife, whose name *was* 3396
2:27 the sons of Ram the firstborn of J were, 3396
2:33 Peleth, and Zaza. These were the sons of J. 3396
2:42 Now the sons of Caleb the brother of J 3396
24:29 Concerning Kish: the son of Kish *was* J. 3396
Jer 36:26 the king commanded J the son of 3396

JERAHMEELITES (2) [JERAHMEEL]
1Sa 27:10 against the south of the J, and against 3397
30:29 to *them* which *were* in the cities of the J, 3397

JERED (2)
1Ch 1: 2 Kenan, Mahalaleel, J, 3382
4:18 his wife Jehudijah bare J the father of 3382

JEREMAI (1)
Ezr 10:33 Zabad, Eliphelet, J, Manasseh, *and* Shimei 3413

JEREMIAH (146) [JEREMIAH'S, JEREMIAS, JEREMIE]
2Ki 23:31 *was* Hamutal, the daughter of J of Libnah. 3414
24:18 *was* Hamutal, the daughter of J of Libnah. 3414
1Ch 5:24 Azriel, and J, and Hodaviah, and Jahdiel, 3414
12: 4 J, and Jahaziel, and Johanan, and 3414
12:10 Mishmannah the fourth, J the fifth, 3414
12:13 J the tenth, Machbanai the eleventh. 3414
2Ch 35:25 J lamented for Josiah: and all the singing 3414
36:12 humbled not himself before J the prophet 3414
36:21 the word of the LORD by the mouth of J, 3414
36:22 by the mouth of J might be accomplished, 3414
Ezr 1: 1 by the mouth of J might be fulfilled, 3414
Ne 10: 2 Seraiah, Azariah, J, 3414
12: 1 of Shealtiel, and Jeshua: Seraiah, J, Ezra, 3414
12:12 of Seraiah, Meraiah; of J, Hananiah; 3414
12:34 Judah, and Benjamin, and Shemaiah, and J, 3414
Jer 1: 1 The words of J the son of Hilkiah, of 3414
1:11 came unto me, saying, J, what seest thou? 3414
7: 1 The word that came to J from the LORD, 3414
11: 1 The word that came to J from the LORD, 3414
14: 1 The word of the LORD that came to J 3414
18: 1 The word which came to J from 3414
18:18 Come, and let us devise devices against J; 3414
19:14 came J from Tophet, whither the LORD 3414
20: 1 heard *that* J prophesied these things. 3414
20: 2 Pashur smote J the prophet, and put him in 3414
20: 3 that Pashur brought forth J out of 3414
20: 3 said J unto him, The LORD hath not 3414
21: 1 The word which came unto J from 3414
21: 3 said J unto them, Thus shall ye say to 3414
24: 3 the LORD unto me, What seest thou, J? 3414
25: 1 The word that came to J concerning all 3414
25: 2 The which J the prophet spake unto all 3414
25:13 which J hath prophesied against all 3414
26: 7 all the people heard J speaking these words 3414
26: 8 when J had made an end of speaking all 3414
26: 9 all the people were gathered against J in 3414
26:12 spake J unto all the princes and to all 3414
26:20 this land according to all the words of J: 3414
26:24 of Ahikam the son of Shaphan was with J, 3414
27: 1 came this word unto J from the LORD, 3414
28: 5 the prophet J said unto the prophet 3414
28: 6 Even the prophet J said, Amen: 3414
28:11 full years. And the prophet J went his way. 3414
28:12 the word of the LORD came unto J 3414
28:12 the yoke from off the neck of the prophet J, 3414
28:15 said the prophet J unto Hananiah 3414
29: 1 Now these *are* the words of the letter that J 3414
29:27 why hast thou not reproved J of Anathoth, 3414
29:29 read this letter in the ears of J the prophet. 3414
29:30 came the word of the LORD unto J, 3414
30: 1 The word that came to J from the LORD, 3414
32: 1 The word that came to J from the LORD 3414
32: 2 J the prophet was shut up in the court of 3414
32: 6 J said, The word of the LORD came unto 3414
32:26 came the word of the LORD unto J, 3414
33: 1 the LORD came unto J the second time, 3414
33:19 the word of the LORD came unto J, 3414
33:23 the word of the LORD came to J, 3414
34: 1 The word which came unto J from 3414
34: 6 J the prophet spake all these words unto 3414
34: 8 *This is* the word that came unto J from 3414
34:12 of the LORD came to J from the LORD, 3414
35: 1 The word which came unto J from 3414
35: 3 I took Jaazaniah the son of J, the son of 3414
35:12 came the word of the LORD unto J, 3414
35:18 J said unto the house of the Rechabites, 3414
36: 1 *that* this word came unto J from 3414
36: 4 J called Baruch the son of Neriah: and 3414
36: 4 Baruch wrote from the mouth of J all 3414
36: 5 J commanded Baruch, saying, I *am* shut 3414
36: 8 to all that J the prophet commanded him, 3414
36:10 read Baruch in the book the words of J *in* 3414
36:19 unto Baruch, Go, hide thee, thou and J; 3414
36:26 to take Baruch the scribe and J the prophet: 3414
36:27 the word of the LORD came to J, 3414
36:27 which Baruch wrote at the mouth of J, 3414
36:32 took J another roll, and gave it to Baruch 3414
36:32 who wrote therein from the mouth of J all 3414
37: 2 which he spake by the prophet J. 3414
37: 3 son of Maaseiah the priest to the prophet J, 3414
37: 4 Now J came in and went out among 3414
37: 6 the word of the LORD unto the prophet J, 3414
37:12 J went forth out of Jerusalem to go *into* 3414
37:13 he took J the prophet, saying, Thou fallest 3414
37:14 said J, *It is* false; I fall not away to 3414
37:14 so Irijah took J, and brought him to 3414
37:15 Wherefore the princes were wroth with J, 3414
37:16 When J was entered into the dungeon, 3414
37:16 and J had remained there many days; 3414
37:17 J said, There is: for, said he, thou shalt be 3414
37:18 Moreover J said unto king Zedekiah, 3414
37:21 commit J into the court of the prison, 3414
37:21 Thus J remained in the court of the prison. 3414
38: 1 heard the words that J had spoken unto all 3414
38: 6 took they J, and cast him into the dungeon 3414
38: 6 they let down J with cords. And in 3414
38: 6 no water, but mire: so J sunk in the mire. 3414
38: 7 heard that they had put J in the dungeon; 3414
38: 9 in all that they have done to J the prophet, 3414
38:10 take up J the prophet out of the dungeon, 3414
38:11 them down by cords into the dungeon to J. 3414
38:12 Ebed-melech the Ethiopian said unto J, 3414
38:12 armholes under the cords. And J did so. 3414
38:13 So they drew up J with cords, and took him 3414
38:13 and J remained in the court of the prison. 3414
38:14 took J the prophet unto him into the third 3414
38:14 the king said unto J, I *will* ask thee a thing; 3414
38:15 J said unto Zedekiah, If I declare *it* unto 3414
38:16 So Zedekiah the king sware secretly unto J, 3414
38:17 said J unto Zedekiah, Thus saith 3414
38:19 Zedekiah the king said unto J, I am afraid 3414
38:20 J said, They shall not deliver *thee.* Obey, 3414
38:24 said Zedekiah unto J, Let no man know of 3414
38:27 came all the princes unto J, and asked him: 3414
38:28 So J abode in the court of the prison until 3414
39:11 J to Nebuzar-adan the captain of the guard, 3414
39:14 took J out of the court of the prison, and 3414
39:15 Now the word of the LORD came unto J, 3414

J

Jer 40: 1 The word which came to J from 3414
40: 2 the captain of the guard took J, and 3414
40: 6 went J unto Gedaliah the son of Ahikam to 3414
42: 2 said unto J the prophet, Let, we beseech 3414
42: 4 J the prophet said unto them, I have heard 3414
42: 5 they said to J, The LORD be a true and 3414
42: 7 that the word of the LORD came unto J. 3414
43: 1 *that* when J had made an end of speaking 3414
43: 2 all the proud men, saying unto J, 3414
43: 6 J the prophet, and Baruch the son of 3414
43: 8 came the word of the LORD unto J in 3414
44: 1 The word that came to J concerning all 3414
44:15 of Egypt, in Pathros, answered J, saying, 3414
44:20 J said unto all the people, to the men, and 3414
44:24 Moreover J said unto all the people, and 3414
45: 1 The word that J the prophet spake unto 3414
45: 1 these words in a book at the mouth of J, 3414
46: 1 The word of the LORD which came to J 3414
46:13 The word that the LORD spake to J 3414
47: 1 The word of the LORD that came to J 3414
49:34 The word of the LORD that came to J 3414
50: 1 against the land of the Chaldeans by J 3414
51:59 The word which J the prophet commanded 3414
51:60 So J wrote in a book all the evil that should 3414
51:61 J said to Seraiah, When thou comest *to* 3414
51:64 shall be weary. Thus far *are* the words of J. 3414
52: 1 *was* Hamutal the daughter of J of Libnah. 3414
Da 9: 2 where*of* the word of the LORD came to J 3414

JEREMIAH'S (1) [JEREMIAH]
Jer 28:10 took the yoke from off the prophet J neck, 3414

JEREMIAS (1) [JEREMIAH]
Mt 16:14 Elias; and others, J, or one of the prophets. *2408*

JEREMIE (2) [JEREMIAH]
Mt 2:17 that which was spoken by J the prophet, *2408*
27: 9 that which was spoken by J the prophet, *2408*

JEREMOTH (5)
1Ch 8:14 And Ahio, Shashak, and J, 3406
23:23 of Mushi; Mahli, and Eder, and J, three. 3406
25:22 The fifteenth to J, *he,* his sons, and 3406
Ezr 10:26 and Jehiel, and Abdi, and J, and Eliah. 3406
10:27 Mattaniah, and J, and Zabad, and Aziza. 3406

JERIAH (2)
1Ch 23:19 J the first, Amariah the second, Jahaziel 3404
24:23 the sons *of Hebron;* J *the first,* Amariah 3404

JERIBAI (1)
1Ch 11:46 Eliel the Mahavite, and J, and Joshaviah, 3403

JERICHO (64)
Nu 22: 1 the plains of Moab on *this* side Jordan *by* J. 3405
26: 3 in the plains of Moab by Jordan *near* J, 3405
26:63 in the plains of Moab by Jordan *near* J. 3405
31:12 of Moab, which *are* by Jordan *near* J. 3405
33:48 in the plains of Moab by Jordan *near* J. 3405
33:50 in the plains of Moab by Jordan *near* J, 3405
34:15 on *this* side Jordan *near* J eastward, 3405
35: 1 in the plains of Moab by Jordan *near* J, 3405
36:13 in the plains of Moab by Jordan *near* J. 3405
Dt 32:49 in the land of Moab, that *is* over against J; 3405
34: 1 *to* the top of Pisgah, that *is* over against J. 3405
34: 3 the south, and the plain of the valley of J, 3405
Jos 2: 1 saying, Go view the land, even J. 3405
2: 2 it was told the king of J, saying, Behold, 3405
2: 3 the king of J sent unto Rahab, saying, 3405
3:16 and the people passed over right against J. 3405
4:13 the LORD unto battle, to the plains of J. 3405
4:19 encamped in Gilgal, in the east border of J. 3405
5:10 day of the month at even in the plains of J. 3405
5:13 And it came to pass, when Joshua was by J, 3405
6: 1 Now J was straitly shut up because of 3405
6: 2 I have given into thine hand J, and the king 3405
6:25 which Joshua sent to spy out J. 3405
6:26 that riseth up and buildeth this city J: 3405
7: 2 Joshua sent men from J *to* Ai, which *is* 3405
8: 2 her king as thou didst unto J and her king: 3405
9: 3 Gibeon heard what Joshua had done unto J 3405
10: 1 as he had done to J and her king, so he had 3405
10:28 of Makkedah as he did unto the king of J. 3405
10:30 king thereof as he did unto the king of J. 3405
12: 9 The king of J, one; the king of Ai, which *is* 3405
13:32 on the *other* side Jordan, *by* J, eastward. 3405
16: 1 children of Joseph fell from Jordan *by* J, 3405
16: 1 *by* Jericho, unto the water of J on the east, 3405
16: 1 *to* the wilderness that goeth up from J 3405
16: 7 and came to J, and went out *at* Jordan. 3405
18:12 the border went up to the side of J on 3405
18:21 according to their families were J, 3405
20: 8 And on the *other* side Jordan *by* J eastward, 3405
24:11 ye went over Jordan, and came unto J: and 3405
24:11 the men of J fought against you, 3405
2Sa 10: 5 Tarry at J until your beards be grown, and 3405
1Ki 16:34 In his days did Hiel the Bethelite build J: 3405
2Ki 2: 4 for the LORD hath sent me *to* J. 3405
2: 4 I will not leave thee. So they came *to* J. 3405
2: 5 the sons of the prophets that *were* at J came 3405
2:15 prophets which *were* to view at J saw him, 3405
2:18 came again to him, (for he tarried at J,) 3405
25: 5 and overtook him in the plains of J: 3405
1Ch 6:78 on the *other* side Jordan *by* J, on the east 3405
19: 5 Tarry at J until your beards be grown, and 3405
2Ch 28:15 brought them *to* J, the city of palm trees, 3405
Ezr 2:34 The children of J, three hundred forty and 3405
Ne 3: 2 next unto him builded the men of J. 3405
7:36 The children of J, three hundred forty and 3405
Jer 39: 5 and overtook Zedekiah in the plains of J: 3405
52: 8 and overtook Zedekiah in the plains of J; 3405
Mt 20:29 And as they departed from J, a great *2410*
Mk 10:46 And they came to J: and as he went out of *2410*
10:46 as he went out of J with his disciples and *2410*
Lk 10:30 man went down from Jerusalem to J, *2410*
18:35 to pass, *that* as he was come nigh unto J, *2410*
19: 1 And *Jesus* entered and passed through J. *2410*
Heb 11:30 By faith the walls of J fell down, after they *2410*

JERIEL (1)
1Ch 7: 2 J, and Jahmai, and Jibsam, and Shemuel, 3400

JERIJAH (1)
1Ch 26:31 Among the Hebronites *was* J the chief, 3404

JERIMOTH (8)
1Ch 7: 7 and Uzzi, and Uzziel, and J, and Iri, five; 3406
7: 8 J, and Abiah, and Anathoth, and Alameth. 3406
12: 5 J, and Bealiah, and Shemariah, and 3406
24:30 sons also of Mushi; Mahli, and Eder, and J. 3406
25: 4 Uzziel, Shebuel, and J, Hananiah, Hanani, 3406
27:19 of Naphtali, J the son of Azriel: 3406
2Ch 11:18 the daughter of J the son of David *to* wife, 3406
31:13 J, and Jozabad, and Eliel, and Ismachiah, 3406

JERIOTH (1)
1Ch 2:18 *children* of Azubah *his* wife, and of J: 3408

JEROBOAM (102) [JEROBOAM'S]
1Ki 11:26 J the son of Nebat, an Ephrathite of Zereda, 3379
11:28 the man J *was* a mighty *man* of valour: 3379
11:29 it came to pass at that time when J went out 3379
11:31 he said to J, Take thee ten pieces: for thus 3379
11:40 Solomon sought therefore to kill J. 3379
11:40 J arose, and fled *into* Egypt, unto Shishak 3379
12: 2 it came to pass, when J the son of Nebat, 3379
12: 2 of king Solomon, and J dwelt in Egypt;) 3379
12: 3 J and all the congregation of Israel came, 3379
12:12 So J and all the people came to Rehoboam 3379
12:15 the Shilonite unto J the son of Nebat. 3379
12:20 when all Israel heard that J was come 3379
12:25 J built Shechem in mount Ephraim, and 3379
12:26 J said in his heart, Now shall the kingdom 3379
12:32 J ordained a feast in the eighth month, 3379
13: 1 and J stood by the altar to burn incense. 3379
13: 4 when king J heard the saying of the man of 3379
13:33 After this thing J returned not from his evil 3379
13:34 this thing became sin unto the house of J, 3379
14: 1 At that time Abijah the son of J fell sick. 3379
14: 2 J said to his wife, Arise, I pray thee, and 3379
14: 2 that thou be not known to be the wife of J; 3379
14: 5 the wife of J cometh to ask a thing of thee 3379
14: 6 that he said, Come in, thou wife of J; 3379
14: 7 Go, tell J, Thus saith the LORD God of 3379
14:10 I will bring evil upon the house of J, and 3379
14:10 will cut off from J *him that* pisseth against 3379
14:10 take away the remnant of the house of J, 3379
14:11 Him that dieth of J in the city shall 3379
14:13 for he only of J shall come to the grave, 3379
14:13 the LORD God of Israel in the house of J. 3379
14:14 who shall cut off the house of J that day: 3379
14:16 shall give Israel up because of the sins of J, 3379
14:19 the rest of the acts of J, how he warred, 3379
14:20 the days which J reigned *were* two and 3379
14:30 between Rehoboam and J all *their* days. 3379
15: 1 Now in the eighteenth year of king J 3379
15: 6 and J all the days of his life. 3379
15: 7 And there was war between Abijam and J. 3379
15: 9 in the twentieth year of J king of Israel 3379
15:25 Nadab the son of J *began* to reign over 3379
15:29 he reigned, *that* he smote all the house of J; 3379
15:29 he left not to J any that breathed, until *he* 3379
15:30 Because of the sins of J which he sinned, 3379
15:34 walked in the way of J and in his sin 3379
16: 2 thou hast walked in the way of J, and 3379
16: 3 will make thy house like the house of J 3379
16: 7 of his hands, in being like the house of J; 3379
16:19 in walking in the way of J, and in his sin 3379
16:26 For he walked in all the way of J the son of 3379
16:31 to walk in the sins of J the son of Nebat, 3379
21:22 will make thine house like the house of J 3379
22:52 in the way of J the son of Nebat, who made 3379
2Ki 3: 3 Nevertheless he cleaved unto the sins of J 3379
9: 9 Ahab like the house of J the son of Nebat, 3379
10:29 Howbeit *from* the sins of J the son of 3379
10:31 *for* he departed not from the sins of J, 3379
13: 2 followed the sins of J the son of Nebat, 3379
13: 6 not from the sins of the house of J, 3379
13:11 he departed not from all the sins of J 3379
13:13 with his fathers; and J sat upon his throne: 3379
14:16 of Israel; and J his son reigned in his stead. 3379
14:23 J the son of Joash king of Israel *began* to 3379
14:24 he departed not from all the sins of J 3379
14:27 he saved them by the hand of J the son of 3379
14:28 Now the rest of the acts of J, and all that he 3379
14:29 J slept with his fathers, *even* with the kings 3379
15: 1 seventh year of J king of Israel *began* 3379
15: 8 J reign over Israel in Samaria six months. 3379
15: 9 he departed not from the sins of J the son 3379
15:18 days from the sins of J the son of Nebat, 3379
15:24 he departed not from the sins of J the son 3379
15:28 he departed not from the sins of J the son 3379
17:21 and they made J the son of Nebat king: 3379
17:21 J drave Israel from following the LORD, 3379
17:22 walked in all the sins of J which he did; 3379
23:15 the high place which J the son of Nebat, 3379
1Ch 5:17 and in the days of J king of Israel. 3379
2Ch 9:29 in the visions of Iddo the seer against J 3379
10: 2 when J the son of Nebat, who *was* in 3379
10: 2 heard *it,* that J returned out of Egypt. 3379
10: 3 So J and all Israel came and spake to 3379
10:12 So J and all the people came to Rehoboam 3379
10:15 Ahijah the Shilonite to J the son of Nebat. 3379
11: 4 and returned from going against J. 3379
11:14 for J and his sons had cast them off from 3379
12:15 wars between Rehoboam and J continually. 3379
13: 1 Now in the eighteenth year of king J *began* 3379
13: 2 And there was war between Abijah and J. 3379
13: 3 J also set the battle in array against him 3379
13: 4 and said, Hear me, *thou* J, and all Israel; 3379
13: 6 Yet J the son of Nebat, the servant of 3379
13: 8 golden calves, which J made you for gods. 3379
13:13 J caused an ambushment to come about 3379
13:15 that God smote J and all Israel before 3379
13:19 Abijah pursued after J, and took cities from 3379
13:20 Neither did J recover strength again in 3379
Hos 1: 1 in the days of J the son of Joash, king of 3379
Am 1: 1 in the days of J the son of Joash king of 3379
7: 9 I will rise against the house of J with 3379
7:10 Amaziah *the* priest of Beth-el sent to J king 3379
7:11 J shall die by the sword, and Israel shall 3379

JEROBOAM'S (2) [JEROBOAM]
1Ki 14: 4 J wife did so, and arose, and went *to* 3379
14:17 J wife arose, and departed, and came to 3379

JEROHAM (10)
1Sa 1: 1 the son of J, the son of Elihu, the son of 3395
1Ch 6:27 Eliab his son, J his son, Elkanah his son. 3395
6:34 the son of J, the son of Eliel, the son of 3395
8:27 and Eliah, and Zichri, the sons of J. 3395
9: 8 Ibneiah the son of J, and Elah the son of 3395
9:12 Adaiah the son of J, the son of Pashur, 3395
12: 7 and Zebadiah, the sons of J of Gedor. 3395
27:22 Of Dan, Azareel the son of J. These *were* 3395
2Ch 23: 1 Azariah the son of J, and Ishmael the son 3395
Ne 11:12 Adaiah the son of J, the son of Pelaliah, 3395

JERUBBAAL (14) [GIDEON, JERUBBESHETH]
Jdg 6:32 Therefore on that day he called him J, 3378
7: 1 J, who *is* Gideon, and all the people that 3378
8:29 J the son of Joash went and dwelt in his 3378
8:35 shewed they kindness to the house of J, 3378
9: 1 Abimelech the son of J went to Shechem 3378
9: 2 either that all the sons of J, *which are* 3378
9: 5 slew his brethren the sons of J, 3378
9: 5 yet Jotham the youngest son of J was left; 3378
9:16 if ye have dealt well with J and his house, 3378
9:19 have dealt truly and sincerely with J and 3378
9:24 and ten sons of J might come, 3378
9:28 *is* not *he* the son of J? and Zebul his 3378
9:57 came the curse of Jotham the son of J. 3378
1Sa 12:11 the LORD sent J, and Bedan, and 3378

JERUBBESHETH (1) [JERUBBAAL]
2Sa 11:21 Who smote Abimelech the son of J? 3380

JERUEL (1)
2Ch 20:16 of the brook, before the wilderness of J. 3385

JERUSALEM (811) [JEBUS, JERUSALEM'S, SALEM]
Jos 10: 1 when Adoni-zedek king of J had heard how 3389
10: 3 Wherefore Adoni-zedek king of J sent unto 3389
10: 5 the king of J, the king of Hebron, the king 3389
10:23 the king of J, the king of Hebron, the king 3389
12:10 The king of J, one; the king of Hebron, 3389
15: 8 the south side of the Jebusite; the same *is* J: 3389
15:63 As for the Jebusites the inhabitants of J, 3389
15:63 the children of Judah at J unto this day. 3389
18:28 Eleph, and Jebusi, which *is* J, Gibeath, *and* 3389
Jdg 1: 7 they brought him *to* J, and there he died. 3389
1: 8 the children of Judah had fought against J, 3389
1:21 not drive out the Jebusites that inhabited J; 3389
1:21 the children of Benjamin in J unto this day. 3389
19:10 and came over against Jebus, which *is* J; 3389
1Sa 17:54 head of the Philistine, and brought it *to* J; 3389
2Sa 5: 5 in J he reigned thirty and three years over 3389
5: 6 and his men went *to* J unto the Jebusites, 3389
5:13 *him* mo concubines and wives out of J, 3389
5:14 of those that were born unto him in J; 3389
8: 7 of Hadadezer, and brought them *to* J. 3389
9:13 So Mephibosheth dwelt in J: for he did eat 3389
10:14 the children of Ammon, and came *to* J. 3389
11: 1 But David tarried *still* at J. 3389
11:12 So Uriah abode in J that day, and 3389
12:31 and all the people returned *unto* J. 3389
14:23 went to Geshur, and brought Absalom *to* J. 3389
14:28 So Absalom dwelt two full years in J, and 3389
15: 8 LORD shall bring me again indeed *to* J, 3389
15:11 Absalom went two hundred men out of J, 3389
15:14 all his servants that *were* with him at J, 3389
15:29 Abiathar carried the ark of God again *to* J: 3389
15:37 *into* the city, and Absalom came *into* J. 3389
16: 3 said unto the king, Behold, he abideth at J: 3389
16:15 came *to* J, and Ahithophel with him. 3389
17:20 and could not find *them,* they returned *to* J. 3389
19:19 the day that my lord the king went out of J, 3389
19:25 when he was come *to* J to meet the king, 3389
19:33 with me, and I will feed thee with me in J. 3389
19:34 that I should go up with the king *unto* J? 3389
20: 2 unto their king, from Jordan even to J. 3389
20: 3 David came to his house at J; and the king 3389
20: 7 all the mighty *men:* and they went out of J, 3389
20:22 And Joab returned *to* J unto the king. 3389
24: 8 they came *to* J at the end of nine months 3389
24:16 stretched out his hand *upon* J to destroy it, 3389
1Ki 2:11 and thirty and three years reigned he in J. 3389
2:36 Build thee a house in J, and dwell there, 3389
2:38 And Shimei dwelt in J many days. 3389
2:41 that Shimei had gone from J *to* Gath, 3389
3: 1 the LORD, and the wall of J round about. 3389
3:15 he came *to* J, and stood before the ark of 3389
8: 1 children of Israel, unto king Solomon *in* J, 3389
9:15 the wall of J, and Hazor, and Megiddo, and 3389
9:19 that which Solomon desired to build in J, 3389
10: 2 she came to J with a very great train, 3389
10:26 cities for chariots, and with the king at J. 3389
10:27 the king made silver *to be* in J as stones, 3389
11: 7 in the hill that *is* before J, and for Molech, 3389
11:29 at that time when Jeroboam went out of J, 3389
11:36 may have a light alway before me in J, 3389
11:42 the time that Solomon reigned in J over all 3389

1Ki 12:18 to get *him* up to *his* chariot, to flee *to* J. 3389
12:21 when Rehoboam was come *to* J, he 3389
12:27 sacrifice in the house of the LORD at J, 3389
12:28 *It is* too much for you to go up *to* J: 3389
14:21 and he reigned seventeen years in J, 3389
14:25 Shishak king of Egypt came up against J: 3389
15: 2 Three years reigned he in J. And his 3389
15: 4 the LORD his God give him a lamp in J, 3389
15: 4 set up his son after him, and to establish J: 3389
15:10 forty and one years reigned he in J. And his 3389
22:42 and he reigned twenty and five years in J. 3389
2Ki 8:17 to reign; and he reigned eight years in J. 3389
8:26 to reign; and he reigned one year in J. 3389
9:28 his servants carried him *in a chariot* to J, 3389
12: 1 to reign; and forty years reigned he in J. 3389
12:17 and Hazael set his face to go up to J. 3389
12:18 king of Syria: and he went away from J. 3389
14: 2 and reigned twenty and nine years in J. 3389
14: 2 his mother's name *was* Jehoaddan of J. 3389
14:13 came *to* J, and brake down the wall of 3389
14:13 brake down the wall of J from the gate of 3389
14:19 they made a conspiracy against him in J: 3389
14:20 he was buried at J with his fathers in 3389
15: 2 and he reigned two and fifty years in J. 3389
15: 2 And his mother's name *was* Jecholiah of J. 3389
15:33 to reign, and he reigned sixteen years in J. 3389
16: 2 reigned sixteen years in J, and did not *that* 3389
16: 5 king of Israel came up *to* J to war: 3389
18: 2 and he reigned twenty and nine years in J. 3389
18:17 king Hezekiah with a great host *against* J. 3389
18:17 they went up and came *to* J. And when 3389
18:22 taken away, and hath said to Judah and J, 3389
18:22 Ye shall worship before this altar in J? 3389
18:35 that the LORD should deliver J out of 3389
19:10 J shall not be delivered into the hand of 3389
19:21 the daughter of J hath shaken her head at 3389
19:31 For out of J shall go forth a remnant, and 3389
21: 1 and reigned fifty and five years in J. 3389
21: 4 the LORD said, In J will I put my name. 3389
21: 7 to Solomon his son, In this house, and in J, 3389
21:12 I *am* bringing *such* evil upon J and Judah, 3389
21:13 I will stretch over J the line of Samaria, 3389
21:13 I will wipe J as *a man* wipeth a dish, 3389
21:16 till he had filled J from one end to another; 3389
21:19 to reign, and he reigned two years in J. 3389
22: 1 and he reigned thirty and one years in J. 3389
22:14 (now she dwelt in J in the college;) and 3389
23: 1 unto him all the elders of Judah and of J. 3389
23: 2 and all the inhabitants of J with him, 3389
23: 4 he burnt them without J in the fields of 3389
23: 5 of Judah, and in the places round about J; 3389
23: 6 without J, unto the brook Kidron, and 3389
23: 9 came not up to the altar of the LORD in J, 3389
23:13 the high places that *were* before J, 3389
23:20 men's bones upon them, and returned *to* J. 3389
23:23 passover was holden to the LORD in J. 3389
23:24 were spied in the land of Judah and in J, 3389
23:27 will cast off this city J which I have 3389
23:30 brought him *to* J, and buried him in his 3389
23:31 to reign; and he reigned three months in J. 3389
23:33 of Hamath, that *he* might not reign in J; 3389
23:36 to reign; and he reigned eleven years in J. 3389
24: 4 for he filled J *with* innocent blood; 3389
24: 8 to reign, and he reigned in J three months. 3389
24: 8 the daughter of Elnathan of J. 3389
24:10 king of Babylon came up *against* J, 3389
24:14 he carried away all J, and all the princes, 3389
24:15 *those* carried he *into* captivity from J to 3389
24:18 to reign, and he reigned eleven years in J. 3389
24:20 anger of the LORD it came to pass in J 3389
25: 1 his host, against J, and pitched against it; 3389
25: 8 a servant of the king of Babylon, *unto* J: 3389
25: 9 all the houses of J, and every great *man's* 3389
25:10 brake down the walls of J round about. 3389
1Ch 3: 4 and in J he reigned thirty and three years. 3389
3: 5 these were born unto him in J; Shimea, 3389
6:10 in the temple that Solomon built in J:) 3389
6:15 and J by the hand of Nebuchadnezzar. 3389
6:32 had built the house of the LORD in J: 3389
8:28 chief *men*. These dwelt in J. 3389
8:32 these also dwelt with their brethren in J, 3389
9: 3 in J dwelt of the children of Judah, and 3389
9:34 their generations; these dwelt at J. 3389
9:38 they also dwelt with their brethren at J, 3389
11: 4 David and all Israel went *to* J, which *is* 3389
14: 3 David took moe wives at J: and 3389
14: 4 names of *his* children which he had in J; 3389
15: 3 David gathered all Israel together to J, 3389
18: 7 of Hadarezer, and brought them *to* J. 3389
19:15 entered into the city. Then Joab came *to* J. 3389
20: 1 David tarried at J. And Joab smote Rabbah, 3389
20: 3 And David and all the people returned *to* J. 3389
21: 4 went throughout all Israel, and came *to* J. 3389
21:15 God sent an angel unto J to destroy it: and 3389
21:16 sword in his hand stretched out over J. 3389
23:25 that they may dwell in J for ever: 3389
28: 1 and with all the valiant men, unto J. 3389
29:27 and thirty and three *years* reigned he in J. 3389
2Ch 1: 4 for it: for he had pitched a tent for it at J. 3389
1:13 to the high place that *was* at Gibeon *to* J, 3389
1:14 in the chariot cities, and with the king at J. 3389
1:15 and gold at J *as plenteous* as stones, 3389
2: 7 *men* that *are* with me in Judah and in J, 3389
2:16 sea *to* Joppa; and thou shalt carry it up *to* J. 3389
3: 1 house of the LORD at J in mount Moriah, 3389
5: 2 the fathers of the children of Israel, unto J, 3389
6: 6 I have chosen J, that my name might be 3389
8: 6 all that Solomon desired to build in J, and 3389
9: 1 to prove Solomon with hard questions at J, 3389
9:25 in the chariot cities, and with the king at J. 3389
9:27 the king made silver in J as stones, and 3389
9:30 Solomon reigned in J over all Israel forty 3389
10:18 to get *him* up to *his* chariot, to flee *to* J. 3389
11: 1 when Rehoboam was come *to* J, he 3389
11: 5 Rehoboam dwelt in J, and built cities for 3389
2Ch 11:14 their possession, and came to Judah and J: 3389
11:16 seek the LORD God of Israel came *to* J, 3389
12: 2 Shishak king of Egypt came up against J, 3389
12: 4 which *pertained* to Judah, and came to J. 3389
12: 5 that were gathered together to J because 3389
12: 7 my wrath shall not be poured out upon J by 3389
12: 9 Shishak king of Egypt came up against J, 3389
12:13 king Rehoboam strengthened himself in J, 3389
12:13 and he reigned seventeen years in J, 3389
13: 2 He reigned three years in J. His mother's 3389
14:15 and camels in abundance, and returned *to* J. 3389
15:10 So they gathered themselves together *at* J 3389
17:13 of war, mighty *men* of valour, *were* in J. 3389
19: 1 Judah returned to his house in peace to J. 3389
19: 4 Jehoshaphat dwelt at J: and he went out 3389
19: 8 Moreover in J did Jehoshaphat set of 3389
19: 8 for controversies, when they returned *to* J. 3389
20: 5 stood in the congregation of Judah and J, 3389
20:15 ye inhabitants of J, and thou king 3389
20:17 of the LORD with you, O Judah and J: 3389
20:18 the inhabitants of J fell before the LORD, 3389
20:20 Hear me, O Judah, and ye inhabitants of J; 3389
20:27 every man of Judah and J, and 3389
20:27 forefront of them, to go again to J with joy; 3389
20:28 they came *to* J with psalteries and harps 3389
20:31 and he reigned twenty and five years in J. 3389
21: 5 to reign, and he reigned eight years in J. 3389
21:11 caused the inhabitants of J to commit 3389
21:13 and the inhabitants of J to go a whoring, 3389
21:20 he reigned in J eight years, and 3389
22: 1 the inhabitants of J made Ahaziah his 3389
22: 2 to reign, and he reigned one year in J. 3389
23: 2 of the fathers of Israel, and they came to J. 3389
24: 1 to reign, and he reigned forty years in J. 3389
24: 6 in out of Judah and out of J the collection, 3389
24: 9 made a proclamation through Judah and J, 3389
24:18 upon Judah and J for this their trespass. 3389
24:23 they came to Judah and J, and destroyed all 3389
25: 1 and he reigned twenty and nine years in J. 3389
25: 1 his mother's name *was* Jehoaddan of J. 3389
25:23 brought him *to* J, and brake down the wall 3389
25:23 brake down the wall of J from the gate of 3389
25:27 they made a conspiracy against him in J; 3389
26: 3 and he reigned fifty and two years in J. 3389
26: 3 His mother's name also *was* Jecoliah of J. 3389
26: 9 Moreover Uzziah built towers in J at 3389
26:15 he made in J engines, invented by cunning 3389
27: 1 to reign, and he reigned sixteen years in J. 3389
27: 8 to reign, and reigned sixteen years in J. 3389
28: 1 to reign, and he reigned sixteen years in J: 3389
28:10 J for bondmen and bondwomen unto you: 3389
28:24 he made him altars in every corner of J. 3389
28:27 and they buried him in the city, *even* in J: 3389
29: 1 and he reigned nine and twenty years in J. 3389
29: 8 of the LORD was upon Judah and J, 3389
30: 1 come to the house of the LORD at J, 3389
30: 2 his princes, and all the congregation in J, 3389
30: 3 people gathered themselves together to J. 3389
30: 5 unto the LORD God of Israel at J: 3389
30:11 humbled themselves, and came to J. 3389
30:13 there assembled *at* J much people to keep 3389
30:14 and took away the altars that *were* in J, 3389
30:21 the children of Israel that were present at J 3389
30:26 So there was great joy in J: for since 3389
30:26 king of Israel *there was* not the like in J. 3389
31: 4 dwelt in J to give the portion of the priests 3389
32: 2 and that he was purposed to fight against J, 3389
32: 9 king of Assyria send his servants to J, 3389
32: 9 and unto all Judah that *were* at J, saying, 3389
32:10 do ye trust, that ye abide in the siege in J? 3389
32:12 and commanded Judah and J, saying, 3389
32:18 unto the people of J that *were* on the wall, 3389
32:19 they spake against the God of J, as against 3389
32:22 the inhabitants of J from the hand of 3389
32:23 many brought gifts unto the LORD to J, 3389
32:25 wrath upon him, and upon Judah and J. 3389
32:26 *both* he and the inhabitants of J, so that 3389
32:33 the inhabitants of J did him honour at his 3389
33: 1 and he reigned fifty and five years in J: 3389
33: 4 had said, In J shall my name be for ever. 3389
33: 7 to Solomon his son, In this house, and in J, 3389
33: 9 made Judah and the inhabitants of J to err, 3389
33:13 brought him again *to* J into his kingdom. 3389
33:15 and in J, and cast *them* out of the city. 3389
33:21 *began* to reign, and reigned two years in J. 3389
34: 1 and he reigned in J one and thirty years. 3389
34: 3 to purge Judah and J from the high places, 3389
34: 5 upon their altars, and cleansed Judah and J. 3389
34: 7 all the land of Israel, he returned to J. 3389
34: 9 and Benjamin; and they returned *to* J. 3389
34:22 (now she dwelt in J in the college:) and 3389
34:29 together all the elders of Judah and J. 3389
34:30 the inhabitants of J, and the priests, and 3389
34:32 he caused all that were present in J and 3389
34:32 of J did according to the covenant of God, 3389
35: 1 kept a passover unto the LORD in J: 3389
35:18 that were present, and the inhabitants of J. 3389
35:24 they brought him *to* J, and he died, and 3389
35:24 And all Judah and J mourned for Josiah. 3389
36: 1 made him king in his father's stead in J. 3389
36: 2 to reign, and he reigned three months in J. 3389
36: 3 the king of Egypt put him down at J, and 3389
36: 4 Eliakim his brother king over Judah and J, 3389
36: 5 to reign, and he reigned eleven years in J: 3389
36: 9 he reigned three months and ten days in J: 3389
36:10 his brother king over Judah and J. 3389
36:11 to reign, and reigned eleven years in J. 3389
36:14 of the LORD which he had hallowed in J. 3389
36:19 brake down the wall of J, and burnt all 3389
36:23 hath charged me to build him a house in J, 3389
Ezr 1: 2 hath charged me to build him a house at J, 3389
1: 3 let him go up to J, which *is* in Judah, and 3389
1: 3 of Israel, (he *is* the God,) which *is* in J 3389
1: 4 offering for the house of God that *is* in J. 3389
1: 5 the house of the LORD which *is* in J. 3389
Ezr 1: 7 Nebuchadnezzar had brought forth out of J, 3389
1:11 that were brought up from Babylon unto J. 3389
2: 1 came again unto J and Judah, every one 3389
2:68 to the house of the LORD which *is* at J, 3389
3: 1 themselves together as one man to J. 3389
3: 8 of their coming unto the house of God at J, 3389
3: 8 that were come out of the captivity *unto* J; 3389
4: 6 against the inhabitants of Judah and J. 3389
4: 8 Shimshai the scribe wrote a letter against J 3390
4:12 came up from thee to us are come unto J, 3390
4:20 There have been mighty kings also over J, 3390
4:23 they went up in haste to J unto the Jews, 3390
4:24 work of the house of the God which *is* at J. 3390
5: 1 and J in the name of the God of Israel, 3390
5: 2 to build the house of God which *is* at J: 3390
5:14 took out of the temple that *was* in J, 3390
5:15 go, carry them into the temple that *is* in J, 3390
5:16 of the house of God which *is* in J: 3390
5:17 the king to build this house of God at J, 3390
6: 3 a decree *concerning* the house of God at J, 3390
6: 5 took forth out of the temple which *is* at J, 3390
6: 5 brought *again* unto the temple which *is* at J, 3390
6: 9 appointment of the priests which *are* at J, 3390
6:12 to destroy this house of God which *is* at J. 3390
6:18 for the service of God, which *is* at J; 3390
7: 7 and the porters, and the Nethinims, unto J, 3389
7: 8 he came *to* J in the fifth month, which *was* 3389
7: 9 first *day* of the fifth month came he to J, 3389
7:13 minded of their own freewill to go *up* to J, 3390
7:14 to inquire concerning Judah and J, 3390
7:15 the God of Israel, whose habitation *is* in J, 3390
7:16 for the house of their God which *is* in J: 3390
7:17 of the house of your God which *is* in J. 3390
7:19 *those* deliver thou before the God of J. 3390
7:27 the house of the LORD which *is* in J: 3389
8:29 and chief of the fathers of Israel, at J, 3389
8:30 to bring *them* to J unto the house of our 3389
8:31 twelfth *day* of the first month, to go *unto* J: 3389
8:32 we came *to* J, and abode there three days. 3389
9: 9 and to give us a wall in Judah and in J. 3389
10: 7 and J unto all the children of the captivity, 3389
10: 7 should gather themselves together *unto* J; 3389
10: 9 together *unto* J within three days. 3389
Ne 1: 2 were left of the captivity, and concerning J. 3389
1: 3 the wall of J also *is* broken down, and 3389
2:11 So I came to J, and was there three days. 3389
2:12 my God had put in my heart to do at J: 3389
2:13 to the dung port, and viewed the walls of J, 3389
2:17 how J *lieth* waste, and the gates thereof are 3389
2:17 come, and let us build *up* the wall of J, 3389
2:20 no portion, nor right, nor memorial, in J. 3389
3: 8 and they fortified J unto the broad wall. 3389
3: 9 son of Hur, the ruler of the half part of J. 3389
3:12 the ruler of the half part of J, he and 3389
4: 7 heard that the walls of J were made up, 3389
4: 8 together to come *and* to fight against J, 3389
4:22 every one with his servant lodge within J, 3389
6: 7 appointed prophets to preach of thee at J, 3389
7: 2 the ruler of the palace, charge over J: 3389
7: 3 Let not the gates of J be opened until 3389
7: 3 and appoint watches of the inhabitants of J, 3389
7: 6 came again to J and to Judah, every one 3389
8:15 in J, saying, Go forth *unto* the mount, and 3389
11: 1 the rulers of the people dwelt at J: the rest 3389
11: 1 to bring one of ten to dwell in J the holy 3389
11: 2 willingly offered themselves to dwell at J. 3389
11: 3 *are* the chief of the province that dwelt in J: 3389
11: 4 at J dwelt *certain* of the children of Judah, 3389
11: 6 All the sons of Perez that dwelt at J *were* 3389
11:22 The overseer also of the Levites at J *was* 3389
12:27 at the dedication of the wall of J they 3389
12:27 to bring them to J, to keep the dedication 3389
12:28 both out of the plain country round about J, 3389
12:29 had builded them villages round about J. 3389
12:43 so that the joy of J was heard even afar off. 3389
13: 6 in all this *time* was not I at J: for in the two 3389
13: 7 I came to J, and understood of the evil that 3389
13:15 which they brought *into* J on the sabbath 3389
13:16 unto the children of Judah, and in J. 3389
13:19 that when the gates of J began to be dark 3389
13:20 sellers of all *kind of* ware lodged without J 3389
Est 2: 6 Who had been carried away from J with 3389
Ps 51:18 unto Zion: build thou the walls of J. 3389
68:29 Because of thy temple at J shall kings bring 3389
79: 1 they defiled; they have laid J on heaps. 3389
79: 3 have they shed like water round about J; 3389
102:21 of the LORD in Zion, and his praise in J; 3389
116:19 LORD'S house, in the midst of thee, O J. 3389
122: 2 Our feet shall stand within thy gates, O J. 3389
122: 3 J *is* builded as a city that is compact 3389
122: 6 Pray for the peace of J: they shall prosper 3389
125: 2 *As* the mountains *are* round about J, so 3389
128: 5 thou shalt see the good of J all the days of 3389
135:21 LORD out of Zion, which dwelleth *at* J. 3389
137: 5 If I forget thee, O J, let my right hand 3389
137: 6 if I prefer not J above my chief joy. 3389
137: 7 the children of Edom *in* the day of J; 3389
147: 2 The LORD doth build up J: he gathereth 3389
147:12 Praise the LORD, O J; praise thy God, 3389
Ecc 1: 1 of the Preacher, the son of David, king in J. 3389
1:12 I the Preacher was king over Israel in J. 3389
1:16 than all *they* that have been before me in J: 3389
2: 7 small cattle above all that were in J before 3389
2: 9 more than all that were before me in J: 3389
SS 1: 5 *am* black, but comely, O ye daughters of J, 3389
2: 7 O ye daughters of J, by the roes, and by 3389
3: 5 O ye daughters of J, by the roes, and by 3389
3:10 paved *with* love, for the daughters of J. 3389
5: 8 I charge you, O daughters of J, if ye find 3389
5:16 and this *is* my friend, O daughters of J. 3389
6: 4 O my love, as Tirzah, comely as J, 3389
8: 4 I charge you, O daughters of J, that ye stir 3389
Isa 1: 1 and J in the days of Uzziah, 3389
2: 1 son of Amoz saw concerning Judah and J. 3389
2: 3 and the word of the LORD from J. 3389

Isa 3: 1 doth take away from J and from Judah 3389
3: 8 For J is ruined, and Judah is fallen: because 3389
4: 3 he that remaineth in J, shall be called holy, 3389
4: 3 one that is written among the living in J: 3389
4: 4 shall have purged the blood of J from 3389
5: 3 O inhabitants of J, and men of Judah, 3389
7: 1 went up *towards* J to war against it, but 3389
8:14 a gin and for a snare to the inhabitants of J. 3389
10:10 whose graven images did excel *them of* J 3389
10:11 and her idols, so do to J and her idols? 3389
10:12 his whole work upon mount Zion and on J, 3389
10:32 mount of the daughter of Zion, the hill of J. 3389
22:10 And ye have numbered the houses of J, and 3389
22:21 he shall be a father to the inhabitants of J, 3389
24:23 and in J, and before his ancients gloriously. 3389
27:13 worship the LORD in the holy mount at J. 3389
28:14 that rule this people which *is* in J. 3389
30:19 For the people shall dwell in Zion at J: 3389
31: 5 so will the LORD of hosts defend J; 3389
31: 9 whose fire *is* in Zion, and his furnace in J. 3389
33:20 thine eyes shall see J a quiet habitation, 3389
36: 2 to J unto king Hezekiah with a great army. 3389
36: 7 said to Judah and to J, Ye shall worship 3389
36:20 that the LORD should deliver J out of my 3389
37:10 J shall not be given into the hand of 3389
37:22 the daughter of J hath shaken her head at 3389
37:32 For out of J shall go forth a remnant, and 3389
40: 2 Speak ye comfortably to J, and cry unto 3389
40: 9 O J, that bringest good tidings, lift up thy 3389
41:27 I will give to J one that bringeth good 3389
44:26 that saith to J, Thou shalt be inhabited; and 3389
44:28 even saying to J, Thou shalt be built; and 3389
51:17 Awake, awake, stand up, O J, which hast 3389
52: 1 thy beautiful garments, O J, the holy city: 3389
52: 2 from the dust; arise, *and* sit down, O J: 3389
52: 9 sing together, ye waste places of J: 3389
52: 9 comforted his people, he hath redeemed J. 3389
62: 6 I have set watchmen upon thy walls, O J, 3389
62: 7 and till he make J a praise in the earth. 3389
64:10 Zion is a wilderness, J a desolation. 3389
65:18 I create J a rejoicing, and her people a joy. 3389
65:19 I will rejoice in J, and joy in my people: 3389
66:10 Rejoice ye with J, and be glad with her, 3389
66:13 and ye shall be comforted in J. 3389
66:20 to my holy mountain J, saith the LORD, 3389
Jer 1: 3 unto the carrying away of J captive in 3389
1:15 his throne *at* the entering of the gates of J, 3389
2: 2 Go and cry in the ears of J, saying, 3389
3:17 At that time they shall call J the throne of 3389
3:17 unto it, to the name of the LORD, to J: 3389
4: 3 the LORD to the men of Judah and J, 3389
4: 4 ye men of Judah and inhabitants of J: 3389
4: 5 Declare ye in Judah, and publish in J; and 3389
4:10 hast greatly deceived this people and J, 3389
4:11 time shall it be said to this people and to J, 3389
4:14 O J, wash thine heart from wickedness, that 3389
4:16 behold, publish against J, *that* watchers 3389
5: 1 Run ye to and fro through the streets of J, 3389
6: 1 yourselves to flee out of the midst of J, 3389
6: 6 ye down trees, and cast a mount against J: 3389
6: 8 Be thou instructed, O J, lest my soul depart 3389
7:17 in the cities of Judah and in the streets of J? 3389
7:29 *O J,* and cast *it* away, and take up a NIH
7:34 from the streets of J, the voice of mirth, 3389
8: 1 the bones of the inhabitants of J, out of 3389
8: 5 is this people of J slidden back *by* a 3389
9:11 I will make J heaps, *and* a den of dragons; 3389
11: 2 men of Judah, and to the inhabitants of J; 3389
11: 6 in the streets of J, saying, Hear ye 3389
11: 9 of Judah, and among the inhabitants of J. 3389
11:12 the cities of Judah and inhabitants of J go, 3389
11:13 *according to* the number of the streets of J 3389
13: 9 the pride of Judah, and the great pride of J. 3389
13:13 the prophets, and all the inhabitants of J, 3389
13:27 Woe unto thee, O J! wilt thou not be made 3389
14: 2 the ground; and the cry of J is gone up. 3389
14:16 prophesy shall be cast out in the streets of J 3389
15: 4 king of Judah, for *that* which he did in J. 3389
15: 5 For who shall have pity upon thee, O J? or 3389
17:19 which they go out, and in all the gates of J; 3389
17:20 and all Judah, and all the inhabitants of J, 3389
17:21 nor bring *it* in by the gates of J; 3389
17:25 the men of Judah, and the inhabitants of J: 3389
17:26 from the places about J, and from the land 3389
17:27 even entering in at the gates of J on 3389
17:27 it shall devour the palaces of J, and it shall 3389
18:11 to the inhabitants of J, saying, Thus saith 3389
19: 3 O kings of Judah, and inhabitants of J; 3389
19: 7 the counsel of Judah and J in this place; 3389
19:13 the houses of J, and the houses of the kings 3389
22:19 drawn and cast forth beyond the gates of J. 3389
23:14 I have seen also in the prophets of J a 3389
23:15 for from the prophets of J is profaneness 3389
24: 1 from J, and had brought them *to* Babylon. 3389
24: 8 his princes, and the residue of J, 3389
25: 2 and to all the inhabitants of J, saying, 3389
25:18 *To wit,* J, and the cities of Judah, and 3389
26:18 J shall become heaps, and the mountain of 3389
27: 3 come *to* J unto Zedekiah king of Judah; 3389
27:18 king of Judah, and at J, go not to Babylon. 3389
27:20 king of Judah from J to Babylon, 3389
27:20 and all the nobles of Judah and J; 3389
27:21 *in* the house of the king of Judah and of J; 3389
29: 1 J unto the residue of the elders which were 3389
29: 1 carried away captive from J to Babylon; 3389
29: 2 the princes of Judah and J, and 3389
29: 2 and the smiths, were departed from J;) 3389
29: 4 to be carried away from J unto Babylon; 3389
29:20 whom I have sent from J to Babylon: 3389
29:25 in thy name unto all the people that *are* at J, 3389
32: 2 the king of Babylon's army besieged J: 3389
32:32 the men of Judah, and the inhabitants of J. 3389
32:44 in the places about J, and in the cities of 3389
33:10 in the streets of J, that are desolate, without 3389
33:13 in the places about J, and in the cities of 3389
Jer 33:16 Judah be saved, and J shall dwell safely: 3389
34: 1 fought against J, and against all the cities 3389
34: 6 words unto Zedekiah king of Judah in J, 3389
34: 7 king of Babylon's army fought against J, 3389
34: 8 with all the people which *were* at J, 3389
34:19 the princes of J, the eunuchs, and 3389
35:11 let us go *to* J for fear of the army of 3389
35:11 the army of the Syrians: so we dwell at J. 3389
35:13 the men of Judah and the inhabitants of J, 3389
35:17 upon all the inhabitants of J all the evil that 3389
36: 9 before the LORD *to* all the people in J, 3389
36: 9 that came from the cities of Judah unto J. 3389
36:31 upon the inhabitants of J, and upon the men 3389
37: 5 when the Chaldeans that besieged J heard 3389
37: 5 tidings of them, they departed from J. 3389
37:11 up from J for fear of Pharaoh's army, 3389
37:12 Jeremiah went forth out of J to go *into* 3389
38:28 of the prison until the day that J was taken: 3389
38:28 and he was *there* when J was taken. 3389
39: 1 king of Babylon and all his army against J, 3389
39: 8 with fire, and brake down the walls of J. 3389
40: 1 all that were carried away captive of J 3389
42:18 been poured forth upon the inhabitants of J; 3389
44: 2 seen all the evil that I have brought upon J, 3389
44: 6 in the cities of Judah and in the streets of J; 3389
44: 9 in the land of Judah, and in the streets of J? 3389
44:13 as I have punished J, by the sword, by 3389
44:17 the cities of Judah, and in the streets of J: 3389
44:21 in the streets of J, ye, and your fathers, 3389
51:35 the inhabitants of Chaldea, shall J say. 3389
51:50 afar off, and let J come into your mind. 3389
52: 1 to reign, and he reigned eleven years in J. 3389
52: 3 anger of the LORD it came to pass in J 3389
52: 4 against J, and pitched against it, and 3389
52:12 *which* served the king of Babylon, into J, 3389
52:13 all the houses of J, and all the houses of 3389
52:14 brake down all the walls of J round about. 3389
52:29 away captive from J eight hundred thirty 3389
La 1: 7 J remembered in the days of her affliction 3389
1: 8 J hath grievously sinned; therefore she is 3389
1:17 J is as a menstruous *woman* among them. 3389
2:10 the virgins of J hang down their heads to 3389
2:13 *thing* shall I liken to thee, O daughter of J? 3389
2:15 and wag their head at the daughter of J, 3389
4:12 should have entered into the gates of J. 3389
Eze 4: 1 and pourtray upon it *the* city, *even* J: 3389
4: 7 shalt set thy face toward the siege of J, 3389
4:16 behold, I will break the staff of bread in J: 3389
5: 5 Thus saith the Lord GOD; This *is* J: 3389
8: 3 and brought me in the visions of God to J, 3389
9: 4 the midst of the city through the midst of J, 3389
9: 8 in thy pouring out of thy fury upon J? 3389
11:15 *are* they unto whom the inhabitants of J 3389
12:10 This burden *concerneth* the prince in J, and 3389
12:19 of the inhabitants of J, *and* of the land of 3389
13:16 of Israel which prophesy concerning J, 3389
14:21 I send my four sore judgments upon J, 3389
14:22 the evil that I have brought upon J, 3389
15: 6 for fuel, so will I give the inhabitants of J. 3389
16: 2 of man, cause J to know her abominations, 3389
16: 3 And say, Thus saith the Lord GOD unto J; 3389
17:12 the king of Babylon is come *to* J, and 3389
21: 2 set thy face toward J, and drop *thy word* 3389
21:20 and to Judah in J the defenced. 3389
21:22 At his right hand was the divination for J, 3389
22:19 I will gather you into the midst of J. 3389
23: 4 Samaria *is* Aholah, and J Aholibah. 3389
24: 2 the king of Babylon set himself against J 3389
26: 2 because that Tyrus hath said against J, Aha, 3389
33:21 *that* one that had escaped out of J came 3389
36:38 as the flock of J in her solemn feasts; 3389
Da 1: 1 Nebuchadnezzar king of Babylon *unto* J, 3389
5: 2 had taken out of the temple which *was* in J; 3390
5: 3 temple of the house of God which *was* at J; 3390
6:10 being open in his chamber toward J, 3390
9: 2 seventy years in the desolations of J. 3389
9: 7 to the inhabitants of J, and unto all Israel, 3389
9:12 not been done as hath been done upon J. 3389
9:16 thy fury be turned away from thy city J, 3389
9:16 J and thy people *are become* a reproach to 3389
9:25 to build J unto the Messiah the Prince *shall* 3389
Joel 2:32 mount Zion and in J shall be deliverance, 3389
3: 1 bring again the captivity of Judah and J, 3389
3: 6 the children of J have ye sold unto 3389
3:16 roar out of Zion, and utter his voice from J; 3389
3:17 shall J be holy, and there shall no strangers 3389
3:20 and J from generation to generation. 3389
Am 1: 2 roar from Zion, and utter his voice from J; 3389
2: 5 and it shall devour the palaces of J. 3389
Ob 1:11 cast lots upon J, even thou *wast* as one of 3389
1:20 the captivity of J, which *is* in Sepharad, 3389
Mic 1: 1 which he saw concerning Samaria and J. 3389
1: 5 the high places of Judah? *are they* not J? 3389
1: 9 come unto the gate of my people, *even* to J. 3389
1:12 down from the LORD unto the gate of J. 3389
3:10 up Zion with blood, and J with iniquity. 3389
3:12 J shall become heaps, and the mountain of 3389
4: 2 and the word of the LORD from J. 3389
4: 8 kingdom shall come to the daughter of J. 3389
Zep 1: 4 and upon all the inhabitants of J; 3389
1:12 *that* I will search J with candles, and 3389
3:14 rejoice with all the heart, O daughter of J. 3389
3:16 In that day it shall be said to J, Fear thou 3389
Zec 1:12 how long wilt thou not have mercy on J 3389
1:14 I am jealous for J and for Zion *with* a great 3389
1:16 I am returned to J with mercies: 3389
1:16 and a line shall be stretched forth upon J. 3389
1:17 yet comfort Zion, and shall yet choose J. 3389
1:19 which have scattered Judah, Israel, and J. 3389
2: 2 he said unto me, To measure J, to see what 3389
2: 4 J shall be inhabited *as* towns without walls 3389
2:12 in the holy land, and shall choose J again. 3389
3: 2 even the LORD that hath chosen J rebuke 3389
7: 7 when J was inhabited and in prosperity, 3389
8: 3 unto Zion, and will dwell in the midst of J: 3389
Zec 8: 3 J shall be called a city of truth; and 3389
8: 4 and old women dwell in the streets of J, 3389
8: 8 and they shall dwell in the midst of J: 3389
8:15 I thought in these days to do well unto J 3389
8:22 come to seek the LORD of hosts in J, 3389
9: 9 O daughter of Zion; shout, O daughter of J: 3389
9:10 the horse from J, and the battle bow shall 3389
12: 2 I *will* make J a cup of trembling unto all 3389
12: 2 the siege both against Judah *and* against J. 3389
12: 3 in that day will I make J a burdensome 3389
12: 5 The inhabitants of J *shall be* my strength in 3389
12: 6 J shall be inhabited again in her own place, 3389
12: 6 inhabited again in her own place, *even* in J. 3389
12: 7 the glory of the inhabitants of J do not 3389
12: 8 the LORD defend the inhabitants of J; 3389
12: 9 destroy all the nations that come against J. 3389
12:10 upon the inhabitants of J, the spirit of grace 3389
12:11 day shall there be a great mourning in J, 3389
13: 1 to the inhabitants of J for sin and 3389
14: 2 For I will gather all nations against J to 3389
14: 4 which *is* before J on the east, and 3389
14: 8 *that* living waters shall go out from J: 3389
14:10 a plain from Geba to Rimmon south of J: 3389
14:11 but J shall be safely inhabited. 3389
14:12 all the people that have fought against J; 3389
14:14 Judah also shall fight at J; and the wealth 3389
14:16 J shall even go up from year to year to 3389
14:17 of the earth unto J to worship the King, 3389
14:21 every pot in J and in Judah shall be 3389
Mal 2:11 is committed in Israel and in J; 3389
3: 4 and J be pleasant unto the LORD, 3389
Mt 2: 1 there came wise men from the east to J, *2414*
2: 3 *things,* he was troubled, and all J with him. *2414*
3: 5 Then went out to him J, and all Judea, and *2414*
4:25 and *from* J, and *from* Judea, and *2414*
5:35 neither by J; for it is the city of the great *2414*
15: 1 and Pharisees, which were of J, saying, *2414*
16:21 how that he must go unto J, and *2414*
20:17 And Jesus going up to J took the twelve *2414*
20:18 Behold, we go up to J; and the Son of man *2414*
21: 1 And when they drew nigh unto J, and *2414*
21:10 And when he was come into J, all the city *2414*
23:37 O J, Jerusalem, *thou* that killest *2419*
23:37 O Jerusalem, J, *thou* that killest *2419*
Mk 1: 5 and they of J, and were all baptized of him *2415*
3: 8 And from J, and from Idumea, and *2414*
3:22 And the scribes which came down from J *2414*
7: 1 certain of the scribes, which came from J. *2414*
10:32 And they were in the way going up to J; *2414*
10:33 *Saying,* Behold, we go up to J; and the Son *2414*
11: 1 And when they came nigh to J, *2419*
11:11 And Jesus entered into J, and into *2414*
11:15 And they come to J: and Jesus went into *2414*
11:27 And they come again to J: and as he was *2414*
15:41 *women* which came up with him unto J. *2414*
Lk 2:22 they brought him to J, to present *him* to *2414*
2:25 And behold, there was a man in J, *2419*
2:38 to all them that looked for redemption in J. *2419*
2:41 Now his parents went to J every year at *2419*
2:42 they went up to J after the custom of *2414*
2:43 the child Jesus tarried behind in J; *2419*
2:45 they turned back again to J, seeking him. *2419*
4: 9 And he brought him to J, and set him on a *2419*
5:17 of every town of Galilee, and Judea, and J: *2419*
6:17 multitude of people out of all Judea and J, *2419*
9:31 decease which he should accomplish at J. *2419*
9:51 he stedfastly set his face to go to J, *2419*
9:53 his face was *as though he* would go to J. *2419*
10:30 A certain man went down from J to *2419*
13: 4 were sinners above all men that dwelt in J? *2419*
13:22 teaching, and journeying towards J. *2419*
13:33 it cannot be that a prophet perish out of J. *2419*
13:34 O J, Jerusalem, which killest the prophets, *2419*
13:34 O Jerusalem, J, which killest the prophets, *2419*
17:11 And it came to pass, as he went to J, that he *2419*
18:31 we go up to J, and all *things* that are *2414*
19:11 because he was nigh to J, and *because* *2419*
19:28 he went before, ascending up to J. *2414*
21:20 And when ye shall see J compassed with *2419*
21:24 J shall be trodden down of the Gentiles, *2419*
23: 7 who himself also was at J at that time. *2414*
23:28 said, Daughters of J, weep not for me, but *2419*
24:13 which was from J *about* threescore *2419*
24:18 Art thou only a stranger in J, and hast not *2419*
24:33 and returned to J, and found the eleven *2419*
24:47 his name among all nations, beginning at J. *2419*
24:49 but tarry ye in the city of J, until ye be *2419*
24:52 and returned to J with great joy: *2419*
Jn 1:19 sent priests and Levites from J to ask him, *2414*
2:13 was at hand, and Jesus went up to J, *2414*
2:23 Now when he was in J at the passover, *2414*
4:20 that in J is the place where *men* ought to *2414*
4:21 nor *yet* at J, worship the Father. *2414*
4:45 having seen all *the things* that he did at J at *2414*
5: 1 a feast of the Jews; and Jesus went up to J. *2414*
5: 2 Now there is at J by the sheep *market* a *2414*
7:25 Then said some of them of J, Is not this he, *2415*
10:22 And it was at J *the feast of* the dedication, *2414*
11:18 Now Bethany was nigh unto J, *2414*
11:55 many went out of the country up to J *2414*
12:12 they heard that Jesus was coming to J, *2414*
Ac 1: 4 them that *they* should not depart from J, *2414*
1: 8 ye shall be witnesses unto me both in J, *2419*
1:12 Then returned they unto J from the mount *2419*
1:12 which is from J a sabbath day's journey. *2419*
1:19 it was known unto all the dwellers at J; *2419*
2: 5 And there were dwelling at J Jews, *2419*
2:14 Ye men of Judea, and all *ye* that dwell at J, *2419*
4: 6 the high priest, were gathered together at J. *2419*
4:16 them *is* manifest to all them that dwell in J; *2419*
5:16 *out* of the cities round about unto J, *2419*
5:28 ye have filled J with your doctrine, and *2419*
6: 7 the number of the disciples multiplied in J *2419*
8: 1 against the church which was at J; *2414*
8:14 Now when the apostles which were at J *2414*

Ac 8:25 returned to J, and preached the gospel in *2419*
8:26 the way that goeth down from J unto Gaza, *2419*
8:27 and had come to J for to worship, *2419*
9: 2 women, he might bring *them* bound unto J. *2419*
9:13 much evil he hath done to thy saints at J: *2419*
9:21 them which called on this name in J, *2419*
9:26 And when Saul was come to J, he assayed *2419*
9:28 with them coming in and going out at J. *2419*
10:39 did both in the land of the Jews, and in J; *2419*
11: 2 And when Peter was come up to J, *2414*
11:22 unto the ears of the church which was in J: *2414*
11:27 And in these days came prophets from J *2414*
12:25 And Barnabas and Saul returned from J, *2419*
13:13 John departing from them returned to J. *2414*
13:27 For they that dwell at J, and their rulers, *2419*
13:31 which came up with him from Galilee to J, *2419*
15: 2 should go up to J unto the apostles and *2419*
15: 4 And when they were come to J, they were *2419*
16: 4 of the apostles and elders which were at J. *2419*
18:21 all means keep *this* feast that cometh in J: *2414*
19:21 and Achaia, to go to J, saying, *2419*
20:16 for him, to be at J the day of Pentecost. *2414*
20:22 now behold, I go bound in the spirit unto J, *2419*
21: 4 the Spirit, that *he* should not go up to J. *2419*
21:11 So shall the Jews at J bind the man that *2419*
21:12 that place, besought him not to go up to J. *2419*
21:13 also to die at J for the name of the Lord *2419*
21:15 we took up our carriages, and went up to J. *2419*
21:17 And when we were come to J, the brethren *2414*
21:31 of the band, that all J was in an uproar. *2419*
22: 5 bound unto J, for to be punished. *2419*
22:17 to pass that, when I was come again to J, *2419*
22:18 Make haste, and get *thee* quickly out of J: *2419*
23:11 for as thou hast testified of me in J, so *2419*
24:11 twelve days since I went up to J for to *2419*
25: 1 three days he ascended from Cesarea to J. *2414*
25: 3 that he would send for him to J, *2419*
25: 7 the Jews which came down from J stood *2414*
25: 9 Wilt thou go up to J, and there be judged of *2414*
25:15 About whom, when I was at J, the chief *2414*
25:20 I asked *him* whether he would go to J, and *2419*
25:24 both at J, and *also* here, crying that he *2414*
26: 4 at the first among mine own nation at J, *2414*
26:10 Which *thing* I also did in J: and many of *2414*
26:20 and at J, and throughout all the coasts of *2414*
28:17 *yet* was I delivered prisoner from J into *2414*
Ro 15:19 so that from J, and round about unto *2419*
15:25 But now I go unto J to minister unto *2419*
15:26 for the poor saints which are at J. *2419*
15:31 that my service which I have for J may be *2419*
1Co 16: 3 will I send to bring your liberality unto J. *2419*
Gal 1:17 Neither went I up to J to them which were *2414*
1:18 Then after three years I went up to J to see *2414*
2: 1 after I went up again to J with Barnabas, *2414*
4:25 and answereth to J which now is, and is in *2419*
4:26 But J which is above is free, which is *2419*
Heb 12:22 the heavenly J, and to an innumerable *2419*
Rev 3:12 of the city of my God, *which is* new J, *2419*
21: 2 And I John saw the holy city, new J, *2419*
21:10 and shewed me *that* great city, the holy J, *2419*

JERUSALEM'S (3) [JERUSALEM]
1Ki 11:13 and for J sake, which I have chosen. 3389
11:32 my servant David's sake, and for J sake, 3389
Isa 62: 1 my peace, and for J sake I will not rest, 3389

JERUSHA (1) [JERUSHAH]
2Ki 15:33 his mother's name *was* J, the daughter of 3388

JERUSHAH (1) [JERUSHA]
2Ch 27: 1 His mother's name also *was* J, the daughter 3388

JESAIAH (2)
1Ch 3:21 the sons of Hananiah; Pelatiah, and J: 3470
Ne 11: 7 of Maaseiah, the son of Ithiel, the son of J. 3470

JESARELAH See JESHARELAH

JESHAIAH (5)
1Ch 25: 3 Gedaliah, and Zeri, and J, Hashabiah, and 3470
25:15 The eighth *to* J, *he*, his sons, and 3470
26:25 J his son, and Joram his son, and Zichri his 3470
Ezr 8: 7 J the son of Athaliah, and with him seventy 3470
8:19 with him J of the sons of Merari, 3470

JESHANAH (1)
2Ch 13:19 J with the towns thereof, and Ephrain with 3466

JESHARELAH (1)
1Ch 25:14 The seventh *to* J, *he*, his sons, and 3480

JESHEBEAB (1)
1Ch 24:13 thirteenth to Huppah, the fourteenth to J, 3428

JESHER (1)
1Ch 2:18 sons *are* these, J, and Shobab, and Ardon. 3475

JESHIMON (6)
Nu 21:20 the top of Pisgah, which looketh toward J. 3452
23:28 *unto* the top of Peor, that looketh toward J. 3452
1Sa 23:19 hill of Hachilah, which *is* on the south of J? 3452
23:24 of Maon, in the plain on the south of J. 3452
26: 1 in the hill of Hachilah, *which is* before J? 3452
26: 3 of Hachilah, which *is* before J, by the way. 3452

JESHISHAI (1)
1Ch 5:14 the son of J, the son of Jahdo, the son of 3454

JESHOHAIAH (1)
1Ch 4:36 J, and Asaiah, and Adiel, and Jesimiel, and 3439

JESHUA (30) [JOSHUA]
1Ch 24:11 The ninth to J, the tenth to Shecaniah, 3442
2Ch 31:15 J, and Shemaiah, Amariah, and Shecaniah, 3442
Ezr 2: 2 J, Nehemiah, Seraiah, Reelaiah, Mordecai, 3442
2: 6 of the children of J *and* Joab, two thousand 3442
2:36 of the house of J, nine hundred seventy and 3442
2:40 the children of J and Kadmiel, of 3442
3: 2 stood up J the son of Jozadak, and 3442
3: 8 J the son of Jozadak, and the remnant of 3442
3: 9 stood J *with* his sons and his brethren, 3442
4: 3 J, and the rest of the chief of the fathers of 3442
5: 2 J the son of Jozadak, and began to build 3443
8:33 with them *was* Jozabad the son of J, and 3442
10:18 *namely*, of the sons of J the son of Jozadak, 3442
Ne 3:19 next to him repaired Ezer the son of J, 3442
7: 7 J, Nehemiah, Azariah, Raamiah, 3442
7:11 of the children of J and Joab, two thousand 3442
7:39 of the house of J, nine hundred seventy and 3442
7:43 the children of J, of Kadmiel, *and* of 3442
8: 7 Also J, and Bani, and Sherebiah, Jamin, 3442
8:17 for since the days of J the son of Nun unto 3442
9: 4 J, and Bani, Kadmiel, Shebaniah, Bunni, 3442
9: 5 J and Kadmiel, Bani, Hashabniah, 3442
10: 9 both J the son of Azaniah, Binnui of 3442
11:26 at J, and at Moladah, and at Beth-phelet, 3442
12: 1 with Zerubbabel the son of Shealtiel, and J: 3442
12: 7 and of their brethren in the days of J. 3442
12: 8 J, Binnui, Kadmiel, Sherebiah, Judah, *and* 3442
12:10 J begat Joiakim, Joiakim also begat 3442
12:24 Sherebiah, and J the son of Kadmiel, 3442
12:26 *were* in the days of Joiakim the son of J, 3442

JESHURUN (4)
Dt 32:15 J waxed fat, and kicked: thou art waxed fat, 3484
33: 5 he was king in J, when the heads of 3484
33:26 *There is* none like unto the God of J, 3484
Isa 44: 2 and *thou*, J, whom I have chosen. 3484

JESIAH (2)
1Ch 12: 6 J, and Azareel, and Joezer, and Jashobeam, 3449
23:20 Michah the first, and J the second. 3449

JESIMIEL (1)
1Ch 4:36 and Asaiah, and Adiel, and J, and Benaiah, 3450

JESSE (47)
Ru 4:17 he *is* the father of J, the father of David. 3448
4:22 And Obed begat J, and Jesse begat David. 3448
4:22 And Obed begat Jesse, and J begat David. 3448
1Sa 16: 1 go, I will send thee to J the Beth-lehemite: 3448
16: 3 call J to the sacrifice, and I will shew thee 3448
16: 5 he sanctified J and his sons, and 3448
16: 8 J called Abinadab, and made him pass 3448
16: 9 J made Shammah to pass by. And he said, 3448
16:10 J made seven of his sons to pass before 3448
16:10 Samuel said unto J, The LORD hath not 3448
16:11 Samuel said unto J, Are here all *thy* 3448
16:11 Samuel said unto J, Send and fetch him: 3448
16:18 I have seen a son of J the Beth-lehemite, 3448
16:19 Wherefore Saul sent messengers unto J, 3448
16:20 J took an ass *laden* with bread, and a bottle 3448
16:22 Saul sent to J, saying, Let David, I pray 3448
17:12 of Beth-lehem-judah, whose name *was* J; 3448
17:13 the three eldest sons of J went *and* 3448
17:17 J said unto David his son, Take now for thy 3448
17:20 took, and went, as J had commanded him; 3448
17:58 *I am* the son of thy servant J 3448
20:27 Wherefore cometh not the son of J to meat, 3448
20:30 chosen the son of J to thine own confusion, 3448
20:31 For as long as the son of J liveth upon 3448
22: 7 will the son of J give every one of you 3448
22: 8 son hath made *a league* with the son of J, 3448
22: 9 said, I saw the son of J coming to Nob, 3448
22:13 thou and the son of J, in that thou hast 3448
25:10 who *is* the son of J? there be many servants 3448
2Sa 20: 1 neither have we inheritance in the son of J: 3448
23: 1 David the son of J said, and the man *who* 3448
1Ki 12:16 neither *have we* inheritance in the son of J: 3448
1Ch 2:12 And Boaz begat Obed, and Obed begat J, 3448
2:13 J begat his firstborn Eliab, and 3448
10:14 the kingdom unto David the son of J. 3448
12:18 *we*, David, and on thy side, thou son of J: 3448
29:26 Thus David the son of J reigned over all 3448
2Ch 10:16 *we have* none inheritance in the son of J: 3448
11:18 Abihail the daughter of Eliab the son of J; 3448
Ps 72:20 The prayers of David the son of J are 3448
Isa 11: 1 shall come forth a rod out of the stem of J, 3448
11:10 in that day there shall be a root of J, 3448
Mt 1: 5 begat Obed of Ruth; and Obed begat J; *2421*
1: 6 And J begat David the king; and David *2421*
Lk 3:32 Which was *the son* of J, which was *the son* *2421*
Ac 13:22 and said, I have found David the *son* of J, *2421*
Ro 15:12 There shall be a root of J, and he that *shall* *2421*

JESTING (1)
Eph 5: 4 Neither filthiness, nor foolish talking, nor j, *2160*

JESUI (1) [ISHUI, JESUITES]
Nu 26:44 of J, the family of the Jesuites: of Beriah, 3440

JESUITES (1) [JESUI]
Nu 26:44 of Jesui, the family of the J: of Beriah, 3441

JESUS (973) [JESUS']
Mt 1: 1 The book of the generation of J Christ, *2424*
1:16 of whom was born J, who is called Christ. *2424*
1:18 Now the birth of J Christ was on this wise: *2424*
1:21 forth a son, and thou shalt call his name J: *2424*
1:25 her firstborn son: and *he* called his name J. *2424*
2: 1 Now when J was born in Bethlehem of *2424*
3:13 Then cometh J from Galilee to Jordan unto *2424*
3:15 And J answering said unto him, Suffer *it to* *2424*
3:16 And J, when he was baptized, went up *2424*
4: 1 Then was J led up of the Spirit into *2424*
4: 7 J said unto him, It is written again, *2424*
4:10 Then saith J unto him, Get thee hence, *2424*
4:12 Now when J had heard that John was cast *2424*
4:17 From that time J began to preach, and *2424*
4:18 And J, walking by the sea of Galilee, *2424*
4:23 And J went about all Galilee, teaching in *2424*
7:28 to pass, when J had ended these sayings, *2424*
8: 3 And J put forth *his* hand, and touched him, *2424*
8: 4 And J saith unto him, See thou tell no *man*; *2424*
8: 5 And when J was entered into Capernaum, *2424*
8: 7 And J saith unto him, I will come and *2424*
8:10 When J heard *it*, he marvelled, and said to *2424*
8:13 And J said unto the centurion, Go thy way; *2424*
8:14 And when J was come into Peter's house, *2424*
8:18 Now when J saw great multitudes about *2424*
8:20 And J saith unto him, The foxes have *2424*
8:22 But J said unto him, Follow me; and let *2424*
8:29 we to do with thee, J, *thou* Son of God? *2424*
8:34 the whole city came out to meet J: *2424*
9: 2 J seeing their faith said unto the sick of *2424*
9: 4 And J knowing their thoughts said, *2424*
9: 9 And as J passed forth from thence, he saw *2424*
9:10 as J[S] sat at meat in the house, behold, *846*
9:12 But when J heard *that*, he said unto them, *2424*
9:15 And J said unto them, Can the children of *2424*
9:19 And J arose, and followed him, and *so* *2424*
9:22 But J turned him about, and when he saw *2424*
9:23 And when J came into the ruler's house, *2424*
9:27 And when J departed thence, two blind *2424*
9:28 and J saith unto them, Believe ye that I am *2424*
9:30 and J straitly charged them, saying, *2424*
9:35 And J went about all the cities and villages, *2424*
10: 5 These twelve J sent forth, and *2424*
11: 1 when J had made an end of commanding *2424*
11: 4 J answered and said unto them, Go and *2424*
11: 7 J began to say unto the multitudes *2424*
11:25 At that time J answered and said, I thank *2424*
12: 1 At that time J went on the sabbath day *2424*
12:15 But when J knew *it*, he withdrew himself *2424*
12:25 And J knew their thoughts, and said unto *2424*
13: 1 The same day went J out of the house, and *2424*
13:34 All these *things* spake J unto the multitude *2424*
13:36 Then J sent the multitude away, and *2424*
13:51 J saith unto them, Have ye understood all *2424*
13:53 *that* when J had finished these parables, *2424*
13:57 But J said unto them, A prophet is not *2424*
14: 1 Herod the tetrarch heard of the fame of J, *2424*
14:12 and buried it, and went and told J. *2424*
14:13 When J heard *of it*, he departed thence by *2424*
14:14 And J went forth, and saw a great *2424*
14:16 But J said unto them, They need not depart; *2424*
14:22 And straightway J constrained his disciples *2424*
14:25 And in the fourth watch of the night J went *2424*
14:27 But straightway J spake unto them, saying, *2424*
14:29 the ship, he walked on the water, to go to J. *2424*
14:31 And immediately J stretched forth *his* *2424*
15: 1 Then came to J scribes and Pharisees, *2424*
15:16 And J said, Are ye also yet without *2424*
15:21 Then J went thence, and departed into *2424*
15:28 Then J answered and said unto her, *2424*
15:29 And J departed from thence, and came nigh *2424*
15:32 Then J called his disciples unto *him*, and *2424*
15:34 And J saith unto them, How many loaves *2424*
16: 6 Then J said unto them, Take heed and *2424*
16: 8 *Which* when J perceived, he said unto *2424*
16:13 When J came into the coasts of Cesarea *2424*
16:17 And J answered and said unto him, *2424*
16:20 should tell no *man* that he was J the Christ. *2424*
16:21 From that time forth began J to shew unto *2424*
16:24 Then said J unto his disciples, If any *man* *2424*
17: 1 And after six days J taketh Peter, James, *2424*
17: 4 answered Peter, and said unto J, Lord, *2424*
17: 7 And J came and touched them, and said, *2424*
17: 8 their eyes, they saw no *man*, save J only. *2424*
17: 9 from the mountain, J charged them, saying, *2424*
17:11 And J answered and said unto them, *2424*
17:17 Then J answered and said, O faithless and *2424*
17:18 And J rebuked the devil; and he departed *2424*
17:19 Then came the disciples to J apart, *2424*
17:20 And J said unto them, Because of your *2424*
17:22 they abode in Galilee, J said unto them, *2424*
17:25 J prevented him, saying, What thinkest *2424*
17:26 J saith unto him, Then are the children free. *2424*
18: 1 At the same time came the disciples unto J, *2424*
18: 2 And J called a little child unto *him*, and *2424*
18:22 J saith unto him, I say not unto thee, *2424*
19: 1 *that* when J had finished these sayings, *2424*
19:14 But J said, Suffer little children, and *2424*
19:18 J said, Thou shalt do no murder, Thou shalt *2424*
19:21 J said unto him, If thou wilt be perfect, go *2424*
19:23 Then said J unto his disciples, Verily I say *2424*
19:26 But J beheld *them*, and said unto them, *2424*
19:28 And J said unto them, Verily I say unto *2424*
20:17 And J going up to Jerusalem took *2424*
20:22 But J answered and said, Ye know not *2424*
20:25 But J called them unto *him*, and said, *2424*
20:30 when they heard that J passed by, cried out, *2424*
20:32 And J stood still, and called them, and said, *2424*
20:34 So J had compassion *on them*, and *2424*
21: 1 mount of Olives, then sent J two disciples, *2424*
21: 6 and did as J commanded them, *2424*
21:11 This is J the prophet of Nazareth of *2424*
21:12 And J went into the temple of God, and *2424*
21:16 And J saith unto them, Yea; have ye never *2424*
21:21 J answered and said unto them, Verily I say *2424*
21:24 And J answered and said unto them, I also *2424*
21:27 And they answered J, and said, We cannot *2424*
21:31 J saith unto them, Verily I say unto you, *2424*
21:42 J saith unto them, Did ye never read in *2424*
22: 1 And J answered and spake unto them again *2424*
22:18 But J perceived their wickedness, and said, *2424*
22:29 J answered and said unto them, Ye do err, *2424*
22:37 J said unto him, Thou shalt love the Lord *2424*
22:41 were gathered together, J asked them, *2424*
23: 1 Then spake J to the multitude, and to his *2424*
24: 1 And J went out, and departed from *2424*
24: 2 And J said unto them, See ye not all these *2424*

J

Mt 24: 4 And J answered and said unto them, 2424
26: 1 when J had finished all these sayings, 2424
26: 4 And consulted that they might take J by 2424
26: 6 Now when J was in Bethany, in the house 2424
26:10 When J understood *it,* he said unto them, 2424
26:17 unleavened bread the disciples came to J, 2424
26:19 And the disciples did as J had appointed 2424
26:26 J took bread, and blessed *it,* and brake *it,* 2424
26:31 Then saith J unto them, All ye shall be 2424
26:34 J said unto him, Verily I say unto thee, 2424
26:36 Then cometh J with them unto a place 2424
26:49 And forthwith he came to J, and said, Hail, 2424
26:50 And J said unto him, Friend, wherefore art 2424
26:50 and laid hands on J, and took him. 2424
26:51 one of them which were with J stretched 2424
26:52 Then said J unto him, Put up again thy 2424
26:55 In that *same* hour said J to the multitudes, 2424
26:57 And they that had laid hold on J led *him* 2424
26:59 the council, sought false witness against J, 2424
26:63 But J held his peace. And the high priest 2424
26:64 J saith unto him, Thou hast said: 2424
26:69 saying, Thou also wast with J of Galilee. 2424
26:71 This *fellow* was also with J of Nazareth. 2424
26:75 And Peter remembered the word of J, 2424
27: 1 elders of the people took counsel against J 2424
27:11 And J stood before the governor: and 2424
27:11 And J said unto him, Thou sayest. 2424
27:17 Barabbas, or J which is called Christ? 2424
27:20 they should ask Barabbas, and destroy J. 2424
27:22 I do then with J which is called Christ? 2424
27:26 and when he had scourged J, he delivered 2424
27:27 Then the soldiers of the governor took J 2424
27:37 THIS IS J THE KING OF THE JEWS. 2424
27:46 And about the ninth hour J cried with a 2424
27:50 J, when he had cried again with a loud 2424
27:54 watching J, saw the earthquake, and 2424
27:55 which followed J from Galilee, 2424
27:58 went to Pilate, and begged the body of J. 2424
28: 5 for I know that ye seek J, which was 2424
28: 9 behold, J met them, saying, *All* hail. 2424
28:10 Then said J unto them, Be not afraid: 2424
28:16 into a mountain where J had appointed 2424
28:18 And J came and spake unto them, saying, 2424
Mk 1: 1 The beginning of the gospel of J Christ, 2424
1: 9 *that* J came from Nazareth of Galilee, and 2424
1:14 John was put in prison, J came into Galilee, 2424
1:17 And J said unto them, Come ye after me, 2424
1:24 we to do with thee, *thou* J of Nazareth? 2424
1:25 And J rebuked him, saying, Hold thy 2424
1:41 And J, moved with compassion, put forth 2424
1:45 insomuch that *J* could no more openly enter NIG
2: 5 When J saw their faith, he said unto 2424
2: 8 when J perceived in his spirit that they so 2424
2:15 that as *J* sat at meat in his house, NIG
2:15 and sinners sat also together with J and 2424
2:17 When J heard *it,* he saith unto them, They 2424
2:19 And J said unto them, Can the children of 2424
3: 7 But J withdrew himself with his disciples 2424
5: 6 But when he saw J afar off, he ran and 2424
5: 7 and said, What have I to do with thee, J, 2424
5:13 And forthwith J gave them leave. And 2424
5:15 And they come to J, and see him that was 2424
5:19 Howbeit J suffered him not, but saith unto 2424
5:20 how great *things* J had done for him: 2424
5:21 And when J was passed over again by ship 2424
5:24 And *J* went with him; and much people NIG
5:27 When she had heard of J, came in the press 2424
5:30 And J immediately knowing in himself that 2424
5:36 As soon as J heard the word *that was* 2424
6: 4 But J said unto them, A prophet is not 2424
6:30 gathered themselves together unto J, 2424
6:34 And J, when he came out, saw much 2424
7:27 But J said unto her, Let the children first be 2424
8: 1 J called his disciples unto *him,* and 2424
8:17 And when J knew *it,* he saith unto them, 2424
8:27 And J went out, and his disciples, into 2424
9: 2 And after six days J taketh with *him* Peter, 2424
9: 4 with Moses: and they were talking with J. 2424
9: 5 And Peter answered and said to J, Master, 2424
9: 8 any more, save J only with themselves. 2424
9:23 J said unto him, If thou canst believe, 2424
9:25 When J saw that the people came running 2424
9:27 But J took him by the hand, and lifted him 2424
9:39 But J said, Forbid him not: for there is no 2424
10: 5 And J answered and said unto them, 2424
10:14 But when J saw *it,* he was much 2424
10:18 And J said unto him, Why callest thou me 2424
10:21 Then J beholding him loved him, and 2424
10:23 And J looked round about, and saith unto 2424
10:24 But J answereth again, and saith unto them, 2424
10:27 And J looking upon them saith, With men 2424
10:29 And J answered and said, Verily I say unto 2424
10:32 up to Jerusalem; and J went before them: 2424
10:38 But J said unto them, Ye know not what ye 2424
10:39 And J said unto them, Ye shall indeed 2424
10:42 But J called them to *him,* and saith unto 2424
10:47 And when he heard that it was J of 2424
10:47 and say, J, *thou* Son of David, have mercy 2424
10:49 And J stood still, and commanded him to 2424
10:50 away his garment, rose, and came to J. 2424
10:51 And J answered and said unto him, 2424
10:52 And J said unto him, Go thy way; thy faith 2424
10:52 his sight, and followed J in the way. 2424
11: 6 And they said unto them even as J had 2424
11: 7 And they brought the colt to J, and 2424
11:11 And J entered into Jerusalem, and into 2424
11:14 And J answered and said unto it, No *man* 2424
11:15 and J went into the temple, and began to 2424
11:22 And J answering saith unto them, 2424
11:29 And J answered and said unto them, I will 2424
11:33 And they answered and said unto J, 2424
11:33 And J answering saith unto them, 2424
12:17 And J answering said unto them, Render to 2424
12:24 And J answering said unto them, Do ye not 2424
12:29 And J answered him, The first of all 2424

Mk 12:34 And when J saw that he answered 2424
12:35 And J answered and said, while he taught 2424
12:41 And J sat over against the treasury, and 2424
13: 2 And J answering said unto him, Seest thou 2424
13: 5 And J answering them began to say, 2424
14: 6 And J said, Let her alone; why trouble you 2424
14:18 And as they sat and did eat, J said, Verily I 2424
14:22 J took bread, and blessed, and brake *it,* and 2424
14:27 And J saith unto them, All ye shall be 2424
14:30 And J saith unto him, Verily I say unto 2424
14:48 And J answered and said unto them, Are ye 2424
14:53 And they led J away to the high priest: and 2424
14:55 all the council sought for witness against J 2424
14:60 and asked J, saying, Answerest thou 2424
14:62 And J said, I am: and ye shall see the Son 2424
14:67 *And* thou also wast with J of Nazareth. 2424
14:72 And Peter called to mind the word that J 2424
15: 1 and bound J, and carried *him* away, and 2424
15: 5 But J yet answered nothing; so that Pilate 2424
15:15 Barabbas unto them, and delivered J, 2424
15:34 And at the ninth hour J cried with a loud 2424
15:37 And J cried with a loud voice, and gave up 2424
15:43 unto Pilate, and craved the body of J. 2424
16: 6 Ye seek J of Nazareth, which was 2424
16: 9 Now when *J* was risen early the first *day* of NIG
Lk 1:31 bring forth a son, and shalt call his name J. 2424
2:21 his name was called J, which was *so* 2424
2:27 and when the parents brought in the child J, 2424
2:43 the child J tarried behind in Jerusalem; 2424
2:52 And J increased in wisdom and stature, and 2424
3:21 *that* J also being baptized, and praying, 2424
3:23 And J himself began *to be* about thirty 2424
4: 1 And J being full of the Holy Ghost 2424
4: 4 And J answered him, saying, It is written, 2424
4: 8 And J answered and said unto him, 2424
4:12 And J answering said unto him, It is said, 2424
4:14 And J returned in the power of the Spirit 2424
4:34 we to do with thee, *thou* J of Nazareth? 2424
4:35 And J rebuked him, saying, Hold thy 2424
5:10 And J said unto Simon, Fear not; 2424
5:12 who seeing J fell on *his* face, and 2424
5:19 with *his* couch into the midst before J. 2424
5:22 But when J perceived their thoughts, 2424
5:31 And J answering said unto them, They that 2424
6: 3 And J answering them said, Have ye not 2424
6: 9 Then said J unto them, I will ask you one 2424
6:11 one with another what they might do to J. 2424
7: 3 And when he heard of J, he sent unto him 2424
7: 4 And when they came to J, they besought 2424
7: 6 Then J went with them. And when he was 2424
7: 9 When J heard these *things,* he marvelled at 2424
7:19 *him* two of his disciples sent *them* to J, 2424
7:22 Then J answering said unto them, Go *your* 2424
7:37 when she knew that *J* sat at meat in NIG
7:40 And J answering said unto him, Simon, 2424
8:28 When he saw J, he cried out, and fell down 2424
8:28 with thee, J, *thou* Son of God most high? 2424
8:30 And J asked him, saying, What is thy 2424
8:35 and came to J, and found the man, out of 2424
8:35 sitting at the feet of J, clothed, and in his 2424
8:38 be with him: but J sent him away, saying, 2424
8:39 city how great *things* J had done unto him. 2424
8:40 it came to pass that, when J was returned, 2424
8:45 And J said, Who touched me? When all 2424
8:46 And J said, Somebody hath touched me: 2424
8:50 But when *J* heard *it,* he answered him, 2424
9:33 from him, Peter said unto J, Master, 2424
9:36 the voice was past, J was found alone. 2424
9:41 And J answering said, O faithless and 2424
9:42 tare *him.* And J rebuked the unclean spirit, 2424
9:43 every one at all *things* which J did, 2424
9:47 And J, perceiving the thought of their 2424
9:50 And J said unto him, Forbid *him* not: for he 2424
9:58 And J said unto him, Foxes have holes, and 2424
9:60 J said unto him, Let the dead bury their 2424
9:62 And J said unto him, No *man* having put 2424
10:21 In that hour J rejoiced in spirit, and said, 2424
10:29 willing to justify himself, said unto J, 2424
10:30 And J answering said, A certain man went 2424
10:37 Then said J unto him, Go, and do thou 2424
10:41 And J answered and said unto her, Martha, 2424
13: 2 And J answering said unto them, 2424
13:12 And when J saw her, he called *her* to *him,* 2424
13:14 that J had healed on the sabbath day, 2424
14: 3 And J answering spake unto the lawyers 2424
17:13 and said, J, Master, have mercy on us. 2424
17:17 And J answering said, Were there not ten 2424
18:16 But J called them unto *him,* and said, 2424
18:19 And J said unto him, Why callest thou me 2424
18:22 Now when J heard these *things,* he said 2424
18:24 And when J saw that he was very 2424
18:37 told him, that J of Nazareth passeth by. 2424
18:38 And he cried, saying, J, *thou* Son of David, 2424
18:40 And J stood, and commanded him to be 2424
18:42 And J said unto him, Receive thy sight: 2424
19: 1 And *J* entered and passed through Jericho. NIG
19: 3 And he sought to see J who he was; and 2424
19: 5 And when J came to the place, he looked 2424
19: 9 And J said unto him, This day is salvation 2424
19:35 And they brought him to J: and they cast 2424
19:35 upon the colt, and they set J thereon. 2424
20: 8 And J said unto them, Neither tell I you by 2424
20:34 And J answering said unto them, 2424
22:47 and drew near unto J to kiss him. 2424
22:48 But J said unto him, Judas, betrayest thou 2424
22:51 And J answered and said, Suffer ye thus 2424
22:52 Then J said unto the chief priests, and 2424
22:63 And the men that held J mocked him, and 2424
23: 8 And when Herod saw J, he was exceeding 2424
23:20 Pilate therefore, willing to release J, spake 2424
23:25 had desired; but he delivered J to their will. 2424
23:26 laid the cross, that *he* might bear *it* after J. 2424
23:28 But J turning unto them, said, Daughters of 2424
23:34 Then said J, Father, forgive them; for they 2424
23:42 And he said unto J, Lord, remember me 2424

Lk 23:43 And J said unto him, Verily I say unto thee, 2424
23:46 And when J had cried with a loud voice, 2424
23:52 went unto Pilate, and begged the body of J. 2424
24: 3 and found not the body of the Lord J. 2424
24:15 J himself drew near, and went with them. 2424
24:19 Concerning J of Nazareth, which was a 2424
24:36 J himself stood in the midst of them, and 2424
Jn 1:17 *but* grace and truth came by J Christ. 2424
1:29 The next day John seeth J coming unto 2424
1:36 And looking upon J as he walked, he saith, 2424
1:37 heard him speak, and they followed J. 2424
1:38 Then J turned, 2424
1:42 And he brought him to J. And when Jesus 2424
1:42 And when J beheld him, he said, Thou art 2424
1:43 The day following J would go forth into 2424
1:45 and the prophets, did write, J of Nazareth, 2424
1:47 J saw Nathanael coming to him, and 2424
1:48 J answered and said unto him, Before that 2424
1:50 J answered and said unto him, Because I 2424
2: 1 of Galilee; and the mother of J was there: 2424
2: 2 And both J was called, and his disciples, 2424
2: 3 the mother of J saith unto him, They have 2424
2: 4 J saith unto her, Woman, what have I to do 2424
2: 7 J saith unto them, Fill the waterpots with 2424
2:11 This beginning of miracles did J in Cana of 2424
2:13 was at hand, and J went up to Jerusalem, 2424
2:19 J answered and said unto them, 2424
2:22 and the word which J had said. 2424
2:24 But J did not commit himself unto them, 2424
3: 2 The same came to J by night, and said unto 2424
3: 3 J answered and said unto him, Verily, 2424
3: 5 J answered, Verily, verily, I say unto thee, 2424
3:10 J answered and said unto him, Art thou a 2424
3:22 After these *things* came J and his disciples 2424
4: 1 how the Pharisees had heard that J made 2424
4: 2 (Though J himself baptized not, but 2424
4: 6 J therefore, being wearied with *his* journey, 2424
4: 7 J saith unto her, Give me to drink. 2424
4:10 J answered and said unto her, If thou 2424
4:13 J answered and said unto her, 2424
4:16 J saith unto her, Go, call thy husband, and 2424
4:17 J said unto her, Thou hast well said, I have 2424
4:21 J saith unto her, Woman, believe me, 2424
4:26 J saith unto her, I that speak unto thee am 2424
4:34 J saith unto them, My meat is to do the will 2424
4:44 For J himself testified, that a prophet hath 2424
4:46 So J came again into Cana of Galilee, 2424
4:47 When he heard that J was come out of 2424
4:48 Then said J unto him, Except ye see signs 2424
4:50 J saith unto him, Go *thy way;* thy son 2424
4:50 And the man believed the word that J had 2424
4:53 in the which J said unto him, Thy son 2424
4:54 This *is* again the second miracle *that* J did, 2424
5: 1 of the Jews; and J went up to Jerusalem. 2424
5: 6 When J saw him lie, and knew that he had 2424
5: 8 J saith unto him, Rise, take up thy bed, and 2424
5:13 for J had conveyed himself away, 2424
5:14 Afterward J findeth him in the temple, and 2424
5:15 and told the Jews that it was J, 2424
5:16 And therefore did the Jews persecute J, and 2424
5:17 But J answered them, My Father worketh 2424
5:19 Then answered J and said unto them, 2424
6: 1 After these *things* J went over the sea of 2424
6: 3 And J went up into a mountain, and 2424
6: 5 When J then lift up *his* eyes, 2424
6:10 And J said, Make the men sit down. 2424
6:11 And J took the loaves; and when he had 2424
6:14 when they had seen the miracle that J did, 2424
6:15 When J therefore perceived that they 2424
6:17 was now dark, and J was not come to them. 2424
6:19 they see J walking on the sea, and drawing 2424
6:22 that J went not with his disciples into 2424
6:24 therefore saw that J was not there, 2424
6:24 and came to Capernaum, seeking for J. 2424
6:26 J answered them and said, Verily, verily, 2424
6:29 J answered and said unto them, This is 2424
6:32 Then J said unto them, Verily, verily, I say 2424
6:35 And J said unto them, I am the bread of 2424
6:42 And they said, Is not this J, the son of 2424
6:43 J therefore answered and said unto them, 2424
6:53 Then J said unto them, Verily, verily, I say 2424
6:61 When J knew in himself that his disciples 2424
6:64 For J knew from the beginning who they 2424
6:67 Then said J unto the twelve, Will ye also 2424
6:70 J answered them, Have not I chosen you 2424
7: 1 After these *things* J walked in Galilee: 2424
7: 6 Then J said unto them, My time is not yet 2424
7:14 Now about the midst of the feast J went up 2424
7:16 J answered them, and said, My doctrine is 2424
7:21 J answered and said unto them, I have done 2424
7:28 Then cried J in the temple as he taught, 2424
7:33 Then said J unto them, Yet a little while 2424
7:37 J stood and cried, saying, If any *man* thirst, 2424
7:39 because that J was not yet glorified.) 2424
7:50 (he that came to *J* by night, being one of NIG
8: 1 J went unto the mount of Olives. 2424
8: 6 But J stooped down, and with *his* finger 2424
8: 9 and J was left alone, and the woman 2424
8:10 When J had lift up *himself,* and saw none 2424
8:11 And J said unto her, Neither do I condemn 2424
8:12 Then spake J again unto them, saying, I am 2424
8:14 J answered and said unto them, Though I 2424
8:19 J answered, Ye neither know me, nor my 2424
8:20 These words spake J in the treasury, as he 2424
8:21 Then said J again unto them, I go my way, 2424
8:25 And J saith unto them, Even the same that I 2424
8:28 Then said J unto them, When ye have lift 2424
8:31 Then said J to those Jews which believed 2424
8:34 J answered them, Verily, verily, I say unto 2424
8:39 J saith unto them, If ye were Abraham's 2424
8:42 J said unto them, If God were your Father, 2424
8:49 J answered, I have not a devil; but I honour 2424
8:54 J answered, If I honour myself, my honour 2424
8:58 J said unto them, Verily, verily, I say unto 2424
8:59 but J hid himself, and went out of 2424

Jn 9: 1 And as J passed by, he saw a man *which* NIG
9: 3 J answered, Neither hath this *man* sinned, 2424
9:11 A man *that is* called J made clay, and 2424
9:14 And it was the sabbath day when J made 2424
9:35 J heard that they had cast him out; 2424
9:37 And J said unto him, Thou hast both seen 2424
9:39 And J said, For judgment I am come into 2424
9:41 J said unto them, If ye were blind, 2424
10: 6 This parable spake J unto them: but 2424
10: 7 Then said J unto them again, Verily, verily, 2424
10:23 And J walked in the temple in Solomon's 2424
10:25 J answered them, I told you, and ye believe 2424
10:32 J answered them, Many good works have I 2424
10:34 J answered them, Is it not written in your 2424
11: 4 When J heard *that*, he said, This sickness is 2424
11: 5 Now J loved Martha, and her sister, and 2424
11: 9 J answered, Are there not twelve hours in 2424
11:13 Howbeit J spake of his death: but 2424
11:14 Then said J unto them plainly, Lazarus is 2424
11:17 Then when J came, he found that he had 2424
11:20 as soon as she heard that J was coming, 2424
11:21 Then said Martha unto J, Lord, if thou 2424
11:23 J saith unto her, Thy brother shall rise 2424
11:25 J said unto her, I am the resurrection, and 2424
11:30 Now J was not yet come into the town, but 2424
11:32 Then when Mary was come where J was, 2424
11:33 When J therefore saw her weeping, and 2424
11:35 J wept. 2424
11:38 J therefore again groaning in himself 2424
11:39 J said, Take ye away the stone. Martha, 2424
11:40 J saith unto her, Said I not unto thee, that, 2424
11:41 And J lift up *his* eyes, and said, Father, 2424
11:44 J saith unto them, Loose him, and let *him* 2424
11:45 and had seen *the things* which J did, 2424
11:46 and told them what *things* J had done. 2424
11:51 he prophesied that J should die for *that* 2424
11:54 J therefore walked no more openly among 2424
11:56 Then sought they for J, and spake among 2424
12: 1 Then J six days before the passover came 2424
12: 3 and anointed the feet of J, and wiped his 2424
12: 7 Then said J, Let her alone: against the day 2424
12:11 of the Jews went away, and believed on J. 2424
12:12 when they heard that J was coming to 2424
12:14 And J, when he had found a young ass, 2424
12:16 but when J was glorified, then 2424
12:21 desired him, saying, Sir, we would see J. 2424
12:22 and again Andrew and Philip tell J. 2424
12:23 And J answered them, saying, The hour is 2424
12:30 J answered and said, This voice came not 2424
12:35 Then J said unto them, Yet a little while is 2424
12:36 These *things* spake J, and departed, and 2424
12:44 J cried and said, He that believeth on me, 2424
13: 1 when J knew that his hour was come that 2424
13: 3 J knowing that the Father had given all 2424
13: 7 J answered and said unto him, What I do 2424
13: 8 J answered him, If I wash thee not, 2424
13:10 J saith to him, He that is washed needeth 2424
13:21 When J had thus said, he was troubled in 2424
13:23 bosom one of his disciples, whom J loved. 2424
13:26 J answered, He it is, to whom I shall give a 2424
13:27 Then said J unto him, That thou doest, 2424
13:29 Judas had the bag, that J had said unto him, 2424
13:31 Therefore, when he was gone out, J said, 2424
13:36 J answered him, Whither I go, thou canst 2424
13:38 J answered him, Wilt thou lay down thy 2424
14: 6 J saith unto him, I am the way, the truth, 2424
14: 9 J saith unto him, Have I been so long time 2424
14:23 J answered and said unto him, If a man 2424
16:19 Now J knew that they were desirous to ask 2424
16:31 J answered them, Do ye now believe? 2424
17: 1 These *words* spake J, and lift up his eyes to 2424
17: 3 and J Christ, whom thou hast sent. 2424
18: 1 When J had spoken these *words*, he went 2424
18: 2 for J ofttimes resorted thither with his 2424
18: 4 J therefore, knowing all *things* that should 2424
18: 5 They answered him, J of Nazareth. 2424
18: 5 J saith unto them, I am *he*. And Judas also, 2424
18: 7 seek ye? And they said, J of Nazareth. 2424
18: 8 J answered, I have told you that I am *he*: if 2424
18:11 Then said J unto Peter, Put up thy sword 2424
18:12 the captain and officers of the Jews took J, 2424
18:15 And Simon Peter followed J, and *so* 2424
18:15 went in with J into the palace of the high 2424
18:19 high priest then asked J of his disciples, 2424
18:20 J answered him, I spake openly to 2424
18:22 one of the officers which stood by stroke J 2424
18:23 J answered him, If I have spoken evil, 2424
18:28 Then led they J from Caiaphas unto 2424
18:32 That the saying of J might be fulfilled, 2424
18:33 and called J, and said unto him, Art thou 2424
18:34 J answered him, Sayest thou this *thing* of 2424
18:36 J answered, My kingdom is not of this 2424
18:37 J answered, Thou sayest that I am a king. 2424
19: 1 Then Pilate therefore took J, and 2424
19: 5 Then came J forth, wearing the crown of 2424
19: 9 and saith unto J, Whence art thou? 2424
19: 9 art thou? But J gave him no answer. 2424
19:11 J answered, Thou couldest have no power 2424
19:13 he brought J forth, and sat down in 2424
19:16 And they took J, and led *him* away. 2424
19:18 on either side one, and J in the midst. 2424
19:19 J OF NAZARETH THE KING OF THE 2424
19:20 for the place where J was crucified was 2424
19:23 the soldiers, when they had crucified J, 2424
19:25 Now there stood by the cross of J his 2424
19:26 When J therefore saw *his* mother, and 2424
19:28 J knowing that all *things* were now 2424
19:30 When J therefore had received the vinegar, 2424
19:33 But when they came to J, and saw that he 2424
19:38 being a disciple of J, but secretly for fear of 2424
19:38 that he might take away the body of J: 2424
19:38 He came therefore, and took the body of J. 2424
19:39 which at the first came to J by night, and 2424
19:40 Then took they the body of J, and wound it 2424
19:42 There laid they J therefore because of 2424
Jn 20: 2 whom J loved, and saith unto them, 2424
20:12 at the feet, where the body of J had lain. 2424
20:14 and saw J standing, and knew not that it 2424
20:14 Jesus standing, and knew not that it was J. 2424
20:15 J saith unto her, Woman, why weepest 2424
20:16 J saith unto her, Mary. She turned herself, 2424
20:17 J saith unto her, Touch me not; for I am not 2424
20:19 came J and stood in the midst, and 2424
20:21 Then said J to them again, Peace *be* unto 2424
20:24 was not with them when J came. 2424
20:26 *then* came J, the doors being shut, 2424
20:29 J saith unto him, Thomas, because 2424
20:30 And many other signs truly did J in 2424
20:31 that ye might believe that J is the Christ, 2424
21: 1 After these *things* J shewed himself again 2424
21: 4 was now come, J stood on the shore: 2424
21: 4 but the disciples knew not that it was J. 2424
21: 5 Then J saith unto them, Children, have ye 2424
21: 7 Therefore that disciple whom J loved saith 2424
21:10 J saith unto them, Bring of the fish which 2424
21:12 J saith unto them, Come *and* dine. 2424
21:13 J then cometh, and taketh bread, and 2424
21:14 This *is* now the third time *that* J shewed 2424
21:15 J saith to Simon Peter, Simon, *son* of 2424
21:17 love thee. J saith unto him, Feed my sheep. 2424
21:20 seeth the disciple whom J loved following; 2424
21:21 Peter seeing him saith to J, Lord, and 2424
21:22 J saith unto him, If I will that he tarry till I 2424
21:23 yet J said not unto him, He shall not die; 2424
21:25 are also many other *things* which J did, 2424
Ac 1: 1 of all that J began both to do and teach, 2424
1:11 this *same* J, which is taken up from you 2424
1:14 and Mary the mother of J, and with his 2424
1:16 which was guide to them that took J. 2424
1:21 with us all the time that the Lord J went in 2424
2:22 J of Nazareth, a man approved of God 2424
2:32 This J hath God raised up, whereof we all 2424
2:36 that God hath made that same J, whom ye 2424
2:38 name of J Christ for the remission of sins, 2424
3: 6 In the name of J Christ of Nazareth rise up 2424
3:13 God of our fathers, hath glorified his Son J; 2424
3:20 And he shall send J Christ, which before 2424
3:26 you first God, having raised up his Son J, 2424
4: 2 preached through J the resurrection from 2424
4:10 that by the name of J Christ of Nazareth, 2424
4:13 of them, that they had been with J. 2424
4:18 to speak at all nor teach in the name of J. 2424
4:27 For of a truth against thy holy child J, 2424
4:30 be done by the name of thy holy child J. 2424
4:33 witness of the resurrection of the Lord J: 2424
5:30 The God of our fathers raised up J, 2424
5:40 that *they* should not speak in the name of J, 2424
5:42 ceased not to teach and preach J Christ. 2424
6:14 that this J of Nazareth shall destroy this 2424
7:45 with J into the possession of the Gentiles, 2424
7:55 and J standing on the right hand of God, 2424
7:59 calling upon *God*, and saying, Lord J, 2424
8:12 and the name of J Christ, they were 2424
8:16 were baptized in the name of the Lord J.) 2424
8:35 same scripture, and preached unto him J. 2424
8:37 I believe that J Christ is the Son of God. 2424
9: 5 Lord said, I am J whom thou persecutest: 2424
9:17 on him said, Brother Saul, the Lord, *even* J, 2424
9:27 boldly at Damascus in the name of J. 2424
9:29 he spake boldly in the name of the Lord J, 2424
9:34 Aeneas, J Christ maketh thee whole: 2424
10:36 of Israel, preaching peace by J Christ: 2424
10:38 How God anointed J of Nazareth with 2424
11:17 unto us, who believed on the Lord J Christ; 2424
11:20 unto the Grecians, preaching the Lord J. 2424
13:23 *his* promise raised unto Israel a Saviour, J: 2424
13:33 in that he hath raised up J again; 2424
15:11 of the Lord J Christ *we* shall be saved, 2424
15:26 lives for the name of our Lord J Christ. 2424
16:18 I command thee in the name of J Christ to 2424
16:31 Believe on the Lord J Christ, and thou shalt 2424
17: 3 and that this J, whom I preach unto you, 2424
17: 7 saying that there is another king, *one* J. 2424
17:18 because he preached unto them J, and 2424
18: 5 and testified to the Jews *that* J *was* Christ. 2424
18:28 shewing by the scriptures that J was Christ. 2424
19: 4 should come after him, that is, on Christ J. 2424
19: 5 were baptized in the name of the Lord J. 2424
19:10 dwelt in Asia heard the word of the Lord J, 2424
19:13 had evil spirits the name of the Lord J, 2424
19:13 We adjure you by J whom Paul preacheth. 2424
19:15 and said, J I know, and Paul I know; 2424
19:17 and the name of the Lord J was magnified. 2424
20:21 and faith toward our Lord J Christ. 2424
20:24 which I have received of the Lord J, 2424
20:35 and to remember the words of the Lord J, 2424
21:13 die at Jerusalem for the name of the Lord J. 2424
22: 8 And he said unto me, I am J of Nazareth, 2424
25:19 and of one J, *which was* dead, whom Paul 2424
26: 9 contrary to the name of J of Nazareth. 2424
26:15 And he said, I am J whom thou persecutest. 2424
28:23 persuading them concerning J, both out of 2424
28:31 *things* which concern the Lord J Christ, 2424
Ro 1: 1 Paul, a servant of J Christ, called *to be* an 2424
1: 3 Concerning his Son J Christ our Lord, 2424
1: 6 Among whom are ye also *the* called of J 2424
1: 7 God our Father, and the Lord J Christ. 2424
1: 8 I thank my God through J Christ for you 2424
2:16 of men by J Christ according to my gospel. 2424
3:22 of God *which is* by faith of J Christ unto all 2424
3:24 through the redemption that is in Christ J: 2424
3:26 the justifier of him which believeth in J. 2424
4:24 if we believe on him that raised up J our 2424
5: 1 peace with God through our Lord J Christ: 2424
5:11 we also joy in God through our Lord J 2424
5:15 by grace, which is by one man, J Christ, 2424
5:17 shall reign in life by one, J Christ. 2424
5:21 unto eternal life by J Christ our Lord. 2424
6: 3 many of us as were baptized into J Christ 2424
6:11 alive unto God through J Christ our Lord. 2424
Ro 6:23 the gift of God *is* eternal life through J 2424
7:25 I thank God through J Christ our Lord. So 2424
8: 1 *are* in Christ J who walk not after the flesh, 2424
8: 2 For the law of the Spirit of life in Christ J 2424
8:11 But if the Spirit of him that raised up J 2424
8:39 love of God, which is in Christ J our Lord. 2424
10: 9 shalt confess with thy mouth the Lord J, 2424
13:14 But put ye on the Lord J Christ, and 2424
14:14 I know, and am persuaded by the Lord J, 2424
15: 5 one towards another according to Christ J: 2424
15: 6 even the Father of our Lord J Christ. 2424
15: 8 Now I say that J Christ was a minister of 2424
15:16 That I should be the minister of J Christ to 2424
15:17 whereof *I* may glory through J Christ *in* 2424
15:30 for the Lord J Christ's sake, and for 2424
16: 3 and Aquila my helpers in Christ J: 2424
16:18 For *they that are* such serve not our Lord J 2424
16:20 The grace of our Lord J Christ *be* with you. 2424
16:24 The grace of our Lord J Christ *be* with you 2424
16:25 and the preaching of J Christ, according to 2424
16:27 *be* glory through J Christ for ever. 2424
1Co 1: 1 called *to be* an apostle of J Christ through 2424
1: 2 to them that are sanctified in Christ J, 2424
1: 2 call upon the name of J Christ our Lord, 2424
1: 3 our Father, and *from* the Lord J Christ. 2424
1: 4 of God which is given you by J Christ; 2424
1: 7 waiting for the coming of our Lord J 2424
1: 8 blameless in the day of our Lord J Christ. 2424
1: 9 the fellowship of his Son J Christ our Lord. 2424
1:10 brethren, by the name of our Lord J Christ, 2424
1:30 But of him are ye in Christ J, who of God 2424
2: 2 save J Christ, and him crucified. 2424
3:11 *man* lay than that is laid, which is J Christ. 2424
4:15 for in Christ J I have begotten you through 2424
5: 4 In the name of our Lord J Christ, when ye 2424
5: 4 with the power of our Lord J Christ, 2424
5: 5 may be saved in the day of the Lord J. 2424
6:11 ye are justified in the name of the Lord J, 2424
8: 6 and one Lord J Christ, by whom *are* all 2424
9: 1 have I not seen J Christ our Lord? are not 2424
11:23 That the Lord J the *same* night in which he 2424
12: 3 by the Spirit of God calleth J accursed: 2424
12: 3 and *that* no *man* can say that J is the Lord, 2424
15:31 rejoicing which I have in Christ J our Lord, 2424
15:57 us the victory through our Lord J Christ. 2424
16:22 If any *man* love not the Lord J Christ, 2424
16:23 The grace of *our* Lord J Christ *be* with you. 2424
16:24 My love *be* with you all in Christ J. Amen. 2424
2Co 1: 1 an apostle of J Christ by the will of God, 2424
1: 2 our Father, and *from* the Lord J Christ. 2424
1: 3 even the Father of our Lord J Christ, 2424
1:14 as ye also *are* ours in the day of the Lord J. 2424
1:19 For the Son of God, J Christ, who was 2424
4: 5 preach not ourselves, but Christ J the Lord; 2424
4: 6 of the glory of God in the face of J Christ. 2424
4:10 about in the body the dying of the Lord J, 2424
4:10 that the life also of J might be made 2424
4:11 that the life also of J might be made 2424
4:14 the Lord J shall raise up us also by Jesus, 2424
4:14 the Lord Jesus shall raise up us also by J, 2424
5:18 who hath reconciled us to himself by J 2424
8: 9 For ye know the grace of our Lord J Christ, 2424
11: 4 For if he that cometh preacheth another J, 2424
11:31 The God and Father of our Lord J Christ, 2424
13: 5 how that J Christ is in you, except ye be 2424
13:14 The grace of the Lord J Christ, and the love 2424
Gal 1: 1 but by J Christ, and God the Father, 2424
1: 3 the Father, and *from* our Lord J Christ, 2424
1:12 I taught *it*, but by the revelation of J Christ. 2424
2: 4 out our liberty which we have in Christ J, 2424
2:16 but by the faith of J Christ, even we have 2424
2:16 even we have believed in J Christ, 2424
3: 1 before whose eyes J Christ hath been 2424
3:14 come on the Gentiles through J Christ; 2424
3:22 that the promise by faith of J Christ might 2424
3:26 all the children of God by faith in Christ J. 2424
3:28 nor female: for ye are all one in Christ J. 2424
4:14 me as an angel of God, *even* as Christ J. 2424
5: 6 For in J Christ neither circumcision 2424
6:14 save in the cross of our Lord J Christ, 2424
6:15 For in Christ J neither circumcision 2424
6:17 I bear in my body the marks of the Lord J. 2424
6:18 the grace of our Lord J Christ *be* with your 2424
Eph 1: 1 an apostle of J Christ by the will of God, 2424
1: 1 at Ephesus, and to the faithful in Christ J: 2424
1: 2 our Father, and *from* the Lord J Christ. 2424
1: 3 *be* the God and Father of our Lord J Christ, 2424
1: 5 adoption of children by J Christ to himself, 2424
1:15 after I heard of your faith in the Lord J, and 2424
1:17 That the God of our Lord J Christ, 2424
2: 6 sit together in heavenly *places* in Christ J: 2424
2: 7 in *his* kindness towards us through Christ J. 2424
2:10 created in Christ J unto good works, 2424
2:13 But now in Christ J ye who sometimes 2424
2:20 J Christ himself being the chief corner 2424
3: 1 the prisoner of J Christ for you Gentiles, 2424
3: 9 in God, who created all *things* by J Christ: 2424
3:11 which he purposed in Christ J our Lord: 2424
3:14 knees unto the Father of our Lord J Christ, 2424
3:21 Unto him *be* glory in the church by Christ J 2424
4:21 been taught by him, as the truth is in J: 2424
5:20 the Father in the name of our Lord J Christ; 2424
6:23 from God the Father and the Lord J Christ. 2424
6:24 Grace *be* with all them that love our Lord J 2424
Php 1: 1 and Timotheus, the servants of J Christ, 2424
1: 1 to all the saints in Christ J which are at 2424
1: 2 our Father, and *from* the Lord J Christ. 2424
1: 6 will perform *it* until the day of J Christ: 2424
1: 8 long after you all in the bowels of J Christ. 2424
1:11 which are by J Christ unto the glory and 2424
1:19 and the supply of the Spirit of J Christ, 2424
1:26 J Christ for me by my coming to you again. 2424
2: 5 mind be in you, which *was* also in Christ J: 2424
2:10 That at the name of J every knee should 2424
2:11 And *that* every tongue should confess that J 2424

Php 2:19 But I trust in the Lord J to send Timotheus 2424
2:21 not the *things which are* J Christ's. 2424
3: 3 and rejoice in Christ J, and have no 2424
3: 8 of the knowledge of Christ J my Lord: 2424
3:12 which also I am apprehended of Christ J. 2424
3:14 prize of the high calling of God in Christ J. 2424
3:20 we look for the Saviour, the Lord J Christ: 2424
4: 7 your hearts and minds through Christ J. 2424
4:19 according to his riches in glory by Christ J. 2424
4:21 Salute every saint in Christ J. The brethren 2424
4:23 The grace of our Lord J Christ *be* with you 2424
Col 1: 1 an apostle of J Christ by the will of God, 2424
1: 2 from God our Father and the Lord J Christ. 2424
1: 3 to God and the Father of our Lord J Christ, 2424
1: 4 Since we heard of your faith in Christ J, 2424
1:28 may present every man perfect in Christ J: 2424
2: 6 therefore received Christ J the Lord, 2424
3:17 or deed, *do* all in the name of the Lord J, 2424
4:11 And J, which is called Justus, who are of 2424
1Th 1: 1 in God the Father and *in* the Lord J Christ: 2424
1: 1 God our Father, and the Lord J Christ. 2424
1: 3 and patience of hope in our Lord J Christ, 2424
1:10 whom he raised from the dead, *even* J, 2424
2:14 of God which in Judea are in Christ J: 2424
2:15 Who both killed the Lord J, and their own 2424
2:19 of our Lord J Christ at his coming? 2424
3:11 and our Father, and our Lord J Christ, 2424
3:13 at the coming of our Lord J Christ with all 2424
4: 1 brethren, and exhort *you* by the Lord J, 2424
4: 2 commandments we gave you by the Lord J. 2424
4:14 For if we believe that J died and rose again, 2424
4:14 them also which sleep in J will God bring 2424
5: 9 to obtain salvation by our Lord J Christ, 2424
5:18 for this *is* the will of God in Christ J 2424
5:23 unto the coming of our Lord J Christ. 2424
5:28 The grace of our Lord J Christ *be* with you. 2424
2Th 1: 1 in God our Father and the Lord J Christ: 2424
1: 2 from God our Father and the Lord J Christ. 2424
1: 7 when the Lord J shall be revealed from 2424
1: 8 that obey not the gospel of our Lord J 2424
1:12 That the name of our Lord J Christ may be 2424
1:12 the grace of our God and the Lord J Christ. 2424
2: 1 by the coming of our Lord J Christ, and 2424
2:14 to the obtaining of the glory of our Lord J 2424
2:16 Now our Lord J Christ himself, and God, 2424
3: 6 brethren, in the name of our Lord J Christ, 2424
3:12 and exhort by our Lord J Christ, 2424
3:18 The grace of our Lord J Christ *be* with you 2424
1Ti 1: 1 an apostle of J Christ by the commandment 2424
1: 1 and Lord J Christ, *which is* our hope; 2424
1: 2 from God our Father and J Christ our Lord. 2424
1:12 And I thank Christ J our Lord, who hath 2424
1:14 with faith and love which is in Christ J. 2424
1:15 that Christ J came into the world to save 2424
1:16 that in me first J Christ might shew forth 2424
2: 5 between God and men, *the* man Christ J; 2424
3:13 boldness in the faith which is in Christ J. 2424
4: 6 thou shalt be a good minister of J Christ, 2424
5:21 and the Lord J Christ, and the elect angels, 2424
6: 3 *even the words* of our Lord J Christ, and 2424
6:13 quickeneth all *things,* and *before* Christ J, 2424
6:14 until the appearing of our Lord J Christ: 2424
2Ti 1: 1 an apostle of J Christ by the will of God, 2424
1: 1 to the promise of life which is in Christ J, 2424
1: 2 from God the Father and Christ J our Lord. 2424
1: 9 which was given us in Christ J before 2424
1:10 by the appearing of our Saviour J Christ, 2424
1:13 in faith and love which is in Christ J. 2424
2: 1 be strong in the grace that is in Christ J. 2424
2: 3 as a good soldier of J Christ. 2424
2: 8 Remember that J Christ of the seed of 2424
2:10 which is in Christ J with eternal glory. 2424
3:12 all that will live godly in Christ J shall 2424
3:15 salvation through faith which is in Christ J. 2424
4: 1 before God, and the Lord J Christ, 2424
4:22 The Lord J Christ *be* with thy spirit. Grace 2424
Tit 1: 1 servant of God, and an apostle of J Christ, 2424
1: 4 and the Lord J Christ our Saviour. 2424
2:13 of the great God and our Saviour J Christ; 2424
3: 6 Which he shed on us abundantly through J 2424
Phm 1: 1 a prisoner of J Christ, and Timothy *our* 2424
1: 3 from God our Father and the Lord J Christ. 2424
1: 5 which thou hast toward the Lord J, and 2424
1: 6 good *thing* which is in you in Christ J. 2424
1: 9 and now also a prisoner of J Christ. 2424
1:23 my fellowprisoner in Christ J; 2424
1:25 The grace of our Lord J Christ *be* with your 2424
Heb 2: 9 But we see J, who was made a little lower 2424
3: 1 and High Priest of our profession, Christ J; 2424
4: 8 For if J had given them rest, *then* would he 2424
4:14 J the Son of God, let us hold fast *our* 2424
6:20 the forerunner is for us entered, *even* J, 2424
7:22 much was J made a surety of a better 2424
10:10 of the body of J Christ once for all. 2424
10:19 to enter into the holiest by the blood of J, 2424
12: 2 Looking unto J the author and finisher of 2424
12:24 And to J the mediator of the new covenant, 2424
13: 8 J Christ the same yesterday, and to day, 2424
13:12 Wherefore J also, that he might sanctify 2424
13:20 brought again from the dead our Lord J, 2424
13:21 well pleasing in his sight, through J Christ; 2424
Jas 1: 1 a servant of God and of the Lord J Christ, 2424
2: 1 have not the faith of our Lord J Christ, 2424
1Pe 1: 1 Peter, an apostle of J Christ, to 2424
1: 2 and sprinkling of the blood of J Christ: 2424
1: 3 *be* the God and Father of our Lord J Christ, 2424
1: 3 the resurrection of J Christ from the dead, 2424
1: 7 and glory at the appearing of J Christ: 2424
1:13 unto you at the revelation of J Christ; 2424
2: 5 acceptable to God by J Christ. 2424
3:21 by the resurrection of J Christ: 2424
4:11 *things* may be glorified through J Christ, 2424
5:10 called us into his eternal glory by Christ J, 2424
5:14 Peace *be* with you all that are in Christ J. 2424
2Pe 1: 1 a servant and an apostle of J Christ, 2424
1: 1 of God and our Saviour J Christ: 2424
1: 2 the knowledge of God, and of J our Lord. 2424
1: 8 in the knowledge of our Lord J Christ. 2424
1:11 kingdom of our Lord and Saviour J Christ. 2424
1:14 even as our Lord J Christ hath shewed me. 2424
1:16 the power and coming of our Lord J Christ, 2424
2:20 of the Lord and Saviour J Christ, 2424
3:18 of our Lord and Saviour J Christ. 2424
1Jn 1: 3 with the Father, and with his Son J Christ. 2424
1: 7 the blood of J Christ his Son cleanseth us 2424
2: 1 with the Father, J Christ *the* righteous: 2424
2:22 but he that denieth that J is the Christ? 2424
3:23 believe on the name of his Son J Christ, 2424
4: 2 Every spirit that confesseth that J Christ is 2424
4: 3 And every spirit that confesseth not that J 2424
4:15 Whosoever shall confess that J is the Son 2424
5: 1 Whosoever believeth that J is the Christ is 2424
5: 5 he that believeth that J is the Son of God? 2424
5: 6 came by water and blood, *even* J Christ; 2424
5:20 in him *that is* true, *even* in his Son J Christ. 2424
2Jn 1: 3 God the Father, and from the Lord J Christ, 2424
1: 7 who confess not that J Christ is come in 2424
Jude 1: 1 the servant of J Christ, and brother of 2424
1: 1 and preserved *in* J Christ, *and* called: 2424
1: 4 the only Lord God, and our Lord J Christ. 2424
1:17 before of the apostles of our Lord J Christ; 2424
1:21 looking for the mercy of our Lord J Christ 2424
Rev 1: 1 The Revelation of J Christ, which God 2424
1: 2 and of the testimony of J Christ, and of all 2424
1: 5 And from J Christ, *who is* the faithful 2424
1: 9 in the kingdom and patience of J Christ, 2424
1: 9 of God, and for the testimony of J Christ. 2424
12:17 of God, and have the testimony of J Christ. 2424
14:12 commandments of God, and the faith of J. 2424
17: 6 and with the blood of the martyrs of J: 2424
19:10 thy brethren that have the testimony of J: 2424
19:10 for the testimony of J is the spirit of 2424
20: 4 that were beheaded for the witness of J, 2424
22:16 I J have sent mine angel to testify unto you 2424
22:20 Amen. Even so, come, Lord J. 2424
22:21 The grace of our Lord J Christ *be* with you 2424

JESUS' (10) [JESUS]
Mt 15:30 many others, and cast them *down* at J feet; 2424
27:57 who also himself was J disciple: 2424
Lk 5: 8 When Simon Peter saw *it,* he fell down at J 2424
8:41 and he fell down at J feet, and 2424
10:39 which also sat at J feet, and heard his word. 2424
Jn 12: 9 and they came not for J sake only, 2424
13:23 Now there was leaning on J bosom one of 2424
13:25 He then lying on J breast saith unto him, 2424
2Co 4: 5 and ourselves your servants for J sake. 2424
4:11 are alway delivered unto death for J sake, 2424

JETHER (8)
Jdg 8:20 he said unto J his firstborn, Up, *and* 3500
1Ki 2: 5 unto Amasa the son of J, whom he slew, 3500
2:32 the host of Israel, and Amasa the son of J, 3500
1Ch 2:17 the father of Amasa *was* J the Ishmeelite. 3500
2:32 the brother of Shammai; J, and Jonathan: 3500
2:32 and Jonathan: and J died without children. 3500
4:17 the sons of Ezra *were,* J, and Mered, and 3500
7:38 the sons of J; Jephunneh, and Pispah, and 3500

JETHETH (2)
Ge 36:40 duke Timnah, duke Alvah, duke J, 3509
1Ch 1:51 duke Timnah, duke Aliah, duke J, 3509

JETHLAH (1)
Jos 19:42 And Shaalabbin, and Aijalon, and J, 3494

JETHRO (10)
Ex 3: 1 Now Moses kept the flock of J his father in 3503
4:18 and returned to J his father in law, 3500
4:18 And J said to Moses, Go in peace. 3503
18: 1 When J, the priest of Midian, Moses' father 3503
18: 2 J, Moses' father in law, took Zipporah, 3503
18: 5 J, Moses' father in law, came with his sons 3503
18: 6 I thy father in law J am come unto thee, 3503
18: 9 J rejoiced for all the goodness which 3503
18:10 J said, Blessed *be* the LORD, who hath 3503
18:12 J, Moses' father in law, took a burnt 3503

JETUR (3)
Ge 25:15 Hadar, and Tema, J, Naphish, and 3195
1Ch 1:31 J, Naphish, and Kedemah. These *are* 3195
5:19 with J, and Nephish, and Nodab. 3195

JEUEL (1)
1Ch 9: 6 J, and their brethren, six hundred and 3262

JEUSH (8)
Ge 36: 5 Aholibamah bare J, and Jaalam, and 3266
36:14 she bare to Esau J, and Jaalam, and Korah. 3266
36:18 duke J, duke Jaalam, duke Korah: 3266
1Ch 1:35 Reuel, and J, and Jaalam, and Korah. 3266
7:10 J, and Benjamin, and Ehud, and 3266
23:10 *were,* Jahath, Zina, and J, and Beriah. 3266
23:11 J and Beriah had not many sons; therefore 3266
2Ch 11:19 J, and Shamariah, and Zaham. 3266

JEUZ (1)
1Ch 8:10 J, and Shachia, and Mirma. These *were* his 3263

JEW (32) [JEWESS, JEWISH, JEWRY, JEWS, JEWS']
Est 2: 5 in Shushan the palace there was a certain J, 3064
3: 4 for he had told them that he *was* a J. 3064
5:13 long as I see Mordecai the J sitting at 3064
6:10 hast said, and do *even* so to Mordecai the J, 3064
8: 7 Esther the queen and to Mordecai the J, 3064
9:29 daughter of Abihail, and Mordecai the J, 3064
9:31 *appointed,* according as Mordecai the J 3064
10: 3 For Mordecai the J *was* next unto king 3064
Jer 34: 9 himself of them, *to wit,* of a J his brother. 3064
Zec 8:23 take hold of the skirt of him that is a J, 3064
Jn 4: 9 *is it that* thou, being a J, askest drink of me, 2453
18:35 Pilate answered, Am I a J? Thine own 2453
Ac 10:28 *thing* for a man *that is* a J to keep company, 2453
13: 6 a false prophet, a J, whose name *was* 2453
18: 2 And found a certain J named Aquila, born 2453
18:24 And a certain J named Apollos, born at 2453
19:14 a J, *and* chief of the priests, which did so. 2453
19:34 But when *they* knew that he was a J, 2453
21:39 I am a man *which am* a J of Tarsus, 2453
22: 3 I am verily a man *which am* a J, born in 2453
Ro 1:16 to the J first, and *also* to the Greek. 2453
2: 9 of the J first, and *also* of the Gentile; 2453
2:10 to the J first, and *also* to the Gentile: 2453
2:17 thou art called a J, and restest in the law, 2453
2:28 For he is not a J, which is one outwardly; 2453
2:29 But he *is* a J, which is one inwardly; 2453
3: 1 What advantage then hath the J? or 2453
10:12 For there is no difference between the J 2453
1Co 9:20 And unto the Jews I became as a J, that I 2453
Gal 2:14 Peter before *them* all, If thou, being a J, 2453
3:28 There is neither J nor Greek, there is 2453
Col 3:11 Where there is neither Greek nor J, 2453

JEWEL (3) [JEWELS]
Pr 11:22 *As* a j of gold in a swine's snout, *so is* a fair 5141
20:15 but the lips of knowledge *are* a precious j. 3627
Eze 16:12 I put a j on thy forehead, and earrings in 5141

JEWELS (25) [JEWEL]
Ge 24:53 the servant brought forth j of silver, and 3627
24:53 j of gold, and raiment, and gave *them* to 3627
Ex 3:22 j of silver, and jewels of gold, and raiment: 3627
3:22 jewels of silver, and j of gold, and raiment: 3627
11: 2 j of silver, and jewels of gold. 3627
11: 2 jewels of silver, and j of gold. 3627
12:35 they borrowed of the Egyptians j of silver, 3627
12:35 jewels of silver, and j of gold, and raiment: 3627
35:22 and rings, and tablets, all j of gold: 3627
Nu 31:50 *of* j of gold, chains, and bracelets, rings, 3627
31:51 took the gold of them, *even* all wrought j. 3627
1Sa 6: 8 put the j of gold, which ye return him *for* a 3627
6:15 wherein the j of gold *were,* and put *them* on 3627
2Ch 20:25 precious j, which they stript off for 3627
32:27 for shields, and for all *manner of* pleasant j; 3627
Job 28:17 the exchange of it *shall not be for* j of fine 3627
SS 1:10 Thy cheeks are comely with rows *of j,* thy NIH
7: 1 the joints of thy thighs *are* like j, the work 2481
Isa 3:21 The rings, and nose j, 5141
61:10 and as a bride adorneth *herself* with her j. 3627
Eze 16:17 Thou hast also taken thy fair j of my gold 3627
16:39 shall take thy fair j, and leave thee naked 3627
23:26 out of thy clothes, and take away thy fair j. 3627
Hos 2:13 decked herself with her earrings and her j, 2484
Mal 3:17 of hosts, in that day when I make up my j; 5459

JEWESS (2) [JEW]
Ac 16: 1 *which was* a J, and believed; 2453
24:24 which was a J, he sent for Paul, and 2453

JEWISH (1) [JEW]
Tit 1:14 Not giving heed to J fables, and 2451

JEWRY (3) [JEW]
Da 5:13 whom the king my father brought out of J? 3061
Lk 23: 5 up the people, teaching throughout all J, 2449
Jn 7: 1 for he would not walk in J, because 2449

JEWS (243) [JEW]
2Ki 16: 6 Elath to Syria, and drave the J from Elath: 3064
25:25 the J and the Chaldees that were with him 3064
Ezr 4:12 that the J which came up from thee to us 3062
4:23 went up in haste to Jerusalem unto the J, 3062
5: 1 prophesied unto the J that *were* in Judah 3062
5: 5 of their God was upon the elders of the J, 3062
6: 7 let the governor of the J and the elders of 3062
6: 7 the elders of the J build this house of God 3062
6: 8 J for the building of this house of God: 3062
6:14 the elders of the J builded, and 3062
Ne 1: 2 I asked them concerning the J that had 3064
2:16 neither had I as yet told *it* to the J, nor to 3064
4: 1 took great indignation, and mocked the J. 3064
4: 2 and said, What do *these* feeble J? 3064
4:12 that when the J which dwelt by them came, 3064
5: 1 of their wives against their brethren the J. 3064
5: 8 ability have redeemed our brethren the J, 3064
5:17 an hundred and fifty of the J and rulers, 3064
6: 6 saith *it, that* thou and the J think to rebel: 3064
13:23 In those days also saw I J *that* had married 3064
Est 3: 6 J that *were* throughout the whole kingdom 3064
3:13 all J, both young and old, little children and 3064
4: 3 *there was* great mourning among the J, and 3064
4: 7 to pay to the king's treasuries for the J, 3064
4:13 *in* the king's house, more than all the J. 3064
4:14 deliverance arise to the J from another 3064
4:16 gather together all the J that are present in 3064
6:13 If Mordecai *be* of the seed of the J, 3064
8: 3 his device that he had devised against the J. 3064
8: 5 which he wrote to destroy the J which *are* 3064
8: 7 because he laid his hand upon the J. 3064
8: 8 Write ye also for the J, as it liketh you, 3064
8: 9 to all that Mordecai commanded unto the J, 3064
8: 9 to the J according to their writing, and 3064
8:11 Where*in* the king granted the J which *were* 3064
8:13 that the J should be ready against that day 3064
8:16 The J had light, and gladness, and joy, and 3064
8:17 the J had joy and gladness, a feast and 3064
8:17 many of the people of the land **became** J; 3054
8:17 for the fear of the J fell upon them. 3064
9: 1 in the day that the enemies of the J hoped 3064
9: 1 the J had rule over them that hated them;) 3064
9: 2 The J gathered themselves together in their 3064
9: 3 and officers of the king, helped the J; 3064
9: 5 Thus the J smote all their enemies *with* 3064

Est 9: 6 in Shushan the palace the J slew and 3064
9:10 the enemy of the J, slew they; 3064
9:12 The J have slain and destroyed five 3064
9:13 let it be granted to the J which *are* in 3064
9:15 For the J that *were* in Shushan gathered 3064
9:16 the other J that *were* in the king's 3064
9:18 the J that *were* at Shushan assembled 3064
9:19 Therefore the J of the villages, that dwelt in 3064
9:20 sent letters unto all the J that *were* in all 3064
9:22 As the days wherein the J rested from their 3064
9:23 the J undertook to do as they had begun, 3064
9:24 the Agagite, the enemy of all the J, 3064
9:24 had devised against the J to destroy them, 3064
9:25 which he devised against the J, 3064
9:27 The J ordained, and took upon them, and 3064
9:28 of Purim should not fail from among the J, 3064
9:30 he sent the letters unto all the J, to 3064
10: 3 great among the J, and accepted of 3064
Jer 32:12 before all the J that sat in the court of 3064
38:19 I am afraid of the J that are fallen to 3064
40:11 Likewise when all the J that *were* in Moab, 3064
40:12 Even all the J returned out of all places 3064
40:15 that all the J which are gathered unto thee 3064
41: 3 Ishmael also slew all the J that were with 3064
44: 1 all the J which dwell in the land of Egypt, 3064
52:28 in the seventh year three thousand J and 3064
52:30 away captive *of* the J seven hundred forty 3064
Da 3: 8 Chaldeans came near, and accused the J. 3062
3:12 There are certain J whom thou hast set over 3062
Mt 2: 2 Where is he that is born King of the J? *2453*
27:11 saying, Art thou the King of the J? *2453*
27:29 mocked him, saying, Hail, King of the J! *2453*
27:37 THIS IS JESUS THE KING OF THE J. *2453*
28:15 reported among the J until this day. *2453*
Mk 7: 3 For the Pharisees, and all the J, except they *2453*
15: 2 asked him, Art thou the King of the J? *2453*
15: 9 ye *that* I release unto you the King of the J? *2453*
15:12 *unto him* whom ye call the King of the J? *2453*
15:18 began to salute him, Hail, King of the J. *2453*
15:26 was written over, THE KING OF THE J. *2453*
Lk 7: 3 he sent unto him *the* elders of the J, *2453*
23: 3 saying, Art thou the King of the J? *2453*
23:37 And saying, If thou be the King of the J, *2453*
23:38 Hebrew, THIS IS THE KING OF THE J. *2453*
23:51 *he was* of Arimathea, a city of the J: *2453*
Jn 1:19 when the J sent priests and Levites from *2453*
2: 6 after the manner of the purifying of the J, *2453*
2:18 Then answered the J and said unto him, *2453*
2:20 Then said the J, Forty and six years was *2453*
3: 1 named Nicodemus, a ruler of the J: *2453*
3:25 John's disciples and the J about purifying. *2453*
4: 9 For the J have no dealings with *2453*
4:22 what we worship: for salvation is of the J. *2453*
5: 1 After this there was a feast of the J; and *2453*
5:10 The J therefore said unto him that was *2453*
5:15 and told the J that it was Jesus, *2453*
5:16 And therefore did the J persecute Jesus, *2453*
5:18 Therefore the J sought the more to kill him, *2453*
6: 4 the passover, a feast of the J, was nigh. *2453*
6:41 The J then murmured at him, because *2453*
6:52 The J therefore strove amongst themselves, *2453*
7: 1 in Jewry, because the J sought to kill him. *2453*
7:11 Then the J sought him at the feast, and *2453*
7:13 *man* spake openly of him for fear of the J. *2453*
7:15 And the J marvelled, saying, How knoweth *2453*
7:35 Then said the J among themselves, *2453*
8:22 Then said the J, Will he kill himself? *2453*
8:31 Then said Jesus to those J which believed *2453*
8:48 Then answered the J, and said unto him, *2453*
8:52 Then said the J unto him, Now we know *2453*
8:57 Then said the J unto him, Thou art not yet *2453*
9:18 But the J did not believe concerning him, *2453*
9:22 his parents, because they feared the J: *2453*
9:22 for the J had agreed already, that if any *2453*
10:19 again among the J for these sayings. *2453*
10:24 Then came the J round about him, and *2453*
10:31 Then the J took up stones again to stone *2453*
10:33 The J answered him, saying, For a good *2453*
11: 8 Master, the J of late sought to stone thee; *2453*
11:19 And many of the J came to Martha and *2453*
11:31 The J then which were with her in *2453*
11:33 the J also weeping which came with her, *2453*
11:36 Then said the J, Behold, how he loved him. *2453*
11:45 Then many of the J which came to Mary, *2453*
11:54 walked no more openly among the J; *2453*
12: 9 Much people of the J therefore knew that *2453*
12:11 by reason of him many of the J went away, *2453*
13:33 and as I said unto the J, Whither I go, *2453*
18:12 the captain and officers of the J took Jesus, *2453*
18:14 was he, which gave counsel to the J, *2453*
18:20 in the temple, whither the J always resort; *2453*
18:31 The J therefore said unto him, It is not *2453*
18:33 said unto him, Art thou the King of the J? *2453*
18:36 that I should not be delivered to the J: *2453*
18:38 he went out again unto the J, and saith unto *2453*
18:39 *that* I release unto you the King of the J? *2453*
19: 3 And said, Hail, King of the J: and *2453*
19: 7 The J answered him, We have a law, and *2453*
19:12 but the J cried out, saying, If thou let this *2453*
19:14 and he saith unto the J, Behold your King. *2453*
19:19 OF NAZARETH THE KING OF THE J. *2453*
19:20 This title then read many of the J: for *2453*
19:21 Then said the chief priests of the J to *2453*
19:21 to Pilate, Write not, The King of the J; *2453*
19:21 but that he said, I am King of the J. *2453*
19:31 The J therefore, because it was *2453*
19:38 of Jesus, but secretly for fear of the J, *2453*
19:40 the spices, as the manner of the J is to bury. *2453*
20:19 disciples were assembled for fear of the J, *2453*
Ac 2: 5 And there were dwelling at Jerusalem J, *2453*
2:10 and strangers of Rome, J and proselytes, *2453*
9:22 confounded the J which dwelt at *2453*
9:23 the J took counsel to kill him: *2453*
10:22 good report among all the nation of the J, *2453*
10:39 which he did both in the land of the J, *2453*

Ac 11:19 the word to none but unto *the* J only. *2453*
12: 3 And because he saw it pleased the J, *2453*
12:11 all the expectation of the people of the J. *2453*
13: 5 the word of God in the synagogues of the J: *2453*
13:42 And when the J were gone out of *2453*
13:43 many of the J and religious proselytes *2453*
13:45 But when the J saw the multitudes, *2453*
13:50 But the J stirred up the devout and *2453*
14: 1 *both* together into the synagogue of the J, *2453*
14: 1 that a great multitude both of the J and *2453*
14: 2 But the unbelieving J stirred up *2453*
14: 4 and part held with the J, and part with *2453*
14: 5 and *also* of the J with their rulers, to use *2453*
14:19 And there came thither *certain* J from *2453*
16: 3 of the J which were in those quarters: *2453*
16:20 saying, These men, being J, do exceedingly *2453*
17: 1 where was a synagogue of the J: *2453*
17: 5 But the J which believed not, moved with *2453*
17:10 *thither* went into the synagogue of the J. *2453*
17:13 But when the J of Thessalonica had *2453*
17:17 disputed he in the synagogue with the J, *2453*
18: 2 that Claudius had commanded all J to *2453*
18: 4 and persuaded *the* J and *the* Greeks. *2453*
18: 5 and testified to the J *that* Jesus *was* Christ. *2453*
18:12 the J made insurrection with one accord *2453*
18:14 Gallio said unto the J, If it were a matter of *2453*
18:14 of wrong or wicked lewdness, O *ye* J, *2453*
18:19 the synagogue, and reasoned with the J. *2453*
18:28 For he mightily convinced the J, *and* *2453*
19:10 word of the Lord Jesus, both J and Greeks. *2453*
19:13 Then certain of the vagabond J, exorcists, *2453*
19:17 And this was known to all the J and *2453*
19:33 of the multitude, the J putting him forward. *2453*
20: 3 and when the J laid wait for him, as he was *2453*
20:19 befell me by the lying in wait of the J: *2453*
20:21 Testifying both to the J, and *also* to *2453*
21:11 So shall the J at Jerusalem bind the man *2453*
21:20 how many thousands of J there are which *2453*
21:21 that thou teachest all the J which are *2453*
21:27 the J which were of Asia, when they saw *2453*
22:12 having a good report of all the J which *2453*
22:30 wherefore he was accused of the J, *2453*
23:12 it was day, certain of the J banded together, *2453*
23:20 The J have agreed to desire thee that thou *2453*
23:27 This man was taken of the J, and *2453*
23:30 And when it was told me how that the J *2453*
24: 5 a mover of sedition among all the J *2453*
24: 9 And the J also assented, saying that these *2453*
24:18 Whereupon certain J from Asia found me *2453*
24:27 and Felix, willing to shew the J a pleasure, *2453*
25: 2 the chief of the J informed him against *2453*
25: 7 the J which came down from Jerusalem *2453*
25: 8 Neither against the law of the J, *2453*
25: 9 But Festus, willing to do the J a pleasure, *2453*
25:10 to the J have I done no wrong, as thou very *2453*
25:15 the elders of the J informed *me*, desiring *to* *2453*
25:24 the multitude of the J have dealt with me, *2453*
26: 2 *the things* whereof I am accused of the J: *2453*
26: 3 and questions which are among the J: *2453*
26: 4 own nation at Jerusalem, know all the J; *2453*
26: 7 king Agrippa, I am accused of the J. *2453*
26:21 For these causes the J caught me in *2453*
28:17 days Paul called the chief of the J together: *2453*
28:19 But when the J spake against *it*, I was *2453*
28:29 And when he had said these *words*, the J *2453*
Ro 3: 9 for we have before proved both J and *2453*
3:29 *Is he* the God of the J only? *is he* not also *2453*
9:24 not of the J only, but also of the Gentiles? *2453*
1Co 1:22 For the J require a sign, and the Greeks *2453*
1:23 unto the J a stumblingblock, and unto *2453*
1:24 both J and Greeks, Christ the power of *2453*
9:20 And unto the J I became as a Jew, that I *2453*
9:20 I became as a Jew, that I might gain *the* J, *2453*
10:32 Give none offence, neither to the J, nor to *2453*
12:13 whether *we be* J or Gentiles, whether *we be* *2453*
2Co 11:24 Of the J five times received I forty *stripes* *2453*
Gal 2:13 And the other J dissembled likewise with *2453*
2:14 manner of Gentiles, and not **as do the J**, *2452*
2:14 thou the Gentiles to **live as do the J**? *2450*
2:15 We *who are* J by nature, and not sinners of *2453*
1Th 2:14 even as they *have* of the J: *2453*
Rev 2: 9 blasphemy of them which say they are J, *2453*
3: 9 which say they are J, and are not, but *2453*

JEWS' (14) [JEW]

2Ki 18:26 talk not with us **in the J language** in 3066
18:28 cried with a loud voice **in the J language**, 3066
2Ch 32:18 **in the J speech** unto the people of 3066
Ne 13:24 could not speak **in the J language**, but 3066
Est 3:10 of Hammedatha the Agagite, the J enemy. 3064
8: 1 Haman the J enemy unto Esther the queen. 3064
Isa 36:11 and speak not to us **in the J language**, 3066
36:13 cried with a loud voice **in the J language**, 3066
Jn 2:13 And the J passover was at hand, and *2453*
7: 2 Now the J feast of tabernacles was at hand. *2453*
11:55 And the J passover was nigh at hand: and *2453*
19:42 of the J preparation *day*; for the sepulchre *2453*
Gal 1:13 conversation in time past in the **J religion**, *2454*
1:14 And profited in the **J religion** above many *2454*

JEZANIAH (2)

Jer 40: 8 J the son of a Maachathite, they and 3153
42: 1 J the son of Hoshaiah, and all the people 3153

JEZEBEL (22) [JEZEBEL'S]

1Ki 16:31 that he took *to* wife J the daughter of 348
18: 4 when J cut off the prophets of the LORD, 348
18:13 Was it not told my lord what I did when J 348
19: 1 Ahab told J all that Elijah had done, and 348
19: 2 Then J sent a messenger unto Elijah, saying, 348
21: 5 J his wife came to him, and said unto him, 348
21: 7 J his wife said unto him, Dost thou now 348
21:11 did as J had sent unto them, *and* as *it was* 348
21:14 they sent to J, saying, Naboth is stoned, 348

1Ki 21:15 when J heard that Naboth was stoned, and 348
21:15 and was dead, that J said to Ahab, Arise, 348
21:23 of J also spake the LORD, saying, 348
21:23 The dogs shall eat J by the wall of Jezreel. 348
21:25 of the LORD, whom J his wife stirred up. 348
2Ki 9: 7 the servants of the LORD, at the hand of J. 348
9:10 the dogs shall eat J in the portion of Jezreel, 348
9:22 so long as the whoredoms of thy mother J 348
9:30 J heard *of it*; and she painted her face, and 348
9:36 of Jezreel shall dogs eat the flesh of J: 348
9:37 the carcase of J shall be as dung upon 348
9:37 *so* that they shall not say, This *is* J. 348
Rev 2:20 because thou sufferest *that* woman J, *2403*

JEZEBEL'S (1) [JEZEBEL]

1Ki 18:19 groves four hundred, which eat *at* J table. 348

JEZER (3) [JEZERITES]

Ge 46:24 Jahzeel, and Guni, and J, and Shillem. 3337
Nu 26:49 Of J, the family of the Jezerites: 3337
1Ch 7:13 Jahziel, and Guni, and J, and Shallum, 3337

JEZERITES (1) [JEZER]

Nu 26:49 Of Jezer, the family of the J: of Shillem, 3340

JEZIAH (1)

Ezr 10:25 J, and Malchiah, and Miamin, and Eleazar, 3150

JEZIEL (1)

1Ch 12: 3 and J, and Pelet, the sons of Azmaveth; and 3149

JEZLIAH (1)

1Ch 8:18 Ishmerai also, and J, and Jobab, the sons of 3152

JEZOAR (1)

1Ch 4: 7 of Helah *were*, Zereth, and J, and Ethnan. 3328

JEZRAHIAH (1)

Ne 12:42 the singers sang loud, with J *their* overseer. 3156

JEZREEL (36) [JEZREELITE, JEZREELITESS]

Jos 15:56 And J, and Jokdeam, and Zanoah, 3157
17:16 and *they* who *are* of the valley of J. 3157
19:18 their border was toward J, and Chesulloth, 3157
Jdg 6:33 went over, and pitched in the valley of J. 3157
1Sa 25:43 David also took Ahinoam of J; and 3157
29: 1 pitched by a fountain which *is* in J. 3157
29:11 And the Philistines went up *to* J. 3157
2Sa 2: 9 over J, and over Ephraim, and 3157
4: 4 tidings came of Saul and Jonathan out of J, 3157
1Ki 4:12 which *is* by Zartanah beneath J, 3157
18:45 a great rain. And Ahab rode, and went to J. 3157
18:46 and ran before Ahab to the entrance of J. 3157
21: 1 Jezreelite had a vineyard, which *was* in J, 3157
21:23 The dogs shall eat Jezebel by the wall of J. 3157
2Ki 8:29 king Joram went back to be healed in J of 3157
8:29 down to see Joram the son of Ahab in J, 3157
9:10 dogs shall eat Jezebel in the portion of J, 3157
9:15 king Joram was returned to be healed in J 3157
9:15 escape out of the city to go to tell *it* in J. 3157
9:16 So Jehu rode *in a chariot*, and went to J; 3157
9:17 there stood a watchman on the tower in J, 3157
9:30 when Jehu was come to J, Jezebel heard *of* 3157
9:36 In the portion of J shall dogs eat the flesh 3157
9:37 the face of the field in the portion of J; 3157
10: 1 unto the rulers of J, to the elders, and 3157
10: 6 come to me to J by to morrow *this* time. 3157
10: 7 heads in baskets, and sent him *them* to J. 3157
10:11 all that remained of the house of Ahab in J, 3157
1Ch 4: 3 father of Etam; J, and Ishma, and Idbash: 3157
2Ch 22: 6 he returned to be healed in J because of 3157
22: 6 down to see Jehoram the son of Ahab at J, 3157
Hos 1: 4 the LORD said unto him, Call his name J; 3157
1: 4 I will avenge the blood of J upon the house 3157
1: 5 break the bow of Israel in the valley of J. 3157
1:11 of the land: for great *shall be* the day of J. 3157
2:22 the wine, and the oil; and they shall hear J. 3157

JEZREELITE (8) [JEZREEL]

1Ki 21: 1 *that* Naboth the J had a vineyard, 3158
21: 4 of the word which Naboth the J had spoken 3158
21: 6 Because I spake unto Naboth the J, and 3158
21: 7 will give thee the vineyard of Naboth the J. 3158
21:15 possession of the vineyard of Naboth the J, 3158
21:16 to go down to the vineyard of Naboth the J, 3158
2Ki 9:21 and met him in the portion of Naboth the J. 3158
9:25 in the portion of the field of Naboth the J: 3158

JEZREELITESS (5) [JEZREEL]

1Sa 27: 3 Ahinoam the J, and Abigail 3159
30: 5 Ahinoam the J, and Abigail the wife of 3159
2Sa 2: 2 Ahinoam the J, and Abigail Nabal's wife 3159
3: 2 firstborn was Amnon, of Ahinoam the J; 3159
1Ch 3: 1 the firstborn Amnon, of Ahinoam the J; 3159

JIBSAM (1)

1Ch 7: 2 and Jeriel, and Jahmai, and J, and Shemuel, 3005

JIDLAPH (1)

Ge 22:22 and Hazo, and Pildash, and J, and Bethuel. 3044

JIMNA (1) [JIMNAH, JIMNITES]

Nu 26:44 of J, the family of the Jimnites: of Jesui, 3232

JIMNAH (1) [JIMNA]

Ge 46:17 J, and Ishuah, and Ishui, and Beriah, and 3232

JIMNITES (1) [JIMNA]

Nu 26:44 of Jimna, the family of the J: of Jesui, 3232

JIPHTAH (1)

Jos 15:43 And J, and Ashnah, and Nezib, 3316

JIPHTHAH-EL (2)
Jos 19:14 the outgoings thereof are *in* the valley of J: 3317
19:27 to the valley of J toward the north side *of* 3317

JOAB (138) [JOAB'S]
1Sa 26: 6 the son of Zeruiah, brother to J, saying, 3097
2Sa 2:13 J the son of Zeruiah, and the servants of 3097
2:14 Abner said to J, Let the young men now 3097
2:14 play before us. And J said, Let them arise. 3097
2:18 Zeruiah there, J, and Abishai, and Asahel: 3097
2:22 should I hold up my face to J thy brother? 3097
2:24 J also and Abishai pursued after Abner: 3097
2:26 Abner called to J, and said, Shall the sword 3097
2:27 J said, *As* God liveth, unless thou hadst 3097
2:28 So J blew a trumpet, and all the people 3097
2:30 J returned from following Abner: and 3097
2:32 J and his men went all night, and they 3097
3:22 of David and J came from *pursuing* a troop, 3097
3:23 When J and all the host that *was* with him 3097
3:23 they told J, saying, Abner the son of Ner 3097
3:24 J came to the king, and said, What hast 3097
3:26 when J was come out from David, he sent 3097
3:27 J took him aside in the gate to speak with 3097
3:29 Let it rest on the head of J, and on all his 3097
3:29 let there not fail from the house of J one 3097
3:30 So J and Abishai his brother slew Abner, 3097
3:31 David said to J, and to all the people that 3097
8:16 And J the son of Zeruiah *was* over the host; 3097
10: 7 when David heard *of it*, he sent J, and all 3097
10: 9 When J saw that the front of the battle was 3097
10:13 J drew nigh, and the people that *were* with 3097
10:14 So J returned from the children of Ammon, 3097
11: 1 kings go forth *to battle*, that David sent J, 3097
11: 6 David sent to J, *saying*, Send me Uriah 3097
11: 6 the Hittite. And J sent Uriah to David. 3097
11: 7 David demanded *of him* how J did, and 3097
11:11 my lord J, and the servants of my lord, 3097
11:14 that David wrote a letter to J, and sent *it* by 3097
11:16 it came to pass, when J observed the city, 3097
11:17 of the city went out, and fought with J: 3097
11:18 J sent and told David all the things 3097
11:22 shewed David all that J had sent him for. 3097
11:25 Thus shalt thou say unto J, Let not this 3097
12:26 J fought against Rabbah of the children of 3097
12:27 J sent messengers to David, and said, 3097
14: 1 Now J the son of Zeruiah perceived that 3097
14: 2 J sent to Tekoah, and fetcht thence a wise 3097
14: 3 unto him. So J put the words in her mouth. 3097
14:19 *Is not* the hand of J with thee in all this? 3097
14:19 for thy servant J, he bade me, and he put all 3097
14:20 speech hath thy servant J done this thing: 3097
14:21 the king said unto J, Behold now, I have 3097
14:22 J fell to the ground on his face, and 3097
14:22 J said, To day thy servant knoweth that I 3097
14:23 So J arose and went to Geshur, and 3097
14:29 Therefore Absalom sent for J, to have sent 3097
14:31 J arose, and came to Absalom unto *his* 3097
14:32 Absalom answered J, Behold, I sent unto 3097
14:33 So J came to the king, and told him: and 3097
17:25 Amasa captain of the host instead of J: 3097
18: 2 third part of the people under the hand of J, 3097
18: 5 the king commanded J and Abishai and 3097
18:10 a certain man saw *it*, and told J, and said, 3097
18:11 J said unto the man that told him, 3097
18:12 the man said unto J, Though I should 3097
18:14 said J, I may not tarry thus with thee. 3097
18:16 J blew the trumpet, and the people returned 3097
18:16 after Israel: for J held back the people. 3097
18:20 J said unto him, Thou *shalt* not bear tidings 3097
18:21 said J to Cushi, Go tell the king what thou 3097
18:21 And Cushi bowed himself unto J, and ran. 3097
18:22 Ahimaaz the son of Zadok yet again to J, 3097
18:22 J said, Wherefore wilt thou run, my son, 3097
18:29 When J sent the king's servant, and *me* thy 3097
19: 1 it was told J, Behold, the king weepeth 3097
19: 5 J came *into* the house to the king, and said, 3097
19:13 before me continually in the room of J. 3097
20: 9 J said to Amasa, *Art* thou in health, 3097
20: 9 J took Amasa by the beard with the right 3097
20:10 So J and Abishai his brother pursued after 3097
20:11 He that favoureth J, and he that *is* for 3097
20:11 and he that *is* for David, *let him go* after J. 3097
20:13 all the people went on after J, to pursue 3097
20:15 all the people that *were* with J battered 3097
20:16 say, I pray you, unto J, Come near hither, 3097
20:17 near unto her, the woman said, *Art* thou J? 3097
20:20 J answered and said, Far be it, far be it 3097
20:21 the woman said unto J, Behold, his head 3097
20:22 Sheba the son of Bichri, and cast *it* out to J. 3097
20:22 And J returned *to* Jerusalem unto the king. 3097
20:23 Now J *was* over all the host of Israel: and 3097
23:18 Abishai, the brother of J, the son of 3097
23:24 Asahel the brother of J *was* one of 3097
23:37 armourbearer to J the son of Zeruiah, 3097
24: 2 For the king said to J the captain of 3097
24: 3 J said unto the king, Now the LORD thy 3097
24: 4 the king's word prevailed against J, 3097
24: 4 and J and the captains of the host went out from 3097
24: 9 J gave *up* the sum of the number of 3097
1Ki 1: 7 And he conferred with J the son of Zeruiah, 3097
1:19 the priest, and J the captain of the host: 3097
1:41 when J heard the sound of the trumpet, 3097
2: 5 Moreover thou knowest also what J the son 3097
2:22 the priest, and for J the son of Zeruiah. 3097
2:28 tidings came to J: for Joab had turned after 3097
2:28 for J had turned after Adonijah, though he 3097
2:28 J fled unto the tabernacle of the LORD, 3097
2:29 it was told king Solomon that J was fled 3097
2:30 Thus said J, and thus he answered me. 3097
2:31 which J shed, from me, and from the house 3097
2:33 therefore return upon the head of J, 3097
11:15 J the captain of the host was gone up to 3097
11:16 (For six months did J remain there with all 3097
11:21 that J the captain of the host was dead, 3097
1Ch 2:16 Abishai, and J, and Asahel, three. 3097
2:54 the house of J, and half of 3097
4:14 Seraiah begat J, the father of the valley of 3097
11: 6 So J the son of Zeruiah went first up, and 3097
11: 8 and J repaired the rest of the city. 3097
11:20 Abishai the brother of J, he was chief of 3097
11:26 of the armies *were*, Asahel the brother of J, 3097
11:39 the armourbearer of J the son of Zeruiah, 3097
18:15 And J the son of Zeruiah *was* over the host; 3097
19: 8 when David heard *of it*, he sent J, and all 3097
19:10 Now when J saw that the battle was set 3097
19:14 So J and the people that *were* with him 3097
19:15 into the city. Then J came *to* Jerusalem. 3097
20: 1 at the time that kings go out *to battle*, J led 3097
20: 1 And J smote Rabbah, and destroyed it. 3097
21: 2 David said to J and to the rulers of 3097
21: 3 J answered, The LORD make his people 3097
21: 4 the king's word prevailed against J. 3097
21: 4 Wherefore J departed, and went throughout 3097
21: 5 J gave the sum of the number of the people 3097
21: 6 for the king's word was abominable to J. 3097
26:28 and J the son of Zeruiah, had dedicated; 3097
27: 7 fourth month *was* Asahel the brother of J, 3097
27:24 J the son of Zeruiah began to number, but 3097
27:34 and the general of the king's army *was* J. 3097
Ezr 2: 6 of the children of Jeshua *and* J, 3097
8: 9 Of the sons of J; Obadiah the son of Jehiel, 3097
Ne 7:11 of the children of Jeshua and J, 3097
Ps 60: T when J returned, and smote of Edom in 3097

JOAB'S (8) [JOAB]
2Sa 14:30 J field is near mine, and he hath barley 3097
17:25 of Nahash, sister to Zeruiah J mother. 3097
18: 2 J brother, and a third part under the hand of 3097
18:15 ten young men that bare J armour 3097
20: 7 there went out after him J men, and 3097
20: 8 J garment that he had put on *was* girded 3097
20:10 no heed to the sword that *was* in J hand: 3097
20:11 one of J men stood by him, and said, 3097

JOAH (11)
2Ki 18:18 and J the son of Asaph the recorder. 3098
18:26 Shebna, and J, unto Rab-shakeh, Speak, 3098
18:37 and J the son of Asaph the recorder, 3098
1Ch 6:21 J his son, Iddo his son, Zerah his son, 3098
26: 4 J the third, and Sacar the fourth, and 3098
2Ch 29:12 J the son of Zimmah, and Eden the son of 3098
29:12 the son of Zimmah, and Eden the son of J: 3098
34: 8 and J the son of Joahaz the recorder, 3098
Isa 36: 3 the scribe, and J, Asaph's son, the recorder. 3098
36:11 and Shebna and J unto Rabshakeh, 3098
36:22 and J, the son of Asaph, the recorder, 3098

JOAHAZ (1)
2Ch 34: 8 the city, and Joah the son of J the recorder, 3099

JOANNA (3)
Lk 3:27 Which was *the son* of J, which was *the son* *2490*
8: 3 And J the wife of Chuza Herod's steward, *2489*
24:10 and J, and Mary *the mother* of James, and *2489*

JOASH (49)
Jdg 6:11 that *pertained* unto J the Abi-ezrite: 3101
6:29 Gideon the son of J hath done this thing. 3101
6:30 the men of the city said unto J, Bring out 3101
6:31 J said unto all that stood against him, Will 3101
7:14 else save the sword of Gideon the son of J, 3101
8:13 Gideon the son of J returned from battle 3101
8:29 Jerubbaal the son of J went and dwelt in his 3101
8:32 Gideon the son of J died in a good old age, 3101
8:32 was buried in the sepulchre of J his father, 3101
1Ki 22:26 of the city, and to J the king's son; 3101
2Ki 11: 2 took J the son of Ahaziah, and stale him 3101
12:19 the rest of the acts of J, and all that he did, 3101
12:20 slew J *in* the house of Millo, 3101
13: 1 twentieth year of J the son of Ahaziah king 3101
13: 9 and J his son reigned in his stead. 3101
13:10 seventh year of J king of Judah *began* 3101
13:12 the rest of the acts of J, and all that he did, 3101
13:13 J slept with his fathers; and Jeroboam sat 3101
13:13 J was buried in Samaria with the kings of 3101
13:14 J the king of Israel came down unto him, 3101
13:25 Three times did J beat him, and 3101
14: 1 In the second year of J son of Jehoahaz 3101
14: 1 Amaziah the son of J king of Judah. 3101
14: 3 he did according to all *things* as J his father 3101
14:17 Amaziah the son of J king of Judah lived 3101
14:23 J king of Judah Jeroboam the son of Joash 3101
14:23 J king of Israel *began* to reign in Samaria, 3101
14:27 them by the hand of Jeroboam the son of J. 3101
1Ch 3:11 Joram his son, Ahaziah his son, J his son, 3101
4:22 the men of Chozeba, and J, and Saraph, 3101
7: 8 J, and Eliezer, and Elioenai, and Omri, and 3135
12: 3 The chief *was* Ahiezer, then J, the sons of 3101
27:28 and over the cellars of oil *was* J: 3135
2Ch 18:25 of the city, and to J the king's son; 3101
22:11 took J the son of Ahaziah, and stole him 3101
24: 1 J *was* seven years old when he *began* to 3101
24: 2 J did *that* which *was* right in the sight of 3101
24: 4 *that* J was minded to repair the house of 3101
24:22 Thus J the king remembered not 3101
24:24 So they executed judgment against J. 3101
25:17 sent to J, the son of Jehoahaz, the son of 3101
25:18 J king of Israel sent to Amaziah king of 3101
25:21 So J the king of Israel went up; and 3101
25:23 J the king of Israel took Amaziah king of 3101
25:23 the son of J, the son of Jehoahaz, 3101
25:25 Amaziah the son of J king of Judah lived 3101
25:25 J son of Jehoahaz king of Israel fifteen 3101
Hos 1: 1 in the days of Jeroboam the son of J, 3101
Am 1: 1 in the days of Jeroboam the son of J king 3101

JOATHAM (2)
Mt 1: 9 And Ozias begat J; and Joatham begat *2488*
Mt 1: 9 and J begat Achaz; and Achaz begat *2488*

JOB (59) [JOB'S]
Ge 46:13 Tola, and Phuvah, and J, and Shimron. 3102
Job 1: 1 a man in the land of Uz, whose name *was* J; 347
1: 5 that J sent and sanctified them, and rose up 347
1: 5 for J said, It may be that my sons have 347
1: 5 God in their hearts. Thus did J continually. 347
1: 8 Hast thou considered my servant J, 347
1: 9 and said, Doth J fear God for nought? 347
1:14 there came a messenger unto J, and said, 347
1:20 J arose, and rent his mantle, and shaved his 347
1:22 In all this J sinned not, nor charged God 347
2: 3 Hast thou considered my servant J, 347
2: 7 smote J with sore boils from the sole of his 347
2:10 In all this did not J sin with his lips. 347
3: 1 After this opened J his mouth, and 347
3: 2 And J spake, and said, 347
6: 1 But J answered and said, 347
9: 1 Then J answered and said, 347
12: 1 And J answered and said, 347
16: 1 Then J answered and said, 347
19: 1 Then J answered and said, 347
21: 1 But J answered and said, 347
23: 1 Then J answered and said, 347
26: 1 But J answered and said, 347
27: 1 Moreover J continued his parable, and said, 347
29: 1 Moreover J continued his parable, and said, 347
31:40 instead of barley. The words of J are ended. 347
32: 1 So these three men ceased to answer J, 347
32: 2 against J was his wrath kindled, because 347
32: 3 found no answer, and *yet* had condemned J. 347
32: 4 Now Elihu had waited till J had spoken, 347
32:12 *there was* none of you that convinced J, *or* 347
33: 1 Wherefore, J, I pray thee, hear my speeches, 347
33:31 Mark well, O J, hearken unto me: hold thy 347
34: 5 For J hath said, I am righteous: and 347
34: 7 What man *is* like J, *who* drinketh up 347
34:35 J hath spoken without knowledge, and 347
34:36 My desire *is that* J may be tried unto the end 347
35:16 Therefore doth J open his mouth in vain; 347
37:14 Hearken unto this, O J: stand still, and 347
38: 1 the LORD answered J out of 347
40: 1 Moreover the LORD answered J, and said, 347
40: 3 Then J answered the LORD, and said, 347
40: 6 answered the LORD unto J out of 347
42: 1 Then J answered the LORD, and said, 347
42: 7 the LORD had spoken these words unto J, 347
42: 7 *the thing that is* right, as my servant J *hath*. 347
42: 8 go to my servant J, and offer up for 347
42: 8 and my servant J shall pray for you: 347
42: 8 *the thing which is* right, like my servant J. 347
42: 9 the LORD also accepted J. 347
42:10 the LORD turned the captivity of J, 347
42:10 also the LORD gave J twice as much as he 347
42:12 So the LORD blessed the latter end of J 347
42:15 women found *so* fair as the daughters of J: 347
42:16 After this lived J an hundred and forty years, 347
42:17 So J died, *being* old and full of days. 347
Eze 14:14 Noah, Daniel, and J, were in it, they should 347
14:20 Daniel, and J, *were* in it, *as* I live, 347
Jas 5:11 Ye have heard of the patience of J, and *2492*

JOB'S (1) [JOB]
Job 2:11 Now when J three friends heard of all this 347

JOBAB (9)
Ge 10:29 Ophir, and Havilah, and J: all these *were* 3103
36:33 J the son of Zerah of Bozrah reigned in his 3103
36:34 J died, and Husham of the land of Temani 3103
Jos 11: 1 *things*, that he sent to J king of Madon, 3103
1Ch 1:23 Ophir, and Havilah, and J. All these *were* 3103
1:44 J the son of Zerah of Bozrah reigned in his 3103
1:45 when J was dead, Husham of the land of 3103
8: 9 J, and Zibia, and Mesha, and Malcham, 3103
8:18 Ishmerai also, and Jezliah, and J, the sons 3103

JOCHEBED (2)
Ex 6:20 Amram took him J his father's sister to 3115
Nu 26:59 the name of Amram's wife *was* J, 3115

JOED (1)
Ne 11: 7 the son of J, the son of Pedaiah, the son of 3133

JOEL (20)
1Sa 8: 2 Now the name of his firstborn was J; and 3100
1Ch 4:35 J, and Jehu the son of Josibiah, the son of 3100
5: 4 The sons of J; Shemaiah his son, Gog his 3100
5: 8 the son of Shema, the son of J, who dwelt 3100
5:12 J the chief, and Shapham the next, and 3100
6:33 Heman a singer, the son of J, the son of 3100
6:36 the son of J, the son of Azariah, 3100
7: 3 Michael, and Obadiah, and J, Ishiah, five: 3100
11:38 J the brother of Nathan, Mibhar the son of 3100
15: 7 J the chief, and his brethren an hundred and 3100
15:11 for Uriel, Asaiah, and J, Shemaiah, and 3100
15:17 the Levites appointed Heman the son of J; 3100
23: 8 chief *was* Jehiel, and Zetham, and J, three. 3100
26:22 Zetham, and J his brother, *which were* over 3100
27:20 tribe of Manasseh, J the son of Pedaiah: 3100
2Ch 29:12 son of Amasai, and J the son of Azariah, 3100
Ezr 10:43 Zabad, Zebina, Jadau, and J, Benaiah. 3100
Ne 11: 9 J the son of Zichri *was* their overseer: 3100
Joel 1: 1 The word of the LORD that came to J 3100
Ac 2:16 is that which was spoken by the prophet J; *2493*

JOELAH (1)
1Ch 12: 7 J, and Zebadiah, the sons of Jeroham of 3132

JOEZER (1)
1Ch 12: 6 Jesiah, and Azareel, and J, and Jashobeam, 3134

JOGBEHAH (2)
Nu 32:35 And Atroth, Shophan, and Jaazer, and J, 3011

Jdg 8:11 dwelt in tents on the east of Nobah and J, 3011

JOGLI (1)
Nu 34:22 of the children of Dan, Bukki the son of J. 3020

JOHA (2)
1Ch 8:16 Michael, and Ispah, and J, the sons of 3109
11:45 son of Shimri, and J his brother, the Tizite, 3109

JOHANAN (27)
2Ki 25:23 J the son of Careah, and Seraiah the son of 3110
1Ch 3:15 the sons of Josiah *were*, the firstborn J, 3110
3:24 and J, and Dalaiah, and Anani, seven. 3110
6: 9 begat Azariah, and Azariah begat J, 3110
6:10 J begat Azariah, (he *it is* that executed 3110
12: 4 and J, and Josabad the Gederathite, 3110
12:12 J the eighth, Elzabad the ninth, 3110
2Ch 28:12 Azariah the son of J, Berechiah the son of 3076
Ezr 8:12 J the son of Hakkatan, and with him an 3110
10: 6 went into the chamber of J the son of 3076
Ne 6:18 his son J had taken the daughter of 3076
12:22 Joiada, and J, and Jaddua, *were* recorded 3110
12:23 even until the days of J the son of Eliashib. 3110
Jer 40: 8 J and Jonathan the sons of Kareah, and 3110
40:13 Moreover J the son of Kareah, and all 3110
40:15 J the son of Kareah spake to Gedaliah in 3110
40:16 Gedaliah the son of Ahikam said unto J 3110
41:11 when J the son of Kareah, and all 3110
41:13 *were* with Ishmael saw J the son of Kareah, 3110
41:14 and went unto J the son of Kareah. 3110
41:15 Nethaniah escaped from J with eight men, 3110
41:16 took J the son of Kareah, and all 3110
42: 1 J the son of Kareah, and Jezaniah the son 3110
42: 8 called he J the son of Kareah, and all 3110
43: 2 J the son of Kareah, and all the proud men, 3110
43: 4 So J the son of Kareah, and all the captains 3110
43: 5 J the son of Kareah, and all the captains of 3110

JOHN (131) [JOHN'S]
Mt 3: 1 In those days came J the Baptist, *2491*
3: 4 And the same J had his raiment of camel's *2491*
3:13 Jesus from Galilee to Jordan unto J, *2491*
3:14 But J forbad him, saying, I have need to be *2491*
4:12 Now when Jesus had heard that J was cast *2491*
4:21 the *son* of Zebedee, and J his brother, *2491*
9:14 Then came to him the disciples of J, *2491*
10: 2 the *son* of Zebedee, and J his brother; *2491*
11: 2 Now when J had heard in the prison *2491*
11: 4 shew J again *those things* which ye do hear *2491*
11: 7 to say unto the multitudes concerning J, *2491*
11:11 hath not risen a greater than J the Baptist: *2491*
11:12 And from the days of J the Baptist until *2491*
11:13 the prophets and the law prophesied until J. *2491*
11:18 For J came neither eating nor drinking, and *2491*
14: 2 said unto his servants, This is J the Baptist; *2491*
14: 3 For Herod had laid hold on J, and *2491*
14: 4 For J said unto him, It is not lawful for thee *2491*
14: 8 Give me here J Baptist's head in a charger. *2491*
14:10 And he sent, and beheaded J in the prison. *2491*
16:14 Some *say that thou art* J the Baptist: *2491*
17: 1 and J his brother, and bringeth them up into *2491*
17:13 that he spake unto them of J the Baptist. *2491*
21:25 The baptism of J, whence was it? *2491*
21:26 fear the people; for all hold J as a prophet. *2491*
21:32 For J came unto you in the way of *2491*
Mk 1: 4 J did baptize in the wilderness, and *2491*
1: 6 And J was clothed with camel's hair, and *2491*
1: 9 of Galilee, and was baptized of J in Jordan. *2491*
1:14 Now after that J was put in prison, Jesus *2491*
1:19 the *son* of Zebedee, and J his brother, *2491*
1:29 of Simon and Andrew, with James and J. *2491*
2:18 And the disciples of J and of the Pharisees *2491*
2:18 Why do the disciples of J and of *2491*
3:17 *son* of Zebedee, and J the brother of James; *2491*
5:37 and James, and J the brother of James. *2491*
6:14 That J the Baptist was risen from the dead, *2491*
6:16 *thereof*, he said, It is J, whom I beheaded: *2491*
6:17 himself had sent forth and laid hold upon J, *2491*
6:18 For J had said unto Herod, It is not lawful *2491*
6:20 For Herod feared J, knowing that he *was* a *2491*
6:24 And she said, The head of J the Baptist. *2491*
6:25 by in a charger the head of J the Baptist. *2491*
8:28 And they answered, J the Baptist: but *2491*
9: 2 and J, and leadeth them up into a high *2491*
9:38 And J answered him, saying, Master, *2491*
10:35 And James and J, the sons of Zebedee, *2491*
10:41 to be much displeased with James and J. *2491*
11:30 The baptism of J, was *it* from heaven, or *2491*
11:32 for all *men* counted J, that he was a prophet *2491*
13: 3 Peter and James and J and Andrew asked *2491*
14:33 he taketh with him Peter and James and J, *2491*
Lk 1:13 thee a son, and thou shalt call his name J. *2491*
1:60 and said, Not *so;* but he shall be called J. *2491*
1:63 and wrote, saying, His name is J. *2491*
3: 2 the word of God came unto J the son of *2491*
3:15 and all *men* mused in their hearts of J, *2491*
3:16 J answered, saying unto *them* all, I indeed *2491*
3:20 this above all, that he shut up J in prison. *2491*
5:10 And so *was* also James, and J, *the* sons of *2491*
5:33 Why do the disciples of J fast often, and *2491*
6:14 and J, Philip and Bartholomew, *2491*
7:18 And the disciples of J shewed him of all *2491*
7:19 And J calling unto *him* two of his disciples *2491*
7:20 J Baptist hath sent us unto thee, saying, *2491*
7:22 and tell J what *things* ye have seen and *2491*
7:24 And when the messengers of J were *2491*
7:24 to speak unto the people concerning J, *2491*
7:28 is not a greater prophet than J the Baptist: *2491*
7:29 being baptized *with* the baptism of J. *2491*
7:33 For J the Baptist came neither eating bread *2491*
8:51 and J, and the father and the mother of *2491*
9: 7 of some, that J was risen from the dead; *2491*
9: 9 And Herod said, J have I beheaded: but *2491*
9:19 They answering said, J the Baptist; but *2491*
Lk 9:28 he took Peter and J and James, and went up *2491*
9:49 And J answered and said, Master, we saw *2491*
9:54 disciples James and J saw *this*, they said, *2491*
11: 1 us to pray, as J also taught his disciples. *2491*
16:16 The law and the prophets *were* until J: *2491*
20: 4 The baptism of J, was it from heaven, or *2491*
20: 6 for they be persuaded that J was a prophet. *2491*
22: 8 And he sent Peter and J, saying, Go and *2491*
Jn 1: 6 a man sent from God, whose name *was* J. *2491*
1:15 J bare witness of him, and cried, saying, *2491*
1:19 And this is the record of J, when the Jews *2491*
1:26 J answered them, saying, I baptize with *2491*
1:28 beyond Jordan, where J was baptizing. *2491*
1:29 The next day J seeth Jesus coming unto *2491*
1:32 And J bare record, saying, I saw the Spirit *2491*
1:35 Again the next day *after* J stood, and *2491*
1:40 One of the two which heard J speak, and *2491*
3:23 And J also was baptizing in Aenon near to *2491*
3:24 For J was not yet cast into prison. *2491*
3:26 And they came unto J, and said unto him, *2491*
3:27 J answered and said, A man can receive *2491*
4: 1 and baptized moe disciples than J, *2491*
5:33 Ye sent unto J, and he bare witness unto *2491*
5:36 But I have greater witness than *that of* J: *2491*
10:40 into the place where J at first baptized; *2491*
10:41 unto him, and said, J did no miracle: *2491*
10:41 all *things* that J spake of this *man* were *2491*
Ac 1: 5 For J truly baptized with water; but ye shall *2491*
1:13 and J, and Andrew, Philip, and Thomas, *2491*
1:22 Beginning from the baptism of J, unto *that* *2491*
3: 1 J went up together into the temple at *2491*
3: 3 and J about to go into the temple, *2491*
3: 4 fastening his eyes upon him with J, said, *2491*
3:11 *man* which was healed held Peter and J, *2491*
4: 6 and J, and Alexander, and as many as were *2491*
4:13 when they saw the boldness of Peter and J, *2491*
4:19 But Peter and J answered and said unto *2491*
8:14 of God, they sent unto them Peter and J: *2491*
10:37 after the baptism which J preached; *2491*
11:16 that he said, J indeed baptized with water; *2491*
12: 2 And he killed James the brother of J with *2491*
12:12 came to the house of Mary the mother of J, *2491*
12:25 and took with *them* J, whose surname was *2491*
13: 5 and they had also J to *their* minister. *2491*
13:13 J departing from them returned to *2491*
13:24 When J had first preached before his *2491*
13:25 And as J fulfilled *his* course, he said, *2491*
15:37 Barnabas determined to take with *them* J, *2491*
18:25 of the Lord, knowing only the baptism of J. *2491*
19: 4 J verily baptized *with* the baptism of *2491*
Gal 2: 9 And when James, Cephas, and J, *2491*
Rev 1: 1 signified *it* by his angel unto his servant J: *2491*
1: 4 J to the seven churches which are in Asia: *2491*
1: 9 I J, who also am your brother, and *2491*
21: 2 And I J saw the holy city, new Jerusalem, *2491*
22: 8 And I J saw these *things*, and heard *them.* *2491*

JOHN'S (2) [JOHN]
Jn 3:25 a question between *some* of J disciples *2491*
Ac 19: 3 And they said, Unto J baptism. *2491*

JOIADA (4)
Ne 12:10 also begat Eliashib, and Eliashib begat J, 3111
12:11 J begat Jonathan, and Jonathan begat 3111
12:22 J, and Johanan, and Jaddua, *were* recorded 3111
13:28 *one* of the sons of J, the son of Eliashib 3111

JOIAKIM (4)
Ne 12:10 Jeshua begat J, Joiakim also begat Eliashib, 3113
12:10 J also begat Eliashib, and Eliashib begat 3113
12:12 in the days of J were priests, the chief of 3113
12:26 These *were* in the days of J the son of 3113

JOIARIB (5)
Ezr 8:16 chief *men;* also for J, and for Elnathan, 3114
Ne 11: 5 of Hazaiah, the son of Adaiah, the son of J, 3114
11:10 Of the priests: Jedaiah the son of J, Jachin, 3114
12: 6 Shemaiah, and J, Jedaiah, 3114
12:19 And of J, Mattenai; of Jedaiah, Uzzi; 3114

JOIN (14) [JOINED, JOINING, JOININGS, JOINT, JOINT-HEIRS, JOINTS]
Ex 1:10 they j also unto our enemies, and 3254
2Ch 20:35 after this did Jehoshaphat king of Judah j 2266
Ezr 9:14 **j in affinity** with the people of these 2859
Pr 11:21 *Though* hand *j* in hand, the wicked shall not NIH
16: 5 *though* hand *j* in hand, he shall not be NIH
Isa 5: 8 Woe unto them that j house to house, 5060
9:11 against him, and j his enemies **together**; 5526
56: 6 that j themselves to the LORD, to serve 3867
Jer 50: 5 let us j ourselves to the LORD *in* a 3867
Eze 37:17 j them one to another into one stick; and 7126
Da 11: 6 of years they shall j themselves **together**; 2266
Ac 5:13 And of the rest durst no *man* j himself to *2853*
8:29 Go near, and j thyself **to** this chariot. *2853*
9:26 he assayed to j himself to the disciples: *2853*

JOINED (43) [JOIN]
Ge 14: 3 All these were j **together** in the vale of 2266
14: 8 they j battle with them in the vale of 6186
29:34 Now *this* time will my husband be j unto 3867
Ex 28: 7 *thereof* j at the two edges thereof; 2266
28: 7 edges thereof; and *so* it shall be j **together**. 2266
Nu 18: 2 that they may be j unto thee, and 3867
18: 4 they shall be j unto thee, and keep 3867
25: 3 Israel j himself **unto** Baal-peor: and 6775
25: 5 Slay ye every one his men that were j unto 6775
1Sa 4: 2 when they j battle, Israel was smitten 5203
1Ki 7:32 the axletrees of the wheels *were* j to 3027
20:29 that in the seventh day the battle was j: 7126
2Ch 18: 1 in abundance, and j **affinity** with Ahab. 2859
20:36 he j himself with him to make ships to go 2266
20:37 Because thou hast j thyself with Ahaziah, 2266
Ezr 4:12 up the walls *thereof*, and j the foundations. 2338
Ne 4: 6 all the wall was j **together** unto the half 7194
Est 9:27 upon all such as j themselves unto them, 3867
Job 3: 6 let it not be j unto the days of the year, let it 2302
41:17 They are j one to another, they stick 1692
41:23 The flakes of his flesh are j **together**: 1692
Ps 83: 8 Assur also is j with them: they have holpen 3867
106:28 They j themselves also unto Baal-peor, and 6775
Ecc 9: 4 For to him that is j to all the living there is 2266
Isa 13:15 every one that is j *unto them* shall fall by 5595
14: 1 the strangers shall be j with them, and 3867
14:20 Thou shalt not be j **with** them in burial, 3161
56: 3 that hath j himself to the LORD, speak, 3867
Eze 1: 9 Their wings *were* j one to another; they 2266
1:11 two *wings* of every one *were* j one to 2266
46:22 *there were* courts j *of* forty *cubits* long 7000
Hos 4:17 Ephraim *is* j **to** idols: let him alone. 2266
Zec 2:11 many nations shall be j to the LORD in 3867
Mt 19: 6 What therefore God hath j **together**, let not *4801*
Mk 10: 9 What therefore God hath j **together**, let not *4801*
Lk 15:15 and j himself **to** a citizen of that country; *2853*
Ac 5:36 of men, about four hundred, j themselves: *4347*
18: 7 whose house j **hard to** the synagogue. *4927*
1Co 1:10 *that* ye be **perfectly** j **together** in the same *2675*
6:16 know ye not that he which is j **to** a harlot is *2853*
6:17 But he that is j unto the Lord is one spirit. *2853*
Eph 4:16 whom the whole body **fitly** j **together** *4883*
5:31 and shall be j unto his wife, and they two *4347*

JOINING (1) [JOIN]
2Ch 3:12 the other wing *was* five cubits *also*, j to 1695

JOININGS (1) [JOIN]
1Ch 22: 3 for the doors of the gates, and for the j; 4226

JOINT (4) [JOIN]
Ge 32:25 the hollow of Jacob's thigh was **out of** j, 3363
Ps 22:14 like water, and all my bones are **out of** j: 6504
Pr 25:19 *is like* a broken tooth, and a foot **out of** j. 4154
Eph 4:16 compacted by that which every j supplieth, *860*

JOINT-HEIRS (1) [HEIR, JOIN]
Ro 8:17 heirs of God, and j **with** Christ; if so be that *4789*

JOINTS (6) [JOIN]
1Ki 22:34 smote the king of Israel between the j of 1694
2Ch 18:33 smote the king of Israel between the j of 1694
SS 7: 1 the j of thy thighs *are* like jewels, the work 2542
Da 5: 6 so that the j of his loins were loosed, and 7001
Col 2:19 from which all the body by j and *860*
Heb 4:12 and of the j and marrow, and *is* a discerner *719*

JOKDEAM (1)
Jos 15:56 And Jezreel, and J, and Zanoah, 3347

JOKIM (1)
1Ch 4:22 J, and the men of Chozeba, and Joash, and 3137

JOKMEAM (1)
1Ch 6:68 J with her suburbs, and Beth-horon with 3361

JOKNEAM (4)
Jos 12:22 one; the king of J of Carmel, one; 3362
19:11 and reached to the river that *is* before J; 3362
21:34 J with her suburbs, and Kartah with her 3362
1Ki 4:12 *even* unto *the place that is* beyond J: 3361

JOKSHAN (4)
Ge 25: 2 J, and Medan, and Midian, and Ishbak, and 3370
25: 3 J begat Sheba, and Dedan. And the sons of 3370
1Ch 1:32 J, and Medan, and Midian, and Ishbak, and 3370
1:32 And the sons of J; Sheba, and Dedan. 3370

JOKTAN (6)
Ge 10:25 and his brother's name *was* J. 3355
10:26 J begat Almodad, and Sheleph, and 3355
10:29 and Jobab: all these *were* the sons of J. 3355
1Ch 1:19 was divided: and his brother's name *was* J. 3355
1:20 J begat Almodad, and Sheleph, and 3355
1:23 and Jobab. All these *were* the sons of J. 3355

JOKTHEEL (2)
Jos 15:38 And Dilean, and Mizpeh, and J, 3371
2Ki 14: 7 and called the name of it J unto this day. 3371

JONA (1)
Jn 1:42 he said, Thou art Simon the son of J: *2495*

JONADAB (12)
2Sa 13: 3 Amnon had a friend, whose name *was* J, 3122
13: 3 and J *was* a very subtil man. 3122
13: 5 J said unto him, Lay *thee* down on thy bed, 3082
13:32 J, the son of Shimeah David's brother, 3122
13:35 J said unto the king, Behold, the king's 3122
Jer 35: 6 for J the son of Rechab our father 3122
35: 8 Thus have we obeyed the voice of J the son 3082
35:10 done according to all that J our father 3122
35:14 The words of J the son of Rechab, that he 3082
35:16 Because the sons of J the son of Rechab 3082
35:18 obeyed the commandment of J your father, 3082
35:19 J the son of Rechab shall not want a man to 3122

JONAH (19) [JONAS]
2Ki 14:25 he spake by the hand of his servant J, 3124
Jnh 1: 1 Now the word of the LORD came unto J 3124
1: 3 J rose up to flee unto Tarshish from 3124
1: 5 J was gone down into the sides of the ship; 3124
1: 7 So they cast lots, and the lot fell upon J. 3124
1:15 So they took up J, and cast him forth into 3124
1:17 had prepared a great fish to swallow up J. 3124
1:17 J was in the belly of the fish three days 3124
2: 1 J prayed unto the LORD his God out of 3124
2:10 and it vomited out J upon the dry *land.* 3124
3: 1 the word of the LORD came unto J 3124

Jnh 3: 3 So J arose, and went unto Nineveh, 3124
3: 4 J began to enter into the city a day's 3124
4: 1 it displeased J exceedingly, and he was 3124
4: 5 So J went out of the city, and sat on 3124
4: 6 a gourd, and made *it* to come up over J, 3124
4: 6 So J was exceeding glad of the gourd. 3124
4: 8 the sun beat upon the head of J, that he 3124
4: 9 God said to J, Doest thou well to be angry 3124

JONAM See JONAN

JONAN (1)

Lk 3:30 *the son* of Joseph, which was *the son* of J, *2494*

JONAS (12) [JONAH]

Mt 12:39 be given to it, but the sign of the prophet J: *2495*
12:40 For as J was three days and three nights in *2495*
12:41 because they repented at the preaching of J; *2495*
12:41 and behold, a greater than J *is* here. *2495*
16: 4 given unto it, but the sign of the prophet J. *2495*
Lk 11:29 be given it, but the sign of J the prophet. *2495*
11:30 For as J was a sign unto the Ninevites, so *2495*
11:32 for they repented at the preaching of J; and *2495*
11:32 and behold, a greater than J *is* here. *2495*
Jn 21:15 Jesus saith to Simon Peter, Simon, *son* of J, *2495*
21:16 Simon, *son* of J, lovest thou me? *2495*
21:17 third time, Simon, *son* of J, lovest thou me? *2495*

JONATHAN (118) [JONATHAN'S]

Jdg 18:30 J, the son of Gershom, the son of 3083
1Sa 13: 2 a thousand were with J in Gibeah of 3129
13: 3 J smote the garrison of the Philistines that 3129
13:16 J his son, and the people that were present 3129
13:22 of the people that *were* with Saul and J: 3129
13:22 and with J his son was there found. 3129
14: 1 that J the son of Saul said unto the young 3129
14: 3 And the people knew not that J was gone. 3129
14: 4 *by* which J sought to go over unto 3129
14: 6 J said to the young man that bare his 3083
14: 8 said J, Behold, we will pass over unto *these* 3083
14:12 the men of the garrison answered J and 3129
14:12 J said unto his armourbearer, Come up 3129
14:13 J climbed up upon his hands and upon his 3129
14:13 they fell before J; and his armourbearer 3129
14:14 which J and his armourbearer made, was 3129
14:17 behold J and his armourbearer *were* not 3129
14:21 the Israelites that *were* with Saul and J. 3129
14:27 J heard not when his father charged 3129
14:29 said J, My father hath troubled the land: 3129
14:39 though it be in J my son, he shall surely 3129
14:40 I and J my son will be on the other side. 3129
14:41 a perfect *lot.* And Saul and J were taken: 3129
14:42 Cast *lots* between me and J my son. 3129
14:42 and Jonathan my son. And J was taken. 3129
14:43 Saul said to J, Tell me what thou hast done. 3129
14:43 J told him, and said, I did but taste a little 3129
14:44 and more also: for thou shalt surely die, J. 3129
14:45 the people said unto Saul, Shall J die, 3129
14:45 So the people rescued J, that he died not. 3129
14:49 Now the sons of Saul were J, and Ishui, 3129
18: 1 that the soul of J was knit with the soul of 3083
18: 1 of David, and J loved him as his own soul. 3083
18: 3 J and David made a covenant, because 3083
18: 4 J stript himself of the robe that *was* upon 3083
19: 1 Saul spake to J his son, and to all his 3129
19: 2 J Saul's son delighted much in David: and 3083
19: 2 J told David, saying, Saul my father 3083
19: 4 J spake good of David unto Saul his father, 3083
19: 6 Saul hearkened unto the voice of J: and 3083
19: 7 J called David, and Jonathan shewed him 3083
19: 7 and J shewed him all those things. 3083
19: 7 J brought David to Saul, and he was in his 3083
20: 1 came and said before J, What have I done? 3083
20: 3 he saith, Let not J know this, lest he be 3083
20: 4 said J unto David, Whatsoever thy soul 3083
20: 5 David said unto J, Behold, to morrow *is* 3083
20: 9 J said, Far be it from thee: for if I knew 3083
20:10 Then said David to J, Who shall tell me? or 3083
20:11 J said unto David, Come, and let us go out 3083
20:12 J said unto David, O LORD God of Israel, 3083
20:13 The LORD do so and much more to J: *but* 3083
20:16 So J made *a covenant* with the house of 3083
20:17 J caused David to swear again, because 3083
20:18 J said to *David,* To morrow *is* the new 3083
20:25 J arose, and Abner sat by Saul's side, and 3083
20:27 Saul said unto J his son, Wherefore cometh 3083
20:28 J answered Saul, David earnestly asked 3083
20:30 Saul's anger was kindled against J, and 3083
20:32 J answered Saul his father, and said unto 3083
20:33 whereby J knew that it was determined of 3083
20:34 So J arose from the table in fierce anger, 3083
20:35 that J went out *into* the field at the time 3083
20:37 to the place of the arrow which J had shot, 3083
20:37 J cried after the lad, and said, *Is* not 3083
20:38 J cried after the lad, Make speed, haste, 3083
20:39 only J and David knew the matter. 3083
20:40 J gave his artillery unto his lad, and 3083
20:42 J said to David, Go in peace, forasmuch as 3083
20:42 and departed: and J went *into* the city. 3083
23:16 J Saul's son arose, and went to David *into* 3083
23:18 abode in the wood, and J went to his house. 3083
31: 2 the Philistines slew J, and Abinadab, and 3083
2Sa 1: 4 dead; and Saul and J his son are dead also. 3083
1: 5 thou that Saul and J his son be dead? 3083
1:12 for J his son, and for the people of 3083
1:17 lamentation over Saul and over J his son: 3083
1:22 the bow of J turned not back, and 3083
1:23 Saul and J *were* lovely and pleasant in their 3083
1:25 O J, *thou wast* slain in thine high places. 3083
1:26 I am distressed for thee, my brother J: 3083
4: 4 J, Saul's son, had a son *that was* lame of 3083
4: 4 tidings came of Saul and J out of Jezreel, 3083
9: 3 J hath yet a son, *which is* lame on *his* feet. 3083
9: 6 the son of J, the son of Saul, was come 3083
2Sa 9: 7 for I will surely shew thee kindness for J 3083
15:27 thy son, and J the son of Abiathar. 3083
15:36 Zadok's *son,* and J Abiathar's *son;* and 3083
17:17 Now J and Ahimaaz stayed by En-rogel; 3083
17:20 they said, Where *is* Ahimaaz and J? 3083
21: 7 the son of J the son of Saul, because of 3083
21: 7 between David and J the son of Saul. 3083
21:12 the bones of J his son from the men of 3083
21:13 bones of Saul and the bones of J his son; 3083
21:14 J his son buried they in the country of 3083
21:21 J the son of Shimea the brother of David 3083
23:32 the Shaalbonite, *of* the sons of Jashen, J, 3083
1Ki 1:42 J the son of Abiathar the priest came: 3129
1:43 J answered and said to Adonijah, 3129
1Ch 2:32 Jada the brother of Shammai; Jether, and J: 3129
2:33 the sons of J; Peleth, and Zaza. These were 3129
8:33 Saul begat J, and Malchishua, and 3083
8:34 the son of J *was* Merib-baal; and 3083
9:39 Saul begat J, and Malchishua, and 3083
9:40 the son of J *was* Merib-baal: and 3083
10: 2 the Philistines slew J, and Abinadab, and 3129
11:34 J the son of Shage the Hararite, 3129
20: 7 J the son of Shimea David's brother slew 3083
27:32 Also J David's uncle *was* a counseller, 3083
Ezr 8: 6 Ebed the son of J, and with him fifty males. 3129
10:15 Only J the son of Asahel and Jahaziah 3129
Ne 12:11 Joiada begat J, and Jonathan begat Jaddua. 3129
12:11 Joiada begat Jonathan, and J begat Jaddua. 3129
12:14 Of Melicu, J; of Shebaniah, Joseph; 3129
12:35 *namely,* Zechariah the son of J, the son of 3129
Jer 37:15 put him *in* prison *in* the house of J 3083
37:20 not to return *to* the house of J the scribe, 3083
40: 8 Johanan and J the sons of Kareah, and 3129

JONATHAN'S (3) [JONATHAN]

1Sa 20:38 J lad gathered up the arrows, and came to 3083
2Sa 9: 1 that I may shew him kindness for J sake? 3083
Jer 38:26 that *he* would not cause me to return *to* J 3083

JONATH-ELEM-RECHOKIM (1)

Ps 56: T To the chief Musician upon J, Michtam of 3128

JOPPA (13)

2Ch 2:16 we will bring it to thee *in* flotes by sea *to* J; 3305
Ezr 3: 7 cedar trees from Lebanon to the sea of J, 3305
Jnh 1: 3 of the LORD, and went down *to* J; 3305
Ac 9:36 Now there was at J a certain disciple *2445*
9:38 And forasmuch as Lydda was nigh to J, *2445*
9:42 And it was known throughout all J; and *2445*
9:43 that he tarried many days in J with one *2445*
10: 5 And now send men to J, and call for *one* *2445*
10: 8 *these things* unto them, he sent them to J. *2445*
10:23 certain brethren from J accompanied him. *2445*
10:32 Send therefore to J, and call hither Simon, *2445*
11: 5 I was in the city of J praying: and in a *2445*
11:13 Send men to J, and call for Simon, *2445*

JORAH (1)

Ezr 2:18 The children of J, an hundred and twelve. 3139

JORAI (1)

1Ch 5:13 J, and Jachan, and Zia, and Heber, seven. 3140

JORAM (29)

2Sa 8:10 Toi sent J his son unto king David, 3141
8:10 *J* brought with him vessels of silver, and NIH
2Ki 8:16 in the fifth year of J the son of Ahab king 3141
8:21 So J went over to Zair, and all the chariots 3141
8:23 the rest of the acts of J, and all that he did, 3141
8:24 J slept with his fathers, and was buried 3141
8:25 In the twelfth year of J the son of Ahab 3141
8:28 he went with J the son of Ahab to the war 3141
8:28 and the Syrians wounded J. 3141
8:29 king J went back to be healed in Jezreel of 3141
8:29 down to see J the son of Ahab in Jezreel, 3141
9:14 the son of Nimshi conspired against J. 3141
9:14 (Now J had kept Ramoth-gilead, he and 3141
9:15 king J was returned to be healed in Jezreel 3088
9:16 and went to Jezreel; for J lay there. 3141
9:16 king of Judah was come down to see J. 3141
9:17 J said, Take a horseman, and send to meet 3088
9:21 J said, Make ready. And his chariot was 3088
9:21 J king of Israel and Ahaziah king of Judah 3088
9:22 when J saw Jehu, that he said, *Is it* peace, 3088
9:23 J turned his hands, and fled, and said to 3088
9:29 in the eleventh year of J the son of Ahab 3141
11: 2 Jehosheba, the daughter of king J, sister of 3141
1Ch 3:11 J his son, Ahaziah his son, Joash his son, 3141
26:25 J his son, and Zichri his son, and 3141
2Ch 22: 5 at Ramoth-gilead: and the Syrians smote J. 3141
22: 7 of Ahaziah was of God by coming to J: 3141
Mt 1: 8 and Josaphat begat J; and Joram begat *2496*
1: 8 Josaphat begat Joram; and J begat Ozias; *2496*

JORDAN (197)

Ge 13:10 up his eyes, and beheld all the plain of J, 3383
13:11 Lot chose him all the plain of J; and 3383
32:10 for with my staff I passed over this J; 3383
50:10 which *is* beyond J, and there they mourned 3383
50:11 called Abel-mizraim, which *is* beyond J. 3383
Nu 13:29 dwell by the sea, and by the coast of J. 3383
22: 1 pitched in the plains of Moab on *this* side J 3383
26: 3 in the plains of Moab by J *near* Jericho, 3383
26:63 in the plains of Moab by J *near* Jericho. 3383
31:12 of Moab, which *are* by J *near* Jericho. 3383
32: 5 for a possession, *and* bring us not over J. 3383
32:19 will not inherit with them on *yonder* side J, 3383
32:19 our inheritance is fallen to us on *this* side J 3383
32:21 will go all of you armed over J before 3383
32:29 of Reuben will pass with you over J, 3383
32:32 our inheritance on *this* side J *may be* ours. 3383
33:48 pitched in the plains of Moab by J *near* 3383
33:49 they pitched by J, from Beth-jesimoth *even* 3383
33:50 in the plains of Moab by J *near* Jericho, 3383
Nu 33:51 When ye are passed over J into the land of 3383
34:12 the border shall go down to J, and 3383
34:15 on *this* side J *near* Jericho eastward, 3383
35: 1 in the plains of Moab by J *near* Jericho, 3383
35:10 When ye be come over J into the land of 3383
35:14 Ye shall give three cities on *this* side J, and 3383
36:13 in the plains of Moab by J *near* Jericho. 3383
Dt 1: 1 all Israel on *this* side J in the wilderness, 3383
1: 5 On *this* side J, in the land of Moab, 3383
2:29 until I shall pass over J into the land which 3383
3: 8 Amorites the land that *was* on *this* side J, 3383
3:17 J, and the coast *thereof,* from Chinnereth 3383
3:20 your God hath given them beyond J: 3383
3:25 and see the good land that *is* beyond J, 3383
3:27 thine eyes: for thou shalt not go over this J. 3383
4:21 sware that I should not go over J, and that *I* 3383
4:22 I *must* die in this land, I *must* not go over J: 3383
4:26 land whereunto you go over J to possess it; 3383
4:41 Moses severed three cities on *this* side J 3383
4:46 On *this* side J, in the valley over against 3383
4:47 which *were* on *this* side J *toward* 3383
4:49 all the plain on *this* side J eastward, even 3383
9: 1 Thou art to pass over J *this* day, to go in to 3383
11:30 *Are* they not on the *other* side J, by the way 3383
11:31 For ye shall pass over J to go in to possess 3383
12:10 *when* ye go over J and dwell in the land 3383
27: 2 J unto the land which the LORD thy God 3383
27: 4 it shall be when ye be gone over J, 3383
27:12 bless the people, when ye are come over J; 3383
30:18 whither thou passest over J to go to possess 3383
31: 2 said unto me, Thou shalt not go over this J. 3383
31:13 the land whither ye go over J to possess it. 3383
32:47 the land, whither ye go over J to possess it. 3383
Jos 1: 2 go over this J, thou, and all this people, 3383
1:11 within three days ye shall pass over this J, 3383
1:14 land which Moses gave you on *this* side J; 3383
1:15 you on *this* side J *toward* the sunrising. 3383
2: 7 the men pursued after them the way to J 3383
2:10 that *were* on the *other* side J, Sihon and Og, 3383
3: 1 came to J, he and all the children of Israel, 3383
3: 8 ye are come to the brink of the water of J, 3383
3: 8 the water of Jordan, ye shall stand still in J. 3383
3:11 all the earth passeth over before you into J. 3383
3:13 of all the earth, shall rest in the waters of J, 3383
3:13 *that* the waters of J shall be cut off *from* 3383
3:14 to pass over J, and the priests bearing 3383
3:15 as they that bare the ark were come unto J, 3383
3:15 (for J overfloweth all his banks all the time 3383
3:17 stood firm on dry *ground* in the midst of J, 3383
3:17 all the people were passed clean over J. 3383
4: 1 all the people were clean passed over J, 3383
4: 3 Take you hence out of the midst of J, 3383
4: 5 the LORD your God into the midst of J, 3383
4: 7 That the waters of J were cut off before 3383
4: 7 when it passed over J, the waters of Jordan 3383
4: 7 over Jordan, the waters of J were cut off: 3383
4: 8 took up twelve stones out of the midst of J, 3383
4: 9 set up twelve stones in the midst of J, 3383
4:10 which bare the ark stood in the midst of J, 3383
4:16 the Testimony, that they come up out of J. 3383
4:17 the priests, saying, Come ye up out of J. 3383
4:18 were come up out of the midst of J, 3383
4:18 the waters of J returned unto their place, 3383
4:19 the people came up out of J on the tenth 3383
4:20 twelve stones, which they took out of J, 3383
4:22 Israel came over this J on dry *land.* 3383
4:23 dried up the waters of J from before you, 3383
5: 1 which *were* on the side of J westward, 3383
5: 1 of J from before the children of Israel, 3383
7: 7 hast thou at all brought this people over J, 3383
7: 7 been content, and dwelt on the *other* side J! 3383
9: 1 all the kings which *were* on *this* side J, 3383
9:10 that *were* beyond J, to Sihon king of 3383
12: 1 possessed their land on the *other* side J 3383
12: 7 the children of Israel smote on *this* side J 3383
13: 8 Moses gave them, beyond J eastward, 3383
13:23 the border of the children of Reuben was J, 3383
13:27 of Sihon king of Heshbon, J and *his* border, 3383
13:27 of Cinnereth on the *other* side J eastward. 3383
13:32 on the *other* side J, *by* Jericho, eastward. 3383
14: 3 and a half tribe on the *other* side J: 3383
15: 5 *was* the salt sea, *even* unto the end of J. 3383
15: 5 the bay of the sea at the uttermost part of J: 3383
16: 1 the lot of the children of Joseph fell from J 3383
16: 7 and came to Jericho, and went out *at* J. 3383
17: 5 which *were* on the *other* side J; 3383
18: 7 have received their inheritance beyond J on 3383
18:12 their border on the north side was from J; 3383
18:19 bay of the salt sea at the south end of J: 3383
18:20 J was the border of it on the east side. 3383
19:22 and the outgoings of their border were *at* J: 3383
19:33 and the outgoings thereof were *at* J: 3383
19:34 and to Judah upon J *toward* the sunrising. 3383
20: 8 on the *other* side J *by* Jericho eastward, 3383
22: 4 of the LORD gave you on the *other* side J. 3383
22: 7 their brethren on *this* side J westward. 3383
22:10 when they came unto the borders of J, 3383
22:10 tribe of Manasseh built there an altar by J, 3383
22:11 in the borders of J, at the passage of 3383
22:25 For the LORD hath made J a border 3383
23: 4 to be an inheritance for your tribes, from J, 3383
24: 8 which dwelt on the *other* side J; 3383
24:11 ye went over J, and came unto Jericho: 3383
Jdg 3:28 took the fords of J toward Moab, and 3383
5:17 Gilead abode beyond J: and why did Dan 3383
7:24 them the waters unto Beth-barah and J. 3383
7:24 and took the waters unto Beth-barah and J. 3383
7:25 and Zeeb to Gideon on the *other* side J. 3383
8: 4 Gideon came to J, *and* passed over, he, 3383
10: 8 the *other* side J in the land of the Amorites, 3383
10: 9 passed over J to fight also against Judah, 3383
11:13 from Arnon even unto Jabbok, and unto J: 3383
11:22 and from the wilderness even unto J. 3383
12: 5 the Gileadites took the passages of J before 3383
12: 6 and slew him at the passages of J: 3383

1Sa 13: 7 *some of the* Hebrews went over J *to* 3383
31: 7 *they* that *were* on the *other* side J, saw that 3383
2Sa 2:29 passed over J, and went *through* all 3383
10:17 and passed over J, and came to Helam. 3383
17:22 that *were* with him, and they passed over J: 3383
17:22 not one *of them* that was not gone over J. 3383
17:24 Absalom passed over J, he and all the men 3383
19:15 So the king returned, and came to J. 3383
19:15 meet the king, to conduct the king over J. 3383
19:17 and they went over J before the king. 3383
19:18 before the king, as he was come over J; 3383
19:31 went over J with the king, to conduct him 3383
19:31 with the king, to conduct him *over* J. 3383
19:36 Thy servant will go a little *way* over J with 3383
19:39 all the people went over J. And when 3383
19:41 and all David's men with him, over J? 3383
20: 2 unto their king, from J even to Jerusalem. 3383
24: 5 they passed over J, and pitched in Aroer, 3383
1Ki 2: 8 he came down to meet me *at* J, and I sware 3383
7:46 In the plain of J did the king cast them, 3383
17: 3 by the brook Cherith, that *is* before J. 3383
17: 5 dwelt by the brook Cherith, that *is* before J. 3383
2Ki 2: 6 here; for the LORD hath sent me to J. 3383
2: 7 to view afar off: and they two stood by J. 3383
2:13 and went back, and stood by the bank of J; 3383
5:10 Go and wash in J seven times, and 3383
5:14 and dipped *himself* seven times in J, 3383
6: 2 unto J, and take thence every man a beam, 3383
6: 4 when they came to J, they cut down wood. 3383
7:15 they went after them unto J: and lo, all 3383
10:33 From J eastward, all the land of Gilead, 3383
1Ch 6:78 on the *other* side J *by* Jericho, on the east 3383
6:78 Jordan *by* Jericho, on the east *side* of J, 3383
12:15 These *are* they that went over J in the first 3383
12:37 on the *other* side of J, of the Reubenites, 3383
19:17 passed over J, and came upon them, and 3383
26:30 J westward in all the business of 3383
2Ch 4:17 In the plain of J did the king cast them, 3383
Job 40:23 he trusteth that he can draw up J into his 3383
Ps 42: 6 will I remember thee from the land of J, 3383
114: 3 The sea saw *it,* and fled: J was driven back. 3383
114: 5 thou J, *that* thou wast driven back? 3383
Isa 9: 1 the sea, beyond J, in Galilee of the nations. 3383
Jer 12: 5 then how wilt thou do in the swelling of J? 3383
49:19 of J against the habitation of the strong: 3383
50:44 of J unto the habitation of the strong: 3383
Eze 47:18 and from the land of Israel *by* J, 3383
Zec 11: 3 of young lions; for the pride of J is spoiled. 3383
Mt 3: 5 all Judea, and all the region round about J, *2446*
3: 6 And were baptized of him in J, *2446*
3:13 Then cometh Jesus from Galilee to J unto *2446*
4:15 *by* the way of the sea, beyond J, Galilee of *2446*
4:25 and *from* Judea, and *from* beyond J. *2446*
19: 1 came into the coasts of Judea beyond J; *2446*
Mk 1: 5 were all baptized of him in the river *of* J, *2446*
1: 9 of Galilee, and was baptized of John in J. *2446*
3: 8 and from Idumea, and *from* beyond J; *2446*
10: 1 the coasts of Judea by the farther side of J: *2446*
Lk 3: 3 And he came into all the country about J, *2446*
4: 1 full of the Holy Ghost returned from J, *2446*
Jn 1:28 *things* were done in Bethabara beyond J, *2446*
3:26 Rabbi, *he* that was with thee beyond J, *2446*
10:40 And went away again beyond J into *2446*

JORIM (1)
Lk 3:29 *the son* of Eliezer, which was *the son* of J, *2497*

JORKEAM See JORKOAM

JORKOAM (1)
1Ch 2:44 Shema begat Raham, the father of J: and 3421

JOSABAD (1)
1Ch 12: 4 and Johanan, and J the Gederathite, 3107

JOSAPHAT (2) [JEHOSHAPHAT]
Mt 1: 8 And Asa begat J; and Josaphat begat *2498*
1: 8 and J begat Joram; and Joram begat Ozias; *2498*

JOSE (1)
Lk 3:29 Which was *the son* of J, which was *the son* *2499*

JOSEDECH (6)
Hag 1: 1 to Joshua the son of J the high priest, 3087
1:12 Joshua the son of J the high priest, with all 3087
1:14 the spirit of Joshua the son of J the high 3087
2: 2 to Joshua the son of J the high priest and 3087
2: 4 be strong, O Joshua, son of J, the high 3087
Zec 6:11 head of Joshua the son of J the high priest; 3087

JOSEPH (228) [JOSEPH'S, JOSES]
Ge 30:24 she called his name J; and said, 3130
30:25 it came to pass, when Rachel had born J, 3130
33: 2 and Rachel and J hindermost. 3130
33: 7 after came J near and Rachel, and 3130
35:24 The sons of Rachel; J, and Benjamin: 3130
37: 2 J, *being* seventeen years old, was feeding 3130
37: 2 J brought unto his father their evil report. 3130
37: 3 Now Israel loved J more than all his 3130
37: 5 J dreamed a dream, and he told *it* his 3130
37:13 Israel said unto J, Do not thy brethren feed 3130
37:17 J went after his brethren, and found them in 3130
37:23 when J was come unto his brethren, 3130
37:23 that they stript J out of his coat, 3130
37:28 they drew and lift up J out of the pit, and 3130
37:28 sold J to the Ishmeelites for twenty *pieces* 3130
37:28 of silver: and they brought J into Egypt. 3130
37:29 behold, J *was* not in the pit; and he rent his 3130
37:33 J is without doubt rent in pieces. 3130
39: 1 J was brought down to Egypt; and 3130
39: 2 the LORD was with J, and he was a 3130
39: 4 J found grace in his sight, and he served 3130
39: 6 J was *a* goodly *person,* and well favoured, 3130
39: 7 that his master's wife cast her eyes upon J; 3130
Ge 39:10 came to pass, as she spake to J day by day, 3130
39:11 that *J* went into the house to do his NIH
39:21 the LORD was with J, and shewed him 3130
40: 3 the prison, the place where J *was* bound. 3130
40: 4 the captain of the guard charged J with 3130
40: 6 J came in unto them in the morning, and 3130
40: 8 J said unto them, *Do* not interpretations 3130
40: 9 the chief butler told his dream to J, and 3130
40:12 J said unto him, This *is* the interpretation of 3130
40:16 he said unto J, I also *was* in my dream, and 3130
40:18 J answered and said, This *is* 3130
40:22 chief baker: as J had interpreted to them. 3130
40:23 Yet did not the chief butler remember J, 3130
41:14 Pharaoh sent and called J, and they brought 3130
41:15 Pharaoh said unto J, I have dreamed a 3130
41:16 J answered Pharaoh, saying, *It is* not in me: 3130
41:17 Pharaoh said unto J, In my dream, behold, 3130
41:25 J said unto Pharaoh, The dream of Pharaoh 3130
41:39 Pharaoh said unto J, Forasmuch as God 3130
41:41 Pharaoh said unto J, See, I have set thee 3130
41:44 Pharaoh said unto J, I *am* Pharaoh, and 3130
41:45 And J went out over *all* the land of Egypt. 3130
41:46 J *was* thirty years old when he stood before 3130
41:46 J went out from the presence of Pharaoh, 3130
41:49 J gathered corn as the sand of the sea, 3130
41:50 unto J were born two sons before the years 3130
41:51 J called the name of the firstborn 3130
41:54 began to come, according as J had said: 3130
41:55 said unto all the Egyptians, Go unto J; 3130
41:56 J opened all the storehouses, and sold unto 3130
41:57 all countries came into Egypt to J for to 3130
42: 6 J *was* the governor over the land, *and* he *it* 3130
42: 7 J saw his brethren, and he knew them, but 3130
42: 8 J knew his brethren, but they knew not 3130
42: 9 J remembered the dreams which he 3130
42:14 J said unto them, That *is it* that I spake unto 3130
42:18 J said unto them the third day, This do, 3130
42:23 they knew not that J understood *them;* for 3130
42:25 J commanded to fill their sacks *with* corn, 3130
42:36 J *is* not, and Simeon *is* not, and ye will take 3130
43:15 went down *to* Egypt, and stood before J. 3130
43:16 when J saw Benjamin with them, he said to 3130
43:17 the man did as J bade; and the man brought 3130
43:25 they made ready the present against J came 3130
43:26 when J came home, they brought him 3130
43:30 J made haste; for his bowels did yern upon 3130
44: 2 he did according to the word that J had 3130
44: 4 not *yet* far off, J said unto his steward, Up, 3130
44:15 J said unto them, What deed *is* this that ye 3130
45: 1 J could not refrain himself before all them 3130
45: 1 while J made himself known unto his 3130
45: 3 J said unto his brethren, I *am* Joseph; doth 3130
45: 3 Joseph said unto his brethren, I *am* J; doth 3130
45: 4 J said unto his brethren, Come near to me, 3130
45: 4 he said, I *am* J your brother, whom ye sold 3130
45: 9 and say unto him, Thus saith thy son J, 3130
45:17 Pharaoh said unto J, Say unto thy brethren, 3130
45:21 J gave them wagons, according to 3130
45:26 J *is* yet alive, and he *is* governor over all 3130
45:27 they told him all the words of J, which he 3130
45:27 when he saw the wagons which J had sent 3130
45:28 *It is* enough; J my son *is* yet alive: 3130
46: 4 and J shall put his hand upon thine eyes. 3130
46:19 of Rachel Jacob's wife; J, and Benjamin. 3130
46:20 unto J in the land of Egypt were born 3130
46:27 the sons of J, which were born him in 3130
46:28 he sent Judah before him unto J, to direct 3130
46:29 J made ready his chariot, and went up to 3130
46:30 Israel said unto J, Now let me die, since I 3130
46:31 J said unto his brethren, and unto his 3130
47: 1 J came and told Pharaoh, and said, 3130
47: 5 Pharaoh spake unto J, saying, Thy father 3130
47: 7 J brought in Jacob his father, and set him 3130
47:11 J placed his father and his brethren, and 3130
47:12 J nourished his father, and his brethren, 3130
47:14 J gathered up all the money that was found 3130
47:14 J brought the money into Pharaoh's house. 3130
47:15 all the Egyptians came unto J, and said, 3130
47:16 J said, Give your cattle; and I will give you 3130
47:17 they brought their cattle unto J: and 3130
47:17 J gave them bread *in exchange* for horses, 3130
47:20 J bought all the land of Egypt for Pharaoh; 3130
47:23 J said unto the people, Behold, I have 3130
47:26 J made it a law over the land of Egypt unto 3130
47:29 he called his son J, and said unto him, 3130
48: 1 that *one* told J, Behold, thy father *is* sick: 3130
48: 2 said, Behold, thy son J cometh unto thee: 3130
48: 3 Jacob said unto J, God Almighty appeared 3130
48: 9 J said unto his father, They *are* my sons, 3130
48:11 Israel said unto J, I had not thought to see 3130
48:12 J brought them out from between his 3130
48:13 J took them both, Ephraim in his right hand 3130
48:15 he blessed J, and said, God, before whom 3130
48:17 when J saw that his father laid his right 3130
48:18 J said unto his father, Not so, my father: 3130
48:21 Israel said unto J, Behold, I die: but 3130
49:22 J *is* a fruitful bough, *even* a fruitful bough 3130
49:26 they shall be on the head of J, and on 3130
50: 1 J fell upon his father's face, and wept upon 3130
50: 2 J commanded his servants the physicians to 3130
50: 4 J spake unto the house of Pharaoh, saying, 3130
50: 7 J went up to bury his father: and with him 3130
50: 8 all the house of J, and his brethren, and 3130
50:14 J returned into Egypt, he, and his brethren, 3130
50:15 J will peradventure hate us, and 3130
50:16 they sent a messenger unto J, saying, 3130
50:17 So shall ye say unto J, Forgive, I pray thee 3130
50:17 And J wept when they spake unto him. 3130
50:19 J said unto them, Fear not: for *am* I in 3130
50:22 J dwelt in Egypt, he, and his father's 3130
50:22 and J lived an hundred and ten years. 3130
50:23 J saw Ephraim's children of the third 3130
50:24 J said unto his brethren, I die: and God will 3130
50:25 And J took an oath of the children of Israel, 3130
50:26 So J died, *being* an hundred and ten years 3130
Ex 1: 5 seventy souls: for J was in Egypt *already.* 3130
1: 6 J died, and all his brethren, and all that 3130
1: 8 a new king over Egypt, which knew not J. 3130
13:19 Moses took the bones of J with him: for he 3130
Nu 1:10 Of the children of J: of Ephraim; 3130
1:32 Of the children of J, *namely,* of 3130
13: 7 Of the tribe of Issachar, Igal the son of J. 3130
13:11 Of the tribe of J, *namely,* of the tribe of 3130
26:28 The sons of J after their families *were* 3130
26:37 These *are* the sons of J after their families. 3130
27: 1 of the families of Manasseh the son of J: 3130
32:33 half the tribe of Manasseh the son of J, 3130
34:23 The prince of the children of J, for the tribe 3130
36: 1 of the families of the sons of J, came near, 3130
36: 5 The tribe of the sons of J hath said well. 3130
36:12 of the sons of Manasseh the son of J, 3130
Dt 27:12 Judah, and Issachar, and J, and Benjamin: 3130
33:13 of J he said, Blessed of the LORD *be* his 3130
33:16 let *the blessing* come upon the head of J, 3130
Jos 14: 4 For the children of J were two tribes, 3130
16: 1 the lot of the children of J fell from Jordan 3130
16: 4 So the children of J, Manasseh and 3130
17: 1 for he *was* the firstborn of J; *to wit,* for 3130
17: 2 of Manasseh the son of J by their families. 3130
17:14 the children of J spake unto Joshua, saying, 3130
17:16 the children of J said, The hill is not 3130
17:17 Joshua spake unto the house of J, *even* to 3130
18: 5 the house of J shall abide in their coasts on 3130
18:11 the children of Judah and the children of J. 3130
24:32 the bones of J, which the children of Israel 3130
24:32 became the inheritance of the children of J. 3130
Jdg 1:22 the house of J, they also went up *against* 3130
1:23 the house of J sent to descry Beth-el. 3130
1:35 yet the hand of the house of J prevailed, so 3130
2Sa 19:20 of J to go down to meet my lord the king. 3130
1Ki 11:28 ruler over all the charge of the house of J. 3130
1Ch 2: 2 Dan, J, and Benjamin, Naphtali, Gad, and 3130
5: 1 his birthright was given unto the sons of J 3130
7:29 In these dwelt the children of J the son of 3130
25: 2 and J, and Nethaniah, and Asarelah, 3130
25: 9 Now the first lot came forth for Asaph to J: 3130
Ezr 10:42 Shallum, Amariah, *and* J. 3130
Ne 12:14 Of Melicu, Jonathan; of Shebaniah, J; 3130
Ps 77:15 thy people, the sons of Jacob and J. 3130
78:67 Moreover he refused the tabernacle of J, 3130
80: 1 of Israel, thou that leadest J like a flock; 3130
81: 5 This he ordained in J *for* a testimony, 3084
105:17 *even* J, *who* was sold for a servant: 3130
Eze 37:16 take another stick, and write upon it, For J, 3130
37:19 Behold, I *will* take the stick of J, which *is* 3130
47:13 tribes of Israel: J *shall have two* portions. 3130
48:32 one gate of J, one gate of Benjamin, 3130
Am 5: 6 lest he break out like fire *in* the house of J, 3130
5:15 will be gracious unto the remnant of J. 3130
6: 6 they are not grieved for the affliction of J. 3130
Ob 1:18 the house of J a flame, and the house of 3130
Zec 10: 6 I will save the house of J, and I will bring 3130
Mt 1:16 And Jacob begat J the husband of Mary, *2501*
1:18 as his mother Mary was espoused to J, *2501*
1:19 Then J her husband, being a just *man,* and *2501*
1:20 saying, J, *thou* son of David, fear not to *2501*
1:24 Then J being raised from sleep did as *2501*
2:13 *the* angel of the Lord appeareth to J in a *2501*
2:19 Lord appeareth in a dream to J in Egypt, *2501*
27:57 came a rich man of Arimathea, named J, *2501*
27:59 And when J had taken the body, *2501*
Mk 15:43 J of Arimathea, an honourable counseller, *2501*
15:45 *it* of the centurion, he gave the body to J. *2501*
Lk 1:27 espoused to a man whose name was J, *2501*
2: 4 And J also went up from Galilee, out of *2501*
2:16 and J, and the babe lying in a manger. *2501*
2:33 And J and his mother marvelled at those *2501*
2:43 and J and his mother knew not *of it.* *2501*
3:23 the son of J, which was *the son* of Heli, *2501*
3:24 *the son* of Janna, which was *the son* of J, *2501*
3:26 which was *the son* of J, which was *the son* *2501*
3:30 *the son* of Juda, which was *the son* of J, *2501*
23:50 And behold, *there was* a man named J, *2501*
Jn 1:45 did write, Jesus of Nazareth, the son of J. *2501*
4: 5 of ground that Jacob gave to his son J. *2501*
6:42 the son of J, whose father and mother we *2501*
19:38 And after this J of Arimathea, being a *2501*
Ac 1:23 And they appointed two, J called Barsabas, *2501*
7: 9 moved with envy, sold J into Egypt: *2501*
7:13 And at the second time J was made known *2501*
7:14 Then sent J, and called his father Jacob to *2501*
7:18 Till another king arose, which knew not J. *2501*
Heb 11:21 he was a dying, blessed both the sons of J; *2501*
11:22 By faith J, when he died, made mention of *2501*
Rev 7: 8 Of the tribe of J *were* sealed twelve *2501*

JOSEPH'S (22) [JOSEPH]
Ge 37:31 they took J coat, and killed a kid of 3130
39: 5 blessed the Egyptian's house for J sake; 3130
39: 6 he left all that he had in J hand; and 3130
39:20 J master took him, and put him into 3130
39:22 the keeper of the prison committed to J 3130
41:42 put it upon J hand, and arrayed him in 3130
41:45 Pharaoh called J name Zaphnath-paaneah; 3130
42: 3 J ten brethren went down to buy corn in 3130
42: 4 Benjamin, J brother, Jacob sent not with 3130
42: 6 J brethren came, and bowed down 3130
43:17 and the man brought the men into J house. 3130
43:18 because they were brought into J house; 3130
43:19 they came near to the steward of J house, 3130
43:24 the man brought the men into J house, and 3130
44:14 and his brethren came to J house; 3130
45:16 saying, J brethren are come: 3130
48: 8 Israel beheld J sons, and said, Who *are* 3130
50:15 when J brethren saw that their father was 3130
50:23 Manasseh were brought up upon J knees. 3130
1Ch 5: 2 the chief ruler; but the birthright *was* J:) 3130
Lk 4:22 his mouth. And they said, Is not this J son? *2501*
Ac 7:13 J kindred was made known unto Pharaoh. *2501*

JOSES (6) [BARNABAS, JOSEPH]
Mt 13:55 and his brethren, James, and J, 2500
27:56 and Mary the mother of James and J, and 2500
Mk 6: 3 of James, and J, and of Juda, and Simon? 2500
15:40 Mary the mother of James the less and of J, 2500
15:47 Mary *the mother* of J beheld where he was 2500
Ac 4:36 And J, who by the apostles was surnamed 2500

JOSHAH (1)
1Ch 4:34 and Jamlech, and J the son of Amaziah, 3144

JOSHAPHAT (1)
1Ch 11:43 the son of Maachah, and J the Mithnite, 3146

JOSHAVIAH (1)
1Ch 11:46 Eliel the Mahavite, and Jeribai, and J, 3145

JOSHBEKASHAH (2)
1Ch 25: 4 J, Mallothi, Hothir, *and* Mahazioth: 3436
25:24 The seventeenth to J, *he,* his sons, and 3436

JOSHIBIAH See JOSIBIAH

JOSHUA (216) [HOSHEA, JEHOSHUA, JESHUA, OSHEA]
Ex 17: 9 Moses said unto J, Choose us out men, 3091
17:10 So J did as Moses had said to him, and 3091
17:13 J discomfited Amalek and his people with 3091
17:14 in a book, and rehearse *it* in the ears of J: 3091
24:13 Moses rose up, and his minister J: and 3091
32:17 when J heard the noise of the people as 3091
33:11 his servant J, the son of Nun, a young man, 3091
Nu 11:28 J the son of Nun, the servant of Moses, 3091
14: 6 J the son of Nun, and Caleb the son of 3091
14:30 the son of Jephunneh, and J the son of Nun. 3091
14:38 J the son of Nun, and Caleb the son of 3091
26:65 the son of Jephunneh, and J the son of Nun. 3091
27:18 Take thee J the son of Nun, a man in whom 3091
27:22 he took J, and set him before Eleazar 3091
32:12 the Kenezite, and J the son of Nun: 3091
32:28 J the son of Nun, and the chief fathers of 3091
34:17 Eleazar the priest, and J the son of Nun. 3091
Dt 1:38 *But* J the son of Nun, which standeth 3091
3:21 I commanded J at that time, saying, 3091
3:28 charge J, and encourage him, and 3091
31: 3 *and* J, he shall go over before thee, as 3091
31: 7 Moses called unto J, and said unto him in 3091
31:14 call J, and present yourselves in 3091
31:14 Moses and J went, and 3091
31:23 And he gave J the son of Nun a charge, and 3091
34: 9 J the son of Nun was full *of* the spirit of 3091
Jos 1: 1 that the LORD spake unto J the son of 3091
1:10 J commanded the officers of the people, 3091
1:12 half the tribe of Manasseh, spake J, saying, 3091
1:16 they answered J, saying, All that thou 3091
2: 1 J the son of Nun sent out of Shittim two 3091
2:23 came to J the son of Nun, and told him all 3091
2:24 they said unto J, Truly the LORD hath 3091
3: 1 J rose early in the morning; and 3091
3: 5 J said unto the people, Sanctify yourselves: 3091
3: 6 J spake unto the priests, saying, Take up 3091
3: 7 the LORD said unto J, This day will I 3091
3: 9 J said unto the children of Israel, 3091
3:10 J said, Hereby ye shall know that the living 3091
4: 1 that the LORD spake unto J, saying, 3091
4: 4 J called the twelve men, whom he had 3091
4: 5 J said unto them, Pass over before the ark 3091
4: 8 children of Israel did so as J commanded, 3091
4: 8 of Jordan, as the LORD spake unto J, 3091
4: 9 J set up twelve stones in the midst of 3091
4:10 commanded J to speak unto the people, 3091
4:10 according to all that Moses commanded J: 3091
4:14 On that day the LORD magnified J in 3091
4:15 And the LORD spake unto J, saying, 3091
4:17 J therefore commanded the priests, saying, 3091
4:20 took out of Jordan, did J pitch in Gilgal. 3091
5: 2 At that time the LORD said unto J, 3091
5: 3 J made him sharp knives, and 3091
5: 4 this *is* the cause why J did circumcise: 3091
5: 7 up in their stead, them J circumcised: 3091
5: 9 the LORD said unto J, *This* day have I 3091
5:13 it came to pass, when J was by Jericho, 3091
5:13 J went unto him, and said unto him, 3091
5:14 J fell on his face to the earth, and 3091
5:15 captain of the LORD'S host said unto J, 3091
5:15 thou standest *is* holy. And J did so. 3091
6: 2 the LORD said unto J, See, I have given 3091
6: 6 And J the son of Nun called the priests, and 3091
6: 8 when J had spoken unto the people, 3091
6:10 J had commanded the people, saying, 3091
6:12 J rose early in the morning, and the priests 3091
6:16 the trumpets, J said unto the people, Shout; 3091
6:22 J had said unto the two men that had spied 3091
6:25 J saved Rahab the harlot alive, and her 3091
6:25 which J sent to spy out Jericho. 3091
6:26 J adjured *them* at that time, saying, 3091
6:27 So the LORD was with J; and his fame 3091
7: 2 J sent men from Jericho *to* Ai, which *is* 3091
7: 3 they returned to J, and said unto him, 3091
7: 6 J rent his clothes, and fell to the earth upon 3091
7: 7 J said, Alas, O Lord GOD, wherefore hast 3091
7:10 the LORD said unto J, Get thee up; 3091
7:16 So J rose up early in the morning, and 3091
7:19 J said unto Achan, My son, give, I pray 3091
7:20 Achan answered J, and said, Indeed I have 3091
7:22 So J sent messengers, and they ran unto 3091
7:23 brought them unto J, and unto all 3091
7:24 J, and all Israel with him, took Achan 3091
7:25 J said, Why hast thou troubled us? 3091
8: 1 the LORD said unto J, Fear not, 3091
8: 3 So J arose, and all the people of war, to go 3091
8: 3 J chose out thirty thousand mighty *men* of 3091
8: 9 J therefore sent them forth: and they went 3091
8: 9 but J lodged that night among the people. 3091
Jos 8:10 J rose up early in the morning, and 3091
8:13 J went that night into the midst of 3091
8:15 J and all Israel *made as if they* were beaten 3091
8:16 they pursued after J, and were drawn away 3091
8:18 the LORD said unto J, Stretch out 3091
8:18 J stretched out the spear that *he had* in his 3091
8:21 when J and all Israel saw that the ambush 3091
8:23 of Ai they took alive, and brought him to J. 3091
8:26 For J drew not his hand back, wherewith he 3091
8:27 of the LORD which he commanded J. 3091
8:28 J burnt Ai, and made it a heap for ever, 3091
8:29 J commanded that they should take his 3091
8:30 J built an altar unto the LORD God of 3091
8:35 which J read not before all 3091
9: 2 to fight with J and with Israel, *with* one 3091
9: 3 Gibeon heard what J had done unto Jericho 3091
9: 6 And they went to J unto the camp *at* Gilgal, 3091
9: 8 they said unto J, We *are* thy servants. 3091
9: 8 J said unto them, Who *are* ye? and 3091
9:15 J made peace with them, and made a 3091
9:22 J called for them, and he spake unto them, 3091
9:24 they answered J, and said, Because it was 3091
9:27 J made them that day hewers of wood and 3091
10: 1 of Jerusalem had heard how J had taken Ai, 3091
10: 4 for it hath made peace with J and with 3091
10: 6 the men of Gibeon sent unto J to the camp 3091
10: 7 So J ascended from Gilgal, he, and all 3091
10: 8 the LORD said unto J, Fear them not: 3091
10: 9 J therefore came unto them suddenly, *and* 3091
10:12 spake J to the LORD in the day when 3091
10:15 J returned, and all Israel with him, unto 3091
10:17 it was told J, saying, The five kings are 3091
10:18 J said, Roll great stones upon the mouth of 3091
10:20 when J and the children of Israel had made 3091
10:21 all the people returned to the camp to J *at* 3091
10:22 said J, Open the mouth of the cave, and 3091
10:24 when they brought out those kings unto J, 3091
10:24 that J called for all the men of Israel, and 3091
10:25 J said unto them, Fear not, nor be 3091
10:26 afterward J smote them, and slew them, 3091
10:27 *that* J commanded, and they took them 3091
10:28 that day J took Makkedah, and smote it 3091
10:29 J passed from Makkedah, and all Israel 3091
10:31 J passed from Libnah, and all Israel with 3091
10:33 J smote him and his people, until *he* had 3091
10:34 from Lachish J passed unto Eglon, and 3091
10:36 J went up from Eglon, and all Israel with 3091
10:38 J returned, and all Israel with him, 3091
10:40 So J smote all the country of the hills, and 3091
10:41 J smote them from Kadesh-barnea even 3091
10:42 and their land did J take *at* one time, 3091
10:43 J returned, and all Israel with him, unto 3091
11: 6 the LORD said unto J, Be not afraid 3091
11: 7 So J came, and all the people of war with 3091
11: 9 J did unto them as the LORD bade him: 3091
11:10 J at that time turned back, and took Hazor, 3091
11:12 did J take, and smote them with the edge of 3091
11:13 of them, save Hazor only; *that* did J burn. 3091
11:15 so did Moses command J, and so 3091
11:15 did Moses command Joshua, and so did J; 3091
11:16 So J took all that land, the hills, and all 3091
11:18 J made war a long time with all those 3091
11:21 at that time came J, and cut off 3091
11:21 J destroyed them utterly with their cities. 3091
11:23 So J took the whole land, according to all 3091
11:23 J gave it for an inheritance unto Israel 3091
12: 7 these *are* the kings of the country which J 3091
12: 7 which J gave unto the tribes of Israel *for* a 3091
13: 1 Now J was old *and* stricken in years; and 3091
14: 1 J the son of Nun, and the heads of 3091
14: 6 the children of Judah came unto J in 3091
14:13 J blessed him, and gave unto Caleb the son 3091
15:13 to the commandment of the LORD to J, 3091
17: 4 before J the son of Nun, and before 3091
17:14 the children of Joseph spake unto J, saying, 3091
17:15 J answered them, If thou *be* a great people, 3091
17:17 J spake unto the house of Joseph, *even* to 3091
18: 3 J said unto the children of Israel, How long 3091
18: 8 J charged them that went to describe 3091
18: 9 and came *again* to J to the host *at* Shiloh. 3091
18:10 J cast lots for them in Shiloh before 3091
18:10 there J divided the land unto the children of 3091
19:49 to J the son of Nun among them: 3091
19:51 J the son of Nun, and the heads of 3091
20: 1 The LORD also spake unto J, saying, 3091
21: 1 unto J the son of Nun, and unto the heads 3091
22: 1 J called the Reubenites, and the Gadites, 3091
22: 6 So J blessed them, and sent them away: 3091
22: 7 unto the *other* half thereof gave J among 3091
22: 7 when J sent them away also unto their 3091
23: 1 that J waxed old *and* stricken in age. 3091
23: 2 J called for all Israel, *and* for their elders, 3091
24: 1 J gathered all the tribes of Israel to 3091
24: 2 J said unto all the people, Thus saith 3091
24:19 J said unto the people, Ye cannot serve 3091
24:21 the people said unto J, Nay; but we will 3091
24:22 J said unto the people, Ye *are* witnesses 3091
24:24 the people said unto J, The LORD our 3091
24:25 So J made a covenant with the people that 3091
24:26 J wrote these words in the book of the law 3091
24:27 J said unto all the people, Behold, this 3091
24:28 So J let the people depart, every man unto 3091
24:29 that J the son of Nun, the servant of 3091
24:31 Israel served the LORD all the days of J, 3091
24:31 all the days of the elders that overlived J, 3091
Jdg 1: 1 Now after the death of J it came to pass, 3091
2: 6 when J had let the people go, the children 3091
2: 7 people served the LORD all the days of J, 3091
2: 7 all the days of the elders that outlived J, 3091
2: 8 J the son of Nun, the servant of 3091
2:21 of the nations which J left when he died: 3091
2:23 delivered he them into the hand of J. 3091
1Sa 6:14 the cart came into the field of J, 3091
6:18 *remaineth* unto this day in the field of J, 3091
1Ki 16:34 which he spake by J the son of Nun. 3091
2Ki 23: 8 in of the gate of J the governor of the city, 3091
Hag 1: 1 and to J the son of Josedech the high priest, 3091
1:12 J the son of Josedech the high priest, 3091
1:14 the spirit of J the son of Josedech the high 3091
2: 2 to J the son of Josedech the high priest and 3091
2: 4 be strong, O J, son of Josedech, the high 3091
Zec 3: 1 he shewed me J the high priest standing 3091
3: 3 Now J was clothed with filthy garments, 3091
3: 6 the angel of the LORD protested unto J, 3091
3: 8 O J the high priest, thou, and thy fellows 3091
3: 9 behold the stone that I have laid before J; 3091
6:11 set *them* upon the head of J the son of 3091

JOSIAH (53) [JOSIAS]
1Ki 13: 2 born unto the house of David, J by name; 2977
2Ki 21:24 the people of the land made J his son king 2977
21:26 of Uzza: and J his son reigned in his stead. 2977
22: 1 J *was* eight years old when he *began* to 2977
22: 3 to pass in the eighteenth year of king J, 2977
23:16 as J turned himself, he spied the sepulchres 2977
23:19 J took away, and did to them according to 2977
23:23 in the eighteenth year of king J, 2977
23:24 of Judah and in Jerusalem, did J put away, 2977
23:28 Now the rest of the acts of J, and all that he 2977
23:29 king J went against him; and he slew him 2977
23:30 of the land took Jehoahaz the son of J, 2977
23:34 Pharaoh-nechoh made Eliakim the son of J 2977
23:34 of Josiah king in the room of J his father, 2977
1Ch 3:14 Amon his son, J his son. 2977
3:15 the sons of J *were,* the firstborn Johanan, 2977
2Ch 33:25 the people of the land made J his son king 2977
34: 1 J *was* eight years old when he *began* to 2977
34:33 J took away all the abominations out of all 2977
35: 1 Moreover J kept a passover unto 2977
35: 7 J gave to the people, *of* the flock, lambs 2977
35:16 according to the commandment of king J. 2977
35:18 of Israel keep such a passover as J kept, 2977
35:19 In the eighteenth year of the reign of J was 2977
35:20 all this, when J had prepared the temple, 2977
35:20 by Euphrates: and J went out against him. 2977
35:22 Nevertheless J would not turn his face from 2977
35:23 the archers shot at king J; and the king said 2977
35:24 all Judah and Jerusalem mourned for J. 2977
35:25 Jeremiah lamented for J: and all the singing 2977
35:25 the singing *women* spake of J in their 2977
35:26 Now the rest of the acts of J, and 2977
36: 1 of the land took Jehoahaz the son of J, 2977
Jer 1: 2 days of J the son of Amon king of Judah, 2977
1: 3 of Jehoiakim the son of J king of Judah, 2977
1: 3 of Zedekiah the son of J king of Judah, 2977
3: 6 said also unto me in the days of J the king, 2977
22:11 Shallum the son of J king of Judah, 2977
22:11 which reigned instead of J his father, 2977
22:18 Jehoiakim the son of J king of Judah; 2977
25: 1 of Jehoiakim the son of J king of Judah, 2977
25: 3 From the thirteenth year of J the son of 2977
26: 1 J king of Judah came this word from 2977
27: 1 J king of Judah came this word unto 2977
35: 1 of Jehoiakim the son of J king of Judah, 2977
36: 1 of Jehoiakim the son of J king of Judah, 2977
36: 2 from the days of J, even unto this day. 2977
36: 9 of Jehoiakim the son of J king of Judah, 2977
37: 1 king Zedekiah the son of J reigned instead 2977
45: 1 in the fourth year of Jehoiakim the son of J 2977
46: 2 of Jehoiakim the son of J king of Judah. 2977
Zep 1: 1 in the days of J the son of Amon, king of 2977
Zec 6:10 go *into* the house of J the son of 2977

JOSIAS (2) [JOSIAH]
Mt 1:10 Manasses begat Amon; and Amon begat J; 2502
1:11 And J begat Jechonias and his brethren, 2502

JOSIBIAH (1)
1Ch 4:35 Joel, and Jehu the son of J, the son of 3143

JOSIPHIAH (1)
Ezr 8:10 the son of J, and with him an hundred and 3131

JOT (1)
Mt 5:18 one j or one tittle shall in no wise pass from 2503

JOTBAH (1)
2Ki 21:19 the daughter of Haruz of J. 3192

JOTBATH (1) [JOTBATHAH]
Dt 10: 7 from Gudgodah to J, a land of rivers of 3193

JOTBATHAH (2) [JOTBATH]
Nu 33:33 went from Hor-hagidgad, and pitched in J. 3193
33:34 they removed from J, and encamped at 3193

JOTHAM (24)
Jdg 9: 5 notwithstanding yet J the youngest son of 3147
9: 7 when they told *it* to J, he went and stood in 3147
9:21 J ran away, and fled, and went to Beer, 3147
9:57 upon them came the curse of J the son of 3147
2Ki 15: 5 J the king's son *was* over the house, 3147
15: 7 of David: and J his son reigned in his stead. 3147
15:30 in the twentieth year of J the son of Uzziah. 3147
15:32 J the son of Uzziah king of Judah to reign. 3147
15:36 Now the rest of the acts of J, and all that he 3147
15:38 J slept with his fathers, and was buried 3147
16: 1 the son of J king of Judah *began* to reign. 3147
1Ch 2:47 J, and Geshan, and Pelet, and Ephah, and 3147
3:12 his son, Azariah his son, J his son, 3147
5:17 genealogies in the days of J king of Judah, 3147
2Ch 26:21 J his son *was* over the king's house, 3147
26:23 a leper: and J his son reigned in his stead. 3147
27: 1 J *was* twenty and five years old when he 3147
27: 6 So J became mighty, because he prepared 3147
27: 7 Now the rest of the acts of J, and all his 3147
27: 9 J slept with his fathers, and they buried him 3147
Isa 1: 1 J, Ahaz, *and* Hezekiah, kings of Judah. 3147
7: 1 to pass in the days of Ahaz the son of J, 3147

Hos 1: 1 J, Ahaz, *and* Hezekiah, kings of Judah, and 3147
Mic 1: 1 to Micah the Morasthite in the days of J, 3147

JOURNEY (60) [JOURNEYED, JOURNEYING, JOURNEYINGS, JOURNEYS]

Ge 24:21 to wit whether the LORD had made his j 1870
29: 1 Jacob **went on** his j, and came into 5375+7272
30:36 he set three days' j betwixt himself and 1870
31:23 and pursued after him seven days' j; 1870
33:12 Let us **take** our j, and let us go, and I will 5265
46: 1 Israel **took** his j with all that he had, and 5265
Ex 3:18 three days' j into the wilderness, 1870
5: 3 three days' j into the desert, and 1870
8:27 We will go three days' j into 1870
13:20 they **took** their j from Succoth, and 5265
16: 1 they **took** their j from Elim, and all 5265
Nu 9:10 or *be* in a j afar off, yet he shall keep 1870
9:13 is not in a j, and forbeareth to keep 1870
10: 6 that lie on the south side shall **take** their j: 5265
10:13 they first **took** their j according to 5265
10:33 the mount of the LORD three days' j: 1870
10:33 went before them *in* the three days' j, 1870
11:31 as it were a day's j on this side, and as it 1870
11:31 as it were a day's j on the other side, 1870
33: 8 went three days' j in the wilderness of 1870
33:12 they **took** their j out of the wilderness of 5265
Dt 1: 2 (*There are* eleven days' *j* from Horeb *by* NIH
1: 7 **take** your j, and go *to* the mount of 5265
1:40 **take** your j into the wilderness *by* the way 5265
2: 1 **took** our j into the wilderness *by* the way of 5265
2:24 **take** your j, and pass over the river Arnon: 5265
10: 6 the children of Israel **took** their j from 5265
10:11 Arise, take thy j before the people, 4550
Jos 9:11 Take victuals with you for the j, and go to 1870
9:13 become old by reason of the very long j. 1870
Jdg 4: 9 notwithstanding the j that thou takest shall 1870
1Sa 15:18 the LORD sent thee on a j, and said, Go 1870
2Sa 11:10 unto Uriah, Camest thou not from *thy* j? 1870
1Ki 18:27 or he is in a j, *or* peradventure he sleepeth, 1870
19: 4 he himself went a day's j into 1870
19: 7 *and* eat; because the j *is* too great for thee. 1870
2Ki 3: 9 they fetcht a compass of seven days' j: and 1870
2Ch 1:13 Solomon came *from his* j to the high place NIH
Ne 2: 6 by him,) For how long shall thy j be? 4109
Pr 7:19 *is* not at home, he is gone a long j: 1870
Jnh 3: 3 an exceeding great city of three days' j. 4109
3: 4 Jonah began to enter into the city a day's j, 4109
Mt 10:10 Nor scrip for *your* j, neither two coats, *3598*
25:15 several ability; and straightway **took** his j. *589*
Mk 6: 8 that they should take nothing for *their* j, *3598*
13:34 *the Son of man is* as a man **taking a far j**, *590*
Lk 2:44 have been in the company, went a day's j; *3598*
9: 3 Take nothing for *your* j, neither staves, *3598*
11: 6 For a friend of mine in *his* j is come to me, *3598*
15:13 and **took** his j into a far country, and *589*
Jn 4: 6 Jesus therefore, being wearied with *his* j, *3597*
Ac 1:12 Jerusalem a **sabbath day's j**. *2192+3598+4521*
10: 9 as they **went on** their j, and drew nigh unto *3596*
22: 6 as I **made** my j, and was come nigh unto *4198*
Ro 1:10 **have a prosperous** j by the will of God to *2137*
15:24 Whensoever I **take** my j into Spain, I will *4198*
15:24 for I trust to see you **in** my j, and to be *1279*
1Co 16: 6 that ye may **bring** me **on** my j *4311*
Tit 3:13 **Bring** Zenas the lawyer and Apollos **on** their j *4311*
3Jn 1: 6 whom if thou **bring forward on** their j *4311*

JOURNEYED (33) [JOURNEY]

Ge 11: 2 And it came to pass, as they j from the east, 5265
12: 9 Abram j, going on still toward the south. 5265
13:11 him all the plain of Jordan; and Lot j east: 5265
20: 1 Abraham j from thence toward the south 5265
33:17 Jacob j to Succoth, and built him a house, 5265
35: 5 they j: and the terror of God was upon 5265
35:16 they j from Beth-el; and there was but 5265
35:21 Israel j, and spread his tent beyond 5265
Ex 12:37 the children of Israel j from Rameses to 5265
17: 1 of Israel j from the wilderness of Sin, 5265
40:37 they j not till the day that it was taken up. 5265
Nu 9:17 then after that the children of Israel j: 5265
9:18 of the LORD the children of Israel j, 5265
9:19 kept the charge of the LORD, and j not. 5265
9:20 to the commandment of the LORD they j. 5265
9:21 was taken up in the morning, then they j: 5265
9:21 by night that the cloud was taken up, they j. 5265
9:22 of Israel abode in their tents, and j not: 5265
9:22 but when it was taken up, they j. 5265
9:23 at the commandment of the LORD they j: 5265
11:35 *And* the people j from Kibroth-hattaavah 5265
12:15 the people j not till Miriam was brought in 5265
20:22 j from Kadesh, and came *unto* mount Hor. 5265
21: 4 they j from mount Hor *by* the way of 5265
21:11 they j from Oboth, and pitched at 5265
33:22 they j from Rissah, and pitched in 5265
Dt 10: 7 From thence they j *unto* Gudgodah; and 5265
Jos 9:17 the children of Israel j, and came unto their 5265
Jdg 17: 8 to the house of Micah, as he j. 1870+6213
Lk 10:33 as he j, came where he was: *3593*
Ac 9: 3 And as *he* j, he came near Damascus: and *4198*
9: 7 And the men which j **with** him stood *4922*
26:13 round about me and them which j with me. *4198*

JOURNEYING (3) [JOURNEY]

Nu 10: 2 of the assembly, and for the j of the camps. 4550
10:29 We *are* j unto the place of which 5265
Lk 13:22 teaching, and j towards Jerusalem. *4160+4197*

JOURNEYINGS (2) [JOURNEY]

Nu 10:28 Thus *were* the j of the children of Israel 4550
2Co 11:26 *In* j often, *in* perils of waters, *in* perils of *3597*

JOURNEYS (9) [JOURNEY]

Ge 13: 3 he went on his j from the south even to 4550
Ex 17: 1 after their j, according to 4550
40:36 children of Israel went onward in all their j: 4550
40:38 the house of Israel, throughout all their j. 4550
Nu 10: 6 they shall blow an alarm for their j. 4550
10:12 the children of Israel took their j out of 4550
33: 1 These *are* the j of the children of Israel, 4550
33: 2 j by the commandment of the LORD: 4550
33: 2 these *are* their j according to their goings 4550

JOY (165) [JOYED, JOYFUL, JOYFULLY, JOYFULNESS, JOYING, JOYOUS]

1Sa 18: 6 with j, and with instruments of musick. 8057
1Ki 1:40 rejoiced *with* great j, so that the earth rent 8057
1Ch 12:40 sheep abundantly: for *there was* j in Israel. 8057
15:16 sounding, by lifting up the voice with j. 8057
15:25 out of the house of Obed-edom with j. 8057
29: 9 David the king also rejoiced *with* great j. 8057
29:17 and now have I seen with j thy people, 8057
2Ch 20:27 of them, to go again to Jerusalem with j; 8057
30:26 So there was great j in Jerusalem: for since 8057
Ezr 3:12 a loud voice; and many shouted aloud for j: 8057
3:13 j from the noise of the weeping of 8057
6:16 the dedication of this house of God with j, 2305
6:22 of unleavened bread seven days with j: 8057
Ne 8:10 for the j of the LORD *is* your strength. 2304
12:43 God had made them rejoice *with* great j: 8057
12:43 that the j of Jerusalem was heard even afar 8057
Est 8:16 had light, and gladness, and j, and honour. 8342
8:17 the Jews had j and gladness, a feast and 8057
9:22 was turned unto them from sorrow to j, 8057
9:22 should make them days of feasting and j, 8057
Job 8:19 this *is* the j of his way, and out of the earth 4885
20: 5 the j of the hypocrite *but* for a moment? 8057
29:13 I **caused** the widow's heart **to sing for** j. 7442
33:26 he shall see his face with j: for he will 8643
38: 7 and all the sons of God **shouted for** j? 7321
41:22 and sorrow is **turned into** j before him. 1750
Ps 5:11 let them ever **shout for** j, because 7442
16:11 in thy presence *is* fulness of j; at thy right 8057
21: 1 The king shall j in thy strength, O LORD; 8055
27: 6 will I offer in his tabernacle sacrifices of j; 8643
30: 5 for a night, but j *cometh* in the morning. 7440
32:11 **shout for** j, all *ye that are* upright in heart. 7442
35:27 Let them **shout for** j, and be glad, 7442
42: 4 with the voice of j and praise, *with* a 7440
43: 4 the altar of God, unto God my exceeding j: 1524
48: 2 the j of the whole earth, *is* mount Zion, 4885
51: 8 Make me to hear j and gladness; *that* 8342
51:12 Restore unto me the j of thy salvation; and 8342
65:13 with corn; they **shout for** j, they also sing. 7321
67: 4 O let the nations be glad and **sing for** j: 7442
105:43 he brought forth his people with j, *and* 8342
126: 5 They that sow in tears shall reap in j. 7440
132: 9 and let thy saints **shout for** j. 7442
132:16 her saints shall **shout aloud for** j. 7442+7444
137: 6 if I prefer not Jerusalem above my chief j. 8057
Pr 12:20 but to the counsellers of peace *is* j. 8057
14:10 a stranger doth not intermeddle with his j. 8057
15:21 Folly *is* j to *him that is* destitute of wisdom: 8057
15:23 A man hath j by the answer of his mouth: 8057
17:21 and the father of a fool **hath** no j. 8055
21:15 *It is* j to the just to do judgment: but 8057
23:24 he that begetteth a wise *child* shall **have** j 8055
Ecc 2:10 I withheld not my heart from any j; 8057
2:26 in his sight wisdom, and knowledge, and j: 8057
5:20 God answereth *him* in the j of his heart. 8057
9: 7 Go *thy way,* eat thy bread with j, and 8057
Isa 9: 3 the nation, *and* not increased the j: 8057
9: 3 they j before thee according to the joy in 8055
9: 3 they joy before thee according to the j in 8057
9:17 Therefore the Lord shall have no j in their 8055
12: 3 Therefore with j shall ye draw water out of 8342
16:10 taken away, and j out of the plentiful field; 1524
22:13 behold j and gladness, slaying oxen, and 8342
24: 8 rejoice endeth, the j of the harp ceaseth. 4885
24:11 all j is darkened, the mirth of the land is 8057
29:19 The meek also shall increase *their* j in 8057
32:13 upon all the houses of j *in* the joyous city: 4885
32:14 a j of wild asses, a pasture of flocks; 4885
35: 2 rejoice even *with* j and singing: 1525
35:10 and everlasting j upon their heads: 8057
35:10 they shall obtain j and gladness, and sorrow 8342
51: 3 j and gladness shall be found therein, 8342
51:11 and everlasting j *shall be* upon their head: 8057
51:11 they shall obtain gladness and j; *and* sorrow 8342
52: 9 Break forth **into** j, **sing** together, ye waste 7442
55:12 For ye shall go out with j, and be led forth 8057
60:15 eternal excellency, a j of many generations. 4885
61: 3 beauty for ashes, the oil of j for mourning, 8342
61: 7 the double: everlasting j shall be unto them. 8057
65:14 my servants shall sing for j of heart, but 2898
65:18 Jerusalem a rejoicing, and her people a j. 4885
65:19 rejoice in Jerusalem, and j in my people: 7797
66: 5 he *shall* appear to your j, and they shall be 8057
66:10 rejoice for j with her, all ye that mourn for 4885
Jer 15:16 thy word was unto me the j and rejoicing of 8342
31:13 for I will turn their mourning into j, and 8342
33: 9 it shall be to me a name of j, a praise and 8342
33:11 The voice of j, and the voice of gladness, 8342
48:27 thou spakest of him, thou **skippedst for** j. 5110
48:33 j and gladness is taken from the plentiful 8057
49:25 the city of praise not left, the city of my j! 4885
La 2:15 of beauty, The j of the whole earth? 4885
5:15 The j of our heart is ceased; our dance is 4885
Eze 24:25 the j of their glory, the desire of their eyes, 4885
36: 5 their possession with the j of all *their* heart, 8057
Hos 9: 1 Rejoice not, O Israel, for j, as *other* people: 1524
Joel 1:12 j is withered away from the sons of men. 8342
1:16 *yea,* j and gladness from the house of our 8057
Hab 3:18 I will j in the God of my salvation. 1523
Zep 3:17 will save, he will rejoice over thee with j; 8057
3:17 in his love, he will j over thee with singing. 1523
Zec 8:19 shall be to the house of Judah j and 8342
Mt 2:10 they rejoiced *with* exceeding great j. *5479*
13:20 the word, and anon with j receiveth it; *5479*
13:44 and for j thereof goeth and selleth all that *5479*
25:21 *things:* enter thou into the j of thy lord. *5479*
25:23 *things:* enter thou into the j of thy lord. *5479*
28: 8 from the sepulchre with fear and great j; *5479*
Lk 1:14 And thou shalt have j and gladness; and *5479*
1:44 mine ears, the babe leaped in my womb for j. *20*
2:10 I bring you good tidings of great j, *5479*
6:23 ye in that day, and leap *for j*: for behold, NIG
8:13 when they hear, receive the word with j; *5479*
10:17 And the seventy returned *again* with j, *5479*
15: 7 that likewise j shall be in heaven over one *5479*
15:10 there is j in the presence of the angels of *5479*
24:41 And while they yet believed not for j, and *5479*
24:52 and returned to Jerusalem with great j: *5479*
Jn 3:29 this my j therefore is fulfilled. *5479*
15:11 that my j might remain in you, and *5479*
15:11 remain in you, and *that* your j might be full. *5479*
16:20 but your sorrow shall be turned into j. *5479*
16:21 for j that a man is born into the world. *5479*
16:22 and your j no *man* taketh from you. *5479*
16:24 ye shall receive, that your j may be full. *5479*
17:13 that they might have my j fulfilled in *5479*
Ac 2:28 thou shalt make me full of j with thy *2167*
8: 8 And there was great j in that city. *5479*
13:52 And the disciples were filled with j, and *5479*
15: 3 they caused great j unto all the brethren. *5479*
20:24 so that *I* might finish my course with j, and *5479*
Ro 5:11 we also j in God through our Lord Jesus *2744*
14:17 and peace, and j in the Holy Ghost. *5479*
15:13 Now the God of hope fill you with all j and *5479*
15:32 That I may come unto you with j by *5479*
2Co 1:24 over your faith, but are helpers of your j: *5479*
2: 3 in you all, that my j is *the joy* of you all. *5479*
2: 3 in you all, that my joy is *the j* of you all. NIG
7:13 exceedingly the more joyed we for the j of *5479*
8: 2 trial of affliction the abundance of their j *5479*
Gal 5:22 j, peace, longsuffering, gentleness, *5479*
Php 1: 4 of mine for you all making request with j, *5479*
1:25 you all for your furtherance and j of faith; *5479*
2: 2 Fulfil ye my j, that ye be likeminded, *5479*
2:17 of your faith, I j, and rejoice with you all. *5463*
2:18 *For* the same *cause* also do ye j, and *5463*
4: 1 my j and crown, so stand fast in the Lord, *5479*
1Th 1: 6 much affliction, with j of the Holy Ghost: *5479*
2:19 *is* our hope, or j, or crown of rejoicing? *5479*
2:20 For ye are our glory and j. *5479*
3: 9 for all the j wherewith we joy for your *5479*
3: 9 for all the joy wherewith we j for your *5463*
2Ti 1: 4 of thy tears, that I may be filled with j; *5479*
Phm 1: 7 For we have great j and consolation in thy *5479*
1:20 brother, let me have j of thee in the Lord: *3685*
Heb 12: 2 who for the j that was set before him *5479*
13:17 that they may do it with j, and not with *5479*
Jas 1: 2 count *it* all j when ye fall into divers *5479*
4: 9 to mourning, and *your* j to heaviness. *5479*
1Pe 1: 8 ye rejoice with j unspeakable and full of *5479*
4:13 ye may be glad also with **exceeding** j. *21*
1Jn 1: 4 write we unto you, that your j may be full. *5479*
2Jn 1:12 speak face to face, that our j may be full. *5479*
3Jn 1: 4 I have no greater j than to hear that my *5479*
Jude 1:24 the presence of his glory with **exceeding** j, *20*

JOYED (1) [JOY]

2Co 7:13 exceedingly the more j we for the joy of *5463*

JOYFUL (25) [JOY]

1Ki 8:66 went unto their tents j and glad of heart for 8056
Ezr 6:22 for the LORD had **made** them j, and 8055
Est 5: 9 went Haman forth that day j and with a 8056
Job 3: 7 be solitary, let no j **voice** come therein. 7445
Ps 5:11 let them also that love thy name be j in 5970
35: 9 my soul shall be j in the LORD: it shall 1523
63: 5 and my mouth shall praise *thee with* j lips: 7445
66: 1 **Make a j noise** unto God, all ye lands: 7321
81: 1 **make a j noise** unto the God of Jacob. 7321
89:15 *is* the people that know the **j sound**: 8643
95: 1 let us **make a j noise** to the rock of our 7321
95: 2 *and* **make a j noise** unto him with psalms. 7321
96:12 Let the field be j, and all that *is* therein: 5937
98: 4 **Make a j noise** unto the LORD, all 7321
98: 6 sound of cornet **make a j noise** before 7321
98: 8 clap *their* hands: let the hills be j together 7442
100: 1 **Make a j noise** unto the LORD, all ye 7321
113: 9 to keep house, *to be* a j mother of children. 8056
149: 2 let the children of Zion be j in their King. 1523
149: 5 Let the saints be j in glory: let them sing 5937
Ecc 7:14 In the day of prosperity be j, but in the day 2896
Isa 49:13 be j, O earth; and break forth *into* singing, 1523
56: 7 and **make** them j in my house of prayer: 8055
61:10 the LORD, my soul shall be j in my God; 1523
2Co 7: 4 I am exceeding j in all our tribulation. *5479*

JOYFULLY (3) [JOY]

Ecc 9: 9 Live j with the wife whom thou lovest all 7200
Lk 19: 6 and came down, and received him j. *5463*
Heb 10:34 took j the spoiling of your goods, *3326+5479*

JOYFULNESS (2) [JOY]

Dt 28:47 servedst not the LORD thy God with j, 8057
Col 1:11 unto all patience and longsuffering with j; *5479*

JOYING (1) [JOY]

Col 2: 5 j and beholding your order, and *5463*

JOYOUS (4) [JOY]

Isa 22: 2 *art* full *of* stirs, a tumultuous city, a j city: 5947
23: 7 *Is* this your j *city*, whose antiquity *is* of 5947
32:13 yea, upon all the houses of joy *in* the j city: 5947
Heb 12:11 chastening for the present seemeth to be j, *5479*

JOZABAD (9)

1Ch 12:20 J, and Jediael, and Michael, and Jozabad, 3107
12:20 and Michael, and J, and Elihu, and Zilthai, 3107
2Ch 31:13 J, and Eliel, and Ismachiah, and Mahath, 3107
35: 9 and Hashabiah and Jeiel and J, 3107
Ezr 8:33 with them *was* J the son of Jeshua, and 3107

Ezr 10:22 Ishmael, Nethaneel, J, and Elasah. 3107
10:23 J, and Shimei, and Kelaiah, (the same *is* 3107
Ne 8: 7 Azariah, J, Hanan, Pelaiah, and the Levites, 3107
11:16 Shabbethai and J, of the chief of 3107

JOZACHAR (1)
2Ki 12:21 For J the son of Shimeath, and 3108

JOZADAK (5)
Ezr 3: 2 stood up Jeshua the son of J, and 3136
3: 8 Jeshua the son of J, and the remnant of 3136
5: 2 Jeshua the son of J, and began to build 3136
10:18 *namely,* of the sons of Jeshua the son of J, 3136
Ne 12:26 the son of J, and in the days of Nehemiah 3136

JUBAL (1)
Ge 4:21 his brother's name *was* J: he was the father 3106

JUBILE (22)
Lev 25: 9 shalt thou cause the trumpet of the j to 8643
25:10 it shall be a j unto you; and ye shall return 3104
25:11 A j shall that fiftieth year be unto you: 3104
25:12 For it *is* the j; it shall be holy unto you: 3104
25:13 In the year of this j ye shall return every 3104
25:15 to the number of years after the j 3104
25:28 him that hath bought it until the year of j: 3104
25:28 in the j it shall go out, and he shall return 3104
25:30 his generations: it shall not go out in the j. 3104
25:31 be redeemed, and they shall go out in the j. 3104
25:33 his possession, shall go out in the *year of* j: 3104
25:40 *and* shall serve thee unto the year of j: 3104
25:50 that he was sold to him unto the year of j: 3104
25:52 but few years unto the year of j, 3104
25:54 then he shall go out in the year of j, 3104
27:17 If he sanctify his field from the year of j, 3104
27:18 if he sanctify his field after the j, then 3104
27:18 *even* unto the year of the j, and it shall be 3104
27:21 the field, when it goeth out in the j, shall be 3104
27:23 thy estimation, *even* unto the year of the j: 3104
27:24 In the year of the j the field shall return 3104
Nu 36: 4 when the j of the children of Israel shall be, 3104

JUBILEE See JUBILE

JUCAL (1)
Jer 38: 1 J the son of Shelemiah, and Pashur the son 3116

JUDA (11) [JUDAH]
Mt 2: 6 And thou Bethlehem, *in* the land of J, art *2448*
2: 6 art not the least among the princes of J: *2448*
Mk 6: 3 of James, and Joses, and of J, and Simon? *2455*
Lk 1:39 the hill country with haste, into a city of J; *2448*
3:26 *the son* of Joseph, which was *the son* of J, *2455*
3:30 which was *the son* of J, which was *the son* *2455*
3:33 *the son* of Phares, which was *the son* of J, *2455*
Heb 7:14 *it is* evident that our Lord sprang out of J; *2455*
8: 8 the house of Israel and with the house of J: *2455*
Rev 5: 5 behold, the Lion of the tribe of J, the root *2455*
7: 5 Of the tribe of J *were* sealed twelve *2455*

JUDAH (811) [BAALE OF JUDAH, BETH-LEHEM-JUDAH, JUDA, JUDAH'S, JUDAS, JUDEA]
Ge 29:35 therefore she called his name J; and 3063
35:23 and Levi, and J, and Issachar, and Zebulun: 3063
37:26 J said unto his brethren, What profit *is it* if 3063
38: 1 that J went down from his brethren, and 3063
38: 2 J saw there a daughter of a certain 3063
38: 6 J took a wife for Er his firstborn, 3063
38: 8 J said unto Onan, Go in unto thy brother's 3063
38:11 said J to Tamar his daughter in law, 3063
38:12 J was comforted, and went up unto his 3063
38:15 When J saw her, he thought her to be a 3063
38:20 J sent the kid by the hand of his friend 3063
38:22 he returned to J, and said, I cannot find her; 3063
38:23 J said, Let her take *it* to her, lest we be 3063
38:24 months after, that it was told J, saying, 3063
38:24 J said, Bring her forth, and let her be burnt. 3063
38:26 J acknowledged *them,* and said, She hath 3063
43: 3 J spake unto him, saying, The man did 3063
43: 8 J said unto Israel his father, Send the lad 3063
44:14 J and his brethren came to Joseph's house; 3063
44:16 J said, What shall we say unto my lord? 3063
44:18 J came near unto him, and said, O my lord, 3063
46:12 the sons of J; Er, and Onan, and Shelah, 3063
46:28 he sent J before him unto Joseph, to direct 3063
49: 8 J, thou *art he* whom thy brethren shall 3063
49: 9 J *is* a lion's whelp: from the prey, my son, 3063
49:10 The sceptre shall not depart from J, nor a 3063
Ex 1: 2 Reuben, Simeon, Levi, and J, 3063
31: 2 son of Uri, the son of Hur, of the tribe of J: 3063
35:30 son of Uri, the son of Hur, of the tribe of J; 3063
38:22 son of Uri, the son of Hur, of the tribe of J, 3063
Nu 1: 7 Of J; Nahshon the son of Amminadab. 3063
1:26 Of the children of J, *by* their generations, 3063
1:27 *even* of the tribe of J, *were* threescore and 3063
2: 3 camp of J pitch throughout their armies: 3063
2: 3 *shall be* captain of the children of J. 3063
2: 9 All that were numbered in the camp of J 3063
7:12 the son of Amminadab, of the tribe of J: 3063
10:14 the children of J according to their armies: 3063
13: 6 Of the tribe of J, Caleb the son of 3063
26:19 The sons of J *were* Er and Onan: and Er 3063
26:20 the sons of J after their families were, 3063
26:22 These *are* the families of J according to 3063
34:19 Of the tribe of J, Caleb the son of 3063
Dt 27:12 J, and Issachar, and Joseph, and Benjamin: 3063
33: 7 this *is the blessing* of J: and he said, Hear, 3063
33: 7 the voice of J, and bring him unto his 3063
34: 2 Manasseh, and all the land of J, unto 3063
Jos 7: 1 of Zabdi, the son of Zerah, of the tribe of J, 3063
7:16 by their tribes; and the tribe of J was taken: 3063
7:17 he brought the family of J; and he took 3063
7:18 son of Zerah, of the tribe of J, was taken. 3063
Jos 11:21 from all the mountains of J, and from all 3063
14: 6 the children of J came unto Joshua in 3063
15: 1 was the lot of the tribe of the children of J 3063
15:12 J round about according to their families. 3063
15:13 he gave a part among the children of J, 3063
15:20 children of J according to their families. 3063
15:21 J toward the coast of Edom southward 3063
15:63 the children of J could not drive them out: 3063
15:63 the Jebusites dwell with the children of J at 3063
18: 5 J shall abide in their coast on the south, and 3063
18:11 lot came forth between the children of J 3063
18:14 *is* Kirjath-jearim, a city of the children of J: 3063
19: 1 within the inheritance of the children of J. 3063
19: 9 Out of the portion of the children of J *was* 3063
19: 9 for the part of the children of J was too 3063
19:34 and to J upon Jordan *toward* the sunrising. 3063
20: 7 which *is* Hebron, in the mountain of J. 3063
21: 4 had by lot out of the tribe of J, and out of 3063
21: 9 gave out of the tribe of the children of J, 3063
21:11 *city is* Hebron, in the hill *country* of J, 3063
Jdg 1: 2 the LORD said, J shall go up: behold, 3063
1: 3 J said unto Simeon his brother, Come up 3063
1: 4 J went up; and the LORD delivered 3063
1: 8 Now the children of J had fought against 3063
1: 9 afterward the children of J went down to 3063
1:10 J went against the Canaanites that dwelt in 3063
1:16 children of J *into* the wilderness of Judah, 3063
1:16 children of Judah *into* the wilderness of J, 3063
1:17 J went with Simeon his brother, and 3063
1:18 Also J took Gaza with the coast thereof, 3063
1:19 the LORD was with J; and he drave out 3063
10: 9 passed over Jordan to fight also against J, 3063
15: 9 pitched in J, and spread themselves in Lehi. 3063
15:10 the men of J said, Why are ye come up 3063
15:11 three thousand men of J went to the top of 3063
17: 7 out of Beth-lehem-judah of the family of J, 3063
18:12 and pitched in Kirjath-jearim, in J: 3063
20:18 And the LORD said, J *shall go up* first. 3063
Ru 1: 7 on the way to return unto the land of J. 3063
4:12 house of Pharez, whom Tamar bare unto J, 3063
1Sa 11: 8 and the men of J thirty thousand. 3063
15: 4 and ten thousand men of J. 3063
17: 1 which *belongeth* to J, and pitched between 3063
17:52 the men of Israel and of J arose, and 3063
18:16 all Israel and J loved David, because 3063
22: 5 depart, and get thee *into* the land of J. 3063
23: 3 unto him, Behold, we *be* afraid here in J: 3063
23:23 him out throughout all the thousands of J. 3063
27: 6 pertaineth unto the kings of J unto this day. 3063
27:10 Against the south of J, and against 3063
30:14 upon *the coast* which *belongeth* to J, and 3063
30:16 of the Philistines, and out of the land of J. 3063
30:26 he sent of the spoil unto the elders of J, 3063
2Sa 1:18 (Also he bade *them* teach the children of J 3063
2: 1 Shall I go up into any of the cities of J? 3063
2: 4 the men of J came, and there they anointed 3063
2: 4 anointed David king over the house of J. 3063
2: 7 also the house of J have anointed me king 3063
2:10 But the house of J followed David. 3063
2:11 over the house of J was seven years 3063
3: 8 which against J do shew kindness *this* day 3063
3:10 the throne of David over Israel and over J, 3063
5: 5 In Hebron he reigned over J seven years 3063
5: 5 and three years over all Israel and J. 3063
11:11 The ark, and Israel, and J, abide in tents; 3063
12: 8 and gave thee the house of Israel and of J; 3063
19:11 Speak unto the elders of J, saying, 3063
19:14 he bowed the heart of all the men of J, 3063
19:15 J came to Gilgal, to go to meet the king, 3063
19:16 came down with the men of J to meet king 3063
19:40 all the people of J conducted the king, and 3063
19:41 Why have our brethren the men of J stolen 3063
19:42 all the men of J answered the men of Israel, 3063
19:43 the men of Israel answered the men of J, 3063
19:43 the words of the men of J were fiercer than 3063
20: 2 the men of J clave unto their king, 3063
20: 4 Assemble me the men of J *within* three 3063
20: 5 So Amasa went to assemble *the men of* J: 3063
21: 2 in his zeal to the children of Israel and J.) 3063
24: 1 them to say, Go, number Israel and J. 3063
24: 7 they went out to the south of J, *even to* 3063
24: 9 the men of J *were* five hundred thousand 3063
1Ki 1: 9 and all the men of J the king's servants: 3063
1:35 him to be ruler over Israel and over J. 3063
2:32 the son of Jether, captain of the host of J. 3063
4:20 J and Israel *were* many, as the sand which 3063
4:25 J and Israel dwelt safely, every man under 3063
12:17 of Israel which dwelt in the cities of J, 3063
12:20 the house of David, but the tribe of J only. 3063
12:21 he assembled all the house of J, with 3063
12:23 king of J, and unto all the house of Judah 3063
12:23 unto all the house of J and Benjamin, and 3063
12:27 *even* unto Rehoboam king of J, and 3063
12:27 and go again to Rehoboam king of J. 3063
12:32 like unto the feast that *is* in J, and 3063
13: 1 there came a man of God out of J by 3063
13:12 the man of God went, which came from J. 3063
13:14 thou the man of God that camest from J? 3063
13:21 unto the man of God that came from J, 3063
14:21 the son of Solomon reigned in J. 3063
14:22 J did evil in the sight of the LORD, and 3063
14:29 book of the chronicles of the kings of J? 3063
15: 1 the son of Nebat reigned Abijam over J. 3063
15: 7 book of the chronicles of the kings of J? 3063
15: 9 Jeroboam king of Israel reigned Asa over J. 3063
15:17 Baasha king of Israel went up against J, 3063
15:17 *any* to go out or come in to Asa king of J. 3063
15:22 Asa made a proclamation throughout all J; 3063
15:23 book of the chronicles of the kings of J? 3063
15:25 Israel in the second year of Asa king of J, 3063
15:28 Even in the third year of Asa king of J did 3063
15:33 In the third year of Asa king of J *began* 3063
16: 8 sixth year of Asa king of J *began* Elah 3063
16:10 and seventh year of Asa king of J, 3063
16:15 seventh year of Asa king of J did Zimri 3063
1Ki 16:23 first year of Asa king of J *began* Omri to 3063
16:29 eighth year of Asa king of J *began* Ahab 3063
19: 3 which *belongeth* to J, and left his servant 3063
22: 2 that Jehoshaphat the king of J came down 3063
22:10 Jehoshaphat the king of J sat each on his 3063
22:29 Jehoshaphat the king of J went up *to* 3063
22:41 J in the fourth year of Ahab king of Israel. 3063
22:45 book of the chronicles of the kings of J? 3063
22:51 seventeenth year of Jehoshaphat king of J, 3063
2Ki 1:17 Jehoram the son of Jehoshaphat king of J; 3063
3: 1 eighteenth year of Jehoshaphat king of J, 3063
3: 7 and sent to Jehoshaphat the king of J, 3063
3: 9 and the king of J, and the king of Edom: 3063
3:14 the presence of Jehoshaphat the king of J, 3063
8:16 of Israel, Jehoshaphat *being* then king of J, 3063
8:16 Jehoram the son of Jehoshaphat king of J 3063
8:19 Yet the LORD would not destroy J for 3063
8:20 Edom revolted from under the hand of J, 3063
8:22 Edom revolted from under the hand of J 3063
8:23 book of the chronicles of the kings of J? 3063
8:25 the son of Jehoram king of J *begin* to reign. 3063
8:29 Ahaziah the son of Jehoram king of J went 3063
9:16 Ahaziah king of J was come down to see 3063
9:21 of Israel and Ahaziah king of J went out, 3063
9:27 when Ahaziah the king of J saw *this,* he 3063
9:29 son of Ahab *began* Ahaziah to reign over J. 3063
10:13 met with the brethren of Ahaziah king of J, 3063
12:18 Jehoash king of J took all the hallowed 3063
12:18 and Ahaziah, his fathers, kings of J, 3063
12:19 book of the chronicles of the kings of J? 3063
13: 1 J Jehoahaz the son of Jehu *began* to reign 3063
13:10 seventh year of Joash king of J *began* 3063
13:12 he fought against Amaziah king of J, 3063
14: 1 Amaziah the son of Joash king of J. 3063
14: 9 king of Israel sent to Amaziah king of J, 3063
14:10 shouldest fall, *even* thou, and J with thee? 3063
14:11 Amaziah king of J looked one another *in* 3063
14:11 at Beth-shemesh, which *belongeth* to J. 3063
14:12 J was put to the worse before Israel; and 3063
14:13 king of Israel took Amaziah king of J, 3063
14:15 and how he fought with Amaziah king of J, 3063
14:17 Amaziah the son of Joash king of J lived 3063
14:18 book of the chronicles of the kings of J? 3063
14:21 all the people of J took Azariah, which *was* 3063
14:22 He built Elath, and restored it to J, 3063
14:23 J Jeroboam the son of Joash king of Israel 3063
14:28 Hamath, *which belonged* to J, for Israel, 3063
15: 1 Azariah son of Amaziah king of J to reign. 3063
15: 6 book of the chronicles of the kings of J? 3063
15: 8 eighth year of Azariah king of J did 3063
15:13 and thirtieth year of Uzziah king of J; 3063
15:17 thirtieth year of Azariah king of J *began* 3063
15:23 In the fiftieth year of Azariah king of J 3063
15:27 fiftieth year of Azariah king of J Pekah 3063
15:32 the son of Uzziah king of J to reign. 3063
15:36 book of the chronicles of the kings of J? 3063
15:37 to send against J Rezin the king of Syria, 3063
16: 1 the son of Jotham king of J *began* to reign. 3063
16:19 book of the chronicles of the kings of J? 3063
17: 1 In the twelfth year of Ahaz king of J *began* 3063
17:13 against J, by all the prophets, *and by* all 3063
17:18 there was none left but the tribe of J only. 3063
17:19 Also J kept not the commandments of 3063
18: 1 *that* Hezekiah the son of Ahaz king of J 3063
18: 5 was none like him among all the kings of J, 3063
18:13 come up against all the fenced cities of J, 3063
18:14 Hezekiah king of J sent to the king of 3063
18:14 king of J three hundred talents of silver 3063
18:16 *from* the pillars which Hezekiah king of J 3063
18:22 and hath said to J and Jerusalem, 3063
19:10 Thus shall ye speak to Hezekiah king of J, 3063
19:30 remnant that is escaped of the house of J 3063
20:20 book of the chronicles of the kings of J? 3063
21:11 Because Manasseh king of J hath done 3063
21:11 and hath made J also to sin with his idols: 3063
21:12 bringing *such* evil upon Jerusalem and J, 3063
21:16 beside his sin where*with* he made J to sin, 3063
21:17 book of the chronicles of the kings of J? 3063
21:25 book of the chronicles of the kings of J? 3063
22:13 for me, and for the people, and for all J, 3063
22:16 of the book which the king of J hath read: 3063
22:18 to the king of J which sent you to inquire 3063
23: 1 they gathered unto him all the elders of J 3063
23: 2 all the men of J and all the inhabitants of 3063
23: 5 whom the kings of J had ordained to burn 3063
23: 5 incense in the high places in the cities of J, 3063
23: 8 brought all the priests out of the cities of J, 3063
23:11 he took away the horses that the kings of J 3063
23:12 which the kings of J had made, and 3063
23:17 which came from J, and proclaimed these 3063
23:22 of the kings of Israel, nor of the kings of J; 3063
23:24 that were spied in the land of J 3063
23:26 where*with* his anger was kindled against J, 3063
23:27 I will remove J also out of my sight, 3063
23:28 book of the chronicles of the kings of J? 3063
24: 2 and sent them against J to destroy it, 3063
24: 3 of the LORD came *this* upon J, 3063
24: 5 book of the chronicles of the kings of J? 3063
24:12 Jehoiachin the king of J went out to 3063
24:20 LORD it came to pass in Jerusalem and J, 3063
25:21 So J was carried away out of their land. 3063
25:22 the people that remained in the land of J, 3063
25:27 of the captivity of Jehoiachin king of J, 3063
25:27 did lift up the head of Jehoiachin king of J 3063
1Ch 2: 1 Reuben, Simeon, Levi, and J, Issachar, and 3063
2: 3 The sons of J; Er, and Onan, and Shelah: 3063
2: 3 Er, the firstborn of J, was evil in the sight 3063
2: 4 and Zerah. All the sons of J *were* five. 3063
2:10 begat Nahshon, prince of the children of J; 3063
4: 1 The sons of J; Pharez, Hezron, and Carmi, 3063
4:21 The sons of Shelah the son of J *were,* Er 3063
4:27 family multiply, like to the children of J. 3063
4:41 came in the days of Hezekiah king of J, 3063
5: 2 For J prevailed above his brethren, and of 3063
5:17 in the days of Jotham king of J, 3063

1Ch 6:15 *captivity,* when the LORD carried away J 3063
6:55 they gave them Hebron in the land of J, 3063
6:57 the sons of Aaron they gave the cities of J, NIH
6:65 by lot out of the tribe of the children of J, 3063
9: 1 in the book of the kings of Israel and J, 3063
9: 3 in Jerusalem dwelt of the children of J, 3063
9: 4 of the children of Pharez the son of J. 3063
12:16 of Benjamin and J to the hold unto David. 3063
12:24 The children of J that bare shield and 3063
13: 6 *is,* to Kirjath-jearim, which *belonged* to J, 3063
21: 5 J *was* four hundred threescore and 3063
27:18 Of J, Elihu, *one* of the brethren of David: 3063
28: 4 for he hath chosen J to be the ruler; and 3063
28: 4 of the house of J, the house of my father; 3063
2Ch 2: 7 with the cunning *men* that *are* with me in J 3063
9:11 none such seen before in the land of J. 3063
10:17 of Israel that dwelt in the cities of J, 3063
11: 1 he gathered *of* the house of J and 3063
11: 3 king of J, and to all Israel in Judah and 3063
11: 3 and to all Israel in J and Benjamin, saying, 3063
11: 5 and built cities for defence in J. 3063
11:10 which *are* in J and in Benjamin, 3063
11:12 having J and Benjamin on his side. 3063
11:14 and came to J and Jerusalem: 3063
11:17 So they strengthened the kingdom of J, and 3063
11:23 children throughout all the countries of J 3063
12: 4 took the fenced cities which *pertained* to J, 3063
12: 5 *to* the princes of J, that were gathered 3063
12:12 and also in J things went well. 3063
13: 1 Jeroboam *began* Abijah to reign over J. 3063
13:13 so they were before J, and the ambushment 3063
13:14 when J looked back, behold, the battle *was* 3063
13:15 the men of J gave a shout: and as the men 3063
13:15 as the men of J shouted, it came to pass, 3063
13:15 and all Israel before Abijah and J. 3063
13:16 the children of Israel fled before J: and 3063
13:18 the children of J prevailed, because 3063
14: 4 commanded J to seek the LORD God of 3063
14: 5 Also he took away out of all the cities of J 3063
14: 6 he built fenced cities in J: for the land had 3063
14: 7 Therefore he said unto J, Let us build these 3063
14: 8 spears, out of J three hundred thousand; 3063
14:12 the Ethiopians before Asa, and before J; 3063
15: 2 Hear ye me, Asa, and all J and Benjamin; 3063
15: 8 the abominable idols out of all the land of J 3063
15: 9 he gathered all J and Benjamin, and 3063
15:15 all J rejoiced at the oath: for they had 3063
16: 1 Baasha king of Israel came up against J, 3063
16: 1 let none go out or come in to Asa king of J. 3063
16: 6 Asa the king took all J; and they carried 3063
16: 7 time Hanani the seer came to Asa king of J, 3063
16:11 *are* written in the book of the kings of J 3063
17: 2 placed forces in all the fenced cities of J, 3063
17: 2 set garrisons in the land of J, and in 3063
17: 5 all J brought to Jehoshaphat presents; and 3063
17: 6 away the high places and groves out of J. 3063
17: 7 and to Michaiah, to teach in the cities of J. 3063
17: 9 they taught in J, and *had* the book of 3063
17: 9 went about throughout all the cities of J, 3063
17:10 of the lands that *were* round about J, 3063
17:12 he built in J castles, and cities of store. 3063
17:13 he had much business in the cities of J: 3063
17:14 Of J, the captains of thousands; Adnah 3063
17:19 put in the fenced cities throughout all J. 3063
18: 3 of Israel said unto Jehoshaphat king of J, 3063
18: 9 Jehoshaphat king of J sat either of them on 3063
18:28 Jehoshaphat the king of J went up to 3063
19: 1 Jehoshaphat the king of J returned to his 3063
19: 5 land throughout all the fenced cities of J, 3063
19:11 the ruler of the house of J, for all the king's 3063
20: 3 and proclaimed a fast throughout all J. 3063
20: 4 J gathered themselves together, to ask *help* 3063
20: 4 even out of all the cities of J they came to 3063
20: 5 Jehoshaphat stood in the congregation of J 3063
20:13 all J stood before the LORD, with their 3063
20:15 all J, and ye inhabitants of Jerusalem, and 3063
20:17 the LORD with you, O J and Jerusalem: 3063
20:18 all J and the inhabitants of Jerusalem fell 3063
20:20 O J, and ye inhabitants of Jerusalem; 3063
20:22 mount Seir, which were come against J; 3063
20:24 when J came toward the watch tower in 3063
20:27 every man of J and Jerusalem, and 3063
20:31 Jehoshaphat reigned over J: *he was* thirty 3063
20:35 after this did Jehoshaphat king of J join 3063
21: 3 of precious things, with fenced cities in J: 3063
21: 8 revolted from under the dominion of J, 3063
21:10 from under the hand of J unto this day. 3063
21:11 he made high places in the mountains of J, 3063
21:11 and compelled J *thereto.* 3063
21:12 thy father, nor in the ways of Asa king of J, 3063
21:13 hast made J and the inhabitants of 3063
21:17 they came up into J, and brake into it, and 3063
22: 1 So Ahaziah the son of Jehoram king of J 3063
22: 6 Azariah the son of Jehoram king of J went 3063
22: 8 found the princes of J, and the sons of 3063
22:10 all the seed royal of the house of J. 3063
23: 2 they went about in J, and gathered 3063
23: 2 the Levites out of all the cities of J, 3063
23: 8 all J did according to all *things* that 3063
24: 5 Go out unto the cities of J, and gather of all 3063
24: 6 required of the Levites to bring in out of J 3063
24: 9 they made a proclamation through J and 3063
24:17 the death of Jehoiada came the princes of J, 3063
24:18 wrath came upon J and Jerusalem for this 3063
24:23 they came to J and Jerusalem, and 3063
25: 5 Moreover Amaziah gathered J together, 3063
25: 5 throughout all J and Benjamin: 3063
25:10 their anger was greatly kindled against J, 3063
25:12 did the children of J carry away captive, 3063
25:13 fell upon the cities of J, from Samaria even 3063
25:17 Amaziah king of J took advice, and sent to 3063
25:18 king of Israel sent to Amaziah king of J, 3063
25:19 shouldest fall, *even* thou, and J with thee? 3063
25:21 *both* he and Amaziah king of J, 3063
25:21 at Beth-shemesh, which *belongeth* to J. 3063

2Ch 25:22 J was put to the worse before Israel, and 3063
25:23 the king of Israel took Amaziah king of J, 3063
25:25 Amaziah the son of Joash king of J lived 3063
25:26 not written in the book of the kings of J 3063
25:28 buried him with his fathers in the city of J. 3063
26: 1 all the people of J took Uzziah, who *was* 3063
26: 2 He built Eloth, and restored it to J, 3063
27: 4 he built cities in the mountains of J, 3063
27: 7 in the book of the kings of Israel and J. 3063
28: 6 For Pekah the son of Remaliah slew in J an 3063
28: 9 God of your fathers was wroth with J, 3063
28:10 ye purpose to keep under the children of J 3063
28:17 the Edomites had come and smitten J, 3063
28:18 of the south of J, and had taken 3063
28:19 For the LORD brought J low because 3063
28:19 for he made J naked, and transgressed sore 3063
28:25 in every several city of J he made high 3063
28:26 *are* written in the book of the kings of J 3063
29: 8 the wrath of the LORD was upon J 3063
29:21 and for the sanctuary, and for J. 3063
30: 1 Hezekiah sent to all Israel and J, and 3063
30: 6 and his princes throughout all Israel and J, 3063
30:12 Also in J the hand of God was to give them 3063
30:24 For Hezekiah king of J did give to 3063
30:25 all the congregation of J, with the priests 3063
30:25 land of Israel, and that dwelt in J, rejoiced. 3063
31: 1 that were present went out to the cities of J, 3063
31: 1 and the altars out of all J and Benjamin, 3063
31: 6 *concerning* the children of Israel and J, 3063
31: 6 and Judah, that dwelt in the cities of J, 3063
31:20 thus did Hezekiah throughout all J, and 3063
32: 1 entered into J, and encamped against 3063
32: 8 upon the words of Hezekiah king of J. 3063
32: 9 unto Hezekiah king of J, and unto all Judah 3063
32: 9 unto all J that *were* at Jerusalem, saying, 3063
32:12 and commanded J and Jerusalem, saying, 3063
32:23 and presents to Hezekiah king of J: 3063
32:25 wrath upon him, and upon J and Jerusalem. 3063
32:32 *and* in the book of the kings of J and Israel. 3063
32:33 all J and the inhabitants of Jerusalem did 3063
33: 9 So Manasseh made J and the inhabitants of 3063
33:14 captains of war in all the fenced cities of J. 3063
33:16 commanded J to serve the LORD God of 3063
34: 3 in the twelfth year he began to purge J and 3063
34: 5 their altars, and cleansed J and Jerusalem. 3063
34: 9 of Israel, and of all J and Benjamin; 3063
34:11 to floor the houses which the kings of J had 3063
34:21 and for them that are left in Israel and in J, 3063
34:24 which they have read before the king of J: 3063
34:26 as for the king of J, who sent you to inquire 3063
34:29 and gathered together all the elders of J and 3063
34:30 all the men of J, and the inhabitants of 3063
35:18 all J and Israel that were present, and 3063
35:21 have I to do with thee, thou king of J? 3063
35:24 all J and Jerusalem mourned for Josiah. 3063
35:27 in the book of the kings of Israel and J. 3063
36: 4 Egypt made Eliakim his brother king over J 3063
36: 8 in the book of the kings of Israel and J: 3063
36:10 made Zedekiah his brother king over J and 3063
36:23 him a house in Jerusalem, which *is* in J. 3063
Ezr 1: 2 him a house at Jerusalem, which *is* in J. 3063
1: 3 which *is* in J, and build the house of 3063
1: 5 rose up the chief of the fathers of J and 3063
1: 8 them unto Sheshbazzar, the prince of J. 3063
2: 1 came again unto Jerusalem and J, 3063
3: 9 Kadmiel and his sons, the sons of J, 3063
4: 1 Now *when* the adversaries of J and 3063
4: 4 land weakened the hands of the people of J, 3063
4: 6 an accusation against the inhabitants of J 3063
5: 1 prophesied unto the Jews that *were* in J and 3061
7:14 to inquire concerning J and Jerusalem, 3061
9: 9 and to give us a wall in J and in Jerusalem. 3063
10: 7 they made proclamation throughout J and 3063
10: 9 all the men of J and Benjamin gathered 3063
10:23 same *is* Kelita,) Pethahiah, J, and Eliezer. 3063
Ne 1: 2 came, he and *certain* men of J; 3063
2: 5 that thou wouldest send me unto J, unto 3063
2: 7 they may convey me over till I come into J; 3063
4:10 J said, The strength of the bearers of 3063
4:16 the rulers *were* behind all the house of J. 3063
5:14 to be their governor in the land of J, 3063
6: 7 at Jerusalem, saying, *There is* a king in J: 3063
6:17 Moreover in those days the nobles of J sent 3063
6:18 For *there were* many in J sworn unto him, 3063
7: 6 came again to Jerusalem and to J, 3063
11: 3 in the cities of J dwelt every one in his 3063
11: 4 dwelt *certain* of the children of J, 3063
11: 4 Of the children of J; Athaiah the son of 3063
11: 9 J the son of Senuah *was* second over 3063
11:20 *and* the Levites, *were* in all the cities of J, 3063
11:24 of the children of Zerah the son of J, 3063
11:25 *some* of the children of J dwelt at 3063
11:36 of the Levites *were* divisions *in* J, *and* 3063
12: 8 Kadmiel, Sherebiah, J, *and* Mattaniah, 3063
12:31 I brought up the princes of J upon the wall, 3063
12:32 went Hoshaiah, and half of the princes of J, 3063
12:34 J, and Benjamin, and Shemaiah, and 3063
12:36 Gilalai, Maai, Nethaneel, and J, Hanani, 3063
12:44 for J rejoiced for the priests and for 3063
13:12 brought all J the tithe of the corn and 3063
13:15 In those days saw I in J *some* treading wine 3063
13:16 sold on the sabbath unto the children of J, 3063
13:17 I contended with the nobles of J, and 3063
Est 2: 6 been carried away with Jeconiah king of J, 3063
Ps 48:11 let the daughters of J be glad, because 3063
60: 7 strength of mine head; J *is* my lawgiver; 3063
63: T when he was in the wilderness of J. 3063
68:27 the princes of J *and* their council, 3063
69:35 save Zion, and will build the cities of J: 3063
76: 1 In J *is* God known: his name *is* great in 3063
78:68 chose the tribe of J, the mount Zion which 3063
97: 8 the daughters of J rejoiced, because of thy 3063
108: 8 strength of mine head; J *is* my lawgiver; 3063
114: 2 J was his sanctuary, *and* Israel his 3063
Pr 25: 1 which the men of Hezekiah king of J 3063

Isa 1: 1 which he saw concerning J and 3063
1: 1 Jotham, Ahaz, *and* Hezekiah, kings of J. 3063
2: 1 Isaiah the son of Amoz saw concerning J 3063
3: 1 and from J the stay and the staff, 3063
3: 8 For Jerusalem is ruined, and J is fallen: 3063
5: 3 and men of J, judge, I pray you, betwixt me 3063
5: 7 and the men of J his pleasant plant: 3063
7: 1 the son of Uzziah king of J, *that* Rezin 3063
7: 6 Let us go up against J, and vex it, and let us 3063
7:17 from the day that Ephraim departed from J; 3063
8: 8 he shall pass through J; he shall overflow 3063
9:21 *and* they together *shall be* against J. For all 3063
11:12 gather together the dispersed of J from 3063
11:13 and the adversaries of J shall be cut off: 3063
11:13 Ephraim shall not envy J, and Judah shall 3063
11:13 envy Judah, and J shall not vex Ephraim. 3063
19:17 the land of J shall be a terror unto Egypt, 3063
22: 8 he discovered the covering of J, and 3063
22:21 of Jerusalem, and to the house of J. 3063
26: 1 day shall this song be sung in the land of J; 3063
36: 1 came up against all the defenced cities of J, 3063
36: 7 said to J and to Jerusalem, Ye shall 3063
37:10 Thus shall ye speak to Hezekiah king of J, 3063
37:31 remnant that is escaped of the house of J 3063
38: 9 king of J, when he had been sick, and 3063
40: 9 say unto the cities of J, Behold your God. 3063
44:26 to the cities of J, Ye shall be built, and 3063
48: 1 and are come forth out of the waters of J, 3063
65: 9 and out of J an inheritor of my mountains: 3063
Jer 1: 2 days of Josiah the son of Amon king of J, 3063
1: 3 of Jehoiakim the son of Josiah king of J, 3063
1: 3 of Zedekiah the son of Josiah king of J, 3063
1:15 round about, and against all the cities of J. 3063
1:18 against the kings of J, against the princes 3063
2:28 the number of thy cities are thy gods, O J. 3063
3: 7 And her treacherous sister J saw *it.* 3063
3: 8 yet her treacherous sister J feared not, but 3063
3:10 yet for all this her treacherous sister J hath 3063
3:11 justified herself more than treacherous J. 3063
3:18 In those days the house of J shall walk with 3063
4: 3 For thus saith the LORD to the men of J 3063
4: 4 ye men of J and inhabitants of Jerusalem: 3063
4: 5 Declare ye in J, and publish in Jerusalem; 3063
4:16 give out their voice against the cities of J. 3063
5:11 the house of J have dealt very 3063
5:20 house of Jacob, and publish it in J, saying, 3063
7: 2 Hear the word of the LORD, all *ye of* J, 3063
7:17 thou not what they do in the cities of J 3063
7:30 For the children of J have done evil in my 3063
7:34 will I cause to cease from the cities of J, 3063
8: 1 shall bring out the bones of the kings of J, 3063
9:11 I will make the cities of J desolate, 3063
9:26 J, and Edom, and the children of Ammon, 3063
10:22 to make the cities of J desolate, *and* a den 3063
11: 2 speak unto the men of J, and to 3063
11: 6 Proclaim all these words in the cities of J, 3063
11: 9 A conspiracy is found among the men of J, 3063
11:10 the house of J have broken my covenant 3063
11:12 shall the cities of J and inhabitants of 3063
11:13 number of thy cities were thy gods, O J; 3063
11:17 of the house of Israel and of the house of J, 3063
12:14 pluck out the house of J from among them. 3063
13: 9 After this manner will I mar the pride of J, 3063
13:11 house of Israel and the whole house of J, 3063
13:19 none shall open *them:* J shall be carried 3063
14: 2 J mourneth, and the gates thereof languish; 3063
14:19 Hast thou utterly rejected J? hath thy soul 3063
15: 4 of Manasseh the son of Hezekiah king of J, 3063
17: 1 The sin of J *is* written with a pen of iron, 3063
17:19 whereby the kings of J come in, and by 3063
17:20 ye kings of J, and all Judah, and all 3063
17:20 all J, and all the inhabitants of Jerusalem, 3063
17:25 the men of J, and the inhabitants of 3063
17:26 they shall come from the cities of J, and 3063
18:11 speak to the men of J, and to 3063
19: 3 O kings of J, and inhabitants of Jerusalem; 3063
19: 4 nor the kings of J, and have filled this place 3063
19: 7 I will make void the counsel of J and 3063
19:13 and the houses of the kings of J, 3063
20: 4 I will give all J into the hand of the king of 3063
20: 5 all the treasures of the kings of J will I give 3063
21: 7 I will deliver Zedekiah king of J, and his 3063
21:11 touching the house of the king of J, 3063
22: 1 Go down *to* the house of the king of J, and 3063
22: 2 Hear the word of the LORD, O king of J, 3063
22: 6 the LORD unto the king's house of J; 3063
22:11 Shallum the son of Josiah king of J, 3063
22:18 Jehoiakim the son of Josiah king of J, 3063
22:24 of J were the signet upon my right hand, 3063
22:30 throne of David, and ruling any more in J. 3063
23: 6 In his days J shall be saved, and Israel shall 3063
24: 1 Jeconiah the son of Jehoiakim king of J, 3063
24: 1 the princes of J, with the carpenters and 3063
24: 5 them that are carried away captive of J, 3063
24: 8 So will I give Zedekiah the king of J, and 3063
25: 1 J in the fourth year of Jehoiakim the son of 3063
25: 1 of Jehoiakim the son of Josiah king of J, 3063
25: 2 the prophet spake unto all the people of J, 3063
25: 3 year of Josiah the son of Amon king of J, 3063
25:18 the cities of J, and the kings thereof, *and* 3063
26: 1 king of J came this word from the LORD, 3063
26: 2 and speak unto all the cities of J, 3063
26:10 When the princes of J heard these things, 3063
26:18 in the days of Hezekiah king of J, 3063
26:18 spake to all the people of J, saying, 3063
26:19 Did Hezekiah king of J and all Judah put 3063
26:19 of Judah and all J put him at all to death? 3063
27: 1 J came this word unto Jeremiah from 3063
27: 3 come *to* Jerusalem unto Zedekiah king of J; 3063
27:12 I spake also to Zedekiah king of J 3063
27:18 *in* the house of the king of J, and 3063
27:20 king of J from Jerusalem to Babylon, 3063
27:20 and all the nobles of J and Jerusalem; 3063
27:21 *in* the house of the king of J and 3063
28: 1 of the reign of Zedekiah king of J, 3063

Jer 28: 4 Jeconiah the son of Jehoiakim king of J, 3063
28: 4 with all the captives of J, that went into 3063
29: 2 the princes of J and Jerusalem, and 3063
29: 3 whom Zedekiah king of J sent unto 3063
29:22 all the captivity of J which *are* in Babylon, 3063
30: 3 the captivity of my people Israel and J, 3063
30: 4 spake concerning Israel and concerning J. 3063
31:23 they shall use this speech in the land of J 3063
31:24 there shall dwell in J itself, and *in* all 3063
31:27 and the house of J *with* the seed of man, 3063
31:31 the house of Israel, and with the house of J: 3063
32: 1 in the tenth year of Zedekiah king of J, 3063
32: 3 For Zedekiah king of J had shut him up, 3063
32: 4 Zedekiah king of J shall not escape out of 3063
32:30 the children of J have only done evil before 3063
32:32 children of Israel and of the children of J, 3063
32:32 the men of J, and the inhabitants of 3063
32:35 do this abomination, to cause J to sin. 3063
32:44 in the cities of J, and in the cities of 3063
33: 4 concerning the houses of the kings of J, 3063
33: 7 I will cause the captivity of J and 3063
33:10 *even* in the cities of J, and in the streets of 3063
33:13 about Jerusalem, and in the cities of J, 3063
33:14 the house of Israel and to the house of J. 3063
33:16 In those days shall J be saved, and 3063
34: 2 Go and speak to Zedekiah king of J, and 3063
34: 4 word of the LORD, O Zedekiah king of J; 3063
34: 6 unto Zedekiah king of J in Jerusalem, 3063
34: 7 against all the cities of J that were left, 3063
34: 7 defenced cities remained of the cities of J. 3063
34:19 The princes of J, and the princes of 3063
34:21 Zedekiah king of J and his princes will I 3063
34:22 I will make the cities of J a desolation 3063
35: 1 of Jehoiakim the son of Josiah king of J, 3063
35:13 Go and tell the men of J and the inhabitants 3063
35:17 I will bring upon J and upon all 3063
36: 1 of Jehoiakim the son of Josiah king of J, 3063
36: 2 against J, and against all the nations, 3063
36: 3 It may be that the house of J will hear all 3063
36: 6 also thou shalt read them in the ears of all J 3063
36: 9 of Jehoiakim the son of Josiah king of J, 3063
36: 9 came from the cities of J unto Jerusalem. 3063
36:28 which Jehoiakim the king of J hath burnt. 3063
36:29 thou shalt say to Jehoiakim king of J, 3063
36:30 saith the LORD of Jehoiakim king of J; 3063
36:31 of Jerusalem, and upon the men of J, 3063
36:32 Jehoiakim king of J had burnt in the fire: 3063
37: 1 king of Babylon made king in the land of J. 3063
37: 7 Thus shall ye say to the king of J, that sent 3063
39: 1 In the ninth year of Zedekiah king of J, 3063
39: 4 *that* when Zedekiah the king of J saw them, 3063
39: 6 king of Babylon slew all the nobles of J. 3063
39:10 in the land of J, and gave them vineyards 3063
40: 1 carried away captive of Jerusalem and J, 3063
40: 5 hath made governor over the cities of J, 3063
40:11 the king of Babylon had left a remnant of J, 3063
40:12 came *to* the land of J, to Gedaliah, unto 3063
40:15 be scattered, and the remnant in J perish? 3063
42:15 the word of the LORD, ye remnant of J; 3063
42:19 said concerning you, O ye remnant of J; 3063
43: 4 of the LORD, to dwell in the land of J. 3063
43: 5 of the forces, took all the remnant of J, 3063
43: 5 had been driven, to dwell in the land of J: 3063
43: 9 in Tahpanhes, in the sight of the men of J; 3064
44: 2 and upon all the cities of J; 3063
44: 6 was kindled in the cities of J and in 3063
44: 7 and woman, child and suckling, out of J, 3063
44: 9 the wickedness of the kings of J, and 3063
44: 9 they have committed in the land of J, 3063
44:11 against you for evil, and to cut off all J. 3063
44:12 I will take the remnant of J, that have set 3063
44:14 So that none of the remnant of J, which are 3063
44:14 that *they* should return *into* the land of J, 3063
44:17 in the cities of J, and in the streets of 3063
44:21 The incense that ye burnt in the cities of J, 3063
44:24 all J that *are* in the land of Egypt: 3063
44:26 all J that dwell in the land of Egypt; 3063
44:26 of any man of J in all the land of Egypt, 3063
44:27 all the men of J that *are* in the land of 3063
44:28 out of the land of Egypt *into* the land of J, 3063
44:28 all the remnant of J, that are gone into 3063
44:30 as I gave Zedekiah king of J into the hand 3063
45: 1 of Jehoiakim the son of Josiah king of J, 3063
46: 2 of Jehoiakim the son of Josiah king of J. 3063
49:34 of the reign of Zedekiah king of J, 3063
50: 4 they and the children of J together, going 3063
50:20 the sins of J, and they shall not be found: 3063
50:33 the children of J *were* oppressed together: 3063
51: 5 nor J of his God, of the LORD of hosts; 3063
51:59 when he went with Zedekiah the king of J 3063
52: 3 LORD it came to pass in Jerusalem and J, 3063
52:10 he slew also all the princes of J in Riblah. 3063
52:27 Thus J was carried away captive out of his 3063
52:31 of the captivity of Jehoiachin king of J, 3063
52:31 lifted up the head of Jehoiachin king of J, 3063
La 1: 3 J is gone into captivity because 3063
1:15 the daughter of J, *as in* a winepress. 3063
2: 2 wrath the strong holds of the daughter of J; 3063
2: 5 hath increased in the daughter of J 3063
5:11 in Zion, *and* the maids in the cities of J. 3063
Eze 4: 6 the iniquity of the house of J forty days: 3063
8: 1 and the elders of J sat before me, 3063
8:17 Is it a light thing to the house of J that *they* 3063
9: 9 the house of Israel and J *is* exceeding great, 3063
21:20 to J in Jerusalem the defenced. 3063
25: 3 against the house of J, when they went into 3063
25: 8 the house of J *is* like unto all the heathen; 3063
25:12 against the house of J by taking vengeance, 3063
27:17 J, and the land of Israel, they *were* thy 3063
37:16 For J, and for the children of Israel his 3063
37:19 *even* with the stick of J, and make them 3063
48: 7 east side unto the west side, a *portion for* J. 3063
48: 8 by the border of J, from the east side unto 3063
48:22 between the border of J and the border of 3063
48:31 of Reuben, one gate of J, one gate of Levi. 3063
Da 1: 1 J came Nebuchadnezzar king of Babylon 3063
1: 2 the Lord gave Jehoiakim king of J into his 3063
1: 6 Now among these were of the children of J, 3063
2:25 I have found a man of the captives of J, 3061
5:13 *art* of the children of the captivity of J, 3061
6:13 *is* of the children of the captivity of J, 3061
9: 7 to the men of J, and to the inhabitants of 3063
Hos 1: 1 kings of J, and in the days of Jeroboam 3063
1: 7 I will have mercy upon the house of J, and 3063
1:11 shall the children of J and the children of 3063
4:15 Israel, play the harlot, *yet* let not J offend; 3063
5: 5 in their iniquity; J also shall fall with them. 3063
5:10 The princes of J were like them that 3063
5:12 a moth, and to the house of J as rottenness. 3063
5:13 J *saw* his wound, then went Ephraim to 3063
5:14 and as a young lion to the house of J: 3063
6: 4 O J, what shall I do unto thee? for your 3063
6:11 Also, O J, he hath set a harvest for thee, 3063
8:14 and J hath multiplied fenced cities: 3063
10:11 J shall plow, *and* Jacob shall break his 3063
11:12 J yet ruleth with God, and is faithful with 3063
12: 2 The LORD hath also a controversy with J, 3063
Joel 3: 1 when I shall bring again the captivity of J 3063
3: 6 The children also of J and the children of 3063
3: 8 daughters into the hand of the children of J, 3063
3:18 all the rivers of J shall flow *with* waters, 3063
3:19 for the violence against the children of J, 3063
3:20 J shall dwell for ever, and Jerusalem from 3063
Am 1: 1 Israel in the days of Uzziah king of J, 3063
2: 4 For three transgressions of J, and for four, 3063
2: 5 I will send a fire upon J, and it shall devour 3063
7:12 go, flee thee away into the land of J, and 3063
Ob 1:12 children of J in the day of their destruction; 3063
Mic 1: 1 Ahaz, *and* Hezekiah, kings of J, which he 3063
1: 5 what *are* the high places of J? *are they* not 3063
1: 9 wound *is* incurable; for it is come unto J; 3063
5: 2 *thou* be little among the thousands of J, 3063
Na 1:15 O J, keep thy solemn feasts, perform thy 3063
Zep 1: 1 days of Josiah the son of Amon, king of J. 3063
1: 4 I will also stretch out mine hand upon J, 3063
2: 7 shall be for the remnant of the house of J; 3063
Hag 1: 1 governor of J, and to Joshua the son of 3063
1:14 governor of J, and the spirit of Joshua 3063
2: 2 governor of J, and to Joshua the son of 3063
2:21 Speak to Zerubbabel, governor of J, saying, 3063
Zec 1:12 mercy on Jerusalem and on the cities of J, 3063
1:19 These *are* the horns which have scattered J, 3063
1:21 These *are* the horns which have scattered J, 3063
1:21 which lift up *their* horn over the land of J 3063
2:12 the LORD shall inherit J his portion in 3063
8:13 O house of J, and house of Israel; 3063
8:15 well unto Jerusalem and to the house of J: 3063
8:19 shall be to the house of J joy and gladness, 3063
9: 7 he shall be as a governor in J, and Ekron as 3063
9:13 When I have bent J for me, filled the bow 3063
10: 3 hosts hath visited his flock the house of J, 3063
10: 6 I will strengthen the house of J, and I will 3063
11:14 I might break the brotherhood between J 3063
12: 2 they shall be in the siege both against J 3063
12: 4 I will open mine eyes upon the house of J, 3063
12: 5 the governors of J shall say in their heart, 3063
12: 6 In that day will I make the governors of J 3063
12: 7 The LORD also shall save the tents of J 3063
12: 7 do not magnify *themselves* against J. 3063
14: 5 earthquake in the days of Uzziah king of J: 3063
14:14 J also shall fight at Jerusalem; and 3063
14:21 in J shall be holiness unto the LORD of 3063
Mal 2:11 J hath dealt treacherously, and 3063
2:11 for J hath profaned the holiness of 3063
3: 4 shall the offering of J and Jerusalem be 3063

JUDAH'S (4) [JUDAH]

Ge 38: 7 Er, J firstborn, was wicked in the sight of 3063
38:12 in process of time the daughter of Shuah J 3063
Jer 32: 2 which *was in* the king of J house. 3063
38:22 all the women that are left in the king of J 3063

JUDAS (33) [JUDAH]

Mt 1: 2 and Jacob begat J and his brethren; *2455*
1: 3 And J begat Phares and Zara of Thamar; *2455*
10: 4 Simon the Canaanite, and J Iscariot, *2455*
13:55 James, and Joses, and Simon, and J? *2455*
26:14 Then one of the twelve, called J Iscariot, *2455*
26:25 Then J, which betrayed him, answered and *2455*
26:47 lo, J, one of the twelve, came, and with him *2455*
27: 3 Then J, which had betrayed him, when he *2455*
Mk 3:19 And J Iscariot, which also betrayed him. *2455*
14:10 And J Iscariot, one of the twelve, *2455*
14:43 cometh J, one of the twelve, and with him a *2455*
Lk 6:16 *And* J *the brother* of James, and *2455*
6:16 and J Iscariot, which also was the traitor. *2455*
22: 3 Then entered Satan into J surnamed *2455*
22:47 and he that was called J, one of the twelve, *2455*
22:48 But Jesus said unto him, J, betrayest thou *2455*
Jn 6:71 He spake of J Iscariot *the son* of Simon: *2455*
12: 4 Then saith one of his disciples, J Iscariot, *2455*
13: 2 the devil having now put into the heart of J *2455*
13:26 he gave *it* to J Iscariot, *the son* of Simon. *2455*
13:29 *of them* thought, because J had the bag, *2455*
14:22 J saith unto him, not Iscariot, Lord, how is *2455*
18: 2 And J also, which betrayed him, knew *2455*
18: 3 J then, having received a band *of men*, and *2455*
18: 5 I am *he*. And J also, which betrayed him, *2455*
Ac 1:13 Simon Zelotes, and J *the brother* of James. *2455*
1:16 mouth of David spake before concerning J, *2455*
1:25 from which J by transgression fell, *2455*
5:37 After this *man* rose up J of Galilee in the *2455*
9:11 inquire in the house of J for *one* called *2455*
15:22 *namely*, J surnamed Barsabas, and Silas, *2455*
15:27 We have sent therefore J and Silas, *2455*
15:32 And J and Silas, being prophets also *2455*

JUDE (1)

Jude 1: 1 J, the servant of Jesus Christ, and *2455*

JUDEA (44) [JUDAH]

Ezr 5: 8 that we went into the province of J, 3061
Mt 2: 1 of J in the days of Herod the king, *2449*
2: 5 And they said unto him, In Bethlehem of J: *2449*
2:22 reign in J in the room of his father Herod, *2449*
3: 1 preaching in the wilderness of J, *2449*
3: 5 and all J, and all the region round about *2449*
4:25 and *from* J, and *from* beyond Jordan. *2449*
19: 1 came into the coasts of J beyond Jordan; *2449*
24:16 Then let them which be in J flee into *2449*
Mk 1: 5 there went out unto him all the land of J, *2449*
3: 7 from Galilee followed him, and from J, *2449*
10: 1 cometh into the coasts of J by the farther *2449*
13:14 let them that be in J flee to the mountains: *2449*
Lk 1: 5 was in the days of Herod, the king of J, *2449*
1:65 abroad throughout all the hill country of J. *2449*
2: 4 of Nazareth, into J, unto the city of David, *2449*
3: 1 Pontius Pilate being governor of J, and *2449*
5:17 town of Galilee, and J, and Jerusalem: *2449*
6:17 a great multitude of people out of all J and *2449*
7:17 rumour of him went forth throughout all J, *2449*
21:21 Then let them which are in J flee to *2449*
Jn 3:22 and his disciples into the land of J; *2453*
4: 3 He left J, and departed again into Galilee. *2449*
4:47 he heard that Jesus was come out of J *2449*
4:54 when he was come out of J into Galilee. *2449*
7: 3 said unto him, Depart hence, and go into J, *2449*
11: 7 he to *his* disciples, Let us go into J again. *2449*
Ac 1: 8 and in all J, and in Samaria, and unto *2449*
2: 9 and in J, and Cappadocia, in Pontus, and *2449*
2:14 Ye men of J, and all *ye* that dwell at *2453*
8: 1 abroad throughout the regions of J *2449*
9:31 Then had the churches rest throughout all J *2449*
10:37 which was published throughout all J, and *2449*
11: 1 brethren that were in J heard that *2449*
11:29 relief unto the brethren which dwelt in J: *2449*
12:19 And he went down from J to Cesarea, and *2449*
15: 1 And certain *men* which came down from J *2449*
21:10 there came down from J a certain prophet, *2449*
26:20 and throughout all the coasts of J, and *then* *2449*
28:21 We neither received letters out of J *2449*
Ro 15:31 from them that do not believe in J; *2449*
2Co 1:16 of you to be brought on *my* way toward J. *2449*
Gal 1:22 the churches of J which were in Christ: *2449*
1Th 2:14 of God which in J are in Christ Jesus: *2449*

JUDEAN See JEHUDIJAH; JUDAH

JUDGE (191) [JUDGED, JUDGES, JUDGEST, JUDGETH, JUDGING, JUDGMENT, JUDGMENTS]

Ge 15:14 that nation, whom they shall serve, will I j: 1777
16: 5 the LORD j between me and thee. 8199
18:25 Shall not the J of all the earth do right? 8199
19: 9 to sojourn, and he will **needs be a j**: 8199+8199
31:37 that they may j betwixt us both. 3198
31:53 the God of their father, j betwixt us. 8199
49:16 Dan shall j his people, as one of the tribes 1777
Ex 2:14 Who made thee a prince and a j over us? 8199
5:21 The LORD look upon you, and j; 8199
18:13 the morrow, that Moses sat to j the people: 8199
18:16 I j between one and another, and I do make 8199
18:22 let them j the people at all seasons: and 8199
18:22 but every small matter they shall j: 8199
Lev 19:15 in righteousness shalt thou j thy neighbour. 8199
Nu 35:24 the congregation shall j between the slayer 8199
Dt 1:16 j righteously between every man and his 8199
16:18 they shall j the people *with* just judgment. 8199
17: 9 unto the j that shall be in those days, 8199
17:12 or unto the j, even that man shall die: 8199
25: 1 unto judgment, that *the judges* may j them; 8199
25: 2 that the j shall cause him to lie down, and 8199
32:36 For the LORD shall j his people, and 1777
Jdg 2:18 the LORD was with the j, and 8199
2:18 hand of their enemies all the days of the j: 8199
2:19 when the j was dead, *that* they returned, 8199
11:27 the LORD the J be judge *this* day between 8199
11:27 the LORD the Judge be j *this* day between 8199
1Sa 2:10 the LORD shall j the ends of the earth; 1777
2:25 sin against another, the j shall judge him: 430
2:25 sin against another, the judge shall j him: 6419
3:13 For I have told him that I will j his house 8199
8: 5 now make us a king to j us like all 8199
8: 6 when they said, Give us a king to j us. 8199
8:20 that our king may j us, and go out before 8199
24:12 The LORD j between me and thee, and 8199
24:15 The LORD therefore be j, and 1781
24:15 j between me and thee, and see, and 8199
2Sa 15: 4 Oh that I were made j in the land, 8199
1Ki 3: 9 thy servant an understanding heart to j thy 8199
3: 9 for who is able to j this thy *so* great a 8199
7: 7 a porch for the throne where he might j, 8199
8:32 do, and j thy servants, condemning 8199
1Ch 16:33 because he cometh to j the earth. 8199
2Ch 1:10 for who can j this thy people, *that is so* 8199
1:11 for thyself, that thou mayest j my people, 8199
6:23 do, and j thy servants, by requiting 8199
19: 6 for ye j not for man, but for the LORD, 8199
20:12 O our God, wilt thou not j them? for we 8199
Ezr 7:25 which may j all the people that *are* beyond 1778
Job 9:15 *but* I would make supplication to my j. 8199
22:13 can he j through the dark *cloud?* 8199
23: 7 so should I be delivered for ever from my j. 8199
31:28 *were* an iniquity *to be punished by* the j: 6416
Ps 7: 8 The LORD shall j the people: judge me, 1777
7: 8 j me, O LORD, according to my 8199
9: 8 he shall j the world in righteousness, 8199
10:18 To j the fatherless and the oppressed, 8199
26: 1 J me, O LORD; for I have walked in mine 8199
35:24 J me, O LORD my God, according to thy 8199
43: 1 J me, O God, and plead my cause against 8199
50: 4 and to the earth, that *he* may j his people. 1777
50: 6 for God *is* j himself. Selah. 8199
54: 1 by thy name, and j me by thy strength. 1777
58: 1 do ye j uprightly, O ye sons of men? 8199

Ps 67: 4 for thou shalt j the people righteously, and 8199
68: 5 of the fatherless, and a j of the widows, 1781
72: 2 He shall j thy people with righteousness, 1777
72: 4 He shall j the poor of the people, he shall 8199
75: 2 receive the congregation I will j uprightly. 8199
75: 7 God *is* the j: he putteth down one, and 8199
82: 2 How long will ye j unjustly, and accept 8199
82: 8 Arise, O God, j the earth: for thou shalt 8199
94: 2 Lift up thyself, thou j of the earth: render a 8199
96:10 be moved: he shall j the people righteously. 1777
96:13 for he cometh, for he cometh to j the earth: 8199
96:13 he shall j the world with righteousness, and 8199
98: 9 the LORD; for he cometh to j the earth: 8199
98: 9 with righteousness shall he j the world, and 8199
110: 6 He shall j among the heathen, he shall fill 1777
135:14 For the LORD will j his people, and 1777
Pr 31: 9 j righteously, and plead the cause of 8199
Ecc 3:17 God shall j the righteous and the wicked: 8199
Isa 1:17 j the fatherless, plead for the widow. 8199
1:23 they j not the fatherless, neither doth 8199
2: 4 he shall j among the nations, and 8199
3: 2 the j, and the prophet, and the prudent, and 8199
3:13 *up* to plead, and standeth to j the people. 1777
5: 3 j, I pray you, betwixt me and my vineyard. 8199
11: 3 he shall not j after the sight of his eyes, 8199
11: 4 with righteousness shall he j the poor, and 8199
33:22 For the LORD *is* our j, the LORD *is* our 8199
51: 5 and mine arms shall j the people; 8199
Jer 5:28 they j not the cause, the cause of 1777
5:28 and the right of the needy do they not j. 8199
La 3:59 thou hast seen my wrong: j thou my cause. 8199
Eze 7: 3 will j thee according to thy ways, and 8199
7: 8 I will j thee according to thy ways, and 8199
7:27 and according to their deserts will I j them; 8199
11:10 I will j you in the border of Israel; and 8199
11:11 *but* I will j you in the border of Israel: 8199
16:38 I will j thee, as *women* that break wedlock 8199
18:30 Therefore I will j you, O house of Israel, 8199
20: 4 Wilt thou j them, son of man, wilt thou 8199
20: 4 wilt thou j *them?* cause them to know 8199
21:30 I will j thee in the place where thou wast 8199
22: 2 Now, thou son of man, wilt thou j, wilt 8199
22: 2 wilt thou judge, wilt thou j the bloody city? 8199
23:24 they shall j thee according to their 8199
23:36 of man, wilt thou j Aholah and Aholibah? 8199
23:45 they shall j them after the manner of 8199
24:14 shall they j thee, saith the Lord GOD. 8199
33:20 I will j you every one after his ways. 8199
34:17 Behold, I j between cattle and cattle, 8199
34:20 will j between the fat cattle and 8199
34:22 and I will j between cattle and cattle. 8199
44:24 they shall j it according to my judgments: 8199
Joel 3:12 for there will I sit to j all the heathen round 8199
Am 2: 3 I will cut off the j from the midst thereof, 8199
Ob 1:21 saviours shall come up on mount Zion to j 8199
Mic 3:11 The heads thereof j for reward, and 8199
4: 3 he shall j among many people, and 8199
5: 1 they shall smite the j of Israel with a rod 8199
7: 3 prince asketh, and the j *asketh* for a reward; 8199
Zec 3: 7 thou shalt also j my house, and shalt also 1777
Mt 5:25 any time the adversary deliver thee to the j, 2923
5:25 and the j deliver thee to the officer, and 2923
7: 1 J not, that ye be not judged. 2919
7: 2 For with what judgment ye j, ye shall be 2919
Lk 6:37 J not, and ye shall not be judged: 2919
12:14 who made me a j or a divider over you? 1348
12:57 why even of yourselves j ye not what *is* 2919
12:58 lest he hale thee to the j, and the judge 2923
12:58 and the j deliver thee to the officer, and 2923
18: 2 Saying, There was in a city a j, 2923
18: 6 the Lord said, Hear what the unjust j saith. 2923
19:22 Out of thine own mouth will I j thee, 2919
Jn 5:30 as I hear, I j: and my judgment is just; 2919
7:24 J not according to the appearance, but 2919
7:24 the appearance, but j righteous judgment. 2919
7:51 Doth our law j any man, before it hear him, 2919
8:15 Ye j after the flesh; I judge no *man.* 2919
8:15 Ye judge after the flesh; I j no *man.* 2919
8:16 And yet if I j, my judgment is true: for I am 2919
8:26 I have many *things* to say and to j of you: 2919
12:47 hear my words, and believe not, I j him not: 2919
12:47 for I came not to j the world, but to save 2919
12:48 the same shall j him in the last day. 2919
18:31 ye him, and j him according to your law. 2919
Ac 4:19 hearken unto you more than unto God, j ye. 2919
7: 7 to whom they shall be in bondage will I j, 2919
7:27 Who made thee a ruler and a j over us? 1348
7:35 saying, Who made thee a ruler and a j? 1348
10:42 was ordained of God *to be* the J of quick 2923
13:46 j yourselves unworthy of everlasting life, 2919
17:31 in the which he will j the world in 2919
18:15 look ye *to it;* for I will be no j of such 2923
23: 3 for sittest thou to j me after the law, and 2919
24:10 been of many years a j unto this nation, 2923
Ro 2:16 In the day when God shall j the secrets of 2919
2:27 j thee, who by the letter and 2919
3: 6 for then how shall God j the world? 2919
14: 3 let not him which eateth not j him that 2919
14:10 But why dost thou j thy brother? or why 2919
14:13 us not therefore j one another any more: 2919
14:13 but j this rather, that no *man* put a 2919
1Co 4: 3 man's judgment: yea, I j not mine own self. 350
4: 5 Therefore j nothing before the time, 2919
5:12 For what have I to do to j them also that are 2919
5:12 do not ye j them that are within? 2919
6: 2 Do ye not know that the saints shall j 2919
6: 2 are ye unworthy to j the smallest matters? 2922
6: 3 Know ye not that we shall j angels? 2919
6: 4 **set** them to j who are least esteemed in 2523
6: 5 not one that shall be able to j between his 1252
10:15 I speak as to wise *men;* j ye what I say. 2919
11:13 J in yourselves: is it comely that a woman 2919
11:31 For if we would j ourselves, we should not 1252
14:29 speak two or three, and let the other j. 1252
2Co 5:14 because we thus j, that if one died for all, 2919
Col 2:16 Let no *man* therefore j you in meat, 2919
2Ti 4: 1 who shall j the quick and the dead at his 2919
4: 8 which the Lord, the righteous j, shall give 2923
Heb 10:30 And again, The Lord shall j his people. 2919
12:23 and to God the J of all, and to the spirits of 2923
13: 4 whoremongers and adulterers God will j. 2919
Jas 4:11 but if thou j the law, thou art not a doer of 2919
4:11 thou art not a doer of the law, but a j. 2923
5: 9 the j standeth before the door. 2923
1Pe 4: 5 account to him that is ready to j the quick 2919
Rev 6:10 dost thou not j and avenge our blood on 2919
19:11 and in righteousness he doth j and 2919

JUDGED (63) [JUDGE]

Ge 30: 6 God hath j me, and hath also heard my 1777
Ex 18:26 they j the people at all seasons: the hard 8199
18:26 but every small matter they j themselves. 8199
Jdg 3:10 and he j Israel, and went out to war: 8199
4: 4 wife of Lapidoth, she j Israel at that time. 8199
10: 2 he j Israel twenty and three years, and died, 8199
10: 3 and j Israel twenty and two years. 8199
12: 7 Jephthah j Israel six years. Then died 8199
12: 8 And after him Ibzan of Beth-lehem j Israel. 8199
12: 9 for his sons. And he j Israel seven years. 8199
12:11 after him Elon, a Zebulonite, j Israel; and 8199
12:11 judged Israel; and he j Israel ten years. 8199
12:13 the son of Hillel, a Pirathonite, j Israel. 8199
12:14 ten ass colts: and he j Israel eight years. 8199
15:20 he j Israel in the days of the Philistines 8199
16:31 his father. And he j Israel twenty years. 8199
1Sa 4:18 and heavy. And he had j Israel forty years. 8199
7: 6 Samuel j the children of Israel in Mizpeh. 8199
7:15 And Samuel j Israel all the days of his life. 8199
7:16 and Mizpeh, and j Israel in all those places. 8199
7:17 there he j Israel; and there he built an altar 8199
1Ki 3:28 heard of the judgment which the king had j; 8199
2Ki 23:22 from the days of the judges that j Israel, 8199
Ps 9:19 let the heathen be j in thy sight. 8199
37:33 in his hand, nor condemn him when he is j. 8199
109: 7 When he shall be j, let him be condemned: 8199
Jer 22:16 He j the cause of the poor and needy; then 1777
Eze 16:38 that break wedlock and shed blood are j; 4941
16:52 Thou also, which hast j thy sisters, 6419
28:23 the wounded shall be j in the midst of her 5307
35:11 known amongst them, when I have j thee. 8199
36:19 and according to their doings I j them. 8199
Da 9:12 against us, and against our judges that j us, 8199
Mt 7: 1 Judge not, that ye be not j. 2919
7: 2 with what judgment ye judge, ye shall be j: 2919
Lk 6:37 Judge not, and ye shall not be j: 2919
7:43 And he said unto him, Thou hast rightly j. 2919
Jn 16:11 because the prince of this world is j. 2919
Ac 16:15 If ye have j me to be faithful to the Lord, 2919
24: 6 and would have j according to our law. 2919
25: 9 and there be j of these *things* before me? 2919
25:10 judgment seat, where I ought to be j: 2919
25:20 and there be j of these *matters.* 2919
26: 6 am j for the hope of the promise made of 2919
Ro 2:12 as many as have sinned in the law shall be j 2919
3: 4 and mightest overcome when thou art j. 2919
3: 7 his glory; why yet am I also j as a sinner? 2919
1Co 2:15 all *things,* yet he himself is j of no *man.* 350
4: 3 a very small *thing* that I should be j of you, 350
5: 3 but present in spirit, have j already, 2919
6: 2 and if the world shall be j by you, are ye 2919
10:29 for why is my liberty j of another *man's* 2919
11:31 would judge ourselves, we should not be j. 2919
11:32 But when we are j, we are chastened of 2919
14:24 he is convinced of all, he is j of all: 350
Heb 11:11 she j him faithful who had promised. 2233
Jas 2:12 as they that shall be j by the law of liberty. 2919
1Pe 4: 6 that they might be j according to men in 2919
Rev 11:18 that *they* should be j, and that *thou* 2919
16: 5 and shalt be, because thou hast j thus. 2919
19: 2 for he hath j the great whore, which did 2919
20:12 the dead were j out of those *things* which 2919
20:13 they were j every man according to their 2919

JUDGES (52) [JUDGE]

Ex 21: 6 his master shall bring him unto the j; he shall 430
21:22 and he shall pay as the j determine. 6414
22: 8 of the house shall be brought unto the j, 430
22: 9 cause of both parties shall come before the j; 430
22: 9 *and* whom the j shall condemn, he shall pay 430
Nu 25: 5 Moses said unto the j of Israel, Slay ye 8199
Dt 1:16 I charged your j at that time, saying, 8199
16:18 J and officers shalt thou make thee in all 8199
19:17 before the priests and the j, which shall be 8199
19:18 the j shall make diligent inquisition: and 8199
21: 2 thy elders and thy j shall come forth, and 8199
25: 1 unto judgment, that *the j* may judge them; NIH
32:31 even our enemies themselves *being* j. 6414
Jos 8:33 and their elders, and officers, and their j, 8199
23: 2 for their j, and for their officers, and 8199
24: 1 and for their j, and for their officers; 8199
Jdg 2:16 Nevertheless the LORD raised up j, 8199
2:17 yet they would not hearken unto their j, 8199
2:18 when the LORD raised them up j, then 8199
Ru 1: 1 Now it came to pass in the days when the j 8199
1Sa 8: 1 was old, that he made his sons j over Israel. 8199
8: 2 Abiah: *they were* j in Beer-sheba. 8199
2Sa 7:11 *as* since the time that I commanded j *to be* 8199
2Ki 23:22 from the days of the j that judged Israel, 8199
1Ch 17: 6 spake I a word to any of the j of Israel, 8199
17:10 since the time that I commanded j *to be* 8199
23: 4 and six thousand *were* officers and j: 8199
26:29 business over Israel, for officers and j. 8199
2Ch 1: 2 to the j, and to every governor in all Israel, 8199
19: 5 he set j in the land throughout all 8199
19: 6 said to the j, Take heed what ye do: for ye 8199
Ezr 7:25 that *is* in thine hand, set magistrates and j, 1782
10:14 the elders of every city, and the j thereof, 8199
Job 9:24 he covereth the faces of the j thereof; if not, 8199
12:17 away spoiled, and maketh the j fools. 8199
31:11 yea, it *is* an iniquity *to be punished by* the j. 6414
Ps 2:10 O ye kings: be instructed, ye j of the earth. 8199
141: 6 When their j are overthrown in stony 8199
148:11 all people; princes, and all j of the earth: 8199
Pr 8:16 and nobles, *even* all the j of the earth. 8199
Isa 1:26 I will restore thy j as at the first, and 8199
40:23 he maketh the j of the earth as vanity. 8199
Da 3: 2 and the captains, the j, the treasurers, 148
3: 3 the governors and captains, the j, 148
9:12 against us, and against our j that judged us, 8199
Hos 7: 7 hot as an oven, and have devoured their j; 8199
13:10 thy j *of* whom thou saidst, Give me a king 8199
Zep 3: 3 *are* roaring lions; her j *are* evening wolves; 8199
Mt 12:27 *them* out? therefore they shall be your j. 2923
Lk 11:19 *them* out? therefore shall they be your j. 2923
Ac 13:20 And after that he gave *unto them* j about 2923
Jas 2: 4 and are become j of evil thoughts? 2923

JUDGEST (8) [JUDGE]

Ps 51: 4 thou speakest, *and* be clear when thou j. 8199
Jer 11:20 that j righteously, that triest the reins and 8199
Ro 2: 1 O man, whosoever thou art that j: 2919
2: 1 for wherein thou j another, 2919
2: 1 for thou that j doest the same *things.* 2919
2: 3 that j them which do such *things,* and 2919
14: 4 Who art thou that j another *man's* servant? 2919
Jas 4:12 and to destroy: who art thou that j another? 2919

JUDGETH (17) [JUDGE]

Job 21:22 seeing he j those that are high. 8199
36:31 For by them j he the people; he giveth meat 1777
Ps 7:11 God j the righteous, and God is angry *with* 8199
58:11 verily he is a God that j in the earth. 8199
82: 1 of the mighty; he j among the gods. 8199
Pr 29:14 The king that faithfully j the poor, 8199
Jn 5:22 For the Father j no *man,* but 2919
8:50 own glory: there is *one* that seeketh and j. 2919
12:48 not my words, hath *one* that j him: 2919
1Co 2:15 But he that is spiritual j all *things,* yet he 350
4: 4 hereby justified: but he that j me is the Lord. 350
5:13 But them that are without God j 2919
Jas 4:11 and j his brother, speaketh evil of the law, 2919
4:11 speaketh evil of the law, and j the law: 2919
1Pe 1:17 who without respect of persons j according 2919
2:23 committed *himself* to him that j 2919
Rev 18: 8 for strong *is* the Lord God who j her. 2919

J

JUDGING (6) [JUDGE]

2Ki 15: 5 over the house, j the people of the land. 8199
2Ch 26:21 the king's house, j the people of the land. 8199
Ps 9: 4 my cause; thou satest in the throne j right. 8199
Isa 16: 5 j, and seeking judgment, and 8199
Mt 19:28 twelve thrones, j the twelve tribes of Israel. 2919
Lk 22:30 sit on thrones j the twelve tribes of Israel. 2919

JUDGMENT (294) [JUDGE]

Ge 18:19 the way of the LORD, to do justice and j; 4941
Ex 12:12 all the gods of Egypt I will execute j: 8201
21:31 according to this j shall it be done unto 4941
23: 2 in a cause to decline after many to wrest *j:* NIH
23: 6 Thou shalt not wrest the j of thy poor in his 4941
28:15 thou shalt make the breastplate of j *with* 4941
28:29 Israel in the breastplate of j upon his heart, 4941
28:30 thou shalt put in the breastplate of j 4941
28:30 Aaron shall bear the j of the children of 4941
Lev 19:15 Ye shall do no unrighteousness in j: 4941
19:35 Ye shall do no unrighteousness in j, 4941
Nu 27:11 be unto the children of Israel a statute of j, 4941
27:21 who shall ask *counsel* for him after the j of 4941
35:12 until he stand before the congregation in j. 4941
35:29 So these *things* shall be for a statute of j 4941
Dt 1:17 Ye shall not respect persons in j; *but* 4941
1:17 afraid of the face of man; for the j *is* God's: 4941
10:18 He doth execute the j of the fatherless and 4941
16:18 and they shall judge the people *with* just j. 4941
16:19 Thou shalt not wrest j; thou shalt not 4941
17: 8 If there arise a matter too hard for thee in j, 4941
17: 9 and they shall shew thee the sentence of j: 4941
17:11 according to the j which they shall tell thee, 4941
24:17 Thou shalt not pervert the j of the stranger, 4941
25: 1 they come unto j, that *the judges* may judge 4941
27:19 Cursed *be* he that perverteth the j of 4941
32: 4 for all his ways *are* j: a God of truth and 4941
32:41 and mine hand take hold on j; 4941
Jos 20: 6 until he stand before the congregation for j, 4941
Jdg 4: 5 the children of Israel came up to her for j. 4941
5:10 ye that sit in j, and walk by the way. 4055
1Sa 8: 3 after lucre, and took bribes, and perverted j. 4941
2Sa 8:15 David executed j and justice unto all his 4941
15: 2 had a controversy came to the king for j, 4941
15: 6 to all Israel that came to the king for j: 4941
1Ki 3:11 for thyself understanding to discern j; 4941
3:28 all Israel heard of the j which the king had 4941
3:28 that the wisdom of God *was* in him, to do j. 4941
7: 7 where he might judge, *even* the porch of j: 4941
10: 9 made he thee king, to do j and justice. 4941
20:40 So *shall* thy j *be;* thyself hast decided *it.* 4941
2Ki 25: 6 to Riblah; and they gave j upon him. 4941
1Ch 18:14 executed j and justice among all his people. 4941
2Ch 9: 8 he thee king over them, to do j and justice. 4941
19: 6 the LORD, who *is* with you in the j. 1697+4941
19: 8 for the j of the LORD, and 4941
20: 9 *as* the sword, j, or pestilence, or famine, 8196
22: 8 that when Jehu was **executing** j upon 8199
24:24 So they executed j against Joash. 8201
Ezr 7:26 let j be executed speedily upon him, 1780
Est 1:13 manner towards all that knew law and j: 1779
Job 8: 3 Doth God pervert j? or doth the Almighty 4941
9:19 if of j, who shall set me a time *to plead?* 4941
9:32 *and* we should come together in j. 4941
14: 3 a one, and bringest me into j with thee? 4941
19: 7 am not heard: I cry aloud, but *there is* no j. 4941
19:29 of the sword, that ye may know *there is* a j. 1779
22: 4 fear of thee? will he enter with thee into j? 4941
27: 2 *As* God liveth, *who* hath taken away my j; 4941

Job 29:14 my j *was* as a robe and a diadem. 4941
32: 9 neither do the aged understand j. 4941
34: 4 Let us choose to us j: let us know among 4941
34: 5 and God hath taken away my j. 4941
34:12 neither will the Almighty pervert j. 4941
34:23 *right;* that *he* should enter into j with God. 4941
35:14 thou shalt not see him, *yet* j *is* before him; 1779
36:17 thou hast fulfilled the j of the wicked: 1779
36:17 the wicked: j and justice take hold on *thee.* 1779
37:23 in power, and *in* j, and *in* plenty of justice: 4941
40: 8 Wilt thou also disannul my j? wilt thou 4941
Ps 1: 5 the ungodly shall not stand in the j, 4941
7: 6 awake for me *to* the j *that* thou hast 4941
9: 7 for ever: he hath prepared his throne for j. 4941
9: 8 he shall **minister** j to the people in 1777
9:16 The LORD is known *by* the j *which* he 4941
25: 9 The meek will he guide in j: and the meek 4941
33: 5 He loveth righteousness and j: the earth is 4941
35:23 Stir up thyself, and awake to my j, 4941
37: 6 as the light, and thy j as the noonday. 4941
37:28 For the LORD loveth j, and forsaketh not 4941
37:30 and his tongue talketh of j. 4941
72: 2 with righteousness, and thy poor with j. 4941
76: 8 Thou didst cause j to be heard from 1779
76: 9 When God arose to j, to save all the meek 4941
89:14 and j *are* the habitation of thy throne: 4941
94:15 j shall return unto righteousness: and all 4941
97: 2 and j *are* the habitation of his throne. 4941
99: 4 The king's strength also loveth j; thou dost 4941
99: 4 thou executest j and righteousness in Jacob. 4941
101: 1 I will sing of mercy and j: unto thee, 4941
103: 6 and j for all that are oppressed. 4941
106: 3 Blessed *are* they that keep j, *and he* that 4941
106:30 stood up Phinehas, and **executed** j: and 6419
111: 7 The works of his hands *are* verity and j; 4941
119:66 Teach me good j and knowledge: for I have 2940
119:84 when wilt thou execute j on them that 4941
119:121 I have done j and justice: leave me not to 4941
119:149 O LORD, quicken me according to thy j. 4941
122: 5 For there are set thrones of j, the thrones of 4941
143: 2 enter not into j with thy servant: for in thy 4941
146: 7 Which executeth j for the oppressed: 4941
149: 9 To execute upon them the j written: 4941
Pr 1: 3 of wisdom, justice, and j, and equity; 4941
2: 8 *He* keepeth the paths of j, and 4941
2: 9 understand righteousness, and j, and equity; 4941
8:20 in the midst of the paths of j: 4941
13:23 but there is *that is* destroyed for want of j. 4941
16:10 the king: his mouth transgresseth not in j. 4941
17:23 out of the bosom to pervert the ways of j. 4941
18: 5 the wicked, to overthrow the righteous in j. 4941
19:28 An ungodly witness scorneth j: and 4941
20: 8 A king that sitteth in the throne of j 1779
21: 3 j *is* more acceptable to the LORD than 4941
21: 7 destroy them; because they refuse to do j. 4941
21:15 *It is* joy to the just to do j: but 4941
24:23 *is* not good to have respect of persons in j. 4941
28: 5 Evil men understand not j: but they that 4941
29: 4 The king by j stablisheth the land: but 4941
29:26 *every* man's j *cometh* from the LORD. 4941
31: 5 and pervert the j of any of the afflicted. 1779
Ecc 3:16 I saw under the sun the place of j, 4941
5: 8 violent perverting of j and justice in a 4941
8: 5 *man's* heart discerneth *both* time and j. 4941
8: 6 to every purpose there is time and j, 4941
11: 9 all these *things* God will bring thee into j. 4941
12:14 For God shall bring every work into j, 4941
Isa 1:17 seek j, relieve the oppressed, judge 4941
1:21 *it was* full of j; righteousness lodged in it; 4941
1:27 Zion shall be redeemed with j, and 4941
3:14 The LORD will enter into j with 4941
4: 4 from the midst thereof by the spirit of j, 4941
5: 7 he looked for j, but behold oppression; 4941
5:16 the LORD of hosts shall be exalted in j, 4941
9: 7 to stablish it with j and with justice from 4941
10: 2 To turn aside the needy from j, and to take 1779
16: 3 Take counsel, execute j; make thy shadow 6415
16: 5 and seeking j, and hasting righteousness. 4941
28: 6 for a spirit of j to him that sitteth in 4941
28: 6 a spirit of judgment to him that sitteth in j, 4941
28: 7 they err in vision, they stumble *in* j. 6417
28:17 J also will I lay to the line, and 4941
30:18 for the LORD *is* a God of j: blessed *are* all 4941
32: 1 in righteousness, and princes shall rule in j. 4941
32:16 j shall dwell in the wilderness, and 4941
33: 5 he hath filled Zion *with* j and 4941
34: 5 and upon the people of my curse, to j. 4941
40:14 taught him in the path of j, and taught him 4941
40:27 and my j is passed over from my God? 4941
41: 1 them speak: let us come near together to j. 4941
42: 1 he shall bring forth j to the Gentiles. 4941
42: 3 not quench: he shall bring forth j unto truth. 4941
42: 4 till he have set j in the earth: 4941
49: 4 *yet* surely my j *is* with the LORD, and 4941
51: 4 I will make my j to rest for a light of 4941
53: 8 He was taken from prison and from j: and 4941
54:17 every tongue *that* shall rise against thee in j 4941
56: 1 saith the LORD, Keep ye j, and do justice: 4941
59: 8 know not; and *there is* no j in their goings: 4941
59: 9 Therefore is j far from us, neither doth 4941
59:11 we look for j, but *there is* none; 4941
59:14 j is turned away backward, and 4941
59:15 and it displeased him that *there was* no j. 4941
61: 8 For I the LORD love j, I hate robbery for 4941
Jer 4: 2 in truth, in j, and in righteousness; 4941
5: 1 find a man, if there be *any* that executeth j, 4941
5: 4 way of the LORD, *nor* the j of their God. 4941
5: 5 way of the LORD, *and* the j of their God: 4941
7: 5 if ye throughly execute j between a man 4941
8: 7 my people know not the j of the LORD. 4941
9:24 j, and righteousness, in the earth: 4941
10:24 O LORD, correct me, but with j; not in 4941
21:12 Execute j in the morning, and deliver *him* 4941
22: 3 Execute ye j and righteousness, and 4941
22:15 do j and justice, *and* then *it was* well with 4941

Jer 23: 5 and shall execute j and justice in the earth. 4941
33:15 he shall execute j and righteousness in 4941
39: 5 land of Hamath, where he gave j upon him. 4941
48:21 j is come upon the plain country; 4941
48:47 saith the LORD. Thus far *is* the j of Moab. 4941
49:12 they whose j *was* not to drink of the cup 4941
51: 9 for her j reacheth unto heaven, and is lifted 4941
51:47 that I will **do** j upon the graven images of 6485
51:52 that I will **do** j upon her graven images: 6485
52: 9 land of Hamath; where he gave j upon him. 4941
Eze 18: 8 hath executed true j between man and man, 4941
23:10 for they had executed j upon her. 8196
23:24 I will set j before them, and they shall 4941
34:16 and the strong; I will feed them with j. 4941
39:21 all the heathen shall see my j that I have 4941
44:24 in controversy they shall stand in j; *and* 4941
45: 9 and spoil, and execute j and justice, 4941
Da 4:37 all whose works *are* truth, and his ways j: 1780
7:10 the j was set, and the books were opened. 1780
7:22 j *was* given to the saints of the most High; 1780
7:26 the j shall sit, and they shall take away his 1780
Hos 2:19 in j, and in lovingkindness, and in mercies. 4941
5: 1 for j *is* toward you, because ye have been a 4941
5:11 Ephraim *is* oppressed *and* broken in j, 4941
10: 4 thus j springeth up as hemlock in 4941
12: 6 keep mercy and j, and wait on thy God 4941
Am 5: 7 *Ye* who turn j to wormwood, and leave off 4941
5:15 love the good, and establish j in the gate: 4941
5:24 let j run down as waters, and 4941
6:12 for ye have turned j into gall, and the fruit 4941
Mic 3: 1 house of Israel; *is it* not for you to know j? 4941
3: 8 *of* j, and *of* might, to declare unto Jacob his 4941
3: 9 that abhor j, and pervert all equity. 4941
7: 9 he plead my cause, and execute j for me: 4941
Hab 1: 4 law is slacked, and j doth never go forth: 4941
1: 4 therefore wrong j proceedeth. 4941
1: 7 their j and their dignity shall proceed of 4941
1:12 O LORD, thou hast ordained them for j; 4941
Zep 2: 3 of the earth, which have wrought his j; 4941
3: 5 every morning doth he bring his j to light, 4941
Zec 7: 9 Execute true j, and shew mercy and 4941
8:16 **execute the** j of truth and peace in 4941+8199
Mal 2:17 in them; or, Where *is* the God of j? 4941
3: 5 I will come near to you to j; and I will be a 4941
Mt 5:21 shall kill shall be in danger of the j: *2920*
5:22 without a cause shall be in danger of the j: *2920*
7: 2 For with what j ye judge, ye shall be *2917*
10:15 of Sodom and Gomorrha in the day of j, *2920*
11:22 tolerable for Tyre and Sidon at the day of j, *2920*
11:24 for the land of Sodom in the day of j, *2920*
12:18 and he shall shew j to the Gentiles. *2920*
12:20 not quench, till he send forth j unto victory. *2920*
12:36 shall give account thereof in the day of j. *2920*
12:41 *The* men of Nineveh shall rise in j with this *2920*
12:42 *The* queen of the south shall rise up in the j *2920*
23:23 *matters* of the law, j, mercy, and faith: *2920*
27:19 When he was set down on the j **seat**, *968*
Mk 6:11 for Sodom and Gomorrha in the day of j, *2920*
Lk 10:14 more tolerable for Tyre and Sidon at the j, *2920*
11:31 *The* queen of the south shall rise up in the j *2920*
11:32 *The* men of Nineveh shall rise up in the j *2920*
11:42 and pass over j and the love of God: *2920*
Jn 5:22 but hath committed all j unto the Son: *2920*
5:27 And hath given him authority to execute j *2920*
5:30 and my j is just; because I seek not mine *2920*
7:24 to the appearance, but judge righteous j. *2920*
8:16 And yet if I judge, my j is true: for I am not *2920*
9:39 Jesus said, For j I am come into this world, *2917*
12:31 Now is the j of this world: now shall *2920*
16: 8 world of sin, and of righteousness, and of j: *2920*
16:11 Of j, because the prince of this world is *2920*
18:28 they Jesus from Caiaphas unto the **hall of** j: *4232*
18:28 they themselves went not into the j **hall**, *4232*
18:33 Then Pilate entered into the j **hall** again, *4232*
19: 9 And went again into the j **hall**, and *4232*
19:13 sat down in the j **seat** in a place *that is* called *968*
Ac 8:33 In his humiliation his j was taken away: *2920*
18:12 against Paul, and brought him to the j **seat**, *968*
18:16 And he drave them from the j **seat**. *968*
18:17 and beat *him* before the j **seat**. *968*
23:35 him to be kept in Herod's j **hall**. *4232*
24:25 and j to come, Felix trembled, *2917*
25: 6 and the next day sitting in the j **seat**, *968*
25:10 Then said Paul, I stand at Cesar's j **seat**, *968*
25:15 *me,* desiring *to have* j against him. *1349*
25:17 on the morrow I sat on the j **seat**, and *968*
Ro 1:32 Who knowing the j of God, that they which *1345*
2: 2 But we are sure that the j of God is *2917*
2: 3 that thou shalt escape the j of God? *2917*
2: 5 and revelation of the **righteous** j of God; *1341*
5:16 for the j *was* by one to condemnation, but *2917*
5:18 Therefore as by the offence of one *j came* NIG
14:10 for we shall all stand before the j **seat** of *968*
1Co 1:10 in the same mind and in the same j. *1106*
4: 3 I should be judged of you, or of man's j: *2250*
7:25 yet I give *my* j, as one that hath obtained *1106*
7:40 she is happier if she so abide, after my j: *1106*
2Co 5:10 For we must all appear before the j **seat** of *968*
Gal 5:10 but he that troubleth you shall bear *his* j, *2917*
Php 1: 9 yet more and more in knowledge and *in* all j; *144*
2Th 1: 5 *Which is* a manifest token of the righteous j *2920*
1Ti 5:24 sins are open beforehand, going before to j; *2920*
Heb 6: 2 of resurrection of the dead, and of eternal j. *2917*
9:27 unto men once to die, but after this the j: *2920*
10:27 But a certain fearful looking for of j and *2920*
Jas 2: 6 and draw you before the j **seats**? *2922*
2:13 For he shall have j without mercy, that hath *2920*
2:13 no mercy; and mercy rejoiceth against j. *2920*
1Pe 4:17 For the time *is come* that j must begin at *2917*
2Pe 2: 3 whose j now of a long time lingereth not, *2917*
2: 4 chains of darkness, *to be* reserved unto j; *2920*
2: 9 to reserve the unjust unto the day of j *to be* *2920*
3: 7 reserved unto fire against the day of j and *2920*
1Jn 4:17 that we may have boldness in the day of j: *2920*
Jude 1: 6 under darkness unto the j of the great day. *2920*

Jude 1:15 To execute j upon all, and to convince all *2920*
Rev 14: 7 glory to him; for the hour of his j is come: *2920*
17: 1 I will shew unto thee the j of the great *2917*
18:10 mighty city! for in one hour is thy j come. *2920*
20: 4 sat upon them, and j was given unto them: *2917*

JUDGMENTS (127) [JUDGE]

Ex 6: 6 with a stretched out arm, and with great j: 8201
7: 4 out of the land of Egypt by great j. 8201
21: 1 Now these *are* the j which thou shalt set 4941
24: 3 all the words of the LORD, and all the j: 4941
Lev 18: 4 Ye shall do my j, and keep mine 4941
18: 5 therefore keep my statutes, and my j: 4941
18:26 therefore keep my statutes and my j, 4941
19:37 all my statutes, and all my j, and do them: 4941
20:22 all my statutes, and all my j, and do them: 4941
25:18 my statutes, and keep my j, and do them; 4941
26:15 or if your soul abhor my j, so that *ye* will 4941
26:43 even because they despised my j, and 4941
26:46 These *are* the statutes and j and laws, 4941
Nu 33: 4 their gods also the LORD executed j. 8201
35:24 the revenger of blood according to these j: 4941
36:13 These *are* the commandments and the j, 4941
Dt 4: 1 O Israel, unto the statutes and unto the j, 4941
4: 5 Behold, I have taught you statutes and j, 4941
4: 8 that hath statutes and j *so* righteous as all 4941
4:14 me at that time to teach you statutes and j, 4941
4:45 the testimonies, and the statutes, and the j, 4941
5: 1 and j which I speak in your ears *this* day, 4941
5:31 the statutes, and the j, which thou shalt 4941
6: 1 the commandments, the statutes, and the j, 4941
6:20 the testimonies, and the statutes, and the j, 4941
7:11 and the statutes, and the j, 4941
7:12 if ye hearken to these j, and keep, and 4941
8:11 his j, and his statutes, which I command 4941
11: 1 and his j, and his commandments alway. 4941
11:32 and j which I set before you *this* day. 4941
12: 1 These *are* the statutes and j, which ye shall 4941
26:16 commanded thee to do these statutes and j: 4941
26:17 and his j, and to hearken unto his voice: 4941
30:16 and his statutes and his j, 4941
33:10 They shall teach Jacob thy j, and Israel thy 4941
33:21 justice of the LORD, and his j with Israel. 4941
2Sa 22:23 For all his j *were* before me: and *as for* his 4941
1Ki 2: 3 and his j, and his testimonies, 4941
6:12 execute my j, and keep all my 4941
8:58 and his statutes, and his j, 4941
9: 4 *and* wilt keep my statutes and my j: 4941
11:33 *to keep* my statutes and my j, as *did* David 4941
1Ch 16:12 his wonders, and the j of his mouth; 4941
16:14 LORD our God; his j *are* in all the earth. 4941
22:13 j which the LORD charged Moses with 4941
28: 7 to do my commandments and my j, 4941
2Ch 7:17 and shalt observe my statutes and my j; 4941
19:10 and commandment, statutes and j, 4941
Ezr 7:10 to do *it,* and to teach in Israel statutes and j. 4941
Ne 1: 7 nor the statutes, nor the j, 4941
9:13 gavest them right j, and true laws, 4941
9:29 sinned against thy j, (which if a man do, 4941
10:29 LORD our Lord, and his j and his statutes; 4941
Ps 10: 5 thy j *are* far above out of his sight: 4941
18:22 For all his j *were* before me, and I did not 4941
19: 9 the j of the LORD *are* true *and* 4941
36: 6 the great mountains; thy j *are* a great deep: 4941
48:11 of Judah be glad, because of thy j. 4941
72: 1 Give the king thy j, O God, and 4941
89:30 forsake my law, and walk not in my j; 4941
97: 8 because of thy j, O LORD. 4941
105: 5 his wonders, and the j of his mouth; 4941
105: 7 LORD our God: his j *are* in all the earth. 4941
119: 7 when I shall have learned thy righteous j. 4941
119:13 With my lips have I declared all the j of thy 4941
119:20 longing *that it hath* unto thy j at all times. 4941
119:30 way of truth: thy j have I laid *before me.* 4941
119:39 reproach which I fear: for thy j *are* good. 4941
119:43 out of my mouth; for I have hoped in thy j. 4941
119:52 I remembered thy j of old, O LORD; and 4941
119:62 thanks unto thee because of thy righteous j. 4941
119:75 that thy j *are* right, and *that* thou *in* 4941
119:102 I have not departed from thy j: for thou hast 4941
119:106 perform *it,* that *I* will keep thy righteous j. 4941
119:108 my mouth, O LORD, and teach me thy j. 4941
119:120 for fear of thee; and I am afraid of thy j. 4941
119:137 *art* thou, O LORD, and upright *are* thy j. 4941
119:156 O LORD: quicken me according to thy j. 4941
119:160 every one of thy righteous j *endureth* for 4941
119:164 do I praise thee because of thy righteous j. 4941
119:175 it shall praise thee; and let thy j help me. 4941
147:19 his statutes and his j unto Israel. 4941
147:20 *as for his* j, they have not known them. 4941
Pr 19:29 J are prepared for scorners, and stripes for 8201
Isa 26: 8 Yea, *in* the way of thy j, O LORD, 4941
26: 9 for when thy j *are* in the earth, 4941
Jer 1:16 I will utter my j against them touching all 4941
12: 1 yet let me talk with thee of *thy* j. 4941
Eze 5: 6 she hath changed my j into wickedness 4941
5: 6 for they have refused my j, and my statutes, 4941
5: 7 in my statutes, neither have kept my j, 4941
5: 7 neither have done according to the j of 4941
5: 8 will execute j in the midst of thee in 4941
5:10 I will execute j in thee, and the whole 8201
5:15 when I shall execute j in thee in anger and 8201
11: 9 of strangers, and will execute j among you. 8201
11:12 neither executed my j, but have done after 4941
14:21 much more when I send my four sore j 8201
16:41 execute j upon thee in the sight of many 8201
18: 9 and hath kept my j, to deal truly; 4941
18:17 hath executed my j, hath walked in my 4941
20:11 shewed them my j, which *if* a man do, he 4941
20:13 they despised my j, which *if* a man do, he 4941
20:16 Because they despised my j, and walked 4941
20:18 neither observe their j, nor defile 4941
20:19 in my statutes, and keep my j, and do them; 4941
20:21 neither kept my j to do them, which *if* a 4941
20:24 Because they had not executed my j, but 4941

Eze 20:25 and j whereby they should not live; 4941
23:24 they shall judge thee according to their j. 4941
25:11 I will execute j upon Moab; and they shall 8201
28:22 when I shall have executed j in her, and 8201
28:26 when I have executed j upon all those that 8201
30:14 set fire in Zoan, and will execute j in No. 8201
30:19 Thus will I execute j in Egypt: and 8201
36:27 and ye shall keep my j, and do them. 4941
37:24 they shall also walk in my j, and 4941
44:24 and they shall judge it according to my j: 4941
Da 9: 5 departing from thy precepts and from thy j: 4941
Hos 6: 5 and thy j are as the light that goeth forth. 4941
Zep 3:15 The LORD hath taken away thy j, he hath 4941
Mal 4: 4 Horeb for all Israel, with the statutes and j. 4941
Ro 11:33 how unsearchable are his j, and his ways 2917
1Co 6: 4 ye have j of things pertaining to this life, 2922
Rev 15: 4 before thee; for thy j are made manifest. 1345
16: 7 God Almighty, true and righteous are thy j. 2920
19: 2 For true and righteous are his j: for he hath 2920

JUDITH (1)
Ge 26:34 to wife J the daughter of Beeri the Hittite, 3067

JUG See CRUSE

JUICE (1)
SS 8: 2 of spiced wine, of the j of my pomegranate. 6071

JULIA (1)
Ro 16:15 and J, Nereus, and his sister, and Olympas, 2456

JULIUS (2)
Ac 27: 1 certain other prisoners unto one named J, 2457
27: 3 And J courteously entreated Paul, and 2457

JUMPING (1)
Na 3: 2 of the pransing horses, and of the j chariots. 7540

JUNIA (1)
Ro 16: 7 Salute Andronicus and J, my kinsmen, and 2458

JUNIAS See JUNIA

JUNIPER (4)
1Ki 19: 4 and came and sat down under a j tree: 7574
19: 5 as he lay and slept under a j tree, 7574
Job 30: 4 by the bushes, and j roots for their meat. 7574
Ps 120: 4 Sharp arrows of the mighty, with coals of j. 7574

JUPITER (3)
Ac 14:12 And they called Barnabas, J; and Paul, 2203
14:13 Then the priest of J, which was before their 2203
19:35 and of the image which fell down from J? 1356

JURISDICTION (1)
Lk 23: 7 he knew that he belonged unto Herod's j, 1849

JUSHABHESED (1)
1Ch 3:20 Ohel, and Berechiah, and Hasadiah, J, five. 3142

JUST (94) [JUSTICE, JUSTIFICATION, JUSTIFIED, JUSTIFIER, JUSTIFIETH, JUSTIFY, JUSTIFYING, JUSTLY, UNJUST]
Ge 6: 9 Noah was a j man and perfect in his 6662
Lev 19:36 J balances, just weights, a just ephah, and 6664
19:36 j weights, a just ephah, and a just hin, 6664
19:36 just weights, a j ephah, and a just hin, 6664
19:36 just weights, a just ephah, and a j hin, 6664
Dt 16:18 they shall judge the people with j 6664
16:20 That which is altogether j shalt thou 6664+6664
25:15 But thou shalt have a perfect and j weight, 6664
25:15 a perfect and j measure shalt thou have: 6664
32: 4 and without iniquity, j and right is he. 6662
2Sa 23: 3 He that ruleth over men must be j, ruling in 6662
Ne 9:33 Howbeit thou art j in all that is brought 6662
Job 4:17 Shall mortal man be more j than God? 6663
9: 2 a truth: but how should man be j with God? 6663
12: 4 the j upright man is laughed to scorn. 6662
27:17 He may prepare it, but the j shall put it on, 6662
33:12 Behold, in this thou art not j: I will answer 6663
34:17 and wilt thou condemn him that is most j? 6662
Ps 7: 9 wicked come to an end; but establish the j: 6662
37:12 The wicked plotteth against the j, and 6662
Pr 3:33 but he blesseth the habitation of the j. 6662
4:18 the path of the j is as the shining light, 6662
9: 9 teach a j man, and he will increase in 6662
10: 6 Blessings are upon the head of the j: but 6662
10: 7 The memory of the j is blessed: but 6662
10:20 The tongue of the j is as choice silver: 6662
10:31 The mouth of the j bringeth forth wisdom: 6662
11: 1 to the LORD: but a j weight is his delight. 8003
11: 9 through knowledge shall the j be delivered. 6662
12:13 his lips: but the j shall come out of trouble. 6662
12:21 There shall no evil happen to the j: but 6662
13:22 the wealth of the sinner is laid up for the j. 6662
16:11 A j weight and balance are the LORD'S: 4941
17:15 the wicked, and he that condemneth the j, 6662
17:26 Also to punish the j is not good, nor to 6662
18:17 He that is first in his own cause seemeth j; 6662
20: 7 The j man walketh in his integrity: 6662
21:15 It is joy to the j to do judgment: but 6662
24:16 For a j man falleth seven times, and 6662
29:10 hate the upright: but the j seek his soul. 3477
29:27 An unjust man is an abomination to the j: 6662
Ecc 7:15 there is a j man that perisheth in his 6662
7:20 For there is not a j man upon earth, 6662
8:14 that there be j men, unto whom it 6662
Isa 26: 7 The way of the j is uprightness: thou, 6662
26: 7 most upright, dost weigh the path of the j. 6662
29:21 and turn aside the j for a thing of nought. 6662
45:21 a j God and a saviour; there is none beside 6662
La 4:13 that have shed the blood of the j in 6662
Eze 18: 5 if a man be j, and do that which is lawful 6662
Eze 18: 9 he is j, he shall surely live, saith the Lord 6662
45:10 Ye shall have j balances, and a just ephah, 6664
45:10 just balances, and a j ephah, and a just bath. 6664
45:10 just balances, and a just ephah, and a j bath. 6664
Hos 14: 9 are right, and the j shall walk in them: 6662
Am 5:12 they afflict the j, they take a bribe, and 6662
Hab 2: 4 in him: but the j shall live by his faith. 6662
Zep 3: 5 The j LORD is in the midst thereof; 6662
Zec 9: 9 he is j, and having salvation; lowly, and 6662
Mt 1:19 being a j man, and not willing to make her 1342
5:45 and sendeth rain on the j and on the unjust. 1342
13:49 and sever the wicked from among the j, 1342
27:19 Have thou nothing to do with that j man: 1342
27:24 I am innocent of the blood of this j person: 1342
Mk 6:20 knowing that he was a j man and a holy, 1342
Lk 1:17 and the disobedient to the wisdom of the j; 1342
2:25 and the same man was j and devout, 1342
14:14 be recompensed at the resurrection of the j. 1342
15: 7 nine j persons which need no repentance. 1342
20:20 which should feign themselves j men, that 1342
23:50 and he was a good man, and a j: 1342
Jn 5:30 and my judgment is j; because I seek not 1342
Ac 3:14 But ye denied the Holy One and the J, and 1342
7:52 shewed before of the coming of the J One; 1342
10:22 a j man, and one that feareth God, and 1342
22:14 and see that J One, and shouldest hear 1342
24:15 of the dead, both of the j and unjust. 1342
Ro 1:17 as it is written, The j shall live by faith. 1342
2:13 (For not the hearers of the law are j before 1342
3: 8 good may come? whose damnation is j. 1738
3:26 that he might be j, and the justifier of him 1342
7:12 the commandment holy, and j, and good. 1342
Gal 3:11 it is evident: for, The j shall live by faith. 1342
Php 4: 8 whatsoever things are j, whatsoever things 1342
Col 4: 1 give unto your servants that which is j and 1342
Tit 1: 8 of good men, sober, j, holy, temperate; 1342
Heb 2: 2 disobedience received a j recompence of 1738
10:38 Now the j shall live by faith: but if any man 1342
12:23 and to the spirits of j men made perfect, 1342
Jas 5: 6 Ye have condemned and killed the j; and 1342
1Pe 3:18 the j for the unjust, that he might bring us 1342
2Pe 2: 7 And delivered j Lot, vexed with the filthy 1342
1Jn 1: 9 he is faithful and j to forgive us our sins, 1342
Rev 15: 3 j and true are thy ways, thou King of saints. 1342

JUSTICE (28) [JUST]
Ge 18:19 way of the LORD, to do j and judgment; 6666
Dt 33:21 he executed the j of the LORD, and 6666
2Sa 8:15 and j unto all his people. 6666
15: 4 might come unto me, and I would do him j. 6663
1Ki 10: 9 made he thee king, to do judgment and j. 6666
1Ch 18:14 and j among all his people. 6666
2Ch 9: 8 thee king over them, to do judgment and j 6666
Job 8: 3 or doth the Almighty pervert j? 6664
36:17 judgment and j take hold on thee. 4941
37:23 and in judgment, and in plenty of j: 6666
Ps 82: 3 fatherless: do j to the afflicted and needy. 6663
89:14 J and judgment are the habitation of thy 6664
119:121 I have done judgment and j: leave me not 6664
Pr 1: 3 of wisdom, j, and judgment, and equity; 6664
8:15 By me kings reign, and princes decree j. 6664
21: 3 To do j and judgment is more acceptable to 6666
Ecc 5: 8 perverting of judgment and j in a province, 6664
Isa 9: 7 and with j from henceforth even for ever. 6666
56: 1 the LORD, Keep ye judgment, and do j: 6666
58: 2 they ask of me the ordinances of j; 6664
59: 4 None calleth for j, nor any pleadeth for 6664
59: 9 far from us, neither doth j overtake us: 6666
59:14 away backward, and j standeth afar off: 6666
Jer 22:15 do judgment and j, and then it was well 6666
23: 5 shall execute judgment and j in the earth. 6666
31:23 O habitation of j, and mountain of holiness. 6664
50: 7 the habitation of j, even the LORD, 6664
Eze 45: 9 and spoil, and execute judgment and j, 6666

JUSTIFICATION (3) [JUST]
Ro 4:25 and was raised again for our j. 1347
5:16 but the free gift is of many offences unto j. 1345
5:18 free gift came upon all men unto j of life. 1347

JUSTIFIED (43) [JUST]
Job 11: 2 and should a man full of talk be j? 6663
13:18 ordered my cause; I know that I shall be j. 6663
25: 4 How then can man be j with God? or 6663
32: 2 because he j himself rather than God. 6663
Ps 51: 4 that thou mightest be j when thou speakest, 6663
143: 2 for in thy sight shall no man living be j. 6663
Isa 43: 9 forth their witnesses, that they may be j: 6663
43:26 declare thou, that thou mayest be j. 6663
45:25 the LORD shall all the seed of Israel be j, 6663
Jer 3:11 The backsliding Israel hath j herself more 6663
Eze 16:51 hast j thy sisters in all thine abominations 6663
16:52 thy shame, in that thou hast j thy sisters. 6663
Mt 11:19 sinners. But wisdom is j of her children. 1344
12:37 For by thy words thou shalt be j, and by thy 1344
Lk 7:29 that heard him, and the publicans, j God, 1344
7:35 But wisdom is j of all her children. 1344
18:14 this man went down to his house j rather 1344
Ac 13:39 And by him all that believe are j from all 1344
13:39 ye could not be j by the law of Moses. 1344
Ro 2:13 but the doers of the law shall be j. 1344
3: 4 That thou mightest be j in thy sayings, and 1344
3:20 the law there shall no flesh be j in his sight: 1344
3:24 Being j freely by his grace through 1344
3:28 Therefore we conclude that a man is j by 1344
4: 2 For if Abraham were j by works, he hath 1344
5: 1 Therefore being j by faith, we have peace 1344
5: 9 Much more then, being now j by his blood, 1344
8:30 and whom he called, them he also j: and 1344
8:30 and whom he j, them he also glorified. 1344
1Co 4: 4 nothing by myself; yet am I not hereby j: 1344
6:11 but ye are j in the name of the Lord Jesus, 1344
Gal 2:16 Knowing that a man is not j by the works 1344
2:16 that we might be j by the faith of Christ, 1344
Gal 2:16 by the works of the law shall no flesh be j. 1344
2:17 But if, while we seek to be j by Christ, 1344
3:11 But that no man is j by the law in the sight 1344
3:24 us unto Christ, that we might be j by faith. 1344
5: 4 whosoever of you are j by the law; 1344
1Ti 3:16 j in the Spirit, seen of angels, 1344
Tit 3: 7 That being j by his grace, we should be 1344
Jas 2:21 Was not Abraham our father j by works, 1344
2:24 Ye see then how that by works a man is j, 1344
2:25 Likewise also was not Rahab the harlot j by 1344

JUSTIFIER (1) [JUST]
Ro 3:26 and the j of him which believeth in Jesus. 1344

JUSTIFIETH (4) [JUST]
Pr 17:15 He that j the wicked, and he that 6663
Isa 50: 8 He is near that j me; who will contend with 6663
Ro 4: 5 but believeth on him that j the ungodly, 1344
8:33 the charge of God's elect? It is God that j: 1344

JUSTIFY (11) [JUST]
Ex 23: 7 slay thou not: for I will not j the wicked. 6663
Dt 25: 1 they shall j the righteous, and condemn 6663
Job 9:20 If I j myself, mine own mouth shall 6663
27: 5 God forbid that I should j you: till I die I 6663
33:32 answer me: speak, for I desire to j thee. 6663
Isa 5:23 Which j the wicked for reward, and 6663
53:11 shall my righteous servant j many; 6663
Lk 10:29 But he, willing to j himself, said unto Jesus, 1344
16:15 Ye are they which j yourselves before men; 1344
Ro 3:30 which shall j the circumcision by faith, and 1344
Gal 3: 8 foreseeing that God would j the heathen 1344

JUSTIFYING (2) [JUST]
1Ki 8:32 j the righteous, to give him according to his 6663
2Ch 6:23 by j the righteous, by giving him according 6663

JUSTLE (1)
Na 2: 4 they shall j one against another in 8264

JUSTLY (3) [JUST]
Mic 6: 8 to do j, and to love mercy, and to walk 4941
Lk 23:41 And we indeed j; for we receive the due 1346
1Th 2:10 and God also, how holily and j and 1346

JUSTUS (3)
Ac 1:23 who was surnamed J, and Matthias. 2459
18: 7 named J, one that worshipped God, 2459
Col 4:11 And Jesus, which is called J, who are of 2459

JUTTAH (2)
Jos 15:55 Maon, Carmel, and Ziph, and J, 3194
21:16 J with her suburbs, and Beth-shemesh with 3194

K

K

KAB (1)
2Ki 6:25 the fourth part of a k of dove's dung for 6894

KABZEEL (3)
Jos 15:21 the coast of Edom southward were K, 6909
2Sa 23:20 the son of a valiant man, of K, who had 6909
1Ch 11:22 the son of a valiant man of K, who had 6909

KADESH (17) [KADESH-BARNEA, MERIBAH-KADESH]
Ge 14: 7 which is K, and smote all the country of 6946
16:14 behold, it is between K and Bered. 6946
20: 1 dwelled between K and Shur, and 6946
Nu 13:26 unto the wilderness of Paran, to K; 6946
20: 1 the people abode in K; and Miriam died 6946
20:14 Moses sent messengers from K unto 6946
20:16 behold, we are in K, a city in the uttermost 6946
20:22 journeyed from K, and came unto mount 6946
27:14 that is the water of Meribah in K in 6946
33:36 in the wilderness of Zin, which is K. 6946
33:37 they removed from K, and pitched in 6946
Dt 1:46 So ye abode in K many days, 6946
Jdg 11:16 unto the Red sea, and came to K; 6946
11:17 would not consent: and Israel abode in K. 6946
Ps 29: 8 the LORD shaketh the wilderness of K. 6946
Eze 47:19 Tamar even to the waters of strife in K, 6946
48:28 from Tamar unto the waters of strife in K, 6946

KADESH-BARNEA (10) [KADESH]
Nu 32: 8 when I sent them from K to see the land. 6947
34: 4 forth thereof shall be from the south to K, 6947
Dt 1: 2 Horeb by the way of mount Seir unto K.) 6947
1:19 God commanded us; and we came to K. 6947
2:14 the space in which we came from K, 6947
9:23 when the LORD sent you from K, 6947
Jos 10:41 Joshua smote them from K even unto Gaza, 6947
14: 6 man of God concerning me and thee in K. 6947
14: 7 sent me from K to espy out the land; 6947
15: 3 ascended up on the south side unto K, and 6947

KADMIEL (8)
Ezr 2:40 the children of Jeshua and K, of 6934
3: 9 his sons and his brethren, K and his sons, 6934
Ne 7:43 of K, and of the children of Hodevah, 6934
9: 4 Jeshua, and Bani, K, Shebaniah, Bunni, 6934
9: 5 Jeshua and K, Bani, Hashabniah, 6934

Ne 10: 9 Binnui of the sons of Henadad, **K**; 6934
12: 8 Jeshua, Binnui, **K**, Sherebiah, Judah, *and* 6934
12:24 Sherebiah, and Jeshua the son of **K**, 6934

KADMONITES (1)
Ge 15:19 The Kenites, and the Kenizzites, and the **K**, 6935

KALLAI (1)
Ne 12:20 Of Sallai, **K**; of Amok, Eber; 7040

KAMON See CAMON

KANAH (3)
Jos 16: 8 from Tappuah westward *unto* the river **K**; 7071
17: 9 the coast descended *unto* the river **K**, 7071
19:28 and Rehob, and Hammon, and **K**, 7071

KAREAH (13)
Jer 40: 8 Johanan and Jonathan the sons of **K**, and 7143
40:13 Moreover Johanan the son of **K**, and all 7143
40:15 Johanan the son of **K** spake to Gedaliah in 7143
40:16 of Ahikam said unto Johanan the son of **K**, 7143
41:11 when Johanan the son of **K**, and all 7143
41:13 with Ishmael saw Johanan the son of **K**, 7143
41:14 and went unto Johanan the son of **K**. 7143
41:16 took Johanan the son of **K**, and all 7143
42: 1 Johanan the son of **K**, and Jezaniah the son 7143
42: 8 called he Johanan the son of **K**, and all 7143
43: 2 Johanan the son of **K**, and all the proud 7143
43: 4 So Johanan the son of **K**, and all 7143
43: 5 Johanan the son of **K**, and all the captains 7143

KARKA See KARKAA

KARKAA (1)
Jos 15: 3 up to Adar, and fetched a compass to **K**: 7173

KARKOR (1)
Jdg 8:10 Now Zebah and Zalmunna *were* in **K**, and 7174

KARNAIM See ASHTEROTH KARNAIM

KARTAH (1)
Jos 21:34 with her suburbs, and **K** with her suburbs, 7177

KARTAN (1)
Jos 21:32 with her suburbs, and **K** with her suburbs; 7178

KATTATH (1)
Jos 19:15 **K**, and Nahallal, and Shimron, and Idalah, 7005

KEBAR See CHEBAR

KEDAR (12)
Ge 25:13 Nebajoth; and **K**, and Adbeel, and Mibsam, 6938
1Ch 1:29 then **K**, and Adbeel, and Mibsam, 6938
Ps 120: 5 *in* Mesech, *that* I dwell in the tents of **K**! 6938
SS 1: 5 as the tents of **K**, as the curtains of 6938
Isa 21:16 a hireling, and all the glory of **K** shall fail: 6938
21:17 the mighty *men* of the children of **K**, 6938
42:11 *their voice*, the villages *that* **K** doth inhabit: 6938
60: 7 All the flocks of **K** shall be gathered 6938
Jer 2:10 send *unto* **K**, and consider diligently, and 6938
49:28 Concerning **K**, and concerning 6938
49:28 go up to **K**, and spoil the men of the east. 6938
Eze 27:21 Arabia, and all the princes of **K**, 6938

KEDEMAH (2)
Ge 25:15 Hadar, and Tema, Jetur, Naphish, and **K**: 6929
1Ch 1:31 Jetur, Naphish, and **K**. These *are* the sons 6929

KEDEMOTH (4)
Dt 2:26 **K** unto Sihon king of Heshbon *with* words 6932
Jos 13:18 And Jahazah, and **K**, and Mephaath, 6932
21:37 **K** with her suburbs, and Mephaath with her 6932
1Ch 6:79 **K** also with her suburbs, and Mephaath 6932

KEDESH (11) [KEDESH-NAPHTALI]
Jos 12:22 The king of **K**, one; the king of Jokneam of 6943
15:23 And **K**, and Hazor, and Ithnan, 6943
19:37 And **K**, and Edrei, and En-hazor, 6943
20: 7 they appointed **K** in Galilee in mount 6943
21:32 of Naphtali, **K** in Galilee with her suburbs, 6943
Jdg 4: 9 Deborah arose, and went with Barak to **K**. 6943
4:10 Barak called Zebulun and Naphtali to **K**; 6943
4:11 unto the plain of Zaanaim, which *is* by **K**. 6943
2Ki 15:29 and **K**, and Hazor, and Gilead, and Galilee, 6943
1Ch 6:72 **K** with her suburbs, Daberath with her 6943
6:76 **K** in Galilee with her suburbs, and 6943

KEDESH-NAPHTALI (1) [KEDESH, NAPHTALI]
Jdg 4: 6 Barak the son of Abinoam out of **K**, 5321+6943

KEDORLAOMER See CHEDORLAOMER

KEEP (362) [DOORKEEPER, DOORKEEPERS, KEEPER, KEEPERS, KEEPEST, KEEPETH, KEEPING, KEPT]
Ge 2:15 the garden of Eden to dress it and to **k** it. 8104
3:24 every way, to **k** the way of the tree of life. 8104
6:19 into the ark, to **k** *them* **alive** with thee; 2421
6:20 *sort* shall come unto thee, to **k** *them* **alive**. 2421
7: 3 to **k** seed **alive** upon the face of all 2421
17: 9 Thou shalt **k** my covenant therefore, thou, 8104
17:10 which ye shall **k**, between me and you and 8104
18:19 they shall **k** the way of the LORD, to do 8104
28:15 will **k** thee in all *places* whither thou goest, 8104
28:20 will **k** me in this way that I go, and 8104
30:31 for me, I will again feed *and* **k** thy flock: 8104
33: 9 my brother; **k** that thou hast unto thyself. 1961
41:35 and let them **k** food in the cities. 8104
Ex 6: 5 whom the Egyptians **k in bondage**; 5647
12: 6 ye shall **k** it *up* until the fourteenth 1961+4931
12:14 you shall **k** it a feast to the LORD 2287
12:14 you shall **k** it **a feast** by an ordinance for 2287
12:25 hath promised, that ye shall **k** this service. 8104
12:47 All the congregation of Israel shall **k** it. 6213
12:48 will **k** the passover to the LORD, let all 6213
12:48 and then let him come near and **k** it; 6213
13: 5 that thou shalt **k** this service in this month. 5647
13:10 **k** this ordinance in his season from year to 8104
15:26 his commandments, and **k** all his statutes, 8104
16:28 How long refuse ye to **k** my 8104
19: 5 **k** my covenant, then ye shall be a peculiar 8104
20: 6 that love me, and **k** my commandments. 8104
20: 8 Remember the sabbath day, to **k** it **holy**. 6942
22: 7 unto his neighbour money or stuff to **k**, 8104
22:10 or an ox, or a sheep, or any beast, to **k**; 8104
23: 7 **K** thee **far** from a false matter; and 7368
23:14 Three times thou shalt **k a feast** unto me in 2287
23:15 Thou shalt **k** the feast of unleavened bread: 8104
23:20 to **k** thee in the way, and to bring thee into 8104
31:13 Verily my sabbaths ye shall **k**: 8104
31:14 Ye shall **k** the sabbath therefore; for it *is* 8104
31:16 Wherefore the children of Israel shall **k** 8104
34:18 The feast of unleavened bread shalt thou **k**: 8104
Lev 6: 2 in **that which was delivered** him **to k**, 6487
6: 4 which was **delivered** him **to k**, 854+6485+6487
8:35 **k** the charge of the LORD, that ye die not: 8104
18: 4 and **k** mine ordinances, to walk therein: 8104
18: 5 Ye shall therefore **k** my statutes, and my 8104
18:26 Ye shall therefore **k** my statutes and my 8104
18:30 Therefore shall ye **k** mine ordinance, 8104
19: 3 and his father, and **k** my sabbaths: 8104
19:19 Ye shall **k** my statutes. Thou shalt not let 8104
19:30 Ye shall **k** my sabbaths, and reverence my 8104
20: 8 ye shall **k** my statutes, and do them: I *am* 8104
20:22 Ye shall therefore **k** all my statutes, and all 8104
22: 9 They shall therefore **k** mine ordinance, 8104
22:31 Therefore shall ye **k** my commandments, 8104
23:39 ye shall **k** a feast unto the LORD seven 2287
23:41 ye shall **k** it **a feast** unto the LORD 2282+2287
25: 2 shall the land **k a sabbath** unto 7673+7676
25:18 and **k** my judgments, and do them; 8104
26: 2 Ye shall **k** my sabbaths, and reverence my 8104
26: 3 and **k** my commandments, and do them; 8104
Nu 1:53 the Levites shall **k** the charge of 8104
3: 7 they shall **k** his charge, and the charge of 8104
3: 8 they shall **k** all the instruments of 8104
3:32 *have* the oversight of them that **k** 8104
6:24 The LORD bless thee, and **k** thee: 8104
8:26 to **k** the charge, and shall do no service. 8104
9: 2 Let the children of Israel also **k** 6213
9: 3 ye shall **k** it in his appointed season: 6213
9: 3 to all the ceremonies thereof, shall ye **k** it. 6213
9: 4 of Israel, that they should **k** the passover. 6213
9: 6 that they could not **k** the passover on that 6213
9:10 yet he shall **k** the passover unto 6213
9:11 of the second month at even they shall **k** it, 6213
9:12 ordinances of the passover they shall **k** it. 6213
9:13 a journey, and forbeareth to **k** the passover, 6213
9:14 and will **k** the passover unto the LORD; 6213
18: 3 they shall **k** thy charge, and the charge of 8104
18: 4 **k** the charge of the tabernacle of 8104
18: 5 ye shall **k** the charge of the sanctuary, and 8104
18: 7 thy sons with thee shall **k** your priest's 8104
29:12 ye shall **k a feast** unto the LORD 2282+2287
31:18 by lying with him, **k alive** for yourselves. 2421
31:30 which **k** the charge of the tabernacle of 8104
36: 7 **k** himself to the inheritance of the tribe of 1692
36: 9 shall **k** himself to his own inheritance. 1692
Dt 4: 2 that *ye* may **k** the commandments of 8104
4: 6 **K** therefore and do *them;* for this *is* your 8104
4: 9 heed to thyself, and **k** thy soul diligently, 8104
4:40 Thou shalt **k** therefore his statutes, and his 8104
5: 1 ye may learn them, and **k**, and do them. 8104
5:10 that love me and **k** my commandments. 8104
5:12 **K** the sabbath day to sanctify it, as 8104
5:15 the LORD thy God commanded thee to **k** 6213
5:29 and **k** all my commandments always, 8104
6: 2 to **k** all his statutes and his commandments, 8104
6:17 You shall **diligently k** 8104+8104
7: 8 he would **k** the oath which he had sworn 8104
7: 9 **k** his commandments to a thousand 8104
7:11 Thou shalt therefore **k** the commandments, 8104
7:12 to these judgments, and **k**, and do them, 8104
7:12 that the LORD thy God shall **k** unto thee 8104
8: 2 whether thou wouldest **k** his 8104
8: 6 Therefore thou shalt **k** the commandments 8104
10:13 To **k** the commandments of the LORD, 8104
11: 1 **k** his charge, and his statutes, and 8104
11: 8 Therefore shall ye **k** all the commandments 8104
11:22 For if ye shall **diligently k** all these 8104+8104
13: 4 **k** his commandments, and obey his voice, 8104
13:18 to **k** all his commandments which I 8104
16: 1 **k** the passover unto the LORD thy God: 6213
16:10 thou shalt **k** the feast of weeks unto 6213
16:15 Seven days shalt thou **k a solemn feast** 2287
17:19 to **k** all the words of this law and 8104
19: 9 If thou shalt **k** all these commandments to 8104
23: 9 then **k** thee from every wicked thing. 8104
23:23 which is gone out of thy lips thou shalt **k** 8104
26:16 thou shalt therefore **k** and do them with all 8104
26:17 to **k** his statutes, and his commandments, 8104
26:18 that *thou* shouldest **k** all his 8104
27: 1 **K** all the commandments which I command 8104
28: 9 if thou shalt **k** the commandments of 8104
28:45 to **k** his commandments and his statutes 8104
29: 9 **K** therefore the words of this covenant, 8104
30:10 to **k** his commandments and his statutes 8104
30:16 to **k** his commandments and his statutes 8104
Jos 6:18 in any wise **k** *yourselves* from the accursed 8104
10:18 of the cave, and set men by it for to **k** them: 8104
22: 5 to **k** his commandments, and to cleave unto 8104
23: 6 Be ye therefore very courageous to **k** and 8104
Jdg 2:22 whether they will **k** the way of the LORD 8104
2:22 as their fathers did **k** *it,* or not. 8104
3:19 who said, **K silence**. And all that stood by 2013
Ru 2:21 Thou shalt **k fast** by my young men, 1692
1Sa 2: 9 He will **k** the feet of his saints, and 8104
7: 1 sanctified Eleazar his son to **k** the ark of 8104
2Sa 8: 2 to death, and *with* one full line to **k alive**. 2421
15:16 *which were* concubines, to **k** the house. 8104
16:21 which he hath left to **k** the house; 8104
18:18 no son to **k** my name **in remembrance**: 2142
20: 3 whom he had left to **k** the house, and 8104
1Ki 2: 3 **k** the charge of the LORD thy God, 8104
2: 3 to **k** his statutes, *and* his commandments, 8104
3:14 to **k** my statutes and my commandments, 8104
6:12 **k** all my commandments to walk in them; 8104
8:25 **k** with thy servant David my father that 8104
8:58 to **k** his commandments, and his statutes, 8104
8:61 and to **k** his commandments, as at this day. 8104
9: 4 *and* wilt **k** my statutes and my judgments: 8104
9: 6 will not **k** my commandments *and* 8104
11:33 *to* **k** my statutes and my judgments, as *did* NIH
11:38 to **k** my statutes and my commandments, 8104
20:39 a man unto me, and said, **K** this man: 8104
2Ki 11: 6 so shall ye **k** the watch of the house, that it 8104
11: 7 even they shall **k** the watch of the house of 8104
17:13 and **k** my commandments *and* my statutes, 8104
23: 3 to **k** his commandments and his testimonies 8104
23:21 **K** the passover unto the LORD your God, 6213
1Ch 4:10 that thou wouldest **k** *me* from evil, that it 6213
12:33 of war, fifty thousand, which could **k rank**: 5737
12:38 All these men of war, that could **k** rank, 5737
22:12 that *thou* mayest **k** the law of the LORD 8104
23:32 that they should **k** the charge of 8104
28: 8 **k** and seek for all the commandments of 8104
29:18 **k** this for ever in the imagination of 8104
29:19 to **k** thy commandments, thy testimonies, 8104
2Ch 6:16 **k** with thy servant David my father *that* 8104
13:11 for we **k** the charge of the LORD our 8104
22: 9 had no power to **k still** the kingdom. 6113
23: 6 all the people shall **k** the watch of 8104
28:10 now ye purpose to **k under** the children of 3533
30: 1 to **k** the passover unto the LORD God of 6213
30: 2 to **k** the passover in the second month. 6213
30: 3 For they could not **k** it at that time, because 6213
30: 5 that *they* should come to **k** the passover 6213
30:13 **k** the feast of unleavened bread in 6213
30:23 the whole assembly took counsel to **k** other 6213
34:31 to **k** his commandments, and 8104
35:16 to **k** the passover, and to offer burnt 6213
35:18 neither did all the kings of Israel **k** such a 6213
Ezr 8:29 **k** *them,* until ye weigh *them* before 8104
Ne 1: 9 and **k** my commandments, and do them; 8104
12:27 to **k** the dedication with gladness, both with 6213
13:22 *that* they should come *and* **k** the gates, 8104
Est 3: 8 all people; neither **k** they the king's laws: 6213
9:21 that they should **k** the fourteenth day of 6213
9:27 that they would **k** these two days according 6213
Job 14:13 that thou wouldest **k** me **secret**, until thy 5641
20:13 it not; but **k** it **still** within his mouth: 4513
Ps 12: 7 Thou shalt **k** them, O LORD, thou shalt 8104
17: 8 **K** me as the apple of the eye, hide me 8104
19:13 **K back** thy servant also from 2820
22:29 and none can **k alive** his own soul. 2421
25:10 truth unto such as **k** his covenant and 5341
25:20 O **k** my soul, and deliver me: let me not be 8104
31:20 thou shalt **k** them **secretly** in a pavilion 6845
33:19 from death, and to **k** them **alive** in famine. 2421
34:13 **K** thy tongue from evil, and thy lips from 5341
35:22 **k** not **silence**: O Lord, be not far from me. 2790
37:34 **k** his way, and he shall exalt thee to inherit 8104
39: 1 I will **k** my mouth with a bridle, while 8104
41: 2 LORD will preserve him, and **k** him **alive**; 2421
50: 3 God shall come, and shall not **k silence**: 2790
78: 7 works of God, but **k** his commandments: 5341
83: 1 **K** not thou **silence**, O God: hold not thy 1824
89:28 My mercy will I **k** for him for evermore, 8104
89:31 my statutes, and **k** not my commandments; 8104
91:11 charge over thee, to **k** thee in all thy ways. 8104
103: 9 neither will he **k** *his anger* for ever. 5201
103:18 To such as **k** his covenant, and to those that 8104
105:45 might observe his statutes, and **k** his laws. 5341
106: 3 Blessed *are* they that **k** judgment, *and* 8104
113: 9 He **maketh** the barren *woman* **to k** house, 3427
119: 2 Blessed *are* they that **k** his testimonies, *and* 5341
119: 4 Thou hast commanded *us* to **k** thy precepts 8104
119: 5 O that my ways were directed to **k** thy 8104
119: 8 I will **k** thy statutes: O forsake me not 8104
119:17 thy servant, *that* I may live, and **k** thy word. 8104
119:33 of thy statutes; and I shall **k** it *unto* the end. 5341
119:34 me understanding, and I shall **k** thy law; 5341
119:44 So shall I **k** thy law continually for ever 8104
119:57 I have said that *I* would **k** thy words. 8104
119:60 and delayed not to **k** thy commandments. 8104
119:63 fear thee, and of them that **k** thy precepts. 8104
119:69 I will **k** thy precepts with *my* whole heart. 5341
119:88 so shall I **k** the testimony of thy mouth. 8104
119:100 than the ancients, because I **k** thy precepts. 5341
119:101 every evil way, that I might **k** thy word. 8104
119:106 I will perform *it,* that *I* will **k** thy righteous 8104
119:115 for I will **k** the commandments of my God. 5341
119:129 therefore doth my soul **k** them. 5341
119:134 oppression of man: so will I **k** thy precepts. 8104
119:136 mine eyes, because they **k** not thy law. 8104
119:145 hear me, O LORD: I will **k** thy statutes. 5341
119:146 save me, and I shall **k** thy testimonies. 8104
127: 1 except the LORD **k** the city, 8104
132:12 If thy children will **k** my covenant and 8104
140: 4 **K** me, O LORD, from the hands of 8104
141: 3 before my mouth; **k** the door of my lips. 5341
141: 9 **K** me from the snare *which* they have laid 8104
Pr 2:11 preserve thee, understanding shall **k** thee: 5341
2:20 good *men,* and **k** the paths of the righteous. 8104
3: 1 but let thine heart **k** my commandments: 5341
3:21 thine eyes: **k** sound wisdom and discretion: 5341
3:26 and shall **k** thy foot from being taken. 8104
4: 4 my words: **k** my commandments, and live. 8104
4: 6 love her, and she shall **k** thee. 5341
4:13 let *her* not go: **k** her; for she *is* thy life. 5341

Pr 4:21 **k** them in the midst of thine heart. 8104
4:23 **K** thy heart with all diligence; for out of it 5341
5: 2 and *that* thy lips may **k** knowledge. 5341
6:20 **k** thy father's commandment, and 5341
6:22 when thou sleepest, it shall **k** thee; and 8104
6:24 To **k** thee from the evil woman, from 8104
7: 1 **k** my words, and lay up my commandments 8104
7: 2 **K** my commandments, and live; and 8104
7: 5 That *they* may **k** thee from the strange 8104
8:32 for blessed *are they that* **k** my ways. 8104
22: 5 he that doth **k** his soul shall be far from 8104
22:18 For *it is* a pleasant *thing* if thou **k** them 8104
28: 4 but such as **k** the law contend with them. 8104
Ecc 3: 6 a time to **k**, and a time to cast away; 8104
3: 7 a time to **k silence**, and a time to speak; 2814
5: 1 **K** thy foot when thou goest to the house of 8104
8: 2 I *counsel thee* to **k** the king's 8104
12:13 Fear God, and **k** his commandments: 8104
SS 8:12 those that **k** the fruit thereof two hundred. 5201
Isa 26: 3 Thou wilt **k** *him in* perfect peace, *whose* 5341
27: 3 I the LORD do **k** it; I will water it every 5341
27: 3 lest *any* hurt it, I will **k** it night and day. 5341
41: 1 **K silence** before me, O islands; and let 2790
42: 6 will **k** thee, and give thee for a covenant of 5341
43: 6 Give *up;* and to the south, **K** not **back**: 3607
56: 1 the LORD, **K** ye judgment, and do justice: 8104
56: 4 unto the eunuchs that **k** my sabbaths, 8104
62: 6 mention of the LORD, **k** not silence, 3807.1
65: 6 I will not **k** silence, but will recompense, NIH
Jer 3: 5 will he **k** *it* to the end? Behold, thou hast 8104
3:12 the LORD, *and* I will not **k** *anger* for ever. 5201
31:10 and **k** him as a shepherd *doth* his flock. 8104
42: 4 unto you; I will **k** nothing **back** from you. 4513
La 2:10 of Zion sit upon the ground, *and* **k silence**: 1826
Eze 11:20 and **k** mine ordinances, and do them: 8104
18:21 **k** all my statutes, and do that which is 8104
20:19 and **k** my judgments, and do them; 8104
36:27 and ye shall **k** my judgments, and do *them*. 8104
43:11 that they may **k** the whole form thereof, 8104
44:16 unto me, and they shall **k** my charge. 8104
44:24 they shall **k** my laws and my statutes in all 8104
Da 9: 4 and to them that **k** his commandments; 8104
Hos 12: 6 **k** mercy and judgment, and wait on thy 8104
Am 5:13 Therefore the prudent shall **k silence** in that 1826
Mic 7: 5 **k** the doors of thy mouth from her that lieth 8104
Na 1:15 O Judah, **k** thy solemn feasts, perform thy 2287
2: 1 **k** the munition, watch the way, make *thy* 5341
Hab 2:20 let all the earth **k silence** before him. 2013
Zec 3: 7 if thou wilt **k** my charge, then thou shalt 8104
3: 7 shalt also **k** my courts, and I will give thee 8104
13: 5 for man taught me *to* **k** *cattle* from my NIH
14:16 of hosts, and to **k** the feast of tabernacles. 2287
14:18 come not up to **k** the feast of tabernacles. 2287
14:19 come not up to **k** the feast of tabernacles. 2287
Mal 2: 7 For the priest's lips should **k** knowledge, 8104
Mt 19:17 wilt enter into life, **k** the commandments. *5083*
26:18 I will **k** the passover at thy house with my *4160*
Mk 7: 9 of God, that ye may **k** your own tradition. *5083*
Lk 4:10 give his angels charge over thee, to **k** thee: *1314*
8:15 **k** *it*, and bring forth fruit with patience. *2722*
11:28 *are* they that hear the word of God, and **k** it. *5442*
19:43 thee round, and **k** thee **in** on every side, *4912*
Jn 8:51 I say unto you, If a man **k** my saying, *5083*
8:52 and thou sayest, If a man **k** my saying, *5083*
8:55 unto you: but I know him, and **k** his saying. *5083*
12:25 he that hateth his life in this world shall **k** it *5442*
14:15 If ye love me, **k** my commandments. *5083*
14:23 If a man love me, he will **k** my words: *5083*
15:10 If ye **k** my commandments, ye shall abide *5083*
15:20 kept my saying, they will **k** yours also. *5083*
17:11 **k** through thine own name those whom *5083*
17:15 that thou shouldest **k** them from the evil. *5083*
Ac 5: 3 and to **k back** *part* of the price of the land? *3557*
10:28 *thing* for a man *that is* a Jew to **k company**, *2853*
12: 4 to four quaternions of soldiers to **k** him; *5442*
15: 5 to command *them* to **k** the law of Moses. *5083*
15:24 *Ye must* be circumcised, and **k** the law: *5083*
15:29 from which if ye **k** yourselves, ye shall do *1301*
16: 4 they delivered them the decrees for to **k**, *5442*
16:23 charging the jailor to **k** them safely: *5083*
18:21 I must by all means **k** *this* feast that cometh *4160*
21:25 **k** themselves **from** things offered to idols, *5442*
24:23 And he commanded a centurion to **k** Paul, *5083*
Ro 2:25 verily profiteth, if thou **k** the law: *4238*
2:26 Therefore if the uncircumcision **k** *5442*
1Co 5: 8 Therefore let us **k the feast**, not with old *1858*
5:11 I have written unto you not to **k company**, *4874*
7:37 decreed in his heart that *he* will **k** his *5083*
9:27 But I **k under** my body, and bring *it* into *5299*
11: 2 me in all *things*, and **k** the ordinances, *2722*
14:28 let him **k silence** in the church; *4601*
14:34 Let your women **k silence** in the churches: *4601*
15: 2 if ye **k in memory** what I preached unto *2722*
2Co 11: 9 burdensome to you, and *so* will I **k** *myself*. *5083*
Gal 6:13 themselves who are circumcised **k** the law; *5442*
Eph 4: 3 Endeavouring to **k** the unity of the Spirit in *5083*
Php 4: 7 shall **k** your hearts and minds through *5432*
2Th 3: 3 shall stablish you, and **k** *you* from evil. *5442*
1Ti 5:22 partaker of other *men's* sins: **k** thyself pure. *5083*
6:14 That thou **k** *this* commandment without *5083*
6:20 **k** that which is committed to *thy* trust, *5442*
2Ti 1:12 I am persuaded that he is able to **k** that *5442*
1:14 **k** by the Holy Ghost which dwelleth in us. *5442*
Jas 1:27 *and* to **k** himself unspotted from the world. *5083*
2:10 For whosoever shall **k** the whole law, and *5083*
1Jn 2: 3 we know him, if we **k** his commandments. *5083*
3:22 because we **k** his commandments, and *5083*
5: 2 we love God, and **k** his commandments. *5083*
5: 3 love of God, that we **k** his commandments: *5083*
5:21 Little children, **k** yourselves from idols. *5442*
Jude 1:21 **K** yourselves in the love of God, *5083*
1:24 Now unto him that is able to **k** you **from** *5442*
Rev 1: 3 **k** those *things* which are written therein: *5083*
3:10 I also will **k** thee from the hour of *5083*
12:17 which **k** the commandments of God, and *5083*
14:12 here *are* they that **k** the commandments of *5083*
22: 9 of them which **k** the sayings of this book: *5083*

KEEPER (21) [KEEP]

Ge 4: 2 Abel was a **k** of sheep, but Cain was a tiller 7462
4: 9 he said, I know not: *Am* I my brother's **k**? 8104
39:21 gave him favour in the sight of the **k** of 8269
39:22 the **k** of the prison committed to Joseph's 8269
39:23 The **k** of the prison looked not to any thing 8269
1Sa 17:20 left the sheep with a **k**, and took, and went, 8104
17:22 David left his carriage in the hand of the **k** 8104
28: 2 Therefore will I make thee **k** of mine head 8104
2Ki 22:14 the son of Harhas, **k** of the wardrobe; 8104
2Ch 34:22 the son of Hasrah, **k** of the wardrobe; 8104
Ne 2: 8 a letter unto Asaph the **k** of the king's 8104
3:29 son of Shechaniah, the **k** of the east gate. 8104
Est 2: 3 the king's chamberlain, **k** of the women; 8104
2: 8 to the custody of Hegai, **k** of the women. 8104
2:15 the **k** of the women, appointed. 8104
Job 27:18 as a moth, and as a booth *that* the **k** maketh. 5341
Ps 121: 5 The LORD *is* thy **k**: the LORD *is* thy 8104
SS 1: 6 they made me the **k** of the vineyards; *but* 5201
Jer 35: 4 the son of Shallum, the **k** of the door: 8104
Ac 16:27 And the **k of the prison** awaking out of his *1200*
16:36 And the **k of the prison** told this saying to *1200*

KEEPERS (21) [KEEP]

2Ki 11: 5 even be **k** of the watch of the king's house; 8104
22: 4 which the **k** of the door have gathered of 8104
23: 4 the **k** of the door, to bring forth out of 8104
25:18 second priest, and the three **k** of the door: 8104
1Ch 9:19 the service, **k** of the gates of the tabernacle: 8104
9:19 the host of the LORD, *were* **k** of the entry. 8104
Est 6: 2 the king's chamberlains, the **k** of the door, 8104
Ecc 12: 3 In the day when the **k** of the house shall 8104
SS 5: 7 the **k** of the walls took away my vail from 8104
8:11 he let out the vineyard unto **k**; 5201
Jer 4:17 As **k** of a field, are they against her round 8104
52:24 second priest, and the three **k** of the door: 8104
Eze 40:45 the priests, the **k** of the charge of the house. 8104
40:46 the priests, the **k** of the charge of the altar: 8104
44: 8 ye have set **k** of my charge in my sanctuary 8104
44:14 I will make them **k** of the charge of 8104
Mt 28: 4 And for fear of him the **k** did shake, and *5083*
Ac 5:23 the **k** standing without before the doors: *5441*
12: 6 and *the* **k** before the door kept the prison. *5441*
12:19 he examined the **k**, and commanded that *5441*
Tit 2: 5 *To be* discreet, chaste, **k at home**, good, *3626*

KEEPEST (4) [KEEP]

1Ki 8:23 who **k** covenant and mercy with thy 8104
2Ch 6:14 which **k** covenant, and *shewest* mercy unto 8104
Ne 9:32 terrible God, who **k** covenant and mercy, 8104
Ac 21:24 thyself also walkest orderly, and **k** the law. *5442*

KEEPETH (46) [KEEP]

Ex 21:18 with *his* fist, and he die not, but **k** *his* bed: 5307
Dt 7: 9 which **k** covenant and mercy with them that 8104
1Sa 16:11 the youngest, and behold, he **k** the sheep. 7462
Ne 1: 5 that **k** covenant and mercy for them that 8104
Job 33:18 He **k back** his soul from the pit, and his life 2820
Ps 34:20 He **k** all his bones: not one of them is 8104
121: 3 be moved: he that **k** thee will not slumber. 8104
121: 4 he that **k** Israel shall neither slumber nor 8104
146: 6 all that therein is: which **k** truth for ever: 8104
Pr 2: 8 *He* **k** the paths of judgment, and 5341
10:17 He *is in* the way of life that **k** instruction: 8104
13: 3 He that **k** his mouth keepeth his life: *but* 5341
13: 3 He that keepeth his mouth **k** his life: *but* 8104
13: 6 Righteousness **k** *him that is* upright in 5341
16:17 he that **k** his way preserveth his soul. 5341
19: 8 he that **k** understanding shall find good. 8104
19:16 He that **k** the commandment keepeth his 8104
19:16 He that keepeth the commandment **k** his 8104
21:23 Whoso **k** his mouth and his tongue keepeth 8104
21:23 and his tongue **k** his soul from troubles. 8104
24:12 the heart consider *it?* and he that **k** thy soul, 5341
27:18 Whoso **k** the fig tree shall eat the fruit 5341
28: 7 Whoso **k** the law *is* a wise son: but he that 5341
29: 3 he that **k company with** harlots spendeth 7462
29:11 but a wise *man* **k** it in *till* afterwards. 7623
29:18 but he that **k** the law, happy *is* he. 8104
Ecc 8: 5 Whoso **k** the commandment shall feel no 8104
Isa 26: 2 that the righteous nation which **k** the truth 8104
56: 2 that **k** the sabbath from polluting it, and 8104
56: 2 and **k** his hand from doing any evil. 8104
56: 6 every one that **k** the sabbath from polluting 8104
Jer 48:10 cursed *be* he that **k back** his sword from 4513
La 3:28 He sitteth alone and **k silence**, because 1826
Hab 2: 5 *he is* a proud man, neither **k at home**, 5115
Lk 11:21 When a strong *man* armed **k** his palace, his *5442*
Jn 7:19 you the law, and *yet* none of you **k** the law? *4160*
9:16 of God, because he **k** not the sabbath day. *5083*
14:21 and **k** them, he it is that loveth me: *5083*
14:24 He that loveth me not **k** not my sayings: *5083*
1Jn 2: 4 and **k** not his commandments, is a liar, and *5083*
2: 5 But whoso **k** his word, in him verily is *5083*
3:24 And he that **k** his commandments dwelleth *5083*
5:18 but he that is begotten of God **k** himself, *5083*
Rev 2:26 and **k** my works unto the end, *5083*
16:15 and **k** his garments, lest he walk naked, and *5083*
22: 7 blessed *is* he that **k** the sayings of *5083*

KEEPING (12) [KEEP]

Ex 34: 7 **K** mercy for thousands, forgiving iniquity 5341
Nu 3:28 six hundred, **k** the charge of the sanctuary. 8104
3:38 **k** the charge of the sanctuary for the charge 8104
Dt 8:11 in not **k** his commandments, and 8104
1Sa 25:16 all the while we were with them **k** 7462
Ne 12:25 *were* porters **k** the ward at the thresholds of 8104
Ps 19:11 *and* in **k** of them *there is* great reward. 8104
Eze 17:14 *but* that by **k** of his covenant it might stand. 8104
Da 9: 4 **k** the covenant and mercy to them that love 8104
Lk 2: 8 **k watch** over their flock by night. *5438+5442*
1Co 7:19 but the **k** of the commandments of God. *5084*
1Pe 4:19 **commit the k** of their souls *to him* in well *3908*

KEHELATHAH (2)

Nu 33:22 journeyed from Rissah, and pitched in **K**. 6954
33:23 they went from **K**, and pitched in mount 6954

KEILAH (18)

Jos 15:44 **K**, and Achzib, and Mareshah; nine cities 7084
1Sa 23: 1 the Philistines fight against **K**, and they rob 7084
23: 2 Go, and smite the Philistines, and save **K**. 7084
23: 3 if we come *to* **K** against the armies of 7084
23: 4 and said, Arise, go down *to* **K**; 7084
23: 5 So David and his men went *to* **K**, and 7084
23: 5 So David saved the inhabitants of **K**. 7084
23: 6 the son of Ahimelech fled to David *to* **K**, 7084
23: 7 it was told Saul that David was come *to* **K**. 7084
23: 8 to go down *to* **K**, to besiege David and his 7084
23:10 heard that Saul seeketh to come to **K**, 7084
23:11 Will the men of **K** deliver me up into his 7084
23:12 Will the men of **K** deliver me and my men 7084
23:13 arose and departed out of **K**, and 7084
23:13 told Saul that David was escaped from **K**; 7084
1Ch 4:19 the father of **K** the Garmite, and 7084
Ne 3:17 the ruler of the half part of **K**, in his part. 7084
3:18 of Henadad, the ruler of the half part of **K**. 7084

KELAIAH (1)

Ezr 10:23 Jozabad, and Shimei, and **K**, (the same *is* 7041

KELAL See CHELAL

KELITA (3)

Ezr 10:23 and Shimei, and Kelaiah, (the same *is* **K**,) 7042
Ne 8: 7 **K**, Azariah, Jozabad, Hanan, Pelaiah, and 7042
10:10 Shebaniah, Hodijah, **K**, Pelaiah, Hanan, 7042

KELUB See CHELUB

KELUHI See CHELLUH

KEMUEL (3)

Ge 22:21 Buz his brother, and **K** the father of Aram, 7055
Nu 34:24 children of Ephraim, **K** the son of Shiphtan. 7055
1Ch 27:17 Of the Levites, Hashabiah the son of **K**: 7055

KENAANAH See CHENAANAH

KENAN (1)

1Ch 1: 2 **K**, Mahalaleel, Jered, 7018

KENANI See CHENANI

KENANIAH See CHENANIAH

KENATH (2)

Nu 32:42 Nobah went and took **K**, and the villages 7079
1Ch 2:23 from them, with **K**, and the towns thereof, 7079

KENAZ (11)

Ge 36:11 Omar, Zepho, and Gatam, and **K**. 7073
36:15 duke Omar, duke Zepho, duke **K**, 7073
36:42 Duke **K**, duke Teman, duke Mibzar, 7073
Jos 15:17 Othniel the son of **K**, the brother of Caleb, 7073
Jdg 1:13 Othniel the son of **K**, Caleb's younger 7073
3: 9 delivered them, *even* Othniel the son of **K**, 7073
3:11 forty years. And Othniel the son of **K** died. 7073
1Ch 1:36 and Gatam, **K**, and Timna, and Amalek. 7073
1:53 Duke **K**, duke Teman, duke Mibzar, 7073
4:13 the sons of **K**; Othniel, and Seraiah: and 7073
4:15 and Naam: and the sons of Elah, even **K**. 7073

KENEZITE (3)

Nu 32:12 Save Caleb the son of Jephunneh the **K**, 7074
Jos 14: 6 Caleb the son of Jephunneh the **K** said unto 7074
14:14 the son of Jephunneh the **K** unto this day, 7074

KENITE (6) [KENITES]

Nu 24:22 Nevertheless the **K** shall be wasted, 7014
Jdg 1:16 the children of the **K**, Moses' father in law, 7017
4:11 Now Heber the **K**, *which was* of 7017
4:17 to the tent of Jael the wife of Heber the **K**: 7017
4:17 of Hazor and the house of Heber the **K**. 7017
5:24 shall Jael the wife of Heber the **K** be, 7017

KENITES (8) [KENITE]

Ge 15:19 The **K**, and the Kenizzites, and 7017
Nu 24:21 he looked on the **K**, and took up his 7017
Jdg 4:11 had severed himself from the **K**, and 7014
1Sa 15: 6 Saul said unto the **K**, Go, depart, get you 7017
15: 6 So the **K** departed from among 7017
27:10 and against the south of the **K**. 7017
30:29 to *them* which *were* in the cities of the **K**, 7017
1Ch 2:55 These *are* the **K** that came of Hemath, 7017

KENIZZITES (1)

Ge 15:19 and the **K**, and the Kadmonites, 7074

KEPHAR AMMONI See CHEPHAR-HAAMMONAI

KEPHIRAH See CHEPHIRAH

KEPT (175) [KEEP]

Ge 26: 5 **k** my charge, my commandments, 8104
29: 9 with her father's sheep: for she **k** them. 7462
39: 9 neither hath he **k back** any thing from me 2820
42:16 your brother, and ye shall be **k in prison**, 631
Ex 3: 1 Now Moses **k** the flock of Jethro his father 7462
16:23 lay up for you to be **k** until the morning. 4931
16:32 Fill an omer of it to be **k** for your 4931
16:33 the LORD, to be **k** for your generations. 4931
16:34 laid it up before the Testimony, to be **k**. 4931

K

Ex 21:29 he hath not **k** him in, but that he hath killed 8104
21:36 time past, and his owner hath not **k** him in; 8104
Nu 5:13 be **k close**, and she be defiled, and *there be* 5641
9: 5 they **k** the passover on the fourteenth day 6213
9: 7 wherefore are we **k back**, that *we* may not 1639
9:19 the children of Israel **k** the charge of 8104
9:23 they **k** the charge of the LORD, at 8104
17:10 to be **k** for a token against the rebels; 4931
19: 9 it shall be **k** for the congregation of 4931
24:11 the LORD hath **k** thee **back** from honour. 4513
31:47 which **k** the charge of the tabernacle of 8104
Dt 32:10 he **k** him as the apple of his eye. 5341
33: 9 observed thy word, and **k** thy covenant. 5341
Jos 5:10 **k** the passover on the fourteenth day of 6213
14:10 the LORD hath **k** me **alive**, as he said, 2421
22: 2 Ye have **k** all that Moses the servant of 8104
22: 3 have **k** the charge of the commandment of 8104
Ru 2:23 So she **k fast** by the maidens of Boaz to 1692
1Sa 9:24 for unto *this* time *hath it* been **k** for thee 8104
13:13 thou hast not **k** the commandment of 8104
13:14 thou hast not **k** *that* which the LORD 8104
17:34 Thy servant **k** his father's sheep, and 7462
21: 4 if the young men have **k** themselves at least 8104
21: 5 Of a truth women *have been* **k** from us 6113
25:21 Surely in vain have I **k** all that this *fellow* 8104
25:33 which hast **k** me this day from coming to 3607
25:34 which hath **k** me **back** from hurting thee, 4513
25:39 of Nabal, and hath **k** his servant from evil: 2820
26:15 then hast thou not **k** thy lord the king? 8104
26:16 to die, because ye have not **k** your master, 8104
2Sa 13:34 the young man that **k** the **watch** lift up his 6822
22:22 For I have **k** the ways of the LORD, and 8104
22:24 and have **k** myself from mine iniquity. 8104
22:44 thou hast **k** me to be head of the heathen: 8104
1Ki 2:43 hast thou not **k** the oath of the LORD, 8104
3: 6 thou hast **k** for him this great kindness, that 8104
8:24 Who hast **k** with thy servant David my 8104
11:10 he **k** not *that* which the LORD 8104
11:11 thou hast not **k** my covenant and 8104
11:34 because he **k** my commandments and 8104
13:21 hast not **k** the commandment which 8104
14: 8 who **k** my commandments, and 8104
14:27 which **k** the door of the king's house. 8104
2Ki 9:14 (Now Joram had **k** Ramoth-gilead, he and 8104
12: 9 the priests that **k** the door put therein all 8104
17:19 Also Judah **k** not the commandments of 8104
18: 6 following him, but **k** his commandments, 8104
1Ch 10:13 which he **k** not, and also for asking *counsel* 8104
12: 1 while he yet **k** himself **close** because 6113
12:29 for hitherto the greatest part of them had **k** 8104
2Ch 6:15 Thou which hast **k** with thy servant David 8104
7: 8 Also at the same time Solomon **k** the feast 6213
7: 9 for they **k** the dedication of the altar seven 6213
12:10 that **k** the entrance of the king's house. 8104
30:21 **k** the feast of unleavened bread seven days 6213
30:23 and they **k** *other* seven days *with* gladness. 6213
34: 9 which the Levites that **k** the doors had 8104
34:21 our fathers have not **k** the word of 8104
35: 1 Moreover Josiah **k** a passover unto 6213
35:17 the children of Israel that were present **k** 6213
35:18 **k** in Israel from the days of Samuel 6213
35:18 of Israel keep such a passover as Josiah **k**, 6213
35:19 of the reign of Josiah was this passover **k**. 6213
36:21 as long as *she* lay desolate she **k sabbath**, 7673
Ezr 3: 4 They **k** also the feast of tabernacles, as it is 6213
6:16 **k** the dedication of this house of God with 5648
6:19 the children of the captivity **k** the passover 6213
6:22 **k** the feast of unleavened bread seven days 6213
Ne 1: 7 have not **k** the commandments, nor 8104
8:18 they **k** the feast seven days; and on 6213
9:34 our priests, nor our fathers, **k** thy law, 6213
11:19 Talmon, and their brethren that **k** the gates, 8104
12:45 and the porters **k** the ward of their God, 8104
Est 2:14 which **k** the concubines: 8104
2:21 and Teresh, of those which **k** the door, 8104
9:28 and **k** throughout every generation, 6213
Job 23:11 his way have I **k**, and not declined. 8104
28:21 and **k close** from the fowls of the air. 5641
29:21 and waited, and **k silence** at my counsel. 1826
31:34 that I **k silence**, *and* went not out *of* 1826
Ps 17: 4 by the word of thy lips I have **k** *me from* 8104
18:21 For I have **k** the ways of the LORD, and 8104
18:23 and I **k** myself from mine iniquity. 8104
30: 3 thou hast **k** me **alive**, that I should not go 2421
32: 3 When I **k silence**, my bones waxed old 2790
42: 4 and praise, *with* a multitude that **k holyday**. 2287
50:21 *things* hast thou done, and I **k silence**; 2790
78:10 They **k** not the covenant of God, and 8104
78:56 most high God, and **k** not his testimonies: 8104
99: 7 they **k** his testimonies, and the ordinance 8104
119:22 and contempt; for I have **k** thy testimonies. 5341
119:55 in the night, and have **k** thy law. 8104
119:56 This I had, because I **k** thy precepts. 5341
119:67 I went astray: but now have I **k** thy word. 8104
119:158 was grieved; because they **k** not thy word. 8104
119:167 My soul hath **k** thy testimonies; and *I* love 8104
119:168 I have **k** thy precepts and thy testimonies: 8104
Ecc 2:10 whatsoever mine eyes desired I **k** not from 680
5:13 *namely,* riches **k** for the owners thereof to 8104
SS 1: 6 *but* mine own vineyard have I not **k**. 5201
Isa 30:29 as *in* the night when a **holy** solemnity is **k**; 6942
Jer 16:11 have forsaken me, and have not **k** my law; 8104
35:18 **k** all his precepts, and done according unto 8104
Eze 5: 7 my statutes, neither have **k** my judgments, 6213
18: 9 and hath **k** my judgments, to deal truly; 8104
18:19 *and* hath **k** all my statutes, and hath done 8104
20:21 neither **k** my judgments to do them, 8104
44: 8 ye have not **k** the charge of mine holy 8104
44:15 that **k** the charge of my sanctuary when 8104
48:11 which have **k** my charge, which went not 8104
Da 5:19 whom he would he **k alive**; and whom he 2418
7:28 in me: but I **k** the matter in my heart. 5202
Hos 12:12 for a wife, and for a wife he **k** *sheep*. 8104
Am 1:11 and he **k** his wrath for ever: 8104
2: 4 have not **k** his commandments, and 8104
Mic 6:16 For the statutes of Omri are **k**, and all 8104
Mal 2: 9 according as ye have not **k** my ways, but 8104
3: 7 have not **k** *them*. Return unto me, and I will 8104
3:14 what profit *is it* that we have **k** his 8104
Mt 8:33 And they that **k** *them* fled, and went their *1006*
13:35 I will utter *things which have been* **k secret** *2928*
14: 6 But when Herod's birthday was **k**, *71*
19:20 All these *things* have I **k** from my youth up: *5442*
Mk 4:22 neither was *any thing* **k secret**, but that it *614*
9:10 And they **k** *that* saying with themselves, *2902*
Lk 2:19 But Mary **k** all these things, and *4933*
2:51 his mother **k** all these sayings in her heart. *1301*
8:29 and he was **k** bound with chains and *5442*
9:36 And they **k** *it* **close**, and told no *man* in *4601*
18:21 All these have I **k** from my youth up. *5442*
19:20 which I have **k** laid up in a napkin: *2192*
Jn 2:10 *but* thou hast **k** the good wine until now. *5083*
12: 7 against the day of my burying hath she **k** *5083*
15:10 even as I have **k** my Father's *5083*
15:20 if they have **k** my saying, they will keep *5083*
17: 6 gavest them me; and they have **k** thy word. *5083*
17:12 them in the world, I **k** them in thy name: *5083*
17:12 *those* that thou gavest me I have **k**, and *5442*
18:16 and spake unto her that **k the door**, and *2377*
18:17 Then saith the damsel that **k the door** unto *2377*
Ac 5: 2 And **k back** *part* of the price, his wife also *3557*
7:53 the disposition of angels, and have not **k** *it*. *5442*
9:33 which had **k** his bed eight years, and *1909+2621*
12: 5 Peter therefore was **k** in prison: but *5083*
12: 6 *the* keepers before the door **k** the prison. *5083*
15:12 Then all the multitude **k silence**, and *4601*
20:20 *And* how I **k back** nothing that was *5288*
22: 2 tongue to them, they **k** the more silence: *3930*
22:20 and **k** the raiment of them that slew him. *5442*
23:35 And he commanded him to be **k** in Herod's *5442*
25: 4 that Paul should be **k** at Cesarea, and *5083*
25:21 I commanded him to be **k** till I might send *5083*
27:43 to save Paul, **k** them **from** *their* purpose; *2967*
28:16 dwell by himself with a soldier that **k** him. *5442*
Ro 16:25 which was **k secret** since the world began, *4601*
2Co 11: 9 in all *things* I have **k** myself from being *5083*
11:32 **k** the city of the Damascenes *with a* *5432*
Gal 3:23 faith came, we were **k** under the law, *5432*
2Ti 4: 7 have finished *my* course, I have **k** the faith: *5083*
Heb 11:28 Through faith he **k** the passover, and *4160*
Jas 5: 4 which is of you **k back by fraud**, crieth: *650*
1Pe 1: 5 Who are **k** by the power of God through *5432*
2Pe 3: 7 are now, by the same word are **k in store**, *2343*
Jude 1: 6 And the angels which **k** not their first *5083*
Rev 3: 8 and hast **k** my word, and hast not denied *5083*
3:10 Because thou hast **k** the word of my *5083*

KERAN See CHERAN

KERCHIEFS (2) [HANDKERCHIEFS]

Eze 13:18 make **k** upon the head of every stature to 4555
13:21 Your **k** also will I tear, and deliver my 4555

KEREN-HAPPUCH (1)

Job 42:14 Kezia; and the name of the third, **K**. 7163

KERETHITES See CHERETHIMS; CHERETHITES

KERIOTH (4)

Jos 15:25 Hazor, Hadattah, and **K**, *and* Hezron, 7152
Jer 48:24 upon **K**, and upon Bozrah, and upon all 7152
48:41 **K** is taken, and the strong holds are 7152
Am 2: 2 and it shall devour the palaces of **K**: 7152

KERITH See CHERITH

KERNELS (1)

Nu 6: 4 the vine tree, from the **k** even to the husk. 2785

KEROS (2)

Ezr 2:44 The children of **K**, the children of Siaha, 7026
Ne 7:47 The children of **K**, the children of Sia, 7026

KESALON See CHESALON

KESED See CHESED

KESIL See CHESIL

KESULLOTH See CHESULLOTH

KETTLE (1)

1Sa 2:14 *it* into the pan, or **k**, or caldron, or pot; 1731

KETURAH (4)

Ge 25: 1 Abraham took a wife, and her name *was* **K**. 6989
25: 4 Eldaah. All these *were* the children of **K**. 6989
1Ch 1:32 Now the sons of **K**, Abraham's concubine: 6989
1:33 and Eldaah. All these *are* the sons of **K**. 6989

KEY (6) [KEYS]

Jdg 3:25 therefore they took a **k**, and opened *them:* 4668
Isa 22:22 the **k** of the house of David will I lay upon 4668
Lk 11:52 for ye have taken away the **k** of knowledge: *2807*
Rev 3: 7 he *that is* true, he that hath the **k** of David, *2807*
9: 1 to him was given the **k** of the bottomless *2807*
20: 1 having the **k** of the bottomless *pit* and *2807*

KEYS (2) [KEY]

Mt 16:19 And I will give unto thee the **k** of *2807*
Rev 1:18 and have the **k** of hell and of death. *2807*

KEZIA (1)

Job 42:14 the name of the second, **K**; and the name of 7103

KEZIAH See KEZIA

KEZIB See CHEZIB

KEZIZ (1)

Jos 18:21 and Beth-hoglah, and the valley of **K**, 7104

KIBROTH-HATTAAVAH (5)

Nu 11:34 he called the name of that place **K**: because 6914
11:35 *And* the people journeyed from **K** *unto* 6914
33:16 from the desert of Sinai, and pitched at **K**. 6914
33:17 they departed from **K**, and encamped at 6914
Dt 9:22 at Taberah, and at Massah, and at **K**, 6914

KIBZAIM (1)

Jos 21:22 **K** with her suburbs, and Beth-horon with 6911

KICK (3) [KICKED]

1Sa 2:29 Wherefore **k** ye at my sacrifice and at mine 1163
Ac 9: 5 *it is* hard for thee to **k** against the pricks. *2979*
26:14 *it is* hard for thee to **k** against the pricks. *2979*

KICKED (1) [KICK]

Dt 32:15 Jeshurun waxed fat, and **k**: thou art waxed 1163

KID (43) [KIDS]

Ge 37:31 killed a **k** of the goats, and dipped the coat 8163
38:17 I will send *thee* a **k** from the flock. 1423+5795
38:20 Judah sent the **k** by the hand of his 1423+5795
38:23 I sent this **k**, and thou hast not found her. 1423
Ex 23:19 Thou shalt not seethe a **k** in his mother's 1423
34:26 Thou shalt not seethe a **k** in his mother's 1423
Lev 4:23 a **k** of the goats, a male without blemish; 8163
4:28 a **k** of the goats, a female without blemish, 8166
5: 6 a lamb or a **k** of the goats, for a sin 8166
9: 3 Take ye a **k** of the goats for a sin offering; 8163
23:19 ye shall sacrifice one **k** of the goats for a 8163
Nu 7:16 One **k** of the goats for a sin offering: 8163
7:22 One **k** of the goats for a sin offering: 8163
7:28 One **k** of the goats for a sin offering: 8163
7:34 One **k** of the goats for a sin offering: 8163
7:40 One **k** of the goats for a sin offering: 8163
7:46 One **k** of the goats for a sin offering: 8163
7:52 One **k** of the goats for a sin offering: 8163
7:58 One **k** of the goats for a sin offering: 8163
7:64 One **k** of the goats for a sin offering: 8163
7:70 One **k** of the goats for a sin offering: 8163
7:76 One **k** of the goats for a sin offering: 8163
7:82 One **k** of the goats for a sin offering: 8163
15:11 or for one ram, or for a lamb, or a **k**. 5795
15:24 and one **k** of the goats for a sin offering. 8163
28:15 one **k** of the goats for a sin offering unto 8163
28:30 *And* one **k** of the goats, to make an 8163
29: 5 one **k** of the goats for a sin offering, 8163
29:11 One **k** of the goats *for* a sin offering; beside 8163
29:16 one **k** of the goats *for* a sin offering; beside 8163
29:19 one **k** of the goats *for* a sin offering; beside 8163
29:25 one **k** of the goats *for* a sin offering; beside 8163
Dt 14:21 Thou shalt not seethe a **k** in his mother's 1423
Jdg 6:19 made ready a **k**, and 1423+5795
13:15 until we shall have made ready a **k** 1423+5795
13:19 So Manoah took a **k** with a meat 1423+5795
14: 6 he rent him as *he* would have rent a **k**, and 1423
15: 1 Samson visited his wife with a **k**; 1423+5795
1Sa 16:20 a **k**, and sent *them* by David his son 1423+5795
Isa 11: 6 and the leopard shall lie down with the **k**; 1423
Eze 43:22 on the second day thou shalt offer a **k** of 8163
45:23 and a **k** of the goats daily *for* a sin offering. 8163
Lk 15:29 and yet thou never gavest me a **k**, that I *2056*

KIDNEYS (18)

Ex 29:13 the two **k**, and the fat that *is* upon them, 3629
29:22 the two **k**, and the fat that *is* upon them, 3629
Lev 3: 4 the two **k**, and the fat that *is* on them, 3629
3: 4 the liver, with the **k**, it shall he take away. 3629
3:10 the two **k**, and the fat that *is* upon them, 3629
3:10 the liver, with the **k**, it shall he take away. 3629
3:15 the two **k**, and the fat that *is* upon them, 3629
3:15 the liver, with the **k**, it shall he take away. 3629
4: 9 the two **k**, and the fat that *is* upon them, 3629
4: 9 the liver, with the **k**, it shall he take away, 3629
7: 4 the two **k**, and the fat that *is* on them, 3629
7: 4 the liver, with the **k**, it shall he take away: 3629
8:16 the two **k**, and their fat, and Moses burned 3629
8:25 the two **k**, and their fat, and the right 3629
9:10 the **k**, and the caul above the liver of the sin 3629
9:19 that which covereth *the inwards*, and the **k**, 3629
Dt 32:14 and goats, with the fat of **k** of wheat; 3629
Isa 34: 6 and goats, with the fat of the **k** of rams: 3629

KIDON See CHIDON

KIDRON (11)

2Sa 15:23 king also *himself* passed over the brook **K**, 6939
1Ki 2:37 goest out, and passest over the brook **K**, 6939
15:13 her idol, and burnt *it* by the brook **K**. 6939
2Ki 23: 4 them without Jerusalem in the fields of **K**, 6939
23: 6 unto the brook **K**, and burnt it at the brook 6939
23: 6 burnt it at the brook **K**, and stamped *it* small 6939
23:12 and cast the dust of them into the brook **K**. 6939
2Ch 15:16 and stamped *it*, and burnt *it* at the brook **K**. 6939
29:16 *it*, to carry *it* out abroad into the brook **K**. 6939
30:14 they away, and cast *them* into the brook **K**. 6939
Jer 31:40 and all the fields unto the brook of **K**, 6939

KIDS (8) [KID]

Ge 27: 9 fetch me from thence two good **k** of 1423
27:16 she put the skins of the **k** of the goats upon 1423
Lev 16: 5 Israel two **k** of the goats for a sin offering, 8163
Nu 7:87 the **k** of the goats for sin offering twelve. 8163
1Sa 10: 3 one carrying three **k**, and another carrying 1423
1Ki 20:27 before them like two little flocks of **k**; 5795
2Ch 35: 7 the people, *of* the flock, lambs and **k**, 1121+5795
SS 1: 8 and feed thy **k** beside the shepherds' tents. 1429

KILEAB See CHILEAB

KILION See CHILION

KILL (126) [KILLED, KILLEDST, KILLEST, KILLETH, KILLING]
Ge 4:15 lest any finding him should **k** him. 5221
12:12 they will **k** me, but they will save thee 2026
26: 7 *said he,* the men of the place should **k** me 2026
27:42 doth comfort himself, *purposing* to **k** thee. 2026
37:21 of their hands; and said, Let us not **k** him. 5221
Ex 1:16 if it *be* a son, then ye shall **k** him: 4191
2:14 intendest thou to **k** me, as thou killedst 2026
4:24 the LORD met him, and sought to **k** him. 4191
12: 6 of Israel shall **k** it in the evening. 7819
12:21 to your families, and **k** the passover. 7819
16: 3 to **k** this whole assembly with hunger. 4191
17: 3 to **k** us and our children and our cattle with 4191
20:13 Thou shalt not **k**. 7523
22: 1 steal an ox, or a sheep, and **k** it, or sell it; 2873
22:24 wax hot, and I will **k** you with the sword; 2026
29:11 thou shalt **k** the bullock before the LORD, 7819
29:20 shalt thou **k** the ram, and take of his blood, 7819
Lev 1: 5 he shall **k** the bullock before the LORD: 7819
1:11 he shall **k** it on the side of the altar 7819
3: 2 **k** it *at* the door of the tabernacle of 7819
3: 8 **k** it before the tabernacle of 7819
3:13 **k** it before the tabernacle of 7819
4: 4 and **k** the bullock before the LORD. 7819
4:24 **k** it in the place where they kill the burnt 7819
4:24 kill it in the place where they **k** the burnt 7819
4:33 the place where they **k** the burnt offering. 7819
7: 2 In the place where they **k** the burnt offering 7819
7: 2 offering shall they **k** the trespass offering: 7819
14:13 the place where he shall **k** the sin offering 7819
14:19 and afterward he shall **k** the burnt offering: 7819
14:25 he shall **k** the lamb of the trespass offering, 7819
14:50 he shall **k** the one of the birds in an earthen 7819
16:11 shall **k** the bullock of the sin offering which 7819
16:15 shall he **k** the goat of the sin offering, 7819
20: 4 of his seed unto Molech, and **k** him not: 4191
20:16 thou shalt **k** the woman and the beast: 2026
22:28 ye shall not **k** it and her young both in one 7819
Nu 11:15 **k** me, I pray thee, **out of hand,** 2026+2026
14:15 Now *if* thou shalt **k** *all* this people as one 4191
16:13 and honey, to **k** us in the wilderness, 4191
22:29 in mine hand, for now would I **k** thee. 2026
31:17 **k** every male among the little ones, 2026
31:17 **k** every woman that hath known man by 2026
35:27 and the revenger of blood **k** the slayer; 7523
Dt 4:42 which should **k** his neighbour unawares, 7523
5:17 Thou shalt not **k**. 7523
12:15 Notwithstanding thou mayest **k** and 2076
12:21 thou shalt **k** of thy herd and of thy flock, 2076
13: 9 thou shalt **surely k** him; thine hand 2026+2026
32:39 I **k**, and I make alive; I wound, and I heal: 4191
Jdg 13:23 If the LORD were pleased to **k** us, 4191
15:13 **surely** we will not **k** thee. And they 4191+4191
16: 2 when it is day, we shall **k** him. 2026
20:31 *and* **k**, as at other times, in the highways, 2491
20:39 **k** of the men of Israel about thirty persons: 2491
1Sa 16: 2 if Saul hear *it,* he will **k** me. And 2026
17: 9 and *to* **k** me, then will we be your servants: 5221
17: 9 **k** him, then shall ye be our servants, and 5221
19: 1 all his servants, that they should **k** David. 4191
19: 2 Saul my father seeketh to **k** thee: 4191
19:17 unto me, Let me go; why should I **k** thee? 4191
24:10 *some* bade *me* **k** thee: but *mine eye* spared 2026
30:15 me by God, that thou wilt neither **k** me, 4191
2Sa 13:28 Smite Amnon; then **k** him, fear not: 4191
14: 7 that smote his brother, that we may **k** him, 4191
14:32 if there be *any* iniquity in me, let him **k** me. 4191
21: 4 neither for us *shalt thou* **k** any man in 4191
1Ki 11:40 Solomon sought therefore to **k** Jeroboam. 4191
12:27 they shall **k** me, and go again to Rehoboam 2026
2Ki 5: 7 and said, *Am* I God, to **k** and to make alive, 4191
7: 4 shall live; and if they **k** us, we shall but die. 4191
11:15 him that followeth her **k** with the sword. 4191
2Ch 35: 6 So **k** the passover, and sanctify yourselves, 7819
Est 3:13 to **k**, and to cause to perish, all Jews, 2026
Ps 59: T and they watcht the house to **k** him. 4191
Ecc 3: 3 A time to **k**, and a time to heal; a time to 2026
Isa 14:30 I will **k** thy root with famine, and he shall 4191
29: 1 add ye year to year; let them **k** sacrifices. 5362
Eze 34: 3 you with the wool, ye **k** them that are fed: 2076
Mt 5:21 said by them of old time, Thou shalt not **k**; *5407*
5:21 whosoever shall **k** shall be in danger of *5407*
10:28 And fear not them which **k** the body, but *615*
10:28 kill the body, but are not able to **k** the soul: *615*
17:23 And they shall **k** him, and the third day he *615*
21:38 let us **k** him, and let us seize on his *615*
23:34 and *some* of them ye shall **k** and crucify; and *615*
24: 9 you up to be afflicted, and shall **k** you: *615*
26: 4 might take Jesus by subtilty, and **k** *him.* *615*
Mk 3: 4 to save life, or to **k**? But they held their *615*
9:31 into the hands of men, and they shall **k** him; *615*
10:19 commit adultery, Do not **k**, Do not steal, *5407*
10:34 and shall spit upon him, and shall **k** him: *615*
12: 7 let us **k** him, and the inheritance shall be *615*
Lk 12: 4 Be not afraid of them that **k** the body, and *615*
13:31 and depart hence: for Herod will **k** thee. *615*
15:23 and **k** *it;* and let us eat, and be merry: *2380*
18:20 commit adultery, Do not **k**, Do not steal, *5407*
20:14 come, let us **k** him, that the inheritance may *615*
22: 2 and scribes sought how they might **k** him; *337*
Jn 5:18 Therefore the Jews sought the more to **k** *615*
7: 1 in Jewry, because the Jews sought to **k** him. *615*
7:19 keepeth the law? Why go ye about to **k** me? *615*
7:20 hast a devil: who goeth about to **k** thee? *615*
7:25 Is not this he, whom they seek to **k**? *615*
8:22 Then said the Jews, Will he **k** himself? *615*
8:37 but ye seek to **k** me, because my word hath *615*
8:40 But now ye seek to **k** me, a man that hath *615*
10:10 but for to steal, and to **k**, and to destroy: *2380*
Ac 7:28 Wilt thou **k** me, as thou didst the Egyptian *337*
9:23 the Jews took counsel to **k** him: *337*
9:24 watched the gates day and night to **k** him. *337*
10:13 came a voice to him, Rise, Peter; **k**, and eat. *2380*
21:31 And as *they* went about to **k** him, *615*
23:15 or ever he come near, are ready to **k** him. *337*
25: 3 laying wait in the way to **k** him. *337*
26:21 me in the temple, and went about to **k** *me.* *1315*
27:42 And the soldiers' counsel was to **k** *615*
Ro 13: 9 Thou shalt not **k**, Thou shalt not steal, *5407*
Jas 2:11 not commit adultery, said also, Do not **k**. *5407*
2:11 if thou commit no adultery, yet *if* thou **k**, *5407*
4: 2 ye **k**, and desire *to have,* and cannot obtain: *5407*
Rev 2:23 And I will **k** her children with death; and *615*
6: 4 and that they should **k** one another: *4969*
6: 8 to **k** with sword, and with hunger, and *615*
9: 5 it was given that they should not **k** them, *615*
11: 7 and shall overcome them, and **k** them. *615*

KILLED (67) [KILL]
Ge 37:31 **k** a kid of the goats, and dipped the coat in 7819
Ex 21:29 but that he hath **k** a man or a woman; 4191
Lev 4:15 the bullock shall be **k** before the LORD. 7819
6:25 In the place where the burnt offering is **k** 7819
6:25 the sin offering be **k** before the LORD: 7819
8:19 he **k** *it;* and Moses sprinkled the blood 7819
14: 5 **k** in an earthen vessel over running water: 7819
14: 6 the bird *that was* **k** over the running water: 7819
Nu 16:41 Ye have **k** the people of the LORD. 4191
31:19 whosoever hath **k** *any* person, and 2026
1Sa 24:11 **k** thee not, know thou and see that *there is* 2026
25:11 my flesh that I have **k** for my shearers, and 2873
28:24 and **k** it, and took flour, and kneaded *it,* and 2076
2Sa 12: 9 thou hast **k** Uriah the Hittite with 5221
21:17 and smote the Philistine, and **k** him. 4191
1Ki 16: 7 house of Jeroboam; and because he **k** him. 5221
16:10 Zimri went in and smote him, and **k** him, 4191
21:19 Hast thou **k**, and also taken possession? 7523
2Ki 15:25 he **k** him, and reigned in his room. 4191
1Ch 19:18 **k** Shophach the captain of the host. 4191
2Ch 18: 2 Ahab **k** sheep and oxen for him in 2076
25: 3 that he slew his servants that had **k** the king 5221
29:22 So they **k** the bullocks, and the priests 7819
29:22 likewise, when they had **k** the rams, they 7819
29:22 they **k** also the lambs, and they sprinkled 7819
29:24 the priests **k** them, and they made 7819
30:15 they **k** the passover on the fourteenth *day* 7819
35: 1 they **k** the passover on the fourteenth *day* 7819
35:11 they **k** the passover, and the priests 7819
Ezr 6:20 **k** the passover for all the children of 7819
Ps 44:22 Yea, for thy sake are we **k** all the day long; 2026
Pr 9: 2 She hath **k** her beasts; she hath mingled her 2873
La 2:21 of thine anger; thou hast **k**, *and* not pitied. 2873
Mt 16:21 and be **k**, and be raised *again* the third day. *615*
21:35 beat one, and **k** another, and stoned another. *615*
22: 4 my oxen and *my* fatlings *are* **k**, and *2380*
23:31 that ye are the children of them which **k** *5407*
Mk 6:19 quarrel against him, and would have **k** him; *615*
8:31 and be **k**, and after three days rise again. *615*
9:31 and after that he is **k**, he shall rise the third *615*
12: 5 and him they **k**, and many others; *615*
12: 8 and **k** *him,* and cast *him* out of the vineyard. *615*
14:12 when they **k** the passover, his disciples said *2380*
Lk 11:47 of the prophets, and your fathers **k** them. *615*
11:48 for they indeed **k** them, and ye build their *615*
12: 5 which after *he* hath **k** hath power to cast into *615*
15:27 and thy father hath **k** the fatted calf, *2380*
15:30 thou hast **k** for him the fatted calf. *2380*
20:15 and **k** *him.* What therefore shall the lord of *615*
22: 7 when the passover must be **k**. *2380*
Ac 3:15 And **k** the Prince of life, whom God hath *615*
12: 2 And he **k** James the brother of John with *337*
16:27 out his sword, and would have **k** himself, *337*
23:12 neither eat nor drink till they had **k** Paul. *615*
23:21 neither eat nor drink till they have **k** him: *337*
23:27 of the Jews, and should have been **k** of them: *337*
Ro 8:36 For thy sake we are **k** all the day long; *2289*
11: 3 they have **k** thy prophets, and digged down *615*
2Co 6: 9 behold, we live; as chastened, and not **k**; *2289*
1Th 2:15 Who both **k** the Lord Jesus, and their own *615*
Jas 5: 6 Ye have condemned *and* **k** the just; *and* *5407*
Rev 6:11 that should be **k** as they *were,* should be *615*
9:18 By these three was the third *part* of men **k**, *615*
9:20 And the rest of the men which were not **k** by *615*
11: 5 will hurt them, he must in this manner be **k**. *615*
13:10 he that killeth with the sword must be **k** with *615*
13:15 worship the image of the beast should be **k**. *615*

KILLEDST (2) [KILL]
Ex 2:14 thou to kill me, as thou **k** the Egyptian? 2026
1Sa 24:18 me into thine hand, thou **k** me not. 2026

KILLEST (2) [KILL]
Mt 23:37 *thou* that **k** the prophets, and stonest them *615*
Lk 13:34 which **k** the prophets, and stonest them that *615*

KILLETH (23) [KILL]
Lev 17: 3 that **k** an ox, or lamb, or goat, in the camp, 7819
17: 3 in the camp, or that **k** *it* out of the camp, 7819
24:17 he that **k** any man shall surely be put 5221+5315
24:18 he that **k** a beast shall make it good; 5221+5315
24:21 he that **k** a beast, he shall restore it: and 5221
24:21 he that **k** a man, he shall be put to death. 5221
Nu 35:11 which **k** *any* person at unawares. 5221
35:15 that every one that **k** *any* person unawares 5221
35:30 Whoso **k** *any* person, the murderer shall be 5221
Dt 19: 4 Whoso **k** his neighbour ignorantly, whom 5221
Jos 20: 3 That the slayer that **k** *any* person unawares 5221
20: 9 that whosoever **k** *any* person at unawares 5221
1Sa 2: 6 The LORD **k**, and maketh alive: 4191
17:25 it shall be, *that* the man who **k** him, 5221
17:26 What shall be done to the man that **k** this 5221
17:27 So shall it be done to the man that **k** him. 5221
Job 5: 2 For wrath **k** the foolish man, and 2026
24:14 The murderer rising with the light **k** 6991
Pr 21:25 The desire of the slothful **k** him; for his 4191
Isa 66: 3 He that **k** an ox *is as if* he slew a man; 7819
Jn 16: 2 that whosoever **k** you will think that he *615*
2Co 3: 6 for the letter **k**, but the spirit giveth life. *615*
Rev 13:10 he that **k** with the sword must be killed with *615*

KILLING (5) [KILL]
Jdg 9:24 which aided him in the **k** of his brethren. 2026
2Ch 30:17 the Levites had the charge of the **k** of 7821
Isa 22:13 **k** sheep, eating flesh, and drinking wine: 7819
Hos 4: 2 **k**, and stealing, and committing adultery, 7523
Mk 12: 5 and many others; beating some, and **k** some. *615*

KILMAD See CHILMAD

KIMHAM See CHIMHAM

KIN (8) [KINDRED, KINDREDS, KINSFOLK, KINSFOLKS, KINSMAN, KINSMAN'S, KINSMEN, KINSWOMAN, KINSWOMEN]
Lev 18: 6 approach to any that is near of **k** to him, 1320
20:19 for he uncovereth his **near k**: they shall 7607
21: 2 for his **k**, that is near unto him, *that is,* for 7607
25:25 *if any of* his **k** come to redeem it, then 7138
25:49 *any* that is nigh of **k** unto him of his family 1320
Ru 2:20 The man *is* **near of k** unto us, one of our 7138
2Sa 19:42 Because the king *is* **near of k** to us: 7138
Mk 6: 4 and among his own **k**, and in his own *4773*

KINAH (1)
Jos 15:22 And **K**, and Dimonah, and Adadah, 7016

KIND (45) [KINDLY, KINDNESS, KINDS, LOVINGKINDNESS, LOVINGKINDNESSES]
Ge 1:11 *and* the fruit tree yielding fruit after his **k**, 4327
1:12 *and* herb yielding seed after his **k**, and 4327
1:12 whose seed *was* in itself, after his **k**: 4327
1:21 after their **k**, and every winged fowl after 4327
1:21 and every winged fowl after his **k**: 4327
1:24 bring forth the living creature after his **k**, 4327
1:24 and beast of the earth after his **k**: 4327
1:25 God made the beast of the earth after his **k**, 4327
1:25 cattle after their **k**, and every thing that 4327
1:25 that creepeth upon the earth after his **k**: 4327
6:20 Of fowls after their **k**, and of cattle after 4327
6:20 after their kind, and of cattle after their **k**, 4327
6:20 every creeping thing of the earth after his **k**, 4327
7:14 every beast after his **k**, and all the cattle 4327
7:14 all the cattle after their **k**, and 4327
7:14 that creepeth upon the earth after his **k**, 4327
7:14 every fowl after his **k**, every bird of every 4327
Lev 11:14 And the vulture, and the kite after his **k**; 4327
11:15 Every raven after his **k**; 4327
11:16 and the cuckow, and the hawk after his **k**, 4327
11:19 the heron after her **k**, and the lapwing, and 4327
11:22 the locust after his **k**, and the bald locust 4327
11:22 the bald locust after his **k**, and the beetle 4327
11:22 the beetle after his **k**, and the grasshopper 4327
11:22 his kind, and the grasshopper after his **k**. 4327
11:29 and the mouse, and the tortoise after his **k**, 4327
19:19 not let thy cattle gender with a **diverse k**: 3610
Dt 14:13 and the kite, and the vulture after his **k**, 4327
14:14 And every raven after his **k**, 4327
14:15 and the cuckow, and the hawk after his **k**, 4327
14:18 the heron after her **k**, and the lapwing, and 4327
1Ch 28:14 of **every k of service**: 5656+5656+2050.1
2Ch 10: 7 If thou be **k** to this people, and please them, 2896
Ne 13:20 sellers of all ***k** of* ware lodged without NIH
Ecc 2: 5 and I planted trees in them of all ***k** of* fruits: NIH
Eze 27:12 by reason of the multitude of all ***k** of* riches; NIH
Mt 13:47 cast into the sea, and gathered of every **k**: *1085*
17:21 Howbeit this **k** goeth not out but by prayer *1085*
Mk 9:29 This **k** can come forth by nothing, but by *1085*
Lk 6:35 for he is **k** unto the unthankful and *to* *5543*
1Co 13: 4 Charity suffereth long, *and* is **k**; *5541*
15:39 but *there is* one ***k** of* flesh of men, NIG
Eph 4:32 And be ye **k** one to another, tenderhearted, *5543*
Jas 1:18 that we should be a **k** of firstfruits of his *5100*
3: 7 For every **k** of beasts, and of birds, and *5449*

KINDLE (19) [KINDLED, KINDLETH]
Ex 35: 3 Ye shall **k** no fire throughout your 1197
Pr 26:21 to fire; so *is* a contentious man to **k** strife. 2787
Isa 9:18 shall **k** in the thickets of the forest, and 3341
10:16 under his glory he shall **k** a burning like 3344
30:33 like a stream of brimstone, doth **k** it. 1197
43: 2 neither shall the flame **k** upon thee. 1197
50:11 Behold, all ye that **k** a fire, that compass 6919
Jer 7:18 the fathers **k** the fire, and the women knead 1197
17:27 will I **k** a fire in the gates thereof, and 3341
21:14 I will **k** a fire in the forest thereof, and 3341
33:18 to **k** meat offerings, and to do sacrifice 6999
43:12 I will **k** a fire in the houses of the gods of 3341
49:27 I will **k** a fire in the wall of Damascus, and 3341
50:32 I will **k** a fire in his cities, and it shall 3341
Eze 20:47 I *will* **k** a fire in thee, and it shall devour 3341
24:10 Heap on wood, **k** the fire, consume 1814
Am 1:14 I will **k** a fire in the wall of Rabbah, and 3341
Ob 1:18 and they shall **k** in them, and devour them; 1814
Mal 1:10 neither do ye **k** *fire on* mine altar for nought. 215

KINDLED (66) [KINDLE]
Ge 30: 2 Jacob's anger was **k** against Rachel: and 2734
39:19 did thy servant to me; that his wrath was **k**. 2734
Ex 4:14 the anger of the LORD was **k** against 2734
22: 6 be consumed *therewith;* he that **k** the fire 1197
Lev 10: 6 the burning which the LORD hath **k**. 8313
Nu 11: 1 the LORD heard *it;* and his anger was **k**; 2734
11:10 the anger of the LORD was **k** greatly; 2734
11:33 the wrath of the LORD was **k** against 2734
12: 9 the anger of the LORD was **k** against 2734
22:22 God's anger was **k** because he went: and 2734
22:27 Balaam's anger was **k**, and he smote the ass 2734
24:10 Balak's anger was **k** against Balaam, and 2734
25: 3 the anger of the LORD was **k** against 2734
32:10 the LORD'S anger was **k** the same time, 2734
32:13 the LORD'S anger was **k** against Israel, 2734

Dt 6:15 lest the anger of the LORD thy God be **k** 2734
7: 4 will the anger of the LORD be **k** against 2734
11:17 *then* the LORD'S wrath be **k** against you, 2734
29:27 the anger of the LORD was **k** against this 2734
31:17 my anger shall be **k** against them in that 2734
32:22 For a fire is **k** in my anger, and shall burn 6919
Jos 7: 1 the anger of the LORD was **k** against 2734
23:16 shall the anger of the LORD be **k** against 2734
Jdg 9:30 of Gaal the son of Ebed, his anger was **k**. 2734
14:19 his anger was **k**, and he went up *to* his 2734
1Sa 11: 6 those tidings, and his anger was **k** greatly. 2734
17:28 Eliab's anger was **k** against David, and 2734
20:30 Saul's anger was **k** against Jonathan, and 2734
2Sa 6: 7 the anger of the LORD was **k** against 2734
12: 5 David's anger was greatly **k** against 2734
22: 9 of his mouth devoured: coals were **k** by it. 1197
22:13 brightness before him were coals of fire **k**. 1197
24: 1 again the anger of the LORD was **k** 2734
2Ki 13: 3 the anger of the LORD was **k** against 2734
22:13 wrath of the LORD that is **k** against us, 3341
22:17 my wrath shall be **k** against this place, 3341
23:26 where*with* his anger was **k** against Judah, 2734
1Ch 13:10 the anger of the LORD was **k** against 2734
2Ch 25:10 their anger was greatly **k** against Judah, 2734
25:15 Wherefore the anger of the LORD was **k** 2734
Job 19:11 He hath also **k** his wrath against me, and 2734
32: 2 was **k** the wrath of Elihu the son of 2734
32: 2 against Job was his wrath **k**, because 2734
32: 3 against his three friends was his wrath **k**, 2734
32: 5 of *these* three men, then his wrath was **k**. 2734
42: 7 My wrath is **k** against thee, and against thy 2734
Ps 2:12 the way, when his wrath is **k** but a little: 1197
18: 8 of his mouth devoured: coals were **k** by it. 1197
78:21 so a fire was **k** against Jacob, and 5400
106:18 a fire was **k** in their company; the flame 1197
106:40 Therefore was the wrath of the LORD **k** 2734
124: 3 when their wrath was **k** against us: 2734
Isa 5:25 Therefore is the anger of the LORD **k** 2734
50:11 your fire, and in the sparks *that* ye have **k**. 1197
Jer 11:16 with the noise of a great tumult he hath **k** 3341
15:14 for a fire is **k** in mine anger, *which* shall 6919
17: 4 for ye have **k** a fire in mine anger, 6919
44: 6 was **k** in the cities of Judah and in 1197
La 4:11 hath **k** a fire in Zion, and it hath devoured 3341
Eze 20:48 all flesh shall see that I the LORD have **k** 1197
Hos 8: 5 cast *thee* off; mine anger is **k** against them: 2734
11: 8 within me, my repentings are **k** together. 3648
Zec 10: 3 Mine anger was **k** against the shepherds, 2734
Lk 12:49 the earth; and what will I, if it be already **k**? *381*
22:55 And when they had **k** a fire in the midst of *681*
Ac 28: 2 for they **k** a fire, and received us every one, *381*

KINDLETH (3) [KINDLE]

Job 41:21 His breath **k** coals, and a flame goeth out of 3857
Isa 44:15 yea, he **k** *it*, and baketh bread; yea, 5400
Jas 3: 5 Behold, how great a matter a little fire **k**. *381*

KINDLY (10) [KIND]

Ge 24:49 now if ye will deal **k** and truly with my 2617
34: 3 and spake **k** unto the damsel. 3820+5921
47:29 my thigh, and deal **k** and truly with me; 2617
50:21 he comforted them, and spake **k** unto them. 3820
Jos 2:14 that we will deal **k** and truly with thee. 2617
Ru 1: 8 the LORD deal **k** with you, as ye have 2617
1Sa 20: 8 Therefore thou shalt deal **k** with thy 2617
2Ki 25:28 he spake **k** to him, and set his throne above 2896
Jer 52:32 spake **k** unto him, and set his throne above 2896
Ro 12:10 *Be* **k affectioned** one to another with *5387*

KINDNESS (48) [KIND]

Ge 20:13 This *is* thy **k** which thou shalt shew unto 2617
21:23 according to the **k** that I have done unto 2617
24:12 and shew **k** unto my master Abraham. 2617
24:14 that thou hast shewed **k** unto my master. 2617
40:14 shew **k**, I pray thee, unto me, and 2617
Jos 2:12 by the LORD, since I have shewed you **k**, 2617
2:12 that ye will also shew **k** unto my father's 2617
Jdg 8:35 Neither shewed they **k** to the house of 2617
Ru 2:20 who hath not left off his **k** to the living and 2617
3:10 *for* thou hast shewed more **k** in the latter 2617
1Sa 15: 6 for ye shewed **k** to all the children of Israel, 2617
20:14 yet I live shew me the **k** of the LORD, 2617
20:15 *also* thou shalt not cut off thy **k** from my 2617
2Sa 2: 5 that ye have shewed this **k** unto your lord, 2617
2: 6 now the LORD shew **k** and truth unto 2617
2: 6 I also will requite you this **k**, because 2896
3: 8 which against Judah do shew **k** *this* day 2617
9: 1 that I may shew him **k** for Jonathan's sake? 2617
9: 3 that I may shew the **k** of God unto him? 2617
9: 7 for I will surely shew thee **k** for Jonathan 2617
10: 2 I will shew **k** unto Hanun the son of 2617
10: 2 of Nahash, as his father shewed **k** unto me. 2617
16:17 said to Hushai, *Is* this thy **k** to thy friend? 2617
1Ki 2: 7 shew **k** unto the sons of Barzillai 2617
3: 6 thou hast kept for him this great **k**, that 2617
1Ch 19: 2 I will shew **k** unto Hanun the son of 2617
19: 2 because his father shewed **k** to me. 2617
2Ch 24:22 Thus Joash the king remembered not the **k** 2617
Ne 9:17 and of great **k**, and forsookest them not. 2617
Est 2: 9 pleased him, and she obtained **k** of him; 2617
Ps 31:21 for he hath shewed me his marvellous **k** in 2617
117: 2 For his **merciful k** is great toward us: and 2617
119:76 thy **merciful k** be for my comfort, 2617
141: 5 Let the righteous smite me; *it shall be* a **k**: 2617
Pr 19:22 The desire of a man *is* his **k**: and a poor 2617
31:26 and in her tongue *is* the law of **k**. 2617
Isa 54: 8 with everlasting **k** will I have mercy on 2617
54:10 my **k** shall not depart from thee, 2617
Jer 2: 2 I remember thee, the **k** of thy youth, 2617
Joel 2:13 of great **k**, and repenteth him of the evil. 2617
Jnh 4: 2 of great **k**, and repentest thee of the evil. 2617
Ac 28: 2 the barbarous people shewed us no little **k**: *5363*
2Co 6: 6 by knowledge, by longsuffering, by **k**, *5544*
Eph 2: 7 in *his* **k** towards us through Christ Jesus. *5544*
Col 3:12 holy and beloved, bowels of mercies, **k**, *5544*
Tit 3: 4 But after that the **k** and love of God our *5544*
2Pe 1: 7 And to godliness **brotherly k**; and *5360*
1: 7 and to **brotherly k** charity. *5360*

KINDRED (28) [KIN]

Ge 12: 1 from thy **k**, and from thy father's house, 4138
24: 4 to my **k**, and take a wife unto my son Isaac. 4138
24: 7 from the land of my **k**, and which spake 4138
24:38 and to my **k**, and take a wife unto my son. 4940
24:40 thou shalt take a wife for my son of my **k**, 4940
24:41 *this* my oath, when thou comest to my **k**; 4940
31: 3 unto the land of thy fathers, and to thy **k**; 4138
31:13 this land, and return unto the land of thy **k**. 4138
32: 9 and to thy **k**, and I will deal well with thee: 4138
43: 7 of our **k**, saying, *Is* your father yet alive? 4138
Nu 10:30 will depart to mine own land, and to my **k**. 4138
Jos 6:23 they brought out all her **k**, and left them 4940
Ru 2: 3 unto Boaz, who *was* of the **k** of Elimelech. 4940
3: 2 now *is* not Boaz of our **k**, with whose 4130
1Ch 12:29 of Benjamin, the **k** of Saul, three thousand: 251
Est 2:10 had not shewed her people nor her **k**: 4138
2:20 Esther had not *yet* shewed her **k** nor her 4138
8: 6 can I endure to see the destruction of my **k**? 4138
Job 32: 2 of Barachel the Buzite, of the **k** of Ram: 4940
Eze 11:15 the men of thy **k**, and all the house of Israel 1353
Lk 1:61 There is none of thy **k** that is called by this *4772*
Ac 4: 6 as many as were of the **k** of the high priest, *1085*
7: 3 and from thy **k**, and come into the land *4772*
7:13 Joseph's **k** was made known unto Pharaoh. *1085*
7:14 called his father Jacob to *him*, and all his **k**, *4772*
7:19 The same dealt subtilly with our **k**, and *1085*
Rev 5: 9 us to God by thy blood out of every **k**, *5443*
14: 6 and **k**, and tongue, and people, *5443*

KINDREDS (8) [KIN]

1Ch 16:28 Give unto the LORD, ye **k** of the people, 4940
Ps 22:27 all the **k** of the nations shall worship before 4940
96: 7 unto the LORD, O ye **k** of the people, 4940
Ac 3:25 And in thy seed shall all the **k** of the earth *3965*
Rev 1: 7 and all **k** of the earth shall wail because *5443*
7: 9 all nations, and **k**, and people, and tongues, *5443*
11: 9 *they* of the people and **k** and tongues and *5443*
13: 7 and power was given him over all **k**, and *5443*

KINDS (10) [KIND]

Ge 8:19 after their **k**, went forth out of the ark. 4940
2Ch 16:14 **divers** *of spices* prepared by 2177
Jer 15: 3 I will appoint over them four **k**, saith 4940
Eze 47:10 their fish shall be according to their **k**, 4327
Da 3: 5 psaltery, dulcimer, and all **k** of musick, 2178
3: 7 sackbut, psaltery, and all **k** of musick, 2178
3:10 psaltery, and dulcimer, and all **k** of musick, 2178
3:15 psaltery, and dulcimer, and all **k** of musick, 2178
1Co 12:10 of spirits; to another *divers* **k** of tongues; *1085*
14:10 so many **k** of voices in the world, and *1085*

KINE (24)

Ge 32:15 forty **k**, and ten bulls, twenty she asses, and 6510
41: 2 up out of the river seven well favoured **k** 6510
41: 3 seven other **k** came up after them out of 6510
41: 3 stood by the *other* **k** upon the brink of 6510
41: 4 leanfleshed **k** did eat up the seven well 6510
41: 4 eat up the seven well favoured and fat **k**. 6510
41:18 there came up out of the river seven **k**, 6510
41:19 seven other **k** came up after them, poor and 6510
41:20 the ill favoured **k** did eat up the first seven 6510
41:20 kine did eat up the first seven fat **k**: 6510
41:26 The seven good **k** *are* seven years; and 6510
41:27 ill favoured **k** that came up after them *are* 6510
Dt 7:13 the increase of thy **k**, and the flocks of thy 504
28: 4 the increase of thy **k**, and the flocks of thy 504
28:18 the increase of thy **k**, and the flocks of thy 504
28:51 *or* the increase of thy **k**, or flocks of thy 504
32:14 Butter of **k**, and milk of sheep, with fat of 1241
1Sa 6: 7 make a new cart, and take two milch **k**, 6510
6: 7 tie the **k** to the cart, and bring their calves 6510
6:10 took two milch **k**, and tied them to the cart, 6510
6:12 the **k** took the straight way to the way of 6510
6:14 offered the **k** a burnt offering unto 6510
2Sa 17:29 butter, and sheep, and cheese of **k**, 1241
Am 4: 1 Hear this word, ye **k** of Bashan, that *are* in 6510

KING (2256) [KING'S, KINGDOM, KINGDOMS, KINGLY, KINGS, KINGS']

Ge 14: 1 it came to pass in the days of Amraphel **k** 4428
14: 1 Arioch **k** of Ellasar, Chedorlaomer king of 4428
14: 1 Chedorlaomer **k** of Elam, and Tidal king of 4428
14: 1 king of Elam, and Tidal **k** of nations; 4428
14: 2 *That these* made war with Bera **k** of 4428
14: 2 with Birsha **k** of Gomorrah, Shinab king of 4428
14: 2 Shinab **k** of Admah, and Shemeber king of 4428
14: 2 Shemeber **k** of Zeboiim, and the king of 4428
14: 2 and the **k** of Bela, which *is* Zoar. 4428
14: 8 there went out the **k** of Sodom, and 4428
14: 8 the **k** of Gomorrah, and the king of Admah, 4428
14: 8 the **k** of Admah, and the king of Zeboiim, 4428
14: 8 the **k** of Zeboiim, and the king of Bela 4428
14: 8 and the **k** of Bela (the same *is* Zoar); 4428
14: 9 With Chedorlaomer the **k** of Elam, and 4428
14: 9 *with* Tidal **k** of nations, and Amraphel king 4428
14: 9 Amraphel **k** of Shinar, and Arioch king of 4428
14: 9 king of Shinar, and Arioch **k** of Ellasar; 4428
14:17 the **k** of Sodom went out to meet him after 4428
14:18 Melchizedek **k** of Salem brought forth 4428
14:21 the **k** of Sodom said unto Abram, Give me 4428
14:22 Abram said to the **k** of Sodom, I have lift 4428
20: 2 Abimelech **k** of Gerar sent, and took Sarah. 4428
26: 1 Isaac went unto Abimelech **k** of 4428
26: 8 that Abimelech **k** of the Philistims looked 4428
36:31 before there reigned *any* **k** over the children 4428
40: 1 *that* the butler of the **k** of Egypt and *his* 4428
40: 1 *his* baker had offended their lord the **k** of 4428
40: 5 the butler and the baker of the **k** of Egypt, 4428
Ge 41:46 when he stood before Pharaoh **k** of Egypt. 4428
Ex 1: 8 Now there arose up a new **k** over Egypt, 4428
1:15 the **k** of Egypt spake to the Hebrew 4428
1:17 did not as the **k** of Egypt commanded them, 4428
1:18 the **k** of Egypt called for the midwives, 4428
2:23 in process of time, that the **k** of Egypt died: 4428
3:18 unto the **k** of Egypt, and you shall say unto 4428
3:19 I am sure that the **k** of Egypt will not let 4428
5: 4 the **k** of Egypt said unto them, Wherefore 4428
6:11 Go in, speak unto Pharaoh **k** of Egypt, 4428
6:13 of Israel, and unto Pharaoh **k** of Egypt, 4428
6:27 *These are* they which spake to Pharaoh **k** of 4428
6:29 speak thou unto Pharaoh **k** of Egypt all that 4428
14: 5 it was told the **k** of Egypt that the people 4428
14: 8 hardened the heart of Pharaoh **k** of Egypt, 4428
Nu 20:14 from Kadesh unto the **k** of Edom, 4428
21: 1 *when* **k** Arad the Canaanite, which dwelt *in* 4428
21:21 Israel sent messengers unto Sihon **k** of 4428
21:26 For Heshbon *was* the city of Sihon the **k** of 4428
21:26 who had fought against the former **k** of 4428
21:29 his daughters into captivity unto Sihon **k** of 4428
21:33 Og the **k** of Bashan went out against them, 4428
21:34 as thou didst unto Sihon **k** of the Amorites, 4428
22: 4 Balak the son of Zippor *was* **k** of 4428
22:10 **k** of Moab, hath sent unto me, *saying*, 4428
23: 7 Balak the **k** of Moab hath brought me from 4428
23:21 and the shout of a **k** *is* among them. 4428
24: 7 his **k** shall be higher than Agag, and 4428
32:33 the kingdom of Sihon **k** of the Amorites, 4428
32:33 the kingdom of Og **k** of Bashan, the land, 4428
33:40 **k** Arad the Canaanite, which dwelt in 4428
Dt 1: 4 After he had slain Sihon the **k** of 4428
1: 4 dwelt in Heshbon, and Og the **k** of Bashan, 4428
2:24 the Amorite, **k** of Heshbon, and his land: 4428
2:26 Sihon **k** of Heshbon *with* words of peace, 4428
2:30 Sihon **k** of Heshbon would not let us pass 4428
3: 1 Og the **k** of Bashan came out against us, 4428
3: 2 as thou didst unto Sihon **k** of the Amorites, 4428
3: 3 the **k** of Bashan, and all his people: 4428
3: 6 as we did unto Sihon **k** of Heshbon, 4428
3:11 For only Og **k** of Bashan remained of 4428
4:46 in the land of Sihon **k** of the Amorites, 4428
4:47 the land of Og **k** of Bashan, two kings of 4428
7: 8 from the hand of Pharaoh **k** of Egypt. 4428
11: 3 of Egypt unto Pharaoh the **k** of Egypt, 4428
17:14 shalt say, I will set a **k** over me, 4428
17:15 Thou shalt in any wise set *him* **k** over thee, 4428
17:15 thy brethren shalt thou set **k** over thee: 4428
28:36 and thy **k** which thou shalt set over thee, 4428
29: 7 Sihon the **k** of Heshbon, and Og the king of 4428
29: 7 king of Heshbon, and Og the **k** of Bashan, 4428
33: 5 he was **k** in Jeshurun, when the heads of 4428
Jos 2: 2 it was told the **k** of Jericho, saying, Behold, 4428
2: 3 the **k** of Jericho sent unto Rahab, saying, 4428
6: 2 the **k** thereof, *and* the mighty *men* of 4428
8: 1 I have given into thy hand the **k** of Ai, and 4428
8: 2 her **k** as thou didst unto Jericho and 4428
8: 2 king as thou didst unto Jericho and her **k**: 4428
8:14 when the **k** of Ai saw *it*, that they hasted 4428
8:23 the **k** of Ai they took alive, and 4428
8:29 the **k** of Ai he hanged on a tree until 4428
9:10 to Sihon **k** of Heshbon, and to Og king of 4428
9:10 to Og **k** of Bashan, which *was* at Ashtaroth. 4428
10: 1 when Adoni-zedek **k** of Jerusalem had 4428
10: 1 as he had done to Jericho and her **k**, so 4428
10: 1 her king, so he had done to Ai and her **k**; 4428
10: 3 Wherefore Adoni-zedek **k** of Jerusalem 4428
10: 3 of Jerusalem sent unto Hoham **k** of Hebron, 4428
10: 3 unto Piram **k** of Jarmuth, and unto Japhia 4428
10: 3 unto Japhia **k** of Lachish, and unto Debir 4428
10: 3 and unto Debir **k** of Eglon, saying, 4428
10: 5 the **k** of Jerusalem, the king of Hebron, 4428
10: 5 the **k** of Hebron, the king of Jarmuth, 4428
10: 5 the king of Hebron, the **k** of Jarmuth, 4428
10: 5 the **k** of Lachish, the king of Eglon, 4428
10: 5 the king of Lachish, the **k** of Eglon, 4428
10:23 the **k** of Jerusalem, the king of Hebron, 4428
10:23 the **k** of Hebron, the king of Jarmuth, 4428
10:23 the king of Hebron, the **k** of Jarmuth, 4428
10:23 the **k** of Lachish, *and* the king of Eglon. 4428
10:23 the king of Lachish, *and* the **k** of Eglon. 4428
10:28 the **k** thereof he utterly destroyed, them, 4428
10:28 he did to the **k** of Makkedah as he did unto 4428
10:28 Makkedah as he did unto the **k** of Jericho. 4428
10:30 the **k** thereof, into the hand of Israel; 4428
10:30 did unto the **k** thereof as he did unto 4428
10:30 king thereof as he did unto the **k** of Jericho. 4428
10:33 Horam **k** of Gezer came up to help 4428
10:37 the **k** thereof, and all the cities thereof, 4428
10:39 and the **k** thereof, and all the cities thereof; 4428
10:39 so he did to Debir, and to the **k** thereof; 4428
10:39 as he had done also to Libnah, and to her **k**. 4428
11: 1 when Jabin **k** of Hazor had heard *those* 4428
11: 1 *things*, that he sent to Jobab **k** of Madon, 4428
11: 1 to the **k** of Shimron, and to the king of 4428
11: 1 king of Shimron, and to the **k** of Achshaph, 4428
11:10 and smote the **k** thereof with the sword: 4428
12: 2 Sihon **k** of the Amorites, who dwelt in 4428
12: 4 the coast of Og **k** of Bashan, *which was* of 4428
12: 5 the border of Sihon **k** of Heshbon. 4428
12: 9 The **k** of Jericho, one; the king of Ai, 4428
12: 9 the **k** of Ai, which *is* beside Beth-el, one; 4428
12:10 The **k** of Jerusalem, one; the king of 4428
12:10 of Jerusalem, one; the **k** of Hebron, one; 4428
12:11 The **k** of Jarmuth, one; the king of Lachish, 4428
12:11 king of Jarmuth, one; the **k** of Lachish, one; 4428
12:12 The **k** of Eglon, one; the king of Gezer, 4428
12:12 king of Eglon, one; the **k** of Gezer, one; 4428
12:13 The **k** of Debir, one; the king of Geder, 4428
12:13 king of Debir, one; the **k** of Geder, one; 4428
12:14 The **k** of Hormah, one; the king of Arad, 4428
12:14 king of Hormah, one; the **k** of Arad, one; 4428
12:15 The **k** of Libnah, one; the king of Adullam, 4428
12:15 king of Libnah, one; the **k** of Adullam, one; 4428
12:16 The **k** of Makkedah, one; the king of 4428

Jos 12:16 of Makkedah, one; the **k** of Beth-el, one; 4428
12:17 The **k** of Tappuah, one; the king of Hepher, 4428
12:17 of Tappuah, one; the **k** of Hepher, one; 4428
12:18 The **k** of Aphek, one; the king of Lasharon, 4428
12:18 king of Aphek, one; the **k** of Lasharon, one; 4428
12:19 The **k** of Madon, one; the king of Hazor, 4428
12:19 king of Madon, one; the **k** of Hazor, one; 4428
12:20 The **k** of Shimron-meron, one; the king of 4428
12:20 one; the **k** of Achshaph, one; 4428
12:21 The **k** of Taanach, one; the king of 4428
12:21 of Taanach, one; the **k** of Megiddo, one; 4428
12:22 The **k** of Kedesh, one; the king of Jokneam 4428
12:22 one; the **k** of Jokneam of Carmel, one; 4428
12:23 The **k** of Dor in the coast of Dor, one; 4428
12:23 one; the **k** of the nations of Gilgal, one; 4428
12:24 The **k** of Tirzah, one: all the kings thirty 4428
13:10 all the cities of Sihon **k** of the Amorites, 4428
13:21 all the kingdom of Sihon **k** of the Amorites, 4428
13:27 the rest of the kingdom of Sihon **k** of 4428
13:30 all the kingdom of Og **k** of Bashan, and 4428
24: 9 **k** of Moab, arose and warred against Israel, 4428
Jdg 3: 8 of Chushan-rishathaim **k** of Mesopotamia: 4428
3:10 LORD delivered Chushan-rishathaim **k** 4428
3:12 the LORD strengthened Eglon the **k** of 4428
3:14 So the children of Israel served Eglon the **k** 4428
3:15 sent a present unto Eglon the **k** of Moab. 4428
3:17 he brought the present unto Eglon **k** of 4428
3:19 said, I have a secret errand unto thee, O **k**: 4428
4: 2 them into the hand of Jabin **k** of Canaan, 4428
4:17 for *there was* peace between Jabin the **k** of 4428
4:23 So God subdued on that day Jabin the **k** of 4428
4:24 prevailed against Jabin the **k** of Canaan, 4428
4:24 until they had destroyed Jabin **k** of Canaan. 4428
8:18 *each* one resembled the children of a **k**. 4428
9: 6 of Millo, and went, and made Abimelech **k**, 4428
9: 8 The trees went forth on a time to anoint a **k** 4428
9:15 If in truth ye anoint me **k** over you, *then* 4428
9:16 in that ye have **made** Abimelech **k**, and 4427
9:18 **made** Abimelech, the son of his
maidservant, **k** 4427
11:12 Jephthah sent messengers unto the **k** of 4428
11:13 the **k** of the children of Ammon answered 4428
11:14 Jephthah sent messengers again unto the **k** 4428
11:17 Israel sent messengers unto the **k** of Edom, 4428
11:17 the **k** of Edom would not hearken *thereto*. 4428
11:17 like manner they sent unto the **k** of Moab: 4428
11:19 Israel sent messengers unto Sihon **k** of 4428
11:19 king of the Amorites, the **k** of Heshbon; 4428
11:25 than Balak the son of Zippor, **k** of Moab? 4428
11:28 Howbeit the **k** of the children of Ammon 4428
17: 6 In those days *there was* no **k** in Israel, *but* 4428
18: 1 In those days *there was* no **k** in Israel: and 4428
19: 1 those days, when *there was* no **k** in Israel, 4428
21:25 In those days *there was* no **k** in Israel: 4428
1Sa 2:10 he shall give strength unto his **k**, and 4428
8: 5 now make us a **k** to judge us like all 4428
8: 6 when they said, Give us a **k** to judge us. 4428
8: 9 shew them the manner of the **k** that shall 4428
8:10 unto the people that asked of him a **k**. 4428
8:11 This will be the manner of the **k** that shall 4428
8:18 of your **k** which ye shall have chosen you; 4428
8:19 Nay, but we will have a **k** over us; 4428
8:20 that our **k** may judge us, and go out before 4428
8:22 unto their voice, and **make** them **a k**. 4427+4428
10:19 said unto him, *Nay*, but set a **k** over us. 4428
10:24 people shouted, and said, God save the **k**. 4428
11:15 there they **made** Saul **k** before the LORD 4427
12: 1 and have **made a k** over you. 4427+4428
12: 2 now behold, the **k** walketh before you: and 4428
12: 9 into the hand of the **k** of Moab, and 4428
12:12 when ye saw that Nahash the **k** of 4428
12:12 unto me, Nay; but a **k** shall reign over us: 4428
12:12 when the LORD your God *was* your **k**. 4428
12:13 behold the **k** whom ye have chosen, 4428
12:13 behold, the LORD hath set a **k** over you. 4428
12:14 also the **k** that reigneth over you continue 4428
12:17 the sight of the LORD, in asking you a **k**. 4428
12:19 unto all our sins *this* evil, to ask us a **k**. 4428
12:25 ye shall be consumed, both ye and your **k**. 4428
15: 1 The LORD sent me to anoint thee to be **k** 4428
15: 8 he took Agag the **k** of the Amalekites alive, 4428
15:11 me that I have **set up** Saul **to be k**: 4427+4428
15:17 the LORD anointed thee **k** over Israel? 4428
15:20 have brought Agag the **k** of Amalek, and 4428
15:23 he hath also rejected thee from *being* **k**. 4428
15:26 the LORD hath rejected thee from being **k** 4428
15:32 Bring you hither to me Agag the **k** of 4428
15:35 that he had **made** Saul **k** over Israel. 4427
16: 1 for I have provided me a **k** among his sons. 4428
17:25 the **k** will enrich him *with* great riches, and 4428
17:55 *As* thy soul liveth, O **k**, I cannot tell. 4428
17:56 the **k** said, Inquire thou whose son 4428
18: 6 singing and dancing, to meet **k** Saul, 4428
18:18 that I should be son in law to the **k**? 4428
18:22 the **k** hath delight in thee, and all his 4428
18:25 The **k** desireth not *any* dowry, but an 4428
18:27 and they gave them in full tale to the **k**, 4428
19: 4 Let not the **k** sin against his servant, 4428
20: 5 I should not fail to sit with the **k** at meat: 4428
20:24 was come, the **k** sat him down to eat meat. 4428
20:25 the **k** sat upon his seat, as at other times, 4428
21: 2 The **k** hath commanded me a business, and 4428
21:10 of Saul, and went to Achish the **k** of Gath. 4428
21:11 *Is* not this David the **k** of the land? 4428
21:12 was sore afraid of Achish the **k** of Gath. 4428
22: 3 he said unto the **k** of Moab, Let my father 4428
22: 4 And he brought them before the **k** of Moab: 4428
22:11 the **k** sent to call Ahimelech the priest, 4428
22:11 in Nob: and they came all of them to the **k**. 4428
22:14 Ahimelech answered the **k**, and said, 4428
22:15 let not the **k** impute *any* thing unto his 4428
22:16 the **k** said, Thou shalt surely die, 4428
22:17 the **k** said unto the footmen that stood 4428
22:17 the servants of the **k** would not put forth 4428
22:18 the **k** said to Doeg, Turn thou, and fall upon 4428

1Sa 23:17 thou shalt be **k** over Israel, and I shall be 4427
23:20 Now therefore, O **k**, come down according 4428
24: 8 and cried after Saul, saying, My lord the **k**. 4428
24:14 After whom is the **k** of Israel come out? 4428
24:20 well that thou shalt **surely be k**, 4427+4427
25:36 a feast in his house, like the feast of a **k**; 4428
26:14 and said, Who *art* thou *that* criest to the **k**? 4428
26:15 then hast thou not kept thy lord the **k**? 4428
26:15 of the people in to destroy the **k** thy lord. 4428
26:17 David said, *It is* my voice, my lord, O **k**. 4428
26:19 let my lord the **k** hear the words of his 4428
26:20 for the **k** of Israel is come out to seek a 4428
27: 2 unto Achish, the son of Maoch, **k** of Gath. 4428
28:13 the **k** said unto her, Be not afraid: for what 4428
29: 3 the servant of Saul the **k** of Israel, 4428
29: 8 fight against the enemies of my lord the **k**? 4428
2Sa 2: 4 there they anointed David **k** over the house 4428
2: 7 also the house of Judah have anointed me **k** 4428
2: 9 he **made** him **k** over Gilead, and over 4427
2:11 the time that David was **k** in Hebron over 4428
3: 3 the daughter of Talmai **k** of Geshur; 4428
3:17 Ye sought for David in times past to be **k** 4428
3:21 will gather all Israel unto my lord the **k**, 4428
3:23 Abner the son of Ner came to the **k**, and 4428
3:24 Joab came to the **k**, and said, What hast 4428
3:31 And **k** David *himself* followed the bier. 4428
3:32 the **k** lift up his voice, and wept at the grave 4428
3:33 the **k** lamented over Abner, and said, Died 4428
3:36 as whatsoever the **k** did, pleased all 4428
3:37 not of the **k** to slay Abner the son of Ner. 4428
3:38 the **k** said unto his servants, Know ye not 4428
3:39 And I *am this* day weak, though anointed **k**; 4428
4: 8 said to the **k**, Behold the head of 4428
4: 8 the LORD hath avenged my lord the **k** 4428
5: 2 Also in time past, when Saul was **k** over us, 4428
5: 3 So all the elders of Israel came to the **k** to 4428
5: 3 **k** David made a league with them in 4428
5: 3 and they anointed David **k** over Israel. 4428
5: 6 the **k** and his men went *to* Jerusalem unto 4428
5:11 Hiram **k** of Tyre sent messengers to David, 4428
5:12 LORD had established him **k** over Israel, 4428
5:17 that they had anointed David **k** over Israel, 4428
6:13 it was told **k** David, saying, The LORD 4428
6:16 saw **k** David leaping and dancing before 4428
6:20 How glorious was the **k** of Israel to day, 4428
7: 1 when the **k** sat in his house, and 4428
7: 2 That the **k** said unto Nathan the prophet, 4428
7: 3 Nathan said to the **k**, Go, do all that *is* in 4428
7:18 went **k** David in, and sat before 4428
8: 3 the son of Rehob, **k** of Zobah, 4428
8: 5 came to succour Hadadezer **k** of Zobah, 4428
8: 8 **k** David took exceeding much brass. 4428
8: 9 When Toi **k** of Hamath heard that David 4428
8:10 Toi sent Joram his son unto **k** David, 4428
8:11 Which also **k** David did dedicate unto 4428
8:12 of Hadadezer, son of Rehob, **k** of Zobah. 4428
9: 2 the **k** said unto him, *Art* thou Ziba? 4428
9: 3 the **k** said, *Is there* not yet any of the house 4428
9: 3 Ziba said unto the **k**, Jonathan hath yet a 4428
9: 4 the **k** said unto him, Where *is* he? And Ziba 4428
9: 4 Ziba said unto the **k**, Behold, he *is in* 4428
9: 5 **k** David sent, and fet him out of the house 4428
9: 9 the **k** called to Ziba, Saul's servant, and 4428
9:11 said Ziba unto the **k**, According to all that 4428
9:11 According to all that my lord the **k** hath 4428
9:11 *said the* **k**, he shall eat at my table, NIH
10: 1 that the **k** of the children of Ammon died, 4428
10: 5 the **k** said, Tarry at Jericho until your 4428
10: 6 of **k** Maacah a thousand men, and 4428
11: 8 followed him a mess *of meat* from the **k**. 4428
11:19 of telling the matters of the war unto the **k**, 4428
12: 7 I anointed thee **k** over Israel, and 4428
13: 6 when the **k** was come to see him, Amnon 4428
13: 6 Amnon said unto the **k**, I pray thee, 4428
13:13 I pray thee, speak unto the **k**; 4428
13:21 when **k** David heard of all these things, he 4428
13:24 Absalom came to the **k**, and said, 4428
13:24 let the **k**, I beseech thee, and his servants go 4428
13:25 the **k** said to Absalom, Nay, my son, let us 4428
13:26 the **k** said unto him, Why should he go with 4428
13:31 the **k** arose, and tare his garments, and 4428
13:33 let not my lord the **k** take the thing to his 4428
13:35 Jonadab said unto the **k**, Behold, the king's 4428
13:36 the **k** also and all his servants wept very 4428
13:37 the son of Ammihud, **k** of Geshur. 4428
13:39 *the soul of* **k** David longed to go forth unto 4428
14: 3 come to the **k**, and speak on this manner 4428
14: 4 when the woman of Tekoah spake to the **k**, 4428
14: 4 and did obeisance, and said, Help, O **k**. 4428
14: 5 the **k** said unto her, What aileth thee? 4428
14: 8 the **k** said unto the woman, Go to thine 4428
14: 9 the woman of Tekoah said unto the **k**, 4428
14: 9 My lord, O **k**, the iniquity *be* on me, and 4428
14: 9 and the **k** and his throne *be* guiltless. 4428
14:10 the **k** said, Whosoever saith *ought* unto 4428
14:11 let the **k** remember the LORD thy God, 4428
14:12 speak *one* word unto my lord the **k**. 4428
14:13 for the **k** doth speak this thing as one which 4428
14:13 in that the **k** doth not fetch *home* again his 4428
14:15 to speak of this thing unto my lord the **k**, 4428
14:15 handmaid said, I will now speak unto the **k**; 4428
14:15 it may be that the **k** will perform 4428
14:16 For the **k** will hear, to deliver his handmaid 4428
14:17 The word of my lord the **k** shall now be 4428
14:17 so *is* my lord the **k** to discern good and bad: 4428
14:18 the **k** answered and said unto the woman, 4428
14:18 woman said, Let my lord the **k** now speak. 4428
14:19 the **k** said, *Is not* the hand of Joab with thee 4428
14:19 and said, *As* thy soul liveth, my lord the **k**, 4428
14:19 to the left from ought that my lord the **k** 4428
14:21 the **k** said unto Joab, Behold now, I have 4428
14:22 and bowed himself, and thanked the **k**: 4428
14:22 my lord, O **k**, in that the king hath fulfilled 4428
14:22 in that the **k** hath fulfilled the request of his 4428
14:24 the **k** said, Let him turn to his own house, 4428

2Sa 14:29 sent for Joab, to have sent him to the **k**; 4428
14:32 that I may send thee to the **k**, to say, 4428
14:33 So Joab came to the **k**, and told him: and 4428
14:33 he came to the **k**, and bowed himself on his 4428
14:33 on his face to the ground before the **k**: 4428
14:33 before the king: and the **k** kissed Absalom. 4428
15: 2 a controversy came to the **k** for judgment, 4428
15: 3 *there is* no man *deputed* of the **k** to hear 4428
15: 6 all Israel that came to the **k** for judgment: 4428
15: 7 that Absalom said unto the **k**, I pray thee, 4428
15: 9 the **k** said unto him, Go in peace. So he 4428
15:15 the king's servants said unto the **k**, Behold, 4428
15:15 *do* whatsoever my lord the **k** shall appoint. 4428
15:16 the **k** went forth, and all his household after 4428
15:16 the **k** left ten women, *which were* 4428
15:17 the **k** went forth, and all the people after 4428
15:18 him from Gath, passed on before the **k**. 4428
15:19 said the **k** to Ittai the Gittite, Wherefore 4428
15:19 return to thy place, and abide with the **k**: 4428
15:21 Ittai answered the **k**, and said, *As* 4428
15:21 LORD liveth, and *as* my lord the **k** liveth, 4428
15:21 surely in what place my lord the **k** shall be, 4428
15:23 the **k** also *himself* passed over the brook 4428
15:25 the **k** said unto Zadok, Carry back the ark 4428
15:27 The **k** said also unto Zadok the priest, *Art* 4428
15:34 unto Absalom, I will be thy servant, O **k**; 4428
16: 2 the **k** said unto Ziba, What meanest thou by 4428
16: 3 the **k** said, And where *is* thy master's son? 4428
16: 3 Ziba said unto the **k**, Behold, he abideth at 4428
16: 4 said the **k** to Ziba, Behold, thine *are* all that 4428
16: 4 I may find grace in thy sight, my lord, O **k**. 4428
16: 5 when **k** David came to Bahurim, behold, 4428
16: 6 at David, and at all the servants of **k** David: 4428
16: 9 said Abishai the son of Zeruiah unto the **k**, 4428
16: 9 should this dead dog curse my lord the **k**? 4428
16:10 And the **k** said, What have I to do with you, 4428
16:14 the **k**, and all the people that *were* with 4428
16:16 God save the **k**, God save the king. 4428
16:16 God save the king, God save the **k**. 4428
17: 2 him shall flee; and I will smite the **k** only: 4428
17:16 lest the **k** be swallowed up, and all 4428
17:17 told them; and they went and told **k** David. 4428
17:21 went and told **k** David, and said unto 4428
18: 2 the **k** said unto the people, I will surely go 4428
18: 4 the **k** said unto them, What seemeth you 4428
18: 4 the **k** stood by the gate side, and all 4428
18: 5 the **k** commanded Joab and Abishai and 4428
18: 5 all the people heard when the **k** gave all 4428
18:12 for in our hearing the **k** charged thee and 4428
18:13 for there is no matter hid from the **k**, and 4428
18:19 Let me now run, and bear the **k** tidings, 4428
18:21 to Cushi, Go tell the **k** what thou hast seen. 4428
18:25 the watchman cried, and told the **k**. And 4428
18:25 the **k** said, If he *be* alone, *there is* tidings in 4428
18:26 And the **k** said, He also bringeth tidings. 4428
18:27 the **k** said, He *is* a good man, and 4428
18:28 and said unto the **k**, All is well. 4428
18:28 to the earth upon his face before the **k**, 4428
18:28 that lift up their hand against my lord the **k**. 4428
18:29 the **k** said, *Is* the young man Absalom safe? 4428
18:30 the **k** said *unto him*, Turn aside, *and* 4428
18:31 and Cushi said, Tidings, my lord the **k**: 4428
18:32 the **k** said unto Cushi, *Is* the young man 4428
18:32 The enemies of my lord the **k**, and all that 4428
18:33 the **k** was much moved, and went up to 4428
19: 1 the **k** weepeth and mourneth for Absalom. 4428
19: 2 for the people heard say that day *how* the **k** 4428
19: 4 the **k** covered his face, and the king cried 4428
19: 4 the **k** cried *with* a loud voice, O my son 4428
19: 5 Joab came *into* the house to the **k**, and said, 4428
19: 8 the **k** rose, and sat in the gate. And they 4428
19: 8 Behold, the **k** doth sit in the gate. 4428
19: 8 all the people came before the **k**: for Israel 4428
19: 9 The **k** saved us out of the hand of our 4428
19:10 why speak ye not a word of bringing the **k** 4428
19:11 **k** David sent to Zadok and to Abiathar 4428
19:11 Why are ye the last to bring the **k** back to 4428
19:11 the speech of all Israel is come to the **k**, 4428
19:12 then are ye the last to bring back the **k**? 4428
19:14 so that they sent *this word* unto the **k**, 4428
19:15 So the **k** returned, and came to Jordan. 4428
19:15 Judah came to Gilgal, to go to meet the **k**, 4428
19:15 the king, to conduct the **k** over Jordan. 4428
19:16 with the men of Judah to meet **k** David. 4428
19:17 and they went over Jordan before the **k**. 4428
19:18 the son of Gera fell down before the **k**, 4428
19:19 said unto the **k**, Let not my lord impute 4428
19:19 that my lord the **k** went out of Jerusalem, 4428
19:19 that the **k** should take *it* to his heart. 4428
19:20 Joseph to go down to meet my lord the **k**. 4428
19:22 for do not I know that I *am this* day **k** over 4428
19:23 Therefore the **k** said unto Shimei, 4428
19:23 shalt not die. And the **k** sware unto him. 4428
19:24 the son of Saul came down to meet the **k**, 4428
19:24 from the day the **k** departed until the day he 4428
19:25 he was come *to* Jerusalem to meet the **k**, 4428
19:25 that the **k** said unto him, Wherefore wentest 4428
19:26 he answered, My lord, O **k**, my servant 4428
19:26 that I may ride thereon, and go to the **k**; 4428
19:27 slandered thy servant unto my lord the **k**; 4428
19:27 but my lord the **k** *is* as an angel of God: 4428
19:28 but dead men before my lord the **k**: 4428
19:28 have I yet to cry any more unto the **k**? 4428
19:29 the **k** said unto him, Why speakest thou any 4428
19:30 Mephibosheth said unto the **k**, Yea, let him 4428
19:30 forasmuch as my lord the **k** is come *again* 4428
19:31 went over Jordan with the **k**, to conduct 4428
19:32 he had provided the **k** of sustenance while 4428
19:33 the **k** said unto Barzillai, Come thou over 4428
19:34 Barzillai said unto the **k**, How long have I 4428
19:34 that I should go up with the **k** *unto* 4428
19:35 servant be yet a burden unto my lord the **k**? 4428
19:36 will go a little *way* over Jordan with the **k**: 4428
19:36 why should the **k** recompense *it* me *with* 4428
19:37 let him go over with my lord the **k**; and 4428

K

2Sa 19:38 the **k** answered, Chimham shall go over 4428
19:39 when the **k** was come over, the king kissed 4428
19:39 the **k** kissed Barzillai, and blessed him; 4428
19:40 the **k** went on to Gilgal, and Chimham went 4428
19:40 all the people of Judah conducted the **k**, 4428
19:41 all the men of Israel came to the **k**, and 4428
19:41 Israel came to the king, and said unto the **k**, 4428
19:41 have brought the **k**, and his household, and 4428
19:42 of Israel, Because the **k** *is* near of kin to us: 4428
19:43 We have ten parts in the **k**, and we have 4428
19:43 not be first had in bringing back our **k**? 4428
20: 2 the men of Judah clave unto their **k**, 4428
20: 3 the **k** took the ten women *his* concubines, 4428
20: 4 said the **k** to Amasa, Assemble me the men 4428
20:21 hath lift up his hand against the **k**, 4428
20:22 And Joab returned *to* Jerusalem unto the **k**. 4428
21: 2 the **k** called the Gibeonites, and said unto 4428
21: 5 they answered the **k**, The man that 4428
21: 6 And the **k** said, I will give *them*. 4428
21: 7 the **k** spared Mephibosheth, the son of 4428
21: 8 the **k** took the two sons of Rizpah 4428
21:14 they performed all that the **k** commanded. 4428
22:51 *He is* the tower of salvation for his **k**: and 4428
24: 2 For the **k** said to Joab the captain of 4428
24: 3 Joab said unto the **k**, Now the LORD thy 4428
24: 3 *that* the eyes of my lord the **k** may see *it*: 4428
24: 3 why doth my lord the **k** delight in this 4428
24: 4 host went out from the presence of the **k**, 4428
24: 9 sum of the number of the people unto the **k**: 4428
24:20 saw the **k** and his servants coming on 4428
24:20 bowed himself before the **k** *on* his face 4428
24:21 Wherefore is my lord the **k** come to his 4428
24:22 Let my lord the **k** take and offer up what 4428
24:23 did Araunah, *as* a **k**, give unto the king. 4428
24:23 did Araunah, *as* a king, give unto the **k**. 4428
24:23 Araunah said unto the **k**, The LORD thy 4428
24:24 the **k** said unto Araunah, Nay; but I will 4428
1Ki 1: 1 Now **k** David was old *and* stricken in years; 4428
1: 2 Let there be sought for my lord the **k** a 4428
1: 2 let her stand before the **k**, and let her 4428
1: 2 thy bosom, that my lord the **k** may get heat. 4428
1: 3 a Shunammite, and brought her to the **k**. 4428
1: 4 and cherished the **k**, and ministered to him: 4428
1: 4 ministered to him: but the **k** knew her not. 4428
1: 5 exalted himself, saying, I will be **k**: 4427
1:13 Go and get thee in unto **k** David, and 4428
1:13 say unto him, Didst not thou, my lord O **k**, 4428
1:14 while thou yet talkest there with the **k**, 4428
1:15 Bath-sheba went in unto the **k** into 4428
1:15 the **k** was very old; and Abishag 4428
1:15 the Shunammite ministered unto the **k**. 4428
1:16 and did obeisance unto the **k**. 4428
1:16 And the **k** said, What wouldest thou? 4428
1:18 now, my lord the **k**, thou knowest *it* not: 4428
1:19 hath called all the sons of the **k**, and 4428
1:20 thou, my lord O **k**, the eyes of all Israel *are* 4428
1:20 sit on the throne of my lord the **k** after him. 4428
1:21 when my lord the **k** shall sleep with his 4428
1:22 lo, while she yet talked with the **k**, 4428
1:23 they told the **k**, saying, Behold Nathan 4428
1:23 when he was come in before the **k**, he 4428
1:23 he bowed himself before the **k** with his face 4428
1:24 Nathan said, My lord O **k**, hast thou said, 4428
1:25 before him, and say, God save **k** Adonijah. 4428
1:27 Is this thing done by my lord the **k**, and 4428
1:27 sit on the throne of my lord the **k** after him? 4428
1:28 **k** David answered and said, Call me 4428
1:28 the king's presence, and stood before the **k**. 4428
1:29 the **k** sware, and said, *As* the LORD 4428
1:31 did reverence to the **k**, and said, Let my 4428
1:31 and said, Let my lord **k** David live for ever. 4428
1:32 **k** David said, Call me Zadok the priest, 4428
1:32 of Jehoiada. And they came before the **k**. 4428
1:33 The **k** also said unto them, Take with you 4428
1:34 Nathan the prophet anoint him there **k** over 4428
1:34 the trumpet, and say, God save **k** Solomon. 4428
1:35 my throne; for he shall be **k** in my stead: 4427
1:36 the son of Jehoiada answered the **k**, 4428
1:36 the LORD God of my lord the **k** say so 4428
1:37 the LORD hath been with my lord the **k**, 4428
1:37 greater than the throne of my lord **k** David. 4428
1:38 caused Solomon to ride upon **k** David's 4428
1:39 all the people said, God save **k** Solomon. 4428
1:43 Verily our lord **k** David hath made 4428
1:43 our lord king David hath **made** Solomon **k**. 4427
1:44 the **k** hath sent with him Zadok the priest, 4428
1:45 Nathan the prophet have anointed him **k** in 4428
1:47 servants came to bless our lord **k** David, 4428
1:47 And the **k** bowed himself upon the bed. 4428
1:48 also thus said the **k**, Blessed *be* the LORD 4428
1:51 Behold, Adonijah feareth **k** Solomon: 4428
1:51 Let **k** Solomon swear unto me to day that 4428
1:53 So **k** Solomon sent, and they brought him 4428
1:53 he came and bowed himself to **k** Solomon: 4428
2:17 Speak, I pray thee, unto Solomon the **k**, 4428
2:18 Well; I will speak for thee unto the **k**. 4428
2:19 Bath-sheba therefore went unto **k** Solomon, 4428
2:19 the **k** rose up to meet her, and 4428
2:20 the **k** said unto her, Ask on, my mother: 4428
2:22 **k** Solomon answered and said unto his 4428
2:23 **k** Solomon sware by the LORD, saying, 4428
2:25 **k** Solomon sent by the hand of Benaiah 4428
2:26 unto Abiathar the priest said the **k**, Get thee 4428
2:29 it was told **k** Solomon that Joab was fled 4428
2:30 unto him, Thus saith the **k**, Come forth. 4428
2:30 Benaiah brought the **k** word again, saying, 4428
2:31 the **k** said unto him, Do as he hath said, 4428
2:35 the **k** put Benaiah the son of Jehoiada in his 4428
2:35 Zadok the priest did the **k** put in the room 4428
2:36 the **k** sent and called for Shimei, and 4428
2:38 Shimei said unto the **k**, The saying *is* good: 4428
2:38 as my lord the **k** hath said, so will thy 4428
2:39 unto Achish son of Maachah **k** of Gath. 4428
2:42 the **k** sent and called for Shimei, and 4428
2:44 The **k** said moreover to Shimei, 4428
1Ki 2:45 **k** Solomon *shall be* blessed, and the throne 4428
2:46 So the **k** commanded Benaiah the son of 4428
3: 1 Solomon made affinity with Pharaoh **k** of 4428
3: 4 the **k** went to Gibeon to sacrifice there; 4428
3: 7 thou hast **made** thy servant **k** instead of 4427
3:16 unto the **k**, and stood before him. 4428
3:22 *is* my son. Thus they spake before the **k**. 4428
3:23 said the **k**, The one saith, This *is* my son 4428
3:24 the **k** said, Bring me a sword. And they 4428
3:24 And they brought a sword before the **k**. 4428
3:25 the **k** said, Divide the living child in two, 4428
3:26 whose the living child *was* unto the **k**, 4428
3:27 the **k** answered and said, Give her 4428
3:28 all Israel heard of the judgment which the **k** 4428
3:28 the king had judged; and they feared the **k**: 4228
4: 1 So **k** Solomon was king over all Israel. 4428
4: 1 So king Solomon was **k** over all Israel. 4428
4: 7 which provided victuals for the **k** and his 4428
4:19 *in* the country of Sihon **k** of the Amorites, 4428
4:19 of the Amorites, and of Og **k** of Bashan; 4428
4:27 those officers provided victual for **k** 4428
4:27 for all that came unto **k** Solomon's table, 4428
5: 1 Hiram **k** of Tyre sent his servants unto 4428
5: 1 anointed him **k** in the room of his father: 4428
5:13 **k** Solomon raised a levy out of all Israel; 4428
5:17 the **k** commanded, and they brought great 4428
6: 2 the house which **k** Solomon built for 4428
7:13 **k** Solomon sent and fet Hiram out of Tyre. 4428
7:14 he came to **k** Solomon, and wrought all his 4428
7:40 **k** Solomon *for* the house of the LORD: 4428
7:45 which Hiram made to **k** Solomon *for* 4428
7:46 In the plain of Jordan did the **k** cast them, 4428
7:51 So was ended all the work that **k** Solomon 4428
8: 1 of Israel, unto **k** Solomon *in* Jerusalem, 4428
8: 2 **k** Solomon at the feast in the month 4428
8: 5 **k** Solomon, and all the congregation of 4428
8:14 the **k** turned his face about, and blessed all 4428
8:62 the **k**, and all Israel with him, 4428
8:63 So the **k** and all the children of Israel 4428
8:64 The same day did the **k** hallow the middle 4428
8:66 they blessed the **k**, and went unto their tents 4428
9:11 (*Now* Hiram the **k** of Tyre had furnished 4428
9:11 **k** Solomon gave Hiram twenty cities in 4428
9:14 Hiram sent to the **k** sixscore talents of gold. 4428
9:15 this *is* the reason of the levy which **k** 4428
9:16 *For* Pharaoh **k** of Egypt had gone up, and 4428
9:26 **k** Solomon made a navy *of ships* in 4428
9:28 and brought *it* to **k** Solomon. 4428
10: 3 there was not *any* thing hid from the **k**, 4428
10: 6 she said to the **k**, It was a true report that I 4428
10: 9 therefore made he thee **k**, to do judgment 4428
10:10 she gave the **k** an hundred and 4428
10:10 the queen of Sheba gave to **k** Solomon. 4428
10:12 the **k** made *of* the almug trees pillars for 4428
10:13 **k** Solomon gave unto the queen of Sheba 4428
10:16 **k** Solomon made two hundred targets *of* 4428
10:17 the **k** put them *in* the house of the forest of 4428
10:18 Moreover the **k** made a great throne of 4428
10:21 all **k** Solomon's drinking vessels *were of* 4428
10:22 For the **k** had at sea a navy of Tharshish 4428
10:23 So **k** Solomon exceeded all the kings of 4428
10:26 for chariots, and with the **k** at Jerusalem. 4428
10:27 the **k** made silver *to be* in Jerusalem as 4428
11: 1 **k** Solomon loved many strange women, 4428
11:18 came *to* Egypt, unto Pharaoh **k** of Egypt; 4428
11:23 which fled from his lord Hadadezer **k** of 4428
11:26 even he lift up *his* hand against the **k**. 4428
11:27 cause that he lift up *his* hand against the **k**: 4428
11:37 thy soul desireth, and shalt be **k** over Israel. 4428
11:40 unto Shishak **k** of Egypt, and was in Egypt 4428
12: 1 were come *to* Shechem to **make** him **k**. 4427
12: 2 was fled from the presence of **k** Solomon, 4428
12: 6 **k** Rehoboam consulted with the old men, 4428
12:12 as the **k** had appointed, saying, Come to me 4428
12:13 the **k** answered the people roughly, and 4428
12:15 Wherefore the **k** hearkened not unto 4428
12:16 So when all Israel saw that the **k** hearkened 4428
12:16 the people answered the **k**, saying, 4428
12:18 **k** Rehoboam sent Adoram, who *was* over 4428
12:18 Therefore **k** Rehoboam made speed to get 4428
12:20 and **made** him **k** over all Israel: 4427
12:23 **k** of Judah, and unto all the house of Judah 4428
12:27 *even* unto Rehoboam **k** of Judah, and 4428
12:27 and go again to Rehoboam **k** of Judah. 4428
12:28 Whereupon the **k** took counsel, and 4428
13: 4 when **k** Jeroboam heard the saying of 4428
13: 6 the **k** answered and said unto the man of 4428
13: 7 the **k** said unto the man of God, 4428
13: 8 the man of God said unto the **k**, If thou wilt 4428
13:11 the words which he had spoken unto the **k**, 4428
14: 2 which told me that I should be **k** over this 4428
14:14 LORD shall raise him up a **k** over Israel, 4428
14:25 it came to pass in the fifth year of **k** 4428
14:25 *that* Shishak **k** of Egypt came up against 4428
14:27 **k** Rehoboam made in their stead brasen 4428
14:28 when the **k** went *into* the house of 4428
15: 1 Now in the eighteenth year of **k** Jeroboam 4428
15: 9 in the twentieth year of Jeroboam **k** of 4428
15:16 and Baasha **k** of Israel all their days. 4428
15:17 Baasha **k** of Israel went up against Judah, 4428
15:17 *any* to go out or come in to Asa **k** of Judah. 4428
15:18 **k** Asa sent them to Ben-hadad, the son of 4428
15:18 of Tabrimon, the son of Hezion, **k** of Syria, 4428
15:19 break thy league with Baasha **k** of Israel, 4428
15:20 So Ben-hadad hearkened unto **k** Asa, and 4428
15:22 **k** Asa made a proclamation throughout all 4428
15:22 **k** Asa built with them Geba of Benjamin, 4428
15:25 Israel in the second year of Asa **k** of Judah, 4428
15:28 Even in the third year of Asa **k** of Judah did 4428
15:32 and Baasha **k** of Israel all their days. 4428
15:33 In the third year of Asa **k** of Judah *began* 4428
16: 8 sixth year of Asa **k** of Judah *began* Elah 4428
16:10 and seventh year of Asa **k** of Judah, 4428
16:15 seventh year of Asa **k** of Judah did Zimri 4428
16:16 hath conspired, and hath also slain the **k**: 4428
1Ki 16:16 Israel **made** Omri, the captain of the host, **k** 4427
16:21 Tibni the son of Ginath, to **make** him **k**; 4427
16:23 first year of Asa **k** of Judah *began* Omri to 4428
16:29 eighth year of Asa **k** of Judah *began* Ahab 4428
16:31 the daughter of Ethbaal **k** of the Zidonians, 4428
19:15 anoint Hazael to be **k** over Syria: 4428
19:16 shalt thou anoint to be **k** over Israel: 4428
20: 1 Ben-hadad the **k** of Syria gathered all his 4428
20: 2 he sent messengers to Ahab **k** of Israel into 4428
20: 4 the **k** of Israel answered and said, My lord, 4428
20: 4 of Israel answered and said, My lord, O **k**, 4428
20: 7 the **k** of Israel called all the elders of 4428
20: 9 of Ben-hadad, Tell my lord the **k**, 4428
20:11 the **k** of Israel answered and said, Tell *him*, 4428
20:13 there came a prophet unto Ahab **k** of Israel, 4428
20:20 Ben-hadad the **k** of Syria escaped on a 4428
20:21 the **k** of Israel went out, and smote 4428
20:22 the prophet came to the **k** of Israel, and 4428
20:22 for at the return of the year the **k** of Syria 4428
20:23 the servants of the **k** of Syria said unto him, 4428
20:28 spake unto the **k** of Israel, and said, 4428
20:31 our heads, and go out to the **k** of Israel: 4428
20:32 and came to the **k** of Israel, and said, 4428
20:38 waited for the **k** by the way, and 4428
20:39 as the **k** passed by, he cried unto the king: 4428
20:39 as the king passed by, he cried unto the **k**: 4428
20:40 the **k** of Israel said unto him, So *shall* thy 4428
20:41 the **k** of Israel discerned him that he *was* of 4428
20:43 the **k** of Israel went to his house heavy and 4428
21: 1 hard by the palace of Ahab **k** of Samaria. 4428
21:10 Thou didst blaspheme God and the **k**. 4428
21:13 Naboth did blaspheme God and the **k**. 4428
21:18 Arise, go down to meet Ahab **k** of Israel, 4428
22: 2 that Jehoshaphat the **k** of Judah came down 4428
22: 2 king of Judah came down to the **k** of Israel. 4428
22: 3 the **k** of Israel said unto his servants, Know 4428
22: 3 take it not out of the hand of the **k** of Syria? 4428
22: 4 Jehoshaphat said to the **k** of Israel, I *am* as 4428
22: 5 Jehoshaphat said unto the **k** of Israel, 4428
22: 6 the **k** of Israel gathered the prophets 4428
22: 6 Lord shall deliver *it* into the hand of the **k**. 4428
22: 8 the **k** of Israel said unto Jehoshaphat, 4428
22: 8 And Jehoshaphat said, Let not the **k** say so. 4428
22: 9 the **k** of Israel called an officer, and said, 4428
22:10 the **k** of Israel and Jehoshaphat the king of 4428
22:10 Jehoshaphat the **k** of Judah sat each on his 4428
22:13 *declare* good unto the **k** *with* one mouth: 4428
22:15 So he came to the **k**. And the king said unto 4428
22:15 the **k** said unto him, Micaiah, shall we go 4428
22:15 shall deliver *it* into the hand of the **k**. 4428
22:16 the **k** said unto him, How many times shall 4428
22:18 the **k** of Israel said unto Jehoshaphat, Did I 4428
22:26 the **k** of Israel said, Take Micaiah, and 4428
22:27 say, Thus saith the **k**, Put this *fellow in* 4428
22:29 So the **k** of Israel and Jehoshaphat the king 4428
22:29 Jehoshaphat the **k** of Judah went up *to* 4428
22:30 the **k** of Israel said unto Jehoshaphat, I will 4428
22:30 the **k** of Israel disguised himself, and 4428
22:31 the **k** of Syria commanded his thirty and 4428
22:31 nor great, save only with the **k** of Israel. 4428
22:32 that they said, Surely it *is* the **k** of Israel. 4428
22:33 perceived that it *was* not the **k** of Israel, 4428
22:34 smote the **k** of Israel between the joints of 4428
22:35 the **k** was stayed up in *his* chariot against 4428
22:37 So the **k** died, and was brought *to* Samaria; 4428
22:37 and they buried the **k** in Samaria. 4428
22:41 in the fourth year of Ahab **k** of Israel. 4428
22:44 Jehoshaphat made peace with the **k** of 4428
22:47 *There was* then no **k** in Edom: a deputy *was* 4428
22:47 then no king in Edom: a deputy *was* **k**. 4428
22:51 year of Jehoshaphat **k** of Judah, 4428
2Ki 1: 3 go up to meet the messengers of the **k** of 4428
1: 6 turn again unto the **k** that sent you, and 4428
1: 9 the **k** sent unto him a captain of fifty with NIH
1: 9 man of God, the **k** hath said, Come down. 4428
1:11 O man of God, thus hath the **k** said, 4428
1:15 and went down with him unto the **k**. 4428
1:17 Jehoram the son of Jehoshaphat **k** of Judah; 4428
3: 1 eighteenth year of Jehoshaphat **k** of Judah, 4428
3: 4 Mesha **k** of Moab was a sheepmaster, and 4428
3: 4 rendered unto the **k** of Israel an hundred 4428
3: 5 that the **k** of Moab rebelled against the king 4428
3: 5 that the king of Moab rebelled against the **k** 4428
3: 6 **k** Jehoram went out of Samaria the same 4428
3: 7 and sent to Jehoshaphat the **k** of Judah, 4428
3: 7 The **k** of Moab hath rebelled against me: 4428
3: 9 So the **k** of Israel went, and the king of 4428
3: 9 and the **k** of Judah, and the king of Edom: 4428
3: 9 and the king of Judah, and the **k** of Edom: 4428
3:10 the **k** of Israel said, Alas, that the LORD 4428
3:11 one of the **k** of Israel's servants answered 4428
3:12 So the **k** of Israel and Jehoshaphat and 4428
3:12 and the **k** of Edom went down to him. 4428
3:13 Elisha said unto the **k** of Israel, What have 4428
3:13 the **k** of Israel said unto him, Nay: for 4428
3:14 the presence of Jehoshaphat the **k** of Judah, 4428
3:26 when the **k** of Moab saw that the battle was 4428
3:26 to break through *even* unto the **k** of Edom: 4428
4:13 wouldest thou be spoken for to the **k**, or 4428
5: 1 captain of the host of the **k** of Syria, 4428
5: 5 the **k** of Syria said, Go to, go, and I will 4428
5: 5 and I will send a letter unto the **k** of Israel. 4428
5: 6 he brought the letter to the **k** of Israel, 4428
5: 7 when the **k** of Israel had read the letter, 4428
5: 8 that the **k** of Israel had rent his clothes, 4428
5: 8 that he sent to the **k**, saying, Wherefore 4428
6: 8 the **k** of Syria warred against Israel, and 4428
6: 9 the man of God sent unto the **k** of Israel, 4428
6:10 the **k** of Israel sent to the place which 4428
6:11 Therefore the heart of the **k** of Syria was 4428
6:11 shew me which of us *is* for the **k** of Israel? 4428
6:12 of his servants said, None, my lord, O **k**: 4428
6:12 telleth the **k** of Israel the words that thou 4428
6:21 the **k** of Israel said unto Elisha, when he 4428
6:24 that Ben-hadad **k** of Syria gathered all his 4428

2Ki 6:26 as the **k** of Israel was passing by upon 4428
6:26 unto him, saying, Help, my lord, O **k**. 4428
6:28 the **k** said unto her, What aileth thee? 4428
6:30 when the **k** heard the words of the woman, 4428
6:32 and *the* **k** sent a man from before him: NIH
7: 2 a lord on whose hand the **k** leaned 4428
7: 6 the **k** of Israel hath hired against us 4428
7:12 the **k** arose in the night, and said unto his 4428
7:14 the **k** sent after the host of the Syrians, 4428
7:15 the messengers returned, and told the **k**. 4428
7:17 the **k** appointed the lord on whose hand he 4428
7:17 who spake when the **k** came down to him. 4428
7:18 as the man of God had spoken to the **k**, 4428
8: 3 she went forth to cry unto the **k** for her 4428
8: 4 the **k** talked with Gehazi the servant of 4428
8: 5 *as* he was telling the **k** how he had restored 4428
8: 5 cried to the **k** for her house and for her 4428
8: 5 Gehazi said, My lord, O **k**, this *is* 4428
8: 6 when the **k** asked the woman, she told him. 4428
8: 6 So the **k** appointed unto her a certain 4428
8: 7 Ben-hadad the **k** of Syria was sick; and 4428
8: 8 the **k** said unto Hazael, Take a present in 4428
8: 9 Thy son Ben-hadad **k** of Syria hath sent me 4428
8:13 shewed me *that* thou *shalt be* **k** over Syria. 4428
8:16 in the fifth year of Joram the son of Ahab **k** 4428
8:16 Jehoshaphat *being* then **k** of Judah, 4428
8:16 Jehoram the son of Jehoshaphat **k** of Judah 4428
8:20 and **made a k** over themselves. 4427+4428
8:25 **k** of Israel did Ahaziah the son of Jehoram 4428
8:25 son of Jehoram **k** of Judah *begin* to reign. 4428
8:26 the daughter of Omri **k** of Israel. 4428
8:28 Hazael **k** of Syria in Ramoth-gilead; 4428
8:29 **k** Joram went back to be healed in Jezreel 4428
8:29 when he fought against Hazael **k** of Syria. 4428
8:29 Ahaziah the son of Jehoram **k** of Judah 4428
9: 3 I have anointed thee **k** over Israel. 4428
9: 6 I have anointed thee **k** over the people of 4428
9:12 I have anointed thee **k** over Israel. 4428
9:13 and blew with trumpets, saying, Jehu is **k**. 4427
9:14 and all Israel, because of Hazael **k** of Syria. 4428
9:15 **k** Joram was returned to be healed in 4428
9:15 when he fought with Hazael **k** of Syria.) 4428
9:16 Ahaziah **k** of Judah was come down to see 4428
9:18 and said, Thus saith the **k**, *Is it* peace? 4428
9:19 and said, Thus saith the **k**, *Is it* peace? 4428
9:21 Joram **k** of Israel and Ahaziah king of 4428
9:21 of Israel and Ahaziah **k** of Judah went out, 4428
9:27 when Ahaziah the **k** of Judah saw *this*, he 4428
10: 5 thou shalt bid us; we will not **make** any **k**: 4427
10:13 Jehu met with the brethren of Ahaziah **k** of 4428
10:13 we go down to salute the children of the **k** 4428
11: 2 Jehosheba, the daughter of **k** Joram, 4428
11: 7 of the house of the LORD about the **k**. 4428
11: 8 ye shall compass the **k** round about, 4428
11: 8 be ye with the **k** as he goeth out and as he 4428
11:10 did the priest give **k** David's spears 4428
11:11 his weapons in his hand, round about the **k**, 4428
11:12 they **made** him **k**, and anointed him; and 4427
11:12 clapt their hands, and said, God save the **k**. 4428
11:14 behold, the **k** stood by a pillar, as 4428
11:14 and the princes and the trumpeters by the **k**, 4428
11:17 the LORD and the **k** and the people, 4428
11:17 between the **k** also and the people. 4428
11:19 they brought down the **k** from the house of 4428
12: 6 twentieth year of **k** Jehoash the priests had 4428
12: 7 **k** Jehoash called for Jehoiada the priest, 4428
12:17 Hazael **k** of Syria went up, and 4428
12:18 Jehoash **k** of Judah took all the hallowed 4428
12:18 and sent *it* to Hazael **k** of Syria: 4428
13: 1 **k** of Judah Jehoahaz the son of Jehu *began* 4428
13: 3 he delivered them into the hand of Hazael **k** 4428
13: 4 because the **k** of Syria oppressed them. 4428
13: 7 for the **k** of Syria had destroyed them, and 4428
13:10 seventh year of Joash **k** of Judah *began* 4428
13:12 he fought against Amaziah **k** of Judah, 4428
13:14 Joash the **k** of Israel came down unto him, 4428
13:16 he said to the **k** of Israel, Put thine hand 4428
13:18 he took *them*. And he said unto the **k** of 4428
13:22 Hazael **k** of Syria oppressed Israel all 4428
13:24 So Hazael **k** of Syria died; and 4428
14: 1 **k** of Israel reigned Amaziah the son of 4428
14: 1 Amaziah the son of Joash **k** of Judah. 4428
14: 5 servants which had slain the **k** his father. 4428
14: 8 son of Jehu, **k** of Israel, saying, Come, 4428
14: 9 Jehoash the **k** of Israel sent to Amaziah 4428
14: 9 king of Israel sent to Amaziah **k** of Judah, 4428
14:11 Therefore Jehoash **k** of Israel went up; and 4428
14:11 Amaziah **k** of Judah looked one another *in* 4428
14:13 Jehoash **k** of Israel took Amaziah king of 4428
14:13 Jehoash king of Israel took Amaziah **k** of 4428
14:15 how he fought with Amaziah **k** of Judah, 4428
14:17 Amaziah the son of Joash **k** of Judah lived 4428
14:17 son of Jehoahaz **k** of Israel fifteen years. 4428
14:21 **made** him **k** instead of his father Amaziah. 4427
14:22 after that the **k** slept with his fathers. 4428
14:23 **k** of Judah Jeroboam the son of Joash king 4428
14:23 Joash **k** of Israel *began* to reign in Samaria, 4428
15: 1 seventh year of Jeroboam **k** of Israel *began* 4428
15: 1 son of Amaziah **k** of Judah to reign. 4428
15: 5 the LORD smote the **k**, so that he was a 4428
15: 8 eighth year of Azariah **k** of Judah did 4428
15:13 thirtieth year of Uzziah **k** of Judah; 4428
15:17 thirtieth year of Azariah **k** of Judah *began* 4428
15:19 *And* Pul the **k** of Assyria came against 4428
15:20 *of* silver, to give to the **k** of Assyria. 4428
15:20 So the **k** of Assyria turned back, and 4428
15:23 In the fiftieth year of Azariah **k** of Judah 4428
15:27 fiftieth year of Azariah **k** of Judah Pekah 4428
15:29 In the days of Pekah **k** of Israel came 4428
15:29 of Israel came Tiglath-pileser **k** of Assyria, 4428
15:32 **k** of Israel *began* Jotham the son of Uzziah 4428
15:32 the son of Uzziah **k** of Judah to reign. 4428
15:37 to send against Judah Rezin the **k** of Syria, 4428
16: 1 son of Jotham **k** of Judah *began* to reign. 4428
16: 5 Rezin **k** of Syria and Pekah son of 4428

2Ki 16: 5 Pekah son of Remaliah **k** of Israel came up 4428
16: 6 At that time Rezin **k** of Syria recovered 4428
16: 7 messengers to Tiglath-pileser **k** of Assyria, 4428
16: 7 save me out of the hand of the **k** of Syria, 4428
16: 7 out of the hand of the **k** of Israel, which rise 4428
16: 8 and sent *it for* a present to the **k** of Assyria. 4428
16: 9 the **k** of Assyria hearkened unto him: 4428
16: 9 for the **k** of Assyria went up against 4428
16:10 **k** Ahaz went *to* Damascus to meet 4428
16:10 to meet Tiglath-pileser **k** of Assyria, 4428
16:10 **k** Ahaz sent to Urijah the priest the fashion 4428
16:11 to all that **k** Ahaz had sent from Damascus: 4428
16:11 Urijah the priest made *it* against **k** Ahaz 4428
16:12 when the **k** was come from Damascus, 4428
16:12 come from Damascus, the **k** saw the altar: 4428
16:12 the **k** approached to the altar, and 4428
16:15 **k** Ahaz commanded Urijah the priest, 4428
16:16 according to all that **k** Ahaz commanded. 4428
16:17 **k** Ahaz cut off the borders of the bases, 4428
16:18 house of the LORD for the **k** of Assyria. 4428
17: 1 In the twelfth year of Ahaz **k** of Judah 4428
17: 3 Against him came up Shalmaneser **k** of 4428
17: 4 the **k** of Assyria found conspiracy in 4428
17: 4 for he had sent messengers to So **k** of 4428
17: 4 brought no present to the **k** of Assyria, 4428
17: 4 therefore the **k** of Assyria shut him up, and 4428
17: 5 the **k** of Assyria came up throughout all 4428
17: 6 the **k** of Assyria took Samaria, and 4428
17: 7 from under the hand of Pharaoh **k** of Egypt, 4428
17:21 they **made** Jeroboam the son of Nebat **k**: 4427
17:24 the **k** of Assyria brought *men* from 4428
17:26 Wherefore they spake to the **k** of Assyria, 4428
17:27 the **k** of Assyria commanded, saying, 4428
18: 1 year of Hoshea son of Elah **k** of Israel, 4428
18: 1 *that* Hezekiah the son of Ahaz **k** of Judah 4428
18: 7 he rebelled against the **k** of Assyria, and 4428
18: 9 it came to pass in the fourth year of **k** 4428
18: 9 year of Hoshea son of Elah **k** of Israel, 4428
18: 9 *that* Shalmaneser **k** of Assyria came up 4428
18:10 that *is* the ninth year of Hoshea **k** of Israel, 4428
18:11 the **k** of Assyria did carry away Israel unto 4428
18:13 Now in the fourteenth year of **k** Hezekiah 4428
18:13 **k** of Assyria come up against all the fenced 4428
18:14 Hezekiah **k** of Judah sent to the king of 4428
18:14 Hezekiah king of Judah sent to the **k** of 4428
18:14 the **k** of Assyria appointed unto Hezekiah 4428
18:14 **k** of Judah three hundred talents of silver 4428
18:16 *from* the pillars which Hezekiah **k** of Judah 4428
18:16 and gave it to the **k** of Assyria. 4428
18:17 the **k** of Assyria sent Tartan and Rabsaris 4428
18:17 Rab-shakeh from Lachish to **k** Hezekiah 4428
18:18 when they had called to the **k**, there came 4428
18:19 Thus saith the great **k**, the king of Assyria, 4428
18:19 Thus saith the great king, the **k** of Assyria, 4428
18:21 *is* Pharaoh **k** of Egypt unto all that trust on 4428
18:23 give pledges to my lord the **k** of Assyria, 4428
18:28 spake, saying, Hear the word of the great **k**, 4428
18:28 the word of the great king, the **k** of Assyria: 4428
18:29 Thus saith the **k**, Let not Hezekiah deceive 4428
18:30 delivered into the hand of the **k** of Assyria. 4428
18:31 for thus saith the **k** of Assyria, Make *an* 4428
18:33 land out of the hand of the **k** of Assyria? 4428
19: 1 when **k** Hezekiah heard *it*, that he rent his 4428
19: 4 whom the **k** of Assyria his master hath sent 4428
19: 5 So the servants of **k** Hezekiah came to 4428
19: 6 *with* which the servants of the **k** of Assyria 4428
19: 8 found the **k** of Assyria warring against 4428
19: 9 when he heard say of Tirhakah **k** of 4428
19:10 Thus shall ye speak to Hezekiah **k** of 4428
19:10 delivered into the hand of the **k** of Assyria. 4428
19:13 Where *is* the **k** of Hamath, and the king of 4428
19:13 the **k** of Arpad, and the king of the city of 4428
19:13 the **k** of the city of Sepharvaim, *of* Hena, 4428
19:20 Sennacherib **k** of Assyria I have heard. 4428
19:32 the LORD concerning the **k** of Assyria, 4428
19:36 So Sennacherib **k** of Assyria departed, and 4428
20: 6 this city out of the hand of the **k** of Assyria; 4428
20:12 **k** of Babylon, sent letters and a present 4428
20:14 came Isaiah the prophet unto **k** Hezekiah, 4428
20:18 they shall be eunuchs in the palace of the **k** 4428
21: 3 and made a grove, as did Ahab **k** of Israel; 4428
21:11 Because Manasseh **k** of Judah hath done 4428
21:23 and slew the **k** in his own house. 4428
21:24 them that had conspired against **k** Amon; 4428
21:24 the land **made** Josiah his son **k** in his stead. 4427
22: 3 it came to pass in the eighteenth year of **k** 4428
22: 3 *that* the **k** sent Shaphan the son of Azaliah, 4428
22: 9 Shaphan the scribe came to the **k**, and 4428
22: 9 and brought the **k** word again, and said, 4428
22:10 Shaphan the scribe shewed the **k**, saying, 4428
22:10 a book. And Shaphan read it before the **k**. 4428
22:11 when the **k** had heard the words of the book 4428
22:12 the **k** commanded Hilkiah the priest, and 4428
22:16 *even* all the words of the book which the **k** 4428
22:18 to the **k** of Judah which sent you to inquire 4428
22:20 And they brought the **k** word again. 4428
23: 1 the **k** sent, and they gathered unto him all 4428
23: 2 the **k** went up *into* the house of 4428
23: 3 the **k** stood by a pillar, and made a 4428
23: 4 the **k** commanded Hilkiah the high priest, 4428
23:12 did the **k** beat down, and brake *them* down 4428
23:13 which Solomon the **k** of Israel had builded 4428
23:13 of the children of Ammon, did the **k** defile. 4428
23:21 the **k** commanded all the people, saying, 4428
23:23 in the eighteenth year of **k** Josiah, 4428
23:25 like unto him was there no **k** before him, 4428
23:29 In his days Pharaoh-nechoh **k** of Egypt 4428
23:29 the **k** of Assyria to the river Euphrates: 4428
23:29 **k** Josiah went against him; and he slew him 4428
23:30 and **made** him **k** in his father's stead. 4427
23:34 **made** Eliakim the son of Josiah **k** in 4427
24: 1 In his days Nebuchadnezzar **k** of Babylon 4428
24: 7 the **k** of Egypt came not again any more out 4428
24: 7 for the **k** of Babylon had taken from 4428
24: 7 all that pertained to the **k** of Egypt. 4428

2Ki 24:10 **k** of Babylon came up *against* Jerusalem, 4428
24:11 Nebuchadnezzar **k** of Babylon came 4428
24:12 Jehoiachin the **k** of Judah went out to 4428
24:12 king of Judah went out to the **k** of Babylon, 4428
24:12 the **k** of Babylon took him in the eighth 4428
24:13 **k** of Israel had made in the temple of 4428
24:16 even them the **k** of Babylon brought 4428
24:17 the **k** of Babylon made Mattaniah his 4428
24:17 **made** Mattaniah his father's brother **k** in 4427
24:20 that Zedekiah rebelled against the **k** of 4428
25: 1 *that* Nebuchadnezzar **k** of Babylon came, 4428
25: 2 unto the eleventh year of **k** Zedekiah. 4428
25: 4 and *the* **k** went the way toward the plain. NIH
25: 5 army of the Chaldees pursued after the **k**, 4428
25: 6 So they took the **k**, and brought him up to 4428
25: 6 brought him up to the **k** of Babylon to 4428
25: 8 which *is* the nineteenth year of **k** 4428
25: 8 year of king Nebuchadnezzar **k** of Babylon, 4428
25: 8 a servant of the **k** of Babylon, 4428
25:11 the fugitives that fell away to the **k** of 4428
25:20 brought them to the **k** of Babylon to 4428
25:21 the **k** of Babylon smote them, and 4428
25:22 whom Nebuchadnezzar **k** of Babylon had 4428
25:23 heard that the **k** of Babylon had made 4428
25:24 in the land, and serve the **k** of Babylon; 4428
25:27 of the captivity of Jehoiachin **k** of Judah, 4428
25:27 *that* Evil-merodach **k** of Babylon, 4428
25:27 did lift up the head of Jehoiachin **k** of 4428
25:30 a continual allowance given him of the **k**, 4428
1Ch 1:43 *any* **k** reigned over the children of Israel; 4428
3: 2 the daughter of Talmai **k** of Geshur: 4428
4:23 there they dwelt with the **k** for his work. 4428
4:41 came in the days of Hezekiah **k** of Judah, 4428
5: 6 whom Tilgath-pilneser **k** of Assyria carried 4428
5:17 in the days of Jotham **k** of Judah, 4428
5:17 and in the days of Jeroboam **k** of Israel. 4428
5:26 stirred up the spirit of Pul **k** of Assyria, 4428
5:26 the spirit of Tilgath-pilneser **k** of Assyria, 4428
11: 2 in time past, even when Saul was **k**, 4428
11: 3 all the elders of Israel to the **k** to Hebron; 4428
11: 3 they anointed David **k** over Israel, 4428
11:10 *and* with all Israel, to **make** him **k**, 4427
12:31 by name, to come and **make** David **k**. 4427
12:38 to Hebron, to **make** David **k** over all Israel: 4427
12:38 Israel *were of* one heart to **make** David **k**. 4427
14: 1 Now Hiram **k** of Tyre sent messengers to 4428
14: 2 LORD had confirmed him **k** over Israel, 4428
14: 8 that David was anointed **k** over all Israel, 4428
15:29 out at a window saw **k** David dancing 4428
17:16 David the **k** came and sat before 4428
18: 3 David smote Hadarezer **k** of Zobah unto 4428
18: 5 came to help Hadarezer **k** of Zobah, 4428
18: 9 Now when Tou **k** of Hamath heard how 4428
18: 9 all the host of Hadarezer **k** of Zobah; 4428
18:10 He sent Hadoram his son to **k** David, 4428
18:11 Them also **k** David dedicated unto 4428
18:17 the sons of David *were* chief about the **k**. 4428
19: 1 that Nahash the **k** of the children of 4428
19: 5 the **k** said, Tarry at Jericho until your 4428
19: 7 and the **k** of Maachah and his people; 4428
20: 2 David took the crown of their **k** from off 4428
21: 3 so many moe as they *be: but*, my lord the **k**, 4428
21:23 let my lord the **k** do *that* which *is* good in 4428
21:24 **k** David said to Ornan, Nay; but I will 4428
23: 1 he **made** Solomon his son **k** over Israel. 4427
24: 6 wrote them before the **k**, and the princes, 4428
24:31 of Aaron in the presence of David the **k**, 4428
25: 2 prophesied according to the order of the **k**. 4428
26:26 of the dedicate *things*, which David the **k**, 4428
26:30 of the LORD, and in the service of the **k**. 4428
26:32 whom **k** David made rulers over 4428
26:32 pertaining to God, and affairs of the **k**. 4428
27: 1 their officers that served the **k** in any matter 4428
27:24 in the account of the chronicles of **k** David. 4428
27:31 of the substance which *was* **k** David's. 4428
28: 1 that ministered to the **k** by course, 4428
28: 1 all the substance and possession of the **k**, 4428
28: 2 David the **k** stood up upon his feet, and 4428
28: 4 of my father to be **k** over Israel for ever: 4428
28: 4 he liked me to **make** *me* **k** over all Israel: 4427
29: 1 Furthermore David the **k** said unto all 4428
29: 9 David the **k** also rejoiced *with* great joy. 4428
29:20 and worshipped the LORD, and the **k**. 4428
29:22 they **made** Solomon the son of David **k** 4427
29:23 LORD as **k** instead of David his father, 4428
29:24 and all the sons likewise of **k** David, 4428
29:24 submitted themselves unto Solomon the **k**. 4428
29:25 had not been on any **k** before him in Israel. 4428
29:29 Now the acts of David the **k**, first and last, 4428
2Ch 1: 9 for thou hast **made** me **k** over a people like 4427
1:11 my people, over whom I have **made** thee **k**: 4427
1:14 chariot cities, and with the **k** at Jerusalem. 4428
1:15 the **k** made silver and gold at Jerusalem *as* 4428
2: 3 Solomon sent to Huram the **k** of Tyre, 4428
2:11 Huram the **k** of Tyre answered in writing, 4428
2:11 his people, he hath made thee **k** over them. 4428
2:12 who hath given to David the **k** a wise son, 4428
4:11 make for **k** Solomon for the house of God; 4428
4:16 did Huram his father make to **k** Solomon 4428
4:17 In the plain of Jordan did the **k** cast them, 4428
5: 3 **k** in the feast which *was in* the seventh 4428
5: 6 Also **k** Solomon, and all the congregation 4428
6: 3 the **k** turned his face, and blessed the whole 4428
7: 4 the **k** and all the people offered sacrifices 4428
7: 5 **k** Solomon offered a sacrifice of twenty 4428
7: 5 so the **k** and all the people dedicated 4428
7: 6 which David the **k** had made to praise 4428
8:10 these *were* the chief of **k** Solomon's 4428
8:11 not dwell in the house of David **k** of Israel, 4428
8:15 the commandment of the **k** unto the priests 4428
8:18 of gold, and brought *them* to **k** Solomon. 4428
9: 5 she said to the **k**, *It was* a true report which 4428
9: 8 his throne, to be **k** for the LORD thy God: 4428
9: 8 therefore made he thee **k** over them, to do 4428
9: 9 she gave the **k** an hundred and 4428

K

2Ch 9: 9 as the queen of Sheba gave **k** Solomon. 4428
9:11 the **k** made *of* the algum trees terraces to 4428
9:12 **k** Solomon gave to the queen of Sheba all 4428
9:12 *that* which she had brought unto the **k**. 4428
9:15 **k** Solomon made two hundred targets *of* 4428
9:16 the **k** put them in the house of the forest of 4428
9:17 Moreover the **k** made a great throne of 4428
9:20 all the drinking vessels of **k** Solomon *were* 4428
9:22 **k** Solomon passed all the kings of the earth 4428
9:25 chariot cities, and with the **k** at Jerusalem. 4428
9:27 the **k** made silver in Jerusalem as stones, 4428
10: 1 were all Israel come to **make** him **k**. 4427
10: 2 fled from the presence of Solomon the **k**, 4428
10: 6 **k** Rehoboam took counsel with the old men 4428
10:12 as the **k** bade, saying, Come again to me on 4428
10:13 the **k** answered them roughly; and king 4428
10:13 **k** Rehoboam forsook the counsel of the old 4428
10:15 So the **k** hearkened not unto the people: 4428
10:16 when all Israel saw that the **k** would not 4428
10:16 the people answered the **k**, saying, 4428
10:18 **k** Rehoboam sent Hadoram that *was* over 4428
10:18 **k** Rehoboam made speed to get *him* up to 4428
11: 3 **k** of Judah, and to all Israel in Judah and 4428
11:22 his brethren: for *he thought* to **make** him **k**. 4427
12: 2 *that* in the fifth year of **k** Rehoboam 4428
12: 2 **k** of Egypt came up against Jerusalem, 4428
12: 6 of Israel and the **k** humbled themselves; 4428
12: 9 So Shishak **k** of Egypt came up against 4428
12:10 Instead of which **k** Rehoboam made shields 4428
12:11 when the **k** entered *into* the house of 4428
12:13 So **k** Rehoboam strengthened himself in 4428
13: 1 Now in the eighteenth year of **k** Jeroboam 4428
15:16 Maachah the mother of Asa the **k**, 4428
16: 1 thirtieth year of the reign of Asa Baasha **k** 4428
16: 1 none go out or come in to Asa **k** of Judah. 4428
16: 2 and sent to Ben-hadad **k** of Syria, 4428
16: 3 break thy league with Baasha **k** of Israel, 4428
16: 4 Ben-hadad hearkened unto **k** Asa, and 4428
16: 6 Asa the **k** took all Judah; and they carried 4428
16: 7 at that time Hanani the seer came to Asa **k** 4428
16: 7 Because thou hast relied on the **k** of Syria, 4428
16: 7 is the host of the **k** of Syria escaped out of 4428
17:19 These waited on the **k**, besides *those* whom 4428
17:19 besides *those* whom the **k** put in the fenced 4428
18: 3 Ahab **k** of Israel said unto Jehoshaphat king 4428
18: 3 Ahab king of Israel said unto Jehoshaphat **k** 4428
18: 4 Jehoshaphat said unto the **k** of Israel, 4428
18: 5 Therefore the **k** of Israel gathered together 4428
18: 7 the **k** of Israel said unto Jehoshaphat, 4428
18: 7 And Jehoshaphat said, Let not the **k** say so. 4428
18: 8 the **k** of Israel called for one *of his* officers, 4428
18: 9 the **k** of Israel and Jehoshaphat king of 4428
18: 9 Jehoshaphat **k** of Judah sat either of them 4428
18:11 shall deliver *it* into the hand of the **k**. 4428
18:12 *declare* good to the **k** with one assent; 4428
18:14 when he was come to the **k**, the king said 4428
18:14 to the king, the **k** said unto him, Micaiah, 4428
18:15 the **k** said to him, How many times shall I 4428
18:17 the **k** of Israel said to Jehoshaphat, Did I 4428
18:19 Who shall entice Ahab **k** of Israel, that he 4428
18:25 the **k** of Israel said, Take ye Micaiah, and 4428
18:26 say, Thus saith the **k**, Put this *fellow in* 4428
18:28 So the **k** of Israel and Jehoshaphat the king 4428
18:28 Jehoshaphat the **k** of Judah went up to 4428
18:29 the **k** of Israel said unto Jehoshaphat, I will 4428
18:29 So the **k** of Israel disguised himself; and 4428
18:30 Now the **k** of Syria had commanded 4428
18:30 or great, save only with the **k** of Israel. 4428
18:31 that they said, It *is* the **k** of Israel. 4428
18:32 perceived that it was not the **k** of Israel, 4428
18:33 smote the **k** of Israel between the joints of 4428
18:34 howbeit the **k** of Israel stayed *himself* up in 4428
19: 1 Jehoshaphat the **k** of Judah returned to his 4428
19: 2 said to **k** Jehoshaphat, Shouldest thou help 4428
20:15 of Jerusalem, and thou **k** Jehoshaphat, 4428
20:35 after this did Jehoshaphat **k** of Judah join 4428
20:35 join himself with Ahaziah **k** of Israel, 4428
21: 2 all these *were* the sons of Jehoshaphat **k** of 4428
21: 8 of Judah, and **made** themselves a **k**. 4427+4428
21:12 nor in the ways of Asa **k** of Judah, 4428
22: 1 **made** Ahaziah his youngest son **k** in his 4427
22: 1 So Ahaziah the son of Jehoram **k** of Judah 4428
22: 5 went with Jehoram the son of Ahab **k** of 4428
22: 5 against Hazael **k** of Syria at Ramoth-gilead: 4428
22: 6 when he fought with Hazael **k** of Syria. 4428
22: 6 Azariah the son of Jehoram **k** of Judah 4428
22:11 Jehoshabeath, the daughter of the **k**, took 4428
22:11 the daughter of **k** Jehoram, 4428
23: 3 a covenant with the **k** in the house of God. 4428
23: 7 the Levites shall compass the **k** round 4428
23: 7 be you with the **k** when he cometh in, and 4428
23: 9 and shields, that *had been* **k** David's, 4428
23:10 and the temple, by the **k** round about. 4428
23:11 *gave him* the Testimony, and **made** him **k**. 4427
23:11 anointed him, and said, God save the **k**. 4428
23:12 of the people running and praising the **k**, 4428
23:13 the **k** stood at his pillar at the entering in, 4428
23:13 and the princes and the trumpets by the **k**: 4428
23:16 between all the people, and between the **k**, 4428
23:20 brought down the **k** from the house of 4428
23:20 set the **k** upon the throne of the kingdom. 4428
24: 6 the **k** called for Jehoiada the chief, and 4428
24:12 the **k** and Jehoiada gave it to such as did 4428
24:14 brought the rest of the money before the **k** 4428
24:17 of Judah, and made obeisance to the **k**. 4428
24:17 the king. Then the **k** hearkened unto them. 4428
24:21 **k** in the court of the house of the LORD. 4428
24:22 Thus Joash the **k** remembered not 4428
24:23 sent all the spoil of them unto the **k** of 4428
25: 3 his servants that had killed the **k** his father. 4428
25: 7 came a man of God to him, saying, O **k**, 4428
25:16 he talked with him, that *the* **k** said unto him, NIH
25:17 Amaziah **k** of Judah took advice, and 4428
25:17 the son of Jehu, **k** of Israel, saying, Come, 4428
25:18 Joash **k** of Israel sent to Amaziah king of 4428

2Ch 25:18 Joash king of Israel sent to Amaziah **k** of 4428
25:21 So Joash the **k** of Israel went up; and 4428
25:21 *both* he and Amaziah **k** of Judah, 4428
25:23 Joash the **k** of Israel took Amaziah king of 4428
25:23 Joash the king of Israel took Amaziah **k** of 4428
25:25 Amaziah the son of Joash **k** of Judah lived 4428
25:25 son of Jehoahaz **k** of Israel fifteen years. 4428
26: 1 **made** him **k** in the room of his father 4427
26: 2 after that the **k** slept with his fathers. 4428
26:13 to help the **k** against the enemy. 4428
26:18 they withstood Uzziah the **k**, and said unto 4428
26:21 Uzziah the **k** was a leper unto the day of his 4428
27: 5 He fought also with the **k** of 4428
28: 5 him into the hand of the **k** of Syria; 4428
28: 5 he was also delivered into the hand of the **k** 4428
28: 7 and Elkanah *that was* next to the **k**. 4428
28:16 At that time did **k** Ahaz send unto the kings 4428
28:19 Judah low because of Ahaz **k** of Israel; 4428
28:20 Tilgath-pilneser **k** of Assyria came unto 4428
28:21 *out* of the house of the **k**, and of 4428
28:21 and gave *it* unto the **k** of Assyria: 4428
28:22 against the LORD: this *is that* **k** Ahaz. 4428
29:15 according to the commandment of the **k**, 4428
29:18 they went in to Hezekiah the **k**, and said, 4428
29:19 which **k** Ahaz in his reign did cast away in 4428
29:20 Hezekiah the **k** rose early, and gathered 4428
29:23 he goats for the sin offering before the **k** 4428
29:24 for the **k** commanded *that* the burnt 4428
29:27 with the instruments ordained by David **k** 4428
29:29 the **k** and all that were present with him 4428
29:30 Moreover Hezekiah the **k** and the princes 4428
30: 2 For the **k** had taken counsel, and 4428
30: 4 the thing pleased the **k** and all 4428
30: 6 the posts went with the letters from the **k** 4428
30: 6 according to the commandment of the **k**, 4428
30:12 one heart to do the commandment of the **k** 4428
30:24 For Hezekiah **k** of Judah did give to 4428
30:26 **k** of Israel *there was* not the like in 4428
31:13 at the commandment of Hezekiah the **k**, 4428
32: 1 the establishment *thereof*, Sennacherib **k** of 4428
32: 7 be not afraid nor dismayed for the **k** of 4428
32: 8 upon the words of Hezekiah **k** of Judah. 4428
32: 9 After this did Sennacherib **k** of Assyria 4428
32: 9 unto Hezekiah **k** of Judah, and unto all 4428
32:10 Thus saith Sennacherib **k** of Assyria, 4428
32:11 us out of the hand of the **k** of Assyria? 4428
32:20 for this *cause* Hezekiah the **k**, and 4428
32:21 captains in the camp of the **k** of Assyria. 4428
32:22 the hand of Sennacherib the **k** of Assyria, 4428
32:23 and presents to Hezekiah **k** of Judah: 4428
33:11 the captains of the host of the **k** of Assyria, 4428
33:25 them that had conspired against **k** Amon; 4428
33:25 the land **made** Josiah his son **k** in his stead. 4427
34:16 Shaphan carried the book to the **k**, and 4428
34:16 brought the **k** word back again, saying, 4428
34:18 Shaphan the scribe told the **k**, saying, 4428
34:18 a book. And Shaphan read it before the **k**. 4428
34:19 when the **k** had heard the words of the law, 4428
34:20 the **k** commanded Hilkiah, and Ahikam 4428
34:22 *they that* the **k** *had appointed*, went to 4428
34:24 which they have read before the **k** of Judah: 4428
34:26 as for the **k** of Judah, who sent you to 4428
34:28 So they brought the **k** word again. 4428
34:29 the **k** sent and gathered together all 4428
34:30 the **k** went up *into* the house of 4428
34:31 the **k** stood in his place, and made a 4428
35: 3 the son of David **k** of Israel did build; 4428
35: 4 according to the writing of David **k** of 4428
35:16 according to the commandment of **k** Josiah. 4428
35:20 Necho **k** of Egypt came up to fight against 4428
35:21 have I to do with thee, thou **k** of Judah? 4428
35:23 the archers shot at **k** Josiah; and the king 4428
35:23 the **k** said to his servants, Have me away; 4428
36: 1 **made** him **k** in his father's stead in 4427
36: 3 the **k** of Egypt put him down at Jerusalem, 4428
36: 4 the **k** of Egypt made Eliakim his brother 4428
36: 4 **made** Eliakim his brother **k** over Judah 4427
36: 6 Against him came up Nebuchadnezzar **k** of 4428
36:10 **k** Nebuchadnezzar sent, and brought him to 4428
36:10 **made** Zedekiah his brother **k** over Judah 4427
36:13 he also rebelled against **k** Nebuchadnezzar, 4428
36:17 Therefore he brought upon them the **k** of 4428
36:18 the treasures of the **k**, and of his princes; 4428
36:22 Now in the first year of Cyrus **k** of Persia, 4428
36:22 the LORD stirred up the spirit of Cyrus **k** 4428
36:23 Thus saith Cyrus **k** of Persia, All 4428
Ezr 1: 1 Now in the first year of Cyrus **k** of Persia, 4428
1: 1 the LORD stirred up the spirit of Cyrus **k** 4428
1: 2 Thus saith Cyrus **k** of Persia, The LORD 4428
1: 7 Also Cyrus the **k** brought forth the vessels 4428
1: 8 Even those did Cyrus **k** of Persia bring 4428
2: 1 whom Nebuchadnezzar the **k** of Babylon 4428
3: 7 the grant that they had of Cyrus **k** of Persia. 4428
3:10 after the ordinance of David **k** of Israel. 4428
4: 2 since the days of Esar-haddon **k** of Assur, 4428
4: 3 as **k** Cyrus the king of Persia hath 4428
4: 3 as king Cyrus the **k** of Persia hath 4428
4: 5 all the days of Cyrus **k** of Persia, 4428
4: 5 even until the reign of Darius **k** of Persia. 4428
4: 7 unto Artaxerxes **k** of Persia; 4428
4: 8 Jerusalem to Artaxerxes the **k** in this sort: 4430
4:11 sent unto him, *even* unto Artaxerxes the **k**: 4430
4:12 Be it known unto the **k**, that the Jews which 4430
4:13 Be it known now unto the **k**, that, if this 4430
4:14 therefore have we sent and certified the **k**; 4430
4:16 We certify the **k** that, if this city be builded 4430
4:17 *Then* sent the **k** an answer unto Rehum 4430
4:23 Now when the copy of **k** Artaxerxes' letter 4430
4:24 year of the reign of Darius **k** of Persia. 4430
5: 6 *this* side the river, sent unto Darius the **k**: 4430
5: 7 written thus: Unto Darius the **k**, all peace. 4430
5: 8 Be it known unto the **k**, that we went into 4430
5:11 which a great **k** of Israel builded and set up. 4430
5:12 hand of Nebuchadnezzar the **k** of Babylon, 4430
5:13 in the first year of Cyrus the **k** of Babylon 4430

Ezr 5:13 **k** Cyrus made a decree to build this house 4430
5:14 those did Cyrus the **k** take out of the temple 4430
5:17 Now therefore, if *it seem* good to the **k**, 4430
5:17 that a decree *was* made of Cyrus the **k** to 4430
5:17 let the **k** send his pleasure to us concerning 4430
6: 1 Darius the **k** made a decree, and search was 4430
6: 3 In the first year of Cyrus the **k** *the same* 4430
6: 3 **k** made a decree *concerning* the house of 4430
6:10 pray for the life of the **k**, and of his sons. 4430
6:13 according to that which Darius the **k** had 4430
6:14 and Darius, and Artaxerxes **k** of Persia. 4430
6:15 the sixth year of the reign of Darius the **k**. 4430
6:22 turned the heart of the **k** of Assyria unto 4428
7: 1 in the reign of Artaxerxes **k** of Persia, 4428
7: 6 the **k** granted him all his request, 4428
7: 7 in the seventh year of Artaxerxes the **k**. 4428
7: 8 which *was* in the seventh year of the **k**. 4428
7:11 Now this *is* the copy of the letter that the **k** 4428
7:12 Artaxerxes, **k** of kings, unto Ezra the priest, 4430
7:14 Forasmuch as *thou art* sent of the **k**, and 4430
7:15 which the **k** and his counsellers have freely 4430
7:21 I, *even* I Artaxerxes the **k**, do make a 4430
7:23 there be wrath against the realm of the **k** 4430
7:26 the law of the **k**, let judgment be executed 4430
7:28 hath extended mercy unto me before the **k**, 4428
8: 1 in the reign of Artaxerxes the **k**. 4428
8:22 For I was ashamed to require of the **k** a 4428
8:22 because we had spoken unto the **k**, saying, 4428
8:25 which the **k**, and his counsellers, and 4428
Ne 2: 1 *in* the twentieth year of Artaxerxes the **k**, 4428
2: 1 I took up the wine, and gave *it* unto the **k**. 4428
2: 2 Wherefore the **k** said unto me, Why *is* thy 4428
2: 3 said unto the **k**, Let the king live for ever: 4428
2: 3 said unto the king, Let the **k** live for ever: 4428
2: 4 the **k** said unto me, For what dost thou 4428
2: 5 I said unto the **k**, If it please the king, and 4428
2: 5 If it please the **k**, and if thy servant have 4428
2: 6 the **k** said unto me, (the queen also sitting 4428
2: 6 So it pleased the **k** to send me; and I set 4428
2: 7 Moreover I said unto the **k**, If it please 4428
2: 7 I said unto the king, If it please the **k**, 4428
2: 8 the **k** granted me, according to the good 4428
2: 9 Now the **k** had sent captains of the army 4428
2:19 that ye do? will ye rebel against the **k**? 4428
5:14 and thirtieth year of Artaxerxes the **k**, 4428
6: 6 that thou mayest be their **k**, according to 4428
6: 7 at Jerusalem, saying, *There is* a **k** in Judah: 4428
6: 7 now shall it be reported to the **k** according 4428
7: 6 whom Nebuchadnezzar the **k** of Babylon 4428
9:22 the land of the **k** of Heshbon, and the land 4428
9:22 and the land of Og **k** of Bashan. 4428
13: 6 thirtieth year of Artaxerxes **k** of Babylon 4428
13: 6 king of Babylon came I unto the **k**, 4428
13: 6 after certain days obtained I *leave* of the **k**: 4428
13:26 Did not Solomon **k** of Israel sin by these 4428
13:26 many nations was there no **k** like him, 4428
13:26 and God made him **k** over all Israel: 4428
Est 1: 2 when the **k** Ahasuerus sat on the throne of 4428
1: 5 the **k** made a feast unto all the people that 4428
1: 7 according to the state of the **k**. 4428
1: 8 the **k** had appointed to all the officers of his 4428
1: 9 house which *belonged* to **k** Ahasuerus. 4428
1:10 when the heart of the **k** was merry with 4428
1:10 served in the presence of Ahasuerus the **k**, 4428
1:11 To bring Vashti the queen before the **k** with 4428
1:12 therefore was the **k** very wroth, and 4428
1:13 the **k** said to the wise *men*, which knew 4428
1:15 of the **k** Ahasuerus by the chamberlains? 4428
1:16 Memucan answered before the **k** and 4428
1:16 queen hath not done wrong to the **k** only, 4428
1:16 *are* in all the provinces of the **k** Ahasuerus. 4428
1:17 The **k** Ahasuerus commanded Vashti 4428
1:19 If it please the **k**, let there go a royal 4428
1:19 That Vashti come no *more* before **k** 4428
1:19 let the **k** give her royal estate unto another 4428
1:21 the saying pleased the **k** and the princes; 4428
1:21 the **k** did according to the word of 4428
2: 1 when the wrath of **k** Ahasuerus was 4428
2: 2 there be fair young virgins sought for the **k**: 4428
2: 3 let the **k** appoint officers in all 4428
2: 4 let the maiden which pleaseth the **k** be 4428
2: 4 And the thing pleased the **k**; and he did so. 4428
2: 6 carried away with Jeconiah **k** of Judah, 4428
2: 6 whom Nebuchadnezzar the **k** of Babylon 4428
2:12 turn was come to go in to **k** Ahasuerus, 4428
2:13 thus came *every* maiden unto the **k**; 4428
2:14 she came in unto the **k** no more, except 4428
2:14 except the **k** delighted in her, and *that* she 4428
2:15 was come to go in unto the **k**, she required 4428
2:16 So Esther was taken unto **k** Ahasuerus into 4428
2:17 the **k** loved Esther above all the women, 4428
2:18 the **k** made a great feast unto all his princes 4428
2:18 gave gifts, according to the state of the **k**. 4428
2:21 and sought to lay hand on the **k** Ahasuerus. 4428
2:22 Esther certified the **k** *thereof* in Mordecai's 4428
2:23 in the book of the chronicles before the **k**. 4428
3: 1 After these things did **k** Ahasuerus promote 4428
3: 2 for the **k** had so commanded concerning 4428
3: 7 in the twelfth year of **k** Ahasuerus, 4428
3: 8 Haman said unto **k** Ahasuerus, There is a 4428
3: 9 If it please the **k**, let it be written that they 4428
3:10 the **k** took his ring from his hand, and 4428
3:11 the **k** said unto Haman, The silver *is* given 4428
3:12 in the name of **k** Ahasuerus was it written, 4428
3:15 the **k** and Haman sat down to drink; but 4428
4: 8 charge her that *she* should go in unto the **k**, 4428
4:11 shall come unto the **k** into the inner court, 4428
4:11 except such to whom the **k** shall hold out 4428
4:11 I have not been called to come in unto the **k** 4428
4:16 so will I go in unto the **k**, which *is* not 4428
5: 1 the **k** sat upon his royal throne in the royal 4428
5: 2 when the **k** saw Esther the queen standing 4428
5: 2 the **k** held out to Esther the golden sceptre 4428
5: 3 said the **k** unto her, What wilt thou, queen 4428
5: 4 If *it seem* good unto the **k**, let the king and 4428

Est 5: 4 let the **k** and Haman come *this* day unto 4428
5: 5 the **k** said, Cause Haman to make haste, 4428
5: 5 So the **k** and Haman came to the banquet 4428
5: 6 the **k** said unto Esther at the banquet of 4428
5: 8 If I have found favour in the sight of the **k**, 4428
5: 8 if it please the **k** to grant my petition, and 4428
5: 8 let the **k** and Haman come to the banquet 4428
5: 8 and I will do to morrow as the **k** hath said. 4428
5:11 all *the things* where*in* the **k** had promoted 4428
5:11 above the princes and servants of the **k**. 4428
5:12 **k** unto the banquet that she had prepared 4428
5:12 *am* I invited unto her also with the **k**. 4428
5:14 to morrow speak thou unto the **k** that 4428
5:14 go thou in merrily with the **k** unto 4428
6: 1 On that night could not the **k** sleep, and 4428
6: 1 and they were read before the **k**. 4428
6: 2 who sought to lay hand on the **k** Ahasuerus. 4428
6: 3 the **k** said, What honour and dignity hath 4428
6: 4 the **k** said, Who *is* in the court? 4428
6: 4 to speak unto the **k** to hang Mordecai on 4428
6: 5 the court. And the **k** said, Let him come in. 4428
6: 6 the **k** said unto him, What shall be done 4428
6: 6 the man whom the **k** delighteth to honour? 4428
6: 6 To whom would the **k** delight to do honour 4428
6: 7 Haman answered the **k**, *For* the man whom 4428
6: 7 *For* the man whom the **k** delighteth to 4428
6: 8 be brought which the **k** *useth* to wear, 4428
6: 8 the horse that the **k** rideth upon, and 4428
6: 9 *withal* whom the **k** delighteth to honour, 4428
6: 9 shall it be done to the man whom the **k** 4428
6:10 the **k** said to Haman, Make haste, *and* 4428
6:11 the man whom the **k** delighteth to honour. 4428
7: 1 So the **k** and Haman came to banquet with 4428
7: 2 the **k** said again unto Esther on the second 4428
7: 3 in thy sight, O **k**, and if it please the king, 4428
7: 3 in thy sight, O king, and if it please the **k**, 4428
7: 5 the **k** Ahasuerus answered and said unto 4428
7: 6 Haman was afraid before the **k** and 4428
7: 7 the **k** arising from the banquet of wine in 4428
7: 7 was evil determined against him by the **k**. 4428
7: 8 the **k** returned out of the palace garden into 4428
7: 8 bed whereon Esther *was*. Then said the **k**, 4428
7: 9 said before the **k**, Behold also, 4428
7: 9 who had spoken good for the **k**, standeth in 4428
7: 9 Then the **k** said, Hang him thereon. 4428
8: 1 On that day did the **k** Ahasuerus give 4428
8: 1 Mordecai came before the **k**; for Esther had 4428
8: 2 the **k** took off his ring, which he had taken 4428
8: 3 Esther spake yet again before the **k**, and 4428
8: 4 the **k** held out the golden sceptre toward 4428
8: 4 So Esther arose, and stood before the **k**, 4428
8: 5 If it please the **k**, and if I have found favour 4428
8: 5 the thing seem right before the **k**, and I *be* 4428
8: 7 the **k** Ahasuerus said unto Esther the queen 4428
8:10 he wrote in the **k** Ahasuerus' name, and 4428
8:11 Where*in* the **k** granted the Jews which *were* 4428
8:12 Upon one day in all the provinces of **k** 4428
8:15 presence of the **k** in royal apparel *of* blue 4428
9: 2 all the provinces of the **k** Ahasuerus, 4428
9: 3 and the deputies, and officers of the **k**, 4428
9:11 the palace was brought before the **k**. 4428
9:12 the **k** said unto Esther the queen, The Jews 4428
9:13 said Esther, If it please the **k**, let it be 4428
9:14 the **k** commanded it so to be done: and 4428
9:20 in all the provinces of the **k** Ahasuerus, 4428
9:25 when *Esther* came before the **k**, 4428
10: 1 the **k** Ahasuerus laid a tribute upon 4428
10: 2 where*unto* the **k** advanced him, 4428
10: 3 For Mordecai the Jew *was* next unto **k** 4428
Job 15:24 against him, as a **k** ready to the battle. 4428
18:14 and it shall bring him to the **k** of terrors. 4428
29:25 and sat chief, and dwelt as a **k** in the army, 4428
34:18 *Is it fit* to say to a **k**, *Thou art* wicked? *and* 4428
41:34 He beholdeth all high *things*: he *is* a **k** over 4428
Ps 2: 6 Yet have I set my **k** upon my holy hill of 4428
5: 2 the voice of my cry, my **K**, and my God: 4428
10:16 The LORD *is* **K** for ever and ever: 4428
18:50 Great deliverance giveth he to his **k**; and 4428
20: 9 LORD: let the **k** hear us when we call. 4428
21: 1 The **k** shall joy in thy strength, O LORD; 4428
21: 7 For the **k** trusteth in the LORD, and 4428
24: 7 and the **K** of glory shall come in. 4428
24: 8 Who *is* this **K** of glory? the LORD strong 4428
24: 9 and the **K** of glory shall come in. 4428
24:10 Who is this **K** of glory? The LORD of 4428
24:10 The LORD of hosts, he *is* the **K** of glory. 4428
29:10 yea, the LORD sitteth **K** for ever. 4428
33:16 There is no **k** saved by the multitude of a 4428
44: 4 Thou *art* my **K**, O God: 4428
45: 1 things which I have made touching *the* **k**: 4428
45:11 So shall the **k** greatly desire thy beauty: 4428
45:14 She shall be brought unto the **k** in raiment 4428
47: 2 *is* terrible; *he is* a great **K** over all the earth. 4428
47: 6 sing *praises*: sing *praises* unto our **K**, 4428
47: 7 For God *is* the **K** of all the earth: sing ye 4428
48: 2 sides of the north, the city of the great **K**. 4428
63:11 the **k** shall rejoice in God; every one that 4428
68:24 goings of my God, my **K**, in the sanctuary. 4428
72: 1 Give the **k** thy judgments, O God, and 4428
74:12 For God *is* my **K** of old, working salvation 4428
84: 3 O LORD of hosts, my **K**, and my God. 4428
89:18 and the Holy One of Israel *is* our **k**. 4428
95: 3 a great God, and a great **K** above all gods. 4428
98: 6 a joyful noise before the LORD, the **K**. 4428
105:20 The **k** sent and loosed him; *even* the ruler 4428
135:11 Sihon **k** of the Amorites, and Og king of 4428
135:11 Og **k** of Bashan, and all the kingdoms of 4428
136:19 Sihon **k** of the Amorites: for his mercy 4428
136:20 Og the **k** of Bashan: for his mercy *endureth* 4428
145: 1 I will extol thee, my God, O **k**; and I will 4428
149: 2 let the children of Zion be joyful in their **K**. 4428
Pr 1: 1 of Solomon the son of David, **k** of Israel, 4428
16:10 A divine sentence *is* in the lips of the **k**: 4428
16:14 The wrath of a **k** *is as* messengers of death: 4428
20: 2 The fear of a **k** *is* as the roaring of a lion: 4428
Pr 20: 8 A **k** that sitteth in the throne of judgment 4428
20:26 A wise **k** scattereth the wicked, and 4428
20:28 Mercy and truth preserve the **k**: and 4428
22:11 *for* the grace of his lips the **k** *shall be* his 4428
24:21 My son, fear thou the LORD and the **k**: 4428
25: 1 which the men of Hezekiah **k** of Judah 4428
25: 5 Take away the wicked *from* before the **k**, 4428
25: 6 not forth thyself in the presence of the **k**, 4428
29: 4 The **k** by judgment stablisheth the land: but 4428
29:14 The **k** that faithfully judgeth the poor, 4428
30:27 The locusts have no **k**, yet go they forth all 4428
30:31 and a **k**, against whom *there is* no rising up. 4428
31: 1 The words of **k** Lemuel, the prophecy that 4428
Ecc 1: 1 the son of David, **k** in Jerusalem. 4428
1:12 I the Preacher was **k** over Israel in 4428
2:12 *can* the man *do* that cometh after the **k**? 4428
4:13 and a wise child than an old and foolish **k**, 4428
5: 9 for all: the **k** *himself* is served by the field. 4428
8: 4 Where the word of a **k** *is, there is* power: 4428
9:14 there came a great **k** against it, and 4428
10:16 when thy **k** *is* a child, and thy princes eat in 4428
10:17 when thy **k** *is* the son of nobles, and 4428
10:20 Curse not the **k**, no not in thy thought; and 4428
SS 1: 4 the **k** hath brought me *into* his chambers: 4428
1:12 While the **k** *sitteth* at his table, 4428
3: 9 **K** Solomon made himself a chariot of 4428
3:11 behold **k** Solomon with the crown 4428
7: 5 like purple; the **k** *is* held in the galleries. 4428
Isa 6: 1 In the year that **k** Uzziah died I saw also 4428
6: 5 for mine eyes have seen the **K**, the LORD 4428
7: 1 the son of Uzziah **k** of Judah, *that* Rezin 4428
7: 1 *that* Rezin the **k** of Syria, and Pekah the son 4428
7: 1 and Pekah the son of Remaliah, **k** of Israel, 4428
7: 6 **set a k** in the midst of it, *even* 4427+4428
7:17 departed from Judah; *even* the **k** of Assyria. 4428
7:20 by the **k** of Assyria, the head, and the hair 4428
8: 4 shall be taken away before the **k** of Assyria. 4428
8: 7 *even* the **k** of Assyria, and all his glory: 4428
8:21 curse their **k** and their God, and 4428
10:12 fruit of the stout heart of the **k** of Assyria, 4428
14: 4 up this proverb against the **k** of Babylon, 4428
14:28 In the year that **k** Ahaz died was this 4428
19: 4 a fierce **k** shall rule over them, saith 4428
20: 1 (when Sargon the **k** of Assyria sent him,) 4428
20: 4 So shall the **k** of Assyria lead away 4428
20: 6 help to be delivered from the **k** of Assyria: 4428
23:15 according to the days of one **k**: 4428
30:33 yea, for the **k** it is prepared; he hath made *it* 4428
32: 1 a **k** shall reign in righteousness, and princes 4428
33:17 Thine eyes shall see the **k** in his beauty: 4428
33:22 *is* our lawgiver, the LORD *is* our **k**; 4428
36: 1 pass in the fourteenth year of **k** Hezekiah, 4428
36: 1 *that* Sennacherib **k** of Assyria came up 4428
36: 2 the **k** of Assyria sent Rabshakeh from 4428
36: 2 unto **k** Hezekiah with a great army. 4428
36: 4 Thus saith the great **k**, the king of Assyria, 4428
36: 4 Thus saith the great king, the **k** of Assyria, 4428
36: 6 *is* Pharaoh **k** of Egypt to all that trust in 4428
36: 8 to my master the **k** of Assyria, and I will 4428
36:13 said, Hear ye the words of the great **k**, 4428
36:13 words of the great king, the **k** of Assyria. 4428
36:14 Thus saith the **k**, Let not Hezekiah deceive 4428
36:15 delivered into the hand of the **k** of Assyria. 4428
36:16 for thus saith the **k** of Assyria, Make *an* 4428
36:18 land out of the hand of the **k** of Assyria? 4428
37: 1 when **k** Hezekiah heard *it*, that he rent his 4428
37: 4 whom the **k** of Assyria his master hath sent 4428
37: 5 So the servants of **k** Hezekiah came to 4428
37: 6 where*with* the servants of the **k** of Assyria 4428
37: 8 found the **k** of Assyria warring against 4428
37: 9 he heard say concerning Tirhakah **k** of 4428
37:10 Thus shall ye speak to Hezekiah **k** of 4428
37:10 be given into the hand of the **k** of Assyria. 4428
37:13 Where *is* the **k** of Hamath, and the king of 4428
37:13 the **k** of Arphad, and the king of the city of 4428
37:13 the **k** of the city of Sepharvaim, Hena, and 4428
37:21 to me against Sennacherib **k** of Assyria: 4428
37:33 the LORD concerning the **k** of Assyria, 4428
37:37 So Sennacherib **k** of Assyria departed, and 4428
38: 6 this city out of the hand of the **k** of Assyria: 4428
38: 9 **k** of Judah, when he had been sick, and 4428
39: 1 **k** of Babylon, sent letters and a present to 4428
39: 3 came Isaiah the prophet unto **k** Hezekiah, 4428
39: 7 they shall be eunuchs in the palace of the **k** 4428
41:21 bring forth your strong *reasons*, saith the **K** 4428
43:15 Holy One, the creator of Israel, your **K**. 4428
44: 6 Thus saith the LORD the **K** of Israel, and 4428
57: 9 thou wentest to the **k** with ointment, and 4428
Jer 1: 2 days of Josiah the son of Amon **k** of Judah, 4428
1: 3 of Jehoiakim the son of Josiah **k** of Judah, 4428
1: 3 of Zedekiah the son of Josiah **k** of Judah, 4428
3: 6 also unto me in the days of Josiah the **k**, 4428
4: 9 *that* the heart of the **k** shall perish, and 4428
8:19 *is* not her **k** in her? Why have they 4428
10: 7 Who would not fear thee, O **K** of nations? 4428
10:10 he *is* the living God, and an everlasting **k**: 4428
13:18 Say unto the **k** and to the queen, 4428
15: 4 of Manasseh the son of Hezekiah **k** of 4428
20: 4 I will give all Judah into the hand of the **k** 4428
21: 1 when **k** Zedekiah sent unto him Pashur 4428
21: 2 for Nebuchadrezzar **k** of Babylon maketh 4428
21: 4 wherewith ye fight against the **k** of 4428
21: 7 I will deliver Zedekiah **k** of Judah, and his 4428
21: 7 into the hand of Nebuchadrezzar **k** of 4428
21:10 it shall be given into the hand of the **k** of 4428
21:11 touching the house of the **k** of Judah, 4428
22: 1 Go down *to* the house of the **k** of Judah, 4428
22: 2 the word of the LORD, O **k** of Judah, 4428
22:11 Shallum the son of Josiah **k** of Judah, 4428
22:18 Jehoiakim the son of Josiah **k** of Judah; 4428
22:24 though Coniah the son of Jehoiakim **k** of 4428
22:25 even into the hand of Nebuchadrezzar **k** of 4428
23: 5 a **K** shall reign and prosper, and 4428
24: 1 after that Nebuchadrezzar **k** of Babylon had 4428
24: 1 Jeconiah the son of Jehoiakim **k** of Judah, 4428
Jer 24: 8 So will I give Zedekiah the **k** of Judah, and 4428
25: 1 of Jehoiakim the son of Josiah **k** of Judah, 4428
25: 1 that *was* the first year of Nebuchadrezzar **k** 4428
25: 3 year of Josiah the son of Amon **k** of Judah, 4428
25: 9 Nebuchadrezzar the **k** of Babylon, 4428
25:11 these nations shall serve the **k** of Babylon 4428
25:12 *that* I will punish the **k** of Babylon, and that 4428
25:19 Pharaoh **k** of Egypt, and his servants, and 4428
25:26 the **k** of Sheshach shall drink after them. 4428
26: 1 **k** of Judah came this word from 4428
26:18 in the days of Hezekiah **k** of Judah, 4428
26:19 Did Hezekiah **k** of Judah and all Judah put 4428
26:21 when Jehoiakim the **k**, with all his mighty 4428
26:21 his words, the **k** sought to put him to death: 4428
26:22 Jehoiakim the **k** sent men *into* Egypt, 4428
26:23 and brought him unto Jehoiakim the **k**; 4428
27: 1 **k** of Judah came this word unto Jeremiah 4428
27: 3 send them to the **k** of Edom, and to the king 4428
27: 3 to the **k** of Moab, and to the king of 4428
27: 3 to the **k** of the Ammonites, and to the king 4428
27: 3 to the **k** of Tyrus, and to the king of Zidon, 4428
27: 3 to the king of Tyrus, and to the **k** of Zidon, 4428
27: 3 *to* Jerusalem unto Zedekiah **k** of Judah; 4428
27: 6 hand of Nebuchadnezzar the **k** of Babylon, 4428
27: 8 same Nebuchadnezzar the **k** of Babylon, 4428
27: 8 neck under the yoke of the **k** of Babylon, 4428
27: 9 saying, Ye shall not serve the **k** of Babylon: 4428
27:11 neck under the yoke of the **k** of Babylon, 4428
27:12 I spake also to Zedekiah **k** of Judah 4428
27:12 Bring your necks under the yoke of the **k** of 4428
27:13 nation that will not serve the **k** of Babylon? 4428
27:14 saying, Ye shall not serve the **k** of Babylon: 4428
27:17 serve the **k** of Babylon, and live: 4428
27:18 *in* the house of the **k** of Judah, and 4428
27:20 Which Nebuchadnezzar **k** of Babylon took 4428
27:20 **k** of Judah from Jerusalem to Babylon, 4428
27:21 *in* the house of the **k** of Judah and 4428
28: 1 in the beginning of the reign of Zedekiah **k** 4428
28: 2 I have broken the yoke of the **k** of Babylon. 4428
28: 3 that Nebuchadnezzar **k** of Babylon took 4428
28: 4 Jeconiah the son of Jehoiakim **k** of Judah, 4428
28: 4 for I will break the yoke of the **k** of 4428
28:11 will I break the yoke of Nebuchadnezzar **k** 4428
28:14 that *they* may serve Nebuchadnezzar **k** of 4428
29: 2 (After that Jeconiah the **k**, and the queen, 4428
29: 3 whom Zedekiah **k** of Judah sent unto 4428
29: 3 Babylon to Nebuchadnezzar **k** of Babylon, 4428
29:16 *Know* that thus saith the LORD of the **k** 4428
29:21 the hand of Nebuchadrezzar **k** of Babylon; 4428
29:22 whom the **k** of Babylon roasted in the fire; 4428
30: 9 David their **k**, whom I will raise up unto 4428
32: 1 in the tenth year of Zedekiah **k** of Judah, 4428
32: 2 the **k** of Babylon's army besieged 4428
32: 2 which *was in* the **k** of Judah's house. 4428
32: 3 For Zedekiah **k** of Judah had shut him up, 4428
32: 3 I *will* give this city into the hand of the **k** of 4428
32: 4 Zedekiah **k** of Judah shall not escape out of 4428
32: 4 delivered into the hand of the **k** of Babylon, 4428
32:28 into the hand of Nebuchadrezzar **k** of 4428
32:36 It shall be delivered into the hand of the **k** 4428
34: 1 when Nebuchadnezzar **k** of Babylon, and 4428
34: 2 Go and speak to Zedekiah **k** of Judah, and 4428
34: 2 I *will* give this city into the hand of the **k** of 4428
34: 3 thine eyes shall behold the eyes of the **k** of 4428
34: 4 of the LORD, O Zedekiah **k** of Judah; 4428
34: 6 unto Zedekiah **k** of Judah in Jerusalem, 4428
34: 7 When the **k** of Babylon's army fought 4428
34: 8 after that the **k** Zedekiah had made a 4428
34:21 Zedekiah **k** of Judah and his princes will I 4428
34:21 into the hand of the **k** of Babylon's army, 4428
35: 1 of Jehoiakim the son of Josiah **k** of Judah, 4428
35:11 when Nebuchadrezzar **k** of Babylon came 4428
36: 1 of Jehoiakim the son of Josiah **k** of Judah, 4428
36: 9 of Jehoiakim the son of Josiah **k** of Judah, 4428
36:16 We will surely tell the **k** of all these words. 4428
36:20 And they went in to the **k** into the court, but 4428
36:20 and told all the words in the ears of the **k**. 4428
36:21 So the **k** sent Jehudi to fet the roll: and 4428
36:21 Jehudi read it in the ears of the **k**, and in 4428
36:21 of all the princes which stood beside the **k**. 4428
36:22 Now the **k** sat *in* the winterhouse in 4428
36:24 nor rent their garments, *neither* the **k**, 4428
36:25 Gemariah had made intercession to the **k** 4428
36:26 the **k** commanded Jerahmeel the son of 4428
36:27 after that the **k** had burnt the roll, and 4428
36:28 which Jehoiakim the **k** of Judah hath burnt. 4428
36:29 And thou shalt say to Jehoiakim **k** of Judah, 4428
36:29 The **k** of Babylon shall certainly come 4428
36:30 saith the LORD of Jehoiakim **k** of Judah; 4428
36:32 Jehoiakim **k** of Judah had burnt in the fire: 4428
37: 1 **k** Zedekiah the son of Josiah reigned 4428
37: 1 whom Nebuchadrezzar **k** of Babylon made 4428
37: 1 of Babylon **made k** in the land of Judah. 4427
37: 3 Zedekiah the **k** sent Jehucal the son of 4428
37: 7 Thus shall ye say to the **k** of Judah, 4428
37:17 Zedekiah the **k** sent, and took him *out*: 4428
37:17 and the **k** asked him secretly in his house, 4428
37:17 delivered into the hand of the **k** of Babylon. 4428
37:18 Moreover Jeremiah said unto **k** Zedekiah, 4428
37:19 The **k** of Babylon shall not come against 4428
37:20 hear now, I pray thee, O my lord the **k**: 4428
37:21 Zedekiah the **k** commanded that they 4428
38: 3 into the hand of the **k** of Babylon's army, 4428
38: 4 Therefore the princes said unto the **k**, 4428
38: 5 Zedekiah the **k** said, Behold, he *is* in your 4428
38: 5 for the **k** *is* not *he that* can do *any* thing 4428
38: 7 the **k** then sitting in the gate of Benjamin; 4428
38: 8 king's house, and spake to the **k**, saying, 4428
38: 9 My lord the **k**, these men have done evil in 4428
38:10 the **k** commanded Ebed-melech 4428
38:11 went *into* the house of the **k** under 4428
38:14 Zedekiah the **k** sent, and took Jeremiah 4428
38:14 the **k** said unto Jeremiah, I *will* ask thee a 4428
38:16 So Zedekiah the **k** sware secretly unto 4428
38:17 If thou wilt assuredly go forth unto the **k** of 4428

K

Book	Ref	Context	Strong's
Jer	38:18	if thou wilt not go forth to the **k** of	4428
	38:19	Zedekiah the **k** said unto Jeremiah, I am	4428
	38:22	all the women that are left in the **k** of	4428
	38:22	brought forth to the **k** of Babylon's princes,	4428
	38:23	shalt be taken by the hand of the **k** of	4428
	38:25	unto us now what thou hast said unto the **k**,	4428
	38:25	to death; also what the **k** said unto thee:	4428
	38:26	I presented my supplication before the **k**,	4428
	38:27	all these words that the **k** had commanded.	4428
	39: 1	In the ninth year of Zedekiah **k** of Judah,	4428
	39: 1	came Nebuchadrezzar **k** of Babylon and	4428
	39: 3	all the princes of the **k** of Babylon came in,	4428
	39: 3	with all the residue of the princes of the **k**	4428
	39: 4	*that* when Zedekiah the **k** of Judah saw	4428
	39: 5	they brought him up to Nebuchadnezzar **k**	4428
	39: 6	the **k** of Babylon slew the sons of Zedekiah	4428
	39: 6	also the **k** of Babylon slew all the nobles of	4428
	39:11	Now Nebuchadrezzar **k** of Babylon gave	4428
	39:13	and all the **k** of Babylon's princes;	4428
	40: 5	whom the **k** of Babylon hath made	4428
	40: 7	heard that the **k** of Babylon had made	4428
	40: 9	in the land and serve the **k** of Babylon,	4428
	40:11	heard that the **k** of Babylon had left a	4428
	40:14	Dost thou certainly know that Baalis the **k**	4428
	41: 1	of the seed royal, and the princes of the **k**,	4428
	41: 2	whom the **k** of Babylon had made governor	4428
	41: 9	*was* it which Asa the **k** had made for fear of	4428
	41: 9	had made for fear of Baasha **k** of Israel:	4428
	41:18	whom the **k** of Babylon made governor in	4428
	42:11	Be not afraid of the **k** of Babylon, of whom	4428
	43:10	and take Nebuchadrezzar the **k** of Babylon,	4428
	44:30	I *will* give Pharaoh-hophra **k** of Egypt into	4428
	44:30	as I gave Zedekiah **k** of Judah into the hand	4428
	44:30	the hand of Nebuchadrezzar **k** of Babylon,	4428
	45: 1	of Jehoiakim the son of Josiah **k** of Judah,	4428
	46: 2	against the army of Pharaoh-necho **k** of	4428
	46: 2	which Nebuchadrezzar **k** of Babylon smote	4428
	46: 2	of Jehoiakim the son of Josiah **k** of Judah.	4428
	46:13	how Nebuchadrezzar **k** of Babylon should	4428
	46:17	Pharaoh **k** of Egypt *is but* a noise;	4428
	46:18	*As* I live, saith the **K**, whose name *is*	4428
	46:26	into the hand of Nebuchadrezzar **k** of	4428
	48:15	saith the **K**, whose name *is* the LORD of	4428
	49: 1	why *then* doth their **k** inherit Gad, and	4428
	49: 3	for their **k** shall go into captivity, *and*	4428
	49:28	which Nebuchadrezzar **k** of Babylon shall	4428
	49:30	for Nebuchadrezzar **k** of Babylon hath	4428
	49:34	of the reign of Zedekiah **k** of Judah,	4428
	49:38	will destroy from thence the **k** and	4428
	50:17	first the **k** of Assyria hath devoured him;	4428
	50:17	last this Nebuchadrezzar **k** of Babylon hath	4428
	50:18	I *will* punish the **k** of Babylon and his land,	4428
	50:18	as I have punished the **k** of Assyria.	4428
	50:43	The **k** of Babylon hath heard the report of	4428
	51:31	to shew the **k** of Babylon that his city is	4428
	51:34	Nebuchadrezzar the **k** of Babylon hath	4428
	51:57	perpetual sleep, and not wake, saith the **K**,	4428
	51:59	when he went with Zedekiah the **k** of Judah	4428
	52: 3	that Zedekiah rebelled against the **k** of	4428
	52: 4	*that* Nebuchadrezzar **k** of Babylon came, he	4428
	52: 5	unto the eleventh year of **k** Zedekiah.	4428
	52: 8	army of the Chaldeans pursued after the **k**,	4428
	52: 9	they took the **k**, and carried him up unto	4428
	52: 9	carried him up unto the **k** of Babylon to	4428
	52:10	the **k** of Babylon slew the sons of Zedekiah	4428
	52:11	the **k** of Babylon bound him in chains, and	4428
	52:12	year of Nebuchadrezzar **k** of Babylon,	4428
	52:12	*which* served the **k** of Babylon,	4428
	52:15	that fell to the **k** of Babylon, and the rest of	4428
	52:20	which **k** Solomon had made in the house of	4428
	52:26	brought them to the **k** of Babylon to Riblah.	4428
	52:27	the **k** of Babylon smote them, and put them	4428
	52:31	of the captivity of Jehoiachin **k** of Judah,	4428
	52:31	*that* Evil-merodach **k** of Babylon in the *first*	4428
	52:31	lifted up the head of Jehoiachin **k** of Judah,	4428
	52:34	diet given him of the **k** of Babylon,	4428
La	2: 6	in the indignation of his anger the **k**	4428
	2: 9	her **k** and her princes *are* among	4428
Eze	1: 2	which *was* the fifth year of **k** Jehoiachin's	4428
	7:27	The **k** shall mourn, and the prince shall be	4428
	17:12	the **k** of Babylon is come *to* Jerusalem, and	4428
	17:12	hath taken the **k** thereof, and the princes	4428
	17:16	surely in the place *where* the **k** *dwelleth*	4428
	17:16	*where* the king *dwelleth* that **made** him **k**,	4427
	19: 9	and brought him to the **k** of Babylon:	4428
	21:19	that the sword of the **k** of Babylon may	4428
	21:21	For the **k** of Babylon stood at the parting of	4428
	24: 2	the **k** of Babylon set himself against	4428
	26: 7	I *will* bring upon Tyrus Nebuchadrezzar **k**	4428
	26: 7	a **k** of kings, from the north, with horses,	4428
	28:12	take up a lamentation upon the **k** of Tyrus,	4428
	29: 2	set thy face against Pharaoh **k** of Egypt,	4428
	29: 3	I *am* against thee, Pharaoh **k** of Egypt,	4428
	29:18	Nebuchadrezzar **k** of Babylon caused his	4428
	29:19	Egypt unto Nebuchadrezzar **k** of Babylon;	4428
	30:10	the hand of Nebuchadrezzar **k** of Babylon.	4428
	30:21	I have broken the arm of Pharaoh **k** of	4428
	30:22	I *am* against Pharaoh **k** of Egypt, and	4428
	30:24	I will strengthen the arms of the **k** of	4428
	30:25	I will strengthen the arms of the **k** of	4428
	30:25	sword into the hand of the **k** of Babylon,	4428
	31: 2	speak unto Pharaoh **k** of Egypt, and to his	4428
	32: 2	take up a lamentation for Pharaoh **k** of	4428
	32:11	The sword of the **k** of Babylon shall come	4428
	37:22	and one **k** shall be king to them all:	4428
	37:22	and one king shall be **k** to them all:	4428
	37:24	David my servant *shall be* **k** over them;	4428
Da	1: 1	In the third year of the reign of Jehoiakim **k**	4428
	1: 1	**k** of Babylon *unto* Jerusalem,	4428
	1: 2	the Lord gave Jehoiakim **k** of Judah into	4428
	1: 3	the **k** spake unto Ashpenaz the master of	4428
	1: 5	the **k** appointed them a daily provision of	4428
	1: 5	end thereof they might stand before the **k**.	4428
	1:10	I fear my lord the **k**, who hath appointed	4428
	1:10	ye make *me* endanger my head to the **k**.	4428
Da	1:18	Now at the end of the days that the **k** had	4428
	1:19	the **k** communed with them; and	4428
	1:19	Azariah: therefore stood they before the **k**.	4428
	1:20	understanding, that the **k** inquired of them,	4428
	1:21	*even* unto the first year of **k** Cyrus.	4428
	2: 2	the **k** commanded to call the magicians,	4428
	2: 2	for to shew the **k** his dreams.	4428
	2: 2	So they came and stood before the **k**.	4428
	2: 3	the **k** said unto them, I have dreamed a	4428
	2: 4	spake the Chaldeans to the **k** in Syriack,	4428
	2: 4	to the king in Syriack, O **k**, live for ever:	4430
	2: 5	The **k** answered and said to the Chaldeans,	4430
	2: 7	Let the **k** tell his servants the dream, and	4430
	2: 8	The **k** answered and said, I know of	4430
	2:10	The Chaldeans answered before the **k**, and	4430
	2:10	therefore *there is* no **k**, lord, nor ruler,	4430
	2:11	*it is* a rare thing that the **k** requireth, and	4430
	2:11	is none other that can shew it before the **k**,	4430
	2:12	For this cause the **k** was angry and	4430
	2:15	Why *is* the decree *so* hasty from the **k**?	4430
	2:16	desired of the **k** that he would give him	4430
	2:16	that *he* would shew the **k** the interpretation.	4430
	2:24	whom the **k** had ordained to destroy	4430
	2:24	bring me in before the **k**, and I will shew	4430
	2:24	I will shew unto the **k** the interpretation.	4430
	2:25	Arioch brought in Daniel before the **k** in	4430
	2:25	that will make known unto the **k**	4430
	2:26	The **k** answered and said to Daniel,	4430
	2:27	Daniel answered in the presence of the **k**,	4430
	2:27	The secret which the **k** hath demanded	4430
	2:27	the soothsayers, shew unto the **k**;	4430
	2:28	maketh known to the **k** Nebuchadnezzar	4430
	2:29	*As for* thee, O **k**, thy thoughts came *into*	4430
	2:30	make known the interpretation to the **k**,	4430
	2:31	Thou, O **k**, sawest, and behold a great	4430
	2:36	tell the interpretation thereof before the **k**.	4430
	2:37	Thou, O **k**, *art* a king of kings: for the God	4430
	2:37	Thou, O king, *art* a **k** of kings: for the God	4430
	2:45	the great God hath made known to the **k**	4430
	2:46	the **k** Nebuchadnezzar fell upon his face,	4430
	2:47	The **k** answered unto Daniel, and said, Of a	4430
	2:48	the **k** made Daniel a great man, and	4430
	2:49	Daniel requested of the **k**, and he set	4430
	2:49	but Daniel *sat* in the gate of the **k**.	4430
	3: 1	Nebuchadnezzar the **k** made an image of	4430
	3: 2	Nebuchadnezzar the **k** sent to gather	4430
	3: 2	which Nebuchadnezzar the **k** had set up.	4430
	3: 3	that Nebuchadnezzar the **k** had set up;	4430
	3: 5	that Nebuchadnezzar the **k** hath set up:	4430
	3: 7	that Nebuchadnezzar the **k** had set up.	4430
	3: 9	and said to the **k** Nebuchadnezzar,	4430
	3: 9	king Nebuchadnezzar, O **k**, live for ever.	4430
	3:10	Thou, O **k**, hast made a decree, that every	4430
	3:12	these men, O **k**, have not regarded thee:	4430
	3:13	Then they brought these men before the **k**.	4430
	3:16	and Abed-nego, answered and said to the **k**,	4430
	3:17	he will deliver *us* out of thine hand, O **k**.	4430
	3:18	if not, be it known unto thee, O **k**, that we	4430
	3:24	Nebuchadnezzar the **k** was astonied, and	4430
	3:24	They answered and said unto the **k**, True, O	4430
	3:24	and said unto the king, True, O **k**.	4430
	3:30	the **k** promoted Shadrach, Meshach, and	4430
	4: 1	Nebuchadnezzar the **k**, unto all people,	4430
	4:18	This dream I **k** Nebuchadnezzar have seen.	4430
	4:19	The **k** spake, and said, Belteshazzar, let not	4430
	4:22	It *is* thou, O **k**, that art grown and	4430
	4:23	whereas the **k** saw a watcher and a holy one	4430
	4:24	O **k**, and this *is* the decree of the most	4430
	4:24	which is come upon my lord the **k**:	4430
	4:27	Wherefore, O **k**, let my counsel be	4430
	4:28	All this came upon the **k** Nebuchadnezzar.	4430
	4:30	The **k** spake, and said, *Is* not this great	4430
	4:31	*saying*, O **k** Nebuchadnezzar, to thee it is	4430
	4:37	and extol and honour the **K** of heaven,	4430
	5: 1	Belshazzar the **k** made a great feast to a	4430
	5: 2	that the **k**, and his princes, his wives, and	4430
	5: 3	the **k**, and his princes, his wives, and	4430
	5: 5	the **k** saw the part of the hand that wrote.	4430
	5: 7	The **k** cried aloud to bring in	4430
	5: 7	*And* the **k** spake, and said to the wise *men*	4430
	5: 8	nor make known to the **k** the interpretation	4430
	5: 9	*was* **k** Belshazzar greatly troubled, and	4430
	5:10	by reason of the words of the **k** and	4430
	5:10	*and* the queen spake and said, O **k**, live for	4430
	5:11	whom the **k** Nebuchadnezzar thy father,	4430
	5:11	the **k**, *I say*, thy father, made master of	4430
	5:12	whom the **k** named Belteshazzar:	4430
	5:13	was Daniel brought in before the **k**.	4430
	5:13	*And* the **k** spake and said unto Daniel,	4430
	5:13	whom the **k** my father brought out of	4430
	5:17	Daniel answered and said before the **k**,	4430
	5:17	yet I will read the writing unto the **k**, and	4430
	5:18	O thou **k**, the most high God gave	4430
	5:30	In that night *was* Belshazzar the **k** of	4430
	6: 2	and the **k** should have no damage.	4430
	6: 3	the **k** thought to set him over the whole	4430
	6: 6	princes assembled *together* to the **k**,	4430
	6: 6	said thus unto him, **K** Darius, live for ever.	4430
	6: 7	or man for thirty days, save of thee, O **k**,	4430
	6: 8	Now, O **k**, establish the decree, and	4430
	6: 9	Wherefore **k** Darius signed the writing and	4430
	6:12	spake before the **k** concerning the king's	4430
	6:12	man within thirty days, save of thee, O **k**,	4430
	6:12	The **k** answered and said, The thing *is* true,	4430
	6:13	answered they and said before the **k**,	4430
	6:13	regardeth not thee, O **k**, nor the decree that	4430
	6:14	the **k**, when he heard *these* words, was sore	4430
	6:15	these men assembled unto the **k**, and	4430
	6:15	said unto the **k**, Know, O king, that the law	4430
	6:15	said unto the king, Know, O **k**, that the law	4430
	6:15	which the **k** establisheth may be changed.	4430
	6:16	the **k** commanded, and they brought	4430
	6:16	*Now* the **k** spake and said unto Daniel,	4430
	6:17	the **k** sealed it with his own signet, and	4430
	6:18	the **k** went to his palace, and passed	4430
Da	6:19	the **k** arose very early in the morning, and	4430
	6:20	*and* the **k** spake and said to Daniel,	4430
	6:21	said Daniel unto the **k**, O king, live for	4430
	6:21	Daniel unto the king, O **k**, live for ever.	4430
	6:22	also before thee, O **k**, have I done no hurt.	4430
	6:23	Then was the **k** exceeding glad for him, and	4430
	6:24	the **k** commanded, and they brought those	4430
	6:25	**k** Darius wrote unto all people, nations,	4430
	7: 1	In the first year of Belshazzar **k** of Babylon	4430
	8: 1	In the third year of the reign of **k**	4428
	8:21	the rough goat *is* the **k** of Grecia: and	4428
	8:21	horn that *is* between his eyes *is* the first **k**.	4428
	8:23	a **k** of fierce countenance, and	4428
	9: 1	which was **made** **k** over the realm of	4427
	10: 1	In the third year of Cyrus **k** of Persia a	4428
	11: 3	a mighty **k** shall stand up, that shall rule	4428
	11: 5	the **k** of the south shall be strong, and	4428
	11: 6	to the **k** of the north to make an agreement:	4428
	11: 7	shall enter into the fortress of the **k** of	4428
	11: 8	he shall continue *more* years than the **k** of	4428
	11: 9	So the **k** of the south shall come into *his*	4428
	11:11	the **k** of the south shall be moved with	4428
	11:11	with him, *even* with the **k** of the north:	4428
	11:13	For the **k** of the north shall return, and	4428
	11:14	many stand up against the **k** of the south:	4428
	11:15	So the **k** of the north shall come, and	4428
	11:25	his courage against the **k** of the south with	4428
	11:25	the **k** of the south shall be stirred up to	4428
	11:36	the **k** shall do according to his will; and	4428
	11:40	at the time of the end shall the **k** of	4428
	11:40	the **k** of the north shall come against him	4428
Hos	1: 1	of Jeroboam the son of Joash, **k** of Israel.	4428
	3: 4	of Israel shall abide many days without a **k**,	4428
	3: 5	the LORD their God, and David their **k**;	4428
	5: 1	of Israel; and give ye ear, O house of the **k**;	4428
	5:13	to the Assyrian, and sent to **k** Jareb:	4428
	7: 3	They make the **k** glad with their	4428
	7: 5	*In* the day of our **k** the princes have made	4428
	8:10	a little for the burden of the **k** of princes.	4428
	10: 3	We have no **k**, because we feared not	4428
	10: 3	the LORD; what then should a **k** do to us?	4428
	10: 6	unto Assyria *for* a present to **k** Jareb:	4428
	10: 7	her **k** is cut off as the foam upon the water.	4428
	10:15	in a morning shall the **k** of Israel utterly be	4428
	11: 5	the Assyrian shall be his **k**, because	4428
	13:10	I will be thy **k**: where *is any other* that may	4428
	13:10	thou saidst, Give me a **k** and princes?	4428
	13:11	I gave thee a **k** in mine anger, and took *him*	4428
Am	1: 1	Israel in the days of Uzziah **k** of Judah,	4428
	1: 1	in the days of Jeroboam the son of Joash **k**	4428
	1:15	their **k** shall go into captivity, he and	4428
	2: 1	he burnt the bones of the **k** of Edom into	4428
	7:10	of Beth-el sent to Jeroboam **k** of Israel,	4428
Jnh	3: 6	For word came unto the **k** of Nineveh, and	4428
	3: 7	through Nineveh by the decree of the **k**	4428
Mic	2:13	their **k** shall pass before them, and	4428
	4: 9	*is there* no **k** in thee? is thy counseller	4428
	6: 5	remember now what Balak **k** of Moab	4428
Na	3:18	Thy shepherds slumber, O **k** of Assyria:	4428
Zep	1: 1	days of Josiah the son of Amon, **k** of Judah.	4428
	3:15	the **k** of Israel, *even* the LORD, *is* in	4428
Hag	1: 1	In the second year of Darius the **k**, in	4428
	1:15	in the second year of Darius the **k**.	4428
Zec	7: 1	it came to pass in the fourth year of **k**	4428
	9: 5	the **k** shall perish from Gaza, and	4428
	9: 9	behold, thy **K** cometh unto thee: he *is* just,	4428
	11: 6	and into the hand of his **k**:	4428
	14: 5	in the days of Uzziah **k** of Judah:	4428
	14: 9	the LORD shall be **k** over all the earth:	4428
	14:16	go up from year to year to worship the **K**,	4428
	14:17	the earth unto Jerusalem to worship the **K**,	4428
Mal	1:14	the Lord a corrupt *thing*: for I *am* a great **K**,	4428
Mt	1: 6	And Jesse begat David the **k**; and David	*935*
	1: 6	David the **k** begat Solomon of *her that had*	*935*
	2: 1	of Judea in the days of Herod the **k**,	*935*
	2: 2	Where is he that is born **K** of the Jews?	*935*
	2: 3	When Herod the **k** had heard *these things*, he	*935*
	2: 9	When they had heard the **k**, they departed;	*935*
	5:35	by Jerusalem; for it is the city of the great **K**.	*935*
	14: 9	And the **k** was sorry: nevertheless for	*935*
	18:23	kingdom of heaven likened unto a certain **k**,	*935*
	21: 5	thy **K** cometh unto thee, meek, and	*935*
	22: 2	kingdom of heaven is like unto a certain **k**,	*935*
	22: 7	But when the **k** heard *thereof*, he was wroth:	*935*
	22:11	And when the **k** came in to see the guests,	*935*
	22:13	Then said the **k** to the servants, Bind him	*935*
	25:34	Then shall the **K** say unto them on his right	*935*
	25:40	And the **K** shall answer and say unto them,	*935*
	27:11	saying, Art thou the **K** of the Jews?	*935*
	27:29	mocked him, saying, Hail, **K** of the Jews!	*935*
	27:37	THIS IS JESUS THE **K** OF THE JEWS.	*935*
	27:42	If he be the **K** of Israel, let him now come	*935*
Mk	6:14	And **k** Herod heard *of him*; (for his name	*935*
	6:22	them that sat with *him*, the **k** said unto	*935*
	6:25	came in straightway with haste unto the **k**,	*935*
	6:26	And the **k** was exceeding sorry; *yet* for his	*935*
	6:27	And immediately the **k** sent an executioner,	*935*
	15: 2	asked him, Art thou the **K** of the Jews?	*935*
	15: 9	Will ye *that* I release unto you the **K** of	*935*
	15:12	*that* I shall do *unto him* whom ye call the **K**	*935*
	15:18	began to salute him, Hail, **K** of the Jews.	*935*
	15:26	was written over, THE **K** OF THE JEWS.	*935*
	15:32	Let Christ the **K** of Israel descend now from	*935*
Lk	1: 5	was in the days of Herod, the **k** of Judea,	*935*
	14:31	Or what **k**, going to make war against	*935*
	14:31	going to make war against another **k**,	*935*
	19:38	Blessed *be* the **K** that cometh in the name of	*935*
	23: 2	saying that he himself is Christ a **K**.	*935*
	23: 3	saying, Art thou the **K** of the Jews?	*935*
	23:37	And saying, If thou be the **K** of the Jews,	*935*
	23:38	Hebrew, THIS IS THE **K** OF THE JEWS.	*935*
Jn	1:49	art the Son of God; thou art the **K** of Israel.	*935*
	6:15	and take him by force, to make him a **k**,	*935*
	12:13	Blessed *is* the **K** of Israel that cometh in	*935*
	12:15	behold, thy **K** cometh, sitting on an ass's	*935*

Jn 18:33 said unto him, Art thou the **K** of the Jews? *935*
18:37 therefore said unto him, Art thou a **k** then? *935*
18:37 Jesus answered, Thou sayest that I am a **k**. *935*
18:39 *that* I release unto you the **K** of the Jews? *935*
19: 3 And said, Hail, **K** of the Jews: and *935*
19:12 whosoever maketh himself a **k** speaketh *935*
19:14 and he saith unto the Jews, Behold your **K**. *935*
19:15 saith unto them, Shall I crucify your **K**? *935*
19:15 priests answered, We have no **k** but Cesar. *935*
19:19 JESUS OF NAZARETH THE **K** OF THE *935*
19:21 Jews to Pilate, Write not, The **K** of the Jews; *935*
19:21 but that he said, I am **K** of the Jews. *935*
Ac 7:10 wisdom in the sight of Pharaoh **k** of Egypt; *935*
7:18 Till another **k** arose, which knew not Joseph. *935*
12: 1 Now about that time Herod the **k** stretched *935*
13:21 And afterward they desired a **k**: and God *935*
13:22 he raised up unto them David to be their **k**; *935*
17: 7 saying that there is another **k**, *one* Jesus. *935*
25:13 And after certain days **k** Agrippa and *935*
25:14 Festus declared Paul's cause unto the **k**, *935*
25:24 **K** Agrippa, and all men which are here *935*
25:26 and specially before thee, O **k** Agrippa, that, *935*
26: 2 **k** Agrippa, because I shall answer for myself *935*
26: 7 For which hope's sake, **k** Agrippa, I am *935*
26:13 At midday, O **k**, I saw in the way a light *935*
26:19 Whereupon, O **k** Agrippa, I was not *935*
26:26 For the **k** knoweth of these *things*, before *935*
26:27 **K** Agrippa, believest thou the prophets? *935*
26:30 thus spoken, the **k** rose up, and the governor, *935*
2Co 11:32 **k** kept the city of the Damascenes *with a* *935*
1Ti 1:17 Now unto the **K** eternal, immortal, invisible, *935*
6:15 the **K** of kings, and Lord of lords; *935*
Heb 7: 1 For this Melchisedec, **k** of Salem, priest of *935*
7: 2 first being by interpretation **K** of *935*
7: 2 and after that also **K** of Salem, which is, *935*
7: 2 also King of Salem, which is, **K** of peace; *935*
11:27 not fearing the wrath of the **k**: *935*
1Pe 2:13 whether *it be* to the **k**, as supreme; *935*
2:17 the brotherhood. Fear God. Honour the **k**. *935*
Rev 9:11 And they had a **k** over them, *which is* *935*
15: 3 just and true *are* thy ways, thou **K** of saints. *935*
17:14 for he is Lord of lords, and **K** of kings: and *935*
19:16 **K** OF KINGS, AND LORD OF LORDS. *935*

KING'S (284) [KING]

Ge 14:17 at the valley of Shaveh, which *is* the **k** dale. 4428
39:20 a place where the **k** prisoners *were* bound: 4428
Nu 20:17 we will go *by* the **k** *high* way, we will not 4428
21:22 *but* we will go along by the **k** *high* way, 4428
1Sa 18:22 now therefore be the **k** son in law. 4428+871.1
18:23 a light *thing* to be a **k** son in law, 4428+871.1
18:25 to be avenged of the **k** enemies. 4428
18:26 it pleased David well to be the **k** son 4428+871.1
18:27 that he might be the **k** son in law. 4428+871.1
20:29 Therefore he cometh not unto the **k** table. 4428
21: 8 because the **k** business required haste. 4428
22:14 which *is* the **k** son in law, and goeth at thy 4428
23:20 our part *shall be* to deliver him into the **k** 4428
26:16 now see where the **k** spear *is*, and the cruse 4428
26:22 and said, Behold, the **k** spear; 4428
2Sa 9:11 shall eat at my table, as one of the **k** sons. 4428
9:13 for he did eat continually at the **k** table; and 4428
11: 2 and walked upon the roof of the **k** house: 4428
11: 8 Uriah departed out of the **k** house, and 4428
11: 9 Uriah slept *at* the door of the **k** house with 4428
11:20 if so be that the **k** wrath arise, and he say 4428
11:24 *some* of the **k** servants be dead, and 4428
12:30 he took their **k** crown from off his head, 4428
13: 4 Why *art* thou, *being* the **k** son, lean from 4428
13:18 for with such robes were the **k** daughters 4428
13:23 and Absalom invited all the **k** sons. 4428
13:27 let Amnon and all the **k** sons go with him. 4428
13:29 all the **k** sons arose, and every man gat him 4428
13:30 Absalom hath slain all the **k** sons, and 4428
13:32 have slain all the young men the **k** sons; 4428
13:33 to think *that* all the **k** sons are dead. 4428
13:35 unto the king, Behold, the **k** sons come: 4428
13:36 the **k** sons came, and lift up their voice and 4428
14: 1 that the **k** heart *was* toward Absalom. 4428
14:24 to his own house, and saw not the **k** face. 4428
14:26 *at* two hundred shekels after the **k** weight. 4428
14:28 years in Jerusalem, and saw not the **k** face. 4428
14:32 now therefore let me see the **k** face; and 4428
15:15 the **k** servants said unto the king, Behold, 4428
15:35 soever thou shalt hear out of the **k** house, 4428
16: 2 The asses *be* for the **k** household to ride on; 4428
18:12 I not put forth mine hand against the **k** son: 4428
18:18 for himself a pillar, which *is* in the **k** dale: 4428
18:20 bear no tidings, because the **k** son is dead. 4428
18:29 When Joab sent the **k** servant, and *me* thy 4428
19:18 a ferry boat to carry over the **k** household, 4428
19:42 have we eaten at all of the **k** *cost*? or 4428
24: 4 Notwithstanding the **k** word prevailed 4428
1Ki 1: 9 called all his brethren the **k** sons, and all 4428
1: 9 and all the men of Judah the **k** servants: 4428
1:25 hath called all the **k** sons, and the captains 4428
1:28 she came into the **k** presence, and 4428
1:44 they have caused him to ride upon the **k** 4428
1:47 moreover the **k** servants came to bless our 4428
2:19 and caused a seat to be set for the **k** mother; 4428
4: 5 *was* principal officer, *and* the **k** friend: 4428
9: 1 the **k** house, and all Solomon's desire 4428
9:10 the house of the LORD, and the **k** house, 4428
10:12 for the **k** house, harps also and 4428
10:28 the **k** merchants received the linen yarn at a 4428
11:14 the Edomite: he *was* of the **k** seed in Edom. 4428
13: 6 the **k** hand was restored him again, and 4428
14:26 and the treasures of the **k** house; 4428
14:27 which kept the door of the **k** house. 4428
15:18 the treasures of the **k** house, and 4428
16:18 that he went into the palace of the **k** house, 4428
16:18 burnt the **k** house over him with fire, and 4428
22:12 for the LORD shall deliver *it* into the **k** 4428
22:26 governor of the city, and to Joash the **k** son; 4428
2Ki 7: 9 that we may go and tell the **k** household. 4428

2Ki 7:11 and they told *it to* the **k** house within. 4428
9:34 and bury her: for she *is* a **k** daughter. 4428
10: 6 Now the **k** sons, *being* seventy persons, 4428
10: 7 that they took the **k** sons, and slew seventy 4428
10: 8 They have brought the heads of the **k** sons. 4428
11: 2 stale him from among the **k** sons which 4428
11: 4 of the LORD, and shewed them the **k** son. 4428
11: 5 be keepers of the watch of the **k** house; 4428
11:12 he brought forth the **k** son, and put 4428
11:16 the which the horses came *into* the **k** house: 4428
11:19 way of the gate of the guard *to* the **k** house. 4428
11:20 Athaliah with the sword *beside* the **k** house. 4428
12:10 that the **k** scribe and the high priest came 4428
12:18 *in* the **k** house, and sent *it* to Hazael king of 4428
13:16 and Elisha put his hands upon the **k** hands. 4428
14:14 in the treasures of the **k** house, and 4428
15: 5 Jotham the **k** son *was* over the house, 4428
15:25 in the palace of the **k** house, with Argob 4428
16: 8 in the treasures of the **k** house, and sent *it* 4428
16:15 the **k** burnt sacrifice, and his meat offering, 4428
16:18 built in the house, and the **k** entry without, 4428
18:15 and in the treasures of the **k** house. 4428
18:36 for the **k** commandment was, saying, 4428
22:12 and Asahiah a servant of the **k**, saying, 4428
24:13 the treasures of the **k** house, and cut in 4428
24:15 and the **k** mother, and the king's wives, and 4428
24:15 the **k** wives, and his officers, and 4428
25: 4 two walls, which *is* by the **k** garden: 4428
25: 9 the **k** house, and all the houses of 4428
25:19 five men of them that were in the **k** 4428
1Ch 9:18 Who hitherto *waited* in the **k** gate eastward: 4428
21: 4 Nevertheless the **k** word prevailed against 4428
21: 6 for the **k** word was abominable to Joab. 4428
25: 5 All these *were* the sons of Heman the **k** 4428
25: 6 according to the **k** order *to* Asaph, 4428
27:25 over the **k** treasures *was* Azmaveth the son 4428
27:32 Jehiel the son of Hachmoni *was* with the **k** 4428
27:33 Ahithophel *was* the **k** counseller: 4428+3807.1
27:33 Hushai the Archite *was* the **k** companion: 4428
27:34 and the general of the **k** army *was* Joab. 4428
29: 6 with the rulers over the **k** work, 4428
2Ch 1:16 the **k** merchants received the linen yarn at a 4428
7:11 the house of the LORD, and the **k** house: 4428
9:11 to the **k** palace, and harps and psalteries for 4428
9:21 For the **k** ships went *to* Tarshish with 4428
12: 9 and the treasures of the **k** house; 4428
12:10 that kept the entrance of the **k** house. 4428
16: 2 house of the LORD and of the **k** house, 4428
18: 5 for God will deliver *it* into the **k** hand. 4428
18:25 governor of the city, and to Joash the **k** son; 4428
19:11 of the house of Judah, for all the **k** matters: 4428
21:17 substance that was found in the **k** house, 4428
22:11 stole him from among the **k** sons that were 4428
23: 3 unto them, Behold, the **k** son shall reign, 4428
23: 5 And a third *part shall be* at the **k** house; and 4428
23:11 they brought out the **k** son, and put upon 4428
23:15 entering of the horse gate *by* the **k** house, 4428
23:20 they came through the high gate *into* the **k** 4428
24: 8 at the **k** commandment they made a chest, 4428
24:11 unto the **k** office by the hand of the Levites, 4428
24:11 the **k** scribe and the high priest's officer 4428
25:16 unto him, Art thou made of the **k** counsel? 4428
25:24 the treasures of the **k** house, the hostages 4428
26:11 hand of Hananiah, *one* of the **k** captains. 4428
26:21 Jotham his son *was* over the **k** house, 4428
28: 7 slew Maaseiah the **k** son, and Azrikam 4428
29:25 of Gad the **k** seer, and Nathan the prophet: 4428
31: 3 *He appointed* also the **k** portion of his 4428
34:20 and Asaiah a servant of the **k**, saying, 4428
35: 7 these *were* of the **k** substance. 4428
35:10 according to the **k** commandment. 4428
35:15 and Heman, and Jeduthun the **k** seer; 4428
Ezr 4:14 we have maintenance from *the* **k** palace, NIH
4:14 *it was* not meet for us to see the **k** 4430
5:17 let there be search made in the **k** treasure 4430
6: 4 let the expences be given out of the **k** 4430
6: 8 that of the **k** goods, *even* of the tribute 4430
7:20 bestow *it* out of the **k** treasure house. 4430
7:27 which hath put *such a thing* as this in the **k** 4428
7:28 and before all the **k** mighty princes. 4428
8:36 they delivered the **k** commissions unto 4428
8:36 king's commissions unto the **k** lieutenants, 4428
Ne 1:11 of this man. For I was the **k** cupbearer. 4428
2: 8 Asaph the keeper of the **k** forest, 4428+3807.1
2: 9 the river, and gave them the **k** letters. 4428
2:14 the gate of the fountain, and to the **k** pool: 4428
2:18 as also the **k** words that he had spoken unto 4428
3:15 the wall of the pool of Siloah by the **k** 4428
3:25 the tower which lieth out from the **k** high 4428
5: 4 We have borrowed money for the **k** tribute, 4428
11:23 For *it was* the **k** commandment concerning 4428
11:24 *was* at the **k** hand in all matters concerning 4428
Est 1: 5 in the court of the garden of the **k** palace; 4428
1:12 the queen Vashti refused to come at the **k** 4428
1:13 *was* the **k** manner towards all that knew 4428
1:14 which saw the **k** face, *and* which sat 4428
1:18 Media say this day unto all the **k** princes. 4428
1:20 when the **k** decree which he shall make 4428
1:22 For he sent letters into all the **k** provinces, 4428
2: 2 said the **k** servants that ministered unto 4428
2: 3 unto the custody of Hege the **k** 4428
2: 8 when the **k** commandment and his decree 4428
2: 8 that Esther was brought *also* unto the **k** 4428
2: 9 meet to be given her, out of the **k** house: 4428
2:13 the house of the women unto the **k** house. 4428
2:14 the **k** chamberlain, which kept 4428
2:15 but what Hegai the **k** chamberlain, 4428
2:19 then Mordecai sat in the **k** gate. 4428
2:21 while Mordecai sat in the **k** gate, 4428
2:21 two of the **k** chamberlains, Bigthan and 4428
3: 2 all the **k** servants, that *were* in the king's 4428
3: 2 that *were* in the **k** gate, bowed, and 4428
3: 3 the **k** servants, which *were* in the king's 4428
3: 3 which *were* in the **k** gate, said unto 4428
3: 3 Why transgressest thou the **k** 4428

Est 3: 8 all people; neither keep they the **k** laws: 4428
3: 8 it *is* not for the **k** profit to suffer them. 4428
3: 9 to bring *it* into the **k** treasuries. 4428
3:12 were the **k** scribes called on the thirteenth 4428
3:12 had commanded unto the **k** lieutenants, 4428
3:12 was it written, and sealed with the **k** ring. 4428
3:13 the letters were sent by posts into all the **k** 4428
3:15 being hastened by the **k** commandment, 4428
4: 2 came even before the **k** gate: for none 4428
4: 2 for none might enter into the **k** gate clothed 4428
4: 3 whithersoever the **k** commandment and 4428
4: 5 for Hatach, *one* of the **k** chamberlains, 4428
4: 6 of the city, which *was* before the **k** gate. 4428
4: 7 to pay to the **k** treasuries for the Jews, 4428
4:11 All the **k** servants, and the people of 4428
4:11 and the people of the **k** provinces, do know, 4428
4:13 that *thou* shalt escape *in* the **k** house, 4428
5: 1 and stood in the inner court of the **k** house, 4428
5: 1 the king's house, over against the **k** house: 4428
5: 9 when Haman saw Mordecai in the **k** gate, 4428
5:13 I see Mordecai the Jew sitting at the **k** gate. 4428
6: 2 and Teresh, two of the **k** chamberlains, 4428
6: 3 said the **k** servants that ministered unto 4428
6: 4 come into the outward court of the **k** house, 4428
6: 5 the **k** servants said unto him, Behold, 4428
6: 9 hand of one of the **k** most noble princes, 4428
6:10 Mordecai the Jew, that sitteth at the **k** gate: 4428
6:12 Mordecai came again to the **k** gate. 4428
6:14 came the **k** chamberlains, and hasted to 4428
7: 4 enemy could not countervail the **k** damage. 4428
7: 8 As the word went out of the **k** mouth, 4428
7:10 Then was the **k** wrath pacified. 4428
8: 5 the Jews which *are* in all the **k** provinces: 4428
8: 8 in the **k** name, and seal *it* with the king's 4428
8: 8 the king's name, and seal *it* with the **k** ring: 4428
8: 8 for the writing which *is* written in the **k** 4428
8: 8 sealed with the **k** ring, may no man reverse. 4428
8: 9 were the **k** scribes called at that time in 4428
8:10 sealed *it* with the **k** ring, and sent letters by 4428
8:14 and pressed on by the **k** commandment, 4428
8:17 whithersoever the **k** commandment and 4428
9: 1 when the **k** commandment and his decree 4428
9: 4 For Mordecai *was* great in the **k** house, and 4428
9:12 what have they done in the rest of the **k** 4428
9:16 the other Jews that *were* in the **k** provinces 4428
Ps 45: 5 Thine arrows *are* sharp in the heart of the **k** 4428
45:13 The **k** daughter *is* all glorious within: 4428
45:15 they shall enter into the **k** palace. 4428
61: 6 Thou wilt prolong the **k** life: *and* his years 4428
72: 1 and thy righteousness unto the **k** son. 4428
99: 4 The **k** strength also loveth judgment; 4428
Pr 14:28 In the multitude of people *is* the **k** honour: 4428
14:35 The **k** favour *is* toward a wise servant: but 4428
16:15 In the light of the **k** countenance *is* life; and 4428
19:12 The **k** wrath *is* as the roaring of a lion; but 4428
21: 1 The **k** heart *is* in the hand of the LORD, 4428
Ecc 8: 2 I *counsel thee* to keep the **k** commandment, 4428
Isa 36:21 for the **k** commandment was, saying, 4428
Jer 22: 6 For thus saith the LORD unto the **k** house 4428
26:10 they came up from the **k** house *unto* 4428
36:12 he went down *into* the **k** house, into 4428
38: 7 one of the eunuchs which *was* in the **k** 4428
38: 8 Ebed-melech went forth out of the **k** house, 4428
39: 4 *by* the way of the **k** garden, by the gate 4428
39: 8 the Chaldeans burnt the **k** house, and 4428
41:10 *even* the **k** daughters, and all the people 4428
43: 6 the **k** daughters, and every person that 4428
52: 7 the two walls, which *was* by the **k** garden; 4428
52:13 the house of the LORD, and the **k** house; 4428
52:25 seven men of them that were near the **k** 4428
Eze 17:13 hath taken of the **k** seed, and made a 4410
Da 1: 3 and of the **k** seed, and of the princes; 4410
1: 4 such as *had* ability in them to stand in the **k** 4428
1: 5 them a daily provision of the **k** meat, 4428
1: 8 himself with the portion of the **k** meat, 4428
1:13 that eat *of* the portion of the **k** meat: 4428
1:15 which did eat the portion of the **k** meat. 4428
2:10 upon the earth that can shew the **k** matter: 4430
2:14 wisdom to Arioch the captain of the **k** 4430
2:15 and said to Arioch the **k** captain, 4430
2:23 hast *now* made known unto us the **k** matter. 4430
3:22 the **k** commandment *was* urgent, 4430
3:27 captains, and the **k** counsellers, 4430
3:28 have changed the **k** word, and yielded their 4430
4:31 While the word *was* in the **k** mouth, 4430
5: 5 the plaister of the wall of the **k** palace: 4430
5: 6 the **k** countenance was changed, and 4430
5: 8 came in all the **k** wise *men*: but they could 4430
6:12 spake before the king concerning the **k** 4430
8:27 afterward I rose up, and did the **k** business; 4428
11: 6 for the **k** daughter of the south shall come 4428
Am 7: 1 *it was* the latter growth after the **k** 4428
7:13 for it *is* the **k** chapel, and it *is* the king's 4428
7:13 it *is* the king's chapel, and it *is* the **k** court. 4467
Zep 1: 8 the **k** children, and all such as are clothed 4428
Zec 14:10 *from* the tower of Hananeel unto the **k** 4428
Ac 12:20 having made Blastus the **k** chamberlain their *935*
12:20 their country was nourished by the **k** *937*
Heb 11:23 they were not afraid of the **k** commandment. *935*

KINGDOM (342) [KING]

Ge 10:10 the beginning of his **k** was Babel, and 4467
20: 9 brought on me and on my **k** a great sin? 4467
Ex 19: 6 ye shall be unto me a **k** of priests, and 4467
Nu 24: 7 than Agag, and his **k** shall be exalted. 4438
32:33 the **k** of Sihon king of the Amorites, and 4467
32:33 the **k** of Og king of Bashan, the land, 4467
Dt 3: 4 the region of Argob, the **k** of Og in Bashan. 4467
3:10 and Edrei, cities of the **k** of Og in Bashan. 4467
3:13 and all Bashan, *being* the **k** of Og, 4467
17:18 when he sitteth upon the throne of his **k**, 4467
17:20 end that he may prolong *his* days in his **k**, 4467
Jos 13:12 All the **k** of Og in Bashan, which reigned in 4468
13:21 all the **k** of Sihon king of the Amorites, 4468
13:27 the rest of the **k** of Sihon king of Heshbon, 4468

K

Jos 13:30 all the **k** of Og king of Bashan, and all 4468
13:31 and Edrei, cities of the **k** of Og in Bashan, 4468
1Sa 10:16 of the matter of the **k**, whereof Samuel 4410
10:25 Samuel told the people the manner of the **k**, 4410
11:14 let us go *to* Gilgal, and renew the **k** there. 4410
13:13 have established thy **k** upon Israel for ever. 4467
13:14 now thy **k** shall not continue: the LORD 4467
14:47 So Saul took the **k** over Israel, and 4410
15:28 The LORD hath rent the **k** of Israel from 4468
18: 8 and *what* can he have more but the **k**? 4410
20:31 thou shalt not be stablished, nor thy **k**. 4438
24:20 *that* the **k** of Israel shall be established in 4467
28:17 for the LORD hath rent the **k** out of thine 4467
2Sa 3:10 To translate the **k** from the house of Saul, 4467
3:28 my **k** *are* guiltless before the LORD for 4467
5:12 that he had exalted his **k** for his people 4467
7:12 out of thy bowels, and I will establish his **k**. 4467
7:13 I will stablish the throne of his **k** for ever. 4467
7:16 thy **k** shall be stablished for ever before 4467
16: 3 of Israel restore me the **k** of my father. 4468
16: 8 the LORD hath delivered the **k** into 4410
1Ki 1:46 also Solomon sitteth on the throne of the **k**. 4410
2:12 and his **k** was established greatly. 4438
2:15 Thou knowest that the **k** was mine, and 4410
2:15 howbeit the **k** is turned about, and 4410
2:22 ask for him the **k** also; for he *is* mine elder 4410
2:46 the **k** was established in the hand of 4467
9: 5 I will establish the throne of thy **k** upon 4467
10:20 there was not the like made in any **k**. 4467
11:11 I will surely rend the **k** from thee, and 4467
11:13 Howbeit I will not rend away all the **k**; *but* 4467
11:31 I will rent the **k** out of the hand of 4467
11:34 Howbeit I will not take the whole **k** out of 4467
11:35 I will take the **k** out of his son's hand, and 4410
12:21 to bring the **k** again to Rehoboam the son 4410
12:26 Now shall the **k** return to the house of 4467
14: 8 rent the **k** away from the house of David, 4467
18:10 thy God liveth, there is no nation or **k**, 4467
18:10 *He is* not *there;* he took an oath of the **k** and 4467
21: 7 Dost thou now govern the **k** of Israel? 4410
2Ki 14: 5 as soon as the **k** was confirmed in his hand, 4467
15:19 be with him to confirm the **k** in his hand. 4467
1Ch 10:14 turned the **k** unto David the son of Jesse. 4410
11:10 strengthened themselves with him in his **k**, 4438
12:23 to Hebron, to turn the **k** of Saul to him, 4438
14: 2 for his **k** *was* lift up on high, because of his 4438
16:20 and from *one* **k** to another people; 4467
17:11 be of thy sons; and I will stablish his **k**. 4438
17:14 him in mine house and in my **k** for ever: 4438
22:10 I will establish the throne of his **k** over 4438
28: 5 throne of the **k** of the LORD over Israel. 4438
28: 7 Moreover I will establish his **k** for ever, 4438
29:11 and in the earth *is thine;* thine *is* the **k**, 4467
2Ch 1: 1 the son of David was strengthened in his **k**, 4438
2: 1 name of the LORD, and a house for his **k**. 4438
2:12 for the LORD, and a house for his **k**. 4438
7:18 will I stablish the throne of thy **k**, 4438
9:19 There was not the like made in any **k**. 4467
11: 1 that *he* might bring the **k** again to 4467
11:17 So they strengthened the **k** of Judah, and 4438
12: 1 when Rehoboam had established the **k**, and 4438
13: 5 gave the **k** over Israel to David for ever, 4467
13: 8 now ye think to withstand the **k** of 4467
14: 5 the images: and the **k** was quiet before him. 4467
17: 5 Therefore the LORD stablished the **k** in 4467
21: 3 the **k** gave he to Jehoram; because he *was* 4467
21: 4 Now when Jehoram was risen up to the **k** 4467
22: 9 of Ahaziah had no power to keep still the **k**. 4467
23:20 and set the king upon the throne of the **k**. 4467
25: 3 to pass, when the **k** was established to him, 4467
29:21 for a sin offering for the **k**, and for 4467
32:15 **k** was able to deliver his people out of mine 4467
33:13 brought him again *to* Jerusalem into his **k**. 4438
36:20 his sons until the reign of the **k** of Persia: 4438
36:22 made a proclamation throughout all his **k**, 4438
Ezr 1: 1 made a proclamation throughout all his **k**, 4438
Ne 9:35 For they have not served thee in their **k**, 4438
Est 1: 2 king Ahasuerus sat on the throne of his **k**, 4438
1: 4 he shewed the riches of his glorious **k** 4438
1:14 *and* which sat the first in the **k**;) 4438
2: 3 officers in all the provinces of his **k**, 4438
3: 6 *were* throughout the whole **k** of Ahasuerus, 4438
3: 8 the people in all the provinces of thy **k**; 4438
4:14 art come to the **k** for *such* a time as this? 4438
5: 3 shall be even given thee to the half of the **k**. 4438
5: 6 even to the half of the **k** it shall be 4438
7: 2 be performed, *even* to the half of the **k**. 4438
9:30 and seven provinces of the **k** of Ahasuerus, 4438
Ps 22:28 For the **k** *is* the LORD'S: and *he is* 4410
45: 6 ever: the sceptre of thy **k** *is* a right sceptre. 4438
103:19 in the heavens; and his **k** ruleth over all. 4438
105:13 to another, from *one* **k** to another people; 4467
145:11 They shall speak of the glory of thy **k**, and 4438
145:12 and the glorious majesty of his **k**. 4438
145:13 Thy **k** *is* an everlasting kingdom, and 4438
145:13 Thy kingdom *is* an everlasting **k**, and 4438
Ecc 4:14 whereas also *he that is* born in his **k** 4438
Isa 9: 7 upon his **k**, to order it, and to stablish it 4467
17: 3 the **k** from Damascus, and the remnant of 4467
19: 2 city against city, *and* **k** against kingdom. 4467
19: 2 city against city, *and* kingdom against **k**. 4467
34:12 They shall call the nobles thereof *to the* **k**, 4410
60:12 and **k** that will not serve thee shall perish; 4467
Jer 18: 7 concerning a nation and concerning a **k**, 4467
18: 9 and concerning a **k**, to build and to plant *it;* 4467
27: 8 **k** which will not serve the same 4467
La 2: 2 he hath polluted the **k** and the princes 4467
Eze 16:13 and thou didst prosper into a **k**. 4410
17:14 That the **k** might be base, that *it* might not 4467
29:14 and they shall be there a base **k**. 4467
Da 2:37 for the God of heaven hath given thee a **k**, 4437
2:39 after thee shall arise another **k** inferior to 4437
2:39 another third **k** of brass, which shall bear 4437
2:40 the fourth **k** shall be strong as iron: 4437
2:41 and part of iron, the **k** shall be divided; 4437
Da 2:42 *so* the **k** shall be partly strong, and 4437
2:44 kings shall the God of heaven set up a **k**, 4437
2:44 the **k** shall not be left to other people, *but* 4437
4: 3 his **k** *is* an everlasting kingdom, and 4437
4: 3 his kingdom *is* an everlasting **k**, and 4437
4:17 that the most High ruleth in the **k** of men, 4437
4:18 forasmuch as all the wise *men* of my **k** are 4437
4:25 that the most High ruleth in the **k** of men, 4437
4:26 thy **k** *shall be* sure unto thee, after that thou 4437
4:29 walked in the palace of the **k** of Babylon. 4437
4:30 that I have built for the house of the **k** by 4437
4:31 it is spoken; The **k** is departed from thee. 4437
4:32 that the most High ruleth in the **k** of men, 4437
4:34 and his **k** *is* from generation to generation: 4437
4:36 for the glory of my **k**, mine honour and 4437
4:36 I was established in my **k**, and 4437
5: 7 and shall be the third ruler in the **k**. 4437
5:11 There is a man in thy **k**, in whom *is* 4437
5:16 and shalt be the third ruler in the **k**. 4437
5:18 God gave Nebuchadnezzar thy father a **k**, 4437
5:21 the most high God ruled in the **k** of men, 4437
5:26 God hath numbered thy **k**, and finished it. 4437
5:28 Thy **k** is divided, and given to the Medes 4437
5:29 that *he* should be the third ruler in the **k**. 4437
5:31 Darius the Median took the **k**, *being* about 4437
6: 1 It pleased Darius to set over the **k** an 4437
6: 1 which should be over the whole **k**; 4437
6: 4 occasion against Daniel concerning the **k**; 4437
6: 7 All the presidents of the **k**, the governors, 4437
6:26 That in every dominion of my **k** *men* 4437
6:26 his **k** *that* which shall not be destroyed, and 4437
7:14 glory, and a **k**, that all people, nations, 4437
7:14 and his **k** *that* which shall not be destroyed. 4437
7:18 the saints of the most High shall take the **k**, 4437
7:18 possess the **k** for ever, even for ever and 4437
7:22 time came that the saints possessed the **k**. 4437
7:23 The fourth beast shall be the fourth **k** upon 4437
7:24 the ten horns out of this **k** *are* ten kings *that* 4437
7:27 the **k** and dominion, and the greatness of 4437
7:27 the greatness of the **k** under the whole 4437
7:27 whose **k** *is* an everlasting kingdom, and 4437
7:27 whose kingdom *is* an everlasting **k**, and 4437
8:23 in the latter time of their **k**, when 4438
10:13 the prince of the **k** of Persia withstood me 4438
11: 4 his **k** shall be broken, and shall be divided 4438
11: 4 for his **k** shall be pluckt up, even for others 4438
11: 9 the king of the south shall come into *his* **k**, 4438
11:17 to enter with the strength of his whole **k**, 4438
11:20 estate a raiser of taxes *in* the glory of the **k**: 4438
11:21 they shall not give the honour of the **k**: 4438
11:21 in peaceably, and obtain the **k** by flatteries. 4438
Hos 1: 4 will cause to cease the **k** of the house of 4468
Am 9: 8 of the Lord GOD *are* upon the sinful **k**, 4467
Ob 1:21 of Esau; and the **k** shall be the LORD'S. 4410
Mic 4: 8 the **k** shall come to the daughter of 4467
Mt 3: 2 Repent ye: for the **k** of heaven is at hand. *932*
4:17 Repent: for the **k** of heaven is at hand. *932*
4:23 and preaching the gospel of the **k**, *932*
5: 3 poor in spirit: for theirs is the **k** of heaven. *932*
5:10 for theirs is the **k** of heaven. *932*
5:19 he shall be called the least in the **k** of *932*
5:19 same shall be called great in the **k** of heaven. *932*
5:20 ye shall in no case enter into the **k** of heaven. *932*
6:10 Thy **k** come. Thy will be done in earth, as *it* *932*
6:13 For thine is the **k**, and the power, and *932*
6:33 But seek ye first the **k** of God, and *932*
7:21 Lord, Lord, shall enter into the **k** of heaven; *932*
8:11 and Isaac, and Jacob, in the **k** of heaven. *932*
8:12 But the children of the **k** shall be cast out *932*
9:35 and preaching the gospel of the **k**, and *932*
10: 7 preach, saying, The **k** of heaven is at hand. *932*
11:11 notwithstanding he that is least in the **k** of *932*
11:12 until now the **k** of heaven suffereth violence, *932*
12:25 Every **k** divided against itself is brought to *932*
12:26 against himself; how shall then his **k** stand? *932*
12:28 of God, then the **k** of God is come unto you. *932*
13:11 to know the mysteries of the **k** of heaven, *932*
13:19 When any one heareth the word of the **k**, and *932*
13:24 The **k** of heaven is likened unto a man which *932*
13:31 The **k** of heaven is like unto a grain of *932*
13:33 The **k** of heaven is like unto leaven, which a *932*
13:38 the good seed are the children of the **k**; but *932*
13:41 they shall gather out of his **k** all things that *932*
13:43 shine forth as the sun in the **k** of their Father. *932*
13:44 the **k** of heaven is like unto treasure hid in a *932*
13:45 the **k** of heaven is like unto a merchant man, *932*
13:47 Again, the **k** of heaven is like unto a net, *932*
13:52 **k** of heaven is like unto a man *that is* a *932*
16:19 And I will give unto thee the keys of the **k** of *932*
16:28 till they see the Son of man coming in his **k**. *932*
18: 1 Who is the greatest in the **k** of heaven? *932*
18: 3 ye shall not enter into the **k** of heaven. *932*
18: 4 the same is greatest in the **k** of heaven. *932*
18:23 Therefore is the **k** of heaven likened unto a *932*
19:12 eunuchs for the **k** of heaven's sake. *932*
19:14 unto me: for of such is the **k** of heaven. *932*
19:23 That a rich *man* shall hardly enter into the **k** *932*
19:24 than for a rich *man* to enter into the **k** of *932*
20: 1 For the **k** of heaven is like unto a man *that is* *932*
20:21 right hand, and the other on the left, in thy **k**. *932*
21:31 the harlots go into the **k** of God before you. *932*
21:43 The **k** of God shall be taken from you, and *932*
22: 2 The **k** of heaven is like unto a certain king, *932*
23:13 for ye shut up the **k** of heaven against men: *932*
24: 7 rise against nation, and **k** against kingdom: *932*
24: 7 rise against nation, and kingdom against **k**: *932*
24:14 And this gospel of the **k** shall be preached in *932*
25: 1 Then shall the **k** of heaven be likened unto *932*
25:14 For *the k of heaven is* as a man travelling NIG
25:34 inherit the **k** prepared for you from *932*
26:29 I drink it new with you in my Father's **k**. *932*
Mk 1:14 preaching the gospel of the **k** of God, *932*
1:15 time is fulfilled, and the **k** of God is at hand: *932*
3:24 And if a **k** be divided against itself, *932*
3:24 be divided against itself, that **k** cannot stand. *932*
Mk 4:11 given to know the mystery of the **k** of God: *932*
4:26 And he said, So is the **k** of God, as if a man *932*
4:30 Whereunto shall we liken the **k** of God? *932*
6:23 I will give *it* thee, unto the half of my **k**. *932*
9: 1 till they have seen the **k** of God come with *932*
9:47 it is better for thee to enter into the **k** of God *932*
10:14 forbid them not: for of such is the **k** of God. *932*
10:15 Whosoever shall not receive the **k** of God as *932*
10:23 they that have riches enter into the **k** of God! *932*
10:24 that trust in riches to enter into the **k** of God! *932*
10:25 than for a rich *man* to enter into the **k** of *932*
11:10 Blessed *be* the **k** of our father David, *932*
12:34 Thou art not far from the **k** of God. *932*
13: 8 rise against nation, and **k** against kingdom: *932*
13: 8 rise against nation, and kingdom against **k**: *932*
14:25 until that day that I drink it new in the **k** of *932*
15:43 which also waited for the **k** of God, came, *932*
Lk 1:33 for ever; and of his **k** there shall be no end. *932*
4:43 I must preach the **k** of God to other cities *932*
6:20 *be ye* poor: for yours is the **k** of God. *932*
7:28 he that is least in the **k** of God is greater than *932*
8: 1 shewing the glad tidings of the **k** of God: *932*
8:10 given to know the mysteries of the **k** of God: *932*
9: 2 And he sent them to preach the **k** of God, *932*
9:11 and spake unto them of the **k** of God, and *932*
9:27 not taste of death, till they see the **k** of God. *932*
9:60 but go thou and preach the **k** of God. *932*
9:62 and looking back, is fit for the **k** of God. *932*
10: 9 The **k** of God is come nigh unto you. *932*
10:11 that the **k** of God is come nigh unto you. *932*
11: 2 Thy **k** come. Thy will be done, as in heaven, *932*
11:17 Every **k** divided against itself is brought to *932*
11:18 against himself, how shall his **k** stand? *932*
11:20 no doubt the **k** of God is come upon you. *932*
12:31 But rather seek ye the **k** of God; *932*
12:32 Father's good pleasure to give you the **k**. *932*
13:18 said he, Unto what is the **k** of God like? *932*
13:20 Whereunto shall I liken the **k** of God? *932*
13:28 in the **k** of God, and you yourselves thrust *932*
13:29 the south, and shall sit down in the **k** of God. *932*
14:15 Blessed *is he* that shall eat bread in the **k** of *932*
16:16 since that time the **k** of God is preached, and *932*
17:20 when the **k** of God should come, *932*
17:20 The **k** of God cometh not with observation: *932*
17:21 for behold, the **k** of God is within you. *932*
18:16 forbid them not: for of such is the **k** of God. *932*
18:17 Whosoever shall not receive the **k** of God as *932*
18:24 they that have riches enter into the **k** of God! *932*
18:25 than for a rich *man* to enter into the **k** of *932*
18:29 or wife, or children, for the **k** of God's sake, *932*
19:11 they thought that the **k** of God should *932*
19:12 into a far country to receive for himself a **k**, *932*
19:15 having received the **k**, then he commanded *932*
21:10 rise against nation, and **k** against kingdom: *932*
21:10 rise against nation, and kingdom against **k**: *932*
21:31 know ye that the **k** of God is nigh at hand. *932*
22:16 until it be fulfilled in the **k** of God. *932*
22:18 of the vine, until the **k** of God shall come. *932*
22:29 And I appoint unto you a **k**, as my Father *932*
22:30 ye may eat and drink at my table in my **k**, *932*
23:42 remember me when thou comest into thy **k**. *932*
23:51 who also himself waited for the **k** of God. *932*
Jn 3: 3 be born again, he cannot see the **k** of God. *932*
3: 5 the Spirit, he cannot enter into the **k** of God. *932*
18:36 Jesus answered, My **k** is not of this world: *932*
18:36 not of this world: if my **k** were of this world, *932*
18:36 to the Jews: but now is my **k** not from hence. *932*
Ac 1: 3 speaking of the *things* pertaining to the **k** of *932*
1: 6 wilt thou at this time restore again the **k** to *932*
8:12 the *things* concerning the **k** of God, *932*
14:22 much tribulation enter into the **k** of God. *932*
19: 8 persuading the *things* concerning the **k** of *932*
20:25 among whom I have gone preaching the **k** of *932*
28:23 he expounded and testified the **k** of God, *932*
28:31 Preaching the **k** of God, and teaching those *932*
Ro 14:17 For the **k** of God is not meat and drink; but *932*
1Co 4:20 For the **k** of God *is* not in word, but *932*
6: 9 unrighteous shall not inherit the **k** of God? *932*
6:10 nor extortioners, shall inherit the **k** of God. *932*
15:24 when he shall have delivered up the **k** to *932*
15:50 and blood cannot inherit the **k** of God; *932*
Gal 5:21 do such *things* shall not inherit the **k** of God. *932*
Eph 5: 5 hath *any* inheritance in the **k** of Christ and *932*
Col 1:13 hath translated *us* into the **k** of his dear Son: *932*
4:11 These only *are my* fellowworkers unto the **k** *932*
1Th 2:12 who hath called you unto his **k** and glory. *932*
2Th 1: 5 that ye may be counted worthy of the **k** of *932*
2Ti 4: 1 and the dead at his appearing and his **k**; *932*
4:18 and will preserve *me* unto his heavenly **k**: *932*
Heb 1: 8 of righteousness *is* the sceptre of thy **k**. *932*
12:28 Wherefore we receiving a **k** which cannot be *932*
Jas 2: 5 heirs of the **k** which he hath promised to *932*
2Pe 1:11 abundantly into the everlasting **k** of our Lord *932*
Rev 1: 9 and in the **k** and patience of Jesus Christ, *932*
12:10 and the **k** of our God, and the power of his *932*
16:10 and his **k** was full of darkness; and *932*
17:12 ten kings, which have received no **k** as yet; *932*
17:17 and to agree, and give their **k** unto the beast, *932*

KINGDOMS (57) [KING]
Dt 3:21 shall the LORD do unto all the **k** whither 4467
28:25 shalt be removed into all the **k** of the earth. 4467
Jos 11:10 beforetime *was* the head of all those **k**. 4467
1Sa 10:18 out of the hand of all **k**, *and* of them that 4467
1Ki 4:21 Solomon reigned over all **k** from the river 4467
2Ki 19:15 *even* thou alone, of all the **k** of the earth; 4467
19:19 that all the **k** of the earth may know that 4467
1Ch 29:30 and over all the **k** of the countries. 4467
2Ch 12: 8 and the service of the **k** of the countries. 4467
17:10 the fear of the LORD fell upon all the **k** of 4467
20: 6 rulest *not* thou over all the **k** of 4467
20:29 the fear of God was on all the **k** of *those* 4467
36:23 All the **k** of the earth hath the LORD God 4467
Ezr 1: 2 heaven hath given me all the **k** of the earth; 4467
Ne 9:22 Moreover thou gavest them **k** and nations, 4467

Ps 46: 6 The heathen raged, the **k** were moved: 4467
68:32 Sing unto God, ye **k** of the earth; O sing 4467
79: 6 upon the **k** that have not called upon thy 4467
102:22 and the **k**, to serve the LORD. 4467
135:11 king of Bashan, and all the **k** of Canaan: 4467
Isa 10:10 As my hand hath found the **k** of the idols, 4467
13: 4 a tumultuous noise of the **k** of nations 4467
13:19 Babylon, the glory of **k**, the beauty of 4467
14:16 made the earth to tremble, that did shake **k**; 4467
23:11 out his hand over the sea, he shook the **k**: 4467
23:17 shall commit fornication with all the **k** of 4467
37:16 *even* thou alone, of all the **k** of the earth: 4467
37:20 that all the **k** of the earth may know that 4467
47: 5 thou shalt no more be called, The lady of **k**. 4467
Jer 1:10 set thee over the nations and over the **k**, 4467
1:15 I will call all the families of the **k** of 4467
10: 7 in all their **k**, *there is* none like unto thee. 4438
15: 4 I will cause them to be removed into all **k** 4467
24: 9 into all the **k** of the earth for *their* hurt, 4467
25:26 one with another, and all the **k** of the world, 4467
28: 8 against great **k**, of war, and of evil, and 4467
29:18 will deliver them to be removed to all the **k** 4467
34: 1 all the **k** of the earth of his dominion, 4467
34:17 to be removed into all the **k** of the earth. 4467
49:28 and concerning the **k** of Hazor, 4467
51:20 the nations, and with thee will I destroy **k**: 4467
51:27 call together against her the **k** of Ararat, 4467
Eze 29:15 It shall be the basest of the **k**; neither shall 4467
37:22 neither shall they be divided into two **k** any 4467
Da 2:44 break in pieces and consume all these **k**, 4437
7:23 which shall be diverse from all **k**, and 4437
8:22 four **k** shall stand up out of the nation, but 4438
Am 6: 2 *be they* better than these **k**? or their border 4467
Na 3: 5 nations thy nakedness, and the **k** thy shame. 4467
Zep 3: 8 that I may assemble the **k**, to pour upon 4467
Hag 2:22 I will overthrow the throne of **k**, and I will 4467
2:22 I will destroy the strength of the **k** of 4467
Mt 4: 8 and sheweth him all the **k** of the world, and *932*
Lk 4: 5 shewed unto him all the **k** of the world in a *932*
Heb 11:33 Who through faith subdued **k**, *932*
Rev 11:15 The **k** of *this* world are become *932*
11:15 of *this* world are become *the k* of our Lord, NIG

KINGLY (1) [KING]

Da 5:20 he was deposed from his **k** throne, and 4437

KINGS (329) [KING]

Ge 14: 5 the **k** that *were* with him, and smote 4428
14: 9 Arioch king of Ellasar; four **k** with five. 4428
14:10 the **k** of Sodom and Gomorrah fled, and 4428
14:17 of the **k** that *were* with him, at the valley of 4428
17: 6 of thee, and **k** shall come out of thee. 4428
17:16 of nations; **k** of people shall be of her. 4428
35:11 of thee, and **k** shall come out of thy loins; 4428
36:31 these *are* the **k** that reigned in the land of 4428
Nu 31: 8 they slew the **k** of Midian, beside *the rest* 4428
31: 8 and Hur, and Reba, five **k** of Midian: 4428
Dt 3: 8 **k** of the Amorites the land that *was* on *this* 4428
3:21 your God hath done unto these two **k**: 4428
4:47 Og king of Bashan, two **k** of the Amorites, 4428
7:24 he shall deliver their **k** into thine hand, and 4428
31: 4 **k** of the Amorites, and unto the land of 4428
Jos 2:10 what you did unto the two **k** of 4428
5: 1 to pass, when all the **k** of the Amorites, 4428
5: 1 all the **k** of the Canaanites, which *were* by 4428
9: 1 when all the **k** which *were* on *this* side 4428
9:10 all that he did to the two **k** of the Amorites, 4428
10: 5 Therefore the five **k** of the Amorites, 4428
10: 6 for all the **k** of the Amorites that dwell in 4428
10:16 these five **k** fled, and hid themselves in a 4428
10:17 The five **k** are found hid in a cave at 4428
10:22 bring out those five **k** unto me out of 4428
10:23 brought forth those five **k** unto him out of 4428
10:24 when they brought out those **k** unto Joshua, 4428
10:24 put your feet upon the necks of these **k**. 4428
10:40 the vale, and of the springs, and all their **k**: 4428
10:42 all these **k** and their land did Joshua take *at* 4428
11: 2 to the **k** that *were* on the north of 4428
11: 5 when all these **k** were met together, 4428
11:12 all the cities of those **k**, and all the kings of 4428
11:12 all the **k** of them, did Joshua take, and 4428
11:17 and all their **k** he took, and smote them, and 4428
11:18 made war a long time with all those **k**. 4428
12: 1 Now these *are* the **k** of the land, which 4428
12: 7 these *are* the **k** of the country which Joshua 4428
12:24 king of Tirzah, one: all the **k** thirty and one. 4428
24:12 before you, *even* the two **k** of the Amorites; 4428
Jdg 1: 7 Threescore and ten **k**, having their thumbs 4428
5: 3 Hear, O ye **k**; give ear, O ye princes; I, 4428
5:19 The **k** came *and* fought, then fought 4428
5:19 fought the **k** of Canaan in Taanach by 4428
8: 5 after Zebah and Zalmunna, **k** of Midian. 4428
8:12 took the two **k** of Midian, Zebah and 4428
8:26 purple raiment that *was* on the **k** of Midian, 4428
1Sa 14:47 against the **k** of Zobah, and against 4428
27: 6 wherefore Ziklag pertaineth unto the **k** of 4428
2Sa 10:19 when all the **k** *that were* servants to 4428
11: 1 at the time when **k** go forth *to battle*, that 4428
1Ki 3:13 that there shall not be any among the **k** like 4428
4:24 over all the **k** on *this* side the river: 4428
4:34 from all **k** of the earth, which had heard of 4428
10:15 *of* all the **k** of Arabia, and *of* the governors 4428
10:23 So king Solomon exceeded all the **k** of 4428
10:29 so for all the **k** of the Hittites, and for 4428
10:29 kings of the Hittites, and for the **k** of Syria, 4428
14:19 the book of the chronicles of the **k** of Israel. 4428
14:29 book of the chronicles of the **k** of Judah? 4428
15: 7 book of the chronicles of the **k** of Judah? 4428
15:23 book of the chronicles of the **k** of Judah? 4428
15:31 book of the chronicles of the **k** of Israel? 4428
16: 5 book of the chronicles of the **k** of Israel? 4428
16:14 book of the chronicles of the **k** of Israel? 4428
16:20 book of the chronicles of the **k** of Israel? 4428
16:27 book of the chronicles of the **k** of Israel? 4428
16:33 all the **k** of Israel that were before him. 4428
1Ki 20: 1 *there were* thirty and two **k** with him, and 4428
20:12 *was* drinking, he and the **k** in the pavilions, 4428
20:16 he and the **k**, the thirty and two kings that 4428
20:16 the thirty and two **k** that helped him. 4428
20:24 do this thing, Take the **k** away, every man 4428
20:31 we have heard that the **k** of the house of 4428
20:31 kings of the house of Israel *are* merciful **k**: 4428
22:39 book of the chronicles of the **k** of Israel? 4428
22:45 book of the chronicles of the **k** of Judah? 4428
2Ki 1:18 book of the chronicles of the **k** of Israel? 4428
3:10 that the LORD hath called these three **k** 4428
3:13 for the LORD hath called these three **k** 4428
3:21 when all the Moabites heard that the **k** were 4428
3:23 the **k** are surely slain, and they have smitten 4428
7: 6 the king of Israel hath hired against us the **k** 4428
7: 6 the **k** of the Egyptians, to come upon us. 4428
8:18 he walked in the way of the **k** of Israel, 4428
8:23 book of the chronicles of the **k** of Judah? 4428
10: 4 said, Behold, two **k** stood not before him: 4428
10:34 book of the chronicles of the **k** of Israel? 4428
11:19 And he sat on the throne of the **k**. 4428
12:18 and Ahaziah, his fathers, **k** of Judah, 4428
12:19 book of the chronicles of the **k** of Judah? 4428
13: 8 book of the chronicles of the **k** of Israel? 4428
13:12 book of the chronicles of the **k** of Israel? 4428
13:13 Joash was buried in Samaria with the **k** of 4428
14:15 book of the chronicles of the **k** of Israel? 4428
14:16 was buried in Samaria with the **k** of Israel; 4428
14:18 book of the chronicles of the **k** of Judah? 4428
14:28 book of the chronicles of the **k** of Israel? 4428
14:29 with his fathers, *even* with the **k** of Israel; 4428
15: 6 book of the chronicles of the **k** of Judah? 4428
15:11 the book of the chronicles of the **k** of Israel. 4428
15:15 the book of the chronicles of the **k** of Israel. 4428
15:21 book of the chronicles of the **k** of Israel? 4428
15:26 the book of the chronicles of the **k** of Israel. 4428
15:31 the book of the chronicles of the **k** of Israel. 4428
15:36 book of the chronicles of the **k** of Judah? 4428
16: 3 he walked in the way of the **k** of Israel, yea, 4428
16:19 book of the chronicles of the **k** of Judah? 4428
17: 2 not as the **k** of Israel that were before him. 4428
17: 8 of the **k** of Israel, which they had made. 4428
18: 5 none like him among all the **k** of Judah, 4428
19:11 thou hast heard what the **k** of Assyria have 4428
19:17 the **k** of Assyria have destroyed the nations 4428
20:20 book of the chronicles of the **k** of Judah? 4428
21:17 book of the chronicles of the **k** of Judah? 4428
21:25 book of the chronicles of the **k** of Judah? 4428
23: 5 whom the **k** of Judah had ordained to burn 4428
23:11 he took away the horses that the **k** of Judah 4428
23:12 which the **k** of Judah had made, and 4428
23:19 which the **k** of Israel had made to provoke 4428
23:22 nor *in* all the days of the **k** of Israel, nor of 4428
23:22 of the kings of Israel, nor of the **k** of Judah; 4428
23:28 book of the chronicles of the **k** of Judah? 4428
24: 5 book of the chronicles of the **k** of Judah? 4428
25:28 set his throne above the throne of the **k** that 4428
1Ch 1:43 Now these *are* the **k** that reigned in the land 4428
9: 1 they *were* written in the book of the **k** of 4428
16:21 yea, he reproved **k** for their sakes, 4428
19: 9 the **k** that were come *were* by themselves in 4428
20: 1 at the time that **k** go out *to battle*, Joab led 4428
2Ch 1:12 such as none of the **k** have had that *have* 4428
1:17 brought they out *horses* for all the **k** of 4428
1:17 and *for* the **k** of Syria, by their means. 4428
9:14 all the **k** of Arabia and governors of 4428
9:22 king Solomon passed all the **k** of the earth 4428
9:23 all the **k** of the earth sought the presence of 4428
9:26 he reigned over all the **k** from the river 4428
16:11 they *are* written in the book of the **k** of 4428
20:34 who is mentioned in the book of the **k** of 4428
21: 6 he walked in the way of the **k** of Israel, 4428
21:13 hast walked in the way of the **k** of Israel, 4428
21:20 of David, but not in the sepulchres of the **k**. 4428
24:16 him in the city of David among the **k**, 4428
24:25 buried him not in the sepulchres of the **k**. 4428
24:27 *are* written in the story of the book of the **k**. 4428
25:26 *are* they not written in the book of the **k** of 4428
26:23 field of the burial which *belonged* to the **k**; 4428
27: 7 lo they *are* written in the book of the **k** of 4428
28: 2 For he walked in the ways of the **k** of 4428
28:16 At that time did king Ahaz send unto the **k** 4428
28:23 Because the gods of the **k** of Syria help 4428
28:26 they *are* written in the book of the **k** of 4428
28:27 not into the sepulchres of the **k** of Israel: 4428
30: 6 that are escaped out of the hand of the **k** of 4428
32: 4 Why should the **k** of Assyria come, and 4428
32:32 *and* in the book of the **k** of Judah and 4428
33:18 they *are written* in the book of the **k** of 4428
34:11 to floor the houses which the **k** of Judah 4428
35:18 neither did all the **k** of Israel keep such a 4428
35:27 they *are* written in the book of the **k** of 4428
36: 8 they *are* written in the book of the **k** of 4428
Ezr 4:13 thou shalt endamage the revenue of the **k**. 4430
4:15 hurtful unto **k** and provinces, and that they 4430
4:19 old time *hath* made insurrection against **k**, 4430
4:20 There have been mighty **k** also over 4430
4:22 should damage grow to the hurt of the **k**? 4430
6:12 caused his name to dwell there destroy all **k** 4430
7:12 Artaxerxes, king of **k**, unto Ezra the priest, 4430
9: 7 iniquities have we, our **k**, *and* our priests, 4428
9: 7 been delivered into the hand of the **k** of 4428
9: 9 unto us in the sight of the **k** of Persia, 4428
Ne 9:24 with their **k**, and the people of the land, 4428
9:32 on our **k**, on our princes, and on our priests, 4428
9:32 since the time of the **k** of Assyria unto this 4428
9:34 Neither have our **k**, our princes, our priests, 4428
9:37 it yieldeth much increase unto the **k** whom 4428
Est 10: 2 book of the chronicles of the **k** of Media 4428
Job 3:14 With **k** and counsellers of the earth, 4428
12:18 He looseth the bond of **k**, and girdeth their 4428
36: 7 with **k** *are they* on the throne; yea, he doth 4428
Ps 2: 2 The **k** of the earth set themselves, and 4428
2:10 Be wise now therefore, O ye **k**: 4428
48: 4 For lo, the **k** were assembled, they passed 4428
Ps 68:12 **K** of armies did flee apace: and she that 4428
68:14 When the Almighty scattered **k** in it, it was 4428
68:29 Because of thy temple at Jerusalem shall **k** 4428
72:10 The **k** of Tarshish and *of* the isles shall 4428
72:10 the **k** of Sheba and Seba shall offer gifts. 4428
72:11 Yea, all **k** shall fall down before him: 4428
76:12 *he is* terrible to the **k** of the earth. 4428
89:27 *my* firstborn, higher than the **k** of the earth. 4428
102:15 and all the **k** of the earth thy glory. 4428
105:14 yea, he reproved **k** for their sakes; 4428
105:30 in abundance, in the chambers of their **k**. 4428
110: 5 strike through **k** in the day of his wrath. 4428
119:46 will speak of thy testimonies also before **k**, 4428
135:10 smote great nations, and slew mighty **k**; 4428
136:17 To him which smote great **k**: for his mercy 4428
136:18 slew famous **k**: for his mercy *endureth* for 4428
138: 4 All the **k** of the earth shall praise thee, 4428
144:10 *It is he* that giveth salvation unto **k**: 4428
148:11 **K** of the earth, and all people; princes, and 4428
149: 8 To bind their **k** with chains, and 4428
Pr 8:15 By me **k** reign, and princes decree justice. 4428
16:12 *It is* an abomination to **k** to commit 4428
16:13 Righteous lips *are* the delight of **k**; and 4428
22:29 he shall stand before **k**; he shall not stand 4428
25: 2 the honour of **k** *is* to search out a matter. 4428
25: 3 and the heart of **k** *is* unsearchable. 4428
31: 3 nor thy ways to *that which* destroyeth **k**. 4428
31: 4 *It is* not for **k**, O Lemuel, *it is* not for kings 4428
31: 4 O Lemuel, *it is* not for **k** to drink wine; 4428
Ecc 2: 8 the peculiar treasure of **k** and of 4428
Isa 1: 1 Jotham, Ahaz, *and* Hezekiah, **k** of Judah. 4428
7:16 abhorrest shall be forsaken of both her **k**. 4428
10: 8 he saith, *Are* not my princes altogether **k**? 4428
14: 9 it hath raised up from their thrones all the **k** 4428
14:18 All the **k** of the nations, *even* all of them, 4428
19:11 the son of the wise, the son of ancient **k**? 4428
24:21 and the **k** of the earth upon the earth. 4428
37:11 thou hast heard what the **k** of Assyria have 4428
37:18 the **k** of Assyria have laid waste all 4428
41: 2 before him, and made *him* rule over **k**? 4428
45: 1 I will loose the loins of **k**, to open before 4428
49: 7 to a servant of rulers, K shall see and arise, 4428
49:23 **k** shall be thy nursing fathers, and 4428
52:15 the **k** shall shut their mouths at him: 4428
60: 3 and **k** to the brightness of thy rising. 4428
60:10 and their **k** shall minister unto thee: 4428
60:11 and *that* their **k** *may be* brought. 4428
60:16 the Gentiles, and shalt suck the breast of **k**: 4428
62: 2 see thy righteousness, and all **k** thy glory: 4428
Jer 1:18 against the **k** of Judah, against the princes 4428
2:26 they, their **k**, their princes, and their priests, 4428
8: 1 they shall bring out the bones of the **k** of 4428
13:13 even the **k** that sit upon David's throne, and 4428
17:19 whereby the **k** of Judah come in, and by 4428
17:20 ye **k** of Judah, and all Judah, and all 4428
17:25 shall there enter into the gates of this city **k** 4428
19: 3 O **k** of Judah, and inhabitants of Jerusalem; 4428
19: 4 nor the **k** of Judah, and have filled this 4428
19:13 and the houses of the **k** of Judah, 4428
20: 5 all the treasures of the **k** of Judah will I 4428
22: 4 house **k** sitting upon the throne of David, 4428
25:14 great **k** shall serve themselves of them also: 4428
25:18 and the **k** thereof, *and* the princes thereof, 4428
25:20 all the **k** of the land of Uz, and all the kings 4428
25:20 all the **k** of the land of the Philistines, and 4428
25:22 all the **k** of Tyrus, and all the kings of 4428
25:22 all the **k** of Zidon, and the kings of the isles 4428
25:22 the **k** of the isles which *are* beyond the sea, 4428
25:24 all the **k** of Arabia, and all the kings of 4428
25:24 all the **k** of the mingled people that dwell in 4428
25:25 all the **k** of Zimri, and all the kings of 4428
25:25 all the **k** of Elam, and all the kings of 4428
25:25 kings of Elam, and all the **k** of the Medes, 4428
25:26 all the **k** of the north, far and near, one with 4428
27: 7 and great **k** shall serve themselves of him. 4428
32:32 they, their **k**, their princes, their priests, and 4428
33: 4 concerning the houses of the **k** of Judah, 4428
34: 5 the former **k** which were before thee, so 4428
44: 9 the wickedness of the **k** of Judah, and 4428
44:17 we, and our fathers, our **k**, and our princes, 4428
44:21 your **k**, and your princes, and the people of 4428
46:25 and Egypt, with their gods, and their **k**; 4428
50:41 many **k** shall be raised up from the coasts 4428
51:11 raised up the spirit of the **k** of the Medes: 4428
51:28 Prepare against her the nations with the **k** 4428
52:32 set his throne above the throne of the **k** that 4428
La 4:12 The **k** of the earth, and all the inhabitants of 4428
Eze 26: 7 a king of **k**, from the north, with horses, 4428
27:33 thou didst enrich the **k** of the earth with 4428
27:35 their **k** shall be sore afraid, they shall be 4428
28:17 I will lay thee before **k**, that *they* may 4428
32:10 and their **k** shall be horribly afraid for thee, 4428
32:29 There *is* Edom, her **k**, and all her princes, 4428
43: 7 *neither* they, nor their **k**, by their 4428
43: 7 nor by the carcases of their **k** *in* their high 4428
43: 9 the carcases of their **k**, far from me, and 4428
Da 2:21 he removeth **k**, and setteth up kings: 4430
2:21 he removeth kings, and setteth up **k**: 4430
2:37 Thou, O king, *art* a king of **k**: for the God 4430
2:44 in the days of these **k** shall the God of 4430
2:47 a Lord of **k**, and a revealer of secrets, 4430
7:17 great beasts, which *are* four, *are* four **k**, 4430
7:24 the ten horns out of this kingdom *are* ten **k** 4430
7:24 from the first, and he shall subdue three **k**. 4430
8:20 sawest having two horns *are* the **k** of Media 4428
9: 6 which spake in thy name to our **k**, 4428
9: 8 to our **k**, to our princes, and to our fathers, 4428
10:13 and I remained there with the **k** of Persia. 4428
11: 2 there *shall* stand up yet three **k** in Persia; 4428
Hos 1: 1 **k** of Judah, and in the days of Jeroboam 4428
7: 7 devoured their judges; all their **k** are fallen: 4428
8: 4 They have **set up k**, but not by me: 4427
Mic 1: 1 Ahaz, *and* Hezekiah, **k** of Judah, which he 4428
1:14 the houses of Achzib *shall be* a lie to the **k** 4428
Hab 1:10 they shall scoff at the **k**, and the princes 4428

K

Mt 10:18 brought before governors and **k** for my sake, *935*
17:25 of whom do the **k** of the earth take custom or *935*
Mk 13: 9 be brought before rulers and **k** for my sake, *935*
Lk 10:24 **k** have desired to see *those things* which ye *935*
21:12 being brought before **k** and rulers for my *935*
22:25 The **k** of the Gentiles exercise lordship over *935*
Ac 4:26 The **k** of the earth stood up, and the rulers *935*
9:15 and **k**, and the children of Israel: *935*
1Co 4: 8 ye are rich, ye have **reigned as k** without us: *936*
1Ti 2: 2 For **k**, and *for* all that are in authority; *935*
6:15 the King of **k**, and Lord of lords; *936*
Heb 7: 1 returning from the slaughter of the **k**, *935*
Rev 1: 5 the dead, and the prince of the **k** of the earth. *935*
1: 6 And hath made us **k** and priests unto God *935*
5:10 And hast made us unto our God **k** and *935*
6:15 And the **k** of the earth, and the great men, *935*
10:11 and nations, and tongues, and **k**. *935*
16:12 that the way of the **k** of the east might be *935*
16:14 which go forth unto the **k** of the earth and *935*
17: 2 With whom the **k** of the earth have *935*
17:10 And there are seven **k**: five are fallen, and *935*
17:12 the ten horns which thou sawest are ten **k**, *935*
17:12 receive power as **k** one hour with the beast. *935*
17:14 for he is Lord of lords, and King of **k**: and *935*
17:18 which reigneth over the **k** of the earth. *935*
18: 3 the **k** of the earth have committed *935*
18: 9 And the **k** of the earth, who have committed *935*
19:16 KING OF **K**, AND LORD OF LORDS. *935*
19:18 That ye may eat the flesh of **k**, and the flesh *935*
19:19 and the **k** of the earth, and their armies, *935*
21:24 the **k** of the earth do bring their glory and *935*

KINGS' (5) [KING]
Ps 45: 9 **K** daughters *were* among thy honourable 4428
Pr 30:28 hold with her hands, and *is* in **k** palaces. 4428
Da 11:27 both these **k** hearts *shall be* to do mischief, 4428
Mt 11: 8 they that wear soft *clothing* are in **k** houses. *935*
Lk 7:25 and live delicately, are in **k courts**. *933*

KINNERETH See CHINNERETH; CINNERETH

KINNEROTH See CINNEROTH

KINSFOLK (2) [FOLK, KIN]
Job 19:14 My **k** have failed, and my familiar friends 7138
Lk 2:44 and they sought him among *their* **k** and *4773*

KINSFOLKS (3) [FOLK, KIN]
1Ki 16:11 a wall, neither *of* his **k**, nor *of* his friends. 1350
2Ki 10:11 all his great *men*, and his **k**, and his priests, 3045
Lk 21:16 and brethren, and **k**, and friends; *4773*

KINSMAN (16) [KIN, MAN]
Nu 5: 8 if the man have no **k** to recompense 1350
27:11 ye shall give his inheritance unto his **k** that 7607
Ru 2: 1 Naomi had a **k** of her husband's, a mighty 4129
3: 9 over thine handmaid; for thou *art* a **near k**. 1350
3:12 now it is true that I *am thy* **near k**: 1350
3:12 howbeit there is a **k** nearer than I. 1350
3:13 he will **perform** unto thee **the part of a k**, 1350
3:13 if he will not **do the part of a k** to thee, 1350
3:13 will I **do the part of a k** to thee, *as* 1350
4: 1 the **k** of whom Boaz spake came by; 1350
4: 3 he said unto the **k**, Naomi, that is come 1350
4: 6 the **k** said, I cannot redeem *it* for myself, 1350
4: 8 Therefore the **k** said unto Boaz, Buy *it* for 1350
4:14 hath not left thee *this* day without a **k**, 1350
Jn 18:26 being *his* **k** whose ear Peter cut off, saith, *4773*
Ro 16:11 Salute Herodion my **k**. Greet them that be *4773*

KINSMAN'S (1) [KIN, MAN]
Ru 3:13 of a kinsman, well; let him **do the k part**: 1350

KINSMEN (7) [KIN, MAN]
Ru 2:20 *is* near of kin unto us, one of our **next k**. 1350
Ps 38:11 from my sore; and my **k** stand afar off. 7138
Lk 14:12 thy friends, nor thy brethren, neither thy **k**, *4773*
Ac 10:24 and had called together his **k** and near *4773*
Ro 9: 3 my brethren, my **k** according to the flesh: *4773*
16: 7 and Junia, my **k**, and my fellowprisoners, *4773*
16:21 and Lucius, and Jason, and Sosipater, my **k**, *4773*

KINSWOMAN (3) [KIN, WOMAN]
Lev 18:12 father's sister: she *is* thy father's **near k**. 7607
18:13 for she *is* thy mother's **near k**. 7607
Pr 7: 4 *art* my sister; and call understanding *thy* **k**: 4129

KINSWOMEN (1) [KIN, WOMAN]
Lev 18:17 her nakedness; *for* they *are* her **near k**: 7608

KIOS See CHIOS

KIR (5) [KIR-HARASETH, KIR-HARESETH, KIR-HARESH, KIR-HERES]
2Ki 16: 9 carried *the people of* it captive to **K**, and 7024
Isa 15: 1 in the night **K** of Moab is laid waste, 7024
22: 6 *and* horsemen, and **K** uncovered the shield. 7024
Am 1: 5 of Syria shall go into captivity unto **K**, 7024
9: 7 from Caphtor, and the Syrians from **K**? 7024

KIR-HARASETH (1) [KIR]
2Ki 3:25 only in **K** left *they* the stones thereof; 7025

KIR-HARESETH (1) [KIR]
Isa 16: 7 for the foundations of **K** shall ye mourn; 7025

KIR-HARESH (1) [KIR]
Isa 16:11 for Moab, and mine inward parts for **K**. 7025

KIR-HERES (2) [KIR]
Jer 48:31 *mine heart* shall mourn for the men of **K**. 7025
48:36 shall sound like pipes for the men of **K**: 7025

KIRIATH See KIRJATH

KIRIATH ARBA See KIRJATH-ARBA

KIRIATH ARIM See KIRJATH-ARIM

KIRIATH BAAL See KIRJATH-BAAL

KIRIATH HUZOTH See KIRJATH-HUZOTH

KIRIATH JEARIM See KIRJATH-JEARIM

KIRIATH SANNAH See KIRJATH-SANNAH

KIRIATH SEPHER See KIRJATH-SEPHER

KIRIATHAIM (3) [SHAVEH KIRIATHAIM]
Jer 48: 1 **K** is confounded *and* taken: Misgab is 7156
48:23 upon **K**, and upon Beth-gamul, and 7156
Eze 25: 9 Beth-jeshimoth, Baal-meon, and **K**, 7156

KIRJATH (1)
Jos 18:28 Jebusi, which *is* Jerusalem, Gibeath, *and* **K**; 7157

KIRJATHAIM (3)
Nu 32:37 Reuben built Heshbon, and Elealeh, and **K**, 7156
Jos 13:19 **K**, and Sibmah, and Zareth-shahar in 7156
1Ch 6:76 with her suburbs, and **K** with her suburbs. 7156

KIRJATH-ARBA (6) [ARBA]
Ge 23: 2 Sarah died in **K**; the same *is* Hebron in 7153
Jos 14:15 the name of Hebron before *was* **K**; 7153
15:54 Humtah, and **K**, which *is* Hebron, and Zior; 7153
20: 7 **K**, which *is* Hebron, in the mountain of 7153
Jdg 1:10 (now the name of Hebron before *was* **K**:) 7153
Ne 11:25 *some* of the children of Judah dwelt at **K**, 7153

KIRJATH-ARIM (1) [KIRJATH-JEARIM]
Ezr 2:25 The children of **K**, Chephirah, and Beeroth, 7157

KIRJATH-BAAL (2) [BAAL]
Jos 15:60 **K**, which *is* Kirjath-jearim, and Rabbah; 7154
18:14 the goings out thereof were at **K**, which *is* 7154

KIRJATH-HUZOTH (1)
Nu 22:39 went with Balak, and they came *unto* **K**. 7155

KIRJATH-JEARIM (18) [JEARIMKIRJATH-ARIM]
Jos 9:17 and Chephirah, and Beeroth, and **K**. 7157
15: 9 border was drawn *to* Baalah, which *is* **K**: 7157
15:60 Kirjath-baal, which *is* **K**, and Rabbah; 7157
18:14 which *is* **K**, a city of the children of Judah: 7157
18:15 the south quarter *was* from the end of **K**, 7157
Jdg 18:12 they went up, and pitched in **K**, in Judah: 7157
18:12 unto this day: behold, *it is* behind **K**. 7157
1Sa 6:21 sent messengers to the inhabitants of **K**, 7157
7: 1 the men of **K** came, and fetched up the ark 7157
7: 2 it came to pass, while the ark abode in **K**, 7157
1Ch 2:50 of Ephratah; Shobal the father of **K**, 7157
2:52 Shobal the father of **K** had sons; Haroeh, 7157
2:53 the families of **K**; the Ithrites, and 7157
13: 5 of Hemath, to bring the ark of God from **K**. 7157
13: 6 and all Israel, to Baalah, *that is*, to **K**, 7157
2Ch 1: 4 **K** to *the place which* David had prepared 7157
Ne 7:29 The men of **K**, Chephirah, and Beeroth, 7157
Jer 26:20 Urijah the son of Shemaiah of **K**, 7157

KIRJATH-SANNAH (1) [DEBIR]
Jos 15:49 And Dannah, and **K**, which *is* Debir, 7158

KIRJATH-SEPHER (4) [DEBIR]
Jos 15:15 and the name of Debir before *was* **K**. 7158
15:16 Caleb said, He that smiteth **K**, and taketh it, 7158
Jdg 1:11 and the name of Debir before *was* **K**. 7158
1:12 Caleb said, He that smiteth **K**, and taketh it, 7158

KISH (21)
1Sa 9: 1 whose name *was* **K**, the son of Abiel, 7027
9: 3 the asses of **K** Saul's father were lost. 7027
9: 3 **K** said to Saul his son, Take now one of 7027
10:11 What *is* this *that* is come unto the son of **K**? 7027
10:21 and Saul the son of **K** was taken: 7027
14:51 **K** *was* the father of Saul; and Ner the father 7027
2Sa 21:14 in Zelah, in the sepulchre of **K** his father: 7027
1Ch 8:30 and Zur, and **K**, and Baal, and Nadab, 7027
8:33 Ner begat **K**, and Kish begat Saul, and 7027
8:33 **K** begat Saul, and Saul begat Jonathan, and 7027
9:36 Zur, and **K**, and Baal, and Ner, and Nadab, 7027
9:39 Ner begat **K**; and Kish begat Saul; and 7027
9:39 **K** begat Saul; and Saul begat Jonathan, and 7027
12: 1 himself close because of Saul the son of **K**: 7027
23:21 Mushi. The sons of Mahli; Eleazar, and **K**. 7027
23:22 and their brethren the sons of **K** took them. 7027
24:29 Concerning **K**: the son of Kish *was* 7027
24:29 the son of **K** *was* Jerahmeel. 7027
26:28 Saul the son of **K**, and Abner the son of 7027
2Ch 29:12 **K** the son of Abdi, and Azariah the son of 7027
Est 2: 5 son of Shimei, the son of **K**, a Benjamite; 7027

KISHI (1)
1Ch 6:44 Ethan the son of **K**, the son of Abdi, 7029

KISHION (1)
Jos 19:20 And Rabbith, and **K**, and Abez, 7191

KISHON (6) [KISON]
Jos 21:28 **K** with her suburbs, Dabareh with her 7191
Jdg 4: 7 I will draw unto thee to the river **K** Sisera, 7028
4:13 of the Gentiles unto the river of **K**. 7028
5:21 The river of **K** swept them away, 7028
5:21 them away, *that* ancient river, the river **K**. 7028
1Ki 18:40 Elijah brought them down to the brook **K**, 7028

KISLEV See CHISLEU

KISLON See CHISLON

KISLOTH TABOR See CHISLOTH-TABOR

KISON (1) [KISHON]
Ps 83: 9 as *to* Sisera, as *to* Jabin, at the brook of **K**: 7028

KISS (20) [KISSED, KISSES]
Ge 27:26 Come near now, and **k** me, my son. 5401
31:28 hast not suffered me to **k** my sons and my 5401
2Sa 20: 9 by the beard with the right hand to **k** him. 5401
1Ki 19:20 **k** my father and my mother, and *then* I will 5401
Ps 2:12 **K** the Son, lest he be angry, and ye perish 5401
Pr 24:26 *Every man* shall **k** *his* lips that giveth a 5401
SS 1: 2 Let him **k** me with the kisses of his mouth: 5401
8: 1 I should find thee without, I would **k** thee; 5401
Hos 13: 2 Let the men that sacrifice **k** the calves. 5401
Mt 26:48 saying, Whomsoever I shall **k**, that *same* is *5368*
Mk 14:44 saying, Whomsoever I shall **k**, *that* same is *5368*
Lk 7:45 Thou gavest me no **k**: but this *woman* since *5370*
7:45 time I came in hath not ceased to **k** my feet. *2705*
22:47 and drew near unto Jesus to **k** him. *5368*
22:48 betrayest thou the Son of man with a **k**? *5370*
Ro 16:16 Salute one another with a holy **k**. The *5370*
1Co 16:20 Greet ye one another with a holy **k**. *5370*
2Co 13:12 Greet one another with a holy **k**. *5370*
1Th 5:26 Greet all the brethren with a holy **k**. *5370*
1Pe 5:14 Greet ye one another with a **k** of charity. *5370*

KISSED (26) [KISS]
Ge 27:27 he came near, and **k** him: and he smelled 5401
29:11 Jacob **k** Rachel, and lifted up his voice, 5401
29:13 and **k** him, and brought him to his house. 5401
31:55 **k** his sons and his daughters, and 5401
33: 4 and fell on his neck, and **k** him: 5401
45:15 Moreover he **k** all his brethren, and 5401
48:10 and he **k** them, and embraced them. 5401
50: 1 and wept upon him, and **k** him. 5401
Ex 4:27 met him in the mount of God, and **k** him. 5401
18: 7 father in law, and did obeisance, and **k** him; 5401
Ru 1: 9 she **k** them; and they lift up their voice, 5401
1:14 Orpah **k** her mother in law; but Ruth clave 5401
1Sa 10: 1 **k** him, and said, *Is it* not because 5401
20:41 they **k** one another, and wept one with 5401
2Sa 14:33 before the king: and the king **k** Absalom. 5401
15: 5 forth his hand, and took him, and **k** him. 5401
19:39 the king **k** Barzillai, and blessed him; 5401
1Ki 19:18 and every mouth which hath not **k** him. 5401
Job 31:27 or my mouth hath **k** my hand: 5401
Ps 85:10 righteousness and peace have **k** *each other*. 5401
Pr 7:13 **k** him, and with an impudent face said unto 5401
Mt 26:49 to Jesus, and said, Hail, master; and **k** him. *2705*
Mk 14:45 and saith, Master, master; and **k** him. *2705*
Lk 7:38 and **k** his feet, and anointed *them* with *2705*
15:20 and ran, and fell on his neck, and **k** him. *2705*
Ac 20:37 and fell on Paul's neck, and **k** him, *2705*

KISSES (2) [KISS]
Pr 27: 6 but the **k** of an enemy *are* deceitful. 5390
SS 1: 2 Let him kiss me with the **k** of his mouth: 5390

KITE (2)
Lev 11:14 And the vulture, and the **k** after his kind; 344
Dt 14:13 and the **k**, and the vulture after his kind, 344

KITHLISH (1)
Jos 15:40 And Cabbon, and Lahmam, and **K**, 3798

KITLISH See KITHLISH

KITRON (1)
Jdg 1:30 did Zebulun drive out the inhabitants of **K**, 7003

KITTIM (2)
Ge 10: 4 Elishah, and Tarshish, **K**, and Dodanim. 3794
1Ch 1: 7 Elishah, and Tarshish, **K**, and Dodanim. 3794

KNEAD (2) [KNEADED, KNEADINGTROUGHS]
Ge 18: 6 **k** *it*, and make cakes upon the hearth. 3888
Jer 7:18 the fire, and the women **k** *their* dough, 3888

KNEADED (3) [KNEAD]
1Sa 28:24 **k** *it*, and did bake unleavened bread 3888
2Sa 13: 8 **k** *it*, and made cakes in his sight, and 3888
Hos 7: 4 *who* ceaseth from raising after *he* hath **k** 3888

KNEADINGTROUGHS (2) [KNEAD, TROUGH]
Ex 8: 3 and into thine ovens, and into thy **k**: 4863
12:34 their **k** being bound up in their clothes upon 4863

KNEE (6) [KNEES]
Ge 41:43 he had; and they cried before him, **Bow the k**: 86
Isa 45:23 not return, That unto me every **k** shall bow, 1290
Mt 27:29 and they **bowed the k** before him, and *1120*
Ro 11: 4 who have not bowed the **k** to *the image of* *1119*
14:11 every **k** shall bow to me, and every tongue *1119*
Php 2:10 That at the name of Jesus every **k** should *1119*

KNEEL (2) [KNEELED, KNEELING]
Ge 24:11 he **made** *his* camels **to k down** without 1288
Ps 95: 6 let us **k** before the LORD our Maker. 1288

KNEELED (8) [KNEEL]
2Ch 6:13 **k** *down* upon his knees before all 1288
Da 6:10 he **k** upon his knees three times a day, and 1289
Mk 10:17 and **k** to him, and asked him, Good Master, *1120*
Lk 22:41 a stone's cast, and **k down**, *1119+3588+5087*
Ac 7:60 And he **k down**, *1119+3588+5087*
9:40 and **k down**, and prayed; *1119+3588+5087*
20:36 **k down**, and prayed with them *1119+3588+5087*
21: 5 **k down** on the shore, and *1119+3588+5087*

KNEELING (3) [KNEEL]
1Ki 8:54 from **k** on his knees with his hands spread 3766
Mt 17:14 a *certain* man, **k down** to him, and saying, *1120*
Mk 1:40 and **k down** to him, and saying unto him, If *1120*

KNEES (30) [KNEE]
Ge 30: 3 she shall bear upon my **k**, that I may also 1290
48:12 brought them out from between his **k**, 1290
50:23 were brought up upon Joseph's **k**. 1290
Dt 28:35 The LORD shall smite thee in the **k**, and 1290
Jdg 7: 5 one that boweth down upon his **k** to drink. 1290
7: 6 bowed down upon their **k** to drink water. 1290
16:19 she made him sleep upon her **k**; and 1290
1Ki 8:54 from kneeling on his **k** with his hands 1290
18:42 the earth, and put his face between his **k**, 1290
19:18 all the **k** which have not bowed unto Baal, 1290
2Ki 1:13 came and fell on his **k** before Elijah, and 1290
4:20 he sat on her **k** till noon, and *then* died. 1290
2Ch 6:13 kneeled *down* upon his **k** before all 1290
Ezr 9: 5 I fell upon my **k**, and spread out my hands 1290
Job 3:12 Why did the **k** prevent me? or why 1290
4: 4 and thou hast strengthened the feeble **k**. 1290
Ps 109:24 My **k** are weak through fasting; and 1290
Isa 35: 3 the weak hands, and confirm the feeble **k**. 1290
66:12 upon *her* sides, and be dandled upon *her* **k**. 1290
Eze 7:17 be feeble, and all **k** shall be weak *as* water. 1290
21: 7 shall faint, and all **k** shall be weak *as* water: 1290
47: 4 the waters; the waters *were to* the **k**. 1290
Da 5: 6 and his **k** smote one against another. 755
6:10 he kneeled upon his **k** three times a day, 1291
10:10 which set me upon my **k** and *upon* 1290
Na 2:10 the **k** smite together, and much pain *is* in all 1290
Mk 15:19 and bowing *their* **k** worshipped him. *1119*
Lk 5: 8 Peter saw *it*, he fell down at Jesus' **k**, *1119*
Eph 3:14 For this cause I bow my **k** unto the Father *1119*
Heb 12:12 hands which hang down, and the feeble **k**; *1119*

KNEW (169) [KNOW]
Ge 3: 7 and they **k** that they *were* naked; 3045
4: 1 Adam **k** Eve his wife; and she conceived, 3045
4:17 Cain **k** his wife; and she conceived, and 3045
4:25 Adam **k** his wife again; and she bare a son, 3045
8:11 Noah **k** that the waters were abated from 3045
9:24 **k** what his younger son had done unto him. 3045
28:16 the LORD is in this place; and I **k** *it* not. 3045
31:32 For Jacob **k** not that Rachel had stolen 3045
37:33 he **k** it, and said, *It is* my son's coat; an evil 5234
38: 9 And Onan **k** that the seed should not be his; 3045
38:16 (for he **k** not that she *was* his daughter in 3045
38:26 my son. And he **k** her again no more. 3045
39: 6 he **k** not ought he had, save the bread 3045
42: 7 he **k** them, but made himself strange unto 5234
42: 8 Joseph **k** his brethren, but they knew not 5234
42: 8 knew his brethren, but they **k** not him. 5234
42:23 they **k** not that Joseph understood *them;* for 3045
Ex 1: 8 a new king over Egypt, which **k** not Joseph. 3045
Nu 22:34 for I **k** not that thou stoodest in the way 3045
24:16 and **k** the knowledge of the most High, 3045
Dt 8:16 which thy fathers **k** not, that he might 3045
9:24 the LORD from the day that I **k** you. 3045
29:26 gods whom they **k** not, and *whom* he had 3045
32:17 to gods whom they **k** not, *to* new *gods that* 3045
33: 9 his brethren, nor **k** his own children: 3045
34:10 whom the LORD **k** face to face, 3045
Jdg 2:10 after them, which **k** not the LORD, 3045
3: 2 at the least such as before **k** nothing 3045
11:39 she **k** no man. And it was a custom in 3045
13:16 For Manoah **k** not that he *was* an angel of 3045
13:21 Manoah **k** that he *was* an angel of 3045
14: 4 his mother **k** not that it *was* of the LORD, 3045
18: 3 they **k** the voice of the young man 5234
19:25 they **k** her, and abused her all the night 3045
20:34 but they **k** not that evil *was* near them. 3045
1Sa 1:19 Elkanah **k** Hannah his wife; and 3045
2:12 *were* sons of Belial; they **k** not the LORD. 3045
3:20 all Israel from Dan even to Beer-sheba **k** 3045
10:11 when all that **k** him beforetime saw that 3045
14: 3 the people **k** not that Jonathan was gone. 3045
18:28 and **k** that the LORD *was* with David, 3045
20: 9 for if I **k certainly** that evil were 3045+3045
20:33 whereby Jonathan **k** that it was determined 3045
20:39 the lad **k** not any thing: only Jonathan and 3045
20:39 only Jonathan and David **k** the matter. 3045
22:15 for thy servant **k** nothing of all this, less or 3045
22:17 because they **k** when he fled, and did not 3045
22:22 David said unto Abiathar, I **k** *it* that day, 3045
23: 9 David **k** that Saul secretly practised 3045
26:12 and no man saw *it*, nor **k** *it*, neither awaked: 3045
26:17 Saul **k** David's voice, and said, *Is* this thy 5234
2Sa 3:26 from the well of Sirah: but David **k** *it* not. 3045
11:16 a place where he **k** that valiant men *were*. 3045
11:20 **k** ye not that they would shoot from 3045
15:11 their simplicity, and they **k** not any thing. 3045
18:29 saw a great tumult, but I **k** not what *it was*. 3045
22:44 a people *which* I **k** not shall serve me. 3045
1Ki 1: 4 ministered to him: but the king **k** her not. 3045
18: 7 he **k** him, and fell on his face, and said, *Art* 5234
2Ki 4:39 into the pot of pottage: for they **k** *them* not. 3045
2Ch 33:13 Manasseh **k** that the LORD he *was* God. 3045
Ne 2:16 the rulers **k** not whither I went, or what I 3045
Est 1:13 the king said to the wise *men*, which **k** 3045
1:13 *was* the king's manner towards all that **k** 3045
Job 2:12 **k** him not, they lifted up their voice, and 5234
23: 3 O that I **k** where I might find him! *that* I 3045
29:16 and the cause *which* I **k** not I searched out. 3045
42: 3 *things* too wonderful for me, which I **k** not. 3045
Ps 35:11 they laid to my charge *things* that I **k** not. 3045
35:15 together against me, and I **k** *it* not; 3045
Pr 24:12 If thou sayest, Behold, we **k** it not; doth not 3045
Isa 42:16 I will bring the blind by a way *that* they **k** 3045
42:25 set him on fire round about, yet he **k** not; 3045
48: 4 Because I **k** that thou *art* obstinate, and 1847
48: 7 lest thou shouldest say, Behold, I **k** them. 3045
48: 8 for I **k** *that* thou wouldest deal very 3045
Isa 55: 5 nations *that* **k** not thee shall run unto thee 3045
Jer 1: 5 Before I formed thee in the belly I **k** thee; 3045
2: 8 they that handle the law **k** me not: 3045
11:19 I **k** not that they had devised devices 3045
32: 8 I **k** that this *was* the word of the LORD. 3045
41: 4 *he* had slain Gedaliah, and no man **k** *it*, 3045
44: 3 whom they **k** not, *neither* they, you, 3045
44:15 all the men which **k** that their wives had 3045
Eze 10:20 and I **k** that they *were the* cherubims. 3045
19: 7 he **k** their desolate palaces, and he laid 3045
Da 5:21 till he **k** that the most high God ruled in 3046
6:10 Now when Daniel **k** that the writing *was* 3046
11:38 a god whom his fathers **k** not shall he 3045
Hos 8: 4 they have made princes, and I **k** *it* not: 3045
11: 3 but they **k** not that I healed them. 3045
Jnh 1:10 For the men **k** that he fled from 3045
4: 2 for I **k** that thou *art* a gracious God, and 3045
Zec 7:14 among all the nations whom they **k** not: 3045
11:11 the poor of the flock that waited upon me **k** 3045
Mt 1:25 And **k** her not till she had brought forth her 1097
7:23 will I profess unto them, I never **k** you: 1097
12:15 But when Jesus **k** *it*, he withdrew himself 1097
12:25 And Jesus **k** their thoughts, and said unto 1492
17:12 and they **k** him not, but have done unto him 1921
24:39 And **k** not until the flood came, and 1097
25:24 Lord, I **k** thee that thou art a hard man, 1097
27:18 For he **k** that for envy they had delivered 1492
Mk 1:34 not the devils to speak, because they **k** him. 1492
6:33 and many **k** him, and ran afoot thither out 1921
6:38 And when they **k**, they say, Five, and 1097
6:54 out of the ship, straightway they **k** him, 1921
8:17 And when Jesus **k** *it*, he saith unto them, 1097
12:12 for they **k** that he had spoken the parable 1097
15:10 For he **k** that the chief priests had delivered 1097
15:45 And when he **k** *it* of the centurion, he gave 1097
Lk 2:43 and Joseph and his mother **k** not *of it*. 1097
4:41 not to speak: for they **k** that he was Christ. 1492
6: 8 But he **k** their thoughts, and said to the man 1492
7:37 when she **k** that *Jesus* sat at meat in 1921
9:11 the people, when they **k** *it*, followed him: 1097
12:47 which **k** his lord's will, and prepared not 1097
12:48 But he that **k** not, and did commit *things* 1097
18:34 neither **k** they the *things* which were 1097
23: 7 And as soon as he **k** that he belonged unto 1921
24:31 their eyes were opened, and they **k** him; 1921
Jn 1:10 was made by him, and the world **k** him not. 1097
1:31 And I **k** him not: but that he should be 1492
1:33 And I **k** him not: but he that sent me to 1492
2: 9 *was* made wine, and **k** not whence it was: 1492
2: 9 (but the servants which drew the water **k**;) 1492
2:24 himself unto them, because he **k** all *men*, 1097
2:25 testify of man: for he **k** what was in man. 1097
4: 1 the Lord **k** how the Pharisees had heard 1097
4:53 So the father **k** that *it was* at the same hour, 1097
5: 6 **k** that he had been now a long time *in that* 1097
6: 6 for he himself **k** what he would do. 1492
6:61 When Jesus **k** in himself that his disciples 1492
6:64 For Jesus **k** from the beginning who they 1492
11:42 And I **k** that thou hearest me always: but 1492
11:57 that, if any *man* **k** where he were, 1097
12: 9 of the Jews therefore **k** that he was there: 1097
13: 1 when Jesus **k** that his hour was come that 1492
13:11 For he **k** who should betray him; therefore 1492
13:28 Now no *man* at the table **k** for what intent 1097
16:19 Now Jesus **k** that they were desirous to ask 1097
18: 2 which betrayed him, **k** the place: 1492
20: 9 For as yet they **k** not the scripture, that he 1492
20:14 Jesus standing, and **k** not that it was Jesus. 1492
21: 4 but the disciples **k** not that it was Jesus. 1492
Ac 3:10 And they **k** that it was he which sat for 1921
7:18 Till another king arose, which **k** not Joseph. 1492
9:30 Which when the brethren **k**, they brought 1921
12:14 And when she **k** Peter's voice, she opened 1921
13:27 and their rulers, because they **k** him **not**, 50
16: 3 for they **k** all that his father was a Greek. 1492
19:32 the more part **k** not wherefore they were 1492
19:34 But when *they* **k** that he was a Jew, all with 1921
22:29 after he **k** that he was a Roman, and 1921
26: 5 Which **k** me from the beginning, if they 4267
27:39 And when it was day, they **k** not the land: 1921
28: 1 they **k** that the island was called Melita. 1921
Ro 1:21 Because that, when they **k** God, 1097
1Co 1:21 of God the world by wisdom **k** not God, 1097
2: 8 Which none of the princes of this world **k**: 1097
2Co 5:21 made him *to be* sin for us, who **k** no sin; 1097
12: 2 I **k** a man in Christ above fourteen years 1492
12: 3 And I **k** such a man, (whether in the body, 1492
Gal 4: 8 Howbeit then, when ye **k** not God, ye did 1492
Col 1: 6 heard of *it*, and **k** the grace of God in truth: 1921
2: 1 For I would that ye **k** what great conflict I 1492
1Jn 3: 1 world knoweth us not, because it **k** him not. 1097
Jude 1: 5 though ye once **k** this, how that the Lord, 1492
Rev 19:12 that no *man* **k**, but he himself. 1492

KNEWEST (10) [KNOW]
Dt 8: 3 and fed thee with manna, which thou **k** not, 3045
Ru 2:11 art come unto a people which thou **k** not 3045
Ne 9:10 for thou **k** that they dealt proudly against 3045
Ps 142: 3 within me, then thou **k** my path. 3045
Isa 48: 8 yea, thou **k** not; yea, from that time *that* 3045
Da 5:22 humbled thine heart, though thou **k** all this; 3046
Mt 25:26 thou **k** that I reap where I sowed not, and 1492
Lk 19:22 Thou **k** that I was an austere man, taking up 1492
19:44 thou **k** not the time of thy visitation. 1097
Jn 4:10 If thou **k** the gift of God, and who it is that 1492

KNIFE (6) [KNIVES]
Ge 22: 6 he took the fire in his hand, and a **k**; and 3979
22:10 his hand, and took the **k** to slay his son. 3979
Jdg 19:29 he took a **k**, and laid hold on his concubine, 3979
Pr 23: 2 put a **k** to thy throat, if thou *be* a man given 7915
Eze 5: 1 thou, son of man, take thee a sharp **k**, 2719
5: 2 a third *part, and* smite about it with a **k**: 2719

KNIT (6)
Jdg 20:11 against the city, **k together** as one man. 2270
1Sa 18: 1 that the soul of Jonathan was **k** with 7194
1Ch 12:17 mine heart shall be **k** unto you: 3162+3807.1
Ac 10:11 as *it had been* a great sheet **k** at the four *1210*
Col 2: 2 being **k together** in love, and unto all *4822*
2:19 and **k together**, increaseth *with* *4822*

KNITTED See WOOF

KNIVES (5) [KNIFE]
Jos 5: 2 Make thee sharp **k**, and circumcise again 2719
5: 3 Joshua made him sharp **k**, and 2719
1Ki 18:28 cut themselves after their manner with **k** 2719
Ezr 1: 9 chargers of silver, nine and twenty **k**, 4252
Pr 30:14 *are as* swords, and their jaw teeth *as* **k**, 3979

KNOCK (4) [KNOCKED, KNOCKETH, KNOCKING]
Mt 7: 7 **k**, and it shall be opened unto you: *2925*
Lk 11: 9 **k**, and it shall be opened unto you. *2925*
13:25 and to **k** at the door, saying, Lord, Lord, *2925*
Rev 3:20 Behold, I stand at the door, and **k**: if any *2925*

KNOCKED (1) [KNOCK]
Ac 12:13 And as Peter **k** at the door of the gate, *2925*

KNOCKETH (4) [KNOCK]
SS 5: 2 *it is* the voice of my beloved that **k** *saying*, 1849
Mt 7: 8 and to him that **k** it shall be opened. *2925*
Lk 11:10 and to him that **k** it shall be opened. *2925*
12:36 that when *he* cometh and **k**, they may open *2925*

KNOCKING (1) [KNOCK]
Ac 12:16 But Peter continued **k**: and when they had *2925*

KNOP (10) [KNOPS]
Ex 25:33 *with* a **k** and a flower in one branch; 3730
25:33 in the other branch, *with* a **k** and a flower: 3730
25:35 *there shall be* a **k** under two branches of 3730
25:35 a **k** under two branches of the same, and 3730
25:35 and a **k** under two branches of the same, 3730
37:19 of almonds in one branch, a **k** and a flower; 3730
37:19 in another branch, a **k** and a flower: 3730
37:21 a **k** under two branches of the same, and 3730
37:21 a **k** under two branches of the same, and 3730
37:21 and a **k** under two branches of the same, 3730

KNOPS (9) [KNOP]
Ex 25:31 his bowls, his **k**, and his flowers, 3730
25:34 *with* their **k** and their flowers. 3730
25:36 Their **k** and their branches shall be of 3730
37:17 his bowls, his **k**, and his flowers, 3730
37:20 made like almonds, his **k**, and his flowers: 3730
37:22 Their **k** and their branches were of 3730
1Ki 6:18 of the house within *was* carved with **k** 6497
7:24 the brim of it round about *there were* **k** 6497
7:24 the **k** *were* cast *in* two rows, when it was 6497

KNOW (763) [FOREKNEW, FOREKNOW, FOREKNOWLEDGE, KNEWEST, KNOWEST, KNOWETH, KNOWING, KNOWLEDGE, KNOWN, UNKNOWN]
Ge 3: 5 For God doth **k** that in the day ye eat 3045
3:22 is become as one of us, to **k** good and evil: 3045
4: 9 he said, I **k** not: *Am* I my brother's keeper? 3045
12:11 I **k** that thou *art* a fair woman to look upon: 3045
15: 8 whereby shall I **k** that I shall inherit it? 3045
15:13 **K of a surety** that thy seed shall be a 3045+3045
18:19 For I **k** him, that he will command his 3045
18:21 which is come unto me; and if not, I will **k**. 3045
19: 5 them out unto us, that we may **k** them. 3045
20: 6 I **k** that thou didst this in the integrity of thy 3045
20: 7 **k** thou that thou shalt surely die, thou, and 3045
22:12 for now I **k** that thou fearest God, 3045
24:14 thereby shall I **k** that thou hast shewed 3045
27: 2 I am old, I **k** not the day of my death: 3045
29: 5 unto them, **K** ye Laban the son of Nahor? 3045
29: 5 son of Nahor? And they said, We **k** *him*. 3045
31: 6 ye **k** that with all my power I have served 3045
37:32 **k** now whether it *be* thy son's coat or no. 5234
42:33 Hereby shall I **k** that ye *are* true *men;* leave 3045
42:34 shall I **k** that ye *are* no spies, but *that* ye *are* 3045
43: 7 could we **certainly k** that he would 3045+3045
44:27 Ye **k** that my wife bare me two *sons:* 3045
48:19 his father refused, and said, I **k** *it*, my son, 3045
48:19 I **k** *it:* he also shall become a people, and 3045
Ex 3: 7 of their taskmasters; for I **k** their sorrows; 3045
4:14 I **k** that he can speak well. And also, 3045
5: 2 I **k** not the LORD, neither will I let Israel 3045
6: 7 ye shall **k** that I *am* the LORD your God, 3045
7: 5 the Egyptians shall **k** that I *am* the LORD, 3045
7:17 In this thou shalt **k** that I *am* the LORD: 3045
8:10 that thou mayest **k** that *there is* none like 3045
8:22 to the end thou mayest **k** that I *am* 3045
9:14 that thou mayest **k** that *there is* none like 3045
9:29 that thou mayest **k** how that the earth *is* 3045
9:30 I **k** that ye will not yet fear the LORD 3045
10: 2 that ye may **k** how that I *am* the LORD. 3045
10:26 we **k** not with what we must serve 3045
11: 7 that ye may **k** how that the LORD doth 3045
14: 4 that the Egyptians may **k** that I *am* 3045
14:18 the Egyptians shall **k** that I *am* the LORD, 3045
16: 6 ye shall **k** that the LORD hath brought 3045
16:12 ye shall **k** that I *am* the LORD your God. 3045
18:11 Now I **k** that the LORD *is* greater than all 3045
18:16 I do **make** *them* **k** the statutes of God, and 3045
23: 9 for ye **k** the heart of a stranger, seeing ye 3045
29:46 they shall **k** that I *am* the LORD their 3045
31:13 that *ye* may **k** that I *am* the LORD that 3045
33: 5 that I may **k** what to do unto thee. 3045
33:12 thou hast not let me **k** whom thou wilt send 3045
33:12 I **k** thee by name, and thou hast also found 3045
33:13 shew me now thy way, that I may **k** thee, 3045

K

Ex 33:17 grace in my sight, and I **k** thee by name. 3045
36: 1 understanding to **k** how to work all *manner* 3045
Lev 23:43 That your generations may **k** that I made 3045
Nu 14:31 they shall **k** the land which ye have 3045
14:34 and ye shall **k** my breach of promise. 3045
16:28 Hereby ye shall **k** that the LORD hath 3045
22:19 that I may **k** what the LORD will say unto 3045
Dt 3:19 (*for* I **k** that ye have much cattle,) 3045
4:35 that thou mightest **k** that the LORD he *is* 3045
4:39 **K** therefore *this* day, and consider *it* in 3045
7: 9 **K** therefore that the LORD thy God, he *is* 3045
8: 2 to prove thee, to **k** what *was* in thine heart, 3045
8: 3 thou knewest not, neither did thy fathers **k**; 3045
8: 3 that he might **make** thee **k** that man doth 3045
11: 2 **k** you *this* day: for *I speak* not with your 3045
13: 3 to **k** whether you love the LORD your 3045
18:21 How shall we **k** the word which 3045
22: 2 or *if* thou **k** him not, then thou shalt bring it 3045
29: 6 that ye might **k** that I *am* the LORD your 3045
29:16 (For ye **k** how we have dwelt in the land of 3045
31:21 for I **k** their imagination which they go 3045
31:27 For I **k** thy rebellion, and thy stiff neck: 3045
31:29 For I **k** that after my death ye will utterly 3045
Jos 2: 9 I **k** that the LORD hath given you 3045
3: 4 that ye may **k** the way by which ye must 3045
3: 7 that they may **k** that, as I was with Moses, 3045
3:10 Hereby ye shall **k** that the living God *is* 3045
4:22 ye shall let your children **k**, saying, 3045
4:24 That all the people of the earth might **k** 3045
22:22 of gods, he knoweth, and Israel he shall **k**; 3045
23:13 **K for a certainty** that the LORD 3045+3045
23:14 ye **k** in all your hearts and in all your souls, 3045
Jdg 3: 2 of the children of Israel might **k**, 3045
3: 4 to **k** whether they would hearken unto 3045
6:37 shall I **k** that thou wilt save Israel by mine 3045
17:13 Now **k** I that the LORD will do me good, 3045
18: 5 that we may **k** whether our way which we 3045
18:14 Do ye **k** that there is in these houses an 3045
19:22 came into thine house, that we may **k** him. 3045
Ru 3:11 for all the city of my people doth **k** that 3045
3:14 she rose up before one could **k** another. 5234
3:18 until thou **k** how the matter will fall: 3045
4: 4 not redeem *it, then* tell me, that I may **k**: 3045
1Sa 3: 7 Now Samuel did not yet **k** the LORD, 3045
6: 9 we shall **k** that *it is* not his hand *that* smote 3045
14:38 **k** and see wherein this sin hath been *this* 3045
17:28 I **k** thy pride, and the naughtiness of thine 3045
17:46 that all the earth may **k** that there is a God 3045
17:47 all this assembly shall **k** that the LORD 3045
20: 3 he saith, Let not Jonathan **k** this, lest he be 3045
20:30 **k** that thou hast chosen the son of Jesse to 3045
21: 2 Let no man **k** any thing of the business 3045
22: 3 with you, till I **k** what God will do for me. 3045
23:22 **k** and see his place where his haunt is, *and* 3045
24:11 **k** thou and see that *there is* neither evil nor 3045
24:20 I **k well** that thou shalt surely be king, 3045
25:11 unto men, whom I **k** not whence they *be?* 3045
25:17 Now therefore **k** and consider what thou 3045
28: 1 said unto David, **K** thou **assuredly**, 3045+3045
28: 2 Surely thou shalt **k** what thy servant can do. 3045
29: 9 to David, I **k** that thou *art* good in my sight, 3045
2Sa 3:25 to **k** thy going out and thy coming in, and 3045
3:25 thy coming in, and to **k** all that thou doest. 3045
3:38 **K** ye not that there is a prince and a great 3045
7:21 great things, to **make** thy servant **k** *them.* 3045
14:20 of God, to **k** all *things* that *are* in the earth. 3045
19:20 For thy servant doth **k** that I have sinned: 3045
19:22 for do not I **k** that I *am this* day king over 3045
24: 2 that I may **k** the number of the people. 3045
1Ki 2:37 thou shalt **k for certain** that thou 3045+3045
2:42 unto thee, saying, **K for a certain**, 3045+3045
3: 7 I **k** not *how* to go out or come in. 3045
8:38 which shall **k** every man the plague of his 3045
8:43 that all people of the earth may **k** thy name, 3045
8:43 that *they* may **k** that this house, which I 3045
8:60 That all the people of the earth may **k** that 3045
17:24 Now *by* this I **k** that thou *art* a man of God, 3045
18:12 the LORD shall carry thee whither I **k** not; 3045
18:37 that this people may **k** that thou *art* 3045
20:13 and thou shalt **k** that I *am* the LORD. 3045
20:28 and ye shall **k** that I *am* the LORD. 3045
22: 3 **K** ye that Ramoth in Gilead *is* ours, and 3045
2Ki 2: 3 he said, Yea, I **k** *it;* hold you your peace. 3045
2: 5 Yea, I **k** *it;* hold you your peace. 3045
5: 8 he shall **k** that there is a prophet in Israel. 3045
5:15 now I **k** that *there is* no God in all the earth, 3045
7:12 They **k** that we *be* hungry; therefore 3045
8:12 Because I **k** the evil that thou wilt do unto 3045
9:11 Ye **k** the man, and his communication. 3045
10:10 **K** now that there shall fall unto the earth 3045
17:26 **k** not the manner of the God of the land: 3045
17:26 they **k** not the manner of the God of 3045
19:19 that all the kingdoms of the earth may **k** 3045
19:27 I **k** thy abode, and thy going out, and 3045
1Ch 12:32 of the times, to **k** what Israel ought to do; 3045
21: 2 the number of them to me, that I may **k** *it.* 3045
28: 9 **k** thou the God of thy father, and serve him 3045
29:17 I **k** also, my God, that thou triest the heart, 3045
2Ch 2: 8 for I **k** that thy servants can skill to cut 3045
6:29 when every one shall **k** his own sore and 3045
6:33 that all people of the earth may **k** thy name, 3045
6:33 may **k** that this house which I have built is 3045
12: 8 that they may **k** my service, and the service 3045
13: 5 Ought you not to **k** that the LORD God of 3045
20:12 cometh against us; neither **k** we what to do: 3045
25:16 I **k** that God hath determined to destroy 3045
32:13 **K** ye not what I and my fathers have done 3045
32:31 that he might **k** all *that was* in his heart. 3045
Ezr 4:15 **k** that this city *is* a rebellious city, and 3046
7:25 the river, all such as **k** the laws of thy God; 3046
7:25 and teach ye them that **k** *them* not. 3046
Ne 4:11 They shall not **k**, neither see, 3045
Est 2:11 to **k** how Esther did, and what should 3045
4: 5 to **k** what it *was,* and why it *was.* 3045
4:11 do **k**, that whosoever, *whether* man or 3045
Job 5:24 thou shalt **k** that thy tabernacle *shall be in* 3045
5:25 Thou shalt **k** also that thy seed *shall be* 3045
5:27 so it *is;* hear it, and **k** thou *it* for thy good. 3045
7:10 neither shall his place **k** him any more. 5234
8: 9 **k** nothing, because our days upon earth *are* 3045
9: 2 I **k** *it is* so of a truth: but how should man 3045
9: 5 removeth the mountains, and they **k** not: 3045
9:21 I *were* perfect, *yet* would I not **k** my soul: 3045
9:28 I **k** that thou wilt not hold me innocent. 3045
10:13 hid in thine heart: I **k** that this *is* with thee. 3045
11: 6 **K** therefore that God exacteth of thee *less* 3045
11: 8 deeper than hell; what canst thou **k**? 3045
13: 2 What ye **k**, *the same* do I know also. I *am* 1847
13: 2 What ye know, *the same* do I **k** also. I *am* 3045
13:18 *my* cause; I **k** that I shall be justified. 3045
13:23 **make** me **to k** my transgression and 3045
15: 9 What knowest thou, that we **k** not? 3045
19: 6 **K** now that God hath overthrown me, and 3045
19:25 For I **k** *that* my Redeemer liveth, and 3045
19:29 that ye may **k** *there is* a judgment. 3045
21:19 he rewardeth him, and he shall **k** *it.* 3045
21:27 I **k** your thoughts, and the devices *which* ye 3045
21:29 by the way? and do ye not **k** their tokens, 5234
22:13 thou sayest, How doth God **k**? can he 3045
23: 5 I would **k** the words *which* he would 3045
24: 1 do they that **k** him not see his days? 3045
24:13 they **k** not the ways thereof, nor abide in 5234
24:16 in the daytime: they **k** not the light. 3045
24:17 if *one* **k** *them, they are in* the terrors of 5234
30:23 For I **k** *that* thou wilt bring me *to* death, and 3045
31: 6 that God may **k** mine integrity. 3045
32:22 For I **k** not to give flattering titles; *in so* 3045
34: 4 let us **k** among ourselves what *is* good. 3045
36:26 Behold, God *is* great, and we **k** *him* not, 3045
37: 7 of every man; that all men may **k** his work. 3045
37:15 Dost thou **k** when God disposed them, and 3045
37:16 Dost thou **k** the balancings of the clouds, 3045
38:12 *and* **caused** the dayspring **to k** his place; 3045
38:20 that thou shouldest **k** the paths to the house 995
42: 2 I **k** that thou canst do every *thing,* and 3045
Ps 4: 3 **k** that the LORD hath set apart *him that is* 3045
9:10 they that **k** thy name will put their trust in 3045
9:20 *that* the nations may **k** themselves *to be but* 3045
20: 6 Now **k** I that the LORD saveth his 3045
36:10 thy lovingkindness unto them that **k** thee; 3045
39: 4 **make** me **to k** mine end, and the measure 3045
39: 4 what it *is; that* I may **k** how frail I *am.* 3045
41:11 By this I **k** that thou favourest me, because 3045
46:10 Be still, and **k** that I *am* God: I will be 3045
50:11 I **k** all the fowls of the mountains: and 3045
51: 6 in the hidden *part* thou shalt **make** me **to k** 3045
56: 9 turn back: this I **k**; for God *is* for me. 3045
59:13 let them **k** that God ruleth in Jacob unto 3045
71:15 all the day; for I **k** not the numbers *thereof.* 3045
73:11 they say, How doth God **k**? and is there 3045
73:16 When I thought to **k** this, it *was* too painful 3045
78: 6 That the generation to come might **k** *them,* 3045
82: 5 They **k** not, neither will they understand; 3045
83:18 That *men* may **k** that thou, whose name 3045
87: 4 of Rahab and Babylon to them that **k** me: 3045
89:15 Blessed *is* the people that **k** the joyful 3045
94:10 teacheth man knowledge, *shall not he* **k**? NIH
100: 3 **K** ye that the LORD he *is* God: *it is* he 3045
101: 4 from me: I will not **k** a wicked *person.* 3045
103:16 and the place thereof shall **k** it no more. 5234
109:27 That they may **k** that this *is* thy hand; 3045
119:75 I **k**, O LORD, that thy judgments *are* 3045
119:125 that I may **k** thy testimonies. 3045
135: 5 For I **k** that the LORD *is* great, and 3045
139:23 Search me, O God, and **k** my heart: try me, 3045
139:23 know my heart: try me, and **k** my thoughts: 3045
140:12 I **k** that the LORD will maintain the cause 3045
142: 4 but *there was* no man that would **k** me: 5234
143: 8 **cause** me **to k** the way wherein I should 3045
Pr 1: 2 To **k** wisdom and instruction; to perceive 3045
4: 1 of a father, and attend to **k** understanding. 3045
4:19 they **k** not at what they stumble. 3045
5: 6 are moveable, *that* thou canst not **k** *them.* 3045
10:32 The lips of the righteous **k** what is 3045
22:21 That *I* might **make** thee **k** the certainty of 3045
24:12 doth *not* he **k** *it?* and shall *not* he render to 3045
25: 8 lest *thou* **k** *not* what to do in the end thereof, NIH
27:23 Be thou **diligent** to **k** the state of thy 3045+3045
29: 7 *but* the wicked regardeth not to **k** *it.* 1847
30:18 wonderful for me, yea, four which I **k** not: 3045
Ecc 1:17 I gave my heart to **k** wisdom, and to know 3045
1:17 know wisdom, and to **k** madness and folly: 3045
3:12 I **k** that *there is* no good in them, but for *a* 3045
3:14 I **k** that, whatsoever God doeth, it shall be 3045
7:25 I applied mine heart to **k**, and to search, and 3045
7:25 *of things,* and to **k** the wickedness of folly, 3045
8:12 yet surely I **k** that it shall be well with them 3045
8:16 When I applied mine heart to **k** wisdom, 3045
8:17 though a wise *man* think to **k** *it,* yet shall 3045
9: 5 For the living **k** that they shall die: but 3045
9: 5 the dead **k** not any thing, neither have they 3045
11: 9 **k** thou, that for all these *things* God will 3045
SS 1: 8 If thou **k** not, O thou fairest among women, 3045
Isa 1: 3 *but* Israel doth not **k**, my people doth not 3045
5:19 draw nigh and come, that we may **k** *it.* 3045
7:15 that he may **k** to refuse the evil, and 3045
7:16 For before the child shall **k** to refuse 3045
9: 9 all the people shall **k**, *even* Ephraim and 3045
19:12 let them **k** what the LORD of hosts hath 3045
19:21 the Egyptians shall **k** the LORD in that 3045
37:20 that all the kingdoms of the earth may **k** 3045
37:28 I **k** thy abode, and thy going out, and thy 3045
41:20 **k**, and consider, and understand together, 3045
41:22 consider *them,* and **k** the latter end of them; 3045
41:23 that we may **k** that ye *are* gods: 3045
41:26 from the beginning, that we may **k**? 3045
43:10 that ye may **k** and believe me, and 3045
43:19 now it shall spring forth; shall ye not **k** it? 3045
44: 8 yea, *there is* no God; I **k** not *any.* 3045
44: 9 they see not, nor **k**; that they may be 3045
Isa 45: 3 that thou mayest **k** that I, the LORD, 3045
45: 6 That they may **k** from the rising of the sun, 3045
47: 8 neither shall I **k** the loss of children: 3045
47:11 thou shalt not **k** from whence it riseth: 3045
47:11 upon thee suddenly, *which* thou shalt not **k**. 3045
48: 6 hidden *things,* and thou didst not **k** them. 3045
49:23 and thou shalt **k** that I *am* the LORD: 3045
49:26 all flesh shall **k** that I the LORD *am* thy 3045
50: 4 that *I* should **k** how to speak a word in 3045
50: 7 a flint, and I **k** that I shall not be ashamed. 3045
51: 7 Hearken unto me, ye that **k** righteousness, 3045
52: 6 Therefore my people shall **k** my name: 3045
52: 6 *they shall* **k** in that day that I *am* he that NIH
58: 2 seek me daily, and delight to **k** my ways, 1847
59: 8 The way of peace they **k** not; and *there is* 3045
59: 8 whosoever goeth therein shall not **k** peace. 3045
59:12 and *as for* our iniquities, we **k** them; 3045
60:16 thou shalt **k** that I the LORD *am* thy 3045
66:18 For I **k** their works and their thoughts: NIH
Jer 2:19 **k** therefore and see that *it is* an evil *thing* 3045
2:23 way in the valley, **k** what thou hast done: 3045
5: 1 and **k**, and seek in the broad places thereof, 3045
5: 4 for they **k** not the way of the LORD, 3045
6:18 Therefore hear, ye nations, and **k**, 3045
6:27 that thou mayest **k** and try their way. 3045
7: 9 and walk after other gods whom ye **k** not; 3045
8: 7 my people **k** not the judgment of 3045
9: 3 and they **k** not me, saith the LORD. 3045
9: 6 through deceit they refuse to **k** me, saith 3045
10:23 I **k** that the way of man *is* not in himself: 3045
10:25 Pour out thy fury upon the heathen that **k** 3045
11:18 I **k** *it:* then thou shewedst me their doings. 3045
13:12 Do we not **certainly k** that every 3045+3045
14:18 the priest go about into a land that they **k** 3045
15:15 **k** that for thy sake I have suffered rebuke. 3045
16:13 out of this land into a land that ye **k** not, 3045
16:21 I *will* this once **cause** them **to k**, 3045
16:21 I will **cause** them **to k** mine hand and my 3045
16:21 they shall **k** that my name *is* The LORD. 3045
17: 9 and desperately wicked: who can **k** it? 3045
22:16 *it was* well *with him: was* not this to **k** me? 1847
22:28 and are cast into a land which they **k** not? 3045
24: 7 I will give them a heart to **k** me, that I *am* 3045
26:15 **k** ye **for certain**, that if ye put me to 3045+3045
29:11 For I **k** the thoughts that I think towards 3045
29:16 *K* that thus saith the LORD of the king NIH
29:23 even I **k**, and *am* a witness, saith 3045
31:34 man his brother, saying, **K** the LORD: 3045
31:34 for they shall all **k** me, from the least of 3045
36:19 Jeremiah; and let no man **k** where ye *be.* 3045
38:24 Let no man **k** of these words, and thou shalt 3045
40:14 Dost thou **certainly k** that Baalis 3045+3045
40:15 no man shall **k** *it:* wherefore should he slay 3045
42:19 **k certainly** that I have admonished 3045+3045
42:22 **k certainly** that ye shall die by 3045+3045
44:28 shall **k** whose words shall stand, mine, or 3045
44:29 that ye may **k** that my words shall surely 3045
48:17 all ye that **k** his name, say, How is 3045
48:30 I **k** his wrath, saith the LORD; but *it shall* 3045
Eze 2: 5 yet shall **k** that there hath been a prophet 3045
5:13 they shall **k** that I the LORD have spoken 3045
6: 7 and ye shall **k** that I *am* the LORD. 3045
6:10 they shall **k** that I *am* the LORD, *and* 3045
6:13 shall ye **k** that I *am* the LORD, when their 3045
6:14 and they shall **k** that I *am* the LORD. 3045
7: 4 and ye shall **k** that I *am* the LORD. 3045
7: 9 ye shall **k** that I *am* the LORD that 3045
7:27 and they shall **k** that I *am* the LORD. 3045
11: 5 for I **k** the things that come into your mind, 3045
11:10 and ye shall **k** that I *am* the LORD. 3045
11:12 ye shall **k** that I *am* the LORD: for ye 3045
12:15 they shall **k** that I *am* the LORD, when I 3045
12:16 and they shall **k** that I *am* the LORD. 3045
12:20 and ye shall **k** that I *am* the LORD. 3045
13: 9 and ye shall **k** that I *am* the Lord GOD. 3045
13:14 and ye shall **k** that I *am* the LORD. 3045
13:21 and ye shall **k** that I *am* the LORD. 3045
13:23 and ye shall **k** that I *am* the LORD. 3045
14: 8 and ye shall **k** that I *am* the LORD. 3045
14:23 ye shall **k** that I have not done without 3045
15: 7 ye shall **k** that I *am* the LORD, when I set 3045
16: 2 **cause** Jerusalem **to k** her abominations, 3045
16:62 and thou shalt **k** that I *am* the LORD: 3045
17:12 **K** ye not what these *things mean?* tell *them,* 3045
17:21 ye shall **k** that I the LORD have spoken 3045
17:24 all the trees of the field shall **k** that I 3045
20: 4 wilt thou judge *them?* **cause** them **to k** 3045
20:12 that *they* might **k** that I *am* the LORD that 3045
20:20 that *ye* may **k** that I *am* the LORD your 3045
20:26 to the end that they might **k** that I *am* 3045
20:38 and ye shall **k** that I *am* the LORD. 3045
20:42 ye shall **k** that I *am* the LORD, when I 3045
20:44 ye shall **k** that I *am* the LORD, when I 3045
21: 5 That all flesh may **k** that I the LORD have 3045
22:16 and thou shalt **k** that I *am* the LORD. 3045
22:22 ye shall **k** that I the LORD have poured 3045
23:49 and ye shall **k** that I *am* the Lord GOD. 3045
24:24 ye shall **k** that I *am* the Lord GOD. 3045
24:27 and they shall **k** that I *am* the LORD. 3045
25: 5 and ye shall **k** that I *am* the LORD. 3045
25: 7 and thou shalt **k** that I *am* the LORD. 3045
25:11 and they shall **k** that I *am* the LORD. 3045
25:14 they shall **k** my vengeance, saith the Lord 3045
25:17 they shall **k** that I *am* the LORD, when I 3045
26: 6 and they shall **k** that I *am* the LORD. 3045
28:19 All they that **k** thee among the people shall 3045
28:22 they shall **k** that I *am* the LORD, when I 3045
28:23 and they shall **k** that I *am* the LORD. 3045
28:24 and they shall **k** that I *am* the Lord GOD. 3045
28:26 they shall **k** that I *am* the LORD their 3045
29: 6 all the inhabitants of Egypt shall **k** that I *am* 3045
29: 9 and they shall **k** that I *am* the LORD: 3045
29:16 but they shall **k** that I *am* the Lord GOD. 3045
29:21 and they shall **k** that I *am* the LORD. 3045
30: 8 they shall **k** that I *am* the LORD, when I 3045

Eze 30:19 and they shall **k** that I *am* the LORD. 3045
30:25 they shall **k** that I *am* the LORD, when I 3045
30:26 and they shall **k** that I *am* the LORD. 3045
32:15 shall they **k** that I *am* the LORD. 3045
33:29 shall they **k** that I *am* the LORD, when I 3045
33:33 shall they **k** that a prophet hath been among 3045
34:27 and shall **k** that I *am* the LORD, 3045
34:30 Thus shall they **k** that I the LORD their 3045
35: 4 and thou shalt **k** that I *am* the LORD. 3045
35: 9 and ye shall **k** that I *am* the LORD. 3045
35:12 thou shalt **k** that I *am* the LORD, *and* 3045
35:15 of it: and they shall **k** that I *am* the LORD. 3045
36:11 and ye shall **k** that I *am* the LORD. 3045
36:23 the heathen shall **k** that I *am* the LORD, 3045
36:36 **k** that I the LORD build the ruined *places,* 3045
36:38 and they shall **k** that I *am* the LORD. 3045
37: 6 and ye shall **k** that I *am* the LORD. 3045
37:13 ye shall **k** that I *am* the LORD, when I 3045
37:14 shall ye **k** that I the LORD have spoken *it,* 3045
37:28 the heathen shall **k** that I the LORD do 3045
38:14 Israel dwelleth safely, shalt thou not **k** *it?* 3045
38:16 my land, that the heathen may **k** me, 3045
38:23 and they shall **k** that I *am* the LORD. 3045
39: 6 and they shall **k** that I *am* the LORD. 3045
39: 7 the heathen shall **k** that I *am* the LORD, 3045
39:22 So the house of Israel shall **k** that I *am* 3045
39:23 the heathen shall **k** that the house of Israel 3045
39:28 shall they **k** that I *am* the LORD their 3045
Da 2: 3 and my spirit was troubled to **k** the dream. 3045
2: 8 I **k** of certainty that ye would gain the time, 3046
2: 9 I shall **k** that ye can shew me 3046
2:21 knowledge to them that **k** understanding: 3046
2:30 *that* thou mightest **k** the thoughts of thy 3046
4: 9 I **k** that the spirit of the holy gods *is* in thee, 3046
4:17 to the intent that the living may **k** that 3046
4:25 till thou **k** that the most High ruleth in 3046
4:32 until thou **k** that the most High ruleth in 3046
5:23 stone, which see not, nor hear, nor **k**: 3046
6:15 said unto the king, **K**, O king, that the law 3046
7:16 **made** me **k** the interpretation of the things. 3046
7:19 I would **k the truth** of the fourth beast, 3321
8:19 I *will* **make** thee **k** what shall be in the last 3045
9:25 **K** therefore and understand, *that* from 3045
11:32 the people that do **k** their God shall be 3045
Hos 2: 8 For she did not **k** that I gave her corn, and 3045
2:20 and thou shalt **k** the LORD. 3045
5: 3 I **k** Ephraim, and Israel is not hid from me: 3045
6: 3 shall we **k**, *if* we follow on to know 3045
6: 3 we know, *if* we follow on to **k** the LORD: 3045
8: 2 shall cry unto me, My God, we **k** thee. 3045
9: 7 Israel shall **k** *it:* the prophet *is* a fool, 3045
13: 4 of Egypt, and thou shalt **k** no god but me: 3045
13: 5 I did **k** thee in the wilderness, in the land of 3045
14: 9 these *things?* prudent, and he shall **k** them? 3045
Joel 2:27 ye shall **k** that I *am* in the midst of Israel, 3045
3:17 So shall ye **k** that I *am* the LORD your 3045
Am 3:10 For they **k** not to do right, saith 3045
5:12 For I **k** your manifold transgressions and 3045
Jnh 1: 7 that we may **k** for whose cause this evil *is* 3045
1:12 for I **k** that for my sake this great tempest *is* 3045
Mic 3: 1 of Israel; *is it* not for you to **k** judgment? 3045
4:12 they **k** not the thoughts of the LORD, 3045
6: 5 that *ye* may **k** the righteousness of 3045
Zec 2: 9 ye shall **k** that the LORD of hosts hath 3045
2:11 thou shalt **k** that the LORD of hosts hath 3045
4: 9 thou shalt **k** that the LORD of hosts hath 3045
6:15 ye shall **k** that the LORD of hosts hath 3045
Mal 2: 4 ye shall **k** that I have sent this 3045
Mt 6: 3 let not thy left hand **k** what thy right hand *1097*
7:11 **k how** to give good gifts unto your *1492*
7:16 Ye shall **k** them by their fruits. Do *men* *1921*
7:20 Wherefore by their fruits ye shall **k** them. *1921*
9: 6 But that ye may **k** that the Son of man hath *1492*
9:30 charged them, saying, See *that* no *man* **k** *it.* *1097*
13:11 Because it is given unto you to **k** *1097*
20:22 and said, Ye **k** not what ye ask. *1492*
20:25 Ye **k** that the princes of the Gentiles *1492*
22:16 we **k** that thou art true, and teachest *1492*
24:32 forth leaves, ye **k** that summer *is* nigh: *1097*
24:33 when ye shall see all these *things,* **k** that it *1097*
24:42 for ye **k** not what hour your Lord doth *1492*
24:43 But **k** this, that if the goodman of the house *1097*
25:12 and said, Verily I say unto you, I **k** you not. *1492*
25:13 for ye **k** neither the day nor the hour *1492*
26: 2 Ye **k** that after two days is *the feast of* *1492*
26:70 *them* all, saying, I **k** not what thou sayest. *1492*
26:72 he denied with an oath, I do not **k** the man. *1492*
26:74 and to swear, *saying,* I **k** not the man. *1492*
28: 5 for I **k** that ye seek Jesus, which was *1492*
Mk 1:24 I **k** thee who thou art, the Holy One of God. *1492*
2:10 But that ye may **k** that the Son of man hath *1492*
4:11 Unto you it is given to **k** the mystery of *1097*
4:13 he said unto them, **K** ye not this parable? *1492*
4:13 and how *then* will ye **k** all parables? *1097*
5:43 them straitly that no *man* should **k** it; *1097*
7:24 and would have no *man* **k** *it:* but he could *1097*
9:30 and he would not that any *man* should **k** *it.* *1097*
10:38 Jesus said unto them, Ye **k** not what ye ask: *1492*
10:42 Ye **k** that they which are accounted to rule *1492*
12:14 we **k** that thou art true, and carest for no *1492*
12:24 because ye **k** not the scriptures, *1492*
13:28 forth leaves, ye **k** that summer is near: *1097*
13:29 to pass, **k** that it is nigh, *even* at the doors. *1097*
13:33 and pray: for ye **k** not when the time is. *1492*
13:35 for ye **k** not when the master of the house *1492*
14:68 But he denied, saying, I **k** not, neither *1492*
14:71 *saying,* I **k** not this man of whom ye speak. *1492*
Lk 1: 4 That thou mightest **k** the certainty of *those* *1921*
1:18 said unto the angel, Whereby shall I **k** this? *1097*
1:34 How shall this be, seeing I **k** not a man? *1097*
4:34 I **k** thee who thou art, the Holy One of God. *1492*
5:24 But that ye may **k** that the Son of man hath *1492*
8:10 Unto you it is given to **k** the mysteries of *1097*
9:55 Ye **k** not what manner of spirit ye are of. *1492*
11:13 **k how** to give good gifts unto your *1492*

Lk 12:39 And this **k**, that if the goodman of *1097*
13:25 say unto you, I **k** you not whence you are: *1492*
13:27 I tell you, I **k** you not whence you are; *1492*
19:15 that he might **k** how much every *man* had *1097*
20:21 we **k** that thou sayest and teachest rightly, *1492*
21:20 then **k** that the desolation thereof is nigh. *1097*
21:30 **k** of your own selves that summer is now *1097*
21:31 **k** ye that the kingdom of God is nigh at *1097*
22:57 denied him, saying, Woman, I **k** him not. *1492*
22:60 Peter said, Man, I **k** not what thou sayest. *1492*
23:34 forgive them; for they **k** not what they do. *1492*
24:16 were holden that *they* should not **k** him. *1921*
Jn 1:26 standeth one among you, whom ye **k** not; *1492*
3: 2 we **k** that thou art a teacher come from *1492*
3:11 We speak that we do **k**, and testify that we *1492*
4:22 Ye worship ye **k** not what: we know what *1492*
4:22 we **k** what we worship: for salvation is of *1492*
4:25 I **k** that Messias cometh, which is called *1492*
4:32 I have meat to eat that ye **k** not of. *1492*
4:42 and **k** that this is indeed the Christ, *1492*
5:32 I **k** that the witness which he witnesseth of *1492*
5:42 But I **k** you, that ye have not the love of *1097*
6:42 of Joseph, whose father and mother we **k**? *1492*
7:17 he shall **k** of the doctrine, whether it be of *1097*
7:26 Do the rulers **k** indeed that this is the very *1097*
7:27 Howbeit we **k** this *man* whence he is: but *1492*
7:28 Ye both **k** me, and ye know whence I am: *1492*
7:28 Ye both know me, and ye **k** whence I am: *1492*
7:28 but he that sent me is true, whom ye **k** not. *1492*
7:29 But I **k** him: for I am from him, and he hath *1492*
7:51 before it hear him, and **k** what he doeth? *1097*
8:14 for I **k** whence I came, and whither I go; *1492*
8:19 Ye neither **k** me, nor my Father: *1492*
8:28 then shall ye **k** that I am *he,* and *that* I do *1097*
8:32 And ye shall **k** the truth, and the truth shall *1097*
8:37 I **k** that ye are Abraham's seed; but ye seek *1492*
8:52 unto him, Now we **k** that thou hast a devil. *1097*
8:55 Yet ye have not known him; but I **k** him: *1492*
8:55 and if I should say, I **k** him not, I shall be a *1492*
8:55 unto you: but I **k** him, and keep his saying. *1492*
9:12 unto him, Where is he? He said, I **k** not. *1492*
9:20 We **k** that this is our son, and that he was *1492*
9:21 But by what means he now seeth, we **k** not; *1492*
9:21 or who hath opened his eyes, we **k** not: *1492*
9:24 the praise: we **k** that this man is a sinner. *1492*
9:25 said, Whether he be a sinner *or no,* I **k** not: *1492*
9:25 one *thing* I **k**, that, whereas I was blind, *1492*
9:29 We **k** that God spake unto Moses: *as for* *1492*
9:29 *as for* this *fellow,* we **k** not from whence he *1492*
9:30 Why herein is a marvellous *thing,* that ye **k** *1492*
9:31 Now we **k** that God heareth not sinners: but *1492*
10: 4 the sheep follow him: for they **k** his voice. *1492*
10: 5 for they **k** not the voice of strangers. *1492*
10:14 and **k** my *sheep,* and am known of mine. *1097*
10:15 Father knoweth me, *even* so **k** I the Father: *1097*
10:27 and I **k** them, and they follow me: *1097*
10:38 that ye may **k**, and believe, that the Father *1097*
11:22 But I **k**, that even now, whatsoever thou *1492*
11:24 I **k** that he shall rise again in *1492*
11:49 said unto them, Ye **k** nothing at all, *1492*
12:50 And I **k** that his commandment is life *1492*
13: 7 not now; but thou shalt **k** hereafter. *1097*
13:12 unto them, **K** ye what I have done to you? *1097*
13:17 If ye **k** these *things,* happy are ye if ye do *1492*
13:18 I **k** whom I have chosen: but that *1492*
13:35 By this shall all *men* **k** that ye are my *1097*
14: 4 And whither I go ye **k**, and the way ye *1492*
14: 4 whither I go ye know, and the way ye **k**. *1492*
14: 5 Lord, we **k** not whither thou goest; *1492*
14: 5 thou goest; and how can we **k** the way? *1492*
14: 7 and from henceforth ye **k** him, and *1097*
14:17 but ye **k** him; for he dwelleth with you, and *1097*
14:20 At that day ye shall **k** that I *am* in my *1097*
14:31 But that the world may **k** that I love *1097*
15:18 ye **k** that it hated me before *it hated* you. *1097*
15:21 because they **k** not him that sent me. *1492*
17: 3 that they might **k** thee the only true God, *1097*
17:23 that the world may **k** that thou hast sent me, *1097*
18:21 said unto them: behold, they **k** what I said. *1492*
19: 4 that ye may **k** that I find no fault in him. *1097*
20: 2 and we **k** not where they have laid him. *1492*
20:13 and I **k** not where they have laid him. *1492*
21:24 and we **k** that his testimony is true. *1492*
Ac 1: 7 It is not for you to **k** *the* times or *1097*
2:22 in the midst of you, as ye yourselves also **k**: *1492*
2:36 Therefore let all the house of Israel **k** *1097*
3:16 made this *man* strong, whom ye see and **k**: *1492*
10:28 Ye **k** how that it is an unlawful *thing* for a *1987*
10:37 *That* word, *I say,* you **k**, which was *1492*
12:11 he said, Now I **k** of a surety, that the Lord *1492*
15: 7 ye **k** how that a good while ago God made *1987*
17:19 saying, May we **k** what this new doctrine, *1097*
17:20 we would **k** therefore what these *things* *1097*
19:15 and said, Jesus I **k**, and Paul I know; *1097*
19:15 and said, Jesus I know, and Paul I **k**; *1987*
19:25 ye **k** that by this craft we have our wealth. *1987*
20:18 were come to him, he said unto them, Ye **k**, *1987*
20:25 And now behold, I **k** that ye all, *1492*
20:29 For I **k** this, that after my departing shall *1492*
20:34 Yea, ye yourselves **k**, that these hands have *1097*
21:24 all may **k** that *those things,* whereof they *1097*
21:34 when he could not **k** the certainty for *1097*
22:14 that *thou* shouldest **k** his will, and see *that* *1097*
22:19 they **k** that I imprisoned and beat in every *1987*
22:24 that he might **k** wherefore they cried so *1921*
24:10 Forasmuch as I **k** that thou hast been of *1987*
24:22 I will **k the uttermost** of your matter. *1231*
26: 3 *I* **k** *thee* to be expert in all customs and NIG
26: 4 own nation at Jerusalem, **k** all the Jews; *2467*
26:27 thou the prophets? I **k** that thou believest. *1492*
28:22 **k** that every where it is spoken *1110+1510*
Ro 3:19 Now we **k** that what *things* soever the law *1492*
6: 3 **K** ye **not**, that so many of us as were baptized *50*
6:16 **K** ye not, that to whom ye yield yourselves *1492*
7: 1 **K** ye **not**, brethren, (for I speak to them that *50*

Ro 7: 1 (for I speak to them that **k** the law,) *1097*
7:14 For we **k** that the law is spiritual: but I am *1492*
7:18 For I **k** that in me (that is, in my flesh,) *1492*
8:22 For we **k** that the whole creation groaneth *1492*
8:26 for we **k** not what we should pray for as we *1492*
8:28 And we **k** that all *things* work together for *1492*
10:19 But I say, Did not Israel **k**? First Moses *1097*
14:14 I **k**, and am persuaded by the Lord Jesus, *1492*
1Co 1:16 I **k** not whether I baptized any other. *1492*
2: 2 For I determined not to **k** any *thing* among *1492*
2:12 that we might **k** the *things* that are freely *1492*
2:14 neither can he **k** *them,* because they are *1097*
3:16 **K** ye not that ye are the temple of God, and *1492*
4: 4 For I **k** nothing by myself; yet am I not *4894*
4:19 to you shortly, if the Lord will, and will **k**, *1097*
5: 6 **K** ye not that a little leaven leaveneth *1492*
6: 2 Do ye not **k** that the saints shall judge *1492*
6: 3 **K** ye not that we shall judge angels? *1492*
6: 9 **K** ye not that the unrighteous shall not *1492*
6:15 **K** ye not that your bodies are the members *1492*
6:16 **k** ye not that he which is joined to a harlot *1492*
6:19 **k** ye not that your body is the temple of *1492*
8: 1 we **k** that we all have knowledge. *1492*
8: 2 he knoweth nothing yet as he ought to **k**. *1097*
8: 4 we **k** that an idol *is* nothing in the world, *1492*
9:13 Do ye not **k** that they which minister about *1492*
9:24 **K** ye not that they which run in a race run *1492*
11: 3 But I would have you **k**, that the head of *1492*
12: 2 Ye **k** that ye were Gentiles, carried away *1492*
13: 9 For we **k** in part, and we prophesy in part. *1097*
13:12 now I **k** in part; but then shall I know even *1097*
13:12 but then shall I **k** even as also I am known. *1921*
14:11 Therefore if I **k** not the meaning of *1492*
15:58 forasmuch as you **k** that your labour is not *1492*
16:15 brethren, (ye **k** the house of Stephanas, *1492*
2Co 2: 4 that ye might **k** the love which I have more *1097*
2: 9 did I write, that I might **k** the proof of you, *1097*
5: 1 For we **k** that if our earthly house of *this* *1492*
5:16 Wherefore henceforth **k** we no *man* after *1492*
5:16 yet now henceforth **k** we *him* no more. *1097*
8: 9 For ye **k** the grace of our Lord Jesus Christ, *1097*
9: 2 For I **k** the forwardness of your mind, *1492*
13: 5 **K** ye not your own selves, how that Jesus *1921*
13: 6 But I trust that ye shall **k** that we are not *1097*
Gal 3: 7 **K** ye therefore that they which are of faith, *1097*
4:13 Ye **k** how through infirmity of the flesh I *1492*
Eph 1:18 that ye may **k** what is the hope of his *1492*
3:19 And to **k** the love of Christ, which passeth *1097*
5: 5 For this ye **k**, that no whoremonger, *1097*
6:21 But that ye also may **k** my affairs, *and* *1492*
6:22 that ye might **k** our affairs, and *that* he *1097*
Php 1:19 For I **k** that this shall turn to my salvation *1492*
1:25 I **k** that I shall abide and continue with you *1492*
2:19 be of good comfort, when I **k** your state. *1097*
2:22 But ye **k** the proof of him, that, as a son *1097*
3:10 That *I* may **k** him, and the power of his *1097*
4:12 I **k** both how to be abased, and I know *how* *1492*
4:12 *how* to be abased, and I **k** *how* to abound: *1492*
4:15 Now ye Philippians **k** also, that in *1492*
Col 4: 6 that *you* may **k** how ye ought to answer *1492*
4: 8 that he might **k** your estate, and *1097*
1Th 1: 5 as ye **k** what manner of *men* we were *1492*
2: 1 brethren, **k** our entrance in unto you, *1492*
2: 2 shamefully entreated, as ye **k**, at Philippi, *1492*
2: 5 as ye **k**, nor a cloke of covetousness; *1492*
2:11 As you **k** how we exhorted and comforted *1492*
3: 3 for yourselves **k** that we are appointed *1492*
3: 4 even as it came to pass, and ye **k**. *1492*
3: 5 no longer forbear, I sent to **k** your faith, *1097*
4: 2 For ye **k** what commandments we gave you *1492*
4: 4 That every one of you should **k** how to *1492*
4: 5 even as the Gentiles which **k** not God: *1492*
5: 2 For yourselves **k** perfectly that the day of *1492*
5:12 to **k** them which labour among you, and *1492*
2Th 1: 8 taking vengeance on them that **k** not God, *1492*
2: 6 And now ye **k** what withholdeth that he *1492*
3: 7 For yourselves **k** how *ye* ought to follow *1492*
1Ti 1: 8 But we **k** that the law *is* good, if a man use *1492*
3: 5 (For if a man **k** not how to rule his own *1492*
3:15 that thou mayest **k** how *thou* oughtest to *1492*
4: 3 of them which believe and **k** the truth. *1921*
2Ti 1:12 for I **k** whom I have believed, and I am *1492*
3: 1 This **k** also, that in the last days perilous *1097*
Tit 1:16 They profess that *they* **k** God; but in works *1492*
Heb 8:11 every man his brother, saying, **K** the Lord: *1097*
8:11 for all shall **k** me, from the least to *1492*
10:30 For we **k** him that hath said, *1492*
12:17 For ye **k** how that afterward, when he *2467*
13:23 **K** ye that *our* brother Timothy is set at *1097*
Jas 2:20 But wilt thou **k**, O vain man, that faith *1097*
4: 4 **k** ye not that the friendship of the world is *1492*
4:14 Whereas ye **k** not what *shall be* on *1987*
5:20 Let him **k**, that he which converteth *1097*
1Pe 1:18 Forasmuch as ye **k** that ye were not *1492*
2Pe 1:12 of these *things,* though ye **k** *them,* *1492*
3:17 beloved, seeing ye **k** *these things* **before**, *4267*
1Jn 2: 3 And hereby we do **k** that we know him, *1097*
2: 3 And hereby we do know that we **k** him, *1097*
2: 4 I **k** him, and keepeth not his *1097*
2: 5 hereby **k** we that we are in him. *1097*
2:18 whereby we **k** that it is the last time. *1097*
2:20 from the Holy One, and ye **k** all *things.* *1492*
2:21 written unto you because ye **k** not the truth, *1492*
2:21 but because ye **k** it, and that no lie is of *1492*
2:29 If ye **k** that he is righteous, ye know that *1492*
2:29 ye **k** that every one which doeth *1097*
3: 2 but we **k** that, when he shall appear, *1492*
3: 5 And ye **k** that he was manifested to take *1492*
3:14 We **k** that we have passed from death unto *1492*
3:15 ye **k** that no murderer hath eternal life *1492*
3:19 And hereby we **k** that we are of the truth, *1097*
3:24 And hereby we **k** that he abideth in us, *1097*
4: 2 Hereby **k** ye the Spirit of God: Every spirit *1097*
4: 6 Hereby **k** we the spirit of truth, and *1097*
4:13 Hereby **k** we that we dwell in him, and *1097*

1Jn 5: 2 By this we **k** that we love the children of *1097*
5:13 that ye may **k** that ye have eternal life, and *1492*
5:15 And if we **k** that he hear us, whatsoever we *1492*
5:15 we **k** that we have the petitions that we *1492*
5:18 We **k** that whosoever is born of God *1492*
5:19 *And* we **k** that we are of God, and *1492*
5:20 And we **k** that the Son of God is come, and *1492*
5:20 that we may **k** him *that is* true, and we are *1097*
3Jn 1:12 and ye **k** that our record is true. *1492*
Jude 1:10 speak evil of those *things* which they **k** not: *1492*
1:10 but what they **k** naturally, as brute beasts, *1987*
Rev 2: 2 I **k** thy works, and thy labour, and *1492*
2: 9 I **k** thy works, *1492*
2: 9 *I* **k** the blasphemy of them which say they NIG
2:13 I **k** thy works, and where thou dwellest, *1492*
2:19 I **k** thy works, and charity, and service, *1492*
2:23 all the churches shall **k** that I am he which *1097*
3: 1 I **k** thy works, that thou hast a name that *1492*
3: 3 thou shalt not **k** what hour I will come upon *1097*
3: 8 I **k** thy works: behold, I have set before *1492*
3: 9 thy feet, and to **k** that I have loved thee. *1097*
3:15 I **k** thy works, that thou art neither cold nor *1492*

KNOWEST (89) [KNOW]

Ge 30:26 for thou **k** my service which I have done 3045
30:29 Thou **k** how I have served thee, and how 3045
47: 6 if thou **k** *any* man of activity amongst them, 3045
Ex 10: 7 **k** thou not yet that Egypt is destroyed? 3045
32:22 thou **k** the people, that they *are set* on 3045
Nu 10:31 forasmuch as thou **k** how we are to encamp 3045
11:16 whom thou **k** to be the elders of the people, 3045
20:14 Thou **k** all the travail that hath befallen us: 3045
Dt 7:15 diseases of Egypt, which thou **k**, upon thee; 3045
9: 2 whom thou **k**, and *of whom* thou hast heard 3045
20:20 Only the trees which thou **k** that they *be* not 3045
28:33 shall a nation which thou **k** not eat up; 3045
Jos 14: 6 Thou **k** the thing that the LORD said unto 3045
Jdg 15:11 **K** thou not that the Philistines *are* rulers 3045
1Sa 28: 9 Behold, thou **k** what Saul hath done, 3045
2Sa 1: 5 How **k** thou that Saul and Jonathan his son 3045
2:26 **k** thou not that it will be bitterness in 3045
3:25 Thou **k** Abner the son of Ner, that he came 3045
7:20 for thou, Lord GOD, **k** thy servant. 3045
17: 8 thou **k** thy father and his men, that they *be* 3045
1Ki 1:18 and now, my lord the king, thou **k** *it* not: 3045
2: 5 Moreover thou **k** also what Joab the son of 3045
2: 9 and **k** what thou oughtest to do unto him; 3045
2:15 Thou **k** that the kingdom was mine, and 3045
2:44 Thou **k** all the wickedness which thine 3045
5: 3 Thou **k** how that David my father could not 3045
5: 6 for thou **k** that *there is* not among us any 3045
8:39 according to his ways, whose heart thou **k**; 3045
8:39 **k** the hearts of all the children of men;) 3045
2Ki 2: 3 **K** thou that the LORD will take away thy 3045
2: 5 **K** thou that the LORD will take away thy 3045
4: 1 thou **k** that thy servant did fear the LORD: 3045
1Ch 17:18 of thy servant? for thou **k** thy servant. 3045
2Ch 6:30 unto all his ways, whose heart thou **k**; 3045
6:30 (for thou only **k** the hearts of the children 3045
Job 10: 7 Thou **k** that I am not wicked; and 1847+5921
15: 9 What **k** thou, that we know not? 3045
20: 4 **K** thou *not* this of old, since man was 3045
34:33 and not I: therefore speak what thou **k**. 3045
38: 5 hath laid the measures thereof, if thou **k**? 3045
38:18 breadth of the earth? declare if thou **k** it all. 3045
38:21 **K** thou *it*, because thou wast then born? or 3045
38:33 **K** thou the ordinances of heaven? canst 3045
39: 1 **K** thou the time when the wild goats of 3045
39: 2 or **k** thou the time when they bring forth? 3045
Ps 40: 9 not refrained my lips, O LORD, thou **k**. 3045
69: 5 O God, thou **k** my foolishness; and my sins 3045
139: 2 Thou **k** my downsitting and mine uprising, 3045
139: 4 *but* lo, O LORD, thou **k** it altogether. 3045
Pr 27: 1 for thou **k** not what a day may bring forth. 3045
Ecc 11: 2 for thou **k** not what evil shall be upon 3045
11: 5 As thou **k** not what *is* the way of the spirit, 3045
11: 5 thou **k** not the works of God who maketh 3045
11: 6 for thou **k** not whether shall prosper, 3045
Isa 55: 5 thou shalt call a nation *that* thou **k** not, and 3045
Jer 5:15 a nation whose language thou **k** not, 3045
12: 3 thou, O LORD, **k** me: thou hast seen me, 3045
15:14 thine enemies into a land *which* thou **k** not: 3045
15:15 O LORD, thou **k**: remember me, and 3045
17: 4 thine enemies in the land which thou **k** not: 3045
17:16 have I desired the woeful day; thou **k**: 3045
18:23 thou **k** all their counsel against me to slay 3045
33: 3 and mighty *things*, which thou **k** not. 3045
Eze 37: 3 And I answered, O Lord GOD, thou **k**. 3045
Da 10:20 **K** thou wherefore I come unto thee? 3045
Zec 4: 5 **K** thou not what these *be?* And I said, No, 3045
4:13 **K** thou not what these *be?* And I said, No, 3045
Mt 15:12 **K** thou that the Pharisees were offended, *1492*
Mk 10:19 Thou **k** the commandments, Do not commit *1492*
Lk 18:20 Thou **k** the commandments, Do not commit *1492*
22:34 that thou shalt thrice deny that *thou* **k** me. *1492*
Jn 1:48 saith unto him, Whence **k** thou me? *1097*
3:10 a master of Israel, and **k** not these *things?* *1097*
13: 7 said unto him, What I do thou **k** not now; *1492*
16:30 Now are we sure that thou **k** all *things*, and *1492*
19:10 **k** thou not that I have power to crucify *1492*
21:15 Yea, Lord; thou **k** that I love thee. *1492*
21:16 Yea, Lord; thou **k** that I love thee. *1492*
21:17 thou **k** all *things;* thou knowest that I love *1492*
21:17 thou knowest all *things;* thou **k** that I love *1097*
Ac 1:24 which **k** the **hearts** of all *men*, shew *2589*
25:10 have I done no wrong, as thou very well **k**. *1921*
Ro 2:18 And **k** *his* will, and approvest the *things* *1097*
1Co 7:16 For what **k** thou, O wife, whether thou shalt *1492*
7:16 or how **k** thou, O man, whether thou shalt *1492*
2Ti 1:15 This thou **k**, that all they which are in Asia *1492*
1:18 *unto me* at Ephesus, thou **k** very well. *1097*
Rev 3:17 and **k** not that thou art wretched, and *1492*
7:14 And I said unto him, Sir, thou **k**. And he *1492*

KNOWETH (104) [KNOW]

Ge 33:13 My lord **k** that the children *are* tender, and 3045
Lev 5: 3 when he **k** *of it*, then he shall be guilty. 3045
5: 4 when he **k** *of it*, then he shall be guilty in 3045
Dt 2: 7 he **k** thy walking *through* this great 3045
34: 6 but no man **k** of his sepulchre unto this day. 3045
Jos 22:22 of gods, he **k**, and Israel he shall know; 3045
1Sa 3:13 house for ever for the iniquity which he **k**; 3045
20: 3 Thy father **certainly k** that I have 3045+3045
23:17 unto thee; and that also Saul my father **k**. 3045
2Sa 14:22 To day thy servant **k** that I have found 3045
17:10 for all Israel **k** that thy father *is* a mighty 3045
1Ki 1:11 doth reign, and David our lord **k** *it* not? 3045
Est 4:14 who **k** whether thou art come to 3045
Job 11:11 For he **k** vain men: he seeth wickedness 3045
12: 3 to you: yea, who **k** not such *things* as these? 854
12: 9 Who **k** not in all these that the hand of 3045
14:21 His sons come to honour, and he **k** *it* not; 3045
15:23 *saying*, Where *is it?* he **k** that the day of 3045
18:21 and this *is* the place *of him that* **k** not God. 3045
23:10 he **k** the way that I take: *when* he hath tried 3045
28: 7 *There is* a path which no fowl **k**, and 3045
28:13 Man **k** not the price thereof; neither is it 3045
28:23 the way thereof, and he **k** the place thereof. 3045
34:25 Therefore he **k** their works, and 5234
35:15 his anger; yet he **k** *it* not in great extremity: 3045
Ps 1: 6 For the LORD **k** the way of the righteous: 3045
37:18 The LORD **k** the days of the upright: and 3045
39: 6 up *riches*, and **k** not who shall gather them. 3045
44:21 this out? for he **k** the secrets of the heart. 3045
74: 9 neither *is there* among us any that **k** how 3045
90:11 Who **k** the power of thine anger? 3045
92: 6 A brutish man **k** not; neither doth a fool 3045
94:11 The LORD **k** the thoughts of man, 3045
103:14 For he **k** our frame; he remembereth that 3045
104:19 for seasons: the sun **k** his going down. 3045
138: 6 unto the lowly: but the proud he **k** afar off. 3045
139:14 thy works; and *that* my soul **k** right well. 3045
Pr 7:23 to the snare, and **k** not that it *is* for his life. 3045
9:13 *is* clamorous: *she is* simple, and **k** nothing. 3045
9:18 he **k** not that the dead *are* there; *and* 3045
14:10 The heart **k** his own bitterness; and 3045
24:22 and who **k** the ruin of them both? 3045
Ecc 2:19 who **k** whether he shall be a wise *man* or 3045
3:21 Who **k** the spirit of man that goeth upward, 3045
6: 8 the poor, that **k** to walk before the living? 3045
6:12 For who **k** what *is* good for man in *this* life, 3045
7:22 For oftentimes also thine own heart **k** that 3045
8: 1 and who **k** the interpretation of a thing? 3045
8: 7 For he **k** not that which shall be: for who 3045
9: 1 no man **k** either love or hatred *by* all *that is* 3045
9:12 For man also **k** not his time: as the fishes 3045
10:15 because he **k** not how to go to the city. 3045
Isa 1: 3 The ox **k** his owner, and the ass his 3045
29:15 and they say, Who seeth us? and who **k** us? 3045
Jer 8: 7 the stork in the heaven **k** her appointed 3045
9:24 in this, that *he* understandeth and **k** me, 3045
Da 2:22 secret *things:* he **k** what *is* in the darkness, 3046
Hos 7: 9 have devoured his strength, and he **k** *it* not: 3045
7: 9 are here and there upon him, yet he **k** not. 3045
Joel 2:14 Who **k** *if* he will return and repent, and 3045
Na 1: 7 of trouble; and he **k** them that trust in him. 3045
Zep 3: 5 he faileth not; but the unjust **k** no shame. 3045
Mt 6: 8 for your Father **k** what *things* ye have need *1492*
6:32 for your heavenly Father **k** that ye have *1492*
11:27 and no *man* **k** the Son, but the Father; *1921*
11:27 neither **k** any *man* the Father, save the Son, *1921*
24:36 But of that day and hour **k** no *man*, no, *1492*
Mk 4:27 should spring and grow up, he **k** not how. *1492*
13:32 But of that day and *that* hour **k** no *man*, no, *1492*
Lk 10:22 and no *man* **k** who the Son is, but *1097*
12:30 your Father **k** that ye have need of these *1492*
16:15 before men; but God **k** your hearts: *1097*
Jn 7:15 saying, How **k** this *man* letters, *1492*
7:27 Christ cometh, no *man* **k** whence he is. *1097*
7:49 But this people who **k** not the law are *1097*
10:15 As the Father **k** me, *even* so know I *1097*
12:35 for he that walketh in darkness **k** not *1492*
14:17 because it seeth him not, neither **k** him: *1097*
15:15 for the servant **k** not what his lord doeth: *1492*
19:35 and he **k** that he saith true, that ye might *1492*
Ac 15: 8 And God, which **k** the **hearts**, bare them *2589*
19:35 what man is there that **k** not how that *1097*
26:26 For the king **k** of these *things*, before whom *1987*
Ro 8:27 And he that searcheth the hearts **k** what *is* *1492*
1Co 2:11 For what man **k** the *things* of a man, *1492*
2:11 even so the *things* of God **k** no *man*, but *1492*
3:20 The Lord **k** the thoughts of the wise, *1097*
8: 2 And if any *man* think that *he* **k** any *thing*, *1492*
8: 2 he **k** nothing yet as he ought to know. *1097*
2Co 11:11 because I love you not? God **k**. *1492*
11:31 is blessed for evermore, **k** that I lie not. *1492*
12: 2 God **k**;) such a one caught up to the third *1492*
12: 3 or out of the body, I cannot tell: God **k**;) *1492*
2Ti 2:19 this seal, The Lord **k** them that are his. *1097*
Jas 4:17 Therefore to him that **k** to do good, and *1492*
2Pe 2: 9 The Lord **k** *how* to deliver the godly out of *1492*
1Jn 2:11 and **k** not whither he goeth, because *1492*
3: 1 therefore the world **k** us not, because *1097*
3:20 is greater than our heart, and **k** all *things*. *1097*
4: 6 he that **k** God heareth us; *he* that is not of *1097*
4: 7 one that loveth is born of God, and **k** God. *1097*
4: 8 He that loveth not, **k** not God; for God is *1097*
Rev 2:17 which no *man* **k** saving he that receiveth *it*. *1097*
12:12 because he **k** that he hath *but* a short time. *1492*

KNOWING (51) [KNOW]

Ge 3: 5 and ye shall be as gods, **k** good and evil. 3045
1Ki 2:32 my father David not **k** *thereof, to wit*, 3045
Mt 9: 4 And Jesus **k** their thoughts said, *1492*
22:29 unto them, Ye do err, not **k** the scriptures, *1492*
Mk 5:30 And Jesus immediately **k** in himself that *1921*
5:33 **k** what was done in her, came and *1492*
6:20 **k** that he *was* a just man and a holy, and *1492*
12:15 But he, **k** their hypocrisy, said unto them, *1492*
Lk 8:53 laughed him to scorn, **k** that she was dead. *1492*
9:33 and one for Elias: not **k** what he said. *1492*
11:17 But he, **k** their thoughts, said unto them, *1492*
Jn 13: 3 Jesus **k** that the Father had given all *things* *1492*
18: 4 **k** all *things* that should come upon him, *1492*
19:28 Jesus **k** that all *things* were now *1492*
21:12 Who art thou? **k** that it was the Lord. *1492*
Ac 2:30 **k** that God had sworn with an oath to him, *1492*
5: 7 his wife, not **k** what was done, came in. *1492*
18:25 of the Lord, **k** only the baptism of John. *1987*
20:22 not **k** the *things* that shall befall me there: *1492*
Ro 1:32 Who **k** the judgment of God, that they *1921*
2: 4 **not k** that the goodness of God leadeth thee to *50*
5: 3 **k** that tribulation worketh patience; *1492*
6: 6 **K** this, that our old man is crucified with *1097*
6: 9 **K** that Christ being raised from the dead *1492*
13:11 And that, **k** the time, that now *it is* high *1492*
2Co 1: 7 And our hope of you *is* stedfast, **k**, that as *1492*
4:14 **K** that he which raised up the Lord Jesus *1492*
5: 6 **k** that, whilst we are at home in the body, *1492*
5:11 **K** therefore the terror of the Lord, *1492*
Gal 2:16 **K** that a man is not justified by the works *1492*
Eph 6: 8 **K** that whatsoever good *thing* any man *1492*
6: 9 **k** that your Master also is in heaven; *1492*
Php 1:17 **k** that I am set for the defence of *1492*
Col 3:24 **K** that of the Lord ye shall receive *1492*
4: 1 **k** that ye also have a Master in heaven. *1492*
1Th 1: 4 **K**, brethren beloved, your election of God. *1492*
1Ti 1: 9 **K** this, that the law is not made for a *1492*
6: 4 **k** nothing, but doting about questions and *1987*
2Ti 2:23 **k** that they do gender strifes. *1492*
3:14 **k** of whom thou hast learned *them;* *1492*
Tit 3:11 **K** that *he that is* such is subverted, and *1492*
Phm 1:21 **k** that thou wilt also do more than I say. *1492*
Heb 10:34 **k** in yourselves that *ye* have in heaven a *1097*
11: 8 and he went out, not **k** whither he went. *1987*
Jas 1: 3 **K** *this*, that the trying of your faith worketh *1097*
3: 1 **k** that we shall receive the greater *1492*
1Pe 3: 9 **k** that ye are thereunto called, that ye *1492*
5: 9 **k** that the same afflictions are *1492*
2Pe 1:14 **K** that shortly *I* must put off *this* my *1492*
1:20 **K** this first, that no prophecy of *1097*
3: 3 **K** this first, that there shall come in the last *1097*

KNOWLEDGE (172) [KNOW]

Ge 2: 9 and the tree of **k** of good and evil. 1847
2:17 of the tree of the **k** of good and evil, 1847
Ex 31: 3 in **k**, and in all *manner of* workmanship, 1847
35:31 in **k**, and in all *manner of* workmanship; 1847
Lev 4:23 wherein he hath sinned, **come to** his **k**, 3045
4:28 **come to** his **k**, then he shall bring his 3045
Nu 15:24 **without** the **k** of the congregation, 4480+5869
24:16 of God, and knew the **k** of the most High, 1847
Dt 1:39 which *in that* day **had no k** between good 3045
Ru 2:10 that *thou* shouldest **take k** of me, seeing I 5234
2:19 blessed be he that did **take k** of thee. 5234
1Sa 2: 3 for the LORD *is* a God of **k**, and by him 1844
23:23 **take k** of all the lurking places where he 3045
1Ki 9:27 shipmen that had **k** of the sea, with 3045
2Ch 1:10 Give me now wisdom and **k**, that I may go 4093
1:11 hast asked wisdom and **k** for thyself, 4093
1:12 Wisdom and **k** *is* granted unto thee; and 4093
8:18 and servants that had **k** of the sea; 3045
30:22 **taught** the good **k** of the LORD: 7919+7922
Ne 10:28 every one **having k**, *and* 3045
Job 15: 2 Should a wise *man* utter vain **k**, and fill his 1847
21:14 for we desire not the **k** of thy ways. 1847
21:22 Shall *any* teach God **k**? seeing he judgeth 1847
33: 3 my heart: and my lips shall utter **k** clearly. 1847
34: 2 and give ear unto me, ye that **have k**. 3045
34:35 Job hath spoken without **k**, and his words 1847
35:16 in vain; he multiplieth words without **k**. 1847
36: 3 I will fetch my **k** from afar, and will ascribe 1843
36: 4 *be* false: *he that is* perfect in **k** *is* with thee. 1844
36:12 by the sword, and they shall die without **k**. 1847
37:16 works of *him which is* perfect in **k**? 1843
38: 2 that darkeneth counsel by words without **k**? 1847
42: 3 Who *is* he that hideth counsel without **k**? 1847
Ps 14: 4 Have all the workers of iniquity no **k**? 3045
19: 2 and night unto night sheweth **k**. 1847
53: 4 Have the workers of iniquity no **k**? who eat 3045
73:11 and is there **k** in the most High? 1844
94:10 he that teacheth man **k**, *shall not he know?* 1847
119:66 Teach me good judgment and **k**: for I have 1847
139: 6 *Such* **k** *is* too wonderful for me; it is high, 1847
144: 3 what *is* man, that thou **takest k** of him? 3045
Pr 1: 4 to the young man **k** and discretion. 1847
1: 7 fear of the LORD *is* the beginning of **k**: 1847
1:22 delight in their scorning, and fools hate **k**? 1847
1:29 For that they hated **k**, and did not choose 1847
2: 3 if thou criest after **k**, *and* liftest up thy voice 998
2: 5 fear of the LORD, and find the **k** of God. 1847
2: 6 out of his mouth *cometh* **k** and 1847
2:10 thine heart, and **k** is pleasant unto thy soul; 1847
3:20 By his **k** the depths are broken up, and 1847
5: 2 and *that* thy lips may keep **k**. 1847
8: 9 and right to them that find **k**. 1847
8:10 not silver; and **k** rather than choice gold. 1847
8:12 and find out **k** of witty inventions. 1847
9:10 and the **k** of the holy *is* understanding. 1847
10:14 Wise *men* lay up **k**: but the mouth of 1847
11: 9 but through **k** shall the just be delivered. 1847
12: 1 Whoso loveth instruction loveth **k**: but 1847
12:23 A prudent man concealeth **k**: but the heart 1847
13:16 Every prudent *man* dealeth with **k**: but 1847
14: 6 but **k** *is* easy unto him that understandeth. 1847
14: 7 thou perceivest not *in him* the lips of **k**. 1847
14:18 but the prudent are crowned *with* **k**. 1847
15: 2 The tongue of the wise useth **k** aright: but 1847
15: 7 The lips of the wise disperse **k**: but 1847
15:14 of him that hath understanding seeketh **k**: 1847
17:27 He that **hath k** spareth his words: 1847+3045
18:15 The heart of the prudent getteth **k**; and 1847
18:15 and the ear of the wise seeketh **k**. 1847

Pr 19: 2 Also, *that* the soul *be* without **k**, *it is* not 1847
19:25 *and* he will understand **k**. 1847
19:27 *that causeth* to err from the words of **k**. 1847
20:15 but the lips of **k** *are* a precious jewel. 1847
21:11 when the wise is instructed, he receiveth **k**. 1847
22:12 The eyes of the LORD preserve **k**, and 1847
22:17 the wise, and apply thine heart unto my **k**. 1847
22:20 to thee excellent things in counsels and **k**, 1847
23:12 and thine ears to the words of **k**. 1847
24: 4 by **k** shall the chambers be filled *with* all 1847
24: 5 yea, a man of **k** increaseth strength. 1847
24:14 So shall the **k** of wisdom be unto thy soul: 3045
28: 2 *and* **k** the state *thereof* shall be prolonged. 3045
30: 3 nor **have** the **k** of the holy. 1847+3045
Ecc 1:16 had great experience of wisdom and **k**. 1847
1:18 and he that increaseth **k** increaseth sorrow. 1847
2:21 *is* in wisdom, and in **k**, and in equity; 1847
2:26 *is* good in his sight wisdom, and **k**, and joy: 1847
7:12 the excellency of **k** *is, that* wisdom giveth 1847
9:10 nor device, nor **k**, nor wisdom, in the grave, 1847
12: 9 was wise, he still taught the people **k**; 1847
Isa 5:13 into captivity, because *they have* no **k**: 1847
8: 4 For before the child shall have **k** to cry, 3045
11: 2 the spirit of **k** and of the fear of 1847
11: 9 for the earth shall be full *of* the **k** of 1844
28: 9 Whom shall he teach **k**? and whom shall he 1844
32: 4 heart also of the rash shall understand **k**, 1847
33: 6 and **k** shall be the stability of thy times, 1847
40:14 taught him **k**, and shewed to him the way 1847
44:19 neither *is there* **k** nor understanding to say, 1847
44:25 *men* backward, and maketh their **k** foolish; 1847
45:20 they have no **k** that set up the wood of their 3045
47:10 Thy wisdom and thy **k**, it hath perverted 1847
53:11 by his **k** shall my righteous servant justify 1847
58: 3 we afflicted our soul, and thou **takest** no **k**? 3045
Jer 3:15 which shall feed you with **k** and 1844
4:22 to do evil, but to do good they have no **k**. 3045
10:14 Every man is brutish in *his* **k**: 1847
11:18 the LORD hath **given** me **k** *of it,* and 3045
51:17 Every man is brutish by *his* **k**; 1847
Da 1: 4 cunning in **k**, and understanding science, 1847
1:17 God gave them **k** and skill in all learning 4093
2:21 and **k** to them that know understanding: 4486
5:12 **k**, and understanding, interpreting of 4486
12: 4 run to and fro, and **k** shall be increased. 1847
Hos 4: 1 nor mercy, nor **k** of God in the land. 1847
4: 6 My people are destroyed for lack of **k**, 1847
4: 6 because thou hast rejected **k**, I will also 1847
6: 6 and the **k** of God more than burnt offerings. 1847
Hab 2:14 For the earth shall be filled with the **k** of 3045
Mal 2: 7 For the priest's lips should keep **k**, and 1847
Mt 14:35 And when the men of that place **had k** of 1921
Lk 1:77 To give **k** of salvation unto his people by 1108
11:52 for ye have taken away the key of **k**: 1108
Ac 4:13 and they **took k** of them, that they had been 1921
17:13 But when the Jews of Thessalonica had **k** 1097
24: 8 **k** of all these *things,* whereof we accuse 1921
24:22 *things,* having more perfect **k** of *that* way, 1492
Ro 1:28 as they did not like to retain God in *their* **k**, 1922
2:20 which hast the form of **k** and of the truth in 1108
3:20 in his sight: for by the law *is* the **k** of sin. 1922
10: 2 have a zeal of God, but not according to **k**. 1922
11:33 riches both of the wisdom and **k** of God! 1108
15:14 also are full of goodness, filled with all **k**, 1108
1Co 1: 5 by him, in all utterance, and *in* all **k**; 1108
8: 1 unto idols, we know that we all have **k**. 1108
8: 1 **K** puffeth up, but charity edifieth. 1108
8: 7 Howbeit *there is* not in every man *that* **k**: 1108
8:10 For if any *man* see thee which hast **k** sit at 1108
8:11 And through thy **k** shall the weak brother 1108
12: 8 to another the word of **k** by the same Spirit; 1108
13: 2 and understand all mysteries, and all **k**; 1108
13: 8 whether *there be* **k**, it shall vanish away. 1108
14: 6 or by **k**, or by prophesying, or by doctrine? 1108
15:34 for some have **not** the **k** of God: I speak *this* 56
2Co 2:14 maketh manifest the savour of his **k** by us 1108
4: 6 to give the light of the **k** of the glory of 1108
6: 6 By pureness, by **k**, by longsuffering, 1108
8: 7 and **k**, and *in* all diligence, and *in* your love 1108
10: 5 that exalteth itself against the **k** of God, 1108
11: 6 though *I be* rude in speech, yet not in **k**; 1108
Eph 1:17 of wisdom and revelation in the **k** of him: 1922
3: 4 ye may understand my **k** in the mystery of 4907
3:19 know the love of Christ, which passeth **k**, 1108
4:13 and of the **k** of the Son of God, unto a 1922
Php 1: 9 and more in **k** and *in* all judgment; 1922
3: 8 loss for the excellency of the **k** of Christ 1108
Col 1: 9 to desire that ye might be filled *with* the **k** 1922
1:10 good work, and increasing in the **k** of God; 1922
2: 3 are hid all the treasures of wisdom and **k**. 1108
3:10 **k** after the image of him that created him: 1922
1Ti 2: 4 and to come unto the **k** of the truth. 1922
2Ti 3: 7 and never able to come to the **k** of the truth. 1922
Heb 10:26 that *we* have received the **k** of the truth, 1922
Jas 3:13 wise *man* and endued with **k** amongst you? 1990
1Pe 3: 7 dwell with *them* according to **k**, 1108
2Pe 1: 2 peace be multiplied unto you through the **k** 1922
1: 3 through the **k** of him that hath called us to 1922
1: 5 add to your faith virtue; and to virtue **k**; 1108
1: 6 And to **k** temperance; and to temperance 1108
1: 8 unfruitful in the **k** of our Lord Jesus Christ. 1922
2:20 of the world through the **k** of the Lord 1922
3:18 and *in* the **k** of our Lord and Saviour Jesus 1108

KNOWN (222) [KNOW]

Ge 19: 8 I have two daughters which have not **k** 3045
24:16 a virgin, neither had any man **k** her: 3045
41:21 it could not be **k** that they had eaten them; 3045
41:31 the plenty shall not be **k** in the land by 3045
45: 1 while Joseph **made** himself **k** unto his 3045
Ex 2:14 and said, Surely *this* thing is **k** 3045
6: 3 *by* my name JEHOVAH was I not **k** to 3045
21:36 Or *if* it be **k** that the ox *hath* used to push in 3045
33:16 For wherein shall it be **k** here that I and 3045
Lev 4:14 is **k**, then the congregation shall offer a 3045
Lev 5: 1 or **k** *of it;* if he do not utter *it,* then 3045
Nu 12: 6 *I* the LORD will **make** myself **k** unto him 3045
31:17 kill every woman that hath **k** man by lying 3045
31:18 that have not **k** a man by lying with him, 3045
31:35 of women that had not **k** man by lying with 3045
Dt 1:13 **k** among your tribes, and I will make them 3045
1:15 and **k**, and made them heads over you, 3045
11: 2 not with your children which have not **k**, 3045
11:28 to go after other gods, which ye have not **k**. 3045
13: 2 which thou hast not **k**, and let us serve 3045
13: 6 which thou hast not **k**, thou, nor thy fathers; 3045
13:13 and serve other gods, which ye have not **k**; 3045
21: 1 *and* it be not **k** who hath slain him: 3045
28:36 which neither thou nor thy fathers have **k**; 3045
28:64 which neither thou nor thy fathers have **k**, 3045
31:13 which have not **k** *any thing,* may hear, and 3045
Jos 24:31 which had **k** all the works of the LORD, 3045
Jdg 3: 1 *even* as many *of Israel* as had not **k** all 3045
16: 9 toucheth the fire. So his strength was not **k**. 3045
21:12 that had **k** no man by lying with *any* male: 3045
Ru 3: 3 *but* **make** not thyself **k** unto the man, 3045
3:14 Let it not be **k** that a woman came *into* 3045
1Sa 6: 3 it shall be **k** to you why his hand is not 3045
28:15 that *thou* mayest **make k** unto me what I 3045
2Sa 17:19 corn thereon; and the thing was not **k**. 3045
1Ki 14: 2 that thou be not **k** to be the wife of 3045
18:36 let it be **k** *this* day that thou *art* God in 3045
1Ch 16: 8 **make k** his deeds among the people. 3045
17:19 in **making k** all *these* great things. 3045
Ezr 4:12 Be it **k** unto the king, that the Jews which 3046
4:13 Be it **k** now unto the king, that, if this city 3046
5: 8 Be it **k** unto the king, that we went into 3046
Ne 4:15 when our enemies heard that it was **k** unto 3045
9:14 **madest k** unto them thy holy sabbath, and 3045
Est 2:22 the thing was **k** to Mordecai, who told *it* 3045
Ps 9:16 The LORD is **k** *by* the judgment *which* he 3045
18:43 a people *whom* I have not **k** shall serve me. 3045
31: 7 thou hast **k** my soul in adversities; 3045
48: 3 God is **k** in her palaces for a refuge. 3045
67: 2 That thy way may be **k** upon earth, 3045
69:19 Thou hast **k** my reproach, and my shame, 3045
76: 1 In Judah *is* God **k**: his name *is* great in 3045
77:19 great waters, and thy footsteps are not **k**. 3045
78: 3 Which we have heard and **k**, and 3045
78: 5 that *they* should **make** them **k** to their 3045
79: 6 upon the heathen that have not **k** thee, 3045
79:10 let him be **k** among the heathen in our sight 3045
88:12 Shall thy wonders be **k** in the dark? and 3045
89: 1 with my mouth will I **make k** thy 3045
91:14 him on high, because he hath **k** my name. 3045
95:10 *their* heart, and they have not **k** my ways: 3045
98: 2 The LORD hath **made k** his salvation: 3045
103: 7 He **made k** his ways unto Moses, his acts 3045
105: 1 **make k** his deeds among the people. 3045
106: 8 *he* might **make** his mighty power **to be k**. 3045
119:79 and those that have **k** thy testimonies. 3045
119:152 I have **k** of old that thou hast founded them 3045
139: 1 thou hast searched me, and **k** *me*. 3045
145:12 To **make k** to the sons of men his mighty 3045
147:20 *as for his* judgments, they have not **k** them. 3045
Pr 1:23 I will **make k** my words unto you. 3045
10: 9 but he that perverteth his ways shall be **k**. 3045
12:16 A fool's wrath is presently **k**: but a prudent 3045
14:33 *which is* in the midst of fools is **made k**. 3045
20:11 Even a child is **k** by his doings, whether his 5234
22:19 I have **made k** to thee *this* day, even *to* 3045
31:23 Her husband is **k** in the gates, when he 3045
Ecc 5: 3 a fool's voice *is* **k** by multitude of words. NIH
6: 5 nor **k** *any thing:* this hath more rest than 3045
6:10 is named already, and *it is* **k** that it *is* man: 3045
Isa 12: 5 excellent things: this *is* **k** in all the earth. 3045
19:21 the LORD shall be **k** to Egypt, and 3045
38:19 the father to the children shall **make k** thy 3045
40:21 Have ye not **k**? have ye not heard? hath it 3045
40:28 Hast thou not **k**? hast thou not heard, 3045
42:16 will lead them in paths *that* they have not **k**: 3045
44:18 They have not **k** nor understood: for he 3045
45: 4 surnamed thee, though thou hast not **k** me. 3045
45: 5 I girded thee though thou hast not **k** me: 3045
61: 9 their seed shall be **k** among the Gentiles, 3045
64: 2 to **make** thy name **k** to thine adversaries, 3045
66:14 the hand of the LORD shall be **k** towards 3045
Jer 4:22 my people *is* foolish, they have not **k** me; 3045
5: 5 for they have **k** the way of the LORD, *and* 3045
9:16 whom neither they nor their fathers have **k**: 3045
19: 4 whom neither they nor their fathers have **k**, 3045
28: 9 *then* shall the prophet be **k**, that the LORD 3045
La 4: 8 than a coal; they are not **k** in the streets: 5234
Eze 20: 5 **made** myself **k** unto them in the land of 3045
20: 9 in whose sight I **made** myself **k** unto them, 3045
32: 9 into the countries which thou hast not **k**. 3045
35:11 I will **make** myself **k** amongst them, 3045
36:32 *this,* saith the Lord GOD, be it **k** unto you: 3045
38:23 I will be **k** in the eyes of many nations, and 3045
39: 7 So will I **make** my holy name **k** in 3045
Da 2: 5 if ye will not **make k** unto me the dream, 3046
2: 9 if ye will not **make k** unto me the dream, 3046
2:15 Then Arioch **made** the thing **k** to Daniel. 3046
2:17 **made** the thing **k** to Hananiah, Mishael, 3046
2:23 hast **made k** unto me now what we desired 3046
2:23 for thou hast *now* **made k** unto us 3046
2:25 that will **make k** unto the king 3046
2:26 Art thou able to **make k** unto me the dream 3046
2:28 **maketh k** to the king Nebuchadnezzar 3046
2:29 he that revealeth secrets **maketh k** to thee 3046
2:30 for *their* sakes that shall **make k** 3046
2:45 the great God hath **made k** to the king what 3046
3:18 if not, be it **k** unto thee, O king, that we 3046
4: 6 that they might **make k** unto me 3046
4: 7 they *did* not **make k** unto me 3046
4:18 able to **make** it **k** unto me the interpretation: 3046
4:26 after that thou shalt have **k** that the heavens 3046
5: 8 nor **make k** to the king the interpretation 3046
5:15 **make k** unto me the interpretation thereof: 3046
5:16 **make k** to me the interpretation thereof, 3046
Da 5:17 and **make k** to him the interpretation. 3046
Hos 5: 4 of them, and they have not **k** the LORD. 3045
5: 9 among the tribes of Israel have I **made k** 3045
Am 3: 2 You only have I **k** of all the families of 3045
Na 3:17 and their place is not **k** where they *are*. 3045
Hab 3: 2 the years, in the midst of the years **make k**; 3045
Zec 14: 7 it shall be one day which shall be **k** to 3045
Mt 10:26 not be revealed; and hid, that shall not be **k**. 1097
12: 7 But if ye had **k** what *this* meaneth, I will 1097
12:16 them that they should not make him **k**: 5318
12:33 fruit corrupt: for the tree is **k** by *his* fruit. 1097
24:43 that if the goodman of the house had **k** in 1492
Mk 3:12 them that they should not make him **k**. 5318
Lk 2:15 which the Lord hath **made k** unto us. 1107
2:17 **made k abroad** the saying which was told 1232
6:44 For every tree is **k** by his own fruit. For of 1097
7:39 would have **k** who and what manner of 1097
8:17 that shall not be **k** and come abroad. 1097
12: 2 be revealed; neither hid, that shall not be **k**. 1097
12:39 that if the goodman of the house had **k** 1492
19:42 Saying, If thou hadst **k**, even thou, at least 1097
24:18 hast not **k** the *things* which are come to 1097
24:35 how he was **k** of them in breaking of bread. 1097
Jn 7: 4 he himself seeketh to be **k openly**. 1722+3954
8:19 if ye had **k** me, ye should have known my 1492
8:19 ye should have **k** my Father also. 1492
8:55 Yet ye have not **k** him; but I know him: and 1097
10:14 and know my *sheep,* and am **k** of mine. 1097
14: 7 If ye had **k** me, ye should have known my 1097
14: 7 ye should have **k** my Father also: 1097
14: 9 and *yet* hast thou not **k** me, Philip? 1097
15:15 of my Father I have **made k** unto you. 1107
16: 3 because they have not **k** the Father, nor me. 1097
17: 7 Now they have **k** that all *things* whatsoever 1097
17: 8 have **k** surely that I came out from thee, 1097
17:25 righteous Father, the world hath not **k** thee: 1097
17:25 but I have **k** thee, and these have known 1097
17:25 and these have **k** that thou hast sent me. 1097
18:15 that disciple was **k** unto the high priest, and 1110
18:16 which was **k** unto the high priest, and 1110
Ac 1:19 And it was **k** unto all the dwellers at 1110
2:14 be this **k** unto you, and hearken to my 1110
2:28 Thou hast **made k** to me the ways of life; 1107
4:10 Be it **k** unto you all, and to all the people of 1110
7:13 And at the second time Joseph was **made k** 319
7:13 Joseph's kindred was made **k** unto Pharaoh. 5318
9:24 But their laying await was **k** of Saul. 1097
9:42 And it was **k** throughout all Joppa; and 1110
13:38 Be it **k** unto you therefore, men *and* 1110
15:18 **K** unto God are all his works from 1110
19:17 And this was **k** to all the Jews and 1110
22:30 he would have **k** the certainty wherefore he 1097
23:28 And when I would have **k** the cause 1097
28:28 Be it **k** therefore unto you, that 1110
Ro 1:19 Because that which may be **k** of God is 1110
3:17 And the way of peace have they not **k**: 1097
7: 7 Nay, I had not **k** sin, but by the law: for I 1097
7: 7 for I had not **k** lust, except the law had said, 1492
9:22 shew *his* wrath, and to **make** his power **k**, 1107
9:23 And that he might **make k** the riches of his 1107
11:34 For who hath **k** the mind of the Lord? or 1097
16:26 **made k** to all nations for the obedience of 1107
1Co 2: 8 for had they **k** *it,* they would not have 1097
2:16 For who hath **k** the mind of the Lord, 1097
8: 3 if any *man* love God, the same is **k** of him. 1097
13:12 but then shall I know even as also I am **k**. 1921
14: 7 how shall it be **k** what is piped or harped? 1097
14: 9 how shall it be **k** what is spoken? 1097
2Co 3: 2 written in our hearts, **k** and read of all men: 1097
5:16 though we have **k** Christ after the flesh, 1097
6: 9 As unknown, and *yet* **well k**; as dying, and 1921
Gal 4: 9 after that ye have **k** God, or rather are 1097
4: 9 or rather are **k** of God, how turn ye again to 1097
Eph 1: 9 Having **made k** unto us the mystery of his 1107
3: 3 How that by revelation he **made k** unto me 1107
3: 5 Which in other ages was not **made k** unto 1107
3:10 powers in heavenly *places* might be **k** by 1107
6:19 to **make k** the mystery of the gospel, 1107
6:21 in the Lord, shall **make k** to you all *things:* 1107
Php 4: 5 Let your moderation be **k** unto all men. 1097
4: 6 let your requests be **made k** unto God. 1107
Col 1:27 To whom God would **make k** what *is* 1107
4: 9 They shall **make k** unto you all *things* 1107
2Ti 3:10 But thou hast **fully k** my doctrine, manner 3877
3:15 And that from a child thou hast **k** the holy 1492
4:17 that by me the preaching might be **fully k**, 4135
Heb 3:10 *their* heart; and they have not **k** my ways. 1097
2Pe 1:16 when we **made k** unto you the power and 1107
2:21 it had been better for them not to have **k** 1921
2:21 after they have **k** *it,* to turn from the holy 1921
1Jn 2:13 ye have **k** him that is from the beginning. 1097
2:13 because ye have **k** the Father. 1097
2:14 ye have **k** him that is from the beginning. 1097
3: 6 sinneth hath not seen him, neither **k** him. 1097
4:16 And we have **k** and believed the love that 1097
2Jn 1: 1 but also all they that have **k** the truth; 1097
Rev 2:24 and which have not **k** the depths of Satan, 1097

KOA (1)

Eze 23:23 all the Chaldeans, Pekod, and Shoa, and **K**, 6970

KOHATH (32) [KOHATHITES]

Ge 46:11 the sons of Levi; Gershon, **K**, and Merari. 6955
Ex 6:16 Gershon, and **K**, and Merari: 6955
6:18 the sons of **K**; Amram, and Izhar, and 6955
6:18 the years of the life of **K** *were* an hundred 6955
Nu 3:17 their names; Gershon, and **K**, and Merari. 6955
3:19 the sons of **K** by their families; Amram, 6955
3:27 of **K** *was* the family of the Amramites, and 6955
3:29 The families of the sons of **K** shall pitch on 6955
4: 2 Take the sum of the sons of **K** from among 6955
4: 4 This *shall be* the service of the sons of **K** in 6955
4:15 the sons of **K** shall come to bear *it:* but 6955
4:15 of **K** in the tabernacle of the congregation. 6955
7: 9 unto the sons of **K** he gave none: because 6955

Nu 16: 1 the son of **K**, the son of Levi, and Dathan 6955
26:57 of **K**, the family of the Kohathites: 6955
26:58 of the Korahites. And **K** begat Amram. 6955
Jos 21: 5 the rest of the children of **K** had by lot out 6955
21:20 the families of the children of **K**, 6955
21:20 which remained of the children of **K**, 6955
21:26 families of the children of **K** that remained. 6955
1Ch 6: 1 The sons of Levi; Gershon, **K**, and Merari. 6955
6: 2 the sons of **K**; Amram, Izhar, and Hebron, 6955
6:16 The sons of Levi; Gershom, **K**, and Merari. 6955
6:18 And the sons of **K** *were*, Amram, and Izhar, 6955
6:22 The sons of **K**; Amminadab his son, 6955
6:38 the son of **K**, the son of Levi, the son of 6955
6:61 unto the sons of **K**, which were left of 6955
6:66 *the residue* of the families of the sons of **K** 6955
6:70 the family of the remnant of the sons of **K**. 6955
15: 5 Of the sons of **K**; Uriel the chief, and 6955
23: 6 of Levi, *namely*, Gershon, **K**, and Merari. 6955
23:12 The sons of **K**; Amram, Izhar, Hebron, and 6955

KOHATHITES (15) [KOHATH]

Nu 3:27 these *are* the families of the **K**. 6956
3:30 the **K** *shall be* Elizaphan the son of Uzziel. 6956
4:18 families of the **K** from among the Levites: 6956
4:34 the sons of the **K** after their families, 6956
4:37 were numbered of the families of the **K**, 6956
10:21 the **K** set forward, bearing the sanctuary: 6956
26:57 of Kohath, the family of the **K**: of Merari, 6956
Jos 21: 4 the lot came out for the families of the **K**: 6956
21:10 of Aaron, *being* of the families of the **K**, 6956
1Ch 6:33 Of the sons of the **K**: Heman a singer, 6956
6:54 the sons of Aaron, of the families of the **K**: 6956
9:32 of the sons of the **K**, *were* over 6956
2Ch 20:19 of the children of the **K**, and of the children 6956
29:12 the son of Azariah, of the sons of the **K**: 6956
34:12 and Meshullam, of the sons of the **K**, 6956

KOLAIAH (2)

Ne 11: 7 of Joed, the son of Pedaiah, the son of **K**, 6964
Jer 29:21 of Ahab the son of **K**, and of Zedekiah, 6964

KORAH (37) [KORAHITE, KORAHITES, KORHITES]

Ge 36: 5 bare Jeush, and Jaalam, and **K**: 7141
36:14 she bare to Esau Jeush, and Jaalam, and **K**. 7141
36:16 Duke **K**, duke Gatam, *and* duke Amalek: 7141
36:18 duke Jeush, duke Jaalam, duke **K**: 7141
Ex 6:21 sons of Izhar; **K**, and Nepheg, and Zichri. 7141
6:24 the sons of **K**; Assir, and Elkanah, and 7141
Nu 16: 1 Now **K**, the son of Izhar, the son of 7141
16: 5 he spake unto **K** and unto all his company, 7141
16: 6 Take you censers, **K**, and all his company; 7141
16: 8 Moses said unto **K**, Hear, I pray you, 7141
16:16 Moses said unto **K**, Be thou and all thy 7141
16:19 **K** gathered all the congregation against 7141
16:24 Get you up from about the tabernacle of **K**, 7141
16:27 So they gat up from the tabernacle of **K**, 7141
16:32 all the men that *appertained* unto **K**, and 7141
16:40 that he be not as **K**, and as his company: 7141
16:49 them that died about the matter of **K**. 7141
26: 9 and against Aaron in the company of **K**, 7141
26:10 swallowed them up together with **K**, 7141
26:11 Notwithstanding the children of **K** died not. 7141
27: 3 against the LORD in the company of **K**; 7141
1Ch 1:35 Reuel, and Jeush, and Jaalam, and **K**. 7141
2:43 **K**, and Tappuah, and Rekem, and Shema. 7141
6:22 his son, **K** his son, Assir his son, 7141
6:37 of Assir, the son of Ebiasaph, the son of **K**, 7141
9:19 of Ebiasaph, the son of **K**, and his brethren, 7141
Ps 42: T chief Musician, Maschil, for the sons of **K**. 7141
44: T To the chief Musician for the sons of **K**, 7141
45: T for the sons of **K**, Maschil, A Song of 7141
46: T To the chief Musician for the sons of **K**, 7141
47: T chief Musician, A Psalm for the sons of **K**. 7141
48: T A Song *and* Psalm for the sons of **K**. 7141
49: T chief Musician, A Psalm for the sons of **K**. 7141
84: T upon Gittith, A Psalm for the sons of **K**. 7141
85: T chief Musician, A Psalm for the sons of **K**. 7141
87: T A Psalm *or* Song for the sons of **K**. 7141
88: T A Song *or* Psalm for the sons of **K**. To 7141

KORAHITE (1) [KORAH]

1Ch 9:31 who *was* the firstborn of Shallum the **K**, 7145

KORAHITES (2) [KORAH]

Nu 26:58 family of the Mushites, the family of the **K**. 7145
1Ch 9:19 of the house of his father, the **K**, 7145

KORAZIN See CHORAZIN

KORE (4)

1Ch 9:19 Shallum the son of **K**, the son of Ebiasaph, 6981
26: 1 Korhites *was* Meshelemiah the son of **K**, 6981
26:19 of the porters among the sons of **K**, 7145
2Ch 31:14 **K** the son of Imnah the Levite, the porter 6981

KORHITES (4) [KORAH]

Ex 6:24 Abiasaph: these *are* the families of the **K**. 7145
1Ch 12: 6 Azareel, and Joezer, and Jashobeam, the **K**, 7145
26: 1 Of the **K** *was* Meshelemiah the son of 7145
2Ch 20:19 and of the children of the **K**, 7145

KOUM See CUMI

KOZ (4)

Ezr 2:61 the children of Habaiah, the children of **K**, 6976
Ne 3: 4 Meremoth the son of Urijah, the son of **K**. 6976
3:21 son of Urijah the son of **K** another piece, 6976
7:63 the children of Habaiah, the children of **K**, 6976

KUSHAIAH (1)

1Ch 15:17 Merari their brethren, Ethan the son of **K**; 6984

L

LAADAH (1)

1Ch 4:21 **L** the father of Mareshah, and the families 3935

LAADAN (7)

1Ch 7:26 **L** his son, Ammihud his son, Elishama his 3936
23: 7 Of the Gershonites *were*, **L**, and Shimei. 3936
23: 8 The sons of **L**; the chief *was* Jehiel, and 3936
23: 9 These *were* the chief of the fathers of **L**. 3936
26:21 *As concerning* the sons of **L**; the sons of 3936
26:21 the sons of the Gershonite **L**, chief fathers, 3936
26:21 *even* of **L** the Gershonite, *were* Jehieli. 3936

LABAN (51) [LABAN'S]

Ge 24:29 had a brother, and his name *was* **L**: 3837
24:29 and **L** ran out unto the man, unto the well. 3837
24:50 **L** and Bethuel answered and said, 3837
25:20 of Padan-aram, the sister to **L** the Syrian. 3837
27:43 arise, flee thou to **L** my brother to Haran; 3837
28: 2 of the daughters of **L** thy mother's brother. 3837
28: 5 he went to Padan-aram unto **L**, son of 3837
29: 5 unto them, Know ye **L** the son of Nahor? 3837
29:10 when Jacob saw Rachel the daughter of **L** 3837
29:10 the sheep of **L** his mother's brother, 3837
29:10 watered the flock of **L** his mother's brother. 3837
29:13 when **L** heard the tidings of Jacob his 3837
29:13 to his house. And he told **L** all these things. 3837
29:14 And **L** said to him, Surely thou *art* my bone 3837
29:15 **L** said unto Jacob, Because thou *art* my 3837
29:16 **L** had two daughters: the name of the elder 3837
29:19 **L** said, *It is* better that I give her to thee, 3837
29:21 Jacob said unto **L**, Give *me* my wife, 3837
29:22 **L** gathered together all the men of 3837
29:24 **L** gave unto his daughter Leah Zilpah his 3837
29:25 he said to **L**, What *is* this thou hast done 3837
29:26 **L** said, It must not be so done in our 3837
29:29 **L** gave to Rachel his daughter Bilhah his 3837
30:25 that Jacob said unto **L**, Send me away, 3837
30:27 **L** said unto him, I pray thee, if I have found 3837
30:34 **L** said, Behold, I would it might be 3837
30:40 and all the brown in the flock of **L**; 3837
31: 2 Jacob beheld the countenance of **L**, and 3837
31:12 for I have seen all that **L** doeth unto thee. 3837
31:19 **L** went to shear his sheep: and Rachel had 3837
31:20 Jacob stale away unawares to **L** the Syrian, 3837
31:22 it was told **L** on the third day that Jacob 3837
31:24 God came to **L** the Syrian in a dream by 3837
31:25 **L** overtook Jacob. Now Jacob had pitched 3837
31:25 **L** with his brethren pitched in the mount of 3837
31:26 **L** said to Jacob, What hast thou done, 3837
31:31 Jacob answered and said to **L**, Because I 3837
31:33 **L** went into Jacob's tent, and into Leah's 3837
31:34 **L** searched all the tent, but found *them* not. 3837
31:36 Jacob was wroth, and chode with **L**: and 3837
31:36 Jacob answered and said to **L**, What *is* my 3837
31:43 **L** answered and said unto Jacob, *These* 3837
31:47 **L** called it Jegar-sahadutha: but 3837
31:48 **L** said, This heap *is* a witness between me 3837
31:51 **L** said to Jacob, Behold this heap, 3837
31:55 early in the morning **L** rose up, and 3837
31:55 **L** departed, and returned unto his place. 3837
32: 4 I have sojourned with **L**, and stayed *there* 3837
46:18 whom **L** gave to Leah his daughter, and 3837
46:25 which **L** gave unto Rachel his daughter, 3837
Dt 1: 1 and **L**, and Hazeroth, and Dizahab. 3837

LABAN'S (4) [LABAN]

Ge 30:36 and Jacob fed the rest of **L** flocks. 3837
30:40 and put them not unto **L** cattle. 3837
30:42 so the feebler were **L**, and the stronger 3837
31: 1 he heard the words of **L** sons, saying, 3837

LABOR See TRAVAIL; TRAVAILED; TRAVAILEST; TRAVAILETH

LABORERS See HIRELING

LABOUR (89) [FELLOWLABOURER, FELLOWLABOURERS, LABOURED, LABOURER, LABOURERS, LABOURETH, LABOURING, LABOURS]

Ge 31:42 seen mine affliction and the **l** of my hands, 3018
35:16 and Rachel travailed, and she had hard **l**. 3205
35:17 it came to pass, when she was in hard **l**, 3205
Ex 5: 9 laid upon the men, that they may **l** therein; 6213
20: 9 Six days shalt thou **l**, and do all thy work: 5647
Dt 5:13 Six days thou shalt **l**, and do all thy work: 5647
26: 7 and our **l**, and our oppression: 5999
Jos 7: 3 *and* **make** not all the people **to l** thither; 3021
24:13 given you a land for which ye did not **l**, 3021
Ne 4:22 they may be a guard to us, and **l** on the day. 4399
5:13 from his **l**, that performeth not this promise, 3018
Job 9:29 *If* I be wicked, why then **l** I in vain? 3021
39:11 *is* great? or wilt thou leave thy **l** to him? 3018
39:16 *were* not hers: her **l** *is* in vain without fear; 3018
Ps 78:46 the caterpillar, and their **l** unto the locust. 3018
90:10 yet *is* their strength **l** and sorrow; 5999
104:23 unto his work and to his **l** until the evening. 5656
105:44 and they inherited the **l** of the people; 5999
107:12 he brought down their heart with **l**; 5999
109:11 he hath; and let the strangers spoil his **l**. 3018
127: 1 build the house, they **l** in vain that build it: 5998
128: 2 For thou shalt eat the **l** of thine hands: 3018
144:14 *That* our oxen *may be* **strong to l**; 5445
Pr 10:16 The **l** of the righteous *tendeth* to life: 6468
13:11 but he that gathereth by **l** shall increase. 3027
14:23 In all **l** there is profit: but the talk of the lips 6089
21:25 killeth him; for his hands refuse to **l**. 6213
23: 4 **L** not to be rich: cease from thine own 3021
Ecc 1: 3 What profit hath a man of all his **l** which he 5999
1: 8 All things *are* **full of l**; man cannot utter *it*: 3023
2:10 any joy; for my heart rejoiced in all my **l**: 5999
2:10 and this was my portion of all my **l**. 5999
2:11 and on the **l** that I had laboured to do: 5999
2:18 I hated all my **l** which I *had* taken under 5999
2:19 yet shall he have rule over all my **l** where*in* 5999
2:20 of all the **l** which I took under the sun. 5999
2:21 For there is a man whose **l** *is* in wisdom, 5999
2:22 For what hath man of all his **l**, and of 5999
2:24 he should make his soul enjoy good in his **l**. 5999
3:13 and drink, and enjoy the good of all his **l**, 5999
4: 8 yet *is there* no end of all his **l**; neither is his 5999
4: 8 neither *saith he*, For whom do I **l**, and 6001
4: 9 because they have a good reward for their **l**. 5999
5:15 shall take nothing of his **l**, which he may 5999
5:18 to enjoy the good of all his **l** that he taketh 5999
5:19 to take his portion, and to rejoice in his **l**; 5999
6: 7 All the **l** of man *is* for his mouth, and 5999
8:15 for that shall abide with him of his **l** 5999
8:17 because though a man **l** to seek *it* out, 5998
9: 9 in thy **l** which thou takest under the sun. 5999
10:15 The **l** of the foolish wearieth every one of 5999
Isa 22: 4 **l** not to comfort me, because of the spoiling 213
45:14 The **l** of Egypt, and merchandise of 3018
55: 2 your **l** for *that which* satisfieth not? hearken 3018
65:23 They shall not **l** in vain, nor bring forth for 3021
Jer 3:24 For shame hath devoured the **l** of our 3018
20:18 came I forth out of the womb to see **l** 5999
51:58 the people shall **l** in vain, and the folk in 3021
La 5: 5 under persecution: we **l**, *and* have no rest. 3021
Eze 23:29 shall take *away* all thy **l**, and shall leave 3018
29:20 I have given him the land of Egypt *for* his **l** 6468
Mic 4:10 Be in pain, and **l to bring forth**, 1518
Hab 2:13 hosts that the people shall **l** in the very fire, 3021
3:17 the **l** of the olive shall fail, and the fields 4639
Hag 1:11 upon cattle, and upon all the **l** of the hands. 3018
Mt 11:28 all *ye* that **l** and are heavy laden, and I will *2872*
Jn 4:38 you to reap *that* whereon ye **bestowed** no **l**: *2872*
6:27 **L** not for the meat which perisheth, but *2038*
Ro 16: 6 Greet Mary, who **bestowed** much **l** on us. *2872*
16:12 and Tryphosa, who **l** in the Lord. *2872*
1Co 3: 8 his own reward according to his own **l**. *2873*
4:12 And **l**, working with our own hands: *2872*
15:58 forasmuch as you know that your **l** is not in *2873*
2Co 5: 9 Wherefore we **l**, that, whether present or *5389*
Gal 4:11 lest I have **bestowed** upon you **l** in vain. *2872*
Eph 4:28 but rather let him **l**, working with *his* hands *2872*
Php 1:22 if *I* live in the flesh, this *is* the fruit of my **l**: *2041*
2:25 and **companion in l**, and fellowsoldier, but *4904*
Col 1:29 Whereunto I also **l**, striving according to *2872*
1Th 1: 3 and **l** of love, and patience of hope in our *2873*
2: 9 ye remember, brethren, our **l** and travail: *2873*
3: 5 have tempted you, and our **l** be in vain. *2873*
5:12 to know them which **l** among you, and *2872*
2Th 3: 8 but wrought with **l** and travail night and *2873*
1Ti 4:10 For therefore we both **l** and *2872*
5:17 especially they who **l** in the word and *2872*
Heb 4:11 Let us **l** therefore to enter into that rest, *4704*
6:10 to forget your work and **l** of love, *2873*
Rev 2: 2 and thy **l**, and thy patience, and how thou *2873*

LABOURED (19) [LABOUR]

Ne 4:21 So we **l** in the work: and half of them held 6213
Job 20:18 **That which** he **l for** shall he restore, and 3022
Ecc 2:11 and on the labour that I had **l** to do: 5998
2:19 rule over all my labour where*in* I have **l**, 5998
2:21 yet to a man that hath not **l** therein shall he 5998
2:22 his heart, wherein he *hath* **l** under the sun? 6001
5:16 what profit hath he that hath **l** for the wind? 5998
Isa 47:12 wherein thou hast **l** from thy youth; 3021
47:15 they be unto thee *with* whom thou hast **l**, 3021
49: 4 I said, I have **l** in vain, I have spent my 3021
62: 8 drink thy wine, for the which thou hast **l**: 3021
Da 6:14 he **l** till the going down of the sun to deliver 7712
Jnh 4:10 for the which thou hast not **l**, neither 5998
Jn 4:38 other *men* **l**, and ye are entered into their *2872*
Ro 16:12 beloved Persis, which **l** much in the Lord. *2872*
1Co 15:10 but I **l** more abundantly than they all: *2872*
Php 2:16 that I have not run in vain, neither **l** in vain. *2872*
4: 3 help those *women* which **l with** me in *4866*
Rev 2: 3 and for my name's sake hast **l**, and hast not *2872*

LABOURER (2) [LABOUR]

Lk 10: 7 for the **l** is worthy of his hire. Go not from *2040*
1Ti 5:18 And, The **l** *is* worthy of his reward. *2040*

LABOURERS (9) [LABOUR]

Mt 9:37 harvest truly is plenteous, but the **l** *are* few; *2040*
9:38 that he will send forth **l** into his harvest. *2040*
20: 1 in the morning to hire **l** into his vineyard. *2040*
20: 2 And when he had agreed with the **l** for a *2040*
20: 8 Call the **l**, and give them *their* hire, *2040*
Lk 10: 2 The harvest truly *is* great, but the **l** *are* few: *2040*
10: 2 that he would send forth **l** into his harvest. *2040*
1Co 3: 9 For we are **l together with** God: ye are *4904*
Jas 5: 4 the hire of the **l** which have reaped *down* *2040*

LABOURETH (5) [LABOUR]

Pr 16:26 He that **l** laboureth for himself; for his 6001
16:26 He that laboureth **l** for himself; for his 5998
Ecc 3: 9 *hath* he that worketh in *that* where*in* he **l**? 6001
1Co 16:16 and to every one that helpeth with *us*, and **l**. *2872*
2Ti 2: 6 The husbandman that **l** must be first *2872*

LABOURING (4) [LABOUR]

Ecc 5:12 The sleep of a **l** *man is* sweet, whether he 5647
Ac 20:35 how that so **l** *ye* ought to support the weak, *2872*
Col 4:12 always **l fervently** for you in prayers, *75*

1Th 2: 9 for l night and day, because *we* would not *2038*

LABOURS (13) [LABOUR]

Ex 23:16 the feast of harvest, the firstfruits of thy l, 4639
23:16 when thou hast gathered in thy l out of 4639
Dt 28:33 The fruit of thy land, and all thy l, shall a 3018
Pr 5:10 and thy l *be* in the house of a stranger; 6089
Isa 58: 3 fast you find pleasure, and exact all your l. 6092
Jer 20: 5 all the l thereof, and all the precious things 3018
Hos 12: 8 *in* all my l they shall find none iniquity in 3018
Hag 2:17 and with hail *in* all the l of your hands; 4639
Jn 4:38 and ye are entered into their l. *2873*
2Co 6: 5 in tumults, in l, in watchings, in fastings; *2873*
10:15 *our* measure, *that is,* of other *men's* l; *2873*
11:23 in l more abundant, in stripes above *2873*
Rev 14:13 the Spirit, that they may rest from their l; *2873*

LACE (4)

Ex 28:28 unto the rings of the ephod with a l of blue, 6616
28:37 thou shalt put it on a blue l, that it may be 6616
39:21 unto the rings of the ephod with a l of blue, 6616
39:31 they tied unto it a l of blue, to fasten *it* on 6616

LACHISH (24)

Jos 10: 3 unto Japhia king of **L**, and unto Debir king 3923
10: 5 the king of **L**, the king of Eglon, 3923
10:23 the king of **L**, *and* the king of Eglon. 3923
10:31 unto **L**, and encamped against it, and 3923
10:32 the LORD delivered **L** into the hand of 3923
10:33 Horam king of Gezer came up to help **L**; 3923
10:34 from **L** Joshua passed unto Eglon, and 3923
10:35 according to all that he had done to **L**. 3923
12:11 king of Jarmuth, one; the king of **L**, one; 3923
15:39 **L**, and Bozkath, and Eglon, 3923
2Ki 14:19 he fled to **L**; but they sent after him to 3923
14:19 they sent after him to **L**, and slew him 3923
18:14 of Judah sent to the king of Assyria to **L**, 3923
18:17 Rab-shakeh from **L** to king Hezekiah with 3923
19: 8 he had heard that he was departed from **L**. 3923
2Ch 11: 9 And Adoraim, and **L**, and Azekah, 3923
25:27 against him in Jerusalem; and he fled to **L**: 3923
25:27 they sent to **L** after him, and slew him 3923
32: 9 (but he *himself laid siege* against **L**, and 3923
Ne 11:30 *at* **L**, and the fields thereof, *at* Azekah, and 3923
Isa 36: 2 the king of Assyria sent Rabshakeh from **L** 3923
37: 8 he had heard that he was departed from **L**. 3923
Jer 34: 7 were left, against **L**, and against Azekah: 3923
Mic 1:13 O thou inhabitant of **L**, bind the chariot to 3923

LACK (15) [LACKED, LACKEST, LACKETH, LACKING]

Ge 18:28 Peradventure there shall l five of the fifty 2637
18:28 wilt thou destroy all the city for *l of* five? NIH
Ex 16:18 and he that gathered little **had** no l; 2637
Dt 8: 9 thou shalt not l any *thing* in it; 2637
Job 4:11 The old lion perisheth for l of prey, and 1097
38:41 cry unto God, they wander for l of meat. 1097
Ps 34:10 The young lions do l, and suffer hunger: 7326
Pr 28:27 He that giveth unto the poor *shall* not l: but 4270
Ecc 9: 8 and let thy head l no ointment. 2637
Hos 4: 6 My people are destroyed for l of 1097
Mt 19:20 have I kept from my youth up: what l I yet? *5302*
2Co 8:15 and he that *had gathered* little **had** no l. *1641*
Php 2:30 to supply your l of service toward me. *5303*
1Th 4:12 and *that* ye may have l of no*thing*. *5532*
Jas 1: 5 If any of you l wisdom, let him ask of God, *3007*

LACKED (11) [LACK]

Dt 2: 7 *hath been* with thee; thou hast l nothing. 2637
2Sa 2:30 there l of David's servants nineteen men 6485
17:22 by the morning light there l not one *of them* 5737
1Ki 4:27 every man *in* his month: they l nothing. 5737
11:22 But what *hast* thou l with me, that behold, 2638
Ne 9:21 in the wilderness, *so that* they l nothing; 2637
Lk 8: 6 withered away, because *it* l moisture. *2192+3361*
22:35 and shoes, l ye any *thing?* And they said, *5302*
Ac 4:34 Neither was there any among them that l: *1729*
1Co 12:24 more abundant honour to that *part* which l: *5302*
Php 4:10 ye were also careful, but ye l **opportunity**. *170*

LACKEST (2) [LACK]

Mk 10:21 and said unto him, One *thing* thou l: *5302*
Lk 18:22 Yet l thou one *thing:* sell all that thou hast, *3007*

LACKETH (5) [LACK]

Nu 31:49 our charge, and there l not one man of us. 6485
2Sa 3:29 or that falleth on the sword, or that l bread. 2638
Pr 6:32 adultery with a woman l understanding: 2638
12: 9 than he that honoureth himself, and l bread. 2638
2Pe 1: 9 But he that l these *things* is blind, *3361+3918*

LACKING (8) [LACK]

Lev 2:13 **suffer** the salt of the covenant of thy God **to be** l 7673
22:23 hath any thing superfluous or l **in** his **parts**, 7038
Jdg 21: 3 that there should be to day one tribe l in 6485
1Sa 30:19 there was nothing l to them, neither small 5737
Jer 23: 4 nor be dismayed, neither shall they be l, 6485
1Co 16:17 for that which was l on your part they have *5303*
2Co 11: 9 l to me the brethren which came from *5303*
1Th 3:10 might perfect that which is l in your faith? *5303*

LAD (33) [LAD'S, LADS]

Ge 21:12 be grievous in thy sight because of the l, 5288
21:17 God heard the voice of the l; and the angel 5288
21:17 for God hath heard the voice of the l where 5288
21:18 lift up the l, and hold him in thine hand; 5288
21:19 the bottle *with* water, and gave the l drink. 5288
21:20 God was with the l; and he grew, and 5288
22: 5 I and the l will go yonder and worship, and 5288
22:12 he said, Lay not thine **hand** upon the l, 5288
37: 2 the l *was* with the sons of Bilhah, and 5288
43: 8 Send the l with me, and we will arise and 5288
44:22 unto my lord, The l cannot leave his father: 5288
44:30 servant my father, and the l *be* not with us; 5288
44:31 when he seeth that the l *is* not *with us,* that 5288
44:32 For thy servant became surety for the l unto 5288
44:33 let thy servant abide instead of the l a 5288
44:33 and let the l go up with his brethren. 5288
44:34 up to my father, and the l *be* not with me? 5288
Jdg 16:26 Samson said unto the l that held him by 5288
1Sa 20:21 behold, I will send a l, *saying,* Go, find out 5288
20:21 If I expressly say unto the l, Behold, 5288
20:35 with David, and a little l with him. 5288
20:36 he said unto his l, Run, find out now 5288
20:36 *And* as the l ran, he shot an arrow beyond 5288
20:37 when the l was come to the place of 5288
20:37 Jonathan cried after the l, and said, *Is* not 5288
20:38 Jonathan cried after the l, Make speed, 5288
20:38 Jonathan's l gathered up the arrows, and 5288
20:39 But the l knew not any thing: only Jonathan 5288
20:40 Jonathan gave his artillery unto his l, and 5288
20:41 *And* as soon as the l was gone, David arose 5288
2Sa 17:18 Nevertheless a l saw them, and 5288
2Ki 4:19 And he said to a l, Carry him to his mother. 5288
Jn 6: 9 There is a l here, which hath five barley *3808*

LAD'S (1) [LAD]

Ge 44:30 seeing that his life *is* bound up in *the l* life; NIH

LADAN See LAADAN

LADDER (1)

Ge 28:12 behold a l set up on the earth, and the top of 5551

LADE (3) [LADED, LADEN, LADETH, LADING, UNLADE]

Ge 45:17 l your beasts, and go, get you unto the land 2943
1Ki 12:11 now whereas my father did l you with a 6006
Lk 11:46 for ye l men *with* burdens grievous to be *5412*

LADED (4) [LADE]

Ge 42:26 they l their asses with the corn, and 5375
44:13 l every man his ass, and returned to 6006
Ne 4:17 they that bare burdens, *with* those that l, 6006
Ac 28:10 they l *us* **with** such *things* as were *2007*

LADEN (6) [LADE]

Ge 45:23 ten asses l with the good things of Egypt, 5375
45:23 ten she asses l with corn and bread and 5375
1Sa 16:20 Jesse took an ass *l* with bread, and a bottle NIH
Isa 1: 4 Ah sinful nation, a people l with iniquity, 3515
Mt 11:28 all *ye* that labour and are **heavy** l, and I will *5412*
2Ti 3: 6 and lead captive silly women l with sins, *4987*

LADETH (1) [LADE]

Hab 2: 6 and to him that l himself **with** thick clay! 3513

LADIES (2) [LADY]

Jdg 5:29 Her wise l answered *her,* yea, she returned 8282
Est 1:18 Likewise shall the l of Persia and 8282

LADING (2) [LADE]

Ne 13:15 and bringing in sheaves, and l asses; 5921+6006
Ac 27:10 not only of the l and ship, but also of our *5414*

LADS (1) [LAD]

Ge 48:16 redeemed me from all evil, bless the l; 5288

LADY (4) [LADIES]

Isa 47: 5 shalt no more be called, The l of kingdoms. 1404
47: 7 thou saidst, I shall be a l for ever: *so* 1404
2Jn 1: 1 The elder unto the elect l and her children, *2959*
1: 5 And now I beseech thee, l, not as though I *2959*

LAEL (1)

Nu 3:24 Gershonites *shall be* Eliasaph the son of **L**. 3815

LAHAD (1)

1Ch 4: 2 and Jahath begat Ahumai, and **L**. 3855

LAHAI-ROI (2) [BEER-LAHAI-ROI]

Ge 24:62 And Isaac came from the way of the **well L**; 883
25:11 his son Isaac; and Isaac dwelt by the **well L**. 883

LAHMAM (1)

Jos 15:40 And Cabbon, and **L**, and Kithlish, 3903

LAHMAS See LAHMAM

LAHMI (1)

1Ch 20: 5 Elhanan the son of Jair slew **L** the brother 3902

LAID (279) [LAY]

Ge 9:23 l *it* upon both their shoulders, and 7760
15:10 and l each piece one against another: 5414
19:16 the men l **hold** upon his hand, and upon 2388
22: 6 burnt offering, and l *it* upon Isaac his son; 7760
22: 9 l the wood **in order**, and bound Isaac his 6186
22: 9 and l him on the altar upon the wood. 7760
30:41 that Jacob l the rods before the eyes of 7760
38:19 l **by** her vail from her, and put on 5493
39:16 she l **up** his garment by her, until his lord 3240
41:48 of Egypt, and l **up** the food in the cities: 5414
41:48 round about every city, l he **up** in the same. 5414
48:14 l *it* upon Ephraim's head, who *was* 7896
48:17 when Joseph saw that his father l his right 7896
Ex 2: 3 she l *it* in the flags by the river's brink. 7760
5: 9 Let there **more** work be l upon the men, 3513
16:24 they l it **up** till the morning, as Moses bade: 4340
16:34 so Aaron l it **up** before the Testimony, 3240
19: 7 l before their faces all these words which 7760
21:30 If there be l **on him** a sum of money, then 7896
21:30 ransom of his life whatsoever is l upon him. 7896
24:11 of the children of Israel he l not his hand: 7971
Lev 8:14 his sons l their hands upon the head of 5564
8:18 his sons l their hands upon the head of 5564
8:22 his sons l their hands upon the head of 5564
Nu 16:18 l incense thereon, and stood *in* the door of 7760
17: 7 Moses l **up** the rods before the LORD in 4340
21:30 we have l *them* **waste** even unto Nophah, 8074
27:23 he l his hands upon him, and gave him a 5564
Dt 26: 6 afflicted us, and l upon us hard bondage: 5414
29:22 the sicknesses which the LORD hath l 2470
32:34 *Is* not this l **up in store** with me, *and* 3647
34: 9 for Moses had l his hands upon him: 5564
Jos 2: 6 which she had l **in order** upon the roof. 6186
2: 8 before they were l **down**, she came up unto 7901
4: 8 where they lodged, and l them **down** there. 3240
7:23 and l them **out** before the LORD. 3332
10:27 l great stones in the cave's mouth, 7760
Jdg 9:24 their blood be l upon Abimelech their 7760
9:34 they l **wait** against Shechem *in* four 693
9:43 l **wait** in the field, and looked, and behold, 693
9:48 l *it* on his shoulder, and said unto 7760
16: 2 l **wait** for him all night in the gate of 693
19:29 l **hold** on his concubine, and divided her, 2388
Ru 3: 7 and uncovered his feet, and l her **down**. 7901
3:15 six *measures* of barley, and l *it* on her: 7896
4:16 l it in her bosom, and became nurse unto it. 7896
1Sa 3: 2 when Eli *was* l **down** in his place, and 7901
3: 3 God *was,* and Samuel was l **down** *to sleep;* 7901
6:11 they l the ark of the LORD upon the cart, 7760
10:25 *it* in a book, and l *it* **up** before the LORD. 3240
15: 2 how he l *wait* for him in the way, when he 7760
15: 5 a city of Amalek, and l **wait** in the valley. 7378
15:27 he l **hold** upon the skirt of his mantle, and 2388
19:13 l *it* in the bed, and put a pillow of goats' 7760
21:12 David l **up** these words in his heart, and 7760
25:18 hundred cakes *of figs,* and l *them* on asses. 7760
2Sa 13: 8 Amnon's house; and he was l **down.** 7901
13:19 l her hand on her head, and went on crying. 7760
18:17 and l a very great heap of stones upon him: 5324
1Ki 3:20 l it in her bosom, and laid her dead child in 7901
3:20 and l her dead child in my bosom. 7901
6:37 **foundation** of the house of the LORD l, 3245
8:31 an oath be l upon him to cause him to 5375
13:29 and l it upon the ass, and brought it back: 3240
13:30 he l his carcase in his own grave; and 3240
15:27 and all Israel l **siege** to Gibbethon. 6696
16:34 he l the **foundation** thereof in Abiram his 3245
17:19 he abode, and l him upon his own bed. 7901
18:33 in pieces, and l *him* on the wood, and said, 7760
19: 6 he did eat and drink, and l him **down** again. 7901
21: 4 he l him **down** upon his bed, and 7901
2Ki 4:21 l him on the bed of the man of God, and 7901
4:31 and l the staff upon the face of the child; 7760
4:32 the child was dead, *and* l upon his bed. 7901
5:23 and l *them* upon two of his servants; 5414
9:25 the LORD l this burden upon him; 5375
11:16 they l hands on her; and she went *by* 7760
12:11 they l it **out** to the carpenters and builders, 3318
12:12 for all that was l **out** for the house to repair 3318
20: 7 they took and l *it* on the boil, and 7760
20:17 *that* which thy fathers have l **up in store** 686
2Ch 6:22 an oath be l upon him to make him swear, 5375
7:22 l **hold** on other gods, and worshipped them, 2388
16:14 l him in the bed which was filled *with* 7901
23:15 So they l hands on her; and when she was 7760
24: 9 of God l **upon** Israel in the wilderness. 5921
24:27 and the greatness of the burdens *l* upon him, NIH
29:23 and l their hands upon them: 5564
31: 6 the LORD their God, and l *them* by heaps. 5414
32: 9 (but he *himself l siege* against Lachish, and NIH
Ezr 3: 6 **foundation** of the temple of the LORD was not *yet* l. 3245
3:10 when the builders l the **foundation** of 3245
3:11 **foundation** of the house of the LORD was l. 3245
3:12 when the **foundation** of this house was l 3245
5: 8 timber *is* l in the walls, and this work goeth 7761
5:16 l the foundation of the house of God which 3052
6: 1 where the treasures were l **up** in Babylon. 5182
6: 3 *let* the foundations thereof *be* **strongly** l; 5446
Ne 3: 3 who *also* l the **beams** thereof, and set up 7136
3: 6 they l the **beams** thereof, and set up 7136
13: 5 where aforetime they l the meat offerings, 5414
Est 8: 7 because he l his hand upon the Jews. 7971
9:10 but on the spoil l they not their hand. 7971
9:15 but on the prey they l not their hand. 7971
9:16 but they l not their hands on the prey, 7971
10: 1 the king Ahasuerus l a tribute upon 7760
Job 6: 2 my calamity l in the balances together! 5375
18:10 The snare *is* l for him in the ground, and 2934
29: 9 and l *their* hand on their mouth. 7760
31: 9 or *if* I have l **wait** at my neighbour's door; 693
38: 4 Where wast thou when I l the **foundations** 3245
38: 5 Who hath l the measures thereof, if thou 7760
38: 6 or who l the corner stone thereof; 3384
Ps 3: 5 I l me **down** and slept; I awaked; for 7901
21: 5 honour and majesty hast thou l upon him. 7737
31: 4 of the net that they have l **privily** for me: 2934
31:19 which thou hast l **up** for them that fear 6845
35:11 they l **to** my **charge** *things* that I knew not. 7592
49:14 Like sheep they are l in the grave; 8371
62: 9 to be l in the balance, they *are* altogether 5927
79: 1 they have l Jerusalem on heaps. 7760
79: 7 and l **waste** his dwelling place. 8074
88: 6 Thou hast l me in the lowest pit, 7896
89:19 I have l help upon *one that is* mighty; 7737
102:25 Of old hast thou l the **foundation** of 3245
104: 5 *Who* l the foundations of the earth, *that* it 3245
105:18 feet they hurt with fetters: he was l *in* iron: 935
119:30 of truth: thy judgments have I l *before me.* 7737
119:110 The wicked have l a snare for me: yet I 5414
139: 5 and before, and l thine hand upon me. 7896
141: 9 Keep me from the snare *which* they have l 3369
142: 3 I walked have they **privily** l a snare for me. 2934
Pr 13:22 the wealth of the sinner *is* l **up** for the just. 6845
SS 7:13 and old, *which* I have l **up** for thee, 6845
Isa 6: 7 he l *it* upon my mouth, and said, Lo, 5060
10:28 at Michmash he hath l **up** his carriages: 6485
14: 8 of Lebanon, *saying,* Since thou art l **down**, 7901

Isa 15: 1 Because in the night Ar of Moab is **l waste**, 7703
15: 1 because in the night Kir of Moab is **l waste**, 7703
15: 7 have gotten, and **that** which they have **l up**, 6486
23: 1 for it is **l waste**, so that *there is* no house, 7703
23:14 of Tarshish: for your strength is **l waste**. 7703
23:18 it shall not be treasured nor **l up**; for her 2630
37:18 the kings of Assyria have **l waste** all 2717
39: 6 *that* which thy fathers have **l up in store** 686
42:25 and it burned him, yet he **l** *it* not to heart. 7760
44:28 *to* the temple, Thy **foundation** shall be **l**. 3245
47: 6 upon the ancient hast thou very **heavily l** 3513
48:13 Mine hand also hath **l** the **foundation** of 3245
51:13 and **l** the **foundations** of the earth; 3245
51:23 thou hast **l** thy body as the ground, and 7760
53: 6 the LORD hath **l** on him the iniquity of us 6293
57:11 not remembered me, nor **l** *it* to thy heart? 7760
64:11 and all our pleasant things are **l waste**. 2723
Jer 4: 7 *and* thy cities shall be **l waste**, without an 5327
27:17 live: wherefore should this city be **l waste**? 2723
36:20 they **l up** the roll in the chamber of 6485
50:24 I have **l a snare** for thee, and thou art also 3369
La 4:19 they **l wait** for us in the wilderness. 693
Eze 4: 5 For I have **l** upon thee the years of their 5414
6: 6 dwelling places the cities shall be **l waste**, 2717
6: 6 that your altars may be **l waste** and 2717
11: 7 Your slain whom ye have **l** in the midst of 7760
12:20 the cities that are inhabited shall be **l waste**, 2717
19: 7 desolate palaces, and he **l waste** their cities; 2717
26: 2 I shall be replenished, *now* she is **l waste**: 2717
29:12 her cities among the cities *that are* **l waste** 2717
32:19 and be thou **l** with the uncircumcised. 7901
32:27 they have **l** their swords under their heads, 5414
32:29 which with their might are **l** by *them that* 5414
32:32 he shall be **l** in the midst of 7901
33:29 when I have **l** the land most desolate 5414
35:12 saying, They are **l desolate**, they are given 8074
39:21 and my hand that I have **l** upon them. 7760
40:42 whereupon also they **l** the instruments 3240
Da 6:17 and **l** upon the mouth of the den; 7761
Hos 11: 4 yoke on their jaws, and I **l** meat unto them. 5186
Joel 1: 7 He hath **l** my vine waste, and barked my fig 7760
1:17 the garners are **l desolate**, the barns are 8074
Am 2: 8 upon clothes **l to pledge** by every altar, 2254
7: 9 the sanctuaries of Israel shall be **l waste**; 2717
Ob 1: 7 *they that eat* thy bread have **l** a wound 7760
1:13 nor have **l** *hands* on their substance in 7971
Jnh 3: 6 he **l** his robe from him, and covered *him* 5674
Mic 5: 1 he hath **l** siege against us: they shall smite 7760
Na 3: 7 flee from thee, and say, Nineveh is **l waste**: 7703
Hab 2:19 it *is* **l over** *with* gold and silver, and *there is* 8610
Hag 2:15 from before a stone was **l** upon a stone in 7760
2:18 **foundation** of the LORD'S temple was **l**, 3245
Zec 3: 9 For behold the stone that I have **l** before 5414
4: 9 have **l** the **foundation** of this house; 3245
7:14 for they **l** the pleasant land desolate. 7760
8: 9 **foundation** of the house of the LORD of hosts was **l**, 3245
Mal 1: 3 **l** his mountains and his heritage waste for 7760
Mt 3:10 And now also the axe is **l** unto the root of *2749*
8:14 he saw his wife's mother **l**, and sick of a *906*
14: 3 For Herod had **l hold on** John, and *2902*
18:28 and he **l hands on** him, and took *him* by *2902*
19:15 And he **l** *his* hands **on** them, and *2007*
26:50 and **l** hands on Jesus, and took him. *1911*
26:55 in the temple, and ye **l** no **hold** on me. *2902*
26:57 And they that had **l hold** on Jesus led *him* *2902*
27:60 And **l** it in his own new tomb, which he had *5087*
Mk 6: 5 save that he **l** *his* hands **upon** a few sick *2007*
6:17 had sent forth and **l hold upon** John, *2902*
6:29 and took up his corpse, and **l** it in a tomb. *5087*
6:56 they **l** the sick in the streets, and *5087*
7:30 gone out, and *her* daughter **l** upon the bed. *906*
14:46 And they **l** their hands on him, and *1911*
14:51 and the young men **l hold on** him: *2902*
15:46 **l** him in a sepulchre which was hewn out of *2698*
15:47 *the mother* of Joses beheld where he was **l**. *5087*
16: 6 not here: behold the place where they **l** him. *5087*
Lk 1:66 And all they that heard *them* **l** *them* **up** in *5087*
2: 7 in swaddling clothes, and **l** him in a manger; *347*
3: 9 And now also the axe is **l** unto the root of *2749*
4:40 and he **l** *his* hands **on** every one of them, *2007*
6:48 and **l** the foundation on a rock: *5087*
12:19 thou hast much goods **l up** for many years; *2749*
13:13 And he **l** *his* hands **on** her: and *2007*
14:29 after he hath **l** the foundation, and is not *5087*
16:20 which was **l** at his gate, full of sores, *906*
19:20 which I have kept **l up** in a napkin: *606*
19:22 taking up that I **l** not **down**, and *5087*
23:26 they **l hold upon** one Simon, a Cyrenian, *1949*
23:26 of the country, and **on** him they **l** the cross, *2007*
23:53 **l** it in a sepulchre *that was* hewn in stone, *5087*
23:53 in stone, wherein never man before was **l**. *2749*
23:55 the sepulchre, and how his body was **l**. *5087*
24:12 he beheld the linen clothes **l** by themselves, *2749*
Jn 7:30 but no *man* **l** hands on him, because *1911*
7:44 have taken him; but no *man* **l** hands on him. *1911*
8:20 and no *man* **l hands on** him; for his hour *4084*
11:34 And said, Where have ye **l** him? They say *5087*
11:41 stone *from the place* where the dead was **l**. *2749*
13: 4 from supper, and **l aside** *his* garments; *5087*
19:41 wherein was never man yet **l**. *5087*
19:42 There **l** they Jesus therefore because of *5087*
20: 2 and we know not where they have **l** him. *5087*
20:13 and I know not where they have **l** him. *5087*
20:15 him *hence*, tell me where thou hast **l** him, *5087*
21: 9 coals there, and fish **l thereon**, and bread. *1945*
Ac 3: 2 whom they **l** daily at the gate of the temple *5087*
4: 3 And they **l** hands **on** them, and put *them* in *1911*
4:35 And **l** *them down* at the apostles' feet: and *5087*
4:37 the money, and **l** *it* at the apostles' feet. *5087*
5: 2 a certain part, and **l** *it* at the apostles' feet. *5087*
5:15 the streets, and **l** *them* on beds and couches, *5087*
5:18 And **l** their hands on the apostles, and *1911*
6: 6 had prayed, they **l** *their* hands **on** them. *2007*
7:16 **l** in the sepulchre that Abraham bought for *5087*
Ac 7:58 the witnesses **l down** their clothes at a young *659*
8:17 Then **l** they *their* hands on them, and *2007*
9:37 they **l** *her* in an upper chamber. *5087*
13: 3 and prayed, and **l** *their* hands **on** them, *2007*
13:29 from the tree, and **l** *him* in a sepulchre. *5087*
13:36 and was **l** unto his fathers, and *4369*
16:23 And when they had **l** many stripes upon *2007*
19: 6 And when Paul had **l** *his* hands **upon** them, *2007*
20: 3 and when the Jews **l wait for** him, *1096+1917*
21:27 up all the people, and **l** hands on him, *1911*
23:29 to have nothing **l to** his **charge** worthy of *1462*
23:30 me how that the Jews **l wait** for the man, *1917*
25: 7 and **l** many and grievous complaints against *5342*
25:16 concerning the **crime l** *against him*. *1462*
25:27 not withal to signify the crimes *l* against NIG
28: 3 and **l** *them* on the fire, there came a viper *2007*
28: 8 and **l** *his* hands **on** him, and healed him. *2007*
Ro 16: 4 Who have for my life **l down** their own *5294*
1Co 3:10 I have **l** the foundation, and *5087*
3:11 foundation can no *man* lay than that is **l**, *2749*
9:16 for necessity is **l upon** me; yea, woe is unto *1945*
Col 1: 5 For the hope which is **l up** for you in heaven, *606*
2Ti 4: 8 Henceforth there is **l up** for me a crown of *606*
4:16 *God* that it may not be **l to** their **charge**. *3049*
Heb 1:10 in the beginning hast **l the foundation** of *2311*
1Jn 3:16 *of God*, because he **l down** his life for us: *5087*
Rev 1:17 And he **l** his right hand upon me, *2007*
20: 2 And he **l hold on** the dragon, *that* old *2902*

LAIDST (1) [LAY]

Ps 66:11 into the net; thou **l** affliction upon our loins. 7760

LAIN (3) [LIE]

Nu 5:19 If no man have **l** with thee, and if thou hast 7901
5:20 *some* man hath **l** with thee beside thine 7903
Jn 20:12 at the feet, where the body of Jesus had **l**. *2749*

LAISH (7)

Jdg 18: 7 came to **L**, and saw the people that *were* 3919
18:14 men that went to spy out the country of **L**, 3919
18:27 the priest which he had, and came unto **L**, 3919
18:29 howbeit the name of the city *was* **L** at 3919
1Sa 25:44 David's wife, to Phalti the son of **L**, 3919
2Sa 3:15 *even* from Phaltiel the son of **L**. 3919
Isa 10:30 cause *it* to be heard unto **L**, O poor 3919

LAKE (10)

Lk 5: 1 of God, he stood by the **l** of Gennesaret, *3041*
5: 2 And saw two ships standing by the **l**: but *3041*
8:22 Let us go over unto the other side of the **l**. *3041*
8:23 there came down a storm of wind on the **l**; *3041*
8:33 ran violently down a steep place into the **l**, *3041*
Rev 19:20 *These* both were cast alive into a **l** of fire *3041*
20:10 deceived them was cast into the **l** of fire *3041*
20:14 and hell were cast into the **l** of fire. *3041*
20:15 in the book of life was cast into the **l** of fire. *3041*
21: 8 shall have their part in the **l** which burneth *3041*

LAKKUM See LAKUM

LAKUM (1)

Jos 19:33 and Adami, Nekeb, and Jabneel, unto **L**; 3946

LAMA (2)

Mt 27:46 saying, ELI, ELI, **L** SABACHTHANI? *2982*
Mk 15:34 saying, ELOI, ELOI, **L** SABACHTHANI? *2982*

LAMB (105) [LAMB'S, LAMBS]

Ge 22: 7 but where *is* the **l** for a burnt offering? 7716
22: 8 God will provide himself a **l** for a burnt 7716
Ex 12: 3 they shall take to them every man a **l**, 7716
12: 3 to the house of *their* fathers, a **l** for a house: 7716
12: 4 if the household be too little for the **l**, 7716
12: 4 his eating shall make your count for the **l**. 7716
12: 5 Your **l** shall be without blemish, a male of 7716
12:21 and take you a **l** according to your families, 6629
13:13 of an ass thou shalt redeem with a **l**; 7716
29:39 The one **l** thou shalt offer in the morning; 3532
29:39 and the other **l** thou shalt offer at even: 3532
29:40 with the one **l** a tenth deal of flour mingled 3532
29:41 the other **l** thou shalt offer at even, *and* 3532
34:20 of an ass thou shalt redeem with a **l**: 7716
Lev 3: 7 If he offer a **l** for his offering, then shall he 3775
4:32 if he bring a **l** for a sin offering, he shall 3532
4:35 as the fat of the **l** is taken away from 3775
5: 6 a **l** or a kid of the goats, for a sin offering; 3776
5: 7 if he be not able to bring a **l**, then he shall 7716
9: 3 a calf and a **l**, both of the first year, 3532
12: 6 she shall bring a **l** of the first year for a 3532
12: 8 if she be not able to bring a **l**, then she shall 7716
14:10 one **ewe l** of the first year without blemish, 3535
14:12 the priest shall take one **he l**, and offer him 3532
14:13 he shall slay the **l** in the place where he 3532
14:21 he shall take one **l** *for* a trespass offering to 3532
14:24 the priest shall take the **l** of the trespass 3532
14:25 he shall kill the **l** of the trespass offering, 3532
17: 3 or **l**, or goat, in the camp, or that killeth *it* 3775
22:23 or a **l** that hath any thing superfluous or 7716
23:12 **he l** without blemish of the first year for a 3532
Nu 6:12 shall bring a **l** of the first year for a trespass 3532
6:14 one **he l** of the first year without blemish 3532
6:14 one **ewe l** of the first year without blemish 3535
7:15 one ram, one **l** of the first year, 3532
7:21 one ram, one **l** of the first year, 3532
7:27 one ram, one **l** of the first year, 3532
7:33 one ram, one **l** of the first year, 3532
7:39 one ram, one **l** of the first year, 3532
7:45 one ram, one **l** of the first year, 3532
7:51 one ram, one **l** of the first year, 3532
7:57 one ram, one **l** of the first year, 3532
7:63 one ram, one **l** of the first year, 3532
7:69 one ram, one **l** of the first year, 3532
7:75 one ram, one **l** of the first year, 3532
7:81 one ram, one **l** of the first year, 3532
Nu 15: 5 the burnt offering or sacrifice, for one **l**. 3532
15:11 or for one ram, or for a **l**, or a kid. 3532+7716
28: 4 The one **l** shalt thou offer in the morning, 3532
28: 4 and the other **l** shalt thou offer at even; 3532
28: 7 *be* the fourth *part* of a hin for the one **l**: 3532
28: 8 the other **l** shalt thou offer at even: as 3532
28:13 with oil *for* a meat offering unto one **l**; 3532
28:14 a ram, and a fourth *part* of a hin unto a **l**: 3532
28:21 tenth deal shalt thou offer for every **l**, 3532
28:29 A several tenth deal unto one **l**, throughout 3532
29: 4 one tenth deal for one **l**, throughout 3532
29:10 A several tenth deal for one **l**, throughout 3532
29:15 a several tenth deal to each **l** of the fourteen 3532
1Sa 7: 9 Samuel took a sucking **l**, and offered it *for* 2924
17:34 and a bear, and took a **l** out of the flock: 7716
2Sa 12: 3 save one little **ewe l**, which he had bought 3535
12: 4 took the poor man's **l**, and dressed it for 3535
12: 6 he shall restore the **l** fourfold, because he 3535
Isa 11: 6 The wolf also shall dwell with the **l**, and 3532
16: 1 Send ye the **l** *to* the ruler of the land from 3733
53: 7 he is brought as a **l** to the slaughter, and 7716
65:25 The wolf and the **l** shall feed together, and 2924
66: 3 he that sacrificeth a **l**, *as if* he cut off a 7716
Jer 11:19 I *was* like a **l** *or* an ox *that* is brought to 3532
Eze 45:15 one **l** out of the flock, out of two hundred, 7716
46:13 *of* a **l** of the first year without blemish: 3532
46:15 Thus shall they prepare the **l**, and the meat 3532
Hos 4:16 now the LORD will feed them as a **l** in a 3532
Jn 1:29 and saith, Behold the **L** of God, which taketh *286*
1:36 as he walked, he saith, Behold the **L** of God. *286*
Ac 8:32 and like a **l** dumb before his shearer, so *286*
1Pe 1:19 as of a **l** without blemish and without spot: *286*
Rev 5: 6 stood a **L** as *it had been* slain, having seven *721*
5: 8 *and* twenty elders fell down before the **L**, *721*
5:12 Worthy is the **L** that was slain to receive *721*
5:13 the throne, and unto the **L** for ever and ever. *721*
6: 1 And I saw when the **L** opened one of *721*
6:16 on the throne, and from the wrath of the **L**: *721*
7: 9 stood before the throne, and before the **L**, *721*
7:10 sitteth upon the throne, and unto the **L**. *721*
7:14 and made them white in the blood of the **L**. *721*
7:17 For the **L** which is in the midst of the throne *721*
12:11 they overcame him by the blood of the **L**, *721*
13: 8 the **L** slain from the foundation of the world. *721*
13:11 and he had two horns like a **l**, and he spake *721*
14: 1 and lo, a **L** stood on the mount Sion, and *721*
14: 4 These are they which follow the **L** *721*
14: 4 *being* the firstfruits unto God and to the **L**. *721*
14:10 the holy angels, and in the presence of the **L**: *721*
15: 3 and the song of the **L**, saying, Great and *721*
17:14 These shall make war with the **L**, and *721*
17:14 the Lamb, and the **L** shall overcome them: *721*
19: 7 for the marriage of the **L** is come, and *721*
19: 9 are called unto the marriage supper of the **L**. *721*
21:14 the names of the twelve apostles of the **L**. *721*
21:22 God Almighty and the **L** are the temple of it. *721*
21:23 did lighten it, and the **L** *is* the light thereof. *721*
22: 1 out of the throne of God and of the **L**. *721*
22: 3 the throne of God and of the **L** shall be in it; *721*

LAMB'S (2) [LAMB]

Rev 21: 9 I will shew thee the bride, the **L** wife. *721*
21:27 they which are written in the **L** book of life. *721*

LAMBS (81) [LAMB]

Ge 21:28 Abraham set seven **ewe l** of the flock by 3535
21:29 What *mean* these seven **ewe l** which thou 3535
21:30 For *these* seven **ewe l** shalt thou take of my 3535
30:40 Jacob did separate the **l**, and set the faces of 3775
Ex 29:38 two **l** of the first year day by day 3532
Lev 14:10 on the eighth day he shall take two **he l** 3532
23:18 ye shall offer with the bread seven **l** 3532
23:19 two **l** of the first year for a sacrifice of 3532
23:20 offering before the LORD, with the two **l**: 3532
Nu 7:17 five he goats, five **l** of the first year: 3532
7:23 five he goats, five **l** of the first year: 3532
7:29 five he goats, five **l** of the first year: 3532
7:35 five he goats, five **l** of the first year: 3532
7:41 five he goats, five **l** of the first year: 3532
7:47 five he goats, five **l** of the first year: 3532
7:53 five he goats, five **l** of the first year: 3532
7:59 five he goats, five **l** of the first year: 3532
7:65 five he goats, five **l** of the first year: 3532
7:71 five he goats, five **l** of the first year: 3532
7:77 five he goats, five **l** of the first year: 3532
7:83 five he goats, five **l** of the first year: 3532
7:87 rams twelve, the **l** of the first year twelve, 3532
7:88 he goats sixty, the **l** of the first year sixty. 3532
28: 3 two **l** of the first year without spot day by 3532
28: 9 on the sabbath day two **l** of the first year 3532
28:11 seven **l** of the first year without spot; 3532
28:19 and one ram, and seven **l** of the first year: 3532
28:21 for every lamb, throughout the seven **l**; 3532
28:27 one ram, seven **l** of the first year; 3532
28:29 deal unto one lamb, throughout the seven **l**; 3532
29: 2 seven **l** of the first year without blemish: 3532
29: 4 deal for one lamb, throughout the seven **l**: 3532
29: 8 one ram, *and* seven **l** of the first year; 3532
29:10 deal for one lamb, throughout the seven **l**: 3532
29:13 two rams, *and* fourteen **l** of the first year; 3532
29:15 tenth deal to each lamb of the fourteen **l**: 3532
29:17 fourteen **l** of the first year without spot: 3532
29:18 for the rams, and for the **l**, *shall be* 3532
29:20 fourteen **l** of the first year without blemish; 3532
29:21 for the rams, and for the **l**, *shall be* 3532
29:23 fourteen **l** of the first year without blemish: 3532
29:24 for the rams, and for the **l**, *shall be* 3532
29:26 *and* fourteen **l** of the first year without spot: 3532
29:27 for the rams, and for the **l**, *shall be* 3532
29:29 fourteen **l** of the first year without blemish: 3532
29:30 for the rams, and for the **l**, *shall be* 3532
29:32 fourteen **l** of the first year without blemish: 3532
29:33 for the rams, and for the **l**, *shall be* 3532
29:36 seven **l** of the first year without blemish: 3532
29:37 for the ram, and for the **l**, *shall be* according 3532

Dt 32:14 with fat of l, and rams of the breed of 3733
1Sa 15: 9 the l, and all *that was* good, and would not 3733
2Ki 3: 4 the king of Israel an hundred thousand l, 3733
1Ch 29:21 a thousand rams, *and* a thousand l, 3532
2Ch 29:21 and seven l, and seven he goats, 3532
29:22 they killed also the l, and they sprinkled 3532
29:32 an hundred rams, *and* two hundred l: 3532
35: 7 gave to the people, *of* the flock, l and kids, 3532
Ezr 6: 9 both young bullocks, and rams, and l, 563
6:17 two hundred rams, four hundred l; 563
7:17 rams, l, with their meat offerings and 563
8:35 ninety and six rams, seventy and seven l, 3532
Ps 37:20 of the LORD *shall be* as the fat of l: 3733
114: 4 like rams, *and* the little hills like l. 1121+6629
114: 6 like rams; *and* ye little hills, like l? 1121+6629
Pr 27:26 The l *are* for thy clothing, and the goats *are* 3532
Isa 1:11 blood of bullocks, or of l, or of he goats. 3532
5:17 Then shall the l feed after their manner, and 3532
34: 6 *and* with the blood of l and goats, 3733
40:11 he shall gather the l with his arm, and 2922
Jer 51:40 I will bring them down like l to 3733
Eze 27:21 they occupied with thee in l, and rams, and 3733
39:18 of rams, of l, and of goats, of bullocks, 3733
46: 4 sabbath day *shall be* six l without blemish, 3532
46: 5 the meat offering for the l as he shall be 3532
46: 6 without blemish, and six l, and a ram: 3532
46: 7 for the l according as his hand shall attain 3532
46:11 to the l as he is able to give, and a hin of oil 3532
Am 6: 4 eat the l out of the flock, and the calves out 3733
Lk 10: 3 behold, I send you forth as l among wolves. *704*
Jn 21:15 I love thee. He saith unto him, Feed my l. *721*

LAME (27)

Lev 21:18 or a l, or he that hath a flat nose, or 6455
Dt 15:21 *as if it be* l, or blind, *or have* any ill 6455
2Sa 4: 4 had a son *that was* l of *his* feet, *and* 5223
4: 4 haste to flee, that he fell, and **became** l. 6452
5: 6 Except thou take away the blind and the l, 6455
5: 8 the Jebusites, and the l and the blind, 6455
5: 8 and the l shall not come into the house. 6455
9: 3 hath yet a son, *which is* l on *his* feet. 5223
9:13 the king's table; and *was* l on both his feet. 6455
19:26 go to the king; because thy servant *is* l. 6455
Job 29:15 eyes to the blind, and feet *was* I to the l. 6455
Pr 26: 7 The legs of the l are not equal: so *is* a 6455
Isa 33:23 of a great spoil divided; the l take the prey. 6455
35: 6 shall the l *man* leap as a hart, and 6455
Jer 31: 8 *and* with them the blind and the l, 6455
Mal 1: 8 if ye offer the l and sick, *is it* not evil? 6455
1:13 *that which was* torn, and the l, and the sick; 6455
Mt 11: 5 and the l walk, the lepers are cleansed, and *5560*
15:30 having with them *those that were* l, blind, *5560*
15:31 the l to walk, and the blind to see: *5560*
21:14 and *the* l came to him in the temple; *5560*
Lk 7:22 how that the blind see, the l walk, the lepers *5560*
14:13 call the poor, the maimed, the l, the blind: *5560*
Ac 3: 2 And a certain man l from his mother's *5560*
3:11 And as the l *man* which was healed held *5560*
8: 7 with palsies, and *that were* l, were healed. *5560*
Heb 12:13 lest *that which is* l be turned out of the way; *5560*

LAMECH (12)

Ge 4:18 begat Methusael: and Methusael begat **L**. 3929
4:19 **L** took unto him two wives: the name of 3929
4:23 **L** said unto his wives, Adah and Zillah, 3929
4:23 ye wives of **L**, hearken unto my speech: 3929
4:24 truly **L** seventy and sevenfold. 3929
5:25 and seven years, and begat **L**: 3929
5:26 Methuselah lived after he begat **L** seven 3929
5:28 **L** lived an hundred eighty and two years, 3929
5:30 **L** lived after he begat Noah five hundred 3929
5:31 all the days of **L** were seven hundred 3929
1Ch 1: 3 Henoch, Methuselah, L, 3929
Lk 3:36 *the son* of Noe, which was *the son* of L, *2984*

LAMENT (21) [LAMENTABLE, LAMENTATION, LAMENTATIONS, LAMENTED]

Jdg 11:40 *That* the daughters of Israel went yearly to l 8567
Isa 3:26 her gates shall l and mourn; and she *being* 578
19: 8 all they that cast angle into the brooks shall l, 56
32:12 They *shall* l for the teats, for the pleasant 5594
Jer 4: 8 this gird you with sackcloth, l and howl: 5594
16: 5 neither go to l nor bemoan them: 5594
16: 6 neither shall *men* l for them, nor cut 5594
22:18 They shall not l for him, *saying,* Ah my 5594
22:18 they shall not l for him, *saying,* Ah lord! or, 5594
34: 5 and they will l thee, *saying,* Ah lord! 5594
49: 3 l, and run to and fro by the hedges; 5594
La 2: 8 he **made** the rampart and the wall **to** l; 56
Eze 27:32 l over thee, *saying,* What *city is* like Tyrus, 6969
32:16 the lamentation wherewith they shall l her: 6969
32:16 the daughters of the nations shall l her: 6969
32:16 they shall l for her, *even* for Egypt, and 6969
Joel 1: 8 **L** like a virgin girded with sackcloth for 421
1:13 Gird yourselves, and l, ye priests: howl, 5594
Mic 2: 4 l with a doleful lamentation, *and* say, 5091
Jn 16:20 That ye shall weep and l, but the world *2354*
Rev 18: 9 with her, shall bewail her, and l for her, *2875*

LAMENTABLE (1) [LAMENT]

Da 6:20 the den, he cried with a l voice unto Daniel: 6088

LAMENTATION (25) [LAMENT]

Ge 50:10 they mourned with a great and very sore l: 4553
2Sa 1:17 David lamented with this l over Saul and 7015
Ps 78:64 by the sword; and their widows **made** no l. 1058
Jer 6:26 *as* for an only *son,* most bitter l: 4553
7:29 cast *it* away, and take up a l on high places; 7015
9:10 and for the habitations of the wilderness a l, 7015
9:20 and every one her neighbour l. 7015
31:15 was heard in Ramah, l, *and* bitter weeping; 5092
48:38 *There shall be* l generally upon all 4553
La 2: 5 in the daughter of Judah mourning and l. 592
Eze 19: 1 Moreover take thou up a l for the princes of 7015
19:14 This *is* a l, and shall be for a lamentation. 7015
19:14 This *is* a lamentation, and shall be for a l. 7015
26:17 they shall take up a l for thee, and say to 7015
27: 2 thou son of man, take up a l for Tyrus; 7015
27:32 in their wailing they shall take up a l for 7015
28:12 take up a l upon the king of Tyrus, and 7015
32: 2 take up a l for Pharaoh king of Egypt, and 7015
32:16 This *is* the l wherewith they shall lament 7015
Am 5: 1 up against you, *even* a l, O house of Israel. 7015
5:16 and such as are skilful of l to wailing. 5092
8:10 into mourning, and all your songs into l; 7015
Mic 2: 4 lament with a **doleful** l, *and* say, We be 5093
Mt 2:18 l, and weeping, and great mourning, *2355*
Ac 8: 2 *to his burial,* and made great l over him. *2870*

LAMENTATIONS (3) [LAMENT]

2Ch 35:25 singing *women* spake of Josiah in their l 7015
35:25 and behold, they *are* written in the l. 7015
Eze 2:10 *there was* written therein l, and mourning, 7015

LAMENTED (11) [LAMENT]

1Sa 6:19 the people l, because the LORD had smitten 56
7: 2 all the house of Israel l after the LORD. 5091
25: 1 l him, and buried him in his house at 5594
28: 3 all Israel had l him, and buried him in 5594
2Sa 1:17 David l with this lamentation over Saul 6969
3:33 the king l over Abner, and said, Died Abner 6969
2Ch 35:25 Jeremiah l for Josiah: and all the singing 6969
Jer 16: 4 they shall not be l; neither shall they be 5594
25:33 they shall not be l, neither gathered, 5594
Mt 11:17 have mourned unto you, and ye have not l. *2875*
Lk 23:27 of women, which also bewailed and l him. *2354*

LAMENTS See LAMENTATIONS

LAMP (13) [LAMPS]

Ge 15:17 a burning l that passed between those 3940
Ex 27:20 for the light, to cause the l to burn always. 5216
1Sa 3: 3 ere the l of God went out in the temple of 5216
2Sa 22:29 For thou *art* my l, O LORD: and 5216
1Ki 15: 4 LORD his God give him a l in Jerusalem, 5216
Job 12: 5 He that is ready to slip with *his* feet *is as* a l 3940
Ps 119:105 Thy word *is* a l unto my feet, and a light 5216
132:17 I have ordained a l for mine anointed. 5216
Pr 6:23 For the commandment *is* a l; and the law *is* 5216
13: 9 but the l of the wicked shall be put out. 5216
20:20 his l shall be put out in obscure darkness. 5216
Isa 62: 1 and the salvation thereof as a l *that* burneth. 3940
Rev 8:10 burning as *it were* a l, and it fell upon *2985*

LAMPS (37) [LAMP]

Ex 25:37 thou shalt make the seven l thereof: and 5216
25:37 they shall light the l thereof, that they may 5216
30: 7 when he dresseth the l, he shall burn 5216
30: 8 when Aaron lighteth the l at even, he shall 5216
35:14 his furniture, and his l, with the oil for 5216
37:23 he made his seven l, and his snuffers, and 5216
39:37 The pure candlestick, *with* the l thereof, 5216
39:37 *even with* the l to be set in order, and all 5216
40: 4 in the candlestick, and light the l thereof. 5216
40:25 he lighted the l before the LORD; as 5216
Lev 24: 2 the light, to cause the l to burn continually. 5216
24: 4 He shall order the l upon the pure 5216
Nu 4: 9 and his l, and his tongs, and his snuffdishes, 5216
8: 2 and say unto him, When thou lightest the l, 5216
8: 2 the seven l shall give light over against 5216
8: 3 he lighted the l thereof over against 5216
Jdg 7:16 empty pitchers, and l within the pitchers. 3940
7:20 held the l in their left hands, and 3940
1Ki 7:49 and the l, and the tongs *of* gold, 5216
1Ch 28:15 *for* their l of gold, by weight for every 5216
28:15 for every candlestick, and *for* the l thereof: 5216
28:15 the candlestick, and *also for* the l thereof, 5216
2Ch 4:20 Moreover the candlesticks with their l, 5216
4:21 the flowers, and the l, and the tongs, 5216
13:11 the candlestick of gold with the l thereof, 5216
29: 7 put out the l, and have not burnt incense 5216
Job 41:19 Out of his mouth go **burning** l, *and* 3940
Eze 1:13 coals of fire, *and* like the appearance of l: 3940
Da 10: 6 his eyes as l of fire, and his arms and 3940
Zec 4: 2 seven l thereon, and seven pipes to 5216
4: 2 and seven pipes to the seven l, 5216
Mt 25: 1 which took their l, and went forth to meet *2985*
25: 3 They that *were* foolish took their l, and *2985*
25: 4 wise took oil in their vessels with their l. *2985*
25: 7 all those virgins arose, and trimmed their l. *2985*
25: 8 Give us of your oil; for our l are gone out. *2985*
Rev 4: 5 *there were* seven l of fire burning before *2985*

LAMPSTAND; LAMPSTANDS See CANDLESTICK; CANDLESTICKS

LANCE (1) [LANCETS]

Jer 50:42 They shall hold the bow and the l: they *are* 3591

LANCETS (1) [LANCE]

1Ki 18:28 after their manner with knives and l, 7420

LAND (1717) [LANDED, LANDING, LANDMARK, LANDMARKS, LANDS]

Ge 1: 9 unto one place, and let the dry *l* appear: NIH
1:10 God called the dry *l* Earth; and NIH
2:11 that *is it* which compasseth the whole l of 776
2:12 the gold of that l *is* good: there *is* bdellium 776
2:13 the same *is it* that compasseth the whole l of 776
4:16 dwelt in the l of Nod, on the east of Eden. 776
7:22 of life, of all that *was* in the dry *l*, died. NIH
10:10 and Accad, and Calneh, in the l of Shinar. 776
10:11 Out of that l went forth Asshur, and 776
11: 2 that they found a plain in the l of Shinar; 776
11:28 Haran died before his father Terah in the l of 776
11:31 of the Chaldees, to go into the l of Canaan; 776
12: 1 father's house, unto a l that I will shew thee: 776
12: 5 they went forth to go into the l of Canaan; 776
12: 5 and into the l of Canaan they came. 776
12: 6 Abram passed through the l unto the place of 776
12: 6 And the Canaanite *was* then in the l. 776
12: 7 and said, Unto thy seed will I give this l: 776
12:10 there was a famine in the l: and Abram went 776
12:10 for the famine *was* grievous in the l. 776
13: 6 the l was not able to bear them, that they 776
13: 7 and the Perizzite dwelled then in the l. 776
13: 9 *Is* not the whole l before thee? 776
13:10 like the l of Egypt, as thou comest unto Zoar. 776
13:12 Abram dwelled in the l of Canaan, and 776
13:15 For all the l which thou seest, to thee will I 776
13:17 walk through the l in the length of it and 776
15: 7 the Chaldees, to give thee this l to inherit it. 776
15:13 shall be a stranger in a l *that is* not theirs, 776
15:18 saying, Unto thy seed have I given this l, 776
16: 3 after Abram had dwelt ten years in the l of 776
17: 8 after thee, the l wherein thou art a stranger, 776
17: 8 all the l of Canaan, for an everlasting 776
19:28 and toward all the l of the plain, and beheld, 776
20:15 Abimelech said, Behold, my l *is* before thee: 776
21:21 his mother took him a wife out of the l of 776
21:23 and to the l wherein thou hast sojourned. 776
21:32 and they returned into the l of the Philistines. 776
21:34 Abraham sojourned in the Philistines' l 776
22: 2 and get thee into the l of Moriah; 776
23: 2 the same *is* Hebron in the l of Canaan: 776
23: 7 and bowed himself to the people of the l, 776
23:12 down himself before the people of the l. 776
23:13 Ephron in the audience of the people of the l, 776
23:15 the l *is worth* four hundred shekels of silver; 776
23:19 the same *is* Hebron in the l of Canaan. 776
24: 5 will not be willing to follow me unto this l: 776
24: 5 must I needs bring thy son again unto the l 776
24: 7 from the l of my kindred, and which spake 776
24: 7 saying, Unto thy seed will I give this l; 776
24:37 of the Canaanites, in whose l I dwell: 776
26: 1 there was a famine in the l, besides the first 776
26: 2 dwell in the l which I shall tell thee of: 776
26: 3 Sojourn in this l, and I will be with thee, and 776
26:12 Isaac sowed in that l, and received in 776
26:22 room for us, and we shall be fruitful in the l. 776
27:46 as these *which are* of the daughters of the l, 776
28: 4 that thou mayest inherit the l wherein thou 776
28:13 the l whereon thou liest, to thee will I give it, 776
28:15 and will bring thee again into this l; 127
29: 1 and came into the l of the people of the east. 776
31: 3 Return unto the l of thy fathers, and to thy 776
31:13 get thee out from this l, and return unto 776
31:13 and return unto the l of thy kindred. 776
31:18 for to go to Isaac his father in the l of 776
32: 3 him to Esau his brother unto the l of Seir, 776
33:18 city of Shechem, which *is* in the l of Canaan, 776
34: 1 went out to see the daughters of the l. 776
34:10 the l shall be before you; dwell and trade you 776
34:21 therefore let them dwell in the l, and 776
34:21 for the l, behold, *it is* large enough for them; 776
34:30 me to stink among the inhabitants of the l, 776
35: 6 which *is* in the l of Canaan, that *is,* Beth-el, 776
35:12 the l which I gave Abraham and Isaac, 776
35:12 and to thy seed after thee will I give the l. 776
35:22 when Israel dwelt in that l, that Reuben went 776
36: 5 which were born unto him in the l of 776
36: 6 which he had got in the l of Canaan; 776
36: 7 the l wherein they were strangers could not 776
36:16 dukes *that came* of Eliphaz in the l of Edom; 776
36:17 dukes *that came* of Reuel in the l of Edom; 776
36:20 sons of Seir the Horite, who inhabited the l; 776
36:21 the children of Seir in the l of Edom. 776
36:30 of Hori, among their dukes in the l of Seir. 776
36:31 these *are* the kings that reigned in the l of 776
36:34 Husham of the l of Temani reigned in his 776
36:43 according to their habitations in the l of their 776
37: 1 Jacob dwelt in the l wherein his father was a 776
37: 1 his father was a stranger, in the l of Canaan. 776
40:15 For indeed I was stolen away out of the l of 776
41:19 such as I never saw in all the l of Egypt for 776
41:29 of great plenty throughout all the l of Egypt: 776
41:30 all the plenty shall be forgotten in the l of 776
41:30 and the famine shall consume the l; 776
41:31 the plenty shall not be known in the l by 776
41:33 and wise, and set him over the l of Egypt. 776
41:34 and let him appoint officers over the l, 776
41:34 take up the fifth *part* of the l of Egypt in 776
41:36 *that* food shall be for store to the l against 776
41:36 of famine, which shall be in the l of Egypt; 776
41:36 that the l perish not through the famine. 776
41:41 See, I have set thee over all the l of Egypt. 776
41:43 he made him *ruler* over all the l of Egypt. 776
41:44 lift up his hand or foot in all the l of Egypt. 776
41:45 And Joseph went out over *all* the l of Egypt. 776
41:46 and went throughout all the l of Egypt. 776
41:48 which were in the l of Egypt, and laid up 776
41:52 me to be fruitful in the l of my affliction. 776
41:53 that was in the l of Egypt, were ended. 776
41:54 but in all the l of Egypt there was bread. 776
41:55 when all the l of Egypt was famished, 776
41:56 and the famine waxed sore in the l of Egypt. 776
42: 5 for the famine was in the l of Canaan. 776
42: 6 And Joseph *was* the governor over the l, *and* 776
42: 6 he *it was* that sold to all the people of the l: 776
42: 7 they said, From the l of Canaan to buy food. 776
42: 9 to see the nakedness of the l you are come. 776
42:12 to see the nakedness of the l you are come. 776
42:13 the sons of one man in the l of Canaan; 776
42:29 they came unto Jacob their father unto the l 776
42:30 The man, *who is* the lord of the l, 776
42:32 *is this* day with our father in the l of Canaan. 776
42:34 your brother, and ye shall traffick in the l. 776
43: 1 And the famine *was* sore in the l. 776
43:11 take of the best fruits in the l in your vessels, 776
44: 8 we brought again unto thee out of the l of 776
45: 6 these two years *hath* the famine *been* in the l: 776
45: 8 and a ruler throughout all the l of Egypt. 776
45:10 And thou shalt dwell in the l of Goshen, and 776

L

Ge 45:17 and go, get you unto the l of Canaan; 776
45:18 I will give you the good of the l of Egypt, 776
45:18 of Egypt, and ye shall eat the fat of the l. 776
45:19 take you wagons out of the l of Egypt for 776
45:20 for the good of all the l of Egypt *is* yours. 776
45:25 came *into* the l of Canaan unto Jacob their 776
45:26 and he *is* governor over all the l of Egypt. 776
46: 6 which they had gotten in the l of Canaan, 776
46:12 Er and Onan died in the l of Canaan. And 776
46:20 unto Joseph in the l of Egypt were born 776
46:28 and they came into the l of Goshen. 776
46:31 which *were* in the l of Canaan, are come 776
46:34 that ye may dwell in the l of Goshen; 776
47: 1 they have, are come out of the l of Canaan; 776
47: 1 and behold, they *are* in the l of Goshen. 776
47: 4 For to sojourn in the l are we come; 776
47: 4 for the famine *is* sore in the l of Canaan: 776
47: 4 let thy servants dwell in the l of Goshen. 776
47: 6 The l of Egypt *is* before thee; in the best of 776
47: 6 in the best of the l make thy father and 776
47: 6 to dwell; in the l of Goshen let them dwell: 776
47:11 and gave them a possession in the l of Egypt, 776
47:11 in the best of the l, in the land of Rameses, 776
47:11 in the best of the land, in the l of Rameses, 776
47:13 *there was* no bread in all the l; for the famine 776
47:13 so that the l of Egypt and *all* the land of 776
47:13 *all* the l of Canaan fainted by reason of 776
47:14 the money that was found in the l of Egypt, 776
47:14 in the l of Canaan, for the corn which they 776
47:15 when money failed in the l of Egypt, and 776
47:15 in the l of Canaan, all the Egyptians came 776
47:19 we die before thine eyes, both we and our l? 127
47:19 buy us and our l for bread, and we and 127
47:19 we and our l will be servants unto Pharaoh: 127
47:19 and not die, that the l be not desolate. 127
47:20 Joseph bought all the l of Egypt for Pharaoh; 127
47:20 over them: so the l became Pharaoh's. 776
47:22 Only the l of the priests bought he not; 127
47:23 bought you *this* day and your l for Pharaoh: 127
47:23 *here is* seed for you, and ye shall sow the l. 127
47:26 Joseph made it a law over the l of Egypt 127
47:26 the fifth *part;* except the l of the priests only, 127
47:27 Israel dwelt in the l of Egypt, in the country 776
47:28 Jacob lived in the l of Egypt seventeen 776
48: 3 appeared unto me at Luz in the l of Canaan, 776
48: 4 will give this l to thy seed after thee *for* an 776
48: 5 which were born unto thee in the l of Egypt 776
48: 7 Rachel died by me in the l of Canaan in 776
48:21 bring you again unto the l of your fathers. 776
49:15 rest *was* good, and the l that *it was* pleasant; 776
49:30 which *is* before Mamre, in the l of Canaan, 776
50: 5 I have digged for me in the l of Canaan, 776
50: 7 and all the elders of the l of Egypt, 776
50: 8 and their herds, they left in the l of Goshen. 776
50:11 when the inhabitants of the l, the Canaanites, 776
50:13 For his sons carried him into the l of Canaan, 776
50:24 bring you out of this l unto the land which he 776
50:24 bring you out of this land unto the l which he 776
Ex 1: 7 and the l was filled with them. 776
1:10 against us, and *so* get them up out of the l. 776
2:15 of Pharaoh, and dwelt in the l of Midian: 776
2:22 he said, I have been a stranger in a strange l. 776
3: 8 to bring them up out of that l unto a good 776
3: 8 bring them up out of that land unto a good l 776
3: 8 unto a l flowing with milk and honey; 776
3:17 of Egypt unto the l of the Canaanites, 776
3:17 unto a l flowing with milk and honey. 776
4: 9 pour *it upon* the dry *l:* and the water which NIH
4: 9 the river shall become blood upon the dry *l.* NIH
4:20 an ass, and he returned to the l of Egypt: 776
5: 5 the people of the l now *are* many, and 776
5:12 l of Egypt to gather stubble instead of straw. 776
6: 1 a strong hand shall he drive them out of his l. 776
6: 4 to give them the l of Canaan, the land of 776
6: 4 the l of their pilgrimage, wherein they were 776
6: 8 I will bring you in unto the l, *concerning* 776
6:11 he let the children of Israel go out of his l. 776
6:13 to bring the children of Israel out of the l of 776
6:26 Bring out the children of Israel from the l of 776
6:28 LORD spake unto Moses in the l of Egypt, 776
7: 2 he send the children of Israel out of his l. 776
7: 3 my signs and my wonders in the l of Egypt. 776
7: 4 out of the l of Egypt by great judgments. 776
7:19 *that* there may be blood throughout all the l 776
7:21 there was blood throughout all the l of 776
8: 5 cause frogs to come up upon the l of Egypt. 776
8: 6 frogs came up, and covered the l of Egypt. 776
8: 7 and brought up frogs upon the l of Egypt. 776
8:14 them together upon heaps: and the l stank. 776
8:16 out thy rod, and smite the dust of the l, 776
8:16 that it may become lice throughout all the l 776
8:17 all the dust of the l became lice throughout 776
8:17 became lice throughout all the l of Egypt. 776
8:22 And I will sever in that day the l of Goshen, 776
8:24 servants' houses, and into all the l of Egypt: 776
8:24 the l was corrupted by reason of the swarm 776
8:25 said, Go ye, sacrifice to your God in the l. 776
9: 5 the LORD shall do this thing in the l. 776
9: 9 it shall become small dust in all the l of 776
9: 9 upon beast, throughout all the l of Egypt. 776
9:22 that there may be hail in all the l of Egypt, 776
9:22 herb of the field, throughout the l of Egypt. 776
9:23 the LORD rained hail upon the l of Egypt. 776
9:24 such as there was none like it in all the l of 776
9:25 the hail smote throughout all the l of Egypt 776
9:26 Only in the l of Goshen, where the children 776
10:12 Stretch out thine hand over the l of Egypt for 776
10:12 that they may come up upon the l of Egypt, 776
10:12 eat every herb of the l, *even* all that the hail 776
10:13 Moses stretched forth his rod over the l of 776
10:13 the LORD brought an east wind upon the l 776
10:14 the locusts went up over all the l of Egypt, 776
10:15 the whole earth, so that the l was darkened; 776
10:15 they did eat every herb of the l, and all 776
10:15 herbs of the field, through all the l of Egypt. 776

Ex 10:21 that there may be darkness over the l of 776
10:22 there was a thick darkness in all the l of 776
11: 3 man Moses *was* very great in the l of Egypt, 776
11: 5 all the firstborn in the l of Egypt shall die, 776
11: 6 there shall be a great cry throughout all the l 776
11: 9 that my wonders may be multiplied in the l 776
11:10 not let the children of Israel go out of his l. 776
12: 1 unto Moses and Aaron in the l of Egypt, 776
12:12 For I will pass through the l of Egypt this 776
12:12 will smite all the firstborn in the l of Egypt, 776
12:13 to destroy *you,* when I smite the l of Egypt. 776
12:17 I brought your armies out of the l of Egypt: 776
12:19 whether he be a stranger, or born in the l. 776
12:25 when ye be come to the l which the LORD 776
12:29 smote all the firstborn in the l of Egypt, 776
12:33 that they might send them out of the l in 776
12:41 of the LORD went out from the l of Egypt. 776
12:42 for bringing them out from the l of Egypt: 776
12:48 and he shall be as one that is born in the l: 776
12:51 Israel out of the l of Egypt by their armies. 776
13: 5 shall bring thee into the l of the Canaanites, 776
13: 5 give thee, a l flowing with milk and honey, 776
13:11 shall bring thee into the l of the Canaanites, 776
13:15 that the LORD slew all the firstborn in the l 776
13:17 *through* the way of the l of the Philistines, 776
13:18 went up harnessed out of the l of Egypt. 776
14: 3 They *are* entangled in the l, the wilderness 776
14:21 made the sea dry *l,* and the waters were NIH
14:29 the children of Israel walked upon dry *l* in NIH
15:19 the children of Israel went on dry *l* in NIH
16: 1 after their departing out of the l of Egypt. 776
16: 3 by the hand of the LORD in the l of Egypt, 776
16: 6 hath brought you out from the l of Egypt: 776
16:32 when I brought you forth from the l of 776
16:35 forty years, until they came to a l inhabited; 776
16:35 until they came unto the borders of the l of 776
18: 3 he said, I have been an alien in a strange l: 776
18:27 and he went his way into his own l. 776
19: 1 Israel were gone forth out of the l of Egypt, 776
20: 2 which have brought thee out of the l of 776
20:12 that thy days may be long upon the l which 127
22:21 for ye were strangers in the l of Egypt. 776
23: 9 seeing ye were strangers in the l of Egypt. 776
23:10 six years thou shalt sow thy l, and 776
23:19 The first of the firstfruits of thy l thou shalt 127
23:26 cast their young, nor be barren, in thy l: 776
23:29 lest the l become desolate, and the beast of 776
23:30 until thou be increased, and inherit the l. 776
23:31 for I will deliver the inhabitants of the l into 776
23:33 They shall not dwell in thy l, lest they make 776
29:46 that brought them forth out of the l of Egypt, 776
32: 1 the man that brought us up out of the l of 776
32: 4 which brought thee up out of the l of Egypt. 776
32: 7 which thou broughtest out of the l of Egypt, 776
32: 8 which have brought thee up out of the l of 776
32:11 which thou hast brought forth out of the l of 776
32:13 all this l that I have spoken of will I give 776
32:23 the man that brought us up out of the l of 776
33: 1 thou hast brought up out of the l of Egypt, 776
33: 1 unto the l which I sware unto Abraham, 776
33: 3 Unto a l flowing with milk and honey: for I 776
34:12 the inhabitants of the l whither thou goest, 776
34:15 a covenant with the inhabitants of the l, 776
34:24 neither shall any man desire thy l, when thou 776
34:26 The first of the firstfruits of thy l thou shalt 127
Lev 11:45 that bringeth you up out of the l of Egypt, 776
14:34 When ye be come into the l of Canaan, 776
14:34 I put the plague of leprosy in a house of the l 776
16:22 him all their iniquities unto a l not inhabited: 776
18: 3 After the doings of the l of Egypt, 776
18: 3 after the doings of the l of Canaan, whither I 776
18:25 the l is defiled: therefore I do visit 776
18:25 and the l *itself* vomiteth out her inhabitants. 776
18:27 abominations have the men of the l done, 776
18:27 which *were* before you, and the l is defiled;) 776
18:28 That the l spue not you out also, when ye 776
19: 9 when ye reap the harvest of your l, thou shalt 776
19:23 when ye shall come into the l, and shall have 776
19:29 lest the l fall to whoredom, and the land 776
19:29 and the l become full of wickedness. 776
19:33 And if a stranger sojourn with thee in your l, 776
19:34 for ye were strangers in the l of Egypt: 776
19:36 which brought you out of the l of Egypt. 776
20: 2 the people of the l shall stone him with 776
20: 4 if the people of the l do any ways hide their 776
20:22 that the l, whither I bring you to dwell 776
20:24 Ye shall inherit their l, and I will give it unto 127
20:24 a l that floweth with milk and honey: 776
22:24 you make *any* offering *thereof* in your l. 776
22:33 That brought you out of the l of Egypt, to be 776
23:10 When ye be come into the l which I give 776
23:22 when ye reap the harvest of your l, thou shalt 776
23:39 when ye have gathered in the fruit of the l, 776
23:43 when I brought them out of the l of Egypt: 776
24:16 well the stranger, as he **that is born in** the l, 249
25: 2 When ye come into the l which I give you, 776
25: 2 shall the l keep a sabbath unto the LORD. 776
25: 4 year shall be a sabbath of rest unto the l, 776
25: 5 *for* it is a year of rest unto the l. 776
25: 6 the sabbath of the l shall be meat for you; 776
25: 7 thy cattle, and for the beast that *are* in thy l, 776
25: 9 the trumpet sound throughout all your l. 776
25:10 proclaim liberty throughout *all* the l unto all 776
25:18 do them; and ye shall dwell in the l in safety. 776
25:19 the l shall yield her fruit, and ye shall eat 776
25:23 The l shall not be sold for ever: for the land 776
25:23 for the l *is* mine; for ye *were* strangers and 776
25:24 in all the l of your possession ye shall grant a 776
25:24 ye shall grant a redemption for the l. 776
25:38 which brought you forth out of the l of 776
25:38 to give you the l of Canaan, *and* to be your 776
25:42 which I brought forth out of the l of Egypt: 776
25:45 that *are* with you, which they begat in your l: 776
25:55 whom I brought forth out of the l of Egypt: 776
26: 1 shall ye set up *any* image of stone in your l, 776

Lev 26: 4 the l shall yield her increase, and the trees of 776
26: 5 bread to the full, and dwell in your l safely. 776
26: 6 I will give peace in the l, and ye shall lie 776
26: 6 I will rid evil beasts out of the l, neither shall 776
26: 6 neither shall the sword go through your l. 776
26:13 which brought you forth out of the l of 776
26:20 for your l shall not yield her increase, neither 776
26:20 neither shall the trees of the l yield their 776
26:32 I will bring the l into desolation: and 776
26:33 your l shall be desolate, and your cities 776
26:34 shall the l enjoy her sabbaths, as long as it 776
26:34 lieth desolate, and ye *be* in your enemies' l; 776
26:34 *even* then shall the l rest, and enjoy her 776
26:38 and the l of your enemies shall eat you up. 776
26:41 have brought them into the l of their 776
26:42 will I remember; and I will remember the l. 776
26:43 The l also shall be left of them, and 776
26:44 when they be in the l of their enemies, 776
26:45 whom I brought forth out of the l of Egypt in 776
27:24 *even* to him to whom the possession of the l 776
27:30 all the tithe of the l, *whether* of the seed of 776
27:30 *whether* of the seed of the l, *or* of the fruit of 776
Nu 1: 1 after they were come out of the l of Egypt, 776
3:13 l of Egypt I hallowed unto me all 776
8:17 that I smote every firstborn in the l of Egypt, 776
9: 1 after they were come out of the l of Egypt, 776
9:14 and for him that was born in the l. 776
10: 9 if ye go *to* war in your l against the enemy 776
10:30 I will depart to mine own l, and to my 776
11:12 unto the l which thou swarest unto their 127
13: 2 that they may search the l of Canaan, 776
13:16 the men which Moses sent to spy out the l. 776
13:17 Moses sent them to spy out the l of Canaan, 776
13:18 see the l, what it *is;* and the people that 776
13:19 what the l *is* that they dwell in, whether it *be* 776
13:20 what the l *is,* whether it *be* fat or lean, 776
13:20 good courage, and bring of the fruit of the l. 776
13:21 searched the l from the wilderness of Zin 776
13:25 they returned from searching of the l after 776
13:26 and shewed them the fruit of the l. 776
13:27 We came unto the l whither thou sentest us, 776
13:28 the people *be* strong that dwell in the l, 776
13:29 The Amalekites dwell in the l of the south: 776
13:32 they brought up an evil report of the l which 776
13:32 saying, The l, through which we have gone 776
13:32 *is* a l that eateth up the inhabitants thereof; 776
14: 2 Would God that we had died in the l of 776
14: 3 *hath* the LORD brought us unto this l, 776
14: 6 *which were* of them that searched the l, 776
14: 7 saying, The l, which we passed through to 776
14: 7 through to search it, *is* an exceeding good l. 776
14: 8 he will bring us into this l, and give it us; 776
14: 8 it us; a l which floweth with milk and honey. 776
14: 9 neither fear ye the people of the l; 776
14:14 they will tell *it* to the inhabitants of this l: 776
14:16 people into the l which he sware unto them, 776
14:23 Surely they shall not see the l which I sware 776
14:24 him will I bring into the l whereinto he went; 776
14:30 Doubtless ye shall not come into the l, 776
14:31 they shall know the l which ye have 776
14:34 of the days *in* which ye searched the l, 776
14:36 the men, which Moses sent to search the l, 776
14:36 by bringing up a slander upon the l, 776
14:37 that did bring up the evil report upon the l, 776
14:38 *were* of the men that went to search the l, 776
15: 2 When ye be come into the l of your 776
15:18 When ye come into the l whither I bring you, 776
15:19 *that* when ye eat of the bread of the l, 776
15:30 *whether he be* **born in the** l, or a stranger, 249
15:41 which brought you out of the l of Egypt, 776
16:13 us up out of a l that floweth with milk 776
16:14 Moreover thou hast not brought us into a l 776
18:13 *And* whatsoever is first ripe in the l, 776
18:20 Thou shalt have no inheritance in their l, 776
20:12 ye shall not bring this congregation into the l 776
20:23 by the coast of the l of Edom, saying, 776
20:24 for he shall not enter into the l which I have 776
21: 4 of the Red sea, to compass the l of Edom: 776
21:22 Let me pass through thy l: we will not turn 776
21:24 and possessed his l from Arnon unto Jabbok, 776
21:26 taken all his l out of his hand, *even* unto 776
21:31 Thus Israel dwelt in the l of the Amorites. 776
21:34 into thy hand, and all his people, and his l; 776
21:35 none left him alive: and they possessed his l. 776
22: 5 which *is* by the river *of* the l of the children 776
22: 6 and *that* I may drive them out of the l: 776
22:13 the princes of Balak, Get you into your l: 776
26: 4 which went forth out of the l of Egypt. 776
26:19 and Er and Onan died in the l of Canaan. 776
26:53 Unto these the l shall be divided for an 776
26:55 Notwithstanding the l shall be divided by lot: 776
27:12 see the l which I have given unto 776
32: 1 when they saw the l of Jazer, and the land of 776
32: 1 the l of Gilead, that behold, the place *was* a 776
32: 4 *is* a l for cattle, and thy servants have cattle: 776
32: 5 let this l be given unto thy servants for a 776
32: 7 the l which the LORD hath given them? 776
32: 8 I sent them from Kadesh-barnea to see the l. 776
32: 9 up unto the valley of Eshcol, and saw the l, 776
32: 9 that *they* should not go into the l which 776
32:11 shall see the l which I sware unto Abraham, 127
32:17 because of the inhabitants of the l. 776
32:22 the l be subdued before the LORD: then 776
32:22 this l shall be your possession before 776
32:29 and the l shall be subdued before you; 776
32:29 ye shall give them the l of Gilead for a 776
32:30 possessions among you in the l of Canaan. 776
32:32 before the LORD *into* the l of Canaan, 776
32:33 the l, with the cities thereof in the coasts, 776
33: 1 which went forth out of the l of Egypt with 776
33:37 in mount Hor, in the edge of the l of Edom. 776
33:38 of Israel were come out of the l of Egypt, 776
33:40 which dwelt in the south in the l of Canaan, 776
33:51 When ye are passed over Jordan into the l of 776
33:52 ye shall drive out all the inhabitants of the l 776

Nu 33:53 ye shall dispossess *the inhabitants of* the l, 776
33:53 for I have given you the l to possess it. 776
33:54 ye shall divide the l by lot for an inheritance 776
33:55 out the inhabitants of the l from before you; 776
33:55 and shall vex you in the l wherein ye dwell. 776
34: 2 When ye come into the l of Canaan; 776
34: 2 (this *is* the l that shall fall unto you for an 776
34: 2 *even* the l of Canaan with the coasts 776
34:12 this shall be your l with the coasts thereof 776
34:13 This *is* the l which ye shall inherit by lot, 776
34:17 of the men which shall divide the l unto you: 776
34:18 of every tribe, to divide the l by inheritance. 776
34:29 unto the children of Israel in the l of Canaan. 776
35:10 When ye be come over Jordan into the l of 776
35:14 three cities shall ye give in the l of Canaan, 776
35:28 shall return into the l of his possession. 776
35:32 that he should come again to dwell in the l, 776
35:33 So ye shall not pollute the l wherein ye *are:* 776
35:33 wherein ye *are:* for blood it defileth the l: 776
35:33 the l cannot be cleansed of the blood that is 776
35:34 therefore the l which ye shall inhabit, 776
36: 2 l for an inheritance by lot to the children of 776
Dt 1: 5 On *this* side Jordan, in the l of Moab, 776
1: 7 *to* the l of the Canaanites, and *unto* Lebanon, 776
1: 8 Behold, I have set the l before you: go in and 776
1: 8 possess the l which the LORD sware unto 776
1:21 the LORD thy God hath set the l before 776
1:22 they shall search us out the l, and bring us 776
1:25 they took of the fruit of the l in their hands, 776
1:25 *It is* a good l which the LORD our God 776
1:27 he hath brought us forth out of the l of 776
1:35 men of this evil generation see that good l, 776
1:36 to him will I give the l that he hath trodden 776
2: 5 for I will not give you of their l, no, not so 776
2: 9 for I will not give thee of their l *for* a 776
2:12 as Israel did unto the l of his possession, 776
2:19 for I will not give thee of the l of 776
2:20 (That also was accounted a l of giants: 776
2:24 the Amorite, king of Heshbon, and his l: 776
2:27 Let me pass through thy l: I will go along by 776
2:29 until I shall pass over Jordan into the l which 776
2:31 begin to give Sihon and his l before thee: 776
2:31 to possess, that *thou* mayest inherit his l. 776
2:37 Only unto the l of the children of Ammon 776
3: 2 and all his people, and his l, into thy hand; 776
3: 8 Amorites the l that *was* on *this* side Jordan, 776
3:12 And this l, *which* we possessed at that time, 776
3:13 all Bashan, which was called the l of giants. 776
3:18 The LORD your God hath given you this l 776
3:20 *until* they also possess the l which 776
3:25 and see the good l that *is* beyond Jordan, 776
3:28 he shall cause them to inherit the l which 776
4: 1 possess the l which the LORD God of your 776
4: 5 so in the l whither ye go to possess it. 776
4:14 that ye might do them in the l whither ye go 776
4:21 and that *I* should not go in unto *that* good l, 776
4:22 I *must* die in this l, I *must* not go over 776
4:22 but ye *shall* go over, and possess that good l. 776
4:25 and ye shall have remained long in the l, and 776
4:26 ye shall soon utterly perish from off the l 776
4:38 to give thee their l *for* an inheritance, as *it is* 776
4:46 in the l of Sihon king of the Amorites, 776
4:47 they possessed his l, and the land of Og king 776
4:47 the l of Og king of Bashan, two kings of 776
5: 6 which brought thee out of the l of Egypt, 776
5:15 remember that thou wast a servant in the l of 776
5:16 in the l which the LORD thy God giveth 127
5:31 that they may do *them* in the l which I give 776
5:33 *that* ye may prolong *your* days in the l which 776
6: 1 that ye might do *them* in the l whither ye go 776
6: 3 *in* the l that floweth with milk and honey. 776
6:10 into the l which he sware unto thy fathers, 776
6:12 which brought thee forth out of the l of 776
6:18 possess the good l which the LORD sware 776
6:23 to give us the l which he sware unto our 776
7: 1 into the l whither thou goest to possess it, 776
7:13 and the fruit of thy l, thy corn, and thy wine, 127
7:13 in the l which he sware unto thy fathers to 127
8: 1 possess the l which the LORD sware unto 776
8: 7 LORD thy God bringeth thee into a good l, 776
8: 7 a l of brooks of water, of fountains and 776
8: 8 A l of wheat, and barley, and vines, and 776
8: 8 pomegranates; a l of oil olive, and honey; 776
8: 9 A l wherein thou shalt eat bread without 776
8: 9 a l whose stones *are* iron, and out of whose 776
8:10 God for the good l which he hath given thee. 776
8:14 which brought thee forth out of the l of 776
9: 4 LORD hath brought me in to possess this l: 776
9: 5 of thine heart, dost thou go to possess their l: 776
9: 6 good l to possess it for thy righteousness; 776
9: 7 that thou didst depart out of the l of Egypt, 776
9:23 and possess the l which I have given you; 776
9:28 Lest the l whence thou broughtest us out say, 776
9:28 them into the l which he promised them, 776
10: 7 Gudgodah to Jotbath, a l of rivers of waters. 776
10:11 that they may go in and possess the l, 776
10:19 for ye were strangers in the l of Egypt. 776
11: 3 Pharaoh the king of Egypt, and unto all his l; 776
11: 8 may be strong, and go in and possess the l, 776
11: 9 that ye may prolong *your* days in the l, 127
11: 9 a l that floweth with milk and honey. 776
11:10 For the l, whither thou goest in to possess it, 776
11:10 *is* not as the l of Egypt, from whence ye 776
11:11 the l, whither ye go to possess it, *is* a land of 776
11:11 *is* a l of hills and valleys, *and* drinketh water 776
11:12 A l which the LORD thy God careth for: 776
11:14 That I will give *you* the rain of your l in his 776
11:17 be no rain, and *that* the l yield not her fruit; 127
11:17 *lest* ye perish quickly from off the good l 776
11:21 in the l which the LORD sware unto your 127
11:25 the dread of you upon all the l that ye shall 776
11:29 in unto the l whither thou goest to possess it, 776
11:30 sun goeth down, in the l of the Canaanites, 776
11:31 l which the LORD your God giveth you, 776
12: 1 which ye shall observe to do in the l, 776
Dt 12:10 dwell in the l which the LORD your God 776
12:29 thou succeedest them, and dwellest in their l; 776
13: 5 which brought you out of the l of Egypt, and 776
13:10 which brought thee out of the l of Egypt, 776
15: 4 l which the LORD thy God giveth thee *for* 776
15: 7 thy l which the LORD thy God giveth thee, 776
15:11 For the poor shall never cease out of the l: 776
15:11 to thy poor, and to thy needy, in thy l. 776
15:15 that thou wast a bondman in the l of Egypt, 776
16: 3 for thou camest forth out of the l of Egypt in 776
16: 3 out of the l of Egypt all the days of thy life. 776
16:20 inherit the l which the LORD thy God 776
17:14 When thou art come unto the l which 776
18: 9 When thou art come into the l which 776
19: 1 whose l the LORD thy God giveth thee, 776
19: 2 three cities for thee in the midst of thy l, 776
19: 3 thee a way, and divide the coasts of thy l, 776
19: 8 give thee all the l which he promised to give 776
19:10 That innocent blood be not shed in thy l, 776
19:14 which thou shalt inherit in the l that 776
20: 1 which brought thee up out of the l of Egypt. 776
21: 1 If *one* be found slain in the l which 127
21:23 that thy l be not defiled, which the LORD 127
23: 7 because thou wast a stranger in his l. 776
23:20 to in the l whither thou goest to possess it. 776
24: 4 thou shalt not cause the l to sin, which 776
24:14 of thy strangers that *are* in thy l within thy 776
24:22 that thou wast a bondman in the l of Egypt: 776
25:15 that thy days may be lengthened in the l 127
25:19 in the l which the LORD thy God giveth 776
26: 1 when thou art come in unto the l which 776
26: 2 which thou shalt bring of thy l that 776
26: 9 hath given us this l, *even* a land that floweth 776
26: 9 *even* a l that floweth with milk and honey. 776
26:10 behold, I have brought the firstfruits of the l, 127
26:15 and the l which thou hast given us, 127
26:15 a l that floweth with milk and honey. 776
27: 2 the l which the LORD thy God giveth thee, 776
27: 3 that thou mayest go in unto the l which 776
27: 3 a l that floweth with milk and honey; 776
28: 8 he shall bless thee in the l which the LORD 776
28:11 in the l which the LORD sware unto thy 127
28:12 the heaven to give the rain unto thy l in his 776
28:18 the fruit of thy l, the increase of thy kine, 127
28:21 until he have consumed thee from off the l, 127
28:24 The LORD shall make the rain of thy l 776
28:33 The fruit of thy l, and all thy labours, shall a 127
28:42 and fruit of thy l shall the locust consume. 127
28:51 and the fruit of thy l, until thou be destroyed: 127
28:52 wherein thou trustedst, throughout all thy l: 776
28:52 thee in all thy gates throughout all thy l, 776
28:63 ye shall be plucked from off the l whither 127
29: 1 with the children of Israel in the l of Moab, 776
29: 2 your eyes in the l of Egypt unto Pharaoh, 776
29: 2 and unto all his servants, and unto all his l; 776
29: 8 we took their l, and gave it for an inheritance 776
29:16 (For ye know how we have dwelt in the l of 776
29:22 and the stranger that shall come from a far l, 776
29:22 when they see the plagues of that l, and 776
29:23 *And that* the whole l thereof *is* brimstone, 776
29:24 hath the LORD done thus unto this l? 776
29:25 he brought them forth out of the l of Egypt: 776
29:27 of the LORD was kindled against this l, 776
29:28 the LORD rooted them out of their l in 127
29:28 and cast them into another l, as *it is* this day. 776
30: 5 the LORD thy God will bring thee into the l 776
30: 9 thy cattle, and in the fruit of thy l, for good: 127
30:16 the LORD thy God shall bless thee in the l 776
30:18 ye shall not prolong *your* days upon the l, 127
30:20 that thou mayest dwell in the l which 127
31: 4 and unto the l of them, whom he destroyed. 776
31: 7 for thou must go with this people unto the l 776
31:13 as long as ye live in the l whither ye go over 127
31:16 after the gods of the strangers of the l, 776
31:20 *For* when I shall have brought them into the l 127
31:21 before I have brought them into the l which I 776
31:23 of Israel into the l which I sware unto them: 776
32:10 He found him in a desert l, and in the waste 776
32:43 will be merciful *unto* his l, *and to* his people. 127
32:47 this thing ye shall prolong *your* days in the l, 127
32:49 *unto* mount Nebo, which *is* in the l of Moab, 776
32:49 behold the l of Canaan, which I give unto 776
32:52 Yet thou shalt see the l before *thee;* but 776
32:52 thou shalt not go thither unto the l which I 776
33:13 he said, Blessed of the LORD *be* his l, 776
33:28 the fountain of Jacob *shall be* upon a l of 776
34: 1 the LORD shewed him all the l of Gilead, 776
34: 2 the l of Ephraim, and Manasseh, and all 776
34: 2 Manasseh, and all the l of Judah, unto 776
34: 4 This *is* the l which I sware unto Abraham, 776
34: 5 of the LORD died there in the l of Moab, 776
34: 6 he buried him in a valley in the l of Moab, 776
34:11 which the LORD sent him to do in the l of 776
34:11 and to all his servants, and to all his l, 776
Jos 1: 2 unto the l which I do give to them, 776
1: 4 all the l of the Hittites, and unto the great sea 776
1: 6 shalt thou divide for an inheritance the l, 776
1:11 over this Jordan, to go in to possess the l, 776
1:13 given you rest, and hath given you this l. 776
1:14 shall remain in the l which Moses gave you 776
1:15 they also have possessed the l which 776
1:15 ye shall return unto the l of your possession, 776
2: 1 saying, Go view the l, even Jericho. 776
2: 9 I know that the LORD hath given you the l, 776
2: 9 that all the inhabitants of the l faint because 776
2:14 when the LORD hath given us the l, 776
2:18 Behold, *when* we come into the l, thou shalt 776
2:24 hath delivered into our hands all the l; 776
4:18 *l,* that the waters of Jordan returned unto NIH
4:22 Israel came over this Jordan on dry *l.* NIH
5: 6 sware that *he* would not shew them the l, 776
5: 6 a l that floweth with milk and honey. 776
5:11 they did eat of the old corn of the l on 776
5:12 after they had eaten of the old corn of the l; 776
5:12 they did eat of the fruit of the l of Canaan 776
Jos 7: 9 all the inhabitants of the l shall hear *of it,* 776
8: 1 of Ai, and his people, and his city, and his l: 776
9:24 his servant Moses to give you all the l, 776
9:24 to destroy all the inhabitants of the l from 776
10:42 and their l did Joshua take *at* one time, 776
11: 3 *to* the Hivite under Hermon in the l of 776
11:16 So Joshua took all that l, the hills, and all 776
11:16 all the south *country,* and all the l of Goshen, 776
11:22 There was none of the Anakims left in the l 776
11:23 So Joshua took the whole l, according to all 776
11:23 by their tribes. And the l rested from war. 776
12: 1 Now these *are* the kings of the l, which 776
12: 1 possessed their l on the *other* side Jordan 776
13: 1 there remaineth *yet* very much l to be 776
13: 2 This is the l that *yet* remaineth: all 776
13: 4 all the l of the Canaanites, and Mearah that 776
13: 5 the l of the Giblites, and all Lebanon, 776
13: 7 divide this l for an inheritance unto the nine 776
13:25 and half the l of the children of Ammon, 776
14: 1 of Israel inherited in the l of Canaan, 776
14: 4 they gave no part unto the Levites in the l, 776
14: 5 children of Israel did, and they divided the l. 776
14: 7 me from Kadesh-barnea to espy out the l; 776
14: 9 Surely the l whereon thy feet have trodden 776
14:15 the Anakims. And the l had rest from war. 776
15:19 a blessing; for thou hast given me a south l; 776
17: 5 beside the l of Gilead and Bashan, 776
17: 6 the rest of Manasseh's sons had the l of 776
17: 8 *Now* Manasseh had the l of Tappuah: but 776
17:12 but the Canaanites would dwell in that l. 776
17:15 cut down for thyself there in the l of 776
17:16 all the Canaanites that dwell in the l of 776
18: 1 And the l was subdued before them. 776
18: 3 long *are* you slack to go to possess the l, 776
18: 4 go through the l, and describe it according to 776
18: 6 therefore describe the l *into* seven parts, 776
18: 8 charged them that went to describe the l, 776
18: 8 Go and walk through the l, and describe it, 776
18: 9 And the men went and passed through the l, 776
18:10 there Joshua divided the l unto the children 776
19:49 When they had made an end of dividing the l 776
21: 2 they spake unto them at Shiloh in the l of 776
21:43 the LORD gave unto Israel all the l which 776
22: 4 your tents, *and* unto the l of your possession, 776
22: 9 which *is* in the l of Canaan, to go unto 776
22: 9 to the l of their possession, whereof they 776
22:10 that *are* in the l of Canaan, the children of 776
22:11 built an altar over against the l of Canaan, 776
22:13 half tribe of Manasseh, into the l of Gilead, 776
22:15 unto the l of Gilead, and they spake with 776
22:19 if the l of your possession *be* unclean, *then* 776
22:19 pass ye over unto the l of the possession of 776
22:32 out of the l of Gilead, unto the land of 776
22:32 unto the l of Canaan, to the children of 776
22:33 to destroy the l wherein the children of 776
23: 5 ye shall possess their l, as the LORD your 776
23:13 until ye perish from off this good l which 127
23:15 l which the LORD your God hath given 127
23:16 ye shall perish quickly from off the good l 776
24: 3 led him throughout all the l of Canaan, and 776
24: 8 And I brought you into the l of the Amorites, 776
24: 8 into your hand, that ye might possess their l; 776
24:13 I have given you a l for which ye did not 776
24:15 gods of the Amorites, in whose l ye dwell: 776
24:17 us up and our fathers out of the l of Egypt, 776
24:18 even the Amorites which dwelt in the l: 776
Jdg 1: 2 behold, I have delivered the l into his hand. 776
1:15 for thou hast given me a south l; give me 776
1:26 the man went *into* the l of the Hittites, and 776
1:27 but the Canaanites would dwell in that l. 776
1:32 the Canaanites, the inhabitants of the l: 776
1:33 the Canaanites, the inhabitants of the l: 776
2: 1 have brought you unto the l which I sware 776
2: 2 make no league with the inhabitants of this l; 776
2: 6 man unto his inheritance to possess the l. 776
2:12 which brought them out of the l of Egypt, 776
3:11 the l had rest forty years. And Othniel 776
3:30 of Israel. And the l had rest fourscore years. 776
5:31 in his might. And the l had rest forty years. 776
6: 5 and they entered into the l to destroy it. 776
6: 9 out from before you, and gave you their l; 776
6:10 gods of the Amorites, in whose l ye dwell: 776
9:37 come people down by the middle of the l, 776
10: 4 unto this day, which *are* in the l of Gilead. 776
10: 8 *other* side Jordan in the l of the Amorites, 776
11: 3 from his brethren, and dwelt in the l of Tob: 776
11: 5 went to fetch Jephthah out of the l of Tob: 776
11:12 thou art come against me to fight in my l? 776
11:13 Because Israel took away my l, when they 776
11:15 Israel took not away the l of Moab, 776
11:15 nor the l of the children of Ammon: 776
11:17 Let me, I pray thee, pass through thy l: 776
11:18 compassed the l of Edom, and the land of 776
11:18 the l of Moab, and came by the east side of 776
11:18 came by the east side of the l of Moab, and 776
11:19 we pray thee, through thy l into my place. 776
11:21 so Israel possessed all the l of the Amorites, 776
12:15 was buried in Pirathon in the l of Ephraim, 776
18: 2 to spy out the l, and to search it; 776
18: 2 and they said unto them, Go, search the l: 776
18: 7 *there was* no magistrate in the l, that might 776
18: 9 for we have seen the l, and behold, it *is* very 776
18: 9 slothful to go, *and* to enter to possess the l. 776
18:10 come unto a people secure, and to a large l: 776
18:17 the five men that went to spy out the l went 776
18:30 of Dan until the day of the captivity of the l. 776
19:30 came up out of the l of Egypt unto this day: 776
20: 1 with the l of Gilead, unto the LORD *in* 776
21:12 camp *to* Shiloh, which *is* in the l of Canaan. 776
21:21 of Shiloh, and go *to* the l of Benjamin. 776
Ru 1: 1 judges ruled, that there was a famine in the l. 776
1: 7 they went on the way to return unto the l of 776
2:11 the l of thy nativity, and art come unto a 776
4: 3 selleth a parcel of l, which *was* our brother 7704
1Sa 6: 5 and images of your mice that mar the l; 776

L

1Sa 6: 5 and from off your l. 776
9: 4 passed through the l of Shalisha, but 776
9: 4 then they passed through the l of Shalim, and 776
9: 4 he passed through the l of the Benjamites, 776
9: 5 *And* when they were come to the l of Zuph, 776
9:16 send thee a man out of the l of Benjamin, 776
12: 6 that brought your fathers up out of the l of 776
13: 3 Saul blew the trumpet throughout all the l, 776
13: 7 Hebrews went over Jordan *to* the l of Gad 776
13:17 that leadeth to Ophrah, unto the l of Shual: 776
13:19 no smith found throughout all the l of Israel: 776
14:14 within as it were a half acre of l, 7704
14:25 all *they of* the l came to a wood; and 776
14:29 said Jonathan, My father hath troubled the l: 776
21:11 unto him, *Is* not this David the king of the l? 776
22: 5 depart, and get thee *into* the l of Judah. 776
23:23 it shall come to pass, if he be in the l, that I 776
23:27 come; for the Philistines have invaded the l. 776
27: 1 speedily escape into the l of the Philistines; 776
27: 8 the inhabitants of the l as thou goest to Shur, 776
27: 8 thou goest to Shur, even unto the l of Egypt. 776
27: 9 David smote the l, and left neither man nor 776
28: 3 familiar spirits, and the wizards, out of the l. 776
28: 9 familiar spirits, and the wizards, out of the l: 776
29:11 to return into the l of the Philistines. 776
30:16 they had taken out of the l of the Philistines, 776
30:16 of the Philistines, and out of the l of Judah. 776
31: 9 sent into the l of the Philistines round about, 776
2Sa 3:12 David on his behalf, saying, Whose *is* the l? 776
5: 6 unto the Jebusites, the inhabitants of the l: 776
7:23 do for you great things and terrible, for thy l, 776
9: 7 will restore thee all the l of Saul thy father; 7704
9:10 shall till the l for him, and thou shalt bring in 127
10: 2 David's servants came *into* the l of 776
15: 4 Oh that I were made judge in the l, 776
17:26 and Absalom pitched *in* the l of Gilead. 776
19: 9 and now he is fled out of the l for Absalom. 776
19:29 I have said, Thou and Ziba divide the l. 7704
21:14 And after that God was intreated for the l. 776
24: 6 to Gilead, and to the l of Tahtim-hodshi; 776
24: 8 So when they had gone through all the l, 776
24:13 years of famine come unto thee in thy l? 776
24:13 that there be three days' pestilence in thy l? 776
24:25 So the LORD was intreated for the l, and 776
1Ki 4:10 *pertained* Sochoh, and all the l of Hepher: 776
4:19 *he was* the only officer which *was* in the l. 776
4:21 from the river *unto* the l of the Philistines, 776
6: 1 of Israel were come out of the l of Egypt, 776
8: 9 when they came out of the l of Egypt. 776
8:21 when he brought them out of the l of Egypt. 776
8:34 bring them again unto the l which thou 127
8:36 give rain upon thy l, which thou hast given 776
8:37 If there be in the l famine, if there be 776
8:37 if their enemy besiege them in the l of their 776
8:40 in the l which thou gavest unto our fathers. 127
8:46 that they carry them away captives unto the l 776
8:47 *Yet* if they shall bethink themselves in the l 776
8:47 make supplication unto thee in the l of them 776
8:48 with all their soul, in the l of their enemies, 776
8:48 and pray unto thee toward their l, 776
9: 7 will I cut off Israel out of the l which I have 127
9: 8 Why hath the LORD done thus unto this l, 776
9: 9 who brought forth their fathers out of the l of 776
9:11 gave Hiram twenty cities in the l of Galilee. 776
9:13 he called them the l of Cabul unto this day. 776
9:18 and Tadmor in the wilderness, in the l, 776
9:19 in Lebanon, and in all the l of his dominion. 776
9:21 children that were left after them in the l, 776
9:26 on the shore of the Red sea, in the l of Edom. 776
10: 6 report that I heard in mine own l of thy acts 776
11:18 and appointed him victuals, and gave him l. 776
12:28 which brought thee up out of the l of Egypt. 776
14:15 and he shall root up Israel out of this good l, 127
14:24 there were also sodomites in the l: *and* 776
15:12 And he took away the sodomites out of the l, 776
15:20 and all Cinneroth, with all the l of Naphtali. 776
17: 7 because there had been no rain in the l. 776
18: 5 Go into the l, unto all fountains of water, and 776
18: 6 So they divided the l between them to pass 776
20: 7 king of Israel called all the elders of the l, 776
22:46 days of his father Asa, he took out of the l. 776
2Ki 2:21 be from thence any more death or barren *l*. NIH
3:19 and mar every good **piece of** l with stones. 2513
3:25 *on* every good **piece of** l cast every man his 2513
3:27 from him, and returned to *their own* l. 776
4:38 *there was* a dearth in the l; and the sons of 776
5: 2 had brought away captive out of the l of 776
5: 4 thus said the maid that *is* of the l of Israel. 776
6:23 of Syria came no more into the l of Israel. 776
8: 1 and it shall also come upon the l seven years. 776
8: 2 sojourned in the l of the Philistines seven 776
8: 3 that the woman returned out of the l of 776
8: 3 unto the king for her house and for her l. 7704
8: 5 cried to the king for her house and for her l. 7704
8: 6 of the field since the day that she left the l, 776
10:33 all the l of Gilead, the Gadites, and 776
11: 3 six years. And Athaliah *did* reign over the l. 776
11:14 all the people of the l rejoiced, and 776
11:18 all the people of the l went *into* the house of 776
11:19 and the guard, and all the people of the l; 776
11:20 all the people of the l rejoiced, and the city 776
13:20 the bands of the Moabites invaded the l *at* 776
15: 5 over the house, judging the people of the l. 776
15:19 Pul the king of Assyria came against the l: 776
15:20 turned back, and stayed not there in the l. 776
15:29 all the l of Naphtali, and carried them 776
16:15 the burnt offering of all the people of the l, 776
17: 5 king of Assyria came up throughout all the l, 776
17: 7 which had brought them up out of the l of 776
17:23 So was Israel carried away out of their own l 127
17:26 know not the manner of the God of the l: 776
17:26 know not the manner of the God of the l. 776
17:27 teach them the manner of the God of the l. 776
17:36 who brought you up out of the l of Egypt 776
18:25 to me, Go up against this l, and destroy it. 776

2Ki 18:32 and take you away to a l like your own land, 776
18:32 and take you away to a land like your own l, 776
18:32 a l of corn and wine, a land of bread and 776
18:32 of corn and wine, a l of bread and vineyards, 776
18:32 and vineyards, a l of oil olive and of honey, 776
18:33 his l out of the hand of the king of Assyria? 776
19: 7 hear a rumour, and shall return to his own l; 776
19: 7 cause him to fall by the sword in his own l. 776
19:37 they escaped *into* the l of Armenia. 776
21: 8 more out of the l which I gave their fathers; 127
21:24 the people of the l slew all them that had 776
21:24 the people of the l made Josiah his son king 776
23:24 all the abominations that were spied in the l 776
23:30 the people of the l took Jehoahaz the son of 776
23:33 him in bands at Riblah in the l of Hamath, 776
23:33 put the l to a tribute of an hundred talents of 776
23:35 he taxed the l to give the money according to 776
23:35 the silver and the gold of the people of the l, 776
24: 7 Egypt came not again any more out of his l: 776
24:14 save the poorest sort of the people of the l. 776
24:15 and his officers, and the mighty of the l, 776
25: 3 there was no bread for the people of the l. 776
25:12 left of the poor of the l to be vinedressers 776
25:19 which mustered the people of the l, and 776
25:19 threescore men of the people of the l that 776
25:21 and slew them at Riblah in the l of Hamath. 776
25:21 So Judah was carried away out of their l. 127
25:22 *as for* the people that remained in the l of 776
25:24 dwell in the l, and serve the king of Babylon; 776
1Ch 1:43 Now these *are* the kings that reigned in the l 776
1:45 Husham of the l of the Temanites reigned in 776
2:22 had three and twenty cities in the l of Gilead. 776
4:40 and the l *was* wide, and quiet, and peaceable; 776
5: 9 their cattle were multiplied in the l of Gilead. 776
5:10 tents throughout all the east *l* of Gilead. NIH
5:11 in the l of Bashan unto Salchah: 776
5:23 of the half tribe of Manasseh dwelt in the l: 776
5:25 whoring after the gods of the people of the l, 776
6:55 they gave them Hebron in the l of Judah, 776
7:21 men of Gath that were born in *that* l slew, 776
10: 9 sent into the l of the Philistines round about, 776
11: 4 the Jebusites *were*, the inhabitants of the l. 776
13: 2 that are left in all the l of Israel, and 776
16:18 Unto thee will I give the l of Canaan, 776
19: 2 So the servants of David came into the l of 776
19: 3 and to overthrow, and to spy out the l? 776
21:12 in the l, and the angel of the LORD 776
22: 2 the strangers that *were* in the l of Israel; 776
22:18 for he hath given the inhabitants of the l into 776
22:18 and the l is subdued before the LORD, and 776
28: 8 that ye may possess *this* good l, and leave *it* 776
2Ch 2:17 all the strangers that *were* in the l of Israel, 776
6: 5 l of Egypt I chose no city among all 776
6:25 bring them again unto the l which thou 127
6:27 send rain upon thy l, which thou hast given 776
6:28 If there be dearth in the l, if there be 776
6:28 enemies besiege them in the cities of their l; 776
6:31 long as they live in the l which thou gavest 127
6:36 they carry them away captives unto a l far 776
6:37 *Yet* if they bethink themselves in the l 776
6:37 and pray unto thee in the l of their captivity, 776
6:38 with all their soul in the l of their captivity, 776
6:38 pray toward their l, which thou gavest unto 776
7:13 or if I command the locusts to devour the l, 776
7:14 will forgive their sin, and will heal their l. 776
7:20 will I pluck them up by the roots out of my l 127
7:21 Why hath the LORD done thus unto this l, 776
7:22 which brought them forth out of the l of 776
8: 6 and throughout all the l of his dominion. 776
8: 8 who were left after them in the l, 776
8:17 and to Eloth, at the sea side in the l of Edom. 776
9: 5 which I heard in mine own l of thine acts, 776
9:11 there were none such seen before in the l of 776
9:12 went away to her own l, she and 776
9:26 the river even unto the l of the Philistines, 776
14: 1 In his days the l was quiet ten years. 776
14: 6 for the l had rest, and he had no war in those 776
14: 7 gates, and bars, *while* the l *is* yet before us; 776
15: 8 put away the abominable idols out of all the l 776
17: 2 set garrisons in the l of Judah, and in 776
19: 3 thou hast taken away the groves out of the l, 776
19: 5 he set judges in the l throughout all 776
20: 7 who didst drive out the inhabitants of this l 776
20:10 when they came out of the l of Egypt, but 776
22:12 six years: and Athaliah reigned over the l. 776
23:13 all the people of the l rejoiced, and 776
23:20 all the people of the l, and brought down 776
23:21 all the people of the l rejoiced: and the city 776
26:21 the king's house, judging the people of the l. 776
30: 9 so that *they shall* come again into this l: 776
30:25 the strangers that came out of the l of Israel, 776
32: 4 the brook that ran through the midst of the l, 776
32:21 he returned with shame of face to his own l. 776
32:31 inquire of the wonder that was *done* in the l, 776
33: 8 l which I have appointed for your fathers; 127
33:25 the people of the l slew all them that had 776
33:25 the people of the l made Josiah his son king 776
34: 7 cut down all the idols throughout all the l of 776
34: 8 when he had purged the l, and the house, 776
36: 1 the people of the l took Jehoahaz the son of 776
36: 3 condemned the l in an hundred talents of 776
36:21 until the l had enjoyed her sabbaths: 776
Ezr 4: 4 the people of the l weakened the hands of 776
6:21 from the filthiness of the heathen of the l, 776
9:11 saying, The l, *unto* which ye go to possess it, 776
9:11 *is* an unclean l with the filthiness of 776
9:12 eat the good of the l, and leave *it* for an 776
10: 2 taken strange wives of the people of the l: 776
10:11 separate yourselves from the people of the l, 776
Ne 4: 4 and give them for a prey in the l of captivity: 776
5:14 to be their governor in the l of Judah, 776
5:16 work of this wall, neither bought we *any* l: 7704
9: 8 madest a covenant with him to give the l of 776
9:10 all his servants, and on all the people of his l: 776
9:11 through the midst of the sea on the dry *l*; NIH

Ne 9:15 the l which thou hadst sworn to give them. 776
9:22 so they possessed the l of Sihon, and 776
9:22 the l of the king of Heshbon, and the land of 776
9:22 of Heshbon, and the l of Og king of Bashan. 776
9:23 broughtest them into the l, *concerning* which 776
9:24 So the children went in and possessed the l, 776
9:24 before them the inhabitants of the l, 776
9:24 with their kings, and the people of the l, 776
9:25 a fat l, and possessed houses full *of* all 127
9:35 and fat l which thou gavest before them, 776
9:36 *for* the l that thou gavest unto our fathers to 776
10:30 give our daughters unto the people of the l, 776
10:31 *if* the people of the l bring ware or 776
Est 8:17 many of the people of the l became Jews; 776
10: 1 the king Ahasuerus laid a tribute upon the l, 776
Job 1: 1 There was a man in the l of Uz, whose name 776
1:10 and his substance is increased in the l. 776
10:21 *even* to the l of darkness and the shadow of 776
10:22 A l of darkness, as darkness itself; *and of* 776
28:13 neither is it found in the l of the living. 776
31:38 If my l cry against me, or that the furrows 127
37:13 for correction, or for his l, or for mercy. 776
39: 6 and the barren *l* his dwellings. NIH
42:15 in all the l were no women found *so* fair as 776
Ps 10:16 ever: the heathen are perished out of his l. 776
27:13 of the LORD in the l of the living. 776
35:20 matters against *them that are* quiet in the l. 776
37: 3 *so* shalt thou dwell in the l, and verily thou 776
37:29 The righteous shall inherit the l, and 776
37:34 and he shall exalt thee to inherit the l: 776
42: 6 will I remember thee from the l of Jordan, 776
44: 3 For they got not the l in possession by their 776
52: 5 and root thee out of the l of the living. 776
63: 1 in a dry and thirsty l, where no water is; 776
66: 6 He turned the sea into dry *l*: they went NIH
68: 6 but the rebellious dwell *in* a dry *l*. NIH
74: 8 burnt up all the synagogues of God in the l. 776
78:12 in the l of Egypt, *in* the field of Zoan. 776
80: 9 cause it to take deep root, and it filled the l. 776
81: 5 when he went out through the l of Egypt: 776
81:10 which brought thee out of the l of Egypt: 776
85: 1 thou hast been favourable unto thy l: 776
85: 9 that fear him; that glory may dwell in our l. 776
85:12 *is* good; and our l shall yield her increase. 776
88:12 thy righteousness in the l of forgetfulness? 776
95: 5 he made it: and his hands formed the dry *l*. NIH
101: 6 Mine eyes *shall be* upon the faithful of the l, 776
101: 8 I will early destroy all the wicked of the l; 776
105:11 Unto thee will I give the l of Canaan, 776
105:16 Moreover, he called *for* a famine upon the l: 776
105:23 and Jacob sojourned in the l of Ham. 776
105:27 among them, and wonders in the l of Ham. 776
105:30 Their l brought forth frogs in abundance, 776
105:32 them hail *for* rain, *and* flaming fire in their l. 776
105:35 did eat up all the herbs in their l, and 776
105:36 He smote also all the firstborn in their l, 776
106:22 Wondrous works in the l of Ham, *and* 776
106:24 Yea, they despised the pleasant l, 776
106:38 and the l was polluted with blood. 776
107:34 A fruitful l into barrenness, for 776
116: 9 I will walk before the LORD in the l of 776
135:12 gave their l *for* an heritage, an heritage unto 776
136:21 gave their l for an heritage: for his mercy 776
137: 4 we sing the LORD'S song in a strange l? 127
142: 5 *and* my portion in the l of the living. 776
143: 6 my soul *thirsteth* after thee, as a thirsty l. 776
143:10 *is* good; lead me into the l of uprightness. 776
Pr 2:21 For the upright shall dwell *in* the l, and 776
12:11 He that tilleth his l shall be satisfied *with* 127
28: 2 For the transgression of a l many *are* 776
28:19 He that tilleth his l shall have plenty *of* 127
29: 4 The king by judgment stablisheth the l: but 776
31:23 when he sitteth among the elders of the l. 776
Ecc 10:16 Woe to thee, O l, when thy king *is* a child, 776
10:17 Blessed *art* thou, O l, when thy king *is* 776
SS 2:12 and the voice of the turtle is heard in our l; 776
Isa 1: 7 your l, strangers devour it in your presence, 127
1:19 and obedient, ye shall eat the good of the l: 776
2: 7 Their l also is full *of* silver and gold, 776
2: 7 their l is also full *of* horses, neither *is there* 776
2: 8 Their l also is full *of* idols; they worship 776
5:30 if *one* look unto the l, behold darkness *and* 776
6:11 without man, and the l be utterly desolate, 127
6:12 *be* a great forsaking in the midst of the l. 776
7:16 the l that thou abhorrest shall be forsaken of 127
7:18 and for the bee that *is* in the l of Assyria. 776
7:22 honey shall every one eat that is left in the l. 776
7:24 all the l shall become briers and thorns. 776
8: 8 out of his wings shall fill the breadth of thy l, 776
9: 1 when at the first he lightly afflicted the l of 776
9: 1 the land of Zebulun and the l of Naphtali, 776
9: 2 they that dwell in the l of the shadow of 776
9:19 of the LORD of hosts is the l darkened, 776
10:23 even determined, *in* the midst of all *the l*. NIH
11:16 the day that he came up out of the l of Egypt. 776
13: 5 of his indignation, to destroy the whole l. 776
13: 9 and fierce anger, to lay the l desolate: 776
13:14 and flee every one into his own l. 776
14: 1 choose Israel, and set them in their own l: 127
14: 2 the house of Israel shall possess them in the l 127
14:20 because thou hast destroyed thy l, *and* 776
14:21 *that* they do not rise, nor possess the l, 776
14:25 That *I* will break the Assyrian in my l, and 776
15: 9 of Moab, and upon the remnant of the l. 127
16: 1 Send ye the lamb *to* the ruler of the l from 776
16: 4 the oppressors are consumed out of the l. 776
18: 1 Woe to the l shadowing with wings, which *is* 776
18: 2 whose l the rivers have spoiled. 776
18: 7 under foot, whose l the rivers have spoiled, 776
19:17 the l of Judah shall be a terror unto Egypt, 127
19:18 In that day shall five cities in the l of Egypt 776
19:19 to the LORD in the midst of the l of Egypt, 776
19:20 unto the LORD of hosts in the l of Egypt: 776
19:24 *even* a blessing in the midst of the l: 776
21: 1 it cometh from the desert, from a terrible l. 776

Isa 21:14 The inhabitants of the **l** of Tema brought 776
23: 1 from the **l** of Chittim it is revealed to them. 776
23:10 Pass through thy **l** as a river, O daughter of 776
23:13 Behold the **l** of the Chaldeans; this people 776
24: 3 The **l** shall be utterly emptied, and 776
24:11 all joy is darkened, the mirth of the **l** is gone. 776
24:13 When thus it shall be in the midst of the **l** 776
26: 1 In that day shall this song be sung in the **l** of 776
26:10 in the **l** of uprightness will he deal unjustly, 776
27:13 were ready to perish in the **l** of Assyria, 776
27:13 the outcasts in the **l** of Egypt, and 776
30: 6 into the **l** of trouble and anguish, 776
32: 2 as the shadow of a great rock in a weary **l**. 776
32:13 Upon the **l** of my people shall come up 127
33:17 they shall behold the **l** that is very far off. 776
34: 6 and a great slaughter in the **l** of Idumea. 776
34: 7 their **l** shall be soaked with blood, and 776
34: 9 and the **l** thereof shall become burning pitch. 776
35: 7 a pool, and the **thirsty l** springs of water: 6774
36:10 the LORD against this **l** to destroy it? 776
36:10 unto me, Go up against this **l**, and destroy it. 776
36:17 and take you away to a **l** like your own land, 776
36:17 and take you away to a land like your own **l**, 776
36:17 a **l** of corn and wine, a land of bread and 776
36:17 of corn and wine, a **l** of bread and vineyards. 776
36:18 his **l** out of the hand of the king of Assyria? 776
36:20 that have delivered their **l** out of my hand, 776
37: 7 shall hear a rumour, and return to his own **l**; 776
37: 7 cause him to fall by the sword in his own **l**. 776
37:38 and they escaped *into* the **l** of Armenia: 776
38:11 *even* the LORD, in the **l** of the living: 776
41:18 pool of water, and the dry **l** springs of water. 776
49:12 from the west; and these from the **l** of Sinim. 776
49:19 desolate places, and the **l** of thy destruction, 776
53: 8 for he was cut off out of the **l** of the living: 776
57:13 putteth his trust in me shall possess the **l**, 776
60:18 Violence shall no more be heard in thy **l**, 776
60:21 they shall inherit the **l** for ever, the branch of 776
61: 7 in their **l** they shall possess the double: 776
62: 4 neither shall thy **l** any more be termed 776
62: 4 shalt be called Hephzi-bah, and thy **l** Beulah: 776
62: 4 delighteth in thee, and thy **l** shall be married. 776
Jer 1: 1 of the priests that *were* in Anathoth in the **l** 776
1:14 break forth upon all the inhabitants of the **l**. 776
1:18 and brasen walls against the whole **l**, 776
1:18 and against the people of the **l**. 776
2: 2 in the wilderness, in a **l** *that was* not sown. 776
2: 6 that brought us up out of the **l** of Egypt, 776
2: 6 through a **l** of deserts and of pits, through a 776
2: 6 through a **l** of drought, and of the shadow of 776
2: 6 through a **l** that no man passed through, and 776
2: 7 ye defiled my **l**, and made mine heritage an 776
2:15 *and* yelled, and they made his **l** waste: 776
2:31 a **l** of darkness? wherefore say my people, 776
3: 1 shall not that **l** be greatly polluted? but 776
3: 2 thou hast polluted the **l** with thy whoredoms 776
3: 9 that she defiled the **l**, and 776
3:16 when ye be multiplied and increased in the **l**, 776
3:18 they shall come together out of the **l** of 776
3:18 **l** that I have given for an inheritance unto 776
3:19 the children, and give thee a pleasant **l**, 776
4: 5 and say, Blow ye the trumpet in the **l**: 776
4: 7 he is gone forth from his place to make thy **l** 776
4:20 is cried; for the whole **l** is spoiled: 776
4:27 LORD said, The whole **l** shall be desolate; 776
5:19 served strange gods in your **l**, so shall ye 776
5:19 shall ye serve strangers in a **l** *that is* not 776
5:30 and horrible thing is committed in the **l**; 776
6: 8 lest I make thee desolate, a **l** not inhabited. 776
6:12 out my hand upon the inhabitants of the **l**, 776
7: 7 in the **l** that I gave to your fathers, for ever 776
7:22 day that I brought them out of the **l** of Egypt, 776
7:25 forth out of the **l** of Egypt unto this day, 776
7:34 voice of the bride: for the **l** shall be desolate. 776
8:16 the whole **l** trembled at the sound of 776
8:16 and have devoured the **l**, and all that is in it; 776
9:12 for what the **l** perisheth *and* is burnt up like a 776
9:19 because we have forsaken the **l**, because 776
10:17 Gather up thy wares out of the **l**, 776
10:18 I will sling out the inhabitants of the **l** at this 776
11: 4 I brought them forth out of the **l** of Egypt, 776
11: 5 to give them a **l** flowing with milk and 776
11: 7 that I brought them up out of the **l** of Egypt, 776
11:19 let us cut him off from the **l** of the living, 776
12: 4 How long shall the **l** mourn, and the herbs of 776
12: 5 *if* in the **l** of peace, *wherein* thou trustedst, 776
12:11 the whole **l** is made desolate, because 776
12:12 end of the **l** even to the *other* end of the land: 776
12:12 end of the land even to the *other* end of the **l**: 776
12:14 I will pluck them out of their **l**, and pluck out 127
12:15 man to his heritage, and every man to his **l**. 776
13:13 Behold, I *will* fill all the inhabitants of this **l**, 776
14: 8 why shouldest thou be as a stranger in the **l**, 776
14:15 Sword and famine shall not be in this **l**; 776
14:18 the priest go about into a **l** that they know 776
15: 7 will fan them with a fan in the gates of the **l**; 776
15:14 enemies into a **l** *which* thou knowest not: 776
16: 3 their fathers that begat them in this **l**; 776
16: 6 the great and the small shall die in this **l**: 776
16:13 Therefore will I cast you out of this **l** into a 776
16:13 you out of this land into a **l** that ye know not, 776
16:14 the children of Israel out of the **l** of Egypt; 776
16:15 the children of Israel from the **l** of the north, 776
16:15 I will bring them again into their **l** that I gave 127
16:18 because they have defiled my **l**, they have 776
17: 4 enemies in the **l** which thou knowest not: 776
17: 6 the wilderness, *in* a salt **l** and not inhabited. 776
17:26 from the **l** of Benjamin, and from the plain, 776
18:16 To make their **l** desolate, *and* a perpetual 776
22:12 led him captive, and shall see this **l** no more. 776
22:27 to the **l** whereunto they desire to return, 776
22:28 and are cast into a **l** which they know not? 776
23: 7 the children of Israel out of the **l** of Egypt; 776
23: 8 and they shall dwell in their own **l**. 127
23:10 For the **l** is full *of* adulterers; for because 776

Jer 23:10 for because of swearing the **l** mourneth; 776
23:15 is profaneness gone forth into all the **l**. 776
24: 5 whom I have sent out of this place *into* the **l** 776
24: 6 and I will bring them again to this **l**: 776
24: 8 that remain in this **l**, and them that dwell in 776
24: 8 and them that dwell in the **l** of Egypt: 776
24:10 till they be consumed from off the **l** that I 127
25: 5 dwell in the **l** that the LORD hath given 127
25: 9 will bring them against this **l**, and against 776
25:11 this whole **l** shall be a desolation, *and* 776
25:12 the **l** of the Chaldeans, and will make it 776
25:13 I will bring upon that **l** all my words which I 776
25:20 all the kings of the **l** of Uz, and all the kings 776
25:20 all the kings of the **l** of the Philistines, and 776
25:38 for their **l** is desolate because of 776
26:17 rose up certain of the elders of the **l**, and 776
26:20 against this **l** according to all the words of 776
27: 7 son's son, until the very time of his **l** come: 776
27:10 lie unto you, to remove you far from your **l**; 127
27:11 those will I let remain still in their own **l**, 127
30: 3 I will cause them to return to the **l** that I gave 776
30:10 and thy seed from the **l** of their captivity; 776
31:16 they shall come again from the **l** of 776
31:23 As yet they shall use this speech in the **l** of 776
31:32 the hand, to bring them out of the **l** of Egypt; 776
32:15 vineyards shall be possessed again in this **l**. 776
32:20 hast set signs and wonders in the **l** of Egypt, 776
32:21 people Israel out of the **l** of Egypt with signs, 776
32:22 hast given them this **l**, which thou didst 776
32:22 give them, a **l** flowing with milk and honey; 776
32:41 I will plant them in this **l** assuredly with my 776
32:43 fields shall be bought in this **l**, whereof ye 776
32:44 and take witnesses in the **l** of Benjamin, 776
33:11 to return the captivity of the **l** as at the first, 776
33:13 in the **l** of Benjamin, and in the places about 776
33:15 execute judgment and righteousness in the **l**. 776
34:13 I brought them forth out of the **l** of Egypt, 776
34:19 and the priests, and all the people of the **l**, 776
35: 7 that ye may live many days in the **l** where ye 127
35:11 king of Babylon came up into the **l**, 776
35:15 ye shall dwell in the **l** which I have given to 127
36:29 shall certainly come and destroy this **l**, 776
37: 1 king of Babylon made king in the **l** of Judah. 776
37: 2 nor his servants, nor the people of the **l**, 776
37: 7 shall return *to* Egypt into their own **l**. 776
37:12 of Jerusalem to go *into* the **l** of Benjamin, 776
37:19 not come against you, nor against this **l**? 776
39: 5 of Babylon to Riblah in the **l** of Hamath, 776
39:10 in the **l** of Judah, and gave them vineyards 776
40: 4 behold, all the **l** *is* before thee: whither it 776
40: 6 him among the people that were left in the **l**. 776
40: 7 the son of Ahikam governor in the **l**, 776
40: 7 and children, and of the poor of the **l**, 776
40: 9 dwell in the **l** and serve the king of Babylon, 776
40:12 came *to* the **l** of Judah, to Gedaliah, unto 776
41: 2 of Babylon had made governor over the **l**. 776
41:18 the king of Babylon made governor in the **l**. 776
42:10 If ye will still abide in this **l**, then will I build 776
42:12 and cause you to return to your own **l**. 127
42:13 if ye say, We will not dwell in this **l**, neither 776
42:14 we will go *into* the **l** of Egypt, where we 776
42:16 shall overtake you there in the **l** of Egypt, 776
43: 4 of the LORD, to dwell in the **l** of Judah. 776
43: 5 had been driven, to dwell in the **l** of Judah: 776
43: 7 So they came *into* the **l** of Egypt: for they 776
43:11 he shall smite the **l** of Egypt, *and* 776
43:12 he shall array himself with the **l** of Egypt, 776
43:13 of Beth-shemesh, that *is* in the **l** of Egypt; 776
44: 1 all the Jews which dwell in the **l** of Egypt, 776
44: 8 burning incense unto other gods in the **l** of 776
44: 9 which they have committed in the **l** of Judah, 776
44:12 that have set their faces to go *into* the **l** of 776
44:12 all be consumed, *and* fall in the **l** of Egypt; 776
44:13 For I will punish them that dwell in the **l** of 776
44:14 which are gone into the **l** of Egypt to sojourn 776
44:14 that *they* should return *into* the **l** of Judah, 776
44:15 even all the people that dwelt in the **l** of 776
44:21 and your princes, and the people of the **l**, 776
44:22 therefore is your **l** a desolation, and an 776
44:24 all Judah that *are* in the **l** of Egypt: 776
44:26 all Judah that dwell in the **l** of Egypt; 776
44:26 of any man of Judah in all the **l** of Egypt, 776
44:27 all the men of Judah that *are* in the **l** of Egypt 776
44:28 out of the **l** of Egypt *into* the land of Judah, 776
44:28 out of the land of Egypt *into* the **l** of Judah, 776
44:28 that are gone into the **l** of Egypt to sojourn 776
45: 4 planted I *will* pluck up, even this whole **l**. 776
46:12 *of* thy shame, and thy cry hath filled the **l**: 776
46:13 should come and smite the **l** of Egypt. 776
46:16 to the **l** of our nativity, from the oppressing 776
46:27 and thy seed from the **l** of their captivity; 776
47: 2 shall overflow the **l**, and all that is therein; 776
47: 2 and all the inhabitants of the **l** shall howl. 776
48:24 upon all the cities of the **l** of Moab, far or 776
48:33 the plentiful field, and from the **l** of Moab; 776
50: 1 against the **l** of the Chaldeans by Jeremiah 776
50: 3 which shall make her **l** desolate, and 776
50: 8 go forth out of the **l** of the Chaldeans, and 776
50:12 *shall be* a wilderness, a **dry l**, and a desert. 6723
50:16 and they shall flee every one to his own **l**. 776
50:18 I *will* punish the king of Babylon and his **l**, 776
50:21 Go up against the **l** of Merathaim, 776
50:22 A sound of battle *is* in the **l**, and of great 776
50:25 GOD of hosts in the **l** of the Chaldeans. 776
50:28 that flee and escape out of the **l** of Babylon, 776
50:34 that he may give rest to the **l**, and 776
50:38 for it *is* the **l** of graven images, and they are 776
50:45 that he hath purposed against the **l** of 776
51: 2 that shall fan her, and shall empty her **l**: 776
51: 4 Thus the slain shall fall in the **l** of 776
51: 5 though their **l** was filled *with* sin against 776
51:27 Set ye up a standard in the **l**, blow 776
51:28 rulers thereof, and all the **l** of his dominion. 776
51:29 the **l** shall tremble and sorrow: for every 776
51:29 to make the **l** of Babylon a desolation 776

Jer 51:43 are a desolation, a dry **l**, and a wilderness, 776
51:43 a wilderness, a **l** wherein no man dwelleth, 776
51:46 for the rumour that shall be heard in the **l**; 776
51:46 and violence in the **l**, ruler against ruler. 776
51:47 her whole **l** shall be confounded, and all her 776
51:52 through all her **l** the wounded shall groan. 776
51:54 great destruction from the **l** of 776
52: 6 there was no bread for the people of the **l**. 776
52: 9 of Babylon to Riblah in the **l** of Hamath; 776
52:16 *certain* of the poor of the **l** for vinedressers 776
52:25 the host, who mustered the people of the **l**; 776
52:25 threescore men of the people of the **l**, 776
52:27 put them to death in Riblah in the **l** of 776
52:27 was carried away captive out of his own **l**. 127
La 4:21 of Edom, that dwellest in the **l** of Uz; 776
Eze 1: 3 in the **l** of the Chaldeans by the river Chebar; 776
6:14 upon them, and make the **l** desolate, yea, 776
7: 2 thus saith the Lord GOD unto the **l** of 127
7: 2 end is come upon the four corners of the **l**. 776
7: 7 come unto thee, O thou that dwellest in the **l**: 776
7:23 for the **l** is full *of* bloody crimes, and the city 776
7:27 the hands of the people of the **l** shall be 776
8:17 for they have filled the **l** *with* violence, and 776
9: 9 the **l** is full *of* blood, and the city full *of* 776
11:15 unto us is this **l** given in possession. 776
11:17 and I will give you the **l** of Israel. 127
12:13 I will bring him to Babylon *to* the **l** of 776
12:19 say unto the people of the **l**, Thus saith 776
12:19 of Jerusalem, *and* of the **l** of Israel; 127
12:19 that her **l** may be desolate from all that is 776
12:20 be laid waste, and the **l** shall be desolate; 776
12:22 what *is* that proverb *that* ye have in the **l** of 127
13: 9 neither shall they enter into the **l** of Israel; 127
14:13 when the **l** sinneth against me by trespassing 776
14:15 I cause noisome beasts to pass through the **l**, 776
14:16 shall be delivered, but the **l** shall be desolate. 776
14:17 Or *if* I bring a sword upon that **l**, and say, 776
14:17 that land, and say, Sword, go through the **l**; 776
14:19 Or *if* I send a pestilence into that **l**, and 776
15: 8 I will make the **l** desolate, because they have 776
16: 3 and thy nativity *is* of the **l** of Canaan; 776
16:29 fornication in the **l** of Canaan unto Chaldea; 776
17: 4 and carried it into a **l** of traffick; 776
17: 5 He took also of the seed of the **l**, and 776
17:13 he hath also taken the mighty of the **l**: 776
18: 2 that ye use this proverb concerning the **l** of 127
19: 4 they brought him with chains unto the **l** of 776
19: 7 the **l** was desolate, and the fulness thereof, 776
20: 5 made myself known unto them in the **l** of 776
20: 6 to bring them forth of the **l** of Egypt into a 776
20: 6 of Egypt into a **l** that I had espied for them, 776
20: 8 against them in the midst of the **l** of Egypt. 776
20: 9 in bringing them forth out of the **l** of Egypt. 776
20:10 caused them to go forth out of the **l** of Egypt, 776
20:15 that *I* would not bring them into the **l** which I 776
20:28 *For* when I had brought them into the **l**, 776
20:36 fathers in the wilderness of the **l** of Egypt, 776
20:38 and they shall not enter into the **l** of Israel: 127
20:40 of Israel, all of them in the **l**, serve me: 776
20:42 when I shall bring you into the **l** of Israel, 127
21: 2 and prophesy against the **l** of Israel, 127
21: 3 say to the **l** of Israel, Thus saith the LORD; 127
21:19 both twain shall come forth out of one **l**: and 776
21:30 thou wast created, in the **l** of thy nativity. 776
21:32 thy blood shall be in the midst of the **l**; 776
22:24 unto her, Thou *art* the **l** that is not cleansed, 776
22:29 The people of the **l** have used oppression, 776
22:30 stand in the gap before me for the **l**, that *I* 776
23:15 of Chaldea, the **l** of their nativity: 776
23:19 wherein she had played the harlot in the **l** of 776
23:27 thy whoredom *brought* from the **l** of Egypt: 776
23:48 will I cause lewdness to cease out of the **l**, 776
25: 3 against the **l** of Israel, when it was desolate; 127
25: 6 with all thy despite against the **l** of Israel; 127
26:20 and I shall set glory in the **l** of the living; 776
27:17 Judah, and the **l** of Israel, they *were* thy 776
27:29 from their ships, they shall stand upon the **l**; 776
28:25 shall they dwell in their **l** that I have given to 127
29: 9 the **l** of Egypt shall be desolate and waste; 776
29:10 I will make the **l** of Egypt utterly waste *and* 776
29:12 I will make the **l** of Egypt desolate in 776
29:14 will cause them to return *into* the **l** of 776
29:14 land of Pathros, into the **l** of their habitation; 776
29:19 I *will* give the **l** of Egypt unto 776
29:20 I have given him the **l** of Egypt *for* his 776
30: 5 Chub, and the men of the **l** that is in league, 776
30:11 the nations, *shall be* brought to destroy the **l**: 776
30:11 against Egypt, and fill the **l** *with* the slain. 776
30:12 and sell the **l** into the hand of the wicked: 776
30:12 I will make the **l** waste, and all that is 776
30:13 there shall be no more a prince of the **l** of 776
30:13 and I will put a fear in the **l** of Egypt. 776
30:25 he shall stretch it out upon the **l** of Egypt. 776
31:12 boughs are broken by all the rivers of the **l**; 776
32: 4 will I leave thee upon the **l**, I will cast thee 776
32: 6 I will also water with thy blood the **l** wherein 776
32: 8 set darkness upon thy **l**, saith the Lord 776
32:15 When I shall make the **l** of Egypt desolate, 776
32:23 which caused terror in the **l** of the living. 776
32:24 which caused their terror in the **l** of 776
32:25 though their terror was caused in the **l** of 776
32:26 though they caused their terror in the **l** of 776
32:27 the terror of the mighty in the **l** of the living. 776
32:32 For I have caused my terror in the **l** of 776
33: 2 unto them, When I bring the sword upon a **l**, 776
33: 2 if the people of the **l** take a man of their 776
33: 3 *If* when he seeth the sword come upon the **l**, 776
33:24 they that inhabit those wastes of the **l** of 127
33:24 Abraham was one, and he inherited the **l**: 776
33:24 *are* many; the **l** is given us for inheritance. 776
33:25 and shed blood: and shall ye possess the **l**? 776
33:26 neighbour's wife: and shall ye possess the **l**? 776
33:28 For I will lay the **l** most desolate, and 776
33:29 when I have laid the **l** most desolate because 776
34:13 will bring them to their own **l**, and feed them 127

Eze 34:25 cause the evil beasts to cease out of the l: 776
34:27 they shall be safe in their l, and shall know 127
34:28 neither shall the beast of the l devour them; 776
34:29 be no more consumed with hunger in the l, 776
36: 5 which have appointed my l into their 776
36: 6 Prophesy therefore concerning the l of Israel, 127
36:13 Thou *l* devourest up men, and hast bereaved NIH
36:17 the house of Israel dwelt in their own l, 127
36:18 for the blood that they had shed upon the l, 776
36:20 the LORD, and are gone forth out of his l. 776
36:24 and will bring you into your own l. 127
36:28 ye shall dwell in the l that I gave to your 776
36:34 the desolate l shall be tilled, whereas it lay 776
36:35 This l that was desolate is become like 776
37:12 and bring you into the l of Israel. 127
37:14 and I shall place you in your own l: 127
37:21 every side, and bring them into their own l: 127
37:22 I will make them one nation in the l upon 776
37:25 they shall dwell in the l that I have given 776
38: 2 set thy face against Gog, the l of Magog, 776
38: 8 in the latter years thou shalt come into the l 776
38: 9 thou shalt be like a cloud to cover the l, thou, 776
38:11 I will go up to the l of unwalled villages; 776
38:12 and goods, that dwell in the midst of the l. 776
38:16 my people of Israel, as a cloud to cover the l; 776
38:16 and I will bring thee against my l, 776
38:18 when Gog shall come against the l of Israel, 127
38:19 shall be a great shaking in the l of Israel; 127
39:12 burying of them, that *they* may cleanse the l. 776
39:13 all the people of the l shall bury *them;* and 776
39:14 passing through the l to bury with 776
39:15 the passengers *that* pass through the l, 776
39:16 *be* Hamonah. Thus shall they cleanse the l. 776
39:26 when they dwelt safely in their l, and 127
39:28 I have gathered them unto their own l, and 127
40: 2 of God brought he me into the l of Israel, 776
45: 1 when ye shall divide *by lot* the l for 776
45: 1 unto the LORD, a holy *portion* of the l: 776
45: 4 The holy *portion* of the l shall be for 776
45: 8 In the l shall be his possession in Israel: and 776
45: 8 *the rest of* the l shall they give to the house 776
45:16 All the people of the l shall give this oblation 776
45:22 for all the people of the l a bullock *for* a sin 776
46: 3 Likewise the people of the l shall worship *at* 776
46: 9 when the people of the l shall come before 776
47:13 whereby ye shall inherit the l according to 776
47:14 and this l shall fall unto you for inheritance. 776
47:15 this *shall be* the border of the l toward 776
47:18 and from the l of Israel *by* Jordan, 776
47:21 So shall ye divide this l unto you according 776
48:12 *this* oblation of the l that is offered shall be 776
48:14 nor alienate the firstfruits of the l: 776
48:29 This *is* the l which ye shall divide *by lot* unto 776
Da 1: 2 which he carried *into* the l of Shinar *to* 776
8: 9 toward the east, and toward the pleasant *l*. NIH
9: 6 and our fathers, and to all the people of the l. 776
9:15 that hast brought thy people forth out of the l 776
11: 9 *his* kingdom, and shall return into his own l. 127
11:16 he shall stand in the glorious l, which by his 776
11:19 turn his face towards the fort of his own l: 776
11:28 shall he return *into* his l with great riches; 776
11:28 he shall do *exploits,* and return to his own l. 776
11:39 over many, and shall divide the l for gain. 127
11:41 He shall enter also into the glorious l, and 776
11:42 and the l of Egypt shall not escape. 776
Hos 1: 2 for the l hath committed great whoredom, 776
1:11 and they shall come up out of the l: 776
2: 3 set her like a dry l, and slay her with thirst. 776
2:15 as *in* the day when she came up out of the l 776
4: 1 a controversy with the inhabitants of the l, 776
4: 1 nor mercy, nor knowledge of God in the l. 776
4: 3 Therefore shall the l mourn, and every one 776
7:16 this *shall be* their derision in the l of Egypt. 776
9: 3 They shall not dwell in the LORD'S l; but 776
10: 1 according to the goodness of his l they have 776
11: 5 He shall not return into the l of Egypt, but 776
11:11 and as a dove out of the l of Assyria: 776
12: 9 I *that am* the LORD thy God from the l of 776
13: 4 Yet I *am* the LORD thy God from the l of 776
13: 5 in the wilderness, in the l of great drought. 776
Joel 1: 2 and give ear, all ye inhabitants of the l. 776
1: 6 For a nation is come up upon my l, strong, 776
1:10 The field is wasted, the l mourneth; for 127
1:14 all the inhabitants of the l *into* the house of 776
2: 1 let all the inhabitants of the l tremble: for 776
2: 3 the l *is* as the garden of Eden before them, 776
2:18 will the LORD be jealous for his l, and 776
2:20 will drive him into a l barren and desolate, 776
2:21 Fear not, O l; be glad and rejoice: for 127
3: 2 among the nations, and parted my l. 776
3:19 they have shed innocent blood in their l. 776
Am 2:10 Also I brought you up from the l of Egypt, 776
2:10 to possess the l of the Amorite. 776
3: 1 which I brought up from the l of Egypt, 776
3: 9 and in the palaces in the l of Egypt, and say, 776
3:11 *there shall be* even round about the l; 776
5: 2 she is forsaken upon her l; *there is* none to 127
7: 2 had made an end of eating the grass of the l, 776
7:10 the l is not able to bear all his words. 776
7:11 surely be led away captive out of their own l. 127
7:12 go, flee thee away into the l of Judah, and 776
7:17 the sword, and thy l shall be divided by line; 127
7:17 by line; and thou shalt die in a polluted l: 127
7:17 shall surely go into captivity forth of his l. 127
8: 4 even to make the poor of the l to fail, 776
8: 8 Shall not the l tremble for this, and 776
8:11 that I will send a famine in the l, 776
9: 5 Lord GOD of hosts *is* he that toucheth the l, 776
9: 7 Have not I brought up Israel out of the l of 776
9:15 I will plant them upon their l, and they shall 127
9:15 they shall no more be pulled up out of their l 127
Jnh 1: 9 which hath made the sea and the dry *l*. NIH
1:13 the men rowed hard to bring *it* to the l; 3004
2:10 and it vomited out Jonah upon the dry *l*. NIH
Mic 5: 5 when the Assyrian shall come into our l: 776
Mic 5: 6 they shall waste the l of Assyria with 776
5: 6 and the l of Nimrod in the entrances thereof: 776
5: 6 when he cometh into our l, and when he 776
5:11 I will cut off the cities of thy l, and 776
6: 4 For I brought thee up out of the l of Egypt, 776
7:13 Notwithstanding the l shall be desolate 776
7:15 l of Egypt will I shew unto him marvellous 776
Na 3:13 the gates of thy l shall be set wide open unto 776
Hab 1: 6 *shall* march through the breadth of the l, 776
2: 8 and *for* the violence of the l, *of* the city, and 776
2:17 and *for* the violence of the l, *of* the city, and 776
3: 7 the curtains of the l of Midian did tremble. 776
3:12 Thou didst march through the l in 776
Zep 1: 2 will utterly consume all *things* from off the l, 127
1: 3 I will cut off man from off the l, saith 127
1:18 the whole l shall be devoured by the fire of 776
1:18 riddance of all them that dwell in the l. 776
2: 5 O Canaan, the l of the Philistines, I will even 776
3:19 fame in every l where they have been put to 776
Hag 1:11 I called *for* a drought upon the l, and 776
2: 4 be strong, all ye people of the l, saith 776
2: 6 and the earth, and the sea, and the dry *l*; NIH
Zec 1:21 which lift up *their* horn over the l of Judah to 776
2: 6 *come forth,* and flee from the l of the north, 776
2:12 shall inherit Judah his portion in the holy l, 127
3: 9 I will remove the iniquity of that l in one 776
5:11 To build it a house in the l of Shinar: 776
7: 5 Speak unto all the people of the l, and to 776
7:14 thus the l was desolate after them, that no 776
7:14 for they laid the pleasant l desolate. 776
9: 1 the word of the LORD in the l of Hadrach, 776
9:16 of a crown, lifted up as an ensign upon his l. 127
10:10 I will bring them again also out of the l of 776
10:10 and I will bring them into the l of Gilead and 776
11: 6 I will no more pity the inhabitants of the l, 776
11: 6 they shall smite the l, and out of their hand I 776
11:16 For lo, I *will* raise up a shepherd in the l, 776
12:12 the l shall mourn, every family apart; 776
13: 2 cut off the names of the idols out of the l, 776
13: 2 and the unclean spirit to pass out of the l. 776
13: 8 to pass, *that* in all the l, saith the LORD, 776
14:10 All the l shall be turned as a plain from Geba 776
Mal 3:12 for ye shall be a delightsome l, saith 776
Mt 2: 6 And thou Bethlehem, *in* the l of Juda, art *1093*
2:20 and his mother, and go into the l of Israel: *1093*
2:21 his mother, and came into the l of Israel. *1093*
4:15 The l of Zabulon, and the l of *1093*
4:15 land of Zabulon, and the l of Nephthalim, *1093*
9:26 the fame hereof went abroad into all that l. *1093*
10:15 It shall be more tolerable for the l of Sodom *1093*
11:24 that it shall be more tolerable for the l of *1093*
14:34 they came into the l of Gennesaret. *1093*
23:15 compass sea and l to make one proselyte, *3584*
27:45 darkness over all the l unto the ninth hour. *1093*
Mk 1: 5 And there went out unto him all the l of *5561*
4: 1 the whole multitude was by the sea on the l. *1093*
6:47 the midst of the sea, and he alone on the l. *1093*
6:53 they came into the l of Genesaret, and *1093*
15:33 there was darkness over the whole l until *1093*
Lk 4:25 when great famine was throughout all the l; *1093*
5: 3 that *he* would thrust out a little from the l. *1093*
5:11 And when they had brought *their* ships to l, *1093*
8:27 And when he went forth to l, there met him *1093*
14:35 It is neither fit for the l, nor yet for *1093*
15:14 there arose a mighty famine in that l; *5561*
21:23 for there shall be great distress in the l, and *1093*
Jn 3:22 and his disciples into the l of Judea; *1093*
6:21 immediately the ship was at the l whither *1093*
21: 8 (for they were not far from l, but as it were *1093*
21: 9 As soon then as they were come to l, *1093*
21:11 and drew the net to l full of great fishes, *1093*
Ac 4:37 Having l, sold *it,* and brought the money, and *68*
5: 3 and to keep back *part* of the price of the l? *5564*
5: 8 Tell me whether ye sold the l for so much? *5564*
7: 3 and come into the l which I shall shew thee. *1093*
7: 4 Then came he out of the l of the Chaldeans, *1093*
7: 4 he removed him into this l, wherein ye now *1093*
7: 6 That his seed should sojourn in a strange l; *1093*
7:11 Now there came a dearth over all the l of *1093*
7:29 and was a stranger in the l of Madian, *1093*
7:36 and signs in the l of Egypt, *1093*
7:40 which brought us out of the l of Egypt, *1093*
10:39 which he did both in the l of the Jews, *5561*
13:17 *they* dwelt as strangers in the l of Egypt, *1093*
13:19 destroyed seven nations in the l of Canaan, *1093*
13:19 of Canaan, he divided their l to them by lot. *1093*
27:39 And when it was day, they knew not the l: *1093*
27:43 *themselves* first into *the sea,* and get to l: *1093*
27:44 came to pass, that *they* escaped all safe to l. *1093*
Heb 8: 9 the hand to lead them out of the l of Egypt; *1093*
11: 9 By faith he sojourned in the l of promise, *1093*
11:29 *l* which the Egyptians assaying to do were NIG
Jude 1: 5 having saved the people out of the l of *1093*

LANDED (2) [LAND]

Ac 18:22 And when he had l at Cesarea, and gone up, *2718*
21: 3 and sailed into Syria, and l at Tyre: *2609*

LANDING (1) [LAND]

Ac 28:12 And l at Syracuse, we tarried *there* three *2609*

LANDMARK (4) [LAND, MARK]

Dt 19:14 Thou shalt not remove thy neighbour's l, 1366
27:17 *be* he that removeth his neighbour's l. 1366
Pr 22:28 Remove not the ancient l, which thy fathers 1366
23:10 Remove not the old l; and enter not into 1366

LANDMARKS (1) [LAND, MARK]

Job 24: 2 *Some* remove the l; they violently take 1367

LANDOWNER See GOODMAN

LANDS (46) [LAND]

Ge 10: 5 the isles of the Gentiles divided in their l; 776
Ge 10:31 their tongues, in their l, after their nations. 776
41:54 the dearth was in all l; but in all the land of 776
41:57 because that the famine was *so* sore in all l. 776
47:18 sight of my lord, but our bodies, and our l: 127
47:22 gave them: wherefore they sold not their l. 127
Lev 26:36 into their hearts in the l of their enemies; 776
26:39 away in their iniquity in your enemies' l; 776
Jdg 11:13 therefore restore those *l* again peaceably. NIH
2Ki 19:11 what the kings of Assyria have done to all l, 776
19:17 have destroyed the nations and their l, 776
1Ch 14:17 the fame of David went out into all l; and 776
2Ch 9:28 horses out of Egypt, and out of all l. 776
13: 9 after the manner of the nations of *other* l? 776
17:10 of the l that *were* round about Judah, 776
32:13 have done unto all the people of *other* l? 776
32:13 were the gods of the nations of *those* l any 776
32:13 able to deliver their l out of mine hand? 776
32:17 As the gods of the nations of *other* l have not 776
Ezr 9: 1 themselves from the people of the l, 776
9: 2 themselves with the people of *those* l: 776
9: 7 delivered into the hand of the kings of the l, 776
9:11 land with the filthiness of the people of the l, 776
Ne 5: 3 We *have* mortgaged our l, vineyards, and 7704
5: 4 *and that upon* our l and vineyards. 7704
5: 5 *to redeem them;* for other men have our l 7704
5:11 I pray you, to them, even *this* day, their l, 7704
9:30 them into the hand of the people of the l. 776
10:28 from the people of the l unto the law of God, 776
Ps 49:11 they call *their* l after their own names. 127
66: 1 Make a joyful noise unto God, all ye l: 776
100: 1 a joyful noise unto the LORD, all ye l. 776
105:44 gave them the l of the heathen: and 776
106:27 the nations, and to scatter them in the l. 776
107: 3 gathered them out of the l, from the east, 776
Isa 36:20 Who *are they* amongst all the gods of these l, 776
37:11 have done to all l by destroying them utterly; 776
Jer 16:15 from all the l whither he had driven them: 776
27: 6 now have I given all these l into the hand of 776
Eze 20: 6 and honey, which *is* the glory of all l: 776
20:15 and honey, which *is* the glory of all l; 776
39:27 gathered them out of their enemies' l, and 776
Mt 19:29 or father, or mother, or wife, or children, or l, *68*
Mk 10:29 or father, or mother, or wife, or children, or l, *68*
10:30 and sisters, and mothers, and children, and l, *68*
Ac 4:34 for as many as were possessors of l or *5564*

LANES (1)

Lk 14:21 out quickly into the streets and l of the city, *4505*

LANGUAGE (27) [LANGUAGES]

Ge 11: 1 the whole earth was *of* one l, and *of* one 8193
11: 6 the people *is* one, and they have all one l; 8193
11: 7 let us go down, and there confound their l, 8193
11: 9 the LORD did there confound the l of all 8193
2Ki 18:26 I pray thee, to thy servants **in the Syrian** l; 762
18:26 talk not with us **in the Jews'** l in the ears of 3066
18:28 and cried with a loud voice **in the Jews'** l, 3066
Ne 13:24 could not speak **in the Jews'** l, but 3066
13:24 but according to the l of each people. 3956
Est 1:22 to every people after their l, that every man 3956
1:22 according to the l of every people. 3956
3:12 and *to* every people after their l; 3956
8: 9 *unto* every people after their l, and to 3956
8: 9 to their writing, and according to their l. 3956
Ps 19: 3 *There is* no speech nor l, *where* their voice 1697
81: 5 *where* I heard a l *that* I understood not. 8193
114: 1 house of Jacob from a people of **strange** l; 3937
Isa 19:18 in the land of Egypt speak the l of Canaan, 8193
36:11 pray thee, unto thy servants **in the Syrian** l; 762
36:11 and speak not to us **in the Jews'** l, 3066
36:13 cried with a loud voice **in the Jews'** l, and 3066
Jer 5:15 a nation whose l thou knowest not, 3956
Eze 3: 5 a people of a strange speech and of a hard l, 3956
3: 6 people of a strange speech and of a hard l, 3956
Da 3:29 a decree, That every people, nation, and l, 3961
Zep 3: 9 For then will I turn to the people a pure l, 8193
Ac 2: 6 every man heard them speak in his own l. *1258*

LANGUAGES (7) [LANGUAGE]

Da 3: 4 it is commanded, O people, nations, and l, 3961
3: 7 the l, fell down *and* worshipped the golden 3961
4: 1 unto all people, nations, and l, that dwell in 3961
5:19 nations, and l, trembled and feared before 3961
6:25 and l, that dwell in all the earth; 3961
7:14 a kingdom, that all people, nations, and l, 3961
Zec 8:23 shall take hold out of all l of the nations, 3956

LANGUISH (5) [LANGUISHED, LANGUISHETH, LANGUISHING]

Isa 16: 8 For the fields of Heshbon l, *and* the vine of 535
19: 8 they that spread nets upon the waters shall l. 535
24: 4 the haughty people of the earth do l. 535
Jer 14: 2 Judah mourneth, and the gates thereof l; 535
Hos 4: 3 every one that dwelleth therein shall l, 535

LANGUISHED (1) [LANGUISH]

La 2: 8 and the wall to lament; they l together. 535

LANGUISHETH (8) [LANGUISH]

Isa 24: 4 fadeth away, the world l *and* fadeth away, 535
24: 7 The new wine mourneth, the vine l, all 535
33: 9 The earth mourneth *and* l: Lebanon is 535
Jer 15: 9 She that hath borne seven l: she hath given 535
Joel 1:10 is wasted, the new wine is dried up, the oil l. 535
1:12 The vine is dried up, and the fig tree l; 535
Na 1: 4 Bashan l, and Carmel, and the flower of 535
1: 4 and Carmel, and the flower of Lebanon l. 535

LANGUISHING (1) [LANGUISH]

Ps 41: 3 will strengthen him upon the bed of l: 1741

LANTERNS (1)

Jn 18: 3 cometh thither with l and torches and *5322*

LAODICEA (6) [LAODICEANS]
Col 2: 1 and *for* them at L, and *for* as many as have 2993
4:13 and them that are in L, and them in 2993
4:15 Salute the brethren which are in L, and 2993
4:16 that ye likewise read the *epistle* from L. 2993
1Ti 6: S The first to Timothy was written from L, 2993
Rev 1:11 and unto Philadelphia, and unto L. 2993

LAODICEANS (2) [LAODICEA]
Col 4:16 that it be read also in the church of the L; 2994
Rev 3:14 And unto the angel of the church of the L 2994

LAP (3) [LAPPED, LAPPETH]
2Ki 4:39 gathered thereof wild gourds his l full, and 899
Ne 5:13 Also I shook my l, and said, So God shake 2684
Pr 16:33 The lot is cast into the l; but the whole 2436

LAPIDOTH (1)
Jdg 4: 4 Deborah, a prophetess, the wife of L, 3941

LAPPED (2) [LAP]
Jdg 7: 6 the number of them that l, putting their 3952
7: 7 By the three hundred men that l will I save 3952

LAPPETH (2) [LAP]
Jdg 7: 5 Every one that l of the water with his 3952
7: 5 as a dog l, him shalt thou set by himself; 3952

LAPPIDOTH See LAPIDOTH

LAPWING (2)
Lev 11:19 heron after her kind, and the l, and the bat. 1744
Dt 14:18 heron after her kind, and the l, and the bat. 1744

LARGE (21) [LARGENESS]
Ge 34:21 behold, *it is* l enough for them; 3027+7342
Ex 3: 8 up out of that land unto a good land and a l, 7342
Jdg 18:10 unto a people secure, and to a l land: 3027+7342
2Sa 22:20 He brought me forth also into a l place: he 4800
Ne 4:19 The work *is* great and l, and we *are* 7342
7: 4 Now the city *was* l and great: but 3027+7342
9:35 in the l and fat land which thou gavest 7342
Ps 18:19 He brought me forth also into a l place; 4800
31: 8 thou hast set my feet in a l room. 4800
118: 5 answered me, *and set me* in a l place. 4800
Isa 22:18 toss thee like a ball into a l country: 3027+7342
30:23 in that day shall thy cattle feed in l 7337
30:33 it is prepared; he hath made *it* deep *and* l: 7337
Jer 22:14 will build me a wide house and l chambers, 7304
Eze 23:32 shalt drink *of* thy sister's cup deep and l: 7342
Hos 4:16 will feed them as a lamb in a l place. 4800
Mt 28:12 they gave l money unto the soldiers, 2425
Mk 14:15 And he will shew you a l upper room 3173
Lk 22:12 And he shall shew you a l upper room 3173
Gal 6:11 Ye see how l a letter I have written unto 4080
Rev 21:16 and the length is as l as the breadth: 5118

LARGENESS (1) [LARGE]
1Ki 4:29 exceeding much, and l of heart, 7341

LASCIVIOUSNESS (6)
Mk 7:22 deceit, l, an evil eye, blasphemy, pride, 766
2Co 12:21 and l which they have committed. 766
Gal 5:19 *these;* Adultery, fornication, uncleanness, l, 766
Eph 4:19 feeling have given themselves over unto l, 766
1Pe 4: 3 when we walked in l, lusts, excess of wine, 766
Jude 1: 4 *men,* turning the grace of our God into l, 766

LASEA (1)
Ac 27: 8 nigh whereunto was the city *of* L. 2996

LASH; LASHES See SCOURGES; SCOURGETH; SCOURGING; SCOURGINGS; STRIPE; STRIPES

LASHA (1)
Ge 10:19 and Admah, and Zeboim, even unto L. 3962

LASHARON (1)
Jos 12:18 The king of Aphek, one; the king of L, one; 8289

LAST (85) [LASTED, LASTING]
Ge 49: 1 you *that* which shall befall you in the l days. 319
49:19 but he shall overcome at the l. 6119
Nu 23:10 of the righteous, and let my l end be like his! 319
2Sa 19:11 Why are ye the l to bring the king back to his 314
19:12 then are ye the l to bring back the king? 314
23: 1 Now these *be* the l words of David. 314
1Ch 23:27 For by the l words of David, the Levites 314
29:29 acts of David the king, first and l, behold, 314
2Ch 9:29 the rest of the acts of Solomon, first and l, 314
12:15 Now the acts of Rehoboam, first and l, *are* 314
16:11 behold, the acts of Asa, first and l, lo, 314
20:34 the rest of the acts of Jehoshaphat, first and l, 314
25:26 of the acts of Amaziah, first and l, behold, 314
26:22 first and l, did Isaiah the prophet, the son of 314
28:26 and of all his ways, first and l, behold, 314
35:27 his deeds, first and l, behold, they *are* written 314
Ezr 8:13 of the l sons of Adonikam, whose names *are* 314
Ne 8:18 day by day, from the first day unto the l day, 314
Pr 5:11 And thou mourn at the l, when thy flesh and 319
23:32 At the l it biteth like a serpent, and 319
Isa 2: 2 it shall come to pass in the l days, *that* 319
41: 4 I the LORD, the first, and with the l; I *am* 314
44: 6 I *am* the first, and I *am* the l; and besides me 314
48:12 I *am* he; I *am* the first, I also *am* the l. 314
Jer 12: 4 because they said, He shall not see our l end. 319
50:17 l this Nebuchadrezzar king of Babylon hath 314
La 1: 9 she remembereth not her l end; therefore 319
Da 4: 8 at the l Daniel came in before me, 318
8: 3 and the higher came up l. 314+871.1+1886.1
8:19 what shall be in the l end of the indignation: 319
Am 9: 1 and I will slay the l of them with the sword: 319
Mic 4: 1 in the l days it shall come to pass, *that* 319
Mt 12:45 the l *state* of that man is worse than 2078
19:30 But many *that are* first shall be l; and 2078
19:30 *are* first shall be last; and *the* l *shall be* first. 2078
20: 8 beginning from the l unto the first. 2078
20:12 These l have wrought *but* one hour, and 2078
20:14 I will give unto this l, even as unto thee. 2078
20:16 So the l shall be first, and the first last: 2078
20:16 So the last shall be first, and the first l: 2078
21:37 But l *of all* he sent unto them his son, 5306
22:27 And l of all the woman died also. 5306
26:60 At the l came two false witnesses, 5306
27:64 so the l error shall be worse than the first. 2078
Mk 9:35 *the same* shall be l of all, and servant of all. 2078
10:31 But many *that are* first shall be l; and 2078
10:31 *that are* first shall be last; and the l first. 2078
12: 6 he sent him also l unto them, saying, 2078
12:22 left no seed: l of all the woman died also. 2078
Lk 11:26 the l *state* of that man is worse than 2078
12:59 till thou hast paid the very l mite. 2078
13:30 there are l which shall be first, and there are 2078
13:30 be first, and there are first which shall be l. 2078
20:32 L of all the woman died also. 5306
Jn 6:39 but should raise it up *again* at the l day. 2078
6:40 and I will raise him up *at* the l day. 2078
6:44 and I will raise him up *at* the l day. 2078
6:54 and I will raise him up *at* the l day. 2078
7:37 In the l day, *that* great *day* of the feast, 2078
8: 9 beginning at the eldest, *even* unto the l: 2078
11:24 rise again in the resurrection at the l day. 2078
12:48 the same shall judge him in the l day. 2078
Ac 2:17 And it shall come to pass in the l days, 2078
1Co 4: 9 that God hath set forth us the apostles l, 2078
15: 8 And l of all he was seen of me also, as of 2078
15:26 The l enemy *that* shall be destroyed *is* 2078
15:45 the l Adam *was made* a quickening spirit. 2078
15:52 in the twinkling of an eye, at the l trump: 2078
Php 4:10 that now at the l your care of me hath 4218
2Ti 3: 1 that in the l days perilous times shall come. 2078
Heb 1: 2 Hath in these l days spoken unto us by *his* 2078
Jas 5: 3 ye have heaped treasure together for the l 2078
1Pe 1: 5 salvation ready to be revealed in the l time. 2078
1:20 but was manifest in *these* l times for you, 2078
2Pe 3: 3 that there shall come in the l days scoffers, 2078
1Jn 2:18 Little children, it is the l time: and as ye 2078
2:18 whereby we know that it is the l time. 2078
Jude 1:18 you there should be mockers in the l time, 2078
Rev 1:11 I am Alpha and Omega, the first and the l: 2078
1:17 unto me, Fear not; I am the first and the l: 2078
2: 8 These *things* saith the first and the l, 2078
2:19 and the l *to be* more than the first. 2078
15: 1 seven angels having the seven l plagues; 2078
21: 9 the seven vials full of the seven l plagues, 2078
22:13 and the end, the first and the l. 2078

LASTED (1) [LAST]
Jdg 14:17 him the seven days, while their feast l: 1961

LASTING (1) [LAST]
Dt 33:15 and for the precious things of the l hills, 5769

LATCHET (4) [SHOELATCHET]
Isa 5:27 nor the l of their shoes be broken: 8288
Mk 1: 7 the l of whose shoes I am not worthy to 2438
Lk 3:16 the l of whose shoes I am not worthy to 2438
Jn 1:27 whose shoe's l I am not worthy to unloose. 2438

LATE (3) [LATELY, LATTER]
Ps 127: 2 to sit up l, to eat the bread of sorrows: 309
Mic 2: 8 Even of l my people is risen up as an enemy: 865
Jn 11: 8 Master, the Jews of l sought to stone thee; 3568

LATELY (1) [LATE]
Ac 18: 2 born in Pontus, l come from Italy, with his 4373

LATIN (2)
Lk 23:38 and L, and Hebrew, THIS IS THE KING 4513
Jn 19:20 was written in Hebrew, *and* Greek, *and* L. 4515

LATRINE See DRAUGHT

LATTER (42) [LATE]
Ex 4: 8 that they will believe the voice of the l sign. 314
Nu 24:14 people shall do to thy people in the l days. 319
24:20 but his l end *shall be* that he perish for ever. 319
Dt 4:30 *even* in the l days, if thou turn to the LORD 319
8:16 prove thee, to do thee good at thy l end; 319
11:14 the first rain and the l rain, that thou 4456
24: 3 *if* the l husband hate her, and write her a bill 314
24: 3 or if the l husband die, which took her *to be* 314
31:29 and evil will befall you in the l days; because 319
32:29 *that* they would consider their l end! 319
Ru 3:10 kindness in the l end than at the beginning, 314
2Sa 2:26 not that it will be bitterness in the l end? 314
Job 8: 7 yet thy l end should greatly increase. 319
19:25 *that* he shall stand *at* the l *day* upon 314
29:23 opened their mouth wide *as* for the l rain. 4456
42:12 So the LORD blessed the l end of Job more 319
Pr 16:15 and his favour *is* as a cloud of the l rain. 4456
19:20 that thou mayest be wise in thy l end. 319
Isa 41:22 consider *them,* and know the l end of them; 319
47: 7 neither didst remember the l end of it. 319
Jer 3: 3 and there hath been no l rain; 4456
5:24 both the former and the l, in his season: 4456
23:20 in the l days ye shall consider it perfectly. 319
30:24 of his heart: in the l days ye shall consider it. 319
48:47 again the captivity of Moab in the l days, 319
49:39 it shall come to pass in the l days, *that* I will 319
Eze 38: 8 in the l years thou shalt come into the land 319
38:16 it shall be in the l days, and I will bring thee 319
Da 2:28 Nebuchadnezzar what shall be in the l days. 320
8:23 in the l time of their kingdom, when 319
10:14 what shall befall thy people in the l days: 319
11:29 but it shall not be as the former, or as the l. 314
Hos 3: 5 the LORD and his goodness in the l days. 319
6: 3 as the l *and* former rain *unto* the earth. 4456
Joel 2:23 and the l rain in the first *month.* 4456
Am 7: 1 of the shooting up of the l growth; 3954
7: 1 *it was* the l growth after the king's 3954
Hag 2: 9 The glory of this l house shall be greater 314
Zec 10: 1 of the LORD rain in the time of the l rain; 4456
1Ti 4: 1 that in the l times some shall depart from 5306
Jas 5: 7 for it, until he receive the early and l rain. 3797
2Pe 2:20 the l *end* is worse with them than 2078

LATTICE (3)
Jdg 5:28 and cried through the l, Why is his chariot *so* 822
2Ki 1: 2 Ahaziah fell down through a l in his upper 7639
SS 2: 9 shewing himself through the l. 2762

LAUD (1)
Ro 15:11 all ye Gentiles; and l him, all ye people. 1867

LAUGH (18) [LAUGHED, LAUGHETH, LAUGHING, LAUGHTER]
Ge 18:13 Wherefore did Sarah l, saying, 6711
18:15 And he said, Nay; but thou didst l. 6711
21: 6 God hath made me to l, *so that* all that hear 6712
21: 6 to laugh, *so that* all that hear will l with me. 6711
Job 5:22 At destruction and famine thou shalt l: 7832
9:23 he will l at the trial of the innocent. 3932
22:19 are glad: and the innocent l them to scorn. 3932
Ps 2: 4 He that sitteth in the heavens shall l: 7832
22: 7 All they that see me l me to scorn: 3932
37:13 The Lord shall l at him: for he seeth that his 7832
52: 6 also shall see, and fear, and shall l at him: 7832
59: 8 thou, O LORD, shalt l at them; thou shalt 7832
80: 6 and our enemies l among themselves. 3932
Pr 1:26 I also will l at your calamity; I will mock 7832
29: 9 whether he rage or l, *there is* no rest. 7832
Ecc 3: 4 A time to weep, and a time to l; a time to 7832
Lk 6:21 *are ye* that weep now: for ye shall l. 1070
6:25 Woe unto you that l now! for ye shall 1070

LAUGHED (13) [LAUGH]
Ge 17:17 upon his face, and l, and said in his heart, 6711
18:12 Therefore Sarah l within herself, saying, 6711
18:15 Sarah denied, saying, I l not; for she was 6711
2Ki 19:21 hath despised thee, *and* l thee to scorn; 3932
2Ch 30:10 but they l them to scorn, and mocked them. 7832
Ne 2:19 heard *it,* they l us to scorn, and 3932
Job 12: 4 the just upright *man is* l to scorn. 7814
29:24 *If* I l on them, they believed *it* not; and 7832
Isa 37:22 hath despised thee, *and* l thee to scorn; 3932
Eze 23:32 thou shalt be l to scorn and had in derision; 6712
Mt 9:24 but sleepeth. And they l him to scorn. 2606
Mk 5:40 And they l him to scorn. But when he had 2606
Lk 8:53 And they l him to scorn, knowing that she 2606

LAUGHETH (1) [LAUGH]
Job 41:29 as stubble: he l at the shaking of a spear. 7832

LAUGHING (1) [LAUGH]
Job 8:21 Till he fill thy mouth *with* l, and thy lips 7814

LAUGHTER (7) [LAUGH]
Ps 126: 2 was our mouth filled *with* l, and our tongue 7814
Pr 14:13 Even in l the heart is sorrowful; and the end 7814
Ecc 2: 2 I said of l, *It is* mad: and of mirth, 7814
7: 3 Sorrow *is* better than l: for by the sadness 7814
7: 6 of thorns under a pot, so *is* the l of the fool: 7814
10:19 A feast is made for l, and wine maketh 7814
Jas 4: 9 let your l be turned to mourning, and 1071

LAUNCH (1) [LAUNCHED]
Lk 5: 4 L out into the deep, and let down your nets 1877

LAUNCHED (4) [LAUNCH]
Lk 8:22 the other side of the lake. And they l forth. 321
Ac 21: 1 after we were gotten from them, and had l, 321
27: 2 we l, meaning to sail by the coasts of Asia; 321
27: 4 And when we had l from thence, we sailed 321

LAUNDERER'S SOAP See SOPE

LAVER (15) [LAVERS]
Ex 30:18 Thou shalt also make a l *of* brass, and 3595
30:28 with all his vessels, and the l and his foot. 3595
31: 9 with all his furniture, and the l and his foot, 3595
35:16 and all his vessels, the l and his foot, 3595
38: 8 he made the l *of* brass, and the foot of it *of* 3595
39:39 and all his vessels, the l and his foot, 3595
40: 7 thou shalt set the l between the tent of 3595
40:11 And thou shalt anoint the l and his foot, and 3595
40:30 he set the l between the tent of 3595
Lev 8:11 and all his vessels, both the l and his foot, 3595
1Ki 7:30 under the l *were* undersetters molten, at 3595
7:38 one l contained forty baths: *and* every laver 3595
7:38 *and* every l was four cubits: *and* upon every 3595
7:38 *and* upon every one of the ten bases one l. 3595
2Ki 16:17 the bases, and removed the l from off them; 3595

LAVERS (5) [LAVER]
1Ki 7:38 made he ten l of brass: one laver contained 3595
7:40 And Hiram made the l, and the shovels, and 3595
7:43 And the ten bases, and ten l on the bases; 3595
2Ch 4: 6 He made also ten l, and put five on the right 3595
4:14 also bases and l made he upon the bases; 3595

LAVISH (1)
Isa 46: 6 They l gold out of the bag, and weigh silver 2107

LAW (523) [LAWFUL, LAWFULLY, LAWGIVER, LAWLESS, LAWS, LAWYER, LAWYERS, UNLAWFUL]
Ge 11:31 Sarai his daughter in l, his son Abram's 3618

Ge 19:12 **son in l**, and thy sons, and thy daughters, 2860
19:14 Lot went out, and spake unto his **sons in l**, 2860
19:14 as one that mocked unto his **sons in l**. 2860
38:11 said Judah to Tamar his **daughter in l**, 3618
38:13 Behold thy **father in l** goeth up to Timnath 2524
38:16 knew not that she *was* his **daughter in l**:) 3618
38:24 Tamar thy **daughter in l** hath played 3618
38:25 she sent to her **father in l**, saying, By 2524
47:26 Joseph made it a l over the land of Egypt 2706
Ex 3: 1 kept the flock of Jethro his **father in l**, 2859
4:18 and returned to Jethro his **father in l**, 2859
12:49 One l shall be to him that is homeborn, and 8451
13: 9 that the LORD'S l may be in thy mouth: 8451
16: 4 whether they will walk in my l, or no. 8451
18: 1 the priest of Midian, Moses' **father in l**, 2859
18: 2 Jethro, Moses' **father in l**, took Zipporah, 2859
18: 5 Jethro, Moses' **father in l**, came with his 2859
18: 6 I thy **father in l** Jethro am come unto thee, 2859
18: 7 Moses went out to meet his **father in l**, 2859
18: 8 Moses told his **father in l** all that 2859
18:12 Jethro, Moses' **father in l**, took a burnt 2859
18:12 to eat bread with Moses' **father in l** before 2859
18:14 when Moses' **father in l** saw all that he did 2859
18:15 Moses said unto his **father in l**, 2859
18:17 Moses' **father in l** said unto him, The thing 2859
18:24 hearkened to the voice of his **father in l**, 2859
18:27 Moses let his **father in l** depart; and 2859
24:12 a l, and commandments which I have 8451
Lev 6: 9 This *is* the l of the burnt offering: 8451
6:14 this *is* the l of the meat offering: the sons of 8451
6:25 This *is* the l of the sin offering: 8451
7: 1 Likewise this *is* the l of the trespass 8451
7: 7 *there is* one l for them: the priest that 8451
7:11 this *is* the l of the sacrifice of peace 8451
7:37 This *is* the l of the burnt offering, of 8451
11:46 This *is* the l of the beasts, and of the fowl, 8451
12: 7 This *is* the l for her that hath born a male or 8451
13:59 This *is* the l of the plague of leprosy in a 8451
14: 2 This shall be the l of the leper in the day of 8451
14:32 This *is* the l *of him* in whom *is* the plague 8451
14:54 This *is* the l for all *manner of* plague of 8451
14:57 and when *it is* clean: this *is* the l of leprosy. 8451
15:32 This *is* the l of him that hath an issue, and 8451
18:15 the nakedness of thy **daughter in l**: 3618
20:12 if a man lie with his **daughter in l**, both of 3618
24:22 Ye shall have one manner of l, as well for 4941
Nu 5:29 This *is* the l of jealousies, when a wife 8451
5:30 the priest shall execute upon her all this l. 8451
6:13 this *is* the l of the Nazarite, when the days 8451
6:21 This *is* the l of the Nazarite who hath 8451
6:21 so he must do after the l of his separation. 8451
10:29 Raguel the Midianite, Moses' **father in l**, 2859
15:16 One l and one manner shall be for you, and 8451
15:29 You shall have one l for him that sinneth 8451
19: 2 This *is* the ordinance of the l which 8451
19:14 This *is* the l, when a man dieth in a tent: 8451
31:21 This *is* the ordinance of the l which 8451
Dt 1: 5 began Moses to declare this l, saying, 8451
4: 8 and judgments *so* righteous as all this l, 8451
4:44 this *is* the l which Moses set before 8451
17:11 According to the sentence of the l which 8451
17:18 that he shall write him a copy of this l in a 8451
17:19 to keep all the words of this l and 8451
27: 3 write upon them all the words of this l, 8451
27: 8 stones all the words of this l very plainly. 8451
27:23 *be* he that lieth with his **mother in l**. 2859
27:26 not *all* the words of this l to do them. 8451
28:58 words of this l that are written in this book, 8451
28:61 which *is* not written in the book of this l, 8451
29:21 that are written in this book of the l: 8451
29:29 that *we* may do all the words of this l. 8451
30:10 which are written in this book of the l, 8451
31: 9 Moses wrote this l, and delivered it unto 8451
31:11 thou shalt read this l before all Israel in 8451
31:12 and observe to do all the words of this l: 8451
31:24 end of writing the words of this l in a book, 8451
31:26 Take this book of the l, and put it in 8451
32:46 to observe to do, all the words of this l. 8451
33: 2 from his right hand *went* a fiery l for them. 1881
33: 4 Moses commanded us a l, *even* 8451
33:10 teach Jacob thy judgments, and Israel thy l: 8451
Jos 1: 7 mayest observe to do according to all the l, 8451
1: 8 This book of the l shall not depart out of 8451
8:31 as it is written in the book of the l of 8451
8:32 upon the stones a copy of the l of Moses, 8451
8:34 afterward he read all the words of the l, 8451
8:34 to all that is written in the book of the l. 8451
22: 5 heed to do the commandment and the l, 8451
23: 6 to do all that is written in the book of the l 8451
24:26 these words in the book of the l of God, 8451
Jdg 1:16 children of the Kenite, Moses' **father in l**, 2859
4:11 children of Hobab the **father in l** of Moses, 2859
15: 6 the **son in l** of the Timnite, because he had 2860
19: 4 his **father in l**, the damsel's father, 2859
19: 5 the damsel's father said unto his **son in l**, 2860
19: 7 rose up to depart, his **father in l** urged him: 2859
19: 9 and his servant, his **father in l**, 2859
Ru 1: 6 she arose with her **daughters in l**, that she 3618
1: 7 and her two **daughters in l** with her; 3618
1: 8 Naomi said unto her two **daughters in l**, 3618
1:14 Orpah kissed her **mother in l**; but 2545
1:15 thy **sister in l** is gone back unto her people, 2994
1:15 her gods: return thou after thy **sister in l**. 2994
1:22 the Moabitess, her **daughter in l**, with her, 3618
2:11 all that thou hast done unto thy **mother in l** 2545
2:18 her **mother in l** saw what she had gleaned: 2545
2:19 her **mother in l** said unto her, Where hast 2545
2:19 she shewed her **mother in l** with whom she 2545
2:20 Naomi said unto her **daughter in l**, 3618
2:22 Naomi said unto Ruth her **daughter in l**, 3618
2:23 and dwelt with her **mother in l**. 2545
3: 1 Naomi her **mother in l** said unto her, 2545
3: 6 did according to all that her **mother in l** 2545
3:16 when she came to her **mother in l**, she said, 2545
3:17 to me, Go not empty unto thy **mother in l**. 2545
Ru 4:15 for thy **daughter in l**, which loveth thee, 3618
1Sa 4:19 his **daughter in l**, Phinehas' wife, was with 3618
4:19 that her **father in l** and her husband were 2524
4:21 because of her **father in l** and her husband. 2524
18:18 that I should be **son in l** to the king? 2860
18:21 Thou shalt *this* day be my **son in l** in 2859
18:22 now therefore be the king's **son in l**. 2859
18:23 to you a light *thing* to be a king's **son in l**, 2859
18:26 David well to be the king's **son in l**: 2859
18:27 that he might be the king's **son in l**. 2859
22:14 which *is* the king's **son in l**, and goeth at 2860
1Ki 2: 3 as *it is* written in the l of Moses, 8451
2Ki 8:27 for he *was* the **son in l** of the house of 2860
10:31 Jehu took no heed to walk in the l of 8451
14: 6 is written in the book of the l of Moses, 8451
17:13 according to all the l which I commanded 8451
17:34 or after the l and commandment which 8451
17:37 and the l, and the commandment, 8451
21: 8 according to all the l that my servant Moses 8451
22: 8 I have found the book of the l in the house 8451
22:11 had heard the words of the book of the l, 8451
23:24 that he might perform the words of the l 8451
23:25 his might, according to all the l of Moses; 8451
1Ch 2: 4 Tamar his **daughter in l** bare him Pharez 3618
16:17 hath confirmed the same to Jacob for a l, 2706
16:40 *to do* according to all that is written in the l 8451
22:12 that *thou* mayest keep the l of the LORD 8451
2Ch 6:16 take heed to their way to walk in my l, 8451
12: 1 he forsook the l of the LORD, and 8451
14: 4 and to do the l and the commandment. 8451
15: 3 and without a teaching priest, and without l. 8451
17: 9 *had* the book of the l of the LORD with 8451
19:10 and blood, between l and commandment, 8451
23:18 as it is written in the l of Moses, 8451
25: 4 *did* as it is written in the l in the book of 8451
30:16 according to the l of Moses the man of 8451
31: 3 as it is written in the l of the LORD. 8451
31: 4 that they might be encouraged in the l of 8451
31:21 in the l, and in the commandments, to seek 8451
33: 8 according to the whole l and the statutes 8451
34:14 Hilkiah the priest found a book of the l of 8451
34:15 I have found the book of the l in the house 8451
34:19 when the king had heard the words of the l, 8451
35:26 according to that which was written in the l 8451
Ezr 3: 2 as it is written in the l of Moses the man of 8451
7: 6 he *was* a ready scribe in the l of Moses, 8451
7:10 his heart to seek the l of the LORD, 8451
7:12 a scribe of the l of the God of heaven, 1882
7:14 according to the l of thy God which *is* in 1882
7:21 the scribe of the l of the God of heaven, 1882
7:26 whosoever will not do the l of thy God, 1882
7:26 the l of the king, let judgment be executed 1882
10: 3 and let it be done according to the l. 8451
Ne 6:18 he *was* the **son in l** of Shechaniah the son 2860
8: 1 scribe to bring the book of the l of Moses, 8451
8: 2 Ezra the priest brought the l before 8451
8: 3 *were attentive* unto the book of the l. 8451
8: 7 caused the people to understand the l: 8451
8: 8 So they read in the book in the l of God 8451
8: 9 when they heard the words of the l. 8451
8:13 even to understand the words of the l. 8451
8:14 they found written in the l which 8451
8:18 he read in the book of the l of God. 8451
9: 3 read in the book of the l of the LORD 8451
9:26 cast thy l behind their backs, and slew thy 8451
9:29 *thou* mightest bring them again unto thy l: 8451
9:34 our priests, nor our fathers, kept thy l, 8451
10:28 the people of the lands unto the l of God, 8451
10:29 and into an oath, to walk in God's l, 8451
10:34 LORD our God, as it is written in the l: 8451
10:36 as it is written in the l, and the firstlings of 8451
12:44 the cities the portions of the l for the priests 8451
13: 3 it came to pass, when they had heard the l, 8451
13:28 *was* **son in l** to Sanballat the Horonite: 2860
Est 1: 8 the drinking *was* according to the l; 1881
1:13 the king's manner towards all that knew l 1881
1:15 *we* do unto the queen Vashti according to l, 1881
4:11 *there is* one l of his to put *him* to death, 1881
4:16 the king, which *is* not according to the l: 1881
Job 22:22 the l from his mouth, and lay up his words 8451
Ps 1: 2 his delight *is* in the l of the LORD; and 8451
1: 2 and in his l doth he meditate day and night. 8451
19: 7 The l of the LORD *is* perfect, 8451
37:31 The l of his God *is* in his heart; none of his 8451
40: 8 O my God: yea, thy l *is* within my heart. 8451
78: 1 Give ear, O my people, to my l: 8451
78: 5 appointed a l in Israel, which he 8451
78:10 of God, and refused to walk in his l; 8451
81: 4 for Israel, *and* a l of the God of Jacob. 4941
89:30 If his children forsake my l, and walk not in 8451
94:12 O LORD, and teachest him out of thy l; 8451
94:20 *with* thee, which frameth mischief by a l? 2706
105:10 confirmed the same unto Jacob for a l, *and* 2706
119: 1 the way, who walk in the l of the LORD. 8451
119:18 I may behold wondrous *things* out of thy l. 8451
119:29 way of lying: and grant me thy l graciously. 8451
119:34 me understanding, and I shall keep thy l; 8451
119:44 So shall I keep thy l continually for ever 8451
119:51 *yet* have I not declined from thy l. 8451
119:53 because of the wicked that forsake thy l. 8451
119:55 in the night, and have kept thy l. 8451
119:61 robbed me: *but* I have not forgotten thy l. 8451
119:70 is as fat as grease; *but* I delight *in* thy l. 8451
119:72 The l of thy mouth *is* better unto me than 8451
119:77 that I may live: for thy l *is* my delight. 8451
119:85 pits for me, which *are* not after thy l. 8451
119:92 Unless thy l *had been* my delights, I should 8451
119:97 O how love I thy l! it *is* my meditation all 8451
119:109 in my hand: yet do I not forget thy l. 8451
119:113 I hate *vain* thoughts: but thy l do I love. 8451
119:126 to work: *for* they have made void thy l. 8451
119:136 mine eyes, because they keep not thy l. 8451
119:142 and thy l *is* the truth. 8451
119:150 after mischief: they are far from thy l. 8451
119:153 and deliver me: for I do not forget thy l. 8451
Ps 119:163 I hate and abhor lying: *but* thy l do I love. 8451
119:165 Great peace have they which love thy l: and 8451
119:174 O LORD; and thy l *is* my delight. 8451
Pr 1: 8 and forsake not the l of thy mother: 8451
3: 1 My son, forget not my l; but let thine heart 8451
4: 2 you good doctrine, forsake you not my l. 8451
6:20 and forsake not the l of thy mother: 8451
6:23 the l *is* light; and reproofs of instruction *are* 8451
7: 2 and live; and my l as the apple of thine eye. 8451
13:14 The l of the wise *is* a fountain of life, 8451
28: 4 They that forsake the l praise the wicked: 8451
28: 4 but such as keep the l contend with them. 8451
28: 7 Whoso keepeth the l *is* a wise son: but 8451
28: 9 that turneth away his ear from hearing the l, 8451
29:18 but he that keepeth the l, happy *is* he. 8451
31: 5 forget the l, and pervert the judgment of 2710
31:26 and in her tongue *is* the l of kindness. 8451
Isa 1:10 give ear unto the l of our God, ye people of 8451
2: 3 for out of Zion shall go forth the l, and 8451
5:24 they have cast away the l of the LORD of 8451
8:16 seal the l among my disciples. 8451
8:20 To the l and to the testimony: if they speak 8451
30: 9 children *that* will not hear the l of 8451
42: 4 the earth: and the isles shall wait for his l. 8451
42:21 he will magnify the l, and make *it* 8451
42:24 neither were they obedient unto his l. 8451
51: 4 for a l shall proceed from me, and I will 8451
51: 7 the people in whose heart *is* my l; 8451
Jer 2: 8 they that handle the l knew me not: 8451
6:19 unto my words, nor *to* my l, but rejected it. 8451
8: 8 and the l of the LORD *is* with us? 8451
9:13 Because they have forsaken my l which I 8451
16:11 have forsaken me, and have not kept my l; 8451
18:18 for the l shall not perish from the priest, 8451
26: 4 to walk in my l, which I have set before 8451
31:33 I will put my l in their inward parts, and 8451
32:11 that which was sealed *according to* the l 4687
32:23 not thy voice, neither walked in thy l; 8451
44:10 nor walked in my l, nor in my statutes, 8451
44:23 nor walked in his l, nor in his statutes, 8451
La 2: 9 the l *is* no *more;* her prophets also find no 8451
Eze 7:26 the l shall perish from the priest, and 8451
22:11 hath lewdly defiled his **daughter in l**; 3618
22:26 Her priests have violated my l, and 8451
43:12 This *is* the l of the house; Upon the top of 8451
43:12 Behold, this *is* the l of the house. 8451
Da 6: 5 *it* against him concerning the l of his God. 1882
6: 8 according to the l of the Medes and 1882
6:12 according to the l of the Medes and 1882
6:15 that the l of the Medes and Persians *is,* That 1882
9:11 Yea, all Israel have transgressed thy l, 8451
9:11 the oath that *is* written in the l of Moses 8451
9:13 As *it is* written in the l of Moses, all this 8451
Hos 4: 6 seeing thou hast forgotten the l of thy God, 8451
8: 1 my covenant, and trespassed against my l. 8451
8:12 written to him the great things of my l, 8451
Am 2: 4 they have despised the l of the LORD, 8451
Mic 4: 2 for the l shall go forth of Zion, and 8451
7: 6 the **daughter in l** against her mother in 3618
7: 6 the daughter in law against her **mother in l**; 2545
Hab 1: 4 Therefore the l is slacked, and 8451
Zep 3: 4 they have done violence to the l. 8451
Hag 2:11 Ask now the priests *concerning* the l, 8451
Zec 7:12 lest *they* should hear the l, and the words 8451
Mal 2: 6 The l of truth was in his mouth, and 8451
2: 7 and they should seek the l at his mouth: 8451
2: 8 ye have caused many to stumble at the l; 8451
2: 9 my ways, but have been partial in the l. 8451
4: 4 Remember ye the l of Moses my servant, 8451
Mt 5:17 Think not that I am come to destroy the l, *3551*
5:18 or one tittle shall in no wise pass from the l, *3551*
5:40 And if any man will **sue** thee **at the l**, and *2919*
7:12 so to them: for this is the l and the prophets. *3551*
10:35 the **daughter in l** against her mother in *3565*
10:35 the daughter in law against her **mother in l**. *3994*
11:13 and the l prophesied until John. *3551*
12: 5 Or have ye not read in the l, how that on *3551*
22:36 which *is* the great commandment in the l? *3551*
22:40 On these two commandments hang all the l *3551*
23:23 have omitted the weightier *matters* of the l, *3551*
Lk 2:22 to the l of Moses were accomplished, *3551*
2:23 (As it is written in the l of the Lord, Every *3551*
2:24 to that which is said in the l of the Lord, *3551*
2:27 to do for him after the custom of the l, *3551*
2:39 all *things* according to the l of the Lord, *3551*
5:17 **doctors of the l** sitting *by,* which were *3547*
10:26 He said unto him, What is written in the l? *3551*
12:53 the **mother in l** against her daughter in law, *3994*
12:53 mother in law against her **daughter in l**, *3565*
12:53 the **daughter in l** against her mother in *3565*
12:53 the daughter in law against her **mother in l**. *3994*
16:16 The l and the prophets *were* until John: *3551*
16:17 earth to pass, than one tittle of the l to fail. *3551*
24:44 which were written in the l of Moses, and *3551*
Jn 1:17 For the l was given by Moses, *but* grace *3551*
1:45 of whom Moses in the l, and the prophets, *3551*
7:19 Did not Moses give you the l, and *yet* none *3551*
7:19 the law, and *yet* none of you keepeth the l? *3551*
7:23 that the l of Moses should not be broken; *3551*
7:49 But this people who knoweth not the l are *3551*
7:51 Doth our l judge any man, before it hear *3551*
8: 5 Now Moses in the l commanded us, *3551*
8:17 It is also written in your l, that *3551*
10:34 Is it not written in your l, I said, Ye are *3551*
12:34 We have heard out of the l that Christ *3551*
15:25 might be fulfilled that is written in their l, *3551*
18:13 for he was **father in l** to Caiaphas, *3995*
18:31 ye him, and judge him according to your l. *3551*
19: 7 We have a l, and by our law he ought to *3551*
19: 7 and by our l he ought to die, because *3551*
Ac 5:34 a Pharisee, named Gamaliel, a **doctor of l**, *3547*
6:13 words against this holy place, and the l: *3551*
7:53 Who have received the l by the disposition *3551*
13:15 And after the reading of the l and *3551*
13:39 ye could not be justified by the l of Moses. *3551*

Ac 15: 5 to command *them* to keep the l of Moses. 3551
15:24 *Ye must* be circumcised, and keep the l: 3551
18:13 men to worship God contrary to the l. 3551
18:15 question of words and names, and *of* your l, 3551
19:38 have a matter against any *man,* the l is open, 60
21:20 and they are all zealous of the l: 3551
21:24 also walkest orderly, and keepest the l. 3551
21:28 against the people, and the l, and this place: 3551
22: 3 to the perfect manner of the l of the fathers, 3551
22:12 a devout man according to the l, 3551
23: 3 for sittest thou to judge me after the l, and 3551
23: 3 me to be smitten **contrary to the** l? 3891
23:29 to be accused of questions of their l, 3551
24: 6 and would have judged according to our l. 3551
24:14 all *things* which are written in the l 3551
25: 8 Neither against the l of the Jews, 3551
28:23 both out of the l of Moses, and *out of* 3551
Ro 2:12 For as many as have sinned **without** l shall 460
2:12 without law shall also perish **without** l: 460
2:12 as many as have sinned in the l shall be 3551
2:12 sinned in the law shall be judged by the l; 3551
2:13 (For not the hearers of the l *are* just before 3551
2:13 but the doers of the l shall be justified. 3551
2:14 when *the* Gentiles, which have not the l, 3551
2:14 do by nature the *things* contained in the l, 3551
2:14 these, having not the l, are a law unto 3551
2:14 having not the law, are a l unto themselves: 3551
2:15 Which shew the work of the l written in 3551
2:17 and restest in the l, and makest thy boast of 3551
2:18 being instructed out of the l; 3551
2:20 form of knowledge and of the truth in the l. 3551
2:23 Thou that makest thy boast of the l, 3551
2:23 through breaking the l dishonourest thou 3551
2:25 verily profiteth, if thou keep the l: 3551
2:25 but if thou be a breaker of the l, 3551
2:26 keep the righteousness of the l, 3551
2:27 if it fulfil the l, judge thee, who by the letter 3551
2:27 and circumcision dost transgress the l? 3551
3:19 Now we know that what *things* soever the l 3551
3:19 it saith to them who are under the l: 3551
3:20 Therefore by the deeds of the l there shall 3551
3:20 for by the l *is* the knowledge of sin. 3551
3:21 of God without the l is manifested, 3551
3:21 being witnessed by the l and the prophets; 3551
3:27 By what l? of works? Nay: but by the law 3551
3:27 of works? Nay: but by the l of faith. 3551
3:28 justified by faith without the deeds of the l. 3551
3:31 Do we then make void the l through faith? 3551
3:31 God forbid: yea, we establish the l. 3551
4:13 through the l, but through the righteousness 3551
4:14 For if they which are of the l *be* heirs, faith 3551
4:15 Because the l worketh wrath: for where no 3551
4:15 for where no l is, *there is* no transgression. 3551
4:16 not to that only which is of the l, but to that 3551
5:13 For until the l sin was in the world: but 3551
5:13 but sin is not imputed when there is no l. 3551
5:20 Moreover the l entered, that the offence 3551
6:14 for ye are not under the l, but under grace. 3551
6:15 because we are not under the l, but 3551
7: 1 (for I speak to them that know the l,) 3551
7: 1 how that the l hath dominion over a man, 3551
7: 2 a husband is bound by the l to *her* husband 3551
7: 2 she is loosed from the l of the husband. 3551
7: 3 *her* husband be dead, she is free from *that* l; 3551
7: 4 ye also are become dead to the l by 3551
7: 5 the motions of sins, which were by the l, 3551
7: 6 But now we are delivered from the l, 3551
7: 7 *Is* the l sin? God forbid. Nay, I had not 3551
7: 7 Nay, I had not known sin, but by the l: for I 3551
7: 7 except the l had said, Thou shalt not covet. 3551
7: 8 For without the l sin *was* dead. 3551
7: 9 For I was alive without the l once: but 3551
7:12 Wherefore the l *is* holy, and 3551
7:14 For we know that the l is spiritual: but I am 3551
7:16 I consent unto the l that *it is* good. 3551
7:21 I find then a l, that, when I would do good, 3551
7:22 For I delight in the l of God after 3551
7:23 But I see another l in my members, 3551
7:23 warring against the l of my mind, and 3551
7:23 bringing me into captivity to the l of sin 3551
7:25 with the mind I myself serve the l of God; 3551
7:25 law of God; but with the flesh the l of sin. 3551
8: 2 For the l of the Spirit of life in Christ Jesus 3551
8: 2 Jesus hath made me free from the l of sin 3551
8: 3 For what the l could not do, in that it was 3551
8: 4 That the righteousness of the l might be 3551
8: 7 for it is not subject to the l of God, 3551
9: 4 and the **giving of the** l, and the service *of* 3548
9:31 which followed *after* the l of righteousness, 3551
9:31 hath not attained to the l of righteousness. 3551
9:32 but as *it were* by the works of the l. 3551
10: 4 For Christ *is* the end of the l for 3551
10: 5 the righteousness which is of the l, 3551
13: 8 he that loveth another hath fulfilled the l. 3551
13:10 therefore love *is* the fulfilling of the l. 3551
1Co 6: 1 **go to** l before the unjust, and not before 2919
6: 6 But brother **goeth to** l with brother, and 2919
6: 7 because ye **go to** l one with another. 2192+2917
7:39 The wife is bound by the l as long as her 3551
9: 8 as a man? or saith not the l the same also? 3551
9: 9 For it is written in the l of Moses, 3551
9:20 to them that are under the l, as under 3551
9:20 them that are under the law, as under the l, 3551
9:20 that I might gain them that are under the l; 3551
9:21 To them *that are* **without** l, as without law, 459
9:21 To them *that are* without law, as **without** l, 459
9:21 (being not **without** l to God, but under 459
9:21 law to God, but **under** the l to Christ,) 1772
9:21 that I might gain them *that are* **without** l. 459
14:21 In the l it is written, With *men* of other 3551
14:34 to be under obedience, as also saith the l. 3551
15:56 death *is* sin; and the strength of sin *is* the l. 3551
Gal 2:16 a man is not justified by the works of the l, 3551
2:16 of Christ, and not by the works of the l: 3551
2:16 for by the works of the l shall no flesh be 3551

Gal 2:19 For I through the l am dead to the law, 3551
2:19 For I through the law am dead to the l, 3551
2:21 for if righteousness *come* by the l, then 3551
3: 2 ye the Spirit by the works of the l, 3551
3: 5 *doeth he it* by the works of the l, or by 3551
3:10 For as many as are of the works of the l are 3551
3:10 are written in the book of the l to do them. 3551
3:11 But that no *man* is justified by the l in 3551
3:12 And the l is not of faith: but, The man that 3551
3:13 hath redeemed us from the curse of the l, 3551
3:17 the l, which was four hundred and 3551
3:18 For if the inheritance *be* of the l, *it is* no 3551
3:19 Wherefore then *serveth* the l? It was added 3551
3:21 *Is* the l then against the promises of God? 3551
3:21 for if there had been a l given which could 3551
3:21 righteousness should have been by the l. 3551
3:23 faith came, we were kept under the l, 3551
3:24 Wherefore the l was our schoolmaster *to* 3551
4: 4 made of a woman, made under the l, 3551
4: 5 To redeem them that were under the l, 3551
4:21 Tell me, ye that desire to be under the l, 3551
4:21 to be under the law, do ye not hear the l? 3551
5: 3 that he is a debtor to do the whole l. 3551
5: 4 whosoever of you are justified by the l; 3551
5:14 For all the l is fulfilled in one word, *even* in 3551
5:18 be led of the Spirit, ye are not under the l. 3551
5:23 against such there is no l. 3551
6: 2 and so fulfil the l of Christ. 3551
6:13 themselves who are circumcised keep the l; 3551
Eph 2:15 *even* the l of commandments *contained* in 3551
Php 3: 5 the Hebrews; as touching the l, a Pharisee; 3551
3: 6 touching the righteousness which is in the l, 3551
3: 9 which is of the l, but that which is through 3551
1Ti 1: 7 Desiring to be **teachers of the** l; 3547
1: 8 But we know that the l *is* good, if a man 3551
1: 9 that the l is not made for a righteous *man,* 3551
Tit 3: 9 and contentions, and strivings **about** the l; 3544
Heb 7: 5 take tithes of the people according to the l, 3551
7:11 (for under it the people **received** the l,) 3549
7:12 is made of necessity a change also of the l. 3551
7:16 not after the l of a carnal commandment, 3551
7:19 For the l made nothing perfect, but 3551
7:28 For the l maketh men high priests which 3551
7:28 which was since the l, *maketh* the Son, 3551
8: 4 are priests that offer gifts according to the l: 3551
9:19 precept to all the people according to the l, 3551
9:22 And almost all *things* are by the l purged 3551
10: 1 For the l having a shadow of good *things* to 3551
10: 8 pleasure *therein;* which are offered by the l; 3551
10:28 He that despised Moses' l died without 3551
Jas 1:25 But whoso looketh into the perfect l of 3551
2: 8 If ye fulfil the royal l according to 3551
2: 9 and are convinced of the l as transgressors. 3551
2:10 For whosoever shall keep the whole l, and 3551
2:11 thou art become a transgressor of the l. 3551
2:12 as they that shall be judged by the l of 3551
4:11 speaketh evil of the l, and judgeth the law: 3551
4:11 speaketh evil of the law, and judgeth the l: 3551
4:11 but if thou judge the l, thou art not a doer of 3551
4:11 thou art not a doer of the l, but a judge. 3551
1Jn 3: 4 sin **transgresseth** also the l: 458+4160
3: 4 the law: for sin is the **transgression of** the l. 458

LAWFUL (39) [LAW]

Ezr 7:24 it *shall* not *be* l to impose toll, tribute, or 7990
Isa 49:24 from the mighty, or the l captive delivered? 6662
Eze 18: 5 be just, and do **that which is** l and right, 4941
18:19 When the son hath done **that which is** l and 4941
18:21 do **that which is** l and right, he shall surely 4941
18:27 doeth **that which is** l and right, he shall 4941
33:14 his sin, and do **that which is** l and right; 4941
33:16 he hath done **that which is** l and right; 4941
33:19 do **that which is** l and right, he shall live 4941
Mt 12: 2 thy disciples do *that* which is not l to do 1832
12: 4 which was not l for him to eat, 1832
12:10 saying, Is it l to heal on the sabbath days? 1832
12:12 Wherefore it is l to do well on the sabbath 1832
14: 4 unto him, It is not l for thee to have her. 1832
19: 3 Is it l for a man to put away his wife for 1832
20:15 Is it not l for me to do what I will with 1832
22:17 Is it l to give tribute unto Cesar, or not? 1832
27: 6 It is not l for to put them into the treasury, 1832
Mk 2:24 they on the sabbath day *that* which is not l? 1832
2:26 which is not l to eat but for the priests, and 1832
3: 4 Is it l to do good on the sabbath days, or 1832
6:18 It is not l for thee to have thy brother's 1832
10: 2 Is it l for a man to put away *his* wife? 1832
12:14 Is it l to give tribute to Cesar, or not? 1832
Lk 6: 2 Why do ye *that* which is not l to do on 1832
6: 4 which it is not l to eat but **for** the priests 1832
6: 9 I will ask you one *thing;* Is it l on 1832
14: 3 saying, Is it l to heal on the sabbath day? 1832
20:22 Is it l for us to give tribute unto Cesar, or 1832
Jn 5:10 it is not l for thee to carry *thy* bed. 1832
18:31 It is not l for us to put any *man* to death: 1832
Ac 16:21 which are not l for us to receive, neither to 1832
19:39 it shall be determined in a l assembly. 1772
22:25 l for you to scourge a man *that is* a Roman, 1832
1Co 6:12 All *things* are l unto me, but all *things* are 1832
6:12 all *things* are l for me, but I will not be 1832
10:23 All *things* are l for me, but all *things* are not 1832
10:23 all *things* are l for me, but all *things* edify 1832
2Co 12: 4 which *it is* not l for a man to utter. 1832

LAWFULLY (2) [LAW]

1Ti 1: 8 know that the law *is* good, if a man use it l; 3545
2Ti 2: 5 *yet* is he not crowned, except he strive l. 3545

LAWGIVER (7) [GIVE, LAW]

Ge 49:10 nor a l from between his feet, until Shiloh 2710
Nu 21:18 by the direction of the l, with their staves. 2710
Dt 33:21 because there, *in* a portion of the l, *was he* 2710
Ps 60: 7 *is* the strength of mine head; Judah *is* my l; 2710
108: 8 *is* the strength of mine head; Judah *is* my l; 2710

Isa 33:22 the LORD *is* our l, the LORD *is* our 2710
Jas 4:12 There is one l, who is able to save and 3550

LAWLESS (1) [LAW]

1Ti 1: 9 righteous *man,* but for the l and disobedient, 459

LAWS (20) [LAW]

Ge 26: 5 my commandments, my statutes, and my l. 8451
Ex 16:28 ye to keep my commandments and my l? 8451
18:16 *them* know the statutes of God, and his l. 8451
18:20 And thou shalt teach them ordinances and l, 8451
Lev 26:46 These *are* the statutes and judgments and l, 8451
Ezr 7:25 the river, all such as know the l of thy God; 1882
Ne 9:13 true l, good statutes and commandments: 8451
9:14 them precepts, statutes, and l, 8451
Est 1:19 let it be written among the l of the Persians 1881
3: 8 their l *are* diverse from all people; 1881
3: 8 all people; neither keep they the king's l: 1881
Ps 105:45 might observe his statutes, and keep his l. 8451
Isa 24: 5 because they have transgressed the l, 8451
Eze 43:11 all the forms thereof, and all the l thereof: 8451
44: 5 house of the LORD, and all the l thereof; 8451
44:24 they shall keep my l and my statutes in all 8451
Da 7:25 most High, and think to change times and l: 1882
9:10 to walk in his l, which he set before us by 8451
Heb 8:10 I will put my l into their mind, and 3551
10:16 I will put my l into their hearts, and in their 3551

LAWYER (3) [LAW]

Mt 22:35 Then one of them, *which was* a l, 3544
Lk 10:25 a certain l stood up, and tempted him, 3544
Tit 3:13 Bring Zenas the l and Apollos on their 3544

LAWYERS (5) [LAW]

Lk 7:30 l rejected the counsel of God against 3544
11:45 Then answered one of the l, and said unto 3544
11:46 And he said, Woe unto you also, *ye* l! 3544
11:52 Woe unto you, l! for ye have taken away 3544
14: 3 And Jesus answering spake unto the l and 3544

LAY (241) [LAID, LAIDST, LAYEDST, LAYEST, LAYETH, LAYING, OVERLAY]

Ge 19: 4 But before they l **down,** the men of the city, 7901
19:33 the firstborn went in, and l with her father; 7901
19:33 he perceived not when she l **down,** 7901
19:34 Behold, I l yesternight with my father: 7901
19:35 the younger arose, and l with him; and 7901
19:35 he perceived not when she l **down,** 7901
22:12 he said, **L** not thine hand upon the lad, 7971
28:11 and l **down** in that place to **sleep.** 7901
30:16 And he l with her that night. 7901
34: 2 he took her, and l with her, and defiled her. 7901
35:22 and l with Bilhah his father's concubine: 7901
37:22 l no hand upon him, that he might rid him 7971
41:35 l **up** corn under the hand of Pharaoh, and 6651
Ex 5: 8 did make heretofore, you shall l upon them; 7760
7: 4 that I may l my hand upon Egypt, and 5414
16:13 in the morning the dew l round about 7902
16:14 when the dew that l was gone up, behold, 7902
16:14 upon the face of the wilderness *there l* a NIH
16:23 that which remaineth over l **up** for you to 3240
16:33 l it **up** before the LORD, to be kept for 3240
21:22 according as the woman's husband will l 7896
22:25 neither shalt thou l upon him usury. 7760
Lev 1: 7 and l the wood **in order** upon the fire: 6186
1: 8 l the parts, the head, and the fat, **in order** 6186
1:12 the priest shall l them **in order** on the wood 6186
2:15 put oil upon it, and l frankincense thereon: 7760
3: 2 he shall l his hand upon the head of his 5564
3: 8 he shall l his hand upon the head of his 5564
3:13 he shall l his hand upon the head of it, and 5564
4: 4 shall l his hand upon the bullock's head, 5564
4:15 the elders of the congregation shall l their 5564
4:24 he shall l his hand upon the head of 5564
4:29 he shall l his hand upon the head of the sin 5564
4:33 he shall l his hand upon the head of the sin 5564
6:12 l the burnt offering **in order** upon it; 6186
16:21 Aaron shall l both his hands upon the head 5564
24:14 let all that heard *him* l their hands upon his 5564
Nu 8:12 the Levites shall l their hands upon 5564
12:11 I beseech thee, l not the sin upon us, 7896
17: 4 thou shalt l them **up** in the tabernacle of 3240
19: 9 l *them* **up** without the camp in a clean 3240
24: 9 he l **down** as a lion, and as a great lion: 7901
27:18 *is* the spirit, and l thine hand upon him; 5564
Dt 7:15 but will l them upon all *them* that hate thee. 5414
11:18 Therefore shall ye l **up** these my words in 7760
11:25 *for* the LORD your God shall l the fear of 5414
14:28 and shalt l *it* **up** within thy gates: 3240
21: 8 l not innocent blood unto thy people of 5414
21:19 his father and his mother l **hold** on him, 8610
22:22 *both* the man that l with the woman, and 7901
22:25 then the man only that l with her shall die: 7901
22:28 l **hold on** her, and lie with her, and they be 8610
22:29 the man that l with her shall give unto 7901
Jos 6:26 he shall l the **foundation** thereof in his 3245
8: 2 l thee an ambush for the city behind it. 7760
15:46 all that *l* near Ashdod, with their villages: NIH
Jdg 4:22 Sisera l dead, and the nail *was* in his 5307
5:27 At her feet he bowed, he fell, he l **down:** 7901
6:20 and l *them* upon this rock, 3240
7:12 all the children of the east l **along in** 5307
7:13 and overturned it, that the tent l **along.** 5307
14:17 he told her, because she l **sore upon** him: 6693
16: 3 Samson l till midnight, and arose at 7901
18:19 l thine hand upon thy mouth, and go with 7760
Ru 3: 4 and uncover his feet, and l thee **down;** 7901
3: 8 and behold, a woman l at his feet. 7901
3:14 she l at his feet until the morning: and 7901
1Sa 2:22 how they l with the women that assembled 7901
3: 5 lie down again. And he went and l **down.** 7901
3: 9 So Samuel went and l **down** in his place. 7901
3:15 Samuel l until the morning, and opened 7901
6: 8 ark of the LORD, and l it upon the cart; 5414

1Sa 11: 2 and l it *for* a reproach upon all Israel. 7760
19:24 l down naked all that day and all *that* night. 5307
26: 5 David beheld the place where Saul l, and 7901
26: 5 Saul l in the trench, and the people pitched 7901
26: 7 Saul l sleeping within the trench, and 7901
26: 7 Abner and the people l round about him. 7901
2Sa 2:21 l thee hold on one of the young men, and 270
4: 5 who l on a bed at noon. 4904+7901
4: 7 he l on his bed in his bedchamber, and 7901
11: 4 she came in unto him, and he l with her; 7901
12: 3 l in his bosom, and was unto him as a 7901
12:16 and went in, and l all night upon the earth. 7901
12:24 and went in unto her, and l with her: 7901
13: 5 L *thee* down on thy bed, and make thyself 7901
13: 6 So Amnon l down, and made himself sick: 7901
13:14 than she, forced her, and l with her. 7901
13:31 and tare his garments, and l on the earth; 7901
19:32 king of sustenance while he l at Mahanaim; 7871
1Ki 5:17 to l the foundation of the house. 3245
7: 3 that l on forty five pillars, fifteen *in* a row. NIH
13: 4 hand from the altar, saying, L hold on him. 8610
13:31 God *is* buried; l my bones beside his bones: 3240
18:23 l *it* on wood, and put no fire *under:* and 7760
18:23 and l *it* on wood, and put no fire *under:* 5414
19: 5 as he l and slept under a juniper tree, 7901
21:27 fasted, and l in sackcloth, and went softly. 7901
2Ki 4:11 he turned into the chamber, and l there. 7901
4:29 and l my staff upon the face of the child. 7760
4:34 l upon the child, and put his mouth upon 7901
9:16 and went to Jezreel; for Joram l there. 7901
10: 8 L ye them *in* two heaps *at* the entering in of 7760
19:25 that thou shouldest be to l waste fenced 7582
2Ch 31: 7 began to l the foundation of the heaps, 3245
36:21 *for* as long as *she* l desolate she kept 8074
Ezr 8:31 and of such as l in wait by the way. 693
Ne 13:21 if ye do *so* again, I will l hands on you. 7971
Est 2:21 and sought to l hand on the king Ahasuerus. 7971
3: 6 he thought scorn to l hands on Mordecai 7971
4: 3 wailing; *and* many l in sackcloth and ashes. 3331
6: 2 who sought to l hand on the king 7971
9: 2 to l hand on such as sought their hurt: 7971
Job 9:33 *that* might l his hand upon us both. 7896
17: 3 L down now, put me in a surety with thee; 7760
21: 5 and l *your* hand upon *your* mouth. 7760
22:22 and l up his words in thine heart. 7760
22:24 shalt thou l up gold as dust, and *the gold of* 7896
29:19 and the dew l all night upon my branch. 3885
34:23 For he will not l upon man more *than right;* 7760
40: 4 I will l my hand upon my mouth. 7760
41: 8 L thine hand upon him, remember 7760
Ps 4: 8 I will both l me down in peace, and sleep: 7901
7: 5 the earth, and l mine honour in the dust. 7931
38:12 They also that seek after my life l snares 5367
71:10 they that l wait for my soul take counsel 8104
84: 3 where she may l her young, *even* thine 7896
104:22 and l them down in their dens. 7257
Pr 1:11 Come with us, let us l wait for blood, 693
1:18 they l wait for their own blood; they lurk 693
3:18 She *is* a tree of life to them that l hold upon 2388
7: 1 and l up my commandments with thee. 6845
10:14 Wise *men* l up knowledge: but the mouth 6845
24:15 L not wait, O wicked *man,* against 693
30:32 thought evil, *l thine* hand upon thy mouth. NIH
Ecc 2: 3 to l hold on folly, till I might see what *was* 270
7: 2 all men; and the living will l *it* to his heart. 5414
Isa 5: 6 I will l it waste: it shall not be pruned, nor 7896
5: 8 that l field to field, till *there be* no place, 7126
5:29 l hold of the prey, and shall carry *it* away 270
11:14 they shall l their hand upon Edom and 4916
13: 9 and fierce anger, to l the land desolate: 7760
13:11 will l low the haughtiness of the terrible. 8213
22:22 the key of the house of David will I l upon 5414
25:12 l low, *and* bring to the ground, *even* to 8213
28:16 I l in Zion for a foundation a stone, 3245
28:17 Judgment also will I l to the line, and 7760
29: 3 will l siege against thee *with* a mount, and 6696
29:21 l a snare for him that reproveth in the gate, 6983
30:32 which the LORD shall l upon him, *it* shall 5117
34:15 l, and hatch, and gather under her shadow: 4422
35: 7 where each l, *shall be* grass with reeds and 7258
37:26 that thou shouldest be to l waste defenced 7582
38:21 l *it* for a plaister upon the boil, and 4799
47: 7 that thou didst not l these *things* to thy 7760
51:16 l the foundations of the earth, and say unto 3245
54:11 I will l thy stones with fair colours, and 7257
54:11 and l thy foundations with sapphires. 3245
Jer 5:26 people are found wicked *men:* they l wait, 7789
6:21 I will l stumblingblocks before this people, 5414
6:23 They shall l hold on bow and spear; 2388
Eze 3:20 I l a stumblingblock before him, he shall 5414
4: 1 l it before thee, and pourtray upon it 5414
4: 2 l siege against it, and build a fort against it, 5414
4: 3 and thou shalt l siege against it. 6696
4: 4 l the iniquity of the house of Israel upon it: 7760
4: 8 I will l bands upon thee, and thou shalt not 5414
6: 5 I will l the dead carcases of the children of 5414
19: 2 she l down among lions, she nourished her 7257
23: 8 for in her youth they l with her, and 7901
25:14 I will l my vengeance upon Edom by 5414
25:17 when I shall l my vengeance upon them. 5414
26:12 they shall l thy stones and thy timber and 7760
26:16 l away their robes, and put off their 5493
28:17 I will l thee before kings, that *they* may 5414
32: 5 I will l thy flesh upon the mountains, and 5414
33:28 For I will l the land most desolate, and 5414
35: 4 I will l thy cities waste, and thou shalt be 7760
36:29 will increase it, and l no famine upon you. 5414
36:34 whereas it l desolate in the sight of all that 1961
37: 6 I will l sinews upon you, and will bring up 5414
42:13 there shall they l the most holy *things,* 3240
42:14 there they shall l their garments wherein 3240
44:19 l them in the holy chambers, and they shall 3240
Am 2: 8 they l *themselves* down upon clothes laid 5186
Jnh 1: 5 of the ship; and he l, and was fast asleep. 7901
1:14 and l not upon us innocent blood: 5414
Mic 1: 7 and all the idols thereof will I l desolate: 7760
7:16 they shall l *their* hand upon *their* mouth, 7760
Zec 14:13 they shall l hold every one on the hand of 2388
Mal 2: 2 will not hear, and if ye will not l *it* to heart, 7760
2: 2 because ye do not l *it* to heart. 7760
Mt 6:19 L not up for yourselves treasures upon 2343
6:20 But l up for yourselves treasures in heaven, 2343
8:20 the Son of man hath not where to l *his* 2827
9:18 but come and l thy hand upon her, and 2007
12:11 will he not l hold on it, and lift *it* out? 2902
21:46 But when they sought to l hands on him, 2902
23: 4 and l *them* on men's shoulders; 2007
28: 6 Come, see the place where the Lord l. 2749
Mk 1:30 But Simon's wife's mother l sick of a fever, 2621
2: 4 the bed wherein the sick of the palsy l. 2621
3:21 heard *of it,* they went out to l hold on him: 2902
5:23 *I pray thee,* come and l *thy* hands on her, 2007
12:12 And they sought to l hold on him, but 2902
15: 7 *which* l bound with them that had made NIG
16:18 they shall l hands on the sick, and 2007
Lk 5:18 to bring him in, and to l *him* before him. 5087
5:25 and took up *that* whereon he l, and 2621
8:42 about twelve years of age, and she l a dying. NIG
9:58 the Son of man hath not where to l *his* 2827
19:44 And shall l thee even with the ground, and 1474
20:19 same hour sought to l hands on him; 1911
21:12 they shall l their hands on you, and 1911
Jn 5: 3 In these l a great multitude of impotent 2621
10:15 and I l down my life for the sheep. 5087
10:17 because I l down my life, that I might take 5087
10:18 taketh it from me, but I l it down of myself. 5087
10:18 I have power to l it down, and I have power 5087
11:38 It was a cave, and a stone l upon it. 1945
13:37 I will l down my life for thy sake. 5087
13:38 Wilt thou l down thy life for my sake? 5087
15:13 that a man l down his life for his friends. 5087
Ac 7:60 Lord, l not this sin to their charge. 2476
8:19 this power, that on whomsoever I l hands, 2007
15:28 to l upon you no greater burden than these 2007
27:20 no small tempest l on *us,* all hope that we 1945
28: 8 that the father of Publius l sick of a fever 2621
Ro 8:33 Who shall l any thing to the charge of 1458
9:33 I l in Sion a stumblingstone and rock of 5087
1Co 3:11 For other foundation can no *man* l than that 5087
16: 2 week let every one of you l by him in store, 5087
2Co 12:14 for the children ought not to l up for 2343
1Ti 5:22 L hands suddenly on no *man,* neither be 2007
6:12 good fight of faith, l hold on eternal life, 1949
6:19 that they may l hold on eternal life. 1949
Heb 6:18 who have fled for refuge to l hold upon 2902
12: 1 let us l aside every weight, and the sin which 659
Jas 1:21 Wherefore l apart all filthiness and 659
1Pe 2: 6 I l in Sion a chief corner stone, elect, 5087
1Jn 3:16 we ought to l down *our* lives for 5087

LAYEDST (1) [LAY]
Lk 19:21 thou takest up that thou l not down, and 5087

LAYEST (2) [LAY]
Nu 11:11 that *thou* l the burden of all this people 7760
1Sa 28: 9 wherefore then l thou a snare for my life, 5367

LAYETH (18) [LAY]
Job 21:19 God l up his iniquity for his children: 6845
24:12 crieth out: yet God l not folly *to them.* 7760
41:26 The sword of him that l at him cannot hold: 5381
Ps 33: 7 as a heap: he l up the depth in storehouses. 5414
104: 3 Who l the beams of his chambers in 7136
Pr 2: 7 He l up sound wisdom for the righteous: 6845
13:16 with knowledge: but a fool l open *his* folly. 6566
26:24 with his lips, and l up deceit within him; 7896
31:19 She l her hands to the spindle, and 7971
Isa 26: 5 the lofty city, he l it low; he layeth it low, 8213
26: 5 it low; he l it low, *even* to the ground; 8213
56: 2 and the son of man *that* l hold on it; 2388
57: 1 and no man l *it* to heart: 7760
Jer 9: 8 with his mouth, but in heart he l his wait. 7760
12:11 made desolate, because no man l *it* to heart. 7760
Zec 12: 1 l the foundation of the earth, and 3245
Lk 12:21 So *is* he that l up treasure for himself, and 2343
15: 5 And when he hath found *it,* he l *it* on his 2007

LAYING (13) [LAY]
Nu 35:20 or hurl at him by l of wait, that he die; 6660
35:22 cast upon him any thing without l of wait, 6660
Ps 64: 5 they commune of l snares privily; they say, 2934
Mk 7: 8 For l aside the commandment of God, 863
Lk 11:54 L wait for him, and seeking to catch 1748
Ac 8:18 And when Simon saw that through l on of 1936
9:24 But their l await was known of Saul. 1917
25: 3 l wait in the way to kill him. 1747+4160
1Ti 4:14 with the l on of the hands of the presbytery. 1936
6:19 L up in store for themselves a good 597
Heb 6: 1 not l again the foundation of repentance 2598
6: 2 and of l on of hands, and of resurrection of 1936
1Pe 2: 1 Wherefore l aside all malice, and all guile, 659

LAZARUS (15)
Lk 16:20 And there was a certain beggar named L, 2976
16:23 Abraham afar off, and L in his bosom. 2976
16:24 have mercy on me, and send L, 2976
16:25 and likewise L evil *things:* but now he is 2976
Jn 11: 1 *named* L, of Bethany, the town of Mary 2976
11: 2 with her hair, whose brother L was sick.) 2976
11: 5 Jesus loved Martha, and her sister, and L. 2976
11:11 he saith unto them, Our friend L sleepeth; 2976
11:14 said Jesus unto them plainly, L is dead. 2976
11:43 he cried with a loud voice, L, come forth. 2976
12: 1 where L was which had been dead, 2976
12: 2 L was one of them that sat at the table with 2976
12: 9 sake only, but that they might see L also, 2976
12:10 that they might put L also to death; 2976
12:17 that was with him when he called L out of 2976

LAZINESS See SLOTHFUL

LAZY See SLOTHFUL

LEAD (60) [LEADER, LEADERS, LEADEST, LEADETH, LED, LEDDEST, RINGLEADER]
Ge 33:14 I will l on softly, according as the cattle 5095
Ex 13:21 day in a pillar of a cloud, to l them the way; 5148
15:10 they sank as l in the mighty waters. 5777
32:34 l the people unto *the place* of which I have 5148
Nu 27:17 which may l them out, and which may 3318
31:22 the brass, the iron, the tin, and the l, 5777
Dt 4:27 whither the LORD shall l you. 5090
20: 9 make captains of the armies to l the people. 7218
28:37 all nations whither the LORD shall l thee. 5090
32:12 *So* the LORD alone did l him, and 5148
Jdg 5:12 arise, Barak, and l thy captivity captive, 7617
1Sa 30:22 that they may l *them* away, and depart. 5090
2Ch 30: 9 before them that l them captive, 7617
Ne 9:19 not from them by day, to l them in the way; 5148
Job 19:24 with an iron pen and l in the rock for ever! 5777
Ps 5: 8 L me, O LORD, in thy righteousness 5148
25: 5 L me in thy truth, and teach me: for thou 1869
27:11 l me in a plain path, because of mine 5148
31: 3 therefore for thy name's sake l me, and 5148
43: 3 let them l me; let them bring me unto thy 5148
60: 9 the strong city? who will l me into Edom? 5148
61: 2 l me to the rock *that* is higher than I. 5148
108:10 the strong city? who will l me into Edom? 5148
125: 5 the LORD shall l them forth with 1980
139:10 Even there shall thy hand l me, and 5148
139:24 way in me, and l me in the way everlasting. 5148
143:10 *is* good; l me into the land of uprightness. 5148
Pr 6:22 When thou goest, it shall l thee; when thou 5148
8:20 I l in the way of righteousness, in the midst 1980
SS 8: 2 I would l thee, *and* bring thee into my 5090
Isa 3:12 they which l thee cause *thee* to err, and 833
11: 6 and a little child shall l them. 5090
20: 4 So shall the king of Assyria l away 5090
40:11 *and* shall gently l those that are with young. 5095
42:16 I will l them in paths *that* they have not 1869
49:10 for he that hath mercy on them shall l them, 5090
57:18 I will l him also, and restore comforts unto 5148
63:14 so didst thou l thy people, to make thyself a 5090
Jer 6:29 are burnt, the l is consumed of the fire; 5777
31: 9 and with supplications will I l them: 2986
32: 5 he shall l Zedekiah *to* Babylon, and 1980
Eze 22:18 all they *are* brass, and tin, and iron, and l, 5777
22:20 and brass, and iron, and l, and tin, 5777
27:12 with silver, iron, tin, and l, they traded in 5777
Na 2: 7 her maids *shall* l *her* as *with* the voice of 5090
Zec 5: 7 behold, there *was* lift up a talent of l: and 5777
5: 8 he cast the weight of l upon the mouth 5777
Mt 6:13 And l us not into temptation, but deliver us 1533
15:14 And if the blind l the blind, both shall fall 3594
Mk 13:11 But when they shall l *you,* and deliver you up, 71
14:44 same is he; take him, and l *him* away safely. 520
Lk 6:39 unto them, Can the blind l the blind? 3594
11: 4 And l us not into temptation; but 1533
13:15 from the stall, and l *him* away to watering? 520
Ac 13:11 about seeking *some* to l him by the hand. 5497
1Co 9: 5 Have we not power to l about a sister, 4013
1Ti 2: 2 that we may l a quiet and peaceable life in 1236
2Ti 3: 6 and l captive silly women laden with sins, 162
Heb 8: 9 the hand to l them out of the land of Egypt; 1806
Rev 7:17 shall l them unto living fountains of waters: 3594

LEADER (3) [LEAD]
1Ch 12:27 Jehoiada *was* the l of the Aaronites, and 5057
13: 1 and hundreds, *and* with every l. 5057
Isa 55: 4 a l and commander to the people. 5057

LEADERS (3) [LEAD]
2Ch 32:21 the l and captains in the camp of the king of 5057
Isa 9:16 For the l of this people cause *them* to err; 833
Mt 15:14 they be blind l of the blind. And if the blind 3595

LEADERSHIP See BISHOPRICK

LEADEST (1) [LEAD]
Ps 80: 1 of Israel, thou that l Joseph like a flock; 5090

LEADETH (14) [LEAD]
1Sa 13:17 one company turned unto the way that l to NIH
Job 12:17 He l counsellers away spoiled, and 1980
12:19 He l princes away spoiled, and 1980
Ps 23: 2 he l me beside the still waters. 5095
23: 3 he l me in the paths of righteousness for his 5148
Pr 16:29 and l him into the way *that is* not good. 1980
Isa 48:17 which l thee by the way *that* thou shouldest 1869
Mt 7:13 that l to destruction, and many there be 520
7:14 which l unto life, and few there be that find 520
Mk 9: 2 l them up into a high mountain apart by 399
Jn 10: 3 his own sheep by name, and l them out. 1806
Ac 12:10 they came unto the iron gate that l unto 5342
Ro 2: 4 not knowing that the goodness of God l thee 71
Rev 13:10 He that l into captivity *shall* go into 4863

LEAF (11) [LEAVES]
Ge 8:11 lo, in her mouth *was* an olive l pluckt off: 5929
Lev 26:36 the sound of a shaken l shall chase them; 5929
Job 13:25 Wilt thou break a l driven to and fro? and 5929
Ps 1: 3 his l also shall not wither; and 5929
Isa 1:30 For ye shall be as an oak whose l fadeth, 5929
34: 4 as the l falleth off from the vine, and as a 5929
64: 6 we all do fade as a l; and our iniquities, 5929
Jer 8:13 nor figs on the fig tree, and the l shall fade; 5929
17: 8 when heat cometh, but her l shall be green; 5929
Eze 47:12 all trees for meat, whose l shall not fade, 5929
47:12 be for meat, and the l thereof for medicine. 5929

LEAGUE (19)
Jos 9: 6 now therefore make ye a l with us. 1285
9: 7 and how shall we make a l with you? 1285

Jos 9:11 therefore now make ye a l with us. 1285
9:15 and made a l with them, to let them live: 1285
9:16 days after they had made a l with them, 1285
Jdg 2: 2 ye shall make no l with the inhabitants of 1285
1Sa 22: 8 my son hath made *a l* with the son of Jesse, NIH
2Sa 3:12 saying *also,* Make thy l with me, and 1285
3:13 he said, Well; I will make a l with thee: 1285
3:21 that they may make a l with thee, and 1285
5: 3 king David made a l with them in Hebron 1285
1Ki 5:12 and they two made a l *together.* 1285
15:19 *There is* a l between me and thee, *and* 1285
15:19 *and* break thy l with Baasha king of Israel, 1285
2Ch 16: 3 *There is* a l between me and thee, as *there* 1285
16: 3 go, break thy l with Baasha king of Israel, 1285
Job 5:23 For thou shalt be **in l** with the stones of 1285
Eze 30: 5 Chub, and the men of the land that is **in l,** 1285
Da 11:23 after the l *made* with him he shall work 2266

LEAH (29) [LEAH'S]

Ge 29:16 the name of the elder *was* L, and the name 3812
29:17 L was tender eyed; but Rachel was 3812
29:23 that he took L his daughter, and 3812
29:24 Laban gave unto his daughter L Zilpah his 3812
29:25 that in the morning, behold, it *was* L: 3812
29:30 he loved also Rachel more than L, and 3812
29:31 when the LORD saw that L *was* hated, 3812
29:32 L conceived, and bare a son, and she called 3812
30: 9 When L saw that she had left bearing, she 3812
30:11 L said, A troop cometh: and she called his 3812
30:13 L said, Happy am I, for the daughters will 3812
30:14 and brought them unto his mother L. 3812
30:14 Rachel said to L, Give me, I pray thee, 3812
30:16 L went out to meet him, and said, 3812
30:17 God hearkened unto L, and she conceived, 3812
30:18 L said, God hath given *me* my hire, 3812
30:19 L conceived again, and bare Jacob the sixth 3812
30:20 L said, God hath endued me with a good 3812
31: 4 and L to the field unto his flock, 3812
31:14 Rachel and L answered and said unto him, 3812
33: 1 he divided the children unto L, and 3812
33: 2 L and her children after, and Rachel and 3812
33: 7 L also with her children came near, and 3812
34: 1 Dinah the daughter of L, which she bare 3812
35:23 The sons of L; Reuben, Jacob's firstborn, 3812
46:15 These *be* the sons of L, which she bare 3812
46:18 whom Laban gave to L his daughter, and 3812
49:31 and Rebekah his wife; and there I buried L. 3812
Ru 4:11 into thine house like Rachel and like L, 3812

LEAH'S (5) [LEAH]

Ge 30:10 And Zilpah L maid bare Jacob a son. 3812
30:12 Zilpah L maid bare Jacob a second son. 3812
31:33 into L tent, and into the two maidservants' 3812
31:33 went he out of L tent, and entered into 3812
35:26 the sons of Zilpah, L handmaid; Gad, and 3812

LEAN (11) [LEANED, LEANETH, LEANFLESHED, LEANING, LEANNESS]

Ge 41:20 the l and the ill favoured kine did eat up 7534
Nu 13:20 what the land *is,* whether it *be* fat or l, 7330
Jdg 16:26 the house standeth, that I may l upon them. 8172
2Sa 13: 4 *being* the king's son, l from day to day? 1800
2Ki 18:21 *even* upon Egypt, on which if a man l, it 5564
Job 8:15 He shall l upon his house, but it shall not 8172
Pr 3: 5 and l not unto thine own understanding. 8172
Isa 17: 4 and the fatness of his flesh shall **wax l.** 7329
36: 6 whereon if a man l, it will go into his hand, 5564
Eze 34:20 the fat cattle and between the l cattle. 7330
Mic 3:11 yet will they l upon the LORD, and say, *Is* 8172

LEANED (6) [LEAN]

2Sa 1: 6 behold, Saul l upon his spear; 8172
2Ki 7: 2 a lord on whose hand the king l answered 8172
7:17 hand he l to have the charge of the gate: 8172
Eze 29: 7 when they l upon thee, thou brakest, and 8172
Am 5:19 l his hand on the wall, and a serpent bit 5564
Jn 21:20 which also l on his breast at supper, and said, *377*

LEANETH (2) [LEAN]

2Sa 3:29 or that l on a staff, or that falleth on 2388
2Ki 5:18 he l on my hand, and I bow myself *in* 8172

LEANFLESHED (3) [FLESH, LEAN]

Ge 41: 3 out of the river, ill favoured and **l;** 1320+1851
41: 4 l kine did eat up the seven well 1320+1851
41:19 poor and very ill favoured and l, 1320+7534

LEANING (3) [LEAN]

SS 8: 5 from the wilderness, l upon her beloved? 7514
Jn 13:23 Now there was l on Jesus' bosom one of his *345*
Heb 11:21 and worshipped, *l* upon the top of his staff. NIG

LEANNESS (5) [LEAN]

Job 16: 8 my l rising up in me beareth witness to my 3585
Ps 106:15 them their request; but sent l into their soul. 7332
Isa 10:16 Lord of hosts, send among his fat ones l; 7332
24:16 I said, My l, my leanness, woe unto me! 7334
24:16 I said, My leanness, my l, woe unto me! 7334

LEANNOTH (1)

Ps 88: T To the chief Musician upon Mahalath L, 6031

LEAP (9) [LEAPED, LEAPING, LEAPT]

Ge 31:12 all the rams which l upon the cattle *are* 5927
Lev 11:21 above their feet, to l withal upon the earth; 5425
Dt 33:22 *is* a lion's whelp: he shall l from Bashan. 2187
Job 41:19 go burning lamps, *and* sparks of fire **l out.** 4422
Ps 68:16 Why l ye, ye high hills? *this is* the hill 7520
Isa 35: 6 shall the lame *man* l as a hart, and 1801
Joel 2: 5 on the tops of mountains shall they l, 7540
Zep 1: 9 I punish all those that l on the threshold, 1801
Lk 6:23 ye in that day, and l *for joy:* for behold, *4640*

LEAPED (6) [LEAP]

Ge 31:10 the rams which l upon the cattle *were* 5927
2Sa 22:30 a troop: by my God have I **l over** a wall. 1801
Ps 18:29 and by my God have I **l over** a wall. 1801
Lk 1:41 salutation of Mary, the babe l in her womb; *4640*
1:44 mine ears, the babe l in my womb for joy. *4640*
Ac 14:10 upright on thy feet. And he l and walked. *242*

LEAPING (4) [LEAP]

2Sa 6:16 saw king David l and dancing before 6339
SS 2: 8 behold, he cometh l upon the mountains, 1801
Ac 3: 8 And he **l up** stood, and walked, and *1814*
3: 8 the temple, walking, and l, and praising God. *242*

LEAPT (2) [LEAP]

1Ki 18:26 And they l upon the altar which was made. 6452
Ac 19:16 whom the evil spirit was **l on** them, *2177*

LEARN (32) [LEARNED, LEARNING, UNLEARNED]

Dt 4:10 that they may l to fear me all the days that 3925
5: 1 that ye may l them, and keep, and do them. 3925
14:23 that thou mayest l to fear the LORD thy 3925
17:19 that he may l to fear the LORD his God, 3925
18: 9 thou shalt not l to do after the abominations 3925
31:12 that they may l, and fear the LORD your 3925
31:13 and l to fear the LORD your God, 3925
Ps 119:71 been afflicted; that I might l thy statutes. 3925
119:73 that I may l thy commandments. 3925
Pr 22:25 Lest thou l his ways, and get a snare to thy 502
Isa 1:17 L to do well; seek judgment, relieve 3925
2: 4 neither shall they l war any more. 3925
26: 9 the inhabitants of the world will l 3925
26:10 the wicked, *yet* will he not l righteousness: 3925
29:24 and they that murmured shall l doctrine. 3925
Jer 10: 2 L not the way of the heathen, and be not 3925
12:16 if they will **diligently** l the ways of 3925+3925
Mic 4: 3 neither shall they l war any more. 3925
Mt 9:13 But go ye and l what *that* meaneth, I will *3129*
11:29 Take my yoke upon you, and l of me; for I *3129*
24:32 Now l a parable of the fig tree; When his *3129*
Mk 13:28 Now l a parable of the fig tree; When her *3129*
1Co 4: 6 that ye might l in us not to think *of men* *3129*
14:31 that all may l, and all may be comforted. *3129*
14:35 And if they will l any *thing,* let them ask *3129*
Gal 3: 2 This only would I l of you, Received ye *3129*
1Ti 1:20 that they may l not to blaspheme. *3811*
2:11 Let the woman l in silence with all *3129*
5: 4 let them l first to shew piety at home, and *3129*
5:13 And withal they l *to be* idle, *3129*
Tit 3:14 And let ours also l to maintain good works *3129*
Rev 14: 3 and no *man* could l *that* song but *3129*

LEARNED (22) [LEARN]

Ge 30:27 *tarry: for* I have **l by experience** that 5172
Ps 106:35 among the heathen, and l their works. 3925
119: 7 when I shall have l thy righteous 3925
Pr 30: 3 I neither l wisdom, nor have the knowledge 3925
Isa 29:11 which *men* deliver to one that is l, 3045+5612
29:12 book is delivered to *him* that is not l, 3045+5612
29:12 I pray thee: and he saith, I am not l. 3045+5612
50: 4 GOD hath given me the tongue of the l, 3928
50: 4 he wakeneth mine ear to hear as the l. 3928
Eze 19: 3 a young lion, and it l to catch the prey; 3925
19: 6 and l to catch the prey, *and* devoured men. 3925
Jn 6:45 that hath heard, and hath l of the Father, *3129*
7:15 knoweth this *man* letters, having never l? *3129*
Ac 7:22 And Moses was l in all the wisdom of *3811*
Ro 16:17 contrary to the doctrine which ye have l; *3129*
Eph 4:20 But ye have not so l Christ; *3129*
Php 4: 9 Those *things,* which ye have both l, and *3129*
4:11 for I have l, in whatsoever *state* I am, *3129*
Col 1: 7 As ye also l of Epaphras our dear *3129*
2Ti 3:14 thou in *the things* which thou hast l *3129*
3:14 knowing of whom thou hast l *them;* *3129*
Heb 5: 8 *yet* l he obedience by *the things* which he *3129*

LEARNING (9) [LEARN]

Pr 1: 5 A wise *man* will hear, and will increase l; 3948
9: 9 teach a just *man,* and he will increase in l. 3948
16:21 and the sweetness of the lips increaseth l. 3948
16:23 teacheth his mouth, and addeth l to his lips. 3948
Da 1: 4 whom *they* might teach the l and the tongue 5612
1:17 and skill in all l and wisdom: 5612
Ac 26:24 beside thyself; much l doth make thee mad. *1121*
Ro 15: 4 written aforetime were written for our l, *1319*
2Ti 3: 7 Ever l, and never able to come to *3129*

LEASING (2)

Ps 4: 2 *long* will ye love vanity, *and* seek after l? 3577
5: 6 Thou shalt destroy them that speak l: 3577

LEAST (39) [LESS]

Ge 24:55 abide with us *a few* days, **at the l** ten; 176
32:10 I am not worthy **of the l** of all the mercies, 4480
Nu 11:32 he that **gathered** l gathered ten homers: and 4591
Jdg 3: 2 **at the l** such as before knew nothing 7535
6:15 and I *am* the l in my father's house. 6810
1Sa 9:21 my family the l of all the families of 6810
21: 4 if the young men have kept themselves **at l** 389
2Ki 18:24 captain of the l of my master's servants, 6996
1Ch 12:14 one of the l *was* over an hundred, and 6996
Isa 36: 9 captain of the l of my master's servants, 6996
Jer 6:13 For from the l of them even unto 6996
8:10 l even unto the greatest is given to 6996
31:34 from the l of them unto the greatest of 6996
42: 1 all the people from the l even unto 6996
42: 8 all the people from the l even to 6996
44:12 from the l even unto the greatest, by 6996
49:20 Surely the l of the flock shall draw them 6810
50:45 Surely the l of the flock shall draw them 6810
Am 9: 9 yet shall not the **l grain** fall *upon* the earth. 6872
Jnh 3: 5 from the greatest of them even to the l of 6996
Mt 2: 6 art not the l among the princes of Juda: *1646*
5:19 shall break one of these l commandments, *1646*
5:19 he shall be called the l in the kingdom of *1646*
11:11 notwithstanding he that is l in the kingdom *3398*
13:32 Which indeed is the l of all seeds: but *3398*
25:40 *it* unto one of the l of these my brethren, *1646*
25:45 Inasmuch as ye did *it* not to one of the l of *1646*
Lk 7:28 he that is l in the kingdom of God is greater *3398*
9:48 for he that is l among you all, the same *3398*
12:26 then be not able *to do that thing which is* l, *1646*
16:10 He that is faithful in *that which is* l is *1646*
16:10 he that is unjust in the l is unjust also in *1646*
19:42 even thou, **at l** in this thy day, 1065+2532
Ac 5:15 that **at the l** the shadow of Peter passing by *2579*
8:10 from the l to the greatest, saying, *3398*
1Co 6: 4 set them to judge who are **l esteemed** in *1848*
15: 9 For I am the l of the apostles, that am not *1646*
Eph 3: 8 *who am* less than the l of all saints, *1647*
Heb 8:11 shall know me, from the l to the greatest. *3398*

LEATHER (1) [LEATHERN]

2Ki 1: 8 girt *with* a girdle of l about his loins. 5785

LEATHERN (1) [LEATHER]

Mt 3: 4 camel's hair, and a l girdle about his loins; *1193*

LEAVE (115) [LEAVED, LEAVETH, LEAVING, LEFT, LEFTEST]

Ge 2:24 Therefore shall a man l his father and his 5800
28:15 for I will not l thee, until I have done *that* 5800
33:15 Let me now l with thee *some* of the folk 3322
42:33 Hereby shall I know that ye *are* true *men;* l 3240
44:22 unto my lord, The lad cannot l his father: 5800
44:22 for *if* he should l his father, *his father* 5800
Ex 16:19 Let no man l of it till the morning. 3498
23:11 what they l the beasts of the field shall eat. 3499
Lev 7:15 he shall not l *any* of it until the morning. 3240
16:23 into the holy *place,* and shall l them there: 3240
19:10 thou shalt l them for the poor and stranger: 5800
22:30 ye shall l none of it until the morrow: 3498
23:22 thou shalt l them unto the poor, and to 5800
Nu 9:12 They shall l none of it unto the morning, 7604
10:31 he said, L us not, I pray thee; forasmuch as 5800
22:13 for the LORD refuseth to **give** me l to go 5414
32:15 he will yet again l them in the wilderness; 3240
Dt 28:51 which *also* shall not l thee *either* corn, 7604
28:54 remnant of his children which he shall l: 3498
Jos 4: 3 l them in the lodging place, where you shall 3240
Jdg 9: 9 tree said unto them, Should I l my fatness, 2308
9:13 Should I l my wine, which cheereth God 2308
Ru 1:16 Intreat me not to l thee, *or* to return from 5800
2:16 l *them,* that she may glean *them,* and 5800
1Sa 9: 5 lest my father l *caring* for the asses, and 2308
14:36 and let us not l a man of them. 7604
20: 6 David earnestly asked *l* of me that *he* might NIH
20:28 David earnestly asked *l* of me *to go* to NIH
25:22 if I l of all that *pertain* to him by 7604
2Sa 14: 7 shall not l to my husband *neither* name nor 7760
1Ki 8:57 our fathers: let him not l us, nor forsake us: 5800
2Ki 2: 2 and *as* thy soul liveth, I will not l thee. 5800
2: 4 and *as* thy soul liveth, I will not l thee. 5800
2: 6 and *as* thy soul liveth, I will not l thee. 5800
4:30 and *as* thy soul liveth, I will not l thee. 5800
4:43 They shall eat, and shall l *thereof.* 3498
13: 7 Neither did he l *of* the people to Jehoahaz 7604
1Ch 28: 8 l *it* **for an inheritance** for your children 5157
Ezr 9: 8 to l us a remnant to escape, and to give us a 7604
9:12 l *it* for **an inheritance** to your children for 3423
Ne 5:10 and corn: I pray you, let us **l off** this usury. 5800
6: 3 whilst I l it, and come down to you? 7503
10:31 *that* we would l the seventh year, and 5203
13: 6 after certain days obtained I *l* of the king: NIH
Job 9:27 I will **l off** my heaviness, and 5800
10: 1 my life; I will l my complaint upon myself; 5800
39:11 *is* great? or wilt thou l thy labour to him? 5800
Ps 16:10 For thou wilt not l my soul in hell; 5800
17:14 l the rest of their *substance* to their babes. 3240
27: 9 l me not, neither forsake me, O God of my 5203
37:33 The LORD will not l him in his hand, 5800
49:10 person perish, and l their wealth to others. 5800
119:121 and justice: l me not to mine oppressors. 3240
141: 8 in thee is my trust; l not my soul **destitute.** 6168
Pr 2:13 Who l the paths of uprightness, to walk in 5800
17:14 therefore **l off** contention, before *it* be 5203
Ecc 2:18 I should l it unto the man that shall be after 3240
2:21 laboured therein shall he l it *for* his portion. 5414
10: 4 ruler rise up against thee, l not thy place; 3240
Isa 10: 3 for help? and where will ye l your glory? 5800
65:15 ye shall l your name for a curse unto my 3240
Jer 9: 2 that I might l my people, and go from 5800
14: 9 and we are called by thy name; l us not. 3240
17:11 shall l them in the midst of his days, and 5800
18:14 Will *a man* l the snow of Lebanon *which* 5800
30:11 not l thee **altogether unpunished.** 5352+5352
44: 7 out of Judah, to l you none to remain; 3498
46:28 will I not l thee **wholly unpunished.** 5352+5352
48:28 l the cities, and dwell in the rock, and 5800
49: 9 would they not l *some* gleaning grapes? 7604
49:11 L thy fatherless children, I will preserve 5800
Eze 6: 8 Yet will I l **a remnant,** that ye may have 3498
12:16 I will l a few men of them from the sword, 3498
16:39 thy fair jewels, and l thee naked and bare. 3240
22:20 and I will l *you there,* and melt you. 3240
23:29 thy labour, and shall l thee naked and bare: 5800
29: 5 I will l thee *thrown* into the wilderness, 5203
32: 4 will I l thee upon the land, I will cast thee 5203
39: 2 l but **the sixth part** of thee, and will cause 8338
Da 4:15 Nevertheless l the stump of his roots in 7662
4:23 yet l the stump of the roots thereof in 7662
4:26 whereas they commanded to l the stump of 7662
Hos 12:14 therefore shall he l his blood upon him, and 5203
Joel 2:14 and repent, and l a blessing behind him; 7604
Am 5: 3 The city that went out *by* a thousand shall l 7604
5: 3 that which went forth *by* an hundred shall l 7604
5: 7 and **l off** righteousness in the earth, 3240
Ob 1: 5 to thee, would they not l *some* grapes? 7604

Zep 3:12 I will also l in the midst of thee an afflicted 7604
Mal 4: 1 that it shall l them neither root nor branch. 5800
Mt 5:24 L there thy gift before the altar, and go thy 863
18:12 doth he not l the ninety and nine, and 863
19: 5 For this cause shall a man l father and 2641
23:23 to have done, and not to l the other **undone**. 863
Mk 5:13 And forthwith Jesus **gave** them l. And 2010
10: 7 For this cause shall a man l his father and 2641
12:19 and l *his* wife *behind him,* and leave no 2641
12:19 leave *his* wife *behind him, shall* l no children, 863
Lk 11:42 to have done, and not to l the other **undone**. 863
15: 4 doth not l the ninety and nine in 2641
19:44 they shall not l in thee one stone upon 863
Jn 14:18 I will not l you comfortless: I will come to 863
14:27 Peace I l with you, my peace I give unto 863
16:28 again, I l the world, and go to the Father. 863
16:32 every man to his own, and shall l me alone: 863
19:38 and Pilate **gave** *him* l. He came therefore, 2010
Ac 2:27 Because thou wilt not l my soul in hell, 1459
6: 2 It is not reason that we should l the word of 2641
18:18 and then **took** his l of the brethren, and 657
21: 6 And when we had **taken** our l one of 782
1Co 7:13 pleased to dwell with her, let her not l him. 863
2Co 2:13 but **taking** my **l of** them, I went from *thence* 657
Eph 5:31 For this cause shall a man l his father and 2641
Heb 13: 5 for he hath said, I will never l thee, 447
Rev 11: 2 But the court which is without the temple l 1544

LEAVED (1) [LEAVE]
Isa 45: 1 to open before him the **two l gates**; 1817

LEAVEN (23) [LEAVENED, LEAVENETH, UNLEAVENED]
Ex 12:15 even the first day ye shall put away l out of 7603
12:19 Seven days shall there be no l found in your 7603
13: 7 neither shall there be l seen with thee in all 7603
34:25 not offer the blood of my sacrifice with l; 2557
Lev 2:11 unto the LORD, shall be made *with* l: 2557
2:11 for ye shall burn no l, nor any honey, *in* any 7603
6:17 It shall not be baken *with* l. I have given it 2557
10:12 by fire, and eat it **without** l beside the altar: 4682
23:17 be *of* fine flour; they shall be baken *with* l; 2557
Am 4: 5 And offer a sacrifice of thanksgiving with l, 2557
Mt 13:33 The kingdom of heaven is like unto l, 2219
16: 6 and beware of the l of the Pharisees and 2219
16:11 that *ye* should beware of the l of 2219
16:12 he bade *them* not beware of the l of bread, 2219
Mk 8:15 beware of the l of the Pharisees, and *of* 2219
8:15 of the Pharisees, and *of* the l of Herod. 2219
Lk 12: 1 *of all,* Beware ye of the l of the Pharisees, 2219
13:21 It is like l, which a woman took and hid in 2219
1Co 5: 6 Know ye not that a little l leaveneth 2219
5: 7 Purge out therefore the old l, that ye may 2219
5: 8 let us keep the feast, not with old l, 2219
5: 8 neither with the l of malice and 2219
Gal 5: 9 A little l leaveneth the whole lump. 2219

LEAVENED (14) [LEAVEN]
Ex 12:15 for whosoever eateth **l bread** from the first 2557
12:19 for whosoever eateth **that which is** l, 2556
12:20 Ye shall eat nothing l; in all your 2556
12:34 the people took their dough before it was l, 2556
12:39 brought forth out of Egypt, for it was not l; 2556
13: 3 this *place:* there shall no **l bread** be eaten. 2557
13: 7 there shall no **l bread** be seen with thee, 2557
23:18 the blood of my sacrifice with **l bread**; 2557
Lev 7:13 he shall offer *for* his offering l bread with 2557
Dt 16: 3 Thou shalt eat no **l bread** with it; 2557
16: 4 there shall be no **l bread** seen with thee in 7603
Hos 7: 4 *he* hath kneaded the dough, until it be l. 2556
Mt 13:33 measures of meal, till the whole was l. 2220
Lk 13:21 measures of meal, till the whole was l. 2220

LEAVENETH (2) [LEAVEN]
1Co 5: 6 Know ye not that a little leaven l the whole 2220
Gal 5: 9 A little leaven l the whole lump. 2220

LEAVES (19) [LEAF]
Ge 3: 7 they sewed fig l together, and 5929
1Ki 6:34 the two l of the one door *were* folding, and 6763
6:34 the two l of the other door *were* folding. 7050
Isa 6:13 when they cast *their l: so* the holy seed *shall* NIH
Jer 36:23 *that* when Jehudi had read three or four l, 1817
Eze 17: 9 it shall wither *in* all the l of her spring, 2964
41:24 the doors had two l *apiece,* two turning 1817
41:24 doors had two leaves *apiece,* two turning l; 1817
41:24 two *l* for the one door, and two leaves for NIH
41:24 the one door, and two l for the other *door.* 1817
Da 4:12 The l thereof *were* fair, and the fruit thereof 6074
4:14 shake off his l, and scatter his fruit: 6074
4:21 Whose l *were* fair, and the fruit thereof 6074
Mt 21:19 but l only, and said unto it, 5444
24:32 and putteth forth l, ye know that summer *is* 5444
Mk 11:13 And seeing a fig tree afar off having l, 5444
11:13 when he came to it, he found nothing but l; 5444
13:28 and putteth forth l, ye know that summer is 5444
Rev 22: 2 the l of the tree *were* for the healing of 5444

LEAVETH (6) [LEAVE]
Job 39:14 Which l her eggs in the earth, and 5800
Pr 13:22 A good *man* l **an inheritance** to *his* 5157
28: 3 *is like* a sweeping rain which l no food. NIH
Zec 11:17 Woe to the idol shepherd that l the flock! 5800
Mt 4:11 Then the devil l him, and behold, 863
Jn 10:12 the wolf coming, and l the sheep, and fleeth: 863

LEAVING (5) [LEAVE]
Mt 4:13 And l Nazareth, he came and dwelt in 2641
Lk 10:30 wounded *him,* and departed, l *him* half dead. 863
Ro 1:27 also the men, l the natural use of the woman, 863
Heb 6: 1 Therefore l the principles of the doctrine of 863
1Pe 2:21 Christ also suffered for us, l us an example, 5277

LEBANA (1) [LEBANAH]
Ne 7:48 The children of L, the children of Hagaba, 3838

LEBANAH (1) [LEBANA]
Ezr 2:45 The children of L, the children of Hagabah, 3838

LEBANON (71)
Dt 1: 7 *unto* L, unto the great river, the river 3844
3:25 that goodly mountain, and L. 3844
11:24 from the wilderness and L, from the river, 3844
Jos 1: 4 and this L even unto the great river, 3844
9: 1 the coasts of the great sea over against L, 3844
11:17 even unto Baal-gad in the valley of L under 3844
12: 7 from Baal-gad in the valley of L even unto 3844
13: 5 and all L, *toward* the sunrising, 3844
13: 6 hill country from L unto Misrephoth-maim, 3844
Jdg 3: 3 and the Hivites that dwelt in mount L, 3844
9:15 of the bramble, and devour the cedars of L. 3844
1Ki 4:33 from the cedar tree that *is* in L even unto 3844
5: 6 thou that they hew me cedar trees out of L; 3844
5: 9 My servants shall bring *them* down from L 3844
5:14 he sent them to L, ten thousand a month *by* 3844
5:14 a month they were in L, *and* two months at 3844
7: 2 He built also the house of the forest of L; 3844
9:19 in L, and in all the land of his dominion. 3844
10:17 put them *in* the house of the forest of L. 3844
10:21 house of the forest of L *were of* pure gold: 3844
2Ki 14: 9 The thistle that *was* in L sent to the cedar 3844
14: 9 in Lebanon sent to the cedar that *was* in L, 3844
14: 9 there passed by a wild beast that *was* in L, 3844
19:23 *to* the sides of L, and will cut down the tall 3844
2Ch 2: 8 fir trees, and algum trees, out of L: 3844
2: 8 thy servants can skill to cut timber in L; 3844
2:16 we will cut wood out of L, as much as thou 3844
8: 6 in L, and throughout all the land of his 3844
9:16 put them in the house of the forest of L. 3844
9:20 house of the forest of L *were of* pure gold: 3844
25:18 The thistle that *was* in L sent to the cedar 3844
25:18 in Lebanon sent to the cedar that *was* in L, 3844
25:18 there passed by a wild beast that *was* in L, 3844
Ezr 3: 7 to bring cedar trees from L to the sea of 3844
Ps 29: 5 yea, the LORD breaketh the cedars of L. 3844
29: 6 a calf; L and Sirion like a young unicorn. 3844
72:16 the fruit thereof shall shake like L: 3844
92:12 palm tree: he shall grow like a cedar in L. 3844
104:16 the LORD are full *of sap;* the cedars of L, 3844
SS 3: 9 made himself a chariot of the wood of L. 3844
4: 8 Come with me from L, *my* spouse, with me 3844
4: 8 from Lebanon, *my* spouse, with me from L: 3844
4:11 smell of thy garments *is* like the smell of L. 3844
4:15 a well of living waters, and streams from L. 3844
5:15 his countenance *is* as L, excellent as 3844
7: 4 thy nose *is* as the tower of L which looketh 3844
Isa 2:13 upon all the cedars of L, that are high and 3844
10:34 with iron, and L shall fall by a mighty one. 3844
14: 8 fir trees rejoice at thee, *and* the cedars of L, 3844
29:17 L shall be turned into a fruitful field, and 3844
33: 9 L is ashamed *and* hewn down: Sharon is 3844
35: 2 the glory of L shall be given unto it, 3844
37:24 height of the mountains, *to* the sides of L; 3844
40:16 L *is* not sufficient to burn, nor the beasts 3844
60:13 The glory of L shall come unto thee, the fir 3844
Jer 18:14 Will *a man* leave the snow of L *which* 3844
22: 6 *art* Gilead unto me, *and* the head of L: 3844
22:20 Go up *to* L, and cry; and lift up thy voice in 3844
22:23 O inhabitant of L, that makest thy nest in 3844
Eze 17: 3 came unto L, and took the highest branch 3844
27: 5 they have taken cedars from L to make 3844
31: 3 the Assyrian *was* a cedar in L with fair 3844
31:15 I caused L to mourn for him, and all 3844
31:16 the choice and best of L, all that drink 3844
Hos 14: 5 as the lily, and cast forth his roots as L. 3844
14: 6 be as the olive tree, and his smell as L. 3844
14: 7 the sent thereof *shall be* as the wine of L. 3844
Na 1: 4 Carmel, and the flower of L languisheth. 3844
Hab 2:17 For the violence of L shall cover thee, and 3844
Zec 10:10 bring them into the land of Gilead and L; 3844
11: 1 Open thy doors, O L, that the fire may 3844

LEBAOTH (1)
Jos 15:32 L, and Shilhim, and Ain, and Rimmon: 3822

LEBBEUS (1)
Mt 10: 3 James the *son* of Alpheus, and L, 3002

LEBONAH (1)
Jdg 21:19 Beth-el to Shechem, and on the south of L. 3829

LECAH (1)
1Ch 4:21 the son of Judah *were,* Er the father of L, 3922

LECTURE HALL See SCHOOL

LED (68) [LEAD]
Ge 24:27 the LORD l me to the house of my 5148
24:48 which had l me in the right way to take my 5148
Ex 3: 1 he l the flock to the backside of the desert, 5090
13:17 that God l them not *through* the way of 5148
13:18 God l the people **about**, *through* the way of 5437
15:13 Thou in thy mercy hast l **forth** the people 5148
Dt 8: 2 l thee these forty years in the wilderness, 1980
8:15 Who l thee through *that* great and terrible 1980
29: 5 I have l you forty years in the wilderness: 1980
32:10 he l him **about**, he instructed him, he kept 5437
Jos 24: 3 l him throughout all the land of Canaan, 1980
1Ki 8:48 which l them **away captive**, and pray unto 7617
2Ki 6:19 whom ye seek. But he l them to Samaria. 1980
1Ch 20: 1 *battle,* Joab l **forth** the power of the army, 5090
2Ch 25:11 l **forth** his people, and went *to* the valley of 5090
Ps 68:18 on high, thou hast l captivity **captive**: 7617
78:14 In the daytime also he l them with a cloud, 5148
78:53 he l them **on** safely, so that they feared not: 5148
106: 9 so he l them through the depths, as *through* 1980
107: 7 he l them **forth** by the right way, that *they* 1869
Ps 136:16 To him which l his people through 1980
Pr 4:11 way of wisdom; I have l thee in right paths. 1869
Isa 9:16 and *they that are* l of them *are* destroyed. 833
48:21 they thirsted not *when* he l them through 1980
55:12 go out with joy, and be l **forth** with peace: 2986
63:12 That l *them* by the right hand of Moses 1980
63:13 That l them through the deep, as a horse in 1980
Jer 2: 6 that l us through the wilderness, through a 1980
2:17 thy God, when he l thee by the way? 1980
22:12 the place whither they have l him **captive**, 1540
23: 8 which l the seed of the house of Israel out of 935
La 3: 2 He hath l me, and brought *me into* 5090
Eze 17:12 and l them with him to Babylon; 935
39:28 which **caused** them **to be l into captivity** 1540
47: 2 l me **about** the way without unto the utter 5437
Am 2:10 l you forty years through the wilderness, 1980
7:11 Israel shall **surely** be l **away captive** 1540+1540
Na 2: 7 Huzzab shall be l **away captive**, she shall 1540
Mt 4: 1 Then was Jesus l **up** of the Spirit into 321
26:57 Jesus l *him* **away** to Caiaphas the high priest, 520
27: 2 they l *him* **away**, and delivered him to 520
27:31 on him, and l him **away** to crucify *him.* 520
Mk 8:23 by the hand, and l him **out** of the town; 1806
14:53 And they l Jesus **away** to the high priest: and 520
15:16 And the soldiers l him **away** into the hall, 520
15:20 on him, and l him **out** to crucify him. 1806
Lk 4: 1 and was l by the Spirit into the wilderness, 71
4:29 l him unto the brow of the hill whereon their 71
21:24 and shall be l **away captive** into all nations: 163
22:54 and l *him,* and brought him into the high 71
22:66 and l him into their council, saying, 321
23: 1 of them arose, and l him unto Pilate. 71
23:26 And as they l him **away**, they laid hold upon 520
23:32 malefactors, l with him to be put to death. 71
24:50 And he l them **out** as far as to 1806
Jn 18:13 And l him **away** to Annas first; for he was 520
18:28 Then l they Jesus from Caiaphas unto the hall 71
19:16 And they took Jesus, and l *him* **away**. 520
Ac 8:32 was this, He was l as a sheep to the slaughter; 71
9: 8 saw no *man:* but they l him **by the hand**, 5496
21:37 And as Paul was to be l **into** 1521
22:11 being l **by the hand** of them that were with 5496
Ro 8:14 For as many as are l by the Spirit of God, 71
1Co 12: 2 unto *these* dumb idols, *even* as ye were l. 71
Gal 5:18 But if ye be l of the Spirit, ye are not under 71
Eph 4: 8 he l captivity **captive**, and gave gifts unto 162
2Ti 3: 6 laden with sins, l **away** with divers lusts, 71
2Pe 3:17 being l **away with** the error of the wicked, 4879

LEDDEST (5) [LEAD]
2Sa 5: 2 thou wast he that l **out** and broughtest in 3318
1Ch 11: 2 thou *wast* he that l **out** and broughtest in 3318
Ne 9:12 Moreover thou l them in the day by a 5148
Ps 77:20 Thou l thy people like a flock by the hand 5148
Ac 21:38 l **out** into the wilderness four thousand men 1806

LEDGES (5)
1Ki 7:28 and the borders *were* between the l: 7948
7:29 on the borders that *were* between the l *were* 7948
7:29 upon the l *there was* a base above: and 7948
7:35 on the top of the base the l thereof and 3027
7:36 For on the plates of the l thereof, and on 3027

LEECH See HORSELEACH

LEEKS (1)
Nu 11: 5 and the l, and the onions, and the garlick: 2682

LEES (4)
Isa 25: 6 a feast of **wines on the l**, of fat things full 8105
25: 6 of marrow, of **wines on the l** well refined. 8105
Jer 48:11 he *hath* settled on his l, and hath not been 8105
Zep 1:12 punish the men that are settled on their l: 8105

LEESE (1)
1Ki 18: 5 and mules alive, that we l not all the beasts. 3772

LEFT (348) [LEAVE, LEFTHANDED]
Ge 11: 8 all the earth: and they l off to build the city. NIH
13: 9 if *thou wilt take* the l **hand**, then I will go 8040
13: 9 *to* the right hand, then I will **go to the l**. 8041
14:15 which *is* on the l **hand** of Damascus. 8040
17:22 he l **off** talking with him, and God went up 3615
18:33 as soon as he had l communing with 3615
24:27 who hath not l **destitute** my master of his 5800
24:49 that I may turn to the right hand, or to the l. 8040
29:35 she called his name Judah; and l bearing. 5975
30: 9 When Leah saw that she had l bearing, she 5975
32: 8 the *other* company which is l shall escape. 7604
32:24 Jacob was l alone; and there wrestled a man 3498
39: 6 he l all that he had in Joseph's hand; and 5800
39:12 he l his garment in her hand, and fled, and 5800
39:13 when she saw that he had l his garment in 5800
39:15 that he l his garment with me, and fled, and 5800
39:18 that he l his garment with me, and fled out. 5800
41:49 of the sea, very much, until he l numbering; 2308
42:38 for his brother is dead, and he is l alone: 7604
44:12 began at the eldest, and l at the youngest: 3615
44:20 he alone is l of his mother, and his father 3498
47:18 there is not ought l in the sight of my lord, 7604
48:13 in his right hand toward Israel's l **hand**, 8040
48:13 Manasseh in his l **hand** towards Israel's 8040
48:14 and his l **hand** upon Manasseh's head, 8040
50: 8 their herds, they l in the land of Goshen. 5800
Ex 2:20 why *is* it *that* ye have l the man? call him, 5800
9:21 not the word of the LORD l his servants 5800
10:12 of the land, *even* all that the hail hath l. 7604
10:15 all the fruit of the trees which the hail had l: 3498
10:26 with us; there shall not a hoof be l **behind**; 7604
14:22 them on their right hand, and on their l. 8040
14:29 them on their right hand, and on their l. 8040
16:20 some of them l of it until the morning, and 3498
34:25 feast of the passover be l unto the morning. 3885
Lev 2:10 that which is l of the meat offering *shall be* 3498

Lev 10:12 and unto Ithamar his sons that were **l**, 3498
10:16 Ithamar the sons of Aaron which were **l** 3498
14:15 and pour *it* into the palm of his own **l** hand: 8042
14:16 right finger in the oil that *is* in his **l** hand, 8042
14:26 of the oil into the palm of his own **l** hand: 8042
14:27 his **l** hand seven times before the LORD: 8042
26:36 *upon* them that are **l** *alive* of you I will send 7604
26:39 they that are **l** of you shall pine away in 7604
26:43 The land also shall be **l** of them, and 5800
Nu 20:17 will not turn *to* the right hand nor *to* the **l**, 8040
21:35 his people, until there was none **l** him alive: 7604
22:26 to turn *either to* the right hand or *to* the **l**. 8040
26:65 there was not **l** a man of them, save Caleb 3498
Dt 2:27 neither turn *unto* the right hand nor *to* the **l**. 8040
2:34 of every city, we **l** none to remain: 7604
3: 3 we smote him until none was **l** to him 7604
4:27 ye shall be **l** few in number among 7604
5:32 not turn aside *to* the right hand or *to* the **l**. 8040
7:20 until they that are **l**, and hide themselves 7604
17:11 shew thee, *to* the right hand, nor *to* the **l**. 8040
17:20 *to* the right hand, or *to* the **l**: 8040
28:14 *to* the right hand, or *to* the **l**, to go after 8040
28:55 because he hath nothing **l** him in the siege, 7604
28:62 ye shall be **l** few in number, whereas ye 7604
32:36 is gone, and *there is* none shut up, or **l**. 5800
Jos 1: 7 turn not from it *to* the right hand or *to* the **l**, 8040
6:23 and **l** them without the camp of Israel. 3240
8:17 there was not a man **l** in Ai or Beth-el, 7604
8:17 they **l** the city open, and pursued after 5800
10:33 until *he* had **l** him none remaining. 7604
10:37 he **l** none remaining, according to all that 7604
10:39 that *were* therein; he **l** none remaining: 7604
10:40 he **l** none remaining, but utterly destroyed 7604
11: 8 until *they* **l** them none remaining. 7604
11:11 utterly destroying *them:* there was not any **l** 3498
11:14 neither **l** they any to breathe. 7604
11:15 he **l** nothing **undone** of all that the LORD 5493
11:22 There was none of the Anakims **l** in 3498
19:27 and goeth out to Cabul on the **l hand**, 8040
22: 3 Ye have not **l** your brethren these many 5800
23: 6 aside therefrom *to* the right hand or *to* the **l**; 8040
Jdg 2:21 of the nations which Joshua **l** when he died: 5800
2:23 Therefore the LORD **l** those nations, 3240
3: 1 these *are* the nations which the LORD **l**, 3240
3:21 Ehud put forth his **l** hand, and took 8040
4:16 of the sword; *and* there was not a man **l**. 7604
6: 4 **l** no sustenance for Israel, neither sheep, 7604
7:20 held the lamps in their **l** hands, and 8040
8:10 about fifteen thousand *men,* all that were **l** 3498
9: 5 the youngest son of Jerubbaal was **l**; 3498
16:29 his right hand, and of the other with his **l**. 8040
Ru 1: 3 and she was **l**, and her two sons. 7604
1: 5 the woman was **l** of her two sons and 7604
1:18 to go with her, then she **l** speaking unto her. 2308
2:11 *how* thou hast **l** thy father and thy mother, 5800
2:14 and she did eat, and was sufficed, and **l**. 3498
2:20 who hath not **l off** his kindness to the living 5800
4:14 which hath not **l** thee *this* day **without** a 7673
1Sa 2:36 *that* every one that is **l** in thine house shall 3498
5: 4 only *the stump of* Dagon was **l** to him. 7604
6:12 not aside *to* the right hand or *to* the **l**; 8040
9:24 *Samuel* said, Behold that which is **l**; set *it* 7604
10: 2 lo, thy father hath **l** the care of the asses, 5203
11:11 so that two of them were not **l** together. 7604
17:20 and **l** the sheep with a keeper, and took, and 5203
17:22 David **l** his carriage in the hand of 5203
17:28 with whom hast thou **l** those few sheep in 5203
25:34 surely there had not been **l** unto Nabal by 3498
27: 9 **l** neither man nor woman **alive**, and 2421
30: 9 where those that were **l behind** stayed. 3498
30:13 my master **l** me, because three days agone I 5800
2Sa 2:19 hand nor to the **l** from following Abner. 8040
2:21 Turn thee aside to thy right hand or to thy **l**, 8040
5:21 there they **l** their images, and David and 5800
9: 1 Is there yet *any* that is **l** of the house of 3498
13:30 king's sons, and there is not one of them **l**. 3498
14: 7 *so* they shall quench my coal which is **l**, 7604
14:19 to the **l** from ought that my lord the king 8041
15:16 the king **l** ten women, *which were* 5800
16: 6 *men were* on his right hand and on his **l**. 8040
16:21 which he hath **l** to keep the house; 3240
17:12 men that *are* with him there shall not be **l** 3498
20: 3 whom he had **l** to keep the house, and 3240
1Ki 7:21 he set up the **l** pillar, and called the name 8042
7:39 and five on the **l** side of the house: 8040
7:47 Solomon **l** all the vessels *unweighed,* 3240
7:49 five on the **l**, before the oracle, with 8040
9:20 *And* all the people that were **l** of 3498
9:21 Their children that were **l** after them in 3498
14:10 *and him that is* shut up and **l** in Israel, and 5800
15:18 the gold that were **l** in the treasures of 3498
15:21 when Baasha heard *thereof,* that he **l off** 2308
15:29 he **l** not to Jeroboam any that breathed, 7604
16:11 he **l** him not *one that* pisseth against a wall, 7604
17:17 so sore, that there was no breath **l** in him. 3498
19: 3 *belongeth* to Judah, and **l** his servant there. 3240
19:10 I, *even* I only, am **l**; and they seek my life, 3498
19:14 I, *even* I only, am **l**; and they seek my life, 3498
19:18 Yet I have **l** *me* seven thousand in Israel, 7604
19:20 he **l** the oxen, and ran after Elijah, and said, 5800
20:30 and seven thousand of the men that were **l**. 3498
21:21 and *him that is* shut up and **l** in Israel, 5800
22:19 by him on his right hand and on his **l**. 8040
2Ki 3:25 only in Kir-haraseth **l** *they* the stones 7604
4:44 **l** *thereof,* according to the word of 3498
7: 7 **l** their tents, and their horses, and their 5800
7:13 that remain, which are **l** in the city, (behold, 7604
7:13 as all the multitude of Israel that are **l** in it: 7604
8: 6 of the field since the day that she **l** the land, 5800
9: 8 and *him that is* shut up and **l** in Israel: 5800
10:11 his priests, until *he* **l** him none remaining. 7604
10:14 and forty men, neither **l** he any of them. 7604
10:21 so that there was not a man **l** that came not. 7604
11:11 from the right corner of the temple to the **l** 8042
14:26 shut up, nor any **l**, nor any helper for Israel. 5800
2Ki 17:16 they **l** all the commandments of the LORD 5800
17:18 there was none **l** but the tribe of Judah only. 7604
19: 4 lift up *thy* prayer for the remnant that are **l**. 4672
20:17 nothing shall be **l**, saith the LORD. 3498
22: 2 turned not aside *to* the right hand or *to* the **l**. 8040
23: 8 which *were* on a man's **l hand** at the gate 8040
25:11 Now the rest of the people that were **l** in 7604
25:12 the captain of the guard **l** of the poor of 7604
25:22 Nebuchadnezzar king of Babylon had **l**, 7604
1Ch 6:44 the sons of Merari *stood* on the **l hand**: 8040
6:61 which were **l** of the family of *that* tribe, 3498
12: 2 right hand and the **l** in *hurling* stones and 8041
13: 2 that are **l** in all the land of Israel, and 7604
14:12 when they had **l** their gods there, David 5800
16:37 So he **l** there before the ark of the covenant 5800
2Ch 3:17 on the right hand, and the other on the **l**; 8040
3:17 and the name of *that on* the **l** Boaz. 8042
4: 6 and five on the **l**, to wash in them: 8040
4: 7 five on the right hand, and five on the **l**. 8040
4: 8 five on the right side, and five on the **l**. 8040
8: 7 *As for* all the people that were **l** of 3498
8: 8 who were **l** after them in the land, 3498
11:14 For the Levites **l** their suburbs and 5800
12: 5 have I also **l** you in the hand of Shishak. 5800
16: 5 when Baasha heard *it,* that he **l off** building 2308
18:18 standing on his right hand and *on* his **l**. 8040
21:17 so that there was never a son **l** him, 7604
23:10 from the right side of the temple to the **l** 8042
24:18 they **l** the house of the LORD God of their 5800
24:25 from him, (for they **l** him in great diseases,) 5800
25:12 *other* ten thousand *l* alive did the children of NIH
28:14 So the armed men **l** the captives and 5800
31:10 have had enough to eat, and have **l** plenty: 3498
31:10 and that which is **l** *is* this great store. 3498
32:31 God **l** him, to try him, that *he* might know 5800
34: 2 neither *to* the right hand, nor *to* the **l**. 8040
34:21 for them that are **l** in Israel and in Judah, 7604
Ne 1: 2 which were **l** of the captivity, and 7604
1: 3 The remnant that are **l** of the captivity there 7604
6: 1 and *that* there was no breach **l** therein; 3498
8: 4 on his **l hand**, Pedaiah, and Mishael, and 8040
Job 20:21 *There shall* none of his meat *be* **l**; therefore 8300
20:26 it shall go ill with him that is **l** in his 8300
23: 9 *On* the **l hand**, where he doth work, but 8040
32:15 no more: they **l off** speaking. 4480+6275
Ps 36: 3 he hath **l off** to be wise, *and* to do good. 2308
106:11 their enemies: there was not one of them **l**. 3498
Pr 3:16 and in her **l hand** riches and honour. 8040
4:27 Turn not *to* the right hand nor *to* the **l**: 8040
29:15 a child **l** *to himself* bringeth his mother to 7971
Ecc 10: 2 at his right hand; but a fool's heart at his **l**. 8040
SS 2: 6 His **l hand** *is* under my head, and his right 8040
8: 3 His **l hand** *should be* under my head, and 8040
Isa 1: 8 the daughter of Zion is **l** as a cottage in a 3498
1: 9 Except the LORD of hosts had **l** unto us a 3498
4: 3 *that* he that is **l** in Zion, and he that 7604
7:22 honey shall every one eat that is **l** in 3498
9:20 he shall eat on the **l hand**, and they shall 8040
10:14 as *one* gathereth eggs *that are* **l**, have I 5800
11:11 which shall be **l** from Assyria, and 7604
11:16 his people, which shall be **l** from Assyria; 7604
17: 6 Yet gleaning grapes shall be **l** in it, as 7604
17: 9 which they **l** because of the children of 5800
18: 6 They shall be **l** together unto the fowls of 5800
24: 6 of the earth are burned, and few men **l**. 7604
24:12 In the city is **l** desolation, and the gate is 7604
27:10 habitation forsaken, and **l** like a wilderness: 5800
30:17 till ye be **l** as a beacon upon the top of a 3498
30:21 the right hand, and when ye **turn to the l**. 8041
32:14 the multitude of the city shall be **l**; the forts 5800
37: 4 lift up *thy* prayer for the remnant that is **l**. 4672
39: 6 nothing shall be **l**, saith the LORD. 3498
49:21 Behold, I was **l** alone; these, where *had* 7604
54: 3 break forth *on* the right hand and *on* the **l**; 8040
Jer 12: 7 mine house, I have **l** mine heritage; 5203
21: 7 such as are **l** in this city from the pestilence, 7604
27:18 that the vessels which are **l** in the house of 3498
31: 2 The people which were **l** of the sword 8300
34: 7 against all the cities of Judah that were **l**, 3498
38:22 all the women that are **l** in the king of 7604
38:27 So they **l off speaking** with him; for 2790
39:10 Nebuzar-adan the captain of the guard **l** of 7604
40: 6 among the people that were **l** in the land. 7604
40:11 heard that the king of Babylon had **l** a 5414
42: 2 (for we are **l** *but* a few of many, as thine 7604
43: 6 **l** with Gedaliah the son of Ahikam the son 3240
44:18 since we **l off** to burn incense to the queen 2308
49:25 How is the city of praise not **l**, the city of 5800
50:26 destroy her utterly: let nothing of her be **l**. 7611
52:16 Nebuzar-adan the captain of the guard **l** 7604
Eze 1:10 four had the face of an ox on the **l side**; 8040
4: 4 Lie thou also upon thy **l** side, and lay 8042
9: 8 I *was* **l**, that I fell upon my face, and cried, 7604
14:22 therein shall be **l** a remnant that shall be 3498
16:46 and her daughters that dwell at thy **l hand**: 8040
21:16 other, *either* on the right hand, *or* **on the l**, 8041
23: 8 Neither **l** she her whoredoms *brought* from 5800
24:21 your daughters whom ye have **l** shall fall by 5800
31:12 have cut him off, and have **l** him: 5203
31:12 down from his shadow, and have **l** him. 5203
36:36 the heathen that are **l** round about you shall 7604
39: 3 I will smite thy bow out of thy **l** hand, and 8040
39:28 and have **l** none of them any more there. 3498
41: 9 *that* which *was* **l** *was* the place of the side 3240
41:11 chambers *were* toward *the place* that *was* **l**, 3240
41:11 the breadth of the place that was **l** *was* five 3240
48:15 that are **l** in the breadth over against 3498
Da 2:44 the kingdom shall not be **l** to other people, 7662
10: 8 Therefore I was **l** alone, and saw this great 7604
10:17 in me, neither is there breath **l** in me. 7604
12: 7 his right hand and his **l hand** unto heaven, 8040
Hos 4:10 they have **l off** to take heed to the LORD. 5800
9:12 *that there shall* not *be* a man *l*: yea, NIH
Joel 1: 4 That which the palmerworm hath **l** hath 3499
1: 4 that which the locust hath **l** hath 3499
Joel 1: 4 that which the cankerworm hath **l** hath 3499
Jnh 4:11 between their right hand and their **l hand**; 8040
Hag 2: 3 Who *is* **l** among you that saw this house in 7604
Zec 4: 3 and the other upon the **l** *side* thereof. 8040
4:11 the candlestick and upon the **l** *side* thereof? 8040
12: 6 round about, on the right hand and on the **l**: 8040
13: 8 *and* die; but the third shall be **l** therein. 3498
14:16 *that* every one that is **l** of all the nations 3498
Mt 4:20 And they straightway **l** *their* nets, and *863*
4:22 And they immediately **l** the ship and *863*
6: 3 let not thy **l hand** know what thy right hand *710*
8:15 he touched her hand, and the fever **l** her: *863*
15:37 they took up of the broken *meat* that was **l** *4052*
16: 4 And he **l** them, and departed. *2641*
20:21 and the other on thy **l**, in thy kingdom. *2176*
20:23 and on my **l**, is not mine to give, but *it shall* *2176*
21:17 And he **l** them, and went out of the city into *2641*
22:22 and **l** him, and went their way. *863*
22:25 having no issue, **l** his wife unto his brother: *863*
23:38 Behold, your house is **l** unto you desolate. *863*
24: 2 There shall not be **l** here one stone upon *863*
24:40 the one shall be taken, and the other **l**. *863*
24:41 *the* one shall be taken, and *the* other **l**. *863*
25:33 on his right hand, but the goats on the **l**. *2176*
25:41 shall he say also unto them on the **l hand**, *2176*
26:44 And he **l** them, and went away again, and *863*
27:38 one on the right hand, and another on the **l**. *2176*
Mk 1:20 they **l** their father Zebedee in the ship with *863*
1:31 and immediately the fever **l** her, and *863*
8: 8 they took up of the broken *meat* that was **l** *4051*
8:13 And he **l** them, and entering into the ship *863*
10:28 Lo, we have **l** all, and have followed thee. *863*
10:29 There is no *man* that hath **l** house, or *863*
10:37 and the other on thy **l hand**, in thy glory. *2176*
10:40 and on my **l hand** is not mine to give; *2176*
12:12 and they **l** him, and went their way. *863*
12:20 and the first took a wife, and dying **l** no seed. *863*
12:21 took her, and died, neither **l** he *any* seed: *863*
12:22 And the seven had her, and **l** no seed: last of *863*
13: 2 there shall not be **l** one stone upon another, *863*
13:34 who **l** his house, and gave authority to his *863*
14:52 And he **l** the linen cloth, and fled from *2641*
15:27 on *his* right hand, and the other on his **l**. *2176*
Lk 4:39 over her, and rebuked the fever; and it **l** her: *863*
5: 4 Now when he had **l** speaking, he said unto *3973*
5:28 And he **l** all, rose up, and followed him. *2641*
10:40 dost thou not care that my sister hath **l** me *2641*
13:35 Behold, your house is **l** unto you desolate: *863*
17:34 one shall be taken, and the other shall be **l**. *863*
17:35 the one shall be taken, and the other **l**. *863*
17:36 the one shall be taken, and the other **l**. *863*
18:28 Then Peter said, Lo, we have **l** all, *863*
18:29 There is no *man* that hath **l** house, or parents, *863*
20:31 seven also: and they **l** no children, and died. *2641*
21: 6 in the which there shall not be **l** one stone *863*
23:33 one on the right hand, and the other on the **l**. *710*
Jn 4: 3 He **l** Judea, and departed again into Galilee. *863*
4:28 The woman then **l** her waterpot, and *863*
4:52 Yesterday at the seventh hour the fever **l** *863*
8: 9 and Jesus was **l** alone, and the woman *2641*
8:29 the Father hath not **l** me alone; for I do *863*
Ac 2:31 of Christ, that his soul was not **l** in hell, *2641*
14:17 Nevertheless he **l** not himself without *863*
18:19 And he came to Ephesus, and **l** them there: *2641*
21: 3 we **l** it on the left hand, and sailed into *2641*
21: 3 we left it on the **l hand**, and sailed into *2176*
21:32 and the soldiers, they **l** beating of Paul. *3973*
23:32 On the morrow they **l** the horsemen to go *1439*
24:27 to shew the Jews a pleasure, **l** Paul bound. *2641*
25:14 There is a certain man **l** in bonds by Felix: *2641*
Ro 9:29 Except the Lord of sabaoth had **l** us a seed, *1459*
11: 3 and I am **l** alone, and they seek my life *5275*
2Co 6: 7 righteousness on the right hand and on the **l**, *710*
1Th 3: 1 we thought it good to be **l** at Athens alone; *2641*
2Ti 4:13 The cloke that I **l** at Troas with Carpus, *620*
4:20 but Trophimus have I **l** at Miletum sick. *620*
Tit 1: 5 For this cause **l** I thee in Crete, that thou *2641*
Heb 2: 8 he **l** nothing *that is* not put under him. *863*
4: 1 a promise being **l** *us* of entering into his *2641*
Jude 1: 6 their first estate, but **l** their own habitation, *620*
Rev 2: 4 because thou hast **l** thy first love. *863*
10: 2 upon the sea, and *his* **l** *foot* on the earth, *2176*

LEFTEST (1) [LEAVE]
Ne 9:28 **l** thou them in the hand of their enemies, 5800

LEFTHANDED (2) [HAND, LEFT]
Jdg 3:15 of Gera, a Benjamite, a man **l**: 334+3027+3225
20:16 seven hundred chosen men **l**; 334+3027+3225

LEG (1) [LEGS]
Isa 47: 2 make bare the **l**, uncover the thigh, 7640

LEGION (3) [LEGIONS]
Mk 5: 9 And he answered, saying, My name *is* **L**: *3003*
5:15 and had the **l**, sitting, and clothed, and *3003*
Lk 8:30 And he said, **L**: because many devils were *3003*

LEGIONS (1) [LEGION]
Mt 26:53 give me more than twelve **l** of angels? *3003*

LEGS (19) [LEG]
Ex 12: 9 his head with his **l**, and with the purtenance 3767
29:17 his **l**, and put *them* unto his pieces, and 3767
Lev 1: 9 and his **l** shall he wash in water: 3767
1:13 shall wash the inwards and the **l** with water: 3767
4:11 with his **l**, and his inwards, and his dung, 3767
8:21 he washed the inwards and the **l** in water; 3767
9:14 he did wash the inwards and the **l**, and 3767
11:21 which have **l** above their feet, to leap withal 3767
Dt 28:35 in the **l**, with a sore botch that cannot be 7785
1Sa 17: 6 *he had* greaves of brass upon his **l**, and 7272
Ps 147:10 he taketh not pleasure in the **l** of a man. 7785
Pr 26: 7 The **l** of the lame are not equal: so *is* a 7785

SS 5:15 His l *are as* pillars of marble, set upon 7785
Isa 3:20 the **ornaments of the l**, and the headbands, 6807
Da 2:33 His l of iron, his feet part of iron and 8243
Am 3:12 taketh out of the mouth of the lion two l, 3767
Jn 19:31 besought Pilate that their l might be broken, *4628*
19:32 and brake the l of the first, and of the other *4628*
19:33 he was dead already, they brake not his l: *4628*

LEHABIM (2)
Ge 10:13 and Anamim, and **L**, and Naphtuhim, 3853
1Ch 1:11 and Anamim, and **L**, and Naphtuhim, 3853

LEHABITES See LEHABIM

LEHI (3) [RAMATH-LEHI]
Jdg 15: 9 in Judah, and spread themselves in **L**. 3896
15:14 *And* when he came unto **L**, the Philistines 3896
15:19 which *is* in **L** unto this day. 3896

LEISURE (1)
Mk 6:31 and they **had** no l so much as to eat. *2119*

LEMUEL (2)
Pr 31: 1 The words of king **L**, the prophecy that his 3927
31: 4 *It is* not for kings, O **L**, *it is* not for kings to 3927

LEND (16) [LENDER, LENDETH, LENT]
Ex 22:25 If thou l money to *any of* my people *that is* 3867
Lev 25:37 nor l him thy victuals for increase. 5414
Dt 15: 6 thou shalt l unto many nations, but 5670
15: 8 **surely** l him sufficient for his need, 5670+5670
23:19 Thou shalt not l **upon usury** to thy brother; 5391
23:20 Unto a stranger thou mayest l **upon usury**; 5391
23:20 thy brother thou shalt not l **upon usury**: 5391
24:10 When thou dost l thy brother any 4859+5383
24:11 the man to whom thou dost l shall bring out 5383
28:12 thou shalt l unto many nations, and 3867
28:44 He shall l to thee, and thou shalt not lend to 3867
28:44 lend to thee, and thou shalt not l to him: 3867
Lk 6:34 And if ye l *to them* of whom ye hope to *1155*
6:34 for sinners also l to sinners, to receive as *1155*
6:35 and do good, and l, hoping for nothing *1155*
11: 5 and say unto him, Friend, l me three loaves; *5531*

LENDER (2) [LEND]
Pr 22: 7 and the borrower *is* servant to the l. 376+3867
Isa 24: 2 as *with* the l, so *with* the borrower; 3867

LENDETH (4) [LEND]
Dt 15: 2 Every creditor that l *ought* unto his 5383
Ps 37:26 *He is* ever merciful, and l; and his seed *is* 3867
112: 5 A good man sheweth favour, and l: he will 3867
Pr 19:17 He that hath pity upon the poor l unto 3867

LENGTH (77) [LENGTHEN, LENGTHENED, LENGTHENING, LONG, LONGER, LONGSUFFERING, LONGWINGED]
Ge 6:15 the l of the ark *shall be* three hundred cubits, 753
13:17 walk through the land in the l of it and in 753
Ex 25:10 two cubits and a half *shall be* the l thereof, 753
25:17 two cubits and a half *shall be* the l thereof, 753
25:23 two cubits *shall be* the l thereof, and a cubit 753
26: 2 The l of one curtain *shall be* eight and 753
26: 8 The l of one curtain *shall be* thirty cubits, 753
26:13 remaineth in the l of the curtains of the tent, 753
26:16 Ten cubits *shall be* the l of a board, and 753
27:11 likewise for the north side in l *there shall be* 753
27:18 The l of the court *shall be* an hundred cubits, 753
28:16 a span *shall be* the l thereof, and a span *shall* 753
30: 2 A cubit *shall be* the l thereof, and a cubit 753
36: 9 The l of one curtain *was* twenty and 753
36:15 The l of one curtain *was* thirty cubits, and 753
36:21 The l of a board *was* ten cubits, and 753
37: 1 two cubits and a half *was* the l of it, and 753
37: 6 two cubits and a half *was* the l thereof, and 753
37:10 two cubits *was* the l thereof, and a cubit 753
37:25 the l of it *was* a cubit, and the breadth of it a 753
38: 1 five cubits *was* the l thereof, and five cubits 753
38:18 twenty cubits *was* the l, and the height in 753
39: 9 a span *was* the l thereof, and a span 753
Dt 3:11 nine cubits *was* the l thereof, and four cubits 753
30:20 for he *is* thy life, and the l of thy days: 753
Jdg 3:16 a dagger which had two edges, of a cubit l; 753
1Ki 6: 2 the l thereof *was* threescore cubits, and 753
6: 3 twenty cubits *was* the l thereof, according to 753
6:20 oracle in the forepart *was* twenty cubits in l, 753
7: 2 the l thereof *was* an hundred cubits, and 753
7: 6 the l thereof *was* fifty cubits, and the breadth 753
7:27 four cubits *was* the l of one base, and 753
2Ch 3: 3 The l *by* cubits after the first measure *was* 753
3: 4 l *of it was* according to the breadth of 753
3: 8 the l whereof *was* according to the breadth 753
4: 1 twenty cubits the l thereof, and twenty cubits 753
Job 12:12 *is* wisdom; and *in* l of days understanding. 753
Ps 21: 4 *it* him, *even* l of days for ever and ever. 753
Pr 3: 2 For l of days, and long life, and peace, 753
3:16 **L** of days *is* in her right hand; and in her left 753
29:21 child shall have him become *his* son at the l. 319
Eze 31: 7 fair in his greatness, in the l of his branches: 753
40:11 *and* the l of the gate, thirteen cubits. 753
40:18 the l of the gates *was* the lower pavement. 753
40:20 he measured the l thereof, and the breadth 753
40:21 the l thereof *was* fifty cubits, and the breadth 753
40:25 the l *was* fifty cubits, and the breadth five 753
40:36 the l *was* fifty cubits, and the breadth five 753
40:49 The l of the porch *was* twenty cubits, and 753
41: 2 he measured the l thereof, forty cubits: and 753
41: 4 So he measured the l thereof, twenty cubits; 753
41:12 round about, and the l thereof ninety cubits. 753
41:15 he measured the l of the building over 753
41:22 cubits high, and the l thereof two cubits; 753
41:22 the l thereof, and the walls thereof, *were of* 753
42: 2 Before the l of an hundred cubits *was* 753
42: 7 the chambers, the l thereof *was* fifty cubits. 753
Eze 42: 8 For the l of the chambers that *were* in 753
45: 1 the l *shall be* the length of five and 753
45: 1 the length *shall be* the l *of* five and 753
45: 2 *l*, with five hundred *in breadth*, square NIH
45: 3 of this measure shalt thou measure the l of 753
45: 5 *the* five and twenty thousand of l, and *the* ten 753
45: 7 the l *shall be* over against one of 753
48: 8 *in* breadth, and *in* l as one of the *other* parts, 753
48: 9 *shall be of* five and twenty thousand *in* l, 753
48:10 the north five and twenty thousand *in l*, and NIH
48:10 the south five and twenty thousand *in* l: 753
48:13 *shall have* five and twenty thousand *in* l, 753
48:13 all the l *shall be* five and twenty thousand, 753
48:18 the residue in l over against the oblation of 753
Zec 2: 2 the breadth thereof, and what *is* the l thereof. 753
5: 2 the l thereof *is* twenty cubits, and the breadth 753
Ro 1:10 if by any means now **at** l I might have a *4218*
Eph 3:18 *is* the breadth, and l, and depth, and height; *3372*
Rev 21:16 and the l is as large as the breadth: *3372*
21:16 The l and the breadth and the height of it *3372*

LENGTHEN (2) [LENGTH]
1Ki 3:14 father David did walk, then I will l thy days. 748
Isa 54: 2 l thy cords, and strengthen thy stakes; 748

LENGTHENED (1) [LENGTH]
Dt 25:15 that thy days may be l in the land which 748

LENGTHENING (1) [LENGTH]
Da 4:27 the poor; if it may be a l of thy tranquillity. 754

LENT (7) [LEND]
Ex 12:36 that they l unto them *such things as they* 7592
Dt 23:19 usury of any thing that is l **upon usury**: 5391
1Sa 1:28 Therefore also I have l him to the LORD; 7592
1:28 as long as he liveth he *shall be* l to 7592
2:20 for the loan which is l to the LORD. 7592
Jer 15:10 I have neither l **on usury**, nor *men* have 5383
15:10 on usury, nor *men* have l to me **on usury**; 5383

LENTILES (4)
Ge 25:34 Jacob gave Esau bread and pottage of l; 5742
2Sa 17:28 and beans, and l, and parched *pulse*, 5742
23:11 where was a piece of ground full *of* l: 5742
Eze 4: 9 l, and millet, and fitches, and put them in 5742

LENTILS See LENTILES

LEOPARD (6) [LEOPARDS]
Isa 11: 6 and the l shall lie down with the kid; 5246
Jer 5: 6 spoil them, a l shall watch over their cities: 5246
13:23 change his skin, or the l his spots? 5246
Da 7: 6 After this I beheld, and lo another, like a l, 5245
Hos 13: 7 as a l by the way will I observe *them:* 5246
Rev 13: 2 the beast which I saw was like unto a l, *3917*

LEOPARDS (2) [LEOPARD]
SS 4: 8 the lions' dens, from the mountains of the l. 5246
Hab 1: 8 Their horses also are swifter than the l, and 5246

LEPER (17) [LEPROSY]
Lev 13:45 the l in whom the plague *is*, his clothes 6879
14: 2 This shall be the law of the l in the day of 6879
14: 3 *if* the plague of leprosy be healed in the l; 6879
22: 4 man soever of the seed of Aaron *is* a l, 6879
Nu 5: 2 that they put out of the camp every l, and 6879
2Sa 3:29 or that is a l, or that leaneth on a staff, or 6879
2Ki 5: 1 also a mighty *man* in valour, *but he was* a l. 6879
5:11 his hand over the place, and recover the l. 6879
5:27 he went out from his presence a l *as white* 6879
15: 5 so that he was a l unto the day of his death, 6879
2Ch 26:21 Uzziah the king was a l unto the day of his 6879
26:21 and dwelt *in* a several house, *being* a l; 6879
26:23 to the kings; for they said, He *is* a l: 6879
Mt 8: 2 there came a l and worshipped him, saying, *3015*
26: 6 in Bethany, in the house of Simon the l, *3015*
Mk 1:40 And there came a l to him, beseeching him, *3015*
14: 3 in Bethany in the house of Simon the l, *3015*

LEPERS (6) [LEPROSY]
2Ki 7: 8 when these l came to the uttermost part of 6879
Mt 10: 8 Heal the sick, cleanse the l, raise the dead, *3015*
11: 5 the l are cleansed, and the deaf hear, *3015*
Lk 4:27 And many l were in Israel in the time of *3015*
7:22 lame walk, the l are cleansed, the deaf hear, *3015*
17:12 there met him ten men *that were* l, *3015*

LEPROSY (39) [LEPER, LEPERS, LEPROUS]
Lev 13: 2 in the skin of his flesh like the plague of l; 6883
13: 3 than the skin of his flesh, it *is* a plague of l: 6883
13: 8 priest shall pronounce him unclean: it *is* a l. 6883
13: 9 When the plague of l is in a man, then 6883
13:11 It *is* an old l in the skin of his flesh, and 6883
13:12 if a l break out abroad in the skin, and 6883
13:12 the l cover all the skin of *him that hath* 6883
13:13 behold, *if* the l have covered all his flesh, 6883
13:15 *for* the raw flesh *is* unclean: it *is* a l. 6883
13:20 it *is* a plague of l broken out of the boil. 6883
13:25 the skin; it *is* a l broken out of the burning: 6883
13:25 him unclean: it *is* the plague of l. 6883
13:27 him unclean: it *is* the plague of l. 6883
13:30 a dry scall, *even* a l upon the head or beard. 6883
13:42 it *is* a l sprung up in his bald head, or his 6883
13:43 as the l appeareth in the skin of the flesh; 6883
13:47 The garment also that the plague of l is in, 6883
13:49 it *is* a plague of l, and shall be shewed unto 6883
13:51 the plague *is* a fretting l; it *is* unclean. 6883
13:52 for it *is* a fretting l; it shall be burnt in 6883
13:59 This *is* the law of the plague of l in a 6883
14: 3 *if* the plague of l be healed in the leper; 6883
14: 7 is to be cleansed from the l seven times, 6883
14:32 the law of *him* in whom *is* the plague of l, 6883
14:34 I put the plague of l in a house of the land 6883
14:44 in the house, it *is* a fretting l in the house: 6883
Lev 14:54 *is* the law for all *manner of* plague of l, 6883
14:55 And for the l of a garment, and of a house, 6883
14:57 and when *it is* clean: this *is* the law of l. 6883
Dt 24: 8 Take heed in the plague of l, that *thou* 6883
2Ki 5: 3 for he would recover him of his l. 6883
5: 6 that thou mayest recover him of his l. 6883
5: 7 send unto me to recover a man of his l? 6883
5:27 The l therefore of Naaman shall cleave unto 6883
2Ch 26:19 the l even rose up in his forehead before 6883
Mt 8: 3 And immediately his l was cleansed. *3014*
Mk 1:42 immediately the l departed from him, and *3014*
Lk 5:12 was in a certain city, behold a man full of l: *3014*
5:13 And immediately the l departed from him. *3014*

LEPROUS (6) [LEPROSY]
Ex 4: 6 took it out, behold, his hand *was* l as snow. 6879
Lev 13:44 He *is* a l man, he *is* unclean: the priest shall 6879
Nu 12:10 behold, Miriam *became* l, *white* as snow: 6879
12:10 looked upon Miriam, and behold, *she was* l. 6879
2Ki 7: 3 there were four l men *at* the entering in of 6879
2Ch 26:20 he *was* l in his forehead, and they thrust 6879

LESHEM (2) [DAN]
Jos 19:47 children of Dan went up to fight against **L**, 3959
19:47 and dwelt therein, and called **L**, Dan, 3959

LESS (27) [LEAST, LESSER]
Ex 16:17 did so, and gathered, some more, some l. 4591
30:15 the poor shall not **give** l than half a shekel, 4591
Nu 22:18 of the LORD my God, to do l or more. 6996
26:54 to few thou shalt **give** the l inheritance: 4591
33:54 to the fewer ye shall **give** the l inheritance: 4591
1Sa 22:15 servant knew nothing of all this, l or more. 6996
25:36 l or more, until the morning light. 6996
1Ki 8:27 **how much** l this house that I have 637+3588
2Ch 6:18 **how much** l this house which I have 637+3588
32:15 **how much** l shall your God 637+3588+3808
Ezr 9:13 seeing that thou our God hast punished us l 4295
Job 4:19 **How much** l *in* them that dwell in houses of 637
9:14 **How much** l shall I answer him, and 637+3588
11: 6 that God exacteth of thee *l* than thine NIH
25: 6 **How much** l man, *that is* a worm? and 637+3588
34:19 *How much l to him* that accepteth not NIH
Pr 17: 7 a fool: **much** l do lying lips a prince. 637+3588
19:10 **much** l **for** a servant to have rule over 637+3588
Isa 40:17 they are counted to him l **than** nothing, and 4480
Eze 15: 5 **how much** l shall it be meet yet for 637+3588
Mk 4:31 is l **than** all the seeds that be in the earth: *3398*
15:40 and Mary the mother of James the l and *3398*
1Co 12:23 which we think to be l **honourable**, *820*
2Co 12:15 abundantly I love you, the l I be loved. *2276*
Eph 3: 8 *who am* l than the least of all saints, NIG
Php 2:28 and *that* I may be the l **sorrowful**. *253*
Heb 7: 7 And without all contradiction the l is *1640*

LESSER (3) [LESS]
Ge 1:16 the day, and the l light to rule the night: 6996
Isa 7:25 of oxen, and for the treading of l **cattle**. 7716
Eze 43:14 from the l settle *even* to the greater settle 6996

LEST (240)
Ge 3: 3 eat of it, neither shall ye touch it, l ye die. 6435
3:22 l he put forth his hand, and take also of 6435
4:15 l any finding him should kill him. 1115+3807.1
11: 4 l we be scattered abroad upon the face of 6435
14:23 l thou shouldest say, I have made 3808+2050.1
19:15 l thou be consumed in the iniquity of 6435
19:17 to the mountain, l thou be consumed. 6435
19:19 l *some* evil take me, and I die: 6435
26: 7 l, *said he*, the men of the place should kill 6435
26: 9 unto him, Because I said, L I die for her. 6435
32:11 l he will come and smite me, *and* 6435
38: 9 l **that** he should give seed to his 1115+3807.1
38:11 for he said, **L peradventure** he die also, 6435
38:23 Let her take *it* to her, l we be shamed: 6435
42: 4 **L peradventure** mischief befall him. 6435
44:34 l **peradventure** I see the evil that shall 6435
45:11 l thou, and thy household, and all that thou 6435
Ex 1:10 l they multiply, and it come to pass, that, 6435
5: 3 l he fall upon us with pestilence, or with 6435
13:17 **L peradventure** the people repent when 6435
19:21 l they break through unto the LORD to 6435
19:22 l the LORD break forth upon them. 6435
19:24 the LORD, l he break forth upon them. 6435
20:19 but let not God speak with us, l we die. 6435
23:29 l the land become desolate, and the beast of 6435
23:33 thy land, l they make thee sin against me: 6435
33: 3 l I consume thee in the way. 6435
34:12 l thou make a covenant with the inhabitants 6435
34:12 l it be for a snare in the midst of thee: 6435
34:15 **L** thou make a covenant with 6435
Lev 10: 6 l you die, and lest wrath come 3808+2050.1
10: 6 and l wrath come upon all the people: NIH
10: 7 tabernacle of the congregation, l you die: 6435
10: 9 of the congregation, l ye die: 3808+2050.1
19:29 l the land fall to whoredom, and 3808+2050.1
22: 9 l they bear sin for it, and 3808+2050.1
Nu 4:15 they shall not touch *any* holy *thing*, l they 2050.1
4:20 the holy *things* are covered, l they die. 2050.1
16:26 of theirs, l ye be consumed in all their sins. 6435
16:34 they said, **L** the earth swallow us up *also*. 6435
18:22 of the congregation, l they bear sin, and die. NIH
18:32 of the children of Israel, l ye die. 3808+2050.1
20:18 l I come out against thee with the sword. 6435
Dt 1:42 l ye be smitten before your 3808+2050.1
4: 9 l thou forget the things which thine eyes 6435
4: 9 l they depart from thy heart all the days of 6435
4:16 **L** ye corrupt *yourselves*, and make you a 6435
4:19 l thou lift up thine eyes unto heaven, and 6435
4:23 l ye forget the covenant of the LORD your 6435
6:12 *Then* beware l thou forget the LORD, 6435
6:15 l the anger of the LORD thy God be 6435
7:22 l the beasts of the field increase upon thee. 6435
7:25 take *it* unto thee, l thou be snared therein: 6435

Dt 7:26 l thou be a cursed thing like it: 2050.1
8:12 L when thou hast eaten and art full, and 6435
9:28 L the land whence thou broughtest us out 6435
11:17 l ye perish quickly from off the good land NIH
19: 6 L the avenger of the blood pursue 6435
20: 5 l he die in the battle, and another man 6435
20: 6 l he die in the battle, and another man eat of 6435
20: 7 l he die in the battle, and another man take 6435
20: 8 l his brethren's heart faint as well 3808+2050.1
22: 9 l the fruit of thy seed which thou hast sown, 6435
24:15 l he cry against thee unto 3808+2050.1
25: 3 l, if he should exceed, and beat him above 6435
29:18 L there should be among you man, or 6435
29:18 l there should be among you a root that 6435
32:27 l their adversaries should behave 6435
32:27 and l they should say, Our hand is high, and 6435
Jos 2:16 to the mountain, l the pursuers meet you; 6435
6:18 l ye make yourselves accursed, when ye 6435
9:20 l wrath be upon us, because of 3808+2050.1
24:27 a witness unto you, l ye deny your God. 6435
Jdg 7: 2 l Israel vaunt themselves against me, 6435
14:15 l we burn thee and thy father's house with 6435
18:25 l angry fellows run upon thee, and thou lose 6435
Ru 4: 6 it for myself, l l mar mine own inheritance: 6435
1Sa 9: 5 l my father leave caring for the asses, and 6435
13:19 L the Hebrews make them swords or 6435
15: 6 the Amalekites, l l destroy you with them: 6435
20: 3 Let not Jonathan know this, l he be grieved: 6435
27:11 saying, L they should tell on us, saying, 6435
29: 4 l in the battle he be an adversary to 3808+2050.1
31: 4 l these uncircumcised come and thrust me 6435
2Sa 1:20 l the daughters of the Philistines rejoice, 6435
1:20 l the daughters of the uncircumcised 6435
12:28 l l take the city, and it be called after my 6435
13:25 l we be chargeable unto thee. 3808+2050.1
14:11 any more, l they destroy my son. 3808+2050.1
15:14 l he overtake us suddenly, and bring evil 6435
17:16 l the king be swallowed up, and all 6435
20: 6 l he get him fenced cities, and escape us. 6435
2Ki 2:16 l peradventure the spirit of the LORD 6435
1Ch 10: 4 l these uncircumcised come and abuse me. 6435
Job 32:13 L ye should say, We have found out 6435
34:30 reign not, l the people be ensnared. 4480
36:18 beware l he take thee away with his stroke: 6435
42: 8 l l deal with you after your folly, 1115+3807.1
Ps 2:12 l he be angry, and ye perish from the way, 6435
7: 2 L he tear my soul like a lion, rending it in 6435
13: 3 mine eyes, l l sleep the sleep of death; 6435
13: 4 L mine enemy say, I have prevailed against 6435
28: 1 l, if thou be silent to me, I become like 6435
32: 9 and bridle, l they come near unto thee. 1077
38:16 Hear me, l otherwise they should rejoice 6435
50:22 l l tear you in pieces, and there be none to 6435
59:11 Slay them not, l my people forget: 6435
91:12 l thou dash thy foot against a stone. 6435
106:23 away his wrath, l he should destroy them. 4480
125: 3 the lot of the righteous; l 3808+4616+3807.1
140: 8 his wicked device; l they exalt themselves. NIH
143: 7 l l be like unto them that go down 5973+2050.1
Pr 5: 6 L thou shouldest ponder the path of life, 6435
5: 9 L thou give thine honour unto others, and 6435
5:10 L strangers be filled with thy wealth; and 6435
9: 8 Reprove not a scorner, l he hate thee: 6435
20:13 Love not sleep, l thou come to poverty; 6435
22:25 L thou learn his ways, and get a snare to 6435
24:18 L the LORD see it, and it displease him, 6435
25: 8 l thou know not what to do in the end 6435
25:10 L he that heareth it put thee to shame, and 6435
25:16 l thou be filled therewith, and vomit it. 6435
25:17 l he be weary of thee, and so hate thee. 6435
26: 4 to his folly, l thou also be like unto him. 6435
26: 5 to his folly, l he be wise in his own conceit. 6435
30: 6 l he reprove thee, and thou be found a liar. 6435
30: 9 L l be full, and deny thee, and say, Who is 6435
30: 9 or l l be poor, and steal, and take the name 6435
30:10 l he curse thee, and thou be found guilty. 6435
31: 5 L they drink, and forget the law, and 6435
Ecc 7:21 l thou hear thy servant curse thee: 834+3808
Isa 6:10 l they see with their eyes, and hear with 6435
27: 3 l any hurt it, I will keep it night and day. 6435
28:22 not mockers, l your bands be made strong: 6435
36:18 Beware l Hezekiah persuade you, saying, 6435
48: 5 l thou shouldest say, Mine idol hath done 6435
48: 7 l thou shouldest say, Behold, I knew them. 6435
Jer 1:17 their faces, l l confound thee before them. 6435
4: 4 l my fury come forth like fire, and burn that 6435
6: 8 O Jerusalem, l my soul depart from thee; 6435
6: 8 l l make thee desolate, a land not inhabited. 6435
10:24 in thine anger, l thou bring me to nothing. 6435
21:12 l my fury go out like fire, and burn that 6435
37:20 of Jonathan the scribe, l l die there. 3808+2050.1
38:19 l they deliver me into their hand, and 6435
51:46 l your heart faint, and ye fear for 6435
Hos 2: 3 L l strip her naked, and set her as in the day 6435
Am 5: 6 l he break out like fire in the house of 6435
Zec 7:12 l they should hear the law, and the words 4480
Mal 4: 6 l l come and smite the earth with a curse. 6435
Mt 4: 6 l at any time thou dash thy foot against a 3379
5:25 l at any time the adversary deliver thee to 3379
7: 6 l they trample them under their feet, and 3379
13:15 l at any time they should see with their 3379
13:29 l while ye gather up the tares, ye root up 3379
15:32 them away fasting, l they faint in the way. 3379
17:27 Notwithstanding, l we should offend them, 3363
25: 9 Not so; l there be not enough for us and 3379
26: 5 Not on the feast day, l there be an uproar 3363
27:64 l his disciples come by night, and steal him 3379
Mk 3: 9 of the multitude, l they should throng him. 3363
4:12 l at any time they should be converted, and 3379
13: 5 to say, Take heed l any man deceive you: 3361
13:36 L coming suddenly he find you sleeping. 3361
14: 2 Not on the feast day, l there be an uproar of 3379
14:38 and pray, l ye enter into temptation. 3363
Lk 4:11 l at any time thou dash thy foot against a 3379
8:12 l they should believe and be saved. 3363
Lk 12:58 l he hale thee to the judge, and the judge 3379
14: 8 l a more honourable man than thou be 3379
14:12 l they also bid thee again, and 3379
14:29 L haply, after he hath laid the foundation, 3379
16:28 l they also come into this place of torment. 3363
18: 5 l by her continual coming she weary me. 3363
21:34 l at any time your hearts be overcharged 3379
22:46 rise and pray, l ye enter into temptation. 3363
Jn 3:20 to the light, l his deeds should be reproved. 3363
5:14 no more, l a worse thing come unto thee. 3363
12:35 have the light, l darkness come upon you: 3363
12:42 of the Pharisees they did not confess him, l 3363
18:28 the judgment hall, l they should be defiled; 3363
Ac 5:26 the people, l they should have been stoned. 3363
5:39 l haply ye be found even to fight against 3379
13:40 Beware therefore, l that come upon you, 3361
23:10 fearing l Paul should have been pulled in 3361
27:17 fearing l they should fall into 3361
27:29 Then fearing l we should have fallen upon 3381
27:42 l any of them should swim out, and escape. 3361
28:27 l they should see with their eyes, and 3379
Ro 11:21 take heed l he also spare not thee. 3381
11:25 l ye should be wise in your own conceits; 3363
15:20 l l should build upon another man's 3363
1Co 1:15 L any should say that I had baptized in 3363
1:17 l the cross of Christ should be made of 3363
8: 9 But take heed l by any means this liberty 3381
8:13 l l make my brother to offend. 3363
9:12 suffer all things, l we should hinder 3363
9:27 l that by any means, when I have preached 3381
10:12 that thinketh he standeth take heed l he fall. 3361
2Co 2: 3 I wrote this same unto you, l, when I came, 3363
2: 7 comfort him, l perhaps such a one should 3381
2:11 L Satan should get an advantage of us: 3363
4: 4 l the light of the glorious 1519+3361+3588
9: 3 l our boasting of you should be in vain in 3363
9: 4 L haply if they of Macedonia come with 3381
11: 3 But I fear, l by any means, as the serpent 3381
12: 6 l any man should think of me above that 3361
12: 7 And l l should be exalted above measure 3363
12: 7 l l should be exalted above measure. 3363
12:20 For I fear, l, when I come, I shall not find 3381
12:20 l there be debates, envyings, wraths, strifes, 3381
12:21 And l, when I come again, my God will 3361
13:10 l being present I should use sharpness, 3363
Gal 2: 2 l by any means I should run, or had run, 3381
4:11 l l have bestowed upon you labour in vain. 3381
6: 1 considering thyself, l thou also be tempted. 3361
6:12 only l they should suffer persecution for 3363
Eph 2: 9 Not of works, l any man should boast. 3363
Php 2:27 l l should have sorrow upon sorrow. 3363
Col 2: 4 l any man should beguile you with enticing 3363
2: 8 Beware l any man spoil you through 3361
3:21 provoke not your children to anger, l they 3363
1Th 3: 5 l by some means the tempter have tempted 3381
1Ti 3: 6 l being lifted up with pride he fall into 3363
3: 7 l he fall into reproach and the snare of 3363
Heb 2: 1 l at any time we should let them slip. 3379
3:12 l there be in any of you an evil heart of 3379
3:13 l any of you be hardened through 3363
4: 1 Let us therefore fear, l, a promise being left 3379
4:11 l any man fall after the same example of 3363
11:28 l he that destroyed the firstborn should 3363
12: 3 l ye be wearied and faint in your minds. 3363
12:13 l that which is lame be turned out of 3363
12:15 Looking diligently l any man fail of 3361
12:15 l any root of bitterness springing up trouble 3361
12:16 L there be any fornicator, or 3361
Jas 5: 9 brethren, l ye be condemned: 3363
5:12 your nay, nay; l ye fall into condemnation. 3363
2Pe 3:17 know these things before, beware l ye also, 3363
Rev 16:15 l he walk naked, and they see his shame. 3363

LET (1511) [LETTEST, LETTETH, LETTING]

Ge 1: 3 God said, L there be light: and there was NIH
1: 6 L there be a firmament in the midst of NIH
1: 6 l it divide the waters from the waters. NIH
1: 9 L the waters under the heaven be gathered NIH
1: 9 unto one place, and l the dry land appear: NIH
1:11 And God said, L the earth bring forth grass, NIH
1:14 L there be lights in the firmament of NIH
1:14 and l them be for signs, and for seasons, and NIH
1:15 l them be for lights in the firmament of NIH
1:20 L the waters bring forth abundantly NIH
1:22 in the seas, and l fowl multiply in the earth. NIH
1:24 L the earth bring forth the living creature NIH
1:26 And God said, L us make man in our image, NIH
1:26 l them have dominion over the fish of NIH
11: 3 l us make brick, and burn them thoroughly. NIH
11: 4 Go to, l us build us a city and a tower, NIH
11: 4 l us make us a name, lest we be scattered NIH
11: 7 l us go down, and there confound their NIH
13: 8 L there be no strife, I pray thee, between me NIH
14:24 and Mamre; l them take their portion. NIH
18: 4 L a little water, I pray you, be fetched, and NIH
18:30 he said unto him, Oh l not the Lord be NIH
18:32 Oh l not the Lord be angry, and I will speak NIH
19: 8 l me, I pray you, bring them out unto you, NIH
19:20 Oh, l me escape thither, (is it not a little NIH
19:32 l us make our father drink wine, and we will NIH
19:34 l us make him drink wine this night also; NIH
21:12 L it not be grievous in thy sight because NIH
21:16 L me not see the death of the child. NIH
24:14 l it come to pass, that the damsel to whom I NIH
24:14 L down thy pitcher, I pray thee, that I may 5186
24:14 l the same be she that thou hast appointed NIH
24:17 ran to meet her, and said, L me, I pray thee, NIH
24:18 l down her pitcher upon her hand, and 3381
24:44 l the same be the woman whom the LORD NIH
24:45 and I said unto her, L me drink, I pray thee. NIH
24:46 l down her pitcher from her shoulder, and 3381
24:51 and go, and l her be thy master's son's wife, NIH
24:55 L the damsel abide with us a few days, NIH
24:60 l thy seed possess the gate of those which NIH
26:28 we said, L there be now an oath betwixt us, NIH
Ge 26:28 and l us make a covenant with thee; NIH
27:29 L people serve thee, and nations bow down NIH
27:29 and l thy mother's sons bow down to thee: NIH
27:31 L my father arise, and eat of his son's NIH
30:26 for whom I have served thee, and l me go: NIH
31:32 thou findest thy gods, l him not live: NIH
31:35 L it not displease my lord that I cannot rise NIH
31:44 l us make a covenant, I and thou; NIH
31:44 l it be for a witness between me and thee. NIH
32:26 he said, L me go, for the day breaketh. 7971
32:26 he said, I will not l thee go, except thou 7971
33:12 L us take our journey, and let us go, and NIH
33:12 and l us go, and I will go before thee. NIH
33:14 L my lord, I pray thee, pass over before his NIH
33:15 L me now leave with thee some of the folk NIH
33:15 l me find grace in the sight of my lord. NIH
34:11 L me find grace in your eyes, and what ye NIH
34:21 therefore l them dwell in the land, and NIH
34:21 l us take their daughters to us for wives, and NIH
34:21 for wives, and l us give them our daughters. NIH
34:23 only l us consent unto them, and they will NIH
35: 3 l us arise, and go up to Beth-el; and I will NIH
37:17 for I heard them say, L us go to Dothan. NIH
37:20 l us slay him, and cast him into some pit, NIH
37:21 of their hands; and said, L us not kill him. NIH
37:27 l us sell him to the Ishmeelites, and let not NIH
37:27 and l not our hand be upon him; NIH
38:16 Go to, I pray thee, l me come in unto thee; NIH
38:23 Judah said, L her take it to her, lest we be NIH
38:24 Bring her forth, and l her be burnt. NIH
41:33 l Pharaoh look out a man discreet and wise, NIH
41:34 L Pharaoh do this, and let him appoint NIH
41:34 and l him appoint officers over the land, NIH
41:35 l them gather all the food of those good NIH
41:35 and l them keep food in the cities. NIH
42:16 l him fetch your brother, and ye shall be NIH
42:19 If ye be true men, l one of your brethren be NIH
43: 9 then l me bear the blame for ever: NIH
44: 9 both l him die, and we also will be my NIH
44:10 Now also l it be according unto your words: NIH
44:18 said, O my lord, l thy servant, I pray thee, NIH
44:18 l not thine anger burn against thy servant: NIH
44:33 l thy servant abide instead of the lad a NIH
44:33 and l the lad go up with his brethren. NIH
46:30 Now l me die, since I have seen thy face, NIH
47: 4 l thy servants dwell in the land of Goshen. NIH
47: 6 in the land of Goshen l them dwell: NIH
47:25 l us find grace in the sight of my lord, and NIH
48:16 l my name be named on them, and the name NIH
48:16 l them grow into a multitude in the midst of NIH
49:21 Naphtali is a hind l loose: he giveth goodly 7971
50: 5 Now therefore l me go up, I pray thee, and NIH
Ex 1:10 Come on, l us deal wisely with them; NIH
3:18 now l us go, we beseech thee, three days' NIH
3:19 I am sure that the king of Egypt will not l 5414
3:20 and after that he will l you go. 7971
4:18 L me go, I pray thee, and return unto my NIH
4:21 his heart, that he shall not l the people go. 7971
4:23 I say unto thee, L my son go, that he may 7971
4:23 if thou refuse to l him go, behold, I will 7971
4:26 So he l him go: then she said, A bloody 7503
5: 1 the LORD God of Israel, L my people go, 7971
5: 2 that I should obey his voice to l Israel go? 7971
5: 2 not the LORD, neither will I l Israel go. 7971
5: 3 l us go, we pray thee, three days' journey NIH
5: 4 and Aaron, l the people from their works? 6544
5: 7 l them go and gather straw for themselves. NIH
5: 8 L us go and sacrifice to our God. NIH
5: 9 L there more work be laid upon the men, NIH
5: 9 and l them not regard vain words. NIH
5:17 L us go and do sacrifice to the LORD. NIH
6: 1 for with a strong hand shall he l them go, 7971
6:11 that he l the children of Israel go out of his 7971
7:14 is hardened, he refuseth to l the people go. 7971
7:16 saying, L my people go, that they may 7971
8: 1 Thus saith the LORD, L my people go, 7971
8: 2 if thou refuse to l them go, behold, I will 7971
8: 8 I will l the people go, that they may do 7971
8:20 Thus saith the LORD, L my people go, 7971
8:21 Else, if thou wilt not l my people go, 7971
8:28 Pharaoh said, I will l you go, that ye may 7971
8:29 l not Pharaoh deal deceitfully any more in NIH
8:32 time also, neither would he l the people go. 7971
9: 1 L my people go, that they may serve me. 7971
9: 2 For if thou refuse to l them go, and wilt 7971
9: 7 and he did not l the people go. 7971
9: 8 l Moses sprinkle it towards the heaven in NIH
9:13 L my people go, that they may serve me. 7971
9:17 my people, that thou wilt not l them go? 7971
9:28 I will l you go, and ye shall stay no longer. 7971
9:35 neither would he l the children of Israel go; 7971
10: 3 l my people go, that they may serve me. 7971
10: 4 Else, if thou refuse to l my people go, 7971
10: 7 l the men go, that they may serve 7971
10:10 L the LORD be so with you, as I will let NIH
10:10 as I will l you go, and your little ones: 7971
10:20 that he would not l the children of Israel go. 7971
10:24 only l your flocks and your herds be stayed: NIH
10:24 l your little ones also go with you. NIH
10:27 and he would not l them go. 7971
11: 1 afterwards he will l you go hence: 7971
11: 1 when he shall l you go, he shall surely 7971
11: 2 l every man borrow of his neighbour, and NIH
11:10 that he would not l the children of Israel go 7971
12: 4 l him and his neighbour next unto his house NIH
12:10 ye shall l nothing of it remain until NIH
12:48 l all his males be circumcised, and then NIH
12:48 and then l him come near and keep it; NIH
13:15 when Pharaoh would hardly l us go, 7971
13:17 to pass, when Pharaoh had l the people go, 7971
14: 5 that we have l Israel go from serving us? 7971
14:12 saying, L us alone, that we may serve NIH
14:25 L us flee from the face of Israel; NIH
16:19 L no man leave of it till the morning. NIH
16:29 l no man go out of his place on the seventh NIH

L

Ex 17:11 when he l **down** his hand, 5117
18:22 l them judge the people at all seasons: and NIH
18:27 Moses l his father in law depart; and NIH
19:10 to morrow, and l them wash their clothes, NIH
19:22 l the priests also, which come near to NIH
19:24 l not the priests and the people break NIH
20:19 but l not God speak with us, lest we die. NIH
21: 8 to himself, then shall he l her be redeemed: NIH
21:26 he shall l him **go** free for his eye's sake. 7971
21:27 he shall l him **go** free for his tooth's sake. 7971
22: 7 if the thief be found, l him pay double. NIH
22:13 *then* l him bring it *for* witness, *and* he shall NIH
23:11 the seventh *year* thou shalt l it rest and NIH
23:13 neither l it be heard out of thy mouth. NIH
24:14 any matters to do, l him come unto them. NIH
25: 8 l them make me a sanctuary; that I may NIH
32:10 Now therefore l me **alone**, that my wrath 3240
32:22 L not the anger of my lord wax hot: NIH
32:24 hath *any* gold, l them break *it* off. NIH
32:26 *l him come* unto me. And all the sons of NIH
33:12 thou hast not l me know whom thou wilt NIH
34: 3 neither l any man be seen throughout all NIH
34: 3 neither l the flocks nor herds feed before NIH
34: 9 O Lord, l my Lord, I pray thee, go amongst NIH
35: 5 l him bring it, an offering of the LORD; NIH
36: 6 L neither man nor woman make any more NIH
Lev 1: 3 l him offer a male without blemish: NIH
4: 3 l him bring for his sin, which he hath NIH
10: 6 l your brethren, the whole house of Israel, NIH
14: 7 shall l the living bird **loose** into the open 7971
14:53 he shall l **go** the living bird out of the city 7971
16:10 to l him **go** for a scapegoat into 7971
16:22 and he shall l **go** the goat in the wilderness. 7971
16:26 he that l **go** the goat for the scapegoat shall 7971
18:21 thou shalt not l *any* of thy seed 5414+3807.1
19:19 Thou shalt not l thy cattle gender with a NIH
21:17 l him not approach to offer the bread of his NIH
24:14 l all that heard *him* lay their hands upon his NIH
24:14 and l all the congregation stone him. NIH
25:27 l him count the years of the sale thereof, NIH
Nu 5: 8 *l* the trespass *be* recompensed unto NIH
6: 5 shall l the locks of the hair of his head grow. NIH
8: 7 l them shave all their flesh, and let them NIH
8: 7 l them wash their clothes, and *so* NIH
8: 8 l them take a young bullock with his meat NIH
9: 2 L the children of Israel also keep NIH
10:35 LORD, and l thine enemies be scattered; NIH
10:35 and l them that hate thee flee before thee. NIH
11:15 and l me not see my wretchedness. NIH
11:31 from the sea, and l *them* fall by the camp, NIH
12:12 L her not be as one dead, of whom the flesh 4994
12:14 l her be shut out from the camp seven days, NIH
12:14 and after *that* l her be received in *again.* NIH
13:30 and said, L us go up at once, and possess it; NIH
14: 4 L us make a captain, and let us return into NIH
14: 4 make a captain, and l us return into Egypt. NIH
14:17 l the power of my Lord be great, NIH
16:38 l them make them broad plates *for* a NIH
20:17 L us pass, I pray thee, through thy country: NIH
21:22 L me pass through thy land: we will not NIH
21:27 l the city of Sihon be built and prepared: NIH
22:16 L nothing, I pray thee, hinder thee from NIH
23:10 L me die the death of the righteous, and NIH
23:10 the righteous, and l my last end be like his! NIH
27:16 L the LORD, the God of the spirits of all NIH
31: 3 l them go against the Midianites, and NIH
32: 5 l this land be given unto thy servants for a NIH
33:55 *that those* which ye l remain of them *shall* NIH
36: 6 L them marry to whom they think best; NIH
Dt 2:27 L me pass through thy land: I will go along NIH
2:30 Sihon king of Heshbon would not l us pass NIH
3:25 l me go over, and see the good land that *is* NIH
3:26 the LORD said unto me, L it suffice thee; NIH
9:14 L me **alone**, that I may destroy them, and 7503
13: 2 saying, L us go after other gods, which thou NIH
13: 2 thou hast not known, and l us serve them; NIH
13: 6 L us go and serve other gods, NIH
13:13 saying, L us go and serve other gods, NIH
15:12 in the seventh year thou shalt l him **go** free 7971
15:13 thou shalt not l him **go away** empty: 7971
18:16 L me not hear again the voice of NIH
18:16 neither l me see this great fire any more, NIH
20: 3 l not your hearts faint, fear not, and do not NIH
20: 5 l him go and return to his house, lest he die NIH
20: 6 l him *also* go and return unto his house, NIH
20: 7 l him go and return unto his house, lest he NIH
20: 8 l him go and return unto his house, lest his NIH
21:14 then thou shalt l her **go** whither she will; 7971
22: 7 thou shalt **in any wise** l the dam **go**, 7971+7971
24: 1 l him write her a bill of divorcement, and NIH
25: 7 l his brother's wife go up to the gate unto NIH
32:38 l them rise up and help you, *and* be your NIH
33: 6 L Reuben live, and not die; and let *not* his NIH
33: 6 and not die; and l *not* his men be few. NIH
33: 7 l his hands *be* sufficient for him; and NIH
33: 8 *L* thy Thummim and thy Urim *be* with thy NIH
33:16 l *the blessing* come upon the head of NIH
33:24 he said, *L* Asher *be* blessed with children; NIH
33:24 l him be acceptable to his brethren, and NIH
33:24 to his brethren, and l him dip his foot in oil. NIH
Jos 2:15 she l them **down** by a cord through 3381
2:18 the window which thou didst l us **down** by: 3381
4:22 ye shall l your children know, saying, NIH
6: 6 l seven priests bear seven trumpets of rams' NIH
6: 7 l him that is armed pass on before the ark of NIH
7: 3 said unto him, L not all the people go up; NIH
7: 3 *but* l about two or three thousand men go up NIH
8:22 so that *they* l none of them remain or 7604
9:15 and made a league with them, to l them live: NIH
9:20 we will even l them live, lest wrath be upon NIH
9:21 the princes said unto them, L them live; NIH
9:21 l them be hewers of wood and drawers of NIH
10:28 souls that *were* therein; he l none remain: 7604
10:30 he l none remain in it; but did unto the king 7604
22:23 l the LORD himself require *it;* NIH
Jos 22:26 L us now prepare to build us an altar, NIH
24:28 So Joshua l the people **depart**, every man 7971
Jdg 1:25 but they l **go** the man and all his family. 7971
2: 6 when Joshua had l the people **go**, 7971
5:31 So l all thine enemies perish, O LORD: but NIH
5:31 *l* them that love him *be* as the sun when he NIH
6:31 l him be put to death whilst *it is yet* NIH
6:31 l him plead for himself, because *one* hath NIH
6:32 saying, L Baal plead against him, because NIH
6:39 L not thine anger be hot against me, and NIH
6:39 l me prove, I pray thee, but *this* once with NIH
6:39 l it now be dry only upon the fleece, NIH
6:39 upon all the ground l there be dew. NIH
7: 3 l him return and depart early from mount NIH
7: 7 l all the *other* people go every man unto his NIH
9:15 l fire come out of the bramble, and NIH
9:19 in Abimelech, and l him also rejoice in you: NIH
9:20 l fire come out from Abimelech, and NIH
9:20 l fire come out from the men of Shechem, NIH
10:14 l them deliver you in the time of your NIH
11:17 saying, L me, I pray thee, pass through thy NIH
11:19 said unto him, L us pass, we pray thee, NIH
11:37 unto her father, L this thing be done for me: NIH
11:37 l me **alone** two months, that I may go up 7503
12: 5 which were escaped said, L me go over; NIH
13: 8 l the man of God which thou didst send 4994
13:12 Now l thy words come to pass. NIH
13:13 Of all that I said unto the woman l her NIH
13:14 neither l her drink wine or strong drink, NIH
13:14 all that I commanded her l her observe. NIH
13:15 I pray thee, l us detain thee, until we shall NIH
15: 5 he l *them* **go** into the standing corn of 7971
16:30 Samson said, L me die with the Philistines. NIH
18:25 L not thy voice be heard among us, NIH
19: 6 tarry all night, and l thine heart be merry. NIH
19:11 l us turn in into this city of the Jebusites, NIH
19:13 l us draw near to one of *these* places to NIH
19:20 howsoever *l* all thy wants *lie* upon me; NIH
19:25 when the day began to spring, they l her **go**. 7971
19:28 And he said unto her, Up, and l us be going. NIH
20:32 L us flee, and draw them from the city unto NIH
Ru 2: 2 L me now go *to* the field, and glean ears of NIH
2: 7 l me glean and gather after the reapers NIH
2: 9 *L* thine eyes *be* on the field that they do NIH
2:13 L me find favour in thy sight, my lord; NIH
2:15 L her glean even among the sheaves, and NIH
2:16 l **fall** also *some* of the handfuls
of purpose 7997+7997
3:13 well; l him do the kinsman's part: NIH
3:14 L it not be known that a woman came *into* NIH
4:12 And l thy house be like the house of Pharez, NIH
1Sa 1:18 L thine handmaid find grace in thy sight. NIH
2: 3 l *not* arrogancy come out of your mouth: NIH
2:16 L them not fail to burn the fat presently, and NIH
3:18 l him do what seemeth him good. NIH
3:19 did l none of his words fall to the ground. NIH
4: 3 L us fetch the ark of the covenant of NIH
5: 8 L the ark of the God of Israel be carried NIH
5:11 l it go again to his own place, that it slay us NIH
6: 6 did they not l the people **go**, and 7971
9: 5 that *was* with him, Come, and l us return; NIH
9: 6 now l us go thither; peradventure he can NIH
9: 9 thus he spake, Come, and l us go to the seer: NIH
9:10 Saul to his servant, Well said; come, l us go. NIH
9:19 to morrow I will l thee **go**, and will tell thee 7971
10: 7 l it be, when these signs are come unto thee, NIH
11:14 l us go *to* Gilgal, and renew the kingdom NIH
13: 3 all the land, saying, L the Hebrews hear. NIH
14: 1 and l us go over to the Philistines' garrison, NIH
14: 6 l us go over unto the garrison of these NIH
14:36 L us go down after the Philistines by night, NIH
14:36 and l us not leave a man of them. NIH
14:36 the priest, L us draw near hither unto God. NIH
16:16 L our lord now command thy servants NIH
16:22 saying, L David, I pray thee, stand before NIH
17: 8 a man for you, and l him come down to me. NIH
17:32 L no man's heart fail because of him; NIH
18: 2 would l him go no more home *to* his 5414
18:17 L not mine hand be upon him, but let NIH
18:17 l the hand of the Philistines be upon him. NIH
19: 4 L not the king sin against his servant, NIH
19:12 So Michal l David **down** through a 3381
19:17 answered Saul, He said unto me, L me **go**; 7971
20: 3 he saith, L not Jonathan know this, lest he NIH
20: 5 l me **go**, that I may hide myself in the fields 7971
20:11 Come, and l us go out *into* the field. NIH
20:16 *saying,* L the LORD even require *it* at NIH
20:29 he said, L me **go**, I pray thee; for our 7971
20:29 l me get away, I pray thee, and see my NIH
21: 2 L no man know any thing of the business NIH
21:13 and l his spittle **fall down** upon his beard. 3381
22: 3 L my father and my mother, I pray thee, NIH
22:15 l not the king impute *any* thing unto his NIH
24:19 find his enemy, will he l him **go** well away? 7971
25: 8 Wherefore l the young men find favour in NIH
25:24 *upon* me *l this* iniquity *be:* and let thine NIH
25:24 *let this* iniquity *be:* and l thine handmaid, NIH
25:25 L not my lord, I pray thee, regard this man NIH
25:26 now l thine enemies, and they that seek evil NIH
25:27 l it even be given unto the young men that NIH
25:41 *l* thine handmaid *be* a servant to wash NIH
26: 8 now therefore l me smite him, I pray thee, NIH
26:11 and the cruse of water, and l us go. NIH
26:19 l my lord the king hear the words of his NIH
26:19 thee up against me, l him accept an offering: NIH
26:20 l not my blood fall to the earth before NIH
26:22 l one of the young men come over and NIH
26:24 l my life be much set by in the eyes of NIH
26:24 and l him deliver me out of all tribulation. NIH
27: 5 l them give me a place in some town in NIH
28:22 and l me set a morsel of bread before thee; NIH
29: 4 l him not go down with us to battle, NIH
2Sa 1:21 Ye mountains of Gilboa, *l there be* no dew, NIH
1:21 *be* no dew, neither *l there be* rain upon you, NIH
2: 7 Therefore now l your hands be NIH
2Sa 2:14 L the young men now arise, and play before NIH
2:14 play before us. And Joab said, L them arise. NIH
3:29 L it rest on the head of Joab, and on all his NIH
3:29 l there not fail from the house of Joab one NIH
5:24 l it be, when thou hearest the sound of a NIH
7:26 l thy name be magnified for ever, saying, NIH
7:26 l the house of thy servant David be NIH
7:29 Therefore now l it please thee to bless NIH
7:29 with thy blessing l the house of thy servant NIH
10:12 l us play the men for our people, and for NIH
11:12 day also, and to morrow I will l thee depart. NIH
11:25 unto Joab, L not this thing displease thee, NIH
13: 5 l my sister Tamar come, and give me meat, NIH
13: 6 l Tamar my sister come, and make *me* a NIH
13:24 l the king, I beseech thee, and his servants NIH
13:25 Nay, my son, l us not all now go, NIH
13:26 I pray thee, l my brother Amnon go with us. NIH
13:27 that he l Amnon and all the king's sons **go** 7971
13:32 L not my lord suppose *that* they have slain NIH
13:33 l not my lord the king take the thing to his NIH
14:11 l the king remember the LORD thy God, NIH
14:12 woman said, L thine handmaid, I pray thee, NIH
14:18 woman said, L my lord the king now speak. NIH
14:24 L him turn to his own house, and let him NIH
14:24 to his own house, and l him not see my face. NIH
14:32 now therefore l me see the king's face; and NIH
14:32 if there be *any* iniquity in me, l him kill me. NIH
15: 7 I pray thee, l me go and pay my vow, NIH
15:14 with him at Jerusalem, Arise, and l us flee; NIH
15:26 l him do to me as seemeth good unto him. NIH
16: 9 l me go over, I pray thee, and take off his NIH
16:10 so l him curse, because the LORD hath NIH
16:11 now *may this* Benjamite *do it?* l him **alone**, 3240
16:11 *do it?* let him alone, and l him curse; NIH
17: 1 L me now choose out twelve thousand men, NIH
17: 5 and l us hear likewise what he saith. NIH
18:19 L me now run, and bear the king tidings, NIH
18:22 howsoever, l me, I pray thee, also run after NIH
18:23 howsoever, *said he,* l me run. And he said NIH
19:19 L not my lord impute iniquity unto me, NIH
19:30 said unto the king, Yea, l him take all, NIH
19:37 L thy servant, I pray thee, turn back again, NIH
19:37 l him go over with my lord the king; and NIH
20:11 and he that *is* for David, *l him go* after Joab. NIH
21: 6 L seven men of his sons be delivered unto NIH
24:14 l us fall now into the hand of the LORD; NIH
24:14 and l me not fall into the hand of man. NIH
24:17 l thine hand, I pray thee, be against me, and NIH
24:22 L my lord the king take and offer up what NIH
1Ki 1: 2 L there be sought for my lord the king a NIH
1: 2 l her stand before the king, and let her NIH
1: 2 l her cherish him, and let her lie in thy NIH
1: 2 her cherish him, and l her lie in thy bosom, NIH
1:12 Now therefore come, l me, I pray thee, NIH
1:31 said, L my lord king David live for ever. NIH
1:34 l Zadok the priest and Nathan the prophet NIH
1:51 L king Solomon swear unto me to day that NIH
2: 6 l not his hoar head go down to the grave in NIH
2: 7 and l them be of *those* that eat at thy table: NIH
2:21 L Abishag the Shunammite be given to NIH
3:26 L it be neither mine nor thine, *but* divide *it.* NIH
8:26 of Israel, l thy word, I pray thee, be verified, NIH
8:57 l him not leave us, nor forsake us: NIH
8:59 l these my words, wherewith I have made NIH
8:61 L your heart therefore be perfect with NIH
11:21 Hadad said to Pharaoh, L me **depart**, that I 7971
11:22 howbeit l me **go in any wise**. 7971+7971
17:21 l this child's soul come into him again. NIH
18:23 L them therefore give us two bullocks; and NIH
18:23 l them choose one bullock for themselves, NIH
18:24 God that answereth by fire, l him be God. NIH
18:36 l it be known *this* day that thou *art* God in NIH
18:40 prophets of Baal; l not one of them escape. NIH
19: 2 So l the gods do *to me,* and more also, NIH
19:20 said, L me, I pray thee, kiss my father and NIH
20:11 Tell *him,* L not him that girdeth on *his* NIH
20:23 l us fight against them in the plain, and NIH
20:31 l us, I pray thee, put sackcloth on our loins, NIH
20:32 Ben-hadad saith, I pray thee, l me live. NIH
20:42 Because thou hast l **go** out of *thy* hand a 7971
21: 7 *and* eat bread, and l thine heart be merry: NIH
22: 8 Jehoshaphat said, L not the king say so. NIH
22:13 l thy word, I pray thee, be like the word of NIH
22:17 l them return every man to his house in NIH
22:49 L my servants go with thy servants in NIH
2Ki 1:10 l fire come down from heaven, and NIH
1:12 l fire come down from heaven, and NIH
1:13 l my life, and the life of these fifty thy NIH
1:14 l my life now be precious in thy sight. NIH
2: 9 l a double portion of thy spirit be upon me. NIH
2:16 l them go, we pray thee, and seek thy NIH
4:10 L us make a little chamber, I pray thee, NIH
4:10 l us set for him there a bed, and a table, and NIH
4:27 the man of God said, L her **alone**; for her 7503
5: 8 l him come now to me, and he shall know NIH
5:24 and he l the men **go**, and they departed. 7971
6: 2 L us go, we pray thee, unto Jordan, and NIH
6: 2 l us make us a place there, where we may NIH
7: 4 and l us fall unto the host of the Syrians: NIH
7:13 servants answered and said, L *some* take, NIH
7:13 that are consumed:) and l us send and see. NIH
9:15 l none go forth *nor* escape out of the city to NIH
9:17 to meet them, and l him say, *Is it* peace? NIH
10:19 and all his priests; l none be wanting: NIH
10:25 Go in, *and* slay them; l none come forth. NIH
11: 8 cometh within the ranges, l him be slain: NIH
11:15 L her not be slain *in* the house of NIH
12: 5 L the priests take *it* to them, every man of NIH
12: 5 l them repair the breaches of the house, NIH
13:21 when the man was l **down**, and touched 1980
14: 8 Come, l us look one another *in* the face. NIH
17:27 l them go and dwell there, and let him teach NIH
17:27 l him teach them the manner of the God of NIH
18:29 saith the king, L not Hezekiah deceive you: NIH
18:30 Neither l Hezekiah make you trust in NIH

2Ki 19:10 L not thy God in whom thou trustest NIH
20:10 l the shadow return backward ten degrees. NIH
22: 5 l them deliver it into the hand of the doers NIH
22: 5 l them give it to the doers of the work which NIH
23:18 he said, L him **alone**; let no man move his 3240
23:18 Let him alone; l no man move his bones. NIH
23:18 So they l his bones **alone**, with the bones of 4422
1Ch 13: 2 l us send abroad unto our brethren every NIH
13: 3 l us bring again the ark of our God to us: NIH
16:10 l the heart of them rejoice that seek NIH
16:31 L the heavens be glad, and let the earth NIH
16:31 the heavens be glad, and l the earth rejoice: NIH
16:31 l *men* say among the nations, The LORD NIH
16:32 L the sea roar, and the fulness thereof: NIH
16:32 l the fields rejoice, and all that *is* therein. NIH
17:23 l the thing that thou hast spoken concerning NIH
17:24 L it even be established, that thy name may NIH
17:24 *l* the house of David thy servant *be* NIH
17:27 l it please thee to bless the house of thy NIH
19:13 l us behave ourselves valiantly for our NIH
19:13 l the LORD do *that* which *is* good in his NIH
21:13 l me fall now into the hand of the LORD; NIH
21:13 but l me not fall into the hand of man. NIH
21:17 l thine hand, I pray thee, O LORD my NIH
21:23 l my lord the king do *that* which *is* good in NIH
2Ch 1: 9 l thy promise unto David my father be NIH
2:15 hath spoken of, l him send unto his servants: NIH
6:17 God of Israel, l thy word be verified, NIH
6:40 Now, my God, l, I beseech thee, thine eyes NIH
6:40 *l* thine ears *be* attent unto the prayer *that is* NIH
6:41 l thy priests, O LORD God, be clothed NIH
6:41 and l thy saints rejoice in goodness. NIH
14: 7 L us build these cities, and make about NIH
14:11 *art* our God; l not man prevail against thee. NIH
15: 7 and l not your hands be weak: NIH
16: 1 to the intent that *he* might l none go out or 5414
16: 5 off building of Ramah, and l his work cease. NIH
18: 7 Jehoshaphat said, L not the king say so. NIH
18:12 l thy word therefore, I pray thee, be like one NIH
18:16 l them return *therefore* every man to his NIH
19: 7 Wherefore now l the fear of the LORD be NIH
20:10 whom thou wouldest not l Israel invade, 5414
23: 6 l none come *into* the house of the LORD, NIH
23:14 followeth her, l him be slain with the sword. NIH
25: 7 l not the army of Israel go with thee; NIH
25:17 Come, l us see one another *in* the face. NIH
32:15 Now therefore l not Hezekiah deceive you, NIH
36:23 his God *be* with him, and l him go up. NIH
Ezr 1: 3 l him go up to Jerusalem, which *is* in Judah, NIH
1: 4 l the men of his place help him with silver, NIH
4: 2 and said unto them, L us build with you: NIH
5:15 l the house of God be builded in his place. NIH
5:17 l there be search made in the king's treasure NIH
5:17 l the king send his pleasure to us NIH
6: 3 L the house be builded, the place where NIH
6: 3 *l* the foundations thereof *be* strongly laid; NIH
6: 4 l the expences be given out of the king's NIH
6: 5 also l the golden and silver vessels of NIH
6: 7 L the work of this house of God alone; NIH
6: 7 l the governor of the Jews and the elders of NIH
6: 9 l *it* be given them day by day without fail: NIH
6:11 l timber be pulled down from his house, and NIH
6:11 and being set up, l him be hanged thereon; NIH
6:11 l his house be made a dunghill for this. NIH
6:12 have made a decree; l it be done with speed. NIH
7:23 l it be diligently done for the house of NIH
7:26 l judgment be executed speedily upon him, NIH
10: 3 l us make a covenant with our God to put NIH
10: 3 and l it be done according to the law. NIH
10:14 L now our rulers of all the congregation NIH
10:14 l all *them* which have taken strange wives in NIH
Ne 1: 6 L thine ear now be attentive, and thine eyes NIH
1:11 l now thine ear be attentive to the prayer of NIH
2: 3 said unto the king, L the king live for ever: NIH
2: 7 l letters be given me to the governors NIH
2:17 and l us build *up* the wall of Jerusalem, NIH
2:18 they said, L us rise up and build. So they NIH
4: 5 l not their sin be blotted out from before NIH
4:22 L every one with his servant lodge within NIH
5:10 corn: I pray you, l us leave off this usury. NIH
6: 2 l us meet together in *some one of* NIH
6: 7 and l us take counsel together. NIH
6:10 L us meet together in the house of God, NIH
6:10 and l us shut the doors of the temple: NIH
7: 3 L not the gates of Jerusalem be opened until NIH
7: 3 l them shut the doors, and bar *them:* and NIH
9:32 l not all the trouble seem little before thee, NIH
Est 1:19 l there go a royal commandment from him, NIH
1:19 l it be written among the laws of NIH
1:19 l the king give her royal estate unto another NIH
2: 2 L there be fair young virgins sought for NIH
2: 3 l the king appoint officers in all NIH
2: 3 l their things for purification be given NIH
2: 4 l the maiden which pleaseth the king be NIH
3: 9 l it be written that they may be destroyed: NIH
5: 4 l the king and Haman come *this* day unto NIH
5: 8 l the king and Haman come to the banquet NIH
5:12 Esther the queen did l no *man* come in with NIH
5:14 L a gallows be made of fifty cubits high, NIH
6: 5 the court. And the king said, L him come in. NIH
6: 8 L the royal apparel be brought which NIH
6: 9 l *this* apparel and horse be delivered to NIH
6:10 l nothing fail of all that thou hast spoken. NIH
7: 3 l my life be given me at my petition, and NIH
8: 5 l it be written to reverse the letters devised NIH
9:13 l it be granted to the Jews which *are* in NIH
9:13 l Haman's ten sons be hanged upon NIH
Job 3: 3 L the day perish wherein I was born, and NIH
3: 4 L that day be darkness; let not God regard it NIH
3: 4 l not God regard it from above, neither let NIH
3: 4 from above, neither l the light shine upon it NIH
3: 5 L darkness and the shadow of death stain it; NIH
3: 5 of death stain it; l a cloud dwell upon it; NIH
3: 5 upon it; l the blackness of the day terrify it. NIH
3: 6 *As for* that night, l darkness seize upon it; NIH

Job 3: 6 l it not be joined unto the days of the year, NIH
3: 6 l it not come into the number of the months. NIH
3: 7 Lo, l that night be solitary, let no joyful NIH
3: 7 be solitary, l no joyful voice come therein. NIH
3: 8 L them curse it that curse the day, who are NIH
3: 9 L the stars of the twilight thereof be dark; NIH
3: 9 l it look for light, but *have* none; neither let NIH
3: 9 neither l it see the dawning of the day: NIH
6: 9 *that* he would l loose his hand, and cut me NIH
6:10 harden myself in sorrow; l him not spare: NIH
6:29 Return, I pray you, l it not be iniquity; yea, NIH
7:16 l me alone; for my days *are* vanity. NIH
7:19 nor l me **alone** till I swallow down my 7503
9:34 L him take his rod away from me, and NIH
9:34 away from me, and l not his fear terrify me: NIH
10:20 cease then, and l **me** alone, that I may 5204.1
11:14 l not wickedness dwell in thy tabernacles. NIH
13:13 l me **alone**, that I may speak, and let come 4480
13:13 I may speak, and l come on me what *will*. NIH
13:21 and l not thy dread make me afraid. NIH
13:22 or l me speak, and answer thou me. NIH
15:31 L not him that is deceived trust in vanity: NIH
16:18 thou my blood, and l my cry have no place. NIH
21: 2 my speech, and l this be your consolations. NIH
27: 6 I hold fast, and will not l it **go**: 7503
27: 7 L mine enemy be as the wicked, and he that NIH
30:11 they have also l loose the bridle before me. NIH
31: 6 L me be weighed in an even balance, NIH
31: 8 *Then* l me sow, and let another eat; yea, NIH
31: 8 *Then* let me sow, and l another eat; yea, NIH
31: 8 yea, l my offspring be rooted out. NIH
31:10 *Then* l my wife grind unto another, and NIH
31:10 and l others bow down upon her. NIH
31:22 *Then* l mine arm fall from *my* shoulder NIH
31:40 L thistles grow instead of wheat, and NIH
32:21 L me not, I pray you, accept *any* man's NIH
32:21 neither l me give flattering titles unto man. NIH
34: 4 L us choose to us judgment: let us know NIH
34: 4 l us know among ourselves what *is* good. NIH
34:34 L men of understanding tell me, and let a NIH
34:34 tell me, and l a wise man hearken unto me. NIH
40: 2 *him?* he that reproveth God, l him answer it. NIH
Ps 2: 3 L us break their bands asunder, and NIH
5:10 O God; l them fall by their own counsels; NIH
5:11 l all those that put their trust in thee rejoice: NIH
5:11 l them ever shout for joy, because NIH
5:11 l them also that love thy name be joyful in NIH
6:10 L all mine enemies be ashamed and NIH
6:10 l them return *and* be ashamed suddenly. NIH
7: 5 L the enemy persecute my soul, and take *it;* NIH
7: 5 l him tread down my life upon the earth, NIH
7: 9 O l the wickedness of the wicked come to NIH
9:19 Arise, O LORD; l not man prevail: let NIH
9:19 l the heathen be judged in thy sight. NIH
10: 2 l them be taken in the devices that they have NIH
17: 2 L my sentence come forth from thy NIH
17: 2 l thine eyes behold the things that are equal. NIH
18:46 and l the God of my salvation be exalted. NIH
19:13 *sins;* l them not have dominion over me: NIH
19:14 L the words of my mouth, and NIH
20: 9 LORD: l the king hear us when we call. NIH
22: 8 l him deliver him, seeing he delighted in NIH
25: 2 l me not be ashamed, let not mine enemies NIH
25: 2 l not mine enemies triumph over me. NIH
25: 3 Yea, l none that wait on thee be ashamed: NIH
25: 3 l them be ashamed which transgress without NIH
25:20 l me not be ashamed; for I put my trust in NIH
25:21 L integrity and uprightness preserve me; NIH
31: 1 do I put my trust; l me never be ashamed: NIH
31:17 L me not be ashamed, O LORD; for I have NIH
31:17 l the wicked be ashamed, *and* let them be NIH
31:17 *and* l them be silent in the grave. NIH
31:18 L the lying lips be put to silence; NIH
33: 8 L all the earth fear the LORD: let all NIH
33: 8 l all the inhabitants of the world stand in NIH
33:22 L thy mercy, O LORD, be upon us, NIH
34: 3 with me, and l us exalt his name together. NIH
35: 4 L them be confounded and put to shame NIH
35: 4 l them be turned back and brought to NIH
35: 5 L them be as chaff before the wind: and NIH
35: 5 and l the angel of the LORD chase *them.* NIH
35: 6 L their way be dark and slippery: and let NIH
35: 6 l the angel of the LORD persecute them. NIH
35: 8 L destruction come upon him at unawares; NIH
35: 8 and l his net that he hath hid catch himself: NIH
35: 8 into that *very* destruction l him fall. NIH
35:19 L not them that are mine enemies NIH
35:19 *neither* l them wink *with* the eye that hate NIH
35:24 and l them not rejoice over me. NIH
35:25 L them not say in their hearts, Ah, so NIH
35:25 l them not say, We have swallowed him up. NIH
35:26 L them be ashamed and brought to NIH
35:26 l them be clothed with shame and NIH
35:27 L them shout for joy, and be glad, NIH
35:27 yea, l them say continually, Let the LORD NIH
35:27 L the LORD be magnified, NIH
36:11 L not the foot of pride come against me, NIH
36:11 l not the hand of the wicked remove me. NIH
40:11 l thy lovingkindness and thy truth NIH
40:14 L them be ashamed and NIH
40:14 l them be driven backward and put to shame NIH
40:15 L them be desolate for a reward of their NIH
40:16 L all those that seek thee rejoice and be glad NIH
40:16 l such as love thy salvation say continually, NIH
43: 3 l them lead me; let them bring me unto thy NIH
43: 3 l them bring me unto thy holy hill, and NIH
48:11 L mount Zion rejoice, let the daughters of NIH
48:11 l the daughters of Judah be glad, because NIH
55:15 L death seize upon them, *and* let them go NIH
55:15 *and* l them go down quick *into* hell: NIH
57: 5 *l* thy glory *be* above all the earth. NIH
57:11 *l* thy glory *be* above all the earth. NIH
58: 7 L them melt away as waters *which* run NIH
58: 7 *shoot* his arrows, l them be as cut in pieces. NIH
58: 8 l *every one of them* pass away: NIH

Ps 59:10 God shall l me see *my desire* upon mine NIH
59:12 the words of their lips l them even be taken NIH
59:13 l them know that God ruleth in Jacob unto NIH
59:14 at evening l them return; *and* let them make NIH
59:14 *and* l them make a noise like a dog, and NIH
59:15 L them wander up and down for meat, and NIH
66: 7 l not the rebellious exalt themselves. Selah. NIH
67: 3 L the people praise thee, O God; let all NIH
67: 3 O God; l all the people praise thee. NIH
67: 4 O l the nations be glad and sing for joy: NIH
67: 5 L the people praise thee, O God; let all NIH
67: 5 O God; l all the people praise thee. NIH
68: 1 L God arise, let his enemies be scattered: NIH
68: 1 Let God arise, l his enemies be scattered: NIH
68: 1 l them also that hate him flee before him. NIH
68: 2 l the wicked perish at the presence of God. NIH
68: 3 l the righteous be glad; let them rejoice NIH
68: 3 be glad; l them rejoice before God: NIH
68: 3 before God: yea, l them exceedingly rejoice. NIH
69: 6 L not them that wait on thee, O Lord GOD NIH
69: 6 l not those that seek thee be confounded for NIH
69:14 me out of the mire, and l me not sink: NIH
69:14 l me be delivered from them that hate me, NIH
69:15 L not the waterflood overflow me, NIH
69:15 neither l the deep swallow me up, and NIH
69:15 and l not the pit shut her mouth upon me. NIH
69:22 L their table become a snare before them: NIH
69:22 *been* for *their* welfare, *l it become* a trap. NIH
69:23 L their eyes be darkened, that *they* see not; NIH
69:24 and l thy wrathful anger take hold of them. NIH
69:25 L their habitation be desolate; *and* let none NIH
69:25 be desolate; *and* l none dwell in their tents. NIH
69:27 and l them not come into thy righteousness. NIH
69:28 L them be blotted out of the book of NIH
69:29 l thy salvation, O God, set me up on high. NIH
69:34 L the heaven and earth praise him, the seas, NIH
70: 2 L them be ashamed and confounded that NIH
70: 2 l them be turned backward, and put to NIH
70: 3 L them be turned back for a reward of their NIH
70: 4 L all those that seek thee rejoice and be glad NIH
70: 4 l such as love thy salvation say continually, NIH
70: 4 say continually, L God be magnified. NIH
71: 1 put my trust: l me never be put to confusion. NIH
71: 8 L my mouth be filled *with* thy praise *and* NIH
71:13 L them be confounded *and* consumed that NIH
71:13 l them be covered *with* reproach and NIH
72:19 l the whole earth be filled *with* his glory; NIH
74: 8 in their hearts, L us destroy them together: NIH
74:21 O l not the oppressed return ashamed: NIH
74:21 l the poor and needy praise thy name. NIH
76:11 l all that be round about him bring presents NIH
78:28 he l *it* fall in the midst of their camp, NIH
79: 8 l thy tender mercies speedily prevent us: NIH
79:10 l him be known among the heathen in our NIH
79:11 L the sighing of the prisoner come before NIH
80:17 L thy hand be upon the man of thy right NIH
83: 4 and l us cut them off from *being* a nation; NIH
83:12 L us take to ourselves the houses of God in NIH
83:17 L them be confounded and troubled for NIH
83:17 yea, l them be put to shame, and perish: NIH
85: 8 his saints: but l them not turn *again* to folly. NIH
88: 2 L my prayer come before thee: incline thine NIH
90:13 and l it repent thee concerning thy servants. NIH
90:16 L thy work appear unto thy servants, and NIH
90:17 l the beauty of the LORD our God be upon NIH
95: 1 O come, l us sing unto the LORD: let us NIH
95: 1 l us make a joyful noise to the rock of our NIH
95: 2 L us come before his presence with NIH
95: 6 O come, l us worship and bow down: let us NIH
95: 6 l us kneel before the LORD our Maker. NIH
96:11 L the heavens rejoice, and let the earth be NIH
96:11 the heavens rejoice, and l the earth be glad; NIH
96:11 l the sea roar, and the fulness thereof. NIH
96:12 L the field be joyful, and all that *is* therein: NIH
97: 1 The LORD reigneth; l the earth rejoice; NIH
97: 1 l the multitude of isles be glad *thereof.* NIH
98: 7 L the sea roar, and the fulness thereof; NIH
98: 8 L the floods clap *their* hands: let the hills NIH
98: 8 *their* hands: l the hills be joyful together NIH
99: 1 The LORD reigneth; l the people tremble: NIH
99: 1 the cherubims; l the earth be moved. NIH
99: 3 L them praise thy great and terrible name; NIH
102: 1 O LORD, and l my cry come unto thee. NIH
104:35 L the sinners be consumed out of the earth, NIH
104:35 of the earth, and l the wicked be no more. NIH
105: 3 l the heart of them rejoice that seek NIH
105:20 the ruler of the people, and l him go free. NIH
106:48 l all the people say, Amen. Praise ye NIH
107: 2 L the redeemed of the LORD say *so,* NIH
107:22 l them sacrifice the sacrifices of NIH
107:32 L them exalt him also in the congregation NIH
109: 6 and l Satan stand at his right hand. NIH
109: 7 he shall be judged, l him be condemned: NIH
109: 7 be condemned: and l his prayer become sin. NIH
109: 8 L his days be few; *and* let another take his NIH
109: 8 days be few; *and* l another take his office. NIH
109: 9 L his children be fatherless, and his wife a NIH
109:10 L his children be continually vagabonds, NIH
109:10 l them seek *their bread* also out of their NIH
109:11 L the extortioner catch all that he hath; and NIH
109:11 he hath; and l the strangers spoil his labour. NIH
109:12 L there be none to extend mercy unto him: NIH
109:12 neither l there be any to favour his NIH
109:13 L his posterity be cut off; *and* in NIH
109:13 in the generation following l their name be NIH
109:14 L the iniquity of his fathers be remembered NIH
109:14 l not the sin of his mother be blotted out. NIH
109:15 L them be before the LORD continually, NIH
109:17 As he loved cursing, so l it come *unto* him: NIH
109:17 not in blessing, so l it be far from him. NIH
109:18 so l it come into his bowels like water, and NIH
109:19 L it be unto him as the garment *which* NIH
109:20 *L* this *be* the reward of mine adversaries NIH
109:28 L them curse, but bless thou: when they NIH
109:28 when they arise, l them be ashamed; but NIH

L

Ps 109:28 them be ashamed; but l thy servant rejoice. NIH
109:29 L mine adversaries be clothed with shame, NIH
109:29 l them cover *themselves with* their own NIH
118: 2 L Israel now say, that his mercy *endureth* NIH
118: 3 L the house of Aaron now say, that his NIH
118: 4 L them now that fear the LORD say, NIH
119:10 O l me not wander from thy NIH
119:41 L thy mercies come also *unto* me, NIH
119:76 L, I pray thee, thy merciful kindness be for NIH
119:77 L thy tender mercies come *unto* me, that I NIH
119:78 L the proud be ashamed; for they dealt NIH
119:79 L those that fear thee turn unto me, and NIH
119:80 L my heart be sound in thy statutes; that I NIH
119:116 and l me not be ashamed of my hope. NIH
119:122 for good: l not the proud oppress me. NIH
119:133 l not any iniquity have dominion over me. NIH
119:169 L my cry come near before thee, O LORD: NIH
119:170 L my supplication come before thee: NIH
119:173 L thine hand help me; for I have chosen thy NIH
119:175 L my soul live, and it shall praise thee; and NIH
119:175 praise thee; and l thy judgments help me. NIH
122: 1 L us go *into* the house of the LORD. NIH
129: 5 L them all be confounded and turned back NIH
129: 6 L them be as the grass upon the housetops, NIH
130: 2 l thine ears be attentive to the voice of my NIH
130: 7 L Israel hope in the LORD: for with NIH
131: 3 L Israel hope in the LORD from NIH
132: 9 L thy priests be clothed *with* righteousness; NIH
132: 9 and l thy saints shout for joy. NIH
137: 5 l my right hand forget *her cunning.* NIH
137: 6 l my tongue cleave to the roof of my mouth; NIH
140: 9 l the mischief of their own lips cover them. NIH
140:10 L burning coals fall upon them: let them be NIH
140:10 l them be cast into the fire; into deep pits, NIH
140:11 L not an evil speaker be established in NIH
141: 2 L my prayer be set forth before thee *as* NIH
141: 4 and l me not eat of their dainties. NIH
141: 5 L the righteous smite me; *it shall be* a NIH
141: 5 l him reprove me; *it shall be* an excellent NIH
141:10 L the wicked fall into their own nets, NIH
145:21 l all flesh bless his holy name for ever and NIH
148: 5 L them praise the name of the LORD: NIH
148:13 L them praise the name of the LORD: NIH
149: 2 L Israel rejoice in him that made him: NIH
149: 2 l the children of Zion be joyful in their NIH
149: 3 L them praise his name in the dance: NIH
149: 3 l them sing *praises* unto him with NIH
149: 5 L the saints be joyful in glory: let them sing NIH
149: 5 in glory: l them sing aloud upon their beds. NIH
149: 6 *L* the high *praises* of God *be* in their mouth, NIH
150: 6 L every *thing that hath* breath praise NIH
Pr 1:11 Come with us, l us lay wait for blood, NIH
1:11 l us lurk privily for the innocent without NIH
1:12 L us swallow them up alive as the grave; NIH
1:14 in thy lot among us; l us all have one purse: NIH
3: 1 but l thine heart keep my commandments: NIH
3: 3 L not mercy and truth forsake thee: NIH
3:21 My son, l not them depart from thine eyes: NIH
4: 4 said unto me, L thine heart retain my words: NIH
4:13 Take fast hold of instruction; l *her* not go: NIH
4:21 L them not depart from thine eyes; NIH
4:25 L thine eyes look right on, and let thine NIH
4:25 and l thine eyelids look straight before thee. NIH
4:26 of thy feet, and l all thy ways be established. NIH
5:16 L thy fountains be dispersed abroad, NIH
5:17 L them be only thine own, and NIH
5:18 L thy fountain be blessed: and rejoice with NIH
5:19 *L her be as* the loving hind and pleasant roe; NIH
5:19 l her breasts satisfy thee at all times; and NIH
6:25 neither l her take thee with her eyelids. NIH
7:18 l us take our fill of love until the morning: NIH
7:18 l us solace ourselves with loves. NIH
7:25 L not thine heart decline to her ways, go not NIH
9: 4 Whoso *is* simple, l him turn in hither: *as for* NIH
9:16 Whoso *is* simple, l him turn in hither: and NIH
17:12 *L* a bear robbed of her whelps meet a man, NIH
19:18 and l not thy soul spare for his crying. NIH
23:17 L not thine heart envy sinners: but *be thou* NIH
23:26 and l thine eyes observe my ways. NIH
24:17 l not thine heart be glad when he stumbleth: NIH
27: 2 L another *man* praise thee, and not thine NIH
28:17 shall flee to the pit; l no man stay him. NIH
31: 7 L him drink, and forget his poverty, and NIH
31:31 and l her own works praise her in the gates. NIH
Ecc 5: 2 l not thine heart be hasty to utter *any* thing NIH
5: 2 upon earth: therefore l thy words be few. NIH
9: 8 L thy garments be always white; and let thy NIH
9: 8 and l thy head lack no ointment. NIH
11: 8 yet l him remember the days of darkness; NIH
11: 9 l thy heart cheer thee in the days of thy NIH
12:13 L us hear the conclusion of the whole NIH
SS 1: 2 L him kiss me with the kisses of his mouth: NIH
2:14 l me see thy countenance, let me hear thy NIH
2:14 see thy countenance, l me hear thy voice; NIH
3: 4 I held him, and would not l him **go**, until I 7503
4:16 L my beloved come into his garden, and NIH
7:11 my beloved, l us go forth *into* the field; NIH
7:11 *into* the field; l us lodge in the villages. NIH
7:12 L us get up early to the vineyards; let us see NIH
7:12 l us see if the vine flourish, *whether* NIH
8:11 he l **out** the vineyard unto keepers; 5414
Isa 1:18 Come now, and l us reason together, NIH
2: 3 l us go up to the mountain of the LORD, NIH
2: 5 and l us walk in the light of the LORD. NIH
3: 6 our ruler, and *l* this ruin *be* under thy hand: NIH
4: 1 only l us be called by thy name, to take NIH
5:19 L him make speed, *and* hasten his work, NIH
5:19 l the counsel of the Holy One of Israel draw NIH
7: 6 L us go up against Judah, and vex it, and NIH
7: 6 l us make a breach therein for us, and set a NIH
8:13 *l* him *be* your fear, and *let* him *be* your NIH
8:13 him *be* your fear, and *l* him *be* your dread. NIH
16: 4 L mine outcasts dwell with thee, Moab; NIH
19:12 *are* thy wise *men?* and l them tell thee now, NIH
19:12 l them know what the LORD of hosts hath NIH

Isa 21: 6 a watchman, l him declare what he seeth. NIH
22:13 l us eat and drink; for to morrow we shall NIH
26:10 L favour be shewed to the wicked, *yet* will NIH
27: 5 Or l him take hold of my strength, *that* he NIH
29: 1 add ye year to year; l them kill sacrifices. NIH
34: 1 l the earth hear, and all that is therein; NIH
36:14 saith the king, L not Hezekiah deceive you: NIH
36:15 Neither l Hezekiah make you trust in NIH
37:10 saying, L not thy God, in whom thou NIH
38:21 L them take a lump of figs, and lay *it* for a NIH
41: 1 and l the people renew *their* strength: NIH
41: 1 l them come near; then let them speak: NIH
41: 1 let them come near; then l them speak: NIH
41: 1 l us come near together to judgment. NIH
41:22 L them bring *them* forth, and shew us what NIH
41:22 l them shew the former *things,* what they NIH
42:11 L the wilderness and the cities thereof lift NIH
42:11 l the inhabitants of the rock sing, let them NIH
42:11 l them shout from the top of the mountains. NIH
42:12 L them give glory unto the LORD, and NIH
43: 9 L all the nations be gathered together, and NIH
43: 9 and l the people be assembled: NIH
43: 9 shew us former *things?* l them bring forth NIH
43: 9 or l them hear, and say, *It is* truth. NIH
43:13 of my hand: I will work, and who shall l it? 7725
43:26 l us plead together: declare thou, that thou NIH
44: 7 and shall come, l them shew unto them. NIH
44:11 l them all be gathered together, let them NIH
44:11 l them stand *up; yet* they shall fear, *and* NIH
45: 8 and l the skies pour down righteousness: NIH
45: 8 l the earth open, and let them bring forth NIH
45: 8 l them bring forth salvation, and NIH
45: 8 and l righteousness spring up together; NIH
45: 9 *L* the potsherd *strive* with the potsherds of NIH
45:13 my city, and he shall l **go** my captives, 7971
45:21 yea, l them take counsel together: NIH
47:13 L now the astrologers, the stargazers, NIH
50: 8 l us stand together: who *is* mine adversary? NIH
50: 8 *is* mine adversary? l him come near to me. NIH
50:10 l him trust in the name of the LORD, and NIH
54: 2 l them stretch forth the curtains of thine NIH
55: 2 and l your soul delight itself in fatness. NIH
55: 7 L the wicked forsake his way, and NIH
55: 7 l him return unto the LORD, and he will NIH
56: 3 Neither l the son of the stranger, that hath NIH
56: 3 neither l the eunuch say, Behold, I *am* a dry NIH
57:13 thou criest, l thy companies deliver thee; NIH
58: 6 to l the oppressed **go** free, and *that* ye break 7971
66: 5 said, L the LORD be glorified: NIH
Jer 2:28 l them arise, if they can save thee in NIH
4: 5 and l us go into the defenced cities. NIH
5:24 L us now fear the LORD our God, NIH
6: 4 against her; arise, and l us go up at noon. NIH
6: 5 l us go by night, and let us destroy her NIH
6: 5 us go by night, and l us destroy her palaces. NIH
8:14 l us enter into the defenced cities, and let us NIH
8:14 the defenced cities, and l us be silent there: NIH
9:18 l them make haste, and take up a wailing for NIH
9:20 l your ear receive the word of his mouth, NIH
9:23 L not the wise *man* glory in his wisdom, NIH
9:23 neither l the mighty *man* glory in his might, NIH
9:23 l not the rich *man* glory in his riches: NIH
9:24 l him that glorieth glory in this, that *he* NIH
11:19 *saying,* L us destroy the tree with the fruit NIH
11:19 l us cut him off from the land of the living, NIH
11:20 the heart, l me see thy vengeance on them: NIH
12: 1 yet l me talk with thee of *thy* judgments. NIH
14:17 L mine eyes run down *with* tears night and NIH
14:17 tears night and day, and l them not cease: NIH
15: 1 *them* out of my sight, and l them go forth. NIH
15:19 l them return unto thee; but return not thou NIH
17:15 *is* the word of the LORD? l it come now. NIH
17:18 L them be confounded that persecute me, NIH
17:18 persecute me, but l not me be confounded: NIH
17:18 l them be dismayed, but let not me be NIH
17:18 be dismayed, but l not me be dismayed: NIH
18:18 and l us devise devices against Jeremiah; NIH
18:18 l us smite him with the tongue, and let us NIH
18:18 and l us not give heed to any of his words. NIH
18:21 l their wives be bereaved of their children, NIH
18:21 *be* widows; and l their men be put to death; NIH
18:21 *l* their young men *be* slain by the sword in NIH
18:22 L a cry be heard from their houses, NIH
18:23 but l them be overthrown before thee; NIH
20:12 the heart, l me see thy vengeance on them: NIH
20:14 l not the day wherein my mother bare me be NIH
20:16 l that man be as the cities which the LORD NIH
20:16 l him hear the cry in the morning, and NIH
23:28 that hath a dream, l him tell a dream; NIH
23:28 my word, l him speak my word faithfully. NIH
27:11 those will I l remain still in their own land, NIH
27:18 l them now make intercession to NIH
29: 8 L not your prophets and your diviners, NIH
31: 6 l us go up *to* Zion unto the LORD our NIH
34: 9 That every man should l his manservant, NIH
34:10 heard that every one should l his NIH
34:10 any more, then they obeyed, and l *them* **go**. 7971
34:11 whom they had l **go** free, to return, and 7971
34:14 At the end of seven years l ye **go** every man 7971
34:14 thou shalt l him **go** free from thee: 7971
35:11 l us go *to* Jerusalem for fear of the army of NIH
36:19 Jeremiah; and l no man know where ye *be.* NIH
37:20 l my supplication, I pray thee, be accepted NIH
38: 4 We beseech thee, l this man be put to death: NIH
38: 6 they l **down** Jeremiah with cords. And in 7971
38:11 l them **down** by cords into the dungeon to 7971
38:24 L no man know of these words, and NIH
40: 1 of the guard had l him **go** from Ramah, 7971
40: 5 him victuals and a reward, and l him **go**. 7971
40:15 saying, L me go, I pray thee, and I will slay NIH
42: 2 Jeremiah the prophet, L, we beseech thee, NIH
46: 6 L not the swift flee away, nor the mighty NIH
46: 9 and l the mighty *men* come forth; NIH
46:16 l us go again to our own people, and to NIH
48: 2 and l us cut it off from *being* a nation. NIH

Jer 49:11 *them* alive; and l thy widows trust in me. NIH
50: 5 l us join ourselves to the LORD *in* a NIH
50:26 destroy her utterly: l nothing of her be left. NIH
50:27 l them go down to the slaughter: NIH
50:29 it round about; l none thereof escape: 1961
50:33 held them fast; they refused to l them **go**. 7971
51: 3 Against *him that* bendeth l the archer bend NIH
51: 9 and l us go every one into his own country: NIH
51:10 l us declare in Zion the work of the LORD NIH
51:50 and l Jerusalem come into your mind. NIH
La 1:22 L all their wickedness come before thee; NIH
2:18 l tears run down like a river day and night: NIH
2:18 no rest; l not the apple of thine eye cease. NIH
3:40 L us search and try our ways, and turn again NIH
3:41 L us lift up our heart with *our* hands unto NIH
Eze 1:24 when they stood, they l **down** their wings. 7503
1:25 they stood, *and* had l **down** their wings. 7503
3:27 He that heareth, l him hear; and he that NIH
3:27 and he that forbeareth, l him forbear: NIH
7:12 l not the buyer rejoice, nor the seller mourn: NIH
9: 5 l not your eye spare, neither have ye pity: NIH
11: 3 Which say, *It is* not near; *l us* build houses: NIH
13:20 from your arms, and will l the souls go, NIH
21:14 l the sword be doubled the third time, NIH
24: 5 l them seethe the bones of it therein. NIH
24: 6 it out piece by piece; l no lot fall upon it. NIH
24:10 and spice it well, and l the bones be burnt. NIH
39: 7 I will not l *them* pollute my holy name any NIH
43: 9 Now l them put away their whoredom, and NIH
43:10 and l them measure the pattern. NIH
44: 6 l it suffice you of all your abominations, NIH
45: 9 L it suffice you, O princes of Israel: NIH
Da 1:12 l them give us pulse to eat, and water to NIH
1:13 l our countenances be looked upon before NIH
2: 7 L the king tell his servants the dream, and NIH
4:14 l the beasts get away from under it, and NIH
4:15 l it be wet with the dew of heaven, and NIH
4:15 *l* his portion *be* with the beasts in the grass NIH
4:16 L his heart be changed from man's, and NIH
4:16 l a beast's heart be given unto him; NIH
4:16 unto him; and l seven times pass over him. NIH
4:19 l not the dream, or the interpretation thereof, NIH
4:23 l it be wet with the dew of heaven, and NIH
4:23 *l* his portion *be* with the beasts of the field, NIH
4:27 l my counsel be acceptable unto thee, and NIH
5:10 l not thy thoughts trouble thee, nor let thy NIH
5:10 nor l thy countenance be changed. NIH
5:12 now l Daniel be called, and he will shew NIH
5:17 L thy gifts be to thyself, and give thy NIH
9:16 l thine anger and thy fury be turned away NIH
10:19 and said, L my lord speak; NIH
Hos 2: 2 l her therefore put away her whoredoms out NIH
4: 4 Yet l no man strive, nor reprove another: NIH
4:15 play the harlot, *yet* l not Judah offend; NIH
4:17 Ephraim *is* joined to idols: l him **alone**. 3240
6: 1 Come and l us return unto the LORD: NIH
13: 2 L the men that sacrifice kiss the calves. NIH
Joel 1: 3 *l* your children *tell* their children, and NIH
2: 1 l all the inhabitants of the land tremble: NIH
2:16 l the bridegroom go forth of his chamber, NIH
2:17 L the priests, the ministers of the LORD, NIH
2:17 the porch and the altar, and l them say, NIH
3: 9 wake up the mighty *men,* l all the men of NIH
3: 9 the men of war draw near; l them come up: NIH
3:10 into spears: l the weak say, I *am* strong. NIH
3:12 L the heathen be wakened, and come up to NIH
Am 4: 1 say to their masters, Bring, and l us drink. NIH
5:24 l judgment run down as waters, and NIH
Ob 1: 1 and l us rise up against her in battle. NIH
Jnh 1: 7 one to his fellow, Come, and l us cast lots, NIH
1:14 l us not perish for this man's life, and NIH
3: 7 his nobles, saying, L neither man nor beast, NIH
3: 7 any thing: l them not feed, nor drink water: NIH
3: 8 l man and beast be covered with sackcloth, NIH
3: 8 l them turn every one from his evil way, and NIH
Mic 1: 2 l the Lord GOD be witness against you, NIH
4: 2 l us go up to the mountain of the LORD, NIH
4:11 L her be defiled, and let our eye look upon NIH
4:11 be defiled, and l our eye look upon Zion. NIH
6: 1 the mountains, and l the hills hear thy voice. NIH
7:14 l them feed *in* Bashan and Gilead, as *in* NIH
Hab 2:16 thou also, and l thy foreskin be uncovered: NIH
2:20 l all the earth keep silence before him. NIH
Zep 3:16 *and to* Zion, L not thine hands be slack. NIH
Zec 3: 5 I said, L them set a fair mitre upon his head. NIH
7:10 l none of you imagine evil against his NIH
8: 9 L your hands be strong, ye that hear in these NIH
8:13 fear not, *but* l your hands be strong. NIH
8:17 l none of you imagine evil in your hearts NIH
8:21 L us go speedily to pray before the LORD, NIH
11: 9 that that dieth, l it die; and that that is to be NIH
11: 9 that that is to be cut off, l it be cut off; and NIH
11: 9 l the rest eat every one the flesh of another. NIH
Mal 2:15 l none deal treacherously against the wife of NIH
Mt 5:16 L your light so shine before men, that they NIG
5:31 l him give her a writing of divorcement: NIG
5:37 But l your communication be, Yea, yea; NIG
5:40 *away* thy coat, l him **have** *thy* cloke also. *863*
6: 3 l not thy left hand know what thy right hand NIG
7: 4 L me pull out the mote out of thine eye; *863*
8:22 Follow me; and l the dead bury their dead. *863*
10:13 house be worthy, l your peace come upon it: NIG
10:13 it be not worthy, l your peace return to you. NIG
11:15 He that hath ears to hear, l him hear. NIG
13: 9 Who hath ears to hear, l him hear. NIG
13:30 L both grow together until the harvest: and *863*
13:43 Who hath ears to hear, l him hear. NIG
15: 4 or mother, l him die the death. NIG
15:14 L them **alone**: they be blind leaders of *863*
16:24 l him deny himself, and take up his cross, NIG
17: 4 thou wilt, l us make here three tabernacles: NIG
18:17 l him be unto thee as a heathen *man* and NIG
19: 6 hath joined together, l not man put asunder. NIG
19:12 He that is able to receive *it,* l him receive *it.* NIG
20:26 be great among you, l him be your minister; NIG

Mt 20:27 be chief among you, l him be your servant: NIG
21:19 L no fruit grow on thee henceforward for NIG
21:33 and l it **out** to husbandmen, and went into a *1554*
21:38 l us kill him, and let us seize on his NIG
21:38 us kill him, and l us seize on his inheritance. NIG
21:41 will l **out** *his* vineyard unto other *1554*
24:15 (whoso readeth, l him understand:) NIG
24:16 Then l them which be in Judea flee into NIG
24:17 L him which is on the housetop not come NIG
24:18 Neither l him which is in the field return NIG
26:39 if it be possible, l this cup pass from me: NIG
26:46 Rise, l us be going: behold, he is at hand NIG
27:22 *They* all say unto him, L him be crucified. NIG
27:23 out the more, saying, L him be crucified. NIG
27:42 l him now come down from the cross, and NIG
27:43 l him deliver him now, if he will have him: NIG
27:49 The rest said, **L be**, let us see whether Elias *863*
27:49 l us see whether Elias will come to save NIG
Mk 1:24 Saying, L *us* **alone**; what have we to do *1436*
1:38 said unto them, L us go into the next towns, NIG
2: 4 they l **down** the bed wherein the sick of *5465*
4: 9 He that hath ears to hear, l him hear. NIG
4:23 If any *man* have ears to hear, l him hear. NIG
4:35 L us pass over unto the other side. NIG
7:10 or mother, l him die the death. NIG
7:16 If any *man* have ears to hear, l him hear. NIG
7:27 said unto her, L the children first be filled: *863*
8:34 l him deny himself, and take up his cross, NIG
9: 5 and l us make three tabernacles; one for NIG
10: 9 hath joined together, l not man put asunder. NIG
11: 6 Jesus had commanded: and they l them **go**. *863*
12: 1 and l it **out** to husbandmen, and went into a *1554*
12: 7 l us kill him, and the inheritance shall be NIG
13:14 it ought not, (l him that readeth understand,) NIG
13:14 l them that be in Judea flee to NIG
13:15 And l him that is on the housetop not go NIG
13:16 And l him that is in the field not turn back NIG
14: 6 And Jesus said, L her **alone**; why trouble *863*
14:42 Rise up, l us go; lo, he that betrayeth me is NIG
15:32 L Christ the King of Israel descend now NIG
15:36 and gave him to drink, saying, **L alone**; *863*
15:36 l us see whether Elias will come to take him NIG
Lk 2:15 L us now go *even* unto Bethlehem, and NIG
3:11 l him impart to him that hath none; NIG
3:11 and he that hath meat, l him do likewise. NIG
4:34 Saying, L *us* **alone**; what have we to do *1436*
5: 4 and l **down** your nets for a draught. *5465*
5: 5 nevertheless at thy word I will l **down** *5465*
5:19 l him **down** through the tiling with *his* *2524*
6:42 l me pull out the mote that is in thine eye, *863*
8: 8 He that hath ears to hear, l him hear. NIG
8:22 L us go over unto the other side of the lake. NIG
9:23 l him deny himself, and take up his cross NIG
9:33 and l us make three tabernacles; one for NIG
9:44 L these sayings sink down into your ears: NIG
9:60 said unto him, L the dead bury their dead: *863*
9:61 but l me first go bid them farewell, *2010*
12:35 L your loins be girded about, and *your* NIG
13: 8 Lord, l it **alone** this year also, till I shall dig *863*
14: 4 he took *him,* and healed him, and l *him* **go**; *630*
14:35 it out. He that hath ears to hear, l him hear. NIG
15:23 and kill *it;* and l us eat, and be merry: NIG
16:29 and the prophets; l them hear them. NIG
17:31 l him not come down to take it away: NIG
17:31 in the field, l him likewise not return back. NIG
20: 9 and l it **forth** to husbandmen, and went into *1554*
20:14 come, l us kill him, that the inheritance may NIG
21:21 Then l them which are in Judea flee to NIG
21:21 l them which are in the midst of it depart NIG
21:21 l not them that are in the countries enter NIG
22:26 among you, l him be as the younger; NIG
22:36 a purse, l him take *it,* and likewise *his* scrip: NIG
22:36 l him sell his garment, and buy one. NIG
22:68 *you,* you will not answer me, nor l me **go**. *630*
23:22 I will therefore chastise him, and l *him* **go**. *630*
23:35 l him save himself, if he be Christ, NIG
Jn 7:37 *man* thirst, l him come unto me, and drink. NIG
8: 7 among you, l him first cast a stone at her. NIG
11: 7 he to *his* disciples, L us go into Judea again. NIG
11:15 may believe; nevertheless l us go unto him. NIG
11:16 unto *his* fellow-disciples, L us also go, NIG
11:44 saith unto them, Loose him, and l *him* **go**. *863*
11:48 If we l him thus **alone**, all *men* will believe *863*
12: 7 Then said Jesus, L her **alone**: against the day *863*
12:26 If any *man* serve me, l him follow me; and NIG
14: 1 L not your heart be troubled: ye believe in NIG
14:27 L not your heart be troubled, neither let it NIG
14:27 your heart be troubled, neither l it be afraid. NIG
14:31 *even* so I do. Arise, l us go hence. NIG
18: 8 therefore ye seek me, l these go their way: *863*
19:12 Jews cried out, saying, If thou l this *man* **go**, *630*
19:24 L us not rent it, but cast lots for it, whose it NIG
Ac 1:20 L his habitation be desolate, and let no man NIG
1:20 be desolate, and l no man dwell therein: *1510*
1:20 and his bishoprick l another take. NIG
2:29 l *me* freely speak unto you of the patriarch *1832*
2:36 Therefore l all the house of Israel know NIG
3:13 when he was determined to l *him* **go**. *630*
4:17 the people, l us straitly threaten them, NIG
4:21 had further threatened *them,* they l them **go**, *630*
4:23 And being l **go**, they went to their own *630*
5:38 Refrain from these men, and l them **alone**: *1439*
5:40 speak in the name of Jesus, and l them **go**. *630*
9:25 l *him* **down** by the wall in a basket. *2524+5465*
10:11 at the four corners, and l **down** to the earth: *2524*
11: 5 l **down** from heaven by four corners; *2524*
15:33 they were l **go** in peace from the brethren *630*
15:36 L us go again and visit our brethren in every NIG
16:35 sent the sergeants, saying, L those men **go**. *630*
16:36 The magistrates have sent to l you **go**: *630*
16:37 but l them come themselves and fetch us NIG
17: 9 of Jason, and *of* the other, they l them **go**. *630*
19:38 are deputies: l them implead one another. NIG
23: 9 spoken to him, l us not fight against God. NIG
23:22 chief captain then l the young man **depart**, *630*
Ac 24:20 Or else l these same *here* say, if they have NIG
24:23 and to l *him* have liberty, and that *he* NIG
25: 5 L them therefore, said he, which among you NIG
27:15 bear up into the wind, we l *her* **drive**. *1929+5342*
27:30 when they had l **down** the boat into the sea, *5465*
27:32 off the ropes of the boat, and l her fall off. *1439*
28:18 would have l *me* **go**, because there was no *630*
Ro 1:13 to come unto you, (but was l hitherto,) *2967*
3: 4 yea, l God be true, but every man a liar; as it NIG
3: 8 we say,) L us do evil, that good may come? NIG
6:12 L not sin therefore reign in your mortal NIG
11: 9 L their table be made a snare, and a trap, NIG
11:10 L their eyes be darkened, that *they* may not NIG
12: 6 *l us prophesy* according to the proportion of NIG
12: 7 Or ministry, *l us wait* on *our* ministering: or NIG
12: 8 he that giveth, *l him do it* with simplicity; NIG
12: 9 *L* love *be* without dissimulation. Abhor *that* NIG
13: 1 L every soul be subject unto the higher NIG
13:12 l us therefore cast off the works of darkness, NIG
13:12 and l us put on the armour of light. NIG
13:13 L us walk honestly, as in the day; not in NIG
14: 3 L not him that eateth despise him that eateth NIG
14: 3 l not him which eateth not judge him that NIG
14: 5 another esteemeth every day *alike.* L every NIG
14:13 L us not therefore judge one another any NIG
14:16 L not then your good be evil spoken of: NIG
14:19 L us therefore follow *after* the *things* which NIG
15: 2 L every one of us please *his* neighbour for NIG
1Co 1:31 He that glorieth, l him glory in the Lord. NIG
3:10 But l every man take heed how he buildeth NIG
3:18 L no *man* deceive himself. If any *man* NIG
3:18 l him become a fool, that he may be wise. NIG
3:21 Therefore l no *man* glory in men. For all NIG
4: 1 L a man so account of us, as of NIG
5: 8 Therefore l us keep the feast, not with old NIG
7: 2 l every man have his own wife, and NIG
7: 2 and l every woman have her own husband. NIG
7: 3 L the husband render unto the wife due NIG
7: 9 But if they cannot contain, l them marry: NIG
7:10 L not the wife depart from *her* husband: NIG
7:11 l her remain unmarried, or be reconciled to NIG
7:11 and l not the husband put away *his* wife. NIG
7:12 to dwell with him, l him not put her away. NIG
7:13 to dwell with her, l her not leave him. NIG
7:15 But if the unbelieving depart, l him depart. NIG
7:17 Lord hath called every one, so l him walk. NIG
7:18 l him not become uncircumcised. Is any NIG
7:18 l him not be circumcised. NIG
7:20 L every man abide in the same calling NIG
7:24 Brethren, l every man, wherein he is called, NIG
7:36 and need so require, l him do what he will, NIG
7:36 what he will, he sinneth not: l them marry. NIG
10: 8 Neither l us commit fornication, as some of NIG
10: 9 Neither l us tempt Christ, as some of them NIG
10:12 Wherefore l him that thinketh he standeth NIG
10:24 L no *man* seek his own, but every man NIG
11: 6 woman be not covered, l her also be shorn: NIG
11: 6 to be shorn or shaven, l her be covered. NIG
11:28 But l a man examine himself, and so let him NIG
11:28 and so l him eat of *that* bread, and drink of NIG
11:34 And if any *man* hunger, l him eat at home; NIG
14:13 Wherefore l him that speaketh in an NIG
14:26 L all *things* be done unto edifying. NIG
14:27 *l it be* by two, or at the most *by* three, and NIG
14:27 and *that* by course; and l one interpret. NIG
14:28 l him keep silence in the church; NIG
14:28 and l him speak to himself, and to God. NIG
14:29 L the prophets speak two or three, and NIG
14:29 speak two or three, and l the other judge. NIG
14:30 that sitteth *by,* l the first hold his peace. NIG
14:34 L your women keep silence in the churches: NIG
14:35 And if they will learn any *thing,* l them ask NIG
14:37 l him acknowledge that *the things* that I NIG
14:38 if any *man* be ignorant, l him be ignorant. NIG
14:40 L all *things* be done decently and in order. NIG
15:32 l us eat and drink; for to morrow we die. NIG
16: 2 Upon the first *day* of the week l every one NIG
16:11 L no *man* therefore despise him: but NIG
16:14 L all your *things* be done with charity. NIG
16:22 l him be anathema, Maran-atha. NIG
2Co 7: 1 l us cleanse ourselves from all filthiness of NIG
9: 7 in *his* heart, *so l him give;* not grudgingly, NIG
10: 7 l him of himself think this again, that, as he NIG
10:11 L such a one think this, that, such as we are NIG
10:17 But he that glorieth, l him glory in the Lord. NIG
11:16 I say again, L no *man* think me a fool; NIG
11:33 in a basket was I l **down** by the wall, *5465*
Gal 1: 8 have preached unto you, l him be accursed. NIG
1: 9 that ye have received, l him be accursed. NIG
5:25 live in the Spirit, l us also walk in the Spirit. NIG
5:26 L us not be desirous of vain glory, NIG
6: 4 But l every man prove his own work, and NIG
6: 6 L him that is taught in the word NIG
6: 9 And l us not be weary in well doing: for in NIG
6:10 l us do good unto all *men,* especially unto NIG
6:17 From henceforth l no *man* trouble me: for I NIG
Eph 4:26 l not the sun go down upon your wrath: NIG
4:28 L him that stole steal no more: but rather let NIG
4:28 but rather l him labour, working with *his* NIG
4:29 L no corrupt communication proceed out of NIG
4:31 L all bitterness, and wrath, and anger, and NIG
5: 3 l it not be once named amongst you, NIG
5: 6 L no *man* deceive you with vain words: for NIG
5:24 *l* the wives *be* to their own husbands in NIG
5:33 Nevertheless l every one of you in particular NIG
Php 1:27 Only l your conversation be as it becometh NIG
2: 3 *L* nothing *be done* through strife or NIG
2: 3 in lowliness of mind *l* each esteem other NIG
2: 5 L this mind be in you, which *was* also in NIG
3:15 L us therefore, as many as *be* perfect, NIG
3:16 *l us* walk by the same rule, *let us* mind NIG
3:16 by the same rule, *l us* mind the same *thing.* NIG
4: 5 L your moderation be known unto all men. NIG
4: 6 supplication with thanksgiving l your NIG
Col 2:16 L no *man* therefore judge you in meat, NIG
Col 2:18 L no *man* beguile you of your reward in a NIG
3:15 And l the peace of God rule in your hearts, NIG
3:16 L the word of Christ dwell in you richly in NIG
4: 6 L your speech *be* alway with grace, NIG
1Th 5: 6 Therefore l us not sleep, as *do* others; but NIG
5: 6 as *do* others; but l us watch and be sober. NIG
5: 8 But l us, who are of the day, be sober, NIG
2Th 2: 3 L no *man* deceive you by any means: NIG
2: 7 only he who now letteth *will l,* until he be NIG
1Ti 2:11 L the woman learn in silence with all NIG
3:10 And l these also first be proved; then NIG
3:10 then l them use the office of a deacon, NIG
3:12 L the deacons be the husbands of one wife, NIG
4:12 L no *man* despise thy youth; but be thou an NIG
5: 4 l them learn first to shew piety at home, and NIG
5: 9 L not a widow be taken into the number NIG
5:16 l them relieve them, and let not the church NIG
5:16 and l not the church be charged; NIG
5:17 L the elders that rule well be counted NIG
6: 1 L as many servants as are under the yoke NIG
6: 2 l them not despise *them,* because they are NIG
6: 8 and raiment l us be therewith content. NIG
2Ti 2:19 L every one that nameth the name of Christ NIG
Tit 2:15 with all authority. L no *man* despise thee. NIG
3:14 And l ours also learn to maintain good NIG
Phm 1:20 brother, l me have joy of thee in the Lord: NIG
Heb 1: 6 And l all the angels of God worship him. NIG
2: 1 lest at any time we should l *them* slip. NIG
4: 1 L us therefore fear, lest, a promise being NIG
4:11 L us labour therefore to enter into that rest, NIG
4:14 Son of God, l us hold fast *our* profession. NIG
4:16 L us therefore come boldly unto the throne NIG
6: 1 of Christ, l us go on unto perfection; NIG
10:22 L us draw near with a true heart in full NIG
10:23 L us hold fast the profession of *our* hope NIG
10:24 And l us consider one another to provoke NIG
12: 1 l us lay aside every weight, and the sin NIG
12: 1 l us run with patience the race that is set NIG
12:13 out of the way; but l it rather be healed. NIG
12:28 l us have grace, whereby we may serve God NIG
13: 1 L brotherly love continue. NIG
13: 5 *L your* conversation *be* without NIG
13:13 L us go forth therefore unto him without NIG
13:15 l us offer the sacrifice of praise to God NIG
Jas 1: 4 But l patience have *her* perfect work, that ye NIG
1: 5 any of you lack wisdom, l him ask of God, NIG
1: 6 But l him ask in faith, nothing wavering: NIG
1: 7 For l not that man think that he shall receive NIG
1: 9 L the brother of low degree rejoice in that NIG
1:13 L no *man* say when he is tempted, I am NIG
1:19 l every man be swift to hear, slow to speak, NIG
3:13 l him shew out of a good conversation his NIG
4: 9 l your laughter be turned to mourning, and NIG
5:12 but l your yea be yea; and *your* nay, nay; NIG
5:13 l him pray. Is any merry? let him sing NIG
5:13 him pray. Is any merry? l him sing psalms. NIG
5:14 l him call for the elders of the church; and NIG
5:14 and l them pray over him, anointing him NIG
5:20 L him know, that he which converteth NIG
1Pe 3: 3 Whose adorning l it not be that outward NIG
3: 4 But *l it be* the hidden man of the heart, NIG
3:10 l him refrain his tongue from evil, and NIG
3:11 L him eschew evil, and do good; let him NIG
3:11 and do good; l him seek peace, and ensue it. NIG
4:11 *l him speak* as the oracles of God; NIG
4:11 *l him do it* as of the ability which God NIG
4:15 But l none of you suffer as a murderer, or NIG
4:16 *suffer* as a Christian, l him not be ashamed; NIG
4:16 but l him glorify God on this behalf. NIG
4:19 Wherefore l them that suffer according to NIG
1Jn 2:24 L *that* therefore abide in you, which ye have NIG
3: 7 Little children, l no *man* deceive you: NIG
3:18 l us not love in word, neither in tongue; NIG
4: 7 Beloved, l us love one another: for love is NIG
Rev 2: 7 l him hear what the Spirit saith unto NIG
2:11 l him hear what the Spirit saith unto NIG
2:17 l him hear what the Spirit saith unto NIG
2:29 l him hear what the Spirit saith unto NIG
3: 6 l him hear what the Spirit saith unto NIG
3:13 l him hear what the Spirit saith unto NIG
3:22 l him hear what the Spirit saith unto NIG
13: 9 If any *man* have an ear, l him hear. NIG
13:18 L him that hath understanding count NIG
19: 7 L us be glad and rejoice, and give honour to NIG
22:11 He that is unjust, l him be unjust still: and NIG
22:11 and he which is filthy, l him be filthy still: NIG
22:11 *he that is* righteous, l him be righteous still: NIG
22:11 and *he that is* holy, l him be holy still. NIG
22:17 And l him that heareth say, Come. And let NIG
22:17 And l him that is athirst come. NIG
22:17 l him take the water of life freely. NIG

LETTER (37) [LETTERS]

2Sa 11:14 that David wrote a l to Joab, and sent *it* by 5612
11:15 he wrote in the l, saying, Set ye Uriah in 5612
2Ki 5: 5 and I will send a l unto the king of Israel. 5612
5: 6 he brought the l to the king of Israel, 5612
5: 6 saying, Now when this l is come unto thee, 5612
5: 7 when the king of Israel had read the l, 5612
10: 2 Now as soon as this l cometh to you, 5612
10: 6 he wrote a l the second time to them, 5612
10: 7 it came to pass, when the l came to them, 5612
19:14 Hezekiah received the l of the hand of 5612
Ezr 4: 7 the writing of the l *was* written in 5406
4: 8 Shimshai the scribe wrote a l against 104
4:11 This *is* the copy of the l that they sent unto 104
4:18 The l which ye sent unto us *hath been* 5407
4:23 Now when the copy of king Artaxerxes' l 5407
5: 5 they returned answer by l concerning this 5407
5: 6 The copy of the l that Tatnai, governor on 104
5: 7 They sent a l unto him, wherein *was* written 6600
7:11 Now this *is* the copy of the l that the king 5406
Ne 2: 8 a l unto Asaph the keeper of the king's 107
6: 5 the fifth time with an open l in his hand; 107
Est 9:26 Therefore for all the words of this l, and 107

L

Est 9:29 to confirm this second l of Purim. 107
Isa 37:14 Hezekiah received the l from the hand of 5612
Jer 29: 1 Now these *are* the words of the l that 5612
29:29 Zephaniah the priest read this l in the ears 5612
Ac 23:25 And he wrote a l after this manner: *1992*
23:34 And when the governor had read *the l*, he NIG
Ro 2:27 who by the l and circumcision dost *1121*
2:29 of the heart, in the spirit, *and* not *in* the l; *1121*
7: 6 of spirit, and not *in* the oldness of the l. *1121*
2Co 3: 6 new testament; not of the l, but of the spirit: *1121*
3: 6 for the l killeth, but the spirit giveth life. *1121*
7: 8 For though I made you sorry with a l, I do *1992*
Gal 6:11 Ye see how large a l I have written unto *1121*
2Th 2: 2 by spirit, nor by word, nor by l as from us, *1992*
Heb 13:22 for I have **written a l** unto you in few *1989*

LETTERS (34) [LETTER]
1Ki 21: 8 So she wrote l in Ahab's name, and 5612
21: 8 sent the l unto the elders and to the nobles 5612
21: 9 she wrote in the l, saying, Proclaim a fast, 5612
21:11 as *it was* written in the l which she had sent 5612
2Ki 10: 1 Jehu wrote l, and sent *to* Samaria, unto 5612
20:12 sent l and a present unto Hezekiah: 5612
2Ch 30: 1 and wrote l also to Ephraim and Manasseh, 107
30: 6 So the posts went with the l from the king 107
32:17 He wrote also l to rail on the LORD God 5612
Ne 2: 7 let l be given me to the governors beyond 107
2: 9 beyond the river, and gave them the king's l. 107
6:17 the nobles of Judah sent many l unto Tobiah, 107
6:17 and *the l* of Tobiah came unto them. NIH
6:19 to him. *And* Tobiah sent l to put me in fear. 107
Est 1:22 For he sent l into all the king's provinces, 5612
3:13 the l were sent by posts into all the king's 5612
8: 5 let it be written to reverse the l devised by 5612
8:10 sent l by posts on horseback, *and* riders on 5612
9:20 sent l unto all the Jews that *were* in all 5612
9:25 he commanded by l *that* his wicked device, 5612
9:30 he sent the l unto all the Jews, to 5612
Isa 39: 1 sent l and a present to Hezekiah: 5612
Jer 29:25 Because thou hast sent l in thy name unto 5612
Lk 23:38 also was written over him in l of Greek, *1121*
Jn 7:15 saying, How knoweth this *man* l, *1121*
Ac 9: 2 And desired of him l to Damascus to *1992*
15:23 And they wrote *l* by them after this manner; NIG
22: 5 from whom also I received l unto *1992*
28:21 We neither received l out of Judea *1121*
1Co 16: 3 whomsoever you shall approve by *your* l, *1992*
2Co 3: 1 to you, or *l* of commendation from you? NIG
10: 9 may not seem as if *I* would terrify you by l. *1992*
10:10 For *his* l, say they, *are* weighty and *1992*
10:11 such as we are in word by l when we are *1992*

L

LETTEST (3) [LET]
Job 15:13 and l *such* words go out of thy mouth? NIH
41: 1 his tongue with a cord *which* thou **l down**? 8257
Lk 2:29 now l thou thy servant depart in peace, NIG

LETTETH (3) [LET]
2Ki 10:24 *he that l him go*, his life *shall be* for the life NIH
Pr 17:14 The beginning of strife *is as* when one **l out** 6362
2Th 2: 7 only he who now l *will let*, until he be *2722*

LETTING (1) [LET]
Ex 8:29 l the people **go** to sacrifice to the LORD. 7971

LETUSHIM (1)
Ge 25: 3 were Asshurim, and L, and Leummim. 3912

LETUSHITES See LETUSHIM

LEUMMIM (1)
Ge 25: 3 were Asshurim, and Letushim, and L. 3817

LEUMMITES See LEUMMIM

LEVI (72) [LEVITE, LEVITES, LEVITICAL]
Ge 29:34 therefore was his name called L. 3878
34:25 Simeon and L, Dinah's brethren, took each 3878
34:30 Jacob said to Simeon and L, Ye have 3878
35:23 L, and Judah, and Issachar, and Zebulun: 3878
46:11 the sons of L; Gershon, Kohath, and 3878
49: 5 Simeon and L *are* brethren; instruments of 3878
Ex 1: 2 Reuben, Simeon, L, and Judah, 3878
2: 1 there went a man of the house of L, and 3878
2: 1 of Levi, and took *to wife* a daughter of L. 3878
6:16 these *are* the names of the sons of L 3878
6:16 the years of the life of L *were* an hundred 3878
6:19 these *are* the families of L according to 3878
32:26 all the sons of L gathered themselves 3878
32:28 the children of L did according to the word 3878
Nu 1:49 Only thou shalt not number the tribe of L, 3878
3: 6 Bring the tribe of L near, and present them 3878
3:15 Number the children of L after the house of 3878
3:17 these were the sons of L by their names; 3878
4: 2 sons of Kohath from among the sons of L, 3878
16: 1 the son of L, and Dathan and Abiram, 3878
16: 7 *ye take* too much upon you, ye sons of L. 3878
16: 8 unto Korah, Hear, I pray you, ye sons of L: 3878
16:10 and all thy brethren the sons of L with thee: 3878
17: 3 write Aaron's name upon the rod of L: 3878
17: 8 the rod of Aaron for the house of L was 3878
18: 2 thy brethren also *of* the tribe of L, the tribe 3878
18:21 I have given the children of L all the tenth 3878
26:59 the daughter of L, whom *her mother* bare to 3878
26:59 whom *her mother* bare to L in Egypt: 3878
Dt 10: 8 time the LORD separated the tribe of L, 3878
10: 9 Wherefore L hath no part nor inheritance 3878
18: 1 priests the Levites, *and* all the tribe of L, 3878
21: 5 the priests the sons of L shall come near; 3878
27:12 and L, and Judah, and Issachar, and Joseph, 3878
31: 9 delivered it unto the priests the sons of L, 3878
33: 8 of L he said, *Let* thy Thummim and 3878
Jos 13:14 Only unto the tribe of L he gave none 3878
13:33 unto the tribe of L Moses gave not *any* 3878
Jos 21:10 *who were* of the children of L, had: 3878
1Ki 12:31 which were not of the sons of L. 3878
1Ch 2: 1 Reuben, Simeon, L, and Judah, Issachar, 3878
6: 1 The sons of L; Gershon, Kohath, and 3878
6:16 The sons of L; Gershom, Kohath, and 3878
6:38 of Kohath, the son of L, the son of Israel. 3878
6:43 the son of Gershom, the son of L. 3878
6:47 of Mushi, the son of Merari, the son of L. 3878
9:18 in the companies of the children of L. 3878
12:26 Of the children of L four thousand and 3878
21: 6 L and Benjamin counted he not among 3878
23: 6 them *into* courses among the sons of L, 3878
23:14 his sons were named of the tribe of L. 3878
23:24 These *were* the sons of L after the house of 3878
24:20 the rest of the sons of L *were these:* Of 3878
Ezr 8:15 and found there none of the sons of L. 3878
8:18 of Mahli, the son of L, the son of Israel; 3878
Ne 10:39 the children of L shall bring the offering of 3878
12:23 The sons of L, the chief of the fathers, 3878
Ps 135:20 Bless the LORD, O house of L: ye that 3878
Eze 40:46 *are* the sons of Zadok among the sons of L, 3878
48:31 one gate of Judah, one gate of L. 3878
Zec 12:13 The family of the house of L apart, 3878
Mal 2: 4 that my covenant might be with L, saith 3878
2: 8 ye have corrupted the covenant of L, 3878
3: 3 he shall purify the sons of L, and 3878
Mk 2:14 he saw L the *son* of Alpheus sitting at *3018*
Lk 3:24 which was *the son* of L, which was *the son* *3017*
3:29 *the son* of Matthat, which was *the son* of L, *3017*
5:27 and saw a publican, named L, sitting at *3018*
5:29 And L made him a great feast in his own *3018*
Heb 7: 5 And verily they that are of the sons of L *3017*
7: 9 And as *I* may so say, L also, who receiveth *3017*
Rev 7: 7 Of the tribe of L *were* sealed twelve *3017*

LEVIATHAN (5)
Job 41: 1 Canst thou draw out l with a hook? or 3882
Ps 74:14 Thou brakest the heads of l in pieces, *and* 3882
104:26 *there is* that l, *whom* thou hast made to play 3882
Isa 27: 1 strong sword shall punish l the piercing 3882
27: 1 even l *that* crooked serpent; 3882

LEVITE (28) [LEVI]
Ex 4:14 and he said, Is not Aaron the L thy brother? 3881
Dt 12:12 and the L that *is* within your gates; 3881
12:18 and the L that *is* within thy gates: 3881
12:19 the L as long as thou livest upon the earth. 3881
14:27 the L that *is* within thy gates; thou shalt not 3881
14:29 the L, (because he hath no part nor 3881
16:11 the L that *is* within thy gates, and 3881
16:14 the L, the stranger, and the fatherless, and 3881
18: 6 if a L come from any of thy gates out of all 3881
26:11 the L, and the stranger that *is* among you. 3881
26:12 hast given *it* unto the L, the stranger, 3881
26:13 also have given them unto the L, and 3881
Jdg 17: 7 who *was* a L, and he sojourned there. 3881
17: 9 I *am* a L of Beth-lehem-judah, and I go to 3881
17:10 and thy victuals. So the L went *in*. 3881
17:11 the L was content to dwell with the man; 3881
17:12 Micah consecrated the L; and the young 3881
17:13 do me good, seeing I have a L to *my* priest. 3881
18: 3 knew the voice of the young man the L: 3881
18:15 came to the house of the young man the L, 3881
19: 1 that there was a certain L sojourning on 3881
20: 4 the L, the husband of the woman that was 3881
2Ch 20:14 son of Mattaniah, a L of the sons of Asaph, 3881
31:12 over which Cononiah the L *was* ruler, and 3881
31:14 Kore the son of Imnah the L, the porter 3881
Ezr 10:15 and Shabbethai the L helped them. 3881
Lk 10:32 And likewise a L, when he was at *3019*
Ac 4:36 a L, *and* of the country of Cyprus, *3019*

LEVITES (265) [LEVI]
Ex 6:25 these *are* the heads of the fathers of the L 3881
38:21 *for* the service of the L, by the hand of 3881
Lev 25:32 Notwithstanding the cities of the L, *and* 3881
25:32 may the L redeem at any time. 3881
25:33 if a man purchase of the L, then the house 3881
25:33 for the houses of the cities of the L *are* their 3881
Nu 1:47 the L after the tribe of their fathers were 3881
1:50 thou shalt appoint the L over the tabernacle 3881
1:51 setteth forward, the L shall take it down: 3881
1:51 is to be pitched, the L shall set it up: 3881
1:53 the L shall pitch round about the tabernacle 3881
1:53 the L shall keep the charge of 3881
2:17 the camp of the L in the midst of the camp: 3881
2:33 the L were not numbered among 3881
3: 9 thou shalt give the L unto Aaron and to his 3881
3:12 I have taken the L from among the children 3881
3:12 of Israel: therefore the L shall be mine; 3881
3:20 These *are* the families of the L according to 3881
3:32 priest *shall be* chief over the chief of the L, 3881
3:39 All that were numbered of the L, 3881
3:41 thou shalt take the L for me (I *am* 3881
3:41 the cattle of the L instead of all 3881
3:45 Take the L instead of all the firstborn 3881
3:45 the cattle of the L instead of their cattle; 3881
3:45 of their cattle; and the L shall be mine: 3881
3:46 of Israel, which are more than the L; 3881
3:49 above them that were redeemed by the L: 3881
4:18 of the Kohathites from among the L: 3881
4:46 All those that were numbered of the L, 3881
7: 5 thou shalt give them unto the L, to every 3881
7: 6 and the oxen, and gave them unto the L. 3881
8: 6 Take the L from among the children of 3881
8: 9 thou shalt bring the L before the tabernacle 3881
8:10 thou shalt bring the L before the LORD: 3881
8:10 of Israel shall put their hands upon the L: 3881
8:11 Aaron shall offer the L before the LORD 3881
8:12 the L shall lay their hands upon the heads 3881
8:12 to make an atonement for the L. 3881
8:13 thou shalt set the L before Aaron, and 3881
8:14 Thus shalt thou separate the L from among 3881
8:14 children of Israel: and the L shall be mine. 3881
Nu 8:15 after that shall the L go in to do the service 3881
8:18 I have taken the L for all the firstborn of 3881
8:19 I have given the L *as* a gift to Aaron and 3881
8:20 did to the L according unto all that 3881
8:20 commanded Moses concerning the L, 3881
8:21 the L were purified, and they washed their 3881
8:22 after that went the L in to do their service 3881
8:22 had commanded Moses concerning the L, 3881
8:24 This *is it* that *belongeth* unto the L: 3881
8:26 Thus shalt thou do unto the L touching 3881
18: 6 I have taken your brethren the L from 3881
18:23 the L shall do the service of the tabernacle 3881
18:24 I have given to the L to inherit: 3881
18:26 Thus speak unto the L, and say unto them, 3881
18:30 it shall be counted unto the L as 3881
26:57 these *are* they that were numbered of the L 3881
26:58 These *are* the families of the L: the family 3881
31:30 *of* beasts, and give them unto the L, 3881
31:47 and of beast, and gave them unto the L, 3881
35: 2 that they give unto the L of the inheritance 3881
35: 2 ye shall give *also* unto the L suburbs for 3881
35: 4 of the cities, which ye shall give unto the L, 3881
35: 6 the L *there shall be* six cities for refuge, 3881
35: 7 *So* all the cities which ye shall give to the L 3881
35: 8 every one shall give of his cities unto the L 3881
Dt 17: 9 thou shalt come unto the priests the L, and 3881
17:18 out of *that which is* before the priests the L: 3881
18: 1 The priests the L, *and* all the tribe of Levi, 3881
18: 7 as all his brethren the L *do*, which stand 3881
24: 8 do according to all that the priests the L 3881
27: 9 and the priests the L spake unto all Israel, 3881
27:14 the L shall speak, and say unto all the men 3881
31:25 That Moses commanded the L, which bare 3881
Jos 3: 3 the priests the L bearing it, then ye shall 3881
8:33 and on that side before the priests the L, 3881
14: 3 unto the L he gave none inheritance among 3881
14: 4 they gave no part unto the L in the land, 3881
18: 7 the L have no part among you; for 3881
21: 1 came near the heads of the fathers of the L 3881
21: 3 the children of Israel gave unto the L out of 3881
21: 4 of Aaron the priest, *which were* of the L, 3881
21: 8 the children of Israel gave by lot unto the L 3881
21:20 the L which remained of the children of 3881
21:27 of Gershon, of the families of the L, 3881
21:34 the rest of the L, out of the tribe of 3881
21:40 were remaining of the families of the L, 3881
21:41 All the cities of the L within the possession 3881
1Sa 6:15 the L took down the ark of the LORD, 3881
2Sa 15:24 lo Zadok also, and all the L *were* with him, 3881
1Ki 8: 4 those did the priests and the L bring up. 3881
1Ch 6:19 these *are* the families of the L according to 3881
6:48 Their brethren also the L *were* appointed 3881
6:64 the children of Israel gave to the L *these* 3881
9: 2 the priests, L, and the Nethinims. 3881
9:14 of the L; Shemaiah the son of Hasshub, 3881
9:26 For these L, the four chief porters, *were* in 3881
9:31 Mattithiah, *one* of the L, who *was* 3881
9:33 *are* the singers, chief of the fathers of the L, 3881
9:34 These chief fathers of the L *were* chief 3881
13: 2 and L *which are* in their cities *and* suburbs, 3881
15: 2 ought to carry the ark of God but the L: 3881
15: 4 the children of Aaron, and the L: 3881
15:11 for the L, for Uriel, Asaiah, and Joel, 3881
15:12 Ye *are* the chief of the fathers of the L: 3881
15:14 the L sanctified themselves to bring up 3881
15:15 the children of the L bare the ark of God 3881
15:16 David spake to the chief of the L to appoint 3881
15:17 So the L appointed Heman the son of Joel; 3881
15:22 chief of the L, *was* for song: 3881
15:26 when God helped the L that bare the ark of 3881
15:27 all the L that bare the ark, and the singers, 3881
16: 4 he appointed *certain* of the L to minister 3881
23: 2 princes of Israel, with the priests and the L. 3881
23: 3 Now the L were numbered from the age of 3881
23:26 also unto the L; *they* shall no *more* carry 3881
23:27 the L *were* numbered from twenty 1121+3878
24: 6 *one* of the L, wrote them before the king, 3881
24: 6 the chief of the fathers of the priests and L: 3881
24:30 These *were* the sons of the L after 3881
24:31 the chief of the fathers of the priests and L, 3881
26:17 Eastward *were* six L, northward four a day, 3881
26:20 *of* the L, Ahijah *was* over the treasures of 3881
27:17 Of the L, Hashabiah the son of Kemuel: 3881
28:13 for the courses of the priests and the L, 3881
28:21 the courses of the priests and the L, 3881
2Ch 5: 4 of Israel came; and the L took up the ark. 3881
5: 5 these did the priests *and* the L bring up. 3881
5:12 Also the L *which were* the singers, all of 3881
7: 6 the L also with instruments of musick of 3881
8:14 the L to their charges, to praise and 3881
8:15 the priests and L concerning any matter, 3881
11:13 the L that *were* in all Israel resorted to him 3881
11:14 For the L left their suburbs and 3881
13: 9 the L, and have made you priests after 3881
13:10 and the L *wait* upon *their* business: 3881
17: 8 with them *he sent* L, *even* Shemaiah, and 3881
17: 8 and Tobijah, and Tob-adonijah, L; 3881
19: 8 in Jerusalem did Jehoshaphat set of the L, 3881
19:11 also the L *shall be* officers before you. 3881
20:19 the L, of the children of the Kohathites, 3881
23: 2 gathered the L out of all the cities of Judah, 3881
23: 4 of the priests and of the L, *shall be* porters 3881
23: 6 the priests, and they that minister of the L; 3881
23: 7 the L shall compass the king round about, 3881
23: 8 So the L and all Judah did according to all 3881
23:18 LORD by the hand of the priests the L, 3881
24: 5 he gathered together the priests and the L, 3881
24: 5 the matter. Howbeit the L hastened *it* not. 3881
24: 6 Why hast thou not required of the L to 3881
24:11 unto the king's office by the hand of the L, 3881
29: 4 he brought in the priests and the L, and 3881
29: 5 said unto them, Hear me, ye L, 3881
29:12 the L arose, Mahath the son of Amasai, 3881
29:16 the L took *it*, to carry *it* out abroad into 3881
29:25 he set the L *in* the house of the LORD 3881

2Ch 29:26 the **L** stood with the instruments of David, 3881
29:30 the princes commanded the **L** to *sing* praise 3881
29:34 wherefore their brethren the **L** did help 3881
29:34 for the **L** *were* more upright in heart to 3881
30:15 the priests and the **L** were ashamed, and 3881
30:16 *which they received* of the hand of the **L**. 3881
30:17 the **L** had the charge of the killing of 3881
30:21 the **L** and the priests praised the LORD 3881
30:22 Hezekiah spake comfortably unto all the **L** 3881
30:25 with the priests and the **L**, and all 3881
30:27 the priests the **L** arose and blessed 3881
31: 2 of the priests and the **L** after their courses, 3881
31: 2 the priests and **L** for burnt offerings and 3881
31: 4 to give the portion of the priests and the **L**, 3881
31: 9 the priests and the **L** concerning the heaps. 3881
31:17 the **L** from twenty years old and upward, 3881
31:19 reckoned by genealogies among the **L**. 3881
34: 9 which the **L** that kept the doors had 3881
34:12 of them *were* Jahath and Obadiah, the **L**, 3881
34:12 *other of* the **L**, all that could skill of 3881
34:13 of the **L** *there were* scribes, and officers, 3881
34:30 the **L**, and all the people, great and small: 3881
35: 3 said unto the **L** that taught all Israel, 3881
35: 5 *after* the division of the families of the **L**. 3881
35: 8 unto the people, to the priests, and to the **L**: 3881
35: 9 and Jeiel and Jozabad, chief of the **L**, 3881
35: 9 gave unto the **L** for passover *offerings* five 3881
35:10 in their place, and the **L** in their courses, 3881
35:11 from their hands, and the **L** flayed *them*. 3881
35:14 therefore the **L** prepared for themselves, 3881
35:15 for their brethren the **L** prepared for them. 3881
35:18 the **L**, and all Judah and Israel that were 3881
Ezr 1: 5 and Benjamin, and the priests, and the **L**, 3881
2:40 The **L**: the children of Jeshua and Kadmiel, 3881
2:70 the **L**, and *some* of the people, and 3881
3: 8 of their brethren the priests and the **L**, 3881
3: 8 appointed the **L** from twenty years old and 3881
3: 9 *with* their sons and their brethren the **L**. 3881
3:10 the **L** the sons of Asaph with cymbals, 3881
3:12 of the priests and **L** and chief of the fathers, 3881
6:16 the **L**, and the rest of the children of 3879
6:18 the **L** in their courses, for the service of 3879
6:20 the priests and the **L** were purified together, 3881
7: 7 the **L**, and the singers, and the porters, and 3881
7:13 and *of* his priests and **L**, in my realm, 3879
7:24 that *touching* any of the priests and **L**, 3879
8:20 had appointed for the service of the **L**, 3881
8:29 before the chief of the priests and the **L**, 3881
8:30 and the **L** the weight of the silver, 3881
8:33 and Noadiah the son of Binnui, **L**; 3881
9: 1 people of Israel, and the priests, and the **L**, 3881
10: 5 made the chief priests, the **L**, and all Israel, 3881
10:23 Also of the **L**; Jozabad, and Shimei, and 3881
Ne 3:17 After him repaired the **L**, Rehum the son of 3881
7: 1 and the singers and the **L** were appointed, 3881
7:43 The **L**: the children of Jeshua, of Kadmiel, 3881
7:73 the **L**, and the porters, and the singers, and 3881
8: 7 Jozabad, Hanan, Pelaiah, and the **L**, 3881
8: 9 the **L** that taught the people, said unto all 3881
8:11 So the **L** stilled all the people, saying, 3881
8:13 the priests, and the **L**, unto Ezra the scribe, 3881
9: 4 stood up upon the stairs of the **L**, Jeshua, 3881
9: 5 the **L**, Jeshua and Kadmiel, Bani, 3881
9:38 write *it*; and our princes, **L**, *and* priests, 3881
10: 9 the **L**: both Jeshua the son of Azaniah, 3881
10:28 the priests, the **L**, the porters, the singers, 3881
10:34 the **L**, and the people, for the wood 3881
10:37 the tithes of our ground unto the **L**, that 3881
10:37 that the same **L** *might* have the tithes in all 3881
10:38 priest the son of Aaron shall be with the **L**, 3881
10:38 be with the Levites, when the **L** take tithes: 3881
10:38 the **L** shall bring up the tithe of the tithes 3881
11: 3 the **L**, and the Nethinims, and the children 3881
11:15 Also of the **L**: Shemaiah the son of Hashub, 3881
11:16 and Jozabad, of the chief of the **L**, 3881
11:18 All the **L** in the holy city *were* two hundred 3881
11:20 residue of Israel, of the priests, *and* the **L**, 3881
11:22 The overseer also of the **L** at Jerusalem *was* 3881
11:36 of the **L** *were* divisions *in* Judah, *and* 3881
12: 1 the **L** that went up with Zerubbabel the son 3881
12: 8 Moreover the **L**: Jeshua, Binnui, Kadmiel, 3881
12:22 The **L** in the days of Eliashib, Joiada, and 3881
12:24 the chief of the **L**: Hashabiah, Sherebiah, 3881
12:27 they sought the **L** out of all their places, 3881
12:30 the priests and the **L** purified themselves, 3881
12:44 portions of the law for the priests and **L**: 3881
12:44 for the priests and for the **L** that waited. 3881
12:47 they sanctified *holy things* unto the **L**; and 3881
12:47 the **L** sanctified *them* unto the children of 3881
13: 5 was commanded *to be given* to the **L**, 3881
13:10 I perceived that the portions of the **L** had 3881
13:10 Levites had not been given *them*: for the **L** 3881
13:13 Zadok the scribe, and of the **L**, Pedaiah: 3881
13:22 I commanded the **L** that they should 3881
13:29 covenant of the priesthood, and of the **L**. 3881
13:30 the wards of the priests and the **L**, 3881
Isa 66:21 will also take of them for priests *and* for **L**, 3881
Jer 33:18 Neither shall the priests the **L** want a man 3881
33:21 and with the **L** the priests, my ministers. 3881
33:22 and the **L** that minister unto me. 3881
Eze 43:19 thou shalt give to the priests the **L** that *be* 3881
44:10 the **L** that are gone away far from me, 3881
44:15 the priests the **L**, the sons of Zadok, 3881
45: 5 shall also the **L**, the ministers of the house, 3881
48:11 of Israel went astray, as the **L** went astray. 3881
48:12 *a thing* most holy by the border of the **L**. 3881
48:13 the **L** *shall have* five and twenty thousand 3881
48:22 Moreover from the possession of the **L**, *and* 3881
Jn 1:19 and **L** from Jerusalem to ask him, *3019*

LEVITICAL (1) [LEVI]
Heb 7:11 perfection were by the **L** priesthood, *3020*

LEVY (6)
Nu 31:28 **l** a tribute unto the LORD of the men of 7311
1Ki 5:13 king Solomon raised a **l** out of all Israel; 4522
5:13 and the **l** was thirty thousand men. 4522
5:14 at home: and Adoniram *was* over the **l**. 4522
9:15 this *is* the reason of the **l** which king 4522
9:21 **upon** those did Solomon **l** a tribute of 5927

LEWD (3) [LEWDLY, LEWDNESS]
Eze 16:27 which are ashamed of thy **l** way. 2154
23:44 and unto Aholibah, the **l** women. 2154
Ac 17: 5 took unto *them* certain **l** fellows of *4190*

LEWDLY (1) [LEWD]
Eze 22:11 hath **l** defiled his daughter in law; 2154+871.1

LEWDNESS (17) [LEWD]
Jdg 20: 6 for they have committed **l** and folly in 2154
Jer 11:15 *seeing* she hath wrought **l** *with* many, and 4209
13:27 the **l** of thy whoredom, *and* 2154
Eze 16:43 thou shalt not commit *this* **l** above all thine 2154
16:58 Thou hast borne thy **l** and thine 2154
22: 9 in the midst of thee they commit **l**. 2154
23:21 Thus thou calledst to remembrance the **l** of 2154
23:27 Thus will I make thy **l** to cease from thee, 2154
23:29 both thy **l** and thy whoredoms. 2154
23:35 therefore bear thou also thy **l** and thy 2154
23:48 Thus will I cause **l** to cease out of the land, 2154
23:48 may be taught not to do after your **l**. 2154
23:49 they shall recompense your **l** upon you, 2154
24:13 In thy filthiness *is* **l**: because I have purged 2154
Hos 2:10 now will I discover her **l** in the sight of her 5040
6: 9 *in* the way by consent: for they commit **l**. 2154
Ac 18:14 If it were a matter of wrong or wicked **l**, *4467*

LIAR (13) [LIE]
Job 24:25 who will **make** me **a l**, and make my 3576
Pr 17: 4 *and* a **l** giveth ear to a naughty tongue. 8267
19:22 and a poor *man is* better than a **l**. 376+3577
30: 6 lest he reprove thee, and thou be **found a l**. 3576
Jer 15:18 wilt thou be altogether unto me as a **l**, *and* 391
Jn 8:44 of his own: for he is a **l**, and the father of it. *5583*
8:55 I know him not, I shall be a **l** like unto you: *5583*
Ro 3: 4 yea, let God be true, but every man a **l**; as it *5583*
1Jn 1:10 we make him a **l**, and his word is not in us. *5583*
2: 4 is a **l**, and the truth is not in him. *5583*
2:22 Who is a **l** but he that denieth that Jesus is *5583*
4:20 I love God, and hateth his brother, he is a **l**: *5583*
5:10 that believeth not God hath made him a **l**; *5583*

LIARS (8) [LIE]
Dt 33:29 thine enemies shall be **found l** unto thee; 3584
Ps 116:11 I said in my haste, All men *are* **l**. 3576
Isa 44:25 That frustrateth the tokens of the **l**, and 907
Jer 50:36 A sword *is* upon the **l**; and they shall dote: 907
1Ti 1:10 for menstealers, for **l**, for perjured *persons*, *5583*
Tit 1:12 said, The Cretians *are* alway **l**, evil beasts, *5583*
Rev 2: 2 and are not, and hast found them **l**: *5571*
21: 8 and sorcerers, and idolaters, and all **l**, *5571*

LIBERAL (6) [LIBERALITY, LIBERALLY, LIBERTINES]
Pr 11:25 The **l** soul shall be made fat: and he that 1293
Isa 32: 5 The vile person shall be no more called **l**, 5081
32: 8 the **l** deviseth liberal *things*; and by liberal 5081
32: 8 the liberal deviseth **l** *things*; and by liberal 5082
32: 8 and by **l** *things* shall he stand. 5082
2Co 9:13 and *for your* **l** distribution unto them, and *572*

LIBERALITY (2) [LIBERAL]
1Co 16: 3 them will I send to bring your **l** unto *5485*
2Co 8: 2 poverty abounded unto the riches of their **l**. *572*

LIBERALLY (2) [LIBERAL]
Dt 15:14 Thou shalt **furnish** him **l** out of thy 6059+6059
Jas 1: 5 that giveth to all *men* **l**, and upbraideth not; *574*

LIBERTINES (1) [LIBERAL]
Ac 6: 9 which is called *the synagogue* of the **L**, and *3032*

LIBERTY (27)
Lev 25:10 proclaim **l** throughout *all* the land unto all 1865
Ps 119:45 And I will walk at **l**: for I seek thy precepts. 7342
Isa 61: 1 to proclaim **l** to the captives, and 1865
Jer 34: 8 *were* at Jerusalem, to proclaim **l** unto them; 1865
34:15 in proclaiming **l** every man to his 1865
34:16 whom ye had set at **l** at their pleasure, 2670
34:17 in proclaiming **l**, every one to his brother, 1865
34:17 behold, I proclaim a **l** for you, saith 1865
Eze 46:17 then it shall be his to the year of **l**; 1865
Lk 4:18 to the blind, to set at **l** *them that are* bruised, *859*
Ac 24:23 and to let *him* have **l**, and *that he* should *425*
26:32 This man might have been **set at l**, *630*
27: 3 **gave** *him* **l** to go unto *his* friends to refresh *2010*
Ro 8:21 into the glorious **l** of the children of God. *1657*
1Co 7:39 she is at **l** to be married to whom she will; *1658*
8: 9 But take heed lest by any means this **l** of *1849*
10:29 for why is my **l** judged of another *man's* *1657*
2Co 3:17 where the Spirit of the Lord *is*, there *is* **l**. *1657*
Gal 2: 4 who came in privily to spy out our **l** which *1657*
5: 1 in the **l** wherewith Christ hath made us free, *1657*
5:13 For, brethren, ye have been called unto **l**; *1657*
5:13 only *use* not **l** for an occasion to the flesh, *1657*
Heb 13:23 Know ye that *our* brother Timothy is **set at l**; *630*
Jas 1:25 But whoso looketh into the perfect law of **l**, *1657*
2:12 as they that shall be judged by the law of **l**. *1657*
1Pe 2:16 not using *your* **l** for a cloke of *1657*
2Pe 2:19 While they promise them **l**, they themselves *1657*

LIBNAH (18)
Nu 33:20 from Rimmon-parez, and pitched in **L**. 3841
33:21 they removed from **L**, and pitched at 3841
Jos 10:29 *unto* **L**, and fought against Libnah: 3841
10:29 *unto* Libnah, and fought against **L**: 3841
10:31 Joshua passed from **L**, and all Israel with 3841
10:32 according to all that he had done to **L**. 3841
10:39 as he had done also to **L**, and to her king. 3841
Jos 12:15 The king of **L**, one; the king of Adullam, 3841
15:42 **L**, and Ether, and Ashan, 3841
21:13 for the slayer; and **L** with her suburbs, 3841
2Ki 8:22 this day. Then **L** revolted at the same time. 3841
19: 8 the king of Assyria warring against **L**: 3841
23:31 the daughter of Jeremiah of **L**. 3841
24:18 the daughter of Jeremiah of **L**. 3841
1Ch 6:57 **L** with her suburbs, and Jattir, and 3841
2Ch 21:10 The same time also did **L** revolt from under 3841
Isa 37: 8 the king of Assyria warring against **L**: 3841
Jer 52: 1 Hamutal the daughter of Jeremiah of **L**. 3841

LIBNI (5) [LIBNITES]
Ex 6:17 **L**, and Shimi, according to their families. 3845
Nu 3:18 Gershon by their families; **L**, and Shimei. 3845
1Ch 6:17 of the sons of Gershom; **L**, and Shimei. 3845
6:20 **L** his son, Jahath his son, Zimmah his son, 3845
6:29 Mahli, **L** his son, Shimei his son, Uzza his 3845

LIBNITES (2) [LIBNI]
Nu 3:21 Of Gershon *was* the family of the **L**, and 3846
26:58 the family of the **L**, the family of 3846

LIBYA (3) [LIBYANS]
Eze 30: 5 **L**, and Lydia, and all the mingled people, 6316
38: 5 Persia, Ethiopia, and **L** with them; all of 6316
Ac 2:10 and in the parts of **L** about Cyrene, and *3033*

LIBYANS (2) [LIBYA]
Jer 46: 9 the Ethiopians and the **L**, that handle 6316
Da 11:43 the **L** and the Ethiopians *shall be* at his 3864

LICE (6)
Ex 8:16 that it may become **l** throughout all the land 3654
8:17 and it became **l** in man, and in beast; 3654
8:17 all the dust of the land became **l** throughout 3654
8:18 so with their enchantments to bring forth **l**, 3654
8:18 so there were **l** upon man, and upon beast. 3654
Ps 105:31 divers sorts of *flies*, *and* **l** in all their coasts. 3654

LICENCE (2)
Ac 21:40 And when he had **given** *him* **l**, Paul stood *2010*
25:16 have **l** to answer for himself concerning *5117*

LICK (5) [LICKED, LICKETH]
Nu 22: 4 Now shall *this* company **l up** all *that are* 3897
1Ki 21:19 the blood of Naboth shall dogs **l** thy blood, 3952
Ps 72: 9 before him; and his enemies shall **l** the dust. 3897
Isa 49:23 the earth, and **l up** the dust of thy feet; 3897
Mic 7:17 They shall **l** the dust like a serpent, 3897

LICKED (4) [LICK]
1Ki 18:38 and **l up** the water that *was* in the trench. 3897
21:19 In the place where dogs **l** the blood of 3952
22:38 the dogs **l up** his blood; and they washed 3952
Lk 16:21 moreover the dogs came and **l** his sores. *621*

LICKETH (1) [LICK]
Nu 22: 4 as the ox **l up** the grass of the field. 3897

LID (1)
2Ki 12: 9 bored a hole in the **l** of it, and set it beside 1817

LIE (155) [LAIN, LIAR, LIARS, LIED, LIEN, LIERS, LIES, LIEST, LIETH, LYING]
Ge 19:32 father drink wine, and we will **l** with him, 7901
19:34 go thou in, *and* **l** with him, that we may 7901
30:15 Therefore he shall **l** with thee to night for 7901
39: 7 eyes upon Joseph; and she said, **L** with me. 7901
39:10 not unto her, to **l** by her, *or* to be with her. 7901
39:12 him by his garment, saying, **L** with me: 7901
39:14 he came in unto me to **l** with me, and 7901
47:30 I will **l** with my fathers, and thou shalt 7901
Ex 21:13 if a man **l** not **in wait**, but God deliver *him* 6658
22:16 **l** with her, he shall surely endow her to be 7901
23:11 seventh *year* thou shalt let it rest and **l still**; 5203
Lev 6: 2 **l** unto his neighbour in that which was 3584
15:18 The woman also with whom man shall **l** 7901
15:24 if any man **l with** her **at all**, 854+7901+7901
18:20 **l carnally** with thy 2233+5414+7903+3807.1
18:22 Thou shalt not **l** with mankind, as with 7901
18:23 Neither shalt thou **l** with any beast to 5414+7903
18:23 stand before a beast to **l down** thereto: 7250
19:11 deal falsely, neither **l** one to another. 8266
20:12 if a man **l** with his daughter in law, both of 7901
20:13 If a man also **l** with mankind, as he lieth 7901
20:15 if a man **l with** a beast, he shall 5414+7903
20:16 **l down** thereto, thou shalt kill the woman 7250
20:18 if a man shall **l** with a woman having her 7901
20:20 if a man shall **l** with his uncle's wife, 7901
26: 6 ye shall **l down**, and none shall make *you* 7901
Nu 5:13 a man **l** with her carnally, and it be hid 7901
10: 5 the camps that **l** on the east parts shall go 2583
10: 6 the camps that **l** on the south side shall take 2583
23:19 God *is* not a man, that he should **l**; 3576
23:24 he shall not **l down** until he eat *of* the prey, 7901
Dt 19:11 **l in wait** for him, and rise up against him, 693
22:23 a man find her in the city, and **l** with her; 7901
22:25 and the man force her, and **l** with her: 7901
22:28 on her, and **l** with her, and they be found; 7901
25: 2 that the judge shall **cause** him **to l down**, 5307
28:30 a wife, and another man shall **l with** her: 7901
29:20 are written in this book shall **l** upon him, 7257
Jos 8: 4 Behold, ye shall **l in wait against** the city, 693
8: 9 they went to **l in ambush**, and 3993
8:12 set them to **l in ambush** between Beth-el 693
Jdg 9:32 that *is* with thee, *and* **l in wait** in the field: 693
19:20 howsoever *let* all thy wants *l* upon me; NIH
21:20 Go and **l in wait** in the vineyards; 693
Ru 3: 4 thou shalt mark the place where he shall **l**, 7901
3: 7 he went to **l down** at the end of the heap *of* 7901
3:13 LORD liveth: **l down** until the morning. 7901
1Sa 3: 5 he said, I called not; **l down** again. And he 7901

L

1Sa 3: 6 I called not, my son; **l down** again. 7901
3: 9 Eli said unto Samuel, Go, **l down**: 7901
15:29 also the Strength of Israel will not l nor 8266
22: 8 against me, to **l in wait**, as at this day? 693
22:13 rise against me, to **l in wait**, as at this day? 693
2Sa 11:11 to eat and to drink, and to l with my wife? 7901
11:13 at even he went out to l on his bed with 7901
12:11 he shall l with thy wives in the sight of this 7901
13:11 said unto her, Come l with me, my sister. 7901
1Ki 1: 2 her cherish him, and let her l in thy bosom, 7901
2Ki 4:16 man of God, do not l unto thine handmaid. 3576
Job 6:28 upon me; for *it is* evident unto you if I l. 3576
7: 4 When I **l down**, I say, When shall I arise, 7901
11:19 Also thou shalt **l down**, and none shall 7257
20:11 which shall **l down** with him in the dust. 7901
21:26 They shall **l down** alike in the dust, and 7901
27:19 The rich *man* shall **l down**, but he shall not 7901
34: 6 Should I l against my right? my wound *is* 3576
38:40 *and* abide in the covert to **l in wait**? 695
Ps 23: 2 He **maketh** me to **l down** in green 7257
57: 4 I l *even among* them that are set on fire, 7901
59: 3 For lo, they **l in wait** for my soul: the mighty 693
62: 9 *are* vanity, *and* men of high degree *are* a **l**: 3577
88: 5 the dead, like the slain that l in the grave, 7901
89:35 by my holiness that I will not l unto David. 3576
119:69 The proud have forged a l against me: *but* 8267
Pr 3:24 thou shalt **l down**, and thy sleep shall be 7901
12: 6 The words of the wicked *are* to **l in wait** *for* 693
14: 5 A faithful witness will not l: but a false 3576
Ecc 4:11 if two **l together**, then they have heat: 7901
SS 1:13 he shall **l all night** betwixt my breasts. 3885
Isa 11: 6 and the leopard shall **l down** with the kid; 7257
11: 7 their young ones shall **l down** together: 7257
13:21 wild beasts of the desert shall l there; and 7257
14:18 of the nations, *even* all of them, l in glory, 7901
14:30 and the needy shall **l down** in safety: 7257
17: 2 which shall **l down**, and none shall make 7257
27:10 there shall he **l down**, and consume 7257
33: 8 The highways **l waste**, the wayfaring man 8074
34:10 generation to generation it shall **l waste**; 2717
43:17 they shall **l down** together, they shall not 7901
44:20 nor say, *Is there* not a l in my right hand? 8267
50:11 of mine hand; ye shall **l down** in sorrow. 7901
51:20 they l at the head of all the streets, as a wild 7901
63: 8 they *are* my people, children *that* will not l: 8266
65:10 of Achor a **place** for the herds **to l down in**, 7258
Jer 3:25 We **l down** in our shame, and 7901
27:10 For they prophesy a l unto you, to remove 8267
27:14 of Babylon: for they prophesy a l unto you. 8267
27:15 yet they prophesy a l in my name; 8267
27:16 for they prophesy a l unto you. 8267
28:15 but thou makest this people to trust in a l. 8267
29:21 which prophesy a l unto you in my name; 8267
29:31 him not, and he caused you to trust in a l: 8267
33:12 shepherds **causing** *their* flocks **to l down**. 7257
La 2:21 and the old l on the ground in the streets: 7901
Eze 4: 4 **L** thou also upon thy left side, and lay 7901
4: 4 shalt l upon it thou shalt bear their iniquity. 7901
4: 6 l again on thy right side, and thou shalt bear 7901
4: 9 of the days that thou shalt l upon thy side, 7901
21:29 unto thee, whiles *they* divine a l unto thee, 3577
31:18 thou shalt l in the midst of 7901
32:21 they l uncircumcised, slain by the sword. 7901
32:27 they shall not l with the mighty *that are* 7901
32:28 shalt l with *them that are* slain with 7901
32:29 they shall l with the uncircumcised, and 7901
32:30 they l uncircumcised with *them that be* 7901
34:14 there shall they l in a good fold, and *in* a fat 7257
34:15 my flock, and I will **cause** them **to l down**, 7257
Hos 2:18 and will **make** them **to l down** safely. 7901
7: 6 heart like an oven, whiles they **l in wait**: 693
Joel 1:13 come, **l all night** in sackcloth, ye ministers 3885
Am 6: 4 That l upon beds of ivory, and 7901
Mic 1:14 the houses of Achzib *shall be* a l to the kings 391
2:11 walking *in* the spirit and falsehood do l, 3576
7: 2 they all **l in wait** for blood; they hunt every 693
Hab 2: 3 but at the end it shall speak, and not l: 3576
Zep 2: 7 Ashkelon shall they **l down** in the evening: 7257
2:14 And flocks shall **l down** in the midst of her, 7257
2:15 a **place** for beasts **to l down in**! 4769
3:13 for they shall feed and **l down**, and 7257
Hag 1: 4 your cieled houses, and this house *l* waste? NIH
Zec 10: 2 the diviners have seen a l, and have told 8267
Jn 5: 6 When Jesus saw him l, and knew that he *2621*
8:44 When he speaketh a l, he speaketh of his *5579*
20: 6 the sepulchre, and seeth the linen clothes l, *2749*
Ac 5: 3 why hath Satan filled thine heart to l to *5574*
23:21 for there **l in wait for** him of them moe *1748*
Ro 1:25 Who changed the truth of God into a l, and *5579*
3: 7 abounded through my l unto his glory; *5582*
9: 1 I say the truth in Christ, I l not, *5574*
2Co 11:31 blessed for evermore, knoweth that I l not. *5574*
Gal 1:20 write unto you, behold, before God, I l not. *5574*
Eph 4:14 whereby they **l in wait** to deceive; *3180*
Col 3: 9 **L** not one to another, seeing that ye have *5574*
2Th 2:11 that they should believe a l: *5579*
1Ti 2: 7 (I speak the truth in Christ, *and* l not;) *5574*
Tit 1: 2 of eternal life, which God, that **cannot l**, *893*
Heb 6:18 in which *it was* impossible for God to l, *5574*
Jas 3:14 glory not, and l *not* against the truth. *5574*
1Jn 1: 6 walk in darkness, we l, and do not the truth: *5574*
2:21 ye know it, and that no l is of the truth. *5579*
2:27 and is no l, and even as it hath taught you, *5579*
Rev 3: 9 say they are Jews, and are not, but do l; *5574*
11: 8 And their dead bodies *shall l* in the street of NIG
21:27 worketh abomination, or *maketh* a l: *5579*
22:15 and whosoever loveth and maketh a l. *5579*

LIED (4) [LIE]

1Ki 13:18 and drink water. *But* he l unto him. 3584
Ps 78:36 and they l unto him with their tongues. 3576
Isa 57:11 that thou hast l, and hast not remembered 3576
Ac 5: 4 thou hast not l unto men, but unto God. *5574*

LIEN (6) [LIE]

Ge 26:10 might lightly have **l with** thy wife, 854+7901
Jdg 21:11 and every woman that hath l by man. 4904
Job 3:13 For now should I have l *still* and 7901
Ps 68:13 Though ye have l among the pots, *yet shall* 7901
Jer 3: 2 and see where thou hast not been l with. 7693
Jn 11:17 he found that he had *l* in the grave four days NIG

LIERS (10) [LIE]

Jos 8:13 and their **l in wait** on the west of the city, 6119
8:14 he wist not that *there were* **l in ambush** 693
Jdg 9:25 the men of Shechem set **l in wait** for him in 693
16:12 *there were* **l in wait** abiding in the chamber. 693
20:29 And Israel set **l in wait** round about Gibeah. 693
20:33 the **l in wait** of Israel came forth out of their 693
20:36 they trusted unto the **l in wait** which they 693
20:37 the **l in wait** hasted, and rushed upon 693
20:37 and the **l in wait** drew *themselves* along, and 693
20:38 between the men of Israel and the **l in wait**, 693

LIES (51) [LIE]

Jdg 16:10 thou hast mocked me, and told me l: 3577
16:13 thou hast mocked me, and told me l: 3577
Job 11: 3 Should thy l make men hold their peace? and 907
13: 4 ye *are* forgers of l, ye *are* all physicians of 8267
Ps 40: 4 not the proud, nor such as turn aside to l. 3577
58: 3 astray as soon as they be born, speaking l. 3577
62: 4 they delight in l: they bless with their 3577
63:11 the mouth of them that speak l shall be 8267
101: 7 he that telleth l shall not tarry in my sight. 8267
Pr 6:19 A false witness *that* speaketh l, and he that 3577
14: 5 will not lie: but a false witness will utter l. 3577
14:25 but a deceitful *witness* speaketh l. 3577
19: 5 and *he that* speaketh l shall not escape. 3577
19: 9 and *he that* speaketh l shall perish. 3577
29:12 If a ruler hearken to l, all his servants 1697+8267
30: 8 Remove far from me vanity and l: 1697+3577
Isa 9:15 the prophet that teacheth l, he *is* the tail. 8267
16: 6 and his wrath: *but* his l *shall* not *be* so. 907
28:15 for we have made l our refuge, and 3577
28:17 the hail shall sweep away the refuge of l, 3577
59: 3 your lips have spoken l, your tongue hath 8267
59: 4 *they* trust in vanity, and speak l; 7723
Jer 9: 3 they bend their tongues *like* their bow *for* l: 8267
9: 5 they have taught their tongue to speak l, 8267
14:14 The prophets prophesy l in my name: 8267
16:19 Surely our fathers have inherited l, vanity, 8267
20: 6 to whom thou hast prophesied l. 8267
23:14 *they* commit adultery, and walk in l: 8267
23:25 that prophesy l in my name, saying, I have 8267
23:26 in the heart of the prophets that prophesy l? 8267
23:32 cause my people to err by their l, and 8267
48:30 *it shall* not *be* so; his l shall not so effect *it*. 907
Eze 13: 8 seen l, therefore behold, I *am* against you, 3577
13: 9 prophets that see vanity, and that divine l: 3577
13:19 your lying to my people that hear *your* l? 3577
13:22 Because *with* l *ye* have made the heart of 8267
22:28 divining l unto them, saying, Thus saith 3577
24:12 She hath wearied *herself with* l, and 8383
Da 11:27 and they shall speak l at one table; 3577
Hos 7: 3 and the princes with their l. 3585
7:13 yet they have spoken l against me. 3577
10:13 reaped iniquity; ye have eaten the fruit of l: 3585
11:12 Ephraim compasseth me about with l, and 3585
12: 1 he daily increaseth l and desolation; and 3577
Am 2: 4 and their l caused them to err, 3577
Mic 6:12 the inhabitants thereof have spoken l, and 8267
Na 3: 1 it *is* all full *of* l *and* robbery; the prey 3585
Hab 2:18 the molten image, and a teacher of l, 8267
Zep 3:13 of Israel shall not do iniquity, nor speak l; 3577
Zec 13: 3 for thou speakest l in the name of 8267
1Ti 4: 2 **Speaking** l in hypocrisy, having their *5573*

LIEST (5) [LIE]

Ge 28:13 the land whereon thou l, to thee will I give 7901
Dt 6: 7 when thou **l down**, and when thou risest up. 7901
11:19 when thou **l down**, and when thou risest up. 7901
Jos 7:10 wherefore l thou thus upon thy face? 5307
Pr 3:24 When thou **l down**, thou shalt not be afraid: 7901

LIETH (59) [LIE]

Ge 4: 7 if thou doest not well, sin l at the door. 7257
49:25 blessings of the deep that l under, 7257
Ex 22:19 Whosoever l with a beast shall surely be 7901
Lev 6: 3 and l concerning it, and sweareth falsely; 3584
14:47 he that l in the house shall wash his clothes; 7901
15: 4 whereon he l that hath the issue, is unclean: 7901
15:20 every *thing* that she l upon in her separation 7901
15:24 all the bed whereon he l shall be unclean. 7901
15:26 Every bed whereon she l all the days of her 7901
15:33 him that **l with** her which is unclean. 5973+7901
19:20 **l carnally with** a woman 854+2233+7901+7902
20:11 the man that l with his father's wife hath 7901
20:13 lie with mankind, as he **l with** a woman, 4904
26:34 as long as it **l desolate**, and ye *be* in your 8074
26:35 As long as it **l desolate** it shall rest; because 8074
26:43 while she **l desolate** without them: 8074
Nu 21:15 of Ar, and l upon the border of Moab. 8172
Dt 27:20 Cursed *be* he that l with his father's wife; 7901
27:21 Cursed *be* he that l with any *manner of* 7901
27:22 Cursed *be* he that l with his sister, 7901
27:23 Cursed *be* he that l with his mother in law. 7901
Jos 15: 8 *l* before the valley of Hinnom westward, NIH
17: 7 *to* Michmethah, that *l* before Shechem; NIH
18:13 near the hill that *l* on the south side of NIH
18:14 from the hill that *l* before Beth-horon NIH
18:16 *l* before the valley of the son of Hinnom, NIH
Jdg 1:16 of Judah, which *l* in the south of Arad; NIH
16: 5 see wherein his great strength *l*, and by what NIH
16: 6 wherein thy great strength *l*, and NIH
16:15 not told me wherein thy great strength *l*. NIH
18:28 and it was in the valley that *l* by Beth-rehob. NIH
Ru 3: 4 it shall be, when he **l down**, that thou shalt 7901
2Sa 2:24 that *l* before Giah *by* the way of NIH
2Sa 24: 5 *on* the right side of the city that *l* in NIH
Ne 2: 3 *l* waste, and the gates thereof are consumed NIH
2:17 how Jerusalem *l* waste, and the gates NIH
3:25 the tower which **l out** from the king's high 3318
3:26 toward the east, and the tower that **l out**. 3318
3:27 over against the great tower that **l out**, 3318
Job 14:12 So man **l down**, and riseth not: till 7901
40:21 He l under the shady trees, in the covert of 7901
Ps 10: 9 He **l in wait** secretly as a lion in his den: 693
10: 9 he **l in wait** to catch the poor: he doth catch 693
41: 8 and *now* that he l he shall rise up no more. 7901
88: 7 Thy wrath **l hard** upon me, and thou hast 5564
Pr 7:12 in the streets, and **l in wait** at every corner.) 693
23:28 She also **l in wait** as *for* a prey, and 693
23:34 thou shalt be as he that **l down** in the midst 7901
23:34 or as he that l upon the top of a mast. 7901
Eze 9: 2 which l toward the north, and every man a 6437
29: 3 the great dragon that l in the midst of his 7257
Mic 7: 5 keep the doors of thy mouth from her that l 7901
Mt 8: 6 Lord, my servant l at home sick of the palsy, *906*
Mk 5:23 daughter **l at the point of death**: *2079+2192*
Ac 14: 6 and *unto* the **region that l round about**: *4066*
27:12 and l toward the south west and north west. *991*
Ro 12:18 If *it be* possible, **as much as l in** you, *1537*
1Jn 5:19 and the whole world l in wickedness. *2749*
Rev 21:16 And the city l foursquare, and the length is *2749*

LIEUTENANTS (4)

Ezr 8:36 the king's commissions unto the king's l, 323
Est 3:12 Haman had commanded unto the king's l, 323
8: 9 to the l, and the deputies and rulers of 323
9: 3 the l, and the deputies, and officers of 323

LIFE (450) [LIVE]

Ge 1:20 abundantly the moving creature that hath l, 2416
1:30 wherein *there is* l, *I have given* every 2416+5315
2: 7 breathed into his nostrils the breath of l; 2416
2: 9 the tree of l also in the midst of the garden, 2416
3:14 and dust shalt thou eat all the days of thy l: 2416
3:17 shalt thou eat *of* it all the days of thy l; 2416
3:22 take also of the tree of l, and eat, and 2416
3:24 every way, to keep the way of the tree of l. 2416
6:17 destroy all flesh, wherein *is* the breath of l, 2416
7:11 In the six hundredth year of Noah's l, in 2416
7:15 two of all flesh, wherein *is* the breath of l. 2416
7:22 All in whose nostrils *was* the breath of l, 2416
9: 4 flesh with the l thereof, *which is* the blood 5315
9: 5 man's brother will I require the l of man. 5315
18:10 return unto thee according to the time of l; 2416
18:14 according to the time of l, and Sarah shall 2416
19:17 forth abroad, that he said, Escape for thy l; 5315
19:19 thou hast shewed unto me in saving my l; 5315
23: 1 *these were* the years of the l of Sarah. 2416
25: 7 of the years of Abraham's l which he lived, 2416
25:17 these *are* the years of the l of Ishmael, 2416
27:46 I am weary of my l because of 2416
27:46 of the land, what good shall my l do me? 2416
32:30 God face to face, and my l is preserved. 5315
42:15 By the l of Pharaoh ye shall not go forth 2416
42:16 else by the l of Pharaoh surely ye *are* spies. 2416
44:30 seeing that his l *is* bound up in *the lad's* 5315
44:30 that his life *is* bound up in *the lad's* l; 5315
45: 5 God did send me before you to **preserve l**. 4241
47: 9 evil have the days of the years of my l 2416
47: 9 l of my fathers in the days of their 2416
48:15 the God which fed me **all my l long** 4480+5750
Ex 4:19 for all the men are dead which sought thy l. 5315
6:16 the years of the l of Levi *were* an hundred 2416
6:18 the years of the l of Kohath *were* an 2416
6:20 the years of the l of Amram *were* an 2416
21:23 then thou shalt give l for life, 5315
21:23 then thou shalt give life for l, 5315
21:30 he shall give *for* the ransom of his l 5315
Lev 17:11 For the l of the flesh *is* in the blood: and 5315
17:14 For *it is* the l of all flesh; the blood of it *is* 5315
17:14 all flesh; the blood of it *is* for the l thereof: 5315
17:14 for the l of all flesh *is* the blood thereof: 5315
18:18 besides the other in her l *time*. 2416
Nu 35:31 take no satisfaction for the l of a murderer, 5315
Dt 4: 9 depart from thy heart all the days of thy l: 2416
6: 2 and thy son's son, all the days of thy l; 2416
12:23 for the blood *is* the l; and thou mayest not 5315
12:23 and thou mayest not eat the l with the flesh. 5315
16: 3 of the land of Egypt all the days of thy l. 2416
17:19 he shall read therein all the days of his l: 2416
19:21 *but* l *shall go* for life, eye for eye, tooth for 5315
19:21 *but* life *shall go* for l, eye for eye, tooth for 5315
20:19 down (for the tree of the field *is* man's *l*) NIH
24: 6 to pledge: for he taketh *a man's* l to pledge. 5315
28:66 thy l shall hang in doubt before thee; and 2416
28:66 and shalt have none assurance of thy l: 2416
30:15 I have set before thee *this* day l and good, 2416
30:19 *that* I have set before you l and death, 2416
30:19 therefore choose l, that *both* thou and 2416
30:20 for he *is* thy l, and the length of thy days: 2416
32:47 a vain thing for you; because it *is* your l: 2416
Jos 1: 5 *to* stand before thee all the days of thy l: 2416
2:14 the men answered her, Our l for yours, if ye 5315
4:14 as they feared Moses, all the days of his l. 2416
Jdg 9:17 adventured his l far, and delivered you out 5315
12: 3 I put my l in my hands, and passed over 5315
16:30 were moe than *they* which he slew in his l. 2416
18:25 thou lose thy l, with the lives of thy 5315
Ru 4:15 And he shall be unto thee a restorer of *thy* l, 5315
1Sa 1:11 him unto the LORD all the days of his l, 2416
7:15 Samuel judged Israel all the days of his l. 2416
18:18 what *is* my l, *or* my father's family in 2416
19: 5 For he did put his l in his hand, and 5315
19:11 saying, If thou save not thy l to night, 5315
20: 1 sin before thy father, that he seeketh my l? 5315
22:23 for he that seeketh my l seeketh thy life: but 5315
22:23 for he that seeketh my life seeketh thy l: but 5315
23:15 saw that Saul was come out to seek his l: 5315
25:29 in the bundle of l with the LORD thy God; 2416
26:24 as thy l was much set by this day in mine 5315

1Sa 26:24 let my l be much set by in the eyes of 5315
28: 9 wherefore then layest thou a snare for my l, 5315
28:21 I have put my l in my hand, and 5315
2Sa 1: 9 upon me, because my l *is* yet whole in me. 5315
4: 8 of Saul thine enemy, which sought thy l; 5315
14: 7 for the l of his brother whom he slew; 5315
15:21 whether in death or l, even there *also* will 2416
16:11 came forth of my bowels, seeketh my l: 5315
18:13 wrought falsehood against mine own l: 5315
19: 5 which *this* day have saved thy l, and 5315
1Ki 1:12 that thou mayest save thine own l, and 5315
1:12 own life, and the l of thy son Solomon. 5315
2:23 not spoken this word against his own l. 5315
3:11 and hast not asked for thyself long l; 3117
3:11 nor hast asked the l of thine enemies; 5315
4:21 and served Solomon all the days of his l. 2416
11:34 I will make him prince all the days of his l 2416
15: 5 he commanded him all the days of his l, 2416
15: 6 and Jeroboam all the days of his l. 2416
19: 2 if I make not thy l as the life of one of them 5315
19: 2 if I make not thy life as the l of one of them 5315
19: 3 went for his l, and came *to* Beer-sheba, 5315
19: 4 now, O LORD, take away my l; 5315
19:10 am left; and they seek my l, to take it away. 5315
19:14 am left; and they seek my l, to take it away. 5315
20:31 of Israel: peradventure he will save thy l. 5315
20:39 shall thy l be for his life, or else thou shalt 5315
20:39 shall thy life be for his l, or else thou shalt 5315
20:42 therefore thy l shall go for his life, and 5315
20:42 therefore thy life shall go for his l, and 5315
2Ki 1:13 let my l, and the life of these fifty thy 5315
1:13 my life, and the l of these fifty thy servants, 5315
1:14 let my l now be precious in thy sight. 5315
4:16 this season, according to the time of l, 2416
4:17 said unto her, according to the time of l. 2416
7: 7 *even* the camp as it *was*, and fled for their l. 5315
8: 1 whose son he had **restored to l**, saying, 2421
8: 5 king how he had **restored** a dead *body* **to l**, 2421
8: 5 whose son he had **restored to l**, 2421
8: 5 this *is* her son, whom Elisha **restored to l**. 2421
10:24 *he that letteth him go,* his l *shall be* for 5315
10:24 *him go,* his life *shall be* for the l of him. 5315
25:29 continually before him all the days of his l. 2416
25:30 rate for every day, all the days of his l. 2416
2Ch 1:11 or honour, nor the l of thine enemies, 5315
1:11 thine enemies, neither yet hast asked long l; 3117
Ezr 6:10 pray for the l of the king, and of his sons. 2417
Ne 6:11 *am,* would go into the temple to **save** his l? 2421
Est 7: 3 let my l be given me at my petition, and 5315
7: 7 Haman stood *up* to make request for his l to 5315
8:11 to stand for their l, to destroy, to slay, and 5315
Job 2: 4 all that a man hath will he give for his l. 5315
2: 6 Behold, he *is* in thine hand; but save his l. 5315
3:20 is in misery, and l unto the bitter in soul; 2416
6:11 *is* mine end, that I should prolong my l? 5315
7: 7 O remember that my l *is* wind: mine eye 2416
7:15 *and* death rather than my l. 6106
9:21 I not know my soul: I would despise my l. 2416
10: 1 My soul is weary of my l; I will leave my 2416
10:12 Thou hast granted me l and favour, and 2416
13:14 in my teeth, and put my l in mine hand? 5315
24:22 he riseth up, and no *man* is sure of l. 2416
31:39 caused the owners thereof to lose their l: 5315
33: 4 the breath of the Almighty hath **given** me l. 2421
33:18 and his l from perishing by the sword. 2416
33:20 So that his l abhorreth bread, and his soul 2416
33:22 unto the grave, and his l to the destroyers. 2416
33:28 into the pit, and his l shall see the light. 2416
36: 6 He **preserveth** not the l of the wicked: but 2421
36:14 in youth, and their l *is* among the unclean. 2416
Ps 7: 5 let him tread down my l upon the earth, and 2416
16:11 Thou wilt shew me the path of l: in thy 2416
17:14 *which have* their portion in *this* l, and 2416
21: 4 He asked l of thee, *and* thou gavest *it* him, 2416
23: 6 mercy shall follow me all the days of my l: 2416
26: 9 with sinners, nor my l with bloody men: 2416
27: 1 the LORD *is* the strength of my l; 2416
27: 4 house of the LORD all the days of my l, 2416
30: 5 *but* a moment; in his favour *is* l: 2416
31:10 For my l is spent with grief, and my years 2416
31:13 against me, they devised to take away my l. 5315
34:12 What man *is he that* desireth l, *and* 2416
36: 9 For with thee *is* the fountain of l: in thy 2416
38:12 They also that seek after my l lay snares *for* 5315
42: 8 *and my* prayer unto the God of my l. 2416
61: 6 wilt **prolong** the king's l: 3117+3117+5921
63: 3 Because thy lovingkindness *is* better than l, 2416
64: 1 preserve my l from fear of the enemy. 2416
66: 9 Which holdeth our soul in l, and 2416
78:50 but gave their l over to the pestilence; 2416
88: 3 and my l draweth nigh unto the grave. 2416
91:16 *With* long l will I satisfy him, and 3117
103: 4 Who redeemeth thy l from destruction; 2416
128: 5 the good of Jerusalem all the days of thy l. 2416
133: 3 the blessing, *even* l for evermore. 2416
143: 3 he hath smitten my l down to the ground; 2416
Pr 1:19 *which* taketh away the l of the owners 5315
2:19 neither take they hold of the paths of l. 2416
3: 2 For length of days, and long l, and peace, 2416
3:18 She *is* a tree of l to them that lay hold upon 2416
3:22 So shall they be l unto thy soul, and 2416
4:10 and the years of thy l shall be many. 2416
4:13 let *her* not go: keep her; for she *is* thy l. 2416
4:22 For they *are* l unto those that find them, and 2416
4:23 all diligence; for out of it *are* the issues of l. 2416
5: 6 Lest thou shouldest ponder the path of l, 2416
6:23 and reproofs of instruction *are* the way of l: 2416
6:26 the adulteress will hunt for the precious l. 5315
7:23 and knoweth not that it *is* for his l. 5315
8:35 For whoso findeth me findeth l, and 2416
9:11 and the years of thy l shall be increased. 2416
10:11 The mouth of a righteous *man is* a well of l: 2416
10:16 The labour of the righteous *tendeth* to l: 2416
10:17 He *is in* the way of l that keepeth 2416
11:19 As righteousness *tendeth* to l: so he that 2416

Pr 11:30 The fruit of the righteous *is* a tree of l; and 2416
12:10 A righteous *man* regardeth the l of his 5315
12:28 In the way of righteousness *is* l; and *in* 2416
13: 3 He that keepeth his mouth keepeth his l: 5315
13: 8 The ransom of a man's l *are* his riches: but 5315
13:12 but *when* the desire cometh, *it is* a tree of l. 2416
13:14 The law of the wise *is* a fountain of l, 2416
14:27 The fear of the LORD *is* a fountain of l, 2416
14:30 A sound heart *is* the l of the flesh: but 2416
15: 4 A wholesome tongue *is* a tree of l: but 2416
15:24 The way of l *is* above to the wise, that *he* 2416
15:31 The ear that heareth the reproof of l abideth 2416
16:15 In the light of the king's countenance *is* l; 2416
16:22 Understanding *is* a wellspring of l unto him 2416
18:21 Death and l *are* in the power of the tongue: 2416
19:23 The fear of the LORD *tendeth* to l: and 2416
21:21 after righteousness and mercy findeth l, 2416
22: 4 the LORD *are* riches, and honour, and l. 2416
31:12 him good and not evil all the days of her l. 2416
Ecc 2: 3 do under the heaven all the days of their l. 2416
2:17 Therefore I hated l; because the work that 2416
3:12 for *a man* to rejoice, and to do good in his l. 2416
5:18 he taketh under the sun all the days of his l, 2416
5:20 shall not much remember the days of his l; 2416
6:12 knoweth what *is* good for man in *this* l, 2416
6:12 all the days of his vain l which he spendeth 2416
7:12 *that* wisdom **giveth** l to them that have it. 2421
7:15 there is a wicked *man* that prolongeth *his l* NIH
8:15 with him of his labour the days of his l, 2416
9: 9 lovest all the days of the l of thy vanity, 2416
9: 9 for that *is* thy portion in *this* l, and in thy 2416
Isa 15: 4 cry out; his l shall be grievous unto him. 5315
38:12 I have cut off like a weaver my l: he will 2416
38:16 and in all these *things is* the l of my spirit: 2416
38:20 days of our l in the house of the LORD. 2416
43: 4 I give men for thee, and people for thy l. 5315
57:10 thou hast found the l of thine hand; 2416
Jer 4:30 will despise thee, they will seek thy l. 5315
8: 3 death shall be chosen rather than l by all 2416
11:21 that seek thy l, saying, Prophesy not in 5315
21: 7 and into the hand of those that seek their l: 5315
21: 8 I set before you the way of l, and the way 2416
21: 9 and his l shall be unto him for a prey. 5315
22:25 thee into the hand of them that seek thy l, 5315
34:20 and into the hand of them that seek their l: 5315
34:21 into the hand of them that seek their l, and 5315
38: 2 for he shall have his l for a prey, and 5315
38:16 into the hand of these men that seek thy l. 5315
39:18 but thy l shall be for a prey unto thee: 5315
44:30 and into the hand of them that seek his l; 5315
44:30 his enemy, and that sought his l. 5315
45: 5 thy l will I give unto thee for a prey in all 5315
49:37 and before them that seek their l: 5315
52:33 eat bread before him all the days of his l. 2416
52:34 the day of his death, all the days of his l. 2416
La 2:19 lift up thy hands toward him for the l of thy 5315
3:53 They have cut off my l in the dungeon, and 2416
3:58 of my soul; thou hast redeemed my l. 2416
Eze 3:18 wicked from his wicked way, to **save** his l; 2421
7:13 strengthen himself in the iniquity of his l. 2416
13:22 from his wicked way, by **promising** him l: 2421
32:10 every man for his own l, in the day of thy 5315
33:15 walk in the statutes of l, 2416
Da 12: 2 some to everlasting l, and some to shame 2416
Jnh 1:14 let us not perish for this man's l, and 5315
2: 6 yet hast thou brought up my l from 2416
4: 3 take, I beseech thee, my l from me; 5315
Mal 2: 5 My covenant was with him of l and peace; 2416
Mt 2:20 are dead which sought the young child's l. 5590
6:25 Take no thought for your l, what ye shall 5590
6:25 ye shall put on. Is not the l more than meat, 5590
7:14 which leadeth unto l, and few there be that 2222
10:39 He that findeth his l shall lose it: and 5590
10:39 he that loseth his l for my sake shall find it. 5590
16:25 For whosoever will save his l shall lose it: 5590
16:25 whosoever will lose his l for my sake shall 5590
18: 8 it is better for thee to enter into l halt or 2222
18: 9 it is better for thee to enter into l with one 2222
19:16 *thing* shall I do, that I may have eternal l? 2222
19:17 but if thou wilt enter into l, keep 2222
19:29 and shall inherit everlasting l. 2222
20:28 and to give his l a ransom for many. 5590
25:46 but the righteous into l eternal. 2222
Mk 3: 4 to save l, or to kill? But they held their 5590
8:35 For whosoever will save his l shall lose it; 5590
8:35 but whosoever shall lose his l for my sake 5590
9:43 it is better for thee to enter into l maimed, 2222
9:45 it is better for thee to enter halt into l, 2222
10:17 what shall I do that I may inherit eternal l? 2222
10:30 and in the world to come eternal l. 2222
10:45 and to give his l a ransom for many. 5590
Lk 1:75 before him, all the days of our l. 2222
6: 9 or to do evil? to save l, or to destroy *it?* 5590
8:14 with cares and riches and pleasures of *this* l, 979
9:24 For whosoever will save his l shall lose it: 5590
9:24 but whosoever will lose his l for my sake, 5590
10:25 Master, what shall I do to inherit eternal l? 2222
12:15 for a man's l consisteth not in 2222
12:22 Take no thought for your l, what ye shall 5590
12:23 The l is more than meat, and the body *is* 5590
14:26 and sisters, yea, and his own l also, 5590
17:33 Whosoever shall seek to save his l shall 5590
17:33 whosoever shall lose *his l* shall preserve it. NIG
18:18 what shall I do to inherit eternal l? 2222
18:30 and in the world to come l everlasting. 2222
21:34 and cares **of** *this* l, and *so* that day come 982
Jn 1: 4 In him was l; and the life was the light of 2222
1: 4 him was life; and the l was the light of men. 2222
3:15 in him should not perish, but have eternal l. 2222
3:16 should not perish, but have everlasting l. 2222
3:36 that believeth on the Son hath everlasting l: 2222
3:36 he that believeth not the Son shall not see l; 2222
4:14 of water springing up into everlasting l. 2222
4:36 and gathereth fruit unto l eternal: 2222
5:24 hath everlasting l, and shall not come into 2222

Jn 5:24 but is passed from death unto l. 2222
5:26 For as the Father hath l in himself; so 2222
5:26 hath he given to the Son to have l in 2222
5:29 have done good, unto the resurrection of l; 2222
5:39 for in them ye think ye have eternal l: 2222
5:40 will not come to me, that ye might have l. 2222
6:27 *that* meat which endureth unto everlasting l, 2222
6:33 from heaven, and giveth l unto the world. 2222
6:35 Jesus said unto them, I am the bread of l: 2222
6:40 believeth on him, may have everlasting l: 2222
6:47 He that believeth on me hath everlasting l. 2222
6:48 I am *that* bread of l. 2222
6:51 which I will give for the l of the world. 2222
6:53 and drink his blood, ye have no l in you. 2222
6:54 and drinketh my blood, hath eternal l; 2222
6:63 unto you, *they* are spirit, and *they* are l. 2222
6:68 we go? thou hast the words of eternal l. 2222
8:12 in darkness, but shall have the light of l. 2222
10:10 I am come that they might have l, and 2222
10:11 the good shepherd giveth his l for 5590
10:15 and I lay down my l for the sheep. 5590
10:17 because I lay down my l, that I might take 5590
10:28 And I give unto them eternal l; and 2222
11:25 unto her, I am the resurrection, and the l: 2222
12:25 He that loveth his l shall lose it; and he that 5590
12:25 he that hateth his l in this world shall keep 5590
12:25 life in this world shall keep it unto l eternal. 2222
12:50 And I know that his commandment is l 2222
13:37 I will lay down my l for thy sake. 5590
13:38 Wilt thou lay down thy l for my sake? 5590
14: 6 unto him, I am the way, the truth, and the l: 2222
15:13 that a man lay down his l for his friends. 5590
17: 2 that he should give eternal l to as many as 2222
17: 3 And this is l eternal, that they might know 2222
20:31 that believing ye might have l through his 2222
Ac 2:28 Thou hast made known to me the ways of l; 2222
3:15 And killed the Prince of l, whom God hath 2222
5:20 temple to the people all the words of this l. 2222
8:33 for his l is taken from the earth. 2222
11:18 to the Gentiles granted repentance unto l. 2222
13:46 judge yourselves unworthy of everlasting l, 2222
13:48 as many as were ordained to eternal l 2222
17:25 needed any *thing,* seeing he giveth to all l, 2222
20:10 Trouble not yourselves; for his l is in him. 5590
20:24 neither count I my l dear unto myself, so 5590
26: 4 My **manner of** l from *my* youth, which was 981
27:22 for there shall be no loss of *any man's* l 5590
Ro 2: 7 and honour and immortality, eternal l: 2222
5:10 we shall be saved by his l. 2222
5:17 of the gift of righteousness shall reign in l 2222
5:18 *came* upon all men unto justification of l. 2222
5:21 unto eternal l by Jesus Christ our Lord. 2222
6: 4 so we also should walk in newness of l. 2222
6:22 unto holiness, and the end everlasting l. 2222
6:23 the gift of God *is* eternal l through Jesus 2222
7:10 which was *ordained* to l, 2222
8: 2 For the law of the Spirit of l in Christ Jesus 2222
8: 6 but to be spiritually minded *is* l and peace. 2222
8:10 but the Spirit *is* l because of righteousness. 2222
8:38 nor l, nor angels, nor principalities, 2222
11: 3 and I am left alone, and they seek my l. 5590
11:15 receiving *of them be,* but l from the dead? 2222
16: 4 Who have for my l laid down their own 5590
1Co 3:22 or l, or death, or *things* present, or *things* to 2222
6: 3 much more *things* **that pertain to** *this* l? 982
6: 4 judgments *of things* **pertaining to** *this* l, 982
14: 7 *And* even *things* **without** l giving sound, 895
15:19 If in this l only we have hope in Christ, 2222
2Co 1: 8 insomuch that we despaired even of l: 2198
2:16 and to the other the savour of l unto life. 2222
2:16 and to the other the savour of life unto l. 2222
3: 6 for the letter killeth, but the spirit **giveth l**. 2227
4:10 that the l also of Jesus might be made 2222
4:11 that the l also of Jesus might be made 2222
4:12 So then death worketh in us, but l in you. 2222
5: 4 that mortality might be swallowed up of l. 2222
Gal 2:20 *the l* which I now live in the flesh I live by NIG
3:21 a law given which could have **given l**, 2227
6: 8 Spirit shall of the Spirit reap l everlasting. 2222
Eph 4:18 being alienated from the l of God through 2222
Php 1:20 in my body, whether *it be* by l, or by death. 2222
2:16 Holding forth the word of l; that I may 2222
2:30 not regarding *his* l, to supply your lack of 5590
4: 3 whose names *are* in the book of l. 2222
Col 3: 3 and your l is hid with Christ in God. 2222
3: 4 *who is* our l, shall appear, then shall ye also 2222
1Ti 1:16 hereafter believe on him to l everlasting. 2222
2: 2 and peaceable l in all godliness and honesty. 979
4: 8 *things,* having promise of the l that now is, 2222
6:12 the good fight of faith, lay hold on eternal l, 2222
6:19 that they may lay hold on eternal l. 2222
2Ti 1: 1 according to the promise of l which is in 2222
1:10 and hath brought l and immortality to light 2222
2: 4 entangleth himself with the affairs of *this* l; 979
3:10 **manner of** l, purpose, faith, longsuffering, 72
Tit 1: 2 In hope of eternal l, which God, that cannot 2222
3: 7 heirs according to the hope of eternal l. 2222
Heb 7: 3 neither beginning of days, nor end of l; 2222
7:16 but after the power of an endless l. 2222
11:35 received their dead **raised to l again**: 386+1537
Jas 1:12 he is tried, he shall receive the crown of l, 2222
4:14 for what *is* your l? It is even a vapour, 2222
1Pe 3: 7 and as *being* heirs together of the grace of l; 2222
3:10 For he that will love l, and see good days, 2222
4: 3 For the time past of *our* l may suffice us to 979
2Pe 1: 3 given unto us all *things* that *pertain* unto l 2222
1Jn 1: 1 our hands have handled, of the Word of l; 2222
1: 2 (For the l was manifested, and we have 2222
1: 2 and shew unto you *that* eternal l, 2222
2:16 and the lust of the eyes, and the pride of l, 979
2:25 that he hath promised us, *even* eternal l. 2222
3:14 that we have passed from death unto l, 2222
3:15 ye know that no murderer hath eternal l 2222
3:16 *of God,* because he laid down his l for us: 5590
5:11 that God hath given to us eternal l, and 2222

1Jn 5:11 to us eternal life, and this **l** is in his Son. 2222
5:12 He that hath the Son hath **l**; *and* he that hath 2222
5:12 he that hath not the Son of God hath not **l**. 2222
5:13 that ye may know that ye have eternal **l**, 2222
5:16 he shall give him **l** for them that sin not 2222
5:20 This is the true God, and eternal **l**. 2222
Jude 1:21 of our Lord Jesus Christ unto eternal **l**. 2222
Rev 2: 7 will I give to eat of the tree of **l**, 2222
2:10 and I will give thee a crown of **l**. 2222
3: 5 not blot out his name out of the book of **l**, 2222
8: 9 which were in the sea, and had **l**, died; 5590
11:11 a half the spirit of **l** from God entered into 2222
13: 8 names are not written in the book of **l** 2222
13:15 And he had power to give **l** unto the image 4151
17: 8 book of **l** from the foundation of the world, 2222
20:12 book was opened, which is *the book* of **l**: 2222
20:15 the book of **l** was cast into the lake of fire. 2222
21: 6 of the fountain of the water of **l** freely. 2222
21:27 which are written in the Lamb's book of **l**. 2222
22: 1 he shewed me a pure river of water of **l**, 2222
22: 2 side of the river, *was there* the tree of **l**, 2222
22:14 that they may have right to the tree of **l**, and 2222
22:17 let him take the water of **l** freely. 2222
22:19 shall take away his part out of the book of **l**, 2222

LIFELESS See DUMB

LIFETIME (3) [LIVE, TIME]

2Sa 18:18 Now Absalom in his **l** had taken and 2416
Lk 16:25 remember that thou in thy **l** receivedst thy 2222
Heb 2:15 of death were all their **l** subject to bondage. 2198

LIFT (193) [LIFTED, LIFTER, LIFTEST, LIFTETH, LIFTING]

Ge 7:17 up the ark, and it was **l up** above the earth. 7311
13:14 **L up** now thine eyes, and look from 5375
14:22 I have **l up** mine hand unto the LORD, 7311
18: 2 he **l up** his eyes and looked, and lo, 5375
21:16 sat over against *him*, and **l up** her voice, 5375
21:18 **l up** the lad, and hold him in thine hand; 5375
22: 4 on the third day Abraham **l up** his eyes, 5375
24:63 he **l up** his eyes, and saw, and behold, 5375
24:64 Rebekah **l up** her eyes, and when she saw 5375
27:38 And Esau **l up** his voice, and wept. 5375
31:12 he said, **L up** now thine eyes, and see, 5375
33: 5 he **l up** his eyes, and saw the women and 5375
37:25 they **l up** their eyes and looked, and behold, 5375
37:28 they drew and **l up** Joseph out of the pit, 5927
39:18 came to pass, as I **l up** my voice and cried, 7311
40:13 Yet within three days shall Pharaoh **l up** 5375
40:19 Yet within three days shall Pharaoh **l up** 5375
41:44 without thee shall no man **l up** his hand or 7311
43:29 he **l up** his eyes, and saw his brother 5375
Ex 7:20 he **l up** the rod, and smote the waters that 7311
14:10 the children of Israel **l up** their eyes, and 5375
14:16 **l** thou **up** thy rod, and stretch out thine 7311
20:25 for if thou **l up** thy tool upon it, thou hast 5130
Lev 9:22 Aaron **l up** his hand towards the people, 5375
Nu 6:26 The LORD **l up** his countenance upon 5375
16: 3 **l** you **up** yourselves above the congregation 5375
20:11 Moses **l up** his hand, and with his rod he 7311
23:24 great lion, and **l up** himself as a young lion: 5375
24: 2 Balaam **l up** his eyes, and he saw Israel 5375
Dt 3:27 **l up** thine eyes westward, and northward, 5375
4:19 lest thou **l up** thine eyes unto heaven, and 5375
22: 4 **surely** help him to **l** *them* **up again**. 6965+6965
27: 5 thou shalt not **l up** *any* iron *tool* upon them. 5130
32:40 For I **l up** my hand to heaven, and say, 5375
Jos 4:18 the soles of the priests' feet were **l up** unto 5423
5:13 that he **l up** his eyes and looked, and 5375
8:31 over which no *man* hath **l up** *any* iron: 5130
Jdg 2: 4 that the people **l up** their voice, and wept. 5375
9: 7 **l up** his voice, and cried, and said unto 5375
19:17 when he had **l up** his eyes, he saw a 5375
21: 2 and **l up** their voices, and wept sore; 5375
Ru 1: 9 and they **l up** their voice, and wept. 5375
1:14 they **l up** their voice, and wept again: and 5375
1Sa 11: 4 all the people **l up** their voices, and wept. 5375
24:16 And Saul **l up** his voice, and wept. 5375
30: 4 the people that *were* with him **l up** their 5375
2Sa 3:32 the king **l up** his voice, and wept at 5375
13:34 the young man that kept the watch **l up** his 5375
13:36 sons came, and **l up** their voice and wept: 5375
18:24 **l up** his eyes, and looked, and behold a man 5375
18:28 which hath delivered up the men that **l up** 5375
20:21 hath **l up** his hand against the king, 5375
23: 8 *he l up his spear* against eight hundred, NIH
23:18 he **l up** his spear against three hundred, 5782
1Ki 11:26 even he **l up** *his* hand against the king. 7311
11:27 this *was* the cause that he **l up** *his* hand 7311
2Ki 9:32 he **l up** his face to the window, and said, 5375
19: 4 wherefore **l up** *thy* prayer for the remnant 5375
19:22 *thy* voice, and **l up** thine eyes on high? 5375
25:27 did **l up** the head of Jehoiachin king of 5375
1Ch 11:11 he **l up** his spear against three hundred 5782
14: 2 for his kingdom *was* **l up** on high, because 5375
21:16 David **l up** his eyes, and saw the angel of 5375
25: 5 seer in the words of God, to **l up** the horn. 7311
2Ch 5:13 when *they* **l up** *their* voice with 7311
17: 6 his heart was **l up** in the ways of 1361
Ezr 9: 6 and blush to **l up** my face to thee, 7311
Job 2:12 when they **l up** their eyes afar off, and 5375
10:15 I be righteous, *yet* will I not **l up** my head. 5375
11:15 then shalt thou **l up** thy face without spot; 5375
22:26 and shalt **l up** thy face unto God. 5375
31:21 If I have **l up** my hand against 5130
31:29 or **l up** myself when evil found him: 5782
38:34 Canst thou **l up** thy voice to the clouds, 7311
Ps 4: 6 **l** thou **up** the light of thy countenance upon 5375
7: 6 **l up** thyself because of the rage of mine 5375
10:12 Arise, O LORD; O God, **l up** thine hand: 5375
24: 4 who hath not **l up** his soul unto vanity, 5375
24: 7 **L up** your heads, O ye gates; and be ye lift 5375
24: 7 be ye **l up**, ye everlasting doors; and 5375
24: 9 **L up** your heads, O ye gates; even lift *them* 5375
24: 9 even **l** *them* **up**, ye everlasting doors; and 5375
25: 1 Unto thee, O LORD, do I **l up** my soul. 5375
28: 2 when I **l up** my hands toward thy holy 5375
28: 9 feed them also, and **l** them **up** for ever. 5375
41: 9 *of* my bread, hath **l up** *his* heel against me. 1431
63: 4 I live: I will **l up** my hands in thy name. 5375
74: 3 **L up** thy feet unto the perpetual 7311
75: 4 and to the wicked, **L** not **up** the horn: 7311
75: 5 **L** not **up** your horn on high: speak *not* with 7311
83: 2 and they that hate thee have **l up** the head. 5375
86: 4 for unto thee, O Lord, do I **l up** my soul. 5375
93: 3 up their voice; the floods **l up** their waves. 5375
94: 2 **L up** thyself, thou judge of the earth: 5375
110: 7 in the way: therefore shall he **l up** the head. 7311
119:48 My hands also will I **l up** unto thy 5375
121: 1 I will **l up** mine eyes unto the hills, 5375
123: 1 Unto thee I **l up** mine eyes, O thou that 5375
134: 2 **L up** your hands *in* the sanctuary, and 5375
143: 8 I should walk; for I **l up** my soul unto thee. 5375
Ecc 4:10 For if they fall, the one will **l up** his fellow: 6965
Isa 2: 4 nation shall not **l up** sword against nation, 5375
5:26 he will **l up** an ensign to the nations from 5375
10:15 should shake *itself against* them that **l** it **up**, 7311
10:15 as if the staff should **l up** *itself, as if it were* 7311
10:24 shall **l up** his staff against thee, after 5375
10:26 shall he **l** it **up** after the manner of Egypt. 5375
10:30 **L up** thy voice, O daughter of Gallim: 6670
13: 2 **L** ye **up** a banner upon the high mountain, 5375
24:14 They shall **l up** their voice, they shall sing, 5375
33:10 will I be exalted; now will I **l up** myself. 5375
37: 4 wherefore **l up** *thy* prayer for the remnant 5375
40: 9 good tidings, **l up** thy voice with strength; 7311
40: 9 **l** *it* **up**, be not afraid; say unto the cities of 7311
40:26 **L up** your eyes on high, and behold who 5375
42: 2 He shall not cry, nor **l up**, nor cause his 5375
42:11 the cities thereof **l up** *their voice*, 5375
49:18 **L up** thine eyes round about, and behold: 5375
49:22 I will **l up** mine hand to the Gentiles, and 5375
51: 6 **L up** your eyes to the heavens, and 5375
52: 8 Thy watchmen shall **l up** the voice; 5375
58: 1 **l up** thy voice like a trumpet, and shew my 7311
59:19 LORD shall **l up a standard** against him. 5127
60: 4 **L up** thine eyes round about, and see: 5375
62:10 the stones; **l up** a standard for the people. 7311
Jer 3: 2 **L up** thine eyes unto the high places, and 5375
7:16 neither **l up** cry nor prayer for them, 5375
11:14 neither **l up** a cry or prayer for them: 5375
13:20 **L up** your eyes, and behold them that come 5375
22:20 **l up** thy voice in Bashan, and cry from 5414
51:14 and they shall **l up** a shout against thee. 6030
La 2:19 **l up** thy hands toward him for the life of 5375
3:41 Let us **l up** our heart with *our* hands unto 5375
Eze 1:19 when the living creatures were **l up** from 5375
1:19 lift up from the earth, the wheels were **l up**. 5375
8: 3 and the spirit **l** me **up** between the earth and 5375
8: 5 **l up** thine eyes now the way towards 5375
8: 5 So I **l up** mine eyes the way toward 5375
10:16 when the cherubims **l up** their wings to 5375
10:17 *these* **l up** themselves *also*: for the spirit of 7426
10:19 the cherubims **l up** their wings, and 5375
11: 1 Moreover the spirit **l** me **up**, and 5375
11:22 did the cherubims **l up** their wings, and 5375
17:14 that *it* might not **l** itself **up**, *but* that by 5375
18: 6 neither hath **l up** his eyes to the idols of 5375
18:12 and hath **l up** his eyes to the idols, 5375
18:15 neither hath **l up** his eyes to the idols of 5375
21:22 to **l up** the voice with shouting, 7311
23:27 that thou shalt not **l up** thine eyes unto 5375
26: 8 and **l up** the buckler against thee. 6965
33:25 **l up** your eyes toward your idols, and 5375
44:12 have I **l up** mine hand against them, 5375
Da 4:34 **l up** mine eyes unto heaven, 5191
10: 5 I **l up** mine eyes, and looked, and behold, 5375
Mic 4: 3 nation shall not **l up** a sword against nation, 5375
5: 9 Thine hand shall be **l up** upon thine 7311
Hab 3:10 his voice, *and* **l up** his hands on high. 5375
Zec 1:18 I **l up** mine eyes, and saw, and behold four 5375
1:21 so that no man did **l up** his head: 5375
1:21 which **l up** *their* horn over the land of 5375
2: 1 I **l up** mine eyes again, and looked, and 5375
5: 1 I **l up** mine eyes, and looked, and behold, 5375
5: 5 **L up** now thine eyes, and see what *is* this 5375
5: 7 behold, there *was* **l up** a talent of lead: and 5375
5: 9 I **l up** mine eyes, and looked, and behold, 5375
5: 9 they **l up** the ephah between the earth and 5375
6: 1 **l up** mine eyes, and looked, and behold, 5375
Mt 12:11 will he not lay hold on it, and **l** *it* **out**? 1453
17: 8 And when they had **l up** their eyes, 1869
Mk 1:31 and took her by the hand, and **l** her **up**; 1453
Lk 11:27 woman of the company **l up** her voice, 1869
13:11 and could in no wise **l up** *herself*. 352
16:23 And in hell he **l up** his eyes, being in 1869
18:13 would not **l up** so much as *his* eyes unto 1869
21:28 to pass, *then* look up, and **l up** your heads; 1869
24:50 and he **l up** his hands, and blessed them. 1869
Jn 4:35 **L up** your eyes, and look on the fields; 1869
6: 5 When Jesus then **l up** *his* eyes, 1869
8: 7 he **l up** *himself*, and said unto them, He that 352
8:10 When Jesus had **l up** *himself*, and saw none 352
8:28 When ye have **l up** the Son of man, then 5312
11:41 And Jesus **l up** *his* eyes, and said, Father, 142
12:34 sayest thou, The Son of man must be **l up**? 5312
13:18 He that eateth bread with me hath **l up** his 1869
17: 1 and **l up** his eyes to heaven, and said, 1869
Ac 2:14 **l up** his voice, and said unto them, Ye men 1869
3: 7 took him by the right hand, and **l** *him* **up**: 1453
4:24 And when they heard *that*, they **l up** their 142
9:41 and **l** her **up**, and when he had called 450
14:11 they **l up** their voices, saying in the speech 1869
22:22 and *then* **l up** their voices, and said, 1869
Heb 12:12 Wherefore **l up** the hands which hang down, 461
Jas 4:10 the sight of the Lord, and he shall **l** you **up**. 5312

LIFTED (69) [LIFT]

Ge 13:10 Lot **l up** his eyes, and beheld all the plain 5375
22:13 Abraham **l up** his eyes, and looked, and 5375
29:11 kissed Rachel, and **l up** his voice, and wept. 5375
31:10 that I **l up** mine eyes, and saw in a dream, 5375
33: 1 Jacob **l up** his eyes, and looked, and 5375
39:15 when he heard that I **l up** my voice and 7311
40:20 he **l up** the head of the chief butler and of 5375
Nu 14: 1 all the congregation **l up** their voice, and 5375
Dt 8:14 thine heart be **l up**, and thou forget 7311
17:20 That his heart be not **l up** above his 7311
Jdg 8:28 so that they **l up** their heads no more. 5375
1Sa 6:13 they **l up** their eyes, and saw the ark, and 5375
2Sa 22:49 thou also hast **l** me **up on high** above them 7311
2Ki 14:10 and thine heart hath **l** thee **up**: 5375
2Ch 26:16 his heart was **l up** to *his* destruction: 1361
32:25 *done* unto him; for his heart was **l up**: 1361
Job 2:12 him not, they **l up** their voice, and wept; 5375
Ps 27: 6 now shall mine head be **l up** above mine 7311
30: 1 for thou hast **l** me **up**, and hast not made 1802
74: 5 *A man* was famous according as he had **l up** 935
93: 3 The floods have **l up**, O LORD, the floods 5375
93: 3 O LORD, the floods have **l up** their voice; 5375
102:10 for thou hast **l** me **up**, and cast me down. 5375
106:26 Therefore he **l up** his hand against them, 5375
Pr 30:13 are their eyes! and their eyelids are **l up**. 5375
Isa 2:12 and lofty, and upon every one that is **l up**; 5375
2:13 that are high and **l up**, and upon all the oaks 5375
2:14 upon all the hills that are **l up**, 5375
6: 1 high and **l up**, and his train filled 5375
26:11 LORD, *when* thy hand is **l up**, they will 7311
37:23 *thy* voice, and **l up** thine eyes on high? 5375
Jer 51: 9 unto heaven, and is **l up** *even* to the skies. 5375
52:31 **l up** the head of Jehoiachin king of Judah, 5375
Eze 1:20 the wheels were **l up** over against them: 5375
1:21 when those were **l up** from the earth, 5375
1:21 the wheels were **l up** over against them: 5375
3:14 So the spirit **l** me **up**, and took me away, 5375
10:15 the cherubims were **l up**. This *is* the living 7426
10:17 when they were **l up**, *these* lift up 7311
20: 5 **l up** mine hand unto the seed of the house 5375
20: 5 when I **l up** mine hand unto them, saying, 5375
20: 6 In the day *that* I **l up** mine hand unto them, 5375
20:15 Yet also I **l up** my hand unto them in 5375
20:23 I **l up** mine hand unto them also in 5375
20:28 *for* the which I **l up** mine hand to give it to 5375
20:42 into the country *for* the which I **l up** mine 5375
28: 2 Because thine heart *is* **l up**, and thou hast 1361
28: 5 thine heart is **l up** because of thy riches: 1361
28:17 Thine heart was **l up** because of thy beauty, 1361
31:10 Because thou hast **l up** thyself in height, 1361
31:10 and his heart is **l up** in his height; 7311
36: 7 I have **l up** mine hand, Surely the heathen 5375
47:14 *concerning* the which I **l up** mine hand to 5375
Da 5:20 when his heart was **l up**, and his mind 7313
5:23 hast **l up** thyself against the Lord of 7313
7: 4 it was **l up** from the earth, and made stand 5191
8: 3 I **l up** mine eyes, and saw, and behold, 5375
11:12 away the multitude, his heart shall be **l up**; 7311
Hab 2: 4 his soul *which* is **l up** is not upright in him: 6075
Zec 9:16 a crown, **l up as an ensign** upon his land. 5264
14:10 it shall be **l up**, and inhabited in her place, 7213
Mk 9:27 Jesus took him by the hand, and **l** him **up**; 1453
Lk 6:20 And he **l up** his eyes on his disciples, and 1869
17:13 And they **l up** *their* voices, and said, Jesus, 142
Jn 3:14 And as Moses **l up** the serpent in 5312
3:14 *even* so must the Son of man be **l up**: 5312
12:32 And I, if I be **l up** from the earth, will draw 5312
1Ti 3: 6 lest being **l up with pride** he fall into 5187
Rev 10: 5 and upon the earth **l up** his hand to heaven, 142

LIFTER (1) [LIFT]

Ps 3: 3 my glory, and the **l up** of mine head. 7311

LIFTEST (4) [LIFT]

Job 30:22 Thou **l** me **up** to the wind; thou causest me 5375
Ps 9:13 thou that **l** me **up** from the gates of death: 7311
18:48 thou **l** me **up** above those that rise up 7311
Pr 2: 3 *and* **l up** thy voice for understanding; 5414

LIFTETH (10) [LIFT]

1Sa 2: 7 and maketh rich: he bringeth low, and **l up**. 7311
2: 8 *and* **l up** the beggar from the dunghill, 7311
2Ch 25:19 and thine heart **l** thee **up** to boast: 5375
Job 39:18 What time she **l up** herself on high, 4754
Ps 107:25 stormy wind, which **l up** the waves thereof. 7311
113: 7 *and* **l** the needy out of the dunghill; 7311
147: 6 The LORD **l up** the meek: he casteth 5749
Isa 18: 3 when *he* **l up** an ensign *on* the mountains; 5375
Jer 51: 3 against *him that* **l** himself **up** in his 5927
Na 3: 3 The horseman **l up** both the bright sword 5927

LIFTING (9) [LIFT]

1Ch 11:20 for **l up** his spear against three hundred, 5782
15:16 sounding, by **l up** the voice with joy. 7311
Ne 8: 6 Amen, Amen, with **l up** their hands: 4607
Job 22:29 then thou shalt say, *There is* **l up**; 1466
Ps 141: 2 the **l up** of my hands *as* the evening 4864
Pr 30:32 If thou hast done foolishly in **l up** thyself, 5375
Isa 9:18 they shall mount up *like* the **l up** of smoke. 1348
33: 3 at the **l up** of thyself the nations were 7427
1Ti 2: 8 **l up** holy hands, without wrath and 1869

LIGHT (272) [ENLIGHTEN, ENLIGHTENED, ENLIGHTENING, LIGHTED, LIGHTEN, LIGHTENED, LIGHTENETH, LIGHTER, LIGHTEST, LIGHTETH, LIGHTING, LIGHTLY, LIGHTNESS, LIGHTS]

Ge 1: 3 God said, Let there be **l**: and there was light. 216
1: 3 God said, Let there be light: and there was **l**. 216
1: 4 God saw the **l**, that *it was* good: and 216
1: 4 and God divided the **l** from the darkness. 216
1: 5 God called the **l** Day, and the darkness he 216

L

Ge 1:15 of the heaven to **give l** upon the earth: 215
1:16 the greater l to rule the day, and the lesser 3974
1:16 the day, and the lesser l to rule the night: 3974
1:17 of the heaven to **give l** upon the earth, 215
1:18 and to divide the l from the darkness: 216
44: 3 As soon as the morning was l, the men were 215
Ex 10:23 all the children of Israel had l in their 216
13:21 by night in a pillar of fire, to **give** them l; 215
14:20 *to them,* but it **gave l** by night *to these:* so 215
25: 6 Oil for the l, spices for anointing oil, and 3974
25:37 they shall l the lamps thereof, that they may 5927
25:37 that they may **give** l over against it. 215
27:20 bring thee pure oil olive beaten for the l, 3974
35: 8 oil for the l, and spices for anointing oil, 3974
35:14 The candlestick also for the l, and his 3974
35:14 and his lamps, with the oil for the l, 3974
35:28 oil for the l, and for the anointing oil, and 3974
39:37 and all the vessels thereof, and the oil for l, 3974
40: 4 in the candlestick, and l the lamps thereof. 5927
Lev 24: 2 unto thee pure oil olive beaten for the l, 3974
Nu 4: 9 cover the candlestick of the l, and his 3974
4:16 Aaron the priest *pertaineth* the oil for the l, 3974
8: 2 the seven lamps shall **give** l over against 215
21: 5 and our soul loatheth *this* l bread. 7052
Dt 27:16 Cursed *be* he that **setteth** l by his father or 7034
Jdg 9: 4 Abimelech hired vain and l persons, 6348
19:26 man's house where her lord *was,* till it was l. 216
Ru 2: 3 her hap was to **l on** a part of the field 7136
1Sa 14:36 spoil them until the morning l, and let us not 216
18:23 Seemeth it to you a l *thing* to be a king's 7043
25:22 morning l *any that* pisseth against the wall. 216
25:34 morning l *any that* pisseth against the wall. 216
25:36 less or more, until the morning l. 216
29:10 up early in the morning, and **have** l, depart. 215
2Sa 2:18 and Asahel *was as* l of foot as a wild roe. 7031
17:12 we *will l* upon him as the dew falleth on NIH
17:22 by the morning l there lacked not one *of* 216
21:17 that thou quench not the l of Israel. 5216
23: 4 *he shall be* as the l of the morning, *when* 216
1Ki 7: 4 and l *was* against light *in* three ranks. 4237
7: 4 and light *was* against l *in* three ranks. 4237
7: 5 and l *was* against light *in* three ranks. 4237
7: 5 and light *was* against l *in* three ranks. 4237
11:36 that David my servant may have a l alway 5216
16:31 as if it had been a l **thing** for him to walk in 7043
2Ki 3:18 *but* a l **thing** in the sight of the LORD: 7043
7: 9 if we tarry till the morning l, *some* mischief 216
8:19 he promised him to give to him alway a l, 5216
20:10 It is a l **thing** for the shadow to go down 7043
2Ch 21: 7 as he promised to give a l to him and to his 5216
Ne 9:12 to **give** them l in the way wherein they 215
9:19 to **shew** them l, and the way wherein they 215
Est 8:16 The Jews had l, and gladness, and joy, and 219
Job 3: 4 it from above, neither let the l shine upon it. 5105
3: 9 let it look for l, but *have* none; neither let it 216
3:16 I had not been; as infants *which* never saw l. 216
3:20 Wherefore is l given to him that is in misery, 216
3:23 *Why is l given* to a man whose way is hid, NIH
10:22 any order, and *where* the l is as darkness. 3313
12:22 and bringeth out to l the shadow of death. 216
12:25 They grope *in* the dark without l, and 216
17:12 into day: the l *is* short, because of darkness. 216
18: 5 the l of the wicked shall be put out, and 216
18: 6 The l shall be dark in his tabernacle, and 216
18:18 He shall be driven from l into darkness, and 216
22:28 and the l shall shine upon thy ways. 216
24:13 They are of those that rebel against the l; 216
24:14 The murderer rising with the l killeth 216
24:16 in the daytime: they know not the l. 216
25: 3 and upon whom doth not his l arise? 216
28:11 the thing that is hid bringeth he forth *to* l. 216
29: 3 *when* by his l I walked *through* darkness; 216
29:24 the l of my countenance they cast not down. 216
30:26 evil came *unto me:* and when I waited for l, 216
33:28 going into the pit, and his life shall see the l. 216
33:30 to be enlightened with the l of the living. 216
36:30 he spreadeth his l upon it, and covereth 216
36:32 With clouds he covereth the l; and 216
37:15 and caused the l of his cloud to shine? 216
37:21 now *men* see not the bright l which *is* in 216
38:15 from the wicked their l is withholden, and 216
38:19 Where *is* the way *where* l dwelleth? and 216
38:24 By what way is the l parted, *which* scattereth 216
41:18 *By* his neesings a l doth shine, and his eyes 216
Ps 4: 6 lift thou up the l of thy countenance upon us. 216
18:28 For thou wilt l my candle: the LORD my 215
27: 1 The LORD *is* my l and my salvation; 216
36: 9 fountain of life: in thy l shall we see light. 216
36: 9 fountain of life: in thy light shall we see l. 216
37: 6 shall bring forth thy righteousness as the l, 216
38:10 as for the l of mine eyes, it also is gone from 216
43: 3 O send out thy l and thy truth: let them lead 216
44: 3 the l of thy countenance, because thou hadst 216
49:19 of his fathers; they shall never see l. 216
56:13 that *I* may walk before God in the l of 216
74:16 thou hast prepared the l and the sun. 3974
78:14 a cloud, and all the night with a l of fire. 216
89:15 O LORD, in the l of thy countenance. 216
90: 8 our secret *sins* in the l of thy countenance. 3974
97:11 L is sown for the righteous, and gladness for 216
104: 2 Who coverest *thyself* with l as *with* a 216
105:39 for a covering; and fire to **give** l in the night. 215
112: 4 Unto the upright there ariseth l in 216
118:27 God *is* the LORD, which hath **shewed** us l: 215
119:105 *is* a lamp unto my feet, and a l unto my path. 216
119:130 The entrance of thy words **giveth** l; it giveth 215
139:11 cover me; even the night *shall be* l about me. 216
139:12 the darkness and the l *are* both alike *to thee.* 219
148: 3 sun and moon: praise him, all ye stars of l. 216
Pr 4:18 the path of the just *is* as the shining l, 216
6:23 the law *is* l; and reproofs of instruction *are* 216
13: 9 The l of the righteous rejoiceth: but the lamp 216
15:30 The l of the eyes rejoiceth the heart: *and* 3974
16:15 In the l of the king's countenance *is* life; and 216
Ecc 2:13 excelleth folly, as far as l excelleth darkness. 216
Ecc 11: 7 Truly the l *is* sweet, and a pleasant *thing it is* 216
12: 2 the sun, or the l, or the moon, or the stars, 216
Isa 2: 5 and let us walk in the l of the LORD. 216
5:20 that put darkness for l, and light for 216
5:20 put darkness for light, and l for darkness; 216
5:30 and the l is darkened in the heavens thereof. 216
8:20 *it is* because *there is* no l in them. 7837
9: 2 that walked in darkness have seen a great l: 216
9: 2 of death, upon them hath the l shined. 216
10:17 the l of Israel shall be for a fire, and his Holy 216
13:10 constellations thereof shall not give their l: 216
13:10 and the moon shall not cause her l to shine. 216
30:26 Moreover the l of the moon shall be as 216
30:26 light of the moon shall be as the l of the sun, 216
30:26 the l of the sun shall be sevenfold, as 216
30:26 shall be sevenfold, as the l of seven days, 216
42: 6 of the people, for a l of the Gentiles; 216
42:16 I will make darkness l before them, and 216
45: 7 I form the l, and create darkness: I make 216
49: 6 It is a l thing that thou shouldest be my 7043
49: 6 I will also give thee for a l to the Gentiles, 216
50:10 that walketh *in* darkness, and hath no l? 5051
50:11 walk in the l of your fire, and in the sparks 217
51: 4 I will make my judgment to rest for a l of 216
58: 8 shall thy l break forth as the morning, and 216
58:10 shall thy l rise in obscurity, and thy darkness 216
59: 9 we wait for l, but behold obscurity; 216
60: 1 for thy l is come, and the glory of 216
60: 3 the Gentiles shall come to thy l, and kings to 216
60:19 The sun shall be no more thy l by day; 216
60:19 neither for brightness shall the moon **give l** 215
60:19 LORD shall be unto thee an everlasting l, 216
60:20 for the LORD shall be thine everlasting l, 216
Jer 4:23 and void; and the heavens, and they *had* no l. 216
13:16 and, while ye look for l, he turn it into 216
25:10 of the millstones, and the l of the candle. 216
31:35 which giveth the sun for a l by day, *and* 216
31:35 of the moon and of the stars for a l by night, 216
La 3: 2 and brought *me into* darkness, but not *into* l. 216
Eze 8:17 Is it a l **thing** to the house of Judah that 7043
22: 7 In thee have they **set** l by father and 7043
32: 7 and the moon shall not **give** her l. 215+216
Da 2:22 the darkness, and the l dwelleth with him. 5094
5:11 in the days of thy father l and 5094
5:14 *that* l and understanding and 5094
Hos 6: 5 thy judgments *are as* the l *that* goeth forth. 216
Am 5:18 the day of the LORD *is* darkness, and not l. 216
5:20 day of the LORD *be* darkness, and not l? 216
Mic 2: 1 when the morning is l, they practise it, 216
7: 8 in darkness, the LORD *shall be* a l unto me. 216
7: 9 he will bring me forth to the l, *and* I shall 216
Hab 3: 4 *his* brightness was as the l; he had horns 216
3:11 at the l of thine arrows they went, *and* at 216
Zep 3: 4 Her prophets *are* l *and* treacherous persons: 6348
3: 5 morning doth he bring his judgment to l, 216
Zec 14: 6 *that* the l shall not be clear, *nor* dark: 216
14: 7 to pass, *that* at evening time it shall be l. 216
Mt 4:16 people which sat in darkness saw great l; *5457*
4:16 and shadow of death l is sprung up. *5457*
5:14 Ye are the l of the world. A city that is set *5457*
5:15 Neither do men l a candle, and put it under *2545*
5:15 and it **giveth** l unto all that are in the house. *2989*
5:16 Let your l so shine before men, that they *5457*
6:22 The l of the body is the eye: if therefore *3088*
6:22 be single, thy whole body shall be **full of l**. *5460*
6:23 If therefore the l that is in thee be darkness, *5457*
10:27 I tell you in darkness, *that* speak ye in l: *5457*
11:30 For my yoke *is* easy, and my burden is l. *1645*
17: 2 the sun, and his raiment was white as the l. *5457*
22: 5 But they **made l of** *it,* and went their ways, *272*
24:29 and the moon shall not give her l, and *5338*
Mk 13:24 and the moon shall not give her l, *5338*
Lk 1:79 To **give** l to them that sit in darkness and *2014*
2:32 A l to lighten the Gentiles, and the glory of *5457*
8:16 that they which enter in may see the l. *5457*
11:33 that they which come in may see the l. *5338*
11:34 The l of the body is the eye: *3088*
11:34 is single, thy whole body also is **full of l**; *5460*
11:35 that the l which is in thee be not darkness. *5457*
11:36 If thy whole body therefore *be* **full of l**, *5460*
11:36 no part dark, the whole shall be **full of l**, *5460*
11:36 bright shining of a candle doth **give** thee l. *5461*
12: 3 spoken in darkness shall be heard in the l; *5457*
15: 8 doth not l a candle, and sweep the house, and *681*
16: 8 their generation wiser than the children of l. *5457*
Jn 1: 4 him was life; and the life was the l of men. *5457*
1: 5 And the l shineth in darkness; and *5457*
1: 7 for a witness, to bear witness of the L, *5457*
1: 8 He was not *that* L, but *was sent* to bear *5457*
1: 8 but *was sent* to bear witness of *that* L. *5457*
1: 9 *That* was the true L, which lighteth every *5457*
3:19 that l is come into the world, and men *5457*
3:19 and men loved darkness rather than l, *5457*
3:20 For every one that doeth evil hateth the l, *5457*
3:20 neither cometh to the l, lest his deeds *5457*
3:21 But he that doeth truth cometh to the l, *5457*
5:35 He was a burning and a shining l: and *3088*
5:35 were willing for a season to rejoice in his l. *5457*
8:12 unto them, saying, I am the l of the world: *5457*
8:12 in darkness, but shall have the l of life. *5457*
9: 5 I am in the world, I am the l of the world. *5457*
11: 9 because he seeth the l of this world. *5457*
11:10 he stumbleth, because there is no l in him. *5457*
12:35 Yet a little while is the l with you. *5457*
12:35 Walk while ye have the l, lest darkness *5457*
12:36 While ye have l, believe in the light, that ye *5457*
12:36 While ye have light, believe in the l, that ye *5457*
12:36 in the light, that ye may be the children of l. *5457*
12:46 I am come a l into the world, *5457*
Ac 9: 3 suddenly there shined round about him a l *5457*
12: 7 upon *him,* and a l shined in the prison: *5457*
13:47 *saying,* I have set thee to be a l of *5457*
16:29 Then he called for a l, and sprang in, and *5457*
22: 6 suddenly there shone from heaven a great l *5457*
22: 9 they that were with me saw indeed the l, *5457*
Ac 22:11 when I could not see for the glory of that l, *5457*
26:13 O king, I saw in the way a l from heaven, *5457*
26:18 *and* to turn *them* from darkness to l, and *5457*
26:23 and should shew l unto the people, and *5457*
Ro 2:19 the blind, a l of them which are in darkness, *5457*
13:12 and let us put on the armour of l. *5457*
1Co 4: 5 who both will **bring to l** the hidden *things* *5461*
2Co 4: 4 lest the l of the glorious gospel of Christ, *5462*
4: 6 who commanded the l to shine out of *5457*
4: 6 to give the l of the knowledge of the glory *5462*
4:17 For our l affliction, which is but for a *1645*
6:14 and what communion hath l with darkness? *5457*
11:14 himself is transformed into an angel of l. *5457*
Eph 5: 8 but now *are ye* l in the Lord: *5457*
5: 8 *ye* light in the Lord: walk as children of l: *5457*
5:13 are reproved are made manifest by the l: *5457*
5:13 for whatsoever doth make manifest is l. *5457*
5:14 from the dead, and Christ shall **give** thee l. *2017*
Col 1:12 of the inheritance of the saints in l: *5457*
1Th 5: 5 Ye are all the children of l, and the children *5457*
1Ti 6:16 dwelling in the l which no *man* can *5457*
2Ti 1:10 hath **brought** life and immortality **to l** *5461*
1Pe 2: 9 you out of darkness into his marvellous l: *5457*
2Pe 1:19 as unto a l that shineth in a dark place, *3088*
1Jn 1: 5 that God is l, and in him is no darkness at *5457*
1: 7 But if we walk in the l, as he is in the light, *5457*
1: 7 But if we walk in the light, as he is in the l, *5457*
2: 8 darkness is past, and the true l now shineth. *5457*
2: 9 He that saith *he* is in the l, and hateth his *5457*
2:10 He that loveth his brother abideth in the l, *5457*
Rev 7:16 neither shall the sun l on them, nor any *4098*
18:23 And the l of a candle shall shine no more at *5457*
21:11 her l *was* like unto a stone most precious, *5458*
21:23 did lighten it, and the Lamb *is* the l thereof. *3088*
21:24 which are saved shall walk in the l of it: *5457*
22: 5 they need no candle, neither l of the sun; *5457*
22: 5 of the sun; for the Lord God **giveth** them l: *5461*

LIGHTED (13) [LIGHT]

Ge 24:64 when she saw Isaac, she l off the camel. 5307
28:11 he l upon a *certain* place, and tarried there 6293
Ex 40:25 he l the lamps before the LORD; as 5927
Nu 8: 3 he l the lamps thereof over against 5927
Jos 15:18 she l **off** *her* ass; and 4480+5921+6795
Jdg 1:14 she l from off *her* ass; and Caleb said unto 6795
4:15 so that Sisera l **down** off *his* chariot, and 3381
1Sa 25:23 l off the ass, and fell before David on her 3381
2Ki 5:21 he l **down** from the chariot to meet him, 5307
10:15 he l **on** Jehonadab the son of Rechab 4672
Isa 9: 8 a word into Jacob, and it hath l upon Israel. 5307
Lk 8:16 No *man,* when he hath l a candle, covereth it *681*
11:33 No *man,* when he hath l a candle, putteth *it* *681*

LIGHTEN (7) [LIGHT]

1Sa 6: 5 peradventure he will l his hand from off 7043
2Sa 22:29 and the LORD will l my darkness. 5050
Ezr 9: 8 that our God may l our eyes, and give us a 215
Ps 13: 3 l mine eyes, lest I sleep the *sleep of* death; 215
Jnh 1: 5 *were* in the ship into the sea, to l *it* of them. 7043
Lk 2:32 A light to l the Gentiles, and the glory of thy *602*
Rev 21:23 for the glory of God did l it, and the Lamb *5461*

LIGHTENED (5) [LIGHT]

Ps 34: 5 They looked unto him, and were l: and 5102
77:18 the lightnings l the world: the earth trembled 215
Ac 27:18 the next *day* they l **the ship**; 1546+4160
27:38 they l the ship, and cast out the wheat into *2893*
Rev 18: 1 and the earth was l with his glory. *5461*

LIGHTENETH (2) [LIGHT]

Pr 29:13 meet together: the LORD l both their eyes. 215
Lk 17:24 that l out of the one *part* under heaven, *797*

LIGHTER (5) [LIGHT]

1Ki 12: 4 **make** thou the grievous service of thy father, and his heavy yoke which he put upon us, l, 7043
12: 9 **Make** the yoke which thy father did put upon us l? 7043
12:10 our yoke heavy, but **make** thou *it* l unto us; 7043
2Ch 10:10 but **make** thou *it* **somewhat** l for us; 7043
Ps 62: 9 they *are* altogether *l* than vanity. NIH

LIGHTEST (1) [LIGHT]

Nu 8: 2 and say unto him, When thou l the lamps, 5927

LIGHTETH (3) [LIGHT]

Ex 30: 8 when Aaron l the lamps at even, he shall 5927
Dt 19: 5 and l **upon** his neighbour, that he die; 4672
Jn 1: 9 which l every man *that* cometh into *5461*

LIGHTING (2) [LIGHT]

Isa 30:30 shall shew the l **down** of his arm, with 5183
Mt 3:16 descending like a dove, and l upon him: *2064*

LIGHTLY (7) [LIGHT]

Ge 26:10 one of the people might l have lien 4592+3509.1
Dt 32:15 and l **esteemed** the Rock of his salvation. 5034
1Sa 2:30 they that despise me shall be l **esteemed**. 7043
18:23 that I *am* a poor man, and l **esteemed**? 7034
Isa 9: 1 when at the first he l **afflicted** the land of 7043
Jer 4:24 lo, they trembled, and all the hills **moved** l. 7043
Mk 9:39 in my name, that can l speak evil of me. *5036*

LIGHTNESS (3) [LIGHT]

Jer 3: 9 it came to pass through the l of her 6963
23:32 people to err by their lies, and by their l; 6350
2Co 1:17 therefore was thus minded, did I use l? *1644*

LIGHTNING (13) [LIGHTNINGS]

2Sa 22:15 scattered them; l, and discomfited them. 1300
Job 28:26 the rain, and a way for the l of the thunder: 2385
37: 3 and his l unto the ends of the earth. 216
38:25 of waters, or a way for the l of thunder; 2385
Ps 144: 6 **Cast forth l**, and scatter them: 1299+1300

Eze 1:13 was bright, and out of the fire went forth **l.** 1300
1:14 returned as the appearance of a **flash of l.** 965
Da 10: 6 his face as the appearance of **l**, and his eyes 1300
Zec 9:14 and his arrow shall go forth as the **l**: 1300
Mt 24:27 For as the **l** cometh out of the east, and *796*
28: 3 His countenance was like **l**, and his raiment *796*
Lk 10:18 I beheld Satan as **l** fall from heaven. *796*
17:24 For as the **l**, that lighteneth out of the one *796*

LIGHTNINGS (14) [LIGHTNING]

Ex 19:16 that there were thunders and **l**, and a thick 1300
20:18 the **l**, and the noise of the trumpet, and 3940
Job 38:35 Canst thou send **l**, that they may go, and 1300
Ps 18:14 and he shot out **l**, and discomfited them. 1300
77:18 the **l** lightened the world: the earth trembled 1300
97: 4 His **l** enlightened the world: the earth saw, 1300
135: 7 he maketh **l** for the rain; he bringeth 1300
Jer 10:13 he maketh **l** with rain, and bringeth forth 1300
51:16 he maketh **l** with rain, and bringeth forth 1300
Na 2: 4 seem like torches, they shall run like the **l**. 1300
Rev 4: 5 And out of the throne proceeded **l** and *796*
8: 5 and thunderings, and **l**, and an earthquake. *796*
11:19 and there were **l**, and voices, and *796*
16:18 And there were voices, and thunders, and **l**; *796*

LIGHTS (10) [LIGHT]

Ge 1:14 Let there be **l** in the firmament of 3974
1:15 let them be for **l** in the firmament of 3974
1:16 God made two great **l**; the greater light to 3974
1Ki 6: 4 the house he made windows of narrow **l.** 8261
Ps 136: 7 To him that made great **l**: for his mercy 216
Eze 32: 8 All the bright **l** of heaven will I make dark 216
Lk 12:35 loins be girded about, and *your* **l** burning; *3088*
Ac 20: 8 And there were many **l** in the upper *2985*
Php 2:15 among whom ye shine as **l** in the world; *5458*
Jas 1:17 and cometh down from the Father of **l**, *5457*

LIGN (1)

Nu 24: 6 as the **trees of l aloes** *which* the LORD 174

LIGURE (2)

Ex 28:19 the third row a **l**, an agate, and an amethyst. 3958
39:12 third row, a **l**, an agate, and an amethyst. 3958

LIKE (669) [ALIKE, LIKED, LIKEMINDED, LIKEN, LIKENED, LIKENESS, LIKETH, LIKEWISE, LIKING]

Ge 13:10 **l** the land of Egypt, as thou comest unto 3509.1
25:25 came out red, all over **l** a hairy garment; 3509.1
Ex 7:11 they also did **in l manner** with their 3651
8:10 *there is* none **l unto** the LORD our God. 3509.1
9:14 that thou mayest know that *there is* none **l** 3644
9:24 such as there was none **l** it in all the land of 3644
11: 6 such as there was none **l** it, nor shall be like 3644
11: 6 was none like it, nor shall be **l** it any more. NIH
15:11 Who *is* **l** unto thee, O LORD, among 3644
15:11 who *is* **l** thee, glorious in holiness, 3644
16:31 it *was* **l** coriander seed, white; and 3509.1
16:31 the taste of it *was* **l** wafers *made* with 3509.1
23:11 **In l manner** thou shalt deal with thy 3651
24:17 the sight of the glory of the LORD *was* **l** 3509.1
25:33 Three bowls **made l unto almonds**, *with* a 8246
25:33 three bowls **made l almonds** in the other 8246
25:34 *shall be* four bowls **made l unto almonds**, 8246
28:11 in stone, *l* the engravings of a signet, NIH
28:21 to their names, *l* the engravings of a signet; NIH
28:36 grave upon it, *l* the engravings of a signet, NIH
30:32 neither shall ye make *any other* **l** it, 3644
30:33 Whosoever compoundeth *any* **l** it, or 3644
30:34 **each** shall there be **a l** *weight:* 905+905+871.1
30:38 Whosoever shall make **l unto** that, to smell 3644
34: 1 Hew thee two tables of stone **l unto** 3509.1
34: 4 he hewed two tables of stone **l unto** 3509.1
37:19 three bowls **made l almonds** in another 8246
37:20 *were* four bowls **made l almonds**, 8246
39: 8 *of* cunning work, **l** the work of the ephod; 3509.1
39:14 *l* the engravings of a signet, every one with NIH
39:30 it a writing, *l to* the engravings of a signet, NIH
Lev 13: 2 it be in the skin of his flesh **l** the plague 3807.1
Nu 23:10 the righteous, and let my last end be **l** his! 3644
Dt 4:32 this great thing *is*, or hath been heard **l** it? 3644
7:26 thine house, lest thou be a cursed thing **l** it: 3644
10: 1 Hew thee two tables of stone **l unto** 3509.1
10: 3 hewed two tables of stone **l unto** the first, 3509.1
17:14 **l as** all the nations that *are* about me; 3509.1
18: 8 They shall have **l** portions to eat, beside 3509.1
18:15 midst of thee, of thy brethren, **l unto** me; 3644
18:18 **l unto** thee, and will put my words in his 3644
22: 3 **In l manner** shalt thou do with his ass; and 3651
25: 7 if the man **l** not to take his brother's wife, 2654
25: 8 *if* he stand *to it*, and say, I **l** not to take her; 2654
29:23 **l** the overthrow of Sodom, and Gomorrah, 3509.1
33:17 His glory *is* *l* the firstling of his bullock, and NIH
33:17 and his horns *are* *l* the horns of unicorns: NIH
33:26 *There is* none **l unto** the God of Jeshurun, 3509.1
33:29 who *is* **l unto** thee, O people saved by 3644
34:10 a prophet since in Israel **l unto** Moses, 3509.1
Jos 10:14 there was no day **l** that before it or 3509.1
Jdg 7:12 in the valley **l** grasshoppers for multitude; 3509.1
11:17 **in l manner** they sent unto the king of 1571
13: 6 his countenance *was* **l** the countenance of 3509.1
16:12 he brake them from off his arms **l** a 3509.1
16:17 become weak, and be **l** any *other* man. 3509.1
Ru 2:13 though I be not **l** unto one of thy 3509.1
4:11 that is come into thine house **l** Rachel 3509.1
4:11 into thine house like Rachel and **l** Leah, 3509.1
4:12 let thy house be **l** the house of Pharez, 3509.1
1Sa 2: 2 neither *is there* any rock **l** our God. 3509.1
4: 9 Be strong, and quit yourselves **l** men, 3807.1
4: 9 to you: quit yourselves **l** men, and fight. 3807.1
8: 5 now make us a king to judge us **l** all 3509.1
8:20 That we also may be **l** all the nations; and 3509.1
10:24 that *there is* none **l** him among all the 3644
17: 7 the staff of his spear *was* **l** a weaver's 3509.1
19:24 and prophesied before Samuel **in l manner**, 1571
1Sa 21: 9 David said, *There is* none **l** that; give it me. 3644
25:36 a feast in his house, **l** the feast of a king; 3509.1
26:15 who *is* **l to** thee in Israel? wherefore then 3644
2Sa 7: 9 **l unto** the name of the great *men* that *are* 3509.1
7:22 for *there is* none **l** thee, neither *is there any* 3644
7:23 what one nation in the earth *is* **l** thy 3509.1
7:23 *even* **l** Israel, whom God went to redeem 3509.1
18:27 **l** the running of Ahimaaz the son of 3509.1
21:19 the staff of whose spear *was* **l** a weaver's 3509.1
22:34 He maketh my feet **l** hinds' *feet:* and 3509.1
1Ki 3:12 so that there was none **l** thee before thee, 3644
3:12 neither after thee shall any arise **l unto** 3644
3:13 among the kings **l unto** thee all thy days. 3644
5: 6 skill to hew timber **l unto** the Sidonians. 3509.1
7: 8 the porch, *which* was of the **l** work. 3509.1
7: 8 whom he had taken *to wife*, **l unto** this 3509.1
7:26 the brim thereof was wrought **l** the brim 3509.1
7:33 the work of the wheels *was* **l** the work of 3509.1
8:23 *there is* no God **l** thee, in heaven above, or 3644
10:20 there was not the **l** made in any kingdom. 3651
12:32 **l unto** the feast that *is* in Judah, and 3509.1
16: 3 will make thy house **l** the house of 3509.1
16: 7 in being **l** the house of Jeroboam; 3509.1
18:44 little cloud out of the sea, **l** a man's hand. 3509.1
20:25 **l** the army that thou hast lost, horse for 3509.1
20:27 before them **l** two little flocks of kids; 3509.1
21:22 will make thine house **l** the house of 3509.1
21:22 **l** the house of Baasha the son of Ahijah, 3509.1
21:25 (But there was none **l unto** Ahab, 3509.1
22:13 be **l** the word of one of them, and 3509.1
2Ki 3: 2 but not **l** his father, and like his mother: 3509.1
3: 2 but not like his father, and **l** his mother: 3509.1
5:14 his flesh came again **l unto** the flesh of a 3509.1
9: 9 I will make the house of Ahab **l** the house 3509.1
9: 9 **l** the house of Baasha the son of Ahijah: 3509.1
9:20 the driving *is* **l** the driving of Jehu the son 3509.1
13: 7 had made them **l** the dust by threshing. 3509.1
14: 3 of the LORD, yet not **l** David his father: 3509.1
16: 2 the LORD his God, **l** David his father. 3509.1
17:14 their necks, **l to** the neck of their fathers, 3509.1
17:15 that *they* should not do **l** them. 3509.1
18: 5 that after him was none **l** him among all 3644
18:32 take you away to a land **l** your own land, 3509.1
23:25 **l unto** him was there no king before him, 3644
23:25 neither after him arose there *any* **l** him. 3644
25:17 **l unto** these had the second pillar with 3509.1
1Ch 4:27 family multiply, **l to** the children of Judah. 5704
11:23 in the Egyptian's hand *was* a spear **l** a 3509.1
12: 8 whose faces *were* *l* the faces of lions, and NIH
12:22 until it was a great host, **l** the host of God. 3509.1
14:11 mine hand **l** the breaking forth of waters: 3509.1
17: 8 have made thee a name **l** the name of 3509.1
17:20 O LORD, *there is* none **l** thee, neither *is* 3644
17:21 what one nation in the earth *is* **l** thy 3509.1
20: 5 whose spear staff *was* **l** a weaver's beam. 3509.1
27:23 Israel **l to** the stars of the heavens. 3509.1
2Ch 1: 9 people **l** the dust of the earth in multitude. 3509.1
1:12 neither shall there any after thee have the **l.** 3651
4: 5 the brim of it **l** the work of the brim of a 3509.1
6:14 *there is* no God **l** thee in the heaven, nor in 3644
9:19 There was not the **l** made in any kingdom. 3651
18:12 be **l** one of theirs, and speak thou good. 3509.1
21: 6 of Israel, **l as** did the house of Ahab: 834+3509.1
21:13 **l to** the whoredoms of the house of Ahab, 3509.1
21:19 for him, **l** the burning of his fathers. 3509.1
22: 4 sight of the LORD, **l** the house of Ahab: 3509.1
28: 1 sight of the LORD, **l** David his father: 3509.1
30: 7 be not ye **l** your fathers, and like your 3509.1
30: 7 ye like your fathers, and **l** your brethren, 3509.1
30:26 of Israel *there was* not the **l** in Jerusalem. 3509.1
33: 2 **l unto** the abominations of the heathen, 3509.1
35:18 there was no passover **l to** that, kept in 3644
Ne 6: 5 sent Sanballat his servant unto me in **l** 2088
13:26 many nations was there no king **l** him, 3644
Est 2:20 **l as when** she was brought up with 834+3509.1
Job 1: 8 that *there is* none **l** him in the earth, 3644
2: 3 that *there is* none **l** him in the earth, 3644
3:24 my roarings are poured out **l** the waters. 3509.1
5:26 **l as** a shock of corn cometh in in his 3509.1
7: 1 *are not* his days also **l** the days of a 3509.1
8: 2 *how long shall* the words of thy mouth *be l* NIH
10:10 out as milk, and cruddled me **l** cheese? 3509.1
11:12 though man be born *l* a wild ass's colt. NIH
12:25 he maketh them to stagger **l** a drunken 3509.1
13:12 Your remembrances *are* **l unto** ashes, 4912
14: 2 He cometh forth **l** a flower, and is cut 3509.1
14: 9 it will bud, and bring forth boughs **l** a plant. 3644
15:16 *is* man, which drinketh iniquity **l** water? 3509.1
16:14 he runneth upon me **l** a giant. 3509.1
19:10 and mine hope hath he removed **l** a tree. 3509.1
20: 7 *Yet* he shall perish for ever **l** his own 3509.1
21:11 They send forth their little ones **l** a flock, 3509.1
30:19 the mire, and I am **become l** dust and ashes. 4911
32:19 no vent; it is ready to burst **l** new bottles. 3509.1
34: 7 What man *is* **l** Job, *who* drinketh up 3509.1
34: 7 *who* drinketh up scorning **l** water? 3509.1
36:22 exalteth by his power: who teacheth **l** him? 3644
38: 3 Gird up now thy loins **l** a man; for I will 3509.1
40: 7 Gird up thy loins now **l** a man: I will 3509.1
40: 9 Hast thou an arm **l** God? or, canst thou 3509.1
40: 9 or, canst thou thunder with a voice **l** him? 3644
40:17 He moveth his tail **l** a cedar: the sinews of 3644
40:18 of brass; his bones *are* **l** bars of iron. 3509.1
41:18 his eyes *are* **l** the eyelids of the morning. 3509.1
41:31 He maketh the deep to boil **l** a pot: 3509.1
41:31 he maketh the sea **l** a pot of ointment. 3509.1
41:33 Upon earth there is not his **l**, who is made 4915
42: 8 *the thing which is* right, **l** my servant Job. 3509.1
Ps 1: 3 he shall be **l** a tree planted by the rivers of 3509.1
1: 4 *are* **l** the chaff which the wind driveth 3509.1
2: 9 thou shalt dash them in pieces **l** a potter's 3509.1
7: 2 Lest he tear my soul **l** a lion, rending *it* in 3509.1
17:12 **L** as a lion *that* is greedy of his prey, and 1825
18:33 He maketh my feet **l** hinds' *feet*, and 3509.1
22:14 I am poured out **l** water, and all my bones 3509.1
Ps 22:14 my heart is **l** wax; it is melted in the midst 3509.1
22:15 My strength is dried up **l** a potsherd; and 3509.1
28: 1 I **become l** them that go down into the pit. 4911
29: 6 He maketh them also to skip **l** a calf; 3644
29: 6 Lebanon and Sirion **l** a young unicorn. 3644
31:12 man out of mind: I am **l** a broken vessel. 3509.1
35:10 shall say, LORD, who *is* **l unto** thee, 3644
36: 6 Thy righteousness *is* **l** the great 3509.1
37: 2 For they shall soon be cut down **l** 3509.1
37:35 and spreading himself **l** a green bay tree. 3509.1
39:11 his beauty to consume away **l** a moth: 3509.1
44:11 Thou hast given us **l** sheep appointed for 3509.1
49:12 abideth not: he is **l** the beasts *that* perish. 4911
49:14 **L** sheep they are laid in the grave; 3509.1
49:20 is **l** the beasts *that* perish. 4911
52: 2 **l** a sharp rasor, working deceitfully. 3509.1
52: 8 I *am* **l** a green olive tree in the house of 3509.1
55: 6 O that I had wings **l** a dove, *for then* 3509.1
58: 4 Their poison *is* **l** the poison of a 1823+3509.1
58: 4 *they are* **l** the deaf adder *that* stoppeth her 3644
58: 8 *l* the untimely birth of a woman, *that* they NIH
59: 6 they make a noise **l** a dog, and go round 3509.1
59:14 *and* let them make a noise **l** a dog, and 3509.1
64: 3 Who whet their tongue **l** a sword, *and* 3509.1
71:19 great *things:* O God, who *is* **l unto** thee! 3644
72: 6 He shall come down **l** rain upon 3509.1
72:16 the fruit thereof shall shake **l** Lebanon: 3509.1
72:16 *they* of the city shall flourish **l** grass of 3509.1
73: 5 neither are they plagued **l** *other* men. 5973
77:20 Thou leddest thy people **l** a flock by 3509.1
78:16 and caused waters to run down **l** rivers. 3509.1
78:27 feathered fowls **l as** the sand of the sea: 3509.1
78:52 made his own people to go forth **l** sheep, 3509.1
78:52 guided them in the wilderness **l** a flock. 3509.1
78:57 and dealt unfaithfully **l** their fathers: 3509.1
78:57 they were turned aside **l** a deceitful bow. 3509.1
78:65 **l** a mighty *man* that shouteth by reason of 3509.1
78:69 he built his sanctuary **l** high *palaces*, like 3644
78:69 he built his sanctuary like high *palaces*, **l** 3509.1
79: 3 Their blood have they shed **l** water round 3509.1
79: 5 for ever? shall thy jealousy burn **l** fire? 3644
80: 1 thou that leadest Joseph **l** a flock; 3509.1
80:10 the boughs thereof *were* *l* the goodly cedars. NIH
82: 7 ye shall die **l** men, and fall like one of 3509.1
82: 7 die like men, and fall **l** one of the princes. 3509.1
83:11 Make their nobles **l** Oreb, and like Zeeb: 3509.1
83:11 Make their nobles like Oreb, and **l** Zeeb: 3509.1
83:13 O my God, make them **l** a wheel; as 3509.1
86: 8 Among the gods *there is* none **l unto** thee, 3644
86: 8 neither *are there any works* **l unto** thy 3509.1
88: 5 the dead, **l** the slain that lie in the grave, 3644
88:17 They came round about me daily **l** water; 3509.1
89: 8 who *is* a strong LORD **l unto** thee? 3644
89:46 for ever? shall thy wrath burn **l** fire? 3644
90: 5 in the morning *they are* **l** grass *which* 3509.1
92:10 my horn shalt thou exalt **l** *the horn of* an 3509.1
92:12 The righteous shall flourish **l** the palm 3509.1
92:12 he shall grow **l** a cedar in Lebanon. 3509.1
97: 5 The hills melted **l** wax at the presence of 3509.1
102: 3 For my days are consumed **l** smoke, and 871.1
102: 4 My heart is smitten, and withered **l** grass; 3509.1
102: 6 I am **l** a pelican of the wilderness: I am like 1819
102: 6 I am **l** an owl of the desert. 3509.1
102: 9 For I have eaten ashes **l** bread, and 3509.1
102:11 My days *are* **l** a shadow that declineth; 3509.1
102:11 that declineth; and I am withered **l** grass. 3509.1
102:26 yea, all of them shall wax old **l** a garment; 3509.1
103: 5 *so that* thy youth is renewed **l** the eagle's. 3509.1
103:13 **L as** a father pitieth *his* children, *so* 3509.1
104: 2 who stretchest out the heavens **l** a curtain: 3509.1
105:41 they ran in the dry *places* *l* a river. NIH
107:27 stagger **l** a drunken *man*, and are at their 3509.1
107:41 and maketh *him* families **l** a flock. 3509.1
109:18 As he clothed himself with cursing **l as** 3509.1
109:18 so let it come into his bowels **l** water, and 3509.1
109:18 like water, and **l** oil into his bones. 3509.1
109:23 I am gone **l** the shadow when it declineth: 3509.1
113: 5 Who *is* **l unto** the LORD our God, who 3509.1
114: 4 The mountains skipped **l** rams, *and* 3509.1
114: 4 like rams, *and* the little hills **l** lambs. 3509.1
114: 6 Ye mountains, *that* ye skipped **l** rams; *and* 3509.1
114: 6 like rams; *and* ye little hills, **l** lambs? 3509.1
115: 8 They that make them are **l unto** them; *so* 3644
118:12 They compassed me about **l** bees; 3509.1
119:83 For I am become **l** a bottle in the smoke; 3509.1
119:119 away all the wicked of the earth *l* dross: NIH
119:176 I have gone astray **l** a lost sheep; seek thy 3509.1
126: 1 of Zion, we were **l** them that dream. 3509.1
128: 3 thy children **l** olive plants round about thy 3509.1
133: 2 *It is* **l** the precious ointment upon 3509.1
135:18 They that make them are **l unto** them: *so* 3644
140: 3 They have sharpened their tongues **l** a 3644
143: 7 lest I be **l unto** them that go down into 4911
144: 4 Man is **l** to vanity: his days *are* as a shadow 1819
147:16 He giveth snow **l** wool: he scattereth 3509.1
147:16 he scattereth the hoarfrost **l** ashes. 3509.1
147:17 He casteth forth his ice **l** morsels: 3509.1
Pr 12:18 There is that speaketh **l** the piercings of a 3509.1
17:22 A merry heart doeth good *l* a medicine: but NIH
18:19 *their* contentions *are* **l** the bars of a castle. 3509.1
20: 5 Counsel in the heart of man *is l* deep water; NIH
23:32 At the last it biteth **l** a serpent, and 3509.1
23:32 like a serpent, and stingeth **l** an adder. 3509.1
25:11 A word fitly spoken *is l* apples of gold in NIH
25:14 Whoso boasteth himself of a false gift *is l* NIH
25:19 *man* in time of trouble *is l* a broken tooth, NIH
25:28 He that *hath* no rule over his own spirit *is l* a NIH
26: 4 to his folly, lest thou also be **l** unto him. 7737
26:17 to him, *is l* one that taketh a dog by the ears. NIH
26:23 a wicked heart *are l* a potsherd covered with NIH
28: 3 A poor man that oppresseth the poor *is l* a NIH
31:14 She is **l** the merchant's ships; 3509.1
SS 2: 9 My beloved *is* **l** a roe or a young hart: 1819
2:17 be thou **l** a roe or a young hart upon 1819
3: 6 out of the wilderness **l** pillars of smoke, 3509.1

SS 4: 2 Thy teeth *are* l a flock of *sheep that are* 3509.1
4: 3 Thy lips *are* l a thread of scarlet, and 3509.1
4: 3 thy temples *are* l a piece of a 3509.1
4: 4 Thy neck *is* l the tower of David builded 3509.1
4: 5 Thy two breasts *are* l two young roes *that* 3509.1
4:11 the smell of thy garments *is* l the smell of 3509.1
5:13 his lips *l* lilies, dropping sweet smelling NIH
6:12 my soul made me *l* the chariots of NIH
7: 1 the joints of thy thighs *are* l jewels, 3644
7: 2 Thy navel *is l* a round goblet, NIH
7: 2 thy belly *is l* a heap of wheat set about with NIH
7: 3 Thy two breasts *are* l two young roes *that* 3509.1
7: 4 thine eyes *l* the *fish*pools in Heshbon, by NIH
7: 5 Thine head upon thee *is* l Carmel, and 3509.1
7: 5 and the hair of thine head l purple; 3509.1
7: 7 This thy stature is l to a palm tree, and 1819
7: 8 and the smell of thy nose l apples; 3509.1
7: 9 the roof of thy mouth l the best wine, 3509.1
8:10 I *am* a wall, and my breasts l towers: then 3509.1
8:14 be thou l to a roe or to a young hart upon 1819
Isa 1: 9 *and* we should have been l unto Gomorrah. 1819
1:18 though they be red l crimson, they shall 3509.1
2: 6 *are* soothsayers l the Philistines, and 3509.1
3:18 and *their* **round tires l the moon**, 7720
5:28 their horses' hoofs shall be counted l 3509.1
5:28 like flint, and their wheels l a whirlwind: 3509.1
5:29 Their roaring *shall be* l a lion, they shall 3509.1
5:29 like a lion, they shall roar l young lions: 3509.1
5:30 in that day they shall roar against them l 3509.1
9:18 they shall mount up *l* the lifting up of NIH
10: 6 tread them down l the mire of the streets. 3509.1
10:13 I have put down the inhabitants l a 3509.1
10:16 under his glory he shall kindle a burning l 3509.1
11: 7 and the lion shall eat straw l the ox. 3509.1
11:16 l as it was to Israel in the day that he 3509.1
13: 4 in the mountains, **l as** of a great people; 1823
14:10 weak as we? art thou **become l** unto us? 4911
14:14 of the clouds; I will be l the most High. 1819
14:19 thou art cast out of thy grave l an 3509.1
16:11 Wherefore my bowels shall sound l a 3509.1
17:12 make a noise l the noise of the seas; 3509.1
17:12 *that* make a rushing l the rushing of 3509.1
17:13 The nations shall rush l the rushing of 3509.1
17:13 and l a rolling thing before the whirlwind. 3509.1
18: 4 I will consider in my dwelling place l a 3509.1
18: 4 l a cloud of dew in the heat of harvest. 3509.1
19:16 In that day shall Egypt be **l unto** women: 3509.1
20: 3 **L as** my servant Isaiah hath walked 834+3509.1
22:18 and toss thee l a ball into a large country: 3509.1
24:20 The earth shall reel to and fro l a 3509.1
24:20 and shall be removed l a cottage; 3509.1
26:17 **L as** a woman with child, *that* draweth near 3644
27:10 and left l a wilderness: 3509.1
29: 5 of thy strangers shall be l small dust, 3509.1
30:33 l a stream of brimstone, doth kindle it. 3509.1
31: 4 **L as** the lion and the young lion 834+3509.1
33: 4 your spoil shall be gathered *l* the gathering NIH
33: 9 Sharon is l a wilderness; and Bashan and 3509.1
36:17 take you away to a land l your own land, 3509.1
38:12 I have cut off l a weaver my life: he will 3509.1
38:14 **L** a crane *or* a swallow, so did I chatter: 3509.1
40:11 He shall feed his flock l a shepherd: 3509.1
42:13 he shall stir up jealousy l a man of war: 3509.1
42:14 *now* will I cry l a travailing woman; I will 3509.1
46: 5 and compare me, that we may be l? 1819
46: 9 *I am* God, and *there is* none l me, 3644
48:19 the offspring of thy bowels l the gravel 3509.1
49: 2 he hath made my mouth l a sharp sword; 3509.1
50: 7 therefore have I set my face l a flint, and 3509.1
51: 3 he will make her wilderness l Eden, and 3509.1
51: 3 her desert l the garden of the LORD; 3509.1
51: 6 for the heavens shall vanish away l 3509.1
51: 6 the earth shall wax old l a garment, and 3509.1
51: 6 they that dwell therein shall die in l 3644
51: 8 For the moth shall eat them up l 3509.1
51: 8 and the worm shall eat them l wool: 3509.1
53: 6 All we l sheep have gone astray; we have 3509.1
57:20 the wicked *are* l the troubled sea, when it 3509.1
58: 1 lift up thy voice l a trumpet, and shew my 3509.1
58:11 thou shalt be l a watered garden, and 3509.1
58:11 l a spring of water, whose waters fail not. 3509.1
59:10 We grope for the wall l the blind, and 3509.1
59:11 We roar all l bears, and mourn sore like 3509.1
59:11 all like bears, and mourn sore l doves: 3509.1
59:19 When the enemy shall come in l a flood, 3509.1
63: 2 thy garments l him that treadeth in 3509.1
64: 6 our iniquities, l the wind, have taken us 3509.1
65:25 and the lion shall eat straw l the bullock: 3509.1
66:12 I will extend peace to her l a river, and 3509.1
66:12 the glory of the Gentiles l a flowing 3509.1
66:14 and your bones shall flourish l an herb: 3509.1
66:15 with his chariots l a whirlwind, to render 3509.1
Jer 2:30 your prophets, l a destroying lion. 3509.1
4: 4 lest my fury come forth l fire, and 3509.1
5:19 **L as** ye have forsaken me, and 834+3509.1
6:23 their voice roareth l the sea; and they ride 3509.1
9: 3 they bend their tongues *l* their bow *for* lies: NIH
9:12 *and* is burnt up l a wilderness, 3509.1
10: 6 Forasmuch as *there is* none **l unto** thee, 3644
10: 7 their kingdoms, *there is* none l **unto** thee. 3644
10:16 The portion of Jacob *is* not l them: for he 3509.1
11:19 I *was* l a lamb *or* an ox *that is* brought to 3509.1
12: 3 pull them out l sheep for the slaughter, 3509.1
14: 6 they snuffed up the wind l dragons; 3509.1
17: 6 For he shall be l the heath in the desert, 3509.1
21:12 lest my fury go out l fire, and burn that 3509.1
23: 9 I am l a drunken man, and like a man 3509.1
23: 9 l a man whom wine hath overcome, 3509.1
23:29 *Is* not my word **l as** a fire? saith 3509.1
23:29 l a hammer *that* breaketh the rock in 3509.1
24: 2 *even* l the figs *that are* first ripe: 3509.1
24: 5 **L** these good figs, so will I acknowledge 3509.1
25:34 And ye shall fall l a pleasant vessel. 3509.1
26: 6 will I make this house l Shiloh, and will 3509.1
26: 9 This house shall be l Shiloh, and this city 3509.1
Jer 26:18 Zion shall be plowed *l* a field, and NIH
29:17 and will make them l vile figs, 3509.1
29:22 The LORD make thee l Zedekiah and 3509.1
29:22 make thee like Zedekiah and l Ahab, 3509.1
30: 7 for that day *is* great, so that none *is* l it: it *is* 3644
31:28 *that* **l as** I have watched over them, 834+3509.1
32:42 **L as** I have brought all this great 834+3509.1
36:32 added besides unto them many l words. 3509.1
38: 9 he is l to die for hunger in the place where NIH
46: 8 Egypt riseth up l a flood, and *his* waters 3509.1
46: 8 and *his* waters are moved l the rivers; 3509.1
46:20 Egypt *is l* a very fair heifer, *but* NIH
46:21 *are* in the midst of her l fatted bullocks; 3509.1
46:22 The voice thereof shall go l a serpent; 3509.1
48: 6 and be l the heath in the wilderness. 3509.1
48:28 be l the dove *that* maketh her nest in 3509.1
48:36 mine heart shall sound for Moab l pipes, 3509.1
48:36 mine heart shall sound l pipes for the men 3509.1
48:38 for I have broken Moab l a vessel 3509.1
49:19 he shall come up l a lion from 3509.1
49:19 for who *is* l me? and who will appoint me 3644
50:42 their voice shall roar l the sea, and 3509.1
50:42 l a man to the battle, against thee, 3509.1
50:44 he shall come up l a lion from 3509.1
50:44 for who *is* l me? and who will appoint me 3644
51:19 The portion of Jacob *is* not l them; for he 3509.1
51:33 The daughter of Babylon *is* l a 3509.1
51:34 he hath swallowed me up l a dragon, 3509.1
51:38 They shall roar together l lions: they shall 3509.1
51:40 I will bring them down l lambs to 3509.1
51:40 to the slaughter, l rams with he goats. 3509.1
51:55 when her waves do roar l great waters, 3509.1
52:22 and the pomegranates *were* **l unto** these. 3509.1
La 1: 6 her princes are become l harts *that* find no 3509.1
1:12 see if there be any sorrow **l unto** my 3509.1
1:21 hast called, and they shall be **l unto** me. 3644
2: 3 he burned against Jacob l a flaming fire, 3509.1
2: 4 He hath bent his bow l an enemy: 3509.1
2: 4 of Zion: he poured out his fury l fire. 3509.1
2:13 for thy breach *is* great l the sea: who can 3509.1
2:18 let tears run down l a river day and night: 3509.1
2:19 pour out thine heart l water before 3509.1
3:52 chased me sore, l a bird, without cause. 3509.1
4: 3 l the ostriches in the wilderness. 3509.1
4: 8 it is withered, it is become l a stick. 3509.1
5:10 Our skin was black l an oven because 3509.1
Eze 1: 7 the sole of their feet *was* l the sole of a 3509.1
1: 7 they sparkled l the colour of burnished 3509.1
1:13 their appearance *was* l burning coals of 3509.1
1:13 of fire, *and* l the appearance of lamps: 3509.1
1:16 work *was* **l unto** the colour of a beryl: 3509.1
1:24 l the noise of great waters, as the voice of 3509.1
2: 8 Be not thou rebellious l *that* rebellious 3509.1
5: 9 whereunto I will not do any more the l, 3644
7:16 shall be on the mountains l doves of 3509.1
12:11 **l as** I have done, so shall it be done 834+3509.1
13: 4 thy prophets are l the foxes in the deserts. 3509.1
16:16 *the l things shall* not come, neither shall it NIH
18:10 *that* doeth the l to *any* one of these *things,* 251
18:14 and considereth, and doeth not **such l**, 3509.1
19:10 Thy mother *is* l a vine in thy blood, 3509.1
20:36 **L as** I pleaded with your fathers in 834+3509.1
22:25 l a roaring lion ravening the prey; 3509.1
22:27 Her princes in the midst thereof *are* l 3509.1
23:18 **l as** my mind was alienated from her 834+3509.1
23:20 and whose issue *is l* the issue of horses. NIH
25: 8 house of Judah *is* **l unto** all the heathen; 3509.1
26: 4 and make her l the top of a rock. 3807.1
26:14 I will make thee l the top of a rock: 3807.1
26:19 l the cities that are not inhabited; 3509.1
27:32 over thee, *saying,* What *city is* l Tyrus, 3509.1
27:32 l the destroyed in the midst of the sea? 3509.1
31: 2 Whom art thou l in thy greatness? 1819
31: 8 the fir trees were not l his boughs, and 1819
31: 8 the chesnut trees were not l his branches; 3509.1
31: 8 nor any tree in the garden of God was l 1819
31:18 To whom art thou thus l in glory and 1819
32: 2 Thou art l a young lion of the nations, and 1819
32:14 cause their rivers to run l oil, saith 3509.1
36:35 This land that was desolate is become l 3509.1
36:37 I will increase them *with* men l a flock. 3509.1
38: 9 Thou shalt ascend and come l a storm, 3509.1
38: 9 thou shalt be l a cloud to cover the land, 3509.1
40: 3 whose appearance *was* l the appearance 3509.1
40:25 thereof round about, l those windows: 3509.1
41:25 **l as** *were* made upon the walls; 834+3509.1
42:11 the way before them *was* l the appearance 3509.1
43: 2 his voice *was* l a noise of many waters: 3509.1
43: 3 the visions *were* l the vision that I saw by 3509.1
45:25 shall he do the l in the feast *of* the seven 3509.1
Da 1:19 among them all was found none l Daniel, 3509.1
2:35 became l the chaff of the summer 3509.4
3:25 the form of the fourth *is* l the Son of God. 1821
4:33 till his hairs were grown l eagles' 3509.4
4:33 and his nails l birds' *claws.* 3509.4
5:11 and wisdom, l the wisdom of the gods, 3509.4
5:21 his heart was made l the beasts, and 5974
5:21 they fed him with grass l oxen, and 3509.4
7: 4 The first *was* l a lion, and had eagle's 3509.4
7: 5 l to a bear, and it raised up itself on one 1821
7: 6 this I beheld, and lo another, l a leopard, 3509.4
7: 8 in this horn *were* eyes l the eyes of man, 3509.4
7: 9 and the hair of his head l the pure wool: 3509.4
7: 9 his throne *was l* the fiery flame, *and* NIH
7:13 *one* l the Son of man came with 3509.4
10: 6 His body also *was* l the beryl, and 3509.1
10: 6 and his feet l in colour to polished brass, 3509.1
10: 6 the voice of his words l the voice of a 3509.1
10:16 *one* l the similitude of the sons of men 3509.1
10:18 me *one* l the appearance of a man, 3509.1
11:40 shall **come** against him **l a whirlwind**, 8175
Hos 2: 3 set her l a dry land, and slay her with 3509.1
4: 9 there shall be, l people, like priest: and 3509.1
4: 9 there shall be, like people, l priest: and 3509.1
5:10 The princes of Judah were l them that 3509.1
Hos 5:10 I will pour out my wrath upon them l 3509.1
6: 7 they l men have transgressed 3509.1
7: 6 For they have made ready their heart l an 3509.1
7:11 Ephraim also is l a silly dove, 3509.1
7:16 they are l a deceitful bow: their princes 3509.1
9:10 I found Israel l grapes in the wilderness; 3509.1
9:11 their glory shall fly away l a bird, 3509.1
11:10 he shall roar l a lion: when he shall roar, 3509.1
13: 8 and there will l devour them l a lion: 3509.1
14: 8 I *am* l a green fir tree. From me is thy 3509.1
Joel 1: 8 Lament l a virgin girded with sackcloth 3509.1
2: 2 there hath not been ever **the l**, neither shall 3644
2: 5 **L** the noise of chariots on the tops of 3509.1
2: 5 l the noise of a flame of fire that 3509.1
2: 7 They shall run l mighty *men;* they shall 3509.1
2: 7 they shall climb the wall l men of war; 3509.1
2: 9 shall enter in at the windows l a thief. 3509.1
Am 2: 9 whose height *was* l the height of 3509.1
5: 6 lest he break out l fire *in* the house of 3509.1
6: 5 instruments of musick, l David; 3509.1
9: 5 it shall rise up wholly l a flood; and 3509.1
9: 9 l as *corn* is sifted in a sieve, yet shall not 3509.1
Jnh 1: 4 the sea, so that the ship was l to be broken. 2803
Mic 1: 8 I will make a wailing l the dragons, and 3509.1
4:10 O daughter of Zion, l a woman in travail: 3509.1
7:17 They shall lick the dust l a serpent, 3509.1
7:17 they shall move out of their holes l 3509.1
7:18 Who *is* a God **l unto** thee, that pardoneth 3644
Na 1: 6 his fury is poured out l fire, and the rocks 3509.1
2: 4 they shall seem l torches, they shall run 3509.1
2: 4 they shall run l the lightnings. 3509.1
2: 8 Nineveh *is* of old l a pool of water: yet 3509.1
3:12 All thy strong holds *shall be l* fig trees with NIH
3:15 it shall eat thee up l the cankerworm: 3509.1
Hab 3:19 he will make my feet l hinds' *feet,* and 3509.1
Zep 1:17 that they shall walk l blind *men,* because 3509.1
2:13 a desolation, *and* dry l a wilderness. 3509.1
Zec 1: 6 **L** as the LORD of hosts thought to do 3509.1
5: 9 for they had wings l the wings of a stork: 3509.1
9:15 they shall be filled l bowls, *and* as 3509.1
10: 7 *they of* Ephraim shall be l a mighty *man,* 3509.1
12: 6 Judah l a hearth of fire among the wood, 3509.1
12: 6 the wood, and l a torch of fire in a sheaf; 3509.1
14: 5 **l as** ye fled from before 834+3509.1
14:20 the pots in the LORD'S house shall be l 3509.1
Mal 3: 2 for he *is* l a refiner's fire, and like fullers' 3509.1
3: 2 *is* like a refiner's fire, and l fullers' sope: 3509.1
Mt 3:16 he saw the Spirit of God descending l a *5616*
6: 8 Be not ye therefore l unto them: for your *3666*
6:29 all his glory was not arrayed l one of these. *5613*
11:16 It is l unto children sitting in the markets, *3664*
12:13 and it was restored whole, *l* as the other. NIG
13:31 The kingdom of heaven is **l unto** a grain of *3664*
13:33 The kingdom of heaven is l unto leaven, *3664*
13:44 the kingdom of heaven is l unto treasure *3664*
13:45 the kingdom of heaven is l unto a merchant *3664*
13:47 the kingdom of heaven is l unto a net, *3664*
13:52 is l unto a man *that is* a householder, *3664*
20: 1 For the kingdom of heaven is l unto a man *3664*
21:24 **I in l wise** will tell you by what authority I *2504*
22: 2 The kingdom of heaven is l unto a certain *3666*
22:39 And the second *is* l unto it, Thou shalt love *3664*
23:27 for ye are l unto whited sepulchres, *3945*
28: 3 His countenance was l lightning, and *5613*
Mk 1:10 the Spirit l a dove descending upon him: *5616*
4:31 *It is* l a grain of mustard seed, which, *5613*
7: 8 cups: and many other such l *things* ye do. *3946*
7:13 and many such l *things* do ye. *3946*
12:31 And the second *is* l, *namely* this, Thou shalt *3664*
13:29 **So** ye **in l manner**, when ye shall see *2532+3779*
Lk 3:22 in a bodily shape l a dove upon him, *5616*
6:23 for **in the l manner** did their *846+3596+3588*
6:47 I will shew you to whom he is l: *3664*
6:48 He is l a man which built a house, and *3664*
6:49 is l a man that without a foundation built a *3664*
7:31 of this generation? and to what are they l? *3664*
7:32 They are l unto children sitting in *3664*
12:27 all his glory was not arrayed l one of these. *5613*
12:36 And ye yourselves l unto men that wait for *3664*
13:18 Unto what is the kingdom of God l? *3664*
13:19 It is l a grain of mustard seed, which a man *3664*
13:21 It is l leaven, which a woman took and *3664*
20:31 took her; and **in l manner** the seven also: *5615*
Jn 1:32 I saw the Spirit descending from heaven l a *5616*
7:46 Never man spake l this man. *5613*
8:55 I know him not, I shall be a liar l unto you: *3664*
9: 9 others *said,* He is l him: *but* he said, I am *3664*
Ac 1:11 come *in* l manner as ye have seen him go *3739*
2: 3 unto them cloven tongues **l as** of fire, *5616*
3:22 up unto you of your brethren, **l unto** me; *5613*
7:37 up unto you of your brethren, **l unto** me; *5613*
8:32 and l a lamb dumb before his shearer, so *5613*
11:17 as God gave them the l gift as *he did* unto *2470*
14:15 We also are men **of l passions with** you, *3663*
17:29 to think that the Godhead is **l unto** gold, *3664*
19:25 together with the workmen of **l occupation**, *5108*
Ro 1:23 into an image made **l to** corruptible man, *3667*
1:28 And even as they did not l to retain God in *1381*
6: 4 that **l as** Christ was raised up from the dead *5618*
9:29 and been **made** l unto Gomorrha. *3666*
1Co 16:13 fast in the faith, **quit** you **l men**, be strong. *407*
Gal 5:21 drunkenness, revellings, and such l: *3664*
Php 3:21 that it may be **fashioned l unto** his glorious *4832*
1Th 2:14 for ye also have suffered l *things* of your *5024*
1Ti 2: 9 **In l manner** also, that women adorn *5615*
Heb 2:17 him to be **made** l unto *his* brethren, *3666*
4:15 was in all *points* tempted **l as** *we are,* *2596+3665*
7: 3 end of life; but **made l unto** the Son of God; *871*
Jas 1: 6 for he that wavereth is l a wave of the sea *1503*
1:23 he is l unto a man beholding his natural *1503*
5:17 Elias was a man **subject to l passions** as *3663*
1Pe 3:21 The **l figure** whereunto *even* baptism doth *499*
2Pe 1: 1 to them that have obtained **l precious** faith *2472*
1Jn 3: 2 when he shall appear, we shall be l him; *3664*
Jude 1: 7 in l manner giving themselves over to *3664*

L

Rev 1:13 candlesticks one l unto the Son of man, NIG
1:14 His head and *his* hairs *were* white l wool, 5616
1:15 And his feet l **unto** fine brass, as if they 3664
2:18 who hath his eyes l **unto** a flame of fire, 5613
2:18 a flame of fire, and his feet *are* l fine brass; 3664
4: 3 And he that sat was to look upon l a jasper 3664
4: 3 the throne, in sight l **unto** an emerald. 3664
4: 6 *there was* a sea of glass l unto crystal: 5613
4: 7 And the first beast *was* l a lion, and 3664
4: 7 And the second beast l a calf, and the third 3664
4: 7 and the fourth beast *was* l a flying eagle. 3664
9: 7 And the shapes of the locusts *were* l unto 3664
9: 7 on their heads *were* as *it were* crowns l 3664
9:10 And they had tails l unto scorpions, and 3664
9:19 for their tails *were* l unto serpents, and 3664
11: 1 And there was given me a reed l unto a rod: 3664
13: 2 And the beast which I saw was l unto a 3664
13: 4 the beast, saying, Who *is* l unto the beast? 3664
13:11 and he had two horns l a lamb, and 3664
14:14 upon the cloud one sat l unto the Son of 3664
16:13 And I saw three unclean spirits l frogs 3664
18:18 saying, What *city is* l unto *this* great city? 3664
18:21 And a mighty angel took up a stone l a 5613
21:11 her light *was* l unto a stone most precious, 3664
21:11 *even* l a jasper stone, clear as crystal; 5613
21:18 the city *was* pure gold, l unto clear glass. 3664

LIKED (1) [LIKE]
1Ch 28: 4 among the sons of my father he l me to 7521

LIKEMINDED (3) [LIKE, MIND]
Ro 15: 5 consolation grant you to be l 846+3588+5426
Php 2: 2 Fulfil ye my joy, that ye be l, 846+3588+5426
2:20 For I have no *man* l, who will naturally 2473

LIKEN (9) [LIKE]
Isa 40:18 To whom then will ye l God? or 1819
40:25 To whom then will ye l me, or shall I be 1819
46: 5 To whom will ye l me, and make *me* equal, 1819
La 2:13 what *thing* shall I l to thee, O daughter of 1819
Mt 7:24 doeth them, I will l him unto a wise man, 3666
11:16 But whereunto shall I l this generation? It is 3666
Mk 4:30 Whereunto shall we l the kingdom of God? 3666
Lk 7:31 then shall I l the men of this generation? 3666
13:20 Whereunto shall I l the kingdom of God? 3666

LIKENED (6) [LIKE]
Ps 89: 6 *who* among the sons of the mighty can be l 1819
Jer 6: 2 I have l the daughter of Zion *to* a comely 1819
Mt 7:26 them not, shall be l unto a foolish man, 3666
13:24 The kingdom of heaven is l unto a man 3666
18:23 Therefore is the kingdom of heaven l unto a 3666
25: 1 Then shall the kingdom of heaven be l unto 3666

LIKENESS (34) [LIKE]
Ge 1:26 Let us make man in our image, after our l: 1823
5: 1 created man, in the l of God made he him; 1823
5: 3 thirty years, and begat *a son* in his own l, 1823
Ex 20: 4 any l *of any thing* that *is* in heaven above, 8544
Dt 4:16 of any figure, the l of male or female, 8403
4:17 The l of any beast that *is* on the earth, 8403
4:17 the l of any winged fowl that flieth in 8403
4:18 The l of any *thing* that creepeth on 8403
4:18 the l of any fish that *is* in the waters 8403
4:23 the l of any *thing*, which the LORD thy 8544
4:25 *or* the l of any *thing*, and shall do evil in 8544
5: 8 any l *of any thing* that *is* in heaven above, 8544
Ps 17:15 shall be satisfied, when *I* awake, *with* thy l. 8544
Isa 40:18 or what l will ye compare unto him? 1823
Eze 1: 5 Also out of the midst thereof *came* the l of 1823
1: 5 their appearance; they had the l of a man. 1823
1:10 As for the l of their faces, they four had 1823
1:13 As for the l of the living creatures, 1823
1:16 they four had one l: and their appearance 1823
1:22 the l of the firmament upon the heads of 1823
1:26 *was* over their heads *was* the l of a throne, 1823
1:26 upon the l of the throne *was* the likeness as 1823
1:26 upon the likeness of the throne *was* the l as 1823
1:28 This *was* the appearance of the l of 1823
8: 2 and lo, a l as the appearance of fire: 1823
10: 1 as the appearance of the l of a throne. 1823
10:10 *for* their appearances, they four had one l, 1823
10:21 the l of the hands of a man *was* under their 1823
10:22 the l of their faces *was* the same faces 1823
Ac 14:11 The gods are come down to us in the l of 3666
Ro 6: 5 if we have been planted together **in** the l 3667
6: 5 we shall be also *in the l* of *his* resurrection: NIG
8: 3 God sending his own Son in the l of sinful 3667
Php 2: 7 of a servant, and was made in the l of men: 3667

LIKETH (3) [LIKE]
Dt 23:16 where it l him **best**: 2896+871.1+1886.1
Est 8: 8 as it l you, in the king's name, 2896+5869+871.1
Am 4: 5 for this l you, O ye children of Israel, 157

LIKEWISE (107) [LIKE]
Ex 22:30 L shalt thou do with thine oxen, *and* 3651
26: 4 l shalt thou make in the uttermost edge of 3651
27:11 l for the north side in length *there shall be* 3651
36:11 l he made in the uttermost side of *another* 3651
Lev 7: 1 L this *is* the law of the trespass offering: 2050.1
Dt 9:23 L when the LORD sent you from 2050.1
12:30 serve their gods? even so will I do l. 1571
15:17 also unto thy maidservant thou shalt do l. 3651
22: 3 and thou hast found, shalt thou do l: NIH
Jdg 1: 3 and I l will go with thee into thy lot. 1571
7: 5 l every one that boweth down upon his 2050.1
7:17 he said unto them, Look on me, and do l: 3651
8: 8 *to* Penuel, and spake unto them l: 2088+3509.1
9:49 all the people l cut down every man his 1571
1Sa 14:22 L all the men of Israel which had hid 2050.1
19:21 other messengers, and they prophesied l. 1571
31: 5 l upon his sword, and died with 1571+2050.1
2Sa 1:11 and l all the men that *were* with him: 1571
17: 5 Archite also, and let us hear l what he saith. 1571
1Ki 11: 8 l did he for all his strange wives, 3651
1Ch 10: 5 was dead, he fell l on the sword, and died. 1571
18: 8 L from Tibhath, and from Chun, cities of 2050.1
19:15 they l fled before Abishai his 1571+2050.1
23:30 and praise the LORD, and l at even; 3651
24:31 These l cast lots over against their brethren 1571
27: 4 in his course l *were* twenty and 2050.1
28:16 and *l* silver for the tables of silver: NIH
28:17 *l silver* by weight for every bason of silver: NIH
29:24 and all the sons l of king David, 1571
2Ch 3:11 the other wing *was l* five cubits, reaching to NIH
29:22 l, **when** they had killed the rams, they 2050.1
Ne 4:22 L at the same time said I unto the people, 1571
5:10 I l, *and* my brethren, and 1571+2050.1
Est 1:18 L shall the ladies of Persia and Media say 2050.1
4:16 I also and my maidens will fast l; and so 3651
Job 31:38 or that the furrows l thereof complain; 3162
37: 6 l *to* the small rain, and *to* the great rain of 2050.1
Ps 49:10 l the fool and the brutish person perish, and 3162
52: 5 God shall l destroy thee for ever, he shall 1571
Ecc 7:22 that thou thyself l hast cursed others. 1571
Isa 30:24 The oxen l and the young asses that ear 2050.1
Jer 40:11 L when all the Jews that *were* in Moab, and 1571
Eze 13:17 L thou son of man, set thy face against 2050.1
40:16 the gate round about, and l to the arches: 3651
46: 3 L the people of the land shall worship *at* 2050.1
Na 1:12 Though *they be* quiet, and l many, yet thus 3651
Mt 17:12 L shall also the Son of man suffer of them. 3779
18:35 So l shall my heavenly Father do *also* unto 3779
20: 5 about the sixth and ninth hour, and did l. 5615
20:10 and they l received every man a penny. 2532
21:30 And he came to the second, and said l. 5615
21:36 moe than the first: and they did unto them l. 5615
22:26 L the second also, and the third, unto 3668
24:33 So l ye, when ye shall see all these *things*, 2532
25:17 And l he that *had received* two, he also 5615
26:35 I not deny thee. L also said all the disciples. 3668
27:41 L also the chief priests mocking *him*, with 3668
Mk 4:16 And these are they l which are sown on 3668
12:21 neither left he *any* seed: and the third l. 5615
14:31 deny thee in any wise. L also said they all. 5615
15:31 L also the chief priests mocking said 3668
Lk 2:38 And she coming in that instant gave thanks *l* NIG
3:11 and he that hath meat, let him do l. 3668
3:14 And *the* soldiers l demanded of him, 2532
5:33 and l the *disciples* of the Pharisees; 3668
6:31 men should do to you, do ye also to them l. 3668
10:32 And l a Levite, when he was at the place, 3668
10:37 said Jesus unto him, Go, and do thou l. 3668
13: 3 but, except ye repent, ye shall all l perish. 5615
13: 5 but except ye repent, ye shall all l perish. 3668
14:33 So l, whosoever *he be* of you that forsaketh 3779
15: 7 that l joy shall be in heaven over one sinner 3779
15:10 L, I say unto you, there is joy in 3779
16:25 and l Lazarus evil *things*: but now he is 3668
17:10 So l ye, when ye shall have done all those 2532
17:28 L also as it was in the days of Lot; they did 3668
17:31 that is in the field, let him l not return back. 3668
19:19 And he said l to him, Be thou also over five 2532
21:31 So l ye, when ye see these *things* come to 2532
22:20 L also the cup after supper, saying, 5615
22:36 hath a purse, let him take *it*, and l *his* scrip: 3668
Jn 5:19 soever he doeth, these also doeth the Son l. 3668
6:11 and l of the fishes as much as they would. 3668
21:13 taketh bread, and giveth them, and fish l. 3668
Ac 3:24 have spoken, have l foretold of these days. 2532
Ro 1:27 And l also the men, leaving the natural use 3668
6:11 L reckon ye also yourselves to be dead 3779
8:26 L the Spirit also helpeth our infirmities: 5615
16: 5 L *greet* the church that is in their house. 2532
1Co 7: 3 and l also the wife unto the husband. 3668
7: 4 l also the husband hath not power of his 3668
7:22 l also he that is called, *being* free, 3668
14: 9 So l you, except ye utter by the tongue 2532
Gal 2:13 And the other Jews dissembled l with him; 2532
Col 4:16 and that ye l read the *epistle* from Laodicea. 2532
1Ti 3: 8 L *must* the deacons *be* grave, 5615
5:25 L also the good works *of some* are manifest 5615
Tit 2: 3 The aged women l, *that they be* in 5615
2: 6 Young *men* l exhort to be sober minded. 5615
Heb 2:14 he also himself l took part of the same; 3898
Jas 2:25 L also was not Rahab the harlot justified by 3668
1Pe 3: 1 L, ye wives, *be* in subjection to your own 3668
3: 7 L, ye husbands, dwell with *them* according 3668
4: 1 arm yourselves l with the same mind: 2532
5: 5 L, *ye* younger, submit yourselves unto 3668
Jude 1: 8 L also these *filthy* dreamers defile 3305+3668
Rev 8:12 not for a third *part* of it, and the night l. 3668

LIKHI (1)
1Ch 7:19 Ahian, and Shechem, and L, and Aniam. 3949

LIKING (2) [LIKE]
Job 39: 4 Their young ones are **in good** l, they grow 2492
Da 1:10 for why should he see your faces **worse** l 2196

LILIES (10) [LILY]
1Ki 7:26 like the brim of a cup, *with* flowers of l: 7799
2Ch 4: 5 of the brim of a cup, *with* flowers of l; 7799
SS 2:16 and I *am* his: he feedeth among the l. 7799
4: 5 roes *that are* twins, which feed among the l. 7799
5:13 his lips *like* l, dropping sweet smelling 7799
6: 2 to feed in the gardens, and to gather l. 7799
6: 3 beloved *is* mine: he feedeth among the l. 7799
7: 2 *is like* a heap of wheat set about with l. 7799
Mt 6:28 Consider the l of the field, how they grow; 2918
Lk 12:27 Consider the l how they grow: they toil not, 2918

LILY (5) [LILIES]
1Ki 7:19 of the pillars *were* of l work in the porch, 7799
7:22 upon the top of the pillars *was* l work: so 7799
SS 2: 1 the rose of Sharon, *and* the l of the valleys. 7799
2: 2 As the l among thorns, so *is* my love 7799
Hos 14: 5 he shall grow as the l, and cast forth his 7799

LIME (2)
Isa 33:12 the people shall be *as* the burnings of l: 7875
Am 2: 1 burnt the bones of the king of Edom into l: 7875

LIMIT (1) [LIMITED, LIMITETH]
Eze 43:12 Upon the top of the mountain the whole l 1366

LIMITED (1) [LIMIT]
Ps 78:41 tempted God, and l the Holy One of Israel. 8428

LIMITETH (1) [LIMIT]
Heb 4: 7 Again he l a certain day, saying in David, 3724

LINE (31) [LINEAGE, LINES, PLUMBLINE]
Jos 2:18 thou shalt bind this l of scarlet thread in 8615
2:21 and she bound the scarlet l in the window. 8615
2Sa 8: 2 smote Moab, and measured them with a l, 2256
8: 2 to death, and *with* one full l to keep alive. 2256
1Ki 7:15 a l of twelve cubits did compass either of 2339
7:23 a l of thirty cubits did compass it round 6957
2Ki 21:13 I will stretch over Jerusalem the l of 6957
2Ch 4: 2 a l of thirty cubits did compass it round 6957
Job 38: 5 or who hath stretched the l upon it? 6957
Ps 19: 4 Their l is gone out through all the earth, 6957
78:55 divided them an inheritance by l, and 2256
Isa 28:10 l upon line, line upon line; here a little, *and* 6957
28:10 line upon l, line upon line; here a little, *and* 6957
28:10 line upon line, l upon line; here a little, *and* 6957
28:10 line upon line, line upon l; here a little, *and* 6957
28:13 l upon line, line upon line; here a little, *and* 6957
28:13 line upon l, line upon line; here a little, *and* 6957
28:13 line upon line, l upon line; here a little, *and* 6957
28:13 line upon line, line upon l; here a little, *and* 6957
28:17 Judgment also will I lay to the l, and 6957
34:11 he shall stretch out upon it the l of 6957
34:17 and his hand hath divided it unto them by l: 6957
44:13 he marketh it out with a l; he fitteth it with 8279
Jer 31:39 the measuring l shall yet go forth over 6957
La 2: 8 he hath stretched out a l, he hath not 6957
Eze 40: 3 with a l of flax in his hand, and a measuring 6616
47: 3 when the man that had the l in his hand 6957
Am 7:17 and thy land shall be divided by l; 2256
Zec 1:16 a l shall be stretched forth upon Jerusalem. 6957
2: 1 a man with a measuring l in his hand. 2256
2Co 10:16 not to boast in another *man's* l of *things* 2583

LINEAGE (1) [LINE]
Lk 2: 4 he was of the house and l of David:) 3965

LINEN (104)
Ge 41:42 arrayed him in vestures of **fine** l, and put a 8336
Ex 25: 4 and scarlet, and **fine** l, and goats' *hair*, 8336
26: 1 *with* ten curtains *of* **fine** twined l, 8336
26:31 scarlet, and **fine** twined l *of* cunning work: 8336
26:36 and purple, and scarlet, and **fine** twined l, 8336
27: 9 **fine** twined l of an hundred cubits long for 8336
27:16 and purple, and scarlet, and **fine** twined l, 8336
27:18 the height five cubits *of* **fine** twined l, and 8336
28: 5 and blue, and purple, and scarlet, and **fine** l. 8336
28: 6 and *of* purple, *of* scarlet, and **fine** twined l, 8336
28: 8 and purple, and scarlet, and **fine** twined l. 8336
28:15 and *of* scarlet, and *of* **fine** twined l, 8336
28:39 thou shalt embroider the coat of **fine** l, and 8336
28:39 thou shalt make the mitre *of* **fine** l, and 8336
28:42 thou shalt make them l breeches to cover 906
35: 6 and scarlet, and **fine** l, and goats' *hair*, 8336
35:23 **fine** l, and goats' *hair*, and red skins of 8336
35:25 and of purple, *and* of scarlet, and of **fine** l. 8336
35:35 in scarlet, and in **fine** l, and of the weaver, 8336
36: 8 made ten curtains *of* **fine** twined l, 8336
36:35 and purple, and scarlet, and **fine** twined l: 8336
36:37 purple, and scarlet, and **fine** twined l, 8336
38: 9 hangings of the court *were of* **fine** twined l, 8336
38:16 the court round about *were of* **fine** twined l. 8336
38:18 and purple, and scarlet, and **fine** twined l: 8336
38:23 and in purple, and in scarlet, and **fine** l. 8336
39: 2 and purple, and scarlet, and **fine** twined l. 8336
39: 3 and in the scarlet, and in the **fine** l, 8336
39: 5 and purple, and scarlet, and **fine** twined l; 8336
39: 8 and purple, and scarlet, and **fine** twined l. 8336
39:24 and purple, and scarlet, *and* twined *l*. NIH
39:27 they made coats *of* **fine** l *of* woven work 8336
39:28 a mitre *of* **fine** l, and goodly bonnets *of* fine 8336
39:28 goodly bonnets *of* **fine** l, and linen breeches 8336
39:28 and l breeches *of* fine twined linen, 906
39:28 and linen breeches *of* **fine** twined l, 8336
39:29 a girdle *of* **fine** twined l, and blue, and 8336
Lev 6:10 And the priest shall put on his l garment, and 906
6:10 *his* l breeches shall he put upon his flesh, 906
13:47 *it be* a woollen garment, or a l garment; 6593
13:48 *be* in the warp, or woof; of l, or of woollen; 6593
13:52 in woollen or in l, or any thing of skin, 6593
13:59 of leprosy in a garment of woollen or l, 6593
16: 4 He shall put on the holy l coat, and he shall 906
16: 4 he shall have the l breeches upon his flesh, 906
16: 4 shall be girded with a l girdle, and with 906
16: 4 and with the l mitre shall he be attired: 906
16:23 shall put off the l garments, which he put on 906
16:32 shall put on the l clothes, *even* the holy 906
19:19 a garment **mingled of l and woollen** 3610+8162
Dt 22:11 of divers sorts, *as* of woollen and l together. 6593
1Sa 2:18 *being* a child, girded *with* a l ephod. 906
22:18 and five persons that did wear a l ephod. 906
2Sa 6:14 and David *was* girded *with* a l ephod. 906
1Ki 10:28 horses brought out of Egypt, and l **yarn**: 4723
10:28 the king's merchants received the l **yarn** at 4723
1Ch 4:21 of the house of them that wrought **fine** l, 948
15:27 And David *was* clothed with a robe of **fine** l, 948
15:27 David also *had* upon him an ephod of l. 906
2Ch 1:16 horses brought out of Egypt, and l **yarn**: 4723
1:16 the king's merchants received the l **yarn** at 4723
2:14 in blue, and in **fine** l, and in crimson; 948

2Ch 3:14 and **fine l**, and wrought cherubims thereon. 948
5:12 and their brethren, *being* arrayed in **white l**, 948
Est 1: 6 blue *hangings,* fastened with cords of **fine l** 948
8:15 and *with* a garment of **fine l** and purple: 948
Pr 7:16 *with* carved *works, with* **fine l** of Egypt. 330
31:24 She maketh **fine l**, and selleth *it;* and 5466
Isa 3:23 and the **fine l**, and the hoods, and the vails. 5466
Jer 13: 1 Go and get thee a **l** girdle, and put it upon 6593
Eze 9: 2 one man among them *was* clothed *with* **l**, 906
9: 3 he called to the man clothed *with* **l**, 906
9:11 behold, the man clothed with **l**, which *had* 906
10: 2 he spake unto the man clothed with **l**, and 906
10: 6 he had commanded the man clothed with **l**, 906
10: 7 into the hands of *him that was* clothed with **l**: 906
16:10 and I girded thee about with **fine l**, 8336
16:13 thy raiment *was of* **fine l**, and silk, and 8336
27: 7 **Fine l** with broidered work from Egypt was 8336
27:16 and **fine l**, and coral, and agate. 948
44:17 they shall be clothed with **l** garments; 6593
44:18 They shall have **l** bonnets upon their heads, 6593
44:18 and shall have **l** breeches upon their loins; 6593
Da 10: 5 and behold, a certain man clothed *in* **l**, 906
12: 6 *one* said to the man clothed in **l**, which *was* 906
12: 7 I heard the man clothed in **l**, which *was* upon 906
Mt 27:59 the body, he wrapped it in a clean **l cloth**, *4616*
Mk 14:51 having a **l cloth** cast about *his* naked *body;* *4616*
14:52 And he left the **l cloth**, and fled from them *4616*
15:46 And he bought **fine l**, and took him down, *4616*
15:46 and wrapped *him* in the **l**, and laid him in a *4616*
Lk 16:19 which was clothed in purple and **fine l**, and *1040*
23:53 and wrapped it in **l**, and laid it in a *4616*
24:12 he beheld the **l clothes** laid by themselves, *3608*
Jn 19:40 and wound it in **l clothes** with the spices, *3608*
20: 5 and looking in, saw the **l clothes** lying; *3608*
20: 6 the sepulchre, and seeth the **l clothes** lie, *3608*
20: 7 not lying with the **l clothes**, but *3608*
Rev 15: 6 clothed in pure and white **l**, and *3043*
18:12 and **fine l**, and purple, and silk, and scarlet, *1040*
18:16 that was clothed in **fine l**, and purple, and *1039*
19: 8 granted that she should be arrayed in **fine l**, *1039*
19: 8 for the **fine l** is the righteousness of saints. *1039*
19:14 clothed in **fine l**, white and clean. *1039*

LINES (2) [LINE]
2Sa 8: 2 even *with* two **l** measured he to put to 2256
Ps 16: 6 The **l** are fallen unto me in pleasant *places;* 2256

LINGERED (2) [LINGERETH]
Ge 19:16 while he **l**, the men laid hold upon his hand, 4102
43:10 For except we had **l**, surely now we had 4102

LINGERETH (1) [LINGERED]
2Pe 2: 3 whose judgment now of a long time **l** not, *691*

LINTEL (4) [LINTELS]
Ex 12:22 strike the **l** and the two side posts with 4947
12:23 and when he seeth the blood upon the **l**, and 4947
1Ki 6:31 the **l** *and* side posts *were* a fifth *part of* 352
Am 9: 1 he said, Smite the **l of the door**, that 3730

LINTELS (1) [LINTEL]
Zep 2:14 the bittern shall lodge in the **upper l** of it; 3730

LINUS (1)
2Ti 4:21 and **L**, and Claudia, and all the brethren. *3044*

LION (98) [LION'S, LIONESS, LIONESSES, LIONLIKE, LIONS, LIONS']
Ge 49: 9 he couched as a **l**, and as an old lion; 738
49: 9 he couched as a lion, and as an **old l**; 3833
Nu 23:24 the people shall rise up as a **great l**, and 3833
23:24 a great lion, and lift up himself as a **young l**: 738
24: 9 he lay down as a **l**, and as a great lion: 738
24: 9 he lay down as a lion, and as a **great l**: 3833
Dt 33:20 he dwelleth as a **l**, and teareth the arm with 3833
Jdg 14: 5 behold, a young **l** roared against him. 738
14: 8 he turned aside to see the carcase of the **l**: 738
14: 8 of bees and honey in the carcase of the **l**. 738
14: 9 taken the honey out of the carcase of the **l**. 738
14:18 what *is* stronger than a **l**? And he said unto 738
1Sa 17:34 there came a **l** and a bear, and took a lamb 738
17:36 Thy servant slew both the **l** and the bear: and 738
17:37 that delivered me out of the paw of the **l**, 738
2Sa 17:10 whose heart *is* as the heart of a **l**, shall utterly 738
23:20 slew a **l** in the midst of a pit in time of snow: 738
1Ki 13:24 a **l** met him by the way, and slew him: 738
13:24 stood by it, the **l** also stood by the carcase. 738
13:25 in the way, and the **l** standing by the carcase: 738
13:26 the LORD hath delivered him unto the **l**, 738
13:28 and the ass and the **l** standing by the carcase: 738
13:28 the **l** had not eaten the carcase, nor torn 738
20:36 thou art departed from me, a **l** shall slay thee. 738
20:36 from him, a **l** found him, and slew him. 738
1Ch 11:22 and slew a **l** in a pit in a snowy day. 738
Job 4:10 The roaring of the **l**, and the voice of 738
4:10 the voice of the **fierce l**, and the teeth of 7826
4:11 The **old l** perisheth for lack of prey, and 3918
10:16 Thou huntest me as a **fierce l**: and 7826
28: 8 not trodden it, nor the **fierce l** passed by it. 7826
38:39 Wilt thou hunt the prey for the **l**? or fill 3833
Ps 7: 2 Lest he tear my soul like a **l**, rending *it* in 738
10: 9 He lieth in wait secretly as a **l** in his den: 738
17:12 Like as a **l** *that* is greedy of his prey, and 738
17:12 as it were a **young l** lurking in secret 3715
22:13 their mouths, *as* a ravening and a roaring **l**. 738
91:13 Thou shalt tread upon the **l** and adder: 7826
91:13 the **young l** and the dragon shalt thou 3715
Pr 19:12 The king's wrath *is* as the roaring of a **l**; but 3715
20: 2 The fear of a king *is* as the roaring of a **l**: 3715
22:13 The slothful *man* saith, *There is* a **l** without, 738
26:13 slothful *man* saith, *There is* a **l** in the way; 7826
26:13 *is* a lion in the way; a **l** *is* in the streets. 738
28: 1 but the righteous are bold as a **l**. 3715
28:15 *As* a roaring **l**, and a ranging bear; *so is* a 738
Pr 30:30 A **l** *which is* strongest among beasts, and 3918
Ecc 9: 4 for a living dog *is* better than a dead **l**. 738
Isa 5:29 Their roaring *shall be* like a **l**, they shall 3833
11: 6 the calf and the **young l** and the fatling 3715
11: 7 and the **l** shall eat straw like the ox. 738
21: 8 he cried, A **l**: My lord, I stand continually 738
30: 6 from whence *come* the young and **old l**, 3918
31: 4 Like as the **l** and the young lion roaring on 738
31: 4 and the **young l** roaring on his prey, 3715
35: 9 No **l** shall be there, nor *any* ravenous beast 738
38:13 *that,* as a **l**, so will he break all my bones: 738
65:25 and the **l** shall eat straw like the bullock: 738
Jer 2:30 devoured your prophets, like a destroying **l**. 738
4: 7 The **l** is come up from his thicket, and 738
5: 6 Wherefore a **l** out of the forest shall slay 738
12: 8 Mine heritage is unto me as a **l** in the forest; 738
25:38 He hath forsaken his covert, as the **l**: 3715
49:19 he shall come up like a **l** from the swelling 738
50:44 he shall come up like a **l** from the swelling 738
La 3:10 bear lying in wait, *and as* a **l** in secret places. 738
Eze 1:10 a man, and the face of a **l**, on the right side: 738
10:14 the third the face of a **l**, and the fourth 738
19: 3 it became a **young l**, and it learned to catch 3715
19: 5 of her whelps, *and* made him a **young l**. 3715
19: 6 he became a **young l**, and learned to catch 3715
22:25 like a roaring **l** ravening the prey; 738
32: 2 Thou art like a **young l** of the nations, and 3715
41:19 the face of a **young l** toward the palm tree 3715
Da 7: 4 The first *was* like a **l**, and had eagle's wings: 744
Hos 5:14 For I *will be* unto Ephraim as a **l**, and as a 7826
5:14 and as a **young l** to the house of Judah: 3715
11:10 he shall roar like a **l**: when he shall roar, then 738
13: 7 Therefore I will be unto them as a **l**: as a 7826
13: 8 and there will I devour them like a **l**: 3833
Joel 1: 6 whose teeth *are* the teeth of a **l**, and he hath 738
1: 6 and he hath the cheek-teeth of a **great l**. 3833
Am 3: 4 Will a **l** roar in the forest, when he hath no 738
3: 4 will a **young l** cry out of his den, if he have 3715
3: 8 The **l** hath roared, who will not fear? 738
3:12 taketh out of the mouth of the **l** two legs, 738
5:19 As if a man did flee from a **l**, and a bear met 738
Mic 5: 8 people as a **l** among the beasts of the forest, 738
5: 8 as a **young l** among the flocks of sheep: 3715
Na 2:11 where the **l**, *even* the old lion, walked, *and* 738
2:11 *even* the **old l**, walked, *and* the lion's 3833
2:12 The **l** did tear in pieces enough for his 738
2Ti 4:17 I was delivered out of the mouth of the **l**. *3023*
1Pe 5: 8 the devil, as a roaring **l**, walketh about, *3023*
Rev 4: 7 And the first beast *was* like a **l**, and *3023*
5: 5 behold, the **L** of the tribe of Juda, the root *3023*
10: 3 cried with a loud voice, as *when* a **l** roareth: *3023*
13: 2 a bear, and his mouth as the mouth of a **l**: *3023*

LION'S (6) [LION]
Ge 49: 9 Judah *is* a **l** whelp: from the prey, my son, 738
Dt 33:22 of Dan he said, Dan *is* a **l** whelp: he shall 738
Job 4:11 and the **stout l** whelps are scattered abroad. 3833
28: 8 The **l** whelps have not trodden it, nor 7830
Ps 22:21 Save me from the **l** mouth: for thou hast 738
Na 2:11 *and* the **l** whelp, and none made *them* afraid? 738

LIONESS (1) [LION]
Eze 19: 2 A **l**: she lay down among lions, 3833

LIONESSES (1) [LION]
Na 2:12 strangled for his **l**, and filled his holes *with* 3833

LIONLIKE (2) [LION]
2Sa 23:20 done many acts, he slew two **l men** of Moab: 739
1Ch 11:22 done many acts; he slew two **l men** of Moab: 739

LIONS (43) [LION]
2Sa 1:23 than eagles, they were stronger than **l**. 738
1Ki 7:29 borders that *were* between the ledges *were* **l**, 738
7:29 beneath the **l** and oxen *were certain* additions 738
7:36 he graved cherubims, **l**, and palm trees, 738
10:19 of the seat, and two **l** stood beside the stays. 738
10:20 And twelve **l** stood there on the one side and 738
2Ki 17:25 therefore the LORD sent **l** among them, 738
17:26 therefore he hath sent **l** among them, 738
1Ch 12: 8 whose faces *were like* the faces of **l**, and 738
2Ch 9:18 sitting place, and two **l** standing by the stays: 738
9:19 And twelve **l** stood there on the one side and 738
Job 4:10 and the teeth of the **young l**, are broken. 3715
38:39 the lion? or fill the appetite of the **young l**, 3715
Ps 34:10 The **young l** do lack, and suffer hunger: 3715
35:17 their destructions, my darling from the **l**. 3715
57: 4 My soul *is* among **l**: *and* I lie *even among* 3833
58: 6 break out the great teeth of the **young l**, 3715
104:21 The **young l** roar after *their* prey, and seek 3715
Isa 5:29 *be* like a lion, they shall roar like **young l**: 3715
15: 9 **l** upon him that escapeth of Moab, and 738
Jer 2:15 The **young l** roared upon him, *and* yelled, 3715
50:17 scattered sheep; the **l** have driven *him* away: 738
51:38 They shall roar together like **l**: they shall 3715
Eze 19: 2 she lay down among **l**, she nourished her 738
19: 2 she nourished her whelps among **young l**. 3715
19: 6 he went up and down among the **l**, 738
38:13 with all the **young l** thereof, shall say unto 3715
Da 6: 7 O king, he shall be cast into the den of **l**. 744
6:12 O king, shall be cast into the den of **l**? 744
6:16 and cast *him* into the den of **l**. 744
6:19 and went in haste unto the den of **l**. 744
6:20 able to deliver thee from the **l**? 744
6:24 they cast *them* into the den of **l**, them, 744
6:24 the **l** had the mastery of them, and brake all 744
6:27 delivered Daniel from the power of the **l**. 744
Na 2:11 Where *is* the dwelling of the **l**, and 738
2:11 the feeding place of the **young l**, where 3715
2:13 and the sword shall devour thy **young l**: 3715
Zep 3: 3 Her princes within her *are* roaring **l**; 738
Zec 11: 3 a voice of the roaring of **young l**; for 3715
Heb 11:33 obtained promises, stopped the mouths of **l**, *3023*
Rev 9: 8 and their teeth were as *the teeth* of **l**. *3023*
Rev 9:17 heads of the horses *were* as the heads of **l**; *3023*

LIONS' (3) [LION]
SS 4: 8 top of Shenir and Hermon, from the **l** dens, 738
Jer 51:38 like lions: they shall yell as **l** whelps, 738
Da 6:22 hath shut the **l** mouths, that they have not 744

LIP (3) [LIPS]
Lev 13:45 he shall put a covering upon *his* **upper l**, 8222
Ps 22: 7 they shoot out the **l**, they shake the head, 8193
Pr 12:19 The **l** of truth shall be established for ever: 8193

LIPS (119) [LIP]
Ex 6:12 hear me, who *am* of uncircumcised **l**? 8193
6:30 I *am* of uncircumcised **l**, and how shall 8193
Lev 5: 4 pronouncing with *his* **l** to do evil, or to do 8193
Nu 30: 6 she vowed, or uttered ought out of her **l**, 8193
30: 8 that which she uttered with her **l**, 8193
30:12 whatsoever proceeded out of her **l** 8193
Dt 23:23 That which is gone out of thy **l** thou shalt 8193
1Sa 1:13 only her **l** moved, but her voice was not 8193
2Ki 19:28 my bridle in thy **l**, and I will turn thee back 8193
Job 2:10 In all this did not Job sin with his **l**. 8193
8:21 *with* laughing, and thy **l** *with* rejoicing. 8193
11: 5 would speak, and open his **l** against thee; 8193
13: 6 and hearken to the pleadings of my **l**. 8193
15: 6 not I; yea, thine own **l** testify against thee. 8193
16: 5 the moving of my **l** should asswage *your* 8193
23:12 gone back from the commandment of his **l**; 8193
27: 4 My **l** shall not speak wickedness, nor my 8193
32:20 be refreshed: I will open my **l** and answer. 8193
33: 3 and my **l** shall utter knowledge clearly. 8193
Ps 12: 2 *with* flattering **l** *and* with a double heart do 8193
12: 3 The LORD shall cut off all flattering **l**, 8193
12: 4 tongue will we prevail; our **l** *are* our own: 8193
16: 4 not offer, nor take up their names into my **l**. 8193
17: 1 my prayer, *that goeth* not out of feigned **l**. 8193
17: 4 by the word of thy **l** I have kept *me from* 8193
21: 2 and hast not withholden the request of his **l**. 8193
31:18 Let the lying **l** be put to silence; 8193
34:13 from evil, and thy **l** from speaking guile. 8193
40: 9 lo, I have not refrained my **l**, O LORD, 8193
45: 2 grace is poured into thy **l**: therefore 8193
51:15 O Lord, open thou my **l**; and my mouth 8193
59: 7 swords *are* in their **l**: for who, *say they,* 8193
59:12 the words of their **l** let them even be taken 8193
63: 3 *is* better than life, my **l** shall praise thee. 8193
63: 5 my mouth shall praise *thee with* joyful **l**: 8193
66:14 Which my **l** have uttered, and my mouth 8193
71:23 My **l** shall greatly rejoice when I sing unto 8193
89:34 nor alter the thing that is gone out of my **l**. 8193
106:33 so that he spake unadvisedly with his **l**. 8193
119:13 With my **l** have I declared all the judgments 8193
119:171 My **l** shall utter praise, when thou hast 8193
120: 2 from lying **l**, *and* from a deceitful tongue. 8193
140: 3 a serpent; adder's poison *is* under their **l**. 8193
140: 9 let the mischief of their own **l** cover them. 8193
141: 3 before my mouth; keep the door of my **l**. 8193
Pr 4:24 and perverse **l** put far from thee. 8193
5: 2 and *that* thy **l** may keep knowledge. 8193
5: 3 For the **l** of a strange *woman* drop *as* a 8193
7:21 with the flattering of her **l** she forced him. 8193
8: 6 the opening of my **l** *shall be* right things. 8193
8: 7 and wickedness *is* an abomination to my **l**. 8193
10:13 In the **l** of him that hath understanding 8193
10:18 He that hideth hatred *with* lying **l**, and 8193
10:19 not sin: but he that refraineth his **l** *is* wise. 8193
10:21 The **l** of the righteous feed many: but 8193
10:32 The **l** of the righteous know what is 8193
12:13 is snared by the transgression of *his* **l**: 8193
12:22 Lying **l** *are* abomination to the LORD: but 8193
13: 3 he that openeth wide his **l** shall have 8193
14: 3 but the **l** of the wise shall preserve them. 8193
14: 7 when thou perceivest not *in him* the **l** of 8193
14:23 but the talk of the **l** *tendeth* only to penury. 8193
15: 7 The **l** of the wise disperse knowledge: but 8193
16:10 A divine sentence *is* in the **l** of the king: 8193
16:13 Righteous **l** *are* the delight of kings; and 8193
16:21 the sweetness of the **l** increaseth learning. 8193
16:23 his mouth, and addeth learning to his **l**. 8193
16:27 and in his **l** *there is* as a burning fire. 8193
16:30 moving his **l** he bringeth evil to pass. 8193
17: 4 A wicked doer giveth heed to false **l**; *and* 8193
17: 7 not a fool: much less do lying **l** a prince. 8193
17:28 he that shutteth his **l** *is esteemed a man* of 8193
18: 6 A fool's **l** enter into contention, and 8193
18: 7 and his **l** *are* the snare of his soul. 8193
18:20 *with* the increase of his **l** shall he be filled. 8193
19: 1 than *he that is* perverse in his **l**, and *is* a 8193
20:15 but the **l** of knowledge *are* a precious jewel. 8193
20:19 not with him that flattereth *with* his **l**. 8193
22:11 *for* the grace of his **l** the king *shall be* his 8193
22:18 they shall withal be fitted in thy **l**. 8193
23:16 shall rejoice, when thy **l** speak right things. 8193
24: 2 and their **l** talk of mischief. 8193
24:26 *Every man* shall kiss *his* **l** that giveth a right 8193
24:28 without cause; and deceive not with thy **l**. 8193
26:23 Burning **l** and a wicked heart *are like* a 8193
26:24 He that hateth dissembleth with his **l**, and 8193
27: 2 own mouth; a stranger, and not thine own **l**. 8193
Ecc 10:12 but the **l** of a fool will swallow up himself. 8193
SS 4: 3 Thy **l** *are* like a thread of scarlet, and 8193
4:11 Thy **l**, O *my* spouse, drop *as* 8193
5:13 his **l** *like* lilies, dropping sweet smelling 8193
7: 9 causing the **l** of *those that are* asleep to 8193
Isa 6: 5 because I *am* a man of unclean **l**, and 8193
6: 5 dwell in the midst of a people of unclean **l**: 8193
6: 7 and said, Lo, this hath touched thy **l**; 8193
11: 4 with the breath of his **l** shall he slay 8193
28:11 For with stammering **l** and another tongue 8193
29:13 with their **l** do honour me, but 8193
30:27 his **l** are full *of* indignation, and his tongue 8193
37:29 my bridle in thy **l**, and I will turn thee back 8193
57:19 I create the fruit of the **l**; Peace, peace to 8193

L

Isa 59: 3 your **l** have spoken lies, your tongue hath 8193
Jer 17:16 that which came out of my **l** was right 8193
La 3:62 The **l** of those that rose up against me, and 8193
Eze 24:17 cover not *thy* **l**, and eat not the bread of 8222
24:22 ye shall not cover *your* **l**, nor eat the bread 8222
36: 3 ye are taken up in the **l** of talkers, and 8193
Da 10:16 similitude of the sons of men touched my **l**: 8193
Hos 14: 2 so will we render the calves of our **l**. 8193
Mic 3: 7 yea, they shall all cover their **l**; for *there is* 8222
Hab 3:16 belly trembled; my **l** quivered at the voice: 8193
Mal 2: 6 and iniquity was not found in his **l**: 8193
2: 7 For the priest's **l** should keep knowledge, 8193
Mt 15: 8 their mouth, and honoureth me with *their* **l**; *5491*
Mk 7: 6 This people honoureth me with *their* **l**, but *5491*
Ro 3:13 the poison of asps *is* under their **l**: *5491*
1Co 14:21 and other **l** will I speak unto this people; *5491*
Heb 13:15 the fruit of *our* **l** giving thanks to his name. *5491*
1Pe 3:10 and his **l** that *they* speak no guile: *5491*

LIQUOR (2) [LIQUORS]

Nu 6: 3 neither shall he drink any **l** of grapes, 4952
SS 7: 2 *is like* a round goblet, *which* wanteth not **l**: 4197

LIQUORS (1) [LIQUOR]

Ex 22:29 *offer the first of* thy ripe fruits, and *of* thy **l**: 1831

LISTED (2) [LISTETH]

Mt 17:12 but have done unto him whatsoever they **l**. *2309*
Mk 9:13 they have done unto him whatsoever they **l**, *2309*

LISTEN (1)

Isa 49: 1 **L**, O isles, unto me; and hearken, 8085

LISTETH (2) [LISTED]

Jn 3: 8 The wind bloweth where it **l**, and *2309*
Jas 3: 4 whithersoever the governor **l**. *1014+2116*

LITTERS (1)

Isa 66:20 in **l**, and upon mules, and upon swift beasts, 6632

LITTLE (242)

Ge 18: 4 Let a **l** water, I pray you, be fetched, and 4592
19:20 city *is* near to flee unto, and it *is* a **l one**: 4705
19:20 Oh, let me escape thither, (*is* it not a **l one**?) 4705
24:17 I pray thee, drink a **l** water of thy pitcher. 4592
24:43 I pray thee, a **l** water of thy pitcher to drink; 4592
30:30 For *it was* **l** which thou hadst before I 4592
34:29 all their **l ones**, and their wives took they 2945
35:16 a **l way** to come to Ephrath: 776+3530+1886.1
43: 2 said unto them, Go again, buy us a **l** food. 4592
43: 8 both we, and thou, *and* also our **l ones**. 2945
43:11 a **l** balm, and a little honey, spices, and 4592
43:11 a **l** honey, spices, and myrrh, nuts, and 4592
44:20 old man, and a child of *his* old age, a **l one**; 6996
44:25 father said, Go again, *and* buy us a **l** food. 4592
45:19 out of the land of Egypt for your **l ones**, 2945
46: 5 and their **l ones**, and their wives, 2945
47:24 and for food for your **l ones**. 2945
48: 7 but a **l** way to come unto Ephrath: 3530
50: 8 only their **l ones**, and their flocks, and 2945
50:21 I will nourish you and your **l ones**. And he 2945
Ex 10:10 as I will let you go, and your **l ones**: 2945
10:24 be stayed: let your **l ones** also go with you. 2945
12: 4 if the household be too **l** for the lamb, 4591
16:18 and he that **gathered l** had no lack; 4591
23:30 By **l** and little I will drive them out from 4592
23:30 I **l** will drive them out from before thee, 4592
Lev 11:17 the **l owl**, and the cormorant, and the great 3563
Nu 14:31 your **l ones**, which ye said should be a prey, 2945
16:27 and their sons, and their **l children**. 2945
31: 9 their **l ones**, and took the spoil of all their 2945
31:17 therefore kill every male among the **l ones**, 2945
32:16 here for our cattle, and cities for our **l ones**: 2945
32:17 our **l ones** shall dwell in the fenced cities 2945
32:24 Build ye cities for your **l ones**, and folds for 2945
32:26 Our **l ones**, our wives, our flocks, and 2945
Dt 1:39 Moreover your **l ones**, which ye said 2945
2:34 the women, and the **l ones**, of every city, 2945
3:19 and your **l ones**, and your cattle, 2945
7:22 nations before thee **by l and little**: 4592+4592
7:22 nations before thee **by little and l**: 4592+4592
14:16 The **l owl**, and the great owl, and the swan, 3563
20:14 the **l ones**, and the cattle, and all that is in 2945
28:38 out *into* the field, and shalt gather *but* **l** in; 4592
29:11 Your **l ones**, your wives, and thy stranger 2945
Jos 1:14 Your wives, your **l ones**, and your cattle, 2945
8:35 the **l ones**, and the strangers that were 2945
19:47 the children of Dan went out *too* **l** for them: NIH
22:17 *Is* the iniquity of Peor *too* **l** for us, from 4592
Jdg 4:19 Give me, I pray thee, a **l** water to drink; 4592
18:21 put the **l ones** and the cattle and 2945
Ru 2: 7 until now, that she tarried a **l** in the house. 4592
1Sa 2:19 Moreover his mother made him a **l** coat, 6996
14:29 because I tasted a **l** of this honey. 4592
14:43 taste a **l** honey with the end of the rod that 4592
15:17 When thou *wast* **l** in thine own sight, 6996
20:35 appointed with David, and a **l** lad with him. 6996
2Sa 12: 3 save one **l** ewe lamb, which he had bought 6996
12: 8 if *that had been* too **l**, I would moreover 4592
15:22 and all the **l ones** that *were* with him. 2945
16: 1 when David was a **l** past the top *of the hill*, 4592
19:36 Thy servant will go a **l** *way* over Jordan 4592
1Ki 3: 7 I *am but* a **l** child: I know not *how* to go out 6996
8:64 *was* too **l** to receive the burnt offerings, 6996
11:17 to go *into* Egypt; Hadad *being yet* a **l** child. 6996
12:10 My **l** *finger* shall be thicker than my 6995
17:10 Fetch me, I pray thee, a **l** water in a vessel, 4592
17:12 of meal in a barrel, and a **l** oil in a cruse: 4592
17:13 make me thereof a **l** cake first, and bring *it* 6996
18:44 there ariseth a **l** cloud out of the sea, 6996
20:27 before them like two **l flocks** of kids; 2835
2Ki 2:23 there came forth **l** children out of the city, 6996
4:10 Let us make a **l** chamber, I pray thee, on 6996
5: 2 captive out of the land of Israel a **l** maid; 6996
2Ki 5:14 came again like unto the flesh of a **l** child, 6996
5:19 in peace. So he departed from him a **l** way. 3530
10:18 and said unto them, Ahab served Baal a **l**; 4592
2Ch 10:10 My **l** *finger* shall be thicker than my 6995
20:13 with their **l ones**, their wives, and 2945
31:18 to the genealogy of all their **l ones**, 2945
Ezr 8:21 for our **l ones**, and for all our substance. 2945
9: 8 now for a **l** space grace hath been *shewed* 4592
9: 8 and give us a **l** reviving in our bondage. 4592
Ne 9:32 let not all the trouble seem **l** before thee, 4591
Est 3:13 both young and old, **l children** and women, 2945
8:11 *both* **l ones** and women, and *to take* 2945
Job 4:12 to me, and mine ear received a **l** thereof. 8102
10:20 let me alone, that I may take comfort a **l**, 4592
21:11 They send forth their **l ones** like a flock, 5759
24:24 They are exalted for a **l while**, but are gone 4592
26:14 how a **l** portion is heard of him? but 8102
36: 2 Suffer me a **l**, and I will shew thee that *I* 2191
Ps 2:12 the way, when his wrath is kindled but a **l**: 4592
8: 5 For thou hast made him a **l** lower than 4592
37:10 For yet a **l while**, and the wicked *shall* not 4592
37:16 A **l** that a righteous *man* hath *is* better than 4592
65:12 and the **l hills** rejoice on every side. 1389
68:27 There *is* **l** Benjamin *with* their ruler, 6810
72: 3 the people, and the **l hills**, by righteousness. 1389
114: 4 like rams, *and* the **l hills** like lambs. 1389
114: 6 like rams; *and* ye **l hills**, like lambs? 1389
137: 9 and dasheth thy **l ones** against the stones. 5768
Pr 6:10 *Yet* a **l** sleep, a little slumber, a little 4592
6:10 *Yet* a little sleep, a **l** slumber, a little 4592
6:10 a **l** folding of the hands to sleep: 4592
10:20 the heart of the wicked *is* **l worth**. 4592+3509.1
15:16 Better *is* **l** with the fear of the LORD than 4592
16: 8 Better *is* a **l** with righteousness than great 4592
24:33 *Yet* a **l** sleep, a little slumber, a little 4592
24:33 *Yet* a little sleep, a **l** slumber, a little 4592
24:33 a **l** folding of the hands to sleep: 4592
30:24 There be four *things which are* **l** upon 6996
Ecc 5:12 *man is* sweet, whether he eat **l** or much: 4592
9:14 *There was* a **l** city, and few men within it; 6996
10: 1 *doth* a **l** folly *him that is* in reputation for 4592
SS 2:15 Take us the foxes, the **l** foxes, that spoil 6996
3: 4 *It was* but a **l** that I passed from them, but I 4592
8: 8 We have a **l** sister, and she hath no breasts: 6996
Isa 10:25 For yet a **very l while**, and 4213+4592
11: 6 and a **l** child shall lead them. 6996
26:20 hide thyself as it were for a **l** moment, 4592
28:10 line upon line; here a **l**, *and* there a little: 2191
28:10 line upon line; here a little, *and* there a **l**: 2191
28:13 line upon line; here a **l**, *and* there a little; 2191
28:13 line upon line; here a little, *and* there a **l**; 2191
29:17 *Is* it not yet a **very l while**, 4213+4592
40:15 he taketh up the isles as a **very l thing**. 1851
54: 8 In a **l** wrath I hid my face from thee for a 8241
60:22 A **l one** shall become a thousand, and 6996
63:18 thy holiness have possessed *it* but a **l while**: 4705
Jer 14: 3 their nobles have sent their **l ones** to 6810
48: 4 her **l ones** have caused a cry to be heard. 6810
51:33 yet a **l while**, and the time of her harvest 4592
Eze 9: 6 both maids, and **l children**, and women: 2945
11:16 yet will I be to them as a **l** sanctuary in 4592
16:47 as *if that were* a **very l** *thing*, thou 4592+6985
31: 4 sent out her **l rivers** unto all the trees of 8585
40: 7 *every* **l chamber** *was* one reed long, and 8372
40: 7 between the **l chambers** *were* five cubits; 8372
40:10 the **l chambers** of the gate eastward *were* 8372
40:12 The space also before the **l chambers** *was* 8372
40:12 the **l chambers** *were* six cubits on this side, 8372
40:13 the gate from the roof of *one* **l chamber** to 8372
40:16 *were* narrow windows to the **l chambers**, 8372
40:21 the **l chambers** thereof *were* three on this 8372
40:29 the **l chambers** thereof, and the posts 8372
40:33 the **l chambers** thereof, and the posts 8372
40:36 The **l chambers** thereof, the posts thereof, 8372
Da 7: 8 there came up among them another **l** horn, 2192
8: 9 out of one of them came forth a **l** horn, 4704
11:34 shall fall, they shall be holpen *with* a **l** help: 4592
Hos 1: 4 for yet a **l** *while*, and I will avenge 4592
8:10 they shall sorrow a **l** for the burden of 4592
Am 6:11 *with* breaches, and the **l** house *with* clefts. 6996
Mic 5: 2 *though thou* be **l** among the thousands of 6810
Hag 1: 6 Ye have sown much, and bring in **l**; *ye* eat, 4592
1: 9 *Ye* looked for much, and lo, *it came* to **l**; 4592
2: 6 it *is* a **l while**, and I *will* shake the heavens, 4592
Zec 1:15 for I was *but* a **l** displeased, and they helped 4592
13: 7 and I will turn mine hand upon the **l ones**. 6819
Mt 6:30 not much more *clothe* you, O ye **of l faith**? *3640*
8:26 Why are ye fearful, O ye **of l faith**? *3640*
10:42 **l ones** a cup of cold *water* only in the name *3398*
14:31 and said unto him, O thou **of l faith**, *3640*
15:34 And they said, Seven, and a few **l fishes**. *2485*
16: 8 he said unto them, O ye **of l faith**, *3640*
18: 2 And Jesus called a **l child** unto *him*, and *3813*
18: 3 ye be converted, and become as **l children**, *3813*
18: 4 shall humble himself as this **l child**, *3813*
18: 5 And whoso shall receive one such **l child** in *3813*
18: 6 But whoso shall offend one of these **l ones** *3398*
18:10 heed that ye despise not one of these **l ones**; *3398*
18:14 that one of these **l ones** should perish. *3398*
19:13 were there brought unto him **l children**, *3813*
19:14 Suffer **l children**, and forbid them not, *3813*
26:39 And he went a **l** further, and fell on his *3398*
Mk 1:19 And when he had gone a **l** further thence, *3641*
4:36 And there were also with him other **l ships**. *4142*
5:23 My **l daughter** lieth at the point of death: *2365*
9:42 one of *these* **l ones** that believe in me, *3398*
10:14 Suffer the **l children** to come unto me, and *3813*
10:15 receive the kingdom of God as a **l child**, *3813*
14:35 And he went forward a **l**, and fell on *3398*
14:70 And a **l** after, they that stood by said again *3398*
Lk 5: 3 prayed him that *he* would thrust out a **l** *3641*
7:47 but to whom **l** is forgiven, *the same* loveth *3641*
7:47 whom little is forgiven, *the same* loveth **l**. *3641*
12:28 more *will he clothe* you, O ye **of l faith**? *3640*
12:32 Fear not, **l** flock; for it is your Father's *3398*
Lk 17: 2 that he should offend one of these **l ones**. *3398*
18:16 Suffer **l children** to come unto me, and *3813*
18:17 as a **l child** shall in no wise enter therein. *3813*
19: 3 for the press, because he was **l** of stature. *3398*
19:17 because thou hast been faithful in a **very l**, *1646*
22:58 And after a **l while** another saw him, and *1024*
Jn 6: 7 that every one of them may take a **l**. *1024*
7:33 Yet a **l** while am I with you, and *then* I go *3398*
12:35 Yet a **l** while is the light with you. *3398*
13:33 **L children**, yet a little while I am with you. *5040*
13:33 Little children, yet a **l while** I am with you. *3398*
14:19 Yet a **l** while, and the world seeth me no *3398*
16:16 A **l while**, and ye shall not see me: and *3398*
16:16 and again, a **l while**, and ye shall see me, *3398*
16:17 unto us, A **l while**, and ye shall not see me: *3398*
16:17 and again, a **l while**, and ye shall see me: *3398*
16:18 What is this that he saith, A **l while**? *3398*
16:19 I said, A **l while**, and ye shall not see me: *3398*
16:19 and again, a **l while**, and ye shall see me? *3398*
21: 8 And the other disciples came in a **l ship**; *4142*
Ac 5:34 to put the apostles forth a **l space**; *1024*
20:12 man alive, and were not a **l** comforted. *3357*
27:28 and when they had gone a **l** further, *1024*
28: 2 And the barbarous people shewed us no **l** *5177*
1Co 5: 6 Know ye not that a **l** leaven leaveneth *3398*
2Co 8:15 and he that *had gathered* **l** had no lack. *3641*
11: 1 Would *to God* you could bear with me a **l** *3398*
11:16 fool receive me, that I may boast myself a **l**. *3398*
Gal 4:19 My **l children**, of whom I travail in birth *5040*
5: 9 A **l** leaven leaveneth the whole lump. *3398*
1Ti 4: 8 For bodily exercise profiteth **l**: *3641*
5:23 but use a **l** wine for thy stomach's sake and *3641*
Heb 2: 7 Thou madest him a **l** lower than the angels; *1024*
2: 9 who was made a **l** lower than the angels, *1024*
10:37 For yet a **l while**, *3398+3745+3745*
Jas 3: 5 Even so the tongue is a **l** member, and *3398*
3: 5 Behold, how great a matter a **l** fire kindleth. *3641*
4:14 that appeareth for a **l** *time*, and then *3641*
1Jn 2: 1 My **l children**, these *things* write I unto *5040*
2:12 **l children**, because *your* sins are forgiven *5040*
2:13 **l children**, because ye have known *3813*
2:18 **L children**, it is the last time: and as ye *3813*
2:28 And now, **l children**, abide in him; that, *5040*
3: 7 **L children**, let no *man* deceive you: he that *5040*
3:18 My **l children**, let us not love in word, *5040*
4: 4 **l children**, and have overcome them: *5040*
5:21 **L children**, keep yourselves from idols. *5040*
Rev 3: 8 for thou hast a **l** strength, and hast kept my *3398*
6:11 that they should rest yet for a **l** season, *3398*
10: 2 And he had in his hand a **l book** open: and *974*
10: 8 take the **l book** which is open in the hand of *974*
10: 9 and said unto him, Give me the **l book**. *974*
10:10 And I took the **l book** out of the angel's *974*
20: 3 and after that he must be loosed a **l** season. *3398*

LIVE (247) [ALIVE, LIFE, LIFETIME, LIVED, LIVELY, LIVES, LIVEST, LIVETH, LIVING, OUTLIVED, OVERLIVED]

Ge 3:22 of the tree of life, and eat, and **l** for ever: 2421
12:13 and my soul shall **l** because of thee. 2421
17:18 O that Ishmael might **l** before thee! 2421
19:20 (*is* it not a little one?) and my soul shall **l**. 2421
20: 7 and he shall pray for thee, and thou shalt **l**: 2421
27:40 by thy sword shalt thou **l**, and shalt serve 2421
31:32 thou findest thy gods, let him not **l**: 2421
42: 2 us from thence; that we may **l**, and not die. 2421
42:18 said unto them the third day, This do, and **l**; 2421
43: 8 that we may **l**, and not die, both we, and 2421
45: 3 I *am* Joseph; doth my father yet **l**? 2416
47:19 give *us* seed, that we may **l**, and not die, 2421
Ex 1:16 but if it *be* a daughter, then she shall **l**. 2421
19:13 whether *it be* beast or man, it shall not **l**: 2421
21:35 they shall sell the **l** ox, and divide 2416
22:18 Thou shalt not **suffer** a witch **to l**. 2421
33:20 for there shall no man see me, and **l**. 2421
Lev 16:20 and the altar, he shall bring the **l** goat: 2416
16:21 both his hands upon the head of the **l** goat, 2416
18: 5 which if a man do, he shall **l** in them: *I am* 2421
25:35 or a sojourner; that he may **l** with thee. 2416
25:36 thy God; that thy brother may **l** with thee. 2416
Nu 4:19 do unto them, that they may **l**, and not die, 2421
14:21 *as* truly *as* I **l**, all the earth shall be filled 2416
14:28 Say unto them, *As truly as* I **l**, saith 2416
21: 8 is bitten, when he looketh upon it, shall **l**. 2421
24:23 Alas, who shall **l** when God doeth this! 2421
Dt 4: 1 for to do *them*, that ye may **l**, and go in and 2421
4:10 all the days that they shall **l** upon the earth, 2416
4:33 midst of the fire, as thou hast heard, and **l**? 2421
4:42 fleeing unto one of these cities he might **l**: 2421
5:33 that ye may **l**, and *that it may be* well with 2421
8: 1 that ye may **l**, and multiply, and go in and 2421
8: 3 know that man doth not **l** by bread only, 2421
8: 3 out of the mouth of the LORD doth man **l**. 2421
12: 1 all the days that ye **l** upon the earth. 2416
16:20 that thou mayest **l**, and inherit the land 2421
19: 4 which shall flee thither, that he may **l**: 2421
19: 5 he shall flee unto one of those cities, and **l**: 2421
30: 6 and with all thy soul, that thou mayest **l**. 2416
30:16 that thou mayest **l** and multiply: 2421
30:19 that *both* thou and thy seed may **l**: 2421
31:13 as long as ye **l** in the land whither ye go 2416
32:40 up my hand to heaven, and say, I **l** for ever. 2416
33: 6 Let Reuben **l**, and not die; and let *not* his 2421
Jos 6:17 only Rahab the harlot shall **l**, she and 2421
9:15 and made a league with them, to let them **l**: 2421
9:20 we will even let them **l**, lest wrath be upon 2421
9:21 the princes said unto them, Let them **l**; but 2421
1Sa 20:14 thou shalt not only while yet I **l** shew me 2416
2Sa 1:10 I was sure that he could not **l** after *that* he 2421
12:22 will be gracious to me, that the child may **l**? 2416
19:34 said unto the king, How long have I to **l**, 2416
1Ki 1:31 and said, Let my lord king David **l** for ever. 2421
8:40 **l** in the land which thou gavest unto our 2416
20:32 Ben-hadad saith, I pray thee, let me **l**. 2421

2Ki 4: 7 and l thou and thy children of the rest. 2421
7: 4 if they save us alive, we shall l; and if they 2421
10:19 whosoever shall be wanting, he shall not l. 2421
18:32 and of honey, that ye may l, and not die: 2421
20: 1 house in order; for thou shalt die, and not l. 2421
2Ch 6:31 long as they l in the land which thou gavest 2416
Ne 2: 3 said unto the king, Let the king l for ever: 2421
5: 2 up corn *for them*, that we may eat, and l. 2421
9:29 (which if a man do, he shall l in them;) 2421
Est 4:11 hold out the golden sceptre, that he may l: 2421
Job 7:16 I loathe *it;* I would not l alway: let me 2421
14:14 shall he l *again?* all the days of my 2421
21: 7 Wherefore do the wicked l, become old, 2421
27: 6 heart shall not reproach *me* so long as I l. 3117
Ps 22:26 that seek him: your heart shall l for ever. 2421
49: 9 That he should still l for ever, *and* not see 2421
55:23 deceitful men shall not **l out half** their 2673
63: 4 Thus will I bless thee while I l: I will lift up 2416
69:32 and your heart shall l that seek God. 2421
72:15 he shall l, and to him shall be given of 2421
104:33 I will sing unto the LORD as long as I l: 2416
116: 2 therefore will I call upon *him* as long as I l. 3117
118:17 but l, and declare the works of the LORD. 2421
119:17 *that* I may l, and keep thy word. 2421
119:77 tender mercies come *unto* me, that I may l: 2421
119:116 me according unto thy word, that I may l: 2421
119:144 give me understanding, and I shall l. 2421
119:175 Let my soul l, and it shall praise thee; and 2421
146: 2 While I l will I praise the LORD: I will 2416
Pr 4: 4 my words: keep my commandments, and l. 2421
7: 2 Keep my commandments, and l; and 2421
9: 6 Forsake the foolish, and l; and go in 2421
15:27 own house; but he that hateth gifts shall l. 2421
Ecc 6: 3 an hundred *children,* and l many years, 2421
6: 6 though he l a thousand years twice *told,* yet 2421
9: 3 madness *is* in their heart while they l, and 2416
9: 9 L joyfully with the wife whom thou lovest 2416
11: 8 if a man l many years, *and* rejoice in them 2421
Isa 6: 6 unto me, having a **l coal** in his hand, 7531
26:14 *They are* dead, they shall not l; *they are* 2421
26:19 Thy dead *men* shall l, *together with* my 2421
38: 1 house in order: for thou shalt die, and not l. 2421
38:16 by these *things* men l, and in all these 2421
38:16 so wilt thou recover me, and **make** me **to** l. 2421
49:18 *As* I l, saith the LORD, thou shalt surely 2416
55: 3 hear, and your soul shall l; and I will make 2421
Jer 21: 9 he shall l, and his life shall be unto him for 2421
22:24 *As* I l, saith the LORD, though Coniah 2416
27:12 and serve him and his people, and l. 2421
27:17 serve the king of Babylon, and l: 2421
35: 7 that ye may l many days in the land where 2421
38: 2 he that goeth forth to the Chaldeans shall l; 2421
38: 2 he shall have his life for a prey, and shall l. 2421
38:17 thy soul shall l, and this city shall not be 2421
38:17 with fire; and thou shalt l, and thine house: 2421
38:20 shall be well unto thee, and thy soul shall l. 2421
46:18 *As* I l, saith the King, whose name *is* 2416
La 4:20 Under his shadow we shall l among 2421
Eze 3:21 shall **surely** l, because he is warned; 2421+2421
5:11 Wherefore, *as* I l, saith the Lord GOD; 2416
13:19 and to save the souls alive that should not l, 2421
14:16 men *were* in it, *as* I l, saith the Lord GOD, 2416
14:18 men *were* in it, *as* I l, saith the Lord GOD, 2416
14:20 Daniel, and Job, *were* in it, *as* I l, 2416
16: 6 unto thee *when thou wast* in thy blood, L; 2421
16: 6 unto thee *when thou wast* in thy blood, L. 2421
16:48 *As* I l, saith the Lord GOD, Sodom thy 2416
17:16 *As* I l, saith the Lord GOD, surely in 2416
17:19 *As* I l, surely mine oath that he hath 2416
18: 3 *As* I l, saith the Lord GOD, ye shall not 2416
18: 9 he *is* just, he shall **surely** l, saith 2421+2421
18:13 shall he then l? he shall not live: he hath 2421
18:13 he shall not l: he hath done all these 2421
18:17 of his father, he shall **surely** l. 2421+2421
18:19 hath done them, he shall **surely** l. 2421+2421
18:21 is lawful and right, he shall **surely** l, 2421+2421
18:22 righteousness that he hath done he shall l. 2421
18:23 that he should return from his ways, and l? 2421
18:24 that the wicked *man* doeth, shall he l? 2421
18:28 he shall **surely** l, he shall not die. 2421+2421
18:32 wherefore turn *yourselves,* and l ye. 2421
20: 3 *As* I l, saith the Lord GOD, I will not be 2416
20:11 which *if* a man do, he shall even l in them. 2421
20:13 which *if* a man do, he shall even l in them; 2421
20:21 which *if* a man do, he shall even l in them; 2421
20:25 and judgments whereby they should not l; 2421
20:31 *As* I l, saith the Lord GOD, I will not be 2416
20:33 *As* I l, saith the Lord GOD, surely with a 2416
33:10 pine away in them, how should we then l? 2421
33:11 Say unto them, *As* I l, saith the Lord 2416
33:11 but that the wicked turn from his way and l: 2421
33:12 neither shall the righteous be able to l for 2421
33:13 the righteous, *that* he shall **surely** l; 2421+2421
33:15 he shall **surely** l, he shall not die. 2421+2421
33:16 is lawful and right; he shall **surely** l. 2421+2421
33:19 is lawful and right, he shall l thereby. 2421
33:27 *As* I l, surely *they* that *are* in the wastes 2416
34: 8 *As* I l, saith the Lord GOD, surely because 2416
35: 6 Therefore, *as* I l, saith the Lord GOD, I 2416
35:11 Therefore, *as* I l, saith the Lord GOD, 2416
37: 3 unto me, Son of man, can these bones l? 2421
37: 5 breath to enter into you, and ye shall l: 2421
37: 6 and put breath in you, and ye shall l; 2421
37: 9 breathe upon these slain, that they may l. 2421
37:14 ye shall l, and I shall place you in your own 2421
47: 9 whithersoever the rivers shall come, shall l: 2421
47: 9 every *thing* shall l whither the river cometh. 2416
Da 2: 4 to the king in Syriack, O king, l for ever: 2418
3: 9 king Nebuchadnezzar, O king, l for ever. 2418
5:10 queen spake and said, O king, l for ever: 2418
6: 6 said thus unto him, King Darius, l for ever 2418
6:21 Daniel unto the king, O king, l for ever. 2418
Hos 6: 2 will raise us up, and we shall l in his sight. 2421
Am 5: 4 house of Israel, Seek ye me, and ye shall l: 2421
5: 6 Seek the LORD, and ye shall l; lest he 2421

Am 5:14 Seek good, and not evil, that ye may l: and 2421
Jnh 4: 3 for *it is* better for me to die than to l. 2416
4: 8 and said, *It is* better for me to die than to l. 2416
Hab 2: 4 in him: but the just shall l by his faith. 2421
Zep 2: 9 Therefore *as* I l, saith the LORD of hosts, 2416
Zec 1: 5 and the prophets, do they l for ever? 2421
10: 9 they shall l with their children, and 2421
13: 3 him shall say unto him, Thou shalt not l; 2421
Mt 4: 4 Man shall not l by bread alone, but *2198*
9:18 and lay thy hand upon her, and she shall l. *2198*
Mk 5:23 that she may be healed; and she shall l. *2198*
Lk 4: 4 That man shall not l by bread alone, but *2198*
7:25 and l delicately, are in kings' courts. *5225*
10:28 answered right: this do, and thou shalt l. *2198*
20:38 but of the living: for all l unto him. *2198*
Jn 5:25 the Son of God: and they that hear shall l. *2198*
6:51 *man* eat of this bread, he shall l for ever: *2198*
6:57 Father hath sent me, and I l by the Father: *2198*
6:57 so he that eateth me, even he shall l by me. *2198*
6:58 he that eateth *of* this bread shall l for ever. *2198*
11:25 in me, though he were dead, *yet* shall he l: *2198*
14:19 ye see me: because I l, ye shall live also. *2198*
14:19 ye see me: because I live, ye shall l also. *2198*
Ac 7:19 young children, to the end *they* might not l. *2225*
17:28 For in him we l, and move, and have our *2198*
22:22 the earth: for it is not fit that he should l. *2198*
25:24 crying that he ought not to l any longer. *2198*
28: 4 the sea, yet Vengeance suffereth not to l. *2198*
Ro 1:17 as it is written, The just shall l by faith. *2198*
6: 2 that are dead to sin, l any longer therein? *2198*
6: 8 we believe that we shall also **l with** him: *4800*
8:12 not to the flesh, to l after the flesh. *2198*
8:13 For if ye l after the flesh, ye shall die: but *2198*
8:13 do mortify the deeds of the body, ye shall l. *2198*
10: 5 which doeth those *things* shall l by them. *2198*
12:18 as lieth in you, **l peaceably** with all men. *1514*
14: 8 For whether we l, we live unto the Lord; *2198*
14: 8 For whether we live, we l unto the Lord; *2198*
14: 8 whether we l therefore, or die, we are *2198*
14:11 For it is written, *As* I l, saith the Lord, *2198*
1Co 9:13 holy *things* l of *the things of* the temple? *2060*
9:14 preach the gospel should l of the gospel. *2198*
2Co 4:11 For we which l are alway delivered unto *2198*
5:15 that they which l should not henceforth live *2198*
5:15 that they which live should not henceforth l *2198*
6: 9 as dying, and behold, we l; as chastened, *2198*
7: 3 you are in our hearts to die and **l with** *you.* *4800*
13: 4 we shall l with him by the power of God *2198*
13:11 good comfort, be of one mind, **l in peace**; *1514*
Gal 2:14 thou the Gentiles to **l as do the Jews**? *2450*
2:19 am dead to the law, that I might l unto God. *2198*
2:20 nevertheless I l; yet not I, but Christ liveth *2198*
2:20 *the life* which I now l in the flesh I live by *2198*
2:20 *the life* which I now live in the flesh I l by *2198*
3:11 *it is* evident: for, The just shall l by faith. *2198*
3:12 The man that doeth them shall l in them. *2198*
5:25 If we l in the Spirit, let us also walk in *2198*
Eph 6: 3 and thou mayest **l long** on the earth. *1510+3118*
Php 1:21 For to me to l *is* Christ, and to die *is* gain. *2198*
1:22 But if *I* l in the flesh, this *is* the fruit of my *2198*
1Th 3: 8 For now we l, if ye stand fast in the Lord. *2198*
5:10 or sleep, we should l together with him. *2198*
2Ti 2:11 be dead with *him,* we shall also **l with** *him:* *4800*
3:12 all that will l godly in Christ Jesus shall *2198*
Tit 2:12 and worldly lusts we should l soberly, *2198*
Heb 10:38 Now the just shall l by faith: but if *any man* *2198*
12: 9 subjection unto the Father of spirits, and l? *2198*
13:18 in all *things* willing to l honestly. *390*
Jas 4:15 Lord will, we shall l, and do this, or that. *2198*
1Pe 2:24 dead to sins, should l unto righteousness: *2198*
4: 2 That *he* no longer should l the rest of *his* *980*
4: 6 but l according to God in the spirit. *2198*
2Pe 2: 6 unto **those that** after should **l ungodly**; *764*
2:18 clean escaped from them who l in error. *390*
1Jn 4: 9 into the world, that we might l through him. *2198*
Rev 13:14 which had the wound by a sword, and did l. *2198*

LIVED (58) [LIVE]

Ge 5: 3 Adam l an hundred and thirty years, and 2421
5: 5 all the days that Adam l were nine hundred 2421
5: 6 Seth l an hundred and five years, and 2421
5: 7 Seth l after he begat Enos eight hundred 2421
5: 9 And Enos l ninety years, and begat Cainan: 2421
5:10 Enos l after he begat Cainan eight hundred 2421
5:12 Cainan l seventy years, and 2421
5:13 Cainan l after he begat Mahalaleel eight 2421
5:15 Mahalaleel l sixty and five years, and 2421
5:16 Mahalaleel l after he begat Jared eight 2421
5:18 And Jared l an hundred sixty and two years, 2421
5:19 Jared l after he begat Enoch eight hundred 2421
5:21 Enoch l sixty and five years, and 2421
5:25 Methuselah l an hundred eighty and seven 2421
5:26 Methuselah l after he begat Lamech seven 2421
5:28 Lamech l an hundred eighty and two years, 2421
5:30 Lamech l after he begat Noah five hundred 2421
9:28 Noah l after the flood three hundred and 2421
11:11 Shem l after he begat Arphaxad five 2421
11:12 Arphaxad l five and thirty years, and 2421
11:13 Arphaxad l after he begat Salah four 2421
11:14 And Salah l thirty years, and begat Eber: 2421
11:15 Salah l after he begat Eber four hundred 2421
11:16 Eber l four and thirty years, and 2421
11:17 Eber l after he begat Peleg four hundred 2421
11:18 And Peleg l thirty years, and begat Reu: 2421
11:19 And Peleg l after he begat Reu two hundred 2421
11:20 Reu l two and thirty years, and begat Serug: 2421
11:21 Reu l after he begat Serug two hundred 2421
11:22 And Serug l thirty years, and begat Nahor: 2421
11:23 Serug l after he begat Nahor two hundred 2421
11:24 Nahor l nine and twenty years, and 2421
11:25 Nahor l after he begat Terah an hundred 2421
11:26 Terah l seventy years, and begat Abram, 2421
25: 6 while he yet l, eastward, unto the east 2416
25: 7 of the years of Abraham's life which he l, 2416
47:28 Jacob l in the land of Egypt seventeen 2421
Ge 50:22 and Joseph l an hundred and ten years. 2421
Nu 14:38 the men that went to search the land, l *still.* 2421
21: 9 when he beheld the serpent of brass, he l. 2421
Dt 5:26 of the midst of the fire, as we *have,* and l? 2421
2Sa 19: 6 that if Absalom had l, and all we had died 2416
1Ki 12: 6 Solomon his father while he *yet* l, 1961+2416
2Ki 14:17 Amaziah the son of Joash king of Judah l 2421
2Ch 10: 6 before Solomon his father while he *yet* l, 2416
25:25 Amaziah the son of Joash king of Judah l 2421
Job 42:16 After this l Job an hundred and forty years, 2421
Ps 49:18 Though whiles he l he blessed his soul: and 2416
Eze 37:10 they l, and stood up upon their feet, 2421
Lk 2:36 had l with a husband seven years from her *2198*
Ac 23: 1 I have l in all good conscience before God *4176*
26: 5 straitest sect of our religion I l a Pharisee. *2198*
Col 3: 7 also walked sometime, when ye l in them. *2198*
Jas 5: 5 Ye have **l in pleasure** on the earth, and *5171*
Rev 18: 7 and **l deliciously**, so much torment and *4763*
18: 9 and **l deliciously** with her, *4763*
20: 4 and they l and reigned with Christ a *2198*
20: 5 But the rest of the dead l not **again** until *326*

LIVELY (5) [LIVE]

Ex 1:19 for they *are* l, and are delivered ere 2422
Ps 38:19 mine enemies *are* l, *and* they are strong: 2416
Ac 7:38 who received *the* l oracles to give unto us: *2198*
1Pe 1: 3 l hope by the resurrection of Jesus Christ *2198*
2: 5 Ye also, as l stones, are built *up* a spiritual *2198*

LIVER (14)

Ex 29:13 the caul *that is* above the l, and the two 3516
29:22 the caul *above* the l, and the two kidneys, 3516
Lev 3: 4 the caul above the l, with the kidneys, 3516
3:10 the caul above the l, with the kidneys, 3516
3:15 the caul above the l, with the kidneys, 3516
4: 9 the caul above the l, with the kidneys, 3516
7: 4 the caul *that is* above the l, with 3516
8:16 the caul *above* the l, and the two kidneys, 3516
8:25 the caul *above* the l, and the two kidneys, 3516
9:10 and the caul above the l of the sin offering, 3516
9:19 and the kidneys, and the caul *above* the l: 3516
Pr 7:23 Till a dart strike through his l; as a bird 3516
La 2:11 are troubled, my l is poured upon the earth, 3516
Eze 21:21 consulted with images, he looked in the l. 3516

LIVES (28) [LIVE]

Ge 9: 5 surely your blood of your l will I require; 5315
45: 7 and to **save** your l by a great deliverance. 2421
47:25 they said, Thou hast **saved** our l: let us find 2421
Ex 1:14 they made their l bitter with hard bondage, 2416
Jos 2:13 that they have, and deliver our l from death. 5315
9:24 we were sore afraid of our l because of you, 5315
Jdg 5:18 l unto the death in the high places of 5315
18:25 lose thy life, with the l of thy household. 5315
2Sa 1:23 *were* lovely and pleasant in their l, 2416
19: 5 the l of thy sons and of thy daughters, and 5315
19: 5 the l of thy wives, and the lives of thy 5315
19: 5 of thy wives, and the l of thy concubines; 5315
23:17 of the men that went in *jeopardy of* their l? 5315
1Ch 11:19 these men that have put their l in jeopardy? 5315
11:19 for with *the jeopardy of* their l they brought 5315
Est 9:16 stood for their l, and had rest from their 5315
Pr 1:18 own blood; they lurk privily for their own l. 5315
Jer 19: 7 and by the hands of them that seek their l: 5315
19: 9 they that seek their l, shall straiten them. 5315
46:26 them into the hand of those that seek their l, 5315
48: 6 save your l, and be like the heath in 5315
La 5: 9 We gat our bread with *the peril of* our l 5315
Da 7:12 yet their l were prolonged for a season and 2417
Lk 9:56 Son of man is not come to destroy men's l, *5590*
Ac 15:26 Men that have hazarded their l for the name *5590*
27:10 of the lading and ship, but also of our l. *5590*
1Jn 3:16 we ought to lay down *our* l for the brethren. *5590*
Rev 12:11 and they loved not their l unto the death. *5590*

LIVEST (4) [LIVE]

Dt 12:19 the Levite as long as thou l upon the earth. 3117
2Sa 11:11 *as* thou l, and *as* thy soul liveth, I will not 2416
Gal 2:14 l after the manner of Gentiles, and not as do *2198*
Rev 3: 1 that thou hast a name that thou l, and *2198*

LIVETH (96) [LIVE]

Ge 9: 3 Every moving thing that l shall be meat for 2416
Dt 5:24 day that God doth talk with man, and he l. 2421
Jdg 8:19 *as* the LORD l, if ye had saved them alive, 2416
Ru 3:13 part of a kinsman to thee, *as* the LORD l: 2416
1Sa 1:26 she said, O my lord, *as* thy soul l, my lord, 2416
1:28 as long as he l he *shall be* lent to 1961
14:39 For, *as* the LORD l, which saveth Israel, 2416
14:45 *as* the LORD l, there shall not one hair of 2416
17:55 *As* thy soul l, O king, I cannot tell. 2416
19: 6 Saul sware, *As* the LORD l, he shall not 2416
20: 3 truly *as* the LORD l, and *as* thy soul 2416
20: 3 *as* thy soul l, *there is* but a step between me 2416
20:21 peace to thee, and no hurt; *as* the LORD l. 2416
20:31 For as long as the son of Jesse l upon 2416
25: 6 thus shall ye say to him that l *in prosperity,* 2416
25:26 *as* the LORD l, and *as* thy soul liveth, 2416
25:26 *as* the LORD liveth, and *as* thy soul l, 2416
25:34 in very deed, *as* the LORD God of Israel l, 2416
26:10 David said furthermore, *As* the LORD l, 2416
26:16 *As* the LORD l, ye *are* worthy to die, 2416
28:10 by the LORD, saying, *As* the LORD l, 2416
29: 6 said unto him, Surely, *as* the LORD l, 2416
2Sa 2:27 Joab said, *As* God l, unless thou hadst 2416
4: 9 and said unto them, *As* the LORD l, 2416
11:11 *as* thou livest, and *as* thy soul l, I will not 2416
12: 5 he said to Nathan, *As* the LORD l, 2416
14:11 he said, *As* the LORD l, there shall not 2416
14:19 woman answered and said, *As* thy soul l, 2416
15:21 *As* the LORD l, and *as* my lord the king 2416
15:21 LORD liveth, and *as* my lord the king l, 2416
22:47 The LORD l; and blessed *be* my rock; and 2416
1Ki 1:29 the king sware, and said, *As* the LORD l, 2416

L

1Ki 2:24 Now therefore, as the LORD l, which hath 2416
3:23 This is my son that l, and thy son is 2416
17: 1 unto Ahab, As the LORD God of Israel l, 2416
17:12 she said, As the LORD thy God l, I have 2416
17:23 his mother: and Elijah said, See, thy son l. 2416
18:10 As the LORD thy God l, there is no nation 2416
18:15 Elijah said, As the LORD of hosts l, 2416
22:14 Micaiah said, As the LORD l, what 2416
2Ki 2: 2 And Elisha said unto him, As the LORD l, 2416
2: 2 and as thy soul l, I will not leave thee. 2416
2: 4 As the LORD l, and as thy soul liveth, 2416
2: 4 and as thy soul l, I will not leave thee. 2416
2: 6 As the LORD l, and as thy soul liveth, 2416
2: 6 and as thy soul l, I will not leave thee. 2416
3:14 Elisha said, As the LORD of hosts l, 2416
4:30 As the LORD l, and as thy soul liveth, 2416
4:30 and as thy soul l, I will not leave thee. 2416
5:16 he said, As the LORD l, before whom I 2416
5:20 but, as the LORD l, I will run after him, 2416
2Ch 18:13 Micaiah said, As the LORD l, even what 2416
Job 19:25 For I know that my Redeemer l, and that he 2416
27: 2 As God l, who hath taken away my 2416
Ps 18:46 The LORD l; and blessed be my rock; and 2416
89:48 What man is he that l, and shall not see 2421
Jer 4: 2 The LORD l, in truth, in judgment, and 2416
5: 2 though they say, The LORD l; surely they 2416
12:16 to swear by my name, The LORD l; 2416
16:14 that it shall no more be said, The LORD l, 2416
16:15 But, The LORD l, that brought up 2416
23: 7 that they shall no more say, The LORD l, 2416
23: 8 But, The LORD l, which brought up and 2416
38:16 saying, As the LORD l, that made us this 2416
44:26 land of Egypt, saying, The Lord GOD l. 2416
Eze 47: 9 that every thing that l, which moveth, 2416
Da 4:34 I praised and honoured him that l for ever, 2417
12: 7 sware by him that l for ever that it shall be 2416
Hos 4:15 up to Beth-aven, nor swear, The LORD l. 2416
Am 8:14 sin of Samaria, and say, Thy god, O Dan, l; 2416
8:14 liveth; and, The manner of Beer-sheba l; 2416
Jn 4:50 Jesus saith unto him, Go thy way; thy son l. 2198
4:51 met him, and told him, saying, Thy son l. 2198
4:53 in the which Jesus said unto him, Thy son l: 2198
11:26 And whosoever l and believeth in me shall 2198
Ro 6:10 but in that he l, he liveth unto God. 2198
6:10 but in that he liveth, he l unto God. 2198
7: 1 hath dominion over a man, as long as he l? 2198
7: 2 by the law to her husband so long as he l; 2198
7: 3 So then if, while her husband l, she be 2198
14: 7 For none of us l to himself, and no man 2198
1Co 7:39 bound by the law as long as her husband l; 2198
2Co 13: 4 yet he l by the power of God. 2198
Gal 2:20 I live; yet not I, but Christ l in me: 2198
1Ti 5: 6 But she that l in pleasure is dead while she 4684
5: 6 that liveth in pleasure is dead while she l. 2198
Heb 7: 8 them, of whom it is witnessed that he l. 2198
7:25 seeing he ever l to make intercession for 2198
9:17 is of no strength at all whilst the testator l. 2198
1Pe 1:23 word of God, which l and abideth for ever. 2198
Rev 1:18 I am he that l, and was dead; and behold, 2198
4: 9 sat on the throne, who l for ever and ever, 2198
4:10 and worship him that l for ever and ever, 2198
5:14 and worshipped him that l for ever and 2198
10: 6 And sware by him that l for ever and ever, 2198
15: 7 the wrath of God, who l for ever and ever. 2198

LIVING (147) [LIVE]

Ge 1:21 and every l creature that moveth, 2416
1:24 Let the earth bring forth the l creature after 2416
1:28 over every l thing that moveth upon 2416
2: 7 the breath of life; and man became a l soul. 2416
2:19 whatsoever Adam called every l creature, 2416
3:20 because she was the mother of all l. 2416
6:19 of every l thing of all flesh, two of every 2416
7: 4 every l substance that I have made will I 3351
7:23 every l substance was destroyed which 3351
8: 1 every l thing, and all the cattle that was 2416
8:17 Bring forth with thee every l thing that is 2416
8:21 will I again smite any more every thing l, 2416
9:10 with every l creature that is with you, of 2416
9:12 and every l creature that is with you, 2416
9:15 and you and every l creature of all flesh; 2416
9:16 every l creature of all flesh that is upon 2416
Lev 11:10 and of any l thing which is in the waters, 2416
11:46 of every l creature that moveth in 2416
14: 6 As for the l bird, he shall take it, and 2416
14: 6 the l bird in the blood of the bird that was 2416
14: 7 shall let the l bird loose into the open field. 2416
14:51 the l bird, and dip them in the blood of 2416
14:52 with the l bird, and with the cedar wood, 2416
14:53 he shall let go the l bird out of the city into 2416
20:25 by any manner of l thing that creepeth on NIH
Nu 16:48 he stood between the dead and the l; and 2416
Dt 5:26 that hath heard the voice of the l God 2416
Jos 3:10 Hereby ye shall know that the l God is 2416
Ru 2:20 who hath not left off his kindness to the l 2416
1Sa 17:26 that he should defy the armies of the l God? 2416
17:36 seeing he hath defied the armies of the l 2416
2Sa 20: 3 unto the day of their death, l in widowhood. 2424
1Ki 3:22 but the l is my son, and the dead is thy son. 2416
3:22 but the dead is thy son, and the l is my son. 2416
3:23 but thy son is the dead, and my son is the l. 2416
3:25 Divide the l child in two, and give half to 2416
3:26 spake the woman whose the l child was 2416
3:26 give her the l child, and in no wise slay it. 2416
3:27 Give her the l child, and in no wise slay it: 2416
2Ki 19: 4 his master hath sent to reproach the l God; 2416
19:16 which hath sent him to reproach the l God. 2416
Job 12:10 In whose hand is the soul of every l thing, 2416
28:13 neither is it found in the land of the l. 2416
28:21 Seeing it is hid from the eyes of all l, and 2416
30:23 and to the house appointed for all l. 2416
33:30 to be enlightened with the light of the l. 2416
Ps 27:13 goodness of the LORD in the land of the l. 2416
42: 2 My soul thirsteth for God, for the l God: 2416
52: 5 and root thee out of the land of the l. 2416
Ps 56:13 I may walk before God in the light of the l? 2416
58: 9 with a whirlwind, both l, and in his wrath. 2416
69:28 Let them be blotted out of the book of the l, 2416
84: 2 and my flesh crieth out for the l God. 2416
116: 9 walk before the LORD in the land of the l. 2416
142: 5 and my portion in the land of the l. 2416
143: 2 for in thy sight shall no man l be justified. 2416
145:16 and satisfiest the desire of every l thing. 2416
Ecc 4: 2 dead more than the l which are yet alive. 2416
4:15 I considered all the l which walk under 2416
6: 8 the poor, that knoweth to walk before the l? 2416
7: 2 of all men; and the l will lay it to his heart. 2416
9: 4 For to him that is joined to all the l there is 2416
9: 4 for a l dog is better than a dead lion. 2416
9: 5 For the l know that they shall die: but 2416
SS 4:15 a well of l waters, and streams from 2416
Isa 4: 3 even every one that is written among the l 2416
8:19 seek unto their God? for the l to the dead? 2416
37: 4 his master hath sent to reproach the l God, 2416
37:17 which hath sent to reproach the l God. 2416
38:11 even the LORD, in the land of the l: 2416
38:19 The l, the living, he shall praise thee, as I 2416
38:19 The living, the l, he shall praise thee, as I 2416
53: 8 for he was cut off out of the land of the l: 2416
Jer 2:13 they have forsaken me the fountain of l 2416
10:10 he is the l God, and an everlasting king: 2416
11:19 and let us cut him off from the land of the l, 2416
17:13 the LORD, the fountain of l waters. 2416
23:36 for ye have perverted the words of the l 2416
La 3:39 Wherefore doth a l man complain, a man 2416
Eze 1: 5 came the likeness of four l creatures. 2416
1:13 As for the likeness of the l creatures, 2416
1:13 went up and down among the l creatures; 2416
1:14 the l creatures ran and returned as 2416
1:15 Now as I beheld the l creatures, behold 2416
1:15 wheel upon the earth by the l creatures, 2416
1:19 when the l creatures went, the wheels went 2416
1:19 when the l creatures were lift up from 2416
1:20 for the spirit of the l creature was in 2416
1:21 for the spirit of the l creature was in 2416
1:22 l creature was as the colour of the terrible 2416
3:13 of the l creatures that touched one another, 2416
10:15 This is the l creature that I saw by the river 2416
10:17 for the spirit of the l creature was in them. 2416
10:20 This is the l creature that I saw under 2416
26:20 and I shall set glory in the land of the l; 2416
32:23 which caused terror in the land of the l. 2416
32:24 caused their terror in the land of the l; 2416
32:25 their terror was caused in the land of the l, 2416
32:26 they caused their terror in the land of the l. 2416
32:27 the terror of the mighty in the land of the l. 2416
32:32 I have caused my terror in the land of the l: 2416
Da 2:30 for any wisdom that I have more than any l, 2417
4:17 to the intent that the l may know that 2417
6:20 O Daniel, servant of the l God, is thy God, 2417
6:26 for he is the l God, and stedfast for ever, 2417
Hos 1:10 unto them, Ye are the sons of the l God. 2416
Zec 14: 8 that l waters shall go out from Jerusalem: 2416
Mt 16:16 Thou art the Christ, the Son of the l God. 2198
22:32 God is not the God of the dead, but of the l. 2198
26:63 said unto him, I adjure thee by the l God, 2198
Mk 12:27 the God of the dead, but the God of the l: 2198
12:44 did cast in all that she had, even all her l. 979
Lk 8:43 which had spent all her l upon physicians, 979
15:12 to me. And he divided unto them his l. 979
15:13 there wasted his substance with riotous l. 2198
15:30 which hath devoured thy l with harlots, 979
20:38 For he is not a God of the dead, but of the l: 2198
21: 4 she of her penury hath cast in all the l that 979
24: 5 Why seek ye the l among the dead? 2198
Jn 4:10 and he would have given thee l water. 2198
4:11 from whence then hast thou that l water? 2198
6:51 I am the l bread which came down from 2198
6:57 As the l Father hath sent me, and I live by 2198
6:69 thou art that Christ, the Son of the l God. 2198
7:38 out of his belly shall flow rivers of l water. 2198
Ac 14:15 turn from these vanities unto the l God, 2198
Ro 9:26 they be called the children of the l God. 2198
12: 1 that ye present your bodies a l sacrifice, 2198
14: 9 he might be Lord both of the dead and l. 2198
1Co 15:45 The first man Adam was made a l soul; 2198
2Co 3: 3 with ink, but with the Spirit of the l God; 2198
6:16 for ye are the temple of the l God; as God 2198
Col 2:20 why, as though l in the world, are ye 2198
1Th 1: 9 ye turned to God from idols to serve the l 2198
1Ti 3:15 which is the church of the l God, the pillar 2198
4:10 because we trust in the l God, 2198
6:17 trust in uncertain riches, but in the l God, 2198
Tit 3: 3 l in malice and envy, hateful, and 1236
Heb 3:12 of unbelief, in departing from the l God. 2198
9:14 from dead works to serve the l God? 2198
10:20 By a new and l way, which he hath 2198
10:31 thing to fall into the hands of the l God. 2198
12:22 and unto the city of the l God, the heavenly 2198
1Pe 2: 4 To whom coming, as unto a l stone, 2198
Rev 7: 2 from the east, having the seal of the l God: 2198
7:17 shall lead them unto l fountains of waters: 2198
16: 3 dead man: and every l soul died in the sea. 2198

LIZARD (1)

Lev 11:30 and the l, and the snail, and the mole. 3911

LO (159)

Ge 8:11 l, in her mouth was an olive leaf pluckt off: 2009
15: 3 and l, one born in my house is mine heir. 2009
15:12 and, l, a horror of great darkness fell upon 2009
18: 2 he lift up his eyes and looked, and l, 2009
18:10 and l, Sarah thy wife shall have a son. 2009
19:28 all the land of the plain, and beheld, and l, 2009
29: 2 and behold a well in the field, and l, 2009
29: 7 he said, L, it is yet high day, neither is it 2005
37: 7 l, my sheaf arose, and also stood upright; 2009
42:28 is restored; and l, it is even in my sack: 2009
47:23 l, here is seed for you, and ye shall sow 1887
48:11 and l, God hath shewed me also thy seed. 2009
Ge 50: 5 My father made me swear, saying, L, I die: 2009
Ex 7:15 l, he goeth out unto the water; and 2009
8:20 l, he cometh forth to the water; and 2009
8:26 l, shall we sacrifice the abomination of 2005
19: 9 L, I come unto thee in a thick cloud, 2009
Nu 14:40 saying, L, we be here, and will go up unto 2009
22:38 said unto Balak, L, I am come unto thee: 2009
23: 6 he returned unto him, and l, he stood by his 2009
23: 9 l, the people shall dwell alone, and shall not 2005
24:11 l, the LORD hath kept thee back from 2009
Dt 22:17 l, he hath given occasions of speech against 2009
Jos 14:10 now l, I am this day fourscore and 2009
Jdg 7:13 and said, Behold, I dreamed a dream, and l, 2009
13: 5 For l, thou shalt conceive, and bear a son; 2009
1Sa 4:13 when he came, l, Eli sat upon a seat by 2009
10: 2 l, thy father hath left the care of the asses, 2009
14:43 rod that was in mine hand, and l, I must die. 2009
21:14 his servants, L, you see the man is mad: 2009
2Sa 1: 6 l, the chariots and horsemen followed hard 2009
15:24 l Zadok also, and all the Levites were with 2009
24:17 said, L, I have sinned, and I have done 2009
1Ki 1:22 l, while she yet talked with the king, 2009
1:51 for l, he hath caught hold on the horns of 2009
3:12 l, I have given thee a wise and 2009
2Ki 7: 6 they said one to another, L, the king of 2009
7:15 l, all the way was full of garments and 2009
1Ch 17: 1 L, I dwell in a house of cedars, but the ark 2009
21:23 l, I give thee the oxen also for burnt 7200
2Ch 16:11 And behold, the acts of Asa, first and last, l, 2009
25:19 Thou sayest, L, thou hast smitten 2009
27: 7 l they are written in the book of the kings 2009
29: 9 For l, our fathers have fallen by the sword, 2009
Ne 5: 5 l, we bring into bondage our sons and our 2009
6:12 l, I perceived that God had not sent him; 2009
Job 3: 7 L, let that night be solitary, let no joyful 2009
5:27 L this, we have searched it, so it is; hear it, 2009
9:11 L, he goeth by me, and I see him not: 2005
9:19 If I speak of strength, l, he is strong: and 2009
13: 1 L, mine eye hath seen all this, mine ear 2005
21:16 L, their good is not in their hand: 2005
26:14 L, these are parts of his ways: but how little 2005
33:29 L, all these things worketh God oftentimes 2005
40:16 L now, his strength is in his loins, and 2009
Ps 11: 2 For l, the wicked bend their bow, 2009
37:36 Yet he passed away, and l, he was not: yea, 2009
40: 7 said I, L, I come: in the volume of the book 2009
40: 9 l, I have not refrained my lips, O LORD, 2009
48: 4 For l, the kings were assembled, 2009
52: 7 L, this is the man that made not God his 2009
55: 7 L, then would I wander far off, and 2009
59: 3 For l, they lie in wait for my soul: 2009
68:33 l, he doth send out his voice, and that a 2005
73:27 For l, they that are far from thee shall 2009
83: 2 For l, thine enemies make a tumult: and 2009
92: 9 For l, thine enemies, O LORD, for lo, 2009
92: 9 For lo, thine enemies, O LORD, for l, 2009
127: 3 L, children are an heritage of the LORD: 2009
132: 6 L, we heard of it at Ephratah: we found it 2009
139: 4 but l, O LORD, thou knowest it 2005
Pr 24:31 l, it was all grown over with thorns, and 2009
Ecc 1:16 saying, L, I am come to great estate, and 2009
7:29 L, this only have I found, that God hath 7200
SS 2:11 For l, the winter is past, the rain is over and 2009
Isa 6: 7 and said, L, this hath touched thy lips; 2009
25: 9 shall be said in that day, L, this is our God; 2009
36: 6 L, thou trustest in the staff of this broken 2009
49:12 l, these from the north and from the west; 2009
50: 9 l, they all shall wax old as a garment; 2005
Jer 1:15 For l, I will call all the families of 2009
4:23 I beheld the earth, and l, it was without 2009
4:24 l, they trembled, and all the hills moved 2009
4:25 I beheld, and l, there was no man, and 2009
4:26 I beheld, and l, the fruitful place was a 2009
5:15 L, I will bring a nation upon you from far, 2009
8: 8 L, certainly in vain made he it; the pen of 2009
8: 9 l, they have rejected the word of 2009
25:29 For l, I begin to bring evil on the city which 2009
30: 3 For l, the days come, saith the LORD, 2009
30:10 for l, I will save thee from afar, and thy 2009
36:12 l, all the princes sat there, even Elishama 2009
49:15 For l, I will make thee small among 2009
50: 9 For l, I will raise and cause to come up 2009
Eze 2: 9 unto me; and l, a roll of a book was therein; 2009
4:15 he said unto me, L, I have given thee cow's 7200
8: 2 I beheld, and l, a likeness as the appearance 2009
8:17 and l, they put the branch to their nose. 2009
13:10 one built up a wall, and l, others daubed it 2009
13:12 L, when the wall is fallen, shall it not be 2009
17:18 when l, he had given his hand, and 2009
18:14 Now l, if he beget a son, that seeth all his 2009
18:18 l, even he shall die in his iniquity. 2009
23:39 l, thus have they done in the midst of mine 2009
23:40 a messenger was sent; and l, they came: 2009
30: 9 as in the day of Egypt: for l, it cometh. 2009
30:21 l, it shall not be bound up to be healed, 2009
33:32 l, thou art unto them as a very lovely song 2009
33:33 when this cometh to pass, (l, it will come) 2009
37: 2 the open valley; and l, they were very dry. 2009
37: 8 l, the sinews and the flesh came up upon 2009
40:17 l, there were chambers, and a pavement 2009
42: 8 l, before the temple were an hundred cubits. 2009
Da 3:25 He answered and said, L, I see four men 1888
7: 6 this I beheld, and l another, like a leopard, 718
10:13 l, Michael, one of the chief princes, came to 2009
10:20 when I am gone forth, l, the prince of 2009
Hos 9: 6 For l, they are gone because of destruction: 2009
Am 4: 2 that l, the days shall come upon you, that he 2009
4:13 For l, he that formeth the mountains, and 2009
7: 1 l, it was the latter growth after the king's 2009
9: 9 For l, I will command, and I will sift 2009
Hab 1: 6 For l, I raise up the Chaldeans, that bitter 2009
Hag 1: 9 Ye looked for much, and l, it came to little; 2009
Zec 2:10 for l, I come, and I will dwell in the midst 2009
11: 6 l, I will deliver the men every one into his 2009
11:16 For l, I will raise up a shepherd in the land, 2009

L

Mt 2: 9 and l, the star, which they saw in the east, 2400
3:16 and l, the heavens were opened unto him, 2400
3:17 And l a voice from heaven, saying, This is 2400
24:23 say unto you, L, here is Christ, or there; 2400
25:25 in the earth: l, there thou hast that is thine. 2396
26:47 l, Judas, one of the twelve, came, and 2400
28: 7 there shall ye see him: l, I have told you. 2400
28:20 and l, I am with you alway, even unto 2400
Mk 10:28 L, we have left all, and have followed thee. 2400
13:21 any man shall say to you, L, here is Christ; 2400
13:21 to you, Lo, here is Christ; or l, he is there; 2400
14:42 let us go; l, he that betrayeth me is at hand. 2400
Lk 1:44 For l, as soon as the voice of thy salutation 2400
2: 9 And l, the angel of the Lord came upon 2400
9:39 And l, a spirit taketh him, and he suddenly 2400
13:16 Satan hath bound, l these eighteen years, 2400
15:29 L, these many years do I serve thee, 2400
17:21 Neither shall they say, L here: or, lo there: 2400
17:21 or, l there: for behold, the kingdom of God 2400
18:28 Then Peter said, L, we have left all, 2400
23:15 and l, nothing worthy of death is done unto 2400
Jn 7:26 But l, he speaketh boldly, and they say 2396
16:29 L, now speakest thou plainly, and 2396
Ac 13:46 everlasting life, l, we turn to the Gentiles. 2400
27:24 and l, God hath given thee all them that sail 2400
Heb 10: 7 Then said I, L, I come (in the volume of 2400
10: 9 Then said he, L, I come to do thy will, 2400
Rev 5: 6 And I beheld, and l, in the midst of 2400
6: 5 And I beheld, and l a black horse; and 2400
6:12 and l, there was a great earthquake; 2400
7: 9 After this I beheld, and l, a great multitude, 2400
14: 1 And I looked, and l, a Lamb stood on 2400

LOAD See LADE; LADED; LADING

LOADEN (1) [LOADETH]
Isa 46: 1 your carriages were **heavy l**; they are a 6006

LOADETH (1) [LOADEN]
Ps 68:19 who daily l us with benefits, even the God 6006

LOAF (3) [LOAVES]
Ex 29:23 one l of bread, and one cake of oiled bread, 3603
1Ch 16: 3 to every one a l of bread, and a good piece 3603
Mk 8:14 they in the ship with them more than one l. 740

LO-AMMI (1) [AMMI]
Hos 1: 9 said God, Call his name L: for ye are not 3818

LOAN (1)
1Sa 2:20 for the l which is lent to the LORD. 7596

LOATHE (1) [LOATHETH, LOATHSOME, LOTHE]
Job 7:16 I l it; I would not live alway: let me alone; 3988

LOATHETH (2) [LOATHE]
Nu 21: 5 any water; and our soul l this light bread. 6973
Pr 27: 7 The full soul l a honeycomb; but to 947

LOATHSOME (4) [LOATHE]
Nu 11:20 out at your nostrils, and it be l unto you: 2214
Job 7: 5 of dust; my skin is broken, and **become l**. 3988
Ps 38: 7 For my loins are filled with a l disease: and 7033
Pr 13: 5 but a wicked man is l, and cometh to shame. 887

LOAVES (32) [LOAF]
Lev 23:17 habitations two wave l of two tenth deals: 3899
Jdg 8: 5 l of bread unto the people that follow me; 3603
1Sa 10: 3 another carrying three l of bread, and 3603
10: 4 salute thee, and give thee two l of bread; NIH
17:17 ephah of this parched corn, and these ten l, 3899
21: 3 give me five l of bread in mine hand, or NIH
25:18 took two hundred l, and two bottles of 3899
2Sa 16: 1 upon them two hundred l of bread, and NIH
1Ki 14: 3 And take with thee ten l, and cracknels, and 3899
2Ki 4:42 twenty l of barley, and full ears of corn in 3899
Mt 14:17 We have here but five l, and two fishes. 740
14:19 and took the five l, and the two fishes, and 740
14:19 and gave the l to his disciples, and 740
15:34 Jesus saith unto them, How many l have ye? 740
15:36 And he took the seven l and the fishes, and 740
16: 9 neither remember the five l of the five 740
16:10 Neither the seven l of the four thousand, and 740
Mk 6:38 He saith unto them, How many l have ye? go 740
6:41 And when he had taken the five l and 740
6:41 and brake the l, and gave them to his 740
6:44 And they that did eat of the l were about five 740
6:52 For they considered not the miracle of the l: 740
8: 5 And he asked them, How many l have ye? 740
8: 6 and he took the seven l, and gave thanks, and 740
8:19 When I brake the five l among five 740
Lk 9:13 We have no more but five l and two fishes; 740
9:16 Then he took the five l and the two fishes, 740
11: 5 and say unto him, Friend, lend me three l; 740
Jn 6: 9 which hath five barley l, and two small 740
6:11 And Jesus took the l; and when he had given 740
6:13 with the fragments of the five barley l, 740
6:26 but because ye did eat of the l, and 740

LOCK (2) [LOCKED, LOCKS]
SS 5: 5 smelling myrrh, upon the handles of the l. 4514
Eze 8: 3 of a hand, and took me by a l of mine head; 6734

LOCKED (2) [LOCK]
Jdg 3:23 doors of the parlour upon him, and l them. 5274
3:24 the doors of the parlour were l, they said, 5274

LOCKS (15) [LOCK]
Nu 6: 5 shall let the l of the hair of his head grow, 6545
Jdg 16:13 If thou weavest the seven l of my head with 4253
16:19 she caused him to shave off the seven l of 4253
Ne 3: 3 the l thereof, and the bars thereof. 4514
3: 6 and the l thereof, and the bars thereof. 4514
3:13 the l thereof, and the bars thereof, and 4514
3:14 the l thereof, and the bars thereof. 4514
3:15 the l thereof, and the bars thereof, and 4514
SS 4: 1 art fair; thou hast doves' eyes within thy l: 6777
4: 3 like a piece of a pomegranate within thy l. 6777
5: 2 and my l with the drops of the night. 6977
5:11 his l are bushy, and black as a raven. 6977
6: 7 a pomegranate are thy temples within thy l. 6777
Isa 47: 2 uncover thy l, make bare the leg, 6777
Eze 44:20 their heads, nor suffer their l to grow long; 6545

LOCUST (11) [LOCUSTS]
Ex 10:19 there remained not one l in all the coasts of 697
Lev 11:22 the l after his kind, and the bald locust after 697
11:22 the **bald l** after his kind, and the beetle after 5556
Dt 28:38 but little in; for the l shall consume it. 697
28:42 and fruit of thy land shall the l consume. 6767
1Ki 8:37 blasting, mildew, l, or if there be caterpillar; 697
Ps 78:46 the caterpillar, and their labour unto the l. 697
109:23 I am tossed up and down as the l. 697
Joel 1: 4 the palmerworm hath left hath the l eaten; 697
1: 4 that which the l hath left hath 697
2:25 I will restore to you the years that the l hath 697

LOCUSTS (17) [LOCUST]
Ex 10: 4 to morrow will I bring the l into thy coast: 697
10:12 thine hand over the land of Egypt for the l, 697
10:13 it was morning, the east wind brought the l. 697
10:14 And the l went up over all the land of Egypt, 697
10:14 before them there were no such l as they, 697
10:19 which took away the l, and cast them into 697
2Ch 6:28 be blasting, or mildew, l, or caterpillars; 697
7:13 or if I command the l to devour the land, or 2284
Ps 105:34 the l came, and caterpillars, and that without 697
Pr 30:27 The l have no king, yet go they forth all of 697
Isa 33: 4 and fro of l shall he run upon them. 1357
Na 3:15 the cankerworm, make thyself many as the l. 697
3:17 Thy crowned are as the l, and thy captains as 697
Mt 3: 4 his loins; and his meat was l and wild honey. 200
Mk 1: 6 his loins; and he did eat l and wild honey; 200
Rev 9: 3 And there came out of the smoke l upon 200
9: 7 And the shapes of the l were like unto horses 200

LOD (4)
1Ch 8:12 and Shamed, who built Ono, and L, 3850
Ezr 2:33 The children of L, Hadid, and Ono, 3850
Ne 7:37 The children of L, Hadid, and Ono, 3850
11:35 L, and Ono, the valley of craftsmen. 3850

LO-DEBAR (3)
2Sa 9: 4 house of Machir, the son of Ammiel, in L. 3810
9: 5 of Machir, the son of Ammiel, from L. 3810
17:27 Machir the son of Ammiel of L, and 3810

LODGE (27) [LODGED, LODGEST, LODGETH, LODGING, LODGINGS]
Ge 24:23 room in thy father's house for us to **l in**? 3885
24:25 and provender enough, and room to **l in**. 3885
Nu 22: 8 L here this night, and I will bring you word 3885
Jos 4: 3 lodging place, where ye shall l this night. 3885
Jdg 19: 9 behold, the day groweth to an end, l here, 3885
19:11 in into this city of the Jebusites, and l in it. 3885
19:13 near to one of these places to **l all night**, 3885
19:15 aside thither, to go in and to l in Gibeah: 3885
19:20 wants lie upon me; only l not in the street. 3885
20: 4 to Benjamin, I and my concubine, to l. 3885
Ru 1:16 I will go; and where thou lodgest, I will l: 3885
2Sa 17: 8 man of war, and will not l with the people. 3885
17:16 L not this night in the plains of 3885
Ne 4:22 Let every one with his servant l within 3885
13:21 said unto them, Why l ye about the wall? 3885
Job 24: 7 They **cause** the naked **to l** without clothing, 3885
31:32 The stranger did not l in the street: but 3885
SS 7:11 forth into the field; let us l in the villages. 3885
Isa 1: 8 as a l in a garden of cucumbers, as a 4412
21:13 In the forest in Arabia shall ye l, O ye 3885
65: 4 l in the monuments, which eat swine's 3885
Jer 4:14 How long shall thy vain thoughts l within 3885
Zep 2:14 the bittern shall l in the upper lintels of it; 3885
Mt 13:32 the air come and l in the branches thereof. 2681
Mk 4:32 that the fowls of the air may l under 2681
Lk 9:12 round about, and l, and get victuals: 2647
Ac 21:16 an old disciple, with whom we should l. 3579

LODGED (21) [LODGE]
Ge 32:13 he l there that same night; and took of that 3885
32:21 and himself l that night in the company. 3885
Jos 2: 1 a harlot's house, named Rahab, and l there. 7901
3: 1 and l there before they passed over. 3885
4: 8 with them unto the **place where** they l, 4411
6:11 they came into the camp, and l in the camp. 3885
8: 9 but Joshua l that night among the people. 3885
Jdg 18: 2 to the house of Micah, they l there. 3885
19: 4 so they did eat and drink, and l there. 3885
19: 7 In law urged him: therefore he l there again. 3885
1Ki 19: 9 he came thither unto a cave, and l there; 3885
1Ch 9:27 they l round about the house of God, 3885
Ne 13:20 sellers of all kind of ware l without 3885
Isa 1:21 righteousness l in it; but now murderers. 3885
Mt 21:17 out of the city into Bethany; and he l there. 835
Lk 13:19 the fowls of the air l in the branches of it. 2681
Ac 10:18 which was surnamed Peter, were l there. 3579
10:23 l them. And on the morrow Peter went 3579
10:32 he is l in the house of one Simon a tanner 3579
28: 7 and l us three days courteously. 3579
1Ti 5:10 up children, if she have **l strangers**, 3580

LODGEST (1) [LODGE]
Ru 1:16 I will go; and where thou l, I will lodge: 3885

LODGETH (1) [LODGE]
Ac 10: 6 He l with one Simon a tanner, whose house 3579

LODGING (6) [LODGE]
Jos 4: 3 leave them in the **l place**, where you shall 4411
Jdg 19:15 no man that took them into his house to l. 3885
Isa 10:29 they have **taken up** their l at Geba; Ramah 4411
Jer 9: 2 O that I had in the wilderness a **l place** of 4411
Ac 28:23 a day, there came many to him into his l; 3578
Phm 1:22 But withal prepare me also a l: for I trust 3578

LODGINGS (1) [LODGE]
2Ki 19:23 and I will enter into the l of his borders, and 4411

LOFT (2)
1Ki 17:19 and carried him up into a l, where he abode, 5944
Ac 20: 9 and fell down from the **third l**, and 5152

LOFTILY (1) [LOFTY]
Ps 73: 8 concerning oppression: they speak l. 4480+4791

LOFTINESS (2) [LOFTY]
Isa 2:17 the l of man shall be bowed down, and 1365
Jer 48:29 his l, and his arrogancy, and his pride, and 1363

LOFTY (8) [LOFTILY, LOFTINESS]
Ps 131: 1 my heart is not haughty, nor mine eyes l: 7311
Pr 30:13 is a generation, O how l are their eyes! 7311
Isa 2:11 The l looks of man shall be humbled, and 1365
2:12 shall be upon every one that is proud and l, 7311
5:15 and the eyes of the l shall be humbled: 1364
26: 5 the l city, he layeth it low; he layeth it low, 7682
57: 7 Upon a l and high mountain hast thou set 1364
57:15 the high and l One that inhabiteth eternity, 5375

LOG (5)
Lev 14:10 mingled with oil, and one l of oil. 3849
14:12 the l of oil, and wave them for a wave 3849
14:15 the priest shall take some of the l of oil, 3849
14:21 with oil for a meat offering, and a l of oil; 3849
14:24 the l of oil, and the priest shall wave them 3849

LOINS (83)
Ge 35:11 of thee, and kings shall come out of thy l; 2504
37:34 put sackcloth upon his l, and mourned for 4975
46:26 which came out of his l, besides Jacob's 3409
Ex 1: 5 all the souls that came out of the l of Jacob 3409
12:11 with your l girded, your shoes on your feet, 4975
28:42 from the l even unto the thighs they shall 4975
Dt 33:11 smite through the l of them that rise against 4975
2Sa 20: 8 fastened upon his l in the sheath thereof; 4975
1Ki 2: 5 of war upon his girdle that was about his l, 4975
8:19 thy son that shall come forth out of thy l, 2504
12:10 finger shall be thicker than my father's l. 4975
18:46 he girded up his l, and ran before Ahab to 4975
20:31 put sackcloth on our l, and ropes upon our 4975
20:32 So they girded sackcloth on their l, and 4975
2Ki 1: 8 girt with a girdle of leather about his l. 4975
4:29 Gird up thy l, and take my staff in thine 4975
9: 1 Gird up thy l, and take this box of oil in 4975
2Ch 6: 9 thy son which shall come forth out of thy l, 2504
10:10 finger shall be thicker than my father's l. 4975
Job 12:18 of kings, and girdeth their l with a girdle. 4975
31:20 If his l have not blessed me, and if he were 2504
38: 3 Gird up now thy l like a man; for I will 2504
40: 7 Gird up thy l now like a man: I will 2504
40:16 his strength is in his l, and his force is in 4975
Ps 38: 7 For my l are filled with a loathsome 3689
66:11 the net; thou laidst affliction upon our l. 4975
69:23 and make their l continually to shake. 4975
Pr 31:17 She girdeth her l with strength, and 4975
Isa 5:27 neither shall the girdle of their l be loosed, 2504
11: 5 righteousness shall be the girdle of his l, 4975
20: 2 Go and loose the sackcloth from off thy l, 4975
21: 3 Therefore are my l filled with pain: 4975
32:11 ye bare, and gird sackcloth upon your l. 2504
45: 1 I will loose the l of kings, to open before 4975
Jer 1:17 Thou therefore gird up thy l, and arise, and 4975
13: 1 put it upon thy l, and put it not in water. 4975
13: 2 the word of the LORD, and put it on my l. 4975
13: 4 which is upon thy l, and arise, go to 4975
13:11 For as the girdle cleaveth to the l of a man, 4975
30: 6 do I see every man with his hands on his l, 2504
48:37 shall be cuttings, and upon the l sackcloth. 4975
Eze 1:27 from the appearance of his l even upward, 4975
1:27 from the appearance of his l even 4975
8: 2 from the appearance of his l even 4975
8: 2 from his l even upward, as the appearance 4975
21: 6 thou son of man, with the breaking of thy l; 4975
23:15 Girded with girdles upon their l, 4975
29: 7 and madest all their l to be at a stand. 4975
44:18 and shall have linen breeches upon their l; 4975
47: 4 me through; the waters were to the l. 4975
Da 5: 6 so that the joints of his l were loosed, and 2783
10: 5 whose l were girded with fine gold of 4975
Am 8:10 I will bring up sackcloth upon all l, and 4975
Na 2: 1 watch the way, make thy l strong, 4975
2:10 much pain is in all l, and the faces of them 4975
Mt 3: 4 and a leathern girdle about his l; 3751
Mk 1: 6 and with a girdle of a skin about his l; 3751
Lk 12:35 Let your l be girded about, and your lights 3751
Ac 2:30 that of the fruit of his l, according to 3751
Eph 6:14 having your l girt about with truth, and 3751
Heb 7: 5 though they come out of the l of Abraham: 3751
7:10 For he was yet in the l of his father, 3751
1Pe 1:13 Wherefore gird up the l of your mind, 3751

LOIS (1)
2Ti 1: 5 which dwelt first in thy grandmother L, and 3090

LONG (211) [LENGTH, LONGED, LONGEDST, LONGETH, LONGING]
Ge 26: 8 to pass, when he had been there a l time, 748
48:15 the God which fed me **all my life l** 4480+5750
Ex 10: 3 LORD God of the Hebrews, **How l** 4970+5704
10: 7 servants said unto him, **How l** 4970+5704

Ex 16:28 said unto Moses, **How l** 575+5704+1886.5
19:13 when the trumpet **soundeth l**, they shall 4900
19:19 when the voice of the trumpet **sounded l**, 1980
20:12 that thy days may be l upon the land which 748
27: 1 five cubits l, and five cubits broad; 753
27: 9 linen of an hundred cubits l for one side: 753
27:11 *shall be* hangings of an hundred *cubits* l, 753
Lev 18:19 **as l as** she is put apart for her uncleanness. 871.1
26:34 **as l as** it lieth desolate, and ye *be* in 3117+3605
26:35 **As l as** it lieth desolate it shall rest; 3117+3605
Nu 9:18 **as l as** the cloud abode upon 3117+3605
9:19 when the cloud **tarried l** upon the tabernacle 748
14:11 said unto Moses, **How l** 575+5704+1886.5
14:11 **how l** will it be ere they 575+5704+1886.5
14:27 **How l** *shall I bear* with this evil 4970+5704
20:15 and we have dwelt in Egypt a l time; 7227
Dt 1: 6 Ye have dwelt **l enough** in this mount: 7227
2: 3 have compassed this mountain **l enough**: 7227
4:25 ye shall have **remained l** in the land, and 3462
12:19 the Levite **as l as** thou livest upon the earth. 3605
14:24 if the way be too l for thee, so that thou art 7235
19: 6 because the way is l, and slay him; 7235
20:19 When thou shalt besiege a city a l time, 7227
28:32 and fail *with longing* for them all the day l: NIH
28:59 of **l continuance**, and sore sicknesses, and 539
28:59 and sore sicknesses, and of **l continuance**. 539
31:13 **as l as** ye live in 834+3117+3605+1886.1
33:12 *the* LORD shall cover him all the day l, NIH
Jos 6: 5 *that* when *they* **make a l blast** with 4900
9:13 become old by reason of the very l journey. 7230
11:18 Joshua made war a l time with all those 7227
18: 3 the children of Israel, **How l** 575+5704+1886.5
23: 1 it came to pass a l time after that 7227
24: 7 and ye dwelt in the wilderness a l season. 7227
Jdg 5:28 Why is his chariot *so* l in coming? 954
1Sa 1:14 Eli said unto her, **How l** wilt thou be 4970+5704
1:28 **as l as** he liveth he *shall* 834+3117+3605+1886.1
7: 2 abode in Kirjath-jearim, that the time was l: 7235
16: 1 the LORD said unto Samuel, **How l** 4970+5704
20:31 For **as l as** the son of Jesse 3117+3605+1886.1
25:15 **as l as** we were conversant with 3117+3605
29: 8 **so l as** I have been with thee unto 3117+4480
2Sa 2:26 be bitterness in the latter end? **how l** 4970+5704
3: 1 Now there was l war between the house of 752
14: 2 be as a woman *that had* a l time mourned 7227
19:34 unto the king, **How l** 3117+4100+8141+3509.1
1Ki 3:11 and hast not asked for thyself l life; 7227
6:17 *is*, the temple before it, was forty cubits *l*. NIH
18:21 **How l** halt ye between two opinions? 4970+5704
2Ki 9:22 **so l as** the whoredoms of thy mother 5704
19:25 Hast thou not heard **l ago** 4480+7350+3807.1
2Ch 1:11 thine enemies, neither yet hast asked l life; 7227
3:11 wings of the cherubims *were* twenty cubits l: 753
6:13 of five cubits l, and five cubits broad, 753
6:31 **so l as** they live in the land 3117+3605+1886.1
15: 3 Now for a l season Israel *hath been* without 7227
26: 5 **as l as** he sought the LORD, God 3117+871.1
30: 5 for they had not done *it* of a l *time in such* 7230
36:21 *for* **as l as** *she* lay desolate she kept 3117+3605
Ne 2: 6 **For how l** shall thy journey be? 4970+5704
Est 5:13 **so l as** I see Mordecai the Jew 3605+871.1
Job 3:21 Which **l for** death, but it *cometh* not; and 2442
6: 8 God would grant *me* the **thing** that I **l for**! 8615
7:19 **How l** wilt thou not depart from 4100+3509.1
8: 2 **How l** wilt thou speak these *things?* 575+5704
8: 2 *how l shall* the words of thy mouth *be like* a NIH
18: 2 **How l** *will it be ere* you make 575+5704+1886.5
19: 2 **How l** will ye vex my soul, 575+5704+1886.5
27: 6 heart shall not reproach me **so l as** I live. 4480
Ps 4: 2 **how l** *will ye turn* my glory into 4100+5704
4: 2 *how l* will ye love vanity, *and* seek after NIH
6: 3 but thou, O LORD, **how l**? 4970+5704
13: 1 **How l** wilt thou forget me, 575+5704+1886.5
13: 1 for ever? **how l** wilt thou hide 575+5704+1886.5
13: 2 **How l** shall I take counsel in 575+5704+1886.5
13: 2 **how l** shall mine enemy be 575+5704+1886.5
32: 3 waxed old through my roaring all the day **l**. NIH
35:17 Lord, **how l** wilt thou look on? 4100+3509.1
35:28 *and of* thy praise all the day **l**. NIH
38: 6 down greatly; I go mourning all the day l. NIH
38:12 and imagine deceits all the day l. NIH
44: 8 In God we boast all the day l, and praise thy NIH
44:22 Yea, for thy sake are we killed all the day l; NIH
62: 3 **How l** will ye imagine 575+5704+1886.5
71:24 shall talk of thy righteousness all the day l: NIH
72: 5 They shall fear thee **as l as** the sun and 5973
72: 7 of peace **so l as** the moon **endureth**. 1097+5704
72:17 his name shall be continued **as l as** 6440+3807.1
73:14 For all the day have I been plagued, and NIH
74: 9 among us any that knoweth **how l**. 4100+5704
74:10 O God, **how l** shall the adversary 4970+5704
79: 5 **How l**, LORD? wilt thou be angry, 4100+5704
80: 4 O LORD God *of* hosts, **how l** wilt 4970+5704
82: 2 **How l** will ye judge unjustly, and 4970+5704
89:46 **How l**, LORD? wilt thou hide 4100+5704
90:13 Return, O LORD, **how l**? and let it 4970+5704
91:16 *With* l life will I satisfy him, and shew him 753
94: 3 LORD, **how l** shall the wicked, 4970+5704
94: 3 **how l** shall the wicked triumph? 4970+5704
94: 4 *How l* shall they utter *and* speak hard NIH
95:10 Forty years l was I grieved with *this* NIH
104:33 I will sing unto the LORD **as l as** I live: 871.1
116: 2 therefore will I call upon *him* **as l as** I live. 871.1
120: 6 My soul hath l dwelt with him that hateth 7227
129: 3 upon my back: they **made l** their furrows. 748
143: 3 in darkness, as those that have been l dead. 5769
Pr 1:22 **How l**, ye simple ones, will ye love 4970+5704
3: 2 For length of days, and l life, and peace, 8141
6: 9 **How l** wilt thou sleep, O sluggard? 4970+5704
7:19 *is* not at home, he is gone a l journey: 4480+7350
21:26 He coveteth greedily all the day l: but NIH
23:17 *thou* in the fear of the LORD all the day l. NIH
23:30 They that **tarry l** at the wine; they that go to 309
25:15 By l forbearing is a prince persuaded, and 753
Ecc 12: 5 because man goeth to his l home, and 5769
Isa 6:11 said I, Lord, **how l**? And he 4970+5704
22:11 unto him that fashioned it **l ago**. 4480+7350
37:26 Hast thou not heard **l ago**, 4480+7350+3807.1
42:14 I have **l time** holden my peace; I have been 5769
65:22 mine elect shall **l enjoy** the work of their 1086
Jer 4:14 that thou mayest be saved. **How l** 4970+5704
4:21 **How l** shall I see the standard, *and* 4970+5704
12: 4 **How l** shall the land mourn, and 4970+5704
23:26 **How l** shall *this* be in the heart of 4970+5704
29:28 us *in* Babylon, saying, This *captivity is* l: 752
31:22 **How l** wilt thou go about, O thou 4970+5704
47: 5 the remnant of their valley: **how l** 4970+5704
47: 6 sword of the LORD, **how l** 575+5704+1886.5
La 2:20 eat their fruit, *and* children of a **span l**? 2949
5:20 forget us for ever, *and* forsake us **so l** time? 753
Eze 31: 5 his branches became l because of 748
40: 5 a measuring reed of six cubits *l* by the cubit NIH
40: 7 And *every* little chamber *was* one reed l, and 753
40:29 *it was* fifty cubits l, and five and 753
40:30 round about *were* five and twenty cubits l, 753
40:33 *it was* fifty cubits l, and five and 753
40:42 of a cubit and a half l, and a cubit and a half 753
40:47 an hundred cubits l, and an hundred cubits 753
41:13 he measured the house, an hundred cubits l; 753
41:13 with the walls thereof, an hundred cubits l; 753
42:11 the north, as l as they, *and* as broad as they: 753
42:20 five hundred *reeds* l, and five hundred broad, 753
43:16 the altar *shall be* twelve *cubits* l, twelve 753
43:17 the settle *shall be* fourteen *cubits* l and 753
44:20 nor **suffer** *their* locks to **grow l**; 7971
45: 6 and five and twenty thousand l, 753
46:22 *there were* courts joined *of* forty *cubits* l 753
Da 8:13 that certain *saint* which spake, **How l** 4970+5704
10: 1 *was* true, but the time appointed *was* l: 1419
12: 6 upon the waters of the river, **How l** 4970+5704
Hos 8: 5 anger is kindled against them: **how l** 4970+5704
13:13 for he should not stay l in *the place of* 6256
Hab 1: 2 O LORD, **how l** shall I cry, 575+5704+1886.5
2: 6 *that which is* not his! **how l**? 4970+5704
Zec 1:12 O LORD of hosts, **how l** wilt thou 4970+5704
Mt 9:15 **as l as** the bridegroom is with them? *1909+3745*
11:21 Sidon they would have repented **l ago** in *3819*
17:17 **how l** shall I be with you? *2193+4219*
17:17 **how l** shall I suffer you? bring him *2193+4219*
23:14 and for a pretence make l prayer: *3117*
25:19 After a l time the lord of those servants *4183*
Mk 2:19 **as l as** they have the bridegroom *3745+5550*
9:19 **how l** shall I be with you? *2193+4219*
9:19 **how l** shall I suffer you? bring him *2193+4219*
9:21 How l is it **ago** since this came unto him? *5550*
12:38 which love to go in **l clothing**, and *4749*
12:40 and for a pretence make l prayers: *3117*
16: 5 the right side, clothed in a l white **garment**; *4749*
Lk 1:21 marvelled that he **tarried** *so* l in the temple. *5549*
8:27 which had devils l time, and ware no *2425*
9:41 **how l** shall I be with you, and *2193+4219*
18: 7 unto him, though he **bear l** with them? *3114*
20: 9 and went into a far country for a l time. *2425*
20:46 which desire to walk in **l robes**, and *4749*
20:47 and for a shew make l prayers: *3117*
23: 8 for he was desirous to see him of a l *season*, *2425*
Jn 5: 6 knew that he had been now a l time *in that* *4183*
9: 5 **As l as** I am in the world, I am the light of *3752*
10:24 **How l** dost thou make us to doubt? *2193+4219*
14: 9 Have I been **so l** time with you, and *5118*
Ac 8:11 that of l time *he* had bewitched them with *2425*
14: 3 L time therefore abode they speaking *2425*
14:28 And there they abode l time with *3641+3756*
20: 9 and as Paul was l preaching, he sunk *1909+4183*
20:11 and eaten, and talked a **l while**, *1909+2425*
27:14 But not l after there arose against it a *4183*
27:21 But after l abstinence Paul stood *forth* in *4183*
Ro 1:11 For I l to see you, that I may impart unto *1971*
7: 1 over a man, **as l as** he liveth? *1909+3745+5550*
7: 2 by the law to *her* husband so l as he liveth; NIG
8:36 For thy sake we are killed all the day l; NIG
10:21 **All** day l have I stretched forth my hands *3650*
1Co 7:39 law **as l as** her husband liveth; *1909+3745+5550*
11:14 that, if a man **have l hair**, it is a shame unto *2863*
11:15 But if a woman **have l hair**, it is a glory to *2863*
13: 4 Charity **suffereth l**, *and* is kind; *3114*
2Co 9:14 which **l after** you for the exceeding grace *1971*
Gal 4: 1 the heir, **as l as** he is a child, *1909+3745+5550*
Eph 6: 3 and thou mayest **live l** on the earth. *1510+3118*
Php 1: 8 how *greatly* I **l after** you all in the bowels *1971*
1Ti 3:15 But if I **tarry l**, that thou mayest know how *1019*
Heb 4: 7 saying in David, To day, after **so l** a time; *5118*
Jas 5: 7 and **hath l patience** for it, until he receive *3114*
1Pe 3: 6 as l as ye do well, and are not afraid *with* NIG
2Pe 1:13 **as l as** I am in this tabernacle, *1909+3745*
2: 3 whose judgment now **of a l time** lingereth *1597*
Rev 6:10 saying, **How l**, O Lord, holy and *2193+4219*

LONGED (8) [LONG]

2Sa 13:39 *the soul of* king David l to go forth unto 3615
23:15 David l, and said, Oh that one would give 183
1Ch 11:17 David l, and said, Oh that one would give 183
Ps 119:40 Behold, I have l after thy precepts: 8373
119:131 and panted: for I l for thy commandments. 2968
119:174 I have l for thy salvation, O LORD; and 8373
Php 2:26 For he **l after** you all, and *was* full of *1971*
4: 1 my brethren dearly beloved and **l for**, *1973*

LONGEDST (1) [LONG]

Ge 31:30 thou **sore l** after thy father's house, 3700+3700

LONGER (17) [LENGTH]

Ex 2: 3 when she could not l hide him, she took for 5750
9:28 and I will let you go, and ye shall stay no l. 3254
Jdg 2:14 that they could not **any l** stand before their 5750
2Sa 20: 5 he **tarried l** than the set time which he had 309
2Ki 6:33 what should I wait for the LORD **any l**? 5750
Job 11: 9 The measure thereof *is* l than the earth, and 752
Jer 44:22 So that the LORD could no l bear, 5750
Lk 16: 2 for thou mayest be no l steward. *2089*
Ac 18:20 When they desired *him* to tarry l *1909+4183*
25:24 crying that he ought not to live **any l**. *3371*
Ro 6: 2 that are dead to sin, live **any l** therein? *2089*
Gal 3:25 is come, we are **no l** under a schoolmaster. *3765*
1Th 3: 1 Wherefore when we could **no l** forbear, *3371*
3: 5 For this cause, when I could **no l** forbear, *3371*
1Ti 5:23 Drink **no l** water, but use a little wine for *3371*
1Pe 4: 2 That *he* **no l** should live the rest of *his* time *3371*
Rev 10: 6 are therein, that there should be time no **l**: *2089*

LONGETH (4) [LONG]

Ge 34: 8 The soul of my son Shechem l for your 2836
Dt 12:20 will eat flesh, because thy soul l to eat flesh; 183
Ps 63: 1 my flesh l for thee, in a dry and 3642
84: 2 My soul l, yea, even fainteth for the courts 3700

LONGING (3) [LONG]

Dt 28:32 and fail *with l* for them all the day long: NIH
Ps 107: 9 For he satisfieth the l soul, and filleth 8264
119:20 My soul breaketh for the l *that it hath* unto 8375

LONGSUFFERING (17) [LENGTH, SUFFER]

Ex 34: 6 l, and abundant in goodness and truth, 639+750
Nu 14:18 The LORD *is* l, and of great mercy, 639+750
Ps 86:15 l, and plenteous in mercy and truth. 639+750
Jer 15:15 take me not away in thy l: 639+750
Ro 2: 4 of his goodness and forbearance and l; *3115*
9:22 endured with much l *the* vessels of wrath *3115*
2Co 6: 6 by knowledge, by l, by kindness, *3115*
Gal 5:22 joy, peace, l, gentleness, goodness, faith, *3115*
Eph 4: 2 With all lowliness and meekness, with l, *3115*
Col 1:11 unto all patience and l with joyfulness; *3115*
3:12 kindness, humbleness of mind, meekness, l; *3115*
1Ti 1:16 me first Jesus Christ might shew forth all l, *3115*
2Ti 3:10 of life, purpose, faith, l, charity, patience, *3115*
4: 2 rebuke, exhort with all l and doctrine. *3115*
1Pe 3:20 when once the l of God waited in the days *3115*
2Pe 3: 9 but is l to us-ward, not willing that any *3114*
3:15 And account *that* the l of our Lord *is* *3115*

LONGWINGED (1) [LENGTH, WING]

Eze 17: 3 l, full *of* feathers, which had divers 83+750

LOOK (155) [LOOKED, LOOKEST, LOOKETH, LOOKING, LOOKING-GLASSES, LOOKS]

Ge 9:16 I will l upon it, that I may remember 7200
12:11 know that thou *art* a fair woman to **l upon**: 4758
13:14 l from the place where thou *art* northward, 7200
15: 5 L now towards heaven, and tell the stars, 5027
19:17 l not behind thee, neither stay thou in all 5027
24:16 the damsel *was* very fair to **l upon**, a virgin, 4758
26: 7 because she *was* fair to **l upon**. 4758
40: 7 Wherefore l ye *so* sadly to day? 6440
41:33 let Pharaoh **l out** a man discreet and wise, 7200
42: 1 his sons, Why do ye l one upon another? 7200
Ex 3: 6 his face; for he was afraid to l upon God. 5027
5:21 The LORD l upon you, and judge; 7200
10:10 little ones: l *to it*; for evil *is* before you. 7200
25:20 and their faces *shall l* one to another; NIH
25:40 l that thou make *them* after their pattern, 7200
39:43 Moses did l upon all the work, and, behold, 7200
Lev 13: 3 the priest shall l on the plague in the skin of 7200
13: 3 the priest shall l on him, and 7200
13: 5 the priest shall l on him the seventh day: 7200
13: 6 the priest shall l on him again the seventh 7200
13:21 if the priest l on it, and behold, *there be* no 7200
13:25 the priest shall l upon it: and behold, *if* 7200
13:26 if the priest l on it, and behold, *there be* no 7200
13:27 the priest shall l upon him the seventh day: 7200
13:31 And if the priest l on the plague of the scall, 7200
13:32 in the seventh day the priest shall l on 7200
13:34 in the seventh day the priest shall l on 7200
13:36 the priest shall l on him: and behold, *if* 7200
13:39 the priest shall l: and behold, *if* the bright 7200
13:43 the priest shall l upon it: and behold, *if* 7200
13:50 the priest shall l upon the plague, and 7200
13:51 he shall l on the plague on the seventh day: 7200
13:53 if the priest shall l, and behold, the plague 7200
13:55 the priest shall l on the plague, after *that* it 7200
13:56 if the priest l, and behold, the plague *be* 7200
14: 3 the priest shall l, and behold, *if* the plague 7200
14:37 he shall l on the plague, and behold, *if* 7200
14:39 come again the seventh day, and shall l: 7200
14:44 the priest shall come and l, and behold, 7200
14:48 shall come in, and l *upon it*, and behold, 7200
Nu 15:39 that ye may l upon it, and remember all 7200
Dt 9:27 l not unto the stubbornness of this people, 6437
26:15 **L down** from thy holy habitation, 8259
28:32 thine eyes shall l, and fail *with longing* for 7200
Jdg 7:17 said unto them, L on me, and do likewise: 7200
1Sa 1:11 if thou wilt **indeed l** on the affliction 7200+7200
16: 7 L not on his countenance, or on the height 5027
16:12 a beautiful countenance, and goodly to **l to**. 7210
17:18 l how thy brethren fare, and take their 6485
2Sa 9: 8 that thou shouldest l upon such a dead dog 6437
11: 2 the woman *was* very beautiful to **l upon**. 4758
16:12 It may be that the LORD will l on mine 7200
1Ki 18:43 to his servant, Go up now, l toward the sea. 5027
2Ki 3:14 I would not l toward thee, nor see thee. 5027
6:32 l, when the messenger cometh, shut 7200
9: 2 **l out** there Jehu the son of Jehoshaphat 7200
10: 3 L even out the best and meetest of your 7200
10:23 l that there be here with you none of 7200
14: 8 Come, let us l one another in the face. 7200
1Ch 12:17 the God of our fathers l *thereon*, and 7200
2Ch 24:22 The LORD l upon *it*, and require *it*. 7200
Est 1:11 princes her beauty: for she *was* fair to **l on**. 4758
Job 3: 9 let it l for light, but *have* none; neither let it 6960
6:28 Now therefore be content, l upon me; for *it* 6437
20:21 therefore shall no *man* **l for** his goods. 2342
35: 5 L unto the heavens, and see; and behold 5027
40:12 L on every one *that is* proud, *and* bring him 7200
Ps 5: 3 I direct *my prayer* unto thee, and will **l up**. 6822

Ps 22:17 tell all my bones: they l *and* stare upon me. 5027
25:18 L upon mine affliction and my pain; and 7200
35:17 Lord, how long wilt thou l on? rescue my 7200
40:12 that I am not able to l *up;* they are more than 7200
80:14 l down from heaven, and behold, and 5027
84: 9 and l upon the face of thine anointed. 5027
85:11 righteousness shall l down from heaven. 8259
101: 5 him that hath a high l and a proud heart will 5869
119:132 L thou upon me, and be merciful unto me, 6437
123: 2 as the eyes of servants *l* unto the hand of NIH
Pr 4:25 Let thine eyes l right on, and let thine 5027
4:25 and let thine eyelids l straight before thee. 3474
6:17 A proud l, a lying tongue, and hands that 5869
21: 4 A high l, and a proud heart, *and* 5869
23:31 L not thou upon the wine when it is red, 7200
27:23 state of thy flocks, *and* l well to thy herds. 7896
Ecc 12: 3 those that l out of the windows be 7200
SS 1: 6 L not upon me, because I *am* black, 7200
4: 8 l from the top of Amana, from the top of 7789
6:13 return, return, that we may l upon thee. 2372
Isa 5:30 if *one* l unto the land, behold darkness *and* 5027
8:17 the house of Jacob, and I will l for him. 6960
8:21 their king and their God, and l upward. 6437
8:22 they shall l unto the earth; and 5027
14:16 They that see thee shall narrowly l upon 7688
17: 7 At that day shall a man l to his Maker, and 8159
17: 8 he shall not l to the altars, the work of his 8159
22: 4 Therefore said I, L away from me; I will 8159
22: 8 thou didst l in that day to the armour of 5027
31: 1 they l not unto the Holy One of Israel, 8159
33:20 L upon Zion, the city of our solemnities: 2372
42:18 ye deaf; and l, ye blind, that *ye* may see. 5027
45:22 L unto me, and be ye saved, all the ends of 6437
51: 1 l unto the rock *whence* ye are hewn, and 5027
51: 2 L unto Abraham your father, and 5027
51: 6 the heavens, and l upon the earth beneath: 5027
56:11 they all l to their own way, every one for 6437
59:11 we l for judgment, but *there is* none; 6960
63:15 L down from heaven, and behold from 5027
66: 2 to this *man* will I l, *even* to *him that is* poor 5027
66:24 l upon the carcases of the men that have 7200
Jer 13:16 and, while ye l for light, he turn it into 6960
39:12 l well to him, and do him no harm; 5869+7760
40: 4 come; and I will l well unto thee: 5869+7760
46: 5 and are fled apace, and l not back: 6437
47: 3 the fathers shall not l back to *their* children 6437
La 3:50 Till the LORD l down, and behold from 8259
Eze 23:15 upon their heads, all of them princes to l to, 4758
29:16 when they shall l after them: 6437
43:17 and his stairs *shall* l toward the east. 6437
Da 7:20 whose l *was* more stout than his fellows. 2376
Hos 3: 1 who l to other gods, and love flagons of 6437
Jnh 2: 4 yet I will l again toward thy holy temple. 5027
Mic 4:11 her be defiled, and let our eye l upon Zion. 2372
7: 7 Therefore I will l unto the LORD; I will 6822
Na 2: 8 stand, *shall they cry;* but none shall l back. 6437
3: 7 *that* all they that l upon thee shall flee from 7200
Hab 1:13 to behold evil, and canst not l on iniquity: 5027
2:15 that thou mayest l on their nakedness! 5027
Zec 12:10 they shall l upon me whom they have 5027
Mt 11: 3 that should come, or do we l for another? 4328
Mk 8:25 again upon his eyes, and made him l up: 308
Lk 7:19 he that should come? or l we for another? 4328
7:20 he that should come? or l we for another? 4328
9:38 I beseech thee, l upon my son: 1914
21:28 to pass, *then* l up, and lift up your heads; 352
Jn 4:35 Lift up your eyes, and l on the fields; 2300
7:52 Search, and l: for out of Galilee ariseth no 2396
19:37 They shall l on *him* whom they pierced. 3700
Ac 3: 4 his eyes upon him with John, said, L on us. 991
3:12 or why l ye *so* earnestly on us, as though by 816
6: 3 l ye out among you seven men of honest 1980
18:15 l ye *to it;* for I will be no judge of such 3700
1Co 16:11 unto me: for I l for him with the brethren. 1551
2Co 3:13 stedfastly l to the end of that which is 816
4:18 While we l not at the *things* which are 4648
10: 7 Do ye l on *things* after the outward 991
Php 2: 4 L not every man on his own *things,* but 4648
3:20 from whence also we l for the Saviour, 553
Heb 9:28 unto them that l for him shall he appear 553
1Pe 1:12 which *things the* angels desire to l into. 3879
2Pe 3:13 l for new heavens and a new earth, 4328
3:14 seeing that ye l for such *things,* be diligent 4328
2Jn 1: 8 L to yourselves, that we lose not *those things* 991
Rev 4: 3 And he that sat was to l upon like a jasper 3706
5: 3 able to open the book, neither to l thereon. 991
5: 4 and to read the book, neither to l thereon. 991

LOOKED (143) [LOOK]

Ge 6:12 God l upon the earth, and behold, it was 7200
8:13 l, and behold, the face of the ground was 7200
16:13 Have I also here l after him that seeth me? 7200
18: 2 he lift up his eyes and l, and lo, three men 7200
18:16 rose up from thence, and l toward Sodom: 8259
19:26 his wife l back from behind him, and 5027
19:28 And he l toward Sodom and Gomorrah, and 8259
22:13 l, and behold behind *him* a ram caught in a 7200
26: 8 that Abimelech king of the Philistims l out 8259
29: 2 And he l, and behold a well in the field, and 7200
29:32 Surely the LORD hath l upon my 7200
33: 1 l, and behold, Esau came, and with him 7200
37:25 and they lift up their eyes and l, and behold, 7200
39:23 The keeper of the prison l not to any thing 7200
40: 6 l upon them, and, behold, they *were* sad. 7200
Ex 2:11 unto his brethren, and l on their burdens: 7200
2:12 he l this way and that way, and when he 6437
2:25 God l upon the children of Israel, and 7200
3: 2 he l, and, behold, the bush burned with fire, 7200
4:31 that he had l upon their affliction, then 7200
14:24 that in the morning watch the LORD l 8259
16:10 that they l toward the wilderness, and 6437
33: 8 man *at* his tent door, and l after Moses, 5027
Nu 12:10 Aaron l upon Miriam, and behold, *she was* 6437
16:42 that they l toward the tabernacle of 6437
17: 9 and they l, and took every man his rod. 7200
24:20 when he l on Amalek, he took up his 7200
24:21 he l on the Kenites, and took up his parable, 7200
Dt 9:16 I l, and behold, ye had sinned against 7200
26: 7 l on our affliction, and our labour, and 7200
Jos 5:13 that he lift up his eyes and l, and behold, 7200
8:20 when the men of Ai l behind them, they 6437
Jdg 5:28 The mother of Sisera l out at a window, 8259
6:14 the LORD l upon him, and said, Go in this 6437
9:43 and laid wait in the field, and l, and behold, 7200
13:19 and Manoah and his wife l on. 7200
13:20 Manoah and his wife l on *it,* and fell on 7200
20:40 the Benjamites l behind them, and behold, 6437
1Sa 6:19 they had l into the ark of the LORD, 7200
9:16 for I have l upon my people, because 7200
14:16 watchmen of Saul in Gibeah of Benjamin l; 7200
16: 6 were come, that he l on Eliab, and said, 7200
17:42 when the Philistine l about, and saw David, 5027
24: 8 when Saul l behind him, David stooped 5027
2Sa 1: 7 when he l behind him, he saw me, and 6437
2:20 Abner l behind him, and said, *Art* thou 6437
6:16 Michal Saul's daughter l through a 8259
13:34 watch lift up his eyes, and l, and behold, 7200
18:24 and l, and behold a man running alone. 7200
22:42 They l, but *there was* none to save; 8159
24:20 Araunah l, and saw the king and his 8259
1Ki 18:43 he went up, and l, and said, *There is* 5027
19: 6 he l, and behold, *there was* a cake baken on 5027
2Ki 2:24 l on them, and cursed them in the name of 7200
6:30 upon the wall, and the people l, and behold, 7200
9:30 and tired her head, and l out at a window. 8259
9:32 there l out to him two *or* three eunuchs. 8259
11:14 when she l, behold, the king stood by a 7200
14:11 Amaziah king of Judah l one another *in* 7200
1Ch 21:21 Ornan l and saw David, and went out of 5027
2Ch 13:14 when Judah l back, behold, the battle *was* 6437
20:24 they l unto the multitude, and, behold, 6437
23:13 she l, and behold, the king stood at his 7200
26:20 and all the priests, l upon him, and behold, 6437
Ne 4:14 I l, and rose up, and said unto the nobles, 7200
Est 2:15 in the sight of all them that l upon her. 7200
Job 6:19 The troops of Tema l, the companies of 5027
30:26 When I l *for* good, then evil came *unto me:* 6960
Ps 14: 2 The LORD l down from heaven upon 8259
34: 5 They l unto him, and were lightened: and 5027
53: 2 God l down from heaven upon the children 8259
69:20 I l *for some* to take pity, but *there was* 6960
102:19 For he hath l down from the height of his 8259
109:25 *when* they l upon me they shaked their 7200
142: 4 I l on *my* right hand, and beheld, but 5027
Pr 7: 6 For at the window of my house I l through 8259
24:32 *it* well: I l upon *it, and* received instruction. 7200
Ecc 2:11 I l on all the works that my hands had 6437
SS 1: 6 I *am* black, because the sun hath l upon me: 7805
Isa 5: 2 he l that *it* should bring forth grapes, and 6960
5: 4 when I l that *it* should bring forth grapes, 6960
5: 7 he l for judgment, but behold oppression; 6960
22:11 ye have not l unto the Maker thereof, 5027
63: 5 I l, and *there was* none to help; and 5027
64: 3 When thou didst terrible things *which* we l 6960
Jer 8:15 *We* l for peace, but no good *came; and* for a 6960
14:19 *we* l for peace, and *there is* no good; and 6960
La 2:16 certainly this *is* the day that we l for; we 6960
Eze 1: 4 I l, and, behold, a whirlwind came out of 7200
2: 9 when I l, behold, a hand *was* sent unto me; 7200
8: 7 and when I l, behold a hole in the wall. 7200
10: 1 I l, and, behold, in the firmament that *was* 7200
10: 9 when I l, behold the four wheels by 7200
10:11 *to* the place whither the head l they 6437
16: 8 I passed by thee, and l upon thee, behold, 7200
21:21 he consulted with images, he l in the liver. 7200
40:20 the gate of the outward court that l toward 6440
44: 4 I l, and behold, the glory of the LORD 7200
46:19 of the priests, which l toward the north: 6437
Da 1:13 let our countenances be l upon before thee, 7200
10: 5 I lift up mine eyes, and l, and behold, 7200
12: 5 I Daniel l, and behold, there stood other 7200
Ob 1:12 thou shouldest not have l on the day of thy 7200
1:13 thou shouldest not have l on their affliction 7200
Hag 1: 9 *Ye* l for much, and lo, *it came* to little; and 6437
Zec 2: 1 I lift up mine eyes again, and l, and behold, 7200
4: 2 I said, I have l, and behold, a candlestick all 7200
5: 1 mine eyes, and l, and behold, a flying roll. 7200
5: 9 lift I up mine eyes, and l, and behold, 7200
6: 1 and lift up mine eyes, and l, and behold, 7200
Mk 3: 5 And when he had l round about on them 4017
3:34 And he l round about on them which sat 4017
5:32 And he l round about to see her that had 4017
6:41 he l up to heaven, and blessed, and brake 308
8:24 And he l up, and said, I see men as trees, 308
8:33 he had turned about and l on his disciples, 1492
9: 8 when they had l round about, 4017
10:23 And Jesus l round about, and saith unto 4017
11:11 when he had l round about upon all *things,* 4017
14:67 warming himself, she l upon him, and said, 1689
16: 4 And when they l, they saw that the stone was 308
Lk 1:25 l on *me,* to take away my reproach among 1896
2:38 spake of him to all them that l for 4327
10:32 came and l *on him,* and passed by on 1492
19: 5 he l up, and saw him, and said unto him, 308
21: 1 And he l up, and saw the rich *men* casting 308
22:56 and earnestly l upon him, and said, 816
22:61 And the Lord turned, and l upon Peter. 1689
Jn 13:22 Then the disciples l one on another, 991
20:11 she stooped down, and l into 3879
Ac 1:10 And while they l stedfastly toward heaven 816
7:55 l up stedfastly into heaven, and saw 816
10: 4 And when he l on him, he was afraid, and 816
22:13 And the same hour I l up upon him. 308
28: 6 Howbeit they l when he should have 4328
28: 6 but after they had l a great while, and 4328
Heb 11:10 For he l for a city which hath foundations, 1551
1Jn 1: 1 which we have l upon, and our hands have 2300
Rev 4: 1 After this I l, and, behold, a door *was* 1492
6: 8 And I l, and behold a pale horse: and 1492
14: 1 And I l, and, lo, a Lamb stood on the mount 1492
14:14 And I l, and behold a white cloud, and 1492
15: 5 And after that I l, and, behold, the temple of 1492

LOOKEST (2) [LOOK]

Job 13:27 and l narrowly unto all my paths; 8104
Hab 1:13 wherefore l thou upon them that deal 5027

LOOKETH (33) [LOOK]

Lev 13:12 to his foot, wheresoever the priest l; 4758+5869
Nu 21: 8 that is bitten, when he l upon it, shall live. 7200
21:20 the top of Pisgah, which l toward Jeshimon. 8259
23:28 the top of Peor, that l toward Jeshimon. 8259
Jos 15: 2 the salt sea, from the bay that l southward: 6437
1Sa 13:18 l to the valley of Zeboim toward 8259
16: 7 for man l on the outward appearance, but 7200
16: 7 but the LORD l on the heart. 7200
Job 7: 2 as a hireling l for the reward of his work: 6960
28:24 For he l to the ends of the earth, *and* 5027
33:27 He l upon men, and *if any* say, I have 7789
Ps 33:13 The LORD l from heaven; he beholdeth 5027
33:14 From the place of his habitation he l upon 7688
104:32 He l on the earth, and it trembleth: 5027
Pr 14:15 but the prudent *man* l well to his going. 995
31:27 She l well to the ways of her household, 6822
SS 2: 9 behind our wall, he l forth at the windows, 7688
6:10 Who *is* she *that* l forth as the morning, 8259
7: 4 thy nose *is* as the tower of Lebanon which l 6822
Isa 28: 4 which *when* he that l upon it seeth, while it 7200
Eze 8: 3 to the door of the inner gate that l toward 6437
11: 1 of the LORD'S house, which l eastward: 6437
40: 6 came he unto the gate which l toward 6440
40:22 *were* after the measure of the gate that l 6440
43: 1 *even* the gate that l toward the east: 6437
44: 1 outward sanctuary which l *toward* the east; 6437
46: 1 The gate of the inner court that l *toward* 6437
46:12 open him the gate that l *toward* the east, 6437
47: 2 the utter gate *by* the way that l east*ward;* 6437
Mt 5:28 That whosoever l on a woman to lust after 991
24:50 shall come in a day when he l not for *him,* 4328
Lk 12:46 will come in a day when he l not for *him,* 4328
Jas 1:25 But whoso l into the perfect law of liberty, 3879

LOOKING (30) [LOOK]

Jos 15: 7 *so* northward, l toward Gilgal, that *is* before 6437
1Ki 7:25 three l toward the north, and three looking 6437
7:25 three l toward the west, and three looking 6437
7:25 three l toward the south, and three looking 6437
7:25 the south, and three l toward the east: 6437
1Ch 15:29 that Michal the daughter of Saul l out at a 8259
2Ch 4: 4 three l toward the north, and three looking 6437
4: 4 three l toward the west, and three looking 6437
4: 4 three l toward the south, and three looking 6437
4: 4 the south, and three l toward the east: 6437
Job 37:18 *which is* strong, *and* as a molten l glass? 7209
Isa 38:14 mine eyes fail *with l* upward: O LORD, NIH
Mt 14:19 and l up to heaven, he blessed, and brake, 308
Mk 7:34 And l up to heaven, he sighed, and 308
10:27 And Jesus l upon them saith, With men *it* 1689
15:40 There were also women l on afar off: 2334
Lk 6:10 And l round about upon them all, he said 4017
9:16 and the two fishes, and l up to heaven, 308
9:62 and l back, is fit for the kingdom of God. 991
21:26 *for* l after those *things* which are coming 4329
Jn 1:36 And l upon Jesus as he walked, he saith, 1689
20: 5 And he stooping down, and l in, saw 3879
Ac 6:15 that sat in the council, l stedfastly on him, 816
23:21 are they ready, l for a promise from thee. 4327
Tit 2:13 L for *that* blessed hope, and the glorious 4327
Heb 10:27 But a certain fearful l for of judgment and 1561
12: 2 L unto Jesus the author and finisher of *our* 872
12:15 L diligently lest any *man* fail of the grace 1983
2Pe 3:12 L for and hasting *unto* the coming of 4328
Jude 1:21 l for the mercy of our Lord Jesus Christ 4327

LOOKING-GLASSES (1) [GLASS, LOOK]

Ex 38: 8 *of* brass, of the l of *the women* assembling, 4759

LOOKS (5) [LOOK]

Ps 18:27 afflicted people; but wilt bring down high l. 5869
Isa 2:11 The lofty l of man shall be humbled, and 5869
10:12 king of Assyria, and the glory of his high l. 5869
Eze 2: 6 of their words, nor be dismayed at their l, 6440
3: 9 them not, neither be dismayed at their l, 6440

LOOPS (13)

Ex 26: 4 thou shalt make l of blue upon the edge of 3924
26: 5 Fifty l shalt thou make in the one curtain, 3924
26: 5 fifty l shalt thou make in the edge of 3924
26: 5 that the l may take hold one of another. 3924
26:10 thou shalt make fifty l on the edge of 3924
26:10 fifty l in the edge of the curtain which 3924
26:11 put the taches into the l, and couple the tent 3924
36:11 he made l of blue on the edge of one 3924
36:12 Fifty l made he in one curtain, and 3924
36:12 fifty l made he in the edge of the curtain 3924
36:12 the l held one *curtain* to another. 3924
36:17 he made fifty l upon the uttermost edge of 3924
36:17 fifty l made he upon the edge of the curtain 3924

LOOSE (29) [LOOSED, LOOSETH, LOOSING, UNLOOSE]

Ge 49:21 Naphtali *is* a hind let l: he giveth goodly 7971
Lev 14: 7 shall let the living bird l into the open field. 7971
Dt 25: 9 l his shoe from off his foot, and spit in his 2502
Jos 5:15 unto Joshua, L thy shoe from off thy foot; 5394
Job 6: 9 *that* he would let l his hand, and cut me off! 5425
30:11 they have also let l the bridle before me. 7971
38:31 or l the bands of Orion? 6605
Ps 102:20 to l those that are appointed to death; 6605
Isa 20: 2 Go and l the sackcloth from off thy loins, 6605
45: 1 I will l the loins of kings, to open before 6605
52: 2 l thyself from the bands of thy neck, 6605
58: 6 to l the bands of wickedness, to undo 6605
Jer 40: 4 I l thee *this* day from the chains which *were* 6605

Da 3:25 He answered and said, Lo, I see four men l, 8271
Mt 16:19 whatsoever thou shalt l on earth shall be 3089
18:18 whatsoever ye shall l on earth shall be 3089
21: 2 with her: l them, and bring them unto me. 3089
Mk 11: 2 never man sat; l him, and bring him. 3089
11: 4 place where two ways met; and they l him. 3089
Lk 13:15 doth not each one of you on the sabbath l 3089
19:30 never man sat: l him, and bring him hither. 3089
19:31 Why do ye l him? thus shall ye say unto 3089
19:33 thereof said unto them, Why l ye the colt? 3089
Jn 11:44 saith unto them, L him, and let him go. 3089
Ac 13:25 shoes of his feet I am not worthy to l. 3089
24:26 given him of Paul, that he might l him: 3089
Rev 5: 2 to open the book, and to l the seals thereof? 3089
5: 5 the book, and to l the seven seals thereof. 3089
9:14 L the four angels which are bound in 3089

LOOSED (32) [LOOSE]

Ex 28:28 that the breastplate be not l from the ephod. 2118
39:21 that the breastplate might not be l from 2118
Dt 25:10 The house of him that hath his shoe l. 2502
Jdg 15:14 and his bands l from off his hands. 4549
Job 30:11 Because he hath l my cord, and 6605
39: 5 or who hath l the bands of the wild ass? 6605
Ps 105:20 The king sent and l him; even the ruler of 5425
116:16 son of thy handmaid: thou hast l my bonds. 6605
Ecc 12: 6 Or ever the silver cord be l, or the golden 7576
Isa 5:27 neither shall the girdle of their loins be l, 6605
33:23 Thy tacklings are l; they could not well 5203
51:14 captive exile hasteneth that he may be l, 6605
Da 5: 6 so that the joints of his loins were l, and 8271
Mt 16:19 shalt loose on earth shall be l in heaven. 3089
18:18 ye shall loose on earth shall be l in heaven. 3089
18:27 and l him, and forgave him the debt. 630
Mk 7:35 and the string of his tongue was l, and 3089
Lk 1:64 and his tongue l, and he spake, and NIG
13:12 Woman, thou art l from thy infirmity. 630
13:16 be l from this bond on the sabbath day? 3089
Ac 2:24 hath raised up, having l the pains of death: 3089
13:13 when Paul and his company l from Paphos, 321
16:26 were opened, and every one's bands were l. 447
22:30 he l him from his bands, and 3089
27:21 and not have l from Crete, and to have 321
27:40 and l the rudder bands, and hoised up 447
Ro 7: 2 she is l from the law of the husband. 2673
1Co 7:27 seek not to be l. Art thou loosed from a 3080
7:27 Art thou l from a wife? seek not a wife. 3089
Rev 9:15 And the four angels were l, which were 3089
20: 3 and after that he must be l a little season. 3089
20: 7 Satan shall be l out of his prison, 3089

LOOSETH (2) [LOOSE]

Job 12:18 He l the bond of kings, and girdeth their 6605
Ps 146: 7 to the hungry. The LORD l the prisoners: 5425

LOOSING (4) [LOOSE]

Mk 11: 5 said unto them, What do ye, l the colt? 3089
Lk 19:33 And as they were l the colt, the owners 3089
Ac 16:11 Therefore l from Troas, we came with a 321
27:13 l thence, they sailed close by Crete. 142

LOP (1)

Isa 10:33 of hosts, shall l the bough with terror: 5586

LORD (1367) [LORD'S, LORDLY, LORDS, LORDSHIP; see also LORD*]

Ge 15: 2 Abram said, L GOD, what wilt thou give 136
15: 8 he said, L GOD, whereby shall I know that 136
18: 3 said, My L, if now I have found favour in 136
18:12 shall I have pleasure, my l being old also? 113
18:27 I have taken upon me to speak unto the L, 136
18:30 he said unto him, Oh let not the L be angry, 136
18:31 I have taken upon me to speak unto the L: 136
18:32 Oh let not the L be angry, and I will speak 136
19:18 And Lot said unto them, Oh, not so, my L: 136
20: 4 he said, L, wilt thou slay also a righteous 136
23: 6 Hear us, my l: thou art a mighty prince 113
23:11 Nay, my l, hear me: the field give I thee, and 113
23:15 My l, hearken unto me: the land is worth 113
24:18 she said, Drink, my l: and she hasted, and 113
27:29 be l over thy brethren, and let thy mother's 1376
27:37 I have made him thy l, and all his brethren 1376
31:35 Let it not displease my l that I cannot rise up 113
32: 4 saying, Thus shall ye speak unto my l Esau; 113
32: 5 I have sent to tell my l, that I may find grace 113
32:18 it is a present sent unto my l Esau: 113
33: 8 These are to find grace in the sight of my l. 113
33:13 My l knoweth that the children are tender, 113
33:14 Let my l, I pray thee, pass over before his 113
33:14 to endure, until I come unto my l unto Seir. 113
33:15 let me find grace in the sight of my l. 113
39:16 up his garment by her, until his l came home. 113
40: 1 his baker had offended their l the king of 113
42:10 my l, but to buy food are thy servants come. 113
42:30 The man, who is the l of the land, 113
42:33 the man, the l of the country, said unto us, 113
44: 5 Is not this it in which my l drinketh, and 113
44: 7 unto him, Wherefore saith my l these words? 113
44:16 Judah said, What shall we say unto my l? 113
44:18 and said, O my l, let thy servant, I pray thee, 113
44:19 My l asked his servants, saying, Have ye a 113
44:20 we said unto my l, We have a father, an old 113
44:22 we said unto my l, The lad cannot leave his 113
44:24 my father, we told him the words of my l. 113
44:33 abide instead of the lad a bondman to my l; 113
45: 8 l of all his house, and a ruler throughout all 113
45: 9 God hath made me l of all Egypt: 113
47:18 said unto him, We will not hide it from my l, 113
47:18 is spent; my l also had our herds of cattle; 113
47:18 there is not ought left in the sight of my l, 113
47:25 let us find grace in the sight of my l, and 113
Ex 4:10 O my L, I am not eloquent, neither 136
4:13 he said, O my L, send, I pray thee, by 136
5:22 said, L, wherefore hast thou so evil entreated 136
15:17 in the Sanctuary, O L, which thy hands have 136
23:17 thy males shall appear before the L GOD. 113
32:22 Let not the anger of my l wax hot: 113
34: 9 O L, let my Lord, I pray thee, go amongst 136
34: 9 O Lord, let my L, I pray thee, go amongst 136
34:23 men children appear before the L GOD, 113
Nu 11:28 answered and said, My l Moses, forbid them. 113
12:11 Alas, my l, I beseech thee, lay not the sin 113
14:17 beseech thee, let the power of my L be great, 136
32:25 Thy servants will do as my l commandeth. 113
32:27 before the LORD to battle, as my l saith. 113
36: 2 The LORD commanded my l to give 113
36: 2 my l was commanded by the LORD to give 113
Dt 3:24 O L GOD, thou hast begun to shew thy 136
9:26 unto the LORD, and said, O L GOD, 136
10:17 L of lords, a great God, a mighty, and 113
Jos 3:11 even the L of all the earth passeth over 113
3:13 the L of all the earth, shall rest in the waters 113
5:14 unto him, What saith my l unto his servant? 113
7: 7 Joshua said, Alas, O L GOD, 136
7: 8 O L, what shall I say, when Israel turneth 136
Jdg 3:25 their l was fallen down dead on the earth. 113
4:18 said unto him, Turn in, my l, turn in to me; 113
6:13 O my l, if the LORD be with us, why then 113
6:15 he said unto him, O my L, wherewith shall I 136
6:22 the LORD, Gideon said, Alas, O L GOD! 136
13: 8 intreated the LORD, and said, O my L, 136
16:28 said, O L GOD, remember me, I pray thee, 136
19:26 house where her l was, till it was light. 113
19:27 her l rose up in the morning, and opened 113
Ru 2:13 Let me find favour in thy sight, my l; 113
1Sa 1:15 Hannah answered and said, No, my l, I am a 113
1:26 she said, O my l, as thy soul liveth, my lord, 113
1:26 she said, O my lord, as thy soul liveth, my l, 113
16:16 Let our l now command thy servants which 113
22:12 And he answered, Here I am, my l. 113
24: 8 and cried after Saul, saying, My l the king. 113
24:10 I will not put forth mine hand against my l; 113
25:24 And fell at his feet, and said, Upon me, my l, 113
25:25 Let not my l, I pray thee, regard this man of 113
25:25 handmaid saw not the young men of my l, 113
25:26 Now therefore, my l, as the LORD liveth, 113
25:26 and they that seek evil to my l, be as Nabal. 113
25:27 thine handmaid hath brought unto my l, 113
25:27 given unto the young men that follow my l. 113
25:28 for the LORD will certainly make my l a 113
25:28 my l fighteth the battles of the LORD, 113
25:29 the soul of my l shall be bound in the bundle 113
25:30 when the LORD shall have done to my l 113
25:31 unto thee, nor offence of heart unto my l, 113
25:31 or that my l hath avenged himself: 113
25:31 the LORD shall have dealt well with my l, 113
25:41 to wash the feet of the servants of my l. 113
26:15 then hast thou not kept thy l the king? 113
26:15 one of the people in to destroy the king thy l. 113
26:17 And David said, It is my voice, my l, O king. 113
26:18 Wherefore doth my l thus pursue after his 113
26:19 let my l the king hear the words of his 113
29: 8 fight against the enemies of my l the king? 113
2Sa 1:10 and have brought them hither unto my l. 113
2: 5 ye have shewed this kindness unto your l, 113
3:21 and will gather all Israel unto my l the king, 113
4: 8 the LORD hath avenged my l the king this 113
7:18 and he said, Who am I, O L GOD? 136
7:19 yet a small thing in thy sight, O L GOD; 136
7:19 And is this the manner of man, O L GOD? 136
7:20 for thou, L GOD, knowest thy servant. 136
7:28 And now, O L GOD, thou art that God, and 136
7:29 for thou, O L GOD, hast spoken it: and 136
9:11 According to all that my l the king hath 113
10: 3 children of Ammon said unto Hanun their l, 113
11: 9 king's house with all the servants of his l, 113
11:11 my l Joab, and the servants of my lord, 113
11:11 my lord Joab, and the servants of my l, 113
11:13 to lie on his bed with the servants of his l, 113
13:32 Let not my l suppose that they have slain all 113
13:33 let not my l the king take the thing to his 113
14: 9 My l, O king, the iniquity be on me, and 113
14:12 speak one word unto my l the king. 113
14:15 to speak of this thing unto my l the king, 113
14:17 The word of my l the king shall now be 113
14:17 so is my l the king to discern good and bad: 113
14:18 woman said, Let my l the king now speak. 113
14:19 and said, As thy soul liveth, my l the king, 113
14:19 to the left from ought that my l the king hath 113
14:20 my l is wise, according to the wisdom of an 113
14:22 my l, O king, in that the king hath fulfilled 113
15:15 thy servants are ready to do whatsoever my l 113
15:21 LORD liveth, and as my l the king liveth, 113
15:21 surely in what place my l the king shall be, 113
16: 4 I may find grace in thy sight, my l, O king. 113
16: 9 Why should this dead dog curse my l 113
18:28 that lift up their hand against my l the king. 113
18:31 and Cushi said, Tidings, my l the king: 113
18:32 The enemies of my l the king, and all that 113
19:19 Let not my l impute iniquity unto me, 113
19:19 day that my l the king went out of Jerusalem, 113
19:20 of Joseph to go down to meet my l the king. 113
19:26 he answered, My l, O king, my servant 113
19:27 he hath slandered thy servant unto my l 113
19:27 but my l the king is as an angel of God: 113
19:28 but dead men before my l the king: 113
19:30 forasmuch as my l the king is come again in 113
19:35 should thy servant be yet a burden unto my l 113
19:37 let him go over with my l the king; and do to 113
24: 3 that the eyes of my l the king may see it: but 113
24: 3 why doth my l the king delight in this thing? 113
24:21 Wherefore is my l the king come to his 113
24:22 Let my l the king take and offer up what 113
1Ki 1: 2 Let there be sought for my l the king a 113
1: 2 thy bosom, that my l the king may get heat. 113
1:11 doth reign, and David our l knoweth it not? 113
1:13 say unto him, Didst not thou, my l O king, 113
1:17 she said unto him, My l, thou swarest by 113
1:18 and now, my l the king, thou knowest it not: 113
1:20 thou, my l O king, the eyes of all Israel are 113
1:20 sit on the throne of my l the king after him. 113
1:21 when my l the king shall sleep with his 113
1:24 Nathan said, My l O king, hast thou said, 113
1:27 Is this thing done by my l the king, and 113
1:27 who should sit on the throne of my l the king 113
1:31 and said, Let my l king David live for ever. 113
1:33 Take with you the servants of your l, and 113
1:36 the LORD God of my l the king say so too. 113
1:37 As the LORD hath been with my l the king, 113
1:37 greater than the throne of my l king David. 113
1:43 Verily our l king David hath made Solomon 113
1:47 servants came to bless our l king David, 113
2:26 thou barest the ark of the L GOD before 136
2:38 as my l the king hath said, so will thy servant 113
3:10 the speech pleased the L, that Solomon had 136
3:17 O my l, I and this woman dwell in one 113
3:26 she said, O my l, give her the living child, 113
8:53 our fathers out of Egypt, O L GOD. 136
11:23 which fled from his l Hadadezer king of 113
12:27 heart of this people turn again unto their l, 113
18: 7 his face, and said, Art thou that my l Elijah? 113
18: 8 I am: go, tell thy l, Behold, Elijah is here. 113
18:10 whither my l hath not sent to seek thee: 113
18:11 Go, tell thy l, Behold, Elijah is here. 113
18:13 Was it not told my l what I did when Jezebel 113
18:14 Go, tell thy l, Behold, Elijah is here: and 113
20: 4 the king of Israel answered and said, My l, 113
20: 9 of Ben-hadad, Tell my l the king, 113
22: 6 for the L shall deliver it into the hand of 136
2Ki 2:19 of this city is pleasant, as my l seeth: 113
4:16 she said, Nay, my l, thou man of God, do not 113
4:28 she said, Did I desire a son of my l? did I not 113
5: 3 Would God my l were with the prophet that 113
5: 4 told his l, saying, Thus and thus said 113
6:12 one of his servants said, None, my l, O king: 113
6:26 unto him, saying, Help, my l, O king. 113
7: 2 a l on whose hand the king leaned 7991
7: 6 For the L had made the host of the Syrians 136
7:17 the king appointed the l on whose hand he 7991
7:19 that l answered the man of God, and said, 7991
8: 5 Gehazi said, My l, O king, this is 113
8:12 Hazael said, Why weepeth my l? And he 113
9:11 Then Jehu came forth to the servants of his l: 113
18:23 give pledges to my l the king of Assyria, and 113
19:23 thy messengers thou hast reproached the L, 136
1Ch 21: 3 so many moe as they be: but, my l the king, 113
21: 3 doth my l require this thing? why will he be 113
21:23 let my l the king do that which is good in his 113
2Ch 2:14 with the cunning men of my l David thy 113
2:15 and the wine, which my l hath spoken of, 113
13: 6 is risen up, and hath rebelled against his l. 113
Ezr 10: 3 according to the counsel of my l, and 113
Ne 1:11 O L, I beseech thee, let now thine ear be 136
3: 5 put not their necks to the work of their L. 113
4:14 remember the L, which is great and terrible, 136
8:10 for this day is holy unto our L: neither be ye 113
10:29 all the commandments of the LORD our L, 113
Job 28:28 Behold, the fear of the L, that is wisdom; 136
Ps 8: 1 O LORD our L, how excellent is thy name 113
8: 9 O LORD our L, how excellent is thy name 113
12: 4 our lips are our own: who is l over us? 113
16: 2 hast said unto the LORD, Thou art my L: 136
22:30 it shall be accounted to the L for a 136
35:17 L, how long wilt thou look on? rescue my 136
35:22 keep not silence: O L, be not far from me. 136
35:23 even unto my cause, my God and my L. 136
37:13 The L shall laugh at him: for he seeth that 136
38: 9 L, all my desire is before thee; and 136
38:15 do I hope: thou wilt hear, O L my God. 136
38:22 Make haste to help me, O L my salvation. 136
39: 7 now, L, what wait I for? my hope is in thee. 136
40:17 and needy; yet the L thinketh upon me: 136
44:23 Awake, why sleepest thou, O L? arise, 136
45:11 for he is thy L; and worship thou him. 113
51:15 O L, open thou my lips; and my mouth shall 136
54: 4 the L is with them that uphold my soul. 136
55: 9 Destroy, O L, and divide their tongues: for I 136
57: 9 I will praise thee, O L, among the people: 136
59:11 and bring them down, O L our shield. 136
62:12 Also unto thee, O L, belongeth mercy: 136
66:18 iniquity in my heart, the L will not hear me: 136
68:11 The L gave the word: great was 136
68:17 the L is among them, as in Sinai, in the holy 136
68:19 Blessed be the L, who daily loadeth us with 136
68:20 unto GOD the L belong the issues from 136
68:22 The L said, I will bring again from Bashan, 136
68:26 even the L, from the fountain of Israel. 136
68:32 the earth; O sing praises unto the L; Selah. 136
69: 6 O L GOD of hosts, be ashamed for my 136
71: 5 For thou art my hope, O L GOD: thou art 136
71:16 I will go in the strength of the L GOD: 136
73:20 so, O L, when thou awakest, thou shalt 136
73:28 I have put my trust in the L GOD, that I 136
77: 2 In the day of my trouble I sought the L: 136
77: 7 Will the L cast off for ever? and will he be 136
78:65 the L awaked as one out of sleep, and like a 136
79:12 wherewith they have reproached thee, O L. 136
86: 3 Be merciful unto me, O L: for I cry unto 136
86: 4 for unto thee, O L, do I lift up my soul. 136
86: 5 For thou, L, art good, and ready to forgive; 136
86: 8 the gods there is none like unto thee, O L; 136
86: 9 shall come and worship before thee, O L; 136
86:12 I will praise thee, O L my God, with all my 136
86:15 But thou, O L, art a God full of compassion, 136
89:49 L, where are thy former lovingkindnesses, 136
89:50 Remember, L, the reproach of thy servants; 136
90: 1 L, thou hast been our dwelling place in all 136
97: 5 at the presence of the L of the whole earth. 113
105:21 He made him l of his house, and ruler of all 113
109:21 do thou for me, O GOD the L, for thy 136
110: 1 The LORD said unto my L, Sit thou at my 113
110: 5 The L at thy right hand shall strike through 136
114: 7 Tremble, thou earth, at the presence of the L, 113
130: 2 L, hear my voice: let thine ears be attentive 136

Ps 130: 3 mark iniquities, O **L**, who shall stand? 136
130: 6 My soul *waiteth* for the **L** more than they 136
135: 5 *is* great, and *that* our **L** *is* above all gods. 113
136: 3 O give thanks to the **L** of lords: for his 113
140: 7 O GOD the **L**, the strength of my salvation, 136
141: 8 But mine eyes *are* unto thee, O GOD the **L**: 136
147: 5 Great *is* our **L**, and of great power: 113
Isa 1:24 Therefore saith the **L**, the LORD of hosts, 113
3: 1 For, behold, the **L**, the LORD of hosts, 113
3:15 of the poor? saith the **L** GOD of hosts. 136
3:17 Therefore the **L** will smite with a scab 136
3:18 In that day the **L** will take away the bravery 136
4: 4 When the **L** shall have washed away the filth 136
6: 1 died I saw also the **L** sitting upon a throne, 136
6: 8 Also I heard the voice of the **L**, saying, 136
6:11 Then said I, **L**, how long? And he answered, 136
7: 7 Thus saith the **L** GOD, It shall not stand, 136
7:14 Therefore the **L** himself shall give you a 136
7:20 In the same day shall the **L** shave with a 136
8: 7 the **L** bringeth up upon them the waters of 136
9: 8 The **L** sent a word into Jacob, and it hath 136
9:17 Therefore the **L** shall have no joy in their 136
10:12 *that* when the **L** hath performed his whole 136
10:16 Therefore shall the **L**, the Lord of hosts, 113
10:16 Therefore shall the Lord, the **L** of hosts, 136
10:23 For the **L** GOD of hosts shall make a 136
10:24 Therefore thus saith the **L** GOD of hosts, 136
10:33 Behold, the **L**, the LORD of hosts, shall lop 113
11:11 *that* the **L** shall set his hand again the second 136
19: 4 will I give over into the hand of a cruel **l**; 113
19: 4 over them, saith the **L**, the LORD of hosts. 113
21: 6 For thus hath the **L** said unto me, Go, set a 136
21: 8 My **l**, I stand continually upon 136
21:16 For thus hath the **L** said unto me, Within a 136
22: 5 of perplexity by the **L** GOD of hosts in 136
22:12 in that day did the **L** GOD of hosts call to 136
22:14 you till ye die, saith the **L** GOD of hosts. 136
22:15 Thus saith the **L** GOD of hosts, Go, 136
25: 8 the **L** GOD will wipe away tears from off 136
28:16 Therefore thus saith the **L** GOD, Behold, 136
28:22 for I have heard from the **L** GOD of hosts a 136
29:13 Wherefore the **L** said, Forasmuch as this 136
30:15 For thus saith the **L** GOD, the Holy One of 136
30:20 *though* the **L** give you the bread of adversity, 136
37:24 By thy servants hast thou reproached the **L**, 136
38:16 O **L**, by these *things men* live, and in all 136
40:10 the **L** GOD will come with strong *hand*, 136
48:16 now the **L** GOD, and his Spirit, hath sent 136
49:14 forsaken me, and my **L** hath forgotten me. 136
49:22 Thus saith the **L** GOD, Behold, I will lift 136
50: 4 The **L** GOD hath given me the tongue of 136
50: 5 The **L** GOD hath opened mine ear, and 136
50: 7 For the **L** GOD will help me; therefore 136
50: 9 Behold, the **L** GOD will help me; who *is* he 136
51:22 Thus saith thy **L** the LORD, and thy God 113
52: 4 For thus saith the **L** GOD, My people went 136
56: 8 The **L** GOD which gathereth the outcasts of 136
61: 1 The Spirit of the **L** GOD *is* upon me; 136
61:11 so the **L** GOD will cause righteousness and 136
65:13 Therefore thus saith the **L** GOD, Behold, 136
65:15 for the **L** GOD shall slay thee, and call his 136
Jer 1: 6 said I, Ah, **L** GOD, behold, I cannot speak: 136
2:19 *is* not in thee, saith the **L** GOD of hosts. 136
2:22 *is* marked before me, saith the **L** GOD. 136
4:10 (Then said I, Ah, **L** GOD! surely thou hast 136
7:20 Therefore thus saith the **L** GOD; Behold, 136
14:13 said I, Ah, **L** GOD! behold, the prophets say 136
22:18 they shall not lament for him, *saying*, Ah **l**! 113
32:17 Ah **L** GOD! behold, thou hast made 136
32:25 thou hast said unto me, O **L** GOD, 136
34: 5 and they will lament thee, *saying*, Ah **l**! 113
37:20 hear now, I pray thee, O my **l** the king: 113
38: 9 My **l** the king, these men have done evil in 113
44:26 land of Egypt, saying, The **L** GOD liveth. 136
46:10 For this *is* the day of the **L** GOD of hosts, 136
46:10 for the **L** GOD of hosts hath a sacrifice in 136
49: 5 a fear upon thee, saith the **L** GOD of hosts, 136
50:25 for this *is* the work of the **L** GOD of hosts 136
50:31 *thou* most proud, saith the **L** GOD of hosts: 136
La 1:14 the **L** hath delivered me into *their* hands, 136
1:15 The **L** hath trodden under foot all my mighty 136
1:15 the **L** hath trodden the virgin, the daughter of 136
2: 1 How hath the **L** covered the daughter of 136
2: 2 The **L** hath swallowed up all the habitations 136
2: 5 The **L** was as an enemy: he hath swallowed 136
2: 7 The **L** hath cast off his altar, he hath 136
2:18 Their heart cried unto the **L**, O wall of 136
2:19 heart like water before the face of the **L**: 136
2:20 prophet be slain in the sanctuary of the **L**? 136
3:31 For the **L** will not cast off for ever: 136
3:36 a man in his cause, the **L** approveth not. 136
3:37 to pass, *when* the **L** commandeth *it* not? 136
3:58 O **L**, thou hast pleaded the causes of my 136
Eze 2: 4 shalt say unto them, Thus saith the **L** GOD. 136
3:11 and tell them, Thus saith the **L** GOD; 136
3:27 shalt say unto them, Thus saith the **L** GOD; 136
4:14 said I, Ah **L** GOD, behold, my soul *hath* 136
5: 5 Thus saith the **L** GOD; This *is* Jerusalem: 136
5: 7 Therefore thus saith the **L** GOD; 136
5: 8 Therefore thus saith the **L** GOD; Behold, I, 136
5:11 Wherefore, *as* I live, saith the **L** GOD; 136
6: 3 of Israel, hear the word of the **L** GOD; 136
6: 3 Thus saith the **L** GOD to the mountains, 136
6:11 Thus saith the **L** GOD; Smite with thine 136
7: 2 thus saith the **L** GOD unto the land of 136
7: 5 Thus saith the **L** GOD; An evil, an only 136
8: 1 that the hand of the **L** GOD fell there upon 136
9: 8 my face, and cried, and said, Ah **L** GOD, 136
11: 7 Therefore thus saith the **L** GOD; Your slain 136
11: 8 bring a sword upon you, saith the **L** GOD. 136
11:13 *with* a loud voice, and said, Ah **L** GOD, 136
11:16 Therefore say, Thus saith the **L** GOD; 136
11:17 Therefore say, Thus saith the **L** GOD; 136
11:21 upon their own heads, saith the **L** GOD. 136
12:10 Say thou unto them, Thus saith the **L** GOD; 136

Eze 12:19 Thus saith the **L** GOD, of the inhabitants of 136
12:23 Tell them therefore, Thus saith the **L** GOD; 136
12:25 and will perform it, saith the **L** GOD. 136
12:28 say unto them, Thus saith the **L** GOD; 136
12:28 spoken shall be done, saith the **L** GOD. 136
13: 3 Thus saith the **L** GOD; Woe unto 136
13: 8 Therefore thus saith the **L** GOD; 136
13: 8 behold, I *am* against you, saith the **L** GOD. 136
13: 9 and ye shall know that I *am* the **L** GOD. 136
13:13 Therefore thus saith the **L** GOD; I will 136
13:16 and *there is* no peace, saith the **L** GOD. 136
13:18 say, Thus saith the **L** GOD; Woe to 136
13:20 Wherefore thus saith the **L** GOD; Behold, 136
14: 4 and say unto them, Thus saith the **L** GOD; 136
14: 6 the house of Israel, Thus saith the **L** GOD; 136
14:11 and I may be their God, saith the **L** GOD. 136
14:14 by their righteousness, saith the **L** GOD. 136
14:16 men *were* in it, *as* I live, saith the **L** GOD, 136
14:18 men *were* in it, *as* I live, saith the **L** GOD, 136
14:20 Job, *were* in it, *as* I live, saith the **L** GOD, 136
14:21 For thus saith the **L** GOD; How much more 136
14:23 all that I have done in it, saith the **L** GOD. 136
15: 6 Therefore thus saith the **L** GOD; As 136
15: 8 committed a trespass, saith the **L** GOD. 136
16: 3 Thus saith the **L** GOD unto Jerusalem; 136
16: 8 saith the **L** GOD, and thou becamest mine. 136
16:14 I had put upon thee, saith the **L** GOD. 136
16:19 and *thus* it was, saith the **L** GOD. 136
16:23 (woe, woe unto thee! saith the **L** GOD;) 136
16:30 How weak is thine heart, saith the **L** GOD, 136
16:36 Thus saith the **L** GOD; Because thy 136
16:43 thy way upon *thine* head, saith the **L** GOD: 136
16:48 *As* I live, saith the **L** GOD, Sodom thy 136
16:59 For thus saith the **L** GOD; I will even deal 136
16:63 all that thou hast done, saith the **L** GOD. 136
17: 3 say, Thus saith the **L** GOD; A great eagle 136
17: 9 Say thou, Thus saith the **L** GOD; Shall it 136
17:16 *As* I live, saith the **L** GOD, surely in 136
17:19 Therefore thus saith the **L** GOD; *As* I live, 136
17:22 Thus saith the **L** GOD; I will also take of 136
18: 3 *As* I live, saith the **L** GOD, ye shall not 136
18: 9 he shall surely live, saith the **L** GOD. 136
18:23 saith the **L** GOD: *and* not that he should 136
18:25 Yet ye say, The way of the **L** is not equal. 136
18:29 of Israel, The way of the **L** is not equal. 136
18:30 according to his ways, saith the **L** GOD. 136
18:32 death of him that dieth, saith the **L** GOD: 136
20: 3 and say unto them, Thus saith the **L** GOD; 136
20: 3 *As* I live, saith the **L** GOD, I will not be 136
20: 5 And say unto them, Thus saith the **L** GOD; 136
20:27 and say unto them, Thus saith the **L** GOD; 136
20:30 the house of Israel, Thus saith the **L** GOD; 136
20:31 *As* I live, saith the **L** GOD, I will not be 136
20:33 *As* I live, saith the **L** GOD, surely with a 136
20:36 so will I plead with you, saith the **L** GOD. 136
20:39 O house of Israel, thus saith the **L** GOD; 136
20:40 saith the **L** GOD, there shall all the house 136
20:44 O ye house of Israel, saith the **L** GOD. 136
20:47 Thus saith the **L** GOD; Behold, I *will* 136
20:49 said I, Ah **L** GOD, they say of me, Doth he 136
21: 7 shall be brought to pass, saith the **L** GOD. 136
21:13 it shall be no *more*, saith the **L** GOD. 136
21:24 Therefore thus saith the **L** GOD; 136
21:26 Thus saith the **L** GOD; Remove 136
21:28 Thus saith the **L** GOD concerning 136
22: 3 say thou, Thus saith the **L** GOD, The city 136
22:12 and hast forgotten me, saith the **L** GOD. 136
22:19 Therefore thus saith the **L** GOD; 136
22:28 unto them, saying, Thus saith the **L** GOD, 136
22:31 upon their heads, saith the **L** GOD. 136
23:22 O Aholibah, thus saith the **L** GOD; 136
23:28 For thus saith the **L** GOD; Behold, I *will* 136
23:32 Thus saith the **L** GOD; Thou shalt drink *of* 136
23:34 for I have spoken *it*, saith the **L** GOD. 136
23:35 Therefore thus saith the **L** GOD; 136
23:46 For thus saith the **L** GOD; *I will* bring up a 136
23:49 and ye shall know that I *am* the **L** GOD. 136
24: 3 and say unto them, Thus saith the **L** GOD; 136
24: 6 Wherefore thus saith the **L** GOD; Woe to 136
24: 9 Therefore thus saith the **L** GOD; Woe to 136
24:14 shall they judge thee, saith the **L** GOD. 136
24:21 the house of Israel, Thus saith the **L** GOD; 136
24:24 ye shall know that I *am* the **L** GOD. 136
25: 3 Hear the word of the **L** GOD; 136
25: 3 Thus saith the **L** GOD; Because thou 136
25: 6 For thus saith the **L** GOD; Because thou 136
25: 8 Thus saith the **L** GOD; Because that Moab 136
25:12 Thus saith the **L** GOD; Because that Edom 136
25:13 Therefore thus saith the **L** GOD; I will also 136
25:14 know my vengeance, saith the **L** GOD. 136
25:15 Thus saith the **L** GOD; Because 136
25:16 Therefore thus saith the **L** GOD; Behold, 136
26: 3 Therefore thus saith the **L** GOD; Behold, 136
26: 5 for I have spoken *it*, saith the **L** GOD: and 136
26: 7 For thus saith the **L** GOD; Behold, I *will* 136
26:14 for I the LORD have spoken *it*, saith the **L** 136
26:15 Thus saith the **L** GOD to Tyrus; Shall not 136
26:19 For thus saith the **L** GOD; When I shall 136
26:21 never be found again, saith the **L** GOD. 136
27: 3 for many isles, Thus saith the **L** GOD; 136
28: 2 the prince of Tyrus, Thus saith the **L** GOD; 136
28: 6 Therefore thus saith the **L** GOD; 136
28:10 for I have spoken *it*, saith the **L** GOD. 136
28:12 and say unto him, Thus saith the **L** GOD; 136
28:22 say, Thus saith the **L** GOD; Behold, I *am* 136
28:24 and they shall know that I *am* the **L** GOD. 136
28:25 Thus saith the **L** GOD; When I shall have 136
29: 3 Speak, and say, Thus saith the **L** GOD; 136
29: 8 Therefore thus saith the **L** GOD; Behold, 136
29:13 Yet thus saith the **L** GOD; At the end of 136
29:16 but they shall know that I *am* the **L** GOD. 136
29:19 Therefore thus saith the **L** GOD; Behold, 136
29:20 they wrought for me, saith the **L** GOD. 136
30: 2 prophesy and say, Thus saith the **L** GOD; 136
30: 6 fall in it by the sword, saith the **L** GOD. 136

Eze 30:10 Thus saith the **L** GOD; I will also make 136
30:13 Thus saith the **L** GOD; I will also destroy 136
30:22 Therefore thus saith the **L** GOD; Behold, 136
31:10 Therefore thus saith the **L** GOD; 136
31:15 Thus saith the **L** GOD; In the day when he 136
31:18 and all his multitude, saith the **L** GOD. 136
32: 3 Thus saith the **L** GOD; I will therefore 136
32: 8 darkness upon thy land, saith the **L** GOD. 136
32:11 For thus saith the **L** GOD; The sword of 136
32:14 their rivers to run like oil, saith the **L** GOD. 136
32:16 and for all her multitude, saith the **L** GOD. 136
32:31 army slain by the sword, saith the **L** GOD. 136
32:32 and all his multitude, saith the **L** GOD. 136
33:11 Say unto them, *As* I live, saith the **L** GOD, 136
33:17 people say, The way of the **L** is not equal: 136
33:20 Yet ye say, The way of the **L** is not equal. 136
33:25 say unto them, Thus saith the **L** GOD; 136
33:27 thus unto them, Thus saith the **L** GOD; 136
34: 2 Thus saith the **L** GOD unto the shepherds; 136
34: 8 saith the **L** GOD, surely because my flock 136
34:10 Thus saith the **L** GOD; Behold, I *am* 136
34:11 For thus saith the **L** GOD; Behold, I, 136
34:15 cause them to lie down, saith the **L** GOD. 136
34:17 *for* you, O my flock, thus saith the **L** GOD; 136
34:20 Therefore thus saith the **L** GOD unto them; 136
34:30 of Israel, *are* my people, saith the **L** GOD. 136
34:31 *and* I *am* your God, saith the **L** GOD. 136
35: 3 say unto it, Thus saith the **L** GOD; Behold, 136
35: 6 Therefore, *as* I live, saith the **L** GOD, I will 136
35:11 Therefore, *as* I live, saith the **L** GOD, I will 136
35:14 Thus saith the **L** GOD; When the whole 136
36: 2 Thus saith the **L** GOD; Because the enemy 136
36: 3 and say, Thus saith the **L** GOD; 136
36: 4 of Israel, hear the word of the **L** GOD; 136
36: 4 Thus saith the **L** GOD to the mountains, 136
36: 5 Therefore thus saith the **L** GOD; Surely in 136
36: 6 and to the valleys, Thus saith the **L** GOD; 136
36: 7 Therefore thus saith the **L** GOD; I have 136
36:13 Thus saith the **L** GOD; Because they say 136
36:14 thy nations any more, saith the **L** GOD. 136
36:15 nations to fall any more, saith the **L** GOD. 136
36:22 the house of Israel, Thus saith the **L** GOD; 136
36:23 that I *am* the LORD, saith the **L** GOD, 136
36:32 Not for your sakes do I *this*, saith the **L** 136
36:33 Thus saith the **L** GOD; In the day that I 136
36:37 Thus saith the **L** GOD; I will yet *for* this be 136
37: 3 And I answered, O **L** GOD, thou knowest. 136
37: 5 Thus saith the **L** GOD unto these bones; 136
37: 9 and say to the wind, Thus saith the **L** GOD; 136
37:12 and say unto them, Thus saith the **L** GOD; 136
37:19 Say unto them, Thus saith the **L** GOD; 136
37:21 And say unto them, Thus saith the **L** GOD; 136
38: 3 say, Thus saith the **L** GOD; Behold, I *am* 136
38:10 Thus saith the **L** GOD; It shall also come to 136
38:14 and say unto Gog, Thus saith the **L** GOD; 136
38:17 Thus saith the **L** GOD; *Art* thou he of 136
38:18 saith the **L** GOD, *that* my fury shall come 136
38:21 all my mountains, saith the **L** GOD: 136
39: 1 and say, Thus saith the **L** GOD; 136
39: 5 for I have spoken *it*, saith the **L** GOD. 136
39: 8 it is come, and it is done, saith the **L** GOD; 136
39:10 those that robbed them, saith the **L** GOD. 136
39:13 that I shall be glorified, saith the **L** GOD. 136
39:17 thou son of man, thus saith the **L** GOD; 136
39:20 and *with* all men of war, saith the **L** GOD. 136
39:25 Therefore thus saith the **L** GOD; Now will 136
39:29 upon the house of Israel, saith the **L** GOD. 136
43:18 Son of man, thus saith the **L** GOD; 136
43:19 to minister unto me, saith the **L** GOD, 136
43:27 and I will accept you, saith the **L** GOD. 136
44: 6 the house of Israel, Thus saith the **L** GOD; 136
44: 9 Thus saith the **L** GOD; No stranger, 136
44:12 saith the **L** GOD, and they shall bear their 136
44:15 me the fat and the blood, saith the **L** GOD: 136
44:27 offer his sin offering, saith the **L** GOD. 136
45: 9 Thus saith the **L** GOD; Let it suffice you, 136
45: 9 from my people, saith the **L** GOD. 136
45:15 reconciliation for them, saith the **L** GOD. 136
45:18 Thus saith the **L** GOD; In the first *month*, 136
46: 1 Thus saith the **L** GOD; The gate of 136
46:16 Thus saith the **L** GOD; If the prince give a 136
47:13 Thus saith the **L** GOD; This *shall be* 136
47:23 give *him* his inheritance, saith the **L** GOD. 136
48:29 these *are* their portions, saith the **L** GOD. 136
Da 1: 2 the **L** gave Jehoiakim king of Judah into his 136
1:10 I fear my **l** the king, who hath appointed 113
2:10 therefore *there is* no king, **l**, nor ruler, 7229
2:47 a **L** of kings, and a revealer of secrets, 4756
4:19 Belteshazzar answered and said, My **l**, 4756
4:24 which is come upon my **l** the king: 4756
5:23 hast lifted up thyself against the **L** of 4756
9: 3 I set my face unto the **L** God, to seek *by* 136
9: 4 and said, O **L**, the great and dreadful God, 136
9: 7 O **L**, righteousness *belongeth* unto thee, but 136
9: 8 O **L**, to us *belongeth* confusion of face, 136
9: 9 To the **L** our God *belong* mercies and 136
9:15 now, O **L** our God, that hast brought thy 136
9:16 O **L**, according to all thy righteousness, 136
9:19 O **L**, hear; O Lord, forgive; O Lord, hearken 136
9:19 O Lord, hear; O **L**, forgive; O Lord, hearken 136
9:19 hear; O Lord, forgive; O **L**, hearken and do; 136
10:16 said unto him that stood before me, O my **l**, 113
10:17 For how can the servant of this my **l** talk 113
10:17 servant of this my lord talk with this my **l**? 113
10:19 I was strengthened, and said, Let my **l** speak; 113
12: 8 said I, O my **l**, what *shall be* the end of these 113
Hos 12:14 and his reproach shall his **L** return unto him. 113
Am 1: 8 Philistines shall perish, saith the **L** GOD. 136
3: 7 Surely the **L** GOD will do nothing, but he 136
3: 8 the **L** GOD hath spoken, who can but 136
3:11 Therefore thus saith the **L** GOD; 136
3:13 saith the **L** GOD, the God of hosts, 136
4: 2 The **L** GOD hath sworn by his holiness, 136
4: 5 O ye children of Israel, saith the **L** GOD. 136
5: 3 For thus saith the **L** GOD; The city that 136

Am 5:16 the God of hosts, the L, saith thus; 136
6: 8 The L GOD hath sworn by himself, saith 136
7: 1 Thus hath the L GOD shewed unto me; and 136
7: 2 I said, O L GOD, forgive, I beseech thee: 136
7: 4 Thus hath the L GOD shewed unto me: and 136
7: 4 the L GOD called to contend by fire, and 136
7: 5 said I, O L GOD, cease, I beseech thee: 136
7: 6 This also shall not be, saith the L GOD. 136
7: 7 the L stood upon a wall made by a 136
7: 8 said the L, Behold, I *will* set a plumbline in 136
8: 1 Thus hath the L GOD shewed unto me: and 136
8: 3 be howlings in that day, saith the L GOD: 136
8: 9 come to pass in that day, saith the L GOD, 136
8:11 Behold, the days come, saith the L GOD, 136
9: 1 I saw the L standing upon the altar: and 136
9: 5 the L GOD of hosts *is* he that toucheth 136
9: 8 the eyes of the L GOD *are* upon the sinful 136
Ob 1: 1 Thus saith the L GOD concerning Edom; 136
Mic 1: 2 and let the L GOD be witness against you, 136
1: 2 against you, the L from his holy temple. 136
4:13 their substance unto the L of the whole 113
Hab 3:19 The L GOD *is* my strength, and he will 136
Zep 1: 7 Hold thy peace at the presence of the L 136
Zec 1: 9 said I, O my l, what *are* these? And the angel 113
4: 4 with me, saying, What *are* these, my l? 113
4: 5 not what these *be?* And I said, No, my l. 113
4:13 not what these *be?* And I said, No, my l. 113
4:14 that stand by the L of the whole earth. 113
6: 4 that talked with me, What *are* these, my l? 113
6: 5 *which* go forth from standing before the L of 113
9: 4 the L will cast her out, and he will smite her 136
9:14 and the L GOD shall blow the trumpet, and 136
Mal 1:14 sacrificeth unto the L a corrupt *thing:* for I 136
Mt 1:20 *the* angel of the L appeared unto him in a 2962
1:22 which was spoken of the L by the prophet, 2962
1:24 did as the angel of the L had bidden him, 2962
2:13 *the* angel of the L appeareth to Joseph in a 2962
2:15 which was spoken of the L by the prophet, 2962
2:19 an angel of the L appeareth in a dream to 2962
3: 3 Prepare ye the way of the L, make his paths 2962
4: 7 Thou shalt not tempt the L thy God. 2962
4:10 Thou shalt worship the L thy God, and 2962
5:33 but shalt perform unto the L thine oaths: 2962
7:21 Not every one that saith unto me, L, Lord, 2962
7:21 Not every one that saith unto me, Lord, L, 2962
7:22 Many will say to me in that day, L, Lord, 2962
7:22 Many will say to me in that day, Lord, L, 2962
8: 2 worshipped him, saying, L, if thou wilt, 2962
8: 6 And saying, L, my servant lieth at home 2962
8: 8 The centurion answered and said, L, I am 2962
8:21 L, suffer me first to go and bury my father. 2962
8:25 to *him,* and awoke him, saying, L, save us: 2962
9:28 to do this? They said unto him, Yea, L. 2962
9:38 Pray ye therefore the L of the harvest, 2962
10:24 *his* master, nor the servant above his l. 2962
10:25 he be as his master, and the servant as his l. 2962
11:25 L of heaven and earth, because thou hast 2962
12: 8 For the Son of man is L even of the sabbath 2962
13:51 these *things?* They say unto him, Yea, L. 2962
14:28 And Peter answered him and said, L, if it 2962
14:30 to sink, he cried, saying, L, save me. 2962
15:22 mercy on me, O L, *thou* Son of David; 2962
15:25 and worshipped him, saying, L, help me. 2962
15:27 And she said, Truth, L: yet the dogs eat of 2962
16:22 rebuke him, saying, Be it far from thee, L: 2962
17: 4 answered Peter, and said unto Jesus, L, 2962
17:15 L, have mercy on my son: for he is 2962
18:21 Then came Peter to him, and said, L, 2962
18:25 his l commanded him to be sold, and 2962
18:26 fell down, and worshipped him, saying, L, 2962
18:27 Then the l of that servant was moved with 2962
18:31 came and told unto their l all that was done. 2962
18:32 Then his l, after that he had called him, 2962
18:34 And his l was wroth, and delivered him to 2962
20: 8 the l of the vineyard saith unto his steward, 2962
20:30 cried out, saying, Have mercy on us, O L, 2962
20:31 saying, Have mercy on us, O L, *thou* Son 2962
20:33 They say unto him, L, that our eyes may be 2962
21: 3 ye shall say, The L hath need of them; 2962
21: 9 *is* he that cometh in the name of the L; 2962
21:40 When the l therefore of the vineyard 2962
22:37 Thou shalt love the L thy God with all thy 2962
22:43 How then doth David in spirit call him L, 2962
22:44 The L said unto my Lord, Sit thou on my 2962
22:44 The LORD said unto my L, Sit thou on my 2962
22:45 If David then call him L, how is he his son? 2962
23:39 is he that cometh in the name of the L. 2962
24:42 for ye know not what hour your L doth 2962
24:45 whom his l hath made ruler over his 2962
24:46 whom his l when he cometh shall find so 2962
24:48 say in his heart, My l delayeth his coming; 2962
24:50 The l of that servant shall come in a day 2962
25:11 other virgins, saying, L, Lord, open to us. 2962
25:11 other virgins, saying, Lord, L, open to us. 2962
25:19 After a long time the l of those servants 2962
25:20 and brought other five talents, saying, L, 2962
25:21 His l said unto him, Well *done, thou* good 2962
25:21 *things:* enter thou into the joy of thy l. 2962
25:22 had received two talents came and said, L, 2962
25:23 His l said unto him, Well *done,* good and 2962
25:23 *things:* enter thou into the joy of thy l. 2962
25:24 received the one talent came and said, L, 2962
25:26 His l answered and said unto him, 2962
25:37 saying, L, when saw we thee a hungred, 2962
25:44 saying, L, when saw we thee a hungred, or 2962
26:22 one of them to say unto him, L, is it I? 2962
27:10 the potter's field, as the L appointed me. 2962
28: 2 for *the* angel of the L descended from 2962
28: 6 Come, see the place where the L lay. 2962
Mk 1: 3 Prepare ye the way of the L, make his paths 2962
2:28 Therefore the Son of man is L also of 2962
5:19 tell them how great *things* the L hath done 2962
7:28 she answered and said unto him, Yes, L: 2962
9:24 cried out, and said with tears, L, I believe; 2962
10:51 unto him, L, that I might receive my sight. 4462
Mk 11: 3 say ye that the L hath need of him; and 2962
11: 9 *is* he that cometh in the name of the L: 2962
11:10 that cometh in the name of the L: 2962
12: 9 therefore the l of the vineyard do? 2962
12:29 O Israel; The L our God is one Lord: 2962
12:29 O Israel; The Lord our God is one L: 2962
12:30 And thou shalt love the L thy God with all 2962
12:36 The L said to my Lord, Sit thou on my 2962
12:36 The LORD said to my L, Sit thou on my 2962
12:37 David therefore himself calleth him L; and 2962
13:20 And except that the L had shortened *those* 2962
16:19 So then after the L had spoken unto them, 2962
16:20 the L working with *them,* and 2962
Lk 1: 6 and ordinances of the L blameless. 2962
1: 9 when he went into the temple of the L. 2962
1:11 L standing on the right side of the altar of 2962
1:15 For he shall be great in the sight of the L, 2962
1:16 of Israel shall he turn to the L their God. 2962
1:17 to make ready a people prepared for the L. 2962
1:25 Thus hath the L dealt with me in the days 2962
1:28 *that art* highly favoured, the L *is* with thee: 2962
1:32 the L God shall give unto him the throne of 2962
1:38 Mary said, Behold the handmaid of the L; 2962
1:43 that the mother of my L should come to 2962
1:45 *things* which were told her from the L. 2962
1:46 Mary said, My soul doth magnify the L, 2962
1:58 her cousins heard how the L had shewed 2962
1:66 And the hand of the L was with him. 2962
1:68 Blessed *be* the L God of Israel; for he hath 2962
1:76 for thou shalt go before the face of the L to 2962
2: 9 *the* angel of the L came upon them, and 2962
2: 9 the glory of the L shone round about them: 2962
2:11 of David a Saviour, which is Christ the L. 2962
2:15 which the L hath made known unto us. 2962
2:22 him to Jerusalem, to present *him* to the L; 2962
2:23 (As it is written in the law of the L, Every 2962
2:23 the womb shall be called holy to the L;) 2962
2:24 to that which is said in the law of the L, 2962
2:29 L, now lettest thou thy servant depart in 1203
2:38 instant gave thanks *likewise* unto the L, 2962
2:39 all *things* according to the law of the L, 2962
3: 4 Prepare ye the way of the L, make his paths 2962
4: 8 Thou shalt worship the L thy God, and 2962
4:12 is said, Thou shalt not tempt the L thy God. 2962
4:18 The Spirit of the L *is* upon me, 2962
4:19 To preach the acceptable year of the L. 2962
5: 8 from me; for I am a sinful man, O L. 2962
5:12 and besought him, saying, L, if thou wilt, 2962
5:17 the power of the L was *present* to heal 2962
6: 5 That the Son of man is L also of 2962
6:46 L, Lord, and do not *the things* which I say? 2962
6:46 Lord, L, and do not *the things* which I say? 2962
7: 6 saying unto him, L, trouble not thyself: 2962
7:13 And when the L saw her, he had 2962
7:31 And the L said, Whereunto then shall I 2962
9:54 and John saw *this,* they said, L, 2962
9:57 a certain *man* said unto him, L, I will 2962
9:59 But he said, L, suffer me first to go and 2962
9:61 And another also said, L, I will follow thee; 2962
10: 1 After these *things* the L appointed other 2962
10: 2 pray ye therefore the L of the harvest, 2962
10:17 seventy returned *again* with joy, saying, L, 2962
10:21 O Father, L of heaven and earth, 2962
10:27 Thou shalt love the L thy God with all thy 2962
10:40 and came to *him,* and said, L, 2962
11: 1 L, teach us to pray, as John also taught his 2962
11:39 And the L said unto him, Now do ye 2962
12:36 like unto men that wait for their l, 2962
12:37 whom the l when he cometh shall find 2962
12:41 Then Peter said unto him, L, speakest thou 2962
12:42 And the L said, Who then is *that* faithful 2962
12:42 whom *his* l shall make ruler over his 2962
12:43 whom his l when he cometh shall find so 2962
12:45 say in his heart, My l delayeth his coming; 2962
12:46 The l of that servant will come in a day 2962
13: 8 L, let it alone this year also, till I shall dig 2962
13:15 The L then answered him, and said, 2962
13:23 Then said one unto him, L, are there few 2962
13:25 at the door, saying, L, Lord, open unto us; 2962
13:25 at the door, saying, Lord, L, open unto us; 2962
13:35 *is* he that cometh in the name of the L. 2962
14:21 shewed his l these *things.* Then the master 2962
14:22 And the servant said, L, it is done as thou 2962
14:23 And the l said unto the servant, Go out into 2962
16: 3 for my l taketh away from me 2962
16: 5 the first, How much owest thou unto my l? 2962
16: 8 And the l commended the unjust steward, 2962
17: 5 And the apostles said unto the L, 2962
17: 6 And the L said, If ye had faith as a grain of 2962
17:37 and said unto him, Where, L? 2962
18: 6 And the L said, Hear what the unjust judge 2962
18:41 And he said, L, that I may receive my 2962
19: 8 And Zacchaeus stood, and said unto the L; 2962
19: 8 Behold, L, the half of my goods I give to 2962
19:16 Then came the first, saying, L, thy pound 2962
19:18 And the second came, saying, L, thy pound 2962
19:20 saying, L, behold, *here is* thy pound, 2962
19:25 they said unto him, L, he hath ten pounds.) 2962
19:31 unto him, Because the L hath need of him. 2962
19:34 And they said, The L hath need of him. 2962
19:38 the King that cometh in the name of the L: 2962
20:13 Then said the l of the vineyard, What shall 2962
20:15 shall the l of the vineyard do unto them? 2962
20:37 when he calleth the L the God of Abraham, 2962
20:42 The L said to my Lord, Sit thou on my 2962
20:42 The LORD said to my L, Sit thou on my 2962
20:44 David therefore calleth him L, how is he 2962
22:31 And the L said, Simon, Simon, behold, 2962
22:33 And he said unto him, L, I am ready to go 2962
22:38 And they said, L, behold, here *are* two 2962
22:49 they said unto him, L, shall we smite with 2962
22:61 And the L turned, and looked upon Peter. 2962
22:61 And Peter remembered the word of the L, 2962
23:42 And he said unto Jesus, L, remember me 2962
24: 3 and found not the body of the L Jesus. 2962
Lk 24:34 The L is risen indeed, and hath appeared to 2962
Jn 1:23 Make straight the way of the L, as said 2962
4: 1 the L knew how the Pharisees had heard 2962
6:23 after that the L had given thanks:) 2962
6:34 Then said they unto him, L, evermore give 2962
6:68 answered him, L, to whom shall we go? 2962
8:11 She said, No *man,* L. And Jesus said unto 2962
9:36 He answered and said, Who is he, L, that I 2962
9:38 And he said, L, I believe. And he 2962
11: 2 (It was *that* Mary which anointed the L 2962
11: 3 saying, L, behold, he whom thou lovest is 2962
11:12 L, if he sleep, he shall do well. 2962
11:21 L, if thou hadst been here, my brother had 2962
11:27 She saith unto him, Yea, L: I believe that 2962
11:32 saying unto him, L, if thou hadst been here, 2962
11:34 They say unto him, L, come and see. 2962
11:39 saith unto him, L, by this time he stinketh: 2962
12:13 of Israel that cometh in the name of the L. 2962
12:38 which he spake, L, who hath believed our 2962
12:38 to whom hath the arm of the L been 2962
13: 6 and *Peter* saith unto him, L, dost thou wash 2962
13: 9 L, not my feet only, but also *my* hands and 2962
13:13 Ye call me Master and L: and ye say well; 2962
13:14 If I then, *your* L and Master, have washed 2962
13:16 The servant is not greater than his l; 2962
13:25 Jesus' breast saith unto him, L, who is it? 2962
13:36 Peter said unto him, L, whither goest thou? 2962
13:37 Peter said unto him, L, why cannot I follow 2962
14: 5 Thomas saith unto him, L, we know not 2962
14: 8 L, shew us the Father, and it sufficeth us. 2962
14:22 Judas saith unto him, not Iscariot, L, how is 2962
15:15 for the servant knoweth not what his l 2962
15:20 The servant is not greater than his l. 2962
20: 2 They have taken away the L out of 2962
20:13 Because they have taken away my L, and 2962
20:18 told the disciples that she had seen the L, 2962
20:20 the disciples glad, when they saw the L. 2962
20:25 said unto him, We have seen the L. 2962
20:28 and said unto him, My L and my God. 2962
21: 7 Jesus loved saith unto Peter, It is the L. 2962
21: 7 when Simon Peter heard that it was the L, 2962
21:12 Who art thou? knowing that it was the L. 2962
21:15 He saith unto him, Yea, L; thou knowest 2962
21:16 He saith unto him, Yea, L; thou knowest 2962
21:17 And he said unto him, L, thou knowest all 2962
21:20 and said, L, which is he that betrayeth 2962
21:21 to Jesus, L, and what *shall* this *man do?* 2962
Ac 1: 6 they asked of him, saying, L, 2962
1:21 with us all the time that the L Jesus went in 2962
1:24 And they prayed, and said, Thou, L, 2962
2:20 *that* great and notable day of the L come: 2962
2:21 call on the name of the L shall be saved. 2962
2:25 I foresaw the L always before my face, 2962
2:34 he saith himself, The L said unto my Lord, 2962
2:34 saith himself, The LORD said unto my L, 2962
2:36 ye have crucified, both L and Christ. 2962
2:39 *even* as many as the L our God shall call. 2962
2:47 And the L added to the church daily such 2962
3:19 shall come from the presence of the L; 2962
3:22 A prophet shall the L your God raise up 2962
4:24 and said, L, thou *art* God, which hast made 1203
4:26 rulers were gathered together against the L, 2962
4:29 And now, L, behold their threatenings: and 2962
4:33 witness of the resurrection of the L Jesus: 2962
5: 9 together to tempt the Spirit of the L? 2962
5:14 believers were the more added to the L, 2962
5:19 But *the* angel of the L by night opened 2962
7:30 angel of the L in a flame of fire in a bush. 2962
7:31 behold *it,* the voice of the L came unto him, 2962
7:33 Then said the L to him, Put off *thy* shoes 2962
7:37 A prophet shall the L your God raise up 2962
7:49 saith the L: or what *is* the place of my rest? 2962
7:59 calling upon *God,* and saying, L Jesus, 2962
7:60 and cried with a loud voice, L, 2962
8:16 were baptized in the name of the L Jesus.) 2962
8:24 and said, Pray ye to the L for me, 2962
8:25 and preached the word of the L, 2962
8:26 And *the* angel of the L spake unto Philip, 2962
8:39 the Spirit of the L caught away Philip, 2962
9: 1 and slaughter against the disciples of the L, 2962
9: 5 And he said, Who art thou, L? And 2962
9: 5 And the L said, I am Jesus whom thou 2962
9: 6 And he trembling and astonished said, L, 2962
9: 6 And the L *said* unto him, Arise, and go into 2962
9:10 and to him said the L in a vision, Ananias. 2962
9:10 And he said, Behold, I *am here,* L. 2962
9:11 And the L *said* unto him, Arise, and go into 2962
9:13 Then Ananias answered, L, I have heard by 2962
9:15 But the L said unto him, Go *thy way:* for he 2962
9:17 him said, Brother Saul, the L, *even* Jesus, 2962
9:27 declared unto them how he had seen the L 2962
9:29 And he spake boldly in the name of the L 2962
9:31 and walking in the fear of the L, and in 2962
9:35 and Saron saw him, and turned to the L. 2962
9:42 all Joppa; and many believed in the L. 2962
10: 4 he was afraid, and said, What is it, L? 2962
10:14 But Peter said, Not so, L; for I have never 2962
10:36 peace by Jesus Christ: (he is L of all:) 2962
10:48 them to be baptized in the name of the L. 2962
11: 8 But I said, Not so, L: for nothing common 2962
11:16 Then remembered I the word of the L, 2962
11:17 who believed on the L Jesus Christ; 2962
11:20 unto the Grecians, preaching the L Jesus. 2962
11:21 And the hand of the L was with them: and 2962
11:21 number believed, and turned unto the L. 2962
11:23 of heart *they* would cleave unto the L. 2962
11:24 and much people was added unto the L. 2962
12: 7 *the* angel of the L came upon *him,* and 2962
12:11 that the L hath sent his angel, and 2962
12:17 declared unto them how the L had brought 2962
12:23 And immediately *the* angel of the L smote 2962
13: 2 As they ministered to the L, and fasted, 2962
13:10 cease to pervert the right ways of the L? 2962
13:11 the hand of the L *is* upon thee, and 2962
13:12 being astonished at the doctrine of the L. 2962

Ac 13:47 For so hath the **L** commanded us, *saying,* I 2962
13:48 were glad, and glorified the word of the **L**: 2962
13:49 And the word of the **L** was published 2962
14: 3 abode they speaking boldly in the **L**, 2962
14:23 they commended them to the **L**, on whom 2962
15:11 of the **L** Jesus Christ *we* shall be saved, 2962
15:17 the residue of men might seek after the **L**, 2962
15:17 saith the **L**, who doeth all these *things.* 2962
15:26 lives for the name of our **L** Jesus Christ. 2962
15:35 teaching and preaching the word of the **L**, 2962
15:36 where we have preached the word of the **L**, 2962
16:10 assuredly gathering that the **L** had called us 2962
16:14 heard *us:* whose heart the **L** opened, 2962
16:15 If ye have judged me to be faithful to the **L**, 2962
16:31 Believe on the **L** Jesus Christ, and 2962
16:32 And they spake unto him the word of the **L**, 2962
17:24 seeing that he is **L** of heaven and earth, 2962
17:27 That *they* should seek the **L**, if haply they 2962
18: 8 believed on the **L** with all his house; 2962
18: 9 Then spake the **L** to Paul in the night by a 2962
18:25 *man* was instructed in the way of the **L**; 2962
18:25 and taught diligently the *things* of the **L**, 2962
19: 5 were baptized in the name of the **L** Jesus. 2962
19:10 in Asia heard the word of the **L** Jesus, 2962
19:13 had evil spirits the name of the **L** Jesus, 2962
19:17 and the name of the **L** Jesus was magnified. 2962
20:19 Serving the **L** with all humility of mind, 2962
20:21 and faith toward our **L** Jesus Christ. 2962
20:24 which I have received of the **L** Jesus, 2962
20:35 and to remember the words of the **L** Jesus, 2962
21:13 at Jerusalem for the name of the **L** Jesus. 2962
21:14 saying, The will of the **L** be done. 2962
21:20 when they heard *it,* they glorified the **L**, 2962
22: 8 And I answered, Who art thou, **L**? And he 2962
22:10 And I said, What shall I do, **L**? And 2962
22:10 And the **L** said unto me, Arise, and go into 2962
22:16 away thy sins, calling on the name of the **L**. 2962
22:19 And I said, **L**, they know that I imprisoned 2962
23:11 And the night following the **L** stood by 2962
25:26 I have no certain *thing* to write unto *my* l. 2962
26:15 And I said, Who art thou, **L**? And he said, 2962
28:31 teaching those *things* which concern the **L** 2962
Ro 1: 3 Concerning his Son Jesus Christ our **L**, 2962
1: 7 God our Father, and the **L** Jesus Christ. 2962
4: 8 Blessed *is* the man to whom the **L** will not 2962
4:24 that raised up Jesus our **L** from the dead; 2962
5: 1 we have peace with God through our **L** 2962
5:11 we also joy in God through our **L** Jesus 2962
5:21 unto eternal life by Jesus Christ our **L**. 2962
6:11 alive unto God through Jesus Christ our **L**. 2962
6:23 *is* eternal life through Jesus Christ our **L**. 2962
7:25 I thank God through Jesus Christ our **L**. So 2962
8:39 love of God, which is in Christ Jesus our **L**. 2962
9:28 a short work will the **L** make upon 2962
9:29 Except the **L** of sabaoth had left us a seed, 2962
10: 9 shalt confess with thy mouth the **L** Jesus, 2962
10:12 for the same **L** over all *is* rich unto all that 2962
10:13 call upon the name of the **L** shall be saved. 2962
10:16 For Esaias saith, **L**, who hath believed our 2962
11: 3 **L**, they have killed thy prophets, and 2962
11:34 For who hath known the mind of the **L**? or 2962
12:11 in business; fervent in spirit; serving the **L**; 2962
12:19 *is* mine; I will repay, saith the **L**. 2962
13:14 But put ye on the **L** Jesus Christ, and 2962
14: 6 regardeth the day, regardeth *it* unto the **L**; 2962
14: 6 to the **L** he doth not regard *it.* He that 2962
14: 6 eateth to the **L**, for he giveth God thanks; 2962
14: 6 to the **L** he eateth not, and giveth God 2962
14: 8 For whether we live, we live unto the **L**; 2962
14: 8 and whether we die, we die unto the **L**: 2962
14: 9 that he might be **L** both of the dead and 2961
14:11 For it is written, *As* I live, saith the **L**, 2962
14:14 I know, and am persuaded by the **L** Jesus, 2962
15: 6 even the Father of our **L** Jesus Christ. 2962
15:11 And again, Praise the **L**, all ye Gentiles; 2962
15:30 for the **L** Jesus Christ's sake, and for 2962
16: 2 That ye receive her in the **L**, as becometh 2962
16: 8 Greet Amplias my beloved in the **L**. 2962
16:11 *household* of Narcissus, which are in the **L**. 2962
16:12 and Tryphosa, who labour in the **L**. 2962
16:12 which laboured much in the **L**. 2962
16:13 Salute Rufus chosen in the **L**, and 2962
16:18 For *they that are* such serve not our **L** Jesus 2962
16:20 The grace of our **L** Jesus Christ *be* with 2962
16:22 who wrote *this* epistle, salute you in the **L**. 2962
16:24 The grace of our **L** Jesus Christ *be* with you 2962
1Co 1: 2 call upon the name of Jesus Christ our **L**, 2962
1: 3 our Father, and *from* the **L** Jesus Christ. 2962
1: 7 waiting for the coming of our **L** Jesus 2962
1: 8 blameless in the day of our **L** Jesus Christ. 2962
1: 9 fellowship of his Son Jesus Christ our **L**. 2962
1:10 by the name of our **L** Jesus Christ, 2962
1:31 He that glorieth, let him glory in the **L**. 2962
2: 8 would not have crucified the **L** of glory. 2962
2:16 For who hath known the mind of the **L**, 2962
3: 5 even as the **L** gave to every man? 2962
3:20 The **L** knoweth the thoughts of the wise, 2962
4: 4 but he that judgeth me is the **L**. 2962
4: 5 nothing before the time, until the **L** come, 2962
4:17 is my beloved son, and faithful in the **L**, 2962
4:19 to you shortly, if the **L** will, and will know, 2962
5: 4 In the name of our **L** Jesus Christ, when ye 2962
5: 4 with the power of our **L** Jesus Christ, 2962
5: 5 may be saved in the day of the **L** Jesus. 2962
6:11 ye are justified in the name of the **L** Jesus, 2962
6:13 body *is* not for fornication, but for the **L**; 2962
6:13 but for the Lord; and the **L** for the body. 2962
6:14 And God hath both raised up the **L**, and 2962
6:17 But he that is joined unto the **L** is one 2962
7:10 married I command, *yet* not I, but the **L**, 2962
7:12 But to the rest speak I, not the **L**: If any 2962
7:17 as the **L** hath called every one, so let him 2962
7:22 For he that is called in the **L**, *being* a 2962
7:25 virgins I have no commandment of the **L**: 2962
7:25 as one that hath obtained mercy of the **L** to 2962

1Co 7:32 careth for the *things* that belong to the **L**, 2962
7:32 to the Lord, how he may please the **L**: 2962
7:34 *woman* careth for the *things* of the **L**, 2962
7:35 that you may attend upon the **L** without 2962
7:39 be married to whom she will; only in the **L**. 2962
8: 6 and one **L** Jesus Christ, by whom *are* all 2962
9: 1 have I not seen Jesus Christ our **L**? are not 2962
9: 1 our Lord? are not you my work in the **L**? 2962
9: 2 the seal of mine apostleship are ye in the **L**. 2962
9: 5 and *as* the brethren of the **L**, and Cephas? 2962
9:14 hath the **L** ordained that they which preach 2962
10:21 Ye cannot drink the cup of the **L**, and 2962
10:22 Do we provoke the **L** to jealousy? are we 2962
11:11 the woman without the man, in the **L**. 2962
11:23 For I have received of the **L** *that* which also 2962
11:23 That the **L** Jesus the *same* night in which he 2962
11:27 and drink *this* cup of the **L** unworthily, 2962
11:27 be guilty of the body and blood of the **L**. 2962
11:32 we are judged, we are chastened of the **L**, 2962
12: 3 and *that* no *man* can say that Jesus is the **L**, 2962
12: 5 of administrations, but the same **L**. 2962
14:21 all that will they not hear me, saith the **L**. 2962
14:37 unto you are the commandments of the **L**. 2962
15:31 which I have in Christ Jesus our **L**, 2962
15:47 the second man *is* the **L** from heaven. 2962
15:57 which giveth us the victory through our **L** 2962
15:58 always abounding in the work of the **L**, 2962
15:58 that your labour is not in vain in the **L**. 2962
16: 7 to tarry a while with you, if the **L** permit. 2962
16:10 for he worketh the work of the **L**, as I also 2962
16:19 and Priscilla salute you much in the **L**, 2962
16:22 If any *man* love not the **L** Jesus Christ, 2962
16:23 The grace of *our* **L** Jesus Christ *be* with 2962
2Co 1: 2 our Father, and *from* the **L** Jesus Christ. 2962
1: 3 even the Father of our **L** Jesus Christ, 2962
1:14 even as ye also *are* ours in the day of the **L** 2962
2:12 and a door was opened unto me of the **L**, 2962
3:16 Nevertheless when *it* shall turn to the **L**, 2962
3:17 Now the **L** is *that* Spirit: and where 2962
3:17 where the Spirit of the **L** *is,* there *is* liberty. 2962
3:18 beholding as in a glass the glory of the **L**, 2962
3:18 to glory, even as by the Spirit of the **L**. 2962
4: 5 not ourselves, but Christ Jesus the **L**; 2962
4:10 about in the body the dying of the **L** Jesus, 2962
4:14 Knowing that he which raised up the **L** 2962
5: 6 in the body, we are absent from the **L**: 2962
5: 8 the body, and to be present with the **L**. 2962
5:11 Knowing therefore the terror of the **L**, 2962
6:17 saith the **L**, and touch not the unclean 2962
6:18 and daughters, saith the **L** Almighty. 2962
8: 5 but first gave their own selves to the **L**, and 2962
8: 9 For ye know the grace of our **L** Jesus 2962
8:19 by us to the glory of the same **L**, 2962
8:21 honest *things,* not only in the sight of the **L**, 2962
10: 8 which the **L** hath given us for edification, 2962
10:17 But he that glorieth, let him glory in the **L**. 2962
10:18 is approved, but whom the **L** commendeth. 2962
11:17 I speak *it* not after the **L**, but as *it were* 2962
11:31 The God and Father of our **L** Jesus Christ, 2962
12: 1 come to visions and revelations of the **L**. 2962
12: 8 For this *thing* I besought the **L** thrice, that it 2962
13:10 according to the power which the **L** hath 2962
13:14 The grace of the **L** Jesus Christ, and 2962
Gal 1: 3 the Father, and *from* our **L** Jesus Christ, 2962
4: 1 from a servant, though he be l of all; 2962
5:10 I have confidence in you through the **L**, 2962
6:14 save in the cross of our **L** Jesus Christ, 2962
6:17 for I bear in my body the marks of the **L** 2962
6:18 the grace of our **L** Jesus Christ *be* with your 2962
Eph 1: 2 our Father, and *from* the **L** Jesus Christ. 2962
1: 3 the God and Father of our **L** Jesus Christ, 2962
1:15 after I heard of your faith in the **L** Jesus, 2962
1:17 That the God of our **L** Jesus Christ, 2962
2:21 groweth unto a holy temple in the **L**: 2962
3:11 which he purposed in Christ Jesus our **L**: 2962
3:14 knees unto the Father of our **L** Jesus Christ, 2962
4: 1 I therefore, the prisoner of the **L**, 2962
4: 5 One **L**, one faith, one baptism, 2962
4:17 This I say therefore, and testify in the **L**, 2962
5: 8 but now *are ye* light in the **L**: 2962
5:10 Proving what is acceptable unto the **L**. 2962
5:17 but understanding what the will of the **L** *is.* 2962
5:19 and making melody in your heart to the **L**; 2962
5:20 the Father in the name of our **L** Jesus 2962
5:22 unto your own husbands, as unto the **L**. 2962
5:29 and cherisheth it, even as the **L** the church: 2962
6: 1 Children, obey your parents in the **L**: 2962
6: 4 up in the nurture and admonition of the **L**. 2962
6: 7 doing service, as to the **L**, and not to men: 2962
6: 8 the same shall he receive of the **L**, 2962
6:10 be strong in the **L**, and in the power of his 2962
6:21 and faithful minister in the **L**, 2962
6:23 from God the Father and the **L** Jesus Christ. 2962
6:24 Grace *be* with all them that love our **L** 2962
Php 1: 2 our Father, and *from* the **L** Jesus Christ. 2962
1:14 And many of the brethren in the **L**, 2962
2:11 should confess that Jesus Christ *is* **L**, 2962
2:19 But I trust in the **L** Jesus to send Timotheus 2962
2:24 But I trust in the **L** that I also myself shall 2962
2:29 therefore in the **L** with all gladness; 2962
3: 1 Finally, my brethren, rejoice in the **L**. 2962
3: 8 of the knowledge of Christ Jesus my **L**: 2962
3:20 we look for the Saviour, the **L** Jesus Christ: 2962
4: 1 my joy and crown, so stand fast in the **L**, 2962
4: 2 that *they* be of the same mind in the **L**. 2962
4: 4 Rejoice in the **L** alway: *and* again I say, 2962
4: 5 be known unto all men. The **L** *is* at hand. 2962
4:10 But I rejoiced in the **L** greatly, that now at 2962
4:23 The grace of our **L** Jesus Christ *be* with you 2962
Col 1: 2 God our Father and the **L** Jesus Christ. 2962
1: 3 and the Father of our **L** Jesus Christ, 2962
1:10 That ye might walk worthy of the **L** unto 2962
2: 6 therefore received Christ Jesus the **L**, 2962
3:16 singing with grace in your hearts to the **L**. 2962
3:17 or deed, *do* all in the name of the **L** Jesus, 2962

Col 3:18 your own husbands, as it is fit in the **L**. 2962
3:20 *things:* for this is well pleasing unto the **L**. 2962
3:23 *it* heartily, as to the **L**, and not unto men; 2962
3:24 Knowing that of the **L** ye shall receive 2962
3:24 of the inheritance: for ye serve the **L** Christ. 2962
4: 7 faithful minister and fellowservant in the **L**: 2962
4:17 ministry which thou hast received in the **L**, 2962
1Th 1: 1 in God the Father and *in* the **L** Jesus Christ: 2962
1: 1 God our Father, and the **L** Jesus Christ. 2962
1: 3 and patience of hope in our **L** Jesus Christ, 2962
1: 6 ye became followers of us, and of the **L**, 2962
1: 8 from you sounded out the word of the **L** 2962
2:15 Who both killed the **L** Jesus, and their own 2962
2:19 *Are* not even ye in the presence of our **L** 2962
3: 8 For now we live, if ye stand fast in the **L**. 2962
3:11 and our Father, and our **L** Jesus Christ, 2962
3:12 And the **L** make you to increase and 2962
3:13 at the coming of our **L** Jesus Christ with all 2962
4: 1 brethren, and exhort *you* by the **L** Jesus, 2962
4: 2 we gave you by the **L** Jesus. 2962
4: 6 that the **L** *is* the avenger of all such, 2962
4:15 this we say unto you by the word of the **L**, 2962
4:15 remain unto the coming of the **L** shall not 2962
4:16 For the **L** himself shall descend from 2962
4:17 them in the clouds, to meet the **L** in the air: 2962
4:17 the air: and so shall we ever be with the **L**. 2962
5: 2 know perfectly that the day of the **L** 2962
5: 9 to obtain salvation by our **L** Jesus Christ, 2962
5:12 and are over you in the **L**, and 2962
5:23 unto the coming of our **L** Jesus Christ. 2962
5:27 I charge you by the **L** that *this* epistle be 2962
5:28 The grace of our **L** Jesus Christ *be* with 2962
2Th 1: 1 in God our Father and the **L** Jesus Christ: 2962
1: 2 God our Father and the **L** Jesus Christ. 2962
1: 7 when the **L** Jesus shall be revealed from 2962
1: 8 that obey not the gospel of our **L** Jesus 2962
1: 9 destruction from the presence of the **L**, 2962
1:12 That the name of our **L** Jesus Christ may be 2962
1:12 grace of our God and the **L** Jesus Christ. 2962
2: 1 by the coming of our **L** Jesus Christ, and 2962
2: 8 whom the **L** shall consume with the spirit 2962
2:13 brethren beloved of the **L**, because God 2962
2:14 to the obtaining of the glory of our **L** Jesus 2962
2:16 Now our **L** Jesus Christ himself, and God, 2962
3: 1 that the word of the **L** may have *free* 2962
3: 3 But the **L** is faithful, who shall stablish 2962
3: 4 And we have confidence in the **L** touching 2962
3: 5 And the **L** direct your hearts into the love 2962
3: 6 brethren, in the name of our **L** Jesus Christ, 2962
3:12 and exhort by our **L** Jesus Christ, 2962
3:16 Now the **L** of peace himself give you peace 2962
3:16 always by all means. The **L** *be* with you all. 2962
3:18 The grace of our **L** Jesus Christ *be* with you 2962
1Ti 1: 1 and **L** Jesus Christ, *which is* our hope; 2962
1: 2 God our Father and Jesus Christ our **L**. 2962
1:12 And I thank Christ Jesus our **L**, who hath 2962
1:14 And the grace of our **L** was exceeding 2962
5:21 and the **L** Jesus Christ, and the elect angels, 2962
6: 3 *even* the *words* of our **L** Jesus Christ, and 2962
6:14 until the appearing of our **L** Jesus Christ: 2962
6:15 the King of kings, and **L** of lords; 2962
2Ti 1: 2 God the Father and Christ Jesus our **L**. 2962
1: 8 ashamed of the testimony of our **L**, 2962
1:16 The **L** give mercy unto the house of 2962
1:18 The **L** grant unto him that *he* may find 2962
1:18 that *he* may find mercy of the **L** in that day: 2962
2: 7 the **L** give thee understanding in all *things.* 2962
2:14 charging *them* before the **L** that *they* strive 2962
2:19 this seal, The **L** knoweth them that are his. 2962
2:22 with them that call on the **L** out of a pure 2962
2:24 And the servant of the **L** must not strive; 2962
3:11 but out of *them* all the **L** delivered me. 2962
4: 1 before God, and the **L** Jesus Christ, 2962
4: 8 which the **L**, the righteous judge, shall give 2962
4:14 the **L** reward him according to his works: 2962
4:17 Notwithstanding the **L** stood with me, and 2962
4:18 And the **L** shall deliver me from every evil 2962
4:22 The **L** Jesus Christ *be* with thy spirit. Grace 2962
Tit 1: 4 and the **L** Jesus Christ our Saviour. 2962
Phm 1: 3 God our Father and the **L** Jesus Christ. 2962
1: 5 which thou hast toward the **L** Jesus, and 2962
1:16 unto thee, both in the flesh, and in the **L**? 2962
1:20 brother, let me have joy of thee in the **L**: 2962
1:20 in the Lord: refresh my bowels in the **L**. 2962
1:25 The grace of our **L** Jesus Christ *be* with 2962
Heb 1:10 And, Thou, **L**, in the beginning hast laid 2962
2: 3 at the first began to be spoken by the **L**, 2962
7:14 For *it is* evident that our **L** sprang out of 2962
7:21 unto him, The **L** sware and will not repent, 2962
8: 2 which the **L** pitched, and not man. 2962
8: 8 Behold, the days come, saith the **L**, 2962
8: 9 and I regarded them not, saith the **L**. 2962
8:10 house of Israel after those days, saith the **L**; 2962
8:11 every man his brother, saying, Know the **L**: 2962
10:16 saith the **L**, I will put my laws into their 2962
10:30 unto me, I will recompense, saith the **L**. 2962
10:30 And again, The **L** shall judge his people. 2962
12: 5 despise not thou the chastening of the **L**, 2962
12: 6 For whom the **L** loveth he chasteneth, and 2962
12:14 without which no *man* shall see the **L**: 2962
13: 6 The **L** *is* my helper, and I will not fear what 2962
13:20 that brought again from the dead our **L** 2962
Jas 1: 1 a servant of God and of the **L** Jesus Christ, 2962
1: 7 that he shall receive any *thing* of the **L**. 2962
1:12 which the **L** hath promised to them that 2962
2: 1 have not the faith of our **L** Jesus Christ, 2962
2: 1 *the* ***L*** of glory, with respect of persons. NIG
4:10 Humble yourselves in the sight of the **L**, 2962
4:15 If the **L** will, we shall live, and do this, or 2962
5: 4 entered into the ears of the **L** of sabaoth. 2962
5: 7 brethren, unto the coming of the **L**. 2962
5: 8 for the coming of the **L** draweth nigh. 2962
5:10 who have spoken in the name of the **L**, 2962
5:11 of Job, and have seen the end of the **L**; 2962
5:11 that the **L** is very pitiful, and of tender 2962

Jas 5:14 anointing him with oil in the name of the **L**: *2962*
5:15 save the sick, and the **L** shall raise him up; *2962*
1Pe 1:3 the God and Father of our **L** Jesus Christ, *2962*
1:25 But the word of the **L** endureth for ever. *2962*
2:3 so be ye have tasted that the **L** *is* gracious. *2962*
3:6 as Sara obeyed Abraham, calling him **l**: *2962*
3:12 For the eyes of the **L** *are* over the righteous, *2962*
3:12 the face of the **L** *is* against them that do *2962*
3:15 But sanctify the **L** God in your hearts: and *2962*
2Pe 1:2 the knowledge of God, and of Jesus our **L**. *2962*
1:8 in the knowledge of our **L** Jesus Christ. *2962*
1:11 into the everlasting kingdom of our **L** *2962*
1:14 even as our **L** Jesus Christ hath shewed me. *2962*
1:16 and coming of our **L** Jesus Christ, *2962*
2:1 even denying the **L** that bought them, and *1203*
2:9 The **L** knoweth *how* to deliver the godly *2962*
2:11 accusation against them before the **L**. *2962*
2:20 the world through the knowledge of the **L** *2962*
3:2 commandment of us the apostles of the **L** *2962*
3:8 one day *is* with the **L** as a thousand years, *2962*
3:9 The **L** is not slack concerning *his* promise, *2962*
3:10 But the day of the **L** will come as a thief in *2962*
3:15 And account *that* the longsuffering of our **L** *2962*
3:18 and *in* the knowledge of our **L** and *2962*
2Jn 1:3 the Father, and from the **L** Jesus Christ, *2962*
Jude 1:4 and denying the only **L** God, and our Lord *1203*
1:4 the only Lord God, and our **L** Jesus Christ. *2962*
1:5 though ye once knew this, how that the **L**, *2962*
1:9 but said, The **L** rebuke thee. *2962*
1:14 the **L** cometh with ten thousands of his *2962*
1:17 before of the apostles of our **L** Jesus Christ; *2962*
1:21 looking for the mercy of our **L** Jesus Christ *2962*
Rev 1:8 saith the **L**, which is, and which was, and *2962*
4:8 saying, Holy, holy, holy, **L** God Almighty, *2962*
4:11 O **L**, to receive glory and honour and *2962*
6:10 saying, How long, O **L**, holy and true, *1203*
11:8 and Egypt, where also our **L** was crucified. *2962*
11:15 world are become *the kingdoms* of our **L**, *2962*
11:17 O **L** God Almighty, which art, and wast, *2962*
14:13 Blessed *are* the dead which die in the **L** *2962*
15:3 *are* thy works, **L** God Almighty; *2962*
15:4 not fear thee, O **L**, and glorify thy name? *2962*
16:5 O **L**, which art, and wast, and shalt be, *2962*
16:7 **L** God Almighty, true and righteous *are* thy *2962*
17:14 for he is **L** of lords, and King of kings: and *2962*
18:8 for strong *is* the **L** God who judgeth her. *2962*
19:1 honour, and power, unto the **L** our God: *2962*
19:6 for the **L** God Omnipotent reigneth. *2962*
19:16 KING OF KINGS, AND **L** OF LORDS. *2962*
21:22 for the **L** God Almighty and the Lamb are *2962*
22:5 of the sun; for the **L** God giveth them light: *2962*
22:6 the **L** God of the holy prophets sent his *2962*
22:20 Amen. Even so, come, **L** Jesus. *2962*
22:21 The grace of our **L** Jesus Christ *be* with you *2962*

L

LORD* (6469) [GOD*, JAH, JEHOVAH, LORD'S*; this is the proper name of God, *Yahweh* or *Jehovah*]

Ge 2:4 in the day that **the L** God made the earth 3068
2:5 for **the L** God had not caused it to rain 3068
2:7 **the L** God formed man *of* the dust of 3068
2:8 **the L** God planted a garden eastward in 3068
2:9 out of the ground made **the L** God to grow 3068
2:15 **the L** God took the man, and put him into 3068
2:16 **the L** God commanded the man, saying, 3068
2:18 **the L** God said, *It is* not good that the man 3068
2:19 out of the ground **the L** God formed every 3068
2:21 **the L** God caused a deep sleep to fall upon 3068
2:22 which **the L** God had taken from man, 3068
3:1 of the field which **the L** God had made. 3068
3:8 they heard the voice of **the L** God walking 3068
3:8 **the L** God amongst the trees of the garden. 3068
3:9 **the L** God called unto Adam, and said unto 3068
3:13 **the L** God said unto the woman, What *is* 3068
3:14 **the L** God said unto the serpent, 3068
3:21 to his wife did **the L** God make coats of 3068
3:22 **the L** God said, Behold, the man is become 3068
3:23 Therefore **the L** God sent him forth from 3068
4:1 and said, I have gotten a man from **the L**. 3068
4:3 fruit of the ground an offering unto **the L**. 3068
4:4 **the L** had respect unto Abel and to his 3068
4:6 **the L** said unto Cain, Why art thou wroth? 3068
4:9 **the L** said unto Cain, Where *is* Abel thy 3068
4:13 Cain said unto **the L**, My punishment *is* 3068
4:15 **the L** said unto him, Therefore whosoever 3068
4:15 **the L** set a mark upon Cain, lest any 3068
4:16 Cain went out from the presence of **the L**, 3068
4:26 began *men* to call upon the name of **the L**. 3068
5:29 of the ground which **the L** hath cursed. 3068
6:3 **the L** said, My spirit shall not always strive 3068
6:6 it repented **the L** that he had made man on 3068
6:7 **the L** said, I will destroy man whom I have 3068
6:8 But Noah found grace in the eyes of **the L**. 3068
7:1 **the L** said unto Noah, Come thou and 3068
7:5 Noah did according unto all that **the L** 3068
7:16 commanded him: and **the L** shut him in. 3068
8:20 Noah builded an altar unto **the L**; and 3068
8:21 **the L** smelled a sweet savour; and 3068
8:21 **the L** said in his heart, I will not again 3068
9:26 he said, Blessed *be* **the L** God of Shem; 3068
10:9 He was a mighty hunter before **the L**: 3068
10:9 as Nimrod the mighty hunter before **the L**. 3068
11:5 **the L** came down to see the city and 3068
11:6 **the L** said, Behold, the people *is* one, and 3068
11:8 So **the L** scattered them abroad from 3068
11:9 **the L** did there confound the language of 3068
11:9 from thence did **the L** scatter them abroad 3068
12:1 Now **the L** had said unto Abram, Get thee 3068
12:4 as **the L** had spoken unto him; 3068
12:7 **the L** appeared unto Abram, and said, 3068
12:7 there builded he an altar unto **the L**, 3068
12:8 there he builded an altar unto **the L**, and 3068
12:8 and called upon the name of **the L**. 3068
12:17 **the L** plagued Pharaoh and his house with 3068
Ge 13:4 there Abram called on the name of **the L**. 3068
13:10 before **the L** destroyed Sodom and 3068
13:10 and Gomorrah, *even* as the garden of **the L**, 3068
13:13 and sinners before **the L** exceedingly. 3068
13:14 **the L** said unto Abram, after that Lot was 3068
13:18 and built there an altar unto **the L**. 3068
14:22 I have lift up mine hand unto **the L**, 3068
15:1 After these things the word of **the L** came 3068
15:4 the word of **the L** *came* unto him, saying, 3068
15:6 he believed in **the L**; and he counted it to 3068
15:7 I *am* **the L** that brought thee out of Ur of 3068
15:18 In the same day **the L** made a covenant 3068
16:2 **the L** hath restrained me from bearing: 3068
16:5 her eyes: **the L** judge between me and thee. 3068
16:7 the angel of **the L** found her by a fountain 3068
16:9 the angel of **the L** said unto her, Return to 3068
16:10 the angel of **the L** said unto her, I will 3068
16:11 the angel of **the L** said unto her, Behold, 3068
16:11 because **the L** hath heard thy affliction. 3068
16:13 she called the name of **the L** that spake 3068
17:1 **the L** appeared to Abram, and said unto 3068
18:1 **the L** appeared unto him in the plains of 3068
18:13 **the L** said unto Abraham, Wherefore did 3068
18:14 Is any thing too hard for **the L**? At the time 3068
18:17 **the L** said, Shall I hide from Abraham *that* 3068
18:19 they shall keep the way of **the L**, to do 3068
18:19 that **the L** may bring upon Abraham that 3068
18:20 **the L** said, Because the cry of Sodom and 3068
18:22 but Abraham stood yet before **the L**. 3068
18:26 **the L** said, If I find in Sodom fifty 3068
18:33 **the L** went his way, as soon as he had left 3068
19:13 is waxen great before the face of **the L**; 3068
19:13 and **the L** hath sent us to destroy it. 3068
19:14 this place; for **the L** will destroy this city. 3068
19:16 **the L** being merciful unto him: 3068
19:24 **the L** rained upon Sodom and 3068
19:24 and fire from **the L** out of heaven; 3068
19:27 to the place where he stood before **the L**: 3068
20:18 For **the L** had fast closed up all the wombs 3068
21:1 **the L** visited Sarah as he had said, and 3068
21:1 and **the L** did unto Sarah as he had spoken. 3068
21:33 called there on the name of **the L**, 3068
22:11 the angel of **the L** called unto him out of 3068
22:14 In the mount of **the L** it shall be seen. 3068
22:15 the angel of **the L** called unto Abraham out 3068
22:16 saith **the L**, for because thou hast done this 3068
24:1 **the L** had blessed Abraham in all things. 3068
24:3 I will make thee swear by **the L**, the God of 3068
24:7 **The L** God of heaven, which took me from 3068
24:12 O **L** God of my master Abraham, I pray 3068
24:21 to wit whether **the L** had made his journey 3068
24:26 down his head, and worshipped **the L**. 3068
24:27 Blessed *be* **the L** God of my master 3068
24:27 **the L** led me to the house of my master's 3068
24:31 he said, Come in, thou blessed of **the L**; 3068
24:35 **the L** hath blessed my master greatly; and 3068
24:40 said unto me, **The L**, before whom I walk, 3068
24:42 and said, O **L** God of my master Abraham, 3068
24:44 *let* the same *be* the woman whom **the L** 3068
24:48 worshipped **the L**, and blessed the LORD 3068
24:48 blessed **the L** God of my master Abraham, 3068
24:50 and said, The thing proceedeth from **the L**: 3068
24:51 master's son's wife, as **the L** hath spoken. 3068
24:52 he worshipped **the L**, *bowing himself* to 3068
24:56 seeing **the L** hath prospered my way; 3068
25:21 Isaac intreated **the L** for his wife, because 3068
25:21 **the L** was intreated of him, and 3068
25:22 I thus? And she went to inquire of **the L**. 3068
25:23 **the L** said unto her, Two nations *are* in thy 3068
26:2 **the L** appeared unto him, and said, Go not 3068
26:12 an hundredfold: and **the L** blessed him. 3068
26:22 For now **the L** hath made room for us, and 3068
26:24 **the L** appeared unto him the same night, 3068
26:25 called upon the name of **the L**, and 3068
26:28 We saw certainly that **the L** was with thee: 3068
26:29 in peace: thou *art* now the blessed of **the L**. 3068
27:7 bless thee before **the L** before my death. 3068
27:20 Because **the L** thy God brought *it* to me. 3068
27:27 smell of a field which **the L** hath blessed: 3068
28:13 behold, **the L** stood above it, and said, I *am* 3068
28:13 I *am* **the L** God of Abraham thy father, and 3068
28:16 and he said, Surely **the L** is in this place; 3068
28:21 in peace; then shall **the L** be my God: 3068
29:31 when **the L** saw that Leah *was* hated, 3068
29:32 Surely **the L** hath looked upon my 3068
29:33 Because **the L** hath heard that I *was* hated, 3068
29:35 she said, Now will I praise **the L**: therefore 3068
30:24 said, **The L** shall add to me another son. 3068
30:27 that **the L** hath blessed me for thy sake. 3068
30:30 **the L** hath blessed thee since my coming: 3068
31:3 **the L** said unto Jacob, Return unto the land 3068
31:49 he said, **The L** watch between me and thee, 3068
32:9 father Isaac, **the L** which saidst unto me, 3068
38:7 was wicked in the sight of **the L**; 3068
38:7 sight of the LORD; and **the L** slew him. 3068
38:10 *the thing* which he did displeased **the L**: 3068
39:2 **the L** was with Joseph, and he was a 3068
39:3 his master saw that **the L** *was* with him, 3068
39:3 *that* **the L** made all that he did to prosper in 3068
39:5 that **the L** blessed the Egyptian's house for 3068
39:5 the blessing of **the L** was upon all that he 3068
39:21 **the L** was with Joseph, and shewed him 3068
39:23 because **the L** *was* with him, and 3068
39:23 *that* which he did, **the L** made *it* to prosper. 3068
49:18 I have waited for thy salvation, O **L**. 3068
Ex 3:2 the angel of **the L** appeared unto him in a 3068
3:4 when **the L** saw that he turned aside to see, 3068
3:7 **the L** said, I have surely seen the affliction 3068
3:15 **The L** God of your fathers, the God of 3068
3:16 say unto them, **The L** God of your fathers, 3068
3:18 **The L** God of the Hebrews hath met with 3068
3:18 that we may sacrifice to **the L** our God. 3068
4:1 **The L** hath not appeared unto thee. 3068
4:2 **the L** said unto him, What *is* that in thine 3068
4:4 **the L** said unto Moses, Put forth thine 3068
Ex 4:5 That they may believe that **the L** God of 3068
4:6 **the L** said furthermore unto him, Put now 3068
4:10 Moses said unto **the L**, O my Lord, I *am* 3068
4:11 **the L** said unto him, Who hath made man's 3068
4:11 the seeing, or the blind? have not I **the L**? 3068
4:14 the anger of **the L** was kindled against 3068
4:19 **the L** said unto Moses in Midian, Go, 3068
4:21 **the L** said unto Moses, When thou goest to 3068
4:22 Thus saith **the L**, Israel *is* my son, *even* my 3068
4:24 that **the L** met him, and sought to kill him. 3068
4:27 **the L** said to Aaron, Go into the wilderness 3068
4:28 Moses told Aaron all the words of **the L** 3068
4:30 Aaron spake all the words which **the L** had 3068
4:31 when they heard that **the L** had visited 3068
5:1 Thus saith **the L** God of Israel, 3068
5:2 Pharaoh said, Who *is* **the L**, that I should 3068
5:2 I know not **the L**, neither will I let Israel 3068
5:3 and sacrifice unto **the L** our God; 3068
5:17 ye say, Let us go *and* do sacrifice to **the L**. 3068
5:21 **The L** look upon you, and judge; 3068
5:22 Moses returned unto **the L**, and said, Lord, 3068
6:1 **the L** said unto Moses, Now shalt thou see 3068
6:2 unto Moses, and said unto him, I *am* **the L**: 3068
6:6 I *am* **the L**, and I will bring you out from 3068
6:7 ye shall know that I *am* **the L** your God, 3068
6:8 will give it you *for* an heritage: I *am* **the L**. 3068
6:10 And **the L** spake unto Moses, saying, 3068
6:12 Moses spake before **the L**, saying, Behold, 3068
6:13 **the L** spake unto Moses and unto Aaron, 3068
6:26 that Aaron and Moses, to whom **the L** said, 3068
6:28 it came to pass on the day *when* **the L** 3068
6:29 That **the L** spake unto Moses, saying, I *am* 3068
6:29 spake unto Moses, saying, I *am* **the L**: 3068
6:30 Moses said before **the L**, Behold, I *am* of 3068
7:1 **the L** said unto Moses, See, I have made 3068
7:5 the Egyptians shall know that I *am* **the L**, 3068
7:6 and Aaron did as **the L** commanded them, 3068
7:8 **the L** spake unto Moses and unto Aaron, 3068
7:10 and they did so as **the L** had commanded: 3068
7:13 hearkened not unto them; as **the L** had said. 3068
7:14 **the L** said unto Moses, Pharaoh's heart *is* 3068
7:16 **The L** God of the Hebrews hath sent me 3068
7:17 Thus saith **the L**, In this thou shalt know 3068
7:17 In this thou shalt know that I *am* **the L**: 3068
7:19 **the L** spake unto Moses, Say unto Aaron, 3068
7:20 and Aaron did so, as **the L** commanded; 3068
7:22 he hearken unto them; as **the L** had said. 3068
7:25 after *that* **the L** had smitten the river. 3068
8:1 **the L** spake unto Moses, Go unto Pharaoh, 3068
8:1 and say unto him, Thus saith **the L**, 3068
8:5 **the L** spake unto Moses, Say unto Aaron, 3068
8:8 and Aaron, and said, Intreat **the L**, 3068
8:8 that they may do sacrifice unto **the L**. 3068
8:10 that *there is* none like unto **the L** our God. 3068
8:12 Moses cried unto **the L** because of 3068
8:13 **the L** did according to the word of Moses; 3068
8:15 hearkened not unto them; as **the L** had said. 3068
8:16 **the L** said unto Moses, Say unto Aaron, 3068
8:19 hearkened not unto them; as **the L** had said. 3068
8:20 **the L** said unto Moses, Rise up early in 3068
8:20 say unto him, Thus saith **the L**, Let my 3068
8:22 that I *am* **the L** in the midst of the earth. 3068
8:24 **the L** did so; and there came a grievous 3068
8:26 of the Egyptians to **the L** our God: 3068
8:27 sacrifice to **the L** our God, as he shall 3068
8:28 that ye may sacrifice to **the L** your God in 3068
8:29 I will intreat **the L** that the swarms *of flies* 3068
8:29 letting the people go to sacrifice to **the L**. 3068
8:30 out from Pharaoh, and intreated **the L**. 3068
8:31 **the L** did according to the word of Moses; 3068
9:1 **the L** said unto Moses, Go in unto Pharaoh, 3068
9:1 Thus saith **the L** God of the Hebrews, 3068
9:3 the hand of **the L** is upon thy cattle which 3068
9:4 **the L** shall sever between the cattle of 3068
9:5 **the L** appointed a set time, saying, 3068
9:5 To morrow **the L** shall do this thing in 3068
9:6 **the L** did that thing on the morrow, and 3068
9:8 **the L** said unto Moses and unto Aaron, 3068
9:12 **the L** hardened the heart of Pharaoh, and 3068
9:12 as **the L** had spoken unto Moses. 3068
9:13 **the L** said unto Moses, Rise up early in 3068
9:13 Thus saith **the L** God of the Hebrews, 3068
9:20 He that feared the word of **the L** amongst 3068
9:21 he that regarded not the word of **the L** left 3068
9:22 **the L** said unto Moses, Stretch forth thine 3068
9:23 **the L** sent thunder and hail, and the fire ran 3068
9:23 **the L** rained hail upon the land of Egypt. 3068
9:27 **the L** *is* righteous, and I and my people *are* 3068
9:28 Intreat **the L** (for *it is* enough) that there be 3068
9:29 I will spread abroad my hands unto **the L**; 3068
9:30 I know that ye will not yet fear **the L** God. 3068
9:33 spread abroad his hands unto **the L**: 3068
9:35 of Israel go; as **the L** had spoken by Moses. 3068
10:1 **the L** said unto Moses, Go in unto Pharaoh: 3068
10:2 that ye may know how that I *am* **the L**. 3068
10:3 Thus saith **the L** God of the Hebrews, 3068
10:7 that they may serve **the L** their God: 3068
10:8 said unto them, Go, serve **the L** your God: 3068
10:9 we go; for we *must hold* a feast unto **the L**. 3068
10:10 Let **the L** be so with you, as I will let you 3068
10:11 go now ye *that are* men, and serve **the L**; 3068
10:12 **the L** said unto Moses, Stretch out thine 3068
10:13 **the L** brought an east wind upon the land 3068
10:16 I have sinned against **the L** your God, and 3068
10:17 only *this* once, and intreat **the L** your God, 3068
10:18 out from Pharaoh, and intreated **the L**. 3068
10:19 **the L** turned a mighty strong west wind, 3068
10:20 **the L** hardened Pharaoh's heart, so that he 3068
10:21 **the L** said unto Moses, Stretch out thine 3068
10:24 unto Moses, and said, Go ye, serve **the L**; 3068
10:25 that we may sacrifice unto **the L** our God. 3068
10:26 for thereof must we take to serve **the L** our 3068
10:26 know not with what we must serve **the L**, 3068
10:27 **the L** hardened Pharaoh's heart, and 3068
11:1 (And **the L** said unto Moses, Yet will I 3068

Ex 11: 3 **the L** gave the people favour in the sight of 3068
11: 4 Moses said, Thus saith **the L**, 3068
11: 7 that ye may know how that **the L** doth put 3068
11: 9 **the L** said unto Moses, Pharaoh shall not 3068
11:10 **the L** hardened Pharaoh's heart, so that he 3068
12: 1 **the L** spake unto Moses and Aaron in 3068
12:12 Egypt I will execute judgment: I *am* **the L**. 3068
12:14 you shall keep it a feast to **the L** throughout 3068
12:23 For **the L** will pass through to smite 3068
12:23 **the L** will pass over the door, and will not 3068
12:25 when ye be come to the land which **the L** 3068
12:28 did as **the L** had commanded Moses and 3068
12:29 that at midnight **the L** smote all 3068
12:31 and go, serve **the L**, as ye have said. 3068
12:36 **the L** gave the people favour in the sight of 3068
12:41 *that* all the hosts of **the L** went out from 3068
12:42 **the L** for bringing them out from the land 3068
12:42 this *is* that night of **the L** to be observed of 3068
12:43 **the L** said unto Moses and Aaron, This *is* 3068
12:48 will keep the passover to **the L**, let all his 3068
12:50 as **the L** commanded Moses and Aaron, so 3068
12:51 *that* **the L** did bring the children of Israel 3068
13: 1 And **the L** spake unto Moses, saying, 3068
13: 3 for by strength of hand **the L** brought you 3068
13: 5 it shall be when **the L** shall bring thee into 3068
13: 6 in the seventh day *shall be* a feast to **the L**. 3068
13: 8 of that *which* **the L** did unto me when I 3068
13: 9 for with a strong hand hath **the L** brought 3068
13:11 it shall be when **the L** shall bring thee into 3068
13:12 That thou shalt set apart unto **the L** all that 3068
13:14 By strength of hand **the L** brought us out 3068
13:15 that **the L** slew all the firstborn in the land 3068
13:15 I sacrifice to **the L** all that openeth 3068
13:16 for by strength of hand **the L** brought us 3068
13:21 **the L** went before them by day in a pillar 3068
14: 1 And **the L** spake unto Moses, saying, 3068
14: 4 the Egyptians may know that I *am* **the L**. 3068
14: 8 **the L** hardened the heart of Pharaoh king 3068
14:10 the children of Israel cried out unto **the L**. 3068
14:13 stand still, and see the salvation of **the L**, 3068
14:14 **The L** shall fight for you, and ye shall hold 3068
14:15 **the L** said unto Moses, Wherefore criest 3068
14:18 the Egyptians shall know that I *am* **the L**. 3068
14:21 **the L** caused the sea to go *back* by a strong 3068
14:24 that in the morning watch **the L** looked 3068
14:25 for **the L** fighteth for them against 3068
14:26 **the L** said unto Moses, Stretch out thine 3068
14:27 **the L** overthrew the Egyptians in the midst 3068
14:30 Thus **the L** saved Israel that day out of 3068
14:31 Israel saw *that* great work which **the L** did 3068
14:31 the people feared **the L**, and believed 3068
14:31 and believed **the L**, and his servant Moses. 3068
15: 1 the children of Israel this song unto **the L**, 3068
15: 1 spake, saying, I will sing unto **the L**, for he 3068
15: 2 **The L** *is* my strength and song, and he is 3050
15: 3 **The L** *is* a man of war: the LORD *is* his 3068
15: 3 LORD *is* a man of war: **the L** *is* his name. 3068
15: 6 Thy right hand, O **L**, is become glorious in 3068
15: 6 thy right hand, O **L**, hath dashed in pieces 3068
15:11 *is* like unto thee, O **L**, among the gods? 3068
15:16 pass over, O **L**, till the people pass over, 3068
15:17 *in* the place, O **L**, *which* thou hast made for 3068
15:18 **The L** shall reign for ever and ever. 3068
15:19 **the L** brought again the waters of the sea 3068
15:21 Miriam answered them, Sing ye to **the L**, 3068
15:25 he cried unto **the L**; and the LORD 3068
15:25 **the L** shewed him a tree, *which* when he 3068
15:26 hearken to the voice of **the L** thy God, 3068
15:26 for I *am* **the L** that healeth thee. 3068
16: 3 by the hand of **the L** in the land of Egypt, 3068
16: 4 said **the L** unto Moses, Behold, I will rain 3068
16: 6 ye shall know that **the L** hath brought you 3068
16: 7 then ye shall see the glory of **the L**; 3068
16: 7 he heareth your murmurings against **the L**: 3068
16: 8 *This shall be,* when **the L** shall give you in 3068
16: 8 for that **the L** heareth your murmurings 3068
16: 8 *are* not against us, but against **the L**. 3068
16: 9 children of Israel, Come near before **the L**: 3068
16:10 the glory of **the L** appeared in the cloud. 3068
16:11 And **the L** spake unto Moses, saying, 3068
16:12 ye shall know that I *am* **the L** your God. 3068
16:15 This *is* the bread which **the L** hath given 3068
16:16 This *is* the thing which **the L** hath 3068
16:23 This *is that* which **the L** hath said, 3068
16:23 *is* the rest of the holy sabbath unto **the L**: 3068
16:25 to day; for to day *is* a sabbath unto **the L**: 3068
16:28 **the L** said unto Moses, How long refuse ye 3068
16:29 for that **the L** hath given you the sabbath, 3068
16:32 This *is* the thing which **the L** commandeth, 3068
16:33 lay it up before **the L**, to be kept for your 3068
16:34 As **the L** commanded Moses, so Aaron laid 3068
17: 1 according to the commandment of **the L**, 3068
17: 2 with me? wherefore do ye tempt **the L**? 3068
17: 4 Moses cried unto **the L**, saying, What shall 3068
17: 5 **the L** said unto Moses, Go on before 3068
17: 7 because they tempted **the L**, saying, Is 3068
17: 7 Is **the L** amongst us, or not? 3068
17:14 **the L** said unto Moses, Write this *for* a 3068
17:16 Because **the L** hath sworn *that* the LORD 3050
17:16 Because the LORD hath sworn *that* **the L** 3068
18: 1 that **the L** had brought Israel out of Egypt; 3068
18: 8 Moses told his father in law all that **the L** 3068
18: 8 by the way, and *how* **the L** delivered them. 3068
18: 9 goodness which **the L** had done to Israel, 3068
18:10 Jethro said, Blessed *be* **the L**, who hath 3068
18:11 Now I know that **the L** *is* greater than all 3068
19: 3 **the L** called unto him out of the mountain, 3068
19: 7 these words which **the L** commanded him. 3068
19: 8 said, All that **the L** hath spoken we will do. 3068
19: 8 the words of the people unto **the L**. 3068
19: 9 **the L** said unto Moses, Lo, I come unto 3068
19: 9 told the words of the people unto **the L**. 3068
19:10 **the L** said unto Moses, Go unto the people, 3068
19:11 for the third day **the L** will come down in 3068
19:18 **the L** descended upon it in fire: 3068

Ex 19:20 **the L** came down upon mount Sinai, on 3068
19:20 **the L** called Moses *up* to the top of 3068
19:21 **the L** said unto Moses, Go down, 3068
19:21 lest they break through unto **the L** to gaze, 3068
19:22 which come near to **the L**, 3068
19:22 lest **the L** break forth upon them. 3068
19:23 Moses said unto **the L**, The people cannot 3068
19:24 **the L** said unto him, Away, get thee down, 3068
19:24 break through to come up unto **the L**, 3068
20: 2 I *am* **the L** thy God, which have brought 3068
20: 5 for I **the L** thy God *am* a jealous God, 3068
20: 7 Thou shalt not take the name of **the L** thy 3068
20: 7 for **the L** will not hold him guiltless that 3068
20:10 the seventh day *is* the sabbath of **the L** thy 3068
20:11 For *in* six days **the L** made heaven and 3068
20:11 wherefore **the L** blessed the sabbath day, 3068
20:12 the land which **the L** thy God giveth thee. 3068
20:22 **the L** said unto Moses, Thus thou shalt say 3068
22:11 *Then* shall an oath of **the L** be between 3068
22:20 save unto **the L** only, he shall be utterly 3068
23:19 shalt bring *into* the house of **the L** thy God. 3068
23:25 ye shall serve **the L** your God, and he shall 3068
24: 1 Come up unto **the L**, thou, and Aaron, 3068
24: 2 Moses alone shall come near **the L**: but 3068
24: 3 and told the people all the words of **the L**, 3068
24: 3 All the words which **the L** hath said will 3068
24: 4 Moses wrote all the words of **the L**, and 3068
24: 5 peace offerings *of* oxen unto **the L**. 3068
24: 7 All that **the L** hath said will we do, and 3068
24: 8 which **the L** hath made with you 3068
24:12 **the L** said unto Moses, Come up to me into 3068
24:16 the glory of **the L** abode upon mount Sinai, 3068
24:17 the sight of the glory of **the L** *was* like 3068
25: 1 And **the L** spake unto Moses, saying, 3068
27:21 it from evening to morning before **the L**: 3068
28:12 Aaron shall bear their names before **the L** 3068
28:29 for a memorial before **the L** continually. 3068
28:30 when he goeth in before **the L**: 3068
28:30 upon his heart before **the L** continually. 3068
28:35 goeth in unto the holy *place* before **the L**, 3068
28:36 of a signet, HOLINESS TO **THE L**. 3068
28:38 that they may be accepted before **the L**. 3068
29:11 thou shalt kill the bullock before **the L**, 3068
29:18 it *is* a burnt offering unto **the L**: it *is* a 3068
29:18 an offering made by fire unto **the L**. 3068
29:23 the unleavened bread that *is* before **the L**: 3068
29:24 them *for* a wave offering before **the L**. 3068
29:25 for a sweet savour before **the L**: 3068
29:25 it *is* an offering made by fire unto **the L**. 3068
29:26 wave it *for* a wave offering before **the L**: 3068
29:28 *even* their heave offering unto **the L**. 3068
29:41 an offering made by fire unto **the L**. 3068
29:42 of the congregation before **the L**: 3068
29:46 they shall know that I *am* **the L** their God, 3068
29:46 dwell amongst them: I *am* **the L** their God. 3068
30: 8 a perpetual incense before **the L** 3068
30:10 it *is* most holy unto **the L**. 3068
30:11 And **the L** spake unto Moses, saying, 3068
30:12 man a ransom for his soul unto **the L**, 3068
30:13 a half shekel *shall be* the offering of **the L**. 3068
30:14 above, shall give an offering unto **the L**. 3068
30:15 when *they* give an offering unto **the L**, 3068
30:16 unto the children of Israel before **the L**, 3068
30:17 And **the L** spake unto Moses, saying, 3068
30:20 to burn offering made by fire unto **the L**: 3068
30:22 Moreover **the L** spake unto Moses, saying, 3068
30:34 **the L** said unto Moses, Take unto thee 3068
30:37 it shall be unto thee holy for **the L**. 3068
31: 1 And **the L** spake unto Moses, saying, 3068
31:12 And **the L** spake unto Moses, saying, 3068
31:13 that *ye* may know that I *am* **the L** that doth 3068
31:15 *is* the sabbath of rest, holy to **the L**: 3068
31:17 for *in* six days **the L** made heaven and 3068
32: 5 and said, To morrow *is* a feast to **the L**. 3068
32: 7 **the L** said unto Moses, Go, get thee down; 3068
32: 9 **the L** said unto Moses, I have seen this 3068
32:11 Moses besought **the L** his God, and said, 3068
32:11 besought the LORD his God, and said, **L**, 3068
32:14 **the L** repented of the evil which he thought 3068
32:27 unto them, Thus saith **the L** God of Israel, 3068
32:29 Consecrate yourselves to day to **the L**, 3068
32:30 now I will go up unto **the L**; peradventure I 3068
32:31 Moses returned unto **the L**, and said, Oh, 3068
32:33 **the L** said unto Moses, Whosoever hath 3068
32:35 **the L** plagued the people, because they 3068
33: 1 **the L** said unto Moses, Depart, *and* go up 3068
33: 5 For **the L** had said unto Moses, Say unto 3068
33: 7 *that* every one which sought **the L** went out 3068
33: 9 the tabernacle, and *the* **L** talked with Moses. NIH
33:11 **the L** spake unto Moses face to face, as a 3068
33:12 Moses said unto **the L**, See, thou sayest 3068
33:17 **the L** said unto Moses, I will do this thing 3068
33:19 I will proclaim the name of **the L** before 3068
33:21 **the L** said, Behold, *there is* a place by me, 3068
34: 1 **the L** said unto Moses, Hew thee two 3068
34: 4 as **the L** had commanded him, and took in 3068
34: 5 **the L** descended in the cloud, and 3068
34: 5 and proclaimed the name of **the L**. 3068
34: 6 **the L** passed by before him, and 3068
34: 6 proclaimed, **The L**, The LORD God, 3068
34: 6 **The L** God, merciful and gracious, 3068
34:10 which thou *art* shall see the work of **the L**: 3068
34:14 for **the L**, whose name *is* Jealous, *is* a 3068
34:24 before **the L** thy God thrice in the year. 3068
34:26 bring *unto* the house of **the L** thy God. 3068
34:27 **the L** said unto Moses, Write thou these 3068
34:28 he was there with **the L** forty days and 3068
34:32 **the L** had spoken with him in mount Sinai. 3068
34:34 when Moses went in before **the L** to speak 3068
35: 1 These *are* the words which **the L** hath 3068
35: 2 you a holy *day*, a sabbath of rest to **the L**: 3068
35: 4 This *is* the thing which **the L** commanded, 3068
35: 5 from amongst you an offering unto **the L**: 3068
35: 5 let him bring it, an offering of **the L**; 3068
35:10 and make all that **the L** hath commanded; 3068

Ex 35:22 *offered* an offering of gold unto **the L**. 3068
35:29 brought a willing offering unto **the L**, 3068
35:29 which **the L** had commanded to be made 3068
35:30 **the L** hath called by name Bezaleel the son 3068
36: 1 in whom **the L** put wisdom and 3068
36: 1 according to all that **the L** had commanded. 3068
36: 2 in whose heart **the L** had put wisdom, 3068
36: 5 which **the L** commanded to make. 3068
38:22 made all that **the L** commanded Moses. 3068
39: 1 for Aaron; as **the L** commanded Moses. 3068
39: 5 twined linen; as **the L** commanded Moses. 3068
39: 7 of Israel; as **the L** commanded Moses. 3068
39:21 the ephod; as **the L** commanded Moses. 3068
39:26 to minister *in;* as **the L** commanded Moses. 3068
39:29 as **the L** commanded Moses. 3068
39:30 of a signet, HOLINESS TO **THE L**. 3068
39:31 the mitre; as **the L** commanded Moses. 3068
39:32 to all that **the L** commanded Moses, 3068
39:42 According to all that **the L** commanded 3068
39:43 they had done it as **the L** had commanded, 3068
40: 1 And **the L** spake unto Moses, saying, 3068
40:16 according to all that **the L** commanded 3068
40:19 above upon it; as **the L** commanded Moses. 3068
40:21 as **the L** commanded Moses. 3068
40:23 set the bread in order upon it before **the L**; 3068
40:23 as **the L** had commanded Moses. 3068
40:25 he lighted the lamps before **the L**; as 3068
40:25 the LORD; as **the L** commanded Moses. 3068
40:27 as **the L** commanded Moses. 3068
40:29 meat offering; as **the L** commanded Moses. 3068
40:32 they washed; as **the L** commanded Moses. 3068
40:34 and the glory of **the L** filled the tabernacle. 3068
40:35 the glory of **the L** filled the tabernacle. 3068
40:38 For the cloud of **the L** *was* upon 3068
Lev 1: 1 **the L** called unto Moses, and spake unto 3068
1: 2 man of you bring an offering unto **the L**, 3068
1: 3 of the congregation before **the L**. 3068
1: 5 he shall kill the bullock before **the L**: and 3068
1: 9 made by fire, of a sweet savour unto **the L**. 3068
1:11 side of the altar northward before **the L**: 3068
1:13 made by fire, of a sweet savour unto **the L**. 3068
1:14 for his offering to **the L** *be* of fowls, 3068
1:17 made by fire, of a sweet savour unto **the L**. 3068
2: 1 any will offer a meat offering unto **the L**, 3068
2: 2 made by fire, of a sweet savour unto **the L**: 3068
2: 3 holy of the offerings of **the L** made by fire. 3068
2: 8 that is made of these *things* unto **the L**: 3068
2: 9 made by fire, of a sweet savour unto **the L**. 3068
2:10 holy of the offerings of **the L** made by fire. 3068
2:11 which ye shall bring unto **the L**, 3068
2:11 *in* any offering of **the L** made by fire. 3068
2:12 ye shall offer them unto **the L**: 3068
2:14 a meat offering of *thy* firstfruits unto **the L**, 3068
2:16 *it is* an offering made by fire unto **the L**. 3068
3: 1 shall offer it without blemish before **the L**. 3068
3: 3 an offering made by fire unto **the L**; 3068
3: 5 made by fire, of a sweet savour unto **the L**. 3068
3: 6 peace offering unto **the L** *be* of the flock, 3068
3: 7 then shall he offer it before **the L**. 3068
3: 9 an offering made by fire unto **the L**; 3068
3:11 of the offering made by fire unto **the L**. 3068
3:12 a goat, then he shall offer it before **the L**. 3068
3:14 *even* an offering made by fire unto the **L**; 3068
4: 1 And **the L** spake unto Moses, saying, 3068
4: 2 **the L** (*concerning things* which ought not 3068
4: 3 blemish unto **the L** for a sin offering. 3068
4: 4 of the congregation before **the L**; 3068
4: 4 and kill the bullock before **the L**. 3068
4: 6 of the blood seven times before **the L**, 3068
4: 7 of the altar of sweet incense before **the L**, 3068
4:13 **the L** *concerning things* which should not 3068
4:15 upon the head of the bullock before **the L**: 3068
4:15 and the bullock shall be killed before **the L**. 3068
4:17 sprinkle *it* seven times before **the L**, 3068
4:18 the horns of the altar which *is* before **the L**, 3068
4:22 **the L** his God *concerning things* which 3068
4:24 they kill the burnt offering before **the L**: 3068
4:27 **the L** *concerning things* which ought not to 3068
4:31 the altar for a sweet savour unto **the L**; 3068
4:35 to the offerings made by fire unto **the L**; 3068
5: 6 unto **the L** for his sin which he hath sinned, 3068
5: 7 or two young pigeons, unto **the L**; 3068
5:12 to the offerings made by fire unto **the L**: 3068
5:14 And **the L** spake unto Moses, saying, 3068
5:15 in the holy *things* of **the L**; 3068
5:15 he shall bring for his trespass unto **the L** a 3068
5:17 to be done by the commandments of **the L**; 3068
5:19 he hath certainly trespassed against **the L**. 3068
6: 1 And **the L** spake unto Moses, saying, 3068
6: 2 commit a trespass against **the L**, and 3068
6: 6 shall bring his trespass offering unto **the L**, 3068
6: 7 make an atonement for him before **the L**: 3068
6: 8 And **the L** spake unto Moses, saying, 3068
6:14 sons of Aaron shall offer it before **the L**, 3068
6:15 *even* the memorial of it, unto **the L**. 3068
6:18 the offerings of **the L** made by fire: 3068
6:19 And **the L** spake unto Moses, saying, 3068
6:20 which they shall offer unto **the L** in the day 3068
6:21 thou offer *for* a sweet savour unto **the L**. 3068
6:22 *it is* a statute for ever unto **the L**; it shall be 3068
6:24 And **the L** spake unto Moses, saying, 3068
6:25 shall the sin offering be killed before **the L**: 3068
7: 5 *for* an offering made by fire unto **the L**: 3068
7:11 which he shall offer unto **the L**. 3068
7:14 oblation *for* a heave offering unto **the L**, 3068
7:20 that *pertain* unto **the L**, having his 3068
7:21 which *pertain* unto **the L**, even that soul 3068
7:22 And **the L** spake unto Moses, saying, 3068
7:25 offer an offering made by fire unto **the L**, 3068
7:28 And **the L** spake unto Moses, saying, 3068
7:29 **the L** shall bring his oblation unto 3068
7:29 **the L** of the sacrifice of his peace offerings. 3068
7:30 bring the offerings of **the L** made by fire, 3068
7:30 be waved *for* a wave offering before **the L**. 3068
7:35 out of the offerings of **the L** made by fire, 3068

L

Lev 7:35 to minister unto **the L** in the priest's office; 3068
7:36 Which **the L** commanded to be given them 3068
7:38 Which **the L** commanded Moses in mount 3068
7:38 of Israel to offer their oblations unto **the L**, 3068
8: 1 And **the L** spake unto Moses, saying, 3068
8: 4 Moses did as **the L** commanded him; and 3068
8: 5 This *is* the thing which **the L** commanded 3068
8: 9 holy crown; as **the L** commanded Moses. 3068
8:13 upon them; as **the L** commanded Moses. 3068
8:17 the camp; as **the L** commanded Moses. 3068
8:21 *and* an offering made by fire unto **the L**; 3068
8:21 the LORD; as **the L** commanded Moses. 3068
8:26 that *was* before **the L**, he took one 3068
8:27 them *for* a wave offering before **the L**. 3068
8:28 it *is* an offering made by fire unto **the L**. 3068
8:29 waved it *for* a wave offering before **the L**: 3068
8:29 Moses' part; as **the L** commanded Moses. 3068
8:34 this day, *so* **the L** hath commanded to do, 3068
8:35 keep the charge of **the L**, that ye die not: 3068
8:36 his sons did all things which **the L** 3068
9: 2 and offer *them* before **the L**. 3068
9: 4 peace offerings, to sacrifice before **the L**; 3068
9: 4 for to day **the L** will appear unto you. 3068
9: 5 drew near and stood before **the L**. 3068
9: 6 This *is* the thing which **the L** commanded 3068
9: 6 the glory of **the L** shall appear unto you. 3068
9: 7 atonement for them; as **the L** commanded. 3068
9:10 the altar; as **the L** commanded Moses. 3068
9:21 waved *for* a wave offering before **the L**; 3068
9:23 the glory of **the L** appeared unto all 3068
9:24 there came a fire out from before **the L**, 3068
10: 1 offered strange fire before **the L**, 3068
10: 2 there went out fire from **the L**, and 3068
10: 2 devoured them, and they died before **the L**. 3068
10: 3 This *is it* that **the L** spake, saying, 3068
10: 6 bewail the burning which **the L** hath 3068
10: 7 for the anointing oil of **the L** *is* upon you. 3068
10: 8 And **the L** spake unto Aaron, saying, 3068
10:11 **the L** hath spoken unto them by the hand of 3068
10:12 of the offerings of **the L** made by fire, 3068
10:13 of the sacrifices of **the L** made by fire: 3068
10:15 to wave *it for* a wave offering before **the L**; 3068
10:15 statute for ever; as **the L** hath commanded. 3068
10:17 to make atonement for them before **the L**? 3068
10:19 and their burnt offering before **the L**; 3068
10:19 it have been accepted in the sight of **the L**? 3068
11: 1 **the L** spake unto Moses and to Aaron, 3068
11:44 For I *am* **the L** your God: ye shall therefore 3068
11:45 For I *am* **the L** that bringeth you up out of 3068
12: 1 And **the L** spake unto Moses, saying, 3068
12: 7 Who shall offer it before **the L**, and 3068
13: 1 **the L** spake unto Moses and Aaron, saying, 3068
14: 1 And **the L** spake unto Moses, saying, 3068
14:11 those *things,* before **the L**, *at* the door of 3068
14:12 them *for* a wave offering before **the L**: 3068
14:16 with his finger seven times before **the L**: 3068
14:18 make an atonement for him before **the L**. 3068
14:23 of the congregation, before **the L**. 3068
14:24 them *for* a wave offering before **the L**: 3068
14:27 *is* in his left hand seven times before **the L**: 3068
14:29 to make an atonement for him before **the L**. 3068
14:31 for him that is to be cleansed before **the L**. 3068
14:33 **the L** spake unto Moses and unto Aaron, 3068
15: 1 **the L** spake unto Moses and to Aaron, 3068
15:14 come before **the L** unto the door of 3068
15:15 for him before **the L** for his issue. 3068
15:30 **the L** for the issue of her uncleanness. 3068
16: 1 **the L** spake unto Moses after the death of 3068
16: 1 when they offered before **the L**, and died; 3068
16: 2 **the L** said unto Moses, Speak unto Aaron 3068
16: 7 present them before **the L** *at* the door of 3068
16: 8 one lot for **the L**, and the other lot for 3068
16:10 shall be presented alive before **the L**, 3068
16:12 coals of fire from off the altar before **the L**, 3068
16:13 put the incense upon the fire before **the L**, 3068
16:18 go out unto the altar that *is* before **the L**, 3068
16:30 be clean from all your sins before **the L**. 3068
16:34 And he did as **the L** commanded Moses. 3068
17: 1 And **the L** spake unto Moses, saying, 3068
17: 2 This *is* the thing which **the L** hath 3068
17: 4 to offer an offering unto **the L** before 3068
17: 4 the LORD before the tabernacle of **the L**; 3068
17: 5 even that they may bring them unto **the L**, 3068
17: 5 offer them *for* peace offerings unto **the L**. 3068
17: 6 **the L** *at* the door of the tabernacle of 3068
17: 6 burn the fat for a sweet savour unto **the L**. 3068
17: 9 of the congregation, to offer it unto **the L**; 3068
18: 1 And **the L** spake unto Moses, saying, 3068
18: 2 and say unto them, I *am* **the L** your God. 3068
18: 4 to walk therein: I *am* **the L** your God. 3068
18: 5 a man do, he shall live in them: I *am* **the L**. 3068
18: 6 to uncover *their* nakedness: I *am* **the L**. 3068
18:21 profane the name of thy God: I *am* **the L**. 3068
18:30 yourselves therein: I *am* **the L** your God. 3068
19: 1 And **the L** spake unto Moses, saying, 3068
19: 2 be holy: for I **the L** your God *am* holy. 3068
19: 3 keep my sabbaths: I *am* **the L** your God. 3068
19: 4 molten gods: I *am* **the L** your God. 3068
19: 5 a sacrifice of peace offerings unto **the L**, 3068
19: 8 hath profaned the hallowed *thing* of **the L**: 3068
19:10 and stranger: I *am* **the L** your God. 3068
19:12 profane the name of thy God: I *am* **the L**. 3068
19:14 but shalt fear thy God: I *am* **the L**. 3068
19:16 the blood of thy neighbour: I *am* **the L**. 3068
19:18 love thy neighbour as thyself: I *am* **the L**. 3068
19:21 shall bring his trespass offering unto **the L**, 3068
19:22 **the L** for his sin which he hath done: 3068
19:24 shall be holy to praise **the L** *withal.* 3068
19:25 the increase thereof: I *am* **the L** your God. 3068
19:28 nor print any marks upon you: I *am* **the L**. 3068
19:30 and reverence my sanctuary: I *am* **the L**. 3068
19:31 be defiled by them: I *am* **the L** your God. 3068
19:32 the old man, and fear thy God: I *am* **the L**. 3068
19:34 in the land of Egypt: I *am* **the L** your God. 3068
19:36 I *am* **the L** your God, which brought you 3068

Lev 19:37 all my judgments, and do them: I *am* **the L**. 3068
20: 1 And **the L** spake unto Moses, saying, 3068
20: 7 and be ye holy: for I *am* **the L** your God. 3068
20: 8 do them: I *am* **the L** which sanctify you. 3068
20:24 I *am* **the L** your God, which have separated 3068
20:26 for I **the L** *am* holy, and have severed you 3068
21: 1 **the L** said unto Moses, Speak unto 3068
21: 6 for the offerings of **the L** made by fire, *and* 3068
21: 8 for I **the L**, which sanctify you, *am* holy. 3068
21:12 oil of his God *is* upon him: I *am* **the L**. 3068
21:15 his people: for I **the L** do sanctify him. 3068
21:16 And **the L** spake unto Moses, saying, 3068
21:21 to offer the offerings of **the L** made by fire: 3068
21:23 for I **the L** do sanctify them. 3068
22: 1 And **the L** spake unto Moses, saying, 3068
22: 2 which they hallow unto me: I *am* **the L**. 3068
22: 3 the children of Israel hallow unto **the L**, 3068
22: 3 be cut off from my presence: I *am* **the L**. 3068
22: 8 eat to defile *himself* therewith: I *am* **the L**. 3068
22: 9 if they profane it: I **the L** do sanctify them. 3068
22:15 of Israel, which they offer unto **the L**; 3068
22:16 when they eat their holy *things:* for I **the L** 3068
22:17 And **the L** spake unto Moses, saying, 3068
22:18 which they will offer unto **the L** for a burnt 3068
22:21 unto **the L** to accomplish *his* vow, 3068
22:22 ye shall not offer these unto **the L**, 3068
22:22 by fire of them upon the altar unto **the L**. 3068
22:24 Ye shall not offer unto **the L** that which is 3068
22:26 And **the L** spake unto Moses, saying, 3068
22:27 for an offering made by fire unto **the L**. 3068
22:29 offer a sacrifice of thanksgiving unto **the L**, 3068
22:30 none of it until the morrow: I *am* **the L**. 3068
22:31 and do them: I *am* **the L**. 3068
22:32 of Israel: I *am* **the L** which hallow you, 3068
22:33 land of Egypt, to be your God: I *am* **the L**. 3068
23: 1 And **the L** spake unto Moses, saying, 3068
23: 2 unto them, *Concerning* the feasts of **the L**, 3068
23: 3 the sabbath of **the L** in all your dwellings. 3068
23: 4 These *are* the feasts of **the L**, *even* holy 3068
23: 6 *is* the feast of unleavened bread unto **the L**: 3068
23: 8 made by fire unto **the L** seven days: 3068
23: 9 And **the L** spake unto Moses, saying, 3068
23:11 he shall wave the sheaf before **the L**, to be 3068
23:12 first year for a burnt offering unto **the L**. 3068
23:13 an offering made by fire unto **the L** *for* a 3068
23:16 shall offer a new meat offering unto **the L**. 3068
23:17 *they are* the firstfruits unto **the L**. 3068
23:18 shall be *for* a burnt offering unto **the L**, 3068
23:18 made by fire, of sweet savour unto **the L**. 3068
23:20 firstfruits *for* a wave offering before **the L**, 3068
23:20 they shall be holy to **the L** for the priest. 3068
23:22 and to the stranger: I *am* **the L** your God. 3068
23:23 And **the L** spake unto Moses, saying, 3068
23:25 offer an offering made by fire unto **the L**. 3068
23:26 And **the L** spake unto Moses, saying, 3068
23:27 offer an offering made by fire unto **the L**. 3068
23:28 to make an atonement for you before **the L** 3068
23:33 And **the L** spake unto Moses, saying, 3068
23:34 of tabernacles *for* seven days unto **the L**. 3068
23:36 offer an offering made by fire unto **the L**: 3068
23:36 offer an offering made by fire unto **the L**: 3068
23:37 These *are* the feasts of **the L**, which ye 3068
23:37 offer an offering made by fire unto **the L**, 3068
23:38 Beside the sabbaths of **the L**, and 3068
23:38 which ye give unto **the L**. 3068
23:39 ye shall keep a feast unto **the L** seven days: 3068
23:40 ye shall rejoice before **the L** your God 3068
23:41 ye shall keep it a feast unto **the L** seven 3068
23:43 of the land of Egypt: I *am* **the L** your God. 3068
23:44 the children of Israel the feasts of **the L**. 3068
24: 1 And **the L** spake unto Moses, saying, 3068
24: 3 unto the morning before **the L** continually: 3068
24: 4 pure candlestick before **the L** continually. 3068
24: 6 on a row, upon the pure table before **the L**. 3068
24: 7 *even* an offering made by fire unto **the L**. 3068
24: 8 set it in order before **the L** continually, 3068
24: 9 him of the offerings of **the L** made by fire, 3068
24:11 son blasphemed the name *of the* **L**, NIH
24:12 that the mind of **the L** might be shewed 3068
24:13 And **the L** spake unto Moses, saying, 3068
24:16 he that blasphemeth the name of **the L**, 3068
24:16 when he blasphemeth the name *of the* **L**, NIH
24:22 own country: for I *am* **the L** your God. 3068
24:23 the children of Israel did as **the L** 3068
25: 1 **the L** spake unto Moses in mount Sinai, 3068
25: 2 shall the land keep a sabbath unto **the L**. 3068
25: 4 of rest unto the land, a sabbath for **the L**: 3068
25:17 fear thy God: for I *am* **the L** your God. 3068
25:38 I *am* **the L** your God, which brought you 3068
25:55 of the land of Egypt: I *am* **the L** your God. 3068
26: 1 bow down unto it: for I *am* **the L** your God. 3068
26: 2 and reverence my sanctuary: I *am* **the L**. 3068
26:13 I *am* **the L** your God, which brought you 3068
26:44 with them: for I *am* **the L** their God. 3068
26:45 that *I* might be their God: I *am* **the L**. 3068
26:46 which **the L** made between him and 3068
27: 1 And **the L** spake unto Moses, saying, 3068
27: 2 the persons *shall be* for **the L** by thy 3068
27: 9 whereof *men* bring an offering unto **the L**, 3068
27: 9 all that *any man* giveth of such unto **the L** 3068
27:11 they do not offer a sacrifice unto **the L**, 3068
27:14 sanctify his house *to be* holy unto **the L**, 3068
27:16 if a man shall sanctify unto **the L** *some part* 3068
27:21 shall be holy unto **the L**, as a field devoted; 3068
27:22 if *a man* sanctify unto **the L** a field which 3068
27:23 in that day, *as* a holy *thing* unto **the L**. 3068
27:28 that a man shall devote unto **the L** of all 3068
27:28 devoted thing *is* most holy unto **the L**. 3068
27:30 *is* the LORD'S: *it is* holy unto **the L**. 3068
27:32 the rod, the tenth shall be holy unto **the L**. 3068
27:34 which **the L** commanded Moses for 3068
Nu 1: 1 **the L** spake unto Moses in the wilderness 3068
1:19 As **the L** commanded Moses, so 3068
1:48 For **the L** had spoken unto Moses, saying, 3068
1:54 to all that **the L** commanded Moses, 3068

Nu 2: 1 **the L** spake unto Moses and unto Aaron, 3068
2:33 of Israel; as **the L** commanded Moses. 3068
2:34 to all that **the L** commanded Moses: 3068
3: 1 Moses in the day that **the L** spake with 3068
3: 4 Nadab and Abihu died before **the L**, 3068
3: 4 they offered strange fire before **the L**, 3068
3: 5 And **the L** spake unto Moses, saying, 3068
3:11 And **the L** spake unto Moses, saying, 3068
3:13 and beast: mine they shall be: I *am* **the L**. 3068
3:14 **the L** spake unto Moses in the wilderness 3068
3:16 them according to the word of **the L**, 3068
3:39 numbered at the commandment of **the L**, 3068
3:40 **the L** said unto Moses, Number all 3068
3:41 shalt take the Levites for me (I *am* **the L**) 3068
3:42 as **the L** commanded him, 3068
3:44 And **the L** spake unto Moses, saying, 3068
3:45 and the Levites shall be mine: I *am* **the L**. 3068
3:51 to his sons, according to the word of **the L**, 3068
3:51 the LORD, as **the L** commanded Moses. 3068
4: 1 **the L** spake unto Moses and unto Aaron, 3068
4:17 **the L** spake unto Moses and unto Aaron, 3068
4:21 And **the L** spake unto Moses, saying, 3068
4:37 of **the L** by the hand of Moses. 3068
4:41 according to the commandment of **the L**. 3068
4:45 to the word of **the L** by the hand of Moses. 3068
4:49 According to the commandment of **the L** 3068
4:49 of him, as **the L** commanded Moses. 3068
5: 1 And **the L** spake unto Moses, saying, 3068
5: 4 as **the L** spake unto Moses, so did 3068
5: 5 And **the L** spake unto Moses, saying, 3068
5: 6 to do a trespass against **the L**, and 3068
5: 8 *let* the trespass *be* recompensed unto **the L**, 3068
5:11 And **the L** spake unto Moses, saying, 3068
5:16 bring her near, and set her before **the L**: 3068
5:18 the priest shall set the woman before **the L**, 3068
5:21 **The L** make thee a curse and an oath 3068
5:21 when **the L** doth make thy thigh to rot, and 3068
5:25 shall wave the offering before **the L**, and 3068
5:30 shall set the woman before **the L**, and 3068
6: 1 And **the L** spake unto Moses, saying, 3068
6: 2 to separate *themselves* unto **the L**: 3068
6: 5 the which he separateth *himself* unto **the L**, 3068
6: 6 unto **the L** he shall come at no dead body. 3068
6: 8 of his separation he *is* holy unto **the L**. 3068
6:12 he shall consecrate unto **the L** the days of 3068
6:14 he shall offer his offering unto **the L**, 3068
6:16 the priest shall bring *them* before **the L**, 3068
6:17 a sacrifice of peace offerings unto **the L**, 3068
6:20 them *for* a wave offering before **the L**: 3068
6:21 *of* his offering unto **the L** for his 3068
6:22 And **the L** spake unto Moses, saying, 3068
6:24 **The L** bless thee, and keep thee: 3068
6:25 **The L** make his face shine upon thee, and 3068
6:26 **The L** lift up his countenance upon thee, 3068
7: 3 they brought their offering before **the L**, 3068
7: 4 And **the L** spake unto Moses, saying, 3068
7:11 **the L** said unto Moses, They shall offer 3068
8: 1 And **the L** spake unto Moses, saying, 3068
8: 3 as **the L** commanded Moses. 3068
8: 4 according unto the pattern which **the L** had 3068
8: 5 And **the L** spake unto Moses, saying, 3068
8:10 thou shalt bring the Levites before **the L**: 3068
8:11 Aaron shall offer the Levites before **the L** 3068
8:11 that they may execute the service of **the L**. 3068
8:12 the other *for* a burnt offering, unto **the L**, 3068
8:13 and offer them *for* an offering unto **the L**. 3068
8:20 **the L** commanded Moses concerning 3068
8:21 offered them *as* an offering before **the L**; 3068
8:22 as **the L** had commanded Moses 3068
8:23 And **the L** spake unto Moses, saying, 3068
9: 1 **the L** spake unto Moses in the wilderness 3068
9: 5 according to all that **the L** commanded 3068
9: 7 that *we* may not offer an offering of **the L** 3068
9: 8 I will hear what **the L** will command 3068
9: 9 And **the L** spake unto Moses, saying, 3068
9:10 yet he shall keep the passover unto **the L**. 3068
9:13 he brought not the offering of **the L** in his 3068
9:14 and will keep the passover unto **the L**; 3068
9:18 At the commandment of **the L** the children 3068
9:18 at the commandment of **the L** they pitched: 3068
9:19 children of Israel kept the charge of **the L**, 3068
9:20 according to the commandment of **the L** 3068
9:20 according to the commandment of **the L** 3068
9:23 At the commandment of **the L** they rested 3068
9:23 at the commandment of **the L** they 3068
9:23 they kept the charge of **the L**, at 3068
9:23 at the commandment of **the L** by the hand 3068
10: 1 And **the L** spake unto Moses, saying, 3068
10: 9 ye shall be remembered before **the L** your 3068
10:10 before your God: I *am* **the L** your God. 3068
10:13 of **the L** by the hand of Moses. 3068
10:29 unto the place of which **the L** said, 3068
10:29 for **the L** hath spoken good concerning 3068
10:32 *that* what goodness **the L** shall do unto us, 3068
10:33 they departed from the mount of **the L** 3068
10:33 the ark of the covenant of **the L** went 3068
10:34 the cloud of **the L** *was* upon them by day, 3068
10:35 **L**, and let thine enemies be scattered; 3068
10:36 when it rested, he said, Return, O **L**, 3068
11: 1 the people complained, it displeased **the L**: 3068
11: 1 **the L** heard *it;* and his anger was kindled; 3068
11: 1 the fire of **the L** burnt among them, and 3068
11: 2 when Moses prayed unto **the L**, the fire 3068
11: 3 the fire of **the L** burnt among them. 3068
11:10 the anger of **the L** was kindled greatly; 3068
11:11 Moses said unto **the L**, Wherefore hast 3068
11:16 **the L** said unto Moses, Gather unto me 3068
11:18 for you have wept in the ears of **the L**, 3068
11:18 therefore **the L** will give you flesh, and 3068
11:20 that ye have despised **the L** which *is* 3068
11:23 **the L** said unto Moses, Is the LORD'S 3068
11:24 told the people the words of **the L**, and 3068
11:25 **the L** came down in a cloud, and 3068
11:29 that **the L** would put his spirit upon them! 3068
11:31 there went forth a wind from **the L**, and 3068

Nu 11:33 the wrath of **the L** was kindled against 3068
11:33 **the L** smote the people *with* a very great 3068
12: 2 Hath **the L** indeed spoken only by Moses? 3068
12: 2 not spoken also by us? And **the L** heard *it.* 3068
12: 4 **the L** spake suddenly unto Moses, and 3068
12: 5 **the L** came down in the pillar of the cloud, 3068
12: 6 *I* **the L** will make myself known unto him 3068
12: 8 and the similitude of **the L** shall he behold: 3068
12: 9 the anger of **the L** was kindled against 3068
12:13 Moses cried unto **the L**, saying, Heal her 3068
12:14 **the L** said unto Moses, If her father had 3068
13: 1 And **the L** spake unto Moses, saying, 3068
13: 3 Moses by the commandment of **the L** sent 3068
14: 3 wherefore *hath* **the L** brought us unto this 3068
14: 8 If **the L** delight in us, then he will bring us 3068
14: 9 Only rebel not ye against **the L**, 3068
14: 9 departed from them, and **the L** *is* with us: 3068
14:10 the glory of **the L** appeared in 3068
14:11 **the L** said unto Moses, How long will this 3068
14:13 Moses said unto **the L**, Then the Egyptians 3068
14:14 *for* they have heard that thou **L** *art* among 3068
14:14 that thou **L** *art* seen face to face, and 3068
14:16 Because **the L** was not able to bring this 3068
14:18 **The L** *is* longsuffering, and of great mercy, 3068
14:20 **the L** said, I have pardoned according to 3068
14:21 earth shall be filled *with* the glory of **the L**. 3068
14:26 **the L** spake unto Moses and unto Aaron, 3068
14:28 unto them, *As truly as* I live, saith **the L**, 3068
14:35 I **the L** have said, I will surely do it unto all 3068
14:37 the land, died by the plague before **the L**. 3068
14:40 will go up unto the place which **the L** hath 3068
14:41 ye transgress the commandment of **the L**? 3068
14:42 Go not up, for **the L** *is* not among you; 3068
14:43 because ye are turned away from **the L**, 3068
14:43 therefore **the L** will not be with you. 3068
14:44 the ark of the covenant of **the L**, 3068
15: 1 And **the L** spake unto Moses, saying, 3068
15: 3 will make an offering by fire unto **the L**, 3068
15: 3 to make a sweet savour unto **the L**, of 3068
15: 4 **the L** bring a meat offering of a tenth deal 3068
15: 7 hin *of* wine, *for* a sweet savour unto **the L**. 3068
15: 8 a vow, or peace offerings unto **the L**: 3068
15:10 made by fire, of a sweet savour unto **the L**. 3068
15:13 made by fire, of a sweet savour unto **the L**. 3068
15:14 made by fire, of a sweet savour unto **the L**; 3068
15:15 so shall the stranger be before **the L**. 3068
15:17 And **the L** spake unto Moses, saying, 3068
15:19 shall offer up a heave offering unto **the L**. 3068
15:21 **the L** a heave offering in your generations. 3068
15:22 which **the L** hath spoken unto Moses, 3068
15:23 *Even* all that **the L** hath commanded you 3068
15:23 from the day that **the L** commanded 3068
15:24 for a sweet savour unto **the L**, with his 3068
15:25 a sacrifice made by fire unto **the L**, and 3068
15:25 their sin offering before **the L**, for their 3068
15:28 when he sinneth by ignorance before **the L**, 3068
15:30 or a stranger, the same reproacheth **the L**; 3068
15:31 he hath despised the word of **the L**, 3068
15:35 **the L** said unto Moses, The man shall be 3068
15:36 and he died; as **the L** commanded Moses. 3068
15:37 And **the L** spake unto Moses, saying, 3068
15:39 remember all the commandments of **the L**, 3068
15:41 I *am* **the L** your God, which brought you 3068
15:41 to be your God: I *am* **the L** your God. 3068
16: 3 one of them, and **the L** *is* among them: 3068
16: 3 above the congregation of **the L**? 3068
16: 5 Even to morrow **the L** will shew who *are* 3068
16: 7 put incense in them before **the L** to 3068
16: 7 it shall be *that* the man whom **the L** doth 3068
16: 9 to do the service of the tabernacle of **the L**, 3068
16:11 *are* gathered together against **the L**: 3068
16:15 was very wroth, and said unto **the L**, 3068
16:16 Be thou and all thy company before **the L**, 3068
16:17 bring ye before **the L** every man his censer, 3068
16:19 the glory of **the L** appeared unto all 3068
16:20 **the L** spake unto Moses and unto Aaron, 3068
16:23 And **the L** spake unto Moses, saying, 3068
16:28 Hereby ye shall know that **the L** hath sent 3068
16:29 of all men; *then* **the L** hath not sent me. 3068
16:30 if **the L** make a new thing, and the earth 3068
16:30 that these men have provoked **the L**. 3068
16:35 there came out a fire from **the L**, and 3068
16:36 And **the L** spake unto Moses, saying, 3068
16:38 for they offered them before **the L**, 3068
16:40 come near to offer incense before **the L**; 3068
16:40 as **the L** said to him by the hand of Moses. 3068
16:41 Ye have killed the people of **the L**. 3068
16:42 covered it, and the glory of **the L** appeared. 3068
16:44 And **the L** spake unto Moses, saying, 3068
16:46 for there is wrath gone out from **the L**; 3068
17: 1 And **the L** spake unto Moses, saying, 3068
17: 7 Moses laid up the rods before **the L** in 3068
17: 9 before **the L** unto all the children of Israel: 3068
17:10 **the L** said unto Moses, Bring Aaron's rod 3068
17:11 Moses did *so:* as **the L** commanded him, 3068
17:13 near unto the tabernacle of **the L** shall die: 3068
18: 1 **the L** said unto Aaron, Thou and thy sons 3068
18: 6 to you *they are* given *as* a gift for **the L**, 3068
18: 8 **the L** spake unto Aaron, Behold, I also 3068
18:12 of them which they shall offer unto **the L**, 3068
18:13 which they shall bring unto **the L**, shall be 3068
18:15 which they bring unto **the L**, *whether it be* 3068
18:17 by fire, for a sweet savour unto **the L**. 3068
18:19 the children of Israel offer unto **the L**, 3068
18:19 it *is* a covenant of salt for ever before **the L** 3068
18:20 **the L** spake unto Aaron, Thou shalt have 3068
18:24 they offer *as* a heave offering unto **the L**, 3068
18:25 And **the L** spake unto Moses, saying, 3068
18:26 offer up a heave offering of it for **the L**, 3068
18:28 heave offering unto **the L** of all your tithes, 3068
18:29 shall offer every heave offering of **the L**, 3068
19: 1 **the L** spake unto Moses and unto Aaron, 3068
19: 2 of the law which **the L** hath commanded, 3068
19:13 defileth the tabernacle of **the L**; 3068
19:20 he hath defiled the sanctuary of **the L**: 3068

Nu 20: 3 died when our brethren died before **the L**! 3068
20: 4 congregation of **the L** into this wilderness, 3068
20: 6 and the glory of **the L** appeared unto them. 3068
20: 7 And **the L** spake unto Moses, saying, 3068
20: 9 Moses took the rod from before **the L**, 3068
20:12 **the L** spake unto Moses and Aaron, 3068
20:13 the children of Israel strove with **the L**, 3068
20:16 when we cried unto **the L**, he heard our 3068
20:23 **the L** spake unto Moses and Aaron in 3068
20:27 Moses did as **the L** commanded: and 3068
21: 2 Israel vowed a vow unto **the L**, and said, 3068
21: 3 **the L** hearkened to the voice of Israel, and 3068
21: 6 **the L** sent fiery serpents among the people, 3068
21: 7 for we have spoken against **the L**, and 3068
21: 7 pray unto **the L**, that he take away 3068
21: 8 **the L** said unto Moses, Make thee a fiery 3068
21:14 it is said in the book of the wars of **the L**, 3068
21:16 that *is* the well whereof **the L** spake unto 3068
21:34 **the L** said unto Moses, Fear him not: for I 3068
22: 8 word again, as **the L** shall speak unto me: 3068
22:13 for **the L** refuseth to give me leave to go 3068
22:18 I cannot go beyond the word of **the L** my 3068
22:19 that I may know what **the L** will say unto 3068
22:22 the angel of **the L** stood in the way for an 3068
22:23 the ass saw the angel of **the L** standing in 3068
22:24 the angel of **the L** stood in a path of 3068
22:25 when the ass saw the angel of **the L**, she 3068
22:26 the angel of **the L** went further, and 3068
22:27 when the ass saw the angel of **the L**, she 3068
22:28 **the L** opened the mouth of the ass, and 3068
22:31 Then **the L** opened the eyes of Balaam, and 3068
22:31 he saw the angel of **the L** standing in 3068
22:32 the angel of **the L** said unto him, 3068
22:34 Balaam said unto the angel of **the L**, I have 3068
22:35 the angel of **the L** said unto Balaam, 3068
23: 3 peradventure **the L** will come to meet me: 3068
23: 5 **the L** put a word in Balaam's mouth, and 3068
23: 8 shall I defy, *whom* **the L** hath not defied? 3068
23:12 that which **the L** hath put in my mouth? 3068
23:15 burnt offering, while I meet *the L* yonder. NIH
23:16 **the L** met Balaam, and put a word in his 3068
23:17 said unto him, What hath **the L** spoken? 3068
23:21 **the L** his God *is* with him, and the shout of 3068
23:26 saying, All that **the L** speaketh, that I must 3068
24: 1 when Balaam saw that it pleased **the L** to 3068
24: 6 as the trees of lign aloes *which* **the L** hath 3068
24:11 lo, **the L** hath kept thee back from honour. 3068
24:13 go beyond the commandment of **the L**, 3068
24:13 *but* what **the L** saith, that will I speak? 3068
25: 3 the anger of **the L** was kindled against 3068
25: 4 **the L** said unto Moses, Take all the heads 3068
25: 4 hang them up before **the L** against the sun, 3068
25: 4 that the fierce anger of **the L** may be turned 3068
25:10 And **the L** spake unto Moses, saying, 3068
25:16 And **the L** spake unto Moses, saying, 3068
26: 1 that **the L** spake unto Moses and 3068
26: 4 as **the L** commanded Moses and 3068
26: 9 of Korah, when they strove against **the L**: 3068
26:52 And **the L** spake unto Moses, saying, 3068
26:61 they offered strange fire before **the L**. 3068
26:65 For **the L** had said of them, They shall 3068
27: 3 against **the L** in the company of Korah; 3068
27: 5 Moses brought their cause before **the L**. 3068
27: 6 And **the L** spake unto Moses, saying, 3068
27:11 of judgment, as **the L** commanded Moses. 3068
27:12 **the L** said unto Moses, Get thee up into 3068
27:15 And Moses spake unto **the L**, saying, 3068
27:16 Let **the L**, the God of the spirits of all flesh, 3068
27:17 that the congregation of **the L** be not as 3068
27:18 **the L** said unto Moses, Take thee Joshua 3068
27:21 after the judgment of Urim before **the L**: 3068
27:22 Moses did as **the L** commanded him: and 3068
27:23 as **the L** commanded by the hand of Moses. 3068
28: 1 And **the L** spake unto Moses, saying, 3068
28: 3 by fire which ye shall offer unto **the L**; 3068
28: 6 a sacrifice made by fire unto **the L**. 3068
28: 7 be poured unto **the L** *for* a drink offering. 3068
28: 8 made by fire, *of* a sweet savour unto **the L**. 3068
28:11 ye shall offer a burnt offering unto **the L**; 3068
28:13 a sacrifice made by fire unto **the L**. 3068
28:15 a sin offering unto **the L** shall be offered, 3068
28:16 of the first month *is* the passover of **the L**. 3068
28:19 by fire *for* a burnt offering unto **the L**; 3068
28:24 made by fire, *of* a sweet savour unto **the L**: 3068
28:26 ye bring a new meat offering unto **the L**, 3068
28:27 offering for a sweet savour unto **the L**; 3068
29: 2 offering for a sweet savour unto **the L**; 3068
29: 6 a sacrifice made by fire unto **the L**. 3068
29: 8 ye shall offer a burnt offering unto **the L** 3068
29:12 ye shall keep a feast unto **the L** seven days: 3068
29:13 made by fire, *of* a sweet savour unto **the L**; 3068
29:36 made by fire, *of* a sweet savour unto **the L**: 3068
29:39 These *things* ye shall do unto **the L** in your 3068
29:40 to all that **the L** commanded Moses. 3068
30: 1 This *is* the thing which **the L** hath 3068
30: 2 If a man vow a vow unto **the L**, or 3068
30: 3 If a woman also vow a vow unto **the L**, and 3068
30: 5 **the L** shall forgive her, because her father 3068
30: 8 of none effect: and **the L** shall forgive her. 3068
30:12 them void; and **the L** shall forgive her. 3068
30:16 which **the L** commanded Moses, between a 3068
31: 1 And **the L** spake unto Moses, saying, 3068
31: 3 and avenge **the L** of Midian. 3068
31: 7 as **the L** commanded Moses; 3068
31:16 to commit trespass against **the L** in 3068
31:16 a plague among the congregation of **the L**. 3068
31:21 *is* the ordinance of the law which **the L** 3068
31:25 And **the L** spake unto Moses, saying, 3068
31:28 levy a tribute unto **the L** of the men of war 3068
31:29 the priest, *for* a heave offering of **the L**. 3068
31:30 keep the charge of the tabernacle of **the L**. 3068
31:31 Eleazar the priest did as **the L** commanded 3068
31:41 the priest, as **the L** commanded Moses. 3068
31:47 kept the charge of the tabernacle of **the L**; 3068
31:47 the LORD; as **the L** commanded Moses. 3068

Nu 31:50 therefore brought an oblation for **the L**, 3068
31:50 an atonement for our souls before **the L**. 3068
31:52 the offering that they offered up to **the L**, 3068
31:54 for the children of Israel before **the L**. 3068
32: 4 *Even* the country which **the L** smote before 3068
32: 7 into the land which **the L** hath given them? 3068
32: 9 into the land which **the L** had given them. 3068
32:12 for they have wholly followed **the L**. 3068
32:13 that had done evil in the sight of **the L**, 3068
32:14 to augment yet the fierce anger of **the L** 3068
32:20 if ye will go armed before **the L** to war, 3068
32:21 all of you armed over Jordan before **the L**, 3068
32:22 And the land be subdued before **the L**: then 3068
32:22 be guiltless before **the L**, and before Israel; 3068
32:22 land shall be your possession before **the L**. 3068
32:23 behold, ye have sinned against **the L**: 3068
32:27 before **the L** to battle, as my lord saith. 3068
32:29 before **the L**, and the land shall be subdued 3068
32:31 As **the L** hath said unto thy servants, so 3068
32:32 We will pass over armed before **the L** *into* 3068
33: 2 journeys by the commandment of **the L**: 3068
33: 4 which **the L** had smitten among them: 3068
33: 4 upon their gods also **the L** executed 3068
33:38 mount Hor at the commandment of **the L**, 3068
33:50 **the L** spake unto Moses in the plains of 3068
34: 1 And **the L** spake unto Moses, saying, 3068
34:13 which **the L** commanded to give unto 3068
34:16 And **the L** spake unto Moses, saying, 3068
34:29 These *are they* whom **the L** commanded to 3068
35: 1 **the L** spake unto Moses in the plains of 3068
35: 9 And **the L** spake unto Moses, saying, 3068
35:34 for I **the L** dwell among the children of 3068
36: 2 **The L** commanded my lord to give the land 3068
36: 2 my lord was commanded by **the L** to give 3068
36: 5 of Israel according to the word of **the L**, 3068
36: 6 This *is* the thing which **the L** doth 3068
36:10 Even as **the L** commanded Moses, so 3068
36:13 which **the L** commanded by the hand of 3068
Dt 1: 3 according unto all that **the L** had given him 3068
1: 6 **The L** our God spake unto us in Horeb, 3068
1: 8 possess the land which **the L** sware unto 3068
1:10 **The L** your God hath multiplied you, and 3068
1:11 (**The L** God of your fathers make you a 3068
1:19 as **the L** our God commanded us; 3068
1:20 which **the L** our God doth give unto us. 3068
1:21 **the L** thy God hath set the land before thee: 3068
1:21 possess *it,* as **the L** God of thy fathers hath 3068
1:25 *It is* a good land which **the L** our God doth 3068
1:26 rebelled against the commandment of **the L** 3068
1:27 and said, Because **the L** hated us, 3068
1:30 **The L** your God which goeth before you, 3068
1:31 where thou hast seen how that **the L** thy 3068
1:32 Yet in this thing ye did not believe **the L** 3068
1:34 **the L** heard the voice of your words, and 3068
1:36 because he hath wholly followed **the L**. 3068
1:37 Also **the L** was angry with me for your 3068
1:41 unto me, We have sinned against **the L**, 3068
1:41 according to all that **the L** our God 3068
1:42 **the L** said unto me, Say unto them, Go not 3068
1:43 against the commandment of **the L**, 3068
1:45 And ye returned and wept before **the L**; but 3068
1:45 **the L** would not hearken to your voice, 3068
2: 1 of the Red sea, as **the L** spake unto me: 3068
2: 2 And **the L** spake unto me, saying, 3068
2: 7 For **the L** thy God hath blessed thee in all 3068
2: 7 these forty years **the L** thy God *hath been* 3068
2: 9 **the L** said unto me, Distress not 3068
2:12 which **the L** gave unto them.) 3068
2:14 among the host, as **the L** sware unto them. 3068
2:15 For indeed the hand of **the L** was against 3068
2:17 That **the L** spake unto me, saying, 3068
2:21 **the L** destroyed them before them; and 3068
2:29 the land which **the L** our God giveth us 3068
2:30 for **the L** thy God hardened his spirit, and 3068
2:31 **the L** said unto me, Behold, I have begun 3068
2:33 **the L** our God delivered him before us; 3068
2:36 for us: **the L** our God delivered all unto us: 3068
2:37 nor *unto* whatsoever **the L** our God forbad 3068
3: 2 **the L** said unto me, Fear him not: for I will 3068
3: 3 So **the L** our God delivered into our hands 3068
3:18 **The L** your God hath given you this land to 3068
3:20 Until **the L** have given rest unto your 3068
3:20 *until* they also possess the land which **the L** 3068
3:21 Thine eyes have seen all that **the L** your 3068
3:21 shall **the L** do unto all the kingdoms 3068
3:22 for **the L** your God he shall fight for you. 3068
3:23 And I besought **the L** at that time, saying, 3068
3:26 **the L** was wroth with me for your sakes, 3068
3:26 **the L** said unto me, Let it suffice thee; 3068
4: 1 possess the land which **the L** God of your 3068
4: 2 of **the L** your God which I command you. 3068
4: 3 Your eyes have seen what **the L** did 3068
4: 3 **the L** thy God hath destroyed them from 3068
4: 4 ye that did cleave unto **the L** your God *are* 3068
4: 5 even as **the L** my God commanded me, 3068
4: 7 as **the L** our God *is* in all *things that* we 3068
4:10 stoodest before **the L** thy God in Horeb, 3068
4:10 when **the L** said unto me, Gather me 3068
4:12 **the L** spake unto you out of the midst of 3068
4:14 **the L** commanded me at that time to teach 3068
4:15 **the L** spake unto you in Horeb out of 3068
4:19 which **the L** thy God hath divided unto all 3068
4:20 **the L** hath taken you, and brought you 3068
4:21 Furthermore **the L** was angry with me for 3068
4:21 which **the L** thy God giveth thee *for* an 3068
4:23 lest ye forget the covenant of **the L** your 3068
4:23 the likeness of any *thing,* which **the L** thy 3068
4:24 For **the L** thy God *is* a consuming fire, 3068
4:25 shall do evil in the sight of **the L** thy God, 3068
4:27 **the L** shall scatter you among the nations, 3068
4:27 the heathen, whither **the L** shall lead you. 3068
4:29 if from thence thou shalt seek **the L** thy 3068
4:30 if thou turn to **the L** thy God, and shalt be 3068
4:31 (For **the L** thy God *is* a merciful God;) 3068
4:34 according to all that **the L** your God did for 3068

Dt	4:35	that thou mightest know that **the L** he *is*	3068
	4:39	that **the L** he *is* God in heaven above, and	3068
	4:40	which **the L** thy God giveth thee, for ever.	3068
	5: 2	**The L** our God made a covenant with us in	3068
	5: 3	**The L** made not this covenant with our	3068
	5: 4	**The L** talked with you face to face in	3068
	5: 5	(I stood between **the L** and you at that	3068
	5: 5	at that time, to shew you the word of **the L**:	3068
	5: 6	I *am* **the L** thy God, which brought thee out	3068
	5: 9	for I **the L** thy God *am* a jealous God,	3068
	5:11	Thou shalt not take the name of **the L** thy	3068
	5:11	for **the L** will not hold *him* guiltless that	3068
	5:12	as **the L** thy God hath commanded thee.	3068
	5:14	the seventh day *is* the sabbath of **the L** thy	3068
	5:15	*that* **the L** thy God brought thee out thence	3068
	5:15	**the L** thy God commanded thee to keep	3068
	5:16	as **the L** thy God hath commanded thee;	3068
	5:16	in the land which **the L** thy God giveth	3068
	5:22	These words **the L** spake unto all your	3068
	5:24	**the L** our God hath shewed us his glory	3068
	5:25	if we hear the voice of **the L** our God any	3068
	5:27	and hear all that **the L** our God shall say:	3068
	5:27	speak thou unto us all that **the L** our God	3068
	5:28	**the L** heard the voice of your words,	3068
	5:28	**the L** said unto me, I have heard the voice	3068
	5:32	as **the L** your God hath commanded you:	3068
	5:33	You shall walk in all the ways which **the L**	3068
	6: 1	which **the L** your God commanded to teach	3068
	6: 2	That thou mightest fear **the L** thy God,	3068
	6: 3	as **the L** God of thy fathers hath promised	3068
	6: 4	O Israel: **The L** our God *is* one LORD:	3068
	6: 4	O Israel: The LORD our God *is* one **L**:	3068
	6: 5	thou shalt love **the L** thy God with all thine	3068
	6:10	when **the L** thy God shall have brought	3068
	6:12	*Then* beware lest thou forget **the L**,	3068
	6:13	Thou shalt fear **the L** thy God, and	3068
	6:15	(For **the L** thy God *is* a jealous God among	3068
	6:15	lest the anger of **the L** thy God be kindled	3068
	6:16	Ye shall not tempt **the L** your God, as ye	3068
	6:17	the commandments of **the L** your God,	3068
	6:18	*is* right and good in the sight of **the L**:	3068
	6:18	possess the good land which **the L** sware	3068
	6:19	from before thee, as **the L** hath spoken.	3068
	6:20	which **the L** our God hath commanded	3068
	6:21	**the L** brought us out of Egypt with a	3068
	6:22	**the L** shewed signs and wonders, great	3068
	6:24	**the L** commanded us to do all these	3068
	6:24	to fear **the L** our God, for our good always,	3068
	6:25	commandments before **the L** our God,	3068
	7: 1	When **the L** thy God shall bring thee into	3068
	7: 2	when **the L** thy God shall deliver them	3068
	7: 4	will the anger of **the L** be kindled against	3068
	7: 6	For thou *art* a holy people unto **the L** thy	3068
	7: 6	**the L** thy God hath chosen thee to be a	3068
	7: 7	**The L** did not set his love upon you,	3068
	7: 8	because **the L** loved you, and because	3068
	7: 8	hath **the L** brought you out with a mighty	3068
	7: 9	Know therefore that **the L** thy God, he *is*	3068
	7:12	that **the L** thy God shall keep unto thee	3068
	7:15	**the L** will take away from thee all sickness,	3068
	7:16	which **the L** thy God shall deliver thee;	3068
	7:18	shalt well remember what **the L** thy God	3068
	7:19	where*by* **the L** thy God brought thee out:	3068
	7:19	shall **the L** thy God do unto all the people	3068
	7:20	Moreover **the L** thy God will send	3068
	7:21	for **the L** thy God *is* among you, a mighty	3068
	7:22	**the L** thy God will put out those nations	3068
	7:23	**the L** thy God shall deliver them unto thee,	3068
	7:25	for it *is* an abomination to **the L** thy God.	3068
	8: 1	possess the land which **the L** sware unto	3068
	8: 2	**the L** thy God led thee these forty years in	3068
	8: 3	out of the mouth of **the L** doth man live.	3068
	8: 5	his son, *so* **the L** thy God chasteneth thee.	3068
	8: 6	keep the commandments of **the L** thy God,	3068
	8: 7	For **the L** thy God bringeth thee into a	3068
	8:10	thou shalt bless **the L** thy God for the good	3068
	8:11	Beware that thou forget not **the L** thy God,	3068
	8:14	be lifted up, and thou forget **the L** thy God,	3068
	8:18	thou shalt remember **the L** thy God: for *it*	3068
	8:19	if thou do at all forget **the L** thy God, and	3068
	8:20	As the nations which **the L** destroyeth	3068
	8:20	obedient unto the voice of **the L** your God.	3068
	9: 3	that **the L** thy God *is* he which goeth over	3068
	9: 3	them quickly, as **the L** hath said unto thee.	3068
	9: 4	after that **the L** thy God hath cast them out	3068
	9: 4	For my righteousness **the L** hath brought	3068
	9: 4	for the wickedness of these nations **the L**	3068
	9: 5	for the wickedness of these nations **the L**	3068
	9: 5	that he may perform the word which **the L**	3068
	9: 6	that **the L** thy God giveth thee not this	3068
	9: 7	how thou provokedst **the L** thy God to	3068
	9: 7	ye have been rebellious against **the L**.	3068
	9: 8	Also in Horeb ye provoked **the L** to wrath,	3068
	9: 8	that **the L** was angry with you to have	3068
	9: 9	*even* the tables of the covenant which **the L**	3068
	9:10	**the L** delivered unto me two tables of stone	3068
	9:10	which **the L** spake with you in the mount	3068
	9:11	*that* **the L** gave me the two tables of stone,	3068
	9:12	**the L** said unto me, Arise, get thee down	3068
	9:13	Furthermore **the L** spake unto me, saying,	3068
	9:16	ye had sinned against **the L** your God, *and*	3068
	9:16	the way which **the L** had commanded you.	3068
	9:18	And I fell down before **the L**, as at the first,	3068
	9:18	in doing wickedly in the sight of **the L**,	3068
	9:19	where*with* **the L** was wroth against you to	3068
	9:19	**the L** hearkened unto me at that time also.	3068
	9:20	**the L** was very angry with Aaron to have	3068
	9:22	ye provoked **the L** to wrath.	3068
	9:23	Likewise when **the L** sent you from	3068
	9:23	the commandment of **the L** your God,	3068
	9:24	You have been rebellious against **the L**	3068
	9:25	Thus I fell down before **the L** forty days	3068
	9:25	**the L** had said he would destroy you.	3068
	9:26	I prayed therefore unto **the L**, and said,	3068
	9:28	Because **the L** was not able to bring them	3068
Dt	10: 1	At that time **the L** said unto me, Hew thee	3068
	10: 4	which **the L** spake unto you in the mount	3068
	10: 4	and **the L** gave them unto me.	3068
	10: 5	and there they be, as **the L** commanded me.	3068
	10: 8	At that time **the L** separated the tribe of	3068
	10: 8	to bear the ark of the covenant of **the L**,	3068
	10: 8	to stand before **the L** to minister unto him,	3068
	10: 9	**the L** *is* his inheritance, according as	3068
	10: 9	according as **the L** thy God promised him.	3068
	10:10	**the L** hearkened unto me at that time also,	3068
	10:10	*and* **the L** would not destroy thee.	3068
	10:11	**the L** said unto me, Arise, take thy journey	3068
	10:12	what doth **the L** thy God require of thee,	3068
	10:12	to fear **the L** thy God, to walk in all his	3068
	10:12	to serve **the L** thy God with all thy heart	3068
	10:13	To keep the commandments of **the L**, and	3068
	10:15	Only **the L** had a delight in thy fathers to	3068
	10:17	For **the L** your God *is* God of gods, and	3068
	10:20	Thou shalt fear **the L** thy God; him shalt	3068
	10:22	now **the L** thy God hath made thee as	3068
	11: 1	Therefore thou shalt love **the L** thy God,	3068
	11: 2	seen the chastisement of **the L** your God,	3068
	11: 4	*how* **the L** hath destroyed them unto this	3068
	11: 7	all the great acts of **the L** which he did.	3068
	11: 9	which **the L** sware unto your fathers to	3068
	11:12	A land which **the L** thy God careth for:	3068
	11:12	the eyes of **the L** thy God *are* always upon	3068
	11:13	to love **the L** your God, and to serve him	3068
	11:17	off the good land which **the L** giveth you.	3068
	11:21	in the land which **the L** sware unto your	3068
	11:22	to do them, to love **the L** your God, to walk	3068
	11:23	will **the L** drive out all these nations from	3068
	11:25	*for* **the L** your God shall lay the fear of you	3068
	11:27	if ye obey the commandments of **the L**	3068
	11:28	the commandments of **the L** your God,	3068
	11:29	when **the L** thy God hath brought thee in	3068
	11:31	the land which **the L** your God giveth you,	3068
	12: 1	which **the L** God of thy fathers giveth thee	3068
	12: 4	Ye shall not do so unto **the L** your God.	3068
	12: 5	unto the place which **the L** your God shall	3068
	12: 7	there ye shall eat before **the L** your God,	3068
	12: 7	where*in* **the L** thy God hath blessed thee.	3068
	12: 9	which **the L** your God giveth you.	3068
	12:10	dwell in the land which **the L** your God	3068
	12:11	there shall be a place which **the L** your	3068
	12:11	choice vows which ye vow unto **the L**:	3068
	12:12	ye shall rejoice before **the L** your God,	3068
	12:14	in the place which **the L** shall choose in	3068
	12:15	according to the blessing of **the L** thy God	3068
	12:18	thou must eat them before **the L** thy God in	3068
	12:18	place which **the L** thy God shall choose,	3068
	12:18	thou shalt rejoice before **the L** thy God in	3068
	12:20	When **the L** thy God shall enlarge thy	3068
	12:21	If the place which **the L** thy God hath	3068
	12:21	of thy flock, which **the L** hath given thee,	3068
	12:25	do *that which is* right in the sight of **the L**.	3068
	12:26	go unto the place which **the L** shall choose:	3068
	12:27	the blood, upon the altar of **the L** thy God:	3068
	12:27	poured out upon the altar of **the L** thy God,	3068
	12:28	and right in the sight of **the L** thy God.	3068
	12:29	When **the L** thy God shall cut off	3068
	12:31	Thou shalt not do so unto **the L** thy God:	3068
	12:31	for every abomination to **the L**, which he	3068
	13: 3	for **the L** your God proveth you, to know	3068
	13: 3	to know whether you love **the L** your God	3068
	13: 4	Ye shall walk after **the L** your God, and	3068
	13: 5	to turn *you* away from **the L** your God,	3068
	13: 5	to thrust thee out of the way which **the L**	3068
	13:10	to thrust thee away from **the L** thy God,	3068
	13:12	which **the L** thy God hath given thee to	3068
	13:16	spoil thereof every whit, for **the L** thy God:	3068
	13:17	that **the L** may turn from the fierceness of	3068
	13:18	shalt hearken to the voice of **the L** thy God,	3068
	13:18	*which is* right in the eyes of **the L** thy God.	3068
	14: 1	Ye *are* the children of **the L** your God:	3068
	14: 2	For thou *art* a holy people unto **the L** thy	3068
	14: 2	**the L** hath chosen thee to be a peculiar	3068
	14:21	for thou *art* a holy people unto **the L** thy	3068
	14:23	thou shalt eat before **the L** thy God, in	3068
	14:23	that thou mayest learn to fear **the L** thy	3068
	14:24	which **the L** thy God shall choose to set his	3068
	14:24	when **the L** thy God hath blessed thee:	3068
	14:25	shalt go unto the place which **the L** thy	3068
	14:26	thou shalt eat there before **the L** thy God,	3068
	14:29	that **the L** thy God may bless thee in all	3068
	15: 4	for **the L** shall greatly bless thee in the land	3068
	15: 4	**the L** thy God giveth thee *for* an	3068
	15: 5	hearken unto the voice of **the L** thy God,	3068
	15: 6	For **the L** thy God blesseth thee, as he	3068
	15: 7	thy land which **the L** thy God giveth thee,	3068
	15: 9	he cry unto **the L** against thee, and it be sin	3068
	15:10	that for this thing **the L** thy God shall bless	3068
	15:14	*of that* where*with* **the L** thy God hath	3068
	15:15	and **the L** thy God redeemed thee:	3068
	15:18	**the L** thy God shall bless thee in all that	3068
	15:19	of thy flock thou shalt sanctify unto **the L**	3068
	15:20	Thou shalt eat it before **the L** thy God year	3068
	15:20	year in the place which **the L** shall choose,	3068
	15:21	thou shalt not sacrifice it unto **the L** thy	3068
	16: 1	and keep the passover unto **the L** thy God:	3068
	16: 1	for in the month of Abib **the L** thy God	3068
	16: 2	sacrifice the passover unto **the L** thy God,	3068
	16: 2	in the place which **the L** shall choose to	3068
	16: 5	thy gates, which **the L** thy God giveth thee:	3068
	16: 6	at the place which **the L** thy God shall	3068
	16: 7	eat *it* in the place which **the L** thy God	3068
	16: 8	*be* a solemn assembly to **the L** thy God:	3068
	16:10	**the L** thy God *with* a tribute of a freewill	3068
	16:10	which thou shalt give *unto the L thy God,*	NIH
	16:10	as **the L** thy God hath blessed thee:	3068
	16:11	thou shalt rejoice before **the L** thy God,	3068
	16:11	in the place which **the L** thy God hath	3068
	16:15	**the L** thy God in the place which	3068
	16:15	God in the place which **the L** shall choose:	3068
	16:15	**the L** thy God shall bless thee in all thy	3068
Dt	16:16	**the L** thy God in the place which he shall	3068
	16:16	they shall not appear before **the L** empty:	3068
	16:17	according to the blessing of **the L** thy God	3068
	16:18	which **the L** thy God giveth thee,	3068
	16:20	inherit the land which **the L** thy God giveth	3068
	16:21	trees near unto the altar of **the L** thy God,	3068
	16:22	up *any* image; which **the L** thy God hateth.	3068
	17: 1	Thou shalt not sacrifice unto **the L** thy God	3068
	17: 1	for that *is* an abomination unto **the L** thy	3068
	17: 2	within any of thy gates which **the L** thy	3068
	17: 2	wickedness in the sight of **the L** thy God,	3068
	17: 8	get thee up into the place which **the L** thy	3068
	17:10	which *they* of that place which **the L** shall	3068
	17:12	to minister there before **the L** thy God,	3068
	17:14	the land which **the L** thy God giveth thee,	3068
	17:15	whom **the L** thy God shall choose:	3068
	17:16	forasmuch as **the L** hath said unto you,	3068
	17:19	that he may learn to fear **the L** his God,	3068
	18: 1	they shall eat the offerings of **the L** made	3068
	18: 2	**the L** *is* their inheritance, as he hath said	3068
	18: 5	For **the L** thy God hath chosen him out of	3068
	18: 5	to stand to minister in the name of **the L**,	3068
	18: 6	unto the place which **the L** shall choose;	3068
	18: 7	he shall minister in the name of **the L** his	3068
	18: 7	Levites *do,* which stand there before **the L**.	3068
	18: 9	the land which **the L** thy God giveth thee,	3068
	18:12	these *things are* an abomination unto **the L**:	3068
	18:12	of these abominations **the L** thy God doth	3068
	18:13	Thou shalt be perfect with **the L** thy God.	3068
	18:14	**the L** thy God hath not suffered thee so	3068
	18:15	**The L** thy God will raise up unto thee a	3068
	18:16	**the L** thy God in Horeb in the day of	3068
	18:16	Let me not hear again the voice of **the L**	3068
	18:17	**the L** said unto me, They have well *spoken*	3068
	18:21	How shall we know the word which **the L**	3068
	18:22	a prophet speaketh in the name of **the L**,	3068
	18:22	that *is* the thing which **the L** hath not	3068
	19: 1	When **the L** thy God hath cut off	3068
	19: 1	whose land **the L** thy God giveth thee,	3068
	19: 2	which **the L** thy God giveth thee to possess	3068
	19: 3	which **the L** thy God giveth thee to inherit,	3068
	19: 8	if **the L** thy God enlarge thy coast, as he	3068
	19: 9	to love **the L** thy God, and to walk ever in	3068
	19:10	which **the L** thy God giveth thee *for* an	3068
	19:14	that **the L** thy God giveth thee to possess it.	3068
	19:17	the controversy *is,* shall stand before **the L**,	3068
	20: 1	for **the L** thy God *is* with thee,	3068
	20: 4	For **the L** your God *is* he that goeth with	3068
	20:13	when **the L** thy God hath delivered it into	3068
	20:14	which **the L** thy God hath given thee.	3068
	20:16	which **the L** thy God doth give thee *for* an	3068
	20:17	as **the L** thy God hath commanded thee:	3068
	20:18	so should ye sin against **the L** your God.	3068
	21: 1	**the L** thy God giveth thee to possess it,	3068
	21: 5	for them **the L** thy God hath chosen to	3068
	21: 5	unto him, and to bless in the name of **the L**;	3068
	21: 8	Be merciful, O **L**, unto thy people Israel,	3068
	21: 9	do *that which is* right in the sight of **the L**.	3068
	21:10	**the L** thy God hath delivered them into	3068
	21:23	which **the L** thy God giveth thee *for* an	3068
	22: 5	so *are* abomination unto **the L** thy God.	3068
	23: 1	not enter into the congregation of **the L**.	3068
	23: 2	not enter into the congregation of **the L**;	3068
	23: 2	he not enter into the congregation of **the L**.	3068
	23: 3	not enter into the congregation of **the L**;	3068
	23: 3	into the congregation of **the L** for ever:	3068
	23: 5	Nevertheless **the L** thy God would not	3068
	23: 5	**the L** thy God turned the curse into a	3068
	23: 5	because **the L** thy God loved thee.	3068
	23: 8	of **the L** *in* their third generation.	3068
	23:14	For **the L** thy God walketh in the midst of	3068
	23:18	*into* the house of **the L** thy God for any	3068
	23:18	these *are* abomination unto **the L** thy God.	3068
	23:20	that **the L** thy God may bless thee in all	3068
	23:21	When thou shalt vow a vow unto **the L** thy	3068
	23:21	for **the L** thy God will surely require it of	3068
	23:23	according as thou hast vowed unto **the L**	3068
	24: 4	for that *is* abomination before **the L**:	3068
	24: 4	which **the L** thy God giveth thee *for* an	3068
	24: 9	Remember what **the L** thy God did unto	3068
	24:13	unto thee before **the L** thy God.	3068
	24:15	lest he cry against thee unto **the L**, and it be	3068
	24:18	and **the L** thy God redeemed thee thence:	3068
	24:19	that **the L** thy God may bless thee in all	3068
	25:15	the land which **the L** thy God giveth thee.	3068
	25:16	*are* an abomination unto **the L** thy God.	3068
	25:19	when **the L** thy God hath given thee rest	3068
	25:19	in the land which **the L** thy God giveth thee	3068
	26: 1	**the L** thy God giveth thee *for* an	3068
	26: 2	thou shalt bring of thy land that **the L**	3068
	26: 2	shalt go unto the place which **the L** thy	3068
	26: 3	I profess *this* day unto **the L** thy God,	3068
	26: 3	**the L** sware unto our fathers for to give us.	3068
	26: 4	set it down before the altar of **the L** thy	3068
	26: 5	shalt speak and say before **the L** thy God,	3068
	26: 7	when we cried unto **the L** God of our	3068
	26: 7	**the L** heard our voice, and looked on our	3068
	26: 8	**the L** brought us forth out of Egypt with a	3068
	26:10	the land, which thou, O **L**, hast given me.	3068
	26:10	thou shalt set it before **the L** thy God, and	3068
	26:10	and worship before **the L** thy God:	3068
	26:11	which **the L** thy God hath given unto thee,	3068
	26:13	thou shalt say before **the L** thy God, I have	3068
	26:14	I have hearkened to the voice of **the L** my	3068
	26:16	This day **the L** thy God hath commanded	3068
	26:17	Thou hast avouched **the L** *this* day to be	3068
	26:18	**the L** hath avouched thee *this* day to be his	3068
	26:19	be a holy people unto **the L** thy God,	3068
	27: 2	the land which **the L** thy God giveth thee,	3068
	27: 3	the land which **the L** thy God giveth thee,	3068
	27: 3	as **the L** God of thy fathers hath promised	3068
	27: 5	there shalt thou build an altar unto **the L**	3068
	27: 6	Thou shalt build the altar of **the L** thy God	3068
	27: 6	burnt offerings thereon unto **the L** thy God:	3068
	27: 7	eat there, and rejoice before **the L** thy God.	3068

Dt 27: 9 art become the people of **the L** thy God. 3068
27:10 therefore obey the voice of **the L** thy God, 3068
27:15 molten image, an abomination unto **the L**, 3068
28: 1 diligently unto the voice of **the L** thy God, 3068
28: 1 that **the L** thy God will set thee on high 3068
28: 2 hearken unto the voice of **the L** thy God. 3068
28: 7 **The L** shall cause thine enemies that rise 3068
28: 8 **The L** shall command the blessing upon 3068
28: 8 he shall bless thee in the land which **the L** 3068
28: 9 **The L** shall establish thee a holy people 3068
28: 9 keep the commandments of **the L** thy God, 3068
28:10 that thou art called by the name of **the L**; 3068
28:11 **the L** shall make thee plenteous in goods, 3068
28:11 in the land which **the L** sware unto thy 3068
28:12 **The L** shall open unto thee his good 3068
28:13 **the L** shall make thee the head, and not 3068
28:13 unto the commandments of **the L** thy God, 3068
28:15 hearken unto the voice of **the L** thy God, 3068
28:20 **The L** shall send upon thee cursing, 3068
28:21 **The L** shall make the pestilence cleave 3068
28:22 **The L** shall smite thee with a consumption, 3068
28:24 **The L** shall make the rain of thy land 3068
28:25 **The L** shall cause thee *to be* smitten before 3068
28:27 **The L** will smite thee with the botch of 3068
28:28 **The L** shall smite thee with madness, and 3068
28:35 **The L** shall smite thee in the knees, and 3068
28:36 **The L** shall bring thee, and thy king which 3068
28:37 among all nations whither **the L** shall lead 3068
28:45 not unto the voice of **the L** thy God, 3068
28:47 Because thou servedst not **the L** thy God 3068
28:48 which **the L** shall send against thee, 3068
28:49 **The L** shall bring a nation against thee 3068
28:52 which **the L** thy God hath given thee. 3068
28:53 which **the L** thy God hath given thee, in 3068
28:58 and fearful name, **THE L** THY GOD; 3068
28:59 **the L** will make thy plagues wonderful, 3068
28:61 them will **the L** bring upon thee, until thou 3068
28:62 thou wouldest not obey the voice of **the L** 3068
28:63 *that* as **the L** rejoiced over you to do you 3068
28:63 **the L** will rejoice over you to destroy you, 3068
28:64 **the L** shall scatter thee among all people, 3068
28:65 **the L** shall give thee there a trembling 3068
28:68 **the L** shall bring thee *into* Egypt again with 3068
29: 1 which **the L** commanded Moses to make 3068
29: 2 Ye have seen all that **the L** did before your 3068
29: 4 Yet **the L** hath not given you a heart to 3068
29: 6 that ye might know that I *am* **the L** your 3068
29:10 Ye stand *this* day all of you before **the L** 3068
29:12 enter into covenant with **the L** thy God, 3068
29:12 which **the L** thy God maketh with thee *this* 3068
29:15 here with us *this* day before **the L** our God, 3068
29:18 turneth away *this* day from **the L** our God, 3068
29:20 **The L** will not spare him, but then 3068
29:20 then the anger of **the L** and his jealousy 3068
29:20 **the L** shall blot out his name from under 3068
29:21 **the L** shall separate him unto evil out of all 3068
29:22 the sicknesses which **the L** hath laid upon 3068
29:23 which **the L** overthrew in his anger, and 3068
29:24 Wherefore hath **the L** done thus unto this 3068
29:25 the covenant of **the L** God of their fathers, 3068
29:27 the anger of **the L** was kindled against this 3068
29:28 **the L** rooted them out of their land in 3068
29:29 The secret *things belong* unto **the L** our 3068
30: 1 whither **the L** thy God hath driven thee, 3068
30: 2 shalt return unto **the L** thy God, and 3068
30: 3 then **the L** thy God will turn thy captivity, 3068
30: 3 whither **the L** thy God hath scattered thee. 3068
30: 4 from thence will **the L** thy God gather thee, 3068
30: 5 **the L** thy God will bring thee into the land 3068
30: 6 **the L** thy God will circumcise thine heart, 3068
30: 6 to love **the L** thy God with all thine heart, 3068
30: 7 **the L** thy God will put all these curses 3068
30: 8 shalt return and obey the voice of **the L**, 3068
30: 9 **the L** thy God will make thee plenteous in 3068
30: 9 for **the L** will again rejoice over thee for 3068
30:10 hearken unto the voice of **the L** thy God, 3068
30:10 if thou turn unto **the L** thy God with all 3068
30:16 thee *this* day to love **the L** thy God, 3068
30:16 **the L** thy God shall bless thee in the land 3068
30:20 That thou mayest love **the L** thy God, *and* 3068
30:20 land which **the L** sware unto thy fathers, 3068
31: 2 also **the L** hath said unto me, Thou shalt 3068
31: 3 **The L** thy God, he will go over before thee, 3068
31: 3 go over before thee, as **the L** hath said. 3068
31: 4 **the L** shall do unto them as he did to Sihon 3068
31: 5 **the L** shall give them up before your face, 3068
31: 6 for **the L** thy God, he *it is* that doth go with 3068
31: 7 **the L** hath sworn unto their fathers to give 3068
31: 8 **the L**, he *it is* that doth go before thee; 3068
31: 9 bare the ark of the covenant of **the L**, 3068
31:11 **the L** thy God in the place which he shall 3068
31:12 fear **the L** your God, and observe to do all 3068
31:13 may hear, and learn to fear **the L** your God, 3068
31:14 **the L** said unto Moses, Behold, thy days 3068
31:15 **the L** appeared in the tabernacle in a pillar 3068
31:16 **the L** said unto Moses, Behold, thou shalt 3068
31:25 bare the ark of the covenant of **the L**, 3068
31:26 the ark of the covenant of **the L** your God, 3068
31:27 ye have been rebellious against **the L**; 3068
31:29 ye will do evil in the sight of **the L**, 3068
32: 3 Because I will publish the name of **the L**: 3068
32: 6 Do ye thus requite **the L**, O foolish people 3068
32:12 *So* **the L** alone did lead him, and *there was* 3068
32:19 when **the L** saw *it*, he abhorred *them*, 3068
32:27 is high, and **the L** hath not done all this. 3068
32:30 sold them, and **the L** had shut them up? 3068
32:36 For **the L** shall judge his people, and 3068
32:48 **the L** spake unto Moses that selfsame day, 3068
33: 2 **The L** came from Sinai, and rose up from 3068
33: 7 he said, Hear, **L**, the voice of Judah, and 3068
33:11 Bless, **L**, his substance, and accept 3068
33:12 The beloved of **the L** shall dwell in safety 3068
33:12 *and the L* shall cover him all the day long, NIH
33:13 he said, Blessed of **the L** *be* his land, 3068
33:21 he executed the justice of **the L**, and 3068

Dt 33:23 and full *with* the blessing of **the L**: 3068
33:29 *is* like unto thee, O people saved by **the L**, 3068
34: 1 **the L** shewed him all the land of Gilead, 3068
34: 4 **the L** said unto him, This *is* the land which 3068
34: 5 So Moses the servant of **the L** died there in 3068
34: 5 of Moab, according to the word of **the L**. 3068
34: 9 and did as **the L** commanded Moses. 3068
34:10 whom **the L** knew face to face, 3068
34:11 which **the L** sent him to do in the land of 3068
Jos 1: 1 Moses the servant of **the L** it came to pass, 3068
1: 1 that **the L** spake unto Joshua the son of 3068
1: 9 for **the L** thy God *is* with thee 3068
1:11 which **the L** your God giveth you to 3068
1:13 the servant of **the L** commanded you, 3068
1:13 **The L** your God hath given you rest, and 3068
1:15 Until **the L** have given your brethren rest, 3068
1:15 land which **the L** your God giveth them: 3068
1:17 only **the L** thy God be with thee, as he was 3068
2: 9 I know that **the L** hath given you the land, 3068
2:10 For we have heard how **the L** dried up 3068
2:11 for **the L** your God, he *is* God in heaven 3068
2:12 I pray you, swear unto me by **the L**, 3068
2:14 shall be, when **the L** hath given us the land, 3068
2:24 Truly **the L** hath delivered into our hands 3068
3: 3 the ark of the covenant of **the L** your God, 3068
3: 5 for to morrow **the L** will do wonders 3068
3: 7 **the L** said unto Joshua, This day will I 3068
3: 9 and hear the words of **the L** your God. 3068
3:13 feet of the priests that bear the ark of **the L**, 3068
3:17 **the L** stood firm on dry *ground* in the midst 3068
4: 1 that **the L** spake unto Joshua, saying, 3068
4: 5 Pass over before the ark of **the L** your God 3068
4: 7 off before the ark of the covenant of **the L**; 3068
4: 8 of Jordan, as **the L** spake unto Joshua, 3068
4:10 until every thing was finished that **the L** 3068
4:11 that the ark of **the L** passed over, and 3068
4:13 war passed over before **the L** unto battle, 3068
4:14 On that day **the L** magnified Joshua in 3068
4:15 And **the L** spake unto Joshua, saying, 3068
4:18 **the L** were come up out of the midst of 3068
4:23 For **the L** your God dried up the waters of 3068
4:23 as **the L** your God did to the Red sea, 3068
4:24 of the earth might know the hand of **the L**, 3068
4:24 that ye might fear **the L** your God for ever. 3068
5: 1 heard that **the L** had dried up the waters of 3068
5: 2 At that time **the L** said unto Joshua, 3068
5: 6 because they obeyed not the voice of **the L**: 3068
5: 6 unto whom **the L** sware that *he* would not 3068
5: 6 which **the L** sware unto their fathers that he 3068
5: 9 **the L** said unto Joshua, *This* day have I 3068
5:14 *as* captain of the host of **the L** am I now 3068
6: 2 **the L** said unto Joshua, See, I have given 3068
6: 6 of rams' horns before the ark of **the L**. 3068
6: 7 is armed pass on before the ark of **the L**. 3068
6: 8 of rams' horns passed on before **the L**, 3068
6: 8 the ark of the covenant of **the L** followed 3068
6:11 So the ark of **the L** compassed the city, 3068
6:12 and the priests took up the ark of **the L**. 3068
6:13 before the ark of **the L** went on continually, 3068
6:13 the rereward came after the ark of **the L**, 3068
6:16 Shout; for **the L** hath given you the city. 3068
6:17 *even* it, and all that *are* therein, to **the L**: 3068
6:19 and iron, *are* consecrated unto **the L**: 3068
6:19 they shall come *into* the treasury of **the L**. 3068
6:24 put *into* the treasury of the house of **the L**. 3068
6:26 saying, Cursed *be* the man before **the L**, 3068
6:27 So **the L** was with Joshua; and his fame 3068
7: 1 the anger of **the L** was kindled against 3068
7: 6 before the ark of **the L** until the eventide, 3068
7:10 **the L** said unto Joshua, Get thee up; 3068
7:13 for thus saith **the L** God of Israel, *There is* 3068
7:14 *that* the tribe which **the L** taketh shall come 3068
7:14 the family which **the L** shall take shall 3068
7:14 the household which **the L** shall take shall 3068
7:15 he hath transgressed the covenant of **the L**, 3068
7:19 glory to **the L** God of Israel, and 3068
7:20 Indeed I have sinned against **the L** God of 3068
7:23 of Israel, and laid them out before **the L**. 3068
7:25 **the L** shall trouble thee this day. And all 3068
7:26 So **the L** turned from the fierceness of his 3068
8: 1 **the L** said unto Joshua, Fear not, neither be 3068
8: 7 for **the L** your God will deliver it into your 3068
8: 8 according to the commandment of **the L** 3068
8:18 **the L** said unto Joshua, Stretch out 3068
8:27 according unto the word of **the L** which he 3068
8:30 Joshua built an altar unto **the L** God of 3068
8:31 As Moses the servant of **the L** commanded 3068
8:31 offered thereon burnt offerings unto **the L**, 3068
8:33 bare the ark of the covenant of **the L**, 3068
8:33 as Moses the servant of **the L** had 3068
9: 9 because of the name of **the L** thy God: 3068
9:14 asked not *counsel* at the mouth of **the L**. 3068
9:18 sworn unto them by **the L** God of Israel. 3068
9:19 We have sworn unto them by **the L** God of 3068
9:24 how that **the L** thy God commanded his 3068
9:27 for the altar of **the L**, *even* unto this day, 3068
10: 8 **the L** said unto Joshua, Fear them not: for I 3068
10:10 **the L** discomfited them before Israel, and 3068
10:11 that **the L** cast down great stones from 3068
10:12 spake Joshua to **the L** in the day when 3068
10:12 **the L** delivered up the Amorites before 3068
10:14 that **the L** hearkened unto the voice of a 3068
10:14 voice of a man: for **the L** fought for Israel. 3068
10:19 for **the L** your God hath delivered them 3068
10:25 for thus shall **the L** do to all your enemies 3068
10:30 **the L** delivered it also, and the king 3068
10:32 **the L** delivered Lachish into the hand of 3068
10:40 as **the L** God of Israel commanded. 3068
10:42 **the L** God of Israel fought for Israel. 3068
11: 6 **the L** said unto Joshua, Be not afraid 3068
11: 8 **the L** delivered them into the hand of 3068
11: 9 Joshua did unto them as **the L** bade him: 3068
11:12 as Moses the servant of **the L** commanded. 3068
11:15 As **the L** commanded Moses his servant, so 3068
11:15 he left nothing undone of all that **the L** 3068

Jos 11:20 For it was of **the L** to harden their hearts, 3068
11:20 destroy them, as **the L** commanded Moses. 3068
11:23 according to all that **the L** said unto Moses; 3068
12: 6 Them did Moses the servant of **the L** and 3068
12: 6 Moses the servant of **the L** gave it *for* a 3068
13: 1 **the L** said unto him, Thou art old *and* 3068
13: 8 *even* as Moses the servant of the L gave 3068
13:14 the sacrifices of **the L** God of Israel made 3068
13:33 **the L** God of Israel *was* their inheritance, 3068
14: 2 as **the L** commanded by the hand of Moses, 3068
14: 5 As **the L** commanded Moses, so 3068
14: 6 Thou knowest the thing that **the L** said 3068
14: 7 **the L** sent me from Kadesh-barnea to espy 3068
14: 8 but I wholly followed **the L** my God. 3068
14: 9 thou hast wholly followed **the L** my God. 3068
14:10 **the L** hath kept me alive, as he said, 3068
14:10 *even* since **the L** spake this word unto 3068
14:12 whereof **the L** spake in that day; 3068
14:12 if so be **the L** *will be* with me, then I shall 3068
14:12 *be able to* drive them out, as **the L** said. 3068
14:14 that he wholly followed **the L** God of 3068
15:13 according to the commandment of **the L** to 3068
17: 4 **The L** commanded Moses to give us an 3068
17: 4 **the L** he gave them an inheritance among 3068
17:14 forasmuch as **the L** hath blessed me 3068
18: 3 which **the L** God of your fathers hath given 3068
18: 6 cast lots for you here before **the L** our God. 3068
18: 7 for the priesthood of **the L** *is* their 3068
18: 7 which Moses the servant of **the L** gave 3068
18: 8 cast lots for you before **the L** in Shiloh. 3068
18:10 cast lots for them in Shiloh before **the L**: 3068
19:50 According to the word of **the L** they gave 3068
19:51 inheritance by lot in Shiloh before **the L**, 3068
20: 1 **The L** also spake unto Joshua, saying, 3068
21: 2 **The L** commanded by the hand of Moses 3068
21: 3 at the commandment of **the L**, these cities 3068
21: 8 as **the L** commanded by the hand of Moses. 3068
21:43 **the L** gave unto Israel all the land which he 3068
21:44 **the L** gave them rest round about, 3068
21:44 **the L** delivered all their enemies into their 3068
21:45 **the L** had spoken unto the house of Israel; 3068
22: 2 the servant of **the L** commanded you, 3068
22: 3 of the commandment of **the L** your God. 3068
22: 4 now **the L** your God hath given rest unto 3068
22: 4 which Moses the servant of **the L** gave you 3068
22: 5 which Moses the servant of **the L** charged 3068
22: 5 to love **the L** your God, and to walk in all 3068
22: 9 according to the word of **the L** by the hand 3068
22:16 saith the whole congregation of **the L**, 3068
22:16 to turn away *this* day from following **the L**, 3068
22:16 that ye might rebel *this* day against **the L**? 3068
22:17 was a plague in the congregation of **the L**, 3068
22:18 turn away *this* day from following **the L**? 3068
22:18 *seeing* ye rebel to day against **the L**, 3068
22:19 unto the land of the possession of **the L**, 3068
22:19 rebel not against **the L**, nor rebel against 3068
22:19 an altar beside the altar of **the L** our God. 3068
22:22 **The L** God of gods, the LORD God of 3068
22:22 **the L** God of gods, he knoweth, and 3068
22:22 or if in transgression against **the L**, 3068
22:23 us an altar to turn from following **the L**; 3068
22:23 let **the L** himself require *it*; 3068
22:24 What have you to do with **the L** God of 3068
22:25 For **the L** hath made Jordan a border 3068
22:25 children of Gad; ye have no part in **the L**: 3068
22:25 our children cease from fearing **the L**: 3068
22:27 that *we* might do the service of **the L** 3068
22:27 in time to come, Ye have no part in **the L**. 3068
22:28 Behold the pattern of the altar of **the L**, 3068
22:29 forbid that we should rebel against **the L**, 3068
22:29 turn *this* day from following **the L**, to build 3068
22:29 besides the altar of **the L** our God that *is* 3068
22:31 *This* day we perceive that **the L** *is* among 3068
22:31 not committed this trespass against **the L**: 3068
22:31 children of Israel out of the hand of **the L**. 3068
22:34 *be* a witness between us that **the L** *is* God. 3068
23: 1 it came to pass a long time after that **the L** 3068
23: 3 ye have seen all that **the L** your God hath 3068
23: 3 for **the L** your God *is* he that hath fought 3068
23: 5 **the L** your God, he shall expel them from 3068
23: 5 as **the L** your God hath promised unto you. 3068
23: 8 cleave unto **the L** your God, as ye have 3068
23: 9 For **the L** hath driven out from before you 3068
23:10 for **the L** your God, he *it is* that fighteth for 3068
23:11 that ye love **the L** your God. 3068
23:13 Know for a certainty that **the L** your God 3068
23:13 land which **the L** your God hath given you. 3068
23:14 **the L** your God spake concerning you; 3068
23:15 which **the L** your God promised you; 3068
23:15 shall **the L** bring upon you all evil things, 3068
23:15 land which **the L** your God hath given you. 3068
23:16 the covenant of **the L** your God, 3068
23:16 shall the anger of **the L** be kindled against 3068
24: 2 the people, Thus saith **the L** God of Israel, 3068
24: 7 when they cried unto **the L**, he put 3068
24:14 Now therefore fear **the L**, and serve him in 3068
24:14 the flood, and in Egypt; and serve ye **the L**. 3068
24:15 if it seem evil unto you to serve **the L**, 3068
24:15 for me and my house, we will serve **the L**. 3068
24:16 God forbid that we should forsake **the L**, 3068
24:17 For **the L** our God, he *it is* that brought us 3068
24:18 **the L** drave out from before us all 3068
24:18 *therefore* will we also serve **the L**; for he *is* 3068
24:19 unto the people, Ye cannot serve **the L**: 3068
24:20 If ye forsake **the L**, and serve strange gods, 3068
24:21 unto Joshua, Nay; but we will serve **the L**. 3068
24:22 yourselves that ye have chosen you **the L**, 3068
24:23 incline your heart unto **the L** God of Israel. 3068
24:24 **The L** our God will we serve, and his voice 3068
24:26 an oak, that *was* by the sanctuary of **the L** 3068
24:27 for it hath heard all the words of **the L** 3068
24:29 the servant of **the L**, died, *being* an 3068
24:31 Israel served **the L** all the days of Joshua, 3068
24:31 which had known all the works of **the L**, 3068
Jdg 1: 1 that the children of Israel asked **the L**, 3068

Jdg 1: 2 **the L** said, Judah shall go up: behold, 3068
1: 4 **the L** delivered the Canaanites and 3068
1:19 **the L** was with Judah; and he drave out 3068
1:22 *against* Beth-el: and **the L** *was* with them. 3068
2: 1 an angel of **the L** came up from Gilgal to 3068
2: 4 when the angel of **the L** spake these words 3068
2: 5 and they sacrificed there unto **the L**. 3068
2: 7 the people served **the L** all the days of 3068
2: 7 who had seen all the great works of **the L**, 3068
2: 8 the servant of **the L**, died, *being* an 3068
2:10 after them, which knew not **the L**, 3068
2:11 of Israel did evil in the sight of **the L**, 3068
2:12 they forsook **the L** God of their fathers, 3068
2:12 unto them, and provoked **the L** to anger. 3068
2:13 they forsook **the L**, and served Baal and 3068
2:14 the anger of **the L** was hot against Israel, 3068
2:15 the hand of **the L** was against them for evil, 3068
2:15 as **the L** had said, and as the LORD had 3068
2:15 and as **the L** had sworn unto them: 3068
2:16 Nevertheless **the L** raised up judges, 3068
2:17 obeying the commandments of **the L**; 3068
2:18 when **the L** raised them up judges, then 3068
2:18 **the L** was with the judge, and 3068
2:18 for it repented **the L** because of their 3068
2:20 the anger of **the L** was hot against Israel; 3068
2:22 whether they will keep the way of **the L** to 3068
2:23 Therefore **the L** left those nations, without 3068
3: 1 Now these *are* the nations which **the L** left, 3068
3: 4 hearken unto the commandments of **the L**, 3068
3: 7 of Israel did evil in the sight of **the L**, 3068
3: 7 forgat **the L** their God, and served Baalim 3068
3: 8 Therefore the anger of **the L** was hot 3068
3: 9 the children of Israel cried unto **the L**, 3068
3: 9 **the L** raised up a deliverer to the children 3068
3:10 the spirit of **the L** came upon him, and 3068
3:10 **the L** delivered Chushan-rishathaim king 3068
3:12 of Israel did evil again in the sight of **the L**: 3068
3:12 **the L** strengthened Eglon the king of Moab 3068
3:12 they had done evil in the sight of **the L**. 3068
3:15 the children of Israel cried unto **the L**, 3068
3:15 **the L** raised them up a deliverer, Ehud 3068
3:28 for **the L** hath delivered your enemies 3068
4: 1 of Israel again did evil in the sight of **the L**, 3068
4: 2 **the L** sold them into the hand of Jabin king 3068
4: 3 the children of Israel cried unto **the L**: 3068
4: 6 Hath not **the L** God of Israel commanded, 3068
4: 9 for **the L** shall sell Sisera into the hand of a 3068
4:14 for this *is* the day in which **the L** hath 3068
4:14 is not **the L** gone out before thee? So Barak 3068
4:15 **the L** discomfited Sisera, and all *his* 3068
5: 2 Praise ye **the L** for the avenging of Israel, 3068
5: 3 ye princes; I, *even* I, will sing unto **the L**; 3068
5: 3 I will sing *praise* to **the L** God of Israel. 3068
5: 4 **L**, when thou wentest out of Seir, 3068
5: 5 The mountains melted from before **the L**, 3068
5: 5 *even* that Sinai from before **the L** God of 3068
5: 9 willingly among the people. Bless ye **the L**. 3068
5:11 they rehearse the righteous acts of **the L**, 3068
5:11 shall the people of **the L** go down to 3068
5:13 **the L** made me have dominion over 3068
5:23 Curse ye Meroz, said the angel of **the L**, 3068
5:23 because they came not to the help of **the L**, 3068
5:23 to the help of **the L** against the mighty. 3068
5:31 So let all thine enemies perish, O **L**: but 3068
6: 1 of Israel did evil in the sight of **the L**: 3068
6: 1 **the L** delivered them into the hand of 3068
6: 6 and the children of Israel cried unto **the L**. 3068
6: 7 when the children of Israel cried unto **the L** 3068
6: 8 That **the L** sent a prophet unto the children 3068
6: 8 unto them, Thus saith **the L** God of Israel, 3068
6:10 I said unto you, I *am* **the L** your God; 3068
6:11 there came an angel of **the L**, and sat under 3068
6:12 the angel of **the L** appeared unto him, and 3068
6:12 said unto him, **The L** *is* with thee, 3068
6:13 if **the L** be with us, why then is all this 3068
6:13 Did not **the L** bring us up from Egypt? 3068
6:13 now **the L** hath forsaken us, and 3068
6:14 **the L** looked upon him, and said, Go in this 3068
6:16 **the L** said unto him, Surely I will be with 3068
6:21 the angel of **the L** put forth the end of 3068
6:21 the angel of **the L** departed out of his sight. 3068
6:22 perceived that he *was* an angel of **the L**, 3068
6:22 I have seen an angel of **the L** face to face. 3068
6:23 **the L** said unto him, Peace *be* unto thee; 3068
6:24 Then Gideon built an altar there unto **the L**, 3068
6:25 that **the L** said unto him, Take thy father's 3068
6:26 build an altar unto **the L** thy God upon 3068
6:27 and did as **the L** had said unto him: 3068
6:34 the spirit of **the L** came upon Gideon, and 3068
7: 2 **the L** said unto Gideon, The people that *are* 3068
7: 4 **the L** said unto Gideon, The people *are* yet 3068
7: 5 **the L** said unto Gideon, Every one that 3068
7: 7 **the L** said unto Gideon, By the three 3068
7: 9 that **the L** said unto him, Arise, get thee 3068
7:15 for **the L** hath delivered into your hand 3068
7:18 say, *The sword* of **the L**, and of Gideon. 3068
7:20 The sword of **the L**, and of Gideon. 3068
7:22 **the L** set every man's sword against his 3068
8: 7 Therefore when **the L** hath delivered Zebah 3068
8:19 *as* **the L** liveth, if ye had saved them alive, 3068
8:23 rule over you: **the L** shall rule over you. 3068
8:34 the children of Israel remembered not **the L** 3068
10: 6 of Israel did evil again in the sight of **the L**, 3068
10: 6 and forsook **the L**, and served not him. 3068
10: 7 the anger of **the L** was hot against Israel, 3068
10:10 the children of Israel cried unto **the L**, 3068
10:11 **the L** said unto the children of Israel, *Did* 3068
10:15 the children of Israel said unto **the L**, 3068
10:16 gods from among them, and served **the L**: 3068
11: 9 **the L** deliver them before me, shall I be 3068
11:10 **The L** be witness between us, if we do not 3068
11:11 Jephthah uttered all his words before **the L** 3068
11:21 **the L** God of Israel delivered Sihon and 3068
11:23 So now **the L** God of Israel hath 3068
11:24 So whomsoever **the L** our God shall drive 3068

Jdg 11:27 **the L** the Judge be judge *this* day between 3068
11:29 the spirit of **the L** came upon Jephthah, 3068
11:30 And Jephthah vowed a vow unto **the L**, and 3068
11:32 and **the L** delivered them into his hands. 3068
11:35 for I have opened my mouth unto **the L**, 3068
11:36 *if* thou hast opened thy mouth unto **the L**, 3068
11:36 forasmuch as **the L** hath taken vengeance 3068
12: 3 and **the L** delivered them into my hand: 3068
13: 1 of Israel did evil again in the sight of **the L**; 3068
13: 1 **the L** delivered them into the hand of 3068
13: 3 the angel of **the L** appeared unto 3068
13: 8 Manoah intreated **the L**, and said, O my 3068
13:13 the angel of **the L** said unto Manoah, Of all 3068
13:15 Manoah said unto the angel of **the L**, I pray 3068
13:16 the angel of **the L** said unto Manoah, 3068
13:16 thou must offer it unto **the L**. 3068
13:16 knew not that he *was* an angel of **the L**. 3068
13:17 Manoah said unto the angel of **the L**, 3068
13:18 the angel of **the L** said unto him, Why 3068
13:19 and offered *it* upon a rock unto **the L**: 3068
13:20 that the angel of **the L** ascended in 3068
13:21 the angel of **the L** did no more appear to 3068
13:21 knew that he *was* an angel of **the L**. 3068
13:23 unto him, If **the L** were pleased to kill us, 3068
13:24 and the child grew, and **the L** blessed him. 3068
13:25 the spirit of **the L** began to move him at 3068
14: 4 his mother knew not that it *was* of **the L**, 3068
14: 6 the spirit of **the L** came mightily upon him, 3068
14:19 the spirit of **the L** came upon him, and 3068
15:14 the spirit of **the L** came mightily upon him, 3068
15:18 sore athirst, and called on **the L**, and said, 3068
16:20 he wist not that **the L** was departed from 3068
16:28 Samson called unto **the L**, and said, O Lord 3068
17: 2 Blessed *be thou* of **the L**, my son. 3068
17: 3 silver unto **the L** from my hand for my son, 3068
17:13 Now know I that **the L** will do me good, 3068
18: 6 before **the L** *is* your way wherein ye go. 3068
19:18 I am *now* going *to* the house of **the L**; 3068
20: 1 the land of Gilead, unto **the L** *in* Mizpeh. 3068
20:18 And **the L** said, Judah *shall go up* first. 3068
20:23 went up and wept before **the L** until even, 3068
20:23 and asked *counsel* of **the L**, saying, 3068
20:23 And **the L** said, Go up against him.) 3068
20:26 sat there before **the L**, and fasted that day 3068
20:26 and peace offerings before **the L**. 3068
20:27 the children of Israel inquired of **the L**, 3068
20:28 **the L** said, Go up; for to morrow I will 3068
20:35 **the L** smote Benjamin before Israel: and 3068
21: 3 said, O **L** God of Israel, why is this come to 3068
21: 5 not up with the congregation unto **the L**? 3068
21: 5 *him* that came not up to **the L** *to* Mizpeh, 3068
21: 7 seeing we have sworn by **the L** that *we* will 3068
21: 8 Israel that came not up *to* Mizpeh to **the L**? 3068
21:15 that **the L** had made a breach in the tribes 3068
21:19 *there is* a feast of **the L** in Shiloh yearly *in* 3068
Ru 1: 6 **the L** had visited his people in giving them 3068
1: 8 **the L** deal kindly with you, as ye have 3068
1: 9 **The L** grant you that ye may find rest, 3068
1:13 the hand of **the L** is gone out against me. 3068
1:17 **the L** do so to me, and more also, *if ought* 3068
1:21 **the L** hath brought me *home* again empty: 3068
1:21 seeing **the L** hath testified against me, and 3068
2: 4 said unto the reapers, **The L** *be* with you. 3068
2: 4 And they answered him, **The L** bless thee. 3068
2:12 **The L** recompense thy work, and a full 3068
2:12 a full reward be given thee of **the L** God of 3068
2:20 her daughter in law, Blessed *be* he of **the L**, 3068
3:10 he said, Blessed *be* thou of **the L**, 3068
3:13 part of a kinsman to thee, *as* **the L** liveth: 3068
4:11 **The L** make the woman that is come into 3068
4:12 of the seed which **the L** shall give thee of 3068
4:13 **the L** gave her conception, and she bare a 3068
4:14 women said unto Naomi, Blessed *be* **the L**, 3068
1Sa 1: 3 to sacrifice unto **the L** of hosts in Shiloh. 3068
1: 3 Hophni and Phinehas, the priests of **the L**, 3068
1: 5 but **the L** had shut up her womb. 3068
1: 6 because **the L** had shut up her womb. 3068
1: 7 when she went up to the house of **the L**, so 3068
1: 9 a seat by a post of the temple of **the L**. 3068
1:10 and prayed unto **the L**, and wept sore. 3068
1:11 she vowed a vow, and said, O **L** of hosts, 3068
1:11 I will give him unto **the L** all the days of 3068
1:12 as she continued praying before **the L**, 3068
1:15 but have poured out my soul before **the L**. 3068
1:19 worshipped before **the L**, and returned, and 3068
1:19 his wife; and **the L** remembered her. 3068
1:20 *saying*, Because I have asked him of **the L**. 3068
1:21 went up to offer unto **the L** the yearly 3068
1:22 that he may appear before **the L**, and 3068
1:23 weaned him; only **the L** establish his word. 3068
1:24 brought him *unto* the house of **the L** *in* 3068
1:26 that stood by thee here, praying unto **the L**. 3068
1:27 **the L** hath given me my petition which I 3068
1:28 Therefore also I have lent him to **the L**; 3068
1:28 long as he liveth he *shall be* lent to **the L**. 3068
1:28 And he worshipped **the L** there. 3068
2: 1 and said, My heart rejoiceth in **the L**, 3068
2: 1 the LORD, mine horn is exalted in **the L**: 3068
2: 2 *There is* none holy as **the L**: for *there is* 3068
2: 3 for **the L** *is* a God of knowledge, and 3068
2: 6 **The L** killeth, and maketh alive: 3068
2: 7 **The L** maketh poor, and maketh rich: 3068
2:10 The adversaries of **the L** shall be broken to 3068
2:10 **the L** shall judge the ends of the earth; and 3068
2:11 the child did minister unto **the L** before Eli 3068
2:12 *were* sons of Belial; they knew not **the L**. 3068
2:17 young men was very great before **the L**: 3068
2:17 for men abhorred the offering of **the L**. 3068
2:18 Samuel ministered before **the L**, *being* a 3068
2:20 **The L** give thee seed of this woman for 3068
2:20 woman for the loan which is lent to **the L**. 3068
2:21 **the L** visited Hannah, so that she 3068
2:21 And the child Samuel grew before **the L**. 3068
2:25 if a man sin against **the L**, who shall intreat 3068
2:25 because **the L** would slay them. 3068

1Sa 2:26 was in favour both with **the L**, and 3068
2:27 and said unto him, Thus saith **the L**, 3068
2:30 Wherefore **the L** God of Israel saith, I said 3068
2:30 now **the L** saith, Be it far from me; 3068
3: 1 the child Samuel ministered unto **the L** 3068
3: 1 the word of **the L** was precious in those 3068
3: 3 of God went out in the temple of **the L**, 3068
3: 4 That **the L** called Samuel: and 3068
3: 6 **the L** called yet again, Samuel. 3068
3: 7 Now Samuel did not yet know **the L**, 3068
3: 7 neither was the word of **the L** yet revealed 3068
3: 8 **the L** called Samuel again the third time. 3068
3: 8 Eli perceived that **the L** had called 3068
3: 9 if he call thee, that thou shalt say, Speak, **L**; 3068
3:10 **the L** came, and stood, and called as at 3068
3:11 **the L** said to Samuel, Behold, I will do a 3068
3:15 and opened the doors of the house of **the L**. 3068
3:17 What *is* the thing that *the L* hath said unto NIH
3:18 he said, It *is* **the L**: let him do what 3068
3:19 **the L** was with him, and did let none of his 3068
3:20 *was* established to be a prophet of **the L**. 3068
3:21 **the L** appeared again in Shiloh: for 3068
3:21 for **the L** revealed himself to Samuel in 3068
3:21 to Samuel in Shiloh by the word of **the L**. 3068
4: 3 Wherefore hath **the L** smitten us to day 3068
4: 3 us fetch the ark of the covenant of **the L** 3068
4: 4 the ark of the covenant of **the L** of hosts, 3068
4: 5 when the ark of the covenant of **the L** came 3068
4: 6 they understood that the ark of **the L** was 3068
5: 3 his face to the earth before the ark of **the L**. 3068
5: 4 face to the ground before the ark of **the L**; 3068
5: 6 the hand of **the L** was heavy upon them of 3068
5: 9 the hand of **the L** was against the city *with* 3068
6: 1 the ark of **the L** was in the country of 3068
6: 2 What shall we do to the ark of **the L**? 3068
6: 8 take the ark of **the L**, and lay it upon 3068
6:11 they laid the ark of **the L** upon the cart, 3068
6:14 the kine a burnt offering unto **the L**. 3068
6:15 the Levites took down the ark of **the L**, 3068
6:15 sacrifices the same day unto **the L**. 3068
6:17 returned *for* a trespass offering unto **the L**; 3068
6:18 whereon they set down the ark of **the L**: 3068
6:19 they had looked into the ark of **the L**, 3068
6:19 **the L** had smitten *many* of the people *with* 3068
6:20 Who is able to stand before this holy **L** 3068
6:21 have brought again the ark of **the L**; 3068
7: 1 fetched up the ark of **the L**, and brought it 3068
7: 1 Eleazar his son to keep the ark of **the L**. 3068
7: 2 all the house of Israel lamented after **the L**. 3068
7: 3 If ye do return unto **the L** with all your 3068
7: 3 prepare your hearts unto **the L**, and 3068
7: 4 and Ashtaroth, and served **the L** only. 3068
7: 5 and I will pray for you unto **the L**. 3068
7: 6 poured *it* out before **the L**, and fasted on 3068
7: 6 said there, We have sinned against **the L**. 3068
7: 8 Cease not to cry unto **the L** our God for us, 3068
7: 9 it *for* a burnt offering wholly unto **the L**: 3068
7: 9 Samuel cried unto **the L** for Israel; and 3068
7: 9 the LORD for Israel; and **the L** heard him. 3068
7:10 **the L** thundered with a great thunder on 3068
7:12 Hitherto hath **the L** helped us. 3068
7:13 the hand of **the L** was against 3068
7:17 and there he built an altar unto **the L**. 3068
8: 6 judge us. And Samuel prayed unto **the L**. 3068
8: 7 **the L** said unto Samuel, Hearken unto 3068
8:10 Samuel told all the words of **the L** unto 3068
8:18 and **the L** will not hear you in that day. 3068
8:21 and he rehearsed them in the ears of **the L**. 3068
8:22 **the L** said to Samuel, Hearken unto their 3068
9:15 Now **the L** had told Samuel in his ear a day 3068
9:17 Samuel saw Saul, **the L** said unto him, 3068
10: 1 **the L** hath anointed thee to be captain over 3068
10: 6 the spirit of **the L** will come upon thee, 3068
10:17 the people together unto **the L** *to* Mizpeh; 3068
10:18 Thus saith **the L** God of Israel, I brought 3068
10:19 present yourselves before **the L** by your 3068
10:22 Therefore they inquired of **the L** further, 3068
10:22 **the L** answered, Behold, he hath hid 3068
10:24 See ye him whom **the L** hath chosen, 3068
10:25 *it* in a book, and laid *it* up before **the L**. 3068
11: 7 the fear of **the L** fell on the people, and 3068
11:13 for to day **the L** hath wrought salvation in 3068
11:15 there they made Saul king before **the L** in 3068
11:15 sacrifices *of* peace offerings before **the L**; 3068
12: 3 here I *am*: witness against me before **the L**, 3068
12: 5 **The L** *is* witness against you, and 3068
12: 6 *It is* **the L** that advanced Moses and Aaron, 3068
12: 7 that I may reason with you before **the L** of 3068
12: 7 LORD of all the righteous acts of **the L**, 3068
12: 8 your fathers cried unto **the L**, then 3068
12: 8 then **the L** sent Moses and Aaron, 3068
12: 9 when they forgat **the L** their God, he sold 3068
12:10 they cried unto **the L**, and said, We have 3068
12:10 because we have forsaken **the L**, and 3068
12:11 **the L** sent Jerubbaal, and Bedan, and 3068
12:12 when **the L** your God *was* your king. 3068
12:13 and behold, **the L** hath set a king over you. 3068
12:14 If ye will fear **the L**, and serve him, and 3068
12:14 rebel against the commandment of **the L**, 3068
12:14 you continue following **the L** your God: 3068
12:15 if ye will not obey the voice of **the L**, but 3068
12:15 rebel against the commandment of **the L**, 3068
12:15 shall the hand of **the L** be against you, as *it* 3068
12:16 which **the L** will do before your eyes. 3068
12:17 I will call unto **the L**, and he shall send 3068
12:17 which ye have done in the sight of **the L**, 3068
12:18 So Samuel called unto **the L**; and 3068
12:18 and **the L** sent thunder and rain that day: 3068
12:18 all the people greatly feared **the L** and 3068
12:19 Pray for thy servants unto **the L** thy God, 3068
12:20 yet turn not aside from following **the L**, but 3068
12:20 but serve **the L** with all your heart; 3068
12:22 For **the L** will not forsake his people for his 3068
12:22 it hath pleased **the L** to make you his 3068
12:23 God forbid that I should sin against **the L** 3068

L

1Sa 12:24 Only fear **the L**, and serve him in truth 3068
13:12 I have not made supplication unto **the L**: 3068
13:13 kept the commandment of **the L** thy God, 3068
13:13 for now would **the L** have established thy 3068
13:14 **the L** hath sought him a man after his own 3068
13:14 **the L** hath commanded him to be captain 3068
13:14 thou hast not kept *that* which **the L** 3068
14: 6 it may be that **the L** will work for us: 3068
14: 6 for *there is* no restraint to **the L** to save by 3068
14:10 for **the L** hath delivered them into our 3068
14:12 for **the L** hath delivered them into the hand 3068
14:23 So **the L** saved Israel that day: and 3068
14:33 Behold, the people sin against **the L**, 3068
14:34 sin not against **the L** in eating with 3068
14:35 Saul built an altar unto **the L**: the same was 3068
14:35 was the first altar that he built unto **the L**. 3068
14:39 For, *as* **the L** liveth, which saveth Israel, 3068
14:41 Therefore Saul said unto **the L** God of 3068
14:45 *as* **the L** liveth, there shall not one hair of 3068
15: 1 **The L** sent me to anoint thee to be king 3068
15: 1 thou unto the voice of the words of **the L**. 3068
15: 2 Thus saith **the L** of hosts, I remember *that* 3068
15:10 came the word of **the L** unto Samuel, 3068
15:11 and he cried unto **the L** all night. 3068
15:13 said unto him, Blessed *be* thou of **the L**: 3068
15:13 performed the commandment of **the L**. 3068
15:15 the oxen, to sacrifice unto **the L** thy God; 3068
15:16 I will tell thee what **the L** hath said to me 3068
15:17 and **the L** anointed thee king over Israel? 3068
15:18 **the L** sent thee on a journey, and said, Go 3068
15:19 didst thou not obey the voice of **the L**, 3068
15:19 and didst evil in the sight of **the L**? 3068
15:20 I have obeyed the voice of **the L**, and 3068
15:20 have gone the way which **the L** sent me, 3068
15:21 to sacrifice unto **the L** thy God in Gilgal. 3068
15:22 Hath **the L** *as great* delight in burnt 3068
15:22 sacrifices, as in obeying the voice of **the L**? 3068
15:23 thou hast rejected the word of **the L**, 3068
15:24 transgressed the commandment of **the L**, 3068
15:25 again with me, that I may worship **the L**. 3068
15:26 for thou hast rejected the word of **the L**, 3068
15:26 **the L** hath rejected thee from being king 3068
15:28 **The L** hath rent the kingdom of Israel from 3068
15:30 with me, that I may worship **the L** thy God. 3068
15:31 after Saul; and Saul worshipped **the L**. 3068
15:33 Samuel hewed Agag in pieces before **the L** 3068
15:35 **the L** repented that he had made Saul king 3068
16: 1 **the L** said unto Samuel, How long wilt 3068
16: 2 **the L** said, Take a heifer with thee, 3068
16: 2 say, I am come to sacrifice to **the L**. 3068
16: 4 Samuel did *that* which **the L** spake, and 3068
16: 5 I am come to sacrifice unto **the L**: 3068
16: 7 **the L** said unto Samuel, Look not on his 3068
16: 7 for *the L seeth* not as man seeth; for man NIH
16: 7 but **the L** looketh on the heart. 3068
16: 8 he said, Neither hath **the L** chosen this. 3068
16: 9 he said, Neither hath **the L** chosen this. 3068
16:10 unto Jesse, **The L** hath not chosen these. 3068
16:12 **the L** said, Arise, anoint him: for this *is* he. 3068
16:13 the spirit of **the L** came upon David from 3068
16:14 the spirit of **the L** departed from Saul, and 3068
16:14 and an evil spirit from **the L** troubled him. 3068
16:18 a comely person, and **the L** *is* with him. 3068
17:37 **The L** that delivered me out of the paw of 3068
17:37 unto David, Go, and **the L** be with thee. 3068
17:45 I come to thee in the name of **the L** of 3068
17:46 This day will **the L** deliver thee into mine 3068
17:47 all this assembly shall know that **the L** 3068
18:12 because **the L** was with him, and 3068
18:14 in all his ways; and **the L** *was* with him. 3068
18:28 and knew that **the L** *was* with David, 3068
19: 5 **the L** wrought a great salvation for all 3068
19: 6 Saul sware, *As* **the L** liveth, he shall not be 3068
19: 9 the evil spirit from **the L** was upon Saul, 3068
20: 3 truly *as* **the L** liveth, and *as* thy soul liveth, 3068
20: 8 servant into a covenant of **the L** with thee: 3068
20:12 said unto David, O **L** God of Israel, 3068
20:13 **The L** do so and much more to Jonathan: 3068
20:13 **the L** be with thee, as he hath been with my 3068
20:14 yet I live shew me the kindness of **the L**, 3068
20:15 not when **the L** hath cut off the enemies of 3068
20:16 *saying,* Let **the L** even require *it* at 3068
20:21 peace to thee, and no hurt; *as* **the L** liveth. 3068
20:22 go *thy way:* for **the L** hath sent thee away. 3068
20:23 **the L** *be* between thee and me for ever. 3068
20:42 have sworn both of us in the name of **the L**, 3068
20:42 **The L** be between me and thee, and 3068
21: 6 that was taken from before **the L**, 3068
21: 7 *was* there that day, detained before **the L**; 3068
22:10 he inquired of **the L** for him, and gave him 3068
22:17 Turn, and slay the priests of **the L**; 3068
22:17 their hand to fall upon the priests of **the L**. 3068
23: 2 Therefore David inquired of **the L**, saying, 3068
23: 2 **the L** said unto David, Go, and smite 3068
23: 4 David inquired of **the L** yet again. And 3068
23: 4 **the L** answered him and said, Arise, 3068
23:10 said David, O **L** God of Israel, thy servant 3068
23:11 O **L** God of Israel, I beseech thee, tell thy 3068
23:11 And **the L** said, He will come down. 3068
23:12 And **the L** said, They will deliver *thee* up. 3068
23:18 they two made a covenant before **the L**: 3068
23:21 Saul said, Blessed *be* ye of **the L**; for ye 3068
24: 4 Behold the day of which **the L** said unto 3068
24: 6 **The L** forbid that I should do this thing 3068
24: 6 seeing he *is* the anointed of **the L**. 3068
24:10 day thine eyes have seen how that **the L** 3068
24:12 **The L** judge between me and thee, and 3068
24:12 and thee, and **the L** avenge me of thee: 3068
24:15 **The L** therefore be judge, and 3068
24:18 forasmuch as when **the L** had delivered me 3068
24:19 wherefore **the L** reward thee good for that 3068
24:21 Swear now therefore unto me by **the L**, 3068
25:26 *as* **the L** liveth, and *as* thy soul liveth, 3068
25:26 seeing **the L** hath withholden thee 3068
25:28 for **the L** will certainly make my lord a 3068

1Sa 25:28 my lord fighteth the battles of **the L**, 3068
25:29 in the bundle of life with **the L** thy God; 3068
25:30 when **the L** shall have done to my lord 3068
25:31 when **the L** shall have dealt well with my 3068
25:32 to Abigail, Blessed *be* **the L** God of Israel, 3068
25:34 in very deed, *as* **the L** God of Israel liveth, 3068
25:38 ten days *after,* that **the L** smote Nabal, 3068
25:39 Nabal was dead, he said, Blessed *be* **the L**, 3068
25:39 for **the L** hath returned the wickedness of 3068
26:10 David said furthermore, *As* **the L** liveth, 3068
26:10 the LORD liveth, **the L** shall smite him; 3068
26:11 **The L** forbid that *I* should stretch forth 3068
26:12 a deep sleep from **the L** was fallen upon 3068
26:16 *As* **the L** liveth, ye *are* worthy to die, 3068
26:19 If **the L** have stirred thee up against me, 3068
26:19 of men, cursed *be* they before **the L**; 3068
26:19 from abiding in the inheritance of **the L**, 3068
26:20 fall to the earth before the face of **the L**: 3068
26:23 **The L** render to every man his 3068
26:23 for **the L** delivered thee into *my* hand to 3068
26:24 my life be much set by in the eyes of **the L**, 3068
28: 6 when Saul inquired of **the L**, the LORD 3068
28: 6 **the L** answered him not, neither by dreams, 3068
28:10 Saul sware to her by **the L**, saying, *As* 3068
28:10 her by the LORD, saying, *As* **the L** liveth, 3068
28:16 seeing **the L** is departed from thee, and 3068
28:17 **the L** hath done to him, as he spake by me: 3068
28:17 for **the L** hath rent the kingdom out of thine 3068
28:18 thou obeyedst not the voice of **the L**, 3068
28:18 hath **the L** done this thing unto thee this 3068
28:19 Moreover **the L** will also deliver Israel 3068
28:19 **the L** also shall deliver the host of Israel 3068
29: 6 said unto him, Surely, *as* **the L** liveth, 3068
30: 6 David encouraged himself in **the L** his 3068
30: 8 David inquired at **the L**, saying, Shall I 3068
30:23 with *that* which **the L** hath given us, 3068
30:26 you of the spoil of the enemies of **the L**; 3068
2Sa 1:12 for the people of **the L**, and for the house 3068
2: 1 that David inquired of **the L**, saying, 3068
2: 1 **the L** said unto him, Go up. And David 3068
2: 5 said unto them, Blessed *be* ye of **the L**, 3068
2: 6 now **the L** shew kindness and truth unto 3068
3: 9 as **the L** hath sworn to David, even so I do 3068
3:18 then do *it:* for **the L** hath spoken of David, 3068
3:28 my kingdom *are* guiltless before **the L** for 3068
3:39 **the L** shall reward the doer of evil 3068
4: 8 **the L** hath avenged my lord the king this 3068
4: 9 and said unto them, *As* **the L** liveth, 3068
5: 2 **the L** said to thee, Thou shalt feed my 3068
5: 3 a league with them in Hebron before **the L**: 3068
5:10 and **the L** God of hosts *was* with him. 3068
5:12 David perceived that **the L** had established 3068
5:19 David inquired of **the L**, saying, Shall I go 3068
5:19 **the L** said unto David, Go up: for I will 3068
5:20 **The L** hath broken forth upon mine 3068
5:23 And when David inquired of **the L**, he said, 3068
5:24 for then shall **the L** go out before thee, 3068
5:25 did so, as **the L** had commanded him; 3068
6: 2 whose name is called *by* the name of **the L** 3068
6: 5 all the house of Israel played before **the L** 3068
6: 7 the anger of **the L** was kindled against 3068
6: 8 **the L** had made a breach upon Uzzah: 3068
6: 9 David was afraid of **the L** that day, 3068
6: 9 How shall the ark of **the L** come to me? 3068
6:10 of **the L** unto him into the city of David: 3068
6:11 the ark of **the L** continued *in* the house of 3068
6:11 **the L** blessed Obed-edom, and all his 3068
6:12 **The L** hath blessed the house of 3068
6:13 that when they that bare the ark of **the L** 3068
6:14 David danced before **the L** with all *his* 3068
6:15 brought up the ark of **the L** with shouting, 3068
6:16 as the ark of **the L** came *into* the city of 3068
6:16 David leaping and dancing before **the L**; 3068
6:17 they brought in the ark of **the L**, and set it 3068
6:17 and peace offerings before **the L**. 3068
6:18 he blessed the people in the name of **the L** 3068
6:21 said unto Michal, *It was* before **the L**, 3068
6:21 appoint me ruler over the people of **the L**, 3068
6:21 therefore will I play before **the L**. 3068
7: 1 **the L** had given him rest round about from 3068
7: 3 that *is* in thine heart; for **the L** *is* with thee. 3068
7: 4 that the word of **the L** came unto Nathan, 3068
7: 5 tell my servant David, Thus saith **the L**, 3068
7: 8 Thus saith **the L** of hosts, I took thee from 3068
7:11 Also **the L** telleth thee that he will make 3068
7:18 sat before **the L**, and he said, Who *am* I, 3068
7:22 Wherefore thou art great, O **L** God: 3068
7:24 for ever; and thou, **L**, art become their God. 3068
7:25 now, O **L** God, the word that thou hast 3068
7:26 **The L** of hosts *is* the God over Israel: 3068
7:27 For thou, O **L** of hosts, God of Israel, 3068
8: 6 **the L** preserved David whithersoever he 3068
8:11 also king David did dedicate unto **the L**, 3068
8:14 **the L** preserved David whithersoever he 3068
10:12 and **the L** do that which seemeth him good. 3068
11:27 thing that David had done displeased **the L**. 3068
12: 1 **the L** sent Nathan unto David. And he 3068
12: 5 he said to Nathan, *As* **the L** liveth, the man 3068
12: 7 Thus saith **the L** God of Israel, I anointed 3068
12: 9 thou despised the commandment of **the L**, 3068
12:11 Thus saith **the L**, Behold, I will raise up 3068
12:13 unto Nathan, I have sinned against **the L**. 3068
12:13 **The L** also hath put away thy sin; 3068
12:14 to the enemies of **the L** to blaspheme, 3068
12:15 **the L** strake the child that Uriah's wife 3068
12:20 came *into* the house of **the L**, and 3068
12:24 his name Solomon: and **the L** loved him. 3068
12:25 called his name Jedidiah, because of **the L**. 3068
14:11 let the king remember **the L** thy God, 3068
14:11 he said, *As* **the L** liveth, there shall not one 3068
14:17 therefore **the L** thy God will be with thee. 3068
15: 7 which I have vowed unto **the L**, in Hebron. 3068
15: 8 If **the L** shall bring me again indeed *to* 3068
15: 8 *to* Jerusalem, then I will serve **the L**. 3068
15:21 *As* **the L** liveth, and *as* my lord the king 3068

2Sa 15:25 if I shall find favour in the eyes of **the L**, 3068
15:31 David said, O **L**, I pray thee, turn 3068
16: 8 **The L** hath returned upon thee all the blood 3068
16: 8 **the L** hath delivered the kingdom into 3068
16:10 because **the L** hath said unto him, 3068
16:11 let him curse; for **the L** hath bidden him. 3068
16:12 It may be that **the L** will look on mine 3068
16:12 that **the L** will requite me good for his 3068
16:18 whom **the L**, and this people, and all 3068
17:14 For **the L** had appointed to defeat the good 3068
17:14 to the intent that **the L** might bring evil 3068
18:19 how that **the L** hath avenged him of his 3068
18:28 and said, Blessed *be* **the L** thy God, 3068
18:31 for **the L** hath avenged thee *this* day of all 3068
19: 7 for I swear by **the L**, if thou go not forth, 3068
20:19 thou swallow up the inheritance of **the L**? 3068
21: 1 after year; and David inquired of **the L**. 3068
21: 1 **the L** answered, *It is* for Saul, and for *his* 3068
21: 3 that ye may bless the inheritance of **the L**? 3068
21: 6 we will hang them up unto **the L** in Gibeah 3068
21: 6 in Gibeah of Saul, whom **the L** did choose. 3068
21: 9 they hanged them in the hill before **the L**: 3068
22: 1 David spake unto **the L** the words of this 3068
22: 1 **the L** had delivered him out of the hand of 3068
22: 2 **The L** *is* my rock, and my fortress, and 3068
22: 4 I will call on **the L**, who is *worthy* to be 3068
22: 7 In my distress I called upon **the L**, and 3068
22:14 **The L** thundered from heaven, and 3068
22:16 at the rebuking of **the L**, at the blast of 3068
22:19 day of my calamity: but **the L** was my stay. 3068
22:21 **The L** rewarded me according to my 3068
22:22 For I have kept the ways of **the L**, and 3068
22:25 Therefore **the L** hath recompensed me 3068
22:29 For thou *art* my lamp, O **L**: and the LORD 3068
22:29 and **the L** will lighten my darkness. 3068
22:31 way *is* perfect; the word of **the L** *is* tried: 3068
22:32 For who *is* God, save **the L**? and who *is* a 3068
22:42 *even* unto **the L**, but he answered them not. 3068
22:47 **The L** liveth; and blessed *be* my rock; and 3068
22:50 O **L**, among the heathen, and I will sing 3068
23: 2 The Spirit of **the L** spake by me, and 3068
23:10 **the L** wrought a great victory that day; 3068
23:12 and **the L** wrought a great victory. 3068
23:16 drink thereof, but poured it out unto **the L**. 3068
23:17 he said, Be it far from me, O **L**, that I 3068
24: 1 again the anger of **the L** was kindled 3068
24: 3 Now **the L** thy God add unto the people, 3068
24:10 David said unto **the L**, I have sinned 3068
24:10 now, I beseech thee, O **L**, take away 3068
24:11 the word of **the L** came unto the prophet 3068
24:12 Go and say unto David, Thus saith **the L**, 3068
24:14 let us fall now into the hand of **the L**; 3068
24:15 So **the L** sent a pestilence upon Israel from 3068
24:16 **the L** repented him of the evil, and said to 3068
24:16 the angel of **the L** was by 3068
24:17 David spake unto **the L** when he saw 3068
24:18 rear an altar unto **the L** in 3068
24:19 of Gad, went up as **the L** commanded. 3068
24:21 of thee, to build an altar unto **the L**, 3068
24:23 unto the king, **The L** thy God accept thee. 3068
24:24 **the L** my God of that which doth cost me 3068
24:25 David built there an altar unto **the L**, and 3068
24:25 So **the L** was intreated for the land, and 3068
1Ki 1:17 thou swarest by **the L** thy God unto thine 3068
1:29 the king sware, and said, *As* **the L** liveth, 3068
1:30 Even as I sware unto thee by **the L** God of 3068
1:36 **the L** God of my lord the king say so *too.* 3068
1:37 As **the L** hath been with my lord the king, 3068
1:48 the king, Blessed *be* **the L** God of Israel, 3068
2: 3 keep the charge of **the L** thy God, to walk 3068
2: 4 That **the L** may continue his word which 3068
2: 8 and I sware to him by **the L**, saying, 3068
2:15 my brother's: for it was his from **the L**. 3068
2:23 king Solomon sware by **the L**, saying, 3068
2:24 Now therefore, *as* **the L** liveth, which hath 3068
2:27 out Abiathar from being priest unto **the L**; 3068
2:27 that *he* might fulfil the word of **the L**, 3068
2:28 Joab fled unto the tabernacle of **the L**, and 3068
2:29 Joab was fled unto the tabernacle of **the L**; 3068
2:30 Benaiah came to the tabernacle of **the L**, 3068
2:32 **the L** shall return his blood upon his own 3068
2:33 shall there be peace for ever from **the L**. 3068
2:42 Did I not make thee to swear by **the L**, and 3068
2:43 then hast thou not kept the oath of **the L**, 3068
2:44 **the L** shall return thy wickedness upon 3068
2:45 shall be established before **the L** for ever. 3068
3: 1 the house of **the L**, and the wall of 3068
3: 2 was no house built unto the name of **the L**, 3068
3: 3 Solomon loved **the L**, walking in 3068
3: 5 In Gibeon **the L** appeared to Solomon in a 3068
3: 7 now, O **L** my God, thou hast made thy 3068
3:15 before the ark of the covenant of **the L**, 3068
5: 3 **the L** his God for the wars which were 3068
5: 3 until **the L** put them under the soles of his 3068
5: 4 now **the L** my God hath given me rest on 3068
5: 5 a house unto the name of **the L** my God, 3068
5: 5 as **the L** spake unto David my father, 3068
5: 7 and said, Blessed *be* **the L** *this* day, 3068
5:12 **the L** gave Solomon wisdom, as he 3068
6: 1 that he *began* to build the house of **the L**. 3068
6: 2 house which king Solomon built for **the L**, 3068
6:11 the word of **the L** came to Solomon, 3068
6:19 set there the ark of the covenant of **the L**. 3068
6:37 the foundation of the house of **the L** laid, 3068
7:12 for the inner court of the house of **the L**, 3068
7:40 made king Solomon *for* the house of **the L**: 3068
7:45 to king Solomon *for* the house of **the L**, 3068
7:48 that *pertained unto* the house of **the L**: 3068
7:51 king Solomon made *for* the house of **the L**. 3068
7:51 among the treasures of the house of **the L**. 3068
8: 1 covenant of **the L** out of the city of David, 3068
8: 4 they brought up the ark of **the L**, and 3068
8: 6 ark of the covenant of **the L** unto his place, 3068
8: 9 when **the L** made *a covenant* with 3068
8:10 that the cloud filled the house of **the L**, 3068

1Ki 8:11 for the glory of **the L** had filled the house 3068
8:11 the LORD had filled the house of **the L.** 3068
8:12 **The L** said that *he* would dwell in the thick 3068
8:15 he said, Blessed *be* **the L** God of Israel, 3068
8:17 house for the name of **the L** God of Israel. 3068
8:18 **the L** said unto David my father, 3068
8:20 **the L** hath performed his word that he 3068
8:20 as **the L** promised, and have built a house 3068
8:20 have built a house for the name of **the L** 3068
8:21 wherein *is* the covenant of **the L,** which he 3068
8:22 Solomon stood before the altar of **the L** in 3068
8:23 he said, **L** God of Israel, *there is* no God 3068
8:25 Therefore now, **L** God of Israel, keep with 3068
8:28 to his supplication, O **L** my God, 3068
8:44 shall pray unto **the L** toward the city which 3068
8:54 all this prayer and supplication unto **the L,** 3068
8:54 he arose from before the altar of **the L,** 3068
8:56 Blessed *be* **the L,** that hath given rest unto 3068
8:57 **The L** our God be with us, as he was with 3068
8:59 I have made supplication before **the L,** 3068
8:59 be nigh unto **the L** our God day and night, 3068
8:60 of the earth may know that **the L** *is* God, 3068
8:61 therefore be perfect with **the L** our God, 3068
8:62 with him, offered sacrifice before **the L.** 3068
8:63 which he offered unto **the L,** two and 3068
8:63 of Israel dedicated the house of **the L.** 3068
8:64 court that *was* before the house of **the L:** 3068
8:64 the brasen altar that *was* before **the L** *was* 3068
8:65 before **the L** our God, seven days and 3068
8:66 glad of heart for all the goodness that **the L** 3068
9: 1 finished the building of the house of **the L,** 3068
9: 2 That **the L** appeared to Solomon the second 3068
9: 3 **the L** said unto him, I have heard thy 3068
9: 8 Why hath **the L** done thus unto this land, 3068
9: 9 Because they forsook **the L** their God, 3068
9: 9 hath **the L** brought upon them all this evil. 3068
9:10 the house of **the L,** and the king's house, 3068
9:15 for to build the house of **the L,** and his own 3068
9:25 upon the altar which he built unto **the L,** 3068
9:25 upon the altar that *was* before **the L.** 3068
10: 1 of Solomon concerning the name of **the L,** 3068
10: 5 which he went up *unto* the house of **the L;** 3068
10: 9 Blessed be **the L** thy God, which delighted 3068
10: 9 because **the L** loved Israel for ever, 3068
10:12 almug trees pillars for the house of **the L,** 3068
11: 2 Of the nations *concerning* which **the L** said 3068
11: 4 his heart was not perfect with **the L** his 3068
11: 6 Solomon did evil in the sight of **the L,** and 3068
11: 6 went not fully after **the L,** as *did* David his 3068
11: 9 **the L** was angry with Solomon, because 3068
11: 9 his heart was turned from **the L** God of 3068
11:10 he kept not *that* which **the L** commanded. 3068
11:11 Wherefore **the L** said unto Solomon, 3068
11:14 **the L** stirred up an adversary unto 3068
11:31 for thus saith **the L,** the God of Israel, 3068
12:15 for the cause was from **the L,** that *he* might 3068
12:15 which **the L** spake by Ahijah the Shilonite 3068
12:24 Thus saith **the L,** Ye shall not go up, 3068
12:24 therefore to the word of **the L,** 3068
12:24 to depart, according to the word of **the L.** 3068
12:27 sacrifice in the house of **the L** at Jerusalem, 3068
13: 1 of Judah by the word of **the L** unto Beth-el: 3068
13: 2 cried against the altar in the word of **the L,** 3068
13: 2 and said, O altar, altar, thus saith **the L;** 3068
13: 3 This *is* the sign which **the L** hath spoken; 3068
13: 5 of God had given by the word of **the L.** 3068
13: 6 Intreat now the face of **the L** thy God, and 3068
13: 6 the man of God besought **the L,** and 3068
13: 9 so was it charged me by the word of **the L,** 3068
13:17 For it was said to me by the word of **the L,** 3068
13:18 angel spake unto me by the word of **the L,** 3068
13:20 that the word of **the L** came unto 3068
13:21 came from Judah, saying, Thus saith **the L,** 3068
13:21 as thou hast disobeyed the mouth of **the L,** 3068
13:21 which **the L** thy God commanded thee, 3068
13:22 of the which *the L* did say to thee, Eat no NIH
13:26 was disobedient unto the word of **the L:** 3068
13:26 **the L** hath delivered him unto the lion, 3068
13:26 slain him, according to the word of **the L,** 3068
13:32 word of **the L** against the altar in Beth-el, 3068
14: 5 **the L** said unto Ahijah, Behold, the wife of 3068
14: 7 Thus saith **the L** God of Israel, 3068
14:11 of the air eat: for **the L** hath spoken *it.* 3068
14:13 **the L** God of Israel in the house of 3068
14:14 Moreover **the L** shall raise him up a king 3068
14:15 For **the L** shall smite Israel, as a reed is 3068
14:15 their groves, provoking **the L** to anger. 3068
14:18 for him, according to the word of **the L,** 3068
14:21 the city which **the L** did choose out of all 3068
14:22 Judah did evil in the sight of **the L,** and 3068
14:24 **the L** cast out before the children of Israel. 3068
14:26 away the treasures of the house of **the L,** 3068
14:28 when the king went *into* the house of **the L,** 3068
15: 3 his heart was not perfect with **the L** his 3068
15: 4 Nevertheless for David's sake did **the L** his 3068
15: 5 *that* which *was* right in the eyes of **the L,** 3068
15:11 *that* which *was* right in the eyes of **the L,** 3068
15:14 heart was perfect with **the L** all his days. 3068
15:15 *into* the house of **the L,** silver, and gold, 3068
15:18 left in the treasures of the house of **the L,** 3068
15:26 he did evil in the sight of **the L,** and 3068
15:29 according unto the saying of **the L,** 3068
15:30 he provoked **the L** God of Israel to anger. 3068
15:34 he did evil in the sight of **the L,** and 3068
16: 1 the word of **the L** came to Jehu the son of 3068
16: 7 came the word of **the L** against Baasha, 3068
16: 7 all the evil that he did in the sight of **the L,** 3068
16:12 of Baasha, according to the word of **the L,** 3068
16:13 in provoking **the L** God of Israel to anger 3068
16:19 sinned in doing evil in the sight of **the L,** 3068
16:25 But Omri wrought evil in the eyes of **the L,** 3068
16:26 to provoke **the L** God of Israel to anger 3068
16:30 of **the L** above all that *were* before him. 3068
16:33 Ahab did more to provoke **the L** God of 3068
16:34 according to the word of **the L,** which he 3068

1Ki 17: 1 unto Ahab, *As* **the L** God of Israel liveth, 3068
17: 2 the word of **the L** came unto him, saying, 3068
17: 5 and did according unto the word of **the L:** 3068
17: 8 the word of **the L** came unto him, saying, 3068
17:12 she said, *As* **the L** thy God liveth, I have 3068
17:14 For thus saith **the L** God of Israel, 3068
17:14 until the day *that* **the L** sendeth rain upon 3068
17:16 according to the word of **the L,** which he 3068
17:20 he cried unto **the L,** and said, O LORD 3068
17:20 unto the LORD, and said, O **L** my God, 3068
17:21 cried unto **the L,** and said, O LORD my 3068
17:21 and said, O **L** my God, I pray thee, 3068
17:22 **the L** heard the voice of Elijah; and 3068
17:24 *that* the word of **the L** in thy mouth *is* truth. 3068
18: 1 that the word of **the L** came to Elijah in 3068
18: 3 (Now Obadiah feared **the L** greatly: 3068
18: 4 when Jezebel cut off the prophets of **the L,** 3068
18:10 *As* **the L** thy God liveth, there is no nation 3068
18:12 that the spirit of **the L** shall carry thee 3068
18:12 but *I* thy servant fear **the L** from my youth. 3068
18:13 when Jezebel slew the prophets of **the L,** 3068
18:15 Elijah said, *As* **the L** of hosts liveth, before 3068
18:18 have forsaken the commandments of **the L,** 3068
18:21 if **the L** *be* God, follow him: but if Baal, 3068
18:22 I, *even* I only, remain a prophet of **the L;** 3068
18:24 and I will call on the name of **the L:** 3068
18:30 he repaired the altar of **the L** that was 3068
18:31 unto whom the word of **the L** came, 3068
18:32 he built an altar in the name of **the L:** 3068
18:36 said, **L** God of Abraham, Isaac, and 3068
18:37 Hear me, O **L,** hear me, that this people 3068
18:37 people may know that thou *art* **the L** God, 3068
18:38 the fire of **the L** fell, and consumed 3068
18:39 they said, **The L,** he *is* the God; 3068
18:39 he *is* the God; **the L,** he *is* the God. 3068
18:46 the hand of **the L** was on Elijah; and 3068
19: 4 *It is* enough; now, O **L,** take away my life; 3068
19: 7 the angel of **the L** came again the second 3068
19: 9 the word of **the L** *came* to him, and he said 3068
19:10 I have been very jealous for **the L** God of 3068
19:11 and stand upon the mount before **the L.** 3068
19:11 **the L** passed by, and a great and 3068
19:11 and brake in pieces the rocks before **the L;** 3068
19:11 the LORD; *but* **the L** *was* not in the wind: 3068
19:11 *but* **the L** *was* not in the earthquake: 3068
19:12 a fire; *but* **the L** *was* not in the fire: 3068
19:14 I have been very jealous for **the L** God of 3068
19:15 **the L** said unto him, Go, return on thy way 3068
20:13 saying, Thus saith **the L,** Hast thou seen all 3068
20:13 and thou shalt know that I *am* **the L.** 3068
20:14 he said, Thus saith **the L,** *Even* by 3068
20:28 king of Israel, and said, Thus saith **the L,** 3068
20:28 **The L** *is* God of the hills, but he *is* not God 3068
20:28 and ye shall know that I *am* **the L.** 3068
20:35 unto his neighbour in the word of **the L,** 3068
20:36 thou hast not obeyed the voice of **the L,** 3068
20:42 he said unto him, Thus saith **the L,** 3068
21: 3 Naboth said to Ahab, **The L** forbid it me, 3068
21:17 the word of **the L** came to Elijah 3068
21:19 saying, Thus saith **the L,** Hast thou killed, 3068
21:19 speak unto him, saying, Thus saith **the L,** 3068
21:20 thyself to work evil in the sight of **the L,** 3068
21:23 of Jezebel also spake **the L,** saying, 3068
21:25 to work wickedness in the sight of **the L,** 3068
21:26 whom **the L** cast out before the children of 3068
21:28 the word of **the L** came to Elijah 3068
22: 5 I pray thee, at the word of **the L** to day. 3068
22: 7 *Is there* not here a prophet of **the L** besides, 3068
22: 8 by whom *we* may inquire of **the L:** 3068
22:11 he said, Thus saith **the L,** With these shalt 3068
22:12 for **the L** shall deliver *it* into the king's 3068
22:14 Micaiah said, *As* **the L** liveth, what 3068
22:14 what **the L** saith unto me, that will I speak. 3068
22:15 for **the L** shall deliver *it* into the hand of 3068
22:16 but *that which is* true in the name of **the L?** 3068
22:17 **the L** said, These have no master: let them 3068
22:19 Hear thou therefore the word of **the L:** 3068
22:19 I saw **the L** sitting on his throne, and all 3068
22:20 **the L** said, Who shall persuade Ahab, 3068
22:21 stood before **the L,** and said, I will 3068
22:22 **the L** said unto him, Wherewith? And he 3068
22:23 **the L** hath put a lying spirit in the mouth of 3068
22:23 **the L** hath spoken evil concerning thee. 3068
22:24 Which way went the spirit of **the L** from 3068
22:28 all in peace, **the L** hath not spoken by me. 3068
22:38 according unto the word of **the L** which he 3068
22:43 *that* which *was* right in the eyes of **the L:** 3068
22:52 he did evil in the sight of **the L,** and 3068
22:53 and provoked to anger **the L** God of Israel, 3068
2Ki 1: 3 the angel of **the L** said to Elijah 3068
1: 4 Now therefore thus saith **the L,** Thou shalt 3068
1: 6 Thus saith **the L,** *Is it* not because *there is* 3068
1:15 the angel of **the L** said unto Elijah, 3068
1:16 he said unto him, Thus saith **the L,** 3068
1:17 So he died according to the word of **the L** 3068
2: 1 when **the L** would take up Elijah *into* 3068
2: 2 for **the L** hath sent me to Beth-el. 3068
2: 2 Elisha said *unto him, As* **the L** liveth, and 3068
2: 3 Knowest thou that **the L** will take away thy 3068
2: 4 for **the L** hath sent me *to* Jericho. 3068
2: 4 *As* **the L** liveth, and *as* thy soul liveth, 3068
2: 5 Knowest thou that **the L** will take away thy 3068
2: 6 here; for **the L** hath sent me to Jordan. 3068
2: 6 *As* **the L** liveth, and *as* thy soul liveth, 3068
2:14 and said, Where *is* **the L** God of Elijah? 3068
2:16 lest peradventure the spirit of **the L** hath 3068
2:21 the salt in there, and said, Thus saith **the L,** 3068
2:24 and cursed them in the name of **the L.** 3068
3: 2 he wrought evil in the sight of **the L;** but 3068
3:10 that **the L** hath called these three kings 3068
3:11 *Is there* not here a prophet of **the L,** 3068
3:11 that we may inquire of **the L** by him? 3068
3:12 The word of **the L** is with him. 3068
3:13 for **the L** hath called these three kings 3068
3:14 Elisha said, *As* **the L** of hosts liveth, before 3068

2Ki 3:15 that the hand of **the L** came upon him. 3068
3:16 he said, Thus saith **the L,** Make this valley 3068
3:17 For thus saith **the L,** Ye shall not see wind, 3068
3:18 this is *but* a light thing in the sight of **the L:** 3068
4: 1 knowest that thy servant did fear **the L:** 3068
4:27 **the L** hath hid *it* from me, and hath not told 3068
4:30 *As* **the L** liveth, and *as* thy soul liveth, 3068
4:33 upon them twain, and prayed unto **the L.** 3068
4:43 for thus saith **the L,** They shall eat, and 3068
4:44 left *thereof,* according to the word of **the L.** 3068
5: 1 by him **the L** had given deliverance unto 3068
5:11 call on the name of **the L** his God, and 3068
5:16 he said, *As* **the L** liveth, before whom I 3068
5:17 sacrifice unto other gods, but unto **the L.** 3068
5:18 In this thing **the L** pardon thy servant, 3068
5:18 **the L** pardon thy servant in this thing. 3068
5:20 but, *as* **the L** liveth, I will run after him, 3068
6:17 said, **L,** I pray thee, open his eyes, that he 3068
6:17 **the L** opened the eyes of the young man; 3068
6:18 Elisha prayed unto **the L,** and said, 3068
6:20 come *into* Samaria, that Elisha said, **L,** 3068
6:20 **the L** opened their eyes, and they saw; and 3068
6:27 he said, *If* **the L** do not help thee, whence 3068
6:33 he said, Behold, this evil *is* of **the L;** 3068
6:33 what should I wait for **the L** any longer? 3068
7: 1 Elisha said, Hear ye the word of **the L;** 3068
7: 1 Thus saith **the L,** To morrow about *this* 3068
7: 2 *if* **the L** would make windows in heaven, 3068
7:16 a shekel, according to the word of **the L.** 3068
7:19 *if* **the L** should make windows in heaven, 3068
8: 1 for **the L** hath called for a famine; and 3068
8: 8 and inquire of **the L** by him, saying, 3068
8:10 howbeit **the L** hath shewed me that he shall 3068
8:13 **The L** hath shewed me *that* thou *shalt be* 3068
8:18 and he did evil in the sight of **the L.** 3068
8:19 Yet **the L** would not destroy Judah for 3068
8:27 did evil in the sight of **the L,** as *did* 3068
9: 3 *it* on his head, and say, Thus saith **the L,** 3068
9: 6 unto him, Thus saith **the L** God of Israel, 3068
9: 6 thee king over the people of **the L,** 3068
9: 7 the blood of all the servants of **the L,** at 3068
9:12 spake he to me, saying, Thus saith **the L,** 3068
9:25 his father, **the L** laid this burden upon him; 3068
9:26 and the blood of his sons, saith **the L;** 3068
9:26 I will requite thee in this plat, saith **the L.** 3068
9:26 *of ground,* according to the word of **the L.** 3068
9:36 he said, This *is* the word of **the L,** which he 3068
10:10 unto the earth nothing of the word of **the L,** 3068
10:10 which **the L** spake concerning the house of 3068
10:10 for **the L** hath done *that* which he spake by 3068
10:16 Come with me, and see my zeal for **the L.** 3068
10:17 according to the saying of **the L,** which he 3068
10:23 with you none of the servants of **the L,** 3068
10:30 **the L** said unto Jehu, Because thou hast 3068
10:31 of **the L** God of Israel with all his heart: 3068
10:32 In those days **the L** began to cut Israel 3068
11: 3 he was with her hid *in* the house of **the L** 3068
11: 4 them to him *into* the house of **the L,** 3068
11: 4 took an oath of them in the house of **the L,** 3068
11: 7 watch of the house of **the L** about the king. 3068
11:10 that *were* in the temple of **the L.** 3068
11:13 to the people *into* the temple of **the L.** 3068
11:15 Let her not be slain *in* the house of **the L.** 3068
11:17 Jehoiada made a covenant between **the L** 3068
11:18 appointed officers over the house of **the L.** 3068
11:19 down the king from the house of **the L,** 3068
12: 2 **the L** all his days where*in* Jehoiada 3068
12: 4 that is brought *into* the house of **the L,** 3068
12: 4 heart to bring *into* the house of **the L,** 3068
12: 9 side as one cometh *into* the house of **the L:** 3068
12: 9 that was brought *into* the house of **the L.** 3068
12:10 that was found *in* the house of **the L.** 3068
12:11 had the oversight *of* the house of **the L:** 3068
12:11 that wrought upon the house of **the L,** 3068
12:12 to repair the breaches of the house of **the L,** 3068
12:13 *for* the house of **the L** bowls of silver, 3068
12:13 that was brought *into* the house of **the L:** 3068
12:14 repaired therewith the house of **the L.** 3068
12:16 was not brought *into* the house of **the L:** 3068
12:18 in the treasures of the house of **the L,** 3068
13: 2 *that* which *was* evil in the sight of **the L,** 3068
13: 3 the anger of **the L** was kindled against 3068
13: 4 Jehoahaz besought **the L,** and the LORD 3068
13: 4 and **the L** hearkened unto him: 3068
13: 5 (And **the L** gave Israel a saviour, so 3068
13:11 *that* which *was* evil in the sight of **the L;** 3068
13:23 **the L** was gracious unto them, and 3068
14: 3 *that* which *was* right in the sight of **the L,** 3068
14: 6 where*in* **the L** commanded, saying, 3068
14:14 that were found *in* the house of **the L,** 3068
14:24 *that* which *was* evil in the sight of **the L:** 3068
14:25 according to the word of **the L** God of 3068
14:26 For **the L** saw the affliction of Israel, *that it* 3068
14:27 **the L** said not that *he* would blot out 3068
15: 3 *that* which *was* right in the sight of **the L,** 3068
15: 5 **the L** smote the king, so that he was a leper 3068
15: 9 *that* which *was* evil in the sight of **the L,** 3068
15:12 This *was* the word of **the L** which he spake 3068
15:18 *that* which *was* evil in the sight of **the L:** 3068
15:24 *that* which *was* evil in the sight of **the L:** 3068
15:28 *that* which *was* evil in the sight of **the L:** 3068
15:34 *that* which *was* right in the sight of **the L:** 3068
15:35 built the higher gate of the house of **the L.** 3068
15:37 In those days **the L** began to send against 3068
16: 2 *was* right in the sight of **the L** his God, 3068
16: 3 whom **the L** cast out from before 3068
16: 8 gold that was found *in* the house of **the L,** 3068
16:14 which *was* before **the L,** from the forefront 3068
16:14 between the altar and the house of **the L,** 3068
16:18 turned he *from* the house of **the L** for 3068
17: 2 *that* which *was* evil in the sight of **the L,** 3068
17: 7 Israel had sinned against **the L** their God, 3068
17: 8 whom **the L** cast out from before 3068
17: 9 that *were* not right against **the L** their God, 3068
17:11 as *did* the heathen whom **the L** carried 3068

2Ki 17:11 wrought wicked things to provoke **the L** to 3068
17:12 whereof **the L** had said unto them, 3068
17:13 Yet **the L** testified against Israel, and 3068
17:14 that did not believe in **the L** their God. 3068
17:15 *concerning* whom **the L** had charged them, 3068
17:16 they left all the commandments of **the L** 3068
17:17 themselves to do evil in the sight of **the L**, 3068
17:18 Therefore **the L** was very angry with Israel, 3068
17:19 not the commandments of **the L** their God, 3068
17:20 **the L** rejected all the seed of Israel, and 3068
17:21 drave Israel from following **the L**, 3068
17:23 Until **the L** removed Israel out of his sight, 3068
17:25 dwelling there, *that* they feared not **the L**: 3068
17:25 therefore **the L** sent lions among them, 3068
17:28 taught them how they should fear **the L**. 3068
17:32 So they feared **the L**, and made unto 3068
17:33 They feared **the L**, and served their own 3068
17:34 they fear not **the L**, neither do they after 3068
17:34 commandment which **the L** commanded 3068
17:35 With whom **the L** had made a covenant, 3068
17:36 **the L**, who brought you up out of the land 3068
17:39 **the L** your God ye shall fear; and he shall 3068
17:41 So these nations feared **the L**, and served 3068
18: 3 *that* which *was* right in the sight of **the L**, 3068
18: 5 He trusted in **the L** God of Israel; so 3068
18: 6 For he clave to **the L**, *and* departed not 3068
18: 6 which **the L** commanded Moses. 3068
18: 7 **the L** was with him; *and* he prospered 3068
18:12 Because they obeyed not the voice of **the L** 3068
18:12 all that Moses the servant of **the L** 3068
18:15 silver that was found *in* the house of **the L**, 3068
18:16 *gold from* the doors of the temple of **the L**, 3068
18:22 ye say unto me, We trust in **the L** our God: 3068
18:25 Am I now come up without **the L** against 3068
18:25 **The L** said to me, Go up against this land, 3068
18:30 let Hezekiah make you trust in **the L**, 3068
18:30 **The L** will surely deliver us, and this city 3068
18:32 saying, **The L** will deliver us. 3068
18:35 that **the L** should deliver Jerusalem out of 3068
19: 1 and went *into* the house of **the L**. 3068
19: 4 It may be **the L** thy God will hear all 3068
19: 4 will reprove the words which **the L** thy 3068
19: 6 ye say to your master, Thus saith **the L**, 3068
19:14 Hezekiah went up *into* the house of **the L**, 3068
19:14 of the LORD, and spread it before **the L**. 3068
19:15 Hezekiah prayed before **the L**, and said, 3068
19:15 said, O **L** God of Israel, which dwellest 3068
19:16 **L**, bow down thine ear, and hear: open, 3068
19:16 open, **L**, thine eyes, and see: and hear 3068
19:17 Of a truth, **L**, the kings of Assyria have 3068
19:19 O **L** our God, I beseech thee, 3068
19:19 earth may know that thou *art* **the L** God, 3068
19:20 Thus saith **the L** God of Israel, 3068
19:21 This *is* the word that **the L** hath spoken 3068
19:31 the zeal of **the L** *of hosts* shall do this. 3068
19:32 Therefore thus saith **the L** concerning 3068
19:33 shall not come into this city, saith **the L**. 3068
19:35 that the angel of **the L** went out, and 3068
20: 1 said unto him, Thus saith **the L**, Set thine 3068
20: 2 to the wall, and prayed unto **the L**, saying, 3068
20: 3 I beseech thee, O **L**, remember now how I 3068
20: 4 that the word of **the L** came to him, saying, 3068
20: 5 Thus saith **the L**, the God of David thy 3068
20: 5 thou shalt go up *unto* the house of **the L**. 3068
20: 8 What *shall be* the sign that **the L** will heal 3068
20: 8 *that* I shall go up *into* the house of **the L** 3068
20: 9 This sign shalt thou have of **the L**, 3068
20: 9 that **the L** will do the thing that he hath 3068
20:11 Isaiah the prophet cried unto **the L**: and 3068
20:16 unto Hezekiah, Hear the word of **the L**. 3068
20:17 nothing shall be left, saith **the L**. 3068
20:19 Good *is* the word of **the L** which thou hast 3068
21: 2 *that* which *was* evil in the sight of **the L**, 3068
21: 2 whom **the L** cast out before the children of 3068
21: 4 he built altars in the house of **the L**, 3068
21: 4 of which **the L** said, In Jerusalem will I put 3068
21: 5 in the two courts of the house of **the L**. 3068
21: 6 much wickedness in the sight of **the L**, 3068
21: 7 of which **the L** said to David, and 3068
21: 9 **the L** destroyed before the children of 3068
21:10 **the L** spake by his servants the prophets, 3068
21:12 Therefore thus saith **the L** God of Israel, 3068
21:16 *that* which *was* evil in the sight of **the L**. 3068
21:20 *that* which *was* evil in the sight of **the L**, 3068
21:22 he forsook **the L** God of his fathers, and 3068
21:22 and walked not in the way of **the L**. 3068
22: 2 *that* which *was* right in the sight of **the L**, 3068
22: 3 the scribe, *to* the house of **the L**, saying, 3068
22: 4 which is brought *into* the house of **the L**, 3068
22: 5 have the oversight of the house of **the L**: 3068
22: 5 of the work which *is* in the house of **the L**, 3068
22: 8 the book of the law in the house of **the L**. 3068
22: 9 have the oversight *of* the house of **the L**. 3068
22:13 inquire of **the L** for me, and for the people, 3068
22:13 for great *is* the wrath of **the L** that is 3068
22:15 unto them, Thus saith **the L** God of Israel, 3068
22:16 Thus saith **the L**, Behold, I will bring evil 3068
22:18 Judah which sent you to inquire of **the L**, 3068
22:18 say to him, Thus saith **the L** God of Israel, 3068
22:19 thou hast humbled thyself before **the L**, 3068
22:19 I also have heard *thee,* saith **the L**. 3068
23: 2 the king went up *into* the house of **the L**, 3068
23: 2 which was found in the house of **the L**. 3068
23: 3 made a covenant before **the L**, to walk after 3068
23: 3 to walk after **the L**, and to keep his 3068
23: 4 to bring forth out of the temple of **the L** all 3068
23: 6 out the grove from the house of **the L**, 3068
23: 7 that *were* by the house of **the L**, where 3068
23: 9 not up to the altar of **the L** in Jerusalem, 3068
23:11 at the entering in of the house of **the L**, 3068
23:12 in the two courts of the house of **the L**, 3068
23:16 according to the word of **the L** which 3068
23:19 Israel had made to provoke *the L* to anger, NIH
23:21 Keep the passover unto **the L** your God, 3068
23:23 *wherein* this passover was holden to **the L** 3068

2Ki 23:24 the priest found *in* the house of **the L**. 3068
23:25 that turned to **the L** with all his heart, and 3068
23:26 Notwithstanding **the L** turned not from 3068
23:27 **the L** said, I will remove Judah also out of 3068
23:32 *that* which *was* evil in the sight of **the L**, 3068
23:37 *that* which *was* evil in the sight of **the L**, 3068
24: 2 **the L** sent against him bands of 3068
24: 2 destroy it, according to the word of **the L**, 3068
24: 3 Surely at the commandment of **the L** came 3068
24: 4 which **the L** would not pardon. 3068
24: 9 *that* which *was* evil in the sight of **the L**, 3068
24:13 all the treasures of the house of **the L**, 3068
24:13 of Israel had made in the temple of **the L**, 3068
24:13 temple of the LORD, as **the L** had said. 3068
24:19 *that* which *was* evil in the sight of **the L**, 3068
24:20 For through the anger of **the L** it came to 3068
25: 9 he burnt the house of **the L**, and the king's 3068
25:13 of brass that *were* in the house of **the L**, 3068
25:13 brasen sea that *was* in the house of **the L**, 3068
25:16 Solomon had made for the house of **the L**; 3068
1Ch 2: 3 of Judah, was evil in the sight of **the L**; 3068
6:15 Jehozadak went *into captivity,* when **the L** 3068
6:31 the service of song *in* the house of **the L**, 3068
6:32 until Solomon had built the house of **the L** 3068
9:19 their fathers, *being* over the host of **the L**, 3068
9:20 them in time past, *and* **the L** *was* with him. 3068
9:23 oversight of the gates of the house of **the L**, 3068
10:13 which he committed against **the L**, 3068
10:13 *even* against the word of **the L**, which he 3068
10:14 inquired not of **the L**: therefore he slew 3068
11: 2 **the L** thy God said unto thee, Thou shalt 3068
11: 3 with them in Hebron before **the L**; 3068
11: 3 according to the word of **the L** by Samuel. 3068
11: 9 greater: for **the L** of hosts *was* with him. 3068
11:10 according to the word of **the L** concerning 3068
11:14 **the L** saved *them by* a great deliverance. 3068
11:18 not drink *of* it, but poured it out to **the L**, 3068
12:23 to him, according to the word of **the L**. 3068
13: 2 unto you, and *that it be* of **the L** our God, 3068
13: 6 to bring up thence the ark of God **the L**, 3068
13:10 the anger of **the L** was kindled against 3068
13:11 **the L** had made a breach upon Uzza: 3068
13:14 **the L** blessed the house of Obed-edom, 3068
14: 2 David perceived that **the L** had confirmed 3068
14:10 **the L** said unto him, Go up; for I will 3068
14:17 **the L** brought the fear of him upon all 3068
15: 2 for them hath **the L** chosen to carry the ark 3068
15: 3 to bring up the ark of **the L** unto his place, 3068
15:12 that you may bring up the ark of **the L** God 3068
15:13 **the L** our God made a breach upon us, 3068
15:14 to bring up the ark of **the L** God of Israel. 3068
15:15 according to the word of **the L**. 3068
15:25 **the L** out of the house of Obed-edom with 3068
15:26 that bare the ark of the covenant of **the L**, 3068
15:28 ark of the covenant of **the L** with shouting, 3068
15:29 *as* the ark of the covenant of **the L** came to 3068
16: 2 he blessed the people in the name of **the L**. 3068
16: 4 Levites to minister before the ark of **the L**, 3068
16: 4 and to thank and praise **the L** God of Israel: 3068
16: 7 to thank **the L** into the hand of Asaph 3068
16: 8 Give thanks unto **the L**, call upon his 3068
16:10 let the heart of them rejoice that seek **the L**. 3068
16:11 Seek **the L** and his strength, seek his face 3068
16:14 He *is* **the L** our God; his judgments *are* in 3068
16:23 Sing unto **the L**, all the earth; shew forth 3068
16:25 For great *is* **the L**, and greatly to be 3068
16:26 *are* idols: but **the L** made the heavens. 3068
16:28 Give unto **the L**, ye kindreds of the people, 3068
16:28 give unto **the L** glory and strength. 3068
16:29 Give unto **the L** the glory due unto his 3068
16:29 worship **the L** in the beauty of holiness. 3068
16:31 say among the nations, **The L** reigneth. 3068
16:33 the wood sing out at the presence of **the L**, 3068
16:34 O give thanks unto **the L**; for *he is* good; 3068
16:36 Blessed *be* **the L** God of Israel for ever and 3068
16:36 the people said, Amen, and praised **the L**. 3068
16:37 the ark of the covenant of **the L** Asaph 3068
16:39 before the tabernacle of **the L** in the high 3068
16:40 To offer burnt offerings unto **the L** upon 3068
16:40 to all that is written in the law of **the L**, 3068
16:41 to give thanks to **the L**, because his mercy 3068
17: 1 the ark of the covenant of **the L** *remaineth* 3068
17: 4 tell David my servant, Thus saith **the L**, 3068
17: 7 Thus saith **the L** of hosts, I took thee from 3068
17:10 Furthermore I tell thee that **the L** will build 3068
17:16 David the king came and sat before **the L**, 3068
17:16 *am* I, O **L** God, and what *is* mine house, 3068
17:17 estate of a man of high degree, O **L** God. 3068
17:19 O **L**, for thy servant's sake, and 3068
17:20 O **L**, *there is* none like thee, neither *is there* 3068
17:22 for ever; and thou, **L**, becamest their God. 3068
17:23 Therefore now, **L**, let the thing that thou 3068
17:24 saying, **The L** of hosts *is* the God of Israel, 3068
17:26 now, **L**, thou *art* God, and hast promised 3068
17:27 O **L**, and *it shall be* blessed for ever. 3068
18: 6 Thus **the L** preserved David whithersoever 3068
18:11 also king David dedicated unto **the L**, 3068
18:13 Thus **the L** preserved David whithersoever 3068
19:13 let **the L** do *that* which *is* good in his sight. 3068
21: 3 **The L** make his people an hundred times 3068
21: 9 **the L** spake unto Gad, David's seer, 3068
21:10 and tell David, saying, Thus saith **the L**, 3068
21:11 unto him, Thus saith **the L**, Choose thee 3068
21:12 or else three days the sword of **the L**, 3068
21:12 the angel of **the L** destroying throughout all 3068
21:13 let me fall now into the hand of **the L**; 3068
21:14 So **the L** sent pestilence upon Israel: and 3068
21:15 **the L** beheld, and he repented him of 3068
21:15 the angel of **the L** stood by 3068
21:16 saw the angel of **the L** stand between 3068
21:17 O **L** my God, be on me, and on my father's 3068
21:18 the angel of **the L** commanded Gad to say 3068
21:18 set up an altar unto **the L** in 3068
21:19 which he spake in the name of **the L**. 3068
21:22 that I may build an altar therein unto **the L**: 3068

1Ch 21:24 I will not take *that* which *is* thine for **the L**, 3068
21:26 David built there an altar unto **the L**, and 3068
21:26 and peace offerings, and called upon **the L**; 3068
21:27 **the L** commanded the angel; and he put up 3068
21:28 At that time when David saw that **the L** 3068
21:29 For the tabernacle of **the L**, which Moses 3068
21:30 of the sword of the angel of **the L**. 3068
22: 1 This *is* the house of **the L** God, and this *is* 3068
22: 5 the house *that is* to be builded for **the L** 3068
22: 6 charged him to build a house for **the L** God 3068
22: 7 a house unto the name of **the L** my God: 3068
22: 8 the word of **the L** came to me, saying, 3068
22:11 Now, my son, **the L** be with thee; and 3068
22:11 and build the house of **the L** thy God, 3068
22:12 Only **the L** give thee wisdom and 3068
22:12 that *thou* mayest keep the law of **the L** thy 3068
22:13 judgments which **the L** charged Moses 3068
22:14 **the L** an hundred thousand talents *of* gold, 3068
22:16 and be doing, and **the L** be with thee. 3068
22:18 *Is* not **the L** your God with you? and 3068
22:18 the land is subdued before **the L**, and 3068
22:19 and your soul to seek **the L** your God; 3068
22:19 and build ye the sanctuary of **the L** God, 3068
22:19 to bring the ark of the covenant of **the L**, 3068
22:19 that is *to be* built to the name of **the L**. 3068
23: 4 set forward the work of the house of **the L**; 3068
23: 5 four thousand praised **the L** with 3068
23:13 sons for ever, to burn incense before **the L**, 3068
23:24 work for the service of the house of **the L**, 3068
23:25 **The L** God of Israel hath given rest unto 3068
23:28 Aaron for the service of the house of **the L**, 3068
23:30 every morning to thank and praise **the L**, 3068
23:31 to offer all burnt sacrifices unto **the L** in 3068
23:31 unto them, continually before **the L**: 3068
23:32 in the service of the house of **the L**. 3068
24:19 service to come into the house of **the L**, 3068
24:19 as **the L** God of Israel had commanded 3068
25: 3 a harp, to give thanks and to praise **the L**. 3068
25: 6 their father for song *in* the house of **the L**, 3068
25: 7 *that were* instructed in the songs of **the L**, 3068
26:12 to minister in the house of **the L**. 3068
26:22 over the treasures of the house of **the L**. 3068
26:27 dedicate to maintain the house of **the L**. 3068
26:30 westward in all the business of **the L**, 3068
27:23 **the L** had said *he* would increase Israel like 3068
28: 2 of rest for the ark of the covenant of **the L**, 3068
28: 4 Howbeit **the L** God of Israel chose me 3068
28: 5 (for **the L** hath given me many sons,) 3068
28: 5 throne of the kingdom of **the L** over Israel. 3068
28: 8 sight of all Israel the congregation of **the L**, 3068
28: 8 seek for all the commandments of **the L** 3068
28: 9 for **the L** searcheth all hearts, and 3068
28:10 for **the L** hath chosen thee to build a house 3068
28:12 of the courts of the house of **the L**, and 3068
28:13 work of the service of the house of **the L**, 3068
28:13 the vessels of service in the house of **the L**. 3068
28:18 covered the ark of the covenant of **the L**. 3068
28:19 All *this, said David,* **the L** made me 3068
28:20 for **the L** God, *even* my God, *will be* with 3068
28:20 work for the service of the house of **the L**. 3068
29: 1 palace *is* not for man, but for **the L** God. 3068
29: 5 consecrate his service *this* day unto **the L**? 3068
29: 8 *them* to the treasure of the house of **the L**, 3068
29: 9 heart they offered willingly to **the L**: 3068
29:10 Wherefore David blessed **the L** before all 3068
29:10 **L** God of Israel our father, for ever and 3068
29:11 Thine, O **L**, *is* the greatness, and the power, 3068
29:11 O **L**, and *thou* art exalted as head above all. 3068
29:16 O **L** our God, all this store that we have 3068
29:18 O **L** God of Abraham, Isaac, and of Israel, 3068
29:20 Now bless **the L** your God. 3068
29:20 all the congregation blessed **the L** God of 3068
29:20 and worshipped **the L**, and the king. 3068
29:21 they sacrificed sacrifices unto **the L**, and 3068
29:21 offered burnt offerings unto **the L**, on 3068
29:22 drink before **the L** on that day with great 3068
29:22 anointed *him* unto **the L** to be the chief 3068
29:23 Solomon sat on the throne of **the L** as king 3068
29:25 **the L** magnified Solomon exceedingly in 3068
2Ch 1: 1 **the L** his God *was* with him, and 3068
1: 3 which Moses the servant of **the L** had 3068
1: 5 he put before the tabernacle of **the L**: 3068
1: 6 up thither to the brasen altar before **the L**, 3068
1: 9 Now, O **L** God, let thy promise unto David 3068
2: 1 to build a house for the name of **the L**, 3068
2: 4 I build a house to the name of **the L** my 3068
2: 4 and on the solemn feasts of **the L** our God. 3068
2:11 Because **the L** hath loved his people, 3068
2:12 Blessed *be* **the L** God of Israel, that made 3068
2:12 that might build a house for **the L**, and 3068
3: 1 Solomon began to build the house of **the L** 3068
3: 1 where *the L* appeared unto David his father, NIH
4:16 for the house of **the L** *of* bright brass. 3068
5: 1 made for the house of **the L** was finished: 3068
5: 2 to bring up the ark of the covenant of **the L** 3068
5: 7 ark of the covenant of **the L** unto his place, 3068
5:10 when **the L** made *a covenant* with 3068
5:13 to be heard in praising and thanking **the L**; 3068
5:13 and praised **the L**, *saying,* For *he is* good; 3068
5:13 *with* a cloud, *even* the house of **the L**; 3068
5:14 for the glory of **the L** had filled the house 3068
6: 1 **The L** hath said that *he* would dwell in 3068
6: 4 he said, Blessed *be* **the L** God of Israel, 3068
6: 7 house for the name of **the L** God of Israel. 3068
6: 8 **the L** said to David my father, 3068
6:10 **The L** therefore hath performed his word 3068
6:10 as **the L** promised, and have built the house 3068
6:10 have built the house for the name of **the L** 3068
6:11 the ark, wherein *is* the covenant of **the L**, 3068
6:12 he stood before the altar of **the L** in 3068
6:14 said, O **L** God of Israel, *there is* no God 3068
6:16 Now therefore, O **L** God of Israel, 3068
6:17 Now then, O **L** God of Israel, let thy word 3068
6:19 to his supplication, O **L** my God, 3068
6:41 Now therefore arise, O **L** God, into thy 3068

L

Ref	Context	Strong's
2Ch 6:41	let thy priests, O **L** God, be clothed *with*	3068
6:42	O **L** God, turn not away the face of thine	3068
7:1	and the glory of **the L** filled the house.	3068
7:2	could not enter into the house of **the L**,	3068
7:2	the glory of **the L** had filled the LORD'S	3068
7:3	and the glory of **the L** upon the house,	3068
7:3	worshipped, and praised **the L**, *saying*, For	3068
7:4	the people offered sacrifices before **the L**.	3068
7:6	also with instruments of musick of **the L**,	3068
7:6	David the king had made to praise **the L**,	3068
7:7	court that *was* before the house of **the L**:	3068
7:10	merry in heart for the goodness that **the L**	3068
7:11	Thus Solomon finished the house of **the L**,	3068
7:11	heart to make in the house of **the L**,	3068
7:12	**the L** appeared to Solomon by night, and	3068
7:21	Why hath **the L** done thus unto this land,	3068
7:22	Because they forsook **the L** God of their	3068
8:1	Solomon had built the house of **the L**,	3068
8:11	whereunto the ark of **the L** hath come.	3068
8:12	Solomon offered burnt offerings unto **the L**	3068
8:12	unto the LORD on the altar of **the L**,	3068
8:16	day of the foundation of the house of **the L**,	3068
8:16	*So* the house of **the L** was perfected.	3068
9:4	which he went up *into* the house of **the L**;	3068
9:8	Blessed be **the L** thy God, which delighted	3068
9:8	on his throne, to be king for **the L** thy God:	3068
9:11	algum trees terraces to the house of **the L**,	3068
10:15	of God, that **the L** might perform his word,	3068
11:2	the word of **the L** came to Shemaiah	3068
11:4	Thus saith **the L**, Ye shall not go up,	3068
11:4	they obeyed the words of **the L**, and	3068
11:14	executing the priest's office unto **the L**:	3068
11:16	**the L** God of Israel came *to* Jerusalem,	3068
11:16	to sacrifice unto **the L** God of their fathers.	3068
12:1	he forsook the law of **the L**, and all Israel	3068
12:2	they had transgressed against **the L**,	3068
12:5	and said unto them, Thus saith **the L**,	3068
12:6	and they said, **The L** *is* righteous.	3068
12:7	when **the L** saw that they humbled	3068
12:7	the word of **the L** came to Shemaiah,	3068
12:9	away the treasures of the house of **the L**,	3068
12:11	the king entered *into* the house of **the L**,	3068
12:12	the wrath of **the L** turned from him,	3068
12:13	the city which **the L** had chosen out of all	3068
12:14	he prepared not his heart to seek **the L**.	3068
13:5	Ought you not to know that **the L** God of	3068
13:8	of **the L** in the hand of the sons of David;	3068
13:9	Have ye not cast out the priests of **the L**,	3068
13:10	**the L** *is* our God, and we have not forsaken	3068
13:10	the priests, which minister unto **the L**,	3068
13:11	they burn unto **the L** every morning	3068
13:11	for we keep the charge of **the L** our God;	3068
13:12	fight ye not against **the L** God of your	3068
13:14	they cried unto **the L**, and the priests	3068
13:18	they relied upon **the L** God of their fathers.	3068
13:20	and **the L** struck him, and he died.	3068
14:2	and right in the eyes of **the L** his God:	3068
14:4	commanded Judah to seek **the L** God of	3068
14:6	because **the L** had given him rest.	3068
14:7	because we have sought **the L** our God,	3068
14:11	Asa cried unto **the L** his God, and said,	3068
14:11	said, **L**, *it is* nothing with thee to help,	3068
14:11	help us, O **L** our God; for we rest on thee,	3068
14:11	O **L**, thou *art* our God; let not man prevail	3068
14:12	So **the L** smote the Ethiopians before Asa,	3068
14:13	for they were destroyed before **the L**, and	3068
14:14	for the fear of **the L** came upon them:	3068
15:2	**The L** *is* with you, while ye be with him;	3068
15:4	trouble did turn unto **the L** God of Israel,	3068
15:8	renewed the altar of **the L**, that *was* before	3068
15:8	that *was* before the porch of **the L**.	3068
15:9	when they saw that **the L** his God *was* with	3068
15:11	they offered unto **the L** the same time,	3068
15:12	they entered into a covenant to seek **the L**	3068
15:13	That whosoever would not seek **the L** God	3068
15:14	they sware unto **the L** with a loud voice,	3068
15:15	and **the L** gave them rest round about.	3068
16:2	out of the treasures of the house of **the L**	3068
16:7	not relied on **the L** thy God, therefore is	3068
16:8	yet, because thou didst rely on **the L**,	3068
16:9	For the eyes of **the L** run to and	3068
16:12	yet in his disease he sought not *to* **the L**,	3068
17:3	**the L** was with Jehoshaphat, because	3068
17:4	sought to the *L* God of his father, and	NIH
17:5	Therefore **the L** stablished the kingdom in	3068
17:6	his heart was lift up in the ways of **the L**:	3068
17:9	*had* the book of the law of **the L** with them,	3068
17:10	the fear of **the L** fell upon all the kingdoms	3068
17:16	who willingly offered himself unto **the L**;	3068
18:4	I pray thee, at the word of **the L** to day.	3068
18:6	*Is there* not here a prophet of **the L** besides,	3068
18:7	by whom *we* may inquire of **the L**:	3068
18:10	said, Thus saith **the L**, With these thou	3068
18:11	for **the L** shall deliver *it* into the hand of	3068
18:13	Micaiah said, *As* **the L** liveth, even what	3068
18:15	but the truth to me in the name of **the L**?	3068
18:16	**the L** said, These have no master; let them	3068
18:18	he said, Therefore hear the word of **the L**;	3068
18:18	I saw **the L** sitting upon his throne, and	3068
18:19	**the L** said, Who shall entice Ahab king of	3068
18:20	stood before **the L**, and said, I will entice	3068
18:20	And **the L** said unto him, Wherewith?	3068
18:21	*the L* said, Thou shalt entice *him*, and	NIH
18:22	**the L** hath put a lying spirit in the mouth of	3068
18:22	and **the L** hath spoken evil against thee.	3068
18:23	Which way went the spirit of **the L** from	3068
18:27	in peace, *then* hath not **the L** spoken by me.	3068
18:31	cried out, and **the L** helped him;	3068
19:2	the ungodly, and love them that hate **the L**?	3068
19:2	*is* wrath upon thee from before **the L**.	3068
19:4	brought them back unto **the L** God of their	3068
19:6	for ye judge not for man, but for **the L**,	3068
19:7	Wherefore now let the fear of **the L** be	3068
19:7	do *it*: for *there is* no iniquity with **the L** our	3068
19:8	for the judgment of **the L**, and	3068
2Ch 19:9	Thus shall ye do in the fear of **the L**,	3068
19:10	them that they trespass not against **the L**,	3068
19:11	priest *is* over you in all matters of **the L**;	3068
19:11	and **the L** shall be with the good.	3068
20:3	set himself to seek **the L**, and proclaimed a	3068
20:4	themselves together, to ask *help* of **the L**:	3068
20:4	the cities of Judah they came to seek **the L**.	3068
20:5	and Jerusalem, in the house of **the L**,	3068
20:6	said, O **L** God of our fathers, *art* not thou	3068
20:13	all Judah stood before **the L**, with their	3068
20:14	came the spirit of **the L** in the midst of	3068
20:15	Thus saith **the L** unto you,	3068
20:17	and see the salvation of **the L** with you,	3068
20:17	against them: for **the L** *will be* with you.	3068
20:18	inhabitants of Jerusalem fell before **the L**,	3068
20:18	fell before the LORD, worshipping **the L**.	3068
20:19	stood up to praise **the L** God of Israel with	3068
20:20	Believe in **the L** your God, so shall you be	3068
20:21	he appointed singers unto **the L**, and	3068
20:21	before the army, and to say, Praise **the L**;	3068
20:22	**the L** set ambushments against the children	3068
20:26	of Berachah; for there they blessed **the L**:	3068
20:27	for **the L** had made them to rejoice over	3068
20:28	harps and trumpets unto the house of **the L**.	3068
20:29	when they had heard that **the L** fought	3068
20:32	*that* which *was* right in the sight of **the L**.	3068
20:37	with Ahaziah, **the L** hath broken thy works.	3068
21:6	*that* which *was* evil in the eyes of **the L**.	3068
21:7	Howbeit **the L** would not destroy the house	3068
21:10	he had forsaken **the L** God of his fathers.	3068
21:12	Thus saith **the L** God of David thy father,	3068
21:14	*with* a great plague will **the L** smite thy	3068
21:16	Moreover **the L** stirred up against Jehoram	3068
21:18	after all this **the L** smote him in his bowels	3068
22:4	Wherefore he did evil in the sight of **the L**,	3068
22:7	whom **the L** had anointed to cut off	3068
22:9	who sought **the L** with all his heart.	3068
23:3	as **the L** hath said of the sons of David.	3068
23:5	*shall be* in the courts of the house of **the L**.	3068
23:6	let none come *into* the house of **the L**,	3068
23:6	the people shall keep the watch of **the L**.	3068
23:12	came to the people *into* the house of **the L**:	3068
23:14	Slay her not *in* the house of **the L**.	3068
23:18	**the L** by the hand of the priests the Levites,	3068
23:18	David had distributed in the house of **the L**,	3068
23:18	to offer the burnt offerings of **the L**, as it is	3068
23:19	porters at the gates of the house of **the L**,	3068
23:20	down the king from the house of **the L**:	3068
24:2	of **the L** all the days of Jehoiada the priest.	3068
24:4	was minded to repair the house of **the L**.	3068
24:6	of Moses the servant of **the L**,	3068
24:7	of **the L** did they bestow upon Baalim.	3068
24:8	it without at the gate of the house of **the L**.	3068
24:9	to bring in to **the L** the collection that	3068
24:12	work of the service of the house of **the L**,	3068
24:12	and carpenters to repair the house of **the L**,	3068
24:12	and brass to mend the house of **the L**.	3068
24:14	were made vessels for the house of **the L**,	3068
24:14	**the L** continually all the days of Jehoiada.	3068
24:18	they left the house of **the L** God of their	3068
24:19	to them, to bring them again unto **the L**;	3068
24:20	transgress ye the commandments of **the L**,	3068
24:20	because ye have forsaken **the L**, he hath	3068
24:21	the king in the court of the house of **the L**.	3068
24:22	he said, **The L** look upon *it*, and require *it*.	3068
24:24	**the L** delivered a very great host into their	3068
24:24	they had forsaken **the L** God of their	3068
25:2	*that* which *was* right in the sight of **the L**,	3068
25:4	where **the L** commanded, saying,	3068
25:7	for **the L** *is* not with Israel, *to wit*, *with* all	3068
25:9	**The L** is able to give thee much more than	3068
25:15	Wherefore the anger of **the L** was kindled	3068
25:27	**the L** they made a conspiracy against him	3068
26:4	*that* which *was* right in the sight of **the L**,	3068
26:5	as long as he sought **the L**, God made him	3068
26:16	for he transgressed against **the L** his God,	3068
26:16	went into the temple of **the L** to burn	3068
26:17	with him fourscore priests of **the L**,	3068
26:18	to burn incense unto **the L**, but to	3068
26:18	*shall it be* for thine honour from **the L** God.	3068
26:19	before the priests in the house of **the L**,	3068
26:20	to go out, because **the L** had smitten him.	3068
26:21	for he was cut off from the house of **the L**:	3068
27:2	*that* which *was* right in the sight of **the L**,	3068
27:2	he entered not into the temple of **the L**.	3068
27:3	built the high gate of the house of **the L**,	3068
27:6	he prepared his ways before **the L** his God.	3068
28:1	*that* which *was* right in the sight of **the L**,	3068
28:3	**the L** had cast out before the children of	3068
28:5	Wherefore **the L** his God delivered him	3068
28:6	they had forsaken **the L** God of their	3068
28:9	a prophet of **the L** was there, whose name	3068
28:9	**the L** God of your fathers was wroth with	3068
28:10	with you, sins against **the L** your God?	3068
28:11	for the fierce wrath of **the L** *is* upon you.	3068
28:13	**the L** *already*, ye intend to add *more* to our	3068
28:19	For **the L** brought Judah low because	3068
28:19	and transgressed sore against **the L**.	3068
28:21	away a portion *out* of the house of **the L**,	3068
28:22	did he trespass yet more against **the L**:	3068
28:24	and shut up the doors of the house of **the L**,	3068
28:25	provoked to anger **the L** God of his fathers.	3068
29:2	*that* which *was* right in the sight of **the L**,	3068
29:3	opened the doors of the house of **the L**, and	3068
29:5	sanctify the house of **the L** God of your	3068
29:6	*was* evil in the eyes of **the L** our God,	3068
29:6	their faces from the habitation of **the L**,	3068
29:8	Wherefore the wrath of **the L** was upon	3068
29:10	make a covenant with **the L** God of Israel,	3068
29:11	for **the L** hath chosen you to stand before	3068
29:15	by the words of **the L**, to cleanse the house	3068
29:15	the LORD, to cleanse the house of **the L**,	3068
29:16	into the inner part *of* the house of **the L**,	3068
29:16	**the L** into the court of the house of	3068
29:16	into the court of the house of **the L**.	3068
2Ch 29:17	the month came they to the porch of **the L**:	3068
29:17	they sanctified the house of **the L** in eight	3068
29:18	We have cleansed all the house of **the L**,	3068
29:19	behold, they *are* before the altar of **the L**.	3068
29:20	the city, and went up *to* the house of **the L**.	3068
29:21	Aaron to offer *them* on the altar of **the L**.	3068
29:25	he set the Levites *in* the house of **the L**	3068
29:25	*was* the commandment of **the L** by his	3068
29:27	the song of **the L** began *also* with	3068
29:30	praise unto **the L** with the words of David,	3068
29:31	ye have consecrated yourselves unto **the L**,	3068
29:31	and thank offerings into the house of **the L**.	3068
29:32	all these *were* for a burnt offering to **the L**.	3068
29:35	So the service of the house of **the L** was set	3068
30:1	that *they* should come to the house of **the L**	3068
30:1	to keep the passover unto **the L** God of	3068
30:5	unto **the L** God of Israel at Jerusalem:	3068
30:6	turn again unto **the L** God of Abraham,	3068
30:7	which trespassed against **the L** God of their	3068
30:8	*but* yield yourselves unto **the L**,	3068
30:8	serve **the L** your God, that the fierceness of	3068
30:9	For if ye turn again unto **the L**,	3068
30:9	for **the L** your God *is* gracious and	3068
30:12	and of the princes, by the word of **the L**.	3068
30:15	the burnt offerings *into* the house of **the L**.	3068
30:17	*was* not clean, to sanctify *them* unto **the L**.	3068
30:18	**The** good **L** pardon every one	3068
30:19	heart to seek God, **the L** God of his fathers,	3068
30:20	**the L** hearkened to Hezekiah, and	3068
30:21	and the priests praised **the L** day by day,	3068
30:21	*singing* with loud instruments unto **the L**.	3068
30:22	that taught the good knowledge of **the L**:	3068
30:22	making confession to **the L** God of their	3068
31:2	to praise in the gates of the tents of **the L**.	3068
31:3	as it is written in the law of **the L**.	3068
31:4	might be encouraged in the law of **the L**.	3068
31:6	were consecrated unto **the L** their God,	3068
31:8	they blessed **the L**, and his people Israel.	3068
31:10	bring the offerings *into* the house of **the L**,	3068
31:10	for **the L** hath blessed his people; and	3068
31:11	to prepare chambers in the house of **the L**;	3068
31:14	to distribute the oblations of **the L**, and	3068
31:16	one that entereth into the house of **the L**,	3068
31:20	and right and truth before **the L** his God.	3068
32:8	but with us *is* **the L** our God to help us, and	3068
32:11	**The L** our God shall deliver us out of	3068
32:16	his servants spake yet *more* against **the L**	3068
32:17	He wrote also letters to rail on **the L** God	3068
32:21	**the L** sent an angel, which cut off all	3068
32:22	Thus **the L** saved Hezekiah and	3068
32:23	many brought gifts unto **the L** to	3068
32:24	sick to the death, and prayed unto **the L**:	3068
32:26	that the wrath of **the L** came not upon them	3068
33:2	*that* which *was* evil in the sight of **the L**,	3068
33:2	whom **the L** had cast out before	3068
33:4	Also he built altars in the house of **the L**,	3068
33:4	whereof **the L** had said, In Jerusalem shall	3068
33:5	in the two courts of the house of **the L**.	3068
33:6	he wrought much evil in the sight of **the L**,	3068
33:9	whom **the L** had destroyed before	3068
33:10	**the L** spake to Manasseh, and to his	3068
33:11	Wherefore **the L** brought upon them	3068
33:12	he besought **the L** his God, and	3068
33:13	Manasseh knew that **the L** he *was* God.	3068
33:15	the idol out of the house of **the L**, and	3068
33:15	built in the mount of the house of **the L**,	3068
33:16	he repaired the altar of **the L**, and	3068
33:16	commanded Judah to serve **the L** God of	3068
33:17	high places, *yet* unto **the L** their God only.	3068
33:18	to him in the name of **the L** God of Israel,	3068
33:22	*that* which *was* evil in the sight of **the L**,	3068
33:23	humbled not himself before **the L**,	3068
34:2	*that* which *was* right in the sight of **the L**,	3068
34:8	to repair the house of **the L** his God.	3068
34:10	had the oversight of the house of **the L**,	3068
34:10	that wrought in the house of **the L**,	3068
34:14	that was brought *into* the house of **the L**,	3068
34:14	a book of the law of **the L** *given* by Moses.	3068
34:15	the book of the law in the house of **the L**.	3068
34:17	that was found in the house of **the L**,	3068
34:21	inquire of **the L** for me, and for them that	3068
34:21	for great *is* the wrath of **the L** that is	3068
34:21	our fathers have not kept the word of **the L**,	3068
34:23	Thus saith **the L** God of Israel,	3068
34:24	Thus saith **the L**, Behold, I will bring evil	3068
34:26	who sent you to inquire of **the L**, so	3068
34:26	Thus saith **the L** God of Israel *concerning*	3068
34:27	I have even heard *thee* also, saith **the L**.	3068
34:30	the king went up *into* the house of **the L**,	3068
34:30	that was found *in* the house of **the L**.	3068
34:31	made a covenant before **the L**, to walk after	3068
34:31	to walk after **the L**, and to keep his	3068
34:33	to serve, *even* to serve **the L** their God.	3068
34:33	they departed not from following **the L**,	3068
35:1	kept a passover unto **the L** in Jerusalem:	3068
35:2	them to the service of the house of **the L**,	3068
35:3	all Israel, which were holy unto **the L**,	3068
35:3	serve now **the L** your God, and his people	3068
35:6	to the word of **the L** by the hand of Moses.	3068
35:12	to offer unto **the L**, as it is written in	3068
35:16	So all the service of **the L** was prepared	3068
35:16	burnt offerings upon the altar of **the L**,	3068
35:26	that which was written in the law of **the L**,	3068
36:5	*was* evil in the sight of **the L** his God.	3068
36:7	vessels of the house of **the L** to Babylon,	3068
36:9	*that* which *was* evil in the sight of **the L**.	3068
36:10	the goodly vessels of the house of **the L**,	3068
36:12	*was* evil in the sight of **the L** his God,	3068
36:12	prophet *speaking* from the mouth of **the L**.	3068
36:13	hardened his heart from turning unto **the L**	3068
36:14	polluted the house of **the L** which he had	3068
36:15	**the L** God of their fathers sent to them by	3068
36:16	until the wrath of **the L** arose against his	3068
36:18	the treasures of the house of **the L**, and	3068
36:21	To fulfil the word of **the L** by the mouth of	3068

2Ch 36:22 that the word of **the L** *spoken* by the mouth 3068
36:22 **the L** stirred up the spirit of Cyrus king of 3068
36:23 All the kingdoms of the earth hath **the L** 3068
36:23 **The L** his God *be* with him, and let him go 3068
Ezr 1: 1 that the word of **the L** by the mouth of 3068
1: 1 **the L** stirred up the spirit of Cyrus king of 3068
1: 2 **The L** God of heaven hath given me all 3068
1: 3 build the house of **the L** God of Israel, 3068
1: 5 to go up to build the house of **the L** which 3068
1: 7 forth the vessels of the house of **the L**, 3068
2:68 when they came to the house of **the L** 3068
3: 3 offered burnt offerings thereon unto **the L**, 3068
3: 5 of all the set feasts of **the L** that were 3068
3: 5 offered a freewill offering unto **the L**. 3068
3: 6 they to offer burnt offerings unto **the L**. 3068
3: 6 the foundation of the temple of **the L** was 3068
3: 8 set forward the work of the house of **the L**. 3068
3:10 laid the foundation of the temple of **the L**, 3068
3:10 to praise **the L**, after the ordinance of 3068
3:11 in praising and giving thanks unto **the L**; 3068
3:11 when they praised **the L**, because 3068
3:11 the foundation of the house of **the L** was 3068
4: 1 the temple unto **the L** God of Israel; 3068
4: 3 we ourselves together will build unto **the L** 3068
6:21 to seek **the L** God of Israel, did eat, 3068
6:22 for **the L** had made them joyful, and 3068
7: 6 which **the L** God of Israel had given: 3068
7: 6 according to the hand of **the L** his God 3068
7:10 prepared his heart to seek the law of **the L**, 3068
7:11 the words of the commandments of **the L**, 3068
7:27 Blessed *be* **the L** God of our fathers, 3068
7:27 to beautify the house of **the L** which *is* in 3068
7:28 I was strengthened as the hand of **the L** my 3068
8:28 I said unto them, Ye *are* holy unto **the L**; 3068
8:28 the gold *are* a freewill offering unto **the L** 3068
8:29 *in* the chambers of the house of **the L**. 3068
8:35 all *this was* a burnt offering unto **the L**. 3068
9: 5 spread out my hands unto **the L** my God, 3068
9: 8 hath been *shewed* from **the L** our God, 3068
9:15 O **L** God of Israel, thou *art* righteous: 3068
10:11 make confession unto **the L** God of your 3068
Ne 1: 5 O **L** God of heaven, the great and terrible 3068
5:13 Amen, and praised **the L**. 3068
8: 1 which **the L** had commanded to Israel. 3068
8: 6 Ezra blessed **the L**, the great God. And all 3068
8: 6 worshipped **the L** *with their* faces to 3068
8: 9 *This* day *is* holy unto **the L** your God; 3068
8:10 for the joy of **the L** *is* your strength. 3068
8:14 they found written in the law which **the L** 3068
9: 3 read in the book of the law of **the L** their 3068
9: 3 and worshipped **the L** their God. 3068
9: 4 cried with a loud voice unto **the L** their 3068
9: 5 *and* bless **the L** your God for ever and ever: 3068
9: 6 Thou, *even* thou, *art* **L** alone; thou hast 3068
9: 7 Thou *art* **the L** the God, who didst choose 3068
10:29 do all the commandments of **the L** our 3068
10:34 to burn upon the altar of **the L** our God, 3068
10:35 year by year, unto the house of **the L**: 3068
Job 1: 6 came to present themselves before **the L**, 3068
1: 7 **the L** said unto Satan, Whence comest 3068
1: 7 Satan answered **the L**, and said, 3068
1: 8 **the L** said unto Satan, Hast thou considered 3068
1: 9 Satan answered **the L**, and said, Doth Job 3068
1:12 **the L** said unto Satan, Behold, all that he 3068
1:12 went forth from the presence of **the L**. 3068
1:21 **the L** gave, and the LORD hath taken 3068
1:21 **the L** hath taken *away;* blessed be the name 3068
1:21 taken *away;* blessed be the name of **the L**. 3068
2: 1 came to present themselves before **the L**, 3068
2: 1 them to present himself before **the L**. 3068
2: 2 **the L** said unto Satan, From whence 3068
2: 2 Satan answered **the L**, and said, 3068
2: 3 **the L** said unto Satan, Hast thou considered 3068
2: 4 Satan answered **the L**, and said, Skin for 3068
2: 6 **the L** said unto Satan, Behold, he *is* in 3068
2: 7 Satan forth from the presence of **the L**, 3068
12: 9 that the hand of **the L** hath wrought this? 3068
38: 1 **the L** answered Job out of the whirlwind, 3068
40: 1 Moreover **the L** answered Job, and said, 3068
40: 3 Then Job answered **the L**, and said, 3068
40: 6 answered **the L** unto Job out of 3068
42: 1 Then Job answered **the L**, and said, 3068
42: 7 that after **the L** had spoken these words 3068
42: 7 **the L** said to Eliphaz the Temanite, 3068
42: 9 did according as **the L** commanded them: 3068
42: 9 commanded them: **the L** also accepted Job. 3068
42:10 **the L** turned the captivity of Job, when he 3068
42:10 also **the L** gave Job twice as much as he 3068
42:11 comforted him over all the evil that **the L** 3068
42:12 So **the L** blessed the latter end of Job more 3068
Ps 1: 2 his delight *is* in the law of **the L**; and in his 3068
1: 6 For **the L** knoweth the way of 3068
2: 2 against **the L**, and against his anointed, 3068
2: 4 **the L** shall have them in derision. 3068
2: 7 **the L** hath said unto me, Thou *art* my Son; 3068
2:11 Serve **the L** with fear, and rejoice with 3068
3: 1 **L**, how are they increased that trouble me! 3068
3: 3 thou, O **L**, *art* a shield for me; my glory, 3068
3: 4 I cried unto **the L** *with* my voice, and 3068
3: 5 slept; I awaked; for **the L** sustained me. 3068
3: 7 Arise, O **L**; save me, O my God: for thou 3068
3: 8 Salvation *belongeth* unto **the L**: 3068
4: 3 know that **the L** hath set apart *him that is* 3068
4: 3 **the L** will hear when I call unto him. 3068
4: 5 and put your trust in **the L**. 3068
4: 6 **L**, lift thou up the light of thy countenance 3068
4: 8 for thou, **L**, only makest me dwell in safety. 3068
5: 1 Give ear to my words, O **L**, consider my 3068
5: 3 voice shalt thou hear *in* the morning, O **L**; 3068
5: 6 **the L** will abhor the bloody and 3068
5: 8 Lead me, O **L**, in thy righteousness because 3068
5:12 For thou, **L**, wilt bless the righteous; 3068
6: 1 O **L**, rebuke me not in thine anger, 3068
6: 2 Have mercy upon me, O **L**; for I *am* weak: 3068
6: 2 O **L**, heal me; for my bones are vexed. 3068

Ps 6: 3 also sore vexed: but thou, O **L**, how long? 3068
6: 4 Return, O **L**, deliver my soul: O save me 3068
6: 8 for **the L** hath heard the voice of my 3068
6: 9 **The L** hath heard my supplication; 3068
6: 9 **the L** will receive my prayer. 3068
7: T of David, which he sang unto **the L**, 3068
7: 1 O **L** my God, in thee do I put my trust: 3068
7: 3 O **L** my God, if I have done this; if there be 3068
7: 6 Arise, O **L**, in thine anger, lift up thyself 3068
7: 8 **The L** shall judge the people: judge me, 3068
7: 8 judge me, O **L**, according to my 3068
7:17 I will praise **the L** according to his 3068
7:17 will sing *praise* to the name of **the L** most 3068
8: 1 O **L** our Lord, how excellent *is* thy name in 3068
8: 9 O **L** our Lord, how excellent *is* thy name in 3068
9: 1 I will praise *thee*, O **L**, with my whole 3068
9: 7 **the L** shall endure for ever: he hath 3068
9: 9 **The L** also will be a refuge for 3068
9:10 for thou, **L**, hast not forsaken them that 3068
9:11 Sing *praises* to **the L**, which dwelleth in 3068
9:13 Have mercy upon me, O **L**; consider my 3068
9:16 **The L** is known *by* the judgment *which* he 3068
9:19 Arise, O **L**; let not man prevail: let 3068
9:20 Put them in fear, O **L**: *that* the nations may 3068
10: 1 Why standest thou afar off, O **L**? 3068
10: 3 the covetous, *whom* **the L** abhorreth. 3068
10:12 Arise, O **L**; O God, lift up thine hand: 3068
10:16 **The L** *is* King for ever and ever: 3068
10:17 **L**, thou hast heard the desire of the humble: 3068
11: 1 In **the L** put I my trust: how say ye to my 3068
11: 4 **The L** *is* in his holy temple, the LORD'S 3068
11: 5 **The L** trieth the righteous: but the wicked 3068
11: 7 For **the** righteous **L** loveth righteousness; 3068
12: 1 Help, **L**; for the godly *man* ceaseth; for 3068
12: 3 **The L** shall cut off all flattering lips, *and* 3068
12: 5 of the needy, now will I arise, saith **the L**; 3068
12: 6 The words of **the L** *are* pure words: 3068
12: 7 Thou shalt keep them, O **L**, thou shalt 3068
13: 1 How long wilt thou forget me, O **L**? 3068
13: 3 Consider *and* hear me, O **L** my God: 3068
13: 6 I will sing unto **the L**, because he hath 3068
14: 2 **The L** looked down from heaven upon 3068
14: 4 *as* they eat bread, *and* call not upon **the L**. 3068
14: 6 of the poor, because **the L** *is* his refuge. 3068
14: 7 when **the L** bringeth back the captivity of 3068
15: 1 **L**, who shall abide in thy tabernacle? 3068
15: 4 but he honoureth them that fear **the L**. 3068
16: 2 *O my soul,* thou hast said unto **the L**, 3068
16: 5 **The L** *is* the portion of mine inheritance 3068
16: 7 I will bless **the L**, who hath given me 3068
16: 8 I have set **the L** always before me: because 3068
17: 1 Hear the right, O **L**, attend unto my cry, 3068
17:13 Arise, O **L**, disappoint him, cast him down: 3068
17:14 *are* thy hand, O **L**, from men of the world, 3068
18: T *A Psalm* of David, the servant of **the L**, 3068
18: T who spake unto **the L** the words of this 3068
18: T **the L** delivered him from the hand of all 3068
18: 1 I will love thee, O **L**, my strength. 3068
18: 2 **The L** *is* my rock, and my fortress, and 3068
18: 3 I will call upon **the L**, who is *worthy* to be 3068
18: 6 In my distress I called upon **the L**, and 3068
18:13 **The L** also thundered in the heavens, and 3068
18:15 O **L**, at the blast of the breath of thy 3068
18:18 day of my calamity: but **the L** was my stay. 3068
18:20 **The L** rewarded me according to my 3068
18:21 For I have kept the ways of **the L**, and 3068
18:24 Therefore hath **the L** recompensed me 3068
18:28 **the L** my God will enlighten my darkness. 3068
18:30 the word of **the L** is tried: he *is* a buckler to 3068
18:31 For who *is* God save **the L**? or who *is* a 3068
18:41 *was* none to save *them: even* unto **the L**, 3068
18:46 **The L** liveth; and blessed *be* my rock; and 3068
18:49 O **L**, among the heathen, and sing *praises* 3068
19: 7 The law of **the L** *is* perfect, converting 3068
19: 7 the testimony of **the L** *is* sure, making wise 3068
19: 8 The statutes of **the L** *are* right, rejoicing 3068
19: 8 the commandment of **the L** *is* pure, 3068
19: 9 The fear of **the L** *is* clean, enduring for 3068
19: 9 the judgments of **the L** *are* true *and* 3068
19:14 O **L**, my strength, and my redeemer. 3068
20: 1 **The L** hear thee in the day of trouble; 3068
20: 5 *our* banners: **the L** fulfil all thy petitions. 3068
20: 6 Now know I that **the L** saveth his anointed; 3068
20: 7 we will remember the name of **the L** our 3068
20: 9 Save, **L**: let the king hear us when we call. 3068
21: 1 The king shall joy in thy strength, O **L**; and 3068
21: 7 For the king trusteth in **the L**, and 3068
21: 9 **the L** shall swallow them up in his wrath, 3068
21:13 Be thou exalted, **L**, in thine own strength: 3068
22: 8 He trusted on **the L** *that* he would deliver 3068
22:19 be not thou far *from me*, O **L**: O my 3068
22:23 Ye that fear **the L**, praise him; all ye 3068
22:26 they shall praise **the L** that seek him: 3068
22:27 world shall remember and turn unto **the L**: 3068
23: 1 **The L** *is* my shepherd; I shall not want. 3068
23: 6 I will dwell in the house of **the L** for ever. 3068
24: 3 Who shall ascend into the hill of **the L**? 3068
24: 5 He shall receive the blessing from **the L**, 3068
24: 8 **the L** strong and mighty, the LORD 3068
24: 8 and mighty, **the L** mighty *in* battle. 3068
24:10 **The L** of hosts, he *is* the King of glory. 3068
25: 1 Unto thee, O **L**, do I lift up my soul. 3068
25: 4 Shew me thy ways, O **L**; teach me thy 3068
25: 6 Remember, O **L**, thy tender mercies and 3068
25: 7 thou me for thy goodness' sake, O **L**. 3068
25: 8 Good and upright *is* **the L**: therefore 3068
25:10 All the paths of **the L** *are* mercy and 3068
25:11 For thy name's sake, O **L**, pardon mine 3068
25:12 What man *is* he that feareth **the L**? 3068
25:14 The secret of **the L** *is* with them that fear 3068
25:15 Mine eyes *are* ever towards **the L**; for he 3068
26: 1 Judge me, O **L**; for I have walked in mine 3068
26: 1 I have trusted also in **the L**; *therefore* 3068
26: 2 Examine me, O **L**, and prove me; try my 3068
26: 6 so will I compass thine altar, O **L**: 3068

Ps 26: 8 **L**, I have loved the habitation of thy house, 3068
26:12 in the congregations will I bless **the L**. 3068
27: 1 **The L** *is* my light and my salvation; whom 3068
27: 1 **the L** *is* the strength of my life; of whom 3068
27: 4 One *thing* have I desired of **the L**, that will 3068
27: 4 that I may dwell in the house of **the L** all 3068
27: 4 to behold the beauty of **the L**, and 3068
27: 6 yea, I will sing *praises* unto **the L**. 3068
27: 7 Hear, O **L**, *when* I cry *with* my voice: 3068
27: 8 said unto thee, Thy face, **L**, will I seek. 3068
27:10 forsake me, then **the L** will take me up. 3068
27:11 O **L**, and lead me in a plain path, because 3068
27:13 goodness of **the L** in the land of the living. 3068
27:14 Wait on **the L**: be of good courage, and 3068
27:14 strengthen thine heart: wait, I say, on **the L**. 3068
28: 1 Unto thee will I cry, O **L**, my rock; be not 3068
28: 5 they regard not the works of **the L**, 3068
28: 6 Blessed *be* **the L**, because he hath heard 3068
28: 7 **The L** *is* my strength and my shield; 3068
28: 8 **The L** *is* their strength, and he *is* the saving 3068
29: 1 Give unto **the L**, O ye mighty, give unto 3068
29: 1 give unto **the L** glory and strength. 3068
29: 2 Give unto **the L** the glory due unto his 3068
29: 2 worship **the L** in the beauty of holiness. 3068
29: 3 The voice of **the L** *is* upon the waters: 3068
29: 3 **the L** *is* upon many waters. 3068
29: 4 The voice of **the L** *is* powerful; the voice of 3068
29: 4 the voice of **the L** *is* full of majesty. 3068
29: 5 The voice of **the L** breaketh the cedars; 3068
29: 5 yea, **the L** breaketh the cedars of Lebanon. 3068
29: 7 The voice of **the L** divideth the flames of 3068
29: 8 The voice of **the L** shaketh the wilderness; 3068
29: 8 **the L** shaketh the wilderness of Kadesh. 3068
29: 9 The voice of **the L** maketh the hinds to 3068
29:10 **The L** sitteth upon the flood; yea, 3068
29:10 the flood; yea, **the L** sitteth King for ever. 3068
29:11 **The L** will give strength unto his people; 3068
29:11 **the L** will bless his people with peace. 3068
30: 1 I will extol thee, O **L**; for thou hast lifted 3068
30: 2 O **L** my God, I cried unto thee, and 3068
30: 3 O **L**, thou hast brought up my soul from 3068
30: 4 Sing unto **the L**, O ye saints of his, and 3068
30: 7 **L**, by thy favour thou hast made my 3068
30: 8 I cried to thee, O **L**; and unto the LORD I 3068
30: 8 and unto **the L** I made supplication. 3068
30:10 Hear, O **L**, and have mercy upon me: 3068
30:10 have mercy upon me: **L**, be thou my helper. 3068
30:12 O **L** my God, I will give thanks unto thee 3068
31: 1 In thee, O **L**, do I put my trust; let me never 3068
31: 5 thou hast redeemed me, O **L** God of truth. 3068
31: 6 regard lying vanities: but I trust in **the L**. 3068
31: 9 mercy upon me, O **L**, for I am in trouble: 3068
31:14 I trusted in thee, O **L**: I said, Thou *art* my 3068
31:17 Let me not be ashamed, O **L**; for I have 3068
31:21 Blessed *be* **the L**: for he hath shewed me 3068
31:23 O love **the L**, all ye his saints: *for* 3068
31:23 *for* **the L** preserveth the faithful, and 3068
31:24 your heart, all ye that hope in **the L**. 3068
32: 2 Blessed *is* the man unto whom **the L** 3068
32: 5 will confess my transgressions unto **the L**; 3068
32:10 he that trusteth in **the L**, mercy shall 3068
32:11 Be glad in **the L**, and rejoice, ye righteous: 3068
33: 1 Rejoice in **the L**, O ye righteous: *for* praise 3068
33: 2 Praise **the L** with harp: sing unto him with 3068
33: 4 For the word of **the L** *is* right; and all his 3068
33: 5 the earth is full *of* the goodness of **the L**. 3068
33: 6 By the word of **the L** were the heavens 3068
33: 8 Let all the earth fear **the L**: let all 3068
33:10 **The L** bringeth the counsel of the heathen 3068
33:11 The counsel of **the L** standeth for ever, 3068
33:12 Blessed *is* the nation whose God *is* **the L**; 3068
33:13 **The L** looketh from heaven; he beholdeth 3068
33:18 the eye of **the L** *is* upon them that fear him, 3068
33:20 Our soul waiteth for **the L**: he *is* our help 3068
33:22 Let thy mercy, O **L**, be upon us, 3068
34: 1 I will bless **the L** at all times: his praise 3068
34: 2 My soul shall make her boast in **the L**: 3068
34: 3 O magnify **the L** with me, and let us exalt 3068
34: 4 I sought **the L**, and he heard me, and 3068
34: 6 **the L** heard *him,* and saved him out of all 3068
34: 7 The angel of **the L** encampeth round about 3068
34: 8 O taste and see that **the L** *is* good: 3068
34: 9 O fear **the L**, ye his saints: for *there is* no 3068
34:10 they that seek **the L** shall not want any 3068
34:11 unto me: I will teach you the fear of **the L**. 3068
34:15 The eyes of **the L** *are* upon the righteous, 3068
34:16 The face of **the L** *is* against them that do 3068
34:17 **the L** heareth, and delivereth them out of 3068
34:18 **The L** *is* nigh unto them that are of a 3068
34:19 but **the L** delivereth him out of them all. 3068
34:22 **The L** redeemeth the soul of his servants: 3068
35: 1 Plead *my cause,* O **L**, with them that strive 3068
35: 5 and let the angel of **the L** chase *them.* 3068
35: 6 and let the angel of **the L** persecute them. 3068
35: 9 my soul shall be joyful in **the L**: it shall 3068
35:10 bones shall say, **L**, who *is* like unto thee, 3068
35:22 *This* thou hast seen, O **L**: keep not silence: 3068
35:24 Judge me, O **L** my God, according to thy 3068
35:27 say continually, Let **the L** be magnified, 3068
36: T *A Psalm* of David the servant of **the L**. 3068
36: 5 Thy mercy, O **L**, *is* in the heavens; *and* 3068
36: 6 O **L**, thou preservest man and beast. 3068
37: 3 Trust in **the L**, and do good; *so* shalt thou 3068
37: 4 Delight thyself also in **the L**; and he shall 3068
37: 5 Commit thy way unto **the L**; trust also in 3068
37: 7 Rest in **the L**, and wait patiently for him: 3068
37: 9 those that wait upon **the L**, they shall 3068
37:17 but **the L** upholdeth the righteous. 3068
37:18 **The L** knoweth the days of the upright: and 3068
37:20 the enemies of **the L** *shall be* as the fat of 3068
37:23 steps of a good man are ordered by **the L**: 3068
37:24 for **the L** upholdeth *him with* his hand. 3068
37:28 For **the L** loveth judgment, and 3068
37:33 **The L** will not leave him in his hand, 3068
37:34 Wait on **the L**, and keep his way, and 3068

Ps	37:39	the salvation of the righteous *is* of **the L**:	3068
	37:40	**the L** shall help them, and deliver them:	3068
	38: 1	O **L**, rebuke me not in thy wrath:	3068
	38:15	For in thee, O **L**, do I hope: thou wilt hear,	3068
	38:21	Forsake me not, O **L**: O my God, be not far	3068
	39: 4	**L**, make me to know mine end, and	3068
	39:12	my prayer, O **L**, and give ear unto my cry;	3068
	40: 1	I waited patiently for **the L**; and he inclined	3068
	40: 3	see *it*, and fear, and shall trust in **the L**.	3068
	40: 4	Blessed *is that* man that maketh **the L** his	3068
	40: 5	Many, O **L** my God, *are* thy wonderful	3068
	40: 9	not refrained my lips, O **L**, thou knowest.	3068
	40:11	not thou thy tender mercies from me, O **L**:	3068
	40:13	Be pleased, O **L**, to deliver me: O LORD,	3068
	40:13	to deliver me: O **L**, make haste to help me.	3068
	40:16	say continually, **The L** be magnified.	3068
	41: 1	**the L** will deliver him in time of trouble.	3068
	41: 2	**The L** will preserve him, and keep him	3068
	41: 3	**The L** will strengthen him upon the bed of	3068
	41: 4	I said, **L**, be merciful unto me: heal my	3068
	41:10	thou, O **L**, be merciful unto me, and	3068
	41:13	Blessed *be* **the L** God of Israel from	3068
	42: 8	*Yet* **the L** will command his	3068
	46: 7	**The L** of hosts *is* with us; the God of Jacob	3068
	46: 8	Come, behold the works of **the L**,	3068
	46:11	**The L** of hosts *is* with us; the God of Jacob	3068
	47: 2	For **the L** most High *is* terrible; *he is* a	3068
	47: 5	a shout, **the L** with the sound of a trumpet.	3068
	48: 1	Great *is* **the L**, and greatly to be praised in	3068
	48: 8	have we seen in the city of **the L** of hosts,	3068
	50: 1	*even* **the L**, hath spoken, and called	3068
	54: 6	I will praise thy name, O **L**; for *it is* good.	3068
	55:16	call upon God; and **the L** shall save me.	3068
	55:22	Cast thy burden upon **the L**, and he shall	3068
	56:10	*his* word: in **the L** will I praise *his* word.	3068
	58: 6	out the great teeth of the young lions, O **L**.	3068
	59: 3	*for* my transgression, nor *for* my sin, O **L**.	3068
	59: 5	Thou therefore, O **L** God *of* hosts, the God	3068
	59: 8	thou, O **L**, shalt laugh at them; thou shalt	3068
	64:10	The righteous shall be glad in **the L**, and	3068
	68:16	yea, **the L** will dwell *in it* for ever.	3068
	68:18	that **the L** God might dwell *among them*.	3050
	69:13	*is* unto thee, O **L**, *in* an acceptable time:	3068
	69:16	Hear me, O **L**; for thy lovingkindness *is*	3068
	69:31	*This* also shall please **the L** better than an	3068
	69:33	For **the L** heareth the poor, and despiseth	3068
	70: 1	to deliver me; make haste to help me, O **L**.	3068
	70: 5	and my deliverer; O **L**, make no tarrying.	3068
	71: 1	In thee, O **L**, do I put my trust: let me never	3068
	72:18	Blessed *be* **the L** God, the God of Israel,	3068
	74:18	O **L**, and *that* the foolish people have	3068
	75: 8	For in the hand of **the L** *there is* a cup, and	3068
	76:11	Vow, and pay unto **the L** your God: let all	3068
	77:11	I will remember the works of **the L**:	3050
	78: 4	the generation to come the praises of **the L**,	3068
	78:21	Therefore **the L** heard *this*, and was wroth:	3068
	79: 5	How long, **L**? wilt thou be angry, for ever?	3068
	80: 4	O **L** God *of* hosts, how long wilt thou be	3068
	80:19	Turn us again, O **L** God *of* hosts, cause thy	3068
	81:10	I *am* **the L** thy God, which brought thee out	3068
	81:15	The haters of **the L** should have submitted	3068
	83:16	that they may seek thy name, O **L**.	3068
	84: 1	amiable *are* thy tabernacles, O **L** of hosts!	3068
	84: 2	yea, even fainteth for the courts of **the L**:	3068
	84: 3	O **L** of hosts, my King, and my God.	3068
	84: 8	O **L** God *of* hosts, hear my prayer: give ear,	3068
	84:11	For **the L** God *is* a sun and shield:	3068
	84:11	**the L** will give grace and glory: no good	3068
	84:12	O **L** of hosts, blessed *is* the man that	3068
	85: 1	**L**, thou hast been favourable unto thy land:	3068
	85: 7	thy mercy, O **L**, and grant us thy salvation.	3068
	85: 8	I will hear what God **the L** will speak:	3068
	85:12	Yea, **the L** shall give *that which is* good;	3068
	86: 1	Bow down thine ear, O **L**, hear me: for I	3068
	86: 6	Give ear, O **L**, unto my prayer; and	3068
	86:11	Teach me thy way, O **L**; I will walk in thy	3068
	86:17	because thou, **L**, hast holpen me, and	3068
	87: 2	**The L** loveth the gates of Zion more than	3068
	87: 6	**The L** shall count, when he writeth *up*	3068
	88: 1	O **L** God of my salvation, I have cried day	3068
	88: 9	**L**, I have called daily upon thee, I have	3068
	88:13	unto thee have I cried, O **L**; and in	3068
	88:14	**L**, why castest thou off my soul?	3068
	89: 1	I will sing of the mercies of **the L** for ever:	3068
	89: 5	the heavens shall praise thy wonders, O **L**:	3068
	89: 6	in the heaven can be compared unto **the L**?	3068
	89: 6	of the mighty can be likened unto **the L**?	3068
	89: 8	O **L** God of hosts, who *is* a strong LORD	3068
	89: 8	of hosts, who *is* a strong **L** like unto thee?	3050
	89:15	they shall walk, O **L**, in the light of thy	3068
	89:18	For **the L** *is* our defence; and the Holy One	3068
	89:46	How long, **L**? wilt thou hide thyself,	3068
	89:51	thine enemies have reproached, O **L**;	3068
	89:52	Blessed *be* **the L** for evermore. Amen, and	3068
	90:13	Return, O **L**, how long? and let it repent	3068
	90:17	let the beauty of **the L** our God be upon us:	3068
	91: 2	I will say of **the L**, *He is* my refuge and	3068
	91: 9	Because thou hast made **the L**, *which is* my	3068
	92: 1	*It is* a good *thing* to give thanks unto **the L**,	3068
	92: 4	For thou, **L**, hast made me glad through thy	3068
	92: 5	O **L**, how great are thy works! *and*	3068
	92: 8	But thou, **L**, *art most* high for evermore.	3068
	92: 9	For lo, thine enemies, O **L**, for lo,	3068
	92:13	Those that be planted in the house of **the L**	3068
	92:15	To shew that **the L** *is* upright: *he is* my	3068
	93: 1	**The L** reigneth, he is clothed with majesty;	3068
	93: 1	**the L** is clothed with strength,	3068
	93: 3	The floods have lifted up, O **L**, the floods	3068
	93: 4	**The L** on high *is* mightier than the noise of	3068
	93: 5	becometh thine house, O **L**, for ever.	3068
	94: 1	O **L** God, to whom vengeance belongeth;	3068
	94: 3	**L**, how long shall the wicked, how long	3068
	94: 5	thy people, O **L**, and afflict thine heritage.	3068
	94: 7	Yet they say, **The L** shall not see,	3050
	94:11	**The L** knoweth the thoughts of man,	3068
Ps	94:12	O **L**, and teachest him out of thy law;	3050
	94:14	For **the L** will not cast off his people,	3068
	94:17	Unless **the L** *had been* my help, my soul	3068
	94:18	foot slippeth; thy mercy, O **L**, held me up.	3068
	94:22	**the L** is my defence; and my God *is*	3068
	94:23	*yea*, **the L** our God shall cut them off.	3068
	95: 1	O come, let us sing unto **the L**: let us make	3068
	95: 3	For **the L** *is* a great God, and a great King	3068
	95: 6	let us kneel before **the L** our Maker.	3068
	96: 1	O sing unto **the L** a new song: sing unto	3068
	96: 1	a new song: sing unto **the L**, all the earth.	3068
	96: 2	Sing unto **the L**, bless his name; shew forth	3068
	96: 4	For **the L** *is* great, and greatly to be	3068
	96: 5	*are* idols: but **the L** made the heavens.	3068
	96: 7	Give unto **the L**, O ye kindreds of	3068
	96: 7	give unto **the L** glory and strength.	3068
	96: 8	Give unto **the L** the glory due unto his	3068
	96: 9	O worship **the L** in the beauty of holiness:	3068
	96:10	Say among the heathen *that* **the L** reigneth:	3068
	96:13	Before **the L**, for he cometh, for he cometh	3068
	97: 1	**The L** reigneth; let the earth rejoice; let	3068
	97: 5	melted like wax at the presence of **the L**,	3068
	97: 8	because of thy judgments, O **L**.	3068
	97: 9	For thou, **L**, *art* High above all the earth:	3068
	97:10	Ye that love **the L**, hate evil: he preserveth	3068
	97:12	Rejoice in **the L**, ye righteous; and	3068
	98: 1	O sing unto **the L** a new song; for he hath	3068
	98: 2	**The L** hath made known his salvation:	3068
	98: 4	Make a joyful noise unto **the L**, all	3068
	98: 5	Sing unto **the L** with the harp; with	3068
	98: 6	of cornet make a joyful noise before **the L**,	3068
	98: 9	Before **the L**; for he cometh to judge	3068
	99: 1	**The L** reigneth; let the people tremble:	3068
	99: 2	**The L** *is* great in Zion; and he *is* high	3068
	99: 5	Exalt ye **the L** our God, and worship at his	3068
	99: 6	they called upon **the L**, and he answered	3068
	99: 8	Thou answeredst them, O **L** our God:	3068
	99: 9	Exalt **the L** our God, and worship at his	3068
	99: 9	at his holy hill; for **the L** our God *is* holy.	3068
	100: 1	Make a joyful noise unto **the L**, all ye	3068
	100: 2	Serve **the L** with gladness: come before his	3068
	100: 3	Know ye that **the L** he *is* God: *it is* he *that*	3068
	100: 5	For **the L** *is* good; his mercy *is* everlasting;	3068
	101: 1	and judgment: unto thee, O **L**, will I sing.	3068
	101: 8	off all wicked doers from the city of **the L**.	3068
	102: T	and poureth out his complaint before **the L**.	3068
	102: 1	O **L**, and let my cry come unto thee.	3068
	102:12	thou, O **L**, shalt endure for ever; and	3068
	102:15	So the heathen shall fear the name of **the L**,	3068
	102:16	When **the L** shall build up Zion, he shall	3068
	102:18	which *shall be* created shall praise **the L**.	3050
	102:19	from heaven did **the L** behold the earth;	3068
	102:21	To declare the name of **the L** in Zion, and	3068
	102:22	and the kingdoms, to serve **the L**.	3068
	103: 1	Bless **the L**, O my soul: and all that is	3068
	103: 2	Bless **the L**, O my soul, and forget not all	3068
	103: 6	**The L** executeth righteousness and	3068
	103: 8	**The L** *is* merciful and gracious, slow to	3068
	103:13	*so* **the L** pitieth them that fear him.	3068
	103:17	the mercy of **the L** *is* from everlasting to	3068
	103:19	**The L** hath prepared his throne in	3068
	103:20	Bless **the L**, ye his angels, that excel in	3068
	103:21	Bless ye **the L**, all ye his hosts;	3068
	103:22	Bless **the L**, all his works in all places of	3068
	103:22	of his dominion: bless **the L**, O my soul.	3068
	104: 1	Bless **the L**, O my soul. O LORD my	3068
	104: 1	O **L** my God, thou art very great; thou art	3068
	104:16	The trees of **the L** are full *of sap*;	3068
	104:24	O **L**, how manifold are thy works!	3068
	104:31	The glory of **the L** shall endure for ever:	3068
	104:31	for ever: **the L** shall rejoice in his works.	3068
	104:33	I will sing unto **the L** as long as I live:	3068
	104:34	him shall be sweet: I will be glad in **the L**.	3068
	104:35	Bless thou **the L**, O my soul. Praise ye	3068
	104:35	the LORD, O my soul. Praise ye **the L**.	3050
	105: 1	O give thanks unto **the L**; call upon his	3068
	105: 3	let the heart of them rejoice that seek **the L**.	3068
	105: 4	Seek **the L**, and his strength: seek his face	3068
	105: 7	He *is* **the L** our God: his judgments *are* in	3068
	105:19	word came: the word of **the L** tried him.	3068
	105:45	and keep his laws. Praise ye **the L**.	3050
	106: 1	Praise ye **the L**. O give thanks unto	3050
	106: 1	O give thanks unto **the L**; for *he is* good:	3068
	106: 2	Who can utter the mighty acts of **the L**?	3068
	106: 4	Remember me, O **L**, with the favour *that*	3068
	106:16	in the camp, *and* Aaron the saint of **the L**.	3068
	106:25	*and* hearkened not unto the voice of **the L**.	3068
	106:34	*concerning* whom **the L** commanded them:	3068
	106:40	Therefore was the wrath of **the L** kindled	3068
	106:47	O **L** our God, and gather us from among	3068
	106:48	Blessed *be* **the L** God of Israel from	3068
	106:48	all the people say, Amen. Praise ye **the L**.	3050
	107: 1	O give thanks unto **the L**, for *he is* good:	3068
	107: 2	Let the redeemed of **the L** say *so*, whom he	3068
	107: 6	they cried unto **the L** in their trouble, *and*	3068
	107: 8	Oh that *men* would praise **the L** *for* his	3068
	107:13	they cried unto **the L** in their trouble, *and*	3068
	107:15	Oh that *men* would praise **the L** *for* his	3068
	107:19	they cry unto **the L** in their trouble,	3068
	107:21	Oh that *men* would praise **the L** *for* his	3068
	107:24	These see the works of **the L**, and	3068
	107:28	they cry unto **the L** in their trouble, and	3068
	107:31	Oh that *men* would praise **the L** *for* his	3068
	107:43	understand the lovingkindness of **the L**.	3068
	108: 3	I will praise thee, O **L**, among the people:	3068
	109:14	of his fathers be remembered with **the L**;	3068
	109:15	Let them be before **the L** continually,	3068
	109:20	the reward of mine adversaries from **the L**,	3068
	109:26	Help me, O **L** my God: O save me	3068
	109:27	this *is* thy hand; *that* thou, **L**, hast done it.	3068
	109:30	I will greatly praise **the L** with my mouth;	3068
	110: 1	**The L** said unto my Lord, Sit thou at my	3068
	110: 2	**The L** shall send the rod of thy strength out	3068
	110: 4	**The L** hath sworn, and will not repent,	3068
	111: 1	Praise ye **the L**. I will praise the LORD	3050
Ps	111: 1	I will praise **the L** with *my* whole heart,	3068
	111: 2	The works of **the L** *are* great, sought out of	3068
	111: 4	**the L** *is* gracious and full of compassion.	3068
	111:10	The fear of **the L** *is* the beginning of	3068
	112: 1	Praise ye **the L**. Blessed *is* the man *that*	3050
	112: 1	Blessed *is* the man *that* feareth **the L**,	3068
	112: 7	his heart is fixed, trusting in **the L**.	3068
	113: 1	Praise ye **the L**. Praise, O ye servants of	3050
	113: 1	Praise, O ye servants of **the L**, praise	3068
	113: 1	of the LORD, praise the name of **the L**.	3068
	113: 2	Blessed be the name of **the L** from this	3068
	113: 4	**The L** *is* high above all nations, *and*	3068
	113: 5	Who *is* like unto **the L** our God, who	3068
	113: 9	joyful mother of children. Praise ye **the L**.	3050
	115: 1	O **L**, not unto us, but unto thy name give	3068
	115: 9	O Israel, trust thou in **the L**: he *is* their help	3068
	115:10	O house of Aaron, trust in **the L**: he *is* their	3068
	115:11	Ye that fear **the L**, trust in the LORD:	3068
	115:11	Ye that fear the LORD, trust in **the L**:	3068
	115:12	**The L** hath been mindful of us: he will	3068
	115:13	He will bless them that fear **the L**, *both*	3068
	115:14	**The L** shall increase you more and more,	3068
	115:15	You *are* blessed of **the L** which made	3068
	115:17	The dead praise not **the L**, neither any that	3050
	115:18	But we will bless **the L** from this time forth	3050
	115:18	time forth and for evermore. Praise **the L**.	3050
	116: 1	I love **the L**, because he hath heard my	3068
	116: 4	called I upon the name of **the L**;	3068
	116: 4	O **L**, I beseech thee, deliver my soul.	3068
	116: 5	Gracious *is* **the L**, and righteous; yea,	3068
	116: 6	**The L** preserveth the simple: I was brought	3068
	116: 7	for **the L** hath dealt bountifully with thee.	3068
	116: 9	I will walk before **the L** in the land of	3068
	116:12	What shall I render unto **the L** *for* all his	3068
	116:13	and call upon the name of **the L**.	3068
	116:14	I will pay my vows unto **the L** now in	3068
	116:15	Precious in the sight of **the L** *is* the death	3068
	116:16	Oh **L**, truly I *am* thy servant; I *am* thy	3068
	116:17	and will call upon the name of **the L**.	3068
	116:18	I will pay my vows unto **the L** now in	3068
	116:19	midst of thee, O Jerusalem. Praise ye **the L**.	3050
	117: 1	O praise **the L**, all ye nations: praise him,	3068
	117: 2	the truth of **the L** *endureth* for ever.	3068
	117: 2	LORD *endureth* for ever. Praise ye **the L**.	3050
	118: 1	O give thanks unto **the L**; for *he is* good:	3068
	118: 4	Let them now that fear **the L** say, that his	3068
	118: 5	I called upon **the L** in distress: the LORD	3050
	118: 5	**the L** answered me, *and set me* in a large	3050
	118: 6	**The L** *is* on my side; I will not fear:	3068
	118: 7	**The L** taketh my part with them that help	3068
	118: 8	*It is* better to trust in **the L** than to put	3068
	118: 9	*It is* better to trust in **the L** than to put	3068
	118:10	in the name of **the L** will I destroy them.	3068
	118:11	in the name of **the L** I will destroy them.	3068
	118:12	for in the name of **the L** I will destroy	3068
	118:13	me that *I* might fall: but **the L** helped me.	3068
	118:14	**The L** *is* my strength and song, and	3050
	118:15	the right hand of **the L** doeth valiantly.	3068
	118:16	The right hand of **the L** is exalted: the right	3068
	118:16	the right hand of **the L** doeth valiantly.	3068
	118:17	but live, and declare the works of **the L**.	3050
	118:18	**The L** hath chastened me sore: but he hath	3050
	118:19	I will go into them, *and* I will praise **the L**:	3050
	118:20	This gate of **the L**, into which the righteous	3068
	118:24	This *is* the day *which* **the L** hath made;	3068
	118:25	Save now, I beseech thee, O **L**: O LORD,	3068
	118:25	O **L**, I beseech thee, send now prosperity.	3068
	118:26	*be* he that cometh in the name of **the L**:	3068
	118:26	have blessed you out of the house of **the L**.	3068
	118:27	God *is* **the L**, which hath shewed us light:	3068
	118:29	O give thanks unto **the L**; for *he is* good:	3068
	119: 1	in the way, who walk in the law of **the L**.	3068
	119:12	Blessed *art* thou, O **L**: teach me thy	3068
	119:31	thy testimonies: O **L**, put me not to shame.	3068
	119:33	Teach me, O **L**, the way of thy statutes; and	3068
	119:41	O **L**, *even* thy salvation, according to thy	3068
	119:52	I remembered thy judgments of old, O **L**;	3068
	119:55	O **L**, in the night, and have kept thy law.	3068
	119:57	*Thou art* my portion, O **L**: I have said that *I*	3068
	119:64	The earth, O **L**, is full *of* thy mercy:	3068
	119:65	thy servant, O **L**, according unto thy word.	3068
	119:75	I know, O **L**, that thy judgments *are* right,	3068
	119:89	For ever, O **L**, thy word *is* settled in	3068
	119:107	quicken me, O **L**, according unto thy word.	3068
	119:108	O **L**, and teach me thy judgments.	3068
	119:126	*It is* time for *thee*, **L**, to work: *for* they have	3068
	119:137	O **L**, and upright *are* thy judgments.	3068
	119:145	I cried with *my* whole heart; hear me, O **L**:	3068
	119:149	O **L**, quicken me according to thy	3068
	119:151	Thou *art* near, O **L**; and all thy	3068
	119:156	Great *are* thy tender mercies, O **L**:	3068
	119:159	quicken me, O **L**, according to thy	3068
	119:166	**L**, I have hoped for thy salvation, and	3068
	119:169	Let my cry come near before thee, O **L**:	3068
	119:174	I have longed for thy salvation, O **L**; and	3068
	120: 1	In my distress I cried unto **the L**, and	3068
	120: 2	O **L**, from lying lips, *and* from a deceitful	3068
	121: 2	My help *cometh* from **the L**, which made	3068
	121: 5	**The L** *is* thy keeper: the LORD *is* thy	3068
	121: 5	**the L** *is* thy shade upon thy right hand.	3068
	121: 7	**The L** shall preserve thee from all evil:	3068
	121: 8	**The L** shall preserve thy going out and	3068
	122: 1	unto me, Let us go *into* the house of **the L**.	3068
	122: 4	the tribes go up, the tribes of **the L**,	3050
	122: 4	to give thanks unto the name of **the L**.	3068
	122: 9	Because of the house of **the L** our God I	3068
	123: 2	so our eyes *wait* upon **the L** our God,	3068
	123: 3	mercy upon us, O **L**, have mercy upon us:	3068
	124: 1	If *it had* not *been* **the L** who was on our	3068
	124: 2	If *it had* not *been* **the L** who was on our	3068
	124: 6	Blessed *be* **the L**, who hath not given us *as*	3068
	124: 8	Our help *is* in the name of **the L**, who made	3068
	125: 1	They that trust in **the L** *shall be* as mount	3068
	125: 2	**the L** *is* round about his people from	3068
	125: 4	Do good, O **L**, unto *those that be* good, and	3068

Ps 125: 5 **the L** shall lead them forth with 3068
126: 1 When **the L** turned again the captivity of 3068
126: 2 **The L** hath done great things for them. 3068
126: 3 **The L** hath done great things for us; 3068
126: 4 Turn again our captivity, O **L**, as 3068
127: 1 Except **the L** build the house, they labour 3068
127: 1 except **the L** keep the city, the watchman 3068
127: 3 Lo, children *are* an heritage of **the L**: *and* 3068
128: 1 Blessed *is* every one that feareth **the L**; 3068
128: 4 shall the man be blessed that feareth **the L**. 3068
128: 5 **The L** shall bless thee out of Zion: and 3068
129: 4 **The L** *is* righteous: he hath cut asunder 3068
129: 8 by say, The blessing of **the L** *be* upon you: 3068
129: 8 we bless you in the name of **the L**. 3068
130: 1 of the depths have I cried unto thee, O **L**. 3068
130: 3 If thou, **L**, shouldest mark iniquities, 3050
130: 5 I wait for **the L**, my soul doth wait, and 3068
130: 7 Let Israel hope in **the L**: for with 3068
130: 7 for with **the L** *there is* mercy, and with him 3068
131: 1 **L**, my heart is not haughty, nor mine eyes 3068
131: 3 Let Israel hope in **the L** from henceforth 3068
132: 1 **L**, remember David, *and* all his afflictions: 3068
132: 2 How he sware unto **the L**, *and* vowed unto 3068
132: 5 Until I find out a place for **the L**, 3068
132: 8 Arise, O **L**, into thy rest; thou, and the ark 3068
132:11 **The L** hath sworn *in* truth unto David; 3068
132:13 For **the L** hath chosen Zion; he hath 3068
133: 3 for there **the L** commanded the blessing, 3068
134: 1 Behold, bless ye **the L**, all ye servants of 3068
134: 1 ye the LORD, all ye servants of **the L**, 3068
134: 1 which by night stand in the house of **the L**. 3068
134: 2 hands *in* the sanctuary, and bless **the L**. 3068
134: 3 **The L** that made heaven and earth bless 3068
135: 1 Praise ye **the L**. Praise ye the name of 3050
135: 1 Praise ye the name of **the L**; praise *him,* O 3068
135: 1 praise *him,* O ye servants of **the L**. 3068
135: 2 Ye that stand in the house of **the L**, in 3068
135: 3 Praise **the L**; for the LORD *is* good: 3050
135: 3 Praise the LORD; for **the L** *is* good: 3068
135: 4 For **the L** hath chosen Jacob unto himself, 3050
135: 5 For I know that **the L** *is* great, and *that* our 3068
135: 6 Whatsoever **the L** pleased, *that* did he in 3068
135:13 Thy name, O **L**, *endureth* for ever; *and* 3068
135:13 *and* thy memorial, O **L**, throughout all 3068
135:14 For **the L** will judge his people, and he will 3068
135:19 Bless **the L**, O house of Israel: bless 3068
135:19 of Israel: bless **the L**, O house of Aaron: 3068
135:20 Bless **the L**, O house of Levi: ye that fear 3068
135:20 ye that fear **the L**, bless the LORD. 3068
135:20 ye that fear the LORD, bless **the L**. 3068
135:21 Blessed *be* **the L** out of Zion, 3068
135:21 dwelleth *at* Jerusalem. Praise ye **the L**. 3050
136: 1 O give thanks unto **the L**; for *he is* good: 3068
137: 7 Remember, O **L**, the children of Edom *in* 3068
138: 4 O **L**, when they hear the words of thy 3068
138: 5 Yea, they shall sing in the ways of **the L**: 3068
138: 5 the LORD: for great *is* the glory of **the L**. 3068
138: 6 Though **the L** *be* high, yet hath he respect 3068
138: 8 **The L** will perfect that which concerneth 3068
138: 8 thy mercy, O **L**, *endureth* for ever: 3068
139: 1 O **L**, thou hast searched me, and 3068
139: 4 *but* lo, O **L**, thou knowest it altogether. 3068
139:21 Do not I hate them, O **L**, that hate thee? 3068
140: 1 Deliver me, O **L**, from the evil man: 3068
140: 4 Keep me, O **L**, from the hands of 3068
140: 6 I said unto **the L**, Thou *art* my God: 3068
140: 6 hear the voice of my supplications, O **L**. 3068
140: 8 Grant not, O **L**, the desires of the wicked: 3068
140:12 I know that **the L** will maintain the cause 3068
141: 1 **L**, I cry unto thee: make haste unto me; 3068
141: 3 Set a watch, O **L**, before my mouth; 3068
142: 1 I cried unto **the L** *with* my voice; *with* my 3068
142: 1 *with* my voice unto **the L** did I make my 3068
142: 5 I cried unto thee, O **L**: I said, Thou *art* my 3068
143: 1 Hear my prayer, O **L**, give ear to my 3068
143: 7 Hear me speedily, O **L**: my spirit faileth: 3068
143: 9 Deliver me, O **L**, from mine enemies: I flee 3068
143:11 Quicken me, O **L**, for thy name's sake: 3068
144: 1 Blessed *be* **the L** my strength, 3068
144: 3 **L**, what *is* man, that thou takest knowledge 3068
144: 5 Bow thy heavens, O **L**, and come down: 3068
144:15 happy *is that* people, whose God *is* **the L**. 3068
145: 3 Great *is* **the L**, and greatly to be praised; 3068
145: 8 **The L** *is* gracious, and full of compassion; 3068
145: 9 **The L** *is* good to all: and his tender mercies 3068
145:10 All thy works shall praise thee, O **L**; and 3068
145:14 **The L** upholdeth all that fall, and raiseth up 3068
145:17 **The L** *is* righteous in all his ways, and 3068
145:18 **The L** *is* nigh unto all them that call upon 3068
145:20 **The L** preserveth all them that love him: 3068
145:21 My mouth shall speak the praise of **the L**: 3068
146: 1 Praise ye **the L**. Praise the LORD, O my 3050
146: 1 ye the LORD. Praise **the L**, O my soul. 3068
146: 2 While I live will I praise **the L**: I will sing 3068
146: 5 his help, whose hope *is* in **the L** his God: 3068
146: 7 to the hungry. **The L** looseth the prisoners: 3068
146: 8 **The L** openeth *the eyes of* the blind: 3068
146: 8 **the L** raiseth them that are bowed down: 3068
146: 8 bowed down: **the L** loveth the righteous: 3068
146: 9 **The L** preserveth the strangers; he relieveth 3068
146:10 **The L** shall reign for ever, *even* thy God, 3068
146:10 unto all generations. Praise ye **the L**. 3050
147: 1 Praise ye **the L**: for *it is* good to sing 3050
147: 2 **The L** doth build up Jerusalem: 3068
147: 6 **The L** lifteth up the meek: he casteth 3068
147: 7 Sing unto **the L** with thanksgiving; 3068
147:11 **The L** taketh pleasure in them that fear 3068
147:12 Praise **the L**, O Jerusalem; praise thy God, 3068
147:20 they have not known them. Praise ye **the L**. 3050
148: 1 Praise ye **the L**. Praise ye the LORD from 3050
148: 1 Praise ye **the L** from the heavens: 3068
148: 5 Let them praise the name of **the L**: for he 3068
148: 7 Praise **the L** from the earth, ye dragons, 3068
148:13 Let them praise the name of **the L**: for his 3068
148:14 a people near unto him. Praise ye **the L**. 3050

Ps 149: 1 Praise ye **the L**. Sing unto the LORD a 3050
149: 1 Sing unto **the L** a new song, *and* his praise 3068
149: 4 For **the L** taketh pleasure in his people: 3068
149: 9 honour have all his saints. Praise ye **the L**. 3050
150: 1 Praise ye **the L**. Praise God in his 3050
150: 6 every *thing that hath* breath praise **the L**. 3050
150: 6 breath praise the LORD. Praise ye **the L**. 3050
Pr 1: 7 The fear of **the L** *is* the beginning of 3068
1:29 and did not choose the fear of **the L**: 3068
2: 5 shalt thou understand the fear of **the L**, 3068
2: 6 For **the L** giveth wisdom: out of his mouth 3068
3: 5 Trust in **the L** with all thine heart; and 3068
3: 7 own eyes: fear **the L**, and depart from evil. 3068
3: 9 Honour **the L** with thy substance, and 3068
3:11 despise not the chastening of **the L**; 3068
3:12 For whom **the L** loveth he correcteth; 3068
3:19 **The L** by wisdom hath founded the earth; 3068
3:26 For **the L** shall be thy confidence, and 3068
3:32 For the froward *is* abomination to **the L**: 3068
3:33 The curse of **the L** *is* in the house of 3068
5:21 ways of man *are* before the eyes of **the L**, 3068
6:16 These six *things* doth **the L** hate: yea, 3068
8:13 The fear of **the L** *is* to hate evil: pride, and 3068
8:22 **The L** possessed me *in* the beginning of his 3068
8:35 and shall obtain favour of **the L**. 3068
9:10 The fear of **the L** *is* the beginning of 3068
10: 3 **The L** will not suffer the soul of 3068
10:22 The blessing of **the L**, it maketh rich, and 3068
10:27 The fear of **the L** prolongeth days: but 3068
10:29 The way of **the L** *is* strength to the upright: 3068
11: 1 A false balance *is* abomination to **the L**: 3068
11:20 froward heart *are* abomination unto **the L**: 3068
12: 2 A good *man* obtaineth favour of **the L**: but 3068
12:22 Lying lips *are* abomination to **the L**: but 3068
14: 2 walketh in his uprightness feareth **the L**: 3068
14:26 In the fear of **the L** *is* strong confidence: 3068
14:27 The fear of **the L** *is* a fountain of life, 3068
15: 3 The eyes of **the L** *are* in every place, 3068
15: 8 of the wicked *is* an abomination to **the L**: 3068
15: 9 the wicked *is* an abomination unto **the L**: 3068
15:11 Hell and destruction *are* before **the L**: 3068
15:16 Better *is* little with the fear of **the L** than 3068
15:25 **The L** will destroy the house of the proud: 3068
15:26 of the wicked *are* an abomination to **the L**: 3068
15:29 **The L** *is* far from the wicked: but 3068
15:33 The fear of **the L** *is* the instruction of 3068
16: 1 the answer of the tongue, *is* from **the L**. 3068
16: 2 own eyes; but **the L** weigheth the spirits. 3068
16: 3 Commit thy works unto **the L**, and 3068
16: 4 **The L** hath made all *things* for himself: 3068
16: 5 proud in heart *is* an abomination to **the L**: 3068
16: 6 by the fear of **the L** *men* depart from evil. 3068
16: 7 When a man's ways please **the L**, 3068
16: 9 his way: but **the L** directeth his steps. 3068
16:20 and whoso trusteth in **the L**, happy *is* he. 3068
16:33 but the whole disposing thereof *is* of **the L**. 3068
17: 3 furnace for gold: but **the L** trieth the hearts. 3068
17:15 even they both *are* abomination to **the L**. 3068
18:10 The name of **the L** *is* a strong tower: 3068
18:22 good *thing*, and obtaineth favour of **the L**. 3068
19: 3 and his heart fretteth against **the L**. 3068
19:14 and a prudent wife *is* from **the L**. 3068
19:17 hath pity upon the poor lendeth unto **the L**; 3068
19:21 nevertheless the counsel of **the L**, that shall 3068
19:23 The fear of **the L** *tendeth* to life: and 3068
20:10 of them *are* alike abomination to **the L**. 3068
20:12 **the L** hath made even both of them. 3068
20:22 *but* wait on **the L**, and he shall save thee. 3068
20:23 weights *are* an abomination unto **the L**; 3068
20:24 Man's goings *are* of **the L**; how can a man 3068
20:27 The spirit of man *is* the candle of **the L**, 3068
21: 1 The king's heart *is* in the hand of **the L**, 3068
21: 2 own eyes: but **the L** pondereth the hearts. 3068
21: 3 judgment *is* more acceptable to **the L** than 3068
21:30 understanding nor counsel against **the L**. 3068
21:31 the day of battle: but safety *is* of **the L**. 3068
22: 2 **the L** *is* the Maker of them all. 3068
22: 4 *and* the fear of **the L** *are* riches, 3068
22:12 The eyes of **the L** preserve knowledge, and 3068
22:14 he that is abhorred of **the L** shall fall 3068
22:19 That thy trust may be in **the L**, I have made 3068
22:23 For **the L** will plead their cause, and 3068
23:17 *be thou* in the fear of **the L** all the day long. 3068
24:18 Lest **the L** see *it*, and it displease him, and 3068
24:21 My son, fear thou **the L** and the king: *and* 3068
25:22 upon his head, and **the L** shall reward thee. 3068
28: 5 they that seek **the L** understand all *things.* 3068
28:25 he that putteth his trust in **the L** shall be 3068
29:13 **the L** lighteneth both their eyes. 3068
29:25 whoso putteth his trust in **the L** shall be 3068
29:26 *every* man's judgment *cometh* from **the L**. 3068
30: 9 and deny *thee*, and say, Who *is* **the L**? 3068
31:30 *but* a woman that feareth **the L**, she shall 3068
Isa 1: 2 for **the L** hath spoken, I have nourished and 3068
1: 4 they have forsaken **the L**, they have 3068
1: 9 Except **the L** of hosts had left unto us a 3068
1:10 Hear the word of **the L**, ye rulers of 3068
1:11 saith **the L**: I am full *of* the burnt offerings 3068
1:18 and let us reason together, saith **the L**: 3068
1:20 for the mouth of **the L** hath spoken *it.* 3068
1:24 Therefore saith the Lord, **the L** of hosts, 3068
1:28 they that forsake **the L** shall be consumed. 3068
2: 3 and let us go up to the mountain of **the L**, 3068
2: 3 and the word of **the L** from Jerusalem. 3068
2: 5 and let us walk in the light of **the L**. 3068
2:10 for fear of **the L**, and for the glory of his 3068
2:11 and **the L** alone shall be exalted in that day. 3068
2:12 For the day of **the L** of hosts *shall be* upon 3068
2:17 and **the L** alone shall be exalted in that day. 3068
2:19 for fear of **the L**, and for the glory of his 3068
2:21 for fear of **the L**, and for the glory of his 3068
3: 1 For behold, the Lord, **the L** of hosts, 3068
3: 8 and their doings *are* against **the L**, 3068
3:13 **The L** standeth *up* to plead, and standeth to 3068
3:14 **The L** will enter into judgment with 3068

Isa 3:16 Moreover **the L** saith, Because 3068
3:17 and **the L** will discover their secret parts. 3068
4: 2 In that day shall the branch of **the L** be 3068
4: 5 **the L** will create upon every dwelling place 3068
5: 7 For the vineyard of **the L** of hosts *is* 3068
5: 9 In mine ears *said* **the L** of hosts, Of a truth 3068
5:12 they regard not the work of **the L**, 3068
5:16 **the L** of hosts shall be exalted in judgment, 3068
5:24 they have cast away the law of **the L** of 3068
5:25 Therefore is the anger of **the L** kindled 3068
6: 3 said, Holy, holy, holy, *is* **the L** of hosts: 3068
6: 5 eyes have seen the King, **the L** of hosts. 3068
6:12 **the L** have removed men far away, and 3068
7: 3 said **the L** unto Isaiah, Go forth now to 3068
7:10 Moreover **the L** spake again unto Ahaz, 3068
7:11 Ask thee a sign of **the L** thy God; ask it 3068
7:12 I will not ask, neither will I tempt **the L**. 3068
7:17 **The L** shall bring upon thee, and upon thy 3068
7:18 *that* **the L** shall hiss for the fly that *is* in 3068
8: 1 Moreover **the L** said unto me, Take thee a 3068
8: 3 said **the L** to me, Call his name 3068
8: 5 **The L** spake also unto me again, saying, 3068
8:11 For **the L** spake thus to me with a strong 3068
8:13 Sanctify **the L** of hosts himself; and *let* him 3068
8:17 I will wait upon **the L**, that hideth his face 3068
8:18 the children whom **the L** hath given me *are* 3068
8:18 for wonders in Israel from **the L** of hosts, 3068
9: 7 The zeal of **the L** of hosts will perform 3068
9:11 Therefore **the L** shall set up the adversaries 3068
9:13 neither do they seek **the L** of hosts. 3068
9:14 Therefore **the L** will cut off from Israel 3068
9:19 Through the wrath of **the L** of hosts is 3068
10:20 shall stay upon **the L**, the Holy One of 3068
10:26 **the L** of hosts shall stir up a scourge for 3068
10:33 Behold, the Lord, **the L** of hosts, shall lop 3068
11: 2 the Spirit of **the L** shall rest upon him, 3068
11: 2 of knowledge and of the fear of **the L**; 3068
11: 3 of quick understanding in the fear of **the L**: 3068
11: 9 shall be full *of* the knowledge of **the L**, 3068
11:15 **the L** shall utterly destroy the tongue of 3068
12: 1 day thou shalt say, O **L**, I will praise thee: 3068
12: 2 for **the L** JEHOVAH *is* my strength and 3050
12: 4 ye say, Praise **the L**, call upon his name, 3068
12: 5 Sing unto **the L**; for he hath done excellent 3068
13: 4 **the L** of hosts mustereth the host of 3068
13: 5 *even* **the L**, and the weapons of his 3068
13: 6 Howl ye; for the day of **the L** *is* at hand; 3068
13: 9 Behold, the day of **the L** cometh, 3068
13:13 in the wrath of **the L** of hosts, and in 3068
14: 1 For **the L** will have mercy on Jacob, and 3068
14: 2 them in the land of **the L** for servants 3068
14: 3 it shall come to pass in the day that **the L** 3068
14: 5 **The L** hath broken the staff of the wicked, 3068
14:22 saith **the L** of hosts, and cut off from 3068
14:22 remnant, and son, and nephew, saith **the L**. 3068
14:23 besom of destruction, saith **the L** of hosts. 3068
14:24 **The L** of hosts hath sworn, saying, 3068
14:27 For **the L** of hosts hath purposed, and 3068
14:32 That **the L** hath founded Zion, and the poor 3068
16:13 This *is* the word that **the L** hath spoken 3068
16:14 now **the L** hath spoken, saying, 3068
17: 3 the children of Israel, saith **the L** of hosts. 3068
17: 6 branches thereof, saith **the L** God of Israel. 3068
18: 4 For so **the L** said unto me, I will take my 3068
18: 7 unto **the L** of hosts *of* a people scattered 3068
18: 7 to the place of the name of **the L** of hosts, 3068
19: 1 **the L** rideth upon a swift cloud, and 3068
19: 4 over them, saith the Lord, **the L** of hosts. 3068
19:12 let them know what **the L** of hosts hath 3068
19:14 **The L** hath mingled a perverse spirit in 3068
19:16 of the shaking of the hand of **the L** of 3068
19:17 because of the counsel of **the L** of hosts, 3068
19:18 of Canaan, and swear to **the L** of hosts: 3068
19:19 In that day shall there be an altar to **the L** 3068
19:19 and a pillar at the border thereof to **the L**. 3068
19:20 for a witness unto **the L** of hosts in the land 3068
19:20 for they shall cry unto **the L** because of 3068
19:21 **the L** shall be known to Egypt, and 3068
19:21 the Egyptians shall know **the L** in that day, 3068
19:21 they shall vow a vow unto **the L**, and 3068
19:22 **the L** shall smite Egypt: *he* shall smite and 3068
19:22 heal *it*: and they shall return *even* to **the L**, 3068
19:25 Whom **the L** of hosts shall bless, saying, 3068
20: 2 At the same time spake **the L** by Isaiah 3068
20: 3 **the L** said, Like as my servant Isaiah hath 3068
21:10 that which I have heard of **the L** of hosts, 3068
21:17 for **the L** God of Israel hath spoken *it.* 3068
22:14 it was revealed in mine ears *by* **the L** of 3068
22:17 **the L** will carry thee away with a mighty 3068
22:25 In that day, saith **the L** of hosts, shall 3068
22:25 it shall be cut off: for **the L** hath spoken *it.* 3068
23: 9 **The L** of hosts hath purposed it, to stain 3068
23:11 **the L** hath given a commandment against 3068
23:17 *that* **the L** will visit Tyre, and she shall turn 3068
23:18 and her hire shall be holiness to **the L**: 3068
23:18 shall be for them that dwell before **the L**, 3068
24: 1 **the L** maketh the earth empty, and 3068
24: 3 for **the L** hath spoken this word. 3068
24:14 they shall sing, for the majesty of **the L**, 3068
24:15 Wherefore glorify ye **the L** in the fires, 3068
24:15 *even* the name of **the L** God of Israel in 3068
24:21 *that* **the L** shall punish the host of the high 3068
24:23 when **the L** of hosts shall reign in mount 3068
25: 1 O **L**, thou *art* my God; I will exalt thee, 3068
25: 6 in this mountain shall **the L** of hosts make 3068
25: 8 off all the earth: for **the L** hath spoken *it.* 3068
25: 9 this *is* **the L**; we have waited for him, 3068
25:10 For in this mountain shall the hand of **the L** 3068
26: 4 Trust ye in **the L** for ever: for in 3068
26: 4 for in **the L** JEHOVAH *is* everlasting 3050
26: 8 O **L**, have we waited for thee; 3068
26:10 and will not behold the majesty of **the L**. 3068
26:11 **L**, *when* thy hand is lifted up, they will not 3068
26:12 **L**, thou wilt ordain peace for us: for thou 3068
26:13 O **L** our God, *other* lords besides thee have 3068

Isa 26:15 O **L**, thou hast increased the nation: 3068
26:16 **L**, in trouble have they visited thee, 3068
26:17 so have we been in thy sight, O **L**. 3068
26:21 **the L** cometh out of his place to punish 3068
27: 1 In that day **the L** with his sore and great 3068
27: 3 I **the L** do keep it; I will water it every 3068
27:12 *that* **the L** shall beat off from the channel of 3068
27:13 shall worship **the L** in the holy mount at 3068
28: 2 **the L** hath a mighty and strong one, 3068
28: 5 In that day shall **the L** of hosts be for a 3068
28:13 the word of **the L** was unto them precept 3068
28:14 Wherefore hear the word of **the L**, 3068
28:21 For **the L** shall rise up as *in* mount 3068
28:29 This also cometh forth from **the L** of hosts, 3068
29: 6 Thou shalt be visited of **the L** of hosts with 3068
29:10 For **the L** hath poured out upon you 3068
29:15 seek deep to hide *their* counsel from **the L**, 3068
29:19 meek also shall increase *their* joy in **the L**, 3068
29:22 Therefore thus saith **the L**, who redeemed 3068
30: 1 saith **the L**, that take counsel, but not of 3068
30: 9 children *that* will not hear the law of **the L**: 3068
30:18 therefore will **the L** wait, that *he* may be 3068
30:18 for **the L** *is* a God of judgment: blessed *are* 3068
30:26 in the day that **the L** bindeth up the breach 3068
30:27 the name of **the L** cometh from far, 3068
30:29 a pipe to come into the mountain of **the L**, 3068
30:30 **the L** shall cause his glorious voice to be 3068
30:31 For through the voice of **the L** shall 3068
30:32 which **the L** shall lay upon him, *it* shall be 3068
30:33 the breath of **the L**, like a stream of 3068
31: 1 the Holy One of Israel, neither seek **the L**. 3068
31: 3 When **the L** shall stretch out his hand, 3068
31: 4 For thus hath **the L** spoken unto me, 3068
31: 4 shall **the L** of hosts come down to fight for 3068
31: 5 so will **the L** of hosts defend Jerusalem; 3068
31: 9 saith **the L**, whose fire *is* in Zion, and his 3068
32: 6 and to utter error against **the L**, 3068
33: 2 O **L**, be gracious unto us; we have waited 3068
33: 5 **The L** *is* exalted; for he dwelleth on high: 3068
33: 6 the fear of **the L** *is* his treasure. 3068
33:10 Now will I rise, saith **the L**; now will I be 3068
33:21 there **the** glorious **L** *will be* unto us a place 3068
33:22 For **the L** *is* our judge, the LORD *is* our 3068
33:22 **the L** *is* our lawgiver, the LORD *is* our 3068
33:22 LORD *is* our lawgiver, **the L** *is* our king; 3068
34: 2 For the indignation of **the L** *is* upon all 3068
34: 6 The sword of **the L** is filled *with* blood, 3068
34: 6 for **the L** hath a sacrifice in Bozrah, and 3068
34:16 Seek ye out of the book of **the L**, and read: 3068
35: 2 they shall see the glory of **the L**, *and* 3068
35:10 the ransomed of **the L** shall return, and 3068
36: 7 thou say to me, We trust in **the L** our God: 3068
36:10 am I now come up without **the L** against 3068
36:10 **the L** said unto me, Go up against this land, 3068
36:15 let Hezekiah make you trust in **the L**, 3068
36:15 **The L** will surely deliver us: 3068
36:18 saying, **The L** will deliver us. 3068
36:20 that **the L** should deliver Jerusalem out of 3068
37: 1 and went *into* the house of **the L**. 3068
37: 4 It may be **the L** thy God will hear 3068
37: 4 will reprove the words which **the L** thy 3068
37: 6 ye say unto your master, Thus saith **the L**, 3068
37:14 Hezekiah went up *unto* the house of **the L**, 3068
37:14 of the LORD, and spread it before **the L**. 3068
37:15 And Hezekiah prayed unto **the L**, saying, 3068
37:16 O **L** of hosts, God of Israel, that dwellest 3068
37:17 Incline thine ear, O **L**, and hear; open thine 3068
37:17 and hear; open thine eyes, O **L**, and see: 3068
37:18 Of a truth, **L**, the kings of Assyria have laid 3068
37:20 Now therefore, O **L** our God, save us from 3068
37:20 of the earth may know that thou *art* **the L**, 3068
37:21 Thus saith **the L** God of Israel, 3068
37:22 This *is* the word which **the L** hath spoken 3068
37:32 the zeal of **the L** of hosts shall do this. 3068
37:33 Therefore thus saith **the L** concerning 3068
37:34 shall not come into this city, saith **the L**. 3068
37:36 the angel of **the L** went forth, and smote in 3068
38: 1 said unto him, Thus saith **the L**, Set thine 3068
38: 2 toward the wall, and prayed unto **the L**, 3068
38: 3 Remember now, O **L**, I beseech thee, 3068
38: 4 came the word of **the L** to Isaiah, saying, 3068
38: 5 Go and say to Hezekiah, Thus saith **the L**, 3068
38: 7 this *shall be* a sign unto thee from **the L**, 3068
38: 7 that **the L** will do this thing that he hath 3068
38:11 I said, I shall not see **the L**, *even* 3050
38:11 *even* **the L**, in the land of the living: 3050
38:14 O **L**, I am oppressed; undertake for me. 3068
38:20 **The L** *was ready* to save me: therefore 3068
38:20 the days of our life in the house of **the L**. 3068
38:22 that I shall go up *to* the house of **the L**? 3068
39: 5 Hear the word of **the L** of hosts: 3068
39: 6 nothing shall be left, saith **the L**. 3068
39: 8 Good *is* the word of **the L** which thou hast 3068
40: 3 Prepare ye the way of **the L**, 3068
40: 5 the glory of **the L** shall be revealed, and 3068
40: 5 for the mouth of **the L** hath spoken *it*. 3068
40: 7 because the spirit of **the L** bloweth upon it: 3068
40:13 Who hath directed the spirit of **the L**, or 3068
40:27 My way is hid from **the L**, and 3068
40:28 not heard, *that* the everlasting God, **the L**, 3068
40:31 they that wait upon **the L** shall renew *their* 3068
41: 4 I **the L**, the first, and with the last; I *am* he. 3068
41:13 For I **the L** thy God will hold thy right 3068
41:14 help thee, saith **the L**, and thy redeemer, 3068
41:16 thou shalt rejoice in **the L**, *and* shalt glory 3068
41:17 faileth for thirst, I **the L** will hear them, 3068
41:20 that the hand of **the L** hath done this, and 3068
41:21 Produce your cause, saith **the L**; bring forth 3068
42: 5 Thus saith God **the L**, he that created 3068
42: 6 I **the L** have called thee in righteousness, 3068
42: 8 I *am* **the L**: that *is* my name: and my glory 3068
42:10 Sing unto **the L** a new song, *and* his praise 3068
42:12 Let them give glory unto **the L**, and 3068
42:13 **The L** shall go forth as a mighty *man*, he 3068
42:21 **The L** is well pleased for his righteousness' 3068

Isa 42:24 did not **the L**, he against whom we have 3068
43: 1 now thus saith **the L** that created thee, 3068
43: 3 For I *am* **the L** thy God, the Holy One of 3068
43:10 saith **the L**, and my servant whom I have 3068
43:11 I, *even* I, *am* **the L**; and beside me *there is* 3068
43:12 my witnesses, saith **the L**, that I *am* God. 3068
43:14 Thus saith **the L**, your redeemer, the Holy 3068
43:15 I *am* **the L**, your Holy One, the creator of 3068
43:16 Thus saith **the L**, which maketh a way in 3068
44: 2 Thus saith **the L** that made thee, and 3068
44: 5 shall subscribe *with* his hand unto **the L**, 3068
44: 6 Thus saith **the L** the King of Israel, and 3068
44: 6 of Israel, and his redeemer **the L** of hosts; 3068
44:23 for **the L** hath done *it*: shout, ye lower parts 3068
44:23 for **the L** hath redeemed Jacob, and 3068
44:24 Thus saith **the L**, thy redeemer, and he that 3068
44:24 I *am* **the L** that maketh all *things*; that 3068
45: 1 Thus saith **the L** to his anointed, to Cyrus, 3068
45: 3 **the L**, which call *thee* by thy name, *am* 3068
45: 5 I *am* **the L**, and *there is* none else, *there is* 3068
45: 6 I *am* **the L**, and *there is* none else. 3068
45: 7 and create evil: I **the L** do all these *things*. 3068
45: 8 spring up together; I **the L** have created it. 3068
45:11 Thus saith **the L**, the Holy One of Israel, 3068
45:13 for price nor reward, saith **the L** of hosts. 3068
45:14 Thus saith **the L**, The labour of Egypt, and 3068
45:17 *But* Israel shall be saved in **the L** *with* an 3068
45:18 For thus saith **the L** that created 3068
45:18 I *am* **the L**; and *there is* none else. 3068
45:19 I **the L** speak righteousness, I declare 3068
45:21 *have* not I **the L**? and *there is* no God else 3068
45:24 in **the L** have I righteousness and strength: 3068
45:25 In **the L** shall all the seed of Israel be 3068
47: 4 our redeemer, **the L** of hosts *is* his name, 3068
48: 1 which swear by the name of **the L**, and 3068
48: 2 God of Israel; **The L** of hosts *is* his name. 3068
48:14 these *things*? **The L** hath loved him: 3068
48:17 Thus saith **the L**, thy redeemer, the Holy 3068
48:17 I *am* **the L** thy God which teacheth thee to 3068
48:20 **The L** hath redeemed his servant Jacob. 3068
48:22 *is* no peace, saith **the L**, unto the wicked. 3068
49: 1 **The L** hath called me from the womb; 3068
49: 4 *yet* surely my judgment *is* with **the L**, and 3068
49: 5 saith **the L** that formed me from the womb 3068
49: 5 yet shall I be glorious in the eyes of **the L**, 3068
49: 7 Thus saith **the L**, the redeemer of Israel, 3068
49: 7 because of **the L** that *is* faithful, *and* 3068
49: 8 Thus saith **the L**, In an acceptable time 3068
49:13 for **the L** hath comforted his people, and 3068
49:14 **The L** hath forsaken me, and my Lord hath 3068
49:18 *As* I live, saith **the L**, thou shalt surely 3068
49:23 and thou shalt know that I *am* **the L**: 3068
49:25 thus saith **the L**, Even the captives of 3068
49:26 all flesh shall know that I **the L** *am* thy 3068
50: 1 Thus saith **the L**, Where *is* the bill of your 3068
50:10 Who *is* among you that feareth **the L**, 3068
50:10 let him trust in the name of **the L**, and 3068
51: 1 after righteousness, ye that seek **the L**: 3068
51: 3 For **the L** shall comfort Zion: he will 3068
51: 3 and her desert like the garden of **the L**; 3068
51: 9 awake, put on strength, O arm of **the L**; 3068
51:11 Therefore the redeemed of **the L** shall 3068
51:13 forgettest **the L** thy Maker, that hath 3068
51:15 I *am* **the L** thy God, that divided the sea, 3068
51:15 waves roared: **The L** of hosts *is* his name. 3068
51:17 which hast drunk at the hand of **the L** 3068
51:20 *they are* full *of* the fury of **the L**, the rebuke 3068
51:22 Thus saith thy Lord **the L**, and thy God *that* 3068
52: 3 For thus saith **the L**, Ye have sold 3068
52: 5 what have I here, saith **the L**, 3068
52: 5 over them make *them* to howl, saith **the L**; 3068
52: 8 to eye, when **the L** shall bring again Zion. 3068
52: 9 for **the L** hath comforted his people, 3068
52:10 **The L** hath made bare his holy arm in 3068
52:11 be ye clean, that bear the vessels of **the L**. 3068
52:12 for **the L** will go before you; and the God 3068
53: 1 and to whom is the arm of **the L** revealed? 3068
53: 6 **the L** hath laid on him the iniquity of us all. 3068
53:10 Yet it pleased **the L** to bruise him; he hath 3068
53:10 the pleasure of **the L** shall prosper in his 3068
54: 1 children of the married wife, saith **the L**. 3068
54: 5 **the L** of hosts *is* his name; and 3068
54: 6 For **the L** hath called thee as a woman 3068
54: 8 mercy on thee, saith **the L** thy redeemer. 3068
54:10 saith **the L** that hath mercy on thee. 3068
54:13 all thy children *shall be* taught of **the L**; 3068
54:17 This *is* the heritage of the servants of **the L**, 3068
54:17 their righteousness *is* of me, saith **the L**. 3068
55: 5 run unto thee because of **the L** thy God, 3068
55: 6 Seek ye **the L** while he may be found, 3068
55: 7 let him return unto **the L**, and he will have 3068
55: 8 *are* your ways my ways, saith **the L**. 3068
55:13 it shall be to **the L** for a name, for an 3068
56: 1 Thus saith **the L**, Keep ye judgment, and 3068
56: 3 that hath joined himself to **the L**, speak, 3068
56: 3 **The L** hath utterly separated me from his 3068
56: 4 For thus saith **the L** unto the eunuchs that 3068
56: 6 that join themselves to **the L**, to serve him, 3068
56: 6 serve him, and to love the name of **the L**, 3068
57:19 far off, and to *him that is* near, saith **the L**; 3068
58: 5 this a fast, and an acceptable day to **the L**? 3068
58: 8 the glory of **the L** shall be thy rereward. 3068
58: 9 shalt thou call, and **the L** shall answer; 3068
58:11 **the L** shall guide thee continually, and 3068
58:13 a delight, the holy of **the L**, honourable; 3068
58:14 shalt thou delight thyself in **the L**; and 3068
58:14 for the mouth of **the L** hath spoken *it*. 3068
59:13 In transgressing and lying against **the L**, 3068
59:15 **the L** saw *it*, and it displeased him that 3068
59:19 So shall they fear the name of **the L** from 3068
59:19 the spirit of **the L** shall lift up a standard 3068
59:20 from transgression in Jacob, saith **the L**. 3068
59:21 this *is* my covenant with them, saith **the L**; 3068
59:21 saith **the L**, from henceforth and for ever. 3068
60: 1 and the glory of **the L** is risen upon thee. 3068

Isa 60: 2 **the L** shall arise upon thee, and his glory 3068
60: 6 they shall shew forth the praises of **the L**. 3068
60: 9 unto the name of **the L** thy God, and to 3068
60:14 they shall call thee, The city of **the L**, 3068
60:16 thou shalt know that I **the L** *am* thy Saviour 3068
60:19 **the L** shall be unto thee an everlasting 3068
60:20 for **the L** shall be thine everlasting light, 3068
60:22 I **the L** will hasten it in his time. 3068
61: 1 **the L** hath anointed me to preach good 3068
61: 2 To proclaim the acceptable year of **the L**, 3068
61: 3 the planting of **the L**, that *he* might be 3068
61: 6 ye shall be named the Priests of **the L**: 3068
61: 8 For I **the L** love judgment, I hate robbery 3068
61: 9 that they *are* the seed *which* **the L** hath 3068
61:10 I will greatly rejoice in **the L**, my soul shall 3068
62: 2 which the mouth of **the L** shall name. 3068
62: 3 be a crown of glory in the hand of **the L**, 3068
62: 4 for **the L** delighteth in thee, and thy land 3068
62: 6 ye that make mention of **the L**, keep not 3068
62: 8 **The L** hath sworn by his right hand, and 3068
62: 9 gathered it shall eat it, and praise **the L**; 3068
62:11 **the L** hath proclaimed unto the end of 3068
62:12 The holy people, The redeemed of **the L**: 3068
63: 7 will mention the lovingkindnesses of **the L**, 3068
63: 7 of the LORD, *and* the praises of **the L**, 3068
63: 7 according to all that **the L** hath bestowed 3068
63:14 the Spirit of **the L** caused him to rest: 3068
63:16 thou, O **L**, *art* our father, our redeemer; 3068
63:17 O **L**, why hast thou made us to err from thy 3068
64: 8 now, O **L**, thou *art* our father; we *are* 3068
64: 9 Be not wroth very sore, O **L**, 3068
64:12 thou refrain thyself for these *things*, O **L**? 3068
65: 7 of your fathers together, saith **the L**, 3068
65: 8 Thus saith **the L**, As the new wine is found 3068
65:11 ye *are* they that forsake **the L**, that forget 3068
65:23 they *are* the seed of the blessed of **the L**, 3068
65:25 in all my holy mountain, saith **the L**. 3068
66: 1 Thus saith **the L**, The heaven *is* my throne, 3068
66: 2 and all those *things* have been, saith **the L**: 3068
66: 5 Hear the word of **the L**, ye that tremble at 3068
66: 5 name's sake, said, Let **the L** be glorified: 3068
66: 6 a voice of **the L** that rendereth recompence 3068
66: 9 saith **the L**: shall I cause to bring forth, and 3068
66:12 For thus saith **the L**, Behold, I will extend 3068
66:14 the hand of **the L** shall be known towards 3068
66:15 **the L** will come with fire, and with his 3068
66:16 by his sword will **the L** plead with all flesh: 3068
66:16 and the slain of **the L** shall be many. 3068
66:17 shall be consumed together, saith **the L**. 3068
66:20 unto **the L** out of all nations upon horses, 3068
66:20 my holy mountain Jerusalem, saith **the L**, 3068
66:20 in a clean vessel *into* the house of **the L**. 3068
66:21 for priests *and* for Levites, saith **the L**. 3068
66:22 saith **the L**, so shall your seed and 3068
66:23 come to worship before me, saith **the L**. 3068
Jer 1: 2 To whom the word of **the L** came in 3068
1: 4 the word of **the L** came unto me, saying, 3068
1: 7 **the L** said unto me, Say not, I *am* a child: 3068
1: 8 I *am* with thee to deliver thee, saith **the L**. 3068
1: 9 **the L** put forth his hand, and touched my 3068
1: 9 **the L** said unto me, Behold, I have put my 3068
1:11 the word of **the L** came unto me, saying, 3068
1:12 said **the L** unto me, Thou hast well seen: 3068
1:13 the word of **the L** came unto me the second 3068
1:14 **the L** said unto me, Out of the north an evil 3068
1:15 of the kingdoms of the north, saith **the L**; 3068
1:19 I *am* with thee, saith **the L**, to deliver thee. 3068
2: 1 Moreover the word of **the L** came to me, 3068
2: 2 ears of Jerusalem, saying, Thus saith **the L**; 3068
2: 3 Israel *was* holiness unto **the L**, *and* 3068
2: 3 evil shall come upon them, saith **the L**. 3068
2: 4 Hear ye the word of **the L**, O house of 3068
2: 5 Thus saith **the L**, What iniquity have your 3068
2: 6 Where *is* **the L** that brought us up out of 3068
2: 8 The priests said not, Where *is* **the L**? and 3068
2: 9 saith **the L**, and with your children's 3068
2:12 be ye very desolate, saith **the L**. 3068
2:17 in that thou hast forsaken **the L** thy God, 3068
2:19 that thou hast forsaken **the L** thy God, and 3068
2:29 have transgressed against me, saith **the L**. 3068
2:31 O generation, see ye the word of **the L**. 3068
2:37 for **the L** hath rejected thy confidences, and 3068
3: 1 yet return again to me, saith **the L**. 3068
3: 6 **The L** said also unto me in the days of 3068
3:10 her whole heart, but feignedly, saith **the L**. 3068
3:11 **the L** said unto me, The backsliding Israel 3068
3:12 Return, thou backsliding Israel, saith **the L**; 3068
3:12 saith **the L**, *and* I will not keep *anger* for 3068
3:13 that thou hast transgressed against **the L** 3068
3:13 ye have not obeyed my voice, saith **the L**. 3068
3:14 Turn, O backsliding children, saith **the L**; 3068
3:16 in the land, in those days, saith **the L**, 3068
3:16 no more, The ark of the covenant of **the L**: 3068
3:17 shall call Jerusalem the throne of **the L**; 3068
3:17 unto it, to the name of **the L**, to Jerusalem: 3068
3:20 with me, O house of Israel, saith **the L**. 3068
3:21 *and* they have forgotten **the L** their God. 3068
3:22 come unto thee; for thou *art* **the L** our God. 3068
3:23 truly in **the L** our God *is* the salvation of 3068
3:25 for we have sinned against **the L** our God, 3068
3:25 have not obeyed the voice of **the L** our 3068
4: 1 O Israel, saith **the L**, return unto me: 3068
4: 2 **The L** liveth, in truth, in judgment, and 3068
4: 3 For thus saith **the L** to the men of Judah 3068
4: 4 Circumcise yourselves to **the L**, and 3068
4: 8 for the fierce anger of **the L** is not turned 3068
4: 9 shall come to pass at that day, saith **the L**, 3068
4:17 been rebellious against me, saith **the L**. 3068
4:26 were broken down at the presence of **the L**, 3068
4:27 For thus hath **the L** said, The whole land 3068
5: 2 though they say, **The L** liveth; surely they 3068
5: 3 O **L**, *are* not thine eyes upon the truth? 3068
5: 4 for they know not the way of **the L**, *nor* 3068
5: 5 for they have known the way of **the L**, *and* 3068
5: 9 I not visit for these *things*? saith **the L**: 3068

L

Jer 5:11 very treacherously against me, saith **the L**. 3068
5:12 They have belied **the L**, and said, *It is* not 3068
5:14 Wherefore thus saith **the L** God of hosts, 3068
5:15 you from far, O house of Israel, saith **the L**: 3068
5:18 Nevertheless in those days, saith **the L**, 3068
5:19 Wherefore doth **the L** our God all these 3068
5:22 saith **the L**: will ye not tremble at my 3068
5:24 Let us now fear **the L** our God, that giveth 3068
5:29 I not visit for these *things?* saith **the L**: 3068
6:6 For thus hath **the L** of hosts said, Hew ye 3068
6:9 Thus saith **the L** of hosts, They shall 3068
6:10 the word of **the L** is unto them a reproach; 3068
6:11 Therefore I am full *of* the fury of **the L**; 3068
6:12 the inhabitants of the land, saith **the L**. 3068
6:15 them they shall be cast down, saith **the L**. 3068
6:16 Thus saith **the L**, Stand ye in the ways, and 3068
6:21 Therefore thus saith **the L**, Behold, I will 3068
6:22 Thus saith **the L**, Behold, a people cometh 3068
6:30 because **the L** hath rejected them. 3068
7:1 word that came to Jeremiah from **the L**, 3068
7:2 say, Hear the word of **the L**, all *ye of* 3068
7:2 enter in at these gates to worship **the L**. 3068
7:3 Thus saith **the L** of hosts, the God of Israel, 3068
7:4 saying, The temple of **the L**, The temple of 3068
7:4 The temple of **the L**, The temple of 3068
7:4 the LORD, The temple of **the L**, *are* these. 3068
7:11 Behold, even I have seen *it*, saith **the L**. 3068
7:13 saith **the L**, and I spake unto you, rising up 3068
7:19 saith **the L**: *do they* not *provoke* 3068
7:21 Thus saith **the L** of hosts, the God of Israel; 3068
7:28 obeyeth not the voice of **the L** their God, 3068
7:29 for **the L** hath rejected and forsaken 3068
7:30 have done evil in my sight, saith **the L**: 3068
7:32 the days come, saith **the L**, 3068
8:1 At that time, saith **the L**, they shall bring 3068
8:3 I have driven them, saith **the L** of hosts. 3068
8:4 thou shalt say unto them, Thus saith **the L**; 3068
8:7 my people know not the judgment of **the L**. 3068
8:8 *are* wise, and the law of **the L** *is* with us? 3068
8:9 lo, they have rejected the word of **the L**; 3068
8:12 they shall be cast down, saith **the L**. 3068
8:13 I will surely consume them, saith **the L**: 3068
8:14 for **the L** our God hath put us to silence, 3068
8:14 because we have sinned against **the L**. 3068
8:17 and they shall bite you, saith **the L**. 3068
8:19 *Is* not **the L** in Zion? *is* not her king in her? 3068
9:3 to evil, and they know not me, saith **the L**. 3068
9:6 deceit they refuse to know me, saith **the L**. 3068
9:7 Therefore thus saith **the L** of hosts, Behold, 3068
9:9 not visit them for these *things?* saith **the L**: 3068
9:12 *who is he* to whom the mouth of **the L** hath 3068
9:13 **the L** saith, Because they have forsaken my 3068
9:15 Therefore thus saith **the L** of hosts, the God 3068
9:17 Thus saith **the L** of hosts, Consider ye, and 3068
9:20 Yet hear the word of **the L**, O ye women, 3068
9:22 Speak, Thus saith **the L**, Even the carcases 3068
9:23 Thus saith **the L**, Let not the wise *man* 3068
9:24 that I *am* **the L** which exercise 3068
9:24 for in these *things* I delight, saith **the L**. 3068
9:25 Behold, the days come, saith **the L**, that I 3068
10:1 Hear ye the word which **the L** speaketh 3068
10:2 Thus saith **the L**, Learn not the way of 3068
10:6 as *there is* none like unto thee, O **L**; 3068
10:10 **the L** *is* the true God, he *is* the living God, 3068
10:16 his inheritance: **The L** of hosts *is* his name. 3068
10:18 For thus saith **the L**, Behold, I will sling 3068
10:21 become brutish, and have not sought **the L**: 3068
10:23 O **L**, I know that the way of man *is* not in 3068
10:24 O **L**, correct me, but with judgment; not in 3068
11:1 word that came to Jeremiah from **the L**, 3068
11:3 unto them, Thus saith **the L** God of Israel; 3068
11:5 Then answered I, and said, So be it, O **L**. 3068
11:6 **the L** said unto me, Proclaim all these 3068
11:9 **the L** said unto me, A conspiracy is found 3068
11:11 Therefore thus saith **the L**, Behold, I *will* 3068
11:16 **The L** called thy name, A green olive tree, 3068
11:17 For **the L** of hosts, that planted thee, 3068
11:18 **the L** hath given me knowledge *of it*, and 3068
11:20 But, O **L** of hosts, that judgest righteously, 3068
11:21 Therefore thus saith **the L** of the men of 3068
11:21 Prophesy not in the name of **the L**, 3068
11:22 Therefore thus saith **the L** of hosts, Behold, 3068
12:1 Righteous *art* thou, O **L**, when I plead with 3068
12:3 thou, O **L**, knowest me: thou hast seen me, 3068
12:12 for the sword of **the L** *shall* devour from 3068
12:13 because of the fierce anger of **the L**. 3068
12:14 Thus saith **the L** against all mine evil 3068
12:16 to swear by my name, **The L** liveth; 3068
12:17 and destroy that nation, saith **the L**. 3068
13:1 Thus saith **the L** unto me, Go and get thee 3068
13:2 according to the word of **the L**, and put *it* 3068
13:3 the word of **the L** came unto me the second 3068
13:5 it by Euphrates, as **the L** commanded me. 3068
13:6 that **the L** said unto me, Arise, go to 3068
13:8 the word of **the L** came unto me, saying, 3068
13:9 Thus saith **the L**, After this manner will I 3068
13:11 and the whole house of Judah, saith **the L**; 3068
13:12 Thus saith **the L** God of Israel, Every bottle 3068
13:13 say unto them, Thus saith **the L**, Behold, 3068
13:14 and the sons together, saith **the L**: 3068
13:15 be not proud: for **the L** hath spoken. 3068
13:16 Give glory to **the L** your God, before he 3068
13:25 of thy measures from me, saith **the L**; 3068
14:1 The word of **the L** that came to Jeremiah 3068
14:7 O **L**, though our iniquities testify against 3068
14:9 yet thou, O **L**, *art* in the midst of us, and 3068
14:10 Thus saith **the L** unto this people, Thus 3068
14:10 therefore **the L** doth not accept them; 3068
14:11 said **the L** unto me, Pray not for this people 3068
14:14 **the L** said unto me, The prophets prophesy 3068
14:15 Therefore thus saith **the L** concerning 3068
14:20 O **L**, our wickedness, *and* the iniquity of 3068
14:22 *art* not thou he, O **L** our God? therefore 3068
15:1 said **the L** unto me, Though Moses and 3068
15:2 thou shalt tell them, Thus saith **the L**; 3068
Jer 15:3 appoint over them four kinds, saith **the L**: 3068
15:6 Thou hast forsaken me, saith **the L**, 3068
15:9 the sword before their enemies, saith **the L**. 3068
15:11 **The L** said, Verily it shall be well with thy 3068
15:15 O **L**, thou knowest: remember me, and 3068
15:16 I am called by thy name, O **L** God of hosts. 3068
15:19 Therefore thus saith **the L**, If thou return, 3068
15:20 to save thee and to deliver thee, saith **the L**. 3068
16:1 The word of **the L** came also unto me, 3068
16:3 For thus saith **the L** concerning the sons 3068
16:5 For thus saith **the L**, Enter not *into* 3068
16:5 saith **the L**, *even* lovingkindness and 3068
16:9 For thus saith **the L** of hosts, the God of 3068
16:10 Wherefore hath **the L** pronounced all this 3068
16:10 we have committed against **the L** our God? 3068
16:11 saith **the L**, and have walked after other 3068
16:14 the days come, saith **the L**, 3068
16:14 that it shall no more be said, **The L** liveth, 3068
16:15 But, **The L** liveth, that brought up 3068
16:16 saith **the L**, and they shall fish them; 3068
16:19 O **L**, my strength, and my fortress, and 3068
16:21 they shall know that my name *is* **The L**. 3068
17:5 Thus saith **the L**; Cursed *be* the man that 3068
17:5 and whose heart departeth from **the L**. 3068
17:7 Blessed *is* the man that trusteth in **the L**, 3068
17:7 in the LORD, and whose hope **the L** is. 3068
17:10 I **the L** search the heart, *I* try the reins, 3068
17:13 O **L**, the hope of Israel, all that forsake thee 3068
17:13 because they have forsaken **the L**, 3068
17:14 Heal me, O **L**, and I shall be healed; 3068
17:15 say unto me, Where *is* the word of **the L**? 3068
17:19 Thus said **the L** unto me; Go and stand in 3068
17:20 Hear ye the word of **the L**, ye kings of 3068
17:21 Thus saith **the L**; Take heed to yourselves, 3068
17:24 ye diligently hearken unto me, saith **the L**, 3068
17:26 *of* praise, *unto* the house of **the L**. 3068
18:1 word which came to Jeremiah from **the L**, 3068
18:5 the word of **the L** came to me, saying, 3068
18:6 saith **the L**. Behold, as the clay *is* in 3068
18:11 of Jerusalem, saying, Thus saith **the L**; 3068
18:13 Therefore thus saith **the L**; Ask ye now 3068
18:19 O **L**, and hearken to the voice of them that 3068
18:23 Yet, **L**, thou knowest all their counsel 3068
19:1 Thus saith **the L**, Go and get a potter's 3068
19:3 say, Hear ye the word of **the L**, O kings of 3068
19:3 Thus saith **the L** of hosts, the God of Israel; 3068
19:6 the days come, saith **the L**, 3068
19:11 say unto them, Thus saith **the L** of hosts; 3068
19:12 saith **the L**, and to the inhabitants thereof, 3068
19:14 whither **the L** had sent him to prophesy; 3068
19:15 Thus saith **the L** of hosts, the God of Israel; 3068
20:1 also chief governor in the house of **the L**, 3068
20:2 which *was* by the house of **the L**. 3068
20:3 **The L** hath not called thy name Pashur, but 3068
20:4 For thus saith **the L**, Behold, I will make 3068
20:7 O **L**, thou hast deceived me, and I was 3068
20:8 the word of **the L** was made a reproach 3068
20:11 **the L** *is* with me as a mighty terrible one: 3068
20:12 But, O **L** of hosts, that triest the righteous, 3068
20:13 Sing unto **the L**, praise ye the LORD: 3068
20:13 Sing unto the LORD, praise ye **the L**: 3068
20:16 let that man be as the cities which **the L** 3068
21:1 which came unto Jeremiah from **the L**, 3068
21:2 Inquire, I pray thee, of **the L** for us; for 3068
21:2 be that **the L** will deal with us according to 3068
21:4 Thus saith **the L** God of Israel; Behold, 3068
21:7 afterward, saith **the L**, I will deliver 3068
21:8 this people thou shalt say, Thus saith **the L**; 3068
21:10 city for evil, and not for good, saith **the L**: 3068
21:11 of Judah, *say*, Hear ye the word of **the L**. 3068
21:12 O house of David, thus saith **the L**; 3068
21:13 *and* rock of the plain, saith **the L**; 3068
21:14 to the fruit of your doings, saith **the L**: 3068
22:1 Thus saith **the L**; Go down *to* the house of 3068
22:2 say, Hear the word of **the L**, O king of 3068
22:3 Thus saith **the L**; Execute ye judgment and 3068
22:5 these words, I swear by myself, saith **the L**, 3068
22:6 For thus saith **the L** unto the king's house 3068
22:8 Wherefore hath **the L** done thus unto this 3068
22:9 forsaken the covenant of **the L** their God, 3068
22:11 For thus saith **the L** touching Shallum 3068
22:16 *him: was* not this to know me? saith **the L**. 3068
22:18 Therefore thus saith **the L** concerning 3068
22:24 *As* I live, saith **the L**, though Coniah 3068
22:29 earth, earth, hear the word of **the L**. 3068
22:30 Thus saith **the L**, Write ye this man 3068
23:1 scatter the sheep of my pasture! saith **the L**. 3068
23:2 Therefore thus saith **the L** God of Israel 3068
23:2 you the evil of your doings, saith **the L**. 3068
23:4 neither shall they be lacking, saith **the L**. 3068
23:5 Behold, the days come, saith **the L**, that I 3068
23:6 **THE L** OUR RIGHTEOUSNESS. 3068
23:7 the days come, saith **the L**, 3068
23:7 that they shall no more say, **The L** liveth, 3068
23:8 But, **The L** liveth, which brought up and 3068
23:9 because of **the L**, and because of the words 3068
23:11 have I found their wickedness, saith **the L**. 3068
23:12 the year of their visitation, saith **the L**. 3068
23:15 Therefore thus saith **the L** of hosts 3068
23:16 Thus saith **the L** of hosts, Hearken not unto 3068
23:16 *and* not out of the mouth of **the L**. 3068
23:17 **The L** hath said, Ye shall have peace; 3068
23:18 For who hath stood in the counsel of **the L**, 3068
23:19 a whirlwind of **the L** is gone forth *in* fury, 3068
23:20 The anger of **the L** shall not return, until he 3068
23:23 saith **the L**, and not a God afar off? 3068
23:24 saith **the L**. Do not I fill heaven and earth? 3068
23:24 Do not I fill heaven and earth? saith **the L**. 3068
23:28 What *is* the chaff to the wheat? saith **the L**. 3068
23:29 saith **the L**; and like a hammer *that* 3068
23:30 I *am* against the prophets, saith **the L**, 3068
23:31 saith **the L**, that use their tongues, and say, 3068
23:32 saith **the L**, and do tell them, and cause my 3068
23:32 not profit this people at all, saith **the L**. 3068
23:33 saying, What *is* the burden of **the L**? 3068
Jer 23:33 I will even forsake you, saith **the L**. 3068
23:34 that shall say, The burden of **the L**, 3068
23:35 to his brother, What hath **the L** answered? 3068
23:35 and, What hath **the L** spoken? 3068
23:36 the burden of **the L** shall ye mention no 3068
23:36 the living God, of **the L** of hosts our God. 3068
23:37 What hath **the L** answered thee? 3068
23:37 and, What hath **the L** spoken? 3068
23:38 sith ye say, The burden of **the L**; therefore 3068
23:38 of the LORD; therefore thus saith **the L**; 3068
23:38 The burden of **the L**, and I have sent unto 3068
23:38 Ye shall not say, The burden of **the L**; 3068
24:1 **The L** shewed me, and behold, two baskets 3068
24:1 of figs *were* set before the temple of **the L**, 3068
24:3 said **the L** unto me, What seest thou, 3068
24:4 Again the word of **the L** came unto me, 3068
24:5 Thus saith **the L**, the God of Israel; 3068
24:7 them a heart to know me, that I *am* **the L**: 3068
24:8 surely thus saith **the L**, So will I give 3068
25:3 the word of **the L** hath come unto me, and 3068
25:4 **the L** hath sent unto you all his servants 3068
25:5 dwell in the land that **the L** hath given unto 3068
25:7 have not hearkened unto me, saith **the L**; 3068
25:8 Therefore thus saith **the L** of hosts; 3068
25:9 saith **the L**, and Nebuchadrezzar the king 3068
25:12 that nation, saith **the L**, for their iniquity, 3068
25:15 For thus saith **the L** God of Israel unto me; 3068
25:17 to drink, unto whom **the L** had sent me: 3068
25:27 Thus saith **the L** of hosts, the God of Israel; 3068
25:28 say unto them, Thus saith **the L** of hosts; 3068
25:29 of the earth, saith **the L** of hosts. 3068
25:30 **The L** shall roar from on high, and utter his 3068
25:31 for **the L** hath a controversy with 3068
25:31 *that are* wicked to the sword, saith **the L**. 3068
25:32 Thus saith **the L** of hosts, Behold, evil *shall* 3068
25:33 the slain of **the L** shall be at that day from 3068
25:36 *shall be heard:* for **the L** *hath* spoiled their 3068
25:37 because of the fierce anger of **the L**. 3068
26:1 king of Judah came this word from **the L**, 3068
26:2 Thus saith **the L**; Stand in the court of 3068
26:4 thou shalt say unto them, Thus saith **the L**; 3068
26:7 speaking these words in the house of **the L**. 3068
26:8 **the L** had commanded *him* to speak unto 3068
26:9 hast thou prophesied in the name of **the L**, 3068
26:9 against Jeremiah in the house of **the L**. 3068
26:10 the king's house *unto* the house of **the L**, 3068
26:12 **The L** sent me to prophesy against this 3068
26:13 and obey the voice of **the L** your God; 3068
26:13 **the L** will repent him of the evil that he 3068
26:15 for of a truth **the L** hath sent me unto you 3068
26:16 spoken to us in the name of **the L** our God. 3068
26:18 of Judah, saying, Thus saith **the L** of hosts; 3068
26:19 did he not fear **the L**, and besought 3068
26:19 besought **the L**, and the LORD repented 3068
26:19 **the L** repented him of the evil which he 3068
26:20 a man that prophesied in the name of **the L**, 3068
27:1 came this word unto Jeremiah from **the L**, 3068
27:2 Thus saith **the L** to me; Make thee bonds 3068
27:4 Thus saith **the L** of hosts, the God of Israel; 3068
27:8 saith **the L**, with the sword, and with 3068
27:11 remain still in their own land, saith **the L**; 3068
27:13 as **the L** hath spoken against the nation that 3068
27:15 For I have not sent them, saith **the L**, 3068
27:16 to all this people, saying, Thus saith **the L**; 3068
27:18 and if the word of **the L** be with them, 3068
27:18 let them now make intercession to **the L** of 3068
27:18 vessels which are left in the house of **the L**, 3068
27:19 For thus saith **the L** of hosts concerning 3068
27:21 Yea, thus saith **the L** of hosts, the God of 3068
27:21 vessels that remain *in* the house of **the L**, 3068
27:22 until the day that I visit them, saith **the L**; 3068
28:1 spake unto me in the house of **the L**, 3068
28:2 Thus speaketh **the L** of hosts, the God of 3068
28:4 that went into Babylon, saith **the L**: 3068
28:5 the people that stood in the house of **the L**, 3068
28:6 **the L** do so: the LORD perform thy words 3068
28:6 **the L** perform thy words which thou hast 3068
28:9 be known, that **the L** hath truly sent him. 3068
28:11 of all the people, saying, Thus saith **the L**; 3068
28:12 the word of **the L** came unto Jeremiah 3068
28:13 and tell Hananiah, saying, Thus saith **the L**; 3068
28:14 For thus saith **the L** of hosts, the God of 3068
28:15 **The L** hath not sent thee; but thou makest 3068
28:16 Therefore thus saith **the L**; Behold, I will 3068
28:16 thou hast taught rebellion against **the L**. 3068
29:4 Thus saith **the L** of hosts, the God of Israel, 3068
29:7 away captives, and pray unto **the L** for it: 3068
29:8 For thus saith **the L** of hosts, the God of 3068
29:9 my name: I have not sent them, saith **the L**. 3068
29:10 For thus saith **the L**, That after seventy 3068
29:11 saith **the L**, thoughts of peace, and not of 3068
29:14 And I will be found of you, saith **the L**: and 3068
29:14 whither I have driven you, saith **the L**; 3068
29:15 **The L** hath raised us up prophets in 3068
29:16 *Know* that thus saith **the L** of the king that 3068
29:17 Thus saith **the L** of hosts; Behold, I will 3068
29:19 not hearkened to my words, saith **the L**, 3068
29:19 but ye would not hear, saith **the L**. 3068
29:20 Hear ye therefore the word of **the L**, all *ye* 3068
29:21 Thus saith **the L** of hosts, the God of Israel, 3068
29:22 **The L** make thee like Zedekiah and 3068
29:23 even I know, and *am* a witness, saith **the L**. 3068
29:25 Thus speaketh **the L** of hosts, the God of 3068
29:26 **The L** hath made thee priest in the stead of 3068
29:26 *ye* should be officers in the house of **the L**, 3068
29:30 came the word of **the L** unto Jeremiah, 3068
29:31 Thus saith **the L** concerning Shemaiah 3068
29:32 Therefore thus saith **the L**; Behold, I will 3068
29:32 that I will do for my people, saith **the L**; 3068
29:32 he hath taught rebellion against **the L**. 3068
30:1 word that came to Jeremiah from **the L**, 3068
30:2 Thus speaketh **the L** God of Israel, saying, 3068
30:3 For lo, the days come, saith **the L**, that I 3068
30:3 of my people Israel and Judah, saith **the L**: 3068
30:4 these *are* the words that **the L** spake 3068

Book	Ref	Context	Strong's
Jer	30: 5	For thus saith **the L**; We have heard a voice	3068
	30: 8	to pass in that day, saith **the L** of hosts,	3068
	30: 9	they shall serve **the L** their God, and David	3068
	30:10	thou not, O my servant Jacob, saith **the L**;	3068
	30:11	I *am* with thee, saith **the L**, to save thee:	3068
	30:12	For thus saith **the L**, Thy bruise *is*	3068
	30:17	I will heal thee of thy wounds, saith **the L**;	3068
	30:18	Thus saith **the L**: Behold, I *will* bring again	3068
	30:21	his heart to approach unto me? saith **the L**.	3068
	30:23	the whirlwind of **the L** goeth forth *with*	3068
	30:24	The fierce anger of **the L** shall not return,	3068
	31: 1	At the same time, saith **the L**, will I be	3068
	31: 2	Thus saith **the L**, The people which were	3068
	31: 3	**The L** hath appeared of old unto me,	3068
	31: 6	let us go up *to* Zion unto **the L** our God.	3068
	31: 7	For thus saith **the L**; Sing with gladness for	3068
	31: 7	publish ye, praise ye, and say, O **L**, save	3068
	31:10	Hear the word of **the L**, O ye nations, and	3068
	31:11	For **the L** hath redeemed Jacob, and	3068
	31:12	flow *together* to the goodness of **the L**,	3068
	31:14	be satisfied with my goodness, saith **the L**.	3068
	31:15	Thus saith **the L**; A voice was heard in	3068
	31:16	Thus saith **the L**, Refrain thy voice from	3068
	31:16	for thy work shall be rewarded, saith **the L**;	3068
	31:17	there is hope in thine end, saith **the L**,	3068
	31:18	shall be turned; for thou *art* **the L** my God.	3068
	31:20	surely have mercy upon him, saith **the L**.	3068
	31:22	for **the L** hath created a new *thing* in	3068
	31:23	Thus saith **the L** of hosts, the God of Israel;	3068
	31:23	**The L** bless thee, O habitation of justice,	3068
	31:27	Behold, the days come, saith **the L**, that I	3068
	31:28	to build, and to plant, saith **the L**.	3068
	31:31	Behold, the days come, saith **the L**, that I	3068
	31:32	I was a husband unto them, saith **the L**:	3068
	31:33	After those days, saith **the L**, I will put my	3068
	31:34	every man his brother, saying, Know **the L**:	3068
	31:34	them unto the greatest of them, saith **the L**:	3068
	31:35	Thus saith **the L**, which giveth the sun for a	3068
	31:35	thereof roar; **The L** of hosts *is* his name:	3068
	31:36	saith **the L**, *then* the seed of Israel also	3068
	31:37	Thus saith **the L**; If heaven above can be	3068
	31:37	for all that they have done, saith **the L**.	3068
	31:38	Behold, the days come, saith **the L**, that	3068
	31:38	that the city shall be built to **the L** from	3068
	31:40	towards the east, *shall be* holy unto **the L**;	3068
	32: 1	The word that came to Jeremiah from **the L**	3068
	32: 3	and say, Thus saith **the L**, Behold,	3068
	32: 5	shall he be until I visit him, saith **the L**:	3068
	32: 6	The word of **the L** came unto me, saying,	3068
	32: 8	the prison according to the word of **the L**,	3068
	32: 8	I knew that this *was* the word of **the L**.	3068
	32:14	Thus saith **the L** of hosts, the God of Israel;	3068
	32:15	For thus saith **the L** of hosts, the God of	3068
	32:16	son of Neriah, I prayed unto **the L**, saying,	3068
	32:18	Mighty God, **the L** of hosts, *is* his name,	3068
	32:26	came the word of **the L** unto Jeremiah,	3068
	32:27	Behold, I *am* **the L**, the God of all flesh: is	3068
	32:28	Therefore thus saith **the L**; Behold, I *will*	3068
	32:30	with the work of their hands, saith **the L**.	3068
	32:36	now therefore thus saith **the L**, the God of	3068
	32:42	For thus saith **the L**; Like as I have brought	3068
	32:44	cause their captivity to return, saith **the L**.	3068
	33: 1	Moreover the word of **the L** came unto	3068
	33: 2	Thus saith **the L** the maker thereof,	3068
	33: 2	**the L** that formed it, to establish it;	3068
	33: 2	formed it, to establish it; **the L** *is* his name;	3068
	33: 4	For thus saith **the L**, the God of Israel,	3068
	33:10	Thus saith **the L**; Again there shall be	3068
	33:11	them that shall say, Praise **the L** of hosts:	3068
	33:11	for **the L** *is* good; for his mercy *endureth*	3068
	33:11	sacrifice of praise *into* the house of **the L**.	3068
	33:11	of the land as at the first, saith **the L**.	3068
	33:12	Thus saith **the L** of hosts, Again in this	3068
	33:13	hands of him that telleth *them*, saith **the L**.	3068
	33:14	Behold, the days come, saith **the L**, that I	3068
	33:16	shall be called, **The L** our righteousness.	3068
	33:17	For thus saith **the L**; David shall never	3068
	33:19	And the word of **the L** came unto Jeremiah,	3068
	33:20	Thus saith **the L**; If you can break my	3068
	33:23	Moreover the word of **the L** came to	3068
	33:24	The two families which **the L** hath chosen,	3068
	33:25	Thus saith **the L**; If my covenant *be* not	3068
	34: 1	which came unto Jeremiah from **the L**,	3068
	34: 2	Thus saith **the L**, the God of Israel; Go and	3068
	34: 2	of Judah, and tell him, Thus saith **the L**;	3068
	34: 4	Yet hear the word of **the L**, O Zedekiah	3068
	34: 4	Thus saith **the L** of thee, Thou shalt not die	3068
	34: 5	I have pronounced the word, saith **the L**.	3068
	34: 8	word that came unto Jeremiah from **the L**,	3068
	34:12	Therefore the word of **the L** came to	3068
	34:12	the LORD came to Jeremiah from **the L**,	3068
	34:13	Thus saith **the L**, the God of Israel; I made	3068
	34:17	Therefore thus saith **the L**; Ye have not	3068
	34:17	saith **the L**, to the sword, to the pestilence,	3068
	34:22	saith **the L**, and cause them to return to this	3068
	35: 1	**the L** in the days of Jehoiakim the son of	3068
	35: 2	and bring them *into* the house of **the L**,	3068
	35: 4	I brought them *into* the house of **the L**,	3068
	35:12	came the word of **the L** unto Jeremiah,	3068
	35:13	Thus saith **the L** of hosts, the God of Israel;	3068
	35:13	to hearken to my words? saith **the L**.	3068
	35:17	Therefore thus saith **the L** God of hosts,	3068
	35:18	Thus saith **the L** of hosts, the God of Israel;	3068
	35:19	Therefore thus saith **the L** of hosts, the God	3068
	36: 1	this word came unto Jeremiah from **the L**,	3068
	36: 4	mouth of Jeremiah all the words of **the L**,	3068
	36: 5	I cannot go *into* the house of **the L**:	3068
	36: 6	the words of **the L** in the ears of the people	3068
	36: 7	will present their supplication before **the L**,	3068
	36: 7	the fury that **the L** hath pronounced against	3068
	36: 8	reading in the book the words of **the L** *in*	3068
	36: 9	*that* they proclaimed a fast before **the L** *to*	3068
	36:10	words of Jeremiah *in* the house of **the L**,	3068
	36:11	out of the book all the words of **the L**,	3068
	36:26	Jeremiah the prophet: but **the L** hid them.	3068
Jer	36:27	the word of **the L** came to Jeremiah,	3068
	36:29	Jehoiakim king of Judah, Thus saith **the L**;	3068
	36:30	Therefore thus saith **the L** of Jehoiakim	3068
	37: 2	did hearken unto the words of **the L**,	3068
	37: 3	Pray now unto **the L** our God for us.	3068
	37: 6	came the word of **the L** unto the prophet	3068
	37: 7	Thus saith **the L**, the God of Israel;	3068
	37: 9	Thus saith **the L**; Deceive not yourselves,	3068
	37:17	and said, Is there *any* word from **the L**?	3068
	38: 2	Thus saith **the L**, He that remaineth in this	3068
	38: 3	Thus saith **the L**, This city shall surely be	3068
	38:14	the third entry that *is* in the house of **the L**:	3068
	38:16	saying, *As* **the L** liveth, that made us this	3068
	38:17	Thus saith **the L**, the God of hosts, the God	3068
	38:20	I beseech thee, the voice of **the L**, which I	3068
	38:21	this *is* the word that **the L** hath shewed me:	3068
	39:15	Now the word of **the L** came unto	3068
	39:16	saying, Thus saith **the L** of hosts, the God	3068
	39:17	I will deliver thee in that day, saith **the L**:	3068
	39:18	thou hast put thy trust in me, saith **the L**.	3068
	40: 1	word which came to Jeremiah from **the L**,	3068
	40: 2	**The L** thy God hath pronounced this evil	3068
	40: 3	Now **the L** hath brought *it*, and	3068
	40: 3	because ye have sinned against **the L**, and	3068
	41: 5	to bring *them to* the house of **the L**.	3068
	42: 2	pray for us unto **the L** thy God, *even* for all	3068
	42: 3	That **the L** thy God may shew us the way	3068
	42: 4	I *will* pray unto **the L** your God according	3068
	42: 4	*that* whatsoever thing **the L** shall answer	3068
	42: 5	**The L** be a true and faithful witness	3068
	42: 5	which **the L** thy God shall send thee to us.	3068
	42: 6	we will obey the voice of **the L** our God,	3068
	42: 6	when we obey the voice of **the L** our God.	3068
	42: 7	that the word of **the L** came unto Jeremiah.	3068
	42: 9	Thus saith **the L**, the God of Israel,	3068
	42:11	*are* afraid; be not afraid of him, saith **the L**:	3068
	42:13	neither obey the voice of **the L** your God,	3068
	42:15	now therefore hear the word of **the L**,	3068
	42:15	Thus saith **the L** of hosts, the God of Israel;	3068
	42:18	For thus saith **the L** of hosts, the God of	3068
	42:19	**The L** hath said concerning you, O ye	3068
	42:20	when ye sent me unto **the L** your God,	3068
	42:20	Pray for us unto **the L** our God;	3068
	42:20	according unto all that **the L** our God shall	3068
	42:21	ye have not obeyed the voice of **the L** your	3068
	43: 1	the people all the words of **the L** their God,	3068
	43: 1	*for* which **the L** their God had sent him to	3068
	43: 2	**the L** our God hath not sent thee to say,	3068
	43: 4	the people, obeyed not the voice of **the L**,	3068
	43: 7	for they obeyed not the voice of **the L**:	3068
	43: 8	came the word of **the L** unto Jeremiah in	3068
	43:10	Thus saith **the L** of hosts, the God of Israel;	3068
	44: 2	Thus saith **the L** of hosts, the God of Israel;	3068
	44: 7	Therefore now thus saith **the L**, the God of	3068
	44:11	Therefore thus saith **the L** of hosts, the God	3068
	44:16	hast spoken unto us in the name of **the L**,	3068
	44:21	did not **the L** remember them, and came it	3068
	44:22	So that **the L** could no longer bear, because	3068
	44:23	because ye have sinned against **the L**, and	3068
	44:23	have not obeyed the voice of **the L**,	3068
	44:24	to all the women, Hear the word of **the L**,	3068
	44:25	Thus saith **the L** of hosts, the God of Israel,	3068
	44:26	Therefore hear ye the word of **the L**,	3068
	44:26	have sworn by my great name, saith **the L**,	3068
	44:29	this *shall be* a sign unto you, saith **the L**,	3068
	44:30	Thus saith **the L**; Behold, I *will* give	3068
	45: 2	Thus saith **the L**, the God of Israel,	3068
	45: 3	for **the L** hath added grief to my sorrow;	3068
	45: 4	shalt thou say unto him, **The L** saith thus;	3068
	45: 5	I *will* bring evil upon all flesh, saith **the L**:	3068
	46: 1	The word of **the L** which came to Jeremiah	3068
	46: 5	*for* fear *was* round about, saith **the L**.	3068
	46:13	The word that **the L** spake to Jeremiah	3068
	46:15	stood not, because **the L** did drive them.	3068
	46:18	the King, whose name *is* **the L** of hosts,	3068
	46:23	saith **the L**, though it cannot be searched;	3068
	46:25	**The L** of hosts, the God of Israel, saith;	3068
	46:26	as *in* the days of old, saith **the L**.	3068
	46:28	thou not, O Jacob my servant, saith **the L**:	3068
	47: 1	The word of **the L** that came to Jeremiah	3068
	47: 2	Thus saith **the L**; Behold, waters rise up	3068
	47: 4	for **the L** *will* spoil the Philistines,	3068
	47: 6	O thou sword of **the L**, how long *will it be*	3068
	47: 7	seeing **the L** hath given it a charge against	3068
	48: 1	Against Moab thus saith **the L** of hosts,	3068
	48: 8	shall be destroyed, as **the L** hath spoken.	3068
	48:10	Cursed *be* he that doeth the work of **the L**	3068
	48:12	the days come, saith **the L**,	3068
	48:15	the King, whose name *is* **the L** of hosts.	3068
	48:25	cut off, and his arm is broken, saith **the L**.	3068
	48:26	for he magnified *himself* against **the L**:	3068
	48:30	I know his wrath, saith **the L**; but *it shall*	3068
	48:35	saith **the L**, him that offereth *in* the high	3068
	48:38	a vessel wherein *is* no pleasure, saith **the L**.	3068
	48:40	For thus saith **the L**; Behold, he shall fly as	3068
	48:42	he hath magnified *himself* against **the L**.	3068
	48:43	O inhabitant of Moab, saith **the L**.	3068
	48:44	the year of their visitation, saith **the L**.	3068
	48:47	of Moab in the latter days, saith **the L**.	3068
	49: 1	the Ammonites, thus saith **the L**;	3068
	49: 2	the days come, saith **the L**,	3068
	49: 2	unto them that were his heirs, saith **the L**.	3068
	49: 6	of the children of Ammon, saith **the L**.	3068
	49: 7	thus saith **the L** of hosts;	3068
	49:12	For thus saith **the L**; Behold, they whose	3068
	49:13	For I have sworn by myself, saith **the L**,	3068
	49:14	I have heard a rumour from **the L**, and	3068
	49:16	bring thee down from thence, saith **the L**.	3068
	49:18	saith **the L**, no man shall abide there,	3068
	49:20	Therefore hear the counsel of **the L**, that he	3068
	49:26	be cut off in that day, saith **the L** of hosts.	3068
	49:28	of Babylon shall smite, thus saith **the L**;	3068
	49:30	O ye inhabitants of Hazor, saith **the L**;	3068
	49:31	that dwelleth without care, saith **the L**,	3068
	49:32	calamity from all sides thereof, saith **the L**.	3068
Jer	49:34	The word of **the L** that came to Jeremiah	3068
	49:35	Thus saith **the L** of hosts; Behold, I *will*	3068
	49:37	*even* my fierce anger, saith **the L**;	3068
	49:38	thence the king and the princes, saith **the L**.	3068
	49:39	again the captivity of Elam, saith **the L**.	3068
	50: 1	The word that **the L** spake against Babylon	3068
	50: 4	In those days, and in that time, saith **the L**,	3068
	50: 4	they shall go, and seek **the L** their God.	3068
	50: 5	let us join ourselves to **the L** *in* a perpetual	3068
	50: 7	because they have sinned against **the L**,	3068
	50: 7	the habitation of justice, even **the L**,	3068
	50:10	that spoil her shall be satisfied, saith **the L**.	3068
	50:13	Because of the wrath of **the L** it shall not	3068
	50:14	for she hath sinned against **the L**.	3068
	50:15	for it *is* the vengeance of **the L**:	3068
	50:18	Therefore thus saith **the L** of hosts, the God	3068
	50:20	In those days, and in that time, saith **the L**,	3068
	50:21	saith **the L**, and do according to all that I	3068
	50:24	because thou hast striven against **the L**.	3068
	50:25	**The L** hath opened his armoury, and	3068
	50:28	to declare in Zion the vengeance of **the L**	3068
	50:29	for she hath been proud against **the L**,	3068
	50:30	war shall be cut off in that day, saith **the L**.	3068
	50:33	Thus saith **the L** of hosts; The children of	3068
	50:34	*is* strong; **the L** of hosts *is* his name:	3068
	50:35	saith **the L**, and upon the inhabitants of	3068
	50:40	the neighbour *cities* thereof, saith **the L**;	3068
	50:45	Therefore hear ye the counsel of **the L**,	3068
	51: 1	Thus saith **the L**; Behold, I *will* raise up	3068
	51: 5	nor Judah of his God, of **the L** of hosts;	3068
	51:10	**The L** hath brought forth our	3068
	51:10	let us declare in Zion the work of **the L** our	3068
	51:11	**the L** hath raised up the spirit of the kings	3068
	51:11	because it *is* the vengeance of **the L**,	3068
	51:12	for **the L** hath both devised and done that	3068
	51:14	**The L** of hosts hath sworn by himself,	3068
	51:19	his inheritance: **the L** of hosts *is* his name.	3068
	51:24	done in Zion in your sight, saith **the L**.	3068
	51:25	O destroying mountain, saith **the L**,	3068
	51:26	thou shalt be desolate for ever, saith **the L**.	3068
	51:29	for every purpose of **the L** shall be	3068
	51:33	For thus saith **the L** of hosts, the God of	3068
	51:36	Therefore thus saith **the L**; Behold, I *will*	3068
	51:39	perpetual sleep, and not wake, saith **the L**.	3068
	51:45	man his soul from the fierce anger of **the L**.	3068
	51:48	come unto her from the north, saith **the L**.	3068
	51:50	remember **the L** afar off, and let Jerusalem	3068
	51:52	the days come, saith **the L**,	3068
	51:53	shall spoilers come unto her, saith **the L**.	3068
	51:55	Because **the L** *hath* spoiled Babylon, and	3068
	51:56	for **the L** God of recompences shall surely	3068
	51:57	the King, whose name *is* **the L** of hosts.	3068
	51:58	Thus saith **the L** of hosts; The broad walls	3068
	51:62	shalt thou say, O **L**, thou hast spoken	3068
	52: 2	*that* which *was* evil in the eyes of **the L**,	3068
	52: 3	For through the anger of **the L** it came to	3068
	52:13	burnt the house of **the L**, and the king's	3068
	52:17	of brass that *were* in the house of **the L**,	3068
	52:17	brasen sea that *was* in the house of **the L**,	3068
	52:20	Solomon had made in the house of **the L**:	3068
La	1: 5	for **the L** hath afflicted her for	3068
	1: 9	O **L**, behold my affliction: for the enemy	3068
	1:11	see, O **L**, and consider; for I am become	3068
	1:12	wherewith **the L** hath afflicted *me* in	3068
	1:17	**the L** hath commanded concerning Jacob,	3068
	1:18	**The L** *is* righteous; for I have rebelled	3068
	1:20	Behold, O **L**; for I *am* in distress: my	3068
	2: 6	**the L** hath caused the solemn feasts and	3068
	2: 7	have made a noise in the house of **the L**,	3068
	2: 8	**The L** hath purposed to destroy the wall of	3068
	2: 9	her prophets also find no vision from **the L**.	3068
	2:17	**The L** hath done *that* which he had	3068
	2:20	O **L**, and consider to whom thou hast done	3068
	3:18	and my hope is perished from **the L**:	3068
	3:24	**The L** *is* my portion, saith my soul;	3068
	3:25	**The L** *is* good unto them that wait for him,	3068
	3:26	and quietly wait for the salvation of **the L**.	3068
	3:40	and try our ways, and turn again to **the L**.	3068
	3:50	Till **the L** look down, and behold from	3068
	3:55	I called upon thy name, O **L**, out of the low	3068
	3:59	O **L**; thou hast seen my wrong: judge thou	3068
	3:61	O **L**, *and* all their imaginations against me;	3068
	3:64	Render unto them a recompence, O **L**,	3068
	3:66	in anger from under the heavens of **the L**.	3068
	4:11	**The L** hath accomplished his fury; he hath	3068
	4:16	The anger of **the L** hath divided them;	3068
	4:20	the anointed of **the L**, was taken in their	3068
	5: 1	Remember, O **L**, what is come upon us:	3068
	5:19	Thou, O **L**, remainest for ever; thy throne	3068
	5:21	us unto thee, O **L**, and we shall be turned;	3068
Eze	1: 3	The word of **the L** came expressly unto	3068
	1: 3	and the hand of **the L** was there upon him.	3068
	1:28	of the likeness of the glory of **the L**.	3068
	3:12	*saying*, Blessed *be* the glory of **the L** from	3068
	3:14	but the hand of **the L** was strong upon me.	3068
	3:16	that the word of **the L** came unto me,	3068
	3:22	the hand of **the L** was there upon me; and	3068
	3:23	behold, the glory of **the L** stood there,	3068
	4:13	**the L** said, Even thus shall the children of	3068
	5:13	they shall know that I **the L** have spoken *it*	3068
	5:15	in furious rebukes. I **the L** have spoken *it*.	3068
	5:17	sword upon thee. I **the L** have spoken *it*.	3068
	6: 1	the word of **the L** came unto me, saying,	3068
	6: 7	of you, and ye shall know that I *am* **the L**.	3068
	6:10	they shall know that I *am* **the L**, *and that* I	3068
	6:13	shall ye know that I *am* **the L**, when their	3068
	6:14	and they shall know that I *am* **the L**.	3068
	7: 1	Moreover the word of **the L** came unto me,	3068
	7: 4	of thee: and ye shall know that I *am* **the L**.	3068
	7: 9	ye shall know that I *am* **the L** that smiteth.	3068
	7:19	them in the day of the wrath of **the L**:	3068
	7:27	and they shall know that I *am* **the L**.	3068
	8:12	for they say, **The L** seeth us not;	3068
	8:12	seeth us not; **the L** hath forsaken the earth.	3068
	8:16	behold, *at* the door of the temple of **the L**,	3068

Eze	8:16	their backs toward the temple of **the L**,	3068
	9: 4	**the L** said unto him, Go through the midst	3068
	9: 9	**The L** hath forsaken the earth, and	3068
	9: 9	forsaken the earth, and **the L** seeth not.	3068
	10: 4	the glory of **the L** went up from the cherub,	3068
	10:18	the glory of **the L** departed from off	3068
	11: 5	the Spirit of **the L** fell upon me, and	3068
	11: 5	and said unto me, Speak; Thus saith **the L**;	3068
	11:10	and ye shall know that I *am* **the L**.	3068
	11:12	ye shall know that I *am* **the L**: for ye have	3068
	11:14	Again the word of **the L** came unto me,	3068
	11:15	Jerusalem have said, Get ye far from **the L**:	3068
	11:23	the glory of **the L** went up from the midst	3068
	11:25	all the things that **the L** had shewed me.	3068
	12: 1	The word of **the L** also came unto me,	3068
	12: 8	in the morning came the word of **the L**	3068
	12:15	they shall know that I *am* **the L**, when I	3068
	12:16	and they shall know that I *am* **the L**.	3068
	12:17	Moreover the word of **the L** came to me,	3068
	12:20	and ye shall know that I *am* **the L**.	3068
	12:21	the word of **the L** came unto me, saying,	3068
	12:25	For I *am* **the L**: I will speak, and the word	3068
	12:26	Again the word of **the L** came to me,	3068
	13: 1	the word of **the L** came unto me, saying,	3068
	13: 2	own hearts, Hear ye the word of **the L**;	3068
	13: 5	to stand in the battle in the day of **the L**.	3068
	13: 6	and lying divination, saying, **The L** saith:	3068
	13: 6	**the L** hath not sent them: and they have	3068
	13: 7	**The L** saith *it;* albeit I have not spoken?	3068
	13:14	and ye shall know that I *am* **the L**.	3068
	13:21	and ye shall know that I *am* **the L**.	3068
	13:23	and ye shall know that I *am* **the L**.	3068
	14: 2	the word of **the L** came unto me, saying,	3068
	14: 4	I **the L** will answer him that cometh	3068
	14: 7	I **the L** will answer him by myself:	3068
	14: 8	and ye shall know that I *am* **the L**.	3068
	14: 9	I **the L** have deceived that prophet, and	3068
	14:12	The word of **the L** came again to me,	3068
	15: 1	the word of **the L** came unto me, saying,	3068
	15: 7	ye shall know that I *am* **the L**, when I set	3068
	16: 1	Again the word of **the L** came unto me,	3068
	16:35	O harlot, hear the word of **the L**:	3068
	16:58	and thine abominations, saith **the L**.	3068
	16:62	and thou shalt know that I *am* **the L**:	3068
	17: 1	the word of **the L** came unto me, saying,	3068
	17:11	Moreover the word of **the L** came unto me,	3068
	17:21	ye shall know that I **the L** have spoken *it*.	3068
	17:24	I **the L** have brought down the high tree,	3068
	17:24	I **the L** have spoken and have done *it*.	3068
	18: 1	the word of **the L** came unto me again,	3068
	20: 1	elders of Israel came to inquire of **the L**,	3068
	20: 2	came the word of **the L** unto me, saying,	3068
	20: 5	unto them, saying, I *am* **the L** your God;	3068
	20: 7	the idols of Egypt: I *am* **the L** your God.	3068
	20:12	that *they* might know that I *am* **the L** that	3068
	20:19	I *am* **the L** your God; walk in my statutes,	3068
	20:20	that *ye* may know that I *am* **the L** your	3068
	20:26	end that they might know that I *am* **the L**.	3068
	20:38	and ye shall know that I *am* **the L**.	3068
	20:42	ye shall know that I *am* **the L**, when I shall	3068
	20:44	ye shall know that I *am* **the L**, when I have	3068
	20:45	Moreover the word of **the L** came unto me,	3068
	20:47	forest of the south, Hear the word of **the L**;	3068
	20:48	all flesh shall see that I **the L** have kindled	3068
	21: 1	the word of **the L** came unto me, saying,	3068
	21: 3	say to the land of Israel, Thus saith **the L**;	3068
	21: 5	That all flesh may know that I **the L** have	3068
	21: 8	Again the word of **the L** came unto me,	3068
	21: 9	prophesy, and say, Thus saith **the L**;	3068
	21:17	cause my fury to rest: I **the L** have said *it*.	3068
	21:18	The word of **the L** came unto me again,	3068
	21:32	for I **the L** have spoken *it*.	3068
	22: 1	Moreover the word of **the L** came unto me,	3068
	22:14	I **the L** have spoken *it*, and will do *it*.	3068
	22:16	and thou shalt know that I *am* **the L**.	3068
	22:17	the word of **the L** came unto me, saying,	3068
	22:22	ye shall know that I **the L** have poured out	3068
	22:23	the word of **the L** came unto me, saying,	3068
	22:28	Lord GOD, when **the L** hath not spoken.	3068
	23: 1	The word of **the L** came again unto me,	3068
	23:36	**The L** said moreover unto me; Son of man,	3068
	24: 1	the word of **the L** came unto me, saying,	3068
	24:14	I **the L** have spoken *it:* it shall come to	3068
	24:15	Also the word of **the L** came unto me,	3068
	24:20	The word of **the L** came unto me, saying,	3068
	24:27	and they shall know that I *am* **the L**.	3068
	25: 1	The word of **the L** came again unto me,	3068
	25: 5	and ye shall know that I *am* **the L**.	3068
	25: 7	and thou shalt know that I *am* **the L**.	3068
	25:11	and they shall know that I *am* **the L**.	3068
	25:17	they shall know that I *am* **the L**, when I	3068
	26: 1	*that* the word of **the L** came unto me,	3068
	26: 6	and they shall know that I *am* **the L**.	3068
	26:14	for I **the L** have spoken *it*, saith the Lord	3068
	27: 1	The word of **the L** came again unto me,	3068
	28: 1	The word of **the L** came again unto me,	3068
	28:11	Moreover the word of **the L** came unto me,	3068
	28:20	Again the word of **the L** came unto me,	3068
	28:22	they shall know that I *am* **the L**, when I	3068
	28:23	and they shall know that I *am* **the L**.	3068
	28:26	they shall know that I *am* **the L** their God.	3068
	29: 1	the word of **the L** came unto me, saying,	3068
	29: 6	of Egypt shall know that I *am* **the L**,	3068
	29: 9	waste; and they shall know that I *am* **the L**:	3068
	29:17	the word of **the L** came unto me, saying,	3068
	29:21	and they shall know that I *am* **the L**.	3068
	30: 1	The word of **the L** came again unto me,	3068
	30: 3	even the day of **the L** *is* near, a cloudy day;	3068
	30: 6	Thus saith **the L**; They also that uphold	3068
	30: 8	they shall know that I *am* **the L**, when I	3068
	30:12	hand of strangers: I **the L** have spoken *it*.	3068
	30:19	and they shall know that I *am* **the L**.	3068
	30:20	*that* the word of **the L** came unto me,	3068
	30:25	they shall know that I *am* **the L**, when I	3068
	30:26	and they shall know that I *am* **the L**.	3068
Eze	31: 1	*that* the word of **the L** came unto me,	3068
	32: 1	*that* the word of **the L** came unto me,	3068
	32:15	shall they know that I *am* **the L**.	3068
	32:17	*that* the word of **the L** came unto me,	3068
	33: 1	Again the word of **the L** came unto me,	3068
	33:22	Now the hand of **the L** was upon me in	3068
	33:23	the word of **the L** came unto me, saying,	3068
	33:29	shall they know that I *am* **the L**, when I	3068
	33:30	*is* the word that cometh forth from **the L**.	3068
	34: 1	the word of **the L** came unto me, saying,	3068
	34: 7	ye shepherds, hear the word of **the L**;	3068
	34: 9	O ye shepherds, hear the word of **the L**;	3068
	34:24	I **the L** will be their God, and my servant	3068
	34:24	among them; I **the L** have spoken *it*.	3068
	34:27	their land, and shall know that I *am* **the L**,	3068
	34:30	Thus shall they know that I **the L** their God	3068
	35: 1	Moreover the word of **the L** came unto me,	3068
	35: 4	and thou shalt know that I *am* **the L**.	3068
	35: 9	and ye shall know that I *am* **the L**.	3068
	35:10	will possess it; whereas **the L** was there:	3068
	35:12	thou shalt know that I *am* **the L**, *and that* I	3068
	35:15	of it: and they shall know that I *am* **the L**.	3068
	36: 1	mountains of Israel, hear the word of **the L**:	3068
	36:11	and ye shall know that I *am* **the L**.	3068
	36:16	Moreover the word of **the L** came unto me,	3068
	36:20	These *are* the people of **the L**, and are gone	3068
	36:23	the heathen shall know that I *am* **the L**,	3068
	36:36	know that I **the L** build the ruined *places*,	3068
	36:36	I **the L** have spoken *it*, and I will do *it*.	3068
	36:38	and they shall know that I *am* **the L**.	3068
	37: 1	The hand of **the L** was upon me, and	3068
	37: 1	carried me out in the spirit of **the L**, and	3068
	37: 4	O ye dry bones, hear the word of **the L**.	3068
	37: 6	and ye shall know that I *am* **the L**.	3068
	37:13	ye shall know that I *am* **the L**, when I have	3068
	37:14	shall ye know that I **the L** have spoken *it*,	3068
	37:14	spoken *it*, and performed *it*, saith **the L**.	3068
	37:15	The word of **the L** came again unto me,	3068
	37:28	the heathen shall know that I **the L** do	3068
	38: 1	the word of **the L** came unto me, saying,	3068
	38:23	and they shall know that I *am* **the L**.	3068
	39: 6	and they shall know that I *am* **the L**.	3068
	39: 7	the heathen shall know that I *am* **the L**,	3068
	39:22	that I *am* **the L** their God from that day	3068
	39:28	shall they know that I *am* **the L** their God,	3068
	40: 1	in the selfsame day the hand of **the L** was	3068
	40:46	which come near to **the L** to minister unto	3068
	41:22	This *is* the table that *is* before **the L**.	3068
	42:13	where the priests that approach unto **the L**	3068
	43: 4	the glory of **the L** came into the house by	3068
	43: 5	behold, the glory of **the L** filled the house.	3068
	43:24	And thou shalt offer them before **the L**, and	3068
	43:24	them up *for* a burnt offering unto **the L**.	3068
	44: 2	said **the L** unto me; This gate shall be shut,	3068
	44: 2	because **the L**, the God of Israel,	3068
	44: 3	he shall sit in it to eat bread before **the L**;	3068
	44: 4	the glory of **the L** filled the house of	3068
	44: 4	of the LORD filled the house of **the L**:	3068
	44: 5	**the L** said unto me, Son of man, mark well,	3068
	44: 5	all the ordinances of the house of **the L**,	3068
	45: 1	ye shall offer an oblation unto **the L**, a holy	3068
	45: 4	shall come near to minister unto **the L**:	3068
	45:23	he shall prepare a burnt offering to **the L**,	3068
	46: 3	of this gate before **the L** in the sabbaths	3068
	46: 4	**the L** in the sabbath day *shall be* six lambs	3068
	46: 9	come before **the L** in the solemn feasts,	3068
	46:12	or peace offerings voluntarily unto **the L**,	3068
	46:13	**the L** *of* a lamb of the first year without	3068
	46:14	*by* a perpetual ordinance unto **the L**.	3068
	48: 9	The oblation that ye shall offer unto **the L**	3068
	48:10	the sanctuary of **the L** shall be in the midst	3068
	48:14	of the land: for *it is* holy unto **the L**.	3068
	48:35	city from *that* day *shall be*, **The L** *is* there.	3068
Da	9: 2	where*of* the word of **the L** came to	3068
	9: 4	I prayed unto **the L** my God, and made my	3068
	9:10	Neither have we obeyed the voice of **the L**	3068
	9:13	yet made we not our prayer before **the L**	3068
	9:14	Therefore hath **the L** watched upon	3068
	9:14	for **the L** our God *is* righteous in all his	3068
	9:20	presenting my supplication before **the L**	3068
Hos	1: 1	The word of **the L** that came unto Hosea,	3068
	1: 2	The beginning of the word of **the L** by	3068
	1: 2	**the L** said to Hosea, Go, take unto thee a	3068
	1: 2	great whoredom, *departing* from **the L**.	3068
	1: 4	**the L** said unto him, Call his name Jezreel;	3068
	1: 7	will save them by **the L** their God, and	3068
	2:13	after her lovers, and forgat me, saith **the L**.	3068
	2:16	it shall be at that day, saith **the L**, *that* thou	3068
	2:20	in faithfulness: and thou shalt know **the L**.	3068
	2:21	I will hear, saith **the L**, I will hear	3068
	3: 1	said **the L** unto me, Go yet, love a woman	3068
	3: 1	according to the love of **the L** toward	3068
	3: 5	seek **the L** their God, and David their king;	3068
	3: 5	shall fear **the L** and his goodness in	3068
	4: 1	Hear the word of **the L**, ye children of	3068
	4: 1	for **the L** hath a controversy with	3068
	4:10	they have left off to take heed to **the L**.	3068
	4:15	up *to* Beth-aven, nor swear, **The L** liveth.	3068
	4:16	now **the L** will feed them as a lamb in a	3068
	5: 4	of them, and they have not known **the L**.	3068
	5: 6	and with their herds to seek **the L**;	3068
	5: 7	have dealt treacherously against **the L**:	3068
	6: 1	Come and let us return unto **the L**: for he	3068
	6: 3	we know, *if* we follow on to know **the L**:	3068
	7:10	they do not return to **the L** their God,	3068
	8: 1	as an eagle against the house of **the L**,	3068
	8:13	and eat *it; but* **the L** accepteth them not;	3068
	9: 4	shall not offer wine *offerings* to **the L**,	3068
	9: 4	soul shall not come *into* the house of **the L**.	3068
	9: 5	and in the day of the feast of **the L**?	3068
	9:14	Give them, O **L**: what wilt thou give?	3068
	10: 3	have no king, because we feared not **the L**;	3068
	10:12	for *it is* time to seek **the L**, till he come and	3068
	11:10	They shall walk after **the L**: he shall roar	3068
	11:11	will place them in their houses, saith **the L**.	3068
Hos	12: 2	**The L** hath also a controversy with Judah,	3068
	12: 5	Even **the L** God of hosts; the LORD *is* his	3068
	12: 5	God of hosts; **the L** *is* his memorial.	3068
	12: 9	I *that am* **the L** thy God from the land of	3068
	12:13	by a prophet **the L** brought Israel out of	3068
	13: 4	Yet I *am* **the L** thy God from the land of	3068
	13:15	the wind of **the L** *shall* come up from	3068
	14: 1	O Israel, return unto **the L** thy God;	3068
	14: 2	Take with you words, and turn to **the L**:	3068
	14: 9	for the ways of **the L** *are* right, and the just	3068
Joel	1: 1	The word of **the L** that came to Joel the son	3068
	1: 9	offering is cut off from the house of **the L**;	3068
	1:14	the land *into* the house of **the L** your God,	3068
	1:14	the LORD your God, and cry unto **the L**,	3068
	1:15	for the day of **the L** *is* at hand, and as a	3068
	1:19	O **L**, to thee will I cry: for the fire hath	3068
	2: 1	for the day of **the L** cometh, for *it is* nigh at	3068
	2:11	**the L** shall utter his voice before his army:	3068
	2:11	for the day of **the L** *is* great and	3068
	2:12	Therefore also now, saith **the L**, turn ye	3068
	2:13	and turn unto **the L** your God:	3068
	2:14	and a drink offering unto **the L** your God?	3068
	2:17	Let the priests, the ministers of **the L**,	3068
	2:17	O **L**, and give not thine heritage to	3068
	2:18	will **the L** be jealous for his land, and	3068
	2:19	**the L** will answer and say unto his people,	3068
	2:21	and rejoice: for **the L** will do great things.	3068
	2:23	of Zion, and rejoice in **the L** your God:	3068
	2:26	and praise the name of **the L** your God,	3068
	2:27	*that* I *am* **the L** your God, and none else:	3068
	2:31	and the terrible day of **the L** come.	3068
	2:32	on the name of **the L** shall be delivered:	3068
	2:32	as **the L** hath said, and in the remnant	3068
	2:32	and in the remnant whom **the L** *shall* call.	3068
	3: 8	a people far off: for **the L** hath spoken *it*.	3068
	3:11	cause thy mighty ones to come down, O **L**.	3068
	3:14	for the day of **the L** *is* near in the valley of	3068
	3:16	**The L** also shall roar out of Zion, and	3068
	3:16	**the L** *will be* the hope of his people, and	3068
	3:17	So shall ye know that I *am* **the L** your God	3068
	3:18	shall come forth of the house of **the L**,	3068
	3:21	not cleansed: for **the L** dwelleth in Zion.	3068
Am	1: 2	**The L** will roar from Zion, and utter his	3068
	1: 3	Thus saith **the L**; For three transgressions	3068
	1: 5	shall go into captivity unto Kir, saith **the L**.	3068
	1: 6	Thus saith **the L**; For three transgressions	3068
	1: 9	Thus saith **the L**; For three transgressions	3068
	1:11	Thus saith **the L**; For three transgressions	3068
	1:13	Thus saith **the L**; For three transgressions	3068
	1:15	he and his princes together, saith **the L**.	3068
	2: 1	Thus saith **the L**; For three transgressions	3068
	2: 3	the princes thereof with him, saith **the L**.	3068
	2: 4	Thus saith **the L**; For three transgressions	3068
	2: 4	they have despised the law of **the L**,	3068
	2: 6	Thus saith **the L**; For three transgressions	3068
	2:11	O ye children of Israel? saith **the L**.	3068
	2:16	flee away naked in that day, saith **the L**.	3068
	3: 1	Hear this word that **the L** hath spoken	3068
	3: 6	evil in a city, and **the L** hath not done *it?*	3068
	3:10	saith **the L**, who store up violence and	3068
	3:12	Thus saith **the L**; As the shepherd taketh	3068
	3:15	great houses shall have an end, saith **the L**.	3068
	4: 3	shall cast *them* into the palace, saith **the L**.	3068
	4: 6	have ye not returned unto me, saith **the L**.	3068
	4: 8	have ye not returned unto me, saith **the L**.	3068
	4: 9	have ye not returned unto me, saith **the L**.	3068
	4:10	have ye not returned unto me, saith **the L**.	3068
	4:11	have ye not returned unto me, saith **the L**.	3068
	4:13	**The L**, The God of hosts, *is* his name.	3068
	5: 4	For thus saith **the L** unto the house of	3068
	5: 6	Seek **the L**, and ye shall live; lest he break	3068
	5: 8	the face of the earth: **The L** *is* his name:	3068
	5:14	so **the L**, the God of hosts, shall be with	3068
	5:15	it may be that **the L** God of hosts will be	3068
	5:16	Therefore **the L**, the God of hosts,	3068
	5:17	for I will pass through thee, saith **the L**.	3068
	5:18	Woe unto *you* that desire the day of **the L**!	3068
	5:18	the day of **the L** *is* darkness, and not light.	3068
	5:20	*Shall* not the day of **the L** *be* darkness, and	3068
	5:27	saith **the L**, whose name *is* The God of	3068
	6: 8	saith **the L** the God of hosts, I abhor	3068
	6:10	not make mention of the name of **the L**.	3068
	6:11	**the L** commandeth, and he will smite	3068
	6:14	of Israel, saith **the L** the God of hosts;	3068
	7: 3	**The L** repented for this: It shall not be,	3068
	7: 3	for this: It shall not be, saith **the L**.	3068
	7: 6	**The L** repented for this: This also shall not	3068
	7: 8	**the L** said unto me, Amos, what seest	3068
	7:15	**the L** took me as I followed the flock, and	3068
	7:15	**the L** said unto me, Go, prophesy unto my	3068
	7:16	Now therefore hear thou the word of **the L**:	3068
	7:17	Therefore thus saith **the L**; Thy wife shall	3068
	8: 2	said **the L** unto me, The end is come upon	3068
	8: 7	**The L** hath sworn by the excellency of	3068
	8:11	but of hearing the words of **the L**:	3068
	8:12	run to and fro to seek the word of **the L**,	3068
	9: 6	the face of the earth: **The L** *is* his name.	3068
	9: 7	saith **the L**. Have not I brought up Israel	3068
	9: 8	destroy the house of Jacob, saith **the L**.	3068
	9:12	by my name, saith **the L** that doeth this.	3068
	9:13	Behold, the days come, saith **the L**, that	3068
	9:15	I have given them, saith **the L** thy God.	3068
Ob	1: 1	We have heard a rumour from **the L**, and	3068
	1: 4	thence will I bring thee down, saith **the L**.	3068
	1: 8	Shall I not in that day, saith **the L**,	3068
	1:15	For the day of **the L** *is* near upon all	3068
	1:18	house of Esau; for **the L** hath spoken *it*.	3068
Jnh	1: 1	Now the word of **the L** came unto Jonah	3068
	1: 3	unto Tarshish from the presence of **the L**,	3068
	1: 3	unto Tarshish from the presence of **the L**.	3068
	1: 4	But **the L** sent out a great wind into the sea,	3068
	1: 9	I fear **the L**, the God of heaven, which hath	3068
	1:10	that he fled from the presence of **the L**,	3068
	1:14	Wherefore they cried unto **the L**, and said,	3068
	1:14	We beseech thee, O **L**, we beseech thee,	3068

Jnh 1:14 for thou, O **L**, hast done as it pleased thee. 3068
1:16 the men feared **the L** exceedingly, and 3068
1:16 offered a sacrifice unto **the L**, and 3068
1:17 Now **the L** had prepared a great fish to 3068
2: 1 Jonah prayed unto **the L** his God out of 3068
2: 2 by reason of mine affliction unto **the L**, 3068
2: 6 up my life from corruption, O **L** my God. 3068
2: 7 soul fainted within me I remembered **the L**: 3068
2: 9 that I have vowed. Salvation *is* of **the L**. 3068
2:10 **the L** spake unto the fish, and it vomited 3068
3: 1 the word of **the L** came unto Jonah 3068
3: 3 according to the word of **the L**. 3068
4: 2 he prayed unto **the L**, and said, I pray thee, 3068
4: 2 said, I pray thee, O **L**, *was* not this my 3068
4: 3 Therefore now, O **L**, take, I beseech thee, 3068
4: 4 said **the L**, Doest thou well to be angry? 3068
4: 6 **the L** God prepared a gourd, and made *it* to 3068
4:10 said **the L**, Thou hast had pity on 3068
Mic 1: 1 The word of **the L** that came to Micah 3068
1: 3 **the L** cometh forth out of his place, and 3068
1:12 evil came down from **the L** unto the gate of 3068
2: 3 Therefore thus saith **the L**; Behold, 3068
2: 5 a cord by lot in the congregation of **the L**. 3068
2: 7 of Jacob, is the spirit of **the L** straitened? 3068
2:13 and **the L** on the head of them. 3068
3: 4 shall they cry unto **the L**, but he will not 3068
3: 5 Thus saith **the L** concerning the prophets 3068
3: 8 I am full *of* power by the spirit of **the L**, 3068
3:11 yet will they lean upon **the L**, and say, *Is* 3068
3:11 and say, *Is* not **the L** among us? 3068
4: 1 *that* the mountain of the house of **the L** 3068
4: 2 let us go up to the mountain of **the L**, and 3068
4: 2 and the word of **the L** from Jerusalem. 3068
4: 4 for the mouth of **the L** of hosts hath 3068
4: 5 we will walk in the name of **the L** our God 3068
4: 6 In that day, saith **the L**, will I assemble her 3068
4: 7 **the L** shall reign over them in mount Zion 3068
4:10 there **the L** shall redeem thee from 3068
4:12 they know not the thoughts of **the L**, 3068
4:13 I will consecrate their gain unto **the L**, and 3068
5: 4 and feed in the strength of **the L**, 3068
5: 4 in the majesty of the name of **the L** his 3068
5: 7 midst of many people as a dew from **the L**, 3068
5:10 shall come to pass in that day, saith **the L**, 3068
6: 1 Hear ye now what **the L** saith; Arise, 3068
6: 2 for **the L** hath a controversy with his 3068
6: 5 *ye* may know the righteousness of **the L**. 3068
6: 6 Wherewith shall I come before **the L**, *and* 3068
6: 7 Will **the L** be pleased with thousands of 3068
6: 8 what doth **the L** require of thee, but to do 3068
7: 7 Therefore I will look unto **the L**; I will wait 3068
7: 8 in darkness, **the L** *shall be* a light unto me. 3068
7: 9 I will bear the indignation of **the L**, 3068
7:10 said unto me, Where is **the L** thy God? 3068
7:17 they shall be afraid of **the L** our God, and 3068
Na 1: 2 God *is* jealous, and **the L** revengeth; 3068
1: 2 **the L** revengeth, and *is* furious; 3068
1: 2 **the L** will take vengeance on his 3068
1: 3 **The L** *is* slow to anger, and great in power, 3068
1: 3 will not at all acquit *the wicked:* **the L** *hath* 3068
1: 7 **The L** *is* good, a strong hold in the day of 3068
1: 9 What do ye imagine against **the L**? he *will* 3068
1:11 that imagineth evil against **the L**, a wicked 3068
1:12 Thus saith **the L**; Though *they be* quiet, 3068
1:14 **the L** hath given a commandment 3068
2: 2 For **the L** hath turned *away* the excellency 3068
2:13 saith **the L** of hosts, and I will burn her 3068
3: 5 I *am* against thee, saith **the L** of hosts; 3068
Hab 1: 2 O **L**, how long shall I cry, and thou wilt not 3068
1:12 O **L** my God, mine Holy One? 3068
1:12 O **L**, thou hast ordained them for judgment; 3068
2: 2 **the L** answered me, and said, Write 3068
2:13 *is it* not of **the L** of hosts that the people 3068
2:14 with the knowledge of the glory of **the L**, 3068
2:20 **the L** *is* in his holy temple: let all the earth 3068
3: 2 O **L**, I have heard thy speech, *and* 3068
3: 2 O **L**, revive thy work in the midst of 3068
3: 8 Was **the L** displeased against the rivers? 3068
3:18 Yet I will rejoice in **the L**, I will joy in 3068
Zep 1: 1 The word of **the L** which came unto 3068
1: 2 all *things* from off the land, saith **the L**. 3068
1: 3 cut off man from off the land, saith **the L**. 3068
1: 5 them that worship *and* that swear by **the L**, 3068
1: 6 them that are turned back from **the L**; and 3068
1: 6 *those* that have not sought **the L**, nor 3068
1: 7 for the day of **the L** *is* at hand: for 3068
1: 7 for **the L** hath prepared a sacrifice, he hath 3068
1:10 shall come to pass in that day, saith **the L**, 3068
1:12 say in their heart, **The L** will not do good, 3068
1:14 The great day of **the L** *is* near, *it is* near, 3068
1:14 *even* the voice of the day of **the L**: 3068
1:17 because they have sinned against **the L**: 3068
2: 2 before the fierce anger of **the L** come upon 3068
2: 3 Seek ye **the L**, all ye meek of the earth, 3068
2: 5 the word of **the L** *is* against you; 3068
2: 7 for **the L** their God shall visit them, and 3068
2: 9 saith **the L** of hosts, the God of Israel, 3068
2:10 against the people of **the L** of hosts. 3068
2:11 **The L** *will be* terrible unto them: for he 3068
3: 2 not correction; she trusted not in **the L**; 3068
3: 5 **The** just **L** *is* in the midst thereof; he will 3068
3: 8 Therefore wait ye upon me, saith **the L**, 3068
3: 9 they may all call upon the name of **the L**, 3068
3:12 and they shall trust in the name of **the L**. 3068
3:15 **The L** hath taken away thy judgments, 3068
3:15 the king of Israel, *even* **the L**, *is* in 3068
3:17 **The L** thy God in the midst of thee *is* 3068
3:20 captivity before your eyes, saith **the L**. 3068
Hag 1: 1 came the word of **the L** by Haggai 3068
1: 2 Thus speaketh **the L** of hosts, saying, This 3068
1: 3 came the word of **the L** by Haggai 3068
1: 5 Now therefore thus saith **the L** of hosts; 3068
1: 7 Thus saith **the L** of hosts; Consider your 3068
1: 8 in it, and I will be glorified, saith **the L**. 3068
1: 9 saith **the L** of hosts. Because of mine house 3068
Hag 1:12 obeyed the voice of **the L** their God, and 3068
1:12 as **the L** their God had sent him, and 3068
1:12 and the people did fear before **the L**. 3068
1:13 saying, I *am* with you, saith **the L**. 3068
1:14 **the L** stirred up the spirit of Zerubbabel 3068
1:14 and did work in the house of **the L** of hosts, 3068
2: 1 came the word of **the L** by the prophet 3068
2: 4 now be strong, O Zerubbabel, saith **the L**; 3068
2: 4 people of the land, saith **the L**, and work: 3068
2: 4 for I *am* with you, saith **the L** of hosts: 3068
2: 6 For thus saith **the L** of hosts; Yet once, it *is* 3068
2: 7 this house *with* glory, saith **the L** of hosts. 3068
2: 8 and the gold *is* mine, saith **the L** of hosts. 3068
2: 9 than of the former, saith **the L** of hosts: 3068
2: 9 place will I give peace, saith **the L** of hosts. 3068
2:10 came the word of **the L** by Haggai 3068
2:11 Thus saith **the L** of hosts; Ask now 3068
2:14 and so *is* this nation before me, saith **the L**; 3068
2:15 laid upon a stone in the temple of **the L**: 3068
2:17 yet ye *turned* not to me, saith **the L**. 3068
2:20 again the word of **the L** came unto Haggai 3068
2:23 In that day, saith **the L** of hosts, will I take 3068
2:23 saith **the L**, and will make thee as a signet: 3068
2:23 for I have chosen thee, saith **the L** of hosts. 3068
Zec 1: 1 came the word of **the L** unto Zechariah, 3068
1: 2 **The L** hath been sore displeased with your 3068
1: 3 thou unto them, Thus saith **the L** of hosts; 3068
1: 3 saith **the L** of hosts, and I will turn unto 3068
1: 3 I will turn unto you, saith **the L** of hosts. 3068
1: 4 saying, Thus saith **the L** of hosts; 3068
1: 4 not hear, nor hearken unto me, saith **the L**. 3068
1: 6 Like as **the L** of hosts thought to do unto 3068
1: 7 came the word of **the L** unto Zechariah, 3068
1:10 These *are they* whom **the L** hath sent to 3068
1:11 they answered the angel of **the L** that stood 3068
1:12 the angel of **the L** answered and said, 3068
1:12 LORD answered and said, O **L** of hosts, 3068
1:13 **the L** answered the angel that talked with 3068
1:14 Cry thou, saying, Thus saith **the L** of hosts; 3068
1:16 Therefore thus saith **the L**; I am returned to 3068
1:16 saith **the L** of hosts, and a line shall be 3068
1:17 Cry yet, saying, Thus saith **the L** of hosts; 3068
1:17 **the L** shall yet comfort Zion, and shall yet 3068
1:20 And **the L** shewed me four carpenters. 3068
2: 5 For I, saith **the L**, will be unto her a wall of 3068
2: 6 flee from the land of the north, saith **the L**: 3068
2: 6 the four winds of the heaven, saith **the L**. 3068
2: 8 For thus saith **the L** of hosts; After 3068
2: 9 ye shall know that **the L** of hosts hath sent 3068
2:10 will dwell in the midst of thee, saith **the L**. 3068
2:11 many nations shall be joined to **the L** in 3068
2:11 thou shalt know that **the L** of hosts hath 3068
2:12 **the L** shall inherit Judah his portion in 3068
2:13 Be silent, O all flesh, before **the L**: for he is 3068
3: 1 priest standing before the angel of **the L**, 3068
3: 2 **the L** said unto Satan, The LORD rebuke 3068
3: 2 unto Satan, **The L** rebuke thee, O Satan; 3068
3: 2 even **the L** that hath chosen Jerusalem 3068
3: 5 And the angel of **the L** stood *by*. 3068
3: 6 the angel of **the L** protested unto Joshua, 3068
3: 7 Thus saith **the L** of hosts; If thou wilt walk 3068
3: 9 saith **the L** of hosts, and I will remove 3068
3:10 In that day, saith **the L** of hosts, shall ye 3068
4: 6 This *is* the word of **the L** unto Zerubbabel, 3068
4: 6 but by my spirit, saith **the L** of hosts. 3068
4: 8 Moreover the word of **the L** came unto me, 3068
4: 9 thou shalt know that **the L** of hosts hath 3068
4:10 they *are* the eyes of **the L**, which run to and 3068
5: 4 saith **the L** of hosts, and it shall enter into 3068
6: 9 the word of **the L** came unto me, saying, 3068
6:12 Thus speaketh **the L** of hosts, saying, 3068
6:12 and he shall build the temple of **the L**: 3068
6:13 Even he shall build the temple of **the L**; 3068
6:14 for a memorial in the temple of **the L**. 3068
6:15 and build in the temple of **the L**, 3068
6:15 ye shall know that **the L** of hosts hath sent 3068
6:15 if ye will diligently obey the voice of **the L** 3068
7: 1 *that* the word of **the L** came unto Zechariah 3068
7: 2 and their men, to pray before **the L**, 3068
7: 3 which *were* in the house of **the L** of hosts, 3068
7: 4 came the word of **the L** of hosts unto me, 3068
7: 7 *Should ye* not *hear* the words which **the L** 3068
7: 8 the word of **the L** came unto Zechariah, 3068
7: 9 Thus speaketh **the L** of hosts, saying, 3068
7:12 the words which **the L** of hosts hath sent in 3068
7:12 came a great wrath from **the L** of hosts. 3068
7:13 and I would not hear, saith **the L** of hosts: 3068
8: 1 Again the word of **the L** of hosts came *to* 3068
8: 2 Thus saith **the L** of hosts; I was jealous for 3068
8: 3 Thus saith **the L**; I am returned unto Zion, 3068
8: 3 the mountain of **the L** of hosts the holy 3068
8: 4 Thus saith **the L** of hosts; There shall yet 3068
8: 6 Thus saith **the L** of hosts; If it be 3068
8: 6 in my eyes? saith **the L** of hosts. 3068
8: 7 Thus saith **the L** of hosts; Behold, I *will* 3068
8: 9 Thus saith **the L** of hosts; Let your hands 3068
8: 9 of the house of **the L** of hosts was laid, 3068
8:11 as *in* the former days, saith **the L** of hosts. 3068
8:14 For thus saith **the L** of hosts; As I thought 3068
8:14 saith **the L** of hosts, and I repented not: 3068
8:17 all these *are things* that I hate, saith **the L**. 3068
8:18 the word of **the L** of hosts came unto me, 3068
8:19 Thus saith **the L** of hosts; The fast of 3068
8:20 Thus saith **the L** of hosts; *It shall* yet *come* 3068
8:21 Let us go speedily to pray before **the L**, 3068
8:21 the LORD, and to seek **the L** of hosts: 3068
8:22 strong nations shall come to seek **the L** of 3068
8:22 in Jerusalem, and to pray before **the L**. 3068
8:23 Thus saith **the L** of hosts; In those days *it* 3068
9: 1 The burden of the word of **the L** in the land 3068
9: 1 the tribes of Israel, *shall be* toward **the L**. 3068
9:14 **the L** shall be seen over them, and 3068
9:15 **The L** of hosts shall defend them; and 3068
9:16 **the L** their God shall save them in that day 3068
10: 1 Ask ye of **the L** rain in the time of the latter 3068
Zec 10: 1 *so* **the L** *shall* make bright clouds, and 3068
10: 3 for **the L** of hosts hath visited his flock 3068
10: 5 because **the L** *is* with them, and the riders 3068
10: 6 for I *am* **the L** their God, and will hear 3068
10: 7 be glad; their heart shall rejoice in **the L**. 3068
10:12 I will strengthen them in **the L**; and 3068
10:12 walk up and down in his name, saith **the L**. 3068
11: 4 Thus saith **the L** my God; Feed the flock of 3068
11: 5 they that sell them say, Blessed *be* **the L**; 3068
11: 6 pity the inhabitants of the land, saith **the L**: 3068
11:11 me knew that it *was* the word of **the L**. 3068
11:13 **the L** said unto me, Cast it unto the potter: 3068
11:13 them to the potter *in* the house of **the L**. 3068
11:15 **the L** said unto me, Take unto thee yet 3068
12: 1 The burden of the word of **the L** for Israel, 3068
12: 1 saith **the L**, which stretcheth forth 3068
12: 4 In that day, saith **the L**, I will smite every 3068
12: 5 *be* my strength in **the L** of hosts their God. 3068
12: 7 **The L** also shall save the tents of Judah 3068
12: 8 In that day shall **the L** defend 3068
12: 8 as God, as the angel of **the L** before them. 3068
13: 2 to pass in that day, saith **the L** of hosts, 3068
13: 3 for thou speakest lies in the name of **the L**: 3068
13: 7 man *that is* my fellow, saith **the L** of hosts: 3068
13: 8 to pass, *that* in all the land, saith **the L**, 3068
13: 9 and they shall say, **The L** *is* my God. 3068
14: 1 the day of **the L** cometh, and thy spoil shall 3068
14: 3 shall **the L** go forth, and fight against those 3068
14: 5 **the L** my God shall come, *and* all the saints 3068
14: 7 be one day which shall be known to **the L**, 3068
14: 9 **the L** shall be king over all the earth: 3068
14: 9 in that day shall there be one **L**, and 3068
14:12 this shall be the plague where*with* **the L** 3068
14:13 *that* a great tumult from **the L** shall be 3068
14:16 **the L** of hosts, and to keep the feast of 3068
14:17 **the L** of hosts, even upon them shall be no 3068
14:18 where*with* **the L** will smite the heathen that 3068
14:20 of the horses, HOLINESS UNTO **THE L**; 3068
14:21 in Judah shall be holiness unto **the L** of 3068
14:21 Canaanite in the house of **the L** of hosts. 3068
Mal 1: 1 The burden of the word of **the L** to Israel 3068
1: 2 I have loved you, saith **the L**. Yet ye say, 3068
1: 2 saith **the L**: yet I loved Jacob, 3068
1: 4 thus saith **the L** of hosts, They shall build, 3068
1: 4 The people *against* whom **the L** hath 3068
1: 5 **The L** will be magnified from the border of 3068
1: 6 saith **the L** of hosts unto you, O priests, 3068
1: 7 ye say, The table of **the L** *is* contemptible. 3068
1: 8 or accept thy person? saith **the L** of hosts. 3068
1: 9 regard your persons? saith **the L** of hosts. 3068
1:10 no pleasure in you, saith **the L** of hosts, 3068
1:11 among the heathen, saith **the L** of hosts. 3068
1:12 that ye say, The table of **the L** *is* polluted; 3068
1:13 ye have snuffed at it, saith **the L** of hosts; 3068
1:13 I accept this of your hand? saith **the L**. 3068
1:14 saith **the L** of hosts, and my name *is* 3068
2: 2 glory unto my name, saith **the L** of hosts, 3068
2: 4 might be with Levi, saith **the L** of hosts. 3068
2: 7 for he *is* the messenger of **the L** of hosts. 3068
2: 8 the covenant of Levi, saith **the L** of hosts. 3068
2:11 the holiness of **the L** which he loved, 3068
2:12 **The L** will cut off the man that doth this, 3068
2:12 him that offereth an offering unto **the L** of 3068
2:13 covering the altar of **the L** *with* tears, *with* 3068
2:14 Because **the L** hath been witness between 3068
2:16 *For* **the L**, the God of Israel, saith that he 3068
2:16 with his garment, saith **the L** of hosts: 3068
2:17 Ye have wearied **the L** with your words. 3068
2:17 that doeth evil *is* good in the sight of **the L**, 3068
3: 1 **the L**, whom ye seek, shall suddenly come 3068
3: 1 behold, he *shall* come, saith **the L** of hosts. 3068
3: 3 that they may offer unto **the L** an offering 3068
3: 4 and Jerusalem be pleasant unto **the L**, 3068
3: 5 and fear not me, saith **the L** of hosts. 3068
3: 6 For I *am* **the L**, I change not; therefore 3068
3: 7 I will return unto you, saith **the L** of hosts. 3068
3:10 me now herewith, saith **the L** of hosts, 3068
3:11 the time in the field, saith **the L** of hosts. 3068
3:12 be a delightsome land, saith **the L** of hosts. 3068
3:13 have been stout against me, saith **the L**. 3068
3:14 walked mournfully before **the L** of hosts? 3068
3:16 they that feared **the L** spake often one to 3068
3:16 **the L** hearkened, and heard *it*, and a book 3068
3:16 before him for them that feared **the L**, 3068
3:17 they shall be mine, saith **the L** of hosts, 3068
4: 1 shall burn them up, saith **the L** of hosts, 3068
4: 3 day that I *shall* do *this*, saith **the L** of hosts. 3068
4: 5 of the great and dreadful day of **the L**: 3068

LORD IS MY BANNER See JEHOVAH-NISSI

LORD IS PEACE See JEHOVAH-SHALOM

LORD WILL PROVIDE See JEHOVAH-JIREH

LORD'S (26) [LORD]

Ge 40: 7 *were* with him in the ward of his **l** house, 113
44: 8 should we steal out of thy **l** house silver or 113
44: 9 and we also will be my **l** bondmen. 113+3807.1
44:16 behold, we *are* my **l** servants, both 113+3807.1
44:18 speak a word in my **l** ears, and let not thine 113
2Sa 20: 6 take thou thy **l** servants, and pursue after 113
1Ch 21: 3 *are* they not all my **l** servants? 113+3807.1
Isa 22:18 thy glory *shall be* the shame of thy **l** house. 113
Da 9:17 thy sanctuary that is desolate, for the **L** sake. 136
Mt 21:42 this is the **L** doing, and it is marvellous in *2962*
25:18 digged in the earth, and hid his **l** money. *2962*
Mk 12:11 This was the **L** doing, and it is marvellous *2962*
Lk 2:26 see death, before he had seen the **L** Christ. *2962*
12:47 which knew his **l** will, and prepared not *2962*
16: 5 So he called every one of his **l** debtors unto *2962*
Ro 14: 8 we live therefore, or die, we are the **L**. *2962*
1Co 7:22 the Lord, *being* a servant, is the **L** freeman: *2962*
10:21 ye cannot be partakers of the **L** table, and *2962*
10:26 For the earth *is* the **L**, and the fulness *2962*

L

1Co 10:28 for conscience sake: for the earth is the L, 2962
11:20 one place, this is not to eat the L supper. 2960
11:26 ye do shew the L death till he come. 2962
11:29 to himself, not discerning the L body. 2962
Gal 1:19 saw I none, save James the L brother. 2962
1Pe 2:13 to every ordinance of man for the L sake: 2962
Rev 1:10 I was in the spirit on the L day, and 2960

LORD'S* (108) [LORD*]
Ex 9:29 know how that the earth is the L. 3068+3807.1
12:11 eat it in haste: it is the L passover. 3068+3807.1
12:27 It is the sacrifice of the L passover, 3068+3807.1
13: 9 that the L law may be in thy mouth: 3068
13:12 thou hast; the males shall be the L. 3068+3807.1
32:26 the camp, and said, Who is on the L side? 3068
35:21 they brought the L offering to the work of 3068
35:24 of silver and brass brought the L offering: 3068
Lev 3:16 a sweet savour: all the fat is the L. 3068+3807.1
16: 9 the goat upon which the L lot fell, 3068+3807.1
23: 5 month at even is the L passover. 3068+3807.1
27:26 which should be the L firstling, no 3068+3807.1
27:26 it be ox, or sheep: it is the L. 3068+3807.1
27:30 or of the fruit of the tree, is the L: 3068+3807.1
Nu 11:23 unto Moses, Is the L hand waxed short? 3068
11:29 would God that all the L people were 3068
18:28 ye shall give thereof the L heave offering 3068
31:37 the L tribute of the sheep was six hundred 3068
31:38 of which the L tribute was threescore and 3068
31:39 of which the L tribute was 3068+3807.1
31:40 of which the L tribute was thirty 3068+3807.1
31:41 which was the L heave offering, 3068
32:10 the L anger was kindled the same time, 3068
32:13 And the L anger was kindled against Israel, 3068
Dt 10:14 of heavens is the L thy God, 3068+3807.1
11:17 then the L wrath be kindled against you, 3068
15: 2 because it is called the L release. 3068+3807.1
32: 9 For the L portion is his people; Jacob is 3068
Jos 1:15 which Moses the L servant gave you on 3068
5:15 the captain of the L host said unto Joshua, 3068
22:19 wherein the L tabernacle dwelleth, and 3068
Jdg 11:31 shall surely be the L, and I will 3068+3807.1
1Sa 2: 8 the pillars of the earth are the L, 3068+3807.1
2:24 I hear: ye make the L people to transgress. 3068
14: 3 the son of Eli, the L priest in Shiloh, 3068
16: 6 said, Surely the L anointed is before him. 3068
17:47 for the battle is the L, and he will 3068+3807.1
18:17 thou valiant for me, and fight the L battles. 3068
22:21 David that Saul had slain the L priests. 3068
24: 6 do this thing unto my master, the L 3068+3807.1
24:10 against my lord; for he is the L anointed. 3068
26: 9 forth his hand against the L anointed, 3068
26:11 forth mine hand against the L anointed: 3068
26:16 have not kept your master, the L anointed. 3068
26:23 forth mine hand against the L anointed. 3068
2Sa 1:14 forth thine hand to destroy the L anointed? 3068
1:16 saying, I have slain the L anointed. 3068
19:21 for this, because he cursed the L anointed? 3068
21: 7 of the L oath that was between them, 3068
1Ki 18:13 how I hid an hundred men of the L 3068
2Ki 11:17 that they should be the L people; 3068+3807.1
13:17 The arrow of the L deliverance, 3068+3807.1
2Ch 7: 2 the glory of the LORD had filled the L 3068
23:16 that they should be the L people. 3068+3807.1
Ps 11: 4 his holy temple, the L throne is in heaven: 3068
22:28 For the kingdom is the L: and he is 3068+3807.1
24: 1 The earth is the L, and the fulness 3068+3807.1
113: 3 of the same the L name is to be praised. 3068
115:16 even the heavens, are the L: 3068+3807.1
116:19 In the courts of the L house, in the midst of 3068
118:23 This is the L doing; it is marvellous in our 3068
137: 4 How shall we sing the L song in a strange 3068
Pr 16:11 just weight and balance are the L: 3068+3807.1
Isa 2: 2 that the mountain of the L house shall be 3068
34: 8 For it is the day of the L vengeance, and 3068
40: 2 for she hath received of the L hand double 3068
42:19 that is perfect, and blind as the L servant? 3068
44: 5 One shall say, I am the L; and 3068+3807.1
59: 1 Behold, the L hand is not shortened, that it 3068
Jer 5:10 for they are not the L. 3068+3807.1
7: 2 Stand in the gate of the L house, and 3068
13:17 the L flock is carried away captive. 3068
19:14 he stood in the court of the L house; and 3068
25:17 took I the cup at the L hand, and made all 3068
26: 2 Stand in the court of the L house, and 3068
26: 2 which come to worship in the L house, 3068
26:10 the entry of the new gate of the L house. 3068
27:16 the vessels of the L house shall now 3068
28: 3 this place all the vessels of the L house, 3068
28: 6 to bring again the vessels of the L house, 3068
36: 6 people in the L house upon the fasting day: 3068
36: 8 the words of the LORD in the L house. 3068
36:10 at the entry of the new gate of the L house, 3068
51: 6 for this is the time of the L vengeance; 3068
51: 7 Babylon hath been a golden cup in the L 3068
51:51 come into the sanctuaries of the L house. 3068
La 2:22 that in the day of the L anger none escaped 3068
3:22 It is of the L mercies that we are not 3068
Eze 8:14 the L house which was towards the north; 3068
8:16 he brought me into the inner court of the L 3068
10: 4 the court was full of the brightness of the L 3068
10:19 at the door of the east gate of the L house; 3068
11: 1 brought me unto the east gate of the L 3068
Hos 9: 3 They shall not dwell in the L land; but 3068
Joel 1: 9 the priests, the L ministers, mourn. 3068
Ob 1:21 and the kingdom shall be the L. 3068+3807.1
Mic 6: 2 the L controversy, and ye strong 3068
6: 9 The L voice crieth unto the city, and 3068
Hab 2:16 the cup of the L right hand shall be turned 3068
Zep 1: 8 it shall come to pass in the day of the L 3068
1:18 to deliver them in the day of the L wrath; 3068
2: 2 before the day of the L anger come upon 3068
2: 3 it may be ye shall be hid in the day of the L 3068
Hag 1: 2 the time that the L house should be built. 3068
1:13 spake Haggai the L messenger in 3068
1:13 in the L message unto the people, 3068
2:18 the foundation of the L temple was laid, 3068
Zec 14:20 the pots in the L house shall be like 3068

LORDLY (1) [LORD]
Jdg 5:25 him milk; she brought forth butter in a l dish. 117

LORDS (42) [LORD]
Ge 19: 2 Behold now, my l, turn in, I pray you, 113
Nu 21:28 and the l of the high places of Arnon. 1167
Dt 10:17 Lord of l, a great God, a mighty, and 113
Jos 13: 3 five l of the Philistines; the Gazathites, and 5633
Jdg 3: 3 Namely, five l of the Philistines, and all 5633
16: 5 the l of the Philistines came up unto her, 5633
16: 8 the l of the Philistines brought up to her 5633
16:18 and called for the l of the Philistines, 5633
16:18 the l of the Philistines came up unto her, 5633
16:23 the l of the Philistines gathered them 5633
16:27 all the l of the Philistines were there; 5633
16:30 the house fell upon the l, and upon all 5633
1Sa 5: 8 gathered all the l of the Philistines unto 5633
5:11 gathered together all the l of the Philistines, 5633
6: 4 according to the number of the l of 5633
6: 4 one plague was on you all, and on your l. 5633
6:12 the l of the Philistines went after them unto 5633
6:16 when the five l of the Philistines had seen 5633
6:18 of the Philistines belonging to the five l, 5633
7: 7 the l of the Philistines went up against 5633
29: 2 the l of the Philistines passed on by 5633
29: 6 this day: nevertheless the l favour thee not. 5633
29: 7 that thou displease not the l of 5633
1Ch 12:19 for the l of the Philistines upon advisement 5633
Ezr 8:25 his l, and all Israel there present, had 8269
Ps 136: 3 O give thanks to the Lord of l: for his mercy 113
Isa 16: 8 the l of the heathen have broken down 1167
26:13 other l besides thee have had dominion over 113
Jer 2:31 wherefore say my people, We are l; we will 7300
Eze 23:23 captains and rulers, great l and renowned, 7991
Da 4:36 my counsellers and my l sought unto me; 7261
5: 1 made a great feast to a thousand of his l, 7261
5: 9 changed in him, and his l were astonied. 7261
5:10 by reason of the words of the king and his l, 7261
5:23 thou, and thy l, thy wives, and 7261
6:17 his own signet, and with the signet of his l; 7261
Mk 6:21 on his birthday made a supper to his l, 3175
1Co 8: 5 (as there be gods many, and l many,) 2962
1Ti 6:15 the King of kings, and Lord of l; 2961
1Pe 5: 3 Neither as being l over God's heritage, but 2634
Rev 17:14 for he is Lord of l, and King of kings: and 2962
19:16 KING OF KINGS, AND LORD OF L. 2962

LORDSHIP (2) [LORD]
Mk 10:42 rule over the Gentiles exercise l over them; 2634
Lk 22:25 The kings of the Gentiles exercise l over 2961

LO-RUHAMAH (2) [RUHAMAH]
Hos 1: 6 God said unto him, Call her name L: for I 3819
1: 8 Now when she had weaned L, 3819

LOSE (23) [LOSETH, LOSS, LOST]
Jdg 18:25 thou l thy life, with the lives of thy 622
Job 31:39 have caused the owners thereof to l their 5301
Pr 23: 8 shalt thou vomit up, and l thy sweet words. 7843
Ecc 3: 6 A time to get, and a time to l; a time to keep, 6
Mt 10:39 He that findeth his life shall l it: and he that 622
10:42 unto you, he shall in no wise l his reward. 622
16:25 For whosoever will save his life shall l it: 622
16:25 whosoever will l his life for my sake shall 622
16:26 gain the whole world, and l his own soul? 2210
Mk 8:35 For whosoever will save his life shall l it; but 622
8:35 but whosoever shall l his life for my sake 622
8:36 gain the whole world, and l his own soul? 2210
9:41 I say unto you, he shall not l his reward. 622
Lk 9:24 For whosoever will save his life shall l it: but 622
9:24 but whosoever will l his life for my sake, 622
9:25 whole world, and l himself, or be cast away? 622
15: 4 if he l one of them, doth not leave the ninety 622
15: 8 if she l one piece, doth not light a candle, 622
17:33 Whosoever shall seek to save his life shall l 622
17:33 whosoever shall l his life shall preserve it. 622
Jn 6:39 that of all which he hath given me I should l 622
12:25 He that loveth his life shall l it; and he that 622
2Jn 1: 8 that we l not those things which we have 622

LOSETH (1) [LOSE]
Mt 10:39 and he that l his life for my sake shall find it. 622

LOSS (10) [LOSE]
Ge 31:39 I bare the l of it; of my hand didst thou 2398
Ex 21:19 only he shall pay for the l of his time, and 7674
Isa 47: 8 neither shall I know the l of children: 7908
47: 9 one day, the l of children, and widowhood: 7908
Ac 27:21 and to have gained this harm and l. 2209
27:22 for there shall be no l of any man's life 580
1Co 3:15 man's work shall be burnt, he shall suffer l: 2210
Php 3: 7 gain to me, those I counted l for Christ. 2209
3: 8 I count all things but l for the excellency of the knowledge of 2209
3: 8 for whom I have suffered the l of all 2210

LOST (33) [LOSE]
Ex 22: 9 for any manner of l thing, which another 9
Lev 6: 3 Or have found that which was l, and 9
6: 4 him to keep, or the l thing which he found, 9
Nu 6:12 the days that were before shall be l, because 5307
Dt 22: 3 with all l thing of thy brother's, which he hath 9
22: 3 which he hath l, and thou hast found, shalt thou 6
1Sa 9: 3 the asses of Kish Saul's father were l. 6
9:20 as for thine asses that were l three days ago, 6
1Ki 20:25 like the army that thou hast l, horse for 5307
Ps 119:176 I have gone astray like a l sheep; seek thy 6
Isa 49:20 after thou hast l the other, shall say again in 7923
49:21 seeing I have l my children, and 7921
Jer 50: 6 My people hath been l sheep: their shepherds 6
Eze 19: 5 and her hope was l, then she took another of 6
34: 4 neither have ye sought that which was l; 6
34:16 I will seek that which was l, and bring again 6
37:11 Our bones are dried, and our hope is l: 6
Mt 5:13 but if the salt have l his savour, 3471
10: 6 But go rather to the l sheep of the house of 622
15:24 but unto the l sheep of the house of Israel. 622
18:11 Son of man is come to save that which was l. 622
Mk 9:50 but if the salt have l his saltness, 358
Lk 14:34 but if the salt have l his savour, 3471
15: 4 and go after that which is l, until he find it? 622
15: 6 for I have found my sheep which was l. 622
15: 9 for I have found the piece which I had l. 622
15:24 and is alive again; he was l, and is found. 622
15:32 and is alive again; and was l, and is found. 622
19:10 is come to seek and to save that which was l. 622
Jn 6:12 the fragments that remain, that nothing be l. 622
17:12 and none of them is l, but the son of 622
18: 9 Of them which thou gavest me have I l none. 622
2Co 4: 3 our gospel be hid, it is hid to them that are l: 622

LOT (111) [LOT'S, LOTS]
Ge 11:27 and Haran; and Haran begat L. 3876
11:31 L the son of Haran his son's son, and Sarai 3876
12: 4 had spoken unto him; and L went with him: 3876
12: 5 L his brother's son, and all their substance 3876
13: 1 that he had, and L with him, into the south. 3876
13: 5 L also, which went with Abram, 3876
13: 8 Abram said unto L, Let there be no strife, 3876
13:10 L lifted up his eyes, and beheld all the plain 3876
13:11 L chose him all the plain of Jordan; and 3876
13:11 the plain of Jordan; and L journeyed east: 3876
13:12 L dwelled in the cities of the plain, and 3876
13:14 after that L was separated from him, Lift up 3876
14:12 they took L, Abram's brother's son, 3876
14:16 also brought again his brother L, and 3876
19: 1 at even; and L sat in the gate of Sodom: 3876
19: 1 L seeing them rose up to meet them; and 3876
19: 5 they called unto L, and said unto him, 3876
19: 6 L went out at the door unto them, and 3876
19: 9 even L, and came near to break the door. 3876
19:10 pulled L into the house to them, and shut to 3876
19:12 the men said unto L, Hast thou here any 3876
19:14 L went out, and spake unto his sons in law, 3876
19:15 the angels hastened L, saying, Arise, 3876
19:18 L said unto them, Oh, not so, my Lord: 3876
19:23 The sun was risen upon the earth when L 3876
19:29 sent L out of the midst of the overthrow, 3876
19:29 overthrew the cities in the which L dwelt. 3876
19:30 L went up out of Zoar, and dwelt in 3876
19:36 Thus were both the daughters of L with 3876
Lev 16: 8 one l for the LORD, and the other lot for 1486
16: 8 and the other l for the scapegoat. 1486
16: 9 the goat upon which the LORD'S l fell, 1486
16:10 on which the l fell to be the scapegoat, 1486
Nu 26:55 the land shall be divided by l: 1486
26:56 According to the l shall the possession 1486
33:54 ye shall divide the land by l for an 1486
33:54 shall be in the place where his l falleth; 1486
34:13 This is the land which ye shall inherit by l, 1486
36: 2 an inheritance by l to the children of Israel: 1486
36: 3 shall it be taken from the l of our 1486
Dt 2: 9 I have given Ar unto the children of L for a 3876
2:19 I have given it unto the children of L for a 3876
32: 9 his people; Jacob is the l of his inheritance. 2256
Jos 13: 6 only divide thou it by l unto the Israelites NIH
14: 2 By l was their inheritance, as the LORD 1486
15: 1 was the l of the tribe of the children of 1486
16: 1 the l of the children of Joseph fell from 1486
17: 1 There was also a l for the tribe of 1486
17: 2 There was also a l for the rest of NIH
17:14 but one l and one portion to inherit, 1486
17:17 thou shalt not have one l only: 1486
18:11 the l of the tribe of the children of 1486
18:11 the coast of their l came forth between 1486
19: 1 the second l came forth to Simeon, even for 1486
19:10 the third l came up for the children of 1486
19:17 And the fourth l came out to Issachar, 1486
19:24 the fifth l came out for the tribe of 1486
19:32 The sixth l came out to the children of 1486
19:40 And the seventh l came out for the tribe of 1486
19:51 divided for an inheritance by l in Shiloh 1486
21: 4 the l came out for the families of 1486
21: 4 had by l out of the tribe of Judah, and 1486
21: 5 the rest of the children of Kohath had by l 1486
21: 6 the children of Gershon had by l out of 1486
21: 8 the children of Israel gave by l unto 1486
21:10 of Levi, had: for theirs was the first l. 1486
21:20 even they had the cities of their l out of 1486
21:40 of the Levites, were by their l twelve cities. 1486
23: 4 I have divided unto you by l these nations NIH
Jdg 1: 3 his brother, Come up with me into my l, 1486
1: 3 and I likewise will go with thee into thy l. 1486
20: 9 do to Gibeah; we will go up by l against it; 1486
1Sa 14:41 Give a perfect l. And Saul and NIH
1Ch 6:54 of the Kohathites: for theirs was the l. 1486
6:61 the half tribe of Manasseh, by l, ten cities. 1486
6:63 Unto the sons of Merari were given by l, 1486
6:65 they gave by l out of the tribe of 1486
16:18 land of Canaan, the l of your inheritance; 2256
24: 5 Thus were they divided by l, one sort with 1486
24: 7 Now the first l came forth to Jehoiarib, 1486
25: 9 Now the first l came forth for Asaph to 1486
26:14 the l eastward fell to Shelemiah. Then for 1486
26:14 cast lots; and his l came out northward. 1486
26:16 and Hosah the l came forth westward, NIH
Est 3: 7 they cast Pur, that is, the l, before Haman 1486
9:24 had cast Pur, that is, the l, to consume 1486
Ps 16: 5 and of my cup: thou maintainest my l. 1486
83: 8 they have holpen the children of L. Selah. 3876
105:11 land of Canaan, the l of your inheritance: 2256
125: 3 shall not rest upon the l of the righteous; 1486
Pr 1:14 Cast in thy l among us; let us all have one 1486
16:33 The l is cast into the lap; but the whole 1486
18:18 The l causeth contentions to cease, and 1486
Isa 17:14 that spoil us, and the l of them that rob us. 1486
34:17 he hath cast the l for them, and his hand 1486

Isa 57: 6 stream *is* thy portion; they, they *are* thy l: 1486
Jer 13:25 This *is* thy l, the portion of thy measures 1486
Eze 24: 6 it out piece by piece; let no l fall upon it. 1486
45: 1 when ye shall divide *by l* the land for NIH
47:22 *that* ye shall divide it *by l* for an inheritance NIH
48:29 This *is* the land which ye shall divide *by l* NIH
Da 12:13 and stand in thy l at the end of the days. 1486
Jnh 1: 7 So they cast lots, and the l fell upon Jonah. 1486
Mic 2: 5 by l in the congregation of the LORD. 1486
Lk 1: 9 his l was to burn incense when he went into *2975*
17:28 Likewise also as it was in the days of L; *3091*
17:29 But the *same* day that L went out of Sodom *3091*
Ac 1:26 and the l fell upon Matthias; and he was *2819*
8:21 Thou hast neither part nor l in this matter: *2819*
13:19 he **divided** their land to them **by l**. *2624*
2Pe 2: 7 And delivered just L, vexed with the filthy *3091*

LOT'S (2) [LOT]
Ge 13: 7 Abram's cattle and the herdmen of L cattle: 3876
Lk 17:32 Remember L wife. *3091*

LOTAN (5) [LOTAN'S]
Ge 36:20 L, and Shobal, and Zibeon, and Anah, 3877
36:22 the children of L were Hori and Hemam; 3877
36:29 duke L, duke Shobal, duke Zibeon, 3877
1Ch 1:38 L, and Shobal, and Zibeon, and Anah, and 3877
1:39 the sons of L; Hori, and Homam: and 3877

LOTAN'S (2) [LOTAN]
Ge 36:22 and Hemam; and L sister *was* Timna. 3877
1Ch 1:39 Hori, and Homam: and Timna *was* L sister. 3877

LOTHE (4) [LOATHE, LOTHED, LOTHETH, LOTHING]
Ex 7:18 the Egyptians shall l to drink of the water 3811
Eze 6: 9 they shall l themselves for the evils which 6962
20:43 ye shall l yourselves in your own sight for 6962
36:31 shall l yourselves in your own sight for 6962

LOTHED (3) [LOTHE]
Jer 14:19 hath thy soul l Zion? why hast thou smitten 1602
Eze 16:45 which l their husbands and their children: 1602
Zec 11: 8 my soul l them, and their soul also abhorred 7114

LOTHETH (1) [LOTHE]
Eze 16:45 that l her husband and her children; 1602

LOTHING (1) [LOTHE]
Eze 16: 5 to the l of thy person, in the day that thou 1604

LOTS (24) [LOT]
Lev 16: 8 Aaron shall cast l upon the two goats; 1486
Jos 18: 6 that I may cast l for you here before 1486
18: 8 that I may here cast l for you before 1486
18:10 Joshua cast l for them in Shiloh before 1486
1Sa 14:42 Cast *l* between me and Jonathan my son. NIH
1Ch 24:31 These likewise cast l over against their 1486
25: 8 they cast l, ward against *ward*, as well 1486
26:13 they cast l, as well the small as the great, 1486
26:14 his son, a wise counseller, they cast l; 1486
Ne 10:34 we cast the l *among* the priests, the Levites, 1486
11: 1 the rest of the people also cast l, to bring 1486
Ps 22:18 among them, and cast l upon my vesture. 1486
Joel 3: 3 they have cast l for my people; and 1486
Ob 1:11 cast l upon Jerusalem, even thou *wast* as 1486
Jnh 1: 7 one to his fellow, Come, and let us cast l, 1486
1: 7 So they cast l, and the lot fell upon Jonah. 1486
Na 3:10 they cast l for her honourable *men*, and 1486
Mt 27:35 and parted his garments, casting l: *2819*
27:35 and upon my vesture did they cast l. *2819*
Mk 15:24 parted his garments, casting l upon them, *2819*
Lk 23:34 And they parted his raiment, and cast l. *2819*
Jn 19:24 Let us not rent it, but **cast l** for it, whose it *2975*
19:24 and for my vesture they did cast l. *2819*
Ac 1:26 And they gave forth their l; and the lot fell *2819*

LOUD (61) [ALOUD, LOUDER]
Ge 39:14 to lie with me, and I cried with a l voice: 1419
Ex 19:16 and the voice of the trumpet exceeding l; 2389
Dt 27:14 say unto all the men of Israel *with* a l voice, 7311
1Sa 28:12 saw Samuel, she cried with a l voice: 1419
2Sa 15:23 And all the country wept *with* a l voice, and 1419
19: 4 the king cried *with* a l voice, O my son 1419
1Ki 8:55 all the congregation of Israel *with* a l voice, 1419
18:28 they cried l, and 1419+6963+871.1
2Ki 18:28 cried with a l voice in the Jews' language, 1419
2Ch 15:14 they sware unto the LORD with a l voice, 1419
20:19 God of Israel with a l voice on high. 1419
30:21 *singing* with l instruments unto 5797
32:18 they cried with a l voice in the Jews' 1419
Ezr 3:12 laid before their eyes, wept with a l voice; 1419
3:13 for the people shouted *with* a l shout, and 1419
10:12 and said *with* a l voice, 1419
Ne 9: 4 cried with a l voice unto the LORD their 1419
12:42 the singers **sang l**, with Jezrahiah *their* 8085
Est 4: 1 the city, and cried *with* a l and a bitter cry; 1419
Ps 33: 3 a new song; play skilfully with a **l noise**. 8643
98: 4 **make a l noise**, and rejoice, and 6476
150: 5 Praise him upon the l cymbals: praise him 8088
Pr 7:11 (She *is* l and stubborn; her feet abide not in 1993
27:14 He that blesseth his friend with a l voice, 1419
Isa 36:13 cried with a l voice in the Jews' language, 1419
Eze 8:18 though they cry in mine ears *with* a l voice, 1419
9: 1 He cried also in mine ears *with* a l voice, 1419
11:13 cried *with* a l voice, and said, Ah Lord 1419
Mt 27:46 the ninth hour Jesus cried with a l voice, *3173*
27:50 when he had cried again with a l voice, *3173*
Mk 1:26 and cried with a l voice, he came out of *3173*
5: 7 And cried with a l voice, and said, *3173*
15:34 And at the ninth hour Jesus cried with a l *3173*
15:37 And Jesus cried with a l voice, and gave up *3173*
Lk 1:42 And she spake out with a l voice, *3173*
4:33 unclean devil, and cried out with a l voice, *3173*
8:28 down before him, and with a l voice said, *3173*
Lk 17:15 and with a l voice glorified God, *3173*
19:37 praise God with a l voice for all the mighty *3173*
23:23 And they were instant with l voices, *3173*
23:46 And when Jesus had cried with a l voice, *3173*
Jn 11:43 he cried with a l voice, Lazarus, *3173*
Ac 7:57 Then they cried out with a l voice, and *3173*
7:60 and cried with a l voice, Lord, *3173*
8: 7 For unclean spirits, crying with l voice, *3173*
14:10 Said with a l voice, Stand upright on thy *3173*
16:28 But Paul cried with a l voice, saying, *3173*
26:24 Festus said with a l voice, Paul, thou art *3173*
Rev 5: 2 a strong angel proclaiming with a l voice, *3173*
5:12 Saying with a l voice, Worthy is the Lamb *3173*
6:10 And they cried with a l voice, saying, *3173*
7: 2 he cried with a l voice to the four angels, *3173*
7:10 And cried with a l voice, saying, Salvation *3173*
8:13 saying with a l voice, Woe, woe, woe, *3173*
10: 3 And cried with a l voice, as *when* a lion *3173*
12:10 And I heard a l voice saying in heaven, *3173*
14: 7 Saying with a l voice, Fear God, and *3173*
14: 9 saying with a l voice, If any *man* worship *3173*
14:15 crying with a l voice to him that sat on *3173*
14:18 cried with a l cry to him that had the sharp *3173*
19:17 and he cried with a l voice, saying to all *3173*

LOUDER (2) [LOUD]
Ex 19:19 **waxed l and louder**, Moses spake, 2390+3966
19:19 **waxed louder and l**, Moses spake, 2390+3966

LOVE (310) [BELOVED, BELOVED'S, LOVE'S, LOVED, LOVEDST, LOVELY, LOVER, LOVERS, LOVES, LOVEST, LOVETH, LOVING, LOVINGKINDNESS, LOVINGKINDNESSES, WELLBELOVED, WELL-BELOVED]
Ge 27: 4 such as I l, and bring *it* to me, that I may eat; 157
29:20 *but* a few days, for the l he had to her. 160
29:32 now therefore my husband will l me. 157
Ex 20: 6 shewing mercy unto thousands of them that l 157
21: 5 I l my master, my wife, and my children; 157
Lev 19:18 but thou shalt l thy neighbour as thyself: 157
19:34 amongst you, and thou shalt l him as thyself; 157
Dt 5:10 shewing mercy unto thousands of them that l 157
6: 5 thou shalt l the LORD thy God with all 157
7: 7 The LORD did not **set** his l upon you, 2836
7: 9 and mercy with them that l him and 157
7:13 he will l thee, and bless thee, and 157
10:12 to l him, and to serve the LORD thy God 157
10:15 had a delight in thy fathers to l them, 157
10:19 L ye therefore the stranger: for ye were 157
11: 1 Therefore thou shalt l the LORD thy God, 157
11:13 to l the LORD your God, and to serve him 157
11:22 to do them, to l the LORD your God, 157
13: 3 to know whether you l the LORD your God 157
19: 9 to l the LORD thy God, and to walk ever in 157
30: 6 to l the LORD thy God with all thine heart, 157
30:16 In that I command thee *this* day to l 157
30:20 That thou mayest l the LORD thy God, *and* 157
Jos 22: 5 to l the LORD your God, and to walk in all 157
23:11 that ye l the LORD your God. 157
Jdg 5:31 *let* them that l him *be* as the sun when he 157
16:15 said unto him, How canst thou say, I l thee, 157
1Sa 18:22 delight in thee, and all his servants l thee: 157
2Sa 1:26 thy l to me was wonderful, passing the love 160
1:26 me was wonderful, passing the l of women. 160
13: 4 Amnon said unto him, I l Tamar, my brother 157
13:15 than the l wherewith he had loved her. 160
1Ki 11: 2 their gods: Solomon clave unto these in l. 157
2Ch 19: 2 and l them that hate the LORD? 157
Ne 1: 5 and mercy for them that l him and 157
Ps 4: 2 *how long* will ye l vanity, *and* seek after 157
5:11 let them also that l thy name be joyful in 157
18: 1 I will l thee, O LORD, my strength. 7355
31:23 O l the LORD, all ye his saints: *for* 157
40:16 let such as l thy salvation say continually, 157
69:36 and they that l his name shall dwell therein. 157
70: 4 let such as l thy salvation say continually, 157
91:14 Because he hath **set** his l upon me, 2836
97:10 Ye that l the LORD, hate evil: 157
109: 4 For my l they are my adversaries: but I *give* 160
109: 5 me evil for good, and hatred for my l. 160
116: 1 I l the LORD, because he hath heard my 157
119:97 O how l I thy law! it *is* my meditation all 157
119:113 I hate *vain* thoughts: but thy law do I l. 157
119:119 earth *like* dross: therefore I l thy testimonies. 157
119:127 Therefore I l thy commandments above 157
119:132 as thou usest to do unto those that l thy 157
119:159 Consider how I l thy precepts: quicken me, 157
119:163 I hate and abhor lying: *but* thy law do I l. 157
119:165 Great peace have they which l thy law: and 157
119:167 thy testimonies; and *I* l them exceedingly. 157
122: 6 of Jerusalem: they shall prosper that l thee. 157
145:20 The LORD preserveth all them that l him: 157
Pr 1:22 ye simple ones, will ye l simplicity? 157
4: 6 preserve thee: l her, and she shall keep thee. 157
5:19 and be thou ravished always with her l. 160
7:18 let us take our fill of l until the morning: 1730
8:17 I l them that love me; and those that seek me 157
8:17 I love them that l me; and those that seek me 157
8:21 That *I* may cause those that l me to inherit 157
8:36 his own soul: all they that hate me l death. 157
9: 8 rebuke a wise *man*, and he will l thee. 157
10:12 stirreth up strifes: but l covereth all sins. 160
15:17 Better *is* a dinner of herbs where l is, than a 160
16:13 of kings; and *they* l him that speaketh right. 157
17: 9 He that covereth a transgression seeketh l; 160
18:21 and they that l it shall eat the fruit thereof. 157
20:13 L not sleep, lest thou come to poverty; 157
27: 5 Open rebuke *is* better than secret l. 160
Ecc 3: 8 A time to l, and a time to hate; a time of war, 157
9: 1 no man knoweth either l or hatred *by* all *that* 160
9: 6 Also their l, and their hatred, and their envy, 160
SS 1: 2 of his mouth: for thy l *is* better than wine. 1730
1: 3 poured forth, therefore do the virgins l thee. 157
1: 4 we will remember thy l more than wine: 1730
SS 1: 4 thy love more than wine: the upright l thee. 157
1: 9 I have compared thee, O my l, to a 7474
1:15 Behold, thou *art* fair, my l; behold, thou *art* 7474
2: 2 so *is* my l among the daughters. 7474
2: 4 and his banner over me *was* l. 160
2: 5 comfort me with apples: for I *am* sick of l. 160
2: 7 ye stir not up, nor awake *my* l, till he please. 160
2:10 Rise up, my l, my fair one, and come away. 7474
2:13 Arise, my l, my fair one, and come away. 7474
3: 5 ye stir not up, nor awake *my* l, till he please. 160
3:10 the midst thereof being paved *with* l, 160
4: 1 Behold, thou *art* fair, my l; behold, thou *art* 7474
4: 7 Thou *art* all fair, my l; *there is* no spot in 7474
4:10 How fair is thy l, my sister, *my* spouse! 1730
4:10 how much better is thy l than wine! and 1730
5: 2 my sister, my l, my dove, my undefiled: 7474
5: 8 that ye tell him, that I *am* sick of l. 160
6: 4 Thou *art* beautiful, O my l, as Tirzah, 7474
7: 6 and how pleasant art thou, O l, for delights! 160
8: 4 stir not up, nor awake *my* l, until he please. 160
8: 6 for l *is* strong as death; jealousy *is* cruel as 160
8: 7 Many waters cannot quench l, neither can 160
8: 7 give all the substance of his house for l, 160
Isa 38:17 thou hast **in l** to my soul *delivered it* from 2836
56: 6 serve him, and to l the name of the LORD, 157
61: 8 For I the LORD l judgment, I hate robbery 157
63: 9 in his l and in his pity he redeemed them; 160
66:10 and be glad with her, all ye that l her: 157
Jer 2: 2 of thy youth, the l of thine espousals, 160
2:33 Why trimmest thou thy way to seek l? 160
5:31 their means; and my people l *to have it* so: 157
31: 3 I have loved thee *with* an everlasting l; 160
Eze 16: 8 behold, thy time *was* the time of l; 1730
23:11 more corrupt in her **inordinate** l than she, 5691
23:17 Babylonians came to her into the bed of l, 1730
33:31 for with their mouth they shew **much** l, *but* 5690
Da 1: 9 and **tender** l with the prince of the eunuchs. 7356
9: 4 the covenant and mercy to them that l him, 157
Hos 3: 1 Go yet, l a woman beloved of *her* friend, 157
3: 1 according to the l of the LORD toward 160
3: 1 look to other gods, and l flagons of wine. 157
4:18 her rulers *with* shame do l, Give ye. 157
9:15 out of mine house, I will l them no more: 160
11: 4 them with cords of a man, with bands of l: 160
14: 4 heal their backsliding, I will l them freely: 157
Am 5:15 l the good, and establish judgment in 157
Mic 3: 2 Who hate the good, and l the evil; who pluck 157
6: 8 to l mercy, and to walk humbly with thy 160
Zep 3:17 he will rest in his l, he will joy over thee 160
Zec 8:17 against his neighbour; and l no false oath: 157
8:19 therefore l the truth and peace. 157
Mt 5:43 Thou shalt l thy neighbour, and hate thine *25*
5:44 But I say unto you, L your enemies, *25*
5:46 For if ye l them which love you, what reward *25*
5:46 For if ye love them which l you, what reward *25*
6: 5 they l to pray standing in the synagogues *5368*
6:24 for either he will hate the one, and l the other; *25*
19:19 and, Thou shalt l thy neighbour as thyself. *25*
22:37 Thou shalt l the Lord thy God with all thy *25*
22:39 unto it, Thou shalt l thy neighbour as thyself. *25*
23: 6 And l the uppermost rooms at feasts, and *5368*
24:12 shall abound, the l of many shall wax cold. *26*
Mk 12:30 And thou shalt l the Lord thy God with all thy *25*
12:31 Thou shalt l thy neighbour as thyself. *25*
12:33 And to l him with all the heart, and with all *25*
12:33 the strength, and to l *his* neighbour as himself, *25*
12:38 which l to go in long clothing, and *2309*
12:38 and *l* salutations in the marketplaces, NIG
Lk 6:27 I say unto you which hear, L your enemies, *25*
6:32 For if ye l them which love you, what thank *25*
6:32 For if ye love them which l you, what thank *25*
6:32 for sinners also l those that love them. *25*
6:32 for sinners also love those that l them. *25*
6:35 But l ye your enemies, and do good, and lend, *25*
7:42 me therefore, which of them will l him most? *25*
10:27 Thou shalt l the Lord thy God with all thy *25*
11:42 and pass over judgment and the l of God: *26*
11:43 for ye l the uppermost seats in *25*
16:13 for either he will hate the one, and l the other; *25*
20:46 and l greetings in the markets, and *5368*
Jn 5:42 that ye have not the l of God in you. *26*
8:42 If God were your Father, ye would l me: *25*
10:17 Therefore doth *my* Father l me, because I lay *25*
13:34 I give unto you, That ye l one another; *25*
13:34 as I have loved you, that ye also l one another. *25*
13:35 are my disciples, if ye have l one to another. *26*
14:15 If ye l me, keep my commandments. *25*
14:21 and I will l him, and will manifest myself to *25*
14:23 and said unto him, If a man l me, *25*
14:23 and my Father will l him, and we will come *25*
14:31 But that the world may know that I l *25*
15: 9 so have I loved you: continue ye in my l. *26*
15:10 my commandments, ye shall abide in my l; *26*
15:10 Father's commandments, and abide in his l. *26*
15:12 That ye l one another, as I have loved you. *25*
15:13 Greater l hath no *man* than this, that a man lay *26*
15:17 *things* I command you, that ye l one another. *25*
15:19 of the world, the world would l his own: *5368*
17:26 will declare *it:* that the l where*with* thou hast *26*
21:15 Yea, Lord; thou knowest that I l thee. *5368*
21:16 Yea, Lord; thou knowest that I l thee. *5368*
21:17 all *things;* thou knowest that I l thee. *5368*
Ro 5: 5 the l of God is shed abroad in our hearts by *26*
5: 8 But God commendeth his l toward us, in that, *26*
8:28 work together for good to them that l God, *25*
8:35 Who shall separate us from the l of Christ? *26*
8:39 shall be able to separate us from the l of God, *26*
12: 9 *Let* l *be* without dissimulation. Abhor *that* *26*
12:10 one to another with **brotherly l**; *5360*
13: 8 Owe no *man* any *thing*, but to l one another: *25*
13: 9 namely, Thou shalt l thy neighbour as thyself. *25*
13:10 L worketh no ill to *his* neighbour: therefore *26*
13:10 therefore l *is* the fulfilling of the law. *26*
15:30 Jesus Christ's sake, and for the l of the Spirit, *26*
1Co 2: 9 which God hath prepared for them that l him. *25*

1Co 4:21 a rod, or in l, and *in* the spirit of meekness? 26
8: 3 But if any *man* l God, the same is known of 25
16:22 If any *man* l not the Lord Jesus Christ, 5368
16:24 My l *be* with you all in Christ Jesus. Amen. 26
2Co 2: 4 that ye might know the l which I have more 26
2: 8 that *you* would confirm *your* l towards him. 26
5:14 For the l of Christ constraineth us; because 26
6: 6 by the Holy Ghost, by l unfeigned, 26
8: 7 and *in* all diligence, and *in* your l to us, 26
8: 8 of others, and to prove the sincerity of your l. 26
8:24 the proof of your l, and of our boasting on 26
11:11 because I l you not? God knoweth. 25
12:15 though the more abundantly I l you, the less I 25
13:11 and the God of l and peace shall be with you. 26
13:14 and the l of God, and the communion of 26
Gal 5: 6 but faith which worketh by l. 26
5:13 to the flesh, but by l serve one another. 26
5:14 *even* in *this;* Thou shalt l thy neighbour as 25
5:22 But the fruit of the Spirit is l, joy, peace, 26
Eph 1: 4 be holy and without blame before him in l: 26
1:15 in the Lord Jesus, and l unto all the saints, 26
2: 4 for his great l wherewith he loved us, 26
3:17 that ye, being rooted and grounded in l, 26
3:19 And to know the l of Christ, which passeth 26
4: 2 forbearing one another in l; 26
4:15 But speaking the truth in l, may grow *up* into 26
4:16 of the body unto the edifying of itself in l. 26
5: 2 And walk in l, as Christ also hath loved us, 26
5:25 Husbands, l your wives, even as Christ also 25
5:28 So ought men to l their wives as their own 25
5:33 you in particular so l his wife even as himself; 25
6:23 and l with faith, from God the Father and 26
6:24 Grace *be* with all them that l our Lord Jesus 25
Php 1: 9 that your l may abound yet more and more in 26
1:17 But the other of l, knowing that I am set for 26
2: 1 any consolation in Christ, if any comfort of l, 26
2: 2 having the same l, *being* of one accord, of one 26
Col 1: 4 and of the l which *ye have* to all the saints, 26
1: 8 Who also declared unto us your l in the Spirit. 26
2: 2 being knit together in l, and unto all riches of 26
3:19 l *your* wives, and be not bitter against them. 25
1Th 1: 3 and labour of l, and patience of hope in our 26
3:12 and abound in l one towards another, 26
4: 9 But as touching **brotherly** l ye need not 5360
4: 9 for ye yourselves are taught of God to l one 25
5: 8 putting on the breastplate of faith and l; 26
5:13 And to esteem them very highly in l for their 26
2Th 2:10 because they received not the l of the truth, 26
3: 5 And the Lord direct your hearts into the l of 26
1Ti 1:14 with faith and l which is in Christ Jesus. 26
6:10 For the **l of money** is the root of all evil: 5365
6:11 godliness, faith, l, patience, meekness. 26
2Ti 1: 7 but of power, and of l, and of a sound mind. 26
1:13 of me, in faith and l which is in Christ Jesus. 26
4: 8 but unto all them also that l his appearing. 25
Tit 2: 4 l their **husbands**, to love their 1510+5362
2: 4 to love their husbands, to l their **children**, 5388
3: 4 l of God our Saviour **toward man** 5363
3:15 Greet them that l us in the faith. Grace *be* 5368
Phm 1: 5 Hearing of thy l and faith, which thou hast 26
1: 7 we have great joy and consolation in thy l, 26
Heb 6:10 to forget your work and labour of l, 26
10:24 let us consider one another to provoke unto l 26
13: 1 Let **brotherly** l continue. 5360
Jas 1:12 which the Lord hath promised to them that l 25
2: 5 which he hath promised to them that l him? 25
2: 8 Thou shalt l thy neighbour as thyself, ye do 25
1Pe 1: 8 Whom having not seen, ye l; in whom, 25
1:22 the Spirit unto unfeigned **l of the brethren**, 5360
1:22 *see that ye* l one another with a pure heart 25
2:17 Honour all *men.* L the brotherhood. Fear God. 25
3: 8 **l as brethren**, *be* pitiful, *be* courteous: 5361
3:10 For he that will l life, and see good days, 25
1Jn 2: 5 in him verily is the l of God perfected: 26
2:15 L not the world, neither the *things* that are in 25
2:15 If any *man* l the world, the love of the Father 25
2:15 the world, the l of the Father is not in him. 26
3: 1 what manner of l the Father hath bestowed 26
3:11 the beginning, that we should l one another. 25
3:14 death unto life, because we l the brethren. 25
3:16 Hereby perceive we the l *of God,* because 26
3:17 from him, how dwelleth the l of God in him? 26
3:18 let us not l in word, neither in tongue; 25
3:23 and l one another, as he gave us 25
4: 7 Beloved, let us l one another: for love is of 25
4: 7 for l is of God; and every one that loveth is 26
4: 8 that loveth not, knoweth not God; for God is l. 26
4: 9 In this was manifested the l of God towards 26
4:10 Herein is l, not that we loved God, but that he 26
4:11 so loved us, we ought also to l one another. 25
4:12 If we l one another, God dwelleth in us, and 25
4:12 dwelleth in us, and his l is perfected in us. 26
4:16 and believed the l that God hath to us. 26
4:16 God is l; and he that dwelleth in love dwelleth 26
4:16 and he that dwelleth in l dwelleth in God, and 26
4:17 Herein is our l made perfect, that we may 26
4:18 There is no fear in l; but perfect love casteth 26
4:18 no fear in love; but perfect l casteth out fear: 26
4:18 He that feareth is not made perfect in l. 26
4:19 We l him, because he first loved us. 25
4:20 I l God, and hateth his brother, he is a liar: 25
4:20 how can he l God whom he hath not seen? 25
4:21 That he who loveth God l his brother also. 25
5: 2 By this we know that we l the children of 25
5: 2 when we l God, and keep his commandments. 25
5: 3 For this is the l of God, that we keep his 26
2Jn 1: 1 and her children, whom I l in the truth; 25
1: 3 the Son of the Father, in truth and l. 26
1: 5 had from the beginning, that we l one another. 25
1: 6 And this is l, that we walk after his 26
3Jn 1: 1 the wellbeloved Gaius, whom I l in the truth. 25
Jude 1: 2 unto you, and peace, and l, be multiplied. 26
1:21 Keep yourselves in the l of God, looking for 26
Rev 2: 4 against thee, because thou hast left thy first l. 26
3:19 As many as I l, I rebuke and chasten: 5368

LOVE'S (1) [LOVE]

Phm 1: 9 *Yet* for l sake I rather beseech *thee,* being 26

LOVED (98) [LOVE]

Ge 24:67 and she became his wife; and he l her: 157
25:28 Isaac l Esau, because he did eat of *his* 157
25:28 did eat of *his* venison: but Rebekah l Jacob. 157
27:14 made savoury meat, such as his father l. 157
29:18 Jacob l Rachel; and said, I will serve thee 157
29:30 he l also Rachel more than Leah, and 157
34: 3 he l the damsel, and spake kindly unto 157
37: 3 Now Israel l Joseph more than all his 157
37: 4 when his brethren saw that their father l him 157
Dt 4:37 because he l thy fathers, therefore he chose 157
7: 8 because the LORD l you, and because 160
23: 5 because the LORD thy God l thee. 157
33: 3 Yea, he l the people; all his saints *are* in thy 2245
Jdg 16: 4 that he l a woman in the valley of Sorek, 157
1Sa 1: 5 he gave a worthy portion; for he l Hannah: 157
16:21 he l him greatly; and he became his 157
18: 1 and Jonathan l him as his own soul. 157
18: 3 because he l him as his own soul. 160
18:16 all Israel and Judah l David, because he went 157
18:20 Michal Saul's daughter l David: and 157
18:28 and *that* Michal Saul's daughter l him. 157
20:17 David to swear again, because he l him: 160
20:17 for he l him as he loved his own soul. 157
20:17 for he loved him as he l his own soul. 160
2Sa 12:24 his name Solomon: and the LORD l him. 157
13: 1 and Amnon the son of David l her. 157
13:15 greater than the love wherewith he had l her. 157
1Ki 3: 3 Solomon l the LORD, walking in 157
10: 9 because the LORD l Israel for ever, 160
11: 1 king Solomon l many strange women, 157
2Ch 2:11 Because the LORD hath l his people, 160
9: 8 because thy God l Israel, to establish them 160
11:21 Rehoboam l Maachah the daughter of 157
26:10 and in Carmel: for he l husbandry. 157
Est 2:17 the king l Esther above all the women, and 157
Job 19:19 and they whom I l are turned against me 157
Ps 26: 8 I have l the habitation of thy house, and 157
47: 4 for us, the excellency of Jacob whom he l. 157
78:68 tribe of Judah, the mount Zion which he l. 157
109:17 As he l cursing, so let it come *unto* him: as 157
119:47 in thy commandments, which I have l. 157
119:48 up unto thy commandments, which I have l; 157
Isa 43: 4 thou hast been honourable, and I have l thee: 157
48:14 these *things?* The LORD hath l him: 157
Jer 2:25 for I have l strangers, and after them will I 157
8: 2 whom they have l, and whom they have 157
14:10 Thus have they l to wander, they have not 157
31: 3 I have l thee *with* an everlasting love; 157
Eze 16:37 all *them* that thou hast l, with all *them* that 157
Hos 9: 1 thou hast l a reward upon every cornfloor. 157
9:10 *their* abominations were according as they l. 157
11: 1 then I l him, and called my son out of Egypt. 157
Mal 1: 2 I have l you, saith the LORD. Yet ye say, 157
1: 2 Yet ye say, Wherein hast thou l us? *was* not 157
1: 2 saith the LORD: yet I l Jacob, 157
2:11 the holiness of the LORD which he l, 157
Mk 10:21 Then Jesus beholding him l him, and 25
Lk 7:47 which are many, are forgiven; for she l much: 25
Jn 3:16 For God so l the world, that he gave his only 25
3:19 and men l darkness rather than light, because 25
11: 5 Now Jesus l Martha, and her sister, and 25
11:36 Then said the Jews, Behold, how he l him. 5368
12:43 For they l the praise of men more than 25
13: 1 having l his own which were in the world, 25
13: 1 were in the world, he l them unto the end. 25
13:23 bosom one of his disciples, whom Jesus l. 25
13:34 as I have l you, that ye also love one another. 25
14:21 and he that loveth me shall be l of my Father, 25
14:28 If ye l me, ye would rejoice, because I said, 25
15: 9 As the Father hath l me, so have I loved you: 25
15: 9 As the Father hath loved me, so have I l you: 25
15:12 That ye love one another, as I have l you. 25
16:27 because ye have l me, and have believed 5368
17:23 and hast l them, as thou hast loved me. 25
17:23 and hast loved them, as thou hast l me. 25
17:26 where*with* thou hast l me may be in them, 25
19:26 and the disciple standing by, whom he l, 25
20: 2 whom Jesus l, and saith unto them, 5368
21: 7 Therefore that disciple whom Jesus l saith 25
21:20 seeth the disciple whom Jesus l following; 25
Ro 8:37 more than conquerors through him that l us. 25
9:13 As it is written, Jacob have I l, 25
2Co 12:15 the more abundantly I love you, the less I be l. 25
Gal 2:20 of God, who l me, and gave himself for me. 25
Eph 2: 4 in mercy, for his great love wherewith he l us, 25
5: 2 as Christ also hath l us, and hath given 25
5:25 even as Christ also l the church, and 25
2Th 2:16 which hath l us, and hath given *us* everlasting 25
2Ti 4:10 having l *this* present world, and is departed 25
Heb 1: 9 Thou hast l righteousness, and hated iniquity; 25
2Pe 2:15 of Bosor, who l the wages of unrighteousness; 25
1Jn 4:10 not that we l God, but that he loved us, and 25
4:10 but that he l us, and sent his Son *to be* 25
4:11 Beloved, if God so l us, we ought also to love 25
4:19 We love him, because he first l us. 25
Rev 1: 5 Unto him that l us, and washed us from our 25
3: 9 before thy feet, and to know that I have l thee. 25
12:11 and they l not their lives unto the death. 25

LOVEDST (2) [LOVE]

Isa 57: 8 thou l their bed where thou sawest *it.* 157
Jn 17:24 for thou l me before the foundation of 25

LOVELY (4) [LOVE]

2Sa 1:23 Saul and Jonathan *were* l and pleasant in 157
SS 5:16 yea, he *is* altogether l. This *is* my beloved, 4261
Eze 33:32 thou *art* unto them as a **very** l song *of* one 5690
Php 4: 8 *things are* pure, whatsoever *things are* l, 4375

LOVER (4) [LOVE]

1Ki 5: 1 his father: for Hiram was ever a l of David. 157
Ps 88:18 L and friend hast thou put far from me, *and* 157
Tit 1: 8 But a **l of hospitality**, a lover of good *men,* 5382
1: 8 a **l of good** *men,* sober, just, holy, 5358

LOVERS (23) [LOVE]

Ps 38:11 My l and my friends stand aloof from my 157
Jer 3: 1 thou hast played the harlot with many l; 7453
4:30 *thy* l will despise thee, they will seek thy 5689
22:20 from the passages: for all thy l are destroyed. 157
22:22 thy pastors, and thy l shall go into captivity: 157
30:14 All thy l have forgotten thee; they seek thee 157
La 1: 2 among all her l she hath none to comfort *her:* 157
1:19 I called for my l, *but* they deceived me: 157
Eze 16:33 thou givest thy gifts to all thy l, and 157
16:36 through thy whoredoms with thy l, 157
16:37 Behold therefore, I will gather all thy l, 157
23: 5 she doted on her l, on the Assyrians *her* 157
23: 9 I have delivered her into the hand of her l, 157
23:22 Behold, I will raise up thy l against thee, 157
Hos 2: 5 for she said, I will go after my l, that give *me* 157
2: 7 she shall follow after her l, but she shall not 157
2:10 I discover her lewdness in the sight of her l, 157
2:12 These *are* my rewards that my l have given 157
2:13 and she went after her l, and forgat me, 157
8: 9 ass alone by himself: Ephraim hath hired l. 158
2Ti 3: 2 For men shall be **l of** their **own selves**, 5367
3: 4 **l of pleasures** more than lovers of God; 5369
3: 4 lovers of pleasures more than **l of God**; 5377

LOVES (3) [LOVE]

Ps 45: T the sons of Korah, Maschil, A Song of l. 3039
Pr 7:18 the morning: let us solace ourselves with l. 159
SS 7:12 bud forth: there will I give thee my l. 1730

LOVEST (12) [LOVE]

Ge 22: 2 whom thou l, and get thee into the land of 157
Jdg 14:16 said, Thou dost but hate me, and l me not: 157
2Sa 19: 6 In that thou l thine enemies, and hatest thy 157
Ps 45: 7 Thou l righteousness, and hatest wickedness: 157
52: 3 Thou l evil more than good; *and* lying rather 157
52: 4 Thou l all devouring words, O thou deceitful 157
Ecc 9: 9 Live joyfully with the wife whom thou l all 157
Jn 11: 3 Lord, behold, he whom thou l is sick. 5368
21:15 *son* of Jonas, l thou me more than these? 25
21:16 second time, Simon, *son* of Jonas, l thou me? 25
21:17 third time, Simon, *son* of Jonas, l thou me? 5368
21:17 he said unto him the third time, L thou me? 5368

LOVETH (65) [LOVE]

Ge 27: 9 savoury meat for thy father, such as he l: 157
44:20 is left of his mother, and his father l him. 157
Dt 10:18 the fatherless and widow, and l the stranger, 157
15:16 because he l thee and thine house, because 157
Ru 4:15 for thy daughter in law, which l thee, 157
Ps 11: 5 and him that l violence his soul hateth. 157
11: 7 For the righteous LORD l righteousness; 157
33: 5 He l righteousness and judgment: the earth is 157
34:12 *and* l *many* days, that *he* may see good? 157
37:28 For the LORD l judgment, and 157
87: 2 The LORD l the gates of Zion more than all 157
99: 4 The king's strength also l judgment; 157
119:140 word *is* very pure: therefore thy servant l it. 157
146: 8 are bowed down: the LORD l the righteous: 157
Pr 3:12 For whom the LORD l he correcteth; 157
12: 1 Whoso l instruction loveth knowledge: but 157
12: 1 Whoso loveth instruction l knowledge: but 157
13:24 but he that l him chasteneth him betimes. 157
15: 9 he l him that followeth after righteousness. 157
15:12 A scorner l not one that reproveth him: 157
17:17 A friend l at all times, and a brother is born 157
17:19 He l transgression that loveth strife: *and* 157
17:19 He loveth transgression that l strife: *and* 157
19: 8 He that getteth wisdom l his own soul: 157
21:17 He that l pleasure *shall be* a poor man: 157
21:17 he that l wine and oil shall not be rich. 157
22:11 He that l pureness of heart, *for* the grace of 157
29: 3 Whoso l wisdom rejoiceth his father: but 157
Ecc 5:10 He that l silver shall not be satisfied *with* 157
5:10 nor he that l abundance *with* increase: 157
SS 1: 7 Tell me, O thou whom my soul l, where thou 157
3: 1 on my bed I sought *him* whom my soul l: 157
3: 2 broad ways, I will seek *him* whom my soul l: 157
3: 3 *whom I said,* Saw ye *him* whom my soul l? 157
3: 4 from them, but I found *him* whom my soul l: 157
Isa 1:23 every one l gifts, and followeth after 157
Hos 10:11 *and* l to tread out *the corn;* but I passed over 157
12: 7 of deceit *are* in his hand: he l to oppress. 157
Mt 10:37 He that l father or mother more than me is 5368
10:37 and he that l son or daughter more than me 5368
Lk 7: 5 For he l our nation, and he hath built us a 25
7:47 but to whom little is forgiven, *the same* l little. 25
Jn 3:35 The Father l the Son, and hath given all *things* 25
5:20 For the Father l the Son, and sheweth him 5368
12:25 He that l his life shall lose it; and he that 5368
14:21 and keepeth them, he it is that l me: 25
14:21 and he that l me shall be loved of my Father, 25
14:24 He that l me not keepeth not my sayings: and 25
16:27 For the Father himself l you, because 5368
Ro 13: 8 for he that l another hath fulfilled the law. 25
2Co 9: 7 or of necessity: for God l a cheerful giver. 25
Eph 5:28 own bodies. He that l his wife loveth himself. 25
5:28 own bodies. He that loveth his wife l himself. 25
Heb 12: 6 For whom the Lord l he chasteneth, and 25
1Jn 2:10 He that l his brother abideth in the light, and 25
3:10 is not of God, neither he that l not his brother. 25
3:14 He that l not *his* brother abideth in death. 25
4: 7 and every one that l is born of God, and 25
4: 8 He that l not, knoweth not God; for God is 25
4:20 for he that l not his brother whom he hath 25
4:21 That he who l God love his brother also. 25
5: 1 every one that l him that begat loveth him also 25
5: 1 every one that loveth him that begat l him also 25

3Jn 1: 9 who l **to have** the **preeminence among** *5383*
Rev 22:15 idolaters, and whosoever l and maketh a lie. *5368*

LOVING (3) [LOVE]
Pr 5:19 *Let her be as* the l hind and pleasant roe; 158
22: 1 *and* l favour rather than silver and gold. 2896
Isa 56:10 sleeping, lying down, l to slumber. 157

LOVINGKINDNESS (26) [KIND, LOVE]
Ps 17: 7 Shew thy marvellous l, O thou that savest 2617
26: 3 For thy l *is* before mine eyes: and I have 2617
36: 7 How excellent *is* thy l, O God! therefore 2617
36:10 O continue thy l unto them that know thee; 2617
40:10 I have not concealed thy l and thy truth 2617
40:11 let thy l and thy truth continually preserve 2617
42: 8 *Yet* the LORD will command his l in 2617
48: 9 We have thought of thy l, O God, in 2617
51: 1 mercy upon me, O God, according to thy l: 2617
63: 3 Because thy l *is* better than life, my lips 2617
69:16 Hear me, O LORD; for thy l *is* good: 2617
88:11 Shall thy l be declared in the grave? *or* 2617
89:33 Nevertheless my l will I not utterly take 2617
92: 2 To shew forth thy l in the morning, and 2617
103: 4 who crowneth thee *with* l and 2617
107:43 they shall understand the l of the LORD. 2617
119:88 Quicken me after thy l; so shall I keep 2617
119:149 Hear my voice according unto thy l: 2617
119:159 quicken me, O LORD, according to thy l. 2617
138: 2 praise thy name for thy l and for thy truth: 2617
143: 8 Cause me to hear thy l in the morning; 2617
Jer 9:24 that I *am* the LORD which exercise l, 2617
16: 5 saith the LORD, *even* l and mercies. 2617
31: 3 therefore *with* l have I drawn thee. 2617
32:18 Thou shewest l unto thousands, and 2617
Hos 2:19 and in judgment, and in l, and in mercies. 2617

LOVINGKINDNESSES (4) [KIND, LOVE]
Ps 25: 6 O LORD, thy tender mercies and thy l; 2617
89:49 Lord, where *are* thy former l, *which* thou 2617
Isa 63: 7 I will mention the l of the LORD, *and* 2617
63: 7 and according to the multitude of his l. 2617

LOW (46) [LOWER, LOWEST, LOWLINESS, LOWLY]
Dt 28:43 thou shalt come down **very** l. 4295+4295
Jdg 11:35 thou hast **brought** me **very** l, 3766+3766
1Sa 2: 7 maketh rich: he **bringeth** l, and lifteth up. 8213
1Ch 27:28 the sycomore trees that *were* in the l **plains** 8219
2Ch 9:27 trees that *are* in the l **plains** in abundance. 8219
26:10 both in the l **country**, and in the plains: 8219
28:18 also had invaded the cities of the l **country**, 8219
28:19 For the LORD **brought** Judah l because 3665
Job 5:11 To set up on high those that be l; that those 8217
14:21 they are **brought** l, but he perceiveth *it* not 6819
24:24 a little while, but are gone and **brought** l, 4355
40:12 on every one *that is* proud, *and* **bring** him l; 3665
Ps 49: 2 Both l[S] and high, rich and poor, 120+1121
62: 9 Surely **men of** l **degree** *are* vanity, 120+1121
79: 8 prevent us: for we are **brought** very l. 1809
106:43 and were **brought** l for their iniquity. 4355
107:39 and **brought** l through oppression, 7817
116: 6 I was **brought** l, and he helped me. 1809
136:23 Who remembered us in our l **estate**: for his 8216
142: 6 unto my cry; for I am **brought** very l: 1809
Pr 29:23 A man's pride shall **bring** him l: but 8213
Ecc 10: 6 in great dignity, and the rich sit in l **place**. 8216
12: 4 when the sound of the grinding is l, and 8217
12: 4 the daughters of musick shall be **brought** l; 7817
Isa 2:12 that is lifted up; and he shall be **brought** l: 8213
2:17 the haughtiness of men shall be **made** l: 8213
13:11 will **lay** l the haughtiness of the terrible. 8213
25: 5 of the terrible ones shall be **brought** l. 6030
25:12 **lay** l, *and* bring to the ground, *even* to 8213
26: 5 the lofty city, he **layeth** it l; he layeth it 8213
26: 5 it low; he **layeth** it l, *even* to the ground; 8213
29: 4 thy speech shall be l out of the dust, and 7817
32:19 and the city shall be l in a low place. 8213
32:19 and the city shall be low in a l **place**. 8218
40: 4 every mountain and hill shall be **made** l: 8213
La 3:55 thy name, O LORD, out of the l dungeon. 8482
Eze 17: 6 and became a spreading vine of l stature, 8217
17:24 have exalted the l tree, have dried up 8217
21:26 exalt *him that is* l, and abase *him that is* 8217
26:20 shall set thee **in** the l **parts** of the earth, 8482
Lk 1:48 For he hath regarded the l **estate** of his *5014*
1:52 *their* seats, and exalted them of l **degree**. *5011*
3: 5 every mountain and hill shall be **brought** l; *5013*
Ro 12:16 *things*, but condescend to *men* **of** l **estate**. *5011*
Jas 1: 9 Let the brother of l **degree** rejoice in that he *5011*
1:10 But the rich, in that he is **made** l: because *5014*

LOWBORN See DEGREE; DEGREES

LOWER (18) [LOW]
Ge 6:16 *with* l, second, and third *stories* shalt thou 8482
Lev 13:20 it *be* in sight l than the skin, and the hair 8217
13:21 *if* it *be* not l than the skin, but *be* somewhat 8217
13:26 it *be* no l than the *other* skin, but *be* 8217
14:37 reddish, which in sight *are* l than the wall; 8217
Ne 4:13 Therefore set I in the l places behind 8482
Ps 8: 5 For thou hast **made** him a little l than 2637
63: 9 to destroy *it*, shall go into the l **parts** of 8482
Pr 25: 7 than that thou shouldest be **put** l in 8213
Isa 22: 9 ye gathered together the waters of the l 8481
44:23 hath done *it*: shout, ye l **parts** of the earth: 8482
Eze 40:18 the length of the gates *was* the l pavement. 8481
40:19 l gate unto the forefront of the inner court 8481
42: 5 than the l, and than the middlemost of 8481
43:14 *even* to the l settle *shall be* two cubits, 8481
Eph 4: 9 that he also descended first into the l parts *2737*
Heb 2: 7 Thou **madest** him a little l than the angels; *1642*
2: 9 who was **made** a little l than the angels, *1642*

LOWEST (11) [LOW]
Dt 32:22 shall burn unto the l hell, and 8482
1Ki 12:31 made priests of the l of the people, 7098
13:33 made again of the l of the people priests of 7098
2Ki 17:32 made unto themselves of the l of them 7098
Ps 86:13 thou hast delivered my soul from the l hell. 8482
88: 6 Thou hast laid me in the l pit, in darkness, 8482
139:15 curiously wrought in the l **parts** of 8482
Eze 41: 7 increased *from* the l *chamber* to the highest 8481
42: 6 *the building* was straitened more than the l 8481
Lk 14: 9 thou begin with shame to take the l room. *2078*
14:10 art bidden, go and sit down in the l room; *2078*

LOWETH (1) [LOWING]
Job 6: 5 he hath grass? or l the ox over his fodder? 1600

LOWING (2) [LOWETH]
1Sa 6:12 l as they went, and turned not aside *to* 1600
15:14 and the l of the oxen which I hear? 6963

LOWLINESS (2) [LOW]
Eph 4: 2 With all l and meekness, with *5012*
Php 2: 3 in l **of mind** *let* each esteem other better *5012*

LOWLY (6) [LOW]
Ps 138: 6 *be* high, yet hath he respect unto the l: 8217
Pr 3:34 the scorners: but he giveth grace unto the l. 6035
11: 2 cometh shame: but with the l *is* wisdom. 6800
16:19 *it is to be* of an humble spirit with the l, 6035
Zec 9: 9 l, and riding upon an ass, and upon a colt 6041
Mt 11:29 learn of me; for I am meek and l in heart: *5011*

LOWRING (1)
Mt 16: 3 for the sky is red and l. O *ye* hypocrites, *4768*

LUBIM (1) [LUBIMS]
Na 3: 9 *it was* infinite; Put and L were thy helpers. 3864

LUBIMS (2) [LUBIM]
2Ch 12: 3 the L, the Sukkiims, and the Ethiopians. 3864
16: 8 not the Ethiopians and the L a huge host, 3864

LUCAS (2)
2Co 13: S *a city* of Macedonia, by Titus and L. *3065*
Phm 1:24 Marcus, Aristarchus, Demas, L, *3065*

LUCIFER (1)
Isa 14:12 from heaven, O L, son of the morning! 1966

LUCIUS (2)
Ac 13: 1 and L of Cyrene, and Manaen, *3066*
Ro 16:21 and L, and Jason, and Sosipater, *3066*

LUCRE (5) [LUCRE'S]
1Sa 8: 3 turned aside after l, and took bribes, and 1215
1Ti 3: 3 to wine, no striker, not **greedy of filthy** l; *146*
3: 8 given to much wine, not **greedy of filthy** l; *146*
Tit 1: 7 to wine, no striker, not **given to filthy** l; *146*
1Pe 5: 2 not **for filthy** l, but of a ready mind; *147*

LUCRE'S (1) [LUCRE]
Tit 1:11 which *they* ought not, for filthy l sake. *2771*

LUD (4)
Ge 10:22 Asshur, and Arphaxad, and L, and Aram. 3865
1Ch 1:17 L, and Aram, and Uz, and Hul, and Gether, 3865
Isa 66:19 *to* Tarshish, Pul, and L, that draw the bow, 3865
Eze 27:10 They of Persia and of L and of Phut were 3865

LUDIM (2)
Ge 10:13 Mizraim begat L, and Anamim, and 3865
1Ch 1:11 Mizraim begat L, and Anamim, and 3865

LUDITES See LUDIM

LUHITH (2)
Isa 15: 5 for *by* the mounting up of L with weeping 3872
Jer 48: 5 For *in* the going up of L continual weeping 3872

LUKE (2)
Col 4:14 L, the beloved physician, and Demas, *3065*
2Ti 4:11 Only L is with me. Take Mark, and *3065*

LUKEWARM (1) [WARM]
Rev 3:16 So *then* because thou art l, and neither cold *5513*

LUMP (7)
2Ki 20: 7 Isaiah said, Take a l of figs. And they took 1690
Isa 38:21 Let them take a l of figs, and lay *it* for a 1690
Ro 9:21 of the same l to make one vessel unto *5445*
11:16 the l *is* also *holy*: and if the root *be* holy, so *5445*
1Co 5: 6 that a little leaven leaveneth the whole l? *5445*
5: 7 the old leaven, that ye may be a new l, *5445*
Gal 5: 9 A little leaven leaveneth the whole l. *5445*

LUNATICK (2)
Mt 4:24 and those which were l, and those that had *4583*
17:15 for he is l, and sore vexed: for ofttimes he *4583*

LURK (2) [LURKING]
Pr 1:11 let us l **privily** for the innocent without 6845
1:18 they l **privily** for their own lives. 6845

LURKING (3) [LURK]
1Sa 23:23 take knowledge of all the l **places** where he 4224
Ps 10: 8 He sitteth in the l **places** of the villages: 3993
17:12 as it were a young lion l in secret places. 3427

LUST (19) [LUSTED, LUSTETH, LUSTING, LUSTS, LUSTY]
Ex 15: 9 the spoil; my l shall be satisfied upon them; 5315
Ps 78:18 in their heart by asking meat for their l. 5315
78:30 They were not estranged from their l. 8378
81:12 So I gave them up unto their own heart's l: 8307
Pr 6:25 L not **after** her beauty in thine heart; 2530
Mt 5:28 l **after** her hath committed adultery with *1937*
Ro 1:27 burned in their l one towards another; *3715*
7: 7 for I had not known l, except the law had *1939*
1Co 10: 6 to the intent we should not l **after** evil *1938*
Gal 5:16 and ye shall not fulfil the l of the flesh. *1939*
1Th 4: 5 Not in the l of concupiscence, even as *3806*
Jas 1:14 when he is drawn away of his own l, and *1939*
1:15 Then when l hath conceived, it bringeth *1939*
4: 2 Ye l, and have not: ye kill, and desire *to* *1937*
2Pe 1: 4 the corruption that is in the world through l: *1939*
2:10 walk after the flesh in the l of uncleanness, *1939*
1Jn 2:16 the l of the flesh, and the lust of the eyes, *1939*
2:16 and the l of the eyes, and the pride of life, *1939*
2:17 the world passeth away, and the l thereof: *1939*

LUSTED (4) [LUST]
Nu 11:34 because there they buried the people that l. 183
Ps 106:14 l **exceedingly** in the wilderness, and 183+8378
1Co 10: 6 not lust after evil *things*, as they also l. *1937*
Rev 18:14 And the fruits that thy soul l **after** are *1939*

LUSTETH (6) [LUST]
Dt 12:15 in all thy gates, whatsoever thy soul l **after**, 185
12:20 mayest eat flesh, whatsoever thy soul l **after**. 185
12:21 eat in thy gates whatsoever thy soul l **after**. 185
14:26 *that* money for whatsoever thy soul l **after**, 183
Gal 5:17 For the flesh l against the Spirit, and *1937*
Jas 4: 5 the spirit that dwelleth in us l to envy? *1971*

LUSTING (1) [LUST]
Nu 11: 4 that *was* among them **fell a** l: 183+8378

LUSTS (24) [LUST]
Mk 4:19 and the l of other *things* entering in, *1939*
Jn 8:44 and the l of your father ye will do. *1939*
Ro 1:24 through the l of their own hearts, *1939*
6:12 that *ye* should obey it in the l thereof. *1939*
13:14 for the flesh, to *fulfil* the l *thereof*. *1939*
Gal 5:24 crucified the flesh with the affections and l. *1939*
Eph 2: 3 in times past in the l of our flesh, *1939*
4:22 is corrupt according to the deceitful l; *1939*
1Ti 6: 9 a snare, and *into* many foolish and hurtful l, *1939*
2Ti 2:22 Flee also youthful l: but *1939*
3: 6 laden with sins, led away with divers l, *1939*
4: 3 after their own l shall they heap to *1939*
Tit 2:12 and worldly l we should live soberly, *1939*
3: 3 deceived, serving divers l and pleasures, *1939*
Jas 4: 1 *even* of your l that war in your members? *2237*
4: 3 that ye may consume *it* upon your l. *2237*
1Pe 1:14 according to the former l in your ignorance: *1939*
2:11 and pilgrims, abstain from fleshly l, *1939*
4: 2 rest of *his* time in the flesh to the l of men, *1939*
4: 3 l, excess of wine, revellings, banquetings, *1939*
2Pe 2:18 they allure through the l of the flesh, *1939*
3: 3 last days scoffers, walking after their own l, *1939*
Jude 1:16 complainers, walking after their own l; *1939*
1:18 who should walk after their own ungodly l. *1939*

LUSTY (1) [LUST]
Jdg 3:29 thousand men, all l, and all men of valour; 8082

LUXURY See SUMPTUOUSLY

LUZ (8)
Ge 28:19 the name of *that* city *was called* L at 3870
35: 6 So Jacob came to L, which *is* in the land of 3870
48: 3 God Almighty appeared unto me at L in 3870
Jos 16: 2 goeth out from Beth-el to L, and 3870
18:13 the border went over from thence toward L, 3870
18:13 to the side of L, which *is* Beth-el, 3870
Jdg 1:23 (Now the name of the city before *was* L.) 3870
1:26 built a city, and called the name thereof L: 3870

LYCAONIA (2)
Ac 14: 6 cities of L, and *unto* the region that lieth *3071*
14:11 up their voices, saying **in the speech of** L, *3072*

LYCIA (1)
Ac 27: 5 Pamphylia, we came to Myra, *a city* of L. *3073*

LYDDA (3)
Ac 9:32 down also to the saints which dwelt at L. *3069*
9:35 And all that dwelt at L and Saron saw him, *3069*
9:38 And forasmuch as L was nigh to Joppa, and *3069*

LYDIA (3) [LYDIANS]
Eze 30: 5 L, and all the mingled people, and Chub, 3865
Ac 16:14 And a certain woman named L, a seller of *3070*
16:40 the prison, and entered into *the house of* L: *3070*

LYDIANS (1) [LYDIA]
Jer 46: 9 and the L, that handle *and* bend the bow. 3865

LYING (57) [LIE]
Ge 29: 2 lo, there *were* three flocks of sheep l by it; 7257
34: 7 he had wrought folly in Israel in l with 7901
Ex 23: 5 If thou see the ass of him that hateth thee l 7257
Nu 31:17 woman that hath known man by l **with** him. 4904
31:18 that have not known a man by l **with** him, 4904
31:35 that had not known man by l **with** him. 4904
Dt 21: 1 l in the field, *and* it be not known who hath 5307
22:22 If a man be found l with a woman married 7901
Jdg 9:35 people that *were* with him, from l **in wait**. 3993
16: 9 Now *there were* men l **in wait**, abiding with 693
21:12 that had known no man by l **with** *any* male: 4904
1Ki 22:22 I will be a l spirit in the mouth of all his 8267
22:23 the LORD hath put a l spirit in the mouth 8267
2Ch 18:21 be a l spirit in the mouth of all his prophets. 8267
18:22 the LORD hath put a l spirit in the mouth 8267
Ps 31: 6 I have hated them that regard l vanities: but 7723
31:18 Let the l lips be put to silence; which speak 8267
52: 3 *and* l rather than to speak righteousness. 8267

Ps 59:12 and for cursing and l which they speak. 3585
109: 2 they have spoken against me with a l 8267
119:29 Remove from me the way of l: and 8267
119:163 I hate and abhor l: but thy law do I love. 8267
120: 2 from l lips, and from a deceitful tongue. 8267
139: 3 Thou compassest my path and my l down, 7252
Pr 6:17 a l tongue, and hands that shed innocent 8267
10:18 He that hideth hatred with l lips, and he that 8267
12:19 for ever: but a l tongue is but for a moment. 8267
12:22 L lips are abomination to the LORD: but 8267
13: 5 A righteous man hateth l: but 1697+8267
17: 7 not a fool: much less do l lips a prince. 8267
21: 6 The getting of treasures by a l tongue is a 8267
26:28 A l tongue hateth those that are afflicted by 8267
Isa 30: 9 That this is a rebellious people, l children, 3586
32: 7 devices to destroy the poor with l words, 8267
56:10 sleeping, l down, loving to slumber. 7901
59:13 In transgressing and l against the LORD, 3584
Jer 7: 4 Trust ye not in l words, saying, The temple 8267
7: 8 Behold, ye trust in l words, that cannot 8267
29:23 have spoken l words in my name, which I 8267
La 3:10 He was unto me as a bear l in wait, and as a 693
Eze 13: 6 They have seen vanity and l divination, 3577
13: 7 have ye not spoken a l divination, 3577
13:19 by your l to my people that hear your lies? 3576
Da 2: 9 for ye have prepared l and corrupt words to 3538
Hos 4: 2 l, and killing, and stealing, and 3584
Jnh 2: 8 They that observe l vanities forsake their 7723
Mt 9: 2 to him a man sick of the palsy, l on a bed: 906
Mk 5:40 and entereth in where the damsel was l. 345
Lk 2:12 in swaddling clothes, l in a manger. 2749
2:16 and Joseph, and the babe l in a manger. 2749
Jn 13:25 He then l on Jesus' breast saith unto him, 1968
20: 5 and looking in, saw the linen clothes l; 2749
20: 7 not l with the linen clothes, but 2749
Ac 20:19 which befell me by the l in wait of 1917
23:16 Paul's sister's son heard of their l in wait, 1747
Eph 4:25 Wherefore putting away l, speak every man 5579
2Th 2: 9 with all power and signs and l wonders, 5579

LYRE See SACKBUT

LYSANIAS (1)
Lk 3: 1 and L the tetrarch of Abilene, 3078

LYSIAS (3)
Ac 23:26 Claudius L unto the most excellent 3079
24: 7 But the chief captain L came upon us, and 3079
24:22 When L the chief captain shall come down, 3079

LYSTRA (6)
Ac 14: 6 were ware of it, and fled unto L and Derbe, 3082
14: 8 And there sat a certain man at L, 3082
14:21 they returned again to L, and to Iconium, 3082
16: 1 Then came he to Derbe and L: and behold, 3082
16: 2 reported of by the brethren that were at L 3082
2Ti 3:11 came unto me at Antioch, at Iconium, at L; 3082

M

MAACAH (3) [MAACHAH]
2Sa 3: 3 Absalom the son of M the daughter of 4601
10: 6 of king M a thousand men, and of Ish-tob 4601
10: 8 of Zoba, and of Rehob, and Ish-tob, and M, 4601

MAACATHITE; MAACATHITES See MAACHATHI; MAACHATHITE; MAACHATHITES

MAACHAH (18) [MAACAH, MAACHATHI, MAACHATHITE, MAACHATHITES]
Ge 22:24 and Gaham, and Thahash, and M. 4601
1Ki 2:39 away unto Achish son of M king of Gath. 4601
15: 2 his mother's name was M, the daughter of 4601
15:10 his mother's name was M, the daughter of 4601
15:13 also M his mother, even her he removed 4601
1Ch 2:48 M, Caleb's concubine, bare Sheber, and 4601
3: 2 Absalom the son of M the daughter of 4601
7:15 and Shuppim, whose sister's name was M;) 4601
7:16 M the wife of Machir bare a son, and 4601
8:29 of Gibeon; whose wife's name was M: 4601
9:35 Jehiel, whose wife's name was M: 4601
11:43 Hanan the son of M, and Joshaphat 4601
19: 7 and the king of M and his people; 4601
27:16 the Simeonites, Shephatiah the son of M: 4601
2Ch 11:20 after her he took M the daughter of 4601
11:21 Rehoboam loved M the daughter of 4601
11:22 Rehoboam made Abijah the son of M 4601
15:16 also concerning M the mother of Asa 4601

MAACHATHI (1) [MAACHAH]
Dt 3:14 of Argob unto the coasts of Geshuri and M; 4602

MAACHATHITE (4) [MAACHAH]
2Sa 23:34 the son of Ahasbai, the son of the M, 4602
2Ki 25:23 Jaazaniah the son of a M, they and 4602
1Ch 4:19 Keilah the Garmite, and Eshtemoa the M. 4602
Jer 40: 8 Jezaniah the son of a M, they and 4602

MAACHATHITES (4) [MAACHAH]
Jos 12: 5 the border of the Geshurites and the M, 4602
13:11 the border of the Geshurites and M, and 4602
13:13 expelled not the Geshurites, nor the M: 4602
13:13 the M dwell among the Israelites until this 4601

MAADAI (1)
Ezr 10:34 Of the sons of Bani; M, Amram, and Uel, 4572

MAADIAH (1)
Ne 12: 5 Miamin, M, Bilgah, 4573

MAAI (1)
Ne 12:36 Shemaiah, and Azarael, Milalai, Gilalai, M, 4597

MAALEH-ACRABBIM (1)
Jos 15: 3 it went out to the south side to M, and 4610

MAARATH (1)
Jos 15:59 M, and Beth-anoth, and Eltekon; six cities 4638

MAASEIAH (25)
1Ch 15:18 M, and Mattithiah, and Elipheleh, and 4641
15:20 and Unni, and Eliab, and M, and Benaiah, 4641
2Ch 23: 1 M the son of Adaiah, and Elishaphat 4641
26:11 the hand of Jeiel the scribe and M the ruler, 4641
28: 7 slew M the king's son, and Azrikam 4641
34: 8 M the governor of the city, and Joah 4641
Ezr 10:18 M, and Eliezer, and Jarib, and Gedaliah. 4641
10:21 M, and Elijah, and Shemaiah, and Jehiel, 4641
10:22 Elioenai, M, Ishmael, Nethaneel, Jozabad, 4641
10:30 Adna, and Chelal, Benaiah, M, Mattaniah, 4641
Ne 3:23 After him repaired Azariah the son of M 4641
8: 4 Anaiah, and Urijah, and Hilkiah, and M, 4641
8: 7 M, Kelita, Azariah, Jozabad, Hanan, 4641
10:25 Rehum, Hashabnah, M, 4641
11: 5 M the son of Baruch, the son of Col-hozeh, 4641
11: 7 the son of M, the son of Ithiel, the son of 4641
12:41 Eliakim, M, Miniamin, Michaiah, Elioenai, 4641
12:42 M, and Shemaiah, and Eleazar, and Uzzi, 4641
Jer 21: 1 Zephaniah the son of M the priest, saying, 4641
29:21 of Kolaiah, and of Zedekiah, the son of M, 4641
29:25 to Zephaniah the son of M the priest, and 4641
32:12 the son of M, in the sight of Hanameel 4271
35: 4 which was above the chamber of M the son 4641
37: 3 Zephaniah the son of M the priest to 4641
51:59 Seraiah the son of Neriah, the son of M, 4271

MAASIAI (1)
1Ch 9:12 M the son of Adiel, the son of Jahzerah, 4640

MAATH (1)
Lk 3:26 Which was the son of M, which was 3092

MAAZ (1)
1Ch 2:27 Jerahmeel were, M, and Jamin, and Eker. 4619

MAAZIAH (2)
1Ch 24:18 to Delaiah, the four and twentieth to M. 4590
Ne 10: 8 M, Bilgai, Shemaiah: these were 4590

MACBANNAI See MACHBANAI

MACBENAH See MACHBENAH

MACEDONIA (28) [MACEDONIAN]
Ac 16: 9 There stood a man of M, and prayed him, 3110
16: 9 Come over into M, and help us. 3109
16:10 immediately we endeavoured to go into M, 3109
16:12 which is the chief city of that part of M, 3109
18: 5 and Timotheus were come from M, 3109
19:21 when he had passed through M and Achaia, 3109
19:22 So he sent into M two of them that 3109
19:29 caught Gaius and Aristarchus, men of M, 3110
20: 1 and departed for to go into M. 3109
20: 3 he purposed to return through M. 3109
Ro 15:26 For it hath pleased them of M and 3109
1Co 16: 5 unto you, when I shall pass through M: 3109
16: 5 for I do pass through M. 3109
2Co 1:16 And to pass by you into M, and to come 3109
1:16 and to come again out of M unto you, and 3109
2:13 leave of them, I went from thence into M. 3109
7: 5 For, when we were come into M, our flesh 3109
8: 1 of God bestowed on the churches of M; 3109
9: 2 for which I boast of you to them of M, 3110
9: 4 Lest haply if they of M come with me, and 3110
11: 9 the brethren which came from M supplied: 3109
13: S a city of M, by Titus and Lucas. 3109
Php 4:15 of the gospel, when I departed from M, 3109
1Th 1: 7 ye were ensamples to all that believe in M 3109
1: 8 out the word of the Lord not only in M 3109
4:10 towards all the brethren which are in all M: 3109
1Ti 1: 3 abide still at Ephesus, when I went into M, 3109
Tit 3: S of the Cretians, from Nicopolis of M. 3109

MACEDONIAN (1) [MACEDONIA]
Ac 27: 2 a M of Thessalonica, being with us. 3110

MACHBANAI (1)
1Ch 12:13 Jeremiah the tenth, M the eleventh. 4344

MACHBENAH (1)
1Ch 2:49 Sheva the father of M, and the father of 4343

MACHI (1)
Nu 13:15 Of the tribe of Gad, Geuel the son of M. 4352

MACHIR (22) [MACHIRITES]
Ge 50:23 M the son of Manasseh were brought up 4353
Nu 26:29 of M, the family of the Machirites: and 4353
26:29 M begat Gilead: of Gilead come the family 4353
27: 1 of Hepher, the son of Gilead, the son of M, 4353
32:39 the children of M the son of Manasseh 4353
32:40 Moses gave Gilead unto M the son of 4353
36: 1 the son of M, the son of Manasseh, of 4353
Dt 3:15 And I gave Gilead unto M. 4353
Jos 13:31 were pertaining unto the children of M 4353
13:31 even to the one half of the children of M by 4353
17: 1 to wit, for M the firstborn of Manasseh, 4353
17: 3 of Hepher, the son of Gilead, the son of M, 4353
Jdg 5:14 out of M came down governors, and out of 4353
2Sa 9: 4 Behold, he is in the house of M, the son of 4353
9: 5 fet him out of the house of M, the son of 4353
17:27 M the son of Ammiel of Lo-debar, and 4353
1Ch 2:21 to the daughter of M the father of Gilead, 4353
2:23 All these belonged to the sons of M 4353
7:14 his concubine the Aramitess bare M 4353
7:15 M took to wife the sister of Huppim and 4353
7:16 Maachah the wife of M bare a son, and 4353
7:17 the son of M, the son of Manasseh. 4353

MACHIRITES (1) [MACHIR]
Nu 26:29 of Machir, the family of the M: and 4354

MACHNADEBAI (1)
Ezr 10:40 M, Shashai, Sharai, 4367

MACHPELAH (6)
Ge 23: 9 That he may give me the cave of M, 4375
23:17 the field of Ephron, which was in M, 4375
23:19 in the cave of the field of M before Mamre: 4375
25: 9 and Ishmael buried him in the cave of M, 4375
49:30 In the cave that is in the field of M, 4375
50:13 buried him in the cave of the field of M, 4375

MACNADEBAI See MACHNADEBAI

MAD (22) [MADNESS]
Dt 28:34 So that thou shalt be m for the sight of 7696
1Sa 21:13 feigned himself m in their hands, and 1984
21:14 unto his servants, Lo, you see the man is m: 7696
21:15 Have I need of m men, that ye have 7696
21:15 fellow to play the m man in my presence? 7696
2Ki 9:11 wherefore came this m fellow to thee? 7696
Ps 102: 8 they that are m against me are sworn 1984
Pr 26:18 As a m man who casteth firebrands, 3856
Ecc 2: 2 I said of laughter, It is m: and of mirth, 1984
7: 7 Surely oppression maketh a wise man m; 1984
Isa 44:25 tokens of the liars, and maketh diviners m; 1984
Jer 25:16 be m, because of the sword that I will send 1984
29:26 for every man that is m, and 7696
50:38 and they are m upon their idols. 1984
51: 7 of her wine; therefore the nations are m. 1984
Hos 9: 7 the spiritual man is m, for the multitude of 7696
Jn 10:20 of them said, He hath a devil, and is m; 3105
Ac 12:15 And they said unto her, Thou art m. 3105
26:11 and being exceedingly m against them, 1693
26:24 learning doth make thee m. 1519+3130+4062
26:25 But he said, I am not m, most noble Festus; 3105
1Co 14:23 will they not say that ye are m? 3105

MADAI (2)
Ge 10: 2 M, and Javan, and Tubal, and Meshech, 4074
1Ch 1: 5 M, and Javan, and Tubal, and Meshech, 4074

MADE (1406) [MAKE]
Ge 1: 7 God m the firmament, and divided 6213
1:16 God m two great lights; the greater light to 6213
1:16 light to rule the night: he m the stars also. NIH
1:25 God m the beast of the earth after his kind, 6213
1:31 God saw every thing that he had m, and 6213
2: 2 day God ended his work which he had m; 6213
2: 2 day from all his work which he had m. 6213
2: 3 all his work which God created and m. 6213
2: 4 in the day that the LORD God m the earth 6213
2: 9 m the LORD God to grow every tree that 6779
2:22 m he a woman, and brought her unto 1129
3: 1 of the field which the LORD God had m. 6213
3: 7 leaves together, and m themselves aprons. 6213
5: 1 in the likeness of God m he him; 6213
6: 6 it repented the LORD that he had m man 6213
6: 7 for it repenteth me that I have m them. 6213
7: 4 every living substance that I have m will I 6213
8: 1 God m a wind to pass over the earth, and 5674
8: 6 the window of the ark which he had m: 6213
9: 6 be shed: for in the image of God m he man. 6213
13: 4 the altar, which he had m there at the first: 6213
14: 2 That these m war with Bera king of Sodom, 6213
14:23 thou shouldest say, I have m Abram rich: 6238
15:18 In the same day the LORD m a covenant 3772
17: 5 for a father of many nations have I m thee. 5414
19: 3 he m them a feast, and did bake unleavened 6213
19:33 they m their father drink wine that night: 8248
19:35 they m their father drink wine that night 8248
21: 6 God hath m me to laugh, so that all that 6213
21: 8 Abraham m a great feast the same day that 6213
21:27 and both of them m a covenant. 3772
21:32 Thus they m a covenant at Beer-sheba: then 3772
23:17 all the borders round about, were m sure 6965
23:20 were m sure unto Abraham for a 6965
24:11 he m his camels to kneel down without 1288
24:21 the LORD had m his journey prosperous 6743
24:37 my master m me swear, saying, Thou shalt 7650
24:46 she m haste, and let down her pitcher from 4116
24:46 I drank, and she m the camels drink also. 8248
26:22 For now the LORD hath m room for us, 7337
26:30 he m them a feast, and they did eat and 6213
27:14 his mother m savoury meat, such as his 6213
27:30 as soon as Isaac had m an end of blessing 3615
27:31 he also had m savoury meat, and brought it 6213
27:37 I have m him thy lord, and all his brethren 7760
29:22 all the men of the place, and m a feast. 6213
30:37 m the white appear which was in the rods. 4286
31:46 and they took stones, and m a heap: 6213
33:17 him a house, and m booths for his cattle: 6213
37: 3 and he m him a coat of many colours. 6213
37: 7 round about, and m obeisance to my sheaf. 7812
37: 9 and the eleven stars m obeisance to me. 7812
39: 3 m all that he did to prosper in his hand. 6743
39: 4 he m him overseer over his house, and 6485

Ge 39: 5 *that* he had **m** him **overseer** in his house, 6485
39:23 which he did, the LORD **m** *it* **to prosper**. 6743
40:20 that he **m** a feast unto all his servants: 6213
41:43 he **m** him **to ride** in the second chariot 7392
41:43 he **m** him *ruler* over all the land of Egypt. 5414
41:51 *said he,* hath **m** me **forget** all my toil, and 5382
42: 7 **m** himself **strange** unto them, and 5234
43:25 they **m ready** the present against Joseph 3559
43:28 bowed down their heads, and **m obeisance**. 7812
43:30 Joseph **m haste**; for his bowels did yern 4116
45: 1 while Joseph **m** himself **known** unto his 3045
45: 8 he hath **m** me a father to Pharaoh, and lord 7760
45: 9 God hath **m** me lord of all Egypt: 7760
46:29 Joseph **m ready** his chariot, and went up to 631
47:26 Joseph **m** it a law over the land of Egypt 7760
49:24 the arms of his hands were **m strong** by 6339
49:33 when Jacob had **m an end** of commanding 3615
50: 5 My father **m** me **swear**, saying, Lo, I die: 7650
50: 6 thy father, according as he **m** thee **swear**. 7650
50:10 he **m** a mourning for his father seven days. 6213
Ex 1:13 **m** the children of Israel **to serve** with 5647
1:14 they **m** their lives **bitter** with hard 4843
1:14 their service, wherein they **m** them **serve**, 5647
1:21 feared God, that he **m** them houses. 6213
2:14 Who **m** thee a prince and a judge over us? 7760
4:11 said unto him, Who hath **m** man's mouth? 7760
5:21 you have **m** our savour **to be abhorred** in 887
7: 1 See, I have **m** thee a god to Pharaoh: 5414
9:20 Pharaoh **m** his servants and his cattle **flee** 5127
14: 6 he **m ready** his chariot, and took his people 631
14:21 **m** the sea dry *land,* and the waters were 7760
15:17 *which* thou hast **m** for thee to dwell in, 6466
15:25 into the waters, the waters were **m sweet**: 4985
15:25 there he **m** for them a statute and 7760
16:31 the taste of it *was* like wafers *m* with honey. NIH
18:25 **m** them heads over the people, rulers of 5414
20:11 For *in* six days the LORD **m** heaven and 6213
24: 8 which the LORD hath **m** with you 3772
25:31 *of* beaten work shall the candlestick be **m**: 6213
25:33 Three bowls **m like unto almonds**, *with* a 8246
25:33 three bowls **m like almonds** in the other 8246
25:34 *shall be* four bowls **m like unto almonds**, 8246
26:31 *with* cherubims shall it be **m**: 6213
29:18 an **offering m by fire** unto the LORD. 801
29:25 it *is* an **offering m by fire** unto the LORD. 801
29:33 *things* wherewith the **atonement** was **m**, 3722
29:36 when thou hast **m an atonement** for it, and 3722
29:41 an **offering m by fire** unto the LORD. 801
30:20 to burn **offering m by fire** unto the LORD: 801
31:17 for *in* six days the LORD **m** heaven and 6213
31:18 when he had **m an end** of communing with 3615
32: 4 after he had **m** it a molten calf: 6213
32: 5 Aaron **m proclamation**, and said, 7121
32: 8 they have **m** them a molten calf, and 6213
32:20 And he took the calf which they had **m**, and 6213
32:20 and **m** the children of Israel **drink** *of it.* 8248
32:25 (for Aaron had **m** them **naked** unto *their* 6544
32:31 a great sin, and have **m** them gods of gold. 6213
32:35 because they **m** the calf, which Aaron 6213
32:35 they made the calf, which Aaron **m**. 6213
34: 8 Moses **m haste**, and bowed his head 4116
34:27 for after the tenor of these words I have **m** 3772
35:21 every one whom his spirit **m willing**, *and* 5068
35:29 whose heart **m** them **willing** to bring for all 5068
35:29 which the LORD had commanded to be **m** 6213
36: 4 every man from his work which they **m**; 6213
36: 8 **m** ten curtains *of* fine twined linen, 6213
36: 8 *with* cherubims *of* cunning work **m** he 6213
36:11 he **m** loops of blue on the edge of one 6213
36:11 likewise he **m** in the uttermost side of 6213
36:12 Fifty loops **m** he in one curtain, and 6213
36:12 fifty loops **m** he in the edge of the curtain 6213
36:13 he **m** fifty taches of gold, and coupled 6213
36:14 he **m** curtains *of* goats' *hair* for the tent 6213
36:14 the tabernacle: eleven curtains he **m** them. 6213
36:17 he **m** fifty loops upon the uttermost edge of 6213
36:17 fifty loops **m** he upon the edge of 6213
36:18 he **m** fifty taches of brass to couple the tent 6213
36:19 he **m** a covering for the tent *of* rams' skins 6213
36:20 he **m** boards for the tabernacle *of* shittim 6213
36:23 he **m** boards for the tabernacle; 6213
36:24 forty sockets of silver he **m** under 6213
36:25 the north corner, he **m** twenty boards, 6213
36:27 the tabernacle westward he **m** six boards. 6213
36:28 two boards **m** he for the corners of 6213
36:31 he **m** bars of shittim wood; five for 6213
36:33 he **m** the middle bar to shoot through 6213
36:34 **m** their rings *of* gold *to be* places for 6213
36:35 he **m** a vail *of* blue, and purple, and scarlet, 6213
36:35 *with* cherubims **m** he it *of* cunning work. 6213
36:36 he **m** thereunto four pillars of shittim *wood,* 6213
36:37 he **m** a hanging for the tabernacle door *of* 6213
37: 1 Bezaleel **m** the ark *of* shittim wood: 6213
37: 2 and **m** a crown *of* gold to it round about. 6213
37: 4 he **m** staves of shittim wood, and 6213
37: 6 he **m** the mercy seat *of* pure gold: 6213
37: 7 he **m** two cherubims *of* gold, beaten out of 6213
37: 7 beaten out of one piece **m** he them, on 6213
37: 8 out of the mercy seat **m** he the cherubims 6213
37:10 he **m** the table *of* shittim wood: two cubits 6213
37:11 **m** thereunto a crown *of* gold round about. 6213
37:12 Also he **m** thereunto a border of a 6213
37:12 **m** a crown of gold for the border thereof 6213
37:15 he **m** the staves *of* shittim wood, and 6213
37:16 he **m** the vessels which *were* upon 6213
37:17 he **m** the candlestick *of* pure gold: 6213
37:17 *of* beaten work **m** he the candlestick; 6213
37:19 **m after the fashion of almonds** in one 8246
37:19 three bowls **m like almonds** in another 8246
37:20 *were* four bowls **m like almonds**, 8246
37:23 he **m** his seven lamps, and his snuffers, 6213
37:24 *Of* a talent *of* pure gold **m** he it, and all 6213
37:25 he **m** the incense altar *of* shittim wood: 6213
37:26 also he **m** unto it a crown *of* gold round 6213
37:27 he **m** two rings of gold for it under 6213
Ex 37:28 he **m** the staves *of* shittim wood, and 6213
37:29 he **m** the holy anointing oil, and the pure 6213
38: 1 he **m** the altar of burnt offering *of* shittim 6213
38: 2 he **m** the horns thereof on the four corners 6213
38: 3 he **m** all the vessels of the altar, the pots, 6213
38: 3 all the vessels thereof **m** he *of* brass. 6213
38: 4 he **m** for the altar a brasen grate of network 6213
38: 6 he **m** the staves *of* shittim wood, and 6213
38: 7 it withal; he **m** *the altar* hollow with boards. 6213
38: 8 he **m** the laver *of* brass, and the foot of it *of* 6213
38: 9 he **m** the court: on the south side southward 6213
38:22 **m** all that the LORD commanded Moses. 6213
38:28 and five *shekels* he **m** hooks for the pillars, 6213
38:30 therewith he **m** the sockets to the door of 6213
39: 1 and scarlet, they **m** clothes of service, 6213
39: 1 and **m** the holy garments for Aaron; 6213
39: 2 he **m** the ephod *of* gold, blue, and purple, 6213
39: 4 They **m** shoulderpieces for it, to couple *it* 6213
39: 8 he **m** the breastplate *of* cunning work, 6213
39: 9 they **m** the breastplate double: 6213
39:15 they **m** upon the breastplate chains at 6213
39:16 they **m** two ouches *of* gold, and two gold 6213
39:19 they **m** two rings of gold, and put *them* on 6213
39:20 they **m** two *other* golden rings, and 6213
39:22 he **m** the robe of the ephod *of* woven work, 6213
39:24 they **m** upon the hems of the robe 6213
39:25 they **m** bells of pure gold, and put the bells 6213
39:27 they **m** coats *of* fine linen *of* woven work 6213
39:30 they **m** the plate of the holy crown *of* pure 6213
39:42 so the children of Israel **m** all the work. 6213
Lev 1: 9 *be* a burnt sacrifice, an **offering m by fire**, 801
1:13 it *is* a burnt sacrifice, an **offering m by fire**, 801
1:17 it *is* a burnt sacrifice, an **offering m by fire**, 801
2: 2 *to be* an **offering m by fire**, of a sweet 801
2: 3 of the **offerings** of the LORD **m by fire**. 801
2: 7 it shall be **m** *of* fine flour with oil. 6213
2: 8 thou shalt bring the meat offering that is **m** 6213
2: 9 *it is* an **offering m by fire**, of a sweet savour 801
2:10 of the **offerings** of the LORD **m by fire**. 801
2:11 unto the LORD, shall be **m** *with* leaven: 6213
2:11 *in* any **offering** of the LORD **m by fire**. 801
2:16 *it is* an **offering m by fire** unto the LORD. 801
3: 3 an **offering m by fire** unto the LORD; 801
3: 5 *it is* an **offering m by fire**, of a sweet savour 801
3: 9 an **offering m by fire** unto the LORD; 801
3:11 *it is* the food of the **offering m by fire** unto 801
3:14 *even* an **offering m by fire** unto 801
3:16 *it is* the food of the **offering m by fire** for a 801
4:35 according to the **offerings m by fire** unto 801
5:12 according to the **offerings m by fire** unto 801
6:17 *for* their portion of my **offerings m by fire**; 801
6:18 the **offerings** of the LORD **m by fire**: 801
6:21 In a pan it shall be **m** with oil; *and when it* 6213
7: 5 *for* an **offering m by fire** unto the LORD: 801
7:25 of which *men* offer an **offering m by fire** 801
7:30 bring the **offerings** of the LORD **m by fire**, 801
7:35 of the **offerings** of the LORD **m by fire**, 801
8:21 *and* an **offering m by fire** unto the LORD; 801
8:28 it *is* an **offering m by fire** unto the LORD. 801
10:12 of the **offerings** of the LORD **m by fire**, 801
10:13 of the **sacrifices** of the LORD **m by fire**: 801
10:15 bring with the **offerings m by fire** of the fat, 801
13:48 whether in a skin, or in any thing **m** of skin; 4399
13:51 in a skin, *or* in any work that is **m** of skin; 6213
14:11 shall present the man that is to be **m clean**, 2891
14:36 that all that *is* in the house be not *m* NIH
16:17 have **m an atonement** for himself, and 3722
16:20 when he hath **m an end** of reconciling 3615
21: 6 for the **offerings** of the LORD **m by fire**, 801
21:21 offer the **offerings** of the LORD **m by fire**: 801
22: 5 whereby he may be **m unclean**, or a man of 2930
22:27 **offering m by fire** unto the LORD. 801+7133
23: 8 ye shall offer an **offering m by fire** unto 801
23:13 an **offering m by fire** unto the LORD *for* a 801
23:18 drink offerings, *even* an **offering m by fire**, 801
23:25 ye shall offer an **offering m by fire** unto 801
23:27 offer an **offering m by fire** unto 801
23:36 an **offering m by fire** unto the LORD: 801
23:36 ye shall offer an **offering m by fire** unto 801
23:37 to offer an **offering m by fire** unto 801
23:43 **m** the children of Israel **to dwell** in booths, 3427
24: 7 *even* an **offering m by fire** unto the LORD. 801
24: 9 of the **offerings** of the LORD **m by fire**, 801
26:13 bands of your yoke, and **m** you **go** upright. 1980
26:46 which the LORD **m** between him and 5414
Nu 4:15 his sons have **m an end** of covering 3615
4:26 of their service, and all that is **m** for them: 6213
5: 8 whereby an **atonement** shall be **m** for him. 3722
5:27 when he hath **m** her **to drink** the water, 8248
6: 4 he eat nothing that is **m** of the vine tree, 6213
8: 4 shewed Moses, so he **m** the candlestick. 6213
8:21 Aaron **m an atonement** for them to cleanse 3722
11: 8 and baked *it* in pans, and **m** cakes *of* it: 6213
14:36 **m** all the congregation **to murmur** against 3885
15:10 *for* an **offering m by fire**, of a sweet savour 801
15:13 in offering an **offering m by fire**, of a sweet 801
15:14 will offer an **offering m by fire**, of a sweet 801
15:25 a **sacrifice m by fire** unto the LORD, and 801
16:31 as he had **m an end** of speaking all these 3615
16:39 they were **m broad** *plates for* a covering of 7554
16:47 and **m an atonement** for the people. 3722
18:17 shalt burn their fat *for* an **offering m by fire**, 801
20: 5 wherefore have ye **m** us **to come up** out of 5927
21: 9 Moses **m** a serpent of brass, and put it upon 6213
25:13 **m an atonement** for the children of Israel. 3722
28: 2 *and* my bread for my **sacrifices m by fire**, 801
28: 3 This *is* the **offering m by fire** which ye shall 801
28: 6 a **sacrifice m by fire** unto the LORD. 801
28: 8 thou shalt offer *it,* a **sacrifice m by fire**, 801
28:13 a **sacrifice m by fire** unto the LORD. 801
28:19 ye shall offer a **sacrifice m by fire** *for* a 801
28:24 the meat of the **sacrifice m by fire**, 801
29: 6 a **sacrifice m by fire** unto the LORD. 801
29:13 offer a burnt offering, a **sacrifice m by fire**, 801
29:36 offer a burnt offering, a **sacrifice m by fire**, 801
Nu 30:12 **utterly m** them **void** on the day he 6565+6565
30:12 her husband hath **m** them **void**; and 6565
31:20 all **that is m** of skins, and all work of 3627
31:20 of goats' *hair,* and all **things m** of wood. 3627
32:13 he **m** them **wander** in the wilderness forty 5128
Dt 1:15 and known, and **m** them heads over you, 5414
2:30 **m** his heart **obstinate**, that he might deliver 553
4:23 which he **m** with you, and make you a 3772
4:36 Out of heaven he **m** thee **to hear** his voice, 8085
5: 2 The LORD our God **m** a covenant with us 3772
5: 3 The LORD **m** not this covenant with our 3772
9: 9 covenant which the LORD **m** with you, 3772
9:12 they have **m** them a molten image. 6213
9:16 your God, *and* had **m** you a molten calf: 6213
9:21 the calf which ye had **m**, and burnt it with 6213
10: 3 I **m** an ark of shittim wood, and hewed two 6213
10: 5 and put the tables in the ark which I had **m**; 6213
10:22 now the LORD thy God hath **m** thee as 7760
11: 4 **m** the water of the Red sea **to overflow** 6687
18: 1 eat the **offerings** of the LORD **m by fire**, 801
20: 9 when the officers have **m an end** of 3615
26:12 When thou hast **m an end** of tithing all 3615
26:19 high above all nations which he hath **m**, 6213
29: 1 beside the covenant which he **m** with them 3772
29:25 which he **m** with them when he brought 3772
31:16 break my covenant which I have **m** with 3772
31:24 when Moses had **m an end** of writing 3615
32: 6 hath he *not* **m** thee, and established thee? 6213
32:13 He **m** him **ride** on the high places of 7392
32:13 he **m** him **to suck** honey out of the rock, 3243
32:15 then he forsook God *which* **m** him, 6213
32:45 Moses **m an end** of speaking all these 3615
Jos 2:17 this thine oath which thou hast **m** us **swear**. 7650
2:20 thine oath which thou hast **m** us **to swear**. 7650
5: 3 Joshua **m** him sharp knives, and 6213
8:15 all Israel *m as if they* were beaten before NIH
8:24 when Israel had **m an end** of slaying all 3615
8:28 Joshua burnt Ai, and **m** it a heap for ever, 7760
9: 4 and **m as if** they had been **ambassadors**, 6737
9:15 Joshua **m** peace with them, and made a 6213
9:15 and **m** a league with them, to let them live: 3772
9:16 days after they had **m** a league with them, 3772
9:27 Joshua **m** them that day hewers of wood 5414
10: 1 how the inhabitants of Gibeon had **m peace** 7999
10: 4 for it hath **m peace** with Joshua and 7999
10: 5 before Gibeon, and **m war** against it. 3898
10:20 the children of Israel had **m an end** of 3615
11:18 Joshua **m** war a long time with all those 6213
11:19 There was not a city that **m peace** with 7999
13:14 **sacrifices** of the LORD God of Israel **m by fire** 801
14: 8 up with me **m** the heart of the people **melt**: 4529
19:49 When they had **m an end** of dividing 3615
19:51 So they **m an end** of dividing the country. 3615
22:25 For the LORD hath **m** Jordan a border 5414
22:28 which our fathers **m**, not for burnt 6213
24:25 So Joshua **m** a covenant with the people 3772
Jdg 2: 1 I **m** you **to go up** out of Egypt, and 5927
3:16 Ehud **m** him a dagger which had two edges, 6213
3:18 when he had **m an end** to offer the present, 3615
5:13 **m** him that remaineth **have dominion over** 7287
5:13 the LORD **m** me **have dominion over** 7287
6: 2 of the Midianites the children of Israel **m** 6213
6:19 **m ready** a kid, and unleavened *cakes of* an 6213
8:27 Gideon **m** an ephod thereof, and put it in 6213
8:33 after Baalim, and **m** Baal-berith their god. 7760
9: 6 of Millo, and went, and **m** Abimelech king, 4427
9:16 in that ye have **m** Abimelech **king**, and 4427
9:18 **m** Abimelech, the son of his maidservant, **king** 4427
9:27 trode *the grapes,* and **m** merry, and 6213
11: 4 that the children of Ammon **m war** against 3898
11: 5 that when the children of Ammon **m war** 3898
11:11 the people **m** him head and captain over 7760
13:10 the woman **m haste**, and ran, and 4116
13:15 until we shall have **m ready** a kid for thee. 6213
14:10 Samson **m** there a feast; for so used 6213
15:17 when he had **m an end** of speaking, 3615
16:19 she **m** him **sleep** upon her knees; and 3462
16:25 of the prison house; and he **m** them **sport**: 6711
16:27 women, that beheld while Samson **m sport**. 7832
17: 4 who **m** thereof a graven image and 6213
17: 5 **m** an ephod, and teraphim, and 6213
18:24 Ye have taken away my gods which I **m**, 6213
18:27 they took *the things* which Micah had **m**, 6213
18:31 up Micah's graven image, which he **m**, 6213
21: 5 For *they* had **m** a great oath concerning *him* 1961
21:15 that the LORD had **m** a breach in 6213
1Sa 2:19 Moreover his mother **m** him a little coat, 6213
2:28 **offerings m by fire** of the children of Israel? 801
3:13 because his sons **m** themselves **vile**, and 7043
4:18 when he **m mention** of the ark of God, 2142
8: 1 that he **m** his sons judges over Israel. 7760
9:22 **m** them **sit** in the chiefest place among 5414
10:13 when he had **m an end** of prophesying, 3615
11:15 there they **m** Saul **king** before the LORD 4427
12: 1 and have **m a king** over you. 4427+4428
12: 8 of Egypt, and **m** them **dwell** in this place. 3427
13:10 that as soon as he had **m an end** of offering 3615
13:12 I have not **m supplication** unto 2470
14:14 **slaughter**, which Jonathan and his armourbearer **m**, 4347+5221
15:17 *wast* thou not *m* the head of the tribes of NIH
15:33 As thy sword hath **m** women **childless**, so 7921
15:35 that he had **m** Saul **king** over Israel. 4427
16: 8 and **m** him **pass** before Samuel. 5674
16: 9 Jesse **m** Shammah **to pass by**. And he said, 5674
16:10 Jesse **m** seven of his sons **to pass** before 5674
18: 1 when he **m an end** of speaking unto Saul, 3615
18: 3 Jonathan and David **m** a covenant, because 3772
18:13 and **m** him his captain over a thousand; 7760
20:16 So Jonathan **m** *a covenant* with the house 3772
22: 8 son hath **m** *a league* with the son of Jesse, 3772
23:18 they two **m** a covenant before the LORD: 3772
23:26 David **m haste** to get away for fear of Saul; 2648
24:16 when David had **m an end** of speaking 3615

M

1Sa 25:18 Abigail **m haste**, and took two hundred 4116
27:10 Whither have ye **m a road** to day? 6584
27:12 **m** his people Israel **utterly to abhor** 887+887
30:11 he did eat; and they **m** him **drink** water; 8248
30:14 We **m an invasion** *upon* the south of 6584
30:21 whom they had **m** also **to abide** at 3427
30:25 that he **m** it a statute and an ordinance for 7760
2Sa 2:9 he **m** him **king** over Gilead, and over 4427
3:6 that Abner **m** himself **strong** for the house 2388
3:20 David **m** Abner and the men that *were* with 6213
4:4 as she **m haste** to flee, that he fell, and 2648
5:3 king David **m** a league with them in 3772
6:5 on all *manner of instruments* **m** *of* fir wood, NIH
6:8 had **m a breach** upon Uzzah: 6555+6556
6:18 as soon as David had **m an end** of offering 3615
7:9 of thy sight, and have **m** thee a great name, 6213
10:19 they **m peace** with Israel, and served them. 7999
11:13 drink before him; and he **m** him **drunk**: 7937
11:19 When thou hast **m an end** of telling 3615
12:31 and **m** them **pass** through the brickkiln: 5674
13:6 So Amnon lay down, and **m** himself **sick**: 2470
13:8 kneaded *it*, and **m cakes** in his sight, and 3823
13:10 Tamar took the cakes which she had **m**, 6213
13:36 as soon as he had **m an end** of speaking, 3615
14:15 *it is* because the people have **m** me **afraid**: 3372
15:4 Oh that I were **m** judge in the land, 7760
17:25 Absalom **m** Amasa captain of the host 7760
22:5 the floods of ungodly men **m** me **afraid**; 1204
22:12 he **m** darkness pavilions round about him, 7896
22:36 and thy gentleness hath **m** me **great**. 7235
23:5 yet he hath **m** with me an everlasting 7760
1Ki 1:41 heard *it* as they had **m an end** of eating. 3615
1:43 our lord king David hath **m** Solomon **king**. 4427
2:24 who hath **m** me a house, as he promised, 6213
3:1 Solomon **m affinity** with Pharaoh king of 2859
3:1 until he had **m an end** of building his own 3615
3:7 thou hast **m** thy servant **king** instead of 4427
3:15 and **m** a feast to all his servants. 6213
4:7 each man *his* month in a year **m provision**. 3557
5:12 and they two **m** a league *together*. 3772
6:4 for the house he **m** windows of narrow 6213
6:5 the oracle: and he **m** chambers round about: 6213
6:6 for without *in the wall* of the house he **m** 5414
6:7 was built *of* stone **m ready** *before it was* 8003
6:21 he **m a partition** by the chains of gold 5674
6:23 within the oracle he **m** two cherubims *of* 6213
6:31 for the entering of the oracle he **m** doors of 6213
6:33 So also **m** he for the door of the temple 6213
7:6 he **m** a porch of pillars; the length thereof 6213
7:7 he **m** a porch for the throne where he might 6213
7:8 Solomon **m** also a house for Pharaoh's 6213
7:16 he **m** two chapiters *of* molten brass, to set 6213
7:18 he **m** the pillars, and two rows round about 6213
7:23 he **m** a molten sea, ten cubits from the one 6213
7:27 he **m** ten bases of brass; four cubits *was* 6213
7:29 oxen *were certain* additions **m** of **thin** 4174
7:37 After this *manner* he **m** the ten bases: all of 6213
7:38 **m** he ten lavers of brass: one laver 6213
7:40 Hiram **m** the lavers, and the shovels, and 6213
7:40 So Hiram **m an end** of doing all the work 3615
7:40 **m** king Solomon *for* the house of 6213
7:45 which Hiram **m** to king Solomon *for* 6213
7:48 Solomon **m** all the vessels that *pertained* 6213
7:51 Solomon **m** *for* the house of the LORD. 6213
8:9 when the LORD **m** *a covenant* with 3772
8:21 the LORD, which he **m** with our fathers, 3772
8:38 and supplication soever be **m** by any man, NIH
8:54 *that* when Solomon had **m an end** of 3615
8:59 wherewith I have **m supplication** before 2603
9:3 thy **supplication**, that thou hast **m** before 8467
9:26 king Solomon **m** a navy *of ships* in 6213
10:9 therefore **m** he thee king, to do judgment 7760
10:12 the king **m** *of* the almug trees pillars for 6213
10:16 king Solomon **m** two hundred targets *of* 6213
10:17 *he* **m** three hundred shields *of* beaten gold; NIH
10:18 Moreover the king **m** a great throne of 6213
10:20 there was not the like **m** in any kingdom. 6213
10:27 the king **m** silver *to be* in Jerusalem as 5414
10:27 cedars **m** he *to be* as the sycomore trees 5414
11:28 he **m** him **ruler** over all the charge of 6485
12:4 Thy father **m** our yoke **grievous**: now 7185
12:10 Thy father **m** our yoke **heavy**, but 3513
12:14 My father **m** your yoke **heavy**, and I will 3513
12:18 Therefore king Rehoboam **m speed** to get 553
12:20 and **m** him **king** over all Israel: 4427
12:28 **m** two calves of gold, and said unto them, 6213
12:31 he **m** a house of high places, and 6213
12:31 **m** priests of the lowest of the people, 6213
12:32 sacrificing unto the calves that he had **m**: 6213
12:32 priests of the high places which he had **m**. 6213
12:33 he offered upon the altar which he had **m** 6213
13:33 **m** again of the lowest of the people priests 6213
14:7 and **m** thee prince over my people Israel, 5414
14:9 for thou hast gone and **m** thee other gods, 6213
14:15 because they have **m** their groves, 6213
14:16 who did sin, and who **m** Israel **to sin**. 2398
14:26 the shields of gold which Solomon had **m**. 6213
14:27 king Rehoboam **m** in their stead brasen 6213
15:12 removed all the idols that his fathers had **m**. 6213
15:13 because she had **m** an idol in a grove; 6213
15:22 king Asa **m** a **proclamation** throughout all 8085
15:26 and in his sin wherewith he **m** Israel **to sin**. 2398
15:30 he sinned, and which he **m** Israel **sin**, 2398
15:34 and in his sin wherewith he **m** Israel **to sin**. 2398
16:2 and **m** thee prince over my people Israel; 5414
16:2 hast **m** my people Israel **to sin**, to provoke 2398
16:13 and *by* which they **m** Israel **to sin**, 2398
16:16 Israel **m** Omri, the captain of the host, **king** 4427
16:26 and in his sin wherewith he **m** Israel **to sin**, 2398
16:33 Ahab **m** a grove; and Ahab did more to 6213
18:26 And they leapt upon the altar which was **m**. 6213
18:32 he **m** a trench about the altar, as great as 6213
20:34 in Damascus, as my father **m** in Samaria. 7760
20:34 So he **m** a covenant with him, and sent him 3772
21:22 provoked *me* to anger, and **m** Israel **to sin**. 2398
1Ki 22:11 Zedekiah the son of Chenaanah **m** him 6213
22:39 the ivory house which he **m**, and all 1129
22:44 Jehoshaphat **m peace** with the king of 7999
22:48 Jehoshaphat **m** ships of Tharshish to go to 6213
22:52 the son of Nebat, who **m** Israel **to sin**: 2398
2Ki 3:2 the image of Baal that his father had **m**. 6213
3:3 the son of Nebat, which **m** Israel **to sin**; 2398
7:6 **m** the host of the Syrians **to hear** a noise of 8085
8:20 and **m a king** over themselves. 4427+4428
9:21 his chariot was **m ready**. And Joram king of 631
10:16 So they **m** him **ride** in his chariot. 7392
10:25 as soon as he had **m an end** of offering 3615
10:27 and **m** it a draught house unto *this* day. 7760
10:29 who **m** Israel **to sin**, Jehu departed not from 2398
10:31 the sins of Jeroboam, which **m** Israel **to sin**. 2398
11:4 **m** a covenant with them, and took an oath 3772
11:12 they **m** him **king**, and anointed him; and 4427
11:17 Jehoiada **m** a covenant between 3772
12:13 Howbeit there were not **m** *for* the house of 6213
12:20 **m a conspiracy**, and slew Joash *in* 7194+7195
13:2 the son of Nebat, which **m** Israel **to sin**; 2398
13:6 who **m** Israel **sin**, *but* walked therein: 2398
13:7 and had **m** them like the dust by threshing. 7760
13:11 the son of Nebat, who **m** Israel **sin**: 2398
14:19 Now they **m a conspiracy** against 7194+7195
14:21 **m** him **king** instead of his father Amaziah. 4427
14:24 the son of Nebat, who **m** Israel **to sin**. 2398
15:9 the son of Nebat, who **m** Israel **to sin**. 2398
15:15 his **conspiracy** which he **m**, behold, 7194+7195
15:18 the son of Nebat, who **m** Israel **to sin**. 2398
15:24 the son of Nebat, who **m** Israel **to sin**. 2398
15:28 the son of Nebat, who **m** Israel **to sin**. 2398
15:30 **m a conspiracy** against Pekah 7194+7195
16:3 yea, and **m** his son **to pass** through the fire, 5674
16:11 Urijah the priest **m** *it* against king Ahaz 6213
17:8 of the kings of Israel, which they had **m**. 6213
17:15 his covenant that he **m** with their fathers, 3772
17:16 **m** them molten images, *even* two calves, 6213
17:16 **m** a grove, and worshipped all the host of 6213
17:19 in the statutes of Israel which they **m**. 6213
17:21 they **m** Jeroboam the son of Nebat **king**: 4427
17:21 the LORD, and **m** them **sin** a great sin. 2398
17:29 Howbeit every nation **m** gods of their own, 6213
17:29 high places which the Samaritans had **m**, 6213
17:30 the men of Babylon **m** Succoth-benoth, 6213
17:30 the men of Cuth **m** Nergal, and the men of 6213
17:30 and the men of Hamath **m** Ashima, 6213
17:31 the Avites **m** Nibhaz and Tartak, and 6213
17:32 **m** unto themselves of the lowest of them 6213
17:35 With whom the LORD had **m** a covenant, 3772
17:38 the covenant that I have **m** with you ye 3772
18:4 the brasen serpent that Moses had **m**: 6213
19:15 of the earth; thou hast **m** heaven and earth. 6213
20:20 how he **m** a pool, and a conduit, and 6213
21:3 and **m** a grove, as did Ahab king of Israel; 6213
21:6 And he **m** his son **pass** through the fire, and 5674
21:7 of the grove that he had **m** in the house, 6213
21:11 and hath **m** Judah also **to sin** with his idols: 2398
21:16 beside his sin where*with* he **m** Judah **to sin**, 2398
21:24 the land **m** Josiah his son **king** in his stead. 4427
22:7 Howbeit there was no **reckoning m** with 2803
23:3 **m** a covenant before the LORD, to walk 3772
23:4 all the vessels that were **m** for Baal, 6213
23:12 which the kings of Judah had **m**, and 6213
23:12 the altars which Manasseh had **m** in 6213
23:15 who **m** Israel **to sin**, had made, both that 2398
23:15 had **m**, both that altar and the high place he 6213
23:19 which the kings of Israel had **m** to provoke 6213
23:30 and **m** him **king** in his father's stead. 4427
23:34 **m** Eliakim the son of Josiah **king** in 4427
24:13 Israel had **m** in the temple of the LORD, 6213
24:17 **m** Mattaniah his father's brother **king** in his 4427
25:16 the bases which Solomon had **m** for 6213
25:22 **m** Gedaliah the son of Ahikam, the son of
Shaphan, **ruler**. 6485
25:23 king of Babylon had **m** Gedaliah **governor**, 6485
1Ch 5:10 in the days of Saul they **m** war with 6213
5:19 they **m** war with the Hagarites, with Jetur, 6213
9:30 *some* of the sons of the priests **m** 7543
9:31 over the **things that were m** in the pans. 4639
11:3 David **m** a covenant with them in Hebron 3772
12:18 and **m** them captains of the band. 5414
13:11 LORD had **m a breach** upon Uzza: 6555+6556
15:1 *David* **m** him houses in the city of David, 6213
15:13 the LORD our God **m a breach** upon us, 6555
16:2 when David had **m an end** of offering 3615
16:5 but Asaph **m a sound** with cymbals; 8085
16:16 *Even of the covenant* which he **m** with 3772
16:26 *are* idols: but the LORD **m** the heavens. 6213
17:8 have **m** thee a name like the name of 6213
18:8 wherewith Solomon **m** the brasen sea, and 6213
19:6 that they had **m** themselves **odious** to David, 887
19:19 they **m peace** with David, and became his 7999
21:29 which Moses **m** in the wilderness, and 6213
22:8 blood abundantly, and hast **m** great wars: 6213
23:1 he **m** Solomon his son **king** over Israel. 4427
23:5 LORD with the instruments which I **m**, 6213
26:10 yet his father **m** him the chief;) 7760
26:32 whom king David **m rulers** over 6485
28:2 our God, and had **m ready** for the building: 3559
28:19 **m** me **understand** in writing by *his* hand 7919
29:2 my God the gold for *things to be* **m** *of* gold, NIH
29:5 for all *manner of* work *to be* **m** by the hands NIH
29:19 *for* the which I have **m provision**. 3559
29:22 they **m** Solomon the son of David **king** 4427
2Ch 1:3 of the LORD had **m** in the wilderness 6213
1:5 the son of Uri, the son of Hur, had **m**, 6213
1:8 and hast **m** me **to reign** in his stead. 4427
1:9 for thou hast **m** me **king** over a people like 4427
1:11 my people, over whom I have **m** thee **king**: 4427
1:15 the king **m** silver and gold at Jerusalem *as* 5414
1:15 cedar trees **m** he as the sycomore trees that 5414
2:11 his people, he hath **m** thee king over them. 5414
2:12 God of Israel, that **m** heaven and earth, 6213
3:8 he **m** the most holy house, the length 6213
2Ch 3:10 in the most holy house he **m** two cherubims 6213
3:14 he **m** the vail *of* blue, and purple, and 6213
3:15 Also he **m** before the house two pillars of 6213
3:16 he **m** chains, *as* in the oracle, and put *them* 6213
3:16 **m** an hundred pomegranates, and put *them* 6213
4:1 Moreover he **m** an altar of brass, 6213
4:2 Also he **m** a molten sea of ten cubits from 6213
4:6 He **m** also ten lavers, and put five on 6213
4:7 he **m** ten candlesticks of gold according to 6213
4:8 He **m** also ten tables, and placed *them* in 6213
4:8 And he **m** an hundred basons of gold. 6213
4:9 Furthermore he **m** the court of the priests, 6213
4:11 Huram **m** the pots, and the shovels, and 6213
4:14 He **m** also bases and lavers made he upon 6213
4:14 also bases and lavers **m** he upon the bases; 6213
4:18 Thus Solomon **m** all these vessels in great 6213
4:19 Solomon **m** all the vessels that *were for* 6213
4:21 **m** *he of* gold, *and* that perfect gold; NIH
5:1 Thus all the work that Solomon **m** for 6213
5:10 when the LORD **m** *a covenant* with 3772
6:11 that he **m** with the children of Israel. 3772
6:13 For Solomon had **m** a brasen scaffold, 6213
6:29 what supplication soever shall be **m** of any NIH
6:40 attent unto the prayer *that is* **m** in this place. NIH
7:1 Now when Solomon had **m an end** of 3615
7:6 which David the king had **m** to praise 6213
7:7 the brasen altar which Solomon had **m** was 6213
7:9 in the eighth day they **m** a solemn 6213
7:15 mine ears attent unto the prayer *that is* **m** in NIH
9:8 therefore **m** he thee king over them, to do 5414
9:11 the king **m** *of* the algum trees terraces to 6213
9:15 king Solomon **m** two hundred targets *of* 6213
9:16 three hundred shields **m** *he of* beaten gold: NIH
9:17 Moreover the king **m** a great throne of 6213
9:19 There was not the like **m** in any kingdom. 6213
9:27 the king **m** silver in Jerusalem as stones, 5414
9:27 cedar trees **m** he as the sycomore trees that 5414
10:4 Thy father **m** our yoke **grievous**: now 7185
10:10 Thy father **m** our yoke **heavy**, but 3513
10:14 My father **m** your yoke **heavy**, but I will 3513
10:18 king Rehoboam **m speed** to get *him* up to *his* 553
11:12 and spears, and **m** them exceeding **strong**, 2388
11:15 and for the calves which he had **m**. 6213
11:17 **m** Rehoboam the son of Solomon **strong**, 553
11:22 Rehoboam **m** Abijah the son of Maachah 5975
12:9 the shields of gold which Solomon had **m**. 6213
12:10 Instead of which king Rehoboam **m** shields 6213
13:8 which Jeroboam **m** you for gods. 6213
13:9 have **m** you priests after the manner of 6213
15:16 because she had **m** an idol in a grove: 6213
16:14 which he had **m** for himself in the city of 3738
16:14 they **m** a very great **burning** for him. 8313+8316
17:10 so that they **m** no **war** against Jehoshaphat. 3898
18:10 Zedekiah the son of Chenaanah had **m** him 6213
20:23 when they had **m an end** of the inhabitants 3615
20:27 for the LORD had **m** them **to rejoice** over 8055
20:36 and they **m** the ships in Ezion-geber. 6213
21:7 of the covenant that he had **m** with David, 3772
21:8 of Judah, and **m** themselves **a king**. 4427+4428
21:11 Moreover he **m** high places in 6213
21:13 **m** Judah and the inhabitants of Jerusalem
to go a whoring, 2181
21:19 his people **m** no burning for him, like 6213
22:1 **m** Ahaziah his youngest son **king** in his 4427
23:3 all the congregation **m** a covenant with 3772
23:11 *gave him* the Testimony, and **m** him **king**. 4427
23:16 Jehoiada **m** a covenant between him, and 3772
24:8 at the king's commandment they **m** a chest, 6213
24:9 they **m** a proclamation through Judah and 5414
24:10 cast into the chest, until *they* had **m an end**. 3615
24:14 whereof were **m** vessels for the house of 6213
24:17 of Judah, and **m obeisance** to the king 7812
25:5 **m** them captains over thousands, and 5975
25:16 unto him, Art thou **m** of the king's counsel? 5414
25:27 **m a conspiracy** against him in 7194+7195
26:1 **m** him **king** in the room of his father 4427
26:5 the LORD, God **m** him **to prosper**. 6743
26:13 that **m** war with mighty power, 6213
26:15 he **m** in Jerusalem engines, invented by 6213
28:2 and **m** also molten images for Baalim. 6213
28:19 for he **m** Judah **naked**, and 6544
28:24 he **m** him altars in every corner of 6213
28:25 in every several city of Judah he **m** high 6213
29:17 day of the first month they **m an end**. 3615
29:24 they **m reconciliation** with their blood 2398
29:24 the sin offering *should be* **m** for all Israel. NIH
29:29 when *they* had **m an end** of offering, 3615
32:5 and **m** darts and shields in abundance. 6213
32:27 he **m** himself treasuries for silver, and 6213
33:3 **m** groves, and worshipped all the host of 6213
33:7 the idol which he had **m**, in the house of 6213
33:9 **m** Judah and the inhabitants of Jerusalem
to err, 8582
33:22 images which Manasseh his father had **m**, 6213
33:25 the land **m** Josiah his son **king** in his stead. 4427
34:4 brake *in pieces*, and **m dust** *of them*, 1854
34:31 **m** a covenant before the LORD, to walk 3772
34:33 **m** all that were present in Israel **to serve**, 5975
35:14 afterward they **m ready** for themselves, 3559
35:25 *this* day, and **m** them an ordinance in Israel: 5414
36:1 **m** him **king** in his father's stead in 4427
36:4 **m** Eliakim his brother **king** over Judah 4427
36:10 **m** Zedekiah his brother **king** over Judah 4427
36:13 who had **m** him **swear** by God: 7650
36:22 that he **m a proclamation** 5674+6963
Ezr 1:1 that he **m a proclamation** 5674+6963
4:15 That **search** may be **m** in the book of 1240
4:19 **search** hath been **m**, and it is found that 1240
4:19 old time *hath* **m insurrection** against kings, 5376
4:19 and sedition *have been* **m** therein. 5648
4:23 and **m** them **to cease** by force and power. 989
5:13 **m** a decree to build this house of God. 7761
5:14 whom he had **m** governor; 7761
5:17 let there be **search m** in the king's treasure 1240
5:17 that a decree *was* **m** of Cyrus the king to 7761

Ezr 6: 1 Darius the king **m** a decree, and search was 7761
6: 1 and **search** was **m** in the house of the rolls, 1240
6: 3 **m** a decree *concerning* the house of God at 7761
6:11 Also I have **m** a decree, that whosoever 7761
6:11 let his house be **m** a dunghill for this. 5648
6:12 I Darius have **m** a decree; let it be done 7761
6:22 for the LORD had **m** them **joyful**, and 8055
10: 5 **m** the chief priests, the Levites, and all Israel, **to swear** 7650
10: 7 they **m proclamation** throughout 5674+6963
10:17 they **m an end** with all the men that had 3615
Ne 3:16 to the pool that was **m**, and unto the house 6213
4: 7 the walls of Jerusalem were **m up**, 724+5927
4: 9 Nevertheless we **m** our **prayer** unto our 6419
6: 9 For they all **m** us **afraid**, saying, 3372
8: 4 of wood, which they had **m** for the purpose; 6213
8:16 brought *them*, and **m** themselves booths, 6213
8:17 come again out of the captivity **m** booths, 6213
9: 6 thou hast **m** heaven, the heaven of heavens, 6213
9:18 when they had **m** them a molten calf, and 6213
10:32 Also we **m** ordinances for us, to charge 5975
12:43 for God had **m** them **rejoice** *with* great joy: 8055
13:13 I **m treasurers** over the treasuries, 686
13:25 off their hair, and **m** them **swear** by God, 7650
13:26 and God **m** him king over all Israel: 5414
Est 1: 3 he **m** a feast unto all his princes and 6213
1: 5 the king **m** a feast unto all the people that 6213
1: 9 Also Vashti the queen **m** a feast for 6213
2:17 and **m** her **queen** instead of Vashti. 4427
2:18 the king **m** a great feast unto all his princes 6213
2:18 he **m** a release to the provinces, and 6213
2:23 And when **inquisition was m** of the matter, 1245
5:14 Let a gallows be **m** of fifty cubits high, and 6213
5:14 and he **caused** the gallows **to be m**. 6213
7: 9 which Haman had **m** for Mordecai, 6213
9:17 and **m** it a day of feasting and gladness. 6213
9:18 and **m** it a day of feasting and gladness. 6213
9:19 **m** the fourteenth day of the month Adar *a* 6213
Job 1:10 Hast not thou **m a hedge** about him, and 7753
1:17 The Chaldeans **m out** three bands, and 7760
2:11 for they had **m an appointment** together to 3259
4:14 trembling, which **m** all my bones **to shake**. 6342
7: 3 So am I **m to possess** months of vanity, and 5157
10: 8 Thine hands have **m** me and fashioned me 6087
10: 9 that thou hast **m** me as the clay; 6213
15: 7 was born? or wast thou **m** before the hills? 2342
16: 7 now he hath **m** me **weary**: thou hast made 3811
16: 7 thou hast **m desolate** all my company. 8074
17: 6 He hath **m** me also a byword of the people; 3322
17:13 I have **m** my bed in the darkness. 7502
28:18 No **mention** shall be **m** of coral, or 2142
28:26 When he **m** a decree for the rain, and a way 6213
31: 1 I **m** a covenant with mine eyes; why then 3772
31:15 Did not he that **m** me in the womb make 6213
31:24 If I have **m** gold my hope, or have said to 7760
33: 4 The Spirit of God hath **m** me, and 6213
38: 9 When I **m** the cloud the garment thereof, 7760
39: 6 Whose house I have **m** the wilderness, and 7760
40:15 now behemoth, which I **m** with thee; 6213
40:19 he that **m** him can make his sword to 6213
41:33 there is not his like, who is **m** without fear. 6213
Ps 7:12 he hath bent his bow, and **m** it **ready**. 3559
7:15 He **m** a pit, and digged it, and is fallen into 3738
7:15 and is fallen into the ditch *which* he **m**. 6466
8: 5 For thou hast **m** him a little **lower** than 2637
9:15 are sunk down in the pit *that* they **m**: 6213
18: 4 the floods of ungodly men **m** me **afraid**. 1204
18:11 He **m** darkness his secret place; his pavilion 7896
18:35 and thy gentleness hath **m** me **great**. 7235
18:43 thou hast **m** me the head of the heathen: 7760
21: 6 For thou hast **m** him most blessed for ever: 7896
21: 6 thou hast **m** him exceeding glad with thy 2302
30: 1 and hast not **m** my foes **to rejoice** over me. 8055
30: 7 thou hast **m** my mountain **to stand** strong: 5975
30: 8 and unto the LORD I **m supplication**. 2603
33: 6 word of the LORD were the heavens **m**; 6213
39: 5 thou hast **m** my days *as* a handbreadth; 5414
45: 1 I speak of the **things** which I have **m** 4639
45: 8 *where*by they have **m** thee **glad**. 8055
46: 8 what desolations he hath **m** in the earth. 7760
49:16 Be not thou afraid when one is **m rich**, 6238
50: 5 those that have **m** a covenant with me by 3772
52: 7 *this is* the man *that* **m** not God his strength; 7760
60: 2 Thou hast **m** the earth **to tremble**; 7493
60: 3 **m** us **to drink** the wine *of* astonishment. 8248
69:11 I **m** sackcloth also my garment; and 5414
72:15 **prayer** also shall be **m** for him continually; 6419
74:17 the earth: thou hast **m** summer and winter. 3335
77: 6 and my spirit **m diligent search**. 2664
78:13 and he **m** the waters **to stand** as a heap. 5324
78:50 He **m** a way to his anger; he spared not 6424
78:52 **m** his own people **to go forth** like sheep, 5265
78:55 **m** the tribes of Israel **to dwell** in their tents. 7931
78:64 and their widows **m** no **lamentation**. 1058
86: 9 All nations whom thou hast **m** shall come 6213
88: 8 thou hast **m** me an abomination unto them: 7896
89: 3 I have **m** a covenant with my chosen, 3772
89:39 Thou hast **m void** the covenant of thy 5010
89:42 thou hast **m** all his enemies **to rejoice**. 8055
89:43 and hast not **m** him **to stand** in the battle. 6965
89:44 Thou hast **m** his glory **to cease**, and cast his 7673
89:47 wherefore hast thou **m** all men in vain? 1254
91: 9 Because thou hast **m** the LORD, *which is* 7760
92: 4 LORD, hast **m** me **glad** through thy work: 8055
95: 5 The sea *is* his, and he **m** it: and his hands 6213
96: 5 *are* idols: but the LORD **m** the heavens. 6213
98: 2 The LORD hath **m known** his salvation: 3045
100: 3 *it is* he *that* hath **m** us, and not we 6213
103: 7 He **m known** his ways unto Moses, his acts 3045
104:24 in wisdom hast thou **m** them all: the earth is 6213
104:26 *whom* thou hast **m** to play therein. 3335
105: 9 Which *covenant* he **m** with Abraham, and 3772
105:21 He **m** him lord of his house, and ruler of all 7760
105:24 and **m** them **stronger** than their enemies. 6105
105:28 He sent darkness, and **m** it **dark**; and 2821

Ps 106:19 They **m** a calf in Horeb, and 6213
106:46 He **m** them also to be pitied of all those that 5414
111: 4 He hath **m** his wonderful works to be 6213
115:15 You *are* blessed of the LORD which **m** 6213
118:24 This *is* the day *which* the LORD hath **m**; 6213
119:60 I **m haste**, and delayed not to keep thy 2363
119:73 Thy hands have **m** me and fashioned me: 6213
119:98 hast **m** me **wiser** than mine enemies: 2449
119:126 to work: *for* they have **m void** thy law. 6565
121: 2 the LORD, which **m** heaven and earth. 6213
124: 8 of the LORD, who **m** heaven and earth. 6213
129: 3 upon my back: they **m long** their furrows. 748
134: 3 The LORD that **m** heaven and earth bless 6213
136: 5 To him that by wisdom **m** the heavens: 6213
136: 7 To him that **m** great lights: for his mercy 6213
136:14 **m** Israel **to pass through** the midst of it: 5674
139:14 for I am fearfully and **wonderfully m**: 6381
139:15 when I was **m** in secret, *and* 6213
143: 3 he hath **m** me **to dwell** in darkness, as those 3427
146: 6 Which **m** heaven, and earth, the sea, and all 6213
148: 6 he hath **m** a decree which shall not pass. 5414
149: 2 Let Israel rejoice in him that **m** him: let 6213
Pr 8:26 While as yet he had not **m** the earth, nor 6213
11:25 The liberal soul shall be **m fat**: and he that 1878
13: 4 but the soul of the diligent shall be **m fat**. 1878
14:33 *which is* in the midst of fools is **m known**. 3045
15:19 but the way of the righteous *is* **m plain**. 5549
16: 4 The LORD hath **m** all *things* for himself: 6466
20: 9 Who can say, I have **m** my heart **clean**, 2135
20:12 the LORD hath **m** even both of them. 6213
21:11 scorner is punished, the simple is **m wise**: 2449
22:19 I have **m known** to thee *this* day, even *to* 3045
28:25 his trust in the LORD shall be **m fat**. 1878
Ecc 1:15 *which is* crooked cannot be **m straight**: 8626
2: 4 I **m** me **great** works; I builded me houses; 1431
2: 5 I **m** me gardens and orchards, and I planted 6213
2: 6 I **m** me pools of water, to water therewith 6213
3:11 He hath **m** every *thing* beautiful in his time: 6213
7: 3 of the countenance the heart is **m better**. 3190
7:13 *that* straight, which he hath **m crooked**? 5791
7:29 have I found, that God hath **m** man upright; 6213
10:19 A feast is **m** for laughter, and wine maketh 6213
SS 1: 6 they **m** me the keeper of the vineyards; *but* 7760
3: 9 King Solomon **m** himself a chariot of 6213
3:10 He **m** the pillars thereof *of* silver, 6213
6:12 my soul **m** me *like* the chariots of 7760
Isa 2: 8 *that* which their own fingers have **m**: 6213
2:17 and the haughtiness of men shall be **m low**: 8213
2:20 which they **m** *each one* for himself to 6213
5: 2 midst of it, and also **m** a winepress therein: 2672
14: 3 bondage wherein thou wast **m to serve**, 5647
14:16 *Is* this the man that **m** the earth **to tremble**, 7264
14:17 *That* **m** the world as a wilderness, and 7760
16:10 I have **m** *their vintage* shouting **to cease**. 7673
17: 4 *that* the glory of Jacob shall be **m thin**, and 1809
17: 8 shall respect *that* which his fingers have **m**, 6213
21: 2 all the sighing thereof have I **m to cease**. 7673
22:11 Ye **m** also a ditch between the two walls 6213
25: 2 For thou hast **m** of a city a heap; *of* a 7760
26:14 and **m** all their memory **to perish**. 6
27:11 he that **m** them will not have mercy on 6213
28:15 We have **m** a covenant with death, and 3772
28:15 for we have **m** lies our refuge, and 7760
28:22 not mockers, lest your bands be **m strong**: 2388
28:25 When he hath **m plain** the face thereof, 7737
29:16 for shall the work say of him that **m** it, 6213
29:16 say of him that made it, He **m** me not? 6213
30:33 it is prepared; he hath **m** *it* **deep** *and* large: 6009
31: 7 which your own hands have **m** unto you *for* 6213
34: 6 it is **m fat** with fatness, *and* with the blood 1878
34: 7 and their dust **m fat** with fatness. 1878
37:16 of the earth: thou hast **m** heaven and earth. 6213
40: 4 every mountain and hill shall be **m low**: 8213
40: 4 the crooked shall be **m straight**, and 4334
41: 2 before him, and **m** *him* **rule over** kings? 7287
43: 7 I have formed him; yea, I have **m** him. 6213
43:24 thou hast **m** me **to serve** with thy sins, 5647
44: 2 Thus saith the LORD that **m** thee, and 6213
45:12 I have **m** the earth, and created man upon 6213
45:18 God himself that formed the earth and **m** it; 6213
46: 4 to hoar hairs will I carry *you*: I have **m**, 6213
49: 1 mother hath he **m mention** of my name. 2142
49: 2 he hath **m** my mouth like a sharp sword; 7760
49: 2 hath he hid me, and **m** me a polished shaft; 7760
49:17 they that **m** thee **waste** shall go forth of 2717
51:10 that hath **m** the depths of the sea a way for 7760
51:12 of the son of man *which* shall be **m** *as* 5414
52:10 The LORD hath **m bare** his holy arm in 2834
53: 9 he **m** his grave with the wicked, and 5414
53:12 and **m intercession** for the transgressors. 6293
57: 8 thy bed, and **m** thee *a covenant* with them; 3772
57:16 before me, and the souls *which* I have **m**. 6213
59: 8 they have **m** them **crooked** paths: 6140
63:17 why hast thou **m** us **to err** from thy ways, 8582
66: 2 For all those *things* hath mine hand **m**, and 6213
66: 8 the earth be **m to bring forth** in one day? 2342
Jer 1:18 I have **m** thee *this* day a defenced city, and 5414
2: 7 and **m** mine heritage an abomination. 7760
2:15 *and* yelled, and they **m** his land waste: 7896
2:28 where *are* thy gods that thou hast **m** thee? 6213
5: 3 they have **m** their faces **harder** than a rock; 2388
8: 8 certainly in vain **m** he *it*; the pen of 6213
10:11 The gods that have not **m** the heavens and 5648
10:12 He hath **m** the earth by his power, he hath 6213
10:25 and have **m** his habitation **desolate**. 8074
11:10 my covenant which I **m** with their fathers. 3772
12:10 they have **m** my pleasant portion a desolate 5414
12:11 They have **m** it desolate, *and being* desolate 7760
12:11 the whole land is **m desolate**, because 8074
13:22 thy skirts discovered, *and* thy heels **m bare**. 2554
13:27 wilt thou not be **m clean**? when *shall it* 2891
14:22 upon thee: for thou hast **m** all these *things*. 6213
17:23 **m** their neck **stiff**, that *they* might not hear, 7185
18: 4 the vessel that he **m** of clay was marred in 6213
18: 4 so he **m** it again another vessel, as seemed 6213

Jer 19:11 that cannot be **m whole** again: 7495
20: 8 the word of the LORD was **m** a reproach 1961
25:17 **m** all the nations **to drink**, unto whom 8248
26: 8 when Jeremiah had **m an end** of speaking 3615
27: 5 I have **m** the earth, the man and the beast 6213
29:26 The LORD hath **m** thee priest in the stead 5414
31:32 Not according to the covenant that I **m** with 3772
32:17 thou hast **m** the heaven and the earth by thy 6213
32:20 and hast **m** thee a name, as *at* this day; 6213
34: 8 after that the king Zedekiah had **m** a 3772
34:13 I **m** a covenant with your fathers in the day 3772
34:15 ye had **m** a covenant before me in 3772
34:18 the covenant which they had **m** before me, 3772
36:25 Gemariah had **m intercession** to the king 6293
37: 1 of Babylon **m king** in the land of Judah. 4427
37:15 the scribe: for they had **m** that the prison. 6213
38:16 *As* the LORD liveth, that **m** us this soul, 6213
40: 5 hath **m governor** over the cities of Judah, 6485
40: 7 **m** Gedaliah the son of Ahikam **governor** in 6485
41: 2 of Babylon had **m governor** over the land. 6485
41: 9 *was* it which Asa the king had **m** for fear of 6213
41:18 whom the king of Babylon **m governor** in 6485
43: 1 *that* when Jeremiah had **m an end** of 3615
46:10 be satiate and **m drunk** with their blood: 7301
46:16 He **m many** to fall, yea, one fell upon 7235
49:10 I have **m** Esau **bare**, I have uncovered his 2834
51: 7 that **m** all the earth **drunken**: 7937
51:15 He hath **m** the earth by his power, he hath 6213
51:34 crushed me, he hath **m** me an empty vessel, 3322
51:63 when thou hast **m an end** of reading this 3615
52:20 which king Solomon had **m** in the house of 6213
La 1:13 he hath **m** me desolate *and* faint all the day. 5414
1:14 he hath **m** my strength to **fall**, the Lord 3782
2: 7 they have **m** a noise in the house of 5414
2: 8 he **m** the rampart and the wall to **lament**; 56
3: 4 My flesh and my skin hath he **m old**; 1086
3: 7 cannot get out: he hath **m** my chain **heavy**. 3513
3: 9 hewn stone, he hath **m** my paths **crooked**. 5753
3:11 pulled me in pieces: he hath **m** me desolate. 7760
3:15 he hath **m** me **drunken** *with* wormwood. 7301
3:45 Thou hast **m** us *as* the offscouring and 7760
Eze 3: 8 I have **m** thy face strong against their faces, 5414
3: 9 As an adamant harder than flint have I **m** 5414
3:17 I have **m** thee a watchman unto the house 5414
6: 6 altars may be laid waste and **m desolate**, 816
7:20 they **m** the images of their abominations 6213
13: 5 neither **m up the hedge** for 1443+1447
13: 6 they have **m** *others* **to hope** that *they* would 3176
13:22 *ye* have **m** the heart of the righteous **sad**, 3512
13:22 the righteous sad, whom I have not **m sad**; 3510
16:24 and hast **m** thee a high place in every street. 6213
16:25 hast **m** thy beauty **to be abhorred**, and 8581
17:13 **m** a covenant with him, and hath taken an 3772
17:16 *where* the king *dwelleth* that **m** him **king**, 4427
17:24 and have **m** the dry tree **to flourish**: 6524
19: 5 of her whelps, *and* **m** him a young lion. 7760
20: 5 **m** myself **known** unto them in the land of 3045
20: 9 whose sight I **m** myself **known** unto them, 3045
20:28 there also they **m** their sweet savour, and 7760
21:15 ah, *it is* **m** bright, *it is* wrapt up for 6213
21:21 he **m** *his* arrows **bright**, he consulted with 7043
21:24 have **m** your iniquity **to be remembered**, 2142
22: 4 *thyself* in thine idols which thou hast **m**; 6213
22: 4 have I **m** thee a reproach unto the heathen, 5414
22:13 at thy dishonest gain which thou hast **m**, 6213
22:25 they have **m** her **many** widows in the midst 7235
26:10 enter into a city wherein is **m a breach**. 1234
26:15 when the **slaughter** is **m** in the midst 2026+2027
27: 5 They have **m** all thy *ship* boards of fir trees 1129
27: 6 *Of* the oaks of Bashan have they **m** thine 6213
27: 6 the company of the Ashurites have **m** thy 6213
27:11 they have **m** thy beauty **perfect**. 3634
27:24 bound with cords, and **m of cedar**, 729
27:25 **m** very **glorious** in the midst of the seas. 3513
29: 3 *is* mine own, and I have **m** *it for* myself. 6213
29: 9 The river *is* mine, and I have **m** *it*. 6213
29:18 every head *was* **m bald**, and every shoulder 7139
31: 4 The waters **m** him **great**, the deep set him 1431
31: 6 All the fowls of heaven **m** their **nests** in his 7077
31: 9 I have **m** him fair by the multitude of his 6213
31:16 I **m** the nations **to shake** at the sound of his 7493
36: 3 Because *they* have **m** *you* **desolate**, and 8074
39:26 in their land, and none **m** *them* **afraid**. 2729
40:14 He **m** also posts *of* threescore cubits, 6213
40:17 a pavement **m** for the court round about: 6213
41:18 *it was* **m** *with* cherubims and palm trees, 6213
41:19 *it was* **m** through all the house round about. 6213
41:20 the door *were* cherubims and palm trees **m**, 6213
41:25 *there were* **m** on them, on the doors of 6213
41:25 palm trees, like as *were* **m** upon the walls; 6213
42:15 Now when he had **m an end** of measuring 3615
43:23 When thou hast **m an end** of cleansing *it*, 3615
46:23 *it was* **m** *with* boiling places under the rows 6213
Da 2: 5 and your houses shall be **m** a dunghill. 7761
2:15 Then Arioch **m** the thing **known** to Daniel. 3046
2:17 **m** the thing **known** to Hananiah, Mishael, 3046
2:23 hast **m known** unto me now what we 3046
2:23 for thou hast *now* **m known** unto us 3046
2:38 and hath **m** thee **ruler** over them all. 7981
2:45 the great God hath **m known** to the king 3046
2:48 the king **m** Daniel a **great** man, and 7236
2:48 **m** him **ruler** over the whole province of 7981
3: 1 Nebuchadnezzar the king **m** an image of 5648
3:10 Thou, O king, hast **m** a decree, that every 7761
3:15 and worship the image which I have **m**; 5648
3:29 and their houses shall be **m** a dunghill: 7739
4: 5 I saw a dream which **m** me **afraid**, and 1763
4: 6 Therefore **m** I a decree to bring in all 7761
5: 1 Belshazzar the king **m** a great feast to a 5648
5:11 **m** master of the magicians, astrologers, 6966
5:21 his heart was **m** like the beasts, and 7739
5:29 and **m a proclamation** concerning him, 3745
7: 4 **m stand** upon the feet as a man, and 6966
7:16 **m** me **know** the interpretation of the things. 3046
7:21 the same horn **m** war with the saints, and 5648

M

Da 9: 1 which was **m king** over the realm of 4427
9: 4 **m** my **confession**, and said, O Lord, 3034
9:13 yet **m** we not our **prayer** before 2470
11:23 after the league ***m*** with him he shall work NIH
12:10 shall be purified, and **m white**, and tried; 3835
Hos 5: 9 among the tribes of Israel have I **m known** 3045
7: 5 have **m** *him* **sick** *with* bottles of wine; 2470
7: 6 For they have **m ready** their heart like an 7126
8: 4 they have **m princes**, and I knew *it* not: 7786
8: 4 and their gold have they **m** them idols, 6213
8: 6 the workman **m** it; therefore it *is* not God: 6213
8:11 Because Ephraim hath **m many** altars to 7235
10: 1 of his land they have **m goodly** images. 2895
12: 4 he wept, and **m supplication** unto him: 2603
13: 2 have **m** them molten images of their silver, 6213
Joel 1: 7 he hath **m** it **clean** bare, and cast *it* away; 2834
1: 7 *it* away; the branches thereof are **m white**. 3835
1:18 yea, the flocks of sheep are **m desolate**. 816
Am 4:10 **m** the stink of your camps **to come up** unto 5927
5:26 star of your god, which ye **m** to yourselves. 6213
7: 2 *that* when they had **m an end** of eating 3615
7: 7 the Lord stood upon a wall **m** by a NIH
Ob 1: 2 I have **m** thee small among the heathen: 5414
Jnh 1: 9 which hath **m** the sea and the dry *land*. 6213
1:16 a sacrifice unto the LORD, and **m** vows. 5087
4: 5 there **m** him a booth, and sat under it in 6213
4: 6 a gourd, and **m** *it* **to come up** over Jonah, 5927
Na 2: 3 The shield of his mighty *men is* **m red**, 119
2:11 the lion's whelp, and none **m** *them* **afraid**? 2729
Hab 2:17 *which* **m** them **afraid**, because of men's 2865
3: 9 Thy bow was **m quite naked**, 5783+6181
Zep 3: 6 I **m** their streets **waste**, that none passeth 2717
Zec 7:12 they **m** their hearts *as* an adamant stone, 7760
9:13 and **m** thee as the sword of a mighty *man*. 7760
10: 3 hath **m** them as his goodly horse in 7760
11:10 covenant which I had **m** with all the people. 3772
Mal 2: 9 Therefore have I also **m** you contemptible 5414
Mt 4: 3 command that these stones be **m** bread. 1096
9:16 from the garment, and the rent is **m** worse. 1096
9:22 good comfort; thy faith hath **m** thee **whole**. 4982
9:22 And the woman was **m whole** from that 4982
11: 1 when Jesus had **m an end** of commanding 5055
14:36 many as touched were **m perfectly whole**. 1295
15: 6 **m** the commandment of God **of none effect** 208
15:28 And her daughter was **m whole** from that 2390
18:25 and all that he had, and **payment** to be **m**. 591
19: 4 that he which **m** *them* at the beginning 2936
19: 4 made *them* at the beginning **m** them male 4160
19:12 which were **m eunuchs** of men: 2134
19:12 which have **m** themselves **eunuchs** for 2134
20:12 and thou hast **m** them equal unto us, 4160
21:13 of prayer; but ye have **m** it a den of thieves. 4160
22: 2 which **m** a marriage for his son, 4160
22: 5 But they **m light of** *it*, and went their ways, 272
23:15 to make one proselyte, and when he is **m**, 1096
24:45 whom his lord hath **m ruler** over his 2525
25: 6 And at midnight there was a cry **m**, Behold, 1096
25:16 the same, and **m** *them* other five talents. 4160
26:19 and they **m ready** the passover. 2090
27:24 but *that* rather a tumult was **m**, he took 1096
27:64 that the sepulchre be **m sure** until the third 805
27:66 So they went, and **m** the sepulchre **sure**, 805
Mk 2:21 away *from* the old, and the rent is **m** worse. 1096
2:27 The sabbath was **m** for man, *and* not man 1096
5:34 Daughter, thy faith hath **m** thee **whole**; 4982
6:21 that Herod on his birthday **m** a supper to 4160
6:56 and as many as touched him were **m whole**. 4982
8:25 again upon his eyes, and **m** him look up: 4160
10: 6 beginning of the creation God **m** them male 4160
10:52 Go thy way; thy faith hath **m** thee **whole**. 4982
11:17 but ye have **m** it a den of thieves. 4160
14: 4 Why was this waste of the ointment **m**? 1096
14:16 unto them: and they **m ready** the passover. 2090
14:58 destroy this temple that is **m with hands**, 5499
14:58 days I will build another **m without hands**. 886
15: 7 **m insurrection with** *him*, who had 4955
Lk 1:62 And they **m signs** to his father, how he 1770
2: 2 (*And* this taxing was first **m** when Cyrenius 1096
2:15 which the Lord hath **m known** unto us. 1107
2:17 **m known abroad** the saying which was 1232
3: 5 and the crooked shall be **m** straight, and NIG
3: 5 and the rough ways *shall be* **m** smooth; NIG
4: 3 command this stone that it be **m** bread. 1096
5:29 And Levi **m** him a great feast in his own 4160
8:17 is secret, that shall not be **m** manifest; 1096
8:48 thy faith hath **m** thee **whole**; go in peace.) 4982
8:50 believe only, and she shall be **m whole**. 4982
9:15 And they did so, and **m** *them* **all sit down**. 347
11:40 did not he that **m** that *which is* without 4160
12:14 who **m** me a judge or a divider over you? 2525
13:13 and immediately she was **m straight**, and 461
14:12 thee again, and a recompence be **m** thee. 1096
14:16 A certain man **m** a great supper, and 4160
17:19 go *thy way*: thy faith hath **m** thee **whole**. 4982
19: 6 And he **m haste**, and came down, and 4692
19:46 of prayer: but ye have **m** it a den of thieves. 4160
22:13 unto them: and they **m ready** the passover. 2090
23:12 Pilate and Herod were **m** friends together: 1096
23:19 (Who for a certain sedition **m** in the city, 1096
24:22 *also* of our company **m** us **astonished**, 1839
24:28 he **m as though** *he* would have gone 4364
Jn 1: 3 All *things* were **m** by him; and without him 1096
1: 3 without him was not any *thing* **m** that was 1096
1: 3 him was not any *thing* made that was **m**. 1096
1:10 and the world was **m** by him, and the world 1096
1:14 And the Word was **m** flesh, and 1096
1:31 but that he should be **m manifest** to Israel, 5319
2: 9 feast had tasted the water *that was* **m** wine, 1096
2:15 And when he had **m** a scourge of small 4160
3:21 that his deeds may be **m manifest**, that they 5319
4: 1 how the Pharisees had heard that Jesus **m** 4160
4:46 of Galilee, where he **m** the water wine. 4160
5: 4 was **m** whole of whatsoever disease he had. 1096
5: 6 he saith unto him, Wilt thou be **m** whole? 1096
5: 9 And immediately the man was **m** whole, 1096
Jn 5:11 He answered them, He that **m** me whole, 4160
5:14 said unto him, Behold, thou art **m** whole: 1096
5:15 that it was Jesus, which had **m** him whole. 4160
7:23 I have **m** a man every whit whole on 4160
8:33 *man*: how sayest thou, Ye shall be **m** free? 1096
9: 3 of God should be **m manifest** in him. 5319
9: 6 and **m** clay of the spittle, and he anointed 4160
9:11 A man *that is* called Jesus **m** clay, and 4160
9:14 And it was the sabbath day when Jesus **m** 4160
9:39 and that they which see might be **m** blind. 1096
12: 2 There they **m** him a supper; and Martha 4160
15:15 of my Father I have **m known** unto you. 1107
17:23 in me, that they may be **m perfect** in one; 5048
18:18 officers stood *there*, who had **m** a fire of 4160
19: 7 because he **m** himself the Son of God. 4160
19:23 took his garments, and **m** four parts, 4160
Ac 1: 1 The former treatise have I **m**, 4160
2:28 Thou hast **m known** to me the ways of life; 1107
2:36 that God hath **m** that same Jesus, whom ye 4160
3:12 or holiness we had **m** this *man* to walk? 4160
3:16 faith in his name hath **m** this *man* **strong**, 4732
3:25 of the covenant which God **m** with our 1303
4: 9 by what *means* he is **m whole**; 4982
4:24 which hast **m** heaven, and earth, and 4160
4:35 distribution was **m** unto every man NIG
7:10 and he **m** him governor over Egypt and 2525
7:13 at the second time Joseph was **m known** 319
7:13 Joseph's kindred was **m** known unto 1096
7:27 Who **m** thee a ruler and a judge over us? 2525
7:35 saying, Who **m** thee a ruler and a judge? 2525
7:41 And they **m a calf** in those days, and 3447
7:43 figures which ye **m** to worship them: 4160
7:48 dwelleth not in temples **m with hands**; 5499
7:50 Hath not my hand **m** all these *things*? 4160
8: 2 and **m** great lamentation over him. 4160
8: 3 As for Saul, he **m havock** of the church, 3075
9:39 the coats and garments which Dorcas **m**, 4160
10:10 but while they **m ready**, he fell into a 3903
10:17 had **m inquiry** for Simon's house, 1331
12: 5 prayer was **m** without ceasing of the church 1096
12:20 **m** Blastus the king's chamberlain their **friend**, 3982
12:21 his throne, and **m an oration** unto them. 1215
13:32 how that the promise which was **m** unto 1096
14: 2 **m** their minds **evil affected** against 2559
14: 5 And when there was an assault **m** both of 1096
14:15 which **m** heaven, and earth, and the sea, 4160
15: 7 a good while ago God **m choice** among us, 1586
16:13 river side, where prayer was wont to be **m**; NIG
16:24 and **m** their feet **fast** in the stocks. 805
17:24 God that **m** the world and all *things* therein, 4160
17:24 dwelleth not in temples **m with hands**; 5499
17:26 And hath **m** of one blood all nations of men 4160
18:12 **m insurrection** with one accord **against** 2721
19:24 which **m** silver shrines for Diana, 4160
19:26 they be no gods, which are **m** with hands: 1096
19:33 would have **m** *his* **defence** unto the people. 626
20:28 over the which the Holy Ghost hath **m** you 5087
21:40 And when there was **m** a great silence, 1096
22: 6 as I **m** my **journey**, and was come nigh 4198
23:13 they were more *than* forty which had **m** 4160
26: 6 am judged for the hope of the promise **m** of 1096
27:40 mainsail to the wind, and **m** toward shore. 2722
Ro 1: 3 which was **m** of the seed of David 1096
1:20 being understood by the **things that are m**, 4161
1:23 into an image **m** like to corruptible man, NIG
2:25 thy circumcision is **m** uncircumcision. 1096
4:14 faith is **m void**, and the promise made of 2758
4:14 and the promise **m of none effect**: 2673
4:17 I have **m** thee a father of many nations,) 5087
5:19 man's disobedience many were **m** sinners, 2525
5:19 by the obedience of one shall many be **m** 2525
6:18 Being then **m free** from sin, ye became 1659
6:22 But now being **m free** from sin, and 1659
7:13 then that which is good **m** death unto me? 1096
8: 2 Jesus hath **m** me **free** from the law of sin 1659
8:20 For the creature was **m subject** to vanity, 5293
9:20 that formed *it*, Why hast thou **m** me thus? 4160
9:29 and been **m like** unto Gomorrha. 3666
10:10 with the mouth **confession** is **m** unto 3670
10:20 I was **m** manifest unto them that asked not 1096
11: 9 Let their table be **m** a snare, and a 1096+1519
14:21 or is offended, or is ***m*** weak. NIG
15: 8 to confirm the promises **m** unto the fathers: NIG
15:27 For if the Gentiles have been **m partakers** 2841
16:26 But now is **m manifest**, and by 5319
16:26 **m known** to all nations for the obedience 1107
1Co 1:17 cross of Christ should be **m of none effect**. 2758
1:20 hath not God **m foolish** the wisdom of this 3471
1:30 who of God is **m** unto us wisdom, and 1096
3:13 Every man's work shall be **m** manifest: 1096
4: 9 for we are **m** a spectacle unto the world, 1096
4:13 we are **m** as the filth of the world, *and* 1096
7:21 but if thou mayest be **m** free, use *it* rather. 1096
9:19 *men*, yet have I **m** myself **servant** unto all, 1402
9:22 I am **m** all *things* to all *men*, that I might by 1096
11:19 that they *which are* approved may be **m** 1096
12:13 have been all **m to drink** into one Spirit. 4222
14:25 And thus are the secrets of his heart **m** 1096
15:22 even so in Christ shall all be **m alive**. 2227
15:45 first man Adam was **m** a living soul; 1096+1519
15:45 the last Adam *was* ***m*** a quickening spirit. NIG
2Co 2: 2 but *the same* which is **m sorry** by me? 3076
3: 6 Who also hath **m** us **able** ministers of 2427
3:10 For even that which was **m glorious** had no 1392
4:10 of Jesus might be **m manifest** in our body. 5319
4:11 might be **m manifest** in our mortal flesh. 5319
5: 1 a house **not m with hand**, eternal in 886
5:11 but we are **m manifest** unto God; and 5319
5:11 I trust also are **m manifest** in your 5319
5:21 For he hath **m** him *to be* sin for us, 4160
5:21 that we might be **m** the righteousness of 1096
7: 8 For though I **m** you **sorry** with a letter, I do 3076
7: 8 that the same epistle hath **m** you **sorry**, 3076
7: 9 not that ye were **m sorry**, but that ye 3076
7: 9 for ye were **m sorry** after a godly manner, 3076
2Co 7:14 so our boasting, which *I* ***m*** before Titus, NIG
10:16 line of *things* **m ready to** our **hand**. 1519+2092
11: 6 we *have been* throughly **m manifest** 5319
12: 9 for my strength is **m perfect** in weakness. 5048
Gal 3: 3 are ye now **m perfect** by the flesh? 2005
3:13 the curse of the law, being **m** a curse for us: 1096
3:16 and his seed were the promises **m**. 3004
3:19 should come to whom the **promise** was **m**; 1861
4: 4 **m** of a woman, made under the law, 1096
4: 4 made of a woman, **m** under the law, 1096
5: 1 liberty wherewith Christ hath **m** us **free**, 1659
Eph 1: 6 wherein he hath **m** us **accepted** in 5487
1: 9 Having **m known** unto us the mystery of 1107
2: 6 **m** *us* **sit together** in heavenly *places* in 4776
2:11 the Circumcision in the flesh **m by hands**; 5499
2:13 far off are **m** nigh by the blood of Christ. 1096
2:14 who hath **m** both one, and hath broken 4160
3: 3 How that by revelation he **m known** unto 1107
3: 5 Which in other ages was not **m known** 1107
3: 7 Whereof I was **m** a minister, according to 1096
5:13 are reproved are **m manifest** by the light: 5319
Php 2: 7 But **m** himself **of no reputation**, and 2758
2: 7 and was **m** in the likeness of men: 1096
3:10 being **m conformable** unto his death; 4833
4: 6 let your requests be **m known** unto God. 1107
Col 1:12 which hath **m** us **meet** to be partakers of 2427
1:20 having **m peace** through the blood of his 1517
1:23 whereof I Paul am **m** a minister; 1096
1:25 Whereof I am **m** a minister, according to 1096
1:26 but now is **m manifest** to his saints: 5319
2:11 with the circumcision **m without hands**, 886
2:15 and powers, he **m a shew** of *them* openly, 1165
1Ti 1: 9 that the law is not **m** for a righteous *man*, 2749
1:19 concerning faith have **m shipwrack**: 3489
2: 1 *and* giving of thanks, be **m** for all men; 4160
2Ti 1:10 But is now **m manifest** by the appearing of 5319
Tit 3: 7 we should be **m** heirs according to the hope 1096
Heb 1: 2 all *things*, by whom also he **m** the worlds; 4160
1: 4 Being **m** so much better than the angels, 1096
2: 9 who was **m** a little **lower** than the angels, 1642
2:17 behoved him to be **m like** unto *his* brethren, 3666
3:14 For we are **m** partakers of Christ, if we 1096
5: 5 So also Christ glorified not himself to be **m** 1096
5: 9 And being **m perfect**, he became the author 5048
6: 4 and were **m** partakers of the Holy Ghost, 1096
6:13 For when God **m promise** to Abraham, 1861
6:20 **m** a high priest for ever after the order of 1096
7: 3 end of life; but **m like unto** the Son of God; 871
7:12 there is **m** of necessity a change also of 1096
7:16 Who is **m**, not after the law of a carnal 1096
7:19 For the law **m** nothing **perfect**, but 5048
7:20 as not without an oath *he was m priest*: NIG
7:21 (For those priests were **m** without an oath; 1096
7:22 much was Jesus **m** a surety of a better 1096
7:26 and **m** higher than the heavens; 1096
8: 9 Not according to the covenant that I **m** with 4160
8:13 A new *covenant*, he hath **m** the first **old**. 3822
9: 2 For there was a tabernacle **m**; the first, 2680
9: 8 the holiest *of all* was not yet **m manifest**, 5319
9:11 not **m with hands**, that is to say, not of this 5499
9:24 entered into the holy *places* **m with hands**, 5499
10: 3 a remembrance *again* ***m*** of sins every year. NIG
10:13 till his enemies be **m** his footstool. 5087
10:33 whilst ye were **m a gazingstock** both by 2301
11: 3 that *things* which are seen were not **m** of 1096
11:22 **m mention** of the departing of the children 3421
11:34 out of weakness were **m strong**, waxed 1743
11:40 they without us should not be **m perfect**. 5048
12:23 and to the spirits of just *men* **m perfect**, 5048
12:27 as of *things* that are **m**, that those *things* 4160
Jas 1:10 But the rich, in that he is **m low**: because 5014
2:22 and by works was faith **m perfect**? 5048
3: 9 which are **m** after the similitude of God. 1096
1Pe 2: 7 the same is **m** the head of the corner, 1096+1519
3:22 and powers being **m subject** unto him. 5293
2Pe 1:16 when we **m known** unto you the power and 1107
2:12 brute beasts, **m** to be taken and destroyed, 1080
1Jn 2:19 be **m manifest** that they were not all of us. 5319
4:17 Herein is our love **m perfect**, that we may 5048
4:18 He that feareth is not **m perfect** in love. 5048
5:10 he that believeth not God hath **m** him a liar; 4160
Rev 1: 6 And hath **m** us kings and priests unto God 4160
5:10 And hast **m** us unto our God kings and 4160
7:14 **m** them **white** in the blood of the Lamb. 3021
8:11 of the waters, because they were **m bitter**. 4087
14: 7 and worship him that **m** heaven, and earth, 4160
14: 8 she **m** all nations **drink** of the wine of 4222
15: 4 for thy judgments are **m manifest**. 5319
17: 2 **m drunk** with the wine of her fornication. 3184
18:15 of these *things*, which were **m rich** by her, 4147
18:19 wherein were **m rich** all that had ships in 4147
18:19 for in one hour is she **m desolate**. 2049
19: 7 is come, and his wife hath **m** herself **ready**. 2090

MADEST (10) [MAKE]

Ne 9: 8 **m** a covenant with him to give the land of 3772
9:14 **m known** unto them thy holy sabbath, and 3045
Ps 8: 6 Thou **m** him **to have dominion** over 4910
80:15 the branch *that* thou **m strong** for thyself. 553
80:17 upon the son of man *whom* thou **m strong** 553
Eze 16:17 **m** to thyself images of men, and 6213
29: 7 and **m** all their loins **to be at a stand**. 5976
Jnh 4:10 thou hast not laboured, neither **m** it **grow**; 1431
Ac 21:38 which before these days **m an uproar**, and 387
Heb 2: 7 Thou **m** him a little **lower** than the angels; 1642

MADIAN (1) [MIDIAN]

Ac 7:29 and was a stranger in the land of **M**, 3099

MADMANNAH (2)

Jos 15:31 And Ziklag, and **M**, and Sansannah, 4089
1Ch 2:49 She bare also Shaaph the father of **M**, 4089

M

MADMEN (1)
Jer 48: 2 Also thou shalt be cut down, O **M**; 4086

MADMENAH (1)
Isa 10:31 **M** is removed; the inhabitants of Gebim 4088

MADNESS (9) [MAD]
Dt 28:28 The LORD shall smite thee with **m**, and 7697
Ecc 1:17 to know wisdom, and to know **m** and folly: 1947
2:12 myself to behold wisdom, and **m**, and folly: 1947
7:25 of folly, even of foolishness *and* **m**: 1947
9: 3 **m** *is* in their heart while they live, and 1947
10:13 and the end of his talk *is* mischievous **m**. 1948
Zec 12: 4 with astonishment, and his rider with **m**: 7697
Lk 6:11 And they were filled with **m**; and *454*
2Pe 2:16 man's voice forbad the **m** of the prophet. *3913*

MADON (2)
Jos 11: 1 *things,* that he sent to Jobab king of **M**, 4068
12:19 The king of **M**, one; the king of Hazor, one; 4068

MAGADAN See MAGDALA

MAGBISH (1)
Ezr 2:30 The children of **M**, an hundred fifty and 4019

MAGDALA (1) [MAGDALENE]
Mt 15:39 took ship, and came into the coasts of **M**. *3093*

MAGDALENE (12) [MAGDALA]
Mt 27:56 Among which was Mary **M**, and Mary *3094*
27:61 And there was Mary **M**, and the other *3094*
28: 1 came Mary **M** and the other Mary to see *3094*
Mk 15:40 among whom was Mary **M**, and Mary *3094*
15:47 And Mary **M** and Mary *the mother* of Joses *3094*
16: 1 Mary **M**, and Mary the *mother* of James, *3094*
16: 9 he appeared first to Mary **M**, out of whom *3094*
Lk 8: 2 evil spirits and infirmities, Mary called **M**, *3094*
24:10 It was Mary **M**, and Joanna, and Mary *3094*
Jn 19:25 Mary the *wife* of Cleophas, and Mary **M**. *3094*
20: 1 The first *day* of the week cometh Mary **M** *3094*
20:18 Mary **M** came and told the disciples that *3094*

MAGDIEL (2)
Ge 36:43 Duke **M**, duke Iram: these *be* the dukes of 4025
1Ch 1:54 Duke **M**, duke Iram. These *are* the dukes of 4025

MAGICIAN (1) [MAGICIANS]
Da 2:10 *that* asked such things at any **m**, or 2749

MAGICIANS (15) [MAGICIAN]
Ge 41: 8 he sent and called for all the **m** of Egypt, 2748
41:24 I told *this* unto the **m**; but *there was* none 2748
Ex 7:11 now the **m** of Egypt, they also did in like 2748
7:22 the **m** of Egypt did so with their 2748
8: 7 the **m** did so with their enchantments, and 2748
8:18 the **m** did so with their enchantments to 2748
8:19 the **m** said unto Pharaoh, This *is* the finger 2748
9:11 the **m** could not stand before Moses 2748
9:11 for the boil was upon the **m**, and upon all 2748
Da 1:20 found them ten times better than all the **m** 2748
2: 2 the king commanded to call the **m**, and 2748
2:27 the **m**, the soothsayers, shew unto the king; 2749
4: 7 came in the **m**, the astrologers, 2749
4: 9 master of the **m**, because I know that 2749
5:11 made master of the **m**, astrologers, 2749

MAGISTRATE (2) [MAGISTRATES]
Jdg 18: 7 *there was* no **m** in the land, 3423+6114
Lk 12:58 thou goest with thine adversary to the **m**, *758*

MAGISTRATES (8) [MAGISTRATE]
Ezr 7:25 that *is* in thine hand, set **m** and judges, 8200
Lk 12:11 and *unto* **m**, and powers, take ye no thought *746*
Ac 16:20 And brought them to the **m**, saying, *4755*
16:22 and the **m** rent off their clothes, and *4755*
16:35 the **m** sent the sergeants, saying, Let those *4755*
16:36 to Paul, The **m** have sent to let you go: *4755*
16:38 the sergeants told these words unto the **m**: *4755*
Tit 3: 1 to principalities and powers, to **obey m**, *3980*

MAGNIFICAL (1) [MAGNIFY]
1Ch 22: 5 for the LORD *must be* exceeding **m**, 1431

MAGNIFICENCE (1) [MAGNIFY]
Ac 19:27 and her **m** should be destroyed, whom all *3168*

MAGNIFIED (21) [MAGNIFY]
Ge 19:19 in thy sight, and thou hast **m** thy mercy, 1431
Jos 4:14 On that day the LORD **m** Joshua in 1431
2Sa 7:26 let thy name be **m** for ever, saying, 1431
1Ch 17:24 that thy name may be **m** for ever, saying, 1431
29:25 the LORD **m** Solomon exceedingly in 1431
2Ch 1: 1 God *was* with him, and **m** him exceedingly. 1431
32:23 that he was **m** in the sight of all nations 5375
Ps 35:27 say continually, Let the LORD be **m**, 1431
40:16 say continually, The LORD be **m**. 1431
70: 4 salvation say continually, Let God be **m**. 1431
138: 2 for thou hast **m** thy word above all thy 1431
Jer 48:26 for he **m** *himself* against the LORD: 1431
48:42 he hath **m** *himself* against the LORD. 1431
La 1: 9 for the enemy hath **m** *himself.* 1431
Da 8:11 he **m** *himself even* to the prince of the host, 1431
Zep 2: 8 and **m** *themselves* against their border. 1431
2:10 **m** *themselves* against the people of 1431
Mal 1: 5 The LORD will be **m** from the border of 1431
Ac 5:13 himself to them: but the people **m** them. *3170*
19:17 and the name of the Lord Jesus was **m**. *3170*
Php 1:20 *so* now also Christ shall be **m** in my body, *3170*

MAGNIFY (19) [MAGNIFICAL, MAGNIFICENCE, MAGNIFIED]
Jos 3: 7 This day will I begin to **m** thee in the sight 1431
Job 7:17 What *is* man, that thou shouldest **m** him? 1431
19: 5 If indeed ye will **m** *yourselves* against me, 1431
36:24 Remember that thou **m** his work, 7679
Ps 34: 3 O **m** the LORD with me, and let us exalt 1431
35:26 dishonour that **m** *themselves* against me. 1431
38:16 they **m** *themselves* against me. 1431
55:12 hated me *that* did **m** *himself* against me; 1431
69:30 a song; and will **m** him with thanksgiving. 1431
Isa 10:15 shall the saw **m** itself against him that 1431
42:21 he will **m** the law, and make *it* honourable. 1431
Eze 38:23 Thus will I **m** myself, and sanctify myself; 1431
Da 8:25 he shall **m** *himself* in his heart, and 1431
11:36 **m** himself above every god, and shall speak 1431
11:37 any god: for he shall **m** himself above all. 1431
Zec 12: 7 do not **m** *themselves* against Judah. 1431
Lk 1:46 And Mary said, My soul doth **m** the Lord, *3170*
Ac 10:46 them speak with tongues, and **m** God. *3170*
Ro 11:13 the apostle of the Gentiles, I **m** mine office: *1392*

MAGOG (5)
Ge 10: 2 **M**, and Madai, and Javan, and Tubal, and 4031
1Ch 1: 5 **M**, and Madai, and Javan, and Tubal, and 4031
Eze 38: 2 set thy face against Gog, the land of **M**, 4031
39: 6 I will send a fire on **M**, and among them 4031
Rev 20: 8 Gog and **M**, to gather them together to *3098*

MAGOR-MISSABIB (1)
Jer 20: 3 hath not called thy name Pashur, but **M**. 4036

MAGPIASH (1)
Ne 10:20 **M**, Meshullam, Hezir, 4047

MAHALAH (1)
1Ch 7:18 bare Ishod, and Abiezer, and **M**. 4244

MAHALALEEL (7)
Ge 5:12 Cainan lived seventy years, and begat **M**: 4111
5:13 Cainan lived after he begat **M** eight 4111
5:15 **M** lived sixty and five years, and 4111
5:16 **M** lived after he begat Jared eight hundred 4111
5:17 all the days of **M** were eight hundred ninety 4111
1Ch 1: 2 Kenan, **M**, Jered, 4111
Ne 11: 4 the son of Shephatiah, the son of **M**, 4111

MAHALALEL See MAHALALEEL; MALELEEL

MAHALATH (4)
Ge 28: 9 took unto the wives which he had **M** 4258
2Ch 11:18 Rehoboam took him **M** the daughter of 4258
Ps 53: T To the chief Musician upon **M**, Maschil, 4257
88: T To the chief Musician upon **M** Leannoth, 4257

MAHALI (1)
Ex 6:19 the sons of Merari; **M** and Mushi: these *are* 4249

MAHANAIM (13)
Ge 32: 2 and he called the name of that place **M**. 4266
Jos 13:26 and from **M** unto the border of Debir; 4266
13:30 their coast was from **M**, all Bashan, all 4266
21:38 for the slayer; and **M** with her suburbs, 4266
2Sa 2: 8 son of Saul, and brought him over *to* **M**; 4266
2:12 son of Saul, went out from **M** to Gibeon. 4266
2:29 *through* all Bithron, and they came *to* **M**. 4266
17:24 David came to **M**. And Absalom passed 4266
17:27 came to pass, when David was come to **M**, 4266
19:32 the king of sustenance while he lay at **M**; 4266
1Ki 2: 8 curse in the day when I went *to* **M**: 4266
4:14 Ahinadab the son of Iddo *had* **M**: 4266
1Ch 6:80 with her suburbs, and **M** with her suburbs, 4266

MAHANEH-DAN (1) [DAN]
Jdg 18:12 wherefore they called that place **M** unto 4265

MAHARAI (3)
2Sa 23:28 Zalmon the Ahohite, **M** the Netophathite, 4121
1Ch 11:30 **M** the Netophathite, Heled the son of 4121
27:13 the tenth month *was* **M** the Netophathite, 4121

MAHATH (3)
1Ch 6:35 the son of **M**, the son of Amasai, 4287
2Ch 29:12 **M** the son of Amasai, and Joel the son of 4287
31:13 Eliel, and Ismachiah, and **M**, and Benaiah, 4287

MAHAVITE (1)
1Ch 11:46 Eliel the **M**, and Jeribai, and Joshaviah, 4233

MAHAZIOTH (2)
1Ch 25: 4 Joshbekashah, Mallothi, Hothir, *and* **M**: 4238
25:30 The three and twentieth to **M**, *he,* his sons, 4238

MAHER-SHALAL-HASH-BAZ (2)
Isa 8: 1 write in it with a man's pen concerning **M**. 4122
8: 3 said the LORD to me, Call his name **M**. 4122

MAHLAH (4)
Nu 26:33 of the daughters of Zelophehad *were* **M**, 4244
27: 1 **M**, Noah, and Hoglah, and Milcah, and 4244
36:11 For **M**, Tirzah, and Hoglah, and Milcah, 4244
Jos 17: 3 **M**, and Noah, Hoglah, Milcah, and Tirzah. 4244

MAHLI (11) [MAHLITES]
Nu 3:20 of Merari by their families; **M**, and Mushi. 4249
1Ch 6:19 The sons of Merari; **M**, and Mushi. 4249
6:29 **M**, Libni his son, Shimei his son, Uzza his 4249
6:47 The son of **M**, the son of Mushi, the son of 4249
23:21 The sons of Merari; **M**, and Mushi. 4249
23:21 Mushi. The sons of **M**; Eleazar, and Kish. 4249
23:23 **M**, and Eder, and Jeremoth, three. 4249
24:26 The sons of Merari *were* **M** and Mushi: 4249
24:28 Of **M** *came* Eleazar, who had no sons. 4249
24:30 also of Mushi; **M**, and Eder, and Jerimoth. 4249
Ezr 8:18 of the sons of **M**, the son of Levi, the son of 4249

MAHLITES (2) [MAHLI]
Nu 3:33 Of Merari *was* the family of the **M**, and 4250
26:58 the family of the **M**, the family of 4250

MAHLON (3) [MAHLON'S]
Ru 1: 2 the name of his two sons **M** and Chilion, 4248
1: 5 **M** and Chilion died also both of them; and 4248
4:10 Ruth the Moabitess, the wife of **M**, 4248

MAHLON'S (1) [MAHLON]
Ru 4: 9 all that *was* Chilion's and **M**, of the hand of 4248

MAHOL (1)
1Ki 4:31 and Chalcol, and Darda, the sons of **M**: 4235

MAID (36) [BONDMAID, BONDMAIDS, HANDMAID, HANDMAIDEN, HANDMAIDENS, HANDMAIDS, MAID'S, MAIDEN, MAIDENS, MAIDS, MAIDSERVANT, MAIDSERVANT'S, MAIDSERVANTS, MAIDSERVANTS']
Ge 16: 2 I pray thee, go in unto my **m**; it may be that 8198
16: 3 Sarai Abram's wife took Hagar her **m** 8198
16: 5 I have given my **m** into thy bosom; and 8198
16: 6 unto Sarai, Behold, thy **m** *is* in thy hand; 8198
16: 8 he said, Hagar, Sarai's **m**, whence camest 8198
29:24 Leah Zilpah his **m** *for* a handmaid. 8198
29:29 daughter Bilhah his handmaid to be her **m**. 8198
30: 3 she said, Behold my **m** Bilhah, go in unto 519
30: 7 Bilhah Rachel's **m** conceived again, and 8198
30: 9 she took Zilpah her **m**, and gave her Jacob 8198
30:10 And Zilpah Leah's **m** bare Jacob a son. 8198
30:12 Zilpah Leah's **m** bare Jacob a second son. 8198
Ex 2: 5 among the flags, she sent her **m** to fetch it. 519
2: 8 the **m** went and called the child's mother. 5959
21:20 or his **m**, with a rod, and he die under his 519
21:26 or the eye of his **m**, that it perish; 519
22:16 if a man entice a **m** that is not betrothed, 1330
Lev 12: 5 if she bear a **m child**, then she shall be 5347
25: 6 and for thy **m**, and for thy hired servant, and 519
Dt 22:14 when I came to her, I found her not a **m**: 1331
22:17 *her,* saying, I found not thy daughter a **m**; 1331
2Ki 5: 2 captive out of the land of Israel a little **m**; 5291
5: 4 thus said the **m** that *is* of the land of Israel. 5291
Est 2: 7 and the **m** *was* fair and beautiful; 5291
Job 31: 1 why then should I think upon a **m**? 1330
Pr 30:19 of the sea; and the way of a man with a **m**. 5959
Isa 24: 2 as *with* the **m**, so *with* her mistress; 8198
Jer 2:32 Can a **m** forget her ornaments, *or* a bride 1330
51:22 I break in pieces the young man and the **m**; 1330
Am 2: 7 and his father will go in unto the *same* **m**, 5291
Mt 9:24 for the **m** is not dead, but sleepeth. *2877*
9:25 and took her by the hand, and the **m** arose. *2877*
26:71 another *m* saw him, and said unto them that NIG
Mk 14:69 And a **m** saw him again, and began to say *3814*
Lk 8:54 by the hand, and called, saying, **M**, arise. *3816*
22:56 But a certain **m** beheld him as he sat by *3814*

MAID'S (1) [MAID]
Est 2:12 Now when **every m** turn was 5291+5291+2050.1

MAIDEN (8) [MAID]
Ge 30:18 because I have given my **m** to my husband: 8198
Jdg 19:24 *here is* my daughter a **m**, and 1330
2Ch 36:17 had no compassion upon young man or **m**, 1330
Est 2: 4 let the **m** which pleaseth the king be queen 5291
2: 9 the **m** pleased him, and she obtained 5291
2:13 thus came *every* **m** unto the king; 5291
Ps 123: 2 as the eyes of a **m** unto the hand of her 8198
Lk 8:51 and the father and the mother of the **m**. *3816*

MAIDENS (19) [MAID]
Ex 2: 5 her **m** walked along by the river's side; and 5291
Ru 2: 8 from hence, but abide here fast by my **m**: 5291
2:22 my daughter, that thou go out with his **m**, 5291
2:23 So she kept fast by the **m** of Boaz to glean 5291
3: 2 of our kindred, with whose **m** thou wast? 5291
1Sa 9:11 they found **young m** going out to draw 5291
Est 2: 8 when many **m** were gathered together unto 5291
2: 9 seven **m**, *which were* meet to be given her, 5291
4:16 I also and my **m** will fast likewise; and so 5291
Job 19:15 and my **m**, count me for a stranger: 519
41: 5 a bird? or wilt thou bind him for thy **m**? 5291
Ps 78:63 and their **m** were not given to marriage. 1330
148:12 Both young men, and **m**; old men, and 1330
Pr 9: 3 She hath sent forth her **m**: she crieth upon 5291
27:27 and *for* the maintenance for thy **m**. 5291
31:15 to her household, and a portion to her **m**. 5291
Ecc 2: 7 I got *me* servants and **m**, and had servants 8198
Eze 44:22 they shall take **m** of the seed of the house 1330
Lk 12:45 shall begin to beat the menservants and **m**, *3814*

MAIDS (8) [MAID]
Ezr 2:65 Beside their servants and their **m**, of whom 519
Est 2: 9 her **m** unto the best *place* of the house of 5291
4: 4 So Esther's **m** and her chamberlains came 5291
La 5:11 in Zion, *and* the **m** in the cities of Judah. 1330
Eze 9: 6 both **m**, and little children, and women: 1330
Na 2: 7 her **m** *shall* lead *her* as *with* the voice of 519
Zec 9:17 young men cheerful, and new wine the **m**. 1330
Mk 14:66 there cometh one of the **m** of the high *3814*

MAIDSERVANT (16) [MAID, SERVE]
Ex 11: 5 *even* unto the firstborn of the **m** that *is* 8198
20:10 thy manservant, nor thy **m**, nor thy cattle, 519
20:17 nor his **m**, nor his ox, nor his ass, 519
21: 7 if a man sell his daughter to be a **m**, she shall 519
21:32 If the ox shall push a manservant or a **m**; 519
Dt 5:14 nor thy **m**, nor thine ox, nor thine ass, 519
5:14 and thy **m** may rest as well as thou. 519
5:21 or his **m**, his ox, or his ass, or any *thing* that 519
12:18 thy **m**, and the Levite that *is* within thy 519
15:17 And also unto thy **m** thou shalt do likewise. 519
16:11 thy **m**, and the Levite that *is* within thy 519

Dt 16:14 thy **m**, and the Levite, the stranger, and 519
Jdg 9:18 and have made Abimelech, the son of his **m**, 519
Job 31:13 the cause of my manservant or of my **m**, 519
Jer 34: 9 every man his **m**, *being* a Hebrew or 8198
34:10 and every one his **m**, go free, 8198

MAIDSERVANT'S (1) [MAID, SERVE]

Ex 21:27 out his manservant's tooth, or his **m** tooth; 519

MAIDSERVANTS (9) [MAID, SERVE]

Ge 12:16 and **m**, and she asses, and camels. 8198
20:17 healed Abimelech, and his wife, and his **m**; 519
24:35 menservants, and **m**, and camels, and asses. 8198
30:43 **m**, and menservants, and camels, and asses. 8198
Dt 12:12 your **m**, and the Levite that *is* within your 519
1Sa 8:16 and your **m**, and your goodliest young men, 8198
2Sa 6:22 of the **m** which thou hast spoken of, of them 519
2Ki 5:26 sheep, and oxen, and menservants, and **m**? 8198
Ne 7:67 Beside their manservants and their **m**, 519

MAIDSERVANTS' (1) [MAID, SERVE]

Ge 31:33 into Leah's tent, and into the two **m** tents; 519

MAIL (2)

1Sa 17: 5 and he *was* armed with a coat of **m**; 7193
17:38 also he armed him with a coat *of* **m**. NIH

MAIMED (7)

Lev 22:22 or **m**, or having a wen, or scurvy, or 2782
Mt 15:30 **m**, and many others, and cast them *down* at *2948*
15:31 the **m** *to be* whole, the lame to walk, and *2948*
18: 8 is better for thee to enter into life halt or **m**, *2948*
Mk 9:43 it is better for thee to enter into life **m**, *2948*
Lk 14:13 call the poor, the **m**, the lame, the blind: *376*
14:21 and the **m**, and the halt, and the blind. *376*

MAINSAIL (1)

Ac 27:40 and hoised up the **m** to the wind, and *736*

MAINTAIN (10) [MAINTAINED, MAINTAINEST, MAINTENANCE]

1Ki 8:45 and their supplication, and **m** their cause. 6213
8:49 thy dwelling place, and **m** their cause, 6213
8:59 that *he* **m** the cause of his servant, and 6213
1Ch 26:27 dedicate to **m** the house of the LORD. 2388
2Ch 6:35 and their supplication, and **m** their cause. 6213
6:39 **m** their cause, and forgive thy people 6213
Job 13:15 but I will **m** mine own ways before him. 3198
Ps 140:12 I know that the LORD will **m** the cause of 6213
Tit 3: 8 in God might be careful to **m** good works. *4291*
3:14 And let ours also learn to **m** good works for *4291*

MAINTAINED (1) [MAINTAIN]

Ps 9: 4 For thou hast **m** my right and my cause; 6213

MAINTAINEST (1) [MAINTAIN]

Ps 16: 5 and of my cup: thou **m** my lot. 8551

MAINTENANCE (2) [MAINTAIN]

Ezr 4:14 we **have m** from *the king's* palace, 4415+4416
Pr 27:27 and *for* the **m** for thy maidens. 2416

MAJESTY (29)

1Ch 29:11 and the glory, and the victory, and the **m**: 1935
29:25 bestowed upon him *such* royal **m** as had 1935
Est 1: 4 the honour of his excellent **m** many days, 1420
Job 37:22 out of the north: with God *is* terrible **m**. 1935
40:10 Deck thyself now with **m** and excellency; 1347
Ps 21: 5 honour and **m** hast thou laid upon him. 1926
29: 4 the voice of the LORD *is* **full of m**. 1926
45: 3 O *most* mighty, *with* thy glory and thy **m**. 1926
45: 4 *in* thy **m** ride prosperously because of truth 1926
93: 1 The LORD reigneth, he is clothed with **m**; 1348
96: 6 Honour and **m** *are* before him: strength and 1926
104: 1 thou art clothed with honour and **m**. 1926
145: 5 will speak of the glorious honour of thy **m**, 1935
145:12 and the glorious **m** of his kingdom. 1926
Isa 2:10 of the LORD, and for the glory of his **m**. 1347
2:19 of the LORD, and for the glory of his **m**, 1347
2:21 of the LORD, and for the glory of his **m**, 1347
24:14 they shall sing, for the **m** of the LORD, 1347
26:10 and will not behold the **m** of the LORD. 1348
Eze 7:20 the beauty of his ornament, he set it in **m**: 1347
Da 4:30 of my power, and for the honour of my **m**? 1923
4:36 and excellent **m** was added unto me. 7238
5:18 a kingdom, and **m**, and glory, and honour: 7238
5:19 for the **m** that he gave him, all people, 7238
Mic 5: 4 in the **m** of the name of the LORD his 1347
Heb 1: 3 sat down on the right hand of the **M** on *3172*
8: 1 hand of the throne of the **M** in the heavens; *3172*
2Pe 1:16 but were eyewitnesses of his **m**. *3168*
Jude 1:25 *be* glory and **m**, dominion and power, *3172*

MAKAZ (1)

1Ki 4: 9 in **M**, and in Shaalbim, and Beth-shemesh, 4739

MAKE (1055) [MADE, MADEST, MAKER, MAKERS, MAKEST, MAKETH, MAKING, TENTMAKERS]

Ge 1:26 God said, Let us **m** man in our image, 6213
2:18 be alone; I will **m** him a help meet for him. 6213
3: 6 a tree to be desired to **m** *one* **wise**, she took 7919
3:21 to his wife did the LORD God **m** coats of 6213
6:14 **M** thee an ark of gopher wood; rooms shalt 6213
6:14 rooms shalt thou **m** *in* the ark, and 6213
6:15 this *is the fashion* which thou shalt **m** it *of*: 6213
6:16 A window shalt thou **m** to the ark, and in a 6213
6:16 second, and third *stories* shalt thou **m** it. 6213
9:12 This *is* the token of the covenant which I **m** 5414
11: 3 **m brick**, and burn *them* thoroughly. 3835+3843
11: 4 let us **m** us a name, lest we be scattered 6213
12: 2 I will **m** of thee a great nation, and I will 6213
12: 2 I will bless thee, and **m** thy name **great**; 1431
13:16 I will **m** thy seed as the dust of the earth: 7760
Ge 17: 2 I will **m** my covenant between me and thee, 5414
17: 6 I will **m** thee exceeding **fruitful**, and I will 6509
17: 6 I will **m** nations of thee, and kings shall 5414
17:20 will **m** him **fruitful**, and will multiply him 6509
17:20 he beget, and I will **m** him a great nation. 5414
18: 6 **M ready quickly** three measures of fine 4116
18: 6 knead *it*, and **m** cakes upon the hearth. 6213
19:32 let us **m** our father **drink** wine, and we will 8248
19:34 let us **m** him **drink** wine this night also; 8248
21:13 also of the son of the bondwoman will I **m** 7760
21:18 thine hand; for I will **m** him a great nation. 7760
24: 3 I will **m** thee **swear** by the LORD, 7650
26: 4 I will **m** thy seed **to multiply** as the stars of 7235
26:28 and thee, and let us **m** a covenant with thee; 3772
27: 4 **m** me savoury meat, such as I love, and 6213
27: 7 and **m** me savoury meat, that I may eat, and 6213
27: 9 I will **m** them savoury meat for thy father, 6213
28: 3 and **m** thee **fruitful**, and multiply thee, 6509
31:44 come thou, let us **m** a covenant, I and thou; 3772
32:12 and **m** thy seed as the sand of the sea, 7760
34: 9 **m** ye **marriages** with us, *and* give your 2859
34:30 Ye have troubled me to **m** me **to stink** 887
35: 1 **m** there an altar unto God, that appeared 6213
35: 3 I will **m** there an altar unto God, 6213
40:14 **m mention** of me unto Pharaoh, and 2142
43:16 *these* men home, and slay, and **m ready**; 3559
46: 3 for I will there **m** of thee a great nation. 7760
47: 6 the land **m** thy father and brethren **to dwell**; 3427
47: 6 then **m** them rulers over my cattle. 7760
48: 4 I will **m** thee **fruitful**, and multiply thee, 6509
48: 4 and I will **m** of thee a multitude of people; 5414
48:20 God **m** thee as Ephraim and as Manasseh: 7760
Ex 5: 5 and you **m** them **rest** from their burdens. 7673
5: 7 give the people straw to **m brick**, 3835+3843
5: 8 which they did **m** heretofore, you shall lay 6213
5:16 thy servants, and they say to us, **M** brick: 6213
12: 4 his eating shall **m** your **count** for the lamb. 3699
18:16 I do **m** *them* **know** the statutes of God, and 3045
20: 4 Thou shalt not **m** unto thee *any* graven 6213
20:23 Ye shall not **m** with me gods of silver, 6213
20:23 neither shall ye **m** unto you gods of gold 6213
20:24 An altar of earth thou shalt **m** unto me, and 6213
20:25 if thou wilt **m** me an altar of stone, 6213
21:34 The owner of the pit shall **m** *it* **good**, *and* 7999
22: 3 *for* he should **m full restitution**; if 7999+7999
22: 5 of his own vineyard, shall he **m restitution**. 7999
22: 6 the fire shall **surely m restitution**. 7999+7999
22:11 accept *thereof*, and he shall not **m** *it* **good**. 7999
22:12 he shall **m restitution** unto the owner 7999
22:13 he shall not **m good** that which was torn. 7999
22:14 not with it, he shall **surely m** *it* **good**. 7999+7999
22:15 thereof *be* with it, he shall not **m** *it* **good**: 7999
23:13 **m** no **mention** of the name of other gods, 2142
23:27 I will **m** all thine enemies turn their backs 5414
23:32 Thou shalt **m** no covenant with them, 3772
23:33 in thy land, lest they **m** thee **sin** against me: 2398
25: 8 let them **m** me a sanctuary; that I may 6213
25: 9 instruments thereof, even so shall ye **m** *it*. 6213
25:10 they shall **m** an ark of shittim wood: 6213
25:11 shalt **m** upon it a crown *of* gold round 6213
25:13 thou shalt **m** staves of shittim wood, and 6213
25:17 thou shalt **m** a mercy seat *of* pure gold: 6213
25:18 thou shalt **m** two cherubims *of* gold, 6213
25:18 *of* beaten work shalt thou **m** them, in 6213
25:19 **m** one cherub on the one end, and the other 6213
25:19 *even* of the mercy seat shall ye **m** 6213
25:23 Thou shalt also **m** a table *of* shittim wood: 6213
25:24 and **m** thereto a crown *of* gold round about. 6213
25:25 thou shalt **m** unto it a border of a 6213
25:25 thou shalt **m** a golden crown to the border 6213
25:26 thou shalt **m** for it four rings of gold, and 6213
25:28 thou shalt **m** the staves *of* shittim wood, 6213
25:29 thou shalt **m** the dishes thereof, and 6213
25:29 *of* pure gold shalt thou **m** them. 6213
25:31 thou shalt **m** a candlestick of pure gold: 6213
25:37 thou shalt **m** the seven lamps thereof: and 6213
25:39 *Of* a talent of pure gold shall he **m** it, 6213
25:40 look that thou **m** *them* after their pattern, 6213
26: 1 Moreover thou shalt **m** the tabernacle *with* 6213
26: 1 *of* cunning work shalt thou **m** them. 6213
26: 4 thou shalt **m** loops of blue upon the edge of 6213
26: 4 likewise shalt thou **m** in the uttermost edge 6213
26: 5 Fifty loops shalt thou **m** in the one curtain, 6213
26: 5 fifty loops shalt thou **m** in the edge of 6213
26: 6 thou shalt **m** fifty taches of gold, and 6213
26: 7 thou shalt **m** curtains *of* goats' *hair* to be a 6213
26: 7 eleven curtains shalt thou **m**. 6213
26:10 thou shalt **m** fifty loops on the edge of 6213
26:11 thou shalt **m** fifty taches of brass, and 6213
26:14 thou shalt **m** a covering for the tent *of* 6213
26:15 thou shalt **m** boards for the tabernacle *of* 6213
26:17 thus shalt thou **m** for all the boards of 6213
26:18 thou shalt **m** the boards for the tabernacle, 6213
26:19 thou shalt **m** forty sockets of silver under 6213
26:22 westward thou shalt **m** six boards. 6213
26:23 two boards shalt thou **m** for the corners of 6213
26:26 thou shalt **m** bars *of* shittim wood; five for 6213
26:29 **m** their rings *of* gold *for* places for the bars: 6213
26:31 thou shalt **m** a vail *of* blue, and purple, and 6213
26:36 thou shalt **m** a hanging for the door of 6213
26:37 thou shalt **m** for the hanging five pillars of 6213
27: 1 thou shalt **m** an altar *of* shittim wood, 6213
27: 2 thou shalt **m** the horns of it upon the four 6213
27: 3 thou shalt **m** his pans to receive his ashes, 6213
27: 3 all the vessels thereof thou shalt **m** *of* brass. 6213
27: 4 thou shalt **m** for it a grate of network *of* 6213
27: 4 upon the net shalt thou **m** four brasen rings 6213
27: 6 thou shalt **m** staves for the altar, staves of 6213
27: 8 Hollow with boards shalt thou **m** it: as it 6213
27: 8 thee in the mount, so shall they **m** *it*. 6213
27: 9 thou shalt **m** the court of the tabernacle: 6213
28: 2 thou shalt **m** holy garments for Aaron thy 6213
28: 3 that they may **m** Aaron's garments to 6213
28: 4 these *are* the garments which they shall **m**; 6213
28: 4 they shall **m** holy garments for Aaron thy 6213
Ex 28: 6 they shall **m** the ephod *of* gold, *of* blue, 6213
28:11 thou shalt **m** them to be set *in* ouches *of* 6213
28:13 And thou shalt **m** ouches *of* gold; 6213
28:14 *of* wreathen work shalt thou **m** them, and 6213
28:15 thou shalt **m** the breastplate of judgment 6213
28:15 after the work of the ephod thou shalt **m** it; 6213
28:15 *of* fine twined linen, shalt thou **m** it. 6213
28:22 thou shalt **m** upon the breastplate chains at 6213
28:23 thou shalt **m** upon the breastplate two rings 6213
28:26 thou shalt **m** two rings of gold, and 6213
28:27 two *other* rings of gold thou shalt **m**, and 6213
28:31 thou shalt **m** the robe of the ephod all of 6213
28:33 *beneath* upon the hem of it thou shalt **m** 6213
28:36 thou shalt **m** a plate *of* pure gold, and 6213
28:39 thou shalt **m** the mitre *of* fine linen, and 6213
28:39 and thou shalt **m** the girdle *of* needlework. 6213
28:40 for Aaron's sons thou shalt **m** coats, and 6213
28:40 thou shalt **m** for them girdles, and 6213
28:40 bonnets shalt thou **m** for them, for glory 6213
28:42 thou shalt **m** them linen breeches to cover 6213
29: 2 *of* wheaten flour shalt thou **m** them. 6213
29:37 Seven days thou shalt **m an atonement** for 3722
30: 1 thou shalt **m** an altar to burn incense upon: 6213
30: 1 *of* shittim wood shalt thou **m** it. 6213
30: 3 thou shalt **m** unto it a crown *of* gold round 6213
30: 4 two golden rings shalt thou **m** to it under 6213
30: 4 upon the two sides of it shalt thou **m** *it*; and 6213
30: 5 thou shalt **m** the staves *of* shittim wood, 6213
30:10 Aaron shall **m an atonement** upon 3722
30:10 **m atonement** upon it throughout your 3722
30:15 to **m an atonement** for your souls. 3722
30:16 to **m an atonement** for your souls. 3722
30:18 Thou shalt also **m** a laver *of* brass, and 6213
30:25 thou shalt **m** it an oil of holy ointment, 6213
30:32 neither shall ye **m** *any other* like it, after 6213
30:35 thou shalt **m** it a perfume, a confection *after* 6213
30:37 *as for* the perfume which thou shalt **m**, 6213
30:37 you shall not **m** to yourselves according to 6213
30:38 Whosoever shall **m** like unto that, to smell 6213
31: 6 that they may **m** all that I have commanded 6213
32: 1 said unto him, Up, **m** us gods, which shall 6213
32:10 and I will **m** of thee a great nation. 6213
32:23 For they said unto me, **M** us gods, 6213
32:30 peradventure I shall **m an atonement** for 3722
33:19 I will **m** all my goodness **pass** before thee, 5674
34:10 he said, Behold, I **m** a covenant: before all 3772
34:12 lest thou **m** a covenant with the inhabitants 3772
34:15 Lest thou **m** a covenant with the inhabitants 3772
34:16 **m** thy sons **go a whoring** after their gods. 2181
34:17 Thou shalt **m** thee no molten gods. 6213
35:10 **m** all that the LORD hath commanded; 6213
35:33 to **m** any *manner of* cunning work. 6213
36: 3 to **m** it *withal*. And they brought yet unto 6213
36: 5 which the LORD commanded to **m**. 6213
36: 6 Let neither man nor woman **m** any more 6213
36: 7 *had* was sufficient for all the work to **m** it, 6213
36:22 thus did he **m** for all the boards of 6213
Lev 1: 4 accepted for him to **m atonement** for him. 3722
4:20 the priest shall **m an atonement** for them, 3722
4:26 the priest shall **m an atonement** for him as 3722
4:31 the priest shall **m an atonement** for him, 3722
4:35 the priest shall **m an atonement** for his sin 3722
5: 6 the priest shall **m an atonement** for him 3722
5:10 the priest shall **m an atonement** for him 3722
5:13 the priest shall **m an atonement** for him as 3722
5:16 he shall **m amends** for the harm that he 7999
5:16 the priest shall **m an atonement** for him 3722
5:18 the priest shall **m an atonement** for him 3722
6: 7 the priest shall **m an atonement** for him 3722
8:15 sanctified it, to **m reconciliation** upon it. 3722
8:34 to do, to **m an atonement** for you. 3722
9: 7 **m an atonement** for thyself, and for 3722
9: 7 the people, and **m an atonement** for them; 3722
10:17 to **m atonement** for them before 3722
11:43 Ye shall not **m** yourselves **abominable** 8262
11:43 neither shall ye **m** yourselves **unclean** with 2933
11:47 To **m a difference** between the unclean and 914
12: 7 the LORD, and **m an atonement** for her; 3722
12: 8 the priest shall **m an atonement** for her, 3722
14:18 the priest shall **m an atonement** for him 3722
14:19 **m an atonement** for him that is to be 3722
14:20 the priest shall **m an atonement** for him, 3722
14:21 to **m an atonement** for him, and one tenth 3722
14:29 to **m an atonement** for him before 3722
14:31 the priest shall **m an atonement** for him 3722
14:53 and **m an atonement** for the house: 3722
15:15 the priest shall **m an atonement** for him 3722
15:30 the priest shall **m an atonement** for her 3722
16: 6 **m an atonement** for himself, and for his 3722
16:10 to **m an atonement** with him, *and* to let 3722
16:11 shall **m an atonement** for himself, and 3722
16:16 he shall **m an atonement** for the holy 3722
16:17 **m an atonement** in the holy *place*, until he 3722
16:18 the LORD, and **m an atonement** for it; 3722
16:24 **m an atonement** for himself, and for 3722
16:27 blood was brought in to **m atonement** 3722
16:30 shall *the priest* **m an atonement** for you, 3722
16:32 shall **m** the **atonement**, and shall put on 3722
16:33 he shall **m an atonement** for the holy 3722
16:33 he shall **m an atonement** for the tabernacle 3722
16:33 he shall **m an atonement** for the priests, 3722
16:34 to **m an atonement** for the children of 3722
17:11 the altar to **m an atonement** for your souls: 3722
19: 4 nor **m** to yourselves molten gods: 6213
19:22 the priest shall **m an atonement** for him 3722
19:28 Ye shall not **m** any cuttings in your flesh 5414
20:25 ye shall not **m** your souls **abominable** by 8262
21: 5 They shall not **m baldness** upon 7139+7144
21: 5 nor **m any cuttings** in their flesh. 8295+8296
22:22 nor **m** an offering by fire of them upon 5414
22:24 neither shall you **m** *any* offering *thereof* in 6213
23:22 thou shalt **m** not **clean riddance** of 3615
23:28 to **m an atonement** for you before 3722
24:18 he that killeth a beast shall **m** it **good**; 7999
25: 9 **m** the trumpet **sound** throughout all your 5674

M

Lev 26: 1 Ye shall **m** you no idols nor graven image, 6213
26: 6 lie down, and none shall **m** *you* **afraid**: 2729
26: 9 **m** you **fruitful**, and multiply you, and 6509
26:19 I will **m** your heaven as iron, and your 5414
26:22 your cattle, and **m** you **few in number**; 4591
26:31 I will **m** your cities waste, and bring your 5414
27: 2 When a man shall **m a singular vow**, 5088+6381
Nu 5:21 **m** thee a curse and an oath 5414
5:21 when the LORD doth **m** thy thigh to rot, 5414
5:22 to **m** *thy* belly **to swell**, and *thy* thigh to rot: 6638
6: 7 He shall not **m** himself **unclean** for his 2930
6:11 and **m an atonement** for him, 3722
6:25 The LORD **m** his face **shine** upon thee, and 215
8: 7 their clothes, and *so* **m** themselves **clean**. 2891
8:12 to **m an atonement** for the Levites. 3722
8:19 to **m an atonement** for the children of 3722
10: 2 **M** thee two trumpets of silver; of a whole 6213
10: 2 of a whole piece thou shalt **m** them: 6213
12: 6 *I* the LORD will **m** myself **known** unto 3045
14: 4 Let us **m** a captain, and let us return into 5414
14:12 will **m** of thee a greater nation and 6213
14:30 *concerning* which I sware to **m** you **dwell** 7931
15: 3 will **m** an offering by fire unto the LORD, 6213
15: 3 to **m** a sweet savour unto the LORD, 6213
15:25 the priest shall **m an atonement** for all 3722
15:28 the priest shall **m an atonement** for 3722
15:28 the LORD, to **m an atonement** for him; 3722
15:38 bid them that they **m** them fringes in 6213
16:13 **m** thyself **altogether a prince** over 8323+8323
16:30 if the LORD **m** a new thing, and the earth 1254
16:38 let them **m** them broad plates *for* a covering 6213
16:46 and **m an atonement** for them: 3722
17: 5 I will **m to cease** from me the murmurings 7918
21: 8 **M** thee a fiery *serpent*, and set it upon a 6213
23:19 hath he spoken, and shall he not **m** it **good**? 6965
28:22 a sin offering, to **m an atonement** for you. 3722
28:30 of the goats, to **m an atonement** for you. 3722
29: 5 a sin offering, to **m an atonement** for you: 3722
30: 8 then he shall **m** her vow which she vowed, NIH
30:13 establish it, or her husband may **m** it **void**. 6565
30:15 if he shall **any ways m** them **void** 6565+6565
31:23 ye shall **m** *it* **go** the fire, and it shall be 5674
31:23 all that abideth not the fire ye shall **m go** 5674
31:50 to **m an atonement** for our souls before 3722
Dt 1:11 **m** you a thousand times **so many moe** 3254
1:13 and I will **m** them rulers over you. 7760
4:10 and I will **m** them **hear** my words, 8085
4:16 and **m** you a graven image, 6213
4:23 **m** you a graven image, *or* the likeness of 6213
4:25 corrupt *yourselves*, and **m** a graven image, 6213
5: 8 Thou shalt not **m** thee *any* graven image, *or* 6213
7: 2 thou shalt **m** no covenant with them, 3772
7: 3 Neither shalt thou **m marriages** with them; 2859
8: 3 that he might **m** thee **know** that man doth 3045
9:14 I will **m** of thee a nation mightier and 6213
10: 1 into the mount, and **m** thee an ark of wood. 6213
13:14 and **m search**, and ask diligently; 2713
14: 1 nor **m** *any* baldness between your eyes for 7760
15: 1 of *every* seven years thou shalt **m** a release. 6213
16:18 officers shalt thou **m** thee in all thy gates, 5414
16:21 LORD thy God, which thou shalt **m** thee. 6213
19:18 the judges shall **m** diligent **inquisition**: 1875
20: 9 that they shall **m** captains of the armies to 6485
20:11 if it **m** thee **answer** of peace, and open unto 6030
20:12 if it will **m** no **peace** with thee, but 7999
20:12 will **m** war against thee, then thou shalt 6213
21:14 thou shalt not **m merchandise** of her, 6014
21:16 **m** the son of the beloved **firstborn** before 1069
22: 8 then thou shalt **m** a battlement for thy roof, 6213
22:12 Thou shalt **m** thee fringes upon the four 6213
26:19 to **m** thee high above all nations which he 5414
28:11 the LORD shall **m** thee **plenteous** in 3498
28:13 the LORD shall **m** thee the head, and 5414
28:21 The LORD shall **m** the pestilence **cleave** 1692
28:24 The LORD shall **m** the rain of thy land 5414
28:59 the LORD will **m** thy plagues **wonderful**, 6381
29: 1 which the LORD commanded Moses to **m** 3772
29:14 Neither with you only do I **m** this covenant 3772
30: 9 the LORD thy God will **m** thee **plenteous** 3498
32:26 **m** the remembrance of them **to cease** from 7673
32:35 things that shall come upon them **m haste**. 2363
32:39 I kill, and I **m alive**; I wound, and I heal: 2421
32:42 I will **m** mine arrows **drunk** with blood, 7937
Jos 1: 8 for then thou shalt **m** thy way **prosperous**, 6743
5: 2 **M** thee sharp knives, and circumcise again 6213
6: 5 *that* when *they* **m a long blast** with 4900
6:10 not shout, nor **m** any **noise** with your voice, 8085
6:18 lest ye **m** *yourselves* **accursed**, when ye 2763
6:18 **m** the camp of Israel a curse, and trouble it. 7760
7: 3 *and* **m** not all the people **to labour** thither; 3021
7:19 God of Israel, and **m** confession unto him; 5414
9: 6 now therefore **m** ye a league with us. 3772
9: 7 and how shall we **m** a league with you? 3772
9:11 therefore now **m** ye a league with us. 3772
22:25 shall your children **m** our children **cease** 7673
23: 7 neither **m mention** of the name of their 2142
23:12 shall **m marriages** with them, and go in 2859
Jdg 2: 2 ye shall **m** no league with the inhabitants of 3772
9:48 me do, **m haste**, *and* do as I *have done*. 4116
16:25 Call for Samson, that he may **m** us **sport**. 7832
17: 3 to **m** a graven image and a molten image: 6213
20:38 **m** a great flame with smoke **rise up** out of 5927
Ru 3: 3 *but* **m** not thyself **known** unto the man, 3045
4:11 The LORD **m** the woman that is come 5414
1Sa 1: 6 for to **m** her **fret**, because the LORD had 7481
2: 8 and to **m** them **inherit** the throne of glory: 5157
2:24 *ye* **m** the LORD'S people **to transgress**. 5674
2:29 to **m** yourselves **fat** with the chiefest of all 1254
3:12 when I begin, I will also **m an end**. 3615
6: 5 Wherefore ye shall **m** images of your 6213
6: 7 Now therefore **m** a new cart, and take two 6213
8: 5 now **m** us a king to judge us like all 7760
8:12 to **m** his instruments of war, and 6213
8:22 unto their voice, and **m** them **a king**. 4427+4428
9:12 **m haste** now, for he came to day to 4116
1Sa 11: 1 **M** a covenant with us, and we will serve 3772
11: 2 On this *condition* will I **m** *a covenant* with 3772
12:22 it hath pleased the LORD to **m** you his 6213
13:19 Lest the Hebrews **m** *them* swords or spears: 6213
17:25 and **m** his father's house free in Israel. 6213
18:25 Saul thought to **m** David **fall** by the hand of 5307
20:38 cried after the lad, **M speed**, haste, stay not. 4120
22: 7 *and* **m** you all captains of thousands, and 7760
25:28 for the LORD will **certainly m** my 6213+6213
28: 2 Therefore will I **m** thee keeper of mine 7760
28:15 for the Philistines **m war** against me, and 3898
28:15 that *thou* mayest **m known** unto me what I 3045
29: 4 **M** *this* fellow **return**, that he may go again 7725
2Sa 3:12 saying *also*, **M** thy league with me, and 3772
3:13 he said, Well; I will **m** a league with thee: 3772
3:21 that they may **m** a league with thee, and 3772
7:11 Also the LORD telleth thee that he will **m** 6213
7:21 great things, to **m** thy servant **know** *them*. 3045
7:23 to **m** him a name, and to do for you great 7760
11:25 **m** thy battle *more* **strong** against the city, 2388
13: 5 *thee* down on thy bed, and **m** thyself **sick**: 2470
13: 6 **m** *me* a couple of **cakes** in my sight, 3823+3834
15:14 **m speed** to depart, lest he overtake us 4116
15:20 should I *this* day **m** thee go up and 5128
17: 2 and weak handed, and will **m** him **afraid**: 2729
21: 3 wherewith shall I **m** the **atonement**, that ye 3722
23: 5 all *my* desire, although he **m** *it* **not to grow**. 6779
1Ki 1:37 **m** his throne **greater** than the throne of my 1431
1:47 God **m** the name of Solomon **better** than 3190
1:47 and **m** his throne **greater** than thy throne. 1431
2:42 Did I not **m** thee **to swear** by the LORD, 7650
8:29 **prayer** which thy servant shall **m** 6419+8605
8:33 and **m supplication** unto thee in this house: 2603
8:47 **m supplication** unto thee in the land of 2603
9:22 of the children of Israel did Solomon **m** no 5414
11:34 I will **m** him prince all the days of his life 7896
12: 1 were come *to* Shechem to **m** him **king**. 4427
12: 4 **m** thou the grievous service of thy father, and
his heavy yoke which he put upon us, **lighter**, 7043
12: 9 **M** the yoke which thy father did put upon us
lighter? 7043
12:10 yoke heavy, but **m** thou *it* **lighter** unto us; 7043
16: 3 will **m** thy house like the house of 5414
16:19 and in his sin which he did, to **m** Israel **sin**. 2398
16:21 Tibni the son of Ginath, to **m** him **king**; 4427
17:13 **m** me thereof a little cake first, and bring *it* 6213
17:13 and after **m** for thee and for thy son. 6213
19: 2 if I **m** not thy life as the life of one of them 7760
20:34 thou shalt **m** streets for thee in Damascus, 7760
21:22 will **m** thine house like the house of 5414
2Ki 3:16 the LORD, **M** this valley full of ditches. 6213
4:10 Let us **m** a little chamber, I pray thee, 6213
5: 7 and said, *Am* I God, to kill and to **m alive**, 2421
6: 2 let us **m** us a place there, where we may 6213
7: 2 *if* the LORD would **m** windows in 6213
7:19 *if* the LORD should **m** windows in 6213
9: 2 **m** him **arise up** from among his brethren, 6965
9: 9 I will **m** the house of Ahab like the house 5414
9:21 Joram said, **M ready**. And his chariot was 631
10: 5 thou shalt bid us; we will not **m** any **king**: 4427
18:30 Neither let Hezekiah **m** you **trust** in 982
18:31 **M** *an agreement* with me *by* a present, and 6213
21: 8 Neither will I **m** the feet of Israel **move** any 5110
23:10 might **m** his son or his daughter **to pass** 5674
1Ch 6:49 and to **m an atonement** for Israel, 3722
11:10 *and* with all Israel, to **m** him **king**, 4427
12:31 by name, to come and **m** David **king**. 4427
12:38 to Hebron, to **m** David **king** over all Israel: 4427
12:38 Israel *were* of one heart to **m** David **king**. 4427
16: 8 **m known** his deeds among the people. 3045
16:42 cymbals for those that should **m a sound**, 8085
17:21 to **m** thee a name of greatness and 7760
17:22 For thy people Israel didst thou **m** thine 5414
21: 3 **m** his people an hundred times **so many moe** 3254
22: 5 I will *therefore* now **m preparation** for it. 3559
28: 4 he liked me to **m** *me* **king** over all Israel: 4427
29:12 in thine hand *it is* to **m great**, and to give 1431
2Ch 4:11 Huram finished the work that he was to **m** 6213
4:16 did Huram his father **m** to king Solomon 6213
5:13 to **m** one sound **to be heard** in praising and 8085
6:21 which they shall **m** towards this place: 6419
6:22 an oath be laid upon him to **m** him **swear**, 422
6:24 **m supplication** before thee in this house; 2603
7:11 all that came into Solomon's heart to **m** in 6213
7:20 will **m** it to be a proverb and a byword 5414
8: 8 them did Solomon **m to pay** tribute until 5927
8: 9 of the children of Israel did Solomon **m** no 5414
10: 1 were all Israel come to **m** him **king**. 4427
10:10 but **m** thou *it* **somewhat lighter** for us; 7043
11:22 his brethren: for *he thought* to **m** him **king**. 4427
14: 7 and **m about** *them* walls, and towers, gates, 5437
20:36 he joined himself with him to **m** ships to go 6213
25: 8 God shall **m** thee **fall** before the enemy: 3782
29:10 Now *it is* in mine heart to **m** a covenant 3772
29:24 the altar, to **m an atonement** for all Israel: 3722
30: 5 **m proclamation** throughout all 5674+6963
35:21 for God commanded me to **m haste**: 926
Ezr 5: 3 to build this house, and to **m up** this wall? 3635
5: 4 What are the names of the men that **m** this 1124
5: 9 build this house, and to **m up** these walls? 3635
6: 8 Moreover I **m** a decree what ye shall do to 7761
7:13 I **m** a decree, that all they of the people of 7761
7:21 do **m** a decree to all the treasurers which 7761
10: 3 let us **m** a covenant with our God to put 3772
10:11 **m** confession unto the LORD God of your 5414
Ne 2: 4 unto me, For what dost thou **m request**? 1245
2: 8 that he may give me timber to **m beams** for 7136
4: 2 will they **m an end** in a day? will they 3615
8:12 to **m** great mirth, because they had 6213
8:15 of thick trees, to **m** booths, as it is written. 6213
9:38 because of all this we **m** a sure **covenant**, 3772
10:33 for the sin offerings to **m an atonement** for 3722
Est 1:20 when the king's decree which he shall **m** 6213
4: 8 to **m supplication** unto him, and to make 2603
4: 8 to **m request** before him for her people. 1245
Est 5: 5 the king said, **Cause** Haman to **m haste**, 4116
6:10 **M haste**, *and* take the apparel and 4116
7: 7 Haman stood *up* to **m request** for his life to 1245
9:22 that *they* should **m** them days of feasting 6213
Job 5:18 he woundeth, and his hands **m whole**. 7495
8: 5 and **m** thy **supplication** to the Almighty; 2603
8: 6 **m** the habitation of thy righteousness
prosperous. 7999
9:15 *but* I would **m supplication** to my judge. 2603
9:30 **m** my hands **never so clean**; 1253+2141+871.1
11: 3 Should thy lies **m** men **hold** their **peace**? 2790
11: 3 shall no man **m** *thee* **ashamed**? 3637
11:19 lie down, and none shall **m** *thee* **afraid**; 2729
11:19 yea, many shall **m suit** unto thee. 2470
13:11 Shall not his excellency **m** you **afraid**? 1204
13:21 and let not thy dread **m** me **afraid**. 1204
13:23 **m** me **to know** my transgression and 3045
15:24 Trouble and anguish shall **m** him **afraid**; 1204
18: 2 How long *will it be ere* you **m** an end of 7760
18:11 Terrors shall **m** him **afraid** on every side, 1204
19: 3 *that* you **m** yourselves **strange** to me. 1970
20: 2 cause me to answer, and for *this* I **m haste**. 2363
22:27 Thou shalt **m** thy **prayer** unto him, and 6279
24:11 *Which* **m oil** within their walls, *and* 6671
24:25 who will **m** me **a liar**, and make my speech 3576
24:25 me a liar, and **m** my speech nothing worth? 7760
28:25 To **m** the weight for the winds; and 6213
31:15 Did not he that made me in the womb **m** 6213
33: 7 Behold, my terror shall not **m** thee **afraid**, 1204
34:29 giveth quietness, who then can **m trouble**? 7561
35: 9 of oppressions they **m** *the oppressed* **to cry**: 2199
39:20 Canst thou **m** him **afraid** as a grasshopper? 7493
39:27 at thy command, and **m** her nest **on high**? 7311
40:19 can **m** his sword **to approach** *unto him*. 5066
41: 3 Will he **m many** supplications unto thee? 7235
41: 4 Will he **m** a covenant with thee? wilt thou 3772
41: 6 Shall the companions **m a banquet** of him? 3739
41:28 The arrow cannot **m** him **flee**: 1272
Ps 5: 8 **m** thy way **straight** before my face. 3474
6: 6 all the night **m** I my bed **to swim**; 7811
11: 2 they **m ready** their arrow upon the string, 3559
21: 9 Thou shalt **m** them as a fiery oven in 7896
21:12 Therefore shalt thou **m** them **turn** their 7896
21:12 *when* thou shalt **m ready** *thine arrows* upon 3559
22: 9 thou didst **m** me **hope** *when I was* upon my 982
31:16 **M** thy face **to shine** upon thy servant: 215
34: 2 My soul shall **m** her **boast** in the LORD: 1984
36: 8 thou shalt **m** them **drink** *of* the river of thy 8248
38:22 **M haste** to help me, O Lord my salvation. 2363
39: 4 **m** me **to know** mine end, and the measure 3045
39: 8 **m** me not the reproach of the foolish. 7760
40:13 deliver me: O LORD, **m haste** to help me. 2363
40:17 my deliverer; **m** no **tarrying**, O my God. 309
41: 3 thou wilt **m** all his bed in his sickness. 2015
45:16 whom thou mayest **m** princes in all 7896
45:17 I will **m** thy name **to be remembered** in all 2142
46: 4 the streams whereof shall **m glad** the city 8055
51: 6 in the hidden *part* thou shalt **m** me **to know** 3045
51: 8 **M** me **to hear** joy and gladness; *that* 8085
55: 2 I mourn in my complaint, and **m a noise**; 1949
57: 1 shadow of thy wings will I **m** my **refuge**, 2620
59: 6 they **m a noise** like a dog, and go round 1993
59:14 *and* let them **m a noise** like a dog, and 1993
64: 8 So they shall **m** their own tongue **to fall** 3782
66: 1 **M a joyful noise** unto God, all ye lands: 7321
66: 2 honour of his name: **m** his praise glorious. 7760
66: 8 and **m** the voice of his praise **to be heard**: 8085
69:23 and **m** their loins continually **to shake**. 4571
70: 1 *M haste*, O God, to deliver me; make haste NIH
70: 1 deliver me; **m haste** to help me, O LORD. 2363
70: 5 **m haste** unto me, O God: thou *art* my help 2363
70: 5 my deliverer; O LORD, **m** no **tarrying**. 309
71:12 from me: O my God, **m haste** for my help. 2363
71:16 I will **m mention** of thy righteousness, 2142
78: 5 that *they* should **m** them **known** to their 3045
81: 1 **m a joyful noise** unto the God of Jacob. 7321
83: 2 For lo, thine enemies **m a tumult**: and 1993
83:11 **M** their nobles like Oreb, and like Zeeb: 7896
83:13 O my God, **m** them like a wheel; as 7896
83:15 and **m** them **afraid** with thy storm. 926
84: 6 *Who* passing through the valley of Baca **m** 7896
87: 4 I will **m mention** of Rahab and Babylon to 2142
89: 1 with my mouth will I **m known** thy 3045
89:27 Also I will **m** him *my* firstborn, higher than 5414
89:29 His seed also will I **m** *to endure* for ever, 7760
90:15 **M** us **glad** according to the days *wherein* 8055
95: 1 let us **m a joyful noise** to the rock of our 7321
95: 2 *and* **m a joyful noise** unto him with psalms. 7321
98: 4 **M a joyful noise** unto the LORD, all 7321
98: 4 **m a loud noise**, and rejoice, and 6476
98: 6 sound of cornet **m a joyful noise** before 7321
100: 1 **M a joyful noise** unto the LORD, all ye 7321
104:15 *and* oil to **m** *his* face **to shine**, and 6670
104:17 Where the birds **m** their **nests**: *as for* 7077
105: 1 **m known** his deeds among the people. 3045
106: 8 *he* might **m** his mighty power **to be known**. 3045
110: 1 until I **m** thine enemies thy footstool. 7896
115: 8 They that **m** them are like unto them; *so* 6213
119:27 **M** me **to understand** the way of thy 995
119:35 **M** me **to go** in the path of thy 1869
119:135 **M** thy face **to shine** upon thy servant; and 215
132:17 There will I **m** the horn of David **to bud**: 6779
135:18 They that **m** them are like unto them: *so* 6213
139: 8 if I **m** my **bed** in hell, behold, thou *art* 3331
141: 1 **m haste** unto me; give ear unto my voice, 2363
142: 1 unto the LORD did I **m** my **supplication**. 2603
145:12 To **m known** to the sons of men his mighty 3045
Pr 1:16 feet run to evil, and **m haste** to shed blood. 4116
1:23 I will **m known** my words unto you. 3045
6: 3 go, humble thyself, and **m sure** thy friend. 7292
14: 9 Fools **m a mock at** sin: but among 3887
20:18 by counsel: and with good advice **m** war. 6213
20:25 *which is* holy, and after vows to **m inquiry**. 1239
22:21 That *I* might **m** thee **know** the certainty of 3045
22:24 **M** no **friendship** with an angry man; and 7462

Pr 23: 5 for *riches* **certainly m** themselves 6213+6213
24: 6 For by wise counsel thou shalt **m** thy war: 6213
24:27 and **m** it **fit** for thyself in the field; 6257
27:11 My son, be wise, and **m** my heart **glad**, 8055
30:26 yet **m** they their houses in the rocks; 7760
Ecc 2:24 *that* he should **m** his soul **enjoy** good in his 7200
7:13 for who can **m** *that* **straight**, which he hath 8626
7:16 over much; neither **m** thyself over **wise**: 2449
SS 1:11 We will **m** thee borders of gold with studs 6213
8:14 **M haste**, my beloved, and be thou like to a 1272
Isa 1:15 yea, when ye **m many** prayers, I will not 7235
1:16 Wash ye, **m** you **clean**; put away the evil of 2135
3: 7 **m** me not a ruler of the people. 7760
5:19 Let him **m speed**, *and* hasten his work, 4116
6:10 **M** the heart of this people **fat**, and 8080
6:10 and **m** their ears **heavy**, and shut their eyes; 3513
7: 6 let us **m a breach** therein for us, and set a 1234
10:23 For the Lord GOD of hosts shall **m** a 6213
11: 3 shall **m** him **of quick understanding** in 7306
11:15 and **m** *men* **go over** dryshod. 1869
12: 4 **m mention** that his name *is* exalted. 2142
13:12 I will **m** a man more **precious** than fine 3365
13:20 neither shall the shepherds **m** their **fold** 7257
14:23 I will also **m** it a possession for the bittern, 7760
16: 3 **m** thy shadow as the night in the midst of 7896
17: 2 lie down, and none shall **m** *them* **afraid**. 2729
17:11 In the day shalt thou **m** thy plant **to grow**, 7735
17:11 morning shalt thou **m** thy seed **to flourish**: 6524
17:12 *which* **m a noise** like the noise of the seas; 1993
17:12 *that* **m a rushing** like the rushing of mighty 7582
19:10 all that **m** sluces *and* ponds for fish. 6213
23:16 **m sweet** melody, sing many songs, that 3190
25: 6 hosts **m** unto all people a feast of fat things, 6213
26:13 by thee only will we **m mention** of thy 2142
27: 5 my strength, *that* he may **m** peace with me; 6213
27: 5 with me; *and* he shall **m** peace with me. 6213
28: 9 whom shall he **m to understand** doctrine? 995
28:16 he that believeth shall not **m haste**. 2363
29:21 That **m** a man **an offender** for a word, and 2398
32: 6 to **m empty** the soul of the hungry, and 7324
32:11 **m** ye **bare**, and gird *sackcloth* upon *your* 6209
33: 1 when thou shalt **m an end** to deal 5239
34:15 There shall the great owl **m** her **nest**, and 7077
36:15 Neither let Hezekiah **m** you **trust** in 982
36:16 **M** *an agreement* with me *by* a present, and 6213
37: 9 He is come forth to **m war** with thee. 3898
38:12 from day *even* to night wilt thou **m an end** 7999
38:13 from day *even* to night wilt thou **m an end** 7999
38:16 so wilt thou recover me, and **m** me **to live**. 2421
38:19 the father to the children shall **m known** 3045
40: 3 **m straight** in the desert a highway for our 3474
41:15 I will **m** thee a new sharp threshing 7760
41:15 *them* small, and shalt **m** the hills as chaff. 7760
41:18 I will **m** the wilderness a pool of water, and 7760
42:15 I will **m waste** mountains and hills, and 2717
42:15 I will **m** the rivers islands, and I will dry up 7760
42:16 I will **m** darkness light before them, and 7760
42:21 will magnify the law, and **m** *it* **honourable**. 142
43:19 I will even **m** a way in the wilderness, *and* 7760
44: 9 They that **m** a graven image *are* all of them 3335
44:19 shall I **m** the residue thereof an 6213
45: 2 and **m** the crooked places **straight**: 3474
45: 7 I **m** peace, and create evil: I the LORD do 6213
45:14 they shall **m supplication** unto thee, 6419
46: 5 **m** *me* **equal**, and compare me, that we may 7737
47: 2 **m bare** the leg, uncover the thigh, 2834
48: 1 **m mention** of the God of Israel, *but* not in 2142
48:15 and he shall **m** his way **prosperous**. 6743
49:11 I will **m** all my mountains a way, and 7760
49:17 Thy children shall **m haste**; thy destroyers 4116
50: 2 I dry up the sea, I **m** the rivers a wilderness: 7760
50: 3 and I **m** sackcloth their covering. 7760
51: 3 and he will **m** her wilderness like Eden, and 7760
51: 4 I will **m** my judgment **to rest** for a light of 7280
52: 5 they that rule over them **m** *them* **to howl**, 3213
53:10 when thou shalt **m** his soul an offering for 7760
54: 3 and **m** the desolate cities **to be inhabited**. 3427
54:12 I will **m** thy windows *of* agates, and 7760
55: 3 I will **m** an everlasting covenant with you, 3772
56: 7 and **m** them **joyful** in my house of prayer: 8055
57: 4 against whom **m** ye a **wide** mouth, *and* 7337
58: 4 to **m** your voice **to be heard** on high. 8085
58:11 thy soul in drought, and **m fat** thy bones: 2502
59: 7 and they **m haste** to shed innocent blood: 4116
60:13 and I will **m** the place of my feet **glorious**. 3513
60:15 that no man went through *thee*, I will **m** 7760
60:17 I will also **m** thy officers peace, and 7760
61: 8 I will **m** an everlasting covenant with them. 3772
62: 6 ye that **m mention** of the LORD, keep not 2142
62: 7 till he **m** Jerusalem a praise in the earth. 7760
63: 6 **m** them **drunk** in my fury, and I will bring 7937
63:12 to **m** himself an everlasting name? 6213
63:14 thy people, to **m** thyself a glorious name. 6213
64: 2 to **m** thy name **known** to thine adversaries, 3045
66:22 and the new earth, which I *will* **m**, 6213
Jer 4: 7 he is gone forth from his place to **m** thy 7760
4:16 **M** ye **mention** to the nations; behold, 2142
4:27 be desolate; yet will I not **m** a full end. 6213
4:30 in vain shalt thou **m** thyself **fair**; 3302
5:10 her walls, and destroy; but **m** not a full end: 6213
5:14 I will **m** my words in thy mouth fire, and 5414
5:18 I will not **m** a full end with you. 6213
6: 8 lest I **m** thee desolate, a land not inhabited. 7760
6:26 **m** thee mourning, *as for* an only *son*, most 6213
7:16 for them, neither **m intercession** to me: 6293
7:18 to **m** cakes to the queen of heaven, and 6213
9:11 I will **m** Jerusalem heaps, *and* a den of 5414
9:11 I will **m** the cities of Judah desolate, 5414
9:18 let them **m haste**, and take up a wailing for 4116
10:22 to **m** the cities of Judah desolate, *and* a den 7760
13:16 shadow of death, *and* **m** *it* gross darkness 7896
15:14 I will **m** *thee* **to pass** with thine enemies 5674
15:20 I will **m** thee unto this people a fenced 5414
16: 6 nor **m** themselves **bald** for them: 7139
16:20 Shall a man **m** gods unto himself, and 6213

Jer 18: 4 as seemed good to the potter to **m** *it*. 6213
18:11 and **m** your ways and your doings **good**. 3190
18:16 To **m** their land desolate, *and* a perpetual 7760
19: 7 I will **m void** the counsel of Judah and 1238
19: 8 I will **m** this city desolate, and a hissing; 7760
19:12 and *even* **m** this city as Tophet: 5414
20: 4 I will **m** thee a terror to thyself, and to all 5414
20: 9 I said, I will not **m mention** of him, 2142
22: 6 *yet* surely I will **m** thee a wilderness *and* 7896
23:15 and **m** them **drink** the water of gall: 8248
23:16 they **m** you **vain**: they speak a vision of 1891
25: 9 **m** them an astonishment, and a hissing, and 7760
25:12 and will **m** it perpetual desolations. 7760
25:18 to **m** them a desolation, an astonishment, a 5414
26: 6 will I **m** this house like Shiloh, and will 5414
26: 6 will **m** this city a curse to all the nations of 5414
27: 2 **M** thee bonds and yokes, and put them 6213
27:18 let them now **m intercession** to the LORD 6293
28:13 but thou shalt **m** for them yokes of iron. 6213
29:17 and will **m** them like vile figs, 5414
29:22 The LORD **m** thee like Zedekiah and 7760
30:10 and be quiet, and none shall **m** *him* **afraid**. 2729
30:11 though I **m** a full end of all nations whither 6213
30:11 yet will I not **m** a full end of thee: 6213
30:19 and the voice of them that **m merry**: 7832
31: 4 forth in the dances of them that **m merry**. 7832
31:13 and **m** them **rejoice** from their sorrow. 8055
31:21 Set thee up waymarks, **m** thee high heaps: 7760
31:31 that I will **m** a new covenant with the house 3772
31:33 this *shall be* the covenant that I will **m** with 3772
32:40 I will **m** an everlasting covenant with them, 3772
34:17 I will **m** you to be removed into all 5414
34:22 I will **m** the cities of Judah a desolation 5414
44:19 did we **m** her cakes to worship her, and 6213
46:27 and at ease, and none shall **m** *him* **afraid**. 2729
46:28 for I will **m** a full end of all the nations 6213
46:28 I will not **m** a full end of thee, but 6213
48:26 **M** ye him **drunken**: for he magnified 7937
49:15 I will **m** thee small among the heathen, *and* 5414
49:16 though thou shouldest **m** thy nest as **high** 1361
49:19 I will suddenly **m** him **run** away from her: 7323
49:20 surely he shall **m** their habitations **desolate** 8074
50: 3 which shall **m** her land desolate, and 7896
50:44 I will **m** them suddenly **run** away from her: 7323
50:45 surely he shall **m** *their* habitation **desolate** 8074
51:11 **M bright** the arrows: gather the shields: 1305
51:12 **m** the watch **strong**, set up the watchmen, 2388
51:25 and will **m** thee a burnt mountain. 5414
51:29 to **m** the land of Babylon a desolation 7760
51:36 will dry up her sea, and **m** her springs **dry**. 3001
51:39 In their heat I will **m** their feasts, and I will 7896
51:39 I will **m** them **drunken**, that they may 7937
51:57 I will **m drunk** her princes, and her wise 7937
La 4:21 be drunken, and shalt **m** thyself **naked**. 6168
Eze 3:26 I will **m** thy tongue **cleave** to the roof of 1692
4: 9 in one vessel, and **m** thee bread thereof, 6213
5:14 Moreover I will **m** thee waste, and 5414
6:14 upon them, and **m** the land desolate, yea, 5414
7:14 blown the trumpet, even to **m** all **ready**; 3559
7:23 **M** a chain: for the land is full *of* bloody 6213
7:24 also **m** the pomp of the strong **to cease**; 7673
11:13 *wilt* thou **m** a full end of the remnant of 6213
12:23 I will **m** this proverb **to cease**, and 7673
13:18 **m** kerchiefs upon the head of every stature 6213
13:20 ye there hunt the souls to **m** *them* **fly**, 6524
13:20 *even* the souls that ye hunt to **m** *them* **fly**. 6524
14: 8 will **m** him a sign and a proverb, and I will 8074
15: 8 I will **m** the land desolate, because 5414
16:42 So will I **m** my fury towards thee **to rest**, 5117
17:17 and great company **m** for him in the war, 6213
18:31 and **m** you a new heart and a new spirit: 6213
20:17 neither did I **m** an end of them in 6213
20:26 that I might **m** them **desolate**, to the end 8074
20:31 when *ye* **m** your sons **to pass** through 5674
21:10 It is sharpened to **m** a sore slaughter; *it is* 1961
21:10 should we then **m mirth**? it contemneth 7797
22:30 that *should* **m up the hedge**, 1443+1447
23:27 Thus will I **m** thy lewdness **to cease** from 7673
24: 5 *and* **m** it **boil well**, and let them 7570+7571
24: 9 I will even **m** the pile for fire **great**. 1431
24:17 to cry, **m** no mourning *for* the dead, 6213
25: 4 in thee, and **m** their dwellings in thee: 5414
25: 5 I will **m** Rabbah a stable for camels, and 5414
25:13 I will **m** it desolate from Teman; and 5414
26: 4 from her, and **m** her like the top of a rock. 5414
26: 8 he shall **m** a fort against thee, and cast a 5414
26:12 they shall **m a spoil** of thy riches, and 7997
26:12 thy riches, and **m a prey** of thy merchandise: 962
26:14 I will **m** thee like the top of a rock: 5414
26:19 When I shall **m** thee a desolate city, like 5414
26:21 I will **m** thee a terror, and thou *shalt be* no 5414
27: 5 they have taken cedars from Lebanon to **m** 6213
27:31 they shall **m** themselves **utterly bald** 7139+7139
29:10 I will **m** the land of Egypt utterly waste *and* 5414
29:12 I will **m** the land of Egypt desolate in 5414
30: 9 ships to **m** the careless Ethiopians **afraid**, 2729
30:10 **m** the multitude of Egypt **to cease** by 7673
30:12 I will **m** the rivers dry, and sell the land 5414
30:12 I will **m** the land **waste**, and all that is 8074
30:14 I will **m** Pathros **desolate**, and will set fire 8074
30:21 to bind it, to **m** it **strong** to hold the sword. 2388
32: 7 the heaven, and **m** the stars thereof **dark**; 6937
32: 8 the bright lights of heaven will I **m dark** 6937
32:10 I will **m** many people **amazed** at thee, and 8074
32:14 will I **m** their waters **deep**, and cause their 8257
32:15 When I shall **m** the land of Egypt desolate, 5414
34:25 I will **m** with them a covenant of peace, 3772
34:26 I will **m** them and the places round about 5414
34:28 dwell safely, and none shall **m** *them* **afraid**. 2729
35: 3 and I will **m** thee most desolate. 5414
35: 7 Thus will I **m** mount Seir most desolate, 5414
35: 9 I will **m** thee perpetual desolations, and 5414
35:11 I will **m** myself **known** amongst them, 3045
35:14 earth rejoiceth, I will **m** thee desolate. 6213
37:19 **m** them one stick, and they shall be one in 6213

Eze 37:22 I will **m** them one nation in the land upon 6213
37:26 Moreover I will **m** a covenant of peace 3772
39: 7 So will I **m** my holy name **known** in 3045
42:20 to **m a separation** between the sanctuary 914
43:18 of the altar in the day when *they* shall **m** it, 6213
43:27 the priests shall **m** your burnt offerings 6213
44:14 I will **m** them keepers of the charge of 5414
45:15 to **m reconciliation** for them, 3722
45:17 to **m reconciliation** for the house of Israel. 3722
Da 1:10 shall ye **m** *me* **endanger** my head to 2325
2: 5 if ye will not **m known** unto me the dream, 3046
2: 9 if ye will not **m known** unto me the dream, 3046
2:25 that will **m known** unto the king 3046
2:26 Art thou able to **m known** unto me 3046
2:30 for *their* sakes that shall **m known** 3046
3:29 Therefore I **m** a decree, That every people, 7761
4: 6 that they might **m known** unto me 3046
4: 7 they *did* not **m known** unto me 3046
4:18 to **m known** unto me the interpretation: 3046
4:25 they shall **m** thee **to eat** grass as oxen, 2939
4:32 they shall **m** thee **to eat** grass as oxen, and 2939
5: 8 nor **m known** to the king the interpretation 3046
5:15 **m known** unto me the interpretation 3046
5:16 that thou canst **m interpretations**, 6590+6591
5:16 **m known** to me the interpretation thereof, 3046
5:17 and **m known** to him the interpretation. 3046
6: 7 to **m** a **firm** decree, that whosoever shall 8631
6:26 I **m** a decree, That in every dominion of my 7761
8:16 **m** this *man* **to understand** the vision. 995
8:19 I *will* **m** thee **know** what shall be in the last 3045
9:24 to **m an end** of sins, and to make 8552
9:24 to **m reconciliation** for iniquity, and 3722
9:27 of abominations he *shall* **m** *it* **desolate**, 8074
10:14 Now I am come to **m** thee **understand** what 995
11: 6 to the king of the north to **m** an agreement: 6213
11:35 and to purge, and to **m** *them* **white**, 3835
11:44 to destroy, and **utterly** to **m away** many. 2763
Hos 2: 3 **m** her as a wilderness, and set her like a dry 7760
2: 6 **m a wall**, that she shall not find her 1443+1447
2:12 I will **m** them a forest, and the beasts of 7760
2:18 in that day will I **m** a covenant for them 3772
2:18 and will **m** them **to lie down** safely. 7901
5: 2 the revolters are **profound to m** slaughter, 6009
7: 3 They **m** the king **glad** with their 8055
10:11 I will **m** Ephraim **to ride**; Judah shall plow, 7392
11: 8 how shall I **m** thee as Admah? *how* shall I 5414
12: 1 they do **m** a covenant with the Assyrians, 3772
12: 9 will yet **m** thee **to dwell** in tabernacles, 3427
Joel 2:19 I will no more **m** you a reproach among 5414
Am 6:10 for *we may* not **m mention** of the name of 2142
8: 4 even to **m** the poor of the land **to fail**, 7673
8:10 I will **m** it as the mourning of an only *son*, 7760
9:14 they shall also **m** gardens, and eat the fruit 6213
Mic 1: 6 Therefore I will **m** Samaria as a heap of 7760
1: 8 I will **m** a wailing like the dragons, and 6213
1:16 **M** thee **bald**, and poll thee for thy delicate 7139
2:12 they shall **m great noise** by reason of 1949
3: 5 the prophets that **m** my people **err**, 8582
4: 4 his fig tree; and none shall **m** *them* **afraid**: 2729
4: 7 I will **m** her that halted a remnant, and 7760
4:13 for I will **m** thine horn iron, and I will make 7760
4:13 horn iron, and I will **m** thy hoofs brass: 7760
6:13 Therefore also will I **m** *thee* **sick** in smiting 2470
6:16 that I should **m** thee a desolation, and 5414
Na 1: 8 with an overrunning flood he will **m** an 6213
1: 9 he *will* **m** an utter end: affliction shall not 6213
1:14 I will **m** thy grave; for thou art vile. 7760
2: 1 watch the way, **m** *thy* loins **strong**, 2388
2: 5 they shall **m haste** *to* the wall thereof, and 4116
3: 6 **m** thee **vile**, and will set thee as a 5034
3:14 tread the morter, **m strong** the brickkiln. 2388
3:15 **m** thyself **many** as the cankerworm, 3513
3:15 **m** thyself **many** as the locusts. 3513
Hab 2: 2 Write the vision, and **m** *it* **plain** upon tables, 874
2:18 his work trusteth therein, to **m** dumb idols? 6213
3: 2 in the midst of the years **m known**; 3045
3:19 he will **m** my feet like hinds' *feet*, and 7760
3:19 he will **m** me **to walk** upon mine high 1869
Zep 1:18 for he shall **m** even a speedy riddance of all 6213
2:13 will **m** Nineveh a desolation, *and* dry like a 7760
3:13 lie down, and none shall **m** *them* **afraid**. 2729
3:20 for I will **m** you a name and a praise among 5414
Hag 2:23 the LORD, and will **m** thee as a signet: 7760
Zec 6:11 **m** crowns, and set *them* upon the head of 6213
9:15 shall drink, *and* **m a noise** as *through* wine; 1993
9:17 corn shall **m** the young men **cheerful**, and 5107
10: 1 *so* the LORD *shall* **m** bright clouds, and 6213
12: 2 I *will* **m** Jerusalem a cup of trembling unto 7760
12: 3 in that day will I **m** Jerusalem a 7760
12: 6 In that day will I **m** the governors of Judah 7760
Mal 2:15 did not he **m** one? Yet had he the residue of 6213
3:17 in that day when I **m** *up my* jewels; 6213
Mt 1:19 not willing to **m** her **a publick example**, *3856*
3: 3 the way of the Lord, **m** his paths straight. *4160*
4:19 and I will **m** you fishers of men. *4160*
5:36 thou canst not **m** one hair white or black. *4160*
8: 2 Lord, if thou wilt, thou canst **m** me **clean**. *2511*
12:16 And charged them that they should not **m** *4160*
12:33 Either **m** the tree good, and his fruit good; *4160*
12:33 or else **m** the tree corrupt, and his fruit *4160*
17: 4 if thou wilt, let us **m** here three tabernacles: *4160*
22:44 till I **m** thine enemies thy footstool? *5087*
23: 5 they **m broad** their phylacteries, and *4115*
23:14 and for a pretence **m** long **prayer**: *4336*
23:15 compass sea and land to **m** one proselyte, *4160*
23:15 ye **m** him twofold more *the* child of hell *4160*
23:25 for ye **m clean** the outside of the cup and *2511*
24:47 That he shall **m** him **ruler** over all his *2525*
25:21 **m** thee **ruler** over many *things:* enter thou *2525*
25:23 **m** thee **ruler** over many *things:* enter thou *2525*
27:65 go your way, **m** *it* as **sure** as you can. *805*
Mk 1: 3 the way of the Lord, **m** his paths straight. *4160*
1:17 and I will **m** you to become fishers of men. *4160*
1:40 If thou wilt, thou canst **m** me **clean**. *2511*
3:12 them that they should not **m** him known. *4160*

M

Mk 5:39 unto them, Why m ye *this* ado, and weep? 2350
6:39 And he commanded them to m all sit down 347
9: 5 and let us m three tabernacles; one for thee, 4160
12:36 till I m thine enemies thy footstool. 5087
12:40 and for a pretence m long prayers: 4336
12:42 she threw in two mites, which m a farthing. 1510
14:15 *and* prepared: there m ready for us. 2090
Lk 1:17 to m ready a people prepared for the Lord. 2090
3: 4 the way of the Lord, m his paths straight. 4160
5:12 Lord, if thou wilt, thou canst m me clean. 2511
5:33 and m prayers, and likewise the *disciples* of 4160
5:34 Can ye m the children of the bridechamber 4160
9:14 M them sit down by fifties in a company. 2625
9:33 and let us m three tabernacles; one for thee, 4160
9:52 of the Samaritans, to m ready for him. 2090
11:39 Now do ye Pharisees m clean the outside 2511
11:40 *is* without m that *which is* within also? 4160
12:37 and m them to sit down to meat, and 347
12:42 whom *his* lord shall m ruler over his 2525
12:44 that he will m him ruler over all that he 2525
14:18 all with one *consent* began to m excuse. 3868
14:31 m war against another king, 1519+4171+4820
15:19 thy son: m me as one of thy hired *servants*. 4160
15:29 that I might m merry with my friends: 2165
15:32 It was meet that *we* should m merry, and 2165
16: 9 M to yourselves friends of the mammon of 4160
17: 8 M ready wherewith I may sup, and 2090
19: 5 Zaccheus, m haste, and come down; 4692
20:43 Till I m thine enemies thy footstool. 5087
20:47 and for a shew m long prayers: 4336
22:12 large upper room furnished: there m ready. 2090
Jn 1:23 M straight the way of the Lord, as said 2116
2:16 m not my Father's house a house of 4160
6:10 And Jesus said, M the men sit down. 4160
6:15 and take him by force, to m him a king, 4160
8:32 the truth, and the truth shall m you free. 1659
8:36 If the Son therefore shall m you free, 1659
10:24 long dost thou m us to doubt? 142+3588+5590
14:23 come unto him, and m our abode with him. 4160
Ac 2:28 thou shalt m me full of joy with thy 4137
2:35 Until I m thy foes thy footstool. 5087
7:40 unto Aaron, M us gods to go before us: 4160
7:44 that *he* should m it according to the fashion 4160
9:34 arise, and m thy bed. And he arose 4766
22: 1 hear ye my defence *which I* m now unto NIG
22:18 M haste, and get *thee* quickly out of 4692
23:23 M ready two hundred soldiers to go to 2090
26:16 thee for this *purpose*, to m thee a minister 4400
26:24 learning doth m thee mad. 1519+3130+4062
Ro 1: 9 that without ceasing I m mention of you, 4160
3: 3 unbelief m the faith of God without effect? 2673
3:31 Do we then m void the law through faith? 2673
9:21 of the same lump to m one vessel unto 4160
9:22 *his* wrath, and to m his power known, 1107
9:23 And that he might m known the riches of 1107
9:28 a short work will the Lord m upon 4160
13:14 and m not provision for the flesh, to *fulfil* 4160
14: 4 holden up: for God is able to m him stand. 2476
14:19 follow *after* the *things* which m for peace, NIG
15:18 to m the Gentiles obedient, by word and 1519
15:26 Achaia to m a certain contribution for 4160
1Co 4: 5 will m manifest the counsels of the hearts: 5319
6:15 and m *them* the members of a harlot? 4160
8:13 if meat m my brother to offend, 4624
8:13 lest I m my brother to offend. 4624
9:15 that any *man* should m my glorying void. 2758
9:18 I may m the gospel of Christ without 5087
10:13 will with the temptation also m a way to 4160
2Co 2: 2 For if I m you sorry, who is he then 3076
9: 5 and m up beforehand your bounty, 4294
9: 8 And God *is* able to m all grace abound 4052
10:12 we dare not m *ourselves* of the number, 1469
12:17 Did I m a gain of you by any of them 4122
12:18 Did Titus m a gain of you? walked we not 4122
Gal 2:18 I destroyed, I m myself a transgressor. 4921
3:17 that *it* should m the promise of none effect. 2673
6:12 As many as desire to m a fair shew in 2146
Eph 2:15 for to m in himself of twain one new man, 2936
3: 9 And to m all *men* see what *is* 5461
5:13 for whatsoever doth m manifest is light. 5319
6:19 to m known the mystery of the gospel, 1107
6:21 the Lord, shall m known to you all *things*: 1107
Col 1:27 To whom God would m known what *is* 1107
4: 4 That I may m it manifest, as I ought to 5319
4: 9 They shall m known unto you all *things* 1107
1Th 3:12 And the Lord m you to increase and 4121
2Th 3: 9 to m ourselves an ensample unto you to 1325
2Ti 3:15 which are able to m thee wise unto 4679
4: 5 an evangelist, m full proof of thy ministry. 4135
Heb 1:13 until I m thine enemies thy footstool? 5087
2:10 to m the captain of their salvation perfect 5048
2:17 to m reconciliation for the sins of 2433
7:25 seeing he ever liveth to m intercession for 1793
8: 5 when he was about to m the tabernacle: 2005
8: 5 saith *he*, *that* thou m all *things* according to 4160
8: 8 when I will m a new covenant with 4931
8:10 For this *is* the covenant that I will m with 1303
9: 9 not m him that did the service perfect, 5048
10: 1 m the comers *thereunto* perfect. 5048
10:16 This *is* the covenant that I will m with them 1303
12:13 And m straight paths for your feet, lest *that* 4160
13:21 M you perfect in every good work to do 2675
Jas 3:18 is sown in peace of them that m peace. 4160
1Pe 5:10 m you perfect, stablish, strengthen, 2675
2Pe 1: 8 they m *you that ye shall* neither *be* barren 2525
1:10 give diligence to m your calling and 4160
2: 3 feigned words m merchandise of you: 1710
1Jn 1:10 we m him a liar, and his word is not in us. 4160
Rev 3: 9 I *will* m *them* of the synagogue of Satan, 1325
3: 9 I will m them to come and worship before 4160
3:12 Him that overcometh will I m a pillar in 4160
10: 9 and it shall m thy belly bitter, but it shall 4087
11: 7 bottomless *pit* shall m war against them, 4160
11:10 and m merry, and shall send gifts one to 2165
12:17 went to m war with the remnant of her 4160
13: 4 the beast? who is able to m war with him? 4170
13: 7 And it was given unto him to m war with 4160
13:14 that *they* should m an image to the beast, 4160
17:14 These shall m war with the Lamb, and 4170
17:16 and shall m her desolate and naked, and 4160
19:11 in righteousness he doth judge and m war. 4170
19:19 gathered together to m war against him that 4160
21: 5 the throne said, Behold, I m all *things* new. 4160

MAKER (20) [MAKE]

Job 4:17 shall a man be more pure than his M? 6213
32:22 *so doing* my M would soon take me away. 6213
35:10 none saith, Where *is* God my M, 6213
36: 3 and will ascribe righteousness to my M. 6466
Ps 95: 6 let us kneel before the LORD our M. 6213
Pr 14:31 that oppresseth the poor reproacheth his M: 6213
17: 5 mocketh the poor reproacheth his M: 6213
22: 2 the LORD *is* the M of them all. 6213
Isa 1:31 the m of it as a spark, and they shall both 6467
17: 7 At that day shall a man look to his M, and 6213
22:11 ye have not looked unto the M thereof, 6213
45: 9 Woe unto him that striveth with his M! 3335
45:11 the Holy One of Israel, and his M, 3335
51:13 forgettest the LORD thy M, that hath 6213
54: 5 For thy M *is* thine husband; the LORD of 6213
Jer 33: 2 Thus saith the LORD the m thereof, 6213
Hos 8:14 For Israel hath forgotten his M, and 6213
Hab 2:18 What profiteth the graven image that the m 3335
2:18 that the m of his work trusteth therein, 3335
Heb 11:10 whose builder and m *is* God. 1217

MAKERS (1) [MAKE]

Isa 45:16 go to confusion together *that are* m of idols. 2796

MAKEST (26) [MAKE]

Jdg 18: 3 what m thou in this *place?* and what hast 6213
Job 13:26 m me to possess the iniquities of my youth. 3423
22: 3 gain *to him*, that thou m thy ways perfect? 8552
Ps 4: 8 LORD, only m me dwell in safety. 3427
39:11 thou m his beauty to consume away like a 4529
44:10 Thou m us to turn back from the enemy: 7725
44:13 Thou m us a reproach to our neighbours, 7760
44:14 Thou m us a byword among the heathen, 7760
65: 8 m the outgoings of the morning and evening to rejoice. 7442
65:10 thou m it soft with showers: thou blessest 4127
80: 6 Thou m us a strife unto our neighbours: 7760
104:20 Thou m darkness, and it is night: 7896
144: 3 son of man, that thou m account of him? 2803
SS 1: 7 where thou m *thy flock* to rest at noon: 7257
Isa 45: 9 say to him that fashioneth it, What m thou? 6213
Jer 22:23 of Lebanon, that m thy nest in the cedars, 7077
28:15 but thou m this people to trust in a lie. 982
Eze 16:31 and m thine high place in every street; 6213
Hab 1:14 m men as the fishes of the sea, as 6213
2:15 thy bottle to *him*, and m *him* drunken also, 7937
Lk 14:12 When thou m a dinner or a supper, call not 4160
14:13 But when thou m a feast, call the poor, 4160
Jn 8:53 prophets are dead: whom m thou thyself? 4160
10:33 that thou, being a man, m thyself God. 4160
Ro 2:17 restest in the law, and m thy boast of God, 2744
2:23 Thou that m thy boast of the law, 2744

MAKETH (126) [MAKE]

Ex 4:11 or who m the dumb, or deaf, or the seeing, 7760
Lev 7: 7 the priest that m atonement therewith 3722
14:11 the priest that m *him* clean shall present 2891
17:11 for it *is* the blood *that* m an atonement for 3722
Dt 18:10 m his son or his daughter to pass through 5674
20:20 against the city that m war with thee, 6213
21:16 when he m his sons to inherit *that* which 5157
24: 7 and m merchandise of him, or selleth him; 6014
27:15 Cursed *be* the man that m *any* graven or 6213
27:18 Cursed *be* he that m the blind to wander 7686
29:12 which the LORD thy God m with thee 3772
1Sa 2: 6 The LORD killeth, and m alive: 2421
2: 7 The LORD m poor, and maketh rich: 3423
2: 7 The LORD maketh poor, and m rich: 6238
2Sa 22:33 *and* power: and he m my way perfect. 5425
22:34 He m my feet like hinds' *feet*: and 7737
Job 5:18 For he m sore, and bindeth up: 3510
9: 9 Which m Arcturus, Orion, and Pleiades, 6213
12:17 away spoiled, and m the judges fools. 1984
12:25 he m them to stagger like a drunken *man*. 8582
15:27 and m collops of fat on *his* flanks. 6213
23:16 For God m my heart soft, and the Almighty 7401
25: 2 *are* with him, he m peace in his high places. 6213
27:18 as a moth, and as a booth *that* the keeper m. 6213
35:11 and m us wiser than the fowls of heaven? 2449
36:27 For he m small the drops of water: 1639
41:31 He m the deep to boil like a pot: he maketh 7570
41:31 a pot: he m the sea like a pot of ointment. 7760
41:32 He m a path to shine after him; *one* would 215
Ps 9:12 When he m inquisition for blood, he 1875
18:32 me *with* strength, and m my way perfect. 5414
18:33 He m my feet like hinds' *feet*, and 7737
23: 2 He m me to lie down in green pastures: 7257
29: 6 He m them also to skip like a calf; 7540
29: 9 voice of the LORD m the hinds to calve, 2342
33:10 m the devices of the people of none effect. 5106
40: 4 Blessed *is that* man that m the LORD his 7760
46: 9 He m wars to cease unto the end of 7673
104: 3 who m the clouds his chariot: who walketh 7760
104: 4 Who m his angels spirits; his ministers a 6213
104:15 And wine *that* m glad the heart of man, *and* 8055
107:29 He m the storm a calm, so that the waves 6965
107:36 there he m the hungry to dwell, that they 3427
107:41 and m *him* families like a flock. 7760
113: 9 He m the barren *woman* to keep house, 3427
135: 7 he m lightnings for the rain; he bringeth 6213
147: 8 who m grass to grow *upon* the mountains. 6779
147:14 He m peace *in* thy borders, *and* filleth thee 7760
Pr 10: 1 A wise son m a glad father: but a foolish 8055
10: 4 but the hand of the diligent m rich. 6238
10:22 it m rich, and he addeth no sorrow with it. 6238
12: 4 she that m ashamed *is* as rottenness in his 954
12:25 Heaviness in the heart of man m it stoop: 7812
12:25 maketh it stoop: but a good word m it glad. 8055
13: 7 There is that m himself rich, yet *hath* 2050.1
13: 7 *there is* that m himself poor, yet *hath* great 7326
13:12 Hope deferred m the heart sick: but 2470
15:13 A merry heart m a cheerful countenance: 3190
15:20 A wise son m a glad father: but a foolish 8055
15:30 *and* a good report m the bones fat. 1878
16: 7 he m even his enemies to be at peace with 7999
18:16 A man's gift m room for him, and 7337
19: 4 Wealth m many friends; but the poor is 3254
28:20 he that m haste to be rich shall not be 213
31:22 She m herself coverings of tapestry; 6213
31:24 She m fine linen, and selleth *it*; and 6213
Ecc 3:11 that God m from the beginning to the end. 6213
7: 7 Surely oppression m a wise *man* mad; and 1984
8: 1 a man's wisdom m his face to shine, and 215
10:19 for laughter, and wine m merry: 2416+8055
11: 5 thou knowest not the works of God who m 6213
Isa 19:17 every one that m mention thereof shall be 2142
24: 1 the LORD m the earth empty, and 1238
24: 1 m it waste, and turneth it upside down, and 1110
27: 9 when he m all the stones of the altar as 7760
40:23 he m the judges of the earth as vanity. 6213
43:16 which m a way in the sea, and a path in 5414
44:13 m it after the figure of a man, according to 6213
44:15 he m a god, and worshippeth *it*; he maketh 6466
44:15 worshippeth *it*; he m it a graven image, and 6213
44:17 the residue thereof he m a god, *even* his 6213
44:24 I *am* the LORD that m all *things*; that 6213
44:25 the tokens of the liars, and m diviners mad; 1984
44:25 and m their knowledge foolish; 5528
46: 6 *and* hire a goldsmith; and he m it a god: 6213
55:10 the earth, and m it bring forth and bud, 3205
59:15 *that* departeth from evil m himself a prey: 7997
Jer 4:19 my heart m a noise in me; I cannot hold 1993
10:13 he m lightnings with rain, and 6213
17: 5 m flesh his arm, and whose heart departeth 7760
21: 2 king of Babylon m war against us; 3898
29:26 man *that is* mad, and m himself a prophet, 5012
29:27 which m himself a prophet to you? 5012
48:28 be like the dove *that* m her nest in the sides 7077
51:16 he m lightnings with rain, and 6213
Eze 22: 3 m idols against herself to defile *herself*. 6213
Da 2:28 m known to the king Nebuchadnezzar 3046
2:29 he that revealeth secrets m known to thee 3046
6:13 but m his petition three times a day. 1156+1159
11:31 place the abomination that m desolate. 8074
12:11 and the abomination that m desolate set up, 8074
Am 4:13 that m the morning darkness, and 6213
5: 8 *Seek him* that m the seven stars and Orion, 6213
5: 8 and m the day dark *with* night: 2821
Na 1: 4 and m it dry, and drieth up all the rivers: 3001
Mt 5:45 for he m his sun to rise on the evil and 393
Mk 7:37 he m both the deaf to hear, and the dumb to 4160
Lk 5:36 *then* both the new m a rent, and the piece 4977
Jn 19:12 whosoever m himself a king speaketh 4160
Ac 9:34 Aeneas, Jesus Christ m thee whole: 2390
Ro 5: 5 And hope m not ashamed; because 2617
8:26 the Spirit itself m intercession for us with 5241
8:27 he m intercession for the saints according 1793
8:34 of God, who also m intercession for us. 1793
11: 2 how he m intercession to God against 1793
1Co 4: 7 For who m thee to differ *from another?* 1252
2Co 2: 2 who is he then that m me glad, but 2165
2:14 m manifest the savour of his knowledge by 5319
Gal 2: 6 they were, it m no matter to me: 1308
Eph 4:16 m increase of the body unto the edifying of 4160
Heb 1: 7 Who m his angels spirits, and his ministers 4160
7:28 For the law m men high priests which have 2525
7:28 which was since the law, *m* the Son, NIG
Rev 13:13 that he m fire come down from heaven on 4160
21:27 worketh abomination, or *m* a lie: NIG
22:15 and whosoever loveth and m a lie. 4160

MAKHELOTH (2)

Nu 33:25 removed from Haradah, and pitched in M. 4722
33:26 they removed from M, and encamped at 4722

MAKI See MACHI

MAKING (30) [MAKE]

Ex 5:14 your task in m brick both yesterday 3835
Dt 20:19 a long time, in m war against it to take it, 3898
Jdg 19:22 *Now as* they were m their hearts merry, 3190
1Ki 4:20 eating and drinking, and m merry. 8056
1Ch 15:28 m a noise with psalteries and harps. 8085
17:19 in m known all *these* great things. 3045
2Ch 30:22 m confession to the LORD God of their 3034
Ps 19: 7 of the LORD *is* sure, m wise the simple. 2449
Ecc 12:12 of m many books *there is* no end; and 6213
Isa 3:16 *as* they go, and m a tinkling with their feet: 5913
Jer 20:15 is born unto thee; m him very glad. 8055+8055
Eze 27:16 of the multitude of the wares of thy m: 4639
27:18 in the multitude of the wares of thy m, 4639
Da 6:11 and m supplication before his God. 2604
Hos 10: 4 swearing falsely in m a covenant: 3772
Am 8: 5 m the ephah small, and the shekel great, 6994
Mic 6:13 in m *thee* desolate because of thy sins. 8074
Mt 9:23 saw the minstrels and the people m a noise, 2350
Mk 7:13 M the word of God of none effect through 208
Jn 5:18 was his Father, m himself equal with God. 4160
Ro 1:10 M request, if by any means now at length I 1189
2Co 6:10 as poor, yet m many rich; as having 4148
Eph 1:16 for you, m mention of you in my prayers; 4160
2:15 himself of twain one new man, *so* m peace; 4160
5:19 and m melody in your heart to the Lord; 5567
Php 1: 4 of mine for you all m request with joy, 4160
1Th 1: 2 you all, m mention of you in our prayers; 4160
Phm 1: 4 m mention of thee always in my prayers, 4160
2Pe 2: 6 m *them* an ensample unto those that after 5087
Jude 1:22 of some have compassion, m a difference: 1252

MAKIR See MACHIR

MAKIRITE See MACHIRITES

MAKKEDAH (9)
Jos 10:10 and smote them to Azekah, and unto **M**. 4719
10:16 and hid themselves in a cave at **M**. 4719
10:17 The five kings are found hid in a cave at **M**. 4719
10:21 to the camp to Joshua *at* **M** in peace: 4719
10:28 that day Joshua took **M**, and smote it with 4719
10:28 he did to the king of **M** as he did unto 4719
10:29 Joshua passed from **M**, and all Israel with 4719
12:16 The king of **M**, one; the king of Beth-el, 4719
15:41 Beth-dagon, and Naamah, and **M**; 4719

MAKTESH (1)
Zep 1:11 Howl, ye inhabitants of **M**, for all 4389

MALACHI (1)
Mal 1: 1 of the word of the LORD to Israel by **M**. 4401

MALCAM See MALCHAM

MALCHAM (2) [MOLOCH]
1Ch 8: 9 Jobab, and Zibia, and Mesha, and **M**, 4445
Zep 1: 5 swear by the LORD, and that swear by **M**; 4445

MALCHIAH (9)
1Ch 6:40 the son of Baaseiah, the son of **M**, 4441
Ezr 10:25 **M**, and Miamin, and Eleazar, and 4441
10:31 Eliezer, Ishijah, **M**, Shemaiah, Shimeon, 4441
Ne 3:14 the dung gate repaired **M** the son of 4441
3:31 After him repaired **M** the goldsmith's son 4441
8: 4 and **M**, and Hashum, and Hashbadana, 4441
11:12 the son of Pashur, the son of **M**, 4441
Jer 38: 1 son of Shelemiah, and Pashur the son of **M**, 4441
38: 6 cast him into the dungeon of **M** the son of 4441

MALCHIEL (3)
Ge 46:17 and the sons of Beriah; Heber, and **M**. 4439
Nu 26:45 of **M**, the family of the Malchielites. 4439
1Ch 7:31 Heber, and **M**, who *is* the father of 4439

MALCHIELITES (1)
Nu 26:45 of Malchiel, the family of the **M**. 4440

MALCHIJAH (6)
1Ch 9:12 the son of **M**, and Maasiai the son of Adiel, 4441
24: 9 The fifth to **M**, the sixth to Mijamin, 4441
Ezr 10:25 Miamin, and Eleazar, and **M**, and Benaiah. 4441
Ne 3:11 **M** the son of Harim, and Hashub the son of 4441
10: 3 Pashur, Amariah, **M**, 4441
12:42 Jehohanan, and **M**, and Elam, and Ezer. 4441

MALCHIRAM (1)
1Ch 3:18 **M** also, and Pedaiah, and Shenazar, 4443

MALCHISHUA (4)
1Sa 31: 2 and Abinadab, and **M**, Saul's sons. 4444
1Ch 8:33 and **M**, and Abinadab, and Eshbaal. 4444
9:39 and **M**, and Abinadab, and Eshbaal. 4444
10: 2 and Abinadab, and **M**, the sons of Saul. 4444

MALCHUS (1)
Jn 18:10 his right ear. The servant's name was **M**. *3124*

MALE (46) [MALES]
Ge 1:27 he him; **m** and female created he them. 2145
5: 2 **M** and female created he them; and 2145
6:19 alive with thee; they shall be **m** and female. 2145
7: 2 take to thee by sevens, the **m** and his female: 376
7: 2 *are* not clean by two, the **m** and his female. 376
7: 3 of the air by sevens, the **m** and the female; 2145
7: 9 Noah into the ark, the **m** and the female, 2145
7:16 went in, went in **m** and female of all flesh, 2145
17:23 every **m** among the men of Abraham's 2145
34:15 If ye will be as we *be*, that every **m** of you 2145
34:22 if every **m** among us be circumcised, 2145
34:24 every **m** was circumcised, all that went out 2145
Ex 12: 5 be without blemish, a **m** of the first year: 2145
34:19 thy cattle, *whether* ox or sheep, *that* is **m**. 2142
Lev 1: 3 the herd, let him offer a **m** without blemish: 2145
1:10 he shall bring it a **m** without blemish. 2145
3: 1 whether *it be* a **m** or female, he shall offer 2145
3: 6 **m** or female, he shall offer it without 2145
4:23 a kid of the goats, a **m** without blemish; 2145
7: 6 Every **m** among the priests shall eat 2145
12: 7 This *is* the law for her that hath born a **m** or 2145
22:19 *Ye shall offer* at your own will a **m** without 2145
27: 3 of the **m** from twenty years old even unto 2145
27: 5 thy estimation shall be of the **m** twenty 2145
27: 6 thy estimation shall be of the **m** five 2145
27: 7 if *it be* a **m**, then thy estimation shall be 2145
Nu 1: 2 of *their* names, every **m** by their polls; 2145
1:20 every **m** from twenty years old and upward, 2145
1:22 every **m** from twenty years old and upward, 2145
3:15 every **m** from a month old and 2145
5: 3 Both **m** and female shall ye put out, 2145
18:10 *place* shalt thou eat it; every **m** shall eat it: 2145
31:17 kill every **m** among the little ones, 2145
Dt 4:16 of any figure, the likeness of **m** or female, 2145
7:14 there shall not be **m**[S] or female barren 6135
20:13 thou shalt smite every **m** thereof with 2138
Jos 17: 2 these *were* the **m** children of Manasseh 2145
Jdg 21:11 Ye shall utterly destroy every **m**, and 2145
21:12 had known no man by lying with *any* **m**: 2145
1Ki 11:15 after he had smitten every **m** in Edom; 2145
11:16 until he had cut off every **m** in Edom;) 2145
Mal 1:14 which hath in his flock a **m**, and voweth, 2145
Mt 19: 4 made *them* at the beginning made them **m** *730*
Mk 10: 6 beginning of the creation God made them **m** *730*
Lk 2:23 Every **m** that openeth the womb shall be *730*
Gal 3:28 bond nor free, there is neither **m** nor female: *730*

MALE PROSTITUTES See EFFEMINATE

MALE SHRINE PROSTITUTES See SODOMITE; SODOMITES

MALEFACTOR (1) [MALEFACTORS]
Jn 18:30 and said unto him, If he were not a **m**, *2555*

MALEFACTORS (3) [MALEFACTOR]
Lk 23:32 And there were also two other, **m**, led with *2557*
23:33 and the **m**, one on the right hand, and *2557*
23:39 And one of the **m** which were hanged *2557*

MALELEEL (1)
Lk 3:37 *the son* of Jared, which was *the son* of **M**, *3121*

MALES (32) [MALE]
Ge 34:25 upon the city boldly, and slew all the **m**. 2145
Ex 12:48 let all his **m** be circumcised, and then 2145
13:12 thou hast; the **m** *shall be* the LORD'S. 2145
13:15 all that openeth the matrix, being **m**; 2145
23:17 Three times in the year all thy **m** shall 2138
Lev 6:18 All the **m** among the children of Aaron 2145
6:29 All the **m** among the priests shall eat 2145
Nu 3:22 according to the number of all the **m**, 2145
3:28 In the number of all the **m**, from a month 2145
3:34 according to the number of all the **m**, 2145
3:39 all the **m** from a month old and upward, 2145
3:40 Number all the firstborn of the **m** of 2145
3:43 all the firstborn **m** by the number of names, 2145
26:62 all **m** from a month old and upward: 2145
31: 7 and they slew all the **m**. 2145
Dt 15:19 All the firstling **m** that come of thy herd 2145
16:16 Three times in a year shall all thy **m** appear 2138
Jos 5: 4 *that were* **m**, *even* all the men of war, 2145
2Ch 31:16 Beside their genealogy of **m**, from three 2145
31:19 to give portions to all the **m** among 2145
Ezr 8: 3 by genealogy of the **m** an hundred 2145
8: 4 of Zerahiah, and with him two hundred **m**. 2145
8: 5 of Jahaziel, and with him three hundred **m**. 2145
8: 6 the son of Jonathan, and with him fifty **m**. 2145
8: 7 son of Athaliah, and with him seventy **m**. 2145
8: 8 son of Michael, and with him fourscore **m**. 2145
8: 9 and with him two hundred and eighteen **m**. 2145
8:10 and with him an hundred and threescore **m**. 2145
8:11 of Bebai, and with him twenty and eight **m**. 2145
8:12 and with him an hundred and ten **m**. 2145
8:13 and Shemaiah, and with them threescore **m**. 2145
8:14 and Zabbud, and with them seventy **m**. 2145

MALICE (6) [MALICIOUS, MALICIOUSNESS]
1Co 5: 8 neither with the leaven of **m** and *2549*
14:20 howbeit in **m** be ye children, *2549*
Eph 4:31 be put away from you, with all **m**: *2549*
Col 3: 8 wrath, **m**, blasphemy, filthy communication *2549*
Tit 3: 3 living in **m** and envy, hateful, *and* *2549*
1Pe 2: 1 Wherefore laying aside all **m**, and all guile, *2549*

MALICIOUS (1) [MALICE]
3Jn 1:10 he doeth, prating against us with **m** words: *4190*

MALICIOUSNESS (2) [MALICE]
Ro 1:29 fornication, wickedness, covetousness, **m**; *2549*
1Pe 2:16 and not using *your* liberty for a cloke of **m**, *2549*

MALIGNITY (1)
Ro 1:29 full of envy, murder, debate, deceit, **m**; *2550*

MALKI-SHUA See MELCHISHUA

MALKIEL See MALCHIEL

MALKIELITE See MALCHIELITES

MALKIJAH See MALCHIAH; MALCHIJAH; MELCHIAH

MALKIRAM See MALCHIRAM

MALLOTHI (2)
1Ch 25: 4 Joshbekashah, **M**, Hothir, *and* Mahazioth: 4413
25:26 The nineteenth to **M**, *he*, his sons, and 4413

MALLOWS (1)
Job 30: 4 Who cut up **m** by the bushes, and 4408

MALLUCH (6)
1Ch 6:44 son of Kishi, the son of Abdi, the son of **M**, 4409
Ezr 10:29 **M**, and Adaiah, Jashub, and Sheal, and 4409
10:32 Benjamin, **M**, *and* Shemariah. 4409
Ne 10: 4 Hattush, Shebaniah, **M**, 4409
10:27 **M**, Harim, Baanah. 4409
12: 2 Amariah, **M**, Hattush, 4409

MALTA See MELITA

MAMMON (4)
Mt 6:24 the other. Ye cannot serve God and **m**. *3126*
Lk 16: 9 Make to yourselves friends of the **m** of *3126*
16:11 have not been faithful in the unrighteous **m**, *3126*
16:13 the other. Ye cannot serve God and **m**. *3126*

MAMRE (10)
Ge 13:18 came and dwelt in the plain of **M**, which *is* 4471
14:13 for he dwelt in the plain of **M** the Amorite, 4471
14:24 which went with me, Aner, Eshcol, and **M**; 4471
18: 1 appeared unto him in the plains of **M**: 4471
23:17 which *was* before **M**, the field, and the cave 4471
23:19 cave of the field of Machpelah before **M**: 4471
25: 9 son of Zohar the Hittite, which *is* before **M**; 4471
35:27 Jacob came unto Isaac his father unto **M**, 4471
49:30 which *is* before **M**, in the land of Canaan, 4471
50:13 of Ephron the Hittite, before **M**. 4471

MAN (2616) [BONDMAN, BONDMEN, BOWMEN, CHAPMEN, COUNTRYMEN, CRAFTSMAN, CRAFTSMEN, DAYSMAN, FISHERMEN, FOOTMEN, FREEMAN, GOODMAN, HARVESTMAN, HERDMAN, HERDMEN, HORSEMAN, HORSEMEN, HUSBANDMAN, HUSBANDMEN, KINSMAN, KINSMAN'S, KINSMEN, MAN'S, MANKIND, MANSERVANT, MANSERVANT'S, MANSERVANTS, MANSLAYER, MANSLAYERS, MEN, MEN'S, MENPLEASERS, MENSERVANTS, MENSTEALERS, NOBLEMAN, PLOWMAN, PLOWMEN, SHIPMEN, SPEARMEN, SPOKESMAN, WATCHMAN, WATCHMAN'S, WATCHMEN, WORKWORKMAN, WORKMANSHIP, WORKMEN, WORKMEN'S]
Ge 1:26 And God said, Let us make **m** in our image, 120
1:27 So God created **m** in his own image, in 120
2: 5 and *there was* not a **m** to till the ground. 120
2: 7 the LORD God formed **m** *of* the dust of 120
2: 7 breath of life; and **m** became a living soul. 120
2: 8 and there he put the **m** whom he had formed. 120
2:15 the LORD God took the **m**, and put him 120
2:16 the LORD God commanded the **m**, saying, 120
2:18 *It is* not good that the **m** should be alone; 120
2:22 which the LORD God had taken from **m**, 120
2:22 he a woman, and brought her unto the **m**. 120
2:23 because she was taken out of **M**. 376
2:24 Therefore shall a **m** leave his father and his 376
2:25 the **m** and his wife, and were not ashamed. 120
3:12 the **m** said, The woman whom thou gavest *to* 120
3:22 Behold, the **m** is become as one of us, 120
3:24 So he drove out the **m**; and he placed at 120
4: 1 said, I have gotten a **m** from the LORD. 376
4:23 for I have slain a **m** to my wounding, and 376
4:23 my wounding, and a **young m** to my hurt. 3206
5: 1 In the day that God created **m**, in 120
6: 3 My spirit shall not always strive with **m**, 120
6: 5 GOD saw that the wickedness of **m** *was* 120
6: 6 it repented the LORD that he had made **m** 120
6: 7 I will destroy **m** whom I have created from 120
6: 7 both **m**, and beast, and the creeping thing, 120
6: 9 Noah was a just **m** *and* perfect in his 376
7:21 that creepeth upon the earth, and every **m**: 120
7:23 both **m**, and cattle, and the creeping things, 120
9: 5 beast will I require it, and at the hand of **m**; 120
9: 5 man's brother will I require the life of **m**. 120
9: 6 man's blood, by **m** shall his blood be shed: 120
9: 6 be shed: for in the image of God made he **m**. 120
13:16 that if a **m** can number the dust of the earth, 376
16:12 he will be a wild **m**; his hand *will be* against 120
16:12 his hand *will be* against **every m**; and 3605
17:10 Every **m** *child* among you shall be 2145
17:12 every **m** *child* in your generations, he that 2145
17:14 the uncircumcised **m** *child* whose flesh of 2145
18: 7 and good, and gave *it* unto a **young m**; 5288
19: 8 two daughters which have not known **m**; 376
19: 9 And they pressed sore upon the **m**, *even* Lot, 376
19:31 *there is* not a **m** in the earth to come in unto 376
20: 3 said to him, Behold, thou *art but* a dead **m**, NIH
20: 7 Now therefore restore the **m** *his* wife; for he 376
24:16 a virgin, neither had **any m** known her: 376
24:21 the **m** wondering at her held his peace, to wit 376
24:22 that the **m** took a golden earring of half a 376
24:26 the **m** bowed down his head, and 376
24:29 and Laban ran out unto the **m**, unto the well. 376
24:30 his sister, saying, Thus spake the **m** unto me; 376
24:30 that he came unto the **m**; and behold, 376
24:32 the **m** came into the house: and he ungirded 376
24:58 and said unto her, Wilt thou go with this **m**? 376
24:61 rode upon the camels, and followed the **m**: 376
24:65 What **m** *is* this that walketh in the field to 376
25: 8 an **old m**, and full *of years*; and 2205
25:27 Esau was a cunning hunter, a **m** of the field; 376
25:27 and Jacob *was* a plain **m**, dwelling in tents. 376
26:11 He that toucheth this **m** or his wife shall 376
26:13 the **m** waxed great, and went forward, 376
27:11 Esau my brother *is* a hairy **m**, and I *am* a 376
27:11 brother *is* a hairy man, and I *am* a smooth **m**: 376
29:19 than that I should give her to another **m**: 376
30:43 the **m** increased exceedingly, and had much 376
31:50 wives beside my daughters, no **m** *is* with us; 376
32:24 there wrestled a **m** with him until 376
34:19 the **young m** deferred not to do the thing, 5288
34:25 took **each m** his sword, and came upon 376
37:15 a *certain* **m** found him, and behold, *he was* 376
37:15 the **m** asked him, saying, What seekest thou? 376
37:17 the **m** said, They are departed hence; for I 376
38:25 sent to her father in law, saying, By the **m**, 376
39: 2 with Joseph, and he was a prosperous **m**; 376
40: 5 both of them, **each m** his dream in one night, 376
40: 5 **each m** according to the interpretation of his 376
41:11 we dreamed **each m** according to 376
41:12 *there was* there with us a **young m**, 5288
41:12 to **each m** according to his dream he did 376
41:33 let Pharaoh look out a **m** discreet and wise, 376
41:38 Can we find *such a one* as this *is*, a **m** in 376
41:44 without thee shall no **m** lift up his hand or 376
42:13 the sons of one **m** in the land of Canaan; 376
42:30 The **m**, *who is* the lord of the land, 376
42:33 the **m**, the lord of the country, said unto us, 376
43: 3 The **m** did solemnly protest unto us, saying, 376
43: 5 for the **m** said unto us, Ye shall not see my 376
43: 6 *as* to tell the **m** whether ye had yet a brother? 376
43: 7 The **m** asked us straitly of our state, and 376
43:11 carry down the **m** a present, a little balm, 376
43:13 your brother, and arise, go again unto the **m**: 376
43:14 God Almighty give you mercy before the **m**, 376
43:17 the **m** did as Joseph bade; and the man 376
43:17 the **m** brought the men into Joseph's house. 376
43:24 the **m** brought the men into Joseph's house, 376
43:27 father well, the **old m** of whom ye spake? 2205
44:11 they speedily took down **every m** his sack to 376

M

Ge 44:11 to the ground, and opened **every m** his sack. 376
44:13 laded **every m** his ass, and returned to 376
44:15 wot ye not that such a **m** as I can certainly 376
44:17 *but* the **m** in whose hand the cup is found, 376
44:20 an **old m**, and a child of *his* old age, a little 2205
45: 1 he cried, Cause every **m** to go out from me. 376
45: 1 there stood no **m** with him, while Joseph 376
45:22 To all of them he gave **each m** changes of 376
47: 6 if thou knowest *any* **m** of activity amongst 376
47:20 for the Egyptians sold **every m** his field, 376
49: 6 for in their anger they slew a **m**, and in their 376
Ex 1: 1 **every m** and his household came with Jacob. 376
2: 1 there went a **m** of the house of Levi, and 376
2:12 and when he saw that *there was* no **m**, 376
2:20 why *is* it *that* ye have left the **m**? call him, 376
2:21 And Moses was content to dwell with the **m**: 376
7:12 For they cast down **every m** his rod, and 376
8:17 and it became lice in **m**, and in beast; 120
8:18 so there were lice upon **m**, and upon beast. 120
9: 9 be a boil breaking forth *with* blains upon **m**, 120
9:10 a boil breaking forth *with* blains upon **m**, 120
9:19 *for upon* every **m** and beast which shall be 120
9:22 upon **m**, and upon beast, and upon every 120
9:25 all that *was* in the field, both **m** and beast; 120
10: 7 How long shall this *m* be a snare unto us? NIH
11: 2 let **every m** borrow of his neighbour, and 376
11: 3 Moreover the **m** Moses *was* very great in 376
11: 7 a dog move his tongue, against **m** or beast: 376
12: 3 they shall take to them **every m** a lamb, 376
12: 4 **every m** according to his eating shall make 376
12:12 in the land of Egypt, both **m** and beast; 120
12:16 save *that* which every **m** must eat, that only 5315
13: 2 children of Israel, *both* of **m** and of beast: 120
13:13 all the firstborn of **m** amongst thy children 120
13:15 both the firstborn of **m**, and the firstborn of 120
15: 3 The LORD *is* a **m** of war: the LORD *is* 376
16:16 Gather of it **every m** according to his eating, 376
16:16 an omer for **every m**, *according to* 1538
16:16 take ye **every m** for *them* which *are* in his 376
16:18 they gathered **every m** according to his 376
16:19 Let no **m** leave of it till the morning. 376
16:21 **every m** according to his eating: 376
16:22 two omers for one *m*: and all the rulers of NIH
16:29 abide ye **every m** in his place, let no man go 376
16:29 let no **m** go out of his place on the seventh 376
19:13 whether *it be* beast or **m**, it shall not live: 376
21: 7 if a **m** sell his daughter to be a maidservant, 376
21:12 He that smiteth a **m**, so that he die, shall be 376
21:13 if a **m**[S] lie not in wait, but God deliver *him* 834
21:14 if a **m** come presumptuously upon his 376
21:16 And he that stealeth a **m**, and selleth him, or 376
21:20 if a **m** smite his servant, or his maid, with a 376
21:26 if a **m** smite the eye of his servant, or the eye 376
21:28 If an ox gore a **m** or a woman, that they die: 376
21:29 but that he hath killed a **m** or a woman; 376
21:33 if a **m** shall open a pit, or if a man shall dig a 376
21:33 or if a **m** shall dig a pit, and not cover it, and 376
22: 1 If a **m** shall steal an ox, or a sheep, and 376
22: 5 If a **m** shall cause a field or vineyard to be 376
22: 7 If a **m** shall deliver unto his neighbour 376
22:10 If a **m** deliver unto his neighbour an ass, or 376
22:10 or be hurt, or driven away, **no m** seeing *it:* 369
22:14 if a **m** borrow *ought* of his neighbour, and 376
22:16 if a **m** entice a maid that is not betrothed, 376
23: 3 Neither shalt thou countenance a poor *m* in NIH
24:14 if any **m** have any matters to do, let him 1167
25: 2 of every **m** that giveth it willingly with his 376
30:12 shall they give **every m** a ransom for his 376
32: 1 the **m** that brought us up out of the land of 376
32:23 the **m** that brought us up out of the land of 376
32:27 Put **every m** his sword by his side, *and* go in 376
32:27 slay **every m** his brother, and every man his 376
32:27 **every m** his companion, and every man his 376
32:27 his companion, and **every m** his neighbour. 376
32:29 even **every m** upon his son, and upon his 376
33: 4 and no **m** did put on him his ornaments. 376
33: 8 stood **every m** *at* his tent door, and 376
33:10 and worshipped, **every m** *in* his tent door. 376
33:11 face to face, as a **m** speaketh unto his friend. 376
33:11 servant Joshua, the son of Nun, a **young m**, 5288
33:20 for there shall no **m** see me, and live. 120
34: 3 no **m** shall come up with thee, neither let any 376
34: 3 neither let **any m** be seen throughout all 376
34:24 neither shall **any m** desire thy land, 376
35:22 every **m** that offered *offered* an offering of 376
35:23 every **m**, with whom was found blue, and 376
35:24 **every m**, with whom was found shittim 3605
35:29 every **m** and woman, whose heart made 376
36: 1 and Aholiab, and every wise hearted **m**, 376
36: 2 and Aholiab, and every wise hearted **m**, 376
36: 4 came **every m** from his work which 376+376
36: 6 Let neither **m** nor woman make any more 376
36: 8 every wise hearted *m* among them that NIH
38:26 A bekah for every **m**, *that is*, half a shekel, 1538
Lev 1: 2 If *any* **m** of you bring an offering unto 120
5: 3 Or if he touch the uncleanness of **m**, 120
5: 3 whatsoever uncleanness *it be* that a **m** shall NIH
5: 4 whatsoever *it be* that a **m** shall pronounce 120
6: 3 in any of all *these* that a **m** doeth, sinning 120
7:21 any unclean *thing, as* the uncleanness of **m**, 120
12: 2 have conceived seed, and born a **m child**: 2145
13: 2 When a **m** shall have in the skin of his flesh 120
13: 9 When the plague of leprosy is in a **m**, then 120
13:29 If a **m** or woman hath a plague upon 376
13:38 If a **m** also or a woman have in the skin of 376
13:40 And the **m** whose hair is fallen off his head, 376
13:44 He *is* a leprous **m**, he *is* unclean: the priest 376
14:11 shall present the **m** that is to be made clean, 376
15: 2 When **any m** hath a running issue out 376+376
15:18 The woman also with whom **m** shall lie *with* 376
15:24 if **any m** lie with her at all, and her flowers 376
15:33 of the **m**, and of the woman, and of him 2145
16:17 there shall be no **m** in the tabernacle of 120
16:21 shall send *him* away by the hand of a fit **m** 376
17: 3 **What m soever** *there be* of the house 376+376
Lev 17: 4 blood shall be imputed unto that **m**; he hath 376
17: 4 that **m** shall be cut off from among his 376
17: 8 **Whatsoever m** *there be* of the house of 376+376
17: 9 even that **m** shall be cut off from among his 376
17:10 **whatsoever m** *there be* of the house of 376+376
17:13 **whatsoever m** *there be* of the children 376+376
18: 5 which if a **m** do, he shall live in them: I *am* 120
19: 3 Ye shall fear **every m** his mother, and 376
19:32 honour the face of the **old m**, and fear thy 2205
20: 3 I will set my face against that **m**, and will cut 376
20: 4 land do any ways hide their eyes from the **m**, 376
20: 5 I will set my face against that **m**, and 376
20:10 the **m** that committeth adultery with *another* 376
20:11 the **m** that lieth with his father's wife hath 376
20:12 if a **m** lie with his daughter in law, both of 376
20:13 If a **m** also lie with mankind, as he lieth with 376
20:14 if a **m** take a wife and her mother, it *is* 376
20:15 if a **m** lie with a beast, he shall surely be put 376
20:17 if a **m** shall take his sister, his father's 376
20:18 if a **m** shall lie with a woman having her 376
20:20 if a **m** shall lie with his uncle's wife, he hath 376
20:21 if a **m** shall take his brother's wife, it *is* an 376
20:27 A **m** also or woman that hath a familiar 376
21: 4 *being* a **chief m** among his people, 1167
21:18 For whatsoever **m** *he be* that hath a blemish, 376
21:18 a blind **m**, or a lame, or he that hath a flat 376
21:19 Or a **m** that is brokenfooted, 376
21:21 No **m** that hath a blemish, of the seed of 376
22: 4 **What m soever** of the seed of Aaron *is* 376+376
22: 4 the dead, or a **m** whose seed goeth from him; 376
22: 5 or a **m** of whom he may take uncleanness, 120
22:14 And if a **m** eat *of* the holy *thing* unwittingly, 376
24:10 a **m** of Israel strove together in the camp; 376
24:17 he that killeth any **m** shall surely be put to 120
24:19 And if a **m** cause a blemish in his neighbour; 376
24:20 as he hath caused a blemish in a **m**, so 120
24:21 he that killeth a **m**, he shall be put to death. 120
25:10 ye shall return **every m** unto his possession, 376
25:10 and ye shall return **every m** unto his family. 376
25:13 ye shall return **every m** unto his possession. 376
25:26 if the **m** have none to redeem *it*, and 376
25:27 restore the overplus unto the **m** to whom he 376
25:29 if a **m** sell a dwelling house in a walled city, 376
25:33 if a **m** purchase of the Levites, then NIH
27: 2 When a **m** shall make a singular vow, 376
27: 9 all that *any* **m** giveth of such unto NIH
27:14 when a **m** shall sanctify his house *to be* holy 376
27:16 if a **m** shall sanctify unto the LORD *some* 376
27:20 or if he have sold the field to another **m**, 376
27:22 if *a* **m** sanctify unto the LORD a field NIH
27:26 LORD'S firstling, no **m** shall sanctify it; 376
27:28 that a **m** shall devote unto the LORD of all 376
27:28 *both* of **m** and beast, and of the field of his 120
27:31 if a **m** will at all redeem *ought* of his tithes, 376
Nu 1: 4 with you there shall be a **m** of every tribe; 376
1:52 **every m** by his own camp, and every man 376
1:52 **every m** by his own standard, 376
2: 2 **Every m** of the children of Israel shall pitch 376
2:17 **every m** in his place by their standards. 376
3:13 all the firstborn in Israel, both **m** and beast: 120
5: 6 When a **m** or woman shall commit any sin 376
5: 8 if the **m** have no kinsman to recompense 376
5:10 whatsoever **any m** giveth the priest, it shall 376
5:13 a **m** lie with her **carnally**, and 376+2233+7902
5:15 shall the **m** bring his wife unto the priest, 376
5:19 If no **m** have lain with thee, and if thou hast 376
5:20 *some* **m** hath lain with thee beside thine 376
5:31 shall the **m** be guiltless from iniquity, and 376
6: 2 When either **m** or woman shall separate 376
6: 9 And if any **m** die very suddenly by him, and NIH
7: 5 to **every m** according to his service. 376
8:17 of Israel *are* mine, *both* **m** and beast: 120
9: 6 who were defiled by the dead body of a **m**, 120
9: 7 We *are* defiled by the dead body of a **m**: 120
9:10 If any **m** of you or of your posterity shall be 376
9:13 the **m** that *is* clean, and is not in a journey, 376
9:13 appointed season, that **m** shall bear his sin. 376
11:10 **every m** in the door of his tent: 376
11:27 there ran a **young m**, and told Moses, and 5288
12: 3 (Now the **m** Moses *was* very meek, above all 376
13: 2 every tribe of their fathers shall ye send a **m**, 376
14:15 *if* thou shalt kill *all* this people as one **m**, 376
15:32 they found a **m** that gathered sticks upon 376
15:35 The **m** shall be surely put to death: 376
16: 7 it shall be *that* the **m** whom the LORD doth 376
16:17 take **every m** his censer, and put incense in 376
16:17 bring ye before the LORD **every m** his 376
16:18 they took **every m** his censer, and put fire in 376
16:22 shall one **m** sin, and wilt thou be wroth with 376
17: 9 and they looked, and took **every m** his rod. 376
18:15 nevertheless the firstborn of **m** shalt thou 120
19: 9 a **m** *that is* clean shall gather up the ashes of 376
19:11 of any **m** shall be unclean seven days. 120+5315
19:13 the dead *body* of *any* **m** that is dead, 120+5315
19:14 This *is* the law, when a **m** dieth in a tent: 120
19:16 or a dead *body*, or a bone of a **m**, or a grave, 120
19:20 the **m** that shall be unclean, and shall not 376
21: 9 to pass, that if a serpent had bitten *any* **m**, 376
23:19 God *is* not a **m**, that he should lie; neither 376
23:19 neither the son of **m**, that he should repent: 120
24: 3 and the **m** whose eyes are open hath said: 1397
24:15 and the **m** whose eyes are open hath said: 1397
25: 8 he went after the **m** of Israel into the tent, 376
25: 8 the **m** of Israel, and the woman through her 376
26:64 among these there was not a **m** of them 376
26:65 there was not left a **m** of them, save Caleb 376
27: 8 If a **m** die, and have no son, then ye shall 376
27:16 of all flesh, set a **m** over the congregation, 376
27:18 a **m** in whom *is* the spirit, and lay thine hand 376
30: 2 If a **m** vow a vow unto the LORD, or 376
30:16 between a **m** and his wife, between 376
31:17 kill every woman that hath known **m** by 376
31:18 that have not known a **m** by lying with him, 2145
31:26 *both* of **m** and of beast, thou, and Eleazar 120
31:35 of women that had not known **m** by lying 2145
Nu 31:47 *both* of **m** and of beast, and gave them unto 120
31:49 and there lacketh not **one m** of us. 376
31:50 what **every m** hath gotten, *of* jewels of gold, 376
31:53 of war had taken spoil, **every m** for himself.) 376
32:18 have inherited **every m** his inheritance. 376
32:27 **every m** armed for war, before the LORD 3605
32:29 **every m** armed to battle, before 3605
35:23 wherewith *a m* may die, seeing *him* not, and NIH
36: 8 enjoy **every m** the inheritance of his fathers. 376
Dt 1:16 and judge righteously between every **m** and 376
1:17 you shall not be afraid of the face of **m**; 376
1:31 as a **m** doth bear his son, in all the way that 376
1:41 when ye had girded on **every m** his weapons 376
3:11 the breadth of it, after the cubit of a **m**. 376
3:20 shall ye return **every m** unto his possession, 376
4:32 since the day that God created **m** upon 120
5:24 seen this day that God doth talk with **m**, 120
7:24 there shall no **m** *be able to* stand before thee, 376
8: 3 that he might make thee know that **m** doth 120
8: 3 out of the mouth of the LORD doth **m** live. 120
8: 5 as a **m** chasteneth his son, *so* the LORD thy 376
11:25 There shall no **m** *be able to* stand before 376
12: 8 **every m** whatsoever *is* right in his own eyes. 376
15: 7 If there be among you a **poor m** of one of thy 34
15:12 a **Hebrew m**, or a Hebrew woman, be sold 5680
16:17 **Every m** *shall give* as he is able, according 376
17: 2 LORD thy God giveth thee, **m** or woman, 376
17: 5 shalt thou bring forth that **m** or that woman, 376
17: 5 *even that* **m** or *that* woman, and shalt stone 376
17:12 And the **m** that will do presumptuously, and 376
17:12 or unto the judge, even that **m** shall die: 376
19: 5 As when *a m* goeth into the wood with his NIH
19:11 if **any m** hate his neighbour, and lie in wait 376
19:15 One witness shall not rise up against a **m** for 376
19:16 If a false witness rise up against **any m** to 376
20: 5 What **m** *is there* that hath built a new house, 376
20: 5 die in the battle, and another **m** dedicate it. 376
20: 6 what **m** *is he* that hath planted a vineyard, 376
20: 6 he die in the battle, and another **m** eat of it. 376
20: 7 what **m** *is there* that hath betrothed a wife, 376
20: 7 he die in the battle, and another **m** take her. 376
20: 8 What **m** *is there that is* fearful and 376
21: 3 *that* the city *which is* next unto the slain *m*, NIH
21: 6 *that are* next unto the slain *m*, shall wash NIH
21:15 If a **m** have two wives, one beloved, and 376
21:18 If a **m** have a stubborn and rebellious son, 376
21:22 if a **m** have committed a sin worthy of death, 376
22: 5 not wear that which pertaineth unto a **m**, 1397
22: 5 neither shall a **m** put on a woman's 1397
22: 8 thine house, if any **m**[S] fall from thence. 5307
22:13 If **any m** take a wife, and go in unto her, and 376
22:16 I gave my daughter unto this **m** to wife, and 376
22:18 the elders of that city shall take *that* **m** and 376
22:22 If a **m** be found lying with a woman married 376
22:22 *both* the **m** that lay with the woman, and 376
22:23 and a **m** find her in the city, and lie with her; 376
22:24 the **m**, because he hath humbled his 376
22:25 if a **m** find a betrothed damsel in the field, 376
22:25 and the **m** force her, and lie with her: 376
22:25 then the **m** only that lay with her shall die: 376
22:26 for as when a **m** riseth against his neighbour, 376
22:28 If a **m** find a damsel *that is* a virgin, which is 376
22:29 the **m** that lay with her shall give unto 376
22:30 A **m** shall not take his father's wife, 376
23:10 If there be among you **any m**, that is not 376
24: 1 When a **m** hath taken a wife, and 376
24: 5 When a **m** hath taken a new wife, he shall 376
24: 6 No *m* shall take the nether or the upper NIH
24: 7 If a **m** be found stealing any of his brethren 376
24:11 the **m** to whom thou dost lend shall bring out 376
24:12 if the **m** *be* poor, thou shalt not sleep with 376
24:16 **every m** shall be put to death for his own 376
25: 2 if the wicked *m be* worthy to be beaten, NIH
25: 7 if the **m** like not to take his brother's wife, 376
25: 9 So shall it be done unto *that* **m** that will not 376
27:15 Cursed *be* the **m** that maketh *any* graven or 376
28:26 of the earth, and **no m** shall fray *them* away. 369
28:29 spoiled evermore, and **no m** shall save *thee*. 369
28:30 a wife, and another **m** shall lie with her: 376
28:54 *So that* the **m** *that is* tender among you, and 376
28:68 and bondwomen, and **no m** shall buy *you*. 369
29:18 Lest there should be among you **m**, or 376
29:20 and his jealousy shall smoke against that **m**, 376
32:25 shall destroy both the **young m** and 970
32:25 the suckling *also* with the **m** of gray hairs. 376
33: 1 wherewith Moses the **m** of God blessed 376
34: 6 no **m** knoweth of his sepulchre unto this day. 376
Jos 1: 5 There shall not **any m** *be able to* stand 376
2:11 there remain any more courage in **any m**, 376
3:12 of the tribes of Israel, out of every tribe a **m**. 376
4: 2 out of the people, out of every tribe a **m**, 376
4: 4 the children of Israel, out of every tribe a **m**: 376
4: 5 take ye up **every m** of you a stone upon his 376
5:13 there stood a **m** over against him with his 376
6: 5 the people shall ascend up **every m** straight 376
6:20 **every m** straight before him, and they took 376
6:21 both **m** and woman, young and old, and ox, 376
6:26 saying, Cursed *be* the **m** before the LORD, 376
7:14 LORD shall take shall come **m** by man. 1397
7:14 LORD shall take shall come man by **m**. NIH
7:17 he brought the family of the Zarhites **m** by 1397
7:17 the family of the Zarhites man by **m**; NIH
7:18 he brought his household **m** by man; and 1397
7:18 he brought his household man by **m**; and NIH
8:17 there was not a **m** left in Ai or Beth-el, 376
8:31 over which no *m* hath lift up *any* iron: NIH
10: 8 there shall not a **m** of them stand before 376
10:14 LORD hearkened unto the voice of a **m**: 376
11:14 every **m** they smote with the edge of 120
14: 6 unto Moses the **m** of God concerning me 376
14:15 which *Arba was* a great **m** among 120
17: 1 because he was a **m** of war, therefore he had 376
21:44 there stood not a **m** of all their enemies 376
22:20 and that **m** perished not alone in his iniquity. 376
23: 9 no **m** hath *been able to* stand before you unto 376

Jos 23:10 One **m** of you shall chase a thousand: for 376
24:28 people depart, **every m** unto his inheritance. 376
Jdg 1:24 the spies saw a **m** come forth out of the city, 376
1:25 but they let go the **m** and all his family. 376
1:26 And the **m** went *into* the land of the Hittites, 376
2: 6 the children of Israel went **every m** unto his 376
3:15 son of Gera, a Benjamite, a **m** lefthanded: 376
3:17 king of Moab: and Eglon *was* a very fat **m**. 376
3:28 and suffered not a **m** to pass over. 376
3:29 all men of valour; and there escaped not a **m**. 376
4:16 of the sword; *and* there was not a **m** left. 259
4:20 when any **m** doth come and inquire of thee, 376
4:20 inquire of thee, and say, Is there any **m** here? 376
4:22 I will shew thee the **m** whom thou seekest. 376
5:30 the prey; to every **m** a damsel *or* two; 1397
6:12 *is* with thee, thou mighty ***m*** of valour. NIH
6:16 thou shalt smite the Midianites as one **m**. 376
7: 7 let all the *other* people go **every m** unto his 376
7: 8 he sent all *the rest of* Israel **every m** unto his 376
7:13 *there was* a **m** that told a dream unto his 376
7:14 of Gideon the son of Joash, a **m** of Israel: 376
7:21 they stood **every m** in his place round about 376
8:14 caught a **young m** of the men of Succoth, 5288
8:21 for as the **m** *is, so is* his strength. 376
8:24 that you would give me **every m** the earrings 376
8:25 did cast therein **every m** the earrings of his 376
9: 9 wherewith by me they honour God and **m**, 376
9:13 which cheereth God and **m**, and go to be 376
9:49 all the people likewise cut down **every m** his 376
9:54 he called hastily unto the **young m** his 5288
9:54 his **young m** thrust him through, and 5288
9:55 they departed **every m** unto his place. 376
10: 1 of Puah, the son of Dodo, a **m** of Issachar; 376
10:18 What **m** *is he* that will begin to fight against 376
11: 1 Now Jephthah the Gileadite was a mighty ***m*** NIH
11:39 she knew no **m**. And it was a custom in 376
13: 2 there was a certain **m** of Zorah, of the family 376
13: 6 A **m** of God came unto me, and 376
13: 8 let the **m** of God which thou didst send come 376
13:10 Behold, the **m** hath appeared unto me, 376
13:11 and came to the **m**, and said unto him, 376
13:11 *Art* thou the **m** that spakest unto the woman? 376
16: 7 then shall I be weak, and be as another **m**. 120
16:11 shall I be weak, and be as another **m**. 120
16:17 shall become weak, and be like any *other* **m**. 120
16:19 she called for a **m**, and she caused *him* to 376
17: 1 there was a **m** of mount Ephraim, whose 376
17: 5 the **m** Micah had a house of gods, and 376
17: 6 **every m** did *that which was* right in his own 376
17: 7 there was a **young m** out of 5288
17: 8 the **m** departed out of the city from 376
17:11 the Levite was content to dwell with the **m**; 376
17:11 the **young m** was unto him as one of his 5288
17:12 the **young m** became his priest, and was in 5288
18: 3 they knew the voice of the **young m** 5288
18: 7 and had no business with *any* **m**. 120
18:15 came to the house of the **young m** 5288
18:19 thee to be a priest unto the house of one **m**, 376
18:28 and they had no business with *any* **m**; 120
19: 6 for the damsel's father had said unto the **m**, 376
19: 7 when the **m** rose up to depart, his father in 376
19: 9 when the **m** rose up to depart, he, and 376
19:10 the **m** would not tarry *that* night, but he rose 376
19:15 for *there was* no **m** that took them into *his* 376
19:16 there came an old **m** from his work out of 376
19:17 he saw a wayfaring **m** in the street of 376
19:17 and the old **m** said, Whither goest thou? and 376
19:18 and there *is* no **m** that receiveth me to house. 376
19:19 for the **young m** *which is* with thy servants: 5288
19:20 the old **m** said, Peace *be* with thee; 376
19:22 the master of the house, the **old m**, saying, 2205
19:22 Bring forth the **m** that came into thine house, 376
19:23 the **m**, the master of the house, went out unto 376
19:23 seeing that this **m** is come into mine house, 376
19:24 but unto this **m** do not so vile a thing. 376
19:25 so the **m** took his concubine, and brought *her* 376
19:28 the **m** took her *up* upon an ass, and the man NIH
19:28 the **m** rose up, and gat him unto his place. 376
20: 1 was gathered together as one **m**, 376
20: 8 all the people arose as one **m**, saying, 376
20:11 against the city, knit together as one **m**. 376
21:11 and every woman that hath lien by **m**. 2145
21:12 that had known no **m** by lying with *any* 376
21:21 catch you **every m** his wife of the daughters 376
21:22 we reserved not to **each m** his wife in 376
21:24 **every m** to his tribe and to his family, and 376
21:24 they went out from thence **every m** to his 376
21:25 **every m** did *that* which *was* right in his own 376
Ru 1: 1 a *certain* **m** of Beth-lehem-judah went to 376
1: 2 the name of the **m** *was* Elimelech, and 376
2: 1 a mighty **m** of wealth, of the family of 376
2:20 The **m** *is* near of kin unto us, one of our next 376
3: 3 *but* make not thyself known unto the **m**, 376
3: 8 that the **m** was afraid, and turned himself: 376
3:16 she told her all that the **m** had done to her. 376
3:18 for the **m** will not be in rest, until he have 376
4: 7 a **m** plucked off his shoe, and gave *it* to his 376
1Sa 1: 1 Now there was a certain **m** of 376
1: 3 this **m** went up out of his city yearly to 376
1:11 but wilt give unto thine handmaid a **m** child, 376
1:21 the **m** Elkanah, and all his house, went up to 376
2: 9 for by strength shall no **m** prevail. 376
2:13 *was, that* when any **m** offered sacrifice, 376
2:15 and said to the **m** that sacrificed, 376
2:16 *if any* **m** said unto him, Let them not fail to 376
2:25 If **one m** sin against another, the judge shall 376
2:25 if a **m** sin against the LORD, who shall 376
2:27 there came a **m** of God unto Eli, and 376
2:31 that there shall not be an **old m** in thine 2205
2:32 there shall not be an **old m** in thine house 2205
2:33 the **m** of thine, *whom* I shall not cut off from 376
4:10 and they fled **every m** into his tent: 376
4:12 there ran a **m** of Benjamin out of the army, 376
4:13 when the **m** came into the city, and told *it*, 376
4:14 And the **m** came in hastily, and told Eli. 376

1Sa 4:16 the **m** said unto Eli, I *am* he that came out of 376
4:18 for he was an old **m**, and heavy. And he had 376
8:22 men of Israel, Go ye **every m** unto his city. 376
9: 1 Now there was a **m** of Benjamin, whose 376
9: 1 a Benjamite, a mighty ***m*** of power. NIH
9: 2 *was* Saul, a choice *young **m***, and a goodly: NIH
9: 6 *there is* in this city a **m** of God, and *he is* an 376
9: 6 a man of God, and *he is* an honourable **m**; 376
9: 7 *if* we go, what shall we bring the **m**? 376
9: 7 *there is* not a present to bring to the **m** of 376
9: 8 *that* will I give to the **m** of God, to tell us our 376
9: 9 when a **m** went to inquire of God, thus he 376
9:10 So they went unto the city where the **m** of 376
9:16 send thee a **m** out of the land of Benjamin, 376
9:17 Behold the **m** whom I spake to thee of: 376
10: 6 and shalt be turned into another **m**. 376
10:22 if the **m** should yet come thither. 376
10:25 all the people away, **every m** to his house. 376
10:27 of Belial said, How shall this ***m*** save us? NIH
11: 3 then, if *there be* **no m** to save us, we will 369
11:13 There shall not a **m** be put to death this day: 376
13: 2 the rest of the people he sent **every m** to his 376
13:14 the LORD hath sought him a **m** after his 376
13:20 to sharpen **every m** his share, and his 376
14: 1 said unto the **young m** that bare his armour, 5288
14: 6 Jonathan said to the **young m** that bare his 5288
14:24 Cursed *be* the **m** that eateth *any* food until 376
14:26 but **no m** put his hand to his mouth: 369
14:28 Cursed *be* the **m** that eateth *any* food *this* 376
14:34 Bring me hither **every m** his ox, and 376
14:34 **every m** his sheep, and slay *them* here, and 376
14:34 all the people brought **every m** his ox with 376
14:36 and let us not leave a **m** of them. 376
14:39 *there was* not a ***m*** among all the people *that* NIH
14:52 when Saul saw any strong **m**, or any valiant 376
14:52 or any valiant **m**, he took him unto him. 1121
15: 3 slay both **m** and woman, infant and suckling, 376
15:29 for he *is* not a **m**, that *he* should repent. 120
16: 7 for *the LORD seeth* not as **m** seeth; for man 120
16: 7 for **m** looketh on the outward appearance, 120
16:16 to seek out a **m**, *who is* a cunning player on 376
16:17 Provide me now a **m** that can play well, and 376
16:18 a mighty valiant ***m***, and a man of war, and NIH
16:18 a mighty valiant *man*, and a **m** of war, and 376
17: 8 choose you a **m** for you, and let him come 376
17:10 give me a **m**, that we may fight together. 376
17:12 the **m** went among men *for* an old man in 376
17:12 the man went among men *for* an **old m** in 2204
17:24 when they saw the **m**, fled from him, and 376
17:25 Have ye seen this **m** that is come up? 376
17:25 it shall be, *that* the **m** who killeth him, 376
17:26 What shall be done to the **m** that killeth this 376
17:27 So shall it be done to the **m** that killeth him. 376
17:33 a youth, and he a **m** of war from his youth. 376
17:41 the **m** that bare the shield *went* before him. 376
17:58 to him, Whose son *art* thou, *thou* **young m**? 5288
18:23 seeing that I *am* a poor **m**, and 376
20:22 if I say thus unto the **young m**, Behold, 5958
21: 1 Why *art* thou alone, and no **m** with thee? 376
21: 2 Let no **m** know any thing of the business 376
21: 7 Now a *certain* **m** of the servants of Saul *was* 376
21:14 unto his servants, Lo, you see the **m** *is* mad: 376
21:15 *fellow* to **play the mad m** in my presence? 7696
24:19 For if a **m** find his enemy, will he let him go 376
25: 2 *there was* a **m** in Maon, whose possessions 376
25: 2 the **m** *was* very great, and he had three 376
25: 3 Now the name of the **m** *was* Nabal; and 376
25: 3 the **m** *was* churlish and evil *in* his doings; 376
25:10 that break away **every m** from his master. 376
25:13 his men, Gird you on **every m** his sword. 376
25:13 And they girded on **every m** his sword; and 376
25:17 son of Belial, that *a **m*** cannot speak to him. NIH
25:25 I pray thee, regard this **m** of Belial, 376
25:29 Yet a **m** is risen to pursue thee, and to seek 120
26:12 **no m** saw *it*, nor knew *it*, neither awaked: 369
26:15 said to Abner, *Art* not thou a *valiant* **m**? 376
26:23 The LORD render to **every m** his 376
27: 3 he and his men, **every m** with his household, 376
27: 9 left neither **m** nor woman alive, and 376
27:11 David saved neither **m** nor woman alive, 376
28:14 she said, An old **m** cometh up; and he *is* 376
30: 6 **every m** for his sons and for his daughters: 376
30:13 he said, I *am* a **young m** of Egypt, 5288
30:17 there escaped not a **m** of them, save four 376
30:22 save *to* **every m** his wife and his children, 376
2Sa 1: 2 a **m** came out of the camp from Saul with his 376
1: 5 David said unto the **young m** that told him, 5288
1: 6 the **young m** that told him said, As I 5288
1:13 David said unto the **young m** that told him, 5288
2: 3 David bring up, **every m** with his household: 376
3:34 as *a **m*** falleth before wicked men, *so* NIH
3:38 and a great ***m*** fallen this day in Israel? NIH
7:19 And *is* this the manner of **m**, O Lord GOD? 120
12: 2 The rich ***m*** had exceeding many flocks and NIH
12: 3 the poor ***m*** had nothing, save one little ewe NIH
12: 4 there came a traveller unto the rich **m**, and 376
12: 4 to dress for the **wayfaring m** that was come 732
12: 4 dressed it for the **m** that was come to him. 376
12: 5 anger was greatly kindled against the **m**; 376
12: 5 the **m** that hath done this *thing* shall surely 376
12: 7 Nathan said to David, Thou *art* the **m**. 376
13: 3 and Jonadab *was* a very subtil **m**. 376
13: 9 And they went out every **m** from him. 376
13:29 and **every m** gat him up upon his mule, and 376
13:34 the **young m** that kept the watch lift up his 5288
14:16 of the hand of the **m** *that would* destroy me 376
14:21 bring the **young m** Absalom again. 5288
15: 2 *that when* any **m** that had a controversy 376
15: 3 *there is* **no m** *deputed* of the king to hear 369
15: 4 that every **m** which hath *any* suit or 376
15: 5 that when **any m** came nigh to *him* to do 376
15:30 that *was* with him covered **every m** his head, 376
16: 5 thence came out a **m** of the family of 376
16: 7 thou bloody **m**, and thou man of Belial: 376
16: 7 thou bloody man, and thou **m** of Belial: 376

2Sa 16: 8 to thy mischief, because thou *art* a bloody **m**. 376
16:23 *was* as if a **m** had inquired at the oracle of 376
17: 3 the **m** whom thou seekest *is* as if all 376
17: 8 thy father *is* a **m** of war, and will not lodge 376
17:10 Israel knoweth that thy father *is* a mighty ***m***, NIH
18: 5 *Deal* gently for my sake with the **young m**, 5288
18:10 a certain **m** saw *it*, and told Joab, and said, 376
18:11 Joab said unto the **m** that told him, 376
18:12 the **m** said unto Joab, Though I should 376
18:12 Beware *that* none *touch* the **young m** 5288
18:24 and looked, and behold a **m** running alone. 376
18:26 the watchman saw another **m** running: and 376
18:26 and said, Behold *another* **m** running alone. 376
18:27 He *is* a good **m**, and cometh with good 376
18:29 king said, *Is* the **young m** Absalom safe? 5288
18:32 unto Cushi, *Is* the **young m** Absalom safe? 5288
18:32 thee to do *thee* hurt, be as *that* **young m** *is*. 5288
19: 8 for Israel had fled **every m** to his tent. 376
19:14 men of Judah, *even* as *the heart of* one **m**; 376
19:22 shall there **any m** be put to death *this* day in 376
19:32 Now Barzillai was a very **aged m**, 2204
19:32 lay at Mahanaim; for he *was* a very great **m**. 376
20: 1 there happened to be there a **m** of Belial, 376
20: 1 son of Jesse: **every m** to his tents, O Israel. 376
20: 2 So every **m** of Israel went up from after 376
20:12 when the **m** saw that all the people stood 376
20:21 a **m** of mount Ephraim, Sheba the son of 376
20:22 retired from the city, **every m** to his tent. 376
21: 4 neither for us *shalt thou* kill **any m** in Israel. 376
21: 5 The **m** that consumed us, and that devised 376
21:20 where was a **m** of *great* stature, that had on 376
22:26 with the upright **m** thou wilt shew thyself 1368
22:49 thou hast delivered me from the violent **m**. 376
23: 1 and the **m** *who* was raised up on high, 1397
23: 7 the **m** *that* shall touch them must be fenced 376
23:20 the son of a valiant **m**, of Kabzeel, who had 376
23:21 he slew an Egyptian, a goodly **m**: and 376
24:14 and let me not fall into the hand of **m**. 120
1Ki 1: 6 he also *was* a very goodly ***m***; and NIH
1:42 for thou *art* a valiant **m**, and bringest good 376
1:49 and rose up, and went **every m** his way. 376
1:52 If he will shew himself a worthy **m**, 1121
2: 2 thou strong therefore, and shew thyself a **m**; 376
2: 4 fail thee (said he) a **m** on the throne of Israel. 376
2: 9 for thou *art* a wise **m**, and knowest what 376
4: 7 **each m** *his* month in a year made provision. 259
4:25 **every m** under his vine and under his fig 376
4:27 king Solomon's table, **every m** *in* his month: 376
4:28 **every m** according to his charge. 376
7:14 his father *was* a **m** of Tyre, a worker in 376
8:25 There shall not fail thee a **m** in my sight to 376
8:31 If **any m** trespass against his neighbour, and 376
8:38 and supplication soever be *made* by any **m**, 120
8:38 which shall know **every m** the plague of his 376
8:39 and give to **every m** according to his ways, 376
8:46 (for *there is* no **m** that sinneth not,) 120
9: 5 There shall not fail thee a **m** upon the throne 376
10:25 they brought **every m** his present, vessels of 376
11:28 the **m** Jeroboam *was* a mighty *man* of 376
11:28 the man Jeroboam *was* a mighty ***m*** of NIH
11:28 Solomon seeing the **young m** that he was 5288
12:22 the word of God came unto Shemaiah the **m** 376
12:24 return **every m** to his house; for this thing is 376
13: 1 there came a **m** of God out of Judah by 376
13: 4 Jeroboam heard the saying of the **m** of God, 376
13: 5 according to the sign which the **m** of God 376
13: 6 king answered and said unto the **m** of God, 376
13: 6 And the **m** of God besought the LORD, and 376
13: 7 the king said unto the **m** of God, 376
13: 8 the **m** of God said unto the king, If thou wilt 376
13:11 told him all the works that the **m** of God had 376
13:12 For his sons had seen what way the **m** of 376
13:14 went after the **m** of God, and found him 376
13:14 *Art* thou the **m** of God that camest from 376
13:21 he cried unto the **m** of God that came from 376
13:26 It *is* the **m** of God, who was disobedient unto 376
13:29 the prophet took up the carcase of the **m** of 376
13:31 bury me in the sepulchre wherein the **m** of 376
14:10 as *a **m*** taketh away dung, till it be all gone. NIH
17:18 have I to do with thee, O thou **m** of God? 376
17:24 Now *by* this I know that thou *art* a **m** of 376
20: 7 and see how this ***m*** seeketh mischief: NIH
20:20 they slew every one his **m**: and the Syrians 376
20:24 **every m** out of his place, and put captains in 376
20:28 there came a **m** of God, and spake unto 376
20:35 a certain **m** of the sons of the prophets said 376
20:35 I pray thee. And the **m** refused to smite him. 376
20:37 he found another **m**, and said, Smite me, 376
20:37 the **m** smote him, so that in smiting he 376
20:39 a **m** turned aside, and brought a man unto 376
20:39 brought a **m** unto me, and said, Keep this 376
20:39 a man unto me, and said, Keep this **m**: 376
20:42 Because thou hast let go out of *thy* hand a **m** 376
22: 8 *There is* yet one **m**, Micaiah the son of 376
22:17 let them return **every m** to his house in 376
22:34 a *certain* **m** drew a bow at a venture, 376
22:36 **Every m** to his city, and every man to his 376
22:36 to his city, and **every m** to his own country. 376
2Ki 1: 6 There came a **m** up to meet us, and said unto 376
1: 7 What manner of **m** *was he* which came up to 376
1: 8 *He was* a hairy **m**, and girt *with* a girdle of 376
1: 9 Thou **m** of God, the king hath said, 376
1:10 If I *be* a **m** of God, then let fire come down 376
1:11 he answered and said unto him, O **m** of God, 376
1:12 and said unto them, If I *be* a **m** of God, 376
1:13 O **m** of God, I pray thee, let my life, and 376
3:25 *on* every good piece of land cast **every m** his 376
4: 7 she came and told the **m** of God. And he 376
4: 9 I perceive that this *is* a holy **m** of God, 376
4:16 And she said, Nay, my lord, *thou* **m** of God, 376
4:21 and laid him on the bed of the **m** of God, and 376
4:22 that I may run to the **m** of God, and 376
4:25 came unto the **m** of God to mount Carmel. 376
4:25 to pass, when the **m** of God saw her afar off, 376
4:27 when she came to the **m** of God to the hill, 376

M

2Ki 4:27 the **m** of God said, Let her alone; for her 376
4:29 go *thy way:* if thou meet **any m**, salute him 376
4:40 they cried out, and said, O thou **m** of God, 376
4:42 And there came a **m** from Baal-shalisha, and 376
4:42 brought the **m** of God bread of the firstfruits, 376
5: 1 was a great **m** with his master, and 376
5: 1 he was also a mighty **m** in valour, *but* NIH
5: 7 that this ***m*** doth send unto me to recover a NIH
5: 7 send unto me to recover a **m** of his leprosy? 376
5: 8 when Elisha the **m** of God had heard that 376
5:14 according to the saying of the **m** of God: 376
5:15 he returned to the **m** of God, he and all his 376
5:20 the servant of Elisha the **m** of God, said, 376
5:26 Went not mine heart *with thee,* when the **m** 376
6: 2 take thence **every m** a beam, and let us make 376
6: 6 the **m** of God said, Where fell it? And he 376
6: 9 the **m** of God sent unto the king of Israel, 376
6:10 to the place which the **m** of God told him 376
6:15 when the servant of the **m** of God was risen 376
6:17 LORD opened the eyes of the **young m**; 5288
6:19 and I will bring you to the **m** whom ye seek. 376
6:32 and *the king* sent a **m** from before him: 376
7: 2 the king leaned answered the **m** of God, 376
7: 5 camp of Syria, behold, *there was* no **m** there. 376
7:10 behold, *there was* no **m** there, neither voice 376
7:10 neither voice of **m**, but horses tied, and asses 120
7:17 and he died, as the **m** of God had said, 376
7:18 it came to pass as the **m** of God had spoken 376
7:19 *that* lord answered the **m** of God, and said, 376
8: 2 and did after the saying of the **m** of God: 376
8: 4 with Gehazi the servant of the **m** of God, 376
8: 7 saying, The **m** of God is come hither. 376
8: 8 go, meet the **m** of God, and inquire of 376
8:11 *he* was ashamed: and the **m** of God wept. 376
9: 4 So the **young m**, *even* the young man 5288
9: 4 young man, *even* the **young m** the prophet, 5288
9:11 Ye know the **m**, and his communication. 376
9:13 took **every m** his garment, and put *it* under 376
10:21 so that there was not a **m** left that came not. 376
11: 8 **every m** with his weapons in his hand: 376
11: 9 they took **every m** his men that were to 376
11:11 **every m** with his weapons in his hand, 376
12: 4 *account,* the money that every **m** is set at, 5315
12: 5 take *it* to them, **every m** of his acquaintance: 376
13:19 And the **m** of God was wroth with him, and 376
13:21 as they were burying a **m**, that behold, 376
13:21 they cast the **m** into the sepulchre of Elisha: 376
13:21 when the **m** was let down, and touched 376
14: 6 **every m** shall be put to death for his own 376
14:12 and they fled **every m** to their tents. 376
15:20 of each **m** fifty shekels *of* silver, to give to 376
18:21 *even* upon Egypt, on which if a **m** lean, it 376
18:31 and *then* eat ye **every m** of his own vine, and 376
21:13 I will wipe Jerusalem as *a* ***m*** wipeth a dish, NIH
22:15 God of Israel, Tell the **m** that sent you to me, 376
23:10 that no **m** might make his son or his 376
23:16 the LORD which the **m** of God proclaimed, 376
23:17 *It is* the sepulchre of the **m** of God, 376
23:18 Let him alone; let no **m** move his bones. 376
1Ch 11:22 the son of a valiant **m** of Kabzeel, who had 376
11:23 a **m** of *great* stature, five cubits *high;* and 376
12: 4 a mighty ***m*** among the thirty, and over NIH
12:28 a **young m** mighty of valour, and *of* his 5288
16: 3 both **m** and woman, to every one a loaf of 376
16:21 He suffered no **m** to do them wrong: yea, 376
16:43 all the people departed **every m** to his house: 376
17:17 to the estate of a **m** of high degree, 120
20: 6 where was a **m** of *great* stature, whose 376
21:13 but let me not fall into the hand of **m**. 120
22: 9 *be* born to thee, who shall be a **m** of rest; 376
23: 3 **m** by man, was thirty and eight thousand. NIH
23: 3 man by **m**, was thirty and eight thousand. 1397
23:14 Now *concerning* Moses the **m** of God, 376
27:32 *was* a counseller, a wise **m**, and a scribe: 376
28: 3 because thou *hast been* a **m** of war, and 376
28:21 willing skilful ***m***, for any *manner of* service: NIH
29: 1 for the palace *is* not for **m**, but for 120
2Ch 2: 7 therefore a **m** cunning to work in gold, 376
2:13 now I have sent a cunning **m**, endued with 376
2:14 his father *was* a **m** of Tyre, skilful to work in 376
6: 5 neither chose I **any m** to be a ruler over my 376
6:16 There shall not fail thee a **m** in my sight to 376
6:22 If a **m** sin against his neighbour, and an oath 376
6:29 supplication soever shall be *made* of any **m**, 120
6:30 render unto **every m** according unto all his 376
6:36 (for *there is* no **m** which sinneth not,) 120
7:18 There shall not fail thee a **m** *to be* ruler in 376
8:14 for so had David the **m** of God commanded. 376
9:24 they brought **every m** his present, vessels of 376
10:16 **every m** to your tents, O Israel: *and* now, 376
11: 2 LORD came to Shemaiah the **m** of God, 376
11: 4 return **every m** to his house, for this thing is 376
14:11 *art* our God; let not **m** prevail against thee. 582
15:13 or great, whether **m** or woman. 376
17:17 Eliada a mighty ***m*** of valour, and with him NIH
18: 7 *There is* yet one **m**, by whom *we* may 376
18:16 *therefore* **every m** to his house in peace. 376
18:33 a *certain* **m** drew a bow at a venture, 376
18:33 therefore he said to *his* **chariot m**, 7395
19: 6 for ye judge not for **m**, but for the LORD, 120
20:27 every **m** of Judah and Jerusalem, and 376
23: 7 **every m** with his weapons in his hand; 376
23: 8 took **every m** his men that were to come in 376
23:10 **every m** having his weapon in his hand, 376
25: 4 but **every m** shall die for his own sin. 376
25: 7 there came a **m** of God to him, saying, 376
25: 9 Amaziah said to the **m** of God, But what 376
25: 9 the **m** of God answered, The LORD is able 376
25:22 and they fled **every m** to his tent. 376
28: 7 Zichri, a mighty ***m*** of Ephraim, slew NIH
30:16 according to the law of Moses the **m** of God: 376
31: 1 **every m** to his possession, into their own 376
31: 2 **every m** according to his service, the priests 376
32:19 *which were* the work of the hands of **m**. 120
34:23 of Israel, Tell ye the **m** that sent you to me, 376
2Ch 36:17 had no compassion upon **young m** or 970
36:17 maiden, **old m**, or him that stooped for age: 2205
Ezr 3: 1 themselves together as one **m** to Jerusalem. 376
3: 2 as it is written in the law of Moses the **m** of 376
8:18 us they brought us a **m** of understanding, 376
Ne 1:11 and grant him mercy in the sight of this **m**. 376
2:10 **m** to seek the welfare of the children of 120
2:12 neither told I *any* **m** what my God had put in 120
5:13 So God shake out every **m** from his house, 376
6:11 I said, Should such a **m** as I flee? and who *is* 376
7: 2 for he *was* a faithful **m**, and feared God 376
8: 1 **m** into the street that *was* before the water 376
9:29 (which if a **m** do, he shall live in them;) 120
12:24 to the commandment of David the **m** of God, 376
12:36 with the musical instruments of David the **m** 376
Est 1:22 that every **m** should bear rule in his own 376
4:11 that whosoever, *whether* **m** or woman, 376
5:12 Esther the queen did let no ***m*** come in with NIH
6: 6 What shall be done unto the **m** whom 376
6: 7 *For* the **m** whom the king delighteth to 376
6: 9 that they may array the **m** *withal* whom 376
6: 9 Thus shall it be done to the **m** whom 376
6:11 Thus shall it be done unto the **m** whom 376
8: 8 with the king's ring, may **no m** reverse. 369
9: 2 no **m** could withstand them; for the fear of 376
9: 4 for *this* **m** Mordecai waxed greater and 376
Job 1: 1 There was a **m** in the land of Uz, 376
1: 1 that **m** was perfect and upright, and one that 376
1: 3 that this **m** was the greatest of all the men of 376
1: 8 a perfect and an upright **m**, one that feareth 376
2: 3 a perfect and an upright **m**, one that feareth 376
2: 4 yea, all that a **m** hath will he give for his life. 376
3: 3 *it was* said, There is a **m child** conceived. 1397
3:23 *Why is light given* to a **m** whose way is 1397
4:17 Shall **mortal m** be more just than God? 582
4:17 shall a **m** be more pure than his Maker? 1397
5: 2 For wrath killeth the **foolish m**, and 191
5: 7 Yet **m** is born unto trouble, as the sparks fly 120
5:17 happy *is* the **m** whom God correcteth: 582
7: 1 *Is there* not an appointed time to **m** upon 582
7:17 What *is* **m**, that thou shouldest magnify him? 582
8:20 God will not cast away a perfect ***m***, neither NIH
9: 2 a truth: but how should **m** be just with God? 582
9:32 For *he is* not a **m**, as I *am, that* I should 376
10: 4 thou eyes of flesh? or seest thou as **m** seeth? 582
10: 5 *Are* thy days as the days of **m**? *are* thy years 582
11: 2 and should a **m** full of talk be justified? 376
11: 3 shall **no m** make *thee* ashamed? 369
11:12 For vain **m** would be wise, though man be 376
11:12 though **m** be born *like* a wild ass's colt. 120
12: 4 the just upright ***m*** *is* laughed to scorn. NIH
12:14 it cannot be built *again:* he shutteth up a **m**, 376
12:25 maketh them to stagger like a drunken ***m***. NIH
13: 9 or as *one* **m** mocketh another, do ye *so* NIH
14: 1 **M** *that is* born of a woman *is* of few days, 120
14:10 **m** dieth, and wasteth away: yea, man giveth 1397
14:10 yea, **m** giveth up the ghost, and where *is* he? 120
14:12 So **m** lieth down, and riseth not: till 376
14:14 If a **m** die, shall he live *again?* all the days 1397
14:19 the earth; and thou destroyest the hope of **m**. 582
15: 2 Should a wise ***m*** utter vain knowledge, and NIH
15: 7 *Art* thou the first **m** *that* was born? or 120
15:14 What *is* **m**, that he should be clean? and 582
15:16 How much more abominable and filthy *is* **m**, 376
15:20 The wicked ***m*** travaileth with pain all his NIH
15:28 *and* in houses which no **m** inhabiteth, NIH
16:21 O that *one* might plead for a **m** with God, 1397
16:21 as a **m** *pleadeth* for his neighbour. 120+1121
17:10 for I cannot find *one* wise ***m*** among you. NIH
20: 4 this of old, since **m** was placed upon earth, 120
20:21 therefore shall no ***m*** look for his goods. NIH
20:29 This *is* the portion of a wicked **m** from God, 120
21: 4 *As for* me, *is* my complaint to **m**? and if *it* 120
21:33 every **m** shall draw after him, as *there are* 120
22: 2 Can a **m** be profitable unto God, as he that 1397
22: 8 *as for* the mighty **m**, he had the earth; and 376
22: 8 the earth; and the honourable ***m*** dwelt in it. NIH
24:22 he riseth up, and no ***m*** is sure of life. NIH
25: 4 How then can **m** be justified with God? or 582
25: 6 How much less **m**, *that is* a worm? and 582
25: 6 a worm? and the son of **m**, *which is* a worm? 120
27:13 This *is* the portion of a wicked **m** with God, 120
27:19 The rich ***m*** shall lie down, but he shall not NIH
28:13 **M** knoweth not the price thereof; neither is it 582
28:28 unto **m** he said, Behold, the fear of the Lord, 120
32: 8 *there is* a spirit in **m**: and the inspiration of 582
32:13 out wisdom: God thrusteth him down, not **m**. 376
32:21 neither let me give flattering titles unto **m**. 120
33:12 will answer thee, that God is greater than **m**. 582
33:14 yea twice, *yet* ***m*** perceiveth it not. NIH
33:17 That *he* may withdraw **m** *from his* purpose, 120
33:17 *from his* purpose, and hide pride from **m**. 1397
33:23 a thousand, to shew unto **m** his uprightness: 120
33:26 for he will render unto **m** his righteousness. 582
33:29 *things* worketh God oftentimes with **m**, 1397
34: 7 What **m** *is* like Job, *who* drinketh up 1397
34: 9 It profiteth a **m** nothing that he should 1397
34:11 For the work of a **m** shall he render unto 120
34:11 cause **every m** to find according to *his* ways. 376
34:14 If he set his heart upon ***m***, *if* he gather unto NIH
34:15 and **m** shall turn again unto dust. 120
34:21 For his eyes *are* upon the ways of **m**, and 376
34:23 For he will not lay upon **m** more *than right;* 376
34:29 *done* against a nation, or against a **m** only: 120
34:34 tell me, and let a wise **m** hearken unto me. 1397
35: 8 Thy wickedness *may hurt* a **m** as thou *art;* 376
35: 8 thy righteousness *may profit* the son of **m**. 120
36:25 Every **m** may see it; man may behold *it* afar 120
36:25 man may see it; **m** may behold *it* afar off. 582
36:28 do drop *and* distil upon **m** abundantly. 120
37: 7 He sealeth up the hand of every **m**; that all 120
37:20 if a **m** speak, surely he shall be swallowed 376
38: 3 Gird up now thy loins like a **m**; for I will 1397
38:26 *where* no **m** *is;* on the wilderness, 376
38:26 *is; on* the wilderness, wherein *there is* no **m**; 120
Jnh 40: 7 Gird up thy loins now like a **m**: I will 1397
42:11 **every m** also gave him a piece of money, 376
Ps 1: 1 Blessed *is* the **m** that walketh not in 376
5: 6 will abhor the bloody and deceitful **m**. 376
8: 4 What *is* **m**, that thou art mindful of him? and 582
8: 4 and the son of **m**, that thou visitest him? 120
9:19 Arise, O LORD; let not **m** prevail: let 582
10:15 the evil ***m***: seek out his wickedness *till* thou NIH
10:18 that the **m** of the earth may no more oppress. 582
12: 1 Help, LORD; for the godly ***m*** ceaseth; NIH
18:25 with an upright **m** thou wilt shew thyself 1399
18:48 thou hast delivered me from the violent **m**. 376
19: 5 *and* rejoiceth as a strong ***m*** to run a race. NIH
22: 6 I *am* a worm, and no **m**; a reproach of men, 376
25:12 What **m** *is* he that feareth the LORD? 376
31:12 I am forgotten as a **dead m** out of mind: 4191
31:20 secret of thy presence from the pride of **m**: 376
32: 2 Blessed *is* the **m** unto whom the LORD 120
33:16 a mighty ***m*** is not delivered by much NIH
34: 6 This poor ***m*** cried, and the LORD heard NIH
34: 8 blessed *is* the **m** *that* trusteth in him. 1397
34:12 What **m** *is he that* desireth life, *and* 376
36: 6 O LORD, thou preservest **m** and beast. 120
37: 7 of the **m** who bringeth wicked devices to 376
37:16 A little that a righteous ***m*** hath *is* better than NIH
37:23 The steps of a *good* **m** are ordered by 1397
37:37 Mark the perfect ***m***, and behold the upright: NIH
37:37 the upright: for the end of *that* **m** *is* peace. 376
38:13 I, as a deaf ***m***, heard not; and *I was* as a NIH
38:13 *I was* as a dumb ***m*** *that* openeth not his NIH
38:14 Thus I was as a **m** that heareth not, and 376
39: 5 verily every **m** at his best state *is* altogether 120
39: 6 Surely **every m** walketh in a vain shew: 376
39:11 When thou with rebukes dost correct **m** for 376
39:11 like a moth: surely every **m** *is* vanity. Selah. 120
40: 4 Blessed *is that* **m** that maketh the LORD 1397
43: 1 deliver me from the deceitful and unjust **m**. 376
49:12 Nevertheless **m** *being* in honour abideth not: 120
49:20 **M** *that is* in honour, and understandeth not, 120
52: 1 O mighty ***m***? the goodness of God *endureth* NIH
52: 7 *this is* the **m** *that* made not God his 1397
55:13 a **m** mine equal, my guide, and 582
56: 1 for **m** would swallow me up; he fighting 582
56:11 I will not be afraid what **m** can do unto me. 120
58:11 So that a **m** shall say, Verily *there is* a 120
60:11 help from trouble: for vain *is* the help of **m**. 120
62: 3 long will ye imagine mischief against a **m**? 376
62:12 for thou renderest to *every* **m** according to 376
65: 4 Blessed *is the* ***m*** *whom* thou choosest, and NIH
71: 4 of the hand of the unrighteous and cruel ***m***. NIH
74: 5 *A* ***m*** was famous according as he had lifted NIH
74:22 remember how the foolish ***m*** reproacheth NIH
76:10 Surely the wrath of **m** shall praise thee: 120
78:25 **M** did eat angels' food: he sent them meat to 376
78:65 like a mighty ***m*** that shouteth by reason of NIH
80:17 Let thy hand be upon the **m** of thy right 376
80:17 upon the son of **m** *whom* thou madest strong 120
84: 5 Blessed *is* the **m** whose strength *is* in thee; 120
84:12 blessed *is* the **m** that trusteth in thee. 120
87: 4 Tyre, with Ethiopia; this ***m*** was born there. NIH
87: 5 be said, This and that **m** was born in her: 376
87: 6 *up* the people, *that* this ***m*** was born there. NIH
88: 4 the pit: I am as a **m** *that hath* no strength: 1397
89:48 What **m** *is he that* liveth, and shall not see 1397
90: T A Prayer of Moses the **m** of God. 376
90: 3 Thou turnest **m** to destruction; and sayest, 582
92: 6 A brutish **m** knoweth not; neither doth a fool 376
94:10 he that teacheth **m** knowledge, *shall not he* 120
94:11 The LORD knoweth the thoughts of **m**, 120
94:12 Blessed *is* the **m** whom thou chastenest, 1397
103:15 *As for* **m**, his days *are* as grass: as a flower 582
104:14 for the cattle, and herb for the service of **m**: 120
104:15 wine *that* maketh glad the heart of **m**, 582
104:23 **M** goeth forth unto his work and to his 120
105:14 He suffered no **m** to do them wrong: yea, 120
105:17 He sent a **m** before them, *even* Joseph, 376
107:27 stagger like a drunken ***m***, and are at their NIH
108:12 help from trouble: for vain *is* the help of **m**. 120
109: 6 Set thou a wicked ***m*** over him: and let Satan NIH
109:16 persecuted the poor and needy **m**, that *he* 376
112: 1 Blessed *is* the **m** *that* feareth the LORD, 376
112: 5 A good **m** sheweth favour, and lendeth: 376
118: 6 I will not fear: what can **m** do unto me? 120
118: 8 in the LORD than to put confidence in **m**. 120
119: 9 Wherewithal shall a **young m** cleanse his 5288
119:134 Deliver me from the oppression of **m**: so 120
127: 4 As arrows *are* in the hand of a mighty ***m***; so NIH
127: 5 Happy *is* the **m** that hath his quiver full of 1397
128: 4 that thus shall the **m** be blessed that feareth 1397
135: 8 the firstborn of Egypt, both of **m** and beast. 120
140: 1 Deliver me, O LORD, from the evil **m**: 120
140: 1 evil man: preserve me from the violent **m**; 376
140: 4 the wicked; preserve me from the violent **m**; 376
140:11 evil shall hunt the violent **m** to overthrow 376
142: 4 but *there was* **no m** that would know me: 369
142: 4 refuge failed me; **no m** cared for my soul. 369
143: 2 for in thy sight shall no ***m*** living be NIH
144: 3 LORD, what *is* **m**, that thou takest 120
144: 3 *or* the son of **m**, that thou makest account of 582
144: 4 **M** is like to vanity: his days *are* as a shadow 120
146: 3 *nor* in the son of **m**, in whom *there is* no 120
147:10 he taketh not pleasure in the legs of a **m**. 376
Pr 1: 4 to the **young m** knowledge and discretion. 5288
1: 5 A wise ***m*** will hear, and will increase NIH
1: 5 a **m** of understanding shall attain unto wise NIH
1:24 stretched out my hand, and no **m** regarded; NIH
2:12 To deliver thee from the way of the evil ***m***, NIH
2:12 from the **m** that speaketh froward things; 376
3: 4 understanding in the sight of God and **m**. 120
3:13 Happy *is* the **m** *that* findeth wisdom, and 120
3:13 and the **m** *that* getteth understanding. 120
3:30 Strive not with a **m** without cause, if he have 120
5:21 For the ways of **m** *are* before the eyes of 376
6:11 that travelleth, and thy want as an armed **m**. 376
6:12 A naughty person, a wicked **m**, walketh *with* 376

Pr 6:26 For by means of a whorish woman *a m is* NIH
6:27 Can a **m** take fire in his bosom, and 376
6:34 For jealousy *is* the rage of a **m**: therefore 1397
7: 7 a **young m** void of understanding, 5288
8: 4 I call; and my voice *is* to the sons of **m**. 120
8:34 Blessed *is* the **m** that heareth me, watching 120
9: 7 he that rebuketh a wicked *m getteth* himself NIH
9: 8 rebuke a wise *m*, and he will love thee. NIH
9: 9 Give *instruction* to a wise *m*, and he will be NIH
9: 9 teach a just *m*, and he will increase in NIH
10:11 The mouth of a righteous *m is* a well of life: NIH
10:23 but a **m** of understanding hath wisdom. 376
11: 7 When a wicked **m** dieth, *his* expectation 120
11:12 but a **m** of understanding holdeth his peace. 376
11:17 The merciful **m** doeth good to his own soul: 376
12: 2 A good *m* obtaineth favour of the LORD: NIH
12: 2 but a **m** of wicked devices will he condemn. 376
12: 3 A **m** shall not be established by wickedness: 120
12: 8 A **m** shall be commended according to his 376
12:10 A righteous *m* regardeth the life of his NIH
12:14 A **m** shall be satisfied *with* good by the fruit 376
12:16 but a prudent *m* covereth shame. NIH
12:23 A prudent **m** concealeth knowledge: but 120
12:25 Heaviness in the heart of **m** maketh it stoop: 376
12:27 The slothful *m* roasteth not that which he NIH
12:27 but the substance of a diligent **m** *is* precious. 120
13: 2 A **m** shall eat good by the fruit of *his* mouth: 376
13: 5 A righteous *m* hateth lying: but a wicked NIH
13: 5 a wicked *m* is loathsome, and cometh to NIH
13:16 Every prudent *m* dealeth with knowledge: NIH
13:22 A good *m* leaveth an inheritance to *his* NIH
14: 7 Go from the presence of a foolish **m**, 376
14:12 is a way which seemeth right unto a **m**, 376
14:14 and a good **m** *shall be satisfied* from himself. 376
14:15 but the prudent *m* looketh well to his going. NIH
14:16 A wise *m* feareth, and departeth from evil: NIH
14:17 and a **m** of wicked devices is hated. 376
15:18 A wrathful **m** stirreth up strife: but *he that is* 376
15:19 The way of the slothful *m is* as a hedge of NIH
15:20 but a foolish **m** despiseth his mother. 120
15:21 but a **m** of understanding walketh uprightly. 376
15:23 A **m** hath joy by the answer of his mouth; 376
16: 1 The preparations of the heart in **m**, and 120
16: 2 All the ways of a **m** *are* clean in his own 376
16:14 of death: but a wise **m** will pacify it. 376
16:25 There is a way that seemeth right unto a **m**, 376
16:27 An ungodly **m** diggeth up evil: and in his 376
16:28 A froward **m** soweth strife: and a whisperer 376
16:29 A violent **m** enticeth his neighbour, and 376
17:10 A reproof entereth more into a wise *m* than NIH
17:11 An evil *m* seeketh only rebellion: therefore NIH
17:12 *Let* a bear robbed of her whelps meet a **m**, 376
17:18 A **m** void of understanding striketh hands, 120
17:23 A wicked *m* taketh a gift out of the bosom NIH
17:27 a **m** of understanding is of an excellent 376
17:28 he that shutteth his lips *is esteemed* a *m* of NIH
18: 1 Through desire a *m*, having separated NIH
18:12 Before destruction the heart of **m** is haughty, 376
18:14 The spirit of a **m** will sustain his infirmity; 376
18:24 A **m** that hath friends must shew himself 376
19: 3 The foolishness of **m** perverteth his way: and 120
19: 6 every *m is* a friend to him that giveth gifts. NIH
19:11 The discretion of a **m** deferreth his anger; 120
19:19 *A m* of great wrath *shall* suffer punishment: NIH
19:22 The desire of a **m** *is* his kindness: and a poor 120
19:22 and a poor *m is* better than a liar. NIH
19:24 A slothful *m* hideth his hand in *his* bosom, NIH
20: 3 *It is* an honour for a **m** to cease from strife: 376
20: 5 Counsel in the heart of **m** *is like* deep water; 376
20: 5 but a **m** of understanding will draw it out. 376
20: 6 but a faithful **m** who can find? 376
20: 7 The just *m* walketh in his integrity: NIH
20:17 Bread of deceit *is* sweet to a **m**; but 376
20:24 how can a **m** then understand his own way? 120
20:25 *It is* a snare to the **m** *who* devoureth *that* 120
20:27 The spirit of **m** *is* the candle of the LORD, 120
21: 2 Every way of a **m** *is* right in his own eyes: 376
21: 8 The way of **m** *is* froward and strange: but 376
21:12 The righteous *m* wisely considereth NIH
21:16 The **m** that wandereth out of the way of 120
21:17 He that loveth pleasure *shall be* a poor **m**: 376
21:20 of the wise; but a foolish **m** spendeth it up. 120
21:22 A wise *m* scaleth the city of the mighty, and NIH
21:28 but the **m** that heareth, speaketh constantly. 376
21:29 A wicked **m** hardeneth his face: but *as for* 376
22: 3 A prudent *m* foreseeth the evil, and NIH
22:13 The slothful *m* saith, *There is* a lion NIH
22:24 Make no friendship with an angry **m**; and 1167
22:24 and with a furious **m** thou shalt not go: 376
22:29 Seest thou a **m** diligent in his business? 376
23: 2 thy throat, if thou *be* a **m** given to appetite. 1167
23:21 and drowsiness shall clothe *a m* with rags. NIH
24: 5 A wise **m** *is* strong; yea, a man of 1397
24: 5 yea, a **m** of knowledge increaseth strength. 376
24:12 shall *not* he render to *every* **m** according to 120
24:15 O wicked *m*, against the dwelling of NIH
24:16 For a just *m* falleth seven *times*, and NIH
24:20 For there shall be no reward to the evil *m*; NIH
24:26 *Every m* shall kiss *his* lips that giveth a NIH
24:29 I will render to the **m** according to his work. 376
24:30 by the vineyard of the **m** void of 120
24:34 that travelleth; and thy want as an armed **m**. 376
25:18 A **m** that beareth false witness against his 376
25:19 Confidence in an unfaithful *m* in time of NIH
25:26 A righteous *m* falling down before NIH
26:12 Seest thou a **m** wise in his own conceit? 376
26:13 The slothful *m* saith, *There is* a lion in NIH
26:18 As a mad *m* who casteth firebrands, arrows, NIH
26:19 So *is* the **m** *that* deceiveth his neighbour, and 376
26:21 to fire; so *is* a contentious **m** to kindle strife. 376
27: 2 Let another *m* praise thee, and not thine NIH
27: 8 so *is* a **m** that wandereth from his place. 376
27:12 A prudent *m* foreseeth the evil, *and* NIH
27:17 a **m** sharpeneth the countenance of his 376
27:19 *answereth* to face, so the heart of **m** to man. 120

Pr 27:19 *answereth* to face, so the heart of man to **m**. 120
27:20 so the eyes of **m** are never satisfied. 120
27:21 the furnace for gold; so *is* a **m** to his praise. 376
28: 1 The wicked flee when **no m** pursueth: but 369
28: 2 by a **m** of understanding *and* knowledge 120
28: 3 A poor **m** that oppresseth the poor *is like* a 1397
28:11 The rich **m** *is* wise in his own conceit; but 376
28:12 but when the wicked rise, a **m** is hidden. 120
28:14 Happy *is* the **m** that feareth alway: but 120
28:17 A **m** that doeth violence to the blood of *any* 120
28:17 shall flee to the pit; let no **m** stay him. NIH
28:20 A faithful **m** shall abound with blessings: but 376
28:21 for for a piece of bread *that* **m** will 1397
28:23 He that rebuketh a **m**, afterwards shall find 120
29: 5 A **m** that flattereth his neighbour spreadeth 1397
29: 6 In the transgression of an evil **m** *there is* a 376
29: 9 If a wise **m** contendeth with a foolish man, 376
29: 9 If a wise man contendeth with a foolish **m**, 376
29:11 but a wise *m* keepeth it in *till* afterwards. NIH
29:13 The poor and the deceitful **m** meet together: 376
29:20 Seest thou a **m** that is hasty in his words? 376
29:22 An angry **m** stirreth up strife, and a furious 376
29:22 and a furious **m** aboundeth in transgression. 1167
29:25 The fear of **m** bringeth a snare: but 120
29:27 An unjust **m** is an abomination to the just: 376
30: 1 the **m** spake unto Ithiel, even unto Ithiel 1397
30: 2 Surely I *am* more brutish than *any* **m**, and 376
30: 2 and have not the understanding of a **m**. 120
30:19 of the sea; and the way of a **m** with a maid. 1397
Ecc 1: 3 What profit hath a **m** of all his labour which 120
1: 8 **m** cannot utter *it*: the eye is not satisfied with 376
1:13 to the sons of **m** to be exercised therewith. 120
2:12 for what *can* the **m** *do* that cometh after 120
2:16 And how dieth the wise *m*? as the fool. NIH
2:18 I should leave it unto the **m** that shall be 120
2:19 who knoweth whether he shall be a wise *m* NIH
2:21 For there is a **m** whose labour *is* in wisdom, 120
2:21 yet to a **m** that hath not laboured therein 120
2:22 For what hath **m** of all his labour, and of 120
2:24 *There is* nothing better for a **m**, *than* that he 120
2:26 For *God* giveth to a **m** that *is* good in his 120
3:11 that no **m** can find out the work that God 120
3:12 for *a m* to rejoice, and to do good in his life. NIH
3:13 And also that every **m** should eat and drink, 120
3:19 that a **m** hath no preeminence above a beast: 120
3:21 Who knoweth the spirit of **m** that 120+1121
3:22 than that a **m** should rejoice in his own 120
4: 4 that for this a **m** is envied of his neighbour. 376
5:12 The sleep of a labouring *m is* sweet, NIH
5:19 Every **m** also to whom God hath given 120
6: 2 A **m** to whom God hath given riches, wealth, 376
6: 3 If a **m** beget an hundred *children*, and 376
6: 7 All the labour of **m** *is* for his mouth, and 120
6:10 named already, and *it is* known that it *is* **m**: 120
6:11 that increase vanity, what *is* **m** the better? 120
6:12 For who knoweth what *is* good for **m** in *this* 120
6:12 for who can tell a **m** what shall be after him 120
7: 5 than for a **m** to hear the song of fools. 376
7: 7 Surely oppression maketh a wise *m* mad; NIH
7:14 to the end that **m** should find nothing after 120
7:15 there is a just *m* that perisheth in his NIH
7:15 there is a wicked *m* that prolongeth *his life* NIH
7:20 For *there is* not a just **m** upon earth, 120
7:28 one **m** among a thousand have I found; but 120
7:29 have I found, that God hath made **m** upright; 120
8: 1 Who *is* as the wise *m*? and who knoweth NIH
8: 6 therefore the misery of **m** *is* great upon him. 120
8: 8 *There is* no **m** that hath power over the spirit 120
8: 9 *there is* a time wherein one **m** ruleth over 120
8:15 a **m** hath no better *thing* under the sun, 120
8:17 that a **m** cannot find out the work that is 120
8:17 because though a **m** labour to seek *it* out, 120
8:17 though a wise *m* think to know *it*, yet shall NIH
9: 1 no **m** knoweth either love or hatred *by* all 120
9:12 For **m** also knoweth not his time: as 120
9:15 Now there was found in it a poor wise **m**, 376
9:15 yet no **m** remembered that *same* poor man. 120
9:15 yet no man remembered that *same* poor **m**. 376
10:14 a **m** cannot tell what shall be; and what shall 120
11: 8 if a **m** live many years, *and* rejoice in them 120
11: 9 Rejoice, O **young m**, in thy youth; and 970
12: 5 because **m** goeth to his long home, and 120
12:13 for this *is* the whole *duty of* **m**. 120
SS 3: 8 **every m** *hath* his sword upon his thigh 376
8: 7 if a **m** would give all the substance of his 376
Isa 2: 9 the mean **m** boweth down, and the great man 120
2: 9 and the great **m** humbleth himself; 376
2:11 The lofty looks of **m** shall be humbled, and 120
2:17 And the loftiness of **m** shall be bowed down, 120
2:20 In that day a **m** shall cast his idols of silver, 120
2:22 Cease ye from **m**, whose breath *is* in his 120
3: 2 The mighty *m*, and the man of war, NIH
3: 2 The mighty *man*, and the **m** of war, 376
3: 3 the honourable *m*, and the counsellor, and NIH
3: 6 When a **m** shall take hold of his brother *of* 376
4: 1 day seven women shall take hold of one **m**, 376
5:15 And the mean **m** shall be brought down, and 120
5:15 the mighty **m** shall be humbled, and the eyes 376
6: 5 because I *am* a **m** of unclean lips, and 376
6:11 the houses without **m**, and the land be utterly 120
7:21 *that* a **m** shall nourish a young cow, and 376
9:19 fuel of the fire: no **m** shall spare his brother. 376
9:20 they shall eat **every m** the flesh of his own 376
10:13 put down the inhabitants like a valiant *m*: NIH
13:12 I will make a **m** more precious than fine 582
13:12 even a **m** than the golden wedge of Ophir. 120
13:14 and as a sheep that no *m* taketh up: NIH
13:14 they shall **every m** turn to his own people, 376
14:16 *saying, Is* this the **m** that made the earth to 376
17: 7 At that day shall a **m** look to his Maker, and 120
19:14 as a drunken *m* staggereth in his vomit. NIH
24:10 house is shut up, that no *m may* come in. NIH
28:20 For the bed is shorter than that *a m* can NIH
29: 8 It shall even be as when a hungry *m* NIH
29: 8 or as when a thirsty *m* dreameth, and NIH

Isa 29:21 That make a **m** an offender for a word, and 120
31: 7 For in that day **every m** shall cast away his 376
31: 8 fall with the sword, not of a mighty **m**; 376
31: 8 the sword, not of a mean **m**, shall devour 120
32: 2 a **m** shall be as a hiding place from the wind, 376
33: 8 lie waste, the **wayfaring m** ceaseth: 734+5674
33: 8 hath despised the cities, he regardeth no **m**. 582
35: 6 shall the lame *m* leap as a hart, and NIH
36: 6 whereon if a **m** lean, it will go into his hand, 376
38:11 I shall behold **m** no more with 120
41: 2 Who raised up the righteous *m* from NIH
41:28 For I beheld, and *there was* no **m**; 376
42:13 The LORD shall go forth as a mighty *m*, NIH
42:13 he shall stir up jealousy like a **m** of war: 376
44:13 maketh it after the figure of a **m**, 376
44:13 of a man, according to the beauty of a **m**; 120
44:15 shall it be for a **m** to burn: for he will take 120
45:12 have made the earth, and created **m** upon it: 120
46:11 the **m** that executeth my counsel from a far 376
47: 3 and I will not meet *thee as* a **m**. 120
49: 7 his Holy One, to him whom **m** despiseth, 5315
50: 2 Wherefore, when I came, *was there* no **m**? 376
51:12 that thou shouldest be afraid of a **m** *that* shall 582
51:12 of the son of **m** *which* shall be made *as* 120
52:14 his visage *was* so marred more than *any* **m**, 376
53: 3 a **m** of sorrows, and acquainted with grief: 376
55: 7 his way, and the unrighteous **m** his thoughts: 376
56: 2 Blessed *is* the **m** *that* doeth this, and the son 582
56: 2 and the son of **m** *that* layeth hold on it; 120
57: 1 and no **m** layeth *it* to heart: 376
58: 5 a day for a **m** to afflict his soul? *is it* to bow 120
59:16 he saw that *there was* no **m**, and 376
60:15 that **no m** went through *thee*, I will make 369
62: 5 For *as* a **young m** marrieth a virgin, *so* 970
65:20 nor an **old m** that hath not filled his days: 2205
66: 2 to this *m* will I look, *even* to *him that is* NIH
66: 3 He that killeth an ox *is as if* he slew a **m**; 376
66: 7 pain came, she was delivered of a **m child**. 2145
Jer 2: 6 through a land that no **m** passed through, and 376
2: 6 man passed through, and where no **m** dwelt? 120
3: 1 If a **m** put away his wife, and she go from 376
4:25 lo, *there was* no **m**, and all the birds of 120
4:29 *shall be* forsaken, and not a **m** dwell therein. 376
5: 1 the broad places thereof, if ye can find a **m**, 376
7: 5 throughly execute judgment between a **m** 376
7:20 upon **m**, and upon beast, and upon the trees 120
8: 6 no **m** repented him of his wickedness, 376
9:12 Who *is* the wise **m**, that may understand 376
9:23 Let not the wise *m* glory in his wisdom, NIH
9:23 neither let the mighty *m* glory in his might, NIH
9:23 let not the rich *m* glory in his riches: NIH
10:14 Every **m** is brutish in *his* knowledge: 120
10:23 I know that the way of **m** *is* not in himself: 120
10:23 *it is* not in **m** that walketh to direct his steps. 376
11: 3 Cursed *be* the **m** that obeyeth not the words 376
12:11 because no **m** layeth *it* to heart. 376
12:15 **every m** to his heritage, and every man to 376
12:15 man to his heritage, and **every m** to his land. 376
13:11 For as the girdle cleaveth to the loins of a **m**, 376
14: 8 as a **wayfaring m** *that* turneth aside to tarry 732
14: 9 Why shouldest thou be as a **m** astonied, as a 376
14: 9 as a mighty *m that* cannot save? NIH
15:10 that thou hast borne me a **m** of strife and 376
15:10 and a **m** of contention to the whole earth! 376
16:20 Shall a **m** make gods unto himself, and 120
17: 5 Cursed *be* the **m** that trusteth in man, and 1397
17: 5 Cursed *be* the man that trusteth in **m**, and 120
17: 7 Blessed *is* the **m** that trusteth in 1397
17:10 even to give **every m** according to his ways, 376
18:14 Will *a m* leave the snow of Lebanon *which* NIH
20:15 Cursed *be* the **m** who brought tidings to my 376
20:15 saying, A **m** child is born unto thee; 2145
20:16 let that **m** be as the cities which the LORD 376
21: 6 the inhabitants of this city, both **m** and beast: 120
22: 8 and they shall say **every m** to his neighbour, 376
22:28 *Is* this **m** Coniah a despised broken idol? 376
22:30 saith the LORD, Write ye this **m** childless, 376
22:30 a **m** *that* shall not prosper in his days: 1397
22:30 for no **m** of his seed shall prosper, 376
23: 9 I am like a drunken **m**, and like a man whom 376
23: 9 like a **m** whom wine hath overcome, 1397
23:27 which they tell **every m** to his neighbour, 376
23:34 I will even punish that **m** and his house. 376
26: 3 and turn **every m** from his evil way, 376
26:11 the people, saying, This **m** *is* worthy to die; 376
26:16 to the prophets; This **m** *is* not worthy to die: 376
26:20 there was also a **m** that prophesied in 376
27: 5 the **m** and the beast that *are* upon the ground, 120
29:26 for every **m** *that is* mad, and maketh himself 376
29:32 he shall not have a **m** to dwell among this 376
30: 6 see whether a **m** doth travail with child? 2145
30: 6 wherefore do I see every **m** *with* his hands 1397
30:17 This *is* Zion, whom **no m** seeketh after. 369
31:22 in the earth, A woman shall compass a **m**. 1397
31:27 and the house of Judah *with* the seed of **m**, 120
31:30 every **m** that eateth the sour grape, his teeth 120
31:34 they shall teach no more **every m** his 376
31:34 **every m** his brother, saying, Know 376
32:43 ye say, *It is* desolate without **m** or beast; 120
33:10 which ye say *shall be* desolate without **m** 120
33:10 without **m**, and without inhabitant, and 120
33:12 *which is* desolate without **m** and 120
33:17 David shall never want a **m** to sit upon 376
33:18 shall the priests the Levites want a **m** 376
34: 9 That **every m** should let his manservant, and 376
34: 9 **every m** his maidservant, *being* a Hebrew 376
34:14 At the end of seven years let ye go **every m** 376
34:15 in proclaiming liberty **every m** to his 376
34:16 caused **every m** his servant, and every man 376
34:16 man his servant, and **every m** his handmaid, 376
34:17 to his brother, and **every m** to his neighbour: 376
35: 4 of Hanan, the son of Igdaliah, a **m** of God, 376
35:15 Return ye now **every m** from his evil way, 376
35:19 not want a **m** to stand before me for ever. 376
36: 3 that they may return **every m** from his evil 376

Jer 36:19 Jeremiah; and let no **m** know where ye *be.* 376
36:29 shall cause to cease from thence **m** and 120
37:10 *yet* should they rise up **every m** in his tent, 376
38: 4 We beseech thee, let this **m** be put to death: 376
38: 4 for this **m** seeketh not the welfare of this 376
38:24 Let no **m** know of these words, and 376
40:15 no **m** shall know *it:* wherefore should he slay 376
41: 4 *he* had slain Gedaliah, and no **m** knew *it,* 376
44: 2 *are* a desolation, and **no m** dwelleth therein, 369
44: 7 to cut off from you **m** and woman, child and 376
44:26 of any **m** of Judah in all the land of Egypt, 376
46: 6 swift flee away, nor the mighty ***m*** escape; NIH
46:12 for the mighty ***m*** hath stumbled against NIH
49: 5 ye shall be driven out **every m** right forth; 376
49:18 saith the LORD, no **m** shall abide there, 376
49:18 neither shall a son of **m** dwell in it. 120
49:19 who *is* a chosen ***m,*** *that* I may appoint over NIH
49:33 there shall no **m** abide there, nor *any* son of 376
49:33 abide there, nor *any* son of **m** dwell in it. 120
50: 3 they shall depart, both **m** and beast. 120
50: 9 mighty expert ***m;*** none shall return in vain. NIH
50:40 *so* shall no **m** abide there, neither shall any 376
50:40 neither shall any son of **m** dwell therein. 120
50:42 in array, like a **m** to the battle, against thee, 376
50:44 who *is* a chosen ***m,*** *that* I may appoint over NIH
51: 6 of Babylon, and deliver **every m** his soul: 376
51:17 Every **m** is brutish by *his* knowledge; 120
51:22 With thee also will I break in pieces **m** and 376
51:22 with thee will I break in pieces the **young m** 970
51:43 a wilderness, a land wherein no **m** dwelleth, 376
51:43 neither doth *any* son of **m** pass thereby. 120
51:45 deliver ye **every m** his soul from the fierce 376
51:62 neither **m** nor beast, but that it shall be 120
La 3: 1 I *am* the **m** *that* hath seen affliction by 1397
3:26 *It is* good *that a* **m** *should* both hope and NIH
3:27 *It is* good for a **m** that he bear the yoke in 1397
3:35 To turn aside the right of a **m** before 1397
3:36 To subvert a **m** in his cause, the Lord 120
3:39 Wherefore doth a living **m** complain, a man 120
3:39 a **m** for the punishment of his sins? 1397
4: 4 ask bread, *and* **no m** breaketh *it* unto them. 369
Eze 1: 5 they had the likeness of a **m**. 120
1: 8 *they had* the hands of a **m** under their wings 120
1:10 they four had the face of a **m**, and the face of 120
1:26 as the appearance of a **m** above upon it. 120
2: 1 Son of **m**, stand upon thy feet, and I will 120
2: 3 he said unto me, Son of **m**, I send thee to 120
2: 6 thou, son of **m**, be not afraid of them, 120
2: 8 thou, son of **m**, hear what I say unto thee; 120
3: 1 said unto me, Son of **m**, eat that thou findest; 120
3: 3 he said unto me, Son of **m**, cause thy belly to 120
3: 4 he said unto me, Son of **m**, go, get thee unto 120
3:10 Moreover he said unto me, Son of **m**, all my 120
3:17 Son of **m**, I have made thee a watchman 120
3:18 the same wicked ***m*** shall die in his iniquity; NIH
3:20 When a righteous ***m*** doth turn from his NIH
3:21 Nevertheless if thou warn the righteous ***m,*** NIH
3:25 thou, O son of **m**, behold, they shall put 120
4: 1 Thou also, son of **m**, take thee a tile, and 120
4:12 shalt bake it with dung that cometh out of **m**, 120
4:16 he said unto me, Son of **m**, behold, 120
5: 1 And thou, son of **m**, take thee a sharp knife, 120
6: 2 Son of **m**, set thy face towards the mountains 120
7: 2 Also, thou son of **m**, thus saith the Lord 120
8: 5 said he unto me, Son of **m**, lift up thine eyes 120
8: 6 unto me, Son of **m**, seest thou what they do? 120
8: 8 he unto me, Son of **m**, dig now in the wall: 120
8:11 with **every m** his censer in his hand; 376
8:12 said he unto me, Son of **m**, hast thou seen 120
8:12 **every m** in the chambers of his imagery? 376
8:15 he unto me, Hast thou seen *this,* O son of **m**? 120
8:17 unto me, Hast thou seen *this,* O son of **m**? 120
9: 1 even **every m** *with* his destroying weapon in 376
9: 2 and **every m** a slaughter weapon in his hand; 376
9: 2 one **m** among them *was* clothed *with* linen, 376
9: 3 he called to the **m** clothed *with* linen, 376
9: 6 come not near any **m** upon whom *is* 376
9:11 behold, the **m** clothed with linen, which *had* 376
10: 2 And he spake unto the **m** clothed with linen, 376
10: 3 right side of the house, when the **m** went in; 376
10: 6 *that* when he had commanded the **m** clothed 376
10:14 and the second face *was* the face of a **m**, and 120
10:21 the likeness of the hands of a **m** *was* under 120
11: 2 said he unto me, Son of **m**, these *are* the men 120
11: 4 against them, prophesy, O son of **m**. 120
11:15 Son of **m**, thy brethren, *even* thy brethren, 120
12: 2 Son of **m**, thou dwellest in the midst of a 120
12: 3 Therefore thou son of **m**, prepare thee stuff 120
12: 9 Son of **m**, hath not the house of Israel, 120
12:18 Son of **m**, eat thy bread with quaking, and 120
12:22 Son of **m**, what *is* that proverb *that* ye have 120
12:27 Son of **m**, behold, *they of* the house of Israel 120
13: 2 Son of **m**, prophesy against the prophets of 120
13:17 Likewise thou son of **m**, set thy face against 120
14: 3 Son of **m**, these men have set up their idols 120
14: 4 **Every m** of the house of Israel that 376+376
14: 8 I will set my face against that **m**, and 376
14:13 Son of **m**, when the land sinneth against me 120
14:13 upon it, and will cut off **m** and beast from it: 120
14:15 that **no m** may pass through because of 1097
14:17 so that I cut off **m** and beast from it: 120
14:19 it in blood, to cut off from it **m** and beast: 120
14:21 to cut off from it **m** and beast? 120
15: 2 Son of **m**, What is the vine tree more than 120
16: 2 Son of **m**, cause Jerusalem to know her 120
17: 2 Son of **m**, put forth a riddle, and speak a 120
18: 5 if a **m** be just, and do that which is lawful 376
18: 8 hath executed true judgment between **m** and 376
18: 8 executed true judgment between man and **m**, 376
18:24 the abominations that the wicked ***m*** doeth, NIH
18:26 When a righteous ***m*** turneth away from his NIH
18:27 when the wicked ***m*** turneth away from his NIH
20: 3 Son of **m**, speak unto the elders of Israel, 120
20: 4 Wilt thou judge them, son of **m**, wilt thou 120
20: 7 Cast ye away **every m** the abominations of 376

Eze 20: 8 they did not **every m** cast away 376
20:11 which *if* a **m** do, he shall even live in them. 120
20:13 which *if* a **m** do, he shall even live in them; 120
20:21 which *if* a **m** do, he shall even live in them; 120
20:27 Therefore, son of **m**, speak unto the house of 120
20:46 Son of **m**, set thy face toward the south, and 120
21: 2 Son of **m**, set thy face toward Jerusalem, and 120
21: 6 Sigh therefore, thou son of **m**, with 120
21: 9 Son of **m**, prophesy, and say, Thus saith 120
21:12 Cry and howl, son of **m**: for it shall be upon 120
21:14 son of **m**, prophesy, and smite *thine* hands 120
21:19 Also, thou son of **m**, appoint thee two ways, 120
21:28 thou, son of **m**, prophesy and say, Thus saith 120
22: 2 Now, thou son of **m**, wilt thou judge, wilt 120
22:18 Son of **m**, the house of Israel is to me 120
22:24 Son of **m**, say unto her, Thou *art* the land 120
22:30 I sought for a **m** among them, that *should* 376
23: 2 Son of **m**, there were two women, 120
23:36 Son of **m**, wilt thou judge Aholah and 120
24: 2 Son of **m**, write thee the name of the day, 120
24:16 Son of **m**, behold, I take away from thee 120
24:25 Also, thou son of **m**, *shall it* not *be* in the day 120
25: 2 Son of **m**, set thy face against 120
25:13 and will cut off **m** and beast from it; 120
26: 2 Son of **m**, because that Tyrus hath said 120
27: 2 Now, thou son of **m**, take up a lamentation 120
28: 2 Son of **m**, say unto the prince of Tyrus, 120
28: 2 yet thou *art* a **m**, and not God, though thou 120
28: 9 thou *shalt be* a **m**, and no God, in the hand of 120
28:12 Son of **m**, take up a lamentation upon 120
28:21 Son of **m**, set thy face against Zidon, and 120
29: 2 Son of **m**, set thy face against Pharaoh king 120
29: 8 and cut off **m** and beast out of thee. 120
29:11 No foot of **m** shall pass through it, nor foot 120
29:18 Son of **m**, Nebuchadrezzar king of Babylon 120
30: 2 Son of **m**, prophesy and say, Thus saith 120
30:21 Son of **m**, I have broken the arm of Pharaoh 120
30:24 *with* the groanings of a deadly wounded ***m.*** NIH
31: 2 Son of **m**, speak unto Pharaoh king of Egypt, 120
32: 2 Son of **m**, take up a lamentation for Pharaoh 120
32:10 **every m** for his own life, in the day of thy 376
32:13 neither shall the foot of **m** trouble them any 120
32:18 Son of **m**, wail for the multitude of Egypt, 120
33: 2 Son of **m**, speak to the children of thy 120
33: 2 if the people of the land take a **m** of their 376
33: 7 So thou, O son of **m**, I have set thee a 120
33: 8 O wicked ***m,*** thou shalt surely die; NIH
33: 8 that wicked ***m*** shall die in his iniquity; NIH
33:10 Therefore, O thou son of **m**, speak unto 120
33:12 Therefore, thou son of **m**, say unto 120
33:24 Son of **m**, they that inhabit those wastes of 120
33:30 Also, thou son of **m**, the children of thy 120
34: 2 Son of **m**, prophesy against the shepherds of 120
35: 2 Son of **m**, set thy face against mount Seir, 120
36: 1 Also, thou son of **m**, prophesy unto 120
36:11 I will multiply upon you **m** and beast; and 120
36:17 Son of **m**, when the house of Israel dwelt in 120
37: 3 unto me, Son of **m**, can these bones live? 120
37: 9 prophesy, son of **m**, and say to the wind, 120
37:11 he said unto me, Son of **m**, these bones *are* 120
37:16 Moreover, thou son of **m**, take thee one 120
38: 2 Son of **m**, set thy face against Gog, the land 120
38:14 son of **m**, prophesy and say unto Gog, 120
39: 1 Therefore thou son of **m**, prophesy against 120
39:17 thou son of **m**, thus saith the Lord GOD; 120
40: 3 me thither, and behold, *there was* a **m**, 376
40: 4 the **m** said unto me, Son of man, behold with 376
40: 4 Son of **m**, behold with thine eyes, and 120
41:19 So that the face of a **m** *was* toward the palm 120
43: 6 me out of the house; and *the* **m** stood by me. 376
43: 7 he said unto me, Son of **m**, the place of my 120
43:10 Thou son of **m**, shew the house to the house 120
43:18 he said unto me, Son of **m**, thus saith 120
44: 2 not be opened, and no **m** shall enter in by it; 376
44: 5 Son of **m**, mark well, and behold with thine 120
46:18 that my people be not scattered **every m** 376
47: 3 when the **m** that had the line in his hand 376
47: 6 he said unto me, Son of **m**, hast thou seen 120
47:20 till *a* ***m*** come over against Hamath. NIH
Da 2:10 There is not a **m** upon the earth that can 606
2:25 I have found a **m** of the captives of Judah, 1400
2:48 the king made Daniel a great **m**, and NIH
3:10 that every **m** that shall hear the sound of 606
5:11 There is a **m** in thy kingdom, in whom *is* 1400
6: 7 a petition of any God or **m** for thirty days, 606
6:12 that every **m** that shall ask *a petition* of any 606
6:12 *petition* of any God or **m** within thirty days, 606
7: 4 made stand upon the feet as a **m**, and 606
7: 8 in this horn *were* eyes like the eyes of **m**, 606
7:13 *one* like the Son of **m** came with the clouds 606
8:15 stood before me as the appearance of a **m**. 1397
8:16 make this ***m*** to understand the vision. NIH
8:17 he said unto me, Understand, O son of **m**: 120
9:21 *was* speaking in prayer, even the **m** Gabriel, 376
10: 5 and behold, a certain **m** clothed *in* linen, 376
10:11 said unto me, O Daniel, a **m** greatly beloved, 376
10:18 touched me *one* like the appearance of a **m**, 120
10:19 said, O **m** greatly beloved, fear not: peace *be* 376
12: 6 *one* said to the **m** clothed in linen, 376
12: 7 I heard the **m** clothed in linen, which *was* 376
Hos 3: 3 and thou shalt not be for *another* **m**: 376
4: 4 Yet let no **m** strive, nor reprove another: 376
6: 9 as troops *of robbers* wait for a **m**, *so* 376
9: 7 the spiritual **m** *is* mad, for the multitude of 376
9:12 *that there shall* not *be* a **m** *left:* yea, 120
11: 4 I drew them with cords of a **m**, with bands of 120
11: 9 for I *am* God, and not **m**; the Holy One in 376
Am 2: 7 a **m** and his father will go in unto the *same* 376
4:13 and declareth unto **m** what *is* his thought, 120
5:19 As if a **m** did flee from a lion, and a bear met 376
Jnh 1: 5 cried **every m** unto his god, and cast forth 376
3: 7 his nobles, saying, Let neither **m** nor beast, 120
3: 8 let **m** and beast be covered with sackcloth, 120
Mic 2: 2 so they oppress a **m** and his house, even a 1397
2: 2 and his house, even a **m** and his heritage. 376

Mic 2:11 If a **m** walking *in* the spirit and falsehood do 376
4: 4 But they shall sit **every m** under his vine and 376
5: 5 this *m* shall be *the* peace, when the Assyrian NIH
5: 7 upon the grass, that tarrieth not for **m**, 376
6: 8 He hath shewed thee, O **m**, what *is* good; 120
6: 9 and *the m of* wisdom shall see thy name: NIH
7: 2 The good **m** is perished out of the earth: and NIH
7: 2 they hunt **every m** his brother *with* a net. 376
7: 3 the great ***m,*** he uttereth his mischievous NIH
Na 3:18 the mountains, and no **m** gathereth *them.* NIH
Hab 1:13 *the m that is* more righteous than he? NIH
2: 5 *he is* a proud **m**, neither keepeth at home, 1397
Zep 1: 3 I will consume **m** and beast; I will consume 120
1: 3 I will cut off **m** from off the land, saith 120
1:14 the mighty ***m*** shall cry there bitterly. NIH
3: 6 cities are destroyed, so that there is no **m**, 376
Hag 1: 9 and ye run **every m** unto his own house. 376
Zec 1: 8 and behold a **m** riding upon a red horse, and 376
1:10 the **m** that stood among the myrtle trees 376
1:21 so that no **m** did lift up his head: 376
2: 1 a **m** with a measuring line in his hand. 376
2: 4 Run, speak to this **young m**, saying, 5288
3:10 shall ye call **every m** his neighbour, under 376
4: 1 as a **m** that is wakened out of his sleep, 376
6:12 Behold the **m** whose name *is* The BRANCH; 376
7: 9 and compassions **every m** to his brother: 376
7:14 that no **m** passed through nor returned: NIH
8: 4 **every m** with his staff in his hand for very 376
8:10 before these days there was no hire for **m**, 120
8:16 Speak ye **every m** the truth to his neighbour; 376
9: 1 when the eyes of **m**, as of all the tribes of 120
9:13 and made thee as the sword of a mighty ***m.*** NIH
10: 7 *they of* Ephraim shall be like a mighty ***m,*** NIH
12: 1 and formeth the spirit of **m** within him. 120
13: 5 for **m** taught me *to keep cattle* from my 120
13: 7 and against the **m** *that is* my fellow, 1397
Mal 2:10 why do we deal treacherously **every m** 376
2:12 The LORD will cut off the **m** that doth this, 376
3: 8 Will a **m** rob God? Yet ye *have* robbed me. 120
3:17 as a **m** spareth his own son that serveth him. 376
Mt 1:19 being a just ***m,*** and not willing to make her NIG
4: 4 **M** shall not live by bread alone, but by every *444*
5:40 And if any **m** will sue thee at the law, and NIG
6:24 No ***m*** can serve two masters: for either he NIG
7: 9 Or what **m** is there of you, whom if his son *444*
7:24 doeth them, I will liken him unto a wise **m**, *435*
7:26 them not, shall be likened unto a foolish **m**, *435*
8: 4 See thou tell no ***m;*** but go thy way, NIG
8: 9 For I am a **m** under authority, *444*
8: 9 and I say to this **m**, Go, and he goeth; and NIG
8:20 the Son of **m** hath not where to lay *his* head. *444*
8:27 saying, **What manner of m** is this, *4217*
8:28 so that no ***m*** might pass by that way. NIG
9: 2 they brought to him a **m sick of the palsy**, *3885*
9: 3 within themselves, This ***m*** blasphemeth. NIG
9: 6 But that ye may know that the Son of **m** hath *444*
9: 9 he saw a **m**, named Matthew, sitting at *444*
9:16 No ***m*** putteth a piece of new cloth unto an NIG
9:30 saying, See *that* no ***m*** know *it.* NIG
9:32 they brought to him a dumb **m** possessed *444*
10:23 the cities of Israel, till the Son of **m** be come. *444*
10:35 For I am come to set a **m** at variance against *444*
10:41 he that receiveth a righteous ***m*** in the name NIG
10:41 ***m*** shall receive a righteous *man's* reward. NIG
11: 8 A **m** clothed in soft raiment? behold, *444*
11:19 The Son of **m** came eating and drinking, and *444*
11:19 Behold a **m** gluttonous, and a winebibber, *444*
11:27 and no ***m*** knoweth the Son, but the Father; NIG
11:27 neither knoweth any ***m*** the Father, save NIG
12: 8 For the Son of **m** is Lord even of the sabbath *444*
12:10 there was a **m** which had *his* hand withered. *444*
12:11 What **m** shall there be among you, *444*
12:12 How much then is a **m** better than a sheep? *444*
12:13 Then saith he to the **m**, Stretch forth thine *444*
12:19 neither shall any ***m*** hear his voice in NIG
12:29 except he first bind the strong ***m?*** and then NIG
12:32 speaketh a word against the Son of **m**, *444*
12:35 A good **m** out of the good treasure of *444*
12:35 an evil **m** out of the evil treasure bringeth *444*
12:40 so shall the Son of **m** be three days and *444*
12:43 When the unclean spirit is gone out of a **m**, *444*
12:45 the last *state* of that **m** is worse than the first. *444*
13:24 The kingdom of heaven is likened unto a **m** *444*
13:31 which a **m** took, and sowed in his field: *444*
13:37 that soweth the good seed is the Son of **m**; *444*
13:41 The Son of **m** shall send forth his angels, *444*
13:44 the which when a **m** hath found, he hideth, *444*
13:45 of heaven is like unto a merchant **m**, *444*
13:52 heaven is like unto a **m** *that is* a householder, *444*
13:54 Whence hath this ***m*** this wisdom, and NIG
13:56 Whence then hath this ***m*** all these *things?* NIG
15:11 which goeth into the mouth defileth a **m**; *444*
15:11 cometh out of the mouth, this defileth a **m**. *444*
15:18 forth from the heart; and they defile the **m**. *444*
15:20 These are *the things* which defile a **m**: but *444*
15:20 to eat with unwashen hands defileth not a **m**. *444*
16:13 Whom do men say that I the Son of **m** am? *444*
16:20 tell no ***m*** that he was Jesus the Christ. NIG
16:24 If any ***m*** will come after me, let him deny NIG
16:26 For what is a **m** profited, if he shall gain *444*
16:26 what shall a **m** give in exchange for his soul? *444*
16:27 For the Son of **m** shall come in the glory of *444*
16:27 he shall reward **every m** according to his *1538*
16:28 till they see the Son of **m** coming in his *444*
17: 8 their eyes, they saw no ***m,*** save Jesus only. NIG
17: 9 Tell the vision to no ***m,*** until the Son of man NIG
17: 9 Tell the vision to no *man,* until the Son of **m** *444*
17:12 Likewise shall also the Son of **m** suffer of *444*
17:14 there came to him a *certain* **m**, *444*
17:22 The Son of **m** shall be betrayed into *444*
18: 7 woe to that **m** by whom the offence cometh. *444*
18:11 For the Son of **m** is come to save that which *444*
18:12 if a **m** have an hundred sheep, and one of *444*
18:17 let him be unto thee as a heathen ***m*** and NIG
19: 3 Is it lawful for a **m** to put away his wife for *444*

Mt 19: 5 For this cause shall a m leave father and 444
19: 6 hath joined together, let not m put asunder. 444
19:10 If the case of the m be so with *his* wife, it is 444
19:20 The young m saith unto him, All these 3495
19:22 But when the young m heard *that* saying, 3495
19:23 That a rich m shall hardly enter into NIG
19:24 than for a rich m to enter into the kingdom NIG
19:28 when the Son of m shall sit in the throne of 444
20: 1 For the kingdom of heaven is like unto a m 444
20: 7 say unto him, Because no m hath hired us. NIG
20: 9 they received every m a penny. 303
20:10 and they likewise received every m a penny. 303
20:18 the Son of m shall be betrayed unto the chief 444
20:28 Even as the Son of m came not to be 444
21: 3 And if any m say ought unto you, ye shall NIG
21:28 A *certain* m had two sons; and he came to 444
22:11 he saw there a m which had not on a 444
22:16 neither carest thou for any *m*: for thou NIG
22:24 Saying, Master, Moses said, If a m die, 5100
22:46 And no m was able to answer him a word, NIG
22:46 neither durst any m from that day forth ask NIG
23: 9 And call no m your father upon the earth: NIG
24: 4 Take heed that no m deceive you. NIG
24:23 Then if any m shall say unto you, Lo, NIG
24:27 so shall also the coming of the Son of m be. 444
24:30 shall appear the sign of the Son of m in 444
24:30 they shall see the Son of m coming in 444
24:36 But of that day and hour knoweth no m, no, NIG
24:37 so shall also the coming of the Son of m be. 444
24:39 so shall also the coming of the Son of m be. 444
24:44 hour as you think not the Son of m cometh. 444
25:13 nor the hour wherein the Son of m cometh. 444
25:14 For *the kingdom of heaven is* as a m 444
25:15 to every m according to his several ability; 1538
25:24 Lord, I knew thee that thou art a hard m, 444
25:31 When the Son of m shall come in his glory, 444
26: 2 and the Son of m is betrayed to be crucified. 444
26:18 Go into the city to such a m, and say unto 1170
26:24 The Son of m goeth as it is written of him: 444
26:24 woe unto that m by whom the Son of man is 444
26:24 woe unto that man by whom the Son of m is 444
26:24 it had been good for that m if he had not 444
26:45 the Son of m is betrayed into the hands of 444
26:64 Hereafter shall ye see the Son of m sitting on 444
26:72 he denied with an oath, I do not know the m. 444
26:74 and to swear, *saying*, I know not the m. 444
27:19 Have thou nothing to do with that just *m*: NIG
27:32 they found a m of Cyrene, Simon by name: 444
27:47 heard *that*, said, This m calleth for Elias. NIG
27:57 there came a rich m of Arimathea, 444
Mk 1:23 And there was in their synagogue a m with 444
1:44 See thou say nothing to any *m*: but go thy NIG
2: 7 Why doth this m thus speak blasphemies? NIG
2:10 But that ye may know that the Son of m hath 444
2:21 No m also seweth a piece of new cloth on NIG
2:22 And no m putteth new wine into old bottles: NIG
2:27 The sabbath was made for m, *and* not man 444
2:27 made for man, *and* not m for the sabbath: 444
2:28 Therefore the Son of m is Lord also of 444
3: 1 there was a m there which had a withered 444
3: 3 And he saith unto the m which had 444
3: 5 he saith unto the m, Stretch forth thine hand. 444
3:27 No m can enter into a strong *man's* house, NIG
3:27 except he will first bind the strong *m*; and NIG
4:23 If any m have ears to hear, let him hear. NIG
4:26 as if a m should cast seed into the ground, 444
4:41 What *manner of* m is this, that even 687+5101
5: 2 out of the tombs a m with an unclean spirit, 444
5: 3 and no m could bind him, no, not with NIG
5: 4 in pieces: neither could any m tame him. NIG
5: 8 Come out of the m, *thou* unclean spirit. 444
5:37 And he suffered no m to follow him, NIG
5:43 And he charged them straitly that no m NIG
6: 2 From whence hath this m these *things?* and NIG
6:20 knowing that he *was* a just m and a holy, and 435
7:11 If a m shall say to *his* father or mother, 444
7:15 There is nothing from without a m, 444
7:15 out of him, those are they that defile the m. 444
7:16 If any m have ears to hear, let him hear. NIG
7:18 *thing* from without entereth into the m, 444
7:20 he said, That which cometh out of the m, 444
7:20 cometh out of the man, that defileth the m. 444
7:23 *things* come from within, and defile the m. 444
7:24 and would have no m know *it*: but he could NIG
7:36 he charged them that they should tell no *m*: NIG
8: 4 From whence can a m satisfy these *men* 5100
8:22 and they bring a blind m unto him, and 5185
8:23 And he took the blind m by the hand, and 5185
8:25 he was restored, and saw every m clearly. NIG
8:30 them that they should tell no m of him. NIG
8:31 that the Son of m must suffer many *things*, 444
8:36 For what shall it profit a m, if he shall gain 444
8:37 Or what shall a m give in exchange for his 444
8:38 of him also shall the Son of m be ashamed, 444
9: 8 they saw no m any more, save Jesus only NIG
9: 9 he charged them that they should tell no m NIG
9: 9 till the Son of m were risen from the dead. 444
9:12 and how it is written of the Son of m, 444
9:30 he would not that any m should know *it*. NIG
9:31 The Son of m is delivered into the hands of 444
9:35 saith unto them, If any m desire to be first, NIG
9:39 for there is no m which shall do a miracle in NIG
10: 2 Is it lawful for a m to put away *his* wife? 435
10: 7 For this cause shall a m leave his father and 444
10: 9 hath joined together, let not m put asunder. 444
10:25 than for a rich m to enter into the kingdom NIG
10:29 There is no m that hath left house, or NIG
10:33 the Son of m shall be delivered unto 444
10:45 For even the Son of m came not to be 444
10:49 And they call the blind m, saying unto 5185
10:51 The blind m said unto him, Lord, that I 5185
11: 2 shall find a colt tied, whereon never m sat; 444
11: 3 And if any m say unto you, Why do ye this? NIG
11:14 No m eat fruit of thee hereafter for ever. NIG
11:16 And would not suffer that any m should NIG

Mk 12: 1 A *certain* m planted a vineyard, and set a 444
12:14 carest for no *m*: for thou regardest not NIG
12:34 And no m after that durst ask him *any* NIG
13: 5 to say, Take heed lest any m deceive you: NIG
13:21 And then if any m shall say to you, Lo, here NIG
13:26 shall they see the Son of m coming in 444
13:32 of that day and *that* hour knoweth no m, no, NIG
13:34 *For the Son of* m *is* as a man taking a far NIG
13:34 *For the Son of man is* as a m taking a far 444
13:34 and to every m his work, and 1538
14:13 there shall meet you a m bearing a pitcher of 444
14:21 The Son of m indeed goeth, as it is written 444
14:21 woe to that m by whom the Son of man is 444
14:21 woe to that man by whom the Son of m is 444
14:21 good were it for that m if he had never been 444
14:41 the Son of m is betrayed into the hands of 444
14:51 And there followed him a certain young m, 3495
14:62 ye shall see the Son of m sitting on the right 444
14:71 *saying*, I know not this m of whom ye speak. 444
15:24 lots upon them, what every m should take. NIG
15:39 he said, Truly this m was the Son of God. 444
16: 5 they saw a young m sitting on the right 3495
16: 8 neither said they any *thing* to any *m*; for NIG
Lk 1:18 for I am an old m, and my wife well 4246
1:27 To a virgin espoused to a m whose name 435
1:34 How shall this be, seeing I know not a m? 435
2:25 And behold, there was a m in Jerusalem, 444
2:25 and the same m *was* just and devout, 444
2:52 and stature, and in favour with God and m. 444
3:14 he said unto them, Do violence to no m, 3367
4: 4 That m shall not live by bread alone, but 444
4:33 And in the synagogue there was a m, 444
5: 8 from me; for I am a sinful m, O Lord. 435
5:12 in a certain city, behold a m full of leprosy: 435
5:14 And he charged him to tell no *m*: but go, NIG
5:18 men brought in a bed a m which was taken 444
5:20 he said unto him, M, thy sins are forgiven 444
5:24 But that ye may know that the Son of m hath 444
5:36 No m putteth a piece of a new garment NIG
5:37 And no m putteth new wine into old bottles; NIG
5:39 No m also having drunk old *wine* NIG
6: 5 That the Son of m is Lord also of 444
6: 6 there was a m whose right hand was 444
6: 8 said to the m which had the withered hand, 444
6:10 he said unto the m, Stretch forth thy hand. 444
6:30 Give to every m that asketh of thee; and 3956
6:45 A good m out of the good treasure of his 444
6:45 an evil m out of the evil treasure of his heart 444
6:48 He is like a m which built a house, and 444
6:49 is like a m that without a foundation built a 444
7: 8 For I also am a m set under authority, 444
7:12 behold, there was a dead m carried out, 2348
7:14 And he said, Young m, I say unto thee, 3495
7:25 A m clothed in soft raiment? Behold, 444
7:34 The Son of m is come eating and drinking; 444
7:34 Behold a gluttonous m, and a winebibber, 444
7:39 saying, This *m*, if he were a prophet, NIG
8:16 No *m*, when he hath lighted a candle, NIG
8:25 one to another, What *manner of* m is this? NIG
8:27 there met him out of the city a certain m, 435
8:29 the unclean spirit to come out of the m. 444
8:33 Then went the devils out of the m, and 444
8:35 and came to Jesus, and found the m, out of 444
8:38 Now the m out of whom the devils were 435
8:41 there came a m named Jairus, and he was a 435
8:51 he suffered no m to go in, save Peter, NIG
8:56 he charged them that they should tell no m NIG
9:21 commanded *them* to tell no m that *thing*; NIG
9:22 The Son of m must suffer many *things*, and 444
9:23 If any m will come after me, let him deny NIG
9:25 For what is a m advantaged, if he gain 444
9:26 of him shall the Son of m be ashamed, 444
9:36 told no m in those days any of *those things* NIG
9:38 a m of the company cried out, saying, 435
9:44 for the Son of m shall be delivered into 444
9:56 For the Son of m is not come to destroy 444
9:57 a certain m said unto him, Lord, I will NIG
9:58 the Son of m hath not where to lay *his* head. 444
9:62 No m having put his hand to the plough, NIG
10: 4 nor shoes: and salute no m by the way. NIG
10:22 and no m knoweth who the Son is, but NIG
10:30 A certain m went down from Jerusalem to 444
11:21 When a strong m armed keepeth his palace, NIG
11:24 When the unclean spirit is gone out of a m, 444
11:26 the last *state* of that m is worse than the first. 444
11:30 shall also the Son of m be to this generation. 444
11:33 No *m*, when he hath lighted a candle, NIG
12: 8 him shall the Son of m also confess before 444
12:10 shall speak a word against the Son of m, 444
12:14 And he said unto him, M, who made me a 444
12:16 The ground of a certain rich m brought forth 444
12:40 for the Son of m cometh at an hour when ye 444
13: 6 A certain m had a fig tree planted in his NIG
13:19 which a m took, and cast into his garden; 444
14: 2 there was a certain m before him, 444
14: 8 When thou art bidden of any m to a NIG
14: 8 lest a more honourable m than thou be NIG
14: 9 and say to thee, Give this m place; NIG
14:16 A certain m made a great supper, and 444
14:26 If any m come to me, and hate not his NIG
14:30 This m began to build, and was not able to 444
15: 2 This m receiveth sinners, and eateth with NIG
15: 4 What m of you, having an hundred sheep, 444
15:11 And he said, A certain m had two sons: 444
15:16 the swine did eat: and no m gave unto him. NIG
16: 1 There was a certain rich m, which had a 444
16:16 is preached, and every m presseth into it. NIG
16:19 There was a certain rich m, which was 444
16:22 the rich m also died, and was buried; NIG
17:22 desire to see one of the days of the Son of m, 444
17:24 so shall also the Son of m be in his day. 444
17:26 shall it be also in the days of the Son of m. 444
17:30 be in the day when the Son of m is revealed. 444
18: 2 which feared not God, neither regarded m: 444
18: 4 Though I fear not God, nor regard m; 444

Lk 18: 8 Nevertheless when the Son of m cometh, 444
18:14 this m went down to his house justified NIG
18:25 than for a rich m to enter into the kingdom NIG
18:29 There is no m that hath left house, or NIG
18:31 the Son of m shall be accomplished. 444
18:35 a certain blind m sat by the way side 5185
19: 2 And behold, *there was* a m named Zaccheus, 435
19: 7 That he was gone to be guest with a m *that is* 435
19: 8 if I have taken any *thing* from any m by NIG
19:10 For the Son of m is come to seek and to save 444
19:14 We will not have this m to reign over us. NIG
19:15 that he might know how much every m had NIG
19:21 I feared thee, because thou art an austere m: 444
19:22 Thou knewest that I was an austere m, 444
19:30 find a colt tied, whereon yet never m sat: 444
19:31 And if any m ask you, Why do ye loose NIG
20: 9 A certain m planted a vineyard, and let it 444
21:27 shall they see the Son of m coming in a 444
21:36 to pass, and to stand before the Son of m. 444
22:10 there shall a m meet you, bearing a pitcher 444
22:22 And truly the Son of m goeth, as it was 444
22:22 woe unto that m by whom he is betrayed. 444
22:48 betrayest thou the Son of m with a kiss? 444
22:56 and said, This m was also with him. NIG
22:58 also of them. And Peter said, M, I am not. 444
22:60 And Peter said, M, I know not what thou 444
22:69 Hereafter shall the Son of m sit on the right 444
23: 4 and *to* the people, I find no fault in this m. 444
23: 6 he asked whether the m were a Galilean. 444
23:14 unto them, Ye have brought this m unto me, 444
23:14 have found no fault in this m *touching those* 444
23:18 Away with this *m*, and release unto us NIG
23:41 but this m hath done nothing amiss. NIG
23:47 saying, Certainly this was a righteous m. 444
23:50 And behold, *there was* a m named Joseph, 435
23:50 *and he was* a good m, and a just: 435
23:52 This m went unto Pilate, and begged NIG
23:53 in stone, wherein never m before was laid. 3762
24: 7 The Son of m must be delivered into 444
Jn 1: 6 There was a m sent from God, whose name 444
1: 9 which lighteth every m *that* cometh into 444
1:13 of the flesh, nor of the will of m, but of God. 435
1:18 No m hath seen God at any time; the only NIG
1:30 After me cometh a m which is preferred 435
1:51 and descending upon the Son of m. 444
2:10 Every m at the beginning doth set forth good 444
2:25 And needed not that any should testify of m: 444
2:25 testify of man: for he knew what was in m. 444
3: 1 There was a m of the Pharisees, 444
3: 2 for no m can do these miracles that thou NIG
3: 3 I say unto thee, Except a m be born again, 5100
3: 4 How can a m be born when he is old? 444
3: 5 Except a m be born of water and *of* 5100
3:13 And no m hath ascended up to heaven, but NIG
3:13 *even* the Son of m which is in heaven. 444
3:14 *even* so must the Son of m be lifted up: 444
3:27 and said, A m can receive nothing, 444
3:32 and no m receiveth his testimony. NIG
4:27 yet no m said, What seekest thou? or, NIG
4:29 Come, see a m, which told me all *things* that 444
4:33 Hath any m brought him *ought* to eat? NIG
4:50 And the m believed the word that Jesus had 444
5: 5 And a certain m was there, which had an 444
5: 7 The impotent m answered him, Sir, I have NIG
5: 7 Sir, I have no m, when the water is troubled, 444
5: 9 And immediately the m was made whole, 444
5:12 What m is that which said unto thee, 444
5:15 The m departed, and told the Jews that it 444
5:22 For the Father judgeth no m, but NIG
5:27 judgment also, because he is the Son of m. 444
5:34 But I receive not testimony from m: 444
6:27 which the Son of m shall give unto you: 444
6:44 No m can come to me, except the Father NIG
6:45 Every m therefore that hath heard, and NIG
6:46 Not that any m hath seen the Father, save he NIG
6:50 from heaven, that a m may eat thereof, 5100
6:51 if any m eat of this bread, he shall live for NIG
6:52 How can this m give us *his* flesh to eat? NIG
6:53 Except ye eat the flesh of the Son of m, and 444
6:62 if ye shall see the Son of m ascend up where 444
6:65 I unto you, that no m can come unto me, NIG
7: 4 For *there is* no m *that* doeth any *thing* in NIG
7:12 He is a good *m*: others said, Nay; NIG
7:13 Howbeit no m spake openly of him for fear NIG
7:15 saying, How knoweth this m letters, NIG
7:17 If any m will do his will, he shall know of NIG
7:22 and ye on the sabbath day circumcise a m. 444
7:23 If a m on the sabbath day receive 444
7:23 I have made a m every whit whole on 444
7:27 Howbeit we know this m whence he is: but NIG
7:27 Christ cometh, no m knoweth whence he is. NIG
7:30 but no m laid hands on him, because NIG
7:31 miracles than these which this m hath done? NIG
7:37 and cried, saying, If any m thirst, NIG
7:44 taken him; but no m laid hands on him. NIG
7:46 Never m spake like this man. 444
7:46 Never man spake like this m. 444
7:51 Doth our law judge any m, before it hear 444
7:53 And every m went unto his own house. 1538
8:10 thine accusers? hath no m condemned thee? NIG
8:11 She said, No *m*, Lord. And Jesus said unto NIG
8:15 Ye judge after the flesh; I judge no *m*. NIG
8:20 and no m laid hands on him; for his hour NIG
8:28 When ye have lift up the Son of m, then 444
8:33 were never in bondage to any *m*: how NIG
8:40 a m that hath told you the truth, which I have 444
8:51 I say unto you, If a m keep my saying, 5100
8:52 and thou sayest, If a m keep my saying, 5100
9: 1 he saw a m *which was* blind from *his* birth. 444
9: 2 Master, who did sin, this *m*, or his parents, NIG
9: 3 Neither hath this m sinned, nor his parents: NIG
9: 4 the night cometh, when no m can work. NIG
9: 6 he anointed the eyes of the blind m with 5185
9:11 A m *that is* called Jesus made clay, and 444
9:16 This m is not of God, because he keepeth 444

M

Jn 9:16 How can a m *that is* a sinner do such 444
9:17 They say unto the blind m again, 5185
9:22 that if any m did confess that he *was* Christ, NIG
9:24 Then again called they the m that was blind, 444
9:24 the praise: we know that this m is a sinner. 444
9:30 The m answered and said unto them, 444
9:31 but if any m be a worshipper of God, and NIG
9:32 m opened the eyes of one that was born NIG
9:33 If this m were not of God, he could do NIG
10: 9 by me if any m enter in, he shall be saved, NIG
10:18 No m taketh it from me, but I lay it down of NIG
10:28 neither shall any m pluck them out of my NIG
10:29 no m is able to pluck *them* out of my NIG
10:33 and because that thou, being a m, 444
10:41 all *things* that John spake of this m were NIG
11: 1 Now a certain m was sick, *named* Lazarus, NIG
11: 9 If any m walk in the day, he stumbleth not, NIG
11:10 But if a m walk in the night, he stumbleth, 5100
11:37 Could not this m, which opened the eyes of NIG
11:37 have caused that even this m should not NIG
11:47 do we? for this m doeth many miracles. 444
11:50 that one m should die for the people, and 444
11:57 that, if any m knew where he were, NIG
12:23 that the Son of m should be glorified. 444
12:26 If any m serve me, let him follow me; and NIG
12:26 if any m serve me, him will *my* Father NIG
12:34 sayest thou, The Son of m must be lift up? 444
12:34 man must be lift up? who is this Son of m? 444
12:47 And if any m hear my words, and NIG
13:28 Now no m at the table knew for what intent NIG
13:31 Now is the Son of m glorified, and God is 444
14: 6 no m cometh unto the Father, but by me. NIG
14:23 and said unto him, If a m love me, 5100
15: 6 If a m abide not in me, he is cast forth as a 5100
15:13 Greater love hath no m than this, that a man NIG
15:13 that a m lay down his life for his friends. 5100
15:24 them the works which none other m did, NIG
16:21 for joy that a m is born into the world. 444
16:22 and your joy no m taketh from you. NIG
16:30 and needest not that any m should ask thee: NIG
16:32 every m to his own, and shall leave me NIG
18:14 that it was expedient that one m should die 444
18:29 What accusation bring you against this m? 444
18:31 It is not lawful for us to put any m to death: NIG
18:40 all again, saying, Not this m, but Barabbas. NIG
19: 5 And *Pilate* saith unto them, Behold the m. 444
19:12 Jews cried out, saying, If thou let this m go, NIG
19:41 wherein was never m yet laid. 3762
21:21 to Jesus, Lord, and what *shall* this m *do?* NIG
Ac 1:18 Now this m purchased a field with NIG
1:20 be desolate, and let no m dwell therein: 3588
2: 6 that every m heard them speak in his own 1520
2: 8 And how hear we every m in our own 1538
2:22 a m approved of God among you by 435
2:45 parted them to all *men,* as every m had NIG
3: 2 And a certain m lame from his mother's 435
3:11 And as the lame m which was healed held NIG
3:12 or holiness we had made this m to walk? NIG
3:16 faith in his name hath made this m strong, NIG
4: 9 of the good deed done to the impotent m, 444
4:10 *even* by him doth this m stand here before NIG
4:14 And beholding the m which was healed 444
4:17 that *they* speak henceforth to no m in this 444
4:22 For the m was above forty years old, 444
4:35 distribution was made unto every m 1538
5: 1 But a certain m named Ananias, 435
5:13 And of the rest durst no m join himself to NIG
5:23 we had opened, we found no m within. NIG
5:37 After this m rose up Judas of Galilee in NIG
6: 5 a m full of faith and of the Holy Ghost, and 435
6:13 This m ceaseth not to speak blasphemous 444
7:56 the Son of m standing on the right hand of 444
8: 9 But there was a certain m, called Simon, 435
8:10 saying, This m is the great power of God. NIG
8:27 and behold, a m of Ethiopia, an eunuch of 435
8:31 can I, except some m should guide me? NIG
8:34 of himself, or of some other m? NIG
9: 7 hearing a voice, but seeing no m. NIG
9: 8 he saw no m: but they led him by the hand, NIG
9:12 And hath seen in a vision a m named 435
9:13 Lord, I have heard by many of this m, 435
9:33 And there he found a certain m named 444
10: 1 There was a certain m in Cesarea called 435
10: 2 A devout m, and one that feared God with NIG
10:22 a just m, and one that feareth God, and 435
10:26 saying, Stand up; I myself also am a m. 444
10:28 *thing* for a m *that is* a Jew to keep company, 435
10:28 me that *I* should not call any m common 444
10:30 a m stood before me in bright clothing, 435
10:47 Can any m forbid water, that these should NIG
11:24 For he was a good m, and full of the Holy 435
11:29 every m according to his ability, 1538
12:22 *It is* the voice of a god, and not of a m. 444
13: 7 *of the country,* Sergius Paulus, a prudent m; 435
13:21 a m of the tribe of Benjamin, *by the space of* 435
13:22 a m after mine own heart, which shall fulfil 435
13:38 that through this m is preached unto you NIG
13:41 though a m declare it unto you. 5100
14: 8 And there sat a certain m at Lystra, 435
16: 9 There stood a m of Macedonia, and 435
17:31 by *that* m whom he hath ordained; 435
18:10 and no m shall set on thee to hurt thee: NIG
18:24 an eloquent m, *and* mighty in the scriptures, 435
18:25 This m was instructed in the way of NIG
19:16 And the m in whom the evil spirit was leapt 444
19:24 For a certain m named Demetrius, NIG
19:35 what m is there that knoweth not how that 444
19:38 have a matter against any m, the law is NIG
20: 9 a certain young m named Eutychus, 3494
20:12 And they brought the young m alive, and 3816
21: 9 And the same m had four daughters, NIG
21:11 So shall the Jews at Jerusalem bind the m 435
21:28 This is the m, that teacheth all *men* every 444
21:39 I am a m *which am* a Jew of Tarsus, 444
22: 3 I am verily a m *which am* a Jew, born in 435

Ac 22:12 a devout m according to the law, 435
22:25 for you to scourge a m *that is* a Roman, 444
22:26 heed what thou doest: for this m is a Roman. 444
23: 9 and strove, saying, We find no evil in this m: 444
23:17 Bring this young m unto the chief captain: 3494
23:18 prayed *me* to bring this young m unto thee, 3494
23:22 chief captain then let the young m depart, 3494
23:22 charged *him, See thou* tell no m that thou NIG
23:27 This m was taken of the Jews, and 435
23:30 me how that the Jews laid wait for the m, 435
24: 5 For we have found this m a pestilent *fellow,* 435
24:12 with any m, neither raising up the people, NIG
25: 5 go down with *me,* and accuse this m, 435
25:11 accuse me, no m may deliver me unto them. NIG
25:14 There is a certain m left in bonds by Felix: 435
25:16 of the Romans to deliver any m to die, 444
25:17 and commanded the m to be brought *forth.* 435
25:22 unto Festus, I would also hear the m myself. 444
25:24 ye see this m, about whom all the multitude NIG
26:31 This m doeth nothing worthy of death or 444
26:32 This m might have been set at liberty, 444
28: 4 No doubt this m is a murderer, whom, 444
28: 7 possessions of the chief m of the island, NIG
28:31 with all confidence, no m forbidding him. NIG
Ro 1:23 into an image made like to corruptible m, 444
2: 1 Therefore thou art inexcusable, O m, 444
2: 3 And thinkest thou this, O m, that judgest 444
2: 6 Who will render to every m according to his NIG
2: 9 upon every soul of m that doeth evil, 444
2:10 and peace, to every m that worketh good, NIG
2:21 thou that preachest a m should not steal, NIG
2:22 Thou that sayest a m should not commit NIG
3: 4 yea, let God be true, but every m a liar; as it 444
3: 5 who taketh vengeance? (I speak as a m) 444
3:28 Therefore we conclude that a m is justified 444
4: 6 also describeth the blessedness of the m, 444
4: 8 Blessed *is* the m to whom the Lord will not 435
5: 7 For scarcely for a righteous m will one die: NIG
5: 7 yet peradventure for a good m some would NIG
5:12 as by one m sin entered into the world, and 444
5:15 by grace, which is by one m, Jesus Christ, 444
6: 6 that our old m is crucified with *him,* that 444
7: 1 how that the law hath dominion over a m, 444
7: 3 husband liveth, she be married to another m, 435
7: 3 though she be married to another m. 435
7:22 delight in the law of God after the inward m: 444
7:24 O wretched m that I am! who shall deliver 444
8: 9 Now if any m have not the Spirit of Christ, NIG
8:24 for what a m seeth, why doth he yet hope 5100
9:20 Nay but, O m, who art thou that repliest 444
10: 5 That the m which doeth those *things* shall 444
10:10 For with the heart m believeth unto NIG
12: 3 unto me, to every m that is among you, NIG
12: 3 according as God hath dealt to every m 1538
12:17 Recompense to no m evil for evil. NIG
13: 8 Owe no m any *thing,* but to love one NIG
14: 5 One m esteemeth one day above another: 3739
14: 5 every m be fully persuaded in his own 1538
14: 7 liveth to himself, and no m dieth to himself. NIG
14:13 that no m put a stumblingblock or NIG
14:20 *it is* evil for *that* m who eateth with offence. 444
1Co 2: 9 neither have entered into the heart of m, 444
2:11 For what m knoweth the *things* of a man, 444
2:11 For what man knoweth the *things* of a m, 444
2:11 a man, save the spirit of m which is in him? 444
2:11 so the *things* of God knoweth no m, but NIG
2:14 But the natural m receiveth not the *things* of 444
2:15 all *things,* yet he himself is judged of no m. NIG
3: 5 even as the Lord gave to every m? 1538
3: 8 every m shall receive his own reward 1538
3:10 But let every m take heed how he buildeth 1538
3:11 For other foundation can no m lay than that NIG
3:12 Now if any m build upon this foundation NIG
3:17 If any m defile the temple of God, him shall NIG
3:18 Let no m deceive himself. If any *man* NIG
3:18 If any m among you seemeth to be wise in NIG
3:21 Therefore let no m glory in men. For all NIG
4: 1 Let a m so account of us, as of the ministers 444
4: 2 in stewards, that a m be found faithful. 5100
4: 5 and then shall every m have praise of God. 1538
5:11 if any m *that is* called a brother be a NIG
6: 5 that there is not a wise m amongst you? NIG
6:18 Every sin that a m doeth is without the body; 444
7: 1 *It is* good for a m not to touch a woman. 444
7: 2 let every m have his own wife, and 1538
7: 7 But every m hath his proper gift of God, 1538
7:16 or how knowest thou, O m, whether thou 435
7:17 But as God hath distributed to every m, 1538
7:18 Is any m called being circumcised? let him NIG
7:20 Let every m abide in the same calling 1538
7:24 Brethren, let every m, wherein he is called, 1538
7:26 *I say,* that *it is* good for a m so to be. 444
7:36 But if any m think that he behaveth himself NIG
8: 2 And if any m think that *he* knoweth any NIG
8: 3 But if any m love God, the same is known NIG
8: 7 Howbeit *there is* not in every m *that* NIG
8:10 For if any m see thee which hast knowledge NIG
9: 8 Say I these *things* as a m? or saith not 444
9:15 than that any m should make my glorying NIG
9:25 And every m that striveth for the mastery is NIG
10:13 taken you but such as is common to m: 442
10:24 Let no m seek his own, but every man NIG
10:24 his own, but every m another's *wealth.* 1538
10:28 But if any m say unto you, This is offered in NIG
11: 3 that the head of every m is Christ; 435
11: 3 and the head of the woman *is* the m; and 435
11: 4 Every m praying or prophesying, having *his* 435
11: 7 For a m indeed ought not to cover *his* head, 435
11: 7 of God: but the woman is the glory of the m. 435
11: 8 For the m is not of the woman; but 435
11: 8 not of the woman; but the woman of the m. 435
11: 9 Neither was the m created for the woman; 435
11: 9 for the woman; but the woman for the m. 435
11:11 Nevertheless neither *is* the m without 435
11:11 neither the woman without the m, in 435

1Co 11:12 For as the woman *is* of the m, *even* so *is* 435
11:12 *even* so *is* the m also by the woman; 435
11:14 that, if a m have long hair, it is a shame unto 435
11:16 But if any m seem to be contentious, NIG
11:28 But let a m examine himself, and so let him 444
11:34 And if any m hunger, let him eat at home; NIG
12: 3 that no m speaking by the Spirit of God NIG
12: 3 and *that* no m can say that Jesus is the Lord, NIG
12: 7 Spirit is given to every m to profit withal. 1538
12:11 dividing to every m severally as he will. 1538
13:11 but when I became a m, I put away childish 435
14: 2 for no m understandeth *him;* howbeit in NIG
14:27 If any m speak in an *unknown* tongue, *let it* NIG
14:37 If any m think himself to be a prophet, or NIG
14:38 But if any m be ignorant, let him be NIG
15:21 For since by m *came* death, by man *came* 444
15:21 by m *came* also the resurrection of the dead. 444
15:23 But every m in his own order: Christ 1538
15:35 But some m will say, How are the dead NIG
15:45 The first m Adam was made a living soul; 444
15:47 The first m *is* of the earth, earthy: the second 444
15:47 the second m *is* the Lord from heaven. 444
16:11 Let no m therefore despise him: but NIG
16:22 If any m love not the Lord Jesus Christ, NIG
2Co 2: 6 Sufficient to such a m *is* this punishment, NIG
4:16 but though our outward m perish, yet 444
4:16 yet the inward m is renewed day by day. NIG
5:16 Wherefore henceforth know we no m after NIG
5:17 Therefore if any m *be* in Christ, *he is* a new NIG
7: 2 we have wronged no m, we have corrupted NIG
7: 2 no m, we have defrauded no *man.* NIG
7: 2 no *man,* we have defrauded no m. NIG
8:12 *it is* accepted according to that a m hath, 5100
8:20 that no m should blame us in this NIG
9: 7 Every m according as he purposeth in *his* 1538
10: 7 If any m trust to himself that *he* is Christ's, NIG
11: 9 I was chargeable to no m: for that which NIG
11:10 no m shall stop me of this boasting in NIG
11:16 I say again, Let no m think me a fool; NIG
11:20 ye suffer, if a m bring you into bondage, 1536
11:20 if a m devour *you,* if a man take *of you,* if a 1536
11:20 if a man devour *you,* if a m take *of you,* if a 1536
11:20 if a man take *of you,* if a m exalt himself, 1536
11:20 exalt himself, if a m smite you on the face. 1536
12: 2 I knew a m in Christ above fourteen years 444
12: 3 And I knew such a m, (whether in the body, 444
12: 4 which *it is* not lawful for a m to utter. 444
12: 6 lest any m should think of me above *that* NIG
Gal 1: 1 neither by m, but by Jesus Christ, and 444
1: 9 If any m preach any other gospel unto you NIG
1:11 which was preached of me is not after m. 444
1:12 For I neither received it of m, neither was I 444
2:16 Knowing that a m is not justified by 444
3:11 But that no m is justified by the law in NIG
3:12 The m that doeth them shall live in them. 444
3:15 no m disannulleth, or added thereto. NIG
5: 3 For I testify again to every m that is 444
6: 1 Brethren, if a m be overtaken in a fault, 444
6: 3 For if a m think himself to be something, 5100
6: 4 But let every m prove his own work, and 1538
6: 5 For every m shall bear his own burden. 1538
6: 7 for whatsoever a m soweth, that shall he also 444
6:17 From henceforth let no m trouble me: for I NIG
Eph 2: 9 Not of works, lest any m should boast. NIG
2:15 for to make in himself of twain one new m, 444
3:16 with might by his Spirit in the inner m; 444
4:13 of the Son of God, unto a perfect m, 435
4:22 the former conversation the old m, 444
4:24 And that *ye* put on the new m, which after 444
4:25 speak every m truth with his neighbour: 1538
5: 5 nor unclean *person,* nor covetous m who is 4123
5: 6 Let no m deceive you with vain words: for NIG
5:29 For no m ever yet hated his own flesh; but NIG
5:31 For this cause shall a m leave his father and 444
6: 8 that whatsoever good *thing* any m doeth, 1538
Php 2: 4 Look not every m on his own *things,* but 1538
2: 4 but every m also on the *things* of others. 1538
2: 8 And being found in fashion as a m, 444
2:20 For I have no m likeminded, who will NIG
3: 4 If any other m thinketh that *he hath whereof* NIG
Col 1:28 warning every m, and teaching every man in 444
1:28 and teaching every m in all wisdom; 444
1:28 that we may present every m perfect in 444
2: 4 lest any m should beguile you with enticing NIG
2: 8 Beware lest any m spoil you through NIG
2:16 Let no m therefore judge you in meat, NIG
2:18 Let no m beguile you of your reward in a NIG
3: 9 seeing that ye have put off the old m with 444
3:10 And have put on the new m, which is NIG
3:13 if any m have a quarrel against any: NIG
4: 6 know how ye ought to answer every m. 1520
1Th 3: 3 That no m should be moved by these NIG
4: 6 That no m go beyond and defraud his NIG
4: 8 that despiseth, despiseth not m, but God, 444
5:15 that none render evil for evil unto any m; NIG
2Th 2: 3 Let no m deceive you by any means: NIG
2: 3 and *that* m of sin be revealed, the son of 444
3:14 And if any m obey not our word by *this* NIG
3:14 note that m, and have no company with NIG
1Ti 1: 8 that the law *is* good, if a m use it lawfully; 5100
1: 9 that the law is not made for a righteous m, NIG
2: 5 between God and men, *the* m Christ Jesus; 444
2:12 nor to usurp authority over the m, but to be 435
3: 1 If a m desire the office of a bishop, 1536
3: 5 (For if a m know not how to rule his own 5100
4:12 Let no m despise thy youth; but be thou an NIG
5: 9 years old, having been the wife of one m, 435
5:16 If any m[S] or woman that believeth have 4103
5:22 Lay hands suddenly on no m, neither be NIG
6: 3 If any m teach otherwise, and consent not to NIG
6:11 But thou, O m of God, flee these *things;* and 444
6:16 dwelling in the light which no m can NIG
6:16 whom no m hath seen, nor can see: 444
2Ti 2: 4 No m that warreth entangleth himself with NIG
2: 5 And if a m also strive for masteries, *yet* is 5100

2Ti 2:21 If a **m** therefore purge himself from these, 5100
3:17 That the **m** of God may be perfect, 444
4:16 At my first answer no **m** stood with me, but NIG
Tit 2:15 with all authority. Let no **m** despise thee. NIG
3: 2 To speak evil of no **m**, to be no brawlers, NIG
3: 4 **love** of God our Saviour **toward m** 5363
3:10 A **m** that is a heretick after the first and 444
Heb 2: 6 saying, What is **m**, that thou art mindful of 444
2: 6 or the son of **m**, that thou visitest him? 444
2: 9 of God should taste death for every **m**. NIG
3: 3 For this **m** was counted worthy of more NIG
3: 4 For every house is builded by some **m**; but NIG
4:11 lest any **m** fall after the same example of NIG
5: 4 And no **m** taketh this honour unto himself, NIG
7: 4 Now consider how great this **m** was, unto NIG
7:13 of which no **m** gave attendance at the altar. NIG
7:24 But this **m**, because he continueth ever, hath NIG
8: 2 which the Lord pitched, and not **m**. 444
8: 3 wherefore it is of necessity that this **m** have NIG
8:11 And they shall not teach **every m** his 1538
8:11 and **every m** his brother, saying, Know 1538
10:12 But this **m**, after he had offered one NIG
10:38 but if any **m** draw back, my soul shall have NIG
12:14 without which no **m** shall see the Lord: NIG
12:15 Looking diligently lest any **m** fail of NIG
13: 6 and I will not fear what **m** shall do unto me. 444
Jas 1: 7 For let not that **m** think that he shall receive 444
1: 8 A double minded **m** is unstable in all his 435
1:11 also shall the rich **m** fade away in his ways. NIG
1:12 Blessed is the **m** that endureth temptation: 435
1:13 Let no **m** say when he is tempted, I am NIG
1:13 with evil, neither tempteth he any **m**: NIG
1:14 But **every m** is tempted, when he is drawn 1538
1:19 let every **m** be swift to hear, slow to speak, 444
1:20 For the wrath of **m** worketh not 435
1:23 he is like unto a **m** beholding his natural face 435
1:24 straightway forgetteth what manner of **m** he NIG
1:25 this **m** shall be blessed in his deed. NIG
1:26 If any **m** among you seem to be religious, NIG
2: 2 For if there come unto your assembly a **m** 435
2: 2 there come in also a poor **m** in vile raiment; NIG
2:14 though a **m** say he hath faith, and have not 5100
2:18 Yea, a **m** may say, Thou hast faith, and I 5100
2:20 But wilt thou know, O vain **m**, that faith 444
2:24 then how that by works a **m** is justified, 444
3: 2 If any **m** offend not in word, the same is a NIG
3: 2 the same is a perfect **m**, and able also to 435
3: 8 But the tongue can no **m** tame; it is an 444
3:13 Who is a wise **m** and endued with NIG
5:16 prayer of a righteous **m** availeth much. NIG
5:17 Elias was a **m** subject to like passions as we 444
1Pe 1:24 and all the glory of **m** as the flower of grass. 444
2:13 Submit yourselves to every ordinance **of m** 442
2:19 if a **m** for conscience toward God endure 5100
3: 4 But let it be the hidden **m** of the heart, in that 444
3:15 **m** that asketh you a reason of the hope that NIG
4:10 As **every m** hath received the gift, even so 1538
4:11 If any **m** speak, let him speak as the oracles NIG
4:11 if any **m** minister, let him do it as of NIG
4:16 Yet if any **m** suffer as a Christian, let him NIG
2Pe 1:21 came not in old time by the will of **m**: 444
2: 8 (For that righteous **m** dwelling among them, NIG
2:19 for of whom a **m** is overcome, of the same 5100
1Jn 2: 1 And if any **m** sin, we have an advocate with NIG
2:15 If any **m** love the world, the love of NIG
2:27 and ye need not that any **m** teach you: NIG
3: 3 And every **m** that hath this hope in him NIG
3: 7 Little children, let no **m** deceive you: he that NIG
4:12 No **m** hath seen God at any time. If we love NIG
4:20 If a **m** say, I love God, and hateth his 5100
5:16 If any **m** see his brother sin a sin which is NIG
Rev 1:13 candlesticks one like unto the Son of **m**, 444
2:17 which no **m** knoweth saving he that NIG
3: 7 he that openeth, and no **m** shutteth; NIG
3: 7 and shutteth, and no **m** openeth; NIG
3: 8 thee an open door, and no **m** can shut it: NIG
3:11 which thou hast, that no **m** take thy crown. NIG
3:20 if any **m** hear my voice, and open the door, NIG
4: 7 and the third beast had a face as a **m**, and 444
5: 3 And no **m** in heaven, nor in earth, NIG
5: 4 no **m** was found worthy to open and NIG
6:15 every free **m**, hid themselves in the dens NIG
7: 9 which no **m** could number, of all nations, NIG
9: 5 torment of a scorpion, when he striketh a **m**. 444
11: 5 And if any **m** will hurt them, fire proceedeth NIG
11: 5 and if any **m** will hurt them, he must in this NIG
12: 5 And she brought forth a **m** child, who was to 730
12:13 the woman which brought forth the **m** child. 730
13: 9 If any **m** have an ear, let him hear. NIG
13:17 And that no **m** might buy or sell, save he NIG
13:18 for it is the number of a **m**; and his number 444
14: 3 and no **m** could learn that song but NIG
14: 9 If any **m** worship the beast and his image, NIG
14:14 the cloud one sat like unto the Son of **m**, 444
15: 8 and no **m** was able to enter into the temple, NIG
16: 3 and it became as the blood of a dead **m**: and NIG
18:11 for no **m** buyeth their merchandise any NIG
19:12 that no **m** knew, but he himself. NIG
20:13 they were judged **every m** according to 1538
21:17 according to the measure of a **m**, that is, 444
22:12 to give **every m** according as his work shall 1538
22:18 For I testify unto every **m** that heareth NIG
22:18 If any **m** shall add unto these things, God NIG
22:19 And if any **m** shall take away from NIG

MAN'S (122) [MAN]

Ge 8:21 again curse the ground any more for **m** sake; 120
8:21 for the imagination of **m** heart is evil from 120
9: 5 at the hand of every **m** brother will I require 376
9: 6 Whoso sheddeth **m** blood, by man shall his 120
16:12 every man, and **every m** hand against him; 3605
20: 3 which thou hast taken; for she is a **m** wife. 1167
42:11 We are all one **m** sons; we are true men, thy 376
42:25 to restore every **m** money into his sack, and 376
42:35 every **m** bundle of money was in his sack: 376
43:21 every **m** money was in the mouth of his 376
44: 1 and put **every m** money in his sack's mouth. 376
44:26 for we may not see the **m** face, except our 376
Ex 4:11 said unto him, Who hath made **m** mouth? 120
12:44 every **m** servant that is bought for money, 376
21:35 if **one m** ox hurt another's, that he die; then 376
22: 5 his beast, and shall feed in **another m** field; 312
22: 7 to keep, and it be stolen out of the **m** house; 376
30:32 Upon **m** flesh shall it not be poured, 120
Lev 7: 8 the priest that offereth any **m** burnt offering, 376
15:16 if **any m** seed of copulation go out from 376
20:10 committeth adultery with another **m** wife, 376
Nu 5:10 every **m** hallowed things shall be his: 376
5:12 If any **m** wife go aside, and commit a 376
17: 2 write thou **every m** name upon his rod. 376
17: 5 that the **m** rod, whom I shall choose, shall 376
33:54 every **m**[S] inheritance shall be in 2050.2+3807.1
Dt 20:19 them down (for the tree of the field is **m** life) 120
24: 2 she may go and be another **m** wife. 376
24: 6 to pledge: for he taketh a **m** life to pledge. NIH
Jdg 7:16 he put a trumpet in every **m**[S] hand, 3963.1
7:22 the LORD set **every m** sword against his 376
19:26 fell down at the door of the **m** house where 376
Ru 2:19 The **m** name with whom I wrought to day is 376
1Sa 12: 4 neither hast thou taken ought of **any m** hand. 376
14:20 **every m** sword was against his fellow, and 376
17:32 to Saul, Let no **m** heart fail because of him; 120
2Sa 12: 4 took the poor **m** lamb, and dressed it for 376
17:18 came to a **m** house in Bahurim, which had a 376
17:25 which Amasa was a **m** son, whose name was 376
1Ki 18:44 a little cloud out of the sea, like a **m** hand. 376
2Ki 12: 4 all the money that cometh into **any m** heart 376
23: 8 which were on a **m** left hand at the gate of 376
25: 9 and every great **m** house burnt he with fire. NIH
Est 1: 8 according to **every m** pleasure. 376+376+2050.1
Job 10: 5 the days of man? are thy years as **m** days, 1397
32:21 Let me not, I pray you, accept any **m** person, 376
Ps 104:15 and bread which strengtheneth **m** heart. 582
Pr 10:15 The rich **m** wealth is his strong city: NIH
12:14 the recompence of a **m** hands shall be 120
13: 8 The ransom of a **m** life are his riches: but 376
16: 7 When a **m** ways please the LORD, 376
16: 9 A **m** heart deviseth his way: but the LORD 120
18: 4 The words of a **m** mouth are as deep waters, 376
18:11 The rich **m** wealth is his strong city, and NIH
18:16 A **m** gift maketh room for him, and 120
18:20 A **m** belly shall be satisfied with the fruit of 376
19:21 There are many devices in a **m** heart; 376
20:24 **M** goings are of the LORD; how can a 1397
27: 9 doth the sweetness of a **m**[S] friend by 1930.2
29:23 A **m** pride shall bring him low: but 120
29:26 every **m** judgment cometh from the LORD. 376
Ecc 2:14 The wise **m** eyes are in his head; but NIH
8: 1 a **m** wisdom maketh his face to shine, and 120
8: 5 and a wise **m** heart discerneth both time and NIH
9:16 nevertheless the poor **m** wisdom is NIH
10: 2 A wise **m** heart is at his right hand; but NIH
10:12 The words of a wise **m** mouth are gracious; NIH
Isa 8: 1 write in it with a **m** pen concerning 582
13: 7 hands be faint, and every **m** heart shall melt: 582
Jer 3: 1 she go from him, and become another **m**, 376
23:36 for **every m** word shall be his 376+3807.1
Eze 4:15 I have given thee cow's dung for **m** dung, 120
10: 8 the form of a **m** hand under their wings. 120
38:21 **every m** sword shall be against his brother. 376
39:15 when any seeth a **m** bone, then shall he set 120
40: 5 in the **m** hand a measuring reed of six cubits 376
Da 4:16 Let his heart be changed from **m**, and let a 606
5: 5 In the same hour came forth fingers of a **m** 606
7: 4 feet as a man, and a **m** heart was given to it. 606
8:16 I heard a **m** voice between the banks of Ulai, 120
Am 6:10 a **m**[S] uncle shall take him up, and he that 2050.2
Jnh 1:14 let us not perish for this **m** life, and lay not 376
Mic 7: 6 a **m** enemies are the men of his own house. 376
Mt 10:36 And a **m** foes shall be they of his own 444
10:41 man shall receive a righteous **m** reward. NIG
12:29 Or else how can one enter into a strong **m** NIG
Mk 3:27 No man can enter into a strong **m** house, NIG
12:19 If a **m** brother die, and leave his wife 5100
Lk 6:22 out your name as evil, for the Son of **m** sake. 444
12:15 for a **m** life consisteth not in the abundance 846
16:12 **m**, who shall give you that which is your NIG
16:21 the crumbs which fell from the rich **m** table: NIG
20:28 If any **m** brother die, having a wife, and NIG
Jn 18:17 Art not thou also one of this **m** disciples? 444
Ac 5:28 and intend to bring this **m** blood upon us. 444
7:58 laid down their clothes at a **young m** feet, 3494
11:12 and we entered into the **m** house: 435
13:23 Of this **m** seed hath God according to his NIG
17:29 silver, or stone, graven by art and **m** device. 444
18: 7 and entered into a certain **m** house, NIG
20:33 I have coveted no **m** silver, or gold, or NIG
27:22 for there shall be no loss of any **m** life NIG
Ro 5:17 For if by one **m** offence death reigned by NIG
5:19 For as by one **m** disobedience many were 444
14: 4 Who art thou that judgest another **m** NIG
15:20 lest I should build upon another **m** NIG
1Co 2: 4 was not with enticing words of **m** wisdom, 442
2:13 not in the words which **m** wisdom teacheth, 442
3:13 **Every m** work shall be made manifest: 1538
3:13 the fire shall try **every m** work of what sort 1538
3:14 If any **m** work abide which he hath built NIG
3:15 If any **m** work shall be burnt, he shall suffer NIG
4: 3 I should be judged of you, or of **m** judgment: 442
10:29 for why is my liberty judged of another **m** NIG
2Co 4: 2 to every **m** conscience in the sight of God. 444
10:16 not to boast in another **m** line of things NIG
Gal 2: 6 God accepteth no **m** person:) for they who 444
3:15 Though it be but a **m** covenant, yet if it be 444
2Th 3: 8 Neither did we eat any **m** bread for nought; NIG
Jas 1:26 his own heart, this **m** religion is vain. NIG
1Pe 1:17 judgeth according to **every m** work, 1538
2Pe 2:16 the dumb ass speaking with **m** voice forbad 444

MANAEN (1)

Ac 13: 1 called Niger, and Lucius of Cyrene, and **M**, 3127

MANAHATH (3) [MANAHETHITES]

Ge 36:23 Alvan, and **M**, and Ebal, Shepho, and 4506
1Ch 1:40 Alian, and **M**, and Ebal, Shephi, and Onam. 4506
8: 6 of Geba, and they removed them to **M**: 4506

MANAHETHITES (2) [MANAHATH]

1Ch 2:52 had sons; Haroeh, and half of the **M**. 2679
2:54 of Joab, and half of the **M**, the Zorites. 2680

MANASSEH (143) [MANASSEH'S, MANASSES, MANASSITES]

Ge 41:51 Joseph called the name of the firstborn **M**: 4519
46:20 Joseph in the land of Egypt were born **M** 4519
48: 1 with him his two sons, **M** and Ephraim. 4519
48: 5 now thy two sons, Ephraim and **M**, 4519
48:13 **M** in his left hand towards Israel's right 4519
48:14 hands wittingly; for **M** was the firstborn. 4519
48:20 God make thee as Ephraim and as **M**: 4519
48:20 as Manasseh: and he set Ephraim before **M**. 4519
50:23 of **M** were brought up upon Joseph's knees. 4519
Nu 1:10 of **M**; Gamaliel the son of Pedahzur. 4519
1:34 Of the children of **M**, by their generations, 4519
1:35 even of the tribe of **M**, were thirty and 4519
2:20 by him shall be the tribe of **M**: and 4519
2:20 the captain of the children of **M** shall be 4519
7:54 of Pedahzur, prince of the children of **M**: 4519
10:23 of **M** was Gamaliel the son of Pedahzur. 4519
13:11 namely, of the tribe of **M**, Gaddi the son of 4519
26:28 sons of Joseph after their families were **M** 4519
26:29 Of the sons of **M**: of Machir, the family of 4519
26:34 These are the families of **M**, and those that 4519
27: 1 of Gilead, the son of Machir, the son of **M**, 4519
27: 1 of the families of **M** the son of Joseph: 4519
32:33 unto half the tribe of **M** the son of Joseph, 4519
32:39 the children of Machir the son of **M** went to 4519
32:40 gave Gilead unto Machir the son of **M**: 4519
32:41 Jair the son of **M** went and took the small 4519
34:14 half the tribe of **M** have received their 4519
34:23 for the tribe of the children of **M**, 4519
36: 1 the son of Machir, the son of **M**, of 4519
36:12 families of the sons of **M** the son of Joseph, 4519
Dt 3:13 of Og, gave I unto the half tribe of **M**; 4519
3:14 Jair the son of **M** took all the country of 4519
29: 8 to the Gadites, and to the half tribe of **M**. 4520
33:17 and they are the thousands of **M**. 4519
34: 2 **M**, and all the land of Judah, unto 4519
Jos 1:12 to half the tribe of **M**, spake Joshua, saying, 4519
4:12 the children of Gad, and half the tribe of **M**, 4519
12: 6 and the Gadites, and the half tribe of **M**. 4519
13: 7 unto the nine tribes, and the half tribe of **M**, 4519
13:29 gave inheritance unto the half tribe of **M**: 4519
13:29 tribe of the children of **M** by their families. 4519
13:31 unto the children of Machir the son of **M**, 4519
14: 4 of Joseph were two tribes, **M** and Ephraim: 4519
16: 4 **M** and Ephraim, took their inheritance. 4519
16: 9 among the inheritance of the children of **M**, 4519
17: 1 There was also a lot for the tribe of **M**; 4519
17: 1 to wit, for Machir the firstborn of **M**, 4519
17: 2 rest of the children of **M** by their families; 4519
17: 2 these were the male children of **M** the son 4519
17: 3 the son of **M**, had no sons, but daughters: 4519
17: 5 there fell ten portions to **M**, beside the land 4519
17: 6 Because the daughters of **M** had an 4519
17: 7 the coast of **M** was from Asher to 4519
17: 8 Now **M** had the land of Tappuah: but 4519
17: 8 Tappuah on the border of **M** belonged to 4519
17: 9 of Ephraim are among the cities of **M**: 4519
17: 9 the coast of **M** also was on the north side of 4519
17:11 **M** had in Issachar and in Asher Beth-shean 4519
17:12 Yet the children of **M** could not drive out 4519
17:17 even to Ephraim and to **M**, saying, Thou art 4519
18: 7 Gad, and Reuben, and half the tribe of **M**, 4519
20: 8 and Golan in Bashan out of the tribe of **M**. 4519
21: 5 and out of the half tribe of **M**, ten cities. 4519
21: 6 out of the half tribe of **M** in Bashan, 4519
21:25 out of the half tribe of **M**, Tanach with her 4519
21:27 out of the other half tribe of **M** they gave 4519
22: 1 and the Gadites, and the half tribe of **M**, 4519
22: 7 Now to the one half of the tribe of **M** 4519
22: 9 of Gad and the half tribe of **M** returned, 4519
22:10 the half tribe of **M** built there an altar by 4519
22:11 the half tribe of **M** have built an altar over 4519
22:13 children of Gad, and to the half tribe of **M**, 4519
22:15 children of Gad, and to the half tribe of **M**, 4519
22:21 of Gad and the half tribe of **M** answered, 4519
22:30 of Gad and the children of **M** spake, 4519
22:31 children of Gad, and to the children of **M**, 4519
Jdg 1:27 Neither did **M** drive out the inhabitants of 4519
6:15 my family is poor in **M**, and I am the least 4519
6:35 he sent messengers throughout all **M**; who 4519
7:23 out of all **M**, and pursued after 4519
11:29 he passed over Gilead and **M**, and 4519
18:30 the son of **M**, he and his sons were priests 4519
1Ki 4:13 pertained the towns of Jair the son of **M**, 4519
2Ki 20:21 and **M** his son reigned in his stead. 4519
21: 1 **M** was twelve years old when he began to 4519
21: 9 **M** seduced them to do more evil than did 4519
21:11 Because **M** king of Judah hath done these 4519
21:16 Moreover **M** shed innocent blood very 4519
21:17 Now the rest of the acts of **M**, and all that 4519
21:18 **M** slept with his fathers, and was buried in 4519
21:20 sight of the LORD, as his father **M** did. 4519
23:12 the altars which **M** had made in the two 4519
23:26 of all the provocations that **M** had 4519
24: 3 for the sins of **M**, according to all that he 4519
1Ch 3:13 Ahaz his son, Hezekiah his son, **M** his son, 4519
5:18 the Gadites, and half the tribe of **M**, 4519
5:23 the children of the half tribe of **M** dwelt in 4519
5:26 the half tribe of **M**, and brought them unto 4519
6:61 namely, out of the half tribe of **M**, by lot, 4519
6:62 out of the tribe of **M** in Bashan, 4519

M

1Ch 6:70 out of the half tribe of **M**; Aner with her 4519
6:71 out of the family of the half tribe of **M**, 4519
7:14 The sons of **M**; Ashriel, whom she bare: 4519
7:17 of Gilead, the son of Machir, the son of **M**. 4519
7:29 by the borders of the children of **M**, 4519
9: 3 and of the children of Ephraim, and **M**; 4519
12:19 there fell *some* of **M** to David, when he 4519
12:20 there fell to him of **M**, Adnah, and Jozabad, 4519
12:20 captains of the thousands that *were* of **M**. 4519
12:31 of the half tribe of **M** eighteen thousand, 4519
12:37 and the Gadites, and of the half tribe of **M**, 4519
26:32 the Gadites, and the half tribe of **M**, 4520
27:20 of the half tribe of **M**, Joel the son of 4519
27:21 Of the half *tribe* of **M** in Gilead, Iddo 4519
2Ch 15: 9 strangers with them out of Ephraim and **M**, 4519
30: 1 and wrote letters also to Ephraim and **M**, 4519
30:10 of Ephraim and **M** even unto Zebulun: 4519
30:11 Nevertheless divers of Asher and **M** and 4519
30:18 of Ephraim, and **M**, Issachar, and Zebulun, 4519
31: 1 and Benjamin, in Ephraim also and **M**, 4519
32:33 And **M** his son reigned in his stead. 4519
33: 1 **M** *was* twelve years old when he *began* to 4519
33: 9 So **M** made Judah and the inhabitants of 4519
33:10 the LORD spake to **M**, and to his people: 4519
33:11 which took **M** among the thorns, and 4519
33:13 Then **M** knew that the LORD he *was* God. 4519
33:18 Now the rest of the acts of **M**, and 4519
33:20 So **M** slept with his fathers, and they buried 4519
33:22 sight of the LORD, as did **M** his father: 4519
33:22 images which **M** his father had made, 4519
33:23 as **M** his father had humbled himself; 4519
34: 6 *so did he* in the cities of **M**, and Ephraim, 4519
34: 9 the doors had gathered of the hand of **M** 4519
Ezr 10:30 Mattaniah, Bezaleel, and Binnui, and **M**. 4519
10:33 Zabad, Eliphelet, Jeremai, **M**, *and* Shimei. 4519
Ps 60: 7 Gilead *is* mine, and **M** *is* mine; 4519
80: 2 and Benjamin and **M** stir up thy strength, 4519
108: 8 Gilead *is* mine; **M** *is* mine; Ephraim also *is* 4519
Isa 9:21 **M**, Ephraim; and Ephraim, Manasseh: *and* 4519
9:21 Manasseh, Ephraim; and Ephraim, **M**: *and* 4519
Jer 15: 4 of **M** the son of Hezekiah king of Judah, 4519
Eze 48: 4 side unto the west side, a *portion for* **M**. 4519
48: 5 by the border of **M**, from the east side unto 4519

MANASSEH'S (4) [MANASSEH]

Ge 48:14 and his left hand upon **M** head, 4519
48:17 to remove it from Ephraim's head unto **M** 4519
Jos 17: 6 the rest of **M** sons had the land of Gilead. 4519
17:10 northward *it was* **M**, and the sea is 4519+3807.1

MANASSES (3) [MANASSEH]

Mt 1:10 And Ezekias begat **M**; and Manasses begat *3128*
1:10 and **M** begat Amon; and Amon begat *3128*
Rev 7: 6 Of the tribe of **M** *were* sealed twelve *3128*

MANASSITES (3) [MANASSEH]

Dt 4:43 and Golan in Bashan, of the **M**. 4520
Jdg 12: 4 among the Ephraimites, *and* among the **M**. 4519
2Ki 10:33 and the Reubenites, and the **M**, from Aroer, 4520

MANDRAKES (6)

Ge 30:14 found **m** in the field, and brought them unto 1736
30:14 Give me, I pray thee, of thy son's **m**. 1736
30:15 wouldest thou take away my son's **m** also? 1736
30:15 shall lie with thee to night for thy son's **m**. 1736
30:16 surely I have hired thee with my son's **m**. 1736
SS 7:13 The **m** give a smell, and at our gates *are* all 1736

MANEH (1)

Eze 45:12 fifteen shekels, shall be your **m**. 4488

MANGER (3)

Lk 2: 7 in swaddling clothes, and laid him in a **m**; *5336*
2:12 wrapped in swaddling clothes, lying in a **m**. *5336*
2:16 and Joseph, and the babe lying in a **m**. *5336*

MANIFEST (39) [MANIFESTATION, MANIFESTED, MANIFESTLY]

Ecc 3:18 that God might **m** them, and that *they* 1305
Lk 8:17 nothing is secret, that shall not be **made m**; *5318*
Jn 1:31 but that he should be **made m** to Israel, *5319*
3:21 that his deeds may be **made m**, that they *5319*
9: 3 that the works of God should be **made m** in *5319*
14:21 I will love him, and will **m** myself to him. *1718*
14:22 how is it that thou wilt **m** thyself unto us, *1718*
Ac 4:16 *is* **m** to all them that dwell in Jerusalem; *5318*
Ro 1:19 which may be known of God is **m** in them; *5318*
10:20 I was made **m** unto them that asked not *1717*
16:26 But now is **made m**, and by the scriptures *5319*
1Co 3:13 Every man's work shall be made **m**: for *5318*
4: 5 and will **make m** the counsels of the hearts: *5319*
11:19 *are* approved may be made **m** among you. *5318*
14:25 thus are the secrets of his heart made **m**; *5318*
15:27 all *things* are put under *him, it is* **m** that he *1212*
2Co 2:14 **maketh m** the savour of his knowledge by *5319*
4:10 that the life also of Jesus might be **made m** *5319*
4:11 that the life also of Jesus might be **made m** *5319*
5:11 but we are **made m** unto God; and I trust *5319*
5:11 I trust also are **made m** in your *5319*
11: 6 we *have been* throughly **made m** among *5319*
Gal 5:19 Now the works of the flesh are **m**, *5318*
Eph 5:13 But all *things* that are reproved are **made m** *5319*
5:13 for whatsoever doth **make m** is light. *5319*
Php 1:13 So that my bonds in Christ are **m** in all *5318*
Col 1:26 but now is **made m** to his saints: *5319*
4: 4 That I may **make** it **m**, as I ought to speak. *5319*
2Th 1: 5 *Which is* a **m token** of the righteous *1730*
1Ti 3:16 God was **m** in the flesh, justified in *5319*
5:25 the good works of *some* are **m beforehand**; *4271*
2Ti 1:10 But is now **made m** by the appearing of our *5319*
3: 9 for their folly shall be **m** unto all *men*, as *1552*
Heb 4:13 Neither is there any creature *that is* **not m** in *852*
9: 8 into the holiest *of all* was not yet **made m**, *5319*
1Pe 1:20 but was **m** in *these* last times for you, *5319*
1Jn 2:19 *they went out*, that they might be **made m** *5319*
3:10 In this the children of God are **m**, and *5318*
Rev 15: 4 before thee; for thy judgments are **made m**. *5319*

MANIFESTATION (3) [MANIFEST]

Ro 8:19 waiteth for the **m** of the sons of God. *602*
1Co 12: 7 But the **m** of the Spirit is given to every *5321*
2Co 4: 2 by **m** of the truth commending ourselves to *5321*

MANIFESTED (10) [MANIFEST]

Mk 4:22 there is nothing hid, which shall not be **m**; *5319*
Jn 2:11 in Cana of Galilee, and **m forth** his glory; *5319*
17: 6 I have **m** thy name unto the men which *5319*
Ro 3:21 righteousness of God without the law is **m**, *5319*
Tit 1: 3 But hath in due times **m** his word through *5319*
1Jn 1: 2 (For the life was **m**, and we have seen *it*, *5319*
1: 2 was with the Father, and was **m** unto us;) *5319*
3: 5 And ye know that he was **m** to take away *5319*
3: 8 For this purpose the Son of God was **m**, *5319*
4: 9 In this was **m** the love of God towards us, *5319*

MANIFESTLY (1) [MANIFEST]

2Co 3: 3 Forasmuch as ye are **m declared** to be *5319*

MANIFOLD (8)

Ne 9:19 Yet thou in thy **m** mercies forsookest them 7227
9:27 according to thy **m** mercies thou gavest 7227
Ps 104:24 O LORD, how **m** are thy works! 7231
Am 5:12 For I know your **m** transgressions and 7227
Lk 18:30 Who shall not receive **m more** in this *4179*
Eph 3:10 by the church the **m** wisdom of God, *4182*
1Pe 1: 6 ye are in heaviness through **m** temptations: *4164*
4:10 as good stewards of the **m** grace of God. *4164*

MANKIND (6) [MAN]

Lev 18:22 Thou shalt not lie with **m**, as with 2145
20:13 If a man also lie with **m**, as he lieth with a 2145
Job 12:10 living *thing*, and the breath of all **m**. 376+1320
1Co 6: 9 nor **abusers** of themselves **with m**, *733*
1Ti 1:10 for **them that defile** themselves **with m**, *733*
Jas 3: 7 the sea, is tamed, and hath been tamed **of m**: *442*

MANNA (19)

Ex 16:15 saw *it*, they said one to another, It *is* **m**: 4478
16:31 house of Israel called the name thereof **M**: 4478
16:33 put an omer full of **m** therein, and lay it up 4478
16:35 the children of Israel did eat **m** forty years, 4478
16:35 they did eat **m**, until they came unto 4478
Nu 11: 6 at all, beside *this* **m**, *before* our eyes. 4478
11: 7 the **m** *was* as coriander seed, and the colour 4478
11: 9 the camp in the night, the **m** fell upon it. 4478
Dt 8: 3 thee to hunger, and fed thee with **m**, 4478
8:16 Who fed thee in the wilderness with **m**, 4478
Jos 5:12 the **m** ceased on the morrow after they had 4478
5:12 neither had the children of Israel **m** any 4478
Ne 9:20 withheldest not thy **m** from their mouth, 4478
Ps 78:24 had rained down **m** upon them to eat, and 4478
Jn 6:31 Our fathers did eat **m** in the desert; as it is *3131*
6:49 Your fathers did eat **m** in the wilderness, *3131*
6:58 not as your fathers did eat **m**, and are dead: *3131*
Heb 9: 4 wherein *was* the golden pot that had **m**, and *3131*
Rev 2:17 will I give to eat of the hidden **m**, *3131*

MANNER (196) [MANNERS]

Ge 18:11 it ceased to be with Sarah after the **m** of 734
18:25 That be far from thee to do after this **m**, to 1697
19:31 come in unto us after the **m** of all the earth: 1870
25:23 two **m** of people shall be separated from thy NIH
32:19 On this **m** shall you speak unto Esau, 1697
39:19 After this **m** did thy servant to me; 1697
40:13 after the former **m** when thou wast his 4941
40:17 in the uppermost basket *there was* of all **m** NIH
45:23 to his father he sent after this **m**; ten asses NIH
Ex 1:14 in brick, and in **all m** of service in the field: 3605
7:11 they also did in **like m** with their 3651
12:16 no ***m*** *of* work shall be done in them, NIH
21: 9 he shall deal with her after the **m** of 4941
22: 9 For all **m** of trespass, *whether it be* for ox, 1697
22: 9 for **any m** of lost *thing*, which *another* 3605
23:11 **In like m** thou shalt deal with thy vineyard, 3651
31: 3 in knowledge, and in all ***m*** *of* workmanship, NIH
31: 5 of timber, to work in all ***m*** *of* workmanship. NIH
35:29 them willing to bring for all ***m*** *of* work, NIH
35:31 in knowledge, and in all ***m*** *of* workmanship; NIH
35:33 of wood, to make any ***m*** *of* cunning work. NIH
35:35 to work all ***m*** *of* work, of the engraver, and NIH
36: 1 understanding to know how to work all ***m*** NIH
Lev 5:10 *for* a burnt offering, according to the **m**: 4941
7:23 Ye shall eat no ***m*** fat, of ox, or of sheep, or NIH
7:26 Moreover ye shall eat no ***m*** *of* blood, NIH
7:27 Whatsoever soul *it be* that eateth any ***m*** *of* NIH
9:16 and offered it according to the **m**. 4941
11:27 among all ***m*** *of* beasts that go on *all* four, NIH
11:44 shall ye defile yourselves with any ***m*** NIH
14:54 This *is* the law for all ***m*** *of* plague of NIH
17:10 among you, that eateth any ***m*** *of* blood; NIH
17:14 Ye shall eat the blood of no ***m*** *of* flesh: NIH
19:23 shall have planted all ***m*** *of* trees for food, NIH
20:25 by any ***m*** *of living thing* that creepeth *on* NIH
23:31 Ye shall do no ***m*** *of* work: *it shall be* a NIH
24:22 Ye shall have **one m** of law, as well for 259
Nu 5:13 neither she be taken *with the* ***m***; NIH
9:14 according to the **m** thereof, so shall he do: 4941
15:13 country shall do these *things* **after this m**, 3602
15:16 One law and one **m** shall be for you, and 4941
15:24 according to the **m**, and one kid of 4941
28:18 ye shall do no ***m*** *of* servile work *therein*: NIH
28:24 **After** this **m** ye shall offer daily, 3509.1
29: 6 according unto their **m**, for a sweet savour, 4941
29:18 *be* according to their number, after the **m**: 4941
29:21 *be* according to their number, after the **m**: 4941
29:24 *be* according to their number, after the **m**: 4941
29:27 *be* according to their number, after the **m**: 4941
29:30 *be* according to their number, after the **m**: 4941
29:33 *be* according to their number, after the **m**: 4941
29:37 *be* according to their number, after the **m**: 4941
31:30 of all ***m*** *of* beasts, and give them unto NIH
Dt 4:15 for ye saw no ***m*** *of* similitude on the day NIH
15: 2 this *is* the **m** of the release: Every creditor 1697
22: 3 **In like m** shalt thou do with his ass; and so 3651
27:21 Cursed *be* he that lieth with any ***m*** *of* beast. NIH
Jos 6:15 compassed the city after the same **m** seven 4941
Jdg 8:18 **What m** of men *were they* whom ye slew at 375
11:17 **in like m** they sent unto the king of Moab: 1571
18: 7 after the **m** of the Zidonians, quiet and 4941
Ru 4: 7 Now this *was the* **m** in former time in Israel NIH
1Sa 8: 9 shew them the **m** of the king that shall 4941
8:11 This will be the **m** of the king that shall 4941
10:25 Samuel told the people the **m** of 4941
17:27 the people answered him after this **m**, 1697
17:30 and spake after the same **m**: 1697
17:30 answered him again after the former **m**. 1697
18:24 told him, saying, On this **m** spake David. 1697
19:24 prophesied before Samuel **in like m**, and 1571
21: 5 and *the bread is in* a **m** common, yea, 1870
27:11 *will be* his **m** all the while he dwelleth in 4941
2Sa 6: 5 on all ***m*** *of instruments made of* fir wood, NIH
7:19 And *is* this the **m** of man, O Lord GOD? 8452
14: 3 to the king, and speak on this **m** unto him. 1697
15: 6 on this **m** did Absalom to all Israel that 1697
17: 6 Ahithophel hath spoken after this **m**: 1697
1Ki 7:28 the work of the bases *was on* this ***m***: they NIH
7:37 After this ***m*** he made the ten bases: all of NIH
18:28 cut themselves after their **m** with knives 4941
22:20 one said on **this m**, and another said on that 3541
22:20 on this manner, and another said on **that m**. 3541
2Ki 1: 7 What **m** of man *was he* which came up to 4941
11:14 as the **m** *was*, and the princes and 4941
17:26 know not the **m** of the God of the land: 4941
17:26 they know not the **m** of the God of the land. 4941
17:27 let him teach them the **m** of the God of 4941
17:33 after the **m** of the nations whom they 4941
17:40 but they did after their former **m**. 4941
1Ch 6:48 ***m*** *of* service of the tabernacle of the house NIH
12:37 with all ***m*** *of* instruments of war for NIH
18:10 *with him* all ***m*** *of* vessels of gold and silver NIH
22:15 all ***m*** *of* cunning *men* for every *manner of* NIH
22:15 all *manner of* cunning *men* for every ***m*** *of* NIH
23:29 is fried, and for all ***m*** *of* measure and size; NIH
24:19 according to their **m**, under Aaron their 4941
28:14 of **all m of service**; 5656+5656+2050.1
28:21 *there shall be* with thee for all ***m*** *of* NIH
28:21 willing skilful *man*, for any ***m*** *of* service: NIH
29: 2 all ***m*** *of* precious stones, and marble stones NIH
29: 5 for all ***m*** *of* work *to be made* by the hands NIH
2Ch 2:14 also to grave any ***m*** *of* graving, and to find NIH
4:20 that they should burn after the **m** before 4941
13: 9 have made you priests **after the m of** 3509.1
18:19 one spake saying **after this m**, and 3602
18:19 and another saying **after that m**. 3602
30:16 they stood in their place after their **m**, 4941
32:15 nor persuade you on this ***m***, neither yet NIH
32:27 for shields, and for all ***m*** *of* pleasant jewels; NIH
32:28 stalls for all ***m*** *of* beasts, and cotes for NIH
34:13 work in **any m of service**: 5656+5656+2050.1
Ezr 5: 4 said we unto them **after this m**, What are 3660
Ne 6: 4 and I answered them after the same **m**. 1697
6: 5 sent Sanballat his servant unto me in like **m** 1697
8:18 a solemn assembly, according unto the **m**. 4941
10:37 the fruit of all ***m*** *of* trees, of wine and of oil, NIH
13:15 grapes, and figs, and all ***m*** *of* burdens, NIH
13:16 all ***m*** *of* ware, and sold on the sabbath unto NIH
Est 1:13 *was* the king's **m** towards all that knew law 1697
2:12 according to the **m** of the women, (for so 1881
Ps 107:18 Their soul abhorreth all ***m*** *of* meat; and NIH
144:13 affording **all m of store**: 413+2177+2177+4480
SS 7:13 at our gates *are* all ***m*** *of* pleasant *fruits*, new NIH
Isa 5:17 shall the lambs feed after their **m**, and 1699
10:24 his staff against thee, after the **m** of Egypt. 1870
10:26 so shall he lift it up after the **m** of Egypt. 1870
51: 6 they that dwell therein shall die in like **m**: 3654
Jer 13: 9 **After this m** will I mar the pride of Judah, 3602
22:21 This *hath been* thy **m** from thy youth, 1870
30:18 the palace shall remain after the **m** thereof. 4941
Eze 20:30 Are ye polluted after the **m** of your fathers? 1870
23:15 *after* the **m** of the Babylonians of Chaldea, 1823
23:45 they shall judge them **after the m** of 4941
23:45 and **after the m** of *women* that shed blood; 4941
Da 6:23 no **m** of hurt was found upon him, because 3606
Am 4:10 you the pestilence after the **m** of Egypt: 1870
8:14 liveth; and, The **m** of Beer-sheba liveth; 1870
Mt 4:23 and healing all ***m*** *of* sickness and NIG
4:23 and all ***m*** *of* disease among the people. NIG
5:11 shall say **all m** of evil against you falsely, *3956*
6: 9 **After this m** therefore pray ye: Our Father *3779*
8:27 saying, **What m of man** is this, that even *4217*
10: 1 and to heal all ***m*** *of* sickness and all *manner* NIG
10: 1 all *manner of* sickness and all ***m*** *of* disease. NIG
12:31 All ***m*** *of* sin and blasphemy shall be NIG
Mk 4:41 What ***m*** *of* man is this, that even the wind NIG
13: 1 see **what m** of stones and what buildings *4217*
13:29 **So** ye **in like m**, when ye shall see *2532+3779*
Lk 1:29 cast in her mind **what m** of salutation this *4217*
1:66 saying, What ***m*** *of* child shall this be! NIG
6:23 for **in the like m** did their *846+2596+3588*
7:39 **what m of** woman *this is* that toucheth *4217*
8:25 one to another, What ***m*** *of man* is this? NIG
9:55 Ye know not **what m** of spirit ye are of. *3634*
11:42 for ye tithe mint and rue and all ***m*** *of* herbs, NIG
20:31 third took her; and **in like m** the seven also: *5615*
24:17 What ***m*** *of* communications *are* these that NIG
Jn 2: 6 **after the m** of the purifying of the Jews, *2596*
7:36 What ***m*** *of* saying is this that he said, NIG
19:40 the spices, as the **m** of the Jews is to bury. *1485*
Ac 1:11 come *in* like **m** as ye have seen him go into *5158*
10:12 Wherein were all ***m*** *of* fourfooted beasts of NIG
15: 1 *said*, Except ye be circumcised after the **m** *1485*
15:23 they wrote *letters* by them **after this m**; *3592*
17: 2 And Paul, as his **m** was, went in unto them, *1486*

Ac 20:18 **after what m** I have been with you at all 4459
22: 3 taught according to the **perfect m** of the law 195
23:25 And he wrote a letter after this **m**: 5179
25:16 It is not the **m** of the Romans to deliver any 1485
25:20 because I doubted of such *m of* questions, NIG
26: 4 My **m of life** from *my* youth, which was at 981
Ro 6:19 I speak **after the m of men** because of 442
7: 8 wrought in me all *m* of concupiscence. NIG
1Co 7: 7 his proper gift of God, one **after this m**, 3779
11:25 **After the same m** also *he took* the cup, 5615
15:32 If **after the m of** men I have fought with 2596
2Co 7: 9 for ye were made sorry **after a** godly **m**, 2596
Gal 2:14 livest **after the m of Gentiles**, and not as 1483
3:15 Brethren, I speak **after the m** of men; 2596
1Th 1: 5 as ye know **what m** of *men* we were among 3634
1: 9 For they themselves shew of us **what m of** 3697
1Ti 2: 9 **In like m** also, that women adorn 5615
2Ti 3:10 **m of life,** purpose, faith, longsuffering, 72
Heb 10:25 as the **m** of some *is;* but exhorting *one* 1485
Jas 1:24 straightway forgetteth **what m of** *man* he 3697
1Pe 1:11 **what m** of time the Spirit of Christ which 4169
1:15 so be ye holy in all *m of* conversation; NIG
3: 5 For **after this m** in the old time the holy 3779
2Pe 3:11 **what m** *of persons* ought ye to be in all 4217
1Jn 3: 1 **what m** of love the Father hath bestowed 4217
Jude 1: 7 in like **m** giving themselves over to 5158
Rev 11: 5 will hurt them, he must **in this m** be killed. 3779
18:12 and all *m* vessels of ivory, and all *manner* NIG
18:12 and all *m* vessels of most precious wood, NIG
21:19 garnished with all *m of* precious stones. NIG
22: 2 which bare twelve *m of* fruits, *and* NIG

MANNERS (6) [MANNER]
Lev 20:23 ye shall not walk in the m of the nation, 2708
2Ki 17:34 Unto this day they do after the former m: 4941
Eze 11:12 have done after the m of the heathen that 4941
Ac 13:18 years **suffered** he their m in the wilderness. 5159
1Co 15:33 evil communications corrupt good m. 2239
Heb 1: 1 in divers m spake in time past unto 4187

MANOAH (18)
Jdg 13: 2 family of the Danites, whose name *was* M; 4495
13: 8 M intreated the LORD, and said, O my 4495
13: 9 God hearkened to the voice of M; and 4495
13: 9 but M her husband *was* not with her. 4495
13:11 M arose, and went after his wife, and 4495
13:12 M said, Now let thy words come to pass. 4495
13:13 the angel of the LORD said unto M, Of all 4495
13:15 M said unto the angel of the LORD, 4495
13:16 the angel of the LORD said unto M, 4495
13:16 For M knew not that he *was* an angel of 4495
13:17 M said unto the angel of the LORD, 4495
13:19 So M took a kid with a meat offering, and 4495
13:19 and M and his wife looked on. 4495
13:20 M and his wife looked on *it,* and fell on 4495
13:21 of the LORD did no more appear to M 4495
13:21 M knew that he *was* an angel of 4495
13:22 M said unto his wife, We shall surely die, 4495
16:31 Eshtaol in the buryingplace of M his father. 4495

MANSERVANT (12) [MAN, SERVE]
Ex 20:10 thou, nor thy son, nor thy daughter, thy m, 5650
20:17 nor his m, nor his maidservant, nor his ox, 5650
21:32 If the ox shall push a m or a maidservant; 5650
Dt 5:14 nor thy son, nor thy daughter, nor thy m, 5650
5:14 that thy m and thy maidservant may rest as 5650
5:21 or his m, or his maidservant, his ox, or 5650
12:18 thy m, and thy maidservant, and the Levite 5650
16:11 thy m, and thy maidservant, and the Levite 5650
16:14 thy m, and thy maidservant, and the Levite, 5650
Job 31:13 If I did despise the cause of my m or of my 5650
Jer 34: 9 That every man should let his m, and 5650
34:10 heard that every one should let his m, and 5650

MANSERVANT'S (1) [MAN, SERVE]
Ex 21:27 if he smite out his m tooth, or 5650

MANSERVANTS (1) [MAN, SERVE]
Ne 7:67 Beside their m and their maidservants, 5650

MANSIONS (1)
Jn 14: 2 In my Father's house are many m: if *it* 3438

MANSLAYER (2) [MAN, SLAY]
Nu 35: 6 which ye shall appoint for the m, that he 7523
35:12 that the m die not, until he stand before 7523

MANSLAYERS (1) [MAN, SLAY]
1Ti 1: 9 of fathers and murderers of mothers, for m, 409

MANTLE (13) [MANTLES]
Jdg 4:18 her into the tent, she covered him with a m. 8063
1Sa 15:27 he laid hold upon the skirt of his m, and 4598
28:14 cometh up; and he *is* covered with a m. 4598
1Ki 19:13 heard *it,* that he wrapped his face in his m, 155
19:19 passed by him, and cast his m upon him. 155
2Ki 2: 8 And Elijah took his m, and wrapt *it* together, 155
2:13 He took up also the m of Elijah that fell 155
2:14 he took the m of Elijah that fell from him, 155
Ezr 9: 3 I rent my garment and my m, and 4598
9: 5 having rent my garment and my m, I fell 4598
Job 1:20 rent his m, and shaved his head, and 4598
2:12 they rent every one his m, and 4598
Ps 109:29 *with* their own confusion, as *with* a m. 4598

MANTLES (1) [MANTLE]
Isa 3:22 the m, and the wimples, and the crisping 4595

MANURE PILE See DUNGHILL

MANY (556)
Ge 17: 4 and thou shalt be a father of m nations. 1995
17: 5 for a father of m nations have I made thee. 1995
21:34 sojourned in the Philistines' land m days. 7227
37: 3 and he made him a coat **of m colours**. 6446
37:23 *his* coat **of m colours** that *was* on him; 6446
37:32 they sent the coat **of m colours**, and 6446
37:34 his loins, and mourned for his son m days. 7227
Ex 5: 5 the people of the land now *are* m, and 7227
19:21 the LORD to gaze, and m of them perish. 7227
23: 2 cause to decline after m to wrest *judgment:* 7227
35:22 **as m as** were willing hearted, *and* 3605
Lev 15:25 if a woman have an issue of her blood m 7227
25:51 If *there be* yet m years *behind,* according 7227
Nu 9:19 tarried long upon the tabernacle m days, 7227
10:36 O LORD, *unto* the m thousands of Israel. 7233
13:18 whether they *be* strong or weak, few or m; 7227
22: 3 afraid of the people, because they *were* m: 7227
24: 7 his seed *shall be* in m waters, and his king 7227
26:54 To m thou shalt give the more inheritance, 7227
26:56 possession thereof be divided between m 7227
35: 8 from *them that have* m ye shall give many; 7227
35: 8 from *them that have* many ye shall **give m**; 7235
Dt 1:11 **make** you a thousand times **so m moe** 3254
1:46 So ye abode in Kadesh m days, 7227
2: 1 and we compassed mount Seir m days. 7227
2:10 a people great, and m, and tall, as 7227
2:21 A people great, and m, and tall, as 7227
3: 5 and bars; beside unwalled towns a great m. 7235
7: 1 hath cast out m nations before thee, 7227
15: 6 thou shalt lend unto m nations, but 7227
15: 6 thou shalt reign over m nations, but 7227
25: 3 beat him above these *with* m stripes, then 7227
28:12 thou shalt lend unto m nations, and 7227
31:17 and m evils and troubles shall befall them; 7227
31:21 when m evils and troubles are befallen 7227
32: 7 the years of **m generations**: 1755+1755+2050.1
Jos 11: 4 with horses and chariots very m. 7227
22: 3 Ye have not left your brethren these m days 7227
Jdg 3: 1 *even* **as m** *of Israel* **as** had not known 834+3605
7: 2 The people that *are* with thee *are* **too m** for 7227
7: 4 unto Gideon, The people *are* yet *too* m; 7227
8:30 of his body begotten: for he had m wives. 7227
9:40 and m were overthrown *and* wounded, 7227
16:24 of our country, which slew m of us. 7235
1Sa 2: 5 she that hath m children is waxed feeble. 7227
6:19 the LORD had smitten *m* of the people NIH
14: 6 *is* no restraint to the LORD to save by m 7227
25:10 there be m servants now a days that break 7231
2Sa 1: 4 m of the people also are fallen and dead; 7235
2:23 that **as m as** came to the place where 3605
12: 2 The rich *man* had exceeding m flocks and 7235
22:17 he took me; he drew me out of m waters; 7227
23:20 of Kabzeel, who had done m acts, 7227
24: 3 how m soever they be, an hundredfold, 1992.1
1Ki 2:38 And Shimei dwelt in Jerusalem m days. 7227
4:20 Judah and Israel *were* m, as the sand which 7227
7:47 because they were exceeding m: 7230
11: 1 king Solomon loved m strange women, 7227
17:15 she, and he, and her house, did eat *m* days. NIH
18: 1 it came to pass *after* m days, that the word 7227
18:25 for ye *are* m; and call on the name of your 7227
22:16 king said unto him, **How m** 4100+5704+3509.1
2Ki 9:22 and her witchcrafts *are so* m? 7227
1Ch 4:27 his brethren had not m children, neither did 7227
5:22 For there fell down m slain, because 7227
7: 4 thirty thousand *men:* for they had m wives 7235
7:22 Ephraim their father mourned m days, and 7227
8:40 archers, and **had m** sons, and sons' sons, 7235
11:22 man of Kabzeel, who had done m acts; 7227
21: 3 **make** his people an hundred times **so m moe** 3254
23:11 Jeush and Beriah had not m sons; therefore 7235
23:17 but the sons of Rehabiah were very m. 7235
28: 5 (for the LORD hath given me m sons,) 7227
2Ch 11:23 in abundance. And he desired m wives. 1995
14:11 *whether* with m, *or* with *them that have* no 7227
16: 8 with very m chariots and horsemen? 7235
18:15 the king said to him, **How m** 4100+5704+3509.1
26:10 towers in the desert, and digged m wells: 7227
29:31 **as m as** were of a free heart burnt 3605
30:17 For *there were* m in the congregation that 7227
30:18 *even* m of Ephraim, and Manasseh, 7227
32:23 m brought gifts unto the LORD to 7227
Ezr 3:12 m of the priests and Levites and chief of 7227
3:12 a loud voice; and m shouted aloud for joy: 7227
5:11 build the house that was builded these m 7690
10:13 the people *are* m, and *it is* a time of much 7227
10:13 for we are m that have transgressed in this 7235
Ne 5: 2 We, our sons, and our daughters, *are* m: 7227
6:17 nobles of Judah sent m letters unto Tobiah, 7235
6:18 For *there were* m in Judah sworn unto him, 7227
7: 2 a faithful man, and feared God above m. 7227
9:28 m times didst thou deliver them according 7227
9:30 Yet m years didst thou forbear them, and 7227
13:26 m nations was there no king like him, 7227
Est 1: 4 the honour of his excellent majesty m days, 7227
2: 8 when m maidens were gathered together 7227
4: 3 wailing; *and* m lay in sackcloth and ashes. 7227
8:17 m of the people of the land became Jews; 7227
Job 4: 3 thou hast instructed m, and thou hast 7227
11:19 yea, m shall make suit unto thee. 7227
13:23 **How m** *are* mine iniquities and 4100+3509.1
16: 2 I have heard m such *things:* miserable 7227
23:14 for me: and m such *things are* with him. 7227
41: 3 Will he **make** m supplications unto thee? 7235
Ps 3: 1 m *are* they that rise up against me. 7227
3: 2 M *there be* which say of my soul, *There is* 7227
4: 6 *There be* m that say, Who will shew us *any* 7227
18:16 he took me, he drew me out of m waters. 7227
22:12 M bulls have compassed me: strong *bulls* 7227
25:19 for they are m; and they hate me *with* cruel 7231
29: 3 the LORD *is* upon m waters. 7227
31:13 For I have heard the slander of m: fear *was* 7227
32:10 M sorrows *shall be* to the wicked: but 7227
34:12 *and* loveth m days, that *he* may see good? NIH
34:19 M *are* the afflictions of the righteous: but 7227
37:16 hath *is* better than the riches of m wicked. 7227
40: 3 m shall see *it,* and fear, and shall trust in 7227
40: 5 M, O LORD my God, *are* thy wonderful 7227
55:18 *was* against me: for there were m with me. 7227
56: 2 for *they be* m that fight against me, O thou 7227
61: 6 his years as **m generations**. 1755+1755+2050.1
71: 7 I am as a wonder unto m; but thou *art* my 7227
78:38 **m a time** turned he his anger away, and 7235
93: 4 high *is* mightier than the noise of m waters, 7227
106:43 M times did he deliver them; but 7227
110: 6 he shall wound the heads over m countries. 7227
119:84 **How m** *are* the days of thy 4100+3509.1
119:157 M *are* my persecutors and mine enemies; 7227
129: 1 **M a time** have they afflicted me from my 7227
129: 2 **M a time** have they afflicted me from my 7227
Pr 4:10 and the years of thy life shall be m. 7235
6:35 he rest content, though thou **givest** m gifts. 7235
7:26 For she hath cast down m wounded: yea, 7227
7:26 yea, m strong *men have been* slain by her. 3605
10:21 The lips of the righteous feed m: but 7227
14:20 own neighbour: but the rich *hath* m friends. 7227
19: 4 Wealth maketh m friends; but the poor is 7227
19: 6 M will intreat the favour of the prince: and 7227
19:21 *There are* m devices in a man's heart; 7227
28: 2 For the transgression of a land m *are* 7227
28:27 he that hideth his eyes shall have m a curse. 7227
29:26 M seek the ruler's favour; but *every* man's 7227
31:29 M daughters have done virtuously, but 7227
Ecc 5: 7 and m words *there are* also *divers* vanities: 7235
6: 3 an hundred *children,* and live m years, 7227
6: 3 so that the days of his years be m, and 7227
6:11 Seeing there be m things that increase 7235
7:29 but they have sought out m inventions. 7227
11: 1 for thou shalt find it after m days. 7230
11: 8 if a man live m years, *and* rejoice in them 7235
11: 8 the days of darkness; for they shall be m. 7235
12: 9 sought out, *and* set in order m proverbs. 7235
12:12 of making m books *there is* no end; and 7235
SS 8: 7 M waters cannot quench love, neither can 7227
Isa 1:15 yea, when ye **make** m prayers, I will not 7235
2: 3 m people shall go and say, Come ye, and 7227
2: 4 the nations, and shall rebuke m people: 7227
5: 9 Of a truth m houses shall be desolate, 7227
8: 7 strong and m, *even* the king of Assyria, and 7227
8:15 m among them shall stumble, and fall, and 7227
17:12 Woe to the multitude of m people, 7227
17:13 The nations shall rush like the rushing of m 7227
22: 9 of the city of David, that they are m: 7231
23:16 make sweet melody, sing m songs, that 7235
24:22 and after m days shall they be visited. 7230
31: 1 and trust in chariots, because *they are* m; 7227
32:10 M days and years shall ye be troubled, NIH
42:20 Seeing m *things,* but thou observest not; 7227
52:14 As m were astonied at thee; his visage *was* 7227
52:15 So shall he sprinkle m nations; the kings 7227
53:11 shall my righteous servant justify m; 7227
53:12 he bare the sin of m, and made intercession 7227
58:12 of **m generations;** 1755+1755+2050.1
60:15 a joy of **m generations**. 1755+1755+2050.1
61: 4 of **m generations**. 1755+1755+2050.1
66:16 and the slain of the LORD shall be m. 7231
Jer 3: 1 thou hast played the harlot with m lovers; 7227
5: 6 because their transgressions are m, *and* 7231
11:15 *seeing* she hath wrought lewdness *with* m, 7227
12:10 M pastors have destroyed my vineyard, 7227
13: 6 it came to pass after m days, that 7227
14: 7 for our backslidings are m; we have sinned 7231
16:16 Behold, I will send for m fishers, saith 7227
16:16 after will I send for m hunters, and 7227
20:10 For I heard the defaming of m, fear on 7227
22: 8 m nations shall pass by this city, and 7227
25:14 For m nations and great kings shall serve 7227
27: 7 *then* m nations and great kings shall serve 7227
28: 8 of old prophesied both against m countries, 7227
32:14 that they may continue m days. 7227
35: 7 that ye may live m days in the land where 7227
36:32 there were added besides unto them m like 7227
37:16 and Jeremiah had remained there m days; 7227
42: 2 (for we are left *but* a few of m, as thine 7235
46:11 in vain shalt thou **use** m medicines; *for* 7235
46:16 He **made** m to fall, yea, one fell upon 7235
50:41 m kings shall be raised up from the coasts 7227
51:13 O thou that dwellest upon m waters, 7227
La 1:22 for my sighs *are* m, and my heart *is* faint. 7227
Eze 3: 6 Not to m people of a strange speech and 7227
12:27 The vision that he seeth *is* for m days *to* 7227
16:41 upon thee in the sight of m women: 7227
17: 7 eagle with great wings and m feathers: 7227
17: 9 m people to pluck it up by the roots 7227
17:17 and building forts, to cut off m persons: 7227
19:10 and full of branches by reason of m waters. 7227
22:25 they have **made** her m widows in the midst 7235
26: 3 will cause m nations to come up against 7227
27: 3 *which art* a merchant of the people for m 7227
27:15 m isles *were* the merchandise of thine 7227
27:33 forth out of the seas, thou filledst m people; 7227
32: 3 net over thee with a company of m people; 7227
32: 9 I will also vex the hearts of m people, 7227
32:10 I will make m people amazed at thee, and 7227
33:24 we *are* m; the land is given us for 7227
37: 2 *there were* very m in the open valley; 7227
38: 6 and all his bands: *and* m people with thee. 7227
38: 8 After m days thou shalt be visited: in 7227
38: 8 *and is* gathered out of m people, against 7227
38: 9 and all thy bands, and m people with thee. 7227
38:15 thou, and m people with thee, all of them 7227
38:17 which prophesied in those days *m* years, NIH
38:22 and upon the m people that *are* with him, 7227
38:23 I will be known in the eyes of m nations, 7227
39:27 am sanctified in them in the sight of m 7227
43: 2 his voice *was* like a noise of m waters: and 7227
47: 7 at the bank of the river *were* very m trees 7227
47:10 as the fish of the great sea, exceeding m. 7227
Da 2:48 gave him m great gifts, and made him ruler 7690
8:25 in his heart, and by peace shall destroy m: 7227
8:26 up the vision; for *it shall be* for m days. 7227
9:27 he shall confirm the covenant with m *for* 7227
10:14 latter days: for yet the vision *is* for *m* days. NIH

Da 11:12 and he shall cast down **m** ten thousands: NIH
11:14 in those times there shall **m** stand up 7227
11:18 his face unto the isles, and shall take **m**: 7227
11:26 shall overflow: and **m** shall fall down slain. 7227
11:33 among the people shall instruct **m**: 7227
11:33 by captivity, and by spoil, **m** days. NIH
11:34 but **m** shall cleave to them with flatteries. 7227
11:39 he shall cause them to rule over **m**, and 7227
11:40 and with horsemen, and with **m** ships; 7227
11:41 and **m** *countries* shall be overthrown: 7227
11:44 to destroy, and utterly to make away **m**. 7227
12: 2 **m** of them that sleep in the dust of the earth 7227
12: 3 they that turn **m** to righteousness as 7227
12: 4 **m** shall run to and fro, and knowledge shall 7227
12:10 **M** shall be purified, and made white, and 7227
Hos 3: 3 unto her, Thou shalt abide for me **m** days; 7227
3: 4 For the children of Israel shall abide **m** 7227
8:11 Because Ephraim hath **made m** altars to 7235
Joel 2: 2 the years of **m generations**. 1755+1755+2050.1
Am 8: 3 *there shall be* **m** dead bodies in every place; 7227
Mic 4: 2 **m** nations shall come, and say, Come, and 7227
4: 3 he shall judge among **m** people, and 7227
4:11 Now also **m** nations are gathered against 7227
4:13 thou shalt beat in pieces **m** people: and 7227
5: 7 of **m** people as a dew from the LORD, 7227
5: 8 **m** people as a lion among the beasts of 7227
Na 1:12 Though *they be* quiet, and likewise **m**, 7227
3:15 **make** thyself **m** as the cankerworm, 3513
3:15 **make** thyself **m** as the locusts. 3513
Hab 2: 8 Because thou hast spoiled **m** nations, all 7227
2:10 to thy house by cutting off **m** people, 7227
Zec 2:11 **m** nations shall be joined to the LORD in 7227
7: 3 as I have done these **so m** years? 4100+3509.1
8:20 and the inhabitants of **m** cities: 7227
8:22 **m** people and strong nations shall come to 7227
Mal 2: 6 and did turn **m** away from iniquity. 7227
2: 8 ye have caused **m** to stumble at the law; 7227
Mt 3: 7 But when he saw **m** of the Pharisees and 4183
7:13 and **m** there be which go in thereat: 4183
7:22 **M** will say to me in that day, Lord, Lord, 4183
7:22 and in thy name done **m** wonderful works? 4183
8:11 That **m** shall come from the east and west, 4183
8:16 they brought unto him **m** *that were* 4183
8:30 off from them a herd of **m** swine feeding. 4183
9:10 **m** publicans and sinners came and sat down 4183
10:31 ye are of more value than **m** sparrows. 4183
13: 3 And he spake **m** *things* unto them in 4183
13:17 That **m** prophets and righteous *men* have 4183
13:58 And he did not **m** mighty works there, 4183
14:36 **as m as** touched were made perfectly 3745
15:30 and **m** others, and cast them *down* at Jesus' 4183
15:34 saith unto them, **How m** loaves have ye? 4214
16: 9 and **how m** baskets ye took up? 4214
16:10 and **how m** baskets ye took up? 4214
16:21 and suffer **m** *things* of the elders and 4183
19:30 But **m** *that are* first shall be last; and 4183
20:16 first last: for **m** be called, but few chosen. 4183
20:28 and to give his life a ransom for **m**. 4183
22: 9 and **as m as** ye shall find, 302+3745
22:10 gathered together all **as m as** they found, 3745
22:14 For **m** are called, but few *are* chosen. 4183
24: 5 For **m** shall come in my name, saying, I am 4183
24: 5 saying, I am Christ; and shall deceive **m**. 4183
24:10 And then shall **m** be offended, and 4183
24:11 And **m** false prophets shall rise, and 4183
24:11 prophets shall rise, and shall deceive **m**. 4183
24:12 shall abound, the love of **m** shall wax cold. 4183
25:21 **m** *things*: enter thou into the joy of thy 4183
25:23 **m** *things*: enter thou into the joy of thy 4183
26:28 which is shed for **m** for the remission of 4183
26:60 yea, though **m** false witnesses came, 4183
27:13 Hearest thou not **how m** things they 4214
27:19 have suffered **m** *things* this day in a dream 4183
27:52 and **m** bodies of saints which slept arose, 4183
27:53 into the holy city, and appeared unto **m**. 4183
27:55 And **m** women were there beholding afar 4183
Mk 1:34 And he healed **m** *that were* sick of divers 4183
1:34 of divers diseases, and cast out **m** devils; 4183
2: 2 And straightway **m** were gathered together, 4183
2:15 **m** publicans and sinners sat also together 4183
2:15 for there were **m**, and they followed him. 4183
3:10 For he had healed **m**; insomuch that *they* 4183
3:10 him for to touch him, **as m as** had plagues. 3745
4: 2 And he taught them **m** *things* by parables, 4183
4:33 And with **m** such parables spake he 4183
5: 9 saying, My name *is* Legion: for we are **m**. 4183
5:26 And had suffered **m** *things* of many 4183
5:26 And had suffered many *things* of **m** 4183
6: 2 and **m** hearing *him* were astonished, 4183
6:13 And they cast out **m** devils, and 4183
6:13 and anointed with oil **m** *that were* sick, and 4183
6:20 he did **m** *things*, and heard him gladly. 4183
6:31 for there were **m** coming and going, and 4183
6:33 and **m** knew him, and ran afoot thither out 4183
6:34 and he began to teach them **m** *things*. 4183
6:38 saith unto them, **How m** loaves have ye? 4214
6:56 **as m as** touched him were made 302+3745
7: 4 And **m** other *things* there be, which they 4183
7: 8 cups: and **m** other such like *things* ye do. 4183
7:13 and **m** such like *things* do ye. 4183
8: 5 he asked them, **How m** loaves have ye? 4214
8:19 **how m** baskets full of fragments took ye 4214
8:20 **how m** baskets full of fragments took ye 4214
8:31 that the Son of man must suffer **m** *things*, 4183
9:12 that he must suffer **m** *things*, and be set at 4183
9:26 insomuch that **m** said, He is dead. 4183
10:31 But **m** *that are* first shall be last; and 4183
10:45 and to give his life a ransom for **m**. 4183
10:48 And **m** charged him that he should hold his 4183
11: 8 And **m** spread their garments in the way: 4183
12: 5 and him they killed, and **m** others; 4183
12:41 and **m** *that were* rich cast in much. 4183
13: 6 For **m** shall come in my name, saying, I am 4183
13: 6 saying, I am *Christ*; and shall deceive **m**. 4183
14:24 of the new testament, which is shed for **m**. 4183
Mk 14:56 For **m** bare false witness against him, but 4183
15: 3 And the chief priests accused him of **m** 4183
15: 4 behold **how m** *things* they witness against 4214
15:41 **m** other *women* which came up with him 4183
Lk 1: 1 Forasmuch as **m** have taken in hand to set 4183
1:14 gladness; and **m** shall rejoice at his birth. 4183
1:16 And **m** of the children of Israel shall he 4183
2:34 for the fall and rising again of **m** in Israel; 4183
2:35 that the thoughts of **m** hearts may be 4183
3:18 And **m** other *things* in his exhortation 4183
4:25 **m** widows were in Israel in the days of 4183
4:27 And **m** lepers were in Israel in the time of 4183
4:41 And devils also came out of **m**, crying out, 4183
7:11 and **m** of his disciples went with him, and 2425
7:21 And in that *same* hour he cured **m** of *their* 4183
7:21 and unto **m** *that were* blind he gave sight. 4183
7:47 Her sins, which are **m**, are forgiven; 4183
8: 3 and Susanna, and **m** others, 4183
8:30 because **m** devils were entered into him. 4183
8:32 And there was there a herd of **m** swine 2425
9:22 The Son of man must suffer **m** *things*, and 4183
10:24 that **m** prophets and kings have desired to 4183
10:41 art careful and troubled about **m** *things*: 4183
11: 8 will rise and give him **as m as** he needeth. 3745
11:53 and to provoke him to speak of **m** *things*: 4183
12: 7 ye are of more value than **m** sparrows. 4183
12:19 thou hast much goods laid up for **m** years; 4183
12:47 to his will, shall be beaten with **m** *stripes*. 4183
13:24 for **m**, I say unto you, will seek to enter in, 4183
14:16 man made a great supper, and bade **m**: 4183
15:13 And not **m** days after the younger son 4183
15:17 **How m** hired *servants* of my father's have 4214
15:29 Lo, **these m** years do I serve thee, 5118
17:25 But first must he suffer **m** *things*, and 4183
21: 8 for **m** shall come in my name, saying, I am 4183
22:65 And **m** other *things* blasphemously spake 4183
23: 8 because *he* had heard **m** *things* of him; 4183
23: 9 Then he questioned *with* him in **m** words; 2425
Jn 1:12 But **as m as** received him, to them gave he 3745
2:12 and they continued there not **m** days. 4183
2:23 in the feast *day*, **m** believed in his name, 4183
4:39 And **m** of the Samaritans of that city 4183
4:41 And **m** moe believed because of his own 4183
6: 9 but what are they among **so m**? 5118
6:60 **M** therefore of his disciples, when they had 4183
6:66 From that *time* **m** of his disciples went 4183
7:31 And **m** of the people believed on him, and 4183
7:40 **M** of the people therefore, when they heard 4183
8:26 I have **m** *things* to say and to judge of you: 4183
8:30 As he spake these *words*, **m** believed on 4183
10:20 And **m** of them said, He hath a devil, and 4183
10:32 **M** good works have I shewed you from my 4183
10:41 And **m** resorted unto him, and said, John 4183
10:42 And **m** believed on him there. 4183
11:19 And **m** of the Jews came to Martha and 4183
11:45 Then **m** of the Jews which came to Mary, 4183
11:47 do we? for this man doeth **m** miracles. 4183
11:55 **m** went out of the country up to Jerusalem 4183
12:11 Because that by reason of him **m** of 4183
12:37 he had done **so m** miracles before them, 5118
12:42 Nevertheless among the *chief* rulers also **m** 4183
14: 2 In my Father's house are **m** mansions: if *it* 4183
16:12 I have yet **m** *things* to say unto you, but 4183
17: 2 life to **as m as** thou hast given him. 3739+3956
19:20 This title then read **m** of the Jews: for 4183
20:30 And **m** other signs truly did Jesus in 4183
21:11 and for **all** there were **so m**, *yet* was not 5118
21:25 And there are also **m** other *things* which 4183
Ac 1: 3 after his passion by **m** infallible proofs, 4183
1: 5 with the Holy Ghost not **m** days hence. 4183
2:39 **as m as** the Lord our God shall call. 302+3745
2:40 And with **m** other words did he testify and 4183
2:43 and **m** wonders and signs were done by 4183
3:24 that follow after, **as m as** have spoken, 3745
4: 4 Howbeit **m** of them which heard the word 4183
4: 6 **as m as** were of the kindred of the high 3745
4:34 for **as m as** were possessors of lands or 3745
5:11 and upon **as m as** heard these *things*. 3956
5:12 And by the hands of the apostles were **m** 4183
5:36 and all, **as m as** obeyed him, 3745
5:37 and all, *even* **as m as** obeyed him, 3745
8: 7 came out of **m** that were possessed *with* 4183
8: 7 *with them*: and **m** taken with palsies, 4183
8:25 preached the gospel in **m** villages of 4183
9:13 Lord, I have heard by **m** of this man, 4183
9:23 And after that **m** days were fulfilled, 2425
9:42 all Joppa; and **m** believed in the Lord. 4183
9:43 that he tarried **m** days in Joppa with one 2425
10:27 and found **m** *that were* come together. 4183
10:45 **as m as** came with Peter, because that on 3745
12:12 where **m** were gathered together praying. 2425
13:31 And he was seen **m** days of them which 4183
13:43 **m** of the Jews and religious proselytes 4183
13:48 **as m as** were ordained to eternal life 3745
14:21 and had taught **m**, they returned *again* to 2425
15:32 exhorted the brethren with **m** words, and 4183
15:35 the word of the Lord, with **m** others also. 4183
16:18 And this did she **m** days. But Paul, 4183
16:23 And when they had laid **m** stripes upon 4183
17:12 Therefore **m** of them believed; also of 4183
18: 8 and **m** of the Corinthians hearing believed, 4183
19:18 And **m** that believed came, and confessed, 4183
19:19 **M** also of them which used curious arts 2425
20: 8 And there were **m** lights in the upper 2425
20:19 of mind, and *with* **m** tears, and temptations, 4183
21:10 And as we tarried *there* **m** days, there came 4183
21:20 **how m** thousands of Jews there are which 4214
24:10 been of **m** years a judge unto this nation, 4183
24:17 Now after **m** years I came to bring alms to 4183
25: 7 and laid **m** and grievous complaints against 4183
25:14 And when they had been there **m** days, 4183
26: 9 that *I* ought to do **m** *things* contrary to 4183
26:10 and **m** of the saints did I shut up in prison, 4183
27: 7 And when we had sailed slowly **m** days, 2425
27:20 And when neither sun nor stars in **m** days 4183
Ac 28:10 Who also honoured us with **m** honours; and 4183
28:23 there came **m** to him into *his* lodging; 4183
Ro 2:12 For **as m as** have sinned without law shall 3745
2:12 **as m as** have sinned in the law shall be 3745
4:17 I have made thee a father of **m** nations,) 4183
4:18 that he might become the father of **m** 4183
5:15 For if through the offence of one **m** be 4183
5:15 Jesus Christ, hath abounded unto **m**. 4183
5:16 the free gift *is* of **m** offences unto 4183
5:19 For as by one man's disobedience **m** were 4183
5:19 by the obedience of one shall **m** be made 4183
6: 3 **so m** of us **as** were baptized into Jesus 3745
8:14 For **as m as** are led by the Spirit of God, 3745
8:29 that he might be the firstborn amongst **m** 4183
12: 4 For as we have **m** members in one body, 4183
12: 5 So we, being **m**, are one body in Christ, 4183
15:23 having a great desire these **m** years to come 4183
16: 2 for she hath been a succourer of **m**, and 4183
1Co 1:26 how that not **m** wise *men* after the flesh, 4183
1:26 not **m** mighty, not many noble, *are called*: 4183
1:26 not many mighty, not **m** noble, *are called*: 4183
4:15 in Christ, yet *have ye* not **m** fathers: 4183
8: 5 (as there be gods **m**, and lords many,) 4183
8: 5 (as there be gods many, and lords **m**,) 4183
10: 5 But with **m** of them God was not well 4183
10:17 For we being **m** are one bread, *and* 4183
10:33 but the *profit* of **m**, that they may be saved. 4183
11:30 For this cause **m** *are* weak and 4183
11:30 and sickly among you, and **m** sleep. 2425
12:12 and hath **m** members, and all the members 4183
12:12 of *that* one body, being **m**, are one body: 4183
12:14 For the body is not one member, but **m**. 4183
12:20 But now *are they* **m** members, yet *but* 4183
14:10 **so m** kinds of voices in the world, and 5118
16: 9 unto me, and *there are* **m** adversaries. 4183
2Co 1:11 **m** persons thanks may be given by many 4183
1:11 thanks may be given by **m** on our behalf. 4183
2: 4 anguish of heart I wrote unto you with **m** 4183
2: 6 this punishment, which *was inflicted* of **m**. 4183
2:17 For we are not as **m**, which corrupt 4183
4:15 of **m** redound to the glory of God. 4183
6:10 as poor, yet making **m** rich; as having 4183
8:22 oftentimes proved diligent in **m** *things*, 4183
9: 2 and your zeal hath provoked **very m**. 4183
9:12 is abundant also by **m** thanksgivings unto 4183
11:18 Seeing that **m** glory after the flesh, I will 4183
12:21 *that* I shall bewail **m** which have sinned 4183
Gal 1:14 And profited in the Jews' religion above **m** 4183
3: 4 Have ye suffered **so m** *things* in vain? if *it* 5118
3:10 For **as m as** are of the works of the law are 3745
3:16 *He* saith not, And to seeds, as of **m**; but 4183
3:27 For **as m** of you **as** have been baptized into 3745
4:27 for the desolate hath **m moe** children than 4183
6:12 **As m as** desire to make a fair shew in 3745
6:16 And **as m as** walk according to this rule, 3745
Php 1:14 And **m** of the brethren in the Lord, 4183
3:15 **as m as** *be* perfect, be thus minded: 3745
3:18 (For **m** walk, of whom I have told you 4183
Col 2: 1 *for* **as m as** have not seen my face in 3745
1Ti 6: 1 Let **as m** servants **as** are under the yoke 3745
6: 9 and *into* **m** foolish and hurtful lusts, 4183
6:10 pierced themselves through with **m** 4183
6:12 hast professed a good profession before **m** 4183
2Ti 1:18 in **how m** *things* he ministered *unto me* at 3745
2: 2 thou hast heard of me among **m** witnesses, 4183
Tit 1:10 For there are **m** unruly and vain talkers and 4183
Heb 2:10 by whom *are* all *things*, in bringing **m** sons 4183
5:11 Of whom we have **m things** to say, and 4183
7:23 And they truly were **m** priests, because 4183
9:28 was once offered to bear the sins of **m**; 4183
11:12 *so* **m** as the stars of the sky in multitude, NIG
12:15 up trouble *you*, and thereby **m** be defiled; 4183
Jas 3: 1 My brethren, be not **m** masters, 4183
3: 2 For *in* **m** *things* we offend all. If any *man* 4183
2Pe 2: 2 And **m** shall follow their pernicious ways; 4183
1Jn 2:18 even now are there **m** antichrists; 4183
4: 1 **m** false prophets are gone out into 4183
2Jn 1: 7 For **m** deceivers are entered into the world, 4183
1:12 Having **m** *things* to write unto you, I would 4183
3Jn 1:13 I had **m** *things* to write, 4183
Rev 1:15 and his voice as the sound of **m** waters. 4183
2:24 **as m as** have not this doctrine, and 3745
3:19 **As m as** I love, I rebuke and chasten: 1437+3745
5:11 I heard the voice of **m** angels round about 4183
8:11 and **m** men died of the waters, because 4183
9: 9 of chariots of **m** horses running to battle. 4183
10:11 Thou must prophesy again before **m** 4183
13:15 cause that **as m as** would not worship 3745
14: 2 as the voice of **m** waters, and as the voice 4183
17: 1 the great whore that sitteth upon **m** waters: 4183
18:17 and sailers, and **as m as** trade by sea, 3745
19: 6 and as the voice of **m** waters, and as 4183
19:12 of fire, and on his head *were* **m** crowns; 4183

MAOCH (1)

1Sa 27: 2 unto Achish, the son of **M**, king of Gath. 4582

MAON (7) [MAONITES]

Jos 15:55 **M**, Carmel, and Ziph, and Juttah, 4584
1Sa 23:24 and his men *were* in the wilderness of **M**, 4584
23:25 a rock, and abode in the wilderness of **M**. 4584
23:25 pursued after David *in* the wilderness of **M**. 4584
25: 2 *there was* a man in **M**, whose possessions 4584
1Ch 2:45 the son of Shammai *was* **M**: and Maon *was* 4584
2:45 and **M** *was* the father of Beth-zur. 4584

MAONITES (1) [MAON]

Jdg 10:12 the Amalekites, and the **M**, did oppress 4584

MAR (6) [MARRED]

Lev 19:27 neither shalt thou **m** the corners of thy 7843
Ru 4: 6 for myself, lest I **m** mine own inheritance: 7843
1Sa 6: 5 and images of your mice that **m** the land; 7843
2Ki 3:19 **m** every good piece of land with stones. 3510

Job 30:13 They m my path, they set forward my 5420
Jer 13: 9 After this manner will I m the pride of 7843

MARA (1)

Ru 1:20 unto them, Call me not Naomi, call me M: 4755

MARAH (5)

Ex 15:23 when they came to M, they could not drink 4785
15:23 they could not drink of the waters of M, 4785
15:23 the name of it was called M. 4785
Nu 33: 8 the wilderness of Etham, and pitched in M. 4785
33: 9 they removed from M, and came unto 4785

MARALAH (1)

Jos 19:11 M, and reached to Dabbasheth, and 4831

MARAN-ATHA (1)

1Co 16:22 Lord Jesus Christ, let him be anathema, M. *3134*

MARBLE (5)

1Ch 29: 2 and m stones in abundance. 7893
Est 1: 6 and purple to silver rings and pillars of m: 8336
1: 6 of red, and blue, and white, and black m. 8336
SS 5:15 His legs *are as* pillars of m, set upon 8336
Rev 18:12 and of brass, and iron, and m, *3139*

MARCH (5) [MARCHED, MARCHEDST]

Ps 68: 7 when thou didst m through the wilderness; 6805
Jer 46:22 for they shall m with an army, and 1980
Joel 2: 7 they shall m every one on his ways, and 1980
Hab 1: 6 which *shall* m through the breadth of 1980
3:12 Thou didst m through the land in 6805

MARCHED (1) [MARCH]

Ex 14:10 and behold, the Egyptians m after them; 5265

MARCHEDST (1) [MARCH]

Jdg 5: 4 when thou m out of the field of Edom, 6805

MARCUS (3) [MARK]

Col 4:10 and M, sister's son to Barnabas, *3138*
Phm 1:24 M, Aristarchus, Demas, Lucas, *3138*
1Pe 5:13 *you,* saluteth you; and *so doth* M my son. *3138*

MARDUK See MERODACH

MARESHAH (8)

Jos 15:44 Keilah, and Achzib, and M; nine cities with 4762
1Ch 2:42 and the sons of M the father of Hebron. 4762
4:21 Laadah the father of M, and the families of 4762
2Ch 11: 8 And Gath, and M, and Ziph, 4762
14: 9 three hundred chariots; and came unto M. 4762
14:10 in array in the valley of Zephathah at M. 4762
20:37 Eliezer the son of Dodavah of M 4762
Mic 1:15 bring an heir unto thee, O inhabitant of M: 4762

MARINERS (5)

Eze 27: 8 of Zidon and Arvad were thy m: 7751
27: 9 all the ships of the sea with their m were in 4419
27:27 thy m, and thy pilots, thy calkers, and 4419
27:29 the oar, the m, *and* all the pilots of the sea, 4419
Jnh 1: 5 the m were afraid, and cried every man 4419

MARISHES (1)

Eze 47:11 and the m thereof shall not be healed; 1360

MARITAL UNFAITHFULNESS See FORNICATION

MARK (37) [LANDMARK, LANDMARKS, MARCUS, MARKED, MARKEST, MARKETH, MARKS, WAYMARKS]

Ge 4:15 the LORD set a m upon Cain, lest any 226
Ru 3: 4 that thou shalt m the place where he shall 3045
1Sa 20:20 on the side *thereof,* as *though* I shot at a m. 4307
2Sa 13:28 M ye now when Amnon's heart is merry 7200
1Ki 20: 7 said, M, I pray you, and see how this *man* 3045
20:22 and m, and see what thou doest: 3045
Job 7:20 why hast thou set me as a m against thee, 4645
16:12 me to pieces, and set me up for his m. 4307
18: 2 of words? m, and afterwards we will speak. 995
21: 5 M me, and be astonished, and 413+6437
33:31 M well, O Job, hearken unto me: hold thy 7181
39: 1 *or* canst thou m when the hinds do calve? 8104
Ps 37:37 M the perfect *man,* and behold the upright: 8104
48:13 M ye well her bulwarks, consider her 7896
56: 6 they hide themselves, they m my steps, 8104
130: 3 LORD, shouldest m iniquities, O Lord, 8104
La 3:12 his bow, and set me as a m for the arrow. 4307
Eze 9: 4 set a m upon the foreheads of 8420+8427
9: 6 not near any man upon whom *is* the m; 8420
44: 5 m well, and behold with thine eyes, 3820+7760
44: 5 m well the entering in of the house, 3820+7760
Ac 12:12 the mother of John, whose surname was M; *3138*
12:25 with *them* John, whose surname was M. *3138*
15:37 with *them* John, whose surname was M. *3138*
15:39 and *so* Barnabas took M, and sailed unto *3138*
Ro 16:17 m them which cause divisions and offences *4648*
Php 3:14 I press toward the m for the prize of *4649*
3:17 and m them which walk so as ye have us *4648*
2Ti 4:11 Take M, and bring *him* with thee: for he is *3138*
Rev 13:16 to receive a m in their right hand, or in their *5480*
13:17 save he that had the m, or the name of *5480*
14: 9 and receive *his* m in his forehead, or in his *5480*
14:11 whosoever receiveth the m of his name. *5480*
15: 2 and over his image, and over his m, *5480*
16: 2 upon the men which had the m of the beast, *5480*
19:20 them that had received the m of the beast, *5480*
20: 4 neither had received *his* m upon their *5480*

MARKED (6) [MARK]

1Sa 1:12 before the LORD, that Eli m her mouth. 8104
Job 22:15 Hast thou m the old way which wicked 8104
24:16 *which* they had m for themselves in 2856
Jer 2:22 *yet* thine iniquity *is* m before me, 3799
23:18 who hath m his word, and heard *it?* 7181
Lk 14: 7 when he m how they chose out the chief *1907*

MARKEST (1) [MARK]

Job 10:14 thou m me, and thou wilt not acquit me 8104

MARKET (7) [MARKETPLACE, MARKET-PLACE, MARKETPLACES, MARKETS]

Eze 27:13 of men and vessels of brass in thy m. 4627
27:17 they traded in thy m wheat of Minnith, and 4627
27:19 cassia, and calamus, were in thy m. 4627
27:25 ships of Tarshish did sing of thee *in* thy m: 4627
Mk 7: 4 And *when they come* from the m, except they *58*
Jn 5: 2 Now there is at Jerusalem by the sheep *m* a NIG
Ac 17:17 in the m daily with them that met with *him.* *58*

MARKETH (3) [MARK]

Job 33:11 my feet in the stocks, he m all my paths. 8104
Isa 44:13 he m it out with a line; he fitteth it with 8388
44:13 he m it out with the compass, and 8388

MARKETPLACE, MARKET-PLACE (3) [MARKET, PLACE]

Mt 20: 3 and saw others standing idle in the m, *58*
Lk 7:32 They are like unto children sitting in the m, *58*
Ac 16:19 and drew *them* into the m unto the rulers, *58*

MARKETPLACES (1) [MARKET, PLACE]

Mk 12:38 long clothing, and *love* salutations in the m, *58*

MARKETS (4) [MARKET]

Mt 11:16 It is like unto children sitting in the m, and *58*
23: 7 And greetings in the m, and to be called of *58*
Lk 11:43 in the synagogues, and greetings in the m. *58*
20:46 and love greetings in the m, and the highest *58*

MARKS (2) [MARK]

Lev 19:28 for the dead, nor print any m upon you: 7085
Gal 6:17 for I bear in my body the m of the Lord *4742*

MAROTH (1)

Mic 1:12 For the inhabitant of M waited carefully for 4796

MARRED (5) [MAR]

Isa 52:14 his visage *was* so m more than *any* man, 4893
Jer 13: 7 behold, the girdle was m, it was profitable 7843
18: 4 the vessel that he made of clay was m in 7843
Na 2: 2 them out, and m their vine branches. 7843
Mk 2:22 the wine is spilled, and the bottles will be m. *622*

MARRIAGE (19) [MARRY]

Ex 21:10 her raiment, and her duty of m, shall he not 5772
Ps 78:63 and their maidens were not given to m. 1984
Mt 22: 2 a certain king, which made a m for his son, *1062*
22: 4 and all *things are* ready: come unto the m. *1062*
22: 9 and as many as ye shall find, bid to the m. *1062*
22:30 they neither marry, nor are given in m, *1547*
24:38 and drinking, marrying and giving in m, *1547*
25:10 *that were* ready went in with him to the m: *1062*
Mk 12:25 they neither marry, nor are given in m; *1061*
Lk 17:27 they married *wives,* they were given in m, *1547*
20:34 of this world marry, and are given in m: *1548*
20:35 the dead, neither marry, nor are given in m: *1548*
Jn 2: 1 And the third day there was a m in Cana of *1062*
2: 2 was called, and his disciples, to the m. *1062*
1Co 7:38 So then he that giveth *her* in m doeth well; *1547*
7:38 but he that giveth *her* not in m doeth better. *1547*
Heb 13: 4 M *is* honourable in all, and the bed *1062*
Rev 19: 7 for the m of the Lamb is come, and his wife *1062*
19: 9 are called unto the m supper of the Lamb. *1062*

MARRIAGES (3) [MARRY]

Ge 34: 9 make ye m with us, *and* give your 2859
Dt 7: 3 Neither shalt thou make m with them; 2859
Jos 23:12 shall make m with them, and go in unto 2859

MARRIED (30) [MARRY]

Ge 19:14 which m his daughters, and said, Up, get ye 3947
Ex 21: 3 if he *were* m, then his wife shall go 802+1167
Lev 22:12 If the priest's daughter also be *m* unto a NIH
Nu 12: 1 of the Ethiopian woman whom he had m: 3947
12: 1 for he had m an Ethiopian woman. 3947
36: 3 *if* they be m to any of the sons of 802+3807.1
36:11 m unto their father's brothers' 802+1961+3807.1
36:12 *And* they were m into 802+1961+3807.1
Dt 22:22 If a man be found lying with a woman m to 1166
24: 1 m her, and it come to pass that she find no 1166
1Ch 2:21 whom he m when he *was* threescore years 3947
2Ch 13:21 m fourteen wives, and 5375+3807.1
Ne 13:23 In those days also saw I Jews *that* had m 3427
Pr 30:23 For an odious *woman* when she is m; and 1166
Isa 54: 1 desolate than the children of the m wife, 1166
62: 4 delighteth in thee, and thy land shall be m. 1166
Jer 3:14 saith the LORD; for I am m unto you: 1166
Mal 2:11 and hath m the daughter of a strange god. 1166
Mt 22:25 when he had m *a wife,* deceased, and, *1060*
Mk 6:17 his brother Philip's wife: for he had m her. *1060*
10:12 and be m to another, she committeth *1060*
Lk 14:20 I have m a wife, and therefore I cannot *1060*
17:27 they m *wives,* they were given in marriage, *1060*
Ro 7: 3 husband liveth, she be m to another man, *1096*
7: 3 though she be m to another man. *1096*
7: 4 that ye should be m to another, *even* to him *1096*
1Co 7:10 And unto the m I command, *yet* not I, but *1060*
7:33 But he that is m careth for the *things that* *1060*
7:34 she that is m careth for the *things* of *1060*
7:39 she is at liberty to be m to whom she will; *1060*

MARRIETH (4) [MARRY]

Isa 62: 5 For *as* a young man m a virgin, *so* shall thy 1166
Mt 19: 9 whoso m her *which is* put away doth *1060*
Lk 16:18 and m another, committeth adultery: *1060*
16:18 whosoever m her that is put away from *her* *1060*

MARROW (5)

Job 21:24 and his bones are moistened with m. 4221
Ps 63: 5 My soul shall be satisfied as *with* m and 2459
Pr 3: 8 be health to thy navel, and m to thy bones. 8250
Isa 25: 6 of wines on the lees, of fat things full of m, 4229
Heb 4:12 and of the joints and m, and *is* a discerner *3452*

MARRY (22) [MARRIAGE, MARRIAGES, MARRIED, MARRIETH, MARRYING, UNMARRIED]

Ge 38: 8 and m her, and raise up seed to thy brother. 2992
Nu 36: 6 m to whom they think best; 802+1961+3807.1
36: 6 of their father shall they m. 802+1961+3807.1
Dt 25: 5 the wife of the dead shall not m without 1961
Isa 62: 5 marrieth a virgin, *so* shall thy sons m thee: 1166
Mt 5:32 whosoever shall m her that is divorced *1060*
19: 9 and shall m another, committeth adultery: *1060*
19:10 so with *his* wife, it is not good to m. *1060*
22:24 his brother shall m his wife, and raise up *1918*
22:30 For in the resurrection they neither m, *1060*
Mk 10:11 and m another, committeth adultery against *1060*
12:25 they neither m, nor are given in marriage; *1060*
Lk 20:34 The children of this world m, and are given *1060*
20:35 neither m, nor are given in marriage: *1060*
1Co 7: 9 But if they cannot contain, let them m: *1060*
7: 9 for it is better to m than to burn. *1060*
7:28 But and if thou m, thou hast not sinned; *1060*
7:28 and if a virgin m, she hath not sinned. *1060*
7:36 do what he will, he sinneth not: let them m. *1060*
1Ti 4: 3 Forbidding to m, *and commanding* to *1060*
5:11 *to* wax wanton against Christ, they will m; *1060*
5:14 I will therefore that the younger *women* m, *1060*

MARRYING (2) [MARRY]

Ne 13:27 to transgress against our God in m strange 3427
Mt 24:38 and drinking, m and giving in marriage, *1060*

MARS' HILL (1) [AREOPAGUS]

Ac 17:22 Then Paul stood in the midst of M, and *697*

MARSENA (1)

Est 1:14 Tarshish, Meres, M, *and* Memucan, 4826

MARSHES See MARISHES

MART (1)

Isa 23: 3 *is* her revenue; and she is a m of nations. 5505

MARTHA (13)

Lk 10:38 a certain woman named M received him *3136*
10:40 But M was cumbered about much serving, *3136*
10:41 and said unto her, M, Martha, *3136*
10:41 and said unto her, Martha, M, *3136*
Jn 11: 1 the town of Mary and her sister M. *3136*
11: 5 Now Jesus loved M, and her sister, and *3136*
11:19 And many of the Jews came to M and *3136*
11:20 Then M, as soon as she heard that Jesus *3136*
11:21 Then said M unto Jesus, Lord, if thou hadst *3136*
11:24 M saith unto him, I know that he shall rise *3136*
11:30 but was in *that* place where M met him. *3136*
11:39 M, the sister of him that was dead, saith *3136*
12: 2 they made him a supper; and M served: *3136*

MARTYR (2) [MARTYRS]

Ac 22:20 And when the blood of thy m Stephen was *3144*
Rev 2:13 days wherein Antipas *was* my faithful m, *3144*

MARTYRS (1) [MARTYR]

Rev 17: 6 and with the blood of the m of Jesus: *3144*

MARVEL (11) [MARVELLED, MARVELLOUS, MARVELLOUSLY, MARVELS]

Ecc 5: 8 justice in a province, m not at the matter: 8539
Mk 5:20 Jesus had done for him: and all *men* did m. *2296*
Jn 3: 7 M not that I said unto thee, Ye must be *2296*
5:20 greater works than these, that ye may m. *2296*
5:28 M not at this: for the hour is coming, in *2296*
7:21 I have done one work, and ye all m. *2296*
Ac 3:12 Ye men of Israel, why m ye at this? *2296*
2Co 11:14 And no m; for Satan himself is transformed *2298*
Gal 1: 6 I m that you are so soon removed from him *2296*
1Jn 3:13 M not, my brethren, if the world hate you. *2296*
Rev 17: 7 said unto me, Wherefore didst thou m? *2296*

MARVELLED (23) [MARVEL]

Ge 43:33 to his youth: and the men m one at another. 8539
Ps 48: 5 They saw *it, and* so they m; they were 8539
Mt 8:10 When Jesus heard *it,* he m, and said to *2296*
8:27 But the men m, saying, What manner of *2296*
9: 8 But when the multitudes saw *it,* they m, *2296*
9:33 and the multitudes m, saying, It was never *2296*
21:20 And when the disciples saw *it,* they m, *2296*
22:22 When they had heard *these words,* they m, *2296*
27:14 insomuch that the governor m greatly. *2296*
Mk 6: 6 And he m because of their unbelief. And he *2296*
12:17 *things* that are God's. And they m at him. *2296*
15: 5 yet answered nothing; so that Pilate m. *2296*
15:44 And Pilate m if he were already dead: and *2296*
Lk 1:21 and m that he tarried *so* long in the temple. *2296*
1:63 saying, His name is John. And they m all. *2296*
2:33 his mother m at those *things* which were *2296*
7: 9 When Jesus heard these *things,* he m at *2296*
11:38 And when the Pharisee saw *it,* he m that he *2296*
20:26 and they m at his answer, and held their *2296*
Jn 4:27 and m that he talked with *the* woman: *2296*
7:15 And the Jews m, saying, How knoweth this *2296*
Ac 2: 7 And they were all amazed and m, *2296*
4:13 were unlearned and ignorant men, they m; *2296*

MARVELLOUS (24) [MARVEL]

1Ch 16:12 Remember his m works that he hath done, 6381

M

1Ch 16:24 his m works among all nations. 6381
Job 5: 9 unsearchable; m things without number: 6381
10:16 and again thou shewest thyself m upon me. 6381
Ps 9: 1 I will shew forth all thy m works. 6381
17: 7 Shew thy m lovingkindness, O thou that 6395
31:21 for he hath shewed me his m kindness in a 6381
78:12 M things did he in the sight of their 6382
98: 1 for he hath done m things: his right hand, 6381
105: 5 Remember his m works that he hath done; 6381
118:23 is the LORD'S doing; it is m in our eyes. 6381
139:14 m are thy works; and that my soul knoweth 6395
Isa 29:14 I will proceed to do a m work amongst this 6381
29:14 this people, even a m work and a wonder: 6381
Da 11:36 shall speak m things against the God of 6381
Mic 7:15 of Egypt will I shew unto him m things. 6381
Zec 8: 6 If it be m in the eyes of the remnant of this 6381
8: 6 these days, should it also be m in my eyes? 6381
Mt 21:42 is the Lord's doing, and it is m in our eyes? 2298
Mk 12:11 the Lord's doing, and it is m in our eyes? 2298
Jn 9:30 Why herein is a m thing, that ye know not 2298
1Pe 2: 9 called you out of darkness into his m light: 2298
Rev 15: 1 I saw another sign in heaven, great and m, 2298
15: 3 saying, Great and m are thy works, 2298

MARVELLOUSLY (3) [MARVEL]
2Ch 26:15 for he was m helped, till he was strong. 6381
Job 37: 5 God thundereth m with his voice; 6381
Hab 1: 5 the heathen, and regard, and wonder m: 8539

MARVELS (1) [MARVEL]
Ex 34:10 before all thy people I will do m, such as 6381

MARY (54)
Mt 1:16 And Jacob begat Joseph the husband of M, 3137
1:18 When as his mother M was espoused to 3137
1:20 fear not to take unto thee M thy wife: 3137
2:11 they saw the young child with M his 3137
13:55 is not his mother called M? and 3137
27:56 Among which was M Magdalene, and 3137
27:56 and M the mother of James and Joses, and 3137
27:61 And there was M Magdalene, and the other 3137
27:61 was Mary Magdalene, and the other M, 3137
28: 1 came M Magdalene and the other Mary to 3137
28: 1 and the other M to see the sepulchre. 3137
Mk 6: 3 the son of M, the brother of James, and 3137
15:40 among whom was M Magdalene, and 3137
15:40 and M the mother of James the less and 3137
15:47 And M Magdalene and Mary the mother of 3137
15:47 M the mother of Joses beheld where he was 3137
16: 1 M Magdalene, and Mary the mother of 3137
16: 1 and M the mother of James, and Salome, 3137
16: 9 he appeared first to M Magdalene, out of 3137
Lk 1:27 of David; and the virgin's name was M. 3137
1:30 And the angel said unto her, Fear not, M: 3137
1:34 Then said M unto the angel, How shall this 3137
1:38 And M said, Behold the handmaid of 3137
1:39 And M arose in those days, and went into 3137
1:41 when Elisabeth heard the salutation of M, 3137
1:46 And M said, My soul doth magnify 3137
1:56 And M abode with her about three months, 3137
2: 5 To be taxed with M his espoused wife, 3137
2:16 and found M, and Joseph, and the babe 3137
2:19 But M kept all these things, and 3137
2:34 and said unto M his mother, Behold, 3137
8: 2 and infirmities, M called Magdalene, 3137
10:39 And she had a sister called M, which also 3137
10:42 and M hath chosen that good part, 3137
24:10 It was M Magdalene, and Joanna, and 3137
24:10 and M the mother of James, and other 3137
Jn 11: 1 the town of M and her sister Martha. 3137
11: 2 (It was that M which anointed the Lord 3137
11:19 many of the Jews came to Martha and M, 3137
11:20 and met him: but M sat still in the house. 3137
11:28 and called M her sister secretly, saying, 3137
11:31 and comforted her, when they saw M, 3137
11:32 Then when M was come where Jesus was, 3137
11:45 Then many of the Jews which came to M, 3137
12: 3 Then took M a pound of ointment of 3137
19:25 M the wife of Cleophas, and 3137
19:25 the wife of Cleophas, and M Magdalene. 3137
20: 1 The first day of the week cometh M 3137
20:11 But M stood without at the sepulchre 3137
20:16 Jesus saith unto her, M. She turned herself, 3137
20:18 M Magdalene came and told the disciples 3137
Ac 1:14 and M the mother of Jesus, and with his 3137
12:12 came to the house of M the mother of John, 3137
Ro 16: 6 Greet M, who bestowed much labour on us. 3137

MASCHIL (13)
Ps 32: T A Psalm of David, M. 4905
42: T chief Musician, M, for the sons of Korah. 4905
44: T chief Musician for the sons of Korah, M. 4905
45: T for the sons of Korah, M, A Song of loves. 4905
52: T the chief Musician, M, A Psalm of David, 4905
53: T upon Mahalath, M, A Psalm of David. 4905
54: T M, A Psalm of David, when the Ziphims 4905
55: T on Neginoth, M, A Psalm of David. 4905
74: T M of Asaph. 4905
78: T M of Asaph. 4905
88: T M of Heman the Ezrahite. 4905
89: T M of Ethan the Ezrahite. 4905
142: T M of David; A Prayer when he was in 4905

MASH (1)
Ge 10:23 of Aram; Uz, and Hul, and Gether, and M. 4851

MASHAL (1)
1Ch 6:74 M with her suburbs, and Abdon with her 4913

MASONS (7)
2Sa 5:11 and carpenters, and m: 68+2796+7023
2Ki 12:12 to m, and hewers of stone, and to buy 1443
22: 6 m, and to buy timber and hewn stone to 1443
1Ch 14: 1 of cedars, with m and carpenters, 2796+7023
1Ch 22: 2 he set m to hew wrought stones to build 2672
2Ch 24:12 hired m and carpenters to repair the house 2672
Ezr 3: 7 They gave money also unto the m, and 2672

MASREKAH (2)
Ge 36:36 and Samlah of M reigned in his stead. 4957
1Ch 1:47 Samlah of M reigned in his stead. 4957

MASSA (2)
Ge 25:14 And Mishma, and Dumah, and M, 4854
1Ch 1:30 and Dumah, M, Hadad, and Tema, 4854

MASSAH (4)
Ex 17: 7 he called the name of the place M, and 4532
Dt 6:16 LORD your God, as ye tempted him in M. 4532
9:22 and at M, and at Kibroth-hattaavah, 4532
33: 8 whom thou didst prove at M, and 4532

MAST (2) [MASTS]
Pr 23:34 or as he that lieth upon the top of a m. 2260
Isa 33:23 they could not well strengthen their m, 8650

MASTER (157) [MASTER'S, MASTERBUILDER, MASTERIES, MASTERS, MASTERS', MASTERY, SCHOOLMASTER, SHEEPMASTER, SHIPMASTER, TASKMASTERS]
Ge 24: 9 his hand under the thigh of Abraham his m, 113
24:10 took ten camels of the camels of his m, 113
24:10 for all the goods of his m were in his hand: 113
24:12 O LORD God of my m Abraham, I pray 113
24:12 and shew kindness unto my m Abraham. 113
24:14 that thou hast shewed kindness unto my m. 113
24:27 Blessed be the LORD God of my m 113
24:27 who hath not left destitute my m of his 113
24:35 And the LORD hath blessed my m greatly; 113
24:36 Sarah my master's wife bare a son to my m 113
24:37 my m made me swear, saying, Thou shalt 113
24:39 I said unto my m, Peradventure the woman 113
24:42 and said, O LORD God of my m Abraham, 113
24:48 blessed the LORD God of my m Abraham, 113
24:49 if ye will deal kindly and truly with my m, 113
24:54 and he said, Send me away unto my m. 113
24:56 send me away that I may go to my m. 113
24:65 the servant had said, It is my m: therefore 113
39: 2 he was in the house of his m the Egyptian. 113
39: 3 his m saw that the LORD was with him, 113
39: 8 my m wotteth not what is with me in 113
39:19 when his m heard the words of his wife, 113
39:20 Joseph's m took him, and put him into 113
Ex 21: 4 If his m have given him a wife, and she have 113
21: 5 I love my m, my wife, and my children; 113
21: 6 Then his m shall bring him unto the judges; 113
21: 6 his m shall bore his ear through with an aul; 113
21: 8 If she please not her m, who hath betrothed 113
21:32 he shall give unto their m thirty shekels of 113
22: 8 the m of the house shall be brought unto 1167
Dt 23:15 Thou shalt not deliver unto his m the servant 113
23:15 which is escaped from his m unto thee: 113
Jdg 19:11 the servant said unto his m, Come, I pray 113
19:12 his m said unto him, We will not turn aside 113
19:22 spake to the m of the house, the old 376+1167
19:23 the man, the m of the house, went out unto 1167
1Sa 20:38 gathered up the arrows, and came to his m. 113
24: 6 forbid that I should do this thing unto my m, 113
25:10 days that break away every man from his m. 113
25:14 out of the wilderness to salute our m; 113
25:17 for evil is determined against our m, and 113
26:16 to die, because ye have not kept your m, 113
29: 4 should he reconcile himself unto his m? 113
30:13 my m left me, because three days agone I 113
30:15 nor deliver me into the hands of my m, and 113
2Sa 2: 7 for your m Saul is dead, and also the house 113
1Ki 22:17 the LORD said, These have no m: let them 113
2Ki 2: 3 will take away thy m from thy head to day? 113
2: 5 will take away thy m from thy head to day? 113
2:16 let them go, we pray thee, and seek thy m: 113
5: 1 was a great man with his m, and honourable, 113
5:18 that when my m goeth into the house of 113
5:20 my m hath spared Naaman this Syrian, 113
5:22 My m hath sent me, saying, Behold, 113
5:25 he went in, and stood before his m. 113
6: 5 he cried, and said, Alas, m, for it was 113
6:15 unto him, Alas, my m, how shall we do? 113
6:22 they may eat and drink, and go to their m. 113
6:23 he sent them away, and they went to their m. 113
8:14 he departed from Elisha, and came to his m; 113
9: 7 thou shalt smite the house of Ahab thy m, 113
9:31 she said, Had Zimri peace, who slew his m? 113
10: 9 I conspired against my m, and slew him: 113
18:27 Hath my m sent me to thy master, and 113
18:27 Hath my master sent me to thy m, and 113
19: 4 whom the king of Assyria his m hath sent to 113
19: 6 Thus shall ye say to your m, Thus saith 113
1Ch 12:19 He will fall to his m Saul to the jeopardy of 113
15:27 Chenaniah the m of the song with 8269
2Ch 18:16 the LORD said, These have no m; let them 113
Job 3:19 are there; and the servant is free from his m. 113
Pr 27:18 he that waiteth on his m shall be honoured. 113
30:10 Accuse not a servant unto his m, lest he 113
Isa 24: 2 the priest; as with the servant, so with his m; 113
36: 8 to my m the king of Assyria, and I will give 113
36:12 Hath my m sent me to thy master and to thee 113
36:12 Hath my master sent me to thy m and to thee 113
37: 4 whom the king of Assyria his m hath sent to 113
37: 6 Thus shall ye say unto your m, Thus saith 113
Da 1: 3 the king spake unto Ashpenaz the m of his 7227
4: 9 m of the magicians, because I know that 7229
5:11 made m of the magicians, astrologers, 7229
Mal 1: 6 honoureth his father, and a servant his m: 113
1: 6 if I be a m, where is my fear? saith 113
2:12 the m and the scholar, out of 5782
Mt 8:19 certain scribe came, and said unto him, M, 1320
9:11 Why eateth your M with publicans and 1320
10:24 The disciple is not above his m, nor 1320
Mt 10:25 enough for the disciple that he be as his m, 1320
10:25 If they have called the m of the house 3617
12:38 and of the Pharisees answered, saying, M, 1320
17:24 and said, Doth not your m pay tribute? 1320
19:16 one came and said unto him, Good M, 1320
22:16 saying, M, we know that thou art true, and 1320
22:24 Saying, M, Moses said, If a man die, 1320
22:36 M, which is the great commandment in 1320
23: 8 for one is your M, even Christ; 2519
23:10 for one is your M, even Christ. 2519
26:18 and say unto him, The M saith, My time is 1320
26:25 betrayed him, answered and said, M, is it I? 4461
26:49 he came to Jesus, and said, Hail, m; 4461
Mk 4:38 and they awake him, and say unto him, M, 1320
5:35 why troublest thou the M any further? 1320
9: 5 And Peter answered and said to Jesus, M, 4461
9:17 one of the multitude answered and said, M, 1320
9:38 And John answered him, saying, M, 1320
10:17 kneeled to him, and asked him, Good M, 1320
10:20 And he answered and said unto him, M, 1320
10:35 of Zebedee, come unto him, saying, M, 1320
11:21 M, behold, the fig tree which thou cursedst 4461
12:14 they say unto him, M, we know that thou 1320
12:19 M, Moses wrote unto us, If a man's brother 1320
12:32 unto him, Well, M, thou hast said the truth: 1320
13: 1 M, see what manner of stones and 1320
13:35 for ye know not when the m of the house 2962
14:14 The M saith, Where is the guestchamber, 1320
14:45 straightway to him, and saith, M, master; 4461
14:45 straightway to him, and saith, Master, m; 4461
Lk 3:12 and said unto him, M, what shall we do? 1320
5: 5 M, we have toiled all the night, and 1988
6:40 The disciple is not above his m: but 1320
6:40 every one that is perfect shall be as his m. 1320
7:40 to say unto thee. And he saith, M, say on. 1320
8:24 awoke him, saying, M, master, we perish. 1988
8:24 awoke him, saying, Master, m, we perish. 1988
8:45 M, the multitude throng thee and 1988
8:49 Thy daughter is dead; trouble not the M. 1320
9:33 from him, Peter said unto Jesus, M, 1988
9:38 saying, M, I beseech thee, look upon my 1320
9:49 And John answered and said, M, we saw 1988
10:25 stood up, and tempted him, saying, M, 1320
11:45 one of the lawyers, and said unto him, M, 1320
12:13 M, speak to my brother, that he divide 1320
13:25 When once the m of the house is risen up, 3617
14:21 m of the house being angry said to his 3617
17:13 and said, Jesus, M, have mercy on us. 1988
18:18 a certain ruler asked him, saying, Good M, 1320
19:39 said unto him, M, rebuke thy disciples. 1320
20:21 And they asked him, saying, M, we know 1320
20:28 Saying, M, Moses wrote unto us, If any 1320
20:39 answering said, M, thou hast well said. 1320
21: 7 And they asked him, saying, M, 1320
22:11 The M saith unto thee, Where is 1320
Jn 1:38 (which is to say, being interpreted, M,) 1320
3:10 Art thou a m of Israel, and knowest not 1320
4:31 his disciples prayed him, saying, M, eat. 4461
8: 4 They say unto him, M, this woman was 1320
9: 2 saying, M, who did sin, this man, or 4461
11: 8 His disciples say unto him, M, the Jews of 4461
11:28 The M is come, and calleth for thee. 1320
13:13 Ye call me M and Lord: and ye say well; 1320
13:14 If I then, your Lord and M, have washed 1320
20:16 unto him, Rabboni; which is to say, M. 1320
Ac 27:11 Nevertheless the centurion believed the m 2942
Ro 14: 4 to his own m he standeth or falleth. Yea, 2962
Eph 6: 9 knowing that your M also is in heaven; 2962
Col 4: 1 knowing that ye also have a M in heaven. 2962

MASTER'S (24) [MASTER]
Ge 24:27 the LORD led me to the house of my m 113
24:36 Sarah my m wife bare a son to my master 113
24:44 LORD hath appointed out for my m son. 113
24:48 take my m brother's daughter unto his son. 113
24:51 and go, and let her be thy m son's wife, 113
39: 7 that his m wife cast her eyes upon Joseph; 113
39: 8 and said unto his m wife, Behold, 113
Ex 21: 4 the wife and her children shall be her m, and 113
1Sa 29:10 with thy m servants that are come with thee: 113
2Sa 9: 9 I have given unto thy m son all that 113
9:10 thou shalt bring in the fruits, that thy m son 113
9:10 Mephibosheth thy m son shall eat bread 113
12: 8 I gave thee thy m house, and thy master's 113
12: 8 thy m wives into thy bosom, and gave thee 113
16: 3 And the king said, And where is thy m son? 113
2Ki 6:32 is not the sound of his m feet behind him? 113
10: 2 seeing your m sons are with you, and 113
10: 3 out the best and meetest of your m sons, 113
10: 3 father's throne, and fight for your m house. 113
10: 6 take ye the heads of the men your m sons, 113
18:24 of one captain of the least of my m servants, 113
Isa 1: 3 knoweth his owner, and the ass his m crib: 1167
36: 9 of one captain of the least of my m servants, 113
2Ti 2:21 and meet for the m use, and prepared unto 1203

MASTERBUILDER (1) [BUILD, MASTER]
1Co 3:10 as a wise m, I have laid the foundation, and 753

MASTERIES (1) [MASTER]
2Ti 2: 5 And if a man also strive for m, yet is he not 118

MASTERS (20) [MASTER]
Ps 123: 2 of servants look unto the hand of their m, 113
Pr 25:13 send him: for he refresheth the soul of his m. 113
Ecc 12:11 as nails fastened by the m of assemblies, 1167
Jer 27: 4 command them to say unto their m, 113
27: 4 of Israel; Thus shall ye say unto your m; 113
Am 4: 1 which say to their m, Bring, and let us drink. 113
Mt 6:24 No man can serve two m: for either he will 2962
23:10 Neither be ye called m: for one is your 2519
Lk 16:13 No servant can serve two m: for either he 2962
Ac 16:16 which brought her m much gain by 2962
16:19 And when her m saw that the hope of their 2962

Eph 6: 5 be obedient to *them that are your* **m** 2962
6: 9 And, ye **m**, do the same *things* unto them, 2962
Col 3:22 obey in all *things your* **m** according to 2962
4: 1 **M**, give unto *your* servants that which is 2962
1Ti 6: 1 count their own **m** worthy of all honour, 1203
6: 2 And they that have believing **m**, let them 1203
Tit 2: 9 servants to be obedient unto their own **m**, 1203
Jas 3: 1 My brethren, be not many **m**, knowing that 1320
1Pe 2:18 Servants, *be* subject to *your* **m** with all fear; 1203

MASTERS' (2) [MASTER]
Zep 1: 9 which fill their **m** houses *with* violence and 113
Mt 15:27 of the crumbs which fall from their **m** table. 2962

MASTERY (3) [MASTER]
Ex 32:18 *It is* not the voice of *them that* shout for **m**, 1369
Da 6:24 the lions had the **m** of them, and brake all 7981
1Co 9:25 And every *man* that **striveth for the m** is 75

MASTS (1) [MAST]
Eze 27: 5 cedars from Lebanon to make **m** for thee. 8650

MATE (2)
Isa 34:15 also be gathered, every one *with* her **m**. 7468
34:16 of these shall fail, none shall want her **m**: 7468

MATERIAL See CARNAL

MATHUSALA (1) [METHUSELAH]
Lk 3:37 Which was *the son* of **M**, which was 3103

MATRED (2)
Ge 36:39 the daughter of **M**, the daughter of 4308
1Ch 1:50 the daughter of **M**, the daughter of 4308

MATRI (1)
1Sa 10:21 the family of **M** was taken, and Saul 4309

MATRIX (5)
Ex 13:12 unto the LORD all that openeth the **m**, 7358
13:15 to the LORD all that openeth the **m**, 7358
34:19 All that openeth the **m** *is* mine; and 7358
Nu 3:12 openeth the **m** among the children of Israel: 7358
18:15 Every thing that openeth the **m** in all flesh, 7358

MATTAN (3)
2Ki 11:18 slew **M** the priest of Baal before the altars. 4977
2Ch 23:17 slew **M** the priest of Baal before the altars. 4977
Jer 38: 1 Shephatiah the son of **M**, and Gedaliah 4977

MATTANAH (2)
Nu 21:18 And from the wilderness *they went to* **M**: 4980
21:19 from **M** *to* Nahaliel: and from Nahaliel *to* 4980

MATTANIAH (16)
2Ki 24:17 the king of Babylon made **M** his father's 4983
1Ch 9:15 Heresh, and Galal, and **M** the son of Micah, 4983
25: 4 **M**, Uzziel, Shebuel, and Jerimoth, 4983
25:16 The ninth *to* **M**, *he*, his sons, and 4983
2Ch 20:14 of Benaiah, the son of Jeiel, the son of **M**, 4983
29:13 of the sons of Asaph; Zechariah, and **M**: 4983
Ezr 10:26 **M**, Zechariah, and Jehiel, and Abdi, and 4983
10:27 **M**, and Jeremoth, and Zabad, and Aziza. 4983
10:30 **M**, Bezaleel, and Binnui, and Manasseh. 4983
10:37 **M**, Mattenai, and Jaasau, 4983
Ne 11:17 **M** the son of Micha, the son of Zabdi, 4983
11:22 the son of **M**, the son of Micha. 4983
12: 8 Binnui, Kadmiel, Sherebiah, Judah, *and* **M**, 4983
12:25 **M**, and Bakbukiah, Obadiah, Meshullam, 4983
12:35 the son of **M**, the son of Michaiah, the son 4983
13:13 *was* Hanan the son of Zaccur, the son of **M**: 4983

MATTATHA (1)
Lk 3:31 *the son* of Menan, which was *the son* of **M**, 3160

MATTATHAH (1)
Ezr 10:33 Mattenai, **M**, Zabad, Eliphelet, Jeremai, 4992

MATTATHIAS (2)
Lk 3:25 Which was *the son* of **M**, which was 3161
3:26 which was *the son* of **M**, which was *the son* 3161

MATTATTAH See MATTATHAH

MATTENAI (3)
Ezr 10:33 **M**, Mattathah, Zabad, Eliphelet, Jeremai, 4982
10:37 Mattaniah, **M**, and Jaasau, 4982
Ne 12:19 And of Joiarib, **M**; of Jedaiah, Uzzi; 4982

MATTER (80) [MATTERS]
Ge 24: 9 and sware to him concerning that **m**. 1697
30:15 *Is it* a **small m** that thou hast taken my 4592
Ex 18:16 When they have a **m**, they come unto me; 1697
18:22 *that* every great **m** they shall bring unto 1697
18:22 but every small **m** they shall judge: 1697
18:26 but every small **m** they judged themselves. 1697
23: 7 Keep thee far from a false **m**; and 1697
Nu 16:49 beside them that died about the **m** of 1697
25:18 wherewith they have beguiled you in the **m** 1697
25:18 in the **m** of Cozbi, the daughter of a prince 1697
31:16 against the LORD in the **m** of Peor, 1697
Dt 3:26 speak no more unto me of this **m**. 1697
17: 8 If there arise a **m** too hard for thee in 1697
19:15 three witnesses, shall the **m** be stablished. 1697
22:26 and slayeth him, even so *is* this **m**: 1697
Ru 3:18 until thou know how the **m** will fall: 1697
1Sa 10:16 of the **m** of the kingdom, whereof Samuel 1697
20:23 *as touching* the **m** which thou and I have 1697
20:39 only Jonathan and David knew the **m**. 1697
30:24 For who will hearken unto you in this **m**? 1697
2Sa 1: 4 David said unto him, How went the **m**? 1697
18:13 for there is no **m** hid from the king, and 1697
19:42 wherefore then be ye angry for this **m**? 1697
2Sa 20:18 *counsel* at Abel: and so they ended *the* **m**. NIH
20:21 The **m** *is* not so: but a man of mount 1697
1Ki 8:59 Israel at all times, **as the m shall require**: 1697
15: 5 save only in the **m** of Urijah the Hittite. 1697
1Ch 26:32 for every **m** pertaining to God, and 1697
27: 1 their officers that served the king in any **m** 1697
2Ch 8:15 the priests and Levites concerning any **m**, 1697
24: 5 year to year, and *see that* ye haste the **m**. 1697
Ezr 5: 5 them to cease, till the **m** came to Darius: 2941
5: 5 answer by letter concerning this **m**. NIH
5:17 send his pleasure to us concerning this **m**. NIH
10: 4 Arise; for *this* **m** *belongeth* unto thee: 1697
10: 9 trembling because of *this* **m**, and for 1697
10:14 until the fierce wrath of our God for this **m** 1697
10:15 son of Tikvah were employed about this **m**: NIH
10:16 day of the tenth month to examine the **m**. 1697
Ne 6:13 *that* they might have **m** for an evil report, NIH
Est 2:23 when inquisition was made of the **m**, it was 1697
9:26 *that* which they had seen concerning this **m**, NIH
Job 19:28 seeing the root of the **m** is found in me; 1697
32:18 For I am full *of* **m**, the spirit within me 4405
Ps 45: 1 My heart is inditing a good **m**: I speak of 1697
64: 5 They encourage themselves *in* an evil **m**: 1697
Pr 11:13 that is of a faithful spirit concealeth the **m**. 1697
16:20 He that handleth a **m** wisely shall find 1697
17: 9 he that repeateth a **m** separateth very 1697
18:13 He that answereth a **m** before he heareth *it*, 1697
25: 2 the honour of kings *is* to search out a **m**. 1697
Ecc 5: 8 justice in a province, marvel not at the **m**: 2656
10:20 and that which hath wings shall tell the **m**. 1697
12:13 Let us hear the conclusion of the whole **m**: 1697
Jer 38:27 with him; for the **m** was not perceived. 1697
Eze 9:11 inkhorn by his side, reported the **m**, saying, 1697
16:20 *Is this* of thy whoredoms a **small m**, 4592
Da 1:14 So he consented to them in this **m**, and 1697
2:10 upon the earth that can shew the king's **m**: 4406
2:23 *now* made known unto us the king's **m**. 4406
3:16 we *are* not careful to answer thee in this **m**. 6600
4:17 *This* **m** *is* by the decree of the watchers, 6600
7:28 Hitherto *is* the end of the **m**. *As for* me 4406
7:28 in me: but I kept the **m** in my heart. 4406
9:23 therefore understand the **m**, and 1697
Mk 1:45 publish *it* much, and to blaze abroad the **m**, 3056
10:10 disciples asked him again of the same **m**. NIG
Ac 8:21 Thou hast neither part nor lot in this **m**: 3056
11: 4 But Peter *rehearsed the* **m** from NIG
15: 6 came together for to consider of this **m**. 3056
17:32 We will hear thee again of this **m**. NIG
18:14 If it were a **m** of wrong or 5100
19:38 have a **m** against any *man*, the law is open, 3056
24:22 I will know the uttermost of your **m**. 2596+3588
1Co 6: 1 any of you, having a **m** against another, 4229
2Co 7:11 approved yourselves to be clear in *this* **m**. 4229
9: 5 as *a* **m** *of* bounty, and not as *of* NIG
Gal 2: 6 they were, it **maketh** no **m** to me: 1308
1Th 4: 6 and defraud his brother in *any* **m**: 4229
Jas 3: 5 Behold, how great a **m** a little fire kindleth. 5208

MATTERS (23) [MATTER]
Ex 24:14 if any man have any **m** to do, let him come 1697
Dt 17: 8 *being* **m** of controversy within thy gates: 1697
1Sa 16:18 and prudent in **m**, and a comely person, and 1697
2Sa 11:19 of telling the **m** of the war unto the king, 1697
15: 3 unto him, See, thy **m** *are* good and right; 1697
19:29 Why speakest thou any more of thy **m**? 1697
2Ch 19:11 priest *is* over you in all **m** of the LORD; 1697
19:11 of the house of Judah, for all the king's **m**: 1697
Ne 11:24 *was* at the king's hand in all **m** concerning 1697
Est 3: 4 to see whether Mordecai's **m** would stand: 1697
9:31 the **m** of the fastings and their cry. 1697
9:32 the decree of Esther confirmed these **m** of 1697
Job 33:13 for he giveth not account of any of his **m**. 1697
Ps 35:20 they devise deceitful **m** against *them that* 1697
131: 1 neither do I exercise myself in great **m**, or NIH
Da 1:20 *in* all **m** of wisdom *and* understanding, 1697
7: 1 wrote the dream, *and* told the sum of the **m**. 4406
Mt 23:23 have omitted the weightier **m** of the law, NIG
Ac 18:15 ye *to it*; for I will be no judge of such **m**. NIG
19:39 **m**, it shall be determined in a lawful NIG
25:20 and there be judged of these **m**. NIG
1Co 6: 2 are ye unworthy to judge the **smallest m**? 1646
1Pe 4:15 or as a **busybody in other men's m**. 244

MATTHAN (2)
Mt 1:15 and Eleazar begat **M**; and Matthan begat 3157
1:15 Eleazar begat Matthan; and **M** begat Jacob; 3157

MATTHAT (2)
Lk 3:24 Which was *the son* of **M**, which was 3158
3:29 which was *the son* of **M**, which was *the son* 3158

MATTHEW (5)
Mt 9: 9 he saw a man, named **M**, sitting at 3156
10: 3 Thomas, and **M** the publican; 3156
Mk 3:18 and **M**, and Thomas, and James the *son* of 3156
Lk 6:15 **M** and Thomas, James the *son* of Alpheus, 3156
Ac 1:13 Philip, and Thomas, Bartholomew, and **M**, 3156

MATTHIAS (2)
Ac 1:23 who was surnamed Justus, and **M**. 3159
1:26 and the lot fell upon **M**; and he was 3159

MATTITHIAH (8)
1Ch 9:31 **M**, *one* of the Levites, who *was* 4993
15:18 **M**, and Elipheleh, and Mikneiah, and 4993
15:21 **M**, and Elipheleh, and Mikneiah, and 4993
16: 5 **M**, and Eliab, and Benaiah, and 4993
25: 3 Zeri, and Jeshaiah, Hashabiah, and **M**, six, 4993
25:21 The fourteenth *to* **M**, *he*, his sons, and 4993
Ezr 10:43 Jeiel, **M**, Zabad, Zebina, Jadau, and Joel, 4993
Ne 8: 4 beside him stood **M**, and Shema, and 4993

MATTOCK (2) [MATTOCKS]
1Sa 13:20 and his coulter, and his axe, and his **m**. 4281
Isa 7:25 *on* all hills that shall be digged with the **m**, 4576

MATTOCKS (2) [MATTOCK]
1Sa 13:21 Yet they had a file for the **m**, and for 4281
2Ch 34: 6 unto Naphtali, with their **m** round about. 2719

MAUL (1)
Pr 25:18 false witness against his neighbour *is* a **m**, 4650

MAULED See TARE

MAW (1)
Dt 18: 3 and the two cheeks, and the **m**. 6896

MAY (1027) [MAYEST]
Ge 1:20 fowl *that* **m** fly above the earth in the open NIH
3: 2 We **m** eat of the fruit of the trees of NIH
8:17 that they **m** breed abundantly in the earth, NIH
9:16 that I **m** remember the everlasting covenant NIH
11: 4 a tower, whose top **m** *reach* unto heaven; NIH
11: 7 that they **m** not understand one another's NIH
12:13 that it **m** be well with me for thy sake; and NIH
16: 2 **it m be that** I may obtain children by her. 194
16: 2 it may be that I **m** obtain children by her. NIH
18:19 that the LORD **m** bring upon Abraham NIH
19: 5 them out unto us, that we **m** know them. NIH
19:32 that we **m** preserve seed of our father. NIH
19:34 that we **m** preserve seed of our father. NIH
21:30 that they **m** be a witness unto me, that I NIH
23: 4 that I **m** bury my dead out of my sight. NIH
23: 9 That he **m** give me the cave of Machpelah, NIH
24:14 thy pitcher, I pray thee, that I **m** drink; NIH
24:49 that I **m** turn to the right hand, or to the left. NIH
24:56 send me away that I **m** go to my master. NIH
27: 4 as I love, and bring *it* to me, that I **m** eat; NIH
27: 4 that my soul **m** bless thee before I die. NIH
27: 7 that I **m** eat, and bless thee before NIH
27:10 that he **m** eat, and that he may bless thee NIH
27:10 that he **m** bless thee before his death. NIH
27:19 eat of my venison, that thy soul **m** bless me. NIH
27:21 I pray thee, that I **m** feel thee, my son, NIH
27:25 son's venison, that my soul **m** bless thee. NIH
27:31 his son's venison, that thy soul **m** bless me. NIH
29:21 days are fulfilled, that I **m** go in unto her. NIH
30: 3 that I **m** also have children by her. NIH
30:25 that I **m** go unto mine own place, and to my NIH
31:37 that they **m** judge betwixt us both. NIH
32: 5 tell my lord, that I **m** find grace in thy sight. NIH
42: 2 us from thence; that we **m** live, and not die. NIH
42:16 in prison, that your words **m** be proved, NIH
43: 8 that we **m** live, and not die, both we, and NIH
43:14 that he **m** send away your other brother, and NIH
43:18 that he **m** seek occasion against us, and fall NIH
44:21 unto me, that I **m** set mine eyes upon him. NIH
44:26 for we **m** not see the man's face, except our 3201
46:34 that ye **m** dwell in the land of Goshen; NIH
47:19 give *us* seed, that we **m** live, and not die, NIH
49: 1 that I **m** tell you *that* which shall befall you NIH
Ex 2: 7 that she **m** nurse the child for thee? NIH
2:20 left the man? call him, that he **m** eat bread. NIH
3:18 that we **m** sacrifice to the LORD our God. NIH
4: 5 That they **m** believe that the LORD God of NIH
4:23 Let my son go, that he **m** serve me: NIH
5: 1 that they **m** hold a feast unto me in NIH
5: 9 upon the men, that they **m** labour therein; NIH
7: 4 that I **m** lay my hand upon Egypt, and NIH
7:16 that they **m** serve me in the wilderness: NIH
7:19 pools of water, that they **m** become blood; NIH
7:19 *that* there **m** be blood throughout all NIH
8: 1 Let my people go, that they **m** serve me. NIH
8: 8 that he **m** take away the frogs from me, and NIH
8: 8 that they **m** do sacrifice unto the LORD. NIH
8: 9 *that* they **m** remain in the river only? NIH
8:16 that it **m** become lice throughout all the land NIH
8:20 Let my people go, that they **m** serve me. NIH
8:28 that ye **m** sacrifice to the LORD your God NIH
8:29 the swarms *of flies* **m** depart from Pharaoh, NIH
9: 1 Let my people go, that they **m** serve me. NIH
9:13 Let my people go, that they **m** serve me. NIH
9:15 that I **m** smite thee and thy people with NIH
9:16 that my name **m** be declared throughout all NIH
9:22 that there **m** be hail in all the land of Egypt, NIH
10: 2 that ye **m** know how that I *am* the LORD. NIH
10: 3 let my people go, that they **m** serve me. NIH
10: 7 that they **m** serve the LORD their God: NIH
10:12 that they **m** come up upon the land of NIH
10:17 that he **m** take away from me this death NIH
10:21 that there **m** be darkness over the land of NIH
10:21 of Egypt, even darkness *which* **m** be felt. NIH
10:25 that we **m** sacrifice unto the LORD our NIH
11: 7 that ye **m** know how that the LORD doth NIH
11: 9 that my wonders **m** be multiplied in the land NIH
12:16 man must eat, that only **m** be done of you. NIH
13: 9 that the LORD'S law **m** be in thy mouth: NIH
14: 4 that the Egyptians **m** know that I *am* NIH
14:12 us alone, that we **m** serve the Egyptians? NIH
14:26 that the waters **m** come again upon NIH
16: 4 certain rate every day, that I **m** prove them, NIH
16:32 that they **m** see the bread wherewith I have NIH
17: 2 and said, Give us water that we **m** drink. NIH
17: 6 water out of it, that the people **m** drink. NIH
19: 9 that the people **m** hear when I speak with NIH
20:12 that thy days **m** be long upon the land which NIH
20:20 that his fear **m** be before your faces, that ye NIH
21:14 take him from mine altar, that he **m** die. NIH
23:11 lie still; that the poor of thy people **m** eat: NIH
23:12 that thine ox and thine ass **m** rest, and NIH
23:12 and the stranger, **m** be refreshed. NIH
25: 8 a sanctuary; that I **m** dwell amongst them. NIH
25:14 the ark, that the ark **m** be borne with them. NIH
25:28 that the table **m** be borne with them. NIH
25:37 that they **m** give light over against it. NIH
26: 5 that the loops **m** take hold one of another. NIH
26:11 couple the tent together, that it **m** be one. NIH

M

Ex 27: 5 that the net **m** be even to the midst of NIH
28: 1 that he **m** minister unto me in the priest's NIH
28: 3 that they **m** make Aaron's garments to NIH
28: 3 that he **m** minister unto me in the priest's NIH
28: 4 that he **m** minister unto me in the priest's NIH
28:28 that *it* **m** be above the curious girdle of NIH
28:37 it on a blue lace, that it **m** be upon the mitre; NIH
28:38 that Aaron **m** bear the iniquity of the holy NIH
28:38 that they **m** be accepted before the LORD. NIH
28:41 that they **m** minister unto me in the priest's NIH
29:46 land of Egypt, that I **m** dwell amongst them: NIH
30:16 that it **m** be a memorial unto the children of NIH
30:29 sanctify them, that they **m** be most holy: NIH
30:30 that *they* **m** minister unto me in the priest's NIH
31: 6 that they **m** make all that I have NIH
31:13 that *ye* **m** know that I *am* the LORD that NIH
31:15 Six days **m** work be done; but in the seventh NIH
32:10 that my wrath **m** wax hot against them, and NIH
32:10 against them, and that I **m** consume them: NIH
32:29 that he **m** bestow upon you a blessing *this* NIH
33: 5 that I **m** know what to do unto thee. NIH
33:13 shew me now thy way, that I **m** know thee, NIH
33:13 know thee, that I **m** find grace in thy sight: NIH
35:34 And he hath put in his heart that *he* **m** teach, NIH
40:13 that he **m** minister unto me in the priest's NIH
40:15 that they **m** minister unto me in the priest's NIH
Lev 7:24 the fat of that which is torn *with beasts,* **m** NIH
7:30 that the breast **m** be waved *for* a wave NIH
10:10 that *ye* **m** put difference between holy and NIH
10:11 that *ye* **m** teach the children of Israel all NIH
11:21 Yet these **m** ye eat of every flying creeping NIH
11:22 *Even* these of them ye **m** eat; the locust NIH
11:34 Of all meat which **m** be eaten, *that* on which NIH
11:34 all drink that **m** be drunk in every *such* NIH
11:39 if any beast, of which ye **m** eat, die; he that NIH
11:47 between the beast that **m** be eaten and NIH
11:47 be eaten and the beast that **m** not be eaten. NIH
14: 8 wash *himself* in water, that he **m** be clean: NIH
16:13 that the cloud of the incense **m** cover NIH
16:30 *that* ye **m** be clean from all your sins before NIH
17: 5 To the end that the children of Israel **m** NIH
17: 5 even that they **m** bring them unto NIH
17:13 catcheth *any* beast or fowl that **m** be eaten; NIH
19:25 that *it* **m** yield unto you the increase thereof: NIH
21: 3 had no husband; for her **m** he be defiled. NIH
22: 5 whereby he **m** be made unclean, or a man of NIH
22: 5 or a man of whom he **m** take uncleanness, NIH
22:12 she **m** not eat of an offering of the holy NIH
23:21 *that* it **m** be a holy convocation unto you: NIH
23:43 That your generations **m** know that I made NIH
24: 7 that it **m** be on the bread for a memorial, NIH
25:27 sold it; that he **m** return unto his possession. NIH
25:29 he **m** redeem it within a whole year after it NIH
25:29 it is sold; *within* a full year **m** he redeem it. NIH
25:31 they **m** be redeemed, and they shall go out NIH
25:32 **m** the Levites redeem at any time. NIH
25:34 the field of the suburbs of their cities **m** not NIH
25:35 or a sojourner; that he **m** live with thee. NIH
25:36 thy God; that thy brother **m** live with thee. NIH
25:48 After *that* he is sold he **m** be redeemed NIH
25:48 one of his brethren **m** redeem him: NIH
25:49 **m** redeem him, or *any* that is nigh of kin NIH
25:49 kin unto him of his family **m** redeem him; NIH
25:49 or if he be able, he **m** redeem himself. NIH
Nu 3: 6 the priest, that they **m** minister unto him. NIH
4:19 do unto them, that they **m** live, and not die, NIH
6:20 and after *that* the Nazarite **m** drink wine. NIH
7: 5 that they **m** be to do the service of NIH
8:11 that they **m** execute the service of NIH
9: 7 that *we* **m** not offer an offering of NIH
10:10 that they **m** be to you for a memorial before NIH
11:13 saying, Give us flesh, that we **m** eat. NIH
11:16 that they **m** stand there with thee. NIH
11:21 them flesh, that they **m** eat a whole month. NIH
13: 2 that they **m** search the land of Canaan, NIH
15:39 that ye **m** look upon it, and remember all NIH
15:40 That ye **m** remember, and do all my NIH
16:21 that I **m** consume them in a moment. NIH
16:45 that I **m** consume them as in a moment. NIH
18: 2 that they **m** be joined unto thee, and NIH
19: 3 that he **m** bring her forth without the camp, NIH
22: 6 *that* we **m** smite them, and *that* I may drive NIH
22: 6 and *that* I **m** drive them out of the land: NIH
22:19 that I **m** know what the LORD will say NIH
25: 4 that the fierce anger of the LORD **m** be NIH
27:17 Which **m** go out before them, and NIH
27:17 which **m** go in before them, and which may NIH
27:17 which **m** lead them out, and which may NIH
27:17 lead them out, and which **m** bring them in; NIH
27:20 of the children of Israel **m** be obedient. NIH
30:13 her husband **m** establish it, or her husband NIH
30:13 establish it, or her husband **m** make it void. NIH
31:23 Every thing that **m** abide the fire, ye shall NIH
32:32 inheritance on *this* side Jordan **m** *be* ours. NIH
35: 6 for the manslayer, that he **m** flee thither: NIH
35:11 that the slayer **m** flee thither, which killeth NIH
35:15 killeth *any* person unawares **m** flee thither. NIH
35:17 wherewith he **m** die, and he die, he *is* a NIH
35:18 wherewith he **m** die, and he die, he *is* a NIH
35:23 wherewith *a man* **m** die, seeing *him* not, and NIH
36: 8 that the children of Israel **m** enjoy every NIH
Dt 2: 6 buy meat of them for money, that ye **m** eat; NIH
2: 6 water of them for money, that ye **m** drink. NIH
2:28 shalt sell me meat for money, that I **m** eat; NIH
2:28 give me water for money, that I **m** drink: NIH
4: 1 for to do *them,* that ye **m** live, and go in and NIH
4: 2 that *ye* **m** keep the commandments of NIH
4:10 that they **m** learn to fear me all the days that NIH
4:10 and *that* they **m** teach their children. NIH
4:40 that it **m** go well with thee, and with thy NIH
5: 1 that ye **m** learn them, and keep, and do NIH
5:14 and thy maidservant **m** rest as well as thou. NIH
5:16 that thy days **m** be prolonged, and that it NIH
5:16 and that it **m** go well with thee, NIH
5:31 that they **m** do *them* in the land which I give NIH
Dt 5:33 that ye **m** live, and *that it may be* well with NIH
5:33 *that it* **m** be well with you, and *that* ye may NIH
5:33 *that* ye **m** prolong *your* days in the land NIH
6: 2 thy life; and that thy days **m** be prolonged. NIH
6: 3 observe to do *it;* that it **m** be well with thee, NIH
6: 3 with thee, and that ye **m** increase mightily, NIH
6:18 that it **m** be well with thee, and *that* thou NIH
7: 4 following me, that they **m** serve other gods: NIH
8: 1 that ye **m** live, and multiply, and go in and NIH
8:18 that he **m** establish his covenant which he NIH
9: 5 that he **m** perform the word which NIH
9:14 that I **m** destroy them, and blot out their NIH
10:11 that they **m** go in and possess the land, NIH
11: 8 that ye **m** be strong, and go in and NIH
11: 9 that ye **m** prolong *your* days in the land, NIH
11:18 that they **m** be as frontlets between your NIH
11:21 That your days **m** be multiplied, and NIH
12:15 the unclean and the clean **m** eat thereof, NIH
12:25 that it **m** go well with thee, and with thy NIH
12:28 that it **m** go well with thee, and with thy NIH
13:17 that the LORD **m** turn from the fierceness NIH
14:10 hath not fins and scales ye **m** not eat; NIH
14:20 *But* of all clean fowls ye **m** eat. NIH
14:21 stranger that *is* in thy gates, that he **m** eat it; NIH
14:29 that the LORD thy God **m** bless thee in all NIH
17:19 that he **m** learn to fear the LORD his God, NIH
17:20 to the end that he **m** prolong *his* days in his NIH
19: 3 three parts, that every slayer **m** flee thither. NIH
19: 4 which shall flee thither, that he **m** live: NIH
19:12 hand of the avenger of blood, that he **m** die. NIH
19:13 from Israel, that *it* **m** *go* well with thee. NIH
21:16 *that* he **m** not make the son of the beloved 3201
22: 7 that it **m** be well with thee, and *that* thou NIH
22:19 he **m** not put her away all his days. 3201
22:29 he **m** not put her away all his days. 3201
23:20 that the LORD thy God **m** bless thee in all NIH
24: 2 she **m** go and be another man's *wife.* NIH
24: 4 **m** not take her again to be his wife, 3201
24:13 that he **m** sleep in his own raiment, and NIH
24:19 that the LORD thy God **m** bless thee in all NIH
25: 1 that *the judges* **m** judge them; NIH
25: 3 Forty stripes he **m** give him, *and* NIH
25:15 that thy days **m** be lengthened in the land NIH
26:12 that they **m** eat within thy gates, and NIH
29: 9 do them, that ye **m** prosper *in* all that ye do. NIH
29:13 That he **m** establish thee to day for a people NIH
29:13 *that* he **m** be unto thee a God, as he hath NIH
29:29 that *we* **m** do all the words of this law. NIH
30:12 bring it unto us, that we **m** hear it, and do it? NIH
30:13 bring it unto us, that we **m** hear it, and do it? NIH
30:19 that *both* thou and thy seed **m** live: NIH
31: 5 that ye **m** do unto them according unto all NIH
31:12 that they **m** hear, and that they may learn, NIH
31:12 that they **m** learn, and fear the LORD your NIH
31:13 which have not known *any thing,* **m** hear, NIH
31:14 that I **m** give him a charge. NIH
31:19 that this song **m** be a witness for me against NIH
31:26 that it **m** be there for a witness against thee. NIH
31:28 that I **m** speak these words in their ears, and NIH
Jos 2:16 and afterward **m** ye go your way. NIH
3: 4 that ye **m** know the way by which ye must NIH
3: 7 that they **m** know that, as I was with Moses, NIH
4: 6 That this **m** be a sign among you, *that* when NIH
9:19 now therefore we **m** not touch them. 3201
10: 4 and help me, that we **m** smite Gibeon: NIH
18: 6 that I **m** cast lots for you here before NIH
18: 8 that I **m** here cast lots for you before NIH
20: 3 *and* unwittingly **m** flee thither: NIH
20: 4 him a place, that he **m** dwell among them. NIH
22:27 *that it* **m** *be* a witness between us, and you, NIH
22:27 that your children **m** not say to our children NIH
22:28 that we **m** say *again,* Behold the pattern of NIH
Jdg 1: 3 that we **m** fight against the Canaanites; NIH
2:22 That through them I **m** prove Israel, NIH
6:30 unto Joash, Bring out thy son, that he **m** die: NIH
9: 7 of Shechem, that God **m** hearken unto you. NIH
11: 6 that we **m** fight with the children of NIH
11:37 that I **m** go up and down upon NIH
13:14 She **m** not eat of any *thing* that cometh of NIH
13:17 that when thy sayings come to pass we **m** NIH
14:13 Put forth thy riddle, that we **m** hear it. NIH
14:15 that he **m** declare unto us the riddle, lest we NIH
15:12 that we **m** deliver thee into the hand of NIH
16: 5 by what *means* we **m** prevail against him, NIH
16: 5 that we **m** bind him to afflict him: NIH
16:25 Call for Samson, that he **m** make us sport. NIH
16:26 Suffer me that I **m** feel the pillars NIH
16:26 the house standeth, that I **m** lean upon them. NIH
16:28 that I **m** be at once avenged of NIH
17: 9 I go to sojourn where I **m** find *a place.* NIH
18: 5 that we **m** know whether our way which we NIH
18: 9 Arise, that we **m** go up against them: NIH
19: 9 lodge here, that thine heart **m** be merry; NIH
19:22 came into thine house, that we **m** know him. NIH
20:10 fetch victual for the people, that *they* **m** do, NIH
20:13 that we **m** put them to death, and put away NIH
21:18 Howbeit we **m** not give them wives of our 3201
Ru 1: 9 The LORD grant you that you **m** find rest, NIH
1:11 in my womb, that they **m** be your husbands? NIH
2:16 leave *them,* that she **m** glean *them,* and NIH
3: 1 rest for thee, that it **m** be well with thee? NIH
4: 4 not redeem *it, then* tell me, that I **m** know: NIH
4:14 that his name **m** be famous in Israel. NIH
1Sa 1:22 that he **m** appear before the LORD, and NIH
2:36 that *I* **m** eat a piece of bread. NIH
4: 3 it **m** save us out of the hand of our enemies. NIH
6: 8 side thereof; and send it away, that it **m** go. NIH
8:20 That we also **m** be like all the nations; and NIH
8:20 that our king **m** judge us, and go out before NIH
9:16 that *he* **m** save my people out of the hand of NIH
9:26 saying, Up, that I **m** send thee away. NIH
9:27 that I **m** shew thee the word of God. NIH
11: 2 that *I* **m** thrust out all your right eyes, and NIH
11: 3 that we **m** send messengers unto all NIH
11:12 bring the men, that we **m** put them to death. NIH
1Sa 12: 7 that I **m** reason with you before the LORD NIH
12:17 that ye **m** perceive and see that your NIH
14: 6 **it m be that** the LORD will work for us: 194
14:24 that I **m** be avenged on mine enemies. NIH
15:25 with me, that I **m** worship the LORD. NIH
15:30 that I **m** worship the LORD thy God. NIH
17:10 give me a man, that we **m** fight together. NIH
17:46 that all the earth **m** know that there is a God NIH
18:21 that she **m** be a snare to him, and that NIH
18:21 that the hand of the Philistines **m** be against NIH
19:15 him up to me in the bed, that I **m** slay him. NIH
20: 5 that I **m** hide myself in the fields unto NIH
27: 5 town in the country, that I **m** dwell there: NIH
28: 7 that I **m** go to her, and inquire of her. NIH
29: 4 that he **m** go again to his place, NIH
29: 8 that I **m** not go fight against the enemies of NIH
30:22 that they **m** lead *them* away, and depart. NIH
2Sa 3:21 that they **m** make a league with thee, and NIH
7:10 that they **m** dwell in a place of their own, NIH
7:29 that *it* **m** continue for ever before thee: NIH
9: 1 that I **m** shew him kindness for Jonathan's NIH
9: 3 that I **m** shew the kindness of God unto NIH
9:10 that thy master's son **m** have food to eat: NIH
11:15 ye from him, that he **m** be smitten, and die. NIH
12:22 be gracious to me, that the child **m** live? NIH
13: 5 that I **m** see *it,* and eat *it* at her hand. NIH
13: 6 cakes in my sight, that I **m** eat at her hand. NIH
13:10 *into* the chamber, that I **m** eat of thine hand. NIH
14: 7 that smote his brother, that we **m** kill him, NIH
14:15 **it m be that** the king will perform 194
14:32 that I **m** send thee to the king, to say, NIH
15:20 seeing I go whither I **m,** return thou, and 1980
16: 2 that such as be faint in the wilderness **m** NIH
16: 4 I humbly beseech thee *that* I **m** find grace in NIH
16:11 how much more now **m** *this* Benjamite *do* NIH
16:12 **It m be that** the LORD will look on mine 194
18:14 Then said Joab, I **m** not tarry thus with thee. NIH
19:26 that I **m** ride thereon, and go to the king; NIH
19:37 that I **m** die in mine own city, *and be buried* NIH
20:16 Come near hither, that I **m** speak with thee. NIH
21: 3 that ye **m** bless the inheritance of NIH
24: 2 that I **m** know the number of the people. NIH
24: 3 *that* the eyes of my lord the king **m** see *it:* NIH
24:12 thee one of them, that I **m** do *it* unto thee. NIH
24:21 that the plague **m** be stayed from the people. NIH
1Ki 1: 2 thy bosom, that my lord the king **m** get heat. NIH
1:35 that he **m** come and sit upon my throne; NIH
2: 4 That the LORD **m** continue his word NIH
3: 9 that *I* **m** discern between good and bad: NIH
8:29 That thine eyes **m** be open toward this NIH
8:40 That they **m** fear thee all the days that they NIH
8:43 that all people of the earth **m** know thy NIH
8:43 that *they* **m** know that this house, which I NIH
8:50 that they **m** have compassion on them: NIH
8:52 That thine eyes **m** be open unto NIH
8:58 That *he* **m** incline our hearts unto him, NIH
8:60 That all the people of the earth **m** know that NIH
11:21 me depart, that I **m** go to mine own country. NIH
11:36 that David my servant **m** have a light alway NIH
12: 6 How do you advise that *I* **m** answer this 7725
12: 9 What counsel give ye that we **m** answer 7725
13: 6 that my hand **m** be restored me again. NIH
13:16 he said, I **m** not return with thee, nor go in 3201
13:18 that he **m** eat bread and drink water. NIH
15:19 king of Israel, that he **m** depart from me. NIH
17:10 a little water in a vessel, that I **m** drink. NIH
17:12 that I **m** go in and dress it for me and my NIH
17:12 and my son, that we **m** eat it, and die. NIH
18: 5 peradventure we **m** find grass to save NIH
18:37 that this people **m** know that thou *art* NIH
20: 9 this thing I **m** not do. And the messengers 3201
21: 2 that I **m** have it for a garden of herbs, NIH
21:10 carry him out, and stone him, that he **m** die. NIH
22: 8 by whom *we* **m** inquire of the LORD: NIH
22:20 that he **m** go up and fall at Ramoth-gilead? NIH
2Ki 3:11 that we **m** inquire of the LORD by him? NIH
3:17 that ye **m** drink, *both* ye, and your cattle, NIH
4:22 that I **m** run to the man of God, and NIH
4:41 Pour out for the people, that they **m** eat. NIH
4:42 Give unto the people, that they **m** eat. NIH
4:43 said again, Give the people, that they **m** eat: NIH
5:12 **m** I not wash in them, and be clean? So he NIH
6: 2 make us a place there, where we **m** dwell. NIH
6:13 Go and spy where he *is,* that I **m** send and NIH
6:17 I pray thee, open his eyes, that he **m** see. NIH
6:20 open the eyes of these *men,* that they **m** see. NIH
6:22 that they **m** eat and drink, and go to their NIH
6:28 that we **m** eat him to day, and we will eat NIH
6:29 next day, Give thy son, that we **m** eat him: NIH
7: 9 that we **m** go and tell the king's household. NIH
9: 7 that I **m** avenge the blood of my servants NIH
18:27 that *they* **m** eat their own dung, and drink NIH
18:32 and of honey, that ye **m** live, and not die: NIH
19: 4 **It m be** the LORD thy God will hear all 194
19:19 that all the kingdoms of the earth **m** know NIH
22: 4 that he **m** sum the silver which is brought NIH
1Ch 4:10 keep *me* from evil, that it **m** not grieve me. NIH
13: 2 that they **m** gather themselves unto us: NIH
15:12 that you **m** bring up the ark of the LORD NIH
16:35 that *we* **m** give thanks to thy holy name, *and* NIH
17:24 that thy name **m** be magnified for ever, NIH
17:27 that *it* **m** be before thee for ever: NIH
21: 2 the number of them to me, that I **m** know *it.* NIH
21:10 thee one of them, that I **m** do *it* unto thee. NIH
21:22 that I **m** build an altar therein unto NIH
21:22 that the plague **m** be stayed from the people. NIH
23:25 that they **m** dwell in Jerusalem for ever: NIH
28: 8 that ye **m** possess *this* good land, and NIH
2Ch 1:10 that I **m** go out and come in before this NIH
6:20 That thine eyes **m** be open upon this house NIH
6:31 That they **m** fear thee, to walk in thy ways, NIH
6:33 that all people of the earth **m** know thy NIH
6:33 **m** know that this house which I have built is NIH
7:16 that my name **m** be there for ever: NIH
10: 9 What advice give ye that we **m** return NIH

2Ch 12: 8 that they m know my service, and NIH
13: 9 the same m be a priest of them that are no NIH
16: 3 king of Israel, that he m depart from me. NIH
18: 7 by whom we m inquire of the LORD: NIH
18:19 that he m go up and fall at Ramoth-gilead? NIH
28:23 will I sacrifice to them, that they m help me. NIH
29:10 that his fierce wrath m turn away from us. NIH
30: 8 that the fierceness of his wrath m turn away NIH
35: 6 that they m do according to the word of NIH
Ezr 4:15 That search m be made in the book of NIH
6:10 That they m offer sacrifices of sweet NIH
7:25 which m judge all the people that are NIH
9: 8 that our God m lighten our eyes, and give NIH
9:12 that ye m be strong, and eat the good of NIH
Ne 2: 5 of my fathers' sepulchres, that I m build it. NIH
2: 7 that they m convey me over till I come into NIH
2: 8 that he m give me timber to make beams for NIH
4:22 that in the night they m be a guard to us, NIH
5: 2 we take up corn for them, that we m eat, NIH
Est 2: 3 that they m gather together all the fair NIH
3: 9 let it be written that they m be destroyed: NIH
4:11 hold out the golden sceptre, that he m live: NIH
5: 5 that he m do as Esther hath said. NIH
5:14 king that Mordecai m be hanged thereon: NIH
6: 9 that they m array the man withal whom NIH
8: 8 with the king's ring, m no man reverse. NIH
Job 1: 5 It m be that my sons have sinned, 194
5:11 that those which mourn m be exalted to NIH
10:20 let me alone, that I m take comfort a little, NIH
13:13 that I m speak, and let come on me what NIH
14: 6 Turn from him, that he m rest, till he shall NIH
19:29 that ye m know there is a judgment. NIH
21: 3 Suffer me that I m speak; and after that I NIH
22: 2 as he that is wise m be profitable unto NIH
27:17 He m prepare it, but the just shall put it on, NIH
31: 6 that God m know mine integrity. NIH
32:20 I will speak, that I m be refreshed: I will NIH
33:17 That he m withdraw man from his purpose, NIH
34:22 where the workers of iniquity m hide NIH
34:36 My desire is that Job m be tried unto NIH
35: 8 Thy wickedness m hurt a man as thou art; NIH
35: 8 thy righteousness m profit the son of man. NIH
36:25 Every man m see it; man may behold it afar NIH
36:25 man may see it; man m behold it afar off. NIH
37: 7 every man; that all men m know his work. NIH
37:12 that they m do whatsoever he commandeth NIH
38:34 that abundance of waters m cover thee? NIH
38:35 that they m go, and say unto thee, Here we NIH
39:15 forgetteth that the foot m crush them, or NIH
39:15 or that the wild beast m break them. NIH
Ps 9:14 That I m shew forth all thy praise in NIH
9:20 that the nations m know themselves to be NIH
10:10 that the poor m fall by his strong ones. NIH
10:18 that the man of the earth m no more NIH
11: 2 that they m privily shoot at the upright in NIH
22:17 I m tell all my bones: they look and NIH
26: 7 That I m publish with the voice of NIH
27: 4 that I m dwell in the house of the LORD NIH
30: 5 weeping m endure for a night, but NIH
30:12 To the end that my glory m sing praise to NIH
34:12 and loveth many days, that he m see good? NIH
39: 4 what it is; that I m know how frail I am. NIH
39:13 O spare me, that I m recover strength, NIH
41:10 and raise me up, that I m requite them. NIH
48:13 that ye m tell it to the generation following. NIH
50: 4 and to the earth, that he m judge his people. NIH
51: 8 that the bones which thou hast broken m NIH
56:13 that I m walk before God in the light of NIH
58: 8 of a woman, that they m not see the sun. NIH
59:13 consume them, that they m not be: and NIH
60: 4 that it m be displayed because of the truth. NIH
60: 5 That thy beloved m be delivered; save with NIH
61: 7 and truth, which m preserve him. NIH
61: 8 for ever, that I m daily perform my vows. NIH
64: 4 That they m shoot in secret at the perfect. NIH
65: 4 causest to approach unto thee, that he m NIH
67: 2 That thy way m be known upon earth, NIH
68:23 That thy foot m be dipped in the blood of NIH
69:35 that they m dwell there, and have it in NIH
71: 3 whereunto I m continually resort: NIH
73:28 Lord GOD, that I m declare all thy works. NIH
76: 7 who m stand in thy sight when once thou art NIH
83: 4 that the name of Israel m be no more in NIH
83:16 that they m seek thy name, O LORD. NIH
83:18 That men m know that thou, whose name NIH
84: 3 where she m lay her young, even thine NIH
85: 6 us again: that thy people m rejoice in thee? NIH
85: 9 fear him; that glory m dwell in our land. NIH
86:17 that they which hate me m see it, and NIH
90:12 that we m apply our hearts unto wisdom. NIH
90:14 that we m rejoice and be glad all our days. NIH
101: 6 of the land, that they m dwell with me: NIH
101: 8 that I m cut off all wicked doers from NIH
104: 9 Thou hast set a bound that they m not pass NIH
104:14 that he m bring forth food out of the earth; NIH
106: 5 That I m see the good of thy chosen, that I NIH
106: 5 that I m rejoice in the gladness of thy NIH
106: 5 that I m glory with thine inheritance. NIH
107:36 that they m prepare a city for habitation; NIH
107:37 which m yield fruits of increase. NIH
108: 6 That thy beloved m be delivered: save with NIH
109:15 that he m cut off the memory of them from NIH
109:27 That they m know that this is thy hand; NIH
111: 6 that he m give them the heritage of NIH
113: 8 That he m set him with princes, even with NIH
119:17 that I m live, and keep thy word. NIH
119:18 that I m behold wondrous things out of thy NIH
119:73 that I m learn thy commandments. NIH
119:77 tender mercies come unto me, that I m live: NIH
119:116 me according unto thy word, that I m live: NIH
119:125 that I m know thy testimonies. NIH
124: 1 who was on our side, now m Israel say, NIH
129: 1 me from my youth, m Israel now say: NIH
142: 7 soul out of prison, that I m praise thy name: NIH
144:12 That our sons m be as plants grown up in NIH
Ps 144:12 that our daughters m be as corner stones, NIH
144:13 That our garners m be full, affording all NIH
144:13 that our sheep m bring forth thousands and NIH
144:14 That our oxen m be strong to labour; NIH
Pr 5: 2 and that thy lips m keep knowledge. NIH
7: 5 That they m keep thee from the strange NIH
8:11 all the things that m be desired are not to be NIH
8:21 That I m cause those that love me to inherit NIH
15:24 that he m depart from hell beneath. NIH
18: 2 but that his heart m discover itself. NIH
20:21 An inheritance m be gotten hastily at NIH
22:19 That thy trust m be in the LORD, I have NIH
27: 1 for thou knowest not what a day m bring NIH
27:11 that I m answer him that reproacheth me. NIH
Ecc 1:10 Is there any thing whereof it m be said, See, NIH
2:26 that he m give to him that is good before NIH
5:15 which he m carry away in his hand. NIH
6:10 neither m he contend with him that is 3201
8: 4 and who m say unto him, What doest thou? NIH
SS 4:16 that the spices thereof m flow out. NIH
6: 1 turned aside? that we m seek him with thee. NIH
6:13 return, return, that we m look upon thee. NIH
Isa 5: 8 that they m be placed alone in the midst of NIH
5:11 that they m follow strong drink; NIH
5:19 that we m see it: and let the counsel of NIH
5:19 draw nigh and come, that we m know it. NIH
7:15 that he m know to refuse the evil, and NIH
10: 2 that widows m be their prey, and that they NIH
10: 2 and that they m rob the fatherless. NIH
10:19 shall be few, that a child m write them. NIH
13: 2 that they m go into the gates of the nobles. NIH
19:15 which the head or tail, branch or rush, m do. NIH
24:10 house is shut up, that no man m come in. NIH
26: 2 nation which keepeth the truth m enter in. NIH
27: 5 my strength, that he m make peace with me; NIH
28:12 This is the rest wherewith ye m cause NIH
28:21 that he m do his work, his strange work; NIH
30: 1 not of my Spirit, that they m add sin to sin: NIH
30: 8 that it m be for the time to come for ever NIH
30:18 that he m be gracious unto you, and NIH
30:18 be exalted, that he m have mercy upon you: NIH
36:12 that they m eat their own dung, and drink NIH
37: 4 It m be the LORD thy God will hear 194
37:20 that all the kingdoms of the earth m know NIH
41:20 That they m see, and know, and consider, NIH
41:22 what they be, that we m consider them, NIH
41:23 that we m know that ye are gods: NIH
41:23 that we m be dismayed, and behold it NIH
41:26 from the beginning, that we m know? NIH
41:26 beforetime, that we m say, He is righteous? NIH
42:18 ye deaf; and look, ye blind, that ye m see. NIH
43: 9 their witnesses, that they m be justified: NIH
43:10 that ye m know and believe me, and NIH
44: 9 see not, nor know; that they m be ashamed. NIH
44:13 of a man; that it m remain in the house. NIH
45: 6 That they m know from the rising of NIH
46: 5 and compare me, that we m be like? NIH
49:15 yea, they m forget, yet will I not forget thee. NIH
49:20 for me: give place to me that I m dwell. NIH
51:14 The captive exile hasteneth that he m be NIH
51:16 that I m plant the heavens, and lay NIH
51:23 to thy soul, Bow down, that we m go over: NIH
55: 6 Seek ye the LORD while he m be found, NIH
55:10 that it m give seed to the sower, and NIH
60:11 that men m bring unto thee the forces of NIH
60:11 and that their kings m be brought. NIH
60:21 the work of my hands, that I m be glorified. NIH
64: 2 that the nations m tremble at thy presence. NIH
65: 8 that I m not destroy them all. NIH
66:11 That ye m suck, and be satisfied with NIH
66:11 that ye m milk out, and be delighted with NIH
Jer 6:10 I speak, and give warning, that they m hear? NIH
7:18 that they m provoke me to anger. NIH
7:23 commanded you, that it m be well unto you. NIH
9:12 is the wise man, that m understand this? NIH
9:12 that he m declare it, for what the land NIH
9:17 call for the mourning women, that they m NIH
9:17 send for cunning women, that they m come: NIH
9:18 that our eyes m run down with tears, and NIH
10:18 will distress them, that they m find it so. NIH
11: 5 That I m perform the oath which I have NIH
11:19 that his name m be no more remembered. NIH
13:23 then m ye also do good, that are 3201
13:26 upon thy face, that thy shame m appear. NIH
16:12 evil heart, that they m not hearken unto me: NIH
21: 2 wondrous works, that he m go up from us. NIH
26: 3 that I m repent me of the evil, which I NIH
28:14 that they m serve Nebuchadnezzar king of NIH
29: 6 that they m bear sons and daughters; NIH
29: 6 that ye m be increased there, and NIH
32:14 that they m continue many days. NIH
32:39 one way, that they m fear me for ever, for NIH
33:21 Then m also my covenant be broken with NIH
35: 7 that ye m live many days in the land where NIH
36: 3 It m be that the house of Judah will hear all 194
36: 3 that they m return every man from his evil NIH
36: 3 that I m forgive their iniquity and their sin. NIH
36: 7 It m be they will present their supplication 194
42: 3 That the LORD thy God m shew us NIH
42: 3 may shew us the way wherein we m walk, NIH
42: 3 we may walk, and the thing that we m do. NIH
42: 6 that it m be well with us, when we obey NIH
42:12 that he m have mercy upon you, and NIH
44:29 that ye m know that my words shall surely NIH
46:10 that he m avenge him of his adversaries: NIH
48: 9 unto Moab, that it m flee and get away: NIH
49:19 who is a chosen man, that I m appoint over NIH
50:34 that he m give rest to the land, and NIH
50:44 who is a chosen man, that I m appoint over NIH
51: 8 balm for her pain, if so be she m be healed. NIH
51:39 that they m rejoice, and sleep a perpetual NIH
La 2:13 shall I equal to thee, that I m comfort thee, NIH
3:29 mouth in the dust; if so be there m be hope. NIH
Eze 4:17 That they m want bread and water, and NIH
6: 6 that your altars m be laid waste and NIH
Eze 6: 6 your idols m be broken and cease, and NIH
6: 6 your images m be cut down, and NIH
6: 6 cut down, and your works m be abolished. NIH
6: 8 that ye m have some that shall escape NIH
11:20 That they m walk in my statutes, and keep NIH
12: 3 it m be they will consider, though they be a 194
12:16 that they m declare all their abominations NIH
12:19 that her land m be desolate from all that is NIH
14: 5 That I m take the house of Israel in their NIH
14:11 That the house of Israel m go no more NIH
14:11 that they m be my people, and I may be NIH
14:11 and I m be their God, saith the Lord GOD. NIH
14:15 that no man m pass through because of NIH
16:33 that they m come unto thee on every side NIH
16:37 that they m see all thy nakedness. NIH
20:20 that ye m know that I am the LORD your NIH
21: 5 That all flesh m know that I the LORD NIH
21:10 it is furbished that it m glitter: NIH
21:11 it to be furbished, that it m be handled: NIH
21:15 that their heart m faint, and their ruins be NIH
21:19 that the sword of the king of Babylon m NIH
21:20 that the sword m come to Rabbath of NIH
21:23 the iniquity, that they m be taken. NIH
22: 3 that her time m come, and maketh idols NIH
23:48 that all women m be taught not to do after NIH
24:11 that the brass of it m be hot, and may burn, NIH
24:11 m burn, and that the filthiness of it may be NIH
24:11 that the filthiness of it m be molten in it, NIH
24:11 in it, that the scum of it m be consumed. NIH
25:10 that the Ammonites m not be remembered NIH
28:17 thee before kings, that they m behold thee. NIH
34:10 that they m not be meat for them. NIH
37: 9 breathe upon these slain, that they m live. NIH
38:16 my land, that the heathen m know me, NIH
39:12 of them, that they m cleanse the land. NIH
39:17 that ye m eat flesh, and drink blood. NIH
43:10 that they m be ashamed of their iniquities: NIH
43:11 that they m keep the whole form thereof, NIH
44:25 had no husband, they m defile themselves. NIH
44:30 that he m cause the blessing to rest in thine NIH
45:11 that the bath m contain the tenth part of a 3807.1
Da 4:17 to the intent that the living m know that NIH
4:27 if it m be a lengthening of thy tranquillity. NIH
6:15 which the king establisheth m be changed. NIH
Hos 8: 4 made them idols, that they m be cut off. NIH
13:10 where is any other that m save thee in all NIH
Am 5:14 Seek good, and not evil, that ye m live: and NIH
5:15 it m be that the LORD God of hosts will 194
6:10 for we m not make mention of the name of NIH
8: 5 the new moon be gone, that we m sell corn? NIH
8: 5 the sabbath, that we m set forth wheat, NIH
8: 6 That we m buy the poor for silver, and NIH
9: 1 lintel of the door, that the posts m shake: NIH
9:12 That they m possess the remnant of Edom, NIH
Ob 1: 9 mount of Esau m be cut off by slaughter. NIH
Jnh 1: 7 that we m know for whose cause this evil is NIH
1:11 unto thee, that the sea m be calm unto us? NIH
Mic 6: 5 that ye m know the righteousness of NIH
7: 3 That they m do evil with both hands NIH
Hab 2: 2 upon tables, that he m run that readeth it. NIH
2: 9 that he m set his nest on high, that he may NIH
2: 9 that he m be delivered from the power of NIH
Zep 2: 3 it m be ye shall be hid in the day of 194
3: 8 that I m assemble the kingdoms, to pour NIH
3: 9 that they m all call upon the name of NIH
Zec 11: 1 that the fire m devour thy cedars. NIH
Mal 3: 2 who m abide the day of his coming? and NIH
3: 3 that they m offer unto the LORD an NIH
3:10 that there m be meat in mine house, and NIH
Mt 2: 8 that I m come and worship him also. NIG
5:16 that they m see your good works, and NIG
5:45 That ye m be the children of your Father NIG
6: 2 the streets, that they m have glory of men. NIG
6: 4 That thine alms m be in secret: and NIG
6: 5 of the streets, that they m be seen of men. 302
6:16 that they m appear unto men to fast. NIG
9: 6 But that ye m know that the Son of man NIG
9:21 If I m but touch his garment, I shall be NIG
14:15 that they m go into the villages, and NIG
18:16 three witnesses every word m be NIG
19:16 thing shall I do, that I m have eternal life? NIG
20:21 Grant that these my two sons m sit, NIG
20:33 unto him, Lord, that our eyes m be opened. NIG
23:26 that the outside of them m be clean also. NIG
23:35 That upon you m come all the righteous NIG
26:42 if this cup m not pass away from me, 1410
Mk 1:38 the next towns, that I m preach there also: NIG
2:10 But that ye m know that the Son of man NIG
4:12 That seeing they m see, and not perceive; NIG
4:12 and hearing they m hear, and NIG
4:32 that the fowls of the air m lodge under 1410
5:12 us into the swine, that we m enter into them. NIG
5:23 lay thy hands on her, that she m be healed; NIG
5:28 For she said, If I m touch but his clothes, NIG
6:36 that they m go into the country round about, NIG
7: 9 of God, that ye m keep your own tradition. NIG
10:17 what shall I do that I m inherit eternal life? NIG
10:37 said unto him, Grant unto us that we m sit, NIG
11:25 that your Father also which is in heaven m NIG
12:15 ye me? bring me a penny, that I m see it. NIG
14: 7 whensoever ye will ye m do them good: 1410
15:32 from the cross, that we m see and believe. NIG
Lk 2:35 that the thoughts of many hearts m be NIG
5:24 But that ye m know that the Son of man NIG
8:16 that they which enter in m see the light. NIG
9:12 that they m go into the towns and NIG
11:33 that they which come in m see the light. NIG
11:50 the world, m be required of this generation; NIG
12:36 they m open unto him immediately. NIG
14:10 he m say unto thee, Friend, go up higher: NIG
14:23 them to come in, that my house m be filled. NIG
16: 4 they m receive me into their houses. NIG
16: 9 they m receive you into everlasting NIG
16:24 that he m dip the tip of his finger in water, NIG
16:28 that he m testify unto them, lest they also NIG

M

Lk 17: 8 Make ready wherewith I **m** sup, and NIG
18:41 he said, Lord, that I **m** receive my sight. NIG
20:13 **it m be** they will reverence *him* 24281
20:14 us kill him, that the inheritance **m** be ours. NIG
21:22 that all *things* which are written **m** be NIG
21:36 that ye **m** be accounted worthy to escape all NIG
22: 8 and prepare us the passover, that we **m** eat. NIG
22:30 That ye **m** eat and drink at my table in my NIG
22:31 *to have* you, that *he* **m** sift *you* as wheat: NIG
Jn 1:22 that we **m** give an answer to them that sent NIG
3:21 that his deeds **m** be made manifest, that they NIG
4:36 and he that reapeth **m** rejoice together. NIG
5:20 greater works than these, that ye **m** marvel. NIG
6: 5 shall we buy bread, that these **m** eat? NIG
6: 7 that every one of them **m** take a little. NIG
6:30 thou then, that we **m** see, and believe thee? NIG
6:40 believeth on him, **m** have everlasting life: NIG
6:50 from heaven, that a man **m** eat thereof, NIG
7: 3 that thy disciples also **m** see the works that NIG
10:38 that ye **m** know, and believe, that the Father NIG
11:11 but I go, that I **m** awake him out of sleep. NIG
11:15 I was not there, to the intent ye **m** believe; NIG
11:16 Let us also go, that we **m** die with him. NIG
11:42 that they **m** believe that thou hast sent me. NIG
12:36 the light, that ye **m** be the children of light. NIG
13:18 but that the scripture **m** be fulfilled, He that NIG
13:19 is come to pass, ye **m** believe that I am *he*. NIG
14: 3 that where I am, *there* ye **m** be also. NIG
14:13 that the Father **m** be glorified in the Son. NIG
14:16 that he **m** abide with you for ever; NIG
14:31 But that the world **m** know that I love NIG
15: 2 purgeth it, that it **m** bring forth more fruit. NIG
15:16 of the Father in my name, he **m** give it you. NIG
16: 4 ye **m** remember that I told you of them. NIG
16:24 and ye shall receive, that your joy **m** be full. NIG
17: 1 thy Son, that thy Son also **m** glorify thee: NIG
17:11 given me, that they **m** be one, as we *are*. NIG
17:21 That they all **m** be one; as thou, Father, NIG
17:21 and I in thee, that they also **m** be one in us: NIG
17:21 that the world **m** believe that thou hast sent NIG
17:22 that they **m** be one, even as we are one: NIG
17:23 in me, that they **m** be made perfect in one; NIG
17:23 that the world **m** know that thou hast sent NIG
17:24 that they **m** behold my glory, which thou NIG
17:26 thou hast loved me **m** be in them, NIG
19: 4 that ye **m** know that I find no fault in him. NIG
Ac 1:25 That *he* **m** take part of this ministry and NIG
3:19 that your sins **m** be blotted out, NIG
4:29 that with all boldness *they* **m** speak thy NIG
4:30 wonders **m** be done by the name of thy holy NIG
6: 3 whom we **m** appoint over this business. NIG
8:19 I lay hands, he **m** receive the Holy Ghost. NIG
8:20 thou hast thought that the gift of God **m** be NIG
8:22 if perhaps the thought of thine heart **m** be NIG
17:19 saying, **M** we know what this new doctrine, 1410
19:40 there being no cause whereby we **m** give an 1410
21:24 with them, that they **m** shave *their* heads: NIG
21:24 all **m** know that *those things*, whereof they NIG
21:37 unto the chief captain, **M** I speak unto thee? 1832
23:24 that they **m** set Paul on, and bring *him* safe NIG
25:11 no *man* **m** deliver me unto them. 1410
26:18 that they **m** receive forgiveness of sins, and NIG
Ro 1:11 that I **m** impart unto you some spiritual gift, NIG
1:11 to the end you **m** be established; NIG
1:12 that *I* **m** be comforted together with you by NIG
1:19 Because that which **m** be known of God is NIG
3: 8 we say,) Let us do evil, that good **m** come? NIG
3:19 that every mouth **m** be stopped, and all NIG
3:19 all the world **m** become guilty before God. NIG
6: 1 we continue in sin, that grace **m** abound? NIG
8:17 be that we suffer with *him*, that we **m** be NIG
11:10 that *they* **m** not see, and bow down their NIG
11:14 If by any means I **m** provoke to emulation NIG
11:31 that through your mercy they also **m** obtain NIG
12: 2 that ye **m** prove what *is that* good, and NIG
14: 2 For one believeth that *he* **m** eat all *things*: NIG
14:19 and *things* wherewith one **m** edify another. NIG
15: 6 That ye **m** with one mind *and* one mouth NIG
15:13 in believing, that ye **m** abound in hope, NIG
15:17 whereof *I* **m** glory through Jesus Christ *in* NIG
15:31 That I **m** be delivered from them that do not NIG
15:31 for Jerusalem **m** be accepted of the saints; NIG
15:32 That I **m** come unto you with joy by the will NIG
15:32 will of God, and **m** with you be refreshed. NIG
1Co 1: 8 *that ye* **m** be blameless in the day of our NIG
2:16 mind of the Lord, that he **m** instruct him? NIG
3:18 let him become a fool, that he **m** be wise. NIG
5: 5 that the spirit **m** be saved in the day of NIG
5: 7 the old leaven, that ye **m** be a new lump, NIG
7: 5 that ye **m** give yourselves to fasting and NIG
7:32 to the Lord, how he **m** please the Lord: NIG
7:33 *are* of the world, how he **m** please *his* wife. NIG
7:34 that she **m** be holy both in body and NIG
7:34 the world, how she **m** please *her* husband. NIG
7:35 not that I **m** cast a snare upon you, but NIG
7:35 that you **m** attend upon the Lord without NIG
9:18 I **m** make the gospel of Christ without NIG
9:24 the prize? So run, that ye **m** obtain. NIG
10:13 way to escape, that ye **m** be able to bear *it*. NIG
10:33 but the *profit* of many, that they **m** be saved. NIG
11:19 that they *which are* approved **m** be made NIG
14: 1 but rather that ye **m** prophesy. NIG
14: 5 that the church **m** receive edifying. 3588
14:10 There are, **it m be**, 1487+5177
14:12 ye **m** excel to the edifying of the church. NIG
14:13 *unknown* tongue pray that he **m** interpret. NIG
14:31 For ye **m** all prophesy one by one, that all 1410
14:31 that all **m** learn, and all may be comforted. NIG
14:31 that all may learn, and all **m** be comforted. NIG
15:28 *things* under him, that God **m** be all in all. NIG
15:37 **it m chance** of wheat, or of some 1487+5177
16: 6 And **it m be** that I will abide, yea, and 5177
16: 6 that ye **m** bring me on my journey NIG
16:10 see that he **m** be with you without fear: NIG
16:11 him forth in peace, that he **m** come unto me: NIG
2Co 1: 4 that we **m** be able to comfort them which NIG
1:11 thanks **m** be given by many on our behalf. NIG
2: 5 but in part: that I **m** not overcharge you all. NIG
4: 7 that the excellency of the power **m** be of NIG
5: 9 or absent, we **m** be accepted of him. NIG
5:10 that every one **m** receive the *things done* in NIG
5:12 that you **m** have *somewhat* to *answer* them NIG
8:11 *there* **m** be a performance also out of that NIG
8:14 *that* now at *this* time your abundance **m** *be a* NIG
8:14 that their abundance also **m** be *a supply* for NIG
8:14 for your want: that there **m** be equality: NIG
9: 3 in this behalf; that, as I said, ye **m** be ready: NIG
9: 8 in all *things*, **m** abound to every good work: NIG
10: 2 But I beseech *you*, that I **m** not be bold NIG
10: 9 That I **m** not seem as if *I* would terrify you NIG
11: 2 that *I* **m** present *you as* a chaste virgin to NIG
11:12 that I **m** cut off occasion from them which NIG
11:12 they glory, they **m** be found even as we. NIG
11:16 receive me, that I **m** boast myself a little. NIG
12: 9 that the power of Christ **m** rest upon me. NIG
Gal 6:13 that they **m** glory in your flesh. NIG
Eph 1:17 **m** give unto you the spirit of wisdom and NIG
1:18 that ye **m** know what is the hope of his NIG
3: 4 ye **m** understand my knowledge in 1410
3:17 That Christ **m** dwell in your hearts by faith; NIG
3:18 **M** be able to comprehend with all saints NIG
4:15 **m** grow *up* into him *in* all *things*, which is NIG
4:28 that he **m** have to give to him that needeth. NIG
4:29 that it **m** minister grace unto the hearers. NIG
6: 3 That it **m** be well with thee, and NIG
6:11 that ye **m** be able to stand against the wiles NIG
6:13 that ye **m** be able to withstand in the evil NIG
6:19 for me, that utterance **m** be given unto me, NIG
6:19 unto me, that *I* **m** open my mouth boldly, NIG
6:20 that therein I **m** speak boldly, as I ought to NIG
6:21 But that ye also **m** know my affairs, *and* NIG
Php 1: 9 that your love **m** abound yet more and NIG
1:10 That ye **m** approve *things* that are excellent; NIG
1:10 that ye **m** be sincere and without offence till NIG
1:26 That your rejoicing **m** be *more* abundant in NIG
1:27 or *else* be absent, I **m** hear of your affairs, NIG
2:15 That ye **m** be blameless and harmless, NIG
2:16 that I **m** rejoice in the day of Christ, that I NIG
2:19 that I also **m** be of good comfort, when I NIG
2:28 ye **m** rejoice, and *that* I may be the less NIG
2:28 and *that* I **m** be the less sorrowful. NIG
3: 8 count *them but* dung, that I **m** win Christ, NIG
3:10 That *I* **m** know him, and the power of his NIG
3:12 I follow *after*, if that I **m** apprehend *that* for NIG
3:21 that it **m** be fashioned like unto his glorious NIG
4:17 I desire fruit that *m* abound to your account. NIG
Col 1:28 that we **m** present every man perfect in NIG
4: 4 That I **m** make it manifest, as I ought to NIG
4: 6 that *you* **m** know how ye ought to answer NIG
4:12 that ye **m** stand perfect and complete in all NIG
1Th 3:13 To the end *he* **m** stablish your hearts NIG
4:12 That ye **m** walk honestly toward them that NIG
4:12 and *that* ye **m** have lack of no*thing*. NIG
2Th 1: 5 that ye **m** be counted worthy of NIG
1:12 That the name of our Lord Jesus Christ **m** NIG
3: 1 that the word of the Lord **m** have *free* NIG
3: 2 And that we **m** be delivered from NIG
3:14 company with him, that he **m** be ashamed. NIG
1Ti 1:20 that they **m** learn not to blaspheme. NIG
2: 2 that we **m** lead a quiet and peaceable life in NIG
4:15 to them; that thy profiting **m** appear to all. 1510
5: 7 give in charge, that they **m** be blameless. NIG
5:16 that it **m** relieve them that are widows NIG
5:20 rebuke before all, that others also **m** fear. NIG
6:19 to come, that they **m** lay hold on eternal life. NIG
2Ti 1: 4 of thy tears, that I **m** be filled with joy; NIG
1:18 The Lord grant unto him that *he* **m** find NIG
2: 4 that he **m** please him who hath chosen *him* NIG
2:10 that they **m** also obtain the salvation which NIG
2:26 And *that* they **m** recover themselves out of NIG
3:17 That the man of God **m** be perfect, NIG
4:16 *I pray God* that it **m** not be laid to their NIG
Tit 1: 9 that he **m** be able by sound doctrine both to NIG
1:13 that they **m** be sound in the faith; NIG
2: 4 That they **m** teach the young *women* to be NIG
2: 8 that he that is of the contrary *part* **m** be NIG
2:10 that they **m** adorn the doctrine of God our NIG
Phm 1: 6 That the communication of thy faith **m** NIG
Heb 4:16 that we **m** obtain mercy, and find grace to NIG
5: 1 that he **m** offer both gifts and sacrifices for NIG
7: 9 And as *I* **m** so say, Levi also, who receiveth NIG
10: 9 the first, that he **m** establish the second. NIG
12:27 that those *things* which cannot be shaken **m** NIG
12:28 whereby we **m** serve God acceptably with NIG
13: 6 So that we **m** boldly say, The Lord *is* my NIG
13:17 that they **m** do it with joy, and not with NIG
13:19 that I **m** be restored to you the sooner. NIG
Jas 1: 4 that ye **m** be perfect and entire, NIG
2:18 Yea, a man **m** say, Thou hast faith, and I NIG
3: 3 in the horses' mouths, that they **m** obey us; NIG
4: 3 that ye **m** consume *it* upon your lusts. NIG
5:16 pray one for another, that ye **m** be healed. NIG
1Pe 2: 2 milk of the word, that ye **m** grow thereby: NIG
2:12 they **m** by *your* good works, *which* they NIG
2:15 that with well doing *ye* **m** put to silence NIG
3: 1 they also **m** without the word be won by NIG
3:16 they **m** be ashamed that falsely accuse your NIG
4: 3 For the time past of *our* life **m** suffice us to NIG
4:11 that God in all *things* **m** be glorified through NIG
4:13 ye **m** be glad also with exceeding joy. NIG
5: 6 of God, that he **m** exalt you in due time: NIG
5: 8 walketh about, seeking whom he **m** devour: NIG
2Pe 1:15 Moreover I will endeavour that you **m** be NIG
3: 2 That *ye* **m** be mindful of the words which NIG
3:14 diligent that ye **m** be found of him in peace, NIG
1Jn 1: 3 that ye also **m** have fellowship with us: NIG
1: 4 write we unto you, that your joy **m** be full. NIG
2:28 we **m** have confidence, and not be ashamed NIG
4:17 that we **m** have boldness in the day of NIG
5:13 that ye **m** know that ye have eternal life, NIG
1Jn 5:13 that ye **m** believe on the name of the Son of NIG
5:20 that we **m** know him *that is* true, and we are NIG
2Jn 1:12 speak face to face, that our joy **m** be full. NIG
Rev 2:10 *some* of you into prison, that ye **m** be tried; NIG
14:13 that they **m** rest from their labours; NIG
19:18 That ye **m** eat the flesh of kings, and NIG
22:14 that they **m** have right to the tree of life, and NIG
22:14 **m** enter in through the gates into the city. NIG

MAYEST (114) [MAY]

Ge 2:16 Of every tree of the garden thou **m** freely NIH
23: 6 but that thou **m** bury thy dead. NIH
28: 3 that thou **m** be a multitude of people; NIH
28: 4 that thou **m** inherit the land wherein thou art NIH
38:16 thou give me, that thou **m** come in unto me? NIH
Ex 3:10 that thou **m** bring forth my people NIH
8:10 that thou **m** know that *there is* none like NIH
8:22 to the end thou **m** know that I *am* NIH
9:14 that thou **m** know that *there is* none like me NIH
9:29 that thou **m** know how that the earth *is* NIH
10: 2 that thou **m** tell in the ears of thy son, and NIH
18:19 that thou **m** bring the causes unto God: NIH
24:12 I have written; that thou **m** teach them. NIH
26:33 that thou **m** bring in thither within the vail NIH
Lev 22:23 that **m** thou offer *for* a freewill offering; NIH
Nu 10: 2 that thou **m** use them for the calling of NIH
10:31 and thou **m** be to us instead of eyes. NIH
23:13 from whence thou **m** see them: NIH
23:27 peradventure it will please God that thou **m** NIH
Dt 2:31 to possess, that *thou* **m** inherit his land. NIH
4:40 that thou **m** prolong *thy* days upon the earth, NIH
6:18 *that* thou **m** go in and possess the good land NIH
7:22 thou **m** not consume them at once, lest 3201
8: 9 and out of whose hills thou **m** dig brass. NIH
11:14 that thou **m** gather in thy corn, and NIH
11:15 for thy cattle, that thou **m** eat and be full. NIH
12:15 Notwithstanding thou **m** kill and eat flesh in NIH
12:17 Thou **m** not eat within thy gates the tithe of 3201
12:20 thou **m** eat flesh, whatsoever thy soul NIH
12:23 and thou **m** not eat the life with the flesh. NIH
14:21 he may eat it; or thou **m** sell *it* unto an alien: NIH
14:23 that thou **m** learn to fear the LORD thy NIH
15: 3 Of a foreigner thou **m** exact *it again*: but NIH
16: 3 that thou **m** remember the day when thou NIH
16: 5 Thou **m** not sacrifice the passover within 3201
16:20 that thou **m** live, and inherit the land which NIH
17:15 thou **m** not set a stranger over thee, 3201
20:19 for thou **m** eat of them, and thou shalt not NIH
22: 3 thou do likewise: thou **m** not hide thyself. 3201
22: 7 with thee, and *that* thou **m** prolong *thy* days. NIH
23:20 Unto a stranger thou **m** lend upon usury; but NIH
23:24 thou **m** eat grapes thy fill at thine own NIH
23:25 then thou **m** pluck the ears with thine hand; NIH
26:19 that thou **m** be a holy people unto NIH
27: 3 that thou **m** go in unto the land which NIH
28:58 that *thou* **m** fear this glorious and fearful NIH
30: 6 and with all thy soul, that thou **m** live. NIH
30:14 and in thy heart, that *thou* **m** do it. NIH
30:16 that thou **m** live and multiply: NIH
30:20 That thou **m** love the LORD thy God, *and* NIH
30:20 *and* that thou **m** obey his voice, and NIH
30:20 his voice, and that thou **m** cleave unto him: NIH
30:20 that thou **m** dwell in the land which NIH
Jos 1: 7 that *thou* **m** observe to do according to all NIH
1: 7 that thou **m** prosper whithersoever thou NIH
1: 8 that thou **m** observe to do according to all NIH
Jdg 9:33 **m** thou do to them as thou shalt find NIH
11: 8 that thou **m** go with us, and fight against NIH
19: 9 early on your way, that thou **m** go home. NIH
1Sa 20:13 send thee away, that thou **m** go in peace: NIH
24: 4 that thou **m** do to him as it shall seem good NIH
28:15 that *thou* **m** make known unto me what I NIH
28:22 eat, that thou **m** have strength, when thou NIH
2Sa 3:21 that thou **m** reign over all that thine heart NIH
15:34 **m** thou for me defeat the counsel of NIH
22:28 the haughty, *that* thou **m** bring *them* down. NIH
1Ki 1:12 that thou **m** save thine own life, and the life NIH
2: 3 that thou **m** prosper *in* all that thou doest, NIH
2:31 that thou **m** take away the innocent blood, NIH
8:29 that *thou* **m** hearken unto the prayer which NIH
2Ki 5: 6 that thou **m** recover him of his leprosy. NIH
8:10 say unto him, Thou **m** certainly recover: NIH
1Ch 22:12 that *thou* **m** keep the law of the LORD thy NIH
22:14 have I prepared; and thou **m** add thereto. NIH
2Ch 1:11 for thyself, that thou **m** judge my people, NIH
18:33 that thou **m** carry me out of the host; NIH
Ezr 7:17 That thou **m** buy speedily with this money NIH
Ne 1: 6 that *thou* **m** hear the prayer of thy servant, NIH
6: 6 that thou **m** be their king, according to these NIH
Job 40: 8 condemn me, that thou **m** be righteous? NIH
Ps 32: 6 unto thee in a time when thou **m** be found: NIH
45:16 whom thou **m** make princes in all the earth. NIH
94:13 That *thou* **m** give him rest from the days of NIH
104:27 that *thou* **m** give *them* their meat in due NIH
130: 4 with thee, that thou **m** be feared. NIH
Pr 2:20 That thou **m** walk in the way of good *men*, NIH
5: 2 That *thou* **m** regard discretion, and *that* thy NIH
19:20 that thou **m** be wise in thy latter end. NIH
Isa 23:16 many songs, that thou **m** be remembered. NIH
43:26 declare thou, that thou **m** be justified. NIH
45: 3 that thou **m** know that I, the LORD, NIH
47:12 be able to profit, if so be thou **m** prevail. NIH
49: 6 that *thou* **m** be my salvation unto the end of NIH
49: 9 That *thou* **m** say to the prisoners, Go forth; NIH
Jer 4:14 from wickedness, that thou **m** be saved. NIH
6:27 that thou **m** know and try their way. NIH
30:13 to plead thy cause, that thou **m** be bound up: NIH
Eze 16:54 That thou **m** bear thine own shame, and NIH
16:54 **m** be confounded in all that thou hast done, NIH
16:63 That thou **m** remember, and be confounded, NIH
Hab 2:15 that thou **m** look on their nakedness! NIH
Mk 14:12 and prepare that thou **m** eat the passover? NIG
Lk 12:58 give diligence that *thou* **m** be delivered NIG
16: 2 for thou **m** be no longer steward. 1410
Ac 8:37 thou believest with all *thine* heart, *thou* **m**. 1832

Ac 24: 8 by examining of whom thyself **m** take 1410
24:11 Because that thou **m** understand, that there 1410
1Co 7:21 but if thou **m** be made free, use *it* rather. 1410
Eph 6: 3 with thee, and thou **m** live long on the earth. NIG
1Ti 3:15 that thou **m** know how *thou* oughtest to NIG
3Jn 1: 2 I wish above all *things* that thou **m** prosper NIG
Rev 3:18 gold tried in the fire, that thou **m** be rich; NIG
3:18 that thou **m** be clothed, and *that* the shame NIG
3:18 thine eyes *with* eyesalve, that thou **m** see. NIG

MAZZAROTH (1)
Job 38:32 Canst thou bring forth **M** in his season? or 4216

ME (4096) [I] See Index of Articles, Etc.

MEADOW (2) [MEADOWS]
Ge 41: 2 and fatfleshed; and they fed in a **m**. 260
41:18 well favoured; and they fed in a **m**: 260

MEADOWS (1) [MEADOW]
Jdg 20:33 their places, *even* out of the **m** of Gibeah. 4629

MEAH (2)
Ne 3: 1 even unto the tower of **M** they sanctified it, 3968
12:39 the tower of Hananeel, and the tower of **M**, 3968

MEAL (12) [MEALTIME]
Ge 18: 6 ready quickly three measures of fine **m**, 7058
Nu 5:15 the tenth *part* of an ephah of barley **m**; 7058
1Ki 4:22 of fine flour, and threescore measures of **m**, 7058
17:12 a handful of **m** in a barrel, and a little oil in 7058
17:14 The barrel of **m** shall not waste, 7058
17:16 *And* the barrel of **m** wasted not, neither did 7058
2Ki 4:41 he said, Then bring **m**. And he cast *it* into 7058
1Ch 12:40 and on mules, and on oxen, *and* meat, **m**, 7058
Isa 47: 2 Take the millstones, and grind **m**: 7058
Hos 8: 7 the bud shall yield no **m**: if so be it yield, 7058
Mt 13:33 and hid in three measures of **m**, 224
Lk 13:21 woman took and hid in three measures of **m**, 224

MEALTIME (1) [MEAL, TIME]
Ru 2:14 At **m** come thou hither, and 400+6256+1886.1

MEAN (22) [MEANEST, MEANETH, MEANING, MEANS, MEANT]
Ge 21:29 What ***m*** these seven ewe lambs which thou NIH
Ex 12:26 unto you, What **m** you by this service? 3807.1
Dt 6:20 What ***m*** the testimonies, and the statutes, NIH
Jos 4: 6 What **m** you by these stones? 3807.1
4:21 time to come, saying, What ***m*** these stones? NIH
1Ki 18:45 **in the m while**, 3541+3541+5704+5704+2050.1
Pr 22:29 he shall not stand before **m** *men*. 2823
Isa 2: 9 the **m** man boweth down, and the great man NIH
3:15 What **m** ye *that* ye beat my people to 3807.1
5:15 the **m** man shall be brought down, and NIH
31: 8 the sword, not of a **m** man, shall devour NIH
Eze 17:12 Know ye not what these *things* ***m***? tell NIH
18: 2 What **m** ye, that ye use this proverb 3807.1
Mk 9:10 what the rising from the dead should **m**. 1510
Lk 12: 1 **In the m time**, when there were 1722+3739
Jn 4:31 In the **m while** *his* disciples prayed him, 3342
Ac 10:17 *this* vision which he had seen should **m**, 1510
17:20 would know therefore what these *things* **m**. 2309
21:13 **What m** ye to weep and to break mine 5101
21:39 *a city* in Cilicia, a citizen of no **m** city: 767
Ro 2:15 and *their* thoughts the **m** while accusing or NIG
2Co 8:13 For *I* **m** not that other *men* be eased, and NIG

MEANEST (4) [MEAN]
Ge 33: 8 **m** thou by all this drove which I met? 3807.1
2Sa 16: 2 said unto Ziba, What **m** thou by these? 3807.1
Eze 37:18 Wilt thou not shew us what thou **m** by 3807.1
Jnh 1: 6 said unto him, What **m** thou, O sleeper? 3807.1

MEANETH (8) [MEAN]
Dt 29:24 what ***m*** the heat of this great anger? NIH
1Sa 4: 6 What ***m*** the noise of this great shout in NIH
4:14 he said, What ***m*** the noise of this tumult? NIH
15:14 What ***m*** then this bleating of the sheep in NIH
Isa 10: 7 Howbeit he **m** not so, neither doth his heart 1819
Mt 9:13 But go ye and learn what *that* **m**, I will 1510
12: 7 But if ye had known what *this* **m**, I will 1510
Ac 2:12 saying one to another, What **m** this? 1510+2309

MEANING (3) [MEAN]
Da 8:15 and sought for the **m**, then behold, 998
Ac 27: 2 **m** to sail by the coasts of Asia; 3195
1Co 14:11 Therefore if I know not the **m** of the voice, 1411

MEANINGLESS See VANITIES; VANITY

MEANS (35) [MEAN]
Ex 34: 7 *that* will **by no m** clear *the guilty;* visiting 3008
Nu 14:18 **by no m** clearing *the guilty,* visiting 3808
Jdg 5:22 were the horsehoofs broken **by the m of** 4480
16: 5 and by what *m* we may prevail against him, NIH
2Sa 14:14 yet doth he devise **m**, that *his* banished be 4284
1Ki 10:29 did they bring *them* out by their **m**. 3027
20:39 if **by any m** he be **missing**, then 6485+6485
2Ch 1:17 and *for* the kings of Syria, by their **m**. 3027
Ezr 4:16 by this **m** thou shalt have no portion on *this* 6903
Ps 49: 7 None *of them* can **by any m redeem** 6299+6299
Pr 6:26 For **by m of** a whorish woman *a man is* 1157
Jer 5:31 and the priests bear rule by their **m**; 3027
Mal 1: 9 this hath been by your **m**: will he regard 3027
Mt 5:26 Thou shalt **by no m** come out thence, 3364
Lk 5:18 and they sought *m* to bring him in, and NIG
8:36 **by what m** he that was possessed of 4459
10:19 and nothing shall **by any m** hurt you, 3364
Jn 9:21 But **by what m** he now seeth, we know 4459
Ac 4: 9 impotent man, by what *m* he is made whole; NIG
18:21 I must **by all m** keep *this* feast that cometh 3843
27:12 **if by any m** they might attain to Phenice, 1513
Ro 1:10 **if by any m** now at length I might have a 1513
11:14 **If by any m** I may provoke to emulation 1513
1Co 8: 9 But take heed **lest by any m** this liberty of 3381
9:22 to all *men,* that I might **by all m** save some. 3843
9:27 **lest that by any m**, when I have preached 3381
2Co 1:11 **by the m of** many persons thanks may be 1537
11: 3 But I fear, **lest by any m**, as the serpent 3381
Gal 2: 2 **lest by any m** I should run, or had run, 3381
Php 3:11 **If by any m** I might attain unto 1513
1Th 3: 5 **lest by some m** the tempter have tempted 3381
2Th 2: 3 Let no *man* deceive you by any **m**: for *that* 5158
3:16 himself give you peace always by all **m**. 5158
Heb 9:15 of the new testament, that by **m** of death, NIG
Rev 13:14 **by the m of** *those* miracles which he had 1223

MEANT (3) [MEAN]
Ge 50:20 *but* God **m** it unto good, to bring to pass, 2803
Lk 15:26 and asked what these *things* **m**. 1510
18:36 the multitude pass by, he asked what it **m**. 1510

MEARAH (1)
Jos 13: 4 **M** that *is* beside the Sidonians, unto Aphek, 4632

MEASURE (69) [MEASURED, MEASURES, MEASURING]
Ex 26: 2 every one of the curtains shall have one **m**. 4060
26: 8 the eleven curtains *shall be all* of one **m**. 4060
Lev 19:35 in meteyard, in weight, or in **m**. 4884
Nu 35: 5 ye shall **m** from without the city *on* the east 4058
Dt 21: 2 they shall **m** unto the cities which *are* round 4058
25:15 a perfect and just **m** shalt thou have: 374
Jos 3: 4 and it, about two thousand cubits by **m**: 4060
1Ki 6:25 both the cherubims *were* of one **m** and 4060
7:37 them had one casting, one **m**, *and* one size. 4060
2Ki 7: 1 To morrow about *this* time *shall* a **m** of fine 5429
7:16 So a **m** of fine flour was *sold* for a shekel, 5429
7:18 a shekel, and a **m** of fine flour for a shekel, 5429
1Ch 23:29 is fried, and for all *manner of* **m** and size; 4884
2Ch 3: 3 The length *by* cubits after the first **m** *was* 4060
Job 11: 9 The **m** thereof *is* longer than the earth, and 4055
28:25 and he weigheth the waters by **m**. 4060
Ps 39: 4 to know mine end, and the **m** of my days, 4060
80: 5 and givest them tears to drink *in great* **m**. 7991
Isa 5:14 and opened her mouth without **m**: 2706
27: 8 In **m**, when it shooteth forth, thou wilt 5432
40:12 comprehended the dust of the earth in a **m**, 7991
65: 7 will I **m** their former work into their 4058
Jer 30:11 I will correct thee in **m**, and will not leave 4941
46:28 a full end of thee, but correct thee in **m**; 4941
51:13 end is come, *and* the **m** of thy covetousness. 520
Eze 4:11 Thou shalt drink also water by **m**, the sixth 4884
4:16 they shall drink water by **m**, and 4884
40:10 on that side; they three *were* of one **m**: 4060
40:10 the posts had one **m** on this side and on that 4060
40:21 the arches thereof were after the **m** of 4060
40:22 *were* after the **m** of the gate that looketh 4060
41:17 wall round about within and without, *by* **m**. 4060
43:10 their iniquities: and let them **m** the pattern. 4058
45: 3 of this **m** shalt thou measure the length of 4060
45: 3 of this measure shalt thou **m** the length of 4058
45:11 The ephah and the bath shall be of one **m**, 8506
45:11 the **m** thereof shall be after the homer. 4971
46:22 these four corners *were* of one **m**. 4060
47:18 the east side ye shall **m** from Hauran, and 4058
Mic 6:10 and the scant **m** *that is* abominable? 374
Zec 2: 2 he said unto me, To **m** Jerusalem, to see 4058
Mt 7: 2 and with what **m** ye mete, it shall be 3358
23:32 Fill ye up then the **m** of your fathers. 3358
Mk 4:24 with what **m** ye mete, it shall be measured 3358
6:51 were sore amazed in themselves beyond **m**, 4053
7:37 And were **beyond m** astonished, saying, 5249
10:26 And they were astonished **out of m**, 4057
Lk 6:38 good **m**, pressed down, and 3358
6:38 For with the same **m** that ye mete withal it 3358
Jn 3:34 for God giveth not the Spirit by **m** *unto* 3358
Ro 12: 3 God hath dealt to every man the **m** of faith. 3358
2Co 1: 8 that we were pressed **out of m**, 2596+5236
10:13 we will not boast of *things* **without** *our* **m**, 280
10:13 according to the **m** of the rule which God 3358
10:13 to us, a **m** to reach even unto you. 3358
10:14 For we stretch not ourselves beyond *our* **m**, NIG
10:15 Not boasting of *things* **without** *our* **m**, 280
11:23 in stripes **above m**, in prisons more 5234
12: 7 And lest I should be **exalted above m** 5229
12: 7 lest I should be **exalted above m**. 5229
Gal 1:13 how that **beyond m** I persecuted 2596+5236
Eph 4: 7 according to the **m** of the gift of Christ. 3358
4:13 unto the **m** of the stature of the fulness of 3358
4:16 according to the effectual working in the **m** 3358
Rev 6: 6 A **m** of wheat for a penny, and 5518
11: 1 and **m** the temple of God, and the altar, and 3354
11: 2 without the temple leave out, and **m** it not; 3354
21:15 with me had a golden reed to **m** the city, 3354
21:17 *according to* the **m** of a man, that is, 3358

MEASURED (46) [MEASURE]
Ru 3:15 he **m** six *measures* of barley, and laid *it* on 4058
2Sa 8: 2 he smote Moab, and **m** them with a line, 4058
8: 2 even *with* two lines **m** he to put to death, 4058
Isa 40:12 Who hath **m** the waters in the hollow of his 4058
Jer 31:37 If heaven above can be **m**, and 4058
33:22 neither the sand of the sea **m**: 3808+4058
Eze 40: 5 so he **m** the breadth of the building, 4058
40: 6 and **m** the threshold of the gate, 4058
40: 8 He **m** also the porch of the gate within, one 4058
40: 9 **m** he the porch of the gate, eight cubits; 4058
40:11 he **m** the breadth of the entry of the gate, 4058
40:13 He **m** then the gate from the roof of *one* 4058
40:19 he **m** the breadth from the forefront of 4058
40:20 he **m** the length thereof, and the breadth 4058
40:23 he **m** from gate to gate an hundred cubits. 4058
40:24 he **m** the posts thereof and the arches 4058
40:27 he **m** from gate to gate toward the south an 4058
40:28 he **m** the south gate according to these 4058
40:32 he **m** the gate according to these measures. 4058
40:35 and **m** *it* according to these measures; 4058
40:47 So he **m** the court, an hundred cubits long, 4058
40:48 **m** *each* post of the porch, five cubits on this 4058
41: 1 **m** the posts, six cubits broad on the one 4058
41: 2 he **m** the length thereof, forty cubits: and 4058
41: 3 **m** the post of the door, two cubits; 4058
41: 4 So he **m** the length thereof, twenty cubits; 4058
41: 5 After he **m** the wall of the house, six cubits; 4058
41:13 So he **m** the house, an hundred cubits long; 4058
41:15 he **m** the length of the building over against 4058
42:15 *is* toward the east, and **m** it round about. 4058
42:16 He **m** the east side with the measuring reed, 4058
42:17 He **m** the north side, five hundred reeds, 4058
42:18 He **m** the south side, five hundred reeds, 4058
42:19 **m** five hundred reeds with the measuring 4058
42:20 He **m** it by the four sides: it had a wall 4058
47: 3 forth east*ward,* he **m** a thousand cubits, 4058
47: 4 Again he **m** a thousand, and brought me 4058
47: 4 Again he **m** a thousand, and brought me 4058
47: 5 Afterward he **m** a thousand; *and it was* a 4058
Hos 1:10 the sea, which cannot be **m** nor numbered; 4058
Hab 3: 6 He stood, and **m** the earth: he beheld, and 4128
Mt 7: 2 measure ye mete, it shall be **m** to you **again**. 488
Mk 4:24 what measure ye mete, it shall be **m** to you: 3354
Lk 6:38 ye mete withal it shall be **m** to you **again**. 488
Rev 21:16 and he **m** the city with the reed, 3354
21:17 And he **m** the wall thereof, an hundred *and* 3354

MEASURES (39) [MEASURE]
Ge 18: 6 Make ready quickly three **m** of fine meal, 5429
Dt 25:14 have in thine house **divers m**, 374+374+2050.1
Ru 3:15 he measured six ***m*** of barley, and laid *it* on NIH
3:17 she said, These six ***m*** of barley gave he me; NIH
1Sa 25:18 five **m** of parched *corn,* and an hundred 5429
1Ki 4:22 for one day was thirty **m** of fine flour, 3734
4:22 of fine flour, and threescore **m** of meal, 3734
5:11 Solomon gave Hiram twenty thousand **m** of 3734
5:11 to his household, and twenty **m** of pure oil: 3734
7: 9 according to the **m** of hewed stones, 4060
7:11 after the **m** of hewed stones, and cedars. 4060
18:32 as great as would contain **two m** of seed. 5429
2Ki 7: 1 **two m** of barley for a shekel, in the gate of 5429
7:16 **two m** of barley for a shekel, according to 5429
7:18 **Two m** of barley for a shekel, and 5429
2Ch 2:10 twenty thousand **m** of beaten wheat, and 3734
2:10 twenty thousand **m** of barley, and 3734
27: 5 ten thousand **m** of wheat, and ten thousand 3734
Ezr 7:22 to an hundred **m** *of* wheat, and to an 3734
Job 38: 5 Who hath laid the **m** thereof, if thou 4461
Pr 20:10 Divers weights, *and* **divers m**, 374+374+2050.1
Jer 13:25 *is* thy lot, the portion of thy **m** from me, 4055
Eze 40:24 the arches thereof according to these **m**. 4060
40:28 the south gate according to these **m**; 4060
40:29 the arches thereof, according to these **m**: 4060
40:32 he measured the gate according to these **m**. 4060
40:33 arches thereof, *were* according to these **m**: 4060
40:35 and measured *it* according to these **m**; 4060
43:13 these *are* the **m** of the altar after the cubits: 4060
48:16 these *shall be* the **m** thereof; the north side 4060
48:30 four thousand and five hundred **m**. 4060
48:33 side four thousand and five hundred **m**: 4060
48:35 *It was* round about eighteen thousand ***m***: NIH
Hag 2:16 when *one* came to a heap of twenty **m**, there NIH
Mt 13:33 a woman took, and hid in three **m** of meal, 4568
Lk 13:21 a woman took and hid in three **m** of meal, 4568
16: 6 And he said, An hundred **m** of oil. And he 943
16: 7 And he said, An hundred **m** of wheat. 2884
Rev 6: 6 a penny, and three **m** of barley for a penny; 5518

MEASURING (11) [MEASURE]
Jer 31:39 the **m** line shall yet go forth over against it 4060
Eze 40: 3 a line of flax in his hand, and a **m** reed; 4060
40: 5 in the man's hand a **m** reed of six cubits 4060
42:15 Now when he had made an end of **m** 4060
42:16 He measured the east side with the **m** reed, 4060
42:16 with the **m** reed round about. 4060
42:17 with the **m** reed round about. 4060
42:18 five hundred reeds, with the **m** reed. 4060
42:19 measured five hundred reeds with the **m** 4060
Zec 2: 1 behold, a man with a **m** line in his hand. 4060
2Co 10:12 but they **m** themselves by themselves, and 3354

MEAT (290) [BAKEMEATS, MEATS]
Ge 1:29 a tree yielding seed; to you it shall be for **m**. 402
1:30 *is* life, *I have given* every green herb for **m**: 402
9: 3 Every moving thing that liveth shall be **m** 402
24:33 there was set ***m*** before him to eat: but NIH
27: 4 make me **savoury m**, such as I love, and 4303
27: 7 make me **savoury m**, that I may eat, and 4303
27: 9 I will make them **savoury m** for thy father, 4303
27:14 his mother made **savoury m**, such as his 4303
27:17 And she gave the **savoury m** and the bread, 4303
27:31 he also had made **savoury m**, and 4303
45:23 and bread and **m** for his father by the way. 4202
Ex 29:41 shalt do thereto according to the **m offering** 4503
30: 9 nor burnt sacrifice, nor **m offering**; 4503
40:29 it the burnt offering and the **m offering**; 4503
Lev 2: 1 when any will offer a **m offering** unto 4503
2: 3 the remnant of the **m offering** *shall be* 4503
2: 4 if thou bring an oblation of a **m offering** 4503
2: 5 if thy oblation *be* a **m offering** *baken* in a 4503
2: 6 and pour oil thereon: it *is* a **m offering**. 4503
2: 7 if thy oblation *be* a **m offering** *baken* in 4503
2: 8 thou shalt bring the **m offering** that is made 4503
2: 9 the priest shall take from the **m offering** a 4503
2:10 that which is left of the **m offering** *shall be* 4503
2:11 No **m offering**, which ye shall bring unto 4503
2:13 every oblation of thy **m offering** shalt thou 4503
2:13 thy God to be lacking from thy **m offering**: 4503
2:14 if thou offer a **m offering** of *thy* firstfruits 4503
2:14 thou shalt offer for the **m offering** of thy 4503
2:15 lay frankincense thereon: it *is* a **m offering**. 4503
5:13 shall be the priest's, as a **m offering**. 4503
6:14 this *is* the law of the **m offering**: the sons 4503

M

Lev 6:15 of the flour of the **m offering**, and of the oil 4503
6:15 frankincense which *is* upon the **m offering**, 4503
6:20 of fine flour *for* a **m offering** perpetual, 4503
6:21 the baken pieces of the **m offering** shalt 4503
6:23 For every **m offering** for the priest shall be 4503
7: 9 all the **m offering** that is baken in the oven, 4503
7:10 every **m offering**, mingled with oil, and 4503
7:37 of the **m offering**, and of the sin offering, 4503
9: 4 and a **m offering** mingled with oil: 4503
9:17 he brought the **m offering**, and took a 4503
10:12 Take the **m offering** that remaineth of 4503
11:34 Of all **m** which may be eaten, *that* on which 400
14:10 tenth deals of fine flour *for* a **m offering**, 4503
14:20 and the **m offering** upon the altar: 4503
14:21 flour mingled with oil for a **m offering**, 4503
14:31 *for* a burnt offering, with the **m offering**: 4503
22:11 is born in his house: they shall eat of his **m**. 3899
22:13 *in* her youth, she shall eat of her father's **m**: 3899
23:13 the **m offering** thereof *shall be* two tenth 4503
23:16 ye shall offer a new **m offering** unto 4503
23:18 with their **m offering**, and their drink 4503
23:37 a **m offering**, a sacrifice, and 4503
25: 6 the sabbath of the land shall be **m** for you; 402
25: 7 thy land, shall all the increase thereof be **m**. 398
Nu 4:16 the daily **m offering**, and the anointing oil, 4503
6:15 their **m offering**, and their drink offerings. 4503
6:17 the priest shall offer also his **m offering**, 4503
7:13 flour mingled with oil for a **m offering**: 4503
7:19 flour mingled with oil for a **m offering**: 4503
7:25 flour mingled with oil for a **m offering**: 4503
7:31 flour mingled with oil for a **m offering**: 4503
7:37 flour mingled with oil for a **m offering**: 4503
7:43 flour mingled with oil for a **m offering**: 4503
7:49 flour mingled with oil for a **m offering**: 4503
7:55 flour mingled with oil for a **m offering**: 4503
7:61 flour mingled with oil for a **m offering**: 4503
7:67 flour mingled with oil for a **m offering**: 4503
7:73 flour mingled with oil for a **m offering**: 4503
7:79 flour mingled with oil for a **m offering**: 4503
7:87 the first year twelve, with their **m offering**: 4503
8: 8 take a young bullock with his **m offering**, 4503
15: 4 **m offering** of a tenth deal *of* flour mingled 4503
15: 6 thou shalt prepare *for* a **m offering** two 4503
15: 9 shall he bring with a bullock a **m offering** 4503
15:24 with his **m offering**, and his drink offering, 4503
18: 9 every **m offering** of theirs, and every sin 4503
28: 5 *part* of an ephah *of* flour for a **m offering**, 4503
28: 8 as the **m offering** of the morning, and 4503
28: 9 two tenth deals *of* flour *for* a **m offering**, 4503
28:12 three tenth deals *of* flour *for* a **m offering**, 4503
28:12 two tenth deals *of* flour *for* a **m offering**, 4503
28:13 with oil *for* a **m offering** unto one lamb; 4503
28:20 their **m offering** *shall be of* flour mingled 4503
28:24 the **m** of the sacrifice made by fire, 3899
28:26 when ye bring a new **m offering** unto 4503
28:28 their **m offering** *of* flour mingled with oil, 4503
28:31 his **m offering**, (they shall be unto you 4503
29: 3 their **m offering** *shall be of* flour mingled 4503
29: 6 his **m offering**, and the daily burnt 4503
29: 6 his **m offering**, and their drink offerings, 4503
29: 9 their **m offering** *shall be of* flour mingled 4503
29:11 the **m offering** of it, and their drink 4503
29:14 their **m offering** *shall be of* flour mingled 4503
29:16 his **m offering**, and his drink offering. 4503
29:18 their **m offering** and their drink offerings 4503
29:19 the **m offering** thereof, and their drink 4503
29:21 their **m offering** and their drink offerings 4503
29:22 and his **m offering**, and his drink offering. 4503
29:24 Their **m offering** and their drink offerings 4503
29:25 his **m offering**, and his drink offering. 4503
29:27 their **m offering** and their drink offerings 4503
29:28 and his **m offering**, and his drink offering. 4503
29:30 their **m offering** and their drink offerings 4503
29:31 his **m offering**, and his drink offering. 4503
29:33 their **m offering** and their drink offerings 4503
29:34 his **m offering**, and his drink offering. 4503
29:37 Their **m offering** and their drink offerings 4503
29:38 and his **m offering**, and his drink offering. 4503
29:39 for your **m offerings**, and for your drink 4503
Dt 2: 6 Ye shall buy **m** of them for money, that ye 400
2:28 Thou shalt sell me **m** for money, that I may 400
20:20 thou knowest that they *be* not trees for **m**, 3978
28:26 thy carcase shall be **m** unto all fowls of 3978
Jos 22:23 offer thereon burnt offering or **m offering**, 4503
22:29 for **m offerings**, or for sacrifices, 4503
Jdg 1: 7 cut off, gathered *their* **m** under my table: NIH
13:19 So Manoah took a kid with a **m offering**, 4503
13:23 and a **m offering** at our hands, 4503
14:14 Out of the eater came forth **m**, and out of 3978
1Sa 20: 5 I should not fail to sit with the king at **m**: 398
20:24 was come, the king sat him down to eat **m**. 3899
20:27 cometh not the son of Jesse to **m**, 3899
20:34 did eat no **m** the second day of the month: 3899
2Sa 3:35 cause David to eat **m** while it was yet day, 3899
11: 8 there followed him a mess *of* **m** from NIH
12: 3 it did eat of his own **m**, and drank of his 6595
13: 5 give me **m**, and dress the meat in my sight, 3899
13: 5 give me meat, and dress the **m** in my sight, 1279
13: 7 brother Amnon's house, and dress him **m**. 1279
13:10 Bring the **m** *into* the chamber, that I may 1279
1Ki 8:64 **m offerings**, and the fat of the peace 4503
8:64 **m offerings**, and the fat of the peace 4503
10: 5 the **m** of his table, and the sitting of his 3978
19: 8 went in the strength of that **m** forty days and 396
2Ki 3:20 when the **m offering** was offered, 4503
16:13 burnt his burnt offering and his **m offering**, 4503
16:15 the evening **m offering**, and the king's 4503
16:15 king's burnt sacrifice, and his **m offering**, 4503
16:15 their **m offering**, and their drink offerings; 4503
1Ch 12:40 and on mules, and on oxen, *and* **m**, meal, 3978
21:23 for wood, and the wheat for the **m offering**; 4503
23:29 for the fine flour for **m offering**, and 4503
2Ch 7: 7 and the **m offerings**, and the fat. 4503
9: 4 the **m** of his table, and the sitting of his 3978
Ezr 3: 7 **m**, and drink, and oil, unto them of Zidon, 3978

Ezr 7:17 with their **m offerings** and their drink 4504
Ne 10:33 *for* the continual **m offering**, and for 4503
13: 5 where aforetime they laid the **m offerings**, 4503
13: 9 with the **m offering** and the frankincense. 4503
Job 6: 7 refused to touch *are* as my sorrowful **m**. 3899
12:11 ear try words? and the mouth taste his **m**? 400
20:14 *Yet* his **m** in his bowels is turned, *it is* 3899
20:21 *There shall* none of his **m** *be* left; therefore 400
30: 4 by the bushes, and juniper roots *for* their **m**. 3899
33:20 life abhorreth bread, and his soul dainty **m**. 3978
34: 3 the ear trieth words, as the mouth tasteth **m**. 398
36:31 he the people; he giveth **m** in abundance. 400
38:41 cry unto God, they wander for lack of **m**. 400
Ps 42: 3 My tears have been my **m** day and night, 3899
44:11 hast given us like sheep appointed for **m**; 3978
59:15 Let them wander up and down for **m**, and 398
69:21 They gave me also gall for my **m**; and 1267
74:14 gavest him *to be* **m** to the people inhabiting 3978
78:18 they tempted God in their heart by asking **m** 400
78:25 eat angels' food: he sent them **m** to the full. 6720
78:30 But while their **m** *was* yet in their mouths, 400
79: 2 given *to be* **m** unto the fowls of the heaven, 3978
104:21 after *their* prey, and seek their **m** from God. 400
104:27 that *thou* mayest give *them* their **m** in due 400
107:18 Their soul abhorreth all *manner of* **m**; and 400
111: 5 He hath given **m** unto them that fear him: 2964
145:15 and thou givest them their **m** in due season. 400
Pr 6: 8 Provideth her **m** in the summer, *and* 3899
23: 3 of his dainties: for they *are* deceitful **m**. 3899
30:22 and a fool when he is filled *with* **m**; 3899
30:25 yet they prepare their **m** in the summer; 3899
31:15 giveth **m** to her household, and a portion to 2964
Isa 57: 6 thou hast offered a **m offering**. 4503
62: 8 Surely I will no more give thy corn *to be* **m** 3978
65:25 dust *shall be* the serpent's **m**. They shall 3899
Jer 7:33 the carcases of this people shall be **m** for 3978
16: 4 their carcases shall be **m** for the fowls of 3978
17:26 **m offerings**, and incense, and 4503
19: 7 their carcases will I give to be **m** for 3978
33:18 to kindle **m offerings**, and to do sacrifice 4503
34:20 their dead bodies shall be for **m** unto 3978
La 1:11 they have given their pleasant things for **m** 400
1:19 while they sought their **m**, to relieve their 400
4:10 they were their **m** in the destruction of 1262
Eze 4:10 thy **m** which thou shalt eat *shall be* by 3978
16:19 My **m** also which I gave thee, fine flour, 3899
29: 5 I have given thee for **m** to the beasts of 402
34: 5 they became **m** to all the beasts of the field, 402
34: 8 my flock became **m** to every beast of 402
34:10 that they may not be **m** for them. 402
42:13 the most holy *things*, and the **m offering**, 4503
44:29 They shall eat the **m offering**, and the sin 4503
45:15 for a **m offering**, and for a burnt offering, 4503
45:17 **m offerings**, and drink offerings, in 4503
45:17 the **m offering**, and the burnt offering, and 4503
45:24 he shall prepare a **m offering** *of* an ephah 4503
45:25 according to the **m offering**, and 4503
46: 5 the **m offering** *shall be* an ephah for a ram, 4503
46: 5 the **m offering** for the lambs as he shall be 4503
46: 7 he shall prepare a **m offering**, an ephah for 4503
46:11 in the solemnities the **m offering** shall be 4503
46:14 thou shalt prepare a **m offering** for it every 4503
46:14 a **m offering** continually *by* a perpetual 4503
46:15 the lamb, and the **m offering**, and the oil, 4503
46:20 where they shall bake the **m offering**; 4503
47:12 and on that side, shall grow all trees for **m**, 3978
47:12 the fruit thereof shall be for **m**, and the leaf 3978
Da 1: 5 them a daily provision of the king's **m**, 6598
1: 8 himself with the **portion of** the king's **m**, 6598
1:10 who hath appointed your **m** and your drink: 3978
1:13 that eat *of* the **portion of** the king's **m**: 6598
1:15 which did eat the **portion of** the king's **m**. 6598
1:16 Melzar took away the **portion of** their **m**, 6598
4:12 fruit thereof much, and in it *was* **m** for all: 4203
4:21 fruit thereof much, and in it *was* **m** for all; 4203
11:26 they that feed of the **portion of** his **m** shall 6598
Hos 11: 4 yoke on their jaws, and I laid **m** unto them. 398
Joel 1: 9 The **m offering** and the drink offering is 4503
1:13 for the **m offering** and the drink offering is 4503
1:16 Is not the **m** cut off before our eyes, *yea*, joy 400
2:14 *even* a **m offering** and a drink offering unto 4503
Am 5:22 me burnt offerings and your **m offerings**, 4503
Hab 1:16 their portion *is* fat, and their **m** plenteous. 3978
3:17 shall fail, and the fields shall yield no **m**; 400
Hag 2:12 or pottage, or wine, or oil, or any **m**, shall it 3978
Mal 1:12 the fruit thereof, *even* his **m**, *is* contemptible. 400
3:10 that there may be **m** in mine house, and 2964
Mt 3: 4 and his **m** was locusts and wild honey. *5160*
6:25 ye shall put on. Is not the life more than **m**, *5160*
9:10 as Jesus **sat at m** in the house, behold, *345*
10:10 for the workman is worthy of his **m**. *5160*
14: 9 and them which **sat with** him **at m**, *4873*
15:37 they took up of the broken *m* that was left NIG
24:45 to give them **m** in due season? *5160*
25:35 For I was a hungred, and ye gave me **m**: *5315*
25:42 For I was a hungred, and ye gave me no **m**: *5315*
26: 7 and poured *it* on his head, as he **sat at m**. *345*
Mk 2:15 that as *Jesus* **sat at m** in his house, *2621*
8: 8 they took up of the broken *m* that was left NIG
14: 3 house of Simon the leper, as he **sat at m**, *2621*
16:14 appeared unto the eleven as they **sat at m**, *345*
Lk 3:11 and he that hath **m**, let him do likewise. *1033*
7:36 the Pharisee's house, and **sat down to m**. *347*
7:37 when she knew that *Jesus* **sat at m** in *345*
7:49 And they that **sat at m with** *him* began to *4873*
8:55 and he commanded to give her **m**. *5315*
9:13 we should go and buy **m** for all this people. *1033*
11:37 and he went in, and **sat down to m**. *377*
12:23 The life is more than **m**, and the body *is* *5160*
12:37 and **make** them to **sit down to m**, and *347*
12:42 to give *them their* **portion of m** in due *4620*
14:10 presence of them that **sit at m with** thee. *4873*
14:15 And when one of them that **sat at m with** *4873*
17: 7 come from the field, Go and **sit down to m**? *377*
22:27 he that **sitteth at m**, or he that serveth? *345*

Lk 22:27 *is* not he that **sitteth at m**? but I am among *345*
24:30 as he **sat at m** with them, he took bread, *2625*
24:41 he said unto them, Have ye here any **m**? *1034*
Jn 4: 8 were gone away unto the city to buy **m**.) *5160*
4:32 I have **m** to eat that ye know not of. *1035*
4:34 My **m** is to do the will of him that sent me, *1033*
6:27 Labour not for the **m** which perisheth, but *1035*
6:27 for *that* **m** which endureth unto everlasting *1035*
6:55 For my flesh is **m** indeed, *1035*
21: 5 saith unto them, Children, have ye any **m**? *4371*
Ac 2:46 did eat *their* **m** with gladness and *5160*
9:19 And when he had received **m**, he was *5160*
16:34 he **set m before** *them*, and rejoiced, *3908+5132*
27:33 Paul besought *them* all to take **m**, saying, *5160*
27:34 Wherefore I pray you to take *some* **m**: *5160*
27:36 of good cheer, and they also took *some* **m**. *5160*
Ro 14:15 But if thy brother be grieved with *thy* **m**, *1033*
14:15 Destroy not him with thy **m**, for whom *1033*
14:17 For the kingdom of God is not **m** and drink; *1035*
14:20 For **m** destroy not the work of God. *1033*
1Co 3: 2 I have fed you with milk, and not with **m**: *1033*
8: 8 But **m** commendeth us not to God: *1033*
8:10 knowledge **sit at m** in the idol's temple, *2621*
8:13 if **m** make my brother to offend, *1033*
10: 3 And did all eat the same spiritual **m**; *1033*
Col 2:16 Let no *man* therefore judge you in **m**, *1035*
Heb 5:12 as have need of milk, and not of strong **m**. *5160*
5:14 But strong **m** belongeth to *them that are* of *5160*
12:16 who for one **morsel of m** sold his *1035*

MEAT MARKET See SHAMBLES

MEATS (8) [MEAT]
Pr 23: 6 evil eye, neither desire thou his **dainty m**: 4303
Mk 7:19 goeth out into the draught, purging all **m**? *1033*
Ac 15:29 That *ye* abstain from **m offered to idols**, *1494*
1Co 6:13 **M** for the belly, and the belly for meats: but *1033*
6:13 Meats for the belly, and the belly for **m**: but *1033*
1Ti 4: 3 *and commanding* to abstain from **m**, *1033*
Heb 9:10 *Which stood* only in **m** and drinks, and *1033*
13: 9 not with **m**, which have not profited them *1033*

MEBUNNAI (1)
2Sa 23:27 Abiezer the Anethothite, **M** the Hushathite, 4012

MECHERATHITE (1)
1Ch 11:36 Hepher the **M**, Ahijah the Pelonite, 4382

MECONAH See MEKONAH

MEDAD (2)
Nu 11:26 *was* Eldad, and the name of the other **M**: 4312
11:27 Eldad and **M** do prophesy in the camp. 4312

MEDAN (2) [MEDANITES]
Ge 25: 2 and **M**, and Midian, and Ishbak, and Shuah. 4091
1Ch 1:32 and **M**, and Midian, and Ishbak, and Shuah. 4091

MEDANITES (1) [MEDAN]
Ge 37:36 the **M** sold him into Egypt unto Potiphar, 4084

MEDDLE (6) [MEDDLED, MEDDLETH, MEDDLING]
Dt 2: 5 **M** not with them; for I will not give you of 1624
2:19 distress them not, nor **m** with them: 1624
2Ki 14:10 for why shouldest thou **m** to *thy* hurt, 1624
2Ch 25:19 why shouldest thou **m** to *thine* hurt, 1624
Pr 20:19 **m** not with him that flattereth *with* his lips. 6148
24:21 **m** not with them that are given to change: 6148

MEDDLED (1) [MEDDLE]
Pr 17:14 leave off contention, before *it* be **m with**. 1566

MEDDLER See BUSYBODY

MEDDLETH (1) [MEDDLE]
Pr 26:17 *and* **m** with strife *belonging* not to him, 5674

MEDDLING (2) [MEDDLE]
2Ch 35:21 forbear thee from **m** with God, who *is* with NIH
Pr 20: 3 cease from strife: but every fool will be **m**. 1566

MEDE (1) [MEDIA]
Da 11: 1 Also I in the first year of Darius the **M**, 4075

MEDEBA (5)
Nu 21:30 even unto Nophah, which *reacheth* unto **M**. 4311
Jos 13: 9 and all the plain of **M** unto Dibon; 4311
13:16 midst of the river, and all the plain by **M**; 4311
1Ch 19: 7 who came and pitched before **M**. 4311
Isa 15: 2 Moab shall howl over Nebo, and over **M**: 4311

MEDES (14) [MEDIA]
2Ki 17: 6 river of Gozan, and in the cities of the **M**. 4074
18:11 river of Gozan, and in the cities of the **M**: 4074
Ezr 6: 2 the palace that *is* in the province of the **M**, 4076
Est 1:19 among the laws of the Persians and the **M**, 4074
Isa 13:17 Behold, I will stir up the **M** against them, 4074
Jer 25:25 kings of Elam, and all the kings of the **M**, 4074
51:11 raised up the spirit of the kings of the **M**: 4074
51:28 her the nations with the kings of the **M**, 4074
Da 5:28 is divided, and given to the **M** and Persians. 4076
6: 8 according to the law of the **M** and Persians, 4076
6:12 according to the law of the **M** and Persians, 4076
6:15 that the law of the **M** and Persians *is*, That 4076
9: 1 the son of Ahasuerus, of the seed of the **M**, 4074
Ac 2: 9 and **M**, and Elamites, and the dwellers in *3370*

MEDIA (6) [MEDE, MEDES, MEDIAN]
Est 1: 3 the power of Persia and **M**, the nobles and 4074
1:14 the seven princes of Persia and **M**, 4074
1:18 **M** say this day unto all the king's princes, 4074
10: 2 book of the chronicles of the kings of **M** 4074
Isa 21: 2 besiege, O **M**; all the sighing thereof have I 4074

Da 8:20 sawest having two horns *are* the kings of **M** 4074

MEDIAN (1) [MEDIA]
Da 5:31 Darius the **M** took the kingdom, 4076

MEDIATOR (7)
Gal 3:19 *was* ordained by angels in the hand of a **m**. *3316*
3:20 Now a **m** is not *a mediator* of one, but God *3316*
3:20 Now a mediator is not *a* **m** of one, but God NIG
1Ti 2: 5 and one **m** between God and men, *3316*
Heb 8: 6 by how much also he is the **m** of a better *3316*
9:15 And for this cause he is the **m** of the new *3316*
12:24 And to Jesus the **m** of the new covenant, *3316*

MEDICINE (2) [MEDICINES]
Pr 17:22 A merry heart doeth good *like* a **m**: but 1456
Eze 47:12 be for meat, and the leaf thereof for **m**. 8644

MEDICINES (2) [MEDICINE]
Jer 30:13 be bound up: thou hast no healing **m**. 7499
46:11 in vain shalt thou use many **m**; *for* thou 7499

MEDITATE (14) [MEDITATION]
Ge 24:63 Isaac went out to **m** in the field at 7742
Jos 1: 8 thou shalt **m** therein day and night, that 1897
Ps 1: 2 and in his law doth he **m** day and night. 1897
63: 6 *and* **m** on thee in the *night* watches. 1897
77:12 I will **m** also of all thy work, and talk of thy 1897
119:15 I will **m** in thy precepts, and have respect 7878
119:23 *but* thy servant did **m** in thy statutes. 7878
119:48 I have loved; and I will **m** in thy statutes. 7878
119:78 a cause: *but* I will **m** in thy precepts. 7878
119:148 *night* watches, that *I* might **m** in thy word. 7878
143: 5 the days of old; I **m** on all thy works; 1897
Isa 33:18 Thine heart shall **m** terror. Where *is* 1897
Lk 21:14 not to **m before** *what ye* shall answer: *4304*
1Ti 4:15 **M upon** these *things;* give thyself wholly *3191*

MEDITATION (6) [MEDITATE]
Ps 5: 1 to my words, O LORD, consider my **m**. 1901
19:14 the **m** of my heart, be acceptable in thy 1902
49: 3 the **m** of my heart *shall be of* 1900
104:34 My **m** of him shall be sweet: I will be glad 7879
119:97 how love I thy law! it *is* my **m** all the day. 7881
119:99 my teachers: for thy testimonies *are* my **m**. 7881

MEEK (17) [MEEKNESS]
Nu 12: 3 (Now the man Moses *was* very **m**, 6035
Ps 22:26 The **m** shall eat and be satisfied: they shall 6035
25: 9 The **m** will he guide in judgment: and 6035
25: 9 and the **m** will he teach his way. 6035
37:11 the **m** shall inherit the earth; and 6035
76: 9 to judgment, to save all the **m** of the earth. 6035
147: 6 The LORD lifteth up the **m**: he casteth 6035
149: 4 he will beautify the **m** with salvation. 6035
Isa 11: 4 reprove with equity for the **m** of the earth: 6035
29:19 The **m** also shall increase *their* joy in 6035
61: 1 me to preach good tidings unto the **m**; 6035
Am 2: 7 the poor, and turn aside the way of the **m**: 6035
Zep 2: 3 Seek ye the LORD, all ye **m** of the earth, 6035
Mt 5: 5 Blessed *are* the **m**: for they shall inherit *4239*
11:29 learn of me; for I am **m** and lowly in heart: *4235*
21: 5 **m**, and sitting upon an ass, and a colt *4239*
1Pe 3: 4 *even the ornament* of a **m** and quiet spirit, *4239*

MEEKNESS (14) [MEEK]
Ps 45: 4 of truth and **m** *and* righteousness; 6037
Zep 2: 3 his judgment; seek righteousness, seek **m**: 6038
1Co 4:21 a rod, or in love, and *in* the spirit of **m**? *4236*
2Co 10: 1 Now I Paul myself beseech you by the **m** *4236*
Gal 5:23 **M**, temperance: against such there is no *4236*
6: 1 restore such a one in the spirit of **m**; *4236*
Eph 4: 2 With all lowliness and **m**, with *4236*
Col 3:12 humbleness of mind, **m**, longsuffering; *4236*
1Ti 6:11 godliness, faith, love, patience, **m**. *4236*
2Ti 2:25 In **m** instructing those that oppose *4236*
Tit 3: 2 *but* gentle, shewing all **m** unto all men. *4236*
Jas 1:21 and receive with **m** the engrafted word, *4240*
3:13 conversation his works with **m** of wisdom. *4240*
1Pe 3:15 a reason of the hope that is in you with **m** *4240*

MEET (132) [MEETEST, MEETETH, MEETING, MET]
Ge 2:18 I will make him a help **m for** him. 5048+3509.1
2:20 was not found a help **m for** him. 5048+3509.1
14:17 the king of Sodom went out to **m** him after 7125
18: 2 when he saw *them,* he ran to **m** them from 7125
19: 1 Lot seeing *them* rose up to **m** them; and 7125
24:17 the servant ran to **m** her, and said, Let me, 7125
24:65 *is* this that walketh in the field to **m** us? 7125
29:13 that he ran to **m** him, and embraced him, 7125
30:16 Leah went out to **m** him, and said, 7125
32: 6 also he cometh to **m** thee, and four hundred 7125
33: 4 And Esau ran to **m** him, and embraced him, 7125
46:29 went up to **m** Israel his father, to Goshen, 7125
Ex 4:14 behold, he cometh forth to **m** thee: 7125
4:27 Go into the wilderness to **m** Moses. 7125
8:26 Moses said, It is not **m** so to do; for we 3559
18: 7 Moses went out to **m** his father in law, and 7125
19:17 the people out of the camp to **m with** God; 7125
23: 4 If thou **m** thine enemy's ox or his ass going 6293
25:22 there I will **m** with thee, and I will 3259
29:42 where I will **m** you, to speak there unto 3259
29:43 there I will **m** with the children of Israel, 3259
30: 6 the Testimony, where I will **m** with thee. 3259
30:36 the congregation, where I will **m** with thee: 3259
Nu 17: 4 the Testimony, where I will **m** with you. 3259
22:36 he went out to **m** him unto a city of Moab, 7125
23: 3 peradventure the LORD will come to **m** 7125
23:15 while I **m** *the* LORD yonder. 7136
31:13 went forth to **m** them without the camp. 7125
Dt 3:18 of Israel, all *that are* **m for the war**. 1121+2428
Jos 2:16 to the mountain, lest the pursuers **m** you; 6293
9:11 go to **m** them, and say unto them, We *are* 7125
Jdg 4:18 Jael went out to **m** Sisera, and said unto 7125
4:22 Jael came out to **m** him, and said unto him, 7125
5:30 **m** for the necks of *them that take* the spoil? NIH
6:35 and they came up to **m** them. 7125
11:31 forth of the doors of my house to **m** me, 7125
11:34 his daughter came out to **m** him with 7125
19: 3 the damsel saw him, he rejoiced to **m** him. 7125
Ru 2:22 that they **m** thee not in *any* other field. 6293
1Sa 10: 3 there shall **m** thee three men going up to 4672
10: 5 that thou shalt **m** a company of prophets 6293
13:10 Saul went out to **m** him, that he might 7125
15:12 when Samuel rose early to **m** Saul in 7125
17:48 came and drew nigh to **m** David, that David 7125
17:48 ran *toward* the army to **m** the Philistine. 7125
18: 6 singing and dancing, to **m** king Saul, 7125
25:32 of Israel, which sent thee this day to **m** me: 7125
25:34 thou hadst hasted and come to **m** me, 7125
30:21 they went forth to **m** David, and to meet 7125
30:21 and to **m** the people that *were* with him: 7125
2Sa 6:20 Michal the daughter of Saul came out to **m** 7125
10: 5 he sent to **m** them, because the men were 7125
15:32 Hushai the Archite *came* to **m** him with his 7125
19:15 Judah came to Gilgal, to go to **m** the king, 7125
19:16 came down with the men of Judah to **m** 7125
19:20 Joseph to go down to **m** my lord the king. 7125
19:24 the son of Saul came down to **m** the king, 7125
19:25 when he was come *to* Jerusalem to **m** 7125
1Ki 2: 8 he came down to **m** me *at* Jordan, and 7125
2:19 the king rose up to **m** her, and 7125
18:16 So Obadiah went to **m** Ahab, and told him: 7125
18:16 and told him: and Ahab went to **m** Elijah. 7125
21:18 Arise, go down to **m** Ahab king of Israel, 7125
2Ki 1: 3 go up to **m** the messengers of the king of 7125
1: 6 There came a man up to **m** us, and 7125
1: 7 of man *was he* which came up to **m** you, 7125
2:15 they came to **m** him, and bowed themselves 7125
4:26 I pray thee, to **m** her, and say unto her, 7125
4:29 go *thy way:* if thou **m** any man, salute him 4672
4:31 Wherefore he went again to **m** him, and 7125
5:21 he lighted down from the chariot to **m** him, 7125
5:26 turned *again* from his chariot to **m** thee? 7125
8: 8 go, **m** the man of God, and inquire of 7125
8: 9 So Hazael went to **m** him, and took a 7125
9:17 send to **m** them, and let him say, *Is it* 7125
9:18 So there went one on horseback to **m** him, 7125
10:15 the son of Rechab *coming* to **m** him: 7125
16:10 king Ahaz went *to* Damascus to **m** 7125
1Ch 12:17 David went out to **m** them, and answered 6440
19: 5 he sent to **m** them: for the men were greatly 7125
2Ch 15: 2 he went out to **m** Asa, and said unto him, 6440
19: 2 son of Hanani the seer went out to **m** him, 6440
Ezr 4:14 *it was* not **m** for us to see the king's 749
Ne 6: 2 let us **m** together in *some one of* 3259
6:10 Let us **m together** in the house of God, 3259
Est 2: 9 *which were* **m** to be given her, 7200
Job 5:14 They **m** with darkness in the daytime, and 6298
34:31 Surely it is **m** *to be* said unto God, I have NIH
39:21 He goeth on to **m** the armed men. 7125
Pr 7:15 Therefore came I forth to **m** thee, 7125
11:24 *there is* that withholdeth more than is **m**, 3476
17:12 *Let* a bear robbed of her whelps **m** a man, 6298
22: 2 The rich and poor **m together**: the LORD 6298
29:13 and the deceitful man **m together**: 6298
Isa 7: 3 Go forth now to **m** Ahaz, thou, and 7125
14: 9 Hell from beneath is moved for thee to **m** 7125
34:14 The wild beasts of the desert shall also **m** 6298
47: 3 and I will not **m** *thee as* a man. 6293
Jer 26:14 with me as seemeth good and **m** unto you. 3477
27: 5 have given it unto whom it seemed **m** unto 3474
41: 6 went forth from Mizpah to **m** them, 7125
51:31 One post shall run to **m** another, and 7125
51:31 and one messenger to **m** another, 7125
Eze 15: 4 midst of it is burnt. Is it **m** for *any* work? 6743
15: 5 when it was whole, it was **m** for no work. 6213
15: 5 how much less shall it be **m** yet for *any* 6213
Hos 13: 8 I will **m** them as a bear *that is* bereaved of 6298
Am 4:12 unto thee, prepare to **m** thy God, O Israel. 7125
Zec 2: 3 and another angel went out to **m** him, 7125
Mt 3: 8 therefore fruits **m for** repentance: *514*
8:34 the whole city came out to **m** Jesus: *4877*
15:26 It is not **m** to take the children's bread, and *2570*
25: 1 and went forth to **m** the bridegroom. *529*
25: 6 the bridegroom cometh; go ye out to **m** him. *529*
Mk 7:27 for it is not **m** to take the children's bread, *2570*
14:13 there shall **m** you a man bearing a pitcher of *528*
Lk 14:31 **m** him that cometh against him with twenty *528*
15:32 It was **m** that *we* should make merry, and *1163*
22:10 there shall a man **m** you, bearing a pitcher *4876*
Jn 12:13 and went forth to **m** him, and cried, *5222*
Ac 26:20 turn to God, and do works **m for** repentance. *514*
28:15 they came to **m** us as far as Appii forum, and *529*
Ro 1:27 recompence of their error which was **m**. *1163*
1Co 15: 9 that am not **m** to be called an apostle, *2425*
16: 4 And if it be **m** that I go also, they shall go *514*
Php 1: 7 Even as it is **m** for me to think this of you *1342*
Col 1:12 which hath **made** us **m** to be partakers of *2427*
1Th 4:17 them in the clouds, to **m** the Lord in the air: *529*
2Th 1: 3 as it is **m**, because that your faith groweth *514*
2Ti 2:21 and **m for** the master's **use**, *and* *2173*
Heb 6: 7 bringeth forth herbs **m** for them by whom it *2111*
2Pe 1:13 Yea, I think it **m**, as long as I am in this *1342*

MEETEST (2) [MEET]
2Ki 10: 3 out the best and **m** of your master's sons, 3477
Isa 64: 5 Thou **m** him that rejoiceth and 6293

MEETETH (3) [MEET]
Ge 32:17 When Esau my brother **m** thee, and 6298
Nu 35:19 when he **m** him, he shall slay him. 6293
35:21 shall slay the murderer, when he **m** him. 6293

MEETING (2) [MEET]
1Sa 21: 1 Ahimelech was afraid at the **m** of David, 7125
Isa 1:13 *it is* iniquity, even the **solemn m**. 6116

MEGIDDO (11) [MEGIDDON]
Jos 12:21 king of Taanach, one; the king of **M**, one; 4023
17:11 and the inhabitants of **M** and her towns, 4023
Jdg 1:27 nor the inhabitants of **M** and her towns: 4023
5:19 of Canaan in Taanach by the waters of **M**; 4023
1Ki 4:12 *to him pertained* Taanach and **M**, and 4023
9:15 and Hazor, and **M**, and Gezer. 4023
2Ki 9:27 And he fled *to* **M**, and died there. 4023
23:29 he slew him at **M**, when he had seen him. 4023
23:30 carried him *in a chariot* dead from **M**, 4023
1Ch 7:29 **M** and her towns, Dor and her towns. 4023
2Ch 35:22 and came to fight in the valley of **M**. 4023

MEGIDDON (1) [MEGIDDO]
Zec 12:11 of Hadadrimmon in the valley of **M**. 4023

MEHETABEEL (1)
Ne 6:10 Shemaiah the son of Delaiah the son of **M**, 4105

MEHETABEL (2)
Ge 36:39 his wife's name *was* **M**, the daughter of 4105
1Ch 1:50 his wife's name *was* **M**, the daughter of 4105

MEHIDA (2)
Ezr 2:52 the children of **M**, the children of Harsha, 4240
Ne 7:54 the children of **M**, the children of Harsha, 4240

MEHIR (1)
1Ch 4:11 Chelub the brother of Shuah begat **M**, 4243

MEHOLATHITE (2)
1Sa 18:19 that she was given unto Adriel the **M** to 4259
2Sa 21: 8 up for Adriel the son of Barzillai the **M**: 4259

MEHUJAEL (2)
Ge 4:18 Irad begat **M**: and Mehujael begat 4232
4:18 **M** begat Methusael: and Methusael begat 4232

MEHUMAN (1)
Est 1:10 he commanded **M**, Biztha, Harbona, 4104

MEHUNIM (1) [MEHUNIMS, MEUNIM]
Ezr 2:50 The children of Asnah, the children of **M**, 4586

MEHUNIMS (1) [MEHUNIM]
2Ch 26: 7 Arabians that dwelt in Gur-baal, and the **M**. 4586

ME-JARKON (1)
Jos 19:46 **M**, and Rakkon, with the border before 4313

MEKERATHITE See MECHERATHITE

MEKONAH (1)
Ne 11:28 and at **M**, and in the villages thereof, 4368

MELATIAH (1)
Ne 3: 7 next unto them repaired **M** the Gibeonite, 4424

MELCHI (2)
Lk 3:24 *the son* of Levi, which was *the son* of **M**, *3197*
3:28 Which was *the son* of **M**, which was *3197*

MELCHIAH (1)
Jer 21: 1 sent unto him Pashur the son of **M**, 4441

MELCHISEDEC (9) [MELCHIZEDEK]
Heb 5: 6 *art* a priest for ever after the order of **M**. *3198*
5:10 of God a high priest after the order of **M**. *3198*
6:20 a high priest for ever after the order of **M**. *3198*
7: 1 For this **M**, king of Salem, priest of *3198*
7:10 in the loins of his father, when **M** met him. *3198*
7:11 priest should rise after the order of **M**, *3198*
7:15 for that after the similitude of **M** there *3198*
7:17 *art* a priest for ever after the order of **M**. *3198*
7:21 *art* a priest for ever after the order of **M**:) *3198*

MELCHISHUA (1)
1Sa 14:49 of Saul were Jonathan, and Ishui, and **M**: 4444

MELCHIZEDEK (2) [MELCHISEDEC]
Ge 14:18 **M** king of Salem brought forth bread and 4442
Ps 110: 4 *art* a priest for ever after the order of **M**. 4442

MELEA (1)
Lk 3:31 Which was *the son* of **M**, which was *3190*

MELECH (2)
1Ch 8:35 *were,* Pithon, and **M**, and Tarea, and Ahaz. 4429
9:41 and **M**, and Tahrea, *and Ahaz.* 4429

MELICU (1)
Ne 12:14 Of **M**, Jonathan; of Shebaniah, Joseph; 4409

MELITA (1)
Ac 28: 1 they knew that the island was called **M**. *3194*

MELKI See MELCHI

MELODY (4)
Isa 23:16 make sweet **m**, sing many songs, that thou 5059
51: 3 thanksgiving, and the voice of **m**. 2172
Am 5:23 for I will not hear the **m** of thy viols. 2172
Eph 5:19 and **making m** in your heart to the Lord; *5567*

MELONS (1)
Nu 11: 5 and the **m**, and the leeks, and the onions, and 20

MELT (17) [MELTED, MELTETH, MELTING, MOLTEN]
Ex 15:15 all the inhabitants of Canaan shall **m away**. 4127
Jos 2:11 had heard *these things,* our hearts did **m**, 4549
14: 8 with me **made** the heart of the people **m**: 4529

M

2Sa 17:10 the heart of a lion, shall **utterly m**: 4549+4549
Ps 58: 7 Let them **m away** as waters *which* run 3988
112:10 he shall gnash *with* his teeth, and **m away**: 4549
Isa 13: 7 be faint, and every man's heart shall **m**: 4549
19: 1 the heart of Egypt shall **m** in the midst of it. 4549
Jer 9: 7 Behold, I will **m** them, and try them; 6884
Eze 21: 7 every heart shall **m**, and all hands shall be 4549
22:20 to **m** *it*; so will I gather *you* in mine anger 5413
22:20 and I will leave *you there*, and **m** you. 5413
Am 9: 5 it shall **m**, and all that dwell therein shall 4127
9:13 drop sweet wine, and all the hills shall **m**. 4127
Na 1: 5 the hills **m**, and the earth is burnt at his 4127
2Pe 3:10 and the elements shall **m** with fervent heat, 3089
3:12 and the elements shall **m** with fervent heat? 5080

MELTED (13) [MELT]

Ex 16:21 and when the sun waxed hot, it **m**. 4549
Jos 5: 1 we were passed over, that their heart **m**, 4549
7: 5 wherefore the hearts of the people **m**, and 4549
Jdg 5: 5 The mountains **m** from before the LORD, 5140
1Sa 14:16 the multitude **m away**, and they went on 4127
Ps 22:14 like wax; it is **m** in the midst of my bowels. 4549
46: 6 he uttered his voice, the earth **m**. 4127
97: 5 The hills **m** like wax at the presence of 4549
107:26 their soul is **m** because of trouble. 4127
Isa 34: 3 the mountains shall be **m** with their blood. 4549
Eze 22:21 and ye shall be **m** in the midst thereof. 5413
22:22 As silver is **m** in the midst of the furnace, 2046
22:22 so shall ye be **m** in the midst thereof; 5413

MELTETH (7) [MELT]

Ps 58: 8 As a snail *which* **m**, let *every one of them* 8557
68: 2 as wax **m** before the fire, *so* let the wicked 4549
119:28 My soul **m** for heaviness: strengthen thou 1811
147:18 He sendeth out his word, and **m** them: 4529
Isa 40:19 The workman **m** a graven image, and 5258
Jer 6:29 of the fire; the founder **m** in vain: 6884
Na 2:10 the heart **m**, and the knees smite together, 4549

MELTING (1) [MELT]

Isa 64: 2 As *when* the **m** fire burneth, the fire 2003

MELZAR (2)

Da 1:11 said Daniel to **M**, whom the prince of 4453
1:16 Thus **M** took away the portion of their 4453

MEMBER (6) [MEMBERS]

Dt 23: 1 in the stones, or hath *his* **privy m** cut off, 8212
1Co 12:14 For the body is not one **m**, but many. 3196
12:19 And if they were all one **m**, where *were* 3196
12:26 And whether one **m** suffer, all the members 3196
12:26 suffer with *it*; or one **m** be honoured, 3196
Jas 3: 5 Even so the tongue is a little **m**, and 3196

MEMBERS (32) [MEMBER]

Job 17: 7 of sorrow, and all my **m** *are* as a shadow. 3338
Ps 139:16 in thy book all *my* **m** were written, *which* in NIH
Mt 5:29 for it is profitable for thee that one of thy **m** 3196
5:30 for it is profitable for thee that one of thy **m** 3196
Ro 6:13 Neither yield ye your **m** *as* instruments of 3196
6:13 your **m** *as* instruments of righteousness 3196
6:19 for as ye have yielded your **m** servants to 3196
6:19 now yield your **m** servants to righteousness 3196
7: 5 did work in our **m** to bring forth fruit unto 3196
7:23 But I see another law in my **m**, 3196
7:23 to the law of sin which is in my **m**. 3196
12: 4 For as we have many **m** in one body, and 3196
12: 4 and all **m** have not the same office: 3196
12: 5 in Christ, and every one **m** one of another. 3196
1Co 6:15 Know ye not that your bodies are the **m** of 3196
6:15 shall I then take the **m** of Christ, and 3196
6:15 of Christ, and make *them* the **m** of a harlot? 3196
12:12 and hath many **m**, and all the members of 3196
12:12 and all the **m** of *that* one body, being many, 3196
12:18 But now hath God set the **m** every one of 3196
12:20 But now *are they* many **m**, yet *but* 3196
12:22 Nay, much more those **m** of the body, 3196
12:23 And those *m* of the body, which we think to NIG
12:25 *that* the **m** should have the same care one 3196
12:26 all the **m** suffer with *it*; or one member be 3196
12:26 be honoured, all the **m** rejoice with *it*. 3196
12:27 are the body of Christ, and **m** in particular. 3196
Eph 4:25 his neighbour: for we are **m** one of another. 3196
5:30 For we are **m** of his body, of his flesh, and 3196
Col 3: 5 therefore your **m** which are upon the earth; 3196
Jas 3: 6 so is the tongue amongst our **m**, that it 3196
4: 1 *even* of your lusts that war in your **m**? 3196

MEMORIAL (32)

Ex 3:15 and this *is* my **m** unto all generations. 2143
12:14 this day shall be unto you for a **m**; and 2146
13: 9 for a **m** between thine eyes, that 2146
17:14 Write this *for* a **m** in a book, and rehearse *it* 2146
28:12 *for* stones of **m** unto the children of Israel: 2146
28:12 LORD upon his two shoulders for a **m**. 2146
28:29 for a **m** before the LORD continually. 2146
30:16 that it may be a **m** unto the children of 2146
39: 7 *that they should be* stones for a **m** to 2146
Lev 2: 2 the priest shall burn the **m** of it upon 234
2: 9 take from the meat offering a **m** thereof, 234
2:16 the priest shall burn the **m** of it, *part* of 234
5:12 *even* a **m** thereof, and burn *it* on the altar, 234
6:15 *even* the **m** of it, unto the LORD. 234
23:24 a **m** of blowing of trumpets, a holy 2146
24: 7 that it may be on the bread for a **m**, *even* an 234
Nu 5:15 *is* an offering of jealousy, an offering of **m**, 2146
5:18 and put the offering of **m** in her hands, 2146
5:26 *even* the **m** thereof, and burn *it* upon 234
10:10 that they may be to you for a **m** before your 2146
16:40 *To be* a **m** unto the children of Israel, that 2146
31:54 *for* a **m** for the children of Israel before 2146
Jos 4: 7 these stones shall be for a **m** unto 2146
Ne 2:20 no portion, nor right, nor **m**, in Jerusalem. 2146
Est 9:28 nor the **m** of them perish from their seed. 2143
Ps 9: 6 their **m** is perished *with* them. 2143
135:13 *and* thy **m**, O LORD, throughout all 2143
Hos 12: 5 LORD God of hosts; the LORD *is* his **m**. 2143
Zec 6:14 for a **m** in the temple of the LORD. 2146
Mt 26:13 *woman* hath done, be told for a **m** of her. 3422
Mk 14: 9 hath done shall be spoken of for a **m** of her. 3422
Ac 10: 4 thine alms are come up for a **m** before God. 3422

MEMORY (6)

Ps 109:15 that he may cut off the **m** of them from 2143
145: 7 They shall abundantly utter the **m** of thy 2143
Pr 10: 7 The **m** of the just *is* blessed: but the name 2143
Ecc 9: 5 a reward; for the **m** of them is forgotten. 2143
Isa 26:14 and made all their **m** to perish. 2143
1Co 15: 2 if ye **keep in m** what I preached unto you, 2722

MEMPHIS (1)

Hos 9: 6 shall gather them up, **M** shall bury them: 4644

MEMUCAN (3)

Est 1:14 Tarshish, Meres, Marsena, *and* **M**, 4462
1:16 **M** answered before the king and 4462
1:21 the king did according to the word of **M**: 4462

MEN (1652) [MAN]

Ge 4:26 began *m* to call upon the name of NIH
6: 1 when **m** began to multiply on the face of 120
6: 2 That the sons of God saw the daughters of **m** 120
6: 4 of God came in unto the daughters of **m**, 120
6: 4 the same *became* mighty **m** which *were* of NIH
6: 4 *men* which *were* of old, **m** of renown. 376
11: 5 the tower, which the children of **m** builded. 120
12:20 Pharaoh commanded *his* **m** concerning him: 376
13:13 the **m** of Sodom *were* wicked and 376
14:24 Save only that which the **young m** have 5288
14:24 the portion of the **m** which went with me, 376
17:23 every male among the **m** of Abraham's 376
17:27 all the **m** of his house, born in the house, 376
18: 2 and looked, and lo, three **m** stood by him: 376
18:16 the **m** rose up from thence, and 376
18:22 the **m** turned their faces from thence, and 376
19: 4 the **m** of the city, *even* the men of Sodom, 376
19: 4 the men of the city, *even* the **m** of Sodom, 376
19: 5 Where *are* the **m** which came in to thee this 376
19: 8 only unto these **m** do nothing; for therefore 376
19:10 the **m** put forth their hand, and pulled Lot 376
19:11 they smote the **m** that *were at* the door of 376
19:12 the **m** said unto Lot, Hast thou here any 376
19:16 the **m** laid hold upon his hand, and upon 376
20: 8 in their ears: and the **m** were sore afraid. 376
22: 3 took two of his **young m** with him, and 5288
22: 5 Abraham said unto his **young m**, 5288
22:19 So Abraham returned unto his **young m**, 5288
24:13 the daughters of the **m** of the city come out 376
24:54 he and the **m** that *were* with him, and 376
24:59 and Abraham's servant, and his **m**. 376
26: 7 the **m** of the place asked *him* of his wife; 376
26: 7 *said he*, the **m** of the place should kill me for 376
29:22 Laban gathered together all the **m** of 376
32: 6 to meet thee, and four hundred **m** with him. 376
32:28 hast thou power with God and with **m**, 376
33: 1 Esau came, and with him four hundred **m**. 376
33:13 if *m* should overdrive them one day, all NIH
34: 7 when they heard *it*: and the **m** were grieved, 376
34:20 communed with the **m** of their city, saying, 376
34:21 These **m** *are* peaceable with us; therefore 376
34:22 Only herein will the **m** consent unto us for to 376
38:21 he asked the **m** of that place, saying, 376
38:22 also the **m** of the place said, *that* there was 376
39:11 *there was* none of the **m** of the house there 376
39:14 That she called unto the **m** of her house, and 376
41: 8 of Egypt, and all the **wise m** thereof: 2450
42:11 we *are* true **m**, thy servants are no spies. NIH
42:19 If ye *be* true **m**, let one of your brethren be NIH
42:31 unto him, We *are* true *m*; we are no spies: NIH
42:33 Hereby shall I know that ye *are* true *m*; NIH
42:34 *that* ye *are* true *m*: *so* will I deliver you your NIH
43:15 the **m** took that present, and they took 376
43:16 Bring *these* **m** home, and slay, and 376
43:16 for *these* **m** shall dine with me at noon. 376
43:17 the man brought the **m** into Joseph's house. 376
43:18 the **m** were afraid, because they were 376
43:24 the man brought the **m** into Joseph's house, 376
43:33 and the **m** marvelled one at another. 376
44: 3 the **m** were sent away, they and their asses. 376
44: 4 unto his steward, Up, follow after the **m**; 376
46:32 the **m** *are* shepherds, for their trade hath 376
47: 2 *even* five **m**, and presented them unto 376
Ex 1:17 but saved the **m children** alive. 3206
1:18 have saved the **m children** alive? 3206
2:13 two **m** of the Hebrews strove together: 376
4:19 for all the **m** are dead which sought thy life. 376
5: 9 Let there more work be laid upon the **m**, 376
7:11 Pharaoh also called the **wise m** and 2450
10: 7 let the **m** go, that they may serve the LORD 376
10:11 go now ye *that are* **m**, and serve 1397
12:33 in haste; for they said, We *be* all dead *m*. NIH
12:37 six hundred thousand on foot *that were* **m**, 1397
15:15 the **mighty m** of Moab, trembling shall take 352
17: 9 Choose us out **m**, and go out, fight with 376
18:21 shalt provide out of all the people able **m**, 376
18:21 such as fear God, **m** of truth, 376
18:25 Moses chose able **m** out of all Israel, and 376
21:18 if **m** strive together, and one smite another 376
21:22 If **m** strive, and hurt a woman with child, so 376
22:31 ye shall be holy **m** unto me: neither shall ye 376
24: 5 he sent **young m** of the children of Israel, 5288
32:28 the people that day about three thousand **m**. 376
34:23 Thrice in the year shall all your **m children** 2138
35:22 they came, both **m** and women, as many as 376
36: 4 all the wise *m*, that wrought all the work of NIH
38:26 and five hundred and fifty *m*. NIH
Lev 7:25 of which *m* offer an offering made by fire NIH
18:27 (For all these abominations have the **m** of 376
27: 9 whereof *m* bring an offering unto NIH
27:29 None devoted, which shall be devoted of **m**, 120
Nu 1: 5 these *are* the names of the **m** that shall stand 376
1:17 Aaron took these **m** which are expressed by 376
1:44 and the princes of Israel, *being* twelve **m**: NIH
5: 6 woman shall commit any sin that **m** commit, 120
9: 6 there were *certain* **m**, who were defiled by 376
9: 7 those **m** said unto him, We *are* defiled by 376
11:16 Gather unto me seventy **m** of the elders of 376
11:24 gathered the seventy **m** of the elders of 376
11:26 there remained two *of the* **m** in the camp, 376
11:28 *one* of his **young m**, answered and said, 979
12: 3 above all the **m** which *were* upon the face of 120
13: 2 Send thou **m**, that they may search the land 376
13: 3 all those **m** *were* heads of the children of 376
13:16 These *are* the names of the **m** which Moses 376
13:21 of Zin unto Rehob, as *m* come to Hamath. NIH
13:31 the **m** that went up with him said, We be not 376
13:32 all the people that we saw in it *are* **m** of a 376
14:22 Because all *those* **m** which have seen my 376
14:36 the **m**, which Moses sent to search the land, 376
14:37 Even *those* **m** that did bring up the evil 376
14:38 *which were* of the **m** that went to search 376
16: 1 the son of Peleth, sons of Reuben, took *m*: NIH
16: 2 famous in the congregation, **m** of renown: 376
16:14 wilt thou put out the eyes of these **m**? 376
16:26 from the tents of these wicked **m**, and 376
16:29 If these **m** die the common death of all men, NIH
16:29 If these *men* die the common death of all **m**, 120
16:29 if they be visited after the visitation of all **m**; 120
16:30 ye shall understand that these **m** have 376
16:32 all the **m** that *appertained* unto Korah, and 120
16:35 and fifty **m** that offered incense. 376
18:15 *whether it be* of **m** or beasts, shall be thine: 120
22: 9 and said, What **m** *are* these with thee? 376
22:20 If the **m** come to call thee, rise up, *and* 376
22:35 LORD said unto Balaam, Go with the **m**: 376
25: 5 Slay ye every one his **m** that were joined 376
26:10 the fire devoured two hundred and fifty **m**: 376
31:11 and all the prey, *both* of **m** and of beasts. 120
31:21 Eleazar the priest said unto the **m** of war 376
31:28 levy a tribute unto the LORD of the **m** of 376
31:32 *being* the rest of the prey which the **m** of 5971
31:42 which Moses divided from the **m** that 376
31:49 Thy servants have taken the sum of the **m** of 376
31:53 (*For* the **m** of war had taken spoil, 376
32:11 Surely none of the **m** that came up out of 376
32:14 your fathers' stead, an increase of sinful **m**, 376
34:17 These *are* the names of the **m** which shall 376
34:19 the names of the **m** *are* these: Of the tribe of 376
Dt 1:13 Take ye wise **m**, and understanding, and 376
1:15 wise **m**, and known, and made them heads 376
1:22 We will send **m** before us, and they shall 376
1:23 I took twelve **m** of you, one of a tribe: 376
1:35 Surely there shall not one of these **m** of this 376
2:14 until all the generation of the **m** of war were 376
2:16 when all the **m** of war were consumed and 376
2:34 utterly destroyed the **m**, and the women, 4962
3: 6 utterly destroying the **m**, women, and 4962
4: 3 for all the **m** that followed Baal-peor, 376
13:13 *Certain* **m**, the children of Belial, are gone 376
19:17 both the **m**, between whom the controversy 376
21:21 all the **m** of his city shall stone him with 376
22:21 the **m** of her city shall stone her with stones 376
25: 1 If there be a controversy between **m**, and 376
25:11 When **m** strive together one with another, 376
27:14 say unto all the **m** of Israel *with* a loud 376
29:10 and your officers, *with* all the **m** of Israel, 376
29:25 *m* shall say, Because they have forsaken NIH
31:12 **m**, and women, and children, and 376
32:26 of them to cease from among **m**: 582
33: 6 and not die; and let *not* his **m** be few. 4962
Jos 1:14 all the mighty *m* of valour, and help them; NIH
2: 1 sent out of Shittim two **m** to spy secretly, 376
2: 2 there came **m** in hither to night of 376
2: 3 Bring forth the **m** that are come to thee, 376
2: 4 the woman took the two **m**, and hid them, 376
2: 4 There came **m** unto me, but I wist not 376
2: 5 when it was dark, that the **m** went out: 376
2: 5 whither the **m** went I wot not: pursue after 376
2: 7 the **m** pursued after them the way to Jordan 376
2: 9 she said unto the **m**, I know that the LORD 376
2:14 And the **m** answered her, Our life for yours, 376
2:17 the **m** said unto her, We *will be* blameless of 376
2:23 So the two **m** returned, and descended from 376
3:12 take ye twelve **m** out of the tribes of Israel, 376
4: 2 Take you twelve **m** out of the people, out of 376
4: 4 Joshua called the twelve **m**, whom he had 376
5: 4 *that were* males, *even* all the **m** of war, 376
5: 6 till all the people *that were* **m** of war, 376
6: 2 king thereof, *and* the mighty *m* of valour. NIH
6: 3 all *ye* **m** of war, *and* go round about the city 376
6: 9 the armed **m** went before the priests that NIH
6:13 the armed **m** went before them; but NIH
6:22 Joshua had said unto the two **m** that had 376
6:23 the **young m** that were spies went in, and 5288
7: 2 Joshua sent **m** from Jericho *to* Ai, which *is* 376
7: 2 And the **m** went up and viewed Ai. 376
7: 3 or three thousand **m** go up and smite Ai; 376
7: 4 thither of the people about three thousand **m**: 376
7: 4 and they fled before the **m** of Ai. 376
7: 5 the **m** of Ai smote of them about thirty and 376
7: 5 of Ai smote of them about thirty and six **m**: 376
8: 3 Joshua chose out thirty thousand mighty **m** NIH
8:12 he took about five thousand **m**, and set them 376
8:14 the **m** of the city went out against Israel to 376
8:20 when the **m** of Ai looked behind them, they 376
8:21 then they turned again, and slew the **m** of Ai. 376
8:25 both of **m** and women, *were* twelve 376
8:25 *were* twelve thousand, *even* all the **m** of Ai. 376
9: 6 said unto him, and to the **m** of Israel, We be 376
9: 7 the **m** of Israel said unto the Hivites, 376
9:14 the **m** took of their victuals, and asked not 376
10: 2 than Ai, and all the **m** thereof *were* mighty. 376
10: 6 the **m** of Gibeon sent unto Joshua to 376

Jos 10: 7 with him, and all the mighty *m* of valour. NIH
10:18 of the cave, and set **m** by it for to keep them: 376
10:24 that Joshua called for all the **m** of Israel, and 376
10:24 said unto the captains of the **m** of war which 376
18: 4 Give out from among you three **m** for *each* 376
18: 8 the **m** arose, and went away: and 376
18: 9 the **m** went and passed through the land, 376
24:11 the **m** of Jericho fought against you, 1167
Jdg 1: 4 they slew *of* them in Bezek ten thousand **m**. 376
3:29 *of* Moab at that time about ten thousand **m**, 376
3:29 thousand men, all lusty, and all **m** of valour; 376
3:31 which slew *of* the Philistines six hundred **m** 376
4: 6 take with thee ten thousand **m** of 376
4:10 he went up with ten thousand **m** at his feet: 376
4:14 mount Tabor, and ten thousand **m** after him. 376
6:27 Then Gideon took ten **m** of his servants, and 376
6:27 the **m** of the city, that *he* could not do *it* by 376
6:28 when the **m** of the city arose early in 376
6:30 the **m** of the city said unto Joash, Bring out 376
7: 6 hand to their mouth, were three hundred **m**: 376
7: 7 By the three hundred **m** that lapped will I 376
7: 8 his tent, and retained *those* three hundred **m**: 376
7:11 of the armed *m* that *were* in the host. NIH
7:16 he divided the three hundred **m** *into* three 376
7:19 and the hundred **m** that *were* with him, 376
7:23 the **m** of Israel gathered themselves together 376
7:24 all the **m** of Ephraim gathered themselves 376
8: 1 the **m** of Ephraim said unto him, Why hast 376
8: 4 and the three hundred **m** that *were* with him, 376
8: 5 he said unto the **m** of Succoth, Give, I pray 376
8: 8 the **m** of Penuel answered him as the men of 376
8: 8 the men of Penuel answered him as the **m** of 376
8: 9 he spake also unto the **m** of Penuel, saying, 376
8:10 about fifteen thousand *m*, all that were left NIH
8:10 and twenty thousand **m** that drew sword. 376
8:14 caught a young man of the **m** of Succoth, 376
8:14 *even* threescore and seventeen **m**. 376
8:15 he came unto the **m** of Succoth, and said, 376
8:15 that we should give bread unto thy **m** *that* 376
8:16 and with them he taught the **m** of Succoth. 376
8:17 tower of Penuel, and slew the **m** of the city. 376
8:18 What manner of **m** *were they* whom ye slew 376
8:22 the **m** of Israel said unto Gideon, Rule thou 376
9: 2 in the ears of all the **m** of Shechem, 1167
9: 3 of all the **m** of Shechem all these words: 1167
9: 6 all the **m** of Shechem gathered together, 1167
9: 7 Hearken unto me, you **m** of Shechem, 1167
9:18 king over the **m** of Shechem, because he *is* 1167
9:20 devour the **m** of Shechem, and the house of 1167
9:20 let fire come out from the **m** of Shechem, 1167
9:23 between Abimelech and the **m** of Shechem; 1167
9:23 the **m** of Shechem dealt treacherously with 1167
9:24 upon the **m** of Shechem, which aided him 1167
9:25 the **m** of Shechem set liers in wait for him 1167
9:26 the **m** of Shechem put their confidence in 1167
9:28 serve the **m** of Hamor the father of 376
9:36 shadow of the mountains as *if they were* **m**. 376
9:39 Gaal went out before the **m** of Shechem, 1167
9:46 when all the **m** of the tower of Shechem 1167
9:47 that all the **m** of the tower of Shechem were 1167
9:49 that all the **m** of the tower of Shechem died 376
9:49 died also, about a thousand **m** and women. 376
9:51 thither fled all the **m** and women, and 376
9:54 and slay me, that *m* say not of me, NIH
9:55 when the **m** of Israel saw that Abimelech 376
9:57 all the evil of the **m** of Shechem did God 376
11: 3 and there were gathered vain **m** to Jephthah, 376
12: 1 the **m** of Ephraim gathered themselves 376
12: 4 Jephthah gathered together all the **m** of 376
12: 4 and the **m** of Gilead smote Ephraim, because 376
12: 5 that the **m** of Gilead said unto him, *Art* thou 376
14:10 there a feast; for so used the **young m** to do. 970
14:18 the **m** of the city said unto him on 376
14:19 slew thirty **m** of them, and took their spoil, 376
15:10 the **m** of Judah said, Why are ye come up 376
15:11 three thousand **m** of Judah went to the top of 376
15:15 took it, and slew a thousand **m** therewith. 376
15:16 the jaw of an ass have I slain a thousand **m**. 376
16: 9 Now *there were* **m** lying in wait, NIH
16:27 Now the house was full *of* **m** and women; 376
16:27 *were* upon the roof about three thousand **m** 376
18: 2 sent of their family five **m** from their coasts, 376
18: 2 **m** of valour, from Zorah and 376+1121
18: 7 the five **m** departed, and came to Laish, 376
18:11 six hundred **m** appointed *with* weapons of 376
18:14 answered the five **m** that went to spy out 376
18:16 the six hundred **m** appointed *with* their 376
18:17 the five **m** that went to spy out the land went 376
18:17 **m** that were appointed *with* weapons of war. 376
18:22 the **m** that *were* in the houses near to 376
19:16 but the **m** of the place *were* Benjamites. 376
19:22 behold, the **m** of the city, certain sons of 376
19:25 the **m** would not hearken to him: so the man 376
20: 5 the **m** of Gibeah rose against me, and 1167
20:10 we will take ten **m** of an hundred throughout 376
20:11 So all the **m** of Israel were gathered against 376
20:12 the tribes of Israel sent **m** through all 376
20:13 Now therefore deliver *us* the **m**, the children 376
20:15 and six thousand **m** that drew sword, 376
20:15 were numbered seven hundred chosen **m**. 376
20:16 *were* seven hundred chosen **m** lefthanded; 376
20:17 the **m** of Israel, beside Benjamin, 376
20:17 were numbered four hundred thousand **m** 376
20:17 that drew sword: all these *were* **m** of war. 376
20:20 the **m** of Israel went out to battle against 376
20:20 the **m** of Israel put *themselves* in array to 376
20:21 that day twenty and two thousand **m**. 376
20:22 the people the **m** of Israel encouraged 376
20:25 of Israel again eighteen thousand **m**; 376
20:31 Gibeah in the field, about thirty **m** of Israel 376
20:33 all the **m** of Israel rose up out of their place, 376
20:34 ten thousand chosen **m** out of all Israel, 376
20:35 and five thousand and an hundred **m**: 376
20:36 for the **m** of Israel gave place to 376
20:38 an appointed sign between the **m** of Israel 376
Jdg 20:39 when the **m** of Israel retired in the battle, 376
20:39 kill of the **m** of Israel about thirty persons: 376
20:41 when the **m** of Israel turned *again*, the men 376
20:41 when the men of Israel turned *again*, the **m** 376
20:42 **m** of Israel unto the way of the wilderness; 376
20:44 there fell of Benjamin eighteen thousand **m**; 376
20:44 thousand men; all these *were* **m** of valour. 376
20:45 of them in the highways five thousand **m**; 376
20:45 and slew two thousand **m** of them. 376
20:46 and five thousand **m** that drew the sword; 376
20:46 drew the sword; all these *were* **m** of valour. 376
20:47 six hundred **m** turned and fled to 376
20:48 the **m** of Israel turned again upon 376
20:48 as well the **m** of *every* city, as the beast, 4974
21: 1 Now the **m** of Israel had sworn in Mizpeh, 376
21:10 thither twelve thousand **m** of the valiantest, 376
Ru 2: 9 have I not charged the **young m** that *they* 5288
2: 9 drink of *that* which the **young m** have 5288
2:15 Boaz commanded his **young m**, saying, 5288
2:21 Thou shalt keep fast by my **young m**, 5288
3:10 inasmuch as *thou* followedst not **young m**, 970
4: 2 he took ten **m** of the elders of the city, and 376
1Sa 2: 4 The bows of the mighty *m are* broken, and NIH
2:17 Wherefore the sin of the **young m** was very 5288
2:17 for **m** abhorred the offering of the LORD. 376
2:26 both with the LORD, and also with **m**. 376
4: 2 the army in the field about four thousand **m**. 376
4: 9 Be strong, and quit yourselves like **m**, O ye 376
4: 9 to you: quit yourselves like **m**, and fight. 376
5: 7 when the **m** of Ashdod saw that *it was* so, 376
5: 9 he smote the **m** of the city, both small and 376
5:12 the **m** that died not were smitten with 376
6:10 the **m** did so; and took two milch kine, and 376
6:15 the **m** of Beth-shemesh offered burnt 376
6:19 he smote the **m** of Beth-shemesh, because 376
6:19 fifty thousand and threescore and ten **m**: 376
6:20 the **m** of Beth-shemesh said, Who is able to 376
7: 1 the **m** of Kirjath-jearim came, and 376
7:11 And the **m** of Israel went out of Mizpeh, and 376
8:16 and your goodliest **young m**, and your asses, 970
8:22 Samuel said unto the **m** of Israel, Go ye 376
10: 2 thou shalt find two **m** by Rachel's sepulchre 376
10: 3 there shall meet thee three **m** going up to 376
10:26 there went with him a **band of m**, 2428
11: 1 all the **m** of Jabesh said unto Nahash, 376
11: 5 they told him the tidings of the **m** of Jabesh. 376
11: 8 and the **m** of Judah thirty thousand. 376
11: 9 Thus shall ye say unto the **m** of 376
11: 9 and shewed *it* to the **m** of Jabesh; 376
11:10 Therefore the **m** of Jabesh said, To morrow 376
11:12 bring the **m**, that we may put them to death. 376
11:15 and all the **m** of Israel rejoiced greatly. 376
13: 2 Saul chose him three thousand *m* of Israel; NIH
13: 6 When the **m** of Israel saw that they were in a 376
13:15 were present with him, about six hundred **m**. 376
14: 2 *were* with him *were* about six hundred **m**; 376
14: 8 we will pass over unto *these* **m**, and we will 376
14:12 the **m** of the garrison answered Jonathan 376
14:14 his armourbearer made, was about twenty **m**, 376
14:22 Likewise all the **m** of Israel which had hid 376
14:24 And the **m** of Israel were distressed that day: 376
15: 4 and ten thousand **m** of Judah. 376
17: 2 and the **m** of Israel were gathered together, 376
17:12 the man went among **m** *for* an old man in 376
17:19 Now Saul, and they, and all the **m** of Israel, 376
17:24 all the **m** of Israel, when they saw the man, 376
17:25 the **m** of Israel said, Have ye seen this man 376
17:26 And David spake to the **m** that stood by him, 376
17:28 brother heard when he spake unto the **m**; 376
17:52 the **m** of Israel and of Judah arose, and 376
18: 5 Saul set him over the **m** of war, and he was 376
18:27 he and his **m**, and slew of the Philistines two 376
18:27 and slew of the Philistines two hundred **m**; 376
21: 4 if the **young m** have kept themselves at 5288
21: 5 the vessels of the **young m** are holy, and 5288
21:15 *Have* I need of **mad m**, that ye have 7696
22: 2 there were with him about four hundred **m**. 376
22: 6 and the **m** that *were* with him, 376
22:19 both **m** and women, children and sucklings, 376
23: 3 David's **m** said unto him, Behold, we *be* 376
23: 5 So David and his **m** went *to* Keilah, and 376
23: 8 down *to* Keilah, to besiege David and his **m**. 376
23:11 Will the **m** of Keilah deliver me up into his 1167
23:12 Will the **m** of Keilah deliver me and my 1167
23:12 deliver me and my **m** into the hand of Saul? 376
23:13 David and his **m**, *which were* about six 376
23:24 and his **m** *were* in the wilderness of Maon, 376
23:25 his **m** went to seek *him*. And they told 376
23:26 and his **m** on that side of the mountain: 376
23:26 for Saul and his **m** compassed David and his 376
23:26 and his **m** round about to take them. 376
24: 2 Saul took three thousand chosen **m** out of all 376
24: 2 and his **m** upon the rocks of the wild goats. 376
24: 3 and his **m** remained in the sides of the cave. 376
24: 4 the **m** of David said unto him, Behold 376
24: 6 he said unto his **m**, The LORD forbid that I 376
24:22 David and his **m** gat them up unto the hold. 376
25: 5 David sent out ten **young m**, and 5288
25: 5 David said unto the **young m**, Get you up 5288
25: 8 Ask thy **young m**, and they will shew thee. 5288
25: 8 Wherefore let the **young m** find favour in 5288
25: 9 when David's **young m** came, they spake 5288
25:11 give *it* unto **m**, whom I know not whence 376
25:12 So David's **young m** turned their way, and 5288
25:13 David said unto his **m**, Gird you on every 376
25:13 went up after David about four hundred **m**; 376
25:14 one of the **young m** told Abigail, 5288
25:15 the **m** *were* very good unto us, and we were 376
25:20 David and his **m** came down against her; 376
25:25 I thine handmaid saw not the **young m** of 5288
25:27 let it even be given unto the **young m** that 5288
26: 2 having three thousand chosen **m** of Israel 376
26:19 if *they be* the children of **m**, cursed *be* they 120
26:22 let one of the **young m** come over and 5288
27: 2 he passed over with the six hundred **m** that 376
1Sa 27: 3 he and his **m**, every man with his household, 376
27: 8 David and his **m** went up, and invaded 376
28: 1 go out with me to battle, thou and thy **m**. 376
28: 8 two **m** with him, and they came to 376
29: 2 his **m** passed on in the rereward with Achish. 376
29: 4 *should it* not *be* with the heads of these **m**? 376
29:11 his **m** rose up early to depart in the morning, 376
30: 1 his **m** were come *to* Ziklag on the third day, 376
30: 3 So David and his **m** came to the city, and 376
30: 9 and the six hundred **m** that *were* with him, 376
30:10 But David pursued, he and four hundred **m**: 376
30:17 save four hundred **young m**, 376+5288
30:21 David came to the two hundred **m**, 376
30:22 answered all the wicked **m** and *men* of 376
30:22 all the wicked men and *m* of Belial, NIH
30:31 David himself and his **m** were wont to haunt. 376
31: 1 the **m** of Israel fled from before 376
31: 6 and his armourbearer, and all his **m**, 376
31: 7 when the **m** of Israel that *were* on the *other* 376
31: 7 saw that the **m** of Israel fled, and that Saul 376
31:12 All the valiant **m** arose, and went all night, 376
2Sa 1:11 and likewise all the **m** that *were* with him: 376
1:15 David called one of the **young m**, and said, 5288
2: 3 his **m** that *were* with him did David bring 376
2: 4 the **m** of Judah came, and there they 376
2: 4 *That* the **m** of Jabesh-gilead *were they* that 376
2: 5 David sent messengers unto the **m** of 376
2:14 Let the **young m** now arise, and play before 5288
2:17 Abner was beaten, and the **m** of Israel, 376
2:21 lay thee hold on one of the **young m**, and 5288
2:29 his **m** walked all that night through the plain, 376
2:30 there lacked of David's servants nineteen **m** 376
2:31 and of Abner's **m**, *so that* three hundred and 376
2:31 *so that* three hundred and threescore **m** died. 376
2:32 Joab and his **m** went all night, and they came 376
3:20 to David *to* Hebron, and twenty **m** with him. 376
3:20 and the **m** that *were* with him a feast. 376
3:34 as *a man* falleth before wicked **m**, *so* 1121
3:39 these **m** the sons of Zeruiah *be* too hard for 376
4: 2 Saul's son had two **m** *that were* captains of 376
4:11 when wicked **m** have slain a righteous 376
4:12 David commanded *his* **young m**, and 5288
5: 6 his **m** went *to* Jerusalem unto the Jebusites, 376
5:21 and David and his **m** burnt them. 376
6: 1 David gathered together all the chosen *m* of NIH
6:19 as well to the women as **m**, to every one a 376
7: 9 like unto the name of the great *m* that *are* in NIH
7:14 I will chasten him with the rod of **m**, and 376
7:14 and with the stripes of the children of **m**: 120
8: 5 of the Syrians two and twenty thousand **m**. 376
8:13 valley of salt, *being* eighteen thousand *m* NIH
10: 5 because the **m** were greatly ashamed: 376
10: 6 of king Maacah a thousand **m**, and of Ish-tob 376
10: 6 and of Ish-tob twelve thousand **m**. 376
10: 7 sent Joab, and all the host *of* the mighty *m*. NIH
10: 9 he chose of all the choice *m* of Israel, and NIH
10:12 let us **play the m** for our people, and 2388
10:18 David slew *the m of* seven hundred chariots NIH
11:16 a place where he knew that valiant **m** *were*. 376
11:17 the **m** of the city went out, and fought with 376
11:23 Surely the **m** prevailed against us, and 376
12: 1 said unto him, There were two **m** in one city; 376
13: 9 Amnon said, Have out all **m** from me. 376
13:32 have slain all the **young m** the king's sons; 5288
15: 1 and horses, and fifty **m** to run before him. 376
15: 6 Absalom stole the hearts of the **m** of Israel. 376
15:11 with Absalom went two hundred **m** out of 376
15:13 The hearts of the **m** of Israel are after 376
15:18 six hundred **m** which came after him from 376
15:22 all his **m**, and all the little ones that *were* 376
16: 2 and summer fruit for the **young m** to eat; 5288
16: 6 all the mighty *m were* on his right hand and NIH
16:13 as David and his **m** went by the way, Shimei 376
16:15 and all the people the **m** of Israel, 376
16:18 this people, and all the **m** of Israel, choose, 376
17: 1 Let me now choose out twelve thousand **m**, 376
17: 8 thou knowest thy father and his **m**, that they 376
17: 8 that they *be* mighty *m*, and they *be* chafed NIH
17:10 and *they* which *be* with him *are* valiant **m**. 1121
17:12 of all the **m** that *are* with him there shall not 376
17:14 Absalom and all the **m** of Israel said, 376
17:24 he and all the **m** of Israel with him. 376
18: 7 slaughter that day *of* twenty thousand *m*. NIH
18:15 ten **young m** that bare Joab's armour 5288
18:28 which hath delivered up the **m** that lift up 376
19:14 he bowed the heart of all the **m** of Judah, 376
19:16 came down with the **m** of Judah to meet king 376
19:17 *there were* a thousand **m** of Benjamin with 376
19:28 but dead **m** before my lord the king: 376
19:35 can I hear any more the voice of singing *m* NIH
19:41 all the **m** of Israel came to the king, and 376
19:41 Why have our brethren the **m** of Judah 376
19:41 and all David's **m** with him, over Jordan? 376
19:42 all the **m** of Judah answered the men of 376
19:42 all the men of Judah answered the **m** of 376
19:43 the **m** of Israel answered the men of Judah, 376
19:43 the men of Israel answered the **m** of Judah, 376
19:43 the words of the **m** of Judah were fiercer 376
19:43 fiercer than the words of the **m** of Israel. 376
20: 2 the **m** of Judah clave unto their king, 376
20: 4 Assemble me the **m** of Judah *within* three 376
20: 5 So Amasa went to assemble *the m of* Judah: NIH
20: 7 there went out after him Joab's **m**, and 376
20: 7 all the mighty *m*: and they went out of NIH
20:11 one of Joab's **m** stood by him, and said, 5288
21: 6 Let seven **m** of his sons be delivered unto us, 376
21:12 the bones of Jonathan his son from the **m** of 1167
21:17 the **m** of David sware unto him, saying, 376
22: 5 the floods of **ungodly m** made me afraid, 1100
23: 3 He that ruleth over **m** *must be* just, ruling *in* 120
23: 8 These *be* the names of the mighty *m* whom NIH
23: 9 *one* of the three mighty *m* with David, NIH
23: 9 and the **m** of Israel were gone away: 376
23:16 the three mighty *m* brake through the host NIH
23:17 *is not this* the blood of the **m** that went in 376

M

2Sa 23:17 These *things* did *these* three mighty ***m***. NIH
23:20 many acts, he slew two **lionlike m** of Moab: 739
23:22 and had the name among three mighty ***m***. NIH
24: 9 thousand valiant **m** that drew the sword; 376
24: 9 the **m** of Judah *were* five hundred thousand 376
24: 9 of Judah *were* five hundred thousand **m**. 376
24:15 Dan even to Beer-sheba seventy thousand **m**. 376
1Ki 1: 5 and horsemen, and fifty **m** to run before him. 376
1: 8 and the mighty ***m*** which *belonged* to David, NIH
1: 9 and all the **m** of Judah the king's servants: 376
1:10 and the mighty ***m***, and Solomon his brother, NIH
2:32 who fell upon two **m** more righteous and 376
4:31 For he was wiser than all **m**; than Ethan 120
5:13 and the levy was thirty thousand **m**. 376
8: 2 all the **m** of Israel assembled themselves 376
8:39 knowest the hearts of all the children of **m**;) 120
9:22 they *were* **m** of war, and his servants, and 376
10: 8 Happy *are* thy **m**, happy *are* these thy 376
11:18 and they took **m** with them out of Paran, and 376
11:24 he gathered **m** unto him, and became captain 376
12: 6 king Rehoboam consulted with the **old m**, 2205
12: 8 he forsook the counsel of the **old m**, 2205
12: 8 consulted with the **young m** that were 3206
12:10 the **young m** that were grown up with him 3206
12:14 to them after the counsel of the **young m**, 3206
12:21 fourscore thousand chosen ***m***, which were NIH
13:25 **m** passed by, and saw the carcase cast in 376
18:13 how I hid an hundred **m** of the LORD'S 376
18:22 prophets *are* four hundred and fifty **m**. 376
20:14 *Even* by the **young m** of the princes of 5288
20:15 he numbered the **young m** of the princes of 5288
20:17 the **young m** of the princes of the provinces 5288
20:17 There are **m** come out of Samaria. 376
20:19 So these **young m** of the princes of 5288
20:30 and seven thousand of the **m** that were left. 376
20:33 Now the **m** did diligently observe whether 376
21:10 set two **m**, sons of Belial, before him, to bear 376
21:11 the **m** of his city, *even* the elders and 376
21:13 And there came in two **m**, children of Belial, 376
21:13 the **m** of Belial witnessed against him, 376
22: 6 about four hundred **m**, and said unto them, 376
2Ki 2: 7 And fifty **m** of the sons of the prophets went, 376
2:16 there be with thy servants fifty strong **m**; 376
2:17 They sent therefore fifty **m**; and they sought 376
2:19 the **m** of the city said unto Elisha, Behold, 376
3:26 he took with him seven hundred **m** that drew 376
4:22 one of the **young m**, and one of the asses, 5288
4:40 So they poured out for the **m** to eat. And it 376
4:43 What, should I set this before an hundred **m**? 376
5:22 two **young m** of the sons of the prophets: 5288
5:24 and he let the **m** go, and they departed. 376
6:20 open the eyes of these ***m***, that they may see. NIH
7: 3 there were four leprous **m** *at* the entering in 376
8:12 their young ***m*** wilt thou slay with the sword, NIH
10: 6 take ye the heads of the **m** your master's 376
10: 6 *were* with the great ***m*** of the city, NIH
10:11 all his great ***m***, and his kinsfolks, and NIH
10:14 of the shearing house, *even* two and forty **m**; 376
10:24 Jehu appointed fourscore **m** without, and 376
10:24 *If* any of the **m** whom I *have* brought into 376
11: 9 they took every man his **m** that were to come 376
12:15 Moreover they reckoned not with the **m**, 376
13:21 they spied a band *of* ***m***; and they cast NIH
15:20 *even* of all the mighty ***m*** of wealth, of each NIH
15:25 and with him fifty **m** of the Gileadites: 376
17:24 the king of Assyria brought ***m*** from NIH
17:30 the **m** of Babylon made Succoth-benoth, 376
17:30 the **m** of Cuth made Nergal, and the men of 376
17:30 and the **m** of Hamath made Ashima, 376
18:27 *hath he* not *sent me* to the **m** which sit on 376
20:14 and said unto him, What said these **m**? 376
23: 2 all the **m** of Judah and all the inhabitants of 376
23:14 and filled their places *with* the bones of **m**. 120
23:17 the **m** of the city told him, *It is* the sepulchre 376
24:14 the princes, and all the mighty ***m*** of valour, NIH
24:16 all the **m** of might, *even* seven thousand, 376
25: 4 all the **m** of war *fled* by night *by* the way of 376
25:19 an officer that was set over the **m** of war, 376
25:19 five **m** of them that were in the king's 376
25:19 threescore **m** of the people of the land that 376
25:23 the captains of the armies, they and *their* **m**, 376
25:23 the son of a Maachathite, they and their **m**. 376
25:24 to them, and to their **m**, and said unto them, 376
25:25 and ten **m** with him, and smote Gedaliah, 376
1Ch 4:12 of Irnahash. These *are* the **m** of Rechah. 376
4:22 the **m** of Chozeba, and Joash, and Saraph, 376
4:42 five hundred **m**, went to mount Seir, 376
5:18 of valiant **m**, men *able to* bear buckler and 1121
5:18 **m** *able to* bear buckler and sword, and 376
5:21 and *of* **m** an hundred thousand. 120+5315
5:24 Hodaviah, and Jahdiel, mighty ***m*** of valour, NIH
5:24 famous **m**, *and* heads of the house of their 376
7: 2 *they were* valiant ***m*** of might in their NIH
7: 3 and Joel, Ishiah, five: all of them chief ***m***. NIH
7: 4 thirty thousand ***m***: for they had many wives NIH
7: 5 the families of Issachar *were* **m** of might, 1368
7: 7 house of *their* fathers, mighty ***m*** of valour; NIH
7: 9 mighty ***m*** of valour, *was* twenty thousand NIH
7:11 mighty ***m*** of valour, *were* seventeen NIH
7:21 whom the **m** of Gath that were born in *that* 376
7:40 choice *and* mighty ***m*** of valour, chief of NIH
7:40 *and* to battle *was* twenty and six thousand **m**. 376
8:28 chief ***m***. These dwelt in Jerusalem. NIH
8:40 the sons of Ulam were mighty **m** of valour, 376
9: 9 All these **m** *were* chief of the fathers in 376
9:13 very able **m** *for* the work of the service of 1368
10: 1 the **m** of Israel fled from before 376
10: 7 when all the **m** of Israel that *were* in 376
10:12 all the valiant **m**, and took away the body of 376
11:10 These also *are* the chief of the mighty ***m*** NIH
11:11 this *is* the number of the mighty ***m*** whom NIH
11:19 these **m** that have put their lives in jeopardy? 376
11:22 many acts; he slew two **lionlike m** of Moab: 739
11:26 Also the valiant ***m*** of the armies *were*, NIH
12: 1 they *were* among the mighty ***m***, helpers of NIH

1Ch 12: 8 into the hold to the wilderness **m** of might, 1368
12: 8 *and* **m** of war *fit* for the battle, that could 376
12:21 for they *were* all mighty ***m*** of valour, NIH
12:25 mighty **m** of valour for the war, NIH
12:30 and eight hundred, mighty ***m*** of valour, NIH
12:32 *which were* **m** that had understanding of NIH
12:38 All these **m** of war, that could keep rank, 376
16:31 let ***m*** say among the nations, The LORD NIH
17: 8 the name of the great ***m*** that *are* in the earth. NIH
18: 5 of the Syrians two and twenty thousand **m**. 376
19: 5 and told David how the **m** were served. 376
19: 5 for the **m** were greatly ashamed. And 376
19: 8 sent Joab, and all the host *of* the mighty ***m***. NIH
19:18 David slew of the Syrians seven thousand ***m*** NIH
21: 5 and an hundred thousand **m** that drew sword: 376
21: 5 and ten thousand **m** that drew sword. 376
21:14 and there fell of Israel seventy thousand **m**. 376
22:15 all *manner of* cunning ***m*** for every *manner* NIH
24: 4 there were moe chief **m** found of the sons 1397
24: 4 sixteen chief ***m*** of the house of *their* fathers, NIH
26: 6 for they *were* mighty ***m*** of valour. NIH
26: 7 whose brethren *were* strong **m**, Elihu, and 1121
26: 8 able **m** for strength for the service, 376
26: 9 had sons and brethren, strong **m**, 1121
26:12 *even* among the chief **m**, *having* wards one 1397
26:30 **m** of valour, a thousand and seven hundred, 1121
26:31 there were found among them mighty ***m*** of NIH
26:32 his brethren, **m** of valour, *were* two 1121
28: 1 *with* the mighty ***m***, and with all the valiant NIH
28: 1 the mighty *men*, and with all the valiant **m**, 1368
29:24 the mighty ***m***, and all the sons likewise of NIH
2Ch 2: 2 and ten thousand **m** to bear burdens, 376
2: 7 that can skill to grave with the cunning ***m*** NIH
2:14 with thy cunning ***m***, and with the cunning NIH
2:14 with the cunning ***m*** of my lord David thy NIH
5: 3 Wherefore all the **m** of Israel assembled 376
6:18 will God in very deed dwell with **m** on 120
6:30 knowest the hearts of the children of **m**:) 120
8: 9 they *were* **m** of war, and chief of his 376
9: 7 Happy *are* thy **m**, and happy *are* these thy 376
10: 6 Rehoboam took counsel with the **old m** 2205
10: 8 he forsook the counsel which the **old m** 2205
10: 8 took counsel with the **young m** that were 3206
10:10 the **young m** that were brought up with him 3206
10:13 forsook the counsel of the **old m**, 2205
10:14 them after the advice of the **young m**, 3206
11: 1 fourscore thousand chosen ***m***, which were NIH
13: 3 in array with an army of valiant ***m*** of war, NIH
13: 3 *even* four hundred thousand chosen **m**: 376
13: 3 him with eight hundred thousand chosen **m**, 376
13: 3 chosen men, *being* mighty ***m*** of valour. NIH
13: 7 there are gathered unto him vain **m**, 376
13:15 the **m** of Judah gave a shout: and as the men 376
13:15 as the **m** of Judah shouted, it came to pass, 376
13:17 of Israel five hundred thousand chosen **m**. 376
14: 8 And Asa had an army *of* ***m*** that bare targets NIH
14: 8 all these *were* mighty ***m*** of valour. NIH
17:13 the **m** of war, mighty *men* of valour, *were* in 376
17:13 the men of war, mighty ***m*** of valour, *were* in NIH
17:14 with him mighty ***m*** of valour three hundred NIH
17:16 with him two hundred thousand mighty ***m*** NIH
17:17 with him armed ***m*** with bow and shield two NIH
18: 5 together *of* prophets four hundred **m**, 376
21: 1 for the band *of* ***m*** that came with NIH
23: 8 took every man his **m** that were to come in 376
24:24 Syrians came with a small *company* of **m**, 376
25: 5 thousand choice ***m***, *able to* go forth *to* war, NIH
25: 6 ***m*** of valour out of Israel for an hundred NIH
26:11 Moreover Uzziah had a host of fighting ***m***, NIH
26:12 the mighty ***m*** of valour *were* two thousand NIH
26:15 invented by cunning ***m***, to be on the towers NIH
26:17 priests of the LORD, *that were* valiant **m**: 1121
28: 6 in one day, *which were* all valiant **m**; 1121
28:14 So the armed **m** left the captives and NIH
28:15 the **m** which were expressed by name rose 376
31:19 the **m** that were expressed by name, 376
32: 3 his mighty ***m*** to stop the waters of NIH
32:21 which cut off all the mighty ***m*** of valour, NIH
34:12 the **m** did the work faithfully: and 376
34:30 all the **m** of Judah, and the inhabitants of 376
35:25 all the singing ***m*** and the singing *women* NIH
36:17 who slew their **young m** with the sword in 970
Ezr 1: 4 let the **m** of his place help him with silver, 376
2: 2 The number of the **m** of the people of Israel: 376
2:22 The **m** of Netophah, fifty and six. 376
2:23 The **m** of Anathoth, an hundred twenty and 376
2:27 The **m** of Michmas, an hundred twenty and 376
2:28 The **m** of Beth-el and Ai, two hundred 376
2:65 *were* among them two hundred singing ***m*** NIH
3:12 *who were* **ancient m** that had seen the first 2205
4:11 Thy servants the **m** *on this* side the river, and 606
4:21 commandment to cause these **m** to cease, 1400
5: 4 What are the names of the **m** that make this 1400
5:10 that we might write the names of the **m** that 1400
6: 8 forthwith expences be given unto these **m**, 1400
7:28 I gathered together out of Israel chief ***m*** to NIH
8:16 chief ***m***; also for Joiarib, and for Elnathan, NIH
8:16 and for Elnathan, ***m*** of understanding. NIH
10: 1 out of Israel a very great congregation *of* **m** 376
10: 9 all the **m** of Judah and Benjamin gathered 376
10:17 they made an end with all the **m** that had 376
Ne 1: 2 came, he and *certain* **m** of Judah; 376
2:12 in the night, I and *some* few **m** with me; 376
3: 2 And next unto him builded the **m** of Jericho. 376
3: 7 the **m** of Gibeon, and of Mizpah, 376
3:22 him repaired the priests, the **m** of the plain. 376
4:23 nor the **m** of the guard which followed me, 376
5: 5 *to redeem them;* for **other m** have our lands 312
7: 7 *I say,* of the **m** of the people of Israel *was* 376
7:26 The **m** of Beth-lehem and Netophah, 376
7:27 The **m** of Anathoth, an hundred twenty and 376
7:28 The **m** of Beth-azmaveth, forty and two. 376
7:29 The **m** of Kirjath-jearim, Chephirah, and 376
7:30 The **m** of Ramah and Geba, six hundred 376
7:31 The **m** of Michmas, an hundred and twenty 376

Ne 7:32 The **m** of Beth-el and Ai, an hundred twenty 376
7:33 The **m** of the other Nebo, fifty and two. 376
7:67 and five singing ***m*** and singing *women*. NIH
8: 2 the law before the congregation both of **m** 376
8: 3 before the **m** and the women, and those that 376
11: 2 the people blessed all the **m**, that willingly 376
11: 6 four hundred threescore and eight valiant **m**. 376
11:14 mighty ***m*** of valour, an hundred twenty and NIH
11:14 *was* Zabdiel, the son of *one of* the great ***m***. NIH
13:16 There dwelt **m of Tyre** also therein, which 6876
Est 1:13 the king said to the wise ***m***, which knew NIH
6:13 said his wise ***m*** and Zeresh his wife unto NIH
9: 6 the Jews slew and destroyed five hundred **m**. 376
9:12 destroyed five hundred **m** in Shushan 376
9:15 and slew three hundred **m** at Shushan; 376
Job 1: 3 that this man was the greatest of all the **m** 1121
1:19 it fell upon the **young m**, and they are 5288
4:13 of the night, when deep sleep falleth on **m**. 376
7:20 shall I do unto thee, O thou preserver of **m**? 120
11: 3 Should thy lies make **m** hold their peace? 4962
11:11 For he knoweth vain **m**: he seeth 4962
15:10 *are* both the grayheaded and **very aged m**, 3453
15:18 Which wise ***m*** have told from their fathers, NIH
17: 8 Upright ***m*** shall be astonied at this, and NIH
22:15 the old way which wicked **m** have trodden? 4962
22:29 When ***m*** are cast down, then thou shalt say, NIH
24:12 **M** groan from out of the city, and the soul 4962
27:23 ***M*** shall clap their hands at him, and NIH
28: 4 are dried up, they are gone away from **m**. 582
29: 8 The **young m** saw me, and hid themselves: 5288
29:21 Unto me ***m*** gave ear, and waited, and NIH
30: 5 They were driven forth from among ***m***, NIH
30: 8 of fools, yea, children of **base m**: 1097+8034
31:31 If the **m** of my tabernacle said not, O that 4962
32: 1 So these three **m** ceased to answer Job, 376
32: 5 no answer in the mouth of *these* three **m**, 376
32: 9 **Great m** are not *always* wise: neither do 7227
33:15 the night, when deep sleep falleth upon **m**, 376
33:16 he openeth the ears of **m**, and sealeth their 376
33:27 He looketh upon **m**, and *if any* say, I have 376
34: 2 O ye wise ***m***; and give ear unto me, NIH
34: 8 of iniquity, and walketh with wicked **m**. 376
34:10 hearken unto me, ye **m** of understanding: 376
34:24 He shall break in pieces mighty ***m*** without NIH
34:26 He striketh them as wicked ***m*** in the open NIH
34:34 Let **m** of understanding tell me, and let a 376
34:36 because of *his* answers for wicked **m**. 376
35:12 because of the pride of **evil m**. 7451
36:24 that thou magnify his work, which **m** behold. 376
37: 7 of every man; that all **m** may know his work. 376
37:21 now ***m*** see not the bright light which *is* in NIH
37:24 **M** do therefore fear him: he respecteth not 376
39:21 He goeth on to meet the **armed m**. 5402
Ps 4: 2 O ye sons of **m**, how long *will ye turn* my 376
9:20 nations may know themselves *to be but* **m**. 582
11: 4 his eyelids try, the children of **m**. 120
12: 1 faithful fail from among the children of **m**. 120
12: 8 when the vilest **m** are exalted. 120+1121
14: 2 down from heaven upon the children of **m**, 120
17: 4 Concerning the works of **m**, by the word of 120
17:14 From **m** *which are* thy hand, O LORD, 4962
17:14 thy hand, O LORD, from **m** of the world, 4962
18: 4 the floods of **ungodly m** made me afraid. 1100
21:10 their seed from among the children of **m**. 120
22: 6 a reproach of **m**, and despised of the people. 120
26: 9 with sinners, nor my life with bloody **m**: 120
31:19 them that trust in thee before the sons of **m**! 120
33:13 from heaven; he beholdeth all the sons of **m**. 120
36: 7 the children of **m** put their trust under 120
45: 2 Thou art fairer than the children of **m**: 120
49:10 For he seeth *that* wise ***m*** die, likewise NIH
49:18 ***m*** will praise thee, when thou doest well to NIH
53: 2 down from heaven upon the children of **m**, 120
55:23 deceitful **m** shall not live out half their days; 376
57: 4 *even* the sons of **m**, whose teeth *are* spears 120
58: 1 do ye judge uprightly, O ye sons of **m**? 120
59: 2 of iniquity, and save me from bloody **m**. 376
62: 9 Surely **m of low degree** *are* vanity, 120+1121
62: 9 *and* **m of high degree** *are* a lie: 376+1121
64: 9 all **m** shall fear, and shall declare the work 120
66: 5 *in his* doing toward the children of **m**. 120
66:12 Thou hast caused **m** to ride over our heads; 582
68:18 thou hast received gifts for **m**; yea, *for* 120
72:17 ***m*** shall be blessed in him: all nations shall NIH
73: 5 They *are* not in trouble *as other* **m**; 582
73: 5 neither are they plagued like *other* **m**. 120
76: 5 none of the **m** of might have found their 376
78:31 and smote down the chosen ***m*** of Israel. NIH
78:60 the tent *which* he placed among **m**; 120
78:63 The fire consumed their **young m**; and 970
82: 7 ye shall die like **m**, and fall like one of 120
83:18 That ***m*** may know that thou, whose name NIH
86:14 the assemblies of violent ***m*** have sought NIH
89:47 hast thou made all **m** in vain? 120+1121
90: 3 and sayest, Return, ye children of **m**. 120
105:12 When they were *but a few* **m** in number; 4962
107: 8 Oh that ***m*** would praise the LORD *for* his NIH
107: 8 his wonderful works to the children of **m**! 120
107:15 Oh that ***m*** would praise the LORD *for* his NIH
107:15 his wonderful works to the children of **m**! 120
107:21 Oh that ***m*** would praise the LORD *for* his NIH
107:21 his wonderful works to the children of **m**! 120
107:31 Oh that ***m*** would praise the LORD *for* his NIH
107:31 his wonderful works to the children of **m**! 120
115:16 the earth hath he given to the children of **m**. 120
116:11 I said in my haste, All **m** *are* liars. 120
124: 2 was on our side, when **m** rose up against us: 120
139:19 depart from me therefore, ye bloody **m**. 376
141: 4 to practise wicked works with **m** that work 376
145: 6 ***m*** shall speak of the might of thy terrible NIH
145:12 To make known to the sons of **m** his mighty 120
148:12 Both **young m**, and maidens; old men, and 970
148:12 and maidens; **old m**, and children: 2205
Pr 2:20 thou mayest walk in the way of good ***m***, NIH
4:14 and go not in the way of evil ***m***. NIH

M

Pr 6:30 *M* do not despise a thief, if he steal to NIH
7:26 yea, many strong **m** *have been* slain by her. NIH
8: 4 Unto you, O **m**, I call; and my voice *is* to 376
8:31 and my delights *were* with the sons of **m**. 120
10:14 Wise *m* lay up knowledge: but the mouth of NIH
11: 7 and the hope of unjust *m* perisheth. NIH
11:16 retaineth honour: and strong *m* retain riches. NIH
12:12 The wicked desireth the net of evil *m*: but NIH
13:20 He that walketh with wise *m* shall be wise: NIH
15:11 then the hearts of the children of **m**? 120
16: 6 by the fear of the LORD *m* depart from NIH
17: 6 Children's children *are* the crown of **old m**; 2205
18:16 for him, and bringeth him before great *m*. NIH
20: 6 Most **m** will proclaim every one his own 120
20:29 The glory of **young m** *is* their strength: and 970
20:29 and the beauty of **old m** *is* the gray head. 2205
22:29 he shall not stand before mean *m*. NIH
23:28 and increaseth the transgressors among **m**. 120
24: 1 Be not thou envious against evil **m**, 376
24: 9 and the scorner *is* an abomination to **m**. 120
24:19 of evil *m*, neither be thou envious at NIH
25: 1 which the **m** of Hezekiah king of Judah 376
25: 6 and stand not in the place of great *m*: NIH
25:27 *for m* to search their own glory *is not* glory. NIH
26:16 than seven *m* that can render a reason. NIH
28: 5 Evil **m** understand not judgment: but 376
28: 7 he that is a companion of riotous *m* shameth NIH
28:12 When righteous *m* do rejoice, *there is* great NIH
28:28 When the wicked rise, **m** hide themselves: 120
29: 8 Scornful **m** bring a city into a snare: but 376
29: 8 into a snare: but wise *m* turn away wrath. NIH
30:14 off the earth, and the needy from *among* **m**. 120
Ecc 2: 3 see what *was* that good for the sons of **m**, 120
2: 8 I gat me *m* singers and *women* singers, and NIH
2: 8 and the delights of the sons of **m**, 120
3:10 which God hath given to the sons of **m** to be 120
3:14 God doeth *it*, that *m* should fear before him. NIH
3:18 heart concerning the estate of the sons of **m**, 120
3:19 For that which befalleth the sons of **m** 120
6: 1 under the sun, and it *is* common among **m**: 120
7: 2 for that *is* the end of all **m**; and the living 120
7:19 than ten mighty *m* which are in the city. NIH
8:11 the heart of the sons of **m** is fully set in them 120
8:14 that there be just *m*, unto whom it NIH
8:14 there be wicked *m*, to whom it happeneth NIH
9: 3 also the heart of the sons of **m** is full *of* evil, 120
9:11 nor yet riches to **m**[S] of understanding, 1886.1
9:11 nor yet favour to **m**[S] of skill; 1886.1
9:12 so *are* the sons of **m** snared in an evil time, 120
9:14 *There was* a little city, and few **m** within it; 376
9:17 The words of wise *m are* heard in quiet, NIH
12: 3 and the strong **m** shall bow themselves, and 376
SS 3: 7 threescore valiant *m are* about it, of NIH
4: 4 thousand bucklers, all shields of mighty *m*. NIH
Isa 2:11 the haughtiness of **m** shall be bowed down, 376
2:17 and the haughtiness of **m** shall be made low: 376
3:25 Thy **m** shall fall by the sword, and 4962
5: 3 **m** of Judah, judge, I pray you, betwixt me 376
5: 7 and the **m** of Judah his pleasant plant: 376
5:13 their honourable **m** *are* famished, and 4962
5:22 and **m** of strength to mingle strong drink: 376
6:12 And the LORD have removed **m** far away, 120
7:13 *Is it* a small thing for you to weary **m**, but 376
7:24 and with bows shall *m* come thither; NIH
9: 3 *and* as *m* rejoice when they divide the spoil. NIH
9:17 the Lord shall have no joy in their **young m**, 970
11:15 and make *m* go over dryshod. NIH
13:18 *Their* bows also shall dash the **young m** to 5288
19:12 where *are* thy wise *m*? and let them tell thee NIH
21: 9 behold, here cometh a chariot of **m**, *with* a 376
21:17 the mighty *m* of the children of Kedar, NIH
22: 2 thy slain *m are* not slain with the sword, nor NIH
22: 6 And Elam bare the quiver with chariots of **m** 120
23: 4 neither do I nourish up **young m**, *nor* bring 970
24: 6 of the earth are burned, and few **m** left. 582
26:19 Thy dead *m* shall live, *together with* my NIH
28:14 hear the word of the LORD, ye scornful **m**, 376
29:11 which *m* deliver to one that is learned, NIH
29:13 towards me is taught *by* the precept of **m**: 376
29:14 for the wisdom of their wise *m* shall perish, NIH
29:14 the understanding of their prudent *m* shall NIH
29:19 the poor among **m** shall rejoice in the Holy 120
31: 3 Now the Egyptians *are* **m**, and not God; and 120
31: 8 and his **young m** shall be discomfited. 970
35: 8 the **wayfaring m**, though fools, 1870+1980
36:12 *hath he* not *sent me* to the **m** that sit upon 376
38:16 by these *things* **m** live, and in all these NIH
39: 3 and said unto him, What said these **m**? 376
40:30 be weary, and the **young m** shall utterly fall: 970
41: 9 and called thee from the **chief m** thereof, and 678
41:14 thou worm Jacob, *and* ye **m** of Israel; 4962
43: 4 therefore will I give **m** for thee, and 120
44:11 the workmen, they *are of* **m**: let them all be 120
44:25 that turneth wise *m* backward, and NIH
45:14 of Ethiopia and of the Sabeans, **m** of stature, 376
45:24 *even* to him shall *m* come; and all that are NIH
46: 8 Remember this, and **shew yourselves m**: 377
51: 7 fear ye not the reproach of **m**, neither be ye 582
52:14 and his form more than the sons of **m**: 120
53: 3 He is despised and rejected of **m**; a man of 376
57: 1 merciful *m are* taken away, none 376
59:10 *we are* in desolate places as dead *m*. NIH
60:11 that *m* may bring unto thee the forces of NIH
61: 6 *m* shall call you the Ministers of our God: NIH
64: 4 For since the beginning of the world *m* have NIH
66:24 look upon the carcases of the **m** that have 376
Jer 4: 3 For thus saith the LORD to the **m** of Judah 376
4: 4 ye **m** of Judah and inhabitants of Jerusalem: 376
5: 5 I will get me unto the **great m**, and 1419
5:16 an open sepulchre, they *are* all mighty *m*. NIH
5:26 For among my people are found wicked *m*: NIH
5:26 setteth snares; they set a trap, they catch **m**. 376
6:11 and upon the assembly of **young m** together: 970
6:23 set in array as **m** for war against thee, 376
6:30 Reprobate silver shall *m* call them, because NIH
Jer 8: 9 The wise *m are* ashamed, they are dismayed NIH
9: 2 wilderness a lodging place of **wayfaring m**; 732
9: 2 an assembly of treacherous *m*. NIH
9:10 neither can *m* hear the voice of the cattle; NIH
9:21 *and* the **young m** from the streets. 970
9:22 Even the carcases of **m** shall fall as dung 120
10: 7 forasmuch as among all the wise *m* of NIH
10: 9 they *are* all the work of cunning *m*. NIH
11: 2 speak unto the **m** of Judah, and to 376
11: 9 A conspiracy is found among the **m** of 376
11:21 Therefore thus saith the LORD of the **m** of 376
11:22 the **young m** shall die by the sword; 970
11:23 for I will bring evil upon the **m** of Anathoth, 376
15: 8 mother of the **young m** a spoiler at noonday: 970
15:10 on usury, nor *m* have lent to me on usury; NIH
16: 6 neither shall *m* lament for them, nor cut NIH
16: 7 Neither shall *m* tear *themselves* for them in NIH
16: 7 neither shall *m* give them the cup of NIH
17:25 the **m** of Judah, and the inhabitants of 376
18:11 speak to the **m** of Judah, and to 376
18:21 *be* widows; and let their **m** be put to death; 376
18:21 *let* their **young m** *be* slain by the sword in 970
19:10 bottle in the sight of the **m** that go with thee. 376
26:21 with all his mighty *m*, and all the princes, NIH
26:22 Jehoiakim the king sent **m** *into* Egypt, 376
26:22 and *certain* **m** with him into Egypt. 376
31:13 in the dance, both **young m** and old together: 970
32:19 *are* open upon all the ways of the sons of **m**: 120
32:20 this day, and in Israel, and amongst *other* **m**; 120
32:32 the **m** of Judah, and the inhabitants of 376
32:44 *M* shall buy fields for money, and NIH
33: 5 *it is* to fill them with the dead bodies of **m**, 120
34:18 I will give the **m** that have transgressed my 376
35:13 Go and tell the **m** of Judah and 376
36:31 of Jerusalem, and upon the **m** of Judah, 376
37:10 there remained *but* wounded **m** among them, 376
38: 4 for thus he weakeneth the hands of the **m** of 376
38: 9 these **m** have done evil in all that they have 376
38:10 Take from hence thirty **m** with thee, and 376
38:11 So Ebed-melech took the **m** with him, and 376
38:16 into the hand of these **m** that seek thy life. 376
39: 4 all the **m** of war, then they fled, and 376
39:17 shalt not be given into the hand of the **m** 376
40: 7 *were* in the fields, *even* they and their **m**, 376
40: 7 and had committed unto him **m**, and women, 376
40: 8 the son of a Maachathite, they and their **m**. 376
40: 9 of Shaphan sware unto them and to their **m**, 376
41: 1 the princes of the king, even ten **m** with him, 376
41: 2 the ten **m** that were with him, and 376
41: 3 that were found there, *and* the **m** of war. 376
41: 5 and from Samaria, *even* fourscore **m**, 376
41: 7 of the pit, he, and the **m** that *were* with him. 376
41: 8 ten **m** were found among them that said unto 376
41: 9 had cast all the dead bodies of the **m**, 376
41:12 they took all the **m**, and went to fight with 376
41:15 escaped from Johanan with eight **m**, 376
41:16 *even* mighty **m** of war, and the women, and 376
42:17 So shall it be with all the **m** that set their 376
43: 2 all the proud **m**, saying unto Jeremiah, 376
43: 6 *Even* **m**, and women, and children, and 1397
43: 9 in Tahpanhes, in the sight of the **m** of Judah; 376
44:15 all the **m** which knew that their wives had 376
44:19 out drink offerings unto her, without our **m**? 376
44:20 to the **m**, and to the women, and to all 1397
44:27 all the **m** of Judah that *are* in the land of 376
46: 9 and let the mighty *m* come forth; NIH
46:15 Why are thy valiant *m* swept away? NIH
46:21 Also her **hired m** *are* in the midst of her 7916
47: 2 the **m** shall cry, and all the inhabitants of 120
48:14 We *are* mighty and strong **m** for the war? 376
48:15 his chosen **young m** are gone down to 970
48:31 *mine heart* shall mourn for the **m** of 376
48:36 mine heart shall sound like pipes for the **m** 376
49:15 among the heathen, *and* despised among **m**. 120
49:22 at that day shall the heart of the mighty *m* NIH
49:26 Therefore her **young m** shall fall in her 970
49:26 all the **m** of war shall be cut off in that day, 376
49:28 go up to Kedar, and spoil the **m** of the east. 1121
50:30 Therefore shall her **young m** fall in 970
50:30 all her **m** of war shall be cut off in that day, 376
50:35 and upon her princes, and upon her wise *m*. NIH
50:36 a sword *is* upon her mighty *m*; and NIH
51: 3 spare ye not her **young m**; destroy ye utterly 970
51:14 *saying,* Surely I will fill thee *with* **m**, as *with* 120
51:30 The mighty *m* of Babylon have forborn to NIH
51:32 with fire, and the **m** of war are affrighted. 376
51:56 upon Babylon, and her mighty *m* are taken, NIH
51:57 and her wise *m*, her captains, and her rulers, NIH
51:57 her mighty *m*: and they shall sleep a NIH
52: 7 all the **m** of war fled, and went forth out of 376
52:13 all the houses of the great *m*, burnt he with NIH
52:25 which had the charge of the **m** of war; 376
52:25 seven **m** of them that were near the king's 376
52:25 threescore **m** of the people of the land, 376
La 1:15 foot all my mighty *m* in the midst of me: NIH
1:15 assembly against me to crush my **young m**: 970
1:18 and my **young m** are gone into captivity. 970
2:15 *saying, Is* this the city that *m* call The NIH
2:21 and my **young m** are fallen by the sword; 970
3:33 afflict willingly nor grieve the children of **m**. 376
4:14 They have wandered *as* blind *m* in NIH
4:14 so that *m* could not touch their garments. NIH
5:13 They took the **young m** to grind, and 970
5:14 the gate, the **young m** from their musick. 970
Eze 6: 4 I will cast down your slain *m* before your NIH
6:13 when their slain *m* shall be among their NIH
8:11 there stood before them seventy **m** of 376
8:16 and the altar, *were* about five and twenty **m**, 376
9: 2 six **m** came from the way of the higher gate, 376
9: 4 set a mark upon the foreheads of the **m** that 376
9: 6 they began at the ancient **m** which *were* 376
11: 1 at the door of the gate five and twenty **m**; 376
11: 2 these *are* the **m** that devise mischief, and 376
11:15 the **m** of thy kindred, and all the house of 376
12:16 I will leave a few **m** of them from the sword, 376
Eze 14: 3 these **m** have set up their idols in their heart, 376
14:14 Though these three **m**, Noah, Daniel, and 376
14:16 *Though* these three **m** *were* in it, *as* I live, 376
14:18 Though these three **m** *were* in it, *as* I live, 376
15: 3 will *m* take a pin of it to hang any vessel NIH
16:17 madest to thyself images of **m**, and 2145
19: 3 it learned to catch the prey; it devoured **m**. 120
19: 6 learned to catch the prey, *and* devoured **m**. 120
21:14 it *is* the sword of the great *m that are* slain, NIH
21:31 deliver thee into the hand of brutish **m**, *and* 376
22: 9 In thee are **m** that carry tales to shed blood: 376
23: 6 and rulers, all of them desirable **young m**, 970
23: 7 *with* all them *that were* the chosen **m** of 1121
23:12 upon horses, all of them desirable **young m**. 970
23:14 for when she saw **m** pourtrayed upon 376
23:23 all of them desirable **young m**, captains and 970
23:40 that ye have sent for **m** to come from far, 376
23:42 with the **m** of the common sort *were* brought 376
23:45 *the* righteous **m**, they shall judge them after 376
24:17 not *thy* lips, and eat not the bread of **m**. 376
24:22 not cover *your* lips, nor eat the bread of **m**. 376
25: 4 I *will* deliver thee to the **m** of the east for a 1121
25:10 Unto the **m** of the east with the Ammonites, 1121
26:10 as *m* enter into a city wherein is made a NIH
26:17 *that wast* inhabited of seafaring *m*, NIH
27: 8 thy wise *m*, O Tyrus, *that* were in thee, NIH
27: 9 the wise *m* thereof were in thee thy calkers: NIH
27:10 of Phut were in thine army, thy **m** of war: 376
27:11 The **m** of Arvad with thine army *were* upon 1121
27:13 they traded the persons of **m** and vessels of 120
27:15 The **m** of Dedan *were* thy merchants; 1121
27:27 all thy **m** of war, that *are* in thee, and in all 376
30: 5 and the **m** of the land that is in league, 1121
30:17 The **young m** of Aven and of Phi-beseth 970
31:14 the earth, in the midst of the children of **m**, 120
34:31 *are* **m**, *and* I *am* your God, saith the Lord 120
35: 8 I will fill his mountains *with* his slain *m*: in NIH
36:10 I will multiply **m** upon you, all the house of 120
36:12 Yea, I will cause **m** to walk upon you, 120
36:12 no more henceforth **bereave** them **of m**. 7921
36:13 Thou *land* devourest up **m**, and 120
36:14 Therefore thou shalt devour **m** no more, 120
36:15 Neither will I cause *m* to hear in thee NIH
36:37 I will increase them *with* **m** like a flock. 120
36:38 the waste cities be filled *with* flocks of **m**: 120
38:20 all the **m** that *are* upon the face of the earth, 120
39:14 they shall sever out **m** of continual 376
39:20 with mighty *m*, and *with* all men of war, NIH
39:20 with mighty *men*, and *with* all **m** of war, 376
47:15 the way of Hethlon, as *m* go to Zedad; NIH
Da 2:12 commanded to destroy all the wise *m* of NIH
2:13 the decree went forth that the wise *m* should NIH
2:14 which was gone forth to slay the wise *m* of NIH
2:18 with the rest of the wise *m* of Babylon. NIH
2:24 ordained to destroy the wise *m* of Babylon: NIH
2:24 Destroy not the wise *m* of Babylon: NIH
2:27 cannot the wise *m*, the astrologians, NIH
2:38 wheresoever the children of **m** dwell, 606
2:43 shall mingle themselves with the seed of **m**: 606
2:48 chief of the governors over all the wise *m* of NIH
3:12 these **m**, O king, have not regarded thee: 1400
3:13 Then they brought these **m** before the king. 1400
3:20 **most mighty m** that *were* in 1400+1401+2429
3:21 these **m** were bound in their coats, 1400
3:22 the flame of the fire slew those **m** that took 1400
3:23 these three **m**, Shadrach, Meshach, and 1400
3:24 Did not we cast three **m** bound into 1400
3:25 and said, Lo, I see four **m** loose, 1400
3:27 being gathered together, saw these **m**, 1400
4: 6 in all the wise *m* of Babylon before me, NIH
4:17 the most High ruleth in the kingdom of **m**, 606
4:17 and setteth up over it the basest of **m**. 606
4:18 forasmuch as all the wise *m* of my kingdom NIH
4:25 That they *shall* drive thee from **m**, and 606
4:25 the most High ruleth in the kingdom of **m**, 606
4:32 they *shall* drive thee from **m**, and 606
4:32 the most High ruleth in the kingdom of **m**, 606
4:33 he *was* driven from **m**, and did eat grass as 606
5: 7 and said to the wise *m* of Babylon, NIH
5: 8 came in all the king's wise *m*: but NIH
5:15 now the wise *m*, the astrologers, have been NIH
5:21 he *was* driven from the sons of **m**; and 606
5:21 most high God ruled in the kingdom of **m**, 606
6: 5 said these **m**, We shall not find any 1400
6:11 these **m** assembled, and found Daniel 1400
6:15 these **m** assembled unto the king, and 1400
6:24 they brought those **m** which had accused 1400
6:26 That in every dominion of my kingdom *m* NIH
9: 7 to the **m** of Judah, and to the inhabitants of 376
10: 7 for the **m** that were with me saw not 376
10:16 *one* like the similitude of the sons of **m** 120
Hos 6: 7 they like **m** have transgressed the covenant: 120
10:13 thy way, in the multitude of thy mighty *m*. NIH
13: 2 Let the **m** that sacrifice kiss the calves. 120
Joel 1: 2 Hear this, ye **old m**, and give ear, all ye 2205
1:12 joy is withered away from the sons of **m**. 120
2: 7 They shall run like mighty *m*; they shall NIH
2: 7 *men;* they shall climb the wall like **m** of war; 376
2:28 your **old m** shall dream dreams, 2205
2:28 your **young m** shall see visions: 970
3: 9 wake up the mighty *m*, let all the men of NIH
3: 9 wake up the mighty *men*, let all the **m** of war 376
Am 2:11 and of your **young m** for Nazarites. 970
4:10 your **young m** have I slain with the sword, 970
6: 9 if there remain ten **m** in one house, that they 376
8:13 the fair virgins and **young m** faint for thirst. 970
Ob 1: 7 All the **m** of thy confederacy have brought 376
1: 7 the **m** that were at peace with thee have 376
1: 8 even destroy the wise *m* out of Edom, and NIH
1: 9 thy mighty *m*, O Teman, shall be dismayed, NIH
Jnh 1:10 were the **m** exceedingly afraid, and said unto 376
1:10 For the **m** knew that he fled from 376
1:13 Nevertheless the **m** rowed hard to bring *it* to 376
1:16 Then the **m** feared the LORD exceedingly, 376
Mic 2: 8 that pass by securely *as* **m** averse from war. NIH

Mic 2:12 great noise by reason of *the multitude of* **m**. 120
5: 5 him seven shepherds, and eight principal **m**. 120
5: 7 not for man, nor waiteth for the sons of **m**. 120
6:12 For the rich **m** thereof are full *of* violence, NIH
7: 2 *there is* none upright among **m**: they all lie in 120
7: 6 a man's enemies *are* the **m** of his own house. 376
Na 2: 3 The shield of his mighty **m** *is* made red, NIH
2: 3 *men is* made red, the valiant **m** *are* in scarlet: 376
3:10 and they cast lots for her honourable **m**, and NIH
3:10 and all her great **m** were bound in chains. NIH
Hab 1:14 makest **m** as the fishes of the sea, as 120
Zep 1:12 punish the **m** that are settled on their lees: 376
1:17 I will bring distress upon **m**, that they shall 120
1:17 that they shall walk like blind **m**, because NIH
2:11 **m** shall worship him, every one from his NIH
Hag 1:11 upon **m**, and upon cattle, and upon all 120
Zec 2: 4 towns without walls for the multitude of **m** 120
3: 8 for they *are* **m** wondered at: for behold, 376
7: 2 and Regemmelech, and their **m**, 376
7: 7 when **m** inhabited the south and the plain? NIH
8: 4 There shall yet **old m** and old women dwell 2205
8:10 for I set all **m** every one against his 120
8:23 **m** shall take hold out of all languages of 376
9:17 corn shall make the **young m** cheerful, and 970
10: 5 they shall be as mighty **m**, which tread NIH
11: 6 I *will* deliver the **m** every one into his 120
14:11 **m** shall dwell in it, and there shall be no NIH
Mt 2: 1 there came **wise m** from the east to *3097*
2: 7 when he had privily called the **wise m**, *3097*
2:16 he saw that he was mocked of the **wise m**, *3097*
2:16 he had diligently inquired of the **wise m**. *3097*
4:19 and I will make you fishers of **m**. *444*
5:11 when **m** shall revile you, and persecute *you*, NIG
5:13 cast out, and to be trodden under foot of **m**. *444*
5:15 Neither do **m** light a candle, and put it under NIG
5:16 Let your light so shine before **m**, that they *444*
5:19 least commandments, and shall teach **m** so, *444*
6: 1 heed that *ye* do not your alms before **m**, *444*
6: 2 in the streets, that they may have glory of **m**. *444*
6: 5 of the streets, that they may be seen of **m**. *444*
6:14 For if ye forgive **m** their trespasses, *444*
6:15 But if ye forgive not **m** their trespasses, *444*
6:16 that they may appear unto **m** to fast. *444*
6:18 That thou appear not unto **m** to fast, but *444*
7:12 ye would that **m** should do to you, *444*
7:16 Do **m** gather grapes of thorns, or figs of NIG
8:27 But the **m** marvelled, saying, What manner *444*
9: 8 which had given such power unto **m**. *444*
9:17 Neither do **m** put new wine into old bottles: NIG
9:27 two **blind m** followed him, crying, and *5185*
9:28 into the house, the **blind m** came to him: *5185*
10:17 But beware of **m**: for they will deliver you *444*
10:22 And ye shall be hated of all **m** for my NIG
10:32 therefore shall confess me before **m**, *444*
10:33 But whosoever shall deny me before **m**, *444*
12:31 and blasphemy shall be forgiven unto **m**: *444*
12:31 the *Holy* Ghost shall not be forgiven unto **m**. *444*
12:36 That every idle word that **m** shall speak, *444*
12:41 *The* **m** of Nineveh shall rise in judgment *435*
13:17 righteous **m** have desired to see *those things* NIG
13:25 But while **m** slept, his enemy came and *444*
14:21 that had eaten were about five thousand **m**, *435*
14:35 And when the **m** of that place had *435*
15: 9 for doctrines the commandments of **m**. *444*
15:38 And they that did eat were four thousand **m**, *435*
16:13 Whom do **m** say that I the Son of man am? *444*
16:23 *things* that be of God, but *those* that be of **m**. *444*
17:22 man shall be betrayed into the hands of **m**: *444*
19:11 unto them, All **m** cannot receive this saying, NIG
19:12 which were made eunuchs of **m**: *444*
19:26 said unto them, With **m** this is unpossible; *444*
20:30 two **blind m** sitting by the way side, *5185*
21:25 from heaven, or of **m**? And they reasoned *444*
21:26 But if we shall say, Of **m**; we fear *444*
21:41 He will miserably destroy those wicked **m**, NIG
22:16 *man:* for thou regardest not the person of **m**. *444*
23: 5 all their works they do for to be seen of **m**: *444*
23: 7 and to be called of **m**, Rabbi, Rabbi. *444*
23:13 ye shut up the kingdom of heaven against **m**: *444*
23:28 ye also outwardly appear righteous unto **m**, *444*
23:34 unto you prophets, and wise **m**, and scribes: NIG
26:33 Though all **m** shall be offended because NIG
28: 4 keepers did shake, and became as dead **m**. NIG
Mk 1:17 and I will make you to become fishers of **m**. *444*
1:37 they said unto him, All **m** seek for thee. NIG
3:28 All sins shall be forgiven unto the sons of **m**, *444*
5:20 had done for him: and all **m** did marvel. NIG
6:12 and preached that **m** should repent. NIG
6:44 *of* the loaves were about five thousand **m**. *435*
7: 7 for doctrines the commandments of **m**. *444*
7: 8 ye hold the tradition of **m**, *as* the washing of *444*
7:21 For from within, out of the heart of **m**, *444*
8: 4 From whence can a man satisfy these **m** NIG
8:24 and said, I see **m** as trees, walking. *444*
8:27 unto them, Whom do **m** say that I am? *444*
8:33 that be of God, but the *things* that be of **m**. *444*
9:31 Son of man is delivered into the hands of **m**, *444*
10:27 With **m** *it is* impossible, but not with God: *444*
11:30 of John, was *it* from heaven, or of **m**? *444*
11:32 But if we shall say, Of **m**; they feared *444*
11:32 for all **m** counted John, that he was a NIG
12:14 *man:* for thou regardest not the person of **m**, *444*
13:13 And ye shall be hated of all **m** for my NIG
14:51 and the **young m** laid hold on him: *3495*
Lk 1:25 on *me*, to take away my reproach among **m**. *444*
2:14 and on earth peace, good will towards **m**. *444*
3:15 and all **m** mused in their hearts of John, NIG
5:10 from henceforth thou shalt catch **m**. *444*
5:18 **m** brought in a bed a man which was taken *435*
6:22 when **m** shall hate you, and when they shall *444*
6:26 when all **m** shall speak well of you: *444*
6:31 And as ye would that **m** should do to you, *444*
6:38 running over, shall **m** give into your bosom. NIG
6:44 For of thorns **m** do not gather figs, nor of a NIG
7:20 When the **m** were come unto him, they said, *435*
Lk 7:31 then shall I liken the **m** of this generation? *444*
9:14 For they were about five thousand **m**. *435*
9:30 And behold, there talked with him two **m**, *435*
9:32 his glory, and the two **m** that stood with him. *435*
9:44 man shall be delivered into the hands of **m**. *444*
11:31 the judgment with the **m** of this generation, *435*
11:32 *The* **m** of Nineveh shall rise up in *435*
11:44 the **m** that walk over *them* are not aware *of* *444*
11:46 for ye lade **m** *with* burdens grievous to be *444*
12: 8 Whosoever shall confess me before **m**, *444*
12: 9 But he that denieth me before **m** shall be *444*
12:36 And ye yourselves like unto **m** that wait for *444*
12:48 and to whom **m** have committed much, NIG
13: 4 think ye that they were sinners above all **m** *444*
13:14 There are six days in which **m** ought to NIG
14:24 That none of those **m** which were bidden *435*
14:35 nor yet for the dunghill; *but* **m** cast it out. NIG
16:15 are they which justify yourselves before **m**; *444*
16:15 for that which is highly esteemed amongst **m** *444*
17:12 there met him ten **m** *that were* lepers, *435*
17:34 in that night there shall be two **m** in one NIG
17:36 Two **m** shall be in the field; the one shall be NIG
18: 1 *to this end*, that **m** ought always to pray, NIG
18:10 Two **m** went up into the temple to pray; *444*
18:11 that I am not as other **m** *are*, extortioners, *444*
18:27 The *things which are* unpossible with **m** are *444*
20: 4 of John, was it from heaven, or of **m**? *444*
20: 6 But *and* if we say, Of **m**; all the people will *444*
20:20 which *should* feign themselves just **m**, that NIG
21: 1 saw the rich **m** casting their gifts into NIG
21:17 And ye shall be hated of all **m** for my NIG
22:63 And the **m** that held Jesus mocked him, and *435*
23:11 And Herod with his **m of war** set him at *4753*
24: 4 two **m** stood by them in shining garments: *435*
24: 7 must be delivered into the hands of sinful **m**, *444*
Jn 1: 4 him was life; and the life was the light of **m**. *444*
1: 7 that all **m** through him might believe. NIG
2:10 and when **m** have well drunk, then NIG
2:24 himself unto them, because he knew all **m**, NIG
3:19 and **m** loved darkness rather than light, *444*
3:26 the same baptizeth, and all **m** come to him. NIG
4:20 that in Jerusalem is the place where **m** NIG
4:28 her way into the city, and saith to the **m**, *444*
4:38 other **m** laboured, and ye are entered into NIG
5:23 That all **m** should honour the Son, even as NIG
5:41 I receive not honour from **m**. *444*
6:10 And Jesus said, Make the **m** sit down. *444*
6:10 So the **m** sat down, *in* number about five *435*
6:14 Then *those* **m**, when they had seen *444*
8:17 your law, that the testimony of two **m** is true. *444*
11:48 him thus alone, all **m** will believe on him: NIG
12:32 up from the earth, will draw all **m** unto me. NIG
12:43 For they loved the praise of **m** more than *444*
13:35 By this shall all **m** know that ye are my NIG
15: 6 and **m** gather them, and cast *them* into NIG
17: 6 I have manifested thy name unto the **m** *444*
18: 3 having received a band *of* **m**, and NIG
Ac 1:10 two **m** stood by them in white apparel; *435*
1:11 Which also said, Ye **m** of Galilee, why stand *435*
1:16 **M** *and* brethren, this scripture must needs *435*
1:21 Wherefore of these **m** which have *435*
1:24 which knowest the hearts of all **m**, shew NIG
2: 5 devout **m**, out of every nation under heaven. *435*
2:13 *These* **m** are full of new wine. NIG
2:14 Ye **m** of Judea, and all *ye* that dwell at *435*
2:17 and your **young m** shall see visions, and *3495*
2:17 and your **old m** shall dream dreams: *4245*
2:22 Ye **m** of Israel, hear these words; Jesus of *435*
2:29 **M** *and* brethren, let *me* freely speak unto you *435*
2:37 **M** *and* brethren, what shall we do? *435*
2:45 parted them to all **m**, as every *man* had NIG
3:12 Ye **m** of Israel, why marvel ye at this? *435*
4: 4 the number of the **m** was about five *435*
4:12 other name under heaven given among **m**, *444*
4:13 that they were unlearned and ignorant **m**, *444*
4:16 Saying, What shall we do to these **m**? *444*
4:21 for all **m** glorified God for that which was NIG
5: 4 thou hast not lied unto **m**, but unto God. *444*
5: 6 And the **young m** arose, wound him up, *3501*
5:10 and the **young m** came in, and found her *3495*
5:14 the Lord, multitudes both of **m** and women.) *435*
5:25 the **m** whom ye put in prison are standing in *435*
5:29 said, We ought to obey God rather than **m**. *444*
5:35 And said unto them, Ye **m** of Israel, *435*
5:35 what ye intend to do as touching these **m**. *444*
5:36 to whom a number of **m**, about four *435*
5:38 Refrain from these **m**, and let them alone: *444*
5:38 for if this counsel or this work be of **m**, *444*
6: 3 look ye out among you seven **m** of honest *435*
6:11 Then they suborned **m**, which said, We have *435*
7: 2 he said, **M**, brethren, and fathers, hearken; *435*
8: 2 And devout **m** carried Stephen *to his burial*, *435*
8: 3 and haling **m** and women committed *them* *435*
8:12 they were baptized, both **m** and women. *435*
9: 2 of *this* way, whether they were **m** or women, *435*
9: 7 And the **m** which journeyed with him stood *435*
9:38 Peter was there, they sent unto him two **m**, *435*
10: 5 And now send **m** to Joppa, and call for *one* *435*
10:17 the **m** which were sent from Cornelius had *435*
10:19 said unto him, Behold, three **m** seek thee: *435*
10:21 Then Peter went down to the **m** which were *435*
11: 3 Thou wentest in to **m** uncircumcised, *435*
11:11 immediately there were three **m** already *435*
11:13 Send **m** to Joppa, and call for Simon, *435*
11:20 And some of them were **m** of Cyprus and *435*
13:15 saying, *Ye* **m** *and* brethren, if ye have *any* *435*
13:16 **M** of Israel, and *ye* that fear God, *435*
13:26 **M** *and* brethren, children of the stock of *435*
13:38 it known unto you therefore, **m** *and* brethren, *435*
13:50 and the chief **m** of the city, and NIG
14:11 are come down to us in the likeness of **m**. *444*
14:15 why do ye these *things?* We also are **m** of *444*
15: 1 And certain **m** which came down from NIG
15: 7 rose up, and said unto them, **M** *and* brethren, *435*
15:13 James answered, saying, **M** *and* brethren, *435*
Ac 15:17 That the residue of **m** might seek after *444*
15:22 to send chosen **m** of their own company to *435*
15:22 and Silas, chief **m** among the brethren: NIG
15:25 to send chosen **m** unto you with our beloved *435*
15:26 **M** that have hazarded their lives for *444*
16:17 These **m** are the servants of the most high *444*
16:20 saying, These **m**, being Jews, do exceedingly *444*
16:35 sent the sergeants, saying, Let those **m** go. *444*
17:12 which were Greeks, and of **m**, not a few. *435*
17:22 of Mars' hill, and said, *Ye* **m** of Athens, *435*
17:26 And hath made of one blood all nations of **m** *444*
17:30 now commandeth all **m** every where to *444*
17:31 *whereof* he hath given assurance unto all **m**, NIG
17:34 Howbeit certain **m** clave unto him, and *435*
18:13 This *fellow* persuadeth **m** to worship God *444*
19: 7 And all the **m** were about twelve. *435*
19:19 and burned *them* before all **m**: and NIG
19:29 and Aristarchus, **m** of Macedonia, NIG
19:35 the people, he said, *Ye* **m** of Ephesus, *435*
19:37 For ye have brought *hither* these **m**, *435*
20:26 that I *am* pure from the blood of all **m**. NIG
20:30 Also of your own selves shall **m** arise, *435*
21:23 We have four **m** which have a vow on them; *435*
21:26 Then Paul took the **m**, and the next day *435*
21:28 Crying out, **M** of Israel, help: This is *435*
21:28 that teacheth all **m** every where against NIG
21:38 four thousand **m** that were murderers? *435*
22: 1 **M**, brethren, and fathers, hear ye my defence *435*
22: 4 and delivering into prisons both **m** and *435*
22:15 For thou shalt be his witness unto all **m** of *444*
23: 1 beholding the council, said, **M** *and* brethren, *435*
23: 6 **M** *and* brethren, I am a Pharisee, the son of a *435*
23:21 lie in wait for him of them moe than forty **m**, *435*
24:16 void of offence toward God, and *toward* **m**. *444*
25:23 chief captains, and principal **m** of the city, *435*
25:24 and all **m** which are here present with us, *435*
28:17 he said unto them, **M** *and* brethren, *435*
Ro 1:18 all ungodliness and unrighteousness of **m**, *444*
1:27 And likewise also the **m**, leaving the natural *730*
1:27 **m** with men working that which is *730*
1:27 men with **m** working that which is *730*
2:16 of **m** by Jesus Christ according to my gospel. *444*
2:29 whose praise *is* not of **m**, but of God. *444*
5:12 and so death passed upon all **m**, for that all *444*
5:18 *judgment came* upon all **m** to condemnation; *444*
5:18 *came* upon all **m** unto justification of life. *444*
6:19 I speak **after the manner of m** because *442*
11: 4 I have reserved to myself seven thousand **m**, *435*
12:16 *things*, but condescend to **m** of low estate. NIG
12:17 Provide *things* honest in the sight of all **m**. *444*
12:18 as lieth in you, live peaceably with all **m**. *444*
14:18 *is* acceptable to God, and approved of **m**. *444*
16:19 is come abroad unto all **m**. I am glad NIG
1Co 1:25 the foolishness of God is wiser than **m**; *444*
1:25 and the weakness of God is stronger than **m**. *444*
1:26 how that not many wise **m** after the flesh, NIG
2: 5 faith should not stand in the wisdom of **m**, *444*
3: 3 divisions, are ye not carnal, and walk as **m**? *444*
3:21 Therefore let no *man* glory in **m**. For all *444*
4: 6 that ye might learn in us not to think *of* **m** NIG
4: 9 unto the world, and to angels, and to **m**. *444*
7: 7 For I would that all **m** were even as I myself. *444*
7:23 with a price; be not ye the servants of **m**. *444*
9:19 For though I be free from all **m**, yet have I NIG
9:22 I am made all *things* to all **m**, that I might NIG
10:15 I speak as to wise **m**; judge ye what I say. NIG
10:33 Even as I please all **m** in all *things*, not NIG
13: 1 Though I speak with the tongues of **m** and *444*
14: 2 in an *unknown* tongue speaketh not unto **m**, *444*
14: 3 But he that prophesieth speaketh unto **m** *to* *444*
14:20 be ye children, but in understanding be **m**. *5046*
14:21 With **m** of other tongues and other lips will NIG
15:19 in Christ, we are of all **m** most miserable. *444*
15:32 If after the manner of **m** I have fought with *444*
15:39 but *there is* one *kind of* flesh of **m**, *444*
16:13 fast in the faith, **quit you like m**, be strong. *407*
2Co 3: 2 in our hearts, known and read of all **m**: *444*
5:11 the terror of the Lord, we persuade **m**; *444*
8:13 For *I mean* not that other **m** be eased, and NIG
8:21 sight of the Lord, but also in the sight of **m**. *444*
9:13 distribution unto them, and unto all **m**; NIG
Gal 1: 1 Paul, an apostle, (not of **m**, neither by man, *444*
1:10 For do I now persuade **m**, or God? or do I *444*
1:10 or do I seek to please **m**? for if I yet pleased *444*
1:10 for if I yet pleased **m**, I should not be *444*
3:15 Brethren, I speak after the manner of **m**; *444*
6:10 let us do good unto all **m**, especially unto NIG
Eph 3: 5 was not made known unto the sons of **m**, *444*
3: 9 And to make all **m** see what *is* NIG
4: 8 led captivity captive, and gave gifts unto **m**. *444*
4:14 every wind of doctrine, by the sleight of **m**, *444*
5:28 So ought **m** to love their wives as their own *435*
6: 7 doing service, as to the Lord, and not to **m**: *444*
Php 2: 7 and was made in the likeness of **m**: *444*
4: 5 Let your moderation be known unto all **m**. *444*
Col 2: 8 and vain deceit, after the tradition of **m**, *444*
2:22 the commandments and doctrines of **m**? *444*
3:23 do *it* heartily, as to the Lord, and not unto **m**; *444*
1Th 1: 5 as ye know what manner of **m** we were NIG
2: 4 not as pleasing **m**, but God, which trieth our *444*
2: 6 Nor of **m** sought we glory, neither of you, *444*
2:13 ye received *it* not as the word of **m**, but as it *444*
2:15 please not God, and are contrary to all **m**: *444*
3:12 towards all **m**, even as we *do* towards you: NIG
5:14 support the weak, be patient toward all **m**. NIG
5:15 both among yourselves, and to all **m**. NIG
2Th 3: 2 delivered from unreasonable and wicked **m**: *444*
3: 2 and wicked men: for all **m** have not faith. NIG
1Ti 2: 1 *and* giving of thanks, be made for all **m**; *444*
2: 4 Who will have all **m** to be saved, and *444*
2: 5 and one mediator between God and **m**, *444*
2: 8 I will therefore that **m** pray every where, *435*
4:10 the living God, who is the Saviour of all **m**, *444*
5: 1 as a father; *and* the younger **m** as brethren; NIG
5:24 to judgment; and some **m** they follow after. NIG

1Ti 6: 5 Perverse disputings of m of corrupt minds, 444
6: 9 which drown m in destruction and perdition. 444
2Ti 2: 2 the same commit thou to faithful m, 444
2:24 but be gentle unto all m, apt to teach, NIG
3: 2 For m shall be lovers of their own selves, 444
3: 8 m of corrupt minds, reprobate concerning 444
3: 9 for their folly shall be manifest unto all m, NIG
3:13 But evil m and seducers shall wax worse and 444
4:16 man stood with me, but all m forsook me: NIG
Tit 1: 8 a lover of good m, sober, just, holy, NIG
1:14 and commandments of m, that turn from 444
2: 2 That the aged m be sober, grave, 4246
2: 6 Young m likewise exhort to be sober NIG
2:11 bringeth salvation hath appeared to all m, 444
3: 2 but gentle, shewing all meekness unto all m. 444
3: 8 These things are good and profitable unto m. 444
Heb 5: 1 For every high priest taken from among m is 444
5: 1 ordained for m in things pertaining to God, 444
6:16 For m verily swear by the greater: and 444
7: 8 And here m that die receive tithes; but 444
7:28 For the law maketh m high priests which 444
9:17 For a testament is of force after m are dead: NIG
9:27 And as it is appointed unto m once to die, 444
12:14 Follow peace with all m, and holiness, NIG
12:23 and to the spirits of just m made perfect, NIG
Jas 1: 5 that giveth to all m liberally, and NIG
2: 6 Do not rich m oppress you, and draw you NIG
3: 9 and therewith curse we m, which are made 444
5: 1 ye rich m, weep and howl for your miseries NIG
1Pe 2: 4 disallowed indeed of m, but chosen of God, 444
2:15 put to silence the ignorance of foolish m: 444
2:17 Honour all m. Love the brotherhood. NIG
4: 2 rest of his time in the flesh to the lusts of m, 444
4: 6 that they might be judged according to m in 444
2Pe 1:21 holy m of God spake as they were moved by 444
3: 7 day of judgment and perdition of ungodly m. 444
3: 9 his promise, as some m count slackness; NIG
1Jn 2:13 young m, because you have overcome 3495
2:14 young m, because ye are strong, and 3495
5: 9 If we receive the witness of m, the witness 444
3Jn 1:12 Demetrius hath good report of all m, and NIG
Jude 1: 4 For there are certain m crept in unawares, 444
1: 4 ungodly m, turning the grace of our God NIG
Rev 6:15 and the great m, and the rich men, and 3175
6:15 and the rich m, and the chief captains, and NIG
6:15 and the mighty m, and every bondman, and NIG
8:11 and many m died of the waters, because 444
9: 4 only those m which have not the seal of God 444
9: 6 And in those days shall m seek death, and 444
9: 7 and their faces were as the faces of m. 444
9:10 and their power was to hurt m five months. 444
9:15 and a year, for to slay the third part of m. 444
9:18 By these three was the third part of m killed, 444
9:20 And the rest of the m which were not killed 444
11:13 in the earthquake were slain of m 444+3686
13:13 from heaven on the earth in the sight of m, 444
14: 4 These were redeemed from among m, 444
16: 2 grievous sore upon the m which had 444
16: 8 power was given unto him to scorch m with 444
16: 9 And m were scorched with great heat, and 444
16:18 such as was not since m were upon the earth, 444
16:21 And there fell upon m a great hail out of 444
16:21 and m blasphemed God because of 444
18:13 and chariots, and slaves, and souls of m. 444
18:23 for thy merchants were the great m of 3175
19:18 and the flesh of mighty m, and the flesh of NIG
19:18 and the flesh of all m, both free and bond, NIG
21: 3 the tabernacle of God is with m, and he will 444

MEN OF TOB See ISH-TOB

MEN'S (24) [MAN]
Ge 24:32 his feet, and the m feet that were with him. 376
44: 1 saying, Fill the m sacks with food, as much 376
Dt 4:28 the work of m hands, wood and stone, 120
1Sa 24: 9 Wherefore hearest thou m words, saying, 120
1Ki 12:13 forsook the old m counsel that they gave 2205
13: 2 and m bones shall be burnt upon thee. 120
2Ki 19:18 but the work of m hands, wood and stone: 120
23:20 burnt m bones upon them, and returned to 120
Ps 115: 4 are silver and gold, the work of m hands. 120
135:15 are silver and gold, the work of m hands. 120
Isa 37:19 but the work of m hands, wood and stone: 120
Jer 48:41 the mighty m hearts in Moab at that day NIH
Hab 2: 8 because of m blood, and for the violence of 120
2:17 because of m blood, and for the violence of 120
Mt 23: 4 to be borne, and lay them on m shoulders; 444
23:27 but are within full of dead m bones, and NIG
Lk 9:56 For the Son of man is not come to destroy m 444
21:26 M hearts failing them for fear, and 444
Ac 17:25 Neither is worshipped with m hands, 444
2Co 10:15 our measure, that is, of other m labours; NIG
1Ti 5:22 no man, neither be partaker of other m sins: NIG
5:24 Some m sins are open beforehand, 444
1Pe 4:15 or as a busybody in other m matters. 244
Jude 1:16 words, having m persons in admiration NIG

MENAHEM (8)
2Ki 15:14 For M the son of Gadi went up from 4505
15:16 M smote Tiphsah, and all that were therein, 4505
15:17 M the son of Gadi to reign over Israel, 4505
15:19 and M gave Pul a thousand talents of silver, 4505
15:20 M exacted the money of Israel, even of all 4505
15:21 the rest of the acts of M, and all that he did, 4505
15:22 M slept with his fathers; and Pekahiah his 4505
15:23 of M began to reign over Israel in Samaria, 4505

MENAN (1)
Lk 3:31 the son of Melea, which was the son of M, 3104

MEND (2) [MENDING]
2Ch 24:12 and brass to m the house of the LORD. 2388
34:10 of the LORD, to repair and m the house: 2388

MENDING (2) [MEND]
Mt 4:21 ship with Zebedee their father, m their nets; 2675
Mk 1:19 who also were in the ship m their nets. 2675

MENE (3)
Da 5:25 M, MENE, TEKEL, UPHARSIN. 4484
5:25 MENE, M, TEKEL, UPHARSIN. 4484
5:26 M; God hath numbered thy kingdom, and 4484

MENNA See MENAN

MENPLEASERS (2) [MAN, PLEASE]
Eph 6: 6 Not with eyeservice, as m; but as 441
Col 3:22 not with eyeservice, as m; but in singleness 441

MENSERVANTS (10) [MAN, SERVE]
Ge 12:16 m, and maidservants, and she asses, and 5650
20:14 m, and womenservants, and gave them 5650
24:35 m, and maidservants, and camels, and 5650
30:43 and m, and camels, and asses. 5650
32: 5 asses, flocks, and m, and womenservants: 5650
Ex 21: 7 she shall not go out as the m do. 5650
Dt 12:12 your m, and your maidservants, and 5650
1Sa 8:16 he will take your m, and your 5650
2Ki 5:26 sheep, and oxen, and m, and maidservants? 5650
Lk 12:45 and shall begin to beat the m and maidens, 3816

MENSTEALERS (1) [MAN, STEAL]
1Ti 1:10 for m, for liars, for perjured persons, and 405

MENSTRUOUS (3)
Isa 30:22 thou shalt cast them away as a m cloth; 1739
La 1:17 Jerusalem is as a m woman among them. 5079
Eze 18: 6 neither hath come near to a m woman, 5079

MENTION (23) [MENTIONED]
Ge 40:14 make m of me unto Pharaoh, and bring me 2142
Ex 23:13 make no m of the name of other gods, 2142
Jos 23: 7 neither make m of the name of their gods, 2142
1Sa 4:18 when he made m of the ark of God, 2142
Job 28:18 No m shall be made of coral, or of pearls: 2142
Ps 71:16 I will make m of thy righteousness, even of 2142
87: 4 I will make m of Rahab and Babylon to 2142
Isa 12: 4 make m that his name is exalted. 2142
19:17 every one that maketh m thereof shall be 2142
26:13 by thee only will we make m of thy name. 2142
48: 1 make m of the God of Israel, but not in 2142
49: 1 of my mother hath he made m of my name. 2142
62: 6 ye that make m of the LORD, keep not 2142
63: 7 I will m the lovingkindnesses of 2142
Jer 4:16 Make ye m to the nations; behold, 2142
20: 9 I said, I will not make m of him, nor speak 2142
23:36 the burden of the LORD shall ye m no 2142
Am 6:10 for we may not make m of the name of 2142
Ro 1: 9 that without ceasing I make m of you, 3417
Eph 1:16 for you, making m of you in my prayers; 3417
1Th 1: 2 you all, making m of you in our prayers; 3417
Phm 1: 4 making m of thee always in my prayers, 3417
Heb 11:22 made m of the departing of the children of 3421

MENTIONED (7) [MENTION]
Jos 21: 9 these cities which are here m by name, 7121
1Ch 4:38 These m by their names were princes in their 935
2Ch 20:34 who is m in the book of the kings of Israel. 5927
Eze 16:56 For thy sister Sodom was not m by thy 8052
18:22 they shall not be m unto him: 2142
18:24 that he hath done shall not be m: 2142
33:16 he hath committed shall be m unto him: 2142

MEONENIM (1)
Jdg 9:37 company come along by the plain of M. 6049

MEONOTHAI (1)
1Ch 4:14 M begat Ophrah: and Seraiah begat Joab, 4587

MEPHAATH (4)
Jos 13:18 And Jahazah, and Kedemoth, and M, 4158
21:37 with her suburbs, and M with her suburbs; 4158
1Ch 6:79 with her suburbs, and M with her suburbs: 4158
Jer 48:21 and upon Jahazah, and upon M, 4158

MEPHIBOSHETH (15) [MERIB-BAAL]
2Sa 4: 4 and became lame. And his name was M. 4648
9: 6 Now when M, the son of Jonathan, the son 4648
9: 6 David said, M. And he answered, 4648
9:10 M thy master's son shall eat bread alway at 4648
9:11 As for M, said the king, he shall eat at my 4648
9:12 M had a young son, whose name was 4648
9:12 in the house of Ziba were servants unto M. 4648
9:13 So M dwelt in Jerusalem: for he did eat 4648
16: 1 Ziba the servant of M met him, with a 4648
16: 4 Behold, thine are all that pertained unto M. 4648
19:24 M the son of Saul came down to meet 4648
19:25 Wherefore wentest not thou with me, M? 4648
19:30 M said unto the king, Yea, let him take all, 4648
21: 7 the king spared M, the son of Jonathan 4648
21: 8 whom she bare unto Saul, Armoni and M; 4648

MERAB (3)
1Sa 14:49 were these; the name of the firstborn M, 4764
18:17 to David, Behold my elder daughter M, 4764
18:19 it came to pass at the time when M Saul's 4764

MERAIAH (1)
Ne 12:12 of Seraiah, M; of Jeremiah, Hananiah; 4811

MERAIOTH (7)
1Ch 6: 6 begat Zerahiah, and Zerahiah begat M, 4812
6: 7 M begat Amariah, and Amariah begat 4812
6:52 M his son, Amariah his son, Ahitub his 4812
9:11 the son of Zadok, the son of M, the son of 4812
Ezr 7: 3 the son of Azariah, the son of M, 4812
Ne 11:11 the son of Zadok, the son of M, the son of 4812
12:15 Of Harim, Adna; of M, Helkai; 4812

MERARI (39) [MERARITES]
Ge 46:11 the sons of Levi; Gershon, Kohath, and M. 4847
Ex 6:16 Gershon, and Kohath, and M: 4847
6:19 the sons of M; Mahali and Mushi: these are 4847
Nu 3:17 their names; Gershon, and Kohath, and M. 4847
3:20 the sons of M by their families; Mahli, and 4847
3:33 Of M was the family of the Mahlites, and 4847
3:33 the Mushites: these are the families of M. 4847
3:35 of M was Zuriel the son of Abihail: 4847
3:36 charge of the sons of M shall be the boards 4847
4:29 As for the sons of M, thou shalt number 4847
4:33 the service of the families of the sons of M, 4847
4:42 numbered of the families of the sons of M, 4847
4:45 numbered of the families of the sons of M, 4847
7: 8 and eight oxen he gave unto the sons of M, 4847
10:17 of Gershon and the sons of M set forward, 4847
26:57 of M, the family of the Merarites. 4847
Jos 21: 7 The children of M by their families had out 4847
21:34 unto the families of the children of M, 4847
21:40 So all the cities for the children of M by 4847
1Ch 6: 1 The sons of Levi; Gershon, Kohath, and M. 4847
6:16 sons of Levi; Gershom, Kohath, and M. 4847
6:19 The sons of M; Mahli, and Mushi. 4847
6:29 The sons of M; Mahli, Libni his son, 4847
6:44 their brethren the sons of M stood on 4847
6:47 of Mushi, the son of M, the son of Levi. 4847
6:63 Unto the sons of M were given by lot, 4847
6:77 Unto the rest of the children of M were 4847
9:14 the son of Hashabiah, of the sons of M; 4847
15: 6 Of the sons of M; Asaiah the chief, and 4847
15:17 of the sons of M their brethren, Ethan 4847
23: 6 of Levi, namely, Gershon, Kohath, and M. 4847
23:21 The sons of M; Mahli, and Mushi. 4847
24:26 The sons of M were Mahli and Mushi: 4847
24:27 The sons of M by Jaaziah; Beno, and 4847
26:10 Also Hosah, of the children of M, had sons; 4847
26:19 the sons of Kore, and among the sons of M. 4847
2Ch 29:12 of the sons of M, Kish the son of Abdi, and 4847
34:12 and Obadiah, the Levites, of the sons of M; 4847
Ezr 8:19 with him Jeshaiah of the sons of M, 4847

MERARITES (1) [MERARI]
Nu 26:57 of Merari, the family of the M. 4848

MERCHANDISE (22) [MERCHANT]
Dt 21:14 thou shalt not make m of her, because thou 6014
24: 7 and maketh m of him, or selleth him; 6014
Pr 3:14 For the m of it is better than 5504
3:14 of it is better than the m of silver, 5505
31:18 She perceiveth that her m is good: 5504
Isa 23:18 her m and her hire shall be holiness to 5504
23:18 for her m shall be for them that dwell 5504
45:14 m of Ethiopia and of the Sabeans, men of 5505
Eze 26:12 of thy riches, and make a prey of thy m: 7404
27: 9 mariners were in thee to occupy thy m. 4627
27:15 many isles were the m of thine hand: 5506
27:24 and made of cedar, among thy m. 4819
27:27 Thy riches, and thy fairs, thy m, 4627
27:27 the occupiers of thy m, and all thy men of 4627
27:33 the multitude of thy riches and of thy m. 4627
27:34 thy m and all thy company in the midst of 4627
28:16 By the multitude of thy m they have filled 7404
Mt 22: 5 one to his farm, another to his m: 1711
Jn 2:16 make not my Father's house a house of m. 1712
2Pe 2: 3 they with feigned words make m of you: 1710
Rev 18:11 for no man buyeth their m any more: 1117
18:12 The m of gold, and silver, and 1117

MERCHANT (12) [MERCHANDISE, MERCHANT'S, MERCHANTMEN, MERCHANTS]
Ge 23:16 of silver, current money with the m. 5503
Pr 31:24 selleth it; and delivereth girdles unto the m. 3669
SS 3: 6 frankincense, with all powders of the m? 7402
Isa 23:11 m city, to destroy the strong holds thereof. 3667
Eze 27: 3 which art a m of the people for many isles, 7402
27:12 Tarshish was thy m by reason of 5503
27:16 Syria was thy m by reason of the multitude 5503
27:18 Damascus was thy m in the multitude of 5503
27:20 Dedan was thy m in precious clothes for 7402
Hos 12: 7 He is a m, the balances of deceit are in his 3667
Zep 1:11 for all the m people are cut down; 3667
Mt 13:45 the kingdom of heaven is like unto a m 1713

MERCHANT'S (1) [MERCHANT]
Pr 31:14 She is like the m ships; she bringeth her 5503

MERCHANTMEN (2) [MERCHANT]
Ge 37:28 there passed by Midianites m; and 376+5503
1Ki 10:15 Besides that he had of the m, and of 376

MERCHANTS (28) [MERCHANT]
1Ki 10:15 of the traffick of the spice m, and of all 7402
10:28 the king's m received the linen yarn at a 5503
2Ch 1:16 the king's m received the linen yarn at a 5503
9:14 that which chapmen and m brought. 5503
Ne 3:31 of the m, over against the gate Miphkad, 7402
3:32 gate repaired the goldsmiths and the m. 7402
13:20 So the m and sellers of all kind of ware 7402
Job 41: 6 of him? shall they part him among the m? 3669
Isa 23: 2 thou whom the m of Zidon, that pass over 5503
23: 8 the crowning city, whose m are princes, 5503
47:15 hast laboured, even thy m, from thy youth: 5503
Eze 17: 4 a land of traffick; he set it in a city of m. 7402
27:13 Tubal, and Meshech, they were thy m: 7402
27:15 The men of Dedan were thy m; many isles 7402
27:17 and the land of Israel, they were thy m: 7402
27:21 rams, and goats: in these were they thy m. 5503
27:22 The m of Sheba and Raamah, they were thy 7402
27:22 of Sheba and Raamah, they were thy m: 7402
27:23 Eden, the m of Sheba, Asshur, and 7402
27:23 Asshur, and Chilmad, were thy m. 7402
27:24 These were thy m in all sorts of things, 7402

Eze 27:36 The **m** among the people shall hiss at thee; 5503
38:13 Sheba, and Dedan, and the **m** of Tarshish, 5503
Na 3:16 Thou hast multiplied thy **m** above the stars 7402
Rev 18: 3 the **m** of the earth are waxed rich through *1713*
18:11 And the **m** of the earth *shall* weep and *1713*
18:15 The **m** of these *things,* which were made *1713*
18:23 for thy **m** were the great men of the earth; *1713*

MERCIES (40) [MERCY]

Ge 32:10 I am not worthy of the least of all the **m**, 2617
2Sa 24:14 hand of the LORD; for his **m** *are* great: 7356
1Ch 21:13 of the LORD; for very great *are* his **m**: 7356
2Ch 6:42 remember the **m** of David thy servant. 2617
Ne 9:19 Yet thou in thy manifold **m** forsookest 7356
9:27 according to thy manifold **m** thou gavest 7356
9:28 didst thou deliver them according to thy **m**; 7356
Ps 25: 6 thy **tender m** and thy lovingkindnesses; 7356
40:11 Withhold not thou thy **tender m** from me, 7356
51: 1 of thy **tender m** blot out my transgressions. 7356
69:16 according to the multitude of thy **tender m**. 7356
77: 9 hath he in anger shut up his **tender m**? 7356
79: 8 let thy **tender m** speedily prevent us: 7356
89: 1 I will sing of the **m** of the LORD for ever: 2617
103: 4 thee *with* lovingkindness and **tender m**; 7356
106: 7 remembered not the multitude of thy **m**; 2617
106:45 according to the multitude of his **m**. 2617
119:41 Let thy **m** come also *unto* me, O LORD, 2617
119:77 Let thy **tender m** come *unto* me, that I may 7356
119:156 Great *are* thy **tender m**, O LORD: 7356
145: 9 and his **tender m** *are* over all his works. 7356
Pr 12:10 but the **tender m** of the wicked *are* cruel. 7356
Isa 54: 7 but with great **m** will I gather thee. 7356
55: 3 with you, *even* the sure **m** of David. 2617
63: 7 hath bestowed on them according to his **m**, 7356
63:15 of thy bowels and of thy **m** towards me? 7356
Jer 16: 5 the LORD, *even* lovingkindness and **m**. 7356
42:12 I will shew **m** unto you, that he may have 7356
La 3:22 *It is of* the LORD'S **m** that we are not 2617
3:32 according to the multitude of his **m**. 2617
Da 2:18 That *they* would desire **m** of the God of 7359
9: 9 To the Lord our God *belong* **m** and 7356
9:18 for our righteousnesses, but for thy great **m**. 7356
Hos 2:19 and in lovingkindness, and in **m**. 7356
Zec 1:16 I am returned to Jerusalem with **m**: 7356
Ac 13:34 I will give you the sure **m** of David. *3741*
Ro 12: 1 you therefore, brethren, by the **m** of God, *3628*
2Co 1: 3 the Father of **m**, and the God of all *3628*
Php 2: 1 of the Spirit, if any bowels and **m**, *3628*
Col 3:12 holy and beloved, bowels of **m**, kindness, *3628*

MERCIES' (1) [MERCY]

Ne 9:31 Nevertheless for thy great **m** sake thou 7356

MERCIFUL (40) [MERCY]

Ge 19:16 the LORD being **m** unto him: 2551
Ex 34: 6 **m** and gracious, longsuffering, 7349
Dt 4:31 (For the LORD thy God *is* a **m** God;) 7349
21: 8 Be **m**, O LORD, unto thy people Israel, 3722
32:43 will be **m** *unto* his land, *and to* his people. 3722
2Sa 22:26 With the **m** thou wilt shew thyself merciful, 2623
22:26 the merciful thou wilt **shew** thyself **m**, 2616
1Ki 20:31 the kings of the house of Israel *are* **m** kings: 2617
2Ch 30: 9 the LORD your God *is* gracious and **m**, 7349
Ne 9:17 gracious and **m**, slow to anger, and of great 7349
9:31 for thou *art* a gracious and **m** God. 7349
Ps 18:25 With the **m** thou wilt shew thyself merciful; 2623
18:25 the merciful thou wilt **shew** thyself **m**; 2616
26:11 redeem me, and be **m** unto me. 2603
37:26 *He is* ever **m**, and lendeth; and his seed *is* 2603
41: 4 I said, LORD, be **m** unto me: heal my 2603
41:10 O LORD, be **m** unto me, and raise me up, 2603
56: 1 Be **m** unto me, O God: for man would 2603
57: 1 Be **m** unto me, O God, be merciful unto 2603
57: 1 merciful unto me, O God, be **m** unto me: 2603
59: 5 be not **m** to any wicked transgressors. 2603
67: 1 God be **m** unto us, and bless us; *and* 2603
86: 3 Be **m** unto me, O Lord: for I cry unto thee 2603
103: 8 The LORD *is* **m** and gracious, slow to 7349
116: 5 and righteous; yea, our God *is* **m**. 7355
117: 2 For his **m kindness** is great toward us: and 2617
119:58 be **m** unto me according to thy word. 2603
119:76 thy **m kindness** be for my comfort, 2617
119:132 Look thou upon me, and be **m** unto me, 2603
Pr 11:17 The **m** man doeth good to his own soul: but 2617
Isa 57: 1 **m** men *are* taken away, none considering 2617
Jer 3:12 for I *am* **m**, saith the LORD, *and* I will not 2623
Joel 2:13 for he *is* gracious and **m**, slow to anger, and 7349
Jnh 4: 2 **m**, slow to anger, and of great kindness, 7349
Mt 5: 7 Blessed *are* the **m**: for they shall obtain *1655*
Lk 6:36 Be ye therefore **m**, as your Father also is *3629*
6:36 therefore merciful, as your Father also is **m**. *3629*
18:13 his breast, saying, God be **m** to me a sinner. *2433*
Heb 2:17 that he might be a **m** and faithful high *1655*
8:12 For I will be **m** to their unrighteousness, *2436*

MERCURIUS (1)

Ac 14:12 and Paul, **M**, because he was the chief *2060*

MERCY (277) [MERCIES, MERCIES', MERCIFUL, MERCY'S, UNMERCIFUL]

Ge 19:19 in thy sight, and thou hast magnified thy **m**, 2617
24:27 hath not left destitute my master of his **m** 2617
39:21 shewed him **m**, and gave him favour in 2617
43:14 God Almighty give you **m** before the man, 7356
Ex 15:13 Thou in thy **m** hast led forth the people 2617
20: 6 shewing **m** unto thousands of them that 2617
25:17 thou shalt make a **m seat** *of* pure gold: 3727
25:18 make them, in the two ends of the **m seat**. 3727
25:19 *even* of the **m seat** shall ye make 3727
25:20 covering the **m seat** with their wings, 3727
25:20 toward the **m seat** shall the faces of 3727
25:21 thou shalt put the **m seat** above upon 3727
25:22 commune with thee from above the **m seat**, 3727
26:34 thou shalt put the **m seat** upon the ark of 3727
Ex 30: 6 before the **m seat** that *is* over 3727
31: 7 the **m seat** that *is* thereupon, and all 3727
33:19 will **shew m** on whom I will shew mercy. 7355
33:19 will shew mercy on whom I will **shew m**. 7355
34: 7 Keeping **m** for thousands, 2617
35:12 *with* the **m seat**, and the vail of 3727
37: 6 he made the **m seat** *of* pure gold: 3727
37: 7 he them, on the two ends of the **m seat**; 3727
37: 8 out of the **m seat** made he the cherubims on 3727
37: 9 covered with their wings over the **m seat**, 3727
37: 9 *even* to the **m seatward** were the faces of 3727
39:35 and the staves thereof, and the **m seat**, 3727
40:20 and put the **m seat** above upon the ark: 3727
Lev 16: 2 *place* within the vail before the **m seat**, 3727
16: 2 I will appear in the cloud upon the **m seat**. 3727
16:13 the **m seat** that *is* upon the Testimony, 3727
16:14 sprinkle *it* with his finger upon the **m seat** 3727
16:14 before the **m seat** shall he sprinkle of 3727
16:15 sprinkle it upon the **m seat**, and before 3727
16:15 upon the mercy seat, and before the **m seat**: 3727
Nu 7:89 **m seat** that *was* upon the ark of Testimony, 3727
14:18 of great **m**, forgiving iniquity and 2617
14:19 according unto the greatness of thy **m**, 2617
Dt 5:10 shewing **m** unto thousands of them that 2617
7: 2 with them, nor **shew m** unto them: 2603
7: 9 and **m** with them that love him and 2617
7:12 and the **m** which he sware unto thy fathers: 2617
13:17 shew thee **m**, and have compassion upon 7356
Jdg 1:24 into the city, and we will shew thee **m**. 2617
2Sa 7:15 my **m** shall not depart away from him, as I 2617
15:20 back thy brethren: **m** and truth *be* with thee. 2617
22:51 sheweth **m** to his anointed, unto David, and 2617
1Ki 3: 6 unto thy servant David my father great **m**, 2617
8:23 **m** with thy servants that walk before thee 2617
1Ch 16:34 for *he is* good; for his **m** *endureth* for ever. 2617
16:41 because his **m** *endureth* for ever; 2617
17:13 I will not take my **m** away from him, as I 2617
28:11 and of the place of the **m seat**, 3727
2Ch 1: 8 Thou hast shewed great **m** unto David my 2617
5:13 For *he is* good; for his **m** *endureth* for ever: 2617
6:14 and *shewest* **m** unto thy servants, 2617
7: 3 For *he is* good; for his **m** *endureth* for ever. 2617
7: 6 because his **m** *endureth* for ever, 2617
20:21 the LORD; for his **m** *endureth* for ever. 2617
Ezr 3:11 for his **m** *endureth* for ever towards Israel. 2617
7:28 hath extended **m** unto me before the king, 2617
9: 9 hath extended **m** unto us in the sight of 2617
Ne 1: 5 and **m** for them that love him and 2617
1:11 and grant him **m** in the sight of this man. 7356
9:32 terrible God, who keepest covenant and **m**, 2617
13:22 me according to the greatness of thy **m**. 2617
Job 37:13 for correction, or for his land, or for **m**. 2617
Ps 4: 1 **have m** upon me, and hear my prayer. 2603
5: 7 *into* thy house in the multitude of thy **m**: 2617
6: 2 **Have m** upon me, O LORD; for I *am* 2603
9:13 **Have m** upon me, O LORD; consider my 2603
13: 5 I have trusted in thy **m**; my heart shall 2617
18:50 sheweth **m** to his anointed, to David, and 2617
21: 7 through the **m** of the most High he shall not 2617
23: 6 **m** shall follow me all the days of my life: 2617
25: 7 according to thy **m** remember thou me for 2617
25:10 All the paths of the LORD *are* **m** and 2617
25:16 Turn thee unto me, and **have m** upon me; 2603
27: 7 **have m** also upon me, and answer me. 2603
30:10 Hear, O LORD, and **have m** upon me: 2603
31: 7 I will be glad and rejoice in thy **m**: for thou 2617
31: 9 **Have m** upon me, O LORD, for I am in 2603
32:10 in the LORD, **m** shall compass him about. 2617
33:18 fear him, upon them that hope in his **m**; 2617
33:22 Let thy **m**, O LORD, be upon us, 2617
36: 5 Thy **m**, O LORD, *is* in the heavens; *and* 2617
37:21 but the righteous **sheweth m**, and giveth. 2603
51: 1 **Have m** upon me, O God, according to thy 2603
52: 8 I trust in the **m** of God for ever and ever. 2617
57: 3 God shall send forth his **m** and his truth. 2617
57:10 For thy **m** *is* great unto the heavens, and 2617
59:10 The God of my **m** shall prevent me: 2617
59:16 I will sing aloud of thy **m** in the morning: 2617
59:17 God *is* my defence, *and* the God of my **m**. 2617
61: 7 O prepare **m** and truth, *which* may preserve 2617
62:12 Also unto thee, O Lord, *belongeth* **m**: 2617
66:20 turned away my prayer, nor his **m** from me. 2617
69:13 O God, in the multitude of thy **m** hear me, 2617
77: 8 Is his **m** clean gone for ever? doth *his* 2617
85: 7 Shew us thy **m**, O LORD, and grant us thy 2617
85:10 **M** and truth are met together; righteousness 2617
86: 5 plenteous in **m** unto all them that call upon 2617
86:13 For great *is* thy **m** toward me: and thou hast 2617
86:15 plenteous in **m** and truth. 2617
86:16 O turn unto me, and **have m** upon me; 2603
89: 2 I have said, **M** shall be built up for ever: 2617
89:14 **m** and truth shall go before thy face. 2617
89:24 and my **m** *shall be* with him: 2617
89:28 My **m** will I keep for him for evermore, 2617
90:14 O satisfy us early *with* thy **m**; that we may 2617
94:18 thy **m**, O LORD, held me up. 2617
98: 3 He hath remembered his **m** and his truth 2617
100: 5 his **m** *is* everlasting; and his truth *endureth* 2617
101: 1 I will sing of **m** and judgment: unto thee, 2617
102:13 Thou shalt arise, *and* **have m** upon Zion: 7355
103: 8 slow to anger, and plenteous in **m**. 2617
103:11 *so* great is his **m** toward them that fear him. 2617
103:17 the **m** of the LORD *is* from everlasting to 2617
106: 1 for *he is* good: for his **m** *endureth* for ever. 2617
107: 1 for *he is* good: for his **m** *endureth* for ever. 2617
108: 4 For thy **m** *is* great above the heavens: and 2617
109:12 Let there be none to extend **m** unto him: 2617
109:16 that he remembered not to shew **m**, 2617
109:21 because thy **m** *is* good, deliver thou me. 2617
109:26 my God: O save me according to thy **m**: 2617
115: 1 for thy **m**, *and* for thy truth's sake. 2617
118: 1 *is* good: because his **m** *endureth* for ever. 2617
118: 2 now say, that his **m** *endureth* for ever. 2617
118: 3 now say, that his **m** *endureth* for ever. 2617
118: 4 LORD say, that his **m** *endureth* for ever. 2617
Ps 118:29 for *he is* good: for his **m** *endureth* for ever. 2617
119:64 The earth, O LORD, is full *of* thy **m**: 2617
119:124 with thy servant according unto thy **m**, 2617
123: 2 our God, until that he **have m** upon us. 2603
123: 3 **Have m** upon us, O LORD, have mercy 2603
123: 3 upon us, O LORD, **have m** upon us: 2603
130: 7 for with the LORD *there is* **m**, and 2617
136: 1 for *he is* good: for his **m** *endureth* for ever. 2617
136: 2 God of gods: for his **m** *endureth* for ever. 2617
136: 3 Lord of lords: for his **m** *endureth* for ever. 2617
136: 4 great wonders: for his **m** *endureth* for ever. 2617
136: 5 the heavens: for his **m** *endureth* for ever. 2617
136: 6 the waters: for his **m** *endureth* for ever. 2617
136: 7 great lights: for his **m** *endureth* for ever: 2617
136: 8 to rule by day: for his **m** *endureth* for ever: 2617
136: 9 to rule by night: for his **m** *endureth* for ever. 2617
136:10 their firstborn: for his **m** *endureth* for ever: 2617
136:11 among them: for his **m** *endureth* for ever: 2617
136:12 out arm: for his **m** *endureth* for ever. 2617
136:13 sea into parts: for his **m** *endureth* for ever: 2617
136:14 the midst of it: for his **m** *endureth* for ever: 2617
136:15 in the Red sea: for his **m** *endureth* for ever. 2617
136:16 the wilderness: for his **m** *endureth* for ever. 2617
136:17 great kings: for his **m** *endureth* for ever: 2617
136:18 famous kings: for his **m** *endureth* for ever: 2617
136:19 the Amorites: for his **m** *endureth* for ever: 2617
136:20 of Bashan: for his **m** *endureth* for ever: 2617
136:21 for an heritage: for his **m** *endureth* for ever: 2617
136:22 his servant: for his **m** *endureth* for ever. 2617
136:23 our low estate: for his **m** *endureth* for ever: 2617
136:24 our enemies: for his **m** *endureth* for ever. 2617
136:25 to all flesh: for his **m** *endureth* for ever. 2617
136:26 God of heaven: for his **m** *endureth* for ever. 2617
138: 8 thy **m**, O LORD, *endureth* for ever: 2617
143:12 of thy **m** cut off mine enemies, and 2617
145: 8 slow to anger, and of great **m**. 2617
147:11 that fear him, in those that hope in his **m**. 2617
Pr 3: 3 Let not **m** and truth forsake thee: bind them 2617
14:21 he that **hath m** on the poor, happy *is* he. 2603
14:22 **m** and truth *shall be to* them that devise 2617
14:31 he that honoureth him **hath m** on the poor. 2603
16: 6 By **m** and truth iniquity is purged: and 2617
20:28 **M** and truth preserve the king: and 2617
20:28 the king: and his throne is upholden by **m**. 2617
21:21 after righteousness and **m** findeth life, 2617
28:13 and forsaketh *them* shall **have m**. 7355
Isa 9:17 neither shall **have m** on their fatherless and 7355
14: 1 For the LORD will **have m** on Jacob, and 7355
16: 5 in **m** shall the throne be established: and 2617
27:11 he that made them will not **have m** on 7355
30:18 be exalted, that *he* may **have m** upon you: 7355
47: 6 thou didst shew them no **m**; upon 7356
49:10 for he that **hath m** on them shall lead them, 7355
49:13 and will **have m** upon his afflicted. 7355
54: 8 with everlasting kindness will I **have m** on 7355
54:10 saith the LORD that **hath m** on thee. 7355
55: 7 the LORD, and he will **have m** upon him; 7355
60:10 but in my favour have I **had m** on thee. 7355
Jer 6:23 and spear; they *are* cruel, and have no **m**; 7355
13:14 nor spare, nor **have m**, but destroy them. 7355
21: 7 spare them, neither have pity, nor **have m**. 7355
30:18 and **have m** on his dwelling places; 7355
31:20 I will **surely have m** upon him, 7355+7355
33:11 *is* good; for his **m** *endureth* for ever: 2617
33:26 captivity to return, and **have m** on them. 7355
42:12 that he may **have m** upon you, and 7355
50:42 they *are* cruel, and will not **shew m**: 7355
Eze 39:25 and **have m** upon the whole house of Israel, 7355
Da 4:27 thine iniquities by **shewing m** to the poor; 2604
9: 4 the covenant and **m** to them that love him, 2617
Hos 1: 6 for I will no more **have m** upon the house 7355
1: 7 I will **have m** upon the house of Judah, and 7355
2: 4 I will not **have m** upon her children; 7355
2:23 I will **have m** upon her that had not 7355
2:23 mercy upon her that had not **obtained m**; 7355
4: 1 because *there is* no truth, nor **m**, 2617
6: 6 For I desired **m**, and not sacrifice; and 2617
10:12 to yourselves in righteousness, reap in **m**; 2617
12: 6 keep **m** and judgment, and wait on thy God 2617
14: 3 for in thee the fatherless **findeth m**. 7355
Jnh 2: 8 observe lying vanities forsake their own **m**. 2617
Mic 6: 8 to love **m**, and to walk humbly with thy 2617
7:18 anger for ever, because he delighteth in **m**. 2617
7:20 the truth to Jacob, *and* the **m** to Abraham, 2617
Hab 3: 2 years make known; in wrath remember **m**. 7355
Zec 1:12 how long wilt thou not **have m** on 7355
7: 9 shew **m** and compassions every man to his 2617
10: 6 to place them; for I **have m** upon them: 7355
Mt 5: 7 *are* the merciful: for they shall **obtain m**. *1653*
9:13 I will have **m**, and not sacrifice: *1656*
9:27 saying, *Thou* Son of David, **have m** on us. *1653*
12: 7 I will have **m**, and not sacrifice, *1656*
15:22 unto him, saying, **Have m** on me, O Lord, *1653*
17:15 Lord, **have m** on my son: for he is lunatick, *1653*
20:30 cried out, saying, **Have m** on us, O Lord, *1653*
20:31 saying, **Have m** on us, O Lord, *thou* Son of *1653*
23:23 *matters* of the law, judgment, **m**, and faith: *1656*
Mk 10:47 Jesus, *thou* Son of David, **have m** on me. *1653*
10:48 *Thou* Son of David, **have m** on me. *1653*
Lk 1:50 And his **m** *is* on them that fear him from *1656*
1:54 his servant Israel, in remembrance of *his* **m**, *1656*
1:58 the Lord had shewed great **m** upon her; *1656*
1:72 To perform the **m** *promised* to our fathers, *1656*
1:78 Through the **tender m** of our God; *1656+4698*
10:37 And he said, He that shewed **m** on him. *1656*
16:24 **have m** on me, and send Lazarus, *1653*
17:13 and said, Jesus, Master, **have m** on us. *1653*
18:38 Jesus, *thou* Son of David, **have m** on me. *1653*
18:39 *Thou* Son of David, **have m** on me. *1653*
Ro 9:15 I will **have m** on whom I will have mercy, *1653*
9:15 I will have mercy on whom I will **have m**. *1653*
9:16 that runneth, but of God that **sheweth m**. *1653*
9:18 Therefore **hath** he **m** on whom he will *have* *1653*
9:18 hath he mercy on whom he will *have m*, NIG
9:23 the riches of his glory on the vessels of **m**, *1656*

Ro 11:30 yet have now **obtained m** through their *1653*
11:31 that through your **m** they also may obtain *1656*
11:31 your mercy they also may **obtain m**. *1653*
11:32 in unbelief, that he might **have m** upon all. *1653*
12: 8 he that **sheweth m**, with cheerfulness. *1653*
15: 9 the Gentiles might glorify God for *his* **m**; *1656*
1Co 7:25 as one that hath **obtained m** of the Lord to *1653*
2Co 4: 1 as we have **received m**, we faint not; *1653*
Gal 6:16 to this rule, peace *be* on them, and **m**, *1656*
Eph 2: 4 But God, who is rich in **m**, for his great *1656*
Php 2:27 but God **had m** on him; and not on him *1653*
1Ti 1: 2 Grace, **m**, *and* peace, from God our Father *1656*
1:13 but I **obtained m**, because I did *it* *1653*
1:16 Howbeit for this cause I **obtained m**, *1653*
2Ti 1: 2 Grace, **m**, *and* peace, from God the Father *1656*
1:16 The Lord give **m** unto the house of *1656*
1:18 Lord grant unto him that *he* may find **m** *1656*
Tit 1: 4 Grace, **m**, *and* peace, from God the Father *1656*
3: 5 but according to his **m** he saved us, by *1656*
Heb 4:16 that we may obtain **m**, and find grace to *1656*
9: 5 cherubims of glory shadowing the **m seat**; *2435*
10:28 Moses' law died without **m** under two *3628*
Jas 2:13 For he shall have judgment **without m**, *448*
2:13 without mercy, that hath shewed no **m**; *1656*
2:13 and **m** rejoiceth against judgment. *1656*
3:17 full of **m** and good fruits, without partiality, *1656*
5:11 the Lord is very pitiful, and of **tender m**. *3629*
1Pe 1: 3 which according to his abundant **m** hath *1656*
2:10 which had not **obtained m**, but now have *1653*
2:10 obtained mercy, but now have **obtained m**. *1653*
2Jn 1: 3 Grace be with you, **m**, *and* peace, from God *1656*
Jude 1: 2 **M** unto you, and peace, and love, *1656*
1:21 looking for the **m** of our Lord Jesus Christ *1656*

MERCY'S (3) [MERCY]
Ps 6: 4 deliver my soul: O save me for thy **m** sake. 2617
31:16 upon thy servant: save me for thy **m** sake. 2617
44:26 for our help, and redeem us for thy **m** sake. 2617

MERED (2)
1Ch 4:17 *were*, Jether, and **M**, and Epher, and Jalon: 4778
4:18 the daughter of Pharaoh, which **M** took. 4778

MEREMOTH (6)
Ezr 8:33 the hand of **M** the son of Uriah the priest; 4822
10:36 Vaniah, **M**, Eliashib, 4822
Ne 3: 4 next unto them repaired **M** the son of 4822
3:21 After him repaired **M** the son of Urijah 4822
10: 5 Harim, **M**, Obadiah, 4822
12: 3 Shechaniah, Rehum, **M**, 4822

MERES (1)
Est 1:14 Tarshish, **M**, Marsena, *and* Memucan, 4825

MERETHAIM (1)
Jer 50:21 Go up against the land of **M**, *even* against 4850

MERIBAH (6) [MERIBAH-KADESH]
Ex 17: 7 **M**, because of the chiding of the children of 4809
Nu 20:13 This *is* the water of **M**; because 4809
20:24 rebelled against my word at the water of **M**. 4809
27:14 that *is* the water of **M** in Kadesh *in* 4809
Dt 33: 8 whom thou didst strive at the waters of **M**; 4809
Ps 81: 7 I proved thee at the waters of **M**. Selah. 4809

MERIBAH-KADESH (1) [MERIBAH, KADESH]
Dt 32:51 the children of Israel at the waters of **M**, 4809

MERIB-BAAL (4) [MEPHIBOSHETH]
1Ch 8:34 the son of Jonathan *was* **M**; and 4807
8:34 *was* Merib-baal; and **M** begat Micah. 4807
9:40 the son of Jonathan *was* **M**: and 4807
9:40 *was* Merib-baal: and **M** begat Micah. 4810

MERODACH (1)
Jer 50: 2 Bel is confounded, **M** is broken in pieces; 4781

MERODACH-BALADAN (1) [BERODACH-BALADAN]
Isa 39: 1 At that time **M**, the son of Baladan, king of 4757

MEROM (2)
Jos 11: 5 and pitched together at the waters of **M**, 4792
11: 7 against them by the waters of **M** suddenly; 4792

MERONOTHITE (2)
1Ch 27:30 and over the asses *was* Jehdeiah the **M**: 4824
Ne 3: 7 Jadon the **M**, the men of Gibeon, and of 4824

MEROZ (1)
Jdg 5:23 Curse ye **M**, said the angel of the LORD, 4789

MERRILY (1) [MERRY]
Est 5:14 go thou in **m** with the king unto 8056

MERRY (28) [MERRILY, MERRYHEARTED]
Ge 43:34 And they drunk, and were **m** with him. 7937
Jdg 9:27 trode *the grapes*, and made **m**, and 1974
16:25 when their hearts were **m**, that they said, 2896
19: 6 and tarry all night, and let thine heart be **m**. 3190
19: 9 lodge here, that thine heart may be **m**; 3190
19:22 *Now* as they were **making** their hearts **m**, 3190
Ru 3: 7 had eaten and drunk, and his heart was **m**, 3190
1Sa 25:36 Nabal's heart *was* **m** within him, for he *was* 2896
2Sa 13:28 Mark ye now when Amnon's heart is **m** 2896
1Ki 4:20 eating and drinking, and **making m**. 8056
21: 7 *and* eat bread, and let thine heart be **m**: 3190
2Ch 7:10 **m** in heart for the goodness that 2896
Est 1:10 when the heart of the king was **m** with 2896
Pr 15:13 A **m** heart maketh a cheerful countenance: 8056
15:15 *he that is* of a **m** heart *hath* a continual 2896
17:22 A **m** heart doeth good *like* a medicine: but 8056
Ecc 8:15 than to eat, and to drink, and to be **m**: 8055
9: 7 and drink thy wine with a **m** heart; 2896
10:19 for laughter, and wine **maketh m**: 2416+8055
Jer 30:19 and the voice of them that **make m**: 7832
31: 4 forth in the dances of them that **make m**. 7832
Lk 12:19 take thine ease, eat, drink, *and* be **m**. *2165*
15:23 and kill *it*; and let us eat, and be **m**: *2165*
15:24 and is found. And they began to be **m**. *2165*
15:29 that I might **make m** with my friends: *2165*
15:32 It was meet that *we* should **make m**, and *2165*
Jas 5:13 let him pray. Is any **m**? let him sing psalms. *2114*
Rev 11:10 and **make m**, and shall send gifts one to *2165*

MERRYHEARTED (1) [HEART, MERRY]
Isa 24: 7 vine languisheth, all the **m** do sigh. 3820+8056

MESECH (1)
Ps 120: 5 Woe is me, that I sojourn *in* **M**, *that* I dwell 4902

MESHA (4)
Ge 10:30 their dwelling was from **M**, as thou goest 4852
2Ki 3: 4 **M** king of Moab was a sheepmaster, and 4338
1Ch 2:42 brother of Jerahmeel *were*, **M** his firstborn, 4337
8: 9 and Zibia, and **M**, and Malcham, 4331

MESHACH (15)
Da 1: 7 to Mishael, of **M**; and to Azariah, 4335
2:49 and he set Shadrach, **M**, and Abed-nego, 4336
3:12 of Babylon, Shadrach, **M**, and Abed-nego; 4336
3:13 to bring Shadrach, **M**, and Abed-nego. 4336
3:14 *Is it* true, O Shadrach, **M**, and Abed-nego, 4336
3:16 **M**, and Abed-nego, answered and said to 4336
3:19 against Shadrach, **M**, and Abed-nego: 4336
3:20 **M**, and Abed-nego, *and* to cast *them* into 4336
3:22 that took up Shadrach, **M**, and Abed-nego. 4336
3:23 three men, Shadrach, **M**, and Abed-nego, 4336
3:26 and said, Shadrach, **M**, and Abed-nego, 4336
3:26 *hither*. Then Shadrach, **M**, and Abed-nego, 4336
3:28 **M**, and Abed-nego, who hath sent his 4336
3:29 **M**, and Abed-nego, shall be cut in pieces, 4336
3:30 **M**, and Abed-nego, in the province of 4336

MESHECH (8)
Ge 10: 2 and Javan, and Tubal, and **M**, and Tiras. 4902
1Ch 1: 5 and Javan, and Tubal, and **M**, and Tiras. 4902
1:17 and Uz, and Hul, and Gether, and **M**. 4902
Eze 27:13 Javan, Tubal, and **M**, they *were* thy 4902
32:26 There *is* **M**, Tubal, and all her multitude: 4902
38: 2 the chief prince of **M** and Tubal, and 4902
38: 3 O Gog, the chief prince of **M** and Tubal: 4902
39: 1 O Gog, the chief prince of **M** and Tubal: 4902

MESHELEMIAH (4)
1Ch 9:21 *And* Zechariah the son of **M** *was* porter of 4920
26: 1 Of the Korhites *was* **M** the son of Kore, 4920
26: 2 the sons of **M** *were*, Zechariah 4920
26: 9 **M** had sons and brethren, strong men, 4920

MESHEZABEEL (3)
Ne 3: 4 the son of Berechiah, the son of **M**. 4898
10:21 **M**, Zadok, Jaddua, 4898
11:24 Pethahiah the son of **M**, of the children of 4898

MESHEZABEL See MESHEZABEEL

MESHILLEMITH (1) [MESHILLEMOTH]
1Ch 9:12 the son of **M**, the son of Immer; 4921

MESHILLEMOTH (2) [MESHILLEMITH]
2Ch 28:12 Berechiah the son of **M**, and Jehizkiah 4919
Ne 11:13 of Ahasai, the son of **M**, the son of Immer, 4919

MESHOBAB (1)
1Ch 4:34 **M**, and Jamlech, and Joshah the son of 4877

MESHULLAM (25)
2Ki 22: 3 the son of **M**, the scribe, *to* the house of 4918
1Ch 3:19 **M**, and Hananiah, and Shelomith their 4918
5:13 **M**, and Sheba, and Jorai, and Jachan, and 4918
8:17 and **M**, and Hezeki, and Heber, 4918
9: 7 Sallu the son of **M**, the son of Hodaviah, 4918
9: 8 **M** the son of Shephathiah, the son of 4918
9:11 the son of **M**, the son of Zadok, the son of 4918
9:12 the son of Jahzerah, the son of **M**, the son 4918
2Ch 34:12 Zechariah and **M**, of the sons of 4918
Ezr 8:16 for Nathan, and for Zechariah, and for **M**, 4918
10:15 **M** and Shabbethai the Levite helped them. 4918
10:29 **M**, Malluch, and Adaiah, Jashub, and 4918
Ne 3: 4 next unto them repaired **M** the son of 4918
3: 6 son of Paseah, and **M** the son of Besodeiah; 4918
3:30 After him repaired **M** the son of Berechiah 4918
6:18 the daughter of **M** the son of Berechiah. 4918
8: 4 and Hashbadana, Zechariah, *and* **M**. 4918
10: 7 **M**, Abijah, Mijamin, 4918
10:20 Magpiash, **M**, Hezir, 4918
11: 7 Sallu the son of **M**, the son of Joed, the son 4918
11:11 the son of **M**, the son of Zadok, the son of 4918
12:13 Of Ezra, **M**; of Amariah, Jehohanan; 4918
12:16 Of Iddo, Zechariah; of Ginnethon, **M**; 4918
12:25 Bakbukiah, Obadiah, **M**, Talmon, Akkub, 4918
12:33 And Azariah, Ezra, and **M**, 4918

MESHULLEMETH (1)
2Ki 21:19 his mother's name *was* **M**, the daughter of 4922

MESOBAITE (1)
1Ch 11:47 Eliel, and Obed, and Jasiel the **M**. 4677

MESOPOTAMIA (7)
Ge 24:10 he arose, and went to **M**, unto the city of 763
Dt 23: 4 thee Balaam the son of Beor of Pethor of **M**, 763
Jdg 3: 8 the hand of Chushan-rishathaim king of **M**: 763
3:10 Chushan-rishathaim king of **M** into his hand; 758
1Ch 19: 6 hire them chariots and horsemen out of **M**, 763
Ac 2: 9 and the dwellers in **M**, and in Judea, and *3318*
7: 2 when he was in **M**, before he dwelt in *3318*

MESS (2) [MESSES]
Ge 43:34 Benjamin's **m** was five times so much as 4864
2Sa 11: 8 there followed him a **m** *of meat* from 4864

MESSAGE (7) [MESSENGER, MESSENGERS]
Jdg 3:20 Ehud said, I have a **m** from God unto thee. 1697
1Ki 20:12 when *Ben-hadad* heard this **m**, as he *was* 1697
Pr 26: 6 He that sendeth a **m** by the hand of a fool 1697
Hag 1:13 in the LORD'S **m** unto the people, 4400
Lk 19:14 hated him, and sent a **m** after him, saying, *4242*
1Jn 1: 5 then is the **m** which we have heard of him, *1860*
3:11 For this is the **m** that ye heard from *31*

MESSENGER (34) [MESSAGE]
Ge 50:16 they **sent a m** unto Joseph, saying, 6680
1Sa 4:17 the **m** answered and said, Israel is fled 1319
23:27 there came a **m** unto Saul, saying, 4397
2Sa 11:19 charged the **m**, saying, When thou hast 4397
11:22 So the **m** went, and came and 4397
11:23 the **m** said unto David, Surely the men 4397
11:25 David said unto the **m**, Thus shalt thou say 4397
15:13 there came a **m** to David, saying, 5046
1Ki 19: 2 Jezebel sent a **m** unto Elijah, saying, So let 4397
22:13 the **m** that was gone to call Micaiah spake 4397
2Ki 5:10 Elisha sent a **m** unto him, saying, Go and 4397
6:32 ere the **m** came to him, he said to 4397
6:32 look, when the **m** cometh, shut the door, 4397
6:33 behold, the **m** came down unto him: 4397
9:18 The **m** came to them, but he cometh not 4397
10: 8 there came a **m**, and told him, saying, 4397
2Ch 18:12 the **m** that went to call Micaiah spake to 4397
Job 1:14 there came a **m** unto Job, and said, 4397
33:23 If there be a **m** with him, an interpreter, 4397
Pr 13:17 A wicked **m** falleth into mischief: but 4397
17:11 a cruel **m** shall be sent against him. 4397
25:13 *so is* a faithful **m** to them that send him: 6735
Isa 42:19 or deaf, as my **m** *that* I sent? who *is* blind 4397
Jer 51:31 meet another, and one **m** to meet another, 5046
Eze 23:40 to come from far, unto whom a **m** *was* sent; 4397
Hag 1:13 spake Haggai the LORD'S **m** in 4397
Mal 2: 7 for he *is* the **m** of the LORD of hosts. 4397
3: 1 I *will* send my **m**, and he shall prepare 4397
3: 1 even the **m** of the covenant, whom ye 4397
Mt 11:10 Behold, I send my **m** before thy face, *32*
Mk 1: 2 Behold, I send my **m** before thy face, *32*
Lk 7:27 Behold, I send my **m** before thy face, *32*
2Co 12: 7 the **m** of Satan to buffet me, lest I should be *32*
Php 2:25 but your **m**, and he that ministered to my *652*

MESSENGERS (79) [MESSAGE]
Ge 32: 3 Jacob sent **m** before him to Esau his 4397
32: 6 the **m** returned to Jacob, saying, We came 4397
Nu 20:14 Moses sent **m** from Kadesh unto the king 4397
21:21 Israel sent **m** unto Sihon king of 4397
22: 5 He sent **m** therefore unto Balaam the son of 4397
24:12 Spake I not also to thy **m** which thou 4397
Dt 2:26 I sent **m** out of the wilderness of Kedemoth 4397
Jos 6:17 because she hid the **m** that we sent. 4397
6:25 because she hid the **m**, which Joshua sent 4397
7:22 So Joshua sent **m**, and they ran unto 4397
Jdg 6:35 he sent **m** throughout all Manasseh; who 4397
6:35 he sent **m** unto Asher, and unto Zebulun, 4397
7:24 Gideon sent **m** throughout all mount 4397
9:31 he sent **m** unto Abimelech privily, saying, 4397
11:12 Jephthah sent **m** unto the king of 4397
11:13 Ammon answered unto the **m** of Jephthah, 4397
11:14 Jephthah sent **m** again unto the king of 4397
11:17 Israel sent **m** unto the king of Edom, 4397
11:19 Israel sent **m** unto Sihon king of 4397
1Sa 6:21 they sent **m** to the inhabitants of 4397
11: 3 that we may send **m** unto all the coasts of 4397
11: 4 came the **m** *to* Gibeah of Saul, and told 4397
11: 7 all the coasts of Israel by the hands of **m**, 4397
11: 9 they said unto the **m** that came, Thus shall 4397
11: 9 the **m** came and shewed *it* to the men of 4397
16:19 Wherefore Saul sent **m** unto Jesse, and 4397
19:11 Saul also sent **m** unto David's house, 4397
19:14 when Saul sent **m** to take David, she said, 4397
19:15 Saul sent the **m** *again* to see David, saying, 4397
19:16 when the **m** were come in, behold *there* 4397
19:20 Saul sent **m** to take David: and when they 4397
19:20 the spirit of God was upon the **m** of Saul, 4397
19:21 he sent other **m**, and they prophesied 4397
19:21 Saul sent **m** again the third time, and 4397
25:14 David sent **m** out of the wilderness to 4397
25:42 she went after the **m** of David, and 4397
2Sa 2: 5 David sent **m** unto the men of 4397
3:12 Abner sent **m** to David on his behalf, 4397
3:14 David sent **m** to Ish-bosheth Saul's son, 4397
3:26 out from David, he sent **m** after Abner, 4397
5:11 Hiram king of Tyre sent **m** to David, and 4397
11: 4 David sent **m**, and took her, and she came 4397
12:27 Joab sent **m** to David, and said, I have 4397
1Ki 20: 2 he sent **m** to Ahab king of Israel into 4397
20: 5 the **m** came again, and said, Thus speaketh 4397
20: 9 Wherefore he said unto the **m** of 4397
20: 9 the **m** departed, and brought him word 4397
2Ki 1: 2 he sent **m**, and said unto them, Go, 4397
1: 3 go up to meet the **m** of the king of Samaria, 4397
1: 5 when the **m** turned back unto him, he said 4397
1:16 Forasmuch as thou hast sent **m** to inquire of 4397
7:15 And the **m** returned, and told the king. 4397
14: 8 Amaziah sent **m** to Jehoash, the son of 4397
16: 7 So Ahaz sent **m** to Tiglath-pileser king of 4397
17: 4 for he had sent **m** to So king of Egypt, and 4397
19: 9 he sent **m** again unto Hezekiah, saying, 4397
19:14 received the letter of the hand of the **m**, 4397
19:23 By thy **m** thou hast reproached the Lord, 4397
1Ch 14: 1 Now Hiram king of Tyre sent **m** to David, 4397
19: 2 David sent **m** to comfort him concerning 4397
19:16 they sent **m**, and drew forth the Syrians that 4397

2Ch 36:15 God of their fathers sent to them by his **m**, 4397
36:16 they mocked the **m** of God, and 4397
Ne 6: 3 I sent **m** unto them, saying, I *am* doing a 4397
Pr 16:14 The wrath of a king *is as* **m** of death: but 4397
Isa 14:32 shall *one* then answer the **m** of the nation? 4397
18: 2 *saying*, Go, ye swift **m**, to a nation 4397
37: 9 when he heard *it*, he sent **m** to Hezekiah, 4397
37:14 received the letter from the hand of the **m**, 4397
44:26 and performeth the counsel of his **m**; 4397
57: 9 didst send thy **m** far off, and didst debase 6735
Jer 27: 3 by the hand of the **m** which come *to* 4397
Eze 23:16 and sent **m** unto them into Chaldea. 4397
30: 9 In that day shall **m** go forth from me in 4397
Na 2:13 the voice of thy **m** shall no more be heard. 4397
Lk 7:24 And when the **m** of John were departed, *32*
9:52 And sent **m** before his face: and they went, *32*
2Co 8:23 our brethren *be inquired of, they are* the **m** *652*
Jas 2:25 when she had received the **m**, and had sent *32*

MESSES (1) [MESS]
Ge 43:34 *and sent* **m** unto them from before him: 4864

MESSIAH (2) [MESSIAS]
Da 9:25 to build Jerusalem unto the **M** the Prince 4899
9:26 and two weeks shall **M** be cut off, 4899

MESSIAS (2) [MESSIAH]
Jn 1:41 unto him, We have found the **M**, which is, *3323*
4:25 I know that **M** cometh, which is called *3323*

MET (45) [MEET]
Ge 32: 1 on his way, and the angels of God **m** him. 6293
33: 8 meanest thou by all this drove which I **m**? 6298
Ex 3:18 The LORD God of the Hebrews hath **m** 7136
4:24 that the LORD **m** him, and sought to kill 6298
4:27 **m** him in the mount of God, and 6298
5: 3 The God of the Hebrews hath **m** with us: 7122
5:20 they **m** Moses and Aaron, who stood in 6293
Nu 23: 4 God **m** Balaam: and he said unto him, I 7136
23:16 the LORD **m** Balaam, and put a word in 7136
Dt 23: 4 Because they **m** you not with bread and 6923
25:18 How he **m** thee by the way, and smote 7136
Jos 11: 5 when all these kings were **m together**, 3259
17:10 they **m together** in Asher on the north, and 6293
1Sa 10:10 behold, a company of prophets **m** him; 7125
25:20 came down against her; and she **m** them. 6298
2Sa 2:13 and **m** together by the pool of Gibeon: 6298
16: 1 Ziba the servant of Mephibosheth **m** him, 7125
18: 9 Absalom **m** the servants of David. 7122
1Ki 13:24 a lion **m** him by the way, and slew him: 4672
18: 7 was in the way, behold Elijah **m** him: 7125
2Ki 9:21 **m** him in the portion of Naboth 4672
10:13 Jehu **m** with the brethren of Ahaziah king 4672
Ne 13: 2 Because they **m** not the children of Israel 6923
Ps 85:10 Mercy and truth are **m together**; 6298
Pr 7:10 there **m** him a woman *with* the attire of a 7125
Jer 41: 6 it came to pass, as he **m** them, he said unto 6298
Am 5:19 man did flee from a lion, and a bear **m** him; 6293
Mt 8:28 there **m** him two possessed with devils, *5221*
28: 9 behold, Jesus **m** them, saying, *All* hail. *528*
Mk 5: 2 immediately there **m** him out of the tombs a *528*
11: 4 door without in a place where two ways **m**; *296*
Lk 8:27 there **m** him out of the city a certain man, *5221*
9:37 down from the hill, much people **m** him. *4876*
17:12 there **m** him ten men *that were* lepers, *528*
Jn 4:51 his servants **m** him, and told *him*, saying, *528*
11:20 that Jesus was coming, **went and m** him: *5221*
11:30 but was in *that* place where Martha **m** him. *5221*
12:18 For this cause the people also **m** him, *5221*
Ac 10:25 Cornelius **m** him, and fell down at *his* feet, *4876*
16:16 possessed with a spirit of divination **m** us, *528*
17:17 in the market daily with them that **m with** *3909*
20:14 And when he **m with** us at Assos, we took *4820*
27:41 And falling into a place **where two seas m**, *1337*
Heb 7: 1 who **m** Abraham returning from *4876*
7:10 of his father, when Melchisedec **m** him. *4876*

METALWORKER See COPPERSMITH

METE (6) [METED]
Ex 16:18 when they did **m** *it* with an omer, he that 4058
Ps 60: 6 and **m out** the valley of Succoth. 4058
108: 7 and **m out** the valley of Succoth. 4058
Mt 7: 2 and with what measure ye **m**, it shall be *3354*
Mk 4:24 with what measure ye **m**, it shall be *3354*
Lk 6:38 For with the same measure that ye **m** withal *3354*

METED (3) [METE]
Isa 18: 2 a nation **m out** and trodden down, 6978+6978
18: 7 a nation **m out** and trodden under 6978+6978
40:12 **m out** heaven with the span, and 8505

METEYARD (1)
Lev 19:35 in **m**, in weight, or in measure. 4060

METHEG-AMMAH (1) [AMMAH]
2Sa 8: 1 David took **M** out of the hand of 4964

METHUSAEL (2)
Ge 4:18 Mehujael begat **M**: and Methusael begat 4967
4:18 begat Methusael: and **M** begat Lamech. 4967

METHUSELAH (6) [MATHUSALA]
Ge 5:21 lived sixty and five years, and begat **M**: 4968
5:22 Enoch walked with God after he begat **M** 4968
5:25 **M** lived an hundred eighty and seven years, 4968
5:26 **M** lived after he begat Lamech seven 4968
5:27 all the days of **M** were nine hundred sixty 4968
1Ch 1: 3 Henoch, **M**, Lamech, 4968

METHUSHAEL See METHUSAEL

MEUNIM (1) [MEHUNIM]
Ne 7:52 The children of Besai, the children of **M**, 4586

MEUNITES See MEHUNIMS

MEZAHAB (2)
Ge 36:39 the daughter of Matred, the daughter of **M**. 4314
1Ch 1:50 the daughter of Matred, the daughter of **M**. 4314

MEZOBAITE See MESOBAITE

MIAMIN (2)
Ezr 10:25 **M**, and Eleazar, and Malchijah, and 4326
Ne 12: 5 **M**, Maadiah, Bilgah, 4326

MIBHAR (1)
1Ch 11:38 brother of Nathan, **M** the son of Haggeri, 4006

MIBSAM (3)
Ge 25:13 Nebajoth; and Kedar, and Adbeel, and **M**, 4017
1Ch 1:29 Nebajoth; then Kedar, and Adbeel, and **M**, 4017
4:25 his son, **M** his son, Mishma his son. 4017

MIBZAR (2)
Ge 36:42 Duke Kenaz, duke Teman, duke **M**, 4014
1Ch 1:53 Duke Kenaz, duke Teman, duke **M**, 4014

MICAH (27) [MICAH'S, MICHA]
Jdg 17: 1 of mount Ephraim, whose name *was* **M**. 4321
17: 4 and they were in the house of **M**. 4321
17: 5 the man **M** had a house of gods, and 4318
17: 8 came *to* mount Ephraim to the house of **M**, 4318
17: 9 **M** said unto him, Whence comest thou? 4318
17:10 **M** said unto him, Dwell with me, and 4318
17:12 **M** consecrated the Levite; and the young 4318
17:12 his priest, and was in the house of **M**. 4318
17:13 said **M**, Now know I that the LORD will 4318
18: 2 to the house of **M**, they lodged there. 4318
18: 3 When they *were* by the house of **M**, they 4318
18: 4 Thus and thus dealeth **M** with me, and 4318
18:13 and came unto the house of **M**. 4318
18:15 *even unto* the house of **M**, and saluted him. 4318
18:22 they were a good way from the house of **M**, 4318
18:23 and said unto **M**, What aileth thee, 4318
18:26 when **M** saw that they *were* too strong for 4318
18:27 they took *the things* which **M** had made, 4318
1Ch 5: 5 **M** his son, Reaia his son, Baal his son, 4318
8:34 *was* Merib-baal; and Merib-baal begat **M**. 4318
8:35 the sons of **M** *were*, Pithon, and Melech, 4318
9:15 and Galal, and Mattaniah the son of **M**, 4316
9:40 *was* Merib-baal: and Merib-baal begat **M**. 4318
9:41 the sons of **M** *were*, Pithon, and Melech, 4318
2Ch 34:20 Abdon the son of **M**, and Shaphan 4318
Jer 26:18 **M** the Morasthite prophesied in the days of 4318
Mic 1: 1 The word of the LORD that came to **M** 4318

MICAH'S (3) [MICAH]
Jdg 18:18 these went *into* **M** house, and fetched 4318
18:22 the men that *were* in the houses near to **M** 4318
18:31 they set them up **M** graven image, which he 4318

MICAIAH (18)
1Ki 22: 8 *There is* yet one man, **M** the son of Imlah, 4321
22: 9 and said, Hasten *hither* **M** the son of Imlah. 4321
22:13 the messenger that was gone to call **M** 4321
22:14 **M** said, *As* the LORD liveth, what 4321
22:15 the king said unto him, **M**, shall we go 4321
22:24 and smote **M** on the cheek, and said, 4321
22:25 **M** said, Behold, thou shalt see in that day, 4321
22:26 Take **M**, and carry him back unto Amon 4321
22:28 **M** said, If thou return at all in peace, 4321
2Ch 18: 7 the same *is* **M** the son of Imla. 4321
18: 8 and said, Fetch quickly **M** the son of Imla. 4321
18:12 the messenger that went to call **M** spake to 4321
18:13 **M** said, *As* the LORD liveth, even what 4321
18:14 to the king, the king said unto him, **M**, 4318
18:23 and smote **M** upon the cheek, and said, 4321
18:24 **M** said, Behold, thou shalt see on that day 4321
18:25 Take ye **M**, and carry him back to Amon 4321
18:27 **M** said, If thou certainly return in peace, 4321

MICE (4) [MOUSE]
1Sa 6: 4 Five golden emerods, and five golden **m**, 5909
6: 5 and images of your **m** that mar the land; 5909
6:11 the coffer with the **m** of gold and 5909
6:18 the golden **m**, *according to* the number of 5909

MICHA (4) [MICAH]
2Sa 9:12 had a young son, whose name *was* **M**. 4316
Ne 10:11 **M**, Rehob, Hashabiah, 4316
11:17 Mattaniah the son of **M**, the son of Zabdi, 4316
11:22 the son of Mattaniah, the son of **M**. 4316

MICHAEL (15)
Nu 13:13 Of the tribe of Asher, Sethur the son of **M**. 4317
1Ch 5:13 of the house of their fathers *were*, **M**, 4317
5:14 of Jaroah, the son of Gilead, the son of **M**, 4317
6:40 The son of **M**, the son of Baaseiah, the son 4317
7: 3 **M**, and Obadiah, and Joel, Ishiah, five: 4317
8:16 **M**, and Ispah, and Joha, the sons of Beriah; 4317
12:20 and **M**, and Jozabad, and Elihu, and Zilthai, 4317
27:18 of David: of Issachar, Omri the son of **M**: 4317
2Ch 21: 2 and Azariah, and **M**, and Shephatiah: 4317
Ezr 8: 8 Zebadiah the son of **M**, and with him 4317
Da 10:13 lo, **M**, one of the chief princes, came to 4317
10:21 with me in these *things*, but **M** your prince. 4317
12: 1 at that time shall **M** stand up, the great 4317
Jude 1: 9 Yet **M** the archangel, when contending *3413*
Rev 12: 7 **M** and his angels fought against the dragon; *3413*

MICHAH (4)
1Ch 23:20 **M** the first, and Jesiah the second. 4318
24:24 *Of* the sons of Uzziel; **M**: of the sons of 4318
24:24 Michah: of the sons of **M**; Shamir. 4318
24:25 The brother of **M** *was* Isshiah: of the sons 4318

MICHAIAH (7)
2Ki 22:12 Achbor the son of **M**, and Shaphan 4320
2Ch 13: 2 His mother's name also *was* **M** 4322
17: 7 to Zechariah, and to Nethaneel, and to **M**, 4322
Ne 12:35 the son of **M**, the son of Zaccur, the son of 4320
12:41 Eliakim, Maaseiah, Miniamin, **M**, Elioenai, 4320
Jer 36:11 When **M** the son of Gemariah, the son of 4321
36:13 **M** declared unto them all the words that he 4321

MICHAL (18)
1Sa 14:49 and the name of the younger **M**: 4324
18:20 **M** Saul's daughter loved David: and 4324
18:27 And Saul gave him **M** his daughter to wife. 4324
18:28 and *that* **M** Saul's daughter loved him. 4324
19:11 **M** David's wife told him, saying, If thou 4324
19:12 So **M** let David down through a window: 4324
19:13 **M** took an image, and laid *it* in the bed, 4324
19:17 Saul said unto **M**, Why hast thou deceived 4324
19:17 **M** answered Saul, He said unto me, Let me 4324
25:44 Saul had given **M** his daughter, 4324
2Sa 3:13 except thou first bring **M** Saul's daughter, 4324
3:14 Saul's son, saying, Deliver *me* my wife **M**, 4324
6:16 **M** Saul's daughter looked through a 4324
6:20 **M** the daughter of Saul came out to meet 4324
6:21 David said unto **M**, *It was* before 4324
6:23 Therefore **M** the daughter of Saul had no 4324
21: 8 the five sons of **M** the daughter of Saul, 4324
1Ch 15:29 that **M** the daughter of Saul looking out at a 4324

MICHMAS (2) [MICHMASH]
Ezr 2:27 The men of **M**, an hundred twenty and two. 4363
Ne 7:31 The men of **M**, an hundred and twenty and 4363

MICHMASH (9) [MICHMAS]
1Sa 13: 2 *whereof* two thousand were with Saul in **M** 4363
13: 5 they came up, and pitched in **M**, 4363
13:11 gathered themselves together *at* **M**; 4363
13:16 but the Philistines encamped in **M**. 4363
13:23 Philistines went out to the passage of **M**. 4363
14: 5 one *was* situate northward over against **M**, 4363
14:31 they smote the Philistines that day from **M** 4363
Ne 11:31 also of Benjamin from Geba *dwelt at* **M**, 4363
Isa 10:28 at **M** he hath laid up his carriages: 4363

MICHMETHAH (2)
Jos 16: 6 the border went out toward the sea *to* **M** on 4366
17: 7 coast of Manasseh was from Asher *to* **M**, 4366

MICHRI (1)
1Ch 9: 8 the son of **M**, and Meshullam the son of 4381

MICHTAM (6)
Ps 16: T **M** of David. 4387
56: T **M** of David, when the Philistines took him 4387
57: T chief Musician, Al-taschith, **M** of David, 4387
58: T chief Musician, Al-taschith, **M** of David. 4387
59: T chief Musician, Al-taschith, **M** of David; 4387
60: T upon Shushan-eduth, **M** of David, to teach; 4387

MICMASH See MICHMAS; MICHMASH

MICMETHATH See MICHMETHAH

MICRI See MICHRI

MIDDAY (3) [DAY, MIDDLE]
1Ki 18:29 when **m** was past, and they prophesied until 6672
Ne 8: 3 from the morning until **m**, 3117+4276+1886.1
Ac 26:13 **At m**, O king, I saw in the way a *2250+3319*

MIDDIN (1)
Jos 15:61 Beth-arabah, **M**, and Secacah, 4081

MIDDLE (18) [MIDDAY, MIDDLEMOST, MIDNIGHT, MIDST]
Ex 26:28 the **m** bar in the midst of the boards shall 8484
36:33 he made the **m** bar to shoot through 8484
Jos 12: 2 *from* the **m** of the river, and *from* half 8432
Jdg 7:19 the camp *in* the beginning of the **m** watch; 8484
9:37 See there come people down by the **m** of 2872
16:29 Samson took hold of the two **m** pillars 8432
1Sa 25:29 them shall he sling out *as out* of the **m** of a 3709
2Sa 10: 4 cut off their garments in the **m**, *even* to 2677
1Ki 6: 6 the **m** *was* six cubits broad, and the third 8484
6: 8 The door for the **m** chamber *was* in 8484
6: 8 they went up with winding stairs into the **m** 8484
6: 8 and out of the **m** into the third. 8484
8:64 The same day did the king hallow the **m** of 8432
2Ki 20: 4 afore Isaiah was gone out *into* the **m** court, 8484
2Ch 7: 7 Moreover Solomon hallowed the **m** of 8432
Jer 39: 3 and sat in the **m** gate, *even* Nergal-sharezer, 8432
Eze 1:16 their work *was* as it were a wheel in the **m** 8432
Eph 2:14 hath broken down the **m wall** of partition *3320*

MIDDLEMOST (2) [MIDDLE]
Eze 42: 5 the lower, and than the **m** of the building. 8484
42: 6 than the lowest and the **m** from the ground. 8484

MIDIAN (39) [MADIAN, MIDIANITE, MIDIANITES, MIDIANITISH]
Ge 25: 2 and Medan, and **M**, and Ishbak, and Shuah. 4080
25: 4 the sons of **M**; Ephah, and Epher, and 4080
36:35 who smote **M** in the field of Moab, 4080
Ex 2:15 of Pharaoh, and dwelt in the land of **M**: 4080
2:16 Now the priest of **M** had seven daughters: 4080
3: 1 of Jethro his father in law, the priest of **M**: 4080
4:19 the LORD said unto Moses in **M**, Go, 4080
18: 1 When Jethro, the priest of **M**, Moses' father 4080
Nu 22: 4 Moab said unto the elders of **M**, Now shall 4080
22: 7 the elders of **M** departed with the rewards 4080
25:15 over a people, *and* of a chief house in **M**. 4080
25:18 the daughter of a prince of **M**, their sister, 4080
31: 3 and avenge the LORD of **M**. 4080

Nu 31: 8 they slew the kings of **M**, beside *the rest of* 4080
31: 8 and Hur, and Reba, five kings of **M**: 4080
31: 9 of Israel took *all* the women of **M** captives, 4080
Jos 13:21 whom Moses smote with the princes of **M**, 4080
Jdg 6: 1 them into the hand of **M** seven years. 4080
6: 2 the hand of **M** prevailed against Israel: *and* 4080
7: 8 the host of **M** was beneath him in 4080
7:13 of barley bread tumbled into the host of **M**, 4080
7:14 *for* into his hand hath God delivered **M**, 4080
7:15 delivered into your hand the host of **M**. 4080
7:25 pursued **M**, and brought the heads of Oreb 4080
8: 3 delivered into your hands the princes of **M**, 4080
8: 5 after Zebah and Zalmunna, kings of **M**. 4080
8:12 took the two kings of **M**, Zebah and 4080
8:22 thou hast delivered us from the hand of **M**. 4080
8:26 purple raiment that *was* on the kings of **M**, 4080
8:28 Thus was **M** subdued before the children of 4080
9:17 and delivered you out of the hand of **M**: 4080
1Ki 11:18 they arose out of **M**, and came *to* Paran: 4080
1Ch 1:32 and Medan, and **M**, and Ishbak, and Shuah. 4080
1:33 the sons of **M**; Ephah, and Epher, and 4080
1:46 which smote **M** in the field of Moab, 4080
Isa 9: 4 the rod of his oppressor, as *in* the day of **M**. 4080
10:26 to the slaughter of **M** at the rock Oreb: 4080
60: 6 the dromedaries of **M** and Ephah; 4080
Hab 3: 7 the curtains of the land of **M** did tremble. 4080

MIDIANITE (1) [MIDIAN]

Nu 10:29 the son of Raguel the **M**, Moses' father in 4084

MIDIANITES (23) [MIDIAN]

Ge 37:28 there passed by **M** merchantmen; and 4084
Nu 25:17 Vex the **M**, and smite them: 4084
31: 2 Avenge the children of Israel of the **M**: 4084
31: 3 let them go against the **M**, and avenge 4080
31: 7 they warred against the **M**, as the LORD 4080
Jdg 6: 2 of the **M** the children of Israel made them 4080
6: 3 that the **M** came up, and the Amalekites, 4080
6: 6 greatly impoverished because of the **M**; 4080
6: 7 cried unto the LORD because of the **M**, 4080
6:11 by the winepress, to hide *it* from the **M**. 4080
6:13 and delivered us into the hands of the **M**. 4080
6:14 shalt save Israel from the hand of the **M**: 4080
6:16 and thou shalt smite the **M** as one man. 4080
6:33 all the **M** and the Amalekites and 4080
7: 1 that the host of the **M** were on the north 4080
7: 2 many for me to give the **M** into their hands, 4080
7: 7 and deliver the **M** into thine hand: 4080
7:12 the **M** and the Amalekites and all 4080
7:23 of all Manasseh, and pursued after the **M**. 4080
7:24 Come down against the **M**, and take before 4080
7:25 they took two princes of the **M**, Oreb and 4080
8: 1 when thou wentest to fight with the **M**? 4080
Ps 83: 9 Do unto them as *unto* the **M**; as *to* Sisera, 4080

MIDIANITISH (3) [MIDIAN]

Nu 25: 6 brought unto his brethren a **M** *woman* in 4084
25:14 *even* that was slain with the **M woman**, 4084
25:15 the name of the **M** woman that was slain 4084

MIDNIGHT (14) [MIDDLE, NIGHT]

Ex 11: 4 About **m** will I go out into 2676+3915+1886.1
12:29 that at **m** the LORD smote 2677+3915+1886.1
Jdg 16: 3 Samson lay till **m**, and 2677+3915+1886.1
16: 3 arose at **m**, and took 2677+3915+1886.1
Ru 3: 8 it came to pass at **m**, that 2677+3915+1886.1
1Ki 3:20 she rose at **m**, and took my 3915+8432+1886.1
Job 34:20 the people shall be troubled **at m**, 2676+3915
Ps 119:62 **At m** I will rise to give thanks unto 2676+3915
Mt 25: 6 And **at m** there was a cry made, *3319+3571*
Mk 13:35 or **at m**, or at the cockcrowing, or in *3317*
Lk 11: 5 and shall go unto him at **m**, and say unto *3317*
Ac 16:25 And at **m** Paul and Silas prayed, and *3317*
20: 7 and continued *his* speech until **m**. *3317*
27:27 about **m** the shipmen deemed *3319+3571+3588*

MIDST (364) [MIDDLE]

Ge 1: 6 Let there be a firmament in the **m** of 8432
2: 9 the tree of life also in the **m** of the garden, 8432
3: 3 of the fruit of the tree which *is* in the **m** of 8432
15:10 divided them in the **m**, and laid each piece 8432
19:29 and sent Lot out of the **m** of the overthrow, 8432
48:16 let them grow into a multitude in the **m** of 7130
Ex 3: 2 in a flame of fire out of the **m** of a bush: 8432
3: 4 God called unto him out of the **m** of 8432
3:20 wonders which I will do in the **m** thereof: 7130
8:22 that I *am* the LORD in the **m** of the earth. 7130
11: 4 About midnight will I go out into the **m** of 8432
14:16 go on dry *ground* through the **m** of the sea. 8432
14:22 the children of Israel went into the **m** of 8432
14:23 went in after them to the **m** of the sea, 8432
14:27 the Egyptians in the **m** of the sea. 8432
14:29 walked upon dry *land* in the **m** of the sea; 8432
15:19 Israel went on dry *land* in the **m** of the sea. 8432
23:25 I will take sickness away from the **m** of 7130
24:16 unto Moses out of the **m** of the cloud. 8432
24:18 Moses went into the **m** of the cloud, and 8432
26:28 the middle bar in the **m** of the boards shall 8432
27: 5 that the net may be even to the **m** of 2677
28:32 be a hole in the top of it, in the **m** thereof: 8432
33: 3 for I will not go up in the **m** of thee; 7130
33: 5 I will come up into the **m** of thee in a 7130
34:12 lest it be for a snare in the **m** of thee: 7130
38: 4 compass thereof beneath unto the **m** of it. 2677
39:23 *there was* a hole in the **m** of the robe, as 8432
Lev 16:16 that remaineth among them in the **m** of 8432
Nu 2:17 camp of the Levites in the **m** of the camp: 8432
5: 3 not their camps, in the **m** whereof I dwell. 8432
16:47 and ran into the **m** of the congregation; 8432
19: 6 cast *it* into the **m** of the burning of 8432
33: 8 passed through the **m** of the sea into 8432+871.1
35: 5 and the city *shall be* in the **m**: 8432
Dt 4:11 the mountain burnt with fire unto the **m** of 3820
4:12 the LORD spake unto you out of the **m** of 8432
Dt 4:15 unto you in Horeb out of the **m** of the fire: 8432
4:33 of God speaking out of the **m** of the fire, 8432
4:34 take him a nation from the **m** of *another* 7130
4:36 thou heardest his words out of the **m** of 8432
5: 4 face in the mount out of the **m** of the fire, 8432
5:22 in the mount out of the **m** of the fire, 8432
5:23 when ye heard the voice out of the **m** of 8432
5:24 we have heard his voice out of the **m** of 8432
5:26 God speaking out of the **m** of the fire, 8432
9:10 the **m** of the fire in the day of the assembly. 8432
10: 4 the **m** of the fire in the day of the assembly: 8432
11: 3 which he did in the **m** of Egypt unto 8432
11: 6 in their possession, in the **m** of all Israel: 7130
13: 5 So shalt thou put the evil away from the **m** 7130
13:16 spoil of it into the **m** of the street thereof, 8432
17:20 he, and his children, in the **m** of Israel. 7130
18:15 up unto thee a Prophet from the **m** of thee, 7130
19: 2 three cities for thee in the **m** of thy land, 8432
23:14 For the LORD thy God walketh in the **m** 7130
32:51 ye sanctified me not in the **m** of 8432
Jos 3:17 firm on dry *ground* in the **m** of Jordan, 8432
4: 3 Take you hence out of the **m** of Jordan, 8432
4: 5 the LORD your God into the **m** of Jordan, 8432
4: 8 took up twelve stones out of the **m** of 8432
4: 9 Joshua set up twelve stones in the **m** of 8432
4:10 bare the ark stood in the **m** of Jordan, 8432
4:18 were come up out of the **m** of Jordan, 8432
7:13 *There is* an accursed thing in the **m** of thee, 7130
7:21 they *are* hid in the earth in the **m** of my 8432
7:23 they took them out of the **m** of the tent, 8432
8:13 Joshua went that night into the **m** of 8432
8:22 so they were in the **m** of Israel, some on 8432
10:13 So the sun stood still in the **m** of heaven, 2677
13: 9 and the city that *is* in the **m** of the river, and 8432
13:16 and the city that *is* in the **m** of the river, and 8432
Jdg 15: 4 put a firebrand in the **m** between two tails. 8432
18:20 and went in the **m** of the people. 7130
20:42 the cities they destroyed in the **m** of them. 8432
1Sa 11:11 they came into the **m** of the host in 8432
16:13 and anointed him in the **m** of his brethren; 7130
18:10 and he prophesied in the **m** of the house: 8432
2Sa 1:25 How are the mighty fallen in the **m** of 8432
4: 6 they came thither into the **m** of the house, 8432
6:17 in the **m** of the tabernacle that David had 8432
18:14 while he *was* yet alive in the **m** of the oak. 3820
20:12 Amasa wallowed in blood in the **m** of 8432
23:12 he stood in the **m** of the ground, and 8432
23:20 slew a lion in the **m** of a pit in time of 8432
24: 5 city that *lieth* in the **m** of the river of Gad, 8432
1Ki 3: 8 thy servant *is* in the **m** of thy people which 8432
6:27 their wings touched one another in the **m** of 8432
8:51 of Egypt, from the **m** of the furnace of iron: 8432
20:39 Thy servant went out into the **m** of 7130
22:35 the blood ran out of the wound into the **m** 2436
2Ki 6:20 and behold, *they were* in the **m** of Samaria. 8432
1Ch 11:14 they set themselves in the **m** of *that* parcel, 8432
16: 1 set it in the **m** of the tent that David had 8432
19: 4 cut off their garments in the **m** hard by *their* 2677
2Ch 6:13 and had set it in the **m** of the court: 8432
20:14 came the spirit of the LORD in the **m** of 8432
32: 4 the brook that ran through the **m** of 8432
Ne 4:11 till we come **in the m** among them, and 413
9:11 that they went through the **m** of 8432+871.1
Est 4: 1 went out into the **m** of the city, and 8432
Job 21:21 number of his months is **cut off in the m**? 2686
Ps 22:14 it is melted in the **m** of my bowels. 8432
22:22 in the **m** of the congregation will I praise 8432
46: 2 though the mountains be carried into the **m** 3820
46: 5 God *is* in the **m** of her; she shall not be 7130
48: 9 O God, in the **m** of thy temple. 7130
55:10 mischief also and sorrow *are* in the **m** of it. 7130
55:11 Wickedness *is* in the **m** thereof: deceit and 7130
57: 6 into the **m** whereof they are fallen 8432
74: 4 Thine enemies roar in the **m** of thy 7130
74:12 working salvation in the **m** of the earth. 7130
78:28 he let *it* fall in the **m** of their camp, 7130
102:24 take me not away in the **m** of my days: 2677
110: 2 rule thou in the **m** of thine enemies. 7130
116:19 in the **m** of thee, O Jerusalem. 8432
135: 9 sent tokens and wonders into the **m** of thee, 8432
136:14 made Israel to pass through the **m** of 8432+871.1
137: 2 harps upon the willows in the **m** thereof. 8432
138: 7 Though I walk in the **m** of trouble, 7130
Pr 4:21 keep them in the **m** of thine heart. 8432
5:14 I was almost in all evil in the **m** of 8432
8:20 in the **m** of the paths of judgment: 8432
14:33 *that which is* in the **m** of fools is made 7130
23:34 thou shalt be as he that lieth down in the **m** 3820
30:19 the way of a ship in the **m** of the sea; and 3820
SS 3:10 the **m** thereof being paved *with* love, 8432
Isa 4: 4 the **m** thereof by the spirit of judgment, 7130
5: 2 built a tower in the **m** of it, and also made a 8432
5: 8 that they may be placed alone in the **m** of 7130
5:25 their carcases were torn in the **m** of 7130
6: 5 I dwell in the **m** of a people of unclean lips: 8432
6:12 *there be* a great forsaking in the **m** of 7130
7: 6 set a king in the **m** of it, *even* the son of 8432
10:23 even determined, *in* the **m** of all *the land*. 7130
12: 6 for great *is* the Holy One of Israel in the **m** 7130
16: 3 make thy shadow as the night in the **m** of 8432
19: 1 the heart of Egypt shall melt in the **m** of it. 7130
19: 3 the spirit of Egypt shall fail in the **m** 7130
19:14 mingled a perverse spirit in the **m** thereof: 7130
19:19 the LORD in the **m** of the land of Egypt, 8432
19:24 *even* a blessing in the **m** of the land: 7130
24:13 When thus it shall be in the **m** of the land 7130
24:18 he that cometh up out of the **m** of the pit 8432
25:11 he shall spread forth his hands in the **m** of 7130
29:23 the work of mine hands, in the **m** of him, 7130
30:28 shall reach to the **m** of the neck, 2673
41:18 and fountains in the **m** of the valleys: 8432
52:11 touch no unclean *thing;* go ye out of the **m** 8432
58: 9 Here I *am*. If thou take away from the **m** of 8432
66:17 in the gardens behind one *tree* in the **m**, 8432
Jer 6: 1 gather yourselves to flee out of the **m** of 7130
Jer 6: 6 she *is* wholly oppression in the **m** of her. 7130
9: 6 Thine habitation *is* in the **m** of deceit; 8432
12:16 shall they be built in the **m** of my people. 8432
14: 9 *art* in the **m** of us, and we are called by thy 7130
17:11 shall leave them in the **m** of his days, and 2677
21: 4 I will assemble them into the **m** of this city. 8432
29: 8 that *be* in the **m** of you, deceive you, 7130
30:21 their governor shall proceed from the **m** of 7130
37:12 to separate himself thence in the **m** of 8432
41: 7 *so*, when they came into the **m** of the city, 8432
41: 7 *and cast them* into the **m** of the pit, he, and 8432
46:21 Also her hired men *are* in the **m** of her like 7130
48:45 a flame from the **m** of Sihon, and 996
50: 8 Remove out of the **m** of Babylon, and 8432
50:37 the mingled people that *are* in the **m** of her; 8432
51: 1 against them that dwell in the **m** of them 3820
51: 6 Flee out of the **m** of Babylon, and 8432
51:45 go ye out of the **m** of her, and deliver ye 8432
51:47 and all her slain shall fall in the **m** of her. 8432
51:63 to it, and cast it into the **m** of Euphrates: 8432
52:25 that were found in the **m** of the city. 8432
La 1:15 foot all my mighty *men* in the **m** of me: 7130
3:45 and refuse in the **m** of the people. 7130
4:13 that *have* shed the blood of the just in the **m** 7130
Eze 1: 4 out of the **m** thereof as the colour of amber, 8432
1: 4 colour of amber, out of the **m** of the fire. 8432
1: 5 Also out of the **m** thereof *came* the likeness 8432
5: 2 with fire a third *part* in the **m** of the city, 8432
5: 4 cast them into the **m** of the fire, and 8432
5: 5 I have set it in the **m** of the nations and 8432
5: 8 will execute judgments in the **m** of thee in 8432
5:10 fathers shall eat the sons in the **m** of thee, 8432
5:12 shall they be consumed in the **m** of thee: 8432
6: 7 the slain shall fall in the **m** of you, and 8432
7: 4 thine abominations shall be in the **m** of 8432
7: 9 thine abominations *that* are in the **m** of 8432
8:11 in the **m** of them stood Jaazaniah the son of 8432
9: 4 Go through the **m** of the city 8432+871.1
9: 4 of the city through the **m** of Jerusalem, 8432
9: 4 abominations that be done in the **m** thereof. 8432
10:10 as if a wheel had been in the **m** of a wheel. 8432
11: 7 Your slain whom ye have laid in the **m** of 8432
11: 7 but *I* will bring you forth out of the **m** of it. 8432
11: 9 I will bring you out of the **m** thereof, and 8432
11:11 neither shall ye be the flesh in the **m** 8432
11:23 the LORD went up from the **m** of the city, 8432
12: 2 thou dwellest in the **m** of a rebellious 8432
13:14 and ye shall be consumed in the **m** thereof: 8432
14: 8 I will cut him off from the **m** of my people; 8432
14: 9 will destroy him from the **m** of my people 8432
15: 4 both the ends of it, and the **m** of it is burnt. 8432
16:53 captivity of thy captives in the **m** of them: 8432
17:16 *even* with him in the **m** of Babylon he shall 8432
20: 8 against them in the **m** of the land of Egypt. 8432
21:32 thy blood shall be in the **m** of the land; 8432
22: 3 The city sheddeth blood in the **m** of it, 8432
22: 7 in the **m** of thee have they dealt by 8432
22: 9 in the **m** of thee they commit lewdness. 8432
22:13 at thy blood which hath been in the **m** of 8432
22:18 and iron, and lead, in the **m** of the furnace; 8432
22:19 I will gather you into the **m** of Jerusalem. 8432
22:20 and lead, and tin, into the **m** of the furnace, 8432
22:21 and ye shall be melted in the **m** thereof. 8432
22:22 As silver is melted in the **m** of the furnace, 8432
22:22 so shall ye be melted in the **m** thereof; 8432
22:25 conspiracy of her prophets in the **m** thereof, 8432
22:25 they have made her many widows in the **m** 8432
22:27 Her princes in the **m** thereof *are* like 7130
23:39 thus have they done in the **m** of mine 8432
24: 7 For her blood is in the **m** of her; she set it 8432
26: 5 the spreading of nets in the **m** of the sea: 8432
26:12 and thy dust in the **m** of the water 8432
26:15 when the slaughter is made in the **m** of 8432
27: 4 Thy borders *are* in the **m** of the seas, 3820
27:25 made very glorious in the **m** of the seas. 3820
27:26 the east wind hath broken thee in the **m** of 3820
27:27 in all thy company which *is* in the **m** of 8432
27:27 shall fall into the **m** of the seas in the day of 3820
27:32 like the destroyed in the **m** of the sea? 8432
27:34 all thy company in the **m** of thee shall fall. 8432
28: 2 I sit *in* the seat of God, in the **m** of the seas; 3820
28: 8 of *them that are* slain in the **m** of the seas. 3820
28:14 and down in the **m** of the stones of fire. 8432
28:16 have filled the **m** of thee *with* violence, 8432
28:16 from the **m** of the stones of fire. 8432
28:18 will I bring forth a fire from the **m** of thee, 8432
28:22 and I will be glorified in the **m** of thee: 8432
28:23 the wounded shall be judged in the **m** of 8432
29: 3 the great dragon that lieth in the **m** of his 8432
29: 4 I will bring thee up out of the **m** of thy 8432
29:12 in the **m** of the countries *that are* desolate, 8432
29:21 the opening of the mouth in the **m** of them; 8432
30: 7 they shall be desolate in the **m** of 8432
30: 7 her cities shall be in the **m** of the cities *that* 8432
31:14 the earth, in the **m** of the children of men, 8432
31:17 *that* dwelt under his shadow in the **m** of 8432
31:18 thou shalt lie in the **m** of the uncircumcised 8432
32:20 They shall fall in the **m** of *them that are* 8432
32:21 of the **m** of hell with them that help him: 8432
32:25 They have set her a bed in the **m** of 8432
32:25 he is put in the **m** of *them that be* slain. 8432
32:28 thou shalt be broken in the **m** of 8432
32:32 he shall be laid in the **m** of 8432
36:23 which ye have profaned in the **m** of them; 8432
37: 1 set me down in the **m** of the valley which 8432
37:26 will set my sanctuary in the **m** of them for 8432
37:28 when my sanctuary shall be in the **m** of 8432
38:12 and goods, that dwell in the **m** of the land. 2872
39: 7 name known in the **m** of my people Israel; 8432
41: 7 the lowest *chamber* to the highest by the **m**. 8484
43: 7 where I will dwell in the **m** of the children 8432
43: 9 and I will dwell in the **m** of them for ever. 8432
46:10 the prince in the **m** of them, when they go 8432
48: 8 and the sanctuary shall be in the **m** of it. 8432
48:10 of the LORD shall be in the **m** thereof. 8432

Eze 48:15 and the city shall be in the **m** thereof. 8432
48:21 the sanctuary of the house *shall be* in the **m** 8432
48:22 *being* in the **m** *of that* which is the prince's, 8432
Da 3: 6 cast into the **m** of a burning fiery furnace. 1459
3:11 *that* he should be cast into the **m** of a 1459
3:15 ye shall be cast the same hour into the **m** of 1459
3:21 were cast into the **m** of the burning fiery 1459
3:23 fell down bound into the **m** of the burning 1459
3:24 Did not we cast three men bound into the **m** 1459
3:25 walking in the **m** of the fire, and they have 1459
3:26 Abed-nego, came forth of the **m** of the fire. 1459
4:10 a tree in the **m** of the earth, and the height 1459
7:15 I Daniel was grieved in my spirit in the **m** 1459
9:27 *in* the **m** of the week he shall cause 2677
Hos 5: 4 for the spirit of whoredoms *is* in the **m** of 7130
11: 9 not man; the Holy One in the **m** of thee: 7130
Joel 2:27 ye shall know that I *am* in the **m** of Israel, 7130
Am 2: 3 I will cut off the judge from the **m** thereof, 7130
3: 9 behold the great tumults in the **m** thereof, 7130
3: 9 and the oppressed in the **m** thereof. 8432
6: 4 and the calves out of the **m** of the stall; 8432
7: 8 I *will* set a plumbline in the **m** of my 7130
7:10 Amos hath conspired against thee in the **m** 7130
Jnh 2: 3 cast me *into* the deep, in the **m** of the seas; 3824
Mic 2:12 as the flock in the **m** of their fold: 8432
5: 7 the remnant of Jacob shall be in the **m** of 7130
5: 8 **m** of many people as a lion among 7130
5:10 that I will cut off thy horses out of the **m** of 7130
5:13 thy standing images out of the **m** of thee; 7130
5:14 I will pluck up thy groves out of the **m** of 7130
6:14 thy casting down *shall be* in the **m** of thee; 7130
7:14 solitarily *in* the wood, in the **m** of Carmel: 8432
Na 3:13 thy people in the **m** of thee *are* women: 7130
Hab 2:19 and *there is* no breath at all in the **m** of it. 7130
3: 2 revive thy work in the **m** of the years, 7130
3: 2 in the **m** of the years make known; 7130
Zep 2:14 flocks shall lie down in the **m** of her, all 8432
3: 5 The just LORD *is* in the **m** thereof; he will 7130
3:11 I will take away out of the **m** of thee them 7130
3:12 I will also leave in the **m** of thee an 7130
3:15 *even* the LORD, *is* in the **m** of thee: 7130
3:17 The LORD thy God in the **m** of thee *is* 7130
Zec 2: 5 and will be the glory in the **m** of her. 8432
2:10 I come, and I will dwell in the **m** of thee, 8432
2:11 I will dwell in the **m** of thee, and thou shalt 8432
5: 4 it shall remain in the **m** of his house, and 8432
5: 7 this *is* a woman that sitteth in the **m** of 8432
5: 8 he cast it into the **m** of the ephah; and 8432
8: 3 and will dwell in the **m** of Jerusalem: 8432
8: 8 and they shall dwell in the **m** of Jerusalem: 8432
14: 1 thy spoil shall be divided in the **m** of thee. 7130
14: 4 the mount of Olives shall cleave in the **m** 2677
Mt 10:16 I send you forth as sheep in the **m** of *3319*
14:24 But the ship was now in the **m** of the sea, *3319*
18: 2 unto *him*, and set him in the **m** of them. *3319*
18:20 in my name, there am I in the **m** of them. *3319*
Mk 6:47 the ship was in the **m** of the sea, and *3319*
7:31 through the **m** of the coasts of Decapolis. *3319*
9:36 took a child, and set him in the **m** of them: *3319*
14:60 And the high priest stood up in the **m**, and *3319*
Lk 2:46 sitting in the **m** of the doctors, both hearing *3319*
4:30 But he passing through the **m** of them went *3319*
4:35 when the devil had thrown him in the **m**, *3319*
5:19 with *his* couch into the **m** before Jesus. *3319*
6: 8 Rise up, and stand *forth* in the **m**. *3319*
17:11 that he passed through the **m** of Samaria *3319*
21:21 let them which are in the **m** of it depart out; *3319*
22:55 And when they had kindled a fire in the **m** *3319*
23:45 the vail of the temple was rent **in the m**. *3319*
24:36 Jesus himself stood in the **m** of them, and *3319*
Jn 7:14 Now about the **m** of the feast Jesus went up *3322*
8: 3 and when they had set her in the **m**, *3319*
8: 9 and the woman standing in the **m**. *3319*
8:59 going through the **m** of them, and so *3319*
19:18 on either side one, and Jesus in the **m**. *3319*
20:19 came Jesus and stood in the **m**, and *3319*
20:26 and stood in the **m**, and said, Peace *be* unto *3319*
Ac 1:15 And in those days Peter stood up in the **m** *3319*
1:18 he burst asunder **in the m**, and all his *3319*
2:22 which God did by him in the **m** of you, *3319*
4: 7 And when they had set them in the **m**, *3319*
17:22 Then Paul stood in the **m** of Mars' hill, and *3319*
27:21 Paul stood *forth* in the **m** of them, *3319*
Php 2:15 in the **m** of a crooked and perverse nation, *3319*
Heb 2:12 in the **m** of the church will I sing praise *3319*
Rev 1:13 And in the **m** of the seven candlesticks one *3319*
2: 1 who walketh in the **m** of the seven golden *3319*
2: 7 which is in the **m** of the paradise of God. *3319*
4: 6 and in the **m** of the throne, and round about *3319*
5: 6 in the **m** of the throne and of the four *3319*
5: 6 the four beasts, and in the **m** of the elders, *3319*
6: 6 And I heard a voice in the **m** of the four *3319*
7:17 For the Lamb which is in the **m** of *3319*
8:13 an angel flying through the **m of heaven**, *3321*
14: 6 I saw another angel fly in the **m of heaven**, *3321*
19:17 to all the fowls that fly in the **m of heaven**, *3321*
22: 2 In the **m** of the street of it, and of either *3319*

MIDWIFE (3) [MIDWIVES]

Ge 35:17 that the **m** said unto her, Fear not; 3205
38:28 the **m** took and bound upon his hand a 3205
Ex 1:16 When ye **do the office of a m** to 3205

MIDWIVES (7) [MIDWIFE]

Ex 1:15 the king of Egypt spake to the Hebrew **m**, 3205
1:17 the **m** feared God, and did not as the king 3205
1:18 And the king of Egypt called for the **m**, and 3205
1:19 the **m** said unto Pharaoh, Because 3205
1:19 are delivered ere the **m** come in unto them. 3205
1:20 Therefore God dealt well with the **m**: and 3205
1:21 it came to pass, because the **m** feared God, 3205

MIGDAL-EL (1)

Jos 19:38 **M**, Horem, and Beth-anath, and 4027

MIGDAL-GAD (1)

Jos 15:37 Zenan, and Hadashah, and **M**, 4028

MIGDOL (4)

Ex 14: 2 between **M** and the sea, over against 4024
Nu 33: 7 and they pitched before **M**. 4024
Jer 44: 1 which dwell at **M**, and at Tahpanhes, and 4024
46:14 publish in **M**, and publish in Noph and 4024

MIGHT (475) [ALMIGHTY, MIGHTEST, MIGHTIER, MIGHTIES, MIGHTIEST, MIGHTILY, MIGHTY]

Ge 12:19 so I **m** have taken her to me to wife: now NIH
13: 6 to bear them, that they **m** dwell together: NIH
17:18 O that Ishmael **m** live before thee! NIH
26:10 one of the people **m** lightly have lien with NIH
30:34 I would it **m** be according to thy word. NIH
30:41 that they **m** conceive among the rods. NIH
31:27 that I **m** have sent thee away with mirth, NIH
36: 7 For their riches were more than that they **m** NIH
37:22 that he **m** rid him out of their hands, NIH
43:32 the Egyptians **m** not eat bread with 3201
49: 3 my **m**, and the beginning of my strength, 3581
Ex 10: 1 that I **m** shew these my signs before him: NIH
12:33 that they **m** send them out of the land in NIH
36:18 to couple the tent together, that *it* **m** be one. NIH
39:21 that *it* **m** be above the curious girdle of NIH
39:21 that the breastplate **m** not be loosed from NIH
Lev 24:12 that the mind of the LORD **m** be shewed NIH
26:45 sight of the heathen, that *I* **m** be their God: NIH
Nu 4:37 all that **m** do service in the tabernacle of NIH
4:41 of all that **m** do service in the tabernacle of NIH
14:13 up this people in thy **m** from among them;) 3581
22:41 that thence he **m** see the utmost part of NIH
Dt 2:30 that he **m** deliver him into thy hand, NIH
3:24 to thy works, and according to thy **m**? 1369
4:14 that ye **m** do them in the land whither ye go NIH
4:36 to hear his voice, that he **m** instruct thee: NIH
4:42 That the slayer **m** flee thither, which should NIH
4:42 that fleeing unto one of these cities he **m** NIH
5:29 that it **m** be well with them, and with their NIH
6: 1 that ye **m** do *them* in the land whither ye go NIH
6: 5 and with all thy soul, and with all thy **m**. 3966
6:23 us out from thence, that he **m** bring us in, NIH
6:24 that he **m** preserve us alive, as *it is at* this NIH
8: 3 that he **m** make thee know that man doth NIH
8:16 that he **m** humble thee, and that he might NIH
8:16 humble thee, and that he **m** prove thee, NIH
8:17 the **m** of mine hand hath gotten me this 6108
28:32 and *there shall be* no **m** in thine hand. 410
29: 6 that ye **m** know that I *am* the LORD your NIH
32:13 that he **m** eat the increase of the fields; NIH
Jos 4:24 That all the people of the earth **m** know NIH
4:24 that ye **m** fear the LORD your God for NIH
11:20 that *he* **m** destroy them utterly, *and* that they NIH
11:20 *and* that they **m** have no favour, but that *he* NIH
11:20 have no favour, but that *he* **m** destroy them, NIH
20: 9 *any* person at unawares **m** flee thither, NIH
22:16 that ye **m** rebel *this* day against NIH
22:24 In time to come your children **m** speak unto NIH
22:27 that *we* **m** do the service of the LORD NIH
24: 8 into your hand, that ye **m** possess their land; NIH
Jdg 3: 2 of the children of Israel **m** know, NIH
5:31 *be* as the sun when he goeth forth in his **m**. 1369
6:14 Go in this thy **m**, and thou shalt save Israel 3581
9:24 and ten sons of Jerubbaal **m** come, NIH
16:30 he bowed *himself* with *all his* **m**; and 3581
18: 7 that **m** put *them* to shame in *any* thing; NIH
Ru 1: 6 that she **m** return from the country of Moab: NIH
1Sa 4: 4 that they **m** bring from thence the ark of NIH
13:10 went out to meet him, that he **m** salute him. NIH
14:14 acre of land, *which* a yoke of *oxen* **m** *plow*. NIH
18:27 the king, that he **m** be the king's son in law. NIH
20: 6 David earnestly asked *leave* of me that *he* **m** NIH
2Sa 6:14 danced before the LORD with all *his* **m**; 5797
10:10 that he **m** put *them* in array against NIH
15: 4 hath *any* suit or cause **m** come unto me, NIH
17:14 to the intent that the LORD **m** bring evil NIH
17:17 for they **m** not be seen to come into 3201
22:41 that I **m** destroy them that hate me. NIH
1Ki 2:27 that *he* **m** fulfil the word of the LORD, NIH
7: 7 he made a porch for the throne where he **m** NIH
8: 1 that *they* **m** bring up the ark of the covenant NIH
8:16 build a house, that my name **m** be therein; NIH
12:15 the LORD, that *he* **m** perform his saying, NIH
15:17 that *he* **m** not suffer *any* to go out or NIH
15:23 all his **m**, and all that he did, and the cities 1369
16: 5 acts of Baasha, and what he did, and his **m**, 1369
16:27 which he did, and his **m** that he shewed, 1369
19: 4 he requested for himself that he **m** die; and NIH
22: 7 LORD besides, that we **m** inquire of him? NIH
22:45 his **m** that he shewed, and how he warred, 1369
2Ki 7: 2 make windows in heaven, **m** this thing be? NIH
7:19 windows in heaven, **m** such a thing be? NIH
10:19 to the intent that *he* **m** destroy NIH
10:34 of Jehu, and all that he did, and all his **m**, 1369
13: 8 of Jehoahaz, and all that he did, and his **m**, 1369
13:12 his **m** where*with* he fought against 1369
14:15 his **m**, and how he fought with Amaziah 1369
14:28 all that he did, and his **m**, how he warred, 1369
15:19 that his hand **m** be with him to confirm NIH
20:20 all his **m**, and how he made a pool, and a 1369
22:17 that they **m** provoke me to anger with all NIH
23:10 that no man **m** make his son or his daughter NIH
23:24 that he **m** perform the words of the law NIH
23:25 with all his soul, and with all his **m**, 3966
23:33 that *he* **m** not reign in Jerusalem; NIH
24:16 all the men of **m**, *even* seven thousand, 2428
1Ch 4:10 that thine hand **m** be with me, and that thou NIH
7: 2 *they were* valiant *men* of **m** in their 2428
7: 5 all the families of Issachar *were* men of **m**, 2428
12: 8 into the hold to the wilderness men of **m**, 2428
13: 8 Israel played before God with all *their* **m**, 5797
29: 2 Now I have prepared with all my **m** for 3581
29:12 in thine hand *is* power and **m**; and in thine 1369
1Ch 29:30 With all his reign and his **m**, and the times 1369
2Ch 2:12 that **m** build a house for the LORD, and NIH
6: 5 build a house *in*, that my name **m** be there; NIH
6: 6 chosen Jerusalem, that my name **m** be there; NIH
10:15 that the LORD **m** perform his word, NIH
11: 1 that *he* **m** bring the kingdom again to NIH
16: 1 to the intent that *he* **m** let none go out or NIH
18: 6 LORD besides, that we **m** inquire of him? NIH
20: 6 in thine hand *is there not* power and **m**, so 1369
20:12 for we have no **m** against this great 3581
25:20 that *he* **m** deliver them into the hand *of their* NIH
31: 4 that they **m** be encouraged in the law of NIH
32:18 to trouble them; that they **m** take the city. NIH
32:31 that *he* **m** know all *that was* in his heart. NIH
34:25 that *they* **m** provoke me to anger with all NIH
35:12 that they **m** give according to the divisions NIH
35:15 they **m** not depart from their service; NIH
35:22 that *he* **m** fight with him, and hearkened not NIH
36:22 the mouth of Jeremiah **m** be accomplished, NIH
Ezr 1: 1 by the mouth of Jeremiah **m** be fulfilled, NIH
5:10 that we **m** write the names of the men that NIH
8:21 that *we* **m** afflict ourselves before our God, NIH
Ne 5: 3 houses, that we **m** buy corn, because of NIH
5:10 **m** exact of them money and corn: NIH
6:13 *that* they **m** have *matter* for an evil report, NIH
6:13 for an evil report, that they **m** reproach me. NIH
7: 5 that *they* **m** be reckoned by genealogy. NIH
9:24 that *they* **m** do with them as they would. NIH
10:37 that the same Levites **m** have the tithes in NIH
Est 4: 2 for none **m** enter into the king's gate NIH
10: 2 all the acts of his power and of his **m**, and 1369
Job 6: 8 O that I **m** have my request; and *that* God NIH
9:33 *that* **m** lay his hand upon us both. NIH
16:21 O that *one* **m** plead for a man with God, as a NIH
23: 3 O that I knew where I **m** find him! *that* I NIH
23: 3 find him! *that* I **m** come *even* to his seat! NIH
23: 7 There the righteous **m** dispute with him; so NIH
30: 2 whereto **m** the strength of their hands profit NIH
38:13 That *it* **m** take hold of the ends of the earth, NIH
38:13 that the wicked **m** be shaken out of it? NIH
Ps 18:40 that I **m** destroy them that hate me. NIH
68:18 that the LORD God **m** dwell *among them*. NIH
76: 5 none of the men of **m** have found their 2428
78: 6 That the generation to come **m** know *them*, NIH
78: 7 That they **m** set their hope in God, and NIH
78: 8 **m** not be as their fathers, a stubborn and NIH
105:45 That they **m** observe his statutes, and NIH
106: 8 that *he* **m** make his mighty power to be NIH
107: 7 that *they* **m** go to a city of habitation. NIH
109:16 that *he* **m** even slay the broken in heart. NIH
118:13 Thou hast thrust sore at me that *I* **m** fall: but NIH
119:11 in mine heart, that I **m** not sin against thee. NIH
119:71 been afflicted; that I **m** learn thy statutes. NIH
119:101 every evil way, that I **m** keep thy word. NIH
119:148 that *I* **m** meditate in thy word. NIH
145: 6 *men* shall speak of the **m** of thy terrible 5807
Pr 22:21 That *I* **m** make thee know the certainty of NIH
Ecc 2: 3 till I **m** see what *was* that good for the sons NIH
3:18 that God **m** manifest them, and that *they* NIH
3:18 that *they* **m** see that they themselves are NIH
9:10 thy hand findeth to do, *do it* with thy **m**; 3581
Isa 11: 2 understanding, the spirit of counsel and **m**, 1369
28:13 that they **m** go, and fall backward, and NIH
33:13 and ye *that are* near, acknowledge my **m**. 1369
40:26 them all by names by the greatness of *his* **m**, 202
40:29 to *them that have* no **m** he increaseth 202
61: 3 that they **m** be called trees of righteousness, NIH
61: 3 of the LORD, that *he* **m** be glorified. NIH
64: 1 that the mountains **m** flow down at thy NIH
Jer 9: 1 that I **m** weep day and night for the slain of NIH
9: 2 that I **m** leave my people, and go from NIH
9:23 neither let the mighty *man* glory in his **m**, 1369
10: 6 thou *art* great, and thy name *is* great in **m**. 1369
13:11 that *they* **m** be unto me for a people, and NIH
16:21 cause them to know mine hand and my **m**; 1369
17:23 made their neck stiff, that *they* **m** not hear, NIH
19:15 their necks, that *they* **m** not hear my words. NIH
20:17 or that my mother **m** have been my grave, NIH
25: 7 that *ye* **m** provoke me to anger with NIH
26:19 Thus **m** we procure great evil against our NIH
27:15 that I **m** drive you out, and that ye might NIH
27:15 that ye **m** perish, ye, and the prophets that NIH
43: 3 that *they* **m** put us to death, and carry us NIH
44: 8 that ye **m** cut yourselves off, and that *ye* NIH
44: 8 that *ye* **m** be a curse and a reproach among NIH
49:35 break the bow of Elam, the chief of their **m**. 1369
51:30 their **m** hath failed; they became as women: 1369
Eze 17: 7 that *he* **m** water it by the furrows of her NIH
17: 8 that *it* **m** bring forth branches, and that *it* NIH
17: 8 that *it* **m** bear fruit, that *it* might be a goodly NIH
17: 8 might bear fruit, that *it* **m** be a goodly vine. NIH
17:14 That the kingdom **m** be base, that *it* might NIH
17:14 that *it* **m** not lift itself up, *but* that by NIH
17:14 that by keeping of his covenant it **m** stand. NIH
17:15 that *they* **m** give him horses and NIH
20:12 that *they* **m** know that I *am* the LORD that NIH
20:26 that I **m** make them desolate, to the end that NIH
20:26 to the end that they **m** know that I *am* NIH
24: 8 That *it* **m** cause fury to come up to take NIH
32:29 which with their **m** are laid by *them that* 1369
32:30 their terror *they are* ashamed of their **m**; 1369
36: 3 that ye **m** be a possession unto the residue NIH
40: 4 for to the intent that *I* **m** shew *them* unto NIH
41: 6 that *they* **m** have hold, but they had not hold NIH
Da 1: 4 whom *they* **m** teach the learning and NIH
1: 5 that at the end thereof they **m** stand before NIH
1: 8 of the eunuchs that he **m** not defile himself. NIH
2:20 and ever: for wisdom and **m** are his: 1370
2:23 who hast given me wisdom and **m**, and 1370
3:28 that they **m** not serve nor worship any god, NIH
4: 6 that they **m** make known unto me NIH
4:30 of the kingdom by the **m** of my power, 8632
5: 2 and his concubines, **m** drink therein. NIH
6: 2 that the princes **m** give accounts unto them, 1934
6:17 that the purpose **m** not be changed NIH

Da 8: 4 so that no beasts **m** stand before him, NIH
9:11 that *they* **m** not obey thy voice; NIH
9:13 that *we* **m** turn from our iniquities, and NIH
Joel 3: 3 and sold a girl for wine, that they **m** drink. NIH
3: 6 that *ye* **m** remove them far from their NIH
Am 1:13 at Gilead, that *they* **m** enlarge their border: NIH
Jnh 4: 5 till he **m** see what would become of the city. NIH
4: 6 that *it* **m** be a shadow over his head, NIH
Mic 3: 8 *of* judgment, and *of* **m**, to declare unto 1369
7:16 shall see and be confounded at all their **m**: 1369
Hab 3:16 in myself, that I **m** rest in the day of trouble: NIH
Zec 4: 6 saying, Not by **m**, nor by power, but by my 2428
6: 7 sought to go that *they* **m** walk to and NIH
8: 9 of hosts was laid, that the temple **m** be built. NIH
11:10 that *I* **m** break my covenant which I had NIH
11:14 that I **m** break the brotherhood between NIH
Mal 2: 4 that my covenant **m** be with Levi, saith NIH
2:15 That he **m** seek a godly seed. Therefore take NIH
Mt 1:22 that it **m** be fulfilled which was spoken of NIG
2:15 that it **m** be fulfilled which was spoken of NIG
2:23 that it **m** be fulfilled which was spoken by NIG
4:14 That it **m** be fulfilled which was spoken by NIG
8:17 That it **m** be fulfilled which was spoken by 3704
8:28 so that no *man* **m** pass by that way. 2480
12:10 the sabbath days? that they **m** accuse him. NIG
12:14 against him, how they **m** destroy him. NIG
12:17 That it **m** be fulfilled which was spoken by NIG
13:35 That it **m** be fulfilled which was spoken by NIG
14:36 And besought him that they **m** only touch NIG
21: 4 that it **m** be fulfilled which was spoken by NIG
21:32 not afterward, that *ye* **m** believe him. NIG
21:34 that *they* **m** receive the fruits of it. NIG
22:15 took counsel how they **m** entangle him in NIG
26: 4 And consulted that they **m** take Jesus by NIG
26: 9 For this ointment **m have** been sold for *1410*
26:56 that the scriptures of the prophets **m** be NIG
27:35 that it **m** be fulfilled which was spoken by NIG
Mk 3: 2 on the sabbath day; that they **m** accuse him. NIG
3: 6 against him, how they **m** destroy him. NIG
3:14 and that he **m** send them forth to preach, NIG
5:18 the devil prayed him that he **m** be with him. NIG
6:56 besought him that they **m** touch if it were NIG
10:51 unto him, Lord, that I **m** receive my sight. NIG
11:13 if haply he **m** find any *thing* thereon: NIG
11:18 and sought how they **m** destroy him: NIG
12: 2 that he **m** receive from the husbandmen of NIG
14: 1 the scribes sought how they **m** take him by NIG
14: 5 For it **m** have been sold for more than three NIG
14:11 And he sought how he **m** conveniently NIG
14:35 it were possible, the hour **m** pass from him. NIG
16: 1 that they **m** come and anoint him. NIG
Lk 1:74 of our enemies **m** serve him without fear, NIG
4:29 that *they* **m** cast him down headlong. NIG
5:19 not find by what *way* they **m** bring him in NIG
6: 7 that they **m** find an accusation against him. NIG
6:11 communed one with another what they **m** do *302*
8: 9 asked him, saying, What **m** this parable be? NIG
8:10 that seeing they **m** not see, and hearing they NIG
8:10 not see, and hearing they **m** not understand. NIG
8:38 besought him that *he* **m** be with him: NIG
11:54 out of his mouth, that they **m** accuse him. NIG
15:29 a kid, that I **m** make merry with my friends: NIG
17: 6 ye **m** say unto this sycamine tree, Be thou *302*
19:15 that he **m** know how much every *man* had NIG
19:23 that at my coming I **m have** required *mine* *302*
19:48 And could not find what they **m** do: for all NIG
20:20 *men,* that they **m** take hold of his words, NIG
20:20 *so they* **m** deliver him unto the power and NIG
22: 2 and scribes sought how they **m** kill him; NIG
22: 4 captains, how he **m** betray him unto them. NIG
23:23 requiring that he **m** be crucified. NIG
23:26 laid the cross, that *he* **m** bear *it* after Jesus. NIG
24:45 that *they* **m** understand the scriptures, NIG
Jn 1: 7 that all *men* through him **m** believe. NIG
3:17 but that the world through him **m** be saved. NIG
5:34 but these *things* I say, that ye **m** be saved. NIG
5:40 ye will not come to me, that ye **m** have life. NIG
6:28 we do, that we **m** work the works of God? NIG
8: 6 that they **m** have to accuse him. NIG
9:36 Who is he, Lord, that I **m** believe on him? NIG
9:39 this world, that they which see not **m** see; NIG
9:39 and that they which see **m** be made blind. NIG
10:10 I am come that they **m** have life, and NIG
10:10 and that they **m** have *it more* abundantly. NIG
10:17 I lay down my life, that I **m** take it again. NIG
11: 4 that the Son of God **m** be glorified thereby. NIG
11:57 he should shew *it,* that they **m** take him. NIG
12: 9 sake only, but that they **m** see Lazarus also, NIG
12:10 But the chief priests consulted that they **m** NIG
12:38 That the saying of Esaias the prophet **m** be NIG
14:29 that, when it is come to pass, ye **m** believe. NIG
15:11 that my joy **m** remain in you, and *that* your NIG
15:11 remain in you, and *that* your joy **m** be full. NIG
15:25 But *this cometh to pass,* that the word **m** be NIG
16:33 unto you, that in me ye **m** have peace. NIG
17: 3 that they **m** know thee the only true God, NIG
17:12 that the scripture **m** be fulfilled. NIG
17:13 that they **m** have my joy fulfilled in NIG
17:19 that they also **m** be sanctified through NIG
18: 9 That the saying **m** be fulfilled, which he NIG
18:28 be defiled; but that they **m** eat the passover. NIG
18:32 That the saying of Jesus **m** be fulfilled, NIG
19:24 that the scripture **m** be fulfilled, which saith, NIG
19:28 that the scripture **m** be fulfilled, saith, NIG
19:31 besought Pilate that their legs **m** be broken, NIG
19:31 be broken, and *that* they **m** be taken away. NIG
19:35 that he saith true, that ye **m** believe. NIG
19:38 besought Pilate that he **m** take away NIG
20:31 that ye **m** believe that Jesus is the Christ, NIG
20:31 that believing ye **m** have life through his NIG
Ac 1:25 that *he* **m** go to his own place. NIG
4:21 finding nothing how they **m** punish them, NIG
5:15 passing by **m** overshadow some of them. NIG
7:19 young children, to the end *they* **m** not live. NIG
8:15 that they **m** receive the Holy Ghost: NIG
Ac 9: 2 he **m** bring *them* bound unto Jerusalem. NIG
9:12 *his* hand on him, that he **m** receive his sight. NIG
9:21 came hither for that *intent,* that he **m** bring NIG
13:42 the Gentiles besought that these words **m** be NIG
15:17 That the residue of men **m** seek after NIG
17:27 if haply they **m** feel after him, and find *him,* NIG
20:24 so that *I* **m** finish my course with joy, and NIG
22:24 that he **m** know wherefore they cried so NIG
24:26 given him of Paul, that he **m** loose him: NIG
25:21 I commanded him to be kept till I **m** send NIG
25:26 I **m** have somewhat to write. NIG
26:32 This man **m have** been set at liberty, *1410*
27:12 if by any means they **m** attain to Phenice, *1410*
Ro 1:10 if by any means now at length I **m** have a NIG
1:13 that I **m** have some fruit among you also, NIG
3:26 that he **m** be just, and the justifier of him NIG
4:11 that he **m** be the father of all them that NIG
4:11 that righteousness **m** be imputed unto them NIG
4:16 *it is* of faith, that *it* **m** *be* by grace; NIG
4:16 to the end the promise **m** be sure to all NIG
4:18 that he **m** become the father of many NIG
5:20 the law entered, that the offence **m** abound. NIG
5:21 **m** grace reign through righteousness unto NIG
6: 6 *him,* that the body of sin **m** be destroyed, NIG
7:13 But sin, that it **m** appear sin, working death NIG
7:13 that sin by the commandment **m** become NIG
8: 4 That the righteousness of the law **m** be NIG
8:29 that he **m** be the firstborn amongst many NIG
9:11 of God according to election **m** stand, NIG
9:17 that I **m** shew my power in thee, and NIG
9:17 that my name **m** be declared throughout all NIG
9:23 And that he **m** make known the riches of his NIG
10: 1 to God for Israel is, that *they* **m** be saved. NIG
11:14 *are* my flesh, and **m** save some of them. NIG
11:19 were broken off, that I **m** be graffed in. NIG
11:32 in unbelief, that he **m** have mercy upon all. NIG
14: 9 that he **m** be Lord both of the dead and NIG
15: 4 and comfort of the scriptures **m** have hope. NIG
15: 9 And that the Gentiles **m** glorify God for *his* NIG
15:16 that the offering up of the Gentiles **m** be NIG
1Co 2:12 that we **m** know the *things* that are freely NIG
4: 6 that ye **m** learn in us not to think *of men* NIG
4: 8 ye did reign, that we also **m** reign with you. NIG
5: 2 that he that hath done this deed **m** be taken NIG
9:19 servant unto all, that I **m** gain the more. NIG
9:20 I became as a Jew, that I **m** gain *the* Jews; NIG
9:20 that I **m** gain them that are under the law; NIG
9:21 that I **m** gain them *that are* without law. NIG
9:22 became I as weak, that I **m** gain the weak: NIG
9:22 I am made all *things* to all *men,* that I **m** by NIG
9:23 that I **m** be partaker thereof with *you.* NIG
14:19 that *by my voice* I **m** teach others also, NIG
2Co 1:15 that you **m** have a second benefit; NIG
2: 4 that ye **m** know the love which I have more NIG
2: 9 did I write, that I **m** know the proof of you, NIG
4:10 that the life also of Jesus **m** be made NIG
4:11 that the life also of Jesus **m** be made NIG
4:15 that the abundant grace **m** through NIG
5: 4 that mortality **m** be swallowed up of life. NIG
5:21 that we **m** be made the righteousness of NIG
7: 9 that ye **m** receive damage by us in nothing. NIG
7:12 that our care for you in the sight of God **m** NIG
8: 9 that ye through his poverty **m** be rich. NIG
9: 5 that the same **m** be ready, as *a matter of* NIG
11: 4 not accepted, ye **m** well bear with *him.* NIG
11: 7 in abasing myself that you **m** be exalted, NIG
12: 8 the Lord thrice, that it **m** depart from me. NIG
Gal 1: 4 that he **m** deliver us from *this* present evil NIG
1:16 that I **m** preach him among the heathen; NIG
2: 4 that they **m** bring us into bondage: NIG
2: 5 that the truth of the gospel **m** continue with NIG
2:16 that we **m** be justified by the faith of Christ, NIG
2:19 am dead to the law, that I **m** live unto God. NIG
3:14 That the blessing of Abraham **m** come on NIG
3:14 that we **m** receive the promise of the Spirit NIG
3:22 that the promise by faith of Jesus Christ **m** NIG
3:24 unto Christ, that we **m** be justified by faith. NIG
4: 5 that we **m** receive the adoption of sons. NIG
4:17 would exclude you, that you **m** affect them. NIG
Eph 1:10 **m** gather together in one all *things* in Christ, NIG
1:21 and **m**, and dominion, and every name that *1411*
2: 7 That in the ages to come he **m** shew NIG
2:16 And *that* he **m** reconcile both unto God in NIG
3:10 powers in heavenly *places* **m** be known by NIG
3:16 to be strengthened with **m** by his Spirit in *1411*
3:19 that ye **m** be filled with all the fulness of NIG
4:10 above all heavens, that he **m** fill all *things.*) NIG
5:26 That he **m** sanctify and cleanse *it* with NIG
5:27 That he **m** present it to himself a glorious NIG
6:10 in the Lord, and in the power of his **m**. *2479*
6:22 that ye **m** know our affairs, and *that* he NIG
6:22 and *that* he **m** comfort your hearts. NIG
Php 3: 4 Though I **m** also have confidence in NIG
3: 4 that *he hath whereof he* **m** trust in the flesh, NIG
3:11 If by any means I **m** attain unto NIG
Col 1: 9 to desire that ye **m** be filled *with* NIG
1:10 That ye **m** walk worthy of the Lord unto all NIG
1:11 Strengthened with all **m**, according to his *1411*
1:18 that in all *things* he **m** have NIG
2: 2 That their hearts **m** be comforted, being knit NIG
4: 8 that he **m** know your estate, and NIG
1Th 2: 6 when we **m** have been burdensome, *1410*
2:16 speak to the Gentiles that they **m** be saved, NIG
3:10 day praying exceedingly that *we* **m** see your NIG
3:10 **m** perfect that which is lacking in your NIG
2Th 2: 6 that he **m** be revealed in his time. NIG
2:10 the love of the truth, that they **m** be saved. NIG
2:12 That they all **m** be damned who believed NIG
3: 8 that *we* **m** not be chargeable to any of you: NIG
1Ti 1:16 that in me first Jesus Christ **m** shew forth all NIG
2Ti 4:17 that by me the preaching **m** be fully known, NIG
4:17 and *that* all the Gentiles **m** hear: NIG
Tit 2:14 that he **m** redeem us from all iniquity, and NIG
3: 8 that they which have believed in God **m** be NIG
Phm 1: 8 though I **m** be much bold in Christ to enjoin NIG
Phm 1:13 that in thy stead he **m** have ministered unto NIG
Heb 2:14 that through death he **m** destroy him that NIG
2:17 that he **m** be a merciful and faithful high NIG
6:18 God to lie, we **m** have a strong consolation, NIG
9:15 they which are called **m** receive the promise NIG
10:36 the will of God, ye **m** receive the promise. NIG
11:15 they **m** have had opportunity to have *302*
11:35 that they **m** obtain a better resurrection: NIG
12:10 that *we* **m** be partakers of his holiness. NIG
12:18 For ye are not come unto the mount that **m** NIG
13:12 that he **m** sanctify the people with his own NIG
Jas 5:17 and he prayed earnestly that it **m** not rain: NIG
1Pe 1: 7 **m** be found unto praise and honour and NIG
1:21 that your faith and hope **m** be in God. NIG
3:18 for the unjust, that he **m** bring us to God, NIG
4: 6 that they **m** be judged according to men in NIG
2Pe 1: 4 that by these you **m** be partakers of NIG
2:11 which are greater in power and **m**, *1411*
1Jn 2:19 *they went out,* that they **m** be made manifest NIG
3: 8 that he **m** destroy the works of the devil. NIG
4: 9 into the world, that we **m** live through him. NIG
3Jn 1: 8 that we **m** be fellowhelpers to the truth. NIG
Rev 7:12 and honour, and power, and **m**, *2479*
12:14 that she **m** fly into the wilderness, into her NIG
12:15 that he **m** cause her to be carried away of NIG
13:17 And that no *man* **m** buy or sell, save he that *1410*
16:12 that the way of the kings of the east **m** be NIG

MIGHTEST (19) [MIGHT]

Dt 4:35 that thou **m** know that the LORD he *is* NIH
6: 2 That thou **m** fear the LORD thy God, NIH
Jdg 16: 6 wherewith thou **m** be bound to afflict thee. NIH
16:10 I pray thee, wherewith thou **m** be bound. NIH
16:13 tell me wherewith thou **m** be bound. And he NIH
1Sa 17:28 for thou art come down that *thou* **m** see NIH
Ne 9:29 that *thou* **m** bring them again unto thy law: NIH
Ps 8: 2 that *thou* **m** still the enemy and the avenger. NIH
51: 4 that thou **m** be justified when thou speakest, NIH
Pr 22:21 that *thou* **m** answer the words *of* truth to NIH
Da 2:30 *that* thou **m** know the thoughts of thy heart. NIH
Mt 15: 5 *by* whatsoever thou **m** be profited by me; NIG
Mk 7:11 *by* whatsoever thou **m** be profited by me; NIG
Lk 1: 4 That thou **m** know the certainty of *those* NIG
Ac 9:17 that thou **m** receive thy sight, and be filled NIG
Ro 3: 4 That thou **m** be justified in thy sayings, and NIG
3: 4 and **m** overcome when thou art judged. NIG
1Ti 1: 3 that thou **m** charge some that *they* teach no NIG
1:18 that thou by them **m** war a good warfare; NIG

MIGHTIER (13) [MIGHT]

Ge 26:16 Go from us; for thou art much **m** than we. 6105
Ex 1: 9 children of Israel *are* moe and **m** than we: 6099
Nu 14:12 of thee a greater nation and **m** than they. 6099
Dt 4:38 and **m** than thou *art,* to bring thee in, 6099
7: 1 seven nations greater and **m** than thou; 6099
9: 1 possess nations greater and **m** than thyself, 6099
9:14 I will make of thee a nation **m** and 6099
11:23 greater nations and **m** than yourselves. 6099
Ps 93: 4 The LORD on high *is* **m** than the noise of 117
Ecc 6:10 neither may he contend with him that *is* **m** 8623
Mt 3:11 but he that cometh after me is **m than** I, *2478*
Mk 1: 7 There cometh one **m than** I after me, *2478*
Lk 3:16 but one **m than** I cometh, the latchet of *2478*

MIGHTIES (2) [MIGHT]

1Ch 11:12 the Ahohite, who *was one* of the three **m**. 1368
11:24 and had the name among the three **m**. 1368

MIGHTIEST (1) [MIGHT]

1Ch 11:19 not drink it. These *things* did *these* three **m**. 1368

MIGHTILY (11) [MIGHT]

Dt 6: 3 well with thee, and that ye may increase **m**, 3966
Jdg 4: 3 twenty years he **m** oppressed 2393+871.1
14: 6 the spirit of the LORD **came m** upon him, 6743
15:14 the spirit of the LORD **came m** upon him, 6743
Jer 25:30 he shall **m roar** upon his habitation; 7580+7580
Jnh 3: 8 with sackcloth, and cry **m** unto God: 2394+871.1
Na 2: 1 make *thy* loins strong, fortify *thy* power **m**. 3966
Ac 18:28 For he **m** convinced the Jews, *and* *2159*
19:20 So **m** grew the word of God and *2596+2904*
Col 1:29 to his working, which worketh in me **m**. *1411*
Rev 18: 2 And he cried **m** with a strong voice, saying, *2479*

MIGHTY (284) [MIGHT]

Ge 6: 4 the same *became* **m** *men* which *were* of 1368
10: 8 he began to be a **m** *one* in the earth. 1368
10: 9 He was a **m** hunter before the LORD: 1368
10: 9 *Even* as Nimrod the **m** hunter before 1368
18:18 shall surely become a great and **m** nation, 6099
23: 6 thou *art* a **m** prince among us: in the choice 430
49:24 strong by the hands of the **m** *God* of Jacob; 46
Ex 1: 7 and multiplied, and **waxed** exceeding **m**; 6105
1:20 the people multiplied, and **waxed** very **m**. 6105
3:19 will not let you go, no, not by a **m** hand. 2389
9:28 that there be no *more* **m** thunderings and 430
10:19 the LORD turned a **m** strong west wind, 3966
15:10 they sank as lead in the **m** waters. 117
15:15 the **m men** of Moab, trembling shall take 352
32:11 with great power, and with a **m** hand? 2389
Lev 19:15 the poor, nor honour the person of the **m**: 1419
Nu 22: 6 me this people; for they *are* too **m** for me: 6099
Dt 3:24 thy servant thy greatness, and thy **m** hand: 2389
4:34 by a **m** hand, and by a stretched out arm, 2389
4:37 brought thee out in his sight with his **m** 1419
5:15 brought thee out thence through a **m** hand 2389
6:21 brought us out of Egypt with a **m** hand: 2389
7: 8 hath the LORD brought you out with a **m** 2389
7:19 and the **m** hand, and the stretched out arm, 2389
7:21 God *is* among you, a **m** God and terrible. 1419
7:23 shall destroy them *with* a **m** destruction, 1419
9:26 brought forth out of Egypt with a **m** hand. 2389
9:29 which thou broughtest out by thy **m** power 1419
10:17 of lords, a great God, a **m**, and a terrible, 1368

Dt 11: 2 his **m** hand, and his stretched out arm, 2389
26: 5 there a nation, great, **m**, and populous: 6099
26: 8 us forth out of Egypt with a **m** hand, 2389
34:12 in all *that* **m** hand, and in all the great terror 2389
Jos 1:14 all the **m** *men* of valour, and help them; 1368
4:24 know the hand of the LORD, that it *is* **m**: 2389
6: 2 the king thereof, *and* the **m** *men* of valour. 1368
8: 3 Joshua chose out thirty thousand **m** *men* of 1368
10: 2 than Ai, and all the men thereof *were* **m**. 1368
10: 7 war with him, and all the **m** *men* of valour. 1368
Jdg 5:13 made me have dominion over the **m**. 1368
5:22 the pransings, the pransings of their **m** *ones*. 47
5:23 to the help of the LORD against the **m**. 1368
6:12 LORD *is* with thee, thou **m** *man* of valour. 1368
11: 1 Now Jephthah the Gileadite was a **m** *man* 1368
Ru 2: 1 a **m** man of wealth, of the family of 1368
1Sa 2: 4 The bows of the **m** *men are* broken, and 1368
4: 8 deliver us out of the hand of these **m** Gods? 117
9: 1 of Aphiah, a Benjamite, a **m** *man* of power. 1368
16:18 and a **m** valiant *man*, and a man of war, and 1368
2Sa 1:19 upon thy high places: how are the **m** fallen! 1368
1:21 for there the shield of the **m** is vilely cast 1368
1:22 the blood of the slain, from the fat of the **m**, 1368
1:25 How are the **m** fallen in the midst of 1368
1:27 How are the **m** fallen, and the weapons of 1368
10: 7 he sent Joab, and all the host *of* the **m** *men*. 1368
16: 6 all the **m** *men were* on his right hand and 1368
17: 8 that they *be* **m** *men*, and they *be* chafed in 1368
17:10 for all Israel knoweth that thy father *is* a **m** 1368
20: 7 all the **m** *men*: and they went out of 1368
23: 8 These *be* the names of the **m** *men* whom 1368
23: 9 *one* of the three **m** *men* with David, 1368
23:16 the three **m** *men* brake through the host of 1368
23:17 These *things* did *these* three **m** *men*. 1368
23:22 and had the name among three **m** *men*. 1368
1Ki 1: 8 and the **m** *men* which *belonged* to David, 1368
1:10 and the **m** *men*, and Solomon his brother, 1368
11:28 the man Jeroboam *was* a **m** *man* of valour: 1368
2Ki 5: 1 he was also a **m** *man* in valour, *but he was* 1368
15:20 *even* of all the **m** *men* of wealth, of each 1368
24:14 all the princes, and all the **m** *men* of valour, 1368
24:15 and his officers, and the **m** of the land, 352
1Ch 1:10 he began to be **m** upon the earth. 1368
5:24 Hodaviah, and Jahdiel, **m** *men* of valour, 1368
7: 7 the house of *their* fathers, **m** *men* of valour; 1368
7: 9 **m** *men* of valour, *was* twenty thousand and 1368
7:11 **m** *men* of valour, *were* seventeen thousand 1368
7:40 choice *and* **m** *men* of valour, chief of 1368
8:40 the sons of Ulam were **m** men of valour, 1368
11:10 These also *are* the chief of the **m** *men* 1368
11:11 this *is* the number of the **m** *men* whom 1368
12: 1 they *were* among the **m** *men*, helpers of 1368
12: 4 a **m** *man* among the thirty, and over 1368
12:21 *rovers*: for they *were* all **m** *men* of valour, 1368
12:25 **m** *men* of valour for the war, 1368
12:28 a young man **m** of valour, and *of* his 1368
12:30 and eight hundred, **m** *men* of valour, 1368
19: 8 he sent Joab, and all the host *of* the **m** *men*. 1368
26: 6 their father: for they *were* **m** *men* of valour. 1368
26:31 there were found among them **m** *men* of 1368
27: 6 *who was* **m** among the thirty, and above 1368
28: 1 *with* the **m** *men*, and with all the valiant 1368
29:24 the **m** *men*, and all the sons likewise of 1368
2Ch 6:32 and thy **m** hand, and thy stretched out arm; 2389
13: 3 chosen men, *being* **m** *men* of valour. 1368
13:21 Abijah **waxed m**, and married fourteen 2388
14: 8 all these *were* **m** *men* of valour. 1368
17:13 the men of war, **m** *men* of valour, *were* in 1368
17:14 with him **m** *men* of valour three hundred 1368
17:16 with him two hundred thousand **m** *men* of 1368
17:17 Eliada a **m** *man* of valour, and with him 1368
25: 6 He hired also an hundred thousand **m** *men* 1368
26:12 of the **m** *men* of valour *were* two thousand 1368
26:13 five hundred, that made war with **m** power, 2428
27: 6 So Jotham **became m**, because he prepared 2388
28: 7 Zichri, a **m** *man* of Ephraim, slew 1368
32: 3 his **m** *men* to stop the waters of 1368
32:21 which cut off all the **m** *men* of valour, and 1368
Ezr 4:20 There have been **m** kings also over 8624
7:28 and before all the king's **m** princes. 1368
Ne 3:16 was made, and unto the house of the **m**. 1368
9:11 into the deeps, as a stone into the **m** waters. 5794
9:32 the great, the **m**, and the terrible God, 1368
11:14 **m** *men* of valour, an hundred twenty and 1368
Job 5:15 their mouth, and from the hand of the **m**. 2389
6:23 or, Redeem me from the hand of the **m**? 6184
9: 4 *He is* wise in heart, and **m** in strength: 533
12:19 away spoiled, and overthroweth the **m**. 386
12:21 and weakeneth the strength of the **m**. 650
21: 7 become old, yea, are **m** *in* power? 1396
22: 8 *as for* the **m** man, he had the earth; and 2220
24:22 He draweth also the **m** with his power: 47
34:20 and the **m** shall be taken away without hand. 47
34:24 He shall break in pieces **m** *men* without 3524
35: 9 they cry out by reason of the arm of the **m**. 7227
36: 5 God *is* **m**, and despiseth not *any*: *he is* 3524
36: 5 despiseth not *any*: *he is* **m** in strength *and* 3524
41:25 When he raiseth up *himself*, the **m** are 352
Ps 24: 8 the LORD strong and **m**, the LORD 1368
24: 8 and mighty, the LORD **m** *in* battle. 1368
29: 1 Give unto the LORD, O ye **m**, give 410+1121
33:16 a **m** *man* is not delivered by much strength. 1368
45: 3 O *most* **m**, *with* thy glory and thy majesty. 1368
50: 1 The **m** God, *even* the LORD, hath spoken, 410
52: 1 O **m** *man*? the goodness of God *endureth* 1368
59: 3 the **m** are gathered against me; not *for* my 5794
68:33 doth send out his voice, *and that* a **m** voice. 5797
69: 4 *being* mine enemies wrongfully, are **m**: 6105
74:15 and the flood: thou driedst up **m** rivers. 386
78:65 like a **m** *man* that shouteth by reason of 1368
82: 1 God standeth in the congregation of the **m**; 410
89: 6 *who* among the sons of the **m** can be likened 410
89:13 Thou hast a **m** arm: strong is thy 1369+5973
89:19 saidst, I have laid help upon *one that is* **m**; 1368
89:50 my bosom *the reproach of* all the **m** people; 7227
Ps 93: 4 *yea, than* the **m** waves of the sea. 117
106: 2 Who can utter the **m acts** of the LORD? 1369
106: 8 that *he* might make his **m power** to be 1369
112: 2 His seed shall be **m** upon earth: 1368
120: 4 Sharp arrows of the **m**, with coals of 1368
127: 4 As arrows *are* in the hand of a **m** *man*; so 1368
132: 2 *and* vowed unto the **m** *God* of Jacob; 46
132: 5 a habitation for the **m** *God* of Jacob. 46
135:10 smote great nations, and slew **m** kings; 6099
145: 4 to another, and shall declare thy **m acts**. 1369
145:12 make known to the sons of men his **m acts**, 1369
150: 2 Praise him for his **m acts**: praise him 1369
Pr 16:32 *that is* slow to anger *is* better than the **m**; 1368
18:18 to cease, and parteth between the **m**. 6099
21:22 A wise *man* scaleth the city of the **m**, and 1368
23:11 For their Redeemer *is* **m**; he shall plead 2389
Ecc 7:19 more than ten **m** *men* which are in the city. 7989
SS 4: 4 a thousand bucklers, all shields of **m** *men*. 1368
Isa 1:24 the LORD of hosts, the **m One** of Israel, Ah, 46
3: 2 The **m** *man*, and the man of war, the judge, 1368
3:25 fall by the sword, and thy **m** in the war. 1369
5:15 the **m** man shall be humbled, and the eyes NIH
5:22 Woe unto *them that are* **m** to drink wine, 1368
9: 6 Counseller, The **m** God, The everlasting 1368
10:21 *even* the remnant of Jacob, unto the **m** God. 1368
10:34 with iron, and Lebanon shall fall by a **m one**. 117
11:15 with his **m** wind shall he shake his hand 5868
13: 3 I have also called my **m ones** for mine 1368
17:12 *that* make a rushing like the rushing of **m** 3524
21:17 the **m** *men* of the children of Kedar, 1368
22:17 the LORD will carry thee away with a **m** 1397
28: 2 the LORD hath a **m** and strong one, 2389
28: 2 as a flood of **m** waters overflowing, 3524
30:29 of the LORD, to the **m One** of Israel. 6697
31: 8 fall with the sword, not of a **m** man; NIH
42:13 The LORD shall go forth as a **m** *man*, he 1368
43:16 way in the sea, and a path in the **m** waters; 5794
49:24 Shall the prey be taken from the **m**, or 1368
49:25 Even the captives of the **m** shall be taken 1368
49:26 and thy redeemer, the **m One** of Jacob. 46
60:16 and thy redeemer, the **m One** of Jacob. 46
63: 1 I that speak in righteousness, **m** to save. 7227
Jer 5:15 it *is* a **m** nation, it *is* an ancient nation, 386
5:16 as an open sepulchre, they *are* all **m** *men*. 1368
9:23 neither let the **m** *man* glory in his might, 1368
14: 9 man astonied, as a **m** *man that* cannot save? 1368
20:11 the LORD *is* with me as a **m** terrible one: 1368
26:21 with all his **m** *men*, and all the princes, 1368
32:18 the Great, the **M** God, the LORD of hosts, 1368
32:19 Great in counsel, and **m** in work: for thine 7227
33: 3 and **m** *things*, which thou knowest not. 1219
41:16 *even* **m** men of war, and the women, and 1397
46: 5 their **m ones** are beaten down, and are fled 1368
46: 6 the swift flee away, nor the **m** *man* escape; 1368
46: 9 ye chariots; and let the **m** *men* come forth; 1368
46:12 for the **m** *man* hath stumbled against 1368
46:12 mighty *man* hath stumbled against the **m**, 1368
48:14 We *are* **m** and strong men for the war? 1368
48:41 the **m** *men's* hearts in Moab at that day 1368
49:22 at that day shall the heart of the **m** *men* of 1368
50: 9 their arrows *shall be* as of a **m** expert *man*; 1368
50:36 a sword *is* upon her **m** *men*; and they shall 1368
51:30 The **m** *men* of Babylon have forborn to 1368
51:56 upon Babylon, and her **m** *men* are taken, 1368
51:57 her **m** *men*: and they shall sleep a perpetual 1368
La 1:15 The Lord hath trodden under foot all my **m** 47
Eze 17:13 of him: he hath also taken the **m** of the land: 352
17:17 Neither shall Pharaoh with *his* **m** army and 1419
20:33 surely with a **m** hand, and with a stretched 2389
20:34 with a **m** hand, and with a stretched out 2389
31:11 delivered him into the hand of the **m one** of 410
32:12 By the swords of the **m** will I cause thy 1368
32:21 The strong among the **m** shall speak to him 1368
32:27 they shall not lie with the **m** *that are* fallen 1368
32:27 though *they were* the terror of the **m** in 1368
38:15 a great company, and a **m** army: 7227
39:18 Ye shall eat the flesh of the **m**, and 1368
39:20 with **m** *men*, and *with* all men of war, 1368
Da 3:20 **most m men** that *were* in his 1400+1401+2429
4: 3 how **m** *are* his wonders! his kingdom *is* an 8624
8:24 his power shall be **m**, but not by his own 6105
8:24 shall destroy the **m** and the holy people. 6099
9:15 out of the land of Egypt with a **m** hand, 2389
11: 3 a **m** king shall stand up, that shall rule *with* 1368
11:25 up to battle with a very great and **m** army; 6099
Hos 10:13 in thy way, in the multitude of thy **m** *men*. 1368
Joel 2: 7 They shall run like **m** *men*; they shall climb 1368
3: 9 wake up the **m** *men*, let all the men of war 1368
3:11 thither cause thy **m ones** to come down, 1368
Am 2:14 neither shall the **m** deliver himself: 1368
2:16 he *that is* courageous among the **m** shall 1368
5:12 manifold transgressions and your **m** sins: 6099
5:24 as waters, and righteousness as a **m** stream. 386
Ob 1: 9 thy **m** *men*, O Teman, shall be dismayed, 1368
Jnh 1: 4 there was a **m** tempest in the sea, so that 1419
Na 2: 3 The shield of his **m** *men is* made red, 1368
Hab 1:12 and, O **m God**, thou hast established them 6697
Zep 1:14 the **m** *man* shall cry there bitterly. 1368
3:17 LORD thy God in the midst of thee *is* **m**; 1368
Zec 9:13 and made thee as the sword of a **m** *man*. 1368
10: 5 they shall be as **m** *men*, which tread down 1368
10: 7 And *they of* Ephraim shall be like a **m** *man*, 1368
11: 2 cedar is fallen; because the **m** are spoiled: 117
Mt 11:20 wherein most of his **m works** were done, *1411*
11:21 for if the **m works** which were done in you, *1411*
11:23 for if the **m works**, which have been done *1411*
13:54 this *man* this wisdom, and *these* **m works**? *1411*
13:58 And he did not many **m works** there, *1411*
14: 2 **m works** do shew forth themselves in him. *1411*
Mk 6: 2 that even such **m works** are wrought by his *1411*
6: 5 And he could there do no **m work**, *1411*
6:14 **m works** do shew forth themselves in him. *1411*
Lk 1:49 For he *that is* **m** hath done to me great *1415*
1:52 He hath put down the **m** from *their* seats, *1413*
9:43 And they were all amazed at the **m power** *3168*
Lk 10:13 for if the **m works** had been done in Tyre *1411*
15:14 there arose a **m** famine in that land; *2478*
19:37 for all the **m works** that they had seen; *1411*
24:19 which was a prophet **m** in deed and *1415*
Ac 2: 2 a sound from heaven as of a rushing **m** wind, *972*
7:22 and was **m** in words and in deeds. *1415*
18:24 an eloquent man, *and* **m** in the scriptures, *1415*
Ro 15:19 Through **m** signs and wonders, by *1411*
1Co 1:26 not many **m**, not many noble, *are called*: *1415*
1:27 world to confound the *things which are* **m**; *2478*
2Co 10: 4 **m** through God to the pulling down of *1415*
12:12 in signs, and wonders, and **m deeds**. *1411*
13: 3 to you-ward is not weak, but is **m** in you. *1414*
Gal 2: 8 *the same* was **m in** me towards *1754*
Eph 1:19 according to the working of his **m** power, *2904*
2Th 1: 7 be revealed from heaven with his **m** angels, *1411*
1Pe 5: 6 therefore under the **m** hand of God, *2900*
Rev 6:13 when she is shaken of a **m** wind. *3173*
6:15 and the **m** *men*, and every bondman, and *1415*
10: 1 And I saw another **m** angel come down *2478*
16:18 the earth, so **m** an earthquake, *and* so great. *5082*
18:10 alas, *that* great city Babylon, *that* **m** city! *2478*
18:21 And a **m** angel took up a stone like a great *2478*
19: 6 and as the voice of **m** thunderings, saying, *2478*
19:18 and the flesh of **m** *men*, and the flesh of *2478*

MIGRON (2)

1Sa 14: 2 under a pomegranate tree which *is* in **M**: 4051
Isa 10:28 He is come to Aiath, he is passed to **M**; 4051

MIJAMIN (2)

1Ch 24: 9 The fifth to Malchijah, the sixth to **M**, 4326
Ne 10: 7 Meshullam, Abijah, **M**, 4326

MIKLOTH (4)

1Ch 8:32 **M** begat Shimeah. And these also dwelt 4732
9:37 and Ahio, and Zechariah, and **M**. 4732
9:38 **M** begat Shimeam. And they also dwelt 4732
27: 4 and *of* his course *was* **M** also the ruler: 4732

MIKNEIAH (2)

1Ch 15:18 and **M**, and Obed-edom, and Jeiel, 4737
15:21 **M**, and Obed-edom, and Jeiel, and 4737

MILALAI (1)

Ne 12:36 Shemaiah, and Azarael, **M**, Gilalai, Maai, 4450

MILCAH (11)

Ge 11:29 **M**, the daughter of Haran, the father of 4435
11:29 the father of **M**, and the father of Iscah. 4435
22:20 it was told Abraham, saying, Behold, **M**, 4435
22:23 these eight **M** did bear to Nahor, 4435
24:15 son of **M**, the wife of Nahor, 4435
24:24 I *am* the daughter of Bethuel the son of **M**, 4435
24:47 Nahor's son, whom **M** bare unto him: 4435
Nu 26:33 and Noah, Hoglah, **M**, and Tirzah. 4435
27: 1 Noah, and Hoglah, and **M**, and Tirzah. 4435
36:11 Tirzah, and Hoglah, and **M**, and Noah, 4435
Jos 17: 3 Mahlah, and Noah, Hoglah, **M**, and Tirzah. 4435

MILCH (3) [MILK]

Ge 32:15 Thirty **m** camels with their colts, forty kine, 3243
1Sa 6: 7 make a new cart, and take two **m** kine, 5763
6:10 took two **m** kine, and tied them to the cart, 5763

MILCOM (3) [MOLOCH]

1Ki 11: 5 after **M** the abomination of the Ammonites. 4445
11:33 **M** the god of the children of Ammon, and 4445
2Ki 23:13 for **M** the abomination of the children of 4445

MILDEW (5)

Dt 28:22 the sword, and with blasting, and with **m**; 3420
1Ki 8:37 **m**, locust, *or* if there be caterpillar; 3420
2Ch 6:28 be blasting, or **m**, locusts, or caterpillars; 3420
Am 4: 9 I have smitten you with blasting and **m**: 3420
Hag 2:17 I smote you with blasting and with **m** and 3420

MILE (1)

Mt 5:41 whosoever shall compel thee to go a **m**, *3400*

MILES See FURLONGS

MILETUM (1) [MILETUS]

2Ti 4:20 but Trophimus have I left at **M** sick. *3399*

MILETUS (2) [MILETUM]

Ac 20:15 and the next *day* we came to **M**. *3399*
20:17 And from **M** he sent to Ephesus, and *3399*

MILK (48) [MILCH]

Ge 18: 8 **m**, and the calf which he had dressed, and 2461
49:12 red with wine, and *his* teeth white with **m**. 2461
Ex 3: 8 unto a land flowing with **m** and honey; 2461
3:17 unto a land flowing with **m** and honey. 2461
13: 5 a land flowing with **m** and honey, 2461
23:19 shalt not seethe a kid in his mother's **m**. 2461
33: 3 Unto a land flowing with **m** and honey: 2461
34:26 shalt not seethe a kid in his mother's **m**. 2461
Lev 20:24 a land that floweth with **m** and honey: 2461
Nu 13:27 and surely it floweth with **m** and honey; 2461
14: 8 a land which floweth with **m** and honey. 2461
16:13 us up out of a land that floweth with **m** 2461
16:14 brought us into a land that floweth with **m** 2461
Dt 6: 3 *in* the land that floweth with **m** and honey. 2461
11: 9 a land that floweth with **m** and honey. 2461
14:21 shalt not seethe a kid in his mother's **m**. 2461
26: 9 *even* a land that floweth with **m** and honey. 2461
26:15 a land that floweth with **m** and honey. 2461
27: 3 a land that floweth with **m** and honey; 2461
31:20 that floweth with **m** and honey; 2461
32:14 Butter of kine, and **m** of sheep, with fat of 2461
Jos 5: 6 a land that floweth with **m** and honey. 2461
Jdg 4:19 she opened a bottle of **m**, and gave him 2461

M

Jdg 5:25 He asked water, *and* she gave *him* **m**; 2461
Job 10:10 Hast thou not poured me out as **m**, and 2461
21:24 His breasts are full *of* **m**, and his bones are 2461
Pr 27:27 *thou shalt have* goats' **m** enough for thy 2461
30:33 Surely the churning of **m** bringeth forth 2461
SS 4:11 honey and **m** *are* under thy tongue; and 2461
5: 1 I have drunk my wine with my **m**: 2461
5:12 of waters, washed with **m**, *and* fitly set. 2461
Isa 7:22 for the abundance of **m** *that they* shall give 2461
28: 9 them that are weaned from the **m**, *and* 2461
55: 1 buy wine and **m** without money and 2461
60:16 Thou shalt also suck the **m** of the Gentiles, 2461
66:11 that ye may **m out**, and be delighted with 4711
Jer 11: 5 to give them a land flowing with **m** and 2461
32:22 a land flowing with **m** and honey; 2461
La 4: 7 purer than snow, they were whiter than **m**, 2461
Eze 20: 6 flowing with **m** and honey, which *is* 2461
20:15 which I had given *them*, flowing with **m** 2461
25: 4 eat thy fruit, and they shall drink thy **m**. 2461
Joel 3:18 the hills shall flow *with* **m**, and all 2461
1Co 3: 2 I have fed you with **m**, and not with meat: 1051
9: 7 and eateth not of the **m** of the flock? 1051
Heb 5:12 and are become such as have need of **m**, 1051
5:13 For every one that useth **m** *is* unskilful in 1051
1Pe 2: 2 desire the sincere **m** of the word, 1051

MILL (2) [MILLS, MILLSTONE, MILLSTONES]
Ex 11: 5 of the maidservant that *is* behind the **m**; 7347
Mt 24:41 Two *women shall be* grinding at the **m**; 3459

MILLET (1)
Eze 4: 9 **m**, and fitches, and put them in one vessel, 1764

MILLIONS (1)
Ge 24:60 be thou *the mother* of thousands of **m**, and 7233

MILLO (10)
Jdg 9: 6 all the house of **M**, and went, and 4407
9:20 the men of Shechem, and the house of **M**; 4407
9:20 from the house of **M**, and 4407
2Sa 5: 9 David built round about from **M** and 4407
1Ki 9:15 **M**, and the wall of Jerusalem, and Hazor, 4407
9:24 had built for her: then did he build **M**. 4407
11:27 Solomon built **M**, *and* repaired the breaches 4407
2Ki 12:20 slew Joash *in* the house of **M**, 4407
1Ch 11: 8 round about, even from **M** round about: 4407
2Ch 32: 5 repaired **M** *in* the city of David, and 4407

MILLS (1) [MILL]
Nu 11: 8 gathered *it*, and ground *it* in **m**, or beat *it* in 7347

MILLSTONE (9) [MILL]
Dt 24: 6 take the nether or the **upper m** to pledge: 7393
Jdg 9:53 a certain woman cast a piece of a **m** upon 7393
2Sa 11:21 did not a woman cast a piece of a **m** upon 7393
Job 41:24 yea, as hard as a piece of the nether *m*. NIH
Mt 18: 6 it were better for him that a **m** were 3458+3684
Mk 9:42 it is better for him that a **m** were 3037+3457
Lk 17: 2 It were better for him that a **m** were 3458+3684
Rev 18:21 angel took up a stone like a great **m**, 3458
18:22 the sound of a **m** shall be heard no more at 3458

MILLSTONES (2) [MILL]
Isa 47: 2 Take the **m**, and grind meal: uncover thy 7347
Jer 25:10 the sound of the **m**, and the light of 7347

MINAH See MANEH

MINCING (1)
Isa 3:16 walking and **m** *as* they go, and making a 2952

MIND (95) [FEEBLEMINDED, HIGHMINDED, HIGH-MINDED, LIKEMINDED, MINDED, MINDFUL, MINDING, MINDS, UNMINDFUL]
Ge 23: 8 If it be your **m** that I should bury my dead 5315
26:35 Which were a grief of **m** unto Isaac and 7307
Lev 24:12 that the **m** of the LORD might be shewed 6310
Nu 16:28 for *I have* not *done them* of mine own **m**. 3820
24:13 to do *either* good or bad of mine own **m**; 3820
Dt 18: 6 come with all the desire of his **m** unto 5315
28:65 and failing of eyes, and sorrow of **m**: 5315
30: 1 thou shalt call *them* to **m** among all 3824
1Sa 2:35 to *that* which *is* in my heart and in my **m**: 5315
9:20 lost three days ago, set not thy **m** on them; 3820
1Ch 22: 7 it was in my **m** to build a house unto 3824
28: 9 with a perfect heart and with a willing **m**: 5315
Ne 4: 6 for the people had a **m** to work. 3820
Job 23:13 he *is* in one *m*, and who can turn him? and NIH
34:33 *Should it be* **according to** thy **m**? 4480+5973
Ps 31:12 I am forgotten as a dead man out of **m**: 3820
Pr 21:27 *when* he bringeth it with a **wicked m**? 2154
29:11 A fool uttereth all his **m**: but a wise *man* 7307
Isa 26: 3 *whose* **m** *is* stayed *on thee*: because 3336
46: 8 bring *it* again to **m**, O ye transgressors. 3820
65:17 shall not be remembered, nor come into **m**. 3820
Jer 3:16 neither shall it come to **m**: neither shall 3820
15: 1 *yet* my **m** *could* not *be* toward this people: 5315
19: 5 nor spake *it*, neither came *it* into my **m**: 3820
32:35 them not, neither came it into my **m**, 3820
44:21 and came it *not* into his **m**? 3820
51:50 and let Jerusalem come into your **m**. 3824
La 3:21 This I recall to my **m**, therefore have I 3820
Eze 11: 5 I know the things that come into your **m**, 7307
20:32 that which cometh into your **m** shall not be 7307
23:17 and her **m** was alienated from them. 5315
23:18 my **m** was alienated from her, like as my 5315
23:18 like as my **m** was alienated from her sister. 5315
23:22 from whom thy **m** is alienated, and I will 5315
23:28 into the hand *of them* from whom thy **m** is 5315
38:10 the same time shall things come into thy **m**, 3824
Da 2:29 thy thoughts came *into thy* **m** upon thy bed, NIH
5:20 was lifted up, and his **m** hardened in pride, 7308
Hab 1:11 shall *his* **m** change, and he shall pass over, 7307
Mt 22:37 and with all thy soul, and with all thy **m**. 1271
Mk 5:15 sitting, and clothed, and **in his right m**: 4993
12:30 and with all thy **m**, and with all thy 1271
14:72 And Peter **called to m** the word that Jesus 363
Lk 1:29 **cast in** her **m** what manner of salutation 1260
8:35 feet of Jesus, clothed, and **in his right m**: 4993
10:27 with all thy strength, and with all thy **m**; 1271
12:29 ye shall drink, neither be ye of **doubtful m**. 3349
Ac 17:11 received the word with all **readiness of m**, 4288
20:19 Serving the Lord with all **humility of m**, 5012
Ro 1:28 God gave them over to a reprobate **m**, to do 3563
7:23 warring against the law of my **m**, and 3563
7:25 with the **m** I myself serve the law of God; 3563
8: 5 For they that are after the flesh do **m** 5426
8: 7 Because the carnal **m** *is* enmity against 5427
8:27 hearts knoweth what *is* the **m** of the Spirit, 5427
11:34 For who hath known the **m** of the Lord? or 3563
12: 2 ye transformed by the renewing of your **m**, 3563
12:16 *Be* of the same **m** one towards another. 5426
12:16 **M** not high *things*, but condescend to *men* 5426
14: 5 every man be fully persuaded in his own **m**. 3563
15: 6 That ye may with **one m** *and* one mouth 3661
15:15 as **putting** you **in m**, because of the grace 1878
1Co 1:10 be perfectly joined together in the same **m** 3563
2:16 For who hath known the **m** of the Lord, 3563
2:16 instruct him? But we have the **m** of Christ. 3563
2Co 7: 7 your mourning, your **fervent m** toward me; 2205
8:12 For if there be first a **willing m**, *it is* 4288
8:19 and *declaration of* your **ready m**: 4288
9: 2 For I know the **forwardness** of your **m**, 4288
13:11 good comfort, be of one **m**, live in peace; 5426
Eph 2: 3 the desires of the flesh and of the **m**; 1271
4:17 Gentiles walk, in the vanity of their **m**, 3563
4:23 And be renewed in the spirit of your **m**; 3563
Php 1:27 with one **m** striving together for the faith of 5590
2: 2 same love, *being* of one accord, of one **m**. 5426
2: 3 in **lowliness of m** *let* each esteem other 5012
2: 5 Let this **m** be in you, which *was* also in 5426
3:16 by the same rule, *let us* **m** the same *thing*. 5426
3:19 *is* in their shame, who **m** earthly *things*.) 5426
4: 2 that *they* be of the same **m** in the Lord. 5426
Col 1:21 and enemies in *your* **m** by wicked works, 1271
2:18 not seen, vainly puft up by his fleshly **m**, 3563
3:12 kindness, **humbleness of m**, meekness, 5012
2Th 2: 2 That ye be not soon shaken in **m**, or 3563
2Ti 1: 7 of power, and of love, and of a **sound m**. 4995
Tit 1:15 but even their **m** and conscience is defiled. 3563
3: 1 **Put** them **in m** to be subject to 5279
Phm 1:14 But without thy **m** would I do nothing; 1106
Heb 8:10 I will put my laws into their **m**, and 1271
1Pe 1:13 Wherefore gird up the loins of your **m**, 1271
3: 8 Finally, *be ye* all **of one m**, 3675
4: 1 arm yourselves likewise with the same **m**: 1771
5: 2 not for filthy lucre, but **of a ready m**; 4290
Rev 17: 9 *And* here *is* the **m** which hath wisdom. 3563
17:13 These have one **m**, and shall give their 1106

MINDED (15) [MIND]
Ru 1:18 When she saw that she *was* **stedfastly m** to 553
2Ch 24: 4 *that* Joash was **m** to repair the house 3820+5973
Ezr 7:13 *which are* **m** of their **own freewill** to go *up* 5069
Mt 1:19 was **m** to put her away privily. 1014
Ac 27:39 into the which they were **m**, if it were 1011
Ro 8: 6 For to be carnally **m** *is* death; 5427
8: 6 but to be spiritually **m** *is* life and peace. 5427
2Co 1:15 And in this confidence I was **m** to come 1014
1:17 When I therefore was thus **m**, did I use 1011
Gal 5:10 that you will be none otherwise **m**: 5426
Php 3:15 as many as *be* perfect, be thus **m**: 5426
3:15 and if in any *thing* ye be otherwise **m**, 5426
Tit 2: 6 Young *men* likewise exhort to be **sober m**. 4993
Jas 1: 8 A **double m** man *is* unstable in all his 1374
4: 8 and purify *your* hearts, *ye* **double m**. 1374

MINDFUL (10) [MIND]
1Ch 16:15 Be ye **m** always of his covenant; the word 2142
Ne 9:17 neither were **m** of thy wonders that thou 2142
Ps 8: 4 What *is* man, that thou art **m** of him? and 2142
111: 5 fear him: he will ever be **m** of his covenant. 2142
115:12 The LORD hath been **m** of us: he will 2142
Isa 17:10 hast not been **m** of the rock of thy strength, 2142
2Ti 1: 4 desiring to see thee, being **m** of thy tears, 3415
Heb 2: 6 What is man, that thou art **m** of him? 3403
11:15 if they had been **m** of that *country* from 3421
2Pe 3: 2 That *ye* may be **m** of the words which were 3415

MINDING (1) [MIND]
Ac 20:13 so had he appointed, **m** himself to go afoot. 3195

MINDS (16) [MIND]
Jdg 19:30 of it, take advice, and speak *your* **m**. NIH
2Sa 17: 8 mighty men, and they *be* chafed in their **m**, 5315
2Ki 9:15 If it be your **m**, *then* let none go forth *nor* 5315
Eze 24:25 that whereupon they set their **m**, their sons 5315
36: 5 with despiteful **m**, to cast it out for a prey. 5315
Ac 14: 2 made their **m** evil affected against 5590
28: 6 they changed *their* **m**, and said that he was a NIG
2Co 3:14 But their **m** were blinded: for until this day 3540
4: 4 blinded the **m** of them which believe not, 3540
11: 3 your **m** should be corrupted from 3540
Php 4: 7 your hearts and **m** through Christ Jesus. 3540
1Ti 6: 5 Perverse disputings of men of corrupt **m**, 3563
2Ti 3: 8 men of corrupt **m**, reprobate concerning 3563
Heb 10:16 and in their **m** will I write them; 1271
12: 3 lest ye be wearied and faint in your **m**. 5590
2Pe 3: 1 in both which I stir up your pure **m** by way 1271

MINE (647) [I]
Ge 14:22 I have lift up **m** hand unto the LORD, 2967.1
15: 3 and lo, one born in my house is **m** heir. 2967.1
24:33 I will not eat, until I have told **m** errand. 2967.1
24:45 before I had done speaking in **m** heart, 2967.1
30:25 that I may go unto **m own** place, and 2967.1
30:30 now when shall I provide for **m own** 2967.1
31:10 that I lifted up **m** eyes, and saw in a 2967.1
31:40 and my sleep departed from **m** eyes. 2967.1
31:42 God hath seen **m** affliction and the labour 2967.1
31:43 and all that thou seest *is* **m**: 2967.1+3807.1
41:13 me he restored unto **m** office, and him he 2967.1
44:21 unto me, that I may set **m** eyes upon him. 2967.1
48: 5 unto thee into Egypt, *are* **m**; 2967.1+3807.1
48: 5 and Simeon, they shall be **m**. 2967.1+3807.1
49: 6 **m** honour, be not thou united: 2967.1
Ex 7: 4 bring forth **m** armies, *and* my people 2967.1
7: 5 when I stretch forth **m** hand upon Egypt, 2967.1
7:17 I will smite with the rod that *is* in **m** hand 2967.1
13: 2 *both* of man and of beast: it *is* **m**. 2967.1+3807.1
17: 9 of the hill with the rod of God in **m** hand. 2967.1
18: 4 *said he, was* **m** help, and delivered me 2967.1
19: 5 all people: for all the earth *is* **m**: 2967.1+3807.1
20:26 Neither shalt thou go up by steps unto **m** 2967.1
21:14 thou shalt take him from **m** altar, that he 2967.1
23:23 For **m** Angel shall go before thee, and 2967.1
32:34 behold, **m** Angel shall go before thee: 2967.1
33:23 I will take away **m** hand, and thou shalt 2967.1
34:19 All that openeth the matrix *is* **m**; 2967.1+3807.1
Lev 18: 4 and keep **m** ordinances, to walk therein: 2967.1
18:30 Therefore ye shall keep **m** ordinance, 2967.1
20:26 that *ye* should be **m**. 2967.1+3807.1
22: 9 They shall therefore keep **m** ordinance, 2967.1
25:23 for the land *is* **m**; for ye *were* 2967.1+3807.1
Nu 3:12 therefore the Levites shall be **m**; 2967.1+3807.1
3:13 Because all the firstborn *are* **m**; 2967.1+3807.1
3:13 and beast: **m** they shall be: 2967.1+3807.1
3:45 and the Levites shall be **m**: 2967.1+3807.1
8:14 and the Levites shall be **m**. 2967.1+3807.1
8:17 of the children of Israel *are* **m**, 2967.1+3807.1
10:30 I will depart to **m own** land, and to my 2967.1
12: 7 *is* not so, who *is* faithful in all **m** house. 2967.1
14:28 as ye have spoken in **m** ears, so will I do 2967.1
16:28 for *I have* not *done them* of **m own** mind. 2967.1
18: 8 I also have given thee the charge of **m** 2967.1
22:29 I would there were a sword in **m** hand, 2967.1
23:11 I took thee to curse **m** enemies, and 2967.1
24:10 I called thee to curse **m** enemies, and 2967.1
24:13 to do *either* good or bad of **m own** mind; 2967.1
Dt 8:17 the might of **m** hand hath gotten me this 2967.1
10: 3 having the two tables in **m** hand. 2967.1
26:13 away the hallowed *things* out of *m* house, NIH
29:19 though I walk in the imagination of **m** 2967.1
32:23 I will spend **m** arrows upon them. 2967.1
32:41 and **m** hand take hold on judgment; 2967.1
32:41 I will render vengeance to **m** enemies, 2967.1
32:42 I will make **m** arrows drunk with blood, 2967.1
Jos 14: 7 I brought him word again as *it was* in **m** 2967.1
Jdg 6:36 If thou wilt save Israel by **m** hand, 2967.1
6:37 that thou wilt save Israel by **m** hand, 2967.1
7: 2 saying, **M own** hand hath saved me. 2967.1
8: 7 and Zalmunna into **m** hand, 2967.1
11:30 the children of Ammon into **m** hands, 2967.1
16:17 hath not come a rasor upon **m** head; 2967.1
17: 2 spakest of also in **m** ears, behold, 2967.1
19:23 seeing that this man is come into **m** 2967.1
Ru 4: 6 for myself, lest I mar **m own** inheritance: 2967.1
1Sa 2: 1 **m** horn is exalted in the LORD: 2967.1
2: 1 my mouth is enlarged over **m** enemies; 2967.1
2:28 to offer upon **m** altar, to burn incense, 2967.1
2:29 kick ye at my sacrifice and at **m** offering, 2967.1
2:33 *whom* I shall not cut off from **m** altar, 2967.1
2:35 he shall walk before **m** anointed for ever. 2967.1
12: 3 *any* bribe to blind **m** eyes therewith? 2967.1
14:24 that I may be avenged on **m** enemies. 2967.1
14:29 how **m** eyes have been enlightened, 2967.1
14:43 the end of the rod that *was* in **m** hand, 2967.1
15:14 then this bleating of the sheep in **m** ears, 2967.1
17:46 will the LORD deliver thee into **m** hand; 2967.1
18:17 Let not **m** hand be upon him, but let 2967.1
19:17 sent away **m** enemy, that he is escaped? 2967.1
20: 1 what *is* **m** iniquity? and what *is* my sin 2967.1
21: 3 give *me* five *loaves of* bread in **m** hand, 2967.1
21: 4 *There is* no common bread under **m** hand, 2967.1
23: 7 God hath delivered him into **m** hand; 2967.1
24: 6 to stretch forth **m** hand against him, 2967.1
24:10 thee to day into **m** hand in the cave: 2967.1
24:10 *m eye* spared thee; and I said, I will not put NIH
24:10 will not put forth **m** hand against my lord; 2967.1
24:11 neither evil nor transgression in **m** hand, 2967.1
24:12 but **m** hand shall not be upon thee. 2967.1
24:13 but **m** hand shall not be upon thee. 2967.1
25:33 *from* avenging myself with **m own** hand. 2967.1
26:11 **m** hand against the LORD'S anointed: 2967.1
26:18 have I done? or what evil *is* in **m** hand? 2967.1
26:23 I would not stretch forth **m** hand against 2967.1
26:24 as thy life was much set by this day in **m** 2967.1
28: 2 Therefore will I make thee keeper of **m** 2967.1
2Sa 5:19 wilt thou deliver them into **m** hand? 2967.1
5:20 The LORD hath broken forth upon **m** 2967.1
6:22 and will be base in **m own** sight: 2967.1
11:11 shall I then go into **m** house, to eat and 2967.1
14: 5 a widow woman, and **m** husband is dead. 2967.1
14:30 Joab's field is near **m**, and he hath barley 2967.1
16:12 It may be that the LORD will look on **m** 2967.1
18:12 a thousand *shekels of* silver in **m** hand, 2967.1
18:12 *yet* would I not put forth **m** hand against 2967.1
18:13 wrought falsehood against **m own** life: 2967.1
19:37 that I may die in **m own** city, *and* 2967.1
22: 4 so shall I be saved from **m** enemies. 2967.1
22:24 and have kept myself from **m** iniquity. 2967.1
22:35 that a bow of steel is broken *by* **m** arms. 2967.1
22:38 I have pursued **m** enemies, and 2967.1
22:41 Thou hast also given me the necks of **m** 2967.1
22:49 that bringeth me forth from **m** enemies: 2967.1
1Ki 1:33 son to ride upon **m own** mule, 2967.1+3807.1
1:48 throne *this* day, **m** eyes even seeing *it*. 2967.1
2:15 knowest that the kingdom was **m**, 2967.1+3807.1
2:22 for he *is* **m** elder brother, even for him, 2967.1
3:26 **m** nor thine, *but* divide *it*. 2967.1+3807.1
9: 3 **m** eyes and mine heart shall be there 2967.1
9: 3 and **m** heart shall be there perpetually. 2967.1
10: 6 It was a true report that I heard in **m own** 2967.1

1Ki 10: 7 and **m** eyes had seen *it:* and behold, 2967.1
11:21 that I may go to **m own** country. 2967.1
11:33 to do *that* which *is* right in **m** eyes, and 2967.1
14: 8 do *that* only which *was* right in **m** eyes; 2967.1
20: 3 Thy silver and thy gold *is* **m**; thy 2967.1+3807.1
20: 3 *even* the goodliest, *are* **m**. 2967.1+3807.1
21:20 Hast thou found me, O **m** enemy? 2967.1
2Ki 4:13 I dwell among **m own** people. 2967.1
5:26 Went not **m** heart *with thee,* when 2967.1
6:32 murderer hath sent to take away **m** head? 2967.1
10: 6 If ye *be* **m**, and *if* ye will hearken 2967.1+3807.1
10:30 in executing *that* which *is* right in **m** eyes, 2967.1
10:30 Ahab according to all that *was* in **m** heart, 2967.1
18:34 have they delivered Samaria out of **m** 2967.1
18:35 that have delivered their country out of **m** 2967.1
18:35 should deliver Jerusalem out of **m** hand? 2967.1
19:28 and thy tumult is come up into **m** ears, 2967.1
19:34 for **m own** sake, and for my servant 2967.1
20: 6 I will defend this city for **m own** sake, 2967.1
20:15 All *the things* that *are* in **m** house have 2967.1
21:14 I will forsake the remnant of **m** 2967.1
1Ch 12:17 peaceably unto me to help me, **m** 2967.1+3807.1
12:17 *if ye be come* to betray me to **m** enemies, 2967.1
12:17 seeing *there is* no wrong in **m** hands, 2967.1
14:10 wilt thou deliver them into **m** hand? 2967.1
14:11 God hath broken in upon **m** enemies by 2967.1
14:11 **m** hand like the breaking forth of waters: 2967.1
16:22 *Saying,* Touch not **m** anointed, and 2967.1
17:14 I will settle him in **m** house and in my 2967.1
17:16 O LORD God, and what *is* **m** house, 2967.1
22:18 the inhabitants of the land into **m** hand; 2967.1
28: 2 *As for me,* I *had* in **m** heart to build a 2967.1
29: 3 I have of **m own** proper good, 2967.1+3807.1
29:17 in the uprightness of **m** heart I have 2967.1
2Ch 7:15 Now **m** eyes shall be open, and mine ears 2967.1
7:15 **m** ears attent unto the prayer *that is made* 2967.1
7:16 **m** eyes and mine heart shall be there 2967.1
7:16 and **m** heart shall be there perpetually. 2967.1
9: 5 I heard in **m own** land of thine acts, 2967.1
9: 6 and **m** eyes had seen *it:* and behold, 2967.1
29:10 Now *it is* in **m** heart to make a covenant 2967.1
32:13 able to deliver their lands out of **m** hand? 2967.1
32:14 that could deliver his people out of **m** 2967.1
32:14 be able to deliver you out of **m** hand? 2967.1
32:15 able to deliver his people out of **m** hand, 2967.1
32:15 your God deliver you out of **m** hand? 2967.1
32:17 not delivered their people out of **m** hand, 2967.1
32:17 deliver his people out of **m** hand. 2967.1
Ne 7: 5 my God put into **m** heart to gather 2967.1
Job 3:10 nor hid sorrow from **m** eyes. 2967.1
4:12 to me, and **m** ear received a little thereof. 2967.1
4:16 an image *was* before **m** eyes, *there was* 2967.1
6:11 what *is* **m** end, that I should prolong my 2967.1
7: 7 *is* wind: **m** eye shall no more see good. 2967.1
7:21 and take away **m** iniquity? 2967.1
9:20 **m own** mouth shall condemn me: 2967.1
9:31 and **m own** clothes shall abhor me. 2967.1
10: 6 That thou inquirest after **m** iniquity, and 2967.1
10:14 thou wilt not acquit me from **m** iniquity. 2967.1
10:15 therefore see thou **m** affliction; 2967.1
13: 1 **m** eye hath seen all *this,* mine ear hath 2967.1
13: 1 mine eye hath seen all *this,* **m** ear hath 2967.1
13:14 in my teeth, and put my life in **m** hand? 2967.1
13:15 I will maintain **m own** ways before him. 2967.1
13:23 How many *are* **m** iniquities and 2967.1+3807.1
14:17 in a bag, and thou sewest up **m** iniquity. 2967.1
16: 4 against you, and shake **m** head at you. 2967.1
16: 9 **m** enemy sharpeneth his eyes upon me. 2967.1
16:16 and on **m** eyelids *is* the shadow of death; 2967.1
16:17 Not for *any* injustice in **m** hands: also my 2967.1
16:20 *but* **m** eye poureth out *tears* unto God. 2967.1
17: 2 *doth not* **m** eye continue in their 2967.1
17: 7 **M** eye also is dim by reason of sorrow, 2967.1
17:13 If I wait, the grave *is* **m** house: I have 2967.1
19: 4 **m** error remaineth with myself. 2967.1
19:10 and **m** hope hath he removed like a tree. 2967.1
19:13 **m** acquaintance are verily estranged from 2967.1
19:15 They that dwell in **m** house, and 2967.1
19:17 for the children's *sake* of **m** *own* body. 2967.1
19:27 and **m** eyes shall behold, and not another; 2967.1
27: 7 Let **m** enemy be as the wicked, and 2967.1
31: 1 I made a covenant with **m** eyes; why then 2967.1
31: 6 that God may know **m** integrity. 2967.1
31: 7 **m** heart walked after mine eyes, and 2967.1
31: 7 mine heart walked after **m** eyes, and 2967.1
31: 9 If **m** heart have been deceived by a 2967.1
31:12 and would root out all **m** increase. 2967.1
31:22 *Then* let **m** arm fall from *my* shoulder 2967.1
31:22 and **m** arm be broken from the bone. 2967.1
31:25 and because **m** hand had gotten much; 2967.1
31:33 by hiding **m** iniquity in my bosom: 2967.1
31:35 and *that* **m** adversary had written a book. 2967.1
32: 6 and durst not shew you **m** opinion. 2967.1
32:10 to me; I also will shew **m** opinion. 2967.1
32:17 also my part, I also will shew **m** opinion. 2967.1
33: 8 Surely thou hast spoken in **m** hearing, 2967.1
41:11 *is* under the whole heaven *is* **m**. 2967.1+3807.1
42: 5 of the ear: but now **m** eye seeth thee. 2967.1
Ps 3: 3 my glory, and the lifter up of **m** head. 2967.1
3: 7 for thou hast smitten all **m** enemies *upon* 2967.1
5: 8 thy righteousness because of **m** enemies; 2967.1
6: 7 **M** eye is consumed because of grief; 2967.1
6: 7 it waxeth old because of all **m** enemies. 2967.1
6:10 Let all **m** enemies be ashamed and 2967.1
7: 4 him that without cause is **m** enemy:) 2967.1
7: 5 the earth, and lay **m** honour in the dust. 2967.1
7: 6 because of the rage of **m** enemies: 2967.1
7: 8 and according to **m** integrity *that is* in me. 2967.1
9: 3 When **m** enemies are turned back, 2967.1
13: 2 how long shall **m** enemy be exalted over 2967.1
13: 3 lighten **m** eyes, lest I sleep the *sleep of* 2967.1
13: 4 Lest **m** enemy say, I have prevailed 2967.1
16: 5 The LORD *is* the portion of **m** 2967.1
17: 3 Thou hast proved **m** heart; thou hast 2967.1
18: 3 so shall I be saved from **m** enemies. 2967.1
18:23 and I kept myself from **m** iniquity. 2967.1
18:34 that a bow of steel is broken *by* **m** arms. 2967.1
18:37 I have pursued **m** enemies, and 2967.1
18:40 Thou hast also given me the necks of **m** 2967.1
18:48 He delivereth me from **m** enemies: yea, 2967.1
23: 5 before me in the presence of **m** enemies: 2967.1
25: 2 let not **m** enemies triumph over me. 2967.1
25:11 O LORD, pardon **m** iniquity; 2967.1+3807.1
25:15 **M** eyes *are* ever towards the LORD; 2967.1
25:18 Look upon **m** affliction and my pain; and 2967.1
25:19 Consider **m** enemies; for they are many; 2967.1
26: 1 for I have walked in **m** integrity: 2967.1
26: 3 For thy lovingkindness *is* before **m** eyes: 2967.1
26: 6 I will wash **m** hands in innocency: so 2967.1
26:11 *as for* me, I will walk in **m** integrity: 2967.1
27: 2 the wicked, *even* **m** enemies and my foes, 2967.1
27: 6 now shall **m** head be lifted up above mine 2967.1
27: 6 now shall mine head be lifted up above **m** 2967.1
27:11 me in a plain path, because of **m** enemies. 2967.1
27:12 Deliver me not over unto the will of **m** 2967.1
31: 9 **m** eye is consumed with grief, *yea,* my 2967.1
31:10 my strength faileth because of **m** iniquity, 2967.1
31:11 I was a reproach among all **m** enemies, 2967.1
31:11 and a fear to **m** acquaintance: 2967.1
31:15 deliver me from the hand of **m** enemies, 2967.1
32: 5 unto thee, and **m** iniquity have I not hid. 2967.1
32: 8 shalt go: I will guide thee with **m** eye. 2967.1
35: 2 and buckler, and stand up for **m** help. 2967.1
35:13 my prayer returned into **m own** bosom. 2967.1
35:15 in **m** adversity they rejoiced, and 2967.1
35:19 Let not them that are **m** enemies 2967.1
35:26 confusion together that rejoice at **m** hurt: 2967.1
38: 4 For **m** iniquities are gone *over* mine head: 2967.1
38: 4 For mine iniquities are gone *over* **m** head: 2967.1
38:10 as for the light of **m** eyes, it also is gone 2967.1
38:18 For I will declare **m** iniquity; I will be 2967.1
38:19 **m** enemies *are* lively, *and* they are strong: 2967.1
38:20 They also that render evil for good are **m** 5204.1
39: 4 make me to know **m** end, and 2967.1
39: 5 and **m** age *is* as nothing before thee: 2967.1
40: 6 offering thou didst not desire; **m** 2967.1+3807.1
40:12 **m** iniquities have taken hold upon me, so 2967.1
40:12 they are moe than the hairs of **m** head: 2967.1
41: 5 **M** enemies speak evil of me, When shall 2967.1
41: 9 Yea, **m own** familiar friend, in whom I 2967.1
41:11 **m** enemy doth not triumph over me. 2967.1
41:12 thou upholdest me in **m** integrity, and 2967.1
42:10 in my bones, **m** enemies reproach me; 2967.1
49: 4 I will incline **m** ear to a parable: I will 2967.1
50:10 For every beast of the forest *is* **m**, 2967.1+3807.1
50:11 the wild beasts of the field *are* **m**. 5978+2967.1
50:12 *is* **m**, and the fulness thereof. 2967.1+3807.1
51: 2 Wash me throughly from **m** iniquity, and 2967.1
51: 9 my sins, and blot out all **m** iniquities. 2967.1
54: 4 Behold, God *is* **m** helper: 2967.1+3807.1
54: 5 He shall reward evil unto **m** enemies: 2967.1
54: 7 **m** eye hath seen *his desire* upon mine 2967.1
54: 7 mine eye hath seen *his desire* upon **m** 2967.1
55:13 a man **m** equal, my guide, and 2967.1
55:13 my guide, and **m** acquaintance. 2967.1
56: 2 **M** enemies would daily swallow *me* up: 2967.1
56: 9 then shall **m** enemies turn back: 2967.1
59: 1 Deliver me from **m** enemies, O my God: 2967.1
59:10 God shall let me see *my desire* upon **m** 2967.1
60: 7 Gilead *is* **m**, and Manasseh *is* 2967.1+3807.1
60: 7 *is* mine, and Manasseh *is* **m**; 2967.1+3807.1
60: 7 Ephraim also *is* the strength of **m** head; 2967.1
69: 3 **m** eyes fail while *I* wait for my God. 2967.1
69: 4 a cause are moe than the hairs of **m** head: 2967.1
69: 4 *being* **m** enemies wrongfully, are mighty: 2967.1
69:18 deliver me because of **m** enemies. 2967.1
69:19 **m** adversaries *are* all before thee. 2967.1
71:10 For **m** enemies speak against me; and 2967.1
77: 4 Thou holdest **m** eyes waking: I am *so* 2967.1
77: 6 I commune with **m own** heart: and 2967.1
88: 8 Thou hast put away **m** acquaintance far 2967.1
88: 9 **M** eye mourneth by reason of affliction: 2967.1
88:18 *and* **m** acquaintance *into* darkness. 2967.1
89:21 **m** arm also shall strengthen him. 2967.1
92:11 **M** eye also shall see *my desire* on mine 2967.1
92:11 Mine eye also shall see *my desire* on **m** 2967.1
92:11 **m** ears shall hear *my desire* of the wicked 2967.1
101: 3 I will set no wicked thing before **m** eyes: 2967.1
101: 6 **M** eyes *shall be* upon the faithful of 2967.1
102: 8 **M** enemies reproach me all the day; *and* 2967.1
105:15 *Saying,* Touch not **m** anointed, and do 2967.1
108: 8 Gilead *is* **m**; Manasseh *is* mine; 2967.1+3807.1
108: 8 Gilead *is* mine; Manasseh *is* **m**; 2967.1+3807.1
108: 8 Ephraim also *is* the strength of **m** head; 2967.1
109:20 *Let* this *be* the reward of **m** adversaries 2967.1
109:29 Let **m** adversaries be clothed with shame, 2967.1
116: 8 **m** eyes from tears, *and* my feet from 2967.1
119:11 Thy word have I hid in **m** heart, that I 2967.1
119:18 Open thou **m** eyes, that I may behold 2967.1
119:37 Turn away **m** eyes from beholding 2967.1
119:82 **M** eyes fail for thy word, saying, 2967.1
119:92 then have perished in **m** affliction. 2967.1
119:98 hast made me wiser than **m** enemies: 2967.1
119:112 I have inclined **m** heart to perform thy 2967.1
119:121 and justice: leave me not to **m** oppressors. 2967.1
119:123 **M** eyes fail for thy salvation, and for 2967.1
119:136 Rivers of waters run down **m** eyes, 2967.1
119:139 **m** enemies have forgotten thy words. 2967.1
119:148 **M** eyes prevent the *night* watches, that *I* 2967.1
119:153 Consider **m** affliction, and deliver me: 2967.1
119:157 Many *are* my persecutors and **m** enemies; 2967.1
121: 1 I will lift up **m** eyes unto the hills, 2967.1
123: 1 Unto thee lift I up **m** eyes, O thou that 2967.1
131: 1 my heart is not haughty, nor **m** eyes lofty: 2967.1
132: 4 I will not give sleep to **m** eyes, *or* 2967.1
132: 4 to mine eyes, *or* slumber to **m** eyelids, 2967.1
132:17 I have ordained a lamp for **m** anointed. 2967.1
138: 7 hand against the wrath of **m** enemies, 2967.1
139: 2 knowest my downsitting and **m** uprising, 2967.1
139:22 perfect hatred: I count them **m** enemies. 2967.1
Ps 141: 8 **m** eyes *are* unto thee, O GOD the Lord: 2967.1
143: 9 Deliver me, O LORD, from **m** enemies: 2967.1
143:12 of thy mercy cut off **m** enemies, and 2967.1
Pr 5:13 nor inclined **m** ear to them that instructed 2967.1
8:14 Counsel *is* **m**, and 2967.1+3807.1
23:15 be wise, my heart shall rejoice, even **m**. 589
Ecc 1:16 I communed with **m own** heart, saying, 2967.1
2: 1 I said in **m** heart, Go to now, I will prove 2967.1
2: 3 I sought in **m** heart to give myself unto 2967.1
2: 3 (yet acquainting **m** heart with wisdom) 2967.1
2:10 whatsoever **m** eyes desired I kept not 2967.1
3:17 I said in **m** heart, God shall judge 2967.1
7:25 I applied **m** heart to know, and to search, 2967.1
8:16 When I applied **m** heart to know wisdom, 2967.1
SS 1: 6 *but* **m own** vineyard have I not kept. 2967.1
2:16 My beloved *is* **m**, and I *am* his: 2967.1+3807.1
6: 3 and my beloved *is* **m**: 2967.1+3807.1
8:12 My vineyard, which *is* **m**, *is* 2967.1+3807.1
Isa 1:15 your hands, I will hide **m** eyes from you: 2967.1
1:16 evil of your doings from before **m** eyes; 2967.1
1:24 I will ease me of **m** adversaries, and 2967.1
1:24 and avenge me of **m** enemies: 2967.1
5: 9 In **m** ears *said* the LORD of hosts, Of a 2967.1
6: 5 for **m** eyes have seen the King, 2967.1
10: 5 the rod of **m** anger, and the staff in their 2967.1
10: 5 the staff in their hand *is* **m** indignation. 2967.1
10:25 and **m** anger in their destruction. 2967.1
13: 3 I have also called my mighty ones for **m** 2967.1
16: 4 Let **m** outcasts dwell with thee, Moab; 2967.1
16:11 and **m** inward parts for Kir-haresh. 2967.1
19:25 of my hands, and Israel **m** inheritance. 2967.1
22:14 it was revealed in **m** ears *by* the LORD 2967.1
29:23 the work of **m** hands, in the midst of him, 2967.1
37:29 is come up into **m** ears, therefore will I 2967.1
37:35 defend this city to save it for **m own** sake, 2967.1
38:12 **M** age is departed, and is removed from 2967.1
38:14 **m** eyes fail *with looking* upward: 2967.1
39: 4 All that *is* in **m** house have they seen: 2967.1
42: 1 **m** elect, *in whom* my soul delighteth; 2967.1
43: 1 *thee* by thy name; thou *art* **m**. 2967.1+3807.1
43:25 out thy transgressions for **m own** sake, 2967.1
45: 4 my servant's sake, and Israel **m** elect, 2967.1
47: 6 I have polluted **m** inheritance, and 2967.1
48: 5 **M** idol hath done them, and my graven 2967.1
48: 9 For my name's sake will I defer **m** anger, 2967.1
48:11 For **m own** sake, *even* for mine own sake, 2967.1
48:11 For mine own sake, *even* for **m own** sake, 2967.1
48:13 **M** hand also hath laid the foundation of 2967.1
49:22 I will lift up **m** hand to the Gentiles, and 2967.1
50: 4 **m** ear to hear as the learned. 2967.1+3807.1
50: 5 The Lord GOD hath opened **m** 2967.1+3807.1
50: 8 who *is* **m** adversary? let him come near to 2967.1
50:11 This shall ye have of **m** hand; ye shall lie 2967.1
51: 5 and **m** arms shall judge the people; 2967.1
51: 5 upon me, and on **m** arm shall they trust. 2967.1
51:16 have covered thee in the shadow of **m** 2967.1
56: 5 Even unto them will I give in **m** house 2967.1
56: 7 their sacrifices *shall be* accepted upon **m** 2967.1
56: 7 for **m** house shall be called a house of 2967.1
60: 7 they shall come up with acceptance on **m** 2967.1
63: 3 for I will tread them in **m** anger, and 2967.1
63: 4 For the day of vengeance *is* in **m** heart, 2967.1
63: 5 **m own** arm brought salvation unto me; 2967.1
63: 6 I will tread down the people in **m** anger, 2967.1
65: 2 I have spread out **m** hands all the day 2967.1
65: 9 **m** elect shall inherit it, and my servants 2967.1
65:12 did evil before **m** eyes, and did choose 2967.1
65:16 and because they are hid from **m** eyes. 2967.1
65:22 **m** elect shall long enjoy the work of their 2967.1
66: 2 For all those *things* hath **m** hand made, 2967.1
66: 4 they did evil before **m** eyes, and 2967.1
Jer 2: 7 and made **m** heritage an abomination. 2967.1
3:12 I will not cause **m** anger to fall upon you: 2967.1
3:15 I will give you pastors according to **m** 2967.1
7:20 **m** anger and my fury *shall be* poured out 2967.1
9: 1 **m** eyes a fountain of tears, that I might 2967.1
11:15 What hath my beloved to do in **m** house, 2967.1
12: 3 seen me, and tried **m** heart towards thee: 2967.1
12: 7 I have forsaken **m** house, I have left mine 2967.1
12: 7 mine house, I have left **m** heritage; 2967.1
12: 8 **M** heritage is unto me as a lion in 2967.1
12: 9 **M** heritage *is* unto me *as* a speckled bird, 2967.1
12:14 Thus saith the LORD against all **m** evil 2967.1
13:17 **m** eye shall weep sore, and run down 2967.1
14:17 Let **m** eyes run down *with* tears night and 2967.1
15:14 for a fire is kindled in **m** anger, 2967.1
15:16 unto me the joy and rejoicing of **m** heart: 2967.1
16:17 For **m** eyes *are* upon all their ways: 2967.1
16:17 neither is their iniquity hid from **m** eyes. 2967.1
16:18 they have filled **m** inheritance with 2967.1
16:21 I will cause them to know **m** hand and 2967.1
17: 4 for ye have kindled a fire in **m** anger, 2967.1
18: 6 so *are* ye in **m** hand, O house of Israel. 2967.1
20: 9 *his word* was in **m** heart as a burning fire 2967.1
23: 9 **M** heart within me is broken because 2967.1
24: 6 For I will set **m** eyes upon them for good, 2967.1
25:15 Take the wine cup of this fury at **m** hand, 2967.1
32: 8 So Hanameel **m** uncle's son came to me 2967.1
32:12 in the sight of Hanameel **m** uncle's *son,* 2967.1
32:31 been to me *as* a provocation of **m** anger 2967.1
32:37 whither I have driven them in **m** anger, 2967.1
33: 5 whom I have slain in **m** anger and in my 2967.1
42:18 As **m** anger and my fury hath been 2967.1
44: 6 my fury and **m** anger was poured forth, 2967.1
44:28 know whose words shall stand, **m**, 4480+5204.1
48:31 *m heart* shall mourn for the men of NIH
48:36 Therefore **m** heart shall sound for Moab 2967.1
48:36 **m** heart shall sound like pipes for the men 2967.1
50:11 O ye destroyers of **m** heritage, because 2967.1
51:25 I will stretch out **m** hand upon thee, and 2967.1
La 1:16 **m** eye, mine eye runneth down *with* 2967.1
1:16 **m** eye runneth down *with* water, because 2967.1
1:19 **m** elders gave up the ghost in the city, 2967.1
1:20 are troubled; **m** heart is turned within me; 2967.1
1:21 all **m** enemies have heard of my trouble; 2967.1

La 2:11 **M** eyes do fail with tears, my bowels are 2967.1
2:22 and brought up hath **m** enemy consumed. 2967.1
3:19 Remembering **m** affliction and 2967.1
3:48 **M** eye runneth down *with* rivers of water 2967.1
3:49 **M** eye trickleth down, and ceaseth not, 2967.1
3:51 **M** eye affecteth mine heart because of all 2967.1
3:51 Mine eye affecteth **m** heart 2967.1+3807.1
3:52 **M** enemies chased me sore, like a bird, 2967.1
3:54 Waters flowed over **m** head; *then* I said, 2967.1
Eze 5:11 will I also diminish *thee;* neither shall **m** 2967.1
5:13 Thus shall **m** anger be accomplished, and 2967.1
6:14 So will I stretch out **m** hand upon them, 2967.1
7: 3 I will send **m** anger upon thee, and 2967.1
7: 4 **m** eye shall not spare thee, neither will I 2967.1
7: 8 and accomplish **m** anger upon thee: 2967.1
7: 9 **m** eye shall not spare, neither will I have 2967.1
8: 1 as I sat in **m** house, and the elders of 2967.1
8: 3 a hand, and took me by a lock of **m** head; 2967.1
8: 5 So I lift up **m** eyes the way toward 2967.1
8:18 **m** eye shall not spare, neither will I have 2967.1
8:18 though they cry in **m** ears *with* a loud 2967.1
9: 1 He cried also in **m** ears *with* a loud voice, 2967.1
9: 5 to the others he said in **m** hearing, Go ye 2967.1
9:10 *as for* me also, **m** eye shall not spare, 2967.1
11:20 and keep **m** ordinances, and do them: 2967.1
12: 7 through the wall with **m** hand; 2967.1+3807.1
13: 9 **m** hand shall be upon the prophets that 2967.1
13:13 be an overflowing shower in **m** anger, 2967.1
14:13 will I stretch out **m** hand upon it, and 2967.1
16: 8 and thou becamest **m**. 2967.1+3807.1
16:18 thou hast set **m** oil and mine incense 2967.1
16:18 set mine oil and **m** incense before them. 2967.1
17:19 surely **m** oath that he hath despised, and 2967.1
18: 4 Behold, all souls *are* **m**; as 2967.1+3807.1
18: 4 so also the soul of the son *is* **m**: 2967.1+3807.1
20: 5 lifted up **m** hand unto the seed of 2967.1
20: 5 when I lifted up **m** hand unto them, 2967.1
20: 6 In the day *that* I lifted up **m** hand unto 2967.1
20:17 Nevertheless **m** eye spared them from 2967.1
20:22 Nevertheless I withdrew **m** hand, and 2967.1
20:23 I lifted up **m** hand unto them also in 2967.1
20:28 *for* the which I lifted up **m** hand to give it 2967.1
20:40 For in **m** holy mountain, in the mountain 2967.1
20:42 lifted up **m** hand to give it to your fathers. 2967.1
21:17 I will also smite **m** hands together, and 2967.1
21:31 I will pour out **m** indignation upon thee, 2967.1
22: 8 Thou hast despised **m** holy *things,* and 2967.1
22:13 I have smitten **m** hand at thy dishonest 2967.1
22:20 so will I gather *you* in **m** anger and 2967.1
22:26 have profaned **m** holy *things:* they have 2967.1
22:31 Therefore have I poured out **m** 2967.1
23: 4 they were **m**, and they bare sons 2967.1+3807.1
23: 5 played the harlot when she was **m**; 8478+2967.1
23:39 thus have they done in the midst of **m** 2967.1
23:41 whereupon thou hast set **m** incense and 2967.1
23:41 thou hast set mine incense and **m** oil. 2967.1
25: 7 I will stretch out **m** hand upon thee, and 2967.1
25:13 I will also stretch out **m** hand upon 2967.1
25:14 they shall do in Edom according to **m** 2967.1
25:16 I *will* stretch out **m** hand upon 2967.1
29: 3 My river *is* **m** own, and I have 2967.1+3807.1
29: 9 river *is* **m**, and I have made *it.* 2967.1+3807.1
35: 3 I will stretch out **m** hand against thee, and 2967.1
35:10 these two countries shall be **m**, 2967.1+3807.1
36: 7 I have lifted up **m** hand, Surely 2967.1
36:21 I had pity for **m** holy name, which 2967.1
36:22 of Israel, but for **m** holy name's sake, 2967.1
37:19 and they shall be one in **m** hand. 2967.1
43: 8 wherefore I have consumed them in **m** 2967.1
44: 8 ye have not kept the charge of **m** holy 2967.1
44:12 have I lift up **m** hand against them, 2967.1
44:24 and my statutes in all **m** assemblies; 2967.1
47:14 *concerning* the which I lifted up **m** hand 2967.1
Da 4: 4 I Nebuchadnezzar was at rest in **m** house, 2967.2
4:10 Thus *were* the visions of **m** head in my 2967.2
4:34 lift up **m** eyes unto heaven, 2967.2
4:34 **m** understanding returned unto me, and 2967.2
4:36 **m** honour and brightness returned unto 2967.2
8: 3 I lifted up **m** eyes, and saw, and behold, 2967.1
10: 5 I lift up **m** eyes, and looked, and behold, 2967.1
Hos 2: 5 and my flax, **m** oil and my drink. 2967.1
2:10 and none shall deliver her out of **m** hand, 2967.1
8: 5 *thee* off; **m** anger is kindled against them: 2967.1
8:13 flesh *for* the sacrifices of **m** offerings, 2967.1
9:15 doings I will drive them out of **m** house, 2967.1
11: 8 **m** heart is turned within me, 2967.1
11: 9 I will not execute the fierceness of **m** 2967.1
13:11 I gave thee a king in **m** anger, and 2967.1
13:14 repentance shall be hid from **m** eyes. 2967.1
14: 4 for **m** anger is turned away from him. 2967.1
Am 1: 8 and I will turn **m** hand against Ekron: 2967.1
9: 2 into hell, thence shall **m** hand take them; 2967.1
9: 4 I will set **m** eyes upon them for evil, and 2967.1
Jnh 2: 2 I cried by reason of **m** affliction 2967.1+3807.1
Mic 7: 8 Rejoice not against me, O **m** enemy: 2967.1
7:10 she *that is* **m** enemy shall see *it,* and 2967.1
7:10 **m** eyes shall behold her: now shall she be 2967.1
Hab 1:12 O LORD my God, **m** Holy One? 2967.1
3:19 he will make me to walk upon **m** high 2967.1
Zep 1: 4 I will also stretch out **m** hand upon Judah, 2967.1
3: 8 to pour upon them **m** indignation, 2967.1
3:10 of my dispersed, shall bring **m** offering. 2967.1
Hag 1: 9 Because of **m** house that *is* waste, and 2967.1
2: 8 The silver *is* **m**, and the gold *is* 2967.1+3807.1
2: 8 silver *is* mine, and the gold *is* **m**, 2967.1+3807.1
Zec 1:18 lift I up **m** eyes, and saw, and behold four 2967.1
2: 1 I lift up **m** eyes again, and looked, and 2967.1
2: 9 I *will* shake **m** hand upon them, and 2967.1
5: 1 lift up **m** eyes, and looked, and behold, 2967.1
5: 9 lift I up **m** eyes, and looked, and behold, 2967.1
6: 1 lift up **m** eyes, and looked, and behold, 2967.1
9: 8 I will encamp about **m** house because 2967.1
9: 8 for now have I seen with **m** eyes. 2967.1
10: 3 **M** anger was kindled against 2967.1
11:14 I cut asunder **m** other staff, *even* Bands, 2967.1
Zec 12: 4 I will open **m** eyes upon the house of 2967.1
13: 7 I will turn **m** hand upon the little ones. 2967.1
Mal 1: 6 if then I *be* a father, where *is* **m** honour? 2967.1
1: 7 *Ye* offer polluted bread upon **m** altar; and 2967.1
1:10 do ye kindle *fire on* **m** altar for nought. 2967.1
3: 7 ye are gone away from **m** ordinances, 2967.1
3:10 that there may be meat in **m** house, and 2967.1
3:17 they shall be **m**, saith the LORD 2967.1+3807.1
Mt 7:24 whosoever heareth these sayings of **m**, *1473*
7:26 every one that heareth these sayings of **m**, *1473*
20:15 for me to do what I will with **m own**? *1699*
20:23 is not **m** to give, but *it shall be given to* *1699*
25:27 I should have received **m own** with usury. *1699*
Mk 9:24 Lord, I believe; help thou **m** unbelief. *1473*
10:40 and on my left hand is not **m** to give; *1699*
Lk 1:44 voice of thy salutation sounded in **m** ears, *1473*
2:30 For **m** eyes have seen thy salvation, *1473*
7:46 **M** head with oil thou didst not anoint: but *1473*
9:38 look upon my son: for he is **m** only child. *1473*
11: 6 For a friend of **m** in *his* journey is come to *1473*
18: 3 saying, Avenge me of **m** adversary. *1473*
19:23 that at my coming I might have required **m** NIG
19:27 But those **m** enemies, which would not that *1473*
Jn 2: 4 I to do with thee? **m** hour is not yet come. *1473*
5:30 I can of **m own self** do nothing: as I hear, *1683*
5:30 is just; because I seek not **m own** will, *1699*
6:38 not to do **m own** will, but the will of him *1699*
7:16 My doctrine is not **m**, but his that sent me. *1699*
8:50 And I seek not **m own** glory: there is *one* *1473*
9:11 and anointed **m** eyes, and said unto me, Go *1473*
9:15 He put clay upon **m** eyes, and I washed, *1473*
9:30 he is, and *yet* he hath opened **m** eyes. *1473*
10:14 and know my *sheep,* and am known of **m**. *1699*
14:24 and the word which you hear is not **m**, but *1699*
16:14 for he shall receive of **m**, and shall shew *it* *1699*
16:15 All *things* that the Father hath are **m**: *1699*
16:15 that he shall take of **m**, and shall shew *it* *1699*
17:10 And all **m** are thine, and thine are mine; *1699*
17:10 And all mine are thine, and thine are **m**; *1699*
Ac 11: 6 Upon the which when I had fastened **m** NIG
13:22 a man after **m own** heart, which shall fulfil *1473*
21:13 mean ye to weep and to break **m** heart? *1473*
26: 4 which was at the first among **m own** nation *1473*
Ro 11:13 apostle of the Gentiles, I magnify **m** office: *1473*
12:19 for it is written, Vengeance *is* **m**; I will *1473*
16:13 chosen in the Lord, and his mother and **m**. *1473*
16:23 Gaius **m** host, and of the whole church, *1473*
1Co 1:15 say that I had baptized in **m own** name. *1699*
4: 3 yea, I judge not **m own self**. *1683*
9: 2 for the seal of **m** apostleship are ye in *1699*
9: 3 **M** answer to them that do examine me is *1699*
10:33 in all *things,* not seeking **m own** profit, *1683*
16:21 The salutation of *me* Paul with **m own** *1699*
2Co 11:30 I will glory of the *things* which concern **m** *1473*
12: 5 myself I will not glory, but in **m** infirmities. *1473*
Gal 1:14 above many *my* equals in **m own** nation, *1473*
6:11 I have written unto you with **m own** hand. *1699*
Php 1: 4 Always in every prayer of **m** for you all *1473*
3: 9 not having **m own** righteousness, which is *1699*
2Th 3:17 The salutation of Paul with **m own** hand, *1699*
Tit 1: 4 **m** own son after the common faith: NIG
Phm 1:12 receive him, that is, **m own** bowels: *1699*
1:18 or oweth *thee* ought, put that on **m** account; *1473*
1:19 I Paul have written *it* with **m own** hand, *1699*
Rev 22:16 I Jesus have sent **m** angel to testify unto *1473*

MINGLE (2) [MINGLED]

Isa 5:22 and men of strength to **m** strong drink: 4537
Da 2:43 they shall **m** themselves with the seed of 6151

MINGLED (55) [MINGLE]

Ex 9:24 and fire **m** with the hail, very grievous, 3947
29:40 with the one lamb a tenth deal of flour **m** 1101
Lev 2: 4 *it shall be* unleavened cakes of fine flour **m** 1101
2: 5 be *of* fine flour unleavened, **m** with oil. 1101
7:10 every meat offering, **m** with oil, and dry, 1101
7:12 thanksgiving unleavened cakes **m** with oil, 1101
7:12 and cakes **m** with oil, of fine flour, fried. 1101
9: 4 and a meat offering **m** with oil: 1101
14:10 **m** with oil, and one log of oil. 1101
14:21 one tenth deal of fine flour **m** with oil for a 1101
19:19 thou shalt not sow thy field with **m** seed: 3610
19:19 a garment **m of linen and woollen** 3610+8162
23:13 *be* two tenth deals *of* fine flour **m** with oil, 1101
Nu 6:15 cakes *of* fine flour **m** with oil, and 1101
7:13 both of them *were* full *of* fine flour **m** with 1101
7:19 both of them full *of* fine flour **m** with oil 1101
7:25 both of them full *of* fine flour **m** with oil 1101
7:31 both of them full *of* fine flour **m** with oil 1101
7:37 both of them full *of* fine flour **m** with oil 1101
7:43 both of them full *of* fine flour **m** with oil 1101
7:49 both of them full *of* fine flour **m** with oil 1101
7:55 both of them full *of* fine flour **m** with oil 1101
7:61 both of them full *of* fine flour **m** with oil 1101
7:67 both of them full *of* fine flour **m** with oil 1101
7:73 both of them full *of* fine flour **m** with oil 1101
7:79 both of them full *of* fine flour **m** with oil 1101
8: 8 *even* fine flour **m** with oil, and 1101
15: 4 flour **m** with the fourth *part* of a hin of oil. 1101
15: 6 *of* flour **m** with the third *part* of a hin of oil. 1101
15: 9 tenth deals *of* flour **m** with half a hin of oil. 1101
28: 5 **m** with the fourth *part* of a hin of beaten 1101
28: 9 **m** with oil, and the drink offering thereof: 1101
28:12 meat offering, **m** with oil, for one bullock; 1101
28:12 a meat offering, **m** with oil, for one ram; 1101
28:13 a several tenth deal of flour **m** with oil *for* a 1101
28:20 their meat offering *shall be of* flour **m** with 1101
28:28 their meat offering *of* flour **m** with oil, 1101
29: 3 their meat offering *shall be of* flour **m** with 1101
29: 9 their meat offering *shall be of* flour **m** with 1101
29:14 their meat offering *shall be of* flour **m** with 1101
Ezr 9: 2 that the holy seed have **m** themselves with 6148
Ps 102: 9 like bread, and **m** my drink with weeping, 4537
106:35 were **m** among the heathen, and 6148
Pr 9: 2 hath killed her beasts; she hath **m** her wine; 4537
Pr 9: 5 and drink of the wine *which* I have **m**. 4537
Isa 19:14 The LORD hath **m** a perverse spirit in 4537
Jer 25:20 All the **m people**, and all the kings of 6153
25:24 all the kings of the **m people** that dwell in 6153
50:37 upon all the **m** people that *are* in the midst NIH
Eze 30: 5 all the **m people**, and Chub, and the men of 6153
Mt 27:34 They gave him vinegar to drink **m** with *3396*
Mk 15:23 gave him to drink wine **m with myrrh**: *4669*
Lk 13: 1 whose blood Pilate had **m** with their *3396*
Rev 8: 7 there followed hail and fire **m** with blood, *3396*
15: 2 And I saw as *it were* a sea of glass **m** with *3396*

MINIAMIN (3)

2Ch 31:15 **M**, and Jeshua, and Shemaiah, Amariah, 4509
Ne 12:17 Of Abijah, Zichri; of **M**, of Moadiah, Piltai; 4509
12:41 Eliakim, Maaseiah, **M**, Michaiah, Elioenai, 4509

MINISH (1) [MINISHED]

Ex 5:19 Ye shall not **m** *ought* from your bricks of 1639

MINISHED (1) [MINISH]

Ps 107:39 they are **m** and brought low through 4591

MINISTER (100) [MINISTERED, MINISTERETH, MINISTERING, MINISTERS, MINISTRATION, MINISTRY]

Ex 24:13 Moses rose up, and his **m** Joshua: and 8334
28: 1 he may **m** unto me **in the priest's office**, 3547
28: 3 he may **m** unto me **in the priest's office**. 3547
28: 4 he may **m** unto me **in the priest's office**. 3547
28:35 it shall be upon Aaron to **m**: and his sound 8334
28:41 they may **m** unto me **in the priest's office**. 3547
28:43 when they come near unto the altar to **m** in 8334
29: 1 to **m** unto me **in the priest's office**: 3547
29:30 of the congregation to **m** in the holy *place.* 8334
29:44 his sons, to **m** to me **in the priest's office**. 3547
30:20 or when they come near to the altar to **m**, 8334
30:30 *they* may **m** unto me **in the priest's office**. 3547
31:10 of his sons, to **m in the priest's office**, 3547
35:19 of his sons, to **m in the priest's office**. 3547
39:26 round about the hem of the robe to **m** *in;* as 8334
39:41 sons' garments, to **m in the priest's office**. 3547
40:13 he may **m** unto me **in the priest's office**. 3547
40:15 they may **m** unto me **in the priest's office**: 3547
Lev 7:35 **m** unto the LORD **in the priest's office**; 3547
16:32 **m in the priest's office** in his father's 3547
Nu 1:50 they shall **m** unto it, and shall encamp 8334
3: 3 he consecrated to **m in the priest's office**. 3547
3: 6 Aaron the priest, that they may **m** unto him. 8334
3:31 vessels of the sanctuary wherewith they **m**, 8334
4: 9 vessels thereof, wherewith they **m** unto it: 8334
4:12 wherewith they **m** in the sanctuary, and 8334
4:14 wherewith they **m** about it, *even* 8334
8:26 shall **m** with their brethren in the tabernacle 8334
16: 9 to stand before the congregation to **m** unto 8334
18: 2 may be joined unto thee, and **m** unto thee: 8334
18: 2 thy sons with thee *shall* **m** before NIH
Dt 10: 8 to stand before the LORD to **m** unto him, 8334
17:12 to **m** there before the LORD thy God, 8334
18: 5 to stand to **m** in the name of the LORD, 8334
18: 7 he shall **m** in the name of the LORD his 8334
21: 5 thy God hath chosen to **m** unto him, 8334
Jos 1: 1 Joshua the son of Nun, Moses' **m**, saying, 8334
1Sa 2:11 the child did **m** unto the LORD before Eli 8334
1Ki 8:11 So that the priests could not stand to **m** 8334
1Ch 15: 2 the ark of God, and to **m** unto him for ever. 8334
16: 4 he appointed *certain* of the Levites to **m** 8334
16:37 to **m** before the ark continually, 8334
23:13 to **m** unto him, and to bless in his name for 8334
26:12 to **m** in the house of the LORD. 8334
2Ch 5:14 So that the priests could not stand to **m** by 8334
8:14 to praise and **m** before the priests, 8334
13:10 the priests, which **m** unto the LORD, 8334
23: 6 the priests, and they that **m** of the Levites; 8334
24:14 *even* vessels to **m**, and to offer *withal,* and 8335
29:11 that *you* should **m** unto him, and 8334
31: 2 to **m**, and to give thanks, and to praise in 8334
Ne 10:36 unto the priests that **m** in the house of our 8334
10:39 the priests that **m**, and the porters, and 8334
Ps 9: 8 he shall **m judgment** to the people in 1777
Isa 60: 7 the rams of Nebajoth shall **m** unto thee: 8334
60:10 thy walls, and their kings shall **m** unto thee: 8334
Jer 33:22 and the Levites that **m** unto me. 8334
Eze 40:46 which come near to the LORD to **m** unto 8334
42:14 shall lay their garments wherein they **m**; 8334
43:19 to **m** unto me, saith the Lord GOD, 8334
44:11 they shall stand before them to **m** unto 8334
44:15 they shall come near to me to **m** unto me, 8334
44:16 to **m** unto me, and they shall keep my 8334
44:17 whiles they **m** in the gates of the inner 8334
44:27 unto the inner court, to **m** in the sanctuary, 8334
45: 4 which shall come near to **m** unto 8334
Mt 20:26 be great among you, let him be your **m**; *1249*
20:28 but to **m**, and to give his life a ransom for *1247*
25:44 sick, or in prison, and did not **m** unto thee? *1247*
Mk 10:43 will be great among you, shall be your **m**: *1249*
10:45 but to **m**, and to give his life a ransom for *1247*
Lk 4:20 and he gave *it* again to the **m**, and *5257*
Ac 13: 5 the Jews: and they had also John to *their* **m**. *5257*
24:23 forbid none of his acquaintance to **m** *5256*
26:16 thee for this *purpose,* to make thee a **m** *5257*
Ro 13: 4 For he is the **m** of God to thee for good. *1249*
13: 4 for he is the **m** of God, a revenger to *1249*
15: 8 Now I say that Jesus Christ was a **m** of *1249*
15:16 That I should be the **m** of Jesus Christ to *3011*
15:25 But now I go unto Jerusalem to **m** unto *1247*
15:27 is also to **m** unto them in carnal *things.* *3008*
1Co 9:13 Do ye not know that they which **m** about *2038*
2Co 9:10 to the sower both **m** bread for *your* food, *5524*
Gal 2:17 *is* therefore Christ the **m** of sin? *1249*
Eph 3: 7 Whereof I was made a **m**, according to *1249*
4:29 that it may **m** grace unto the hearers. *1325*
6:21 beloved brother and faithful **m** in the Lord, *1249*
Col 1: 7 who is for you a faithful **m** of Christ; *1249*

M

Col 1:23 whereof I Paul am made a **m**; *1249*
1:25 Whereof I am made a **m**, according to *1249*
4: 7 and a faithful **m** and fellowservant in *1249*
1Th 3: 2 and **m** of God, and our fellowlabourer in *1249*
1Ti 1: 4 endless genealogies, which **m** questions, *3930*
4: 6 thou shalt be a good **m** of Jesus Christ, *1249*
Heb 1:14 sent forth to **m** for them who shall be heirs *1248*
6:10 ye have ministered to the saints, and do **m**. *1247*
8: 2 A **m** of the sanctuary, and of the true *3011*
1Pe 1:12 but unto us they did **m** the things, *1247*
4:10 *the* gift, *even so* **m** the same one to another, *1247*
4:11 if any *man* **m**, *let him do it* as of the ability *1247*

MINISTERED (37) [MINISTER]

Nu 3: 4 Ithamar **m in the priest's office** in the sight 3547
Dt 10: 6 Eleazar his son **m in the priest's office** in 3547
1Sa 2:18 Samuel **m** before the LORD, *being* a 8334
3: 1 the child Samuel **m** unto the LORD before 8334
2Sa 13:17 he called his servant that **m** unto him, and 8334
1Ki 1: 4 and cherished the king, and **m** to him: 8334
1:15 Abishag the Shunammite **m** unto the king. 8334
19:21 and went after Elijah, and **m** unto him. 8334
2Ki 25:14 all the vessels of brass wherewith they **m**, 8334
1Ch 6:32 they **m** before the dwelling place of 8334
28: 1 the captains of the companies that **m** to 8334
2Ch 22: 8 that **m** to Ahaziah, he slew them. 8334
Est 2: 2 said the king's servants that **m** unto him, 8334
6: 3 said the king's servants that **m** unto him, 8334
Jer 52:18 all the vessels of brass wherewith they **m**, 8334
Eze 44:12 Because they **m** unto them before their 8334
44:19 put off their garments wherein they **m**, 8334
Da 7:10 thousand thousands **m** unto him, and 8120
Mt 4:11 and behold, angels came and **m** unto him. *1247*
8:15 left her: and she arose, and **m** unto them. *1247*
20:28 Even as the Son of man came not to be **m** *1247*
Mk 1:13 the wild beasts; and the angels **m** unto him. *1247*
1:31 the fever left her, and she **m** unto them. *1247*
10:45 For even the Son of man came not to be **m** *1247*
15:41 in Galilee, followed him, and **m** unto him;) *1247*
Lk 4:39 immediately she arose and **m** unto them. *1247*
8: 3 which **m** unto him of their substance. *1247*
Ac 13: 2 As they **m** to the Lord, and fasted, the Holy *3008*
19:22 Macedonia two of them that **m** unto him, *1247*
20:34 that these hands have **m** unto my *5256*
2Co 3: 3 declared to be the epistle of Christ **m** by us, *1247*
Php 2:25 and he that **m** to my wants. *3011*
Col 2:19 and bands having **nourishment m**, *2023*
2Ti 1:18 in how many *things* he **m** *unto me* at *1247*
Phm 1:13 that in thy stead he might have **m** unto me *1247*
Heb 6:10 in that ye have **m** to the saints, and *1247*
2Pe 1:11 an entrance shall be **m** unto you abundantly *2023*

MINISTERETH (2) [MINISTER]

2Co 9:10 Now he that **m** seed to the sower both *2023*
Gal 3: 5 He therefore that **m** to you the Spirit, and *2023*

MINISTERING (9) [MINISTER]

1Ch 9:28 *certain* of them had the charge of the **m** 5656
Eze 44:11 the gates of the house, and **m** to the house: 8334
Mt 27:55 followed Jesus from Galilee, **m** unto him: *1247*
Ro 12: 7 Or ministry, *let us wait* on *our* **m**: or he that *1248*
15:16 **m** the gospel of God, that the offering up of *2418*
2Co 8: 4 *take upon us* the fellowship of the **m** to *1248*
9: 1 For as touching the **m** to the saints, it is *1248*
Heb 1:14 Are they not all **m** spirits, sent forth to *3010*
10:11 And every priest standeth daily **m** and *3008*

MINISTERS (26) [MINISTER]

1Ki 10: 5 the attendance of his **m**, and their apparel, 8334
2Ch 9: 4 the attendance of his **m**, and their apparel; 8334
Ezr 7:24 or **m** of this house of God, 6399
8:17 that *they* should bring unto us **m** for 8334
Ps 103:21 his hosts; ye **m** of his, that do his pleasure. 8334
104: 4 his angels spirits; his **m** a flaming fire: 8334
Isa 61: 6 *men* shall call you the **M** of our God: 8334
Jer 33:21 and with the Levites the priests, my **m**. 8334
Eze 44:11 Yet they shall be **m** in my sanctuary, 8334
45: 4 be for the priests the **m** of the sanctuary, 8334
45: 5 the **m** of the house, have for themselves, 8334
46:24 where the **m** of the house shall boil 8334
Joel 1: 9 the priests, the LORD'S **m**, mourn. 8334
1:13 howl, ye **m** of the altar: come, lie all night 8334
1:13 lie all night in sackcloth, ye **m** of my God; 8334
2:17 Let the priests, the **m** of the LORD, 8334
Lk 1: 2 were eyewitnesses, and **m** of the word; *5257*
Ro 13: 6 for they are God's **m**, *3011*
1Co 3: 5 *is* Apollos, but **m** by whom ye believed, *1249*
4: 1 as of the **m** of Christ, and stewards of *5257*
2Co 3: 6 Who also hath made us able **m** of the new *1249*
6: 4 approving ourselves as the **m** of God, *1249*
11:15 Therefore *it is* no great *thing* if his **m** also *1249*
11:15 be transformed as the **m** of righteousness; *1249*
11:23 Are they **m** of Christ? (I speak as a fool) *1249*
Heb 1: 7 his angels spirits, and his **m** a flame of fire. *3011*

MINISTRATION (7) [MINISTER]

Lk 1:23 as the days of his **m** were accomplished, *3009*
Ac 6: 1 their widows were neglected in the daily **m**. *1248*
2Co 3: 7 But if the **m** of death, written *and* *1248*
3: 8 How shall not the **m** of the spirit be rather *1248*
3: 9 For if the **m** of condemnation *be* glory, *1248*
3: 9 much more doth the **m** of righteousness *1248*
9:13 Whiles by the experiment of this **m** they *1248*

MINISTRY (22) [MINISTER]

Nu 4:12 they shall take all the instruments of **m**, 8335
4:47 one that came to do the service of the **m**, 5656
2Ch 7: 6 for ever, when David praised by their **m**; 3027
Hos 12:10 used similitudes by the **m** of the prophets. 3027
Ac 1:17 with us, and had obtained part of this **m**. *1248*
1:25 That *he* may take part of this **m** and *1248*
6: 4 to prayer, and to the **m** of the word. *1248*
12:25 when they had fulfilled *their* **m**, and *1248*
20:24 might finish my course with joy, and the **m**, *1248*
Ac 21:19 had wrought among the Gentiles by his **m**. *1248*
Ro 12: 7 Or **m**, *let us wait on our* ministering: or *1248*
1Co 16:15 *that* they have addicted themselves to the **m** *1248*
2Co 4: 1 Therefore seeing we have this **m**, as we *1248*
5:18 hath given to us the **m** of reconciliation; *1248*
6: 3 Giving no offence in any *thing*, that the **m** *1248*
Eph 4:12 of the saints for the work of the **m**, *1248*
Col 4:17 Take heed to the **m** which thou hast *1248*
1Ti 1:12 counted me faithful, putting *me* into the **m**; *1248*
2Ti 4: 5 of an evangelist, make full proof of thy **m**. *1248*
4:11 for he is profitable to me for the **m**. *1248*
Heb 8: 6 now hath he obtained a more excellent **m**, *3009*
9:21 the tabernacle, and all the vessels of the **m**. *3009*

MINNI (1)

Jer 51:27 kingdoms of Ararat, **M**, and Ashchenaz; 4508

MINNITH (2)

Jdg 11:33 even till thou come *to* **M**, *even* twenty 4511
Eze 27:17 they traded in thy market wheat of **M**, and 4511

MINSTREL (2) [MINSTRELS]

2Ki 3:15 now bring me a **m**. And it came to pass, 5059
3:15 it came to pass, when the **m** played, that 5059

MINSTRELS (1) [MINSTREL]

Mt 9:23 and saw the **m** and the people making a *834*

MINT (2)

Mt 23:23 for ye pay tithe of **m** and anise and *2238*
Lk 11:42 for ye tithe **m** and rue and all *manner of* *2238*

MIPHKAD (1)

Ne 3:31 over against the gate **M**, and to the going 4662

MIRACLE (10) [MIRACLES]

Ex 7: 9 speak unto you, saying, Shew a **m** for you: 4159
Mk 6:52 For they considered not *the* **m** of the loaves: NIG
9:39 for there is no *man* which shall do a **m** in *1411*
Lk 23: 8 he hoped to have seen some **m** done by *4592*
Jn 4:54 This *is* again the second **m** *that* Jesus did, *4592*
6:14 when they had seen the **m** that Jesus did, *4592*
10:41 resorted unto him, and said, John did no **m**: *4592*
12:18 for that they heard that he had done this **m**. *4592*
Ac 4:16 for that indeed a notable **m** hath been done *4592*
4:22 on whom this **m** of healing was shewed. *4592*

MIRACLES (27) [MIRACLE]

Nu 14:22 my **m**, which I did in Egypt and in 226
Dt 11: 3 his **m**, and his acts, which he did in the midst 226
29: 3 have seen, the signs, and those great **m**: 4159
Jdg 6:13 where *be* all his **m** which our fathers told us 6381
Jn 2:11 This beginning of **m** did Jesus in Cana of *4592*
2:23 when they saw the **m** which he did. *4592*
3: 2 for no *man* can do these **m** that thou doest, *4592*
6: 2 they saw his **m** which he did on them that *4592*
6:26 not because ye saw *the* **m**, but because *4592*
7:31 will he do moe **m** than these which this *4592*
9:16 How can a man that *is* a sinner do such **m**? *4592*
11:47 What do we? for this man doeth many **m**. *4592*
12:37 he had done so many **m** before them, *4592*
Ac 2:22 a man approved of God among you by **m** *1411*
6: 8 did great wonders and **m** among the people. *4592*
8: 6 hearing and seeing the **m** which he did. *4592*
8:13 beholding *the* **m** and signs *which were* *1411*
15:12 declaring what **m** and wonders God had *4592*
19:11 And God wrought special **m** by the hands *1411*
1Co 12:10 To another the working of **m**; to another *1411*
12:28 after that **m**, then gifts of healings, helps, *1411*
12:29 *are* all teachers? *are* all **workers of m**? *1411*
Gal 3: 5 you the Spirit, and worketh **m** among you, *1411*
Heb 2: 4 and with divers **m**, and gifts of the Holy *1411*
Rev 13:14 **m** which he had power to do in the sight of *4592*
16:14 they are the spirits of devils, working **m**, *4592*
19:20 with him the false prophet that wrought **m** *4592*

MIRE (15) [MIRY]

2Sa 22:43 I did stamp them as the **m** of the street, *and* 2916
Job 8:11 Can the rush grow up without **m**? can 1207
30:19 He hath cast me into the **m**, and I am 2563
41:30 spreadeth sharp pointed *things* upon the **m**. 2916
Ps 69: 2 I sink in deep **m**, where *there is* no 3121
69:14 Deliver me out of the **m**, and let me not 2916
Isa 10: 6 to tread them down like the **m** of 2563
57:20 whose waters cast up **m** and dirt. 7516
Jer 38: 6 in the dungeon *there was* no water, but **m**: 2916
38: 6 but mire: so Jeremiah sunk in the **m**. 2916
38:22 thy feet are sunk in the **m**, *and* they are 1206
Mic 7:10 now shall she be trodden down as the **m** of 2916
Zec 9: 3 and fine gold as the **m** of the streets. 2916
10: 5 *enemies* in the **m** of the streets in the battle: 2916
2Pe 2:22 that was washed to *her* wallowing in the **m**. *1004*

MIRIAM (15)

Ex 15:20 **M** the prophetess, the sister of Aaron, took 4813
15:21 **M** answered them, Sing ye to the LORD, 4813
Nu 12: 1 **M** and Aaron spake against Moses because 4813
12: 4 unto Moses, and unto Aaron, and unto **M**, 4813
12: 5 of the tabernacle, and called Aaron and **M**: 4813
12:10 behold, **M** *became* leprous, *white* as snow: 4813
12:10 Aaron looked upon **M**, and behold, *she was* 4813
12:15 **M** was shut out from the camp seven days: 4813
12:15 the people journeyed not till **M** was 4813
20: 1 and **M** died there, and was buried there. 4813
26:59 and Moses, and **M** their sister. 4813
Dt 24: 9 LORD thy God did unto **M** by the way, 4813
1Ch 4:17 she bare **M**, and Shammai, and Ishbah 4813
6: 3 of Amram; Aaron, and Moses, and **M**. 4813
Mic 6: 4 I sent before thee Moses, Aaron, and **M**. 4813

MIRMA (1)

1Ch 8:10 Jeuz, and Shachia, and **M**. These *were* his 4821

MIRROR See GLASSES; LOOKINGGLASSES

MIRTH (15)

Ge 31:27 that I might have sent thee away with **m**, 8057
Ne 8:12 to make great **m**, because they had 8057
Ps 137: 3 they that wasted us *required of us* **m**, 8057
Pr 14:13 and the end of that **m** *is* heaviness. 8057
Ecc 2: 1 I will prove thee with **m**, therefore 8057
2: 2 *It is* mad: and of **m**, What doeth it? 8057
7: 4 but the heart of fools *is* in the house of **m**. 8057
8:15 I commended **m**, because a man hath no 8057
Isa 24: 8 The **m** of tabrets ceaseth, the noise of them 4885
24:11 joy is darkened, the **m** of the land is gone. 4885
Jer 7:34 the voice of **m**, and the voice of gladness, 8342
16: 9 the voice of **m**, and the voice of gladness, 8342
25:10 I will take from them the voice of **m**, 8342
Eze 21:10 should we then **make m**? it contemneth 7797
Hos 2:11 I will also cause all her **m** to cease, 4885

MIRY (4) [MIRE]

Ps 40: 2 out of the **m** clay, and set my feet upon a 3121
Eze 47:11 the **m places** thereof and the marishes 1207
Da 2:41 as thou sawest the iron mixed with **m** clay. 2917
2:43 whereas thou sawest iron mixt with **m** clay, 2917

MISCARRYING (1)

Hos 9:14 give them a **m** womb and dry breasts. 7921

MISCHIEF (47) [MISCHIEFS, MISCHIEVOUS]

Ge 42: 4 for he said, Lest peradventure **m** befall him. 611
42:38 if **m** befall him by the way in the which ye 611
44:29 ye take this also from me, and **m** befall him, 611
Ex 21:22 fruit depart *from her*, and yet no **m** follow: 611
21:23 if *any* **m** follow, then thou shalt give life for 611
32:12 say, For **m** did he bring them out, to slay 7451
32:22 knowest the people, that they *are set* on **m**. 7451
1Sa 23: 9 David knew that Saul secretly practised **m** 7451
2Sa 16: 8 and, behold, thou *art taken* to thy **m**, 7451
1Ki 11:25 beside the **m** that Hadad *did:* and 7451
20: 7 pray you, and see how this *man* seeketh **m**: 7451
2Ki 7: 9 morning light, *some* **m** will come upon us: 5771
Ne 6: 2 plain of Ono. But they thought to do me **m**. 7451
Est 8: 3 besought him with tears to put away the **m** 7451
Job 15:35 They conceive **m**, and bring forth vanity, 5999
Ps 7:14 hath conceived **m**, and brought forth 5999
7:16 His **m** shall return upon his own head, and 5999
10: 7 fraud: under his tongue *is* **m** and vanity. 5999
10:14 Thou hast seen *it;* for thou beholdest **m** and 5999
26:10 In whose hands *is* **m**, and their right hand is 2154
28: 3 to their neighbours, but **m** *is* in their hearts. 7451
36: 4 He deviseth **m** upon his bed; he setteth 205
52: 1 Why boastest thou thyself in **m**, O mighty 7451
55:10 **m** also and sorrow *are* in the midst of it. 205
62: 3 How long will ye **imagine m** against a 2050
94:20 *with* thee, which frameth **m** by a law? 5999
119:150 They draw nigh that follow after **m**: 2154
140: 9 let the **m** of their own lips cover them. 5999
Pr 4:16 they sleep not, except they have **done m**; 7489
6:14 *is* in his heart, he deviseth **m** continually; 7451
6:18 feet that be swift in running to **m**, 7451
10:23 *It is* as sport to a fool to do **m**: but a man of 2154
11:27 he that seeketh **m**, it shall come *unto* him. 7451
12:21 but the wicked shall be filled *with* **m**. 7451
13:17 A wicked messenger falleth into **m**: but 7451
17:20 that hath a perverse tongue falleth into **m**. 7451
24: 2 and their lips talk of **m**. 5999
24:16 up *again:* but the wicked shall fall into **m**. 7451
28:14 he that hardeneth his heart shall fall into **m**. 7451
Isa 47:11 **m** shall fall upon thee; thou shalt not be 1943
59: 4 *they* conceive **m**, and bring forth iniquity. 5999
Eze 7:26 **M** shall come upon mischief, and 1943
7:26 Mischief shall come upon **m**, and 1943
11: 2 these *are* the men that devise **m**, and give 205
Da 11:27 both these kings' hearts *shall be* to **do m**, 4827
Hos 7:15 yet do they imagine **m** against me. 7451
Ac 13:10 And said, O full of all subtilty and all **m**, *4468*

MISCHIEFS (3) [MISCHIEF]

Dt 32:23 I will heap **m** upon them; I will spend mine 7451
Ps 52: 2 Thy tongue deviseth **m**; like a sharp rasor, 1942
140: 2 Which imagine **m** in *their* heart; 7451

MISCHIEVOUS (5) [MISCHIEF]

Ps 21:11 they imagined a **m device**, *which* they are 4209
38:12 and they that seek my hurt speak **m things**, 1942
Pr 24: 8 to do evil shall be called a **m** person. 4209
Ecc 10:13 and the end of his talk *is* **m** madness. 7451
Mic 7: 3 and the great *man*, he uttereth his **m** desire: 1942

MISERABLE (3) [MISERY]

Job 16: 2 I have heard many such *things:* **m** 5999
1Co 15:19 hope in Christ, we are of all men **most m**. *1652*
Rev 3:17 and **m**, and poor, and blind, and naked: *1652*

MISERABLY (1) [MISERY]

Mt 21:41 He will **m** destroy those wicked *men*, and *2560*

MISERIES (2) [MISERY]

La 1: 7 of her **m** all her pleasant things that she had 4788
Jas 5: 1 howl for your **m** that shall come upon *you*. *5004*

MISERY (7) [MISERABLE, MISERABLY, MISERIES]

Jdg 10:16 his soul was grieved for the **m** of Israel. 5999
Job 3:20 is light given to him that is **in m**, 6001
11:16 Because thou shalt forget *thy* **m**, *and* 5999
Pr 31: 7 his poverty, and remember his **m** no more. 5999
Ecc 8: 6 therefore the **m** of man *is* great upon him. 7451
La 3:19 Remembering mine affliction and my **m**, 4788
Ro 3:16 Destruction and **m** *are* in their ways: *5004*

MISFORTUNE See TRAVAIL; TRAVAILED; TRAVAILEST; TRAVAILETH

MISGAB (1)

Jer 48: 1 *and* taken: **M** is confounded and dismayed. 4869

MISHAEL (8)

Ex 6:22 of Uzziel; **M**, and Elzaphan, and Zithri. 4332
Lev 10: 4 Moses called **M** and Elzaphan, the sons of 4332
Ne 8: 4 **M**, and Malchiah, and Hashum, and 4332
Da 1: 6 Daniel, Hananiah, **M**, and Azariah: 4332
1: 7 to **M**, of Meshach; and to Azariah, 4332
1:11 set over Daniel, Hananiah, **M**, and Azariah, 4332
1:19 like Daniel, Hananiah, **M**, and Azariah: 4332
2:17 **M**, and Azariah, his companions: 4333

MISHAL (1)

Jos 21:30 **M** with her suburbs, Abdon with her 4861

MISHAM (1)

1Ch 8:12 Eber, and **M**, and Shamed, who built Ono, 4936

MISHEAL (1)

Jos 19:26 Alammelech, and Amad, and **M**; and 4861

MISHMA (4)

Ge 25:14 And **M**, and Dumah, and Massa, 4927
1Ch 1:30 **M**, and Dumah, Massa, Hadad, and Tema, 4927
4:25 his son, Mibsam his son, **M** his son. 4927
4:26 the sons of **M**; Hamuel his son, Zacchur his 4927

MISHMANNAH (1)

1Ch 12:10 **M** the fourth, Jeremiah the fifth, 4925

MISHRAITES (1)

1Ch 2:53 and the Shumathites, and the **M**; 4954

MISPAR See MIZPAR

MISPERETH (1)

Ne 7: 7 Bilshan, **M**, Bigvai, Nehum, Baanah. 4559

MISREPHOTH-MAIM (2)

Jos 11: 8 unto **M**, and unto the valley of Mizpeh 4956
13: 6 of the hill country from Lebanon unto **M**, 4956

MISS (2) [AMISS, MISSED, MISSING]

Jdg 20:16 sling stones at a hair *breadth*, and not **m**. 2398
1Sa 20: 6 If thy father **at all m** me, then say, 6485+6485

MISSED (3) [MISS]

1Sa 20:18 thou shalt be **m**, because thy seat will be 6485
25:15 we were not hurt, neither **m** we any thing, 6485
25:21 that nothing was **m** of all that *pertained* 6485

MISSING (2) [MISS]

1Sa 25: 7 neither was there ought **m** unto them, 6485
1Ki 20:39 if **by any means** he be **m**, then 6485+6485

MIST (3)

Ge 2: 6 there went up a **m** from the earth, and 108
Ac 13:11 And immediately there fell on him a **m** and *887*
2Pe 2:17 to whom the **m** of darkness is reserved for *2217*

MISTREAT; MISTREATED See VEX; VEXATION; VEXED

MISTRESS (9)

Ge 16: 4 her **m** was despised in her eyes. 1404
16: 8 I flee from the face of my **m** Sarai. 1404
16: 9 Return to thy **m**, and submit thyself under 1404
1Ki 17:17 of the woman, the **m** of the house, fell sick; 1172
2Ki 5: 3 she said unto her **m**, Would God my lord 1404
Ps 123: 2 eyes of a maiden unto the hand of her **m**; 1404
Pr 30:23 and a handmaid that is heir to her **m**. 1404
Isa 24: 2 his master; as *with* the maid, so *with* her **m**; 1404
Na 3: 4 the **m** of witchcrafts, that selleth nations 1172

MISUSED (1)

2Ch 36:16 despised his words, and **m** his prophets, 8591

MITE (1) [MITES]

Lk 12:59 till thou hast paid the very last **m**. *3016*

MITES (2) [MITE]

Mk 12:42 and she threw in two **m**, which make a *3016*
Lk 21: 2 poor widow casting in thither two **m**. *3016*

MITHCAH (2)

Nu 33:28 removed from Tarah, and pitched in **M**. 4989
33:29 they went from **M**, and pitched in 4989

MITHNITE (1)

1Ch 11:43 the son of Maachah, and Joshaphat the **M**, 4981

MITHREDATH (2)

Ezr 1: 8 bring forth by the hand of **M** the treasurer, 4990
4: 7 **M**, Tabeel, and the rest of their 4990

MITRE (13)

Ex 28: 4 and a broidered coat, a **m**, and a girdle: 4701
28:37 it on a blue lace, that it may be upon the **m**; 4701
28:37 upon the forefront of the **m** it shall be. 4701
28:39 thou shalt make the **m** *of* fine linen, and 4701
29: 6 thou shalt put the **m** upon his head, and 4701
29: 6 and put the holy crown upon the **m**. 4701
39:28 a **m** *of* fine linen, and goodly bonnets *of* 4701
39:31 of blue, to fasten *it* on high upon the **m**; 4701
Lev 8: 9 he put the **m** upon his head; also upon 4701
8: 9 also upon the **m**, *even* upon his forefront, 4701
16: 4 and with the linen **m** shall he be attired: 4701
Zec 3: 5 I said, Let them set a fair **m** upon his head. 6797
3: 5 So they set a fair **m** upon his head, and 6797

MITYLENE (1)

Ac 20:14 at Assos, we took him in, and came to **M**. *3412*

MIXED (6) [MIXTURE]

Ex 12:38 a **m** multitude went up also with them; and 6154
Ne 13: 3 separated from Israel all the **m multitude**. 6154
Da 2:41 forasmuch as thou sawest the iron **m** with 6151
2:43 to another, even as iron is not **m** with clay. 6151
Hos 7: 8 he hath **m** himself among the people; 1101
Heb 4: 2 not being **m** with faith in them that heard *4786*

MIXT (4) [MIXTURE]

Nu 11: 4 the **m multitude** that *was* among them fell a 628
Pr 23:30 at the wine; they that go to seek **m wine**. 4469
Isa 1:22 is become dross, thy wine **m** with water: 4107
Da 2:43 whereas thou sawest iron **m** with miry clay, 6151

MIXTURE (3) [MIXED, MIXT]

Ps 75: 8 it is full *of* **m**; and he poureth out of 4538
Jn 19:39 and brought a **m** of myrrh and aloes, *3395*
Rev 14:10 which is poured out **without m** into the cup *194*

MIZAR (1)

Ps 42: 6 and of the Hermonites, from the hill **M**. 4706

MIZPAH (23) [MIZPEH]

Ge 31:49 **M**; for he said, The LORD watch between 4709
1Ki 15:22 built with them Geba of Benjamin, and **M**. 4709
2Ki 25:23 there came to Gedaliah *to* **M**, even Ishmael 4709
25:25 and the Chaldees that were with him at **M**. 4709
2Ch 16: 6 and he built therewith Geba and **M**. 4709
Ne 3: 7 the men of Gibeon, and of **M**, 4709
3:15 son of Col-hozeh, the ruler of part of **M**; 4709
3:19 Ezer the son of Jeshua, the ruler of **M**, 4709
Jer 40: 6 unto Gedaliah the son of Ahikam to **M**; 4708
40: 8 they came to Gedaliah to **M**, even Ishmael 4708
40:10 I *will* dwell at **M** to serve the Chaldeans, 4709
40:12 unto **M**, and gathered wine and 4708
40:13 *were* in the fields, came to Gedaliah to **M**, 4708
40:15 of Kareah spake to Gedaliah in **M** secretly, 4709
41: 1 unto Gedaliah the son of Ahikam to **M**; 4708
41: 1 and there they did eat bread together in **M**. 4708
41: 3 *even* with Gedaliah at **M**, and 4709
41: 6 went forth from **M** to meet them, 4709
41:10 all the residue of the people that *were* in **M**, 4709
41:10 and all the people that remained in **M**, 4709
41:14 carried away captive from **M** cast about 4709
41:16 from **M**, after *that* he had slain Gedaliah 4709
Hos 5: 1 because ye have been a snare on **M**, and 4709

MIZPAR (1)

Ezr 2: 2 Bilshan, **M**, Bigvai, Rehum, Baanah. 4558

MIZPEH (23) [MIZPAH, RAMATH-MIZPEH]

Jos 11: 3 the Hivite under Hermon in the land of **M** 4709
11: 8 and unto the valley of **M** eastward; 4708
15:38 And Dilean, and **M**, and Joktheel, 4708
18:26 And **M**, and Chephirah, and Mozah, 4708
Jdg 10:17 themselves together, and encamped in **M**. 4709
11:11 all his words before the LORD in **M**. 4709
11:29 passed over **M** of Gilead, and from Mizpeh 4708
11:29 from **M** of Gilead he passed over *unto* 4708
11:34 Jephthah came *to* **M** unto his house, and 4709
20: 1 the land of Gilead, unto the LORD *in* **M**. 4709
20: 3 the children of Israel were gone up *to* **M**.) 4709
21: 1 Now the men of Israel had sworn in **M**, 4709
21: 5 *him* that came not up to the LORD *to* **M**, 4709
21: 8 that came not up *to* **M** to the LORD? 4709
1Sa 7: 5 Gather all Israel to **M**, and I will pray for 4708
7: 6 they gathered together to **M**, and 4709
7: 6 Samuel judged the children of Israel in **M**. 4708
7: 7 of Israel were gathered together to **M**, 4708
7:11 the men of Israel went out of **M**, and 4709
7:12 set *it* between **M** and Shen, and called 4709
7:16 **M**, and judged Israel in all those places. 4709
10:17 the people together unto the LORD *to* **M**, 4709
22: 3 David went thence *to* **M** of Moab: and 4708

MIZRAIM (4)

Ge 10: 6 Cush, and **M**, and Phut, and Canaan. 4714
10:13 **M** begat Ludim, and Anamim, and 4714
1Ch 1: 8 of Ham; Cush, and **M**, Put, and Canaan. 4714
1:11 **M** begat Ludim, and Anamim, and 4714

MIZZAH (3)

Ge 36:13 Nahath, and Zerah, Shammah, and **M**: 4199
36:17 duke Zerah, duke Shammah, duke **M**: 4199
1Ch 1:37 of Reuel; Nahath, Zerah, Shammah, and **M**. 4199

MNASON (1)

Ac 21:16 and brought *with them* one **M** of Cyprus, *3416*

MO (1) [= MORE]

2Sa 5:13 David took *him* **m** concubines and 5750

MOAB (168) [MOABITE, MOABITES, MOABITESS, MOABITISH]

Ge 19:37 bare a son, and called his name **M**: 4124
36:35 who smote Midian in the field of **M**, 4124
Ex 15:15 the mighty men of **M**, trembling shall take 4124
Nu 21:11 in the wilderness which *is* before **M**, 4124
21:13 for Arnon *is* the border of **M**, 4124
21:13 of Moab, between **M** and the Amorites. 4124
21:15 of Ar, and lieth upon the border of **M**. 4124
21:20 that *is* in the country of **M**, *to* the top of 4124
21:26 had fought against the former king of **M**, 4124
21:28 it hath consumed Ar of **M**, *and* the lords of 4124
21:29 Woe to thee, **M**! thou art undone, O people 4124
22: 1 pitched in the plains of **M** on *this* side 4124
22: 3 **M** was sore afraid of the people, because 4124
22: 3 **M** was distressed because of the children of 4124
22: 4 **M** said unto the elders of Midian, 4124
22: 7 the elders of **M** and the elders of Midian 4124
22: 8 and the princes of **M** abode with Balaam. 4124
22:10 king of **M**, hath sent unto me, *saying*, 4124
22:14 the princes of **M** rose up, and they went 4124
22:21 his ass, and went with the princes of **M**. 4124
22:36 he went out to meet him unto a city of **M**, 4124
23: 6 burnt sacrifice, he, and all the princes of **M**. 4124
23: 7 Balak the king of **M** hath brought me from 4124
23:17 and the princes of **M** with him. 4124
24:17 shall smite the corners of **M**, and 4124
25: 1 whoredom with the daughters of **M**. 4124
26: 3 in the plains of **M** by Jordan *near* Jericho, 4124
26:63 in the plains of **M** by Jordan *near* Jericho. 4124
31:12 unto the camp at the plains of **M**, which *are* 4124
33:44 pitched in Ije-abarim, in the border of **M**. 4124
33:48 pitched in the plains of **M** by Jordan *near* 4124
33:49 *even* unto Abel-shittim in the plains of **M**. 4124
33:50 in the plains of **M** by Jordan *near* Jericho, 4124
35: 1 in the plains of **M** by Jordan *near* Jericho, 4124
36:13 in the plains of **M** by Jordan *near* Jericho. 4124
Dt 1: 5 On *this* side Jordan, in the land of **M**, 4124
2: 8 passed *by* the way of the wilderness of **M**. 4124
2:18 over *through* Ar, the coast of **M**, *this* day: 4124
29: 1 with the children of Israel in the land of **M**, 4124
32:49 mount Nebo, which *is* in the land of **M**, 4124
34: 1 Moses went up from the plains of **M** unto 4124
34: 5 of the LORD died there in the land of **M**, 4124
34: 6 he buried him in a valley in the land of **M**, 4124
34: 8 for Moses in the plains of **M** thirty days: 4124
Jos 13:32 distribute for inheritance in the plains of **M**, 4124
24: 9 king of **M**, arose and warred against Israel, 4124
Jdg 3:12 Eglon the king of **M** against Israel, 4124
3:14 served Eglon the king of **M** eighteen years. 4124
3:15 sent a present unto Eglon the king of **M**. 4124
3:17 brought the present unto Eglon king of **M**: 4124
3:28 took the fords of Jordan toward **M**, and 4124
3:29 they slew *of* **M** at that time about ten 4124
3:30 So **M** was subdued that day under the hand 4124
10: 6 the gods of **M**, and the gods of the children 4124
11:15 Israel took not away the land of **M**, 4124
11:17 like manner they sent unto the king of **M**: 4124
11:18 the land of **M**, and came by the east side of 4124
11:18 came by the east side of the land of **M**, and 4124
11:18 but came not within the border of **M**: 4124
11:18 of Moab: for Arnon *was* the border of **M**. 4124
11:25 than Balak the son of Zippor, king of **M**? 4124
Ru 1: 1 went to sojourn in the country of **M**, 4124
1: 2 they came *into* the country of **M**, and 4124
1: 4 they took them wives of the **women of M**; 4125
1: 6 she might return from the country of **M**: 4124
1: 6 for she had heard in the country of **M** how 4124
1:22 which returned out of the country of **M**: 4124
2: 6 back with Naomi out of the country of **M**: 4124
4: 3 that is come again out of the country of **M**, 4124
1Sa 12: 9 into the hand of the king of **M**, and 4124
14:47 against **M**, and against the children of 4124
22: 3 David went thence *to* Mizpeh of **M**: and 4124
22: 3 he said unto the king of **M**, Let my father 4124
22: 4 he brought them before the king of **M**: and 4124
2Sa 8: 2 he smote **M**, and measured them with a 4124
8:12 of **M**, and of the children of Ammon, and 4124
23:20 many acts, he slew two lionlike men of **M**: 4124
1Ki 11: 7 the abomination of **M**, in the hill that *is* 4124
2Ki 1: 1 **M** rebelled against Israel after the death of 4124
3: 4 Mesha king of **M** was a sheepmaster, and 4124
3: 5 that the king of **M** rebelled against the king 4124
3: 7 The king of **M** hath rebelled against me: 4124
3: 7 wilt thou go with me against **M** to battle? 4124
3:10 to deliver them into the hand of **M**. 4124
3:13 to deliver them into the hand of **M**. 4124
3:23 one another: now therefore, **M**, to the spoil. 4124
3:26 when the king of **M** saw that the battle was 4124
1Ch 1:46 which smote Midian in the field of **M**, 4124
4:22 who had the dominion in **M**, and 4124
8: 8 begat *children* in the country of **M**, 4124
11:22 many acts; he slew two lionlike men of **M**: 4124
18: 2 he smote **M**; and the Moabites became 4124
18:11 from **M**, and from the children of Ammon, 4124
2Ch 20: 1 *that* the children of **M**, and the children of 4124
20:10 children of Ammon and **M** and mount Seir, 4124
20:22 **M**, and mount Seir, which were come 4124
20:23 **M** stood up against the inhabitants of 4124
Ne 13:23 wives of Ashdod, of Ammon, *and* **of M**: 4125
Ps 60: 8 **M** *is* my washpot; over Edom will I cast 4124
83: 6 the Ishmaelites; of **M**, and the Hagarenes; 4124
108: 9 **M** *is* my washpot; over Edom will I cast 4124
Isa 11:14 shall lay their hand upon Edom and **M**; 4124
15: 1 The burden of **M**. Because in the night Ar 4124
15: 1 Because in the night Ar of **M** is laid waste, 4124
15: 1 because in the night Kir of **M** is laid waste, 4124
15: 2 **M** shall howl over Nebo, and over Medeba: 4124
15: 4 the armed soldiers of **M** shall cry out; 4124
15: 5 My heart shall cry out for **M**; his fugitives 4124
15: 8 cry is gone round about the borders of **M**; 4124
15: 9 lions upon him that escapeth of **M**, and 4124
16: 2 the daughters of **M** shall be *at* the fords of 4124
16: 4 Let mine outcasts dwell with thee, **M**; 4124
16: 6 We have heard of the pride of **M**; *he is* very 4124
16: 7 Therefore shall **M** howl for Moab, 4124
16: 7 Therefore shall Moab howl for **M**, 4124
16:11 my bowels shall sound like a harp for **M**, 4124
16:12 when it is seen that **M** is weary on the high 4124
16:13 hath spoken concerning **M** since that time. 4124
16:14 and the glory of **M** shall be contemned, 4124
25:10 **M** shall be trodden down under him, 4124
Jer 9:26 **M**, and all *that are* in the utmost corners, 4124
25:21 Edom, and **M**, and the children of Ammon, 4124
27: 3 to the king of **M**, and to the king of 4124
40:11 Likewise when all the Jews that *were* in **M**, 4124
48: 1 Against **M** thus saith the LORD of hosts, 4124
48: 2 *There shall be* no more praise of **M**: 4124
48: 4 **M** is destroyed; her little ones have caused 4124
48: 9 Give wings unto **M**, that it may flee and 4124
48:11 **M** hath been at ease from his youth, and 4124
48:13 **M** shall be ashamed of Chemosh, as 4124
48:15 **M** is spoiled, and gone up *out of* her cities, 4124
48:16 The calamity of **M** *is* near to come, and 4124
48:18 for the spoiler of **M** shall come upon thee, 4124
48:20 **M** is confounded; for it is broken down: 4124

Jer 48:20 cry; tell ye *it* in Arnon, that **M** is spoiled, 4124
48:24 upon all the cities of the land of **M**, far or 4124
48:25 The horn of **M** is cut off, and his arm is 4124
48:26 **M** also shall wallow in his vomit, and 4124
48:28 O ye that dwell in **M**, leave the cities, and 4124
48:29 We have heard the pride of **M**; *he is* 4124
48:31 Therefore will I howl for **M**, and I will cry 4124
48:31 howl for Moab, and I will cry out for all **M**; 4124
48:33 the plentiful field, and from the land of **M**; 4124
48:35 Moreover I will cause to cease in **M**, 4124
48:36 Therefore mine heart shall sound for **M** like 4124
48:38 generally upon all the housetops of **M**, 4124
48:38 for I have broken **M** like a vessel wherein 4124
48:39 how hath **M** turned the back with shame! 4124
48:39 so shall **M** be a derision and a dismaying to 4124
48:40 and shall spread his wings over **M**. 4124
48:41 the mighty *men's* hearts in **M** at that day 4124
48:42 **M** shall be destroyed from *being* a people, 4124
48:43 O inhabitant of **M**, saith the LORD. 4124
48:44 for I will bring upon it, *even* upon **M**, 4124
48:45 shall devour the corner of **M**, and 4124
48:46 Woe be unto thee, O **M**! the people of 4124
48:47 Yet will I bring again the captivity of **M** in 4124
48:47 the LORD. Thus far *is* the judgment of **M**. 4124
Eze 25: 8 Because that **M** and Seir do say, Behold, 4124
25: 9 I *will* open the side of **M** from the cities, 4124
25:11 I will execute judgments upon **M**; and 4124
Da 11:41 **M**, and the chief of the children of Ammon. 4124
Am 2: 1 For three transgressions of **M**, and for four, 4124
2: 2 I will send a fire upon **M**, and it shall 4124
2: 2 **M** shall die with tumult, with shouting, *and* 4124
Mic 6: 5 remember now what Balak king of **M** 4124
Zep 2: 8 I have heard the reproach of **M**, and 4124
2: 9 Surely **M** shall be as Sodom, and 4124

MOABITE (3) [MOAB]
Dt 23: 3 **M** shall not enter into the congregation of 4125
1Ch 11:46 the sons of Elnaam, and Ithmah the **M**, 4125
Ne 13: 1 the **M** should not come into 4125

MOABITES (19) [MOAB]
Ge 19:37 *the same is* the father of the **M** unto *this* 4124
Nu 22: 4 Balak the son of Zippor *was* king of the **M** 4124
Dt 2: 9 LORD said unto me, Distress not the **M**, 4124
2:11 the Anakims; but the **M** call them Emims. 4125
2:29 and the **M** which dwell in Ar, did unto me;) 4125
Jdg 3:28 your enemies the **M** into your hand. 4124
2Sa 8: 2 *so* the **M** became David's servants, and 4124
1Ki 11: 1 *women of the* **M**, Ammonites, Edomites, 4125
11:33 Chemosh the god of the **M**, and Milcom 4124
2Ki 3:18 he will deliver the **M** also into your hand. 4124
3:21 when all the **M** heard that the kings were 4124
3:22 the **M** saw the water on the other side *as* 4124
3:24 the Israelites rose up and smote the **M**, so 4124
3:24 they went forward smiting the **M**, even in 4124
13:20 the bands of the **M** invaded the land *at* 4124
23:13 for Chemosh the abomination of the **M**, 4124
24: 2 bands of the **M**, and bands of the children 4124
1Ch 18: 2 the **M** became David's servants, and 4124
Ezr 9: 1 the **M**, the Egyptians, and the Amorites. 4125

MOABITESS (6) [MOAB]
Ru 1:22 So Naomi returned, and Ruth the **M**, 4125
2: 2 Ruth the **M** said unto Naomi, Let me now 4125
2:21 And Ruth the **M** said, He said unto me also, 4125
4: 5 thou must buy *it* also of Ruth the **M**, 4125
4:10 Moreover Ruth the **M**, the wife of Mahlon, 4125
2Ch 24:26 and Jehozabad the son of Shimrith a **M**. 4125

MOABITISH (1) [MOAB]
Ru 2: 6 It *is* the **M** damsel that came back with 4125

MOADIAH (1)
Ne 12:17 Zichri; of Miniamin, of **M**, Piltai; 4153

MOCK (12) [MOCKED, MOCKER, MOCKERS, MOCKEST, MOCKETH, MOCKING, MOCKINGS]
Ge 39:14 he hath brought in a Hebrew unto us to **m** 6711
39:17 brought unto us, came in unto me to **m** me: 6711
Job 13: 9 *one* man mocketh another, do ye *so* **m** him? 2048
21: 3 and after that I have spoken, **m** on. 3932
Pr 1:26 I will **m** when your fear cometh; 3932
14: 9 Fools **make a m at** sin: but among 3887
Jer 38:19 deliver me into their hand, and they **m** me. 5953
La 1: 7 saw her, *and* did **m** at her sabbaths. 7832
Eze 22: 5 shall **m** thee, *which art* infamous *and* 7046
Mt 20:19 And shall deliver him to the Gentiles to **m**, *1702*
Mk 10:34 And they shall **m** him, and shall scourge *1702*
Lk 14:29 finish *it*, all that behold *it* begin to **m** him, *1702*

MOCKED (21) [MOCK]
Ge 19:14 he seemed as one that **m** unto his sons in 6711
Nu 22:29 said unto the ass, Because thou hast **m** me: 5953
Jdg 16:10 Behold, thou hast **m** me, and told me lies: 2048
16:13 Hitherto thou hast **m** me, and told me lies: 2048
16:15 thou hast **m** me these three times, and 2048
1Ki 18:27 that Elijah **m** them, and said, Cry aloud: 2048
2Ki 2:23 **m** him, and said unto him, Go up, thou bald 7046
2Ch 30:10 they laughed them to scorn, and **m** them. 3932
36:16 they **m** the messengers of God, and 3931
Ne 4: 1 took great indignation, and **m** the Jews. 3932
Job 12: 4 I am *as* **one m** of his neighbour, 7814
Mt 2:16 when he saw that he was **m** of the wise *1702*
27:29 and **m** him, saying, Hail, King of the Jews! *1702*
27:31 And after that they had **m** him, they took *1702*
Mk 15:20 And when they had **m** him, they took off *1702*
Lk 18:32 and shall be **m**, and spitefully entreated, *1702*
22:63 And the men that held Jesus **m** him, and *1702*
23:11 and **m** *him*, and arrayed him in a gorgeous *1702*
23:36 And the soldiers also **m** him, coming to *1702*
Ac 17:32 of the resurrection of the dead, some **m**: *5512*
Gal 6: 7 Be not deceived; God is not **m**: *3456*

MOCKER (1) [MOCK]
Pr 20: 1 Wine *is* a **m**, strong drink *is* raging: and 3887

MOCKERS (5) [MOCK]
Job 17: 2 *Are there* not **m** with me? and *doth not* 2049
Ps 35:16 With hypocritical **m** in feasts, *they* gnashed 3934
Isa 28:22 Now therefore be ye not **m**, lest your bands 3887
Jer 15:17 I sat not in the assembly of the **m**, 7832
Jude 1:18 How that they told you there should be **m** *1703*

MOCKEST (1) [MOCK]
Job 11: 3 when thou **m**, shall no man make *thee* 3932

MOCKETH (5) [MOCK]
Job 13: 9 or as *one* man **m** another, do ye *so* 2048
39:22 He **m** at fear, and is not affrighted; 7832
Pr 17: 5 Whoso **m** the poor reproacheth his Maker: 3932
30:17 The eye *that* **m** at *his* father, and 3932
Jer 20: 7 I am in derision daily, every one **m** me. 3932

MOCKING (5) [MOCK]
Ge 21: 9 which she had born unto Abraham, **m**. 6711
Eze 22: 4 unto the heathen, and a **m** to all countries. 7048
Mt 27:41 Likewise also the chief priests **m** *him*, with *1702*
Mk 15:31 Likewise also the chief priests **m** said *1702*
Ac 2:13 Others **m** said, *These men* are full of new *5512*

MOCKINGS (1) [MOCK]
Heb 11:36 And others had trial of *cruel* **m** and *1701*

MODEL See ENSAMPLE

MODERATELY (1) [MODERATION]
Joel 2:23 hath given you the former rain **m**, 6666+3807.1

MODERATION (1) [MODERATELY]
Php 4: 5 Let your **m** be known unto all men. *1933*

MODEST (1)
1Ti 2: 9 that women adorn themselves in **m** apparel, *2887*

MOE (28) [= MORE]
Ex 1: 9 the people of the children of Israel *are* **m** 7227
Lev 26:21 I will bring seven *times* **m** plagues upon NIH
Nu 33:54 to the **m** ye shall give the more inheritance, 7227
Dt 1:11 **make** you a thousand times **so many m** 3254
7: 7 ye were **m** in number **than** any people; 4480
7:17 in thine heart, These nations *are* **m** than I; 7227
19: 9 shalt thou add three cities **m** for thee, 5750
Jos 10:11 *they were* **m** which died with hailstones 7227
Jdg 16:30 were **m** than *they* which he slew in his life. 7227
Ru 1:11 *are there* yet *any* **m** sons in my womb, NIH
2Ki 6:16 for *they* that *be* with us *are* **m** than *they* that 7227
1Ch 14: 3 David took **m** wives at Jerusalem: and 5750
14: 3 and David begat **m** sons and daughters. 5750
21: 3 **make** his people an hundred times
so many m 3254
24: 4 there were **m** chief men found of the sons 7227
2Ch 32: 7 for *there be* **m** with us than with him: 7227
Ps 40: 5 speak *of them*, they are **m** than can be 6105
40:12 that I am not able to look *up*; they are **m** 6105
69: 4 They that hate me without a cause are **m** 7231
139:18 they are **m** in number **than** the sand: 4480
Mt 21:36 he sent other servants **m than** the first: *4183*
22:46 that day forth ask him **any m** *questions*. *3765*
25:20 I have gained besides them five talents **m**. *243*
Jn 4: 1 and baptized **m** disciples than John, *4183*
4:41 And many **m** believed because of his own *4183*
7:31 will he do **m** miracles than these which this *4183*
Ac 23:21 for there lie in wait for him of them **m** *than* *4183*
Gal 4:27 for the desolate hath **many m** children than *4183*

MOIST (1) [MOISTENED, MOISTURE]
Nu 6: 3 liquor of grapes, nor eat **m** grapes, or dried. 3892

MOISTENED (1) [MOIST]
Job 21:24 *of* milk, and his bones are **m** with marrow. 8248

MOISTURE (2) [MOIST]
Ps 32: 4 my **m** is turned into the drought of summer. 3955
Lk 8: 6 it withered away, because *it* lacked **m**. *2429*

MOLADAH (4)
Jos 15:26 Amam, and Shema, and **M**, 4137
19: 2 inheritance Beer-sheba, or Sheba, and **M**, 4137
1Ch 4:28 at Beer-sheba, and **M**, and Hazar-shual, 4137
Ne 11:26 at Jeshua, and at **M**, and at Beth-phelet, 4137

MOLDY See MOULDY

MOLE (1) [MOLES]
Lev 11:30 and the lizard, and the snail, and the **m**. 8580

MOLECH (8)
Lev 18:21 *any* of thy seed pass through *the fire* to **M**, 4432
20: 2 that giveth *any* of his seed unto **M**; 4432
20: 3 because he hath given of his seed unto **M**, 4432
20: 4 when he giveth of his seed unto **M**, and 4432
20: 5 to commit whoredom with **M**, from among 4432
1Ki 11: 7 the hill that *is* before Jerusalem, and for **M**, 4432
2Ki 23:10 his daughter to pass through the fire to **M**. 4432
Jer 32:35 daughters to pass through *the fire* unto **M**; 4432

MOLES (1) [MOLE]
Isa 2:20 to worship, to the **m** and to the bats; 2661+6512

MOLID (1)
1Ch 2:29 and she bare him Ahban, and **M**. 4140

MOLLIFIED (1)
Isa 1: 6 neither bound up, neither **m** with ointment. 7401

MOLOCH (2) [MALCHAM, MILCOM]
Am 5:26 ye have borne the tabernacle of your **M** and 4429
Ac 7:43 ye took up the tabernacle of **M**, and the star *3434*

MOLTEN (39) [MELT]
Ex 32: 4 graving tool, after he had made it a **m** calf: 4541
32: 8 they have made them a **m** calf, and 4541
34:17 Thou shalt make thee no **m** gods. 4541
Lev 19: 4 unto idols, nor make to yourselves **m** gods: 4541
Nu 33:52 destroy all their **m** images, and quite pluck 4541
Dt 9:12 they have made them a **m image**. 4541
9:16 your God, *and* had made you a **m** calf: 4541
27:15 man that maketh *any* graven or **m image**, 4541
Jdg 17: 3 to make a graven image and a **m image**: 4541
17: 4 thereof a graven image and a **m image**: 4541
18:14 and a graven image, and a **m image**? 4541
18:17 and the teraphim, and the **m image**: 4541
18:18 and the teraphim, and the **m image**. 4541
1Ki 7:16 he made two chapiters *of* **m** brass, to set 3332
7:23 he made a **m** sea, ten cubits from the one 3332
7:30 under the laver *were* undersetters **m**, at 3332
7:33 their felloes, and their spokes, *were* all **m**. 3332
14: 9 and made thee other gods, and **m images**, 4541
2Ki 17:16 and made them **m images**, *even* two calves, 4541
2Ch 4: 2 Also he made a **m** sea of ten cubits from 3332
28: 2 and made also **m images** for Baalim. 4541
34: 3 and the carved images, and the **m images**. 4541
34: 4 the **m images**, he brake *in pieces*, and 4541
Ne 9:18 when they had made them a **m** calf, and 4541
Job 28: 2 of the earth, and brass *is* **m** *out of* the stone. 6694
37:18 *which is* strong, *and* as a **m** looking glass? 3332
Ps 106:19 in Horeb, and worshipped the **m image**. 4541
Isa 30:22 and the ornament of thy **m images** of gold: 4541
41:29 their **m images** *are* wind and confusion. 5262
42:17 that say to the **m images**, Ye *are* our gods. 4541
44:10 **m** a graven image *that is* profitable for 5258
48: 5 my graven image, and my **m image**, 5262
Jer 10:14 for his **m image** *is* falsehood, and *there is* 5262
51:17 for his **m image** *is* falsehood, and *there is* 5262
Eze 24:11 and *that* the filthiness of it may be **m** in it, 5413
Hos 13: 2 have made them **m images** of their silver, 4541
Mic 1: 4 the mountains shall be **m** under him, and 4549
Na 1:14 cut off the graven image and the **m image**: 4541
Hab 2:18 the **m image**, and a teacher of lies, that 4541

MOMENT (22)
Ex 33: 5 will come up into the midst of thee in a **m**, 7281
Nu 16:21 that I may consume them **in a m**. 7281+3509.1
16:45 that I may consume them as **in a m**. 7281
Job 7:18 him every morning, *and* try him every **m**? 7281
20: 5 and the joy of the hypocrite *but* for a **m**? 7281
21:13 in wealth, and in a **m** go down *to* the grave. 7281
34:20 *In* a **m** shall they die, and the people shall 7281
Ps 30: 5 For his anger *endureth but* a **m**; in his 7281
73:19 are they *brought* into desolation, as *in* a **m**! 7281
Pr 12:19 for ever: but a lying tongue *is* but for a **m**. 7280
Isa 26:20 hide thyself as it were for a little **m**, 7281
27: 3 do keep it; I will water it **every m**: 7281+3807.1
47: 9 these two *things* shall come to thee *in* a **m** 7281
54: 7 For a small **m** have I forsaken thee; but 7281
54: 8 little wrath I hid my face from thee for a **m**; 7281
Jer 4:20 my tents spoiled, *and* my curtains in a **m**. 7281
La 4: 6 that was overthrown as **in a m**, and 7281
Eze 26:16 shall tremble at every **m**, and be astonished 7281
32:10 they shall tremble at every **m**, every man 7281
Lk 4: 5 the kingdoms of the world in a **m** of time. *4743*
1Co 15:52 In a **m**, in the twinkling of an eye, at the last *823*
2Co 4:17 our light affliction, which is but **for a m**, *3910*

MONEY (140) [MONEYCHANGERS, MONEY-CHANGERS]
Ge 17:12 or bought with **m** of any stranger, which *is* 3701
17:13 he that is bought with thy **m**, must needs be 3701
17:23 and all that were bought with his **m**, 3701
17:27 and bought with **m** of the stranger, 3701
23: 9 for as much **m** as it is worth he shall give it 3701
23:13 I will give *thee* **m** for the field; take *it* of 3701
23:16 of silver, current **m** with the merchant. NIH
31:15 and hath quite devoured also our **m**. 3701
33:19 for an hundred **pieces of m**. 7192
42:25 to restore every man's **m** into his sack, and 3701
42:27 ass provender in the inn, he espied his **m**; 3701
42:28 he said unto his brethren, My **m** is restored; 3701
42:35 every man's bundle of **m** *was* in his sack: 3701
42:35 and their father saw the bundles of **m**, 3701
43:12 take double **m** in your hand; and the money 3701
43:12 the **m** that was brought again in the mouth 3701
43:15 they took double **m** in their hand, and 3701
43:18 Because of the **m** that was returned in our 3701
43:21 every man's **m** *was* in the mouth of his 3701
43:21 the mouth of his sack, our **m** in full weight: 3701
43:22 other **m** have we brought down in our 3701
43:22 we cannot tell who put our **m** in our sacks. 3701
43:23 I had your **m**. And he brought Simeon out 3701
44: 1 and put every man's **m** in his sack's mouth. 3701
44: 2 mouth of the youngest, and his corn **m**. 3701
44: 8 Behold, the **m**, which we found in our 3701
47:14 Joseph gathered up all the **m** that was 3701
47:14 Joseph brought the **m** into Pharaoh's house. 3701
47:15 when **m** failed in the land of Egypt, and 3701
47:15 we die in thy presence? for the **m** faileth. 3701
47:16 and I will give you for your cattle, if **m** fail. 3701
47:18 *it* from my lord, how that our **m** is spent; 3701
Ex 12:44 every man's servant that is bought for **m**, 3701
21:11 then shall she go out free without **m**. 3701
21:21 he shall not be punished: for he *is* his **m**. 3701
21:30 If there be laid on him a **sum of m**, then 3724
21:34 *and* give **m** unto the owner of them; 3701
21:35 shall sell the live ox, and divide the **m** of it; 3701
22: 7 If a man shall deliver unto his neighbour **m** 3701
22:17 he shall pay **m** according to the dowry of 3701
22:25 If thou lend **m** to *any of* my people *that is* 3701
30:16 thou shalt take the atonement **m** of 3701
Lev 22:11 if the priest buy *any* soul with his **m**, 3701

Lev 25:37 Thou shalt not give him thy **m** upon usury, 3701
25:51 out of the **m** that he was bought for. 3701
27:15 he shall add the fifth *part* of the **m** of thy 3701
27:18 the priest shall reckon unto him the **m** 3701
27:19 he shall add the fifth *part* of the **m** of thy 3701
Nu 3:48 thou shalt give the **m**, wherewith the odd 3701
3:49 Moses took the redemption **m** of them that 3701
3:50 of the children of Israel took he the **m**; 3701
3:51 Moses gave the **m** of them that were 3701
18:16 thine estimation, *for* the **m** of five shekels, 3701
Dt 2: 6 Ye shall buy meat of them for **m**, that ye 3701
2: 6 ye shall also buy water of them for **m**, 3701
2:28 Thou shalt sell me meat for **m**, that I may 3701
2:28 and give me water for **m**, that I may drink: 3701
14:25 shalt thou turn *it* into **m**, and bind up 3701
14:25 bind up the **m** in thine hand, and shalt go 3701
14:26 thou shalt bestow *that* **m** for whatsoever thy 3701
21:14 thou shalt not sell her at all for **m**, 3701
23:19 usury of **m**, usury of victuals, usury of any 3701
Jdg 5:19 waters of Megiddo; they took no gain of **m**. 3701
16:18 up unto her, and brought **m** in their hand. 3701
17: 4 Yet he restored the **m** unto his mother; and 3701
1Ki 21: 2 to thee, I will give thee the worth of it *in* **m**. 3701
21: 6 said unto him, Give me thy vineyard for **m**; 3701
21:15 which he refused to give thee for **m**: 3701
2Ki 5:26 *Is it* a time to receive **m**, and to receive 3701
12: 4 All the **m** of the dedicated *things* that is 3701
12: 4 *even* the **m** of every one that passeth 3701
12: 4 *the account,* the **m** that every man is set at, 3701
12: 4 all the **m** that cometh into any man's heart 3701
12: 7 receive no *more* **m** of your acquaintance, 3701
12: 8 the priests consented to receive no *more* **m** 3701
12: 9 **m** that was brought *into* the house of 3701
12:10 when they saw that *there was* much **m** in 3701
12:10 told the **m** that was found *in* the house of 3701
12:11 they gave the **m**, being told, into the hands 3701
12:13 of the **m** that was brought *into* the house of 3701
12:15 into whose hand they delivered the **m** to be 3701
12:16 The trespass **m** and sin money was not 3701
12:16 sin **m** was not brought *into* the house of 3701
15:20 Menahem exacted the **m** of Israel, *even* of 3701
22: 7 of the **m** that was delivered into their hand, 3701
22: 9 Thy servants have gathered the **m** that was 3701
23:35 he taxed the land to give the **m** according to 3701
2Ch 24: 5 gather of all Israel **m** to repair the house of 3701
24:11 when they saw that *there was* much **m**, 3701
24:11 day by day, and gathered **m** in abundance. 3701
24:14 brought the rest of the **m** before the king 3701
34: 9 they delivered the **m** that was brought *into* 3701
34:14 when they brought out the **m** that was 3701
34:17 they have gathered together the **m** that was 3701
Ezr 3: 7 They gave **m** also unto the masons, and 3701
7:17 That thou mayest buy speedily with this **m** 3702
Ne 5: 4 We have borrowed **m** for the king's tribute, 3701
5:10 *might* exact of them **m** and corn: 3701
5:11 also the hundredth *part* of the **m**, and *of* 3701
Est 4: 7 of the sum of the **m** that Haman had 3701
Job 31:39 If I have eaten the fruits thereof without **m**, 3701
42:11 every man also gave him a **piece of m**, and 7192
Ps 15: 5 *He that* putteth not out his **m** to usury, 3701
Pr 7:20 He hath taken a bag of **m** with him, 3701
Ecc 7:12 wisdom *is* a defence, *and* **m** *is* a defence: 3701
10:19 maketh merry: but **m** answereth all *things*. 3701
Isa 43:24 hast bought me no sweet cane with **m**, 3701
52: 3 and ye shall be redeemed without **m**. 3701
55: 1 ye to the waters, and he that hath no **m**; 3701
55: 1 buy wine and milk without **m** and without 3701
55: 2 Wherefore do ye spend **m** for *that which is* 3701
Jer 32: 9 *was* in Anathoth, and weighed him the **m**, 3701
32:10 weighed *him* the **m** in the balances. 3701
32:25 Buy thee the field for **m**, and 3701
32:44 *Men* shall buy fields for **m**, and 3701
La 5: 4 We have drunken our water for **m**; 3701
Mic 3:11 and the prophets thereof divine for **m**: 3701
Mt 17:24 they that received **tribute m** came to Peter, *1323*
17:27 his mouth, thou shalt find a **piece of m**: *4715*
22:19 Shew me the tribute **m**. And they brought *3546*
25:18 and digged in the earth, and hid his lord's **m**. *694*
25:27 to have put my **m** to the exchangers, *694*
28:12 they gave large **m** unto the soldiers, *694*
28:15 So they took the **m**, and did as they were *694*
Mk 6: 8 no scrip, no bread, no **m** in *their* purse: *5475*
12:41 beheld how the people cast **m** into *5475*
14:11 they were glad, and promised to give him **m**. *694*
Lk 9: 3 nor scrip, neither bread, neither **m**; *694*
19:15 unto him, to whom he had given the **m**, *694*
19:23 then gavest not thou my **m** into the bank, *694*
22: 5 were glad, and covenanted to give him **m**. *694*
Jn 2:14 and doves, and the **changers of m** sitting: *2773*
2:15 and poured out the changers' **m**, and *2772*
Ac 4:37 sold *it*, and brought the **m**, and laid *it* at *5536*
7:16 **m** of the sons of Emmor the *father* of *694*
8:18 Holy Ghost was given, he offered them **m**, *5536*
8:20 Thy **m** perish with thee, because thou hast *694*
8:20 the gift of God may be purchased with **m**. *5536*
24:26 He hoped also that **m** should have been *5536*
1Ti 6:10 For the **love of m** is the root of all evil: *5365*

MONEYCHANGERS, MONEY-CHANGERS (2)
[MONEY]

Mt 21:12 and overthrew the tables of the **m**, and *2855*
Mk 11:15 and overthrew the tables of the **m**, and *2855*

MONEYLENDER See USURER

MONSTER See WHALE; WHALE'S; WHALES

MONSTERS (1)

La 4: 3 Even the **sea m** draw out the breast, 8577

MONTH (250) [MONTHLY, MONTHS]

Ge 7:11 in the second **m**, the seventeenth day of 2320
7:11 the seventeenth day of the **m**, 2320
8: 4 the ark rested in the seventh **m**, on 2320
8: 4 on the seventeenth day of the **m**, upon 2320
8: 5 decreased continually until the tenth **m**: 2320
8: 5 in the tenth ***m***, on the first *day* of the month, NIH
8: 5 the tenth *month*, on the first *day* of the **m**, 2320
8:13 in the first ***m***, the first *day* of the month, NIH
8:13 in the first *month*, the first *day* of the **m**, 2320
8:14 in the second **m**, on the seven and 2320
8:14 on the seven and twentieth day of the **m**, 2320
29:14 And he abode with him the space of a **m**. 2320
Ex 12: 2 This **m** *shall be* unto you the beginning of 2320
12: 2 it *shall be* the first **m** of the year to you. 2320
12: 3 In the tenth *day* of this **m** they shall take to 2320
12: 6 *up* until the fourteenth day of the same **m**: 2320
12:18 In the first ***m***, on the fourteenth day of NIH
12:18 on the fourteenth day of the **m** at even, 2320
12:18 the one and twentieth day of the **m** at even. 2320
13: 4 *This* day came ye out in the **m** Abib. 2320
13: 5 that thou shalt keep this service in this **m**. 2320
16: 1 on the fifteenth day of the second **m** after 2320
19: 1 In the third **m**, when the children of Israel 2320
23:15 in the time appointed of the **m** Abib; 2320
34:18 in the time of the **m** Abib: 2320
34:18 for in the **m** Abib thou camest out from 2320
40: 2 On the first day of the first **m** shalt thou set 2320
40:17 it came to pass in the first **m** in the second 2320
40:17 on the first *day* of the **m**, *that* the tabernacle 2320
Lev 16:29 *that* in the seventh **m**, on the tenth *day* of 2320
16:29 on the tenth *day* of the **m**, ye shall afflict 2320
23: 5 In the fourteenth *day* of the first **m** at even 2320
23: 6 on the fifteenth day of the same **m** *is* 2320
23:24 saying, In the seventh **m**, in the first *day* of 2320
23:24 the seventh month, in the first *day* of the **m**, 2320
23:27 Also on the tenth *day* of this seventh **m** 2320
23:32 in the ninth *day* of the **m** at even, from even 2320
23:34 The fifteenth day of this seventh **m** *shall be* 2320
23:39 Also in the fifteenth day of the seventh **m**, 2320
23:41 ye shall celebrate it in the seventh **m**. 2320
25: 9 to sound on the tenth *day* of the seventh **m**, 2320
27: 6 if *it be* from a **m** old even unto five years 2320
Nu 1: 1 on the first *day* of the second **m**, 2320
1:18 together on the first *day* of the second **m**, 2320
3:15 every male from a **m** old and upward shalt 2320
3:22 of all the males, from a **m** old and upward, 2320
3:28 from a **m** old and upward, *were* eight 2320
3:34 from a **m** old and upward, *were* six 2320
3:39 all the males from a **m** old and upward, 2320
3:40 males of the children of Israel from a **m** old 2320
3:43 from a **m** old and upward, of those that 2320
9: 1 in the first **m** of the second year after they 2320
9: 3 In the fourteenth day of this **m**, at even, 2320
9: 5 first **m** at even in the wilderness of Sinai: 2320
9:11 The fourteenth day of the second **m** at even 2320
9:22 *whether it were* two days, or a **m**, or a year, 2320
10:11 pass on the twentieth *day* of the second **m**, 2320
11:20 *But* even a whole **m**, until it come out at 2320
11:21 them flesh, that they may eat a whole **m**. 2320
18:16 those that are *to be* redeemed from a **m** old 2320
20: 1 *into* the desert of Zin in the first **m**: 2320
26:62 all males from a **m** old and upward: 2320
28:14 **every m** throughout 2320+2320+871.1
28:16 in the fourteenth day of the first **m** *is* 2320
28:17 in the fifteenth day of this **m** *is* the feast: 2320
29: 1 in the seventh **m**, on the first *day* of 2320
29: 1 seventh month, on the first *day* of the **m**, 2320
29: 6 Beside the burnt offering of the **m**, and 2320
29: 7 *day* of this seventh **m** a holy convocation; 2320
29:12 on the fifteenth day of the seventh **m** ye 2320
33: 3 they departed from Rameses in the first **m**, 2320
33: 3 on the fifteenth day of the first **m**; 2320
33:38 of Egypt, in the first *day* of the fifth **m**. 2320
Dt 1: 3 in the eleventh **m**, on the first *day* of 2320
1: 3 eleventh month, on the first *day* of the **m**, 2320
16: 1 Observe the **m** of Abib, and keep 2320
16: 1 for in the **m** of Abib the LORD thy God 2320
21:13 her father and her mother a **full m**: 3117+3391
Jos 4:19 of Jordan on the tenth *day* of the first **m**, 2320
5:10 of the **m** at even in the plains of Jericho. 2320
1Sa 20:27 *which was* the second *day* of the **m**, 2320
20:34 did eat no meat the second day of the **m**: 2320
1Ki 4: 7 each man *his* **m** in a year made provision. 2320
4:27 king Solomon's table, every man *in* his **m**: 2320
5:14 to Lebanon, ten thousand a **m** *by* courses: 2320
5:14 a **m** they were in Lebanon, *and* two months 2320
6: 1 in the **m** Zif, which *is* the second month, 2320
6: 1 in the month Zif, which *is* the second **m**, 2320
6:37 the house of the LORD laid, in the **m** Zif: 3391
6:38 in the eleventh year, in the **m** Bul, which *is* 3391
6:38 in the month Bul, which *is* the eighth **m**, 2320
8: 2 Solomon at the feast in the **m** Ethanim, 3391
8: 2 month Ethanim, which *is* the seventh **m**. 2320
12:32 Jeroboam ordained a feast in the eighth **m**, 2320
12:32 on the fifteenth day of the **m**, like unto 2320
12:33 in Beth-el the fifteenth day of the eighth **m**, 2320
12:33 *even* in the **m** which he had devised of his 2320
2Ki 15:13 and he reigned a **full m** in Samaria. 3117+3391
25: 1 in the tenth **m**, in the tenth *day* of 2320
25: 1 the tenth month, in the tenth *day* of the **m**, 2320
25: 3 on the ninth *day* of the *fourth* **m** the famine 2320
25: 8 in the fifth **m**, on the seventh *day* of 2320
25: 8 fifth month, on the seventh *day* of the **m**, 2320
25:25 it came to pass in the seventh **m**, 2320
25:27 in the twelfth **m**, on the seven and 2320
25:27 on the seven and twentieth *day* of the **m**, 2320
1Ch 12:15 they that went over Jordan in the first **m**, 2320
27: 1 went out **m** by month throughout all 2320
27: 1 went out month by **m** throughout all 2320
27: 2 Over the first course for the first **m** *was* 2320
27: 3 all the captains of the host for the first **m**. 2320
27: 4 over the course of the second **m** *was* Dodai 2320
27: 5 The third captain of the host for the third **m** 2320
27: 7 The fourth *captain* for the fourth **m** *was* 2320
27: 8 The fifth captain for the fifth **m** *was* 2320
27: 9 The sixth *captain* for the sixth **m** *was* Ira 2320
27:10 The seventh *captain* for the seventh **m** *was* 2320
27:11 The eighth *captain* for the eighth **m** *was* 2320
27:12 The ninth *captain* for the ninth **m** *was* 2320
27:13 The tenth *captain* for the tenth **m** *was* 2320
27:14 The eleventh *captain* for the eleventh **m** 2320
27:15 The twelfth *captain* for the twelfth **m** *was* 2320
2Ch 3: 2 to build in the second *day* of the second **m**, 2320
5: 3 in the feast which *was in* the seventh **m**. 2320
7:10 twentieth day of the seventh **m** he sent 2320
15:10 together *at* Jerusalem in the third **m**, 2320
29: 3 in the first year of his reign, in the first **m**, 2320
29:17 on the first *day* of the first **m** to sanctify, 2320
29:17 on the eighth day of the **m** came they to 2320
29:17 in the sixteenth day of the first **m** they 2320
30: 2 to keep the passover in the second **m**. 2320
30:13 feast of unleavened bread in the second **m**, 2320
30:15 on the fourteenth *day* of the second **m**: 2320
31: 7 In the third **m** they began to lay 2320
31: 7 and finished *them* in the seventh **m**. 2320
35: 1 on the fourteenth *day* of the first **m**. 2320
Ezr 3: 1 when the seventh **m** was come, and 2320
3: 6 From the first day of the seventh **m** began 2320
3: 8 in the second **m**, began Zerubbabel the son 2320
6:15 finished on the third day of the **m** Adar, 3393
6:19 upon the fourteenth *day* of the first **m**. 2320
7: 8 he came *to* Jerusalem in the fifth **m**, 2320
7: 9 For upon the first *day* of the first **m** began 2320
7: 9 on the first *day* of the fifth **m** came he to 2320
8:31 of Ahava on the twelfth *day* of the first **m**, 2320
10: 9 It *was* the ninth **m**, on the twentieth *day* of 2320
10: 9 ninth month, on the twentieth *day* of the **m**; 2320
10:16 sat down in the first day of the tenth **m** to 2320
10:17 strange wives by the first day of the first **m**. 2320
Ne 1: 1 it came to pass in the **m** Chisleu, *in* 2320
2: 1 it came to pass in the **m** Nisan, *in* 2320
6:15 in the twenty and fifth *day of the* **m** Elul, NIH
7:73 when the seventh **m** came, the children of 2320
8: 2 upon the first day of the seventh **m**. 2320
8:14 in booths in the feast of the seventh **m**: 2320
9: 1 fourth day of this **m** the children of Israel 2320
Est 2:16 into his house royal in the tenth **m**, 2320
2:16 which *is* the **m** Tebeth, in the seventh year 2320
3: 7 In the first **m**, that *is*, the month Nisan, 2320
3: 7 In the first month, that *is*, the **m** Nisan, 2320
3: 7 from day to day, and from **m** to month, 2320
3: 7 from day to day, and from month to **m**, 2320
3: 7 *to* the twelfth ***m***, that *is*, the month Adar. NIH
3: 7 *to* the twelfth *month*, that *is*, the **m** Adar. 2320
3:12 called on the thirteenth day of the first **m**, 2320
3:13 upon the thirteenth *day* of the twelfth **m**, 2320
3:13 which *is* the **m** Adar, and *to take* the spoil 2320
8: 9 scribes called at that time in the third **m**, 2320
8: 9 that *is*, the **m** Sivan, on the three and 2320
8:12 upon the thirteenth *day* of the twelfth **m**, 2320
8:12 of the twelfth month, which *is* the **m** Adar. 2320
9: 1 Now in the twelfth **m**, that *is*, the month 2320
9: 1 in the twelfth month, that *is*, the **m** Adar, 2320
9:15 on the fourteenth day also of the **m** Adar, 2320
9:17 On the thirteenth day of the **m** Adar; and 2320
9:19 made the fourteenth day of the **m** Adar *a* 2320
9:21 keep the fourteenth day of the **m** Adar, 2320
9:22 the **m** which was turned unto them from 2320
Jer 1: 3 away of Jerusalem captive in the fifth **m**. 2320
2:24 in her **m** they shall find her. 2320
28: 1 in the fourth year, *and* in the fifth **m**, 2320
28:17 died the same year in the seventh **m**. 2320
36: 9 in the ninth **m**, *that* they proclaimed a fast 2320
36:22 king sat *in* the winterhouse in the ninth **m**: 2320
39: 1 in the tenth **m**, came Nebuchadrezzar king 2320
39: 2 in the fourth **m**, the ninth *day* of the month, 2320
39: 2 in the fourth month, the ninth *day* of the **m**, 2320
41: 1 Now it came to pass in the seventh **m**, 2320
52: 4 in the tenth **m**, in the tenth *day* of 2320
52: 4 the tenth month, in the tenth *day* of the **m**, 2320
52: 6 in the fourth **m**, in the ninth *day* of 2320
52: 6 the fourth month, in the ninth *day* of the **m**, 2320
52:12 Now in the fifth **m**, in the tenth *day* of 2320
52:12 the fifth month, in the tenth *day* of the **m**, 2320
52:31 in the twelfth **m**, in the five and 2320
52:31 in the five and twentieth *day* of the **m**, 2320
Eze 1: 1 in the fourth ***m***, in the fifth *day* of NIH
1: 1 the fourth *month*, in the fifth *day* of the **m**, 2320
1: 2 In the fifth *day* of the **m**, which *was* 2320
8: 1 in the sixth ***m***, in the fifth *day* of the month, NIH
8: 1 in the sixth *month*, in the fifth *day* of the **m**, 2320
20: 1 in the fifth ***m***, the tenth *day* of the month, NIH
20: 1 in the fifth *month*, the tenth *day* of the **m**, 2320
24: 1 Again in the ninth year, in the tenth **m**, 2320
24: 1 the tenth month, in the tenth *day* of the **m**, 2320
26: 1 the eleventh year, in the first *day* of the **m**, 2320
29: 1 in the tenth ***m***, in the twelfth *day* of NIH
29: 1 tenth *month*, in the twelfth *day* of the **m**, 2320
29:17 in the first ***m***, in the first *day* of the month, NIH
29:17 in the first *month*, in the first *day* of the **m**, 2320
30:20 in the first ***m***, in the seventh *day* of NIH
30:20 the first *month*, in the seventh *day* of the **m**, 2320
31: 1 in the third ***m***, in the first *day* of the month, NIH
31: 1 in the third *month*, in the first *day* of the **m**, 2320
32: 1 in the twelfth **m**, in the first *day* of 2320
32: 1 the twelfth month, in the first *day* of the **m**, 2320
32:17 twelfth year, in the fifteenth *day* of the **m**, 2320
33:21 in the tenth ***m***, in the fifth *day* of the month, NIH
33:21 the tenth *month*, in the fifth *day* of the **m**, 2320
40: 1 of the year, in the tenth *day* of the **m**, 2320
45:18 In the first ***m***, in the first *day* of the month, NIH
45:18 In the first *month*, in the first *day* of the **m**, 2320
45:20 thou shalt do the seventh *day* of the **m** for 2320
45:21 In the first ***m***, in the fourteenth day of NIH
45:21 first *month*, in the fourteenth day of the **m**, 2320
45:25 In the seventh ***m***, in the fifteenth day of NIH
45:25 *month*, in the fifteenth day of the **m**, 2320
Da 10: 4 in the four and twentieth day of the first **m**, 2320
Hos 5: 7 now shall a **m** devour them with their 2320
Joel 2:23 and the latter rain in the first ***m***. NIH
Hag 1: 1 in the sixth **m**, in the first day of the month, 2320
1: 1 in the sixth month, in the first day of the **m**, 2320
1:15 the four and twentieth day of the sixth **m**, 2320

Hag 2: 1 In the seventh *m*, in the one and NIH
2: 1 in the one and twentieth *day* of the **m**, 2320
2:10 twentieth *day* of the ninth *m*, in the second NIH
2:18 twentieth day of the ninth *m*, *even* from NIH
2:20 in the four and twentieth *day* of the **m**, 2320
Zec 1: 1 In the eighth **m**, in the second year of 2320
1: 7 and twentieth day of the eleventh **m**, 2320
1: 7 which *is* the **m** Sebat, in the second year of 2320
7: 1 Zechariah in the fourth *day* of the ninth **m**, 2320
7: 3 Should I weep in the fifth **m**, 2320
7: 5 and seventh *m*, even those seventy years, NIH
8:19 The fast of the fourth *m*, and the fast of NIH
11: 8 Three shepherds also I cut off in one **m**; 3391
Lk 1:26 And in the sixth **m** the angel Gabriel was *3376*
1:36 and this is the sixth **m** with her, who was *3376*
Rev 9:15 and a day, and a **m**, and a year, for to slay *3376*
22: 2 *of* fruits, *and* yielded her fruit every **m**: *3376*

MONTHLY (1) [MONTH]

Isa 47:13 the **m** prognosticators, stand *up*, and 2320

MONTHS (59) [MONTH]

Ge 38:24 it came to pass about three **m** after, that it 2320
Ex 2: 2 he *was a* goodly *child*, she hid him three **m**. 3391
12: 2 *shall be* unto you the beginning of **m**: 2320
Nu 10:10 and in the beginnings of your **m**, 2320
28:11 in the beginnings of your **m** ye shall offer a 2320
28:14 every month throughout the **m** of the year. 2320
Jdg 11:37 let me alone two **m**, that I may go up and 2320
11:38 he sent her away *for* two **m**: and she went 2320
11:39 it came to pass at the end of two **m**, that she 2320
19: 2 was there four whole **m**. 2320
20:47 and abode in the rock Rimmon four **m**. 2320
1Sa 6: 1 in the country of the Philistines seven **m**. 2320
27: 7 the Philistines was a full year and four **m**. 2320
2Sa 2:11 house of Judah was seven years and six **m**. 2320
5: 5 reigned over Judah seven years and six **m**: 2320
6:11 house of Obed-edom the Gittite three **m**: 2320
24: 8 came *to* Jerusalem at the end of nine **m** 2320
24:13 wilt thou flee three **m** before thine enemies, 2320
1Ki 5:14 they were in Lebanon, *and* two **m** at home: 2320
11:16 (For six **m** did Joab remain there with all 2320
2Ki 15: 8 reign over Israel in Samaria six **m**. 2320
23:31 and he reigned three **m** in Jerusalem. 2320
24: 8 and he reigned in Jerusalem three **m**. 2320
1Ch 3: 4 and there he reigned seven years and six **m**: 2320
13:14 family of Obed-edom in his house three **m**. 2320
21:12 or three **m** to be destroyed before thy foes, 2320
27: 1 by month throughout all the **m** of the year, 2320
2Ch 36: 2 and he reigned three **m** in Jerusalem. 2320
36: 9 he reigned three **m** and ten days in 2320
Est 2:12 after that she had been twelve **m**, 2320
2:12 *to wit,* six **m** with oil of myrrh, and 2320
2:12 six **m** with sweet odours, and with *other* 2320
Job 3: 6 let it not come into the number of the **m**. 3391
7: 3 So am I made to possess **m** of vanity, and 3391
14: 5 the number of his **m** *are* with thee, 2320
21:21 when the number of his **m** is cut off in 2320
29: 2 O that I were as *in* **m** past, as *in* the days 3391
39: 2 Canst thou number the **m** *that* they fulfil? 3391
Eze 39:12 seven **m** shall the house of Israel be 2320
39:14 after the end of seven **m** shall they search. 2320
47:12 bring forth new fruit according to his **m**, 2320
Da 4:29 At the end of twelve **m** he walked in 3393
Am 4: 7 when *there were* yet three **m** to the harvest: 2320
Lk 1:24 and hid herself five **m**, saying, *3376*
1:56 And Mary abode with her about three **m**, *3376*
4:25 heaven was shut up three years and six **m**, *3376*
Jn 4:35 There are yet **four m**, and *then* cometh *5072*
Ac 7:20 nourished up in his father's house three **m**: *3376*
18:11 And he continued *there* a year and six **m**, *3376*
19: 8 and spake boldly for the space of three **m**, *3376*
20: 3 And *there* abode three **m**: and when *3376*
28:11 And after three **m** we departed in a ship of *3376*
Gal 4:10 observe days, and **m**, and times, and years. *3376*
Heb 11:23 was hid **three m** of his parents, because *5150*
Jas 5:17 earth *by the space of* three years and six **m**. *3376*
Rev 9: 5 but that they should be tormented five **m**: *3376*
9:10 and their power *was* to hurt men five **m**. *3376*
11: 2 shall they tread under foot forty *and* two **m**. *3376*
13: 5 unto him to continue forty *and* two **m**. *3376*

MONUMENTS (1)

Isa 65: 4 lodge in the **m**, which eat swine's flesh, 5341

MOON (51) [MOONS]

Ge 37: 9 the sun and the **m** and the eleven stars 3394
Dt 4:19 thou seest the sun, and the **m**, and the stars, 3394
17: 3 the sun, or **m**, or any of the host of heaven, 3394
33:14 for the precious things put forth by the **m**, 3391
Jos 10:12 and thou, **M**, in the valley of Ajalon. 3394
10:13 the sun stood still, and the **m** stayed, 3394
1Sa 20: 5 to morrow *is* the **new m**, and I should not 2320
20:18 said to *David,* To morrow *is* the **new m**: 2320
20:24 when the **new m** was come, the king sat 2320
2Ki 4:23 *it is* neither **new m**, nor sabbath. And she 2320
23: 5 to the **m**, and to the planets, and to all 3394
Job 25: 5 Behold *even* to the **m**, and it shineth not; 3394
31:26 it shined, or the **m** walking *in* brightness; 3394
Ps 8: 3 the work of thy fingers, the **m** and the stars, 3394
72: 5 fear thee as long as the sun and **m** endure, 3394
72: 7 of peace so long as the **m** endureth. 3394
81: 3 Blow up the trumpet in the **new m**, in 2320
89:37 It shall be established for ever as the **m**, 3394
104:19 He appointed the **m** for seasons: the sun 3394
121: 6 not smite thee by day, nor the **m** by night. 3394
136: 9 The **m** and stars to rule by night: for his 3394
148: 3 Praise ye him, sun and **m**: praise him, all ye 3394
Ecc 12: 2 the sun, or the light, or the **m**, or the stars, 3394
SS 6:10 fair as the **m**, clear as the sun, *and* 3842
Isa 3:18 and *their* **round tires like the m**, 7720
13:10 and the **m** shall not cause her light to shine. 3394
24:23 the **m** shall be confounded, and the sun 3842
30:26 Moreover the light of the **m** shall be as 3842
Isa 60:19 neither for brightness shall the **m** give light 3394
60:20 neither shall thy **m** withdraw itself: 3391
66:23 *that* from one **new m** to another, and 2320
Jer 8: 2 the **m**, and all the host of heaven, 3394
31:35 *and* the ordinances of the **m** and of the stars 3394
Eze 32: 7 a cloud, and the **m** shall not give her light. 3394
46: 1 in the day of the **new m** it shall be opened. 2320
46: 6 in the day of the **new m** *it shall be* a young 2320
Joel 2:10 the sun and the **m** shall be dark, and 3394
2:31 the **m** into blood, before the great and 3394
3:15 The sun and the **m** shall be darkened, and 3394
Am 8: 5 Saying, When will the **new m** be gone, 2320
Hab 3:11 *and* **m** stood still in *their* habitation: 3394
Mt 24:29 and the **m** shall not give her light, and *4582*
Mk 13:24 and the **m** shall not give her light, *4582*
Lk 21:25 in the sun, and in the **m**, and in the stars; *4582*
Ac 2:20 and the **m** into blood, before *that* great and *4582*
1Co 15:41 and another glory of the **m**, and *4582*
Col 2:16 or of the **new m**, or of the sabbath days: *3561*
Rev 6:12 of hair, and the **m** became as blood; *4582*
8:12 and the third *part* of the **m**, and the third *4582*
12: 1 and the **m** under her feet, and upon her *4582*
21:23 of the sun, neither of the **m**, to shine in it: *4582*

MOONS (11) [MOON]

1Ch 23:31 in the **new m**, and on the set feasts, 2320
2Ch 2: 4 on the **new m**, and on the solemn feasts of 2320
8:13 on the **new m**, and on the solemn feasts, 2320
31: 3 and for the **new m**, and for the set feasts, 2320
Ezr 3: 5 both of the **new m**, and of all the set feasts 2320
Ne 10:33 of the sabbaths, of the **new m**, for the set 2320
Isa 1:13 the **new m** and sabbaths, the calling of 2320
1:14 Your **new m** and your appointed feasts my 2320
Eze 45:17 in the **new m**, and in the sabbaths in all 2320
46: 3 LORD in the sabbaths and in the **new m**. 2320
Hos 2:11 her feast *days*, her **new m**, and 2320

MORASTHITE (2) [MORESHETH-GATH]

Jer 26:18 Micah the **M** prophesied in the days of 4183
Mic 1: 1 to Micah the **M** in the days of Jotham, 4183

MORDECAI (58) [MORDECAI'S]

Ezr 2: 2 **M**, Bilshan, Mizpar, Bigvai, Rehum, 4782
Ne 7: 7 **M**, Bilshan, Mispereth, Bigvai, Nehum, 4782
Est 2: 5 whose name *was* **M**, the son of Jair, the son 4782
2: 7 whom **M**, when her father and mother were 4782
2:10 for **M** had charged her that she should not 4782
2:11 **M** walked every day before the court of 4782
2:15 the daughter of Abihail the uncle of **M**, 4782
2:19 second time, then **M** sat in the king's gate. 4782
2:20 nor her people; as **M** had charged her: 4782
2:20 for Esther did the commandment of **M**, 4782
2:21 those days, while **M** sat in the king's gate, 4782
2:22 the thing was known to **M**, who told *it* unto 4782
3: 2 But **M** bowed not, nor did *him* reverence. 4782
3: 3 which *were* in the king's gate, said unto **M**, 4782
3: 5 when Haman saw that **M** bowed not, 4782
3: 6 he thought scorn to lay hands on **M** alone; 4782
3: 6 for they had shewed him the people of **M**: 4782
3: 6 of Ahasuerus, *even* the people of **M**. 4782
4: 1 When **M** perceived all that was done, 4782
4: 1 **M** rent his clothes, and put on sackcloth 4782
4: 4 she sent raiment to clothe **M**, and to take 4782
4: 5 gave him a commandment to **M**, to know 4782
4: 6 So Hatach went forth to **M** unto the street 4782
4: 7 **M** told him of all that had happened unto 4782
4: 9 and told Esther the words of **M**. 4782
4:10 and gave him commandment unto **M**: 4782
4:12 And they told to **M** Esther's words. 4782
4:13 **M** commanded to answer Esther, Think not 4782
4:15 Esther bade *them* return **M** *this answer:* 4782
4:17 So **M** went his way, and did according to 4782
5: 9 when Haman saw **M** in the king's gate, 4782
5: 9 he was full *of* indignation against **M**. 4782
5:13 long as I see **M** the Jew sitting at the king's 4782
5:14 to morrow speak thou unto the king that **M** 4782
6: 2 that **M** had told of Bigthana and Teresh, 4782
6: 3 and dignity hath been done to **M** for this? 4782
6: 4 to speak unto the king to hang **M** on 4782
6:10 hast said, and do *even* so to **M** the Jew, 4782
6:11 arrayed **M**, and brought him on horseback 4782
6:12 **M** came again to the king's gate. 4782
6:13 unto him, If **M** *be* of the seed of the Jews, 4782
7: 9 cubits high, which Haman had made for **M**, 4782
7:10 on the gallows that he had prepared for **M**. 4782
8: 1 **M** came before the king; for Esther had 4782
8: 2 had taken from Haman, and gave it unto **M**. 4782
8: 2 Esther set **M** over the house of Haman. 4782
8: 7 unto Esther the queen and to **M** the Jew, 4782
8: 9 it was written according to all that **M** 4782
8:15 **M** went out from the presence of the king 4782
9: 3 because the fear of **M** fell upon them. 4782
9: 4 For **M** *was* great in the king's house, and 4782
9: 4 for *this* man **M** waxed greater and greater. 4782
9:20 **M** wrote these things, and sent letters unto 4782
9:23 and as **M** had written unto them; 4782
9:29 the daughter of Abihail, and **M** the Jew, 4782
9:31 times *appointed*, according as **M** the Jew 4782
10: 2 and the declaration of the greatness of **M**, 4782
10: 3 For **M** the Jew *was* next unto king 4782

MORDECAI'S (2) [MORDECAI]

Est 2:22 Esther certified the king *thereof* in **M** 4782
3: 4 to see whether **M** matters would stand: 4782

MORE (657) [= MO, = MOE, MOREOVER, MUCH]

Ge 3: 1 Now the serpent was **m** subtil **than** any 4480
8:12 which returned not again unto him **any m**. 5750
8:21 I will not again curse the ground **any m** for 5750
8:21 neither will I again smite **any m** every 5750
9:11 neither shall all flesh be cut off **any m** by 5750
9:11 neither shall there **any m** be a flood to 5750
9:15 the waters shall no **m** become a flood to 5750
17: 5 Neither shall thy name **any m** be called 5750
Ge 29:30 he loved also Rachel **m than** Leah, and 4480
32:28 Thy name shall be called no **m** Jacob, but 5750
34:19 he *was* **m** honourable **than** all the house of 4480
35:10 thy name shall not be called **any m** Jacob, 5750
36: 7 For their riches were **m** than that they 7227
37: 3 Now Israel loved Joseph **m than** all his 4480
37: 4 father loved him **m than** all his brethren, 4480
37: 5 and they hated him **yet the m**. 3254+5750
37: 8 they hated him **yet the m** for his 3254+5750
37: 9 said, Behold, I have dreamed a dream **m**; 5750
38:26 and said, She hath been **m** righteous **than** I; 4480
38:26 my son. And he knew her again no **m**. 5750
44:23 down with you, ye shall see my face no **m**. 3254
Ex 1:12 **the m** they afflicted them, the more 834+3509.1
1:12 **the m** they multiplied and grew. 3651
5: 7 Ye shall no **m** give the people straw to 3254
5: 9 Let there **m** work be **laid** upon the men, 3513
8:29 let not Pharaoh deal deceitfully **any m** in 3254
9:28 that there be no *m* mighty thunderings and NIH
9:29 neither shall there be **any m** hail; 5750
9:34 he sinned yet **m**, and hardened his heart, he 3254
10:28 take heed to thyself, see my face no **m**; 3254
10:29 spoken well, I will see thy face again no **m**. 5750
11: 1 Yet will I bring one plague *m* upon NIH
11: 6 was none like it, nor shall be like it **any m**. 3254
14:13 ye shall see them again no **m** for ever. 5750
16:17 did so, and gathered, some **m**, some less. 7235
30:15 The rich shall not **give m**, and the poor 7235
36: 5 The people bring **much m** than enough for 7235
36: 6 Let neither man nor woman make **any m** 5750
Lev 6: 5 shall add the fifth *part* **m** thereto, *and* 5921
11:42 whatsoever hath **m** feet among all creeping 7235
13: 5 the priest shall shut him up seven days **m**: 8145
13:33 up *him that hath* the scall seven days **m**: 8145
13:54 and he shall shut it up seven days **m**: 8145
17: 7 they shall no **m** offer their sacrifices unto 5750
26:18 I will punish you seven *times* **m** for your 3254
27:20 it shall not be redeemed **any m**. 5750
Nu 3:46 of Israel, which are **m** than the Levites; 5736
8:25 the service *thereof*, and shall serve no **m**: 5750
18: 5 that there be no wrath **any m** upon 5750
22:15 **m**, and more honourable than they. 7227
22:15 more, and **m** honourable **than** they. 4480
22:18 of the LORD my God, to do less or **m**. 1419
22:19 know what the LORD will say unto me **m**. 3254
26:54 To many thou shalt **give** the **m** inheritance, 7235
33:54 to the moe ye shall **give** the **m** inheritance, 7235
Dt 3:26 speak no **m** unto me of this matter. 3254+5750
5:22 he **added** no **m**. And he wrote them in two 3254
5:25 voice of the LORD our God **any m**, 3254+5750
10:16 of your heart, and be no **m** stiffnecked. 5750
13:11 shall do no **m** any such wickedness as this 3254
17:13 and fear, and do no **m** presumptuously. 5750
17:16 Ye shall henceforth return no **m** that way. 5750
18:16 neither let me see this great fire **any m**, 5750
19:20 shall henceforth commit no **m** any such evil 5750
20: 1 and chariots, *and* a people **m** than thou, 7227
28:68 unto thee, Thou shalt see it no **m** again: 3254
31: 2 *this* day; I can no **m** go out and come in: 5750
31:27 and **how much m** after my death? 637+3588
Jos 2:11 neither did there remain **any m** courage in 5750
5: 1 neither was there spirit in them **any m**, 5750
5:12 had the children of Israel manna **any m**; 5750
7:12 neither will I be with you **any m**, except ye 3254
23:13 **m** drive out *any of* these nations from 3254
Jdg 2:19 corrupted *themselves* **m than** their fathers, 4480
8:28 so that they lifted up their heads no **m**. 3254
10:13 wherefore I will deliver you no **m**. 3254
13:21 the angel of the LORD did no **m** 3254+5750
15: 3 Now shall I be **m** blameless **than** 4480
18:24 what have I **m**? and what *is* this *that* ye say 5750
Ru 1:17 the LORD do so to me, and **m** also, 3254
3:10 *for* thou hast **shewed m** kindness in 3190
1Sa 1:18 and her countenance was no **m** *sad*. 5750
2: 3 Talk no **m** *so* exceeding proudly; let *not* 7235
3:17 God do so to thee, and **m** also, if thou hide 3254
7:13 came no **m** into the coast of Israel: 3254+5750
14:30 **How much m**, if haply the people had 637+3588
14:44 Saul answered, God do so and **m** also: 3254
15:35 Samuel **came** no **m** to see Saul until 3254
18: 2 would let him go **no m** home *to* his father's 3808
18: 8 and *what* can he have **m** but the kingdom? 5750
18:29 Saul was yet the **m** afraid of David; and 3254
18:30 *that* David behaved himself **m** wisely **than** 4480
20:13 LORD do so and much **m** to Jonathan: 3254
22:15 servant knew nothing of all this, less or **m**. 1419
23: 3 **how much m** then if we come *to* Keilah 637
24:17 said to David, Thou *art* **m** righteous **than** I: 4480
25:22 **m** also do God unto the enemies of David, 3254
25:36 less or **m**, until the morning light. 1419
26:21 for I will no **m** do thee harm, because my 5750
27: 1 to seek me **any m** in any coast of Israel: 5750
27: 4 *to* Gath: and he sought no **m** again for him. 5750
28:15 answereth me no **m**, neither by prophets, 5750
30: 4 wept, until they had **no m** power to weep. 369
2Sa 2:28 stood still, and pursued after Israel no **m**, 3254
2:28 Israel no more, neither fought they **any m**. 5750
3: 9 So do God to Abner, and **m** also, except, 3254
3:35 and **m** also, if I taste bread, or ought else, 3254
4:11 **How much m**, when wicked men have slain 637
6:22 I will yet be **m** vile **than** thus, and will be 4480
7:10 in a place of their own, and move no **m**; 5750
7:10 children of wickedness afflict them **any m**, 3254
7:20 what can David say **m** unto thee? 3254+5750
10:19 to help the children of Ammon **any m**. 5750
11:25 make thy battle *m* strong against the city, NIH
14:10 and he shall not touch thee **any m**. 3254+5750
14:11 the revengers of blood to destroy **any m**, 7235
16:11 **how much m** now *may this* Benjamite 637+3588
18: 8 the wood devoured **m** people that day than 7235
19:13 God do so to me, and **m also**, if thou 3254+3541
19:28 have I yet to cry **any m** unto the king? 5750
19:29 Why speakest thou **any m** of thy matters? 5750
19:35 can I hear **any m** the voice of singing *men* 5750
19:43 and we have also **m** *right* in David **than** ye: 4480

2Sa 20: 6 of Bichri do us m harm than did Absalom: 4480
21:17 Thou shalt go no m out with us to battle, 5750
23:23 He was m honourable than the thirty, but 4480
1Ki 2:23 God do so to me, and m also, 3254
2:32 upon two men m righteous and better than 4480
10: 5 of the LORD; there was no m spirit in her. 5750
10:10 there came no m such abundance of spices 5750
16:33 Ahab did m to provoke the LORD God of 3254
19: 2 So let the gods do to me, and m also, 3254
20:10 said, The gods do so unto me, and m also, 3254
2Ki 2:12 he saw him no m: and he took hold of his 5750
2:21 there shall not be from thence any m death 5750
4: 6 he said unto her, There is not a vessel m. 5750
6:23 So the bands of Syria came no m 3254+5750
6:31 he said, God do so and m also to me, if 3254
9:35 they found no m of her than the skull, and 3808
12: 7 receive no m money of your acquaintance, NIH
12: 8 the priests consented to receive no m money NIH
21: 8 any m out of the land which I gave their 3254
21: 9 Manasseh seduced them to do m evil than 4480
24: 7 the king of Egypt came not again any m 5750
1Ch 4: 9 Jabez was m honourable than his brethren: 4480
11:21 he was m honourable than the two; 871.1
17: 9 in their place, and shall be moved no m; 5750
17: 9 children of wickedness waste them any m, 3254
17:18 What can David speak m to thee for 3254+5750
19:19 help the children of Ammon any m. 5750
23:26 they shall no m carry the tabernacle, NIH
2Ch 9: 4 of the LORD; there was no m spirit in her. 5750
10:11 yoke upon you, I will put m to your yoke: 3254
15:19 there was no m war unto the five and NIH
20:25 m than they could carry away: 369+3807.1
25: 9 The LORD is able to give thee much m 7235
28:13 already, ye intend to add m to our sins NIH
28:22 did he trespass yet m against the LORD: 3254
29:34 m upright in heart to sanctify themselves than 4480
32:16 his servants spake yet m against the LORD NIH
33: 8 Neither will I any m remove the foot of 3254
33:23 but Amon trespassed m and more. 7235
33:23 but Amon trespassed more and m. 7235
Ezr 7:20 whatsoever m shall be needful for 7606
Ne 2:17 of Jerusalem, that we be no m a reproach. 5750
13:18 yet ye bring m wrath upon Israel by 3254
13:21 From that time forth came they no m on NIH
Est 1:19 That Vashti come no m before king NIH
2:14 she came in unto the king no m, except 5750
2:17 favour in his sight m than all the virgins; 4480
4:13 in the king's house, m than all the Jews. 4480
6: 6 delight to do honour m than to myself? 3148
Job 3:21 and dig for it m than for hid treasures; 4480
4:17 Shall mortal man be m just than God? 4480
4:17 shall a man be m pure than his Maker? 4480
7: 7 life is wind: mine eye shall no m see good. 7725
7: 8 shall see me no m: thine eyes are upon me, NIH
7: 9 down to the grave shall come up no m. NIH
7:10 He shall return no m to his house, 5750
7:10 neither shall his place know him any m. 5750
14:12 till the heavens be no m, they shall not 1115
15:16 How much m abominable and 637+3588
20: 9 also which saw him shall see him no m; 3254
20: 9 neither shall his place any m behold him. 5750
23:12 of his mouth m than my necessary food. 4480
24:20 he shall be no m remembered; and 5750
32:15 They were amazed, they answered no m: 5750
32:16 but stood still, and answered no m:) 5750
34:19 the rich m than the poor? 6440+3807.1
34:23 For he will not lay upon man m than right; 5750
34:31 chastisement, I will not offend any m: NIH
34:32 if I have done iniquity, I will do no m. 3254
35: 2 My righteousness is m than God's? 4480
35:11 Who teacheth us m than the beasts of 4480
41: 8 upon him, remember the battle, do no m. 3254
42:12 the latter end of Job m than his beginning: 4480
Ps 4: 7 m than in the time that their corn and 4480
10:18 that the man of the earth may no m 3254+5750
19:10 M to be desired are they than gold, yea, 4480
39:13 before I go hence, and be no m. 369
41: 8 and now that he lieth he shall rise up no m. 3254
52: 3 Thou lovest evil m than good; and 4480
71:14 yet praise thee m and more. 3254+3605+5921
71:14 yet praise thee more and m. 3254+3605+5921
73: 7 they have m than heart could wish. 5674
74: 9 there is no m any prophet: neither is there 5750
76: 4 Thou art m glorious and excellent than 4480
77: 7 and will he be favourable no m? 3254+5750
78:17 they sinned yet m against him by 3254+5750
83: 4 that the name of Israel may be no m in 5750
87: 2 of Zion m than all the dwellings of Jacob. 4480
88: 5 the grave, whom thou rememberest no m: 5750
103:16 and the place thereof shall know it no m. 5750
104:35 of the earth, and let the wicked be no m. 5750
115:14 LORD shall increase you m and more, 3254
115:14 LORD shall increase you more and m, 3254
119:99 I have m understanding than all my 4480
119:100 I understand m than the ancients, because 4480
130: 6 My soul waiteth for the Lord m than they 4480
130: 6 I say, m than they that watch for NIH
Pr 3:15 She is m precious than rubies: and all 4480
4:18 that shineth m and more unto the perfect 1980
4:18 that shineth more and m unto the perfect 1980
10:25 so is the wicked no m: but the righteous is NIH
11:24 there is that withholdeth m than is meet, 4480
11:31 much m the wicked and the sinner. 637+3588
12:26 The righteous is m excellent than his 4480
15:11 how much m then the hearts of 637+3588
17:10 A reproof entereth m into a wise man than 4480
19: 7 how much m do his friends go far 637+3588
21: 3 m acceptable to the LORD than sacrifice. 4480
21:27 how much m, when he bringeth it 637+3588
26:12 there is m hope of a fool than of him. 4480
28:23 afterwards shall find m favour than he that 4480
29:20 there is m hope of a fool than of him. 4480
30: 2 Surely I am m brutish than any man, and 4480
31: 7 and remember his misery no m. 5750
Ecc 1:16 have gotten m wisdom than all they that 3254

Ecc 2: 9 increased m than all that were before me 3254
2:15 even to me; and why was I then m wise? 3148
2:16 of the wise m than of the fool for ever; 5973
2:25 or who else can hasten hereunto, m than I? 2351
4: 2 dead m than the living which are yet alive. 4480
4:13 who will no m be admonished. 5750
5: 1 be m ready to hear, than to give 4480
6: 5 nor known any thing: this hath m rest than 4480
6: 8 For what hath the wise m than the fool? 3148
7:19 Wisdom strengtheneth the wise m than ten 4480
7:26 I find m bitter than death the woman, 4480
9: 5 neither have they any m a reward; 5750
9: 6 neither have they any m a portion for ever 5750
9:17 m than the cry of him that ruleth among 4480
10:10 the edge, then must he put to m strength: 1396
SS 1: 4 we will remember thy love m than wine: 4480
5: 9 What is thy beloved m than another 4480
5: 9 what is thy beloved m than another 4480
Isa 1: 5 Why should ye be stricken any m? ye will 5750
1: 5 ye will revolt m and more: the whole head 3254
1: 5 ye will revolt more and m: the whole head 3254
1:13 Bring no m vain oblations; incense is an 3254
2: 4 neither shall they learn war any m. 5750
5: 4 What could have been done m to my 5750
9: 1 afterward did m grievously afflict her by 3513
10:20 shall no m again stay upon him that smote 3254
13:12 I will make a man m precious than fine 4480
15: 9 for I will bring m upon Dimon, lions upon 3254
19: 7 shall wither, be driven away, and be no m. NIH
23:10 of Tarshish: there is no m strength. 5750
23:12 he said, Thou shalt no m rejoice, 3254+5750
26:21 her blood, and shall no m cover her slain. 5750
30:19 thou shalt weep no m: he will be 1058+1058
30:20 teachers be removed into a corner any m, 5750
32: 5 The vile person shall be no m called liberal, 5750
38:11 I shall behold man no m with 5750
47: 1 for thou shalt no m be called tender and 3254
47: 5 for thou shalt no m be called, The lady of 3254
51:22 of my fury; thou shalt no m drink it again: 3254
52: 1 for henceforth there shall no m come into 5750
52:14 his visage was so marred m than any man, 4480
52:14 and his form m than the sons of men: 4480
54: 1 for m are the children of the desolate than 7227
54: 4 the reproach of thy widowhood any m. 5750
54: 9 of Noah should no m go over the earth; 5750
56:12 shall be as this day, and much m abundant. 1419
60:18 Violence shall no m be heard in thy land, 5750
60:19 The sun shall be no m thy light by day; 5750
60:20 Thy sun shall no m go down; neither shall 5750
62: 4 Thou shalt no m be termed Forsaken; 5750
62: 4 neither shall thy land any m be termed 5750
62: 8 Surely I will no m give thy corn to be meat 5750
65:19 the voice of weeping shall be no m heard in 5750
65:20 There shall be no m thence an infant of 5750
Jer 2:31 are lords; we will come no m unto thee? 5750
3:11 justified herself m than treacherous Judah. 4480
3:16 saith the LORD, they shall say no m, 5750
3:16 visit it; neither shall that be done any m. 5750
3:17 neither shall they walk any m after 5750
7:32 that it shall no m be called Tophet, 5750
10:20 is none to stretch forth my tent any m, 5750
11:19 that his name may be no m remembered. 5750
16:14 saith the LORD, that it shall no m be said, 5750
19: 6 that this place shall no m be called Tophet, 5750
20: 9 of him, nor speak any m in his name. 5750
22:10 for he shall return no m, nor see his native 5750
22:11 He shall not return thither any m: 5750
22:12 him captive, and shall see this land no m. 5750
22:30 of David, and ruling any m in Judah. 5750
23: 4 they shall fear no m, nor be dismayed, 5750
23: 7 saith the LORD, that they shall no m say, 5750
23:36 of the LORD shall ye mention no m: 5750
26:27 spue, and fall, and rise no m, because of 4480
30: 8 strangers shall no m serve themselves of 5750
31:12 they shall not sorrow any m at all. 3254+5750
31:29 In those days they shall say no m, 5750
31:34 they shall teach no m every man his 5750
31:34 and I will remember their sin no m. 5750
31:40 nor thrown down any m for ever. 5750
33:24 that they should be no m a nation before 5750
34:10 should serve themselves of them any m, 5750
38: 9 he is: for there is no m bread in the city. 5750
42:18 and ye shall see this place no m. 5750
44:26 that my name shall no m be named in 5750
46:23 because they are m than the grasshoppers, 7231
48: 2 There shall be no m praise of Moab: 5750
49: 7 of hosts; Is wisdom no m in Teman? 5750
50:39 it shall be no m inhabited for ever; 5750
51:44 not flow together any m unto him: yea, 1571
La 2: 9 the law is no m; her prophets also find no NIH
4: 7 they were m ruddy in body than rubies, 4480
4:15 They shall no m sojourn there. 3254
4:16 divided them; he will no m regard them: 3254
4:22 he will no m carry thee away into captivity: 3254
Eze 5: 6 into wickedness m than the nations, 4480
5: 6 my statutes m than the countries that are 4480
5: 7 Because ye multiplied m than the nations 4480
5: 9 whereunto I will not do any m the like, 5750
6:14 m desolate than the wilderness toward 4480
12:23 they shall no m use it as a proverb in Israel; 5750
12:24 For there shall be no m any vain vision nor 5750
12:25 come to pass; it shall be no m prolonged: 5750
12:28 none of my words be prolonged any m, 5750
13:15 The wall is no m, neither they that daubed NIH
13:21 they shall be no m in your hand to be 5750
13:23 Therefore ye shall see no m vanity, 5750
14:11 That the house of Israel may go no m 5750
14:11 neither be polluted any m with all their 5750
14:21 How much m when I send my four 637+3588
15: 2 What is the vine tree m than any tree, or 4480
16:41 and thou also shalt give no hire any m. 5750
16:42 and I will be quiet, and will be no m angry. 5750
16:47 wast corrupted m than they in all thy ways. 4480
16:51 multiplied thine abominations m than they, 4480
16:52 hast committed m abominable than they: 4480

Eze 16:52 they are m righteous than thou: yea, 4480
16:63 never open thy mouth any m, because 5750
18: 3 ye shall not have occasion any m to use 5750
19: 9 that his voice should no m be heard upon 5750
20:39 pollute ye my holy name no m with your 5750
21: 5 out of his sheath: it shall not return any m. 5750
21:13 it shall be no m, saith the Lord GOD. NIH
21:27 it shall be no m, until he come whose right NIH
21:32 of the land; thou shalt be no m remembered: NIH
23:11 m corrupt in her inordinate love than she, NIH
23:11 in her whoredoms m than her sister in her 4480
23:27 unto them, nor remember Egypt any m. 5750
24:13 not be purged from thy filthiness any m, 5750
24:27 and thou shalt speak, and be no m dumb: 5750
26:13 the sound of thy harps shall be no m heard. 5750
26:14 spread nets upon; thou shalt be built no m: 5750
26:21 thou shalt be no m: though thou be sought NIH
27:36 be a terror, and never shalt be any m. 5704+5769
28:19 and never shalt thou be any m. 5704+5769
28:24 there shall be no m a pricking brier unto 5750
29:15 neither shall it exalt itself any m above 5750
29:15 that they shall no m rule over 1115+3807.1
29:16 it shall be no m the confidence of the house 5750
30:13 there shall be no m a prince of the land of 5750
32:13 shall the foot of man trouble them any m, 5750
33:22 mouth was opened, and I was no m dumb. 5750
34:10 shall the shepherds feed themselves any m; 5750
34:22 my flock, and they shall no m be a prey; 5750
34:28 they shall no m be a prey to the heathen, 5750
34:29 they shall be no m consumed with hunger 5750
34:29 bear the shame of the heathen any m. 5750
36:12 thou shalt no m henceforth bereave them of 5750
36:14 Therefore thou shalt devour men no m, 5750
36:14 neither bereave thy nations any m, saith 5750
36:15 in thee the shame of the heathen any m, 5750
36:15 thou bear the reproach of the people any m, 5750
36:15 shalt thou cause thy nations to fall any m, 5750
36:30 that ye shall receive no m reproach of 5750
37:22 they shall be no m two nations, 5750
37:22 into two kingdoms any m at all: 5750+5750
37:23 Neither shall they defile themselves any m 5750
39: 7 not let them pollute my holy name any m: 5750
39:28 and have left none of them any m there. 5750
39:29 Neither will I hide my face any m from 5750
42: 6 the building was straitened m than 4480
43: 7 shall the house of Israel no m defile, 5750
45: 8 my princes shall no m oppress my people; 5750
Da 2:30 any wisdom that I have m than any living, 871.2
3:19 seven times m than it was wont to be heat. 5922
7:20 whose look was m stout than his fellows. 4481
11: 8 he shall continue m years than the king of NIH
Hos 1: 6 for I will no m have mercy upon 3254+5750
2:16 call me Ishi; and shalt call me no m Baali. 5750
2:17 they shall no m be remembered by their 5750
6: 6 the knowledge of God m than burnt 4480
9:15 out of mine house, I will love them no m: 3254
13: 2 now they sin m and more, and have made 3254
13: 2 now they sin more and m, and have made 3254
14: 3 neither will we say any m to the work of 5750
14: 8 shall say, What have I to do any m 5750
Joel 2: 2 ever the like, neither shall be any m after it, 3254
2:19 I will no m make you a reproach among 5750
3:17 shall no strangers pass through her any m. 5750
Am 5: 2 of Israel is fallen; she shall no m rise: 3254
7: 8 I will not again pass by them any m: 5750
7:13 prophesy not again any m at Beth-el: for it 5750
8: 2 I will not again pass by them any m. 5750
9:15 they shall no m be pulled up out of their 5750
Jnh 4:11 wherein are m than sixscore thousand 7235
Mic 4: 3 neither shall they learn war any m. 5750
5:12 and thou shalt have no m soothsayers: NIH
5:13 thou shalt no m worship the work of thine 5750
Na 1:12 have afflicted thee, I will afflict thee no m. 5750
1:14 that no m of thy name be sown: 5750
1:15 for the wicked shall no m pass 3254+5750
2:13 the voice of thy messengers shall no m be 5750
Hab 1: 8 and are m fierce than the evening wolves: 4480
1:13 the man that is m righteous than he? 4480
Zep 3:11 thou shalt no m be haughty 3254+5750+3807.1
3:15 of thee: thou shalt not see evil any m. 5750
Zec 9: 8 oppressor shall pass through them any m: 5750
11: 6 For I will no m pity the inhabitants of 5750
13: 2 and they shall no m be remembered: 5750
14:11 and there shall be no m utter destruction; 5750
14:21 in that day there shall be no m 5750
Mal 2:13 that he regardeth not the offering any m, 5750
Mt 5:37 for whatsoever is m than these cometh of 4053
5:47 what do ye m than others? do not even 4053
6:25 ye shall put on. Is not the life m than meat, 4183
6:30 shall he not much m clothe you, O ye of 3123
7:11 how much m shall your Father which is in 3123
10:15 It shall be m tolerable for the land of Sodom 414
10:25 how much m shall they call them of his 3123
10:31 ye are of m value than many sparrows. 1308
10:37 or mother m than me is not worthy of me: 5228
10:37 daughter m than me is not worthy of me. 5228
11: 9 yea, I say unto you, and m than a prophet. 4053
11:22 It shall be m tolerable for Tyre and Sidon at 414
11:24 that it shall be m tolerable for the land of 414
12:45 seven other spirits m wicked than himself, 4191
13:12 be given, and he shall have m abundance: NIG
18:13 he rejoiceth m of that sheep, than of 3123
18:16 hear thee, then take with thee one or two m, 2089
19: 6 Wherefore they are no m twain, but 3765
20:10 supposed that they should have received m; 4183
20:31 but they cried the m, saying, Have mercy 3187
23:15 twofold m the child of hell than 1362
26:53 he shall presently give me m than twelve 4183
27:23 But they cried out the m, saying, Let him 4057
Mk 1:45 insomuch that Jesus could no m openly 3371
4:24 and unto you that hear shall m be given. 4369
6:11 It shall be m tolerable for Sodom and 414
7:12 And ye suffer him no m to do ought for his 3765
7:36 tell no man: but the m he charged them, 3745
7:36 much the m a great deal they published it; 3123

M

Mk 8:14 they in the ship with them m than one loaf. 1508
9: 8 they saw no man any m, save Jesus only 3765
9:25 come out of him, and enter no m into him. 3371
10: 8 so then they are no m twain, but one flesh. 3765
10:48 but he cried the m a great deal, Thou Son 3123
12:33 is m than all whole burnt offerings and 4183
12:43 That this poor widow hath cast m in, than 4183
14: 5 For it might have been sold for m than 1883
14:25 I will drink no m of the fruit of the vine, 3765
14:31 But he spake the m vehemently, If I should 3123
15:14 And they cried out the m exceedingly, 4056
Lk 3:13 Exact no m than that which is appointed 4183
5:15 much the m went there a fame abroad of 3123
7:26 say unto you, and much m than a prophet. 4054
9:13 We have no m but five loaves and 4183
10:12 that it shall be m tolerable in that day for 414
10:14 But it shall be m tolerable for Tyre and 414
10:35 and whatsoever thou spendest m, when I 4325
11:13 how much m shall your heavenly Father 3123
11:26 seven other spirits m wicked than himself; 4191
12: 4 after that have no m that they can do. 4055+5100
12: 7 ye are of m value than many sparrows. 1308
12:23 The life is m than meat, and the body is 4183
12:23 than meat, and the body is m than raiment. NIG
12:24 how much m are ye better than the fowls? 3123
12:28 how much m will he clothe you, O ye of 3123
12:48 of him they will ask the m. 4054
14: 8 lest a m honourable man than thou be 1784
15: 7 m than over ninety and nine just persons NIG
15:19 And am no m worthy to be called thy son: 3765
15:21 and am no m worthy to be called thy son. 3765
18:30 Who shall not receive manifold m in this 4179
18:39 but he cried so much the m, Thou Son of 3123
20:36 Neither can they die any m: for they are 2089
21: 3 that this poor widow hath cast in m than 4183
22:16 I say unto you, I will not any m eat thereof, 3765
22:44 being in an agony he prayed m earnestly: 1617
23: 5 And they were the m fierce, saying, He 2001
Jn 5:14 sin no m, lest a worse thing come unto 3371
5:18 Therefore the Jews sought the m to kill 3123
6:66 went back, and walked no m with him. 3765
8:11 do I condemn thee: go, and sin no m. 3371
10:10 and that they might have it m abundantly. NIG
11:54 walked no m openly among the Jews; 3765
12:43 For they loved the praise of men m than 3123
14:19 a little while, and the world seeth me no m; 3765
15: 2 purgeth it, that it may bring forth m fruit. 4183
15: 4 no m can ye, except ye abide in me. 3761
16:10 I go to my Father, and ye see me no m; 3765
16:21 she remembereth no m the anguish, 3765
16:25 when I shall no m speak unto you in 3765
17:11 And now I am no m in the world, but 3765
19: 8 heard that saying, he was the m afraid; 3123
21:15 son of Jonas, lovest thou me m than these? 4183
Ac 4:19 God to hearken unto you m than unto God, 3123
5:14 And believers were the m added to 3123
8:39 that the eunuch saw him no m: 3765
9:22 But Saul increased the m in strength, and 3123
13:34 now no m to return to corruption, he said 3371
17:11 These were m noble than those in 2104
18:26 unto him the way of God m perfectly. 197
19:32 the m part knew not wherefore they were 4183
20:25 kingdom of God, shall see my face no m. 3765
20:35 It is m blessed to give than to receive. 3123
20:38 that they should see his face no m. 3765
22: 2 tongue to them, they kept the m silence: 3123
23:13 And they were m than forty which had 4183
23:15 something m perfectly concerning him: 197
23:20 inquire somewhat of him m perfectly. 197
24:10 I do the m cheerfully answer for myself: 2115
24:22 having m perfect knowledge of that way, 197
25: 6 And when he had tarried among them m 4183
27:11 m than those things which were spoken by 3123
27:12 the m part advised to depart thence also, 4183
Ro 1:25 and served the creature m than the Creator, 3844
2:18 approvest the things that are m excellent, 1308
3: 7 For if the truth of God hath m abounded NIG
5: 9 Much m then, being now justified by his 3123
5:10 much m, being reconciled, we shall be 3123
5:15 much m the grace of God, and the gift by 3123
5:17 much m they which receive abundance of 3123
5:20 sin abounded, grace did much m abound: 5248
6: 9 being raised from the dead dieth no m; 3765
6: 9 death hath no m dominion over him. 3765
7:17 Now then it is no m I that do it, but sin that 3765
7:20 it is no m I that do it, but sin that dwelleth 3765
8:37 m than conquerors through him that loved 5245
11: 6 And if by grace, then is it no m of works: 3765
11: 6 otherwise grace is no m grace. But if it be 3765
11: 6 But if it be of works, then is it no m grace: 3765
11: 6 more grace: otherwise work is no m work. 3765
11:12 of the Gentiles; how much m their fulness? 3123
11:24 how much m shall these, which be 3123
12: 3 not to think of himself m highly than he 3844
14:13 us not therefore judge one another any m: 3371
15:15 I have written the m boldly unto you in 5112
15:23 But now having no m place in these parts, 3371
1Co 6: 3 how much m things that pertain to this 3386
9:19 servant unto all, that I might gain the m. 4183
12:22 Nay, much m those members of the body, 3123
12:22 which seem to be m feeble, are necessary: 772
12:23 upon these we bestow m abundant 4055
12:23 our uncomely parts have m abundant 4055
12:24 having given m abundant honour to that 4055
12:31 shew I unto you a m excellent way. 2596+5236
14:18 I speak with tongues m than you all: 3123
15:10 but I laboured m abundantly than they all: 4054
2Co 1:12 and m abundantly to you-wards. 4056
2: 4 love which I have m abundantly unto you. 4056
3: 9 much m doth the ministration of 3123
3:11 much m that which remaineth is glorious. 3123
4:17 us a far m exceeding 1519+2596+5236+5236
5:16 yet now henceforth know we him no m. 3765
7: 7 mind toward me; so that I rejoiced the m. 3123
7:13 exceedingly the m joyed we for the joy of 3123
2Co 7:15 And his inward affection is m abundant 4056
8:17 but being m forward, of his own accord he 4707
8:22 in many things, but now much m diligent, NIG
10: 8 For though I should boast somewhat m of 4054
11:23 (I speak as a fool) I am m; in labours more 5228
11:23 in labours m abundant, in stripes above 4056
11:23 in prisons m frequent, in deaths oft. 4056
12:15 though the m abundantly I love you, 4056
Gal 1:14 being m exceedingly zealous of 4056
3:18 be of the law, it is no m of promise: 3765
4: 7 Wherefore thou art no m a servant, but 3765
Eph 2:19 Now therefore ye are no m strangers and 3765
4:14 That we henceforth be no m children, 3371
4:28 Let him that stole steal no m: but rather let 3371
Php 1: 9 that your love may abound yet m and 3123
1: 9 and m in knowledge and in all judgment; 3123
1:14 are much m bold to speak the word 4056
1:24 to abide in the flesh is m needful for you. 316
1:26 That your rejoicing may be m abundant in NIG
2:12 but now much m in my absence, 3123
2:28 I sent him therefore the m carefully, that, 4708
3: 4 whereof he might trust in the flesh, I m: 3123
1Th 2:17 endeavoured the m abundantly to see your 4056
4: 1 so ye would abound m and more. 3123
4: 1 so ye would abound more and m. NIG
4:10 brethren, that ye increase m and more; 3123
4:10 brethren, that ye increase more and m; NIG
2Ti 2:16 for they will increase unto m ungodliness. 4183
3: 4 lovers of pleasures m than lovers of God; 3123
Phm 1:16 specially to me, but how much m unto thee, 3123
1:21 knowing that thou wilt also do m than I 5228
Heb 1: 4 obtained a m excellent name than they. 1313
2: 1 Therefore we ought to give the m earnest 4056
3: 3 For this man was counted worthy of m 4183
3: 3 the house hath m honour than the house. 4183
6:17 willing m abundantly to shew unto 4054
7:15 And it is yet far m evident: for that after 4054
8: 6 But now hath he obtained a m excellent 1313
8:12 and their iniquities will I remember no m. 2089
9:11 by a greater and m perfect tabernacle, 5046
9:14 How much m shall the blood of Christ, 3123
10: 2 have had no m conscience of sins. 2089+3367
10:17 and iniquities will I remember no m. 2089
10:18 of these is, there is no m offering for sin. 3765
10:25 exhorting one another: and so much the m, 3123
10:26 there remaineth no m sacrifice for sins, 3765
11: 4 unto God a m excellent sacrifice than Cain, 4183
11:32 And what shall I m say? for the time would 2089
12:19 word should not be spoken to them any m: 4369
12:25 much m shall not we escape, if we turn 3123
12:26 Yet once m I shake not the earth only, but NIG
12:27 And this word, Yet once m, signifieth NIG
Jas 4: 6 But he giveth m grace. Wherefore he saith, 3187
1Pe 1: 7 being much m precious than of gold that 5093
2Pe 1:19 We have also a m sure word of prophecy; 949
Rev 2:19 and the last to be m than the first. 4183
3:12 of my God, and he shall go no m out: 2089
7:16 They shall hunger no m, neither thirst any 2089
7:16 shall hunger no more, neither thirst any m; 2089
9:12 behold, there come two woes m hereafter. 2089
12: 8 neither was their place found any m in 2089
18:11 no man buyeth their merchandise any m: 3765
18:14 shalt find them no m at all. 3361+3756+3765
18:21 and shall be found no m at all. 2089
18:22 shall be heard no m at all in thee; 2089
18:22 craft he be, shall be found any m in thee; 2089
18:22 millstone shall be heard no m at all in thee; 2089
18:23 And the light of a candle shall shine no m 2089
18:23 of the bride shall be heard no m at all in 2089
20: 3 that he should deceive the nations no m, 2089
21: 1 were passed away; and there was no m sea. 2089
21: 4 and there shall be no m death, 2089
21: 4 neither shall there be any m pain: 2089
22: 3 And there shall be no m curse: but 2089

MOREH (3)

Ge 12: 6 the place of Sichem, unto the plain of M. 4176
Dt 11:30 over against Gilgal, beside the plains of M? 4176
Jdg 7: 1 side of them, by the hill of M, in the valley. 4176

MOREOVER (171) [MORE]

Ge 24:25 She said m unto him, We have both straw 2050.1
32:20 say ye m, Behold, thy servant Jacob is 1571
45:15 M he kissed all his brethren, and 2050.1
47: 4 They said m unto Pharaoh, For to sojourn 2050.1
48:22 M I have given to thee one portion above 2050.1
Ex 3: 6 M he said, I am the God of thy father, 2050.1
3:15 God said m unto Moses, Thus shalt thou 5750
11: 3 M the man Moses was very great in 1571
18:21 M thou shalt provide out of all the people 2050.1
26: 1 M thou shalt make the tabernacle with 2050.1
30:22 M the LORD spake unto Moses, saying, 2050.1
Lev 7:21 M the soul that shall touch any unclean 2050.1
7:26 M ye shall eat no manner of blood, 2050.1
14:46 M he that goeth into the house all 2050.1
18:20 M thou shalt not lie carnally with thy 2050.1
25:45 M of the children of the strangers 1571+2050.1
Nu 13:28 and m we saw the children of Anak there. 1571
16:14 M thou hast not brought us into a land that 637
33:56 M it shall come to pass, that I shall do 2050.1
35:31 M ye shall take no satisfaction for the life 2050.1
Dt 1:28 m we have seen the sons of the Anakims 1571
1:39 M your little ones, which ye said should 2050.1
7:20 M the LORD thy God will send 1571+2050.1
28:45 M all these curses shall come upon thee, 2050.1
28:60 M he will bring upon thee all the diseases 2050.1
Jdg 10: 9 M the children of Ammon passed over 2050.1
Ru 4:10 M Ruth the Moabitess, the wife of 1571+2050.1
1Sa 2:19 M his mother made him a little coat, and 2050.1
12:23 M as for me, God forbid that I should sin 1571
14:21 M the Hebrews that were with 2050.1
17:37 David said m, The LORD that delivered 2050.1
20: 3 David sware m, and said, Thy father 5750
24:11 M, my father, see, yea see the skirt of thy 2050.1
28:19 M the LORD will also deliver Israel 2050.1
2Sa 7:10 M I will appoint a place for my people 2050.1
12: 8 I would m have given unto thee such 3254
15: 4 Absalom said m, Oh that I were made 2050.1
17: 1 M Ahithophel said unto Absalom, Let me 2050.1
17:13 M, if he be gotten into a city, then 2050.1
21:15 M the Philistines had yet war again with 2050.1
1Ki 1:47 m the king's servants came to bless our 1571
2: 5 M thou knowest also what Joab the son 2050.1
2:14 He said m, I have somewhat to say unto 2050.1
2:44 The king said m to Shimei, Thou knowest 2050.1
8:41 M concerning a stranger, that is not 1571+2050.1
10:18 M the king made a great throne of ivory, 2050.1
14:14 M the LORD shall raise him up a king 2050.1
2Ki 12:15 M they reckoned not with the men, 2050.1
21:16 M Manasseh shed innocent blood 1571+2050.1
23:15 M the altar that was at Beth-el, and 1571+2050.1
23:24 M the workers with familiar 1571+2050.1
1Ch 11: 2 And m in time past, even when Saul was 1571
12:40 M they that were nigh them, 1571+2050.1
17:10 M I will subdue all thine enemies. 2050.1
18:12 M Abishai the son of Zeruiah slew of 2050.1
22:15 M there are workmen with thee in 2050.1
23: 5 M four thousand were porters; and 2050.1
25: 1 M David and the captains of the host 2050.1
26: 4 M the sons of Obed-edom were, 2050.1
28: 7 M I will establish his kingdom for ever, 2050.1
29: 3 M, because I have set my affection to 5750
2Ch 1: 5 M the brasen altar, that Bezaleel the son 2050.1
2:12 Huram said m, Blessed be the LORD 2050.1
4: 1 M he made an altar of brass, 2050.1
4:20 M the candlesticks with their lamps, 2050.1
6:32 M concerning the stranger, 1571+2050.1
7: 7 M Solomon hallowed the middle of 2050.1
9:17 M the king made a great throne of ivory, 2050.1
17: 6 m he took away the high places 5750+2050.1
19: 8 M in Jerusalem did Jehoshaphat set 1571+2050.1
21:11 M he made high places in the mountains of 1571
21:16 M the LORD stirred up against Jehoram 2050.1
23: 9 M Jehoiada the priest delivered to 2050.1
25: 5 M Amaziah gathered Judah together, and 2050.1
26: 9 M Uzziah built towers in Jerusalem at 2050.1
26:11 M Uzziah had a host of fighting men, that 2050.1
27: 4 M he built cities in the mountains of 2050.1
28: 3 M he burnt incense in the valley of 2050.1
29:19 M all the vessels, which king Ahaz in his 2050.1
29:30 M Hezekiah the king and the princes 2050.1
31: 4 M he commanded the people that dwelt 2050.1
32:29 M he provided him cities, and 2050.1
35: 1 M Josiah kept a passover unto 2050.1
36:14 M all the chief of the priests, and 1571
Ezr 6: 8 M I make a decree what ye shall do to 2050.3
10:25 M of Israel: of the sons of Parosh; 2050.1
Ne 2: 7 M I said unto the king, If it please 2050.1
3: 6 M the old gate repaired Jehoiada the son 2050.1
3:26 M the Nethinims dwelt in Ophel, unto 2050.1
5:14 M from the time that I was appointed to be 1571
5:17 M there were at my table an hundred and 2050.1
6:17 M in those days the nobles of Judah sent 1571
9:12 M thou leddest them in the day by a 2050.1
9:22 M thou gavest them kingdoms and 2050.1
11:19 M the porters, Akkub, Talmon, and 2050.1
12: 8 M the Levites: Jeshua, Binnui, Kadmiel, 2050.1
Est 5:12 Haman said m, Yea, Esther the queen did 2050.1
Job 27: 1 M Job continued his parable, and said, 2050.1
29: 1 M Job continued his parable, and said, 2050.1
35: 1 Elihu spake m, and said, 2050.1
40: 1 M the LORD answered Job, and said, 2050.1
Ps 19:11 M by them is thy servant warned: and 1571
78:67 M he refused the tabernacle of Joseph, 2050.1
105:16 M, he called for a famine upon the land: 2050.1
Ecc 3:16 m I saw under the sun the place of 5750
5: 9 M the profit of the earth is for all: 2050.1
6: 5 M he hath not seen the sun, nor known any 1571
12: 9 m, because the Preacher was wise, he still 3148
Isa 3:16 M the LORD saith, Because 2050.1
7:10 M the LORD spake again unto Ahaz, 2050.1
8: 1 M the LORD said unto me, Take thee a 2050.1
19: 9 M they that work in fine flax, and 2050.1
29: 5 M the multitude of thy strangers shall be 2050.1
30:26 M the light of the moon shall be as 2050.1
39: 8 He said m, For there shall be peace and 3588
Jer 1:11 M, the word of the LORD came unto 2050.1
2: 1 M the word of the LORD came to me, 2050.1
8: 4 M thou shalt say unto them, Thus saith 2050.1
20: 5 M I will deliver all the strength of this 2050.1
25:10 M I will take from them the voice of 2050.1
33: 1 M the word of the LORD came unto 2050.1
33:23 M the word of the LORD came to 2050.1
37:18 M Jeremiah said unto king Zedekiah, 2050.1
39: 7 M he put out Zedekiah's eyes, and 2050.1
40:13 M Johanan the son of Kareah, and all 2050.1
44:24 M Jeremiah said unto all the people, and 2050.1
48:35 M I will cause to cease in Moab, saith 2050.1
Eze 3: 1 M he said unto me, Son of man, eat that 2050.1
3:10 M he said unto me, Son of man, all my 2050.1
4: 3 M take thou unto thee an iron pan, and 2050.1
4:16 M he said unto me, Son of man, behold, 2050.1
5:14 M I will make thee waste, and a reproach 2050.1
7: 1 M the word of the LORD came unto 2050.1
11: 1 M the spirit lift me up, and brought me 2050.1
12:17 M the word of the LORD came to me, 2050.1
16:20 M thou hast taken thy sons and thy 2050.1
16:29 Thou hast m multiplied thy fornication in 2050.1
17:11 M the word of the LORD came unto 2050.1
19: 1 M take thou up a lamentation for 2050.1
20:12 M also I gave them my sabbaths, to be a 2050.1
20:45 M the word of the LORD came unto 2050.1
22: 1 M the word of the LORD came unto 2050.1
23:36 The LORD said m unto me; Son of 2050.1
23:38 M this they have done unto me: they have 5750
28:11 M the word of the LORD came unto 2050.1
35: 1 M the word of the LORD came unto 2050.1
36:16 M the word of the LORD came unto 2050.1
37:16 M, thou son of man, take thee one stick, 2050.1
37:26 M I will make a covenant of peace with 2050.1

Eze 45: 1 **M**, when ye shall divide *by lot* the land 2050.1
46:18 **M** the prince shall not take of 2050.1
48:22 **M** from the possession of the Levites, *and* 2050.1
Zec 4: 8 **M** the word of the LORD came unto 2050.1
5: 6 He said, **M**, This *is* their resemblance 2050.1
Mt 6:16 **M** when ye fast, be not as the hypocrites, *1161*
18:15 **M** if thy brother shall trespass against thee, *1161*
Lk 16:21 **m** the dogs came and licked his sores. *235+2532*
Ac 2:26 **m** also my flesh shall rest in hope: *1161+2089*
11:12 **M** these six brethren accompanied me, and *2532*
19:26 **M** ye see and hear, that not alone at *2532*
Ro 5:20 **M** the law entered, that the offence might *1161*
8:30 **M** whom he did predestinate, them he also *1161*
1Co 4: 2 **M** it is required in stewards, *1161+3062+3739*
10: 1 **M**, brethren, I would not that ye should be *1161*
15: 1 **M**, brethren, I declare unto you the gospel *1161*
2Co 1:23 **M** I call God for a record upon my soul, *1161*
8: 1 **M**, brethren, we do you to wit of the grace *1161*
1Ti 3: 7 **M** he must have a good report of them *1161*
Heb 9:21 **M** he sprinkled with blood both *3668*
11:36 yea, **m** of bonds and imprisonment: *2089*
2Pe 1:15 **M** I will endeavour that you may be able *2532*

MORESHETH-GATH (1) [GATH, MORASTHITE]

Mic 1:14 Therefore shalt thou give presents to **M**: 4182

MORIAH (2)

Ge 22: 2 thou lovest, and get thee into the land of **M**; 4179
2Ch 3: 1 of the LORD at Jerusalem in mount **M**, 4179

MORNING (227)

Ge 1: 5 the evening and the **m** were the first day. 1242
1: 8 the evening and the **m** were the second day. 1242
1:13 the evening and the **m** were the third day. 1242
1:19 the evening and the **m** were the fourth day. 1242
1:23 the evening and the **m** were the fifth day. 1242
1:31 the evening and the **m** were the sixth day. 1242
19:15 when the **m** arose, then the angels hastened 7837
19:27 Abraham gat up early in the **m** to the place 1242
20: 8 Therefore Abimelech rose early in the **m**, 1242
21:14 Abraham rose up early in the **m**, and 1242
22: 3 Abraham rose up early in the **m**, and 1242
24:54 they rose up in the **m**, and he said, Send me 1242
26:31 they rose up betimes in the **m**, and 1242
28:18 Jacob rose up early in the **m**, and took 1242
29:25 to pass, that in the **m**, behold, it *was* Leah: 1242
31:55 early in the **m** Laban rose up, and 1242
40: 6 Joseph came in unto them in the **m**, and 1242
41: 8 it came to pass in the **m** that his spirit was 1242
44: 3 As soon as the **m** was light, the men were 1242
49:27 in the **m** he shall devour the prey, and 1242
Ex 7:15 Get thee unto Pharaoh in the **m**; lo, 1242
8:20 Rise up early in the **m**, and stand before 1242
9:13 Rise up early in the **m**, and stand before 1242
10:13 *and* when it was **m**, the east wind brought 1242
12:10 ye shall let nothing of it remain until the **m**; 1242
12:10 that which remaineth of it until the **m** ye 1242
12:22 go out at the door of his house until the **m**. 1242
14:24 that in the **m** watch the LORD looked 1242
14:27 the sea returned to his strength when the **m** 1242
16: 7 in the **m**, then ye shall see the glory of 1242
16: 8 flesh to eat, and in the **m** bread to the full; 1242
16:12 and in the **m** ye shall be filled *with* bread; 1242
16:13 in the **m** the dew lay round about the host. 1242
16:19 Let no man leave of it till the **m**. 1242
16:20 some of them left of it until the **m**, and 1242
16:21 they gathered it **every m**,
1242+1242+871.1+871.1+1886.1+1886.1
16:23 over lay up for you to be kept until the **m**. 1242
16:24 they laid it up till the **m**, as Moses bade: 1242
18:13 the people stood by Moses from the **m** unto 1242
18:14 all the people stand by thee from **m** unto 1242
19:16 it came to pass on the third day in the **m**, 1242
23:18 the fat of my sacrifice remain until the **m**. 1242
24: 4 rose up early in the **m**, and builded an altar 1242
27:21 his sons shall order it from evening to **m** 1242
29:34 remain unto the **m**, then thou shalt burn 1242
29:39 The one lamb thou shalt offer in the **m**; and 1242
29:41 according to the meat offering of the **m**, 1242
30: 7 burn thereon sweet incense **every m**:
1242+1242+871.1+871.1+1886.1+1886.1
34: 2 be ready in the **m**, and come up in 1242
34: 2 come up in the **m** unto mount Sinai, and 1242
34: 4 Moses rose up early in the **m**, and went up 1242
34:25 the feast of the passover be left unto the **m**. 1242
36: 3 free offerings **every m**.
1242+1242+871.1+871.1+1886.1+1886.1
Lev 6: 9 burning upon the altar all night unto the **m**, 1242
6:12 burn wood on it **every m**,
1242+1242+871.1+871.1+1886.1+1886.1
6:20 half of it in the **m**, and half thereof at night. 1242
7:15 he shall not leave *any* of it until the **m**. 1242
9:17 beside the burnt sacrifice of the **m**. 1242
19:13 not abide with thee all night until the **m**. 1242
24: 3 unto the **m** before the LORD continually: 1242
Nu 9:12 They shall leave none of it unto the **m**, 1242
9:15 it were the appearance of fire, until the **m**. 1242
9:21 the cloud abode from even unto the **m**, 1242
9:21 *that* the cloud was taken up in the **m**, then 1242
14:40 they rose up early in the **m**, and gat them 1242
22:13 Balaam rose up in the **m**, and said unto 1242
22:21 Balaam rose up in the **m**, and saddled his 1242
28: 4 The one lamb shalt thou offer in the **m**, and 1242
28: 8 as the meat offering of the **m**, and as 1242
28:23 these beside the burnt offering in the **m**, 1242
Dt 16: 4 day at even, remain all night until the **m**. 1242
16: 7 thou shalt turn in the **m**, and go unto thy 1242
28:67 In the **m** thou shalt say, Would God it were 1242
28:67 even thou shalt say, Would God it were **m**! 1242
Jos 3: 1 Joshua rose early in the **m**; and 1242
6:12 Joshua rose early in the **m**, and the priests 1242
7:14 In the **m** therefore ye shall be brought 1242
7:16 So Joshua rose up early in the **m**, and 1242
8:10 Joshua rose up early in the **m**, and 1242
Jdg 6:28 the men of the city arose early in the **m**, 1242
6:31 let him be put to death whilst *it is yet* **m**: 1242
9:33 it shall be, *that* in the **m**, as soon as the sun 1242
16: 2 saying, In the **m**, when it is day, we shall 1242
19: 5 when they arose early in the **m**, that he rose 1242
19: 8 he arose early in the **m** on the fifth day to 1242
19:25 and abused her all the night until the **m**: 1242
19:27 her lord rose up in the **m**, and opened 1242
20:19 the children of Israel rose up in the **m**, and 1242
Ru 2: 7 hath continued even from the **m** until now, 1242
3:13 Tarry this night, and it shall be in the **m**, 1242
3:13 *as* the LORD liveth: lie down until the **m**. 1242
3:14 she lay *at* his feet until the **m**: and she rose 1242
1Sa 1:19 they rose up in the **m** early, and 1242
3:15 Samuel lay until the **m**, and opened 1242
5: 4 when they arose early on the morrow **m**, 1242
11:11 into the midst of the host in the **m** watch, 1242
14:36 spoil them until the **m** light, and let us not 1242
15:12 Samuel rose early to meet Saul in the **m**, 1242
17:16 the Philistine drew near **m** and evening, 7925
17:20 David rose up early in the **m**, and left 1242
19: 2 take heed to thyself until the **m**, and 1242
19:11 to watch him, and to slay him in the **m**: 1242
20:35 it came to pass in the **m**, that Jonathan went 1242
25:22 if I leave of all that *pertain* to him by the **m** 1242
25:34 **m** light *any that* pisseth against the wall. 1242
25:36 him nothing, less or more, until the **m** light. 1242
25:37 it came to pass in the **m**, when the wine 1242
29:10 Wherefore now rise up early in the **m** with 1242
29:10 as soon as ye be up early in the **m**, and 1242
29:11 his men rose up early to depart in the **m**, 1242
2Sa 2:27 in the **m** the people had gone up every one 1242
11:14 it came to pass in the **m**, that David wrote a 1242
17:22 by the **m** light there lacked not one *of them* 1242
23: 4 *he shall be* as the light of the **m**, *when* 1242
23: 4 the sun riseth, *even* a **m** without clouds; 1242
24:11 For when David was up in the **m**, the word 1242
24:15 from the **m** even to the time appointed: 1242
1Ki 3:21 when I rose in the **m** to give my child suck, 1242
3:21 when I had considered it in the **m**, behold, 1242
17: 6 brought him bread and flesh in the **m**, 1242
18:26 called on the name of Baal from **m** even 1242
2Ki 3:20 it came to pass in the **m**, when the meat 1242
3:22 they rose up early in the **m**, and the sun 1242
7: 9 if we tarry till the **m** light, *some* mischief 1242
10: 8 *at* the entering in of the gate until the **m**. 1242
10: 9 it came to pass in the **m**, that he went out, 1242
16:15 Upon the great altar burn the **m** burnt 1242
19:35 and when they arose early in the **m**, behold, 1242
1Ch 9:27 the opening *thereof* **every m**
1242+1242+1886.1+1886.1+3807.1+3807.1
16:40 the altar of the burnt offering continually **m** 1242
23:30 **every m** to thank and praise the LORD,
1242+1242+871.1+871.1+1886.1+1886.1
2Ch 2: 4 *for* the burnt offerings **m** and evening, 1242
13:11 burn unto the LORD **every m**
1242+1242+871.1+871.1+1886.1+1886.1
20:20 they rose early in the **m**, and went forth 1242
31: 3 *to wit*, for the **m** and evening burnt 1242
Ezr 3: 3 *even* burnt offerings **m** and evening. 1242
Ne 4:21 the rising of the **m** till the stars appeared. 7837
8: 3 the water gate from the **m** until midday, 216
Job 1: 5 rose up early in the **m**, and offered burnt 1242
4:20 They are destroyed from **m** to evening: 1242
7:18 *that* thou shouldest visit him every **m**, *and* 1242
7:21 thou shalt **seek** me **in the m**, but I *shall* not 7836
11:17 shalt shine forth, thou shalt be as the **m**. 1242
24:17 For the **m** *is* to them even as the shadow of 1242
38: 7 When the **m** stars sang together, and all 1242
38:12 Hast thou commanded the **m** since thy 1242
41:18 and his eyes *are* like the eyelids of the **m**. 7837
Ps 5: 3 My voice shalt thou hear in the **m**, 1242
5: 3 *in* the **m** will I direct *my prayer* unto thee, 1242
30: 5 endure for a night, but joy *cometh* in the **m**. 1242
49:14 shall have dominion over them in the **m**; 1242
55:17 Evening, and **m**, and at noon, will I pray, 1242
59:16 I will sing aloud of thy mercy in the **m**: 1242
65: 8 thou makest the outgoings of the **m** and 1242
73:14 I been plagued, and chastened every **m**. 1242
88:13 and in the **m** shall my prayer prevent thee. 1242
90: 5 in the **m** *they are* like grass *which* groweth 1242
90: 6 In the **m** it flourisheth, and groweth up; 1242
92: 2 To shew forth thy lovingkindness in the **m**, 1242
110: 3 of holiness from the womb of the **m**: 4891
119:147 I prevented the **dawning of the m**, and 5399
130: 6 Lord more than they that watch for the **m**: 1242
130: 6 *I say, more than* they that watch for the **m**. 1242
139: 9 *If* I take the wings of the **m**, *and* dwell in 7837
143: 8 me to hear thy lovingkindness in the **m**; 1242
Pr 7:18 let us take our fill of love until the **m**: 1242
27:14 rising early in the **m**, it shall be counted a 1242
Ecc 10:16 king *is* a child, and thy princes eat in the **m**. 1242
11: 6 In the **m** sow thy seed, and in the evening 1242
SS 6:10 Who *is* she that looketh forth as the **m**, 7837
Isa 5:11 Woe unto them that rise up early in the **m**, 1242
14:12 from heaven, O Lucifer, son of the **m**! 7837
17:11 in the **m** shalt thou make thy seed to 1242
17:14 *and* before the **m** he *is* not 1242
21:12 The **m** cometh, and also the night: 1242
28:19 for **m** by morning shall it pass over, by day 1242
28:19 for morning by **m** shall it pass over, by day 1242
33: 2 be thou their arm every **m**, our salvation 1242
37:36 and when they arose early in the **m**, behold, 1242
38:13 I reckoned till **m**, *that*, as a lion, so will he 1242
50: 4 he wakeneth **m** by morning, he wakeneth 1242
50: 4 he wakeneth morning by **m**, he wakeneth 1242
58: 8 shall thy light break forth as the **m**, and 7837
Jer 5: 8 They were *as* fed horses in the **m**: 7904
20:16 let him hear the cry in the **m**, and 1242
21:12 Execute judgment in the **m**, and 1242
La 3:23 *They are* new every **m**: great *is* thy 1242
Eze 7: 7 The **m** is come unto thee, O thou that 6843
7:10 the **m** is gone forth; the rod hath 6843
12: 8 in the **m** came the word of the LORD unto 1242
24:18 So I spake unto the people in the **m**: and 1242
Eze 24:18 and I did in the **m** as I was commanded. 1242
33:22 my mouth, until *he* came to me in the **m**; 1242
46:13 thou shalt prepare it **every m**.
1242+1242+871.1+871.1+1886.1+1886.1
46:14 a meat offering for it **every m**,
1242+1242+871.1+871.1+1886.1+1886.1
46:15 **every m** *for* a continual burnt offering.
1242+1242+871.1+871.1+1886.1+1886.1
Da 6:19 the king arose very early in the **m**, and 5053
8:26 and the **m** which was told *is* true: 1242
Hos 6: 3 his going forth *is* prepared as the **m**; and 7837
6: 4 for your goodness *is* as a **m** cloud, and 1242
7: 6 *in* the **m** it burneth as a flaming fire. 1242
10:15 in a **m** shall the king of Israel utterly be cut 7837
13: 3 Therefore they shall be as the **m** cloud, and 1242
Joel 2: 2 as the **m** spread upon the mountains: 7837
Am 4: 4 bring your sacrifices *every* **m**, *and* 1242
4:13 that maketh the **m** darkness, and 7837
5: 8 turneth the shadow of death into the **m**, and 1242
Jnh 4: 7 God prepared a worm when the **m** rose 7837
Mic 2: 1 when the **m** is light, they practise it, 1242
Zep 3: 5 **every m** doth he bring his judgment
1242+1242+871.1+871.1+1886.1+1886.1
Mt 16: 3 And **in the m**, *It will be* foul weather to *4404*
20: 1 which went out **early in the m** to hire *260+4404*
21:18 Now **in the m** as he returned into the city, *4405*
27: 1 When the **m** was come, all the chief priests *4405*
Mk 1:35 And **in the m**, rising up a great while *4404*
11:20 And **in the m**, as they passed by, they saw *4404*
13:35 or at the cockcrowing, or **in the m**: *4404*
15: 1 And straightway in the **m** the chief priests *4404*
16: 2 And very **early in the m** the first *day* of *4404*
Lk 21:38 And all the people **came early in the m** to *3719*
24: 1 **very early in the m**, they came unto *901+3722*
Jn 8: 2 And **early in the m** he came again into *3722*
21: 4 But when the **m** was now come, *4405*
Ac 5:21 into the temple **early in the m**, *3588+3722+5259*
28:23 *out of* the prophets, from **m** till evening. *4404*
Rev 2:28 And I will give him the **m** star. *4407*
22:16 of David, *and* the bright and **m** star. *3720*

MORROW (103)

Ge 19:34 it came to pass on the **m**, that the firstborn 4283
Ex 8:10 he said, **To m**. And he said, *Be it* according 4279
8:23 and thy people: **to m** shall this sign be. 4279
8:29 his servants, and from his people, **to m**. 4279
9: 5 **To m** the LORD shall do this thing in 4279
9: 6 the LORD did that thing on the **m**, and 4283
9:18 **to m** about *this* time I will cause it to rain a 4279
10: 4 **to m** will I bring the locusts into thy coast: 4279
16:23 **To m** *is* the rest of the holy sabbath unto 4279
17: 9 **to m** I will stand on the top of the hill with 4279
18:13 it came to pass on the **m**, that Moses sat to 4283
19:10 sanctify them to day and **to m**, and let them 4279
32: 5 and said, **To m** *is* a feast to the LORD. 4279
32: 6 they rose up early on the **m**, and 4283
32:30 it came to pass on the **m**, that Moses said 4283
Lev 7:16 on the **m** also the remainder of it shall be 4283
19: 6 the *same* day ye offer it, and on the **m**: 4283
22:30 ye shall leave none of it until the **m**: 1242
23:11 on the **m** after the sabbath the priest shall 4283
23:15 ye shall count unto you from the **m** after 4283
23:16 Even unto the **m** after the seventh sabbath 4283
Nu 11:18 Sanctify yourselves against **to m**, and 4279
14:25 **To m** turn you, and get you *into* 4279
16: 5 Even **to m** the LORD will shew who *are* 1242
16: 7 incense in them before the LORD **to m**: 4279
16:16 thou, and they, and Aaron, **to m**: 4279
16:41 on the **m** all the congregation of 4283
17: 8 that on the **m** Moses went into 4283
22:41 it came to pass on the **m**, that Balak took 1242
33: 3 on the **m** after the passover the children of 4283
Jos 3: 5 for **to m** the LORD will do wonders 4279
5:11 of the land on the **m after** the passover, 4283
5:12 the manna ceased on the **m after** they had 4283
7:13 and say, Sanctify yourselves against **to m**: 4279
11: 6 for **to m** about this time will I deliver them 4279
22:18 that **to m** he will be wroth with the whole 4279
Jdg 6:38 for he rose up early on the **m**, and thrust 4283
9:42 it came to pass on the **m**, that the people 4283
19: 9 **to m** get you early on your way, that thou 4279
20:28 for **to m** I will deliver them into thine hand. 4279
21: 4 it came to pass on the **m**, that the people 4283
1Sa 5: 3 when they of Ashdod arose early on the **m**, 4283
5: 4 when they arose early on the **m** morning, 4283
9:16 **To m** about *this* time I will send thee a man 4279
9:19 **to m** I will let thee go, and 1242+871.1+1886.1
11: 9 **To m**, by *that time* the sun be hot, ye shall 4279
11:10 **To m** we will come out unto you, and 4279
11:11 it was *so* on the **m**, that Saul put the people 4283
18:10 it came to pass on the **m**, that the evil spirit 4283
19:11 thy life to night, **to m** thou *shalt be* slain. 4279
20: 5 **to m** *is* the new moon, and I should not fail 4279
20:12 when I have sounded my father about **to m** 4279
20:18 Jonathan said to *David*, **To m** *is* the new 4279
20:27 it came to pass on the **m**, *which was* 4283
28:19 **to m** *shalt* thou and thy sons *be* with me: 4279
31: 8 it came to pass on the **m**, when 4283
2Sa 11:12 to day also, and **to m** I will let thee depart. 4279
11:12 abode in Jerusalem that day, and the **m**. 4283
1Ki 19: 2 life of one of them *by* **to m** about *this* time. 4279
20: 6 Yet I will send my servants unto thee **to m** 4279
2Ki 6:28 him to day, and we will eat my son **to m**. 4279
7: 1 **To m** about this time *shall* a measure of 4279
7:18 shall be **to m** about *this* time in the gate of 4279
8:15 it came to pass on the **m**, that he took a 4283
10: 6 come to me to Jezreel by **to m** *this* time. 4279
1Ch 10: 8 it came to pass on the **m**, when 4283
29:21 on the **m after** that day, *even* a thousand 4283
2Ch 20:16 **To m** go ye down against them: behold, 4279
20:17 nor be dismayed; **to m** go out against them: 4279
Est 2:14 on the **m** she returned into the second 1242
5: 8 and I will do **to m** as the king hath said. 4279
5:12 **to m** *am* I invited unto her also with 4279
5:14 **to m** speak thou unto the king that 1242

M

Est 9:13 to m also according unto *this* day's decree, 4279
Pr 3:28 and come again, and to m I will give; 4279
27: 1 Boast not thyself of to m; for thou 3117+4279
Isa 22:13 let us eat and drink; for to m we shall die. 4279
56:12 to m shall be as this day, *and* much more 4279
Jer 20: 3 it came to pass on the m, that Pashur 4283
Zep 3: 3 they gnaw not the bones till the m. 1242
Mt 6:30 to day is, and to m is cast into the oven, *839*
6:34 Take therefore no thought for the m: for *839*
6:34 for the m shall take thought for the *things* of *839*
Mk 11:12 And on the m, when they were come from *1887*
Lk 10:35 And on the m when he departed, he took out *839*
12:28 in the field, and to m is cast into the oven; *839*
13:32 and I do cures to day and to m, and the third *839*
13:33 to day, and to m, and the *day* following: *839*
Ac 4: 5 And it came to pass on the m, that their *839*
10: 9 On the m, as they went on their journey, *1887*
10:23 lodged *them.* And on the m Peter went *1887*
10:24 And the m *after* they entered into Cesarea. *1887*
20: 7 unto them, ready to depart on the m; *1887*
22:30 On the m, because he would have known *1887*
23:15 that he bring him down unto you to m, *839*
23:20 bring down Paul to m into the council, *839*
23:32 On the m they left the horsemen to go with *1887*
25:17 on the m I sat on the judgment seat, and *1836*
25:22 To m, said he, thou shalt hear him. *839*
25:23 And on the m, when Agrippa was come, *1887*
1Co 15:32 let us eat and drink; for to m we die. *839*
Jas 4:13 To day or to m we will go into such a city, *839*
4:14 ye know not what *shall be* on the m: *839*

MORSEL (10) [MORSELS]
Ge 18: 5 I will fetch a m of bread, and comfort ye 6595
Jdg 19: 5 Comfort thine heart *with* a m of bread, and 6595
Ru 2:14 of the bread, and dip thy m in the vinegar. 6595
1Sa 2:36 him for a piece of silver and a m of bread, 3603
28:22 and let me set a m of bread before thee; 6595
1Ki 17:11 I pray thee, a m of bread in thine hand. 6595
Job 31:17 Or have eaten my m myself alone, and 6595
Pr 17: 1 Better *is* a dry m, and quietness therewith, 6595
23: 8 The m *which* thou hast eaten shalt thou 6595
Heb 12:16 who for one m of meat sold his birthright. *1035*

MORSELS (1) [MORSEL]
Ps 147:17 He casteth forth his ice like m: who can 6595

MORTAL (6) [MORTALITY, MORTALLY]
Job 4:17 Shall m man be more just than God? shall a 582
Ro 6:12 Let not sin therefore reign in your m body, *2349*
8:11 m bodies by his Spirit that dwelleth in you. *2349*
1Co 15:53 and this m *must* put on immortality. *2349*
15:54 and this m shall have put on immortality, *2349*
2Co 4:11 might be made manifest in our m flesh. *2349*

MORTALITY (1) [MORTAL]
2Co 5: 4 that m might be swallowed up of life. *2349*

MORTALLY (1) [MORTAL]
Dt 19:11 smite him m that he die, and fleeth into one 5315

MORTAR (2) [MORTER]
Nu 11: 8 or beat *it* in a m, and baked *it* in pans, and 4085
Pr 27:22 Though thou shouldest bray a fool in a m 4388

MORTER (11) [MORTAR]
Ge 11: 3 brick for stone, and slime had they for m. 2563
Ex 1:14 in m, and in brick, and in all manner of 2563
Lev 14:42 he shall take other m, and shall plaister 6083
14:45 timber thereof, and all the m of the house; 6083
Isa 41:25 he shall come *upon* princes as *upon* m, and 2563
Eze 13:10 lo, others daubed it *with* untempered *m:* NIH
13:11 daub *it with* untempered *m,* that it shall fall: NIH
13:14 that ye have daubed *with* untempered *m,* NIH
13:15 that have daubed it *with* untempered *m,* NIH
22:28 them *with* untempered *m,* seeing vanity, NIH
Na 3:14 go into clay, and tread the m, make strong 2563

MORTGAGED (1)
Ne 5: 3 We *have* m our lands, vineyards, and 6148

MORTIFY (2)
Ro 8:13 if ye through the Spirit do m the deeds of *2289*
Col 3: 5 M therefore your members which are upon *3499*

MOSERA (1)
Dt 10: 6 Beeroth of the children of Jaakan *to* M: 4149

MOSEROTH (2)
Nu 33:30 from Hashmonah, and encamped at M. 4149
33:31 they departed from M, and pitched in 4149

MOSES (829) [MOSES']
Ex 2:10 she called his name M: and she said, 4872
2:11 to pass in those days, when M was grown, 4872
2:14 M feared, and said, Surely *this* thing is 4872
2:15 heard this thing, he sought to slay M. 4872
2:15 M fled from the face of Pharaoh, and 4872
2:17 M stood up and helped them, and 4872
2:21 M was content to dwell with the man: and 4872
2:21 and he gave M Zipporah his daughter. 4872
3: 1 Now M kept the flock of Jethro his father 4872
3: 3 M said, I will now turn aside, and see this 4872
3: 4 the midst of the bush, and said, M, Moses. 4872
3: 4 the midst of the bush, and said, Moses, M. 4872
3: 6 M hid his face; for he was afraid to look 4872
3:11 M said unto God, Who *am* I, that I should 4872
3:13 M said unto God, Behold, *when* I come 4872
3:14 God said unto M, I AM THAT I AM: and 4872
3:15 God said moreover unto M, Thus shalt thou 4872
4: 1 M answered and said, But behold, they will 4872
4: 3 a serpent; and M fled from before it. 4872
4: 4 the LORD said unto M, Put forth thine 4872
4:10 M said unto the LORD, O my Lord, I *am* 4872
Ex 4:14 of the LORD was kindled against M, 4872
4:18 M went and returned to Jethro his father in 4872
4:18 And Jethro said to M, Go in peace. 4872
4:19 the LORD said unto M in Midian, Go, 4872
4:20 M took his wife and his sons, and set them 4872
4:20 and M took the rod of God in his hand. 4872
4:21 the LORD said unto M, When thou goest 4872
4:27 Go into the wilderness to meet M. 4872
4:28 M told Aaron all the words of the LORD 4872
4:29 M and Aaron went and gathered together 4872
4:30 which the LORD had spoken unto M, 4872
5: 1 afterward M and Aaron went in, and 4872
5: 4 Wherefore do ye, M and Aaron, let 4872
5:20 they met M and Aaron, who stood in 4872
5:22 And M returned unto the LORD, and said, 4872
6: 1 the LORD said unto M, Now shalt thou 4872
6: 2 God spake unto M, and said unto him, I *am* 4872
6: 9 M spake so unto the children of Israel: but 4872
6: 9 they hearkened not unto M for anguish of 4872
6:10 And the LORD spake unto M, saying, 4872
6:12 M spake before the LORD, saying, 4872
6:13 the LORD spake unto M and unto Aaron, 4872
6:20 to wife; and she bare him Aaron and M: 4872
6:26 *These are* that Aaron and M, to whom 4872
6:27 from Egypt: *these are* that M and Aaron. 4872
6:28 LORD spake unto M in the land of Egypt, 4872
6:29 That the LORD spake unto M, saying, 4872
6:30 M said before the LORD, Behold, I *am* of 4872
7: 1 the LORD said unto M, See, I have made 4872
7: 6 M and Aaron did as the LORD 4872
7: 7 M *was* fourscore years old, and 4872
7: 8 the LORD spake unto M and unto Aaron, 4872
7:10 M and Aaron went in unto Pharaoh, and 4872
7:14 the LORD said unto M, Pharaoh's heart *is* 4872
7:19 the LORD spake unto M, Say unto Aaron, 4872
7:20 M and Aaron did so, as the LORD 4872
8: 1 the LORD spake unto M, Go unto 4872
8: 5 the LORD spake unto M, Say unto Aaron, 4872
8: 8 Pharaoh called for M and Aaron, and said, 4872
8: 9 M said unto Pharaoh, Glory over me: when 4872
8:12 M and Aaron went out from Pharaoh: and 4872
8:12 M cried unto the LORD because of 4872
8:13 LORD did according to the word of M; 4872
8:16 the LORD said unto M, Say unto Aaron, 4872
8:20 the LORD said unto M, Rise up early in 4872
8:25 Pharaoh called for M and for Aaron, and 4872
8:26 M said, It is not meet so to do; for we shall 4872
8:29 M said, Behold, I go out from thee, and 4872
8:30 M went out from Pharaoh, and intreated 4872
8:31 LORD did according to the word of M; 4872
9: 1 the LORD said unto M, Go in unto 4872
9: 8 the LORD said unto M and unto Aaron, 4872
9: 8 let M sprinkle it towards the heaven in 4872
9:10 M sprinkled it *up* toward heaven; and 4872
9:11 the magicians could not stand before M 4872
9:12 as the LORD had spoken unto M. 4872
9:13 the LORD said unto M, Rise up early in 4872
9:22 the LORD said unto M, Stretch forth thine 4872
9:23 M stretched forth his rod toward heaven: 4872
9:27 called for M and Aaron, and said unto 4872
9:29 M said unto him, As soon as I am gone out 4872
9:33 M went out of the city from Pharaoh, 4872
9:35 Israel go; as the LORD had spoken by M. 4872
10: 1 the LORD said unto M, Go in unto 4872
10: 3 M and Aaron came in unto Pharaoh, and 4872
10: 8 M and Aaron were brought again unto 4872
10: 9 M said, We will go with our young and 4872
10:12 the LORD said unto M, Stretch out thine 4872
10:13 M stretched forth his rod over the land of 4872
10:16 Pharaoh called for M and Aaron in haste; 4872
10:21 the LORD said unto M, Stretch out thine 4872
10:22 M stretched forth his hand toward heaven; 4872
10:24 Pharaoh called unto M, and said, Go ye, 4872
10:25 M said, Thou must give us also sacrifices 4872
10:29 M said, Thou hast spoken well, I will see 4872
11: 1 (And the LORD said unto M, Yet will I 4872
11: 3 Moreover the man M *was* very great in 4872
11: 4 M said, Thus saith the LORD, 4872
11: 9 the LORD said unto M, Pharaoh shall not 4872
11:10 M and Aaron did all these wonders before 4872
12: 1 the LORD spake unto M and Aaron in 4872
12:21 M called for all the elders of Israel, and 4872
12:28 did as the LORD had commanded M and 4872
12:31 he called for M and Aaron by night, and 4872
12:35 of Israel did according to the word of M; 4872
12:43 the LORD said unto M and Aaron, This *is* 4872
12:50 as the LORD commanded M and Aaron, 4872
13: 1 And the LORD spake unto M, saying, 4872
13: 3 M said unto the people, Remember this 4872
13:19 M took the bones of Joseph with him: 4872
14: 1 And the LORD spake unto M, saying, 4872
14:11 they said unto M, Because *there were* no 4872
14:13 M said unto the people, Fear ye not, 4872
14:15 the LORD said unto M, Wherefore criest 4872
14:21 M stretched out his hand over the sea; and 4872
14:26 the LORD said unto M, Stretch out thine 4872
14:27 M stretched forth his hand over the sea, 4872
14:31 believed the LORD, and his servant M. 4872
15: 1 sang M and the children of Israel this song 4872
15:22 So M brought Israel from the Red sea, and 4872
15:24 the people murmured against M, saying, 4872
16: 2 the children of Israel murmured against M 4872
16: 4 said the LORD unto M, Behold, I will 4872
16: 6 M and Aaron said unto all the children of 4872
16: 8 M said, *This shall be,* when the LORD 4872
16: 9 M spake unto Aaron, Say unto all 4872
16:11 And the LORD spake unto M, saying, 4872
16:15 for they wist not what it *was.* And M said 4872
16:19 M said, Let no man leave of it till 4872
16:20 they hearkened not unto M; 4872
16:20 and stank: and M was wroth with them. 4872
16:22 of the congregation came and told M. 4872
16:24 they laid it up till the morning, as M bade: 4872
16:25 M said, Eat that to day; for to day *is* a 4872
16:28 the LORD said unto M, How long refuse 4872
Ex 16:32 M said, This *is* the thing which the LORD 4872
16:33 M said unto Aaron, Take a pot, and put an 4872
16:34 As the LORD commanded M, so 4872
17: 2 Wherefore the people did chide with M, 4872
17: 2 M said unto them, Why chide you with 4872
17: 3 the people murmured against M, and said, 4872
17: 4 M cried unto the LORD, saying, 4872
17: 5 the LORD said unto M, Go on before 4872
17: 6 M did so in the sight of the elders of Israel. 4872
17: 9 M said unto Joshua, Choose us out men, 4872
17:10 So Joshua did as M had said to him, and 4872
17:10 M, Aaron, and Hur went up *to* the top of 4872
17:11 it came to pass, when M held up his hand, 4872
17:14 the LORD said unto M, Write this *for* a 4872
17:15 M built an altar, and called the name of it 4872
18: 1 heard of all that God had done for M, and 4872
18: 5 and his wife unto M into the wilderness, 4872
18: 6 he said unto M, I thy father in law Jethro 4872
18: 7 M went out to meet his father in law, and 4872
18: 8 M told his father in law all that the LORD 4872
18:13 the morrow, that M sat to judge the people: 4872
18:13 the people stood by M from the morning 4872
18:15 M said unto his father in law, Because 4872
18:24 So M hearkened to the voice of his father 4872
18:25 M chose able men out of all Israel, and 4872
18:26 the hard causes they brought unto M, but 4872
18:27 M let his father in law depart; and he went 4872
19: 3 M went up unto God, and the LORD 4872
19: 7 M came and called for the elders of 4872
19: 8 M returned the words of the people unto 4872
19: 9 the LORD said unto M, Lo, I come unto 4872
19: 9 M told the words of the people unto 4872
19:10 the LORD said unto M, Go unto 4872
19:14 M went down from the mount unto 4872
19:17 M brought forth the people out of the camp 4872
19:19 M spake, and God answered him by a 4872
19:20 the LORD called M *up* to the top of 4872
19:20 *up* to the top of the mount; and M went up. 4872
19:21 the LORD said unto M, Go down, 4872
19:23 M said unto the LORD, The people 4872
19:25 So M went down unto the people, and 4872
20:19 they said unto M, Speak thou with us, and 4872
20:20 M said unto the people, Fear not: for God 4872
20:21 M drew near unto the thick darkness 4872
20:22 the LORD said unto M, Thus thou shalt 4872
24: 1 he said unto M, Come up unto the LORD, 4872
24: 2 M alone shall come near the LORD: but 4872
24: 3 M came and told the people all the words 4872
24: 4 M wrote all the words of the LORD, and 4872
24: 6 M took half of the blood, and put *it* in 4872
24: 8 M took the blood, and sprinkled *it* on 4872
24: 9 went up M, and Aaron, Nadab, and Abihu, 4872
24:12 the LORD said unto M, Come up to me 4872
24:13 M rose up, and his minister Joshua: and 4872
24:13 and M went up into the mount of God. 4872
24:15 M went up into the mount, and a cloud 4872
24:16 the seventh day he called unto M out of 4872
24:18 M went into the midst of the cloud, and 4872
24:18 M was in the mount forty days and 4872
25: 1 And the LORD spake unto M, saying, 4872
30:11 And the LORD spake unto M, saying, 4872
30:17 And the LORD spake unto M, saying, 4872
30:22 Moreover the LORD spake unto M, 4872
30:34 the LORD said unto M, Take unto thee 4872
31: 1 And the LORD spake unto M, saying, 4872
31:12 And the LORD spake unto M, saying, 4872
31:18 he gave unto M, when he had made an end 4872
32: 1 when the people saw that M delayed to 4872
32: 1 for *as for* this M, the man that brought us 4872
32: 7 the LORD said unto M, Go, get thee 4872
32: 9 the LORD said unto M, I have seen this 4872
32:11 M besought the LORD his God, and said, 4872
32:15 M turned, and went down from the mount, 4872
32:17 he said unto M, *There is* a noise of war in 4872
32:21 M said unto Aaron, What did this people 4872
32:23 for *as for* this M, the man that brought us 4872
32:25 when M saw that the people *were* naked; 4872
32:26 M stood in the gate of the camp, and said, 4872
32:28 of Levi did according to the word of M: 4872
32:29 For M had said, Consecrate yourselves to 4872
32:30 that M said unto the people, Ye have 4872
32:31 And M returned unto the LORD, and said, 4872
32:33 the LORD said unto M, Whosoever hath 4872
33: 1 the LORD said unto M, Depart, *and* go up 4872
33: 5 For the LORD had said unto M, Say unto 4872
33: 7 M took the tabernacle, and pitched it 4872
33: 8 when M went out unto the tabernacle, 4872
33: 8 man *at* his tent door, and looked after M, 4872
33: 9 to pass, as M entered into the tabernacle, 4872
33: 9 and *the LORD* talked with M. 4872
33:11 And the LORD spake unto M face to face, 4872
33:12 M said unto the LORD, See, thou sayest 4872
33:17 the LORD said unto M, I will do this 4872
34: 1 the LORD said unto M, Hew thee two 4872
34: 4 M rose up early in the morning, and 4872
34: 8 M made haste, and bowed his head toward 4872
34:27 the LORD said unto M, Write thou these 4872
34:29 when M came down from mount Sinai with 4872
34:29 that M wist not that the skin of his face 4872
34:30 and all the children of Israel saw M, 4872
34:31 M called unto them; and Aaron and all 4872
34:31 returned unto him: and M talked with them. 4872
34:33 *till* M had done speaking with them, he put 4872
34:34 when M went in before the LORD to 4872
34:35 the children of Israel saw the face of M, 4872
34:35 M put the vail upon his face again, until he 4872
35: 1 M gathered all the congregation of 4872
35: 4 M spake unto all the congregation of 4872
35:20 of Israel departed from the presence of M. 4872
35:29 commanded to be made by the hand of M. 4872
35:30 And M said unto the children of Israel, See, 4872
36: 2 M called Bezaleel and Aholiab, and every 4872
36: 3 they received of M all the offering, 4872
36: 5 they spake unto M, saying, The people 4872
36: 6 M gave commandment, and they caused it 4872

Ex 38:21 according to the commandment of **M**, 4872
38:22 made all that the LORD commanded **M**. 4872
39: 1 for Aaron; as the LORD commanded **M**. 4872
39: 5 as the LORD commanded **M**. 4872
39: 7 of Israel; as the LORD commanded **M**. 4872
39:21 the ephod; as the LORD commanded **M**. 4872
39:26 minister *in;* as the LORD commanded **M**. 4872
39:29 as the LORD commanded **M**. 4872
39:31 the mitre; as the LORD commanded **M**. 4872
39:32 to all that the LORD commanded **M**, 4872
39:33 they brought the tabernacle unto **M**, 4872
39:42 to all that the LORD commanded **M**, 4872
39:43 **M** did look upon all the work, and behold, 4872
39:43 so had they done it: and **M** blessed them. 4872
40: 1 And the LORD spake unto **M**, saying, 4872
40:16 Thus did **M**: according to all that 4872
40:18 **M** reared up the tabernacle, and 4872
40:19 upon it; as the LORD commanded **M**. 4872
40:21 as the LORD commanded **M**. 4872
40:23 as the LORD had commanded **M**. 4872
40:25 the LORD; as the LORD commanded **M**. 4872
40:27 as the LORD commanded **M**. 4872
40:29 as the LORD commanded **M**. 4872
40:31 **M** and Aaron and his sons washed their 4872
40:32 as the LORD commanded **M**. 4872
40:33 of the court gate. So **M** finished the work. 4872
40:35 **M** was not able to enter into the tent of 4872
Lev 1: 1 the LORD called unto **M**, and spake unto 4872
4: 1 And the LORD spake unto **M**, saying, 4872
5:14 And the LORD spake unto **M**, saying, 4872
6: 1 And the LORD spake unto **M**, saying, 4872
6: 8 And the LORD spake unto **M**, saying, 4872
6:19 And the LORD spake unto **M**, saying, 4872
6:24 And the LORD spake unto **M**, saying, 4872
7:22 And the LORD spake unto **M**, saying, 4872
7:28 And the LORD spake unto **M**, saying, 4872
7:38 Which the LORD commanded **M** in 4872
8: 1 And the LORD spake unto **M**, saying, 4872
8: 4 **M** did as the LORD commanded him; 4872
8: 5 **M** said unto the congregation, This *is* 4872
8: 6 **M** brought Aaron and his sons, and 4872
8: 9 holy crown; as the LORD commanded **M**. 4872
8:10 **M** took the anointing oil, and anointed 4872
8:13 **M** brought Aaron's sons, and put coats 4872
8:13 upon them; as the LORD commanded **M**. 4872
8:15 he slew *it;* and **M** took the blood, and put *it* 4872
8:16 their fat, and **M** burned *it* upon the altar. 4872
8:17 the camp; as the LORD commanded **M**. 4872
8:19 **M** sprinkled the blood upon the altar round 4872
8:20 **M** burnt the head, and the pieces, and 4872
8:21 and **M** burnt the whole ram upon the altar: 4872
8:21 the LORD; as the LORD commanded **M**. 4872
8:23 he slew *it;* and **M** took of the blood of it, 4872
8:24 **M** put of the blood upon the tip of their 4872
8:24 **M** sprinkled the blood upon the altar round 4872
8:28 **M** took them from off their hands, and 4872
8:29 **M** took the breast, and waved it *for* a wave 4872
8:29 as the LORD commanded **M**. 4872
8:30 **M** took of the anointing oil, and of 4872
8:31 **M** said unto Aaron and to his sons, Boil 4872
8:36 the LORD commanded by the hand of **M**. 4872
9: 1 *that* **M** called Aaron and his sons, and 4872
9: 5 they brought *that* which **M** commanded 4872
9: 6 **M** said, This *is* the thing which the LORD 4872
9: 7 **M** said unto Aaron, Go unto the altar, and 4872
9:10 the altar; as the LORD commanded **M**. 4872
9:21 before the LORD; as **M** commanded. 4872
9:23 **M** and Aaron went into the tabernacle of 4872
10: 3 **M** said unto Aaron, This *is it* that 4872
10: 4 **M** called Mishael and Elzaphan, the sons of 4872
10: 5 their coats out of the camp; as **M** had said. 4872
10: 6 **M** said unto Aaron, and unto Eleazar and 4872
10: 7 And they did according to the word of **M**. 4872
10:11 hath spoken unto them by the hand of **M**. 4872
10:12 **M** spake unto Aaron, and unto Eleazar and 4872
10:16 **M** diligently sought the goat of the sin 4872
10:19 Aaron said unto **M**, Behold, *this* day have 4872
10:20 And when **M** heard *that,* he was content. 4872
11: 1 the LORD spake unto **M** and to Aaron, 4872
12: 1 And the LORD spake unto **M**, saying, 4872
13: 1 the LORD spake unto **M** and Aaron, 4872
14: 1 And the LORD spake unto **M**, saying, 4872
14:33 the LORD spake unto **M** and unto Aaron, 4872
15: 1 the LORD spake unto **M** and to Aaron, 4872
16: 1 the LORD spake unto **M** after the death of 4872
16: 2 the LORD said unto **M**, Speak unto Aaron 4872
16:34 And he did as the LORD commanded **M**. 4872
17: 1 And the LORD spake unto **M**, saying, 4872
18: 1 And the LORD spake unto **M**, saying, 4872
19: 1 And the LORD spake unto **M**, saying, 4872
20: 1 And the LORD spake unto **M**, saying, 4872
21: 1 the LORD said unto **M**, Speak unto 4872
21:16 And the LORD spake unto **M**, saying, 4872
21:24 **M** told *it* unto Aaron, and to his sons, and 4872
22: 1 And the LORD spake unto **M**, saying, 4872
22:17 And the LORD spake unto **M**, saying, 4872
22:26 And the LORD spake unto **M**, saying, 4872
23: 1 And the LORD spake unto **M**, saying, 4872
23: 9 And the LORD spake unto **M**, saying, 4872
23:23 And the LORD spake unto **M**, saying, 4872
23:26 And the LORD spake unto **M**, saying, 4872
23:33 And the LORD spake unto **M**, saying, 4872
23:44 **M** declared unto the children of Israel 4872
24: 1 And the LORD spake unto **M**, saying, 4872
24:11 they brought him unto **M**: (and 4872
24:13 And the LORD spake unto **M**, saying, 4872
24:23 **M** spake to the children of Israel, that they 4872
24:23 of Israel did as the LORD commanded **M**. 4872
25: 1 the LORD spake unto **M** in mount Sinai, 4872
26:46 of Israel in mount Sinai by the hand of **M**. 4872
27: 1 And the LORD spake unto **M**, saying, 4872
27:34 which the LORD commanded **M** for 4872
Nu 1: 1 the LORD spake unto **M** in the wilderness 4872
1:17 **M** and Aaron took these men which are 4872
1:19 As the LORD commanded **M**, so 4872

Nu 1:44 which **M** and Aaron numbered, and 4872
1:48 For the LORD had spoken unto **M**, 4872
1:54 to all that the LORD commanded **M**, 4872
2: 1 the LORD spake unto **M** and unto Aaron, 4872
2:33 of Israel; as the LORD commanded **M**. 4872
2:34 to all that the LORD commanded **M**: 4872
3: 1 **M** in the day that the LORD spake with 4872
3: 1 the LORD spake with **M** in mount Sinai. 4872
3: 5 And the LORD spake unto **M**, saying, 4872
3:11 And the LORD spake unto **M**, saying, 4872
3:14 the LORD spake unto **M** in the wilderness 4872
3:16 **M** numbered them according to the word of 4872
3:38 *shall be* **M**, and Aaron and his sons, 4872
3:39 which **M** and Aaron numbered at 4872
3:40 the LORD said unto **M**, Number all 4872
3:42 **M** numbered, as the LORD commanded 4872
3:44 And the LORD spake unto **M**, saying, 4872
3:49 **M** took the redemption money of them that 4872
3:51 **M** gave the money of them that were 4872
3:51 the LORD, as the LORD commanded **M**. 4872
4: 1 the LORD spake unto **M** and unto Aaron, 4872
4:17 the LORD spake unto **M** and unto Aaron, 4872
4:21 And the LORD spake unto **M**, saying, 4872
4:34 **M** and Aaron and the chief of 4872
4:37 which **M** and Aaron did number according 4872
4:37 of the LORD by the hand of **M**. 4872
4:41 whom **M** and Aaron did number according 4872
4:45 whom **M** and Aaron numbered according 4872
4:45 the word of the LORD by the hand of **M**. 4872
4:46 whom **M** and Aaron and the chief of Israel 4872
4:49 they were numbered by the hand of **M**, 4872
4:49 of him, as the LORD commanded **M**. 4872
5: 1 And the LORD spake unto **M**, saying, 4872
5: 4 as the LORD spake unto **M**, so did 4872
5: 5 And the LORD spake unto **M**, saying, 4872
5:11 And the LORD spake unto **M**, saying, 4872
6: 1 And the LORD spake unto **M**, saying, 4872
6:22 And the LORD spake unto **M**, saying, 4872
7: 1 it came to pass on the day that **M** had fully 4872
7: 4 And the LORD spake unto **M**, saying, 4872
7: 6 **M** took the wagons and the oxen, and 4872
7:11 the LORD said unto **M**, They shall offer 4872
7:89 when **M** was gone into the tabernacle of 4872
8: 1 And the LORD spake unto **M**, saying, 4872
8: 3 as the LORD commanded **M**. 4872
8: 4 pattern which the LORD had shewed **M**, 4872
8: 5 And the LORD spake unto **M**, saying, 4872
8:20 **M**, and Aaron, and all the congregation of 4872
8:20 commanded **M** concerning the Levites, 4872
8:22 as the LORD had commanded **M** 4872
8:23 And the LORD spake unto **M**, saying, 4872
9: 1 the LORD spake unto **M** in the wilderness 4872
9: 4 **M** spake unto the children of Israel, 4872
9: 5 to all that the LORD commanded **M**, 4872
9: 6 they came before **M** and before Aaron on 4872
9: 8 **M** said unto them, Stand still, and I will 4872
9: 9 And the LORD spake unto **M**, saying, 4872
9:23 of the LORD by the hand of **M**. 4872
10: 1 And the LORD spake unto **M**, saying, 4872
10:13 of the LORD by the hand of **M**. 4872
10:29 **M** said unto Hobab, the son of Raguel 4872
10:35 that **M** said, Rise up, LORD, and let thine 4872
11: 2 the people cried unto **M**; and when Moses 4872
11: 2 when **M** prayed unto the LORD, the fire 4872
11:10 **M** heard the people weep throughout their 4872
11:10 kindled greatly; **M** also was displeased. 4872
11:11 **M** said unto the LORD, Wherefore hast 4872
11:16 the LORD said unto **M**, Gather unto me 4872
11:21 **M** said, The people, amongst whom I *am,* 4872
11:23 the LORD said unto **M**, Is the LORD'S 4872
11:24 **M** went out, and told the people the words 4872
11:27 told **M**, and said, Eldad and Medad do 4872
11:28 the servant of **M**, *one* of his young men, 4872
11:28 answered and said, My lord **M**, 4872
11:29 **M** said unto him, Enviest thou for my sake? 4872
11:30 **M** gat him into the camp, he and the elders 4872
12: 1 and Aaron spake against **M** because 4872
12: 2 the LORD indeed spoken only by **M**? 4872
12: 3 (Now the man **M** *was* very meek, above all 4872
12: 4 the LORD spake suddenly unto **M**, and 4872
12: 7 My servant **M** *is* not so, who *is* faithful in 4872
12: 8 not afraid to speak against my servant **M**? 4872
12:11 Aaron said unto **M**, Alas, my lord, 4872
12:13 **M** cried unto the LORD, saying, Heal her 4872
12:14 the LORD said unto **M**, If her father had 4872
13: 1 And the LORD spake unto **M**, saying, 4872
13: 3 **M** by the commandment of the LORD 4872
13:16 These *are* the names of the men which **M** 4872
13:16 **M** called Oshea the son of Nun, Jehoshua. 4872
13:17 **M** sent them to spy out the land of Canaan, 4872
13:26 they went and came to **M**, and to Aaron, 4872
13:30 Caleb stilled the people before **M**, and said, 4872
14: 2 the children of Israel murmured against **M** 4872
14: 5 **M** and Aaron fell on their faces before all 4872
14:11 the LORD said unto **M**, How long will 4872
14:13 **M** said unto the LORD, Then 4872
14:26 the LORD spake unto **M** and unto Aaron, 4872
14:36 the men, which **M** sent to search the land, 4872
14:39 **M** told these sayings unto all the children 4872
14:41 **M** said, Wherefore now do ye transgress 4872
14:44 and **M**, departed not out of the camp. 4872
15: 1 And the LORD spake unto **M**, saying, 4872
15:17 And the LORD spake unto **M**, saying, 4872
15:22 which the LORD hath spoken unto **M**, 4872
15:23 hath commanded you by the hand of **M**, 4872
15:23 the day that the LORD commanded *M,* NIH
15:33 him gathering sticks brought him unto **M** 4872
15:35 the LORD said unto **M**, The man shall be 4872
15:36 and he died; as the LORD commanded **M**. 4872
15:37 And the LORD spake unto **M**, saying, 4872
16: 2 they rose up before **M**, with certain of 4872
16: 3 gathered themselves together against **M** 4872
16: 4 And when **M** heard *it,* he fell upon his face: 4872
16: 8 **M** said unto Korah, Hear, I pray you, 4872
16:12 **M** sent to call Dathan and Abiram, the sons 4872

Nu 16:15 **M** was very wroth, and said unto 4872
16:16 **M** said unto Korah, Be thou and all thy 4872
16:18 the tabernacle of the congregation with **M** 4872
16:20 the LORD spake unto **M** and unto Aaron, 4872
16:23 And the LORD spake unto **M**, saying, 4872
16:25 **M** rose up and went unto Dathan and 4872
16:28 **M** said, Hereby ye shall know that 4872
16:36 And the LORD spake unto **M**, saying, 4872
16:40 the LORD said to him by the hand of **M**. 4872
16:41 the children of Israel murmured against **M** 4872
16:42 the congregation was gathered against **M** 4872
16:43 **M** and Aaron came before the tabernacle of 4872
16:44 And the LORD spake unto **M**, saying, 4872
16:46 **M** said unto Aaron, Take a censer, and 4872
16:47 Aaron took as **M** commanded, and ran into 4872
16:50 Aaron returned unto **M** unto the door of 4872
17: 1 And the LORD spake unto **M**, saying, 4872
17: 6 **M** spake unto the children of Israel, and 4872
17: 7 **M** laid up the rods before the LORD in 4872
17: 8 that on the morrow **M** went into 4872
17: 9 **M** brought out all the rods from before 4872
17:10 the LORD said unto **M**, Bring Aaron's 4872
17:11 **M** did *so:* as the LORD commanded him, 4872
17:12 the children of Israel spake unto **M**, saying, 4872
18:25 And the LORD spake unto **M**, saying, 4872
19: 1 the LORD spake unto **M** and unto Aaron, 4872
20: 2 gathered themselves together against **M** 4872
20: 3 the people chode with **M**, and spake, 4872
20: 6 **M** and Aaron went from the presence of 4872
20: 7 And the LORD spake unto **M**, saying, 4872
20: 9 **M** took the rod from before the LORD, 4872
20:10 **M** and Aaron gathered the congregation 4872
20:11 **M** lift up his hand, and with his rod he 4872
20:12 the LORD spake unto **M** and Aaron, 4872
20:14 **M** sent messengers from Kadesh unto 4872
20:23 the LORD spake unto **M** and Aaron in 4872
20:27 And **M** did as the LORD commanded: and 4872
20:28 And **M** stripped Aaron of his garments, and 4872
20:28 **M** and Eleazar came down from the mount. 4872
21: 5 people spake against God, and against **M**, 4872
21: 7 Therefore the people came to **M**, and said, 4872
21: 7 from us. And **M** prayed for the people. 4872
21: 8 the LORD said unto **M**, Make thee a fiery 4872
21: 9 **M** made a serpent of brass, and put it upon 4872
21:16 well whereof the LORD spake unto **M**, 4872
21:32 **M** sent to spy out Jaazer, and they took 4872
21:34 the LORD said unto **M**, Fear him not: 4872
25: 4 the LORD said unto **M**, Take all the heads 4872
25: 5 **M** said unto the judges of Israel, Slay ye 4872
25: 6 a Midianitish *woman* in the sight of **M**, 4872
25:10 And the LORD spake unto **M**, saying, 4872
25:16 And the LORD spake unto **M**, saying, 4872
26: 1 that the LORD spake unto **M** and 4872
26: 3 **M** and Eleazar the priest spake with them 4872
26: 4 as the LORD commanded **M** and 4872
26: 9 who strove against **M** and against Aaron in 4872
26:52 And the LORD spake unto **M**, saying, 4872
26:59 she bare unto Amram Aaron and **M**, and 4872
26:63 These *are* they that were numbered by **M** 4872
26:64 these there was not a man of them whom **M** 4872
27: 2 they stood before **M**, and before Eleazar 4872
27: 5 **M** brought their cause before the LORD. 4872
27: 6 And the LORD spake unto **M**, saying, 4872
27:11 as the LORD commanded **M**. 4872
27:12 the LORD said unto **M**, Get thee up into 4872
27:15 And **M** spake unto the LORD, saying, 4872
27:18 the LORD said unto **M**, Take thee Joshua 4872
27:22 **M** did as the LORD commanded him: 4872
27:23 the LORD commanded by the hand of **M**. 4872
28: 1 And the LORD spake unto **M**, saying, 4872
29:40 **M** told the children of Israel according to 4872
29:40 to all that the LORD commanded **M**. 4872
30: 1 **M** spake unto the heads of the tribes 4872
30:16 which the LORD commanded **M**, 4872
31: 1 And the LORD spake unto **M**, saying, 4872
31: 3 **M** spake unto the people, saying, 4872
31: 6 **M** sent them to the war, a thousand of 4872
31: 7 as the LORD commanded **M**; 4872
31:12 unto **M**, and Eleazar the priest, and unto 4872
31:13 **M**, and Eleazar the priest, and all 4872
31:14 **M** was wroth with the officers of the host, 4872
31:15 **M** said unto them, Have ye saved all 4872
31:21 the law which the LORD commanded **M**; 4872
31:25 And the LORD spake unto **M**, saying, 4872
31:31 **M** and Eleazar the priest did as the LORD 4872
31:31 priest did as the LORD commanded **M**. 4872
31:41 **M** gave the tribute, *which was* 4872
31:41 the priest, as the LORD commanded **M**. 4872
31:42 which **M** divided from the men that warred, 4872
31:47 **M** took one portion of fifty, *both* of man 4872
31:47 the LORD; as the LORD commanded **M**. 4872
31:48 captains of hundreds, came near unto **M**: 4872
31:49 they said unto **M**, Thy servants have taken 4872
31:51 **M** and Eleazar the priest took the gold of 4872
31:54 **M** and Eleazar the priest took the gold of 4872
32: 2 of Reuben came and spake unto **M**, 4872
32: 6 **M** said unto the children of Gad and to 4872
32:20 **M** said unto them, If ye will do this thing, 4872
32:25 and the children of Reuben spake unto **M**, 4872
32:28 So concerning them **M** commanded Eleazar 4872
32:29 **M** said unto them, If the children of Gad 4872
32:33 **M** gave unto them, *even* to the children of 4872
32:40 **M** gave Gilead unto Machir the son of 4872
33: 1 with their armies under the hand of **M** 4872
33: 2 **M** wrote their goings out according to their 4872
33:50 the LORD spake unto **M** in the plains of 4872
34: 1 And the LORD spake unto **M**, saying, 4872
34:13 **M** commanded the children of Israel, 4872
34:16 And the LORD spake unto **M**, saying, 4872
35: 1 the LORD spake unto **M** in the plains of 4872
35: 9 And the LORD spake unto **M**, saying, 4872
36: 1 and spake before **M**, and before the princes, 4872
36: 5 **M** commanded the children of Israel 4872
36:10 Even as the LORD commanded **M**, so 4872
36:13 **M** unto the children of Israel in the plains 4872

Dt 1: 1 These be the words which M spake unto all 4872
1: 3 that M spake unto the children of Israel, 4872
1: 5 began M to declare this law, saying, 4872
4:41 M severed three cities on this side Jordan 4872
4:44 this is the law which M set before 4872
4:45 which M spake unto the children of Israel, 4872
4:46 whom M and the children of Israel smote, 4872
5: 1 M called all Israel, and said unto them, 4872
27: 1 M with the elders of Israel commanded 4872
27: 9 M and the priests the Levites spake unto all 4872
27:11 M charged the people the same day, saying, 4872
29: 1 which the LORD commanded M to make 4872
29: 2 M called unto all Israel, and said unto 4872
31: 1 M went and spake these words unto all 4872
31: 7 M called unto Joshua, and said unto him in 4872
31: 9 M wrote this law, and delivered it unto 4872
31:10 M commanded them, saying, At the end of 4872
31:14 the LORD said unto M, Behold, thy days 4872
31:14 M and Joshua went, and 4872
31:16 the LORD said unto M, Behold, thou shalt 4872
31:22 M therefore wrote this song the same day, 4872
31:24 when M had made an end of writing 4872
31:25 That M commanded the Levites, 4872
31:30 M spake in the ears of all the congregation 4872
32:44 M came and spake all the words of this 4872
32:45 M made an end of speaking all these words 4872
32:48 the LORD spake unto M that selfsame 4872
33: 1 wherewith M the man of God blessed 4872
33: 4 M commanded us a law, even 4872
34: 1 M went up from the plains of Moab unto 4872
34: 5 So M the servant of the LORD died there 4872
34: 7 M was an hundred and twenty years old 4872
34: 8 the children of Israel wept for M in 4872
34: 8 and mourning for M were ended. 4872
34: 9 for M had laid his hands upon him: 4872
34: 9 and did as the LORD commanded M. 4872
34:10 not a prophet since in Israel like unto M, 4872
34:12 in all the great terror which M shewed in 4872
Jos 1: 1 Now after the death of M the servant of 4872
1: 2 M my servant is dead; now therefore arise, 4872
1: 3 have I given unto you, as I said unto M. 4872
1: 5 as I was with M, so I will be with thee: 4872
1: 7 which M my servant commanded thee: 4872
1:13 Remember the word which M the servant 4872
1:14 shall remain in the land which M gave you 4872
1:15 which M the LORD'S servant gave you 4872
1:17 According as we hearkened unto M in all 4872
1:17 thy God be with thee, as he was with M. 4872
3: 7 as I was with M, so I will be with thee. 4872
4:10 according to all that M commanded Joshua: 4872
4:12 children of Israel, as M spake unto them: 4872
4:14 they feared him, as they feared M, all 4872
8:31 As M the servant of the LORD 4872
8:31 as it is written in the book of the law of M, 4872
8:32 upon the stones a copy of the law of M, 4872
8:33 as M the servant of the LORD had 4872
8:35 There was not a word of all that M 4872
9:24 his servant M to give you all the land, 4872
11:12 as M the servant of the LORD 4872
11:15 As the LORD commanded M his servant, 4872
11:15 so did M command Joshua, and so 4872
11:15 of all that the LORD commanded M. 4872
11:20 as the LORD commanded M. 4872
11:23 to all that the LORD said unto M; 4872
12: 6 Them did M the servant of the LORD and 4872
12: 6 M the servant of the LORD gave it for a 4872
13: 8 which M gave them, beyond Jordan 4872
13: 8 even as M the servant of the LORD gave 4872
13:12 for these did M smite, and cast them out. 4872
13:15 M gave unto the tribe of the children of 4872
13:21 whom M smote with the princes of Midian, 4872
13:24 M gave inheritance unto the tribe of Gad, 4872
13:29 M gave inheritance unto the half tribe of 4872
13:32 These are the countries which M did 4872
13:33 unto the tribe of Levi M gave not any 4872
14: 2 the LORD commanded by the hand of M, 4872
14: 3 For M had given the inheritance of two 4872
14: 5 As the LORD commanded M, so 4872
14: 6 said unto M the man of God concerning me 4872
14: 7 Forty years old was I when M the servant 4872
14: 9 M sware on that day, saying, Surely 4872
14:10 since the LORD spake this word unto M, 4872
14:11 this day as I was in the day that M sent me: 4872
17: 4 The LORD commanded M to give us an 4872
18: 7 which M the servant of the LORD gave 4872
20: 2 I spake unto you by the hand of M: 4872
21: 2 The LORD commanded by the hand of M 4872
21: 8 the LORD commanded by the hand of M. 4872
22: 2 Ye have kept all that M the servant of 4872
22: 4 which M the servant of the LORD gave 4872
22: 5 which M the servant of the LORD 4872
22: 7 M had given possession in Bashan: 4872
22: 9 the word of the LORD by the hand of M. 4872
23: 6 that is written in the book of the law of M, 4872
24: 5 I sent M also and Aaron, and I plagued 4872
Jdg 1:20 they gave Hebron unto Caleb, as M said: 4872
3: 4 commanded their fathers by the hand of M. 4872
4:11 children of Hobab the father in law of M, 4872
1Sa 12: 6 It is the LORD that advanced M and 4872
12: 8 then the LORD sent M and Aaron, 4872
1Ki 2: 3 as it is written in the law of M, 4872
8: 9 of stone, which M put there at Horeb, 4872
8:53 as thou spakest by the hand of M thy 4872
8:56 which he promised by the hand of M his 4872
2Ki 14: 6 is written in the book of the law of M, 4872
18: 4 brake in pieces the brasen serpent that M 4872
18: 6 which the LORD commanded M. 4872
18:12 all that M the servant of the LORD 4872
21: 8 according to all the law that my servant M 4872
23:25 all his might, according to all the law of M; 4872
1Ch 6: 3 of Amram; Aaron, and M, and Miriam. 4872
6:49 according to all that M the servant of God 4872
15:15 as M commanded according to the word of 4872
21:29 which M made in the wilderness, and 4872
22:13 judgments which the LORD charged M 4872
1Ch 23:13 The sons of Amram; Aaron and M: and 4872
23:14 Now concerning M the man of God, 4872
23:15 The sons of M were, Gershom, and Eliezer. 4872
26:24 the son of M, was ruler of the treasures. 4872
2Ch 1: 3 which M the servant of the LORD had 4872
5:10 two tables which M put therein at Horeb, 4872
8:13 according to the commandment of M, 4872
23:18 as it is written in the law of M, 4872
24: 6 according to the commandment of M 4872
24: 9 M the servant of God laid upon Israel in 4872
25: 4 as it is written in the law in the book of M, 4872
30:16 according to the law of M the man of God: 4872
33: 8 and the ordinances by the hand of M. 4872
34:14 book of the law of the LORD given by M. 4872
35: 6 the word of the LORD by the hand of M. 4872
35:12 as it is written in the book of M. 4872
Ezr 3: 2 as it is written in the law of M the man of 4872
6:18 as it is written in the book of M. 4873
7: 6 he was a ready scribe in the law of M, 4872
Ne 1: 7 which thou commandedst thy servant M. 4872
1: 8 that thou commandedst thy servant M, 4872
8: 1 scribe to bring the book of the law of M, 4872
8:14 which the LORD had commanded by M, 4872
9:14 and laws, by the hand of M thy servant: 4872
10:29 which was given by M the servant of God, 4872
13: 1 On that day they read in the book of M in 4872
Ps 77:20 thy people like a flock by the hand of M 4872
90: T A Prayer of M the man of God. 4872
99: 6 M and Aaron among his priests, and 4872
103: 7 He made known his ways unto M, his acts 4872
105:26 He sent M his servant; and Aaron whom he 4872
106:16 They envied M also in the camp, and 4872
106:23 had not M his chosen stood before him in 4872
106:32 so that it went ill with M for their sakes: 4872
Isa 63:11 the days of old, M, and his people, 4872
63:12 That led them by the right hand of M with 4872
Jer 15: 1 Though M and Samuel stood before me, 4872
Da 9:11 the oath that is written in the law of M 4872
9:13 As it is written in the law of M, all this evil 4872
Mic 6: 4 I sent before thee M, Aaron, and Miriam. 4872
Mal 4: 4 Remember ye the law of M my servant, 4872
Mt 8: 4 offer the gift that M commanded for a 3475
17: 3 there appeared unto them M and 3475
17: 4 for thee, and one for M, and one for Elias. 3475
19: 7 Why did M then command to give a 3475
19: 8 M because of the hardness of your hearts 3475
22:24 Saying, Master, M said, If a man die, 3475
Mk 1:44 those things which M commanded, 3475
7:10 For M said, Honour thy father and 3475
9: 4 there appeared unto them Elias with M: 3475
9: 5 for thee, and one for M, and one for Elias. 3475
10: 3 unto them, What did M command you? 3475
10: 4 M suffered to write a bill of divorcement, 3475
12:19 Master, M wrote unto us, If a man's 3475
12:26 have ye not read in the book of M, how in 3475
Lk 2:22 to the law of M were accomplished, 3475
5:14 thy cleansing, according as M commanded, 3475
9:30 him two men, which were M and Elias: 3475
9:33 for thee, and one for M, and one for Elias: 3475
16:29 unto him, They have M and the prophets; 3475
16:31 If they hear not M and the prophets, 3475
20:28 Saying, Master, M wrote unto us, If any 3475
20:37 are raised, even M shewed at the bush, 3475
24:27 And beginning at M and all the prophets, 3475
24:44 which were written in the law of M, and 3475
Jn 1:17 For the law was given by M, but grace and 3475
1:45 of whom M in the law, and the prophets, 3475
3:14 And as M lifted up the serpent in 3475
5:45 accuseth you, even M, in whom ye trust. 3475
5:46 For had ye believed M, ye would have 3475
6:32 M gave you not that bread from heaven; 3475
7:19 Did not M give you the law, and yet none 3475
7:22 M therefore gave unto you circumcision, 3475
7:22 not because it is of M, but of the fathers; 3475
7:23 that the law of M should not be broken; 3475
8: 5 Now M in the law commanded us, 3475
9:29 We know that God spake unto M: as for 3475
Ac 3:22 For M truly said unto the fathers, A prophet 3475
6:11 him speak blasphemous words against M, 3475
6:14 shall change the customs which M 3475
7:20 In which time M was born, and 3475
7:22 And M was learned in all the wisdom of 3475
7:29 Then fled M at this saying, and was a 3475
7:31 When M saw it, he wondered at the sight: 3475
7:32 and the God of Jacob. Then M trembled, 3475
7:35 This M whom they refused, saying, 3475
7:37 This is that M, which said unto the children 3475
7:40 for as for this M, which brought us out of 3475
7:44 as he had appointed, speaking unto M, 3475
13:39 ye could not be justified by the law of M. 3475
15: 1 ye be circumcised after the manner of M, 3475
15: 5 to command them to keep the law of M. 3475
15:21 For M of old time hath in every city them 3475
21:21 are among the Gentiles to forsake M, 3475
26:22 the prophets and M did say should come: 3475
28:23 both out of the law of M, and out of 3475
Ro 5:14 death reigned from Adam to M, 3475
9:15 For he saith to M, I will have mercy on 3475
10: 5 For M describeth the righteousness which 3475
10:19 First M saith, I will provoke you to 3475
1Co 9: 9 For it is written in the law of M, Thou shalt 3475
10: 2 And were all baptized unto M in the cloud 3475
2Co 3: 7 face of M for the glory of his countenance; 3475
3:13 And not as M, which put a vail over his 3475
3:15 But even unto this day, when M is read, 3475
2Ti 3: 8 Now as Jannes and Jambres withstood M, 3475
Heb 3: 2 as also M was faithful in all his house. 3475
3: 3 was counted worthy of more glory than M, 3475
3: 5 And M verily was faithful in all his house, 3475
3:16 not all that came out of Egypt by M. 3475
7:14 of which tribe M spake nothing concerning 3475
8: 5 shadow of heavenly things, as M was 3475
9:19 For when M had spoken every precept to 3475
11:23 By faith M, when he was born, was hid 3475
11:24 By faith M, when he was come to years, 3475
Heb 12:21 that M said, I exceedingly fear and quake;) 3475
Jude 1: 9 the devil he disputed about the body of M, 3475
Rev 15: 3 And they sing the song of M the servant of 3475

MOSES' (19) [MOSES]

Ex 17:12 M hands were heavy; and they took a 4872
18: 1 the priest of Midian, M father in law, 4872
18: 2 Jethro, M father in law, took Zipporah, 4872
18: 2 father in law, took Zipporah, M wife, 4872
18: 5 Jethro, M father in law, came with his sons 4872
18:12 Jethro, M father in law, took a burnt 4872
18:12 to eat bread with M father in law before 4872
18:14 when M father in law saw all that he did to 4872
18:17 M father in law said unto him, The thing 4872
32:19 M anger waxed hot, and he cast the tables 4872
34:29 the two tables of Testimony in M hand, 4872
34:35 of Moses, that the skin of M face shone: 4872
Lev 8:29 ram of consecration it was M part; 4872+3807.1
Nu 10:29 of Raguel the Midianite, M father in law, 4872
Jos 1: 1 Joshua the son of Nun, M minister, saying, 4872
Jdg 1:16 the children of the Kenite, M father in law, 4872
Mt 23: 2 The scribes and the Pharisees sit in M seat: 3475
Jn 9:28 art his disciple; but we are M disciples. 3475
Heb 10:28 He that despised M law died without mercy 3475

MOST (135) [MUCH]

Ge 14:18 and he was the priest of the m high God. 5945
14:19 said, Blessed be Abram of the m high God, 5945
14:20 blessed be the m high God, which hath 5945
14:22 the m high God, the possessor of heaven 5945
Ex 26:33 the holy place and the m holy. 6944+6944
26:34 the Testimony in the m holy place. 6944+6944
29:37 and it shall be an altar m holy: 6944+6944
30:10 it is m holy unto the LORD. 6944+6944
30:29 that they may be m holy: 6944+6944
30:36 it shall be unto you m holy. 6944+6944
40:10 and it shall be an altar m holy. 6944+6944
Lev 2: 3 it is a thing m holy of the offerings 6944+6944
2:10 it is a thing m holy of the offerings 6944+6944
6:17 it is m holy, as is the sin offering, 6944+6944
6:25 before the LORD: it is m holy. 6944+6944
6:29 priests shall eat thereof: it is m holy. 6944+6944
7: 1 of the trespass offering: it is m holy. 6944+6944
7: 6 eaten in the holy place: it is m holy. 6944+6944
10:12 beside the altar: for it is m holy: 6944+6944
10:17 seeing it is m holy, and God hath 6944+6944
14:13 is the trespass offering: it is m holy: 6944+6944
21:22 both of the m holy, and of the holy. 6944+6944
24: 9 for it is m holy unto him of 6944+6944
27:28 every devoted thing is m holy unto 6944+6944
Nu 4: 4 about the m holy things: 6944+6944
4:19 unto the m holy things: Aaron 6944+6944
18: 9 This shall be thine of the m holy 6944+6944
18: 9 be m holy for thee and for thy sons. 6944+6944
18:10 In the m holy place shalt thou eat it; 6944+6944
24:16 and knew the knowledge of the m High, 5945
Dt 32: 8 When the m High divided to the nations 5945
2Sa 22:14 and the m High uttered his voice. 5945
23:19 Was he not m honourable of three? 3588
1Ki 6:16 even for the m holy place. 6944+6944
7:50 the m holy place, and for the doors 6944+6944
8: 6 to the m holy place, even under 6944+6944
1Ch 6:49 for all the work of the place m holy, 6944+6944
23:13 should sanctify the m holy things, he 6944+6944
2Ch 3: 8 he made the m holy house, 6944+6944
3:10 in the m holy house he made two 6944+6944
4:22 doors thereof for the m holy place, 6944+6944
5: 7 into the m holy place, even under 6944+6944
31:14 the LORD, and the m holy things. 6944+6944
Ezr 2:63 m holy things till there stood up a 6944+6944
Ne 7:65 m holy things, till there stood up a 6944+6944
Est 6: 9 hand of one of the king's m noble princes, 6579
Job 34:17 and wilt thou condemn him that is m just? 3524
Ps 7:17 praise to the name of the LORD m High. 5945
9: 2 sing praise to thy name, O thou m High. 5945
21: 6 For thou hast made him m blessed for ever: NIH
21: 7 through the mercy of the m High he shall 5945
45: 3 O m mighty, with thy glory and NIH
46: 4 place of the tabernacles of the m High. 5945
47: 2 For the LORD m High is terrible; he is a 5945
50:14 and pay thy vows unto the m High: 5945
56: 2 many that fight against me, O thou m High. NIH
57: 2 I will cry unto God m High; unto God that 5945
73:11 and is there knowledge in the m High? 5945
77:10 the years of the right hand of the m High. 5945
78:17 by provoking the m High in the wilderness. 5945
78:56 and provoked the m high God, 5945
82: 6 and all of you are children of the m High. 5945
83:18 art the m High over all the earth. 5945
91: 1 m High shall abide under the shadow of 5945
91: 9 even the m High, thy habitation; 5945
92: 1 to sing praises unto thy name, O m High: 5945
92: 8 But thou, LORD, art m high for evermore. NIH
107:11 and contemned the counsel of the m High: 5945
Pr 20: 6 M men will proclaim every one his own 7230
SS 5:11 His head is as the m fine gold, his locks are 3800
5:16 His mouth is m sweet: yea, he is altogether 4477
8: 6 of fire, which hath a m vehement flame. 7957
Isa 14:14 of the clouds; I will be like the m High. 5945
26: 7 thou, m upright, dost weigh the path of 3477
Jer 6:26 as for an only son, m bitter lamentation: NIH
50:31 Behold, I am against thee, O thou m proud, NIH
50:32 the m proud shall stumble and fall, and 2087
La 3:35 of a man before the face of the m High, 5945
3:38 Out of the mouth of the m High proceedeth 5945
4: 1 how is the m fine gold changed! the stones 2896
Eze 2: 7 they will forbear: for they are m rebellious. NIH
23:12 captains and rulers clothed m gorgeously, 4358
33:28 will lay the land m desolate, 4923+8077+2050.1
33:29 laid the land m desolate 4923+8077+2050.1
35: 3 I will make thee m desolate. 4923+8077+2050.1
35: 7 mount Seir m desolate, 8077+8077+2050.1
41: 4 unto me, This is the m holy place. 6944+6944
42:13 m holy things: there shall they lay 6944+6944
42:13 shall they lay the m holy things, 6944+6944

Eze 43:12 thereof round about *shall be* **m holy**. 6944+6944
44:13 my holy *things,* in the **m holy** *place:* 6944+6944
45: 3 the sanctuary *and* the **m holy** *place.* 6944+6944
48:12 **m holy** by the border of the Levites. 6944+6944
Da 3:20 **m mighty men** that *were* in 1400+1401+2429
3:26 ye servants of the **m high** God, come forth, 5943
4:17 the **m High** ruleth in the kingdom of men, 5943
4:24 and this *is* the decree of the **m High**, 5943
4:25 till thou know that the **m High** ruleth in 5943
4:32 until thou know that the **m High** ruleth in 5943
4:34 and I blessed the **m High**, and I praised and 5943
5:18 the **m high** God gave Nebuchadnezzar thy 5943
5:21 till he knew that the **m high** God ruled in 5943
7:18 the saints of the **m High** shall take 5946
7:22 *was* given to the saints of the **m High**; 5946
7:25 speak *great* words against the **m High**, 5943
7:25 and shall wear out the saints of the **m High**, 5946
7:27 to the people of the saints of the **m High**, 5946
9:24 prophecy, and to anoint the **m Holy**. 6944+6944
11:15 up a mount, and take the **m fenced** cities: 4013
11:39 Thus shall he do in the **m strong** holds with 4581
Hos 7:16 They return, *but* not *to* the **m High**: 5920
11: 7 though they called them to the **m High**, 5920
12:14 Ephraim provoked *him* to anger **m bitterly**: 8563
Mic 7: 4 the **m** upright *is sharper* than a thorn hedge: NIH
Mt 11:20 wherein **m** of his mighty works were done, *4183*
Mk 5: 7 Jesus, *thou* Son of the **m high** God? *5310*
Lk 1: 1 which are **m surely believed** among us, *4135*
1: 3 unto thee in order, **m excellent** Theophilus, *2903*
7:42 which of them will love him **m**? *4183*
7:43 I suppose that *he,* to whom he forgave **m**. *4183*
8:28 with thee, Jesus, *thou* Son of God **m high**? *5310*
Ac 7:48 Howbeit the **m High** dwelleth not in *5310*
16:17 These men are the servants of the **m high** *5310*
20:38 Sorrowing **m** *of all* for the words which he *3122*
23:26 Claudius Lysias unto the **m excellent** *2903*
24: 3 *it* always, and in all places, **m noble** Felix, *2903*
26: 5 that after the **m straitest** sect of our religion *196*
26:25 But he said, I am not mad, **m noble** Festus; *2903*
1Co 14:27 or at the **m** *by* three, and *that* by course; *4183*
15:19 in Christ, we are of all men **m miserable**. *1652*
2Co 12: 9 **M gladly** therefore will I rather glory in my *2236*
Heb 7: 1 king of Salem, priest of the **m high** God, *5310*
Jude 1:20 building up yourselves on your **m holy** faith, *40*
Rev 18:12 all *manner* vessels of **m precious** wood, *5093*
21:11 her light *was* like unto a stone **m precious**, *5093*

MOTE (6)

Mt 7: 3 And why beholdest thou the **m** that is in thy *2595*
7: 4 Let me pull out the **m** out of thine eye; *2595*
7: 5 shalt thou see clearly to cast out the **m** out *2595*
Lk 6:41 And why beholdest thou the **m** that is in thy *2595*
6:42 let me pull out the **m** that is in thine eye, *2595*
6:42 shalt thou see clearly to pull out the **m** that *2595*

MOTH (9) [MOTHEATEN, MOTH-EATEN]

Job 4:19 the dust, which are crushed before the **m**? 6211
27:18 He buildeth his house as a **m**, and as a 6211
Ps 39:11 his beauty to consume away like a **m**: 6211
Isa 50: 9 old as a garment; the **m** shall eat them up. 6211
51: 8 For the **m** shall eat them up like a garment, 6211
Hos 5:12 Therefore *will* I *be* unto Ephraim as a **m**, 6211
Mt 6:19 where **m** and rust doth corrupt, and *4597*
6:20 where neither **m** nor rust doth corrupt, and *4597*
Lk 12:33 no thief approacheth, neither **m** corrupteth. *4597*

MOTHEATEN, MOTH-EATEN (2) [MOTH]

Job 13:28 consumeth, as a garment that is **m**. 398+6211
Jas 5: 2 are corrupted, and your garments are **m**. *4598*

MOTHER (245) [GRANDMOTHER, MOTHER'S, MOTHERS, MOTHERS']

Ge 2:24 shall a man leave his father and his **m**, 517
3:20 because she was the **m** of all living. 517
17:16 bless her, and she shall be *a m* of nations; NIH
20:12 of my father, but not the daughter of my **m**; 517
21:21 his **m** took him a wife out of the land of 517
24:53 to her brother and to her **m** precious things. 517
24:55 her brother and her **m** said, Let the damsel 517
24:60 be thou *the m* of thousands of millions, and NIH
24:67 Isaac brought her into his **m** Sarah's tent, 517
27:11 Jacob said to Rebekah his **m**, Behold, 517
27:13 his **m** said unto him, Upon me *be* thy curse, 517
27:14 and fetched, and brought *them* to his **m**: 517
27:14 his **m** made savoury meat, such as his father 517
28: 5 brother of Rebekah, Jacob's and Esau's **m**. 517
28: 7 And that Jacob obeyed his father and his **m**, 517
30:14 the field, and brought them unto his **m** Leah. 517
32:11 and smite me, *and* the **m** with the children. 517
37:10 Shall I and thy **m** and thy brethren indeed 517
44:20 he alone is left of his **m**, and his father 517
Ex 2: 8 And the maid went and called the child's **m**. 517
20:12 Honour thy father and thy **m**: that thy days 517
21:15 or his **m**, shall be surely put to death. 517
21:17 or his **m**, shall surely be put to death. 517
Lev 18: 7 or the nakedness of thy **m**, shalt thou not 517
18: 7 she *is* thy **m**; thou shalt not uncover her 517
18: 9 daughter of thy father, or daughter of thy **m**, 517
19: 3 Ye shall fear every man his **m**, and 517
20: 9 or his **m** shall be surely put to death: 517
20: 9 he hath cursed his father or his **m**; his blood 517
20:14 if a man take a wife and her **m**, it *is* 517
21: 2 *that is,* for his **m**, and for his father, and 517
21:11 nor defile himself for his father, or for his **m**; 517
Nu 6: 7 or for his **m**, for his brother, or for his sister, 517
26:59 of Levi, whom *her m* bare to Levi in Egypt: NIH
Dt 5:16 Honour thy father and thy **m**, as the LORD 517
13: 6 the son of thy **m**, or thy son, or thy daughter, 517
21:13 bewail her father and her **m** a full month: 517
21:18 or the voice of his **m**, and *that,* when they 517
21:19 shall his father and his **m** lay hold on him, 517
22:15 her **m**, take and bring forth *the tokens of* 517
27:16 *be* he that setteth light by his father or his **m**. 517
27:22 of his father, or the daughter of his **m**. 517
Dt 27:23 Cursed *be* he that lieth with his **m in law**. 2859
33: 9 Who said unto his father and to his **m**, I have 517
Jos 2:13 And my **m**, and my brethren, and my sisters, 517
2:18 thy **m**, and thy brethren, and all thy father's 517
6:23 her **m**, and her brethren, and all that she had; 517
Jdg 5: 7 I Deborah arose, that I arose a **m** in Israel. 517
5:28 The **m** of Sisera looked out at a window, and 517
8:19 *were* my brethren, *even* the sons of my **m**: 517
14: 2 and told his father and his **m**, and said, 517
14: 3 his father and his **m** said unto him, *Is there* 517
14: 4 his **m** knew not that it *was* of the LORD, 517
14: 5 his father and his **m**, *to* Timnath, and 517
14: 6 not his father or his **m** what he had done. 517
14: 9 came to his father and **m**, and he gave them, 517
14:16 I have not told *it* my father nor my **m**, and 517
17: 2 he said unto his **m**, The eleven hundred 517
17: 2 his **m** said, Blessed *be thou* of the LORD, 517
17: 3 eleven hundred *shekels* of silver to his **m**, 517
17: 3 his **m** said, I had wholly dedicated the silver 517
17: 4 Yet he restored the money unto his **m**; and 517
17: 4 his **m** took two hundred *shekels* of silver, 517
Ru 1:14 Orpah kissed her **m in law**; but Ruth clave 2545
2:11 all that thou hast done unto thy **m in law** 2545
2:11 and *how* thou hast left thy father and thy **m**, 517
2:18 her **m in law** saw what she had gleaned: 2545
2:19 her **m in law** said unto her, Where hast 2545
2:19 she shewed her **m in law** with whom she 2545
2:23 and dwelt with her **m in law**. 2545
3: 1 Naomi her **m in law** said unto her, 2545
3: 6 did according to all that her **m in law** bade 2545
3:16 when she came to her **m in law**, she said, 2545
3:17 to me, Go not empty unto thy **m in law**. 2545
1Sa 2:19 Moreover his **m** made him a little coat, and 517
15:33 so shall thy **m** be childless among women. 517
22: 3 Let my father and my **m**, I pray thee, 517
2Sa 17:25 of Nahash, sister to Zeruiah Joab's **m**. 517
19:37 by the grave of my father and of my **m**. 517
20:19 seekest to destroy a city and a **m** in Israel: 517
1Ki 1: 6 and *his m* bare him after Absalom. NIH
1:11 spake unto Bath-sheba the **m** of Solomon, 517
2:13 came to Bath-sheba the **m** of Solomon. 517
2:19 and caused a seat to be set for the king's **m**; 517
2:20 the king said unto her, Ask on, my **m**: for I 517
2:22 king Solomon answered and said unto his **m**, 517
3:27 and in no wise slay it: she *is* the **m** thereof. 517
15:13 also Maachah his **m**, even her he removed 517
17:23 the house, and delivered him unto his **m**: 517
19:20 kiss my father and my **m**, and *then* I will 517
22:52 in the way of his **m**, and in the way of 517
2Ki 3: 2 but not like his father, and like his **m**: 517
3:13 of thy father, and to the prophets of thy **m**. 517
4:19 And he said to a lad, Carry him to his **m**. 517
4:20 brought him to his **m**, he sat on her knees till 517
4:30 the **m** of the child said, *As* the LORD 517
9:22 so long as the whoredoms of thy **m** Jezebel 517
11: 1 when Athaliah the **m** of Ahaziah saw that 517
24:12 he, and his **m**, and his servants, and 517
24:15 the king's **m**, and the king's wives, and his 517
1Ch 2:26 name *was* Atarah; she *was* the **m** of Onam. 517
4: 9 his **m** called his name Jabez, saying, 517
2Ch 15:16 also *concerning* Maachah the **m** of Asa 517
22: 3 for his **m** was his counseller to do wickedly. 517
22:10 when Athaliah the **m** of Ahaziah saw that 517
Est 2: 7 for she had neither father nor **m**, and 517
2: 7 when her father and **m** were dead, 517
Job 17:14 to the worm, *Thou art* my **m**, and my sister. 517
Ps 27:10 When my father and my **m** forsake me, then 517
35:14 as one that mourneth for his **m**. 517
51: 5 and in sin did my **m** conceive me. 517
109:14 and let not the sin of his **m** be blotted out. 517
113: 9 to keep house, *to be* a joyful **m** of children. 517
131: 2 as a child that is weaned of his **m**: 517
Pr 1: 8 thy father, and forsake not the law of thy **m**: 517
4: 3 and only *beloved* in the sight of my **m**. 517
6:20 and forsake not the law of thy **m**: 517
10: 1 but a foolish son *is* the heaviness of his **m**. 517
15:20 but a foolish man despiseth his **m**. 517
19:26 wasteth *his* father, *and* chaseth away *his* **m**, 517
20:20 Whoso curseth his father or his **m**, his lamp 517
23:22 and despise not thy **m** when she is old. 517
23:25 Thy father and thy **m** shall be glad, and 517
28:24 Whoso robbeth his father or his **m**, and saith, 517
29:15 a child left *to himself* bringeth his **m** to 517
30:11 their father, and doth not bless their **m**. 517
30:17 at *his* father, and despiseth to obey *his* **m**, 517
31: 1 the prophecy that his **m** taught him. 517
SS 3:11 **m** crowned him in the day of his espousals, 517
6: 9 she *is* the *only* one of her **m**, she *is* 517
8: 1 my brother, that sucked the breasts of my **m**! 517
8: 5 there thy **m** brought thee forth: there she 517
Isa 8: 4 My father, and my **m**, the riches of 517
49: 1 from the bowels of my **m** hath he made 517
50: 1 for your transgressions *is* your **m** put away. 517
66:13 As one whom his **m** comforteth, so will I 517
Jer 15: 8 I have brought upon them against the **m** of 517
15:10 Woe is me, my **m**, that thou hast borne me a 517
16: 7 to drink for their father or for their **m**. 517
20:14 let not the day wherein my **m** bare me be 517
20:17 or that my **m** might have been my grave, and 517
22:26 thy **m** that bare thee, into another country, 517
50:12 Your **m** shall be sore confounded; she that 517
Eze 16: 3 father *was* an Amorite, and thy **m** a Hittite. 517
16:44 saying, As *is* the **m**, *so is* her daughter. 517
16:45 your **m** *was* a Hittite, and your father an 517
19: 2 say, What *is* thy **m**? A lioness: she lay down 517
19:10 Thy **m** *is* like a vine in thy blood, planted by 517
22: 7 In thee have they set light by father and **m**: 517
23: 2 were two women, the daughters of one **m**: 517
44:25 or for **m**, or for son, or for daughter, 517
Hos 2: 2 Plead with your **m**, plead: for she *is* not my 517
2: 5 For their **m** hath played the harlot: she that 517
4: 5 thee *in* the night, and I will destroy thy **m**. 517
10:14 the **m** was dashed in pieces upon *her* 517
Mic 7: 6 the daughter riseth up against her **m**, 517
7: 6 the daughter in law against her **m in law**; 2545
Zec 13: 3 and his **m** that begat him shall say unto him, 517
13: 3 his **m** that begat him shall thrust him through 517
Mt 1:18 When as his **m** Mary was espoused to *3384*
2:11 they saw the young child with Mary his **m**, *3384*
2:13 and take the young child and his **m**, and *3384*
2:14 he took the young child and his **m** by night, *3384*
2:20 and take the young child and his **m**, and *3384*
2:21 and took the young child and his **m**, and *3384*
8:14 he saw his **wife's m** laid, and sick of a *3994*
10:35 and the daughter against her **m**, and *3384*
10:35 the daughter in law against her **m in law**. *3994*
10:37 or **m** more than me is not worthy of me: *3384*
12:46 *his* **m** and his brethren stood without, *3384*
12:47 thy **m** and thy brethren stand without, *3384*
12:48 said unto him that told him, Who is my **m**? *3384*
12:49 and said, Behold my **m** and my brethren. *3384*
12:50 the same is my brother, and sister, and **m**. *3384*
13:55 is not his **m** called Mary? and his brethren, *3384*
14: 8 being before instructed of her **m**, said, *3384*
14:11 to the damsel: and she brought *it* to her **m**. *3384*
15: 4 saying, Honour thy father and **m**: *3384*
15: 4 and, He that curseth father or **m**, let him die *3384*
15: 5 Whosoever shall say to *his* father or *his* **m**, *3384*
15: 6 And honour not his father or his **m**, *he shall* *3384*
19: 5 this cause shall a man leave father and **m**, *3384*
19:19 Honour thy father and *thy* **m**: and, *3384*
19:29 father, or **m**, or wife, or children, or lands, *3384*
20:20 Then came to him the **m** of Zebedee's *3384*
27:56 and Mary the **m** of James and Joses, and *3384*
27:56 and Joses, and the **m** of Zebedee's children. *3384*
Mk 1:30 But Simon's **wife's m** lay sick of a fever, *3994*
3:31 There came then *his* brethren and his **m**, *3384*
3:32 thy **m** and thy brethren without seek for *3384*
3:33 saying, Who is my **m**, or my brethren? *3384*
3:34 and said, Behold my **m** and my brethren. *3384*
3:35 same is my brother, and my sister, and **m**. *3384*
5:40 taketh the father and the **m** of the damsel, *3384*
6:24 and said unto her **m**, What shall I ask? *3384*
6:28 and the damsel gave it to her **m**. *3384*
7:10 Moses said, Honour thy father and thy **m**; *3384*
7:10 and, Whoso curseth father or **m**, let him die *3384*
7:11 ye say, If a man shall say to *his* father or **m**, *3384*
7:12 no more to do ought for his father or his **m**; *3384*
10: 7 cause shall a man leave his father and **m**, *3384*
10:19 Defraud not, Honour thy father and **m**. *3384*
10:29 father, or **m**, or wife, or children, or lands, *3384*
15:40 and Mary the **m** of James the less and *3384*
15:47 Mary *the m* of Joses beheld where he was NIG
16: 1 and Mary the *m* of James, and Salome, NIG
Lk 1:43 that the **m** of my Lord should come to me? *3384*
1:60 And his **m** answered and said, Not *so;* but *3384*
2:33 his **m** marvelled at those *things* which were *3384*
2:34 and said unto Mary his **m**, Behold, *3384*
2:43 and Joseph and his **m** knew not *of it.* *3384*
2:48 and his **m** said unto him, Son, why hast *3384*
2:51 his **m** kept all these sayings in her heart. *3384*
4:38 And Simon's **wife's m** was taken with a *3994*
7:12 the only son of his **m**, and she was a *3384*
7:15 to speak. And he delivered him to his **m**. *3384*
8:19 Then came to him *his* **m** and his brethren, *3384*
8:20 Thy **m** and thy brethren stand without, *3384*
8:21 My **m** and my brethren are these which *3384*
8:51 and the father and the **m** of the maiden. *3384*
12:53 the **m** against the daughter, and *3384*
12:53 and the daughter against the **m**; *3384*
12:53 the **m in law** against her daughter in law, *3994*
12:53 the daughter in law against her **m in law**. *3994*
14:26 and **m**, and wife, and children, and *3384*
18:20 false witness, Honour thy father and thy **m**. *3384*
24:10 and Mary *the m* of James, and other *women* NIG
Jn 2: 1 of Galilee; and the **m** of Jesus was there: *3384*
2: 3 the **m** of Jesus saith unto him, They have *3384*
2: 5 His **m** saith unto the servants, *3384*
2:12 he, and his **m**, and his brethren, and *3384*
6:42 of Joseph, whose father and **m** we know? *3384*
19:25 there stood by the cross of Jesus his **m**, *3384*
19:26 When Jesus therefore saw *his* **m**, and *3384*
19:26 he saith unto his **m**, Woman, behold thy *3384*
19:27 Then saith he to the disciple, Behold thy **m**. *3384*
Ac 1:14 and Mary the **m** of Jesus, and with his *3384*
12:12 came to the house of Mary the **m** of John, *3384*
Ro 16:13 chosen in the Lord, and his **m** and mine. *3384*
Gal 4:26 is above is free, which is the **m** of us all. *3384*
Eph 5:31 cause shall a man leave his father and **m**, *3384*
6: 2 Honour thy father and **m**; (which is the first *3384*
2Ti 1: 5 in thy grandmother Lois, and thy **m** Eunice; *3384*
Heb 7: 3 Without father, **without m**, without descent, *282*
Rev 17: 5 THE **M** OF HARLOTS AND *3384*

MOTHER'S (75) [MOTHER]

Ge 24:28 and told *them of* her **m** house these things. 517
24:67 and Isaac was comforted after his **m** *death.* 517
27:29 and let thy **m** sons bow down to thee: 517
28: 2 to the house of Bethuel thy **m** father; 517
28: 2 of the daughters of Laban thy **m** brother. 517
29:10 Rachel the daughter of Laban his **m** brother, 517
29:10 the sheep of Laban his **m** brother, that Jacob 517
29:10 watered the flock of Laban his **m** brother. 517
43:29 his brother Benjamin, his **m** son, and said, 517
Ex 23:19 Thou shalt not seethe a kid in his **m** milk. 517
34:26 Thou shalt not seethe a kid in his **m** milk. 517
Lev 18:13 not uncover the nakedness of thy **m** sister: 517
18:13 for she *is* thy **m** near kinswoman. 517
20:17 or his **m** daughter, and see her nakedness, 517
20:19 not uncover the nakedness of thy **m** sister, 517
24:11 (and his **m** name *was* Shelomith, 517
Nu 12:12 when he cometh out of his **m** womb. 517
Dt 14:21 Thou shalt not seethe a kid in his **m** milk. 517
Jdg 9: 1 went to Shechem unto his **m** brethren, 517
9: 1 with all the family of the house of his **m** 517
9: 3 his **m** brethren spake of him in the ears of all 517
16:17 *been* a Nazarite unto God from my **m** womb: 517
Ru 1: 8 in law, Go, return each to her **m** house: 517
1Sa 20:30 and unto the confusion of thy **m** nakedness? 517
1Ki 11:26 whose **m** name *was* Zeruah, a widow 517

1Ki 14:21 his **m** name *was* Naamah an Ammonitess. 517
14:31 his **m** name *was* Naamah an Ammonitess. 517
15: 2 his **m** name *was* Maachah, the daughter of 517
15:10 his **m** name *was* Maachah, the daughter of 517
22:42 his **m** name *was* Azubah the daughter of 517
2Ki 8:26 his **m** name *was* Athaliah, the daughter of 517
12: 1 And his **m** name *was* Zibiah of Beer-sheba. 517
14: 2 his **m** name *was* Jehoaddan of Jerusalem. 517
15: 2 And his **m** name *was* Jecholiah of Jerusalem. 517
15:33 his **m** name *was* Jerusha, the daughter of 517
18: 2 His **m** name also *was* Abi, the daughter of 517
21: 1 And his **m** name *was* Hephzi-bah. 517
21:19 his **m** name *was* Meshullemeth, the daughter 517
22: 1 his **m** name *was* Jedidah, the daughter of 517
23:31 his **m** name *was* Hamutal, the daughter of 517
23:36 his **m** name *was* Zebudah, the daughter of 517
24: 8 his **m** name *was* Nehushta, the daughter of 517
24:18 his **m** name *was* Hamutal, the daughter of 517
2Ch 12:13 his **m** name *was* Naamah an Ammonitess. 517
13: 2 His **m** name also *was* Michaiah the daughter 517
20:31 his **m** name *was* Azubah the daughter of 517
22: 2 His **m** name also *was* Athaliah the daughter 517
24: 1 His **m** name also *was* Zibiah of Beer-sheba. 517
25: 1 his **m** name *was* Jehoaddan of Jerusalem. 517
26: 3 His **m** name also *was* Jecoliah of Jerusalem. 517
27: 1 His **m** name also *was* Jerushah, the daughter 517
29: 1 his **m** name *was* Abijah, the daughter of 517
Job 1:21 Naked came I out of my **m** womb, and 517
3:10 Because it shut not up the doors of my *m* NIH
31:18 and I have guided her from my **m** womb;) 517
Ps 22: 9 me hope *when I was* upon my **m** breasts. 517
22:10 thou *art* my God from my **m** belly. 517
50:20 thou slanderest thine own **m** son. 517
69: 8 and an alien unto my **m** children. 517
71: 6 thou art he that took me out of my **m** 517
139:13 thou hast covered me in my **m** womb. 517
Ecc 5:15 As he came forth of his **m** womb, 517
SS 1: 6 my **m** children were angry with me; 517
3: 4 until I had brought him into my **m** house, 517
8: 2 lead thee, *and* bring thee into my **m** house, 517
Isa 50: 1 Where *is* the bill of your **m** divorcement, 517
Jer 52: 1 his **m** name *was* Hamutal the daughter of 517
Eze 16:45 Thou *art* thy **m** daughter, that lotheth her 517
Mt 19:12 which were so born from *their* **m** womb: *3384*
Lk 1:15 the Holy Ghost, even from his **m** womb. *3384*
Jn 3: 4 can he enter the second time into his **m** *3384*
19:25 and his **m** sister, Mary the *wife* of *3384*
Ac 3: 2 And a certain man lame from his **m** womb *3384*
14: 8 *his* feet, being a cripple from his **m** womb, *3384*
Gal 1:15 who separated me from my **m** womb, and *3384*

MOTHERS (7) [MOTHER]

Isa 49:23 and their queens thy **nursing m**: 3243
Jer 16: 3 concerning their **m** that bare them, and 517
La 2:12 They say to their **m**, Where *is* corn and 517
5: 3 and fatherless, our **m** *are* as widows. 517
Mk 10:30 and sisters, and **m**, and children, and lands, *3384*
1Ti 1: 9 murderers of fathers and **murderers of m**, *3389*
5: 2 The elder *women* as **m**; the younger as *3384*

MOTHERS' (1) [MOTHER]

La 2:12 when their soul was poured out into their **m** 517

MOTHS See MOTHEATEN

MOTIONS (1) [MOVE]

Ro 7: 5 the **m** of sins, which were by the law, *3804*

MOULDY (2)

Jos 9: 5 the bread of their provision was dry *and* **m**. 5350
9:12 but now, behold, it is dry, and it is **m**: 5350

MOUND; MOUNDS See EMINENT

MOUNT (263) [MOUNTAIN, MOUNTED, MOUNTING, MOUNTS]

Ge 10:30 as thou goest unto Sephar, a **m** of the east. 2022
14: 6 the Horites in their **m** Seir, unto El-paran, 2042
22:14 In the **m** of the LORD it shall be seen. 2022
31:21 and set his face *toward* the **m** Gilead. 2022
31:23 and they overtook him in the **m** Gilead. 2022
31:25 Now Jacob had pitched his tent in the **m**: 2022
31:25 Laban with his brethren pitched in the **m** of 2022
31:54 Jacob offered sacrifice upon the **m**, and 2022
31:54 did eat bread, and tarried all night in the **m**. 2022
36: 8 Thus dwelt Esau in **m** Seir: Esau *is* Edom. 2022
36: 9 Esau the father of the Edomites in **m** Seir: 2022
Ex 4:27 met him in the **m** of God, and kissed him. 2022
18: 5 where he encamped *at* the **m** of God: 2022
19: 2 and there Israel camped before the **m**. 2022
19:11 in the sight of all the people upon **m** Sinai. 2022
19:12 *that ye* go *not* up into the **m**, or touch 2022
19:12 whosoever toucheth the **m** shall be surely 2022
19:13 soundeth long, they shall come up to the **m**. 2022
19:14 Moses went down from the **m** unto 2022
19:16 a thick cloud upon the **m**, and the voice of 2022
19:17 and they stood at the nether part of the **m**. 2022
19:18 **m** Sinai was altogether on a smoke, 2022
19:18 a furnace, and the whole **m** quaked greatly. 2022
19:20 the LORD came down upon **m** Sinai, 2022
19:20 upon mount Sinai, on the top of the **m**: 2022
19:20 called Moses *up* to the top of the **m**; 2022
19:23 The people cannot come up to **m** Sinai: 2022
19:23 Set bounds about the **m**, and sanctify it. 2022
24:12 Come up to me into the **m**, and be there: 2022
24:13 and Moses went up into the **m** of God. 2022
24:15 Moses went up into the **m**, and a cloud 2022
24:15 into the mount, and a cloud covered the **m**. 2022
24:16 the glory of the LORD abode upon **m** 2022
24:17 the **m** in the eyes of the children of Israel. 2022
24:18 of the cloud, and gat him up into the **m**: 2022
24:18 Moses was in the **m** forty days and 2022
25:40 which was shewed thee in the **m**. 2022
26:30 thereof which was shewed thee in the **m**. 2022
Ex 27: 8 as it was shewed thee in the **m**, so 2022
31:18 end of communing with him upon **m** Sinai, 2022
32: 1 Moses delayed to come down out of the **m**, 2022
32:15 went down from the **m**, and the two tables 2022
32:19 his hands, and brake them beneath the **m**. 2022
33: 6 of their ornaments by the **m** Horeb. 2022
34: 2 come up in the morning unto **m** Sinai, and 2022
34: 2 thyself there to me in the top of the **m**. 2022
34: 3 let any man be seen throughout all the **m**; 2022
34: 3 let the flocks nor herds feed before that **m**. 2022
34: 4 in the morning, and went up unto **m** Sinai, 2022
34:29 when Moses came down from **m** Sinai with 2022
34:29 when he came down from the **m**, 2022
34:32 LORD had spoken with him in **m** Sinai. 2022
Lev 7:38 the LORD commanded Moses in **m** Sinai, 2022
25: 1 the LORD spake unto Moses in **m** Sinai, 2022
26:46 the children of Israel in **m** Sinai by 2022
27:34 Moses for the children of Israel in **m** Sinai. 2022
Nu 3: 1 the LORD spake with Moses in **m** Sinai. 2022
10:33 they departed from the **m** of the LORD 2022
20:22 from Kadesh, and came *unto* **m** Hor. 2022
20:23 spake unto Moses and Aaron in **m** Hor, 2022
20:25 his son, and bring them up *unto* **m** Hor: 2022
20:27 they went up into **m** Hor in the sight of all 2022
20:28 and Aaron died there in the top of the **m**: 2022
20:28 Moses and Eleazar came down from the **m**. 2022
21: 4 they journeyed from **m** Hor *by* the way of 2022
27:12 Get thee up into this **m** Abarim, and see 2022
28: 6 which was ordained in **m** Sinai for a sweet 2022
33:23 and pitched in **m** Shapher. 2022
33:24 they removed from **m** Shapher, and 2022
33:37 pitched in **m** Hor, in the edge of the land of 2022
33:38 Aaron the priest went up into **m** Hor at 2022
33:39 and three years old when he died in **m** Hor. 2022
33:41 they departed from **m** Hor, and pitched in 2022
34: 7 great sea you shall point out for you **m** Hor: 2022
34: 8 From **m** Hor ye shall point out *your border* 2022
Dt 1: 2 *by* the way of **m** Seir unto Kadesh-barnea.) 2022
1: 6 Ye have dwelt long enough in this **m**: 2022
1: 7 go *to* the **m** of the Amorites, and unto all 2022
2: 1 and we compassed **m** Seir many days. 2022
2: 5 I have given **m** Seir unto Esau *for* a 2022
3: 8 from the river of Arnon unto **m** Hermon; 2022
3:12 half **m** Gilead, and the cities thereof, gave I 2022
4:48 even unto **m** Sion, which *is* Hermon, 2022
5: 4 to face in the **m** out of the midst of the fire, 2022
5: 5 of the fire, and went not up into the **m**;) 2022
5:22 in the **m** out of the midst of the fire, 2022
9: 9 When I was gone up into the **m** to receive 2022
9: 9 I abode in the **m** forty days and 2022
9:10 which the LORD spake with you in the **m** 2022
9:15 So I turned and came down from the **m**, 2022
9:15 the mount, and the **m** burned with fire: 2022
9:21 into the brook that descended out of the **m**. 2022
10: 1 come up unto me into the **m**, and make thee 2022
10: 3 went up into the **m**, having the two tables 2022
10: 4 which the LORD spake unto you in the **m** 2022
10: 5 turned myself and came down from the **m**, 2022
10:10 I stayed in the **m**, according to the first 2022
11:29 that thou shalt put the blessing upon **m** 2022
11:29 mount Gerizim, and the curse upon **m** Ebal. 2022
27: 4 in **m** Ebal, and thou shalt plaister them with 2022
27:12 These shall stand upon **m** Gerizzim to bless 2022
27:13 these shall stand upon **m** Ebal to curse; 2022
32:49 *unto* **m** Nebo, which *is* in the land of Moab, 2022
32:50 die in the **m** whither thou goest up, and 2022
32:50 as Aaron thy brother died in **m** Hor, 2022
33: 2 he shined forth from **m** Paran, and he came 2022
Jos 8:30 unto the LORD God of Israel in **m** Ebal, 2022
8:33 half of them over against **m** Gerizim, and 2022
8:33 and half of them over against **m** Ebal; 2022
11:17 *Even* from the **m** Halak, that goeth up *to* 2022
11:17 in the valley of Lebanon under **m** Hermon: 2022
12: 1 from the river Arnon unto **m** Hermon, and 2022
12: 5 reigned in **m** Hermon, and in Salcah, and 2022
12: 7 valley of Lebanon even unto the **m** Halak, 2022
13: 5 from Baal-gad under **m** Hermon unto 2022
13:11 all **m** Hermon, and all Bashan unto Salcah; 2022
13:19 and Zareth-shahar in the **m** of the valley, 2022
15: 9 and went out to the cities of **m** Ephron; 2022
15:10 from Baalah westward unto **m** Seir, 2022
15:10 and passed along unto the side of **m** Jearim, 2022
15:11 passed along *to* **m** Baalah, and went out 2022
16: 1 up from Jericho throughout **m** Beth-el, 2022
17:15 if **m** Ephraim be too narrow for thee. 2022
19:50 *even* Timnath-serah in **m** Ephraim: 2022
20: 7 they appointed Kedesh in Galilee in **m** 2022
20: 7 Shechem in **m** Ephraim, and Kirjath-arba, 2022
21:21 Shechem with her suburbs in **m** Ephraim, 2022
24: 4 I gave unto Esau **m** Seir, to possess it; 2022
24:30 which *is* in **m** Ephraim, on the north side of 2022
24:33 which was given him in **m** Ephraim. 2022
Jdg 1:35 the Amorites would dwell in **m** Heres in 2022
2: 9 in the **m** of Ephraim, on the north side of 2022
3: 3 and the Hivites that dwelt in **m** Lebanon, 2022
3: 3 from **m** Baal-hermon unto the entering in 2022
3:27 of Israel went down with him from the **m**, 2022
4: 5 between Ramah and Beth-el in **m** Ephraim: 2022
4: 6 *saying*, Go and draw toward **m** Tabor, and 2022
4:12 son of Abinoam was gone up *to* **m** Tabor. 2022
4:14 So Barak went down from **m** Tabor, and 2022
7: 3 him return and depart early from **m** Gilead. 2022
7:24 Gideon sent messengers throughout all **m** 2022
9: 7 he went and stood in the top of **m** Gerizim, 2022
9:48 Abimelech gat him up *to* **m** Zalmon, he 2022
10: 1 and he dwelt in Shamir in **m** Ephraim. 2022
12:15 of Ephraim, in the **m** of the Amalekites. 2022
17: 1 there was a man of **m** Ephraim, whose 2022
17: 8 he came *to* **m** Ephraim to the house of 2022
18: 2 who when they came *to* **m** Ephraim, to 2022
18:13 they passed thence *unto* **m** Ephraim, and 2022
19: 1 sojourning on the side of **m** Ephraim, 2022
19:16 at even, which *was* also of **m** Ephraim; 2022
19:18 toward the side of **m** Ephraim; 2022
1Sa 1: 1 of **m** Ephraim, and his name *was* Elkanah, 2022
1Sa 9: 4 he passed through **m** Ephraim, and 2022
13: 2 with Saul in Michmash and in **m** Beth-el, 2022
14:22 which had hid themselves in **m** Ephraim, 2022
31: 1 and fell down slain in **m** Gilboa. 2022
31: 8 and his three sons fallen in **m** Gilboa. 2022
2Sa 1: 6 As I happened by chance upon **m** Gilboa, 2022
15:30 David went up by the ascent of *m* Olivet, NIH
15:32 the top *of the m*, where he worshipped God, NIH
20:21 a man of **m** Ephraim, Sheba the son of 2022
1Ki 4: 8 their names: The son of Hur, in **m** Ephraim: 2022
12:25 Jeroboam built Shechem in **m** Ephraim, 2022
18:19 *and* gather to me all Israel unto **m** Carmel, 2022
18:20 gathered the prophets together unto **m** 2022
19: 8 and forty nights unto Horeb the **m** of God. 2022
19:11 and stand upon the **m** before the LORD. 2022
2Ki 2:25 he went from thence to **m** Carmel, and 2022
4:25 came unto the man of God to **m** Carmel. 2022
5:22 even now there be come to me from **m** 2022
19:31 and they that escape out of **m** Zion: 2022
23:13 which *were* on the right hand of the **m** of 2022
23:16 the sepulchres that *were* there in the **m**, 2022
1Ch 4:42 five hundred men, went to **m** Seir, 2022
5:23 and Senir, and *unto* **m** Hermon. 2022
6:67 Shechem in **m** Ephraim with her suburbs; 2022
10: 1 and fell down slain in **m** Gilboa. 2022
10: 8 found Saul and his sons fallen in **m** Gilboa. 2022
2Ch 3: 1 of the LORD at Jerusalem in **m** Moriah, 2022
13: 4 Abijah stood up upon **m** Zemaraim, 2022
13: 4 which *is* in **m** Ephraim, and said, Hear me, 2022
15: 8 out of the cities which he had taken from **m** 2022
19: 4 the people from Beer-sheba to **m** Ephraim, 2022
20:10 children of Ammon and Moab and **m** Seir, 2022
20:22 Moab, and **m** Seir, which were come 2022
20:23 Moab stood up against the inhabitants of **m** 2022
33:15 all the altars that he had built in the **m** of 2022
Ne 8:15 Go forth *unto* the **m**, and fetch olive 2022
9:13 Thou camest down also upon **m** Sinai, and 2022
Job 20: 6 Though his excellency **m up** to 5927
39:27 Doth the eagle **m up** at thy command, and 1361
Ps 48: 2 *is* **m** Zion, *on* the sides of the north, the city 2022
48:11 Let **m** Zion rejoice, let the daughters of 2022
74: 2 this **m** Zion, wherein thou hast dwelt. 2022
78:68 tribe of Judah, the **m** Zion which he loved. 2022
107:26 They **m up** *to* the heaven, they go down 5927
125: 1 They that trust in the LORD *shall be* as **m** 2022
SS 4: 1 a flock of goats, that appear from **m** Gilead. 2022
Isa 4: 5 upon every dwelling place of **m** Zion, 2022
8:18 of hosts, which dwelleth in **m** Zion. 2022
9:18 they shall **m up** *like* the lifting up of smoke. 55
10:12 performed his whole work upon **m** Zion 2022
10:32 he shall shake his hand *against* the **m** of 2022
14:13 I will sit also upon the **m** of 2022
16: 1 unto the **m** of the daughter of Zion. 2022
18: 7 name of the LORD of hosts, the **m** Zion. 2022
24:23 when the LORD of hosts shall reign in **m** 2022
27:13 shall worship the LORD in the holy **m** at 2022
28:21 For the LORD shall rise up as *in* **m** 2022
29: 3 will lay siege against thee *with* a **m**, and 4674
29: 8 all the nations be, that fight against **m** Zion. 2022
31: 4 of hosts come down to fight for **m** Zion, 2022
37:32 and they that escape out of **m** Zion: 2022
40:31 they shall **m up** *with* wings as eagles; 5927
Jer 4:15 and publisheth affliction from **m** Ephraim. 2022
6: 6 down trees, and cast a **m** against Jerusalem: 5550
31: 6 *that* the watchmen upon the **m** Ephraim 2022
50:19 his soul shall be satisfied upon **m** Ephraim 2022
51:53 Though Babylon should **m up** *to* heaven, 5927
Eze 4: 2 a fort against it, and cast a **m** against it; 5550
10:16 lift up their wings to **m up** from the earth, 7311
21:22 the gates, to cast a **m**, *and* to build a fort. 5550
26: 8 cast a **m** against thee, and lift up 5550
35: 2 set thy face against **m** Seir, and 2022
35: 3 Behold, O **m** Seir, I *am* against thee, and 2022
35: 7 Thus will I make **m** Seir most desolate, 2022
35:15 O **m** Seir, and all Idumea, *even* all of it: 2022
Da 11:15 cast up a **m**, and take the most fenced 5550
Joel 2:32 for in **m** Zion and in Jerusalem shall be 2022
Ob 1: 8 and understanding out of the **m** of Esau? 2022
1: 9 to the end that every one of the **m** of Esau 2022
1:17 upon **m** Zion shall be deliverance, and 2022
1:19 *they of* the south shall possess the **m** of 2022
1:21 saviours shall come up on **m** Zion to judge 2022
1:21 up on mount Zion to judge the **m** of Esau; 2022
Mic 4: 7 the LORD shall reign over them in **m** 2022
Hab 3: 3 and the Holy One from **m** Paran. 2022
Zec 14: 4 his feet shall stand in that day upon the **m** 2022
14: 4 the **m** of Olives shall cleave in the midst 2022
Mt 21: 1 unto the **m** of Olives, then sent Jesus two *3735*
24: 3 And as he sat upon the **m** of Olives, *3735*
26:30 a hymn, they went out into the **m** of Olives. *3735*
Mk 11: 1 and Bethany, at the **m** of Olives, *3735*
13: 3 And as he sat upon the **m** of Olives over *3735*
14:26 a hymn, they went out into the **m** of Olives. *3735*
Lk 19:29 at the **m** called *the mount of* Olives, *3735*
19:29 at the mount called *the* **m** of Olives, NIG
19:37 *even* now at the descent of the **m** of Olives, *3735*
21:37 abode in the **m** that is called *the mount of* *3735*
21:37 abode in the mount that is called *the* **m** of NIG
22:39 went, as he was wont, to the **m** of Olives; *3735*
Jn 8: 1 Jesus went unto the **m** of Olives. *3735*
Ac 1:12 unto Jerusalem from the **m** called Olivet, *3735*
7:30 **m** Sina an angel of the Lord in a flame of *3735*
7:38 the angel which spake to him in the **m** Sina, *3735*
Gal 4:24 the one from the **m** Sinai, which gendereth *3735*
4:25 For *this* Agar is **m** Sinai in Arabia, and *3735*
Heb 8: 5 to the pattern shewed to thee in the **m**. *3735*
12:18 For ye are not come unto the **m** that might *3735*
12:22 But ye are come unto **m** Sion, and unto *3735*
2Pe 1:18 when we were with him in the holy **m**. *3735*
Rev 14: 1 and lo, a Lamb stood on the **m** Sion, and *3735*

MOUNTAIN (137) [MOUNT, MOUNTAINS]

Ge 12: 8 he removed from thence unto a **m** on 2022
14:10 and they that remained fled to the **m**. 2022
19:17 escape to the **m**, lest thou be consumed. 2022

Ge 19:19 I cannot escape to the **m**, lest *some* evil 2022
19:30 dwelt in the **m**, and his two daughters with 2022
Ex 3: 1 and came to the **m** of God, *even* to Horeb. 2022
3:12 of Egypt, ye shall serve God upon this **m**. 2022
15:17 plant them in the **m** of thine inheritance, 2022
19: 3 the LORD called unto him out of the **m**, 2022
20:18 noise of the trumpet, and the **m** smoking: 2022
Nu 13:17 this *way* southward, and go up into the **m**: 2022
14:40 gat them up into the top of the **m**, saying, 2022
Dt 1:19 which you saw *by* the way of the **m** of 2022
1:20 Ye are come unto the **m** of the Amorites, 2022
1:24 they turned and went up into the **m**, and 2022
1:44 the Amorites, which dwelt in that **m**, came 2022
2: 3 Ye have compassed this **m** long enough: 2022
3:25 that goodly **m**, and Lebanon. 2022
4:11 ye came near and stood under the **m**; and 2022
4:11 the **m** burnt with fire unto the midst of 2022
5:23 the darkness, (for the **m** did burn with fire,) 2022
32:49 Get thee up into this **m** Abarim, *unto* mount 2022
33:19 They shall call the people *unto* the **m**; 2022
34: 1 the plains of Moab unto the **m** of Nebo, 2022
Jos 2:16 she said unto them, Get you to the **m**, 2022
2:22 came unto the **m**, and abode there three 2022
2:23 descended from the **m**, and passed over, 2022
11:16 the **m** of Israel, and the valley of the same; 2022
14:12 Now therefore give me this **m**, whereof 2022
15: 8 the border went up to the top of the **m** that 2022
17:18 the **m** shall be thine; for it *is* a wood, 2022
18:16 the border came down to the end of the **m** 2022
20: 7 which *is* Hebron, in the **m** of Judah. 2022
Jdg 1: 9 that dwelt in the **m**, and in the south, and 2022
1:19 he drave out *the inhabitants of* the **m**; but 2022
1:34 forced the children of Dan into the **m**: 2022
3:27 that he blew a trumpet in the **m** of Ephraim, 2022
1Sa 17: 3 the Philistines stood on a **m** on the one 2022
17: 3 and Israel stood on a **m** on the other side: 2022
23:14 remained in a **m** in the wilderness of Ziph. 2022
23:26 Saul went on this side of the **m**, and David 2022
23:26 David and his men on that side of the **m**: 2022
2Ki 2:16 cast him upon some **m**, or into some valley. 2022
6:17 the **m** was full *of* horses and chariots of fire 2022
2Ch 2: 2 fourscore thousand to hew in the **m**, and 2022
2:18 fourscore thousand *to be* hewers in the **m**, 2022
Job 14:18 surely the **m** falling cometh to nought, and 2022
Ps 11: 1 say ye to my soul, Flee *as* a bird *to* your **m**? 2022
30: 7 by thy favour thou hast made my **m** to 2042
48: 1 city of our God, *in* the **m** of his holiness. 2022
78:54 *even to* this **m**, *which* his right hand had 2022
SS 4: 6 I will get me to the **m** of myrrh, and to 2022
Isa 2: 2 *that* the **m** of the LORD'S house shall be 2022
2: 3 and let us go up to the **m** of the LORD, 2022
11: 9 shall not hurt nor destroy in all my holy **m**: 2022
13: 2 Lift ye up a banner upon the high **m**, 2022
25: 6 in this **m** shall the LORD of hosts make 2022
25: 7 he will destroy in this **m** the face of 2022
25:10 For in this **m** shall the hand of the LORD 2022
30:17 ye be left as a beacon upon the top of a **m**, 2022
30:25 there shall be upon every high **m**, and 2022
30:29 a pipe to come into the **m** of the LORD, 2022
40: 4 and every **m** and hill shall be made low: 2022
40: 9 good tidings, get thee up into the high **m**; 2022
56: 7 Even them will I bring to my holy **m**, and 2022
57: 7 a lofty and high **m** hast thou set thy bed: 2022
57:13 the land, and shall inherit my holy **m**; 2022
65:11 that forget my holy **m**, that prepare a table 2022
65:25 shall not hurt nor destroy in all my holy **m**, 2022
66:20 to my holy **m** Jerusalem, saith the LORD, 2022
Jer 3: 6 she is gone up upon every high **m** and 2022
16:16 and they shall hunt them from every **m**, and 2022
17: 3 O my **m** in the field, I will give thy 2042
26:18 the **m** of the house as the high places of a 2022
31:23 O habitation of justice, *and* **m** of holiness. 2022
50: 6 they have gone from **m** to hill, they have 2022
51:25 Behold, I *am* against thee, O destroying **m**, 2022
51:25 the rocks, and will make thee a burnt **m**. 2022
La 5:18 Because of the **m** of Zion, which is 2022
Eze 11:23 stood upon the **m** which *is* on the east side 2022
17:22 will plant *it* upon a high **m** and eminent: 2022
17:23 In the **m** of the height of Israel will I plant 2022
20:40 For in mine holy **m**, in the mountain of 2022
20:40 in the **m** of the height of Israel, saith 2022
28:14 *so:* thou wast upon the holy **m** of God; 2022
28:16 I will cast thee as profane out of the **m** of 2022
40: 2 set me upon a very high **m**, by which *was* 2022
43:12 Upon the top of the **m** the whole limit 2022
Da 2:35 that smote the image became a great **m**, 2906
2:45 stone was cut out of the **m** without hands, 2906
9:16 away from thy city Jerusalem, thy holy **m**: 2022
9:20 LORD my God for the holy **m** of my God; 2022
11:45 between the seas in the glorious holy **m**; 2022
Joel 2: 1 in Zion, and sound an alarm in my holy **m**: 2022
3:17 your God dwelling in Zion, my holy **m**: 2022
Am 4: 1 of Bashan, that *are* in the **m** of Samaria, 2022
6: 1 ease in Zion, and trust in the **m** of Samaria, 2022
Ob 1:16 For as ye have drunk upon my holy **m**, *so* 2022
Mic 3:12 the **m** of the house as the high places of 2022
4: 1 *that* the **m** of the house of the LORD shall 2022
4: 2 let us go up to the **m** of the LORD, and 2022
7:12 from sea *to* sea, and *from* **m** *to* mountain. 2022
7:12 from sea *to* sea, and *from* mountain *to* **m**. 2022
Zep 3:11 no more be haughty because of my holy **m**. 2022
Hag 1: 8 Go up *to* the **m**, and bring wood, and 2022
Zec 4: 7 Who *art* thou, O great **m**? 2022
8: 3 the **m** of the LORD of hosts the holy 2022
8: 3 of the LORD of hosts the holy **m**. 2022
14: 4 half of the **m** shall remove toward 2022
Mt 4: 8 taketh him *up* into an exceeding high **m**, 3735
5: 1 seeing the multitudes, he went up into a **m**: 3735
8: 1 When he was come down from the **m**, 3735
14:23 he went up into a **m** apart to pray: 3735
15:29 and went up into a **m**, and sat down there. 3735
17: 1 and bringeth them up into a high **m** apart, 3735
17: 9 And as they came down from the **m**, Jesus 3735
17:20 ye shall say unto this **m**, Remove hence to 3735
21:21 but also if ye shall say unto this **m**, Be thou 3735
Mt 28:16 into a **m** where Jesus had appointed them. 3735
Mk 3:13 And he goeth up into a **m**, and calleth unto 3735
6:46 them away, he departed into a **m** to pray. 3735
9: 2 leadeth them up into a high **m** apart by 3735
9: 9 And as they came down from the **m**, 3735
11:23 That whosoever shall say unto this **m**, 3735
Lk 3: 5 and every **m** and hill shall be brought low; 3735
4: 5 And the devil, taking him up into a high **m**, 3735
6:12 *that* he went out into a **m** to pray, and 3735
8:32 a herd of many swine feeding on the **m**: 3735
9:28 and James, and went up into a **m** to pray. 3735
Jn 4:20 Our fathers worshipped in this **m**; and 3735
4:21 when ye shall neither in this **m**, 3735
6: 3 And Jesus went up into a **m**, and there he 3735
6:15 he departed again into a **m** himself alone. 3735
Heb 12:20 And if *so much as* a beast touch the **m**, 3735
Rev 6:14 and every **m** and island were moved out of 3735
8: 8 as *it were* a great **m** burning with fire was 3735
21:10 me away in the spirit to a great and high **m**, 3735

MOUNTAIN GOAT See HIND

MOUNTAIN SHEEP See CHAMOIS

MOUNTAINS (177) [MOUNTAIN]

Ge 7:20 the waters prevail; and the **m** were covered. 2022
8: 4 day of the month, upon the **m** of Ararat. 2022
8: 5 of the month, were the tops of the **m** seen. 2022
22: 2 upon one of the **m** which I will tell thee of. 2022
Ex 32:12 to slay them in the **m**, and to consume them 2022
Nu 13:29 and the Amorites, dwell in the **m**: 2022
23: 7 out of the **m** of the east, *saying*, Come, 2042
33:47 pitched in the **m** of Abarim, before Nebo. 2022
33:48 they departed from the **m** of Abarim, and 2022
Dt 2:37 river Jabbok, nor *unto* the cities in the **m**, 2022
12: 2 upon the high **m**, and upon the hills, and 2022
32:22 and set on fire the foundations of the **m**. 2022
33:15 for the chief things of the ancient **m**, and 2042
Jos 10: 6 in the **m** are gathered together against us. 2022
11: 2 to the kings that *were* on the north of the **m**, 2022
11: 3 the Jebusite in the **m**, and *to* the Hivite 2022
11:21 cut off the Anakims from the **m**, 2022
11:21 from all the **m** of Judah, and from all 2022
11:21 of Judah, and from all the **m** of Israel: 2022
12: 8 In the **m**, and in the valleys, and in 2022
15:48 in the **m**, Shamir, and Jattir, and Socoh, 2022
18:12 and went up through the **m** westward; 2022
Jdg 5: 5 The **m** melted from before the LORD, 2022
6: 2 made them the dens which *are* in the **m**, 2022
9:25 set liers in wait for him in the top of the **m**, 2022
9:36 come people down from the top of the **m** 2022
9:36 Thou seest the shadow of the **m** as *if they* 2022
11:37 that I may go up and down upon the **m**, and 2022
11:38 and bewailed her virginity upon the **m**. 2022
1Sa 26:20 as when *one* doth hunt a partridge in the **m**. 2022
2Sa 1:21 Ye **m** of Gilboa, *let there be* no dew, 2022
1Ki 5:15 and fourscore thousand hewers in the **m**; 2022
19:11 a great and strong wind rent the **m**, and 2022
2Ki 19:23 I am come up *to* the height of the **m**, 2022
1Ch 12: 8 and *were* as swift as the roes upon the **m**: 2022
2Ch 18:16 I did see all Israel scattered upon the **m**, 2022
21:11 Moreover he made high places in the **m** of 2022
26:10 and vinedressers in the **m**, 2022
27: 4 Moreover he built cities in the **m** of Judah, 2022
Job 9: 5 Which removeth the **m**, and they know not: 2022
24: 8 They are wet with the showers of the **m**, 2022
28: 9 the rock; he overturneth the **m** by the roots. 2022
39: 8 The range of the **m** *is* his pasture, and 2022
40:20 Surely the **m** bring him forth food, 2022
Ps 36: 6 Thy righteousness *is* like the great **m**; 2042
46: 2 though the **m** be carried into the midst of 2022
46: 3 *though* the **m** shake with the swelling 2022
50:11 I know all the fowls of the **m**: and the wild 2022
65: 6 Which by his strength setteth fast the **m**; 2022
72: 3 The **m** shall bring peace to the people, and 2022
72:16 of corn in the earth upon the top of the **m**; 2022
76: 4 *and* excellent than the **m** of prey. 2042
83:14 and as the flame setteth the **m** on fire; 2022
87: 1 His foundation *is* in the holy **m**. 2042
90: 2 Before the **m** were brought forth, or 2022
104: 6 a garment: the waters stood above the **m**. 2022
104: 8 They go up *by* the **m**; they go down *by* 2022
114: 4 The **m** skipped like rams, *and* the little hills 2022
114: 6 Ye **m**, *that* ye skipped like rams; *and* 2022
125: 2 *As* the **m** *are* round about Jerusalem, so 2022
133: 3 *as the dew* that descended upon the **m** of 2042
144: 5 touch the **m**, and they shall smoke. 2022
147: 8 who maketh grass to grow *upon* the **m**. 2022
148: 9 **M**, and all hills; fruitful trees, and 2022
Pr 8:25 Before the **m** were settled, before the hills 2022
27:25 and herbs of the **m** are gathered. 2022
SS 2: 8 behold, he cometh leaping upon the **m**, 2022
2:17 a roe or a young hart upon the **m** of Bether. 2022
4: 8 the lions' dens, from the **m** of the leopards. 2042
8:14 or to a young hart upon the **m** of spices. 2022
Isa 2: 2 shall be established in the top of the **m**, 2022
2:14 upon all the high **m**, and upon all the hills 2022
13: 4 The noise of a multitude in the **m**, like as of 2022
14:25 and upon my **m** tread him under foot: 2022
17:13 shall be chased as the chaff of the **m** before 2022
18: 3 when *he* lifteth up an ensign *on* the **m**; 2022
18: 6 be left together unto the fowls of the **m**, 2022
22: 5 down the walls, and of crying to the **m**. 2022
34: 3 and the **m** shall be melted with their blood. 2022
37:24 am I come up *to* the height of the **m**, 2022
40:12 weighed the **m** in scales, and the hills in a 2022
41:15 thou shalt thresh the **m**, and beat *them* 2022
42:11 let them shout from the top of the **m**. 2022
42:15 I will make waste **m** and hills, and dry up 2022
44:23 ye **m**, O forest, and every tree therein: 2022
49:11 I will make all my **m** a way, and 2022
49:13 O earth; and break forth *into* singing, O **m**: 2022
52: 7 How beautiful upon the **m** are the feet of 2022
54:10 For the **m** shall depart, and the hills be 2022
55:12 the **m** and the hills shall break forth before 2022
Isa 64: 1 that the **m** might flow down at thy 2022
64: 3 the **m** flowed down at thy presence. 2022
65: 7 which have burnt incense upon the **m**, and 2022
65: 9 and out of Judah an inheritor of my **m**: 2022
Jer 3:23 from the hills, *and from* the multitude of **m**: 2022
4:24 I beheld the **m**, and lo, they trembled, and 2022
9:10 For the **m** will I take up a weeping and 2022
13:16 before your feet stumble upon the dark **m**, 2022
17:26 and from the **m**, and from the south, 2022
31: 5 Thou shalt yet plant vines upon the **m** of 2022
32:44 in the cities of the **m**, and in the cities of 2022
33:13 In the cities of the **m**, in the cities of 2022
46:18 Surely as Tabor *is* among the **m**, and 2022
50: 6 they have turned them away *on* the **m**: 2022
La 4:19 they pursued us upon the **m**, they laid wait 2022
Eze 6: 2 set thy face towards the **m** of Israel, and 2022
6: 3 say, Ye **m** of Israel, hear the word of 2022
6: 3 Thus saith the Lord GOD to the **m**, and 2022
6:13 in all the tops of the **m**, and under every 2022
7: 7 and not the sounding again of the **m**. 2022
7:16 shall be on the **m** like doves of the valleys, 2022
18: 6 *And* hath not eaten upon the **m**, 2022
18:11 but even hath eaten upon the **m**, 2022
18:15 *That* hath not eaten upon the **m**, 2022
19: 9 no more be heard upon the **m** of Israel. 2022
22: 9 in thee they eat upon the **m**: in the midst of 2022
31:12 upon the **m** and in all the valleys his 2022
32: 5 I will lay thy flesh upon the **m**, and fill 2022
32: 6 wherein thou swimmest, *even* to the **m**; 2022
33:28 the **m** of Israel shall be desolate, that none 2022
34: 6 My sheep wandered through all the **m**, and 2022
34:13 feed them upon the **m** of Israel by 2022
34:14 upon the high **m** of Israel shall their fold 2022
34:14 *in* a fat pasture shall they feed upon the **m** 2022
35: 8 I will fill his **m** *with* his slain *men:* in thy 2022
35:12 thou hast spoken against the **m** of Israel, 2022
36: 1 prophesy unto the **m** of Israel, and say, 2022
36: 1 say, Ye **m** of Israel, hear the word of 2022
36: 4 Therefore, ye **m** of Israel, hear the word of 2022
36: 4 Thus saith the Lord GOD to the **m**, and 2022
36: 6 say unto the **m**, and to the hills, to 2022
36: 8 ye, O **m** of Israel, ye shall shoot forth your 2022
37:22 one nation in the land upon the **m** of Israel; 2022
38: 8 against the **m** of Israel, which have been 2022
38:20 the **m** shall be thrown down, and the steep 2022
38:21 a sword against him throughout all my **m**, 2022
39: 2 and will bring thee upon the **m** of Israel: 2022
39: 4 Thou shalt fall upon the **m** of Israel, thou, 2022
39:17 *even* a great sacrifice upon the **m** of Israel, 2022
Hos 4:13 They sacrifice upon the tops of the **m**, and 2022
10: 8 they shall say to the **m**, Cover us; and to 2022
Joel 2: 2 as the morning spread upon the **m**: 2022
2: 5 Like the noise of chariots on the tops of **m** 2022
3:18 *that* the **m** shall drop down new wine, and 2022
Am 3: 9 Assemble yourselves upon the **m** of 2022
4:13 he that formeth the **m**, and createth 2022
9:13 the **m** shall drop sweet wine, and all 2022
Jnh 2: 6 I went down to the bottoms of the **m**; 2022
Mic 1: 4 the **m** shall be molten under him, and 2022
4: 1 shall be established in the top of the **m**, 2022
6: 1 contend thou before the **m**, and let the hills 2022
6: 2 Hear ye, O **m**, the LORD'S controversy, 2022
Na 1: 5 The **m** quake at him, and the hills melt, and 2022
1:15 Behold upon the **m** the feet of him that 2022
3:18 *dust:* thy people is scattered upon the **m**, 2022
Hab 3: 6 the everlasting **m** were scattered, 2042
3:10 The **m** saw thee, *and* they trembled: 2022
Hag 1:11 upon the **m**, and upon the corn, and 2022
Zec 6: 1 four chariots out from between two **m**; 2022
6: 1 and the **m** *were* mountains of brass. 2022
6: 1 and the mountains *were* **m** of brass. 2022
14: 5 ye shall flee *to* the valley of the **m**; for 2022
14: 5 for the valley of the **m** shall reach unto 2022
Mal 1: 3 laid his **m** and his heritage waste for 2022
Mt 18:12 and goeth into the **m**, and seeketh that 3735
24:16 let them which be in Judea flee into the **m**: 3735
Mk 5: 5 and day, he was in the **m**, and in the tombs, 3735
5:11 Now there was there nigh unto the **m** a 3735
13:14 then let them that be in Judea flee to the **m**: 3735
Lk 21:21 let them which are in Judea flee to the **m**; 3735
23:30 Then shall they begin to say to the **m**, 3735
1Co 13: 2 so that *I* could remove **m**, and have no 3735
Heb 11:38 and *in* **m**, and *in* dens and caves of 3735
Rev 6:15 in the dens and in the rocks of the **m**; 3735
6:16 And said to the **m** and rocks, Fall on us, 3735
16:20 fled *away*, and the **m** were not found. 3735
17: 9 The seven heads are seven **m**, on which 3735

MOUNTED (1) [MOUNT]

Eze 10:19 and **m up** from the earth in my sight: 7426

MOUNTING (1) [MOUNT]

Isa 15: 5 for *by* the **m up** of Luhith with weeping 4608

MOUNTS (3) [MOUNT]

Jer 32:24 Behold the **m**, they are come *unto* the city 5550
33: 4 which are thrown down by the **m**, and 5550
Eze 17:17 by casting up **m**, and building forts, to cut 5550

MOURN (45) [MOURNED, MOURNER, MOURNERS, MOURNETH, MOURNFULLY, MOURNING]

Ge 23: 2 Abraham came to **m** for Sarah, and to weep 5594
1Sa 16: 1 unto Samuel, How long wilt thou **m** for Saul, 56
2Sa 3:31 you with sackcloth, and **m** before Abner. 5594
1Ki 13:29 came to the city, to **m** and to bury him. 5594
14:13 all Israel shall **m** for him, and bury him: 5594
Ne 8: 9 unto the LORD your God; **m** not, nor weep. 56
Job 2:11 together to come to **m** with him 5110
5:11 that those which **m** may be exalted *to* 6937
14:22 have pain, and his soul within him shall **m**. 56
Ps 55: 2 I **m** in my complaint, and make a noise; 7300
Pr 5:11 thou **m** at the last, when thy flesh and 5098
29: 2 when the wicked beareth rule, the people **m**. 584

M

Ecc 3: 4 to laugh; a time to **m**, and a time to dance; 5594
Isa 3:26 her gates shall lament and **m**; and she *being* 56
16: 7 the foundations of Kir-hareseth shall ye **m**; 1897
19: 8 The fishers also shall **m**, and all they that 578
38:14 I did **m** as a dove: mine eyes fail *with* 1897
59:11 all like bears, and **m sore** like doves: 1897+1897
61: 2 vengeance of our God; to comfort all that **m**; 57
61: 3 To appoint unto them that **m** in Zion, to give 57
66:10 rejoice for joy with her, all ye that **m** for her: 56
Jer 4:28 For this shall the earth **m**, and the heavens 56
12: 4 How long shall the land **m**, and the herbs of 56
48:31 *mine heart* shall **m** for the men of 1897
La 1: 4 The ways of Zion do **m**, because none come 57
Eze 7:12 let not the buyer rejoice, nor the seller **m**: 56
7:27 The king shall **m**, and the prince shall be 56
24:16 yet neither shalt thou **m** nor weep, 5594
24:23 ye shall not **m** nor weep; but ye shall pine 5594
24:23 your iniquities, and **m** one towards another. 5098
31:15 I **caused** Lebanon **to m** for him, and all 6937
Hos 4: 3 Therefore shall the land **m**, and every one that 56
10: 5 for the people thereof shall **m** over it, and 56
Joel 1: 9 the priests, the LORD'S ministers, **m**. 56
Am 1: 2 and the habitations of the shepherds shall **m**, 56
8: 8 and every one **m** that dwelleth therein? 56
9: 5 shall melt, and all that dwell therein shall **m**: 56
Zec 12:10 they shall **m** for him, as one mourneth for 5594
12:12 the land shall **m**, every family apart; 5594
Mt 5: 4 Blessed *are* they that **m**: for they shall be *3996*
9:15 Can the children of the bridechamber **m**, *3996*
24:30 and then shall all the tribes of the earth **m**, *2875*
Lk 6:25 that laugh now: for ye shall **m** and weep. *3996*
Jas 4: 9 Be afflicted, and **m**, and weep: let your *3996*
Rev 18:11 of the earth *shall* weep and **m** over her; *3996*

MOURNED (22) [MOURN]

Ge 37:34 upon his loins, and **m** for his son many days. 56
50: 3 and the Egyptians **m** for him threescore and 1058
50:10 there they **m** with a great and very sore 5594
Ex 33: 4 the people heard these evil tidings, they **m**: 56
Nu 14:39 children of Israel: and the people **m** greatly. 56
20:29 they **m** for Aaron thirty days, *even* all 1058
1Sa 15:35 nevertheless Samuel **m** for Saul: and 56
2Sa 1:12 they **m**, and wept, and fasted until even, 5594
11:26 husband was dead, she **m** for her husband. 5594
13:37 And *David* **m** for his son every day. 56
14: 2 be as a woman *that had* a long time **m** for 56
1Ki 13:30 they **m** over him, *saying*, Alas, my brother. 5594
14:18 all Israel **m** for him, according to the word 5594
1Ch 7:22 And Ephraim their father **m** many days, and 56
2Ch 35:24 And all Judah and Jerusalem **m** for Josiah. 56
Ezr 10: 6 for he **m** because of the transgression of them 56
Ne 1: 4 **m** *certain* days, and fasted, and prayed before 56
Zec 7: 5 When ye fasted and **m** in the fifth and 5594
Mt 11:17 we have **m** unto you, and ye have not *2354*
Mk 16:10 had been with him, as they **m** and wept. *3996*
Lk 7:32 we have **m** to you, and ye have not wept. *2354*
1Co 5: 2 ye are puffed up, and have not rather **m**, *3996*

MOURNER (1) [MOURN]

2Sa 14: 2 **feign** thyself **to be a m**, and put on now 56

MOURNERS (4) [MOURN]

Job 29:25 in the army, as *one that* comforteth the **m**. 57
Ecc 12: 5 long home, and the **m** go about the streets: 5594
Isa 57:18 and restore comforts unto him and to his **m**. 57
Hos 9: 4 *shall be* unto them as the bread of **m**; 205

MOURNETH (11) [MOURN]

2Sa 19: 1 Behold, the king weepeth and **m** for Absalom. 56
Ps 35:14 down heavily, as one that **m** for his mother. 57
88: 9 Mine eye **m** by reason of affliction: 1669
Isa 24: 4 The earth **m** *and* fadeth away, the world 56
24: 7 The new wine **m**, the vine languisheth, all 56
33: 9 The earth **m** *and* languisheth: Lebanon is 56
Jer 12:11 it desolate, *and being* desolate it **m** unto me; 56
14: 2 Judah **m**, and the gates thereof languish; 56
23:10 for because of swearing the land **m**; 56
Joel 1:10 The field is wasted, the land **m**; for the corn is 56
Zec 12:10 as one **m** for *his* only *son*, and shall be in 4553

MOURNFULLY (1) [MOURN]

Mal 3:14 that we have walked **m** before the LORD 6941

MOURNING (51) [MOURN]

Ge 27:41 The days of **m** for my father are at hand; 60
37:35 I will go down into the grave unto my son **m**. 57
50: 4 when the days of his **m** were past, 1068
50:10 and he made a **m** for his father seven days. 60
50:11 saw the **m** in the floor of Atad, they said, 60
50:11 This *is* a grievous **m** to the Egyptians: 60
Dt 26:14 I have not eaten thereof in my **m**, 205
34: 8 of weeping *and* **m** for Moses were ended. 60
2Sa 11:27 when the **m** was past, David sent and fet her 60
14: 2 put on now **m** apparel, and anoint not *thyself* 60
19: 2 the victory that day was *turned* into **m** unto all 60
Est 4: 3 *there was* great **m** among the Jews, and 60
6:12 Haman hasted to his house **m**, and having his 57
9:22 sorrow to joy, and from **m** into a good day: 60
Job 3: 8 the day, who are ready to raise up their **m**. 3882
30:28 I went **m** without the sun: I stood up, *and* 6937
30:31 My harp also is *turned* to **m**, and my organ 60
Ps 30:11 Thou hast turned for me my **m** into 4553
38: 6 down greatly; I go **m** all the day long. 6937
42: 9 why go I **m** because of the oppression of 6937
43: 2 why go I **m** because of the oppression of 6937
Ecc 7: 2 *It is* better to go to the house of **m**, than to go 60
7: 4 The heart of the wise *is* in the house of **m**; but 60
Isa 22:12 to **m**, and to baldness, and to girding with 4553
51:11 and joy; *and* sorrow and **m** shall flee away. 585
60:20 and the days of thy **m** shall be ended. 60
61: 3 them beauty for ashes, the oil of joy for **m**, 60
Jer 6:26 make thee **m**, *as* for an only *son*, most bitter 60
9:17 call for the *m* *women*, that they may come; 6969
16: 5 the LORD, Enter not *into* the house of **m**, 4798
Jer 16: 7 shall *men* tear *themselves* for them in **m**, 60
31:13 for I will turn their **m** into joy, and 60
La 2: 5 hath increased in the daughter of Judah **m** 8386
5:15 heart is ceased; our dance is turned into **m**. 60
Eze 2:10 therein lamentations, and **m**, and woe. 1899
7:16 all of them **m**, every one for his iniquity. 1993
24:17 Forbear to cry, make no **m** *for* the dead, 60
31:15 he went down to the grave I **caused a m**: 56
Da 10: 2 In those days I Daniel was **m** three full weeks. 56
Joel 2:12 and with weeping, and with **m**: 4553
Am 5:16 and they shall call the husbandman to **m**, and 60
8:10 I will turn your feasts into **m**, and all your 60
8:10 and I will make it as the **m** of an only *son*, and 60
Mic 1: 8 a wailing like the dragons, and **m** as the owls. 60
1:11 came not forth *in* the **m** of Beth-ezel; 4553
Zec 12:11 In that day shall there be a great **m** in 4553
12:11 as the **m** of Hadadrimmon in the valley of 4553
Mt 2:18 lamentation, and weeping, and great **m**, *3602*
2Co 7: 7 your **m**, your fervent mind toward me; *3602*
Jas 4: 9 let your laughter be turned to **m**, and *3997*
Rev 18: 8 come in one day, death, and **m**, and famine; *3997*

MOUSE (2) [MICE]

Lev 11:29 and the **m**, and the tortoise after his kind, 5909
Isa 66:17 and the abomination, and the **m**, 5909

MOUTH (424) [MOUTHS]

Ge 4:11 which hath opened her **m** to receive thy 6310
8:11 lo, in her **m** *was* an olive leaf pluckt off: 6310
24:57 will call the damsel, and inquire at her **m**. 6310
29: 2 and a great stone *was* upon the well's **m**. 6310
29: 3 and they rolled the stone from the well's **m**, 6310
29: 3 put the stone again upon the well's **m** in his 6310
29: 8 *till* they roll the stone from the well's **m**; 6310
29:10 rolled the stone from the well's **m**, and 6310
42:27 for behold, it *was* in his sack's **m**. 6310
43:12 the money that was brought again in the **m** 6310
43:21 every man's money *was* in the **m** of his 6310
44: 1 put every man's money in his sack's **m**. 6310
44: 2 in the sack's **m** of the youngest, and 6310
45:12 that *it is* my **m** that speaketh unto you. 6310
Ex 4:11 said unto him, Who hath made man's **m**? 6310
4:12 Now therefore go, and I will be with thy **m**, 6310
4:15 speak unto him, and put words in his **m**: 6310
4:15 I will be with thy **m**, and with his mouth, 6310
4:15 with his **m**, and will teach you what ye 6310
4:16 *even* he shall be to thee instead of a **m**, and 6310
13: 9 that the LORD'S law may be in thy **m**: 6310
23:13 neither let it be heard out of thy **m**. 6310
Nu 12: 8 With him will I speak **m** to mouth, 6310
12: 8 With him will I speak mouth to **m**, 6310
16:30 the earth open her **m**, and swallow them up, 6310
16:32 the earth opened her **m**, and 6310
22:28 the LORD opened the **m** of the ass, and 6310
22:38 the word that God putteth in my **m**, that 6310
23: 5 And the LORD put a word in Balaam's **m**, 6310
23:12 that which the LORD hath put in my **m**? 6310
23:16 put a word in his **m**, and said, Go again 6310
26:10 the earth opened her **m**, and 6310
30: 2 to all that proceedeth out of his **m**. 6310
32:24 that which hath proceeded out of your **m**. 6310
35:30 the murderer shall be put to death by the **m** 6310
Dt 8: 3 by every *word* that proceedeth out of the **m** 6310
11: 6 how the earth opened her **m**, and 6310
17: 6 At the **m** of two witnesses, or 6310
17: 6 at the **m** of one witness he shall not be put 6310
18:18 unto thee, and will put my words in his **m**; 6310
19:15 at the **m** of two witnesses, or at the mouth 6310
19:15 or at the **m** of three witnesses, shall 6310
23:23 which thou hast promised with thy **m**. 6310
30:14 in thy **m**, and in thy heart, that *thou* mayest 6310
32: 1 and hear, O earth, the words of my **m**. 6310
Jos 1: 8 of the law shall not depart out of thy **m**; 6310
6:10 shall *any* word proceed out of your **m**, 6310
9:14 asked not *counsel* at the **m** of the LORD. 6310
10:18 Roll great stones upon the **m** of the cave, 6310
10:22 Open the **m** of the cave, and bring out those 6310
10:27 laid great stones in the cave's **m**, 6310
Jdg 7: 6 putting their hand to their **m**, were three 6310
9:38 Where *is* now thy **m**, wherewith thou 6310
11:35 for I have opened my **m** unto the LORD, 6310
11:36 *if* thou hast opened thy **m** unto the LORD, 6310
11:36 to that which hath proceeded out of thy **m**; 6310
18:19 lay thine hand upon thy **m**, and go with us, 6310
1Sa 1:12 before the LORD, that Eli marked her **m**. 6310
2: 1 my **m** is enlarged over mine enemies; 6310
2: 3 let *not* arrogancy come out of your **m**: 6310
14:26 but no man put his hand to his **m**: 6310
14:27 in a honeycomb, and put his hand to his **m**; 6310
17:35 smote him, and delivered *it* out of his **m**: 6310
2Sa 1:16 for thy **m** hath testified against thee, saying, 6310
14: 3 unto him. So Joab put the words in her **m**. 6310
14:19 he put all these words in the **m** of thine 6310
17:19 and spread a covering over the well's **m**, 6440
18:25 If he *be* alone, *there is* tidings in his **m**. 6310
22: 9 his nostrils, and fire out of his **m** devoured: 6310
1Ki 7:31 the **m** of it within the chapiter and 6310
7:31 the **m** thereof *was* round *after* the work of 6310
7:31 also upon the **m** of it *were* gravings with 6310
8:15 which spake with his **m** unto David my 6310
8:24 thou spakest also with thy **m**, and 6310
13:21 Forasmuch as thou hast disobeyed the **m** of 6310
17:24 *that* the word of the LORD in thy **m** *is* 6310
19:18 and every **m** which hath not kissed him. 6310
22:13 *declare* good unto the king *with* one **m**: 6310
22:22 I will be a lying spirit in the **m** of all his 6310
22:23 the LORD hath put a lying spirit in the **m** 6310
2Ki 4:34 put his **m** upon his mouth, and his eyes 6310
4:34 put his mouth upon his **m**, and his eyes 6310
1Ch 16:12 his wonders, and the judgments of his **m**; 6310
2Ch 6: 4 he spake with his **m** to my father David, 6310
6:15 spakest with thy **m**, and hast fulfilled *it* 6310
18:21 be a lying spirit in the **m** of all his prophets. 6310
18:22 the LORD hath put a lying spirit in the **m** 6310
35:22 the words of Necho from the **m** of God, 6310
2Ch 36:12 *speaking* from the **m** of the LORD. 6310
36:21 To fulfil the word of the LORD by the **m** 6310
36:22 the **m** of Jeremiah might be accomplished, 6310
Ezr 1: 1 that the word of the LORD by the **m** of 6310
Ne 9:20 withheldest not thy manna from their **m**, 6310
Est 7: 8 As the word went out of the king's **m**, 6310
Job 3: 1 After this opened Job his **m**, and cursed his 6310
5:15 from their **m**, and from the hand of 6310
5:16 hath hope, and iniquity stoppeth her **m**. 6310
7:11 Therefore I will not refrain my **m**; I will 6310
8: 2 *how long shall* the words of thy **m** *be like* a 6310
8:21 Till he fill thy **m** *with* laughing, and 6310
9:20 mine own **m** shall condemn me: 6310
12:11 the ear try words? and the **m** taste his meat? 2441
15: 5 For thy **m** uttereth thine iniquity, and 6310
15: 6 Thine own **m** condemneth thee, and not I; 6310
15:13 and lettest *such* words go out of thy **m**? 6310
15:30 by the breath of his **m** shall he go away. 6310
16: 5 *But* I would strengthen you with my **m**, and 6310
16:10 They have gaped upon me with their **m**; 6310
19:16 *me* no answer; I intreated him with my **m**. 6310
20:12 Though wickedness be sweet in his **m**, 6310
20:13 forsake it not; but keep it still within his **m**: 2441
21: 5 and lay *your* hand upon *your* **m**. 6310
22:22 the law from his **m**, and lay up his words in 6310
23: 4 before him, and fill my **m** *with* arguments. 6310
23:12 I have esteemed the words of his **m** more 6310
29: 9 and laid *their* hand on their **m**. 6310
29:10 their tongue cleaved to the **roof of** their **m**. 2441
29:23 they opened their **m** wide *as* for the latter 6310
31:27 or my **m** hath kissed my hand: 6310
31:30 (Neither have I suffered my **m** to sin by 2441
32: 5 *was* no answer in the **m** of *these* three men, 6310
33: 2 Behold now I have opened my **m**, 6310
33: 2 my tongue hath spoken in my **m**. 2441
34: 3 the ear trieth words, as the **m** tasteth meat. 2441
35:16 Therefore doth Job open his **m** in vain; 6310
37: 2 and the sound *that* goeth out of his **m**. 6310
40: 4 I will lay my hand upon my **m**. 6310
40:23 that he can draw up Jordan into his **m**. 6310
41:19 Out of his **m** go burning lamps, *and* 6310
41:21 and a flame goeth out of his **m**. 6310
Ps 5: 9 For *there is* no faithfulness in their **m**; 6310
8: 2 Out of the **m** of babes and sucklings hast 6310
10: 7 His **m** is full *of* cursing and deceit and 6310
17: 3 I am purposed *that* my **m** shall not 6310
17:10 own fat: *with* their **m** they speak proudly. 6310
18: 8 his nostrils, and fire out of his **m** devoured: 6310
19:14 Let the words of my **m**, and the meditation 6310
22:21 Save me from the lion's **m**: for thou hast 6310
32: 9 whose **m** must be held in with bit and 5716
33: 6 all the host of them by the breath of his **m**. 6310
34: 1 his praise *shall* continually *be* in my **m**. 6310
35:21 they opened their **m** wide against me, *and* 6310
36: 3 The words of his **m** *are* iniquity and deceit: 6310
37:30 The **m** of the righteous speaketh wisdom, 6310
38:13 *was* as a dumb *man that* openeth not his **m**. 6310
38:14 and in whose **m** *are* no reproofs. 6310
39: 1 I will keep my **m** with a bridle, while 6310
39: 9 I was dumb, I opened not my **m**; because 6310
40: 3 he hath put a new song in my **m**, 6310
49: 3 My **m** shall speak of wisdom; and 6310
50:16 thou shouldest take my covenant in thy **m**? 6310
50:19 Thou givest thy **m** to evil, and thy tongue 6310
51:15 and my **m** shall shew forth thy praise. 6310
54: 2 O God; give ear to the words of my **m**. 6310
55:21 *The words of* his **m** were smoother than 6310
58: 6 Break their teeth, O God, in their **m**: 6310
59: 7 Behold, they belch out with their **m**: 6310
59:12 *For* the sin of their **m** *and* the words of their 6310
62: 4 they bless with their **m**, but they curse 6310
63: 5 and my **m** shall praise *thee with* joyful lips: 6310
63:11 the **m** of them that speak lies shall be 6310
66:14 my **m** hath spoken, when I was in trouble. 6310
66:17 I cried unto him *with* my **m**, and *he was* 6310
69:15 and let not the pit shut her **m** upon me. 6310
71: 8 Let my **m** be filled *with* thy praise *and* 6310
71:15 My **m** shall shew forth thy righteousness 6310
73: 9 They set their **m** against the heavens, and 6310
78: 1 incline your ears to the words of my **m**. 6310
78: 2 I will open my **m** in a parable: I will utter 6310
78:36 they did flatter him with their **m**, 6310
81:10 of Egypt: open thy **m** wide, and I will fill it. 6310
89: 1 with my **m** will I make known thy 6310
103: 5 Who satisfieth thy **m** with good *things; so* 5716
105: 5 his wonders, and the judgments of his **m**; 6310
107:42 rejoice: and all iniquity shall stop her **m**. 6310
109: 2 For the **m** of the wicked and the mouth of 6310
109: 2 the **m** of the deceitful are opened against 6310
109:30 will greatly praise the LORD with my **m**; 6310
119:13 have I declared all the judgments of thy **m**. 6310
119:43 not the word of truth utterly out of my **m**; 6310
119:72 The law of thy **m** *is* better unto me than 6310
119:88 so shall I keep the testimony of thy **m**. 6310
119:103 my taste! *yea, sweeter* than honey to my **m**! 6310
119:108 the freewill offerings of my **m**, O LORD, 6310
119:131 I opened my **m**, and panted: for I longed 6310
126: 2 was our **m** filled *with* laughter, and 6310
137: 6 let my tongue cleave to the **roof of** my **m**; 2441
138: 4 when they hear the words of thy **m**. 6310
141: 3 Set a watch, O LORD, before my **m**; 6310
141: 7 Our bones are scattered at the grave's **m**, 6310
144: 8 Whose **m** speaketh vanity, and their right 6310
144:11 whose **m** speaketh vanity, and their right 6310
145:21 My **m** shall speak the praise of the LORD: 6310
149: 6 *Let* the high *praises* of God *be* in their **m**, 1627
Pr 2: 6 out of his **m** *cometh* knowledge and 6310
4: 5 neither decline from the words of my **m**. 6310
4:24 Put away from thee a froward **m**, and 6310
5: 3 and her **m** *is* smoother than oil: 2441
5: 7 and depart not from the words of my **m**. 6310
6: 2 Thou art snared with the words of thy **m**, 6310
6: 2 thou art taken with the words of thy **m**, 6310
6:12 a wicked man, walketh *with* a froward **m**. 6310
7:24 and attend to the words of my **m**. 6310

M

Pr 8: 7 For my **m** shall speak truth; and 2441
8: 8 All the words of my **m** *are* in 6310
8:13 the evil way, and the froward **m**, do I hate. 6310
10: 6 but violence covereth the **m** of the wicked. 6310
10:11 The **m** of a righteous *man is* a well of life: 6310
10:11 but violence covereth the **m** of the wicked. 6310
10:14 but the **m** of the foolish *is* near destruction. 6310
10:31 The **m** of the just bringeth forth wisdom: 6310
10:32 the **m** of the wicked *speaketh* frowardness. 6310
11: 9 A hypocrite with *his* **m** destroyeth his 6310
11:11 it is overthrown by the **m** of the wicked. 6310
12: 6 but the **m** of the upright shall deliver them. 6310
12:14 be satisfied *with* good by the fruit of *his* **m**: 6310
13: 2 A man shall eat good by the fruit of *his* **m**: 6310
13: 3 He that keepeth his **m** keepeth his life: *but* 6310
14: 3 In the **m** of the foolish *is* a rod of pride: but 6310
15: 2 but the **m** of fools poureth out foolishness. 6310
15:14 but the **m** of fools feedeth on foolishness. 6310
15:23 A man hath joy by the answer of his **m**: and 6310
15:28 the **m** of the wicked poureth out evil 6310
16:10 his **m** transgresseth not in judgment. 6310
16:23 The heart of the wise teacheth his **m**, and 6310
16:26 for himself; for his **m** craveth it of him. 6310
18: 4 The words of a man's **m** *are as* deep 6310
18: 6 and his **m** calleth for strokes. 6310
18: 7 A fool's **m** *is* his destruction, and his lips 6310
18:20 shall be satisfied with the fruit of his **m**; 6310
19:24 will not so much as bring it to his **m** again. 6310
19:28 and the **m** of the wicked devoureth iniquity. 6310
20:17 afterwards his **m** shall be filled *with* gravel. 6310
21:23 Whoso keepeth his **m** and his tongue 6310
22:14 The **m** of strange *women is* a deep pit: 6310
24: 7 for a fool: he openeth not his **m** in the gate. 6310
26: 7 not equal: so *is* a parable in the **m** of fools. 6310
26: 9 so *is* a parable in the **m** of fools. 6310
26:15 it grieveth him to bring it again to his **m**. 6310
26:28 by it; and a flattering **m** worketh ruin. 6310
27: 2 *man* praise thee, and not thine own **m**; 6310
30:20 she eateth, and wipeth her **m**, and saith, 6310
30:32 thought evil, *lay thine* hand upon thy **m**. 6310
31: 8 Open thy **m** for the dumb in the cause of all 6310
31: 9 Open thy **m**, judge righteously, and 6310
31:26 She openeth her **m** with wisdom; and in her 6310
Ecc 5: 2 Be not rash with thy **m**, and let not thine 6310
5: 6 Suffer not thy **m** to cause thy flesh to sin; 6310
6: 7 All the labour of man *is* for his **m**, and 6310
10:12 The words of a wise *man's* **m** *are* gracious; 6310
10:13 The beginning of the words of his **m** *is* 6310
SS 1: 2 Let him kiss me with the kisses of his **m**: 6310
5:16 His **m** *is* most sweet: yea, he *is* altogether 2441
7: 9 the **roof of** thy **m** like the best wine, for my 2441
Isa 1:20 for the **m** of the LORD hath spoken *it*. 6310
5:14 and opened her **m** without measure: 6310
6: 7 he laid *it* upon my **m**, and said, Lo, 6310
9:12 they shall devour Israel with open **m**. 6310
9:17 an evildoer, and every **m** speaketh folly. 6310
10:14 the wing, or opened the **m**, or peeped. 6310
11: 4 shall smite the earth with the rod of his **m**, 6310
19: 7 by the **m** of the brooks, and every thing 6310
29:13 as this people draw near *me* with their **m**, 6310
30: 2 *into* Egypt, and have not asked *at* my **m**; 6310
34:16 for my **m** it hath commanded, and his spirit 6310
40: 5 for the **m** of the LORD hath spoken *it*. 6310
45:23 the word is gone out of my **m** *in* 6310
48: 3 they went forth out of my **m**, and I shewed 6310
49: 2 he hath made my **m** like a sharp sword; 6310
51:16 I have put my words in thy **m**, and 6310
53: 7 he was afflicted, yet he opened not his **m**: 6310
53: 7 shearers is dumb, so he openeth not his **m**. 6310
53: 9 neither *was any* deceit in his **m**. 6310
55:11 my word be that goeth forth out of my **m**: 6310
57: 4 against whom make ye a wide **m**, *and* 6310
58:14 for the **m** of the LORD hath spoken *it*. 6310
59:21 and my words which I have put in thy **m**, 6310
59:21 shall not depart out of thy **m**, nor out of 6310
59:21 of thy mouth, nor out of the **m** of thy seed, 6310
59:21 nor out of the **m** of thy seed's seed, 6310
62: 2 which the **m** of the LORD shall name. 6310
Jer 1: 9 put forth his hand, and touched my **m**. 6310
1: 9 Behold, I have put my words in thy **m**. 6310
5:14 I will make my words in thy **m** fire, and 6310
7:28 is perished, and is cut off from their **m**. 6310
9: 8 peaceably to his neighbour with his **m**, 6310
9:12 *who is he* to whom the **m** of the LORD 6310
9:20 let your ear receive the word of his **m**, and 6310
12: 2 thou *art* near in their **m**, and far from their 6310
15:19 from the vile, thou shalt be as my **m**: 6310
23:16 *and* not out of the **m** of the LORD. 6310
32: 4 shall speak with him **m** to mouth, and 6310
32: 4 shall speak with him mouth to **m**, and 6310
34: 3 he shall speak with thee **m** to mouth, and 6310
34: 3 he shall speak with thee mouth to **m**, and 6310
36: 4 Baruch wrote from the **m** of Jeremiah all 6310
36: 6 which thou hast written from my **m**, 6310
36:17 didst thou write all these words at his **m**? 6310
36:18 all these words unto me with his **m**, 6310
36:27 the words which Baruch wrote at the **m** of 6310
36:32 who wrote therein from the **m** of Jeremiah 6310
44:17 thing goeth forth out of our own **m**, 6310
44:26 **m** of any man of Judah in all the land of 6310
45: 1 these words in a book at the **m** of Jeremiah, 6310
48:28 her nest in the sides of the hole's **m**. 6310
51:44 I will bring forth out of his **m** that which he 6310
La 2:16 All thine enemies have opened their **m** 6310
3:29 He putteth his **m** in the dust; if so be there 6310
3:38 Out of the **m** of the most High proceedeth 6310
4: 4 cleaveth to the **roof of** his **m** for thirst: 2441
Eze 2: 8 open thy **m**, and eat that I give thee. 6310
3: 2 So I opened my **m**, and he caused me to eat 6310
3: 3 and it was in my **m** as honey for sweetness. 6310
3:17 therefore hear the word at my **m**, and 6310
3:26 thy tongue cleave to the **roof of** thy **m**, 2441
3:27 I will open thy **m**, and thou shalt say unto 6310
4:14 came there abominable flesh into my **m**. 6310
16:56 mentioned by thy **m** in the day of thy pride, 6310
Eze 16:63 never open thy **m** any more, because of thy 6310
21:22 to open the **m** in the slaughter, 6310
24:27 In that day shall thy **m** be opened to him 6310
29:21 I will give thee the opening of the **m** in 6310
33: 7 therefore thou shalt hear the word at my **m**, 6310
33:22 had opened my **m**, until *he* came to me in 6310
33:22 my **m** was opened, and I was no more 6310
33:31 for with their **m** they shew much love, *but* 6310
34:10 for I will deliver my flock from their **m**, 6310
35:13 Thus with your **m** ye have boasted against 6310
Da 3:26 Nebuchadnezzar came near to the **m** of 8651
4:31 While the word *was* in the king's **m**, 6433
6:17 and laid upon the **m** of the den; 6433
7: 5 *it had* three ribs in the **m** of it between 6433
7: 8 of man, and a **m** speaking great *things*. 6433
7:20 a **m** that spake very great *things*, whose 6433
10: 3 neither came flesh nor wine in my **m**, 6310
10:16 I opened my **m**, and spake, and said unto 6310
Hos 2:17 away the names of Baalim out of her **m**, 6310
6: 5 I have slain them by the words of my **m**: 6310
8: 1 *Set* the trumpet to thy **m**. *He shall come* as 2441
Joel 1: 5 the new wine, for it is cut off from your **m**. 6310
Am 3:12 As the shepherd taketh out of the **m** of 6310
Mic 4: 4 for the **m** of the LORD of hosts hath 6310
6:12 and their tongue *is* deceitful in their **m**. 6310
7: 5 keep the doors of thy **m** from her that lieth 6310
7:16 they shall lay *their* hand upon *their* **m**, 6310
Na 3:12 they shall even fall into the **m** of the eater. 6310
Zep 3:13 shall a deceitful tongue be found in their **m**: 6310
Zec 5: 8 he cast the weight of lead upon the **m** 6310
8: 9 days these words by the **m** of the prophets, 6310
9: 7 I will take away his blood out of his **m**, 6310
14:12 their tongue shall consume away in their **m**. 6310
Mal 2: 6 The law of truth was in his **m**, and 6310
2: 7 and they should seek the law at his **m**: 6310
Mt 4: 4 by every word that proceedeth out of the **m** *4750*
5: 2 And he opened his **m**, and taught them, *4750*
12:34 the abundance of the heart the **m** speaketh. *4750*
13:35 saying, I will open my **m** in parables; *4750*
15: 8 people draweth nigh unto me with their **m**, *4750*
15:11 Not that which goeth into the **m** defileth a *4750*
15:11 but that which cometh out of the **m**, *4750*
15:17 that whatsoever entereth in at the **m** goeth *4750*
15:18 out of the **m** come forth from the heart; *4750*
17:27 and when thou hast opened his **m**, *4750*
18:16 that in the **m** of two or three witnesses *4750*
21:16 Out of the **m** of babes and sucklings thou *4750*
Lk 1:64 And his **m** was opened immediately, and *4750*
1:70 (As he spake by the **m** of his holy prophets, *4750*
4:22 words which proceeded out of his **m**. *4750*
6:45 for of the abundance of the heart his **m** *4750*
11:54 seeking to catch something out of his **m**, *4750*
19:22 Out of thine own **m** will I judge thee, *4750*
21:15 For I will give you a **m** and wisdom, *4750*
22:71 for we ourselves have heard of his own **m**. *4750*
Jn 19:29 and put *it* upon hyssop, and put *it* to his **m**. *4750*
Ac 1:16 which the Holy Ghost by the **m** of David *4750*
3:18 had shewed by the **m** of all his prophets, *4750*
3:21 **m** of all his holy prophets since the world *4750*
4:25 Who by the **m** of thy servant David hast *4750*
8:32 before his shearer, so opened he not his **m**: *4750*
8:35 Then Philip opened his **m**, *4750*
10:34 Then Peter opened *his* **m**, and said, Of a *4750*
11: 8 hath at any time entered into my **m**. *4750*
15: 7 that the Gentiles by my **m** should hear *4750*
15:27 shall also tell *you* the same *things* by **m**. *3056*
18:14 when Paul was *now* about to open *his* **m**, *4750*
22:14 and shouldest hear the voice of his **m**. *4750*
23: 2 that stood by him to smite him on the **m**. *4750*
Ro 3:14 Whose **m** is full of cursing and bitterness: *4750*
3:19 that every **m** may be stopped, and all *4750*
10: 8 nigh thee, *even* in thy **m**, and in thy heart: *4750*
10: 9 That if thou shalt confess with thy **m** *4750*
10:10 with the **m** confession is made unto *4750*
15: 6 may with one mind *and* one **m** glorify God, *4750*
1Co 9: 9 Thou shalt not muzzle the **m** of the ox that NIG
2Co 6:11 O *ye* Corinthians, our **m** is open unto you, *4750*
13: 1 In the **m** of two or three witnesses shall *4750*
Eph 4:29 communication proceed out of your **m**, *4750*
6:19 unto me, that *I* may open my **m** boldly, *4750*
Col 3: 8 filthy communication out of your **m**. *4750*
2Th 2: 8 Lord shall consume with the spirit of his **m**, *4750*
2Ti 4:17 and I was delivered out of the **m** of the lion. *4750*
Jas 3:10 Out of the same **m** proceedeth blessing and *4750*
1Pe 2:22 no sin, neither was guile found in his **m**: *4750*
Jude 1:16 their **m** speaketh great swelling *words*, *4750*
Rev 1:16 out of his **m** went a sharp twoedged sword: *4750*
2:16 fight against them with the sword of my **m**. *4750*
3:16 cold nor hot, I will spue thee out of my **m**. *4750*
9:19 For their power is in their **m**, and in their *4750*
10: 9 but it shall be in thy **m** sweet as honey. *4750*
10:10 it up; and it was in my **m** sweet as honey: *4750*
11: 5 fire proceedeth out of their **m**, and *4750*
12:15 And the serpent cast out of his **m** water as a *4750*
12:16 and the earth opened her **m**, and *4750*
12:16 flood which the dragon cast out of his **m**. *4750*
13: 2 of a bear, and his **m** as the mouth of a lion: *4750*
13: 2 of a bear, and his mouth as the **m** of a lion: *4750*
13: 5 And there was given unto him a **m** *4750*
13: 6 And he opened his **m** in blasphemy against *4750*
14: 5 And in their **m** was found no guile: for they *4750*
16:13 like frogs *come* out of the **m** of the dragon, *4750*
16:13 and out of the **m** of the beast, and out of *4750*
16:13 and out of the **m** of the false prophet. *4750*
19:15 And out of his **m** goeth a sharp sword, *4750*
19:21 which *sword* proceeded out of his **m**: *4750*

MOUTHS (18) [MOUTH]

Ge 44: 8 which we found in our sacks' **m**, 6310
Dt 31:19 put it in their **m**, that this song may be a 6310
31:21 for it shall not **be forgotten** out of the **m** of 6310
Ps 22:13 They gaped upon me *with* their **m**, *as* a 6310
78:30 But while their meat *was* yet in their **m**, 6310
115: 5 They have **m**, but they speak not: eyes have 6310
135:16 They have **m**, but they speak not; eyes have 6310
Ps 135:17 neither is there *any* breath in their **m**. 6310
Isa 52:15 the kings shall shut their **m** at him: 6310
Jer 44:25 your wives have both spoken with your **m**, 6310
La 3:46 All our enemies have opened their **m** 6310
Da 6:22 hath shut the lions' **m**, that they have not 6433
Mic 3: 5 he that putteth not into their **m**, they even 6310
Tit 1:11 Whose **m** must be **stopped**, who subvert *1993*
Heb 11:33 obtained promises, stopped the **m** of lions, *4750*
Jas 3: 3 Behold, we put bits in the horses' **m**, *4750*
Rev 9:17 and out of their **m** issued fire and smoke *4750*
9:18 the brimstone, which issued out of their **m**. *4750*

MOVE (13) [MOTIONS, MOVEABLE, MOVED, MOVEDST, MOVER, MOVETH, MOVING, UNMOVEABLE]

Ex 11: 7 of Israel shall not a dog **m** his tongue, 2782
Lev 11:10 of all that **m** in the waters, and of any living 8318
Dt 23:25 thou shalt not **m** a sickle unto thy 5130
32:21 I will **m** them **to jealousy** with *those which* 7065
Jdg 13:25 to **m** him **at times** in the camp of Dan, 6470
2Sa 7:10 in a place of their own, and **m** no more; 7264
2Ki 21: 8 Neither will I **make** the feet of Israel **m** any 5110
23:18 Let him alone; let no man **m** his bones. 5128
Jer 10: 4 with nails and with hammers, that it **m** not. 6328
Mic 7:17 they shall **m** out of their holes like worms 7264
Mt 23: 4 they *themselves* will not **m** them with *one* *2795*
Ac 17:28 in him we live, and **m**, and have our being; *2795*
20:24 But none of these *things* **m** me, *4160*

MOVEABLE (1) [MOVE]

Pr 5: 6 her ways are **m**, *that* thou canst not know 5128

MOVED (75) [MOVE]

Ge 1: 2 the Spirit of God **m** upon the face of 7363
7:21 all flesh died that **m** upon the earth, *both* of 7430
Dt 32:21 They have **m** me **to jealousy** with *that* 7065
Jos 10:21 none **m** his tongue against any of 2782
15:18 as she came *unto him*, that she **m** him to 5496
Jdg 1:14 when she came *to him*, that she **m** him to 5496
Ru 1:19 that all the city was **m** about them, and 1949
1Sa 1:13 only her lips **m**, but her voice was not 5128
2Sa 18:33 the king was **much m**, and went up to 7264
22: 8 the foundations of heaven **m** and shook, 7264
24: 1 he **m** David against them to say, Go, 5496
1Ch 16:30 world also shall be stable, that it be not **m**. 4131
17: 9 in their place, and shall be **m** no more; 7264
2Ch 18:31 and God **m** them **to depart** from him. 5496
Ezr 4:15 that they have **m** sedition within the same 5648
Est 5: 9 that he stood not up, nor **m** for him, he was 2111
Job 37: 1 heart trembleth, and is **m** out of his place. 5425
41:23 are firm in themselves; they cannot be **m**. 4131
Ps 10: 6 He hath said in his heart, I shall not be **m**: 4131
13: 4 those that trouble me rejoice when I am **m**. 4131
15: 5 He that doeth these *things* shall never be **m**. 4131
16: 8 *he is* at my right hand, I shall not be **m**. 4131
18: 7 the foundations also of the hills **m** and 7264
21: 7 mercy of the most High he shall not be **m**. 4131
30: 6 in my prosperity I said, I shall never be **m**. 4131
46: 5 *is* in the midst of her; she shall not be **m**: 4131
46: 6 The heathen raged, the kingdoms were **m**: 4131
55:22 he shall never suffer the righteous to be **m**. 4131
62: 2 *he is* my defence; I shall not be greatly **m**. 4131
62: 6 *he is* my defence; I shall not be **m**. 4131
66: 9 in life, and suffereth not our feet to be **m**. 4132
68: 8 *even* Sinai itself *was* **m** at the presence of NIH
78:58 **m** him **to jealousy** with their graven 7065
93: 1 also is stablished, *that* it cannot be **m**. 4131
96:10 shall be established *that* it shall not be **m**: 4131
99: 1 *between* the cherubims; let the earth be **m**. 5120
112: 6 Surely he shall not be **m** for ever: 4131
121: 3 He will not suffer thy foot to be **m**: he that 4132
Pr 12: 3 but the root of the righteous shall not be **m**. 4131
SS 5: 4 *the door*, and my bowels were **m** for him. 1993
Isa 6: 4 the posts of the door **m** at the voice of him 5128
7: 2 his heart was **m**, and the heart of his 5128
7: 2 as the trees of the wood are **m** with 5128
10:14 there was none that **m** the wing, or 5074
14: 9 Hell from beneath is **m** for thee to meet 7264
19: 1 the idols of Egypt shall be **m** at his 5128
24:19 the earth is **m exceedingly**. 4131+4131
40:20 prepare a graven image, *that* shall not be **m**. 4131
41: 7 it with nails, *that* it should not be **m**. 4131
Jer 4:24 they trembled, and all the hills **m lightly**. 7043
25:16 be **m**, and be mad, because of the sword 1607
46: 7 a flood, whose waters are **m** as the rivers? 1607
46: 8 and *his* waters are **m** like the rivers; 1607
49:21 The earth is **m** at the noise of their fall, 7493
50:46 of the taking of Babylon the earth is **m**, 7493
Da 8: 7 he was **m with choler** against him, and 4843
11:11 king of the south shall be **m with choler**, 4843
Mt 9:36 he was **m with compassion** on them, *4697*
14:14 and was **m with compassion** toward them, *4697*
18:27 of that servant was **m with compassion**, *4697*
20:24 **m with indignation** against the two brethren. *23*
21:10 all the city was **m**, saying, Who is this? *4579*
Mk 1:41 And Jesus, **m with compassion**, put forth *4697*
6:34 and was **m with compassion** toward them, *4697*
15:11 But the chief priests **m** the people, that he *383*
Ac 2:25 is on my right hand, that I should not be **m**: *4531*
7: 9 And the patriarchs, **m with envy**, *2206*
17: 5 the Jews which believed not, **m with envy**, *2206*
21:30 And all the city was **m**, and the people ran *2795*
Col 1:23 *be* not **m away** from the hope of the gospel, *3334*
1Th 3: 3 That no *man* should be **m** by these *4525*
Heb 11: 7 **m with fear**, prepared an ark to the saving *2125*
12:28 we receiving a kingdom which **cannot be m**, *761*
2Pe 1:21 holy men of God spake *as they were* **m** by *5342*
Rev 6:14 and island were **m** out of their places. *2795*

MOVEDST (1) [MOVE]

Job 2: 3 although thou **m** me against him, to destroy 5496

MOVER (1) [MOVE]

Ac 24: 5 a **m** of sedition among all the Jews *2795*

M

MOVETH (8) [MOVE]
Ge 1:21 and every living creature that **m**, 7430
1:28 over every living thing that **m** upon 7430
9: 2 upon all that **m** *upon* the earth, and upon all 7430
Lev 11:46 of every living creature that **m** in 7430
Job 40:17 He **m** his tail like a cedar: the sinews of his 2654
Ps 69:34 the seas, and every *thing* that **m** therein. 7430
Pr 23:31 colour in the cup, *when* it **m** itself aright. 1980
Eze 47: 9 *that* every thing that liveth, which **m**, 8317

MOVING (5) [MOVE]
Ge 1:20 abundantly the **m creature** that hath life, 5315
9: 3 Every **m thing** that liveth shall be meat for 7431
Job 16: 5 the **m** of my lips should asswage *your* 5205
Pr 16:30 **m** his lips he bringeth evil to pass. 7169
Jn 5: 3 withered, waiting for the **m** of the water. *2796*

MOWER (1) [MOWINGS, MOWN]
Ps 129: 7 Where*with* the **m** filleth not his hand; 7114

MOWINGS (1) [MOWER]
Am 7: 1 *it was* the latter growth after the king's **m**. 1488

MOWN (1) [MOWER]
Ps 72: 6 come down like rain upon the **m grass**: 1488

MOZA (5)
1Ch 2:46 bare Haran, and **M**, and Gazez: 4162
8:36 and Zimri; and Zimri begat **M**, 4162
8:37 **M** begat Binea: Rapha *was* his son, 4162
9:42 and Zimri; and Zimri begat **M**; 4162
9:43 **M** begat Binea; and Rephaiah his son, 4162

MOZAH (1)
Jos 18:26 And Mizpeh, and Chephirah, and **M**, 4681

MUCH (287) [FORASMUCH, FORSOMUCH, INASMUCH, INSOMUCH, MORE, MOST, OVERMUCH]
Ge 23: 9 **for as m** money **as** it is worth he shall give 871.1
26:16 from us; for thou art **m** mightier than we. 3966
30:43 had **m** cattle, and maidservants, and 7227
34:12 **Ask** me **never so m** dowry and gift, 3966+7235
41:49 of the sea, very **m**, until he left numbering; 7235
43:34 was five times **so m as** any of theirs. 4480+7235
44: 1 **as m as** they can carry, and 834+3509.1
50:20 as *it is* this day, to save **m** people alive. 7227
Ex 12:38 and flocks, and herds, *even* very **m** cattle. 3515
12:42 It *is* a night to be **m observed** unto 8107
14:28 there remained not **so m as** one of them. 5704
16: 5 be twice **as m as** they gather daily. 834+5921
16:18 he that **gathered m** had nothing over, and 7235
16:22 sixth day they gathered **twice as m** bread, 4932
30:23 and of sweet cinnamon **half so m**, 4276
36: 5 The people bring **m more** than enough for 7235
36: 7 for all the work to make it, and **too m**. 3498
Lev 7:10 sons of Aaron have, one *as* **m** as another. NIH
13: 7 if the scab **spread m abroad** in 6581+6581
13:22 if it **spread m abroad** in the skin, 6581+6581
13:27 *and* if it be **spread m abroad** in 6581+6581
13:35 if the scall **spread m** in the skin after 6581+6581
14:21 cannot get *so m*; then he shall take one lamb NIH
Nu 16: 3 said unto them, *Ye take* **too m** upon you, 7227
16: 7 *ye take* **too m** upon you, ye sons of Levi. 7227
20:20 Edom came out against him with **m** people, 3515
21: 4 the soul of the people was **m** discouraged NIH
21: 6 bit the people; and **m** people of Israel died. 7227
Dt 2: 5 their land, no, not **so m as** a foot breadth; 5704
3:19 (*for* I know that ye have **m** cattle,) 7227
28:38 Thou shalt carry **m** seed out *into* the field, 7227
31:27 and **how m more** after my death? 637+3588
Jos 11: 4 and all their hosts with them, **m** people, 7227
13: 1 there remaineth *yet* very **m** land to be 7235
19: 9 the children of Judah was **too m** for them: 7227
22: 8 Return with **m** riches unto your tents, and 7227
22: 8 with very **m** cattle, with silver, and 7227
22: 8 and with iron, and with very **m** raiment: 7235
Ru 1:13 for it grieveth me **m** for your sakes that 3966
1Sa 2:16 *then* take *as* **m** as thy soul desireth; NIH
14:30 **How m more**, if haply the people had 637+3588
14:30 for had there not been now a **m greater** 7235
18:30 of Saul; so that his name was **m** set by. 3966
19: 2 Jonathan Saul's son delighted **m** in David: 3966
20:13 LORD do so and **m** more to Jonathan: 3541
23: 3 **how m more** then if we come *to* Keilah 637
26:24 as thy life was **m set by** this day in mine 1431
26:24 let my life be **m set by** in the eyes of 1431
2Sa 4:11 **How m more**, when wicked men have slain 637
8: 8 king David took exceeding **m** brass. 7235
13:34 there came **m** people by the way of the hill 7227
14:25 **so m** praised as Absalom for his beauty: 3966
16:11 **how m more** now *may this* Benjamite 637+3588
17:12 with him there shall not be left **so m as** one. 1571
18:33 the king was **m moved**, and went up to 7264
1Ki 4:29 and understanding exceeding **m**, 7235
8:27 **how m less** this house that I have 637+3588
10: 2 and very **m** gold, and precious stones: 7227
12:28 *It is* too **m** for you to go up *to* Jerusalem: 7227
2Ki 5:13 thou not have done *it?* **how m rather** then, 637
10:18 Baal a little; *but* Jehu shall serve him **m**. 7235
12:10 when they saw that *there was* **m** money in 7227
21: 6 he wrought **m** wickedness in the sight of 7235
21:16 Manasseh shed innocent blood very **m**, 7235
1Ch 18: 8 of Hadarezer, brought David very **m** brass, 7227
20: 2 he brought also exceeding **m** spoil *out* of 7235
22: 4 they of Tyre brought **m** cedar wood to 7230
22: 8 thou hast shed **m** blood upon the earth in 7227
2Ch 2:16 **as m as** thou shalt need: 3605+3509.1
6:18 **how m less** this house which I have 637+3588
14:13 and they carried away very **m** spoil. 7235
14:14 for there was *exceeding* **m** spoil in them. 7227
17:13 he had **m** business in the cities of Judah: 7227
20:25 days in gathering of the spoil, it was so **m**. 7227
2Ch 24:11 when they saw that *there was* **m** money, 7227
25: 9 The LORD is able to give thee **m more** 7235
25:13 three thousand of them, and took **m** spoil. 7227
26:10 for he had **m** cattle, both in the low 7227
27: 3 on the wall of Ophel he built **m**. 7230+3807.1
27: 5 **So m** did the children of Ammon pay unto 2063
28: 8 took also away **m** spoil from them, and 7227
30:13 there assembled *at* Jerusalem **m** people to 7227
32: 4 So there was gathered **m** people together, 7227
32: 4 kings of Assyria come, and find **m** water? 7227
32:15 **how m less** shall your God 637+3588+3808
32:27 Hezekiah had exceeding **m** riches and 7235
32:29 for God had given him substance very **m**. 7227
33: 6 he wrought **m** evil in the sight of 7235
36:14 **transgressed** very **m** after all 4603+4604
Ezr 7:22 *of* oil, and salt without prescribing *how* **m**. NIH
10:13 *it is* a time of **m rain**, and *we are* not able 1653
Ne 4:10 burdens is decayed, and *there is* **m** rubbish; 7235
6:16 they were **m** cast down in their own eyes: 3966
9:37 it yieldeth **m** increase unto the kings whom 7235
Est 1:18 Thus *shall there arise* too **m** contempt and 1767
Job 4:19 **How m less** *in* them that dwell in houses of 637
9:14 **How m less** shall I answer him, *and* 637+3588
15:10 and very aged men, **m** elder than thy father. 3524
15:16 **How m more** abominable and filthy *is* 637+3588
25: 6 **How m less** man, *that is* a worm? and 637+3588
31:25 and because mine hand had gotten **m**; 3524
34:19 *How* **m** *less to him* that accepteth not NIH
42:10 gave Job twice **as m as** he had before. 834+3605
Ps 19:10 *are they* than gold, yea, than **m** fine gold: 7227
33:16 a mighty *man* is not delivered by **m** 7230
35:18 I will praise thee among **m** people. 6099
119:14 way of thy testimonies, as *m as* in all riches. NIH
119:107 I am afflicted **very m**: quicken me, 3966+5704
Pr 7:21 With her **m** fair speech she caused him to 7230
11:31 **m more** the wicked and the sinner. 637+3588
13:23 **M** food *is in* the tillage of the poor: but 7230
14: 4 but **m** increase *is* by the strength of the ox. 7230
15: 6 *In* the house of the righteous *is* **m** treasure: 7227
15:11 **how m more then** the hearts of 637+3588
16:16 **How m** better *is it* to get wisdom than gold! 4100
17: 7 a fool: **m less** do lying lips a prince. 637+3588
19: 7 **how m more** do his friends go far 637+3588
19:10 **m less for** a servant to have rule over 637+3588
19:24 **and** will not **so m as** bring it to his mouth 1571
21:27 **how m more**, *when* he bringeth it 637+3588
25:16 eat **so m as is sufficient** for thee, lest thou 1767
25:27 *It is* not good to eat **m** honey: so *for men* to 7235
Ecc 1:18 For in **m** wisdom *is* much grief: and he that 7230
1:18 For in much wisdom *is* **m** grief: and he that 7230
5:12 *man is* sweet, whether he eat little or **m**: 7235
5:17 *he hath* **m** sorrow and wrath with his 7235
5:20 For he shall not **m** remember the days of 7235
7:16 Be not righteous **over m**; neither make 7235
7:17 Be not **over m** wicked, neither be thou 7235
9:18 of war: but one sinner destroyeth **m** good. 7235
10:18 By **m slothfulness** the building decayeth; 6103
12:12 and **m** study *is* a weariness of the flesh. 7235
SS 4:10 **how m** better is thy love than wine! and 4100
Isa 21: 7 and he hearkened diligently *with* **m** heed: 7227
30:33 the pile thereof *is* fire and **m** wood; 7235
56:12 shall be as this day, *and* **m** more abundant. 3966
Jer 2:22 wash thee with nitre, and **take** thee **m** sope, 7235
2:36 thou about *so* **m** to change thy way? 3966
40:12 gathered wine and summer fruits very **m**. 7235
Eze 14:21 **How m more** when I send my four 637+3588
15: 5 **how m less** shall it be meet yet for 637+3588
17:15 *they* might give him horses and **m** people. 7227
22: 5 *which art* infamous *and* **m** vexed. 7227
23:32 and had in derision; *it* containeth **m**. 4767
26: 7 and companies, and **m** people. 7227
33:31 for with their mouth they shew **m love**, *but* 5690
Da 4:12 the fruit thereof **m**, and in it *was* meat for 7690
4:21 the fruit thereof **m**, and in it *was* meat for 7690
7: 5 said thus unto it, Arise, devour **m** flesh. 7690
7:28 my cogitations **m** troubled me, and 7690
11:13 years with a great army and with **m** riches. 7227
Joel 2: 6 their face *the* people shall be **m pained**: 2342
Jnh 4:11 and their left hand; and *also* **m** cattle? 7227
Na 2:10 **m pain** *is* in all loins, and the faces of them 2479
Hag 1: 6 Ye have sown **m**, and bring in little; *ye* eat, 7235
1: 9 *Ye* looked for **m**, and lo, *it came* to little; 7235
Mal 3:13 What have we spoken so **m** against thee? NIH
Mt 6: 7 they shall be heard for their **m speaking**. *4180*
6:26 Are ye not **m** better than they? *3123*
6:30 *shall he* not **m** more *clothe* you, O ye of *4183*
7:11 **how m** more shall your Father which is in *4214*
10:25 **how m** more *shall they call* them of his *4214*
12:12 **How m** then is a man better than a sheep? *4214*
13: 5 stony *places*, where they had not **m** earth: *4183*
15:33 we have **so m** bread in the wilderness, *5118*
26: 9 this ointment might have been sold for **m**, *4183*
Mk 1:45 and began to publish *it* **m**, and to blaze *4183*
2: 2 *them*, no, **not so m as** about the door: *3366*
3:20 so that they could not **so m as** eat bread. *3383*
4: 5 on stony ground, where it had not **m** earth; *4183*
5:10 And he besought him **m** that he would not *4183*
5:21 the other side, **m** people gathered unto him: *4183*
5:24 and **m** people followed him, and *4183*
6:31 **and** they had **no** leisure **so m as** to *2532+3761*
6:34 saw **m** people, and was moved with *4183*
7:36 **m** the **more** a great deal they published *it*; *3123*
10:14 But when Jesus saw *it*, he was **m displeased**, *23*
10:41 *it*, they began to be **m displeased** with James *23*
12:41 and many *that were* rich cast in **m**. *4183*
Lk 5:15 *m* the more went there a fame abroad of NIG
6: 3 Have ye not read so **m** as this, what David NIG
6:34 to sinners, to receive **as m** again. *2470+3588*
7:11 his disciples went with him, and **m** people. *4183*
7:12 and **m** people of the city was with her. *2425*
7:26 say unto you, and **m more than** a prophet. *4054*
7:47 are many, are forgiven; for she loved **m**: *4183*
8: 4 And when **m** people were gathered *4183*
9:37 down from the hill, **m** people met him. *4183*
10:40 But Martha was cumbered about **m** serving, *4183*
Lk 11:13 **how m** more shall *your* heavenly Father *4214*
12:19 thou hast **m** goods laid up for many years; *4183*
12:24 **how m** more are ye better than the fowls? *4214*
12:28 **how m** more *will he clothe* you, O ye of *4214*
12:48 *stripes*. For unto whomsoever **m** is given, *4183*
12:48 much is given, of him shall be **m** required: *4183*
12:48 and to whom *men* have committed **m**, *4183*
16: 5 the first, **How m** owest thou unto my lord? *4214*
16: 7 said he to another, And **how m** owest thou? *4214*
16:10 in *that which is* least is faithful also in **m**: *4183*
16:10 that is unjust in the least is unjust also in **m**. *4183*
18:13 would **not** lift up **so m as** *his* eyes unto *3761*
18:39 but he cried *so* **m** the more, *Thou* Son of *4183*
19:15 that he might know **how m** every *man* had *5101*
24: 4 as they were *m* perplexed thereabout, NIG
Jn 3:23 to Salim, because there was **m** water there: *4183*
6:10 Now there was **m** grass in the place. So *4183*
6:11 likewise of the fishes **as m as** they would. *3745*
7:12 And there was **m** murmuring among *4183*
12: 9 **M** people of the Jews therefore knew that *4183*
12:12 On the next day **m** people that were come *4183*
12:24 but if it die, it bringeth forth **m** fruit. *4183*
14:30 Hereafter I will not talk **m** with you: for *4183*
15: 5 I in him, the same bringeth forth **m** fruit: *4183*
15: 8 is my Father glorified, that ye bear **m** fruit; *4183*
Ac 5: 8 Tell me whether ye sold the land for **so m**? *5118*
5: 8 so much? And she said, Yea, for **so m**. *5118*
5:37 and drew away **m** people after him: *2425*
7: 5 in it, **no, not so m** as to set his foot on: *3761*
9:13 how **m** evil he hath done to thy saints at *3745*
10: 2 which gave **m** alms to the people, and *4183*
11:24 and **m** people was added unto the Lord. *2425*
11:26 and taught **m** people, and the disciples were *2425*
14:22 that we must through **m** tribulation enter *4183*
15: 7 And when there had been **m** disputing, *4183*
16:16 which brought her masters **m** gain by *4183*
18:10 hurt thee: for I have **m** people in this city. *4183*
18:27 helped them **m** which had believed through *4183*
19: 2 We have **not so m as** heard whether *235+3761*
19:26 hath persuaded and turned away **m** people, *2425*
20: 2 and had given them **m** exhortation, he came *4183*
26:24 **m** learning doth make thee mad. *4183*
27: 9 Now when **m** time was spent, and *2425*
27:10 voyage will be with hurt and **m** damage, *4183*
27:16 we **had m work** to come by the boat: *2480+3433*
Ro 1:15 So, **as m as** in me is, I am ready to preach *2596*
3: 2 **M** every way: chiefly, because that unto *4183*
5: 9 **M** more then, being now justified by his *4183*
5:10 **m** more, being reconciled, we shall be *4183*
5:15 **m** more the grace of God, and the gift by *4183*
5:17 **m** more they which receive abundance of *4183*
5:20 sin abounded, grace did **m more abound**: *5248*
9:22 endured with **m** longsuffering *the* vessels *4183*
11:12 of the Gentiles; **how m** more their fulness? *4214*
11:24 **how m** more shall these, which be *4214*
12:18 If *it be* possible, **as m as lieth in** you, *1537*
15:22 For which cause also I have been **m** *4183*
16: 6 Greet Mary, who bestowed **m** labour on us. *4183*
16:12 which laboured **m** in the Lord. *4183*
1Co 2: 3 and in fear, and in **m** trembling. *4183*
5: 1 such fornication as is **not so m as** named *3761*
6: 3 **how m more** *things* that pertain to *this* life? *3386*
12:22 Nay, **m** more those members of the body, *4183*
16:19 and Priscilla salute you **m** in the Lord, *4183*
2Co 2: 4 For out of **m** affliction and anguish of heart *4183*
3: 9 **m** more doth the ministration of *4183*
3:11 **m** more that which remaineth *is* glorious. *4183*
6: 4 in **m** patience, in afflictions, in necessities, *4183*
8: 4 Praying us with **m** intreaty that we would *4183*
8:15 He that *had gathered* **m** had nothing over; *4183*
8:22 in many *things*, but now **m** more diligent, *4183*
Php 1:14 are **m more** bold to speak the word without *4056*
2:12 but now **m** more in my absence, *4183*
1Th 1: 5 and in the Holy Ghost, and in **m** assurance; *4183*
1: 6 having received the word in **m** affliction, *4183*
2: 2 you the gospel of God with **m** contention. *4183*
1Ti 3: 8 not doubletongued, not given to **m** wine, *4183*
2Ti 4:14 Alexander the coppersmith did me **m** evil: *4183*
Tit 2: 3 not false accusers, not given to **m** wine, *4183*
Phm 1: 8 though I might be **m** bold in Christ to *4183*
1:16 specially to me, but **how m** more unto thee, *4214*
Heb 1: 4 Being made **so m** better than the angels, *5118*
7:22 **so m** was Jesus made a surety of a better *5118*
8: 6 by **how m** also he is the mediator of a *3745*
9:14 **How m** more shall the blood of Christ, *4214*
10:25 exhorting *one another*: and **so m** the more, *5118*
10:29 Of **how m** sorer punishment, suppose ye, *4214*
12: 9 shall we not **m** rather be in subjection unto *4183*
12:20 And if *so m as* a beast touch the mountain, NIG
12:25 **m** more *shall not* we *escape*, if we turn *4183*
Jas 5:16 prayer of a righteous *man* availeth **m**. *4183*
1Pe 1: 7 *being* **m** more precious than of gold that *4183*
2Pe 2:18 lusts of the flesh, through **m** wantonness, NIG
Rev 5: 4 And I wept **m**, because no *man* was found *4183*
8: 3 and there was given unto him **m** incense, *4183*
18: 7 **How m** she hath glorified herself, and *3745*
18: 7 **so m** torment and sorrow give her: *5118*
19: 1 heard a great voice of **m** people in heaven, *4183*

MUDDY See FOUL

MUFFLERS (1)
Isa 3:19 The chains, and the bracelets, and the **m**, 7479

MULBERRY (4)
2Sa 5:23 come upon them over against the **m trees**. 1057
5:24 sound of a going in the tops of the **m trees**, 1057
1Ch 14:14 come upon them over against the **m trees**. 1057
14:15 a sound of going in the tops of the **m trees**, 1057

MULE (9) [MULES, MULES']
2Sa 13:29 every man gat him up upon his **m**, and fled. 6505
18: 9 Absalom rode upon a **m**, and the mule went 6505
18: 9 the **m** went under the thick boughs of a 6505

2Sa 18: 9 and the **m** that *was* under him went away. 6505
1Ki 1:33 Solomon my son to ride upon mine own **m**, 6506
1:38 Solomon to ride upon king David's **m**, 6506
1:44 have caused him to ride upon the king's **m**: 6506
Ps 32: 9 Be ye not as the horse, *or* as the **m**, 6505
Zec 14:15 of the **m**, of the camel, and of the ass, and 6505

MULES (11) [MULE]

Ge 36:24 this *was that* Anah that found the **m** in 3222
1Ki 10:25 and armour, and spices, horses, and **m**, 6505
18: 5 find grass to save the horses and **m** alive, 6505
1Ch 12:40 and on **m**, and on oxen, *and* meat, meal, 6505
2Ch 9:24 raiment, harness, and spices, horses, and **m**, 6505
Ezr 2:66 six; their **m**, two hundred forty and five; 6505
Ne 7:68 six: their **m**, two hundred forty and five: 6505
Est 8:10 *and* riders on **m**, camels, *and* 7409
8:14 *So* the posts that rode upon **m** *and* 7409
Isa 66:20 and upon **m**, and upon swift beasts, 6505
Eze 27:14 thy fairs with horses and horsemen and **m**. 6505

MULES' (1) [MULE]

2Ki 5:17 be given to thy servant two **m** burden of 6505

MULTIPLIED (44) [MULTIPLY]

Ge 47:27 and grew, and **m** exceedingly. 7235
Ex 1: 7 and **m**, and waxed exceeding mighty; 7235
1:12 afflicted them, the more they **m** and grew. 7235
1:20 and the people **m**, and waxed very mighty. 7235
11: 9 that my wonders may be **m** in the land of 7235
Dt 1:10 The LORD your God hath **m** you, and 7235
8:13 thy silver and thy gold is **m**, and all that 7235
8:13 is multiplied, and all that thou hast is **m**; 7235
11:21 That your days may be **m**, and the days of 7235
Jos 24: 3 and **m** his seed, and gave him Isaac. 7235
1Ch 5: 9 their cattle were **m** in the land of Gilead. 7235
Job 27:14 If his children be **m**, *it is* for the sword: and 7235
35: 6 or *if* thy transgressions be **m**, what doest 7231
Ps 16: 4 Their sorrows shall be **m** *that* hasten *after* 7235
38:19 and they that hate me wrongfully are **m**. 7231
107:38 them also, so that they are **m** greatly; 7235
Pr 9:11 For by me thy days shall be **m**, and 7235
29:16 When the wicked are **m**, 7235
Isa 9: 3 Thou hast **m** the nation, *and* not increased 7235
59:12 For our transgressions are **m** before thee, 7231
Jer 3:16 when ye be **m** and increased in the land, 7235
Eze 5: 7 Because ye **m** more than the nations that 1995
11: 6 Ye have **m** your slain in this city, and 7235
16:25 one that passed by, and **m** thy whoredoms. 7235
16:29 Thou hast moreover **m** thy fornication in 7235
16:51 thou hast **m** thine abominations more than 7235
21:15 *their* heart may faint, and *their* ruins be **m**: 7235
23:19 Yet she **m** her whoredoms, in calling to 7235
31: 5 his boughs were **m**, and his branches 7235
35:13 and have **m** your words against me: 6280
Da 4: 1 dwell in all the earth; Peace be **m** unto you. 7680
6:25 dwell in all the earth; Peace be **m** unto you. 7680
Hos 2: 8 and oil, and **m** her silver and gold, 7235
8:14 and Judah hath **m** fenced cities: 7235
12:10 I have **m** visions, and used similitudes by 7235
Na 3:16 Thou hast **m** thy merchants above the stars 7235
Ac 6: 1 when the number of the disciples was **m**, *4129*
6: 7 the number of the disciples **m** in Jerusalem *4129*
7:17 the people grew and **m** in Egypt, *4129*
9:31 in the comfort of the Holy Ghost, were **m**. *4129*
12:24 But the word of God grew and **m**. *4129*
1Pe 1: 2 Grace unto you, and peace, be **m**. *4129*
2Pe 1: 2 peace be **m** unto you through *4129*
Jude 1: 2 Mercy unto you, and peace, and love, be **m**. *4129*

MULTIPLIEDST (1) [MULTIPLY]

Ne 9:23 Their children also **m** thou as the stars of 7235

MULTIPLIETH (3) [MULTIPLY]

Job 9:17 and **m** my wounds without cause. 7235
34:37 amongst us, and **m** his words against God. 7235
35:16 in vain; he **m** words without knowledge. 3527

MULTIPLY (46) [MULTIPLIED, MULTIPLIEDST, MULTIPLIETH, MULTIPLYING]

Ge 1:22 **m**, and fill the waters in the seas, and let 7235
1:22 in the seas, and let fowl **m** in the earth. 7235
1:28 **m**, and replenish the earth, and subdue it: 7235
3:16 I will **greatly m** thy sorrow and 7235+7235
6: 1 when men began to **m** on the face of 7231
8:17 and be fruitful, and **m** upon the earth. 7235
9: 1 Be fruitful, and **m**, and replenish the earth. 7235
9: 7 you, be ye fruitful, and **m**; bring forth 7235
9: 7 abundantly in the earth, and **m** therein. 7235
16:10 I will **m** thy seed **exceedingly**, that it 7235+7235
17: 2 and thee, and will **m** thee exceedingly. 7235
17:20 him fruitful, and will **m** him exceedingly; 7235
22:17 in multiplying I will **m** thy seed as the stars 7235
26: 4 I will **make** thy seed **to m** as the stars of 7235
26:24 **m** thy seed for my servant Abraham's sake. 7235
28: 3 and make thee fruitful, and **m** thee, 7235
35:11 be fruitful and **m**; a nation and a company 7235
48: 4 **m** thee, and I will make of thee a multitude 7235
Ex 1:10 lest they **m**, and it come to pass, that, 7235
7: 3 **m** my signs and my wonders in the land of 7235
23:29 and the beast of the field **m** against thee. 7227
32:13 I will **m** your seed as the stars of heaven, 7235
Lev 26: 9 **m** you, and establish my covenant with 7235
Dt 7:13 will love thee, and bless thee, and **m** thee: 7235
8: 1 **m**, and go in and possess the land which 7235
8:13 *when* thy herds and thy flocks **m**, and thy 7235
13:17 have compassion upon thee, and **m** thee, 7235
17:16 he shall not **m** horses to himself, nor cause 7235
17:16 to the end that he should **m** horses: 7235
17:17 Neither shall he **m** wives to himself, 7235
17:17 neither shall he greatly **m** to himself silver 7235
28:63 over you to do you good, and to **m** you; 7235
30: 5 do thee good, and **m** thee above thy fathers. 7235
30:16 his judgments, that thou mayest live and **m**: 7235
1Ch 4:27 neither did all their family **m**, like to 7235
Job 29:18 my nest, and I shall **m** *my* days as the sand. 7235
Jer 30:19 I will **m** them, and they shall not be few; 7235
33:22 so will I **m** the seed of David my servant, 7235
Eze 16: 7 I have caused thee to **m** as the bud of 7233
36:10 I will **m** men upon you, all the house of 7235
36:11 I will **m** upon you man and beast; and 7235
36:30 I will **m** the fruit of the tree, and 7235
37:26 **m** them, and will set my sanctuary in 7235
Am 4: 4 *at* Gilgal **m** transgression; and bring your 7235
2Co 9:10 and **m** your seed sown, and increase *4129*
Heb 6:14 bless thee, and multiplying I will **m** thee. *4129*

MULTIPLYING (2) [MULTIPLY]

Ge 22:17 in **m** I will multiply thy seed as the stars of 7235
Heb 6:14 I will bless thee, and **m** I will multiply thee. *4129*

MULTITUDE (243) [MULTITUDES]

Ge 16:10 that it shall not be numbered for **m**. 7230
28: 3 that thou mayest be a **m** of people; 6951
30:30 I *came,* and it is *now* increased unto a **m**; 7230
32:12 the sea, which cannot be numbered for **m**. 7230
48: 4 and I will make of thee a **m** of people; 6951
48:16 let them grow into a **m** in the midst of 7230
48:19 and his seed shall become a **m** of nations. 4393
Ex 12:38 a mixed **m** went up also with them; and 7227
23: 2 Thou shalt not follow a **m** to *do* evil; 7227
Lev 25:16 According to the **m** of years thou shalt 7230
Nu 11: 4 the **mixt m** that *was* among them fell a 628
32: 1 the children of Gad had a very great **m** of 7227
Dt 1:10 *are this* day as the stars of heaven for **m**. 7230
10:22 made thee as the stars of heaven for **m**. 7230
28:62 ye were as the stars of heaven for **m**; 7230
Jos 11: 4 as the sand that *is* upon the sea shore in **m**, 7230
Jdg 4: 7 Jabin's army, with his chariots and his **m**; 1995
6: 5 and they came as grasshoppers for **m**; 7230
7:12 along in the valley like grasshoppers for **m**; 7230
7:12 as the sand by the sea side for **m**. 7230
1Sa 13: 5 as the sand which *is* on the sea shore in **m**: 7230
14:16 the **m** melted away, and they went on 1995
2Sa 6:19 *even* among the whole **m** of Israel, as well 1995
17:11 as the sand that *is* by the sea for **m**; 7230
1Ki 3: 8 cannot be numbered nor counted for **m**. 7230
4:20 as the sand which *is* by the sea in **m**, eating 7230
8: 5 that could not be told nor numbered for **m**. 7230
20:13 Hast thou seen all this great **m**? 1995
20:28 will I deliver all this great **m** into thine 1995
2Ki 7:13 they *are* as all the **m** of Israel that are left in 1995
7:13 *I say,* they *are even* as all the **m** of 1995
19:23 With the **m** of my chariots I am come up *to* 7230
25:11 of Babylon, with the remnant of the **m**, 1995
2Ch 1: 9 a people like the dust of the earth **in m**. 7227
5: 6 could not be told nor numbered for **m**. 7230
13: 8 ye *be* a great **m**, and *there are* with you 1995
14:11 and in thy name we go against this **m**. 1995
20: 2 There cometh a great **m** against thee from 1995
20:15 nor dismayed by reason of this great **m**; 1995
20:24 they looked unto the **m**, and, behold, 1995
28: 5 carried away a **great m** of them captives, 1419
30:18 For a **m** of the people, *even* many of 4768
32: 7 nor for all the **m** that *is* with him: 1995
Ne 13: 3 they separated from Israel all the **mixed m**. 6154
Est 5:11 the **m** of his children, and all *the things* 7230
10: 3 and accepted of the **m** of his brethren, 7230
Job 11: 2 Should not the **m** of words be answered? 7230
31:34 Did I fear a great **m**, or did the contempt of 1995
32: 7 and **m** of years should teach wisdom. 7230
33:19 and the **m** of his bones *with* strong *pain:* 7379
35: 9 By reason of the **m** of oppressions they 7230
39: 7 He scorneth the **m** of the city, 1995
Ps 5: 7 I will come *into* thy house in the **m** of thy 7230
5:10 cast them out in the **m** of their 7230
33:16 There is no king saved by the **m** of a host: 7230
42: 4 for I had gone with the **m**, I went with them 5519
42: 4 and praise, *with* a **m** that kept holyday. 1995
49: 6 boast themselves in the **m** of their riches; 7230
51: 1 according unto the **m** of thy tender mercies 7230
68:30 the **m** of the bulls, with the calves of 5712
69:13 O God, in the **m** of thy mercy hear me, 7230
69:16 turn unto me according to the **m** of thy 7230
74:19 **m** *of the wicked:* forget not 2416
94:19 In the **m** of my thoughts within me thy 7230
97: 1 let the **m** of isles be glad *thereof.* 7227
106: 7 they remembered not the **m** of thy mercies; 7230
106:45 repented according to the **m** of his mercies. 7230
109:30 yea, I will praise him among the **m**. 7227
Pr 10:19 In the **m** of words there wanteth not sin: but 7230
11:14 but in the **m** of counsellers *there is* safety. 7230
14:28 In the **m** of people *is* the king's honour: but 7230
15:22 in the **m** of counsellers *they* are established. 7230
20:15 There is gold, and a **m** of rubies: but 7230
24: 6 and in **m** of counsellers *there is* safety. 7230
Ecc 5: 3 For a dream cometh through the **m** of 7230
5: 3 and a fool's voice *is known* by **m** of words. 7230
5: 7 For in the **m** of dreams and many words 7230
Isa 1:11 To what purpose *is* the **m** of your sacrifices 7230
5:13 and their **m** dried up with thirst. 1995
5:14 their **m**, and their pomp, and he that 1995
13: 4 The noise of a **m** in the mountains, like as 1995
16:14 shall be contemned, with all *that* great **m**; 1995
17:12 Woe to the **m** of many people, *which* make 1995
29: 5 Moreover the **m** of thy strangers shall be 1995
29: 5 the **m** of the terrible ones *shall be* as chaff 1995
29: 7 the **m** of all the nations that fight against 1995
29: 8 so shall the **m** of all the nations be, 1995
31: 4 when a **m** of shepherds is called forth 4393
32:14 the **m** of the city shall be left; the forts and 1995
37:24 By the **m** of my chariots am I come up *to* 7230
47: 9 their perfection for the **m** of thy sorceries, 7230
47:12 and with the **m** of thy sorceries, 7230
47:13 Thou art wearied in the **m** of thy counsels. 7230
60: 6 The **m** of camels shall cover thee, 8229
63: 7 according to the **m** of his lovingkindnesses. 7230
Jer 3:23 the hills, *and from* the **m** of mountains: 1995
10:13 *there is* a **m** of waters in the heavens, and 1995
12: 6 yea, they have called a **m** after thee: 4392
30:14 of a cruel one, for the **m** of thine iniquity; 7230
30:15 thy sorrow *is* incurable for the **m** of thine 7230
44:15 all the women that stood *by,* a great **m**, 6951
46:25 I will punish the **m** of No, and Pharaoh, and 527
49:32 be a booty, and the **m** of their cattle a spoil: 1995
51:16 *there is* a **m** of waters in the heavens; 1995
51:42 she is covered with the **m** of the waves 1995
52:15 to the king of Babylon, and the rest of the **m**. 527
La 1: 5 for the LORD hath afflicted her for the **m** 7230
3:32 according to the **m** of his mercies. 7230
Eze 7:11 none of them *shall remain,* nor of their **m**, 1995
7:12 for wrath *is* upon all the **m** thereof. 1995
7:13 for the vision *is* touching the whole **m** 1995
7:14 for my wrath *is* upon all the **m** thereof. 1995
14: 4 that cometh according to the **m** of his idols; 7230
19:11 she appeared in her height with the **m** of 7230
23:42 a voice of a **m** being at ease *was* with her: 1995
27:12 by reason of the **m** of all *kind of* riches; 7230
27:16 Syria *was* thy merchant by reason of the **m** 7230
27:18 Damascus *was* thy merchant in the **m** of 7230
27:18 of thy making, for the **m** of all riches; 7230
27:33 kings of the earth with the **m** of thy riches 7230
28:16 By the **m** of thy merchandise they have 7230
28:18 Thou hast defiled thy sanctuaries by the **m** 7230
29:19 he shall take her **m**, and take her spoil, 1995
30: 4 they shall take *away* her **m**, and 1995
30:10 I will also make the **m** of Egypt to cease by 1995
30:15 of Egypt; and I will cut off the **m** of No. 1995
31: 2 unto Pharaoh king of Egypt, and to his **m**; 1995
31: 5 became long because of the **m** of waters, 7227
31: 9 I have made him fair by the **m** of his 7230
31:18 This *is* Pharaoh and all his **m**, saith 1995
32:12 of the mighty will I cause thy **m** to fall, 1995
32:12 and all the **m** thereof shall be destroyed. 1995
32:16 *even* for Egypt, and for all her **m**, saith 1995
32:18 wail for the **m** of Egypt, and cast them 1995
32:24 and all her **m** round about her grave, 1995
32:25 bed in the midst of the slain with all her **m**: 1995
32:26 There *is* Meshech, Tubal, and all her **m**: 1995
32:31 shall be comforted over all his **m**, 1995
32:32 *even* Pharaoh and all his **m**, saith the Lord 1995
39:11 and there shall they bury Gog and all his **m**: 1995
47: 9 there shall be a very **great m** of fish, 7227
Da 10: 6 the voice of his words like the voice of a **m**. 1995
11:10 and shall assemble a **m** of great forces: 1995
11:11 he shall set forth a great **m**; but 1995
11:11 but the **m** shall be given into his hand. 1995
11:12 *And* when he hath taken away the **m**, his 1995
11:13 shall set forth a **m** greater than the former, 1995
Hos 9: 7 for the **m** of thine iniquity, and the great 7230
10: 1 according to the **m** of his fruit he hath 7230
10:13 in thy way, in the **m** of thy mighty *men.* 7230
Mic 2:12 great noise by reason of *the* **m** *of* men. NIH
Na 3: 3 *there is* a **m** of slain, and a great number of 7230
3: 4 Because of the **m** of the whoredoms of 7230
Zec 2: 4 *as* towns without walls for the **m** of men 7230
Mt 13: 2 sat; and the whole **m** stood on the shore. *3793*
13:34 All these *things* spake Jesus unto the **m** in *3793*
13:36 Then Jesus sent the **m** away, and went into *3793*
14: 5 he feared the **m**, because they counted him *3793*
14:14 and saw a great **m**, and was moved with *3793*
14:15 send the **m** away, that they may go into *3793*
14:19 And he commanded the **m** to sit down on *3793*
14:19 to *his* disciples, and the disciples to the **m**. *3793*
15:10 And he called the **m**, and said unto them, *3793*
15:31 Insomuch that the **m** wondered, when they *3793*
15:32 and said, I have compassion on the **m**, *3793*
15:33 in the wilderness, as to fill so great a **m**? *3793*
15:35 And he commanded the **m** to sit down on *3793*
15:36 to his disciples, and the disciples to the **m**. *3793*
15:39 And he sent away the **m**, and took ship, and *3793*
17:14 And when they were come to the **m**, *3793*
20:29 from Jericho, a great **m** followed him. *3793*
20:31 And the **m** rebuked them, because *3793*
21: 8 And a very great **m** spread their garments *3793*
21:11 And the **m** said, This is Jesus the prophet of *3793*
21:46 they feared the **m**, because they took him *3793*
22:33 And when the **m** heard *this,* they were *3793*
23: 1 Then spake Jesus to the **m**, and to his *3793*
26:47 and with him a great **m** with swords and *3793*
27:20 elders persuaded the **m** that they should ask *3793*
27:24 and washed *his* hands before the **m**, saying, *3793*
Mk 2:13 and all the **m** resorted unto him, and *3793*
3: 7 and a great **m** from Galilee followed him, *4128*
3: 8 and they about Tyre and Sidon, a great **m**, *4128*
3: 9 ship should wait on him because of the **m**, *3793*
3:20 And the **m** cometh together again, so *3793*
3:32 And *the* **m** sat about him, and they said *3793*
4: 1 and there was gathered unto him a great **m**, *3793*
4: 1 the whole **m** was by the sea on the land. *3793*
4:36 And when they had sent away the **m**, *3793*
5:31 Thou seest the **m** thronging thee, and *3793*
7:33 And he took him aside from the **m**, and *3793*
8: 1 In those days the **m** being very great, *3793*
8: 2 I have compassion on the **m**, because *3793*
9:14 he saw a great **m** about them, and *3793*
9:17 And one of the **m** answered and said, *3793*
14:43 and with him a great **m** with swords and *3793*
15: 8 And the **m** crying aloud began to desire *3793*
Lk 1:10 And the whole **m** of the people were *4128*
2:13 And suddenly there was with the angel a **m** *4128*
3: 7 Then said he to the **m** that came forth to be *3793*
5: 6 this done, they inclosed a great **m** of fishes: *4128*
5:19 they might bring him in because of the **m**, *3793*
6:17 and a great **m** of people out of all Judea and *4128*
6:19 And the whole **m** sought to touch him: *3793*
8:37 Then the whole **m** of the country of *4128*
8:45 the **m** throng thee and press *thee,* and *3793*
9:12 and said unto him, Send the **m** away, *3793*
9:16 gave to the disciples to set before the **m**. *3793*
12: 1 together an **innumerable m** of people, *3461*
18:36 And hearing the **m** pass by, he asked what *3793*
19:37 the whole **m** of the disciples began to *4128*
19:39 Pharisees from among the **m** said unto him, *3793*
22: 6 him unto them in the absence of the **m**. *3793*

Lk 22:47 behold a **m**, and he that was called Judas, *3793*
23: 1 And the whole **m** of them arose, and *4128*
Jn 5: 3 In these lay a great **m** of impotent *folk*, of *4128*
5:13 himself away, a **m** being in *that* place. *3793*
6: 2 And a great **m** followed him, because *3793*
21: 6 now they were not able to draw it for the **m** *4128*
Ac 2: 6 the **m** came together, and were confounded, *4128*
4:32 And the **m** of them that believed were of *4128*
5:16 There came also a **m** *out* of the cities round *4128*
6: 2 Then the twelve called the **m** of *4128*
6: 5 And the saying pleased the whole **m**: and *4128*
14: 1 that a great **m** both of the Jews and *also* of *4128*
14: 4 But the **m** of the city was divided: and *4128*
15:12 Then all the **m** kept silence, and *4128*
15:30 and when they had gathered the **m** together, *4128*
16:22 And the **m** rose up together against them: *3793*
17: 4 and of the devout Greeks a great **m**, and *4128*
19: 9 but spake evil of *that* way before the **m**, *4128*
19:33 And they drew Alexander out of the **m**, *3793*
21:22 the **m** must needs come together: for they *4128*
21:34 one *thing*, some another, among the **m**: *3793*
21:36 For the **m** of the people followed *after*, *4128*
23: 7 and the Sadducees: and the **m** was divided. *4128*
24:18 the temple, neither with **m**, nor with tumult. *3793*
25:24 ye see this *man*, about whom all the **m** of *4128*
Heb 11:12 *so many* as the stars of the sky in **m**, and *4128*
Jas 5:20 soul from death, and shall hide a **m** of sins. *4128*
1Pe 4: 8 for charity shall cover the **m** of sins. *4128*
Rev 7: 9 After this I beheld, and lo, a great **m**, *3793*
19: 6 I heard as *it were* the voice of a great **m**, *3793*

MULTITUDES (24) [MULTITUDE]

Eze 32:20 *to* the sword: draw her and all her **m**. 1995
Joel 3:14 **M**, multitudes in the valley of decision: 1995
3:14 Multitudes, **m** in the valley of decision: 1995
Mt 4:25 And there followed him great **m** *of people* *3793*
5: 1 And seeing the **m**, he went up into a *3793*
8: 1 from the mountain, great **m** followed him. *3793*
8:18 Now when Jesus saw great **m** about him, *3793*
9: 8 But when the **m** saw *it*, they marvelled, *3793*
9:33 and the **m** marvelled, saying, It was never *3793*
9:36 But when he saw the **m**, he was moved *3793*
11: 7 Jesus began to say unto the **m** concerning *3793*
12:15 and great **m** followed him, and he healed *3793*
13: 2 And great **m** were gathered together unto *3793*
14:22 the other side, while he sent the **m** away. *3793*
14:23 And when he had sent the **m** away, he went *3793*
15:30 And great **m** came unto him, having with *3793*
19: 2 And great **m** followed him; and he healed *3793*
21: 9 And the **m** that went before, *3793*
26:55 In that *same* hour said Jesus to the **m**, *3793*
Lk 5:15 and great **m** came together to hear, and *3793*
14:25 And there went great **m** with him: and *3793*
Ac 5:14 to the Lord, **m** both of men and women.) *4128*
13:45 But when the Jews saw the **m**, they were *3793*
Rev 17:15 and **m**, and nations, and tongues. *3793*

MUNITION (2) [MUNITIONS]

Isa 29: 7 even all that fight against her and her **m**, 4685
Na 2: 1 keep the **m**, watch the way, make *thy* loins 4694

MUNITIONS (1) [MUNITION]

Isa 33:16 his place of defence *shall be* the **m** of 4679

MUPPIM (1)

Ge 46:21 Ehi, and Rosh, **M**, and Huppim, and Ard. 4649

MURDER (9) [MURDERER, MURDERERS, MURDERS]

Ps 10: 8 in the secret places doth he **m** the innocent: 2026
94: 6 and the stranger, and **m** the fatherless. 7523
Jer 7: 9 **m**, and commit adultery, and swear falsely, 7523
Hos 6: 9 the company of priests **m** *in* the way by 7523
Mt 19:18 Jesus said, Thou shalt do no **m**, Thou shalt *5407*
Mk 15: 7 who had committed **m** in the insurrection. *5408*
Lk 23:19 in the city, and *for* **m**, was cast into prison.) *5408*
23:25 that for sedition and **m** was cast into prison, *5408*
Ro 1:29 full of envy, **m**, debate, deceit, malignity; *5408*

MURDERER (20) [MURDER]

Nu 35:16 instrument of iron, so that he die, he *is* a **m**: 7523
35:16 the **m** shall surely be put to death. 7523
35:17 he may die, and he die, he *is* a **m**: 7523
35:17 the **m** shall surely be put to death. 7523
35:18 he may die, and he die, he *is* a **m**: 7523
35:18 the **m** shall surely be put to death. 7523
35:19 revenger of blood himself shall slay the **m**: 7523
35:21 shall surely be put to death; *for* he *is* a **m**: 7523
35:21 the revenger of blood shall slay the **m**, 7523
35:30 the **m** shall be put to death by the mouth of 7523
35:31 shall take no satisfaction for the life of a **m**, 7523
2Ki 6:32 See ye how this son of a **m** hath sent to take 7523
Job 24:14 The **m** rising with the light killeth the poor 7523
Hos 9:13 *shall* bring forth his children to the **m**. 2026
Jn 8:44 He was a **m** from the beginning, and *443*
Ac 3:14 desired a **m** to be granted unto you; *435+5406*
28: 4 No doubt this man is a **m**, whom, *5406*
1Pe 4:15 But let none of you suffer as a **m**, or *as* a *5406*
1Jn 3:15 Whosoever hateth his brother is a **m**: and *443*
3:15 ye know that no **m** hath eternal life abiding *443*

MURDERERS (10) [MURDER]

2Ki 14: 6 the children of the **m** he slew not: 5221
Isa 1:21 righteousness lodged in it; but now **m**. 7523
Jer 4:31 for my soul is wearied because of **m**. 2026
Mt 22: 7 and destroyed those **m**, and burnt up their *5406*
Ac 7:52 ye have been now the betrayers and **m**: *5406*
21:38 wilderness four thousand men that were **m**? *4607*
1Ti 1: 9 for **m of fathers** and murderers of mothers, *3964*
1: 9 for murderers of fathers and **m of mothers**, *3389*
Rev 21: 8 and **m**, and whoremongers, and sorcerers, *5406*
22:15 and **m**, and idolaters, and whosoever loveth *5406*

MURDERS (4) [MURDER]

Mt 15:19 **m**, adulteries, fornications, thefts, *5408*
Mk 7:21 evil thoughts, adulteries, fornications, **m**, *5408*
Gal 5:21 Envyings, **m**, drunkenness, revellings, and *5408*
Rev 9:21 Neither repented they of their **m**, nor of *5408*

MURMUR (9) [MURMURED, MURMURERS, MURMURING, MURMURINGS]

Ex 16: 7 and what *are* we, that ye **m** against us? 3885
16: 8 your murmurings which ye **m** against him: 3885
Nu 14:27 evil congregation, which **m** against me? 3885
14:27 of Israel, which they **m** against me. 3885
14:36 **made** all the congregation **to m** against 3885
16:11 and what *is* Aaron, that ye **m** against him? 3885
17: 5 of Israel, whereby they **m** against you. 3885
Jn 6:43 said unto them, **M** not among yourselves. *1111*
1Co 10:10 Neither **m** ye, as some of them also *1111*

MURMURED (19) [MURMUR]

Ex 15:24 the people **m** against Moses, saying, 3885
16: 2 of the children of Israel **m** against Moses 3885
17: 3 the people **m** against Moses, and said, 3885
Nu 14: 2 all the children of Israel **m** against Moses 3885
14:29 and upward, which have **m** against me, 3885
16:41 of the children of Israel **m** against Moses 3885
Dt 1:27 ye **m** in your tents, and said, Because 7279
Jos 9:18 all the congregation **m** against the princes. 3885
Ps 106:25 **m** in their tents, *and* hearkened not unto 7279
Isa 29:24 and they that **m** shall learn doctrine. 7279
Mt 20:11 And when they had received *it*, they **m** *1111*
Mk 14: 5 given to the poor. And they **m against** her. *1690*
Lk 5:30 and Pharisees **m** against his disciples, *1111*
15: 2 And the Pharisees and scribes **m**, saying, *1234*
19: 7 And when they saw *it*, they all **m**, saying, *1234*
Jn 6:41 The Jews then **m** at him, because he said, *1111*
6:61 knew in himself that his disciples **m** at it, *1111*
7:32 The Pharisees heard that the people **m** such *1111*
1Co 10:10 as some of them also **m**, and *1111*

MURMURERS (1) [MURMUR]

Jude 1:16 These are **m**, complainers, walking after *1113*

MURMURING (2) [MURMUR]

Jn 7:12 And there was much **m** among the people *1112*
Ac 6: 1 there arose a **m** of the Grecians against *1112*

MURMURINGS (9) [MURMUR]

Ex 16: 7 for that he heareth your **m** against 8519
16: 8 for that the LORD heareth your **m** which 8519
16: 8 your **m** *are* not against us, but against 8519
16: 9 the LORD: for he hath heard your **m**. 8519
16:12 I have heard the **m** of the children of Israel: 8519
Nu 14:27 I have heard the **m** of the children of Israel, 8519
17: 5 I will make to cease from me the **m** of 8519
17:10 thou shalt quite take away their **m** from me, 8519
Php 2:14 Do all *things* without **m** and disputings: *1112*

MURRAIN (1)

Ex 9: 3 the sheep: *there shall be* a very grievous **m**. 1698

MUSE (1) [MUSED, MUSING]

Ps 143: 5 thy works; I **m** on the work of thy hands. 7878

MUSED (1) [MUSE]

Lk 3:15 and all *men* **m** in their hearts of John, *1260*

MUSHI (8) [MUSHITES]

Ex 6:19 the sons of Merari; Mahali and **M**: 4187
Nu 3:20 of Merari by their families; Mahli, and **M**. 4187
1Ch 6:19 The sons of Merari; Mahli, and **M**. 4187
6:47 the son of **M**, the son of Merari, the son of 4187
23:21 The sons of Merari; Mahli, and **M**. 4187
23:23 The sons of **M**; Mahli, and Eder, and 4187
24:26 The sons of Merari *were* Mahli and **M**: 4187
24:30 The sons also of **M**; Mahli, and Eder, and 4187

MUSHITES (2) [MUSHI]

Nu 3:33 of the Mahlites, and the family of the **M**: 4188
26:58 family of the Mahlites, the family of the **M**, 4188

MUSICAL (3) [MUSICK]

1Ch 16:42 a sound, and with **m** instruments of God. 7892
Ne 12:36 with the **m** instruments of David the man of 7892
Ecc 2: 8 **m instruments**, and that **of all sorts**. 7705+7705

MUSICIAN (55) [MUSICK]

Ps 4: T To the **chief M** on Neginoth, A Psalm of 5329
5: T To the **chief M** upon Nehiloth, A Psalm of 5329
6: T To the **chief M** on Neginoth upon 5329
8: T To the **chief M** upon Gittith, A Psalm of 5329
9: T To the **chief M** upon Muth-labben, A 5329
11: T To the **chief M**, *A Psalm* of David. 5329
12: T To the **chief M** upon Sheminith, A Psalm 5329
13: T To the **chief M**, A Psalm of David. 5329
14: T To the **chief M**, *A Psalm* of David. 5329
18: T To the **chief M**, *A Psalm* of David, 5329
19: T To the **chief M**, A Psalm of David. 5329
20: T To the **chief M**, A Psalm of David. 5329
21: T To the **chief M**, A Psalm of David. 5329
22: T To the **chief M** upon Aijeleth Shahar, 5329
31: T To the **chief M**, A Psalm of David. 5329
36: T To the **chief M**, *A Psalm* of David 5329
39: T To the **chief M**, *even* to Jeduthun, A Psalm 5329
40: T To the **chief M**, A Psalm of David. 5329
41: T To the **chief M**, A Psalm of David. 5329
42: T To the **chief M**, Maschil, for the sons of 5329
44: T To the **chief M** for the sons of Korah, 5329
45: T To the **chief M** upon Shoshannim, for 5329
46: T To the **chief M** for the sons of Korah, 5329
47: T To the **chief M**, A Psalm for the sons of 5329
49: T To the **chief M**, A Psalm for the sons of 5329
51: T To the **chief M**, A Psalm of David, 5329
52: T To the **chief M**, Maschil, *A Psalm* of 5329
53: T To the **chief M** upon Mahalath, Maschil, 5329
54: T To the **chief M** on Neginoth, Maschil, 5329
55: T To the **chief M** on Neginoth, Maschil, 5329
56: T To the **chief M** upon 5329
57: T To the **chief M**, Al-taschith, Michtam of 5329
58: T To the **chief M**, Al-taschith, Michtam of 5329
59: T To the **chief M**, Al-taschith, Michtam of 5329
60: T To the **chief M** upon Shushan-eduth, 5329
61: T To the **chief M** upon Neginah, *A Psalm* of 5329
62: T To the **chief M**, to Jeduthun, A Psalm of 5329
64: T To the **chief M**, A Psalm of David. 5329
65: T To the **chief M**, A Psalm *and* Song of 5329
66: T To the **chief M**, A Song *or* Psalm. 5329
67: T To the **chief M** on Neginoth, A Psalm *or* 5329
68: T To the **chief M**, A Psalm *or* Song of David. 5329
69: T To the **chief M** upon Shoshannim, *A Psalm* 5329
70: T To the **chief M**, *A Psalm* of David, to bring 5329
75: T To the **chief M**, Al-taschith, A Psalm *or* 5329
76: T To the **chief M** on Neginoth, A Psalm *or* 5329
77: T To the **chief M**, to Jeduthun, A Psalm of 5329
80: T To the **chief M** upon Shoshannim-Eduth, A 5329
81: T To the **chief M** upon Gittith, *A Psalm* of 5329
84: T To the **chief M** upon Gittith, A Psalm for 5329
85: T To the **chief M**, A Psalm for the sons of 5329
88: T To the **chief M** upon Mahalath Leannoth, 5329
109: T To the **chief M**, A Psalm of David. 5329
139: T To the **chief M**, A Psalm of David. 5329
140: T To the **chief M**, A Psalm of David. 5329

MUSICIANS (1) [MUSICK]

Rev 18:22 and **m**, and of pipers, and trumpeters, *3451*

MUSICK (16) [MUSICAL, MUSICIAN, MUSICIANS]

1Sa 18: 6 with joy, and with **instruments of m**. 7991
1Ch 15:16 *to be* the singers with instruments of **m**, 7892
2Ch 5:13 and cymbals and instruments of **m**, 7892
7: 6 the Levites also with instruments of **m** of 7892
23:13 also the singers with instruments of **m**, and 7892
34:12 all that could skill of instruments of **m**. 7892
Ecc 12: 4 all the daughters of **m** shall be brought low; 7892
La 3:63 and their rising up; I *am* their **m**. 4485
5:14 from the gate, the young men from their **m**. 5058
Da 3: 5 psaltery, dulcimer, and all kinds of **m**, 2170
3: 7 sackbut, psaltery, and all kinds of **m**, 2170
3:10 psaltery, and dulcimer, and all kinds of **m**, 2170
3:15 psaltery, and dulcimer, and all kinds of **m**, 2170
6:18 neither were **instruments of m** brought 1761
Am 6: 5 *and* invent to themselves instruments of **m**, 7892
Lk 15:25 nigh to the house, he heard **m** and dancing. *4858*

MUSING (1) [MUSE]

Ps 39: 3 within me, while I was **m** the fire burned: 1901

MUST (132)

Ge 17:13 **m needs be circumcised**: 4135+4135
24: 5 **m** I **needs bring** thy son **again** unto 7725+7725
29:26 It **m** not be so done in our country, NIH
30:16 and said, Thou **m** come in unto me; NIH
43:11 said unto them, If *it m* be so now, do this; NIH
47:29 the time drew nigh that Israel **m** die: and 3807.1
Ex 10: 9 for we **m** *hold* a feast unto the LORD. NIH
10:25 Thou **m** give us also sacrifices and NIH
10:26 for thereof **m** we take to serve the LORD NIH
10:26 we know not with what we **m** serve NIH
12:16 save *that* which every man **m** eat, that only NIH
18:20 shalt shew them the way *wherein* they **m** NIH
18:20 must walk, and the work that they **m** do. NIH
Lev 11:32 it **m** be put into water, and it shall be NIH
23: 6 seven days ye **m** eat unleavened bread. NIH
Nu 6:21 so he **m** do after the law of his separation. NIH
18:22 Neither **m** the children of Israel henceforth NIH
20:10 **m** we fetch you water out of this rock? NIH
23:12 **M** I not take heed to speak that which NIH
23:26 All that the LORD speaketh, that I **m** do? NIH
Dt 1:22 bring us word again by what way we **m** go NIH
4:22 I **m** die in this land, I *must* not go over NIH
4:22 die in this land, I **m** not go over Jordan: NIH
12:18 thou **m** eat them before the LORD thy God NIH
31: 7 for thou **m** go with this people unto the land NIH
31:14 Behold, thy days approach that *thou* **m** die: NIH
Jos 3: 4 that ye may know the way by which ye **m** NIH
22:18 that ye **m** turn away *this* day from following NIH
Jdg 13:16 thou **m** offer it unto the LORD. NIH
21:17 *There* **m** *be* an inheritance for them that be NIH
Ru 4: 5 thou **m** buy *it* also of Ruth the Moabitess, NIH
1Sa 14:43 rod that *was* in mine hand, *and* lo, I **m** die. NIH
2Sa 14:14 For we **m needs die**, and *are* as 4191+4191
23: 3 He that ruleth over men *m be* just, ruling *in* NIH
23: 7 the man *that* shall touch them **m** be fenced NIH
1Ki 18:27 peradventure he sleepeth, and **m** be awaked. NIH
1Ch 17:11 when thy days be expired that *thou* **m** go *to* NIH
22: 5 for the LORD *m be* exceeding magnifical, NIH
Ezr 10:12 a loud voice, As thou hast said, so **m** we do. NIH
Ps 32: 9 whose mouth **m** be held in with bit and NIH
Pr 18:24 A man that hath friends **m** shew himself NIH
19:19 for if thou deliver *him*, yet thou **m** do *it* NIH
Ecc 10:10 the edge, then **m** he put to more strength: NIH
SS 8:12 *m have* a thousand, and those that keep NIH
Isa 28:10 For precept *m be* upon precept, NIH
Jer 10: 5 they **m needs be borne**, because 5375+5375
10:19 I said, Truly this *is* a grief, and I **m** bear it. NIH
Eze 34:18 ye **m** tread down with your feet the residue NIH
34:18 but ye **m** foul the residue with your feet? NIH
Mt 16:21 how that he **m** go unto Jerusalem, and *1163*
17:10 say the scribes that Elias **m** first come? *1163*
18: 7 for it **m needs** be that offences come; but *318*
24: 6 for all *these things* **m** come to pass, but *1163*
26:54 the scriptures be fulfilled, that thus it **m** be? *1163*
Mk 2:22 but new wine **m** be put into new bottles. NIG
8:31 that the Son of man **m** suffer many *things*, *1163*
9:11 Why say the scribes that Elias **m** first *1163*
9:12 that he **m** suffer many *things*, and be set at NIG
13: 7 for *such things* **m needs** be; but the end *1163*
13:10 And the gospel **m** first be published among *1163*

Mk 14:49 me not: but the scriptures **m** be fulfilled. *2443*
Lk 2:49 wist ye not that I **m** be about my Father's *1163*
4:43 I **m** preach the kingdom of God to other *1163*
5:38 But new wine **m be put** into new bottles; *992*
9:22 The Son of man **m** suffer many *things,* and *1163*
13:33 Nevertheless I **m** walk to day, and *1163*
14:18 of ground, and I **m** needs go and see it: *2192*
17:25 But first **m** he suffer many *things,* and *1163*
19: 5 for to day I **m** abide at thy house. *1163*
21: 9 for these *things* **m** first come to pass; but *1163*
22: 7 when the passover **m** be killed. *1163*
22:37 that this that is written **m** yet be *1163*
23:17 (For of necessity he **m** release one unto *2192*
24: 7 The Son of man **m** be delivered into *1163*
24:44 yet with you, that all *things* **m** be fulfilled, *1163*
Jn 3: 7 that I said unto thee, Ye **m** be born again. *1163*
3:14 *even* so **m** the Son of man be lifted up: *1163*
3:30 He **m** increase, but I *must* decrease. *1163*
3:30 He must increase, but I *m* decrease. NIG
4: 4 And he **m needs** go through Samaria. *1163*
4:24 they that worship him **m** worship *him* in *1163*
9: 4 I **m** work the works of him that sent me, *1163*
10:16 them also I **m** bring, and they shall hear my *1163*
12:34 sayest thou, The Son of man **m** be lift up? *1163*
20: 9 that he **m** rise again from the dead. *1163*
Ac 1:16 this scripture **m needs** have been fulfilled, *1163*
1:22 **m** one be ordained *to be* a witness with us *1163*
3:21 Whom the heaven **m** receive until the times *1163*
4:12 given among men, whereby we **m** be saved. *1163*
9: 6 and it shall be told thee what thou **m** do. *1163*
9:16 For I will shew him how great *things* he **m** *1163*
14:22 that we **m** through much tribulation enter *1163*
15:24 *Ye* **m** be circumcised, and keep the law: NIG
16:30 and said, Sirs, what **m** I do to be saved? *1163*
17: 3 that Christ **m needs** have suffered, and *1163*
18:21 I **m** by all means keep *this* feast that *1163*
19:21 After I have been there, I **m** also see Rome. *1163*
21:22 the multitude **m needs** come *1163+3843*
23:11 so **m** thou bear witness also at Rome. *1163*
27:24 Paul; thou **m** be brought before Cesar: *1163*
27:26 Howbeit we **m** be cast upon a certain *1163*
Ro 13: 5 Wherefore *ye* **m needs** be subject, not only *318*
1Co 5:10 for then **m** ye **needs** go out of the world. *3784*
11:19 For there **m** be also heresies among you, *1163*
15:25 For he **m** reign, till he hath put all enemies *1163*
15:53 For this corruptible **m** put on incorruption, *1163*
15:53 and this mortal *m* put on immortality. NIG
2Co 5:10 For we **m** all appear before the judgment *1163*
11:30 If I **m needs** glory, I will glory of the *things* *1163*
1Ti 3: 2 A bishop then **m** be blameless, the husband *1163*
3: 7 Moreover he **m** have a good report of them *1163*
3: 8 Likewise *m* the deacons *be* grave, NIG
3:11 Even so **m** *their* wives *be* grave, NIG
2Ti 2: 6 The husbandman that laboureth **m** be first *1163*
2:24 And the servant of the Lord **m** not strive; *1163*
Tit 1: 7 For a bishop **m** be blameless, as *1163*
1:11 Whose mouths **m** be stopped, who subvert *1163*
Heb 4: 6 it remaineth that some *m* enter therein, NIG
9:16 For where a testament *is,* there **m** also of NIG
9:26 **m** he often have suffered since *1163*
11: 6 he that cometh to God **m** believe that he is, *1163*
13:17 as they that **m** give account, that they may NIG
1Pe 4:17 For the time *is come* that judgment **m** begin NIG
2Pe 1:14 Knowing that shortly *I* **m** put off *this* my *1510*
Rev 1: 1 to shew unto his servants *things* which **m** *1163*
4: 1 I will shew thee *things* which **m** be *1163*
10:11 Thou **m** prophesy again before many *1163*
11: 5 hurt them, he **m** in this manner be killed. *1163*
13:10 he that killeth with the sword **m** be killed *1163*
17:10 he cometh, he **m** continue a short *space.* *1163*
20: 3 and after that he **m** be loosed a little season. *1163*
22: 6 *the things* which **m** shortly be done. *1163*

MUSTARD (5)

Mt 13:31 of heaven is like unto a grain of **m** seed, *4615*
17:20 If ye have faith as a grain of **m** seed, *4615*
Mk 4:31 *It is* like a grain of **m** seed, which, when it *4615*
Lk 13:19 It is like a grain of **m** seed, which a man *4615*
17: 6 If ye had faith as a grain of **m** seed, *4615*

MUSTERED (2) [MUSTERETH]

2Ki 25:19 which **m** the people of the land, and 6633
Jer 52:25 of the host, who **m** the people of the land; 6633

MUSTERETH (1) [MUSTERED]

Isa 13: 4 the LORD of hosts **m** the host of 6485

MUTE See DUMB

MUTH-LABBEN (1)

Ps 9: T Musician upon **M**, 1121+4192+1886.1+3807.1

MUTILATORS OF THE FLESH See CONCISION

MUTTER (1) [MUTTERED]

Isa 8:19 and unto wizards that peep, and that **m**: 1897

MUTTERED (1) [MUTTER]

Isa 59: 3 your tongue hath **m** perverseness. 1897

MUTUAL (1)

Ro 1:12 together with you by the **m** faith both of you *240*

MUZZLE (3)

Dt 25: 4 Thou shalt not **m** the ox when he treadeth 2629
1Co 9: 9 Thou shalt not **m** the mouth of the ox that *5392*
1Ti 5:18 Thou shalt not **m** the ox that treadeth out *5392*

MY (4370) [I] See Index of Articles, Etc.

MYRA (1)

Ac 27: 5 of Cilicia and Pamphylia, we came to **M**, *3460*

MYRRH (17)

Ge 37:25 camels bearing spicery and balm and **m**, 3910
43:11 spices, and **m**, nuts, and almonds: 3910
Ex 30:23 of pure **m** five hundred *shekels,* and 4753
Est 2:12 *to wit,* six months with oil of **m**, and 4753
Ps 45: 8 All thy garments *smell of* **m**, and aloes, *and* 4753
Pr 7:17 I have perfumed my bed *with* **m**, aloes, and 4753
SS 1:13 A bundle of **m** *is* my well-beloved unto me; 4753
3: 6 perfumed *with* **m** and frankincense, with all 4753
4: 6 I will get me to the mountain of **m**, and 4753
4:14 **m** and aloes, with all the chief spices: 4753
5: 1 I have gathered my **m** with my spice; 4753
5: 5 my hands dropped *with* **m**, and my fingers 4753
5: 5 my fingers *with* sweet smelling **m**, 4753
5:13 lips *like* lilies, dropping sweet smelling **m**. 4753
Mt 2:11 him gifts; gold, and frankincense, and **m**. *4666*
Mk 15:23 gave him to drink wine **mingled with m**: *4669*
Jn 19:39 and brought a mixture of **m** and aloes, *4666*

MYRTLE (6)

Ne 8:15 **m** branches, and palm branches, and 1918
Isa 41:19 the shittah tree, and the **m**, and the oil tree; 1918
55:13 of the brier shall come up the **m tree**: 1918
Zec 1: 8 he stood among the **m trees** that *were* in 1918
1:10 the man that stood among the **m trees** 1918
1:11 the LORD that stood among the **m trees**, 1918

MYSELF (118) [I]

Ge 3:10 because I *was* naked; and I hid **m**. NIH
22:16 said, By **m** have I sworn, saith 2967.1
Ex 19: 4 eagles' wings, and brought you unto **m**. 2967.1
Nu 8:17 land of Egypt, I sanctified them for **m**. 2967.1
12: 6 *I* the LORD will make **m** known unto him NIH
Dt 1: 9 I am not able to bear you **m** alone: 2967.1
1:12 How can I **m** alone bear your cumbrance, 2967.1
10: 5 I turned **m** and came down from the mount, NIH
Jdg 16:20 out as at other times *before,* and shake **m**. NIH
Ru 4: 6 kinsman said, I cannot redeem *it* for **m**, 2967.1
1Sa 13:12 I forced **m** therefore, and offered a burnt NIH
20: 5 that I may hide **m** in the fields unto the third NIH
25:33 *from* avenging **m** with mine own hand. 2967.1
2Sa 18: 2 I will surely go forth with you **m** also. 589
22:24 and have kept **m** from mine iniquity. NIH
1Ki 18:15 I will surely shew **m** unto him to day. NIH
22:30 I will disguise **m**, and enter into the battle; NIH
2Ki 5:18 and I bow **m** *in* the house of Rimmon: NIH
5:18 when I bow down **m** *in* the house of NIH
2Ch 7:12 have chosen this place to **m** for a house 2967.1
18:29 I will disguise **m**, and will go to the battle; NIH
Ne 5: 7 I consulted with **m**, and I rebuked 3820+2967.1
Est 5:12 the banquet that she had prepared but **m**; 2967.1
6: 6 delight to do honour more than to **m**? 5204.1
Job 6:10 yea, I would harden **m** in sorrow; let him NIH
7:20 against thee, so that I am a burden to **m**? 2967.1
9:20 If I justify **m**, mine own mouth shall NIH
9:27 will leave off my heaviness, and comfort **m**: NIH
9:30 If I wash **m** with snow water, and make my NIH
10: 1 I will leave my complaint upon **m**; 2967.1
13:20 unto me: then will I not hide **m** from thee. NIH
19: 4 have erred, mine error remaineth with **m**. 2967.1
19:27 Whom I shall see for **m**, and mine eyes 2967.1
31:17 Or have eaten my morsel **m** alone, 905+2967.1
31:29 hated me, or lift up **m** when evil found him: NIH
42: 6 Wherefore I abhor *m,* and repent in dust and NIH
Ps 18:23 and I kept **m** from mine iniquity. NIH
35:14 I behaved **m** as though *he had been* my NIH
55:12 then I would have hid **m** from him: NIH
57: 8 and harp: I *m* will awake early. NIH
101: 2 I will behave **m** wisely in a perfect way. NIH
108: 2 and harp: I *m* will awake early. NIH
109: 4 my adversaries: but I *give* **m** *unto* prayer. NIH
119:16 I will delight **m** in thy statutes: I will not NIH
119:47 And I will delight **m** in thy commandments, NIH
119:52 of old, O LORD; and have comforted **m**. NIH
131: 1 neither do I exercise **m** in great *matters,* or NIH
131: 2 I have behaved and quieted **m**, 5315+2967.1
Ecc 2: 3 I sought in mine heart to give **m** 1320+2967.1
2:12 I turned **m** to behold wisdom, and madness, NIH
2:14 **I m** perceived also that one event happeneth 589
2:19 where*in* I have shewed **m** wise under NIH
Isa 33:10 now will I be exalted; now will I lift up **m**. NIH
42:14 I have been still, *and* refrained **m**: NIH
43:21 This people have I formed for **m**; 2967.1
44:24 that spreadeth abroad the earth by **m**; 2967.1
45:23 I have sworn by **m**, the word is gone out 2967.1
Jer 8:18 *When* I would comfort **m** against sorrow, 2967.1
21: 5 I **m** will fight against you with an 589
22: 5 I swear by **m**, saith the LORD, 2967.1
49:13 For I have sworn by **m**, saith the LORD, 2967.1
Eze 14: 7 I the LORD will answer him by **m**: 2967.1
20: 5 made **m** known unto them in the land of NIH
20: 9 in whose sight I made **m** known unto them, NIH
29: 3 *is* mine own, and I have made *it* for **m**. 5204.1
35:11 I will make **m** known amongst them, when I NIH
38:23 Thus will I magnify **m**, and sanctify myself; NIH
38:23 Thus will I magnify myself, and sanctify **m**; NIH
Da 10: 3 neither did I anoint **m** at all, till three whole NIH
Mic 6: 6 *and* bow **m** before the high God? NIH
Hab 3:16 into my bones, and I trembled in **m**, 2967.1
Zec 7: 3 separating **m**, as I have done these so NIH
Lk 7: 7 Wherefore neither thought I **m** worthy to *1683*
24:39 Behold my hands and my feet, that it is I **m**: *846*
Jn 5:31 If I bear witness of **m**, my witness is not *1683*
7:17 it be of God, or *whether* I speak of **m**. *1683*
7:28 and I am not come of **m**, but he that sent *1683*
8:14 said unto them, Though I bear record of **m**, *1683*
8:18 I am *one* that bear witness of **m**, and *1683*
8:28 that I am *he,* and *that* I do nothing of **m**; *1683*
8:42 and came from God; neither came I of **m**, *1683*
8:54 Jesus answered, If I honour **m**, my honour *1683*
10:18 taketh it from me, but I lay it down of **m**. *1683*
12:49 For I have not spoken of **m**; but the Father *1683*
14: 3 I will come again, and receive you unto **m**; *1683*
14:10 that I speak unto you, I speak not of **m**: *1683*
Jn 14:21 I will love him, and will manifest **m** to him. *1683*
17:19 And for their sakes I sanctify **m**, that they *1683*
Ac 10:26 saying, Stand up; I **m** also am a man. *846*
20:24 neither count I my life dear unto **m**, so *1683*
24:10 I do the more cheerfully answer for **m**: *1683*
24:16 And herein do I exercise **m**, to have always a *846*
25:22 unto Festus, I would also hear the man **m**. *846*
26: 2 I think **m** happy, king Agrippa, because *1683*
26: 2 I shall answer for **m** this day before thee NIG
26: 9 I verily thought with **m**, that *I* ought to do *1683*
Ro 7:25 then with the mind I **m** serve the law of God; *846*
9: 3 For I could wish that **m** were accursed from *846*
11: 4 I have reserved to **m** seven thousand men, *1683*
15:14 And I **m** also am persuaded of you, *846*
16: 2 a succourer of many, and of **m** *also.* *846+1473*
1Co 4: 4 For I know nothing by **m**; yet am I not *1683*
4: 6 I have in a figure transferred to **m** and *1683*
7: 7 For I would that all men were even as I **m**. *1683*
9:19 all *men,* yet have I made **m** servant unto all, *1683*
9:27 to others, I **m** should be a castaway. *846*
2Co 2: 1 But I determined this with **m**, that *I* would *1683*
10: 1 Now I Paul **m** beseech you by the meekness *846*
11: 7 Have I committed an offence in abasing **m** *1683*
11: 9 in all *things* I have kept **m** from being *1683*
11: 9 burdensome to you, and *so* will I keep *m.* NIG
11:16 fool receive me, that I may boast **m** a little. NIG
12: 5 yet of **m** I will not glory, but in mine *1683*
12:13 except *it be* that I **m** was not burdensome to *846*
Gal 2:18 which I destroyed, I make **m** a transgressor. *1683*
Php 2:24 But I trust in the Lord that I also **m** shall *846*
3:13 I count not **m** to have apprehended: *1683*
Phm 1:17 therefore a partner, receive him as **m**. *1473*

MYSIA (2)

Ac 16: 7 After they were come to **M**, they assayed to *3465*
16: 8 And they passing by **M** came down to *3465*

MYSTERIES (5) [MYSTERY]

Mt 13:11 Because it is given unto you to know the **m** *3466*
Lk 8:10 Unto you it is given to know the **m** of *3466*
1Co 4: 1 of Christ, and stewards of the **m** of God. *3466*
13: 2 and understand all **m**, and all knowledge; *3466*
14: 2 *him;* howbeit in the spirit he speaketh **m**. *3466*

MYSTERY (22) [MYSTERIES]

Mk 4:11 Unto you it is given to know the **m** of *3466*
Ro 11:25 that ye should be ignorant of this **m**, *3466*
16:25 according to the revelation of the **m**, *3466*
1Co 2: 7 But we speak the wisdom of God in a **m**, *3466*
15:51 Behold, I shew you a **m**; We shall not all *3466*
Eph 1: 9 Having made known unto us the **m** of his *3466*
3: 3 revelation he made known unto me the **m**; *3466*
3: 4 ye may understand my knowledge in the **m** *3466*
3: 9 all *men* see what *is* the fellowship of the **m**, *3466*
5:32 This is a great **m**: but I speak concerning *3466*
6:19 to make known the **m** of the gospel, *3466*
Col 1:26 *Even* the **m** which hath been hid from ages *3466*
1:27 of the glory of this **m** among the Gentiles; *3466*
2: 2 to the acknowledgement of the **m** of God *3466*
4: 3 to speak the **m** of Christ, for which I am *3466*
2Th 2: 7 For the **m** of iniquity doth already work: *3466*
1Ti 3: 9 Holding the **m** of the faith in a pure *3466*
3:16 And without controversy great is the **m** of *3466*
Rev 1:20 The **m** of the seven stars which thou sawest *3466*
10: 7 to sound, the **m** of God should be finished, *3466*
17: 5 **M**, BABYLON THE GREAT, *3466*
17: 7 I will tell thee the **m** of the woman, and *3466*

MYTHS See FABLES

N

N

NAAM (1)

1Ch 4:15 the son of Jephunneh; Iru, Elah, and **N**: 5277

NAAMAH (5)

Ge 4:22 iron: and the sister of Tubal-cain *was* **N**. 5279
Jos 15:41 Beth-dagon, and **N**, and Makkedah; 5279
1Ki 14:21 his mother's name *was* **N** an Ammonitess. 5279
14:31 his mother's name *was* **N** an Ammonitess. 5279
2Ch 12:13 his mother's name *was* **N** an Ammonitess. 5279

NAAMAN (16) [NAAMAN'S, NAAMITES]

Ge 46:21 and Ashbel, Gera, and **N**, Ehi, and Rosh, 5283
Nu 26:40 the sons of Bela were Ard and **N**: *of Ard,* 5283
26:40 *and* of **N**, the family of the Naamites. 5283
2Ki 5: 1 Now **N**, captain of the host of the king of 5283
5: 6 I have *therewith* sent **N** my servant to thee, 5283
5: 9 So **N** came with his horses and with his 5283
5:11 **N** was wroth, and went away, and said, 5283
5:17 **N** said, Shall there not then, I pray thee, 5283
5:20 my master hath spared **N** this Syrian, 5283
5:21 So Gehazi followed after **N**. And when 5283
5:21 when **N** saw *him* running after him, he 5283
5:23 **N** said, Be content, take two talents. And he 5283
5:27 therefore of **N** shall cleave unto thee, 5283
1Ch 8: 4 And Abishua, and **N**, and Ahoah, 5283
8: 7 **N**, and Ahiah, and Gera, he removed them, 5283
Lk 4:27 of them was cleansed, saving **N** the Syrian. *3497*

NAAMAN'S (1) [NAAMAN]

2Ki 5: 2 a little maid; and she waited on **N** wife. 5283

NAAMATHITE (4)
Job 2:11 and Bildad the Shuhite, and Zophar the **N**: 5284
11: 1 Then answered Zophar the **N**, and said, 5284
20: 1 Then answered Zophar the **N**, and said, 5284
42: 9 Bildad the Shuhite *and* Zophar the **N** went, 5284

NAAMITES (1) [NAAMAN]
Nu 26:40 *and* of Naaman, the family of the **N**. 5280

NAARAH (3)
1Ch 4: 5 of Tekoa had two wives, Helah and **N**. 5292
4: 6 **N** bare him Ahuzam, and Hepher, and 5292
4: 6 and Haahashtari. These *were* the sons of **N**. 5292

NAARAI (1)
1Ch 11:37 Hezro the Carmelite, **N** the son of Ezbai, 5293

NAARAN (1)
1Ch 7:28 and eastward **N**, and westward Gezer, 5295

NAARATH (1)
Jos 16: 7 to **N**, and came to Jericho, and went out *at* 5292

NAASHON (1)
Ex 6:23 of Amminadab, sister of **N**, to wife; 5177

NAASSON (3)
Mt 1: 4 and Aminadab begat **N**; and Naasson begat *3476*
1: 4 begat Naasson; and **N** begat Salmon; *3476*
Lk 3:32 *the son* of Salmon, which was *the son* of **N**, *3476*

NABAL (18) [NABAL'S]
1Sa 25: 3 Now the name of the man *was* **N**; and 5037
25: 4 David heard in the wilderness that **N** did 5037
25: 5 go to **N**, and greet him in my name: 5037
25: 9 they spake to **N** according to all those 5037
25:10 **N** answered David's servants, and said, 5037
25:19 after you. But she told not her husband **N**. 5037
25:25 regard this man of Belial, even **N**: 5037
25:25 *is* he; **N** *is* his name, and folly *is* with him: 5037
25:26 and they that seek evil to my lord, be as **N**. 5037
25:34 surely there had not been left unto **N** by 5037
25:36 Abigail came to **N**; and behold, he held a 5037
25:37 when the wine was gone out of **N**, and 5037
25:38 ten days *after,* that the LORD smote **N**, 5037
25:39 when David heard that **N** was dead, he said, 5037
25:39 cause of my reproach from the hand of **N**, 5037
25:39 the wickedness of **N** upon his own head. 5037
30: 5 and Abigail the wife of **N** the Carmelite. 5037
2Sa 3: 3 of Abigail the wife of **N** the Carmelite; 5037

NABAL'S (4) [NABAL]
1Sa 25:14 men told Abigail, **N** wife, saying, Behold, 5037
25:36 **N** heart *was* merry within him, for he *was* 5037
27: 3 and Abigail the Carmelitess, **N** wife. 5037
2Sa 2: 2 and Abigail **N** wife the Carmelite. 5037

NABOTH (22) [NACHON'S]
1Ki 21: 1 *that* **N** the Jezreelite had a vineyard, 5022
21: 2 Ahab spake unto **N**, saying, Give me thy 5022
21: 3 **N** said to Ahab, The LORD forbid it me, 5022
21: 4 of the word which **N** the Jezreelite had 5022
21: 6 Because I spake unto **N** the Jezreelite, and 5022
21: 7 I will give thee the vineyard of **N** 5022
21: 8 that *were* in his city, dwelling with **N**. 5022
21: 9 a fast, and set **N** on high among the people: 5022
21:12 a fast, and set **N** on high among the people. 5022
21:13 *even* against **N**, in the presence of 5022
21:13 **N** did blaspheme God and the king. 5022
21:14 to Jezebel, saying, **N** is stoned, and is dead. 5022
21:15 when Jezebel heard that **N** was stoned, and 5022
21:15 take possession of the vineyard of **N** 5022
21:15 thee for money: for **N** is not alive, but dead. 5022
21:16 to pass, when Ahab heard that **N** was dead, 5022
21:16 go down to the vineyard of **N** the Jezreelite, 5022
21:18 behold, *he is* in the vineyard of **N**, 5022
21:19 the blood of **N** shall dogs lick thy blood, 5022
2Ki 9:21 met him in the portion of **N** the Jezreelite. 5022
9:25 cast him in the portion of the field of **N** 5022
9:26 I have seen yesterday the blood of **N**, 5022

NACHON'S (1) [NABOTH]
2Sa 6: 6 when they came to **N** threshingfloor, 5225

NACHOR (2) [NAHOR]
Jos 24: 2 the father of Abraham, and the father of **N**: 5152
Lk 3:34 *the son* of Thara, which was *the son* of **N**, *3493*

NACON See NACHON'S

NADAB (20)
Ex 6:23 she bare him **N**, and Abihu, Eleazar, and 5070
24: 1 **N**, and Abihu, and seventy of the elders of 5070
24: 9 **N**, and Abihu, and seventy of the elders of 5070
28: 1 **N** and Abihu, Eleazar and Ithamar, 5070
Lev 10: 1 **N** and Abihu, the sons of Aaron, took either 5070
Nu 3: 2 **N** the firstborn, and Abihu, Eleazar, and 5070
3: 4 **N** and Abihu died before the LORD, 5070
26:60 unto Aaron was born **N**, and Abihu, 5070
26:61 **N** and Abihu died, when they offered 5070
1Ki 14:20 and **N** his son reigned in his stead. 5070
15:25 **N** the son of Jeroboam *began* to reign over 5070
15:27 for **N** and all Israel laid siege to Gibbethon. 5070
15:31 Now the rest of the acts of **N**, and all that 5070
1Ch 2:28 And the sons of Shammai; **N**, and Abishur. 5070
2:30 the sons of **N**; Seled, and Appaim: but 5070
6: 3 **N**, and Abihu, Eleazar, and Ithamar. 5070
8:30 and Zur, and Kish, and Baal, and **N**, 5070
9:36 Zur, and Kish, and Baal, and Ner, and **N**, 5070
24: 1 **N**, and Abihu, Eleazar, and Ithamar. 5070
24: 2 **N** and Abihu died before their father, and 5070

NAGGAI See NAGGE

NAGGE (1)
Lk 3:25 *the son* of Esli, which was *the son* of **N**, *3477*

NAHALAL (1)
Jos 21:35 with her suburbs, **N** with her suburbs; 5096

NAHALIEL (2)
Nu 21:19 from Mattanah *to* **N**: and from Nahaliel *to* 5160
21:19 *to* Nahaliel: and from **N** *to* Bamoth: 5160

NAHALLAL (1)
Jos 19:15 **N**, and Shimron, and Idalah, and 5096

NAHALOL (1)
Jdg 1:30 of Kitron, nor the inhabitants of **N**; 5096

NAHAM (1)
1Ch 4:19 the sons of *his* wife Hodiah the sister of **N**, 5163

NAHAMANI (1)
Ne 7: 7 Azariah, Raamiah, **N**, Mordecai, Bilshan, 5167

NAHARAI (2)
2Sa 23:37 Zelek the Ammonite, **N** the Beerothite, 5171
1Ch 11:39 Zelek the Ammonite, **N** the Berothite, 5171

NAHASH (9)
1Sa 11: 1 **N** the Ammonite came up, and 5176
11: 1 all the men of Jabesh said unto **N**, Make a 5176
11: 2 **N** the Ammonite answered them, On this 5176
12:12 when ye saw that **N** the king of the children 5176
2Sa 10: 2 shew kindness unto Hanun the son of **N**, 5176
17:25 that went in to Abigail the daughter of **N**, 5176
17:27 that Shobi the son of **N** of Rabbah of 5176
1Ch 19: 1 that **N** the king of the children of Ammon 5176
19: 2 shew kindness unto Hanun the son of **N**, 5176

NAHATH (5)
Ge 36:13 **N**, and Zerah, Shammah, and Mizzah: 5184
36:17 duke **N**, duke Zerah, duke Shammah, 5184
1Ch 1:37 of Reuel; **N**, Zerah, Shammah, and Mizzah. 5184
6:26 of Elkanah; Zophai his son, and **N** his son, 5184
2Ch 31:13 **N**, and Asahel, and Jerimoth, and Jozabad, 5184

NAHBI (1)
Nu 13:14 the tribe of Naphtali, **N** the son of Vophsi. 5147

NAHOR (15) [NACHOR, NAHOR'S]
Ge 11:22 And Serug lived thirty years, and begat **N**: 5152
11:23 Serug lived after he begat **N** two hundred 5152
11:24 **N** lived nine and twenty years, and 5152
11:25 **N** lived after he begat Terah an hundred 5152
11:26 and begat Abram, **N**, and Haran. 5152
11:27 Terah begat Abram, **N**, and Haran; and 5152
11:29 Abram and **N** took them wives: the name of 5152
22:20 hath also born children unto thy brother **N**; 5152
22:23 these eight Milcah did bear to **N**, 5152
24:10 went to Mesopotamia, unto the city of **N**. 5152
24:15 son of Milcah, the wife of **N**, 5152
24:24 the son of Milcah, which she bare unto **N**. 5152
29: 5 unto them, Know ye Laban the son of **N**? 5152
31:53 The God of Abraham, and the God of **N**, 5152
1Ch 1:26 Serug, **N**, Terah, 5152

NAHOR'S (2) [NAHOR]
Ge 11:29 the name of **N** wife, Milcah, the daughter 5152
24:47 she said, The daughter of Bethuel, **N** son, 5152

NAHSHON (9)
Nu 1: 7 Of Judah; **N** the son of Amminadab. 5177
2: 3 **N** the son of Amminadab *shall be* captain 5177
7:12 the first day was **N** the son of Amminadab, 5177
7:17 this *was* the offering of **N** the son of 5177
10:14 over his host *was* **N** the son of Amminadab. 5177
Ru 4:20 Amminadab begat **N**, and Nahshon begat 5177
4:20 begat Nahshon, and **N** begat Salmon, 5177
1Ch 2:10 Amminadab begat **N**, prince of the children 5177
2:11 And **N** begat Salma, and Salma begat Boaz, 5177

NAHUM (1)
Na 1: 1 The book of the vision of **N** the Elkoshite. 5151

NAIL (8) [NAILING, NAILS]
Jdg 4:21 Jael Heber's wife took a **n** of the tent, and 3489
4:21 smote the **n** into his temples, and fastened *it* 3489
4:22 lay dead, and the **n** *was* in his temples. 3489
5:26 She put her hand to the **n**, and her right 3489
Ezr 9: 8 and to give us a **n** in his holy place, 3489
Isa 22:23 I will fasten him *as* a **n** in a sure place; and 3489
22:25 shall the **n** that is fastened in the sure place 3489
Zec 10: 4 out of him the **n**, out of him the battle bow, 3489

NAILING (1) [NAIL]
Col 2:14 and took it out of the way, **n** it to *his* cross; *4338*

NAILS (10) [NAIL]
Dt 21:12 she shall shave her head, and pare her **n**; 6856
1Ch 22: 3 David prepared iron in abundance for the **n** 4548
2Ch 3: 9 the weight of the **n** *was* fifty shekels of 4548
Ecc 12:11 as **n** fastened *by* the masters of assemblies, 4930
Isa 41: 7 he fastened it with **n**, *that* it should not be 4548
Jer 10: 4 they fasten it with **n** and with hammers, 4548
Da 4:33 and his **n** like birds' *claws.* 2953
7:19 teeth *were of* iron, and his **n** *of* brass; 2953
Jn 20:25 I shall see in his hands the print of the **n**, *2247*
20:25 and put my finger into the print of the **n**, *2247*

NAIN (1)
Lk 7:11 *day* after, *that* he went into a city called **N**; *3484*

NAIOTH (6)
1Sa 19:18 And he and Samuel went and dwelt in **N**. 5121
19:19 Behold, David *is* at **N** in Ramah. 5121
19:22 *one* said, Behold, *they be* at **N** in Ramah. 5121
19:23 he went thither to **N** in Ramah: and 5121
19:23 prophesied, until he came to **N** in Ramah. 5121
20: 1 David fled from **N** in Ramah, and came 5121

NAKED (47) [NAKEDNESS]
Ge 2:25 they were both **n**, the man and his wife, 6174
3: 7 and they knew that they *were* **n**; 5903
3:10 and I was afraid, because I *was* **n**; 5903
3:11 he said, Who told thee that thou *wast* **n**? 5903
Ex 32:25 when Moses saw that the people *were* **n**; 6544
32:25 (for Aaron had **made** them **n** unto *their* 6544
1Sa 19:24 lay down **n** all that day and all *that* night. 6174
2Ch 28:15 with the spoil clothed all *that were* **n** 4636
28:19 for he **made** Judah **n**, and transgressed sore 6544
Job 1:21 **N** came I out of my mother's womb, and 6174
1:21 mother's womb, and **n** shall I return thither: 6174
22: 6 and stripped the **n** of their clothing. 6174
24: 7 They cause the **n** to lodge without clothing, 6174
24:10 They cause *him* to go **n** without clothing, 6174
26: 6 Hell *is* **n** before him, and destruction hath 6174
Ecc 5:15 **n** shall he return to go as he came, and 6174
Isa 20: 2 And he did so, walking **n** and barefoot. 6174
20: 3 Like as my servant Isaiah hath walked **n** 6174
20: 4 young and old, **n** and barefoot, 6174
58: 7 when thou seest the **n**, that thou cover him; 6174
La 4:21 shalt be drunken, and shalt **make** thyself **n**. 6168
Eze 16: 7 is grown, whereas thou *wast* **n** and bare. 5903
16:22 when thou wast **n** and bare, *and* 5903
16:39 thy fair jewels, and leave thee **n** and bare. 5903
18: 7 and hath covered the **n** with a garment; 5903
18:16 and hath covered the **n** with a garment, 5903
23:29 thy labour, and shall leave thee **n** and bare: 5903
Hos 2: 3 Lest I strip her **n**, and set her as *in* the day 6174
Am 2:16 the mighty shall flee away **n** in that day, 6174
Mic 1: 8 I will wail and howl, I will go stript and **n**: 6174
1:11 inhabitant of Saphir, having *thy* shame **n**: 6181
Hab 3: 9 Thy bow was **made quite n**, 5783+6181
Mt 25:36 **N**, and ye clothed me: I was sick, and *1131*
25:38 and took *thee* in? or **n**, and clothed *thee?* *1131*
25:43 **n**, and ye clothed me not: sick, and *1131*
25:44 or **n**, or sick, or in prison, and did not *1131*
Mk 14:51 having a linen cloth cast about *his* **n** *body;* *1131*
14:52 left the linen cloth, and fled from them **n**. *1131*
Jn 21: 7 *his* fisher's coat unto him, (for he was **n**,) *1131*
Ac 19:16 so that *they* fled out of that house **n** and *1131*
1Co 4:11 and are **n**, and are buffeted, and have no *1130*
2Co 5: 3 that being clothed we shall not be found **n**. *1131*
Heb 4:13 but all *things are* **n** and opened unto *1131*
Jas 2:15 If a brother or sister be **n**, and destitute of *1131*
Rev 3:17 and miserable, and poor, and blind, and **n**: *1131*
16:15 lest he walk **n**, and they see his shame. *1131*
17:16 and shall make her desolate and **n**, and *1131*

NAKEDNESS (57) [NAKED]
Ge 9:22 saw the **n** of his father, and told his two 6172
9:23 and covered the **n** of their father; 6172
9:23 and they saw not their father's **n**. 6172
42: 9 to see the **n** of the land you are come. 6172
42:12 but to see the **n** of the land you are come. 6172
Ex 20:26 that thy **n** be not discovered thereon. 6172
28:42 them linen breeches to cover *their* **n**; 1320+6172
Lev 18: 6 is near of kin to him, to uncover *their* **n**: 6172
18: 7 The **n** of thy father, or the nakedness of thy 6172
18: 7 or the **n** of thy mother, shalt thou not 6172
18: 7 *is* thy mother; thou shalt not uncover her **n**. 6172
18: 8 The **n** of thy father's wife shalt thou not 6172
18: 8 shalt thou not uncover: it *is* thy father's **n**. 6172
18: 9 The **n** of thy sister, the daughter of thy 6172
18: 9 *even* their **n** thou shalt not uncover. 6172
18:10 The **n** of thy son's daughter, or of thy 6172
18:10 *even* their **n** thou shalt not uncover: 6172
18:10 shalt not uncover: for theirs *is* thine own **n**. 6172
18:11 The **n** of thy father's wife's daughter, 6172
18:11 *is* thy sister, thou shalt not uncover her **n**. 6172
18:12 Thou shalt not uncover the **n** of thy father's 6172
18:13 Thou shalt not uncover the **n** of thy 6172
18:14 Thou shalt not uncover the **n** of thy father's 6172
18:15 Thou shalt not uncover the **n** of thy 6172
18:15 son's wife; thou shalt not uncover her **n**. 6172
18:16 Thou shalt not uncover the **n** of thy 6172
18:16 of thy brother's wife: it *is* thy brother's **n**. 6172
18:17 Thou shalt not uncover the **n** of a woman 6172
18:17 her daughter's daughter, to uncover her **n**; 6172
18:18 to vex *her,* to uncover her **n**, besides 6172
18:19 approach unto a woman to uncover her **n**, 6172
20:11 father's wife hath uncovered his father's **n**: 6172
20:17 and see her **n**, and she see his nakedness; 6172
20:17 and see her nakedness, and she see his **n**; 6172
20:17 he hath uncovered his sister's **n**; he shall 6172
20:18 her sickness, and shall uncover her **n**; 6172
20:19 thou shalt not uncover the **n** of thy 6172
20:20 he hath uncovered his uncle's **n**: 6172
20:21 he hath uncovered his brother's **n**; 6172
Dt 28:48 in **n**, and in want of all *things:* and he shall 5903
1Sa 20:30 and unto the confusion of thy mother's **n**? 6172
Isa 47: 3 Thy **n** shall be uncovered, yea, thy shame 6172
La 1: 8 despise her, because they have seen her **n**: 6172
Eze 16: 8 my skirt over thee, and covered thy **n**: 6172
16:36 thy **n** discovered through thy whoredoms 6172
16:37 will discover thy **n** unto them, that they 6172
16:37 unto them, that they may see all thy **n**. 6172
22:10 thee have they discovered their father's **n**: 6172
23:10 These discovered her **n**: they took her sons 6172
23:18 her whoredoms, and discovered her **n**: 6172
23:29 the **n** of thy whoredoms shall be 6172
Hos 2: 9 my wool and my flax *given* to cover her **n**. 6172
Na 3: 5 I will shew the nations thy **n**, and 4626
Hab 2:15 that thou mayest look on their **n**! 4589
Ro 8:35 or famine, or **n**, or peril, or sword? *1132*
2Co 11:27 and thirst, in fastings often, in cold and **n**. *1132*
Rev 3:18 and *that* the shame of thy **n** do not appear; *1132*

NAME (928) [NAME'S, NAMED, NAMELY, NAMES, NAMETH]

Ge 2:11 The **n** of the first *is* Pison: that *is it* which 8034
2:13 the **n** of the second river *is* Gihon: the same 8034
2:14 the **n** of the third river *is* Hiddekel: that *is it* 8034
2:19 living creature, that *was* the **n** thereof. 8034
3:20 And Adam called his wife's **n** Eve; because 8034
4:17 builded a city, and called the **n** of the city, 8034
4:17 of the city, after the **n** of his son, Enoch. 8034
4:19 the **n** of the one *was* Adah, and the name of 8034
4:19 *was* Adah, and the **n** of the other Zillah. 8034
4:21 his brother's **n** *was* Jubal: he was the father 8034
4:25 she bare a son, and called his **n** Seth: 8034
4:26 he called his **n** Enos; then began *men* to 8034
4:26 began *men* to call upon the **n** of 8034
5:2 blessed them, and called their **n** Adam, 8034
5:3 after his image; and called his **n** Seth: 8034
5:29 he called his **n** Noah, saying, This *same* 8034
10:25 the **n** of one *was* Peleg; for in his days was 8034
10:25 and his brother's **n** *was* Joktan. 8034
11:4 let us make us a **n**, lest we be scattered 8034
11:9 Therefore is the **n** of it called Babel; 8034
11:29 the **n** of Abram's wife *was* Sarai; and 8034
11:29 the **n** of Nahor's wife, Milcah, the daughter 8034
12:2 and I will bless thee, and make thy **n** great; 8034
12:8 and called upon the **n** of the LORD. 8034
13:4 there Abram called on the **n** of the LORD. 8034
16:1 an Egyptian, whose **n** *was* Hagar. 8034
16:11 bear a son, and shalt call his **n** Ishmael; 8034
16:13 she called the **n** of the LORD that spake 8034
16:15 Abram called his son's **n**, which Hagar 8034
17:5 Neither shall thy **n** any more be called 8034
17:5 called Abram, but thy **n** shall be Abraham; 8034
17:15 thou shalt not call her **n** Sarai, but 8034
17:15 her name Sarai, but Sarah *shall* her **n** *be.* 8034
17:19 son indeed; and thou shalt call his **n** Isaac: 8034
19:22 Therefore the **n** of the city was called Zoar. 8034
19:37 firstborn bare a son, and called his **n** Moab: 8034
19:38 also bare a son, and called his **n** Ben-ammi: 8034
21:3 Abraham called the **n** of his son that was 8034
21:33 called there on the **n** of the LORD, 8034
22:14 Abraham called the **n** of that place 8034
22:24 his concubine, whose **n** *was* Reumah, she 8034
24:29 had a brother, and his **n** *was* Laban: 8034
25:1 took a wife, and her **n** *was* Keturah. 8034
25:25 a hairy garment; and they called his **n** Esau. 8034
25:26 on Esau's heel; and his **n** was called Jacob: 8034
25:30 I *am* faint: therefore was his **n** called Edom. 8034
26:20 he called the **n** of the well Esek; because 8034
26:21 that also: and he called the **n** of it Sitnah. 8034
26:22 he called the **n** of it Rehoboth; and he said, 8034
26:25 called upon the **n** of the LORD, and 8034
26:33 the **n** of the city *is* Beer-sheba unto this 8034
28:19 he called the **n** of that place Beth-el: but 8034
28:19 the **n** of *that* city *was called* Luz at the first. 8034
29:16 the **n** of the elder *was* Leah, and the name 8034
29:16 and the **n** of the younger *was* Rachel. 8034
29:32 bare a son, and she called his **n** Reuben: 8034
29:33 this *son* also: and she called his **n** Simeon. 8034
29:34 three sons: therefore was his **n** called Levi. 8034
29:35 therefore she called his **n** Judah; and 8034
30:6 me a son: therefore called she his **n** Dan. 8034
30:8 and she called his **n** Naphtali. 8034
30:11 A troop cometh: and she called his **n** Gad. 8034
30:13 call me blessed: and she called his **n** Asher. 8034
30:18 my husband: and she called his **n** Issachar. 8034
30:20 him six sons: and she called his **n** Zebulun. 8034
30:21 bare a daughter, and called her **n** Dinah. 8034
30:24 she called his **n** Joseph; and said, 8034
31:48 Therefore was the **n** of it called Galeed; 8034
32:2 and he called the **n** of that place Mahanaim. 8034
32:27 he said unto him, What *is* thy **n**? And he 8034
32:28 Thy **n** shall be called no more Jacob, but 8034
32:29 and said, Tell *me,* I pray thee, thy **n**. 8034
32:29 *is* it *that* thou dost ask after my **n**? 8034
32:30 Jacob called the **n** of the place Peniel: for I 8034
33:17 the **n** of the place is called Succoth. 8034
35:8 and the **n** of it was called Allon-bachuth. 8034
35:10 God said unto him, Thy **n** *is* Jacob: 8034
35:10 thy **n** shall not be called any more Jacob, 8034
35:10 any more Jacob, but Israel shall be thy **n**: 8034
35:10 be thy name: and he called his **n** Israel. 8034
35:15 Jacob called the **n** of the place where God 8034
35:18 (for she died) that she called his **n** Ben-oni: 8034
36:32 and the **n** of his city *was* Dinhabah. 8034
36:35 in his stead: and the **n** of his city *was* Avith. 8034
36:39 the **n** of his city *was* Pau; and his wife's 8034
36:39 his wife's **n** *was* Mehetabel, the daughter of 8034
38:1 a certain Adullamite, whose **n** *was* Hirah. 8034
38:2 of a certain Canaanite, whose **n** *was* Shuah; 8034
38:3 and bare a son; and he called his **n** Er. 8034
38:4 and bare a son; and she called his **n** Onan. 8034
38:5 and bare a son; and called his **n** Shelah: 8034
38:6 for Er his firstborn, whose **n** *was* Tamar. 8034
38:29 therefore his **n** was called Pharez. 8034
38:30 upon his hand: and his **n** was called Zarah. 8034
41:45 Pharaoh called Joseph's **n** 8034
41:51 Joseph called the **n** of the firstborn 8034
41:52 the **n** of the second called he Ephraim: 8034
48:6 shall be called after the **n** of their brethren 8034
48:16 let my **n** be named on them, and the name 8034
48:16 and the **n** of my fathers Abraham and Isaac; 8034
50:11 wherefore the **n** of it was called 8034
Ex 1:15 of which the **n** of the one *was* Shiphrah, 8034
1:15 *was* Shiphrah, and the **n** of the other Puah: 8034
2:10 she called his **n** Moses: and she said, 8034
2:22 *him* a son, and he called his **n** Gershom: 8034
3:13 and they shall say to me, What *is* his **n**? 8034
3:15 this *is* my **n** for ever, and this *is* my 8034
5:23 since I came to Pharaoh to speak in thy **n**, 8034
6:3 by *the* **n** *of* God Almighty, but *by* my name NIH
6:3 *by* my **n** JEHOVAH was I not known to 8034
9:16 that my **n** may be declared throughout all 8034
Ex 15:3 *is* a man of war: the LORD *is* his **n**. 8034
15:23 the **n** of it was called Marah. 8034
16:31 the house of Israel called the **n** thereof 8034
17:7 he called the **n** of the place Massah, and 8034
17:15 and called the **n** of it Jehovah-nissi: 8034
18:3 of which the **n** of the one *was* Gershom; 8034
18:4 the **n** of the other *was* Eliezer; for the God 8034
20:7 Thou shalt not take the **n** of the LORD thy 8034
20:7 hold him guiltless that taketh his **n** in vain. 8034
20:24 in all places where I record my **n** I will 8034
23:13 make no mention of the **n** of other gods, 8034
23:21 your transgressions: for my **n** *is* in him. 8034
28:21 every one with his **n** shall they be 8034
31:2 I have called by **n** Bezaleel the son of Uri, 8034
33:12 I know thee by **n**, and thou hast also found 8034
33:17 grace in my sight, and I know thee by **n**. 8034
33:19 I will proclaim the **n** of the LORD before 8034
34:5 and proclaimed the **n** of the LORD. 8034
34:14 for the LORD, whose **n** *is* Jealous, *is* a 8034
35:30 the LORD hath called by **n** Bezaleel 8034
39:14 every one with his **n**, according to 8034
Lev 18:21 neither shalt thou profane the **n** of thy God: 8034
19:12 ye shall not swear by my **n** falsely, 8034
19:12 neither shalt thou profane the **n** of thy God: 8034
20:3 my sanctuary, and to profane my holy **n**. 8034
21:6 and not profane the **n** of their God: 8034
22:2 that they profane not my holy **n** *in those* 8034
22:32 Neither shall ye profane my holy **n**; but 8034
24:11 son blasphemed the **n** *of the LORD,* 8034
24:11 (and his mother's **n** *was* Shelomith, 8034
24:16 he that blasphemeth the **n** of the LORD, 8034
24:16 when he blasphemeth the **n** *of the LORD,* 8034
Nu 4:32 by **n** ye shall reckon the instruments of 8034
6:27 they shall put my **n** upon the children of 8034
11:3 he called the **n** of the place Taberah: 8034
11:26 the **n** of the one *was* Eldad, and the name of 8034
11:26 *was* Eldad, and the **n** of the other Medad: 8034
11:34 he called the **n** of that place 8034
17:2 write thou every man's **n** upon his rod. 8034
17:3 thou shalt write Aaron's **n** upon the rod of 8034
21:3 and he called the **n** of the place Hormah. 8034
25:14 Now the **n** of the Israelite that was slain, 8034
25:15 the **n** of the Midianitish woman that was 8034
26:46 the **n** of the daughter of Asher *was* Sarah. 8034
26:59 the **n** of Amram's wife *was* Jochebed, 8034
27:4 Why should the **n** of our father be done 8034
32:42 and called it Nobah, after his own **n**. 8034
Dt 3:14 called them after his own **n**, 8034
5:11 Thou shalt not take the **n** of the LORD thy 8034
5:11 hold *him* guiltless that taketh his **n** in vain. 8034
6:13 and serve him, and shalt swear by his **n**. 8034
7:24 thou shalt destroy their **n** from under 8034
9:14 and blot out their **n** from under heaven: 8034
10:8 and to bless in his **n**, unto this day. 8034
10:20 him shalt thou cleave, and swear by his **n**. 8034
12:5 out of all your tribes to put his **n** there, 8034
12:11 shall choose to cause his **n** to dwell there; 8034
12:21 to put his **n** there be too far from thee, 8034
14:23 which he shall choose to place his **n** there, 8034
14:24 thy God shall choose to set his **n** there,' 8034
16:2 LORD shall choose to place his **n** there. 8034
16:6 **n** *in,* there thou shalt sacrifice the passover 8034
16:11 thy God hath chosen to place his **n** there. 8034
18:5 to stand to minister in the **n** of the LORD, 8034
18:7 he shall minister in the **n** of the LORD his 8034
18:19 my words which he shall speak in my **n**, 8034
18:20 shall presume to speak a word in my **n**, 8034
18:20 or that shall speak in the **n** of other gods, 8034
18:22 When a prophet speaketh in the **n** of 8034
21:5 and to bless in the **n** of the LORD; 8034
22:14 bring up an evil **n** upon her, and say, I took 8034
22:19 he hath brought up an evil **n** upon a virgin 8034
25:6 in the **n** of his brother which is dead, 8034
25:6 is dead, that his **n** be not put out of Israel. 8034
25:7 to raise up unto his brother a **n** in Israel, 8034
25:10 his **n** shall be called in Israel, The house of 8034
26:2 thy God shall choose to place his **n** there. 8034
26:19 in praise, and in **n**, and in honour; 8034
28:10 that thou art called by the **n** of the LORD; 8034
28:58 *thou* mayest fear this glorious and fearful **n**, 8034
29:20 the LORD shall blot out his **n** from under 8034
32:3 Because I will publish the **n** of the LORD: 8034
Jos 5:9 Wherefore the **n** of the place is called 8034
7:9 us round, and cut off our **n** from the earth: 8034
7:9 and what wilt thou do unto thy great **n**? 8034
7:26 Wherefore the **n** of that place was called, 8034
9:9 because of the **n** of the LORD thy God: 8034
14:15 the **n** of Hebron before *was* Kirjath-arba; 8034
15:15 the **n** of Debir before *was* Kirjath-sepher. 8034
19:47 Dan, after the **n** of Dan their father. 8034
21:9 these cities which are *here* mentioned by **n**, 8034
23:7 neither make mention of the **n** of their 8034
Jdg 1:10 (now the **n** of Hebron before *was* 8034
1:11 the **n** of Debir before *was* Kirjath-sepher: 8034
1:17 and the **n** of the city was called Hormah. 8034
1:23 (Now the **n** of the city before *was* Luz.) 8034
1:26 built a city, and called the **n** thereof Luz: 8034
1:26 which *is* the **n** thereof unto this day. 8034
2:5 And they called the **n** of that place Bochim: 8034
8:31 him a son, whose **n** he called Abimelech. 8034
13:2 of the Danites, whose **n** *was* Manoah; 8034
13:6 whence he *was,* neither told he me his **n**: 8034
13:17 the angel of the LORD, What *is* thy **n**, 8034
13:18 Why askest thou thus after my **n**, seeing it 8034
13:24 bare a son, and called his **n** Samson: 8034
15:19 wherefore he called the **n** thereof 8034
16:4 the valley of Sorek, whose **n** *was* Delilah. 8034
17:1 of mount Ephraim, whose **n** *was* Micah. 8034
18:29 they called the **n** of the city Dan, after 8034
18:29 after the **n** of Dan their father, who was 8034
18:29 howbeit the **n** of the city *was* Laish at 8034
Ru 1:2 the **n** of the man *was* Elimelech, and 8034
1:2 the **n** of his wife Naomi, and the name of 8034
1:2 the **n** of his two sons Mahlon and Chilion, 8034
1:4 the **n** of the one *was* Orpah, and the name 8034
Ru 1:4 one *was* Orpah, and the **n** of the other Ruth: 8034
2:1 family of Elimelech; and his **n** *was* Boaz. 8034
2:19 The man's **n** with whom I wrought to day 8034
4:5 to raise up the **n** of the dead upon his 8034
4:10 to raise up the **n** of the dead upon his 8034
4:10 that the **n** of the dead be not cut off from 8034
4:14 that his **n** may be famous in Israel. 8034
4:17 the *women her* neighbours gave it a **n**, 8034
4:17 born to Naomi; and they called his **n** Obed: 8034
1Sa 1:1 of mount Ephraim, and his **n** *was* Elkanah, 8034
1:2 the **n** of the one *was* Hannah, and the name 8034
1:2 and the **n** of the other Peninnah: 8034
1:20 she bare a son, and called his **n** Samuel, 8034
7:12 and Shen, and called the **n** of it Eben-ezer, 8034
8:2 Now the **n** of his firstborn was Joel; and 8034
8:2 was Joel; and the **n** of his second, Abiah: 8034
9:1 whose **n** *was* Kish, the son of Abiel, the son 8034
9:2 he had a son, whose **n** *was* Saul, a choice 8034
14:4 the **n** of the one *was* Bozez, and the name 8034
14:4 *was* Bozez, and the **n** of the other Seneh. 8034
14:49 *were these;* the **n** of the firstborn Merab, 8034
14:49 and the **n** of the younger Michal: 8034
14:50 the **n** of Saul's wife *was* Ahinoam, 8034
14:50 the **n** of the captain of his host *was* Abner, 8034
16:3 thou shalt anoint unto me *him* whom I **n** 559
17:12 of Beth-lehem-judah, whose **n** *was* Jesse; 8034
17:23 the Philistine of Gath, Goliath by **n**, 8034
17:45 I come to thee in the **n** of the LORD of 8034
18:30 of Saul; so that his **n** was much set by. 8034
20:42 sworn both of us in the **n** of the LORD, 8034
21:7 his **n** *was* Doeg, an Edomite, the chiefest of 8034
24:21 that thou wilt not destroy my **n** out of my 8034
25:3 Now the **n** of the man *was* Nabal; and 8034
25:3 *was* Nabal; and the **n** of his wife Abigail: 8034
25:5 go to Nabal, and greet him in my **n**: 8034
25:9 to all those words in the **n** of David, 8034
25:25 for as his **n** *is,* so *is* he; Nabal *is* his name, 8034
25:25 *is* he; Nabal *is* his **n**, and folly *is* with him: 8034
28:8 bring me *him* up, whom I shall **n** unto thee. 559
2Sa 3:7 whose **n** *was* Rizpah, the daughter of Aiah: 8034
4:2 the **n** of the one *was* Baanah, and the name 8034
4:2 *was* Baanah, and the **n** of the other Rechab, 8034
4:4 And his **n** *was* Mephibosheth. 8034
5:20 Therefore he called the **n** of that place 8034
6:2 whose **n** is called *by* the name of 8034
6:2 whose name is called *by* the **n** of 8034
6:8 he called *the* **n** of the place Perez-uzzah to NIH
6:18 he blessed the people in the **n** of 8034
7:9 of thy sight, and have made thee a great **n**, 8034
7:9 like unto the **n** of the great *men* that *are* in 8034
7:13 He shall build a house for my **n**, and I will 8034
7:23 to make him a **n**, and to do for you great 8034
7:26 And let thy **n** be magnified for ever, saying, 8034
8:13 David gat *him* a **n** when he returned from 8034
9:2 house of Saul a servant whose **n** *was* Ziba. 8034
9:12 had a young son, whose **n** *was* Micha. 8034
12:24 bare a son, and he called his **n** Solomon: 8034
12:25 he called his **n** Jedidiah, because of 8034
12:28 I take the city, and it be called after my **n**. 8034
13:1 had a fair sister, whose **n** *was* Tamar; 8034
13:3 Amnon had a friend, whose **n** *was* Jonadab, 8034
14:7 shall not leave to my husband *neither* **n** nor 8034
14:27 and one daughter, whose **n** *was* Tamar: 8034
16:5 whose **n** *was* Shimei, the son of Gera: 8034
17:25 a man's son, whose **n** *was* Ithra an Israelite, 8034
18:18 I have no son to keep my **n** in 8034
18:18 he called the pillar after his own **n**: and it is 8034
20:1 whose **n** *was* Sheba, the son of Bichri, 8034
20:21 Sheba the son of Bichri by **n**, 8034
22:50 and I will sing praises unto thy **n**. 8034
23:18 and slew them, and had the **n** among three. 8034
23:22 and had the **n** among three mighty *men.* 8034
1Ki 1:47 God make the **n** of Solomon better than thy 8034
1:47 the name of Solomon better than thy **n**, 8034
3:2 there was no house built unto the **n** of 8034
5:3 **n** of the LORD his God for the wars 8034
5:5 I purpose to build a house unto the **n** of 8034
5:5 thy room, he shall build a house unto my **n**. 8034
7:21 right pillar, and called the **n** thereof Jachin: 8034
7:21 left pillar, and called the **n** thereof Boaz. 8034
8:16 build a house, that my **n** might be therein; 8034
8:17 for the **n** of the LORD God of Israel. 8034
8:18 in thine heart to build a house unto my **n**, 8034
8:19 he shall build the house unto my **n**. 8034
8:20 have built a house for the **n** of the LORD 8034
8:29 which thou hast said, My **n** shall be there: 8034
8:33 confess thy **n**, and pray, and 8034
8:35 confess thy **n**, and turn from their sin, 8034
8:42 (For they shall hear of thy great **n**, and of 8034
8:43 that all people of the earth may know thy **n**, 8034
8:43 which I have builded, is called by thy **n**. 8034
8:44 *toward* the house that I have built for thy **n**: 8034
8:48 and the house which I have built for thy **n**: 8034
9:3 thou hast built, to put my **n** there for ever; 8034
9:7 which I have hallowed for my **n**, 8034
10:1 Solomon concerning the **n** of the LORD, 8034
11:26 whose mother's **n** *was* Zeruah, a widow 8034
11:36 which I have chosen me to put my **n** there. 8034
13:2 born unto the house of David, Josiah by **n**; 8034
14:21 of all the tribes of Israel, to put his **n** there. 8034
14:21 his mother's **n** *was* Naamah an 8034
14:31 his mother's **n** *was* Naamah an 8034
15:2 his mother's **n** *was* Maachah, the daughter 8034
15:10 his mother's **n** *was* Maachah, the daughter 8034
16:24 and called the **n** of the city which he built, 8034
16:24 after the **n** of Shemer, owner of the hill, 8034
18:24 call ye on the **n** of your gods, and I will call 8034
18:24 and I will call on the **n** of the LORD: 8034
18:25 call on the **n** of your gods, but put no fire 8034
18:26 called on the **n** of Baal from morning even 8034
18:31 LORD came, saying, Israel shall be thy **n**: 8034
18:32 *with* the stones he built an altar in the **n** of 8034
21:8 So she wrote letters in Ahab's **n**, and 8034
22:16 *that which is* true in the **n** of the LORD? 8034
22:42 his mother's **n** *was* Azubah the daughter of 8034

N

Book	Ref	Context	Number
2Ki	2:24	and cursed them in the **n** of the LORD.	8034
	5:11	call on the **n** of the LORD his God, and	8034
	8:26	his mother's **n** *was* Athaliah, the daughter	8034
	12:1	his mother's **n** *was* Zibiah of Beer-sheba.	8034
	14:2	his mother's **n** *was* Jehoaddan of	8034
	14:7	and called the **n** of it Joktheel unto this day.	8034
	14:27	blot out the **n** of Israel from under heaven:	8034
	15:2	his mother's **n** *was* Jecholiah of Jerusalem.	8034
	15:33	his mother's **n** *was* Jerusha, the daughter of	8034
	18:2	His mother's **n** also *was* Abi, the daughter	8034
	21:1	And his mother's **n** *was* Hephzi-bah.	8034
	21:4	LORD said, In Jerusalem will I put my **n**.	8034
	21:7	all tribes of Israel, will I put my **n** for ever:	8034
	21:19	his mother's **n** *was* Meshullemeth,	8034
	22:1	his mother's **n** *was* Jedidah, the daughter of	8034
	23:27	house of which I said, My **n** shall be there.	8034
	23:31	his mother's **n** *was* Hamutal, the daughter	8034
	23:34	turned his **n** *to* Jehoiakim, and took	8034
	23:36	his mother's **n** *was* Zebudah, the daughter	8034
	24:8	his mother's **n** *was* Nehushta, the daughter	8034
	24:17	in his stead, and changed his **n** *to* Zedekiah.	8034
	24:18	his mother's **n** *was* Hamutal, the daughter	8034
1Ch	1:19	the **n** of the one *was* Peleg; because in his	8034
	1:19	and his brother's **n** *was* Joktan.	8034
	1:43	and the **n** of his city *was* Dinhabah.	8034
	1:46	in his stead: and the **n** of his city *was* Avith.	8034
	1:50	the **n** of his city *was* Pai; and his wife's	8034
	1:50	his wife's **n** *was* Mehetabel, the daughter of	8034
	2:26	had also another wife, whose **n** *was* Atarah;	8034
	2:29	the **n** of the wife of Abishur *was* Abihail,	8034
	2:34	a servant, an Egyptian, whose **n** *was* Jarha.	8034
	4:3	and the **n** of their sister *was* Hazelelponi:	8034
	4:9	his mother called his **n** Jabez, saying,	8034
	4:41	these written by **n** came in the days of	8034
	7:15	whose sister's **n** *was* Maachah;)	8034
	7:15	and the **n** of the second *was* Zelophehad:	8034
	7:16	bare a son, and she called his **n** Peresh;	8034
	7:16	the **n** of his brother *was* Sheresh; and	8034
	7:23	he called his **n** Beriah, because it went evil	8034
	8:29	of Gibeon; whose wife's **n** *was* Maachah:	8034
	9:35	Jehiel, whose wife's **n** *was* Maachah:	8034
	11:20	he slew *them*, and had a **n** among the three.	8034
	11:24	and had the **n** among the three mighties.	8034
	12:31	which were expressed by **n**, to come and	8034
	13:6	the cherubims, whose **n** is called *on it*.	8034
	14:11	they called the **n** of that place	8034
	16:2	he blessed the people in the **n** of	8034
	16:8	thanks unto the LORD, call upon his **n**,	8034
	16:10	Glory ye in his holy **n**: let the heart of them	8034
	16:29	unto the LORD the glory due unto his **n**:	8034
	16:35	that *we* may give thanks to thy holy **n**,	8034
	16:41	were chosen, who were expressed by **n**,	8034
	17:8	have made thee a **n** like the name of	8034
	17:8	have made thee a name like the **n** of	8034
	17:21	to make thee a **n** of greatness and	8034
	17:24	that thy **n** may be magnified for ever,	8034
	21:19	which he spake in the **n** of the LORD.	8034
	22:7	a house unto the **n** of the LORD my God:	8034
	22:8	thou shalt not build a house unto my **n**,	8034
	22:9	for his **n** shall be Solomon, and I will give	8034
	22:10	He shall build a house for my **n**; and	8034
	22:19	into the house that is *to be* built to the **n** of	8034
	23:13	unto him, and to bless in his **n** for ever.	8034
	28:3	Thou shalt not build a house for my **n**,	8034
	29:13	we thank thee, and praise thy glorious **n**.	8034
	29:16	for thine holy **n** *cometh* of thine hand,	8034
2Ch	2:1	to build a house for the **n** of the LORD,	8034
	2:4	I build a house to the **n** of the LORD my	8034
	3:17	called the **n** of *that on* the right hand	8034
	3:17	and the **n** of *that on* the left Boaz.	8034
	6:5	build a house *in*, that my **n** might be there;	8034
	6:6	that my **n** might be there;	8034
	6:7	for the **n** of the LORD God of Israel.	8034
	6:8	in thine heart to build a house for my **n**,	8034
	6:9	thy loins, he shall build the house for my **n**.	8034
	6:10	have built the house for the **n** of	8034
	6:20	hast said that *thou* wouldest put thy **n** there;	8034
	6:24	shall return and confess thy **n**, and pray and	8034
	6:26	confess thy **n**, *and* turn from their sin,	8034
	6:33	that all people of the earth may know thy **n**,	8034
	6:33	house which I have built is called by thy **n**.	8034
	6:34	the house which I have built for thy **n**;	8034
	6:38	the house which I have built for thy **n**:	8034
	7:14	If my people, which are called by my **n**,	8034
	7:16	this house, that my **n** may be there for ever:	8034
	7:20	which I have sanctified for my **n**,	8034
	12:13	of all the tribes of Israel, to put his **n** there.	8034
	12:13	his mother's **n** *was* Naamah an	8034
	13:2	His mother's **n** also *was* Michaiah	8034
	14:11	and in thy **n** we go against this multitude.	8034
	18:15	but the truth to me in the **n** of the LORD?	8034
	20:8	built thee a sanctuary therein for thy **n**,	8034
	20:9	in thy presence, (for thy **n** *is* in this house,)	8034
	20:26	the **n** of the same place was called,	8034
	20:31	his mother's **n** *was* Azubah the daughter of	8034
	22:2	His mother's **n** also *was* Athaliah	8034
	24:1	His mother's **n** also *was* Zibiah of	8034
	25:1	his mother's **n** *was* Jehoaddan of	8034
	26:3	His mother's **n** also *was* Jecoliah of	8034
	26:8	his **n** spread abroad even to the entering in	8034
	26:15	his **n** spread far abroad; for he was	8034
	27:1	His mother's **n** also *was* Jerushah,	8034
	28:9	the LORD was there, whose **n** *was* Oded:	8034
	28:15	the men which were expressed by **n** rose	8034
	29:1	his mother's **n** *was* Abijah, the daughter of	8034
	31:19	the men that were expressed by **n**,	8034
	33:4	In Jerusalem shall my **n** be for ever.	8034
	33:7	the tribes of Israel, will I put my **n** for ever:	8034
	33:18	him in the **n** of the LORD God of Israel,	8034
	36:4	Jerusalem, and turned his **n** *to* Jehoiakim.	8034
Ezr	2:61	the Gileadite, and was called after their **n**:	8034
	5:1	and Jerusalem in the **n** of the God of Israel,	8036
	5:14	they *were* delivered unto *one*, whose **n** *was*	8036
	6:12	the God that hath caused his **n** to dwell	8036
	8:20	all of them were expressed by **n**.	8034
Ne	1:9	place that I have chosen to set my **n** there.	8034
	1:11	of thy servants, who desire to fear thy **n**:	8034
	7:63	*to* wife, and was called after their **n**.	8034
	9:5	blessed be thy glorious **n**, which *is* exalted	8034
	9:7	and gavest him the **n** of Abraham;	8034
	9:10	So didst thou get thee a **n**, as *it is* this day.	8034
Est	2:5	whose **n** *was* Mordecai, the son of Jair,	8034
	2:14	in her, and *that* she were called by **n**.	8034
	2:22	certified the king *thereof* in Mordecai's **n**.	8034
	3:12	in the **n** of king Ahasuerus was it written,	8034
	8:8	in the king's **n**, and seal *it* with the king's	8034
	8:8	the writing which *is* written in the king's **n**,	8034
	8:10	And he wrote in the king Ahasuerus' **n**, and	8034
	9:26	called these days Purim after the **n** of Pur.	8034
Job	1:1	a man in the land of Uz, whose **n** *was* Job;	8034
	1:21	*away;* blessed be the **n** of the LORD.	8034
	18:17	and he shall have no **n** in the street.	8034
	42:14	he called the **n** of the first, Jemima; and	8034
	42:14	the **n** of the second, Kezia; and the name of	8034
	42:14	and the **n** of the third, Keren-happuch.	8034
Ps	5:11	let them also that love thy **n** be joyful in	8034
	7:17	will sing *praise* to the **n** of the LORD	8034
	8:1	how excellent *is* thy **n** in all the earth!	8034
	8:9	how excellent *is* thy **n** in all the earth!	8034
	9:2	I will sing *praise* to thy **n**, O thou most	8034
	9:5	thou hast put out their **n** for ever and ever.	8034
	9:10	they that know thy **n** will put their trust in	8034
	18:49	the heathen, and sing *praises* unto thy **n**.	8034
	20:1	the **n** of the God of Jacob defend thee;	8034
	20:5	in the **n** of our God we will set up *our*	8034
	20:7	we will remember the **n** of the LORD our	8034
	22:22	I will declare thy **n** unto my brethren: in	8034
	29:2	unto the LORD the glory due unto his **n**;	8034
	33:21	because we have trusted in his holy **n**.	8034
	34:3	with me, and let us exalt his **n** together.	8034
	41:5	of me, When shall he die, and his **n** perish?	8034
	44:5	through thy **n** will we tread them under that	8034
	44:8	all the day long, and praise thy **n** for ever.	8034
	44:20	If we have forgotten the **n** of our God, or	8034
	45:17	I will make thy **n** to be remembered in all	8034
	48:10	According to thy **n**, O God, so *is* thy praise	8034
	52:9	thou hast done *it*: and I will wait on thy **n**;	8034
	54:1	by thy **n**, and judge me by thy strength.	8034
	54:6	I will praise thy **n**, O LORD; for *it is*	8034
	61:5	*me* the heritage of those that fear thy **n**.	8034
	61:8	So will I sing *praise* unto thy **n** for ever,	8034
	63:4	I live: I will lift up my hands in thy **n**.	8034
	66:2	Sing forth the honour of his **n**: make his	8034
	66:4	sing unto thee; they shall sing *to* thy **n**.	8034
	68:4	Sing unto God, sing *praises to* his **n**:	8034
	68:4	that rideth upon the heavens by his **n** JAH,	8034
	69:30	I will praise the **n** of God with a song; and	8034
	69:36	and they that love his **n** shall dwell therein.	8034
	72:17	His **n** shall endure for ever: his name shall	8034
	72:17	his **n** shall be continued as long as the sun:	8034
	72:19	blessed *be* his glorious **n** for ever: and	8034
	74:7	the dwelling place of thy **n** to the ground.	8034
	74:10	shall the enemy blaspheme thy **n** for ever?	8034
	74:18	the foolish people have blasphemed thy **n**.	8034
	74:21	let the poor and needy praise thy **n**.	8034
	75:1	for *that* thy **n** *is* near thy wondrous works	8034
	76:1	*is* God known: his **n** *is* great in Israel.	8034
	79:6	kingdoms that have not called upon thy **n**.	8034
	79:9	God of our salvation, for the glory of thy **n**:	8034
	80:18	quicken us, and we will call upon thy **n**.	8034
	83:4	that the **n** of Israel may be no more in	8034
	83:16	that they may seek thy **n**, O LORD.	8034
	83:18	that thou, whose **n** alone *is* JEHOVAH,	8034
	86:9	before thee, O Lord; and shall glorify thy **n**.	8034
	86:11	in thy truth: unite my heart to fear thy **n**.	8034
	86:12	and I will glorify thy **n** for evermore.	8034
	89:12	Tabor and Hermon shall rejoice in thy **n**.	8034
	89:16	In thy **n** shall they rejoice all the day: and	8034
	89:24	and in my **n** shall his horn be exalted.	8034
	91:14	him on high, because he hath known my **n**.	8034
	92:1	to sing *praises* unto thy **n**, O most High:	8034
	96:2	Sing unto the LORD, bless his **n**;	8034
	96:8	unto the LORD the glory due unto his **n**:	8034
	99:3	Let them praise thy great and terrible **n**;	8034
	99:6	Samuel among them that call upon his **n**;	8034
	100:4	be thankful unto him, *and* bless his **n**.	8034
	102:15	So the heathen shall fear the **n** of	8034
	102:21	To declare the **n** of the LORD in Zion,	8034
	103:1	and all that is within me, *bless* his holy **n**.	8034
	105:1	thanks unto the LORD; call upon his **n**:	8034
	105:3	Glory ye in his holy **n**: let the heart of them	8034
	106:47	to give thanks unto thy holy **n**, *and*	8034
	109:13	in the generation following let their **n** be	8034
	111:9	for ever: holy and reverend *is* his **n**.	8034
	113:1	of the LORD, praise the **n** of the LORD.	8034
	113:2	Blessed be the **n** of the LORD from this	8034
	113:3	the same the LORD'S **n** *is* to be praised.	8034
	115:1	not unto us, but unto thy **n** give glory,	8034
	116:4	called I upon the **n** of the LORD;	8034
	116:13	and call upon the **n** of the LORD.	8034
	116:17	and will call upon the **n** of the LORD.	8034
	118:10	in the **n** of the LORD will I destroy them.	8034
	118:11	in the **n** of the LORD I will destroy them.	8034
	118:12	for in the **n** of the LORD I will destroy	8034
	118:26	Blessed *be* he that cometh in the **n** of	8034
	119:55	I have remembered thy **n**, O LORD, in	8034
	119:132	thou usest to do unto those that love thy **n**.	8034
	122:4	to give thanks unto the **n** of the LORD.	8034
	124:8	Our help *is* in the **n** of the LORD,	8034
	129:8	we bless you in the **n** of the LORD.	8034
	135:1	Praise ye the **n** of the LORD; praise *him*,	8034
	135:3	sing *praises* unto his **n**; for *it is* pleasant.	8034
	135:13	Thy **n**, O LORD, *endureth* for ever; *and*	8034
	138:2	praise thy **n** for thy lovingkindness and	8034
	138:2	hast magnified thy word above all thy **n**.	8034
	139:20	*and* thine enemies take *thy* **n** in vain.	NIH
	140:13	the righteous shall give thanks unto thy **n**:	8034
	142:7	soul out of prison, that *I* may praise thy **n**:	8034
	145:1	and I will bless thy **n** for ever and ever.	8034
	145:2	and I will praise thy **n** for ever and ever.	8034
Ps	145:21	let all flesh bless his holy **n** for ever and	8034
	148:5	Let them praise the **n** of the LORD: for he	8034
	148:13	Let them praise the **n** of the LORD:	8034
	148:13	for his **n** alone *is* excellent; his glory *is*	8034
	149:3	Let them praise his **n** in the dance: let them	8034
Pr	10:7	*is* blessed: but the **n** of the wicked shall rot.	8034
	18:10	The **n** of the LORD *is* a strong tower:	8034
	21:24	Proud *and* haughty scorner *is* his **n**,	8034
	22:1	A *good* **n** *is* rather to be chosen than great	8034
	30:4	what *is* his **n**, and what *is* his son's name,	8034
	30:4	and what *is* his son's **n**, if thou canst tell?	8034
	30:9	steal, and take the **n** of my God *in vain*.	8034
Ecc	6:4	and his **n** shall be covered with darkness.	8034
	7:1	A *good* **n** *is* better than precious ointment;	8034
SS	1:3	ointments thy **n** *is as* ointment poured forth,	8034
Isa	4:1	only let us be called by thy **n**, to take away	8034
	7:14	bear a Son, and shall call his **n** Immanuel.	8034
	8:3	to me, Call his **n** Maher-shalal-hash-baz.	8034
	9:6	his **n** shall be called Wonderful,	8034
	12:4	ye say, Praise the LORD, call upon his **n**,	8034
	12:4	make mention that his **n** *is* exalted.	8034
	14:22	cut off from Babylon the **n**, and remnant,	8034
	18:7	to the place of the **n** of the LORD of	8034
	24:15	*even* the **n** of the LORD God of Israel in	8034
	25:1	I will exalt thee, I will praise thy **n**;	8034
	26:8	the desire of *our* soul *is* to thy **n**, and to	8034
	26:13	thee only will we make mention of thy **n**.	8034
	29:23	they shall sanctify my **n**, and sanctify	8034
	30:27	the **n** of the LORD cometh from far,	8034
	41:25	rising of the sun shall he call upon my **n**:	8034
	42:8	that *is* my **n**: and my glory will I not give to	8034
	43:1	redeemed thee, I have called *thee* by thy **n**;	8034
	43:7	*Even* every one that is called by my **n**: for I	8034
	44:5	another shall call *himself* by the **n** of Jacob;	8034
	44:5	and surname *himself* by the **n** of Israel.	8034
	45:3	the LORD, which call *thee* by thy **n**,	8034
	45:4	I have even called thee by thy **n**:	8034
	47:4	our redeemer, the LORD of hosts *is* his **n**,	8034
	48:1	which are called by the **n** of Israel, and	8034
	48:1	which swear by the **n** of the LORD, and	8034
	48:2	of Israel; The LORD of hosts *is* his **n**.	8034
	48:11	will I do *it*: for how should my **n** be	NIH
	48:19	his **n** should not have been cut off nor	8034
	49:1	my mother hath he made mention of my **n**.	8034
	50:10	let him trust in the **n** of the LORD, and	8034
	51:15	The LORD of hosts *is* his **n**.	8034
	52:5	my **n** continually every day *is* blasphemed.	8034
	52:6	Therefore my people shall know my **n**:	8034
	54:5	the LORD of hosts *is* his **n**; and	8034
	55:13	it shall be to the LORD for a **n**, for an	8034
	56:5	a **n** better than *of* sons and *of* daughters:	8034
	56:5	I will give them an everlasting **n**, that shall	8034
	56:6	serve him, and to love the **n** of the LORD,	8034
	57:15	that inhabiteth eternity, whose **n** *is* Holy;	8034
	59:19	So shall they fear the **n** of the LORD from	8034
	60:9	unto the **n** of the LORD thy God, and	8034
	62:2	thou shalt be called by a new **n**, which	8034
	62:2	which the mouth of the LORD shall **n**.	5344
	63:12	to make himself an everlasting **n**?	8034
	63:14	thy people, to make thyself a glorious **n**.	8034
	63:16	our redeemer; thy **n** *is* from everlasting.	8034
	63:19	over them; they were not called by thy **n**.	8034
	64:2	to make thy **n** known to thine adversaries,	8034
	64:7	*there is* none that calleth upon thy **n**,	8034
	65:1	unto a nation *that* was not called by my **n**.	8034
	65:15	ye shall leave your **n** for a curse unto my	8034
	65:15	and call his servants by another **n**:	8034
	66:22	so shall your seed and your **n** remain.	8034
Jer	3:17	to the **n** of the LORD, to Jerusalem:	8034
	7:10	which is called by my **n**, and say,	8034
	7:11	Is this house, which is called by my **n**,	8034
	7:12	where I set my **n** at the first, and see what I	8034
	7:14	which is called by my **n**, wherein ye trust,	8034
	7:30	in the house which is called by my **n**,	8034
	10:6	thou *art* great, and thy **n** *is* great in might.	8034
	10:16	The LORD of hosts *is* his **n**.	8034
	10:25	and upon the families that call not on thy **n**:	8034
	11:16	The LORD called thy **n**, A green olive	8034
	11:19	that his **n** may be no more remembered.	8034
	11:21	Prophesy not in the **n** of the LORD,	8034
	12:16	to swear by my **n**, The LORD liveth;	8034
	13:11	for a **n**, and for a praise, and for a glory:	8034
	14:9	the midst of us, and we are called by thy **n**;	8034
	14:14	The prophets prophesy lies in my **n**:	8034
	14:15	the prophets that prophesy in my **n**,	8034
	15:16	for I am called by thy **n**, O LORD God of	8034
	16:21	they shall know that my **n** *is* The LORD.	8034
	20:3	The LORD hath not called thy **n** Pashur,	8034
	20:9	of him, nor speak any more in his **n**.	8034
	23:6	this *is* his **n** whereby he shall be called,	8034
	23:25	that prophesy lies in my **n**, saying, I have	8034
	23:27	**n** by their dreams which they tell every	8034
	23:27	as their fathers have forgotten my **n** for	8034
	25:29	evil on the city which is called by my **n**,	8034
	26:9	Why hast thou prophesied in the **n** of	8034
	26:16	for he hath spoken to us in the **n** of	8034
	26:20	that prophesied in the **n** of the LORD,	8034
	27:15	yet they prophesy a lie in my **n**;	8034
	29:9	they prophesy falsely unto you in my **n**:	8034
	29:21	which prophesy a lie unto you in my **n**;	8034
	29:23	have spoken lying words in my **n**, which I	8034
	29:25	Because thou hast sent letters in thy **n** unto	8034
	31:35	thereof roar; The LORD of hosts *is* his **n**:	8034
	32:18	Mighty God, the LORD of hosts, *is* his **n**,	8034
	32:20	and hast made thee a **n**, as *at* this day;	8034
	32:34	which is called by my **n**, to defile it.	8034
	33:2	to establish it; the LORD *is* his **n**;	8034
	33:9	it shall be to me a **n** of joy, a praise and	8034
	33:16	this *is the* **n** wherewith she shall be called,	NIH
	34:15	me in the house which is called by my **n**.	8034
	34:16	ye turned and polluted my **n**, and	8034
	37:13	whose **n** *was* Irijah, the son of Shelemiah,	8034
	44:16	hast spoken unto us in the **n** of the LORD,	8034
	44:26	Behold, I have sworn by my great **n**,	8034
	44:26	that my **n** shall no more be named in	8034

Jer 46:18 the King, whose **n** *is* the LORD of hosts, 8034
48:15 the King, whose **n** *is* the LORD of hosts. 8034
48:17 all ye that know his **n**, say, How is 8034
50:34 *is* strong; the LORD of hosts *is* his **n**: 8034
51:19 the LORD of hosts *is* his **n**. 8034
51:57 the King, whose **n** *is* the LORD of hosts. 8034
52: 1 his mother's **n** *was* Hamutal the daughter of 8034
La 3:55 I called upon thy **n**, O LORD, out of 8034
Eze 20:29 the **n** thereof is called Bamah unto this day. 8034
20:39 pollute ye my holy **n** no more with your 8034
24: 2 Son of man, write thee the **n** of the day, 8034
36:20 they went, they profaned my holy **n**, 8034
36:21 I had pity for mine holy **n**, which the house 8034
36:23 I will sanctify my great **n**, which was 8034
39: 7 So will I make my holy **n** known in 8034
39: 7 I will not let *them* pollute my holy **n** any 8034
39:16 also the **n** of the city *shall be* Hamonah. 8034
39:25 of Israel, and will be jealous for my holy **n**; 8034
43: 7 my holy **n**, shall the house of Israel no 8034
43: 8 they have even defiled my holy **n** by their 8034
48:35 the **n** of the city from *that* day *shall be*, The 8034
Da 1: 7 for he gave unto Daniel *the* **n** *of* NIH
2:20 Blessed be the **n** of God for ever and ever: 8036
2:26 said to Daniel, whose **n** *was* Belteshazzar, 8036
4: 8 whose **n** *was* Belteshazzar, according to 8036
4: 8 according to the **n** of my god, and in whom 8036
4:19 Daniel, whose **n** *was* Belteshazzar, 8036
9: 6 which spake in thy **n** to our kings, 8034
9:18 and the city which is called by thy **n**: 8034
9:19 thy city and thy people are called by thy **n**. 8034
10: 1 whose **n** was called Belteshazzar; 8034
Hos 1: 4 LORD said unto him, Call his **n** Jezreel; 8034
1: 6 *God* said unto him, Call her **n** Lo-ruhamah: 8034
1: 9 said *God*, Call his **n** Lo-ammi: for ye *are* 8034
2:17 shall no more be remembered by their **n**. 8034
Joel 2:26 and praise the **n** of the LORD your God, 8034
2:32 *that* whosoever shall call on the **n** of 8034
Am 2: 7 unto the *same* maid, to profane my holy **n**: 8034
4:13 The LORD, The God of hosts, *is* his **n**. 8034
5: 8 the face of the earth: The LORD *is* his **n**: 8034
5:27 the LORD, whose **n** *is* The God of hosts. 8034
6:10 for *we may* not make mention of the **n** of 8034
9: 6 the face of the earth: The LORD *is* his **n**. 8034
9:12 all the heathen, which are called by my **n**, 8034
Mic 4: 5 For all people will walk every one in the **n** 8034
4: 5 we will walk in the **n** of the LORD our 8034
5: 4 in the majesty of the **n** of the LORD his 8034
6: 9 and *the man of* wisdom shall see thy **n**: 8034
Na 1:14 *that* no more of thy **n** be sown: 8034
Zep 1: 4 the **n** of the Chemarims with the priests; 8034
3: 9 that they may all call upon the **n** of 8034
3:12 and they shall trust in the **n** of the LORD. 8034
3:20 for I will make you a **n** and a praise among 8034
Zec 5: 4 house of him that sweareth falsely by my **n**: 8034
6:12 Behold the man whose **n** *is* The BRANCH; 8034
10:12 they shall walk up and down in his **n**, 8034
13: 3 for thou speakest lies in the **n** of 8034
13: 9 they shall call on my **n**, and I will hear 8034
14: 9 shall there be one LORD, and his **n** one. 8034
Mal 1: 6 unto you, O priests, that despise my **n**. 8034
1: 6 ye say, Wherein have we despised thy **n**? 8034
1:11 my **n** *shall be* great among the Gentiles; 8034
1:11 place incense *shall be* offered unto my **n**, 8034
1:11 for my **n** *shall be* great among the heathen, 8034
1:14 and my **n** *is* dreadful among the heathen. 8034
2: 2 to give glory unto my **n**, saith the LORD 8034
2: 5 he feared me, and was afraid before my **n**. 8034
3:16 the LORD, and that thought upon his **n**. 8034
4: 2 unto you that fear my **n** shall the Sun of 8034
Mt 1:21 a son, and thou shalt call his **n** JESUS: *3686*
1:23 a son, and they shall call his **n** Emmanuel, *3686*
1:25 firstborn son: and *he* called his **n** JESUS. *3686*
6: 9 which art in heaven, Hallowed be thy **n**. *3686*
7:22 Lord, have we not prophesied in thy **n**? *3686*
7:22 and in thy **n** have cast out devils? *3686*
7:22 and in thy **n** done many wonderful works? *3686*
10:41 He that receiveth a prophet in the **n** of a *3686*
10:41 he that receiveth a righteous *man* in the **n** *3686*
10:42 of cold *water* only in the **n** of a disciple, *3686*
12:21 And in his **n** shall the Gentiles trust. *3686*
18: 5 one such little child in my **n** receiveth me. *3686*
18:20 or three are gathered together in my **n**, *3686*
21: 9 Blessed *is* he that cometh in the **n** of *3686*
23:39 Blessed is he that cometh in the **n** of *3686*
24: 5 For many shall come in my **n**, saying, I am *3686*
27:32 they found a man of Cyrene, Simon by **n**: *3686*
28:19 baptizing them in the **n** of the Father, and *3686*
Mk 5: 9 And he asked him, What *is* thy **n**? And he *3686*
5: 9 And he answered, saying, My **n** *is* Legion: *3686*
5:22 of the rulers of the synagogue, Jairus by **n**; *3686*
6:14 And king Herod heard *of him;* (for his **n** *3686*
9:37 shall receive one of such children in my **n**, *3686*
9:38 we saw one casting out devils in thy **n**, and *3686*
9:39 is no *man* which shall do a miracle in my **n**, *3686*
9:41 give you a cup of water to drink in my **n**, *3686*
11: 9 Blessed *is* he that cometh in the **n** of *3686*
11:10 that cometh in the **n** of the Lord: *3686*
13: 6 For many shall come in my **n**, saying, I am *3686*
16:17 In my **n** shall they cast out devils; *3686*
Lk 1: 5 of Aaron, and her **n** *was* Elisabeth. *3686*
1:13 thee a son, and thou shalt call his **n** John. *3686*
1:27 To a virgin espoused to a man whose **n** was *3686*
1:27 of David; and the virgin's **n** *was* Mary. *3686*
1:31 forth a son, and shalt call his **n** JESUS. *3686*
1:49 done to me great things; and holy *is* his **n**. *3686*
1:59 him Zacharias, after the **n** of his father. *3686*
1:61 none of thy kindred that is called by this **n**. *3686*
1:63 and wrote, saying, His **n** is John. *3686*
2:21 his **n** was called JESUS, which was *so* *3686*
2:25 a man in Jerusalem, whose **n** *was* Simeon; *3686*
6:22 reproach *you*, and cast out your **n** as evil, *3686*
8:30 Jesus asked him, saying, What is thy **n**? *3686*
9:48 Whosoever shall receive this child in my **n** *3686*
9:49 we saw one casting out devils in thy **n**; *3686*
10:17 the devils are subject unto us through thy **n**. *3686*
Lk 11: 2 which art in heaven, Hallowed be thy **n**. *3686*
13:35 Blessed *is* he that cometh in the **n** of *3686*
19:38 Blessed *be* the King that cometh in the **n** of *3686*
21: 8 for many shall come in my **n**, saying, I am *3686*
24:18 And the one *of them*, whose **n** *was* *3686*
24:47 be preached in his **n** among all nations, *3686*
Jn 1: 6 a man sent from God, whose **n** *was* John. *3686*
1:12 of God, *even* to them that believe on his **n**: *3686*
2:23 in the feast *day*, many believed in his **n**, *3686*
3:18 he hath not believed in the **n** of the only *3686*
5:43 I am come in my Father's **n**, and ye receive *3686*
5:43 if another shall come in his own **n**, him ye *3686*
10: 3 and he calleth his own sheep by **n**, and *3686*
10:25 the works that I do in my Father's **n**, *3686*
12:13 of Israel that cometh in the **n** of the Lord. *3686*
12:28 Father, glorify thy **n**. Then came there a *3686*
14:13 And whatsoever ye shall ask in my **n**, *3686*
14:14 If ye shall ask any *thing* in my **n**, I will do *3686*
14:26 whom the Father will send in my **n**, *3686*
15:16 ye shall ask of the Father in my **n**, *3686*
16:23 Whatsoever ye shall ask the Father in my **n**, *3686*
16:24 Hitherto have ye asked nothing in my **n**: *3686*
16:26 At that day ye shall ask in my **n**: and I say *3686*
17: 6 I have manifested thy **n** unto the men *3686*
17:11 keep through thine own **n** those whom thou *3686*
17:12 them in the world, I kept them in thy **n**: *3686*
17:26 And I have declared unto them thy **n**, and *3686*
18:10 his right ear. The servant's **n** was Malchus. *3686*
20:31 believing ye might have life through his **n**. *3686*
Ac 2:21 *that* whosoever shall call on the **n** of *3686*
2:38 be baptized every one of you in the **n** of *3686*
3: 6 In the **n** of Jesus Christ of Nazareth rise up *3686*
3:16 And his **n** through faith in his name hath *3686*
3:16 And his name through faith in his **n** hath *3686*
4: 7 they asked, By what power, or by what **n**, *3686*
4:10 that by the **n** of Jesus Christ of Nazareth, *3686*
4:12 for there is none other **n** under heaven *3686*
4:17 *they* speak henceforth to no man in this **n**. *3686*
4:18 to speak at all nor teach in the **n** of Jesus. *3686*
4:30 wonders may be done by the **n** of thy holy *3686*
5:28 you that *you* should not teach in this **n**? *3686*
5:40 that *they* should not speak in the **n** of Jesus, *3686*
5:41 counted worthy to suffer shame for his **n**. *3686*
7:58 at a young man's feet, whose **n** was Saul. *2564*
8:12 and the **n** of Jesus Christ, they were *3686*
8:16 only they were baptized in the **n** of *3686*
9:14 chief priests to bind all that call on thy **n**. *3686*
9:15 to bear my **n** before the Gentiles, and kings, *3686*
9:21 them which called on this **n** in Jerusalem, *3686*
9:27 boldly at Damascus in the **n** of Jesus. *3686*
9:29 And he spake boldly in the **n** of the Lord *3686*
10:43 that through his **n** whosoever believeth in *3686*
10:48 them to be baptized in the **n** of the Lord. *3686*
13: 6 a Jew, whose **n** *was* Bar-jesus: *3686*
13: 8 sorcerer (for so is his **n** by interpretation) *3686*
15:14 to take out of them a people for his **n**. *3686*
15:17 upon whom my **n** is called, saith the Lord, *3686*
15:26 Men that have hazarded their lives for the **n** *3686*
16:18 I command thee in the **n** of Jesus Christ to *3686*
19: 5 were baptized in the **n** of the Lord Jesus. *3686*
19:13 had evil spirits the **n** of the Lord Jesus, *3686*
19:17 and the **n** of the Lord Jesus was magnified. *3686*
21:13 also to die at Jerusalem for the **n** of *3686*
22:16 away thy sins, calling on the **n** of the Lord. *3686*
26: 9 contrary to the **n** of Jesus of Nazareth. *3686*
28: 7 *man* of the island, whose **n** was Publius; *3686*
Ro 1: 5 to the faith among all nations, for his **n**: *3686*
2:24 For the **n** of God is blasphemed among *3686*
9:17 that my **n** might be declared throughout all *3686*
10:13 For whosoever shall call upon the **n** of *3686*
15: 9 among the Gentiles, and sing unto thy **n**. *3686*
1Co 1: 2 with all that in every place call upon the **n** *3686*
1:10 brethren, by the **n** of our Lord Jesus Christ, *3686*
1:13 or were ye baptized in the **n** of Paul? *3686*
1:15 say that I had baptized in mine own **n**. *3686*
5: 4 In the **n** of our Lord Jesus Christ, when ye *3686*
6:11 ye are justified in the **n** of the Lord Jesus, *3686*
Eph 1:21 and dominion, and every **n** that is named, *3686*
5:20 the Father in the **n** of our Lord Jesus Christ; *3686*
Php 2: 9 given him a **n** which is above every name: *3686*
2: 9 given him a name which is above every **n**: *3686*
2:10 That at the **n** of Jesus every knee should *3686*
Col 3:17 or deed, *do* all in the **n** of the Lord Jesus, *3686*
2Th 1:12 That the **n** of our Lord Jesus Christ may be *3686*
3: 6 brethren, in the **n** of our Lord Jesus Christ, *3686*
1Ti 6: 1 that the **n** of God and *his* doctrine be not *3686*
2Ti 2:19 Let every one that nameth the **n** of Christ *3686*
Heb 1: 4 obtained a more excellent **n** than they. *3686*
2:12 I will declare thy **n** unto my brethren, *3686*
6:10 which ye have shewed toward his **n**, *3686*
13:15 the fruit of *our* lips giving thanks to his **n**. *3686*
Jas 2: 7 Do not they blaspheme *that* worthy **n** by *3686*
5:10 who have spoken in the **n** of the Lord, *3686*
5:14 anointing him with oil in the **n** of the Lord: *3686*
1Pe 4:14 If ye be reproached for the **n** of Christ, *3686*
1Jn 3:23 That we should believe on the **n** of his Son *3686*
5:13 that believe on the **n** of the Son of God; *3686*
5:13 that ye may believe on the **n** of the Son of *3686*
3Jn 1:14 friends salute thee. Greet the friends by **n**. *3686*
Rev 2:13 Satan's seat *is:* and thou holdest fast my **n**, *3686*
2:17 and in the stone a new **n** written, *3686*
3: 1 that thou hast a **n** that thou livest, and *3686*
3: 5 I will not blot out his **n** out of the book of *3686*
3: 5 but I will confess his **n** before my Father, *3686*
3: 8 kept my word, and hast not denied my **n**. *3686*
3:12 and I will write upon him the **n** of my God, *3686*
3:12 and the **n** of the city of my God, *which is* *3686*
3:12 and *I will write upon him* my new **n**. *3686*
6: 8 and his **n** that sat on him *was* Death, and *3686*
8:11 And the **n** of the star is called Wormwood: *3686*
9:11 whose **n** in the Hebrew tongue *is* Abaddon, *3686*
9:11 in the Greek *tongue* hath *his* **n** Apollyon. *3686*
11:18 and them that fear thy **n**, small and great; *3686*
13: 1 and upon his heads the **n** of blasphemy. *3686*
13: 6 to blaspheme his **n**, and his tabernacle, and *3686*
Rev 13:17 or the **n** of the beast, or the number of his *3686*
13:17 name of the beast, or the number of his **n**. *3686*
14: 1 having his Father's **n** written in their *3686*
14:11 and whosoever receiveth the mark of his **n**. *3686*
15: 2 his mark, *and* over the number of his **n**, *3686*
15: 4 not fear thee, O Lord, and glorify thy **n**? *3686*
16: 9 and blasphemed the **n** of God, which hath *3686*
17: 5 And upon her forehead *was* a **n** written, *3686*
19:12 and he had a **n** written, that no *man* knew, *3686*
19:13 and his **n** is called The Word of God. *3686*
19:16 on *his* vesture and on his thigh a **n** written, *3686*
22: 4 and his **n** *shall be* in their foreheads. *3686*

NAME'S (30) [NAME]

1Sa 12:22 not forsake his people for his great **n** sake: 8034
1Ki 8:41 cometh out of a far country for thy **n** sake; 8034
2Ch 6:32 is come from a far country for thy great **n** 8034
Ps 23: 3 in the paths of righteousness for his **n** sake. 8034
25:11 For thy **n** sake, O LORD, pardon mine 8034
31: 3 therefore for thy **n** sake lead me, and 8034
79: 9 and purge away our sins, for thy **n** sake. 8034
106: 8 Nevertheless he saved them for his **n** sake, 8034
109:21 for me, O GOD the Lord, for thy **n** sake: 8034
143:11 Quicken me, O LORD, for thy **n** sake: 8034
Isa 48: 9 For my **n** sake will I defer mine anger, and 8034
66: 5 that cast you out for my **n** sake, said, 8034
Jer 14: 7 testify against us, do thou *it* for thy **n** sake: 8034
14:21 Do not abhor *us*, for thy **n** sake, do not 8034
Eze 20: 9 I wrought for my **n** sake, that *it* should not 8034
20:14 I wrought for my **n** sake, that *it* should not 8034
20:22 mine hand, and wrought for my **n** sake, 8034
20:44 when I have wrought with you for my **n** 8034
36:22 O house of Israel, but for mine holy **n** sake, 8034
Mt 10:22 And ye shall be hated of all *men* for my **n** *3686*
19:29 wife, or children, or lands, for my **n** sake, *3686*
24: 9 ye shall be hated of all nations for my **n** *3686*
Mk 13:13 And ye shall be hated of all *men* for my **n** *3686*
Lk 21:12 before kings and rulers for my **n** sake. *3686*
21:17 And ye shall be hated of all *men* for my **n** *3686*
Jn 15:21 *things* will they do unto you for my **n** sake, *3686*
Ac 9:16 great *things* he must suffer for my **n** sake. *3686*
1Jn 2:12 *your* sins are forgiven you for his **n** sake. *3686*
3Jn 1: 7 Because that for his **n** sake they went forth, *3686*
Rev 2: 3 and for my **n** sake hast laboured, and *3686*

NAMED (57) [NAME]

Ge 23:16 which he had **n** in the audience of the sons 1696
27:36 he said, Is not he rightly **n** Jacob? 7121+8034
48:16 let my name be **n** on them, and the name of 7121
Jos 2: 1 harlot's house, **n** Rahab, and lodged there. 8034
1Sa 4:21 she **n** the child Ichabod, saying, The glory 7121
17: 4 **n** Goliath, of Gath, whose height *was* six 8034
22:20 **n** Abiathar, escaped, and fled after David. 8034
2Ki 17:34 children of Jacob, whom he **n** Israel; 7760+8034
1Ch 23:14 of God, his sons were **n** of the tribe of Levi. 7121
Ecc 6:10 That which hath been is **n** already, 7121+8034
Isa 61: 6 ye shall be **n** the Priests of the LORD: 7121
Jer 44:26 that my name shall no more be **n** in 7121
Da 5:12 whom the king **n** Belteshazzar: 7761+8036
Am 6: 1 *which are* **n** chief of the nations, 5344
Mic 2: 7 O *thou that art* **n** the house of Jacob, is 559
Mt 9: 9 he saw a man, **n** Matthew, sitting at *3004*
27:57 came a rich man of Arimathea, **n** Joseph, *5122*
Mk 14:32 And they came to a place which was **n** *3686*
15: 7 And there was *one* **n** Barabbas, *which lay* *3004*
Lk 1: 5 king of Judea, a certain priest **n** Zacharias, *3686*
1:26 God unto a city of Galilee, **n** Nazareth, *3686*
2:21 **n** of the angel before he was conceived in *2564*
5:27 and saw a publican, **n** Levi, sitting at *3686*
6:13 he chose twelve, whom also he **n** apostles; *3687*
6:14 Simon, (whom he also **n** Peter,) and *3687*
8:41 there came a man **n** Jairus, and he was a *3686*
10:38 a certain woman **n** Martha received him *3686*
16:20 And there was a certain beggar **n** Lazarus, *3686*
19: 2 And behold, *there was* a man **n** Zaccheus, *3686*
23:50 And behold, *there was* a man **n** Joseph, *3686*
Jn 3: 1 **n** Nicodemus, a ruler of the Jews: *3686*
11: 1 *n* Lazarus, of Bethany, the town of Mary NIG
11:49 And one of them, *n* Caiaphas, being NIG
Ac 5: 1 But a certain man **n** Ananias, with Sapphira *3686*
5:34 a Pharisee, **n** Gamaliel, a doctor of law, *3686*
9:10 a certain disciple at Damascus, **n** Ananias; *3686*
9:12 And hath seen in a vision a man **n** Ananias *3686*
9:33 And there he found a certain man **n** *3686*
9:36 Now there was at Joppa a certain disciple **n** *3686*
11:28 And there stood up one of them **n** Agabus, *3686*
12:13 a damsel came to hearken, **n** Rhoda. *3686*
16: 1 **n** Timotheus, the son of a certain woman, *3686*
16:14 And a certain woman **n** Lydia, a seller of *3686*
17:34 and a woman **n** Damaris, and others with *3686*
18: 2 And found a certain Jew **n** Aquila, born in *3686*
18: 7 **n** Justus, one that worshipped God, *3686*
18:24 And a certain Jew **n** Apollos, born at *3686*
19:24 For a certain *man* **n** Demetrius, *3686*
20: 9 a window a certain young man **n** Eutychus, *3686*
21:10 from Judea a certain prophet, **n** Agabus. *3686*
24: 1 and *with* a certain orator *n* Tertullus, NIG
27: 1 certain other prisoners unto *one* **n** Julius, *3686*
Ro 15:20 preach the gospel, not where Christ was **n**, *3687*
1Co 5: 1 is not so much as **n** amongst the Gentiles, *3687*
Eph 1:21 and dominion, and every name that is **n**, *3687*
3:15 the whole family in heaven and earth is **n**, *3687*
5: 3 let it not be once **n** amongst you, *3687*

NAMELY (23) [NAME]

Lev 1:10 *n*, of the sheep, or of the goats, for a burnt NIH
Nu 1:32 *n*, of the children of Ephraim, *by* their NIH
9:15 the tabernacle, *n*, the tent of the Testimony: NIH
13:11 *n*, of the tribe of Manasseh, Gaddi the son NIH
31: 8 *n*, Evi, and Rekem, and Zur, and Hur, and NIH
Dt 4:43 *N*, Bezer in the wilderness, in the plain NIH
13: 7 *N*, of the gods of the people which *are* NIH
20:17 *n*, the Hittites, and the Amorites, NIH
Jdg 3: 3 *N*, five lords of the Philistines, and all NIH

Jdg 8:35 to the house of Jerubbaal, ***n***, Gideon, NIH
1Ch 6:57 ***n***, Hebron, *the city* of refuge, and Libnah NIH
6:61 ***n***, *out of* the half *tribe* of Manasseh, by lot, NIH
9:23 ***n***, the house of the tabernacle, by wards. NIH
23: 6 of Levi, ***n***, Gershon, Kohath, and Merari. NIH
Ezr 10:18 ***n***, of the sons of Jeshua the son of Jozadak, NIH
Ne 12:35 ***n***, Zechariah the son of Jonathan, the son of NIH
Est 8:12 ***n***, upon the thirteenth *day* of the twelfth NIH
Ecc 5:13 ***n***, riches kept for the owners thereof to their NIH
Isa 7:20 ***n***, by them beyond the river, by the king of NIH
Jer 26:22 ***n***, Elnathan the son of Achbor, and NIH
Mk 12:31 And the second *is* like, ***n*** this, Thou shalt NIG
Ac 15:22 ***n***, Judas surnamed Barsabas, and Silas, NIG
Ro 13: 9 **n**, Thou shalt love thy neighbour as *1722+3588*

NAMES (97) [NAME]

Ge 2:20 Adam gave **n** to all cattle, and to the fowl 8034
25:13 these *are* the **n** of the sons of Ishmael, 8034
25:13 by their **n**, according to their generations: 8034
25:16 these *are* their **n**, by their towns, and 8034
26:18 he called their **n** after the names by which 8034
26:18 he called their names after the **n** by which 8034
36:10 These *are* the **n** of Esau's sons; Eliphaz 8034
36:40 these *are* the **n** of the dukes *that came* of 8034
36:40 their families, after their places, by their **n**; 8034
46: 8 these *are* the **n** of the children of Israel, 8034
Ex 1: 1 Now these *are* the **n** of the children of 8034
6:16 these *are* the **n** of the sons of Levi 8034
28: 9 grave on them the **n** of the children of 8034
28:10 Six of their **n** on one stone, and the *other* 8034
28:10 the *other* six **n** of the rest on the other 8034
28:11 stones with the **n** of the children of Israel: 8034
28:12 Aaron shall bear their **n** before the LORD 8034
28:21 the stones shall be with the **n** of 8034
28:21 twelve, according to their **n**, *like* 8034
28:29 Aaron shall bear the **n** of the children of 8034
39: 6 with the **n** of the children of Israel. 8034
39:14 the stones *were* according to the **n** of 8034
39:14 twelve, according to their **n**, *like* 8034
Nu 1: 2 with the number of *their* **n**, every male by 8034
1: 5 these *are* the **n** of the men that shall stand 8034
1:17 these men which are expressed by *their* **n**: 8034
1:18 according to the number of the **n**, 8034
1:20 according to the number of the **n**, by their 8034
1:22 according to the number of the **n**, by their 8034
1:24 according to the number of the **n**, 8034
1:26 according to the number of the **n**, 8034
1:28 according to the number of the **n**, 8034
1:30 according to the number of the **n**, 8034
1:32 according to the number of the **n**, 8034
1:34 according to the number of the **n**, 8034
1:36 according to the number of the **n**, 8034
1:38 according to the number of the **n**, 8034
1:40 according to the number of the **n**, 8034
1:42 according to the number of the **n**, 8034
3: 2 these *are* the **n** of the sons of Aaron; 8034
3: 3 These *are* the **n** of the sons of Aaron, 8034
3:17 these were the sons of Levi by their **n**; 8034
3:18 these *are* the **n** of the sons of Gershon by 8034
3:40 and upward, and take the number of their **n**. 8034
3:43 all the firstborn males by the number of **n**, 8034
13: 4 these *were* their **n**: of the tribe of Reuben, 8034
13:16 These *are* the **n** of the men which Moses 8034
26:33 the **n** of the daughters of Zelophehad *were* 8034
26:53 inheritance according to the number of **n**. 8034
26:55 according to the **n** of the tribes of their 8034
27: 1 these *are* the **n** of his daughters; Mahlah, 8034
32:38 and Baal-meon, (*their* **n** being changed,) 8034
32:38 gave **other n** unto the cities which 8034+8034
34:17 These *are* the **n** of the men which shall 8034
34:19 the **n** of the men *are* these: Of the tribe of 8034
Dt 12: 3 and destroy the **n** of them out of that place. 8034
Jos 17: 3 these *are* the **n** of his daughters, Mahlah, 8034
1Sa 14:49 the **n** of his two daughters *were these;* 8034
17:13 the **n** of his three sons that went to 8034
2Sa 5:14 these *be* the **n** of those that were born unto 8034
23: 8 These *be* the **n** of the mighty *men* whom 8034
1Ki 4: 8 these *are* their **n**: The son of Hur, in mount 8034
1Ch 4:38 These mentioned by *their* **n** *were* princes in 8034
6:17 these *be* the **n** of the sons of Gershom; 8034
6:65 these cities, which are called by *their* **n**. 8034
8:38 whose **n** *are* these, Azrikam, Bocheru, and 8034
9:44 whose **n** *are* these, Azrikam, Bocheru, and 8034
14: 4 Now these *are* the **n** of *his* children which 8034
23:24 as they were counted by number of **n** by 8034
Ezr 5: 4 What are the **n** of the men that make this 8036
5:10 We asked their **n** also, to certify thee, 8036
5:10 that we might write the **n** of the men that 8036
8:13 whose **n** *are* these, Eliphelet, Jeiel, and 8034
10:16 all of them by *their* **n**, were separated, and 8034
Ps 16: 4 I not offer, nor take up their **n** into my lips. 8034
49:11 they call *their* lands after their own **n**. 8034
147: 4 of the stars; he calleth them all *by their* **n**. 8034
Isa 40:26 he calleth them all by **n** by the greatness of 8034
Eze 23: 4 the **n** of them *were* Aholah the elder, and 8034
23: 4 Thus *were* their **n**; Samaria *is* Aholah, and 8034
48: 1 Now these *are* the **n** of the tribes. From 8034
48:31 the gates of the city *shall be* after the **n** of 8034
Da 1: 7 whom the prince of the eunuchs gave **n**: 8034
Hos 2:17 For I will take away the **n** of Baalim out of 8034
Zec 13: 2 *that* I will cut off the **n** of the idols out of 8034
Mt 10: 2 Now the **n** of the twelve apostles are these; *3686*
Lk 10:20 because your **n** are written in heaven. *3686*
Ac 1:15 (the number of **n** together were about an *3686*
18:15 But if it be a question of words and **n**, and *3686*
Php 4: 3 whose **n** *are* in the book of life. *3686*
Rev 3: 4 Thou hast a few **n** even in Sardis, *3686*
13: 8 whose **n** are not written in the book of life *3686*
17: 3 full of **n** of blasphemy, having seven heads *3686*
17: 8 whose **n** were not written in the book of life *3686*
21:12 gates twelve angels, and **n** written *thereon*, *3686*
21:12 which are *the* **n** of the twelve tribes of NIG
21:14 in them the **n** of the twelve apostles of *3686*

NAMETH (1) [NAME]

2Ti 2:19 Let every one that **n** the name of Christ *3687*

NAOMI (20) [NAOMI'S]

Ru 1: 2 the name of his wife **N**, and the name of his 5281
1: 8 **N** said unto her two daughters in law, Go, 5281
1:11 **N** said, Turn again, my daughters: why will 5281
1:19 moved about them, and they said, *Is* this **N**? 5281
1:20 unto them, Call me not **N**, call me Mara: 5281
1:21 why *then* call ye me **N**, seeing the LORD 5281
1:22 So **N** returned, and Ruth the Moabitess, 5281
2: 1 **N** had a kinsman of her husband's, 5281
2: 2 Ruth the Moabitess said unto **N**, Let me 5281
2: 6 back with **N** out of the country of Moab: 5281
2:20 **N** said unto her daughter in law, Blessed *be* 5281
2:20 **N** said unto her, The man *is* near of kin 5281
2:22 **N** said unto Ruth her daughter in law, *It is* 5281
3: 1 **N** her mother in law said unto her, 5281
4: 3 he said unto the kinsman, **N**, that is come 5281
4: 5 day thou buyest the field of the hand of **N**, 5281
4: 9 and Mahlon's, of the hand of **N**. 5281
4:14 the women said unto **N**, Blessed *be* 5281
4:16 **N** took the child, and laid it in her bosom, 5281
4:17 it a name, saying, There is a son born to **N**; 5281

NAOMI'S (1) [NAOMI]

Ru 1: 3 Elimelech **N** husband died; and she was 5281

NAPHISH (2)

Ge 25:15 Hadar, and Tema, Jetur, **N**, and Kedemah: 5305
1Ch 1:31 Jetur, **N**, and Kedemah. These *are* the sons 5305

NAPHTALI (50) [KEDESH-NAPHTALI, NEPHTHALIM]

Ge 30: 8 have prevailed: and she called his name **N**. 5321
35:25 of Bilhah, Rachel's handmaid; Dan, and **N**: 5321
46:24 the sons of **N**; Jahzeel, and Guni, and Jezer, 5321
49:21 **N** *is* a hind let loose: he giveth goodly 5321
Ex 1: 4 Dan, and **N**, Gad, and Asher. 5321
Nu 1:15 Of **N**; Ahira the son of Enan. 5321
1:42 *Of* the children of **N**, *throughout* their 5321
1:43 *even* of the tribe of **N**, *were* fifty and 5321
2:29 the tribe of **N**: and the captain of 5321
2:29 the captain of the children of **N** *shall be* 5321
7:78 prince of the children of **N**, *offered:* 5321
10:27 children of **N** *was* Ahira the son of Enan. 5321
13:14 Of the tribe of **N**, Nahbi the son of Vophsi. 5321
26:48 *Of* the sons of **N** after their families: 5321
26:50 These *are* the families of **N** according to 5321
34:28 the prince of the tribe of the children of **N**, 5321
Dt 27:13 Gad, and Asher, and Zebulun, Dan, and **N**. 5321
33:23 of **N** he said, O Naphtali, satisfied with 5321
33:23 O **N**, satisfied with favour, and full *with* 5321
34: 2 all **N**, and the land of Ephraim, and 5321
Jos 19:32 The sixth lot came out to the children of **N**, 5321
19:32 *even* for the children of **N** according to 5321
19:39 children of **N** according to their families, 5321
20: 7 appointed Kedesh in Galilee in mount **N**, 5321
21: 6 out of the tribe of **N**, and out of the half 5321
21:32 out of the tribe of **N**, Kedesh in Galilee 5321
Jdg 1:33 Neither did **N** drive out the inhabitants of 5321
4: 6 thee ten thousand men of the children of **N** 5321
4:10 Barak called Zebulun and **N** to Kedesh; 5321
5:18 **N** *were* a people *that* jeoparded their lives 5321
6:35 unto Asher, and unto Zebulun, and unto **N**; 5321
7:23 gathered themselves together out of **N**, 5321
1Ki 4:15 Ahimaaz *was* in **N**; he also took Basmath 5321
7:14 He *was* a widow's son of the tribe of **N**, 5321
15:20 and all Cinneroth, with all the land of **N**. 5321
2Ki 15:29 all the land of **N**, and carried them captive 5321
1Ch 2: 2 Joseph, and Benjamin, **N**, Gad, and Asher. 5321
6:62 out of the tribe of **N**, and out of the tribe of 5321
6:76 out of the tribe of **N**; Kedesh in Galilee 5321
7:13 The sons of **N**; Jahziel, and Guni, and 5321
12:34 of **N** a thousand captains, and with them 5321
12:40 *even* unto Issachar and Zebulun and **N**, 5321
27:19 of **N**, Jerimoth the son of Azriel: 5321
2Ch 16: 4 and all the store cities of **N**. 5321
34: 6 and Ephraim, and Simeon, even unto **N**, 5321
Ps 68:27 princes of Zebulun, *and* the princes of **N**. 5321
Isa 9: 1 the land of Zebulun and the land of **N**, 5321
Eze 48: 3 even unto the west side, a *portion for* **N**. 5321
48: 4 by the border of **N**, from the east side unto 5321
48:34 of Gad, one gate of Asher, one gate of **N**. 5321

NAPHTUHIM (2)

Ge 10:13 and Anamim, and Lehabim, and **N**, 5320
1Ch 1:11 and Anamim, and Lehabim, and **N**, 5320

NAPHTUHITES See NAPHTUHIM

NAPKIN (3)

Lk 19:20 thy pound, which I have kept laid up in a **n**: *4676*
Jn 11:44 and his face was bound about with a **n**. *4676*
20: 7 And the **n**, that was about his head, *4676*

NARCISSUS (1)

Ro 16:11 Greet them that be of the *household* of **N**, *3488*

NARD See SPIKENARD

NARROW (9) [NARROWED, NARROWER, NARROWLY]

Nu 22:26 went further, and stood in a **n** place, 6862
Jos 17:15 if mount Ephraim be too **n** for thee. 213
1Ki 6: 4 for the house he made windows of **n** lights. 331
Pr 23:27 deep ditch; and a strange *woman is* a **n** pit. 6862
Isa 49:19 shall even now be too **n** by reason of 3334
Eze 40:16 *there were* **n** windows to the little chambers, 331
41:16 the **n** windows, and the galleries round about 331
41:26 *there were* **n** windows and palm trees on 331
Mt 7:14 and **n** *is* the way, which leadeth unto life, *2346*

NARROWED (1) [NARROW]

1Ki 6: 6 of the house he made **n rests** round about, 4052

NARROWER (1) [NARROW]

Isa 28:20 the covering **n** than that *he* can wrap 6887

NARROWLY (2) [NARROW]

Job 13:27 the stocks, and **lookest n** unto all my paths; 8104
Isa 14:16 They that see thee shall **n look** upon thee, 7688

NATHAN (43)

2Sa 5:14 and Shobab, and **N**, and Solomon, 5416
7: 2 That the king said unto **N** the prophet, 5416
7: 3 **N** said to the king, Go, do all that *is* in thine 5416
7: 4 that the word of the LORD came unto **N**, 5416
7:17 all this vision, so did **N** speak unto David. 5416
12: 1 the LORD sent **N** unto David. And he 5416
12: 5 he said to **N**, *As* the LORD liveth, the man 5416
12: 7 **N** said to David, Thou *art* the man. 5416
12:13 David said unto **N**, I have sinned against 5416
12:13 **N** said unto David, The LORD also hath 5416
12:15 **N** departed unto his house. And 5416
12:25 he sent by the hand of **N** the prophet; and 5416
23:36 Igal the son of **N** of Zobah, Bani 5416
1Ki 1: 8 **N** the prophet, and Shimei, and Rei, and 5416
1:10 **N** the prophet, and Benaiah, and the mighty 5416
1:11 Wherefore **N** spake unto Bath-sheba 5416
1:22 with the king, **N** the prophet also came in. 5416
1:23 told the king, saying, Behold **N** the prophet. 5416
1:24 And **N** said, My lord O king, hast thou said, 5416
1:32 **N** the prophet, and Benaiah the son of 5416
1:34 **N** the prophet anoint him there king over 5416
1:38 **N** the prophet, and Benaiah the son of 5416
1:44 **N** the prophet, and Benaiah the son of 5416
1:45 **N** the prophet have anointed him king in 5416
4: 5 Azariah the son of **N** *was* over the officers: 5416
4: 5 Zabud the son of **N** *was* principal officer, 5416
1Ch 2:36 Attai begat **N**, and Nathan begat Zabad, 5416
2:36 Attai begat Nathan, and **N** begat Zabad, 5416
3: 5 and Shobab, and **N**, and Solomon, four, 5416
11:38 Joel the brother of **N**, Mibhar the son of 5416
14: 4 Shammua, and Shobab, **N**, and Solomon, 5416
17: 1 that David said to **N** the prophet, Lo, 5416
17: 2 **N** said unto David, Do all that *is* in thine 5416
17: 3 that the word of God came to **N**, saying, 5416
17:15 all this vision, so did **N** speak unto David. 5416
29:29 in the book of **N** the prophet, and in 5416
2Ch 9:29 *are* they not written in the book of **N** 5416
29:25 of Gad the king's seer, and **N** the prophet: 5416
Ezr 8:16 for **N**, and for Zechariah, and 5416
10:39 And Shelemiah, and **N**, and Adaiah, 5416
Ps 51: T when **N** the prophet came unto him, 5416
Zec 12:12 the family of the house of **N** apart, and 5416
Lk 3:31 which was *the son* of **N**, which was *the son* *3481*

NATHANAEL (6)

Jn 1:45 Philip findeth **N**, and saith unto him, *3482*
1:46 And **N** said unto him, Can there any good *3482*
1:47 Jesus saw **N** coming to him, and saith of *3482*
1:48 **N** saith unto him, Whence knowest thou *3482*
1:49 **N** answered and saith unto him, Rabbi, *3482*
21: 2 and **N** of Cana in Galilee, and the *sons* of *3482*

NATHAN-MELECH (1)

2Ki 23:11 by the chamber of **N** the chamberlain, 5419

NATION (145) [NATIONS]

Ge 12: 2 I will make of thee a great **n**, and I will 1471
15:14 also that **n**, whom they shall serve, will I 1471
17:20 he beget, and I will make him a great **n**. 1471
18:18 shall surely become a great and mighty **n**, 1471
20: 4 Lord, wilt thou slay also a righteous **n**? 1471
21:13 the son of the bondwoman will I make a **n**, 1471
21:18 in thine hand; for I will make him a great **n**. 1471
35:11 a **n** and a company of nations shall be of 1471
46: 3 for I will there make of thee a great **n**. 1471
Ex 9:24 in all the land of Egypt since it became a **n**. 1471
19: 6 unto me a kingdom of priests, and a holy **n**. 1471
21: 8 to sell her unto a strange **n** he shall have no 5971
32:10 and I will make of thee a great **n**. 1471
33:13 and consider that this **n** *is* thy people. 1471
34:10 not been done in all the earth, nor in any **n**: 1471
Lev 18:26 *neither* any of **your own n**, nor any stranger 249
20:23 ye shall not walk in the manners of the **n**, 1471
Nu 14:12 will make of thee a greater **n** and 1471
Dt 4: 6 Surely this great **n** *is* a wise and 1471
4: 7 For what **n** *is there so* great, who hath God 1471
4: 8 what **n** *is there so* great, that hath statutes 1471
4:34 take him a **n** from the midst of *another* 1471
4:34 him a nation from the midst of *another* **n**, 1471
9:14 I will make of thee a **n** mightier and 1471
26: 5 became there a **n**, great, mighty, and 1471
28:33 shall a **n** which thou knowest not eat up; 5971
28:36 unto a **n** which neither thou nor thy fathers 1471
28:49 The LORD shall bring a **n** against thee 1471
28:49 a **n** whose tongue thou shalt not 1471
28:50 A **n** of fierce countenance, which shall not 1471
32:21 provoke them to anger with a foolish **n**. 1471
32:28 For they *are* a **n** void of counsel, neither *is* 1471
2Sa 7:23 what one **n** in the earth *is* like thy people, 1471
1Ki 18:10 thy God liveth, there is no **n** or kingdom, 1471
18:10 he took an oath of the kingdom and **n**, 1471
2Ki 17:29 Howbeit **every n** made gods of their 1471+1471
17:29 **every n** in their cities wherein they 1471+1471
1Ch 16:20 *when* they went from **n** to nation, and 1471
16:20 *when* they went from nation to **n**, and 1471
17:21 what one **n** in the earth *is* like thy people 1471
2Ch 15: 6 **n** was destroyed of nation, and city of city: 1471
15: 6 nation was destroyed of **n**, and city of city: 1471
32:15 for no god of any **n** or kingdom was able to 1471
Job 34:29 whether *it be done* against a **n**, or against a 1471
Ps 33:12 Blessed *is* the **n** whose God *is* the LORD; 1471
43: 1 and plead my cause against an ungodly **n**: 1471
83: 4 and let us cut them off from *being* a **n**; 1471

N

Ps 105:13 When they went from one **n** to another, 1471
106: 5 that *I* may rejoice in the gladness of thy **n**, 1471
147:20 He hath not dealt so with any **n**: and *as for* 1471
Pr 14:34 Righteousness exalteth a **n**: but sin *is* a 1471
Isa 1: 4 Ah sinful **n**, a people laden with iniquity, 1471
2: 4 **n** shall not lift up sword against nation, 1471
2: 4 nation shall not lift up sword against **n**, 1471
9: 3 Thou hast multiplied the **n**, *and* 1471
10: 6 I will send him against a hypocritical **n**, and 1471
14:32 then answer the messengers of the **n**? 1471
18: 2 to a **n** scattered and peeled, 1471
18: 2 a **n** meted out and trodden down, 1471
18: 7 a **n** meted out and trodden under foot, 1471
26: 2 that the righteous **n** which keepeth the truth 1471
26:15 Thou hast increased the **n**, O LORD, 1471
26:15 O LORD, thou hast increased the **n**: 1471
49: 7 to him whom the **n** abhorreth, to a servant 1471
51: 4 my people; and give ear unto me, O my **n**: 3816
55: 5 thou shalt call a **n** *that* thou knowest not, 1471
58: 2 as a **n** that did righteousness, and 1471
60:12 For the **n** and kingdom that will not serve 1471
60:22 a thousand, and a small one a strong **n**: 1471
65: 1 unto a **n** *that* was not called by my name. 1471
66: 8 *or* shall a **n** be born at once? for as soon as 1471
Jer 2:11 Hath a **n** changed *their* gods, which *are* yet 1471
5: 9 shall not my soul be avenged on such a **n** as 1471
5:15 Lo, I will bring a **n** upon you from far, 1471
5:15 it *is* a mighty **n**, it *is* an ancient nation, 1471
5:15 it *is* a mighty nation, it *is* an ancient **n**, 1471
5:15 a **n** whose language thou knowest not, 1471
5:29 shall not my soul be avenged on such a **n** as 1471
6:22 a great **n** shall be raised from the sides of 1471
7:28 This *is* a **n** that obeyeth not the voice of 1471
9: 9 shall not my soul be avenged on such a **n** as 1471
12:17 I will utterly pluck up and destroy that **n**, 1471
18: 7 *At what* instant I shall speak concerning a **n** 1471
18: 8 If that **n**, against whom I have pronounced, 1471
18: 9 *at what* instant I shall speak concerning a **n**, 1471
25:12 that **n**, saith the LORD, for their iniquity, 1471
25:32 evil *shall* go forth from **n** to nation, and 1471
25:32 evil *shall* go forth from nation to **n**, and 1471
27: 8 *that* the **n** and kingdom which will not 1471
27: 8 that **n** will I punish, saith the LORD, 1471
27:13 as the LORD hath spoken against the **n** 1471
31:36 cease from being a **n** before me for ever. 1471
33:24 that *they* should be no more a **n** before 1471
48: 2 come, and let us cut it off from *being* a **n**. 1471
49:31 Arise, get you up unto the wealthy **n**, 1471
49:36 there shall be no **n** whither the outcasts of 1471
50: 3 For out of the north there cometh up a **n** 1471
50:41 a great **n**, and many kings shall be raised up 1471
La 4:17 in our watching we have watched for a **n** 1471
Eze 2: 3 to a rebellious **n** that hath rebelled against 1471
37:22 I will make them one **n** in the land upon 1471
Da 3:29 That every people, **n**, and language, 524
8:22 four kingdoms shall stand up out of the **n**, 1471
12: 1 such as never was since there was a **n** *even* 1471
Joel 1: 6 For a **n** is come up upon my land, strong, 1471
Am 6:14 behold, I *will* raise up against you a **n**, 1471
Mic 4: 3 **n** shall not lift up a sword against nation, 1471
4: 3 nation shall not lift up a sword against **n**, 1471
4: 7 and her that was cast far off a strong **n**: 1471
Hab 1: 6 up the Chaldeans, *that* bitter and hasty **n**, 1471
Zep 2: 1 yea, gather together, O **n** not desired; 1471
2: 5 of the sea coast, the **n** of the Cherethites! 1471
Hag 2:14 *is* this people, and so *is* this **n** before me, 1471
Mal 3: 9 for ye *have* robbed me, *even* this whole **n**. 1471
Mt 21:43 given to a **n** bringing forth the fruits *1484*
24: 7 For **n** shall rise against nation, and *1484*
24: 7 For nation shall rise against **n**, and *1484*
Mk 7:26 woman was a Greek, a Syrophenician by **n**; *1085*
13: 8 For **n** shall rise against nation, and *1484*
13: 8 For nation shall rise against **n**, and *1484*
Lk 7: 5 For he loveth our **n**, and he hath built us a *1484*
21:10 **N** shall rise against nation, and *1484*
21:10 Nation shall rise against **n**, and *1484*
23: 2 We found this *fellow* perverting the **n**, and *1484*
Jn 11:48 and take away both our place and **n**. *1484*
11:50 the people, and *that* the whole **n** perish not. *1484*
11:51 prophesied that Jesus should die for *that* **n**; *1484*
11:52 And not for *that* **n** only, but that also he *1484*
18:35 Thine own **n** and the chief priests have *1484*
Ac 2: 5 devout men, out of every **n** under heaven. *1484*
7: 7 And the **n** to whom they shall be in *1484*
10:22 of good report among all the **n** of the Jews, *1484*
10:28 or come unto **one of another n**; *246*
10:35 But in every **n** he that feareth him, and *1484*
24: 2 that very worthy deeds are done unto this **n** *1484*
24:10 been of many years a judge unto this **n**, *1484*
24:17 many years I came to bring alms to my **n**, *1484*
26: 4 which was at the first among mine own **n** at *1484*
28:19 not that I had ought to accuse my **n** of. *1484*
Ro 10:19 *and* by a foolish **n** I will anger you. *1484*
Gal 1:14 above many *my* equals in mine own **n**, *1085*
Php 2:15 in the midst of a crooked and perverse **n**, *1074*
1Pe 2: 9 a holy **n**, a peculiar people; *1484*
Rev 5: 9 and tongue, and people, and **n**; *1484*
14: 6 and to every **n**, and kindred, and tongue, *1484*

NATIONS (336) [NATION]

Ge 10: 5 his tongue, after their families, in their **n**. 1471
10:20 in their countries, *and* in their **n**. 1471
10:31 their tongues, in their lands, after their **n**. 1471
10:32 of Noah, after their generations, in their **n**: 1471
10:32 by these were the **n** divided in the earth 1471
14: 1 king of Elam, and Tidal king of **n**; 1471
14: 9 *with* Tidal king of **n**, and Amraphel king of 1471
17: 4 and thou shalt be a father of many **n**. 1471
17: 5 for a father of many **n** have I made thee. 1471
17: 6 I will make **n** of thee, and kings shall come 1471
17:16 bless her, and she shall be *a mother of* **n**; 1471
18:18 all the **n** of the earth shall be blessed in 1471
22:18 in thy seed shall all the **n** of the earth be 1471
25:16 twelve princes according to their **n**. 523
25:23 Two **n** *are* in thy womb, and two manner of 1471
Ge 26: 4 in thy seed shall all the **n** of the earth be 1471
27:29 people serve thee, and **n** bow down to thee: 3816
35:11 and a company of **n** shall be of thee, 1471
48:19 and his seed shall become a multitude of **n**. 1471
Ex 34:24 For I will cast out the **n** before thee, and 1471
Lev 18:24 **n** are defiled which I cast out before you: 1471
18:28 as it spued out the **n** that *were* before you. 1471
Nu 14:15 the **n** which have heard the fame of thee 1471
23: 9 and shall not be reckoned among the **n**. 1471
24: 8 he shall eat up the **n** his enemies, and 1471
24:20 and said, Amalek *was* the first of the **n**; 1471
Dt 2:25 the fear of thee upon the **n** *that are* under 5971
4: 6 your understanding in the sight of the **n**, 5971
4:19 divided unto all **n** under the whole heaven. 5971
4:27 the LORD shall scatter you among the **n**, 5971
4:38 To drive out **n** from before thee greater and 1471
7: 1 hath cast out many **n** before thee, 1471
7: 1 seven **n** greater and mightier than thou; 1471
7:17 say in thine heart, These **n** *are* moe than I; 1471
7:22 the LORD thy God will put out those **n** 1471
8:20 As the **n** which the LORD destroyeth 1471
9: 1 to go in to possess **n** greater and 1471
9: 4 for the wickedness of these **n** the LORD 1471
9: 5 for the wickedness of these **n** the LORD 1471
11:23 will the LORD drive out all these **n** from 1471
11:23 ye shall possess greater **n** and mightier than 1471
12: 2 wherein the **n** which ye shall possess 1471
12:29 God shall cut off the **n** from before thee, 1471
12:30 How did these **n** serve their gods? 1471
14: 2 above all the **n** that *are* upon the earth. 5971
15: 6 thou shalt lend unto many **n**, but thou shalt 1471
15: 6 thou shalt reign over many **n**, but they shall 1471
17:14 over me, like as all the **n** that *are* about me; 1471
18: 9 to do after the abominations of those **n**. 1471
18:14 For these **n**, which thou shalt possess, 1471
19: 1 the LORD thy God hath cut off the **n**, 1471
20:15 which *are* not of the cities of these **n**. 1471
26:19 to make thee high above all **n** which he 1471
28: 1 set thee on high above all **n** of the earth: 1471
28:12 thou shalt lend unto many **n**, and thou shalt 1471
28:37 among all **n** whither the LORD shall lead 5971
28:65 among these **n** shalt thou find no ease, 1471
29:16 how we came through the **n** which ye 1471
29:18 to go *and* serve the gods of these **n**; 1471
29:24 Even all **n** shall say, Wherefore hath 1471
30: 1 shalt call *them* to mind among all the **n**, 1471
30: 3 will return and gather thee from all the **n**, 5971
31: 3 he will destroy these **n** from before thee, 1471
32: 8 When the most High divided to the **n** their 1471
32:43 Rejoice, O ye **n**, *with* his people: for he will 1471
Jos 12:23 one; the king of the **n** of Gilgal, one; 1471
23: 3 your God hath done unto all these **n** 1471
23: 4 I have divided unto you *by lot* these **n** that 1471
23: 4 with all the **n** that I have cut off, 1471
23: 7 That *ye* come not among these **n**, these that 1471
23: 9 hath driven out from before you great **n** 1471
23:12 cleave unto the remnant of these **n**, 1471
23:13 drive out *any of* these **n** from before you; 1471
Jdg 2:21 of the **n** which Joshua left when he died: 1471
2:23 Therefore the LORD left those **n**, without 1471
3: 1 Now these *are* the **n** which the LORD left, 1471
1Sa 8: 5 make us a king to judge us like all the **n**. 1471
8:20 That we also may be like all the **n**; and 1471
27: 8 for those **n** *were* of old the inhabitants of NIH
2Sa 7:23 thee from Egypt, *from* the **n** and their gods? 1471
8:11 gold that he had dedicated of all **n** which he 1471
1Ki 4:31 and his fame was in all **n** round about. 1471
11: 2 Of the **n** *concerning* which the LORD said 1471
14:24 **n** which the LORD cast out before 1471
2Ki 17:26 The **n** which thou hast removed, and 1471
17:33 after the manner of the **n** whom they 1471
17:41 So these **n** feared the LORD, and served 1471
18:33 Hath any of the gods of the **n** delivered at 1471
19:12 Have the gods of the **n** delivered them 1471
19:17 the kings of Assyria have destroyed the **n** 1471
21: 9 **n** whom the LORD destroyed before 1471
1Ch 14:17 LORD brought the fear of him upon all **n**. 1471
16:24 his marvellous works among all **n**. 5971
16:31 let *men* say among the **n**, The LORD 1471
17:21 by driving out **n** from before thy people, 1471
18:11 the gold that he brought from all *these* **n**; 1471
2Ch 7:20 to be a proverb and a byword among all **n**. 5971
13: 9 after the manner of the **n** of *other* lands? 5971
32:13 were the gods of the **n** of *those* lands any 1471
32:14 of those **n** that my fathers utterly destroyed, 1471
32:17 As the gods of the **n** of *other* lands have not 1471
32:23 that he was magnified in the sight of all **n** 1471
Ezr 4:10 the rest of the **n** whom the great and 524
Ne 1: 8 I will scatter you abroad among the **n**: 5971
9:22 thou gavest them kingdoms and **n**, 5971
13:26 among many **n** was there no king like him, 1471
Job 12:23 He increaseth the **n**, and destroyeth them: 1471
12:23 he enlargeth the **n**, and straiteneth them 1471
Ps 9:17 into hell, *and* all the **n** that forget God. 1471
9:20 *that* the **n** may know themselves *to be but* 1471
22:27 all the kindreds of the **n** shall worship 1471
22:28 and *he is* the governor among the **n**. 1471
47: 3 people under us, and the **n** under our feet. 3816
57: 9 I will sing unto thee among the **n**. 3816
66: 7 his power for ever; his eyes behold the **n**: 1471
67: 2 upon earth, thy saving health among all **n**. 1471
67: 4 O let the **n** be glad and sing for joy: 3816
67: 4 and govern the **n** upon earth. 3816
72:11 fall down before him: all **n** shall serve him. 1471
72:17 blessed in him: all **n** shall call him blessed. 1471
82: 8 judge the earth: for thou shalt inherit all **n**. 1471
86: 9 All **n** whom thou hast made shall come and 1471
96: 5 For all the gods of the **n** *are* idols: but 5971
106:27 To overthrow their seed also among the **n**, 1471
106:34 They did not destroy the **n**, 5971
108: 3 I will sing *praises* unto thee among the **n**. 3816
113: 4 The LORD *is* high above all **n**, *and* 1471
117: 1 O praise the LORD, all ye **n**: praise him, 1471
118:10 All **n** compassed me about: but in the name 1471
135:10 Who smote great **n**, and slew mighty kings; 1471
Pr 24:24 shall the people curse, **n** shall abhor him: 3816
Isa 2: 2 above the hills; and all **n** shall flow unto it. 1471
2: 4 he shall judge among the **n**, and 1471
5:26 he will lift up an ensign to the **n** from far, 1471
9: 1 the sea, beyond Jordan, in Galilee of the **n**. 1471
10: 7 his heart to destroy and cut off **n** not a few. 1471
11:12 he shall set up an ensign for the **n**, and 1471
13: 4 a tumultuous noise of the kingdoms of **n** 1471
14: 6 he that ruled the **n** in anger, *is* persecuted, 1471
14: 9 up from their thrones all the kings of the **n**. 1471
14:12 to the ground, which didst weaken the **n**! 1471
14:18 All the kings of the **n**, *even* all of them, 1471
14:26 the hand that is stretched out upon all the **n**. 1471
17:12 to the rushing of **n**, *that* make a rushing like 3816
17:13 The **n** shall rush like the rushing of many 3816
23: 3 *is* her revenue; and she is a mart of **n**. 1471
25: 3 the city of the terrible **n** shall fear thee. 1471
25: 7 and the vail that is spread over all **n**. 1471
29: 7 the multitude of all the **n** that fight against 1471
29: 8 so shall the multitude of all the **n** be, 1471
30:28 to sift the **n** with the sieve of vanity: 1471
33: 3 at the lifting up of thyself the **n** were 1471
34: 1 Come near, ye **n**, to hear; and hearken, 1471
34: 2 the indignation of the LORD *is* upon all **n**, 1471
36:18 Hath any of the gods of the **n** delivered his 1471
37:12 Have the gods of the **n** delivered them 1471
37:18 kings of Assyria have laid waste all the **n**, 776
40:15 the **n** *are* as a drop of a bucket, and 1471
40:17 All **n** before him *are* as nothing; and 1471
41: 2 gave the **n** before him, and made *him* rule 1471
43: 9 Let all the **n** be gathered together, and 1471
45: 1 I have holden, to subdue **n** before him; 1471
45:20 near together, ye *that are* escaped of the **n**: 1471
52:10 bare his holy arm in the eyes of all the **n**; 1471
52:15 So shall he sprinkle many **n**; the kings shall 1471
55: 5 and **n** *that* knew not thee shall run unto thee 1471
60:12 yea, *those* **n** shall be utterly wasted. 1471
61:11 and praise to spring forth before all the **n**. 1471
64: 2 *that* the **n** may tremble at thy presence. 1471
66:18 that *I* will gather all **n** and tongues; 1471
66:19 send those that escape of them unto the **n**, 1471
66:20 unto the LORD out of all **n** upon horses, 1471
Jer 1: 5 *and* I ordained thee a prophet unto the **n**. 1471
1:10 I have this day set thee over the **n** and 1471
3:17 all the **n** shall be gathered unto it, to 1471
3:19 a goodly heritage of the hosts of **n**? 1471
4: 2 and the **n** shall bless themselves in him, and 1471
4:16 Make ye mention to the **n**; behold, 1471
6:18 Therefore hear, ye **n**, and know, 1471
9:26 for all *these* **n** *are* uncircumcised, and 1471
10: 7 Who would not fear thee, O King of **n**? 1471
10: 7 as among all the wise *men* of the **n**, 1471
10:10 the **n** shall not be able to abide his 1471
22: 8 many **n** shall pass by this city, and 1471
25: 9 against all these **n** round about, and 1471
25:11 these **n** shall serve the king of Babylon 1471
25:13 Jeremiah hath prophesied against all the **n**. 1471
25:14 For many **n** and great kings shall serve 1471
25:15 cause all the **n**, to whom I send thee, 1471
25:17 made all the **n** to drink, unto whom 1471
25:31 the LORD hath a controversy with the **n**, 1471
26: 6 will make this city a curse to all the **n** of 1471
27: 7 all **n** shall serve him, and his son, and his 1471
27: 7 *then* many **n** and great kings shall serve 1471
27:11 the **n** that bring their neck under the yoke 1471
28:11 of all **n** within the space of two full years. 1471
28:14 a yoke of iron upon the neck of all these **n**, 1471
29:14 I will gather you from all the **n**, and 1471
29:18 among all the **n** whither I have driven 1471
30:11 though I make a full end of all **n** whither I 1471
31: 7 and shout among the chief of the **n**: 1471
31:10 O ye **n**, and declare *it* in the isles afar off, 1471
33: 9 and an honour before all the **n** of the earth, 1471
36: 2 against Judah, and against all the **n**, 1471
43: 5 that were returned from all **n**, whither they 1471
44: 8 a reproach among all the **n** of the earth? 1471
46:12 The **n** have heard *of* thy shame, and thy cry 1471
46:28 for I will make a full end of all the **n** 1471
50: 2 Declare ye among the **n**, and publish, and 1471
50: 9 assembly of great **n** from the north country: 1471
50:12 the hindermost of the **n** *shall be* a 1471
50:23 Babylon become a desolation among the **n**! 1471
50:46 is moved, and the cry is heard among the **n**. 1471
51: 7 the **n** have drunken of her wine; therefore 1471
51: 7 of her wine; therefore the **n** are mad. 1471
51:20 for with thee will I break in pieces the **n**, 1471
51:27 blow the trumpet among the **n**, prepare 1471
51:27 the nations, prepare the **n** against her, 1471
51:28 Prepare against her the **n** with the kings of 1471
51:41 become an astonishment among the **n**! 1471
51:44 the **n** shall not flow *together* any more unto 1471
La 1: 1 she *that was* great among the **n**, *and* 1471
Eze 5: 5 I have set it in the midst of the **n** and 1471
5: 6 into wickedness more than the **n**, 1471
5: 7 Because ye multiplied more than the **n** that 1471
5: 7 of the **n** that *are* round about you; 1471
5: 8 in the midst of thee in the sight of the **n**. 1471
5:14 a reproach among the **n** that *are* round 1471
5:15 an astonishment unto the **n** that *are* round 1471
6: 8 that shall escape the sword among the **n**, 1471
6: 9 the **n** whither they shall be carried captives, 1471
12:15 when I shall scatter them among the **n**, and 1471
19: 4 The **n** also heard of him; he was taken in 1471
19: 8 the **n** set against him on every side from 1471
25:10 may not be remembered among the **n**. 1471
26: 3 will cause many **n** to come up against thee, 1471
26: 5 and it shall become a spoil to the **n**. 1471
28: 7 strangers upon thee, the terrible of the **n**: 1471
29:12 I will scatter the Egyptians among the **n**, 1471
29:15 shall it exalt itself any more above the **n**: 1471
29:15 that *they* shall no more rule over the **n**. 1471
30:11 his people with him, the terrible of the **n**, 1471
30:23 I will scatter the Egyptians among the **n**, 1471
30:26 I will scatter the Egyptians among the **n**, 1471
31: 6 and under his shadow dwelt all great **n**. 1471

N

Eze 31:12 strangers, the terrible of the **n**, have cut him 1471
31:16 I made the **n** to shake at the sound of his 1471
32: 2 Thou art like a young lion of the **n**, and 1471
32: 9 I shall bring thy destruction among the **n**, 1471
32:12 to fall, the terrible of the **n**, all of them: 1471
32:16 the daughters of the **n** shall lament her: 1471
32:18 and the daughters of the famous **n**, 1471
35:10 These two **n** and these two countries shall 1471
36:13 devourest up men, and hast bereaved thy **n**; 1471
36:14 neither bereave thy **n** any more, saith 1471
36:15 neither shalt thou cause thy **n** to fall any 1471
37:22 they shall be no more two **n**, neither shall 1471
38: 8 it is brought forth out of the **n**, and they 5971
38:12 the people *that are* gathered out of the **n**, 1471
38:23 I will be known in the eyes of many **n**, and 1471
39:27 sanctified in them in the sight of many **n**; 1471
Da 3: 4 is commanded, O people, **n**, and languages, 524
3: 7 the **n**, and the languages, fell down *and* 524
4: 1 unto all people, **n**, and languages, that dwell 524
5:19 **n**, and languages, trembled and feared before 524
6:25 **n**, and languages, that dwell in all the earth; 524
7:14 a kingdom, that all people, **n**, and languages, 524
Hos 8:10 Yea, though they have hired among the **n**, 1471
9:17 and they shall be wanderers among the **n**. 1471
Joel 3: 2 I will also gather all **n**, and will bring them 1471
3: 2 whom they have scattered among the **n**, 1471
Am 6: 1 of Samaria, *which are* named chief of the **n**, 1471
9: 9 I will sift the house of Israel among all **n**, 1471
Mic 4: 2 many **n** shall come, and say, Come, and 1471
4: 3 many people, and rebuke strong **n** afar off; 1471
4:11 Now also many **n** are gathered against thee, 1471
7:16 The **n** shall see and be confounded at all 1471
Na 3: 4 that selleth **n** through her whoredoms, and 1471
3: 5 I will shew the **n** thy nakedness, and 1471
Hab 1:17 and not spare continually to slay the **n**? 1471
2: 5 gathereth unto him all **n**, and heapeth unto 1471
2: 8 Because thou hast spoiled many **n**, all 1471
3: 6 he beheld, and drove asunder the **n**; and 1471
Zep 2:14 in the midst of her, all the beasts of the **n**: 1471
3: 6 I have cut off *the* **n**: their towers are 1471
3: 8 for my determination *is* to gather the **n**, 1471
Hag 2: 7 I will shake all **n**, and the desire of all 1471
2: 7 and the desire of all **n** shall come: 1471
Zec 2: 8 After the glory hath he sent me unto the **n** 1471
2:11 many **n** shall be joined to the LORD in 1471
7:14 among all the **n** whom they knew not: 1471
8:22 strong **n** shall come to seek the LORD of 1471
8:23 shall take hold out of all languages of the **n**, 1471
12: 9 *that* I will seek to destroy all the **n** that 1471
14: 2 For I will gather all **n** against Jerusalem to 1471
14: 3 LORD go forth, and fight against those **n**, 1471
14:16 *that* every one that is left of all the **n** which 1471
14:19 the punishment of all **n** that come not up to 1471
Mal 3:12 all **n** shall call you blessed: for ye shall be a 1471
Mt 24: 9 ye shall be hated of all **n** for my name's *1484*
24:14 in all the world for a witness unto all **n**; *1484*
25:32 And before him shall be gathered all **n**: and *1484*
28:19 Go ye therefore, and teach all **n**, *1484*
Mk 11:17 My house shall be called of all **n** the house *1484*
13:10 gospel must first be published among all **n**. *1484*
Lk 12:30 For all these *things* do the **n** of the world *1484*
21:24 and shall be led away captive into all **n**: *1484*
21:25 and upon the earth distress of **n**, *1484*
24:47 be preached in his name among all **n**, *1484*
Ac 13:19 And when he had destroyed seven **n** in *1484*
14:16 Who in times past suffered all **n** to walk in *1484*
17:26 And hath made of one blood all **n** of men *1484*
Ro 1: 5 for obedience to the faith among all **n**, *1484*
4:17 I have made thee a father of many **n**,) *1484*
4:18 that he might become the father of many **n**; *1484*
16:26 made known to all **n** for the obedience of *1484*
Gal 3: 8 *saying*, In thee shall all **n** be blessed. *1484*
Rev 2:26 to him will I give power over the **n**: *1484*
7: 9 of all **n**, and kindreds, and people, and *1484*
10:11 and **n**, and tongues, and kings. *1484*
11: 9 **n** shall see their dead bodies three days and *1484*
11:18 And the **n** were angry, and thy wrath is *1484*
12: 5 who was to rule all **n** with a rod of iron: *1484*
13: 7 him over all kindreds, and tongues, and **n**. *1484*
14: 8 she made all **n** drink of the wine of *1484*
15: 4 for all **n** shall come and worship before *1484*
16:19 into three parts, and the cities of the **n** fell: *1484*
17:15 and multitudes, and **n**, and tongues. *1484*
18: 3 For all **n** have drunk of the wine of *1484*
18:23 for by thy sorceries were all **n** deceived. *1484*
19:15 that with it he should smite the **n**: *1484*
20: 3 that he should deceive the **n** no more, *1484*
20: 8 And shall go out to deceive the **n** which are *1484*
21:24 And the **n** of them which are saved shall *1484*
21:26 bring the glory and honour of the **n** into it. *1484*
22: 2 of the tree *were* for the healing of the **n**. *1484*

NATIVE (1)
Jer 22:10 shall return no more, nor see his **n** country. 4138

NATIVITY (7)
Ge 11:28 before his father Terah in the land of his **n**, 4138
Ru 2:11 the land of thy **n**, and art come unto a 4138
Jer 46:16 to the land of our **n**, from the oppressing 4138
Eze 16: 3 and thy **n** *is* of the land of Canaan; 4138
16: 4 *as for* thy **n**, in the day thou wast born thy 4138
21:30 thou wast created, in the land of thy **n**. 4351
23:15 Babylonians of Chaldea, the land of their **n**: 4138

NATURAL (13) [NATURE]
Dt 34: 7 his eye was not dim, nor his **n force** abated. 3893
Ro 1:26 for even their women did change the **n** use *5446*
1:27 the men, leaving the **n** use of the woman, *5446*
1:31 **without n affection**, implacable, *794*
11:21 For if God spared not the **n** branches, *2596+5449*
11:24 which be the **n** *branches*, be graffed *2596+5449*
1Co 2:14 But the **n** man receiveth not the *things* of *5591*
15:44 It is sown a **n** body; it is raised a spiritual *5591*
15:44 There is a **n** body, and there is a spiritual *5591*
1Co 15:46 first *which is* spiritual, but *that which is* **n**; *5591*
2Ti 3: 3 **Without n affection**, trucebreakers, *794*
Jas 1:23 he is like unto a man beholding his **n** face *1078*
2Pe 2:12 But these, as **n** brute beasts, made to be *5446*

NATURALLY (2) [NATURE]
Php 2:20 who will **n** care for your state. *1104*
Jude 1:10 but what they know **n**, as brute beasts, *5447*

NATURE (12) [NATURAL, NATURALLY]
Ro 1:26 the natural use into that which is against **n**: *5449*
2:14 do by **n** the *things* contained in the law, *5449*
2:27 shall not uncircumcision which is by **n**, *5449*
11:24 cut out of the olive tree which is wild by **n**, *5449*
11:24 wert graffed contrary to **n** into a good olive *5449*
1Co 11:14 Doth not even **n** itself teach you, that, if a *5449*
Gal 2:15 We *who are* Jews by **n**, and not sinners of *5449*
4: 8 ye did service unto them which by **n** are no *5449*
Eph 2: 3 and were by **n** the children of wrath, *5449*
Heb 2:16 For verily he took not on *him the* **n** *of* NIG
Jas 3: 6 and setteth on fire the course of **n**; *1078*
2Pe 1: 4 you might be partakers of the divine **n**, *5449*

NAUGHT (3) [NOUGHT]
2Ki 2:19 but the water *is* **n**, and the ground barren. 7451
Pr 20:14 *It is* **n**, *it is* naught, saith the buyer: but 7451
20:14 *It is* naught, *it is* **n**, saith the buyer: but 7451

NAUGHTINESS (3) [NAUGHTY]
1Sa 17:28 I know thy pride, and the **n** of thine heart; 7455
Pr 11: 6 transgressors shall be taken in their own **n**. 1942
Jas 1:21 lay apart all filthiness and superfluity of **n**, *2549*

NAUGHTY (3) [NAUGHTINESS]
Pr 6:12 A **n** person, a wicked man, walketh *with* a 1100
17: 4 *and* a liar giveth ear to a **n** tongue. 1942
Jer 24: 2 the other basket *had* very **n** figs, 7451

NAUM (1)
Lk 3:25 which was *the son* of **N**, which was *the son* *3486*

NAVEL (4)
Job 40:16 and his force *is* in the **n** of his belly. 8306
Pr 3: 8 It shall be health to thy **n**, and marrow to 8270
SS 7: 2 Thy **n** *is like* a round goblet, *which* wanteth 8326
Eze 16: 4 in the day thou wast born thy **n** was not cut, 8270

NAVES (1)
1Ki 7:33 their **n**, and their felloes, and their spokes, 1354

NAVY (6)
1Ki 9:26 king Solomon made a **n** *of ships* in 590
9:27 Hiram sent in the **n** his servants, 590
10:11 the **n** also of Hiram, that brought gold from 590
10:22 For the king had at sea a **n** of Tharshish with 590
10:22 sea a navy of Tharshish with the **n** of Hiram: 590
10:22 once in three years came the **n** of Tharshish, 590

NAY (55)
Ge 18:15 And he said, **N**; but thou didst laugh. 3808
19: 2 they said, **N**; but we will abide in the street 3808
23:11 **N**, my lord, hear me: the field give I thee, 3808
33:10 Jacob said, **N**, I pray thee, if now I have 408
42:10 **N**, my lord, but to buy food are thy servants 3808
42:12 **N**, but to see the nakedness of the land you 3808
Nu 22:30 wont to do so unto thee? And he said, **N**. 3808
Jos 5:14 he said, **N**; but *as* captain of the host of 3808
24:21 the people said unto Joshua, **N**; but we will 3808
Jdg 12: 5 *Art* thou an Ephraimite? If he said, **N**; 3808
19:23 said unto them, **N**, my brethren, *nay*, I pray 408
19:23 **n**, I pray you, do not *so* wickedly; NIH
Ru 1:13 **n**, my daughters; for it grieveth me much for 408
1Sa 2:16 *N*; but thou shalt give *it me* now: NIH
2:24 **N**, my sons; for *it is* no good report that I 408
8:19 **N**; but we will have a king over us; 3808
10:19 said unto him, *N*, but set a king over us. NIH
12:12 came against you, ye said unto me, **N**; 3808
2Sa 13:12 **N**, my brother, do not force me; 408
13:25 **N**, my son, let us not all now go, 408
16:18 Hushai said unto Absalom, **N**; but 3808
24:24 the king said unto Araunah, **N**; but I will 3808
1Ki 2:17 the king, (for he will not **say** thee **n**,) 6440+7725
2:20 of thee; *I pray thee*, **say** me not **n**. 6440+7725
2:20 my mother: for I will not **say** thee **n**. 6440+7725
2:30 he said, **N**; but I will die here. And Benaiah 3808
3:22 the other woman said, **N**; but the living *is* 3808
3:23 the other saith, **N**; but thy son *is* the dead, 3808
2Ki 3:13 the king of Israel said unto him, **N**: for 408
4:16 And she said, **N**, my lord, thou man of God, 408
20:10 **n**, but let the shadow return backward ten 3808
1Ch 21:24 king David said to Ornan, **N**; but I will 3808
Jer 6:15 **n**, they were not at all ashamed, neither 1571
8:12 **n**, they were not at all ashamed, neither 1571
Mt 5:37 your communication be, Yea, yea; **N**, nay: *3756*
5:37 your communication be, Yea, yea; Nay, **n**: *3756*
13:29 But he said, **N**; lest while ye gather up *3756*
Lk 12:51 on earth? I tell you, **N**; but rather division: *3780*
13: 3 I tell you, **N**: but, except ye repent, ye shall *3780*
13: 5 I tell you, **N**: but except ye repent, ye shall *3780*
16:30 And he said, **N**, father Abraham: but if one *3780*
Jn 7:12 He is a good *man*: others said, **N**; *3756*
Ac 16:37 **n** verily; but let them come themselves and *3756*
Ro 3:27 of works? **N**: but by the law of faith. *3780*
7: 7 **N**, I had not known sin, but by the law: for I *235*
8:37 **N**, in all these *things* we are more than *235*
9:20 **N but**, O man, who art thou that repliest *3304*
1Co 6: 8 **N**, you do wrong, and defraud, and that *your* *235*
12:22 **N**, much more those members of the body, *235*
2Co 1:17 me there should be yea yea, and **n** nay? *3756*
1:17 me there should be yea yea, and nay **n**? *3756*
1:18 our word toward you was not yea and **n**. *3756*
1:19 was not yea and **n**, but in him was yea. *3756*
Jas 5:12 but let your yea be yea; and *your* **n**, nay; *3756*
5:12 but let your yea be yea; and *your* nay, **n**; *3756*

NAZARENE (1) [NAZARETH]
Mt 2:23 by the prophets, He shall be called a **N**. *3480*

NAZARENES (1) [NAZARETH]
Ac 24: 5 and a ringleader of the sect of the **N**: *3480*

NAZARETH (29) [NAZARENE, NAZARENES]
Mt 2:23 And he came and dwelt in a city called **N**: *3478*
4:13 And leaving **N**, he came and dwelt in *3478*
21:11 This is Jesus the prophet of **N** of Galilee. *3478*
26:71 This *fellow* was also with Jesus **of N**. *3480*
Mk 1: 9 *that* Jesus came from **N** of Galilee, and *3478*
1:24 have we to do with thee, *thou* Jesus **of N**? *3479*
10:47 And when he heard that it was Jesus **of N**, *3480*
14:67 said, *And* thou also wast with Jesus **of N**. *3479*
16: 6 Ye seek Jesus of **N**, which was crucified: *3479*
Lk 1:26 from God unto a city of Galilee, named **N**, *3478*
2: 4 out of the city of **N**, into Judea, unto *3478*
2:39 returned into Galilee, to their own city **N**. *3478*
2:51 and came to **N**, and was subject unto them: *3478*
4:16 And he came to **N**, where he had been *3478*
4:34 have we to do with thee, *thou* Jesus **of N**? *3479*
18:37 they told him, that Jesus **of N** passeth by. *3480*
24:19 Concerning Jesus **of N**, which was a *3480*
Jn 1:45 and the prophets, did write, Jesus of **N**, *3478*
1:46 Can there any good *thing* come out of **N**? *3478*
18: 5 They answered him, Jesus **of N**. Jesus saith *3480*
18: 7 Whom seek ye? And they said, Jesus **of N**. *3480*
19:19 JESUS **OF N** THE KING OF THE JEWS. *3480*
Ac 2:22 Jesus **of N**, a man approved of God among *3480*
3: 6 In the name of Jesus Christ **of N** rise up and *3480*
4:10 that by the name of Jesus Christ **of N**, *3480*
6:14 that this Jesus **of N** shall destroy this place, *3480*
10:38 How God anointed Jesus of **N** with *3478*
22: 8 And he said unto me, I am Jesus **of N**, *3480*
26: 9 *things* contrary to the name of Jesus **of N**. *3480*

NAZARITE (9) [NAZARITES]
Nu 6: 2 separate *themselves* to vow a vow of a **N**, 5139
6:13 this *is* the law of the **N**, when the days of 5139
6:18 the **N** shall shave the head of his separation 5139
6:19 and shall put *them* upon the hands of the **N**, 5139
6:20 and after *that* the **N** may drink wine. 5139
6:21 This *is* the law of the **N** who hath vowed, 5139
Jdg 13: 5 for the child shall be a **N** unto God from 5139
13: 7 **N** to God from the womb to the day of his 5139
16:17 for I *have been* a **N** unto God from my 5139

NAZARITES (3) [NAZARITE]
La 4: 7 Her **N** were purer than snow, they were 5139
Am 2:11 for prophets, and of your young men for **N**. 5139
2:12 ye gave the **N** wine to drink; 5139

NAZIRITE See NAZARITE

NEAH (1)
Jos 19:13 and goeth out *to* Remmon-methoar *to* **N**; 5269

NEAPOLIS (1)
Ac 16:11 to Samothracia, and the next *day* to **N**; *3496*

NEAR (211) [NEARER]
Ge 12:11 when he was **come n** to enter into Egypt, 7126
18:23 Abraham **drew n**, and said, Wilt thou also 5066
19: 9 *even* Lot, and **came n** to break the door. 5066
19:20 this city *is* **n** to flee unto, and it *is* a little 7138
20: 4 Abimelech had not **come n** her: and 7126
27:21 **Come n**, I pray thee, that I may feel thee, 5066
27:22 Jacob **went n** unto Isaac his father; and 5066
27:25 **Bring** *it* **n** to me, and I will eat of my son's 5066
27:25 he **brought** *it* **n** to him, and he did eat: and 5066
27:26 **Come n** now, and kiss me, my son. 5066
27:27 he **came n**, and kissed him: and he smelled 5066
29:10 that Jacob **went n**, and rolled the stone 5066
33: 3 seven times, until he **came n** to his brother. 5066
33: 6 the handmaidens **came n**, they and 5066
33: 7 Leah also with her children **came n**, and 5066
33: 7 after **came** Joseph **n** and Rachel, and 5066
37:18 afar off, even before he **came n** unto them, 7126
43:19 they **came n** to the steward of Joseph's 5066
44:18 Judah **came n** unto him, and said, O my 5066
45: 4 his brethren, **Come n** to me, I pray you. 5066
45: 4 they **came n**. And he said, I *am* Joseph 5066
45:10 thou shalt be **n** unto me, thou, and 7138
48:10 he **brought** them **n** unto him; and he kissed 5066
48:13 right hand, and **brought** *them* **n** unto him. 5066
Ex 12:48 and then let him **come n** and keep it; 7126
13:17 land of the Philistines, although that *was* **n**; 7138
14:20 that the one **came** not **n** the other all 7126
16: 9 of Israel, **Come n** before the LORD: 7126
19:22 which **come n** to the LORD, 5066
20:21 Moses **drew n** unto the thick darkness 5066
24: 2 Moses alone shall **come n** the LORD: 5066
28:43 when they **come n** unto the altar to minister 5066
30:20 when they **come n** to the altar to minister, 5066
40:32 when they **came n** unto the altar, 7126
Lev 9: 5 all the congregation **drew n** and 7126
10: 4 of Aaron, and said unto them, **Come n**, 7126
10: 5 So they **went n**, and carried them in their 7126
18: 6 None of you shall approach to any that is **n** 7607
18:12 she *is* thy father's **n kinswoman**. 7607
18:13 for she *is* thy mother's **n kinswoman**. 7607
18:17 *for* they *are* her **n kinswomen**: 7608
20:19 for he uncovereth his **n kin**: they shall bear 7607
21: 2 for his kin, that is **n** unto him, *that is*, for 7138
Nu 3: 6 **Bring** the tribe of Levi **n**, and present them 7126
5:16 the priest shall **bring** her **n**, and set her 7126
16: 5 and will **cause** *him* **to come n** unto him: 7126
16: 5 chosen will he **cause to come n** unto him. 7126
16: 9 to **bring** you **n** to himself to do the service 7126
16:10 he hath **brought** thee **n** *to him*, and all thy 7126
16:40 **come n** to offer incense before the LORD; 7126
17:13 Whosoever **cometh** any thing **n** unto 7131+7131
26: 3 in the plains of Moab by Jordan **n** Jericho, NIH

Nu 26:63 in the plains of Moab by Jordan *n* Jericho. NIH
31:12 of Moab, which *are* by Jordan *n* Jericho. NIH
31:48 captains of hundreds, **came n** unto Moses: 7126
32:16 they **came n** unto him, and said, We will 5066
33:48 pitched in the plains of Moab by Jordan *n* NIH
33:50 in the plains of Moab by Jordan *n* Jericho, NIH
34:15 on *this* side Jordan *n* Jericho eastward, NIH
35: 1 in the plains of Moab by Jordan *n* Jericho, NIH
36: 1 **came n**, and spake before Moses, and 7126
36:13 in the plains of Moab by Jordan *n* Jericho. NIH
Dt 1:22 ye **came n** unto me every one of you, and 7126
4:11 ye **came n** and stood under the mountain; 7126
5:23 that ye **came n** unto me, *even* all the heads 7126
5:27 **Go** thou **n**, and hear all that the LORD our 7126
16:21 **n unto** the altar of the LORD thy God, 681
21: 5 the priests the sons of Levi shall **come n**; 5066
25:11 the wife of the one **draweth n** for to deliver 7126
Jos 3: 4 **come** not **n** unto it, that ye may know 7126
10:24 **Come n**, put your feet upon the necks of 7126
10:24 they **came n**, and put their feet upon 7126
15:46 *lay* **n** Ashdod, with their villages: 3027+5921
17: 4 they **came n** before Eleazar the priest, and 7126
18:13 **n** the hill that *lieth* on the south side of 5921
21: 1 **came n** the heads of the fathers of 5066
Jdg 18:22 the men that *were* in the houses **n** to 5973
19:13 let us **draw n** to one of *these* places to 7126
20:24 the children of Israel **came n** against 7126
20:34 but they knew not that evil *was* **n** them. 5060
Ru 2:20 The man *is* **n of kin** unto us, one of our 7138
3: 9 thine handmaid; for thou *art* a **n kinsman**. 1350
3:12 And now it is true that I *am* thy **n kinsman**: 1350
1Sa 4:19 was with child, *n* to be delivered: NIH
7:10 the Philistines **drew n** to battle against 5066
9:18 Saul **drew n** to Samuel in the gate, and 5066
10:20 **caused** all the tribes of Israel **to come n**, 7126
10:21 **caused** the tribe of Benjamin **to come n** by 7126
14:36 the priest, Let us **draw n** hither unto God. 7126
14:38 Saul said, **Draw** ye **n** hither, all the chief of 5066
17:16 the Philistine **drew n** morning and evening, 5066
17:40 in his hand: and he **drew n** to the Philistine. 5066
17:41 Philistine came on and **drew n** unto David; 7131
20:21 when David **came n** to the people, he 5066
2Sa 1:15 and said, **Go n**, *and* fall upon him. 5066
14:30 Joab's field is **n** mine, and he hath 413+3027
18:25 And he came apace, and **drew n**. 7131
19:42 of Israel, Because the king *is* **n of kin** to us: 7138
20:16 say, I pray you, unto Joab, **Come n** hither, 7126
20:17 when he was **come n** unto her, the woman 7126
1Ki 8:46 unto the land of the enemy, far or **n**; 7138
18:30 said unto all the people, **Come n** unto me. 5066
18:30 all the people **came n** unto him. And he 5066
18:36 that Elijah the prophet **came n**, and said, 5066
21: 2 of herbs, because it *is* **n** unto my house. 7138
22:24 Zedekiah the son of Chenaanah **went n**, 5066
2Ki 4:27 Gehazi **came n** to thrust her away. And 5066
5:13 his servants **came n**, and spake unto him, 5066
2Ch 6:36 them away captives unto a land far off or **n**; 7138
18:23 Zedekiah the son of Chenaanah **came n**, 5066
21:16 that *were* **n** the Ethiopians: 3027+5921
29:31 **come n** and bring sacrifices and 5066
Est 5: 2 So Esther **drew n**, and touched the top of 7126
9: 1 his decree **drew n** to be put in execution, 5060
Job 31:37 as a prince would I **go n** unto him. 7126
33:22 his soul **draweth n** unto the grave, and 7126
41:16 One is so **n** to another, that no air can come 5066
Ps 22:11 Be not far from me; for trouble *is* **n**; 7138
32: 9 and bridle, lest *they* **come n** unto thee. 7126
73:28 *it is* good for me to **draw n** to God: I have 7132
75: 1 for *that* thy name *is* **n** thy wondrous works 7138
107:18 and they **draw n** unto the gates of death. 5060
119:151 Thou *art* **n**, O LORD; and all thy 7138
119:169 Let my cry **come n** before thee, O LORD: 7126
148:14 the children of Israel, a people **n unto** him. 7138
Pr 7: 8 Passing through the street **n** her corner; and 681
10:14 the mouth of the foolish *is* **n** destruction. 7138
27:10 *for* better *is* a neighbour *that is* **n** than a 7138
Isa 13:22 her time *is* **n** to come, and her days shall 7138
26:17 *that* **draweth n the time** of her delivery, 7126
29:13 Forasmuch as this people **draw n** *me* with 5066
33:13 and ye *that are* **n**, acknowledge my might. 7138
34: 1 **Come n**, ye nations, to hear; and hearken, 7126
41: 1 let them **come n**; then let them speak: let us 5066
41: 1 let us **come n** together to judgment. 7126
41: 5 of the earth were afraid, **drew n**, and came. 7126
45:20 **draw n** together, ye *that are* escaped of 5066
45:21 Tell ye, and **bring** *them* **n**; yea, let them 5066
46:13 I **bring n** my righteousness; it shall not be 7126
48:16 **Come** ye **n** unto me, hear ye this; I have 7126
50: 8 *He is* **n** that justifieth me; who will contend 7138
50: 8 *is* mine adversary? let him **come n** to me. 5066
51: 5 My righteousness *is* **n**; my salvation is gone 7138
54:14 from terror; for it shall not **come n** thee. 7126
55: 6 be found, call ye upon him while he is **n**: 7138
56: 1 for my salvation *is* **n** to come, and 7138
57: 3 But **draw n** hither, ye sons of the sorceress, 7126
57:19 and to *him that is* **n**, saith the LORD; 7138
65: 5 Stand by thyself, **come** not **n** to me; 5066
Jer 12: 2 thou *art* **n** in their mouth, and far from their 7138
25:26 far and **n**, one with another, and all 7138
30:21 I will **cause** him **to draw n**, and he shall 7126
42: 1 the least even **unto** the greatest, came **n**, 5704
46: 3 and shield, and **draw n** to battle. 5066
48:16 The calamity of Moab *is* **n** to come, and 7138
48:24 all the cities of the land of Moab, far or **n**. 7138
52:25 seven men of them that were **n** the king's 7200
La 3:57 Thou **drewest n** in the day *that* I called 7126
4:18 our end is **n**, our days are fulfilled; for our 7126
Eze 6:12 *he* that *is* **n** shall fall by the sword; and 7138
7: 7 the day of trouble *is* **n**, and not 7138
7:12 The time is come, the day **draweth n**: 5060
9: 1 **Cause** them that have charge over the city
to draw n, 7126
9: 6 **come** not **n** any man upon whom *is* 5066
11: 3 Which say, *It is* not **n**; *let us* build 7138+871.1
18: 6 neither hath **come n** to a menstruous 7126
Eze 22: 4 thou hast **caused** thy days **to draw n**, and 7126
22: 5 *Those that be* **n**, and *those that be* far from 7138
30: 3 For the day *is* **n**, even the day of 7138
30: 3 even the day of the LORD *is* **n**, a cloudy 7138
40:46 which **come n** to the LORD to minister 7131
44:13 they shall not **come n** unto me, to do 5066
44:13 nor to **come n** to any of my holy *things*, in 5066
44:15 they shall **come n** to me to minister unto 7126
44:16 they shall **come n** to my table, to minister 7126
45: 4 which shall **come n** to minister unto 7131
Da 3: 8 at that time certain Chaldeans **came n**, 7127
3:26 Nebuchadnezzar **came n** to the mouth of 7127
6:12 they **came n**, and spake before the king 7127
7:13 and they **brought** him **n** before him. 7127
7:16 I **came n** unto one of them that stood *by*, 7127
8:17 So he came **n** where I stood: and when he 681
9: 7 all Israel, *that are* **n**, and *that are* far off, 7138
Joel 3: 9 mighty *men*, let all the men of war **draw n**; 5066
3:14 for the day of the LORD *is* **n** in the valley 7138
Am 6: 3 and **cause** the seat of violence **to come n**; 5066
Ob 1:15 For the day of the LORD *is* **n** upon all 7138
Zep 1:14 The great day of the LORD *is* **n**, *it is* near, 7138
1:14 LORD *is* near, *it is* **n**, and hasteth greatly, 7138
3: 2 in the LORD; she **drew** not **n** to her God. 7126
Mal 3: 5 I will **come n** to you to judgment; and 7126
Mt 21:34 And when the time of the fruit **drew n**, *1448*
24:33 shall see all these *things*, know that it is **n**, *1451*
Mk 13:28 forth leaves, ye know that summer is **n**: *1451*
Lk 15: 1 Then **drew n** unto him all the publicans *1448*
18:40 and when he was **come n**, he asked him, *1448*
19:41 And when he was **come n**, he beheld *1448*
21: 8 I am *Christ;* and the time **draweth n**: *1448*
22:47 and **drew n** unto Jesus to kiss him. *1448*
24:15 Jesus himself **drew n**, and went with them. *1448*
Jn 3:23 And John also was baptizing in Aenon **n** to *1451*
4: 5 **n** to the parcel of ground that Jacob gave to *4139*
11:54 went thence unto a country **n to** *1451*
Ac 7:31 as he **drew n** to behold *it*, the voice of *4334*
8:29 **Go n**, and join thyself to this chariot. *4334*
9: 3 as *he* journeyed, he **came n** Damascus: *1448*
10:24 called together his kinsmen and **n** friends, *316*
21:33 Then the chief captain **came n**, and *1448*
23:15 and we, or ever he **come n**, are ready to kill *1448*
27:27 deemed that they **drew n** to some country; *4317*
Heb 10:22 Let us **draw n** with a true heart in full *4334*

NEARER (2) [NEAR]

Ru 3:12 howbeit there is a kinsman **n** than I. 7138
Ro 13:11 for now *is* our salvation **n** than when we *1452*

NEARIAH (3)

1Ch 3:22 Igeal, and Bariah, and **N**, and Shaphat, six. 5294
3:23 the sons of **N**; Elioenai, and Hezekiah, and 5294
4:42 **N**, and Rephaiah, and Uzziel, the sons of 5294

NEBAI (1)

Ne 10:19 Hariph, Anathoth, **N**, 5109

NEBAIOTH See NEBAJOTH

NEBAJOTH (5)

Ge 25:13 the firstborn of Ishmael, **N**; and Kedar, and 5032
28: 9 the sister of **N**, to be his wife. 5032
36: 3 Bashemath Ishmael's daughter, sister of **N**. 5032
1Ch 1:29 The firstborn of Ishmael, **N**; then Kedar, 5032
Isa 60: 7 the rams of **N** shall minister unto thee: 5032

NEBALLAT (1)

Ne 11:34 Hadid, Zeboim, **N**, 5041

NEBAT (25)

1Ki 11:26 Jeroboam the son of **N**, an Ephrathite of 5028
12: 2 came to pass, when Jeroboam the son of **N**, 5028
12:15 the Shilonite unto Jeroboam the son of **N**. 5028
15: 1 the son of **N** reigned Abijam over Judah. 5028
16: 3 like the house of Jeroboam the son of **N**. 5028
16:26 in all the way of Jeroboam the son of **N**, 5028
16:31 walk in the sins of Jeroboam the son of **N**, 5028
21:22 like the house of Jeroboam the son of **N**, 5028
22:52 in the way of Jeroboam the son of **N**, 5028
2Ki 3: 3 unto the sins of Jeroboam the son of **N**, 5028
9: 9 like the house of Jeroboam the son of **N**, 5028
10:29 *from* the sins of Jeroboam the son of **N**, 5028
13: 2 followed the sins of Jeroboam the son of **N**, 5028
13:11 from all the sins of Jeroboam the son of **N**, 5028
14:24 from all the sins of Jeroboam the son of **N**, 5028
15: 9 not from the sins of Jeroboam the son of **N**, 5028
15:18 from the sins of Jeroboam the son of **N**, 5028
15:24 not from the sins of Jeroboam the son of **N**, 5028
15:28 not from the sins of Jeroboam the son of **N**, 5028
17:21 and they made Jeroboam the son of **N** king: 5028
23:15 high place which Jeroboam the son of **N**, 5028
2Ch 9:29 the seer against Jeroboam the son of **N**? 5028
10: 2 when Jeroboam the son of **N**, who *was* in 5028
10:15 the Shilonite to Jeroboam the son of **N**. 5028
13: 6 Yet Jeroboam the son of **N**, the servant of 5028

NEBO (13)

Nu 32: 3 and Elealeh, and Shebam, and **N**, and Beon, 5015
32:38 **N**, and Baal-meon, (*their* names being 5015
33:47 in the mountains of Abarim, before **N**. 5015
Dt 32:49 *unto* mount **N**, which *is* in the land of 5015
34: 1 the plains of Moab unto the mountain of **N**, 5015
1Ch 5: 8 in Aroer, even unto **N** and Baal-meon: 5015
Ezr 2:29 The children of **N**, fifty and two. 5015
10:43 Of the sons of **N**; Jeiel, Mattithiah, Zabad, 5015
Ne 7:33 The men of the other **N**, fifty and two. 5015
Isa 15: 2 Moab shall howl over **N**, and over Medeba. 5015
46: 1 Bel boweth down, **N** stoopeth, their idols 5015
Jer 48: 1 of hosts, the God of Israel; Woe unto **N**! 5015
48:22 and upon **N**, and upon Beth-diblathaim, 5015

NEBO-SARSEKIM See SARSECHIM

NEBUCHADNEZZAR (60) [NEBUCHADREZZAR]

2Ki 24: 1 In his days **N** king of Babylon came up, 5019
24:10 At that time the servants of **N** king of 5019
24:11 **N** king of Babylon came against the city, 5019
25: 1 *that* **N** king of Babylon came, he, and 5019
25: 8 which *is* the nineteenth year of king **N** king 5019
25:22 whom **N** king of Babylon had left, 5019
1Ch 6:15 and Jerusalem by the hand of **N**. 5019
2Ch 36: 6 Against him came up **N** king of Babylon, 5019
36: 7 **N** also carried of the vessels of the house of 5019
36:10 king **N** sent, and brought him to Babylon, 5019
36:13 he also rebelled against king **N**, who had 5019
Ezr 1: 7 which **N** had brought forth out of 5019
2: 1 whom **N** the king of Babylon had carried 5019
5:12 he gave them into the hand of **N** the king of 5020
5:14 which **N** took out of the temple that *was* in 5020
6: 5 which **N** took forth out of the temple which 5020
Ne 7: 6 whom **N** the king of Babylon had carried 5019
Est 2: 6 whom **N** the king of Babylon had carried 5019
Jer 27: 6 into the hand of **N** the king of Babylon, 5019
27: 8 kingdom which will not serve the same **N** 5019
27:20 Which **N** king of Babylon took not, 5019
28: 3 that **N** king of Babylon took away from this 5019
28:11 will I break the yoke of **N** king of Babylon 5019
28:14 that *they* may serve **N** king of Babylon; 5019
29: 1 to all the people whom **N** had carried away 5019
29: 3 sent unto Babylon to **N** king of Babylon, 5019
34: 1 when **N** king of Babylon, and all his army, 5019
39: 5 they brought him up to **N** king of Babylon 5019
Da 1: 1 came **N** king of Babylon *unto* Jerusalem, 5019
1:18 of the eunuchs brought them in before **N**. 5019
2: 1 in the second year of the reign of **N**, 5019
2: 1 **N** dreamed dreams, wherewith his spirit 5019
2:28 maketh known to the king **N** what shall be 5020
2:46 the king **N** fell upon his face, and 5020
3: 1 **N** the king made an image of gold, 5020
3: 2 **N** the king sent to gather together 5020
3: 2 of the image which **N** the king had set up. 5020
3: 3 of the image that **N** the king had set up; 5020
3: 3 they stood before the image that **N** had set 5020
3: 5 worship the golden image that **N** the king 5020
3: 7 worshipped the golden image that **N** 5020
3: 9 They spake and said to the king **N**, O king, 5020
3:13 **N** in *his* rage and fury commanded to bring 5020
3:14 **N** spake and said unto them, *Is it* true, 5020
3:16 answered and said to the king, O **N**, 5020
3:19 was **N** full *of* fury, and the form of his 5020
3:24 **N** the king was astonied, and rose up in 5020
3:26 **N** came near to the mouth of the burning 5020
3:28 *Then* **N** spake, and said, Blessed *be* 5020
4: 1 **N** the king, unto all people, nations, 5020
4: 4 I **N** was at rest in mine house, and 5020
4:18 This dream I king **N** have seen. Now thou, 5020
4:28 All this came upon the king **N**. 5020
4:31 *saying*, O king **N**, to thee it is spoken; 5020
4:33 same hour was the thing fulfilled upon **N**: 5020
4:34 at the end of the days I **N** lift up mine eyes 5020
4:37 Now I **N** praise and extol and honour 5020
5: 2 silver vessels which his father **N** had taken 5020
5:11 whom the king **N** thy father, the king, *I say*, 5020
5:18 the most high God gave **N** thy father a 5020

NEBUCHADREZZAR (31) [NEBUCHADNEZZAR]

Jer 21: 2 for **N** king of Babylon maketh war against 5019
21: 7 into the hand of **N** king of Babylon, and 5019
22:25 even into the hand of **N** king of Babylon, 5019
24: 1 after that **N** king of Babylon had carried 5019
25: 1 that *was* the first year of **N** king of 5019
25: 9 and **N** the king of Babylon, my servant, and 5019
29:21 I will deliver them into the hand of **N** king 5019
32: 1 which *was* the eighteenth year of **N**. 5019
32:28 into the hand of **N** king of Babylon, and 5019
35:11 when **N** king of Babylon came up into 5019
37: 1 whom **N** king of Babylon made king in 5019
39: 1 came **N** king of Babylon and all his army 5019
39:11 Now **N** king of Babylon gave charge 5019
43:10 I *will* send and take **N** the king of Babylon, 5019
44:30 Judah into the hand of **N** king of Babylon, 5019
46: 2 which **N** king of Babylon smote in 5019
46:13 how **N** king of Babylon should come 5019
46:26 into the hand of **N** king of Babylon, and 5019
49:28 which **N** king of Babylon shall smite, 5019
49:30 for **N** king of Babylon hath taken counsel 5019
50:17 last this **N** king of Babylon hath broken his 5019
51:34 **N** the king of Babylon hath devoured me, 5019
52: 4 *that* **N** king of Babylon came, he and all his 5019
52:12 which *was* the nineteenth year of **N** king of 5019
52:28 This *is* the people whom **N** carried away 5019
52:29 In the eighteenth year of **N** he carried away 5019
52:30 twentieth year of **N** Nebuzar-adan 5019
Eze 26: 7 I *will* bring upon Tyrus **N** king of Babylon, 5019
29:18 **N** king of Babylon caused his army to serve 5019
29:19 I *will* give the land of Egypt unto **N** king of 5019
30:10 to cease by the hand of **N** king of Babylon. 5019

NEBUSHASBAN (1)

Jer 39:13 **N**, Rab-saris, and Nergal-sharezer, 5021

NEBUSHAZBAN See NEBUSHASBAN

NEBUZAR-ADAN (15)

2Ki 25: 8 came **N**, captain of the guard, a servant of 5018
25:11 did **N** the captain of the guard carry away. 5018
25:20 **N** captain of the guard took these, and 5018
Jer 39: 9 **N** the captain of the guard carried away 5018
39:10 **N** the captain of the guard left of the poor 5018
39:11 Jeremiah to **N** the captain of the guard, 5018
39:13 So **N** the captain of the guard sent, and 5018
40: 1 after that **N** the captain of the guard had let 5018
41:10 whom **N** the captain of the guard had 5018
43: 6 every person that **N** the captain of the guard 5018
52:12 came **N**, captain of the guard, *which* served 5018
52:15 **N** the captain of the guard carried away 5018
52:16 **N** the captain of the guard left *certain* of 5018

Jer 52:26 So N the captain of the guard took them, 5018
52:30 twentieth year of Nebuchadrezzar N 5018

NECESSARY (9) [NECESSITY]
Job 23:12 words of his mouth more than my *n food.* *2706*
Ac 13:46 It was n that the word of God should first *316*
15:28 you no greater burden than these n *things;* *1876*
28:10 they laded *us* with such *things* as were n. *5532*
1Co 12:22 which seem to be more feeble, are n: *316*
2Co 9: 5 Therefore I thought it n to exhort *316*
Php 2:25 Yet I supposed it n to send to you *316*
Tit 3:14 also learn to maintain good works for n uses, *316*
Heb 9:23 n that the patterns of *things* in the heavens *318*

NECESSITIES (3) [NECESSITY]
Ac 20:34 these hands have ministered unto my n, *5532*
2Co 6: 4 in afflictions, in n, in distresses, *318*
12:10 in reproaches, in n, in persecutions, *318*

NECESSITY (10) [NECESSARY, NECESSITIES]
Lk 23:17 (For of n he must release one unto them at *318*
Ro 12:13 Distributing to the n of saints; given to *5532*
1Co 7:37 having no n, but hath power over his own *318*
9:16 for n is laid upon me; yea, woe is unto me, *318*
2Co 9: 7 *so let him give;* not grudgingly, or of n: *318*
Php 4:16 ye sent once and again unto my n. *5532*
Phm 1:14 that thy benefit should not be as *it were* of n, *318*
Heb 7:12 there is made of n a change also of the law. *318*
8: 3 wherefore *it is* of n that this *man* have *316*
9:16 must also of n be the death of the testator. *318*

NECHO (3)
2Ch 35:20 N king of Egypt came up to fight against 5224
35:22 hearkened not unto the words of N from 5224
36: 4 N took Jehoahaz his brother, and 5224

NECK (62) [NECKS, STIFFNECKED]
Ge 27:16 his hands, and upon the smooth of his n: 6677
27:40 thou shalt break his yoke from off thy n. 6677
33: 4 and fell on his n, and kissed him: 6677
41:42 fine linen, and put a gold chain about his n; 6677
45:14 he fell upon his brother Benjamin's n, and 6677
45:14 and wept; and Benjamin wept upon his n. 6677
46:29 he fell on his n, and wept on his neck a 6677
46:29 his neck, and wept on his n a good while. 6677
49: 8 thy hand *shall be* in the n of thine enemies; 6203
Ex 13:13 not redeem *it,* then thou shalt **break** his n: 6202
34:20 *him* not, then shalt thou **break** his n. 6202
Lev 5: 8 wring off his head from his n, but shall not 6203
Dt 21: 4 shall **strike off** the heifer's n there in 6202
28:48 and he shall put a yoke of iron upon thy n, 6677
31:27 For I know thy rebellion, and thy stiff n: 6203
1Sa 4:18 of the gate, and his n brake, and he died: 4665
2Ki 17:14 their necks, like to the n of their fathers, 6203
2Ch 36:13 he stiffened his n, and hardened his heart 6203
Ne 9:29 and hardened their n, and would not hear. 6203
Job 15:26 He runneth upon him, *even* on *his* n, 6677
16:12 he hath also taken *me* by my n, and 6203
39:19 hast thou clothed his n with thunder? 6677
41:22 In his n remaineth strength, and sorrow is 6677
Ps 75: 5 your horn on high: speak *not* with a stiff n. 6677
Pr 1: 9 unto thy head, and chains about thy n. 1621
3: 3 bind them about thy n; write them upon 1621
3:22 be life unto thy soul, and grace to thy n. 1621
6:21 upon thine heart, *and* tie them about thy n. 1621
29: 1 that being often reproved hardeneth *his* n, 6203
SS 1:10 rows *of jewels,* thy n with chains *of gold.* 6677
4: 4 Thy n *is* like the tower of David builded for 6677
4: 9 one of thine eyes, with one chain of thy n. 6677
7: 4 Thy n *is* as a tower of ivory; thine eyes *like* 6677
Isa 8: 8 and go over, he shall reach *even* to the n; 6677
10:27 his yoke from off thy n, and the yoke shall 6677
30:28 shall reach to the midst of the n, 6677
48: 4 thy n *is* an iron sinew, and thy brow brass: 6203
52: 2 loose thyself from the bands of thy n, 6677
66: 3 a lamb, *as if* he **cut off** a dog's n; 6202
Jer 7:26 nor inclined their ear, but hardened their n: 6203
17:23 made their n stiff, that *they* might not hear, 6203
27: 2 and yokes, and put them upon thy n, 6677
27: 8 that will not put their n under the yoke of 6677
27:11 the nations that bring their n under the yoke 6677
28:10 the yoke from off the prophet Jeremiah's n, 6677
28:11 n of all nations within the space of two full 6677
28:12 from off the n of the prophet Jeremiah, 6677
28:14 I have put a yoke of iron upon the n of all 6677
30: 8 *that* I will break his yoke from off thy n, 6677
La 1:14 they are wreathed, *and* come up upon my n: 6677
Eze 16:11 upon thine hands, and a chain on thy n. 1627
Da 5: 7 *have* a chain of gold about his n, and 6676
5:16 *have* a chain of gold about thy n, and 6676
5:29 *put* a chain of gold about his n, and made a 6676
Hos 10:11 *the corn;* but I passed over upon her fair n: 6677
Hab 3:13 by discovering the foundation unto the n. 6677
Mt 18: 6 that a millstone were hanged about his n, *5137*
Mk 9:42 that a millstone were hanged about his n, *5137*
Lk 15:20 and ran, and fell on his n, and kissed him. *5137*
17: 2 that a millstone were hanged about his n, *5137*
Ac 15:10 to put a yoke upon the n of the disciples, *5137*
20:37 and fell on Paul's n, and kissed him, *5137*

NECKLACES See TIRES

NECKS (18) [NECK]
Jos 10:24 put your feet upon the n of these kings. 6677
10:24 and put their feet upon the n of them. 6677
Jdg 5:30 *meet* for the n of *them that take* the spoil? 6677
8:21 the ornaments that *were* on their camels' n. 6677
8:26 the chains that *were* about their camels' n. 6677
2Sa 22:41 Thou hast also given me the n of mine 6203
2Ki 17:14 hardened their n, like to the neck of their 6203
Ne 3: 5 their nobles put not their n to the work of 6677
9:16 hardened their n, and hearkened not to thy 6203
9:17 hardened their n, and in their rebellion 6203
Ps 18:40 Thou hast also given me the n of mine 6203

Isa 3:16 walk with stretched forth n and 1627
Jer 19:15 because they have hardened their n, 6203
27:12 Bring your n under the yoke of the king of 6677
La 5: 5 Our n *are* under persecution: we labour, 6677
Eze 21:29 to bring thee upon the n of *them that are* 6677
Mic 2: 3 from which ye shall not remove your n; 6677
Ro 16: 4 have for my life laid down their own n: *5137*

NECO See NECHO

NECROMANCER (1)
Dt 18:11 or a wizard, or a n. 413+1875+1886.1

NEDABIAH (1)
1Ch 3:18 and Shenazar, Jecamiah, Hoshama, and N. 5072

NEED (49) [NEEDED, NEEDEST, NEEDETH, NEEDFUL, NEEDS, NEEDY]
Dt 15: 8 shalt surely lend him sufficient for his n, 4270
1Sa 21:15 *Have* I n of mad men, that ye have brought 2638
2Ch 2:16 out of Lebanon, as much as thou shalt n: 6878
20:17 Ye shall not n to fight in this *battle:* set NIH
Ezr 6: 9 that which *they* **have n of,** both young 2818
Pr 31:11 in her, so that he shall **have** no n of spoil. 2637
Mt 3:14 I have n to be baptized of thee, and *5532*
6: 8 Father knoweth what *things* ye have n of, *5532*
6:32 knoweth that ye **have** n of all these *things.* *5535*
9:12 They that be whole n not a *2192+5532*
14:16 said unto them, They n not depart; *2192+5532*
21: 3 ye shall say, The Lord hath n of them; *5532*
26:65 what further n have we of witnesses? *5532*
Mk 2:17 They that are whole have no n of *5532*
2:25 when he had n, and was a hungred, he, and *5532*
11: 3 say ye that the Lord hath n of him; and *5532*
14:63 What n we any further witnesses? *2192+5532*
Lk 5:31 that are whole n not a physician; *2192+5532*
9:11 and healed them that had n of healing. *5532*
12:30 your Father knoweth that ye **have** n of *5535*
15: 7 just *persons* which n no repentance. *2192+5532*
19:31 unto him, Because the Lord hath n of him. *5532*
19:34 And they said, The Lord hath n of him. *5532*
22:71 What n we any further witness? *2192+5532*
Jn 13:29 Buy *those things* that we have n of against *5532*
Ac 2:45 parted them to all *men,* as every *man* had n. *5532*
4:35 unto every man according as he had n. *5532*
Ro 16: 2 in whatsoever business she hath n of you: *5535*
1Co 7:36 and n so require, let him do what he will, *3784*
12:21 say unto the hand, I have no n of thee: *5532*
12:21 the head to the feet, I have no n of you. *5532*
12:24 For our comely *parts* have no n: *5532*
2Co 3: 1 or n we, as some *others,* epistles of *5535*
Php 4:12 be hungry, both to abound and to **suffer** n. *5302*
4:19 But my God shall supply all your n *5532*
1Th 1: 8 so that we n not to speak any *thing.* *2192+5532*
4: 9 But as touching brotherly love ye n *2192+5532*
5: 1 ye have no n that *I* write unto you. *5532*
Heb 4:16 and find grace to help in **time of** n. *2121*
5:12 ye have n that *one* teach you again which *5532*
5:12 and are become such as have n of milk, and *5532*
7:11 what further n *was there* that another priest *5532*
10:36 For ye have n of patience, that, after ye *5532*
1Pe 1: 6 though now for a season, if n be, *1163*
1Jn 2:27 and ye n not that any *man* teach you: *2192+5532*
3:17 and seeth his brother hath n, and *5532*
Rev 3:17 with goods, and have n of nothing; *5532*
21:23 And the city had no n of the sun, neither of *5532*
22: 5 and they n no candle, neither light of *2192+5532*

NEEDED (2) [NEED]
Jn 2:25 And n not that any should testify of *2192+5532*
Ac 17:25 as though he n any *thing,* seeing he giveth *4326*

NEEDEST (1) [NEED]
Jn 16:30 n not that any *man* should ask thee: *2192+5532*

NEEDETH (6) [NEED]
Ge 33:15 he said, What n it? let me find grace in NIH
Lk 11: 8 he will rise and give him as many as he n. *5535*
Jn 13:10 He that is washed n not save to wash *2192+5532*
Eph 4:28 he may have to give to him that n. *2192+5532*
2Ti 2:15 a workman that **n not to be ashamed,** *422*
Heb 7:27 Who n not daily, as *those* high priests, *318+2250*

NEEDFUL (6) [NEED]
Ezr 7:20 whatsoever more *shall be* n for the house of 2819
Lk 10:42 But one *thing* is n: and Mary hath chosen *5532*
Ac 15: 5 That it was n to circumcise them, and *1163*
Php 1:24 Nevertheless to abide in the flesh *is* **more n** *316*
Jas 2:16 not those *things* which *are* n to the body; *2006*
Jude 1: 3 it was n for me to write unto you, and *318+2192*

NEEDLE (2) [NEEDLE'S, NEEDLEWORK]
Mt 19:24 for a camel to go through the eye of a n, *4476*
Mk 10:25 for a camel to go through the eye of a n, *4476*

NEEDLE'S (1) [NEEDLE]
Lk 18:25 For it is easier for a camel to go through a n *4476*

NEEDLEWORK (9) [NEEDLE, WORK]
Ex 26:36 fine twined linen, **wrought with n.** 4639+7551
27:16 fine twined linen, wrought with n: 7551
28:39 and thou shalt make the girdle *of* n. 4639+7551
36:37 scarlet, and fine twined linen, *of* n; 4639+7551
38:18 for the gate of the court *was* n, 4639+7551
39:29 blue, and purple, and scarlet, *of* n; 4639+7551
Jdg 5:30 a prey of divers colours of n, 7553
5:30 of divers colours of n on both sides, 7553
Ps 45:14 be brought unto the king in **raiment of n:** 7553

NEEDS (16) [NEED]
Ge 17:13 thy money, **must n be circumcised:** 4135+4135
19: 9 to sojourn, and he will **n be a judge:** 8199+8199
24: 5 **must** I **n bring** thy son **again** unto 7725+7725

31:30 *though* thou wouldest **n be gone,** 1980+1980
2Sa 14:14 For we **must n die,** and *are* as water 4191+4191
Jer 10: 5 they **must n be borne,** because 5375+5375
Mt 18: 7 for it **must** n be that offences come; but *318*
Mk 13: 7 for *such things* **must** n be; but the end *shall* *1163*
Lk 14:18 a piece of ground, and I must n go and see it: *318*
Jn 4: 4 And he **must** n go through Samaria. *1163*
Ac 1:16 this scripture **must** n have been fulfilled, *1163*
17: 3 that Christ **must** n have suffered, and *1163*
21:22 the multitude **must** n come together: *1163+3843*
Ro 13: 5 Wherefore *ye* **must** n be subject, not only *318*
1Co 5:10 for then **must** ye n go out of the world. *3784*
2Co 11:30 If I **must** n glory, I will glory of the *things* *1163*

NEEDY (38) [NEED]
Dt 15:11 to thy poor, and to thy n, in thy land. 34
24:14 not oppress a hired servant *that is* poor and n, 34
Job 24: 4 They turn the n out of the way: the poor of 34
24:14 rising with the light killeth the poor and n, 34
Ps 9:18 For the n shall not alway be forgotten: 34
12: 5 for the sighing of the n, now will I arise, 34
35:10 and the n from him that spoileth him? 34
37:14 to cast down the poor and n, *and* to slay such 34
40:17 I *am* poor and n; *yet* the Lord thinketh upon 34
70: 5 I *am* poor and n: make haste unto me, O God: 34
72: 4 he shall save the children of the n, and 34
72:12 For he shall deliver the n when he crieth; 34
72:13 He shall spare the poor and n, and shall save 34
72:13 and needy, and shall save the souls of the n. 34
74:21 let the poor and n praise thy name. 34
82: 3 fatherless: do justice to the afflicted and n. 7326
82: 4 Deliver the poor and n: rid *them* out of 34
86: 1 O LORD, hear me: for I *am* poor and n. 34
109:16 persecuted the poor and n man, that *he* might 34
109:22 For I *am* poor and n, and my heart is wounded 34
113: 7 the dust, *and* lifteth the n out of the dunghill; 34
Pr 30:14 off the earth, and the n from *among* men. 34
31: 9 and plead the cause of the poor and n. 34
31:20 yea, she reacheth forth her hands to the n. 34
Isa 10: 2 To turn aside the n from judgment, and 1800
14:30 shall feed, and the n shall lie down in safety: 34
25: 4 a strength to the n in his distress, a refuge 34
26: 6 the feet of the poor, *and* the steps of the n. 1800
32: 7 lying words, even when the n speaketh right. 34
41:17 *When* the poor and n seek water, and *there is* 34
Jer 5:28 and the right of the n do they not judge. 34
22:16 He judged the cause of the poor and n; then 34
Eze 16:49 did she strengthen the hand of the poor and n. 34
18:12 Hath oppressed the poor and n, hath spoiled 34
22:29 and have vexed the poor and n: 34
Am 4: 1 which oppress the poor, which crush the n, 34
8: 4 Hear this, O ye that swallow up the n, even to 34
8: 6 poor for silver, and the n for a pair of shoes; 34

NEESED (1) [NEESINGS]
2Ki 4:35 the child n seven times, and the child 2237

NEESINGS (1) [NEESED]
Job 41:18 *By* his n a light doth shine, and his eyes *are* 5846

NEGINAH (1)
Ps 61: T To the chief Musician upon N, *A Psalm* of 5058

NEGINOTH (6)
Ps 4: T To the chief Musician on N, A Psalm of 5058
6: T To the chief Musician on N upon 5058
54: T To the chief Musician on N, Maschil, 5058
55: T To the chief Musician on N, Maschil, 5058
67: T To the chief Musician on N, A Psalm *or* 5058
76: T To the chief Musician on N, A Psalm *or* 5058

NEGLECT (4) [NEGLECTED, NEGLECTING, NEGLIGENT]
Mt 18:17 And if he shall **n to hear** them, tell *it* unto *3878*
18:17 but if he **n to hear** the church, let him be *3878*
1Ti 4:14 N not the gift that is in thee, which was *272*
Heb 2: 3 shall we escape, if we n so great salvation; *272*

NEGLECTED (1) [NEGLECT]
Ac 6: 1 their widows were n in the daily *3865*

NEGLECTING (1) [NEGLECT]
Col 2:23 and humility, and n of the body, not in any *857*

NEGLIGENT (2) [NEGLECT]
2Ch 29:11 My sons, be not now n: for the LORD 7952
2Pe 1:12 Wherefore I will not be n to put you always *272*

NEHELAMITE (3)
Jer 29:24 shalt thou also speak to Shemaiah the N, 5161
29:31 the LORD concerning Shemaiah the N; 5161
29:32 I will punish Shemaiah the N, and his seed: 5161

NEHEMIAH (8)
Ezr 2: 2 Jeshua, N, Seraiah, Reelaiah, Mordecai, 5166
Ne 1: 1 The words of N the son of Hachaliah. 5166
3:16 After him repaired N the son of Azbuk, 5166
7: 7 Jeshua, N, Azariah, Raamiah, Nahamani, 5166
8: 9 N, which *is* the Tirshatha, and Ezra 5166
10: 1 Now those that sealed *were,* N, 5166
12:26 in the days of N the governor, and of Ezra 5166
12:47 in the days of N, gave the portions of 5166

NEHILOTH (1)
Ps 5: T To the chief Musician upon N, A Psalm of 5155

NEHUM (1)
Ne 7: 7 Bilshan, Mispereth, Bigvai, N, Baanah. 5149

NEHUSHTA (1)
2Ki 24: 8 his mother's name *was* N, the daughter of 5179

NEHUSHTAN (1)

2Ki 18: 4 did burn incense to it: and he called it **N**. 5180

NEIEL (1)

Jos 19:27 **N**, and goeth out to Cabul on the left hand, 5272

NEIGHBOUR (106) [NEIGHBOUR'S, NEIGHBOURS, NEIGHBOURS']

Ex 3:22 every woman shall borrow of her **n**, and 7934
11: 2 let every man borrow of his **n**, and 7453
11: 2 every woman of her **n**, jewels of silver, and 7468
12: 4 his **n** next unto his house take *it* according 7934
20:16 shalt not bear false witness against thy **n**. 7453
21:14 if a man come presumptuously upon his **n**, 7453
22: 7 If a man shall deliver unto his **n** money or 7453
22: 9 he shall pay double unto his **n**. 7453
22:10 If a man deliver unto his **n** an ass, or an ox, 7453
22:14 if a man borrow *ought* of his **n**, and it be 7453
32:27 man his companion, and every man his **n**. 7138
Lev 6: 2 lie unto his **n** in that which was delivered 5997
6: 2 away by violence, or hath deceived his **n**; 5997
19:13 Thou shalt not defraud thy **n**, neither rob 7453
19:15 *but* in righteousness shalt thou judge thy **n**. 5997
19:16 shalt thou stand against the blood of thy **n**: 7453
19:17 thou shalt in any wise rebuke thy **n**, and 5997
19:18 but thou shalt love thy **n** as thyself: 7453
24:19 if a man cause a blemish in his **n**; as he 5997
25:14 if thou sell ought unto thy **n**, or 5997
25:15 after the jubile thou shalt buy of thy **n**, 5997
Dt 4:42 which should kill his **n** unawares, and 7453
5:20 shalt thou bear false witness against thy **n**. 7453
15: 2 Every creditor that lendeth *ought* unto his **n** 7453
15: 2 shall release *it*; he shall not exact *it* of his **n**, 7453
19: 4 Whoso killeth his **n** ignorantly, whom he 7453
19: 5 into the wood with his **n** to hew wood, 7453
19: 5 and lighteth upon his **n**, that he die; 7453
19:11 if any man hate his **n**, and lie in wait for 7453
22:26 for as when a man riseth against his **n**, and 7453
27:24 Cursed *be* he that smiteth his **n** secretly. 7453
Jos 20: 5 because he smote his **n** unwittingly, 7453
Ru 4: 7 plucked off his shoe, and gave *it* to his **n**: 7453
1Sa 15:28 hath given it to a **n** of thine, *that is* better 7453
28:17 and given it to thy **n**, *even* to David: 7453
2Sa 12:11 give *them* unto thy **n**, and he shall lie with 7453
1Ki 8:31 If any man trespass against his **n**, and 7453
20:35 said unto his **n** in the word of the LORD, 7453
2Ch 6:22 If a man sin against his **n**, and an oath be 7453
Job 12: 4 I am *as* one mocked of his **n**, who calleth 7453
16:21 man with God, as a man *pleadeth* for his **n**. 7453
Ps 12: 2 They speak vanity every one with his **n**: 7453
15: 3 not with his tongue, nor doeth evil to his **n**, 7453
15: 3 nor taketh up a reproach against his **n**. 7138
101: 5 Whoso privily slandereth his **n**, him will I 7453
Pr 3:28 Say not unto thy **n**, Go, and come again, 7453
3:29 Devise not evil against thy **n**, seeing he 7453
11: 9 hypocrite with *his* mouth destroyeth his **n**: 7453
11:12 He that is void of wisdom despiseth his **n**: 7453
12:26 The righteous *is* more excellent than his **n**: 7453
14:20 The poor is hated even of his own **n**: but 7453
14:21 He that despiseth his **n** sinneth: but he that 7453
16:29 A violent man enticeth his **n**, and 7453
18:17 but his **n** cometh and searcheth him. 7453
19: 4 but the poor is separated from his **n**. 7453
21:10 his **n** findeth no favour in his eyes. 7453
24:28 Be not a witness against thy **n** without 7453
25: 8 when thy **n** hath put thee to shame. 7453
25: 9 Debate thy cause with thy **n** *himself*; and 7453
25:18 false witness against his **n** *is* a maul, 7453
26:19 So *is* the man *that* deceiveth his **n**, and 7453
27:10 *for* better *is* a **n** *that is* near than a brother 7934
29: 5 A man that flattereth his **n** spreadeth a net 7453
Ecc 4: 4 that for this a man is envied of his **n**. 7453
Isa 3: 5 one by another, and every one by his **n**: 7453
19: 2 his brother, and every one against his **n**, 7453
41: 6 They helped every one his **n**; and *every one* 7453
Jer 6:21 the **n** and his friend shall perish. 7934
7: 5 execute judgment between a man and his **n**; 7453
9: 4 Take ye heed every one of his **n**, and trust 7453
9: 4 every **n** will walk *with* slanders. 7453
9: 5 they will deceive every one his **n**, and 7453
9: 8 *one* speaketh peaceably to his **n** with his 7453
9:20 and every one her **n** lamentation. 7468
22: 8 and they shall say every man to his **n**, 7453
23:27 dreams which they tell every man to his **n**, 7453
23:30 that steal my words every one from his **n**. 7453
23:35 Thus shall ye say every one to his **n**, and 7453
31:34 they shall teach no more every man his **n**, 7453
34:15 in proclaiming liberty every man to his **n**; 7453
34:17 one to his brother, and every man to his **n**: 7453
49:18 and Gomorrah and the **n** *cities* thereof, 7934
50:40 and Gomorrah and the **n** *cities* thereof, 7934
Hab 2:15 Woe unto him that giveth his **n** drink, 7453
Zec 3:10 shall ye call every man his **n**, under 7453
8:10 for I set all men every one against his **n**. 7453
8:16 Speak ye every man the truth to his **n**; 7453
8:17 imagine evil in your hearts against his **n**; 7453
14:13 lay hold every one on the hand of his **n**, 7453
14:13 hand shall rise up against the hand of his **n**. 7453
Mt 5:43 Thou shalt love thy **n**, and hate thine *4139*
19:19 and, Thou shalt love thy **n** as thyself. *4139*
22:39 unto it, Thou shalt love thy **n** as thyself. *4139*
Mk 12:31 Thou shalt love thy **n** as thyself. *4139*
12:33 the strength, and to love *his* **n** as himself, *4139*
Lk 10:27 and with all thy mind; and thy **n** as thyself. *4139*
10:29 said unto Jesus, And who is my **n**? *4139*
10:36 was **n** unto him that fell among the thieves? *4139*
Ac 7:27 But he that did his **n** wrong thrust him *4139*
Ro 13: 9 namely; Thou shalt love thy **n** as thyself. *4139*
13:10 Love worketh no ill to his **n**: therefore love *4139*
15: 2 Let every one of us please *his* **n** for *his* *4139*
Gal 5:14 *even* in *this*; Thou shalt love thy **n** as *4139*
Eph 4:25 speak every man truth with his **n**: *4139*
Heb 8:11 And they shall not teach every man his **n**, *4139*
Jas 2: 8 Thou shalt love thy **n** as thyself, ye do well: *4139*

NEIGHBOUR'S (29) [NEIGHBOUR]

Ex 20:17 Thou shalt not covet thy **n** house, thou shalt 7453
20:17 thou shalt not covet thy **n** wife, nor his 7453
20:17 nor his ass, nor any thing that *is* thy **n**. 7453
22: 8 he have put his hand unto his **n** goods. 7453
22:11 that he hath not put his hand unto his **n** 7453
22:26 If thou at all take thy **n** raiment to pledge, 7453
Lev 18:20 thou shalt not lie carnally with thy **n** wife, 5997
20:10 *even he* that committeth adultery with his **n** 7453
25:14 or buyest *ought* of thy **n** hand, ye shall not 5997
Dt 5:21 Neither shalt thou desire thy **n** wife, 7453
5:21 neither shalt thou covet thy **n** house, 7453
5:21 his ass, or any *thing* that *is* thy **n**. 7453+3807.1
19:14 Thou shalt not remove thy **n** landmark, 7453
22:24 because he hath humbled his **n** wife: 7453
23:24 When thou comest into thy **n** vineyard, 7453
23:25 thou comest into the standing corn of thy **n**, 7453
23:25 thou shalt not move a sickle unto thy **n** 7453
27:17 Cursed *be* he that removeth his **n** landmark. 7453
Job 31: 9 or *if* I have laid wait at my **n** door; 7453
Pr 6:29 So he that goeth in to his **n** wife; 7453
25:17 Withdraw thy foot from thy **n** house; 7453
Jer 5: 8 every one neighed after his **n** wife. 7453
22:13 *that* useth his **n** service without wages, and 7453
Eze 18: 6 neither hath defiled his **n** wife, neither hath 7453
18:11 upon the mountains, and defiled his **n** wife, 7453
18:15 house of Israel, hath not defiled his **n** wife, 7453
22:11 one hath committed abomination with his **n** 7453
33:26 and ye defile every one his **n** wife: 7453
Zec 11: 6 I *will* deliver the men every one into his **n** 7453

NEIGHBOURS (21) [NEIGHBOUR]

Jos 9:16 that they heard that they *were* their **n**, and 7138
Ru 4:17 the *women her* **n** gave it a name, saying, 7934
2Ki 4: 3 Go, borrow thee vessels abroad of all thy **n**, 7934
Ps 28: 3 which speak peace to their **n**, but 7453
31:11 especially among my **n**, and a fear to mine 7934
44:13 Thou makest us a reproach to our **n**, a scorn 7934
79: 4 We are become a reproach to our **n**, a scorn 7934
79:12 render unto our **n** sevenfold into their 7934
80: 6 Thou makest us a strife unto our **n**: and 7934
89:41 the way spoil him: he is a reproach to his **n**. 7934
Jer 12:14 saith the LORD against all mine evil **n**, 7934
49:10 and his brethren, and his **n**, and he *is* not. 7934
Eze 16:26 fornication with the Egyptians thy **n**, 7934
22:12 thou hast greedily gained of thy **n** by 7453
23: 5 doted on her lovers, on the Assyrians *her* **n**, 7138
23:12 She doted upon the Assyrians *her* **n**, 7138
Lk 1:58 And *her* **n** and her cousins heard how *4040*
14:12 neither thy kinsmen, nor *thy* rich **n**; *1069*
15: 6 he calleth together *his* friends and **n**, *1069*
15: 9 she calleth *her* friends and *her* **n** together, *1069*
Jn 9: 8 The **n** therefore, and they which before had *1069*

NEIGHBOURS' (1) [NEIGHBOUR]

Jer 29:23 have committed adultery with their **n** 7453

NEIGHED (1) [NEIGHING]

Jer 5: 8 every one **n** after his neighbour's wife. 6670

NEIGHING (1) [NEIGHED, NEIGHINGS]

Jer 8:16 at the sound of the **n** of his strong ones; 4684

NEIGHINGS (1) [NEIGHING]

Jer 13:27 I have seen thine adulteries, and thy **n**, 4684

NEITHER (879)

Ge 3: 3 of it, **n** shall ye touch it, lest ye die. 3808+2050.1
8:21 **n** will I again smite any more every 3808+2050.1
9:11 **n** shall all flesh be cut off any more 3808+2050.1
9:11 **n** shall there any more be a flood to 3808+2050.1
17: 5 **N** shall thy name any more be 3808+2050.1
19:17 **n** stay thou in all the plain; 408+2050.1
21:26 **n** didst thou tell me, 1571+3808+2050.1
21:26 **n yet** heard I *of it*, but to 1571+3808+2050.1
22:12 **n** do thou any thing unto him: 408+2050.1
24:16 **n** had any man known her: 3808+2050.1
29: 7 **n** *is it* time that the cattle should be 3808
39: 9 none greater in this house than I; **n** 3808+2050.1
45: 6 *in* the which *there shall* **n** *be* earing nor 369
Ex 4: 8 **n** hearken to the voice of the first 3808+2050.1
4: 9 **n** hearken unto thy voice, 3808+2050.1
4:10 my Lord, I *am* not eloquent, **n** heretofore, 1571
5: 2 **n** will I let Israel go. 1571+3808+2050.1
5:23 **n** hast thou delivered thy people at 3808+2050.1
7:22 **n** did he hearken unto them; 3808+2050.1
7:23 **n** did he set his heart to this also. 3808+2050.1
8:32 **n** would he let the people go. 3808+2050.1
9:29 **n** shall there be any more hail; 3808+2050.1
9:35 **n** would he let the children of 3808+2050.1
10: 6 which **n** thy fathers, nor thy fathers' fathers 3808
10:14 as they, **n** after them shall be such. 3808+2050.1
10:23 **n** rose any from his place for three 3808+2050.1
12:39 **n** had they prepared for 1571+3808+2050.1
12:46 **n** shall ye break a bone thereof. 3808+2050.1
13: 7 **n** shall there be leaven seen with 3808+2050.1
16:24 **n** was there any worm therein. 3808+2050.1
20:23 **n** shall ye make unto you gods of 3808+2050.1
20:26 **N** shalt thou go up by steps unto 3808+2050.1
22:21 Thou shalt **n** vex a stranger, 3808+2050.1
22:25 an usurer, **n** shalt thou lay upon him usury. 3808
22:31 **n** shall ye eat *any* flesh *that is* torn 3808+2050.1
23: 2 **n** shalt thou speak in a cause to 3808+2050.1
23: 3 **N** shalt thou countenance a poor 3808+2050.1
23:13 **n** let it be heard out of thy mouth. 3808
23:18 **n** shall the fat of my sacrifice 3808+2050.1
24: 2 **n** shall the people go up with him. 3808+2050.1
30: 9 **n** shall ye pour drink offering 3808+2050.1
30:32 **n** shall ye make *any other* like it, 3808+2050.1
32:18 **n** *is it* the voice of *them that* cry for 369+2050.1
34: 3 **n** let any man be seen 408+1571+2050.1
34: 3 **n** let the flocks nor herds feed before 408+1571
34:24 **n** shall any man desire thy land, 3808+2050.1
34:25 **n** shall the sacrifice of the feast of 3808+2050.1
Ex 34:28 he did **n** eat bread, nor drink water. 3808
36: 6 Let **n** man nor woman make any more work 408
Lev 2:13 **n** shalt thou suffer the salt of 3808+2050.1
3:17 your dwellings, *that* ye eat **n** fat nor blood. 3808
5:11 **n** shall he put *any* frankincense 3808+2050.1
7:18 **n** shall it be imputed unto him that offereth 3808
10: 6 your heads, **n** rend your clothes; 3808+2050.1
11:43 **n** shall ye make yourselves unclean 3808+2050.1
11:44 **n** shall ye defile yourselves with 3808+2050.1
17:12 No soul of you shall eat blood, **n** 3808+2050.1
18: 3 **n** shall ye walk in their ordinances. 3808+2050.1
18:17 **n** shalt thou take her son's daughter, or 3808
18:18 **N** shalt thou take a wife to her 3808+2050.1
18:21 **n** shalt thou profane the name of 3808+2050.1
18:23 **N** shalt thou lie with any beast to 3808+2050.1
18:23 **n** shall any woman stand before a 3808+2050.1
18:26 *n* any of your own nation, nor any stranger NIH
19: 9 **n** shalt thou gather the gleanings of 3808+2050.1
19:10 **n** shalt thou gather *every* grape of 3808+2050.1
19:11 Ye shall not steal, **n** deal falsely, 3808+2050.1
19:11 deal falsely, **n** lie one to another. 3808+2050.1
19:12 **n** shalt thou profane the name of thy God: 2050.1
19:13 **n** rob *him*: the wages of him that is 3808+2050.1
19:16 **n** shalt thou stand against the blood of thy 3808
19:19 **n** shall a garment mingled of linen 3808+2050.1
19:26 **n** shall ye use enchantment, nor observe 3808
19:27 **n** shalt thou mar the corners of thy 3808+2050.1
19:31 **n** seek after wizards, to be defiled 408+2050.1
21: 5 **n** shall they shave off the corner of 3808+2050.1
21: 7 **n** shall they take a woman put 3808+2050.1
21:11 **N** shall he go in to any dead body, 3808+2050.1
21:12 **N** shall he go out of the sanctuary, 3808+2050.1
21:15 **N** shall he profane his seed among 3808+2050.1
22:24 **n** shall you make *any* offering 3808+2050.1
22:25 **N** from a stranger's hand shall ye 3808+2050.1
22:32 **N** shall ye profane my holy name; 3808+2050.1
23:14 ye shall eat **n** bread, nor parched *corn*, nor 3808
23:22 **n** shalt thou gather *any* gleaning of 3808+2050.1
25: 4 thou shalt **n** sow thy field, nor prune thy 3808
25: 5 **n** gather the grapes of thy vine 3808+2050.1
25:11 **n** reap that which groweth of itself 3808+2050.1
26: 1 **n** rear you up a standing image, 2050.1
26: 1 **n** shall ye set up *any* image of 3808+2050.1
26: 6 **n** shall the sword go through your 3808+2050.1
26:20 land shall not yield her increase, **n** 3808+2050.1
26:44 **n** will I abhor them, to destroy 3808+2050.1
27:33 or bad, **n** shall he change it: 3808+2050.1
Nu 1:49 **n** take the sum of them among 3808+2050.1
5:13 **n** she be taken *with the manner*; 3808+2050.1
6: 3 **n** shall he drink any liquor of 3808+2050.1
11:19 nor two days, nor five days, **n** ten 3808+2050.1
14: 9 **n** fear ye the people of the land; 408+2050.1
14:23 **n** shall any of them that provoked 3808+2050.1
16:15 **n** have I hurt one of them. 3808+2050.1
18: 3 of the sanctuary and the altar, that **n** they, 3808
18:20 **n** shalt thou have any part among 3808+2050.1
18:22 **N** must the children of Israel 3808+2050.1
18:32 **n** shall ye pollute the holy *things* of 3808+2050.1
20: 5 **n** *is there any* water to drink. 369+2050.1
20:17 **n** will we drink *of* the water of 3808+2050.1
21: 5 for *there is* no bread, **n** *is there any* 369+2050.1
23:19 **n** the son of man, that he should repent: 2050.1
23:21 **n** hath he seen perverseness in 3808+2050.1
23:23 **n** *is there* any divination against 3808+2050.1
23:25 Balak said unto Balaam, **N** curse 1571+3808
35:23 not his enemy, **n** sought his harm: 3808+2050.1
36: 9 **N** shall the inheritance remove 3808+2050.1
Dt 1:21 fear not, **n** be discouraged. 408+2050.1
1:29 Dread not, **n** be afraid of them. 3808+2050.1
1:42 Say unto them, Go not up, **n** fight; 3808+2050.1
2: 9 **n** contend with them *in* battle: 408+2050.1
2:27 I will **n** turn *unto* the right hand nor *to* 3808
4: 2 **n** shall you diminish *ought* from it, 3808+2050.1
4:28 wood and stone, which **n** see, nor hear, 3808
4:31 he will not forsake thee, **n** destroy 3808+2050.1
5:18 **N** shalt thou commit adultery. 3808+2050.1
5:19 **N** shalt thou steal. 3808+2050.1
5:20 **N** shalt thou bear false witness 3808+2050.1
5:21 **N** shalt thou desire thy neighbour's 3808+2050.1
5:21 **n** shalt thou covet thy neighbour's 3808+2050.1
7: 3 **N** shalt thou make marriages with 3808+2050.1
7:16 **n** shalt thou serve their gods; 3808+2050.1
7:26 **N** shalt thou bring an abomination 3808+2050.1
8: 3 **n** did thy fathers know; 3808+2050.1
8: 4 **n** did thy foot swell, these forty 3808+2050.1
9: 9 I **n** did eat bread nor drink water: 3808
9:18 I did **n** eat bread, nor drink water, 3808+2050.1
13: 8 **n** shall thine eye pity him, 3808+2050.1
13: 8 **n** shalt thou spare, neither shalt 3808+2050.1
13: 8 **n** shalt thou conceal him: 3808+2050.1
16: 4 **n** shall there *any thing* of the flesh, 3808+2050.1
16:19 not respect persons, **n** take a gift: 3808+2050.1
16:22 **N** shalt thou set thee up *any* image; 3808+2050.1
17:17 **N** shall he multiply wives to 3808+2050.1
17:17 **n** shall he greatly multiply to 3808+2050.1
18:16 **n** let me see this great fire any 3808+2050.1
20: 3 **n** be ye terrified because of them; 408+2050.1
21: 4 which is **n** eared nor sown, and shall strike 3808
21: 7 this blood, **n** have our eyes seen *it*. 3808+2050.1
22: 5 **n** shall a man put on a woman's 3808+2050.1
24: 5 **n** shall he be charged with any 3808+2050.1
24:15 **n** shall the sun go down upon it; 3808+2050.1
24:16 **n** shall the children be put to death 3808+2050.1
26:13 **n** have I forgotten *them*: 3808+2050.1
26:14 **n** have I taken away *ought* thereof 3808+2050.1
28:36 unto a nation which **n** thou nor thy fathers 3808
28:39 dress *them*, but shalt **n** drink *of* the wine, 3808
28:64 which **n** thou nor thy fathers have known, 3808
28:65 **n** shall the sole of thy foot have 3808+2050.1
29: 6 **n** have you drunk wine or 3808+2050.1
29:14 **N** with you only do I make this 3808+2050.1
30:11 not hidden from thee, **n** *is* it far off. 3808+2050.1
30:13 **N** *is* it beyond the sea, that *thou* 3808+2050.1
31: 8 he will not fail thee, **n** forsake thee: 3808+2050.1
31: 8 fear not, **n** be dismayed. 3808+2050.1

N

Dt 32:28 **n** *is there any* understanding in 369+2050.1
32:39 **n** *is there any* that can deliver out of 369+2050.1
33: 9 **n** did he acknowledge his brethren, 3808+2050.1
Jos 1: 9 be not afraid, **n** be thou dismayed: 408+2050.1
2:11 **n** did there remain any more 3808+2050.1
5: 1 **n** was there spirit in them any 3808+2050.1
5:12 **n** had the children of Israel manna 3808+2050.1
6:10 **n** shall *any* word proceed out of 3808+2050.1
7:12 **n** will I be with you any more, except ye 3808
8: 1 Fear not, **n** be thou dismayed: 408+2050.1
11:14 destroyed them, **n** left they any to breathe. 3808
23: 7 **n** make mention of the name of 3808+2050.1
23: 7 nor cause to swear *by them,* **n** 3808+2050.1
Jdg 1:27 **N** did Manasseh drive out 3808+2050.1
1:29 **N** did Ephraim drive out 3808+2050.1
1:30 **N** did Zebulun drive out the inhabitants of 3808
1:31 **N** did Asher drive out the inhabitants of 3808
1:33 **N** did Naphtali drive out the inhabitants of 3808
2:23 **n** delivered he them into the hand 3808+2050.1
6: 4 for Israel, **n** sheep, nor ox, nor ass. 2050.1
8:23 **n** shall my son rule over you: 3808+2050.1
8:35 **N** shewed they kindness to 3808+2050.1
11:34 beside her he had **n** son nor daughter. 369
13: 6 I asked him not whence he *was,* **n** 3808+2050.1
13: 7 **n** eat any unclean *thing:* for the child 408+2050.1
13:14 **n** let her drink wine or strong drink, 408+2050.1
13:23 **n** would he have shewed us all 3808+2050.1
20: 8 **n** will we any *of us* turn into his 3808+2050.1
Ru 2: 8 **n** go from hence, but 1571+3808+2050.1
1Sa 1:15 I have drunk **n** wine nor strong drink, but 2050.1
2: 2 **n** *is there* **any** rock like our God. 369+2050.1
3: 7 **n** was the word of the LORD **yet** 2962+2050.1
4:20 answered not, **n** did she regard *it.* 3808+2050.1
5: 5 Therefore **n** the priests of Dagon, nor any 3808
12: 4 **n** hast thou taken ought of any 3808+2050.1
13:22 that there was **n** sword nor spear 3808+2050.1
16: 8 **N** hath the LORD chosen this. 1571+3808
16: 9 **N** hath the LORD chosen this. 1571+3808
20:27 of Jesse to meat, **n** yesterday, nor to day? 1571
21: 8 for I have **n** brought my sword nor my 1571
24:11 see that *there is* **n** evil nor transgression in 369
25: 7 **n** was there ought missing unto 3808+2050.1
25:15 not hurt, **n** missed we any thing, 3808+2050.1
26:12 man saw *it,* nor knew *it,* **n** awaked: 369+2050.1
27: 9 left **n** man nor woman alive, and took away 3808
27:11 David saved **n** man nor woman alive, 3808
28: 6 **n** by dreams, nor by Urim, nor by prophets. 1571
28:15 me no more, **n** by prophets, nor by dreams: 1571
30:15 unto me by God, that thou wilt **n** kill me, 518
30:19 **n** small nor great, neither sons nor 4480
30:19 **n** sons nor daughters, neither spoil, 2050.1
30:19 neither sons nor daughters, **n** spoil, 2050.1
2Sa 1:21 *let there be* no dew, **n** *let there be* 408+2050.1
2:28 pursued after Israel no more, **n** 3808+2050.1
7:10 **n** shall the children of wickedness 3808+2050.1
7:22 **n** *is there any* God beside thee, 369+2050.1
12:17 **n** did he eat bread with them. 3808+2050.1
13:22 Absalom spake unto his brother Amnon **n** 3808
14: 7 shall not leave to my husband **n** name nor NIH
14:14 **n** doth God respect *any* person: 3808+2050.1
18: 3 **n** if half of us die, will they care 3808+2050.1
19: 6 that thou regardest **n** princes nor servants: 369
19:19 **n** do thou remember *that* which thy 408+2050.1
19:24 had **n** dressed his feet, nor trimmed his 3808
20: 1 **n** have we inheritance in the son of 3808+2050.1
21: 4 nor of his house; **n** for us *shalt thou* 369+2050.1
21:10 suffered **n** the birds of the air to rest on 3808
24:24 **n** will I offer burnt offerings unto 3808+2050.1
1Ki 3:11 **n** hast asked riches for thyself, 3808+2050.1
3:12 **n** after thee shall any arise like 3808+2050.1
3:26 Let it be **n** mine nor thine, *but* divide *it.* 1571
5: 4 *that there is* **n** adversary nor evil occurrent. 369
6: 7 that there was **n** hammer nor axe *nor* any NIH
7:47 **n** was the weight of the brass found out. 3808
11: 2 **n** shall they come in unto you: 3808+2050.1
12:16 **n** *have we* inheritance in the son of 3808+2050.1
13: 8 **n** will I eat bread nor drink water 3808+2050.1
13:16 **n** will I eat bread nor drink water 3808+2050.1
16:11 **n** *of* his kinsfolks, nor *of* his friends. 2050.1
17:14 **n** shall the cruse of oil fail, 3808+2050.1
17:16 **n** did the cruse of oil fail, 3808+2050.1
18:29 that *there was* **n** voice, nor any to 369+2050.1
22:31 saying, Fight **n** with small nor great, 3808
2Ki 3:17 not see wind, **n** shall ye see rain; 3808+2050.1
4:23 *it is* **n** new moon, nor sabbath. And she 3808
4:31 the child; but *there was* **n** voice, nor hearing. 369
5:17 for thy servant will henceforth offer **n** burnt 3808
6:19 *is* not the way, **n** *is* this the city: 3808+2050.1
7:10 **n** voice of man, but horses tied, and asses 2050.1
10:14 forty men; **n** left he any of them. 3808+2050.1
12: 8 **n** to repair the breaches of 1115+2050.1
13: 7 **N** did he leave *of* the people to 3588+3808
13:23 **n** cast he them from his presence as 3808+2050.1
17:34 they fear not the LORD, **n** do they 369+2050.1
17:38 **n** shall ye fear other gods. 3808+2050.1
18:30 **N** let Hezekiah make you trust in 408+2050.1
21: 8 **N** will I make the feet of Israel 3808+2050.1
23:25 **n** after him arose there *any* like 3808+2050.1
1Ch 4:27 **n** did all their family multiply, 3808+2050.1
17: 9 **n** shall the children of wickedness 3808+2050.1
17:20 **n** *is there any* God besides thee, 369+2050.1
19:19 **n** would the Syrians help 3808+2050.1
27:24 **n** was the number put in 3808+2050.1
2Ch 1:11 **n** yet hast asked long life; 3808+2050.1
1:12 **n** shall there **any** after thee have 3808+2050.1
6: 5 *in,* that my name might be there; **n** 3808+2050.1
9: 9 **n** was there **any** such spice as 3808+2050.1
13:20 **N** did Jeroboam recover strength 3808+2050.1
20:12 against us; **n** know we what to do: 3808+2050.1
25: 4 shall not die for the children, **n** 3808+2050.1
26:18 **n** *shall it be* for thine honour from 3808+2050.1
30: 3 **n** had the people gathered 3808+2050.1
32:15 on this *manner,* **n yet** believe him: 408+2050.1
33: 8 **N** will I any more remove the foot 3808+2050.1
34: 2 declined **n** *to* the right hand, nor *to* the left. 3808

2Ch 34:28 **n** shall thine eyes see all the evil 3808+2050.1
35:18 **n** did all the kings of Israel keep 3808+2050.1
Ezr 9:12 **n** take their daughters unto your 408+2050.1
10:13 **n** *is this* a work of one day or two: 3808+2050.1
Ne 2:12 **n** told I *any* man what my God had 3808+2050.1
2:12 **n** *was there any* beast with me, 369+2050.1
2:16 **n** had I as yet told *it* to the Jews, 3808+2050.1
4:11 They shall not know, **n** see, 3808+2050.1
4:23 So **n** I, nor my brethren, nor my servants, 369
5: 5 **n** *is it* in our power *to redeem them;* 369+2050.1
5:16 of this wall, **n** bought we *any* land: 3808+2050.1
8:10 **n** be ye sorry; for the joy of 408+2050.1
8:11 for the day *is* holy; **n** be ye grieved. 408+2050.1
9:17 **n** were mindful of thy wonders that 3808+2050.1
9:19 **n** the pillar of fire by night, to shew them 2050.1
9:34 **N** have our kings, our princes, our priests, 2050.1
9:35 **n** turned they from their wicked 3808+2050.1
Est 2: 7 for she had **n** father nor mother, and 369
3: 8 **n** keep they the king's laws: 369+2050.1
4:16 and **n** eat nor drink three days, night or day; 408
Job 3: 4 **n** let the light shine upon it. 408+2050.1
3: 9 **n** let it see the dawning of the day: 408+2050.1
3:26 I was not in safety, **n** had I rest, 3808+2050.1
3:26 neither had I rest, **n** was I quiet; 3808+2050.1
5: 4 **n** *is there* **any** to deliver *them.* 369+2050.1
5: 6 **n** doth trouble spring out of 3808+2050.1
5:21 **n** shalt thou be afraid of 3808+2050.1
5:22 **n** shalt thou be afraid of the beasts 408+2050.1
7:10 **n** shall his place know him any 3808+2050.1
8:20 *man,* **n** will he help the evil doers: 3808+2050.1
9:33 **N** is there *any* daysman betwixt us, 3863
15:29 **n** shall his substance continue, 3808+2050.1
15:29 **n** shall he prolong the perfection 3808+2050.1
18:19 He shall **n** have son nor nephew among his 3808
20: 9 **n** shall his place any more behold 3808+2050.1
21: 9 **n** *is* the rod of God upon them. 3808+2050.1
23:12 **N** have I gone back from 3808+2050.1
23:17 **n** hath he covered the darkness from my NIH
28:13 **n** is it found in the land of 3808+2050.1
28:15 **n** shall silver be weighed *for* 3808+2050.1
28:19 equal it, **n** shall it be valued with pure gold. 3808
31:30 (**N** have I suffered my mouth to sin 3808+2050.1
32: 9 **n** do the aged understand judgment. 2050.1
32:14 **n** will I answer him with your 3808+2050.1
32:21 **n** let me give flattering titles unto 3808+2050.1
33: 7 **n** shall my hand be heavy upon 3808+2050.1
33: 9 **n** *is there* iniquity in me. 3808+2050.1
34:12 **n** will the Almighty pervert 3808+2050.1
35:13 **n** will the Almighty regard it. 3808+2050.1
36:26 **n** can the number of his years be 3808+2050.1
39: 7 **n** regardeth he the crying of the driver. 3808
39:17 **n** hath he imparted to her 3808+2050.1
39:22 **n** turneth he back from the sword. 3808+2050.1
39:24 **n** believeth he that *it is* the sound 3808+2050.1
Ps 5: 4 in wickedness: **n** shall evil dwell *with* thee. 3808
6: 1 **n** chasten me in thy hot displeasure. 408+2050.1
16:10 **n** wilt thou suffer thine Holy One to see 3808
18:37 **n** did I turn again till they were 3808+2050.1
22:24 **n** hath he hid his face from him; 3808+2050.1
26: 4 **n** will I go in with dissemblers. 3808+2050.1
27: 9 leave me not, **n** forsake me, O God 408+2050.1
33:17 **n** shall he deliver *any* by his great 3808+2050.1
35:19 **n** let them wink *with* the eye that hate me NIH
37: 1 **n** be thou envious against the workers of 408
38: 1 **n** chasten me in thy hot displeasure. 2050.1
38: 3 **n** *is there any* rest in my bones because 369
44: 3 **n** did their own arm save them: 3808+2050.1
44: 6 **n** shall my sword save me. 3808+2050.1
44:17 **n** have we dealt falsely in thy 3808+2050.1
44:18 **n** have our steps declined from thy way; 2050.1
55:12 I could have borne *it:* **n** *was it* he that hated 3808
69:15 **n** let the deep swallow me up, and 408+2050.1
73: 5 **n** are they plagued like *other* men. 3808+2050.1
74: 9 **n** *is there* among us any that 3808+2050.1
75: 6 For promotion *cometh* **n** from the east, 3808
78:37 **n** were they stedfast in his 3808+2050.1
81: 9 **n** shalt thou worship *any* strange 3808+2050.1
82: 5 They know not, **n** will they 3808+2050.1
86: 8 **n** *are there any works* like unto thy 369+2050.1
91:10 **n** shall *any* plague come nigh thy 3808+2050.1
92: 6 **n** doth a fool understand this. 3808+2050.1
94: 7 **n** shall the God of Jacob regard *it.* 3808+2050.1
94:14 **n** will he forsake his inheritance. 3808+2050.1
103: 9 **n** will he keep *his anger* for ever. 3808+2050.1
109:12 **n** let there be any to favour his 408+2050.1
115: 7 walk not: **n** speak they through their throat. 3808
115:17 **n** any that go down into silence. 3808+2050.1
121: 4 he that keepeth Israel shall **n** slumber nor 3808
129: 8 **N** do they which go by say, 3808+2050.1
131: 1 **n** do I exercise myself in great 3808+2050.1
135:17 they hear not; **n** is there *any* breath in 369+637
Pr 2:19 **n** take they hold of the paths of 3808+2050.1
3:11 **n** be weary of his correction: 408+2050.1
3:25 **n** of the desolation of the wicked, when it 2050.1
4: 5 **n** decline from the words of my 408+2050.1
6:25 **n** let her take thee with her eyelids. 408+2050.1
6:35 **n** will he rest content, though thou 3808+2050.1
15:12 reproveth him: **n** will he go unto the wise. 3808
22:22 **n** oppress the afflicted in the gate: 408+2050.1
23: 6 **n** desire thou his dainty meats: 408+2050.1
24: 1 evil men, **n** desire to be with them. 408+2050.1
24:19 of evil *men,* **n** be thou envious at the wicked; 408
27:10 **n** go *into* thy brother's house in 408+2050.1
30: 3 I **n** learned wisdom, nor have 3808+2050.1
30: 8 give me **n** poverty nor riches; feed me with 408
Ecc 1:11 **n** shall there be *any* 1571+3808+2050.1
4: 8 a second; yea, he hath **n** child nor brother: 369
4: 8 **n** is his eye satisfied *with* riches; 1571+3808
4: 8 **n** *saith he,* For whom do I labour, and 2050.1
5: 6 **n** say thou before the angel, that it 408+2050.1
6:10 **n** may he contend with him that *is* 3808+2050.1
7:16 Be not righteous over much; **n** make 408+2050.1
7:17 much wicked, **n** be thou foolish: 408+2050.1
8: 8 **n** *hath he* power in the day of death: 369+2050.1
8: 8 **n** shall wickedness deliver those 3808+2050.1

Ecc 8:13 **n** shall he prolong *his* days, 3808+2050.1
8:16 (for also *there is that* **n** day nor night seeth 369
9: 5 **n** have they any more a reward; 369+2050.1
9: 6 **n** have they any more a portion for 369+2050.1
9:11 the strong, **n** yet bread to the wise, 3808+2050.1
SS 8: 7 **n** can the floods drown it: 3808+2050.1
Isa 1: 6 they have not been closed, **n** bound 3808+2050.1
1: 6 **n** mollified with ointment. 3808+2050.1
1:23 **n** doth the cause of the widow 3808+2050.1
2: 4 not lift up sword against nation, **n** 3808+2050.1
2: 7 **n** *is there any* end of their treasures; 369+2050.1
2: 7 **n** *is there any* end of their chariots: 369+2050.1
3: 7 for in my house *is* **n** bread nor clothing: 369
5:12 **n** consider the operation of his 3808+2050.1
5:27 **n** shall the girdle of their loins be 3808+2050.1
7: 4 **n** be fainthearted for the two tails of 408+2050.1
7: 7 not stand, **n** shall it come to pass. 3808+2050.1
7:12 not ask, **n** will I tempt the LORD. 3808+2050.1
8:12 **n** fear ye their fear, nor be afraid. 3808+2050.1
9:13 **n** do they seek the LORD of 3808+2050.1
9:17 **n** shall have mercy on their 3808+2050.1
10: 7 not so, **n** doth his heart think so; 3808+2050.1
11: 3 **n** reprove after the hearing of his 3808+2050.1
13:20 **n** shall it be dwelt in from 3808+2050.1
13:20 **n** shall the Arabian pitch tent there; 3808+2050.1
13:20 **n** shall the shepherds make their 3808+2050.1
16:10 be no singing, **n** shall there be shouting: 3808
17: 8 **n** shall respect *that* which his 3808+2050.1
19:15 **N** shall there be *any* work for 3808+2050.1
22:11 **n** had respect unto him that 3808+2050.1
23: 4 **n** do I nourish up young men, 3808+2050.1
26:18 **n** have the inhabitants of the world 1077+2050.1
28:27 **n** is a cart wheel turned about upon 2050.1
29:22 **n** shall his face now wax pale. 3808+2050.1
31: 1 One of Israel, **n** seek the LORD. 3808+2050.1
33:20 thereof shall ever be removed, **n** 1077+2050.1
33:21 **n** shall gallant ship pass thereby. 3808+2050.1
36:15 **N** let Hezekiah make you trust in 408+2050.1
40:28 the earth, fainteth not, **n** is weary? 3808+2050.1
42: 8 to another, **n** my praise to graven images. 2050.1
42:24 **n** were they obedient unto his law. 3808+2050.1
43: 2 **n** shall the flame kindle upon thee. 3808+2050.1
43:10 **n** shall there be after me. 3808+2050.1
43:18 *things,* **n** consider the *things* of old. 408+2050.1
43:23 **n** hast thou honoured me *with* thy 3808+2050.1
43:24 **n** hast thou filled me *with* the fat of 3808+2050.1
44: 8 Fear ye not, **n** be afraid: have not I 408+2050.1
44:19 **n** *is there* knowledge nor 3808+2050.1
47: 7 **n** didst remember the latter end of it. 3808
47: 8 **n** shall I know the loss of children: 3808+2050.1
49:10 They shall not hunger nor thirst; **n** 3808+2050.1
50: 5 I was not rebellious, **n** turned away back. 3808
51: 7 **n** be ye afraid of their revilings. 408+2050.1
51:18 **n** *is there any* that taketh her by 369+2050.1
53: 9 **n** *was any* deceit in his mouth. 3808+2050.1
54: 4 **n** be thou confounded; for thou shalt 408+2050.1
54:10 **n** shall the covenant of my peace 3808+2050.1
55: 8 **n** *are* your ways my ways, saith 3808+2050.1
56: 3 **N** let the son of the stranger, 408+2050.1
56: 3 **n** let the eunuch say, Behold, I *am* a 408+2050.1
57:16 For I will not contend for ever, **n** 3808+2050.1
59: 1 that *it* cannot save; **n** his ear heavy, 3808+2050.1
59: 6 **n** shall they cover themselves with 3808+2050.1
59: 9 from us, **n** doth justice overtake us: 3808+2050.1
60:19 be no more thy light by day; **n** 3808+2050.1
60:20 **n** shall thy moon withdraw itself: 3808+2050.1
62: 4 **n** shall thy land any more be 3808+2050.1
64: 4 **n** hath the eye seen, O God, besides thee, 3808
64: 9 **n** remember iniquity for ever: 408+2050.1
66:19 my fame, **n** have seen my glory; 3808+2050.1
66:24 **n** shall their fire be quenched; 3808+2050.1
Jer 2: 6 **N** said they, Where *is* the LORD 3808+2050.1
3:16 **n** shall it come to mind: 3808+2050.1
3:16 **n** shall they remember it; 3808+2050.1
3:16 **n** shall they visit *it;* neither shall 3808+2050.1
3:16 neither shall they visit *it;* **n** shall 3808+2050.1
3:17 **n** shall they walk any more after 3808+2050.1
4:28 **n** will I turn back from it. 3808+2050.1
5:12 not he; **n** shall evil come upon us; 3808+2050.1
5:12 **n** shall we see sword nor famine: 3808+2050.1
5:15 **n** understandest what they say. 3808+2050.1
5:24 **N** say they in their heart, Let us 3808+2050.1
6:15 at all ashamed, **n** could they blush: 1571+3808
7: 6 **n** walk after other gods to your 3808+2050.1
7:16 pray not thou for this people, **n** 408+2050.1
7:16 for them, **n** make intercession to me: 408+2050.1
7:31 which I commanded *them* not, **n** 3808+2050.1
8:12 at all ashamed, **n** could they blush: 3808+2050.1
9:10 that none can pass through *them;* **n** 3808+2050.1
9:13 my voice, **n** walked therein; 3808+2050.1
9:16 whom **n** they nor their fathers have known: 3808
9:23 **n** let the mighty *man* glory in his 408+2050.1
10: 5 **n** also *is it* in them to do good. 369+2050.1
11:14 pray not thou for this people, **n** 408+2050.1
14:13 the sword, **n** shall ye have famine; 3808+2050.1
14:14 I sent them not, **n** have I 3808+2050.1
14:14 **n** spake unto them: 3808+2050.1
15:10 I have **n** lent on usury, nor *men* have lent to 3808
16: 2 **n** shalt thou have sons nor 3808+2050.1
16: 4 **n** shall they be buried; *but* 3808+2050.1
16: 5 **n** go to lament nor bemoan them: 408+2050.1
16: 6 **n** shall *men* lament for them, 3808+2050.1
16: 7 **N** shall *men* tear *themselves* for 3808+2050.1
16: 7 **n** shall *men* give them the cup of 3808+2050.1
16:13 that ye know not, **n** ye nor your fathers; NIH
16:17 they are not hid from my face, **n** is 3808+2050.1
17: 8 **n** shall cease from yielding fruit. 3808+2050.1
17:16 **n** have I desired the woeful day; 3808+2050.1
17:22 **N** carry forth a burden out of your 3808+2050.1
17:22 **n** do ye any work, but hallow ye 3808+2050.1
17:23 **n** inclined their ear, but made their 3808+2050.1
18:23 **n** blot out their sin from thy sight, 408+2050.1
19: 4 whom **n** they nor their fathers have known, 3808
19: 5 spake *it,* **n** came *it* into my mind: 3808+2050.1
21: 7 **n** have pity, nor have mercy. 3808+2050.1

N

Jer 22: 3 n shed innocent blood in this place. 408+2050.1
22:10 Weep ye not for the dead, n bemoan 408+2050.1
23: 4 nor be dismayed, n shall they be 3808+2050.1
25:33 n gathered, nor buried; 3808+2050.1
29: 8 n hearken to your dreams which ye 408+2050.1
29:32 man to dwell among this people; n 3808+2050.1
30:10 n be dismayed, O Israel: 408+2050.1
32:23 not thy voice, n walked in thy law; 3808+2050.1
32:35 them not, n came it into my mind, 3808+2050.1
33:18 N shall the priests the Levites want 3808+2050.1
33:22 n the sand of the sea measured: 2050.1
34:14 not unto me, n inclined their ear. 3808+2050.1
35: 6 drink no wine, *n* ye, nor your sons for ever: NIH
35: 7 N shall ye build house, nor sow 3808+2050.1
35: 9 n have we vineyard, nor field, nor seed: 2050.1
36:24 nor rent their garments, *n* the king, NIH
37: 2 n he, nor his servants, nor the people of 3808
38:16 I will not put thee to death, n will I 518+2050.1
42:13 n obey the voice of the LORD your God, 1115
44: 3 knew not, *n* they, you, nor your fathers. NIH
44:10 n have they feared, nor walked in 3808+2050.1
48:11 n hath he gone into captivity: 3808+2050.1
49:18 n shall a son of man dwell in it. 3808+2050.1
49:31 the LORD, which have n gates nor bars, 3808
50:39 n shall it be dwelt in from 3808+2050.1
50:40 n shall **any** son of man dwell 3808+2050.1
51:43 n doth *any* son of man pass 3808+2050.1
51:62 n man nor beast, but that it shall be 4480+3807.1
Eze 2: 6 n be afraid of their words, 408+2050.1
3: 9 fear them not, n be dismayed at 3808+2050.1
4:14 n came there abominable flesh into 3808+2050.1
5: 7 n have kept my judgments, 3808+2050.1
5: 7 n have done according to 3808+2050.1
5:11 will I also diminish *thee;* n shall 3808+2050.1
5:11 eye spare, n will I have any pity. 3808+2050.1
7: 4 not spare thee, n will I have pity: 3808+2050.1
7: 9 shall not spare, n will I have pity: 3808+2050.1
7:11 n *shall there be* wailing for them. 3808+2050.1
7:13 n shall any strengthen himself in 3808+2050.1
7:19 their souls, n fill their bowels: 3808+2050.1
8:18 mine eye shall not spare, n will I 3808+2050.1
9: 5 not your eye spare, n have ye pity: 408+2050.1
9:10 n will I have pity, *but* I will 3808+2050.1
11:11 n shall ye be the flesh in the midst 2050.1
11:12 n executed my judgments, but 3808+2050.1
13: 5 n made up the hedge for the house of 2050.1
13: 9 n shall they be written in 3808+2050.1
13: 9 n shall they enter into the land of 3808+2050.1
13:15 *is* no *more,* n they that daubed it; 369+2050.1
14:11 n be polluted any more with all 3808+2050.1
14:16 they shall deliver n sons nor daughters; 518
14:18 they shall deliver n sons nor daughters, but 3808
14:20 they shall deliver n son nor daughter; 518
16: 4 n wast thou washed in water to 3808+2050.1
16:16 *the like things shall* not come, n 3808+2050.1
16:49 n did she strengthen the hand of 3808+2050.1
16:51 N hath Samaria committed half of 3808+2050.1
17:17 N shall Pharaoh with *his* mighty 3808+2050.1
18: 6 n hath lift up his eyes to the idols 3808+2050.1
18: 6 n hath defiled his neighbour's 3808+2050.1
18: 6 n hath come near to a menstruous 3808+2050.1
18: 8 n hath taken any increase, 3808+2050.1
18:15 n hath lift up his eyes to the idols 3808+2050.1
18:16 N hath oppressed any, hath not 3808+2050.1
18:16 n hath spoiled by violence, *but* 3808+2050.1
18:20 n shall the father bear the iniquity 3808+2050.1
20: 8 n did they forsake the idols of 3808+2050.1
20:17 n did I make an end of them in 3808+2050.1
20:18 n observe their judgments, 408+2050.1
20:21 n kept my judgments to do them, 3808+2050.1
22:26 n have they shewed *difference* 3808+2050.1
23: 8 N left she her whoredoms *brought* 3808+2050.1
24:14 n will I spare, neither will I repent; 3808+2050.1
24:14 neither will I spare, n will I repent; 3808+2050.1
24:16 **yet** n shalt thou mourn nor weep, 3808+2050.1
24:16 n shall thy tears run down. 3808+2050.1
29:11 n shall it be inhabited forty years. 3808+2050.1
29:15 n shall it exalt itself any more 3808+2050.1
31:14 n shoot up their top among 3808+2050.1
31:14 n their trees stand up in their 3808+2050.1
32:13 n shall the foot of man trouble 3808+2050.1
33:12 n shall the righteous be able to live 3808+2050.1
34: 4 n have ye healed that which was 3808+2050.1
34: 4 n have ye bound up that which was 3808+2050.1
34: 4 n have ye brought again that which 3808+2050.1
34: 4 n have ye sought that which was 3808+2050.1
34: 8 n did my shepherds search for my 3808+2050.1
34:10 n shall the shepherds feed 3808+2050.1
34:28 n shall the beast of the land devour 3808+2050.1
34:29 n bear the shame of the heathen 3808+2050.1
36:14 n bereave thy nations any more, 3808+2050.1
36:15 N will I cause *men* to hear in thee 3808+2050.1
36:15 n shalt thou bear the reproach of 3808+2050.1
36:15 n shalt thou cause thy nations to 3808+2050.1
37:22 n shall they be divided into two 3808+2050.1
37:23 N shall they defile themselves any 3808+2050.1
38:11 without walls, and having n bars nor gates, 369
39:10 n cut down *any* out of the forests; 3808+2050.1
39:29 N will I hide my face any more 3808+2050.1
43: 7 *n* they, nor their kings, by their whoredom, NIH
44:20 N shall they shave their heads, 3808+2050.1
44:21 N shall any priest drink wine, 3808+2050.1
44:22 N shall they take for their wives a 3808+2050.1
47:12 n shall the fruit thereof be 3808+2050.1
48:14 they shall not sell of it, n exchange, 3808+2050.1
Da 3:27 n were their coats changed, 3809+2050.3
6: 4 n was there any error or fault found 3809+2050.3
6:18 n were instruments of musick 3809+2050.3
8: 4 n *was there any* that could deliver 369+2050.1
9: 6 N have we hearkened unto thy 3808+2050.1
9:10 N have we obeyed the voice of 3808+2050.1
10: 3 n came flesh nor wine in my 3808+2050.1
10: 3 n did I anoint myself at all, till 3808+2050.1
10:17 in me, n is there breath left in me. 3808+2050.1
11: 6 n shall he stand, nor his arm: 3808+2050.1

Da 11:15 shall not withstand, n his chosen people, 2050.1
11:15 n *shall there be any* strength to 369+2050.1
11:17 she shall not stand *on his side,* n be 3808+2050.1
11:20 n in anger, nor in battle. 3808+2050.1
11:37 N shall he regard the God of his 5921+2050.1
Hos 2: 2 for she *is* not my wife, n *am* I her 3808+2050.1
4:15 n go ye up *to* Beth-aven, nor swear, 408+2050.1
9: 4 n shall they be pleasing unto him: 3808+2050.1
14: 3 n will we say any more to the work 3808+2050.1
Joel 2: 7 n shall be any more after it, 3808+2050.2
2: 8 N shall one thrust another; 3808+2050.1
Am 2:14 n shall the mighty deliver himself: 3808+2050.1
2:15 N shall he stand that handleth 3808+2050.1
2:15 n shall he that rideth the horse 3808+2050.1
5:22 I will not accept *them:* n will I 3808+2050.1
7:14 n *was* I a prophet's son; 3808+2050.1
Ob 1:12 n shouldest thou have rejoiced over 408+2050.1
1:12 n shouldest thou have spoken 408+2050.1
1:14 N shouldest thou have stood in 408+2050.1
1:14 n shouldest thou have delivered up 408+2050.1
Jnh 3: 7 and his nobles, saying, Let n man nor beast, 408
4:10 not laboured, n madest it grow; 3808+2050.1
Mic 2: 3 n shall ye go haughtily: 3808+2050.1
4: 3 n shall they learn war any more. 3808+2050.1
4:12 n understand they his counsel: 3808+2050.1
Hab 2: 5 *is* a proud man, n keepeth at home, 3808+2050.1
3:17 n *shall* fruit *be* in the vines; 369+2050.1
Zep 1:12 will not do good, n will he do evil. 3808+2050.1
1:18 N their silver nor their gold shall be 1571+3808
3:13 n shall a deceitful tongue be found 3808+2050.1
Zec 8:10 n *was there any* peace to him that 369+2050.1
11:16 n shall seek the young one, nor heal that 3808
13: 4 n shall they wear a rough garment 3808+2050.1
Mal 1:10 n do ye kindle *fire on* mine altar 3808+2050.1
1:10 n will I accept an offering at your 3808+2050.1
3:11 n shall your vine cast her fruit 3808+2050.1
4: 1 that it shall leave them n root nor branch. 3808
Mt 5:15 N do men light a candle, and put it under a *3761*
5:34 say unto you, Swear not at all; n by heaven; *3383*
5:35 n by Jerusalem; for it is the city of the great *3383*
5:36 N shalt thou swear by thy head, because *3383*
6:15 n will your Father forgive your trespasses. *3761*
6:20 where n moth nor rust doth corrupt, and *3777*
6:26 for they sow not, n do they reap, nor gather *3761*
6:28 they grow; they toil not, n do they spin: *3761*
7: 6 n cast ye your pearls before swine, lest they *3366*
7:18 n *can* a corrupt tree bring forth good fruit. *3761*
9:17 N do *men* put new wine into old bottles: *3761*
10: 9 Provide n gold, nor silver, nor brass in your *3361*
10:10 n two coats, neither shoes, nor yet staves: *3366*
10:10 neither two coats, n shoes, nor yet staves: *3366*
11:18 For John came n eating nor drinking, and *3383*
11:27 n knoweth any *man* the Father, save *3761*
12: 4 n for them which were with him, but only *3761*
12:19 n shall any *man* hear his voice in *3761*
12:32 it shall not be forgiven him, n in this world, *3777*
12:32 in this world, n in the *world* to come. *3777*
13:13 they hear not, n do they understand. *3761*
16: 9 n remember the five loaves of the five *3761*
16:10 N the seven loaves of the four thousand, *3761*
21:27 N tell I you by what authority I do these *3761*
22:16 n carest thou for any *man:* for thou *2532+3756*
22:30 For in the resurrection they n marry, *3777*
22:46 n durst any *man* from that day forth ask *3761*
23:10 N be ye called masters: for one is your *3366*
23:13 for ye n go in yourselves, neither suffer ye *3756*
23:13 n suffer ye them that are entering to go in. *3761*
24:18 N let him which is in the field return *2532+3361*
24:20 be not in the winter, n on the sabbath day: *3366*
25:13 for ye know n the day nor the hour wherein *3756*
Mk 4:22 n was *any thing* kept secret, but that it *3761*
5: 4 in pieces: n could any *man* tame him. *2532*
8:14 n had they in the ship with them *2532+3756*
8:17 perceive ye not yet, n understand? have ye *3761*
8:26 saying, N go into the town, nor tell *it* to any *3366*
11:26 n will your Father which is in heaven *3761*
11:33 N do I tell you by what authority I do these *3761*
12:21 took her, and died, n left he *any* seed: *3761*
12:24 not the scriptures, n the power of God? *3366*
12:25 they n marry, nor are given in marriage; *3777*
13:11 what ye shall speak, n do ye premeditate: *3366*
13:15 n enter *therein,* to take any *thing* out of his *3366*
13:19 created unto this time, n shall be. *2532+3364*
13:32 are in heaven, n the Son, but the Father. *3761*
14:40 n wist they what to answer him. *2532+3756*
14:59 But n so did their witness agree together. *3761*
14:68 know not, n understand I what thou sayest. *3761*
16: 8 n said they **any** *thing* to any *man;* for *2532+3762*
16:13 *it* unto the residue: n believed they them. *3761*
Lk 1:15 and shall drink n wine nor strong drink; *3364*
3:14 violence to no man, n accuse *any* falsely; *3366*
6:43 n doth a corrupt tree bring forth good fruit. *3761*
7: 7 Wherefore n thought I myself worthy to *3761*
7:33 For John the Baptist came n eating bread *3383*
8:17 n *any thing* hid, that shall not be known *3761*
8:27 n abode in *any* house, but in *2532+3756*
8:43 n could be healed of **any**, *3756+3762*
9: 3 n staves, nor scrip, neither bread, *3383*
9: 3 neither staves, nor scrip, n bread, *3383*
9: 3 nor scrip, neither bread, n money; *3383*
9: 3 neither money; n have two coats apiece. *3383*
10: 4 Carry n purse, nor scrip, nor shoes: and *3361*
11:33 n under a bushel, but on a candlestick, *3761*
12: 2 be revealed; n hid, that shall not be known. *2532*
12:22 n for the body, what ye shall put on. *3366*
12:24 for they n sow nor reap; which neither have *3756*
12:24 which n have storehouse nor barn; and God *3756*
12:29 shall drink, n be ye of doubtful mind. *2532+3361*
12:33 no thief approacheth, n moth corrupteth. *3761*
12:47 prepared not *himself,* n did according to his *3366*
14:12 nor thy brethren, n thy kinsmen, *3366*
14:35 It is n fit for the land, nor yet for *3777*
15:29 n transgressed I **at any time** thy *2532+3763*
16:26 n can they pass to us, that *would come* *3366*
16:31 and the prophets, n will they be persuaded, *3761*

Lk 17:21 N shall they say, Lo here: or, lo there: *3761*
18: 2 feared not God, n regarded man: *2532+3361*
18:34 n knew they the *things* which were *2532+3756*
20: 8 N tell I you by what authority I do these *3761*
20:21 n acceptest thou the person *of any,* *2532+3756*
20:35 n marry, nor are given in marriage: *3777*
20:36 N can they die any more: for they are equal *3777*
Jn 1:25 be not *that* Christ, nor Elias, n *that* prophet? *3777*
3:20 n cometh to the light, lest his deeds *2532+3756*
4:15 that I thirst not, n come hither to draw. *3366*
4:21 when ye shall n in this mountain, *3777*
5:37 Ye have n heard his voice at any time, *3777*
6:24 n his disciples, they also took shipping, *3761*
7: 5 For n did his brethren believe in him. *3761*
8:11 Jesus said unto her, N do I condemn thee: *3761*
8:19 Ye n know me, nor my Father: *3777*
8:42 and came from God; n came I of myself, *3761*
9: 3 N hath this *man* sinned, nor his parents: *3777*
10:28 n shall any *man* pluck them out of *2532+3756*
13:16 n he that is sent greater than he that sent *3761*
14:17 because it seeth him not, n knoweth him: *3761*
14:27 not your heart be troubled, n let it be afraid. *3366*
17:20 N pray I for these alone, but for them *1161+3756*
Ac 2:27 n wilt thou suffer thine Holy One to see *3761*
2:31 left in hell, n his flesh did see corruption. *3761*
4:12 N is there salvation in any other: *2532+3756*
4:32 n said any *of them* that ought of *2532+3761*
4:34 N was there any among them that lacked: *3761*
8:21 Thou hast n part nor lot in this matter: *3756*
9: 9 days without sight, and n did eat nor drink. *3756*
15:10 which n our fathers nor we were able to *3777*
16:21 us to receive, n to observe, being Romans. *3761*
17:25 N is worshipped with men's hands, *3761*
19:37 *which are* n robbers of churches, nor yet *3777*
20:24 n count I my life dear unto myself, so that *I* *3761*
21:21 *their* children, n to walk after the customs. *3366*
23: 8 there is no resurrection, n angel nor spirit: *3366*
23:12 saying that *they* would n eat nor drink till *3383*
23:21 that *they* will n eat nor drink till they have *3383*
24:12 And they n found me in the temple *3777*
24:12 with any *man,* n raising up the people, *2228*
24:12 n in the synagogues, nor in the city: *3777*
24:13 N can they prove *the things* whereof they *3777*
24:18 n with multitude, nor with tumult. *3756*
25: 8 N against the law of the Jews, *3777*
25: 8 n against the temple, nor *yet* against Cesar, *3777*
27:20 And when n sun nor stars in many days *3383*
28:21 We n received letters out of Judea *3777*
28:21 n any of the brethren that came shewed or *3777*
Ro 1:21 glorified *him* not as God, n were thankful; *2228*
2:28 n *is that* circumcision, which is outward in *3761*
4:19 n *yet* the deadness of Sara's womb: *2532*
6:13 N yield ye your members *as* instruments of *3366*
8: 7 subject to the law of God, n indeed can be. *3761*
8:38 that n death, nor life, nor angels, *3777*
9: 7 N, because they are the seed of Abraham, *3761*
9:11 yet born, n having done any good or evil, *3366*
14:21 *It is* good n to eat flesh, nor to drink wine, *3361*
1Co 2: 9 n have entered into the heart of man, *2532+3756*
2:14 n can he know *them,* because *2532+3756*
3: 2 for hitherto ye were not able *to bear it,* n *3777*
3: 7 n is he that planteth any *thing,* neither he *3777*
3: 7 neither is he that planteth any *thing,* n he *3777*
5: 8 n with the leaven of malice and *3366*
6: 9 n fornicators, nor idolaters, nor adulterers, *3777*
8: 8 for n, if we eat, are we the better; neither, *3777*
8: 8 n, if we eat not, are we the worse. *3777*
9:15 n have I written these *things,* that it *1161+3756*
10: 7 N be ye idolaters, as *were* some of them; *3366*
10: 8 N let us commit fornication, as some of *3366*
10: 9 N let us tempt Christ, as some of them also *3366*
10:10 N murmur ye, as some of them also *3366*
10:32 Give none offence, n to the Jews, nor to *2532*
11: 9 N was the man created for *2532+3756*
11:11 Nevertheless n *is* the man without *3777*
11:11 n the woman without the man, in the Lord. *3777*
11:16 no such custom, n the churches of God. *3761*
15:50 n doth corruption inherit incorruption. *3761*
Gal 1: 1 n by man, but by Jesus Christ, and God *3761*
1:12 For I n received it of man, neither was I *3761*
1:12 n was I taught *it,* but by the revelation of *3777*
1:17 N went I up to Jerusalem to them which *3761*
2: 3 But n Titus, who was with me, being a *3761*
3:28 There is n Jew nor Greek, there is neither *3756*
3:28 Jew nor Greek, there is n bond nor free, *3756*
3:28 bond nor free, there is n male nor female: *3756*
5: 6 For in Jesus Christ n circumcision availeth *3777*
6:13 For n they themselves who are circumcised *3761*
6:15 For in Christ Jesus n circumcision availeth *3777*
Eph 4:27 N give place to the devil. *3383*
5: 4 N filthiness, nor foolish talking, nor jesting, *2532*
6: 9 n is there respect of persons with *2532+3756*
Php 2:16 I have not run in vain, n laboured in vain *3761*
Col 3:11 Where there is n Greek nor Jew, *3756*
1Th 2: 5 For n at any time used we flattering words, *3777*
2: 6 we glory, n of you, nor *yet* of others, *3777*
2Th 2: 2 or be troubled, n by spirit, nor by word, *3383*
3: 8 N did we eat any *man's* bread for nought; *3761*
3:10 that if any would not work, n should he eat. *3366*
1Ti 1: 4 N give heed to fables and *3366*
1: 7 understanding n what they say, nor whereof *3383*
5:22 Lay hands suddenly on no *man,* n be *3366*
Heb 4:13 N is there any creature *that is* not *2532+3756*
7: 3 having n beginning of days, nor end of life; *3383*
9:12 N by the blood of goats and calves, *3761*
9:18 Whereupon n the first *testament* was *3761*
10: 8 n hadst pleasure *therein;* which are offered *3761*
Jas 1:13 with evil, n tempteth he **any** *man:* *1161+3762*
1:17 is no variableness, n shadow of turning. *2228*
5:12 swear not, n by heaven, neither by *3383*
5:12 neither by heaven, n by the earth, *3383*
5:12 neither by the earth, n by any other oath: *3383*
1Pe 2:22 did no sin, n was guile found in his mouth: *3761*
3:14 be not afraid of their terror, n be troubled; *3366*
5: 3 N as being lords over *God's* heritage, but *3366*

N

2Pe 1: 8 they make you that ye shall n be barren nor 3756
1Jn 2:15 the world, n the things that are in the world. 3366
3: 6 sinneth hath not seen him, n known him. 3761
3:10 not of God, n he that loveth not his brother. 2532
3:18 let us not love in word, n in tongue; 3366
2Jn 1:10 your house, n bid him God speed: 2532+3361
3Jn 1:10 n doth he himself receive the brethren, and 3777
Rev 3:15 thy works, that thou art n cold nor hot: 3777
3:16 thou art lukewarm, and n cold nor hot, 3777
5: 3 in heaven, nor in earth, n under the earth, 3761
5: 3 able to open the book, n to look thereon. 3761
5: 4 and to read the book, n to look thereon. 3777
7: 3 Hurt not the earth, n the sea, nor the trees, 3383
7:16 shall hunger no more, n thirst any more; 3761
7:16 n shall the sun light on them, nor any heat. 3761
9: 4 n any green thing, neither any tree; 3761
9: 4 neither any green thing, n any tree; 3761
9:20 which n can see, nor hear, nor walk: 3777
9:21 N repented they of their murders, 2532+3756
12: 8 n was their place found any more in 3777
20: 4 had not worshipped the beast, n his image, 3777
20: 4 n had received his mark upon their 2532+3756
21: 4 be no more death, n sorrow, nor crying, 3777
21: 4 nor crying, n shall there be any more pain: 3777
21:23 of the sun, n of the moon, to shine in it: 3761
21:27 n whatsoever worketh abomination, or 2532
22: 5 and they need no candle, n light of the sun; 2532

NEKEB (1)
Jos 19:33 and Adami, N, and Jabneel, unto Lakum; 5346

NEKODA (4)
Ezr 2:48 The children of Rezin, the children of N, 5353
2:60 the children of N, six hundred fifty and 5353
Ne 7:50 the children of Rezin, the children of N, 5353
7:62 the children of N, six hundred forty and 5353

NEMUEL (3) [NEMUELITES]
Nu 26: 9 sons of Eliab; N, and Dathan, and Abiram. 5241
26:12 of N, the family of the Nemuelites: 5241
1Ch 4:24 The sons of Simeon were, N, and Jamin, 5241

NEMUELITE See NEMUELITES

NEMUELITES (1) [NEMUEL]
Nu 26:12 of Nemuel, the family of the N: of Jamin, 5242

NEPHEG (4)
Ex 6:21 the sons of Izhar; Korah, and N, and Zichri. 5298
2Sa 5:15 Ibhar also, and Elishua, and N, and Japhia, 5298
1Ch 3: 7 And Nogah, and N, and Japhia, 5298
14: 6 And Nogah, and N, and Japhia, 5298

NEPHEW (2) [NEPHEWS]
Job 18:19 He shall neither have son nor n among his 5220
Isa 14:22 remnant, and son, and n, saith the LORD. 5220

NEPHEWS (2) [NEPHEW]
Jdg 12:14 he had forty sons and thirty n, that 1121+1121
1Ti 5: 4 But if any widow have children or n, 1549

NEPHISH (1)
1Ch 5:19 with Jetur, and N, and Nodab. 5305

NEPHISHESIM (1) [NEPHUSIM]
Ne 7:52 the children of Meunim, the children of N, 5300

NEPHTHALIM (3) [NAPHTALI]
Mt 4:13 sea coast, in the borders of Zabulon and N: 3508
4:15 The land of Zabulon, and the land of N, 3508
Rev 7: 6 Of the tribe of N were sealed twelve 3508

NEPHTOAH (2)
Jos 15: 9 the hill unto the fountain of the water of N, 5318
18:15 and went out to the well of waters of N: 5318

NEPHUSIM (1) [NEPHISHESIM]
Ezr 2:50 the children of Mehunim, the children of N, 5300

NEPHUSSIM See NEPHISHESIM; NEPHUSIM

NER (16)
1Sa 14:50 host was Abner, the son of N, Saul's uncle. 5369
14:51 N the father of Abner was the son of Abiel. 5369
26: 5 Abner the son of N, the captain of his host: 5369
26:14 to Abner the son of N, saying, Answerest 5369
2Sa 2: 8 Abner the son of N, captain of Saul's host, 5369
2:12 Abner the son of N, and the servants of 5369
3:23 Abner the son of N came to the king, and 5369
3:25 Thou knowest Abner the son of N, that he 5369
3:28 ever from the blood of Abner the son of N: 5369
3:37 not of the king to slay Abner the son of N. 5369
1Ki 2: 5 unto Abner the son of N, and unto Amasa 5369
2:32 thereof, to wit, Abner the son of N, 5369
1Ch 8:33 N begat Kish, and Kish begat Saul, and 5369
9:36 Zur, and Kish, and Baal, and N, and Nadab, 5369
9:39 N begat Kish; and Kish begat Saul; and 5369
26:28 Abner the son of N, and Joab the son of 5369

NEREUS (1)
Ro 16:15 N, and his sister, and Olympas, and all 3517

NERGAL (1)
2Ki 17:30 the men of Cuth made N, and the men of 5370

NERGAL-SHAREZER (3)
Jer 39: 3 even N, Samgar-nebo, Sarsechim, 5371
39: 3 Sarsechim, Rab-saris, N, Rab-mag, 5371
39:13 N, Rab-mag, and all the king of Babylon's 5371

NERI (1)
Lk 3:27 son of Salathiel, which was the son of N, 3518

NERIAH (10)
Jer 32:12 of the purchase unto Baruch the son of N, 5374
32:16 of the purchase unto Baruch the son of N, 5374
36: 4 Jeremiah called Baruch the son of N: and 5374
36: 8 Baruch the son of N did according to all 5374
36:14 So Baruch the son of N took the roll in his 5374
36:32 gave it to Baruch the scribe, the son of N; 5374
43: 3 Baruch the son of N setteth thee on against 5374
43: 6 the prophet, and Baruch the son of N. 5374
45: 1 prophet spake unto Baruch the son of N, 5374
51:59 prophet commanded Seraiah the son of N, 5374

NERO (1)
2Ti 4: S when Paul was brought before N 3505

NEST (15) [NESTS]
Nu 24:21 and thou puttest thy n in a rock. 7064
Dt 22: 6 If a bird's n chance to be before thee in 7064
32:11 As an eagle stirreth up her n, fluttereth over 7064
Job 29:18 I shall die in my n, and I shall multiply my 7064
39:27 at thy command, and make her n on high? 7064
Ps 84: 3 the swallow a n for herself, where she may 7064
Pr 27: 8 As a bird that wandereth from her n, so is a 7064
Isa 10:14 my hand hath found as a n the riches of 7064
16: 2 that, as a wandering bird cast out of the n, 7064
34:15 There shall the great owl make her n, and 7077
Jer 22:23 that makest thy n in the cedars, 7077
48:28 be like the dove that maketh her n in 7077
49:16 though thou shouldest make thy n as high 7064
Ob 1: 4 though thou set thy n among the stars, 7064
Hab 2: 9 that he may set his n on high, that he may 7064

NESTS (4) [NEST]
Ps 104:17 Where the birds make their n: as for 7077
Eze 31: 6 All the fowls of heaven made their n in his 7077
Mt 8:20 have holes, and the birds of the air have n; 2682
Lk 9:58 have holes, and birds of the air have n; 2682

NET (39) [NETS, NETWORK, NETWORKS]
Ex 27: 4 upon the n shalt thou make four brasen 7568
27: 5 that the n may be even to the midst of 7568
Job 18: 8 For he is cast into a n by his own feet, and 7568
19: 6 and hath compassed me with his n. 4686
Ps 9:15 in the n which they hid is their own foot 7568
10: 9 the poor, when he draweth him into his n. 7568
25:15 for he shall pluck my feet out of the n. 7568
31: 4 Pull me out of the n that they have laid 7568
35: 7 cause have they hid for me their n in a pit, 7568
35: 8 and let his n that he hath hid catch himself: 7568
57: 6 They have prepared a n for my steps; 7568
66:11 Thou broughtest us into the n; thou laidst 4686
140: 5 they have spread a n by the way side; 7568
Pr 1:17 Surely in vain the n is spread in the sight of 7568
12:12 The wicked desireth the n of evil men: but 4685
29: 5 his neighbour spreadeth a n for his feet. 7568
Ecc 9:12 as the fishes that are taken in an evil n, and 4685
Isa 51:20 head of all the streets, as a wild bull in a n: 4364
La 1:13 he hath spread a n for my feet, he hath 7568
Eze 12:13 My n also will I spread upon him, and he 7568
17:20 I will spread my n upon him, and he shall 7568
19: 8 the provinces, and spread their n over him: 7568
32: 3 spread out my n over thee with a company 7568
32: 3 and they shall bring thee up in my n. 2764
Hos 5: 1 on Mizpah, and a n spread upon Tabor. 7568
7:12 shall go, I will spread my n upon them; 7568
Mic 7: 2 they hunt every man his brother with a n. 2764
Hab 1:15 they catch them in their n, and gather them 2764
1:16 Therefore they sacrifice unto their n, and 2764
1:17 Shall they therefore empty their n, and 2764
Mt 4:18 Andrew his brother, casting a n into the sea: 293
13:47 the kingdom of heaven is like unto a n, 4522
Mk 1:16 Andrew his brother casting a n into the sea: 293
Lk 5: 5 at thy word I will let down the n. 1350
5: 6 great multitude of fishes: and their n brake. 1350
Jn 21: 6 Cast the n on the right side of the ship, and 1350
21: 8 hundred cubits,) dragging the n with fishes. 1350
21:11 and drew the n to land full of great fishes, 1350
21:11 so many, yet was not the n broken. 1350

NETHANEEL (14)
Nu 1: 8 Of Issachar; N the son of Zuar. 5417
2: 5 N the son of Zuar shall be captain of 5417
7:18 On the second day N the son of Zuar, 5417
7:23 this was the offering of N the son of Zuar. 5417
10:15 children of Issachar was N the son of Zuar. 5417
1Ch 2:14 N the fourth, Raddai the fifth, 5417
15:24 N, and Amasai, and Zechariah, and 5417
24: 6 Shemaiah the son of N the scribe, one of 5417
26: 4 and Sacar the fourth, and N the fifth, 5417
2Ch 17: 7 to Zechariah, and to N, and to Michaiah, 5417
35: 9 Shemaiah and N, his brethren, and 5417
Ezr 10:22 Maaseiah, Ishmael, N, Jozabad, and Elasah. 5417
Ne 12:21 Of Hilkiah, Hashabiah; of Jedaiah, N. 5417
12:36 Gilalai, Maai, N, and Judah, Hanani, 5417

NETHANEL See NETHANEEL

NETHANIAH (20)
2Ki 25:23 even Ishmael the son of N, and Johanan 5418
25:25 that Ishmael the son of N, the son of 5418
1Ch 25: 2 Zaccur, and Joseph, and N, and Asarelah, 5418
25:12 The fifth to N, he, his sons, and 5418
2Ch 17: 8 N, and Zebadiah, and Asahel, and 5418
Jer 36:14 all the princes sent Jehudi the son of N, 5418
40: 8 even Ishmael the son of N, and Johanan 5418
40:14 hath sent Ishmael the son of N to slay thee? 5418
40:15 I will slay Ishmael the son of N, and 5418
41: 1 that Ishmael the son of N the son of 5418
41: 2 arose Ishmael the son of N, and the ten men 5418
41: 6 Ishmael the son of N went forth from 5418
41: 7 that Ishmael the son of N slew them, and 5418
41: 9 Ishmael the son of N filled it with them that 5418
41:10 Ishmael the son of N carried them away 5418
41:11 the evil that Ishmael the son of N had done, 5418
Jer 41:12 went to fight with Ishmael the son of N, 5418
41:15 Ishmael the son of N escaped from Johanan 5418
41:16 had recovered from Ishmael the son of N, 5418
41:18 Ishmael the son of N had slain Gedaliah 5418

NETHER (15) [NETHERMOST]
Ex 19:17 and they stood at the n part of the mount. 8482
Dt 24: 6 No man shall take the n or the upper 7347
Jos 15:19 her the upper springs, and the n springs. 8482
16: 3 unto the coast of Beth-horon the n, and 8481
18:13 lieth on the south side of the n Beth-horon. 8481
Jdg 1:15 her the upper springs and the n springs. 8482
1Ki 9:17 built Gezer, and Beth-horon the n, 8481
1Ch 7:24 who built Beth-horon the n, and the upper, 8481
2Ch 8: 5 Beth-horon the n, fenced cities, with walls, 8481
Job 41:24 yea, as hard as a piece of the n millstone. 8482
Eze 31:14 to the n parts of the earth, in the midst of 8482
31:16 shall be comforted in the n parts of 8482
31:18 trees of Eden unto the n parts of the earth: 8482
32:18 unto the n parts of the earth, with them 8482
32:24 uncircumcised into the n parts of the earth, 8482

NETHERMOST (1) [NETHER]
1Ki 6: 6 The n chamber was five cubits broad, 8481

NETHINIMS (18)
1Ch 9: 2 the priests, Levites, and the N. 5411
Ezr 2:43 The N: the children of Ziha, the children of 5411
2:58 All the N, and the children of Solomon's 5411
2:70 and the singers, and the porters, and the N, 5411
7: 7 and the singers, and the porters, and the N, 5411
7:24 N, or ministers of this house of God, 5412
8:17 and to his brethren the N, at the place 5411
8:20 Also of the N, whom David and the princes 5411
8:20 of the Levites, two hundred and twenty N: 5411
Ne 3:26 Moreover the N dwelt in Ophel, unto 5411
3:31 the goldsmith's son unto the place of the N, 5411
7:46 The N: the children of Ziha, the children of 5411
7:60 All the N, and the children of Solomon's 5411
7:73 of the people, and the N, and all Israel, 5411
10:28 the N, and all they that had separated 5411
11: 3 the N, and the children of Solomon's 5411
11:21 the N dwelt in Ophel: and Ziha and 5411
11:21 and Ziha and Gispa were over the N. 5411

NETOPHAH (2)
Ezr 2:22 The men of N, fifty and six. 5199
Ne 7:26 The men of Beth-lehem and N, an hundred 5199

NETOPHATHI (1)
Ne 12:28 and from the villages of N; 5200

NETOPHATHITE (8)
2Sa 23:28 Zalmon the Ahohite, Maharai the N, 5200
23:29 Heleb the son of Baanah, a N, Ittai the son 5200
2Ki 25:23 Seraiah the son of Tanhumeth the N, and 5200
1Ch 11:30 Maharai the N, Heled the son of Baanah 5200
11:30 Heled the son of Baanah the N, 5200
27:13 for the tenth month was Maharai the N, 5200
27:15 for the twelfth month was Heldai the N, 5200
Jer 40: 8 the sons of Ephai the N, and Jezaniah 5200

NETOPHATHITES (2)
1Ch 2:54 Beth-lehem, and the N, Ataroth, the house 5200
9:16 that dwelt in the villages of the N. 5200

NETS (13) [NET]
1Ki 7:17 And n of checker work, and wreaths of 7639
Ps 141:10 Let the wicked fall into their own n, 4364
Ecc 7:26 whose heart is snares and n, and her hands 2764
Isa 19: 8 they that spread n upon the waters shall 4365
Eze 26: 5 It shall be a place for the spreading of n in 2764
26:14 thou shalt be a place to spread n upon; 2764
47:10 they shall be a place to spread forth n; 2764
Mt 4:20 And they straightway left their n, and 1350
4:21 with Zebedee their father, mending their n; 1350
Mk 1:18 And straightway they forsook their n, and 1350
1:19 who also were in the ship mending their n. 1350
Lk 5: 2 out of them, and were washing their n. 1350
5: 4 the deep, and let down your n for a draught. 1350

NETTLES (5)
Job 30: 7 under the n they were gathered together. 2738
Pr 24:31 and n had covered the face thereof, and 2738
Isa 34:13 n and brambles in the fortresses thereof: 7057
Hos 9: 6 places for their silver, n shall possess them: 7057
Zep 2: 9 even the breeding of n, and saltpits, and 2738

NETWORK (7) [NET, WORK]
Ex 27: 4 thou shalt make for it a grate of n of 4639+7568
38: 4 n under the compass thereof beneath 4639+7568
1Ki 7:18 and two rows round about upon the one n, 7639
7:20 over against the belly which was by the n: 7639
7:42 even two rows of pomegranates for one n, 7639
Jer 52:22 with n and pomegranates upon 7639
52:23 all the pomegranates upon the n were an 7639

NETWORKS (3) [NET, WORK]
1Ki 7:41 the two n, to cover the two bowls of 7639
7:42 four hundred pomegranates for the two n, 7639
Isa 19: 9 and they that weave n, shall be confounded. 2355

NEVER (86)
Ge 34:12 Ask me n so much dowry and gift, 3966+7235
41:19 such as I n saw in all the land of Egypt for 3808
Lev 6:13 be burning upon the altar; it shall n go out. 3808
Nu 19: 2 no blemish, and upon which n came yoke: 3808
Dt 15:11 For the poor shall n cease out of the land: 3808
Jdg 2: 1 n break my covenant with 3808+5769+3807.1
14: 3 Is there n a woman among the daughters of 369
16: 7 with seven green withs that were n dried, 3808
16:11 If they bind me fast with new ropes that n 3808
2Sa 12:10 n depart from thine house, 3808+5704+5769

2Ch 18: 7 for he **n** prophesied good unto me, 369
21:17 so that there was **n** a son left him, 3808
Job 3:16 I had not been; as infants *which* **n** saw light. 3808
9:30 **make** my hands **n so clean**; 1253+2141+871.1
21:25 of his soul, and **n** eateth with pleasure. 3808
Ps 10: 6 *shall* **n** *be* in adversity. 1755+1755+3808+2050.1
10:11 his face; he will **n** see *it*. 1077+5331+3807.1
15: 5 *things* shall **n** be moved. 3808+5769+3807.1
30: 6 I said, I shall **n** be moved. 1097+5769+3807.1
31: 1 let me **n** be ashamed: 408+5769+3807.1
49:19 they shall **n** see light. 3808+5331+5704
55:22 **n** suffer the righteous to be 3808+5769+3807.1
58: 5 voice of charmers, charming ***n*** *so* wisely. NIH
71: 1 let me **n** be put to confusion. 408+5769+3807.1
119:93 I will **n** forget thy precepts: 3808+5769+3807.1
Pr 10:30 The righteous shall **n** be 1077+5769+3807.1
27:20 Hell and destruction are **n** full; so the eyes 3808
27:20 so the eyes of man are **n** satisfied. 3808
30:15 There are three *things that* are **n** satisfied, 3808
Isa 13:20 It shall **n** be inhabited, 3808+5331+3807.1
14:20 shall **n** be renowned. 3808+5769+3807.1
25: 2 be no city; it shall **n** be built. 3808+5769+3807.1
56:11 *they are* greedy dogs *which* can **n** have 3808
62: 6 *which* shall **n** hold their peace day 3808+8548
63:19 We are *thine:* thou **n** barest 3808+4480+5769
Jer 20:11 *their* everlasting confusion shall **n** be 3808
33:17 David shall **n** want a man to sit upon 3808
Eze 16:63 **n** open thy mouth any more, because of thy 3808
26:21 yet shalt thou **n** be found 3808+5769+3807.1
27:36 shalt be a terror, and **n** *shalt be* any more. 369
28:19 be a terror, and **n** *shalt* thou *be* any more. 369
Da 2:44 which shall **n** be destroyed: 3809+5957+3807.2
12: 1 such as **n** was since there was a nation *even* 3808
Joel 2:26 people shall **n** be ashamed. 3808+5769+3807.1
2:27 people shall **n** be ashamed. 3808+5769+3807.1
Am 8: 7 **Surely** I will **n** forget any of 518+5331+3807.1
8:14 they shall fall, and **n** rise up **again**. 3808+5750
Hab 1: 4 judgment doth **n** go forth: 3808+5331+3807.1
Mt 7:23 will I profess unto them, I **n** knew you: *3763*
9:33 saying, It was **n** so seen in Israel. *3763*
21:16 have ye **n** read, Out of the mouth of babes *3763*
21:42 unto them, Did ye **n** read in the scriptures, *3763*
26:33 because of thee, *yet* will I **n** be offended. *3763*
27:14 And he answered him to **n** a word; *3761*
Mk 2:12 saying, We **n** saw *it* on this fashion. *3763*
2:25 Have ye **n** read what David did, when he *3763*
3:29 Ghost hath **n** forgiveness, *165+1519+3588+3756*
9:43 into the fire that **n** shall **be quenched**: *762*
9:45 into the fire that **n** shall **be quenched**: *762*
11: 2 find a colt tied, whereon **n** man sat; *3762+3768*
14:21 good were it for that man if he had **n** been *3756*
Lk 15:29 and yet thou **n** gavest me a kid, that I might *3763*
19:30 a colt tied, whereon **yet n** man sat: *3762+4455*
23:29 and the wombs that **n** bare, and the paps *3756*
23:29 and the paps which **n** gave suck. *3756*
23:53 wherein **n** man **before** was laid. *3756+3764*
Jn 4:14 him shall **n** thirst; *165+1487+1519+3588+3756*
6:35 he that cometh to me shall **n** hunger; and *3364*
6:35 believeth on me shall **n** thirst. *3361+3756+4455*
7:15 knoweth this *man* letters, having **n** learned? *3361*
7:46 **N** man spake like this man. *3763*
8:33 were **n** in bondage to any *man:* how sayest *4455*
8:51 shall **n** see death. *165+1519+3361+3588+3756*
8:52 **n** taste of death. *165+1519+3361+3588+3756*
10:28 and they shall **n** *165+1519+3361+3588+3756*
11:26 in me shall **n** die. *165+1519+3361+3588+3756*
13: 8 **n** wash my feet. *165+1519+3361+3588+3756*
19:41 new sepulchre, wherein was **n** man **yet** laid. *3764*
Ac 10:14 for I have **n** eaten any *thing that is* common *3763*
14: 8 his mother's womb, who **n** had walked: *3763*
1Co 13: 8 Charity **n** faileth: *3763*
2Ti 3: 7 **n** able to come to the knowledge of *3368*
Heb 10: 1 can **n** with those sacrifices which they *3763*
10:11 which can **n** take away sins: *3763*
13: 5 for he hath said, I will **n** leave thee, *3364*
2Pe 1:10 do these *things,* ye shall **n** fall: *3361+3756+4218*

NEVERTHELESS (97)

Ex 32:34 **n** in the day when I visit, I will visit their 2050.1
Lev 11: 4 **N** these shall ye not eat of them that chew 389
11:36 **N** a fountain or pit, *wherein there is* plenty 389
Nu 13:28 **N** the people *be* strong that dwell in 657+3588
14:44 **n** the ark of the covenant of the LORD, 2050.1
18:15 **n** the firstborn of man shalt thou surely 389
24:22 **N** the Kenite shall be wasted, 518+3588
31:23 **n** it shall be purified with the water of 389
Dt 14: 7 **N** these ye shall not eat of them that chew 389
23: 5 **N** the LORD thy God would not 2050.1
Jos 13:13 (**N** the children of Israel expelled not 2050.1
14: 8 **N** my brethren that went up with me 2050.1
Jdg 1:33 **n** the inhabitants of Beth-shemesh and 2050.1
2:16 **N** the LORD raised up judges, 2050.1
1Sa 8:19 **N** the people refused to obey the voice of 2050.1
15:35 **n** Samuel mourned for Saul: and 3588
20:26 **N** Saul spake not any thing that day: for 2050.1
29: 6 unto this day: **n** the lords favour thee not. 2050.1
2Sa 5: 7 **N** David took the strong hold of Zion: 2050.1
17:18 **N** a lad saw them, and told Absalom: but 2050.1
23:16 **n** he would not drink thereof, but 3808+2050.1
1Ki 8:19 **N** thou shalt not build the house; but thy 7535
15: 4 **N** for David's sake did the LORD his God 3588
15:14 **n** Asa's heart was perfect with the LORD 7535
15:23 **N** in the time of his old age he was diseased 7535
22:43 **n** the high places were not taken away; 389
2Ki 2:10 ***n***, if thou see me *when I am* taken from NIH
3: 3 **N** he cleaved unto the sins of Jeroboam 7535
13: 6 **N** they departed not from the sins of 389
23: 9 **N** the priests of the high places came not up 389
1Ch 11: 5 **N** David took the castle of Zion, which *is* 2050.1
21: 4 **N** the king's word prevailed against Joab. 2050.1
2Ch 12: 8 **N** they shall be his servants; that they may 3588
15:17 **n** the heart of Asa was perfect all his days. 7535
19: 3 **N** there are good things found in thee, in that 61
30:11 **N** divers of Asher and Manasseh and 389
33:17 **N** the people did sacrifice still in the high 61
2Ch 35:22 **N** Josiah would not turn his face from 2050.1
Ne 4: 9 **N** we made our prayer unto our God, and 2050.1
9:26 **N** they were disobedient, and 2050.1
9:31 **N** for thy great mercies' sake thou didst 2050.1
13:26 ***n*** even him did outlandish women cause to NIH
Est 5:10 **N** Haman refrained himself: and when he 2050.1
Ps 31:22 **n** thou heardest the voice of my 403
49:12 **N** man *being* in honour abideth not: he is 2050.1
73:23 **N** I *am* continually with thee: thou hast 2050.1
78:36 **N** they did flatter him with their mouth, 2050.1
89:33 **N** my lovingkindness will I not utterly 2050.1
106: 8 **N** he saved them for his name's sake, 2050.1
106:44 **N** he regarded their affliction, when he 2050.1
Pr 19:21 **n** the counsel of the LORD, that shall 2050.1
Ecc 9:16 **n** the poor *man's* wisdom *is* despised, and 2050.1
Isa 9: 1 **N** the dimness *shall* not *be* such as *was* in 3588
Jer 5:18 **N** in those days, saith the LORD, 1571+2050.1
26:24 **N** the hand of Ahikam the son of Shaphan 389
28: 7 **N** hear thou now this word that I speak in 389
36:25 **N** Elnathan and Delaiah and 1571+2050.1
Eze 3:21 **N** if thou warn the righteous *man,* that 2050.1
16:60 **N** I will remember my covenant with thee 2050.1
20:17 **N** mine eye spared them from destroying 2050.1
20:22 **N** I withdrew mine hand, and wrought for 2050.1
33: 9 **N**, if thou warn the wicked of his way to 2050.1
Da 4:15 **N** leave the stump of his roots in the earth, 1297
Jnh 1:13 **N** the men rowed hard to bring *it* to 2050.1
Mt 14: 9 **n** for the oaths' sake, and them which sat *1161*
26:39 from me: **n** not as I will, but as thou *wilt*. *4133*
26:64 **n** I say unto you, Hereafter shall ye see *4133*
Mk 14:36 **n** not that I will, but what thou *wilt*. *235*
Lk 5: 5 **n** at thy word I will let down the net. *1161*
13:33 **N** I must walk to day, and to morrow, and *4133*
18: 8 **N** when the Son of man cometh, shall he *4133*
22:42 from me: **n** not my will, but thine, be done. *4133*
Jn 11:15 intent ye may believe; **n** let us go unto him. *235*
12:42 **N** among the *chief* rulers also many *3305+3676*
16: 7 **N** I tell you the truth; It is expedient for you *235*
Ac 14:17 **N** he left not himself without witness, *2544*
27:11 **N** the centurion believed the master and *1161*
Ro 5:14 **N** death reigned from Adam to Moses, *235*
15:15 **N**, brethren, I have written the more boldly *1161*
1Co 7: 2 **N**, to avoid fornication, let every man have *1161*
7:28 **N** such shall have trouble in the flesh: but *1161*
7:37 **N** he that standeth stedfast in *his* heart, *1161*
9:12 **N** we have not used this power; but suffer all *235*
11:11 **N** neither *is* the man without the woman, *4133*
2Co 3:16 **N** when *it* shall turn to the Lord, the vail *1161*
7: 6 **N** God, that comforteth *those that are* cast *235*
12:16 **n**, being crafty, I caught you with guile. *235*
Gal 2:20 **n** I live; yet not I, but Christ liveth in me: *1161*
4:30 **N** what saith the scripture? Cast out *235*
Eph 5:33 **N** let every one of you in particular *2532+4133*
Php 1:24 **N** to abide in the flesh *is* more needful for *1161*
3:16 **N**, whereto we have *already* attained, *let us* *4133*
2Ti 1:12 also suffer these *things:* **n** I am not ashamed: *235*
2:19 **N** the foundation of God standeth sure, *3305*
Heb 12:11 **n** afterward it yieldeth the peaceable fruit *1161*
2Pe 3:13 **N** we, according to his promise, look for *1161*
Rev 2: 4 **N** I have *somewhat* against thee, because *235*

NEW (150) [NEWBORN, NEWLY, NEWNESS]

Ex 1: 8 Now there arose up a **n** king over Egypt, 2319
Lev 23:16 ye shall offer a **n** meat offering unto 2319
26:10 bring forth the old because of the **n**. 2319
Nu 16:30 if the LORD make a **n thing**, and 1278
28:26 when ye bring a **n** meat offering unto 2319
Dt 20: 5 What man *is there* that hath built a **n** house, 2319
22: 8 When thou buildest a **n** house, then 2319
24: 5 When a man hath taken a **n** wife, he shall 2319
32:17 knew not, *to* **n** *gods that* came newly up, 2319
Jos 9:13 bottles of wine, which we filled, *were* **n**; 2319
Jdg 5: 8 They chose **n** gods; then *was* war in 2319
15:13 they bound him with two **n** cords, and 2319
15:15 he found a **n** jawbone of an ass, and 2961
16:11 If they bind me fast with **n** ropes that never 2319
16:12 Delilah therefore took **n** ropes, and 2319
1Sa 6: 7 Now therefore make a **n** cart, and take two 2319
20: 5 to morrow *is* the **n moon**, and I should not 2320
20:18 said to *David,* To morrow *is* the **n moon**: 2320
20:24 when the **n moon** was come, the king sat 2320
2Sa 6: 3 they set the ark of God upon a **n** cart, and 2319
6: 3 the sons of Abinadab, drave the **n** cart. 2319
21:16 he being girded *with* a **n** *sword,* thought to 2319
1Ki 11:29 he had clad himself with a **n** garment; and 2319
11:30 Ahijah caught the **n** garment that *was* on 2319
2Ki 2:20 Bring me a **n** cruse, and put salt therein. 2319
4:23 *it is* neither **n moon**, nor sabbath. And she 2320
1Ch 13: 7 they carried the ark of God in a **n** cart out 2319
23:31 in the **n moons**, and on the set feasts, 2320
2Ch 2: 4 on the **n moons**, and on the solemn feasts 2320
8:13 on the **n moons**, and on the solemn feasts, 2320
20: 5 house of the LORD, before the **n** court, 2319
31: 3 and for the **n moons**, and for the set feasts, 2320
Ezr 3: 5 both of the **n moons**, and of all the set 2320
6: 4 rows of great stones, and a row of **n** timber: 2323
Ne 10:33 of the sabbaths, of the **n moons**, for the set 2320
10:39 of the **n wine**, and the oil, unto 8492
13: 5 tithes of the corn, the **n wine**, and the oil, 8492
13:12 the **n wine** and the oil unto the treasuries. 8492
Job 32:19 no vent; it is ready to burst like **n** bottles. 2319
Ps 33: 3 Sing unto him a **n** song; play skilfully with 2319
40: 3 he hath put a **n** song in my mouth, 2319
81: 3 Blow up the trumpet in the **n moon**, in 2320
96: 1 O sing unto the LORD a **n** song: sing unto 2319
98: 1 O sing unto the LORD a **n** song; for he 2319
144: 9 I will sing a **n** song unto thee, O God: 2319
149: 1 Sing unto the LORD a **n** song, *and* 2319
Pr 3:10 and thy presses shall burst out with **n wine**. 8492
Ecc 1: 9 and *there is* no **n** *thing* under the sun. 2319
1:10 thing whereof it may be said, See, this *is* **n**? 2319
SS 7:13 gates *are* all *manner of* pleasant *fruits,* **n** 2319
Isa 1:13 the **n moons** and sabbaths, the calling of 2320
1:14 Your **n moons** and your appointed feasts 2320
24: 7 The **n wine** mourneth, the vine languisheth, 8492
Isa 41:15 I will make thee a **n** sharp threshing 2319
42: 9 are come to pass, and **n** *things* do I declare: 2319
42:10 Sing unto the LORD a **n** song, *and* 2319
43:19 I will do a **n** *thing;* now it shall spring 2319
48: 6 will not ye declare *it?* I have shewed thee **n** 2319
62: 2 thou shalt be called by a **n** name, which 2319
65: 8 As the **n wine** is found in the cluster, and 8492
65:17 behold, I create **n** heavens and a new earth: 2319
65:17 behold, I create new heavens and a **n** earth: 2319
66:22 For as the **n** heavens and the new earth, 2319
66:22 For as the new heavens and the **n** earth, 2319
66:23 *that* from one **n moon** to another, and 2320
Jer 26:10 sat down in the entry of the **n** gate of 2319
31:22 for the LORD hath created a **n** *thing* in 2319
31:31 that I will make a **n** covenant with 2319
36:10 in the higher court *at* the entry of the **n** gate 2319
La 3:23 *They are* **n** every morning: great *is* thy 2319
Eze 11:19 and I will put a **n** spirit within you; 2319
18:31 and make you a **n** heart and a new spirit: 2319
18:31 and make you a new heart and a **n** spirit: 2319
36:26 A **n** heart also will I give you, and a new 2319
36:26 and a **n** spirit will I put within you: 2319
45:17 in the **n moons**, and in the sabbaths in all 2320
46: 1 in the day of the **n moon** it shall be opened. 2320
46: 3 in the sabbaths and in the **n moons**. 2320
46: 6 in the day of the **n moon** *it shall be* a young 2320
47:12 it shall **bring forth n fruit** according to his 1069
Hos 2:11 her feast *days,* her **n moons**, and 2320
4:11 and wine and **n wine** take *away* the heart. 8492
9: 2 feed them, and the **n wine** shall fail in her. 8492
Joel 1: 5 ye drinkers of wine, because of the **n wine**, 6071
1:10 the **n wine** is dried up, the oil languisheth. 8492
3:18 *that* the mountains shall drop down **n wine**, 6071
Am 8: 5 Saying, When will the **n moon** be gone, 2320
Hag 1:11 upon the **n wine**, and upon the oil, and 8492
Zec 9:17 young men cheerful, and **n wine** the maids. 8492
Mt 9:16 No *man* putteth a piece of **n** cloth unto an old *46*
9:17 Neither do *men* put **n** wine into old bottles: *3501*
9:17 but they put **n** wine into new bottles, and *3501*
9:17 but they put new wine into **n** bottles, and *2537*
13:52 bringeth forth out of his treasure *things* **n** *2537*
26:28 For this is my blood of the **n** testament, *2537*
26:29 until that day when I drink it **n** with you in *2537*
27:60 And laid it in his own **n** tomb, which he *2537*
Mk 1:27 what **n** doctrine *is* this? for with authority *2537*
2:21 No *man* also seweth a piece of **n** cloth on an *46*
2:21 else the **n** piece that filled it up taketh away *2537*
2:22 And no *man* putteth **n** wine into old bottles: *3501*
2:22 else the **n** wine doth burst the bottles, and *3501*
2:22 but **n** wine must be put into new bottles. *3501*
2:22 but new wine must be put into **n** bottles. *2537*
14:24 This is my blood of the **n** testament, *2537*
14:25 until that day that I drink it **n** in *2537*
16:17 out devils; they shall speak with **n** tongues; *2537*
Lk 5:36 No *man* putteth a piece of a **n** garment *2537*
5:36 *then* both the **n** maketh a rent, and the piece *2537*
5:36 the piece that was *taken* out of the **n** *2537*
5:37 And no *man* putteth **n** wine into old bottles; *3501*
5:37 else the **n** wine will burst the bottles, and *3501*
5:38 But **n** wine must be put into new bottles; *3501*
5:38 But new wine must be put into **n** bottles; *2537*
5:39 drunk old *wine* straightway desireth **n**: *3501*
22:20 This cup *is* the **n** testament in my blood, *2537*
Jn 13:34 A **n** commandment I give unto you, That ye *2537*
19:41 and in the garden a **n** sepulchre, *2537*
Ac 2:13 *These men* are full of **n wine**. *1098*
17:19 saying, May we know what this **n** doctrine, *2537*
17:21 but *either* to tell, or to hear some **n** *thing.*) *2537*
1Co 5: 7 the old leaven, that ye may be a **n** lump, *3501*
11:25 This cup is the **n** testament in my blood: *2537*
2Co 3: 6 made us able ministers of the **n** testament; *2537*
5:17 if any *man be* in Christ, *he is* a **n** creature: *2537*
5:17 past away; behold, all *things* are become **n**. *2537*
Gal 6:15 *thing,* nor uncircumcision, but a **n** creature. *2537*
Eph 2:15 for to make in himself of twain one **n** man, *2537*
4:24 And that *ye* put on the **n** man, which after *2537*
Col 2:16 or of the **n moon**, or of the sabbath days: *3561*
3:10 And have put on the **n** *man,* which is *3501*
Heb 8: 8 when I will make a **n** covenant with *2537*
8:13 A **n** *covenant,* he hath made the first old. *2537*
9:15 cause he is the mediator of the **n** testament, *2537*
10:20 *By* a **n** and living way, which he hath *4372*
12:24 And to Jesus the mediator of the **n** *3501*
2Pe 3:13 look for **n** heavens and a new earth, *2537*
3:13 look for new heavens and a **n** earth, *2537*
1Jn 2: 7 I write no **n** commandment unto you, but *2537*
2: 8 Again, a **n** commandment I write unto you, *2537*
2Jn 1: 5 not as though I wrote a **n** commandment *2537*
Rev 2:17 and in the stone a **n** name written, *2537*
3:12 the city of my God, *which is* **n** Jerusalem, *2537*
3:12 and *I will write upon him* my **n** name. *2537*
5: 9 And they sung a **n** song, saying, Thou art *2537*
14: 3 And they sung as *it were* a **n** song before *2537*
21: 1 And I saw a **n** heaven and a new earth: *2537*
21: 1 And I saw a new heaven and a **n** earth: *2537*
21: 2 And I John saw the holy city, **n** Jerusalem, *2537*
21: 5 the throne said, Behold, I make all *things* **n**. *2537*

NEWBORN (1) [BEAR, NEW]

1Pe 2: 2 As **n** babes, desire the sincere milk of *738*

NEWLY (2) [NEW]

Dt 32:17 *to* new *gods that* came **n** up, 4480+7138
Jdg 7:19 *and* they had but **n set** the watch: 6965+6965

NEWNESS (2) [NEW]

Ro 6: 4 *even* so we also should walk in **n** of life. *2538*
7: 6 that we should serve in **n** of spirit, and *2538*

NEWS (1)

Pr 25:25 so *is* good **n** from a far country. 8052

NEXT (60)

Ge 17:21 bear unto thee at this set time in the **n** year. 312

N

Ex 12: 4 his neighbour n unto his house take it 7138
Nu 2: 5 those that do pitch n unto him shall be 5921
11:32 all the n day, and they gathered the quails: 4283
27:11 his kinsman that is n to him of his family, 7138
Dt 21: 3 that the city which is n unto the slain man, 7138
21: 6 that are n unto the slain man, shall wash 7138
Ru 2:20 near of kin unto us, one of our n kinsmen. 1350
1Sa 17:13 n unto him Abinadab, and the third 4932
23:17 king over Israel, and I shall be n unto thee; 4932
30:17 even unto the evening of the n day: 4283
2Ki 6:29 I said unto her on the n day, Give thy son, 312
1Ch 5:12 Shapham the n, and Jaanai, and Shaphat in 4932
16: 5 n to him Zechariah, Jeiel, and 4932
2Ch 17:15 n to him was Jehohanan the captain, 3027+5921
17:16 n him was Amasiah the son of 3027+5921
17:18 n him was Jehozabad, and with him 3027+5921
28: 7 and Elkanah that was n to the king. 4932
31:12 and Shimei his brother was the n. 4932
31:15 n him were Eden, and Miniamin, and 3027+5921
Ne 3: 2 n unto him builded the men of 3027+5921
3: 2 n to them builded Zaccur the son of 3027+5921
3: 4 n unto them repaired Meremoth 3027+5921
3: 4 n unto them repaired Meshullam 3027+5921
3: 4 n unto them repaired Zadok the son 3027+5921
3: 5 n unto them the Tekoites repaired; 3027+5921
3: 7 n unto them repaired Melatiah 3027+5921
3: 8 N unto him repaired Uzziel the son 3027+5921
3: 8 N unto him also repaired Hananiah 3027+5921
3: 9 n unto them repaired Rephaiah 3027+5921
3:10 n unto them repaired Jedaiah the son 3027+5921
3:10 n unto him repaired Hattush the son 3027+5921
3:12 n unto him repaired Shallum the son 3027+5921
3:17 N unto him repaired Hashabiah, 3027+5921
3:19 n to him repaired Ezer the son of 3027+5921
13:13 n to them was Hanan the son of 3027+5921
Est 1:14 the n unto him was Carshena, Shethar, 7138
10: 3 For Mordecai the Jew was n unto king 4932
Jnh 4: 7 a worm when the morning rose the n day, 4283
Mt 27:62 Now the n day, that followed the day of 1887
Mk 1:38 said unto them, Let us go into the n towns, 2192
Lk 9:37 And it came to pass, that on the n day, 1836
Jn 1:29 The n day John seeth Jesus coming unto 1887
1:35 Again the n day after John stood, and 1887
12:12 On the n day much people that were come 1887
Ac 4: 3 and put them in hold unto the n day: 839
7:26 And the n day he shewed himself unto 1966
13:42 might be preached to them the n sabbath. 3342
13:44 And the n sabbath day came almost 2064
14:20 the n day he departed with Barnabas to 1887
16:11 to Samothracia, and the n day to Neapolis; 1966
20:15 and came the n day over against Chios; 1966
20:15 and the n day we arrived at Samos, and 2087
20:15 and the n day we came to Miletus. 2192
21: 8 And the n day we that were of Paul's 1887
21:26 the n day purifying himself with them 2192
25: 6 and the n day sitting in the judgment seat, 1887
27: 3 And the n day we touched at Sidon. 2087
27:18 the n day they lightened the ship; 1836
28:13 and we came the n day to Puteoli: 1206

NEZIAH (2)
Ezr 2:54 The children of N, the children of Hatipha. 5335
Ne 7:56 The children of N, the children of Hatipha. 5335

NEZIB (1)
Jos 15:43 And Jiphtah, and Ashnah, and N, 5334

NIBHAZ (1)
2Ki 17:31 the Avites made N and Tartak, and 5026

NIBSHAN (1)
Jos 15:62 N, and the city of salt, and En-gedi; 5044

NICANOR (1)
Ac 6: 5 and N, and Timon, and Parmenas, and 3527

NICODEMUS (5)
Jn 3: 1 the Pharisees, named N, a ruler of the Jews: 3530
3: 4 N saith unto him, How can a man be born 3530
3: 9 N answered and said unto him, How can 3530
7:50 N saith unto them, (he that came to Jesus 3530
19:39 And there came also N, which at the first 3530

NICOLAITANS (2)
Rev 2: 6 that thou hatest the deeds of the N, which I 3531
2:15 also them that hold the doctrine of the N, 3531

NICOLAS (1)
Ac 6: 5 Parmenas, and N a proselyte of Antioch: 3532

NICOPOLIS (2)
Tit 3:12 be diligent to come unto me to N: 3533
3: S of the Cretians, from N of Macedonia. 3533

NIGER (1)
Ac 13: 1 and Simeon that was called N, and 3526

NIGH (100)
Ge 47:29 the time drew n that Israel must die: and 7126
Ex 3: 5 he said, Draw not n hither: put off thy 7126
14:10 when Pharaoh drew n, the children of 7126
24: 2 they shall not come n; neither shall 5066
32:19 as soon as he came n unto the camp, 7126
34:30 and they were afraid to come n him. 5066
34:32 afterward all the children of Israel came n: 5066
Lev 10: 3 I will be sanctified in them that come n me, 7138
21: 3 for his sister a virgin, that is n unto him, 7138
21:21 shall come n to offer the offerings of 5066
21:21 he shall not come n to offer the bread of his 5066
21:23 nor come n unto the altar, because he hath 5066
25:49 any that is n of kin unto him of his family 7607
Nu 1:51 the stranger that cometh n shall be put to 7131
3:10 the stranger that cometh n shall be put to 7131
3:38 the stranger that cometh n shall be put to 7131
8:19 when the children of Israel come n unto 5066
18: 3 only they shall not come n the vessels of 7126
18: 4 and a stranger shall not come n unto you. 7126
18: 7 the stranger that cometh n shall be put to 7131
18:22 come n the tabernacle of the congregation, 7126
24:17 I shall behold him, but not n: there shall 7138
Dt 1: 7 unto all the places n thereunto, in the plain, 7934
2:19 when thou comest n over against 7126
4: 7 so great, who hath God so n unto them, 7138
13: 7 about you, n unto thee, or far off from thee, 7138
20: 2 when ye are come n unto the battle, 7126
20:10 When thou comest n unto a city to fight 7126
22: 2 if thy brother be not n unto thee, or if thou 7138
30:14 the word is very n unto thee, in thy mouth, 7138
Jos 8:11 drew n, and came before the city, and 5066
1Sa 17:48 came and drew n to meet David, 7126
2Sa 10:13 Joab drew n, and the people that were with 5066
11:20 Wherefore approached ye so n unto 5066
11:21 why went ye n the wall? 5066
15: 5 that when any man came n to him to do 7126
1Ki 2: 1 Now the days of David drew n that he 7126
8:59 be n unto the LORD our God day and 7138
1Ch 12:40 Moreover they that were n them, even unto 7138
19:14 the people that were with him drew n 5066
Est 9:20 of the king Ahasuerus, both n and far, 7138
Ps 32: 6 waters they shall not come n unto him. 5060
34:18 The LORD is n unto them that are of a 7138
69:18 Draw n unto my soul, and redeem it: 7126
73: 2 my steps had well n slipt. 369+3509.1
85: 9 Surely his salvation is n them that fear him; 7138
88: 3 and my life draweth n unto the grave. 5060
91: 7 thy right hand; but it shall not come n thee. 5066
91:10 neither shall any plague come n thy 7126
119:150 They draw n that follow after mischief: 7126
145:18 The LORD is n unto all them that call 7138
Pr 5: 8 and come not n the door of her house: 7126
Ecc 12: 1 nor the years draw n, when thou shalt say, 5060
Isa 5:19 counsel of the Holy One of Israel draw n 7126
Joel 2: 1 of the LORD cometh, for it is n at hand; 7138
Mt 15: 8 This people draweth n unto me with their 1448
15:29 and came n unto the sea of Galilee; 3844
21: 1 And when they drew n unto Jerusalem, and 1448
24:32 forth leaves, ye know that summer is n: 1451
Mk 2: 4 And when they could not come n unto him 4331
5:11 Now there was there n unto the mountains 4314
5:21 unto him: and he was n unto the sea. 3844
11: 1 And when they came n to Jerusalem, 1448
13:29 to pass, know that it is n, even at the doors. 1451
Lk 7:12 Now when he came n to the gate of 1448
10: 9 The kingdom of God is come n unto you. 1448
10:11 that the kingdom of God is come n unto 1448
15:25 and as he came and drew n to the house, 1448
18:35 to pass, that as he was come n unto Jericho, 1448
19:11 because he was n to Jerusalem, and 1451
19:29 when he was come n to Bethphage and 1448
19:37 And when he was come n, even now at 1448
21:20 then know that the desolation thereof is n. 1448
21:28 for your redemption draweth n. 1448
21:30 own selves that summer is now n at hand. 1451
21:31 ye that the kingdom of God is n at hand. 1451
22: 1 Now the feast of unleavened bread drew n, 1448
24:28 And they drew n unto the village, 1448
Jn 6: 4 the passover, a feast of the Jews, was n. 1451
6:19 on the sea, and drawing n unto the ship: 1451
6:23 n unto the place where they did eat bread, 1451
11:18 Now Bethany was n unto Jerusalem, 1451
11:55 And the Jews' passover was n at hand: and 1451
19:20 Jesus was crucified was n to the city: 1451
19:42 day; for the sepulchre was n at hand. 1451
Ac 7:17 But when the time of the promise drew n, 1448
9:38 And forasmuch as Lydda was n to Joppa, 1451
10: 9 on their journey, and drew n unto the city, 1448
22: 6 was come n unto Damascus about noon, 1448
27: 8 n whereunto was the city of Lasea. 1451
Ro 10: 8 The word is n thee, even in thy mouth, and 1451
Eph 2:13 far off are made n by the blood of Christ. 1451
2:17 were afar off, and to them that were n; 1451
Php 2:27 For indeed he was sick n unto death: but 3897
2:30 Because for the work of Christ he was n 1448
Heb 6: 8 and briers is rejected, and is n unto cursing; 1451
7:19 did; by the which we draw n unto God. 1448
Jas 4: 8 Draw n to God, and he will draw nigh to 1448
4: 8 nigh to God, and he will draw n to you. 1448
5: 8 for the coming of the Lord draweth n. 1448

NIGHT (307) [MIDNIGHT, NIGHTS, YESTERNIGHT]
Ge 1: 5 the light Day, and the darkness he called N. 3915
1:14 of the heaven to divide the day from the n; 3915
1:16 the day, and the lesser light to rule the n: 3915
1:18 to rule over the day and over the n, and 3915
8:22 and winter, and day and n shall not cease. 3915
14:15 by n, and smote them, and pursued them 3915
19: 2 tarry all n, and wash your feet, and 3885
19: 2 Nay; but we will abide in the street all n. 3885
19: 5 are the men which came in to thee this n? 3915
19:33 they made their father drink wine that n: 3915
19:34 let us make him drink wine this n also; and 3915
19:35 they made their father drink wine that n 3915
20: 3 God came to Abimelech in a dream by n, 3915
24:54 men that were with him, and tarried all n; 3885
26:24 the LORD appeared unto him the same n, 3915
28:11 tarried there all n, because the sun was set; 3885
30:15 thee to n for thy son's mandrakes. 3915+1886.1
30:16 And he lay with her that n. 3915
31:24 came to Laban the Syrian in a dream by n, 3915
31:39 whether stolen by day, or stolen by n. 3915
31:40 drought consumed me, and the frost by n; 3915
31:54 eat bread, and tarried all n in the mount. 3885
32:13 he lodged there that same n; and took of 3915
32:21 and himself lodged that n in the company. 3915
32:22 he rose up that n, and took his two wives, 3915
40: 5 both of them, each man his dream in one n, 3915
41:11 we dreamed a dream in one n, I and he; 3915
46: 2 spake unto Israel in the visions of the n, 3915
49:27 the prey, and at n he shall divide the spoil. 6153
Ex 10:13 upon the land all that day, and all that n; 3915
12: 8 they shall eat the flesh in that n, roast with 3915
12:12 I will pass through the land of Egypt this n, 3915
12:30 Pharaoh rose up in the n, he, and all his 3915
12:31 he called for Moses and Aaron by n, and 3915
12:42 It is a n to be much observed unto 3915
12:42 this is that n of the LORD to be observed 3915
13:21 by n in a pillar of fire, to give them light; 3915
13:21 to give them light; to go by day and n: 3915
13:22 nor the pillar of fire by n, from before 3915
14:20 to them, but it gave light by n to these: so 3915
14:20 the one came not near the other all the n. 3915
14:21 to go back by a strong east wind all that n, 3915
40:38 fire was on it by n, in the sight of all 3915
Lev 6: 9 of the burning upon the altar all n unto 3915
6:20 of it in the morning, and half thereof at n. 6153
8:35 of the congregation day and n seven days, 3915
11:16 the n hawk, and the cuckow, and the hawk 8464
19:13 not abide with thee all n until the morning. 3885
Nu 9:16 it by day, and the appearance of fire by n. 3915
9:21 by day or by n that the cloud was taken up, 3915
11: 9 when the dew fell upon the camp in the n, 3915
11:32 all that n, and all the next day, and 3915
14: 1 and cried; and the people wept that n. 3915
14:14 pillar of a cloud, and in a pillar of fire by n. 3915
22: 8 Lodge here this n, and I will bring you 3915
22:19 I pray you, tarry ye also here this n, 3915
22:20 God came unto Balaam at n, and said unto 3915
Dt 1:33 a place to pitch your tents in, in fire by n, 3915
14:15 the n hawk, and the cuckow, and the hawk 8464
16: 1 God brought thee forth out of Egypt by n. 3915
16: 4 at even, remain all n until the morning. 3885
21:23 His body shall not remain all n upon 3885
23:10 of uncleanness that chanceth him by n, 3915
28:66 thou shalt fear day and n, and shalt have 3915
Jos 1: 8 thou shalt meditate therein day and n, that 3915
2: 2 there came men in hither to n of 3915
4: 3 lodging place, where you shall lodge this n. 3915
8: 3 men of valour, and sent them away by n. 3915
8: 9 but Joshua lodged that n among the people. 3915
8:13 Joshua went that n into the midst of 3915
10: 9 and went up from Gilgal all n. 3915
Jdg 6:25 it came to pass the same n, that the LORD 3915
6:27 could not do it by day, that he did it by n. 3915
6:40 God did so that n: for it was dry upon 3915
7: 9 it came to pass the same n, that the LORD 3915
9:32 Now therefore up by n, thou and the people 3915
9:34 by n, and they laid wait against Shechem in 3915
16: 2 laid wait for him all n in the gate of 3915
16: 2 were quiet all the n, saying, In the morning, 3915
19: 6 tarry all n, and let thine heart be merry. 3885
19: 9 towards evening, I pray you tarry all n: 3885
19:10 the man would not tarry that n, but he rose 3885
19:13 near to one of these places to lodge all n, 3885
19:25 and abused her all the n until the morning: 3915
20: 5 beset the house round about upon me by n, 3915
Ru 1:12 I should have a husband also to n, 3915+1886.1
3: 2 he winnoweth barley to n in 3915+1886.1
3:13 Tarry this n, and it shall be in the morning, 3915
1Sa 14:34 brought every man his ox with him that n, 3915
14:36 Let us go down after the Philistines by n, 3915
15:11 and he cried unto the LORD all n. 3915
15:16 what the LORD hath said to me this n. 3915
19:10 and David fled, and escaped that n. 3915
19:11 If thou save not thy life to n, 3915+1886.1
19:24 lay down naked all that day and all that n. 3915
25:16 They were a wall unto us both by n and 3915
26: 7 and Abishai came to the people by n: 3915
28: 8 and they came to the woman by n: 3915
28:20 had eaten no bread all the day, nor all the n. 3915
28:25 Then they arose up, and went away that n. 3915
31:12 went all n, and took the body of Saul and 3915
2Sa 2:29 his men walked all that n through the plain, 3915
2:32 Joab and his men went all n, and they came 3915
4: 7 and gat them away through the plain all n. 3915
7: 4 it came to pass that n, that the word of 3915
12:16 and went in, and lay all n upon the earth. 3885
17: 1 I will arise and pursue after David this n: 3915
17:16 Lodge not this n in the plains of 3915
19: 7 there will not tarry one with thee this n: 3915
21:10 by day, nor the beasts of the field by n. 3915
1Ki 3: 5 appeared to Solomon in a dream by n: 3915
3:19 this woman's child died in the n; because 3915
8:29 thine eyes may be open toward this house n 3915
8:59 nigh unto the LORD our God day and n, 3915
2Ki 6:14 they came by n, and compassed the city 3915
7:12 the king arose in the n, and said unto his 3915
8:21 he rose by n, and smote the Edomites 3915
19:35 it came to pass that n, that the angel of 3915
25: 4 all the men of war fled by n by the way of 3915
1Ch 9:33 were employed in that work day and n. 3915
17: 3 it came to pass the same n, that the word of 3915
2Ch 1: 7 In that n did God appear unto Solomon, 3915
6:20 may be open upon this house day and n, 3915
7:12 the LORD appeared to Solomon by n, 3915
21: 9 he rose up by n, and smote the Edomites 3915
35:14 of burnt offerings and the fat until n; 3915
Ne 1: 6 which I pray before thee now, day and n, 3915
2:12 I arose in the n, I and some few men with 3915
2:13 I went out by n by the gate of the valley, 3915
2:15 went I up in the n by the brook, and viewed 3915
4: 9 set a watch against them day and n, 3915
4:22 that in the n they may be a guard to us, and 3915
6:10 yea, in the n will they come to slay thee. 3915
9:12 in the n by a pillar of fire, to give them 3915
9:19 neither the pillar of fire by n, to shew them 3915
Est 4:16 neither eat nor drink three days, n or day; 3915
6: 1 On that n could not the king sleep, and 3915
Job 3: 3 the n in which it was said, There is a man 3915
3: 6 As for that n, let darkness seize upon it; 3915
3: 7 Lo, let that n be solitary, let no joyful voice 3915
4:13 In thoughts from the visions of the n, 3915
5:14 and grope in the noonday as in the n. 3915
7: 4 When shall I arise, and the n be gone? 6153
17:12 They change the n into day: the light is 3915

Job 20: 8 shall be chased away as a vision of the **n**. 3915
24:14 and needy, and in the **n** is as a thief. 3915
26:10 until the day and **n** come to an end. 2822
27:20 a tempest stealeth him away in the **n**. 3915
29:19 and the dew **lay all n** upon my branch. 3885
30:17 bones are pierced in me in the **n season**: 3915
33:15 In a dream, *in* a vision of the **n**, when deep 3915
34:25 he overturneth *them* in the **n**, so that they 3915
35:10 God my Maker, who giveth songs in the **n**; 3915
36:20 Desire not the **n**, when people are cut off in 3915
Ps 1: 2 and in his law doth he meditate day and **n**. 3915
6: 6 all the **n** make I my bed to swim; 3915
16: 7 my reins also instruct me *in* the **n seasons**. 3915
17: 3 thou hast visited *me* in the **n**; thou hast tried 3915
19: 2 and **n** unto night sheweth knowledge. 3915
19: 2 and night unto **n** sheweth knowledge. 3915
22: 2 and in the **n season**, and am not silent. 3915
30: 5 weeping may endure for a **n**, but 6153
32: 4 and **n** thy hand was heavy upon me: 3915
42: 3 My tears have been my meat day and **n**, 3915
42: 8 in the **n** his song *shall be* with me, *and* 3915
55:10 **n** they go about it upon the walls thereof: 3915
63: 6 *and* meditate on thee in the **n** watches. NIH
74:16 The day *is* thine, the **n** also *is* thine: 3915
77: 2 my sore ran in the **n**, and ceased not: 3915
77: 6 I call to remembrance my song in the **n**: 3915
78:14 a cloud, and all the **n** with a light of fire. 3915
88: 1 I have cried day *and* **n** before thee: 3915
90: 4 when it is past, and *as* a watch in the **n**. 3915
91: 5 Thou shalt not be afraid for the terror by **n**; 3915
92: 2 the morning, and thy faithfulness every **n**, 3915
104:20 Thou makest darkness, and it is **n**: 3915
105:39 a covering; and fire to give light in the **n**. 3915
119:55 O LORD, in the **n**, and have kept thy law. 3915
119:148 Mine eyes prevent the *n* watches, that *I* NIH
121: 6 not smite thee by day, nor the moon by **n**. 3915
134: 1 which by **n** stand in the house of 3915
136: 9 The moon and stars to rule by **n**: for his 3915
139:11 even the **n** *shall be* light about me. 3915
139:12 not from thee; but the **n** shineth as the day: 3915
Pr 7: 9 in the evening, in the black and dark **n**: 3915
31:15 She riseth also while *it is* yet **n**, and 3915
31:18 *is* good: her candle goeth not out by **n**. 3915
Ecc 2:23 yea, his heart taketh not rest in the **n**. 3915
8:16 (for also *there is that* neither day nor **n** 3915
SS 1:13 he shall **lie all n** betwixt my breasts. 3885
3: 1 By **n** on my bed I sought *him* whom my 3915
3: 8 upon his thigh because of fear in the **n**. 3915
5: 2 *and* my locks *with* the drops of the **n**. 3915
Isa 4: 5 and the shining of a flaming fire by **n**: 3915
5:11 that continue until **n**, *till* wine inflame 5399
15: 1 Because in the **n** Ar of Moab is laid waste, 3915
15: 1 because in the **n** Kir of Moab is laid waste, 3915
16: 3 make thy shadow as the **n** in the midst of 3915
21: 4 the **n** of my pleasure hath he turned into 5399
21:11 me out of Seir, Watchman, what of the **n**? 3915
21:11 of the night? Watchman, what of the **n**? 3915
21:12 The morning cometh, and also the **n**: 3915
26: 9 *With* my soul have I desired thee in the **n**; 3915
27: 3 lest *any* hurt it, I will keep it **n** and day. 3915
28:19 morning shall it pass over, by day and by **n**: 3915
29: 7 shall be as a dream of a **n** vision. 3915
30:29 as *in* the **n** when a holy solemnity is kept; 3915
34:10 It shall not be quenched **n** nor day; 3915
38:12 from day *even* to **n** wilt thou make an end 3915
38:13 from day *even* to **n** wilt thou make an end 3915
59:10 we stumble at noonday as *in* the **n**; *we are* 5399
60:11 they shall not be shut day nor **n**; 3915
62: 6 shall never hold their peace day nor **n**: 3915
Jer 6: 5 let us go by **n**, and let us destroy her 3915
9: 1 **n** for the slain of the daughter of my 3915
14: 8 man *that* turneth aside to **tarry for a n**? 3885
14:17 Let mine eyes run down *with* tears **n** and 3915
16:13 there shall ye serve other gods day and **n**; 3915
31:35 the moon and of the stars for a light by **n**, 3915
33:20 my covenant of the **n**, and that there should 3915
33:20 should not be day and **n** in their season; 3915
33:25 If my covenant *be* not with day and **n**, *and* 3915
36:30 the day to the heat, and in the **n** to the frost. 3915
39: 4 and went forth out of the city by **n**, 3915
49: 9 if thieves by **n**, they will destroy till they 3915
52: 7 went forth out of the city by **n** *by* the way 3915
La 1: 2 She weepeth sore in the **n**, and her tears *are* 3915
2:18 let tears run down like a river day and **n**: 3915
2:19 Arise, cry out in the **n**: in the beginning of 3915
Da 2:19 *was* the secret revealed unto Daniel in a **n** 3916
5:30 In that **n** *was* Belshazzar the king of 3916
6:18 went to his palace, and **passed the n** fasting: 956
7: 2 said, I saw in my vision by **n**, and behold, 3916
7: 7 After this I saw in the **n** visions, and 3916
7:13 I saw in the **n** visions, and behold, *one* like 3916
Hos 4: 5 prophet also shall fall with thee *in* the **n**, 3915
7: 6 their baker sleepeth all the **n**; *in* 3915
Joel 1:13 come, **lie all n** in sackcloth, ye ministers of 3885
Am 5: 8 and maketh the day dark *with* **n**: 3915
Ob 1: 5 if robbers by **n**, (how art thou cut off!) 3915
Jnh 4:10 which came up **in a n**, and 1121+3915
4:10 up in a night, and perished **in a n**: 1121+3915
Mic 3: 6 Therefore **n** *shall be* unto you, that *ye* shall 3915
Zec 1: 8 I saw by **n**, and behold a man riding upon a 3915
14: 7 be known to the LORD, not day, nor **n**: 3915
Mt 2:14 took the young child and his mother by **n**, *3571*
14:25 And in the fourth watch of the **n** Jesus went *3571*
26:31 ye shall be offended because of me this **n**: *3571*
26:34 That this **n**, before *the* cock crow, *3571*
27:64 lest his disciples come by **n**, and steal him *3571*
28:13 His disciples came by **n**, and stole him *3571*
Mk 4:27 and rise **n** and day, and the seed should *3571*
5: 5 And always, **n** and day, he was in *3571*
6:48 about the fourth watch of the **n** he cometh *3571*
14:27 ye shall be offended because of me this **n**: *3571*
14:30 say unto thee, That this day, *even* in this **n**, *3571*
Lk 2: 8 keeping watch over their flock by **n**. *3571*
2:37 *God* with fastings and prayers **n** and day. *3571*
5: 5 we have toiled all the **n**, and have taken *3571*
Lk 6:12 and continued **all n** in prayer to God. *1273*
12:20 this **n** thy soul shall be required of thee: *3571*
17:34 in that **n** there shall be two *men* in one bed; *3571*
18: 7 which cry day and **n** unto him, though he *3571*
21:37 and at **n** he went out, and abode in *3571*
Jn 3: 2 The same came to Jesus by **n**, and said unto *3571*
7:50 (he that came to *Jesus* by **n**, being one of *3571*
9: 4 the **n** cometh, when no *man* can work. *3571*
11:10 But if a man walk in the **n**, he stumbleth, *3571*
13:30 the sop went immediately out: and it was **n**. *3571*
19:39 which at the first came to Jesus by **n**, and *3571*
21: 3 and that **n** they caught nothing. *3571*
Ac 5:19 But *the* angel of the Lord by **n** opened *3571*
9:24 watched the gates day and **n** to kill him. *3571*
9:25 Then the disciples took him by **n**, and *3571*
12: 6 the same **n** Peter was sleeping between two *3571*
16: 9 And a vision appeared to Paul in the **n**; *3571*
16:33 And he took them the same hour of the **n**, *3571*
17:10 sent away Paul and Silas by **n** unto Berea: *3571*
18: 9 Then spake the Lord to Paul in the **n** by a *3571*
20:31 years I ceased not to warn every one **n** *3571*
23:11 And the **n** following the Lord stood by him, *3571*
23:23 two hundred, at the third hour of the **n**; *3571*
23:31 and brought *him* by **n** to Antipatris. *3571*
26: 7 instantly serving *God* day and **n**, hope to *3571*
27:23 For there stood by me this **n** *the* angel of *3571*
27:27 But when the fourteenth **n** was come, as we *3571*
Ro 13:12 The **n** is far spent, the day is at hand: let us *3571*
1Co 11:23 That the Lord Jesus the *same* **n** in which he *3571*
2Co 11:25 **a n and a day** I have been in the deep; *3574*
1Th 2: 9 for labouring **n** and day, because *we* would *3571*
3:10 **N** and day praying exceedingly that *we* *3571*
5: 2 of the Lord so cometh as a thief in the **n**. *3571*
5: 5 we are not of the **n**, nor of darkness. *3571*
5: 7 For they that sleep sleep in the **n**; and *3571*
5: 7 they that be drunken are drunken in the **n**. *3571*
2Th 3: 8 wrought with labour and travail **n** and day, *3571*
1Ti 5: 5 in supplications and prayers **n** and day. *3571*
2Ti 1: 3 have remembrance of thee in my prayers **n** *3571*
2Pe 3:10 of the Lord will come as a thief in the **n**; *3571*
Rev 4: 8 and they rest not day and **n**, saying, Holy, *3571*
7:15 and serve him day and **n** in his temple: *3571*
8:12 not for a third *part* of it, and the **n** likewise. *3571*
12:10 accused them before our God day and **n**. *3571*
14:11 and they have no rest day nor **n**, *3571*
20:10 be tormented day and **n** for ever and ever. *3571*
21:25 at all by day: for there shall be no **n** there. *3571*
22: 5 And there shall be no **n** there; and *3571*

NIGHTS (18) [NIGHT]

Ge 7: 4 rain upon the earth forty days and forty **n**; 3915
7:12 was upon the earth forty days and forty **n**. 3915
Ex 24:18 was in the mount forty days and forty **n**. 3915
34:28 with the LORD forty days and forty **n**; 3915
Dt 9: 9 I abode in the mount forty days and forty **n**, 3915
9:11 to pass at the end of forty days and forty **n**, 3915
9:18 as at the first, forty days and forty **n**: 3915
9:25 before the LORD forty days and forty **n**, 3915
10:10 to the first time, forty days and forty **n**; 3915
1Sa 30:12 drunk *any* water, three days and three **n**. 3915
1Ki 19: 8 and forty **n** unto Horeb the mount of God. 3915
Job 2:13 upon the ground seven days and seven **n**, 3915
7: 3 and wearisome **n** are appointed to me. 3915
Isa 21: 8 and I *am* set in my ward whole **n**: 3915
Jnh 1:17 the belly of the fish three days and three **n**. 3915
Mt 4: 2 when he had fasted forty days and forty **n**, *3571*
12:40 three days and three **n** in the whale's belly; *3571*
12:40 and three **n** in the heart of the earth. *3571*

NIMRAH (1) [BETH-NIMRAH]

Nu 32: 3 **N**, and Heshbon, and Elealeh, and Shebam, 5247

NIMRIM (2)

Isa 15: 6 For the waters of **N** shall be desolate: 5249
Jer 48:34 for the waters also of **N** shall be desolate. 5249

NIMROD (4)

Ge 10: 8 Cush begat **N**: he began to be a mighty *one* 5248
10: 9 *Even* as **N** the mighty hunter before 5248
1Ch 1:10 Cush begat **N**: he began to be mighty upon 5248
Mic 5: 6 and the land of **N** in the entrances thereof: 5248

NIMSHI (5)

1Ki 19:16 Jehu the son of **N** shalt thou anoint to be 5250
2Ki 9: 2 Jehu the son of Jehoshaphat the son of **N**, 5250
9:14 the son of **N** conspired against Joram. 5250
9:20 *is* like the driving of Jehu the son of **N**; 5250
2Ch 22: 7 out with Jehoram against Jehu the son of **N**, 5250

NINE (50) [NINTH]

Ge 5: 5 all the days that Adam lived were **n** 8672
5: 8 all the days of Seth were **n** hundred 8672
5:11 all the days of Enos were **n** hundred 8672
5:14 all the days of Cainan were **n** hundred 8672
5:20 all the days of Jared were **n** hundred sixty 8672
5:27 all the days of Methuselah were **n** hundred 8672
5:27 were nine hundred sixty and **n** years: 8672
9:29 all the days of Noah were **n** hundred and 8672
11:19 he begat Reu two hundred and **n** years, 8672
11:24 Nahor lived **n** and twenty years, and 8672
17: 1 when Abram was ninety years old and **n**, 8672
17:24 Abraham *was* ninety years old and **n**, 8672
Ex 38:24 was twenty and **n** talents, and 8672
Lev 25: 8 years shall be unto thee forty and **n** years. 8672
Nu 1:23 *were* fifty and **n** thousand and 8672
2:13 *were* fifty and **n** thousand and 8672
29:26 on the fifth day **n** bullocks, two rams, *and* 8672
34:13 commanded to give unto the **n** tribes, 8672
Dt 3:11 **n** cubits *was* the length thereof, and 8672
Jos 13: 7 land for an inheritance unto the **n** tribes, 8672
14: 2 for the **n** tribes, and *for* the half tribe. 8672
15:32 all the cities *are* twenty and **n**, with their 8672
15:44 and Mareshah; **n** cities with their villages. 8672
15:54 and Zior; **n** cities with their villages. 8672
Jos 21:16 her suburbs; **n** cities out of those two tribes. 8672
Jdg 4: 3 for he had **n** hundred chariots of iron; and 8672
4:13 *even* **n** hundred chariots of iron, and all 8672
2Sa 24: 8 they came *to* Jerusalem at the end of **n** 8672
2Ki 14: 2 reigned twenty and **n** years in Jerusalem. 8672
15:13 the son of Jabesh *began* to reign in the **n** 8672
15:17 In the **n** and thirtieth year of Azariah king 8672
17: 1 to reign in Samaria over Israel **n** years. 8672
18: 2 he reigned twenty and **n** years in Jerusalem. 8672
1Ch 3: 8 And Elishama, and Eliada, and Eliphelet, **n**. 8672
9: 9 **n** hundred and fifty and six. 8672
2Ch 25: 1 he reigned twenty and **n** years in Jerusalem. 8672
29: 1 he reigned **n** and twenty years in Jerusalem. 8672
Ezr 1: 9 chargers of silver, **n** and twenty knives, 8672
2: 8 children of Zattu, **n** hundred forty and five. 8672
2:36 of Jeshua, **n** hundred seventy and three. 8672
2:42 of Shobai, *in* all an hundred thirty and **n**. 8672
Ne 7:38 three thousand **n** hundred and thirty. 8672
7:39 of Jeshua, **n** hundred seventy and three. 8672
11: 1 and **n** parts *to dwell* in *other* cities. 8672
11: 8 Sallai, **n** hundred twenty and eight. 8672
Mt 18:12 doth he not leave the ninety and **n**, and *1767*
18:13 of the ninety and **n** which went not astray. *1767*
Lk 15: 4 leave the ninety and **n** in the wilderness, *1767*
15: 7 **n** just *persons* which need no repentance. *1767*
17:17 there not ten cleansed? but where *are* the **n**? *1767*

NINETEEN (3) [NINETEENTH]

Ge 11:25 begat Terah an hundred and **n** years, 6240+8672
Jos 19:38 **n** cities with their villages. 6240+8672
2Sa 2:30 there lacked of David's servants **n** 6240+8672

NINETEENTH (4) [NINETEEN]

2Ki 25: 8 which *is* the **n** year of king 6240+8672
1Ch 24:16 The **n** to Pethahiah, the twentieth to 6240+8672
25:26 The **n** to Mallothi, *he*, his sons, and 6240+8672
Jer 52:12 which *was* the **n** year of 6240+8672

NINETY (24)

Ge 5: 9 And Enos lived **n** years, and begat Cainan: 8673
5:17 days of Mahalaleel were eight hundred **n** 8673
5:30 lived after he begat Noah five hundred **n** 8673
17: 1 And when Abram was **n** years old and nine, 8673
17:17 and shall Sarah, that is **n** years old, bear? 8673
17:24 Abraham *was* **n** years old and nine, 8673
1Sa 4:15 Now Eli *was* **n** and eight years old; and 8673
1Ch 9: 6 and their brethren, six hundred and **n**. 8673
Ezr 2:16 children of Ater of Hezekiah, **n** and eight. 8673
2:20 The children of Gibbar, **n** and five. 8673
2:58 *were* three hundred **n** and two. 8673
8:35 **n** and six rams, seventy and seven lambs, 8673
Ne 7:21 children of Ater of Hezekiah, **n** and eight. 8673
7:25 The children of Gibeon, **n** and five. 8673
7:60 *were* three hundred **n** and two. 8673
Jer 52:23 there were **n** and six pomegranates on a 8673
Eze 4: 5 of the days, three hundred and **n** days: 8673
4: 9 and **n** days shalt thou eat thereof. 8673
41:12 and the length thereof **n** cubits. 8673
Da 12:11 *be* a thousand two hundred and **n** days. 8673
Mt 18:12 doth he not leave the **n** and nine, and *1768*
18:13 rejoiceth more of that *sheep*, than of the **n** *1768*
Lk 15: 4 doth not leave the **n** and nine in *1768*
15: 7 *more* than over **n** and nine just *persons* *1768*

NINEVEH (19) [NINEVITES]

Ge 10:11 builded **N**, and the city Rehoboth, and 5210
10:12 Resen between **N** and Calah: the same *is* a 5210
2Ki 19:36 and went and returned, and dwelt at **N**. 5210
Isa 37:37 and went and returned, and dwelt at **N**. 5210
Jnh 1: 2 Arise, go to **N**, *that* great city, and 5210
3: 2 Arise, go unto **N**, *that* great city, and 5210
3: 3 So Jonah arose, and went unto **N**, 5210
3: 3 Now **N** was an exceeding great city of three 5210
3: 4 Yet forty days, and **N** *shall be* overthrown. 5210
3: 5 So the people of **N** believed God, and 5210
3: 6 For word came unto the king of **N**, and 5210
3: 7 published through **N** by the decree of 5210
4:11 should not I spare **N**, *that* great city, 5210
Na 1: 1 The burden of **N**. The book of the vision of 5210
2: 8 **N** *is* of old like a pool of water: yet they 5210
3: 7 flee from thee, and say, **N** is laid waste: 5210
Zep 2:13 will make **N** a desolation, *and* dry like a 5210
Mt 12:41 *The* men **of N** shall rise in judgment with *3536*
Lk 11:32 *The* men of **N** shall rise up in the judgment *3535*

NINEVITES (1) [NINEVEH]

Lk 11:30 For as Jonas was a sign unto the **N**, so *3536*

NINTH (34) [NINE]

Lev 23:32 in the **n** *day* of the month at even, 8672
25:22 and eat *yet* of old fruit until the **n** year; 8671
Nu 7:60 On the **n** day Abidan the son of Gideoni, 8671
2Ki 17: 6 In the **n** year of Hoshea, the king of Assyria 8671
18:10 that *is* the **n** year of Hoshea king of Israel, 8672
25: 1 it came to pass in the **n** year of his reign, 8671
25: 3 on the **n** *day* of the *fourth* month the famine 8672
1Ch 12:12 Johanan the eighth, Elzabad the **n**, 8671
24:11 The **n** to Jeshua, the tenth to Shecaniah, 8671
25:16 The **n** to Mattaniah, *he*, his sons, and 8671
27:12 The **n** *captain* for the ninth month *was* 8671
27:12 The ninth *captain* for the **n** month *was* 8671
2Ch 16:12 **n** year of his reign was diseased in his feet, 8672
Ezr 10: 9 It *was* the **n** month, on the twentieth *day* of 8671
Jer 36: 9 in the **n** month, *that* they proclaimed a fast 8671
36:22 king sat *in* the winterhouse in the **n** month: 8671
39: 1 In the **n** year of Zedekiah king of Judah, 8671
39: 2 in the fourth month, the **n** *day* of the month, 8672
52: 4 it came to pass in the **n** year of his reign, 8671
52: 6 the fourth month, in the **n** *day* of the month, 8672
Eze 24: 1 Again in the **n** year, in the tenth month, 8671
Hag 2:10 twentieth *day* of the **n** *month*, in the second 8671
2:18 twentieth day of the **n** *month*, *even* from 8671
Zec 7: 1 Zechariah in the fourth *day* of the **n** month, 8671
Mt 20: 5 he went out about the sixth and **n** hour, *1766*

N

Mt 27:45 darkness over all the land unto the **n** hour. *1766*
27:46 And about the **n** hour Jesus cried with a *1766*
Mk 15:33 over the whole land until the **n** hour. *1766*
15:34 And at the **n** hour Jesus cried with a loud *1766*
Lk 23:44 darkness over all the earth until the **n** hour. *1766*
Ac 3: 1 at the hour of prayer, *being* the **n** *hour.* *1766*
10: 3 about the **n** hour of the day, *1766*
10:30 and at the **n** hour I prayed in my house, and *1766*
Rev 21:20 the eighth, beryl; the **n**, a topaz; the tenth, *1766*

NISAN (2)

Ne 2: 1 it came to pass in the month **N**, *in* 5212
Est 3: 7 In the first month, that *is,* the month **N**, 5212

NISROCH (2)

2Ki 19:37 as he was worshipping *in* the house of **N** 5268
Isa 37:38 as he was worshipping *in* the house of **N** 5268

NITRE (2)

Pr 25:20 *and as* vinegar upon **n**, so *is* he that singeth 5427
Jer 2:22 For though thou wash thee with **n**, and 5427

NO (1393) [NONE, NOR, NOT]

Ge 8: 9 the dove found **n** rest for the sole of her 3808
9:15 the waters shall **n** more become a flood to 3808
11:30 But Sarai was barren; she had **n** child. 369
13: 8 Let there be **n** strife, I pray thee, between me 408
15: 3 Behold, to me thou hast given **n** seed: 3808
16: 1 Now Sarai Abram's wife bare him **n** 3808
26:29 That thou wilt do us **n** hurt, as we have not 518
30: 1 when Rachel saw that she bare Jacob **n** 3808
31:50 beside my daughters, **n** man *is* with us; 369
32:28 Thy name shall be called **n** more Jacob, but 3808
37:22 Shed **n** blood, *but* cast him into this pit that 408
37:22 lay **n** hand upon him, that he might rid him 408
37:24 the pit *was* empty, *there was* **n** water in it. 369
37:32 now whether it *be* thy son's coat or **n**. 3808
38:21 they said, There was **n** harlot in this *place.* 3808
38:22 *that* there was **n** harlot in this *place.* 3808
38:26 my son. And he knew her again **n** more. 3808
40: 8 a dream, and *there is* **n** interpreter of it. 369
41:44 without thee shall **n** man lift up his hand or 3808
42:11 we *are* true *men,* thy servants are **n** spies. 3808
42:31 unto him, We *are* true *men;* we are **n** spies: 3808
42:34 shall I know that ye *are* **n** spies, but *that* ye 3808
44:23 with you, ye shall see my face **n** more. 3808
45: 1 there stood **n** man with him, while Joseph 3808
47: 4 for thy servants have **n** pasture for their 369
47:13 *there was* **n** bread in all the land; for 369
Ex 2:12 and when he saw that *there was* **n** man, 369
3:19 will not let you go, **n**, not by a mighty hand. NIH
5: 7 Ye shall **n** more give the people straw to 3808
5:16 *There is* **n** straw given unto thy servants, and 369
5:18 for there shall **n** straw be given you, 3808
8:22 that **n** swarms *of flies* shall be there; 1115
9:26 children of Israel *were,* was there **n** hail. 3808
9:28 that there be **n** *more* mighty thunderings 4480
9:28 I will let you go, and ye shall stay **n** longer. 3808
10:14 them there were **n** such locusts as they, 3808
10:28 take heed to thyself, see my face **n** more; 408
10:29 I will see thy face again **n** more. 3808
12:16 **n** *manner of* work shall be done in 3605+3808
12:19 Seven days shall there be **n** leaven found in 3808
12:43 There shall **n** stranger eat thereof: 3605+3808
12:48 for **n** uncircumcised person shall eat 3605+3808
13: 3 there shall **n** leavened bread be eaten. 3808
13: 7 there shall **n** leavened bread be seen with 3808
14:11 Because *there were* **n** graves in Egypt, 369+1097
14:13 ye shall see them again **n** more for ever. 3808
15:22 days in the wilderness, and found **n** water. 3808
16: 4 whether they will walk in my law, or **n**. 3808
16:18 and he that gathered little had **n** lack; 3808
16:19 Let **n** man leave of it till the morning. 408
16:29 let **n** man go out of his place on the seventh 408
17: 1 *there was* **n** water for the people to drink. 369
20: 3 Thou shalt have **n** other gods before me. 3808
21: 8 a strange nation he shall have **n** power, 3808
21:22 depart *from her,* and yet **n** mischief follow: 3808
22: 2 he die, *there shall* **n** blood *be shed* for him. 369
22:10 or be hurt, or driven away, **n man** seeing *it:* 369
23: 8 thou shalt take **n** gift: for the gift blindeth 3808
23:13 make **n** mention of the name of other gods, 3808
23:32 Thou shalt make **n** covenant with them, 3808
30: 9 Ye shall offer **n** strange incense thereon, 3808
30:12 that there be **n** plague amongst them, 3808
33: 4 and **n** man did put on him his ornaments. 3808
33:20 for there shall **n** man see me, and live. 3808
34: 3 **n** man shall come up with thee, neither let 3808
34: 7 *that* will **by n means** clear *the guilty;* 3808
34:14 For thou shalt worship **n** other god: for 3808
34:17 Thou shalt make thee **n** molten gods. 3808
35: 3 Ye shall kindle **n** fire throughout your 3808
Lev 2:11 **N** meat offering, which ye shall 3605+3808
2:11 for ye shall burn **n** leaven, nor any 3605+3808
5:11 he shall put **n** oil upon it, neither shall he 3808
6:30 **n** sin offering, whereof *any* of 3605+3808
7:23 Ye shall eat **n** *manner* fat, of ox, or 3605+3808
7:24 but ye shall **in n wise eat** of it. 398+398+3808
7:26 Moreover ye shall eat **n** *manner of* 3605+3808
11:12 Whatsoever hath **n** fins nor scales in 369
12: 4 she shall touch **n** hallowed *thing,* nor 3605+3808
13:21 *there be* **n** white hairs therein, and *if* it *be* not 369
13:26 *there be* **n** white hair in the bright spot, and 369
13:26 it *be* **n** lower than the *other* skin, but *be* 369
13:31 the skin, and *that there is* **n** black hair in it; 369
13:32 there be in it **n** yellow hair, and the scall *be* 3808
16:17 there shall be **n** man in the tabernacle 3605+3808
16:29 do **n** work *at all, whether it be* one of 3605+3808
17: 7 they shall **n** more offer their sacrifices unto 3808
17:12 I said unto the children of Israel, **N** 3605+3808
17:14 eat the blood of **n** *manner of* flesh: 3605+3808
19:15 Ye shall do **n** unrighteousness in judgment: 3808
19:35 Ye shall do **n** unrighteousness in judgment, 3808
20:14 that there be **n** wickedness among you. 3808
Lev 21: 3 nigh unto him, which hath had **n** husband; 3808
21:21 **N** man that hath a blemish, of 3605+3808
22:10 There shall **n** stranger eat *of* the holy 3605+3808
22:13 have **n** child, and is returned unto her 369
22:13 but there shall **n** stranger eat thereof. 3605+3808
22:21 there shall be **n** blemish therein. 3605+3808
23: 3 ye shall do **n** work *therein:* it *is* 3605+3808
23: 7 ye shall do **n** servile work *therein.* 3605+3808
23: 8 ye shall do **n** servile work *therein.* 3605+3808
23:21 ye shall do **n** servile work *therein: it* 3605+3808
23:25 Ye shall do **n** servile work *therein:* 3605+3808
23:28 ye shall do **n** work in that same day: 3605+3808
23:31 Ye shall do **n** *manner of* work: 3605+3808
23:35 ye shall do **n** servile work *therein.* 3605+3808
23:36 ye shall do **n** servile work *therein.* 3605+3808
25:31 the houses of the villages which have **n** wall 369
25:36 Take thou **n** usury of him, or increase: but 408
26: 1 Ye shall make you **n** idols nor graven 3808
26:37 ye shall have **n** power to stand before your 3808
27:26 LORD'S firstling, **n** man shall sanctify it; 3808
27:28 Notwithstanding **n** devoted thing, 3605+3808
Nu 1:53 that there be **n** wrath upon the congregation 3808
3: 4 of Sinai, and they had **n** children: 3808
5: 8 if the man have **n** kinsman to recompense 369
5:13 and *there be* **n** witness against her, 369
5:15 he shall pour **n** oil upon it, nor put 3808
5:19 If **n** man have lain with thee, and if thou 3808
6: 3 *and* shall drink **n** vinegar of wine, or NIH
6: 5 there shall **n** rasor come upon his head: 3808
6: 6 the LORD he shall come at **n** dead body. 3808
8:19 that there be **n** plague among the children 3808
8:25 the service *thereof,* and shall serve **n** more: 3808
8:26 to keep the charge, and shall do **n** service. 3808
14:18 **by n means** clearing *the guilty,* visiting 3808
16:40 that **n** stranger, which *is* not of the seed of 3808
18: 5 that there be **n** wrath any more upon 3808
18:20 Thou shalt have **n** inheritance in their land, 3808
18:23 children of Israel they have **n** inheritance. 3808
18:24 of Israel they shall have **n** inheritance. 3808
18:32 ye shall bear **n** sin by reason of it, when ye 3808
19: 2 wherein *is* **n** blemish, *and* upon which never 369
19:15 which hath **n** covering bound upon it, 369
20: 2 there was **n** water for the congregation: 3808
20: 5 it *is* **n** place of seed, or of figs, or vines, or 3808
21: 5 for *there is* **n** bread, neither *is there any* 369
22:26 where *was* **n** way to turn *either to* the right 369
23:23 Surely *there is* **n** enchantment against 3808
26:33 Zelophehad the son of Hepher had **n** sons, 3808
26:62 there was **n** inheritance given them among 3808
27: 3 but died in his own sin, and had **n** sons. 3808
27: 4 among his family, because he hath **n** son? 369
27: 8 have **n** son, then ye shall cause his 369
27: 9 if he have **n** daughter, then ye shall give his 369
27:10 if he have **n** brethren, then ye shall give his 369
27:11 if his father have **n** brethren, then ye shall 369
27:17 be not as sheep which have **n** shepherd. 369
28:18 ye shall do **n** *manner of* servile work 3605+3808
28:25 ye shall do **n** servile work. 3605+3808
28:26 ye shall do **n** servile work: 3605+3808
29: 1 ye shall do **n** servile work: 3605+3808
29:12 ye shall do **n** servile work, and 3605+3808
29:35 ye shall do **n** servile work *therein:* 3605+3808
33:14 where was **n** water for the people to drink. 3808
35:31 Moreover ye shall take **n** satisfaction for 3808
35:32 ye shall take **n** satisfaction for him that is 3808
Dt 1:39 which *in that* day had **n** knowledge 3808
2: 5 their land, **n**, not so much as a foot breadth; NIH
3:26 speak **n** more unto me of this matter. 408
4:12 the voice of the words, but saw **n** similitude; 369
4:15 for ye saw **n** *manner of* similitude on 3605+3808
5:22 he added **n** more. And he wrote them in 3808
7: 2 thou shalt make **n** covenant with them, 3808
7:16 thine eye shall have **n** pity upon them: 3808
7:24 there shall **n** man *be able to* stand before 3808
8: 2 wouldest keep his commandments, or **n**. 3808
8:15 and drought, where *there was* **n** water; 369
10: 9 Wherefore Levi hath **n** part nor inheritance 3808
10:16 of your heart, and be **n** more stiffnecked. 3808
11:17 that there be **n** rain, and *that* the land yield 3808
11:25 There shall **n** man *be able to* stand before 3808
12:12 forasmuch as he hath **n** part nor inheritance 369
13:11 shall do **n** more any such wickedness as 3808
14:27 for he hath **n** part nor inheritance with thee. 369
14:29 he hath **n** part nor inheritance with thee,) 369
15: 4 Save when there shall be **n** poor among 3808
15:19 thou shalt do **n** work with the firstling of 3808
16: 3 Thou shalt eat **n** leavened bread with it; 3808
16: 4 there shall be **n** leavened bread seen with 3808
16: 8 thy God: thou shalt do **n** work *therein.* 3808
17:13 and fear, and do **n** more presumptuously. 3808
17:16 Ye shall henceforth return **n** more that way. 3808
18: 1 shall have **n** part nor inheritance with 3808
18: 2 Therefore shall they have **n** inheritance 3808
19:20 shall henceforth commit **n** more any such 3808
20:12 if it will make **n** peace with thee, but 3808
21:14 if thou have **n** delight in her, then thou shalt 3808
22:26 *there is* in the damsel **n** sin *worthy* of death: 369
23:14 that he see **n** unclean thing in thee, and 3808
23:17 There shall be **n** whore of the daughters of 3808
23:22 forbear to vow, it shall be **n** sin in thee. 3808
24: 1 it come to pass that she find **n** favour in his 3808
24: 6 **N** *man* shall take the nether or the upper 3808
25: 5 and one of them die, and have **n** child, 369
28:26 the earth, and **n man** shall fray *them* away. 369
28:29 and **n man** shall save *thee.* 369
28:32 and *there shall be* **n** might in thine hand. 369
28:65 among these nations shalt thou find **n** ease, 3808
28:68 unto thee, Thou shalt see it **n** more again: 3808
28:68 and bondwomen, and **n man** shall buy *you.* 369
31: 2 *this* day; I can **n** more go out and come in: 3808
32:12 and *there was* **n** strange god with him. 369
32:20 children in whom *is* **n** faith. 3808
32:39 *even* I, *am* he, and *there is* **n** god with me: 369
34: 6 **n** man knoweth of his sepulchre unto this 3808
Jos 8:20 they had **n** power to flee this way or 3808
Jos 8:31 over which **n** *man* hath lift up *any* iron: 3808
10:14 there was **n** day like that before it or 3808
11:20 *and* that they might have **n** favour, 1115+3807.1
14: 4 they gave **n** part unto the Levites in 3808
17: 3 of Manasseh, had **n** sons, but daughters: 3808
18: 7 the Levites have **n** part among you; for 369
22:25 of Gad; ye have **n** part in the LORD: 369
22:27 time to come, Ye have **n** part in the LORD. 369
23: 9 **n** man hath *been able to* stand before you 3808
23:13 **n** more drive out *any of* these nations from 3808
Jdg 2: 2 ye shall make **n** league with the inhabitants 3808
4:20 Is there any man here? that thou shalt say, **N**. 369
5:19 of Megiddo; they took **n** gain of money. 3808
6: 4 left **n** sustenance for Israel, neither sheep, 3808
8:28 so that they lifted up their heads **n** more. 3808
10:13 wherefore I will deliver you **n** more. 3808
11:39 she knew **n** man. And it was a custom in 3808
13: 5 a son; and **n** rasor shall come on his head: 3808
13: 7 now drink **n** wine nor strong drink, 408
13:21 the angel of the LORD did **n** more appear 3808
15:13 they spake unto him, saying, **N**; but we will 3808
17: 6 In those days *there was* **n** king in Israel, *but* 369
18: 1 In those days *there was* **n** king in Israel: and 369
18: 7 *there was* **n** magistrate in the land, that might 369
18: 7 and had **n** business with *any* man. 369
18:10 a place where *there is* **n** want of any thing 369
18:28 *there was* **n** deliverer, because it *was* far 369
18:28 and they had **n** business with *any* man; 369
19: 1 those days, when *there was* **n** king in Israel, 369
19:15 for *there was* **n** man that took them into *his* 369
19:18 there *is* **n** man that receiveth me to house. 369
19:19 thy servants: *there is* **n** want of any thing. 369
19:30 There was **n** such *deed* done nor seen from 3808
21:12 that had known **n** man by lying with *any* 3808
21:25 In those days *there was* **n** king in Israel: 369
1Sa 1: 2 had children, but Hannah had **n** children. 369
1:11 and there shall **n** rasor come upon his head. 3808
1:15 Hannah answered and said, **N**, my lord, 3808
1:18 and her countenance was **n** more *sad.* 3808
2: 3 Talk **n** more *so* exceeding proudly; let *not* 408
2: 9 for by strength shall **n** man prevail. 3808
2:24 my sons; for *it is* **n** good report that I hear: 3808
3: 1 in those days; *there was* **n** open vision. 369
6: 7 on which there hath come **n** yoke, and 3808
7:13 they came **n** more into the coast of Israel: 3808
10:14 when we saw that *they were* **n where**, we 369
10:27 despised him, and brought him **n** presents. 3808
11: 3 then, if *there be* **n man** to save us, we will 369
13:19 Now there was **n** smith found throughout 3808
14: 6 for *there is* **n** restraint to the LORD to save 369
14:26 but **n man** put his hand to his mouth: 369
15:35 Samuel came **n** more to see Saul until 3808
17:32 Let **n** man's heart fail because of him; 408
17:50 but *there was* **n** sword in the hand of David. 369
18: 2 would let him go **n more** home to his 3808
20:15 **n**, not when the LORD hath cut off NIH
20:21 for *there is* peace to thee, and **n** hurt; *as* 369
20:34 did eat **n** meat the second day of the month: 3808
21: 1 Why *art* thou alone, and **n** man with thee? 369
21: 2 Let **n** man know any thing of the business 408
21: 4 *There is* **n** common bread under mine hand, 369
21: 6 hallowed *bread:* for there was **n** bread there 3808
21: 9 take *it:* for *there is* **n** other save that here. 369
25:31 That this shall be **n** grief unto thee, 3808
26:12 **n man** saw *it,* nor knew *it,* neither awaked: 369
26:21 for I will **n** more do thee harm, because my 3808
27: 4 and he sought **n** more again for him. 3808
28:10 there shall **n** punishment happen to thee for 518
28:15 answereth me **n** more, neither by prophets, 3808
28:20 there was **n** strength in him; for he had 3808
28:20 for he had eaten **n** bread all the day, nor all 3808
29: 3 I have found **n** *fault* in him since he 3808+3972
30: 4 wept, until they had **n more** power to weep. 369
30:12 for he had eaten **n** bread, nor drunk *any* 3808
2Sa 1:21 Ye mountains of Gilboa, *let there be* **n** dew, 408
2:28 stood still, and pursued after Israel **n** more, 3808
6:23 Saul had **n** child unto the day of her death. 3808
7:10 in a place of their own, and move **n** more; 3808
12: 6 he did this thing, and because he had **n** pity. 3808
13:12 for **n** such thing ought to be done in Israel: 3808
13:16 she said unto him, *There is* **n** cause: this evil 408
14:25 of his head there was **n** blemish in him. 3808
15: 3 *there is* **n man** *deputed* of the king to hear 369
15:26 if he thus say, I have **n** delight in thee; 3808
18:13 for there is **n** matter hid from 3605+3808
18:18 I have **n** son to keep my name in 369
18:20 this day thou shalt bear **n** tidings, because 3808
18:22 seeing that thou hast **n** tidings ready? 369
20: 1 and said, We have **n** part in David, 369
20:10 Amasa took **n** heed to the sword that *was* in 3808
21: 4 We will have **n** silver nor gold of Saul, 369
21:17 Thou shalt go **n** more out with us to battle, 3808
1Ki 1: 1 covered him with clothes, but he gat **n** heat. 3808
3: 2 there was **n** house built unto the name of 3808
3:18 *there was* **n** stranger with us in the house, 369
3:22 this said, **N**; but the dead *is* thy son, and 3808
3:26 her the living child, and in **n** wise slay it. 408
3:27 her the living child, and in **n** wise slay it: 3808
6:18 all *was* cedar; there was **n** stone seen. 369
8:16 I chose **n** city out of all the tribes of Israel 3808
8:23 *there is* **n** God like thee, in heaven above, or 369
8:35 there is **n** rain, because they have sinned 3808
8:46 (for *there is* **n** man that sinneth not,) 369
9:22 of Israel did Solomon make **n** bondman: 3808
10: 5 the LORD; there was **n** more spirit in her. 3808
10:10 there came **n** more such abundance of 3808
10:12 there came **n** such almug trees, nor were 3808
13: 9 Eat **n** bread, nor drink water, 3808
13:17 Thou shalt eat **n** bread nor drink water 3808
13:22 say to thee, Eat **n** bread, and drink no water; 408
13:22 say to thee, Eat no bread, and drink **n** water; 408
17: 7 because there had been **n** rain in the land. 3808
17:17 so sore, that there was **n** breath left in him. 3808
18:10 thy God liveth, there is **n** nation or kingdom, 518
18:23 put **n** fire *under:* and I will dress the other 3808

1Ki 18:23 and lay *it* on wood, and put **n** fire *under:* 3808
18:25 name of your gods, but put **n** fire *under.* 3808
18:26 *there was* **n** voice, nor any that answered. 369
21: 4 away his face, and would eat **n** bread. 3808
21: 5 is thy spirit so sad, that thou eatest **n** bread? 369
22:17 the LORD said, These have **n** master: 3808
22:18 Did I not tell thee that he would prophesy **n** 3808
22:47 *There was* then **n** king in Edom: a deputy 369
2Ki 1:16 *there is* **n** God in Israel to inquire of his 369
1:17 king of Judah; because he had **n** son. 3808
2:12 he saw him **n** more: and he took hold of his 3808
3: 9 there was **n** water for the host, and for 3808
4:14 Verily she hath **n** child, and her husband is 369
4:41 And there was **n** harm in the pot. 1697+3808
5:15 now I know that *there is* **n** God in all 369
5:25 And he said, Thy servant went **n** whither. 3808
6:23 So the bands of Syria came **n** more into 3808
7: 5 of Syria, behold, *there was* **n** man there. 369
7:10 behold, *there was* **n** man there, neither voice 369
9:35 they found **n** *more* of her than the skull, 3808
10:31 Jehu took **n** heed to walk in the law of 3808
12: 7 receive **n** *more* money of your acquaintance, 408
12: 8 the priests consented to receive **n** *more* 1115
17: 4 brought **n** present to the king of Assyria, 3808
19:18 for they *were* **n** gods, but the work of 3808
22: 7 Howbeit there was **n** reckoning made with 3808
23:10 that **n** man might make his son or his 1115
23:18 Let him alone; let **n** man move his bones. 408
23:25 like unto him was there **n** king before him, 3808
25: 3 there was **n** bread for the people of 3808
1Ch 2:34 Now Sheshan had **n** sons, but daughters. 3808
12:17 seeing *there is* **n** wrong in mine hands, 3808
16:21 He suffered **n** man to do them wrong: yea, 3808
16:22 mine anointed, and do my prophets **n** harm. 408
17: 9 in their place, and shall be moved **n** more; 3808
22:16 the brass, and the iron, *there is* **n** number. 369
23:22 and had **n** sons, but daughters: 3808
23:26 *they* shall **n** *more* carry the tabernacle, 369
24: 2 died before their father, and had **n** children: 3808
24:28 Of Mahli *came* Eleazar, who had **n** sons. 3808
2Ch 6: 5 **n** city among all the tribes of Israel to build 3808
6:14 *there is* **n** God like thee in the heaven, nor in 369
6:26 there is **n** rain, because they have sinned 3808
6:36 (for *there is* **n** man which sinneth not,) 369
7:13 If I shut up heaven that there be **n** rain, or 3808
8: 9 did Solomon make **n** servants for his work; 3808
9: 4 the LORD; there was **n** more spirit in her. 3808
13: 9 *the same* may be a priest of *them that are* **n** 3808
14: 6 had rest, and he had **n** war in those years; 369
14:11 with many, *or* with *them that have* **n** power: 369
15: 5 in those times *there was* **n** peace to him that 369
15:19 there was **n** *more* war unto the five and 3808
17:10 that they made **n** war against Jehoshaphat. 3808
18:16 as sheep that have **n** shepherd: 369
18:16 the LORD said, These have **n** master; 3808
19: 7 do *it:* for *there is* **n** iniquity with the LORD 369
20:12 for we have **n** might against this great 369
21:19 his people made **n** burning for him, like 3808
22: 9 So the house of Ahaziah had **n** power to 369
32:15 for **n** god of any nation or 3605+3808
35:18 there was **n** passover like to that, kept in 3808
36:16 against his people, till *there was* **n** remedy. 369
36:17 had **n** compassion upon young man or 3808
Ezr 4:16 by this means thou shalt have **n** portion on 3809
9:14 that *there should be* **n** remnant nor escaping? 369
10: 6 he did eat **n** bread, nor drink water: 3808
Ne 2:14 *there was* **n** place for the beast *that was* 369
2:17 of Jerusalem, that we be **n** more a reproach. 3808
2:20 you have **n** portion, nor right, nor memorial, 369
6: 1 and *that* there was **n** breach left therein; 3808
6: 8 There are **n** such things *done* as thou 3808
13:19 *that* there should **n** burden be brought in on 3808
13:21 From that time forth came they **n** *more* on 3808
13:26 many nations was there **n** king like him, 3808
Est 1:19 That Vashti come **n** *more* before king 3808
2:14 she came in unto the king **n** more, 3808
5:12 Esther the queen did let **n** *man* come in 3808
8: 8 with the king's ring, may **n** *man* reverse. 369
9: 2 **n** man could withstand them; for the fear of 3808
Job 3: 7 be solitary, let **n** joyful voice come therein. 408
4:18 Behold, he put **n** trust in his servants; and 3808
5:19 yea, in seven there shall **n** evil touch thee. 3808
7: 7 *is* wind: mine eye shall **n** more see good. 3808
7: 8 see me **n** *more:* thine eyes *are* upon me, 3808
7: 9 down *to* the grave shall come up **n** *more.* 3808
7:10 He shall return **n** more to his house, 3808
9:25 a post: they flee away, they see **n** good. 3808
10:18 given up the ghost, and **n** eye had seen me! 3808
11: 3 shall **n** *man* make *thee* ashamed? 369
12: 2 **N doubt** but ye *are* the people, and 551
12:14 up a man, and there can be **n** opening. 3808
12:24 in a wilderness *where there is* **n** way. 3808
13: 4 of lies, ye *are* all physicians **of n value**. 457
14:12 till the heavens *be* **n more**, they shall not 1115
15: 3 *with* speeches wherewith he can do **n** 3808
15:15 Behold, he putteth **n** trust in his saints; yea, 3808
15:19 and **n** stranger passed among them. 3808
15:28 *and* in houses which **n** man inhabiteth, 3808
16:18 thou my blood, and let my cry have **n** place. 408
18:17 and he shall have **n** name in the street. 3808
19: 7 I cry aloud, but *there is* **n** judgment. 369
19:16 my servant, and he gave *me* **n** answer; 3808
20: 9 also *which* saw him shall *see him* **n** more; 3808
20:21 therefore shall **n** *man* look for his goods. 3808
23: 6 **N**; but he would put *strength* in me. 3808
24: 7 that *they have* **n** covering in the cold. 369
24:15 for the twilight, saying, **N** eye shall see me: 3808
24:20 he shall be **n** more remembered; and 3808
24:22 he riseth up, and **n** *man* is sure of life. 3808
26: 2 *how* savest thou the arm *that hath* **n** 3808
26: 3 How hast thou counselled *him that hath* **n** 3808
26: 6 before him, and destruction hath **n** covering. 369
28: 7 *There is* a path which **n** fowl knoweth, and 3808
28:18 **N** mention shall be made of coral, or 3808
30:13 forward my calamity, they have **n** helper. 3808

Job 30:17 the night season: and my sinews take **n** rest. 3808
32: 3 because they had found **n** answer, and 3808
32: 5 When Elihu saw that *there was* **n** answer in 369
32:15 They were amazed, they answered **n** more: 3808
32:16 but stood still, *and* answered **n** more:) 3808
32:19 my belly *is* as wine *which* hath **n** vent; 3808
34:22 *There is* **n** darkness, nor shadow of death, 369
34:32 if I have done iniquity, I will do **n** more. 3808
36:16 a broad place, where *there is* **n** straitness; 3808
36:19 *n*, not gold, nor all the forces of strength. NIH
38:11 Hitherto shalt thou come, but **n** further: 3808
38:26 *where* **n** man *is; on* the wilderness, 3808
38:26 *on* the wilderness, wherein *there is* **n** man; 3808
40: 5 yea, twice; but I will proceed **n** further. 3808
41: 8 upon him, remember the battle, do **n** more. 408
41:16 that **n** air can come between them. 3808
42: 2 *that* **n** thought can be withholden from thee. 3808
42:15 in all the land were **n** women found *so* 3808
Ps 3: 2 of my soul, *There is* **n** help for him in God. 369
5: 9 For *there is* **n** faithfulness in their mouth; 369
6: 5 For in death *there is* **n** remembrance of thee: 369
10:18 that the man of the earth may **n** more 1077
14: 1 fool hath said in his heart, *There is* **n** God. 369
14: 3 *there is* none that doeth good, **n**, not one. 369
14: 4 Have all the workers of iniquity **n** 3808
19: 3 *There is* **n** speech nor language, *where* their 369
22: 6 I *am* a worm, and **n** man; a reproach of 3808
23: 4 of the shadow of death, I will fear **n** evil: 3808
32: 2 and in whose spirit *there is* **n** guile. 369
32: 9 *or* as the mule, *which have* **n** understanding: 369
33:16 There is **n** king saved by the multitude of a 369
34: 9 for *there is* **n** want to them that fear him. 369
36: 1 *that there is* **n** fear of God before his eyes. 369
38: 3 *There is* **n** soundness in my flesh because 369
38: 7 and *there is* **n** soundness in my flesh. 369
38:14 and in whose mouth *are* **n** reproofs. 369
39:13 before I go hence, and be **n more**. 369
40:17 my deliverer; make **n** tarrying, O my God. 408
41: 8 *now* that he lieth he shall rise up **n** more. 3808
50: 9 I will take **n** bullock out of thy house, 3808
53: 1 fool hath said in his heart, *There is* **n** God. 369
53: 3 *there is* none that doeth good, **n**, not one. 369
53: 4 Have the workers of iniquity **n** knowledge? 3808
53: 5 were they in great fear, *where* **n** fear was: 3808
55:19 Because they have **n** changes, therefore 369
63: 1 in a dry and thirsty land, where **n** water is; 1097
69: 2 sink in deep mire, where *there is* **n** standing: 369
70: 5 my deliverer; O LORD, make **n** tarrying. 408
72:12 the poor also, and *him* that hath **n** helper. 369
73: 4 For *there are* **n** bands in their death: but 369
74: 9 *there is* **n** more any prophet: neither *is there* 369
77: 7 for ever? and will he be favourable **n** more? 3808
78:64 and their widows made **n** lamentation. 3808
81: 9 There shall **n** strange god be in thee; 3808
83: 4 that the name of Israel may be **n** more in 3808
84:11 **n** good *thing* will he withhold from them 3808
88: 4 the pit: I am as a man *that hath* **n** strength: 369
88: 5 the grave, whom thou rememberest **n** more: 3808
91:10 There shall **n** evil befall thee, neither shall 3808
92:15 and *there is* **n** unrighteousness in him. 3808
101: 3 I will set **n** wicked thing before mine eyes: 3808
102:27 the same, and thy years shall have **n** end. 3808
103:16 and the place thereof shall know it **n** more. 3808
104:35 of the earth, and let the wicked be **n** more. 369
105:14 He suffered **n** man to do them wrong: yea, 3808
105:15 mine anointed, and do my prophets **n** harm. 408
107: 4 solitary way; they found **n** city to dwell in. 3808
107:40 in the wilderness, *where there is* **n** way. 3808
119: 3 They also do **n** iniquity: they walk in his 3808
142: 4 but *there was* **n man** that would know me: 369
142: 4 refuge failed me; **n man** cared for my soul. 369
143: 2 for in thy sight shall **n** *man* living be 3605+3808
144:14 *that there be* **n** breaking in, nor going out; 369
144:14 that *there be* **n** complaining in our streets. 369
146: 3 in the son of man, in whom *there is* **n** help. 369
Pr 1:24 stretched out my hand, and **n** man regarded; 369
3:30 without cause, if he have done thee **n** harm. 3808
6: 7 Which having **n** guide, overseer, or ruler, 369
8:24 When *there were* **n** depths, I was brought 369
8:24 when *there were* **n** fountains abounding with 369
10:22 and he addeth **n** sorrow with it. 3808
10:25 so *is* the wicked **n** *more:* but the righteous *is* 369
11:14 Where **n** counsel *is*, the people fall: but 369
12:21 There shall **n** evil happen to the just: 3605+3808
12:28 and *in* the pathway *thereof there is* **n** death. 408
14: 4 Where **n** oxen *are*, the crib *is* clean: but 369
17:16 to get wisdom, seeing *he hath* **n** heart *to it?* 369
17:20 He that hath a froward heart findeth **n** 3808
17:21 and the father of a fool hath **n** joy. 3808
18: 2 A fool hath **n** delight in understanding, but 3808
21:10 his neighbour findeth **n** favour in his eyes. 3808
21:30 *There is* **n** wisdom nor understanding nor 369
22:24 Make **n** friendship with an angry man; and 408
24:20 For there shall be **n** reward to the evil *man;* 3808
25:28 He that *hath* **n** rule over his own spirit *is like* 369
26:20 Where **n** wood is, *there* the fire goeth out: so 657
26:20 so where *there is* **n** talebearer, the strife 369
28: 1 The wicked flee when **n man** pursueth: but 369
28: 3 *is like* a sweeping rain which leaveth **n** food. 369
28:17 shall flee to the pit; let **n** man stay him. 408
28:24 or his mother, and saith, *It is* **n** transgression; 369
29: 9 whether he rage or laugh, *there is* **n** rest. 369
29:18 Where *there is* **n** vision, the people perish: 369
30:20 and saith, I have done **n** wickedness. 3808
30:27 The locusts have **n** king, yet go they forth all 369
30:31 a king, against whom *there is* **n rising up**. 510
31: 7 and remember his misery **n** more. 3808
31:11 in her, so that he shall have **n** need of spoil. 3808
Ecc 1: 9 *there is* **n** new *thing* under the sun. 369+3605
1:11 *There is* **n** remembrance of former *things;* 369
2:11 and *there was* **n** profit under the sun. 369
2:16 For *there is* **n** remembrance of the wise more 369
3:11 that **n** man can find out the work that God 3808
3:12 I know that *there is* **n** good in them, but for *a* 369
3:19 that a man hath **n** preeminence above a 369

Ecc 4: 1 were oppressed, and they had **n** comforter; 369
4: 1 *there was* power; but they had **n** comforter. 369
4: 8 yet *is there* **n** end of all his labour; neither is 369
4:13 who will **n** more be admonished. 3808
4:16 *There is* **n** end of all the people, *even* of all 369
5: 4 not to pay it; for *he hath* **n** pleasure in fools: 369
6: 3 with good, and also *that* he have **n** burial; 3808
6: 6 years twice *told*, yet hath he seen **n** good: 3808
7:21 Also take **n** heed unto all words that are 408
8: 5 the commandment shall feel **n** evil thing: 3808
8: 8 *There is* **n** man that hath power over 369
8: 8 *there is* **n** discharge in *that* war; neither shall 369
8:15 a man hath **n** better *thing* under the sun, 369
9: 1 **n** man knoweth either love or hatred *by* all 369
9: 8 and let thy head lack **n** ointment. 408
9:10 for *there is* **n** work, nor device, 369
9:15 yet **n** man remembered that *same* poor 3808
10:11 and a babbler is **n** better. 369
10:20 Curse not the king, **n not** in thy thought; 1571
12: 1 thou shalt say, I have **n** pleasure in them; 369
12:12 of making many books *there is* **n** end; and 369
SS 4: 7 *art* all fair, my love; *there is* **n** spot in thee. 369
5: 6 I called him, but he gave me **n** answer. 3808
8: 8 have a little sister, and she hath **n** breasts: 369
Isa 1: 6 even unto the head *there is* **n** soundness in it; 369
1:13 Bring **n** more vain oblations; incense *is* an 3808
1:30 and as a garden that hath **n** water. 369
5: 6 the clouds that they rain **n** rain upon it. 4480
5: 8 *that* lay field to field, till *there be* **n** place, 657
5:13 because *they have* **n** knowledge: 1097
8:20 *it is* because *there is* **n** light in them. 369
9: 7 and peace *there shall be* **n** end, 369
9:17 Therefore the Lord shall have **n** joy in their 3808
9:19 of the fire: **n** man shall spare his brother. 3808
10:15 should lift up *itself, as if it were* **n** wood. 3808
10:20 shall **n** more again stay upon him that 3808
13:14 and as a sheep that **n** *man* taketh up: 369
13:18 they shall have **n** pity on the fruit of 3808
14: 8 laid down, **n** feller is come up against us. 3808
15: 6 the grass faileth, there is **n** green thing. 3808
16:10 in the vineyards there shall be **n** singing, 3808
16:10 the treaders shall tread out **n** wine in *their* 3808
19: 7 shall wither, be driven away, and *be* **n** *more.* 369
23: 1 so that *there is* **n** house, no entering in: 4480
23: 1 so that *there is* no house, **n** entering in: 4480
23:10 of Tarshish: *there is* **n** more strength. 369
23:12 he said, Thou shalt **n** more rejoice, O thou 3808
23:12 *to* Chittim; there also shalt thou have **n** rest. 3808
24:10 house is shut up, that **n** *man may* come in. 4480
25: 2 a palace of strangers to be **n** city; it shall 4480
26:21 her blood, and shall **n** more cover her slain. 3808
27:11 for it *is* a people of **n** understanding: 3808
27:11 he that formed them will shew them **n** 3808
28: 8 filthiness, *so that there is* **n** place *clean.* 1097
29:16 that framed it, He had **n** understanding? 3808
30: 7 shall help in vain, and to **n purpose**: 7385
30:16 ye said, **N**; for we will flee upon horses; 3808
30:19 thou shalt weep **n** more: he will be very 3808
32: 5 The vile person shall be **n** more called 3808
33: 8 despised the cities, he regardeth **n** man. 3808
33:21 wherein shall go **n** galley with oars, 1077
34:16 **n** one of these shall fail, none shall want 3808
35: 9 **N** lion shall be there, nor *any* ravenous 3808
37:19 for they *were* **n** gods, but the work of 3808
38:11 I shall behold man **n** more with 3808
40:20 impoverished that he hath **n** oblation NIH
40:28 *there is* **n** searching of his understanding. 369
40:29 to *them that have* **n** might he increaseth 369
41:28 For I beheld, and *there was* **n** man; 369
41:28 and *there was* **n** counseller, that, 369
43:10 before me there was **n** God formed, 3808
43:11 and beside me *there is* **n** saviour. 369
43:12 when *there was* **n** strange *god* among you: 369
43:24 Thou hast bought me **n** sweet cane with 3808
44: 6 I *am* the last; and besides me *there is* **n** God. 369
44: 8 yea, *there is* **n** God; I know not *any.* 369
44:12 he drinketh **n** water, and is faint. 3808
45: 5 *there is* none else, *there is* **n** God besides me: 369
45: 9 makest thou? or thy work, He hath **n** hands? 369
45:14 and *there is* none else, *there is* **n** God. 657
45:20 they have **n** knowledge that set up 3808
45:21 *there is* **n** God else beside me; a just God 369
47: 1 *there is* **n** throne, O daughter of 369
47: 1 for thou shalt **n** more be called tender and 3808
47: 5 for thou shalt **n** more be called, The lady of 3808
47: 6 thou didst shew them **n** mercy; upon 3808
48:22 *There is* **n** peace, saith the LORD, unto 369
50: 2 Wherefore, when I came, *was there* **n** man? 369
50: 2 or have I **n** power to deliver? behold, at my 369
50: 2 because *there is* **n** water, and dieth for thirst. 369
50:10 that walketh *in* darkness, and hath **n** light? 369
51:22 my fury; thou shalt **n** more drink it again: 3808
52: 1 for henceforth there shall **n** more come into 3808
52:11 touch **n** unclean *thing;* go ye out of the midst 408
53: 2 he hath **n** form nor comeliness; and 3808
53: 2 *there is* **n** beauty that we should desire him. 3808
53: 9 because he had done **n** violence, 3808
54: 9 of Noah should **n** more go over the earth; 4480
54:17 **N** weapon *that* is formed against thee 3605+3808
55: 1 ye to the waters, and he that hath **n** money; 369
57: 1 and **n** man layeth *it* to heart: 369
57:10 *yet* saidst thou not, There is **n hope**: 2976
57:21 *There is* **n** peace, saith my God, to 369
58: 3 our soul, and thou takest **n** knowledge? 3808
59: 8 and *there is* **n** judgment in their goings: 369
59:10 the blind, and we grope as if *we had* **n** eyes: 369
59:15 it displeased him that *there was* **n** judgment. 369
59:16 he saw that *there was* **n** man, and 369
59:16 and wondered that *there was* **n** intercessor: 369
60:15 that **n man** went through *thee*, I will make 369
60:18 Violence shall **n** more be heard in thy land, 3808
60:19 The sun shall be **n** more thy light by day; 3808
60:20 Thy sun shall **n** more go down; 3808
62: 4 Thou shalt **n** more be termed Forsaken; 3808
62: 7 give him **n** rest, till he establish, and till he 408

N

Isa 62: 8 Surely I will n more give thy corn to be 518
65:19 the voice of weeping shall be n more heard 3808
65:20 There shall be n more thence an infant of 3808
Jer 2: 6 through a land that n man passed through, 3808
2: 6 passed through, and where n man dwelt? 3808
2:11 changed their gods, which are yet n gods? 3808
2:13 broken cisterns, that can hold n water. 3808
2:25 thou saidst, There is n hope: no; for I have 2976
2:25 n; for I have loved strangers, and after them 3808
2:30 your children; they received n correction: 3808
2:31 are lords; we will come n more unto thee? 3808
3: 3 and there hath been n latter rain; 3808
3:16 saith the LORD, they shall say n more, 3808
4:22 but to do good they have n knowledge. 3808
4:23 void; and the heavens, and they had n light. 369
4:25 lo, there was n man, and all the birds of 369
5: 7 and sworn by them that are n gods: 3808
6:10 them a reproach; they have n delight in it. 3808
6:14 saying, Peace, peace; when there is n peace. 369
6:23 spear; they are cruel, and have n mercy; 3808
7:32 that it shall n more be called Tophet, 3808
7:32 shall bury in Tophet, till there be n place. 369
8: 6 n man repented him of his wickedness, 369
8:11 saying, Peace, peace; when there is n peace. 369
8:13 there shall be n grapes on the vine, nor figs 369
8:15 n good came; and for a time of health, and 369
8:22 Is there n balm in Gilead; is there no 369
8:22 balm in Gilead; is there n physician there? 369
10:14 is falsehood, and there is n breath in them. 3808
11:19 that his name may be n more remembered. 3808
11:23 there shall be n remnant of them: for I will 3808
12:11 because n man layeth it to heart. 369
12:12 n flesh shall have peace. 369+3605+3807.1
14: 3 they came to the pits, and found n water; 3808
14: 4 for there was n rain in the earth, 3808
14: 5 and forsook it, because there was n grass. 3808
14: 6 their eyes did fail, because there was n grass. 369
14:19 smitten us, and there is n healing for us? 369
14:19 we looked for peace, and there is n good; 369
16:14 the LORD, that it shall n more be said, 3808
16:19 vanity, and things wherein there is n profit. 369
16:20 gods unto himself, and they are n gods? 3808
17:21 bear n burden on the sabbath day, 408
17:24 to bring in n burden through the gates of 1115
17:24 sabbath day, to do n work therein; 1115+3605
18:12 they said, There is n hope: but we will 2976
19: 6 that this place shall n more be called 3808
19:11 them in Tophet, till there be n place to bury. 369
22: 3 do n wrong, do no violence, to the stranger, 408
22: 3 do no wrong, do n violence, to the stranger, 408
22:10 for he shall return n more, nor see his 3808
22:12 him captive, and shall see this land n more. 3808
22:28 is he a vessel wherein is n pleasure? 369
22:30 for n man of his seed shall prosper, 3808
23: 4 they shall fear n more, nor be dismayed, 3808
23: 7 the LORD, that they shall n more say, 3808
23:17 his own heart, N evil shall come upon you. 3808
23:36 of the LORD shall ye mention n more: 3808
25: 6 of your hands; and I will do you n hurt. 3808
25:27 spue, and fall, and rise n more, because 3808
25:35 the shepherds shall have n way to flee, 6+4480
30: 8 strangers shall n more serve themselves of 3808
30:13 be bound up: thou hast n healing medicines. 369
30:17 This is Zion, whom n man seeketh after. 369
31:29 In those days they shall say n more, 3808
31:34 they shall teach n more every man his 3808
31:34 and I will remember their sin n more. 3808
33:24 that they should be n more a nation before 4480
35: 6 they said, We will drink n wine: 3808
35: 6 saying, Ye shall drink n wine, neither ye, 3808
35: 8 to drink n wine all our days, we, our wives, 1115
36:19 Jeremiah; and let n man know where ye be. 408
38: 6 in the dungeon there was n water, but mire: 369
38: 9 he is: for there is n more bread in the city. 369
38:24 Let n man know of these words, and 408
39:12 look well to him, and do him n harm; 408+3972
40:15 n man shall know it: wherefore should he 3808
41: 4 he had slain Gedaliah, and n man knew it, 3808
42:14 Saying, N; but we will go into the land of 3808
42:14 land of Egypt, where we shall see n war, 3808
42:18 and ye shall see this place n more. 3808
44: 2 a desolation, and n man dwelleth therein, 369
44: 5 to burn n incense unto other gods. 1115
44:17 of victuals, and were well, and saw n evil. 3808
44:22 So that the LORD could n longer bear, 3808
44:26 that my name shall n more be named in 518
45: 3 I fainted in my sighing, and I find n rest. 3808
46:25 I will punish the multitude of N, and 4996
48: 2 There shall be n more praise of Moab: 369
48: 8 upon every city, and n city shall escape: 3808
48:33 their shouting shall be n shouting. 3808
48:38 Moab like a vessel wherein is n pleasure, 369
49: 1 thus saith the LORD; Hath Israel n sons? 369
49: 1 Hath he n heir? why then doth their king 369
49: 7 of hosts; Is wisdom n more in Teman? 369
49:18 saith the LORD, n man shall abide there, 3808
49:33 there shall n man abide there, nor any son 3808
49:36 there shall be n nation whither the outcasts 3808
50:14 bend the bow, shoot at her, spare n arrows: 408
50:39 it shall be n more inhabited for ever; 3808
50:40 so shall n man abide there, neither shall any 3808
51:17 is falsehood, and there is n breath in them. 3808
51:43 a land wherein n man dwelleth, 3605+3808
52: 6 that there was n bread for the people of 3808
La 1: 3 among the heathen, she findeth n rest: 3808
1: 6 are become like harts that find n pasture, 3808
1: 9 she had n comforter. O LORD, behold my 369
2: 9 the law is n more; her prophets also find no 369
2: 9 the law is no more; her prophets also find n 3808
2:18 give thyself n rest; let not the apple of thine 408
4: 4 ask bread, and n man breaketh it unto them. 369
4: 6 as in a moment, and n hands stayed on her. 3808
4:15 They shall n more sojourn there. 3808
4:16 divided them; he will n more regard them: 3808
4:22 he will n more carry thee away into 3808
La 5: 5 we labour, and have n rest. 3808
Eze 12:23 they shall n more use it as a proverb in 3808
12:24 For there shall be n more any vain vision 3808
12:25 come to pass; it shall be n more prolonged: 3808
13:10 there was n peace; and one built up a wall, 369
13:15 The wall is n more, neither they that daubed 369
13:16 and there is n peace, saith the Lord GOD. 369
13:21 they shall be n more in your hand to be 3808
13:23 Therefore ye shall see n more vanity, 3808
14:11 That the house of Israel may go n more 3808
14:15 that n man may pass through because of 1097
15: 5 when it was whole, it was meet for n work: 3808
16:34 n reward is given unto thee, therefore 3808
16:41 and thou also shalt give n hire any more. 3808
16:42 I will be quiet, and will be n more angry. 3808
18:32 For I have n pleasure in the death of him 3808
19: 9 that his voice should n more be heard upon 3808
19:14 that she hath n strong rod to be a sceptre to 3808
20:39 pollute ye my holy name n more with your 3808
21:13 it shall be n more, saith the Lord GOD. 3808
21:27 it shall be n more, until he come whose 3808
21:32 the land; thou shalt be n more remembered: 3808
22:26 they have put n difference between the holy 3808
24: 6 it out piece by piece; let n lot fall upon it. 3808
24:17 to cry, make n mourning for the dead, 3808
24:27 and thou shalt speak, and be n more dumb: 3808
26:13 the sound of thy harps shall be n more 3808
26:14 nets upon; thou shalt be built n more: 3808
26:21 thou shalt be n more: though thou be sought 369
28: 3 there is n secret that they can hide 3605+3808
28: 9 thou shalt be a man, and n God, in the hand 3808
28:24 there shall be n more a pricking brier unto 3808
29:11 N foot of man shall pass through it, 3808
29:15 that they shall n more rule over 1115+3807.1
29:16 it shall be n more the confidence of 3808
29:18 yet had he n wages, nor his army, 3808
30:13 there shall be n more a prince of the land of 3808
30:14 in Zoan, and will execute judgments in N. 4996
30:15 and I will cut off the multitude of N. 4996
30:16 N shall be rent asunder, and Noph shall 4996
33:11 I have n pleasure in the death of the wicked; 518
33:22 was opened, and I was n more dumb. 3808
34: 5 were scattered, because there is n shepherd: 1097
34: 8 because there was n shepherd, neither did 369
34:22 my flock, and they shall n more be a prey; 3808
34:28 they shall n more be a prey to the heathen, 3808
34:29 they shall be n more consumed with hunger 3808
36:12 thou shalt n more henceforth bereave them 3808
36:14 Therefore thou shalt devour men n more, 3808
36:29 will increase it, and lay n famine upon you. 3808
36:30 that ye shall receive n more reproach of 3808
37: 8 them above: but there was n breath in them. 369
37:22 they shall be n more two nations, 3808
39:10 So that they shall take n wood out of 3808
43: 7 shall the house of Israel n more defile, 3808
44: 2 be opened, and n man shall enter in by it; 3808
44: 9 Thus saith the Lord GOD; N 3605+3808
44:17 n wool shall come upon them, whiles they 3808
44:25 they shall come at n dead person to defile 3808
44:25 or for sister that hath had n husband, 3808
44:28 ye shall give them n possession in Israel: 3808
45: 8 my princes shall n more oppress my 3808
Da 1: 4 Children in whom was n blemish, but 369+3605
2:10 therefore there is n king, lord, 3606+3809
2:35 that n place was found for them: 3606+3809
3:25 the midst of the fire, and they have n hurt; 3809
3:27 upon whose bodies the fire had n power, 3809
3:29 there is n other God that can deliver after 3809
4: 9 is in thee, and n secret troubleth thee, 3606+3809
6: 2 and the king should have n damage. 3809
6:15 Persians is, That n[S] decree nor statute 3606
6:22 before thee, O king, have I done n hurt. 3809
6:23 n manner of hurt was found upon him, 3809
8: 4 so that n beasts might stand before 3605+3808
8: 7 there was n power in the ram to stand 3808
10: 3 I ate n pleasant bread, neither came flesh 3808
10: 8 and there remained n strength in me: 3808
10: 8 into corruption, and I retained n strength. 3808
10:16 upon me, and I have retained n strength. 3808
10:17 straightway there remained n strength in 3808
Hos 1: 6 for I will n more have mercy upon 3808
2:16 me Ishi; and shalt call me n more Baali. 3808
2:17 they shall n more be remembered by their 3808
4: 1 because there is n truth, nor mercy, 369
4: 4 Yet let n man strive, nor reprove another: 408
4: 6 reject thee, that thou shalt be n priest to me: NIH
8: 7 it hath n stalk: the bud shall yield no meal: if 369
8: 7 the bud shall yield n meal: if so be it yield, 1097
8: 8 Gentiles as a vessel wherein is n pleasure. 369
9:15 out of mine house, I will love them n more: 3808
9:16 their root is dried up, they shall bear n fruit: 1077
10: 3 We have n king, because we feared not 369
13: 4 and thou shalt know n god but me: 3808
13: 4 but me: for there is n saviour beside me. 369
Joel 1:18 are perplexed, because they have n pasture; 369
2:19 I will n more make you a reproach among 3808
3:17 there shall n strangers pass through her any 3808
Am 3: 4 lion roar in the forest, when he hath n prey? 369
3: 5 snare upon the earth, where n gin is for him? 369
5: 2 of Israel is fallen; she shall n more rise: 3808
5:20 even very dark, and n brightness in it? 3808
6:10 he shall say, N. Then shall he say, Hold thy 657
7:14 and said to Amaziah, I was n prophet, 3808
9:15 they shall n more be pulled up out of their 3808
Mic 3: 7 cover their lips; for there is n answer of God. 369
4: 9 is there n king in thee? is thy counseller 369
5:12 and thou shalt have n more soothsayers: 3808
5:13 thou shalt n more worship the work of 3808
7: 1 there is n cluster to eat: my soul desired 369
Na 1:12 afflicted thee, I will afflict thee n more. 3808
1:14 that n more of thy name be sown: 3808
1:15 for the wicked shall n more pass through 3808
2:13 the voice of thy messengers shall n more be 3808
3: 8 Art thou better than populous N, that was 4996
3:18 the mountains, and n man gathereth them. 369
Na 3:19 There is n healing of thy bruise; thy wound 369
Hab 1:14 that have n ruler over them? 3808
2:19 and there is n breath at all in the midst of it. 369
3:17 shall fail, and the fields shall yield n meat; 3808
3:17 and there shall be n herd in the stalls: 369
Zep 2: 5 that there shall be n inhabitant. 369+4480
3: 5 but the unjust knoweth n shame. 3808
3: 6 are destroyed, so that there is n man, 1097+4480
3:11 thou shalt n more be haughty because 3808
Hag 2:12 And the priests answered and said, N. 3808
Zec 1:21 so that n man did lift up his head: 3808
4: 5 not what these be? And I said, N, my lord. 3808
4:13 not what these be? And I said, N, my lord. 3808
7:14 that n man passed through nor returned: 4480
8:10 For before these days there was n hire for 3808
8:17 against his neighbour; and love n false oath: 408
9: 8 n oppressor shall pass through them any 3808
9:11 prisoners out of the pit wherein is n water. 369
10: 2 because there was n shepherd. 369
11: 6 For I will n more pity the inhabitants of 3808
13: 2 and they shall n more be remembered: 3808
13: 5 he shall say, I am n prophet, I am a 3808
14:11 and there shall be n more utter destruction; 3808
14:17 of hosts, even upon them shall be n rain. 3808
14:18 that have n rain; there shall be the plague, 3808
14:21 in that day there shall be n more 3808
Mal 1:10 I have n pleasure in you, saith the LORD of 369
Mt 5:18 one tittle shall in n wise pass from the law, 3364
5:20 ye shall in n case enter into the kingdom of 3364
5:26 Thou shalt by n means come out thence, 3364
6: 1 otherwise ye have n reward of your Father 3756
6:24 N man can serve two masters: for either he 3762
6:25 Take n thought for your life, what ye shall 3361
6:31 Therefore take n thought, saying, 3361
6:34 Take therefore n thought for the morrow: 3361
8: 4 See thou tell n man; but go thy way, 3367
8:10 have not found so great faith, n not in Israel. NIG
8:28 so that n man might pass by that way. 3361
9:16 N man putteth a piece of new cloth unto an 3762
9:30 saying, See that n man know it. 3367
9:36 as sheep having n shepherd. 3361
10:19 take n thought how or what ye shall speak: 3361
10:42 he shall in n wise lose his reward. 3364
11:27 and n man knoweth the Son, but the Father; 3762
12:39 and there shall n sign be given to it, but 3756
13: 5 because they had n deepness of earth: 3361
16: 4 and there shall n sign be given unto it, but 3756
16: 7 saying, It is because we have taken n bread. 3756
16: 8 because ye have brought n bread? 3756
16:20 tell n man that he was Jesus the Christ. 3367
17: 8 their eyes, they saw n man, save Jesus only. 3762
17: 9 Tell the vision to n man, until the Son of 3367
19: 6 Wherefore they are n more twain, but 3765
19:18 Jesus said, Thou shalt do n murder, 3756
20: 7 say unto him, Because n man hath hired us. 3762
20:13 and said, Friend, I do thee n wrong: 3756
21:19 Let n fruit grow on thee henceforward for 3371
22:23 which say that there is n resurrection, and 3361
22:24 Moses said, If a man die, having n children, 3361
22:25 and, having n issue, left his wife unto his 3361
22:46 And n man was able to answer him a 3762
23: 9 And call n man your father upon the earth: 3361
24: 4 Take heed that n man deceive you. 3361
24:21 the world to this time, n, nor ever shall be. 3761
24:22 there should n flesh be saved: 3756+3956
24:36 of that day and hour knoweth n man, no, 3762
24:36 of that day and hour knoweth no man, n, NIG
25: 3 took their lamps, and took n oil with them: 3756
25:42 I was a hungred, and ye gave me n meat: 3756
25:42 I was thirsty, and ye gave me n drink: 3756
26:55 in the temple, and ye laid n hold on me. 3756
Mk 1:45 insomuch that Jesus could n more openly 3371
2: 2 insomuch that there was n room to receive 3371
2: 2 that there was no room to receive them, n, NIG
2:17 They that are whole have n need of 3756
2:21 N man also seweth a piece of new cloth on 3762
2:22 And n man putteth new wine into old 3762
3:27 N man can enter into a strong man's house, 3762
4: 5 sprang up, because it had n depth of earth: 3361
4: 6 and because it had n root, it withered away. 3361
4: 7 and choked it, and it yielded n fruit. 3756
4:17 And have n root in themselves, and so 3756
4:40 so fearful? how is it that you have n faith? 3756
5: 3 and n man could bind him, no, not with 3762
5: 3 no man could bind him, n, not with chains: NIG
5:37 And he suffered n man to follow him, 3762
5:43 And he charged them straitly that n man 3367
6: 5 And he could there do n mighty work, 3762
6: 8 n scrip, no bread, no money in their purse: 3361
6: 8 no scrip, n bread, no money in their purse: 3361
6: 8 no scrip, no bread, n money in their purse: 3361
6:31 and they had n leisure so much as to 2532+3761
7:12 And ye suffer him n more to do ought for 3765
7:24 and would have n man know it: but 3762
7:36 And he charged them that they should tell n 3367
8:12 There shall n sign be given unto this 1487
8:16 saying, It is because we have n bread. 3756
8:17 Why reason ye, because ye have n bread? 3756
8:30 And he charged them that they should tell n 3367
9: 3 so as n fuller on earth can white them. 3756
9: 8 they saw n man any more, save Jesus only 3762
9: 9 he charged them that they should tell n man 3367
9:25 out of him, and enter n more into him. 3371
9:39 for there is n man which shall do a miracle 3762
10: 8 so then they are n more twain, but 3765
10:29 There is n man that hath left house, or 3762
11:14 N man eat fruit of thee hereafter for ever. 3367
12:14 carest for n man: for thou regardest not 3762
12:18 which say there is n resurrection; 3361
12:19 his wife behind him, and leave n children, 3361
12:20 the first took a wife, and dying left n seed. 3756
12:22 And the seven had her, and left n seed: 3756
12:34 And n man after that durst ask him any 3762
13:11 take n thought beforehand what ye shall 3361
13:20 those days, n flesh should be saved: 3756+3956

N

Mk 13:32 that day and *that* hour knoweth **n** *man,* no, *3762*
13:32 that day and *that* hour knoweth no *man,* **n**, NIG
14:25 I will drink **n** more of the fruit of the vine, *3364*
Lk 1: 7 And they had **n** child, because *3756*
1:33 and of his kingdom there shall be **n** end. *3756*
2: 7 there was **n** room for them in the inn. *3756*
3:13 Exact **n** more than that which is appointed *3367*
3:14 he said unto them, Do violence to **n man,** *3367*
4:24 **N** prophet is accepted in his own country. *3762*
5:14 And he charged him to tell **n** *man:* but go, *3367*
5:36 **N** *man* putteth a piece of a new garment *3762*
5:37 And **n** *man* putteth new wine into old *3762*
5:39 **N** *man* also having drunk old *wine* *3762*
7: 9 I have not found so great faith, **n**, not in NIG
7:44 thou gavest me **n** water for my feet: *3756*
7:45 Thou gavest me **n** kiss: but this *woman* *3756*
8:13 and these have **n** root, which for a while *3756*
8:14 of *this* life, and bring **n** fruit to perfection. *3756*
8:16 **N** *man,* when he hath lighted a candle, *3762*
8:27 and ware **n** clothes, neither abode in *any* *3756*
8:51 he suffered **n** *man* to go in, save Peter, *3762*
8:56 he charged them that they should tell **n** *man* *3367*
9:13 We have **n** more but five loaves and *3756*
9:21 commanded *them* to tell **n** *man* that *thing;* *3367*
9:36 told **n** *man* in those days any of *those* *3762*
9:62 **N** *man* having put his hand to the plough, *3762*
10: 4 nor shoes: and salute **n** *man* by the way. *3367*
10:22 and **n** *man* knoweth who the Son is, but *3762*
11:20 **n doubt** the kingdom of God is come upon *686*
11:29 and there shall **n** sign be given it, but *3756*
11:33 **N** *man,* when he hath lighted a candle, *3762*
11:36 *be* full of light, having **n** part dark, *3361+5100*
12: 4 and after that have **n** more that *they* can do. *3361*
12:11 take ye **n** thought how or what *thing* ye *3361*
12:17 I have **n** room where to bestow my fruits? *3756*
12:22 Take **n** thought for your life, what ye shall *3361*
12:33 where **n** thief approacheth, neither moth *3756*
13:11 **in n wise** lift up *herself.* *1519+3361+3588+3838*
15: 7 nine just *persons* which need **n** repentance. *3756*
15:16 swine did eat: and **n** *man* gave unto him. *3762*
15:19 And am **n more** worthy to be called thy *3765*
15:21 and am **n more** worthy to be called thy son. *3765*
16: 2 for thou mayest be **n** longer steward. *3756*
16:13 **N** servant can serve two masters: for either *3762*
18:17 as a little child shall **in n wise** enter therein. *3364*
18:29 There is **n** *man* that hath left house, or *3762*
20:22 for us to give tribute unto Cesar, or **n**? *3756*
20:31 and they left **n** children, and died. *3756*
22:36 and he that hath **n** sword, let him sell his *3361*
22:53 ye stretched forth **n** hands against me: *3756*
23: 4 and *to* the people, I find **n** fault in this man. *3762*
23:14 have found **n** fault in this man *touching* *3762*
23:15 **N**, nor yet Herod: for I sent you to him; *235*
23:22 I have found **n** cause of death in him: I will *3762*
Jn 1:18 **N** *man* hath seen God at any time; the only *3762*
1:21 Art thou *that* prophet? And he answered, **N.** *3756*
1:47 an Israelite indeed, in whom is **n** guile. *3756*
2: 3 of Jesus saith unto him, They have **n** wine. *3756*
3: 2 for **n** *man* can do these miracles that thou *3762*
3:13 And **n** *man* hath ascended up to heaven, but *3762*
3:32 and **n** *man* receiveth his testimony. *3762*
4: 9 For the Jews have **n** dealings with *3756*
4:17 and said, I have **n** husband. *3756*
4:17 Thou hast well said, I have **n** husband: *3756*
4:27 yet **n** *man* said, What seekest thou? or, *3762*
4:38 to reap *that* whereon ye bestowed **n** labour: *3756*
4:44 that a prophet hath **n** honour in his own *3756*
5: 7 Sir, I have **n** man, when the water is *3756*
5:14 sin **n more**, lest a worse *thing* come unto *3371*
5:22 For the Father judgeth **n** *man,* but *3762*
6:37 him that cometh to me I will **in n wise** cast *3364*
6:44 **N** *man* can come to me, except the Father *3762*
6:53 and drink his blood, ye have **n** life in you. *3756*
6:65 I unto you, that **n** *man* can come unto me, *3762*
6:66 went back, and walked **n more** with him. *3765*
7: 4 For *there is* **n** *man that* doeth any *thing* in *3762*
7:13 Howbeit **n** *man* spake openly of him for *3762*
7:18 is true, and **n** unrighteousness is in him. *3756*
7:27 **n** *man* knoweth whence he is. *3762*
7:30 but **n** *man* laid hands on him, because *3762*
7:44 taken him; but **n** *man* laid hands on him. *3762*
7:52 look: for out of Galilee ariseth **n** prophet. *3756*
8:10 hath **n** *man* condemned thee? *3762*
8:11 She said, **N** *man,* Lord. And Jesus said unto *3762*
8:11 do I condemn thee: go, and sin **n more.** *3371*
8:15 Ye judge after the flesh; I judge **n** *man.* *3762*
8:20 and **n** *man* laid hands on him; for his hour *3762*
8:37 because my word hath **n** place in you. *3756*
8:44 in the truth, because there is **n** truth in him. *3756*
9: 4 the night cometh, when **n** *man* can work. *3762*
9:25 Whether he be a sinner *or* **n**, I know not: NIG
9:41 If ye were blind, ye should have **n** sin: *3756*
10:18 **N** *man* taketh it from me, but I lay it down *3762*
10:29 **n** *man* is able to pluck *them* out of my *3762*
10:41 unto him, and said, John did **n** miracle. *3762*
11:10 because there is **n** light in him. *3756*
11:54 walked **n more** openly among the Jews; *3765*
13: 8 If I wash thee not, thou hast **n** part with me. *3756*
13:28 Now **n** *man* at the table knew for what *3762*
14: 6 **n** *man* cometh unto the Father, but by me. *3762*
14:19 and the world seeth me **n more;** *3765*
15: 4 **n more** can ye, except ye abide in me. *3761*
15:13 Greater love hath **n** *man* than this, that a *3762*
15:22 but now they have **n** cloke for their sin. *3756*
16:10 I go to my Father, and ye see me **n more;** *3765*
16:21 she remembereth **n more** the anguish, *3765*
16:22 and your joy **n** *man* taketh from you. *3762*
16:25 when I shall **n more** speak unto you in *3765*
16:29 thou plainly, and speakest **n** proverb. *3762*
17:11 And *now* I am **n more** in the world, but *3765*
18:38 saith unto them, I find in him **n** fault *at all.* *3762*
19: 4 that ye may know that I find **n** fault in him. *3762*
19: 6 and crucify *him:* for I find **n** fault in him. *3756*
19: 9 art thou? But Jesus gave him **n** answer. *3756*
19:11 Thou couldest have **n** power *at all* against *3756*

Jn 19:15 We have **n** king but Cesar. *3756*
21: 5 have ye any meat? They answered him, **N.** *3756*
Ac 1:20 be desolate, and let **n** man dwell therein: *3361*
4:17 But that it spread **n** further among *3361*
4:17 that *they* speak henceforth to **n** man in this *3367*
5:13 And of the rest durst **n** *man* join himself to *3762*
5:23 we had opened, we found **n** *man* within. *3762*
7: 5 in it, **n, not so much** as to set his foot on: *3761*
7: 5 seed after him, when *as yet* he had **n** child. *3756*
7:11 and our fathers found **n** sustenance. *3756*
8:39 that the eunuch saw him **n more:** *3765*
9: 7 hearing a voice, but seeing **n** *man.* *3367*
9: 8 he saw **n** *man:* but they led him by *3762*
10:34 Of a truth I perceive that God is **n** respecter *3756*
12:18 there was **n** small stir among the soldiers, *3756*
13:28 And though they found **n** cause of death *in* *3367*
13:34 *now* **n more** to return to corruption, he said *3371*
13:37 whom God raised *again,* saw **n** corruption. *3756*
13:41 a work which you shall **in n wise** believe, *3364*
15: 2 and Barnabas had **n** small dissension and *3756*
15: 9 And put **n** difference between us and them, *3762*
15:24 to whom we gave **n** *such* commandment: *3756*
15:28 to lay upon you **n** greater burden than *3367*
16:28 a loud voice, saying, Do thyself **n** harm: *3367*
18:10 and **n** *man* shall set on thee to hurt thee: *3762*
18:15 look ye *to it;* for I will be **n** judge of such *3756*
19:23 And the same time there arose **n** small stir *3756*
19:24 brought **n** small gain unto the craftsmen; *3756*
19:26 much people, saying that they be **n** gods, *3756*
19:40 there being **n** cause whereby we may give *3367*
20:25 kingdom of God, shall see my face **n more.** *3765*
20:33 I have coveted **n** *man's* silver, or gold, or *3762*
20:38 that they should see his face **n more.** *3765*
21:25 concluded that they observe **n** such *thing,* *3367*
21:39 *a city* in Cilicia, a citizen of **n** mean city: *3756*
23: 8 For the Sadducees say that there is **n** *3361*
23: 9 strove, saying, We find **n** evil in this man: *3762*
23:22 charged *him, See thou* tell **n** *man* that thou *3367*
25:10 to the Jews have I done **n** wrong, as thou *3762*
25:11 **n** *man* may deliver me unto them. *3762*
25:26 Of whom I have **n** certain *thing* to write *3756*
27:20 **n** small tempest lay on *us,* all hope that we *3756*
27:22 for there shall be **n** loss of *any man's* life *3762*
28: 2 And the barbarous people shewed us **n** little *3756*
28: 4 **N doubt** this man is a murderer, whom, *3843*
28: 5 off the beast into the fire, and felt **n** harm. *3762*
28: 6 and saw **n** harm come to him, they changed *3367*
28:18 because there was **n** cause of death in me. *3367*
28:31 with all confidence, **n** man **forbidding** him. *209*
Ro 2:11 For there is **n** respect of persons with God. *3756*
3: 9 are we better *than they?* **N**, in no wise: *3756*
3: 9 are we better *than they?* No, **in n wise:** *3843*
3:10 There is none righteous, **n**, not one: NIG
3:12 that doeth good, **n, not one.** *1520+2193+3756*
3:18 There is **n** fear of God before their eyes. *3756*
3:20 shall **n** flesh be justified in his sight: *3756+3956*
3:22 them that believe: for there is **n** difference: *3756*
4:15 for where **n** law is, *there is* no *3756*
4:15 where no law is, *there is* **n** transgression. *3761*
5:13 but sin is not imputed when there is **n** law. *3361*
6: 9 being raised from the dead dieth **n more;** *3765*
6: 9 death hath **n more** dominion over him. *3765*
7: 3 so that she is **n** adulteress, though she be *3361*
7:17 Now then it is **n more** I that do it, but *3765*
7:18 dwelleth **n** good *thing:* for to will is present *3756*
7:20 it is **n more** I that do it, but sin that *3765*
8: 1 now **n** condemnation to them *which are* in *3762*
10:12 For there is **n** difference between the Jew *3756*
10:19 you to jealousy by *them that are* **n** people, *3756*
11: 6 And if by grace, *then is it* **n more** of works: *3765*
11: 6 otherwise grace is **n more** grace. But if *it* *3765*
11: 6 if *it be* of works, *then* is it **n more** grace: *3765*
11: 6 otherwise work is **n more** work *3765*
12:17 Recompense to **n** *man* evil for evil. *3367*
13: 1 For there is **n** power but of God: the powers *3756*
13: 8 Owe **n** *man* any *thing,* but to love one *3367*
13:10 Love worketh **n** ill to *his* neighbour: *3756*
14: 7 to himself, and **n** *man* dieth to himself. *3762*
14:13 that **n** *man* put a stumblingblock or *3361*
15:23 But now having **n more** place in these *3371*
1Co 1: 7 So that ye come behind in **n** gift; *3367*
1:10 and *that* there be **n** divisions among you; *3361*
1:29 That **n** flesh should glory in his *3361+3956*
2:11 so the *things* of God knoweth **n** *man,* but *3762*
2:15 *things,* yet he himself is judged of **n** *man.* *3762*
3:11 For other foundation can **n** *man* lay than *3762*
3:18 Let **n** *man* deceive himself. If any *man* *3367*
3:21 Therefore let **n** *man* glory in men. For all *3367*
4: 6 that **n** one of you be puffed up for one *3361*
4:11 and **have n certain dwelling place;** *790*
5:11 an extortioner; with such a one **n not** to eat. *3366*
6: 5 **n**, not one that shall be able to judge NIG
7:25 Now concerning virgins I have **n** *3756*
7:37 having **n** necessity, but hath power over his *3361*
8:13 I will eat **n** flesh while the world standeth, *3364*
9:10 For our sakes, **n doubt,** *this* is written: *1063*
10:13 There hath **n** temptation taken you but such *3756*
10:24 Let **n** *man* seek his own, but every man *3367*
10:25 asking **n** question for conscience sake: *3367*
10:27 eat, asking **n** question for conscience sake. *3367*
11:16 we have **n** such custom, neither *3756*
12: 3 that **n** *man* speaking by the Spirit of God *3762*
12: 3 *that* **n** *man* can say that Jesus is the Lord, *3762*
12:21 say unto the hand, I have **n** need of thee: *3756*
12:21 the head to the feet, I have **n** need of you. *3756*
12:24 For our comely *parts* have **n** need: *3756*
12:25 That there should be **n** schism in the body; *3361*
13: 2 and have **n** charity, I am nothing. *3361*
13: 5 is not easily provoked, thinketh **n** evil; *3756*
14: 2 for **n** *man* understandeth *him;* howbeit in *3762*
14:28 But if there be **n** interpreter, let him keep *3361*
15:12 how say some among you that there is **n** *3756*
15:13 But if there be **n** resurrection of the dead, *3756*
16: 2 that there be **n** gatherings when I come. *3361*
16:11 Let **n** *man* therefore despise him: but *3361*

2Co 2:13 I had **n** rest in my spirit, because I found *3756*
3:10 made glorious had **n** glory in this respect, *3761*
5:16 Wherefore henceforth know we **n** *man* after *3762*
5:16 yet now henceforth know we *him* **n more.** *3765*
5:21 made him *to be* sin for us, who knew **n** sin; *3361*
6: 3 Giving **n** offence in any *thing,* that *3367*
7: 2 we have wronged **n** *man,* we have *3762*
7: 2 **n** *man,* we have defrauded no *man.* *3762*
7: 2 no *man,* we have defrauded **n** *man.* *3762*
7: 5 our flesh had **n** rest, but *we were* troubled *3762*
8:15 and he that *had gathered* little had **n** lack. *3756*
8:20 that **n** *man* should blame us in this *3361*
11: 9 I was chargeable to **n** *man:* for that which *3762*
11:10 **n** *man* shall stop me of this boasting in *3756*
11:14 And **n** marvel; for Satan himself is *3756*
11:15 Therefore *it is* **n** great *thing* if his ministers *3756*
11:16 I say again, Let **n** *man* think me a fool; *3361*
13: 7 Now I pray to God that ye do **n** evil; *3367*
Gal 2: 5 gave place by subjection, **n**, not for an hour; NIG
2: 6 they were, it maketh **n** matter to me: *3762*
2: 6 God accepteth **n** man's person:) for they *3756*
2:16 for by the works of the law shall **n** flesh be *3756*
3:11 But that **n** *man* is justified by the law in *3762*
3:15 **n** *man* disannulleth, or added thereto. *3762*
3:18 *be* of the law, *it is* **n more** of promise: *3765*
3:25 we are **n longer** under a schoolmaster. *3765*
4: 7 Wherefore thou art **n more** a servant, but *3765*
4: 8 unto them which by nature are **n** gods. *3361*
5: 4 Christ is **become of n effect** unto you, *2673*
5:23 against such there is **n** law. *3756*
6:17 From henceforth let **n** *man* trouble me: for I *3367*
Eph 2:12 having **n** hope, and without God in *3361*
2:19 Now therefore ye are **n more** strangers and *3765*
4:14 That we *henceforth* be **n more** children, *3371*
4:28 Let him that stole steal **n more:** but *3371*
4:29 Let **n** corrupt communication *3361+3956*
5: 5 For this ye know, that **n** whoremonger, *3756*
5: 6 Let **n** *man* deceive you with vain words: for *3367*
5:11 And have **n** fellowship with the unfruitful *3361*
5:29 For **n** *man* ever yet hated his own flesh; but *3762*
Php 2: 7 But **made** himself **of n reputation,** and *2758*
2:20 For I have **n** *man* likeminded, who will *3762*
3: 3 and have **n** confidence in the flesh. *3756*
4:15 **n** church communicated with me as *3762*
Col 2:16 Let **n** *man* therefore judge you in meat, *3361*
2:18 Let **n** *man* beguile you of your reward in a *3367*
3:25 hath done: and there is **n** respect of persons. *3756*
1Th 3: 1 Wherefore when we could **n longer** *3371*
3: 3 That **n** *man* should be moved by these *3367*
3: 5 this cause, when I could **n longer** forbear, *3371*
4: 6 That **n** *man* go beyond and defraud his *3361*
4:13 even as others which have **n** hope. *3361*
5: 1 ye have **n** need that *I* write unto you. *3756*
2Th 2: 3 Let **n** *man* deceive you by any means: *3361*
3:14 that *man,* and have **n** company with him, *3361*
1Ti 1: 3 some that *they* teach **n** other doctrine, *3361*
3: 3 Not given to wine, **n** striker, not greedy of *3361*
4:12 Let **n** *man* despise thy youth; but be thou an *3367*
5:22 Lay hands suddenly on **n** *man,* neither be *3367*
5:23 Drink **n longer** water, but use a little wine *3371*
6:16 the light **which n** *man* **can approach unto;** *676*
6:16 whom **n** man hath seen, nor can see: *3762*
2Ti 2: 4 **N** *man* that warreth entangleth himself with *3762*
2:14 that *they* strive not about words to **n** profit, *3762*
3: 9 But they shall proceed **n** further: for their *3756*
4:16 At my first answer **n** *man* stood with me, *3762*
Tit 1: 7 not soon angry, not given to wine, **n** striker, *3361*
2: 8 having **n** evil *thing* to say of you. *3367*
2:15 with all authority. Let **n** *man* despise thee. *3367*
3: 2 To speak evil of **n** *man,* to be no brawlers, *3367*
3: 2 To speak evil of no *man,* to be **n brawlers,** *269*
Heb 5: 4 And **n** *man* taketh *this* honour unto himself, *3756*
6:13 because he could swear by **n** greater, *3762*
7:13 of which **n** *man* gave attendance at *3762*
8: 7 should **n** place have been sought for *3756*
8:12 and their iniquities will I remember **n** more. *3364*
9:17 otherwise it is of **n** strength **at all** whilst *3379*
9:22 without shedding of blood is **n** remission. *3756*
10: 2 have had **n more** conscience of sins. *2089+3367*
10: 6 *sacrifices* for sin thou hast had **n** pleasure. *3756*
10:17 and iniquities will I remember **n** more. *3364*
10:18 of these *is, there is* **n more** offering for sin. *3765*
10:26 there remaineth **n more** sacrifice for sins, *3765*
10:38 my soul shall have **n** pleasure in him. *3756*
12:11 Now **n** chastening for the present *3756+3956*
12:14 without which **n** *man* shall see the Lord: *3762*
12:17 for he found **n** place of repentance, *3756*
13:10 whereof they have **n** right to eat which *3756*
13:14 For here have we **n** continuing city, but *3756*
Jas 1:11 For the sun is **n** sooner risen with a burning NIG
1:13 Let **n** *man* say when he is tempted, I am *3367*
1:17 with whom is **n** variableness, *3756*
2:11 Now if thou commit **n** adultery, yet *if* thou *3756*
2:13 without mercy, that hath shewed **n** mercy; *3361*
3: 8 But the tongue can **n** man tame; *it is* an *3762*
3:12 so *can* **n** fountain *both* yield salt water and *3762*
1Pe 2:22 Who did **n** sin, neither was guile found in *3756*
3:10 and his lips that *they* speak **n** guile: *3361*
4: 2 That *he* **n longer** should live the rest of *his* *3371*
2Pe 1:20 that **n** prophecy of the scripture is of *3756+3956*
1Jn 1: 5 God is light, and in him is **n** darkness at all. *3756*
1: 8 If we say that we have **n** sin, we deceive *3756*
2: 7 I write **n** new commandment unto you, but *3756*
2:19 they would *n doubt* have continued with us: NIG
2:21 know it, and that **n** lie is of the truth. *3756+3956*
2:27 and is **n** lie, and even as it hath taught you, *3756*
3: 5 to take away our sins; and in him is **n** sin. *3756*
3: 7 Little children, let **n** *man* deceive you: *3367*
3:15 ye know that **n** murderer hath eternal *3756+3956*
4:12 **N** *man* hath seen God at any time. If we *3762*
4:18 There is **n** fear in love; but perfect love *3756*
3Jn 1: 4 I have **n** greater joy than to hear that my *3756*
Rev 2:17 which **n** *man* knoweth saving he that *3762*
3: 7 he that openeth, and **n** *man* shutteth; *3762*
3: 7 and shutteth, and **n** *man* openeth; *3762*

N

Rev 3: 8 thee an open door, and **n** *man* can shut it: *3762*
3:11 which thou hast, that **n** *man* take thy crown. *3367*
3:12 of my God, and he shall go **n** more out: *3364*
5: 3 And **n** *man* in heaven, nor in earth, *3762*
5: 4 **n** *man* was found worthy to open and *3762*
7: 9 which **n** *man* could number, of all nations, *3762*
7:16 They shall hunger **n** more, neither thirst *3756*
10: 6 that there should be time **n** longer: *3756*
13:17 And that **n** *man* might buy or sell, save he *3361*
14: 3 and **n** *man* could learn *that* song but *3762*
14: 5 And in their mouth was found **n** guile: *3756*
14:11 and they have **n** rest day nor night, *3756*
15: 8 **n** *man* was able to enter into the temple, *3762*
17:12 which have received **n** kingdom **as yet**; *3768*
18: 7 and am **n** widow, and shall see no sorrow. *3756*
18: 7 and am no widow, and shall see **n** sorrow. *3364*
18:11 for **n** *man* buyeth their merchandise any *3762*
18:14 shalt find them **n more at all**. *3361+3756+3765*
18:21 and shall be found **n** more **at all**. *3364*
18:22 shall be heard **n** more **at all** in thee; *3364*
18:22 and **n** craftsman, of whatsoever craft *he be*, *3364*
18:22 shall be heard **n** more **at all** in thee; *3364*
18:23 a candle shall shine **n** more **at all** in thee; *3364*
18:23 of the bride shall be heard **n** more **at all** in *3364*
19:12 that **n** *man* knew, but he himself. *3762*
20: 3 that he should deceive the nations **n** more, *3361*
20: 6 on such the second death hath **n** power, but *3756*
20:11 and there was found **n** place for them. *3756*
21: 1 passed away; and there was **n** more sea. *3756*
21: 4 and there shall be **n** more death, *3756*
21:22 And I saw **n** temple therein: for the Lord *3756*
21:23 And the city had **n** need of the sun, *3756*
21:25 all by day: for there shall be **n** night there. *3756*
21:27 And there shall **in n wise** enter into it any *3364*
22: 3 And there shall be **n** more curse: but *3756*
22: 5 And there shall be **n** night there; and *3756*
22: 5 and they need **n** candle, neither light of *3756*

NOADIAH (2)

Ezr 8:33 of Jeshua, and **N** the son of Binnui, Levites; 5129
Ne 6:14 on the prophetess **N**, and the rest of 5129

NOAH (51) [NOAH'S, NOE]

Ge 5:29 he called his name **N**, saying, This *same* 5146
5:30 Lamech lived after he begat **N** five hundred 5146
5:32 **N** was five hundred years old: and 5146
5:32 and **N** begat Shem, Ham, and Japheth. 5146
6: 8 **N** found grace in the eyes of the LORD. 5146
6: 9 These *are* the generations of **N**: Noah was a 5146
6: 9 **N** was a just man *and* perfect in his 5146
6: 9 in his generations, *and* **N** walked with God. 5146
6:10 **N** begat three sons, Shem, Ham, and 5146
6:13 God said unto **N**, The end of all flesh is 5146
6:22 Thus did **N**; according to all that God 5146
7: 1 the LORD said unto **N**, Come thou and 5146
7: 5 **N** did according unto all that the LORD 5146
7: 6 **N** *was* six hundred years old when 5146
7: 7 **N** went in, and his sons, and his wife, and 5146
7: 9 went in two and two unto **N** into the ark, 5146
7: 9 and the female, as God had commanded **N**. 5146
7:13 In the selfsame day entered **N**, and Shem, 5146
7:13 the sons of **N**, and Noah's wife, and 5146
7:15 they went in unto **N** into the ark, two and 5146
7:23 **N** only remained *alive*, and *they that were* 5146
8: 1 God remembered **N**, and every living thing, 5146
8: 6 that **N** opened the window of the ark which 5146
8:11 **N** knew that the waters were abated from 5146
8:13 **N** removed the covering of the ark, and 5146
8:15 And God spake unto **N**, saying, 5146
8:18 **N** went forth, and his sons, and his wife, 5146
8:20 **N** builded an altar unto the LORD; and 5146
9: 1 God blessed **N** and his sons, and said unto 5146
9: 8 God spake unto **N**, and to his sons with 5146
9:17 God said unto **N**, This *is* the token of 5146
9:18 the sons of **N**, that went forth of the ark, 5146
9:19 These *are* the three sons of **N**: and of them 5146
9:20 **N** began *to be* a husbandman, and 5146
9:24 **N** awoke from his wine, and knew what his 5146
9:28 **N** lived after the flood three hundred and 5146
9:29 all the days of **N** were nine hundred and 5146
10: 1 these *are* the generations of the sons of **N**, 5146
10:32 These *are* the families of the sons of **N**, 5146
Nu 26:33 and **N**, Hoglah, Milcah, and Tirzah. 5270
27: 1 **N**, and Hoglah, and Milcah, and Tirzah. 5270
36:11 Tirzah, and Hoglah, and Milcah, and **N**, 5270
Jos 17: 3 and **N**, Hoglah, Milcah, and Tirzah. 5270
1Ch 1: 4 **N**, Shem, Ham, and Japheth. 5146
Isa 54: 9 For this *is as* the waters of **N** unto me: 5146
54: 9 for *as* I have sworn that the waters of **N** 5146
Eze 14:14 **N**, Daniel, and Job, were in it, they should 5146
14:20 Though **N**, Daniel, and Job, *were* in it, *as* I 5146
Heb 11: 7 By faith **N**, being warned of God of *things* *3575*
1Pe 3:20 of God waited in the days of **N**, *3575*
2Pe 2: 5 saved **N** the eighth *person*, a preacher of *3575*

NOAH'S (2) [NOAH]

Ge 7:11 In the six hundredth year of **N** life, in 5146
7:13 **N** wife, and the three wives of his sons with 5146

NOB (6)

1Sa 21: 1 came David to **N** to Ahimelech the priest: 5011
22: 9 said, I saw the son of Jesse coming to **N**, 5011
22:11 father's house, the priests that *were* in **N**: 5011
22:19 **N**, the city of the priests, smote he with 5011
Ne 11:32 *And at* Anathoth, **N**, Ananiah, 5011
Isa 10:32 As yet shall *he* remain at **N** *that* day: 5011

NOBAH (3)

Nu 32:42 **N** went and took Kenath, and the villages 5025
32:42 and called it **N**, after his own name. 5025
Jdg 8:11 of them that dwelt in tents on the east of **N** 5025

NOBLE (7) [NOBLEMAN, NOBLES]

Ezr 4:10 the great and **n** Asnappar brought over, 3358
Est 6: 9 hand of one of the king's **most n** princes, 6579
Jer 2:21 Yet I had planted thee a **n vine**, wholly a 8321
Ac 17:11 These were **more n than** those in *2104*
24: 3 *it* always, and in all places, **most n** Felix, *2903*
26:25 But he said, I am not mad, **most n** Festus; *2903*
1Co 1:26 not many mighty, not many **n**, *are called*: *2104*

NOBLEMAN (3) [MAN, NOBLE]

Lk 19:12 A certain **n** went into a far country to *444+2104*
Jn 4:46 And there was a certain **n**, whose son was *937*
4:49 The **n** saith unto him, Sir, come down ere *937*

NOBLES (30) [NOBLE]

Ex 24:11 upon the **n** of the children of Israel he laid 678
Nu 21:18 the well, the **n** of the people digged it, 5081
Jdg 5:13 have dominion over the **n** *among* the people: 117
1Ki 21: 8 the elders and to the **n** that *were* in his city, 2715
21:11 the **n** who *were* the inhabitants in his city, 2715
2Ch 23:20 the **n**, and the governors of the people, and 117
Ne 2:16 to the priests, nor to the **n**, nor to the rulers, 2715
3: 5 their **n** put not their necks to the work of 117
4:14 said unto the **n**, and to the rulers, and to 2715
4:19 I said unto the **n**, and to the rulers, and 2715
5: 7 I rebuked the **n**, and the rulers, and 2715
6:17 Moreover in those days the **n** of Judah sent 2715
7: 5 put into mine heart to gather together the **n**, 2715
10:29 their **n**, and entered into a curse, and into an 117
13:17 I contended with the **n** of Judah, and 2715
Est 1: 3 Media, the **n** and princes of the provinces, 6579
Job 29:10 The **n** held their peace, and their tongue 5057
Ps 83:11 Make their **n** like Oreb, and like Zeeb: yea, 5081
149: 8 with chains, and their **n** with fetters of iron; 3513
Pr 8:16 By me princes rule, and **n**, *even* all 5081
Ecc 10:17 when thy king *is* the son of **n**, and 2715
Isa 13: 2 that they may go *into* the gates of the **n**. 5081
34:12 They shall call the **n** thereof *to* 2715
43:14 have brought down all their **n**, and 1281
Jer 14: 3 their **n** have sent their little ones to 117
27:20 and all the **n** of Judah and Jerusalem; 2715
30:21 their **n** shall be of themselves, and 117
39: 6 also the king of Babylon slew all the **n** of 2715
Jnh 3: 7 by the decree of the king and his **n**, 1419
Na 3:18 thy **n** shall dwell *in the dust*: thy people is 117

NOD (1)

Ge 4:16 dwelt in the land of **N**, on the east of Eden. 5113

NODAB (1)

1Ch 5:19 with Jetur, and Nephish, and **N**. 5114

NOE (5) [NOAH]

Mt 24:37 But as the days of **N** *were*, so shall also *3575*
24:38 until the day that **N** entered into the ark, *3575*
Lk 3:36 *the son* of Sem, which was *the son* of **N**, *3575*
17:26 And as it was in the days of **N**, so shall it be *3575*
17:27 until the day that **N** entered into the ark, *3575*

NOGAH (2)

1Ch 3: 7 And **N**, and Nepheg, and Japhia, 5052
14: 6 And **N**, and Nepheg, and Japhia, 5052

NOHAH (1)

1Ch 8: 2 **N** the fourth, and Rapha the fifth. 5119

NOISE (88) [NOISED]

Ex 20:18 the **n** of the trumpet, and the mountain 6963
32:17 when Joshua heard the **n** of the people as 6963
32:17 *There is* a **n** of war in the camp. 6963
32:18 *but* the **n** of *them that* sing do I hear. 6963
Jos 6:10 not shout, nor **make** any **n** with your voice, 8085
Jdg 5:11 *They that are delivered* from the **n** of 6963
1Sa 4: 6 when the Philistines heard the **n** of 6963
4: 6 What *meaneth* the **n** of this great shout in 6963
4:14 when Eli heard the **n** of the crying, he said, 6963
4:14 he said, What *meaneth* the **n** of this tumult? 6963
14:19 that the **n** that *was* in the host of 1995
1Ki 1:41 Wherefore *is this* **n** of the city being in an 6963
1:45 rang again. This *is* the **n** that ye have heard. 6963
2Ki 7: 6 host of the Syrians to hear a **n** of chariots, 6963
7: 6 a **n** of horses, *even* the noise of a great host: 6963
7: 6 a noise of horses, *even* the **n** of a great host: 6963
11:13 when Athaliah heard the **n** of the guard 6963
1Ch 15:28 **making a n** with psalteries and harps. 8085
2Ch 23:12 Now when Athaliah heard the **n** of 6963
Ezr 3:13 So that the people could not discern the **n** 6963
3:13 from the **n** of the weeping of the people: 6963
3:13 a loud shout, and the **n** was heard afar off. 6963
Job 36:29 of the clouds, *or* the **n** of his tabernacle? 8663
36:33 The **n** thereof sheweth concerning it, 7452
37: 2 Hear attentively the **n** of his voice, and 7267
Ps 33: 3 a new song; play skilfully with a **loud n**. 8643
42: 7 Deep calleth unto deep at the **n** of thy 6963
55: 2 I mourn in my complaint, and **make a n**; 1949
59: 6 they **make a n** like a dog, and go round 1993
59:14 *and* let them **make a n** like a dog, and 1993
65: 7 Which stilleth the **n** of the seas, the noise of 7588
65: 7 the **n** of their waves, and the tumult of 7588
66: 1 **Make a joyful n** unto God, all ye lands: 7321
81: 1 **make a joyful n** unto the God of Jacob. 7321
93: 4 The LORD on high *is* mightier than the **n** 6963
95: 1 let us **make a joyful n** to the rock of our 7321
95: 2 *and* **make a joyful n** unto him with psalms. 7321
98: 4 **Make a joyful n** unto the LORD, all 7321
98: 4 **make a loud n**, and rejoice, and 6476
98: 6 sound of cornet **make a joyful n** before 7321
100: 1 **Make a joyful n** unto the LORD, all ye 7321
Isa 9: 5 battle of the warrior *is* with **confused n**, 7494
13: 4 The **n** of a multitude in the mountains, 6963
13: 4 a tumultuous **n** of the kingdoms of nations 6963
14:11 down *to* the grave, *and* the **n** of thy viols: 1998
17:12 *which* **make a n** like the noise of the seas; 1993
17:12 *which* make a noise like the **n** of the seas; 1993
24: 8 the **n** of them that rejoice endeth, the joy of 7588
24:18 *that* he who fleeth from the **n** of the fear 6963
Isa 25: 5 Thou shalt bring down the **n** of strangers, 7588
29: 6 great **n**, *with* storm and tempest, and 6963
31: 4 nor abase himself for the **n** of them: 1995
33: 3 At the **n** of the tumult the people fled; 6963
66: 6 A voice of **n** from the city, a voice from 7588
Jer 4:19 my heart **maketh a n** in me; I cannot hold 1993
4:29 The whole city shall flee for the **n** of 6963
10:22 the **n** of the bruit is come, and a great 6963
11:16 with the **n** of a great tumult he hath kindled 6963
25:31 A **n** shall come *even* to the ends of 7588
46:17 cry there, Pharaoh king of Egypt *is but* a **n**; 7588
47: 3 At the **n** of the stamping of the hoofs of his 6963
49:21 The earth is moved at the **n** of their fall, 6963
49:21 the **n** thereof was heard in the Red sea. 6963
50:46 At the **n** of the taking of Babylon the earth 6963
51:55 great waters, a **n** of their voice is uttered: 7588
La 2: 7 they have made a **n** in the house of 6963
Eze 1:24 they went, I heard the **n** of their wings, 6963
1:24 like the **n** of great waters, as the voice of 6963
1:24 the voice of speech, as the **n** of a host: 6963
3:13 *I heard* also the **n** of the wings of the living 6963
3:13 the **n** of the wheels over against them, and 6963
3:13 against them, and a **n** of a great rushing. 6963
19: 7 the fulness thereof, by the **n** of his roaring. 6963
26:10 thy walls shall shake at the **n** of 6963
26:13 I will cause the **n** of thy songs to cease; 1995
37: 7 there was a **n**, and behold a shaking, and 6963
43: 2 his voice *was* like a **n** of many waters: and 6963
Joel 2: 5 Like the **n** of chariots on the tops of 6963
2: 5 like the **n** of a flame of fire that devoureth 6963
Am 5:23 Take thou away from me the **n** of thy 1995
Mic 2:12 they shall **make great n** by reason of 1949
Na 3: 2 The **n** of a whip, and the noise of 6963
3: 2 the **n** of the rattling of the wheels, and 6963
Zep 1:10 *that there shall be* the **n** of a cry from 6963
Zec 9:15 shall drink, *and* **make a n** as *through* wine; 1993
Mt 9:23 the minstrels and the people **making a n**, *2350*
2Pe 3:10 the heavens shall pass away with a **great n**, *4500*
Rev 6: 1 and I heard, as *it were* the **n** of thunder, *5456*

NOISED (4) [NOISE]

Jos 6:27 his fame was ***n*** throughout all the country. NIH
Mk 2: 1 and it was **n** that he was in the house. *191*
Lk 1:65 all these sayings were **n abroad** throughout *1255*
Ac 2: 6 Now when this **was n abroad**, *1096+3588+5456*

NOISOME (4)

Ps 91: 3 of the fowler, *and* from the **n** pestilence. 1942
Eze 14:15 If I cause **n** beasts to pass through the land, 7451
14:21 and the **n** beast, and the pestilence, 7451
Rev 16: 2 and there fell a **n** and grievous sore upon *2556*

NOISY See CONCOUSE

NON (1)

1Ch 7:27 **N** his son, Jehoshua his son. 5126

NON-GREEKS See BARBARIANS

NONE (358) [NO]

Ge 23: 6 **n** of us shall withhold from thee his 376+3808
28:17 this *is* **n other** but the house of God, and 369
39: 9 *There is* **n** greater in this house than I; 369
39:11 *there was* **n** of the men of the house there 369
41: 8 *there was* **n** that could interpret them unto 369
41:15 a dream, and *there is* **n** that can interpret it: 369
41:24 but *there was* **n** that could declare *it* to me. 369
41:39 *there is* **n** so discreet and wise as thou *art*: 369
Ex 8:10 that thou mayest know that *there is* **n** like 369
9:14 that thou mayest know that *there is* **n** like me 369
9:24 such as there was **n** like it in all the land of 3808
11: 6 such as there was **n** like it, nor shall be like 3808
12:22 **n** of you shall go out at the door of his 376+3808
15:26 put **n** of *these* diseases upon thee, 3605+3808
16:26 *which is* the sabbath, in it there shall be **n**. 3808
16:27 seventh day for to gather, and they found **n**. 3808
23:15 and **n** shall appear before me empty: 3808
34:20 and **n** shall appear before me empty. 3808
Lev 18: 6 **N** of you shall approach to any 376+376+3808
21: 1 There shall **n** be defiled for the dead among 3808
22:30 ye shall leave **n** of it until the morrow: 3808
25:26 if the man have **n** to redeem *it*, and 3808+2050.2
26: 6 shall lie down, and **n** shall make *you* afraid: 369
26:17 and ye shall flee when **n** pursueth you. 369
26:36 a sword; and they shall fall when **n** pursueth. 369
26:37 as it were before a sword, when **n** pursueth: 369
27:29 **N** devoted, which shall be devoted of 3605+3808
Nu 7: 9 unto the sons of Kohath he gave **n**: because 3808
9:12 They shall leave **n** of it unto the morning, 3808
21:35 his people, until there was **n** left him alive: 1115
30: 8 wherewith she bound her soul, of **n effect**: 6565
32:11 **Surely n** of the men that came up out of 518
Dt 2:34 of every city, we left **n** to remain: 3808
3: 3 we smote him until **n** was left to him 1115
4:35 he *is* God; *there is* **n** else besides him. 369
4:39 and upon the earth beneath: *there is* **n** else. 369
5: 7 Thou shalt have **n** other gods before me. 3808
7:15 will put **n** of the evil diseases of 3605+3808
22:27 damsel cried, and *there was* **n** to save her. 369
28:31 and thou shalt have **n** to rescue *them*. 369
28:66 and shalt have **n** assurance of thy life: 3808
32:36 power is gone, and *there is* **n** shut up, or left. 657
33:26 *There is* **n** like unto the God of Jeshurun, 369
Jos 6: 1 of Israel: **n** went out, and none came in. 369
6: 1 of Israel: none went out, and **n** came in. 369
8:22 so that *they* let **n** of them remain or escape. 1115
9:23 there shall **n** of you be freed from being 3808
10:21 **n** moved his tongue against 376+3808+3807.1
10:28 the souls that *were* therein; he let **n** remain: 3808
10:30 he let **n** remain in it; but did unto the king 3808
10:33 until *he* had left him **n** remaining. 1115
10:37 he left **n** remaining, according to all that he 3808
10:39 souls that *were* therein; he left **n** remaining: 3808
10:40 he left **n** remaining, but utterly destroyed 3808

N

Jos 11: 8 until they left them n remaining. 1115
11:13 burned n of them, save Hazor only; 3605+3808
11:22 There was n of the Anakims left in the land 3808
13:14 Only unto the tribe of Levi he gave n 3808
14: 3 unto the Levites he gave n inheritance 3808
Jdg 19:28 n answered. Then the man took her up upon 369
21: 8 there came n to the camp from 376+3808
21: 9 there were n of the inhabitants of 369+376
Ru 4: 4 for there is n to redeem it besides thee; and 369
1Sa 2: 2 There is n holy as the LORD: for there is 369
2: 2 for there is n beside thee: neither is there any 369
3:19 let n of his words fall to the ground. 3605+3808
10:24 that there is n like him among all the people? 369
14:24 So n of the people tasted any food. 3605+3808
21: 9 David said, There is n like that; give it me. 369
22: 8 there is n that sheweth me that my son hath 369
22: 8 there is n of you that is sorry for me, or 369
2Sa 7:22 for there is n like thee, neither is there any 369
14: 6 there was n to part them, but the one smote 369
14:19 n can turn to the right hand or to the left 518
14:25 in all Israel there was n to be so 376+3808
18:12 Beware that n touch the young man 4310
22:42 They looked, but there was n to save; 369
1Ki 3:12 so that there was n like thee before thee, 3808
8:60 the LORD is God, and that there is n else. 369
10:21 n were of silver: it was nothing accounted of 369
12:20 there was n that followed the house of 3808
15:22 throughout all Judah; n was exempted: 369
21:25 (But there was n like unto Ahab, which did 3808
2Ki 5:16 before whom I stand, I will receive n. 518
6:12 of his servants said, N, my lord, O king: 3808
9:10 there shall be n to bury her. And he opened 369
9:15 let n go forth nor escape out of the city to go 408
10:11 his priests, until he left him n remaining. 1115
10:19 and all his priests; let n be wanting: 376+408
10:23 look that there be here with you n of 6435
10:25 Go in, and slay them; let n come forth. 376+408
17:18 there was n left but the tribe of Judah only. 3808
18: 5 that after him was n like him among all 3808
24:14 n remained, save the poorest sort of 3808
1Ch 15: 2 N ought to carry the ark of God but 3808
17:20 O LORD, there is n like thee, neither is 369
23:17 Eliezer had n other sons; but the sons of 3808
29:15 earth are as a shadow, and there is n abiding. 369
2Ch 1:12 such as n of the kings have had that 834+3808
9:11 there were n such seen before in the land of 3808
9:20 n were of silver; it was not any thing 369
10:16 we have n inheritance in the son of Jesse: 3808
16: 1 to the intent that he might let n go out or 1115
20: 6 might, so that n is able to withstand thee? 369
20:24 bodies fallen to the earth, and n escaped. 369
23: 6 But let n come into the house of the LORD, 408
23:19 that n which was unclean in any thing 3808
Ezr 8:15 found there n of the sons of Levi. 3808+4480
Ne 4:23 followed me, n of us put off our clothes, 369
Est 1: 8 was according to the law; n did compel: 369
4: 2 for n might enter into the king's gate clothed 369
Job 1: 8 that there is n like him in the earth, a perfect 369
2: 3 that there is n like him in the earth, a perfect 369
2:13 seven nights, and n spake a word unto him: 369
3: 9 let it look for light, but have n; neither let it 369
10: 7 there is n that can deliver out of thine hand. 369
11:19 shalt lie down, and n shall make thee afraid; 369
18:15 in his tabernacle, because it is n of his: 1097
20:21 There shall n of his meat be left; therefore 369
29:12 and him that had n to help him. 3808
32:12 there was n of you that convinced Job, or 369
35:10 n saith, Where is God my Maker, 3808
35:12 n giveth answer, because of the pride of 3808
41:10 N is so fierce that dare stir him up: who 3808
Ps 7: 2 it in pieces, while there is n to deliver. 369
10:15 seek out his wickedness till thou find n. 1077
14: 1 there is n that doeth good. 369
14: 3 there is n that doeth good, no, not one. 369
18:41 there was n to save them: even unto 369
22:11 for trouble is near; for there is n to help. 369
22:29 and n can keep alive his own soul. 3808
25: 3 Yea, let n that wait on thee be 3605+3808
33:10 **maketh** the devices of the people **of n effect.** 5106
34:22 n of them that trust in him shall be 3605+3808
37:31 is in his heart; n of his steps shall slide. 3808
49: 7 N of them can by any means redeem 376+3808
50:22 tear you in pieces, and there be n to deliver. 369
53: 1 there is n that doeth good. 369
53: 3 there is n that doeth good, no, not one. 369
69:20 for some to take pity, but there was n; 369
69:20 and for comforters, but I found n. 3808
69:25 be desolate; and let n dwell in their tents. 408
71:11 and take him; for there is n to deliver him. 369
73:25 there is n upon earth that I desire beside 3808
76: 5 n of the men of might have found 3605+3808
79: 3 and there was n to bury them. 369
81:11 to my voice; and Israel would n of me. 3808
86: 8 Among the gods there is n like unto thee, 369
107:12 they fell down, and there was n to help. 369
109:12 Let there be n to extend mercy unto him: 408
139:16 when as yet there was n of them. 259+3808
Pr 1:25 all my counsel, and would n of my reproof: 3808
1:30 They would n of my counsel: they despised 3808
2:19 N that go unto her return again, 3605+3808
3:31 choose n of his ways. 408+3605+871.1
SS 4: 2 beareth twins, and n is barren among them. 369
Isa 1:31 burn together, and n shall quench them. 369
5:27 N shall be weary nor stumble amongst them; 369
5:27 n shall slumber nor sleep; neither shall 3808
5:29 carry it away safe, and n shall deliver it. 369
10:14 there was n that moved the wing, or 3808
14: 6 in anger, is persecuted, and n hindereth. 1097
14:31 and n shall be alone in his appointed times. 369
17: 2 shall lie down, and n shall make them afraid. 369
22:22 so he shall open, and n shall shut; and 369
22:22 and he shall shut, and n shall open. 369
34:10 n shall pass through it for ever and ever. 369
34:12 n shall be there, and all her princes shall be 369
34:16 shall fail, n[s] shall want her mate: 802+3808

Isa 41:17 there is n, and their tongue faileth for thirst, 369
41:26 yea, there is n that sheweth, yea, there is 369
41:26 yea, there is n that declareth, yea, 369
41:26 yea, there is n that heareth your words. 369
42:22 they are for a prey, and n delivereth; for a 369
42:22 for a spoil, and n saith, Restore. 369
43:13 there is n that can deliver out of my hand: 369
44:19 n considereth in his heart, neither is there 3808
45: 5 I am the LORD, and there is n else, there is 369
45: 6 and from the west, that there is n besides me. 657
45: 6 I am the LORD, and there is n else. 369
45:14 in thee; and there is n else, there is no God. 369
45:18 I am the LORD; and there is n else. 369
45:21 just God and a saviour; there is n beside me. 369
45:22 the earth: for I am God, and there is n else. 369
46: 9 for I am God, and there is n else; I am God, 369
46: 9 none else; I am God, and there is n like me, 657
47: 8 in thine heart, I am, and n **else** besides me; 657
47:10 thou hast said, N seeth me. Thy wisdom and 369
47:10 in thine heart, I am, and n **else** besides me. 657
47:15 every one to his quarter; n shall save thee. 369
50: 2 when I called, was there n to answer? Is my 369
51:18 There is n to guide her among all the sons 369
57: 1 n considering that the righteous is taken 369
59: 4 N calleth for justice, nor any pleadeth for 369
59:11 we look for judgment, but there is n; 369
63: 3 of the people there was n with me: 369+376
63: 5 I looked, and there was n to help; and 369
63: 5 and I wondered that there was n to uphold: 369
64: 7 there is n that calleth upon thy name, 369
66: 4 because when I called, n did answer; when I 369
Jer 4: 4 burn that n can quench it, because of the evil 369
4:22 and they have n understanding: 3808
7:33 of the earth; and n shall fray them away. 369
9:10 that n can pass through them; neither 376+1097
9:12 a wilderness, that n passeth through? 1097+4480
9:22 the harvestman, and n shall gather them. 369
10: 6 Forasmuch as there is n like unto thee, 369
10: 7 there is n like unto thee. 369+4480
10:20 there is n to stretch forth my tent any more, 369
13:19 n shall open them: Judah shall be carried 369
14:16 they shall have n to bury them, them, 369
21:12 burn that n can quench it, because of the evil 369
23:14 n doth return from his wickedness: 376+1115
30: 7 for that day is great, so that n is like it: it is 369
30:10 and be quiet, and n shall make him afraid. 369
30:13 There is n to plead thy cause, that thou 369
34: 9 that n should serve himself of them, 376+1115
34:10 that n should serve themselves of them any 1115
35:14 for unto this day they drink n, but 3808
36:30 He shall have n to sit upon the throne of 3808
42:17 n of them shall remain or escape from 3808
44: 7 out of Judah, to leave you n to remain; 1115
44:14 So that n of the remnant of Judah, 3808
44:14 for n shall return but such as shall escape. 3808
46:27 and at ease, and n shall make him afraid. 369
48:33 n shall tread with shouting; their shouting 3808
49: 5 n shall gather up him that wandereth. 369
50: 3 her land desolate, and n shall dwell therein: 3808
50: 9 a mighty expert man; n shall return in vain. 3808
50:20 shall be sought for, and there shall be n; 369
50:29 against it round about; let n thereof escape: 408
50:32 and fall, and n shall raise him up: 369
51:62 to cut it off, that n shall remain in it, 1115
La 1: 2 among all her lovers she hath n to comfort 369
1: 4 because n come to the solemn feasts: 1097
1: 7 the hand of the enemy, and n did help her: 369
1:17 her hands, and there is n to comfort her: 369
1:21 heard that I sigh; there is n to comfort me: 369
2:22 that in the day of the LORD'S anger n 3808
5: 8 there is n that doth deliver us out of their 369
Eze 7:11 n of them shall remain, nor of their 3808
7:14 to make all ready; but n goeth to the battle: 369
7:25 they shall seek peace, and there shall be n. 369
12:28 There shall n of my words be 3605+3808
16: 5 N eye pitied thee, to do any of these unto 3808
16:34 whereas n followeth thee to commit 3808
18: 7 hath spoiled n by violence, hath given his 3808
22:30 that I should not destroy it: but I found n. 3808
31:14 To the end that n of all the trees by 3808
33:16 N of his sins that he hath committed 3605+3808
33:28 shall be desolate, that n shall pass through. 369
34: 6 and n did search or seek after them. 369
34:28 dwell safely, and n shall make them afraid. 369
39:26 safely in their land, and n made them afraid. 369
39:28 and have left n of them any more there. 3808
Da 1:19 among them all was found n like Daniel, 3808
2:11 there is n other that can shew it before 3809
4:35 n can stay his hand, or say unto 383+1768+3809
6: 4 they could find n occasion nor fault; 3606+3809
8: 7 there was n that could deliver the ram out 3808
8:27 astonished at the vision, but n understood it. 369
10:21 there is n that holdeth with me in these 259+369
11:16 his own will, and n shall stand before him: 369
11:45 shall come to his end, and n shall help him. 369
12:10 n of the wicked shall understand; but 3605+3808
Hos 2:10 n shall deliver her out of mine hand, 376+3808
5:14 I will take away, and n shall rescue him. 369
7: 7 there is n among them that calleth unto me. 369
11: 7 to the most High, n at all would exalt him. 3808
12: 8 in all my labours they shall find n iniquity 3808
Joel 2:27 that I am the LORD your God, and n else: 369
Am 5: 2 upon her land; there is n to raise her up 369
5: 6 and there be n to quench it in Beth-el. 369
Ob 1: 7 under thee: there is n understanding in him. 369
Mic 2: 5 Therefore thou shalt have n that shall cast a 3808
3:11 among us? n evil can come upon us. 3808
4: 4 his fig tree; and n shall make them afraid: 369
5: 8 and teareth in pieces, and n can deliver. 369
7: 2 there is n upright among men: they all lie in 369
Na 2: 8 stand, shall they cry; but n shall look back. 369
2: 9 for there is n end of the store and glory out 369
2:11 the lion's whelp, and n made them afraid? 369
3: 3 and there is n end of their corpses; 369
Zep 2:15 in her heart, I am, and there is n beside me: 657

Zep 3: 6 their streets waste, that n passeth by: 1097+4480
3: 6 is no man, that there is n inhabitant. 369+4480
3:13 and lie down, and n shall make them afraid. 369
Hag 1: 6 ye clothe you, but **there is n** warm; and he 369
Zec 7:10 let n of you imagine evil against his 376+408
8:17 let n of you imagine evil in your hearts 376+408
Mal 2:15 let n deal treacherously against the wife of 408
Mt 12:43 dry places, seeking rest, and findeth n. 3756
15: 6 **made** the commandment of God **of n effect** 208
19:17 there is n good but one, that is, God: but 3762
26:60 But found n: yea, though many false 3756
26:60 false witnesses came, yet found they n. 3756
Mk 7:13 **Making** the word of God **of n effect** through 208
10:18 there is n good but one, that is, God. 3762
12:31 There is n other commandment greater than 3756
12:32 is one God; and there is n other but he: 3756
14:55 Jesus to put him to death; and found n. 3756
Lk 1:61 There is n of thy kindred that is called by 3762
3:11 let him impart to him that hath n; 3361
4:26 But unto n of them was Elias sent, 3762
4:27 and n of them was cleansed, 3762
11:24 and finding n, he saith, I will return unto 3361
13: 6 and sought fruit thereon, and found n. 3756
13: 7 seeking fruit on this fig tree, and find n: 3756
14:24 That n of those men which were bidden 3762
18:19 me good? n is good, save one, that is, God. 3762
18:34 And they understood n of these things: and 3762
Jn 6:22 sea saw that there was n other boat there, 3756
7:19 the law, and yet n of you keepeth the law? 3762
8:10 lift up himself, and saw n but the woman, 3367
15:24 them the works which n other man did, 3762
16: 5 and n of you asketh me, Whither goest 3762
17:12 and n of them is lost, but the son of 3762
18: 9 them which thou gavest me have I lost n. 3762
21:12 And n of the disciples durst ask him, 3762
Ac 3: 6 Then Peter said, Silver and gold have I n; 3756
4:12 for there is n other name under heaven 3777
7: 5 And he gave him n inheritance in it, no, not 3756
8:16 (For as yet he was fallen upon n of them: 3762
8:24 that n of these things which ye have spoken 3367
11:19 preaching the word to n but unto the Jews 3367
18:17 And Gallio cared for n of those things. 3762
20:24 But n of these things move me, 3056+3762
24:23 that he should forbid n of his acquaintance 3367
25:11 if there be n of these things whereof these 3762
25:18 n accusation of such things as I supposed: 3762
26:22 saying n other things than those which 3762
26:26 for I am persuaded that n of these things 3762
Ro 3:10 is written, There is n righteous, no, not one: 3756
3:11 There is n that understandeth, there is none 3756
3:11 there is n that seeketh after God. 3756
3:12 there is n that doeth good, no, not one. 3756
4:14 and the promise **made of n effect**: 2673
8: 9 have not the Spirit of Christ, he is n of his. 3756
9: 6 the word of God hath **taken n effect.** 1601
14: 7 For n of us liveth to himself, and no man 3762
1Co 1:14 I thank God that I baptized n of you, but 3762
1:17 cross of Christ should be **made of n effect.** 2758
2: 8 Which n of the princes of this world knew: 3762
7:29 that have wives be as though they had n; 3361
8: 4 and that there is n other God but one. 3762
9:15 But I have used n of these things: 3756+3762
10:32 Give n **offence**, neither to the Jews, nor to 677
14:10 and n of them is without signification. 3762
2Co 1:13 For we write n other things unto you, 3756
Gal 1:19 But other of the apostles saw I n, 3756
3:17 that it should **make** the promise **of n effect.** 2673
5:10 that you will be n otherwise minded: 3762
1Th 5:15 See that n render evil for evil unto 3361+5100
1Ti 5:14 give n occasion to the adversary to speak 3367
1Pe 4:15 But let n of you suffer as a murderer, 3361+5100
1Jn 2:10 and there is n occasion of stumbling in him. 3756
Rev 2:10 Fear n of those things which thou shalt 3367
2:24 I will put upon you n other burden. 3756

NOON (13) [NOONDAY, NOONDAYS, NOONTIDE]

Ge 43:16 for these men shall dine with me at n. 6672
43:25 ready the present against Joseph came at n: 6672
2Sa 4: 5 of Ish-bosheth, who lay on a bed at n. 6672
1Ki 18:26 name of Baal from morning even until n, 6672
18:27 it came to pass at n, that Elijah mocked 6672
20:16 they went out at n. But Ben-hadad was 6672
2Ki 4:20 he sat on her knees till n, and then died. 6672
Ps 55:17 Evening, and morning, and at n, will I pray, 6672
SS 1: 7 where thou makest thy flock to rest at n: 6672
Jer 6: 4 war against her; arise, and let us go up at n. 6672
Am 8: 9 that I will cause the sun to go down at n, 6672
Zep 2: 4 they shall drive out Ashdod at the **n day,** 6672
Ac 22: 6 was come nigh unto Damascus about n, 3314

NOONDAY (8) [DAY, NOON]

Job 5:14 and grope in the n as in the night. 6672
11:17 thine age shall be clearer than the n; 6672
Ps 37: 6 as the light, and thy judgment as the n. 6672
91: 6 nor for the destruction that wasteth at n. 6672
Isa 16: 3 shadow as the night in the midst of the n; 6672
58:10 in obscurity, and thy darkness be as the n: 6672
59:10 we stumble at n as in the night; we are in 6672
Jer 15: 8 the mother of the young men a spoiler at n: 6672

NOONDAYS (1) [DAY, NOON]

Dt 28:29 thou shalt grope at n, as the blind gropeth 6672

NOONTIDE (1) [NOON]

Jer 20:16 the morning, and the shouting at n; 6256+6672

NOPH (7)

Isa 19:13 the princes of N are deceived; 5297
Jer 2:16 Also the children of N and Tahapanes have 5297
44: 1 at N, and in the country of Pathros, saying, 5297
46:14 and publish in N and in Tahpanhes: 5297
46:19 for N shall be waste and desolate without 5297
Eze 30:13 I will cause their images to cease out of N; 5297
30:16 and N shall have distresses daily. 5297

N

NOPHAH (1)

Nu 21:30 we have laid *them* waste even unto **N**, 5302

NOR (758) [NO]

Ge 19:33 when she lay down, **n** when she arose. 2050.1
19:35 when she lay down, **n** when she arose. 2050.1
21:23 **n** with my son, nor with my son's son: 2050.1
21:23 nor with my son, **n** with my son's son: 2050.1
45: 5 **n** angry with yourselves, 408+2050.1
45: 6 *there shall* neither *be* earing **n** harvest. 2050.1
49:10 **n** a lawgiver from between his feet, 2050.1
Ex 4: 1 **n** hearken unto my voice: 3808+2050.1
4:10 **n** since thou hast spoken unto thy servant: 1571
10: 6 **n** thy fathers' fathers have seen, 2050.1
11: 6 like it, **n** shall be like it any more. 3808+2050.1
12: 9 **n** sodden at all with water, but roast with 2050.1
13:22 **n** the pillar of fire by night, *from* before 2050.1
20: 5 thyself to them, **n** serve them: 3808+2050.1
20:10 thou, **n** thy son, nor thy daughter, 2050.1
20:10 thou, nor thy son, **n** thy daughter, 2050.1
20:10 **n** thy maidservant, nor thy cattle, 2050.1
20:10 nor thy maidservant, **n** thy cattle, 2050.1
20:10 **n** thy stranger that *is* within thy gates: 2050.1
20:17 **n** his manservant, nor his maidservant, 2050.1
20:17 **n** his maidservant, nor his ox, nor his ass, 2050.1
20:17 nor his maidservant, **n** his ox, nor his ass, 2050.1
20:17 nor his maidservant, nor his ox, **n** his ass, 2050.1
20:17 **n** any thing that *is* thy neighbour's. 2050.1
22:21 vex a stranger, **n** oppress him: 3808+2050.1
22:28 **n** curse the ruler of thy people. 3808+2050.1
23:24 **n** serve them, nor do after their 3808+2050.1
23:24 serve them, **n** do after their works: 3808+2050.1
23:26 cast their young, **n** be barren, in thy land: 2050.1
23:32 no covenant with them, **n** with their gods. 2050.1
30: 9 **n** burnt sacrifice, nor meat offering; 2050.1
30: 9 nor burnt sacrifice, **n** meat offering; 2050.1
34: 3 neither let the flocks **n** herds feed before 2050.1
34:10 done in all the earth, **n** in any nation: 2050.1
34:28 neither eat bread, **n** drink water. 3808+2050.1
36: 6 Let neither man **n** woman make any more 2050.1
Lev 2:11 for ye shall burn no leaven, **n** any honey, 2050.1
3:17 *that* ye eat neither fat **n** blood. 3605+2050.1
10: 9 Do not drink wine **n** strong drink, thou, 2050.1
10: 9 strong drink, thou, **n** thy sons with thee, 2050.1
11:10 all that have not fins **n** scales in the seas, 2050.1
11:12 Whatsoever hath no fins **n** scales in 2050.1
11:26 *is* not clovenfooted, **n** cheweth 369+2050.1
12: 4 *thing,* **n** come into the sanctuary, 3808+2050.1
13:34 **n** *be* in sight deeper than the skin; 369+2050.1
17:16 if he wash *them* not, **n** bathe his 3808+2050.1
18:26 **n** any stranger that sojourneth among 2050.1
19: 4 **n** make to yourselves molten gods: 3808+2050.1
19:14 **n** put a stumblingblock before 3808+2050.1
19:15 **n** honour the person of the mighty: 3808+2050.1
19:18 **n** bear any grudge against 3808+2050.1
19:20 at all redeemed, **n** freedom given her; 176+3808
19:26 use enchantment, **n** observe times. 3808+2050.1
19:28 **n** print any marks upon you: 3808+2050.1
20:19 mother's sister, **n** of thy father's sister: 2050.1
21: 5 **n** make any cuttings in their flesh. 3808+2050.1
21:10 his head, **n** rend his clothes; 3808+2050.1
21:11 **n** defile himself for his father, or for his 3808
21:12 **n** profane the sanctuary of his God; 3808+2050.1
21:23 **n** come nigh unto the altar, because 3808+2050.1
22:22 **n** make an offering by fire of them 3808+2050.1
23:14 **n** parched *corn,* nor green ears, 2050.1
23:14 nor parched *corn,* **n** green ears, 2050.1
25: 4 thy field, **n** prune thy vineyard. 3808+2050.1
25:11 **n** gather *the grapes* in it of thy vine 3808+2050.1
25:20 not sow, **n** gather in our increase: 3808+2050.1
25:37 **n** lend him thy victuals for 3808+2050.1
26: 1 Ye shall make you no idols **n** 3808+2050.1
27:10 **n** change it, a good for a bad, or 3808+2050.1
Nu 5:15 **n** put frankincense thereon; 3808+2050.1
6: 3 **n** eat moist grapes, or dried. 3808+2050.1
9:12 **n** break any bone of it: 3808+2050.1
11:19 **n** two days, nor five days, 3808+2050.1
11:19 nor two days, **n** five days, 3808+2050.1
11:19 neither ten days, **n** twenty days; 3808+2050.1
18: 3 the altar, that neither they, **n** you also, die. 1571
20:17 we will not turn *to* the right hand **n** *to* 2050.1
23:25 curse them at all, **n** bless them at all. 1571+3808
Dt 1:45 to your voice, **n** give ear unto you. 3808+2050.1
2:19 them not, **n** meddle with them: 408+2050.1
2:27 I will neither turn *unto* the right hand **n** *to* 2050.1
2:37 **n** *unto* any place of the river Jabbok, NIH
2:37 **n** *unto* the cities in the mountains, 2050.1
2:37 **n** *unto* whatsoever the LORD our God 2050.1
4:28 **n** hear, nor eat, nor smell. 3808+2050.1
4:28 nor hear, **n** eat, nor smell. 3808+2050.1
4:28 nor hear, nor eat, **n** smell. 3808+2050.1
4:31 **n** forget the covenant of thy fathers 3808+2050.1
5: 9 thyself unto them, **n** serve them: 3808+2050.1
5:14 thou, **n** thy son, nor thy daughter, nor thy 2050.1
5:14 thou, nor thy son, **n** thy daughter, nor thy 2050.1
5:14 nor thy daughter, **n** thy manservant, 2050.1
5:14 **n** thy maidservant, nor thine ox, nor thine 2050.1
5:14 thy maidservant, **n** thine ox, nor thine ass, 2050.1
5:14 thy maidservant, nor thine ox, **n** thine ass, 2050.1
5:14 thine ox, nor thine ass, **n** any of thy cattle, 2050.1
5:14 **n** thy stranger that *is* within thy gates; 2050.1
7: 2 **n** shew mercy unto them: 3808+2050.1
7: 3 **n** his daughter shalt thou take unto 3808+2050.1
7: 7 **n** choose you, because ye were moe in 2050.1
7:25 gold *that is* on them, **n** take *it* unto thee, 2050.1
9: 9 neither did eat bread **n** drink water: 3808+2050.1
9:18 **n** drink water, because of all your sins 3808
9:23 him not, **n** hearkened to his voice. 3808+2050.1
9:27 **n** to their wickedness, nor to their sin: 2050.1
9:27 nor to their wickedness, **n** to their sin: 2050.1
10: 9 Wherefore Levi hath no part **n** 2050.1
10:17 not persons, **n** taketh reward: 3808+2050.1
12:12 forasmuch as he hath no part **n** 2050.1
12:17 **n** any of thy vows which thou vowest, 2050.1
Dt 12:17 **n** thy freewill offerings, or heave offering 2050.1
12:32 not add thereto, **n** diminish from it. 3808+2050.1
13: 6 thou hast not known, thou, **n** thy fathers; 2050.1
13: 8 unto him, **n** hearken unto him; 3808+2050.1
14: 1 **n** make any baldness between your 3808+2050.1
14: 8 **n** touch their dead carcase. 3808+2050.1
14:27 he hath no part **n** inheritance with thee. 2050.1
14:29 he hath no part **n** inheritance with thee,) 2050.1
15: 7 **n** shut thine hand from thy poor 3808+2050.1
15:19 **n** shear the firstling of thy sheep. 3808+2050.1
17:11 shew thee, *to* the right hand, **n** *to* the left. 2050.1
17:16 **n** cause the people to return to 3808+2050.1
18: 1 have no part **n** inheritance with Israel: 2050.1
18:22 if the thing follow not, **n** come to 3808+2050.1
21: 4 which is neither eared **n** sown, and 3808+2050.1
22:30 **n** discover his father's skirt. 3808+2050.1
23: 6 Thou shalt not seek their peace **n** their 2050.1
23:17 **n** a sodomite of the sons of Israel. 3808+2050.1
24:17 judgment of the stranger, *n* of the fatherless; NIH
24:17 **n** take a widow's raiment to 3808+2050.1
26:14 **n** given *ought* thereof for the dead: 3808+2050.1
28:36 unto a nation which neither thou **n** thy 2050.1
28:39 **n** gather *the grapes;* for the worms 3808+2050.1
28:50 **n** shew favour to the young: 3808+2050.1
28:64 which neither thou **n** thy fathers have 2050.1
29:23 *that* it is not sown, **n** beareth, 3808+2050.1
29:23 **n** any grass groweth therein, 3808+2050.1
31: 6 fear not, **n** be afraid of them: 408+2050.1
31: 6 he will not fail thee, **n** forsake thee. 3808+2050.1
33: 9 **n** knew his own children: 3808+2050.1
34: 7 not dim, **n** his natural force abated. 3808+2050.1
Jos 1: 5 I will not fail thee, **n** forsake thee. 3808+2050.1
6:10 **n** make any noise with your voice, 3808+2050.1
10:25 Fear not, **n** be dismayed, be strong 408+2050.1
13:13 not the Geshurites, **n** the Maachathites: 2050.1
22:19 the LORD, **n** rebel against us, 408+2050.1
22:26 for burnt offering, **n** for sacrifice: 3808+2050.1
22:28 for burnt offerings, **n** for sacrifices; 3808+2050.1
23: 7 **n** cause to swear *by them,* neither 3808+2050.1
23: 7 **n** bow yourselves unto them. 3808+2050.1
24:12 with thy sword, **n** with thy bow. 3808+2050.1
24:19 he will not forgive your transgressions **n** 2050.1
Jdg 1:27 and her towns, **n** Taanach and her towns, 2050.1
1:27 **n** the inhabitants of Dor and her towns, 2050.1
1:27 **n** the inhabitants of Ibleam and her 2050.1
1:27 **n** the inhabitants of Megiddo and her 2050.1
1:30 of Kitron, **n** the inhabitants of Nahalol; 2050.1
1:31 **n** the inhabitants of Zidon, nor of Ahlab, 2050.1
1:31 **n** of Ahlab, nor of Achzib, nor of Helbah, 2050.1
1:31 nor of Ahlab, **n** of Achzib, nor of Helbah, 2050.1
1:31 **n** of Helbah, nor of Aphik, nor of Rehob: 2050.1
1:31 nor of Helbah, **n** of Aphik, nor of Rehob: 2050.1
1:31 nor of Helbah, nor of Aphik, **n** of Rehob: 2050.1
1:33 **n** the inhabitants of Beth-anath; 2050.1
2:10 **n** yet the works which he had done for 2050.1
2:19 own doings, **n** from their stubborn way. 2050.1
6: 4 for Israel, neither sheep, **n** ox, nor ass. 2050.1
6: 4 for Israel, neither sheep, nor ox, **n** ass. 2050.1
11:15 **n** the land of the children of Ammon: 2050.1
11:34 beside her he had neither son **n** daughter. 176
13: 4 drink not wine **n** strong drink, and 2050.1
13: 7 now drink no wine **n** strong drink, 2050.1
13:14 **n** eat any unclean *thing:* all that I 408+2050.1
13:23 **n** would as *at this* time have told us *such* 2050.1
14:16 I have not told *it* my father **n** my mother, 2050.1
19:30 There was no such *deed* done **n** 3808+2050.1
1Sa 1:15 I have drunk neither wine **n** strong 3808+2050.1
3:14 purged with sacrifice **n** offering for ever. 2050.1
5: 5 **n** any that come *into* Dagon's house, 2050.1
12: 4 not defrauded us, **n** oppressed us, 3808+2050.1
12:21 which cannot profit **n** deliver; 3808+2050.1
13:22 that there was neither sword **n** spear 2050.1
15:29 of Israel will not lie **n** repent: 3808+2050.1
20:27 Jesse to meat, neither yesterday, **n** to day? 1571
20:31 shalt not be stablished, **n** thy kingdom. 2050.1
21: 8 **n** my weapons with me, 1571+3808+2050.1
22:15 his servant, **n** to all the house of my father: NIH
24:11 see that *there is* neither evil **n** 2050.1
25:31 **n** offence of heart unto my lord, 2050.1
26:12 saw *it,* **n** knew *it,* neither awaked: 369+2050.1
27: 9 left neither man **n** woman alive, and 2050.1
27:11 David saved neither man **n** woman alive, 2050.1
28: 6 by dreams, **n** by Urim, nor by prophets. 1571
28: 6 by dreams, nor by Urim, **n** by prophets. 1571
28:15 no more, neither by prophets, **n** by dreams: 1571
28:18 **n** executedst his fierce wrath upon 3808+2050.1
28:20 eaten no bread all the day, **n** all the night. 2050.1
30:12 **n** drunk *any* water, three days and 3808+2050.1
30:15 **n** deliver me into the hands of my 518+2050.1
30:19 neither small **n** great, neither sons nor 2050.1
30:19 neither sons **n** daughters, neither spoil, 2050.1
30:19 **n** any *thing* that they had taken to them: 2050.1
2Sa 1:21 *be* rain upon you, **n** fields of offerings: 2050.1
2:19 in going he turned not to the right hand **n** 2050.1
3:34 **n** thy feet put into fetters: 3808+2050.1
13:22 neither good **n** bad: 4480+5704+2050.1+3807.1
14: 7 *neither* name **n** remainder upon the earth. 2050.1
19: 6 that thou regardest neither princes **n** 2050.1
19:24 **n** trimmed his beard, nor washed 3808+2050.1
19:24 his beard, **n** washed his clothes, 3808+2050.1
21: 4 We will have no silver **n** gold of Saul, 2050.1
21: 4 no silver nor gold of Saul, **n** of his house; 2050.1
21:10 by day, **n** the beasts of the field by night. 2050.1
1Ki 3: 8 that cannot be numbered **n** counted 3808+2050.1
3:11 **n** hast asked the life of thine 3808+2050.1
3:26 Let it be neither mine **n** thine, *but* 1571+3808
5: 4 *that there is* neither adversary **n** evil 369+2050.1
6: 7 that there was neither hammer **n** 3808+2050.1
6: 7 that there was neither hammer nor axe *n* NIH
8: 5 that could not be told **n** numbered 3808+2050.1
8:57 let him not leave us, **n** forsake us: 408+2050.1
10:12 **n** were seen unto this day. 3808+2050.1
12:24 **n** fight against your brethren 3808+2050.1
13: 8 neither will I eat bread **n** drink 3808+2050.1
13: 9 Eat no bread, **n** drink water, 3808+2050.1
1Ki 13: 9 **n** turn again by the *same* way that 3808+2050.1
13:16 not return with thee, **n** go in with thee: 2050.1
13:16 neither will I eat bread **n** drink 3808+2050.1
13:17 Thou shalt eat no bread **n** drink 3808+2050.1
13:17 **n** turn again to go by the way that thou 3808
13:28 lion had not eaten the carcase, **n** 3808+2050.1
16:11 neither *of* his kinsfolks, **n** *of* his friends. 2050.1
17: 1 there shall not be dew **n** rain these years, 2050.1
18:26 *there was* no voice, **n** any that answered. 2050.1
18:29 **n any** to answer, nor any that 369+2050.1
18:29 any to answer, **n any** that regarded. 369+2050.1
20: 8 Hearken not *unto him,* **n** consent. 3808+2050.1
22:31 saying, Fight neither with small **n** great, 2050.1
2Ki 3:14 not look toward thee, **n** see thee. 518+2050.1
4:23 *it is* neither new moon, **n** sabbath. 3808+2050.1
4:31 *there was* neither voice, **n** hearing. 369+2050.1
5:17 burnt offering **n** sacrifice unto other gods, 2050.1
6:10 himself there, not once **n** twice. 3808+2050.1
9:15 let none go forth *n* escape out of the city to NIH
14: 6 be put to death for the children, **n** 3808+2050.1
14:26 for *there was* not any shut up, **n any** 657+2050.1
14:26 nor any left, **n any** helper for Israel. 369+2050.1
17:35 **n** bow yourselves to them, 3808+2050.1
17:35 **n** serve them, nor sacrifice to them: 3808+2050.1
17:35 nor serve them, **n** sacrifice to them: 3808+2050.1
18: 5 of Judah, **n** *any* that were before him. 2050.1
18:12 would not hear *them,* **n** do *them.* 3808+2050.1
19:32 **n** shoot an arrow there, nor come 3808+2050.1
19:32 **n** come before it *with* shield, 3808+2050.1
19:32 **n** cast a bank against it. 3808+2050.1
20:13 in his house, **n** in all his dominion, 2050.1
23:22 **n** *in* all the days of the kings of Israel, 2050.1
23:22 kings of Israel, **n** of the kings of Judah; 2050.1
1Ch 21:24 **n** offer burnt offerings without cost. 2050.1
22:13 dread not, **n** be dismayed. 408+2050.1
23:26 **n** any vessels of it for the service thereof. 2050.1
28:20 and do *it:* fear not, **n** be dismayed: 408+2050.1
28:20 he will not fail thee, **n** forsake thee, 3808+2050.1
2Ch 1:11 or honour, **n** the life of thine enemies, 2050.1
5: 6 which could not be told **n** 3808+2050.1
6:14 like thee in the heaven, **n** in the earth; 2050.1
11: 4 **n** fight against your brethren: 3808+2050.1
15: 5 **n** to him that came in, but great vexations 2050.1
19: 7 **n** respect of persons, nor taking of gifts. 2050.1
19: 7 nor respect of persons, **n** taking of gifts. 2050.1
20:15 Be not afraid **n** dismayed by reason 408+2050.1
20:17 fear not, **n** be dismayed; to morrow 408+2050.1
21:12 **n** in the ways of Asa king of Judah, 2050.1
29: 7 have not burnt incense **n** offered 3808+2050.1
32: 7 be not afraid **n** dismayed for 408+2050.1
32: 7 **n** for all the multitude that *is* with him: 2050.1
32:15 **n** persuade you on this *manner,* 408+2050.1
34: 2 neither to the right hand, **n** *to* the left. 2050.1
Ezr 9:12 **n** seek their peace or their wealth 3808+2050.1
9:14 that *there should be* no remnant **n** 2050.1
10: 6 he did eat no bread, **n** drink water: 3808+2050.1
Ne 1: 7 **n** the statutes, nor the judgments, 2050.1
1: 7 nor the statutes, **n** the judgments, 2050.1
2:16 **n** to the priests, nor to the nobles, nor to 2050.1
2:16 **n** to the nobles, nor to the rulers, 2050.1
2:16 nor to the nobles, **n** to the rulers, 2050.1
2:16 the rulers, **n** to the rest that did the work. 2050.1
2:20 **n** right, nor memorial, in Jerusalem. 2050.1
2:20 nor right, **n** memorial, in Jerusalem. 2050.1
4:23 So neither I, **n** my brethren, nor my 2050.1
4:23 neither I, nor my brethren, **n** my servants, 2050.1
4:23 **n** the men of the guard which followed 2050.1
7:61 **n** their seed, whether they *were* of Israel. 2050.1
8: 9 your God; mourn not, **n** weep. 408+2050.1
9:31 consume them, **n** forsake them; 3808+2050.1
9:34 our priests, **n** our fathers, 3808+2050.1
9:34 **n** hearkened unto thy 3808+2050.1
10:30 **n** take their daughters for our sons: 3808+2050.1
13:25 **n** take their daughters unto your 518+2050.1
Est 2: 7 for she had neither father **n** mother, and 2050.1
2:10 Esther had not shewed her people **n** her 2050.1
2:20 Esther had not *yet* shewed her kindred **n** 2050.1
3: 2 bowed not, **n** did *him* reverence. 3808+2050.1
3: 5 **n** did him reverence, *then* was Haman full 2050.1
4:16 neither eat **n** drink three days, night 408+2050.1
5: 9 that he stood not up, **n** moved for 3808+2050.1
9:28 **n** the memorial of them perish 3808+2050.1
Job 1:22 **n** charged God foolishly. 3808+2050.1
3:10 **n** hid sorrow from mine eyes. 2050.1
7:19 **n** let me alone till I swallow down my 3808
14:12 **n** be raised out of their sleep. 3808+2050.1
18:19 He shall neither have son **n** 3808+2050.1
18:19 **n** *any* remaining in his dwellings. 369+2050.1
24:13 **n** abide in the paths thereof. 3808+2050.1
27: 4 **n** my tongue utter deceit. 518+2050.1
28: 8 not trodden it, **n** the fierce lion passed by it. 3808
34:19 **n** regardeth the rich more than 3808+2050.1
34:22 *There is* no darkness, **n** shadow of 369+2050.1
36:19 *no,* not gold, **n** all the forces of strength. 2050.1
41:12 **n** *his* power, nor his comely proportion. 2050.1
41:12 nor *his* power, **n** his comely proportion. 2050.1
41:26 the spear, the dart, **n** the habergeon. 2050.1
Ps 1: 1 **n** standeth in the way of sinners, 3808+2050.1
1: 1 **n** sitteth in the seat of the scornful. 3808+2050.1
1: 5 **n** sinners in the congregation of 2050.1
15: 3 his tongue, **n** doeth evil to his neighbour, 3808
15: 3 **n** taketh up a reproach against his 3808+2050.1
15: 5 **n** taketh reward against 3808+2050.1
16: 4 **n** take up their names into my lips. 1077+2050.1
19: 3 *There is* no speech **n** language, 369+2050.1
22:24 For he hath not despised **n** 3808+2050.1
24: 4 unto vanity, **n** sworn deceitfully. 3808+2050.1
25: 7 sins of my youth, **n** my transgressions: 2050.1
26: 9 with sinners, **n** my life with bloody men: 2050.1
28: 5 **n** the operation of his hands, he shall 2050.1
37:25 **n** his seed begging bread. 2050.1
37:33 **n** condemn him when he is judged. 3808+2050.1
40: 4 not the proud, **n** such as turn aside to lies. 2050.1
49: 7 **n** give to God a ransom for him: 3808
50: 9 out of thy house, *n* he goats out of thy folds. NIH

Ps 59: 3 **n** for my sin, O LORD. 3808+2050.1
66:20 away my prayer, **n** his mercy from me. 2050.1
75: 6 **n** from the west, nor from the south. 2050.1
75: 6 from the west, **n** from the south. 3808+2050.1
78:42 **n** the day when he delivered them from NIH
89:22 **n** the son of wickedness afflict 3808+2050.1
89:33 will I not utterly take from him, **n** 3808+2050.1
89:34 **n** alter the thing that is gone out of 3808+2050.1
91: 5 by night; **n** for the arrow that flieth by day; NIH
91: 6 **N** for the pestilence that walketh in NIH
91: 6 **n** for the destruction that wasteth at NIH
103:10 **n** rewarded us according to our 3808+2050.1
121: 4 Israel shall neither slumber **n** sleep. 3808+2050.1
121: 6 smite thee by day, **n** the moon by night. 2050.1
129: 7 **n** he that bindeth sheaves his bosom. 2050.1
131: 1 is not haughty, **n** mine eyes lofty: 3808+2050.1
132: 3 of my house, **n** go up into my bed; 518
144:14 there be no breaking in, **n** going out; 369+2050.1
146: 3 **n** in the son of man, in whom there is no NIH
Pr 4:27 Turn not to the right hand **n** to the left: 2050.1
5:13 **n** inclined mine ear to them that 3808+2050.1
6: 4 to thine eyes, **n** slumber to thine eyelids. 2050.1
8:26 he had not made the earth, **n** the fields, 2050.1
8:26 **n** the highest part of the dust of the world. 2050.1
17:26 is not good, **n** to strike princes for equity. NIH
21:30 There is no wisdom **n** understanding 369+2050.1
21:30 **n** counsel against the LORD. 369+2050.1
30: 3 **n** have the knowledge of the holy. 2050.1
30: 8 give me neither poverty **n** riches; feed me 2050.1
31: 3 **n** thy ways to that which destroyeth 2050.1
31: 4 to drink wine; **n** for princes strong drink: 176
Ecc 1: 8 eye is not satisfied with seeing, **n** 3808+2050.1
3:14 put to it, **n any thing** taken from it: 369+2050.1
4: 8 yea, he hath neither child **n** brother: 2050.1
5:10 **n** he that loveth abundance with 3808+2050.1
6: 5 **n** known any thing: this hath more 3808+2050.1
8:16 (for also there is that neither day **n** night 2050.1
9:10 **n** device, nor knowledge, nor wisdom, 2050.1
9:10 nor device, **n** knowledge, nor wisdom, 2050.1
9:10 nor knowledge, **n** wisdom, in the grave, 2050.1
9:11 **n** the battle to the strong, 3808+2050.1
9:11 **n** yet riches to men of 3808+2050.1
9:11 **n** yet favour to men of skill; 3808+2050.1
11: 5 **n** how the bones do grow in the womb of NIH
12: 1 **n** the years draw nigh, when thou shalt 2050.1
12: 2 **n** the clouds return after the rain: 2050.1
SS 2: 7 **n** awake my love, till he please. 518+2050.1
3: 5 **n** awake my love, till he please. 518+2050.1
8: 4 **n** awake my love, until he please. 4100+2050.1
Isa 3: 7 house is neither bread **n** clothing: 369+2050.1
5: 6 it shall not be pruned, **n** digged; 3808+2050.1
5:27 None shall be weary **n** stumble 369+2050.1
5:27 none shall slumber **n** sleep; 3808+2050.1
5:27 **n** the latchet of their shoes be 3808+2050.1
8:12 fear ye their fear, **n** be afraid. 3808+2050.1
11: 9 They shall not hurt **n** destroy in all 3808+2050.1
14:21 that they do not rise, **n** possess the land, 2050.1
14:21 **n** fill the face of the world with cities. 2050.1
22: 2 men are not slain with the sword, **n** 3808+2050.1
23: 4 I travail not, **n** bring forth children, 3808+2050.1
23: 4 I nourish up young men, **n** bring up virgins. NIH
23:18 it shall not be treasured **n** laid up; 3808+2050.1
28:28 **n** break it with the wheel of his cart, 2050.1
28:28 **n** bruise it with his horsemen. 3808+2050.1
30: 5 **n** be a help nor profit, but a shame, and 3808
30: 5 nor be a help **n** profit, but a shame, 3808+2050.1
31: 4 **n** abase himself for the noise of 3808+2050.1
32: 5 shall be no more called liberal, **n** 3808+2050.1
34:10 It shall not be quenched night **n** day; 2050.1
35: 9 No lion shall be there, **n** any 1077+2050.1
37:33 **n** shoot an arrow there, nor come 3808+2050.1
37:33 **n** come before it with shields, 3808+2050.1
37:33 **n** cast a bank against it. 3808+2050.1
39: 2 in his house, **n** in all his dominion, 2050.1
40:16 Lebanon is not sufficient to burn, **n** 369+2050.1
42: 2 He shall not cry, **n** lift up, 3808+2050.1
42: 2 **n** cause his voice to be heard in 3808+2050.1
42: 4 He shall not fail **n** be discouraged, 3808+2050.1
43:23 thee to serve with an offering, **n** 3808+2050.1
44: 9 they see not, **n** know; that they 1077+2050.1
44:18 They have not known **n** 3808+2050.1
44:19 neither is there knowledge **n** 3808+2050.1
44:20 that he cannot deliver his soul, **n** 3808+2050.1
45:13 not for price **n** reward, saith 3808+2050.1
45:17 ye shall not be ashamed **n** 3808+2050.1
46: 7 not answer, **n** save him out of his trouble. 3808
47:14 be a coal to warm at, **n** fire to sit before it. NIH
48: 1 but not in truth, **n** in righteousness. 3808+2050.1
48:19 off **n** destroyed from before me. 3808+2050.1
49:10 They shall not hunger **n** thirst; 3808+2050.1
49:10 neither shall the heat **n** sun smite them: 2050.1
51:14 that he should not die in the pit, **n** 3808+2050.1
52:12 go out with haste, **n** go by flight: 3808+2050.1
53: 2 he hath no form **n** comeliness; and 3808+2050.1
54: 9 be wroth with thee, **n** rebuke thee. 4480+2050.1
57:11 not remembered me, **n** laid it to thy heart? 3808
58:13 own ways, **n** finding thine own pleasure, 4480
58:13 **n** speaking thine own words: 2050.1
59: 4 for justice, **n any** pleadeth for truth: 369+2050.1
59:21 **n** out of the mouth of thy seed, 2050.1
59:21 **n** out of the mouth of thy seed's seed, 2050.1
60:11 they shall not be shut day **n** night; 2050.1
60:18 wasting **n** destruction within thy borders; 2050.1
62: 6 which shall never hold their peace day **n** 2050.1
64: 4 **n** perceived by the ear, neither hath the eye 3808
65:17 former shall not be remembered, **n** 3808+2050.1
65:19 more heard in her, **n** the voice of crying. 2050.1
65:20 **n** an old man that hath not filled his days: 2050.1
65:23 in vain, **n** bring forth for trouble; 3808+2050.1
65:25 They shall not hurt **n** destroy in all 3808+2050.1
Jer 4:11 my people, not to fan, **n** to cleanse, 3808+2050.1
5: 4 of the LORD, **n** the judgment of their God. NIH
5:12 neither shall we see sword **n** famine: 2050.1
6:19 my words, **n** to my law, but rejected it. 2050.1
6:20 **n** your sacrifices sweet unto me. 3808+2050.1
Jer 6:25 forth into the field, **n** walk by the way; 2050.1
7:16 neither lift up cry **n** prayer for them, 2050.1
7:22 **n** commanded them in the day that 3808+2050.1
7:24 **n** inclined their ear, but walked in 3808+2050.1
7:26 **n** inclined their ear, but 3808+2050.1
7:28 their God, **n** receiveth correction: 3808+2050.1
7:32 **n** the valley of the son of Hinnom, but 2050.1
8: 2 they shall not be gathered, **n** be 3808+2050.1
8:13 **n** figs on the fig tree, and the leaf 369+2050.1
9:16 whom neither they **n** their fathers have 2050.1
11: 8 **n** inclined their ear, but 3808+2050.1
13:14 I will not pity, **n** spare, nor have 3808+2050.1
13:14 **n** have mercy, but destroy them. 3808+2050.1
14:16 them, their wives, **n** their sons, nor their 2050.1
14:16 nor their sons, **n** their daughters: 2050.1
15:10 I have neither lent on usury, **n** men 3808+2050.1
15:17 the assembly of the mockers, **n** rejoiced; 2050.1
16: 2 neither shalt thou have sons **n** daughters 2050.1
16: 5 go to lament **n** bemoan them: 408+2050.1
16: 6 lament for them, **n** cut themselves, 3808+2050.1
16: 6 **n** make themselves bald for them: 3808+2050.1
16:13 ye know not, neither ye **n** your fathers; 2050.1
17:21 **n** bring it in by the gates of Jerusalem; 2050.1
17:23 **n** receive instruction. 1115+2050.1+3807.1
18:18 **n** counsel from the wise, nor the word 2050.1
18:18 the wise, **n** the word from the prophet. 2050.1
19: 4 whom neither they **n** their fathers have 2050.1
19: 4 **n** the kings of Judah, and have filled this 2050.1
19: 5 **n** spake it, neither came it into my 3808+2050.1
19: 6 **n** The valley of the son of Hinnom, but 2050.1
20: 9 **n** speak any more in his name. 3808+2050.1
21: 7 neither have pity, **n** have mercy. 3808+2050.1
22: 3 the stranger, the fatherless, **n** the widow, 2050.1
22:10 return no more, **n** see his native country. 2050.1
23: 4 shall fear no more, **n** be dismayed, 3808+2050.1
23:32 sent them not, **n** commanded them: 3808+2050.1
25: 4 **n** inclined your ear to hear. 3808+2050.1
25:33 neither gathered, **n** buried; 3808+2050.1
25:35 **n** the principal of the flock to 4480+2050.1
27: 9 **n** to your diviners, nor to your dreamers, 2050.1
27: 9 nor to your diviners, **n** to your dreamers, 2050.1
27: 9 **n** to your enchanters, nor to your 2050.1
27: 9 **n** to your sorcerers, which speak unto 2050.1
31:40 **n** thrown down any more for ever. 3808+2050.1
35: 6 no wine, neither ye, **n** your sons for ever: 2050.1
35: 7 **n** sow seed, nor plant vineyard, 3808+2050.1
35: 7 **n** plant vineyard, nor have any: but 3808+2050.1
35: 7 **n** have any: but all your days ye 3808+2050.1
35: 8 we, our wives, our sons, **n** our daughters; 2050.1
35: 9 **N** to build houses for us to 1115+2050.1+3807.1
35: 9 have we vineyard, **n** field, nor seed: 2050.1
35: 9 we vineyard, nor field, **n** seed: 3808+2050.1
35:15 your ear, **n** hearkened unto me. 3808+2050.1
36:24 Yet they were not afraid, **n** rent 3808+2050.1
36:24 **n** any of his servants that heard all these 2050.1
37: 2 neither he, **n** his servants, nor the people 2050.1
37: 2 nor his servants, **n** the people of the land, 2050.1
37:19 not come against you, **n** against this land? 2050.1
42:14 **n** hear the sound of the trumpet, 3808+2050.1
42:14 **n** have hunger of bread; 3808+2050.1
42:21 **n** any thing for the which he hath sent me 2050.1
44: 3 neither they, you, **n** your fathers. 2050.1
44: 5 **n** inclined their ear to turn from 3808+2050.1
44:10 **n** walked in my law, nor in my 3808+2050.1
44:10 **n** in my statutes, that I set before you and 2050.1
44:23 **n** walked in his law, nor in his statutes, 2050.1
44:23 nor walked in his law, **n** in his statutes, 2050.1
44:23 in his statutes, **n** in his testimonies; 3808+2050.1
46: 6 flee away, **n** the mighty man escape; 408+2050.1
49:31 which have neither gates **n** bars, 3808+2050.1
49:33 **n** any son of man dwell in it. 3808+2050.1
51: 5 **n** Judah of his God, of the LORD of 2050.1
51:26 for a corner, **n** a stone for foundations; 2050.1
51:62 neither man **n** beast, but that it 5704+2050.1
La 2:22 anger none escaped **n** remained: 2050.1
3:33 For he doth not afflict willingly **n** grieve 2050.1
Eze 2: 6 **n** be dismayed at their looks, 408+2050.1
3:18 **n** speakest to warn the wicked 3808+2050.1
3:19 **n** from his wicked way, he shall die in his 2050.1
7:11 none of them shall remain, **n** of 3808+2050.1
7:11 their multitude, **n** of any of theirs: 3808+2050.1
7:12 let not the buyer rejoice, **n** the seller 408+2050.1
12:24 **n** flattering divination within the house of 2050.1
13:23 more vanity, **n** divine divinations: 3808+2050.1
14:16 deliver neither sons **n** daughters; 518+2050.1
14:18 they shall deliver neither sons **n** 2050.1
14:20 they shall deliver neither son **n** daughter; 518
16: 4 not salted at all, **n** swaddled at all. 3808+2050.1
16:47 **n** done after their abominations: 2050.1
16:48 she **n** her daughters, as thou hast done, 2050.1
18:17 that hath not received usury **n** 3808+2050.1
20:18 **n** defile yourselves with their idols: 408+2050.1
20:44 **n** according to your corrupt doings, O ye 2050.1
22:24 **n** rained upon in the day of indignation. 3808
23:27 **n** remember Egypt any more. 3808+2050.1
24:16 yet neither shalt thou mourn **n** 3808+2050.1
24:22 your lips, **n** eat the bread of men. 3808+2050.1
24:23 ye shall not mourn **n** weep; but 3808+2050.1
28:24 **n** any grieving thorn of all that are round 2050.1
29: 5 be brought together, **n** gathered: 3808+2050.1
29:11 **n** foot of beast shall pass through 3808+2050.1
29:18 yet had he no wages, **n** his army, 2050.1
31: 8 **n** any tree in the garden of God was like 3808
32:13 **n** the hoofs of beasts trouble them. 3808+2050.1
37:23 **n** with their detestable things, nor with 2050.1
37:23 **n** with any of their transgressions: 2050.1
38:11 and having neither bars **n** gates, 2050.1
43: 7 neither they, **n** their kings, by their 2050.1
43: 7 **n** by the carcases of their kings in their 2050.1
44: 9 in heart, **n** uncircumcised in flesh, 2050.1
44:13 **n** to come near to any of my holy things, 2050.1
44:20 **n** suffer their locks to grow long; 3808+2050.1
44:22 wives a widow, **n** her that is put away: 2050.1
48:14 **n** alienate the firstfruits of the land: 3808+2050.1
Da 1: 8 **n** with the wine which he drank: 2050.1
Da 2:10 therefore there is no king, lord, **n** ruler, 2050.3
3:12 **n** worship the golden image which 3809+2050.3
3:14 **n** worship the golden image which 3809+2050.3
3:18 **n** worship the golden image which thou 3809
3:27 **n** was a hair of their head singed, 3809+2050.3
3:27 **n** the smell of fire had passed on 3809+2050.3
3:28 that they might not serve **n** worship 3809+2050.3
5: 8 **n** make known to the king 2050.3
5:10 **n** let thy countenance be changed. 409+2050.3
5:23 stone, which see not, **n** hear, nor know: 3809
5:23 which see not, nor hear, **n** know: 3809+2050.3
6: 4 they could find none occasion **n** fault; 2050.3
6:13 **n** the decree that thou hast signed, 5922+2050.3
6:15 Persians is, That no decree **n** 3809+2050.3
10: 3 neither came flesh **n** wine in my mouth, 2050.1
11: 4 not to his posterity, **n** according to 3808+2050.1
11: 6 the arm; neither shall he stand, **n** his arm: 2050.1
11:20 neither in anger, **n** in battle. 3808+2050.1
11:24 have not done, **n** his fathers' fathers; 2050.1
11:37 **n** the desire of women, nor regard 3808+2050.1
11:37 desire of women, **n** regard any god: 3808+2050.1
Hos 1: 7 **n** by sword, nor by battle, by horses, 2050.1
1: 7 nor by sword, **n** by battle, by horses, 2050.1
1: 7 nor by battle, by horses, **n** by horsemen. 2050.1
1:10 cannot be measured **n** numbered; 3808+2050.1
4: 1 because there is no truth, **n** mercy, 369+2050.1
4: 1 **n** knowledge of God in the land. 369+2050.1
4: 4 Yet let no man strive, **n** reprove 408+2050.1
4:14 **n** your spouses when they commit 2050.1
4:15 **n** swear, The LORD liveth. 408+2050.1
5:13 yet could he not heal you **n** cure 3808+2050.1
7:10 their God, **n** seek him for all this. 3808+2050.1
Am 5: 5 **n** enter into Gilgal, and pass not to 3808+2050.1
8:11 **n** a thirst for water, but of hearing 3808+2050.1
9:10 The evil shall not overtake **n** prevent us. 2050.1
Ob 1:13 **n** have laid hands on their substance 408+2050.1
Jnh 3: 7 saying, Let neither man **n** beast, 2050.1
3: 7 nor beast, herd **n** flock, taste any thing: 2050.1
3: 7 let them not feed, **n** drink water: 408+2050.1
Mic 5: 7 **n** waiteth for the sons of men. 3808+2050.1
Zep 1: 6 that have not sought the LORD, **n** 3808+2050.1
1:18 Neither their silver **n** their gold shall be 1571
3:13 shall not do iniquity, **n** speak lies; 3808+2050.1
Zec 1: 4 they did not hear, **n** hearken unto 3808+2050.1
4: 6 Not by might, **n** by power, but by 3808+2050.1
7:10 **n** the fatherless, the stranger, nor 2050.1
7:10 the fatherless, the stranger, **n** the poor; 2050.1
7:14 no man passed through **n** returned: 4480+2050.1
8:10 hire for man, **n any** hire for beast; 369+2050.1
11:16 **n** heal that that is broken, nor feed 3808+2050.1
11:16 that is broken, feed that that standeth still: 3808
14: 6 that the light shall not be clear, **n** dark: NIH
14: 7 to the LORD, not day, **n** night: 3808+2050.1
Mal 4: 1 that it shall leave them neither root **n** 2050.1
Mt 5:35 **N** by the earth; for it is his footstool: 3383
6:20 where neither moth **n** rust doth corrupt, and 3777
6:20 where thieves do not break through **n** steal: 3761
6:25 **n yet** for your body, what ye shall put on. 3366
6:26 neither do they reap, **n** gather into barns; 3761
10: 9 Provide neither gold, **n** silver, nor brass in 3366
10: 9 nor silver, **n** brass in your purses; 3366
10:10 **N** scrip for your journey, neither two coats, 3361
10:10 two coats, neither shoes, **n yet** staves: 3366
10:14 **n** hear your words, when ye depart out of 3366
10:24 his master, **n** the servant above his lord. 3761
11:18 For John came neither eating **n** drinking, 3383
12:19 He shall not strive, **n** cry; neither shall any 3761
22:29 the scriptures, **n** the power of God. 3366
22:30 they neither marry, **n** are given in marriage, 3777
24:21 the world to this time, no, **n ever** shall be. 3364
25:13 for ye know neither the day **n** the hour 3761
Mk 6:11 **n** hear you, when ye depart thence, 3366
8:26 into the town, **n** tell it to any in the town. 3366
12:25 they neither marry, **n** are given in marriage; 3777
Lk 1:15 and shall drink neither wine **n** strong drink; 2532
6:44 **n** of a bramble bush gather they grapes. 3761
7:33 came neither eating bread **n** drinking wine; 3383
9: 3 neither staves, **n** scrip, neither bread, 3383
10: 4 Carry neither purse, **n** scrip, nor shoes: and 3361
10: 4 Carry neither purse, nor scrip, **n** shoes: and 3366
12:24 for they neither sow **n** reap; which neither 3761
12:24 which neither have storehouse **n** barn; and 3761
14:12 call not thy friends, **n** thy brethren, 3366
14:12 neither thy kinsmen, **n** thy rich neighbours; 3366
14:35 fit for the land, **n yet** for the dunghill; 3777
17:23 see there: go not after them, **n** follow them. 3366
18: 4 I fear not God, **n** regard man; 2532+3756
20:35 neither marry, **n** are given in marriage: 3777
21:15 shall not be able to gainsay **n** resist. 3761
22:68 you, you will not answer me, **n** let me go. 2228
23:15 No, **n yet** Herod: for I sent you to him; 3761
Jn 1:13 not of blood, **n** of the will of the flesh, 3761
1:13 the flesh, **n** of the will of man, but of God. 3761
1:25 that Christ, **n** Elias, neither that prophet? 3777
4:21 **n** yet at Jerusalem, worship the Father. 3777
5:37 his voice at any time, **n** seen his shape. 3777
8:19 Ye neither know me, **n** my Father: 3777
9: 3 Neither hath this man sinned, **n** his parents: 3777
11:50 **N** consider that it is expedient for us, that 3761
12:40 **n** understand with their heart, and 2532
16: 3 they have not known the Father, **n** me. 3761
Ac 4:18 commanded them not to speak at all **n** 3366
8:21 Thou hast neither part **n** lot in this matter: 3761
9: 9 without sight, and neither did eat **n** drink. 3761
13:27 **n** yet the voices of the prophets which are 2532
15:10 which neither our fathers **n** we were able to 3777
19:37 **n yet** blasphemers of your goddess. 3777
23: 8 is no resurrection, neither angel **n** spirit: 3383
23:12 saying that they would neither eat **n** drink 3383
23:21 that they will neither eat **n** drink till they 3383
24:12 neither in the synagogues, **n** in the city: 3777
24:18 neither with multitude, **n** with tumult. 3761
25: 8 against the temple, **n** yet against Cesar, 3777
27:20 And when neither sun **n** stars in many days 3383
Ro 8:38 **n** life, nor angels, nor principalities, 3777

Ro 8:38 nor life, **n** angels, nor principalities, 3777
8:38 nor life, nor angels, **n** principalities, 3777
8:38 nor angels, nor principalities, **n** powers, 3777
8:38 nor powers, **n** *things* present, 3777
8:38 nor *things* present, **n** *things* to come, 3777
8:39 **N** height, nor depth, nor any other creature, 3777
8:39 Nor height, **n** depth, nor any other creature, 3777
8:39 Nor height, nor depth, **n** any other creature, 3777
9:16 **n** of him that runneth, but of God that 3761
14:21 *is* good neither to eat flesh, **n** to drink wine, 3366
14:21 **n** *any thing* whereby thy brother stumbleth, 3366
1Co 2:6 **n** of the princes of this world, that come to 3761
2:9 Eye hath not seen, **n** ear heard, 2532+3756
6:9 **n** idolaters, nor adulterers, nor effeminate, 3777
6:9 nor idolaters, **n** adulterers, nor effeminate, 3777
6:9 nor idolaters, nor adulterers, **n** effeminate, 3777
6:9 **n** abusers of themselves with mankind, 3777
6:10 **N** thieves, nor covetous, nor drunkards, 3777
6:10 Nor thieves, **n** covetous, nor drunkards, 3777
6:10 nor covetous, **n** drunkards, nor revilers, 3777
6:10 nor covetous, nor drunkards, **n** revilers, 3756
6:10 nor drunkards, nor revilers, **n** extortioners, 3756
10:32 neither to the Jews, **n** to the Gentiles, 2532
10:32 nor to the Gentiles, **n** to the church of God: 2532
12:21 **n** again the head to the feet, I have no need 2228
2Co 4:2 **n** handling the word of God deceitfully; 3366
7:12 **n** for his cause that suffered wrong, but 3761
Gal 3:28 There is neither Jew **n** Greek, there is 3761
3:28 Jew nor Greek, there is neither bond **n** free, 3761
3:28 nor free, there is neither male **n** female: 2532
4:14 was in my flesh ye despised not, **n** rejected; 3761
5:6 availeth any *thing,* **n** uncircumcision; 3777
6:15 availeth any *thing,* **n** uncircumcision, 3777
Eph 5:4 **n** foolish talking, nor jesting, 2532
5:4 nor foolish talking, **n** jesting, 2228
5:5 **n** unclean *person,* nor covetous man who is 2228
5:5 nor unclean *person,* **n** covetous man who is 2228
Col 3:11 Where there is neither Greek **n** Jew, 2532
3:11 circumcision **n** uncircumcision, barbarian, 2532
3:11 barbarian, Scythian, bond **n** free: NIG
1Th 2:3 of deceit, **n** of uncleanness, nor in guile: 3761
2:3 of deceit, nor of uncleanness, **n** in guile: 3777
2:5 as ye know, **n** a cloke of covetousness; 3777
2:6 **N** of men sought we glory, neither of you, 3777
2:6 we glory, neither of you, **n** *yet* of others, 3777
5:5 we are not of the night, **n** of darkness. 3761
2Th 2:2 or be troubled, neither by spirit, **n** by word, 3383
2:2 nor by word, **n** by letter as from us, 3383
1Ti 1:7 what they say, **n** whereof they affirm. 3383
2:12 **n** to usurp authority over the man, but to be 3761
6:16 whom no man hath seen, **n** can see: 3761
6:17 **n** trust in uncertain riches, but in the living 3366
2Ti 1:8 of our Lord, **n** of me his prisoner: 3366
Heb 7:3 neither beginning of days, **n** end of life; 3383
9:25 **N yet** that he should offer himself often, 3761
12:5 **n** faint when thou art rebuked of him: 3366
12:18 with fire, **n** unto blackness, and darkness, 2532
13:5 I will never leave thee, **n** forsake thee. 3761
2Pe 1:8 **n** unfruitful in the knowledge of our Lord 3761
Rev 3:15 thy works, that thou art neither cold **n** hot: 3777
3:16 thou art lukewarm, and neither cold **n** hot, 3777
5:3 **n** in earth, neither under the earth, 3761
7:1 on the earth, **n** on the sea, nor on any tree. 3383
7:1 on the earth, nor on the sea, **n** on any tree. 3383
7:3 not the earth, neither the sea, **n** the trees, 3383
7:16 shall the sun light on them, **n** any heat. 3761
9:20 which neither can see, **n** hear, nor walk: 3777
9:20 which neither can see, nor hear, **n** walk: 3777
9:21 **n** of their sorceries, nor of their fornication, 3777
9:21 **n** of their fornication, nor of their thefts. 3777
9:21 nor of their fornication, **n** of their thefts. 3777
14:11 and they have no rest day **n** night, 2532
21:4 be no more death, neither sorrow, **n** crying, 3777

NORTH (132) [NORTHERN, NORTHWARD, NORTHWARDS]

Ge 28:14 to the east, and to the **n**, and to the south: 6828
Ex 26:20 on the **n** side *there shall be* twenty boards: 6828
26:35 and thou shalt put the table on the **n** side. 6828
27:11 likewise for the **n** side in length *there shall* 6828
36:25 *which is* toward the **n** corner, he made 6828
38:11 for the **n** side *the hangings were* an hundred 6828
Nu 2:25 Dan *shall be* on the **n side** by their armies: 6828
34:7 this shall be your **n** border: from the great 6828
34:9 at Hazar-enan: this shall be your **n** border. 6828
35:5 and *on* the **n** side two thousand cubits; 6828
Jos 8:11 the city, and pitched on the **n side** of Ai: 6828
8:13 *even* all the host that *was* on the **n** of 6828
11:2 to the kings that *were* on the **n** of 6828
15:5 *their* border in the **n** quarter *was* 6828+1886.5
15:6 and passed along by the **n** of Beth-arabah; 6828
15:10 on the **n side**, and went down *to* 6828+1886.5
16:6 the sea *to* Michmethah on the **n side**; 6828
17:9 also *was* on the **n side** of the river, 6828
17:10 they met together in Asher on the **n**, and 6828
18:5 Joseph shall abide in their coasts on the **n**. 6828
18:12 their border on the **n** side was from Jordan; 6828
18:12 went up to the side of Jericho on the **n side**, 6828
18:16 which *is* in the valley of the giants on the **n**, 6828
18:17 was drawn from the **n**, and went forth *to* 6828
18:19 the outgoings of the border were at the **n** 6828
19:14 the border compasseth it on the **n side** *to* 6828
19:27 toward the **n side** *of* Beth-emek, 6828
24:30 on the **n** side of the hill of Gaash. 6828
Jdg 2:9 of Ephraim, on the **n side** of the hill Gaash. 6828
7:1 the Midianites were on the **n side** of them, 6828
21:19 which *is* on the **n side** of Beth-el, 4480+6828
1Ki 7:25 three looking toward the **n**, and 6828
2Ki 16:14 and put it on the **n** side of the altar. 6828+1886.5
1Ch 9:24 toward the east, west, **n**, and south. 6828
2Ch 4:4 three looking toward the **n**, and 6828
Job 26:7 He stretcheth out the **n** over the empty 6828
37:9 the whirlwind: and cold out of the **n**. 4215
37:22 Fair weather cometh out of the **n**: with God 6828
Ps 48:2 *is* mount Zion, *on* the sides of the **n**, 6828
89:12 The **n** and the south thou hast created them: 6828
107:3 the west, from the **n**, and from the south. 6828
Pr 25:23 The **n** wind driveth away rain: so *doth* an 6828
Ecc 1:6 the south, and turneth about unto the **n**; 6828
11:3 tree fall toward the south, or toward the **n**, 6828
SS 4:16 Awake, O **n wind**; and come thou south; 6828
Isa 14:13 of the congregation, in the sides of the **n**: 6828
14:31 for there shall come from the **n** a smoke, 6828
41:25 I have raised up *one* from the **n**, and 6828
43:6 I will say to the **n**, Give *up;* and to 6828
49:12 lo, these from the **n** and from the west; and 6828
Jer 1:13 the face thereof *is* towards the **n**. 6828+1886.5
1:14 Out of the **n** an evil shall break forth upon 6828
1:15 families of the kingdoms of the **n**, 6828+1886.5
3:12 Go and proclaim these words toward the **n**, 6828
3:18 **n** to the land that I have given for an 6828
4:6 for I will bring evil from the **n**, and a great 6828
6:1 for evil appeareth out of the **n**, and 6828
6:22 a people cometh from the **n** country, and 6828
10:22 a great commotion out of the **n** country, 6828
13:20 and behold them that come from the **n**: 6828
16:15 the children of Israel from the land of the **n**, 6828
23:8 of Israel out of the **n** country, 6828+1886.5
25:9 will send and take all the families of the **n**, 6828
25:26 all the kings of the **n**, far and near, one with 6828
31:8 I *will* bring them from the **n** country, and 6828
46:6 fall toward the **n** by the river Euphrates. 6828
46:10 in the **n** country by the river Euphrates. 6828
46:20 destruction cometh; it cometh out of the **n**. 6828
46:24 into the hand of the people of the **n**. 6828
47:2 waters rise up out of the **n**, and shall be an 6828
50:3 For out of the **n** there cometh up a nation 6828
50:9 of great nations from the **n** country: 6828
50:41 a people shall come from the **n**, and a great 6828
51:48 the spoilers shall come unto her from the **n**, 6828
Eze 1:4 behold, a whirlwind came out of the **n**, 6828
8:3 of the inner gate that looketh toward the **n**; 6828
8:5 up thine eyes now the way towards the **n**. 6828
8:5 So I lift up mine eyes the way toward the **n**, 6828
8:14 LORD'S house which *was* towards the **n**; 6828
9:2 which lieth toward the **n**, and every man a 6828
20:47 all faces from the south to the **n** shall be 6828
21:4 against all flesh from the south *to* the **n**: 6828
26:7 from the **n**, with horses, and with chariots, 6828
32:30 There *be* the princes of the **n**, all of them, 6828
38:6 the house of Togarmah *of* the **n** quarters, 6828
38:15 thou shalt come from thy place out of the **n** 6828
39:2 will cause thee to come up from the **n** parts, 6828
40:20 the outward court that looked toward the **n**, 6828
40:23 *was* over against the gate toward the **n**, 6828
40:35 he brought me to the **n** gate, and 6828
40:40 one goeth up to the entry of the **n** 6828+1886.5
40:44 which *was* at the side of the **n** gate; 6828
40:44 east gate *having* the prospect toward the **n**. 6828
40:46 the chamber whose prospect *is* toward the **n** 6828
41:11 one door toward the **n**, and another door 6828
42:1 into the utter court, the way toward the **n**: 6828
42:1 *was* before the building toward the **n**. 6828
42:2 length of an hundred cubits *was* the **n** door, 6828
42:4 of one cubit; and their doors toward the **n**. 6828
42:11 of the chambers which *were* toward the **n**, 6828
42:13 The **n** chambers *and* the south chambers, 6828
42:17 He measured the **n** side, five hundred reeds, 6828
44:4 brought he me the way of the **n** gate before 6828
46:9 he that entereth in *by* the way of the **n** gate 6828
46:9 go forth *by* the way of the **n** gate: 6828+1886.5
46:19 which looked toward the **n**: 6828+1886.5
47:15 of the land toward the **n** side, 6828+1886.5
47:17 the **n** northward, and the border of Hamath. 6828
47:17 border of Hamath. And *this is* the **n** side. 6828
48:1 From the **n** end to the coast of 6828+1886.5
48:10 toward the **n** five and twenty thousand *in* 6828
48:16 the **n** side four thousand and five hundred, 6828
48:17 the suburbs of the city shall be toward the **n** 6828
48:30 on the **n** side, four thousand and 6828
Da 11:6 to the king of the **n** to make an agreement: 6828
11:7 enter into the fortress of the king of the **n**, 6828
11:8 continue *more* years than the king of the **n**. 6828
11:11 fight with him, *even* with the king of the **n**: 6828
11:13 For the king of the **n** shall return, and 6828
11:15 So the king of the **n** shall come, and cast up 6828
11:40 the king of the **n** shall come against him 6828
11:44 the east and out of the **n** shall trouble him: 6828
Am 8:12 from the **n** even to the east, they shall run 6828
Zep 2:13 he will stretch out his hand against the **n**, 6828
Zec 2:6 *come forth,* and flee from the land of the **n**, 6828
6:6 *are* therein go forth into the **n** country; 6828
6:8 these that go toward the **n** country have 6828
6:8 have quieted my spirit in the **n** country. 6828
14:4 of the mountain shall remove toward the **n**, 6828
Lk 13:29 and from the **n**, and *from* the south, and 1005
Ac 27:12 and lieth toward the south west and **n west**. 5566
Rev 21:13 the east three gates; on the **n** three gates; 1005

NORTHEASTER See EUROCLYDON

NORTHERN (2) [NORTH]

Jer 15:12 Shall iron break the **n** iron and 4480+6828
Joel 2:20 I will remove far off from you the **n** *army,* 6830

NORTHWARD (23) [NORTH]

Ge 13:14 from the place where thou *art* **n**, 6828+1886.5
Ex 40:22 upon the side of the tabernacle **n**, 6828+1886.5
Lev 1:11 of the altar **n** before the LORD: 6828+1886.5
Dt 2:3 mountain long enough: turn you **n**. 6828+1886.5
3:27 **n**, and southward, and eastward, 6828+1886.5
Jos 13:3 even unto the borders of Ekron **n**, 6828+1886.5
15:7 *so* **n**, looking toward Gilgal, that *is* 6828+1886.5
15:8 end of the valley of the giants **n**: 6828+1886.5
15:11 went out unto the side of Ekron **n**: 6828+1886.5
17:10 **n** *it was* Manasseh's, and the sea is 6828+1886.5
18:18 the side over against Arabah **n**: 6828+1886.5
18:19 along to the side of Beth-hoglah **n**: 6828+1886.5
Jdg 12:1 went **n**, and said unto Jephthah, 6828+1886.5
1Sa 14:5 situate **n** over against Michmash, 4480+6828
1Ch 26:14 cast lots; and his lot came out **n**. 6828+1886.5
26:17 **n** four a day, southward four a day, 6828+1886.5
Eze 8:5 behold, **n** at the gate of the altar this 4480+6828
40:19 an hundred cubits east*ward* and **n**. 6828
47:2 he me out *of* the way of the gate **n**, 6828+1886.5
47:17 north **n**, and the border of Hamath. 6828+1886.5
48:1 the border of Damascus **n**, 6828+1886.5
48:31 three gates **n**; one gate of Reuben, 6828+1886.5
Da 8:4 and **n**, and southward; 6828+1886.5

NORTHWARDS (1) [NORTH]

Nu 3:35 on the side of the tabernacle **n**. 6828+1886.5

NOSE (12) [NOSES]

Lev 21:18 or he that hath a **flat n**, or any thing 2763
2Ki 19:28 therefore I will put my hook in thy **n**, and 639
Job 40:24 with his eyes: *his* **n** pierceth through snares. 639
41:2 Canst thou put a hook into his **n**? or bore his 639
Pr 30:33 the wringing of the **n** bringeth forth blood: 639
SS 7:4 thy **n** *is* as the tower of Lebanon which 639
7:8 the vine, and the smell of thy **n** like apples; 639
Isa 3:21 The rings, and **n** jewels, 639
37:29 therefore will I put my hook in thy **n**, and 639
65:5 These *are* a smoke in my **n**, a fire that 639
Eze 8:17 and lo, they put the branch to their **n**. 639
23:25 they shall take away thy **n** and thine ears; 639

NOSES (2) [NOSE]

Ps 115:6 hear not: **n** have they, but they smell not: 639
Eze 39:11 and it *shall* stop the **n** *of the* passengers: and NIH

NOSTRILS (15)

Ge 2:7 and breathed into his **n** the breath of life; 639
7:22 All in whose **n** *was* the breath of life, of all 639
Ex 15:8 with the blast of thy **n** the waters were 639
Nu 11:20 until it come out at your **n**, and it be 639
2Sa 22:9 There went up a smoke out of his **n**, and 639
22:16 at the blast of the breath of his **n**. 639
Job 4:9 by the breath of his **n** are they consumed. 639
27:3 *is* in me, and the spirit of God *is* in my **n**; 639
39:20 a grasshopper? the glory of his **n** *is* terrible. 5170
41:20 Out of his **n** goeth smoke, as *out of* a 5156
Ps 18:8 There went up a smoke out of his **n**, and 639
18:15 O LORD, at the blast of the breath of thy **n**. 639
Isa 2:22 Cease ye from man, whose breath *is* in his **n**: 639
La 4:20 The breath of our **n**, the anointed of 639
Am 4:10 stink of your camps to come up unto your **n**: 639

NOT (6596) [NO] See Index of Articles, Etc.

NOTABLE (5) [NOTE]

Da 8:5 and the goat *had* a **n** horn between his eyes. 2380
8:8 for it came up four **n ones** toward the four 2380
Mt 27:16 And they had then a **n** prisoner, 1978
Ac 2:20 *that* great and **n** day of the Lord come: 2016
4:16 *that* indeed a **n** miracle hath been done 1110

NOTE (3) [NOTABLE, NOTED]

Isa 30:8 it before them in a table, and **n** it in a book, 2710
Ro 16:7 who are of **n** among the apostles, 1978
2Th 3:14 **n** that *man,* and have no company with 4593

NOTED (1) [NOTE]

Da 10:21 I will shew thee that which is **n** in 7559

NOTHING (225) [THING]

Ge 11:6 now **n** will be restrained from them, 3605+3808
19:8 only unto these men do **n**; for 408+1697
26:29 as we have done unto thee **n but** good, and 7535
40:15 here also have I done **n** that they 3808+3972
Ex 9:4 there shall **n** die of all *that is* 1697+3808
12:10 ye shall let **n** of it remain until the morning; 3808
12:20 Ye shall eat **n** leavened; in all your 3605+3808
16:18 he that gathered much had **n** over, and 3808
21:2 in the seventh he shall go out free **for n**. 2600
22:3 if he have **n**, then he shall be sold for his 369
23:26 There shall **n** cast their young, nor be 3808
Nu 6:4 he eat **n** that is made of the vine tree, 3605+3808
11:6 *there is* **n** at all, beside *this* manna, 369
16:26 wicked men, and touch **n** of theirs, 408+3605
22:16 Let **n**, I pray thee, hinder thee from coming 408
Dt 2:7 *been* with thee; thou hast lacked **n**. 1697+3808
20:16 thou shalt save alive **n** that breatheth: 3605+3808
22:26 unto the damsel thou shalt do **n**; 1697+3808
28:55 because he hath **n** left him in 1097+3605
Jos 11:15 he left **n** undone of all that 1697+3808
Jdg 3:2 at the least such as before knew **n** thereof: 3808
7:14 This *is* **n else** save the sword of 369+1115
14:6 rent a kid, and *he had* **n** in his hand: 369+3972
1Sa 3:18 told him every whit, and hid **n** from him. 3808
20:2 my father will do **n** *either* great or 1697+3808
22:15 for thy servant knew **n** of all this, 1697+3808
25:21 that **n** was missed of all that 3808+3972
25:36 wherefore she told him **n**, less or 1697+3808
27:1 *there is* **n** better for me than that I should 369
30:19 there was **n** lacking to them, neither small 3808
2Sa 12:3 the poor *man* had **n**, save one little 369+3605
24:24 my God of that which doth **cost** me **n**. 2600
1Ki 4:27 man *in* his month: they lacked **n**. 1697+3808
8:9 *There was* **n** in the ark save the two tables of 369
10:21 it was **n** accounted of in the days of 3808+3972
11:22 he answered, **N**: howbeit let me go in any 3808
18:43 and looked, and said, *There is* **n**. 369+3972
22:16 times shall I adjure thee that thou tell me **n** 3808
2Ki 10:10 unto the earth **n** of the word of the LORD, 3808
20:13 there was **n** in his house, nor in all 1697+3808
20:15 there is **n** among my treasures that I 1697+3808
20:17 **n** shall be left, saith the LORD. 1697+3808
2Ch 5:10 *There was* **n** in the ark save the two tables 369
9:2 there was **n** hid from Solomon which 1697+3808
14:11 said, LORD, *it is* **n** with thee to help, 369
18:15 times shall I adjure thee that thou say **n** 3808
Ezr 4:3 You have **n** to do with us to build a house 3808
Ne 2:2 this *is* **n** *else* but sorrow of heart. Then I was 369

Ne 5: 8 their peace, and found **n** *to answer.* 1697+3808
5:12 restore *them,* and will require **n** of them; 3808
8:10 send portions unto *them* for whom **n** is 369
9:21 in the wilderness, *so that* they lacked **n**; 3808
Est 2:15 she required **n** but what Hegai 1697+3808
5:13 Yet all this availeth me **n**, so long as I see 369
6: 3 unto him, There is **n** done for him. 1697+3808
6:10 let **n** fail of all that thou hast spoken. 408+1697
Job 6:18 are turned aside; they go to **n**, and perish. 8414
6:21 For now ye are **n**; ye see *my* casting down, 3808
8: 9 know **n**, because our days upon earth *are* a 3808
24:25 me a liar, and make my speech **n** worth? 408
26: 7 *and* hangeth the earth upon **n**. 1097+4100
34: 9 It profiteth a man **n** that he should delight 3808
Ps 17: 3 thou hast tried me, *and* shalt find **n**; 1077
19: 6 of it: and there is **n** hid from the heat thereof. 369
39: 5 and mine age *is* as **n** before thee: 369
49:17 he dieth he shall carry **n** 3605+3808+1886.1
119:165 which love thy law: and **n** *shall* offend them. 369
Pr 8: 8 *there is* **n** froward or perverse in them. 369
9:13 *she is* simple, and knoweth **n**. 1077+4100
10: 2 Treasures of wickedness profit **n**: but 3808
13: 4 soul of the sluggard desireth, and *hath* **n**: 369
13: 7 is that maketh himself rich, yet *hath* **n**: 369+3605
20: 4 therefore shall he beg in harvest, and *have* **n**. 369
22:27 If thou hast **n** to pay, why should he take 369
Ecc 2:24 *There is* **n** better for a man, *than* that he 369
3:14 **n** can be put to it, nor any thing taken from 369
3:22 Wherefore I perceive that *there is* **n** better, 369
5:14 a son, and *there is* **n** in his hand. 369+3972
5:15 shall take **n** of his labour, which he 3808+3972
6: 2 that he wanteth **n** for his soul of all that he 369
7:14 end that man should find **n** after him. 3808+3972
Isa 34:12 *shall be* there, and all her princes shall be **n**. 657
39: 2 there was **n** in his house, nor in all 1697+3808
39: 4 there is **n** among my treasures that I 1697+3808
39: 6 **n** shall be left, saith the LORD. 1697+3808
40:17 All nations before him *are* as **n**; and they are 369
40:17 and they are counted to him less than **n**, and 657
40:23 That bringeth the princes to **n**; he maketh 369
41:11 they shall be as **n**; and they that strive with 369
41:12 they that war against thee shall be as **n**, and 369
41:24 ye *are* of **n**, and your work of nought: 369
41:29 they *are* all vanity; their works *are* **n**: 657
44:10 a graven image *that* is profitable for **n**? 1115
Jer 10:24 not in thine anger, lest thou **bring** me **to n**. 4591
13: 7 it was profitable for **n**. 3605+3808+1886.1
13:10 which is good for **n**. 3605+3808+1886.1
32:17 there is **n** too hard for thee: 1697+3605+3808
32:23 they have done **n** of all that thou 3808
38:14 *will* ask thee a thing; hide **n** from me. 408+1697
39:10 which had **n**, in the land of Judah, and 369+3972
42: 4 I will keep **n** back from you. 1697+3808
50:26 and destroy her utterly: let **n** of her be left. 408
La 1:12 *Is it* **n** to you, all ye that pass by? behold, 3808
Eze 13: 3 follow their own spirit, and have seen **n**! 1115
Da 4:35 the inhabitants of the earth *are* reputed as **n**: 3809
Joel 2: 3 yea, and **n** shall escape them. 3808
Am 3: 4 lion cry out of his den, if he have taken **n**? 1115
3: 5 from the earth, and have taken **n** at all? 3808
3: 7 Surely the Lord GOD will do **n**, 1697+3808
Hag 2: 3 *it* not in your eyes in comparison of it as **n**? 369
Mt 5:13 it is thenceforth good for **n**, but to be cast *3762*
10:26 for there is **n** covered, that shall not be *3762*
15:32 now three days, and have **n** to eat: *3756+5101*
17:20 and **n** shall be unpossible unto you. *3762*
21:19 he came to it, and found **n** thereon, *3762*
23:16 shall swear by the temple, it is **n**; *3762*
23:18 Whosoever shall swear by the altar, it is **n**; *3762*
26:62 and said unto him, Answerest thou **n**? *3762*
27:12 the chief priests and elders, he answered **n**. *3762*
27:19 Have thou **n** to do with that just *man:* for I *3367*
27:24 When Pilate saw that he could prevail **n**, *3762*
Mk 1:44 See thou say **n** to any *man:* but go thy way, *3367*
4:22 For there is **n** hid, which shall not be *3756*
5:26 and was **n** bettered, but rather grew worse, *3367*
6: 8 that they should take **n** for *their* journey, *3367*
6:36 for they have **n** to eat. *3756+5101*
7:15 There is **n** from without a man, *3762*
8: 1 and having **n** to eat, Jesus called his *3361+5101*
8: 2 me three days, and have **n** to eat: *3756+5101*
9:29 This kind can come forth by **n**, but by *3762*
11:13 when he came to it, he found **n** but leaves; *3762*
14:60 and asked Jesus, saying, Answerest thou **n**? *3762*
14:61 But he held his peace, and answered **n**. *3762*
15: 3 him of many *things:* but he answered **n**. *3762*
15: 4 him again, saying, Answerest thou **n**? *3762*
15: 5 But Jesus yet answered **n**; so that Pilate *3762*
Lk 1:37 For with God **n** shall be *3756+3956+4487*
4: 2 And in those days he did eat **n**: and *3762*
5: 5 have toiled all the night, and have taken **n**: *3762*
6:35 and do good, and lend, hoping for **n** again; *3367*
7:42 And when they had **n** to pay, he frankly *3361*
8:17 For **n** is secret, that shall not be made *3756*
9: 3 Take **n** for *your* journey, neither staves, *3367*
10:19 and **n** shall by any means hurt you. *3762*
11: 6 to me, and I have **n** to set before him: *3739+3756*
12: 2 For there is **n** covered, that shall not be *3762*
22:35 lacked ye any *thing?* And they said, **N**. *3762*
23: 9 in many words; but he answered him **n**. *3762*
23:15 and lo, **n** worthy of death is done unto him. *3762*
23:41 our deeds: but this *man* hath done **n** amiss. *3762*
Jn 3:27 and said, A man can receive **n**, *3762*
4:11 Sir, thou hast **n** to draw with, and the well *3777*
5:19 The Son can do **n** of himself, but what he *3762*
5:30 I can of mine own self do **n**: as I hear, *3762*
6:12 fragments that remain, that **n** be lost. *3361+5100*
6:39 hath given me I should lose **n**, *846+1537+3361*
6:63 spirit that quickeneth; the flesh profiteth **n**: *3762*
7:26 speaketh boldly, and they say **n** unto him. *3762*
8:28 that I am *he,* and *that* I do **n** of myself; *3762*
8:54 If I honour myself, my honour is **n**: *3762*
9:33 If this *man* were not of God, he could do **n**. *3762*
11:49 said unto them, Ye know **n at all**, *3756+3762*
12:19 Perceive ye how ye prevail **n**? *3762*
Jn 14:30 of this world cometh, and hath **n** in me. *3762*
15: 5 much fruit: for without me ye can do **n**. *3762*
16:23 And in that day ye shall ask me **n**. Verily, *3762*
16:24 Hitherto have ye asked **n** in my name: ask, *3762*
18:20 always resort; and in secret have I said **n**. *3762*
21: 3 and that night they caught **n**. *3762*
Ac 4:14 with them, they could say **n** against *it.* *3762*
4:21 finding **n** how they might punish them, *3367*
10:20 *thee* down, and go with them, doubting **n**: *3367*
11: 8 **n** common or unclean hath **at any time** *3763+3956*
11:12 Spirit bade me go with them, **n** doubting. *3367*
17:21 which were there spent their time in **n** else, *3762*
19:36 ye ought to be quiet, and to do **n** rashly. *3367*
20:20 *And* how I kept back **n** that was profitable *3762*
21:24 they were informed concerning thee, are **n**; *3762*
23:14 that *we* will eat **n** until we have slain Paul. *3367*
23:29 to have **n** laid to his charge worthy of death *3762*
25:25 But when I found that he had committed **n** *3367*
26:31 This man doeth **n** worthy of death or *3762*
27:33 and continued fasting, having taken **n**. *3367*
28:17 though I have committed **n** against *3762*
Ro 14:14 Lord Jesus, that *there is* **n** unclean of itself: *3762*
1Co 1:19 will **bring to n** the understanding of *114*
4: 4 For I know **n** by myself; yet am I not *3762*
4: 5 Therefore judge **n** before the time, *3361+5100*
7:19 Circumcision is **n**, and uncircumcision is *3762*
7:19 and uncircumcision is **n**, but the keeping of *3762*
8: 2 he knoweth **n** yet as he ought to know. *3762*
8: 4 we know that an idol *is* **n** in the world, and *3762*
9:16 I preach the gospel, I have **n** to glory of: *3756*
13: 2 and have no charity, I am **n**. *3762*
13: 3 and have not charity, it profiteth me **n**. *3762*
2Co 6:10 as having **n**, and *yet* possessing all *things.* *3367*
7: 9 that ye might receive damage by us in **n**. *3367*
8:15 He that *had gathered* much had **n** over; *3756*
12:11 for *in* **n** am I behind the very chiefest *3762*
12:11 the very chiefest apostles, though I be **n**. *3762*
13: 8 For we can do **n** against the truth, but *3756+5100*
Gal 2: 6 *be somewhat* in conference added **n** to me: *3762*
4: 1 as he is a child, differeth **n** from a servant, *3762*
5: 2 ye be circumcised, Christ shall profit you **n**. *3762*
6: 3 when he is **n**, he deceiveth himself. *3367*
Php 1:20 that in **n** I shall be ashamed, but *that* with *3762*
1:28 And in **n** terrified by *your* adversaries: *3367*
2: 3 *Let* **n** *be done* through strife or vainglory; *3367*
4: 6 Be careful for **n**; but in every *thing* by *3367*
1Th 4:12 and *that* ye may have lack of **n**. *3367*
1Ti 4: 4 of God *is* good, and **n** to be refused, *3762*
5:21 *one before another,* doing **n** by partiality. *3367*
6: 4 knowing **n**, but doting about questions and *3367*
6: 7 For we brought **n** into *this* world, *and it is* *3762*
6: 7 *and it is* certain we can carry **n** out. *3761+5100*
Tit 1:15 that are defiled and unbelieving *is* **n** pure; *3762*
3:13 that **n** be wanting unto them. *3367*
Phm 1:14 But without thy mind would I do **n**; that thy *3762*
Heb 2: 8 he left **n** *that is* not put under him. *3762*
7:14 of which tribe Moses spake **n** concerning *3762*
7:19 For the law made **n** perfect, but *3762*
Jas 1: 4 ye may be perfect and entire, wanting **n**. *3367*
1: 6 But let him ask in faith, **n** wavering. For he *3367*
3Jn 1: 7 they went forth, taking **n** of the Gentiles. *3367*
Rev 3:17 increased with goods, and have need of **n**; *3762*

NOTICE (2)

2Sa 3:36 all the people **took n** *of it,* and it pleased 5234
2Co 9: 5 whereof *ye* **had n before**, that the same *4293*

NOTWITHSTANDING (36)

Ex 16:20 **N** they hearkened not unto Moses; but 2050.1
21:21 **N**, if he continue a day or two, he shall not 389
Lev 25:32 **N** the cities of the Levites, *and* the houses 2050.1
27:28 **N** no devoted thing, that a man shall devote 389
Nu 26:11 **N** the children of Korah died not. 2050.1
26:55 **N** the land shall be divided by lot: 389
Dt 1:26 **N** ye would not go up, but 2050.1
12:15 **N** thou mayest kill and eat flesh in all thy 7535
Jos 22:19 **N**, if the land of your possession *be* 389+2050.1
Jdg 4: 9 **n** the journey that thou takest shall not 657+3588
9: 5 **n yet** Jotham the youngest son of 2050.1
1Sa 2:25 **N** they hearkened not unto 3808+2050.1
20: 8 **n**, if there be in me iniquity, slay me 2050.1
29: 9 **n** the princes of the Philistines have said, 389
2Sa 24: 4 **N** the king's word prevailed against Joab, 2050.1
1Ki 11:12 **N** in thy days I will not do it for David thy 389
2Ki 17:14 **N** they would not hear, but hardened their 2050.1
23:26 **N** the LORD turned not from the fierceness 389
2Ch 6: 9 **N** thou shalt not build the house; but 7535
32:26 **N** Hezekiah humbled himself for 2050.1
Jer 35:14 **n** I have spoken unto you, rising early 2050.1
Eze 20:21 **N** the children rebelled against me: 2050.1
Mic 7:13 **N** the land shall be desolate because 2050.1
Mt 2:22 **n**, being warned of God in a dream, *1161*
11:11 **n** he that is least in the kingdom of heaven *1161*
17:27 **N**, lest we should offend them, go thou to *1161*
Lk 10:11 **n** be ye sure of this, that the kingdom of *4133*
10:20 **N** in this rejoice not, that the spirits are *4133*
Ac 15:34 **N** it pleased Silas to abide there *still.* *1161*
24: 4 **N**, that I be not further tedious unto thee, *1161*
Php 1:18 **n**, every way, whether in pretence, or *4133*
4:14 **N** ye have well done, that ye did *4133*
1Ti 2:15 **N** she shall be saved in childbearing, if they *1161*
2Ti 4:17 **N** the Lord stood with me, and *1161*
Jas 2:16 **n** ye give them not those *things which are* *1161*
Rev 2:20 **N** I have a few *things* against thee, because *235*

NOUGHT (36) [NAUGHT]

Ge 29:15 shouldest thou therefore serve me **for n**? 2600
Dt 13:17 there shall cleave **n** of the cursed 3808+3972
15: 9 thy poor brother, and thou givest him **n**; 3808
28:63 you to destroy you, and to **bring** you **to n**; 8045
Ne 4:15 God had **brought** their counsel **to n**, 6565
Job 1: 9 and said, Doth Job fear God **for n**? 2600
8:22 place of the wicked shall **come to n**. 369
14:18 surely the mountain falling **cometh to n**, 5034
Job 22: 6 hast taken a pledge from thy brother **for n**, 2600
Ps 33:10 **bringeth** the counsel of the heathen **to n**: 6331
44:12 Thou sellest thy people for **n**, and 1952+3808
Pr 1:25 ye have **set at n** all my counsel, and 6544
Isa 8:10 counsel together, and it shall **come to n**; 6565
29:20 For the **terrible one** is brought to **n**, and 6184
29:21 and turn aside the just for a **thing of n**. 8414
41:12 thee shall be as nothing, and as a **thing of n**. 657
41:24 ye *are* of nothing, and your work of **n**: 659
49: 4 I have spent my strength for **n**, and in vain: 8414
52: 3 the LORD, Ye have sold yourselves **for n**; 2600
52: 5 that my people is taken away **for n**? 2600
Jer 14:14 a **thing of n**, and the deceit of their heart. 457
Am 5: 5 into captivity, and Beth-el shall come to **n**. 205
6:13 *Ye* which rejoice in a thing of **n**, which say, 3808
Mal 1:10 **n**? neither do ye kindle *fire on* mine altar for NIH
1:10 do ye kindle *fire on* mine altar **for n**. 2600
Mk 9:12 he must suffer many *things,* and be **set at n**. *1847*
Lk 23:11 Herod with his men of war **set** him **at n**, *1848*
Ac 4:11 This is the stone which was **set at n** of you *1848*
5:36 were scattered, and brought to **n**. *3762*
5:38 or this work be of men, it will **come to n**: *2647*
19:27 only this our craft is in danger to be set at **n**; *557*
Ro 14:10 or why dost thou **set at n** thy brother? *1848*
1Co 1:28 which are not, to **bring to n** *things* that are: *2673*
2: 6 of the princes of this world, that **come to n**: *2673*
2Th 3: 8 Neither did we eat any *man's* bread **for n**; *1432*
Rev 18:17 in one hour so great riches is **come to n**. *2049*

NOURISH (5) [NOURISHED, NOURISHER, NOURISHETH, NOURISHING, NOURISHMENT]

Ge 45:11 there will I **n** thee; for yet *there are* five 3557
50:21 I will **n** you and your little ones. And he 3557
Isa 7:21 *that* a man shall **n** a young cow, and 2421
23: 4 neither do I **n up** young men, *nor* bring up 1431
44:14 he planteth an ash, and the rain doth **n** *it.* 1431

NOURISHED (10) [NOURISH]

Ge 47:12 Joseph **n** his father, and his brethren, and 3557
2Sa 12: 3 ewe lamb, which he had bought and **n up**: 2421
Isa 1: 2 I have **n** and brought up children, and 1431
Eze 19: 2 she **n** her whelps among young lions. 7235
Ac 7:20 and **n up** in his father's house three months: *397*
7:21 took him up, and **n** him for her own son. *397*
12:20 their country was **n** by the king's *country.* *5142*
1Ti 4: 6 **n up** in the words of faith and of good *1789*
Jas 5: 5 ye have **n** your hearts, as in a day of *5142*
Rev 12:14 where she is **n** for a time, and times, and *5142*

NOURISHER (1) [NOURISH]

Ru 4:15 restorer of *thy* life, and a **n** of thine old age: 3557

NOURISHETH (1) [NOURISH]

Eph 5:29 but **n** and cherisheth it, even as the Lord *1625*

NOURISHING (1) [NOURISH]

Da 1: 5 so **n** them three years, that at the end 1431

NOURISHMENT (1) [NOURISH]

Col 2:19 by joints and bands having **n ministered**, *2023*

NOVICE (1)

1Ti 3: 6 Not a **n**, lest being lifted up with pride he *3504*

NOW (1356)

Ge 2:23 This *is* **n** bone of my bones, and flesh of 6471
3: 1 **N** the serpent was more subtil than any 2050.1
3:22 **n**, lest he put forth his hand, and take also 6258
4:11 **n** *art* thou cursed from the earth, which hath 6258
10: 1 **N** these *are* the generations of the sons of 2050.1
11: 6 **n** nothing will be restrained from them, 6258
11:27 **N** these *are* the generations of Terah: 2050.1
12: 1 **N** the LORD had said unto Abram, 2050.1
12:11 that he said unto Sarai his wife, Behold **n**, 4994
12:19 **n** therefore behold thy wife, take *her,* and 6258
13:14 Lift up **n** thine eyes, and look from 4994
15: 5 Look **n** towards heaven, and tell the stars, 4994
16: 1 **N** Sarai Abram's wife bare him no 2050.1
16: 2 Sarai said unto Abram, Behold **n**, 4994
18: 3 if **n** I have found favour in thy sight, 4994
18:11 **N** Abraham and Sarah *were* old *and* 2050.1
18:21 I will go down **n**, and see whether they 4994
18:27 Abraham answered and said, Behold **n**, 4994
18:31 he said, Behold **n**, I have taken upon me to 4994
19: 2 Behold **n**, my lords, turn in, I pray you, 4994
19: 8 Behold **n**, I have two daughters which have 4994
19: 9 **n** will we deal worse with thee, than with 6258
19:19 Behold **n**, thy servant hath found grace in 4994
19:20 Behold **n**, this city *is* near to flee unto, and 4994
20: 7 **N** therefore restore the man *his* wife; for he 6258
21:23 **N** therefore swear unto me here by God 6258
22: 2 he said, Take **n** thy son, thine only *son* 4994
22:12 for **n** I know that thou fearest God, 6258
24:42 if **n** thou do prosper my way which I go: 4994
24:49 **n** if ye will deal kindly and truly with my 6258
25:12 **N** these *are* the generations of Ishmael, 2050.1
26:22 For **n** the LORD hath made room for us, 6258
26:28 we said, Let there be **n** an oath betwixt us, 4994
26:29 thou *art* **n** the blessed of the LORD. 6258
27: 2 he said, Behold **n**, I am old, I know not 4994
27: 3 **N** therefore take, I pray thee, thy weapons, 6258
27: 8 **N** therefore, my son, obey my voice 6258
27: 9 Go **n** to the flock, and fetch me from thence 4994
27:26 Come near **n**, and kiss me, my son. 4994
27:36 behold, **n** he hath taken away my blessing. 6258
27:37 and what shall I do **n** unto thee, my son? 645
27:43 **N** therefore, my son, obey my voice; and 6258
29:32 **n** therefore my husband will love me. 6258
29:34 **N** *this* time will my husband be joined unto 6258
29:35 she said, **N** will I praise 6471+1886.1
30:20 **n** will my husband dwell with me, because 6471
30:30 and it is *n* increased unto a multitude; NIH
30:30 **n** when shall I provide for mine own house 6258
31:12 he said, Lift up **n** thine eyes, and see, all 4994

Ge 31:13 n arise, get thee out from this land, 6258
31:16 n then, whatsoever God hath said unto thee, 6258
31:25 N Jacob had pitched his tent in 2050.1
31:28 thou hast n done foolishly in so doing. 6258
31:30 n, though thou wouldest needs be gone, 6258
31:34 N Rachel had taken the images, and 2050.1
31:42 surely thou hadst sent me away n empty. 6258
31:44 N therefore come thou, let us make a 2050.1
32: 4 with Laban, and stayed there until n: 6258
32:10 this Jordan; and n I am become two bands. 6258
33:10 if n I have found grace in thy sight, then 4994
33:15 Let me n leave with thee some of the folk 4994
34: 5 n his sons were with his cattle in 2050.1
35:22 Israel heard it. N the sons of Jacob were 2050.1
36: 1 N these are the generations of Esau, 2050.1
37: 3 N Israel loved Joseph more than all his 2050.1
37:20 Come n therefore, and let us slay him, and 6258
37:32 know n whether it be thy son's coat or no. 4994
41:33 N therefore let Pharaoh look out a man 6258
42: 1 N when Jacob saw that there was corn in 2050.1
43:10 surely n we had returned this second time. 6258
43:11 said unto them, If it must be so n, do this; 645
44:10 N also let it be according unto your words: 6258
44:30 N therefore when I come to thy servant my 6258
44:33 N therefore, I pray thee, let thy servant 6258
45: 5 N therefore be not grieved, nor angry with 6258
45: 8 So n it was not you that sent me hither, but 6258
45:19 N thou art commanded, this do ye; 2050.1
46:30 Israel said unto Joseph, N let me 6471+1886.1
46:34 about cattle from our youth even until n, 6258
47: 4 n therefore, we pray thee, let thy servants 6258
47:29 If n I have found grace in thy sight, put, 4994
48: 5 n thy two sons, Ephraim and Manasseh, 6258
48:10 N the eyes of Israel were dim for age, so 2050.1
50: 4 If n I have found grace in your eyes, speak, 4994
50: 5 N therefore let me go up, I pray thee, and 6258
50:17 Forgive, I pray thee n, the trespass of thy 4994
50:17 n, we pray thee, forgive the trespass of 6258
50:21 N therefore fear ye not: I will nourish you 6258
Ex 1: 1 N these are the names of the children of 2050.1
1: 8 N there arose up a new king over Egypt, 2050.1
2:15 N when Pharaoh heard this thing, he 2050.1
2:16 N the priest of Midian had seven 2050.1
3: 1 N Moses kept the flock of Jethro his 2050.1
3: 3 I will n turn aside, and see this great sight, 4994
3: 9 N therefore, behold, the cry of the children 6258
3:10 Come n therefore, and I will send thee unto 6258
3:18 n let us go, we beseech thee, three days' 6258
4: 6 unto him, Put n thine hand into thy bosom. 4994
4:12 N therefore go, and I will be with thy 6258
5: 5 the people of the land n are many, and 6258
5:18 Go therefore n, and work; for there shall no 6258
6: 1 N shalt thou see what I will do to Pharaoh: 6258
7:11 n the magicians of Egypt, they also did in 2050.1
9:15 For n I will stretch out my hand, that I may 6258
9:18 since the foundation thereof even until n. 6258
9:19 Send therefore n, and gather thy cattle, and 6258
10:11 go n ye that are men, and serve 4994
10:17 N therefore forgive, I pray thee, my sin 6258
11: 2 Speak n in the ears of the people, and 4994
12:40 N the sojourning of the children of Israel, 2050.1
16:36 N an omer is the tenth part of an ephah. 2050.1
18:11 N I know that the LORD is greater than 6258
18:19 Hearken n unto my voice, I will give thee 6258
19: 5 N therefore, if ye will obey my voice 6258
21: 1 N these are the judgments which thou 2050.1
29:38 N this is that which thou shalt offer upon 2050.1
32:10 N therefore let me alone, that my wrath 6258
32:30 n I will go up unto the LORD; 6258
32:32 Yet n, if thou wilt forgive their sin; and 6258
32:34 Therefore n go, lead the people unto 6258
33: 5 n put off thy ornaments from thee, 6258
33:13 N therefore, I pray thee, if I have found 6258
33:13 shew me n thy way, that I may know thee, 4994
34: 9 If n I have found grace in thy sight, 4994
Nu 11: 6 n our soul is dried away: there is nothing at 6258
11:23 thou shalt see n whether my word shall 6258
12: 3 (N the man Moses was very meek, 2050.1
12: 6 he said, Hear n my words: If there be a 4994
12:13 Heal her n, O God, I beseech thee. 4994
13:20 N the time was the time of the first ripe 2050.1
13:22 were. (N Hebron was built seven years 2050.1
14:15 N if thou shalt kill all this people as one 2050.1
14:17 n, I beseech thee, let the power of my Lord 6258
14:19 this people, from Egypt even until n. 2008
14:22 have tempted me n these ten times, and NIH
14:25 (N the Amalekites and the Canaanites 2050.1
14:41 Wherefore n do ye transgress 2088
16: 1 N Korah, the son of Izhar, the son of 2050.1
16:49 N they that died in the plague were 2050.1
20:10 and he said unto them, Hear n, ye rebels; 4994
22: 4 N shall this company lick up all that are 6258
22: 6 Come n therefore, I pray thee, curse me 6258
22:11 come n, curse me them; peradventure I 6258
22:19 N therefore, I pray you, tarry ye also here 6258
22:22 N he was riding upon his ass, and his two 2050.1
22:29 sword in mine hand, for n would I kill thee. 6258
22:33 surely n also I had slain thee, and saved her 6258
22:34 n therefore, if it displease thee, I will get 6258
22:38 have I n any power at all to say any thing? 6258
24:11 Therefore n flee thou to thy place: 6258
24:14 n behold, I go unto my people: come 6258
24:17 I shall see him, but not n: I shall behold 6258
25:14 N the name of the Israelite that was slain, 2050.1
31:17 N therefore kill every male among the little 6258
31:43 (N the half that pertained unto 2050.1
32: 1 N the children of Reuben and the children 2050.1
Dt 2:13 N rise up, said I, and get you over 6258
4: 1 N therefore hearken, O Israel, unto 6258
4:32 For ask n of the days that are past, 4994
5:25 N therefore why should we die? for this 6258
6: 1 N these are the commandments, 2050.1
10:12 n, Israel, what doth the LORD thy God 6258
10:22 n the LORD thy God hath made thee as 6258
26:10 n, behold, I have brought the firstfruits of 6258

Dt 31:19 N therefore write ye this song for you, 6258
31:21 which they go about, even n, 3117+1886.1
32:39 See n that I, even I, am he, and there is no 6258
Jos 1: 1 N after the death of Moses the servant of 2050.1
1: 2 n therefore arise, go over this Jordan, thou, 6258
2:12 N therefore, I pray you, swear unto me by 6258
3:12 N therefore take ye twelve men out of 6258
5: 5 N all the people that came out were 3588
5:14 as captain of the host of the LORD am I n 6258
6: 1 N Jericho was straitly shut up because of 2050.1
7:19 tell me n what thou hast done; hide it not 4994
8:11 n there was a valley between them and 2050.1
9: 6 n therefore make ye a league with us. 2050.1
9:11 therefore n make ye a league with us. 2050.1
9:12 but n, behold, it is dry, and it is mouldy: 6258
9:17 N their cities were Gibeon, and 2050.1
9:19 n therefore we may not touch them. 2050.1
9:23 N therefore ye are cursed, and there shall 2050.1
9:25 n, behold, we are in thine hand: as it 6258
10: 1 N it came to pass, when Adoni-zedek 2050.1
12: 1 N these are the kings of the land, 2050.1
13: 1 N Joshua was old and stricken in years; 2050.1
13: 7 N therefore divide this land for an 2050.1
14:10 n behold, the LORD hath kept me alive, 6258
14:10 n lo, I am this day fourscore and five years 6258
14:11 even so is my strength n, for war, both to 6258
14:12 N therefore give me this mountain, 6258
17: 8 N Manasseh had the land of Tappuah: but NIH
18:21 N the cities of the tribe of the children of 2050.1
22: 4 n the LORD your God hath given rest 6258
22: 4 therefore n return ye, and get ye unto your 6258
22: 7 N to the one half of the tribe of Manasseh 2050.1
22:26 Let us n prepare to build us an altar, 4994
22:31 n ye have delivered the children of Israel out 227
24:14 N therefore fear the LORD, and serve him 6258
24:23 N therefore put away, said he, the strange 6258
Jdg 1: 1 N after the death of Joshua it came to 2050.1
1: 8 N the children of Judah had fought 2050.1
1:10 (n the name of Hebron before was 2050.1
1:23 (N the name of the city before was Luz.) 2050.1
3: 1 N these are the nations which the LORD 2050.1
4:11 N Heber the Kenite, which was of 2050.1
6:13 n the LORD hath forsaken us, and 6258
6:17 If n I have found grace in thy sight, then 4994
6:39 let it n be dry only upon the fleece, 4994
7: 3 N therefore go to, proclaim in the ears of 6258
8: 2 What have I done n in comparison of you? 6258
8: 6 of Zebah and Zalmunna n in thine hand, 6258
8:10 N Zebah and Zalmunna were in Karkor, 2050.1
8:15 of Zebah and Zalmunna n in thine hand, 6258
9:16 N therefore, if ye have done truly and 6258
9:32 N therefore up by night, thou and 6258
9:38 Where is n thy mouth, wherewith thou 645
9:38 go out, I pray n, and fight with them. 6258
11: 1 N Jephthah the Gileadite was a mighty 2050.1
11: 7 why are ye come unto me n when ye are in 6258
11: 8 Therefore we turn again to thee n, that thou 6258
11:13 n therefore restore those lands again 6258
11:23 So n the LORD God of Israel hath 6258
11:25 n art thou any thing better than Balak 6258
12: 6 said they unto him, Say n Shibboleth: and 4994
13: 3 said unto her, Behold n, thou art barren, 4994
13: 4 N therefore beware, I pray thee, and 6258
13: 7 n drink no wine nor strong drink, 6258
13:12 Manoah said, N let thy words come to pass. 6258
14: 2 n therefore get her for me to wife. 6258
14:12 I will n put forth a riddle unto you: 4994
15: 3 N shall I be more blameless than 6471
15:18 n shall I die for thirst, and fall into the hand 6258
16: 9 N there were men lying in wait, 2050.1
16:10 n tell me, I pray thee, wherewith thou 6258
16:27 N the house was full of men and women; 2050.1
17: 3 n therefore I will restore it unto thee. 6258
17:13 N know I that the LORD will do me good, 6258
18:14 n therefore consider what ye have to do. 6258
19: 9 damsel's father, said unto him, Behold n, 4994
19:18 I am n going to the house of the LORD; NIH
19:22 N as they were making their hearts merry, NIH
19:24 them I will bring out n, and humble ye 4994
20: 3 (N the children of Benjamin heard that 2050.1
20: 9 n this shall be the thing which we will do to 6258
20:13 N therefore deliver us the men, the children 6258
20:38 N there was an appointed sign between 2050.1
21: 1 N the men of Israel had sworn in Mizpeh, 2050.1
Ru 1: 1 N it came to pass in the days when 2050.1
2: 2 Let me n go to the field, and glean ears of 4994
2: 7 continued even from the morning until n, 6258
3: 2 n is not Boaz of our kindred, with whose 6258
3:11 n, my daughter, fear not; I will do to thee 6258
3:12 n it is true that I am thy near 3588+6258
4: 7 N this was the manner in former time in 2050.1
4:18 N these are the generations of Pharez: 2050.1
1Sa 1: 1 N there was a certain man of 2050.1
1: 9 N Eli the priest sat upon a seat by a post 2050.1
1:13 N Hannah, she spake in her heart; 2050.1
2:12 N the sons of Eli were sons of Belial; 2050.1
2:16 Nay; but thou shalt give it me n: 6258
2:22 N Eli was very old, and heard all that his 2050.1
2:30 n the LORD saith, Be it far from me; 6258
3: 7 N Samuel did not yet know the LORD, 2050.1
4: 1 N Israel went out against the Philistines 2050.1
4:15 N Eli was ninety and eight years old; and 2050.1
6: 7 N therefore make a new cart, and take two 6258
8: 2 N the name of his firstborn was Joel; and 2050.1
8: 5 n make us a king to judge us like all 6258
8: 9 N therefore hearken unto their voice: 6258
9: 1 N there was a man of Benjamin, whose 2050.1
9: 3 Take n one of the servants with thee, 4994
9: 6 he said unto him, Behold n, there is in this 4994
9: 6 n let us go thither; peradventure he can 6258
9: 9 for he that is n called a Prophet was 3117
9:12 make haste n, for he came to day to 6258
9:13 N therefore get you up; for about this time 6258
9:15 N the LORD had told Samuel in his ear 2050.1
10:19 N therefore present yourselves before 6258

1Sa 12: 2 And n behold, the king walketh before you: 6258
12: 7 N therefore stand still, that I may reason 6258
12:10 n deliver us out of the hand of our enemies, 6258
12:13 N therefore behold the king whom ye have 6258
12:16 N therefore stand and see this great thing, 6258
13:12 The Philistines will come down n upon me 6258
13:13 for n would the LORD have established 6258
13:14 n thy kingdom shall not continue: 6258
13:19 N there was no smith found throughout 2050.1
14: 1 N it came to pass upon a day, 2050.1
14:17 Number n, and see who is gone from us. 4994
14:30 for had there not been n a much greater 6258
14:49 N the sons of Saul were Jonathan, and 2050.1
15: 1 n therefore hearken thou unto the voice of 6258
15: 3 N go and smite Amalek, and utterly destroy 6258
15:25 N therefore, I pray thee, pardon my sin, and 6258
15:30 yet honour me n, I pray thee, before 6258
16:12 N he was ruddy, and withal of a beautiful 2050.1
16:15 Saul's servants said unto him, Behold n, 4994
16:16 Let our lord n command thy servants which 4994
16:17 Provide me n a man that can play well, and 4994
17: 1 N the Philistines gathered together their 2050.1
17:12 N David was the son of that Ephrathite of 2050.1
17:17 Take n for thy brethren an ephah of this 4994
17:19 N Saul, and they, and all the men of 2050.1
17:29 David said, What have I n done? Is there 6258
18:22 n therefore be the king's son in law. 6258
19: 2 n therefore, I pray thee, take heed to thyself 6258
20:29 he hath commanded me to be there: and n, 6258
20:31 Wherefore n send and fetch him unto me, 6258
20:36 Run, find out n the arrows which I shoot. 4994
21: 3 N therefore what is under thine hand? 6258
21: 7 N a certain man of the servants of Saul 2050.1
22: 6 (n Saul abode in Gibeah under a tree in 2050.1
22: 7 stood about him, Hear n, ye Benjamites; 4994
22:12 Saul said, Hear n, thou son of Ahitub. 4994
23:20 N therefore, O king, come down according 6258
24:20 n behold, I know well that thou shalt surely 6258
24:21 Swear n therefore unto me by the LORD, 6258
25: 3 N the name of the man was Nabal; and 2050.1
25: 7 n I have heard that thou hast shearers: 6258
25: 7 n thy shepherds which were with us, 6258
25:10 there be many servants n a days 3117+1886.1
25:17 N therefore know and consider what thou 6258
25:21 N David had said, Surely in vain have I 2050.1
25:26 N therefore, my lord, as the LORD liveth, 6258
25:26 n let thine enemies, and they that seek evil 6258
25:27 n this blessing which thine handmaid hath 6258
26: 8 n therefore let me smite him, I pray thee, 6258
26:11 take thou n the spear that is at his bolster, 4994
26:16 n see where the king's spear is, and 6258
26:19 N therefore, I pray thee, let my lord 6258
26:20 N therefore, let not my blood fall to 6258
27: 1 I shall n perish one day by the hand of 6258
27: 5 If I have n found grace in thine eyes, 4994
28: 3 N Samuel was dead, and all Israel had 2050.1
28:22 N therefore, I pray thee, hearken thou also 6258
29: 1 N the Philistines gathered together all 2050.1
29: 7 Wherefore n return, and go in peace, 6258
29:10 Wherefore n rise up early in the morning 6258
31: 1 N the Philistines fought against Israel: 2050.1
2Sa 1: 1 N it came to pass after the death of Saul, 2050.1
2: 6 n the LORD shew kindness and truth unto 6258
2: 7 Therefore n let your hands be strengthened, 6258
2:14 Let the young men n arise, and play before 4994
3: 1 N there was long war between the house 2050.1
3:18 N then do it: for the LORD hath spoken of 6258
4:11 therefore n require his blood of your hand, 6258
7: 2 See n, I dwell in a house of cedar, but 4994
7: 8 N therefore so shalt thou say unto my 6258
7:25 n, O LORD God, the word that thou hast 6258
7:28 n, O Lord GOD, thou art that God, and 6258
7:29 Therefore n let it please thee to bless 6258
9: 6 N when Mephibosheth, the son of 2050.1
9:10 N Ziba had fifteen sons and 2050.1
12:10 N therefore the sword shall never depart 6258
12:23 n he is dead, wherefore should I fast? can I 6258
12:28 N therefore gather the rest of the people 6258
13: 7 Go n to thy brother Amnon's house, and 4994
13:13 N therefore, I pray thee, speak unto 6258
13:17 Put n this woman out from me, and bolt 4994
13:20 hold n thy peace, my sister: he is thy 6258
13:24 said, Behold n, thy servant hath 4994
13:25 Nay, my son, let us not all n go, 4994
13:28 N Absalom had commanded his servants, 2050.1
13:28 Mark ye n when Amnon's heart is merry 4994
13:33 N therefore let not my lord the king take 6258
14: 1 N Joab the son of Zeruiah perceived that 2050.1
14: 2 put on n mourning apparel, and anoint not 4994
14:15 N therefore that I am come to speak of this 6258
14:15 handmaid said, I will n speak unto the king; 4994
14:17 The word of my lord the king shall n be 4994
14:18 woman said, Let my lord the king n speak. 4994
14:21 unto Joab, Behold n, I have done this thing: 4994
14:32 n therefore let me see the king's face; and 6258
15:34 so will I n also be thy servant: 6258
16:11 how much more n may this Benjamite do 6258
17: 1 Let me n choose out twelve thousand men, 4994
17: 5 Call n Hushai the Archite also, and let us 4994
17: 9 he is hid n in some pit, or in some other 6258
17:16 N therefore send quickly, and tell David, 6258
17:17 N Jonathan and Ahimaaz stayed by 2050.1
18: 3 n thou art worth ten thousand of us: 6258
18: 3 n it is better that thou succour us out of 6258
18:18 N Absalom in his lifetime had taken and 2050.1
18:19 Let me n run, and bear the king tidings, 4994
19: 7 N therefore arise, go forth, and 6258
19: 7 evil that befell thee from thy youth until n. 6258
19: 9 n he is fled out of the land for Absalom. 6258
19:10 N therefore why speak ye not a word of 6258
19:32 N Barzillai was a very aged man, 2050.1
20: 6 N shall Sheba the son of Bichri do us more 6258
20:23 N Joab was over all the host of Israel: and 2050.1
21: 2 (n the Gibeonites were not of the children 2050.1
23: 1 N these be the last words of David. 2050.1

N

2Sa 24: 2 Go **n** through all the tribes of Israel, 4994
24: 3 **N** the LORD thy God add unto 2050.1
24:10 **n**, I beseech thee, O LORD, take away 6258
24:13 **n** advise, and see what answer I shall return 6258
24:14 let us fall **n** into the hand of the LORD; 4994
24:16 stay **n** thine hand. And the angel of 6258
1Ki 1: 1 **N** king David was old *and* stricken in 2050.1
1:12 **N** therefore come, let me, I pray thee, 6258
1:18 **n** behold, Adonijah reigneth; and now, 6258
1:18 **n**, my lord the king, thou knowest *it* not: 6258
2: 1 **N** the days of David drew nigh that *he* 2050.1
2: 9 **N** therefore hold him not guiltless: for thou 6258
2:16 **n** I ask one petition of thee, deny me not. 6258
2:24 **N** therefore, *as* the LORD liveth, 6258
3: 7 **n**, O LORD my God, thou hast made thy 6258
5: 4 **n** the LORD my God hath given me rest 6258
5: 6 **N** therefore command thou that they hew 6258
8:25 Therefore **n**, LORD God of Israel, 6258
8:26 **n**, O God of Israel, let thy word, I pray 6258
9:11 (*N* Hiram the king of Tyre had furnished NIH
10:14 **N** the weight of gold that came to 2050.1
12: 4 **n** therefore make thou the grievous service 6258
12:11 **n** whereas my father did lade you with a 6258
12:16 **n** see to thine own house, David. So Israel 6258
12:26 **N** shall the kingdom return to the house of 6258
13: 6 Intreat **n** the face of the LORD thy God, 4994
13:11 **N** there dwelt an old prophet in Beth-el; 2050.1
14:14 of Jeroboam that day: but what? even **n**. 6258
14:29 **N** the rest of the acts of Rehoboam, and 2050.1
15: 1 **N** in the eighteenth year of king 2050.1
15: 7 **N** the rest of the acts of Abijam, and 2050.1
15:31 **N** the rest of the acts of Nadab, and 2050.1
16: 5 **N** the rest of the acts of Baasha, and 2050.1
16:14 **N** the rest of the acts of Elah, and all that 2050.1
16:20 **N** the rest of the acts of Zimri, and 2050.1
16:27 **N** the rest of the acts of Omri which he 2050.1
17:24 **N** *by* this I know that thou *art* a man of 6258
18: 3 (**N** Obadiah feared the LORD greatly: 2050.1
18:11 **n** thou sayest, Go, tell thy lord, Behold, 6258
18:14 **n** thou sayest, Go, tell thy lord, Behold, 6258
18:19 **N** therefore send, *and* gather to me all Israel 6258
18:43 his servant, Go up **n**, look toward the sea. 4994
19: 4 *is* enough; **n**, O LORD, take away my life; 6258
20:31 his servants said unto him, Behold **n**, 4994
20:33 **N** the men did diligently observe whether 2050.1
21: 7 Dost thou **n** govern the kingdom of Israel? 6258
22:13 Micaiah spake unto him, saying, Behold **n** 4994
22:23 **N** therefore behold, the LORD hath put a 6258
22:39 **N** the rest of the acts of Ahab, and all that 2050.1
22:45 **N** the rest of the acts of Jehoshaphat, and 2050.1
2Ki 1: 4 **N** therefore thus saith the LORD, 2050.1
1: 5 said unto them, Why are ye **n** turned back? 2088
1:14 let my life **n** be precious in thy sight. 6258
1:18 **N** the rest of the acts of Ahaziah which he 2050.1
2:16 they said unto him, Behold **n**, there be with 4994
3: 1 **N** Jehoram the son of Ahab *began* to 2050.1
3:15 **n** bring me a minstrel. And it came to pass, 6258
3:23 **n** therefore, Moab, to the spoil. 6258
4: 1 **N** there cried a certain woman of 2050.1
4: 9 she said unto her husband, Behold **n**, 4994
4:13 he said unto him, Say **n** unto her, Behold, 4994
4:26 Run **n**, I pray thee, to meet her, and 6258
5: 1 **N** Naaman, captain of the host of the king 2050.1
5: 6 **N** when this letter is come unto thee, 6258
5: 8 let him come **n** to me, and he shall know 4994
5:15 **n** I know that *there is* no God in all 4994
5:15 **n** therefore, I pray thee, take a blessing of 6258
5:22 **even n** there be come to me from 2088+6258
6: 1 of the prophets said unto Elisha, Behold **n**, 4994
7: 4 **N** therefore come, and let us fall unto 6258
7: 9 **n** therefore come, that we may go and 6258
7:12 I will **n** shew you what the Syrians have 4994
7:19 the man of God, and said, **N**, behold, 2050.1
8: 6 the day that she left the land, even until **n**. 6258
9:12 they said, *It is* false; tell us **n**. And he said, 4994
9:14 (**N** Joram had kept Ramoth-gilead, he and 2050.1
9:26 **N** therefore take *and* cast him into the plat 6258
9:34 Go, see **n** this cursed *woman*, and bury her: 4994
10: 2 **N** as soon as this letter cometh to you, 6258
10: 6 **N** the king's sons, *being* seventy persons, 2050.1
10:10 Know **n** that there shall fall unto the earth 645
10:19 **N** therefore call unto me all the prophets of 6258
10:34 **N** the rest of the acts of Jehu, and all that 2050.1
12: 7 **n** therefore receive no *more* money of your 6258
13: 8 **N** the rest of the acts of Jehoahaz, and 2050.1
13:14 **N** Elisha was fallen sick of his sickness 2050.1
13:19 *it*: whereas **n** thou shalt smite Syria 6258
14:15 **N** the rest of the acts of Jehoash which he 2050.1
14:19 **N** they made a conspiracy against him in 2050.1
14:28 **N** the rest of the acts of Jeroboam, and 2050.1
15:36 **N** the rest of the acts of Jotham, and 2050.1
16:19 **N** the rest of the acts of Ahaz which he 2050.1
18: 1 **N** it came to pass in the third year of 2050.1
18:13 **N** in the fourteenth year of king Hezekiah 2050.1
18:19 Speak ye **n** to Hezekiah, Thus saith 4994
18:20 **N** on whom dost thou trust, that thou 6258
18:21 **N** behold, thou trustest upon the staff of 6258
18:23 **N** therefore, I pray thee, give pledges to my 6258
18:25 Am I **n** come up without the LORD 6258
19:19 **N** therefore, O LORD our God, I beseech 6258
19:25 **n** have I brought it to pass, that thou 6258
20: 3 remember **n** how I have walked before thee 4994
21:17 **N** the rest of the acts of Manasseh, and 2050.1
21:25 **N** the rest of the acts of Amon which he 2050.1
22:14 (**n** she dwelt in Jerusalem in the college;) 2050.1
23:28 **N** the rest of the acts of Josiah, and 2050.1
24: 5 **N** the rest of the acts of Jehoiakim, and 2050.1
25: 4 (**n** the Chaldees *were* against the city 2050.1
25:11 **N** the rest of the people that were left in 2050.1
1Ch 1:32 **N** the sons of Keturah, 2050.1
1:43 **N** these *are* the kings that reigned in 2050.1
2:34 **N** Sheshan had no sons, but daughters. 2050.1
2:42 **N** the sons of Caleb the brother of 2050.1
3: 1 **N** these were the sons of David, 2050.1
5: 1 **N** the sons of Reuben the firstborn of 2050.1

1Ch 6:54 **N** these *are* their dwelling places 2050.1
7: 1 **N** the sons of Issachar *were*, Tola, and 2050.1
8: 1 **N** Benjamin begat Bela his firstborn, 2050.1
9: 2 **N** the first inhabitants that *dwelt* in their 2050.1
10: 1 **N** the Philistines fought against Israel; 2050.1
11:15 **N** three of the thirty captains went down 2050.1
12: 1 **N** these *are* they that came to David to 2050.1
14: 1 **N** Hiram king of Tyre sent messengers to 2050.1
14: 4 **N** these *are* the names of *his* children 2050.1
17: 1 **N** it came to pass, as David sat in his 2050.1
17: 7 **N** therefore thus shalt thou say unto my 6258
17:23 Therefore **n**, LORD, let the thing that thou 6258
17:26 **n**, LORD, thou *art* God, and 6258
17:27 **N** therefore let it please thee to bless 6258
18: 1 **N** after this it came to pass, that David 2050.1
18: 9 **N when** Tou king of Hamath heard how 2050.1
19: 1 **N** it came to pass after this, that Nahash 2050.1
19:10 **N when** Joab saw that the battle was set 2050.1
21: 8 **n**, I beseech thee, do away the iniquity of 6258
21:12 **N** therefore advise thyself what word I shall 6258
21:13 let me fall **n** into the hand of the LORD; 4994
21:15 *It is* enough, stay **n** thine hand. 6258
21:20 **N** Ornan was threshing wheat. 2050.1
22: 5 I will *therefore* **n** make preparation for it. 4994
22:11 **N**, my son, the LORD be with thee; and 6258
22:14 **N**, behold, in my trouble I have prepared 2050.1
22:19 **N** set your heart and your soul to seek 6258
23: 3 **N** the Levites were numbered from 2050.1
23:14 **N** *concerning* Moses the man of God, 2050.1
24: 1 **N** *these are* the divisions of the sons of 2050.1
24: 7 **N** the first lot came forth to Jehoiarib, 2050.1
25: 9 **N** the first lot came forth for Asaph to 2050.1
27: 1 **N** the children of Israel after their 2050.1
28: 8 **N** therefore in the sight of all Israel 6258
28:10 Take heed **n**; for the LORD hath chosen 6258
29: 2 **N** I have prepared with all my might for 2050.1
29:13 **N** therefore, our God, we thank thee, and 6258
29:17 and **n** have I seen with joy thy people, 6258
29:20 **N** bless the LORD your God. 4994
29:29 **N** the acts of David the king, first and 2050.1
2Ch 1: 9 **N**, O LORD God, let thy promise unto 6258
1:10 Give me **n** wisdom and knowledge, that I 6258
2: 7 Send me **n** therefore a man cunning to 6258
2:13 **n** I have sent a cunning man, endued with 6258
2:15 **N** therefore the wheat, and the barley, 6258
3: 3 **N** these *are the things wherein* Solomon 2050.1
6: 7 **N** it was in the heart of David my father 2050.1
6:16 **N** therefore, O LORD God of Israel, 6258
6:17 **N** then, O LORD God of Israel, let thy 6258
6:40 **N**, my God, let, I beseech thee, thine eyes 6258
6:41 **N** therefore arise, O LORD God, into thy 6258
7: 1 **N** when Solomon had made an end of 2050.1
7:15 **N** mine eyes shall be open, and mine ears 6258
7:16 For **n** have I chosen and sanctified this 6258
8:16 **N** all the work of Solomon was prepared 2050.1
9:13 **N** the weight of gold that came to 2050.1
9:29 **N** the rest of the acts of Solomon, first 2050.1
10: 4 **n** therefore ease thou somewhat 6258
10:16 *and* **n**, David, see to thine own house. 6258
12:15 **N** the acts of Rehoboam, first and last, *are* 2050.1
13: 1 **N** in the eighteenth year of king Jeroboam NIH
13: 8 **n** ye think to withstand the kingdom of 6258
15: 3 **N** for a long season Israel *hath been* 2050.1
18: 1 **N** Jehoshaphat had riches and honour in 2050.1
18:22 **N** therefore behold, the LORD hath put a 6258
18:30 **N** the king of Syria had commanded 2050.1
19: 7 Wherefore **n** let the fear of the LORD be 6258
20:10 **n** behold, the children of Ammon and 6258
20:34 **N** the rest of the acts of Jehoshaphat, first 2050.1
21: 1 **N** Jehoshaphat slept with his fathers, and 2050.1
21: 4 **N when** Jehoram was risen up to 2050.1
23:12 **N when** Athaliah heard the noise of 2050.1
24:11 **N** it came to pass, that at *what* time 2050.1
24:17 **N** after the death of Jehoiada came 2050.1
24:27 **N** *concerning* his sons, and the greatness 2050.1
25: 3 **N** it came to pass, when the kingdom was 2050.1
25:14 **N** it came to pass, after that Amaziah was 2050.1
25:19 abide **n** at home; why shouldest thou 6258
25:26 **N** the rest of the acts of Amaziah, first 2050.1
25:27 **N** after the time that Amaziah did turn 2050.1
26:22 **N** the rest of the acts of Uzziah, first and 2050.1
27: 7 **N** the rest of the acts of Jotham, and 2050.1
28:10 **n** ye purpose to keep under the children of 6258
28:11 **N** hear me therefore, and deliver 6258
28:26 **N** the rest of his acts and of all his ways, 2050.1
29: 5 sanctify **n** yourselves, and sanctify 6258
29:10 **N** *it is* in mine heart to make a covenant 6258
29:11 My sons, be not **n** negligent: for 6258
29:17 **N** they began on the first *day* of the first 2050.1
29:31 **N** ye have consecrated yourselves unto 6258
30: 8 **N** be ye not stiffnecked, as your fathers 6258
31: 1 **N** when all this was finished, all Israel 2050.1
32:15 **N** therefore let not Hezekiah deceive you, 6258
32:32 **N** the rest of the acts of Hezekiah, and 2050.1
33:14 **N** after this he built a wall without 2050.1
33:18 **N** the rest of the acts of Manasseh, and 2050.1
34: 8 **N** in the eighteenth year of his reign, 2050.1
34:22 (**n** she dwelt in Jerusalem in the college:) 2050.1
35: 3 serve **n** the LORD your God, and his 6258
35:26 **N** the rest of the acts of Josiah, and 2050.1
36: 8 **N** the rest of the acts of Jehoiakim, and 2050.1
36:22 **N** in the first year of Cyrus king of Persia, 2050.1
Ezr 1: 1 **N** in the first year of Cyrus king of Persia, 2050.1
2: 1 **N** these *are* the children of the province 2050.1
3: 8 **N** in the second year of their coming unto 2050.1
4: 1 **N** *when* the adversaries of Judah and 2050.1
4:13 Be it known **n** unto the king, that, if this 3705
4:14 **N** because we have maintenance from 3705
4:21 Give ye **n** commandment to cause these 3705
4:22 Take heed **n** that ye fail not to do this: 2050.3
4:23 **N** when the copy of king Artaxerxes' 116+1768
5:16 since that time even until **n** *hath it been* in 3705
5:17 **N** therefore, if *it seem* good to the king, 3705
6: 6 **N** *therefore*, Tatnai, governor beyond 3705
7: 1 **N** after these things, in the reign of 2050.1

Ezr 7:11 **N** this *is* the copy of the letter that 2050.1
8: 1 These *are* **n** the chief of their fathers, and 2050.1
8:33 **N** on the fourth day was the silver and 2050.1
9: 1 **N** when these *things* were done, 2050.1
9: 8 **n** for a little space grace hath been *shewed* 6258
9:10 **n**, O our God, what shall we say after this? 6258
9:12 **N** therefore give not your daughters unto 2050.1
10: 1 **N** when Ezra had prayed, and when he 2050.1
10: 2 yet **n** there is hope in Israel concerning this 6258
10: 3 **N** therefore let us make a covenant with our 6258
10:11 **N** therefore make confession unto 6258
10:14 Let **n** our rulers of all the congregation 4994
Ne 1: 6 Let thine ear **n** be attentive, and thine eyes 4994
1: 6 which I pray before thee **n**, day and night, 3117
1:10 **N** these *are* thy servants and thy people, 2050.1
1:11 let **n** thine ear be attentive to the prayer of 4994
2: 1 **N** I had not been *beforetime* sad in his 2050.1
2: 9 **N** the king had sent captains of the army 2050.1
4: 3 **N** Tobiah the Ammonite *was* by him, and 2050.1
5: 5 Yet **n** our flesh *is* as the flesh of our 6258
5:18 **N** *that* which was prepared *for me* daily 2050.1
6: 1 **N** it came to pass, when Sanballat, and 2050.1
6: 7 **n** shall it be reported to the king according 6258
6: 7 Come **n** therefore, and let us take counsel 6258
6: 9 **N** therefore, *O God*, strengthen my hands. 6258
7: 1 **N** it came to pass, when the wall was 2050.1
7: 4 **N** the city *was* large and great: but 2050.1
9: 1 **N** in the twenty and fourth day of this 2050.1
9:32 **N** therefore, our God, the great, the mighty, 6258
10: 1 **N** those that sealed *were*, Nehemiah, 2050.1
11: 3 **N** these *are* the chief of the province that 2050.1
12: 1 **N** these *are* the priests and the Levites 2050.1
13: 3 **N** it came to pass, when they had heard 2050.1
Est 1: 1 **N** it came to pass in the days of 2050.1
2: 5 *N* in Shushan the palace there was a certain NIH
2:12 **N** when every maid's turn was come to 2050.1
2:15 **N** when the turn of Esther, the daughter 2050.1
3: 4 **N** it came to pass, when they spake daily 2050.1
5: 1 **N** it came to pass on the third day, 2050.1
6: 4 **N** Haman was come into the outward 2050.1
6: 6 **N** Haman thought in his heart, To whom 2050.1
9: 1 **N** in the twelfth month, that *is*, the month 2050.1
9:12 **n** what *is* thy petition? and it shall be 2050.1
Job 1: 6 **N** there was a day when the sons of God 2050.1
1:11 put forth thine hand **n**, and touch all that he 4994
2: 5 put forth thine hand **n**, and touch his bone 4994
2:11 **N when** Job's three friends heard of all 2050.1
3:13 For **n** should I have lien *still* and 6258
4: 5 **n** it is come upon thee, and thou faintest; 6258
4:12 **N** a thing was secretly brought to me, and 2050.1
5: 1 Call **n**, if there be *any* that will answer thee; 4994
6: 3 For **n** it would be heavier than the sand of 6258
6:21 For **n** ye are nothing; ye see *my* casting 6258
6:28 **N** therefore be content, look upon me; for *it* 6258
7:21 for **n** shall I sleep in the dust; and thou shalt 6258
8: 6 surely **n** he would awake for thee, and 6258
9:25 **N** my days are swifter than a post: 2050.1
12: 7 ask **n** the beasts, and they shall teach thee; 4994
13: 6 Hear **n** my reasoning, and hearken to 4994
13:18 Behold **n**, I have ordered *my* cause; I know 4994
13:19 for **n**, if I hold my tongue, I shall give up 6258
14:16 For **n** thou numberest my steps: dost thou 6258
16: 7 **n** he hath made me weary: thou hast made 6258
16:19 Also **n**, behold my witness *is* in heaven, 6258
17: 3 Lay down **n**, put me in a surety with thee; 4994
17:10 *as for* you all, do you return, and come **n**: 4994
17:15 where *is* **n** my hope? as for my hope, 645
19: 6 Know **n** that God hath overthrown me, and 645
19:23 O that my words were **n** written! O that they 645
22:21 Acquaint **n** thyself with him, and be at 4994
24:25 if *it be* not so **n**, who will make me a liar, 645
30: 1 **n** *they that are* younger than I have me in 6258
30: 9 **n** am I their song, yea, I am their byword. 6258
30:16 **n** my soul is poured out upon me; the days 6258
32: 4 **N** Elihu had waited till Job had spoken, 2050.1
32:14 **N** he hath not directed *his* words against 2050.1
33: 2 Behold **n** I have opened my mouth, 4994
34:16 If **n** *thou hast* understanding, hear this: 2050.1
35:15 **n**, because *it is* not *so*, he hath visited *in* his 6258
37:21 **n** *men* see not the bright light which *is* in 6258
38: 3 Gird up **n** thy loins like a man; for I will 4994
40: 7 Gird up thy loins **n** like a man: I will 4994
40:10 Deck thyself **n** with majesty and 4994
40:15 Behold **n** behemoth, which I made with 4994
40:16 Lo **n**, his strength *is* in his loins, and 4994
42: 5 of the ear: but **n** mine eye seeth thee. 6258
42: 8 Therefore take unto you **n** seven bullocks 6258
Ps 2:10 Be wise **n** therefore, O ye kings: 6258
12: 5 the needy, **n** will I arise, saith the LORD; 6258
17:11 They have **n** compassed us *in* our steps: 6258
20: 6 **N** know I that the LORD saveth his 6258
27: 6 **n** shall mine head be lifted up above mine 6258
37:25 I have been young, and *n* am old; yet have I NIH
39: 7 **n**, Lord, what wait I for? my hope *is* in 6258
41: 8 and **n** that he lieth he shall rise up no more. NIH
50:22 **N** consider this, ye that forget God, lest I 4994
71:18 **N** also when I am old and grayheaded, 2050.1
74: 6 **n** they break down the carved work thereof 6258
115: 2 the heathen say, Where *is* **n** their God? 4994
116:14 I will pay my vows unto the LORD **n** in 4994
116:18 I will pay my vows unto the LORD **n** in 4994
118: 2 Let Israel **n** say, that his mercy *endureth* for 4994
118: 3 Let the house of Aaron **n** say, that his 4994
118: 4 Let them **n** that fear the LORD say, 4994
118:25 Save **n**, I beseech thee, O LORD: 4994
118:25 I beseech thee, send **n** prosperity. 4994
119:67 I went astray: but **n** have I kept thy word. 6258
122: 8 and companions' sakes, I will **n** say, 4994
124: 1 who was on our side, **n** may Israel say; 4994
129: 1 me from my youth, may Israel **n** say: 4994
Pr 5: 7 Hear me **n** therefore, O ye children, and 6258
6: 3 Do this **n**, my son, and deliver thyself, 645
7:12 **N** *is she* without, now in the streets, and 6471
7:12 **n** in the streets, and lieth in wait at every 6471
7:24 Hearken unto me **n** therefore, O ye 6258

Pr 8:32 **N** therefore hearken unto me, O ye 6258
Ecc 2: 1 I said in mine heart, Go to **n**, I will prove 4994
2:16 seeing *that* which **n** *is, in* the days to come 3528
3:15 That which hath been, *is* **n**; and *that* which 3528
9: 6 their hatred, and their envy, is **n** perished; 3528
9: 7 for God **n** accepteth thy works. 3528
9:15 **N** there was found in it a poor wise man, 2050.1
12: 1 Remember **n** thy Creator in the days of 2050.1
SS 3: 2 I will rise **n**, and go about the city in 4994
7: 8 **n also** thy breasts shall be as clusters of 2050.1
Isa 1:18 Come **n**, and let us reason together, 4994
1:21 righteousness lodged in it; but **n** murderers. 6258
5: 1 **N** will I sing to my wellbeloved a song of 4994
5: 3 **n**, O inhabitants of Jerusalem, and men of 6258
5: 5 **n** go to, I will tell you what I *will* do to my 6258
7: 3 Go forth **n** to meet Ahaz, thou, and 4994
7:13 he said, Hear ye **n**, O house of David; *Is it* a 4994
8: 7 **N** therefore behold, the Lord bringeth up 2050.1
16:14 **n** the LORD hath spoken, saying, 6258
19:12 *are* thy wise *men?* and let them tell thee **n**, 4994
22: 1 What aileth thee **n**, that thou art wholly gone 645
28:22 **N** therefore be ye not mockers, lest your 6258
29:22 of Jacob, Jacob shall not **n** be ashamed, 6258
29:22 neither shall his face **n** wax pale. 6258
30: 8 **N** go, write it before them in a table, and 6258
31: 3 **N** the Egyptians *are* men, and not God; 2050.1
33:10 **N** will I rise, saith the LORD; now will I 6258
33:10 I rise, saith the LORD; **n** will I be exalted; 6258
33:10 will I be exalted; **n** will I lift up myself. 6258
36: 1 **N** it came to pass in the fourteenth year of 2050.1
36: 4 Say ye **n** to Hezekiah, Thus saith the great 4994
36: 5 **n** on whom dost thou trust, that thou 6258
36: 8 **N** therefore give pledges, I pray thee, to my 6258
36:10 am I **n** come up without the LORD 6258
37:20 **N** therefore, O LORD our God, save us 6258
37:26 **n** have I brought it to pass, that thou 6258
38: 3 said, Remember **n**, O LORD, I beseech 577
42:14 ***n*** will I cry like a travailing woman; I will NIH
43: 1 **n** thus saith the LORD that created thee, 6258
43:19 I will do a new *thing;* **n** it shall spring forth; 6258
44: 1 Yet **n** hear, O Jacob my servant; and Israel, 6258
47: 8 Therefore hear **n** this, *thou that art* given to 6258
47:12 Stand **n** with thine enchantments, and 4994
47:13 Let **n** the astrologers, the stargazers, 4994
48: 7 They are created **n**, and not from 6258
48:16 **n** the Lord GOD, and his Spirit, hath sent 6258
49: 5 **n**, saith the LORD that formed me from 6258
49:19 shall even **n** be too narrow by reason of 6258
51:21 Therefore hear **n** this, thou afflicted, and 4994
52: 5 **N** therefore, what have I here, saith 6258
64: 8 **n**, O LORD, thou *art* our father; we *are* 6258
Jer 2:18 **n** what hast thou to do in the way of Egypt, 6258
4:12 **n** also will I give sentence against them. 6258
4:31 spreadeth her hands, *saying,* Woe *is* me **n**! 4994
5: 1 see **n**, and know, and seek in the broad 4994
5:21 Hear **n** this, O foolish people, and 4994
5:24 Let us **n** fear the LORD our God, 4994
7:12 go ye **n** unto my place which *was* in Shiloh, 4994
7:13 **n**, because ye have done all these works, 6258
14:10 he will **n** remember their iniquity, and 6258
17:15 *is* the word of the LORD? let it come **n**. 4994
18:11 **N** therefore go to, speak to the men of 6258
18:11 return ye **n** every one from his evil way, 4994
18:13 Ask ye **n** among the heathen, who hath 4994
20: 1 **N** Pashur the son of Immer the priest, 2050.1
25: 5 Turn ye again **n** every one from his evil 4994
26: 8 **N** it came to pass, when Jeremiah had 2050.1
26:13 Therefore **n** amend your ways and 6258
27: 6 **n** have I given all these lands into the hand 6258
27:16 the vessels of the LORD'S house *shall* **n** 6258
27:18 let them **n** make intercession to the LORD 4994
28: 7 Nevertheless hear thou **n** this word that I 4994
28:15 Hananiah the prophet, Hear **n**, Hananiah; 4994
29: 1 **N** these *are* the words of the letter that 2050.1
29:27 **N** therefore why hast thou not reproved 2050.1
30: 6 Ask ye **n**, and see whether a man doth 4994
32:16 **N** when I had delivered the evidence of 2050.1
32:36 **n** therefore thus saith the LORD, the God 6258
34:10 ***N*** when all the princes, and all the people, NIH
34:15 ye were **n** turned, and had done 3117+1886.1
35:15 Return ye **n** every man from his evil way, 4994
36:15 Sit down **n**, and read it in our ears. 4994
36:16 **N** it came to pass when they had heard all 2050.1
36:17 they asked Baruch, saying, Tell us **n**, 4994
36:22 **N** the king sat *in* the winterhouse in 2050.1
37: 3 Pray **n** unto the LORD our God for us. 4994
37: 4 **N** Jeremiah came in and went out among 2050.1
37:19 Where *are* **n** your prophets which 2050.1
37:20 Therefore hear **n**, I pray thee, O my lord 6258
38: 7 **N when** Ebed-melech the Ethiopian, 2050.1
38:12 Put **n** *these* old cast clouts and rotten rags 4994
38:25 Declare unto us **n** what thou hast said unto 4994
39:11 **N** Nebuchadrezzar king of Babylon gave 2050.1
39:15 **N** the word of the LORD came unto 2050.1
40: 3 **N** the LORD hath brought *it,* and 2050.1
40: 4 **n** behold, I loose thee *this* day from 6258
40: 5 **N** while he was not yet gone back, 2050.1
40: 7 ***N*** when all the captains of the forces which NIH
41: 1 **N** it came to pass in the seventh month, 2050.1
41: 9 **N** the pit wherein Ishmael had cast all 2050.1
41:13 **N** it came to pass, *that* when all 2050.1
42:15 **n** therefore hear the word of the LORD, 6258
42:21 And **n** I have *this* day declared *it* to you; but NIH
42:22 **N** therefore know certainly that ye shall die 6258
44: 7 Therefore **n** thus saith the LORD, the God 6258
45: 3 Thou didst say, Woe is me **n**! for 4994
52: 7 (**n** the Chaldeans *were* by the city round 2050.1
52:12 **N** in the fifth month, in the tenth *day* of 2050.1
Eze 1: 1 **N** it came to pass in the thirtieth year, 2050.1
1:15 **N as** I beheld the living creatures, behold 2050.1
4:14 for from my youth up even till **n** have I not 6258
7: 3 **N** *is* the end *come* upon thee, and I will 6258
7: 8 **N** will I shortly pour out my fury upon 6258
8: 5 lift up thine eyes **n** the way towards 4994
8: 8 he unto me, Son of man, dig **n** in the wall: 4994

Eze 10: 3 **N** the cherubims stood on the right side of 2050.1
16: 8 **N when** I passed by thee, and 2050.1
17:12 Say **n** to the rebellious house, Know ye not 4994
18:14 **N** lo, *if* he beget a son, that seeth all his 2050.1
18:25 Hear **n**, O house of Israel; Is not my way 4994
19: 5 **N when** she saw that she had waited, *and* 2050.1
19:13 **n** she *is* planted in the wilderness, in a dry 6258
22: 2 **N**, thou son of man, wilt thou judge, wilt 2050.1
23:43 Will they **n** commit whoredoms with her, 6258
26: 2 I shall be replenished, ***n*** she is laid waste: NIH
26:18 **N** shall the isles tremble *in* the day of thy 6258
27: 2 **N**, thou son of man, take up a lamentation 2050.1
33:22 **N** the hand of the LORD was upon me 2050.1
38:12 the desolate places *that are* ***n*** inhabited, NIH
39:25 **N** will I bring again the captivity of Jacob, 6258
41:12 **N** the building that *was* before 2050.1
42: 5 **N** the upper chambers *were* shorter: 2050.1
42:15 **N when** he had made an end of 2050.1
43: 9 **N** let them put away their whoredom, and 6258
46:12 **N** when the prince shall prepare a 2050.1
47: 7 **N** when I had returned, behold, at 2050.1
48: 1 **N** these *are* the names of the tribes. 2050.1
Da 1: 6 **N** among these were of the children of 2050.1
1: 9 **N** God had brought Daniel into favour 2050.1
1:18 **N** at the end of the days that the king had 2050.1
2:23 hast made known unto me **n** what we 3705
2:23 for thou hast ***n*** made known unto us NIH
3:15 **N** if ye be ready that at what time ye hear 3705
4:18 **N** thou, O Belteshazzar, declare 2050.3
4:37 **N** I Nebuchadnezzar praise and extol and 3705
5:10 ***N*** the queen, by reason of the words of NIH
5:12 **n** let Daniel be called, and he will shew 3705
5:15 **n** the wise *men,* the astrologers, have been 3705
5:16 **n** if thou canst read the writing, and 3705
6: 8 **N**, O king, establish the decree, and 3705
6:10 **N** when Daniel knew that the writing *was* 2050.3
6:16 ***N*** the king spake and said unto Daniel, NIH
8:18 **N** as he was speaking with me, I was in a 2050.1
8:22 **N** that being broken, whereas four stood 2050.1
9:15 **n**, O Lord our God, that hast brought thy 6258
9:17 **N** therefore, O our God, hear the prayer of 6258
9:22 I am **n** come forth to give thee skill and 6258
10:11 for unto thee am I **n** sent. And when he had 6258
10:14 **N** I am come to make thee understand 2050.1
10:20 **n** will I return to fight with the prince of 6258
11: 2 **n** will I shew thee the truth. Behold, 6258
11:34 **N** when they shall fall, they shall be 2050.1
Hos 1: 8 **N when** she had weaned Lo-ruhamah, 2050.1
2: 7 for then *was it* better with me than **n**. 6258
2:10 **n** will I discover her lewdness in the sight 6258
4:16 **n** the LORD will feed them as a lamb in a 6258
5: 3 for **n**, O Ephraim, thou committest 6258
5: 7 **n** shall a month devour them with their 6258
7: 2 **n** their own doings have beset them about; 6258
8: 8 **n** shall they be among the Gentiles as a 6258
8:10 **n** will I gather them, and they shall sorrow 6258
8:13 **n** will he remember their iniquity, and 6258
10: 2 is divided; **n** shall they be found faulty: 6258
10: 3 For **n** they shall say, We have no king, 6258
13: 2 **n** they sin more and more, and have made 6258
Joel 2:12 Therefore also **n**, saith the LORD, turn ye 6258
Am 6: 7 Therefore **n** shall they go captive with 6258
7:16 **N** therefore hear thou the word of 6258
Jnh 1: 1 **N** the word of the LORD came unto 2050.1
1:17 **N** the LORD had prepared a great fish to 2050.1
3: 3 **N** Nineveh was an exceeding great city of 2050.1
4: 3 Therefore **n**, O LORD, take, I beseech 6258
Mic 4: 9 **N** why dost thou cry out aloud? *is there* no 6258
4:10 for **n** shalt thou go forth out of the city, and 6258
4:11 **N** also many nations are gathered against 6258
5: 1 **N** gather thyself in troops, O daughter of 6258
5: 4 for **n** shall he be great unto the ends of 6258
6: 1 Hear ye **n** what the LORD saith; Arise, 4994
6: 5 remember **n** what Balak king of Moab 4994
7: 4 **n** shall be their perplexity. 6258
7:10 **n** shall she be trodden down as the mire of 6258
Na 1:13 For **n** will I break his yoke from off thee, 6258
Hag 1: 5 **N** therefore thus saith the LORD of hosts; 6258
2: 2 Speak **n** to Zerubbabel the son of Shealtiel, 4994
2: 3 how do ye see it **n**? *is it* not in your eyes in 6258
2: 4 Yet **n** be strong, O Zerubbabel, saith 6258
2:11 Ask **n** the priests *concerning* the law, 4994
2:15 **n**, I pray you, consider from this day and 6258
2:18 Consider **n** from this day and upward, from 4994
Zec 1: 4 Turn ye **n** from your evil ways, and 4994
3: 3 **N** Joshua was clothed with filthy 2050.1
3: 8 Hear **n**, O Joshua the high priest, thou, and 4994
5: 5 Lift up **n** thine eyes, and see what *is* this 4994
8:11 **n** I *will* not *be* unto the residue of this 6258
9: 8 any more: for **n** have I seen with mine eyes. 6258
Mal 1: 8 offer it **n** unto thy governor; will he be 4994
1: 9 **n**, I pray you, beseech God that he will be 6258
2: 1 **n**, O ye priests, this commandment *is* for 6258
3:10 prove me **n** herewith, saith the LORD of 4994
3:15 **n** we call the proud happy; yea, they that 6258
Mt 1:18 **N** the birth of Jesus Christ was on this wise: *1161*
1:22 **N** all this was done, that it might be *1161*
2: 1 **N** when Jesus was born in Bethlehem of *1161*
3:10 And **n** also the axe is laid unto the root of *2235*
3:15 answering said unto him, Suffer *it to be so* **n**: *737*
4:12 **N** when Jesus had heard that John was cast *1161*
8:18 **N** when Jesus saw great multitudes about *1161*
9:18 saying, My daughter is **even n** dead: *737*
10: 2 **N** the names of the twelve apostles are *1161*
11: 2 **N** when John had heard in the prison *1161*
11:12 from the days of John the Baptist until **n** *737*
14:15 is a desert place, and the time is **n** past; *2235*
14:24 But the ship was **n** in the midst of the sea, *2235*
15:32 they continue with me **n** three days, *2235*
21:18 **N** in the morning as he returned into *1161*
22:25 **N** there were with us seven brethren: and the *1161*
24:32 **N** learn a parable of the fig tree; When his *1161*
26: 6 **N** when Jesus was in Bethany, in the house *1161*
26:17 **N** the first *day* of the *feast of* unleavened *1161*
26:20 **N** when the even was come, he sat down *1161*

Mt 26:45 Sleep on **n**, and take your rest: *3062+3588*
26:48 **N** he that betrayed him gave them a sign, *1161*
26:53 Thinkest thou that I cannot **n** pray to my NIG
26:59 **N** the chief priests, and elders, and all *1161*
26:65 behold, **n** ye have heard his blasphemy. *3568*
26:69 **N** Peter sat without in the palace: and *1161*
27:15 **N** at *that* feast the governor was wont to *1161*
27:42 let him **n** come down from the cross, and *3568*
27:43 let him deliver him **n**, if he will have him: *3568*
27:45 **N** from the sixth hour there was darkness *1161*
27:54 **N** when the centurion, and they that were *1161*
27:62 **N** the next day, that followed the *day of* *1161*
28:11 **N** when they were going, behold, some of *1161*
Mk 1:14 **N** after that John was put in prison, Jesus *1161*
1:16 **N** as he walked by the sea of Galilee, *1161*
4:37 beat into the ship, so that it was **n** full. *2235*
5:11 **N** there was there nigh unto the mountains *1161*
6:35 And when the day was **n** far spent, *2235*
6:35 a desert place, and **n** the time *is* far passed: *2235*
8: 2 they have **n** been with me three days, *2235*
8:14 **N** *the disciples* had forgotten to take bread, *2532*
10:30 But he shall receive an hundredfold **n** in *3568*
11:11 all *things,* and **n** the eventide was come, *2235*
12:20 **N** there were seven brethren: and the first NIG
13:12 **N** the brother shall betray the brother to *1161*
13:28 **N** learn a parable of the fig tree; When her *1161*
14:41 Sleep on **n**, and take your rest: *3062+3588*
15: 6 **N** at *that* feast he released unto them one *1161*
15:32 Let Christ the King of Israel descend **n** *3568*
15:42 And **n** when the even was come, because *2235*
16: 9 **N** when *Jesus* was risen early the first *day* *1161*
Lk 1: 7 and they both were ***n*** well stricken in years. NIG
1:57 **N** Elisabeth's full time came that she *1161*
2:15 Let us **n** go *even* unto Bethlehem, and *1211*
2:29 **n** lettest thou thy servant depart in peace, *3568*
2:41 **N** his parents went to Jerusalem every year *2532*
3: 1 **N** in the fifteenth year of the reign of *1161*
3: 9 And **n** also the axe is laid unto the root of *2235*
3:21 **N** when all the people were baptized, *1161*
4:40 **N** when the sun was setting, all they that *1161*
5: 4 **N** when he had left speaking, he said unto *1161*
6:21 Blessed *are ye* that hunger **n**: for ye shall be *3568*
6:21 Blessed *are ye* that weep **n**: for ye shall *3568*
6:25 Woe unto you that laugh **n**: for ye shall *3568*
7: 1 **N** when he had ended all his sayings in *1161*
7: 6 And when he was **n** not far from the house, *2235*
7:12 **N** when he came nigh to the gate of *1161*
7:39 **N** when the Pharisee which had bidden him *1161*
8:11 **N** the parable is this: The seed is the word *1161*
8:22 **N** it came to pass on a certain day, that he *1161*
8:38 **N** the man out of whom the devils were *1161*
9: 7 **N** Herod the tetrarch heard of all that was *1161*
10:36 Which **n** of these three, thinkest thou, *3767*
10:38 **N** it came to pass, as they went, that he *1161*
11: 7 the door is **n** shut, and my children are with *2235*
11:39 **N** do ye Pharisees make clean the outside *3568*
14:17 Come; for all *things* are **n** ready. *2235*
15:25 **N** his elder son was in the field: and as he *1161*
16:25 Lazarus evil *things:* but **n** he is comforted, *3568*
18:22 **N** when Jesus heard these *things,* he said *1161*
19:37 *even* **n** at the descent of the mount of *2235*
19:42 but **n** they are hid from thine eyes. *3568*
20:37 **N** that the dead are raised, even Moses *1161*
21:30 When they **n** shoot forth, ye see and *2235*
21:30 know of your own selves that summer is **n** *2235*
22: 1 **N** the feast of unleavened bread drew nigh, *1161*
22:36 But **n**, he that hath a purse, let him take *it,* *3568*
23:47 **N** when the centurion saw what was done, *1161*
24: 1 **N** upon the first *day* of the week, very early *1161*
Jn 1:44 **N** Philip was of Bethsaida, the city of *1161*
2: 8 Draw out **n**, and bear unto the governor of *3568*
2:10 *but* thou hast kept the good wine until **n**. *737*
2:23 **N** when he was in Jerusalem at *1161*
4: 6 **N** Jacob's well was there. Jesus therefore, *1161*
4:18 he whom thou **n** hast is not thy husband: *3568*
4:23 But the hour cometh, and **n** is, when *3568*
4:42 ***N*** we believe, not because of thy saying: NIG
4:43 **N** after two days he departed thence, and *1161*
4:51 And as he was **n** going down, his servants *2235*
5: 2 **N** there is at Jerusalem by the sheep *market* *1161*
5: 6 knew that he had been **n** a long time *in that* *2235*
5:25 say unto you, The hour is coming, and **n** is, *3568*
6:10 **N** there was much grass in the place. So *1161*
6:16 And when even was ***n*** come, his disciples NIG
6:17 And it was **n** dark, and Jesus was not come *2235*
7: 2 **N** the Jews' feast of tabernacles was at *1161*
7:14 **N about** the midst of the feast Jesus *1161+2235*
8: 5 **N** Moses in the law commanded us, *1161*
8:40 But **n** ye seek to kill me, a man that hath *3568*
8:52 unto him, **N** we know that thou hast a devil. *3568*
9:19 say was born blind? how then doth he **n** see? *737*
9:21 But by what means he **n** seeth, we know *3568*
9:25 I know, that, whereas I was blind, **n** I see. *737*
9:31 **N** we know that God heareth not sinners: *1161*
9:41 but **n** ye say, We see; therefore your sin *3568*
11: 1 **N** a certain *man* was sick, *named* Lazarus, *1161*
11: 5 **N** Jesus loved Martha, and her sister, and *1161*
11:18 **N** Bethany was nigh unto Jerusalem, *1161*
11:22 But I know, that even **n**, whatsoever thou *3568*
11:30 **N** Jesus was not yet come into the town, *1161*
11:57 **N** both the chief priests and the Pharisees *1161*
12:27 **N** is my soul troubled; and what shall I say? *3568*
12:31 **N** is the judgment of this world: now shall *3568*
12:31 **n** shall the prince of this world be cast out. *3568*
13: 1 **N** before the feast of the passover, *1161*
13: 2 the devil having **n** put into the heart of *2235*
13: 7 unto him, What I do thou knowest not **n**; *737*
13:19 **N** I tell you before it come, that, *575+737*
13:23 **N** there was leaning on Jesus' bosom one *1161*
13:28 **N** no *man* at the table knew for what intent *1161*
13:31 **N** is the Son of man glorified, and God is *3568*
13:33 I go, ye cannot come; so **n** I say to you. *737*
13:36 Whither I go, thou canst not follow me **n**; *3568*
13:37 unto him, Lord, why cannot I follow thee **n**? *737*
14:29 And **n** I have told you before it come to *3568*

Jn 15: 3 N ye are clean through the word which I 2235
15:22 but n they have no cloke for their sin. 3568
15:24 but n have they both seen and hated both 3568
16: 5 But n I go my way to him that sent me; and 3568
16:12 to say unto you, but ye cannot bear *them* n. 737
16:19 N Jesus knew that they were desirous to 3767
16:22 And ye n therefore have sorrow: but I will 3568
16:29 Lo, n speakest thou plainly, and 3568
16:30 N are we sure that thou knowest all *things,* 3568
16:31 Jesus answered them, Do ye n believe? 737
16:32 Behold, the hour cometh, yea, is n come, 3568
17: 5 And n, O Father, glorify thou me with thine 3568
17: 7 N they have known that all *things* 3568
17:11 And *n* I am no more in the world, but NIG
17:13 And n come I to thee; and these *things* I 3568
18:14 N Caiaphas was he, which gave counsel to 1161
18:24 N Annas had sent him bound unto Caiaphas 3767
18:36 but n is my kingdom not from hence. 3568
18:40 but Barabbas. N Barabbas was a robber. 1161
19:23 n the coat was without seam, woven from 1161
19:25 N there stood by the cross of Jesus his 1161
19:28 Jesus knowing that all *things* were n 2235
19:29 N there was set a vessel full of vinegar: and 3767
19:41 N in the place where he was crucified there 1161
21: 4 But when the morning was n come, 2235
21: 6 n they were **not** able to draw it for 3765
21: 7 N when Simon Peter heard that it was 3767
21:10 Bring of the fish which ye have n caught. 3568
21:14 This *is* n the third time that Jesus shewed 2235
Ac 1:18 N this *man* purchased a field with 3767
2: 6 N when this was noised abroad, 1161
2:33 shed forth this, which ye n see and hear. 3568
2:37 N when they heard *this,* they were pricked 1161
3: 1 N Peter and John went up together into 1161
3:17 And n, brethren, I wot that through 3568
4: 3 unto the next day: for it was n eventide. 2235
4:13 N when they saw the boldness of Peter and 1161
4:29 And n, Lord, behold their threatenings: and 3569
5:24 N when the *high* priest and the captain of 1161
5:38 And n I say unto you, Refrain from these 3569
7: 4 him into this land, wherein ye n dwell. 3568
7:11 N there came a dearth over all the land of 1161
7:34 And n come, I will send thee into Egypt. 3568
7:52 of whom ye have been n the betrayers and 3568
8:14 N when the apostles which were at 1161
9:36 N there was at Joppa a certain disciple 1161
10: 5 And n send men to Joppa, and call for *one* 3568
10:17 N while Peter doubted in himself what *this* 1161
10:33 N therefore are we all here present before 3568
11:19 N they which were scattered abroad upon 3767
12: 1 N about that time Herod the king stretched 1161
12:11 he said, N I know of a surety, that the Lord 3568
12:18 N as soon as it was day, there was no small 1161
13: 1 N there were in the church that was at 1161
13:11 And n behold, the hand of the Lord *is* upon 3568
13:13 N when Paul and his company loosed from 1161
13:34 *n* no more to return to corruption, he said on NIG
13:43 N when the congregation was broken up, 1161
15:10 N therefore why tempt ye God, to put a 3568
16: 6 N when they had gone throughout Phrygia 1161
16:36 you go: n therefore depart, and go in peace. 3568
16:37 and n do they thrust us out privily? 3568
17: 1 N when they had passed through 1161
17:16 N while Paul waited for them at Athens, his 1161
17:30 n commandeth all men every where to 3569
18:14 And when Paul was *n* about to open *his* NIG
20:22 And n, behold, I go bound in the spirit unto 3568
20:25 And n behold, I know that ye all, 3568
20:32 And n, brethren, I commend you to God, 3569
21: 3 N when we had discovered Cyprus, we left 1161
22: 1 hear ye my defence *which I make* n unto 3568
22:16 And n why tarriest thou? arise, and 3568
23:15 N therefore ye with the council signify to 3568
23:21 and n are they ready, looking for a promise 3568
24:13 prove *the things* whereof they n accuse me. 3568
24:17 N after many years I came to bring alms to 1161
25: 1 N when Festus was come into the province, 3767
26: 6 And n I stand and am judged for the hope 3568
26:17 the Gentiles, unto whom n I send thee, 3568
27: 9 N when much time was spent, and 1161
27: 9 and when sailing was n dangerous, because 2235
27: 9 because the fast was n **already** past, Paul 2235
27:22 And n I exhort you to be of good cheer: 3569
Ro 1:10 if by any means n at length I might have a 2235
1:13 N I would not have you ignorant, brethren, 1161
3:19 N we know that what *things* soever the law 1161
3:21 But n the righteousness of God without 3570
4: 4 N to him that worketh is the reward not 1161
4:19 he considered not his own body n dead, 2235
4:23 N it was not written for his sake alone, 1161
5: 9 more then, being n justified by his blood, 3568
5:11 by whom we have n received 3568
6: 8 N if we be dead with Christ, we believe 1161
6:19 n yield your members servants to 3568
6:21 *in those things* whereof ye are n ashamed? 3568
6:22 But n being made free from sin, and 3570
7: 6 But n we are delivered from the law, 3570
7:17 N then it is no more I that do it, but sin that 3570
7:20 N if I do that I would not, it is no more I 1161
8: 1 n no condemnation to them *which are* in 3568
8: 9 N if any *man* have not the Spirit of Christ, 1161
8:22 and travaileth in pain together until n. 3568
11:12 N if the fall of them *be* the riches of 1161
11:30 yet have n obtained mercy through their 3568
11:31 *Even* so have these also n not believed, 3568
13:11 n *it is* **high time** to awake out of 2235+5610
13:11 for n *is* our salvation nearer than when we 3568
14:15 *thy* meat, n walkest thou **not** charitably. 3765
15: 5 N the God of patience and consolation 1161
15: 8 N I say that Jesus Christ was a minister of 1161
15:13 N the God of hope fill you with all joy and 1161
15:23 But n having no more place in these parts, 3570
15:25 But n I go unto Jerusalem to minister unto 3570
15:30 N I beseech you, brethren, for the Lord 1161
15:33 N the God of peace *be* with you all. Amen. 1161

Ro 16:17 N I beseech you, brethren, mark them 1161
16:25 N to him that is of power to stablish you 1161
16:26 But n is made manifest, and by 3568
1Co 1:10 N I beseech you, brethren, by the name of 1161
1:12 N this I say, that every one of you saith, I 1161
2:12 N we have received, not the spirit of 1161
3: 2 *to bear it,* neither yet n are ye able. 2089+3568
3: 8 N he that planteth and he that watereth are 1161
3:12 N if any *man* build upon this foundation 1161
4: 7 n if thou didst receive *it,* why dost thou 1161
4: 8 N ye are full, now ye are rich, ye have 2235
4: 8 Now ye are full, n ye are rich, ye have 2235
4:18 N some are puffed up, as though I would 1161
5:11 But n I have written unto you not to keep 3570
6: 7 N therefore there is utterly a fault among 2235
6:13 N the body *is* not for fornication, but 1161
7: 1 N concerning *the things* whereof ye wrote 1161
7:14 your children unclean; but n are they holy. 3568
7:25 N concerning virgins I have no 1161
8: 1 N as touching things offered unto idols, 1161
9:25 N they *do it* to obtain a corruptible crown; 3767
10: 6 N these *things* were our examples, to 1161
10:11 N all these *things* happened unto them for 1161
11: 2 N I praise you, brethren, that you remember 1161
11:17 N in this that I declare *unto you* I praise 1161
12: 1 N concerning spiritual *gifts,* brethren, 1161
12: 4 N there are diversities of gifts, but the same 1161
12:18 But n hath God set the members every one 3570
12:20 But n *are they* many members, yet *but* 3568
12:27 N ye are the body of Christ, and 1161
13:12 For n we see through a glass, darkly; 737
13:12 n I know in part; but then shall I know even 737
13:13 And n abideth faith, hope, charity, 3570
14: 6 N, brethren, if I come unto you speaking 3570
15:12 N if Christ be preached that he rose from 1161
15:20 But n is Christ risen from the dead, *and* 3570
15:50 N this I say, brethren, that flesh and 1161
16: 1 N concerning the collection for the saints, 1161
16: 5 N I will come unto you, when I shall pass 1161
16: 7 For I will not see you n by the way; but I 737
16:10 N if Timotheus come, see that he may be 1161
2Co 1:21 N he which stablisheth us with you in 1161
2:14 N thanks *be* unto God, which always 1161
3:17 N the Lord is *that* Spirit: and where 1161
5: 5 N he that hath wrought us for the selfsame 1161
5:16 yet n **henceforth** know we *him* no more. 3568
5:20 *N* then we are ambassadors for Christ, NIG
6: 2 behold, n *is* the accepted time; behold, 3568
6: 2 behold, n *is* the day of salvation.) 3568
6:13 N for a recompence in the same, (I speak as 1161
7: 9 N I rejoice, not that ye were made sorry, 3568
8:11 N therefore perform the doing *of it;* that as 3570
8:14 *that* n at *this* time your abundance *may be a* 3568
8:22 in many *things,* but n much more diligent, 3570
9:10 N he that ministereth seed to the sower 1161
10: 1 N I Paul myself beseech you by 1161
12: 6 but *n* I forbear, lest any *man* should think of NIG
13: 2 being absent n I write to them which 3568
13: 7 N I pray to God that ye do no evil; not that 1161
Gal 1: 9 As we said before, so say I n again, If any 737
1:10 For do I n persuade men, or God? or do I 737
1:20 N *the things* which I write unto you, 1161
1:23 That he which persecuted us in times past n 3568
2:20 *the life* which I n live in the flesh I live by 3568
3: 3 are ye n made perfect by the flesh? 3568
3:16 N to Abraham and his seed were 1161
3:20 N a mediator is not *a mediator* of one, but 1161
4: 1 N I say, *That* the heir, as long as he is a 1161
4: 9 But n, after that ye have known God, or 3568
4:20 I desire to be present with you n, and 737
4:25 and answereth to Jerusalem which n is, and 3568
4:28 N we, brethren, as Isaac was, are 1161
4:29 was *born* after the Spirit, even so *it is* n. 3568
5:19 N the works of the flesh are manifest, 1161
Eph 2: 2 the spirit that n worketh in the children of 3568
2:13 But n in Christ Jesus ye who sometimes 3570
2:19 N therefore ye are no more strangers and 686
3: 5 as it is n revealed unto his holy apostles 3568
3:10 To the intent that n unto the principalities 3568
3:20 N unto him that is able to do exceeding 1161
4: 9 (N that he ascended, what is it but that he 1161
5: 8 but n *are ye* light in the Lord: 3568
Php 1: 5 in the gospel from the first day until n; 3568
1:20 n also Christ shall be magnified in my 3568
1:30 ye saw in me, and n hear *to be* in me. 3568
2:12 but n much more in my absence, 3568
3:18 you often, and n tell *you* even weeping, 3568
4:10 that n at the last your care of me hath 2235
4:15 N ye Philippians know also, that in 1161
4:20 N unto God and our Father *be* glory for 1161
Col 1:21 by wicked works, yet n hath he reconciled 3570
1:24 Who n rejoice in my sufferings for you, 3568
1:26 but n is made manifest to his saints: 3570
3: 8 But n you also put off all *these;* anger, 3570
1Th 3: 6 But n when Timotheus came from you unto 737
3: 8 For n we live, if ye stand fast in the Lord. 3568
3:11 N God himself and our Father, and 1161
5:14 N we exhort you, brethren, warn *them that* 1161
2Th 2: 1 N we beseech you, brethren, by the coming 1161
2: 6 And n ye know what withholdeth that he 3568
2: 7 only he who n letteth *will let,* until he be 737
2:16 N our Lord Jesus Christ himself, and God, 1161
3: 6 N we command you, brethren, in the name 1161
3:12 N *them that are* such we command and 1161
3:16 N the Lord of peace himself give you peace 1161
1Ti 1: 5 N the end of the commandment is charity 1161
1:17 N unto the King eternal, immortal, 1161
4: 1 N the Spirit speaketh expressly, that in 1161
4: 8 *things,* having promise of the life that n is, 3568
5: 5 N she that is a widow indeed, and desolate, 1161
2Ti 1:10 But is n made manifest by the appearing of 3568
3: 8 N as Jannes and Jambres withstood Moses, 1161
4: 6 For I am n **ready** to be offered, and 2235
Phm 1: 9 and n also a prisoner of Jesus Christ. 3570
1:11 but n profitable to thee and to me: 3570

Phm 1:16 **Not** n as a servant, but above a servant, 3765
Heb 2: 8 But n we see not yet all *things* put under 3568
7: 4 N consider how great this *man was,* unto 1161
8: 1 N of the *things* which we have spoken *this* 1161
8: 6 But n hath he obtained a more excellent 3570
8:13 N that which decayeth and waxeth old *is* 1161
9: 5 of which *we* cannot n speak particularly. 3568
9: 6 N when these *things* were thus ordained, 1161
9:24 n to appear in the presence of God for us: 3568
9:26 n once in the end of the world hath he 3568
10:18 N where remission of these *is, there is* no 1161
10:38 N the just shall live by faith: but if *any man* 1161
11: 1 N faith is the substance of *things* hoped for, 1161
11:16 But n they desire a better *country,* that is, 3570
12:11 N no chastening for the present seemeth to 1161
12:26 but n he hath promised, saying, Yet once 3568
13:20 N the God of peace, that brought again 1161
Jas 2:11 N if thou commit no adultery, yet *if* thou 1161
4:13 Go to n, ye that say, To day or to morrow 3568
4:16 But n ye rejoice in your boastings: all such 3568
5: 1 Go to n, *ye* rich *men,* weep and howl for 3568
1Pe 1: 6 though n for a season, if need be, 737
1: 8 in whom, though n ye see *him* not, 737
1:12 which are n reported unto you by them that 3568
2:10 not a people, but *are* n the people of God: 3568
2:10 but n have obtained mercy. 3568
2:25 but are n returned unto the Shepherd and 3568
3:21 n save us (not the putting away of the filth 3568
2Pe 2: 3 whose judgment n of a long time lingereth NIG
3: 1 second epistle, beloved, I n write unto you; 2235
3: 7 But the heavens and the earth, which are n, 3568
3:18 To him *be* glory both n and for ever. Amen. 3568
1Jn 2: 8 is past, and the true light n shineth. 2235
2: 9 his brother, is in darkness *even* until n. 737
2:18 even n are there many antichrists; 3568
2:28 And n, little children, abide in him; that, 3568
3: 2 n are we the sons of God, and it doth not 3568
4: 3 and *even* n already is it in the world. 3568
2Jn 1: 5 And n I beseech thee, lady, not as though I 3568
Jude 1:24 N unto him that is able to keep you from 1161
1:25 dominion and power, both n and ever. 3568
Rev 12:10 N is come salvation, and strength, and 737

NULLIFIES See VOID

NULLIFY See NOUGHT; VOID

NUMBER (178) [NUMBERED, NUMBEREST, NUMBERING, NUMBERS]

Ge 13:16 so that if a man can n the dust of the earth, 4487
15: 5 and tell the stars, if thou be able to n them: 5608
34:30 I *being* few in n, they shall gather 4557
41:49 he left numbering; for *it was* without n. 4557
Ex 12: 4 take *it* according to the n of the souls; 4373
16:16 *according to* the n of your persons; 4557
23:26 in thy land: the n of thy days I will fulfil. 4557
30:12 sum of the children of Israel after their n, 6485
Lev 15:13 he shall n to himself seven days for his 5608
15:28 she shall n to herself seven days, and 5608
23:16 the seventh sabbath shall ye n fifty days; 5608
25: 8 thou shalt n seven sabbaths of years unto 5608
25:15 According to the n of years after the jubile 4557
25:15 according unto the n of years of the fruits 4557
25:16 for *according to* the n *of the years* of 4557
25:50 sale shall be according unto the n of years, 4557
26:22 your cattle, and **make** you **few in** n; 4591
Nu 1: 2 with the n of *their* names, every male by 4557
1: 3 and Aaron shall n them by their armies. 6485
1:18 according to the n of the names, 4557
1:20 according to the n of the names, by their 4557
1:22 according to the n of the names, by their 4557
1:24 according to the n of the names, 4557
1:26 according to the n of the names, 4557
1:28 according to the n of the names, 4557
1:30 according to the n of the names, 4557
1:32 according to the n of the names, 4557
1:34 according to the n of the names, 4557
1:36 according to the n of the names, 4557
1:38 according to the n of the names, 4557
1:40 according to the n of the names, 4557
1:42 according to the n of the names, 4557
1:49 Only thou shalt not n the tribe of Levi, 6485
3:15 N the children of Levi after the house of 6485
3:15 a month old and upward shalt thou n them. 6485
3:22 according to the n of all the males, from a 4557
3:28 In the n of all the males, from a month old 4557
3:34 according to the n of all the males, from a 4557
3:40 N all the firstborn of the males of 6485
3:40 and upward, and take the n of their names. 4557
3:43 all the firstborn males by the n of names, 4557
3:48 wherewith the **odd** n of them is *to be* 5736
4:23 upward until fifty years old shalt thou n 6485
4:29 thou shalt n them after their families, 6485
4:30 even unto fifty years old shalt thou n them, 6485
4:37 Aaron did n according to 6485
4:41 Aaron did n according to 6485
14:29 according to your whole n, from twenty 4557
14:34 After the n of the days *in* which ye 4557
15:12 According to the n that ye shall prepare, so 4557
15:12 ye do to *every* one according to their n 4557
23:10 and the n *of* the fourth part of Israel? 4557
26:53 an inheritance according to the n of names. 4557
29:18 for the lambs, *shall be* according to their n, 4557
29:21 for the lambs, *shall be* according to their n, 4557
29:24 for the lambs, *shall be* according to their n, 4557
29:27 for the lambs, *shall be* according to their n, 4557
29:30 for the lambs, *shall be* according to their n, 4557
29:33 for the lambs, *shall be* according to their n, 4557
29:37 for the lambs, *shall be* according to their n, 4557
31:36 was *in* n three hundred thousand and seven 4557
Dt 4:27 ye shall be left few in n among the heathen, 4557
7: 7 because ye were moe in n than any people; 7230
16: 9 Seven weeks shalt thou n unto thee: 5608
16: 9 begin to n the seven weeks from *such time* 5608
25: 2 according to his fault, by a *certain* n. 4557

Dt 28:62 ye shall be left few in n, whereas ye were 4962
32: 8 according to the n of the children of Israel. 4557
Jos 4: 5 according unto the n of the tribes of 4557
4: 8 according to the n of the tribes of 4557
Jdg 6: 5 both they and their camels were without n: 4557
7: 6 the n of them that lapped, putting their 4557
7:12 their camels *were* without n, as the sand by 4557
21:23 took *them* wives, according to their n, 4557
1Sa 6: 4 *according to* the n of the lords of 4557
6:18 *according to* the n of all the cities of 4557
14:17 N now, and see who is gone from us. 6485
2Sa 2:15 and went over by n twelve of Benjamin, 4557
21:20 on every foot six toes, four and twenty *in* n; 4557
24: 1 against them to say, Go, n Israel and Judah. 4487
24: 2 even to Beer-sheba, and n ye the people, 6485
24: 2 that I may know the n of the people. 4557
24: 4 of the king, to n the people *of* Israel. 6485
24: 9 Joab gave *up* the sum of the n of the people 4662
1Ki 18:31 according to the n of the tribes of the sons 4557
20:25 n thee an army, like the army that thou hast 4487
1Ch 7: 2 whose n *was* in the days of David two and 4557
7: 9 the n of them, **after** their **genealogy** by 3187
7:40 the n throughout the genealogy of them *that* 4557
11:11 this *is* the n of the mighty *men* whom 4557
21: 1 and provoked David to n Israel. 4487
21: 2 Go, n Israel from Beer-sheba even to Dan; 5608
21: 2 bring the n of them to me, that I may know 4557
21: 5 Joab gave the sum of the n of the people 4662
22:16 and the brass, and the iron, *there is* no n. 4557
23: 3 their n by their polls, man by man, 4557
23:24 as they were counted by n of names by 4557
23:31 the new moons, and on the set feasts, by n, 4557
25: 1 the n of the workmen according to their 4557
25: 7 So the n of them, with their brethren *that* 4557
27: 1 Now the children of Israel after their n, 4557
27:23 David took not the n of them from twenty 4557
27:24 Joab the son of Zeruiah began to n, but 4487
27:24 neither was the n put in the account of 4557
2Ch 12: 3 the people *were* without n that came with 4557
26:11 according to the n of their account by 4557
26:12 The whole n of the chief of the fathers of 4557
29:32 the n of the burnt offerings, which 4557
30:24 **great** n of priests sanctified 7230+3807.1
35: 7 to the n of thirty thousand, and 4557
Ezr 1: 9 this *is* the n of them: thirty chargers of 4557
2: 2 The n of the men of the people of Israel: 4557
3: 4 and *offered* the daily burnt offerings by n, 4557
6:17 according to the n of the tribes of Israel. 4510
8:34 By n *and* by weight of every one: and 4557
Ne 7: 7 The n, *I say,* of the men of the people of 4557
Est 9:11 On that day the n of those that were slain in 4557
Job 1: 5 offered burnt offerings *according to* the n 4557
3: 6 let it not come into the n of the months. 4557
5: 9 unsearchable; marvellous *things* without n: 4557
9:10 finding out; yea, and wonders without n. 4557
14: 5 the n of his months *are* with thee, 4557
15:20 the n of years is hidden to the oppressor. 4557
21:21 when the n of his months is cut off in 4557
25: 3 Is there *any* n of his armies? and 4557
31:37 I would declare unto him the n of my steps; 4557
34:24 shall break in pieces mighty *men* without n, 2714
36:26 neither can the n of his years be searched 4557
38:21 born? or *because* the n of thy days *is* great? 4557
38:37 Who can n the clouds in wisdom? or 5608
39: 2 Canst thou n the months *that* they fulfil? or 5608
Ps 90:12 So teach *us* to n our days, that we may 4487
105:12 When they were *but a few* men in n; yea, 4557
105:34 and caterpillars, and that without n, 4557
139:18 they are moe in n than the sand: 7235
147: 4 He telleth the n of the stars; he calleth them 4557
SS 6: 8 and virgins without n. 4557
Isa 21:17 the residue of the n of archers, the mighty 4557
40:26 *things,* that bringeth out their host by n: 4557
65:11 that furnish the drink offering unto *that* n. 4507
65:12 Therefore will I n you to the sword, and 4487
Jer 2:28 for *according* to the n of thy cities are thy 4557
2:32 people have forgotten me days without n. 4557
11:13 For *according to* the n of thy cities were thy 4557
11:13 *according to* the n of the streets of 4557
44:28 Yet a small n that escape the sword shall 4557
Eze 4: 4 *according to* the n of the days that thou 4557
4: 5 according to the n of the days, 4557
4: 9 *according to* the n of the days that thou 4557
5: 3 Thou shalt also take thereof a few in n, and 4557
Da 9: 2 understood by books the n of the years, 4557
Hos 1:10 Yet the n of the children of Israel shall be 4557
Joel 1: 6 strong, and without n, whose teeth *are* 4557
Na 3: 3 of slain, and a **great** n of carcases; 3514
Mk 10:46 with his disciples and a **great** n of people, *2425*
Lk 22: 3 being of the n of the twelve. *706*
Jn 6:10 the men sat down, *in* n about five thousand. *706*
Ac 1:15 (the n of names together were about an *3793*
4: 4 the n of the men was about five thousand. *706*
5:36 to whom a n of men, about four hundred, *706*
6: 1 when the n of the disciples was multiplied, NIG
6: 7 the n of the disciples multiplied in Jerusalem *706*
11:21 and a great n believed, and turned unto *706*
16: 5 in the faith, and increased in n daily. *706*
Ro 9:27 Though the n of the children of Israel be as *706*
2Co 10:12 For we dare not **make** *ourselves* **of the** n, *1469*
1Ti 5: 9 Let not a widow be **taken into the** n under *2639*
Rev 5:11 the n of them was ten thousand times ten *706*
7: 4 And I heard the n of them which were *706*
7: 9 which no *man* could n, of all nations, and *705*
9:16 And the n of the army of the horsemen *were* *706*
9:16 and I heard the n of them. *706*
13:17 the name of the beast, or the n of his name. *706*
13:18 Let him that hath understanding count the n *706*
13:18 for it is the n of a man; and his number *is* *706*
13:18 and his n *is* Six hundred threescore *and* six. *706*
15: 2 over his mark, *and* over the n of his name, *706*
20: 8 the n of whom *is* as the sand of the sea. *706*

NUMBERED (128) [NUMBER]
Ge 13:16 of the earth, *then* shall thy seed also be n. 4487
16:10 that it shall not be n for multitude. 5608
32:12 of the sea, which cannot be n for multitude. 5608
Ex 30:13 one that passeth among them that are n, 6485
30:14 one that passeth among them that are n, 6485
38:25 the silver of them that were n of 6485
38:26 for every one that went to be n, 6485
Nu 1:19 so he n them in the wilderness of Sinai. 6485
1:21 Those that were n of them, *even* of the tribe 6485
1:22 of their fathers, those that were n of them, 6485
1:23 Those that were n of them, *even* of the tribe 6485
1:25 Those that were n of them, *even* of the tribe 6485
1:27 Those that were n of them, *even* of the tribe 6485
1:29 Those that were n of them, *even* of the tribe 6485
1:31 Those that were n of them, *even* of the tribe 6485
1:33 Those that were n of them, *even* of the tribe 6485
1:35 Those that were n of them, *even* of the tribe 6485
1:37 Those that were n of them, *even* of the tribe 6485
1:39 Those that were n of them, *even* of the tribe 6485
1:41 Those that were n of them, *even* of the tribe 6485
1:43 Those that were n of them, *even* of the tribe 6485
1:44 These *are* those that were n, which Moses 6485
1:44 which Moses and Aaron n, and the princes 6485
1:45 So were all those that were n of 6485
1:46 Even all they that were n were six hundred 6485
1:47 of their fathers were not n among them. 6485
2: 4 his host, and those that were n of them, 6485
2: 6 those that were n thereof, *were* fifty and 6485
2: 8 those that were n thereof, *were* fifty and 6485
2: 9 All that were n in the camp of Judah *were* 6485
2:11 those that were n thereof, *were* forty and 6485
2:13 those that were n of them, *were* fifty and 6485
2:15 those that were n of them, *were* forty and 6485
2:16 All that were n in the camp of Reuben *were* 6485
2:19 his host, and those that were n of them, 6485
2:21 those that were n of them, *were* thirty and 6485
2:23 those that were n of them, *were* thirty and 6485
2:24 All that were n of the camp of Ephraim 6485
2:26 his host, and those that were n of them, 6485
2:28 those that were n of them, *were* forty and 6485
2:30 those that were n of them, *were* fifty and 6485
2:31 All they that were n in the camp of Dan 6485
2:32 These *are* those which were n of 6485
2:32 all those that were n of the camps 6485
2:33 the Levites were not n among the children 6485
3:16 Moses n them according to the word of 6485
3:22 Those that were n of them, according to 6485
3:22 *even* those that were n of them *were* seven 6485
3:34 those that were n of them, according to 6485
3:39 All that were n of the Levites, which Moses 6485
3:39 Aaron n at the commandment of 6485
3:42 Moses n, as the LORD commanded him, 6485
3:43 and upward, of those that were n of them, 6485
4:34 the chief of the congregation n the sons of 6485
4:36 those that were n of them by their families 6485
4:37 These *were* they that were n of the families 6485
4:38 those that were n of the sons of Gershon, 6485
4:40 Even those that were n of them, 6485
4:41 These *are* they that were n of the families 6485
4:42 those that were n of the families of the sons 6485
4:44 Even those that were n of them after their 6485
4:45 These *be* those that were n of the families 6485
4:45 Aaron n according to the word of 6485
4:46 All those that were n of the Levites, 6485
4:46 and Aaron and the chief of Israel n, 6485
4:48 Even those that were n of them, were eight 6485
4:49 LORD they were n by the hand of Moses, 6485
4:49 thus *were they* n of him, as the LORD 6485
7: 2 and were over them that were n, offered: 6485
14:29 all that were n of you, according to your 6485
26: 7 and they that were n of them were forty and 6485
26:18 Gad according to those that were n of them, 6485
26:22 according to those that were n of them, 6485
26:25 according to those that were n of them, 6485
26:27 according to those that were n of them, 6485
26:34 those that were n of them, fifty and 6485
26:37 according to those that were n of them, 6485
26:41 and they that were n of them *were* forty and 6485
26:43 according to those that were n of them, 6485
26:47 according to those that were n of them; 6485
26:50 and they that were n of them *were* forty and 6485
26:51 These *were* the n of the children of Israel, 6485
26:54 according to those that were n of him. 6485
26:57 these *are* they that were n of the Levites 6485
26:62 those that were n of them were twenty and 6485
26:62 for they were not n among the children of 6485
26:63 These *are* they that were n by Moses and 6485
26:63 who n the children of Israel in the plains of 6485
26:64 them whom Moses and Aaron the priest n, 6485
26:64 when they n the children of Israel in 6485
Jos 8:10 n the people, and went up, he and the elders 6485
Jdg 20:15 the children of Benjamin were n at that 6485
20:15 *which* were n seven hundred chosen men. 6485
20:17 were n four hundred thousand men that 6485
21: 9 For the people were n, and behold, 6485
1Sa 11: 8 when he n them in Bezek, the children of 6485
13:15 Saul n the people that were present with 6485
14:17 when they had n, behold Jonathan and 6485
15: 4 n them in Telaim, two hundred thousand 6485
2Sa 18: 1 David n the people that *were* with him, 6485
24:10 David's heart smote him after that he had n 5608
1Ki 3: 8 that cannot be n nor counted for multitude. 4487
8: 5 that could not be told nor n for multitude. 4487
20:15 he n the young men of the princes of 6485
20:15 after them he n all the people, *even* all 6485
20:26 that Ben-hadad n the Syrians, and went up 6485
20:27 the children of Israel were n, and were all 6485
2Ki 3: 6 of Samaria the same time, and n all Israel. 6485
1Ch 21:17 *it* not I *that* commanded the people to be n? 4487
23: 3 Now the Levites were n from the age of 5608
23:27 the Levites *were* n from twenty years old 4557
2Ch 2:17 Solomon n all the strangers that *were* in 5608
2:17 where*with* David his father had n them; 5608
5: 6 which could not be told nor n for multitude. 4487
25: 5 he n them from twenty years old and 6485
Ezr 1: 8 n them unto Sheshbazzar, the prince of 5608
Ps 40: 5 speak *of them,* they are moe than can be n. 5608
Ecc 1:15 and that which is wanting cannot be n. 4487
Isa 22:10 And ye have n the houses of Jerusalem, and 5608
53:12 he was n with the transgressors; and 4487
Jer 33:22 As the host of heaven cannot be n, 5608
Da 5:26 God hath n thy kingdom, and finished it. 4483
Hos 1:10 the sea, which cannot be measured nor n; 5608
Mt 10:30 But the very hairs of your head are all n. *705*
Mk 15:28 And he was n with the transgressors. *3049*
Lk 12: 7 even the *very* hairs of your head are all n. *705*
Ac 1:17 For he was n with us, and had obtained part *2674*
1:26 and he was n with the eleven apostles. *4785*

NUMBEREST (3) [NUMBER]
Ex 30:12 soul unto the LORD, when *thou* n them; 6485
30:12 plague amongst them, when *thou* n them. 6485
Job 14:16 For now thou n my steps: dost thou not 5608

NUMBERING (2) [NUMBER]
Ge 41:49 sand of the sea, very much, until he left n; 5608
2Ch 2:17 after the n where*with* David his father had 5610

NUMBERS (3) [NUMBER]
1Ch 12:23 these *are* the n of the bands that were ready 4557
2Ch 17:14 these *are* the n of them according to 6486
Ps 71:15 all the day; for I know not the n *thereof.* 5615

NUMEROUS See POPULOUS

NUN (29)
Ex 33:11 servant Joshua, the son of N, a young man, 5126
Nu 11:28 Joshua the son of N, the servant of Moses, 5126
13: 8 the tribe of Ephraim, Oshea the son of N. 5126
13:16 Moses called Oshea the son of N, Jehoshua. 5126
14: 6 Joshua the son of N, and Caleb the son of 5126
14:30 son of Jephunneh, and Joshua the son of N. 5126
14:38 Joshua the son of N, and Caleb the son of 5126
26:65 son of Jephunneh, and Joshua the son of N. 5126
27:18 Take thee Joshua the son of N, a man in 5126
32:12 the Kenezite, and Joshua the son of N: 5126
32:28 Joshua the son of N, and the chief fathers 5126
34:17 Eleazar the priest, and Joshua the son of N. 5126
Dt 1:38 *But* Joshua the son of N, which standeth 5126
31:23 he gave Joshua the son of N a charge, 5126
32:44 of the people, he and Hoshea the son of N. 5126
34: 9 Joshua the son of N was full *of* the spirit of 5126
Jos 1: 1 LORD spake unto Joshua the son of N, 5126
2: 1 Joshua the son of N sent out of Shittim two 5126
2:23 came to Joshua the son of N, and told him 5126
6: 6 Joshua the son of N called the priests, and 5126
14: 1 Joshua the son of N, and the heads of 5126
17: 4 before Joshua the son of N, and before 5126
19:49 to Joshua the son of N among them: 5126
19:51 Joshua the son of N, and the heads of 5126
21: 1 unto Joshua the son of N, and unto 5126
24:29 that Joshua the son of N, the servant of 5126
Jdg 2: 8 Joshua the son of N, the servant of 5126
1Ki 16:34 which he spake by Joshua the son of N. 5126
Ne 8:17 for since the days of Jeshua the son of N 5126

NURSE (10) [NURSED, NURSING]
Ge 24:59 her n, and Abraham's servant, and his men. 3243
35: 8 Deborah Rebekah's n died, and she was 3243
Ex 2: 7 and call to thee a n of the Hebrew women, 3243
2: 7 that she may n the child for thee? 3243
2: 9 n it for me, and I will give *thee* thy wages. 3243
Ru 4:16 laid it in her bosom, and became n unto it. 539
2Sa 4: 4 of Jezreel, and his n took him up, and fled: 539
2Ki 11: 2 they hid him, *even* him and his n, in 3243
2Ch 22:11 and put him and his n in a bedchamber. 3243
1Th 2: 7 *even* as a n cherisheth her children: *5162*

NURSED (2) [NURSE]
Ex 2: 9 And the woman took the child, and n it. 5134
Isa 60: 4 and thy daughters shall be n at *thy* side. 539

NURSING (3) [NURSE]
Nu 11:12 as a n **father** beareth the sucking child, 539
Isa 49:23 kings shall be thy n **fathers**, and 539
49:23 and their queens thy n **mothers**: 3243

NURTURE (1)
Eph 6: 4 but bring them up in the n and *3809*

NUTS (2)
Ge 43:11 spices, and myrrh, n, and almonds: 992
SS 6:11 I went down into the garden of n to see 93

NYMPHA See NYMPHAS

NYMPHAS (1)
Col 4:15 and N, and the church which is in his *3564*

O

O (1086) [OH] See Index of Articles, Etc.

OAK (15) [OAKS]
Ge 35: 4 Jacob hid them under the o which *was* by 424
35: 8 she was buried beneath Beth-el under an o: 437
Jos 24:26 a great stone, and set it up there under an o, 427
Jdg 6:11 sat under an o which *was* in Ophrah, 424
6:19 and brought *it* out unto him under the o, and 424

2Sa 18: 9 went under the thick boughs of a great **o**, 424
18: 9 his head caught hold of the **o**, and he was 424
18:10 said, Behold, I saw Absalom hanged in an **o**. 424
18:14 while he *was* yet alive in the midst of the **o**. 424
1Ki 13:14 of God, and found him sitting under an **o**: 424
1Ch 10:12 and buried their bones under the **o** in Jabesh, 424
Isa 1:30 For ye shall be as an **o** whose leaf fadeth, 424
6:13 as a teil tree, and as an **o**, whose substance *is* 437
44:14 and taketh the cypress and the **o**, 437
Eze 6:13 every green tree, and under every thick **o**, 424

OAKS (6) [OAK]

Isa 1:29 For they shall be ashamed of the **o** which ye 352
2:13 and lifted up, and upon all the **o** of Bashan, 437
Eze 27: 6 *Of* the **o** of Bashan have they made thine 437
Hos 4:13 under **o** and poplars and elms, because 437
Am 2: 9 of the cedars, and he *was* strong as the **o**; 437
Zec 11: 2 howl, O ye **o** of Bashan; for the forest of 437

OAR (1) [OARS]

Eze 27:29 all that handle the **o**, the mariners, *and* 4880

OARS (2) [OAR]

Isa 33:21 wherein shall go no galley with **o**, 7885
Eze 27: 6 the oaks of Bashan have they made thine **o**; 4880

OARSMEN See ROWERS

OATH (59) [OATHS, OATHS']

Ge 24: 8 then thou shalt be clear from this my **o**: 7621
24:41 shalt thou be clear from *this* my **o**, 423
24:41 not thee *one*, thou shalt be clear from my **o**. 423
26: 3 I will perform the **o** which I sware unto 7621
26:28 we said, Let there be now an **o** betwixt us, 423
50:25 Joseph **took an o** of the children of Israel, 7650
Ex 22:11 *Then* shall an **o** of the LORD be between 7621
Lev 5: 4 *it be* that a man shall pronounce with an **o**, 7621
Nu 5:19 the priest shall **charge** her **by an o**, 7650
5:21 **charge** the woman **with an o** 7621+7650+871.1
5:21 thee a curse and an **o** among thy people, 7621
30: 2 or swear an **o** to bind his soul with a bond; 7621
30:10 or bound her soul by a bond with an **o**; 7621
30:13 and every binding **o** to afflict the soul, 7621
Dt 7: 8 he would keep the **o** which he had sworn 7621
29:12 into his **o**, which the LORD thy God 423
29:14 you only do I make this covenant and this **o**; 423
Jos 2:17 We *will be* blameless of this thine **o** which 7621
2:20 we will be quit of thine **o** which thou hast 7621
9:20 of the **o** which we sware unto them. 7621
Jdg 21: 5 For *they* had made a great **o** concerning 7621
1Sa 14:26 to his mouth: for the people feared the **o**. 7621
14:27 his father **charged** the people **with the o**: 7650
14:28 **straitly charged** the people **with an o**, 7650+7650
2Sa 21: 7 of the LORD'S **o** that *was* between them, 7621
1Ki 2:43 hast thou not kept the **o** of the LORD, 7621
8:31 an **o** be laid upon him to cause him to swear, 423
8:31 the **o** come before thine altar in this house: 423
18:10 *He is* not *there;* he **took an o** of 7650
2Ki 11: 4 **took an o** of them in the house of 7650
1Ch 16:16 with Abraham, and of his **o** unto Isaac; 7621
2Ch 6:22 an **o** be laid upon him to make him swear, 423
6:22 the **o** come before thine altar in this house; 423
15:15 all Judah rejoiced at the **o**: for they had 7621
Ne 5:12 I called the priests, and **took an o** of them, 7650
10:29 and entered into a curse, and into an **o**, 7621
Ps 105: 9 made with Abraham, and his **o** unto Isaac; 7621
Ecc 8: 2 and *that* in regard of the **o** of God. 7621
9: 2 he that sweareth, as he that feareth an **o**. 7621
Jer 11: 5 That *I* may perform the **o** which I have 7621
Eze 16:59 which hast despised the **o** in breaking 423
17:13 with him, and hath taken an **o** of him: 423
17:16 whose **o** he despised, and whose covenant he 423
17:18 Seeing he despised the **o** by breaking 423
17:19 surely mine **o** that he hath despised, and 423
Da 9:11 the **o** that *is* written in the law of Moses 7621
Zec 8:17 against his neighbour; and love no false **o**: 7621
Mt 14: 7 Whereupon he promised with an **o** to give *3727*
26:72 And again he denied with an **o**, I do not *3727*
Lk 1:73 The **o** which he sware to our father *3727*
Ac 2:30 knowing that God had sworn with an **o** to *3727*
23:21 which have **bound** themselves **with an o**, *332*
Heb 6:16 an **o** for confirmation *is* to them an end of *3727*
6:17 of his counsel, confirmed *it* by an **o**: *3727*
7:20 And inasmuch as not without an **o** *he was* *3728*
7:21 (For those priests were made without an **o**; *3728*
7:21 this with an **o** by him that said unto him, *3728*
7:28 but the word of the **o**, which was since *3728*
Jas 5:12 neither by the earth, neither by any other **o**: *3727*

OATHS (3) [OATH]

Eze 21:23 in their sight, to them that have sworn **o**: 7621
Hab 3: 9 *according to* the **o** of the tribes, *even thy* 7621
Mt 5:33 but shalt perform unto the Lord thine **o**: *3727*

OATHS' (2) [OATH]

Mt 14: 9 nevertheless for the **o** sake, and them which *3727*
Mk 6:26 *yet* for his **o** sake, and for their sakes which *3727*

OBADIAH (20)

1Ki 18: 3 Ahab called **O**, which *was* the governor of 5662
18: 3 (Now **O** feared the LORD greatly: 5662
18: 4 that **O** took an hundred prophets, and 5662
18: 5 Ahab said unto **O**, Go into the land, unto all 5662
18: 6 **O** went another way by himself. 5662
18: 7 as **O** was in the way, behold Elijah met 5662
18:16 So **O** went to meet Ahab, and told him: and 5662
1Ch 3:21 the sons of Arnan, the sons of **O**, 5662
7: 3 Michael, and **O**, and Joel, Ishiah, five: 5662
8:38 Ishmael, and Sheariah, and **O**, and Hanan. 5662
9:16 **O** the son of Shemaiah, the son of Galal, 5662
9:44 Ishmael, and Sheariah, and **O**, and Hanan: 5662
12: 9 Ezer the first, **O** the second, Eliab the third, 5662
27:19 Of Zebulun, Ishmaiah the son of **O**: 5662
2Ch 17: 7 to **O**, and to Zechariah, and to Nethaneel, 5662
34:12 the overseers of them *were* Jahath and **O**, 5662
Ezr 8: 9 **O** the son of Jehiel, and with him two 5662
Ne 10: 5 Harim, Meremoth, **O**, 5662
12:25 Mattaniah, and Bakbukiah, **O**, Meshullam, 5662
Ob 1: 1 The vision of **O**. Thus saith the Lord GOD 5662

OBAL (1)

Ge 10:28 And **O**, and Abimael, and Sheba, 5745

OBED (13)

Ru 4:17 born to Naomi; and they called his name **O**: 5744
4:21 Salmon begat Boaz, and Boaz begat **O**, 5744
4:22 And **O** begat Jesse, and Jesse begat David. 5744
1Ch 2:12 And Boaz begat **O**, and Obed begat Jesse, 5744
2:12 And Boaz begat Obed, and **O** begat Jesse, 5744
2:37 Zabad begat Ephlal, and Ephlal begat **O**, 5744
2:38 And **O** begat Jehu, and Jehu begat Azariah, 5744
11:47 Eliel, and **O**, and Jasiel the Mesobaite. 5744
26: 7 Othni, and Rephael, and **O**, Elzabad, 5744
2Ch 23: 1 Azariah the son of **O**, and Maaseiah the son 5744
Mt 1: 5 and Booz begat **O** of Ruth; and Obed begat *5601*
1: 5 begat Obed of Ruth; and **O** begat Jesse; *5601*
Lk 3:32 which was *the son* of **O**, which was *the son* *5601*

OBED-EDOM (20)

2Sa 6:10 David carried it aside *into* the house of **O** 5654
6:11 *in* the house of **O** the Gittite three months: 5654
6:11 the LORD blessed **O**, and all his 5654
6:12 The LORD hath blessed the house of **O**, 5654
6:12 of **O** *into* the city of David with gladness. 5654
1Ch 13:13 carried it aside into the house of **O** 5654
13:14 the family of **O** in his house three months. 5654
13:14 the LORD blessed the house of **O**, and 5654
15:18 Elipheleh, and Mikneiah, and **O**, and Jeiel, 5654
15:21 Mikneiah, and **O**, and Jeiel, and Azaziah, 5654
15:24 **O** and Jehiah *were* doorkeepers for the ark. 5654
15:25 the LORD out of the house of **O** with joy. 5654
16: 5 Mattithiah, and Eliab, and Benaiah, and **O**: 5654
16:38 **O** with their brethren, threescore and eight; 5654
16:38 **O** also the son of Jeduthun and Hosah to be 5654
26: 4 Moreover the sons of **O** *were,* Shemaiah 5654
26: 8 All these of the sons of **O**: they and 5654
26: 8 the service, *were* threescore and two of **O**. 5654
26:15 To **O** southward; and to his sons the house 5654
2Ch 25:24 were found in the house of God with **O**, 5654

OBEDIENCE (12) [OBEY]

Ro 1: 5 for **o** to the faith among all nations, *5218*
5:19 by the **o** of one shall many be made *5218*
6:16 sin unto death, or of **o** unto righteousness? *5218*
16:19 For your **o** is come abroad unto all *men.* I *5218*
16:26 made known to all nations for the **o** of *5218*
1Co 14:34 but *they are commanded* to be **under o**, *5293*
2Co 7:15 whilst he remembereth the **o** of you all, *5218*
10: 5 captivity every thought to the **o** of Christ; *5218*
10: 6 all disobedience, when your **o** is fulfilled. *5218*
Phm 1:21 Having confidence in thy **o** I wrote unto *5218*
Heb 5: 8 *yet* learned he **o** by *the things* which he *5218*
1Pe 1: 2 unto **o** and sprinkling of the blood of Jesus *5218*

OBEDIENT (16) [OBEY]

Ex 24: 7 the LORD hath said will we do, and be **o**. 8085
Nu 27:20 of the children of Israel may be **o**. 8085
Dt 4:30 thy God, and shalt be **o** unto his voice; 8085
8:20 ye would not be **o** unto the voice of 8085
2Sa 22:45 soon as they hear, they shall be **o** unto me. 8085
Pr 25:12 *so is* a wise reprover upon an **o** ear. 8085
Isa 1:19 If ye be willing and **o**, ye shall eat the good 8085
42:24 his ways, neither were they **o** unto his law. 8085
Ac 6: 7 a great company of the priests were **o** to *5219*
Ro 15:18 to make the Gentiles **o**, by word and deed, *5218*
2Co 2: 9 proof of you, whether ye be **o** in all *things.* *5255*
Eph 6: 5 be **o** to *them that are your* masters *5219*
Php 2: 8 humbled himself, and became **o** unto death, *5255*
Tit 2: 5 at home, good, **o** to their own husbands, *5293*
2: 9 *Exhort* servants to be **o** unto their own *5293*
1Pe 1:14 As **o** children, not fashioning yourselves *5218*

OBEISANCE (9) [OBEY]

Ge 37: 7 round about, and **made o** to my sheaf. 7812
37: 9 and the eleven stars **made o** to me. 7812
43:28 they bowed down their heads, and **made o**. 7812
Ex 18: 7 his father in law, and **did o**, and kissed him; 7812
2Sa 1: 2 to David, that he fell to the earth, and did **o**. 7812
14: 4 and did **o**, and said, Help, O king. 7812
15: 5 any man came nigh *to him* to do him **o**, 7812
1Ki 1:16 Bath-sheba bowed, and **did o** unto the king. 7812
2Ch 24:17 princes of Judah, and **made o** to the king. 7812

OBEY (69) [OBEDIENCE, OBEDIENT, OBEISANCE, OBEYED, OBEYEDST, OBEYETH, OBEYING]

Ge 27: 8 **o** my voice according to *that* which I 8085+871.1
27:13 **o** my voice, and go fetch me *them.* 8085+871.1
27:43 Now therefore, my son, **o** my voice; 8085+871.1
Ex 5: 2 I should **o** his voice to let Israel go? 8085+871.1
19: 5 if ye will **o** my voice **indeed**, 8085+8085+871.1
23:21 Beware of him, and **o** his voice, 8085+871.1
23:22 if thou shalt **indeed o** his voice, and 8085+8085
Dt 11:27 if ye **o** the commandments of the LORD 8085
11:28 if ye will not **o** the commandments of 8085
13: 4 **o** his voice, and ye shall serve him, and 8085
21:18 which will not **o** the voice of his 8085+871.1
21:20 rebellious, he will not **o** our voice; 8085+871.1
27:10 **o** the voice of the LORD thy God, 8085+871.1
28:62 thou wouldest not **o** the voice of 8085+871.1
30: 2 shalt **o** his voice according to all that 8085+871.1
30: 8 and **o** the voice of the LORD, 8085+871.1
30:20 *and* that thou mayest **o** his voice, 8085+871.1
Jos 24:24 God will we serve, and his voice will we **o**. 8085
1Sa 8:19 Nevertheless the people refused to **o** 8085+871.1
12:14 **o** his voice, and not rebel against 8085+871.1
12:15 if ye will not **o** the voice of 8085+871.1
15:19 thou not **o** the voice of the LORD, 8085+871.1
15:22 to **o** *is* better than sacrifice, *and* to hearken 8085
Ne 9:17 refused to **o**, neither were mindful of thy 8085
Job 36:11 If they **o** and serve *him,* they shall spend 8085
36:12 if they **o** not, they shall perish by the sword, 8085
Ps 18:44 As soon as they hear *of me,* they shall **o** 8085
Pr 30:17 at *his* father, and despiseth to **o** *his* mother, 3349
Isa 11:14 and the children of Ammon shall **o** them. 4928
Jer 7:23 **O** my voice, and I will be your God, 8085+871.1
11: 4 **O** my voice, and do them, 8085+871.1
11: 7 and protesting, saying, **O** my voice. 8085+871.1
12:17 But if they will not **o**, I will utterly pluck up 8085
18:10 that *it* **o** not my voice, then I will 8085+871.1
26:13 **o** the voice of the LORD your God; 8085+871.1
35:14 but **o** their father's commandment: 8085
38:20 They shall not deliver *thee.* **O**, I 8085+871.1
42: 6 **o** the voice of the LORD our God, 8085+871.1
42: 6 when we **o** the voice of the LORD 8085+871.1
42:13 neither **o** the voice of the LORD 8085+871.1
Da 7:27 and all dominions shall serve and **o** him. 8086
9:11 that *they* might not **o** thy voice; 8085+871.1
Zec 6:15 if ye will **diligently o** the voice of 8085+8085
Mt 8:27 that even the winds and the sea **o** him? *5219*
Mk 1:27 even the unclean spirits, and they do **o** him. *5219*
4:41 that even the wind and the sea **o** him? *5219*
Lk 8:25 even the winds and water, and they **o** him. *5219*
17: 6 thou planted in the sea; and it should **o** you. *5219*
Ac 5:29 said, We ought to **o** God rather than men. *3980*
5:32 whom God hath given to them that **o** him. *3980*
7:39 To whom our fathers would not **o**, *1096+5255*
Ro 2: 8 and do **not o** the truth, but *544*
2: 8 but **o** unrighteousness, indignation and *3982*
6:12 that *ye* should **o** it in the lusts thereof. *5219*
6:16 to whom ye yield yourselves servants to **o**, *5218*
6:16 to obey, *his* servants ye are to whom ye **o**; *5219*
Gal 3: 1 that *you* should not **o** the truth, *3982*
5: 7 who did hinder you that *ye* should not **o** *3982*
Eph 6: 1 Children, **o** your parents in the Lord: *5219*
Col 3:20 **o** *your* parents in all *things:* for this is well *5219*
3:22 **o** in all *things your* masters according to *5219*
2Th 1: 8 that **o** not the gospel of our Lord Jesus *5219*
3:14 And if any *man* **o** not our word by *this* *5219*
Tit 3: 1 and powers, to **o magistrates**, *3980*
Heb 5: 9 eternal salvation unto all them that **o** him; *5219*
13:17 **O** them that have the rule over you, and *3982*
Jas 3: 3 in the horses' mouths, that they may **o** us; *3982*
1Pe 3: 1 that, if any **o not** the word, they also may *544*
4:17 what *shall* the end *be* of them that **o not** *544*

OBEYED (11) [OBEY]

Ge 22:18 because thou hast **o** my voice. 8085+871.1
26: 5 Because that Abraham **o** my voice, 8085+871.1
28: 7 that Jacob **o** his father and his mother, and 8085
Jos 5: 6 they **o** not the voice of the LORD: 8085+871.1
22: 2 have **o** my voice in all that I commanded 8085
Jdg 2: 2 ye have not **o** my voice: why have ye done 8085
6:10 but ye have not **o** my voice. 8085+871.1
1Sa 15:20 I have **o** the voice of the LORD, 8085+871.1
15:24 feared the people, and **o** their voice. 8085+871.1
28:21 thine handmaid hath **o** thy voice, 8085+871.1
1Ki 20:36 Because thou hast not **o** the voice of 8085+871.1
2Ki 18:12 Because they **o** not the voice of 8085+871.1
1Ch 29:23 and prospered; and all Israel **o** him. 8085
2Ch 11: 4 they **o** the words of the LORD, and 8085
Pr 5:13 have not **o** the voice of my teachers, 8085+871.1
Jer 3:13 ye have not **o** my voice, saith the LORD. 8085
3:25 have not **o** the voice of the LORD 8085+871.1
9:13 have not **o** my voice, neither walked 8085+871.1
11: 8 Yet they **o** not, nor inclined their ear, but 8085
17:23 they **o** not, neither inclined their ear, but 8085
32:23 they **o** not thy voice, neither walked 8085+871.1
34:10 any more, then they **o**, and let *them* go. 8085
35: 8 Thus have we **o** the voice of 8085+871.1
35:10 have **o**, and done according to all that 8085
35:18 Because ye have **o** the commandment of 8085
40: 3 have not **o** his voice, therefore this 8085+871.1
42:21 ye have not **o** the voice of 8085+871.1
43: 4 the people, **o** not the voice of the LORD, 8085
43: 7 for they **o** not the voice of 8085+871.1
44:23 have not **o** the voice of the LORD, 8085+871.1
Da 9:10 Neither have we **o** the voice of 8085+871.1
9:14 he doeth: for we **o** not his voice. 8085+871.1
Zep 3: 2 She **o** not the voice; she received not 8085
Hag 1:12 **o** the voice of the LORD their God, and 8085
Ac 5:36 and all, as many as **o** him, were scattered, *3982*
5:37 and all, *even* as many as **o** him, *3982*
Ro 6:17 ye have **o** from the heart *that* form of *5219*
10:16 But they have not all **o** the gospel. *5219*
Php 2:12 my beloved, as ye have always **o**, *5219*
Heb 11: 8 should after receive for an inheritance, **o**; *5219*
1Pe 3: 6 *Even* as Sara **o** Abraham, calling him lord: *5219*

OBEYEDST (2) [OBEY]

1Sa 28:18 Because thou **o** not the voice of 8085+871.1
Jer 22:21 thy youth, that thou **o** not my voice. 8085+871.1

OBEYETH (3) [OBEY]

Isa 50:10 that **o** the voice of his servant, 8085+871.1
Jer 7:28 This *is* a nation that **o** not the voice 8085+871.1
11: 3 Cursed *be* the man that **o** not the words of 8085

OBEYING (3) [OBEY]

Jdg 2:17 **o** the commandments of the LORD; 8085
1Sa 15:22 as in **o** the voice of the LORD? 8085+871.1
1Pe 1:22 Seeing ye have purified your souls in **o** *5218*

OBIL (1)

1Ch 27:30 Over the camels also *was* **O** the Ishmaelite: 179

OBJECT (1)

Ac 24:19 and **o**, if they had ought against me. *2723*

OBLATION (35) [OBLATIONS]

Lev 2: 4 if thou bring an **o** of a meat offering baken 7133
2: 5 if thy **o** *be* a meat offering *baken* in a pan, 7133
2: 7 if thy **o** *be* a meat offering *baken* in 7133

Lev 2:12 *As for* the **o** of the firstfruits, ye shall offer 7133
2:13 every **o** of thy meat offering shalt thou 7133
3: 1 if his **o** *be* a sacrifice of peace offering, 7133
7:14 of it he shall offer one out of the whole **o** 7133
7:29 **o** unto the LORD of the sacrifice of his 7133
22:18 that will offer his **o** for all his vows, and 7133
Nu 18: 9 every **o** of theirs, every meat offering of 7133
31:50 therefore brought an **o** for the LORD, 7133
Isa 19:21 in that day, and shall do sacrifice and **o**; 4503
40:20 impoverished that he hath no **o** chooseth a 8641
66: 3 he that offereth an **o**, *as if he offered* 4503
Jer 14:12 when they offer burnt offering and an **o**, 4503
Eze 44:30 firstfruits of all *things,* and every **o** of all, 8641
45: 1 ye shall offer an **o** unto the LORD, a holy 8641
45: 6 over against the **o** of the holy *portion:* it 8641
45: 7 on the other side of the **o** of the holy 8641
45: 7 before the **o** of the holy *portion,* and 8641
45:13 This *is* the **o** that ye shall offer; the sixth 8641
45:16 All the people of the land shall give this **o** 8641
48: 9 The **o** that ye shall offer unto the LORD 8641
48:10 *even* for the priests, shall be *this* holy **o**; 8641
48:12 *this* **o** of the land that is offered shall be 8642
48:18 the residue in length over against the **o** of 8641
48:18 it shall be over against the **o** of the holy 8641
48:20 All the **o** *shall be* five and twenty thousand 8641
48:20 ye shall offer the holy **o** foursquare, 8641
48:21 the one side and on the other of the holy **o**, 8641
48:21 twenty thousand of the **o** toward the east 8641
48:21 it shall be the holy **o**; and the sanctuary of 8641
Da 2:46 commanded that *they* should offer an **o** and 4504
9:21 touched me about the time of the evening **o**. 4503
9:27 shall cause the sacrifice and the **o** to cease, 4503

OBLATIONS (5) [OBLATION]
Lev 7:38 of Israel to offer their **o** unto the LORD, 7133
2Ch 31:14 to distribute the **o** of the LORD, and 8641
Isa 1:13 Bring no more vain **o**; incense *is* an 4503
Eze 20:40 the firstfruits of your **o**, with all your holy 4864
44:30 of every *sort* of your **o**, shall be the priests': 8641

OBOTH (4)
Nu 21:10 of Israel set forward, and pitched in **O**. 88
21:11 they journeyed from **O**, and pitched at 88
33:43 they departed from Punon, and pitched in **O**. 88
33:44 they departed from **O**, and pitched in 88

OBSCURE (1) [OBSCURITY]
Pr 20:20 his lamp shall be put out in **o** darkness. 380

OBSCURITY (3) [OBSCURE]
Isa 29:18 the eyes of the blind shall see out of **o**, and 652
58:10 shall thy light rise in **o**, and thy darkness *be* 2822
59: 9 we wait for light, but behold **o**; 2822

OBSERVATION (1) [OBSERVE]
Lk 17:20 The kingdom of God cometh not with **o**: *3907*

OBSERVE (55) [OBSERVATION, OBSERVED, OBSERVER, OBSERVERS, OBSERVEST, OBSERVETH]
Ex 12:17 ye shall **o** the *feast of* unleavened bread; 8104
12:17 shall ye **o** this day in your generations by 8104
12:24 ye shall **o** this thing for an ordinance to thee 8104
31:16 to **o** the sabbath throughout their 6213
34:11 **O** thou that which I command thee *this* 8104
34:22 thou shalt **o** the feast of weeks, of 6213
Lev 19:26 shall ye use enchantment, nor **o times**. 6049
19:37 Therefore shall ye **o** all my statutes, and all 8104
Nu 28: 2 shall ye **o** to offer unto me in their due 8104
Dt 5:32 Ye shall **o** to do therefore as the LORD 8104
6: 3 **o** to do *it;* that it may be well with thee, and 8104
6:25 if we **o** to do all these commandments 8104
8: 1 I command thee *this* day shall ye **o** to do, 8104
11:32 ye shall **o** to do all the statutes and 8104
12: 1 which ye shall **o** to do in the land, 8104
12:28 **O** and hear all these words which I 8104
12:32 thing soever I command you, **o** to do it: 8104
15: 5 to **o** to do all these commandments which I 8104
16: 1 **O** the month of Abib, and keep 8104
16:12 and thou shalt **o** and do these statutes. 8104
16:13 Thou shalt **o** the feast of tabernacles seven 6213
17:10 thou shalt **o** to do according to all that they 8104
24: 8 that *thou* **o** diligently, and do according to 8104
24: 8 as I commanded them, *so* ye shall **o** to do. 8104
28: 1 to **o** *and* to do all his commandments which 8104
28:13 thee *this* day, to **o** and to do *them:* 8104
28:15 to **o** to do all his commandments and 8104
28:58 If thou wilt not **o** to do all the words of this 8104
31:12 and **o** to do all the words of this law: 8104
32:46 which ye shall command your children to **o** 8104
Jos 1: 7 that *thou* mayest **o** to do according to all 8104
1: 8 that thou mayest **o** to do according to all 8104
Jdg 13:14 *thing:* all that I commanded her let her **o**. 8104
1Ki 20:33 Now the men did **diligently o** whether *any* 5172
2Ki 17:37 for you, ye shall **o** to do for evermore; 8104
21: 8 only if they will **o** to do according to all 8104
2Ch 7:17 and shalt **o** my statutes and my judgments; 8104
Ne 1: 5 that love him and **o** his commandments: 8104
10:29 to **o** and do all the commandments of 8104
Ps 105:45 That they might **o** his statutes, and keep his 8104
107:43 will **o** these *things,* even they shall 8104
119:34 yea, I shall **o** it with *my* whole heart. 8104
Pr 23:26 thine heart, and let thine eyes **o** my ways. 5341
Jer 8: 7 and the swallow **o** the time of their coming; 8104
Eze 20:18 neither **o** their judgments, nor defile 8104
37:24 and **o** my statutes, and do them. 8104
Hos 13: 7 as a leopard by the way will I **o** *them:* 7789
Jnh 2: 8 They that **o** lying vanities forsake their own 8104
Mt 23: 3 All therefore whatsoever they bid you **o**, *5083*
23: 3 they bid you observe, *that* **o** and do; *5083*
28:20 Teaching them to **o** all *things* whatsoever I *5083*
Ac 16:21 us to receive, neither to **o**, being Romans. *4160*
21:25 concluded that they **o** no such *thing,* save *5083*
Gal 4:10 Ye **o** days, and months, and times, and *3906*
1Ti 5:21 that thou **o** these *things* without preferring *5442*

OBSERVED (11) [OBSERVE]
Ge 37:11 envied him; but his father **o** the saying. 8104
Ex 12:42 It *is* a night to be **much o** unto the LORD 8107
12:42 this *is* that night of the LORD to be **o** of 8107
Nu 15:22 and not **o** all these commandments, 6213
Dt 33: 9 for they have **o** thy word, and kept thy 8104
2Sa 11:16 it came to pass, when Joab **o** the city, 8104
2Ki 21: 6 **o times**, and used enchantments, and 6049
2Ch 33: 6 also he **o times**, and used enchantments, 6049
Hos 14: 8 I have heard *him,* and **o** him: I *am* like a 7789
Mk 6:20 he *was* a just man and a holy, and **o** him; *4933*
10:20 Master, all these have I **o** from my youth. *5442*

OBSERVER (1) [OBSERVE]
Dt 18:10 *or* an **o of times**, or an enchanter, or 6049

OBSERVERS (1) [OBSERVE]
Dt 18:14 hearkened unto **o of times**, and 6049

OBSERVEST (1) [OBSERVE]
Isa 42:20 Seeing many *things,* but thou **o** not; 8104

OBSERVETH (1) [OBSERVE]
Ecc 11: 4 He that **o** the wind shall not sow; and 8104

OBSTINATE (2)
Dt 2:30 **made** his heart **o**, that he might deliver him 553
Isa 48: 4 Because I knew that thou *art* **o**, and 7186

OBTAIN (15) [OBTAINED, OBTAINETH, OBTAINING]
Ge 16: 2 it may be that I may **o children** by her. 1129
Pr 8:35 and shall **o** favour of the LORD. 6329
Isa 35:10 they shall **o** joy and gladness, and sorrow 5381
51:11 they shall **o** gladness and joy; *and* sorrow 5381
Da 11:21 and **o** the kingdom by flatteries. 2388
Mt 5: 7 *are* the merciful: for they shall **o mercy**. *1653*
Lk 20:35 shall be accounted worthy to **o** that world, *5177*
Ro 11:31 your mercy they also may **o mercy**. *1653*
1Co 9:24 receiveth the prize? So run, that ye may **o**. *2638*
9:25 Now they *do it* to **o** a corruptible crown; *2983*
1Th 5: 9 but to **o** salvation by our Lord Jesus Christ, *4047*
2Ti 2:10 that they may also **o** the salvation which is *5177*
Heb 4:16 that we may **o** mercy, and find grace to *2983*
11:35 that they might **o** a better resurrection: *5177*
Jas 4: 2 ye kill, and desire *to have,* and cannot **o**: *2013*

OBTAINED (28) [OBTAIN]
Ne 13: 6 and after certain days **o** I *leave* of the king: 7592
Est 2: 9 pleased him, and she **o** kindness of him; 5375
2:15 Esther **o** favour in the sight of all them that 5375
2:17 she **o** grace and favour in his sight more 5375
5: 2 in the court, *that* she **o** favour in his sight: 5375
Hos 2:23 have mercy upon her that had not **o mercy**; 7355
Ac 1:17 with us, and had **o** part of this ministry. *2975*
22:28 With a great sum **o** I this freedom. *2932*
26:22 Having therefore **o** help of God, I continue *5177*
27:13 supposing that *they* had **o** *their* purpose, *2902*
Ro 11: 7 Israel hath not **o** that which he seeketh for; *2013*
11: 7 but the election hath **o** *it,* and the rest were *2013*
11:30 yet have now **o mercy** through their *1653*
1Co 7:25 as one that hath **o mercy** of the Lord to be *1653*
Eph 1:11 In whom also we have **o an inheritance**, *2820*
1Ti 1:13 but I **o mercy**, because I did *it* ignorantly in *1653*
1:16 Howbeit for this cause I **o mercy**, that in *1653*
Heb 1: 4 as he hath by **inheritance o** a more *2816*
6:15 he had patiently endured, he **o** the promise. *2013*
8: 6 But now hath he **o** a more excellent *5177*
9:12 *place,* having **o** eternal redemption *for us.* *2147*
11: 2 For by it the elders **o a good report**. *3140*
11: 4 by which he **o witness** that he was *3140*
11:33 wrought righteousness, **o** promises, *2013*
11:39 having **o a good report** through faith, *3140*
1Pe 2:10 which had not **o mercy**, but now have *1653*
2:10 not obtained mercy, but now have **o mercy**. *1653*
2Pe 1: 1 to them that have **o** like precious faith with *2975*

OBTAINETH (2) [OBTAIN]
Pr 12: 2 A good *man* **o** favour of the LORD: but 6329
18:22 a good *thing,* and **o** favour of the LORD. 6329

OBTAINING (1) [OBTAIN]
2Th 2:14 to the **o** of the glory of our Lord Jesus *4047*

OCCASION (21) [OCCASIONED, OCCASIONS]
Ge 43:18 that he may **seek o** against us, and fall upon 1556
Jdg 9:33 thou do to them as thou shalt **find o**. 4672
14: 4 that he sought an **o** against the Philistines: 8385
1Sa 10: 7 *that* thou do as **o serve** thee; 3027+4672
2Sa 12:14 **given great o** to the enemies of the LORD **to blaspheme**, 5006+5006
Ezr 7:20 which thou shalt **have o** to bestow, 5308
Jer 2:24 *in* her **o** who can turn her away? 8385
Eze 18: 3 ye shall not have **o** any more to use this NIH
Da 6: 4 princes sought to find **o** against Daniel 5931
6: 4 they could find none **o** nor fault; 5931
6: 5 We shall not find any **o** against this Daniel, 5931
Ro 7: 8 But sin, taking **o** by the commandment, *874*
7:11 For sin, taking **o** by the commandment, *874*
14:13 or an **o to fall** in *his* brother's way. *4625*
2Co 5:12 but give you **o** to glory on our behalf, *874*
8: 8 but **by o** of the forwardness of others, and *1223*
11:12 that I may cut off **o** from them which desire *874*
11:12 cut off occasion from them which desire **o**; *874*
Gal 5:13 only *use* not liberty for an **o** to the flesh, but *874*
1Ti 5:14 give none **o** to the adversary to speak *874*
1Jn 2:10 and there is none **o of stumbling** in him. *4625*

OCCASIONED (1) [OCCASION]
1Sa 22:22 I have **o** *the death* of all the persons of thy 5437

OCCASIONS (3) [OCCASION]
Dt 22:14 give **o** of speech against her, and bring up 5949
22:17 he hath given **o** of speech *against her,* 5949
Job 33:10 Behold, he findeth **o** against me, 8569

OCCUPATION (5) [OCCUPY]
Ge 46:33 call you, and shall say, What *is* your **o**? 4639
47: 3 said unto his brethren, What *is* your **o**? 4639
Jnh 1: 8 cause this evil *is* upon us; What *is* thine **o**? 4399
Ac 18: 3 for *by* their **o** they were tentmakers. *5078*
19:25 called together with the workmen of **like o**, *5108*

OCCUPIED (7) [OCCUPY]
Ex 38:24 All the gold that was **o** for the work in all 6213
Jdg 16:11 with new ropes that never were **o**, 4399+6213
Eze 27:16 they **o** in thy fairs with emeralds, purple, 5414
27:19 and Javan going to and fro **o** in thy fairs: 5414
27:21 they **o** with thee in lambs, and rams, 3027+5503
27:22 they **o** in thy fairs with chief of all spices, 5414
Heb 13: 9 not profited them that have been **o therein**. *4043*

OCCUPIERS (1) [OCCUPY]
Eze 27:27 the **o** of thy merchandise, and all thy men 6148

OCCUPIETH (1) [OCCUPY]
1Co 14:16 how shall he that **o** the room of *378*

OCCUPY (2) [OCCUPATION, OCCUPIED, OCCUPIERS, OCCUPIETH, UNOCCUPIED]
Eze 27: 9 mariners were in thee to **o** thy merchandise. 6148
Lk 19:13 and said unto them, **O** till I come. *4231*

OCCURRENT (1)
1Ki 5: 4 *so that there is* neither adversary nor evil **o**. 6294

OCRAN (5)
Nu 1:13 Of Asher; Pagiel the son of **O**. 5918
2:27 of Asher *shall be* Pagiel the son of **O**. 5918
7:72 On the eleventh day Pagiel the son of **O**, 5918
7:77 this *was* the offering of Pagiel the son of **O**. 5918
10:26 children of Asher *was* Pagiel the son of **O**. 5918

ODD (1)
Nu 3:48 wherewith the **o number** of them is *to be* 5736

ODED (3)
2Ch 15: 1 of God came upon Azariah the son of **O**: 5752
15: 8 the prophecy *of* **O** the prophet, he took 5752
28: 9 the LORD was there, whose name *was* **O**: 5752

ODIOUS (2) [ODOUR]
1Ch 19: 6 that they had **made** themselves **o** to David, 887
Pr 30:23 For an **o** *woman* when she is married; and 8130

ODOUR (2) [ODIOUS, ODOURS]
Jn 12: 3 the house was filled with the **o** of *3744*
Php 4:18 an **o** of a sweet smell, a sacrifice *3744*

ODOURS (7) [ODOUR]
Lev 26:31 I will not smell the savour of your **sweet o**. 5207
2Ch 16:14 in the bed which was filled *with* **sweet o** 1314
Est 2:12 six months with **sweet o**, and with *other* 1314
Jer 34: 5 before thee, so shall they burn **o** for thee; NIH
Da 2:46 offer an oblation and **sweet o** unto him. 5208
Rev 5: 8 and golden vials full of **o**, which are *2368*
18:13 and **o**, and ointments, and frankincense, and *2368*

OF (34750) [HEREOF, THEREOF, WHEREOF]
See Index of Articles, Etc.

OFF (507)
Ge 7: 4 will I destroy from **o** the face of the earth. 5921
8: 3 the waters returned from **o** the earth 5921
8: 7 until the waters were dried up from **o** 5921
8: 8 to see if the waters were abated from **o** 5921
8:11 lo, in her mouth *was* an olive leaf **pluckt o**: 2965
8:11 the waters were abated from **o** the earth. 5921
8:13 the waters were dried up from **o** the earth: 5921
9:11 neither shall all flesh be **cut o** any more by 3772
11: 8 the earth: and they left **o** to build the city. 2308
17:14 that soul shall be **cut o** from his people; 3772
17:22 he **left o** talking with him, and God went up 3615
21:16 her down over against *him* a **good way o**, 7368
22: 4 his eyes, and saw the place **afar o**. 4480+7350
24:64 saw Isaac, she lighted **o** the camel. 4480+5921
27:40 that thou shalt break his yoke from **o** thy 5921
37:18 when they saw him **afar o**, even 4480+7350
38:14 she **put** her widow's garments **o** from her, 5493
40:19 shall Pharaoh lift up thy head from **o** thee, 5921
40:19 and the birds shall eat thy flesh from **o** thee. 5921
41:42 Pharaoh **took o** his ring from his hand, and 5493
44: 4 *and* not *yet* **far o**, Joseph said unto his 7368
Ex 2: 4 his sister stood **afar o**, to wit what 4480+7350
3: 5 **put o** thy shoes from off thy feet, for 5394
3: 5 put off thy shoes from **o** thy feet, for 5921
4:25 **cut o** the foreskin of her son, and cast *it* at 3772
9:15 and thou shalt be **cut o** from the earth. 3582
12:15 that soul shall be **cut o** from Israel. 3772
12:19 even that soul shall be **cut o** from 3772
14:25 **took o** their chariot wheels, that they drave 5493
20:18 *it,* they removed, and stood **afar o**. 4480+7350
20:21 the people stood **afar o**, and 4480+7350
23:23 and the Jebusites: and I will **cut** them **o**. 3582
24: 1 of Israel; and worship ye **afar o**. 4480+7350
30:33 shall even be **cut o** from his people. 3772
30:38 shall even be **cut o** from his people. 3772
31:14 that soul shall be **cut o** from amongst his 3772
32: 2 unto them, **Break o** the golden earrings, 6561
32: 3 all the people **brake o** the golden earrings 6561
32:24 hath *any* gold, let them **break** *it* **o**. 6561
33: 5 now **put o** thy ornaments from thee, 3381
33: 7 **afar o** from the camp, and called it 7368
34:34 he **took** the vail **o**, until he came out. 5493

Lev 1:15 **wring o** his head, and burn *it* on the altar; 4454
3: 9 it shall he **take o** hard by the back bone; 5493
4: 8 he shall **take o** from it all the fat of 7311
4:10 As it was **taken o** from the bullock of 7311
4:31 as the fat is taken away from **o** the sacrifice 5921
5: 8 **wring o** his head from his neck, but 4454
6:11 he shall **put o** his garments, and put on 6584
7:20 even that soul shall be **cut o** from his 3772
7:21 even that soul shall be **cut o** from his 3772
7:25 even the soul that eateth *it* shall be **cut o** 3772
7:27 even that soul shall be **cut o** from his 3772
7:34 **from o** the sacrifices of their peace 4480
8:28 Moses took them from **o** their hands, and 5921
13:40 the man whose **hair** is **fallen o** his head, 4803
13:41 he that hath his **hair fallen o** from the part 4803
14: 8 **shave o** all his hair, and wash *himself* in 1548
14: 9 *that* he shall **shave** all his hair **o** his head 1548
14: 9 even all his hair he shall **shave o**: 1548
14:41 **scrape o** without the city into an unclean 7096
16:12 of fire from **o** the altar before the LORD, 5921
16:23 shall **put o** the linen garments, which he 6584
17: 4 that man shall be **cut o** from among his 3772
17: 9 even that man shall be **cut o** from among 3772
17:10 and will **cut** him **o** from among his people. 3772
17:14 whosoever eateth it shall be **cut o**. 3772
18:29 shall be **cut o** from among their people. 3772
19: 8 that soul shall be **cut o** from among his 3772
20: 3 and will **cut** him **o** from among his people; 3772
20: 5 will **cut** him **o**, and all that go a whoring 3772
20: 6 and will **cut** him **o** from among his people. 3772
20:17 they shall be **cut o** in the sight of their 3772
20:18 both of them shall be **cut o** from among 3772
21: 5 neither shall they **shave o** the corner of 1548
22: 3 that soul shall be **cut o** from my presence: 3772
23:29 he shall be **cut o** from among his people. 3772
Nu 2: 2 **far o** about the tabernacle of 4480+5048
4:18 **Cut** ye not **o** the tribe of the families of 3772
7:89 **o** the mercy seat that *was* upon the ark of 5921
9:10 or *be* in a journey **afar o**, yet he shall keep 7350
9:13 even the same soul shall be **cut o** from 3772
10:11 *that* the cloud was taken up from **o** 5921
12:10 the cloud departed from **o** the tabernacle; 5921
15:30 that soul shall be **cut o** from among his 3772
15:31 that soul shall **utterly** be **cut o**; 3772+3772
16:46 put fire therein from **o** the altar, and put on 5921
19:13 and that soul shall be **cut o** from Israel: 3772
19:20 that soul shall be **cut o** from among 3772
Dt 4:26 that ye shall soon utterly perish from **o** 5921
6:15 destroy thee from **o** the face of the earth. 5921
11:17 *lest* ye perish quickly from **o** the good land 5921
12:29 When the LORD thy God shall **cut o** 3772
13: 7 nigh unto thee, or **far o** from thee, 7350
19: 1 When the LORD thy God hath **cut o** 3772
20:15 the cities *which are* very **far o** from thee, 7350
21: 4 shall **strike o** the heifer's **neck** there in 6202
21:13 put the raiment of her captivity from **o** her, 5921
23: 1 the stones, or hath *his* privy member **cut o**, 3772
25: 9 loose his shoe from **o** his foot, and spit in 5921
25:12 thou shalt **cut o** her hand, thine eye shall 7112
28:21 until he have consumed thee from **o** 5921
28:63 ye shall be plucked from **o** the land whither 5921
30:11 *is* not hidden from thee, neither *is* it **far o**. 7350
Jos 3:13 *that* the waters of Jordan shall be **cut o** 3772
3:16 *even* the salt sea, failed, *and* were **cut o**: 3772
4: 7 That the waters of Jordan were **cut o** before 3772
4: 7 the waters of Jordan were **cut o**: 3772
5: 9 away the reproach of Egypt from **o** you. 5921
5:15 Loose thy shoe from **o** thy foot; 5921
7: 9 and **cut o** our name from the earth: 3772
10:27 they took them down **o** the trees, and 4480+5921
11:21 **cut o** the Anakims from the mountains, 3772
15:18 she **lighted o** *her* ass; and 4480+5921+6795
23: 4 with all the nations that I have **cut o**, 3772
23:13 until ye perish from **o** this good land which 5921
23:15 until he have destroyed you from **o** this 5921
23:16 ye shall perish quickly from **o** the good 5921
Jdg 1: 6 and **cut o** his thumbs and his great toes. 7112
1: 7 their thumbs and their great toes **cut o**, 7112
1:14 she lighted from **o** *her* ass; and Caleb said 5921
4:15 so that Sisera lighted down **o** *his* 4480+5921
5:26 she **smote o** his head, when she had pierced 4277
13:20 went up toward heaven from **o** the altar, 5921
15:14 and his bands loosed from **o** his hands. 5921
16:12 he brake them from **o** his arms like a 5921
16:19 she **caused** *him* **to shave o** the seven locks 1548
21: 6 There is one tribe **cut o** from Israel *this* 1438
Ru 2:20 who hath not **left o** his kindness to 5800
4: 7 a man **plucked o** his shoe, and gave *it* to 8025
4: 8 Buy *it* for thee. So he **drew o** his shoe. 8025
4:10 that the name of the dead be not **cut o** from 3772
1Sa 2:31 that I will **cut o** thine arm, and the arm of 1438
2:33 *whom* I shall not **cut o** from mine altar, 3772
4:18 that he fell from **o** the seat backward by 5921
5: 4 both the palms of his hands *were* **cut o** 3772
6: 5 he will lighten his hand from **o** you, 5921
6: 5 from **o** your gods, and from off your land. 5921
6: 5 from off your gods, and from **o** your land. 5921
17:39 proved *them.* And David **put** them **o** him. 5493
17:51 and slew him, and **cut o** his head therewith. 3772
19:24 he **stript o** his clothes also, and 6584
20:15 *also* thou shalt not **cut o** thy kindness from 3772
20:15 not when the LORD hath **cut o** 3772
24: 4 and **cut o** the skirt of Saul's robe privily. 3772
24: 5 because he had **cut o** Saul's skirt. 3772
24:11 for in that I **cut o** the skirt of thy robe, and 3772
24:21 that thou wilt not **cut o** my seed after me, 3772
25:23 lighted **o** the ass, and fell before 4480+5921
26:13 and stood on the top of a hill **afar o**; 4480+7350
28: 9 how he hath **cut o** those that have familiar 3772
31: 9 they **cut o** his head, and stripped off his 3772
31: 9 **stripped o** his armour, and sent into 6584
2Sa 4:12 **cut o** their hands and their feet, and 7112
7: 9 have **cut o** all thine enemies out of thy 3772
10: 4 **shaved o** the *one* half of their beards, and 1548
10: 4 **cut o** their garments in the middle, *even* to 3772

2Sa 11: 2 that David arose from **o** his bed, and 5921
11:24 the shooters shot from **o** the wall upon thy 5921
12:30 he took their king's crown from **o** his head, 5921
15:17 and tarried *in* a place that *was* **far o**. 4801
16: 9 go over, I pray thee, and **take o** his head. 5493
20:22 they **cut o** the head of Sheba the son of 3772
1Ki 9: 7 will I **cut o** Israel out of the land which I 3772
11:16 until he had **cut o** every male in Edom:) 3772
13:34 even to **cut** *it* **o**, and to destroy *it* from off 3582
13:34 to destroy *it* from **o** the face of the earth. 5921
14:10 will **cut o** from Jeroboam *him that* pisseth 3772
14:14 who shall **cut o** the house of Jeroboam that 3772
15:21 when Baasha heard *thereof,* that he **left o** 2308
18: 4 when Jezebel **cut o** the prophets of 3772
20:11 boast himself as he that **putteth** *it* **o**. 6605
21:21 will **cut o** from Ahab *him that* pisseth 3772
2Ki 1:16 thou shalt not come down **o** *that* bed on 4480
2: 7 and stood to view **afar o**: 4480+7350
4:25 the man of God saw her **afar o**, 4480+5048
9: 8 I will **cut o** from Ahab *him that* pisseth 3772
16:17 king Ahaz **cut o** the borders of the bases, 7112
16:17 and removed the laver from **o** them; 5921
16:17 took down the sea from **o** the brasen oxen 5921
18:16 At that time did Hezekiah **cut o** *the gold* 7112
23:27 will **cast o** this city Jerusalem which I have 3988
1Ch 17: 8 have **cut o** all thine enemies from before 3772
19: 4 **cut o** their garments in the midst hard by 3772
20: 2 David took the crown of their king from **o** 5921
28: 9 forsake him, he will **cast** thee **o** for ever. 2186
2Ch 6:36 carry them away captives unto a land **far o** 7350
11:14 his sons had **cast** them **o** from executing 2186
16: 5 when Baasha heard *it,* that he **left o** 2308
20:25 which they **stript o** for themselves, 5337
22: 7 whom the LORD had anointed to **cut o** 3772
26:21 for he was **cut o** from the house of 1504
32:21 which **cut o** all the mighty *men* of valour, 3582
Ezr 3:13 was heard **afar o**. 4480+5704+7350+3807.1
9: 3 **pluckt o** the hair of my head and of my 4803
Ne 4:23 followed me, none of us **put o** our clothes, 6584
4:23 *saving that* every one **put** them **o** *for* 7973
5:10 corn: I pray you, let us **leave o** this usury. 5800
12:43 of Jerusalem was heard **even afar o**. 4480+7350
13:25 **pluckt o** their **hair**, and made them swear 4803
Est 8: 2 the king **took o** his ring, which he had 5493
Job 2:12 when they lifted up their eyes **afar o**, 4480+7350
4: 7 or where were the righteous **cut o**? 3582
6: 9 he would let loose his hand, and **cut** me **o**! 1214
8:14 Whose hope shall be **cut o**, and whose trust 6990
9:27 I will **leave o** my heaviness, and 5800
11:10 If he **cut o**, and shut up, or gather together, 2498
15: 4 thou **castest o** fear, and restrainest prayer 6565
15:33 He shall **shake o** his unripe grape as 2554
15:33 and shall **cast o** his flower as the olive. 7993
17:11 days are past, my purposes are **broken o**, 5423
18:16 above shall his branch be **cut o**. 5243
21:21 of his months is **cut o in the midst**? 2686
23:17 Because I was not **cut o** before 6789
24:24 and **cut o** as the tops of the ears of corn. 5243
32:15 no more: they **left o** speaking. 4480+6275
36:20 when people are **cut o** in their place. 5927
36:25 see it; man may behold *it* **afar o**. 4480+7350
39:25 he smelleth the battle **afar o**, 4480+7350
39:29 the prey, *and* her eyes behold **afar o**. 4480+7350
Ps 10: 1 Why standest thou **afar o**, 7350+871.1
12: 3 The LORD shall **cut o** all flattering lips, 3772
30:11 thou hast **put o** my sackcloth, and 6605
31:22 I am **cut o** from before thine eyes: 1629
34:16 to **cut o** the remembrance of them from 3772
36: 3 he hath **left o** to be wise, *and* to do good. 2308
37: 9 For evildoers shall be **cut o**: but those that 3772
37:22 they that be cursed of him shall be **cut o**. 3772
37:28 but the seed of the wicked shall be **cut o**. 3772
37:34 when the wicked are **cut o**, thou shalt see 3772
37:38 the end of the wicked shall be **cut o**. 3772
38:11 and my kinsmen stand **afar o**. 4480+7350
43: 2 why dost thou **cast** me **o**? why go I 2186
44: 9 thou hast **cast o**, and put us to shame; and 2186
44:23 O Lord? arise, **cast** *us* not **o** for ever. 2186
54: 5 unto mine enemies: **cut** them **o** in thy truth. 6789
55: 7 Lo, *then* would I wander **far o**, *and* 7368
60: 1 O God, thou hast **cast** us **o**, thou hast 2186
60:10 not thou, O God, *which* hadst **cast** us **o**? 2186
65: 5 and *of* them that are **afar o** *upon* the sea: 7350
71: 9 **Cast** me not **o** in the time of old age; 7993
74: 1 O God, why hast thou **cast** *us* **o** for ever? 2186
75:10 the horns of the wicked also will I **cut o**; 1438
76:12 He shall **cut o** the spirit of princes: *he is* 1219
77: 7 Will the Lord **cast o** for ever? and will he 2186
83: 4 and let us **cut** them **o** from *being* a nation; 3582
88: 5 no more: and they are **cut o** from thy hand. 1504
88:14 LORD, why **castest** thou **o** my soul? 2186
88:16 goeth over me; thy terrors have **cut** me **o**. 6789
89:38 thou hast **cast o** and abhorred, thou hast 2186
90:10 for it is soon **cut o**, and we fly away. 1468
94:14 For the LORD will not **cast o** his people, 5203
94:23 shall **cut** them **o** in their own wickedness; 6789
94:23 *yea,* the LORD our God shall **cut** them **o**. 6789
101: 5 slandereth his neighbour, him will I **cut o**: 6789
101: 8 that *I* may **cut o** all wicked doers from 3772
108:11 *Wilt* not *thou,* O God, *who* hast **cast** us **o**? 2186
109:13 Let his posterity be **cut o**; *and* in 3772
109:15 that he may **cut o** the memory of them from 3772
138: 6 but the proud he knoweth **afar o**. 4480+4801
139: 2 understandest my thought **afar o**. 4480+7350
143:12 of thy mercy **cut o** mine enemies, and 6789
Pr 2:22 the wicked shall be **cut o** from the earth, 3772
17:14 therefore **leave o** contention, before *it* be 5203
23:18 and thine expectation shall not be **cut o**. 3772
24:14 and thy expectation shall not be **cut o**. 3772
26: 6 by the hand of a fool **cutteth o** the feet, 7096
27:10 neighbour *that is* near than a brother **far o**. 7350
30:14 to devour the poor **from o** the earth, and 4480
Ecc 7:24 That which is **far o**, and exceeding deep, 7350
SS 5: 3 I have **put o** my coat; how shall I put it on? 6584
Isa 6: 6 *which* he had taken with the tongs from **o** 5921

Isa 9:14 Therefore the LORD will **cut o** from 3772
10: 7 to destroy and **cut o** nations not a few. 3772
10:27 *that* his burden shall be taken away from **o** 5921
10:27 his yoke from **o** thy neck, and the yoke 5921
11:13 and the adversaries of Judah shall be **cut o**: 3772
14:22 **cut o** from Babylon the name, and remnant, 3772
14:25 shall his yoke depart from **o** them, and 5921
14:25 his burden depart from **o** their shoulders. 5921
15: 2 *shall be* baldness, *and* every beard **cut o**. 1438
17:13 they shall flee **far o**, and shall be 4480+4801
18: 5 he shall both **cut o** the sprigs with pruning 3772
20: 2 and loose the sackcloth from **o** thy loins, 5921
20: 2 thy loins, and **put o** thy shoe from thy foot. 2502
22:25 the burden that *was* upon it shall be **cut o**: 3772
23: 7 her own feet shall carry her **afar o** to 4480+7350
25: 8 will wipe away tears from **o** all faces; 5921
25: 8 shall he take away from **o** all the earth: 5921
27:11 are withered, they shall be **broken o**: 7665
27:12 *that* the LORD shall **beat o** from 2251
29:20 and all that watch for iniquity are **cut o**: 3772
33: 9 Bashan and Carmel **shake o** *their fruits.* 5287
33:13 Hear, ye *that are* **far o**, what I have done; 7350
33:17 shall behold the land that is **very far o**. 4801
34: 4 as the leaf **falleth o** from the vine, and as a 5034
38:10 I said, in the **cutting o** of my days, I shall 1824
38:12 I have **cut o** like a weaver my life: he will 7088
38:12 he will **cut** me **o** with pining sickness: 1214
46:13 it shall not be **far o**, and my salvation shall 7368
47:11 upon thee; thou shalt not be able to **put** it **o**: 3722
48: 9 will I refrain for thee, that *I* **cut** thee not **o**. 3772
48:19 his name should not have been **cut o** nor 3772
50: 6 my cheeks to them that **plucked o** the **hair**: 4803
53: 8 for he was **cut o** out of the land of 1504
55:13 an everlasting sign *that* shall not be **cut o**. 3772
56: 5 an everlasting name, that shall not be **cut o**. 3772
57: 9 didst send thy messengers **far o**, and 4480+7350
57:19 peace to *him that is* **far o**, and to *him that is* 7350
59:11 for salvation, *but* it is **far o** from us. 7368
59:14 and justice standeth **afar o**: 4480+7350
66: 3 a lamb, *as if* he **cut o** a dog's **neck**; 6202
66:19 *to* Tubal, and Javan, *to* the isles **afar o**, 7350
Jer 7:28 is perished, and is **cut o** from their mouth. 3772
7:29 **Cut o** thine hair, *O Jerusalem,* and cast *it* 1494
9:21 to **cut o** the children from without, *and* 3772
11:19 let us **cut** him **o** from the land of the living, 3772
23:23 the LORD, and not a God **afar o**? 4480+7350
24:10 till they be consumed from **o** the land that I 5921
28:10 Hananiah the prophet took the yoke from **o** 5921
28:12 from **o** the neck of the prophet Jeremiah, 5921
28:16 I will cast thee from **o** the face of the earth: 5921
30: 8 *that* I will break his yoke from **o** thy neck, 5921
31:10 declare *it* in the isles **afar o**, and say, 4480+4801
31:37 I will also **cast o** all the seed of Israel for 3988
33:24 hath chosen, he hath even **cast** them **o**? 3988
38:27 So they **left o speaking** with him; for 2790
44: 7 to **cut o** from you man and woman, child 3772
44: 8 that ye might **cut** yourselves **o**, and that *ye* 3772
44:11 against you for evil, and to **cut o** all Judah. 3772
44:18 since we **left o** to burn incense to the queen 2308
46:27 I *will* save thee from **afar o**, and thy seed 7350
47: 4 *and* to **cut o** from Tyrus and Zidon every 3772
47: 5 Ashkelon is **cut o** *with* the remnant of their 1820
48: 2 and let us **cut** it **o** from *being* a nation. 3772
48:25 The horn of Moab is **cut o**, and his arm is 1438
49:26 all the men of war shall be **cut o** in that 1826
49:30 Flee, get you **far o**, dwell deep, O ye 3966
50:16 **Cut o** the sower from Babylon, and 3772
50:30 all her men of war shall be **cut o** in that 1826
51: 6 be not **cut o** in her iniquity; for this *is* 1826
51:50 remember the LORD **afar o**, and 4480+7350
51:62 to **cut** it **o**, that none shall remain in it, 3772
La 2: 3 He hath **cut o** in *his* fierce anger all 1438
2: 7 The Lord hath **cast o** his altar, he hath 2186
3:17 thou hast **removed** my soul **far o** from 2186
3:31 For the Lord will not **cast o** for ever: 2186
3:53 They have **cut o** my life in the dungeon, 6789
3:54 over mine head; *then* I said, I am **cut o**. 1504
Eze 6:12 *He* that *is* **far o** shall die of the pestilence; 7350
8: 6 that *I* should **go far o** from my sanctuary? 7368
10:18 the glory of the LORD departed from **o** 5921
11:16 Although I have **cast** them **far o** among 7368
12:27 he prophesieth of the times *that are* **far o**. 7350
14: 8 I will **cut** him **o** from the midst of my 3772
14:13 and will **cut o** man and beast from it: 3772
14:17 so that I **cut o** man and beast from it: 3772
14:19 it in blood, to **cut o** from it man and beast: 3772
14:21 to **cut o** from it man and beast? 3772
17: 4 He **cropt o** the top of his young twigs, and 6998
17: 9 and **cut o** the fruit thereof, that it wither? 7082
17:17 and building forts, to **cut o** many persons: 3772
17:22 will set *it;* I will **crop o** from the top of his 6998
18:17 *That* hath **taken o** his hand from the poor, 7725
21: 3 will **cut o** from thee the righteous and 3772
21: 4 that I will **cut o** from thee the righteous and 3772
21:26 Remove the diadem, and **take o** the crown: 7311
23:34 and **pluck o** thine own breasts: 5423
25: 7 I will **cut** thee **o** from the people, and I will 3772
25:13 and will **cut o** man and beast from it; 3772
25:16 I will **cut o** the Cherethims, and destroy 3772
26:16 and **put o** their broidered garments: 6584
29: 8 and **cut o** man and beast out of thee. 3772
30:15 and I will **cut o** the multitude of No. 3772
31:12 have **cut** him **o**, and have left him: 3772
35: 7 **cut o** from it him that passeth out and 3772
37:11 our hope is lost: we are **cut o** for our parts. 1504
44:19 they shall **put o** their garments wherein 6584
Da 4:14 Hew down the tree, and **cut o** his branches, 7113
4:14 **shake o** his leaves, and scatter his fruit: 5426
4:27 **break o** thy sins by righteousness, and 6562
9: 7 all Israel, *that are* near, and *that are* **far o**, 7350
9:26 and two weeks shall Messiah be **cut o**, 3772
Hos 4:10 they have **left o** to take heed to the LORD. 5800
8: 3 Israel hath **cast o** *the thing that is* good: 2186
8: 4 made them idols, that they may be **cut o**. 3772
8: 5 Thy calf, O Samaria, hath **cast** *thee* **o**; 2186

Hos 10: 7 her king is cut o as the foam upon 1820
10:15 the king of Israel utterly be cut o. 1820+1820
11: 4 I was to them as they that take o the yoke 7311
Joel 1: 5 new wine, for it is cut o from your mouth. 3772
1: 9 the drink offering is cut o from the house 3772
1:16 Is not the meat cut o before our eyes, 3772
2:20 I will remove far o from you the northern 7368
3: 8 sell them to the Sabeans, to a people far o: 7350
Am 1: 5 cut o the inhabitant from the plain of Aven, 3772
1: 8 I will cut o the inhabitant from Ashdod, 3772
1:11 did cast o all pity, and his anger did tear 7843
2: 3 I will cut o the judge from the midst 3772
3:14 and the horns of the altar shall be cut o, and 1438
5: 7 and leave o righteousness in the earth, 3240
9: 8 I will destroy it from o the face of the earth; 5921
Ob 1: 5 if robbers by night, (how art thou cut o!) 1820
1: 9 mount of Esau may be cut o by slaughter. 3772
1:10 cover thee, and thou shalt be cut o for ever. 3772
1:14 to cut o those of his that did escape; 3772
Mic 2: 8 ye pull o the robe with the garment 4136+4480
3: 2 who pluck o their skin from off them, and 1497
3: 2 who pluck off their skin from o them, and 5921
3: 2 off them, and their flesh from o their bones; 5921
3: 3 my people, and flay their skin from o them; 5921
4: 3 and rebuke strong nations afar o; 5704+7350
4: 7 and her that was cast far o a strong nation: 1972
5: 9 and all thine enemies shall be cut o. 3772
5:10 that I will cut o thy horses out of the midst 3772
5:11 I will cut o the cities of thy land, and 3772
5:12 I will cut o witchcrafts out of thine hand; 3772
5:13 Thy graven images also will I cut o, and 3772
Na 1:13 For now will I break his yoke from o thee, 5921
1:14 out of the house of thy gods will I cut o 3772
1:15 more pass through thee; he is utterly cut o. 3772
2:13 and I will cut o thy prey from the earth, and 3772
3:15 the sword shall cut thee o, it shall eat thee 3772
Hab 2:10 to thy house by cutting o many people, 7096
3:17 the flock shall be cut o from the fold, and 1504
Zep 1: 2 all things from o the land, 4480+5921+6440
1: 3 I will cut o man from off the land, saith 3772
1: 3 I will cut off man from o 4480+5921+6440
1: 4 I will cut o the remnant of Baal from this 3772
1:11 cut down; all they that bear silver are cut o. 3772
3: 6 I have cut o the nations: their towers are 3772
3: 7 so their dwelling should not be cut o, 3772
Zec 5: 3 for every one that stealeth shall be cut o as 5352
5: 3 every one that sweareth shall be cut o as on 5352
6:15 they that are far o shall come and build in 7350
9: 6 and I will cut o the pride of the Philistines. 3772
9:10 I will cut o the chariot from Ephraim, and 3772
9:10 and the battle bow shall be cut o: 3772
10: 6 shall be as though I had not cast them o: 2186
11: 8 Three shepherds also I cut o in one month; 3582
11: 9 that that is to be cut o, let it be cut off; and 3582
11: 9 that that is to be cut off, let it be cut o; and 3582
11:16 which shall not visit those that be cut o, 3582
13: 2 that I will cut o the names of the idols out 3772
13: 8 two parts therein shall be cut o and die; 3772
14: 2 the residue of the people shall not be cut o 3772
Mal 2:12 The LORD will cut o the man that doth 3772
Mt 5:30 offend thee, cut it o, and cast it from thee: 1581
8:30 And there was a good way o from them a 3112
10:14 or city, shake o the dust of your feet. 1621
18: 8 cut them o, and cast them from thee: 1581
26:51 of the high priest's, and smote o his ear. 851
26:58 But Peter followed him afar o unto the high 575
27:31 they took the robe o from him, and put his 1562
27:55 many women were there beholding afar o, 575
Mk 5: 6 But when he saw Jesus afar o, he ran and 575
6:11 shake o the dust under your feet for a 1621
9:43 And if thy hand offend thee, cut it o: it is 609
9:45 And if thy foot offend thee, cut it o: it is 609
11: 8 and others cut down branches o the trees, 1537
11:13 And seeing a fig tree afar o having leaves, 3113
14:47 a servant of the high priest, and cut o his ear. 851
14:54 And Peter followed him afar o, even into 575
15:20 they took o the purple from him, and 1562
15:40 There were also women looking on afar o: 575
Lk 9: 5 shake o the very dust from your feet for a 660
10:11 cleaveth on us, we do wipe o against you: 631
14:32 while the other is yet a great way o, 4206
15:20 But when he was yet a great way o, 568
16:23 and seeth Abraham afar o, and 575+3113
17:12 men that were lepers, which stood afar o: 4207
18:13 standing afar o, would not lift up so 3113
22:50 of the high priest, and cut o his right ear. 851
22:54 priest's house. And Peter followed afar o. 3113
23:49 stood afar o, beholding these things. 575+3113
Jn 11:18 unto Jerusalem, about fifteen furlongs o: 575
18:10 high priest's servant, and cut o his right ear. 609
18:26 being his kinsman whose ear Peter cut o, 609
Ac 2:39 and to all that are afar o, 1519+3112
7:33 Lord to him, Put o thy shoes from thy feet: 3089
12: 7 And his chains fell o from his hands. 1601
13:51 But they shook o the dust of their feet 1621
16:22 and the magistrates rent o their clothes, 4048
22:23 and cast o their clothes, and threw dust into NIG
27:32 Then the soldiers cut o the ropes of the boat, 609
27:32 off the ropes of the boat, and let her fall o. 1601
28: 5 And he shook o the beast into the fire, and 660
Ro 11:17 And if some of the branches be broken o, 1575
11:19 wilt say then, The branches were broken o, 1575
11:20 because of unbelief they were broken o, 1575
11:22 otherwise thou also shalt be cut o. 1581
13:12 let us therefore cast o the works of darkness, 659
2Co 11:12 that I may cut o occasion from them which 1581
Gal 5:12 I would they were even cut o which trouble 609
Eph 2:13 far o are made nigh by the blood of Christ. 3112
2:17 preached peace to you which were afar o, 3112
4:22 That ye put o concerning the former 659
Col 2:11 in putting o the body of the sins of the flesh, 555
3: 8 But now you also put o all these; anger, 659
3: 9 seeing that ye have put o the old man with 554
1Ti 5:12 because they have cast o their first faith. 114
Heb 11:13 but having seen them afar o, and 4207
2Pe 1: 9 and cannot see far o, and hath forgotten 3467
1:14 Knowing that shortly I must put o this my 595
Rev 18:10 Standing afar o for the fear of her 575+3113
18:15 shall stand afar o for the fear of her 575+3113
18:17 as many as trade by sea, stood afar o, 575+3113

OFFENCE (19) [OFFEND]

1Sa 25:31 grief unto thee, nor o of heart unto my lord, 4383
Isa 8:14 for a rock of o to both the houses of Israel, 4383
Hos 5:15 till they acknowledge their o, and seek my 816
Mt 16:23 thou art an o unto me: for thou savourest 4625
18: 7 woe to that man by whom the o cometh. 4625
Ac 24:16 to have always a conscience void of o 677
Ro 5:15 But not as the o, so also is the free gift. 3900
5:15 For if through the o of one many be dead, 3900
5:17 For if by one man's o death reigned by one; 3900
5:18 Therefore as by the o of one judgment 3900
5:20 the law entered, that the o might abound. 3900
9:33 lay in Sion a stumblingstone and rock of o: 4625
14:20 but it is evil for that man who eateth with o. 4348
1Co 10:32 Give none o, neither to the Jews, nor to 677
2Co 6: 3 Giving no o in any thing, that the ministry 4349
11: 7 Have I committed an o in abasing myself 266
Gal 5:11 then is the o of the cross ceased. 4625
Php 1:10 and without o till the day of Christ; 677
1Pe 2: 8 And a stone of stumbling, and a rock of o, 4625

OFFENCES (7) [OFFEND]

Ecc 10: 4 not thy place; for yielding pacifieth great o. 2399
Mt 18: 7 Woe unto the world because of o: for it 4625
18: 7 for it must needs be that o come; but woe to 4625
Lk 17: 1 It is impossible but that o will come: 4625
Ro 4:25 Who was delivered for our o, and 3900
5:16 the free gift is of many o unto justification. 3900
16:17 o contrary to the doctrine which ye have 4625

OFFEND (25) [OFFENCE, OFFENCES, OFFENDED, OFFENDER, OFFENDERS]

Job 34:31 I have borne chastisement, I will not o any 2254
Ps 73:15 I should o against the generation of thy 898
119:165 love thy law: and nothing shall o them. 4383
Jer 2: 3 all that devour him shall o; evil shall come 816
50: 7 We o not, because they have sinned against 816
Hos 4:15 Israel, play the harlot, yet let not Judah o; 816
Hab 1:11 mind change, and he shall pass over, and o, 816
Mt 5:29 And if thy right eye o thee, pluck it out, and 4624
5:30 And if thy right hand o thee, cut it off, and 4624
13:41 gather out of his kingdom all things that o, 4625
17:27 Notwithstanding, lest we should o them, 4624
18: 6 But whoso shall o one of these little ones 4624
18: 8 Wherefore if thy hand or thy foot o thee, 4624
18: 9 And if thine eye o thee, pluck it out, and 4624
Mk 9:42 And whosoever shall o one of these little 4624
9:43 And if thy hand o thee, cut it off: it is better 4624
9:45 And if thy foot o thee, cut it off: it is better 4624
9:47 And if thine eye o thee, pluck it out: it is 4624
Lk 17: 2 than that he should o one of these little 4624
Jn 6:61 at it, he said unto them, Doth this o you? 4624
1Co 8:13 Wherefore, if meat make my brother to o, 4624
8:13 lest I make my brother to o. 4624
Jas 2:10 and yet o in one point, he is guilty of all. 4417
3: 2 For in many things we o all. If any man 4417
3: 2 If any man o not in word, the same is a 4417

OFFENDED (25) [OFFEND]

Ge 20: 9 what have I o thee, that thou hast brought 2398
40: 1 his baker had o their lord the king of Egypt. 2398
2Ki 18:14 of Assyria to Lachish, saying, I have o; 2398
2Ch 28:13 for whereas we have o against the LORD 819
Pr 18:19 A brother o is harder to be won than a 6586
Jer 37:18 What have I o against thee, or against thy 2398
Eze 25:12 hath greatly o, and revenged himself 816+816
Hos 13: 1 in Israel; but when he o in Baal, he died. 816
Mt 11: 6 And blessed is he, whosoever shall not be o 4624
13:21 because of the word, by and by he is o. 4624
13:57 And they were o in him. But Jesus said 4624
15:12 Knowest thou that the Pharisees were o, 4624
24:10 And then shall many be o, and shall betray 4624
26:31 All ye shall be o because of me this night: 4624
26:33 Though all men shall be o because of thee, 4624
26:33 because of thee, yet will I never be o. 4624
Mk 4:17 the word's sake, immediately they are o. 4624
6: 3 here with us? And they were o at him. 4624
14:27 All ye shall be o because of me this night: 4624
14:29 Although all shall be o, yet will not I. 4624
Lk 7:23 And blessed is he, whosoever shall not be o 4624
Jn 16: 1 I spoken unto you, that ye should not be o. 4624
Ac 25: 8 yet against Cesar, have I o any thing at all. 264
Ro 14:21 brother stumbleth, or is o, or is made weak. 4624
2Co 11:29 I am not weak? who is o, and I burn not? 4624

OFFENDER (2) [OFFEND]

Isa 29:21 That make a man an o for a word, and 2398
Ac 25:11 For if I be an o, or have committed any thing 91

OFFENDERS (1) [OFFEND]

1Ki 1:21 and my son Solomon shall be counted o. 2400

OFFER (236) [OFFERED, OFFERETH, OFFERING, OFFERINGS]

Ge 22: 2 o him there for a burnt offering upon one of 5927
Ex 22:29 Thou shalt not delay to o the first of thy ripe NIH
23:18 Thou shalt not o the blood of my sacrifice 2076
29:36 thou shalt o every day a bullock for a sin 6213
29:38 Now this is that which thou shalt o upon 6213
29:39 The one lamb thou shalt o in the morning; 6213
29:39 and the other lamb thou shalt o at even: 6213
29:41 the other lamb thou shalt o at even, and 6213
30: 9 Ye shall o no strange incense thereon, nor 5927
34:25 Thou shalt not o the blood of my sacrifice 7819
35:24 Every one that did o an offering of silver 7311
Lev 1: 3 the herd, let him o a male without blemish: 7126
1: 3 he shall o it of his own voluntary will at 7126
2: 1 when any will o a meat offering unto 7126
2:12 ye shall o them unto the LORD: 7126
2:13 with all thine offerings thou shalt o salt. 7126
2:14 if thou o a meat offering of thy firstfruits 7126
2:14 thou shalt o for the meat offering of thy 7126
3: 1 of peace offering, if he o it of the herd; 7126
3: 1 he shall o it without blemish before 7126
3: 3 he shall o of the sacrifice of the peace 7126
3: 6 or female, he shall o it without blemish. 7126
3: 7 If he o a lamb for his offering, then shall he 7126
3: 7 then shall he o it before the LORD. 7126
3: 9 he shall o of the sacrifice of the peace 7126
3:12 a goat, then he shall o it before the LORD. 7126
3:14 he shall o thereof his offering, even an 7126
4:14 the congregation shall o a young bullock 7126
5: 8 who shall o that which is for the sin 7126
5:10 he shall o the second for a burnt offering, 6213
6:14 the sons of Aaron shall o it before 7126
6:20 which they shall o unto the LORD in 7126
6:21 thou o for a sweet savour unto the LORD. 7126
6:22 sons that is anointed in his stead shall o it: 6213
7: 3 he shall o of it all the fat thereof; the rump, 7126
7:11 which he shall o unto the LORD. 7126
7:12 If he o it for a thanksgiving, then he shall 7126
7:12 he shall o with the sacrifice of thanksgiving 7126
7:13 he shall o for his offering leavened bread 7126
7:14 of it he shall o one out of the whole 7126
7:25 of which men o an offering made by fire 7126
7:38 Israel to o their oblations unto the LORD, 7126
9: 2 and o them before the LORD. 7126
9: 7 o thy sin offering, and thy burnt offering, 6213
9: 7 o the offering of the people, and make an 6213
12: 7 Who shall o it before the LORD, and 7126
14:12 o him for a trespass offering, and the log of 7126
14:19 the priest shall o the sin offering, and 6213
14:20 And the priest shall o the burnt offering and 5927
14:30 And he shall o the one of the turtledoves, or 6213
15:15 the priest shall o them, the one for a sin 6213
15:30 the priest shall o the one for a sin offering, 6213
16: 6 Aaron shall o his bullock of the sin 7126
16: 9 lot fell, and o him for a sin offering. 6213
16:24 o his burnt offering, and the burnt offering 6213
17: 4 to o an offering unto the LORD before 7126
17: 5 which they o in the open field, even that 2076
17: 5 o them for peace offerings unto 2076
17: 7 they shall no more o their sacrifices unto 2076
17: 9 the congregation, to o it unto the LORD; 6213
19: 5 if ye o a sacrifice of peace offerings 2076+2077
19: 5 the LORD, ye shall o it at your own will. 2076
19: 6 It shall be eaten the same day ye o it, and 2077
21: 6 and the bread of their God, they do o: 7126
21:17 let him not approach to o the bread of his 7126
21:21 shall come nigh to o the offerings of 7126
21:21 he shall not come nigh to o the bread of his 7126
22:15 of Israel, which they o unto the LORD; 7311
22:18 that will o his oblation for all his vows, and 7126
22:18 which they will o unto the LORD for a 7126
22:19 Ye shall o at your own will a male without NIH
22:20 hath a blemish, that shall ye not o: 7126
22:22 ye shall not o these unto the LORD, 7126
22:23 that mayest thou o for a freewill offering; 6213
22:24 Ye shall not o unto the LORD that which 7126
22:25 Neither from a stranger's hand shall ye o 7126
22:29 when ye will o a sacrifice of thanksgiving 2076
22:29 unto the LORD, o it at your own will. 2076
23: 8 ye shall o an offering made by fire unto 7126
23:12 ye shall o that day when ye wave the sheaf 6213
23:16 ye shall o a new meat offering unto 7126
23:18 ye shall o with the bread seven lambs 7126
23:25 ye shall o an offering made by fire unto 7126
23:27 o an offering made by fire unto 7126
23:36 Seven days ye shall o an offering made by 7126
23:36 ye shall o an offering made by fire unto 7126
23:37 to o an offering made by fire unto 7126
27:11 of which they do not o a sacrifice unto 7126
Nu 5:25 before the LORD, and o it upon the altar: 7126
6:11 the priest shall o the one for a sin offering, 6213
6:14 he shall o his offering unto the LORD, 7126
6:16 shall o his sin offering, and his burnt 6213
6:17 he shall o the ram for a sacrifice of peace 6213
6:17 the priest shall o also his meat offering, and 6213
7:11 They shall o their offering, each prince on 7126
7:18 the son of Zuar, prince of Issachar, did o: 7126
7:24 prince of the children of Zebulun, did o: NIH
7:30 prince of the children of Reuben, did o: NIH
7:36 prince of the children of Simeon, did o: NIH
8:11 Aaron shall o the Levites before 5130
8:12 thou shalt o the one for a sin offering, and 6213
8:13 o them for an offering unto the LORD. 5130
8:15 cleanse them, and o them for an offering. 5130
9: 7 that we may not o an offering of 7126
15: 7 for a drink offering thou shalt o the third 7126
15:14 will o an offering made by fire, of a sweet 6213
15:19 ye shall o up a heave offering unto 7311
15:20 Ye shall o up a cake of the first of your 7311
15:24 that all the congregation shall o one young 6213
16:40 come near to o incense before the LORD; 6999
18:12 the firstfruits of them which they shall o 5414
18:19 the children of Israel o unto the LORD, 7311
18:24 which they o as a heave offering unto 7311
18:26 ye shall o up a heave offering of it for 7311
18:28 Thus you also shall o a heave offering unto 7311
18:29 Out of all your gifts ye shall o every heave 7311
28: 2 shall ye observe to o unto me in their due 7126
28: 3 by fire which ye shall o unto the LORD; 7126
28: 4 The one lamb shalt thou o in the morning, 6213
28: 4 and the other lamb shalt thou o at even; 6213
28: 8 the other lamb shalt thou o at even: as 6213
28: 8 thou shalt o it, a sacrifice made by fire, 6213
28:11 in the beginnings of your months ye shall o 7126
28:19 ye shall o a sacrifice made by fire for a 7126
28:20 three tenth deals shall ye o for a bullock, 6213
28:21 A several tenth deal shalt thou o for every 6213
28:23 Ye shall o these beside the burnt offering in 6213
28:24 After this manner ye shall o daily, 6213
28:27 ye shall o the burnt offering for a sweet 7126

Nu 28:31 Ye shall **o** *them* besides the continual burnt 6213
29: 2 ye shall **o** a burnt offering for a sweet 6213
29: 8 ye shall **o** a burnt offering unto the LORD 7126
29:13 ye shall **o** a burnt offering, a sacrifice made 7126
29:17 on the second day *ye shall* **o** twelve young NIH
29:36 ye shall **o** a burnt offering, a sacrifice made 7126
Dt 12:13 Take heed to thyself that thou **o** not thy 5927
12:14 there thou shalt **o** thy burnt offerings, and 5927
12:27 thou shalt **o** thy burnt offerings, the flesh 6213
18: 3 from them that **o** a sacrifice, whether *it be* 2076
27: 6 thou shalt **o** burnt offerings thereon unto 5927
27: 7 thou shalt **o** peace offerings, and shalt eat 2076
33:19 there they shall **o** sacrifices of 2076
Jos 22:23 or if to **o** thereon burnt offering or 5927
22:23 or if to **o** peace offerings thereon, 6213
Jdg 3:18 when he had made an end to **o** the present, 7126
6:26 **o** a burnt sacrifice with the wood of 5927
11:31 and I will **o** it **up** *for* a burnt offering. 5927
13:16 if thou wilt **o** a burnt offering, thou must 6213
13:16 thou must **o** it unto the LORD. 5927
16:23 to **o** a great sacrifice unto Dagon their god, 2076
1Sa 1:21 went up to **o** unto the LORD the yearly 2076
2:19 when she came up with her husband to **o** 2076
2:28 to **o** upon mine altar, to burn incense, 5927
10: 8 to **o** burnt offerings, *and* to sacrifice 5927
2Sa 24:12 I **o** thee three *things;* choose thee one of 5190
24:22 and **o up** what seemeth good unto him: 5927
24:24 neither will I **o** burnt offerings unto 5927
1Ki 3: 4 thousand burnt offerings did Solomon **o up** 5927
9:25 three times in a year did Solomon **o** burnt 5927
13: 2 upon thee shall he **o** the priests of the high 2076
2Ki 5:17 for thy servant will henceforth **o** neither 6213
10:24 when they went in to **o** sacrifices and 6213
1Ch 16:40 To **o** burnt offerings unto the LORD upon 5927
21:10 I **o** thee three *things:* choose thee one of 5186
21:24 nor **o** burnt offerings without cost. 5927
23:31 to **o** all burnt sacrifices unto the LORD in 5927
29:14 that we should be able to **o** *so* **willingly** 5068
29:17 are present here, to **o willingly** unto thee. 5068
2Ch 23:18 to **o** the burnt offerings of the LORD, as it 5927
24:14 to **o** *withal,* and spoons, and vessels of gold 5927
29:21 Aaron to **o** *them* on the altar of the LORD. 5927
29:27 Hezekiah commanded to **o** the burnt 5927
35:12 to **o** unto the LORD, as it is written in 7126
35:16 to **o** burnt offerings upon the altar of 5927
Ezr 3: 2 God of Israel, to **o** burnt offerings thereon, 5927
3: 6 they to **o** burnt offerings unto the LORD. 5927
6:10 That they may **o** sacrifices of sweet savours 1934
7:17 **o** them upon the altar of the house of your 7127
Job 42: 8 and **o up** for yourselves a burnt offering; 5927
Ps 4: 5 **O** the sacrifices of righteousness, and 2076
16: 4 their drink offerings of blood will I not **o**, 5258
27: 6 will I **o** in his tabernacle sacrifices of joy; 2076
50:14 **O** unto God thanksgiving; and pay thy 2076
51:19 then shall they **o** bullocks upon thine altar. 5927
66:15 I will **o** unto thee burnt sacrifices of 5927
66:15 of rams; I will **o** bullocks with goats. 6213
72:10 the kings of Sheba and Seba shall **o** gifts. 7126
116:17 I will **o** to thee the sacrifice of 2076
Isa 57: 7 even thither wentest thou up to **o** sacrifice. 2076
Jer 11:12 unto the gods unto whom they **o incense**: 6999
14:12 when they **o** burnt offering and an oblation, 5927
33:18 want a man before me to **o** burnt offerings, 5927
Eze 6:13 the place where they did **o** sweet savour to 5414
20:31 For when *ye* **o** your gifts, when *ye* make 5375
43:18 to **o** burnt offerings thereon, and to sprinkle 5927
43:22 on the second day thou shalt **o** a kid of 7126
43:23 shalt **o** a young bullock without blemish, 7126
43:24 thou shalt **o** them before the LORD, and 7126
43:24 they shall **o** them **up** *for* a burnt offering 5927
44: 7 when ye **o** my bread, the fat and the blood, 7126
44:15 they shall stand before me to **o** unto me 7126
44:27 he shall **o** his sin offering, saith the Lord 7126
45: 1 ye shall **o** an oblation unto the LORD, 7311
45:13 This *is* the oblation that ye shall **o**; the sixth 7311
45:14 *ye shall* **o** the tenth part of a bath out of NIH
46: 4 the burnt offering that the prince shall **o** 7126
48: 8 shall be the offering which ye shall **o** *of* 7311
48: 9 The oblation that ye shall **o** unto 7311
48:20 ye shall **o** the holy oblation foursquare, 7311
Da 2:46 commanded that *they* should **o** an oblation 5260
Hos 9: 4 They shall not **o** wine *offerings* to 5258
Am 4: 5 **o** a sacrifice of thanksgiving with leaven, 6999
5:22 Though ye **o** me burnt offerings and 5927
Hag 2:14 and *that* which they **o** there *is* unclean. 7126
Mal 1: 7 *Ye* **o** polluted bread upon mine altar; and 5066
1: 8 if ye **o** the blind for sacrifice, *is it* not evil? 5066
1: 8 if ye **o** the lame and sick, *is it* not evil? 5066
1: 8 **o** it now unto thy governor; will he be 7126
3: 3 that they may **o** unto the LORD an 5066
Mt 5:24 thy brother, and then come and **o** thy gift. *4374*
8: 4 **o** the gift that Moses commanded for a *4374*
Mk 1:44 **o** for thy cleansing *those things* which *4374*
Lk 2:24 And to **o** a sacrifice according to that which *1325*
5:14 to the priest, and **o** for thy cleansing, *4374*
6:29 thee on the *one* cheek **o** also the other; *3930*
11:12 shall ask an egg, will he **o** him a scorpion? *1929*
Heb 5: 1 that he may **o** both gifts and sacrifices for *4374*
5: 3 the people, so also for himself, to **o** for sins. *4374*
7:27 as *those* high priests, to **o up** sacrifice, *399*
8: 3 For every high priest is ordained to **o** gifts *4374*
8: 3 that this *man* have somewhat also to **o**. *4374*
8: 4 seeing that there are priests that **o** gifts *4374*
9:25 Nor yet that he should **o** himself often, *4374*
13:15 let us **o** the sacrifice of praise to God *399*
1Pe 2: 5 holy priesthood, to **o up** spiritual sacrifices, *399*
Rev 8: 3 that he should **o** *it* with the prayers of all *1325*

OFFERED (143) [OFFER]

Ge 8:20 and **o** burnt offerings on the altar. 5927
22:13 **o** him **up** for a burnt offering in the stead of 5927
31:54 Jacob **o** sacrifice upon the mount, and 2076
46: 1 **o** sacrifices unto the God of his father 2076
Ex 24: 5 which **o** burnt offerings, and 5927
32: 6 **o** burnt offerings, and brought peace 5927
Ex 35:22 every man that **o** *offered* an offering of 5130
35:22 every man that offered **o** an offering of gold NIH
40:29 **o** upon it the burnt offering and the meat 5927
Lev 7: 8 skin of the burnt offering which he hath **o**. 7126
7:15 shall be eaten the same day that it is **o**; 7133
9:15 and slew it, and **o** it **for sin**, as the first. 2398
9:16 and **o** it according to the manner. 6213
10: 1 **o** strange fire before the LORD, 7126
10:19 *this* day have they **o** their sin offering and 7126
16: 1 when they **o** before the LORD, and died; 7126
Nu 3: 4 when they **o** strange fire before 7126
7: 2 and were over them that were numbered, **o**: 7126
7:10 the princes **o** *for* dedicating of the altar in 7126
7:10 even the princes **o** their offering before 7126
7:12 he that **o** his offering the first day was 7126
7:19 He **o** *for* his offering one silver charger, 7126
7:42 of Deuel, prince of the children of Gad, **o**: NIH
7:48 prince of the children of Ephraim, **o**: NIH
7:54 On the eighth day **o** Gamaliel the son of NIH
7:60 prince of the children of Benjamin, **o**: NIH
7:66 prince of the children of Dan, **o**: NIH
7:72 prince of the children of Asher, **o**: NIH
7:78 prince of the children of Naphtali, **o**: NIH
8:21 Aaron **o** them *as* an offering before 5130
16:35 two hundred and fifty men that **o** incense. 7126
16:38 for they **o** them before the LORD, 7126
16:39 wherewith they that were burnt had **o**; 7126
22:40 Balak **o** oxen and sheep, and sent to 2076
23: 2 and Balaam **o** on *every* altar a bullock and 5927
23: 4 I have **o** upon *every* altar a bullock and 5927
23:14 and **o** a bullock and a ram on *every* altar. 5927
23:30 and **o** a bullock and a ram on *every* altar. 5927
26:61 when they **o** strange fire before 7126
28:15 a sin offering unto the LORD shall be **o**, 6213
28:24 it shall be **o** beside the continual burnt 6213
31:52 all the gold of the offering that they **o up** to 7311
Jos 8:31 they **o** thereon burnt offerings unto 5927
Jdg 5: 2 when the people **willingly o** themselves. 5068
5: 9 that **o** themselves **willingly** among 5068
6:28 the second bullock was **o** upon the altar that 5927
13:19 and **o** *it* upon a rock unto the LORD: 5927
20:26 **o** burnt offerings and peace offerings 5927
21: 4 and **o** burnt offerings and peace offerings. 5927
1Sa 1: 4 when the time was that Elkanah **o**, he gave 2076
2:13 people *was, that* when any man **o** sacrifice, 2076
6:14 **o** the kine a burnt offering unto 5927
6:15 the men of Beth-shemesh **o** burnt offerings 5927
7: 9 **o** it *for* a burnt offering wholly unto 5927
13: 9 And he **o** the burnt offering. 5927
13:12 myself therefore, and **o** a burnt offering. 5927
2Sa 6:17 David **o** burnt offerings and peace offerings 5927
15:12 *even* from Giloh, while he **o** sacrifices. 2076
24:25 and **o** burnt offerings and peace offerings. 5927
1Ki 3:15 **o up** burnt offerings, and offered peace 5927
3:15 **o** peace offerings, and made a feast to all 6213
8:62 with him, **o** sacrifice before the LORD. 2076
8:63 Solomon **o** a sacrifice of peace offerings, 2076
8:63 which he **o** unto the LORD, two and 2076
8:64 for there he **o** burnt offerings, and meat 6213
12:32 he **o** upon the altar (so did he in Beth-el,) 5927
12:33 So he **o** upon the altar which he had made 5927
12:33 and he **o** upon the altar, and burnt incense. 5927
22:43 *for* the people **o** and burnt incense yet in 2076
2Ki 3:20 when the meat offering was **o**, that, behold, 5927
3:27 **o** him *for* a burnt offering upon the wall. 5927
16:12 king approached to the altar, and **o** thereon. 5927
1Ch 6:49 his sons **o** upon the altar of the burnt 6999
15:26 that they **o** seven bullocks and seven rams. 2076
16: 1 they **o** burnt sacrifices and peace offerings 7126
21:26 **o** burnt offerings and peace offerings, and 5927
29: 6 the rulers over the king's work, **o willingly**, 5068
29: 9 for that they **o willingly**, because 5068
29: 9 with perfect heart they **o willingly** to 5068
29:17 heart I have **willingly o** all these *things:* 5068
29:21 **o** burnt offerings unto the LORD, on 5927
2Ch 1: 6 and **o** a thousand burnt offerings upon it. 5927
4: 6 such **things** as they **o** for the burnt offering 4639
7: 4 all the people **o** sacrifices before 2076
7: 5 king Solomon **o** a sacrifice of twenty and 2076
7: 7 for there he **o** burnt offerings, and the fat of 6213
8:12 Solomon **o** burnt offerings unto the LORD 5927
15:11 they **o** unto the LORD the same time, 2076
17:16 who **willingly o** himself unto the LORD; 5068
24:14 they **o** burnt offerings in the house of 5927
29: 7 have not burned incense nor **o** burnt offerings 5927
Ezr 1: 6 beside all *that* was **willingly o**. 5068
2:68 **o freely** for the house of God to set it up in 5068
3: 3 they **o** burnt offerings thereon unto 5927
3: 4 and **o** the daily burnt offerings by number, NIH
3: 5 afterward **o** the continual burnt offering, NIH
3: 5 of every one that **willingly o** a freewill 5068
6: 3 the place where they **o** sacrifices, and 1684
6:17 **o** at the dedication of this house of God an 7127
7:15 his counsellers have **freely o** unto the God 5069
8:25 his lords, and all Israel *there* present, had **o**: 7311
8:35 **o** burnt offerings unto the God of Israel, 7126
10:19 *they* **o** a ram of the flock for their trespass. NIH
Ne 11: 2 that **willingly o** themselves to dwell at 5068
12:43 Also that day they **o** great sacrifices, and 2076
Job 1: 5 **o** burnt offerings *according to* the number 5927
Isa 57: 6 drink offering, thou hast **o** a meat offering. 5927
66: 3 an oblation, *as if he* **o** swine's blood; NIH
Jer 32:29 upon whose roofs they have **o incense** unto 6999
Eze 20:28 they **o** there their sacrifices, and there they 2076
48:12 *this* oblation of the land that is **o** shall be 8641
Da 11:18 cause the reproach **o by** him to cease; 3807.1
Am 5:25 Have ye **o** unto me sacrifices and 5066
Jnh 1:16 **o** a sacrifice unto the LORD, and 2076
Mal 1:11 in every place incense *shall be* **o** unto my 5066
Ac 7:41 and **o** sacrifice unto the idol, and rejoiced in *321*
7:42 have ye **o** to me slain beasts and *4374*
8:18 Holy Ghost was given, he **o** them money, *4374*
15:29 That *ye* abstain from **meats o to idols**, and *1494*
21:25 keep themselves from **things o to idols**, *1494*
21:26 until that an offering should be **o** for every *4374*
1Co 8: 1 Now as touching **things o unto idols**, *1494*
8: 4 **things** that are **o in sacrifice unto idols**, *1494*
8: 7 this hour, eat *it* as a **thing o unto an idol**; *1494*
8:10 to eat those **things** which are **o to idols**; *1494*
10:19 that which is **o in sacrifice to idols** is any *1494*
10:28 unto you, This is **o in sacrifice unto idols**, *1494*
Php 2:17 and if I be **o** upon the sacrifice and *4689*
2Ti 4: 6 For I am now ready to be **o**, and the time of *4689*
Heb 5: 7 when he had **o up** prayers and *4374*
7:27 for this he did once, when he **o up** himself. *399*
9: 7 which he **o** for himself, and *for* the errors of *4374*
9: 9 in which were **o** both gifts and sacrifices, *4374*
9:14 who through the eternal Spirit **o** himself *4374*
9:28 So Christ was once **o** to bear the sins of *4374*
10: 1 never with those sacrifices which they **o** *4374*
10: 2 then would they not have ceased to be **o**? *4374*
10: 8 neither hadst pleasure *therein:* which are **o** *4374*
10:12 But this *man,* after he had **o** one sacrifice *4374*
11: 4 By faith Abel **o** unto God a more excellent *4374*
11:17 when he was tried, **o up** Isaac: *4374*
11:17 he that had received the promises **o up** *his* *4374*
Jas 2:21 when he had **o** Isaac his son upon the altar? *399*

OFFERETH (15) [OFFER]

Lev 6:26 The priest that **o** it **for sin** shall eat it: in 2398
7: 8 the priest that **o** *any* man's burnt offering, 7126
7: 9 and in the pan, shall be the priest's that **o** it. 7126
7:16 it shall be eaten the *same* day that he **o** his 7126
7:18 neither shall it be imputed unto him that **o** 7126
7:29 He that **o** the sacrifice of his peace 7126
7:33 that **o** the blood of the peace offerings, and 7126
17: 8 that **o** a burnt offering or sacrifice, 5927
21: 8 for he **o** the bread of thy God: 7126
22:21 whosoever **o** a sacrifice of peace offerings 7126
Nu 15: 4 shall he that **o** his offering unto the LORD 7126
Ps 50:23 Whoso **o** praise glorifieth me: and to him 2076
Isa 66: 3 he that **o** an oblation, *as if he offered* 5927
Jer 48:35 him that **o** *in* the high places, and him that 5927
Mal 2:12 him that **o** an offering unto the LORD of 5066

OFFERING (724) [OFFER]

Ge 4: 3 fruit of the ground an **o** unto the LORD. 4503
4: 4 LORD had respect unto Abel and to his **o**: 4503
4: 5 unto Cain and to his **o** he had not respect. 4503
22: 2 offer him there for a **burnt o** upon one of 5930
22: 3 clave the wood for the **burnt o**, and 5930
22: 6 Abraham took the wood of the **burnt o**, 5930
22: 7 but where *is* the lamb for a **burnt o**? 5930
22: 8 will provide himself a lamb for a **burnt o**: 5930
22:13 offered him up for a **burnt o** in the stead of 5930
35:14 he poured a **drink o** thereon, and he poured 5262
Ex 18:12 took a **burnt o** and sacrifices for God: 5930
25: 2 children of Israel, that they bring me an **o**: 8641
25: 2 willingly with his heart ye shall take my **o**. 8641
25: 3 this *is* the **o** which ye shall take of them; 8641
29:14 with fire without the camp: it *is* a **sin o**. 2403
29:18 it *is* a **burnt o** unto the LORD: it *is* a 5930
29:18 an **o made by fire** unto the LORD. 801
29:24 shalt wave them *for* a **wave o** before 8573
29:25 burn *them* upon the altar for a **burnt o**, 5930
29:25 it *is* an **o made by fire** unto the LORD. 801
29:26 wave it *for* a **wave o** before the LORD: 8573
29:27 thou shalt sanctify the breast of the **wave o**, 8573
29:27 the shoulder of the **heave o**, which is 8641
29:28 for it *is* a **heave o**: and it shall be a heave 8641
29:28 it shall be a **heave o** from the children of 8641
29:28 *even* their **heave o** unto the LORD. 8641
29:36 day a bullock *for* a **sin o** for atonement: 2403
29:40 fourth *part* of a hin of wine *for* a **drink o**. 5262
29:41 shalt do thereto according to the **meat o** of 4503
29:41 according to the **drink o** thereof, for a 5262
29:41 an **o made by fire** unto the LORD. 801
29:42 *This shall be* a continual **burnt o** 5930
30: 9 nor burnt sacrifice, nor **meat o**; 4503
30: 9 neither shall ye pour **drink o** thereon. 5262
30:10 with the blood of the **sin o** of atonements: 2403
30:13 a half shekel *shall be* the **o** of the LORD. 8641
30:14 above, shall give an **o** unto the LORD. 8641
30:15 when *they* give an **o** unto the LORD, 8641
30:20 to burn **o made by fire** unto the LORD: 801
30:28 the altar of **burnt o** with all his vessels, 5930
31: 9 the altar of **burnt o** with all his furniture, 5930
35: 5 Take ye from amongst you an **o** unto 8641
35: 5 let him bring it, an **o** of the LORD; 8641
35:16 The altar of **burnt o** with his brasen grate, 5930
35:21 they brought the LORD'S **o** to the work of 8641
35:22 every man that offered *offered* an **o** of gold 8573
35:24 Every one that did offer an **o** of silver and 8641
35:24 of silver and brass brought the LORD'S **o**: 8641
35:29 The children of Israel brought a **willing o** 5071
36: 3 they received of Moses all the **o**, which 8641
36: 6 any more work for the **o** of the sanctuary. 8641
38: 1 he made the altar of **burnt o** *of* shittim 5930
38:24 of the holy *place,* even the gold of the **o**, 8573
38:29 the brass of the **o** *was* seventy talents, and 8573
40: 6 thou shalt set the altar of the **burnt o** before 5930
40:10 thou shalt anoint the altar of the **burnt o**, 5930
40:29 he put the altar of **burnt o** *by* the door of 5930
40:29 offered upon it the **burnt o** and the meat 5930
40:29 upon it the burnt offering and the **meat o**; 4503
Lev 1: 2 If *any* man of you bring an **o** unto 7133
1: 2 ye shall bring your **o** of the cattle, *even* of 7133
1: 3 If his **o** *be* a burnt sacrifice of the herd, 7133
1: 4 put his hand upon the head of the **burnt o**; 5930
1: 6 he shall flay the **burnt o**, and cut it into his 5930
1: 9 *to be* a burnt sacrifice, an **o made by fire**, 801
1:10 if his **o** *be* of the flocks, *namely,* of 7133
1:13 it *is* a burnt sacrifice, an **o made by fire**, of a 801
1:14 if the burnt sacrifice for his **o** to 7133
1:14 he shall bring his **o** of turtledoves, or 7133
1:17 it *is* a burnt sacrifice, an **o made by fire**, of a 801
2: 1 when any will offer a **meat o** unto 4503
2: 1 the LORD, his **o** shall be *of* fine flour; 7133
2: 2 *to be* an **o made by fire**, of a sweet savour 801
2: 3 the remnant of the **meat o** *shall be* Aaron's 4503

O

Lev 2: 4 if thou bring an oblation of a **meat o** baken 4503
2: 5 if thy oblation *be* a **meat o** *baken* in a pan, 4503
2: 6 and pour oil thereon: it *is* a **meat o**. 4503
2: 7 if thy oblation *be* a **meat o** *baken* in 4503
2: 8 thou shalt bring the **meat o** that is made of 4503
2: 8 the priest, he shall take from the **meat o** a 4503
2: 9 *it is* an **o made by fire**, of a sweet savour 801
2:10 that which is left of the **meat o** *shall be* 4503
2:11 No **meat o**, which ye shall bring unto 4503
2:11 *in* any **o** of the LORD **made by fire**. 801
2:13 every oblation of thy **meat o** shalt thou 4503
2:13 of thy God to be lacking from thy **meat o**: 4503
2:14 if thou offer a **meat o** of *thy* firstfruits unto 4503
2:14 thou shalt offer for the **meat o** of thy 4503
2:15 and lay frankincense thereon: it *is* a **meat o**. 4503
2:16 *it is* an **o made by fire** unto the LORD. 801
3: 1 if his oblation *be* a sacrifice of **peace o**, 8002
3: 2 he shall lay his hand upon the head of his **o**, 7133
3: 3 he shall offer of the sacrifice of the **peace o** 8002
3: 3 offering an **o made by fire** unto the LORD; 801
3: 5 *it is* an **o made by fire**, of a sweet savour 801
3: 6 if his **o** for a sacrifice of peace offering 7133
3: 6 if his offering for a sacrifice of **peace o** 8002
3: 7 If he offer a lamb for his **o**, then shall he 7133
3: 8 he shall lay his hand upon the head of his **o**, 7133
3: 9 he shall offer of the sacrifice of the **peace o** 8002
3: 9 offering an **o made by fire** unto the LORD; 801
3:11 *it is* the food of the **o made by fire** unto 801
3:12 if his **o** *be* a goat, then he shall offer it 7133
3:14 he shall offer thereof his **o**, *even* an offering 7133
3:14 *even* an **o made by fire** unto the LORD; 801
3:16 *it is* the food of the **o made by fire** for a 801
4: 3 blemish unto the LORD for a **sin o**. 2403
4: 7 at the bottom of the altar of the **burnt o**, 5930
4: 8 it all the fat of the bullock *for* the **sin o**; 2403
4:10 burn them upon the altar of the **burnt o**. 5930
4:18 at the bottom of the altar of the **burnt o**, 5930
4:20 as he did with the bullock for a **sin o**, 2403
4:21 it *is* a **sin o** for the congregation. 2403
4:23 he shall bring his **o**, a kid of the goats, 7133
4:24 they kill the **burnt o** before the LORD: 5930
4:24 offering before the LORD: it *is* a **sin o**. 2403
4:25 of the blood of the **sin o** with his finger, 2403
4:25 *it* upon the horns of the altar of **burnt o**, 5930
4:25 blood at the bottom of the altar of **burnt o**. 5930
4:28 he shall bring his **o**, a kid of the goats, 7133
4:29 lay his hand upon the head of the **sin o**, 2403
4:29 slay the **sin o** in the place of the burnt 2403
4:29 the sin offering in the place of the **burnt o**. 5930
4:30 *it* upon the horns of the altar of **burnt o**, 5930
4:32 if he bring a lamb for a sin **o**, he shall bring 7133
4:33 lay his hand upon the head of the **sin o**, 2403
4:33 slay it for a **sin o** in the place where they 2403
4:33 in the place where they kill the **burnt o**. 5930
4:34 of the blood of the **sin o** with his finger, 2403
4:34 *it* upon the horns of the altar of **burnt o**, 5930
5: 6 he shall bring his **trespass o** unto 817
5: 6 a lamb or a kid of the goats, for a **sin o**; 2403
5: 7 one for a **sin o**, and the other for a burnt 2403
5: 7 a sin offering, and the other for a **burnt o**. 5930
5: 8 who shall offer *that* which *is* for the **sin o** 2403
5: 9 he shall sprinkle of the blood of the **sin o** 2403
5: 9 out at the bottom of the altar: it *is* a **sin o**. 2403
5:10 And he shall offer the second *for* a **burnt o**, 5930
5:11 he that sinned shall bring for his **o** the tenth 7133
5:11 *part* of an ephah of fine flour for a **sin o**; 2403
5:11 *any* frankincense thereon: for it *is* a **sin o**. 2403
5:12 made by fire unto the LORD: it *is* a **sin o**. 2403
5:13 *remnant* shall be the priest's, as a **meat o**. 4503
5:15 the shekel of the sanctuary, for a **trespass o**: 817
5:16 for him with the ram of the **trespass o**, 817
5:18 for a **trespass o**, unto the priest: 817
5:19 It *is* a **trespass o**: he hath certainly 817
6: 5 it appertaineth, in the day of his **trespass o**. 819
6: 6 he shall bring his **trespass o** unto 817
6: 6 for a **trespass o**, unto the priest: 817
6: 9 saying, This *is* the law of the **burnt o**: 5930
6: 9 It *is* the **burnt o**, because of the burning 5930
6:10 consumed with the **burnt o** on the altar, 5930
6:12 lay the **burnt o** in order upon it; 5930
6:14 this *is* the law of the **meat o**: the sons of 4503
6:15 of the flour of the **meat o**, and of the oil 4503
6:15 the frankincense which *is* upon the **meat o**, 4503
6:17 as *is* the **sin o**, and as the trespass offering. 2403
6:17 as *is* the sin offering, and as the **trespass o**. 817
6:20 This *is* the **o** of Aaron and of his sons, 7133
6:20 ephah of fine flour *for* a **meat o** perpetual, 4503
6:21 the baken pieces of the **meat o** shalt thou 4503
6:23 For every **meat o** for the priest shall be 4503
6:25 saying, This *is* the law of the **sin o**: 2403
6:25 In the place where the **burnt o** is killed 5930
6:25 shall the **sin o** be killed before the LORD: 2403
6:30 no **sin o**, whereof *any* of the blood is 2403
7: 1 Likewise this *is* the law of the **trespass o**: 817
7: 2 In the place where they kill the **burnt o** 5930
7: 2 burnt offering shall they kill the **trespass o**: 817
7: 5 altar *for* an **o made by fire** unto the LORD: 801
7: 5 by fire unto the LORD: it *is* a **trespass o**. 817
7: 7 As the **sin o** *is*, so *is* the trespass offering: 2403
7: 7 As the sin offering *is*, so *is* the **trespass o**: 817
7: 8 the priest that offereth *any* man's **burnt o**, 5930
7: 8 skin of the **burnt o** which he hath offered. 5930
7: 9 all the **meat o** that is baken in the oven, 4503
7:10 every **meat o**, mingled with oil, and dry, 4503
7:13 he shall offer *for* his **o** leavened bread with 7133
7:14 oblation *for* a **heave o** unto the LORD, 8641
7:16 if the sacrifice of his **o** *be* a vow, or 7133
7:16 of his offering *be* a vow, or a **voluntary o**, 5071
7:25 of which *men* offer an **o made by fire** unto 801
7:30 that the breast may be waved *for* a **wave o** 8573
7:32 **heave o** of the sacrifices of your peace 8641
7:37 This *is* the law of the **burnt o**, of the meat 5930
7:37 of the **meat o**, and of the sin offering, and 4503
7:37 of the **sin o**, and of the trespass offering, 2403
7:37 of the **trespass o**, and of the consecrations, 817

Lev 8: 2 a bullock *for* the **sin o**, and two rams, and 2403
8:14 he brought the bullock *for* the **sin o**: and 2403
8:14 upon the head of the bullock *for* the **sin o**. 2403
8:18 he brought the ram for the **burnt o**: and 5930
8:21 *and* an **o made by fire** unto the LORD; 801
8:27 waved them *for* a **wave o** before 8573
8:28 burnt *them* on the altar upon the **burnt o**: 5930
8:28 it *is* an **o made by fire** unto the LORD. 801
8:29 waved it *for* a **wave o** before the LORD: 8573
9: 2 Take thee a young calf for a **sin o**, and 2403
9: 2 a ram for a **burnt o**, without blemish, and 5930
9: 3 Take ye a kid of the goats for a **sin o**; 2403
9: 3 first year, without blemish, for a **burnt o**; 5930
9: 4 and a **meat o** mingled with oil: 4503
9: 7 offer thy **sin o**, and thy burnt offering, and 2403
9: 7 thy **burnt o**, and make an atonement for 5930
9: 7 offer the **o** of the people, and make an 7133
9: 8 unto the altar, and slew the calf of the **sin o**, 2403
9:10 and the caul above the liver of the **sin o**, 2403
9:12 he slew the **burnt o**; and Aaron's sons 5930
9:13 they presented the **burnt o** unto him, 5930
9:14 burnt *them* upon the **burnt o** on the altar. 5930
9:15 he brought the people's **o**, and took 7133
9:15 which *was* the **sin o** for the people, and 2403
9:16 he brought the **burnt o**, and offered it 5930
9:17 he brought the **meat o**, and took a handful 4503
9:21 waved *for* a **wave o** before the LORD; 8573
9:22 came down from **o** of the sin offering, and 6213
9:22 came down from offering of the **sin o**, and 2403
9:22 and the **burnt o**, and peace offerings. 5930
9:24 consumed upon the altar the **burnt o** and 5930
10:12 Take the **meat o** that remaineth of 4503
10:15 to wave *it for* a **wave o** before the LORD; 8573
10:16 diligently sought the goat of the **sin o**, 2403
10:17 Wherefore have ye not eaten the **sin o** in 2403
10:19 *this* day have they offered their **sin o** 2403
10:19 and their **burnt o** before the LORD; 5930
10:19 *if* I had eaten the **sin o** to day, should it 2403
12: 6 bring a lamb of the first year for a **burnt o**, 5930
12: 6 a young pigeon, or a turtledove, for a **sin o**, 2403
12: 8 the one for the **burnt o**, and the other for a 5930
12: 8 the burnt offering, and the other for a **sin o**: 2403
14:10 three tenth deals of fine flour *for* a **meat o**, 4503
14:12 offer him for a **trespass o**, and the log of oil, 817
14:12 wave them *for* a **wave o** before 8573
14:13 in the place where he shall kill the **sin o** 2403
14:13 shall kill the sin offering and the **burnt o**, 5930
14:13 for as the **sin o** *is* the priest's, *so is* 2403
14:13 offering *is* the priest's, *so is* the **trespass o**: 817
14:14 take *some* of the blood of the **trespass o**, 817
14:17 right foot, upon the blood of the **trespass o**: 817
14:19 the priest shall offer the **sin o**, and make an 2403
14:19 and afterward he shall kill the **burnt o**: 5930
14:20 the priest shall offer the **burnt o** and 5930
14:20 and the **meat o** upon the altar: 4503
14:21 he shall take one lamb *for* a **trespass o** to be 817
14:21 of fine flour mingled with oil for a **meat o**, 4503
14:22 the one shall be a **sin o**, and the other a 2403
14:22 be a sin offering, and the other a **burnt o**. 5930
14:24 priest shall take the lamb of the **trespass o**, 817
14:24 the priest shall wave them *for* a **wave o** 8573
14:25 And he shall kill the lamb of the **trespass o**, 817
14:25 take *some* of the blood of the **trespass o**, 817
14:28 the place of the blood of the **trespass o**: 817
14:31 the one *for* a **sin o**, and the other *for* a burnt 2403
14:31 the other *for* a **burnt o**, with the meat 5930
14:31 other *for* a burnt offering, with the **meat o**: 4503
15:15 the one *for* a **sin o**, and the other *for* a burnt 2403
15:15 a sin offering, and the other *for* a **burnt o**; 5930
15:30 the priest shall offer the one *for* a **sin o**, 2403
15:30 a sin offering, and the other *for* a **burnt o**; 5930
16: 3 *place:* with a young bullock for a **sin o**, 2403
16: 3 for a sin offering, and a ram for a **burnt o**. 5930
16: 5 of Israel two kids of the goats for a **sin o**, 2403
16: 5 a sin offering, and one ram for a **burnt o**. 5930
16: 6 Aaron shall offer *his* bullock of the **sin o**, 2403
16: 9 LORD'S lot fell, and offer him *for* a **sin o**. 2403
16:11 Aaron shall bring the bullock of the **sin o**, 2403
16:11 shall kill the bullock of the **sin o** which *is* 2403
16:15 shall he kill the goat of the **sin o**, that *is* for 2403
16:24 offer his **burnt o**, and the burnt offering of 5930
16:24 the **burnt o** of the people, and make an 5930
16:25 the fat of the **sin o** shall he burn upon 2403
16:27 the bullock for the **sin o**, and the goat for 2403
16:27 the sin offering, and the goat for the **sin o**, 2403
17: 4 to offer an **o** unto the LORD before 7133
17: 8 that offereth a **burnt o** or sacrifice, 5930
19:21 he shall bring his **trespass o** unto 817
19:21 *even* a ram for a **trespass o**. 817
19:22 **trespass o** before the LORD for his sin 817
22:12 she may not eat of an **o** of the holy *things*. 8641
22:18 will offer unto the LORD for a **burnt o**; 5930
22:21 or a **freewill o** in beeves or sheep, it shall 5071
22:22 nor make an **o by fire** of them upon the altar 801
22:23 that mayest thou offer *for* a **freewill o**; 5071
22:24 neither shall you make *any* **o** *thereof* in your NIH
22:27 an **o made by fire** unto the LORD. 801+7133
23: 8 ye shall offer an **o made by fire** unto 801
23:12 first year for a **burnt o** unto the LORD. 5930
23:13 the **meat o** thereof *shall be* two tenth deals 4503
23:13 an **o made by fire** unto the LORD *for* a 801
23:13 the **drink o** thereof *shall be of* wine, 5262
23:14 that ye have brought an **o** unto your God: 7133
23:15 day that ye brought the sheaf of the **wave o**; 8573
23:16 ye shall offer a new **meat o** unto 4503
23:18 they shall be *for* a **burnt o** unto 5930
23:18 with their **meat o**, and their drink offerings, 4503
23:18 drink offerings, *even* an **o made by fire**, 801
23:19 sacrifice one kid of the goats for a **sin o**, 2403
23:20 firstfruits *for* a **wave o** before the LORD, 8573
23:25 ye shall offer an **o made by fire** unto 801
23:27 offer an **o made by fire** unto the LORD. 801
23:36 Seven days ye shall offer an **o made by fire** 801
23:36 ye shall offer an **o made by fire** unto 801
23:37 to offer an **o made by fire** unto the LORD, 801

Lev 23:37 a **burnt o**, and a meat offering, a sacrifice, 5930
23:37 a **meat o**, a sacrifice, and drink offerings, 4503
24: 7 *even* an **o made by fire** unto the LORD. 801
27: 9 whereof *men* bring an **o** unto the LORD, 7133
Nu 4:16 the daily **meat o**, and the anointing oil, *and* 4503
5: 9 every **o** of all the holy *things* of the children 8641
5:15 he shall bring her **o** for her, the tenth *part* of 7133
5:15 for it *is* an **o** of jealousy, an offering of 4503
5:15 an offering of jealousy, an **o** of memorial, 4503
5:18 and put the **o** of memorial in her hands, 4503
5:18 in her hands, which *is* the jealousy **o**: 4503
5:25 the priest shall take the jealousy **o** out of 4503
5:25 shall wave the **o** before the LORD, and 4503
5:26 the priest shall take a handful of the **o**, *even* 4503
6:11 the priest shall offer the one for a **sin o**, 2403
6:11 the other for a **burnt o**, and make an 5930
6:12 a lamb of the first year for a **trespass o**: 817
6:14 he shall offer his **o** unto the LORD, one he 7133
6:14 the first year without blemish for a **burnt o**, 5930
6:14 of the first year without blemish for a **sin o**, 2403
6:15 and their **meat o**, and their drink offerings. 4503
6:16 shall offer his **sin o**, and his burnt offering: 2403
6:16 shall offer his sin offering, and his **burnt o**: 5930
6:17 the priest shall offer also his **meat o**, and 4503
6:17 also his meat offering, and his **drink o**. 5262
6:20 the priest shall wave them *for* a **wave o** 8573
6:21 *of* his **o** unto the LORD for his separation, 7133
7: 3 they brought their **o** before the LORD, 7133
7:10 even the princes offered their **o** before 7133
7:11 They shall offer their **o**, each prince on *his* 7133
7:12 he that offered his **o** the first day was 7133
7:13 his **o** *was* one silver charger, the weight 7133
7:13 *of* fine flour mingled with oil for a **meat o**: 4503
7:15 one lamb of the first year, for a **burnt o**: 5930
7:16 One kid of the goats for a **sin o**: 2403
7:17 this *was* the **o** of Nahshon the son of 7133
7:19 He offered *for* his **o** one silver charger, 7133
7:19 *of* fine flour mingled with oil for a **meat o**: 4503
7:21 one lamb of the first year, for a **burnt o**: 5930
7:22 One kid of the goats for a **sin o**: 2403
7:23 this *was* the **o** of Nethaneel the son of Zuar. 7133
7:25 His **o** *was* one silver charger, the weight 7133
7:25 *of* fine flour mingled with oil for a **meat o**: 4503
7:27 one lamb of the first year, for a **burnt o**: 5930
7:28 One kid of the goats for a **sin o**: 2403
7:29 this *was* the **o** of Eliab the son of Helon. 7133
7:31 His **o** *was* one silver charger of the weight 7133
7:31 *of* fine flour mingled with oil for a **meat o**: 4503
7:33 one lamb of the first year, for a **burnt o**: 5930
7:34 One kid of the goats for a **sin o**: 2403
7:35 this *was* the **o** of Elizur the son of Shedeur. 7133
7:37 His **o** *was* one silver charger, the weight 7133
7:37 *of* fine flour mingled with oil for a **meat o**: 4503
7:39 one lamb of the first year, for a **burnt o**: 5930
7:40 One kid of the goats for a **sin o**: 2403
7:41 this *was* the **o** of Shelumiel the son of 7133
7:43 His **o** *was* one silver charger of the weight 7133
7:43 *of* fine flour mingled with oil for a **meat o**: 4503
7:45 one lamb of the first year, for a **burnt o**: 5930
7:46 One kid of the goats for a **sin o**: 2403
7:47 this *was* the **o** of Eliasaph the son of Deuel. 7133
7:49 His **o** *was* one silver charger, the weight 7133
7:49 *of* fine flour mingled with oil for a **meat o**: 4503
7:51 one lamb of the first year, for a **burnt o**: 5930
7:52 One kid of the goats for a **sin o**: 2403
7:53 this *was* the **o** of Elishama the son of 7133
7:55 His **o** *was* one silver charger of the weight 7133
7:55 *of* fine flour mingled with oil for a **meat o**: 4503
7:57 one lamb of the first year, for a **burnt o**: 5930
7:58 One kid of the goats for a **sin o**: 2403
7:59 this *was* the **o** of Gamaliel the son of 7133
7:61 His **o** *was* one silver charger, the weight 7133
7:61 *of* fine flour mingled with oil for a **meat o**: 4503
7:63 one lamb of the first year, for a **burnt o**: 5930
7:64 One kid of the goats for a **sin o**: 2403
7:65 this *was* the **o** of Abidan the son of 7133
7:67 His **o** *was* one silver charger, the weight 7133
7:67 *of* fine flour mingled with oil for a **meat o**: 4503
7:69 one lamb of the first year, for a **burnt o**: 5930
7:70 One kid of the goats for a **sin o**: 2403
7:71 this *was* the **o** of Ahiezer the son of 7133
7:73 His **o** *was* one silver charger, the weight 7133
7:73 *of* fine flour mingled with oil for a **meat o**: 4503
7:75 one lamb of the first year, for a **burnt o**: 5930
7:76 One kid of the goats for a **sin o**: 2403
7:77 this *was* the **o** of Pagiel the son of Ocran. 7133
7:79 His **o** *was* one silver charger, the weight 7133
7:79 *of* fine flour mingled with oil for a **meat o**: 4503
7:81 one lamb of the first year, for a **burnt o**: 5930
7:82 One kid of the goats for a **sin o**: 2403
7:83 this *was* the **o** of Ahira the son of Enan. 7133
7:87 All the oxen for the **burnt o** *were* twelve 5930
7:87 of the first year twelve, with their **meat o**: 4503
7:87 and the kids of the goats for **sin o** twelve. 2403
8: 8 them take a young bullock with his **meat o**, 4503
8: 8 young bullock shalt thou take for a **sin o**. 2403
8:11 LORD *for* an **o** of the children of Israel, 8573
8:12 thou shalt offer the one *for* a **sin o**, and 2403
8:12 the other *for* a **burnt o**, unto the LORD, 5930
8:13 and offer them *for* an **o** unto the LORD. 8573
8:15 shalt cleanse them, and offer them *for* an **o**. 8573
8:21 Aaron offered them *as* an **o** before 8573
9: 7 that *we* may not offer an **o** of the LORD 7133
9:13 he brought not the **o** of the LORD in his 7133
15: 3 will make an **o by fire** unto the LORD, 801
15: 3 a **burnt o**, or a sacrifice in performing a 5930
15: 3 or in a **freewill o**, or in your solemn feasts, 5071
15: 4 shall he that offereth his **o** unto the LORD 7133
15: 4 **meat o** of a tenth deal *of* flour mingled 4503
15: 5 **drink o** shalt thou prepare with the burnt 5262
15: 5 offering shalt thou prepare with the **burnt o** 5930
15: 6 thou shalt prepare *for* a **meat o** two tenth 4503
15: 7 for a **drink o** thou shalt offer the third *part* 5262
15: 8 thou preparest a bullock *for* a **burnt o**, 5930
15: 9 shall he bring with a bullock a **meat o** of 4503

Nu 15:10 thou shalt bring for a **drink o** half a hin *of* 5262
15:10 *for* an **o made by fire**, of a sweet savour 801
15:13 in **o** an offering made by fire, of a sweet 7126
15:13 in offering an **o made by fire**, of a sweet 801
15:14 and will offer an **o made by fire**, of a sweet 801
15:19 ye shall offer up a **heave o** unto 8641
15:20 *of* the first of your dough *for* a **heave o**: 8641
15:20 as *ye do* the **heave o** of the threshingfloor, 8641
15:21 the LORD a **heave o** in your generations. 8641
15:24 shall offer one young bullock for a **burnt o**, 5930
15:24 with his **meat o**, and his drink offering, 4503
15:24 with his meat offering, and his **drink o**, 5262
15:24 and one kid of the goats for a **sin o**. 2403
15:25 they shall bring their **o**, a sacrifice made by 7133
15:25 their **sin o** before the LORD, for their 2403
15:27 bring a she goat of the first year for a **sin o**. 2403
16:15 unto the LORD, Respect not thou their **o**: 4503
18: 9 every **meat o** of theirs, and every sin 4503
18: 9 every **sin o** of theirs, and every trespass 2403
18: 9 of theirs, and every **trespass o** of theirs, 817
18:11 the **heave o** of their gift, with all the wave 8641
18:17 shalt burn their fat *for* an **o made by fire**, 801
18:24 which they offer *as* a **heave o** unto 8641
18:26 ye shall offer up a **heave o** of it for 8641
18:27 *this* your **heave o** shall be reckoned unto 8641
18:28 Thus you also shall offer a **heave o** unto 8641
18:28 ye shall give thereof the LORD'S **heave o** 8641
18:29 ye shall offer every **heave o** of the LORD, 8641
23: 3 Stand by thy **burnt o**, and I will go: 5930
23:15 said unto Balak, Stand here by thy **burnt o**, 5930
23:17 he stood by his **burnt o**, and the princes of 5930
28: 2 My **o**, *and* my bread for my sacrifices made 7133
28: 3 This *is* the **o made by fire** which ye shall 801
28: 3 spot day by day, *for* a continual **burnt o**. 5930
28: 5 tenth *part* of an ephah *of* flour for a **meat o**, 4503
28: 6 *It is* a continual **burnt o**, which was 5930
28: 7 the **drink o** thereof *shall be* the fourth *part* 5262
28: 7 be poured unto the LORD *for* a **drink o**. 5262
28: 8 as the **meat o** of the morning, and as 4503
28: 8 of the morning, and as the **drink o** thereof, 5262
28: 9 two tenth deals *of* flour *for* a **meat o**, 4503
28: 9 mingled with oil, and the **drink o** thereof: 5262
28:10 *This is* the **burnt o** of every sabbath, beside 5930
28:10 beside the continual **burnt o**, and his drink 5930
28:10 continual burnt offering, and his **drink o**. 5262
28:11 ye shall offer a **burnt o** unto the LORD; 5930
28:12 three tenth deals *of* flour *for* a **meat o**, 4503
28:12 two tenth deals *of* flour *for* a **meat o**, 4503
28:13 with oil *for* a **meat o** unto one lamb; 4503
28:13 *for* a **burnt o** *of* a sweet savour, a sacrifice 5930
28:14 this *is* the **burnt o** of every month 5930
28:15 one kid of the goats for a **sin o** unto 2403
28:15 besides the continual **burnt o**, and his drink 5930
28:15 continual burnt offering, and his **drink o**. 5262
28:19 by fire *for* a **burnt o** unto the LORD; 5930
28:20 their **meat o** *shall be of* flour mingled with 4503
28:22 one goat for a **sin o**, to make an atonement 2403
28:23 Ye shall offer these beside the **burnt o** in 5930
28:23 which *is* for a continual **burnt o**. 5930
28:24 be offered beside the continual **burnt o**, 5930
28:24 continual burnt offering, and his **drink o**. 5262
28:26 when ye bring a new **meat o** unto 4503
28:27 ye shall offer the **burnt o** for a sweet 5930
28:28 their **meat o** *of* flour mingled with oil, 4503
28:31 offer *them* besides the continual **burnt o**, 5930
28:31 his **meat o**, (they shall be unto you without 4503
29: 2 ye shall offer a **burnt o** for a sweet savour 5930
29: 3 their **meat o** *shall be of* flour mingled with 4503
29: 5 one kid of the goats for a **sin o**, to make an 2403
29: 6 Beside the **burnt o** of the month, and 5930
29: 6 his **meat o**, and the daily burnt offering, 4503
29: 6 the daily **burnt o**, and his meat offering, 5930
29: 6 and his **meat o**, and their drink offerings, 4503
29: 8 ye shall offer a **burnt o** unto the LORD 5930
29: 9 their **meat o** *shall be of* flour mingled with 4503
29:11 One kid of the goats *for* a **sin o**; beside 2403
29:11 beside the **sin o** of atonement, and 2403
29:11 the continual **burnt o**, and the meat 5930
29:11 the **meat o** of it, and their drink offerings. 4503
29:13 ye shall offer a **burnt o**, a sacrifice made 5930
29:14 their **meat o** *shall be of* flour mingled with 4503
29:16 one kid of the goats *for* a **sin o**; beside 2403
29:16 beside the continual **burnt o**, his meat 5930
29:16 his **meat o**, and his drink offering. 4503
29:16 his meat offering, and his **drink o**. 5262
29:18 their **meat o** and their drink offerings for 4503
29:19 one kid of the goats *for* a **sin o**; beside 2403
29:19 beside the continual **burnt o**, and the meat 5930
29:19 the **meat o** thereof, and their drink 4503
29:21 their **meat o** and their drink offerings for 4503
29:22 one goat for a **sin o**; beside the continual 2403
29:22 beside the continual **burnt o**, and his meat 5930
29:22 and his **meat o**, and his drink offering. 4503
29:22 and his meat offering, and his **drink o**. 5262
29:24 Their **meat o** and their drink offerings for 4503
29:25 one kid of the goats *for* a **sin o**; beside 2403
29:25 beside the continual **burnt o**, his meat 5930
29:25 his **meat o**, and his drink offering. 4503
29:25 his meat offering, and his **drink o**. 5262
29:27 their **meat o** and their drink offerings for 4503
29:28 one goat for a **sin o**; beside the continual 2403
29:28 beside the continual **burnt o**, and his meat 5930
29:28 and his **meat o**, and his drink offering. 4503
29:28 and his meat offering, and his **drink o**. 5262
29:30 their **meat o** and their drink offerings for 4503
29:31 one goat for a **sin o**; beside the continual 2403
29:31 beside the continual **burnt o**, his meat 5930
29:31 his **meat o**, and his drink offering. 4503
29:31 his meat offering, and his **drink o**. 5262
29:33 their **meat o** and their drink offerings for 4503
29:34 one goat for a **sin o**; beside the continual 2403
29:34 beside the continual **burnt o**, his meat 5930
29:34 his **meat o**, and his drink offering. 4503
29:34 his meat offering, and his **drink o**. 5262
29:36 ye shall offer a **burnt o**, a sacrifice made 5930
Nu 29:37 Their **meat o** and their drink offerings for 4503
29:38 one goat for a **sin o**; beside the continual 2403
29:38 beside the continual **burnt o**, and his meat 5930
29:38 and his **meat o**, and his drink offering. 4503
29:38 and his meat offering, and his **drink o**. 5262
31:29 the priest, *for* a **heave o** of the LORD. 8641
31:41 *which was* the LORD'S **heave o**, 8641
31:52 all the gold of the **o** that they offered up to 8641
Dt 12:11 the **heave o** of your hand, and all your 8641
12:17 freewill offerings, or **heave o** of thine hand: 8641
16:10 *with* a tribute of a **freewill o** of thine hand, 5071
23:23 *even* a **freewill o**, according as thou hast 5071
Jos 22:23 or if to offer thereon **burnt o** or 5930
22:23 if to offer thereon burnt offering or **meat o**, 4503
22:26 an altar, not for **burnt o**, nor for sacrifice: 5930
Jdg 11:31 and I will offer it up *for* a **burnt o**. 5930
13:16 if thou wilt offer a **burnt o**, thou must offer 5930
13:19 So Manoah took a kid with a **meat o**, and 4503
13:23 he would not have received a **burnt o** and 5930
13:23 a burnt offering and a **meat o** at our hands, 4503
1Sa 2:17 for men abhorred the **o** of the LORD. 4503
2:29 kick ye at my sacrifice and at mine **o**, 4503
3:14 not be purged with sacrifice nor **o** for ever. 4503
6: 3 but in any wise return him a **trespass o**: 817
6: 4 What *shall be* the **trespass o** which we shall 817
6: 8 which ye return him *for* a **trespass o**, 817
6:14 offered the kine a **burnt o** unto 5930
6:17 returned *for* a **trespass o** unto the LORD; 817
7: 9 offered it *for* a **burnt o** wholly unto 5930
7:10 And as Samuel was **o up** the burnt offering, 5927
7:10 as Samuel was offering up the **burnt o**, 5930
13: 9 Bring hither a **burnt o** to me, and peace 5930
13: 9 And he offered the **burnt o**. 5930
13:10 that as soon as he had made an end of **o** 5927
13:10 had made an end of offering the **burnt o**, 5930
13:12 myself therefore, and offered a **burnt o**. 5930
26:19 thee up against me, let him accept an **o**: 4503
2Sa 6:18 as soon as David had made an end of **o** 5927
1Ki 18:29 they prophesied until *the time* of the **o** of 5927
18:36 it came to pass at *the time of* the **o** of 5927
2Ki 3:20 when the **meat o** was offered, that behold, 4503
3:27 offered him *for* a **burnt o** upon the wall. 5930
5:17 **burnt o** nor sacrifice unto other gods, 5930
10:25 as soon as he had made an end of **o** 6213
10:25 had made an end of offering the **burnt o**, 5930
16:13 he burnt his **burnt o** and his meat offering, 5930
16:13 he burnt his burnt offering and his **meat o**, 4503
16:13 poured his **drink o**, and sprinkled the blood 5262
16:15 the great altar burn the morning **burnt o**, 5930
16:15 the evening **meat o**, and the king's burnt 4503
16:15 the king's burnt sacrifice, and his **meat o**, 4503
16:15 with the **burnt o** of all the people of 5930
16:15 and their **meat o**, and their drink offerings; 4503
16:15 upon it all the blood of the **burnt o**, 5930
1Ch 6:49 sons offered upon the altar of the **burnt o**, 5930
16: 2 when David had made an end of **o** the burnt 5927
16:29 bring an **o**, and come before him: 4503
16:40 altar of the **burnt o** continually morning 5930
21:23 for wood, and the wheat for the **meat o**; 4503
21:26 heaven by fire upon the altar of **burnt o**. 5930
21:29 the wilderness, and the altar of the **burnt o**, 5930
22: 1 this *is* the altar of the **burnt o** for Israel. 5930
23:29 for the fine flour for **meat o**, and for 4503
2Ch 4: 6 such things as they offered for the **burnt o** 5930
7: 1 consumed the **burnt o** and the sacrifices; 5930
8:13 **o** according to the commandment of Moses, 5927
29:18 the altar of **burnt o**, with all the vessels 5930
29:21 for a **sin o** for the kingdom, and for 2403
29:23 they brought forth the he goats for the **sin o** 2403
29:24 for the king commanded *that* the **burnt o** 5930
29:24 and the **sin o** *should be made* for all Israel. 2403
29:27 Hezekiah commanded to offer the **burnt o** 5930
29:27 when the **burnt o** began, the song of 5930
29:28 all *this continued* until the **burnt o** was 5930
29:29 when *they* had made an end of **o**, the king 5927
29:32 all these *were* for a **burnt o** to the LORD. 5930
29:35 and the drink offerings for *every* **burnt o**. 5930
30:22 **o** peace offerings, and making confession 2076
35:14 Aaron *were busied* in **o** of burnt offerings 5927
Ezr 1: 4 besides the **freewill o** for the house of God 5071
3: 5 afterward *offered* the continual **burnt o**, 5930
3: 5 offered a **freewill o** unto the LORD. 5071
6:17 for a **sin o** for all Israel, twelve he goats, 2409
7:16 with the **freewill o** of the people, and of 5069
7:16 **o willingly** for the house of their God 5069
8:25 *even* the **o** of the house of our God, 8641
8:28 the gold *are* a **freewill o** unto the LORD 5071
8:35 seven lambs, twelve he goats *for* a **sin o**: 2403
8:35 all *this was* a **burnt o** unto the LORD. 5930
Ne 10:33 *for* the continual **meat o**, and for 4503
10:33 for the continual **burnt o**, of the sabbaths, 5930
10:34 the Levites, and the people, for the wood **o**, 7133
10:39 the children of Levi shall bring the **o** of 8641
13: 9 with the **meat o** and the frankincense. 4503
13:31 for the wood **o**, at times appointed, and 7133
Job 42: 8 and offer up for yourselves a **burnt o**; 5930
Ps 40: 6 Sacrifice and **o** thou didst not desire; mine 4503
40: 6 **burnt o** and sin offering hast thou not 5930
40: 6 and **sin o** hast thou not required. 2401
51:16 I give *it*: thou delightest not in **burnt o**. 5930
51:19 with **burnt o** and whole *burnt offering*: 5930
51:19 with burnt offering and whole *burnt o*: then NIH
96: 8 bring an **o**, and come into his courts. 4503
Isa 40:16 the beasts thereof sufficient *for* a **burnt o**. 5930
43:23 I have not caused thee to serve with an **o**, 4503
53:10 when thou shalt make his soul an **o for sin**, 817
57: 6 even to them hast thou poured a **drink o**, 5262
57: 6 drink offering, thou hast offered a **meat o**. 4503
61: 8 love judgment, I hate robbery for **burnt o**; 5930
65:11 that furnish the **drink o** unto *that* number. 4469
66:20 they shall bring all your brethren *for* an **o** 4503
66:20 as the children of Israel bring an **o** in a 4503
Jer 11:17 me to anger in **o incense** unto Baal. 6999
14:12 when they offer **burnt o** and an oblation, 5930
Eze 20:28 they presented the provocation of their **o**: 7133
Eze 40:38 the gates, where they washed the **burnt o**. 5930
40:39 to slay thereon the **burnt o** and the sin 5930
40:39 and the **sin o** and the trespass offering. 2403
40:39 and the sin offering and the **trespass o**. 817
40:42 tables *were* of hewn stone for the **burnt o**, 5930
40:42 wherewith they slew the **burnt o** 5930
40:43 upon the tables *was* the flesh of the **o**. 7133
42:13 lay the most holy *things*, and the **meat o**, 4503
42:13 and the **sin o**, and the trespass offering; 2403
42:13 and the sin offering, and the **trespass o**; 817
43:19 Lord GOD, a young bullock for a **sin o**. 2403
43:21 shalt take the bullock also of the **sin o**, 2403
43:22 kid of the goats without blemish for a **sin o**; 2403
43:24 they shall offer them up *for* a **burnt o** unto 5930
43:25 thou prepare every day a goat *for* a **sin o**: 2403
44:11 they shall slay the **burnt o** and the sacrifice 5930
44:27 he shall offer his **sin o**, saith the Lord 2403
44:29 They shall eat the **meat o**, and the sin 4503
44:29 and the **sin o**, and the trespass offering; 2403
44:29 and the sin offering, and the **trespass o**; 817
45:15 for a **meat o**, and for a burnt offering, and 4503
45:15 and for a **burnt o**, and for peace offerings, 5930
45:17 he shall prepare the **sin o**, and the meat 2403
45:17 the **meat o**, and the burnt offering, and 4503
45:17 and the **burnt o**, and the peace offerings, 5930
45:19 priest shall take of the blood of the **sin o**, 2403
45:22 the people of the land a bullock *for* a **sin o**. 2403
45:23 he shall prepare a **burnt o** to the LORD, 5930
45:23 and a kid of the goats daily *for* a **sin o**. 2403
45:24 he shall prepare a **meat o** *of* an ephah for a 4503
45:25 according to the **sin o**, according to 2403
45:25 according to the **burnt o**, and according to 5930
45:25 according to the **meat o**, and according to 4503
46: 2 the priests shall prepare his **burnt o** and 5930
46: 4 the **burnt o** that the prince shall offer unto 5930
46: 5 the **meat o** *shall be* an ephah for a ram, 4503
46: 5 the **meat o** for the lambs as he shall be able 4503
46: 7 he shall prepare a **meat o**, an ephah for a 4503
46:11 in the solemnities the **meat o** shall be an 4503
46:12 the prince shall prepare a voluntary **burnt o** 5930
46:12 he shall prepare his **burnt o** and his peace 5930
46:13 Thou shalt daily prepare a **burnt o** unto 5930
46:14 thou shalt prepare a **meat o** for it every 4503
46:14 a **meat o** continually *by* a perpetual 4503
46:15 the lamb, and the **meat o**, and the oil, 4503
46:15 every morning *for* a continual **burnt o**. 5930
46:20 where the priests shall boil the **trespass o** 817
46:20 boil the trespass offering and the **sin o**, 2403
46:20 where they shall bake the **meat o**; 4503
48: 8 shall be the **o** which ye shall offer *of* five 8641
Joel 1: 9 The **meat o** and the drink offering is cut off 4503
1: 9 the **drink o** is cut off from the house of 5262
1:13 for the **meat o** and the drink offering is 4503
1:13 the **drink o** is withholden from the house 5262
2:14 *even* a **meat o** and a drink offering unto 4503
2:14 and a **drink o** unto the LORD your God? 5262
Zep 3:10 of my dispersed, shall bring mine **o**. 4503
Mal 1:10 neither will I accept an **o** at your hand. 4503
1:11 *be* offered unto my name, and a pure **o**: 4503
1:13 and the sick; thus ye brought an **o**: 4503
2:12 him that offereth an **o** unto the LORD of 4503
2:13 insomuch that *he* regardeth not the **o** any 4503
3: 3 that they may offer unto the LORD an **o** in 4503
3: 4 shall the **o** of Judah and Jerusalem be 4503
Lk 23:36 coming to *him*, and **o** him vinegar, *4374*
Ac 21:26 until that an **o** should be offered for every *4376*
Ro 15:16 that the **o up** of the Gentiles might be *4376*
Eph 5: 2 and hath given himself for us an **o** and *4376*
Heb 10: 5 Sacrifice and **o** thou wouldest not, but *4376*
10: 8 Sacrifice and **o** and burnt offerings and *4376*
10: 8 and **o** for sin thou wouldest not, NIG
10:10 **o** of the body of Jesus Christ once for all. *4376*
10:11 and **o** oftentimes the same sacrifices, *4374*
10:14 For by one **o** he hath perfected for ever *4376*
10:18 of these *is, there is* no more **o** for sin. *4376*

OFFERINGS (265) [OFFER]

Ge 8:20 and offered **burnt o** on the altar. 5930
Ex 10:25 must give us also sacrifices and **burnt o**, 5930
20:24 shalt sacrifice thereon thy **burnt o**, and thy 5930
20:24 and thy **peace o**, thy sheep, and thine oxen: 8002
24: 5 which offered **burnt o**, and 5930
24: 5 sacrificed peace **o** *of* oxen unto 2077
29:28 of Israel of the sacrifice of their **peace o**, 8002
32: 6 offered **burnt o**, and brought peace 5930
32: 6 burnt offerings, and brought **peace o**; 8002
36: 3 brought yet unto him **free o** every morning. 5071
Lev 2: 3 holy of the **o** of the LORD **made by fire**. 801
2:10 holy of the **o** of the LORD **made by fire**. 801
2:13 with all thine **o** thou shalt offer salt. 7133
4:10 the bullock of the sacrifice of **peace o**: 8002
4:26 as the fat of the sacrifice of **peace o**: 8002
4:31 away from off the sacrifice of **peace o**; 8002
4:35 away from the sacrifice of the **peace o**; 8002
4:35 according to the **o made by fire** unto 801
5:12 according to the **o made by fire** unto 801
6:12 he shall burn thereon the fat of the **peace o**. 8002
6:17 *them for* their portion of my **o made by fire**; 801
6:18 the **o** of the LORD **made by fire**: 801
7:11 this *is* the law of the sacrifice of **peace o**, 8002
7:13 the sacrifice of thanksgiving of his **peace o**. 8002
7:14 that sprinkleth the blood of the **peace o**. 8002
7:15 the flesh of the sacrifice of his **peace o** for 8002
7:18 his **peace o** be eaten at all on the third day, 8002
7:20 *of* the flesh of the sacrifice of **peace o**, 8002
7:21 eat of the flesh of the sacrifice of **peace o**, 8002
7:29 He that offereth the sacrifice of his **peace o** 8002
7:29 the LORD of the sacrifice of his **peace o**. 8002
7:30 bring the **o** of the LORD **made by fire**, 801
7:32 offering of the sacrifices of your **peace o**. 8002
7:33 that offereth the blood of the **peace o**, and 8002
7:34 from off the sacrifices of their **peace o**, 8002
7:35 out of the **o** of the LORD **made by fire**, 801
7:37 and of the sacrifice of the **peace o**; 8002
9: 4 Also a bullock and a ram for **peace o**, 8002

Lev 9:18 and the ram *for* a sacrifice of **peace o**, 8002
9:22 and the burnt offering, and **peace o**. 8002
10:12 of the **o** of the LORD **made by fire**, 801
10:14 of **peace o** of the children of Israel. 8002
10:15 they bring with the **o made by fire** of the fat, 801
17: 5 offer them *for* peace **o** unto the LORD. 2077
19: 5 if ye offer a sacrifice of **peace o** unto 8002
21: 6 for the **o** of the LORD **made by fire**, *and* 801
21:21 to offer the **o** of the LORD **made by fire**: 801
22:18 for all his vows, and for all his **freewill o**, 5071
22:21 whosoever offereth a sacrifice of **peace o** 8002
23:18 with their meat offering, and their **drink o**, 5262
23:19 of the first year for a sacrifice of **peace o**. 8002
23:37 a meat offering, a sacrifice, and **drink o**, 5262
23:38 your vows, and beside all your **freewill o**, 5071
24: 9 him of the **o** of the LORD **made by fire**, 801
Nu 6:14 and one ram without blemish for **peace o**, 8002
6:15 and their meat offering, and their **drink o**. 5262
6:17 *for* a sacrifice of **peace o** unto the LORD, 8002
6:18 which *is* under the sacrifice of the **peace o**. 8002
7:17 for a sacrifice of **peace o**, two oxen, 8002
7:23 for a sacrifice of **peace o**, two oxen, 8002
7:29 for a sacrifice of **peace o**, two oxen, 8002
7:35 for a sacrifice of **peace o**, two oxen, 8002
7:41 for a sacrifice of **peace o**, two oxen, 8002
7:47 for a sacrifice of **peace o**, two oxen, 8002
7:53 for a sacrifice of **peace o**, two oxen, 8002
7:59 for a sacrifice of **peace o**, two oxen, 8002
7:65 for a sacrifice of **peace o**, two oxen, 8002
7:71 for a sacrifice of **peace o**, two oxen, 8002
7:77 for a sacrifice of **peace o**, two oxen, 8002
7:83 for a sacrifice of **peace o**, two oxen, 8002
7:88 all the oxen for the sacrifice of the **peace o** 8002
10:10 blow with the trumpets over your **burnt o**, 5930
10:10 and over the sacrifices of your **peace o**; 8002
15: 8 a vow, or **peace o** unto the LORD: 8002
18: 8 **heave o** of all the hallowed *things* of 8641
18:11 with all the **wave o** of the children of Israel: 8573
18:19 All the **heave o** of the holy *things*, which 8641
28:14 their **drink o** shall be half a hin of wine 5262
28:31 you without blemish) and their **drink o**. 5262
29: 6 and his meat offering, and their **drink o**, 5262
29:11 the meat offering of it, and their **drink o**. 5262
29:18 and their **drink o** for the bullocks, 5262
29:19 meat offering thereof, and their **drink o**. 5262
29:21 and their **drink o** for the bullocks, 5262
29:24 and their **drink o** for the bullocks, 5262
29:27 and their **drink o** for the bullocks, 5262
29:30 and their **drink o** for the bullocks, 5262
29:33 and their **drink o** for the bullocks, 5262
29:37 and their **drink o** for the bullock, 5262
29:39 besides your vows, and your **freewill o**, 5071
29:39 for your **burnt o**, and for your meat 5930
29:39 for your **meat o**, and for your drink 4503
29:39 for your **drink o**, and for your peace 5262
29:39 your drink offerings, and for your **peace o**. 8002
Dt 12: 6 thither ye shall bring your **burnt o**, and 5930
12: 6 **heave o** of your hand, and your vows, and 8641
12: 6 your **freewill o**, and the firstlings of your 5071
12:11 your **burnt o**, and your sacrifices, 5930
12:13 thy **burnt o** in every place that thou seest: 5930
12:14 there thou shalt offer thy **burnt o**, and 5930
12:17 nor thy **freewill o**, or heave offering of 5071
12:27 thou shalt offer thy **burnt o**, the flesh and 5930
18: 1 shall eat the **o** of the LORD **made by fire**, 801
27: 6 thou shalt offer **burnt o** thereon unto 5930
27: 7 thou shalt offer **peace o**, and shalt eat there, 8002
32:38 *and* drank the wine of their **drink o**? 5257
Jos 8:31 they offered thereon **burnt o** unto 5930
8:31 unto the LORD, and sacrificed **peace o**. 8002
22:23 or if to offer peace **o** thereon, 2077
22:27 the LORD before him with our **burnt o**, 5930
22:27 with our sacrifices, and with our **peace o**; 8002
22:28 not for **burnt o**, nor for sacrifices; 5930
22:29 to build an altar for **burnt o**, for meat 5930
22:29 for **meat o**, or for sacrifices, 4503
Jdg 20:26 offered **burnt o** and peace offerings before 5930
20:26 and **peace o** before the LORD. 8002
21: 4 and offered **burnt o** and peace offerings. 5930
21: 4 and offered burnt offerings and **peace o**. 8002
1Sa 2:28 the **o made by fire** of the children of Israel? 801
2:29 the chiefest of all the **o** of Israel my people? 4503
6:15 the men of Beth-shemesh offered **burnt o** 5930
10: 8 to offer **burnt o**, *and* to sacrifice sacrifices 5930
10: 8 *and* to sacrifice sacrifices of **peace o**: 8002
11:15 there they sacrificed sacrifices *of* peace **o** 8002
13: 9 hither a burnt offering to me, and **peace o**. 8002
15:22 the LORD *as great* delight in **burnt o** 5930
2Sa 1:21 *let there be* rain upon you, nor fields of **o**: 8641
6:17 David offered **burnt o** and peace offerings 5930
6:17 and **peace o** before the LORD. 8002
6:18 David had made an end of offering **burnt o** 5930
6:18 end of offering burnt offerings and **peace o**, 8002
24:24 neither will I offer **burnt o** unto 5930
24:25 and offered **burnt o** and peace offerings. 5930
24:25 and offered burnt offerings and **peace o**. 8002
1Ki 3: 4 a thousand **burnt o** did Solomon offer up 5930
3:15 offered up **burnt o**, and offered peace 5930
3:15 offered **peace o**, and made a feast to all his 8002
8:63 Solomon offered a sacrifice of **peace o**, 8002
8:64 for there he offered **burnt o**, and meat 5930
8:64 **meat o**, and the fat of the peace offerings: 4503
8:64 meat offerings, and the fat of the **peace o**: 8002
8:64 *was* too little to receive the **burnt o**, 5930
8:64 **meat o**, and the fat of the peace offerings. 4503
8:64 meat offerings, and the fat of the **peace o**. 8002
9:25 times in a year did Solomon offer **burnt o** 5930
9:25 **peace o** upon the altar which he built unto 8002
2Ki 10:24 they went in to offer sacrifices and **burnt o**, 5930
16:13 sprinkled the blood of his **peace o**, upon 8002
16:15 and their meat offering, and their **drink o**; 5262
1Ch 16: 1 burnt sacrifices and **peace o** before God. 8002
16: 2 had made an end of offering the **burnt o** 5930
16: 2 the burnt offerings and the **peace o**, 8002
16:40 To offer **burnt o** unto the LORD upon 5930

1Ch 21:23 lo, I give *thee* the oxen *also* for **burnt o**, 5930
21:24 the LORD, nor offer **burnt o** without cost. 5930
21:26 offered **burnt o** and peace offerings, and 5930
21:26 offered burnt offerings and **peace o**, and 8002
29:21 offered **burnt o** unto the LORD, on 5930
29:21 with their **drink o**, and sacrifices in 5262
2Ch 1: 6 and offered a thousand **burnt o** upon it. 5930
2: 4 *for* the **burnt o** morning and evening, 5930
7: 7 for there he offered **burnt o**, and the fat of 5930
7: 7 the fat of the **peace o**, because the brasen 8002
7: 7 made was not able to receive the **burnt o**, 5930
7: 7 burnt offerings, and the **meat o**, and the fat. 4503
8:12 Solomon offered **burnt o** unto the LORD 5930
23:18 to offer the **burnt o** of the LORD, as it is 5930
24:14 they offered **burnt o** in the house of 5930
29: 7 have not burnt incense nor offered **burnt o** 5930
29:31 and **thank o** into the house of the LORD. 8426
29:31 brought in sacrifices and **thank o**; 8426
29:31 as many as were of a free heart **burnt o**. 5930
29:32 the number of the **burnt o**, which 5930
29:34 so that they could not flay all the **burnt o**: 5930
29:35 also the **burnt o** *were* in abundance, 5930
29:35 with the fat of the **peace o**, and the drink 8002
29:35 and the **drink o** for *every* burnt offering. 5262
30:15 brought in the **burnt o** *into* the house of 5930
30:22 offering peace **o**, and making confession to 2077
31: 2 the priests and Levites for **burnt o** and 5930
31: 2 Levites for burnt offerings and for **peace o**, 8002
31: 3 portion of his substance for the **burnt o**, 5930
31: 3 *wit*, for the morning and evening **burnt o**, 5930
31: 3 the **burnt o** for the sabbaths, and for 5930
31:10 Since *the people* began to bring the **o** *into* 8641
31:12 brought in the **o** and the tithes and 8641
31:14 the east, *was* over the **freewill o** of God, 5071
33:16 sacrificed thereon peace **o** and 2077
33:16 thereon peace offerings and **thank o**, 8426
35: 7 all for the passover ***o***, for all that were NIH
35: 8 gave unto the priests for the passover ***o*** two NIH
35: 9 gave unto the Levites for passover ***o*** five NIH
35:12 they removed the **burnt o**, that they might 5930
35:13 the *other* holy ***o*** sod they in pots, and NIH
35:14 Aaron *were busied* in offering of **burnt o** 5930
35:16 to offer **burnt o** upon the altar of 5930
Ezr 3: 2 God of Israel, to offer **burnt o** thereon, 5930
3: 3 they offered **burnt o** thereon unto 5930
3: 3 *even* **burnt o** morning and evening. 5930
3: 4 and *offered* the daily **burnt o** by number, 5930
3: 6 they to offer **burnt o** unto the LORD. 5930
6: 9 for the **burnt o** of the God of heaven, 5928
7:17 with their **meat o** and their drink offerings, 4504
7:17 with their meat offerings and their **drink o**, 5261
8:35 offered **burnt o** unto the God of Israel, 5930
Ne 10:33 for the **sin o** to make an atonement for 2403
10:37 our **o**, and the fruit of all *manner of* trees, 8641
12:44 for the **o**, for the firstfruits, and for 8641
13: 5 where aforetime they laid the **meat o**, 4503
13: 5 and the porters; and the **o** of the priests. 8641
Job 1: 5 offered **burnt o** *according to* the number of 5930
Ps 16: 4 *god*: their **drink o** of blood will I not offer, 5262
20: 3 Remember all thy **o**, and accept thy burnt 4503
50: 8 thee for thy sacrifices or thy **burnt o**, 5930
66:13 I will go *into* thy house with **burnt o**: I will 5930
119:108 the **freewill o** of my mouth, O LORD, and 5071
Pr 7:14 *I have* peace **o** with me; *this* day have I 2077
Isa 1:11 I am full *of* the **burnt o** of rams, and the fat 5930
43:23 brought me the small cattle of thy **burnt o**; 5930
56: 7 their **burnt o** and their sacrifices *shall be* 5930
Jer 6:20 your **burnt o** *are* not acceptable, nor your 5930
7:18 to pour out **drink o** unto other gods, that 5262
7:21 Put your **burnt o** unto your sacrifices, and 5930
7:22 of Egypt, concerning **burnt o** or sacrifices: 5930
17:26 bringing **burnt o**, and sacrifices, and 5930
17:26 **meat o**, and incense, and 4503
19: 5 to burn their sons with fire *for* **burnt o** unto 5930
19:13 have poured out **drink o** unto other gods. 5262
32:29 poured out **drink o** unto other gods, 5262
33:18 want a man before me to offer **burnt o**, 5930
33:18 to kindle **meat o**, and to do sacrifice 4503
41: 5 with **o** and incense in their hand, 4503
44:17 to pour out **drink o** unto her, as we have 5262
44:18 to pour out **drink o** unto her, we have 5262
44:19 poured out **drink o** unto her, did we make 5262
44:19 pour out **drink o** unto her, without our 5262
44:25 and to pour out **drink o** unto her: 5262
Eze 20:28 and poured out there their **drink o**. 5262
20:40 there will I require your **o**, and 8641
43:18 to offer **burnt o** thereon, and to sprinkle 5930
43:27 the priests shall make your **burnt o** upon 5930
43:27 offerings upon the altar, and your **peace o**; 8002
45:15 and for a burnt offering, and for **peace o**, 8002
45:17 it shall be the prince's part *to give* **burnt o**, 5930
45:17 **meat o**, and drink offerings, in the feasts, 4503
45:17 **drink o**, in the feasts, and in the new 5262
45:17 and the burnt offering, and the **peace o**, 8002
46: 2 prepare his burnt offering and his **peace o**, 8002
46:12 or **peace o** voluntarily unto the LORD, 8002
46:12 prepare his burnt offering and his **peace o**, 8002
Hos 6: 6 the knowledge of God more than **burnt o**. 5930
8:13 sacrifice flesh *for* the sacrifices of mine **o**, 1890
9: 4 They shall not offer wine ***o*** to the LORD, NIH
Am 4: 5 and proclaim *and* publish the **free o**: 5071
5:22 Though ye offer me **burnt o** and your meat 5930
5:22 offer me burnt offerings and your **meat o**, 4503
5:22 will I regard the **peace o** of your fat beasts. 8002
5:25 and **o** in the wilderness forty years, 4503
Mic 6: 6 shall I come before him with **burnt o**, 5930
Mal 3: 8 have we robbed thee? *In* tithes and **o**. 8641
Mk 12:33 is more than all **whole burnt o** and *3646*
Lk 21: 4 their abundance cast in unto the **o** of God: *1435*
Ac 24:17 I came to bring alms to my nation, and **o**. *4376*
Heb 10: 6 In **burnt o** and *sacrifices* for sin thou hast *3646*
10: 8 Sacrifice and offering and **burnt o** and *3646*

OFFICE (46) [OFFICER, OFFICERS, OFFICES]

Ge 41:13 me he restored unto mine **o**, and him he 3653
Ex 1:16 When ye **do the o of a midwife** to 3205
28: 1 he may **minister** unto me **in the priest's o**, 3547
28: 3 he may **minister** unto me **in the priest's o**. 3547
28: 4 he may **minister** unto me **in the priest's o**. 3547
28:41 may **minister** unto me **in the priest's o**. 3547
29: 1 to **minister** unto me **in the priest's o**: 3547
29: 9 the **priest's o** shall be theirs for a perpetual 3550
29:44 to **minister** to me **in the priest's o**. 3547
30:30 may **minister** unto me **in the priest's o**. 3547
31:10 of his sons, to **minister in the priest's o**, 3547
35:19 of his sons, to **minister in the priest's o**. 3547
39:41 to **minister in the priest's o**. 3547
40:13 he may **minister** unto me **in the priest's o**. 3547
40:15 may **minister** unto me **in the priest's o**: 3547
Lev 7:35 **minister** unto the LORD **in the priest's o**; 3547
16:32 **minister in the priest's o** in his father's 3547
Nu 3: 3 consecrated to **minister in the priest's o**. 3547
3: 4 Ithamar **ministered in the priest's o** in 3547
3:10 and they shall wait on their **priest's o**: 3550
4:16 *to* the **o** of Eleazar the son of Aaron 6486
18: 7 your **priest's o** for every thing of the altar, 3550
18: 7 I have given your **priest's o** *unto you as a* 3550
Dt 10: 6 **ministered in the priest's o** in his stead. 3547
1Ch 6:10 (he *it is* that **executed the priest's o** in 3547
6:32 they waited on their **o** according to their 5656
9:22 and Samuel the seer did ordain in their **set o**. 530
9:26 *were* in *their* **set o**, and were over 530
9:31 had the **set o** over the things that were made 530
23:28 Because their **o** *was* to wait on the sons of 4612
24: 2 and Ithamar **executed the priest's o**. 3547
2Ch 11:14 **executing the priest's o** unto the LORD: 3547
24:11 the king's **o** by the hand of the Levites, 6486
31:15 in the cities of the priests, in *their* **set o**, 530
31:18 for in their **set o** they sanctified themselves 530
Ne 13:13 their **o** *was* to distribute unto their brethren. 5921
Ps 109: 8 his days be few; *and* let another take his **o**. 6486
Eze 44:13 unto me, to **do the o of a priest** unto me, 3547
Lk 1: 8 *that* while he **executed the priest's o** *2407*
1: 9 According to the custom of the **priest's o**, *2405*
Ro 11:13 apostle of the Gentiles, I magnify mine **o**: *1248*
12: 4 and all members have not the same **o**: *4234*
1Ti 3: 1 If a man desire the **o of a bishop**, *1984*
3:10 then let them **use the o of a deacon**, *1247*
3:13 For they that have **used the o of a deacon** *1247*
Heb 7: 5 **o of the priesthood** have a commandment *2405*

OFFICER (12) [OFFICE]

Ge 37:36 an **o** of Pharaoh's, *and* captain of the guard. 5631
39: 1 Potiphar, an **o** of Pharaoh, captain of 5631
Jdg 9:28 Zebul his **o**? serve the men of Hamor 6496
1Ki 4: 5 Zabud the son of Nathan *was* **principal o**, 3548
4:19 *he was* the only **o** which *was* in the land. 5333
22: 9 the king of Israel called an **o**, and said, 5631
2Ki 8: 6 So the king appointed unto her a certain **o**, 5631
25:19 out of the city he took an **o** that was set 5631
2Ch 24:11 and the high priest's **o** came and 6496
Mt 5:25 and the judge deliver thee to the **o**, and *5257*
Lk 12:58 and the judge deliver thee to the **o**, and *4233*
12:58 the officer, and the **o** cast thee into prison. *4233*

OFFICERS (58) [OFFICE]

Ge 40: 2 Pharaoh was wroth against two *of* his **o**, 5631
40: 7 he asked Pharaoh's **o** that *were* with him in 5631
41:34 do *this*, and let him appoint **o** over the land, 6496
Ex 5: 6 of the people, and their **o**, saying, 7860
5:10 their **o**, and they spake to the people, 7860
5:14 the **o** of the children of Israel, 7860
5:15 the **o** of the children of Israel came and 7860
5:19 the **o** of the children of Israel did see *that* 7860
Nu 11:16 the elders of the people, and **o** over them; 7860
31:14 Moses was wroth with the **o** of the host, 6485
31:48 the **o** which *were* over thousands of 6485
Dt 1:15 over tens, and **o** among your tribes. 7860
16:18 and **o** shalt thou make thee in all thy gates, 7860
20: 5 the **o** shall speak unto the people, saying, 7860
20: 8 the **o** shall speak further unto the people, 7860
20: 9 when the **o** have made an end of speaking 7860
29:10 your elders, and your **o**, *with* all the men of 7860
31:28 your **o**, that I may speak these words in 7860
Jos 1:10 Joshua commanded the **o** of the people, 7860
3: 2 three days, that the **o** went through the host; 7860
8:33 and their elders, and **o**, and their judges, 7860
23: 2 for their **o**, and said unto them, I am old 7860
24: 1 and for their judges, and for their **o**; 7860
1Sa 8:15 and give to his **o**, and to his servants. 5631
1Ki 4: 5 Azariah the son of Nathan *was* over the **o**: 5324
4: 7 Solomon had twelve **o** over all Israel, 5324
4:27 those **o** provided victual for king Solomon, 5324
4:28 they unto the place where *the o* were, NIH
5:16 Besides the chief of Solomon's **o** which 5324
9:23 These *were* the chief of the **o** that *were* over 5324
2Ki 11:15 the **o** of the host, and said unto them, 6485
11:18 the priest appointed **o** over the house of 6485
24:12 and his servants, and his princes, and his **o**: 5631
24:15 and his **o**, and the mighty of the land, 5631
1Ch 23: 4 and six thousand *were* **o** and judges: 7860
26:29 business over Israel, for **o** and judges. 7860
26:30 *were* **o** among them of Israel on *this* side 6486
27: 1 their **o** that served the king in any matter of 7860
28: 1 with the **o**, and *with* the mighty *men*, and 5631
2Ch 8:10 these *were* the chief of king Solomon's **o**, 5324
18: 8 the king of Israel called for one *of* his **o**, 5631
19:11 also the Levites *shall be* **o** before you. 7860
34:13 *there were* scribes, and **o**, and porters. 7860
Est 1: 8 the king had appointed to all the **o** of his 7227
2: 3 let the king appoint **o** in all the provinces of 6496
9: 3 and **o** of the king, 4399+6213+1886.1
Isa 60:17 I will also make thy **o** peace, and 6486
Jer 29:26 that *ye* should be **o** in the house of 6496
Jn 7:32 and the chief priests sent **o** to take him. *5257*
7:45 Then came the **o** to the chief priests and *5257*
7:46 The **o** answered, Never man spake like this *5257*
18: 3 and **o** from the chief priests and Pharisees, *5257*
18:12 the captain and **o** of the Jews took Jesus, *5257*
18:18 **o** stood *there*, who had made a fire of coals; *5257*

Jn 18:22 one of the o which stood by stroke Jesus *5257*
19: 6 the chief priests therefore and o saw him, *5257*
Ac 5:22 But when the o came, and found them not *5257*
5:26 Then went the captain with the o, and *5257*

OFFICES (5) [OFFICE]
1Sa 2:36 I pray thee, into one of the **priests'** o, 3550
1Ch 24: 3 according to their o in their service. 6486
2Ch 7: 6 the priests waited on their o: the Levites 4931
23:18 Also Jehoiada appointed the o of the house 6486
Ne 13:14 the house of my God, and for the o thereof. 4929

OFFSCOURING (2)
La 3:45 Thou hast made us *as* the o and refuse in 5501
1Co 4:13 *and are* the o of all *things* unto this day. *4067*

OFFSPRING (12)
Job 5:25 and thine o as the grass of the earth. 6631
21: 8 with them, and their o before their eyes. 6631
27:14 and his o shall not be satisfied *with* bread. 6631
31: 8 let another eat; yea, let my o be rooted out. 6631
Isa 22:24 the o and the issue, all vessels of small 6631
44: 3 thy seed, and my blessing upon thine o: 6631
48:19 the o of thy bowels like the gravel thereof; 6631
61: 9 the Gentiles, and their o among the people: 6631
65:23 of the LORD, and their o with them. 6631
Ac 17:28 own poets have said, For we are also his o. *1085*
17:29 Forasmuch then as we are the o of God, *1085*
Rev 22:16 I am the root and the o of David, *and* *1085*

OFT (13) [OFTEN]
2Ki 4: 8 *so* it was, *that* **as o as** he passed by, 1767+4480
Job 21:17 **How o** is the candle of the wicked 4100+3509.1
21:17 *how* o cometh their destruction upon them! NIH
Ps 78:40 **How o** did they provoke him in 4100+3509.1
Mt 9:14 Why do we and the Pharisees fast o, but *4183*
17:15 he falleth into the fire, and o into the water. *4178*
18:21 **how o** shall my brother sin against me, and *4212*
Mk 7: 3 except they wash *their* hands o, eat not, *4435*
Ac 26:11 And I punished them o in every synagogue, *4178*
1Co 11:25 **as o as** ye drink *it*, in remembrance of *302+3740*
2Co 11:23 in prisons more frequent, in deaths o. *4178*
2Ti 1:16 for he o refreshed me, and was not ashamed *4178*
Heb 6: 7 drinketh *in* the rain that cometh o upon it, *4178*

OFTEN (15) [OFT, OFTENER, OFTENTIMES, OFTTIMES]
Pr 29: 1 that being o reproved hardeneth *his* neck, NIH
Mal 3:16 they that feared the LORD spake o one to NIH
Mt 23:37 **how o** would I have gathered thy children *4212*
Mk 5: 4 Because that he had been o bound with *4178*
Lk 5:33 Why do the disciples of John fast o, and *4437*
13:34 **how o** would I have gathered thy children *4212*
1Co 11:26 For **as o as** ye eat this bread, and *302+3740*
2Co 11:26 *In* journeyings o, *in* perils of waters, *4178*
11:27 in watchings o, in hunger and thirst, *4178*
11:27 in hunger and thirst, in fastings o, in cold *4178*
Php 3:18 of whom I have told you o, and now tell *4178*
1Ti 5:23 thy stomach's sake and thine o infirmities. *4437*
Heb 9:25 Nor yet that he should offer himself o, *4178*
9:26 must he o have suffered since *4178*
Rev 11: 6 with all plagues, **as o as** they will. *1437+3740*

OFTENER (1) [OFTEN]
Ac 24:26 wherefore he sent for him the o, and *4437*

OFTENTIMES (6) [OFTEN, TIME]
Job 33:29 *things* worketh God o with man, 6471+7969
Ecc 7:22 For o also thine own heart knoweth 6471+7227
Lk 8:29 For o it had caught him: and he was *4183+5550*
Ro 1:13 that o I purposed to come unto you, (but *4178*
2Co 8:22 whom we have o proved diligent in many *4178*
Heb 10:11 and offering o the same sacrifices, *4178*

OFTTIMES (3) [OFTEN, TIME]
Mt 17:15 for o he falleth into the fire, and oft into *4178*
Mk 9:22 And o it hath cast him into the fire, and *4178*
Jn 18: 2 for Jesus o resorted thither with his *4178*

OG (22)
Nu 21:33 O the king of Bashan went out against 5747
32:33 the kingdom of O king of Bashan, the land, 5747
Dt 1: 4 in Heshbon, and O the king of Bashan, 5747
3: 1 O the king of Bashan came out against us, 5747
3: 3 our God delivered into our hands O also, 5747
3: 4 of Argob, the kingdom of O in Bashan. 5747
3:10 cities of the kingdom of O in Bashan. 5747
3:11 For only O king of Bashan remained of 5747
3:13 and all Bashan, *being* the kingdom of O, 5747
4:47 the land of O king of Bashan, two kings of 5747
29: 7 of Heshbon, and O the king of Bashan, 5747
31: 4 do unto them as he did to Sihon and to O, 5747
Jos 2:10 and O, whom ye utterly destroyed. 5747
9:10 to O king of Bashan, which *was* at 5747
12: 4 the coast of O king of Bashan, *which was* 5747
13:12 All the kingdom of O in Bashan, 5747
13:30 all the kingdom of O king of Bashan, and 5747
13:31 cities of the kingdom of O in Bashan, 5747
1Ki 4:19 of the Amorites, and of O king of Bashan; 5747
Ne 9:22 and the land of O king of Bashan. 5747
Ps 135:11 O king of Bashan, and all the kingdoms of 5747
136:20 O the king of Bashan: for his mercy 5747

OH (17) [O]
Ge 18:30 he said *unto him*, O let not the Lord be 4994
18:32 O let not the Lord be angry, and I will 4994
19:18 Lot said unto them, O, not so, my Lord: 4994
19:20 O, let me escape thither, (*is* it not a little 4994
Ex 32:31 said, O, this people have sinned a great sin, 577
2Sa 15: 4 **O that** I were made judge in the land, 4310
23:15 **O that** one would give me drink *of* 4310
1Ch 4:10 **O that** thou wouldest bless me indeed, 518
11:17 **O that** one would give me drink *of* 4310
Job 6: 2 **O that** my grief were throughly weighed, 3863
10:18 **O** *that* I had given up the ghost, and no eye NIH
Ps 107: 8 O that *men* would praise the LORD *for* his NIH
107:15 O that *men* would praise the LORD *for* his NIH
107:21 O that *men* would praise the LORD *for* his NIH
107:31 O that *men* would praise the LORD *for* his NIH
116:16 O LORD, truly I *am* thy servant; I *am* thy 577
Jer 44: 4 rising early and sending *them*, saying, O, 4994

OHAD (2)
Ge 46:10 O, and Jachin, and Zohar, and Shaul the son 161
Ex 6:15 O, and Jachin, and Zohar, and Shaul the son 161

OHEL (1)
1Ch 3:20 O, and Berechiah, and Hasadiah, 169

OHOLAH See AHOLAH

OHOLIAB See AHOLIAB

OHOLIBAH See AHOLIBAH

OHOLIBAMAH See AHOLIBAMAH

OIL (202) [OILED]
Ge 28:18 *for* a pillar, and poured o upon the top of it. 8081
35:14 offering thereon, and he poured o thereon. 8081
Ex 25: 6 O for the light, spices for anointing oil, and 8081
25: 6 spices for anointing o, and for sweet 8081
27:20 that they bring thee pure o olive beaten for 8081
29: 2 cakes unleavened tempered with o, and 8081
29: 2 and wafers unleavened anointed with o: 8081
29: 7 shalt thou take the anointing o, and pour *it* 8081
29:21 of the anointing o, and sprinkle *it* upon 8081
29:40 with the fourth part of a hin of beaten o; 8081
30:24 of the sanctuary, and of o olive a hin: 8081
30:25 thou shalt make it an o of holy ointment, 8081
30:25 it shall be a holy anointing o. 8081
30:31 This shall be a holy anointing o unto me 8081
31:11 the anointing o, and sweet incense for 8081
35: 8 o for the light, and spices for anointing oil, 8081
35: 8 spices for anointing o, and for the sweet 8081
35:14 and his lamps, with the o for the light, 8081
35:15 the anointing o, and the sweet incense, and 8081
35:28 and o for the light, and for the anointing oil, 8081
35:28 for the anointing o, and for the sweet 8081
37:29 he made the holy anointing o, and the pure 8081
39:37 all the vessels thereof, and the o for light, 8081
39:38 the anointing o, and the sweet incense, and 8081
40: 9 thou shalt take the anointing o, and 8081
Lev 2: 1 he shall pour o upon it, and 8081
2: 2 of the o thereof, with all the frankincense 8081
2: 4 cakes of fine flour mingled with o, 8081
2: 4 or unleavened wafers anointed with o. 8081
2: 5 *of* fine flour unleavened, mingled with o. 8081
2: 6 shalt part it in pieces, and pour o thereon. 8081
2: 7 it shall be made *of* fine flour with o. 8081
2:15 thou shalt put o upon it, and 8081
2:16 corn thereof, and *part* of the o thereof, 8081
5:11 he shall put no o upon it, neither shall he 8081
6:15 of the o thereof, and all the frankincense 8081
6:21 In a pan it shall be made with o; *and* 8081
7:10 meat offering, mingled with o, and dry, 8081
7:12 unleavened cakes mingled with o, 8081
7:12 and unleavened wafers anointed with o, and 8081
7:12 cakes mingled with o, of fine flour, fried. 8081
8: 2 the anointing o, and a bullock *for* the sin 8081
8:10 Moses took the anointing o, and 8081
8:12 he poured of the anointing o upon Aaron's 8081
8:30 Moses took of the anointing o, and of 8081
9: 4 and a meat offering mingled with o: 8081
10: 7 for the anointing o of the LORD *is* upon 8081
14:10 mingled with o, and one log of oil. 8081
14:10 mingled with oil, and one log of o. 8081
14:12 the log of o, and wave them *for* a wave 8081
14:15 the priest shall take *some* of the log of o, 8081
14:16 the priest shall dip his right finger in the o 8081
14:16 shall sprinkle of the o with his finger seven 8081
14:17 of the rest of the o that *is* in his hand shall 8081
14:18 the remnant of the o that *is* in the priest's 8081
14:21 one tenth deal of fine flour mingled with o 8081
14:21 with oil for a meat offering, and a log of o; 8081
14:24 the log of o, and the priest shall wave them 8081
14:26 the priest shall pour of the o into the palm 8081
14:27 o that *is* in his left hand seven times before 8081
14:28 the priest shall put of the o that *is* in his 8081
14:29 the rest of the o that *is* in the priest's hand 8081
21:10 upon whose head the anointing o was 8081
21:12 for the crown of the anointing o of his God 8081
23:13 tenth deals *of* fine flour mingled with o, 8081
24: 2 that they bring unto thee pure o olive 8081
Nu 4: 9 and all the o vessels thereof, 8081
4:16 the priest *pertaineth* the o for the light, 8081
4:16 the anointing o, *and* the oversight of all 8081
5:15 he shall pour no o upon it, nor put 8081
6:15 cakes *of* fine flour mingled with o, and 8081
6:15 of unleavened bread anointed with o, 8081
7:13 flour mingled with o for a meat offering: 8081
7:19 flour mingled with o for a meat offering: 8081
7:25 flour mingled with o for a meat offering: 8081
7:31 flour mingled with o for a meat offering: 8081
7:37 flour mingled with o for a meat offering: 8081
7:43 flour mingled with o for a meat offering: 8081
7:49 flour mingled with o for a meat offering: 8081
7:55 flour mingled with o for a meat offering: 8081
7:61 flour mingled with o for a meat offering: 8081
7:67 flour mingled with o for a meat offering: 8081
7:73 flour mingled with o for a meat offering: 8081
7:79 flour mingled with o for a meat offering: 8081
8: 8 *even* fine flour mingled with o, and 8081
11: 8 the taste of it was as the taste of fresh o. 8081
15: 4 mingled with the fourth *part* of a hin of o. 8081
15: 6 mingled with the third *part* of a hin of o. 8081
15: 9 deals *of* flour mingled with half a hin of o. 8081
18:12 All the best of the o, and all the best of 3323
28: 5 with the fourth *part* of a hin of beaten o. 8081
28: 9 mingled with o, and the drink offering 8081
28:12 mingled with o, for one bullock; 8081
28:12 meat offering, mingled with o, for one ram; 8081
28:13 a several tenth deal of flour mingled with o 8081
28:20 offering *shall be of* flour mingled with o: 8081
28:28 their meat offering *of* flour mingled with o, 8081
29: 3 offering *shall be of* flour mingled with o, 8081
29: 9 offering *shall be of* flour mingled with o, 8081
29:14 offering *shall be of* flour mingled with o, 8081
35:25 which was anointed with the holy o. 8081
Dt 7:13 thy corn, and thy wine, and thine o, 3323
8: 8 pomegranates; a land of o olive, and honey; 8081
11:14 in thy corn, and thy wine, and thine o. 3323
12:17 or of thy o, or the firstlings of thy herds or 3323
14:23 of thine o, and the firstlings of thy herds 3323
18: 4 of thy o, and the first of the fleece of thy 3323
28:40 but thou shalt not anoint *thyself with* the o; 8081
28:51 or o, *or* the increase of thy kine, or 3323
32:13 out of the rock, and o out of the flinty rock; 8081
33:24 his brethren, and let him dip his foot in o. 8081
1Sa 10: 1 Samuel took a vial of o, and poured *it* upon 8081
16: 1 fill thine horn *with* o, and go, I will send 8081
16:13 Samuel took the horn of o, and 8081
2Sa 1:21 *as though he had* not *been* anointed with o. 8081
14: 2 anoint not *thyself with* o, but be as a 8081
1Ki 1:39 Zadok the priest took a horn of o out of 8081
5:11 and twenty measures of pure o: 8081
17:12 of meal in a barrel, and a little o in a cruse: 8081
17:14 not waste, neither shall the cruse of o fail, 8081
17:16 wasted not, neither did the cruse of o fail, 8081
2Ki 4: 2 not any thing in the house, save a pot of o. 8081
4: 6 *is* not a vessel more. And the o stayed. 8081
4: 7 sell the o, and pay thy debt, and live thou 8081
9: 1 take this box of o in thine hand, and go *to* 8081
9: 3 take the box of o, and pour *it* on his head, 8081
9: 6 he poured the o on his head, and said unto 8081
18:32 vineyards, a land of o olive and of honey, 3323
1Ch 9:29 the o, and the frankincense, and the spices. 8081
12:40 and o, and oxen, and sheep abundantly: 8081
27:28 and over the cellars of o *was* Joash: 8081
2Ch 2:10 of wine, and twenty thousand baths of o. 8081
2:15 and the barley, the o, and the wine, 8081
11:11 and store of victual, and *of* o and wine. 8081
31: 5 o, and honey, and of all the increase of 3323
32:28 for the increase of corn, and wine, and o; 3323
Ezr 3: 7 meat, and drink, and o, unto them of Zidon, 8081
6: 9 the God of heaven, wheat, salt, wine, and o, 4887
7:22 to an hundred baths *of* o, and salt without 4887
Ne 5:11 *of* the corn, the wine, and the o, that ye 3323
10:37 *of* trees, of wine and of o, unto the priests, 3323
10:39 of the new wine, and the o, unto 3323
13: 5 tithes of the corn, the new wine, and the o, 3323
13:12 the new wine and the o unto the treasuries. 3323
Est 2:12 *to wit*, six months with o of myrrh, and 8081
Job 24:11 *Which* **make** o within their walls, *and* 6671
29: 6 and the rock poured me out rivers of o; 8081
Ps 23: 5 thou anointest my head with o; my cup 8081
45: 7 hath anointed thee *with* the o of gladness 8081
55:21 his words were softer than o, yet *were* they 8081
89:20 with my holy o have I anointed him. 8081
92:10 an unicorn: I shall be anointed with fresh o. 8081
104:15 *and* o to make *his* face to shine, and 8081
109:18 bowels like water, and like o into his bones. 8081
141: 5 *it shall be* an excellent o, *which* shall not 8081
Pr 5: 3 and her mouth *is* smoother than o: 8081
21:17 he that loveth wine and o shall not be rich. 8081
21:20 and o in the dwelling of the wise; 8081
Isa 41:19 shittah tree, and the myrtle, and the o tree; 8081
61: 3 beauty for ashes, the o of joy for mourning, 8081
Jer 31:12 for o, and for the young of the flock and 3323
40:10 o, and put *them* in your vessels, and 8081
41: 8 and *of* barley, and *of* o, and *of* honey. 8081
Eze 16: 9 blood from thee, and I anointed thee with o. 8081
16:13 thou didst eat fine flour, and honey, and o: 8081
16:18 thou hast set mine o and mine incense 8081
16:19 fine flour, and o, and honey, *wherewith* I 8081
23:41 thou hast set mine incense and mine o. 8081
27:17 and Pannag, and honey, and o, and balm. 8081
32:14 cause their rivers to run like o, saith 8081
45:14 Concerning the ordinance of o, the bath *of* 8081
45:14 the ordinance of oil, the bath *of* o, 8081
45:24 for a ram, and a hin of o for an ephah. 8081
45:25 to the meat offering, and according to the o. 8081
46: 5 be able to give, and a hin of o to an ephah. 8081
46: 7 shall attain unto, and a hin of o to an ephah. 8081
46:11 is able to give, and a hin of o to an ephah. 8081
46:14 of an ephah, and the third *part* of a hin of o, 8081
46:15 the lamb, and the meat offering, and the o, 8081
Hos 2: 5 and my flax, mine o and my drink. 8081
2: 8 and o, and multiplied her silver and gold, 3323
2:22 shall hear the corn, and the wine, and the o; 3323
12: 1 the Assyrians, and o is carried into Egypt. 8081
Joel 1:10 the new wine is dried up, the o languisheth. 3323
2:19 and o, and ye shall be satisfied therewith: 3323
2:24 and the fats shall overflow *with* wine and o. 3323
Mic 6: 7 *or* with ten thousands of rivers of o? 8081
6:15 but thou shalt not anoint *thee with* o; 8081
Hag 1:11 upon the o, and upon *that* which the ground 3323
2:12 or pottage, or wine, or o, or any meat, 8081
Zec 4:12 pipes empty the golden *o* out of themselves? NIH
Mt 25: 3 took their lamps, and took no o with them: *1637*
25: 4 But the wise took o in their vessels with *1637*
25: 8 said unto the wise, Give us of your o; *1637*
Mk 6:13 and anointed with o many *that were* sick, *1637*
Lk 7:46 Mine head with o thou didst not anoint: but *1637*
10:34 pouring in o and wine, and set him on his *1637*
16: 6 And he said, An hundred measures of o. *1637*
Heb 1: 9 hath anointed thee *with* the o of gladness *1637*
Jas 5:14 anointing him with o in the name of *1637*
Rev 6: 6 and *see* thou hurt not the o and the wine. *1637*
18:13 and o, and fine flour, and wheat, and *1637*

OILED (2) [OIL]
Ex 29:23 one cake of o bread, and one wafer out of 8081
Lev 8:26 a cake of o bread, and one wafer, and 8081

O

OINTMENT (27) [OINTMENTS]

Ex 30:25 thou shalt make it an oil of holy **o**, 4888
30:25 an **o** compound *after* the art of 7545
2Ki 20:13 the precious **o**, and all the house of his 8081
1Ch 9:30 *some* of the sons of the priests made the **o** 4842
Job 41:31 like a pot: he maketh the sea like a **pot of o**. 4841
Ps 133: 2 *It is* like the precious **o** upon the head, 8081
Pr 27: 9 **O** and perfume rejoice the heart: so 8081
27:16 hideth the wind, and the **o** of his right hand, 8081
Ecc 7: 1 A *good* name *is* better than precious **o**; and 8081
9: 8 be always white; and let thy head lack no **o**. 8081
10: 1 Dead flies cause the **o** of the apothecary to 8081
SS 1: 3 ointments thy name *is as* **o** poured forth, 8081
Isa 1: 6 neither bound up, neither mollified with **o**. 8081
39: 2 the precious **o**, and all the house of his 8081
57: 9 thou wentest to the king with **o**, and 8081
Mt 26: 7 having an alabaster box of very precious **o**, *3464*
26: 9 For this **o** might have been sold for much, *3464*
26:12 For in that she hath poured this **o** on my *3464*
Mk 14: 3 box of **o** of spikenard very precious; *3464*
14: 4 said, Why was this waste of the **o** made? *3464*
Lk 7:37 brought an alabaster box of **o**, *3464*
7:38 his feet, and anointed *them* with the **o**. *3464*
7:46 this *woman* hath anointed my feet with **o**. *3464*
Jn 11: 2 *that* Mary which anointed the Lord with **o**, *3464*
12: 3 Then took Mary a pound of **o** of spikenard, *3464*
12: 3 house was filled with the odour of the **o**. *3464*
12: 5 Why was not this **o** sold for three hundred *3464*

OINTMENTS (5) [OINTMENT]

SS 1: 3 Because of the savour of thy good **o** thy 8081
4:10 and the smell of thine **o** than all spices! 8081
Am 6: 6 and anoint themselves *with* the chief **o**: 8081
Lk 23:56 they returned, and prepared spices and **o**; *3464*
Rev 18:13 and **o**, and frankincense, and wine, and oil, *3464*

OLD (380) [ELDER, ELDERS, ELDEST, OLDNESS]

Ge 5:32 Noah was five hundred years **o**: and 1121
6: 4 same *became* mighty *men* which *were* of **o**, 5769
7: 6 Noah *was* six hundred years **o** when 1121
11:10 Shem *was* an hundred years **o**, and 1121
12: 4 five years **o** when he departed out of Haran. 1121
15: 9 Take me a heifer of **three years o**, and 8027
15: 9 a she goat of **three years o**, and a ram of 8027
15: 9 a ram of **three years o**, and a turtle-dove, 8027
15:15 thou shalt be buried in a good **o age**. 7872
16:16 Abram *was* fourscore and six years **o**, 1121
17: 1 when Abram was ninety years **o** and nine, 1121
17:12 he that is eight days **o** shall be circumcised 1121
17:17 born unto him that is an hundred years **o**? 1121
17:17 and shall Sarah, that is ninety years **o**, bear? 1323
17:24 Abraham *was* ninety years **o** and nine, 1121
17:25 Ishmael his son *was* thirteen years **o**, 1121
18:11 Now Abraham and Sarah *were* **o** *and* 2205
18:12 After I am **waxed o** shall I have pleasure, 1086
18:12 shall I have pleasure, my lord being **o** also? 2204
18:13 I of a surety bear *a child*, which am **o**? 2204
19: 4 the house round, both **o** and young, 2205
19:31 Our father *is* **o**, and *there is* not a man in 2204
21: 2 and bare Abraham a son in his **o age**, 2208
21: 4 his son Isaac being eight days **o**, 1121
21: 5 Abraham *was* an hundred years **o**, when his 1121
21: 7 for I have born *him* a son in his **o age**. 2208
23: 1 an hundred and seven and twenty **years o**: 8141
24: 1 Abraham was **o**, *and* well stricken in age: 2204
24:36 bare a son to my master when she was **o**: 2209
25: 8 died in a good **o age**, an old man, and 7872
25: 8 an **o man**, and full *of years;* and 2205
25:20 Isaac was forty years **o** when he took 1121
25:26 Isaac *was* threescore years **o** when she bare 1121
26:34 Esau was forty years **o** when he took to 1121
27: 1 that when Isaac was **o**, and his eyes were 2204
27: 2 he said, Behold now, I am **o**, I know not 2204
35:29 unto his people, *being* **o** and full of days: 2205
37: 2 Joseph, *being* seventeen years **o**, 1121
37: 3 because he *was* the son of his **o age**: 2208
41:46 Joseph *was* thirty years **o** when he stood 1121
43:27 father well, the **o man** of whom ye spake? 2205
44:20 an **o man**, and a child of *his* old age, a little 2205
44:20 and a child of *his* **o age**, a little one; 2208
47: 8 unto Jacob, How **o** *art* thou? 2416+3117+8141
49: 9 he couched as a lion, and as an **o lion**; 3833
50:26 *being* an hundred and ten years **o**: 1121
Ex 7: 7 Moses *was* fourscore years **o**, and 1121
7: 7 Aaron fourscore and three years **o**, 1121
10: 9 We will go with our young and with our **o**, 2205
30:14 from twenty years **o** and above, shall give 1121
38:26 from twenty years **o** and upward, for six 1121
Lev 13:11 It *is* an **o** leprosy in the skin of his flesh, 3462
19:32 honour the face of the **o man**, and fear thy 2205
25:22 and eat *yet* of **o** fruit until the ninth year; 3465
25:22 until her fruits come in ye shall eat *of* the **o** 3465
26:10 ye shall eat **o store**, and bring forth 3462+3465
26:10 bring forth the **o** because of the new. 3465
27: 3 of the male from twenty years **o** even unto 1121
27: 3 twenty years old even unto sixty years **o**, 1121
27: 5 if *it be* from five years **o** even unto twenty 1121
27: 5 five years old even unto twenty years **o**, 1121
27: 6 if *it be* from a month **o** even unto five years 1121
27: 6 *be* from a month old even unto five years **o**, 1121
27: 7 if *it be* from sixty years **o** and above; if *it be* 1121
Nu 1: 3 From twenty years **o** and upward, all that 1121
1:18 from twenty years **o** and upward, by their 1121
1:20 every male from twenty years **o** and 1121
1:22 every male from twenty years **o** and 1121
1:24 from twenty years **o** and upward, all that 1121
1:26 from twenty years **o** and upward, all that 1121
1:28 from twenty years **o** and upward, all that 1121
1:30 from twenty years **o** and upward, all that 1121
1:32 from twenty years **o** and upward, all that 1121
1:34 from twenty years **o** and upward, all that 1121
1:36 from twenty years **o** and upward, all that 1121
1:38 from twenty years **o** and upward, all that 1121
1:40 from twenty years **o** and upward, all that 1121
Nu 1:42 from twenty years **o** and upward, all that 1121
1:45 from twenty years **o** and upward, 1121
3:15 every male from a month **o** and 1121
3:22 all the males, from a month **o** and upward, 1121
3:28 from a month **o** and upward, *were* eight 1121
3:34 from a month **o** and upward, *were* six 1121
3:39 all the males from a month **o** and upward, 1121
3:40 of the children of Israel from a month **o** 1121
3:43 from a month **o** and upward, of those that 1121
4: 3 From thirty years **o** and upward even until 1121
4: 3 and upward even until fifty years **o**, 1121
4:23 From thirty years **o** and upward until fifty 1121
4:23 upward until fifty years **o** shalt thou 1121
4:30 From thirty years **o** and upward even unto 1121
4:30 upward even unto fifty years **o** shalt thou 1121
4:35 From thirty years **o** and upward even unto 1121
4:35 and upward even unto fifty years **o**, 1121
4:39 From thirty years **o** and upward even unto 1121
4:39 and upward even unto fifty years **o**, 1121
4:43 From thirty years **o** and upward even unto 1121
4:43 and upward even unto fifty years **o**, 1121
4:47 From thirty years **o** and upward even unto 1121
4:47 and upward even unto fifty years **o**, 1121
8:24 from twenty and five years **o** and 1121
14:29 from twenty years **o** and upward, 1121
18:16 from a month **o** shalt thou redeem, 1121
26: 2 from twenty years **o** and upward, 1121
26: 4 *the sum of the people*, from twenty years **o** 1121
26:62 all males from a month **o** and upward: 1121
32:11 from twenty years **o** and upward, shall see 1121
33:39 three years **o** when he died in mount Hor. 1121
Dt 2:20 giants dwelt therein **in o time**; and 6440+3807.1
8: 4 Thy raiment **waxed** not **o** upon thee, 1086
19:14 which they of **o time** have set in thine 7223
28:50 which shall not regard the person of the **o**, 2205
29: 5 your clothes are not **waxen o** upon you, and 1086
29: 5 and thy shoe is not **waxen o** upon thy foot. 1086
31: 2 *am* an hundred and twenty years **o** *this* day; 1121
32: 7 Remember the days **of o**, consider the years 5769
34: 7 and twenty years **o** when he died: 1121
Jos 5:11 they did eat of the **o corn** of the land on 5669
5:12 they had eaten of the **o corn** of the land; 5669
6:21 and **o**, and ox, and sheep, and ass, 2205
9: 4 took **o** sacks upon their asses, and 1087
9: 4 and wine bottles, **o**, and rent, and bound up; 1087
9: 5 **o** shoes and clouted upon their feet, and 1087
9: 5 upon their feet, and **o** garments upon them; 1087
9:13 our shoes are **become o** by reason of 1086
13: 1 Now Joshua was **o** *and* stricken in years; 2204
13: 1 Thou art **o** *and* stricken in years, and 2204
14: 7 Forty years **o** *was* I when Moses the servant 1121
14:10 I *am this* day fourscore and five years **o**. 1121
23: 1 that Joshua **waxed o** *and* stricken in age. 2204
23: 2 said unto them, I am **o** *and* stricken in age: 2204
24: 2 on the *other* side of the flood in **o time**, 5769
24:29 died, *being* an hundred and ten years **o**. 1121
Jdg 2: 8 died, *being* an hundred and ten years **o**. 1121
6:25 even the second bullock of seven **years o**, 8141
8:32 the son of Joash died in a good **o age**, 7872
19:16 there came an **o** man from his work out of 2205
19:17 the **o** man said, Whither goest thou? and 2205
19:20 the **o** man said, Peace *be* with thee; 2205
19:22 the master of the house, the **o man**, saying, 2205
Ru 1:12 go *your way;* for I am too **o** to have a 2204
4:15 of *thy* life, and a nourisher of thine **o age**: 7872
1Sa 2:22 Now Eli was very **o**, and heard all that his 2204
2:31 that there shall not be an **o man** in thine 2205
2:32 there shall not be an **o man** in thine house 2205
4:15 Now Eli *was* ninety and eight years **o**; and 1121
4:18 for he was an **o** man, and heavy. And he 2204
8: 1 it came to pass, when Samuel was **o**, that he 2204
8: 5 thou art **o**, and thy sons walk not in thy 2204
12: 2 I am **o** and grayheaded; and behold, 2204
17:12 the man went among men *for* an **o man** in 2204
27: 8 for those *nations were* of **o** the inhabitants 5769
28:14 she said, An **o** man cometh up; and he *is* 2205
2Sa 2:10 Ish-bosheth Saul's son *was* forty years **o** 1121
4: 4 was five years **o** when the tidings came of 1121
5: 4 David *was* thirty years **o** when he *began* to 1121
19:32 a very aged man, *even* fourscore years **o**: 1121
19:35 I *am this* day fourscore years **o**: *and* can I 1121
20:18 They were wont to speak in **o time**, saying, 7223
1Ki 1: 1 Now king David was **o** *and* stricken in 2204
1:15 the king was very **o**; and Abishag 2204
11: 4 For it came to pass, when Solomon was **o**, 2209
12: 6 king Rehoboam consulted with the **o men**, 2205
12: 8 he forsook the counsel of the **o men**, 2205
12:13 forsook the **o men's** counsel that they gave 2205
13:11 Now there dwelt an **o** prophet in Beth-el; 2205
13:25 told *it* in the city where the **o** prophet dwelt. 2205
13:29 the **o** prophet came to the city, to mourn 2205
14:21 and one years **o** when he *began* to reign, 1121
15:23 Nevertheless in the time of his **o age** he 2209
22:42 and five years **o** when he *began* to reign; 1121
2Ki 4:14 she hath no child, and her husband is **o**. 2204
8:17 two years **o** was he when he *began* to reign; 1121
8:26 twenty years **o** *was* Ahaziah when he *began* 1121
11:21 Seven years **o** *was* Jehoash when he *began* 1121
14: 2 and five years **o** when he *began* to reign, 1121
14:21 which *was* sixteen years **o**, and made him 1121
15: 2 Sixteen years **o** was he when he *began* to 1121
15:33 twenty years **o** was he when he *began* to 1121
16: 2 Twenty years **o** *was* Ahaz when he *began* 1121
18: 2 five years **o** was he when he *began* to reign; 1121
21: 1 Manasseh *was* twelve years **o** when he 1121
21:19 and two years **o** when he *began* to reign, 1121
22: 1 Josiah *was* eight years **o** when he *began* to 1121
23:31 and three years **o** when he *began* to reign; 1121
23:36 and five year **o** when he *began* to reign; 1121
24: 8 Jehoiachin *was* eighteen years **o** when he 1121
24:18 and one years **o** when he *began* to reign, 1121
1Ch 2:21 he married when he *was* threescore years **o**; 1121
4:40 *they* of Ham had dwelt there **of o**. 6440+3807.1
23: 1 So when David was **o** and full *of* days, 2204
23:27 *were* numbered from twenty years **o** 1121
1Ch 27:23 the number of them from twenty years **o** 1121
29:28 he died in a good **o age**, full of days, riches, 7872
2Ch 10: 6 Rehoboam took counsel with the **o men** 2205
10: 8 he forsook the counsel which the **o men** 2205
10:13 forsook the counsel of the **o men**, 2205
12:13 and forty years **o** when he *began* to reign, 1121
20:31 and five years **o** when he *began* to reign, 1121
21: 5 and two years **o** when he *began* to reign, 1121
21:20 two *years* **o** was he when he *began* to reign, 1121
22: 2 two years **o** *was* Ahaziah when he *began* to 1121
24: 1 Joash *was* seven years **o** when he *began* to 1121
24:15 Jehoiada **waxed o**, and was full *of* days 2204
24:15 and thirty years **o** *was he* when he died. 1121
25: 1 and five years **o** *when he* began to reign, 1121
25: 5 he numbered them from twenty years **o** and 1121
26: 1 who *was* sixteen years **o**, and made him 1121
26: 3 Sixteen years **o** *was* Uzziah when he *began* 1121
27: 1 and five years **o** when he *began* to reign, 1121
27: 8 and twenty years **o** when he *began* to reign, 1121
28: 1 Ahaz *was* twenty years **o** when he *began* to 1121
29: 1 reign *when he was* five and twenty years **o**, 1121
31:16 of males, from three years **o** and upward, 1121
31:17 the Levites from twenty years **o** and 1121
33: 1 Manasseh *was* twelve years **o** when he 1121
33:21 and twenty years **o** when he *began* to reign, 1121
34: 1 Josiah *was* eight years **o** when he *began* to 1121
36: 2 and three years **o** when he *began* to reign, 1121
36: 5 and five years **o** when he *began* to reign, 1121
36: 9 Jehoiachin *was* eight years **o** when he 1121
36:11 and twenty years **o** when he *began* to reign, 1121
36:17 **o man**, or him that stooped for age: 2205
Ezr 3: 8 appointed the Levites from twenty years **o** 1121
4:15 moved sedition within the same of **o** time: 5957
4:19 it is found that this city of **o** time *hath* made 5957
Ne 3: 6 Moreover the **o** gate repaired Jehoiada 3465
9:21 their clothes **waxed** not **o**, and their feet 1086
12:39 above the **o** gate, and above the fish gate, 3465
12:46 Asaph of **o** *there were* chief of the singers, 6924
Est 3:13 all Jews, both young and **o**, little children 2205
Job 4:11 The **o lion** perisheth for lack of prey, and 3918
14: 8 Though the root thereof **wax o** in the earth, 2204
20: 4 Knowest thou *not* this of **o**, since man was 5703
21: 7 **become o**, yea, are mighty *in* power? 6275
22:15 Hast thou marked the **o** way which wicked 5769
30: 2 profit me, in whom **o age** was perished? 3624
32: 6 and said, I *am* young, and ye *are* **very o**; 3453
42:17 So Job died, *being* **o** and full of days. 2205
Ps 6: 7 it **waxeth o** because of all mine enemies. 6275
25: 6 for they *have been* **ever of o**. 4480+5769
32: 3 my bones **waxed o** through my roaring all 1086
37:25 I have been young, and *now* am **o**; yet have 2204
44: 1 thou didst in their days, in the times of **o**. 6924
55:19 and afflict them, even he that abideth of **o**. 6924
68:33 the heavens of heavens, *which were* of **o**; 6924
71: 9 Cast me not off in the time of **o age**; 2209
71:18 Now also when I am **o** and grayheaded, 2209
74: 2 *which* thou hast purchased of **o**; 6924
74:12 For God *is* my King of **o**, working salvation 6924
77: 5 I have considered the days of **o**, the years 6924
77:11 surely I will remember thy wonders of **o**. 6924
78: 2 in a parable: I will utter dark sayings of **o**: 6924
92:14 They shall still bring forth fruit in **o age**; 7872
93: 2 Thy throne is established of **o**: thou *art* from 227
102:25 **Of o** hast thou laid the foundation 6440+3807.1
102:26 yea, all of them shall **wax o** like a garment; 1086
119:52 I remembered thy judgments of **o**, 5769
119:152 I have known **of o** that thou hast founded 6924
143: 5 I remember the days of **o**; I meditate on all 6924
148:12 and maidens; **o men**, and children: 2205
Pr 8:22 beginning of his way, before his works of **o**. 227
17: 6 children *are* the crown of **o men**; 2205
20:29 and the beauty of **o men** *is* the gray head. 2205
22: 6 and when he is **o**, he will not depart from it. 2204
23:10 Remove not the **o** landmark; and enter not 5769
23:22 and despise not thy mother when she is **o**. 2204
Ecc 1:10 it hath been already of **o time**, 5769+3807.1
4:13 and a wise child than an **o** and foolish king, 2205
SS 7:13 *are* all *manner* of pleasant *fruits*, new and **o**, 3465
Isa 15: 5 *flee* unto Zoar, a heifer of **three years o**: 7992
20: 4 young and **o**, naked and barefoot, 2205
22:11 the two walls for the water of the **o** pool: 3465
25: 1 *thy* counsels of **o** *are* faithfulness *and* truth. 7350
30: 6 from whence *come* the young and **o lion**, 3918
30:33 For Tophet *is* ordained of **o**; yea, for the king 865
43:18 *things*, neither consider the *things* **of o**. 6931
46: 4 *even* to *your* **o age** I *am* he; and *even* to 2209
46: 9 Remember the former *things* of **o**: for I *am* 5769
50: 9 lo, they all shall **wax o** as a garment; 1086
51: 6 the earth shall **wax o** like a garment, and 1086
51: 9 *in* the ancient days, *in* the generations **of o**. 5769
57:11 have not I held my peace even of **o**, and 5769
58:12 *they that shall be* of thee shall build the **o** 5769
61: 4 they shall build the **o** wastes, they shall 5769
63: 9 and carried them all the days of **o**. 5769
63:11 he remembered the days **of o**, Moses, *and* 5769
65:20 nor an **o man** that hath not filled his days: 2205
65:20 for the child shall die an hundred years **o**; 1121
65:20 the sinner *being* an hundred years **o** shall be 1121
Jer 2:20 For **of o time** I have broken thy 4480+5769
6:16 the ways, and see, and ask for the **o** paths, 5769
28: 8 before thee of **o** prophesied both against 5769
31: 3 The LORD hath appeared of **o** unto me, 7350
31:13 the dance, both young men and **o** together: 2205
38:11 took thence **o** cast clouts and old rotten 1094
38:11 thence old cast clouts and **o** rotten rags, 1094
38:12 Put now *these* **o** cast clouts and rotten rags 1094
46:26 as *in* the days of **o**, saith the LORD. 6924
48:34 *as* a heifer of **three years o**: 7992
51:22 with thee will I break in pieces **o** and 2205
52: 1 and twenty year **o** when he *began* to reign, 1121
La 1: 7 things that she had in the days **of o**, 6924
2:17 that he had commanded in the days **of o**: 6924
2:21 and the **o** lie on the ground in the streets: 2205
3: 4 My flesh and my skin hath he **made o**; 1086
3: 6 me in dark places, as they that be dead of **o**. 5769

La 5:21 we shall be turned; renew our days as **of o.** 6924
Eze 9: 6 Slay utterly **o** *and* young, both maids, and 2205
23:43 said I unto *her that was* **o** *in* adulteries, 1087
25:15 to destroy *it for* the **o** hatred; 5769
26:20 with the people of **o time**, and shall set thee 5769
26:20 in places desolate of **o**, with them that go 5769
36:11 I will settle you after your **o estates**, and 6927
38:17 *Art* thou he of whom I have spoken in **o** 6931
Da 5:31 *being* about threescore and two year **o**. 1247
Joel 1: 2 Hear this, ye **o men**, and give ear, all ye 2205
2:28 your **o men** shall dream dreams, 2205
Am 9:11 and I will build it as *in* the days of **o**: 5769
Mic 5: 2 whose goings forth *have been* from **of o**, 6924
6: 6 burnt offerings, with calves of a year **o**? 1121
7:14 *in* Bashan and Gilead, as *in* the days of **o**. 5769
7:20 sworn unto our fathers from the days **of o**. 6924
Na 2: 8 Nineveh *is* of **o** like a pool of water: yet 3117
2:11 *even* the **o lion**, walked, *and* the lion's 3833
Zec 8: 4 There shall yet **o men** and old women 2205
8: 4 **o women** dwell in the streets of Jerusalem, 2205
Mal 3: 4 as *in* the days of **o**, and as *in* former years. 5769
Mt 2:16 coasts thereof, from **two years o** and under, *1332*
5:21 heard that it was said by them **of o time**, *744*
5:27 heard that it was said by them **of o time**, *744*
5:33 that it hath been said by them **of o time**, *744*
9:16 a piece of new cloth unto an **o** garment; *3820*
9:17 Neither do *men* put new wine into **o** *3820*
13:52 forth out of his treasure *things* new and **o**. *3820*
Mk 2:21 a piece of new cloth on an **o** garment: *3820*
2:21 that filled it up taketh away *from* the **o**, *3820*
2:22 And no *man* putteth new wine into **o** *3820*
Lk 1:18 for I am an **o man**, and my wife well *4246*
1:36 she hath also conceived a son in her **o age**: *1094*
2:42 And when he was twelve **years o**, *2094*
5:36 putteth a piece of a new garment upon an **o**; *3820*
5:36 *taken* out of the new agreeth not with the **o**. *3820*
5:37 And no *man* putteth new wine into **o** *3820*
5:39 No *man* also having drunk **o** *wine* *3820*
5:39 desireth new: for he saith, The **o** is better. *3820*
9: 8 that one of the **o** prophets was risen again. *744*
9:19 others *say,* that one of the **o** prophets is risen *744*
12:33 provide yourselves bags which **wax** not **o**, *3822*
Jn 3: 4 How can a man be born when he is **o**? *1088*
8:57 Thou art not yet fifty **years o**, and hast thou *2094*
21:18 but when thou shalt be **o**, thou shalt stretch *1095*
Ac 2:17 and your **o men** shall dream dreams: *4245*
4:22 For the man was above forty **years o**, *2094*
7:23 And when he was full forty years **o**, it came *5550*
15:21 For Moses of **o** time hath in every city them *744*
21:16 an **o** disciple, with whom we should lodge. *744*
Ro 4:19 when he was about an **hundred year o**, *1541*
6: 6 that our **o** man is crucified with *him,* that *3820*
1Co 5: 7 Purge out therefore the **o** leaven, that ye *3820*
5: 8 let us keep the feast, not with **o** leaven, *3820*
2Co 3:14 away in the reading of the **o** testament; *3820*
5:17 **o** *things* are past away; behold, all *things* are *744*
Eph 4:22 the former conversation the **o** man, *3820*
Col 3: 9 seeing that ye have put off the **o** man with *3820*
1Ti 4: 7 But refuse profane and **o wives'** fables, and *1126*
5: 9 into the number under threescore **years o**, *2094*
Heb 1:11 and they all shall **wax o** as *doth* a garment; *3822*
8:13 A new *covenant,* he hath **made** the first **o**. *3822*
8:13 and **waxeth o** *is* ready to vanish away. *1095*
1Pe 3: 5 For after this manner **in** the **o time** the holy *4218*
2Pe 1: 9 that *he* was purged from his **o** sins. *3819*
1:21 For the prophecy came not **in o time** by *4218*
2: 5 And spared not the **o** world, but saved Noah *744*
3: 5 by the word of God the heavens were **of o**, *1597*
1Jn 2: 7 an **o** commandment which ye had from *3820*
2: 7 The **o** commandment is the word which ye *3820*
Jude 1: 4 who were before **of o** ordained to this *3819*
Rev 12: 9 And the great dragon was cast *out,* that **o** *744*
20: 2 *that* **o** serpent, which is the devil, and Satan, *744*

OLDNESS (1) [OLD]

Ro 7: 6 of spirit, and not *in* the **o** of the letter. *3821*

OLIVE (38) [OLIVES, OLIVET, OLIVEYARD, OLIVEYARDS]

Ge 8:11 lo, in her mouth *was* an **o** leaf pluckt off: 2132
Ex 27:20 that they bring thee pure oil **o** beaten for 2132
30:24 shekel of the sanctuary, and of oil **o** a hin: 2132
Lev 24: 2 that they bring unto thee pure oil **o** beaten 2132
Dt 6:11 thou diggedst not, vineyards and **o trees**, 2132
8: 8 pomegranates; a land of oil **o**, and honey; 2132
24:20 When thou beatest thine **o tree**, thou shalt 2132
28:40 Thou shalt have **o trees** throughout all thy 2132
28:40 *with* the oil; for thine **o** shall cast *his fruit*. 2132
Jdg 9: 8 they said unto the **o tree**, Reign thou over 2132
9: 9 the **o tree** said unto them, Should I leave 2132
1Ki 6:23 the oracle he made two cherubims *of* **o** tree, 8081
6:31 of the oracle he made doors of **o** tree: 8081
6:32 The two doors also *were* of **o** tree; and 8081
6:33 he for the door of the temple posts of **o** tree, 8081
2Ki 18:32 and vineyards, a land of oil **o** and of honey, 2132
1Ch 27:28 over the **o trees** and the sycomore trees that 2132
Ne 8:15 fetch **o** branches, and pine branches, and 2132
Job 15:33 and shall cast off his flower as the **o**. 2132
Ps 52: 8 I *am* like a green **o tree** in the house of 2132
128: 3 thy children like **o** plants round about thy 2132
Isa 17: 6 as the shaking of an **o tree**, two *or* 2132
24:13 *there shall be* as the shaking of an **o tree**, 2132
Jer 11:16 A green **o tree**, fair, *and* of goodly fruit: 2132
Hos 14: 6 his beauty shall be as the **o tree**, and his 2132
Am 4: 9 your fig trees and your **o trees** increased, 2132
Hab 3:17 the labour of the **o** shall fail, and the fields 2132
Hag 2:19 and the pomegranate, and the **o** tree, 2132
Zec 4: 3 two **o trees** by it, one upon the right *side* of 2132
4:11 What *are* these two **o trees** upon the right 2132
4:12 What *be these* two **o** branches which 2132
Ro 11:17 and thou, being a **wild o tree**, wert graffed in *65*
11:17 of the root and fatness of the **o tree**; *1636*
11:24 cut out of the **o tree which is wild** by nature, *65*
11:24 contrary to nature into a **good o tree**: *2565*
11:24 *branches,* be graffed into their own **o tree**? *1636*
Jas 3:12 the fig tree, my brethren, bear **o berries**? *1636*
Rev 11: 4 These are the two **o trees**, and the two *1636*

OLIVE GROVES See OLIVEYARD

OLIVES (15) [OLIVE]

Jdg 15: 5 the standing corn, with the vineyards *and* **o**. 2132
Mic 6:15 thou shalt tread the **o**, but thou shalt not 2132
Zec 14: 4 stand in that day upon the mount of **O**, 2132
14: 4 the mount of **O** shall cleave in the midst 2132
Mt 21: 1 unto the mount of **O**, then sent Jesus two *1636*
24: 3 And as he sat upon the mount of **O**, *1636*
26:30 a hymn, they went out into the mount of **O**. *1636*
Mk 11: 1 and Bethany, at the mount of **O**, *1636*
13: 3 And as he sat upon the mount of **O** over *1636*
14:26 a hymn, they went out into the mount of **O**. *1636*
Lk 19:29 at the mount called *the mount* of **O**, *1636*
19:37 *even* now at the descent of the mount of **O**, *1636*
21:37 in the mount that is called *the mount* of **O**. *1636*
22:39 went, as he was wont, to the mount of **O**; *1636*
Jn 8: 1 Jesus went unto the mount of **O**. *1636*

OLIVET (2) [OLIVE]

2Sa 15:30 David went up by the ascent of *mount* **O**, 2132
Ac 1:12 unto Jerusalem from the mount called **O**, *1638*

OLIVEYARD (1) [OLIVE]

Ex 23:11 deal with thy vineyard, *and* with thy **o**. 2132

OLIVEYARDS (5) [OLIVE]

Jos 24:13 and **o** which ye planted not do ye eat. 2132
1Sa 8:14 your vineyards, and your **o**, *even* the best *of* 2132
2Ki 5:26 **o**, and vineyards, and sheep, and oxen, and 2132
Ne 5:11 their vineyards, their **o**, and their houses, 2132
9:25 and **o**, and fruit trees in abundance: 2132

OLYMPAS (1)

Ro 16:15 and **O**, and all the saints which are with *3652*

OMAR (3)

Ge 36:11 **O**, Zepho, and Gatam, and Kenaz. 201
36:15 duke **O**, duke Zepho, duke Kenaz, 201
1Ch 1:36 **O**, Zephi, and Gatam, Kenaz, and Timna, 201

OMEGA (4)

Rev 1: 8 I am Alpha and **O**, the beginning and *5598*
1:11 Saying, I am Alpha and **O**, the first and *5598*
21: 6 I am Alpha and **O**, the beginning and *5598*
22:13 I am Alpha and **O**, the beginning and *5598*

OMER (5) [OMERS]

Ex 16:16 an **o** for every man, *according to* 6016
16:18 when they did mete *it* with an **o**, he that 6016
16:32 Fill an **o** of it to be kept for your 6016
16:33 put an **o** full of manna therein, and lay it up 6016
16:36 Now an **o** *is* the tenth *part* of an ephah. 6016

OMERS (1) [OMER]

Ex 16:22 two **o** for one *man:* and all the rulers of 6016

OMITTED (1)

Mt 23:23 and have **o** the weightier *matters* of the law, *863*

OMNIPOTENT (1)

Rev 19: 6 Alleluia: for the Lord God **O** reigneth. *3841*

OMRI (18)

1Ki 16:16 wherefore all Israel made **O**, the captain of 6018
16:17 **O** went up from Gibbethon, and all Israel 6018
16:21 to make him king; and half followed **O**. 6018
16:22 the people that followed **O** prevailed 6018
16:22 of Ginath: so Tibni died, and **O** reigned. 6018
16:23 first year of Asa king of Judah *began* **O** to 6018
16:25 **O** wrought evil in the eyes of the LORD, 6018
16:27 Now the rest of the acts of **O** which he did, 6018
16:28 So **O** slept with his fathers, and was buried 6018
16:29 Ahab the son of **O** to reign over Israel: 6018
16:29 Ahab the son of **O** reigned over Israel in 6018
16:30 Ahab the son of **O** did evil in the sight of 6018
2Ki 8:26 the daughter of **O** king of Israel. 6018
1Ch 7: 8 **O**, and Jerimoth, and Abiah, and Anathoth, 6018
9: 4 the son of **O**, the son of Imri, the son of 6018
27:18 of Issachar, **O** the son of Michael: 6018
2Ch 22: 2 name also *was* Athaliah the daughter of **O**. 6018
Mic 6:16 For the statutes of **O** are kept, and all 6018

ON (2016) [THEREON, WHEREON]

Ge 2: 2 **o** the seventh day God ended his work 871.1
2: 2 he rested **o** the seventh day from all his 871.1
4:15 vengeance shall be taken **o** him sevenfold. NIH
4:16 dwelt in the land of Nod, **o** the east of Eden. NIH
6: 1 when men began to multiply **o** the face of 5921
6: 6 LORD that he had made man **o** the earth, 871.1
8: 4 **o** the seventeenth day of the month, 871.1
8: 5 in the tenth *month,* **o** the first *day* of 871.1
8: 9 for the waters *were* **o** the face of the whole 5921
8:14 **o** the seven and twentieth day of 871.1
8:20 and offered burnt offerings **o** the altar. 871.1
12: 8 he removed from thence unto a mountain **o** 4480
12: 8 *having* Beth-el **o** the west, and Hai on 4480
12: 8 Beth-el on the west, and Hai **o** the east: 4480
12: 9 **going o** still toward the south. 1980
13: 3 he went **o** his journeys from the south 3807.1
13: 4 there Abram called **o** the name of 871.1
14:15 which *is* **o** the left hand of Damascus. 4480
17: 3 Abram fell **o** his face: and God talked with 5921
18: 5 ye your hearts; after *that* you shall **pass o**: 5674
18:16 went with them to **bring** them **o** the **way**. 7971
19: 2 shall rise up early, and go **o** your ways. 3807.1
19:34 it came to pass **o** the morrow, that 4480
20: 9 that thou hast brought **o** me and on my 5921
20: 9 on me and **o** my kingdom a great sin? 5921
21:14 putting *it* **o** her shoulder, and the child, and 5921
21:33 called there **o** the name of the LORD, 871.1
22: 4 **o** the third day Abraham lift up his eyes, 871.1
22: 9 and laid him **o** the altar upon the wood. 5921
24:33 told mine errand. And he said, **Speak o.** 1696
24:45 Rebekah came forth with her pitcher **o** her 5921
25:26 and his hand took hold **o** Esau's heel; 871.1
28:12 behold a ladder set up **o** the earth, and 1886.5
28:12 of God ascending and descending **o** it. 871.1
28:20 give me bread to eat, and raiment to **put o**, 3847
29: 1 Jacob **went o** his **journey**, and 5375+7272
31:22 it was told Laban **o** the third day that Jacob 871.1
32: 1 Jacob went **o** his way, and the angels of 3807.1
32:19 **O** this manner shall you speak unto Esau, 3509.1
33: 4 and fell **o** his neck, and kissed him: 5921
33:14 I will **lead o** softly, according as the cattle 5095
33:16 So Esau returned that day **o** his way unto 3807.1
34:25 it came to pass **o** the third day, when they 871.1
37:23 *his* coat of many colours that *was* **o** him; 5921
38: 9 that he spilled *it* **o** the ground, 1886.5
38:19 and **put o** the garments of her widowhood. 3847
40:14 **think o** me when it shall be well with thee, 2142
40:16 *I had* three white baskets **o** my head: 5921
40:19 from off thee, and shall hang thee **o** a tree; 5921
41:45 the daughter of Poti-pherah priest of **O**. 204
41:50 of Poti-pherah priest of **O** bare unto him. 204
43:31 refrained himself, and said, **Set o** bread. 7760
43:32 they **set o** for him by himself, and for them 7760
44:14 and they fell before him **o** the ground. 1886.5
44:34 I see the evil that shall **come o** my father. 4672
46:20 of Poti-pherah priest of **O** bare unto him. 204
46:29 he fell **o** his neck, and wept on his neck a 5921
46:29 his neck, and wept **o** his neck a good while. 5921
48:16 let my name be named **o** them, and 871.1
49:26 they shall be **o** the head of Joseph, and 3807.1
49:26 **o** the crown of the head of him *that was* 3807.1
Ex 1:10 **Come o**, let us deal wisely with them; 3051
2: 6 she had compassion **o** him, and said, This *is* 5921
2:11 his brethren, and looked **o** their burdens: 871.1
4: 3 he said, Cast it **o** the ground. And he cast 1886.5
4: 3 he cast it **o** the ground, and it became a 1886.5
6:28 it came to pass **o** the day *when* the LORD 871.1
8: 4 the frogs shall come up *both* **o** thee, and 871.1
9: 6 the LORD did that thing **o** the morrow, 4480
12: 7 strike *it* **o** the two side posts and on 5921
12: 7 and **o** the upper door post of the houses, 5921
12:11 your shoes **o** your feet, and your staff in 871.1
12:18 In the first *month,* **o** the fourteenth day of 871.1
12:23 **o** the two side posts, the LORD will pass 5921
12:29 from the firstborn of Pharaoh that sat **o** his 5921
12:37 about six hundred thousand **o foot** *that* 7273
14:16 the children of Israel shall go **o** dry *ground* 871.1
14:22 the waters *were* a wall unto them **o** their 4480
14:22 them on their right hand, and **o** their left. 4480
14:29 the waters *were* a wall unto them **o** their 4480
14:29 them on their right hand, and **o** their left. 4480
15:14 sorrow shall take hold **o** the inhabitants of NIH
15:19 the children of Israel went **o** dry *land* in 871.1
16: 1 **o** the fifteenth day of the second month 871.1
16: 5 that **o** the sixth day they shall prepare *that* 871.1
16:14 *as* small as the hoar frost **o** the ground. 5921
16:22 *that* **o** the sixth day they gathered twice as 871.1
16:26 **o** the seventh day, *which is* the sabbath, 871.1
16:27 *that* there went out *some* of the people **o** 871.1
16:29 he giveth you **o** the sixth day the bread of 871.1
16:29 let no man go out of his place **o** 871.1
16:30 So the people rested **o** the seventh day. 871.1
17: 5 **Go o** before the people, and take with thee 5674
17: 9 to morrow I will stand **o** the top of the hill 5921
17:12 the one **o** the one side, and the other on 4480
17:12 the one side, and the other **o** the other side; 4480
18:13 it came to pass **o** the morrow, that Moses 4480
19: 4 *how* I bare you **o** eagles' wings, and 5921
19:16 it came to pass **o** the third day in 871.1
19:18 mount Sinai was altogether **o** a smoke, NIH
19:20 upon mount Sinai, **o** the top of the mount: 413
21:30 If there be laid **o** him a sum of money, then 5921
22:30 **o** the eighth day thou shalt give it me. 871.1
23:12 and **o** the seventh day thou shalt rest: 871.1
24: 6 half of the blood he sprinkled **o** the altar. 5921
24: 8 and sprinkled *it* **o** the people, and said, 5921
24:17 **o** the top of the mount in the eyes of 871.1
25:19 make one cherub **o** the one end, and 4480
25:19 and the other cherub **o** the other end: 4480
25:19 make the cherubims **o** the two ends thereof. 5921
25:20 forth *their* wings **o high**, 4605+1886.5+3807.1
25:26 put the rings in the four corners that *are* **o** 3807.1
26:10 thou shalt make fifty loops **o** the edge of 5921
26:13 a cubit **o** the one side, and a cubit on 4480
26:13 a cubit **o** the other side of that which 4480
26:13 over the sides of the tabernacle **o** this side 4480
26:13 the tabernacle on this side and **o** that side, 4480
26:18 twenty boards **o** the south side southward. 3807.1
26:20 for the second side of the tabernacle **o** 3807.1
26:35 the candlestick over against the table **o** 5921
26:35 and thou shalt put the table **o** the north side. 5921
27:12 *for* the breadth of the court **o** the west 3807.1
27:13 the breadth of the court **o** the east side 1886.5
27:15 **o** the other side *shall be* hangings, 3807.1
27:21 **o the behalf of** the children of Israel. 854+4480
28: 9 grave **o** them the names of the children of 5921
28:10 Six of their names **o** one stone, and 5921
28:10 the *other* six names of the rest **o** the other 5921
28:23 shalt put the two rings **o** the two ends of 5921
28:24 rings *which are* **o** the ends of the breastplate. 413
28:25 put *them* **o** the shoulderpieces of the ephod 5921
28:27 shalt put them **o** the two sides of the ephod 5921
28:37 thou shalt put it **o** a blue lace, that it may be 5921
29: 9 and his sons, and put the bonnets **o** them: 3807.1
29:30 in his stead shall **put** them **o** seven days, 3847
31:17 **o** the seventh day he rested, and 871.1
32: 6 they rose up early **o** the morrow, and 4480
32:15 the tables *were* written **o** both their sides; 4480
32:15 **o** the one side and on the other *were* they 4480
32:15 one side and **o** the other *were* they written. 4480

O

Ex 32:22 the people, that they *are set* **o** mischief. 871.1
32:26 and said, Who *is* **o** the LORD'S **side**? 3807.1
32:30 it came to pass **o** the morrow, that Moses 4480
33: 4 and no man did put **o** him his ornaments. 5921
33:19 will shew mercy **o** whom I will shew mercy. NIH
34:21 but **o** the seventh day thou shalt rest: 871.1
34:33 speaking with them, he put a vail **o** his face. 5921
35: 2 **o** the seventh day there shall be to you a 871.1
36:11 he made loops of blue **o** the edge of one 5921
37: 7 he them, **o** the two ends of the mercy seat; 4480
37: 8 One cherub **o** the end on this side, and 4480
37: 8 One cherub on the end **o** this side, and 4480
37: 8 another cherub **o** the *other* end on that side: 4480
37: 8 another cherub on the *other* end **o** that side: 4480
37: 8 he the cherubims **o** the two ends thereof. 4480
37: 9 out *their* wings **o high**, 4605+1886.5+3807.1
38: 2 he made the horns thereof **o** the four 5921
38: 7 he put the staves into the rings **o** the sides 5921
38: 9 **o** the south side southward the hangings 3807.1
38:15 **o** this hand and that hand, *were* hangings of 4480
39: 7 he put them **o** the shoulders of the ephod, 5921
39:17 the two rings **o** the ends of the breastplate. 5921
39:18 put them **o** the shoulderpieces of the ephod, 5921
39:19 put *them* **o** the two ends of the breastplate, 5921
39:19 which *was* **o** the side of the ephod inward. 413
39:20 put them **o** the two sides of the ephod 5921
39:31 **o high** upon 4480+4605+1886.5+3807.1
40: 2 **O** the first day of the first month shalt thou 871.1
40:17 **o** the first *day* of the month, *that* 871.1
40:20 set the staves **o** the ark, and put the mercy 5921
40:24 **o** the side of the tabernacle southward. 5921
40:38 fire was **o** it by night, in the sight of all 871.1
Lev 1: 8 in order upon the wood that *is* **o** the fire 5921
1: 9 the priest shall burn all **o** the altar, *to be* a 1886.5
1:11 he shall kill it **o** the side of the altar 5921
1:12 the priest shall lay them in order **o** 5921
1:12 that *is* **o** the fire which *is* upon the altar: 5921
1:15 wring off his head, and burn *it* **o** the altar; 1886.5
1:16 cast it beside the altar **o** the east part, 1886.5
2:12 they shall not be burnt **o** the altar for a sweet 413
3: 4 the two kidneys, and the fat that *is* **o** them, 5921
3: 5 Aaron's sons shall burn it **o** the altar upon 1886.5
3: 5 which *is* upon the wood that *is* **o** the fire: 5921
4:12 and burn him **o** the wood with fire: 5921
5:12 memorial thereof, and burn *it* **o** the altar, 1886.5
6:10 the priest shall **put o** his linen garment, 3847
6:10 with the burnt offering **o** the altar, 5921
6:11 **put o** other garments, and carry forth 3847
6:12 the priest shall burn wood **o** it every 5921
7: 4 the two kidneys, and the fat that *is* **o** them, 5921
7:16 **o** the morrow also the remainder of it shall 4480
7:17 the remainder of the flesh of the sacrifice **o** 871.1
7:18 offerings be eaten at all **o** the third day, 871.1
8:26 put *them* **o** the fat, and upon the right 5921
8:28 burnt *them* **o** the altar upon the burnt 1886.5
9: 1 it came to pass **o** the eighth day, *that* 871.1
9:14 burnt *them* upon the burnt offering **o** 1886.5
9:24 they shouted, and fell **o** their faces. 5921
11: 2 eat among all the beasts that *are* **o** the earth. 5921
11:27 among all *manner of* beasts that go **o** *all* 5921
11:34 *that* **o** which *such* water cometh shall be 5921
13: 3 the priest shall look **o** the plague in the skin NIH
13: 3 the priest shall look **o** him, and NIH
13: 5 the priest shall look **o** him the seventh day: 871.1
13: 6 the priest shall look **o** him again 871.1
13:21 if the priest look **o** it, and behold, *there be* NIH
13:26 if the priest look **o** it, and behold, *there be* NIH
13:31 if the priest look **o** the plague of the scall, NIH
13:32 in the seventh day the priest shall look **o** NIH
13:34 in the seventh day the priest shall look **o** NIH
13:36 the priest shall look **o** him: and behold, NIH
13:51 he shall look **o** the plague on the seventh NIH
13:51 he shall look on the plague **o** the seventh 871.1
13:55 the priest shall look **o** the plague, after *that* NIH
14: 9 it shall be **o** the seventh day, *that* he shall 871.1
14:10 **o** the eighth day he shall take two he lambs 871.1
14:23 he shall bring them **o** the eighth day for his 871.1
14:37 he shall look **o** the plague, and behold, *if* NIH
15: 6 he that sitteth **o** *any* thing whereon he sat 5921
15:14 **o** the eighth day he shall take to him two 871.1
15:23 if it *be* **o** *her* bed, or on *any* thing whereon 5921
15:23 or **o** *any* thing whereon she sitteth, when he 5921
15:29 **o** the eighth day she shall take unto her 871.1
16: 4 He shall **put o** the holy linen coat, and 3847
16: 4 and *so* **put** them **o**. 3847
16:10 **o** which the lot fell to be the scapegoat, NIH
16:23 which he **put o** when he went into the holy 3847
16:24 **put o** his garments, and come forth, and 3847
16:29 **o** the tenth *day* of the month, ye shall 871.1
16:30 For **o** that day shall *the priest* make an 871.1
16:32 shall **put o** the linen clothes, *even* the holy 3847
19: 6 the *same* day ye offer it, and **o** the morrow: 4480
19: 7 if it be eaten at all **o** the third day, it *is* 871.1
20:25 *of living thing* that creepeth **o** the ground, NIH
21:10 that is consecrated to **put o** the garments, 3847
22:30 **O** the same day it shall be eaten up; 871.1
23: 6 **o** the fifteenth day of the same month *is* 871.1
23:11 **o** the morrow after the sabbath the priest 4480
23:21 ye shall proclaim **o** the selfsame day, 871.1
23:27 Also **o** the tenth *day* of this seventh month 871.1
23:35 **O** the first day *shall be* a holy 871.1
23:36 **o** the eighth day shall be a holy 871.1
23:39 **o** the first day *shall be* a sabbath, and 871.1
23:39 and **o** the eighth day *shall be* a sabbath. 871.1
23:40 ye shall take you **o** the first day the boughs 871.1
24: 6 thou shalt set them *in* two rows, six **o** a row, NIH
24: 7 that it may be **o** the bread for a memorial, 3807.1
25: 9 **o** the tenth *day* of the seventh month, 871.1
Nu 1: 1 **o** the first *day* of the second month, 871.1
1:18 **o** the first *day* of the second month, 871.1
2: 3 **o** the east side toward the rising of 1886.5
2:10 **O** the south side *shall be* the standard of 1886.5
2:18 **O** the west side *shall be* the standard of 1886.5
2:25 *shall be* **o** the north side by their armies: 1886.5
3:10 and they shall **wait o** their priest's office: 8104
Nu 3:13 *for* **o** the day that I smote all the firstborn 871.1
3:29 **o** the side of the tabernacle southward. 5921
3:35 *these* shall pitch **o** the side of the tabernacle 5921
4:12 badgers' skins, and shall put *them* **o** a bar: 5921
6: 9 **o** the seventh day shall he shave it. 871.1
6:10 **o** the eighth day he shall bring two turtles, 871.1
6:23 **O this wise** ye shall bless the children of 3541
7: 1 it came to pass **o** the day that Moses had 871.1
7:11 each prince **o** *his* day, for the dedicating 3807.1
7:18 **O** the second day Nethaneel the son of 871.1
7:24 **O** the third day Eliab the son of Helon, 871.1
7:30 **O** the fourth day Elizur the son of Shedeur, 871.1
7:36 **O** the fifth day Shelumiel the son of 871.1
7:42 **O** the sixth day Eliasaph the son of Deuel, 871.1
7:48 **O** the seventh day Elishama the son of 871.1
7:54 **O** the eighth day *offered* Gamaliel the son 871.1
7:60 **O** the ninth day Abidan the son of 871.1
7:66 **O** the tenth day Ahiezer the son of 871.1
7:72 **O** the eleventh day Pagiel the son of 871.1
7:78 **O** the twelfth day Ahira the son of Enan, 871.1
8:17 **o** the day that I smote every firstborn in 871.1
9: 5 they kept the passover **o** the fourteenth day 871.1
9: 6 that they could not keep the passover **o** that 871.1
9: 6 before Moses and before Aaron **o** that day: 871.1
9:15 **o** the day that the tabernacle was reared up, 871.1
10: 5 the camps that lie **o** the east parts shall go 1886.5
10: 6 the camps that lie **o** the south side shall 1886.5
10:11 it came to pass **o** the twentieth *day* of 871.1
11:31 as it were a day's journey **o this side**, and 3541
11:31 as it were a day's journey **o the other side**, 3541
14: 5 Aaron fell **o** their faces before all 5921
16: 1 **O**, the son of Peleth, sons of Reuben, 203
16:27 Dathan, and Abiram, **o** every side: 4480
16:41 **o** the morrow all the congregation of 4480
16:46 **put o** incense, and go quickly unto 7760
16:47 he **put o** incense, and made an atonement 5414
17: 8 that **o** the morrow Moses went into 4480
19:12 He shall purify himself with it **o** the third 871.1
19:12 and **o** the seventh day he shall be clean: 871.1
19:19 sprinkle upon the unclean **o** the third day, 871.1
19:19 on the third day, and **o** the seventh day: 871.1
19:19 **o** the seventh day he shall purify him*self*, 871.1
20:19 without *doing any* thing *else*, go through **o** 871.1
21:13 and pitched **o** the *other* side of Arnon, 4480
22: 1 pitched in the plains of Moab **o** *this side* 4480
22:24 a wall *being* **o** this side, and a wall on that 4480
22:24 *being* on this side, and a wall **o** that side. 4480
22:31 down his head, and fell flat **o** his face. 3807.1
22:41 it came to pass **o** the morrow, that Balak 871.1
23: 2 Balaam offered **o** *every* altar a bullock and 871.1
23:14 offered a bullock and a ram **o** *every* altar. 871.1
23:30 offered a bullock and a ram **o** *every* altar. 871.1
24:20 when he looked **o** Amalek, he took up his NIH
24:21 he looked **o** the Kenites, and took up his NIH
28: 9 **o** the sabbath day two lambs of the first 871.1
28:25 **o** the seventh day ye shall have a holy 871.1
29: 1 **o** the first *day* of the month, 871.1
29: 7 ye shall have **o** the tenth *day* of this 871.1
29:12 **o** the fifteenth day of the seventh month ye 871.1
29:17 **o** the second day *ye shall offer* twelve 871.1
29:20 **o** the third day eleven bullocks, two rams, 871.1
29:23 **o** the fourth day ten bullocks, two rams, 871.1
29:26 **o** the fifth day nine bullocks, two rams, 871.1
29:29 **o** the sixth day eight bullocks, two rams, 871.1
29:32 **o** the seventh day seven bullocks, 871.1
29:35 **O** the eighth day ye shall have a solemn 871.1
30: 8 if her husband disallow her **o** the day that 871.1
30:12 made them void **o** the day he heard *them;* 871.1
31:19 and your captives **o** the third day, 871.1
31:19 on the third day, and **o** the seventh day. 871.1
31:24 ye shall wash your clothes **o** the seventh 871.1
32:19 For we will not inherit with them **o** *yonder* 4480
32:19 our inheritance is fallen to us **o** *this* side 4480
32:32 that the possession of our inheritance **o** *this* 4480
33: 3 **o** the fifteenth day of the first month; 871.1
33: 3 **o** the morrow after the passover 4480
34: 4 the ascent of Akrabbim, and **pass o** to Zin: 5674
34: 4 shall **go o** *to* Hazar-addar, and pass on to 3318
34: 4 on *to* Hazar-addar, and **pass o** to Azmon: 5674
34: 9 the border shall **go o** to Ziphron, and 3318
34:11 Shepham *to* Riblah, **o** the east side of Ain; 4480
34:15 **o** *this* side Jordan *near* Jericho eastward, 4480
35: 5 ye shall measure from without the city **o** NIH
35: 5 ***o*** the south side two thousand cubits, and NIH
35: 5 and ***o*** the west side two thousand cubits, and NIH
35: 5 and **o** the north side two thousand cubits; NIH
35:14 Ye shall give three cities **o** *this* side Jordan, 4480
Dt 1: 1 Israel **o** *this* side Jordan in the wilderness, 871.1
1: 3 **o** the first *day* of the month, 871.1
1: 5 **O** *this* side Jordan, in the land of Moab, 871.1
1:41 when ye had **girded o** every man his 2296
2:28 only I will pass through **o** my feet; 871.1
3: 8 the land that *was* **o** *this* side Jordan, 871.1
4:15 for ye saw no *manner of* similitude **o** 871.1
4:17 The likeness of any beast that *is* **o** 871.1
4:18 The likeness of any *thing* that creepeth **o** 871.1
4:41 Moses severed three cities **o** *this* side 871.1
4:46 **O** *this* side Jordan, in the valley over 871.1
4:47 which *were* **o** *this* side Jordan *toward* 871.1
4:49 all the plain **o** *this* side Jordan eastward, NIH
6: 9 the posts of thy house, and **o** thy gates. 871.1
7:25 not desire the silver or gold *that is* **o** them, 5921
9:10 **o** them *was written* according to all 5921
10: 2 I will write **o** the tables the words that were 5921
10: 4 he wrote **o** the tables, according to the first 5921
11:30 *Are* they not **o** the *other* side Jordan, by 871.1
16: 8 **o** the seventh day *shall be* a solemn 871.1
21:19 his father and his mother lay hold **o** him, 871.1
21:22 *be* put to death, and thou hang him **o** a tree: 5921
22: 5 neither shall a man **put o** a woman's 3847
22: 6 or **o** the ground, *whether they be* young 5921
22:28 **lay hold o** her, and lie with her, and they be 8610
23:11 it shall be, when evening **cometh o**, 6437
26: 7 looked **o** our affliction, and our labour, and NIH
27: 2 it shall be **o** the day when you shall pass 871.1
Dt 28: 1 thee **o high** above all nations of the earth: 5945
28: 2 all these blessings shall come **o** thee, and 5921
30: 7 **o** them that hate thee, which persecuted 5921
32:11 taketh them, beareth them **o** her wings: 5921
32:13 He made him ride **o** the high places of 5921
32:22 **set o fire** the foundations of the mountains. 3857
32:41 and mine hand take hold **o** judgment; 871.1
33:26 in thy help, and in his excellency **o** the sky. NIH
Jos 1:14 which Moses gave you **o** *this* side Jordan; 871.1
1:15 **o** *this* side Jordan *toward* the sunrising. 871.1
2:10 that *were* **o** the *other* side Jordan, Sihon 871.1
2:19 his blood *shall be* **o** our head, if *any* hand 871.1
3:17 firm **o** dry *ground* in the midst of Jordan, 871.1
3:17 all the Israelites passed over **o** dry *ground*, 871.1
4:14 **O** that day the LORD magnified Joshua 871.1
4:19 the people came up out of Jordan **o** 871.1
4:22 Israel came over this Jordan **o** dry *land*. 871.1
5: 1 which *were* **o** the side of Jordan westward, 871.1
5:10 kept the passover **o** the fourteenth day of 871.1
5:11 they did eat of the old corn of the land **o** 4480
5:12 the manna ceased **o** the morrow after they 4480
5:14 Joshua fell **o** his face to the earth, and 413
6: 7 **Pass o**, and compass the city, and let him 5674
6: 7 let him that is armed **pass o** before the ark 5674
6: 8 rams' horns **passed o** before the LORD, 5674
6: 9 *the priests* **going o**, and blowing with 1980
6:13 of the LORD **went o continually**, 1980+1980
6:13 *the priests* **going o**, and blowing with 1980
6:15 it came to pass **o** the seventh day, that they 871.1
6:15 only **o** that day they compassed the city 871.1
7: 2 **o** the east side of Beth-el, and spake unto 4480
7: 7 and dwelt **o** the *other* side Jordan! 871.1
8: 8 the city, *that* ye shall set the city **o** fire: 871.1
8: 9 and Ai, **o** the west side of Ai: 4480
8:11 the city, and pitched **o** the north side of Ai: 4480
8:12 and Ai, **o** the west side of the city. 4480
8:13 *even* all the host that *was* **o** the north of 4480
8:13 and their liers in wait **o** the west of the city, 4480
8:19 took it, and hasted and set the city **o** fire. 871.1
8:22 some **o** this **side**, and some on that side: 4480
8:22 some on this side, and some **o** that **side**: 4480
8:24 *when* they were all fallen **o** the edge of 3807.1
8:29 the king of Ai he hanged **o** a tree until 5921
8:33 stood **o** this **side** the ark and on that side 4480
8:33 **o** that side before the priests the Levites, 4480
9: 1 when all the kings which *were* **o** *this* side 871.1
9:12 **o** the day we came forth to go unto you; 871.1
9:17 and came unto their cities **o** the third day. 871.1
10:26 slew them, and hanged them **o** five trees: 5921
10:32 which took it **o** the second day, and 871.1
10:35 they took it **o** that day, and smote it with 871.1
11: 2 to the kings that *were* **o** the north of 4480
11: 2 and in the borders of Dor **o** the west, 4480
11: 3 *And to* the Canaanite **o** the east and on 4480
11: 3 *to* the Canaanite on the east and **o** the west, 4480
12: 1 possessed their land **o** the *other* side Jordan 871.1
12: 1 and all the plain **o** the east: 1886.5
12: 3 *from* the plain to the sea of Cinneroth **o** 1886.5
12: 3 of the plain, *even* the salt sea **o** the east, 1886.5
12: 7 the children of Israel smote **o** *this* side 871.1
12: 7 smote on *this* side Jordan **o** the west, 1886.5
13:16 that *is* **o** the bank of the river Arnon, and 5921
13:27 *even* unto the edge of the sea of Cinnereth **o** NIH
13:32 **o** the *other* side Jordan, *by* Jericho, 4480
14: 3 and a half tribe **o** the *other* side Jordan: 4480
14: 9 Moses sware **o** that day, saying, Surely 871.1
15: 3 ascended up **o** the south side unto 4480
15: 7 which *is* **o** the south side of the river: 4480
15:10 **o** the north side, and went down *to* 4480
15:10 *to* Beth-shemesh, and **passed o** *to* Timnah: 5674
16: 1 unto the water of Jericho **o** the east, 1886.5
16: 5 **o** the east side was Ataroth-addar, 1886.5
16: 6 the sea *to* Michmethah **o** the north side; 4480
16: 6 and passed by it **o** the east *to* Janohah; 4480
17: 5 which *were* **o** the *other* side Jordan; 4480
17: 7 the border went *along* **o** the right hand unto 413
17: 8 Tappuah **o** the border of Manasseh *belonged* 413
17: 9 the coast of Manasseh also *was* **o** the north 4480
17:10 they met together in Asher **o** the north, and 4480
17:10 on the north, and in Issachar **o** the east. 4480
18: 5 Judah shall abide in their coast **o** the south, 4480
18: 5 shall abide in their coasts **o** the north. 4480
18: 7 inheritance beyond Jordan **o** the east, 1886.5
18:12 their border **o** the north side was from 3807.1
18:12 the border went up to the side of Jericho **o** 4480
18:13 near the hill that *lieth* **o** the south side of 4480
18:15 the border went out **o** the west, and 1886.5
18:16 which *is* in the valley of the giants **o** 1886.5
18:16 to the side of Jebusi **o** the south, and 1886.5
18:20 Jordan was the border of it **o** the east side. 3807.1
19:13 from thence **passeth o along** on the east to 5674
19:13 from thence passeth on along **o** the east to 1886.5
19:14 the border compasseth it **o** the north side *to* 4480
19:27 and goeth out to Cabul **o** the left hand, 4480
19:34 reacheth to Zebulun **o** the south side, and 4480
19:34 reacheth to Asher **o** the west side, and 4480
20: 8 **o** the *other* side Jordan *by* Jericho eastward, 4480
22: 4 LORD gave you **o** the *other* side Jordan. 871.1
22: 7 their brethren **o** *this* side Jordan westward. 871.1
22:20 wrath fell **o** all the congregation of Israel? 5921
24: 2 Your fathers dwelt **o** the *other* side of 871.1
24: 8 which dwelt **o** the *other* side Jordan; 871.1
24:14 fathers served **o** the *other* side of the flood, 871.1
24:15 that *were* **o** the *other* side of the flood, 871.1
24:30 **o** the north side of the hill of Gaash. 4480
Jdg 1: 8 edge of the sword, and set the city **o** fire. 871.1
2: 9 **o** the north side of the hill Gaash. 4480
3:25 lord *was* fallen down dead **o** the earth. 1886.5
4:15 off *his* chariot, and fled away **o** his feet. 871.1
4:17 Howbeit Sisera fled away **o** his feet to 871.1
4:23 So God subdued **o** that day Jabin the king 871.1
5: 1 and Barak the son of Abinoam **o** that day, 871.1
5:10 Speak, ye that **ride o** white asses, ye that sit 7392
5:15 he was sent **o** foot into the valley. For 871.1
5:17 Asher continued **o** the sea shore, and 3807.1

O

Jdg 5:30 of divers colours of needlework o both NIH
6:32 Therefore o that day he called him 871.1
6:37 and if the dew be o the fleece only, and 5921
6:38 for he rose up early o the morrow, and 4480
6:40 and there was dew o all the ground. 5921
7: 1 that the host of the Midianites were o 4480
7:17 unto them, Look o me, and do likewise: 4480
7:18 blow ye the trumpets also o every side of 5439
7:25 and Zeeb to Gideon o the other side Jordan. 4480
8:11 them that dwelt in tents o the east of Nobah 4480
8:21 took away the ornaments that were o their 871.1
8:26 purple raiment that was o the kings of 5921
8:34 of all their enemies o every side: 4480+5439
9: 8 The trees went forth o a time to 1980+1980
9:42 it came to pass o the morrow, that 4480
9:48 laid it o his shoulder, and said unto 5921
9:49 the hold, and set the hold o fire upon them; 871.1
10: 4 he had thirty sons that rode o thirty ass 5921
10: 8 all the children of Israel that were o 871.1
11:18 pitched o the other side of Arnon, but 871.1
12:14 that rode o threescore and ten ass colts: 5921
13: 5 a son; and no rasor shall come o his head: 5921
13:19 and Manoah and his wife looked o. 7200
13:20 Manoah and his wife looked o it, and 7200
13:20 on it, and fell o their faces to the ground. 5921
14: 9 went o eating, and came to his father 1980+1980
14:15 it came to pass o the seventh day, that they 871.1
14:17 it came to pass o the seventh day, that he 871.1
14:18 the men of the city said unto him o 871.1
15: 5 when he had set the brands o fire, he let 871.1
15:18 and called o the LORD, and said, 413
16:29 o which it was borne up, of the one with his 5921
19: 1 that there was a certain Levite sojourning o 871.1
19: 5 it came to pass o the fourth day, when they 871.1
19: 8 he arose early in the morning o the fifth 871.1
19: 9 to morrow get you early o your way, that 3807.1
19:14 they passed o and went their way; and 5674
19:29 laid hold o his concubine, and divided her, 871.1
20:30 the children of Benjamin o the third day, 871.1
20:48 also they set o fire all the cities that they 871.1
21: 4 it came to pass o the morrow, that 4480
21:19 place which is o the north side of Beth-el, 1886.5
21:19 o the east side of the highway that goeth 1886.5
21:19 to Shechem, and o the south of Lebonah. 4480
Ru 1: 7 they went o the way to return unto the land 871.1
2: 3 her hap was to light o a part of the field 7136
2: 9 Let thine eyes be o the field that they do 871.1
2:10 she fell o her face, and bowed herself to 5921
3:15 six measures of barley, and laid it o her: 5921
1Sa 1:11 if thou wilt indeed look o the affliction of 871.1
2:26 the child Samuel grew o, and was in favour 1980
2:34 upon thy two sons, o Hophni and Phinehas; 413
5: 3 when they of Ashdod arose early o 4480
5: 4 when they arose early o the morrow 4480
5: 5 tread o the threshold of Dagon in Ashdod 5921
6: 4 for one plague was o you all, and on your 3807.1
6: 4 plague was on you all, and o your lords. 3807.1
6: 7 o which there hath come no yoke, and 5921
6:15 of gold were, and put them o the great stone: 413
7: 6 and fasted o that day, and said there, 871.1
7:10 thunder o that day upon the Philistines, 871.1
9:20 three days ago, set not thy mind o them; 3807.1
9:20 o whom is all the desire of Israel? Is it not 3807.1
9:20 Is it not o thee, and on all thy father's 3807.1
9:20 not on thee, and o all thy father's house? 3807.1
9:27 Bid the servant pass o before us, (and 5674
9:27 pass on before us, (and he passed o,) 5674
10: 3 shalt thou go o forward from thence, and 2498
11: 2 O this condition will I make a covenant 871.1
11: 7 The fear of the LORD fell o the people, 5921
11:11 it was so o the morrow, that Saul put 4480
12:11 of the hand of your enemies o every side, 4480
13: 5 people as the sand which is o the sea shore 5921
14: 1 Philistines' garrison, that is o the other side. 4480
14: 4 there was a sharp rock o the one side, and 4480
14: 4 one side, and a sharp rock o the other side: 4480
14:16 and they went o beating down one another. 1980
14:19 in the host of the Philistines went o 1980+1980
14:24 that I may be avenged o mine enemies. 4480
14:32 and calves, and slew them o the ground: 1886.5
14:40 Be ye o one side, and I and Jonathan my 3807.1
14:40 Jonathan my son will be o the other side. 3807.1
14:47 fought against all his enemies o every side, 5439
15:12 and passed o, and gone down to Gilgal. 5674
15:16 me this night. And he said unto him, Say o. 1696
15:18 the LORD sent thee o a journey, and said, 871.1
16: 6 were come, that he looked o Eliab, and said, NIH
16: 7 Look not o his countenance, or on the height 413
16: 7 or o the height of his stature; 413
16: 7 for man looketh o the outward 3807.1
16: 7 but the LORD looketh o the heart. 3807.1
16:16 a man, who is a cunning player o a harp: 871.1
17: 3 the Philistines stood o a mountain on the one 413
17: 3 the Philistines stood on a mountain o 4480
17: 3 Israel stood o a mountain on the other side: 413
17: 3 Israel stood on a mountain o the other side: 4480
17:41 the Philistine came o and drew near 1980+1980
18:10 it came to pass o the morrow, that the evil 4480
18:24 saying, O this manner spake David. 3509.1
19:23 he went o, and prophesied, until he 1980+1980
20:20 I will shoot three arrows o the side 1886.5
20:21 Behold, the arrows are o this side of thee, 2008
20:27 it came to pass o the morrow, which was 4480
20:41 fell o his face to the ground, and 3807.1
21:13 scrabled o the doors of the gate, and let his 5921
22:18 slew o that day fourscore and five persons 871.1
23:19 which is o the south of Jeshimon? 4480
23:21 the LORD; for ye have compassion o me. 5921
23:24 in the plain o the south of Jeshimon. 413
23:26 Saul went o this side of the mountain, and 4480
23:26 and his men o that side of the mountain: 4480
24: 7 up out of the cave, and went o his way. 871.1
25:13 his men, Gird you o every man his sword. 2296
25:13 they girded o every man his sword; and 2296
25:13 and David also girded o his sword: 2296
1Sa 25:14 to salute our master; and he railed o them. 871.1
25:18 cakes of figs, and laid them o asses. 5921
25:19 she said unto her servants, Go o before me; 5674
25:20 it was so, as she rode o the ass, that she 5921
25:23 fell before David o her face, and 5921
25:41 bowed herself o her face to the earth, and NIH
26:13 and stood o the top of a hill afar off; 5921
26:25 So David went o his way, and 3807.1
27:11 saying, Lest they should tell o us, saying, 5921
28: 8 put o other raiment, and he went, and 3847
28:20 Saul fell straightway all along o the earth, 1886.5
28:22 have strength, when thou goest o thy way. 871.1
29: 2 the lords of the Philistines passed o by 5674
29: 2 his men passed o in the rereward with 5674
30: 1 his men were come to Ziklag o the third 871.1
30: 2 carried them away, and went o their way. 3807.1
31: 7 when the men of Israel that were o 871.1
31: 7 they that were o the other side Jordan, 871.1
31: 8 it came to pass o the morrow, when 4480
2Sa 1: 2 It came even to pass o the third day, that 871.1
1:10 the bracelet that was o his arm, and 5921
1:11 David took hold o his clothes, and 871.1
1:24 who put o ornaments of gold upon your 5927
2:13 the one o the one side of the pool, and 5921
2:13 and the other o the other side of the pool. 5921
2:21 lay thee hold o one of the young men, and 270
2:25 one troop, and stood o the top of a hill. 5921
3:12 sent messengers to David o his behalf, 8478
3:29 Let it rest o the head of Joab, and on all his 5921
3:29 the head of Joab, and o all his father's house; 413
3:29 or that leaneth o a staff, or that falleth on 871.1
3:29 or that falleth o the sword, or that lacketh 871.1
4: 5 who lay o a bed at noon. 4904+7901
4: 7 he lay o his bed in his bedchamber, 5921
5: 8 David said o that day, Whosoever getteth 871.1
5:10 David went o, and grew great, and 1980
6: 5 o all manner of instruments made of fir 871.1
6: 5 even o harps, and on psalteries, and 871.1
6: 5 o psalteries, and on timbrels, and 871.1
6: 5 o timbrels, and on cornets, and 871.1
6: 5 and o cornets, and on cymbals. 871.1
6: 5 and on cornets, and o cymbals. 871.1
8: 7 David took the shields of gold that were o 413
9: 3 hath yet a son, which is lame o his feet. NIH
9: 6 he fell o his face, and did reverence. 5921
9:13 king's table; and was lame o both his feet. NIH
11:13 at even he went out to lie o his bed with 871.1
12:18 it came to pass o the seventh day, that 871.1
12:30 it was set o David's head. And he brought 5921
13: 5 Lay thee down o thy bed, and make thyself 5921
13:19 Tamar put ashes o her head, and rent her 5921
13:19 garment of divers colours that was o her, 5921
13:19 laid her hand o her head, and went on 5921
13:19 her hand on her head, and went o crying. 1980
13:31 and tare his garments, and lay o the earth; 1886.5
14: 2 put o now mourning apparel, and 3847
14: 3 and speak o this manner unto him. 3509.1
14: 4 she fell o her face to the ground, and 5921
14: 9 the iniquity be o me, and on my father's 5921
14: 9 iniquity be on me, and o my father's house: 5921
14:12 unto my lord the king. And he said, Say o. 1696
14:14 and are as water spilt o the ground, 1886.5
14:22 Joab fell to the ground o his face, and 413
14:26 polled it: because the hair was heavy o him, 5921
14:30 he hath barley there; go and set it o fire. 871.1
14:30 Absalom's servants set the field o fire. 871.1
14:31 Wherefore have thy servants set my field o 871.1
14:33 bowed himself o his face to the ground. 5921
15: 6 o this manner did Absalom to all Israel 3509.1
15:18 all his servants passed o beside him; and 5674
15:18 him from Gath, passed o before the king. 5674
15:33 If thou passest o with me, then thou shalt 5674
16: 2 asses be for the king's household to ride o; 7392
16: 6 all the mighty men were o his right hand 4480
16: 6 men were on his right hand and o his left. 4480
16:12 It may be that the LORD will look o mine 871.1
16:13 Shimei went along o the hill's side over 871.1
17:12 we will light upon him as the dew falleth o 5921
19:40 the king went o to Gilgal, and 5674
19:40 to Gilgal, and Chimham went o with him: 5674
20: 8 Joab's garment that he had put o was 3830
20:13 all the people went o after Joab, to pursue 5674
21:10 suffered neither the birds of the air to rest o 5921
21:20 that had o every hand six fingers, and NIH
21:20 o every foot six toes, four and twenty in NIH
22: 4 I will call o the LORD, who is worthy to 7121
22:49 thou also hast lifted me up o high above 7311
23: 1 and the man who was raised up o high, 5920
24: 5 o the right side of the city that lieth in NIH
24:20 and his servants coming o toward him: 5674
24:20 bowed himself before the king o his face NIH
1Ki 1:20 that thou shouldest tell them who shall sit o 5921
1:27 who should sit o the throne of my lord 5921
1:46 also Solomon sitteth o the throne of 5921
1:48 which hath given one to sit o my throne this 5921
1:50 and caught hold o the horns of the altar. 871.1
1:51 hath caught hold o the horns of the altar, 871.1
2: 4 (said he) a man o the throne of Israel. 4480+5921
2: 5 and in his shoes that were o his feet. 871.1
2:14 to say unto thee. And she said, Say o. 1696
2:15 that all Israel set their faces o me, that I 5921
2:16 deny me not. And she said unto him, Say o. 1696
2:19 sat down o his throne, and caused a seat to 5921
2:19 and she sat o his right hand. 3807.1
2:20 the king said unto her, Ask o, my mother: 7592
2:24 set me o the throne of David my father, and 5921
2:28 and caught hold o the horns of the altar. 871.1
2:37 that o the day thou goest out, and 871.1
2:42 o the day thou goest out, and 871.1
3: 4 offerings did Solomon offer up o that altar. 5921
3: 6 that thou hast given him a son to sit o his 5921
4:24 For he had dominion over all the region o NIH
4:24 over all the kings o this side the river: NIH
4:24 he had peace o all sides round about him. 4480
4:29 even as the sand that is o the sea shore. 5921
1Ki 5: 3 wars which were about him o every side, 5437
5: 4 my God hath given me rest o every side, 4480
6:10 they rested o the house with timber of cedar. NIH
6:15 he covered them o the inside with wood, 4480
6:16 he built twenty cubits o the sides of 4480
7: 3 that lay o forty five pillars, fifteen in a row. 5921
7: 9 and so o the outside toward the great court. 4480
7:28 the work of the bases was o this manner: NIH
7:29 o the borders that were between the ledges 5921
7:35 o the top of the base the ledges thereof and 5921
7:36 For o the plates of the ledges thereof, and 5921
7:36 o the borders thereof, he graved cherubims, 5921
7:39 he put five bases o the right side of 5921
7:39 and five o the left side of the house: 5921
7:39 he set the sea o the right side of the house 4480
7:41 the two bowls of the chapiters that were o 5921
7:43 the ten bases, and ten lavers o the bases; 5921
7:49 five o the right side, and five on the left, 4480
7:49 five o the left, before the oracle, with 4480
8:20 sit o the throne of Israel, as the LORD 5921
8:23 in heaven above, or o earth beneath, 5921
8:25 man in my sight to sit o the throne of Israel; 5921
8:27 will God indeed dwell o the earth? behold, 5921
8:50 that they may have compassion o them: NIH
8:54 from kneeling o his knees with his hands 5921
8:66 O the eighth day he sent the people away: 871.1
9:26 o the shore of the Red sea, in the land of 5921
10: 9 in thee, to set thee o the throne of Israel: 5921
10:19 o either side on 2088+2088+4480+4480+2050.1
10:19 there were stays on either side o the place of 413
10:20 twelve lions stood there o the one side and 4480
10:20 one side and o the other upon the six steps: 4480
11:30 Ahijah caught the new garment that was o 5921
12:32 o the fifteenth day of the month, like unto 871.1
13: 4 from the altar, saying, Lay hold o him. 8610
14:23 o every high hill, and under every green 5921
16:11 to reign, as soon as he sat o his throne, 5921
16:24 built o the hill, and called the name of NIH
18: 7 he knew him, and fell o his face, and said, 5921
18:23 lay it o wood, and put no fire under: and 5921
18:23 and lay it o wood, and put no fire under: 5921
18:24 call ye o the name of your gods, and I will 871.1
18:24 and I will call o the name of the LORD: 871.1
18:25 call o the name of your gods, but put no 871.1
18:26 called o the name of Baal from morning 871.1
18:33 and laid him o the wood, and said, 5921
18:33 pour it o the burnt sacrifice, and on 5921
18:33 it on the burnt sacrifice, and o the wood. 5921
18:39 when all the people saw it, they fell o their 5921
18:46 the hand of the LORD was o Elijah; and 413
19: 6 there was a cake baken o the coals, and 7529
19:15 return o thy way to the wilderness of 3807.1
20:11 Tell him, Let not him that girdeth o his 2296
20:20 Ben-hadad the king of Syria escaped o a 5921
20:31 put sackcloth o our loins, and ropes upon 871.1
20:32 So they girded sackcloth o their loins, and 871.1
20:32 put ropes o their heads, and came to 871.1
21: 9 and set Naboth o high among the people: 871.1
21:12 and set Naboth o high among the people. 871.1
22: 2 it came to pass o the third year, that 871.1
22:10 Jehoshaphat the king of Judah sat each o 5921
22:10 on his throne, having put o their robes, 3847
22:19 I saw the LORD sitting o his throne, and 5921
22:19 all the host of heaven standing by him o his 4480
22:19 by him on his right hand and o his left. 4480
22:20 one said o this manner, and another said on 871.1
22:20 and another said o that manner. 871.1
22:24 and smote Micaiah o the cheek, and said, 5921
22:30 into the battle; but put thou o thy robes. 3847
2Ki 1: 4 Thou shalt not come down from that bed o 8033
1: 6 thou shalt not come down from that bed o 8033
1: 9 behold, he sat o the top of a hill. And he 5921
1:13 came and fell o his knees before Elijah, and 5921
1:16 thou shalt not come down off that bed o 8033
2: 6 I will not leave thee. And they two went o. 1980
2: 8 so that they two went over o dry ground. 871.1
2:11 as they still went o, and talked, 1980+1980
2:15 The spirit of Elijah doth rest o Elisha. 5921
2:24 looked o them, and cursed them in the name NIH
3:11 which poured water o the hands of Elijah. 5921
3:21 all that were able to put o armour, 2290+2296
3:22 o the other side as red as blood: 4480+5048
3:25 o every good piece of land cast every man NIH
4: 8 it fell o a day, that Elisha passed to 1961
4:10 a little chamber, I pray thee, o the wall; NIH
4:11 it fell o a day, that he came thither, 1961
4:18 when the child was grown, it fell o a day, 1961
4:20 he sat o her knees till noon, and then died. 5921
4:21 laid him o the bed of the man of God, and 5921
4:31 Gehazi passed o before them, and laid 5674
4:38 Set o the great pot, and seethe pottage for 8239
5: 2 waited o Naaman's wife. 1961+6440+3807.1
5:11 call o the name of the LORD his God, 871.1
5:18 he leaneth o my hand, and I bow myself in 5921
6:29 I said unto her o the next day, Give thy 871.1
6:31 son of Shaphat shall stand o him this day. 5921
7: 2 a lord o whose hand the king leaned 5921
7:17 the king appointed the lord o whose hand 5921
8:12 their strong holds wilt thou set o fire, and 871.1
8:15 it came to pass o the morrow, that he took a 4480
8:15 and spread it o his face, so that he died: 5921
9: 3 pour it o his head, and say, Thus saith 5921
9: 6 he poured the oil o his head, and said unto 413
9:13 put it under him o the top of the stairs, and 413
9:17 there stood a watchman o the tower in 5921
9:18 So there went one o horseback to 5483+7392
9:19 he sent out a second o horseback, 5483+7392
9:32 to the window, and said, Who is o my side? 854
9:33 some of her blood was sprinkled o the wall, 413
9:33 was sprinkled on the wall, and o the horses: 413
10: 3 set him o his father's throne, and fight for 5921
10:15 he lighted o Jehonadab the son of Rechab 4672
10:30 generation shall sit o the throne of Israel. 5921
11: 5 A third part of you that enter in o NIH
11: 7 two parts of all you that go forth o NIH

O

2Ki 11: 9 his men that were to come in **o** the sabbath, NIH
11: 9 with them that should go out **o** the sabbath, NIH
11:16 they laid hands **o** her; and she went *by* 3807.1
11:19 And he sat **o** the throne of the kings. 5921
12: 9 **o** the right side as one cometh *into* 4480
12:15 the money to be bestowed **o** workmen: 3807.1
13:21 he revived, and stood up **o** his feet. 5921
13:23 had compassion **o** them, and had respect NIH
14: 4 and burnt incense **o** the high places. 871.1
14:20 they brought him **o** horses: and he was 5921
15: 4 and burnt incense still **o** the high places. 871.1
15:12 Thy sons shall sit **o** the throne of Israel unto 5921
16: 4 and **o** the hills, and under every green tree. 5921
16:14 and put it **o** the north side of the altar. 5921
18:14 *that* which thou puttest **o** me will I bear. 5921
18:20 Now **o** whom dost thou trust, that thou 5921
18:21 *even* upon Egypt, **o** which if a man lean, it NIH
18:21 king of Egypt unto all that trust **o** him. 5921
18:23 if thou be able **o** thy **part** to set riders 3807.1
18:24 put thy trust **o** Egypt for chariots and 5921
18:26 in the ears of the people that *are* **o** the wall. 5921
18:27 *hath he* not *sent me* to the men which sit **o** 5921
19:22 *thy* voice, and lift up thine eyes **o high**? 4791
19:26 *as* the grass **o** the housetops, and *as* corn NIH
20: 5 **o** the third day thou shalt go up *unto* 871.1
20: 7 they took and laid *it* **o** the boil, and 5921
23: 8 which *were* **o** a man's left hand at the gate 5921
23:12 the altars that *were* **o** the top of the upper 5921
23:13 which *were* **o** the right hand of the mount 4480
25: 3 **o** the ninth *day* of the *fourth* month 871.1
25: 8 **o** the seventh *day* of the month, 871.1
25:27 **o** the seven and twentieth *day* of 871.1
1Ch 4:10 Jabez called **o** the God of Israel, saying, 3807.1
6:32 they waited **o** their office according to their 5921
6:39 brother Asaph, who stood **o** his right hand, 5921
6:44 their brethren the sons of Merari *stood* **o** 5921
6:49 **o** the altar of incense, *and were appointed* 5921
6:78 **o** the *other* side Jordan *by* Jericho, on 4480
6:78 *by* Jericho, **o** the east *side* of Jordan, 3807.1
10: 5 he fell likewise **o** the sword, and died. 5921
10: 8 it came to pass **o** the morrow, when 4480
12:18 and **o** thy **side**, thou son of Jesse: 5973
12:37 **o** the *other* side of Jordan, of 4480
12:40 brought bread **o** asses, and on camels, and 871.1
12:40 **o** camels, and on mules, and on oxen, *and* 871.1
12:40 and **o** mules, and on oxen, *and* meat, meal, 871.1
12:40 and on mules, and **o** oxen, *and* meat, meal, 871.1
13: 6 the cherubims, whose name is called *o it.* NIH
14: 2 *was* lift up **o high**, 4605+1886.5+3807.1
15:20 and Benaiah, with psalteries **o** Alamoth; 5921
15:21 with harps **o** the Sheminith to excel. 5921
16: 7 **o** that day David delivered first *this psalm* 871.1
18: 7 David took the shields of gold that were **o** 5921
20: 6 six *o each hand,* and six *on each foot:* and NIH
20: 6 six *on each hand,* and six *o each foot:* and NIH
21:17 be **o** me, and on my father's house; 871.1
21:17 be on me, and **o** my father's house; 871.1
21:17 not **o** thy people, that *they* should be 871.1
22:18 he *not* given you rest **o every side**? 4480+5439
23:28 Because their office *was* to **wait o** the sons 3027
23:31 and **o** the set feasts, by number, 3807.1
26:30 *were* officers among them of Israel **o** *this* 4480
29:15 our days **o** the earth *are* as a shadow, and 5921
29:21 **o** the morrow after that day, *even* a 3807.1
29:22 drink before the LORD **o** that day with 871.1
29:23 Solomon sat **o** the throne of the LORD as 5921
29:25 not been **o** any king before him in Israel. 5921
2Ch 2: 4 **o** the sabbaths, and on the new moons, 3807.1
2: 4 **o** the new moons, and on the solemn 3807.1
2: 4 **o** the solemn feasts of the LORD our 3807.1
3: 7 and graved cherubims **o** the walls. 5921
3:13 they stood **o** their feet, and their faces *were* 5921
3:15 the chapiter that *was* **o** the top *of each* of 5921
3:16 and put *them* **o** the heads of the pillars; 5921
3:16 and put *them* **o** the chains. 871.1
3:17 one **o** the right hand, and the other on 4480
3:17 on the right hand, and the other **o** the left; 4480
3:17 called the name of *that* **o** the right hand NIH
3:17 and the name of *that* **o** the left Boaz. NIH
4: 6 put five **o** the right hand, and five on 4480
4: 6 and five **o** the left, to wash in them: 4480
4: 7 five **o** the right hand, and five on the left. 4480
4: 7 five on the right hand, and five **o** the left. 4480
4: 8 five **o** the right side, and five on the left. 4480
4: 8 five on the right side, and five **o** the left. 4480
4:10 he set the sea **o** the right side of the east 4480
4:12 the chapiters *which were* **o** the top of 5921
4:12 which *were* **o** the top of the pillars; 5921
4:13 four hundred pomegranates **o** the two 3807.1
4:13 two rows *of* pomegranates **o** each wreath, 3807.1
6:10 am set **o** the throne of Israel, as the LORD 5921
6:18 will God in very deed dwell with men **o** 5921
7: 6 the priests **waited o** their offices: 5975
7:10 **o** the three and twentieth day of 871.1
7:22 laid hold **o** other gods, and 871.1
8:12 unto the LORD **o** the altar of the LORD, 5921
8:13 **o** the sabbaths, and on the new moons, 3807.1
8:13 **o** the new moons, and on the solemn 3807.1
8:13 the new moons, and **o** the solemn feasts, 3807.1
9: 8 which delighted in thee to set thee **o** his 5921
9:18 **o each side** 2088+2088+4480+4480+2050.1
9:19 twelve lions stood there **o** the one side and 5921
9:19 one side and **o** the other upon the six steps. 4480
10:12 all the people came to Rehoboam **o** 871.1
10:12 saying, Come again to me **o** the third day. 871.1
11:12 having Judah and Benjamin **o** his **side**. 3807.1
14: 7 he hath given us rest **o every side**. 4480+5439
14:11 for we rest **o** thee, and in thy name we go 5921
16: 7 Because thou hast relied **o** the king of 5921
16: 7 not relied **o** the LORD thy God, therefore 5921
16: 8 yet, because thou didst rely **o** the LORD, 5921
17:19 These **waited o** the king, besides *those* 8334
18: 9 of Judah sat either of them **o** his throne, 5921
18:18 all the host of heaven standing **o** his right 5921
18:18 standing on his right hand and *o* his left. NIH
2Ch 18:24 thou shalt see **o** that day when thou shalt 871.1
18:29 go to the battle; but **put** thou **o** thy robes. 3847
20: 2 thee from beyond the sea **o** this side Syria; 4480
20:19 with a loud voice **o high**. 4605+1886.5+3807.1
20:26 **o** the fourth day they assembled 871.1
20:29 the fear of God was **o** all the kingdoms of 5921
23: 4 A third *part* of you entering **o** the sabbath, NIH
23: 8 his men that were to come in **o** the sabbath, NIH
23: 8 with them that were to go out **o** the sabbath: NIH
23:15 So they laid hands **o** her; and when she 3807.1
24:25 and slew him **o** his bed, and he died: 5921
26:15 invented by cunning *men,* to be **o** 5921
27: 3 and **o** the wall of Ophel he built much. 871.1
28: 4 and **o** the hills, and under every green tree. 5921
29:17 Now they began **o** the first *day* of the first 871.1
29:17 **o** the eighth day of the month came they to 871.1
29:21 to offer *them* **o** the altar of the LORD. 5921
29:22 the blood, and sprinkled *it* **o** the altar: 1886.5
30:15 they killed the passover **o** the fourteenth 871.1
32:15 nor persuade you **o** this *manner,* neither 3509.1
32:17 He wrote also letters to rail **o** the LORD 3807.1
32:18 people of Jerusalem that *were* **o** the wall, 5921
32:22 and guided them **o every side**. 4480+5439
33:14 **o** the west *side* of Gihon, in the valley, 1886.5
34: 4 *were* **o high** above them, 4605+1886.5+3807.1
35: 1 they killed the passover **o** the fourteenth 871.1
36:15 because he had compassion **o** his people, 5921
36:15 on his people, and **o** his dwelling place: 5921
Ezr 4:10 and the rest *that are o this* side the river, and NIH
4:11 Thy servants the men **o** *this* side the river, NIH
4:16 by this means thou shalt have no portion **o** 871.2
5: 3 governor **o** *this* side the river, and NIH
5: 6 governor **o** *this* side the river, and NIH
5: 6 which *were* **o** *this* side the river, sent unto 871.2
5: 8 this work **goeth** fast **o**, and prospereth in 5648
6:13 Tatnai, governor **o** *this* side the river, NIH
6:15 this house was finished **o** the third day of 5705
7: 9 **o** the first *day* of the fifth month came he 871.1
8:31 we departed from the river of Ahava **o** 871.1
8:33 Now **o** the fourth day was the silver and 871.1
8:36 and *to* the governors **o** *this* side the river: NIH
10: 9 **o** the twentieth *day* of the month; 871.1
Ne 2:14 I **went o** to the gate of the fountain, and 5674
3: 7 unto the throne of the governor **o** *this* side NIH
3:13 a thousand cubits **o** the wall unto the dung 871.1
4:13 behind the wall, *and* **o** the higher places, 871.1
4:17 They which builded **o** the wall, and 871.1
4:22 may be a guard to us, and labour **o** the day. NIH
6:14 **o** the prophetess Noadiah, and the rest of 3807.1
8: 4 Hilkiah, and Maaseiah, **o** his right hand; 5921
8: 4 **o** his left hand, Pedaiah, and Mishael, and 4480
8:13 **o** the second day were gathered together 871.1
8:18 **o** the eighth day *was* a solemn assembly, 871.1
9:10 **o** all his servants, and on all the people of 871.1
9:10 and **o** all the people of his land: 871.1
9:11 through the midst of the sea **o** the dry *land;* 871.1
9:32 **o** our kings, on our princes, and on our 3807.1
9:32 **o** our princes, and on our priests, and 3807.1
9:32 **o** our priests, and on our prophets, and 3807.1
9:32 **o** our prophets, and on our fathers, and 3807.1
9:32 and **o** our fathers, and on all thy people, 3807.1
9:32 and on our fathers, and **o** all thy people, 3807.1
10:31 or any victuals **o** the sabbath day to sell, 871.1
10:31 *that* we would not buy *it* of them **o** 871.1
10:31 of them on the sabbath, or **o** the holy day: 871.1
12:31 whereof *one* went **o** the right hand upon 3807.1
13: 1 **O** that day they read in the book of Moses 871.1
13:15 *some* treading wine presses **o** the sabbath, 871.1
13:15 which they brought *into* Jerusalem **o** 871.1
13:16 sold **o** the sabbath unto the children of 871.1
13:19 *that* there should no burden be brought in **o** 871.1
13:21 if ye do *so* again, I will lay hands **o** you. 871.1
13:21 From that time forth came they no *more* **o** 871.1
Est 1: 2 when the king Ahasuerus sat **o** the throne 5921
1:10 **O** the seventh day, when the heart of 871.1
1:11 her beauty: for she *was* fair to **look o**. 4758
2:14 **o** the morrow she returned into the second 871.1
2:21 sought to lay hand **o** the king Ahasuerus. 871.1
2:23 therefore they were both hanged **o** a tree: 5921
3: 6 he thought scorn to lay hands **o** Mordecai 871.1
3:12 were the king's scribes called **o** 871.1
4: 1 **put o** sackcloth with ashes, and went out 3847
5: 1 Now it came to pass **o** the third day, 871.1
5: 1 that Esther **put o** *her* royal *apparel,* and 3847
6: 1 **O** that night could not the king sleep, and 871.1
6: 2 who sought to lay hand **o** the king 871.1
6: 4 to speak unto the king to hang Mordecai **o** 5921
6: 9 bring him **o** horseback through the street of 5921
6:11 **brought** him **o horseback** through 7392
7: 2 the king said again unto Esther **o** 871.1
7:10 So they hanged Haman **o** the gallows that 5921
8: 1 **O** that day did the king Ahasuerus give 871.1
8: 9 **o** the three and twentieth *day* thereof; 871.1
8:10 sent letters by posts **o** horseback, *and* 871.1
8:10 *and* riders **o** mules, camels, *and* NIH
8:13 day to avenge themselves **o** their enemies. 4480
8:14 and **pressed o** by the king's commandment, 1765
9: 1 **o** the thirteenth day of the same, 871.1
9: 2 to lay hand **o** such as sought their hurt: 871.1
9:10 but **o** the spoil laid they not their hand. 871.1
9:11 **O** that day the number of those that were 871.1
9:15 **o** the fourteenth day also of the month 871.1
9:15 but **o** the prey they laid not their hand. 871.1
9:16 but they laid not their hands **o** the prey, 871.1
9:17 **O** the thirteenth day of the month Adar; 871.1
9:17 **o** the fourteenth day of the same rested 871.1
9:18 together **o** the thirteenth *day* thereof, 871.1
9:18 *day* thereof, and **o** the fourteenth thereof; 871.1
9:18 **o** the fifteenth *day* of the same they rested, 871.1
9:25 his sons should be hanged **o** the gallows. 5921
Job 1:10 about all that he hath **o every side**? 4480+5439
4:13 of the night, when deep sleep falleth **o** men. 5921
5:11 To set up **o** high those that be low; 3807.1
9:11 he **passeth o** also, but I perceive him not. 2498
13:13 I may speak, and let come **o** me what *will.* 5921
Job 15:26 He runneth upon him, *even* **o** *his* neck, 871.1
15:27 and maketh collops of fat **o** *his* flanks. 5921
16:16 and **o** mine eyelids *is* the shadow of death; 5921
16:19 *is* in heaven, and my record *is* **o** high. 871.1
17: 9 The righteous also shall **hold o** his way, and 270
18:11 Terrors shall make him afraid **o every side**, 5439
19:10 He hath destroyed me **o every side**, and 5439
21: 3 and after that I have spoken, mock **o**. NIH
21: 6 and trembling **taketh hold o** my flesh. 270
23: 9 *O* the left hand, where he doth work, but NIH
23: 9 I cannot behold *him:* he hideth *himself* **o** NIH
24:20 the worm shall **feed sweetly o** him; 4988
27:17 may prepare *it,* but the just shall **put** *it* **o**, 3847
27:20 Terrors **take hold o** him as waters, 5381
29: 9 and laid *their* hand **o** their mouth. 3807.1
29:14 I **put o** righteousness, and it clothed me: 3847
29:24 *If* I laughed **o** them, they believed *it* not; and 413
31: 2 inheritance of the Almighty from **o high**? 4791
36: 2 that *I have* yet to speak **o** God's **behalf**. 3807.1
36: 7 with kings *are they* **o** the throne; yea, 3807.1
36:16 **that which** should **be set o** thy table *should* 5183
36:17 judgment and justice **take hold o** *thee.* 8551
37: 6 he saith to the snow, Be thou *o* the earth; NIH
38:26 To cause it to rain **o** the earth, *where* no 5921
38:26 *where* no man *is;* **o** the wilderness, NIH
39:18 What time she lifteth up herself **o** high, 871.1
39:21 He **goeth o** to meet the armed men. 3318
39:27 thy command, and **make** her nest **o high**? 7311
39:28 She dwelleth and abideth **o** the rock, NIH
40:12 Look **o** every one *that is* proud, *and* NIH
Ps 4: T To the chief Musician **o** Neginoth, 871.1
6: T To the chief Musician **o** Neginoth upon 871.1
7: 7 their sakes therefore return thou **o** high. 3807.1
12: 8 The wicked walk **o every side**, when 5439
21: 3 thou settest a crown of pure gold **o** his 3807.1
22: 8 He trusted **o** the LORD *that* he would 413
25: 3 Yea, let none that **wait o** thee be ashamed: 6960
25: 5 of my salvation; **o** thee do I wait all the day. NIH
25:21 uprightness preserve me; for I **wait o** thee. 6960
27:14 Wait **o** the LORD: be of good courage, and 413
27:14 thine heart: wait, I say, **o** the LORD. 413
31:13 fear *was* **o every side**: while they 4480+5439
35:17 Lord, how long wilt thou look **o**? rescue my NIH
37:34 Wait **o** the LORD, and keep his way, and 413
48: 2 *is* mount Zion, *o* the sides of the north, NIH
49:14 death shall feed *o* them; and the upright NIH
52: 9 hast done *it:* and I will **wait o** thy name; 6960
54: T To the chief Musician **o** Neginoth, 871.1
55: T To the chief Musician **o** Neginoth, 871.1
57: 4 I lie *even among* them that are **set o fire**, 3857
63: 6 *and* meditate **o** thee in the *night* watches. 871.1
65:12 and the little hills rejoice **o every side**. 2296
66: 6 *land:* they went through the flood **o** foot: 871.1
67: T To the chief Musician **o** Neginoth, 871.1
68:18 Thou hast ascended **o** high, thou hast led 3807.1
68:21 such a one as **goeth o still** in his trespasses. 1980
68:25 the **players o instruments** *followed* after; 5059
69: 6 Let not them that **wait o** thee, O Lord 6960
69:29 let thy salvation, O God, **set me up o high**. 7682
71:21 my greatness, and comfort me **o every side**. 5437
75: 5 Lift not up your horn **o** high: speak *not* 3807.1
76: T To the chief Musician **o** Neginoth, 871.1
78:53 he **led** them **o** safely, so that they feared 5148
79: 1 they have laid Jerusalem **o** heaps. 3807.1
81: 3 time appointed, **o** our solemn feast day. 3807.1
82: 5 they understand; they **walk o** in darkness: 1980
83:14 as the flame **setteth** the mountains **o fire**; 3857
87: 7 **players o instruments** *shall be there:* all 2490
91:14 I will **set** him **o high**, because he hath 7682
92:11 Mine eye also shall see *my desire* **o** mine 871.1
93: 4 The LORD **o high** *is* 4791+871.1+1886.1
104:32 He looketh **o** the earth, and it trembleth: 3807.1
107:41 Yet **setteth** he the poor **o high** from 7682
113: 5 the LORD our God, who dwelleth **o high**, 1361
118: 6 The LORD *is* **o** my **side**; I will not fear: 3807.1
119:59 I **thought o** my ways, and turned my feet 2803
119:84 when wilt thou execute judgment **o** them 871.1
119:143 and anguish have **taken hold o** me: 4672
124: 1 not *been* the LORD who was **o** our **side**, 3807.1
124: 2 not *been* the LORD who was **o** our **side**, 3807.1
142: 4 I looked *o my* right hand, and beheld, but NIH
143: 5 the days of old; I meditate **o** all thy works; 871.1
143: 5 thy works; I muse **o** the work of thy hands. 871.1
Pr 4:25 Let thine eyes look **right o**, and 5227+3807.1
5: 5 go down *to* death; her steps take hold **o** hell. NIH
9:14 **o** a seat in the high places of the city, 5921
9:15 To call passengers who go right *o* their NIH
14:21 he that hath mercy **o** the poor, happy *is* he. NIH
14:31 he that honoureth him hath mercy **o** NIH
15:14 the mouth of fools **feedeth o** foolishness. 7462
20:22 *but* wait **o** the LORD, and he shall save 3807.1
22: 3 but the simple **pass o**, and are punished. 5674
27:12 *but* the simple **pass o**, *and* are punished. 5674
27:18 he that **waiteth o** his master shall be 8104
Ecc 2: 3 to lay hold **o** folly, till I might see what 871.1
2:11 I looked **o** all the works that my hands had 871.1
2:11 and **o** the labour that I had laboured to do: 871.1
4: 1 **o** the side of their oppressors *there was* 4480
SS 2:12 The flowers appear **o** the earth; the time of 871.1
3: 1 By night **o** my bed I sought *him* whom my 5921
5: 3 I have put off my coat; how shall I **put** it **o**? 3847
Isa 7:25 *o* all hills that shall be digged with NIH
9:17 neither shall have mercy **o** their fatherless NIH
9:20 he shall snatch **o** the right hand, and 5921
9:20 he shall eat **o** the left hand, and they shall 5921
10:12 work upon mount Zion and **o** Jerusalem, 871.1
11: 8 the sucking child shall play **o** the hole of 5921
11: 8 the weaned child shall put his hand **o** 5921
13:18 they shall have no pity **o** the fruit of 5921
14: 1 For the LORD will have mercy **o** Jacob, NIH
15: 2 **o** all their heads *shall be* baldness, *and* 871.1
15: 3 **o** the tops of their houses, and in their 5921
16:12 when it is seen that Moab is weary **o** 5921
18: 3 the world, and dwellers **o** the earth, see ye, NIH
18: 3 when *he* lifteth up an ensign *o* NIH

Isa 22:16 he that heweth him out a sepulchre **o high**, 4791
24:18 for the windows from **o high** are open, and 4791
24:21 the host of the high ones *that are* **o** high, 871.1
25: 6 a feast of **wines o the lees**, of fat things full 8105
25: 6 of **wines o the lees** well refined. 8105
26: 3 *whose* mind *is* stayed *o thee:* because NIH
26: 5 he bringeth down them that dwell **o high**; 4791
27:11 the women come, *and* **set** them **o fire**: for it 215
27:11 he that made them will not have mercy **o** NIH
28: 1 which *are* **o** the head of the fat valleys of 5921
28: 4 which *is* **o** the head of the fat valley, 5921
28:20 than that *a man* can stretch himself *o it:* NIH
30:17 top of a mountain, and as an ensign **o** a hill. 5921
31: 1 stay **o** horses, and trust in chariots, because 5921
31: 4 and the young lion roaring **o** his prey, 5921
32:15 the spirit be poured upon us from **o high**, 4791
32:19 it shall hail, coming down **o** the forest; NIH
33: 5 LORD *is* exalted; for he dwelleth **o high**: 4791
33:16 He shall dwell **o high**: his place of defence 4791
36: 5 now **o** whom dost thou trust, that thou 5921
36: 6 in the staff of this broken reed, **o** Egypt; 5921
36: 8 if thou be able **o** thy **part** to set riders 3807.1
36: 9 put thy trust **o** Egypt for chariots and 5921
36:11 in the ears of the people that *are* **o** the wall. 5921
37:23 *thy* voice, and lifted up thine eyes **o high**? 4791
37:27 *as* the grass **o** the housetops, and *as* corn NIH
40:26 Lift up your eyes **o high**, and behold who 4791
42:25 it hath **set** him **o fire** round about, yet he 3857
44:20 He **feedeth o** ashes: a deceived heart hath 7462
47: 1 daughter of Babylon, sit **o** the ground: 3807.1
48:14 he will do his pleasure **o** Babylon, and 871.1
48:14 and his arm *shall be o* the Chaldeans. NIH
49:10 for he that hath mercy **o** them shall lead NIH
49:15 that *she* should not have compassion **o** NIH
49:18 and bind them *o thee*, as a bride *doth*. NIH
51: 5 upon me, and **o** mine arm shall they trust. 413
51: 9 Awake, awake, **put o** strength, O arm of 3847
52: 1 Awake, awake; **put o** thy strength, O Zion; 3847
52: 1 **put o** thy beautiful garments, O Jerusalem, 3847
53: 6 the LORD hath laid **o** him the iniquity of 871.1
54: 3 For thou shalt break forth **o** the right hand NIH
54: 3 break forth *on* the right hand and *o* the left; NIH
54: 8 kindness will I have mercy **o** thee, NIH
54:10 saith the LORD that hath mercy **o** thee. NIH
56: 2 and the son of man *that* layeth hold **o** it; 871.1
57:17 he **went o** frowardly in the way of his 1980
58: 4 to make your voice to be heard **o** high. 871.1
58:13 *from* doing thy pleasure **o** my holy day; 871.1
59:17 For he **put o** righteousness as a breastplate, 3847
59:17 **Put o** the garments of vengeance *for* **clothing**, 3847+8516
60: 7 they shall come up with acceptance **o** mine NIH
60:10 but in my favour have I had mercy **o** thee. NIH
63: 7 to all that the LORD hath **bestowed o** us, 1580
63: 7 which he hath **bestowed o** them according 1580
Jer 4: 7 the destroyer of the Gentiles is **o** his **way**; 5265
5: 9 shall not my soul be avenged **o** such a 871.1
5:29 shall not my soul be avenged **o** such a 871.1
6:23 They shall **lay hold o** bow and spear; 2388
6:25 the enemy *and* fear *is* **o every side**. 4480+5439
7:29 and take up a lamentation **o** high places; 5921
8:13 *there shall be* no grapes **o** the vine, nor figs 871.1
8:13 nor figs **o** the fig tree, and the leaf shall 2050.1
8:21 astonishment hath **taken hold o** me. 2388
9: 9 shall not my soul be avenged **o** such a 871.1
10:25 upon the families that call not **o** thy name: 871.1
11:20 the heart, let me see thy vengeance **o** them: 4480
12:15 have compassion **o** them, and will bring NIH
13: 2 word of the LORD, and put *it* **o** my loins. 5921
13:27 thine abominations **o** the hills in the fields. 5921
15:10 I have neither **lent o usury**, nor *men* have 5383
15:10 on usury, nor *men* have **lent** to me **o usury**; 5383
17:11 *As* the partridge sitteth *o eggs*, and NIH
17:21 bear no burden **o** the sabbath day, 871.1
17:22 out of your houses **o** the sabbath day, 871.1
17:24 the gates of this city **o** the sabbath day, 871.1
17:25 riding in chariots and **o** horses, they, and 871.1
17:27 even entering in at the gates of Jerusalem **o** 871.1
18: 3 behold, he wrought a work **o** the wheels. 5921
20: 3 it came to pass **o** the morrow, that Pashur 4480
20:10 defaming of many, fear **o every side**. 4480+5439
20:10 and we shall take our revenge **o** him. 4480
20:12 the heart, let me see thy vengeance **o** them: 4480
22: 4 riding in chariots and **o** horses, he, and 871.1
23:12 they shall be **driven o**, and fall therein: 1760
25:29 I begin to bring evil **o** the city which is 871.1
25:30 The LORD shall roar from **o high**, and 4791
30: 6 I see every man *with* his hands **o** his loins, 5921
30:18 and have mercy **o** his dwelling places; NIH
31:29 and the children's teeth are **set o edge**. 6949
31:30 the sour grape, his teeth shall be **set o edge**. 6949
32:29 shall come and **set** fire **o** this city, and 3341
33:26 captivity to return, and have mercy **o** them. NIH
36:22 *there was a fire o* the hearth burning before NIH
36:23 and cast *it* into the fire that *was* **o** the hearth, 413
36:23 consumed in the fire that *was* **o** the hearth. 5921
38:22 Thy friends have **set** thee **o**, and 5496
43: 3 Baruch the son of Neriah **setteth** thee **o** 5496
43:12 as a shepherd **putteth o** his garment; 5844
46: 4 the spears, *and* **put o** the brigandines. 3847
48:11 he *hath* settled **o** his lees, and hath not been 413
49:23 *is* sorrow **o** the sea; it cannot be quiet. 871.1
49:24 fear hath seized **o** *her:* anguish and NIH
49:29 cry unto them, Fear *is* **o every side**. 4480+5439
50: 6 they have turned them away *o* NIH
50:19 and he shall feed **o** Carmel and Bashan, and NIH
52:23 and six pomegranates **o** a side; 1886.5
La 1: 2 in the night, and her tears *are* **o** her cheeks: 5921
2:21 and the old lie **o** the ground in the streets: 3807.1
4: 6 as in a moment, and no hands stayed **o** her. 871.1
Eze 1: 8 a man under their wings **o** their four sides; 5921
1:10 a man, and the face of a lion, **o** the right side: 413
1:10 they four had the face of an ox **o** the left 4480
1:23 which covered **o** this *side*, and every one 3807.1
1:23 which covered **o** that *side*, their bodies. 3807.1

Eze 3:23 by the river of Chebar: and I fell **o** my face. 5921
4: 6 lie again **o** thy right side, and thou shalt 5921
7:16 shall be **o** the mountains like doves of 413
10: 3 Now the cherubims stood **o** the right side of 4480
11:23 stood upon the mountain which *is* **o** the east 4480
16:11 upon thine hands, and a chain **o** thy neck. 5921
16:12 I put a jewel **o** thy forehead, and earrings in 5921
16:15 pouredst out thy fornications **o** every one 5921
16:33 thee **o every side** for thy whoredom. 4480+5439
18: 2 and the children's teeth are **set o edge**? 6949
19: 8 the nations set against him **o every side** 5439
21:16 *either* **o the right hand**, *or* on the left, 3231
21:16 other, *either* on the right hand, *or* **o the left**, 8041
23: 5 she doted **o** her lovers, on the Assyrians *her* 5921
23: 5 her lovers, **o** the Assyrians *her* neighbours, 413
23: 7 of Assyria, and with all *o* whom she doted: NIH
23:22 bring them against thee **o every side**; 4480+5439
24: 3 **Set o** a pot, set *it* on, and also pour water 8239
24: 3 a pot, **set** *it* **o**, and also pour water into it: 8239
24:10 Heap **o** wood, kindle the fire, consume NIH
24:17 **put o** thy shoes upon thy feet, and 7760
25: 9 from his cities *which are* **o** his frontiers, 4480
26:17 which cause their terror *to be* **o** all that 3807.1
28:23 by the sword upon her **o every side**; 4480+5439
31: 4 the deep **set** him **up o high** with her rivers 7311
33:32 and can **play** well **o an instrument**: 5059
36: 3 and swallowed you up **o every side**, 4480+5439
37:21 will gather them **o every side**, and 4480+5439
39: 6 I will send a fire **o** Magog, and 871.1
39: 9 shall **set o fire** and burn the weapons, 1197
39:11 the valley of the passengers *o* the east of NIH
39:17 gather yourselves **o every side** to my 4480+5439
40: 2 by which *was* as the frame of a city **o** 4480
40: 5 behold a wall **o** the outside of the house 4480
40:10 of the gate eastward *were* three **o** this side, 4480
40:10 three on this side, and three **o** that side; 4480
40:10 the posts had one measure **o** this side and 4480
40:10 one measure on this side and **o** that side. 4480
40:12 the little chambers *was* one cubit *o this side,* NIH
40:12 and the space *was* one cubit **o** that side: 4480
40:12 the little chambers *were* six cubits **o** this 4480
40:12 on this side, and six cubits **o** that side. 4480
40:21 the little chambers thereof *were* three **o** this 4480
40:21 *were* three on this side and three **o** that side; 4480
40:26 one **o** this side, and another on that side, 4480
40:26 one on this side, and another **o** that side, 4480
40:34 posts thereof, **o** this side, and on that side: 4480
40:34 posts thereof, on this side, and **o** that side: 4480
40:37 posts thereof, **o** this side, and on that side: 4480
40:37 posts thereof, on this side, and **o** that side: 4480
40:39 in the porch of the gate *were* two tables **o** 4480
40:39 two tables **o** that side, to slay thereon 4480
40:40 **o** the other side, which *was* at the porch of 413
40:41 Four tables *were* **o** this side, and four tables 4480
40:41 four tables **o** that side, by the side of 4480
40:48 five cubits **o** this side, and five cubits on 4480
40:48 on this side, and five cubits **o** that side: 4480
40:48 the breadth of the gate *was* three cubits **o** 4480
40:48 on this side, and three cubits **o** that side. 4480
40:49 one **o** this side, and another on that side. 4480
40:49 one on this side, and another **o** that side. 4480
41: 1 six cubits broad **o** the one side, and 4480
41: 1 and six cubits broad **o** the other side, 4480
41: 2 the sides of the door *were* five cubits **o** 4480
41: 2 one side, and five cubits **o** the other side: 4480
41: 5 round about the house **o every side**. 5439
41:10 round about the house **o every side**. 5439+5439
41:15 the galleries thereof **o** the one side and 4480
41:15 thereof on the one side and **o** the other side, 4480
41:16 the galleries round about **o** their three 3807.1
41:19 *was* toward the palm tree **o** the one side, 4480
41:19 lion toward the palm tree **o** the other side: 4480
41:20 trees made, and *o* the wall of the temple. NIH
41:25 *there were* made **o** them, on the doors of 413
41:25 **o** the doors of the temple, cherubims and 413
41:26 palm trees **o** the one side and on the other 4480
41:26 trees on the one side and **o** the other side, 4480
41:26 **o** the sides of the porch, and *upon* the side 413
42: 7 towards the utter court **o** the forepart of 413
42: 9 from under these chambers *was* the entry **o** 4480
42:14 shall **put o** other garments, and 3847
43:20 put *it* **o** the four horns of it, and on the four 5921
43:20 **o** the four corners of the settle, and upon 413
43:22 **o** the second day thou shalt offer a kid of 871.1
44:19 and they shall **put o** other garments; 3847
45: 7 *a portion shall be* for the prince **o** the one 4480
45: 7 **o** the other side of the oblation of the holy 4480
46: 1 **o** the sabbath it shall be opened, and in 871.1
46:12 as he did **o** the sabbath day: 871.1
46:19 *was* a place **o** the two sides westward. 871.1
47: 2 there ran out waters **o** the right side. 4480
47: 7 river *were* very many trees **o** the one side 4480
47: 7 many trees on the one side and **o** the other. 4480
47:12 **o** this side and on that side, shall grow all 4480
47:12 on this side and **o** that side, shall grow all 4480
48:16 **o** the east side four thousand and 4480
48:21 **o** the one side and on the other of the holy 4480
48:21 and **o** the other of the holy oblation, 4480
48:30 **o** the north side, four thousand and 4480
Da 3:27 nor the smell of fire had passed **o** them. 871.2
6:14 and set *his* heart **o** Daniel to deliver him: 5922
7: 5 it raised up itself **o** one side, and *it had* 3807.2
8: 5 a he goat came from the west **o** the face of 5921
8:18 I was in a deep sleep **o** my face toward 5921
10: 9 was I in a deep sleep **o** my face, and 5921
11:17 she shall not stand *o his side*, neither be for NIH
11:31 arms shall stand **o** his **part**, and they shall 4480
12: 5 the one **o** this side of the bank of 3807.1
12: 5 the other **o** that side of the bank of 3807.1
Hos 4: 8 and they set their heart **o** their iniquity. 413
5: 1 because ye have been a snare **o** Mizpah, 3807.1
6: 3 *if* we follow **o** to know the LORD: NIH
10: 5 the priests thereof *that* rejoiced **o** it, for 5921
10: 8 and the thistle shall come up **o** their altars; 5921
10: 8 Cover us; and to the hills, Fall **o** us. 5921

Hos 11: 4 as they that take off the yoke **o** their jaws, 5921
11: 6 the sword shall abide **o** his cities, and 871.1
12: 1 Ephraim **feedeth o** wind, and 7462
12: 6 judgment, and wait **o** thy God continually. 413
Joel 2: 5 Like the noise of chariots **o** the tops of 5921
2: 7 they shall march every one **o** his ways, and 871.1
2:32 *that* whosoever shall call **o** the name of 871.1
Am 1: 7 I will send a fire **o** the wall of Gaza, 871.1
1:10 I will send a fire **o** the wall of Tyrus, 871.1
2: 7 That pant after the dust of the earth **o** 871.1
5:19 leaned his hand **o** the wall, and a serpent bit 5921
Ob 1:11 In the day that thou stoodest **o** the other 4480
1:12 thou shouldest not have looked **o** the day of NIH
1:13 thou shouldest not have looked **o** their NIH
1:13 nor have laid *hands* **o** their substance in 871.1
1:21 saviours shall come up **o** mount Zion to 871.1
Jnh 3: 5 and proclaimed a fast, and **put o** sackcloth, 3847
4: 5 sat **o** the east side of the city, and 4480
4:10 Thou hast had pity **o** the gourd, 5921
Mic 2:13 and the LORD **o** the head of them. 871.1
Na 1: 2 the LORD will take vengeance **o** his 3807.1
Hab 1:13 to behold evil, and canst not look **o** iniquity: 413
2: 9 that *he* may set his nest **o** high, that *he* may 871.1
2:15 that thou mayest look **o** their nakedness! 5921
2:16 and shameful spuing *shall be* **o** thy glory. 5921
3:10 his voice, *and* lift up his hands **o high**. 7315
3:19 To the chief singer **o** my stringed 871.1
Zep 1: 9 I punish all those that leap **o** the threshold, 5921
1:12 punish the men that are settled **o** their lees: 5921
Zec 1:12 how long wilt thou not have mercy **o** NIH
1:12 on Jerusalem and **o** the cities of Judah, NIH
5: 3 be cut off *as* **o** this *side* according to it; 4480
5: 3 every one that sweareth shall be cut off *as* **o** 4480
10: 5 and the riders **o** horses shall be confounded. NIH
12: 6 **o** the right hand and on the left: 5921
12: 6 on the right hand and **o** the left: 5921
13: 9 they shall call **o** my name, and I will hear 871.1
14: 4 which *is* before Jerusalem **o** the east, and 4480
14:13 they shall lay hold every one **o** the hand of NIH
Mal 1:10 do ye kindle *fire* **o** mine altar for nought. NIH
Mt 1:18 the birth of Jesus Christ was **o this wise**: *3779*
1:20 But while he **thought o** these *things*, *1760*
4: 5 and setteth him **o** a pinnacle of the temple, *1909*
4:21 And **going o** from thence, he saw other two *4260*
5:14 A city that is set **o** a hill cannot be hid. *1883*
5:15 put it under a bushel, but **o** a candlestick; *1909*
5:28 That whosoever **looketh o** a woman to lust *991*
5:39 whosoever shall smite thee **o** thy right *1909*
5:45 for he maketh his sun to rise **o** the evil and *1909*
5:45 his sun to rise on the evil and *o* the good, NIG
5:45 and sendeth rain **o** the just and *on* *1909*
5:45 sendeth rain on the just and *o* the unjust. NIG
6:25 nor yet for your body, what ye shall **put o**. *1746*
9: 2 him a man sick of the palsy, lying **o** a bed: *1909*
9: 6 of man hath power **o** earth to forgive sins, *1909*
9:27 *Thou* Son of David, have mercy **o** us. NIG
9:36 he was moved with compassion **o** them, *4012*
10:29 one of them shall not fall **o** the ground *1909*
10:34 Think not that I am come to send peace **o** *1909*
12: 1 At that time Jesus went **o** the sabbath day NIG
12: 5 how that **o** the sabbath days the priests in NIG
12:10 Is it lawful to heal **o** the sabbath days? NIG
12:11 and if it fall into a pit **o** the sabbath day, NIG
12:11 will he not **lay hold o** it, and lift *it* out? *2902*
12:12 Wherefore it is lawful to do well **o** NIG
13: 2 and the whole multitude stood **o** the shore. *1909*
14: 3 For Herod had **laid hold o** John, and *2902*
14:13 they followed him **o foot** out of the cities. *3979*
14:19 the multitude to sit down **o** the grass, *1909*
14:25 Jesus went unto them, walking **o** the sea. *1909*
14:26 And when the disciples saw him walking **o** *1909*
14:28 be thou, bid me come unto thee **o** the water. *1909*
14:29 he walked **o** the water, to go to Jesus. *1909*
15:22 saying, Have mercy **o** me, O Lord, NIG
15:32 said, I have compassion **o** the multitude, *1909*
15:35 the multitude to sit down **o** the ground. *1909*
16:19 whatsoever thou shalt bind **o** earth shall be *1909*
16:19 whatsoever thou shalt loose **o** earth shall be *1909*
17: 6 And when the disciples heard *it*, they fell **o** *1909*
17:15 Lord, have mercy **o** my son: for he is NIG
18:18 Whatsoever ye shall bind **o** earth shall be *1909*
18:18 whatsoever ye shall loose **o** earth shall be *1909*
18:19 That if two of you shall agree **o** earth as *1909*
18:28 and he **laid hands o** him, and took *him* by *2902*
18:33 have had compassion **o** thy fellowservant, NIG
18:33 thy fellowservant, even as I had pity **o** thee? NIG
19:13 that he should **put** *his* hands **o** them, and *2007*
19:15 And he **laid** *his* hands **o** them, and *2007*
20:21 the one **o** thy right hand, and the other on *1537*
20:21 and the other **o** the left, in thy kingdom. *1537*
20:23 baptized *with:* but to sit **o** my right hand, *1537*
20:23 and **o** my left, is not mine to give, but *1537*
20:30 cried out, saying, Have mercy **o** us, O Lord, NIG
20:31 saying, Have mercy **o** us, O Lord, *thou* Son NIG
20:34 So Jesus had compassion **o** *them*, and NIG
21: 7 and the colt, and put **o** them their clothes, *1883*
21:19 Let no fruit grow **o** thee henceforward for *1537*
21:38 kill him, and let us seize **o** his inheritance. NIG
21:44 And whosoever shall fall **o** this stone shall *1909*
21:44 but **o** whomsoever it shall fall, it will grind *1909*
21:46 But when they sought to **lay hands o** him, *2902*
22:11 he saw there a man which **had** not **o** a *1746*
22:40 **O** these two commandments hang all *1722*
22:44 unto my Lord, Sit thou **o** my right hand, *1537*
23: 4 and **lay** *them* **o** men's shoulders; *2007*
24:17 Let him which is **o** the housetop not come *1909*
24:20 not in the winter, neither **o** the sabbath day: *1722*
25:33 And he shall set the sheep **o** his right hand, *1537*
25:33 on his right hand, but the goats **o** the left. *1537*
25:34 Then shall the King say unto them **o** his *1537*
25:41 Then shall he say also unto them **o** the left *1537*
26: 5 Not **o** the feast *day*, lest there be an uproar *1722*
26: 7 and poured *it* **o** his head, as he sat at meat. *1909*
26:12 For in that she hath poured this ointment **o** *1909*
26:39 and fell **o** his face, and prayed, saying, *1909*

O

Mt 26:45 unto them, Sleep **o** now, and take your rest: NIG
26:50 and laid hands **o** Jesus, and took him. *1909*
26:55 in the temple, and ye laid no hold **o** me. NIG
26:57 And they that had laid hold **o** Jesus led *him* NIG
26:64 of man sitting **o** the right hand of power, *1537*
27:19 When he was set down **o** the judgment seat, *1909*
27:25 His blood *be* **o** us, and on our children. *1909*
27:25 His blood *be* on us, and **o** our children. *1909*
27:28 stripped him, and **put o** him a scarlet robe. *4060*
27:30 took the reed, and smote him **o** the head. *1519*
27:31 and **put** his own raiment **o** him, and *1746*
27:38 one **o** the right hand, and another on *1537*
27:38 on the right hand, and another **o** the left. *1537*
27:48 and **put** *it* **o** a reed, and gave him to drink. *4060*
Mk 1:21 straightway **o** the sabbath day he entered NIG
2:10 of man hath power **o** earth to forgive sins, *1909*
2:12 saying, We never saw *it* **o this fashion**. *3779*
2:21 No *man* also seweth a piece of new cloth **o** *1909*
2:23 that he went through the corn fields **o** *1722*
2:24 why do they **o** the sabbath day *that* which is *1722*
3: 2 whether he would heal him **o** the sabbath NIG
3: 4 Is it lawful to do good **o** the sabbath days, or NIG
3: 5 And when he had looked round about **o** NIG
3: 9 that a small ship should **wait o** him because *4342*
3:21 heard *of it,* they went out to **lay hold o** him: *2902*
3:34 And he looked round about **o** them which NIG
4: 1 the whole multitude was by the sea **o** *1909*
4: 5 And some fell **o** stony ground, where it had *1909*
4: 8 And other fell **o** good ground, and did yield *1519*
4:16 likewise which are sown **o** stony ground; *1909*
4:20 And these are they which are sown **o** good *1909*
4:21 a bed? *and* not to be set **o** a candlestick? *1909*
4:38 hinder part of the ship, asleep **o** a pillow: *1909*
5:19 for thee, and hath had compassion **o** thee. NIG
5:23 *I pray thee,* come and **lay** *thy* hands **o** her, *2007*
6: 9 shod with sandals; and not **put o** two coats. *1746*
6:21 that Herod **o** his birthday made a supper to NIG
6:47 midst of the sea, and he alone **o** the land. *1909*
8: 2 I have compassion **o** the multitude, because *1909*
8: 6 the people to sit down **o** the ground: *1909*
8:23 and when he had spit **o** his eyes, and put *his* *1519*
8:33 turned about and **looked o** his disciples, *1492*
9: 3 so as no fuller **o** earth can white *them.* *1909*
9:20 and he fell **o** the ground, and *1909*
9:22 canst do any *thing,* have compassion **o** us, *1909*
9:40 For he that is not against us is **o** our **part**. *5228*
10:37 one **o** thy right hand, and the other on thy *1537*
10:37 and the other **o** thy left hand, in thy glory. *1537*
10:40 But to sit **o** my right hand and on my left *1537*
10:40 and **o** my left hand is not mine to give; *1537*
10:47 Jesus, *thou* Son of David, have mercy **o** me. NIG
10:48 *Thou* Son of David, have mercy **o** me. NIG
11: 7 colt to Jesus, and **cast** their garments **o** him; *1911*
11:12 And **o** the **morrow**, when they were come *1887*
12:12 And they sought to **lay hold o** him, but *2902*
12:36 said to my Lord, Sit thou **o** my right hand, *1537*
13:15 And let him that is **o** the housetop not go *1909*
14: 2 Not **o** the feast *day,* lest there be an uproar *1722*
14: 3 she brake the box, and poured *it* **o** his head. *2596*
14: 6 she hath wrought a good work **o** me. *1519*
14:35 and fell **o** the ground, and prayed that, if it *1909*
14:41 unto them, Sleep **o** now, and take your rest: NIG
14:46 And they laid their hands **o** him, and *1909*
14:51 and the young men **laid hold o** him: *2902*
14:62 ye shall see the Son of man sitting **o** *1537*
14:65 And some began to **spit o** him, and to cover *1716*
15:19 And they smote him **o** the head with a reed, NIG
15:20 and **put** his own clothes **o** him, and led him *1746*
15:27 the one **o** *his* right hand, and the other on *1537*
15:27 on *his* right hand, and the other **o** his left. *1537*
15:29 And they that passed by **railed o** him, *987*
15:36 and **put** *it* **o** a reed, and gave him to drink, *4060*
15:40 There were also women **looking o** afar off: *2334*
16: 5 they saw a young man sitting **o** the right *1722*
16:18 they shall lay hands **o** the sick, and *1909*
16:19 and sat **o** the right hand of God. *1537*
Lk 1:11 **o** the right side of the altar of incense. *1537*
1:25 **looked o** *me,* to take away my reproach *1896*
1:50 And his mercy *is* **o** them that fear him from NIG
1:59 *that* **o** the eighth day they came to *1722*
1:65 And fear came **o** all that dwelt round about *1909*
1:78 whereby the dayspring from **o high** hath *5311*
2:14 and **o** earth peace, good will towards men. *1909*
4: 9 and set him **o** a pinnacle of the temple, and *1909*
4:16 he went into the synagogue **o** the sabbath *1722*
4:20 *were* in the synagogue were fastened **o** him. NIG
4:31 and taught them **o** the sabbath days. *1722*
4:40 and he **laid** *his* hands **o** every one of them, *2007*
5:12 who seeing Jesus fell **o** *his* face, and *1909*
5:17 And it came to pass **o** a certain day, as he *1722*
6: 1 And it came to pass **o** the second sabbath *1722*
6: 2 Why do ye *that* which is not lawful to do **o** *1722*
6: 6 And it came to pass also **o** another sabbath, *1722*
6: 7 whether he would heal **o** the sabbath day; *1722*
6: 9 I will ask you one *thing;* Is it lawful **o** NIG
6:20 And he lifted up his eyes **o** his disciples, *1519*
6:29 *And* unto him that smiteth thee **o** the *one* *1909*
6:48 and laid the foundation **o** a rock: *1909*
7:13 he had compassion **o** her, and said unto her, *1909*
7:16 And there came a fear **o** all: NIG
7:40 say unto thee. And he saith, Master, say ***o.*** NIG
8: 8 And other fell **o** good ground, and *1909*
8:13 They **o** the rock *are they,* which, when they *1909*
8:15 But that **o** the good ground are they, *1722*
8:16 but **setteth** *it* **o** a candlestick, *2007*
8:22 Now it came to pass **o** a certain day, that he *1722*
8:23 there came down a storm of wind **o** *1519*
8:32 of many swine feeding **o** the mountain: *1722*
9:37 And it came to pass, *that* **o** the next day, *1722*
10:11 which **cleaveth o** us, we do wipe off *2853*
10:19 I give unto you power to tread **o** serpents *1883*
10:31 he saw him, he **passed by o the other side**. *492*
10:32 came and looked **o** *him,* and passed by on NIG
10:32 *on him,* and **passed by o the other side**. *492*
10:33 he saw him, he had compassion ***o*** *him,* NIG

Lk 10:34 and **set** him **o** his own beast, and *1913*
10:35 And **o** the morrow when he departed, *1909*
10:37 And he said, He that shewed mercy **o** him. *3326*
11:33 neither under a bushel, but **o** a candlestick, *1909*
12:22 neither for the body, what ye shall **put o**. *1746*
12:49 I am come to send fire **o** the earth; and *1519*
12:51 Suppose ye that I am come to give peace **o** *1722*
13: 7 *these* three years I come seeking fruit **o** this *1722*
13:10 in one of the synagogues **o** the sabbath. *1722*
13:13 And he **laid** *his* hands **o** her: and *2007*
13:14 that Jesus had healed **o** the sabbath day, NIG
13:14 and be healed, and not **o** the sabbath day. NIG
13:15 doth not each one of you **o** the sabbath loose NIG
13:16 be loosed from this bond **o** the sabbath day? NIG
14: 1 Pharisees to eat bread **o** the sabbath day, NIG
14: 3 Is it lawful to heal **o** the sabbath day? NIG
14: 5 will not straightway pull him out **o** *1722*
15: 5 And when he hath found *it,* he layeth *it* **o** *1909*
15:20 and ran, and fell **o** his neck, and kissed him. *1909*
15:22 Bring forth the best robe, and **put** *it* **o** him; *1746*
15:22 and put *it* on him; and put a ring **o** his hand, *1519*
15:22 put a ring on his hand, and shoes **o** *his* feet: *1519*
16:24 have mercy **o** me, and send Lazarus, NIG
17:13 and said, Jesus, Master, have mercy **o** us. NIG
17:16 And fell down **o** *his* face at his feet, *1909*
18: 8 man cometh, shall he find faith **o** the earth? *1909*
18:32 and spitefully entreated, and **spitted o**: *1716*
18:38 Jesus, *thou* Son of David, have mercy **o** me. NIG
18:39 *Thou* Son of David, have mercy **o** me. NIG
19:43 thee round, and keep thee in **o every side**, *3840*
20: 1 it came to pass, *that* **o** one of those days, *1722*
20:18 but **o** whomsoever it shall fall, it will grind *1909*
20:19 hour sought to **lay** hands **o** him; *1911*
20:42 said to my Lord, Sit thou **o** my right hand, *1537*
21:12 they shall **lay** their hands **o** you, and *1911*
21:26 those *things* which are **coming o** the earth: *1904*
21:35 For as a snare shall it **come o** all *1904*
21:35 that dwell **o** the face of the whole earth. *1909*
22:21 that betrayeth me *is* with me **o** the table. *1909*
22:30 sit **o** thrones judging the twelve tribes of *1909*
22:64 they stroke him **o** the face, and asked him, NIG
22:69 Hereafter shall the Son of man sit **o** *1537*
23:26 the country, and **o** him they **laid** the cross, *2007*
23:30 begin to say to the mountains, Fall **o** us; *1909*
23:33 one **o** the right hand, and the other on *1537*
23:33 on the right hand, and the other **o** the left. *1537*
23:39 which were hanged railed **o** him, NIG
23:54 the preparation, and the sabbath **drew o**. *2020*
24:49 until ye be endued with power from **o high**. *5311*
Jn 1:12 *even* to them that believe **o** his name: *1519*
1:33 the Spirit descending, and remaining **o** him, *1909*
2:11 his glory; and his disciples believed **o** him. *1519*
3:18 He that believeth **o** him is not condemned: *1519*
3:36 He that believeth **o** the Son hath everlasting *1519*
3:36 but the wrath of God abideth **o** him. *1909*
4: 6 with *his* journey, sat thus **o** the well: *1909*
4:35 Lift up your eyes, and **look o** the fields; *2300*
4:39 **o** him for the saying of the woman, *1519*
5: 9 and **o** the same day was the sabbath. *1722*
5:16 he had done these *things* **o** the sabbath day. *1722*
5:24 and believeth **o** him that sent me, NIG
6: 2 they saw his miracles which he did **o** them *1909*
6:19 they see Jesus walking **o** the sea, and *1909*
6:22 **o the other side** of the sea saw that there *4008*
6:25 had found him **o the other side** of the sea, *4008*
6:29 that ye believe **o** *him* whom he hath sent. *1519*
6:35 he that believeth **o** me shall never thirst. *1519*
6:40 and believeth **o** him, may have everlasting *1519*
6:47 He that believeth **o** me hath everlasting life. *1519*
7:22 and ye **o** the sabbath day circumcise a man. *1722*
7:23 If a man **o** the sabbath day receive *1722*
7:23 I have made a man every whit whole **o** *1722*
7:30 but no *man* laid hands **o** him, because *1909*
7:31 And many of the people believed **o** him, *1519*
7:38 He that believeth **o** me, as the scripture hath *1519*
7:39 which they that believe **o** him should *1519*
7:44 taken him; but no *man* laid hands **o** him. *1909*
7:48 or of the Pharisees believed **o** him? *1519*
8: 6 and with *his* finger wrote **o** the ground, *1519*
8: 8 he stooped down, and wrote **o** the ground. *1519*
8:20 and no *man* **laid hands o** him; for his hour *4084*
8:30 As he spake these *words,* many believed **o** *1519*
8:31 Jesus to those Jews which believed **o** him, NIG
9: 6 he spat **o the ground**, and made clay of *5476*
9:35 Dost thou believe **o** the Son of God? *1519*
9:36 is he, Lord, that I might believe **o** him? *1519*
10:42 And many believed **o** him there. *1519*
11:45 *the things* which Jesus did, believed **o** him. *1519*
11:48 him thus alone, all *men* will believe **o** him: *1519*
12:11 the Jews went away, and believed **o** Jesus. *1519*
12:12 **O** the next day much people that were come NIG
12:15 thy King cometh, sitting **o** an ass's colt. *1909*
12:37 before them, *yet* they believed not **o** him: *1519*
12:42 the *chief* rulers also many believed **o** him; *1519*
12:44 and said, He that believeth **o** me, *1519*
12:44 believeth not **o** me, but on him that sent me. *1519*
12:44 believeth not on me, but **o** him that sent me. *1519*
12:46 that whosoever believeth **o** me should not *1519*
13:22 Then the disciples looked one **o** another, *1519*
13:23 Now there was leaning **o** Jesus' bosom one *1722*
13:25 then lying **o** Jesus' breast saith unto him, *1909*
14:12 I say unto you, He that believeth **o** me, *1519*
16: 9 Of sin, because they believe not **o** me; *1519*
17: 4 I have glorified thee **o** the earth: I have *1909*
17:20 for them also which shall believe **o** me *1519*
19: 2 and **put** *it* **o** his head, and they put on him a *2007*
19: 2 his head, and they **put o** him a purple robe, *4016*
19:18 with him, **o either side one**, *1782+1782+2532*
19:19 Pilate wrote a title, and put *it* **o** the cross. *1909*
19:31 remain upon the cross **o** the sabbath day, *1722*
19:37 They shall look **o** *him* whom they pierced. *1519*
20:22 he **breathed o** *them,* and saith unto them, *1720*
21: 1 and **o this wise** shewed he *himself.* *3779*
21: 4 was now come, Jesus stood **o** the shore: *1519*
21: 6 Cast the net **o** the right side of the ship, and *1519*

Jn 21:20 which also leaned **o** his breast at supper, *1909*
Ac 2:18 And **o** my servants and on my *1909*
2:18 **o** my handmaidens I will pour out in those *1909*
2:21 *that* whosoever shall **call o** the name of *1941*
2:25 for he is **o** my right hand, that I should not *1537*
2:30 *he* would raise up Christ to sit **o** his throne; *1909*
2:34 unto my Lord, Sit thou **o** my right hand, *1537*
3: 4 eyes upon him with John, said, Look **o** us. *1519*
3:12 or why look ye *so* earnestly **o** us, as though NIG
4: 3 And they **laid** hands **o** them, and put *them* *1911*
4: 5 And it came to pass **o** the morrow, *1909*
4:22 **o** whom this miracle of healing was *1909*
5: 5 great fear came **o** all them that heard these *1909*
5:15 and laid *them* **o** beds and couches, *1909*
5:18 And laid their hands **o** the apostles, and *1909*
5:30 whom ye slew and hanged **o** a tree. *1909*
6: 6 had prayed, they **laid** *their* hands **o** them. *2007*
6:15 sat in the council, looking stedfastly **o** him, *1519*
7: 5 in it, no, not so much as to **set** his foot **o**: *968*
7: 6 And God spake **o this wise**, That his seed *3779*
7:54 and they gnashed **o** him with *their* teeth. *1909*
7:55 and Jesus standing **o** the right hand of God, *1537*
7:56 the Son of man standing **o** the right hand of *1537*
8:17 Then **laid** they *their* hands **o** them, *2007*
8:18 And when Simon saw that through **laying o** *1936*
8:19 this power, that **o** whomsoever I **lay** hands, *2007*
8:36 And as they went **o** *their* way, they came *2596*
8:39 no more: and he went ***o*** his way rejoicing. NIG
9:12 and **putting** *his* hand **o** him, that he might *2007*
9:14 priests to bind all that **call o** thy name. *1941*
9:17 and **putting** his hands **o** him said, *2007*
9:21 which **called o** this name in Jerusalem, *1941*
10: 4 And when he looked **o** him, he was afraid, NIG
10: 7 of them that **waited o** him **continually**; *4342*
10: 9 **O the morrow**, as they went on their *1887*
10: 9 as they **went o** their **journey**, and *3596*
10:19 While Peter thought **o** the vision, the Spirit *4012*
10:23 lodged *them.* And **o** the **morrow** Peter *1887*
10:39 whom they slew and hanged **o** a tree: *1909*
10:44 the Holy Ghost **fell o** all them which *1968*
10:45 that **o** the Gentiles also was poured out *1909*
11:15 to speak, the Holy Ghost **fell o** them, *1968*
11:15 fell on them, as **o** us at the beginning. *1909*
11:17 who believed **o** the Lord Jesus Christ; *1909*
12: 7 and he smote Peter **o** the side, and NIG
12: 8 Gird thyself, and **bind o** thy sandals. *5265*
12:10 went out, and **passed o** through one street; *4281*
13: 3 and prayed, and **laid** *their* hands **o** them, *2007*
13: 9 with the Holy Ghost, set his eyes **o** him, *1519*
13:11 And immediately there **fell o** him a *1968*
13:14 went into the synagogue **o** the sabbath day, NIG
13:15 word of exhortation for the people, say ***o.*** NIG
13:34 to return to corruption, he said **o this wise**, *3779*
13:36 **fell o sleep**, and was laid unto his fathers, *2837*
14:10 with a loud voice, Stand upright **o** thy feet. *1909*
14:23 them to the Lord, **o** whom they believed. *1519*
15: 3 And being **brought o** their **way** by *4311*
16:13 And **o** the sabbath we went out of the city NIG
16:31 Believe **o** the Lord Jesus Christ, and *1909*
17: 5 and **set** all the city **o an uproar**, and *2350*
17:26 men for to dwell **o** all the face of the earth, *1909*
18: 8 believed **o** the Lord with all his house; NIG
18:10 and no *man* shall **set o** thee to hurt thee: *2007*
19: 4 that they should believe **o** him which *1519*
19: 4 come after him, that is, **o** Christ Jesus. *1519*
19: 6 upon them, the Holy Ghost came **o** them; *1909*
19:16 the evil spirit was **leapt o** them, *2177*
19:17 and fear **fell o** them all, and the name *1968*
20: 7 unto them, ready to depart **o** the **morrow**; *1887*
20:10 and **fell o** him, and embracing *him* said, *1968*
20:37 and fell **o** Paul's neck, and kissed him, *1909*
21: 3 we left it **o** the left hand, and sailed into *1909*
21: 5 and *they* all **brought** us **o** our way, *4311*
21: 5 and we kneeled down **o** the shore, and *1909*
21:23 We have four men which have a vow **o** *1909*
21:27 up all the people, and laid hands **o** him, *1909*
21:40 Paul stood **o** the stairs, and beckoned with *1909*
22:16 thy sins, **calling o** the name of the Lord. *1941*
22:19 every synagogue them that believed **o** thee: *1909*
22:30 **O** the **morrow**, because he would have *1887*
23: 2 that stood by him to smite him **o** the mouth. NIG
23:24 that they may **set** Paul **o**, and bring *him* *1913*
23:32 **O** the **morrow** they left the horsemen to go *1887*
25:17 **o** the **morrow** I sat on the judgment seat, *1836*
25:17 on the morrow I sat **o** the judgment seat, *1909*
25:23 And **o** the **morrow**, when Agrippa was *1887*
27:20 no small tempest **lay o** *us,* all hope that we *1945*
27:33 And while the day was **coming o**, Paul *3195*
27:44 some **o** boards, and some on broken pieces *1909*
27:44 and some **o** broken pieces of the ship. *1909*
28: 3 and laid *them* **o** the fire, there came a viper *1909*
28: 3 out of the heat, and fastened **o** his hand. NIG
28: 4 saw the *venomous* beast hang **o** his hand, *1537*
28: 8 and **laid** *his* hands **o** him, and healed him. *2007*
Ro 4: 5 believeth **o** him that justifieth the ungodly, *1909*
4:24 if we believe **o** him that raised up Jesus our *1909*
9:15 I will have mercy **o** whom I will have NIG
9:15 I will have compassion **o** whom I will have NIG
9:18 Therefore hath he mercy **o** whom he will NIG
9:23 riches of his glory **o** the vessels of mercy, *1909*
9:33 whosoever believeth **o** him shall not be *1909*
10: 6 which is of faith speaketh **o this wise**, *3779*
10:11 Whosoever believeth **o** him shall not be *1909*
10:14 shall they **call o** *him* in whom they have not *1941*
11:22 **o** them which fell, severity; but toward *1909*
12: 7 Or ministry, *let us wait* **o** *our* ministering: *1722*
12: 7 or he that teacheth, **o** teaching; *1722*
12: 8 Or he that exhorteth, **o** exhortation: he that *1722*
12:20 doing thou shalt heap coals of fire **o** his *1909*
13:12 and let us **put o** the armour of light. *1746*
13:14 But **put** ye **o** the Lord Jesus Christ, and *1746*
15: 3 of them that reproached thee fell **o** me. *1909*
15:24 to be **brought o** my way thitherward by *4311*
16: 6 who bestowed much labour **o** us. *1519*
16:19 all *men.* I am glad therefore **o** your **behalf**: *1909*

1Co 1: 4 I thank my God always o your behalf, 4012
11:10 ought the woman to have power o her head 1909
14:25 falling down o his face he will worship 1909
15:53 For this corruptible must put o 1746
15:53 and this mortal must put o immortality. 1746
15:54 So when this corruptible shall have put o 1746
15:54 this mortal shall have put o immortality, 1746
16: 6 that ye may bring me o my journey 4311
16:17 for that which was lacking o your part 4771
2Co 1:11 thanks may be given by many o our behalf. 5228
1:16 of you to be brought o my way toward 4311
4: 8 We are troubled o every side, yet not 1722
5:12 give you occasion to glory o our behalf, 5228
6: 7 by the armour of righteousness o the right NIG
6: 7 on the right hand and o the left, NIG
7: 5 we were troubled o every side; without 1722
8: 1 bestowed o the churches of Macedonia; 1722
8:24 and of our boasting o your behalf. 5228
10: 7 Do ye look o things after the outward 991
11:20 exalt himself, if a man smite you o the face. 1519
Gal 3:13 Cursed is every one that hangeth o a tree: 1909
3:14 come o the Gentiles through Jesus Christ; 1519
3:27 been baptized into Christ have put o Christ. 1746
6:16 to this rule, peace be o them, and mercy, 1909
Eph 1:10 which are in heaven, and which are o earth; 1909
4: 8 he saith, When he ascended up o high, 1519
4:24 And that ye put o the new man, which after 1746
6: 3 and thou mayest live long o the earth. 1909
6:11 Put o the whole armour of God, that ye 1746
6:14 having o the breastplate of righteousness; 1746
Php 1:29 not only to believe o him, but also to suffer 1519
2: 4 Look not every man o his own things, but NIG
2: 4 but every man also o the things of others. NIG
2:27 but God had mercy o him; and not on him NIG
2:27 and not o him only, but on me also, lest I NIG
2:27 and not on him only, but o me also, lest I NIG
4: 8 if there be any praise, think o these things. NIG
Col 3: 1 where Christ sitteth o the right hand of 1722
3: 2 Set your affection o things above, not on 5426
3: 2 on things above, not o things on the earth. NIG
3: 2 on things above, not on things o the earth. 1909
3: 6 God cometh o the children of disobedience: 1909
3:10 And have put o the new man, which is 1746
3:12 Put o therefore, as the elect of God, holy 1746
3:14 And above all these things put o charity, NIG
1Th 5: 8 putting o the breastplate of faith and love; 1746
2Th 1: 8 taking vengeance o them that know not NIG
1Ti 1:16 hereafter believe o him to life everlasting. 1909
1:18 to the prophecies which went before o thee, 1909
3:16 believed o in the world, received up into NIG
4:14 with the laying o of the hands of 1936
5:22 Lay hands suddenly o no man, neither be 2007
6:12 good fight of faith, lay hold o eternal life, 1949
6:19 that they may lay hold o eternal life. 1949
2Ti 1: 6 which is in thee by the putting o of my 1936
2:22 with them that call o the Lord out of a pure 1941
Tit 3: 6 Which he shed o us abundantly through 1909
3:13 Bring Zenas the lawyer and Apollos o their journey 4311
Phm 1:18 oweth thee ought, put that o mine account; 1677
Heb 1: 3 sat down o the right hand of the Majesty on 1722
1: 3 sat down on the right hand of the Majesty o 1722
1:13 Sit o my right hand, until I make thine 1537
2:16 For verily he took not o him the nature of 1949
2:16 but he took o him the seed of Abraham. 1949
4: 4 certain place of the seventh day o this wise, 3779
5: 2 Who can have compassion o the ignorant, NIG
5: 2 and o them that are out of the way; NIG
6: 1 of Christ, let us go o unto perfection; 5342
6: 2 and of laying o of hands, and 1936
8: 1 who is set o the right hand of the throne of 1722
8: 4 For if he were o earth, he should not be a 1909
9:10 imposed o them until the time of NIG
10:12 for ever, sat down o the right hand of God; 1722
11:13 were strangers and pilgrims o the earth. 1909
12:25 not who refused him that spake o earth, 1909
Jas 3: 6 and setteth o fire the course of nature; 5394
3: 6 course of nature; and it is set o fire of hell. 5394
4:14 ye know not what shall be o the morrow: 839
5: 5 Ye have lived in pleasure o the earth, and 1909
5:17 it rained not o the earth by the space of 1909
1Pe 1:17 And if ye call o the Father, who without 1941
2: 6 he that believeth o him shall not be 1909
2:24 bare our sins in his own body o the tree, 1909
3: 3 wearing of gold, or of putting o of apparel; 1745
3:22 into heaven, and is o the right hand of God; 1722
4:14 o their part he is evil spoken of, but 2596
4:14 spoken of, but o your part he is glorified. 2596
4:16 but let him glorify God o this behalf. 1722
2Pe 3:12 wherein the heavens being o fire shall be 4448
1Jn 3:23 That we should believe o the name of his NIG
5:10 He that believeth o the Son of God hath 1519
5:13 that believe o the name of the Son of God; 1519
5:13 that ye may believe o the name of the Son 1519
3Jn 1: 6 bring forward o their journey after a 4311
Jude 1:20 building up yourselves o your most holy NIG
Rev 1:10 I was in the spirit o the Lord's day, and 1722
3: 3 I will come o thee as a thief, and thou shalt 1909
4: 2 was set in heaven, and one sat o the throne. 1909
4: 4 and they had o their heads crowns of gold. 1909
4: 9 and thanks to him that sat o the throne, 1909
4:10 fall down before him that sat o the throne, 1909
5: 1 that sat o the throne a book written within 1909
5: 1 a book written within and o the backside, 3693
5:10 and priests: and we shall reign o the earth. 1909
5:13 and o the earth, and under the earth, and 1722
6: 2 and he that sat o him had a bow; and 1909
6: 5 he that sat o him had a pair of balances in 1909
6: 8 and his name that sat o him was Death, and 1883
6:10 avenge our blood o them that dwell on 575
6:10 avenge our blood on them that dwell o 1909
6:16 Fall o us, and hide us from the face of him 1909
6:16 hide us from the face of him that sitteth o 1909
7: 1 standing o the four corners of the earth, 1909
7: 1 that the wind should not blow o the earth, 1909
Rev 7: 1 on the earth, nor o the sea, nor on any tree. 1909
7: 1 on the earth, nor on the sea, nor o any tree. 1909
7:11 and fell before the throne o their faces, and 1909
7:15 he that sitteth o the throne shall dwell 1909
7:16 neither shall the sun light o them, nor any 1909
9: 7 o their heads were as it were crowns like 1909
9:17 and them that sat o them, 1909
10: 2 upon the sea, and his left foot o the earth, 1909
11:10 tormented them that dwelt o the earth. 1909
11:16 which sat before God o their seats, 1909
13:13 from heaven o the earth in the sight of men, 1519
13:14 And deceiveth them that dwell o the earth 1909
13:14 saying to them that dwell o the earth, 1909
14: 1 and lo, a Lamb stood o the mount Sion, and 1909
14: 6 to preach unto them that dwell o the earth, 1909
14:14 having o his head a golden crown, and 1909
14:15 crying with a loud voice to him that sat o 1909
14:16 And he that sat o the cloud thrust in his 1909
14:16 on the cloud thrust in his sickle o the earth; 1909
15: 2 stand o the sea of glass, having the harps of 1909
17: 8 they that dwell o the earth shall wonder, 1909
17: 9 o which the woman sitteth. 1909
18:19 And they cast dust o their heads, and cried, 1909
18:20 for God hath avenged you o her. 1537
19: 4 and worshipped God that sat o the throne, 1909
19:12 of fire, and o his head were many crowns; 1909
19:16 And he hath o his vesture and on his thigh a 1909
19:16 his vesture and o his thigh a name written, 1909
19:18 and of them that sit o them, and the flesh of 1909
19:19 make war against him that sat o the horse, 1909
20: 2 And he laid hold o the dragon, that old 2902
20: 6 o such the second death hath no power, but 1909
20: 9 And they went up o the breadth of 1909
20:11 and him that sat o it, from whose face 1909
21:13 O the east three gates; on the north three 575
21:13 the east three gates; o the north three gates; 575
21:13 o the south three gates; and on the west three 575
21:13 south three gates; and o the west three gates. 575

ONAM (4)

Ge 36:23 and Manahath, and Ebal, Shepho, and O. 208
1Ch 1:40 and Manahath, and Ebal, Shephi, and O. 208
2:26 name was Atarah; she was the mother of O. 208
2:28 And the sons of O were, Shammai, and Jada. 208

ONAN (8)

Ge 38: 4 and bare a son; and she called his name O. 209
38: 8 Judah said unto O, Go in unto thy brother's 209
38: 9 And O knew that the seed should not be his; 209
46:12 Er, and O, and Shelah, and Pharez, and 209
46:12 Er and O died in the land of Canaan. 209
Nu 26:19 The sons of Judah were Er and O: and Er 209
26:19 and Er and O died in the land of Canaan. 209
1Ch 2: 3 The sons of Judah; Er, and O, and Shelah: 209

ONCE (59) [ONE]

Ge 18:32 be angry, and I will speak yet but this o: 6471
Ex 10:17 my sin only this o, and intreat the LORD 6471
30:10 o in a year with the blood of the sin offering 259
30:10 o in the year shall he make atonement upon 259
Lev 16:34 children of Israel for all their sins o a year. 259
Nu 13:30 Let us go up at o, and possess it; 5927+5927
Dt 7:22 thou mayest not consume them at o, 4118
Jos 6: 3 of war, and go round about the city o. 259+6471
6:11 compassed the city, going about it o: 259+6471
6:14 second day they compassed the city o, 259+6471
Jdg 6:39 hot against me, and I will speak but this o: 6471
6:39 I pray thee, but this o with the fleece; 6471
16:18 saying, Come up this o, for he hath shewed 6471
16:28 I pray thee, only this o, O God, 6471
16:28 that I may be at o avenged of the Philistines 259
1Sa 26: 8 with the spear even to the earth at o, 259+6471
1Ki 10:22 o in three years came the navy of Tharshish, 259
2Ki 6:10 and saved himself there, not o nor twice. 259
2Ch 9:21 every three years o came the ships of 259
Ne 5:18 and o in ten days store of all sorts of wine: 996
13:20 all kind of ware lodged without Jerusalem o 6471
Job 33:14 For God speaketh o, yea twice, 259+871.1
40: 5 O have I spoken; but I will not answer: yea, 259
Ps 62:11 God hath spoken o; twice have I heard this; 259
74: 6 the carved work thereof at o with axes 3162
76: 7 who may stand in thy sight when o 227+4480
89:35 O have I sworn by my holiness that I will 259
Pr 28:18 he that is perverse in his ways shall fall at o. 259
Isa 42:14 I will destroy and devour at o. 3162
66: 8 or shall a nation be born at o? for as 259+6471
Jer 10:18 out the inhabitants of the land at this o, 6471
13:27 not be made clean? when shall it o be? 5750
16:21 this o cause them to know, 6471+871.1+1886.1
Hag 2: 6 Yet o, it is a little while, and I will shake 259
Lk 13:25 When o the master of the house 302+575+3739
23:18 And they cried out all at o, saying, 3826
Ro 6:10 For in that he died, he died unto sin o: but 2178
7: 9 For I was alive without the law o: but 4218
1Co 15: 6 seen of above five hundred brethren at o; 2178
2Co 11:25 o was I stoned, thrice I suffered shipwreck, 530
Gal 1:23 preacheth the faith which o he destroyed. 4218
Eph 5: 3 let it not be o named amongst you, 3366
Php 4:16 For even in Thessalonica ye sent o and again 530
1Th 2:18 come unto you, even I Paul, o and again; 530
Heb 6: 4 For it is impossible for those who were o 530
7:27 for this he did o, when he offered up 2178
9: 7 went the high priest alone o every year, 530
9:12 by his own blood he entered in o into 2178
9:26 now o in the end of the world hath he 530
9:27 And as it is appointed unto men o to die, but 530
9:28 So Christ was o offered to bear the sins of 530
10: 2 that the worshippers o purged should have 530
10:10 of the body of Jesus Christ o for all. 2178
12:26 Yet o more I shake not the earth only, but 530
12:27 And this word, Yet o more, signifieth 530
1Pe 3:18 For Christ also hath o suffered for sins, 530
3:20 when o the longsuffering of God waited in 530
Jude 1: 3 faith which was o delivered unto the saints. 530
Jude 1: 5 though ye o knew this, how that the Lord, 530

ONE (1967) [ONCE, ONE'S, ONES]

Ge 1: 9 heaven be gathered together unto o place, 259
2:21 he took o of his ribs, and closed up the flesh 259
2:24 unto his wife: and they shall be o flesh. 259
3: 6 a tree to be desired to make o wise, she took NIH
3:22 Behold, the man is become as o of us, 259
4:14 that every o that findeth me shall slay me. 3605
4:19 the name of the o was Adah, and the name of 259
10: 5 every o after his tongue, after their families, 376
10: 8 he began to be a mighty o in the earth. NIH
10:25 the name of o was Peleg; for in his days was 259
11: 1 And the whole earth was of o language, and 259
11: 1 earth was of one language, and of o speech. 259
11: 3 they said o to another, Go to, let us make 376
11: 6 the people is o, and they have all one 259
11: 6 people is one, and they have all o language; 259
11: 7 that they may not understand o another's 376
13:11 they separated themselves the o from 376
14:13 there came o that had escaped, and NIH
15: 3 and lo, o born in my house is mine heir. 1121
15:10 and laid each piece o[S] against another: 2050.2
19: 9 they said again, This o fellow came in to 259
19:14 he seemed as o that mocked unto his sons in NIH
19:20 city is near to flee unto, and it is a little o: 4705
19:20 let me escape thither, (is it not a little o?) 4705
21:15 and she cast the child under o of the shrubs. 259
22: 2 offer him there for a burnt offering upon o of 259
24:41 if they give not thee o, thou shalt be clear NIH
25:23 the o people shall be stronger than the other NIH
26:10 o of the people might lightly have lien with 259
26:26 Ahuzzath o of his friends, and Phichol NIH
26:31 in the morning, and sware o to another: 376
27:29 cursed be every o that curseth thee, and NIH
27:38 Hast thou but o blessing, my father? 259
27:45 I be deprived also of you both in o day? 259
30:33 every o that is not speckled and 3605
30:35 and every o that had some white in it, and 3605
31:49 when we are absent o from another. 376
32: 8 If Esau come to the o company, and smite it, 259
33:13 if men should overdrive them o day, all 259
34:14 to give our sister to o that is uncircumcised; 376
34:16 with you, and we will become o people. 259
34:22 to be o people, if every male among us be 259
37:19 they said o to another, Behold, this dreamer 376
38:28 she travailed, that the o put out his hand: NIH
40: 5 both of them, each man his dream in o night, 259
41: 5 seven ears of corn came up upon o stalk, 259
41:11 we dreamed a dream in o night, I and he; 259
41:22 seven ears came up in o stalk, full and good: 259
41:25 unto Pharaoh, The dream of Pharaoh is o: 259
41:26 good ears are seven years: the dream is o. 259
41:38 Can we find such a o as this is, a man in NIH
42: 1 his sons, Why do ye look o upon another? NIH
42:11 We are all o man's sons; we are true men, 259
42:13 the sons of o man in the land of Canaan; 259
42:13 is this day with our father, and o is not. 259
42:16 Send o of you, and let him fetch your 259
42:19 If ye be true men, let o of your brethren be 259
42:21 they said o to another, We are verily guilty 376
42:27 as o of them opened his sack to give his ass 259
42:28 and they were afraid, saying o to another, 376
42:32 o is not, and the youngest is this day with 259
42:33 men; leave o of your brethren here with me, 259
43:33 and the men marvelled o at another. 376
44:20 and a child of his old age, a little o; 6996
44:28 the o went out from me, and I said, Surely he 259
47:21 he removed them to cities from o end of NIH
48: 1 that o told Joseph, Behold, thy father is NIH
48: 2 o told Jacob, and said, Behold, thy son NIH
48:22 Moreover I have given to thee o portion 259
49:16 judge his people, as o of the tribes of Israel. 259
49:28 every o according to his blessing he blessed 376
Ex 1:15 of which the name of the o was Shiphrah, 259
2: 6 and said, This is o of the Hebrews' children. NIH
2:11 smiting a Hebrew, o of his brethren. NIH
6:25 Eleazar Aaron's son took him o of NIH
8:31 and from his people; there remained not o. 259
9: 6 the cattle of the children of Israel died not o. 259
9: 7 there was not o of the cattle of the Israelites 259
10: 5 that o cannot be able to see the earth: NIH
10:19 there remained not o locust in all the coasts 259
10:23 They saw not o another, neither rose any 376
11: 1 Yet will I bring o plague more upon 259
12:18 until the o and twentieth day of the month at 259
12:30 was not a house where there was not o dead. NIH
12:46 In o house shall it be eaten; thou shalt not 259
12:48 and he shall be as o that is born in the land: NIH
12:49 O law shall be to him that is homeborn, and 259
14: 7 and captains over every o of them. 3605
14:20 that the o came not near the other all 2088
14:28 there remained not so much as o of them. 259
16:15 of Israel saw it, they said o to another, 376
16:22 two omers for o man: and all the rulers of 259
17:12 the o on the one side, and the other on 259
17:12 the one on the o side, and the other on 2088
18: 3 of which the name of the o was Gershom; 259
18:16 I judge between o and another, and I do 376
21:18 o smite another with a stone, or with his fist, 376
21:35 if o man's ox hurt another's, that he die; 376
23:29 drive them out from before thee in o year; 259
24: 3 all the people answered with o voice, and 259
25:12 and two rings shall be in the o side of it, and 259
25:19 make o cherub on the one end, and the other 259
25:19 make one cherub on the o end, and 2088
25:20 their faces shall look o to another; 376
25:32 three branches of the candlestick out of the o 259
25:33 with a knop and a flower in o branch; 259
25:36 all it shall be o beaten work of pure gold. 259
26: 2 The length of o curtain shall be eight and 259
26: 2 and the breadth of o[S] curtain four cubits: 1886.1
26: 2 every o of the curtains shall have one 259
26: 2 every one of the curtains shall have o 259
26: 3 The five curtains shall be coupled together o 802

O

Ex 26: 3 *other* five curtains *shall be* coupled **o** to 802
26: 4 **o** curtain from the selvedge in the coupling; 259
26: 5 Fifty loops shalt thou make in the **o** curtain, 259
26: 5 that the loops may take hold **o** of another. 802
26: 6 with the taches: and it shall be **o** tabernacle. 259
26: 8 The length of **o** curtain *shall be* thirty cubits, 259
26: 8 and the breadth of **o** curtain four cubits: 259
26: 8 the eleven curtains *shall be all* of **o** measure. 259
26:10 the **o** curtain *that is* outmost in the coupling, 259
26:11 and couple the tent together, that it may be **o**. 259
26:13 a cubit on the **o side**, and a cubit on 2088
26:16 and a half *shall be* the breadth of **o** board. 259
26:17 Two tenons *shall there be* in **o** board, set in 259
26:17 in one board, set in order **o** against another: 802
26:19 two sockets under **o** board for his two 259
26:21 two sockets under **o** board, and two sockets 259
26:24 together above the head of it unto **o** ring: 259
26:25 two sockets under **o** board, and two sockets 259
26:26 five for the boards of the **o** side of 259
27: 9 linen of an hundred cubits long for **o** side: 259
27:14 The hangings of ***o*** side *of the gate shall be* NIH
28:10 Six of their names on **o** stone, and the *other* 259
28:21 **every o** with his name shall they be 376
29: 1 Take **o** young bullock, and two rams without 259
29: 3 thou shalt put them into **o** basket, and 259
29:15 Thou shalt also take **o** ram; and Aaron and 259
29:23 **o** loaf of bread, and one cake of oiled bread, 259
29:23 **o** cake of oiled bread, and one wafer out of 259
29:23 **o** wafer out of the basket of the unleavened 259
29:39 The **o** lamb thou shalt offer in the morning; 259
29:40 with the **o** lamb a tenth deal of flour mingled 259
30:13 **every o** that passeth among them that are 3605
30:14 **Every o** that passeth among them that are 3605
31:14 *every* **o** that defileth it shall surely be put to NIH
32:15 on **the o side** and on the other *were* they 2088
33: 7 *that* **every o** which sought the LORD went 3605
34:15 and ***o*** call thee, and thou eat of his sacrifice; NIH
35:21 every **o** whose heart stirred him up, and 376
35:21 **every o** whom his spirit made willing, *and* 3605
35:24 **Every o** that did offer an offering of silver 3605
36: 2 *even* **every o** whose heart stirred him up to 3605
36: 9 The length of **o** curtain *was* twenty and 259
36: 9 the breadth of **o** curtain four cubits: 259
36: 9 four cubits: the curtains *were* all of **o** size. 259
36:10 he coupled the five curtains **o** unto another: 259
36:10 *the other* five curtains he coupled **o** unto 259
36:11 he made loops of blue on the edge of **o** 259
36:12 Fifty loops made he in **o** curtain, and 259
36:12 the loops held **o** *curtain* to another. 259
36:13 coupled the curtains **o** unto another with 259
36:13 with the taches: so it became **o** tabernacle. 259
36:15 The length of **o** curtain *was* thirty cubits, and 259
36:15 and four cubits *was* the breadth of **o** curtain: 259
36:15 the eleven curtains *were* of **o** size. 259
36:18 to couple the tent together, that *it* might be **o**. 259
36:21 and the breadth of a board **o** cubit and a half. 259
36:22 **O** board had two tenons, equally distant one 259
36:22 two tenons, equally distant **o** from another: 259
36:24 two sockets under **o** board for his two 259
36:26 two sockets under **o** board, and two sockets 259
36:29 together at the head thereof, to **o** ring: 259
36:31 five for the boards of the **o** side of 259
36:33 the boards from **the o** end to the other. 1886.1
37: 3 even two rings upon the **o** side of it, and 259
37: 6 and **o** cubit and a half the breadth thereof. NIH
37: 7 **beaten out of o piece** made he them, on 4749
37: 8 **O** cherub on the end on this side, and 259
37: 9 the mercy seat, with their faces **o** to another; 376
37:18 three branches of the candlestick out of the **o** 259
37:19 after the fashion of almonds in **o** branch, 259
37:22 all of it *was* **o** beaten work *of* pure gold. 259
38:14 The hangings of the ***o*** side *of the gate were* NIH
38:26 for **every o** that went to be numbered, 3605
39:14 **every o** with his name, according to 376
Lev 4:27 if any **o** of the common people sin through 5315
5: 4 *of it,* then he shall be guilty in **o** of these. 259
5: 5 when he shall be guilty in **o** of these *things,* 259
5: 7 **o** for a sin offering, and the other for a burnt 259
5:13 his sin that he hath sinned in **o** of these, 259
6:18 **every o** that toucheth them shall be holy. 3605
7: 7 *there is* **o** law for them: the priest that 259
7:10 sons of Aaron have, **o** *as much* as another. 376
7:14 of it he shall offer **o** out of the whole 259
8:26 he took **o** unleavened cake, and a cake of 259
8:26 **o** wafer, and put *them* on the fat, and 259
11:26 **every o** that toucheth them shall be 3605
12: 8 the **o** for the burnt offering, and the other for 259
13: 2 the priest, or unto **o** of his sons the priests: 259
14: 5 the priest shall command that **o** of the birds 259
14:10 **o** ewe lamb of the first year without blemish, 259
14:10 mingled with oil, and **o** log of oil. 259
14:12 the priest shall take **o** he lamb, and offer him 259
14:21 he shall take **o** lamb *for* a trespass offering to 259
14:21 **o tenth deal** of fine flour mingled 259+6241
14:22 the **o** shall be a sin offering, and the other a 259
14:30 And he shall offer the **o** of the turtledoves, or 259
14:31 the **o** *for* a sin offering, and the other *for* a 259
14:50 he shall kill the **o** of the birds in an earthen 259
15:15 the **o** *for* a sin offering, and the other *for* a 259
15:30 the priest shall offer the **o** *for* a sin offering, 259
16: 5 a sin offering, and **o** ram for a burnt offering. 259
16: 8 **o** lot for the LORD, and the other lot for 259
16:27 *place,* shall ***o*** carry forth without the camp; NIH
16:29 do no work *at all, whether it be* **o**S of your 1886.1
17:15 *whether it be* **o** of your own country, 1886.1
18:30 that *ye* commit not *any* **o** *of these* NIH
19: 8 Therefore *every* **o** that eateth it shall bear NIH
19:11 neither deal falsely, neither lie **o** to another. 376
19:34 shall be unto you as **o born amongst** you, 249
20: 9 For **every o** that curseth his father or 376+376
22:28 shall not kill it and her young both in **o** day. 259
23:18 and **o** young bullock, and two rams: 259
23:19 ye shall sacrifice **o** kid of the goats for a sin 259
24: 5 two tenth deals shall be *in* **o** cake. 259
24:22 Ye shall have **o manner** of law, as well for 259

Lev 24:22 the stranger, as for **o of** your **own country**: 249
25:14 ye shall not oppress **o** another: 376
25:17 Ye shall not therefore oppress **o** another; but 376
25:46 ye shall not rule **o** over another with rigour. 376
25:48 **o** of his brethren may redeem him: 259
26:26 ten women shall bake your bread in **o** oven, 259
26:37 they shall fall **o** upon another, as it were 376
Nu 1: 4 every **o** head of the house of his fathers. 376
1:41 *were* forty and **o** thousand and five hundred. 259
1:44 each **o** was for the house of his fathers. 259
2:16 fifty and **o** thousand and four hundred and 259
2:28 *were* forty and **o** thousand and five hundred. 259
2:34 they set forward, **every o** after their families, 376
4:19 appoint them **every o** to his service and 376+376
4:30 **every o** that entereth into the service, to do 3605
4:35 **every o** that entereth into the service, 3605
4:39 **every o** that entereth into the service, 3605
4:43 **every o** that entereth into the service, 3605
4:47 **every o** that came to do the service of 3605
4:49 **every o** according to his service, and 376+376
5: 2 **every o** that hath an issue, and 3605
6:11 the priest shall offer the **o** for a sin offering, 259
6:14 **o** he lamb of the first year without blemish 259
6:14 **o** ewe lamb of the first year without blemish 259
6:14 **o** ram without blemish for peace offerings, 259
6:19 and **o** unleavened cake out of the basket, and 259
6:19 **o** unleavened wafer, and shall put *them* upon 259
7: 3 for two of the princes, and for *each* **o** an ox: 259
7:13 his offering *was* **o** silver charger, the weight 259
7:13 thirty *shekels,* **o** silver bowl of seventy 259
7:14 **O** spoon of ten *shekels* of gold, full *of* 259
7:15 **O** young bullock, one ram, one lamb of 259
7:15 One young bullock, **o** ram, one lamb of 259
7:15 one ram, **o** lamb of the first year, 259
7:16 **O** kid of the goats for a sin offering: 259
7:19 He offered *for* his offering **o** silver charger, 259
7:19 thirty *shekels,* **o** silver bowl of seventy 259
7:20 **O** spoon of gold of ten *shekels,* full *of* 259
7:21 **O** young bullock, one ram, one lamb of 259
7:21 One young bullock, **o** ram, one lamb of 259
7:21 one ram, **o** lamb of the first year, 259
7:22 **O** kid of the goats for a sin offering: 259
7:25 His offering *was* **o** silver charger, the weight 259
7:25 thirty *shekels,* **o** silver bowl of seventy 259
7:26 **O** golden spoon of ten *shekels,* full *of* 259
7:27 **O** young bullock, one ram, one lamb of 259
7:27 One young bullock, **o** ram, one lamb of 259
7:27 one ram, **o** lamb of the first year, 259
7:28 **O** kid of the goats for a sin offering: 259
7:31 His offering *was* **o** silver charger of 259
7:31 thirty *shekels,* **o** silver bowl of seventy 259
7:32 **O** golden spoon *of* ten *shekels,* full *of* 259
7:33 **O** young bullock, one ram, one lamb of 259
7:33 One young bullock, **o** ram, one lamb of 259
7:33 one ram, **o** lamb of the first year, 259
7:34 **O** kid of the goats for a sin offering: 259
7:37 His offering *was* **o** silver charger, the weight 259
7:37 thirty *shekels,* **o** silver bowl of seventy 259
7:38 **O** golden spoon of ten *shekels,* full *of* 259
7:39 **O** young bullock, one ram, one lamb of 259
7:39 One young bullock, **o** ram, one lamb of 259
7:39 one ram, **o** lamb of the first year, 259
7:40 **O** kid of the goats for a sin offering: 259
7:43 His offering *was* **o** silver charger of 259
7:44 **O** golden spoon of ten *shekels,* full *of* 259
7:45 **O** young bullock, one ram, one lamb of 259
7:45 One young bullock, **o** ram, one lamb of 259
7:45 one ram, **o** lamb of the first year, 259
7:46 **O** kid of the goats for a sin offering: 259
7:49 His offering *was* **o** silver charger, the weight 259
7:49 thirty *shekels,* **o** silver bowl of seventy 259
7:50 **O** golden spoon of ten *shekels,* full *of* 259
7:51 **O** young bullock, one ram, one lamb of 259
7:51 One young bullock, **o** ram, one lamb of 259
7:51 one ram, **o** lamb of the first year, 259
7:52 **O** kid of the goats for a sin offering: 259
7:55 His offering *was* **o** silver charger of 259
7:55 thirty *shekels,* **o** silver bowl of seventy 259
7:56 **O** golden spoon of ten *shekels,* full *of* 259
7:57 **O** young bullock, one ram, one lamb of 259
7:57 One young bullock, **o** ram, one lamb of 259
7:57 one ram, **o** lamb of the first year, 259
7:58 **O** kid of the goats for a sin offering: 259
7:61 His offering *was* **o** silver charger, the weight 259
7:61 thirty *shekels,* **o** silver bowl of seventy 259
7:62 **O** golden spoon of ten *shekels,* full *of* 259
7:63 **O** young bullock, one ram, one lamb of 259
7:63 One young bullock, **o** ram, one lamb of 259
7:63 one ram, **o** lamb of the first year, 259
7:64 **O** kid of the goats for a sin offering: 259
7:67 His offering *was* **o** silver charger, the weight 259
7:67 thirty *shekels,* **o** silver bowl of seventy 259
7:68 **O** golden spoon of ten *shekels,* full *of* 259
7:69 **O** young bullock, one ram, one lamb of 259
7:69 One young bullock, **o** ram, one lamb of 259
7:69 one ram, **o** lamb of the first year, 259
7:70 **O** kid of the goats for a sin offering: 259
7:73 His offering *was* **o** silver charger, the weight 259
7:73 thirty *shekels,* **o** silver bowl of seventy 259
7:74 **O** golden spoon of ten *shekels,* full *of* 259
7:75 **O** young bullock, one ram, one lamb of 259
7:75 One young bullock, **o** ram, one lamb of 259
7:75 one ram, **o** lamb of the first year, 259
7:76 **O** kid of the goats for a sin offering: 259
7:79 His offering *was* **o** silver charger, the weight 259
7:79 thirty *shekels,* **o** silver bowl of seventy 259
7:80 **O** golden spoon of ten *shekels,* full *of* 259
7:81 **O** young bullock, one ram, one lamb of 259
7:81 One young bullock, **o** ram, one lamb of 259
7:81 one ram, **o** lamb of the first year, 259
7:82 **O** kid of the goats for a sin offering: 259
7:89 he heard the voice of **o** speaking unto him NIH
8:12 thou shalt offer the **o** *for* a sin offering, and 259
9:14 ye shall have **o** ordinance, both for 259
10: 4 *but* with **o** *trumpet,* then the princes, 259

Nu 11:19 Ye shall not eat **o** day, nor two days, nor five 259
11:26 the name of the **o** *was* Eldad, and the name 259
11:28 ***o*** of his young men, answered and said, NIH
12:12 Let her not be as **o** dead, of whom 1886.1
13: 2 ye send a man, **every o** a ruler among them. 3605
13:23 cut down from thence a branch with **o** 259
14: 4 they said **o** to another, Let us make a captain, 376
14:15 Now *if* thou shalt kill *all* this people as **o** 259
15: 5 the burnt offering or sacrifice, for **o** lamb. 259
15:11 Thus shall it be done for **o** bullock, or 259
15:11 or for **o** ram, or for a lamb, or a kid. 259
15:12 shall ye do to *every* **o** according to their 259
15:15 **O** ordinance *shall be both* for you *of* 259
15:16 **O** law and one manner shall be for you, and 259
15:16 One law and **o** manner shall be for you, and 259
15:24 that all the congregation shall offer **o** young 259
15:24 and **o** kid of the goats for a sin offering. 259
15:29 You shall have **o** law for him that sinneth 259
16: 3 **every o** of them, and the LORD *is* among 3605
16:15 I have not taken **o** ass from them, 259
16:15 ass from them, neither have I hurt **o** of them. 259
16:22 shall **o** man sin, and wilt thou be wroth with 259
17: 2 take of every **o** of them a rod according to NIH
17: 3 for **o** rod *shall be* for the head of the house of 259
17: 6 **every o** of their princes gave him a rod 3605
17: 6 for each prince **o**, according to their fathers' 259
18:11 **every o** *that is* clean in thy house shall eat 3605
18:13 **every o** *that is* clean in thine house shall eat 3605
19: 3 and ***o*** shall slay her before his face: NIH
19: 5 ***o*** shall burn the heifer in his sight; her skin, NIH
19:16 whosoever toucheth **o** that is slain with a 1886.1
19:18 a bone, or **o** slain, or one dead, or a grave: 1886.1
19:18 a bone, or one slain, or **o** dead, or a grave: 1886.1
21: 8 come to pass, that **every o** that is bitten, 3605
25: 5 Slay ye **every o** his men that were joined 376
25: 6 **o** of the children of Israel came and 376
26:54 *to* **every o** shall his inheritance be given 376
28: 4 The **o** lamb shalt thou offer in the morning, 259
28: 7 *be* the fourth *part* of a hin for the **o** lamb: 259
28:11 two young bullocks, and **o** ram, seven lambs 259
28:12 mingled with oil, for **o** bullock; 259
28:12 a meat offering, mingled with oil, for **o** ram; 259
28:13 with oil *for* a meat offering unto **o** lamb; 259
28:15 **o** kid of the goats for a sin offering unto 259
28:19 and **o** ram, and seven lambs of the first year: 259
28:22 **o** goat for a sin offering, to make an 259
28:27 two young bullocks, **o** ram, seven lambs of 259
28:28 three tenth deals unto **o** bullock, two tenth 259
28:28 one bullock, two tenth deals unto **o** ram, 259
28:29 A several tenth deal unto **o** lamb, throughout 259
28:30 *And* **o** kid of the goats, to make an 259
29: 2 **o** young bullock, one ram, *and* seven lambs 259
29: 2 **o** ram, *and* seven lambs of the first year 259
29: 4 **o** tenth deal for one lamb, throughout 259
29: 4 one tenth deal for **o** lamb, throughout 259
29: 5 **o** kid of the goats for a sin offering, to make 259
29: 8 **o** young bullock, one ram, *and* seven lambs 259
29: 8 **o** ram, *and* seven lambs of the first year; 259
29: 9 to a bullock, *and* two tenth deals to **o** ram, 259
29:10 A several tenth deal for **o** lamb, throughout 259
29:11 **O** kid of the goats *for* a sin offering; beside 259
29:16 **o** kid of the goats *for* a sin offering; beside 259
29:19 **o** kid of the goats *for* a sin offering; beside 259
29:22 **o** goat for a sin offering; beside the continual 259
29:25 **o** kid of the goats *for* a sin offering; beside 259
29:28 **o** goat for a sin offering; beside the continual 259
29:31 **o** goat for a sin offering; beside the continual 259
29:34 **o** goat for a sin offering; beside the continual 259
29:36 **o** bullock, one ram, seven lambs of the first 259
29:36 one bullock, **o** ram, seven lambs of the first 259
29:38 **o** goat for a sin offering; beside the continual 259
31:28 **o** soul of five hundred, *both* of the persons, 259
31:30 thou shalt take **o** portion of fifty, of 259
31:34 And threescore and **o** thousand asses, 259
31:39 tribute *was* **threescore and o**. 259+8346+2050.1
31:47 Moses took **o** portion of fifty, *both* of man 259
31:49 and there lacketh not **o man** of us. 376
34:18 ye shall take **o** prince of every tribe, 259
35: 8 **every o** shall give of his cities unto 376
35:15 that **every o** that killeth *any* person 3605
35:30 **o** witness shall not testify against *any* person 259
36: 7 for **every o** of the children of Israel shall 376
36: 8 shall be wife unto **o** of the family of the tribe 259
36: 9 Neither shall the inheritance remove from ***o*** NIH
36: 9 **every o** of the tribes of the children of Israel 376
Dt 1:22 ye came near unto me **every o** of you, and 3605
1:23 I took twelve men of you, **o** of a tribe: 259
1:35 Surely there shall not **o** of these men of this 376
2:36 there was not **o** city too strong for us: NIH
4: 4 your God *are* alive **every o** of you *this* day. 3605
4:32 *ask* from the **o** side of heaven unto NIH
4:42 that fleeing unto **o** of these cities he might 259
6: 4 O Israel: The LORD our God *is* **o** LORD: 259
12:14 the LORD shall choose in **o** of thy tribes, 259
13: 7 from the ***o*** end of the earth even unto NIH
13:12 If thou shalt hear *say* in **o** of thy cities, 259
15: 7 If there be among you a poor man of **o** of thy 259
17: 6 at the mouth of **o** witness he shall not be put 259
17:15 ***o*** from among thy brethren shalt thou set NIH
18:10 There shall not be found among you *any* ***o*** NIH
19: 5 he shall flee unto **o** of those cities, and live: 259
19:11 that he die, and fleeth into **o** of these cities: 259
19:15 **O** witness shall not rise up against a man for 259
21: 1 If ***o*** be found slain in the land which NIH
21:15 **o** beloved, and another hated, and they have 259
23:16 in *that* place which he shall choose in **o** of 259
24: 5 *but* he shall be free at home **o** year, and 259
25: 5 and **o** of them die, and have no child, 259
25:11 When men strive together **o** with another, 376
25:11 the wife of the **o** draweth near for to deliver 259
28: 7 they shall come out against thee **o** way, and 259
28:25 thou shalt go out **o** way against them, and 259
28:57 towards her **young o** that cometh out from 7988
28:64 from the **o** end of the earth even unto NIH
32:30 How should **o** chase a thousand, and two put 259

Dt 33: 3 thy feet; *every* **o** shall receive of thy words. NIH
33: 8 and thy Urim *be* with thy holy **o**, 376
Jos 9: 2 with Joshua and with Israel, *with* **o** accord. 259
10: 2 as **o** of the royal cities, and because it *was* 259
10:42 and their land did Joshua take *at* **o** time, 259
12: 9 The king of Jericho, **o**; the king of Ai, 259
12: 9 the king of Ai, which *is* beside Beth-el, **o**; 259
12:10 The king of Jerusalem, **o**; the king of 259
12:10 of Jerusalem, one; the king of Hebron, **o**; 259
12:11 The king of Jarmuth, **o**; the king of Lachish, 259
12:11 king of Jarmuth, one; the king of Lachish, **o**; 259
12:12 The king of Eglon, **o**; the king of Gezer, one; 259
12:12 The king of Eglon, one; the king of Gezer, **o**; 259
12:13 The king of Debir, **o**; the king of Geder, one; 259
12:13 The king of Debir, one; the king of Geder, **o**; 259
12:14 The king of Hormah, **o**; the king of Arad, 259
12:14 king of Hormah, one; the king of Arad, **o**; 259
12:15 The king of Libnah, **o**; the king of Adullam, 259
12:15 king of Libnah, one; the king of Adullam, **o**; 259
12:16 The king of Makkedah, **o**; the king of 259
12:16 of Makkedah, one; the king of Beth-el, **o**; 259
12:17 The king of Tappuah, **o**; the king of Hepher, 259
12:17 king of Tappuah, one; the king of Hepher, **o**; 259
12:18 The king of Aphek, **o**; the king of Lasharon, 259
12:18 king of Aphek, one; the king of Lasharon, **o**; 259
12:19 The king of Madon, **o**; the king of Hazor, 259
12:19 king of Madon, one; the king of Hazor, **o**; 259
12:20 The king of Shimron-meron, **o**; the king of 259
12:20 one; the king of Achshaph, **o**; 259
12:21 The king of Taanach, **o**; the king of 259
12:21 of Taanach, one; the king of Megiddo, **o**; 259
12:22 The king of Kedesh, **o**; the king of Jokneam 259
12:22 one; the king of Jokneam of Carmel, **o**; 259
12:23 The king of Dor in the coast of Dor, **o**; 259
12:23 one; the king of the nations of Gilgal, **o**; 259
12:24 The king of Tirzah, **o**: all the kings thirty and 259
12:24 of Tirzah, one: all the kings thirty and **o**. 259
13:31 *even* to the **o half** of the children of Machir 2677
17:14 given me *but* **o** lot and one portion to inherit, 259
17:14 given me *but* one lot and **o** portion to inherit, 259
17:17 great power: thou shalt not have **o** lot *only:* 259
20: 4 when he that doth flee unto **o** of those cities 259
21:42 These **cities** were **every o** with their 5892+5892
22: 7 Now to the **o** half of the tribe of Manasseh NIH
22:14 **each o** *was* a head of the house of their 376
23:10 **O** man of you shall chase a thousand: for 259
23:14 that not **o** thing hath failed of all the good 259
23:14 unto you, *and* not **o** thing hath failed thereof. 259
Jdg 6:16 and thou shalt smite the Midianites as **o** man. 259
6:29 they said **o** to another, Who hath done this 376
6:31 because **o** hath cast down his altar. NIH
7: 5 **Every o** that lappeth of the water with his 3605
7: 5 likewise **every o** that boweth down upon 3605
8:18 *each* **o** resembled the children of a king. 259
9: 2 reign over you, or that **o** reign over you? 259
9: 5 and ten persons, upon **o** stone: 259
9:18 upon **o** stone, and have made Abimelech, 259
10:18 *and* princes of Gilead said **o** to another, 376
11:35 and thou art **o** of them that trouble me: NIH
12: 7 and was buried in **o** *of* the cities of Gilead. NIH
16: 5 we will give thee **every o** *of us* eleven 376
16:29 of the **o** with his right hand, and of the other 259
17: 5 and teraphim, and consecrated **o** of his sons, 259
17:11 the young man was unto him as **o** of his 259
18:19 thee to be a priest unto the house of **o** man, 259
19:13 let us draw near to **o** of *these* places to lodge 259
20: 1 the congregation was gathered together as **o** 259
20: 8 all the people arose as **o** man, saying, 259
20:11 against the city, knit together as **o** man. 259
20:16 every **o** could sling stones at a hair *breadth,* 2088
20:31 *of* which **o** goeth up *to* the house of God, and 259
21: 3 that there should be to day **o** tribe lacking in 259
21: 6 There is **o** tribe cut off from Israel *this* day. 259
21: 8 What **o** *is there* of the tribes of Israel that 259
Ru 1: 4 the name of the **o** *was* Orpah, and the name 259
2:13 though I be not like unto **o** of thy 259
2:20 near of kin unto us, **o of** our next kinsmen. 4480
3:14 she rose up before **o** could know another. 376
4: 1 **such a o**, turn aside, sit down here. 492+6423
1Sa 1: 2 the name of the **o** *was* Hannah, and the name 259
1:24 **o** ephah of flour, and a bottle of wine, and 259
2:25 If **o man** sin against another, the judge shall 376
2:34 in **o** day they shall die both of them. 259
2:36 *that* **every o** that is left in thine house shall 3605
2:36 I pray thee, into **o** of the priests' offices, 259
3:11 *at* which both the ears of **every o** that 3605
6: 4 for **o** plague *was* on you all, and on your 259
6:17 for Ashdod **o**, for Gaza one, for Askelon 259
6:17 for Ashdod one, for Gaza **o**, for Askelon 259
6:17 for Gaza one, for Askelon **o**, for Gath one, 259
6:17 for Askelon one, for Gath **o**, for Ekron one; 259
6:17 for Askelon one, for Gath one, for Ekron **o**; 259
9: 3 Take now **o** of the servants with thee, 259
10: 3 **o** carrying three kids, and another carrying 259
10:11 then the people said **o** to another, 376
10:12 And **o** of the same place answered and said, 376
11: 7 and they came out with **o** consent. 259
13: 1 Saul reigned **o** year; and when he had 1121
13:17 **o** company turned unto the way that leadeth 259
14: 4 *there was* a sharp rock on the **o** side, and 2088
14: 4 the name of the **o** *was* Bozez, and the name 259
14: 5 The forefront of the **o** *was* situate northward 259
14:16 and they went on beating down **o** *another.* NIH
14:28 answered **o** of the people, and said, 376
14:40 Be ye on **o** side, and I and Jonathan my son 259
14:45 there shall not **o** hair **of** his head fall to 4480
16:18 answered **o** of the servants, and said, Behold, 259
17: 3 stood on a mountain on the **o side**, 2088
17: 7 and **o** bearing a shield went before him. NIH
17:36 this uncircumcised Philistine shall be as **o** of 259
18: 7 the women answered **o** *another* as they NIH
18:21 day be my son in law in *the* **o** *of* the twain. NIH
19:22 **o** said, Behold, *they be* at Naioth in Ramah. NIH
20:15 of David **every o** from the face of the earth. 376
20:41 they kissed **o** another, and wept one with 376

1Sa 20:41 wept **o** with another, until David exceeded. 376
21:11 did they not sing **o** to another of him in NIH
22: 2 every **o** *that was* in distress, and every one 376
22: 2 every **o** that was in debt, and every one *that* 376
22: 2 in debt, and every **o** *that was* discontented, 376
22: 7 will the son of Jesse give **every o** of you 3605
22:20 **o** of the sons of Ahimelech the son of 259
25:14 **o** of the young men told Abigail, 259
26:15 for there came **o** of the people in to destroy 259
26:20 as when **o** doth hunt a partridge in NIH
26:22 let **o** of the young men come over and 259
27: 1 I shall now perish **o** day by the hand of Saul: 259
29: 5 of whom they sang **o** to another in dances, NIH
2Sa 1:15 David called **o** of the young men, and said, 259
2:13 the **o** on the one side of the pool, and 428
2:13 the one on the **o side** of the pool, 2088+4480
2:16 they caught **every o** his fellow by the head, 376
2:21 and lay thee hold on **o** of the young men, and 259
2:25 became **o** troop, and stood on the top of a 259
2:27 gone up **every o** from following his brother. 376
3:13 **o** thing I require of thee, that is, Thou shalt 259
3:29 let there not fail from the house of Joab **o** NIH
4: 2 the name of the **o** *was* Baanah, and the name 259
4:10 When **o**[S] told me, saying, Behold, Saul is 1886.1
6:19 to **every o** a cake of bread, and a good piece 376
6:19 all the people departed **every o** to his house. 376
6:20 as **o** of the vain *fellows* shamelessly 259
7:23 what **o** nation in the earth *is* like thy people, 259
8: 2 and *with* **o**[S] full line to keep alive. 1886.1
9:11 shall eat at my table, as **o** of the king's sons. 259
10: 4 shaved off the **o** half of their beards, and NIH
11: 3 **o** said, *Is* not this Bath-sheba, the daughter NIH
11:25 for the sword devoureth **o** as well as 2090
12: 1 said unto him, There were two men in **o** city; 259
12: 1 in one city; the **o** rich, and the other poor. 259
12: 3 save **o** little ewe lamb, which he had bought 259
13:13 thou shalt be as **o** of the fools in Israel. 259
13:30 king's sons, and there is not **o** of them left. 259
14: 6 but the **o** smote the other, and slew him. 259
14:11 there shall not **o** hair **of** thy son fall to 4480
14:12 speak **o** word unto my lord the king. NIH
14:13 for the king doth speak this thing as **o** which NIH
14:27 and **o** daughter, whose name *was* Tamar: 259
15: 2 Thy servant *is* of **o** of the tribes of Israel. 259
15:31 **o** told David, saying, Ahithophel *is* among NIH
17:12 with him there shall not be left so much as **o**. 259
17:13 until there be not **o** small stone found there. NIH
17:22 by the morning light there lacked not **o** *of* 259
18:17 and all Israel fled **every o** to his tent. 376
19: 7 there will not tarry **o** with thee *this* night: 376
19:14 men of Judah, *even* as *the heart of* **o** man; 259
20:11 And **o** of Joab's men stood by him, and said, 376
20:12 when he saw that **every o** that came by him 3605
20:19 I *am* **o** *of them that are* peaceable *and* NIH
23: 8 eight hundred, whom he slew at **o** time. 259
23: 9 **o** of the three mighty *men* with David, NIH
23:15 Oh that **o** would give me drink *of* the water NIH
23:24 Asahel the brother of Joab *was* **o of** 871.1
24:12 I offer thee three *things;* choose thee **o** of 259
1Ki 1:48 which hath given **o** to sit on my throne *this* NIH
2:16 now I ask **o** petition of thee, deny me not 259
2:20 she said, I desire **o** small petition of thee; 259
3:17 the **o** woman said, O my lord, I and 259
3:17 my lord, I and this woman dwell in **o** house; 259
3:23 said the king, **The o** saith, This *is* my son 2063
3:25 and give half to the **o**, and half to the other. 259
4:22 Solomon's provision for **o** day was thirty 259
6:24 five cubits *was* the **o** wing of the cherub, 259
6:24 from the uttermost part of the **o**[S] wing 2050.2
6:25 both the cherubims *were* of **o** measure and 259
6:25 cherubims *were* of one measure and **o** size. 259
6:26 The height of the **o** cherub *was* ten cubits, 259
6:27 that the wing of the **o** touched the *one* wall, 259
6:27 that the wing of the one touched the **o** wall, NIH
6:27 their wings touched **o another** 413+3671+3671
6:34 the two leaves of the **o** door *were* folding, 259
7: 7 *it was* covered with cedar **from o side of** 4480
7:16 the height of the **o** chapiter *was* five cubits, 259
7:17 seven for the **o** chapiter, and seven for 259
7:18 two rows round about upon the **o** network, 259
7:23 ten cubits from the **o**[S] brim to the other: 2050.2
7:27 four cubits *was* the length of **o** base, and 259
7:34 undersetters to the four corners of **o** base: 259
7:36 according to the proportion of **every o**, and 376
7:37 all of them had **o** casting, one measure, *and* 259
7:37 had one casting, **o** measure, *and* one size. 259
7:37 had one casting, one measure, *and* **o** size. 259
7:38 **o** laver contained forty baths: *and* 259
7:38 *and* upon every **o** of the ten bases one laver. 259
7:38 *and* upon every one of the ten bases **o** laver. 259
7:42 *even* two rows *of* pomegranates for **o** 259
7:44 And **o** sea, and twelve oxen under the sea; 259
8:56 there hath not failed **o** word of all his good 259
9: 8 **every o** that passeth by it shall be 3605
10:14 in **o** year was six hundred threescore 259
10:16 six hundred *shekels* of gold went to **o** target. 259
10:17 three pound *of* gold went to **o** shield: 259
10:20 twelve lions stood there on **the o side** and 2088
11:13 will give **o** tribe to thy son for David my 259
11:32 (But he shall have **o** tribe for my servant 259
11:36 unto his son will I give **o** tribe, that David 259
12:29 he set the **o** in Beth-el, and the other put he 259
12:30 for the people went *to worship* before the **o**, 259
13:33 he became **o** *of* the priests of the high NIH
14:21 and **o** years old when he *began* to reign, 259
15:10 and **o** years reigned he in Jerusalem. 259
16:11 he left him not **o** *that* pisseth against a wall, NIH
18: 6 Ahab went **o** way by himself, and 259
18:23 let them choose **o** bullock for themselves, 259
18:25 Choose you **o** bullock for yourselves, and 259
18:40 prophets of Baal; let not **o** of them escape. 376
19: 2 if I make not thy life as the life of **o** of them 259
20:20 they slew **every o** his man: and the Syrians 376
20:29 they pitched **o** over against the other seven 428
20:29 an hundred thousand footmen in **o** day. 259

1Ki 22: 8 *There is* yet **o** man, Micaiah the son of 259
22:13 *declare* good unto the king *with* **o** mouth: 259
22:13 be like the word of **o** of them, and speak *that* 259
22:20 **o** said on this manner, and another said on 2088
22:28 he said, Hearken, O people, **every o** of you. 3605
22:38 **o** washed the chariot in the pool of Samaria; NIH
2Ki 3:11 **o** of the king of Israel's servants answered 259
3:23 and they have smitten **o** another: 376
4:22 **o** of the young men, and one of the asses, 259
4:22 one of the young men, and **o** of the asses, 259
4:39 And **o** went out into the field to gather herbs, 259
5: 4 **o** went in, and told his lord, saying, Thus NIH
6: 3 **o** said, Be content, I pray thee, and go with 259
6: 5 as **o** was felling a beam, the axe head fell 259
6:12 **o** of his servants said, None, my lord, 259
7: 3 they said **o** to another, Why sit we here until 376
7: 6 they said **o** to another, Lo, the king of Israel 376
7: 8 they went into **o** tent, and did eat and drink, 259
7: 9 Then they said **o** to another, We do not well: 376
7:13 **o** of his servants answered and said, Let 259
8:26 to reign; and he reigned **o** year in Jerusalem. 259
9: 1 Elisha the prophet called **o** of the children of 259
9:11 **o** said unto him, *Is all* well? wherefore came NIH
9:18 So there went **o** on horseback to meet him, NIH
10:21 the house of Baal was full from **o end** to 6310
12: 4 *even* the money of **every o** that passeth 376
12: 9 on the right side as **o** cometh *into* the house 376
14: 8 Come, let us look **o** another *in* the face. NIH
14:11 Amaziah king of Judah looked **o** another *in* NIH
14:23 in Samaria, *and reigned* forty and **o** years. 259
17:27 Carry thither **o** of the priests whom ye 259
17:28 **o** of the priests whom they had carried away 259
18:24 wilt thou turn away the face of **o** captain of 259
18:31 **every o** of his fig tree, and drink ye every 376
18:31 drink ye **every o** the waters of his cistern: 376
19:22 on high? *even* against the **Holy O** of Israel. 6918
21:16 till he had filled Jerusalem from **o end** to 6310
22: 1 he reigned thirty and **o** years in Jerusalem. 259
23:35 of **every o** according to his taxation, to give 376
24:18 and **o** years old when he *began* to reign, 259
25:16 **o** sea, and the bases which Solomon had 259
25:17 The height of the **o** pillar *was* eighteen 259
1Ch 1:19 the name of the **o** *was* Peleg; because in his 259
9:31 Mattithiah, **o** of the Levites, who *was* NIH
10:13 also for asking *counsel of* **o** *that had a* NIH
11:11 against three hundred slain *by him* at **o** time. 259
11:12 who *was* **o** of the three mighties. NIH
11:17 Oh that **o** would give me drink *of* the water NIH
12:14 **o** of the least *was* over an hundred, and 259
12:25 the war, seven thousand and **o hundred.** 3967
12:38 all the rest also of Israel *were of* **o** heart to 259
16: 3 he dealt to every **o** of Israel, both man and 376
16: 3 to **every o** a loaf of bread, and a good piece 376
16:20 and from **o** kingdom to another people; NIH
17: 5 to tent, and from **o** tabernacle *to another.* NIH
17:21 what **o** nation in the earth *is* like thy people 259
21:10 I offer thee three *things:* choose thee **o** of 259
23:11 therefore they were in **o** reckoning, 259
24: 5 they divided by lot, **o** *sort* with another, 428
24: 6 **o** of the Levites, wrote them before NIH
24: 6 **o** principal household being taken for 259
24: 6 taken for Eleazar, and **o** taken for Ithamar. NIH
24:17 The **o** and twentieth to Jachin, the two and 259
25:28 The **o** and twentieth to Hothir, *he,* his sons, 259
26:12 chief men, *having* wards **o** against another, NIH
27:18 Of Judah, Elihu, **o** of the brethren of David: NIH
29: 7 and **o hundred** thousand talents *of* iron. 3967
2Ch 3:11 **o** wing of the one *cherub was* five cubits, NIH
3:11 *one* wing of the **o** *cherub was* five cubits, 259
3:12 **o** wing of the other cherub *was* five cubits, NIH
3:17 **o** on the right hand, and the other on the left; 259
4:15 **O** sea, and twelve oxen under it. 259
5:13 as the trumpeters and singers *were* as **o**, 259
5:13 to make **o** sound to be heard in praising and 259
6:29 when **every o** shall know his own sore and 376
7:21 shall be an astonishment to **every o** that 3605
9: 6 *the* **o** half of the greatness of thy wisdom NIH
9:13 came to Solomon in **o** year was six hundred 259
9:15 six hundred *shekels* of beaten gold went to **o** 259
9:16 three hundred *shekels* of gold went to **o** 259
9:19 lions stood there on the **o side** 2088+4480
12:13 for Rehoboam *was* **o** and forty years old 259
16:13 died in the **o** and fortieth year of his reign. 259
18: 7 *There is* yet **o** man, by whom *we* may 259
18: 8 the king of Israel called for **o** *of his* officers, 259
18:12 *declare* good to the king with **o** assent; 259
18:12 be like **o** of theirs, and speak thou good. 259
18:19 **o** spake saying after this manner, and 2088
20:23 of Seir, **every o** helped to destroy another. 376
22: 2 to reign, and he reigned **o** year in Jerusalem. 259
25:17 Come, let us see **o** another *in* the face. NIH
25:21 they saw **o** another *in* the face, *both* he and NIH
26:11 hand of Hananiah, **o** of the king's captains. NIH
28: 6 an hundred and twenty thousand in **o** day, 259
30:12 **o** heart to do the commandment of the king 259
30:17 passovers for **every o** *that was* not clean, 3605
30:18 The good LORD pardon **every o** 3605
31:16 *even* unto **every o** that entereth into 3605
32:12 Ye shall worship before **o** altar, and 259
34: 1 he reigned in Jerusalem **o** and thirty years. 259
35:24 was buried in **o** *of the* sepulchres of his NIH
36:11 Zedekiah *was* **o** and twenty years old when 259
Ezr 2: 1 and Judah, **every o** unto his city; 376
2:26 and Gaba, six hundred twenty and **o**. 259
2:69 **threescore and o thousand**
505+7239+8337+2050.1
2:69 *of* silver, and **o hundred** priests' garments. 3967
3: 1 the people gathered themselves together as **o** 259
3: 5 of **every o** that willingly offered a freewill 3605
5:14 they *were* delivered unto **o**, whose name NIH
6: 5 *every* **o** to his place, and place *them* in NIH
8:34 By number *and* by weight of **every o**: and 3605
9: 4 were assembled unto me **every o** that 3605
9:11 which have filled it from **o** end to another NIH
10: 2 **o** of the sons of Elam, answered and NIH

Ezr 10:13 neither *is this* a work of **o** day or two: 259
Ne 1: 2 **o** of my brethren, came, he and *certain* men 259
3: 8 Hananiah the son of *o of* the apothecaries, NIH
3:28 the priests, **every o** over against his house. 376
4:15 all of us to the wall, **every o** unto his work. 376
4:17 *every o* with one of his hands wrought in NIH
4:17 *every one* with **o** of his hands wrought in 259
4:18 **every o** had his sword girded by his side, 376
4:19 separated upon the wall, **o** far from another. 376
4:22 Let **every o** with his servant lodge within 376
4:23 *saving that* **every o** put them off *for* 376
5: 7 You exact usury, **every o** of his brother. 376
5:18 which was prepared *for me* daily *was* **o** ox 259
6: 2 let us meet together in *some o of* NIH
7: 3 **every o** in his watch, and every one *to be* 376
7: 3 and **every o** *to be* over against his house. 376
7: 6 and to Judah, **every o** unto his city; 376
7:30 and Geba, six hundred twenty and **o**. 259
7:37 and Ono, seven hundred twenty and **o**. 259
7:63 which took *o* of the daughters of Barzillai NIH
8: 1 **o** man into the street that *was* before 259
8:16 **every o** upon the roof of his house, and 376
9: 3 LORD their God *o* fourth *part* of the day; NIH
10:28 **every o** having knowledge, *and* 3605
11: 1 to bring **o** of ten to dwell in Jerusalem 259
11: 3 in the cities of Judah dwelt **every o** in his 376
11:14 *was* Zabdiel, the son of *o of* the great *men*. NIH
11:20 cities of Judah, **every o** in his inheritance. 376
12:31 whereof *o* went on the right hand upon NIH
13:10 did the work, were fled **every o** to his field. 376
13:28 *o* of the sons of Joiada, the son of Eliashib NIH
13:30 and the Levites, **every o** in his business; 376
Est 1: 7 (the vessels being diverse **o** from **another**,) 3627
3:13 and old, little children and women, in **o** day, 259
4: 5 for Hatach, *o* of the king's chamberlains, NIH
4:11 *there is* **o** law of his to put *him* to death, 259
6: 9 horse be delivered to the hand of **o** of 376
7: 9 Harbonah, **o** of the chamberlains, said before 259
8:12 Upon **o** day in all the provinces of king 259
9:19 and *of* sending portions **o** to another. 376
9:22 of sending portions **o** to another, and gifts to 376
Job 1: 1 and **o that feared** God, and eschewed evil. 3373
1: 4 and feasted *in their* houses, **every o** his day; 376
1: 8 **o that feareth** God, and escheweth evil? 3373
2: 3 **o that feareth** God, and escheweth evil? 3373
2:10 Thou speakest as **o** of the foolish *women* 259
2:11 they came **every o** from his own place; 376
2:12 they rent **every o** his mantle, and 376
5: 2 foolish man, and envy slayeth the **silly o**. 6601
6:10 not concealed the words of the **Holy O**. 6918
6:26 the speeches of **o** that is desperate, NIH
9: 3 he cannot answer him **o** of a thousand. 259
9:22 This *is* **o** *thing*, therefore I said *it*, He 259
12: 4 I am *as* **o mocked** of his neighbour, 7814
13: 9 or as *o* man mocketh another, do ye *so* NIH
14: 3 dost thou open thine eyes upon **such a o**, 2088
14: 4 bring a clean *thing* out of an unclean? not **o**. 259
16:21 O that *o* might plead for a man with God, NIH
17:10 for I cannot find *o* wise *man* among you. NIH
19:11 he counteth me unto him as *o of* his NIH
21:23 **O** dieth in his full strength, *being* wholly 2088
23:13 he *is* in **o** *mind*, and who can turn him? and 259
24: 6 They reap *every o* his corn in the field: and NIH
24:17 if *o* know *them, they are in* the terrors of NIH
29:25 the army, as *o that* comforteth the mourners. NIH
31:15 and did not **o** fashion us in the womb? 259
31:35 O that *o* would hear me! behold, my desire NIH
33:23 an interpreter, **o** among a thousand, 259
40:11 behold **every o** *that is* proud, and 3605
40:12 Look on **every o** *that is* proud, *and* 3605
41: 9 shall *not o* be cast down even at the sight of NIH
41:16 **O** is so near to another, that no air can come 259
41:17 They are joined **o** to another, they stick 376
41:32 *o* would think the deep to be hoary. NIH
42:11 of money, and **every o** an earring of gold. 376
Ps 12: 2 They speak vanity **every o** with his 376
14: 3 *there is* none that doeth good, no, not **o**. 259
16:10 neither wilt thou suffer thine **Holy O** to see 2623
27: 4 **O** *thing* have I desired of the LORD, that 259
29: 9 in his temple doth every *o* speak of *his* 2050.2
32: 6 For this shall **every o** *that is* godly pray 3605
34:20 all his bones: not **o** of them is broken. 259
35:14 as *o* that mourneth for his mother. NIH
49:16 Be not thou afraid when *o* is made rich, 376
50:21 that I was altogether *such a o* as thyself: NIH
53: 3 **Every o** of them is gone back, they are 3605
53: 3 *there is* none that doeth good, no, not **o**. 259
58: 8 let *every o of them* pass away: NIH
63:11 **every o** that sweareth by him shall glory: 3605
64: 6 both the inward *thought* of **every o** *of them*, 376
68:21 the hairy scalp of such a *o* as goeth on still NIH
68:30 *till every o* submit himself with pieces of NIH
71:18 *and* thy power to **every o** *that is* to come. 3605
71:22 sing with the harp, O thou **Holy O** of Israel. 6918
73:20 As a dream when *o* awaketh; *so*, O Lord, NIH
75: 7 he putteth down **o**, and setteth up another. 2088
78:41 and limited the **Holy O** of Israel. 6918
78:65 Then the Lord awaked as *o* out of sleep, *and* NIH
82: 7 die like men, and fall like *o* of the princes. 259
83: 5 For they have consulted together *with o* NIH
84: 7 *every o of them* in Zion appeareth before NIH
89:10 broken Rahab in pieces, as *o* that is slain; NIH
89:18 and the **Holy O** of Israel *is* our king. 6918
89:19 thou spakest in vision to thy **holy o**, and 2623
89:19 I have laid help upon *o that is* mighty; NIH
89:19 I have exalted *o* chosen out of the people. NIH
105:13 When they went from *o* nation to another, NIH
105:13 from *o* kingdom to another people; NIH
105:37 *there was* not *o* feeble *person* among their NIH
106:11 their enemies: there was not **o** of them left. 259
115: 8 *so is* **every o** that trusteth in them. 3605
119:160 **every o** of thy righteous judgments 3605
119:162 at thy word, as *o* that findeth great spoil. NIH
128: 1 Blessed *is* **every o** that feareth the LORD; 3605
135:18 *so is* **every o** that trusteth in them. 3605

Ps 137: 3 *saying,* Sing us **o** of the songs of Zion. NIH
141: 7 as when *o* cutteth and cleaveth *wood* upon NIH
145: 4 **O** generation shall praise thy works to NIH
Pr 1:14 in thy lot among us; let us all have **o** purse: 259
1:19 So *are* the ways of **every o** that is greedy of 3605
3:18 and happy *is* every *o* that retaineth her. NIH
6:11 So shall thy poverty come as *o* that NIH
6:28 Can **o** go upon hot coals, and his feet not be 376
8:30 *as* **o brought up** *with him:* and I was daily 525
15:12 A scorner loveth not *o* that reproveth him: NIH
16: 5 **Every o** *that is* proud in heart *is* an 3605
17:14 The beginning of strife *is as* when *o* letteth NIH
19:25 reprove *o* that hath understanding, *and* NIH
20: 6 Most men will proclaim **every o** his own 376
21: 5 but *of* **every o** that is hasty only to want. 3605
22:26 Be not thou *o* of them that strike hands, *or* NIH
24:34 So shall thy poverty come *as o* that NIH
26:17 *is like o* that taketh a dog by the ears. NIH
Ecc 1: 4 *O* generation passeth away, and NIH
2:14 I myself perceived also that **o** event 259
3:19 even **o thing** befalleth them: 259
3:19 as **the o** dieth, so dieth the other; yea, 2088
3:19 yea, they have all **o** breath; so that a man 259
3:20 All go unto **o** place; all are of the dust, and 259
4: 8 There is **o** *alone*, and *there is* not a second; 259
4: 9 Two *are* better than **o**; because they have a 259
4:10 For if they fall, the **o** will lift up his fellow: 259
4:11 have heat: but how can **o** be warm *alone?* 259
4:12 if **o** prevail against him, two shall withstand 259
5:18 *is* good and comely *for o* to eat and to drink, NIH
6: 6 he seen no good: do not all go to **o** place? 259
7:14 God also hath set **the o** over against 2088
7:27 saith the Preacher, *counting* **o** by one, 259
7:27 saith the Preacher, *counting* one by **o**, 259
7:28 **o** man among a thousand have I found; but 259
8: 9 *there is* a time wherein *o* man ruleth over 1886.1
9: 2 *there is* **o** event to the righteous, and to 259
9: 3 under the sun, that *there is* **o** event unto all: 259
9:18 of war: but **o** sinner destroyeth much good. 259
10: 3 and he saith to **every o** *that* he *is* a fool. 3605
10:15 of the foolish wearieth **every o of them**, 5105.2
12:11 *which* are given from **o** shepherd. 259
SS 1: 7 for why should I be as *o* that turneth aside NIH
2:10 my love, my **fair o**, and come away. 3303
2:13 Arise, my love, my **fair o**, and come away. 3303
4: 2 whereof **every o** beareth twins, and none *is* 3605
4: 9 thou hast ravished my heart with **o** of thine 259
4: 9 one of thine eyes, with **o** chain of thy neck. 259
6: 6 whereof **every o** beareth twins, and *there is* 3605
6: 6 and *there is* not **o** barren among them. NIH
6: 9 My dove, my undefiled *is but o*; she *is* 259
6: 9 she *is* the *only o* of her mother, she *is* 259
6: 9 she *is* the choice *o* of her that bare her. NIH
8:10 was I in his eyes as *o* that found favour. NIH
8:11 **every o** for the fruit thereof was to bring a 376
Isa 1: 4 they have provoked the **Holy O** of Israel 6918
1:23 **every o** loveth gifts, and followeth after 3605
1:24 LORD of hosts, the **mighty O** of Israel, Ah, 46
2:12 of hosts *shall be* upon **every o** *that is* proud 3605
2:12 lofty, and upon **every o** that is lifted up; 3605
2:20 which they made *each o* for himself to NIH
3: 5 **every o** by another, and every one by his 376
3: 5 by another, and **every o** by his neighbour: 376
4: 1 in that day seven women shall take hold of **o** 259
4: 3 *even* **every o** that is written among 3605
5:10 ten acres of vineyard shall yield **o** bath, and 259
5:19 let the counsel of the **Holy O** of Israel draw 6918
5:24 despised the word of the **Holy O** of Israel. 6918
5:30 and if *o* look unto the land, behold darkness NIH
6: 2 **each o** had six wings; with twain he covered 259
6: 3 **o** cried unto another, and said, Holy, holy, 2088
6: 6 flew **o** of the seraphims unto me, having a 259
7:22 honey shall **every o** eat that is left in 3605
9:14 and tail, branch and rush, *in* **o** day. 259
9:17 for **every o** *is* a hypocrite and an evildoer, 3605
10:14 as *o* gathereth eggs *that are* left, have I NIH
10:17 be for a fire, and his **Holy O** for a flame: 6918
10:17 and devour his thorns and his briers in **o** day; 259
10:20 the LORD, the **Holy O** of Israel, in truth. 6918
10:34 and Lebanon shall fall by a **mighty o**. 117
12: 6 for great *is* the **Holy O** of Israel in 6918
13: 8 they shall be amazed **o** at another; their 376
13:14 and flee **every o** into his own land. 376
13:15 **Every o** that is found shall be thrust 3605
13:15 **every o** that is joined *unto them* shall fall 3605
14:18 lie in glory, **every o** in his own house. 376
14:32 What shall *o* then answer the messengers of NIH
15: 3 in their streets, every *o* shall howl, 1886.4
16: 7 Moab howl for Moab, every *o* shall howl: 1886.4
17: 7 his eyes shall have respect to the **Holy O** of 6918
19: 2 they shall fight **every o** against his brother, 376
19: 2 and **every o** against his neighbour; 376
19:17 **every o** that maketh mention thereof shall 3605
19:18 **o** shall be called, The city of destruction. 259
19:20 and a **great o**, and he shall deliver them. 7227
23:15 according to the days of **o** king: 259
27:12 ye shall be gathered **o** by one, O ye children 259
27:12 ye shall be gathered one by **o**, O ye children 259
28: 2 the LORD hath a mighty and strong *o*, NIH
29: 4 as of *o* that hath a familiar spirit, out of NIH
29:11 which *men* deliver to *o* that is learned, NIH
29:19 men shall rejoice in the **Holy O** of Israel. 6918
29:20 For the **terrible o** is brought **to nought**, 6184
29:23 sanctify the **Holy O** of Jacob, and shall fear 6918
30:11 cause the **Holy O** of Israel to cease from 6918
30:12 Wherefore thus saith the **Holy O** of Israel, 6918
30:15 saith the Lord GOD, the **Holy O** of Israel; 6918
30:17 **O** thousand *shall flee* at the rebuke of one; 259
30:17 One thousand *shall flee* at the rebuke of **o**; 259
30:29 as when *o*[S] goeth with a pipe to come into 1886.1
30:29 of the LORD, to the **mighty O** of Israel. 6697
31: 1 they look not unto the **Holy O** of Israel, 6918
33:20 not **o** of the stakes thereof shall ever be NIH
34:15 also be gathered, **every o** *with* her mate. 802
34:16 no **o** of these shall fail, none shall want her 259

Isa 36: 9 wilt thou turn away the face of **o** captain of 259
36:16 eat ye **every o** *of* his vine, and every one *of* 376
36:16 **every o** *of* his fig tree, and drink ye every 376
36:16 drink ye **every o** the waters of his own 376
37:23 on high? *even* against the **Holy O** of Israel. 6918
40:25 or shall I be equal? saith the **Holy O**. 6918
40:26 for that *he is* strong in power; not **o** faileth. 376
41: 6 They helped **every o** his neighbour; and 376
41: 6 *every o* said to his brother, Be of good NIH
41:14 and thy redeemer, the **Holy O** of Israel. 6918
41:16 *and* shalt glory in the **Holy O** of Israel. 6918
41:20 and the **Holy O** of Israel hath created it. 6918
41:25 I have raised up *o* from the north, and NIH
41:27 I will give to Jerusalem *o* that bringeth good NIH
43: 3 thy God, the **Holy O** of Israel, thy Saviour: 6918
43: 7 *Even* **every o** that is called by my name: 3605
43:14 your redeemer, the **Holy O** of Israel; 6918
43:15 I *am* the LORD, your **Holy O**, the creator 6918
44: 5 **O** shall say, I *am* the LORD'S; and 2088
45:11 the **Holy O** of Israel, and his maker, 6918
45:24 Surely, shall *o* say, in the LORD have I NIH
46: 7 yea, *o* shall cry unto him, yet can he not NIH
47: 4 of hosts *is* his name, the **Holy O** of Israel. 6918
47: 9 shall come to thee *in* a moment in **o** day, 259
47:15 they shall wander **every o** to his quarter; 376
48:17 thy redeemer, the **Holy O** of Israel; 6918
49: 7 the redeemer of Israel, *and* his **Holy O**, 6918
49: 7 *and* the **Holy O** of Israel, and he shall 6918
49:26 and thy redeemer, the **mighty O** of Jacob. 46
53: 6 we have turned **every o** to his own way; and 376
54: 5 and thy redeemer the **Holy O** of Israel; 6918
55: 1 Ho, **every o** that thirsteth, come ye to 3605
55: 5 thy God, and for the **Holy O** of Israel; 6918
56: 6 **every o** that keepeth the sabbath from 3605
56:11 **every o** for his gain, from his quarter. 376
57: 2 *each o* walking *in* his uprightness. NIH
57:15 the high and lofty *O* that inhabiteth eternity, NIH
60: 9 to the **Holy O** of Israel, because he hath 6918
60:14 The Zion of the **Holy O** of Israel. 6918
60:16 and thy redeemer, the **mighty O** of Jacob. 46
60:22 A **little o** shall become a thousand, and 6996
60:22 a thousand, and a **small o** a strong nation: 6810
65: 8 in the cluster, and *o* saith, Destroy it not; NIH
66: 8 the earth be made to bring forth in **o** day? 259
66:13 As **o** whom his mother comforteth, so will I 376
66:17 purify themselves in the gardens behind **o** 259
66:23 *that* from **o** new moon to another, and NIH
66:23 to another, and from **o** sabbath to another, NIH
Jer 1:15 they shall set **every o** his throne *at* 376
3:14 I will take you **o** of a city, and two of a 259
5: 6 **every o** that goeth out thence shall be torn 3605
5: 8 **every o** neighed after his neighbour's wife. 376
6: 3 they shall feed **every o** *in* his place. 376
6:13 of them **every o** *is* given to covetousness; 3605
6:13 unto the priest every *o* dealeth falsely. 2050.2
8: 6 **every o** turned to his course, as the horse 3605
8:10 **every o** from the least even unto 3605
8:10 even unto the priest **every o** dealeth falsely. 3605
9: 4 Take ye heed **every o** of his neighbour, and 376
9: 5 they will deceive **every o** his neighbour, 376
9: 8 *o* speaketh peaceably to his neighbour with NIH
9:20 and **every o** her neighbour lamentation. 802
10: 3 for *o* cutteth a tree out of the forest, NIH
11: 8 walked **every o** in the imagination of their 376
12:12 *o* end of the land even to the *other* end of NIH
13:14 I will dash them **o** against another, even 376
15:10 *yet* **every o** of them doth curse me. 3605
16:12 ye walk **every o** after the imagination of his 376
18:11 return ye now **every o** from his evil way, 376
18:12 we will **every o** do the imagination of his 376
18:16 **every o** that passeth thereby shall be 3605
19: 8 **every o** that passeth thereby shall be 3605
19: 9 they shall eat **every o** the flesh of his friend 376
19:11 and this city, as *o* breaketh a potter's vessel, NIH
20: 7 in derision daily, every *o* mocketh me. 1886.4
20:11 LORD *is* with me as a mighty **terrible o**: 6184
22: 7 against thee, **every o** with his weapons: 376
23:17 they say *unto* **every o** that walketh after 3605
23:30 that steal my words **every o** from his 376
23:35 Thus shall ye say **every o** to his neighbour, 376
23:35 **every o** to his brother, What hath 376
24: 2 **O** basket *had* very good figs, *even* like 259
25: 5 Turn ye again now **every o** from his evil 376
25:26 **o** with another, and all the kingdoms of 376
25:33 *o* end of the earth even unto the *other* end of NIH
30:14 *with* the chastisement of a **cruel o**, for 394
30:16 all thine adversaries, **every o** of them, 3605
31:30 **every o** shall die for his own iniquity: 376
32:19 to give **every o** according to his ways, and 376
32:39 I will give them **o** heart, and one way, 259
32:39 **o** way, that *they* may fear me for ever, for 259
34:10 heard that **every o** should let his manservant, 376
34:10 and **every o** his maidservant, go free, 376
34:17 **every o** to his brother, and every man to his 376
35: 2 into **o** of the chambers, and give them wine 259
36: 7 and will return **every o** from his evil way: 376
36:16 they were afraid both **o** and other, and 376
38: 7 **o** of the eunuchs which *was* in the king's 376
46:16 made many to fall, yea, **o** fell upon another: 376
49:17 **every o** that goeth by it shall be astonished, 3605
50:13 **every o** that goeth by Babylon shall be 3605
50:16 sword they shall turn **every o** to his people, 376
50:16 and they shall flee **every o** to his own land. 376
50:29 the LORD, against the **Holy O** of Israel. 6918
50:42 *every o* put in array, like a man to the battle, NIH
51: 5 filled *with* sin against the **Holy O** of Israel. 6918
51: 9 and let us go **every o** into his own country: 376
51:31 **O** post shall run to meet another, and NIH
51:31 and **o** messenger to meet another, NIH
51:31 of Babylon that his city is taken at *o* end, NIH
51:46 a rumour shall both come *o* year, and NIH
51:56 are taken, *every o of* their bows is broken: NIH
52: 1 Zedekiah *was* **o** and twenty year old when he 259
52:20 **o** sea, and twelve brasen bulls that *were* 259
52:21 the height of **o** pillar *was* eighteen cubits; 259

Jer 52:22 the height of o chapiter was five cubits, 259
Eze 1: 6 every o had four faces, and every one had 259
1: 6 had four faces, and every o had four wings. 259
1: 9 Their wings were joined o to another; they 802
1: 9 they went every o straight forward. 376
1:11 two wings of every o were joined one to 376
1:11 two wings of every one were joined o to NIH
1:12 they went every o straight forward: whither 376
1:15 behold o wheel upon the earth by the living 259
1:16 they four had o likeness: and 259
1:23 their wings straight, the o toward the other: 802
1:23 every o had two, which covered on this side, 376
1:23 covered on this side, and every o had two, 376
1:28 my face, and I heard a voice of o that spake. NIH
3:13 the living creatures that touched o another, 802
4: 8 thou shalt not turn thee from o side to NIH
4: 9 put them in o vessel, and make thee bread 259
4:17 be astonied o with another, and 376
7:16 of them mourning, every o for his iniquity. 376
9: 2 o man among them was clothed with linen, 259
10: 7 o cherub stretched forth his hand from NIH
10: 9 o wheel by one cherub, and another wheel 259
10: 9 one wheel by o cherub, and another wheel 259
10:10 their appearances, they four had o likeness, 259
10:14 every o had four faces: the first face was 259
10:19 every o stood at the door of the east gate of NIH
10:21 Every o had four faces apiece, and every 259
10:21 four faces apiece, and every o four wings; 259
10:22 they went every o straight forward. 376
11: 5 that come into your mind, every o of them. NIH
11:19 I will give them o heart, and I will put a new 259
13:10 o built up a wall, and lo, others daubed it 1931
14: 7 For every o of the house of Israel, or 376+376
15: 7 they shall go out from o fire, and another NIH
16:15 pouredst out thy fornications on every o 3605
16:25 hast opened thy feet to every o that passed 3605
16:44 every o that useth proverbs shall use this 3605
17:22 from the top of his young twigs a tender o, 7390
18:10 that doeth the like to any o of these things, 259
18:30 of Israel, every o according to his ways, 376
19: 3 she brought up o of her whelps: it became a 259
20:39 serve ye every o his idols, and 376
21:16 Go thee o way or other, either on the right 258
21:19 both twain shall come forth out of o land: 259
22: 6 every o were in thee to their power to shed 376
22:11 o hath committed abomination with his 376
23: 2 were two women, the daughters of o mother: 259
23:13 she was defiled, that they took both o way, 259
24:23 and mourn o towards another. 376
31:11 delivered him into the hand of the mighty o 410
33:20 I will judge you every o after his ways. 376
33:21 that o that had escaped out of Jerusalem 6412
33:24 Abraham was o, and he inherited the land: 259
33:26 and ye defile every o his neighbour's wife: 376
33:30 speak o to another, every one to his brother, 2297
33:30 every o to his brother, saying, Come, I pray 376
33:32 lovely song of o that hath a pleasant voice, NIH
34:23 And I will set up o shepherd over them, and 259
37:16 take thee o stick, and write upon it, 259
37:17 join them o to another into one stick; and 259
37:17 join them one to another into o stick; and 259
37:17 and they shall become o in thine hand. 259
37:19 make them o stick, and they shall be one in 259
37:19 one stick, and they shall be o in mine hand. 259
37:22 I will make them o nation in the land upon 259
37:22 and o king shall be king to them all: 259
37:24 and they all shall have o shepherd: 259
39: 7 that I am the LORD, the Holy O in Israel. 6918
40: 5 measured the breadth of the building, o reed; 259
40: 5 one reed; and the height, o reed. 259
40: 6 of the gate, which was o reed broad; 259
40: 6 the other threshold of the gate, which was o 259
40: 7 every little chamber was o reed long, and 259
40: 7 was one reed long, and o reed broad; 259
40: 7 by the porch of the gate within was o reed. 259
40: 8 also the porch of the gate within, o reed. 259
40:10 on that side; they three were of o measure: 259
40:10 and the posts had o measure on this side and 259
40:12 the little chambers was o cubit on this side, 259
40:12 and the space was o cubit on that side: 259
40:13 the gate from the roof of o little chamber to NIH
40:26 o on this side, and another on that side, 259
40:40 as o goeth up to the entry of the north 1886.1
40:42 a cubit and a half broad, and o cubit high: 259
40:44 o at the side of the east gate having 259
40:49 o on this side, and another on that side. 259
41: 1 six cubits broad on the o side, and 6311
41: 2 of the door were five cubits on the o side, 6311
41: 6 o[S] over another, and thirty in order; 6763
41:11 o door toward the north, and another door 259
41:15 the galleries thereof on the o side and 6311
41:19 was toward the palm tree on the o side, 6311
41:21 the appearance of the o as the appearance NIH
41:24 two leaves for the o door, and two leaves for 259
41:26 palm trees on the o side and on the other 6311
42: 4 ten cubits breadth inward, a way of o cubit; 259
42: 9 as o goeth into them from the utter court. 2050.2
42:12 toward the east, as o entereth into them. NIH
43:14 shall be two cubits, and the breadth o cubit; 259
43:14 shall be four cubits, and the breadth o cubit. NIH
45: 7 for the prince on the o side 2088
45: 7 the length shall be over against o of 259
45:11 and the bath shall be of o measure, 259
45:15 o lamb out of the flock, out of two hundred, 259
45:20 day of the month for every o that erreth, 376
46:12 o shall then open him the gate that looketh NIH
46:12 after his going forth o shall shut the gate. NIH
46:17 if he give a gift of his inheritance to o of his 259
46:22 these four corners were of o measure. 259
47: 7 river were very many trees on the o side 2088
47:14 ye shall inherit it, o as well as another: 376
48: 1 as o goeth to Hamath, Hazar-enan, NIH
48: 8 and in length as o of the other parts, 259
48:21 on the o side and on the other of the holy 2088
48:31 o gate of Reuben, one gate of Judah, 259
Eze 48:31 of Reuben, o gate of Judah, one gate of Levi. 259
48:31 of Reuben, one gate of Judah, o gate of Levi. 259
48:32 and o gate of Joseph, one gate of Benjamin, 259
48:32 o gate of Benjamin, one gate of Dan. 259
48:32 one gate of Benjamin, o gate of Dan. 259
48:33 o gate of Simeon, one gate of Issachar, 259
48:33 one gate of Simeon, o gate of Issachar, 259
48:33 one gate of Issachar, o gate of Zebulun. 259
48:34 o gate of Gad, one gate of Asher, one gate of 259
48:34 one gate of Gad, o gate of Asher, one gate of 259
48:34 one gate of Asher, o gate of Naphtali. 259
Da 2: 9 me the dream, there is but o decree for you: 2298
2:43 they shall not cleave o to another, even as 1836
3:19 o seven times more than it was wont to be 2298
4:13 and a holy o came down from heaven; 6922
4:19 was astonied for o hour, and his thoughts 2298
4:23 and a holy o coming down from heaven, 6922
5: 6 and his knees smote o against another. 1668
7: 3 up from the sea, diverse o from another. 1668
7: 5 it raised up itself on o side, and it had three 2298
7:13 o like the Son of man came with the clouds NIH
7:16 I came near unto o of them that stood by, 2298
8: 3 o was higher than the other, and the higher 259
8: 9 And out of o of them came forth a little horn, 259
8:13 I heard o saint speaking, and another saint 259
9:27 confirm the covenant with many for o week: 259
10:13 of the kingdom of Persia withstood me o 259
10:13 lo, Michael, o of the chief princes, came to 259
10:16 o like the similitude of the sons of men NIH
10:18 touched me o like the appearance of a man, NIH
11: 5 south shall be strong, and o of his princes; NIH
11: 7 out of a branch of her roots shall o stand up NIH
11:10 o shall certainly come, and overflow, and NIH
11:27 and they shall speak lies at o table; 259
12: 1 every o that shall be found written in 3605
12: 5 the o on this side of the bank of the river, 259
12: 6 o said to the man clothed in linen, NIH
Hos 1:11 appoint themselves o head, and they shall 259
4: 3 every o that dwelleth therein shall languish, 3605
11: 9 not man; the Holy O in the midst of thee: 6918
Joel 2: 7 they shall march every o on his ways, and 376
2: 8 Neither shall o thrust another; they shall 376
2: 8 they shall walk every o in his path: 1397
Am 3: 5 shall o take up a snare from the earth, and NIH
4: 7 I caused it to rain upon o city, and caused it 259
4: 7 o piece was rained upon, and the piece 259
4: 8 So two or three cities wandered unto o city, 259
6: 9 if there remain ten men in o house, that they 259
6:12 will o plow there with oxen? for ye have NIH
8: 8 and every o mourn that dwelleth therein? 3605
Ob 1: 9 to the end that every o of the mount of Esau 376
1:11 even thou wast as o of them. 259
Jnh 1: 7 they said every o to his fellow, Come, and 376
3: 8 let them turn every o from his evil way, and 376
Mic 2: 4 In that day shall o take up a parable against NIH
4: 5 For all people will walk every o in the name 376
Na 1:11 There is o come out of thee, that imagineth NIH
2: 4 they shall justle o against another in NIH
Hab 1:12 O LORD my God, mine Holy O? 6918
3: 3 and the Holy O from mount Paran. 6918
Zep 2:11 shall worship him, every o from his place, 376
2:15 every o that passeth by her shall hiss, and 3605
3: 9 of the LORD, to serve him with o consent. 259
Hag 2: 1 In the seventh month, in the o and 259
2:12 If o bear holy flesh in the skirt of his 376
2:13 If o that is unclean by a dead body touch NIH
2:16 when o came to a heap of twenty measures, NIH
2:16 when o came to the pressfat for to draw out NIH
2:22 every o by the sword of his brother. 376
Zec 3: 9 upon o stone shall be seven eyes: 259
3: 9 I will remove the iniquity of that land in o 259
4: 3 o upon the right side of the bowl, and 259
5: 3 for every o that stealeth shall be cut off as 3605
5: 3 every o that sweareth shall be cut off as on 3605
8:10 for I set all men every o against his 376
8:21 the inhabitants of o city shall go to another, 259
10: 1 showers of rain, to every o grass in the field. 376
11: 6 I will deliver the men every o into his 376
11: 7 the o I called Beauty, and the other I called 259
11: 8 Three shepherds also I cut off in o month; 259
11: 9 let the rest eat every o the flesh of another. 802
11:16 neither shall seek the young o, nor heal that 5289
12:10 as o mourneth for his only son, and shall be NIH
12:10 as o that is in bitterness for his firstborn. NIH
13: 4 that the prophets shall be ashamed every o 376
13: 6 o shall say unto him, What are these NIH
14: 7 it shall be o day which shall be known to 259
14: 9 in that day shall there be o LORD, and 259
14: 9 shall there be one LORD, and his name o. 259
14:13 they shall lay hold every o on the hand of 376
14:16 that every o that is left of all the nations 3605
Mal 2: 3 and o shall take you away with it. NIH
2:10 Have we not all o father? hath not one God 259
2:10 hath not o God created us? why do we deal 259
2:15 did not he make o? Yet had he the residue of 259
2:15 wherefore o? That he might seek a godly 259
2:16 for o covereth violence with his garment, NIH
2:17 Every o that doeth evil is good in the sight 3605
3:16 they that feared the LORD spake often o to 376
Mt 3: 3 The voice of o crying in the wilderness, NIG
5:18 o jot or one tittle shall in no wise pass from 1520
5:18 o tittle shall in no wise pass from the law, 1520
5:19 shall break o of these least commandments, 1520
5:29 for it is profitable for thee that o of thy 1520
5:30 for it is profitable for thee that o of thy 1520
5:36 thou canst not make o hair white or black. 1520
6:24 for either he will hate the o, and love 1520
6:24 or else he will hold to the o, and despise 1520
6:27 Which of you by taking thought can add o 1520
6:29 all his glory was not arrayed like o of these. 1520
7: 8 For every o that asketh receiveth; and 3956
7:21 Not every o that saith unto me, Lord, Lord, 3956
7:26 And every o that heareth these sayings of 3956
7:29 For he taught them as o having authority, NIG
10:29 o of them shall not fall on the ground 1520
Mt 10:42 And whosoever shall give to drink unto o 1520
12: 6 That in this place is o greater than NIG
12:11 that shall have o sheep, and if it fall into a 1520
12:22 brought unto him o possessed with a devil, 1139
12:29 Or else how can o enter into a strong man's 5100
12:47 Then o said unto him, Behold, thy mother 5100
13:19 When any o heareth the word of 3956
13:19 then cometh the wicked o, and 4190
13:38 the tares are the children of the wicked o; 4190
13:46 when he had found o pearl of great price, 1520
16:14 and others, Jeremias, or o of the prophets. 1520
17: 4 o for thee, and one for Moses, and one for 1520
17: 4 and o for Moses, and one for Elias. 1520
17: 4 and one for Moses, and o for Elias. 1520
18: 5 And whoso shall receive o such little child 1520
18: 6 But whoso shall offend o of these little 1520
18: 9 better for thee to enter into life with o eye, 3442
18:10 Take heed that ye despise not o of these 1520
18:12 and o of them be gone astray, doth he not 1520
18:14 that o of these little ones should perish. 1520
18:16 then take with thee o or two more, 1520
18:24 begun to reckon, o was brought unto him, 1520
18:28 went out, and found o of his fellowservants, 1520
18:35 if ye from your hearts forgive not every o 1538
19: 5 to his wife: and they twain shall be o flesh? 1520
19: 6 they are no more twain, but o flesh. 1520
19:16 And behold, o came and said unto him, 1520
19:17 there is none good but o, that is, God: but 1520
19:29 And every o that hath forsaken houses, or 3956
20:12 These last have wrought but o hour, and 1520
20:13 But he answered o of them, and said, 1520
20:21 the o on thy right hand, and the other on 1520
21:24 said unto them, I also will ask you o thing, 1520
21:35 husbandmen took his servants, and beat o, 3739
22: 5 of it, and went their ways, o to his farm, 3739
22:35 Then o of them, which was a lawyer, 1520
23: 4 they themselves will not move them with o NIG
23: 8 for o is your Master, even Christ; 1520
23: 9 for o is your Father, which is in heaven. 1520
23:10 for o is your Master, even Christ. 1520
23:15 compass sea and land to make o proselyte, 1520
24: 2 There shall not be left here o stone upon NIG
24:10 and shall betray o another, and shall hate 240
24:10 betray one another, and shall hate o another. 240
24:31 from o end of heaven to the other. NIG
24:40 the o shall be taken, and the other left. 1520
24:41 the o shall be taken, and the other left. 1520
25:15 And unto o he gave five talents, to another 3739
25:15 to another two, and to another o; 1520
25:18 But he that had received o went and 1520
25:24 Then he which had received the o talent 1520
25:29 For unto every o that hath shall be given, 3956
25:32 and he shall separate them o from another, 240
25:40 Inasmuch as ye have done it unto o of 1520
25:45 Inasmuch as ye did it not to o of the least of 1520
26:14 Then o of the twelve, called Judas Iscariot, 1520
26:21 say unto you, that o of you shall betray me. 1520
26:22 and began every o of them to say unto him, 1538
26:40 What, could ye not watch with me o hour? 1520
26:47 o of the twelve, came, and with him a great 1520
26:51 o of them which were with Jesus stretched 1520
26:73 said to Peter, Surely thou also art o of them; NIG
27:38 o on the right hand, and another on the left. 1520
27:48 And straightway o of them ran, and took a 1520
Mk 1: 3 The voice of o crying in the wilderness, NIG
1: 7 There cometh o mightier than I after me, 3588
1:22 for he taught them as o that had authority, NIG
1:24 I know thee who thou art, the Holy O of God. 40
2: 3 bringing o sick of the palsy, which was 3885
4:41 and said o to another, What manner of man 240
5:22 there cometh o of the rulers of 1520
6:15 That it is a prophet, or as o of the prophets. 1520
7:14 Hearken unto me every o of you, and 3956
7:32 And they bring unto him o that was deaf, NIG
8:14 they in the ship with them more than o loaf. 1520
8:28 say, Elias; and others, O of the prophets. 1520
9: 5 o for thee, and one for Moses, and one for 1520
9: 5 and o for Moses, and one for Elias. 1520
9: 5 and one for Moses, and o for Elias. 1520
9:10 questioning o with another what the rising NIG
9:17 And o of the multitude answered and said, 1520
9:26 came out of him: and he was as o dead; 3498
9:37 Whosoever shall receive o of such children 1520
9:38 we saw o casting out devils in thy name, 5100
9:42 And whosoever shall offend o of these little 1520
9:47 enter into the kingdom of God with o eye, 3442
9:49 For every o shall be salted with fire, and 3956
9:50 and have peace o with another. 240
10: 8 And they twain shall be o flesh: so then 1520
10: 8 so then they are no more twain, but o flesh. 1520
10:17 there came o running, and kneeled to him, 1520
10:18 there is none good but o, that is, God. 1520
10:21 and said unto him, O thing thou lackest: 1520
10:37 o on thy right hand, and the other on thy 1520
11:29 I will also ask of you o question, and 1520
12: 6 Having yet therefore o son, 1520
12:28 And o of the scribes came, and 1520
12:29 O Israel; The Lord our God is o Lord: 1520
12:32 for there is o God; and there is none other 1520
13: 1 o of his disciples saith unto him, Master, 1520
13: 2 there shall not be left o stone upon another, 3364
14:10 And Judas Iscariot, o of the twelve, 1520
14:18 O of you which eateth with me shall betray 1520
14:19 and to say unto him o by one, Is it I? 1527
14:19 and to say unto him one by o, Is it I? 1527
14:20 and said unto them, It is o of the twelve, 1520
14:37 couldest not thou watch o hour? 1520
14:43 o of the twelve, and with him a great 1520
14:47 And o of them that stood by drew a 1520+5100
14:66 there cometh o of the maids of the high 1520
14:69 say to them that stood by, This is o of them. NIG
14:70 again to Peter, Surely thou art o of them: NIG
15: 6 Now at that feast he released unto them o 1520
15: 7 And there was o named Barabbas, NIG
15:21 And they compel o Simon a Cyrenian, 5100

Mk 15:27 the **o** on *his* right hand, and the other on his *1520*
15:36 And **o** ran and filled a spunge *full* of *1520*
Lk 2: 3 went to be taxed, **every o** into his own city. *1538*
2:15 the shepherds said **o** to **another**, Let us now *240*
2:36 And there was **o** Anna, a prophetess, NIG
3: 4 The voice of **o** crying in the wilderness, NIG
3:16 but **o** mightier than I cometh, the latchet of *3588*
4:34 I know thee who thou art, the **Holy O** of God. *40*
4:40 and he laid *his* hands on every **o** of them, *1520*
5: 3 And he entered into **o** of the ships, *1520*
6: 9 I will ask you **o** *thing;* Is it lawful on *5101*
6:11 communed **o** with **another** what they might *240*
6:29 *And* unto him that smiteth thee on the *o* NIG
6:40 **every o** *that is* perfect shall be as his *3956*
7: 8 and I say unto **o**, Go, and he goeth; *3778*
7:32 and calling **o** to **another**, and saying, *240*
7:36 And **o** of the Pharisees desired him that he *5100*
7:41 the **o** ought five hundred pence, and *1520*
8:25 saying **o** to **another**, What *manner of man* is *240*
8:42 For he had **o only** daughter, about twelve *3439*
8:49 there cometh **o** from the ruler of *5100*
9: 8 that **o** of the old prophets was risen again. *1520*
9:19 others *say,* that **o** of the old prophets is *5100*
9:33 **o** for thee, and one for Moses, and one for *1520*
9:33 and **o** for Moses, and one for Elias: *1520*
9:33 and one for Moses, and **o** for Elias: *1520*
9:43 But while they wondered **every o** at all *3956*
9:49 we saw **o** casting out devils in thy name; *5100*
10:42 But **o** *thing* is needful: and Mary hath *1520*
11: 1 **o** of his disciples said unto him, Lord, *5100*
11: 4 for we also forgive **every o** *that is* indebted *3956*
11:10 For **every o** that asketh receiveth; and *3956*
11:45 Then answered **o** of the lawyers, and *5100*
11:46 ye yourselves touch not the burdens with **o** *1520*
12: 1 insomuch that *they* trode **o** upon **another**, *240*
12: 6 and not **o** of them is forgotten before God? *1520*
12:13 And **o** of the company said unto him, *5100*
12:25 thought can add to his stature **o** cubit? *1520*
12:27 all his glory was not arrayed like **o** of these. *1520*
12:52 For from henceforth there shall be five in **o** *1520*
13:10 And he was teaching in **o** of *1520*
13:15 doth not **each o** of you on the sabbath loose *1538*
13:23 Then said **o** unto him, Lord, are there few *5100*
14: 1 as he went into the house of **o** of the chief *5100*
14:15 And when **o** of them that sat at meat with *5100*
14:18 And they all with **o** *consent* began to make *1520*
15: 4 if he lose **o** of them, doth not leave *1520*
15: 7 that likewise joy shall be in heaven over **o** *1520*
15: 8 if she lose **o** piece, doth not light a candle, *1520*
15:10 angels of God over **o** sinner that repenteth. *1520*
15:19 make me as **o** of thy hired *servants.* *1520*
15:26 And he called **o** of the servants, and *1520*
16: 5 So he called every **o** of his lord's debtors *1520*
16:13 for either he will hate the **o**, and love *1520*
16:13 or else he will hold to the **o**, and despise *1520*
16:17 earth to pass, than **o** tittle of the law to fail. *1520*
16:30 but if **o** went unto them from the dead, *5100*
16:31 be persuaded, though **o** rose from the dead. *5100*
17: 2 than that he should offend **o** of these little *1520*
17:15 And **o** of them, when he saw that he was *1520*
17:22 when ye shall desire to see **o** of the days of *1520*
17:24 that lighteneth out of **the o** *part* under *3588*
17:34 in that night there shall be two *men* in **o** *1520*
17:34 the **o** shall be taken, and the other shall be *1520*
17:35 the **o** shall be taken, and the other left. *1520*
17:36 the **o** shall be taken, and the other left. *1520*
18:10 the **o** a Pharisee, and the other a publican. *1520*
18:14 for **every o** that exalteth himself shall be *3956*
18:19 none *is* good, save **o**, *that is,* God. *1520*
18:22 Yet lackest thou **o** *thing:* sell all that thou *1520*
19:26 That unto **every o** which hath shall be *3956*
19:44 they shall not leave in thee **o** stone upon NIG
20: 1 it came to pass, *that* on **o** of those days, *1520*
20: 3 said unto them, I will also ask you **o** thing; *1520*
21: 6 in the which there shall not be left **o** stone NIG
22:36 let him sell his garment, and buy **o**. NIG
22:47 **o** of the twelve, went before them, and *1520*
22:50 And **o** of them smote the servant of *1520+5100*
22:59 And about the space of **o** hour after another *1520*
23:14 unto me, as **o** that perverteth the people: NIG
23:17 (For of necessity he must release **o** unto *1520*
23:26 they laid hold upon **o** Simon, a Cyrenian, *5100*
23:33 **o** on the right hand, and the other on *3739*
23:39 And **o** of the malefactors which were *1520*
24:17 *are* these that ye have **o** to **another**, *240*
24:18 And the **o** *of them,* whose name *was* *1520*
24:32 And they said **o** to **another**, Did not our *240*
Jn 1:23 I *am* the voice of **o** crying in the wilderness, NIG
1:26 but there standeth **o** among you, whom ye NIG
1:40 **O** of the two which heard John speak, and *1520*
3: 8 so is **every o** that is born of the Spirit. *3956*
3:20 For **every o** that doeth evil hateth the light, *3956*
4:33 Therefore said the disciples **o** to **another**, *240*
4:37 And herein is *that* saying true, **O** soweth, *243*
5:44 which receive honour **o** of **another**, and *240*
5:45 there is *o* that accuseth you, *even* Moses, NIG
6: 7 that **every o** of them may take a little. *1538*
6: 8 **O** of his disciples, Andrew, Simon Peter's *1520*
6:22 save that **o** whereinto his disciples were *1520*
6:40 that **every o** which seeth the Son, and *3956*
6:70 chosen you twelve, and **o** of you is a devil? *1520*
6:71 should betray him, being **o** of the twelve. *1520*
7:21 I have done **o** work, and ye all marvel. *1520*
7:50 came to *Jesus* by night, being **o** of them,) *1520*
8: 9 went out **o by one**, beginning at the eldest, *1527*
8: 9 went out **one by o**, beginning at the eldest, *1527*
8:18 I am *o* that bear witness of myself, and NIG
8:41 of fornication; we have **o** Father, *even* God. *1520*
8:50 there is *o* that seeketh and judgeth. NIG
9:25 **o** *thing* I know, that, whereas I was blind, *1520*
9:32 opened the eyes of **o** that was born blind. NIG
10:16 and there shall be **o** fold, *and* one shepherd. *1520*
10:16 and there shall be one fold, *and* **o** shepherd. *1520*
10:30 I and *my* Father are **o**. *1520*
11:49 And **o** of them, *named* Caiaphas, being *1520*
Jn 11:50 that **o** man should die for the people, and *1520*
11:52 that also he should gather together in **o** *1520*
12: 2 Lazarus was **o** of them that sat at the table *1520*
12: 4 Then saith **o** of his disciples, Judas Iscariot, *1520*
12:48 not my words, hath *o* that judgeth him: NIG
13:14 ye also ought to wash **o another's** feet. *240*
13:21 say unto you, that **o** of you shall betray me. *1520*
13:22 Then the disciples looked **o** on **another**, *240*
13:23 Now there was leaning on Jesus' bosom **o** *1520*
13:34 I give unto you, That ye love **o another**; *240*
13:34 have loved you, that ye also love **o another**. *240*
13:35 my disciples, if ye have love **o** to **another**. *240*
15:12 That ye love **o another**, as I have loved you. *240*
15:17 I command you, that ye love **o another**. *240*
17:11 given me, that they may be **o**, as we *are.* *1520*
17:21 That they all may be **o**; as thou, Father, *1520*
17:21 and I in thee, that they also may be **o** in us: *1520*
17:22 that they may be **o**, even as we are one: *1520*
17:22 that they may be one, even as we are **o**: *1520*
17:23 in me, that they may be made perfect in **o**; *1520*
18:14 that it was expedient that **o** man should die *1520*
18:17 Art not thou also *o* of this man's disciples? NIG
18:22 **o** of the officers which stood by struck *1520*
18:25 Art not thou also *o* of his disciples? NIG
18:26 **O** of the servants of the high priest, *1520*
18:37 **Every o** that is of the truth heareth my *3956*
18:39 that I should release unto you **o** at *1520*
19:18 with him, **on either side o**, *1782+1782+2532*
19:34 But **o** of the soldiers with a spear pierced *1520*
20:12 the **o** at the head, and the other at the feet, *1520*
20:24 But Thomas, **o** of the twelve, *1520*
21:25 if they should be written every **o**, *1520*
Ac 1:14 These all continued **with o accord** in *3661*
1:22 must **o** be ordained *to be* a witness with us *1520*
2: 1 they were all **with o accord** in one place. *3661*
2: 1 all with one accord **in o place**. *846+1909+3588*
2: 7 and marvelled, saying **o** to **another**, Behold, *240*
2:12 and were in doubt, saying **o** to another, *243*
2:27 neither wilt thou suffer thine **Holy O** to see *3741*
2:38 be baptized **every o** of you in the name of *1538*
2:46 continuing daily **with o accord** in *3661*
3:14 But ye denied the **Holy O** and the Just, and *40*
3:26 in turning away **every o** of you from *his* *1538*
4:24 lift up their voice to God **with o accord**, *3661*
4:32 of them that believed were of **o** heart *1520*
4:32 believed were of one heart and of **o** soul: NIG
5:12 they were all **with o accord** in Solomon's *3661*
5:16 and they were healed **every o**. *537*
5:25 Then came **o** and told them, saying, *5100*
5:34 Then stood there up **o** in the council, *5100*
7:24 And seeing **o** *of them* suffer wrong, *5100*
7:26 **set** them **at o** *again,* saying, *1515+1519+4900*
7:26 why do ye wrong **o** to **another**? *240*
7:52 shewed before of the coming of the **Just O**; *1342*
7:57 their ears, and ran upon him **with o accord**, *3661*
8: 6 And the people **with o accord** gave heed *3661*
8: 9 giving out that himself was some **great o**: *3173*
9:11 inquire in the house of Judas for **o** called NIG
9:43 that he tarried many days in Joppa with **o** *5100*
10: 2 and **o** that feared God with all his house, NIG
10: 5 and call for *o* Simon, whose surname is NIG
10: 6 He lodgeth with **o** Simon a tanner, *5100*
10:22 and **o** that feareth God, and of good report NIG
10:28 or come unto **o of another nation**; *246*
10:32 he is lodged in the house of *o* Simon a NIG
11:28 And there stood up **o** of them named *1520*
12:10 went out, and passed on through **o** street; *1520*
12:20 but they came **with o accord** to him, and, *3661*
13:25 not *he.* But behold, there cometh **o** after me, NIG
13:35 not suffer thine **Holy O** to see corruption. *3741*
15:25 unto us, being assembled **with o accord**, *3661*
15:39 that they departed asunder **o** from **the other**: *240*
17: 7 saying that there is another king, *o* Jesus. NIG
17:26 And hath made of **o** blood all nations of *1520*
17:27 find *him,* though he be not far from every **o** *1520*
18: 7 named Justus, **o** that worshipped God, NIG
18:12 the Jews made insurrection **with o accord** *3661*
19: 9 disputing daily in the school of **o** Tyrannus. *5100*
19:14 And there were seven sons of *o* Sceva, NIG
19:29 they rushed **with o accord** into the theatre. *3661*
19:32 Some therefore cried **o** *thing,* and *5100*
19:34 all with **o** voice about the space of two *1520*
19:38 are deputies: let them implead **o another**. *240*
20:31 years I ceased not to warn every **o** night *1520*
21: 6 when we had taken our leave **o** of **another**, *240*
21: 7 the brethren, and abode with them **o** day. *1520*
21: 8 the evangelist, which was *o* of the seven; NIG
21:16 brought *with them* **o** Mnason of Cyprus, *5100*
21:26 should be offered for every **o** of them. *1520*
21:34 And some cried **o** *thing,* some another, *5100*
22:12 And **o** Ananias, a devout man according to *5100*
22:14 and see *that* **Just O**, and shouldest hear *1342*
23: 6 But when Paul perceived that the **o** part *1520*
23:17 Then Paul called **o** of the centurions unto *1520*
24:21 Except *it be* for this **o** voice, that I cried *1520*
25:19 and of **o** Jesus, *which was* dead, whom Paul *5100*
27: 1 certain other prisoners unto **o** named Julius, NIG
27: 2 *o* Aristarchus, a Macedonian of NIG
28: 2 and received us **every o**, because of *3956*
28:13 and after **o** day the south wind blew, and *1520*
28:25 after that Paul had spoken **o** word, *1520*
Ro 1:16 unto salvation to **every o** that believeth; *3956*
1:27 burned in their lust **o** towards **another**; *240*
2:15 while accusing or else excusing **o another**;) *240*
2:28 For he is not a Jew, which is **o** outwardly; NIG
2:29 But he *is* a Jew, which is **o** inwardly; NIG
3:10 There is none righteous, no, not **o**: *1520*
3:12 that doeth good, **no, not o**. *1520+2193+3756*
3:30 Seeing *it is* **o** God, which shall justify *1520*
5: 7 For scarcely for a righteous *man* will **o** die: *5100*
5:12 as by **o** man sin entered into the world, and *1520*
5:15 For if through the offence of **o** many be *1520*
5:15 by grace, which is by **o** man, Jesus Christ, *1520*
5:16 And not as *it was* by **o** that sinned, *so is* *1520*
5:16 for the judgment *was* by **o** to *1520*
Ro 5:17 For if by **o** man's offence death reigned by *1520*
5:17 by one man's offence death reigned by **o**; *1520*
5:17 gift of righteousness shall reign in life by **o**, *1520*
5:18 Therefore as by the offence of **o** *judgment* *1520*
5:18 by the righteousness of **o** *the free gift came* *1520*
5:19 For as by **o** man's disobedience many were *1520*
5:19 by the obedience of **o** shall many be made *1520*
9:10 but when Rebecca also had conceived by **o**, *1520*
9:21 of the same lump to make **o** vessel unto *3739*
10: 4 for righteousness to **every o** that believeth. *3956*
12: 4 For as we have many members in **o** body, *1520*
12: 5 are **o** body in Christ, and every one *1520*
12: 5 and every **o** members one of another. *1520*
12: 5 and every one members **o** of **another**. *240*
12:10 *Be* kindly affectioned **o** to **another** with *240*
12:10 in honour preferring **o another**; *240*
12:16 *Be* of the same mind **o** towards **another**. *240*
13: 8 no *man* any *thing,* but to love **o another**: *240*
14: 2 For **o** believeth that *he* may eat all *things:* *3739*
14: 5 **O man** esteemeth one day above another: *3739*
14: 5 One man esteemeth **o** day above another: NIG
14:12 **every o** of us shall give account of himself *1538*
14:13 us not therefore judge **o another** any more: *240*
14:19 and *things* wherewith **o** may edify **another**. *240*
15: 2 Let **every o** of us please *his* neighbour for *1538*
15: 5 **o** towards **another** according to Christ Jesus: *240*
15: 6 That ye may with **o mind** *and* one mouth *3661*
15: 6 with one mind *and* **o** mouth glorify God, *1520*
15: 7 Wherefore receive ye **o another**, as Christ *240*
15:14 able also to admonish **o another**. *240*
16:16 Salute **o another** with a holy kiss. The *240*
1Co 1:12 that **every o** of you saith, I am of Paul; *1538*
3: 4 For while **o** saith, I am of Paul; and *5100*
3: 8 he that planteth and he that watereth are **o**: *1520*
4: 6 that no **o** of you be puffed up for one *1520*
4: 6 that no one of you be puffed up for **o** *1520*
5: 1 that **o** should have *his* father's wife. *5100*
5: 5 To deliver **such a o** unto Satan for *5108*
5:11 an extortioner; with **such a o** no not to eat. *5108*
6: 5 not **o** that shall be able to judge between his *1520*
6: 7 because ye go to law **o** with **another**. *1438*
6:16 he which is joined to a harlot is **o** body? *1520*
6:16 for two, saith *he,* shall be **o** flesh. *1520*
6:17 But he that is joined unto the Lord is **o** *1520*
7: 5 Defraud you not **o** the **other**, except *it be* *240*
7: 7 gift of God, **o** after this manner, *3303+3739*
7:17 as the Lord hath called **every o**, so let him *1538*
7:25 as **o** that hath obtained mercy of the Lord to NIG
8: 4 and that *there is* none other God but **o**. *1520*
8: 6 But to us *there is but* **o** God, the Father, *1520*
8: 6 and **o** Lord Jesus Christ, by whom *are* all *1520*
9:24 in a race run all, but **o** receiveth the prize? *1520*
9:26 so fight I, not as **o** that beateth the air: NIG
10: 8 and fell in **o** day three and twenty thousand. *1520*
10:17 For we being many are **o** bread, *and* *1520*
10:17 we being many are one bread, *and* **o** body: *1520*
10:17 for we are all partakers of *that* **o** bread. *1520*
11: 5 **even all o as if** she were *846+1520+2532+3588*
11:20 therefore **into o place**, *846+1909+3588*
11:21 For in eating **every o** taketh before *other* *1538*
11:21 and **o** is hungry, and another is drunken. *3739*
11:33 ye come together to eat, tarry **o** for **another**. *240*
12: 8 For to **o** is given by the Spirit the word of *3739*
12:11 But all these worketh *that* **o** and *1520*
12:12 For as the body is **o**, and hath many *1520*
12:12 and all the members of *that* **o** body, *1520*
12:12 of *that* one body, being many, are **o** body: *1520*
12:13 For by **o** Spirit are we all baptized into one *1520*
12:13 For by one Spirit are we all baptized into **o** *1520*
12:13 have been all made to drink into **o** Spirit. *1520*
12:14 For the body is not **o** member, but many. *1520*
12:18 But now hath God set the members every **o** *1520*
12:19 And if they were all **o** member, where *were* *1520*
12:20 *are they* many members, yet *but* **o** body. *1520*
12:25 should have the same care **o** for **another**. *240*
12:26 And whether **o** member suffer, all *1520*
12:26 suffer with *it;* or **o** member be honoured, *1520*
14:23 be come together **into o place**, *846+1909+3588*
14:24 and there come in **o** that believeth not, or *5100*
14:24 or *o* unlearned, he is convinced of all, he is NIG
14:26 **every o** of you hath a psalm, hath a *1538*
14:27 and *that* by course; and let **o** interpret. *1520*
14:31 For ye may all prophesy **o by one**, *1520+2596*
14:31 For ye may all prophesy **one by o**, *1520+2596*
15: 8 of me also, as of **o** born out of due time. *3588*
15:39 but *there is* **o** *kind of* flesh of men, *243*
15:40 but the glory of the celestial *is* **o**, and *2087*
15:41 *There is* **o** glory of the sun, and *243*
15:41 for **o** star differeth from *another* star in NIG
16: 2 Upon the first *day* of the week let **every o** *1538*
16:16 and to **every o** that helpeth with *us,* and *3956*
16:20 Greet ye **o another** with a holy kiss. *240*
2Co 2: 7 comfort *him,* lest perhaps **such a o** should *5108*
2:16 To the **o** *we are* the savour of death unto *3739*
5:10 that **every o** may receive the *things done* in *1538*
5:14 that if **o** died for all, then were all dead: *1520*
10:11 Let **such a o** think this, that, such as we are *5108*
11: 2 for I have espoused you to **o** husband, that *I* *1520*
11:24 five times received I forty *stripes* save **o**. *1520*
12: 2 **such a o** caught up to the third heaven. *5108*
12: 5 Of **such a o** will I glory: yet of myself I *5108*
13:11 of good comfort, be of **o** mind, live in peace; *846*
13:12 Greet **o another** with a holy kiss. *240*
Gal 3:10 Cursed *is* **every o** that continueth not in all *3956*
3:13 Cursed *is* **every o** that hangeth on a tree: *3956*
3:16 but as of **o**, And to thy seed, which is *1520*
3:20 Now a mediator is not *a mediator* of **o**, but *1520*
3:20 is not *a mediator* of one, but God is **o**. *1520*
3:28 nor female: for ye are all **o** in Christ Jesus. *1520*
4:22 the **o** by a bondmaid, the other by a *1520*
4:24 the **o** from the mount Sinai, *1520*
5:13 to the flesh, but by love serve **o another**. *240*
5:14 For all the law is fulfilled in **o** word, *1520*
5:15 But if ye bite and devour **o another**, *240*
5:15 take heed ye be not consumed **o** of **another**. *240*

O

Gal 5:17 and these are contrary the **o to the other**: so *240*
5:26 provoking **o another**, envying one another. *240*
5:26 provoking one another, envying **o another**. *240*
6: 1 restore **such a o** in the spirit of meekness; *5108*
6: 2 Bear ye **o another's** burdens, and so *240*
Eph 1:10 **gather together in o** all *things* in Christ, *346*
2:14 who hath made both **o**, and hath broken *1520*
2:15 for to make in himself of twain **o** new man, *1520*
2:16 both unto God in **o** body by the cross, *1520*
2:18 For through him we both have access by **o** *1520*
4: 2 forbearing **o another** in love; *240*
4: 4 *There is* **o** body, and one Spirit, even as ye *1520*
4: 4 *There is* one body, and **o** Spirit, even as ye *1520*
4: 4 even as ye are called in **o** hope of your *1520*
4: 5 **O** Lord, one faith, one baptism, *1520*
4: 5 One Lord, **o** faith, one baptism, *1520*
4: 5 One Lord, one faith, **o** baptism, *1520*
4: 6 **O** God and Father of all, who *is* above all, *1520*
4: 7 But unto every **o** of us is given grace *1520*
4:25 for we are members **o** of **another**. *240*
4:32 And be ye kind **o** to **another**, tenderhearted, *240*
4:32 tenderhearted, forgiving **o another**, *1438*
5:21 Submitting yourselves **o** to **another** in *240*
5:31 unto his wife, and they two shall be **o** flesh. *1520*
5:33 Nevertheless let every **o** of you in particular *1520*
Php 1:16 The **o** preach Christ of contention, *3303*
1:27 of your affairs, that ye stand fast in **o** spirit, *1520*
1:27 with **o** mind striving together for the faith *1520*
2: 2 same love, *being* **of o accord**, of one mind. *4861*
2: 2 same love, *being* of one accord, of **o** mind. *1520*
3:13 *this* **o** *thing I do*, forgetting those *things* *1520*
Col 3: 9 Lie not **o** to **another**, seeing that ye have put *240*
3:13 Forbearing **o another**, and forgiving one *240*
3:13 one another, and forgiving **o another**, *1438*
3:15 to the which also ye are called in **o** body; *1520*
3:16 and admonishing **o another** in psalms and *1438*
4: 9 and beloved brother, who is *o* of you. NIG
4:12 Epaphras, who is *o* of you, a servant of NIG
1Th 2:11 and comforted and charged every **o** of you, *1520*
3:12 and abound in love **o** towards **another**, *240*
4: 4 That **every o** of you should know how to *1538*
4: 9 are taught of God to love **o another**. *240*
4:18 Wherefore comfort **o another** with these *240*
5:11 **o another**, even as also ye do. *1520+1520+3588*
2Th 1: 3 the charity of every **o** of you all towards *1520*
1Ti 2: 5 For *there is* **o** God, and one mediator *1520*
2: 5 and **o** mediator between God and men, *1520*
3: 2 the husband of **o** wife, vigilant, sober, *1520*
3: 4 **O** that ruleth well his own house, having *his* NIG
3:12 Let the deacons be the husbands of **o** wife, *1520*
5: 9 years old, having been the wife of **o** man, *1520*
5:21 *o before another*, doing nothing by NIG
2Ti 2:19 Let **every o** that nameth the name of Christ *3956*
Tit 1: 6 If any be blameless, the husband of **o** wife, *1520*
1:12 **O** of themselves, *even* a prophet of their *5100*
3: 3 and envy, hateful, *and* hating **o another**. *240*
Phm 1: 9 *thee*, being **such a o** as Paul the aged, *5108*
Heb 2: 6 But **o** in a certain place testified, saying, *5100*
2:11 and they who are sanctified *are* all of **o**: *1520*
3:13 But exhort **o another** daily, while it is *1438*
5:12 ye have need that *o* teach you again which NIG
5:13 For **every o** that useth milk *is* unskilful in *3956*
6:11 And we desire that **every o** of you do shew *1538*
10:12 But this *man*, after he had offered **o** *1520*
10:14 For by **o** offering he hath perfected for ever *1520*
10:24 And let us consider **o another** to provoke *240*
10:25 but exhorting *o another*: and so much NIG
11:12 Therefore sprang there even of **o**, and *1520*
12:16 who for **o** morsel of meat sold his *1520*
13:14 no continuing city, but we seek **o** to come. *3588*
Jas 2:10 and *yet* offend in **o** *point*, he is guilty of all. *1520*
2:16 And **o** of you say unto them, Depart in *5100*
2:19 Thou believest that there is **o** God; *1520*
4:11 Speak not evil **o** of **another**, brethren. *240*
4:12 There is **o** lawgiver, who is able to save and *1520*
5: 9 Grudge not **o** against **another**, brethren, *240*
5:16 Confess *your* faults **o** to **another**, and *240*
5:16 and pray **o** for **another**, that ye may be *240*
5:19 do err from the truth, and **o** convert him; *5100*
1Pe 1:22 *see that ye* love **o another** with a pure heart *240*
3: 8 Finally, *be ye* all of **o mind**, *3675*
3: 8 having **compassion o of another**, love as *4835*
4: 9 Use hospitality **o** to **another** without *240*
4:10 *even so* minister the same **o** to **another**, *1438*
5: 5 all *of you* be subject **o** to **another**, and *240*
5:14 Greet ye **o another** with a kiss of charity. *240*
2Pe 3: 8 be not ignorant of this **o** *thing*, that one day *1520*
3: 8 be not ignorant of this one *thing*, that **o** day *1520*
3: 8 and a thousand years as **o** day. *1520*
1Jn 1: 7 we have fellowship **o** with **another**, and *240*
2:13 because you have overcome the **wicked o**. *4190*
2:14 and ye have overcome the **wicked o**. *4190*
2:20 But ye have an unction from the **Holy O**, and *40*
2:29 ye know that **every o** which doeth *3956*
3:11 that we should love **o another**. *240*
3:12 *who* was of *that* **wicked o**, and slew his *4190*
3:23 and love **o another**, as he gave us *240*
4: 7 Beloved, let us love **o another**: for love is of *240*
4: 7 and **every o** that loveth is born of God, and *3956*
4:11 loved us, we ought also to love **o another**. *240*
4:12 If we love **o another**, God dwelleth in us, *240*
5: 1 **every o** that loveth him that begat loveth *3956*
5: 7 and the Holy Ghost: and these three are **o**. *1520*
5: 8 and the blood: and *these* three agree in **o**. *1520*
5:18 and *that* **wicked o** toucheth him not. *4190*
2Jn 1: 5 from the beginning, that we love **o another**. *240*
Rev 1:13 And in the midst of the seven candlesticks *o* NIG
2:23 I will give unto **every o** of you according to *1538*
4: 2 was set in heaven, and *o* sat on the throne. NIG
5: 5 And **o** of the elders saith unto me, *1520*
5: 8 having **every o** *of them* harps, and *1538*
6: 1 And I saw when the Lamb opened **o** of *1520*
6: 1 **o** of the four beasts saying, Come and see. *1520*
6: 4 and that they should kill **o another**: *240*
6:11 And white robes were given unto **every o** *1538*
Rev 7:13 And **o** of the elders answered, saying unto *1520*
9:12 **O** woe is past; *and* behold, there come two *1520*
11:10 and shall send gifts **o** to **another**; *240*
13: 3 And I saw **o** of his heads as *it were* *1520*
14:14 upon the cloud *o* sat like unto the Son of NIG
15: 7 And **o** of the four beasts gave unto *1520*
17: 1 And there came **o** of the seven angels *1520*
17:10 and **o** is, *and* the other is not yet come; *1520*
17:12 receive power as kings **o** hour with *1520*
17:13 These have **o** mind, and shall give their *1520*
18: 8 Therefore shall her plagues come in **o** day, *1520*
18:10 for in **o** hour is thy judgment come. *1520*
18:17 For in **o** hour so great riches is come to *1520*
18:19 for in **o** hour is she made desolate. *1520*
21: 9 And there came unto me **o** of the seven *1520*
21:21 every several gate was of **o** pearl: *1520*

ONE'S (2) [ONE]

Ecc 7: 1 the day of death than the day of **o** birth. 2050.2
Ac 16:26 and **every o** bands were loosed. *3956*

ONES (77) [ONE]

Ge 34:29 all their **little o**, and their wives took they 2945
43: 8 both we, and thou, *and* also our **little o**. 2945
45:19 out of the land of Egypt for your **little o**, 2945
46: 5 and their **little o**, and their wives, 2945
47:24 and for food for your **little o**. 2945
50: 8 only their **little o**, and their flocks, and 2945
50:21 I will nourish you and your **little o**. And he 2945
Ex 10:10 as I will let you go, and your **little o**: 2945
10:24 be stayed: let your **little o** also go with you. 2945
Nu 14:31 your **little o**, which ye said should be a 2945
31: 9 their **little o**, and took the spoil of all their 2945
31:17 therefore kill every male among the **little o**, 2945
32:16 for our cattle, and cities for our **little o**: 2945
32:17 our **little o** shall dwell in the fenced cities 2945
32:24 Build ye cities for your **little o**, and 2945
32:26 Our **little o**, our wives, our flocks, and 2945
Dt 1:39 Moreover your **little o**, which ye said 2945
2:34 the women, and the **little o**, of every city, 2945
3:19 and your **little o**, and your cattle, 2945
20:14 the **little o**, and the cattle, and all that is in 2945
22: 6 *whether they be* **young o**, or eggs, and 667
29:11 Your **little o**, your wives, and thy stranger 2945
Jos 1:14 Your wives, your **little o**, and your cattle, 2945
8:35 the **little o**, and the strangers that were 2945
Jdg 5:22 the pransings of their mighty *o*. NIH
18:21 put the **little o** and the cattle and 2945
2Sa 15:22 and all the **little o** that *were* with him. 2945
1Ch 16:13 ye children of Jacob, his chosen *o*. NIH
2Ch 20:13 with their **little o**, their wives, and 2945
31:18 to the genealogy of all their **little o**, 2945
Ezr 8:21 for our **little o**, and for all our substance. 2945
Est 8:11 *both* **little o** and women, and *to take* 2945
Job 21:11 They send forth their **little o** like a flock, 5759
38:41 when his **young o** cry unto God, 3206
39: 3 they bring forth their **young o**, 3206
39: 4 Their **young o** are in good liking, 1121
39:16 She is hardened against her **young o**, 1121
39:30 Her **young o** also suck up blood: and where 667
Ps 10:10 that the poor may fall by his strong *o*. NIH
83: 3 and consulted against thy **hidden o**. 6845
137: 9 and dasheth thy **little o** against the stones. 5768
Pr 1:22 How long, ye **simple o**, will ye love 6612
7: 7 beheld among the **simple o**, I discerned 6612
Isa 5:17 the waste places of the **fat o** shall strangers 4220
10:16 of hosts, send among his **fat o** leanness; 4924
10:33 the **high o** of stature *shall be* hewn down, 7311
11: 7 their **young o** shall lie down together: 3206
13: 3 I have commanded my **sanctified o**, I have 6942
13: 3 I have also called my **mighty o** for mine 1368
14: 9 for thee, *even* all the **chief o** of the earth; 6260
24:21 the host of the **high o** *that are* on high, 4791
25: 4 when the blast of the **terrible o** *is* as a 6184
25: 5 the branch of the **terrible o** shall be 6184
29: 5 the multitude of the **terrible o** *shall be* as 6184
32:11 that are at ease; be troubled, ye careless *o*: NIH
33: 7 Behold, their **valiant o** shall cry without: 691
57:15 and to revive the heart of the **contrite o**. 1792
Jer 2:33 hast thou also taught the **wicked o** thy 7451
8:16 at the sound of the neighing of his **strong o**; 47
14: 3 their nobles have sent their **little o** to 6810
46: 5 their **mighty o** are beaten down, and 1368
48: 4 her **little o** have caused a cry to be heard. 6810
48:45 the crown of the head of the tumultuous **o**. 1121
La 4: 3 the breast, they give suck to their **young o**: 1482
Da 4:17 and the demand *by* the word of the **holy o**: 6922
8: 8 for it came up four **notable o** toward 2380
11:17 whole kingdom, and **upright o** with him; 3477
Joel 3:11 thither cause thy **mighty o** to come down, 1368
Zec 4:14 said he, These *are* the two anointed **o**, 1121
13: 7 and I will turn mine hand upon the **little o**. 6819
Mt 10:42 **little o** a cup of cold *water* only in the name *3398*
18: 6 But whoso shall offend one of these **little o** *3398*
18:10 that ye despise not one of these **little o**; *3398*
18:14 that one of these **little o** should perish. *3398*
Mk 9:42 one of *these* **little o** that believe in me, *3398*
10:42 their **great o** exercise authority upon them. *3173*
Lk 17: 2 that he should offend one of these **little o**. *3398*

ONESIMUS (4)

Col 4: 9 With **O**, a faithful and beloved brother, *3682*
4: S to the Colossians by Tychicus and **O**. *3682*
Phm 1:10 I beseech thee for my son **O**, whom I have *3682*
1: S from Rome to Philemon, by **O** a servant. *3682*

ONESIPHORUS (2)

2Ti 1:16 The Lord give mercy unto the house of **O**; *3683*
4:19 and Aquila, and the household of **O**. *3683*

ONIONS (1)

Nu 11: 5 and the leeks, and the **o**, and the garlick: 1211

ONLY (253)

Ge 6: 5 thoughts of his heart *was* **o** evil continually. 7535
7:23 Noah **o** remained *alive*, and *they* that *were* 389
14:24 Save **o** that which the young men have 7535
19: 8 **o** unto these men do nothing; for therefore 7535
22: 2 Take now thy son, thine **o** *son* Isaac, 3173
22:12 not withheld thy son, thine **o** *son* from me. 3173
22:16 hast not withheld thy son, thine **o** *son*: 3173
24: 8 my oath: **o** bring not my son thither again. 7535
27:13 **o** obey my voice, and go fetch me *them*. 389
34:22 **O** herein will the men consent unto us for to 389
34:23 **o** let us consent unto them, and they will 389
41:40 **o** *in* the throne will I be greater than thou. 7535
47:22 **O** the land of the priests bought he not; 7535
47:26 *part;* except the land of the priests **o**, 905+3807.1
50: 8 **o** their little ones, and their flocks, and 7535
Ex 8: 9 *that* they may remain in the river **o**? 7535
8:11 thy people; they shall remain in the river **o**. 7535
8:28 **o** you shall not go very far away: 7535
9:26 **O** in the land of Goshen, where the children 7535
10:17 my sin **o** *this* once, and intreat the LORD 389
10:17 he may take away from me this death **o**. 7535
10:24 **o** let your flocks and your herds be stayed: 7535
12:16 must eat, that **o** may be done of you. 905+3807.1
21:19 **o** he shall pay *for* the loss of his time, and 7535
22:20 save unto the LORD **o**, he shall be 905+3807.1
22:27 For that *is* his covering **o**, it *is* his 905+3807.1
Lev 21:23 **O** he shall not go in unto the vail, nor come 389
27:26 **O** the firstling of the beasts, which should be 389
Nu 1:49 **O** thou shalt not number the tribe of Levi, 389
12: 2 Hath the LORD **indeed** spoken **o** by 389+7535
14: 9 **O** rebel not ye against the LORD, 389
18: 3 **o** they shall not come nigh the vessels of 389
20:19 I will **o**, without *doing any* thing *else*, go 7535
22:35 **o** the word that I shall speak unto thee, 657
31:22 **O** the gold, and the silver, the brass, the iron, 389
36: 6 **o** to the family of the tribe of their father 389
Dt 2:28 **o** I will pass through on my feet; 7535
2:35 **O** the cattle we took for a prey unto 7535
2:37 **O** unto the land of the children of Ammon 7535
3:11 For **o** Og king of Bashan remained of 7535
4: 9 **O** take heed to thyself, and keep thy soul 7535
4:12 but saw no similitude; **o** *ye heard* a voice. 2108
8: 3 that man doth not live by bread **o**, 905+3807.1
10:15 **O** the LORD had a delight in thy fathers 7535
12:16 **O** ye shall not eat the blood; ye shall pour it 7535
12:23 **O** be sure that thou eat not the blood: 7535
12:26 **O** thy holy *things* which thou hast, and 7535
15: 5 **O** if thou carefully hearken unto the voice 7535
15:23 **O** thou shalt not eat the blood thereof; 7535
20:20 **O** the trees which thou knowest that they 7535
22:25 the man **o** that lay with her shall die: 905+3807.1
28:13 thou shalt be above **o**, and thou shalt not be 7535
28:29 thou shalt be **o** oppressed and 389
28:33 thou shalt be **o** oppressed and 7535
29:14 Neither with you **o** do I make this 905+3807.1
Jos 1: 7 **O** be thou strong and very courageous, 7535
1:17 **o** the LORD thy God be with thee, as he 7535
1:18 to death: **o** be strong and of a good courage. 7535
6:15 **o** on that day they compassed the city seven 7535
6:17 **o** Rahab the harlot shall live, she and 7535
6:24 **o** the silver, and the gold, and the vessels of 7535
8: 2 **o** the spoil thereof, and the cattle thereof, 7535
8:27 **O** the cattle and the spoil of that city Israel 7535
11:13 burned none of them, save Hazor **o**; 905+3807.1
11:22 **o** in Gaza, in Gath, and in Ashdod, 7535
13: 6 **o** divide thou it *by lot* unto the Israelites for 7535
13:14 **O** unto the tribe of Levi he gave none 7535
17:17 great power: thou shalt not have one lot *o*: NIH
Jdg 3: 2 **O** that the generations of the children of 7535
6:37 *and* if the dew be on the fleece **o**, 905+3807.1
6:39 let it now be dry **o** upon the fleece, 905+3807.1
6:40 for it was dry upon the fleece **o**, 905+3807.1
10:15 deliver us **o**, we pray thee, this day. 389
11:34 she *was his* **o** child; beside her he had 7535
16:28 I pray thee, **o** this once, O God, 389
19:20 wants *lie* upon me; **o** lodge not in the street. 7535
1Sa 1:13 **o** her lips moved, but her voice was not 7535
1:23 **o** the LORD establish his word. 389
5: 4 **o** *the stump of* Dagon was left to him. 7535
7: 3 unto the LORD, and serve him **o**: 905+3807.1
7: 4 and served the LORD **o**. 905+3807.1
12:24 **O** fear the LORD, and serve him in truth 389
18:17 **o** be thou valiant for me, and fight 389
20:14 thou shalt not **o** while yet I live shew me 518
20:39 **o** Jonathan and David knew the matter. 389
2Sa 13:32 king's sons; for Amnon **o** is dead: 905+3807.1
13:33 sons are dead: for Amnon **o** is dead. 905+3807.1
17: 2 and I will smite the king **o**: 905+3807.1
20:21 deliver him **o**, and I will depart from 905+3807.1
23:10 and the people returned after him **o** to spoil. 389
1Ki 3: 2 **O** the people sacrificed in high places, 7535
3: 3 **o** he sacrificed and burnt incense in high 7535
4:19 *he was* the **o** officer which *was* in the land. 259
8:39 (for thou, *even* thou **o**, knowest 905+3807.1
12:20 of David, but the tribe of Judah **o**. 905+3807.1
14: 8 to do *that* **o** which *was* right in mine eyes; 7535
14:13 for he **o** of Jeroboam shall come to 905+3807.1
15: 5 **save o** in the matter of Urijah the Hittite. 7535
18:22 I, *even* I **o**, remain a prophet of 905+3807.1
19:10 I, *even* I **o**, am left; and they seek 905+3807.1
19:14 I, *even* I **o**, am left; and they seek 905+3807.1
22:31 save **o** with the king of Israel. 905+3807.1
2Ki 3:25 **o** in Kir-haraseth left *they* the stones 7535
10:23 but the worshippers of Baal **o**. 905+3807.1
17:18 none left but the tribe of Judah **o**. 905+3807.1
19:19 *art* the LORD God, *even* thou **o**. 905+3807.1
21: 8 **o** if they will observe to do according to all 7535
1Ch 22:12 **O** the LORD give thee wisdom and 389
2Ch 2: 6 **save o** to burn sacrifice before him? 518+3588
6:30 (for thou **o** knowest the hearts of 905+3807.1
18:30 save **o** with the king of Israel. 905+3807.1
33:17 *yet* unto the LORD their God **o**. 7535
Ezr 10:15 **O** Jonathan the son of Asahel and 389

O

Est 1:16 hath not done wrong to the king o, 905+3807.1
Job 1:12 o upon himself put not forth thine hand. 7535
1:15 and I o am escaped alone to tell thee. 7535
1:16 and I o am escaped alone to tell thee. 7535
1:17 and I o am escaped alone to tell thee. 7535
1:19 and I o am escaped alone to tell thee. 7535
13:20 O do not two *things* unto me: then will I not 389
34:29 *done* against a nation, or against a man o: 3162
Ps 4: 8 o makest me dwell in safety. 910+3807.1
51: 4 Against thee, thee o, have I sinned, 905+3807.1
62: 2 He o *is* my rock and my salvation; *he is* my 389
62: 4 They o consult to cast *him* down from his 389
62: 5 My soul, wait thou o upon God; for my 389
62: 6 He o *is* my rock and my salvation: *he is* my 389
71:16 thy righteousness, *even* of thine o. 905+3807.1
72:18 who o doeth wondrous *things*. 905+3807.1
91: 8 O with thine eyes shalt thou behold and 7535
Pr 4: 3 and o *beloved* in the sight of my mother. 3173
5:17 Let them be o thine own, and 905+3807.1
11:23 The desire of the righteous *is* o good: *but* 389
13:10 O by pride cometh contention: but with 7535
14:23 but the talk of the lips *tendeth* o to penury. 389
17:11 An evil *man* seeketh o rebellion: therefore 389
21: 5 The thoughts of the diligent *tend* o to 389
21: 5 but *of* every one that is hasty o to want. 389
Ecc 7:29 Lo, this o have I found, that God 905+3807.1
SS 6: 9 she *is* the *o* one of her mother, she *is* NIH
Isa 4: 1 o let us be called by thy name, to take away 7535
26:13 by thee o will we make mention of 905+3807.1
28:19 it shall be a vexation o *to* understand 7535
37:20 thou *art* the LORD, *even* thou o. 905+3807.1
Jer 3:13 O acknowledge thine iniquity, that thou hast 389
6:26 *as for* an o *son*, most bitter lamentation: 3173
32:30 the children of Judah have o done evil before 389
32:30 for the children of Israel have o provoked 389
Eze 7: 5 An evil, an o evil, behold, is come. 259
14:16 they o shall be delivered, but 905+3807.1
14:18 they o shall be delivered themselves. 905+3807.1
44:20 they shall o **poll** their heads. 3697+3697
Am 3: 2 You o have I known of all the families of 7535
8:10 I will make it as the mourning of an o *son*, 3173
Zec 12:10 as one mourneth for *his* o *son*, and shall be 3173
Mt 4:10 Lord thy God, and him o shalt thou serve. *3441*
5:47 And if ye salute your brethren o, what do *3440*
8: 8 but speak the word o, and my servant shall *3440*
10:42 of cold *water* o in the name of a disciple, *3440*
12: 4 which were with him, but o for the priests? *3441*
14:36 And besought him that they might o touch *3440*
17: 8 their eyes, they saw no *man*, save Jesus o. *3441*
21:19 but leaves o, and said unto it, *3440*
21:21 ye shall not o do this which is done to *3440*
24:36 not the angels of heaven, but my Father o. *3441*
Mk 2: 7 who can forgive sins but God o? *1520*
5:36 of the synagogue, Be not afraid, o believe. *3440*
6: 8 nothing for *their* journey, save a staff o; *3440*
9: 8 any more, save Jesus o with themselves. *3441*
Lk 4: 8 Lord thy God, and him o shalt thou serve. *3441*
7:12 the o son of his mother, and she was a *3439*
8:42 For he had **one** o daughter, about twelve *3439*
8:50 believe o, and she shall be made whole. *3440*
9:38 look upon my son: for he is mine o **child**. *3439*
24:18 Art thou o a stranger in Jerusalem, and *3441*
Jn 1:14 the glory as of the o **begotten** of *3439*
1:18 the o **begotten** Son, which is in the bosom *3439*
3:16 the world, that he gave his o **begotten** Son, *3439*
3:18 in the name of the o **begotten** Son of God. *3439*
5:18 because he not o had broken the sabbath, *3440*
5:44 not the honour that *cometh* from God o? *3441*
11:52 And not for *that* nation o, but that also he *3440*
12: 9 and they came not for Jesus' sake o, *3440*
13: 9 not my feet o, but also *my* hands and *3440*
17: 3 that they might know thee the o true God, *3441*
Ac 8:16 o they were baptized in the name of *3440*
11:19 the word to none but unto *the* Jews o. *3440*
18:25 the Lord, knowing o the baptism of John. *3440*
19:27 So *that* not o this our craft is in danger to be *3440*
21:13 for I am ready not to be bound o, but *3440*
21:25 **save** o that they keep themselves from *1508*
26:29 that not o thou, but also all that hear me this *3440*
27:10 not o of the lading and ship, but also of our *3440*
Ro 1:32 not o do the same, but have pleasure in *3440*
3:29 *Is he* the God of the Jews o? *is he* not also *3440*
4: 9 then upon the circumcision *o*, or NIG
4:12 to them who are not of the circumcision o, *3440*
4:16 not to that o which is of the law, but to that *3440*
5: 3 And not o *so*, but we glory in tribulations *3440*
5:11 And not o *so*, but we also joy in God *3440*
8:23 And not o *they*, but ourselves also, *3440*
9:10 And not o *this*; but when Rebecca also had *3440*
9:24 not of the Jews o, but also of the Gentiles? *3440*
13: 5 not o for wrath, but also for conscience *3440*
16: 4 unto whom not o I give thanks, but also all *3441*
16:27 To God o wise, *be* glory through Jesus *3441*
1Co 7:39 be married to whom she will; o in the Lord. *3440*
9: 6 Or I o and Barnabas, have not we power to *3441*
14:36 God out from you? or came it unto you o? *3441*
15:19 If in this life o we have hope in Christ, *3440*
2Co 7: 7 And not by his coming o, but by *3440*
8:10 not o to do, but also to be forward a year *3440*
8:19 And not *that* o, but who was also chosen of *3440*
8:21 Providing *for* honest *things*, not o in *3440*
9:12 For the administration of this service not o *3440*
Gal 1:23 But they had heard o, That he which *3440*
2:10 O *they would* that we should remember *3440*
3: 2 This o would I learn of you, Received ye *3440*
4:18 and not o when I am present with you. *3440*
5:13 o *use* not liberty for an occasion to *3440*
6:12 o lest they should suffer persecution for *3440*
Eph 1:21 not o in this world, but also in that which is *3440*
Php 1:27 O let your conversation be as it becometh *3440*
1:29 not o to believe on him, but also to suffer *3440*
2:12 not as in my presence o, but now much *3440*
2:27 and not on him o, but on me also, lest I *3440*
4:15 concerning giving and receiving, but ye o. *3441*
Col 4:11 These o *are my* fellowworkers unto *3441*
1Th 1: 5 our gospel came not unto you in word o, *3440*
1: 8 the word of the Lord not o in Macedonia *3440*
2: 8 not the gospel of God o, but also our own *3440*
2Th 2: 7 o he who now letteth *will let*, until he be *3440*
1Ti 1:17 immortal, invisible, the o wise God, *3441*
5:13 and not o idle, but tattlers also and *3440*
6:15 *who is* the blessed and o Potentate, *3441*
6:16 Who o hath immortality, dwelling in *3441*
2Ti 2:20 But in a great house there are not o vessels *3440*
4: 8 and not to me o, but unto all them also that *3440*
4:11 O Luke is with me. Take Mark, and *3441*
Heb 9:10 *Which stood* o in meats and drinks, and *3440*
11:17 promises offered up *his* o **begotten** *son*, *3439*
12:26 Yet once *more* I shake not the earth o, but *3440*
Jas 1:22 and not hearers o, deceiving your own *3440*
2:24 works a man is justified, and not by faith o. *3440*
1Pe 2:18 not o to the good and gentle, but also to *3440*
1Jn 2: 2 and not for ours o, but also for *the sins of* *3440*
4: 9 that God sent his o **begotten** Son into *3439*
5: 6 not by water o, but by water and blood. *3440*
2Jn 1: 1 and not I o, but also all they that have *3441*
Jude 1: 4 and denying the o Lord God, and our Lord *3441*
1:25 To the o wise God our Saviour, *be* glory *3441*
Rev 9: 4 o *those* men which have not the seal of God *3441*
15: 4 for *thou* o *art* holy: for all nations shall *3441*

ONO (5)

1Ch 8:12 Misham, and Shamed, who built O, and Lod, 207
Ezr 2:33 The children of Lod, Hadid, and O, 207
Ne 6: 2 in *some one of* the villages in the plain of O. 207
7:37 The children of Lod, Hadid, and O, 207
11:35 Lod, and O, the valley of craftsmen. 207

ONWARD (1)

Ex 40:36 the children of Israel **went** o in all their 5265

ONYCHA (1)

Ex 30:34 sweet spices, stacte, and o, and galbanum; 7827

ONYX (11)

Ge 2:12 *is* good: there *is* bdellium and the o stone. 7718
Ex 25: 7 O stones, and stones to be set in the ephod, 7718
28: 9 thou shalt take two o stones, and grave on 7718
28:20 fourth row a beryl, and an o, and a jasper: 7718
35: 9 o stones, and stones to be set for the ephod, 7718
35:27 the rulers brought o stones, and stones to be 7718
39: 6 they wrought o stones inclosed *in* ouches *of* 7718
39:13 the fourth row, a beryl, an o, and a jasper: 7718
1Ch 29: 2 o stones, and *stones* to be set, 7718
Job 28:16 with the precious o, or the sapphire. 7718
Eze 28:13 the beryl, the o, and the jasper, 7718

OPEN (124) [OPENED, OPENEST, OPENETH, OPENING, OPENINGS, OPENLY]

Ge 1:20 fowl *that* may fly above the earth in the o 6440
38:14 and sat in an o **place**, 5869+6607
Ex 21:33 if a man shall o a pit, or if a man shall dig a 6605
Lev 14: 7 shall let the living bird loose into the o 6440
14:53 living bird out of the city into the o fields, 6440
17: 5 which they offer in the o field, even that 6440
Nu 8:16 instead of such as o every womb, 6363
16:30 the earth o her mouth, and swallow them 6475
19:15 every o vessel, which hath no covering 6605
19:16 that is slain with a sword in the o fields, 6440
24: 3 and the man whose eyes are o hath said: 8365
24: 4 falling *into a trance*, but having his eyes o: 1540
24:15 and the man whose eyes are o hath said: 8365
24:16 falling *into a trance*, but having his eyes o: 1540
Dt 15: 8 thou shalt o thine hand **wide** unto 6605+6605
15:11 Thou shalt o thine hand **wide** unto 6605+6605
20:11 of peace, and o unto thee, then it shall be, 6605
28:12 The LORD shall o unto thee his good 6605
Jos 8:17 they left the city o, and pursued after Israel. 6605
10:22 O the mouth of the cave, and bring out 6605
1Sa 3: 1 in those days; *there was* no o vision. 6555
2Sa 11:11 of my lord, are encamped in the o fields; 6440
1Ki 6:18 *was* carved with knops and o flowers: 6358
6:29 of cherubims and palm trees and o flowers, 6358
6:32 of cherubims and palm trees and o flowers, 6358
6:35 and palm trees and o flowers: 6358
8:29 That thine eyes may be o toward this house 6605
8:52 That thine eyes may be o unto 6605
2Ki 6:17 said, LORD, I pray thee, o his eyes, 6491
6:20 o the eyes of these *men*, that they may see. 6491
9: 3 Then o the door, and flee, and tarry not. 6605
13:17 he said, O the window eastward. And he 6605
19:16 o, LORD, thine eyes, and see: and 6491
2Ch 6:20 That thine eyes may be o upon this house 6605
6:40 thine eyes be o, and *let* thine ears *be* attent 6605
7:15 Now mine eyes shall be o, and mine ears 6605
Ne 1: 6 thine ear now be attentive, and thine eyes o, 6605
6: 5 the fifth time with an o letter in his hand; 6605
Job 11: 5 would speak, and o his lips against thee; 6605
14: 3 dost thou o thine eyes upon such a one, 6491
32:20 be refreshed: I will o my lips and answer. 6605
34:26 He striketh them as wicked *men* in the o 4725
35:16 Therefore doth Job o his mouth in vain; 6475
41:14 Who can o the doors of his face? his teeth 6605
Ps 5: 9 their throat *is* an o sepulchre; they flatter 6605
34:15 and his ears *are* o unto their cry. NIH
49: 4 I will o my dark saying upon the harp. 6605
51:15 O Lord, o thou my lips; and my mouth 6605
78: 2 I will o my mouth in a parable: I will utter 6605
81:10 o thy mouth **wide**, and I will fill it. 7337
118:19 O to me the gates of righteousness: I will 6605
119:18 O thou mine eyes, that I may behold 1540
Pr 13:16 but a fool **layeth** o *his* folly. 6566
20:13 o thine eyes, *and* thou shalt be satisfied 6491
27: 5 O rebuke *is* better than secret love. 1540
31: 8 O thy mouth for the dumb in the cause of 6605
31: 9 O thy mouth, judge righteously, and 6605
SS 5: 2 my beloved *that* knocketh *saying*, O to me, 6605
5: 5 I rose up to o to my beloved; and my hands 6605
Isa 9:12 they shall devour Israel with o mouth. 3605
Isa 22:22 so he shall o, and none shall shut; and 6605
22:22 and he shall shut, and none shall o. 6605
24:18 for the windows from on high are o, and 6605
26: 2 O ye the gates, that the righteous nation 6605
28:24 doth he o and break the clods of his 6605
37:17 and hear; o thine eyes, O LORD, and see: 6491
41:18 I will o rivers in high places, and 6605
42: 7 To o the blind eyes, to bring out 6491
45: 1 to o before him the two leaved gates; 6605
45: 8 let the earth o, and let them bring forth 6605
60:11 Therefore thy gates shall be o continually; 6605
Jer 5:16 Their quiver *is* as an o sepulchre, they *are* 6605
9:22 of men shall fall as dung upon the o field, 6440
13:19 none shall o *them*: Judah shall be carried 6605
32:11 the law and custom, and that which was o: 1540
32:14 is sealed, and this evidence which is o; 1540
32:19 for thine eyes *are* o upon all the ways of 6491
50:26 from the utmost border, o her storehouses: 6605
Eze 2: 8 o thy mouth, and eat that I give thee. 6475
3:27 I will o thy mouth, and thou shalt say unto 6605
16: 5 thou wast cast out in the o field, to 6440
16:63 never o thy mouth any more, because of thy 6610
21:22 to o the mouth in the slaughter, 6605
25: 9 I *will* o the side of Moab from the cities, 6605
29: 5 thou shalt fall upon the o fields; thou shalt 6440
32: 4 I will cast thee forth upon the o field, and 6440
33:27 him that *is* in the o field will I give to 6440
37: 2 *there were* very many in the o valley; 6440
37:12 I *will* o your graves, and cause you to come 6605
39: 5 Thou shalt fall upon the o field: for I have 6440
46:12 o him the gate that looketh *toward* the east, 6605
Da 6:10 his windows being o in his chamber toward 6606
9:18 o thine eyes, and behold our desolations, 6491
Na 3:13 the gates of thy land shall be set wide o 6605
Zec 11: 1 O thy doors, O Lebanon, that the fire may 6605
12: 4 I will o mine eyes upon the house of Judah, 6491
Mal 3:10 if I will not o you the windows of heaven, 6605
Mt 13:35 saying, I will o my mouth in parables; *455*
25:11 the other virgins, saying, Lord, Lord, o to us. *455*
Lk 12:36 knocketh, they may o unto him immediately. *455*
13:25 at the door, saying, Lord, Lord, o unto us; *455*
Jn 1:51 Hereafter ye shall see heaven o, and *455*
10:21 a devil. Can a devil o the eyes of the blind? *455*
Ac 16:27 and seeing the prison doors o, he drew out *455*
18:14 And when Paul was *now* about to o *his* *455*
19:38 have a matter against any *man*, the law is o, *71*
26:18 To o their eyes, *and* to turn *them* from *455*
Ro 3:13 Their throat *is* an o sepulchre; with their *455*
2Co 3:18 with o face beholding as in a glass the glory *343*
6:11 O *ye* Corinthians, our mouth is o unto you, *455*
Eph 6:19 unto me, that *I* may o my mouth boldly, *457*
Col 4: 3 that God would o unto us a door of *455*
1Ti 5:24 Some men's sins are o **beforehand**, *4271*
Heb 6: 6 of God afresh, and **put** *him* to an o **shame**. *3856*
1Pe 3:12 and his ears *are* o unto their prayers: NIG
Rev 3: 8 I have set before thee an o door, and no *man* *455*
3:20 and o the door, I will come in to him, and *455*
5: 2 Who is worthy to o the book, and to loose *455*
5: 3 under the earth, was able to o the book, *455*
5: 4 because no *man* was found worthy to o and *455*
5: 5 hath prevailed to o the book, and to loose *455*
5: 9 to take the book, and to o the seals thereof: *455*
10: 2 And he had in his hand a little book o: and *455*
10: 8 take the little book which is o in the hand of *455*

OPENED (137) [OPEN]

Ge 3: 5 your eyes shall be o, and ye shall be as 6491
3: 7 the eyes of them both were o, and 6491
4:11 which hath o her mouth to receive thy 6475
7:11 and the windows of heaven were o. 6605
8: 6 that Noah o the window of the ark which he 6605
21:19 God o her eyes, and she saw a well of 6491
29:31 saw that Leah *was* hated, he o her womb: 6605
30:22 and God hearkened to her, and o her womb. 6605
41:56 Joseph o all the storehouses, and sold unto 6605
42:27 as one *of them* o his sack to give his ass 6605
43:21 to the inn, that we o our sacks, and behold, 6605
44:11 to the ground, and o every man his sack. 6605
Ex 2: 6 when she had o *it*, she saw the child: and 6605
Nu 16:32 the earth o her mouth, and swallowed them 6605
22:28 the LORD o the mouth of the ass, and 6605
22:31 Then the LORD o the eyes of Balaam, and 1540
26:10 the earth o her mouth, and swallowed them 6605
Dt 11: 6 how the earth o her mouth, and 6475
Jdg 3:25 behold, he o not the doors of the parlour; 6605
3:25 they took a key, and o *them*: and behold, 6605
4:19 she o a bottle of milk, and gave him drink, 6605
11:35 for I have o my mouth unto the LORD, 6475
11:36 *if* thou hast o thy mouth unto the LORD, 6475
19:27 o the doors of the house, and went out to go 6605
1Sa 3:15 and o the doors of the house of the LORD. 6605
2Ki 4:35 seven times, and the child o his eyes. 6491
6:17 the LORD o the eyes of the young man; 6491
6:20 And the LORD o their eyes, and they saw; 6491
9:10 *there shall be* none to bury *her*. And he o 6605
13:17 he o *it*. Then Elisha said, Shoot. And he 6605
15:16 because they o not *to him*, therefore 6605
2Ch 29: 3 o the doors of the house of the LORD, and 6605
Ne 7: 3 Let not the gates of Jerusalem be o until 6605
8: 5 Ezra o the book in the sight of all 6605
8: 5 and when he o *it*, all the people stood *up*: 6605
13:19 charged that they should not be o till after 6605
Job 3: 1 After this o Job his mouth, and cursed his 6605
29:23 they o their mouth **wide** *as* for the latter 6473
31:32 the street: *but* I o my doors to the traveller. 6605
33: 2 Behold now I have o my mouth, my tongue 6605
38:17 Have the gates of death been o unto thee? 1540
Ps 35:21 they o their mouth **wide** against me, *and* 7337
39: 9 I was dumb, I o not my mouth; because 6605
40: 6 thou didst not desire; mine ears hast thou o: 3738
78:23 from above, and o the doors of heaven, 6605
105:41 He o the rock, and the waters gushed out; 6605
106:17 The earth o and swallowed up Dathan, and 6605
109: 2 the mouth of the deceitful are o against me: 6605
119:131 I o my mouth, and panted: for I longed for 6473

SS 5: 6 I **o** to my beloved; but my beloved had 6605
Isa 5:14 and **o** her mouth without measure: 6473
10:14 moved the wing, or **o** the mouth, or peeped. 6475
14:17 *that* **o** not the house of his prisoners? 6605
35: 5 the eyes of the blind shall be **o**, and the ears 6491
48: 8 yea, from that time *that* thine ear was not **o**: 6605
50: 5 The Lord GOD hath **o** mine ear, and I was 6605
53: 7 he was afflicted, yet he **o** not his mouth: 6605
Jer 20:12 on them: for unto thee have I **o** my cause. 1540
50:25 The LORD hath **o** his armoury, and 6605
La 2:16 All thine enemies have **o** their mouth 6475
3:46 All our enemies have **o** their mouths 6475
Eze 1: 1 *that* the heavens were **o**, and I saw visions 6605
3: 2 So I **o** my mouth, and he caused me to eat 6605
16:25 hast **o** thy feet to every one that passed by, 6589
24:27 In that day shall thy mouth be **o** to him 6605
33:22 had **o** my mouth, until *he* came to me in 6605
33:22 my mouth was **o**, and I was no more dumb. 6605
37:13 when I have **o** your graves, O my people, 6605
44: 2 it shall not be **o**, and no man shall enter in 6605
46: 1 on the sabbath it shall be **o**, and in the day 6605
46: 1 in the day of the new moon it shall be **o**. 6605
Da 7:10 judgment was set, and the books were **o**. 6606
10:16 I **o** my mouth, and spake, and said unto him 6605
Na 2: 6 The gates of the rivers shall be **o**, and 6605
Zec 13: 1 In that day there shall be a fountain **o** to 6605
Mt 2:11 and when they had **o** their treasures, *455*
3:16 and lo, the heavens were **o** unto him, and *455*
5: 2 And he **o** his mouth, and taught them, *455*
7: 7 shall find; knock, and it shall be **o** unto you: *455*
7: 8 and to him that knocketh it shall be **o**. *455*
9:30 And their eyes were **o**; and Jesus straitly *455*
17:27 and when thou hast **o** his mouth, thou shalt *455*
20:33 say unto him, Lord, that our eyes may be **o**. *455*
27:52 And the graves were **o**; and many bodies of *455*
Mk 1:10 he saw the heavens **o**, and the Spirit like a *4977*
7:34 unto him, EPHPHATHA, that is, Be **o**. *1272*
7:35 And straightway his ears were **o**, *1272*
Lk 1:64 And his mouth was **o** immediately, and *455*
3:21 and praying, the heaven was **o**, *455*
4:17 And when he had **o** the book, he found *380*
11: 9 shall find; knock, and it shall be **o** unto you. *455*
11:10 and to him that knocketh it shall be **o**. *455*
24:31 And their eyes were **o**, and they knew him; *1272*
24:32 and while he **o** to us the scriptures? *1272*
24:45 Then **o** he their understanding, that *they* *1272*
Jn 9:10 said they unto him, How were thine eyes **o**? *455*
9:14 when Jesus made the clay, and **o** his eyes. *455*
9:17 sayest thou of him, that he hath **o** thine eyes? *455*
9:21 or who hath **o** his eyes, we know not: *455*
9:26 What did he to thee? how **o** he thine eyes? *455*
9:30 whence he is, and *yet* he hath **o** mine eyes. *455*
9:32 *man* **o** the eyes of one that was born blind. *455*
11:37 Could not this *man*, which **o** the eyes of *455*
Ac 5:19 But *the* angel of the Lord by night **o** *455*
5:23 but when we had **o**, we found no *man* within. *455*
7:56 And said, Behold, I see the heavens **o**, *455*
8:32 before his shearer, so **o** he not his mouth: *455*
8:35 Then Philip **o** his mouth, *455*
9: 8 and when his eyes were **o**, he saw no *man*: *455*
9:40 And she **o** her eyes: and when she saw Peter, *455*
10:11 And saw heaven **o**, and a certain vessel *455*
10:34 Then Peter **o** *his* mouth, and said, Of a truth *455*
12:10 the city; which **o** to them of his own accord: *455*
12:14 she **o** not the gate for gladness, but ran in, *455*
12:16 and when they had **o** *the door*, and saw him, *455*
14:27 how he had **o** *the* door of faith unto *455*
16:14 heard *us*: whose heart the Lord **o**, *1272*
16:26 and immediately all the doors were **o**, and *455*
1Co 16: 9 For a great door and effectual is **o** unto me, *455*
2Co 2:12 and a door was **o** unto me of the Lord, *455*
Heb 4:13 **o** unto the eyes of him with whom we have *5136*
Rev 4: 1 and behold, a door *was* **o** in heaven: *455*
6: 1 And I saw when the Lamb **o** one of the seals, *455*
6: 3 And when he had **o** the second seal, I heard *455*
6: 5 And when he had **o** the third seal, I heard *455*
6: 7 And when he had **o** the fourth seal, I heard *455*
6: 9 And when he had **o** the fifth seal, I saw *455*
6:12 And I beheld when he had **o** the sixth seal, *455*
8: 1 And when he had **o** the seventh seal, *455*
9: 2 And he **o** the bottomless pit; and there arose *455*
11:19 And the temple of God was **o** in heaven, and *455*
12:16 and the earth **o** her mouth, and swallowed up *455*
13: 6 And he **o** his mouth in blasphemy against *455*
15: 5 tabernacle of the testimony in heaven was **o**: *455*
19:11 And I saw heaven **o**, and behold a white *455*
20:12 stand before God; and the books were **o**: *455*
20:12 and another book was **o**, which is *the book* *455*

OPENEST (2) [OPEN]

Ps 104:28 thou **o** thine hand, they are filled *with* good. 6605
145:16 Thou **o** thine hand, and satisfiest the desire 6605

OPENETH (21) [OPEN]

Ex 13: 2 whatsoever **o** the womb among the children 6363
13:12 apart unto the LORD all that **o** the matrix, 6363
13:15 I sacrifice to the LORD all that **o** 6363
34:19 All that **o** the matrix *is* mine; and 6363
Nu 3:12 **o** the matrix among the children of Israel: 6363
18:15 Every thing **that** **o** the matrix in all flesh, 6363
Job 27:19 be gathered: he **o** his eyes, and he *is* not. 6491
33:16 he **o** the ears of men, and sealeth their 1540
36:10 He **o** also their ear to discipline, and 1540
36:15 his affliction, and **o** their ears in oppression. 1540
Ps 38:13 *I was* as a dumb *man that* **o** not his mouth. 6605
146: 8 The LORD **o** *the eyes of* the blind: 6491
Pr 13: 3 he that **o** wide his lips shall have 6589
24: 7 for a fool: he **o** not his mouth in the gate. 6605
31:26 She **o** her mouth with wisdom; and in her 6605
Isa 53: 7 her shearers is dumb, so he **o** not his mouth. 6605
Eze 20:26 pass through *the fire* all **that** **o** the womb, 6363
Lk 2:23 Every male that **o** the womb shall be called *1272*
Jn 10: 3 To him the porter **o**; and the sheep hear his *455*
Rev 3: 7 key of David, he that **o**, and no *man* shutteth; *455*
3: 7 no *man* shutteth; and shutteth, and no *man* **o**; *455*

OPENING (7) [OPEN]

1Ch 9:27 the **o** *thereof* every morning pertained to 4668
Job 12:14 he shutteth up a man, and there can be no **o**. 6605
Pr 8: 6 and the **o** of my lips *shall be* right things. 4669
Isa 42:20 **o** the ears, but he heareth not. 6491
61: 1 the **o of the prison** to *them that are* bound; 6495
Eze 29:21 I will give thee the **o** of the mouth in 6610
Ac 17: 3 **O** and alleging, that Christ must needs have *1272*

OPENINGS (1) [OPEN]

Pr 1:21 place of concourse, in the **o** of the gates: 6607

OPENLY (15) [OPEN]

Ge 38:21 that *was* **o** by the way side? 5869+871.1+1886.1
Ps 98: 2 his righteousness hath he **o** **shewed** in 1540
Mt 6: 4 in secret himself shall reward thee **o**. *1722+5318*
6: 6 seeth in secret shall reward thee **o**. *1722+5318*
6:18 seeth in secret, shall reward thee **o**. *1722+5318*
Mk 1:45 insomuch that *Jesus* could no more **o** enter *5320*
8:32 And he spake *that* saying **o**. And Peter took *3954*
Jn 7: 4 he himself seeketh to be **known** **o**. *1722+3954*
7:10 the feast, not **o**, but as it were in secret. *5320*
7:13 Howbeit no *man* spake **o** of him for fear of *3954*
11:54 walked no more **o** among the Jews; *3954*
18:20 Jesus answered him, I spake **o** to the world; *3954*
Ac 10:40 raised up the third day, and shewed him **o**; *1717*
16:37 They have beaten us **o** uncondemned, *1219*
Col 2:15 he made a shew of *them* **o**, *1722+3954*

OPERATION (3) [OPERATIONS]

Ps 28: 5 nor the **o** of his hands, he shall destroy 4639
Isa 5:12 neither consider the **o** of his hands. 4639
Col 2:12 with *him* through the faith of the **o** of God, *1753*

OPERATIONS (1) [OPERATION]

1Co 12: 6 And there are diversities of **o**, but it is *1755*

OPHEL (5)

2Ch 27: 3 and on the wall of **O** he built much. 6077
33:14 compassed about **O**, and raised it up a very 6077
Ne 3:26 Moreover the Nethinims dwelt in **O**, 6077
3:27 that lieth out, even unto the wall of **O**. 6077
11:21 the Nethinims dwelt in **O**: and Ziha and 6077

OPHIR (13)

Ge 10:29 **O**, and Havilah, and Jobab: all these *were* 211
1Ki 9:28 they came to **O**, and fet from thence gold, 211
10:11 also of Hiram, that brought gold from **O**, 211
10:11 brought in from **O** great plenty of almug 211
22:48 made ships of Tharshish to go to **O** for gold: 211
1Ch 1:23 **O**, and Havilah, and Jobab. All these *were* 211
29: 4 of the gold of **O**, and seven thousand talents 211
2Ch 8:18 went with the servants of Solomon to **O**, 211
9:10 which brought gold from **O**, brought algum 211
Job 22:24 *the gold of* **O** as the stones of the brooks. 211
28:16 It cannot be valued with the gold of **O**, 211
Ps 45: 9 right hand did stand the queen in gold of **O**. 211
Isa 13:12 even a man than the golden wedge of **O**. 211

OPHNI (1)

Jos 18:24 and **O**, and Gaba; 6078

OPHRAH (8)

Jos 18:23 And Avim, and Parah, and **O**, 6084
Jdg 6:11 sat under an oak which *was* in **O**, 6084
6:24 unto this day it *is* yet in **O** of 6084
8:27 and put it in his city, *even* in **O**: 6084
8:32 of Joash his father, in **O** of the Abi-ezrites. 6084
9: 5 he went unto his father's house at **O**, and 6084
1Sa 13:17 turned unto the way that leadeth to **O**, 6084
1Ch 4:14 Meonothai begat **O**: and Seraiah begat 6084

OPINION (3) [OPINIONS]

Job 32: 6 was afraid, and durst not shew you mine **o**. 1843
32:10 Hearken to me; I also will shew mine **o**. 1843
32:17 also my part, I also will shew mine **o**. 1843

OPINIONS (1) [OPINION]

1Ki 18:21 and said, How long halt ye between two **o**? 5587

OPPORTUNITY (5)

Mt 26:16 And from that time he sought **o** to betray *2120*
Lk 22: 6 sought **o** to betray him unto them in *2120*
Gal 6:10 As we have therefore **o**, let us do good unto *2540*
Php 4:10 ye were also careful, but ye **lacked** **o**. *170*
Heb 11:15 they might have had **o** to have returned. *2540*

OPPOSE (1) [OPPOSED, OPPOSEST, OPPOSETH, OPPOSITIONS]

2Ti 2:25 instructing those that **o** **themselves**; *475*

OPPOSED (1) [OPPOSE]

Ac 18: 6 And when they **o** themselves, and *498*

OPPOSEST (1) [OPPOSE]

Job 30:21 with thy strong hand thou **o** thyself against 7852

OPPOSETH (1) [OPPOSE]

2Th 2: 4 Who **o** and exalteth himself above all that is *480*

OPPOSITIONS (1) [OPPOSE]

1Ti 6:20 and **o** of science falsely so called: *477*

OPPRESS (23) [OPPRESSED, OPPRESSETH, OPPRESSING, OPPRESSION, OPPRESSIONS, OPPRESSOR, OPPRESSORS]

Ex 3: 9 wherewith the Egyptians **o** them. 3905
22:21 shalt neither vex a stranger, nor **o** him: 3905
23: 9 Also thou shalt not **o** a stranger: for ye 3905
Lev 25:14 ye shall not **o** one another: 3238
25:17 Ye shall not therefore **o** one another; 3238
Dt 23:16 it liketh him best: thou shalt not **o** him. 3238
24:14 Thou shalt not **o** a hired servant *that is* poor 6231
Jdg 10:12 and the Maonites, did **o** you; 3905
Job 10: 3 *Is it* good unto thee that thou shouldest **o**, 6231
Ps 10:18 that the man of the earth may no more **o**. 6206
17: 9 From the wicked that **o** me, *from* my 7703
119:122 servant for good: let not the proud **o** me. 6231
Pr 22:22 *is* poor: neither **o** the afflicted in the gate: 1792
Isa 49:26 I will feed them that **o** thee with their own 3238
Jer 7: 6 *If* ye **o** not the stranger, the fatherless, and 6231
30:20 before me, and I will punish all that **o** them. 3905
Eze 45: 8 my princes shall no more **o** my people; and 3238
Hos 12: 7 of deceit *are* in his hand: he loveth to **o**. 6231
Am 4: 1 which **o** the poor, which crush the needy, 6231
Mic 2: 2 so they **o** a man and his house, even a man 6231
Zec 7:10 **o** not the widow, nor the fatherless, 6231
Mal 3: 5 against those that **o** the hireling in *his* 6231
Jas 2: 6 Do not rich *men* **o** you, and draw you *2616*

OPPRESSED (38) [OPPRESS]

Dt 28:29 thou shalt be only **o** and spoiled evermore, 6231
28:33 and thou shalt be only **o** and crushed alway: 6231
Jdg 2:18 of their groanings by reason of them that **o** 3905
4: 3 twenty years he mightily **o** the children of 3905
6: 9 out of the hand of all that **o** you, and 3905
10: 8 they vexed and **o** the children of Israel: 7533
1Sa 10:18 of all kingdoms, *and* of them that **o** you: 3905
12: 3 whom have I **o**? or of whose hand have I 7533
12: 4 Thou hast not defrauded us, nor **o** us, 7533
2Ki 13: 4 of Israel, because the king of Syria **o** them. 3905
13:22 Hazael king of Syria **o** Israel all the days of 3905
2Ch 16:10 of this *thing*. And Asa **o** *some* of the people 7533
Job 20:19 Because he hath **o** *and* hath forsaken 7533
35: 9 of oppressions they make *the* **o** to cry: NIH
Ps 9: 9 The LORD also will be a refuge for the **o**, 1790
10:18 To judge the fatherless and the **o**, that 1790
74:21 O let not the **o** return ashamed: let the poor 1790
103: 6 and judgment for all that are **o**. 6231
106:42 Their enemies also **o** them, and they were 3905
146: 7 Which executeth judgment for the **o**: 6231
Ecc 4: 1 the tears of such as were **o**, and they had no 6231
Isa 1:17 seek judgment, relieve the **o**, judge 2541
3: 5 the people shall be **o**, every one by another, 5065
23:12 O thou **o** virgin, daughter of Zidon: 6231
38:14 O LORD, I am **o**; undertake for me. 6234
52: 4 and the Assyrian **o** them without cause. 6231
53: 7 He was **o**, and he was afflicted, yet he 5065
58: 6 to let the **o** go free, and *that* ye break every 7533
Jer 50:33 and the children of Judah *were* **o** together: 6231
Eze 18: 7 hath not **o** any, *but* hath restored *to* 3238
18:12 Hath **o** the poor and needy, hath spoiled by 3238
18:16 Neither hath **o** any, hath not withholden 3238
18:18 *for* his father, because he **cruelly** **o**, 6231+6233
22:29 they have **o** the stranger wrongfully. 6231
Hos 5:11 Ephraim *is* **o** *and* broken in judgment, 6231
Am 3: 9 and the **o** in the midst thereof. 6217
Ac 7:24 defended *him*, and avenged him that was **o**, *2669*
10:38 and healing all that were **o** of the devil; *2616*

OPPRESSETH (5) [OPPRESS]

Nu 10: 9 in your land against the enemy that **o** you, 6887
Ps 56: 1 swallow me up; he fighting daily **o** me. 3905
Pr 14:31 He that **o** the poor reproacheth his Maker: 6231
22:16 He that **o** the poor to increase his *riches*, 6231
28: 3 A poor man that **o** the poor *is like* a 6231

OPPRESSING (3) [OPPRESS]

Jer 46:16 the land of our nativity, from the **o** sword. 3238
50:16 for fear of the **o** sword they shall turn every 3238
Zep 3: 1 her that is filthy and polluted, to the **o** city! 3238

OPPRESSION (24) [OPPRESS]

Ex 3: 9 I have also seen the **o** wherewith 3906
Dt 26: 7 on our affliction, and our labour, and our **o**: 3906
2Ki 13: 4 for he saw the **o** of Israel, because the king 3906
Job 36:15 in his affliction, and openeth their ears in **o**. 3906
Ps 12: 5 For the **o** of the poor, for the sighing of 7701
42: 9 I mourning because of the **o** of the enemy? 3906
43: 2 I mourning because of the **o** of the enemy? 3906
44:24 *and* forgettest our affliction and our **o**? 3906
55: 3 the enemy, because of the **o** of the wicked: 6125
62:10 Trust not in **o**, and become not vain in 6233
73: 8 and speak wickedly *concerning* **o**: 6233
107:39 are minished and brought low through **o**, 6115
119:134 Deliver me from the **o** of man: so will I 6233
Ecc 5: 8 If thou seest the **o** of the poor, and 6233
7: 7 Surely **o** maketh a wise *man* mad; and a gift 6233
Isa 5: 7 he looked for judgment, but behold **o**; 4939
30:12 trust in **o** and perverseness, and 6233
54:14 thou shalt be far from **o**; for thou shalt not 6233
59:13 speaking **o** and revolt, conceiving and 6233
Jer 6: 6 she *is* wholly **o** in the midst of her. 6233
22:17 and for **o**, and for violence, to do *it*. 6233
Eze 22: 7 in the midst of thee have they dealt by **o** 6233
22:29 The people of the land have **used** **o**, 6231+6233
46:18 by **o** to thrust them out of their possession; 3238

OPPRESSIONS (3) [OPPRESS]

Job 35: 9 By reason of the multitude of **o** they make 6217
Ecc 4: 1 considered all the **o** that *are* done under 6217
Isa 33:15 he that despiseth the gain of **o**, that shaketh 4642

OPPRESSOR (14) [OPPRESS]

Job 3:18 they hear not the voice of the **o**. 5065
15:20 and the number of years is hidden to the **o**. 6184
Ps 72: 4 the needy, and shall break in pieces the **o**. 6231
Pr 3:31 Envy thou not the **o**, and choose none 376+2555
28:16 that wanteth understanding *is* also a great **o**: 4642
Isa 9: 4 the rod of his **o**, as *in* the day of Midian. 5065
14: 4 and say, How hath the **o** ceased! 5065
51:13 every day because of the fury of the **o**, 6693
51:13 to destroy? and where *is* the fury of the **o**? 6693
Jer 21:12 *him that is* spoiled out of the hand of the **o**, 6231
22: 3 deliver the spoiled out of the hand of the **o**; 6216
25:38 because of the fierceness of the **o**, 3238

O

Zec 9: 8 no o shall pass through them any more: 5065
10: 4 the battle bow, out of him every o together. 5065

OPPRESSORS (8) [OPPRESS]

Job 27:13 the heritage of o, *which* they shall receive 6184
Ps 54: 3 up against me, and o seek after my soul: 6184
119:121 and justice: leave me not to mine o. 6231
Ecc 4: 1 on the side of their o *there was* power; but 6231
Isa 3:12 children *are* their o, and women rule over 5065
14: 2 they were; and they shall rule over their o. 5065
16: 4 the o are consumed out of the land. 7429
19:20 shall cry unto the LORD because of the o, 3905

OR (1130)

Ge 13: 9 o if *thou depart to* the right hand, then 2050.1
17:12 o bought with money of any stranger, 2050.1
24:21 had made his journey prosperous o not. 518
24:49 that I may turn to the right hand, o to the left. 176
24:50 we cannot speak unto thee bad o good. 176
26:11 He that toucheth this man o his wife shall 2050.1
27:21 whether thou *be* my very son Esau o not. 518
30: 1 Give me children, o else I die. 518+2050.1
31:14 *Is there* yet any portion o inheritance for 2050.1
31:24 thou speak not to Jacob either good o bad. 5704
31:29 thou speak not to Jacob either good o bad. 5704
31:39 *whether* stolen by day, o stolen by night. 2050.1
31:43 o unto their children which they have born? 176
31:50 o if thou shalt take *other* wives beside my 2050.1
37: 8 o shalt thou indeed have dominion over us? 518
37:32 know now **whether** it *be* thy son's coat o no. 518
39:10 not unto her, to lie by her, o to be with her. NIH
41:44 his hand o foot in all the land of Egypt. 2050.1
42:16 o else by the life of Pharaoh surely ye *are* 2050.1
44: 8 steal out of thy lord's house silver o gold? 176
44:16 o how shall we clear ourselves? God hath 2050.1
44:19 Have ye a father, o a brother? 176
Ex 4:11 o who maketh the dumb, or deaf, or 176
4:11 the dumb, o deaf, or the seeing, or the blind? 176
4:11 the dumb, or deaf, o the seeing, or the blind? 176
4:11 the dumb, or deaf, or the seeing, o the blind? 176
5: 3 upon us with pestilence, o with the sword. 176
10:15 o in the herbs of the field, through all 2050.1
11: 7 move his tongue, against man o beast: 2050.1
12: 5 *it* out from the sheep, o from the goats: 2050.1
12:19 he be a stranger, o born in the land. 2050.1
16: 4 whether they will walk in my law, o no. 518
17: 7 Is the LORD amongst us, o not? 518
19:12 into the mount, o touch the border of it: 2050.1
19:13 but he shall surely be stoned, o shot through; 176
19:13 whether *it be* beast o man, it shall not live: 518
20: 4 o any likeness *of any thing* that *is* in 2050.1
20: 4 o that *is* in the earth beneath, or that *is* in 2050.1
20: 4 o that *is* in the water under the earth: 2050.1
21: 4 and she have born him sons o daughters; 176
21: 6 bring him to the door, o unto the door post; 176
21:15 o his mother, shall be surely put to death. 2050.1
21:16 selleth him, o if he be found in his hand, 2050.1
21:17 o his mother, shall surely be put to death. 2050.1
21:18 o with *his* fist, and he die not, but 176
21:20 o his maid, with a rod, and he die under his 176
21:21 Notwithstanding, if he continue a day o two, 176
21:26 o the eye of his maid, that it perish; 176
21:27 o his maidservant's tooth; 176
21:28 If an ox gore a man o a woman, that they 176
21:29 but that he hath killed a man o a woman; 176
21:31 have gored a son, o have gored a daughter, 176
21:32 ox shall push a manservant o a maidservant; 176
21:33 o if a man shall dig a pit, and not cover it, 176
21:33 not cover it, and an ox o an ass fall therein; 176
21:36 O *if* it be known that the ox *hath* used to 176
22: 1 steal an ox, o a sheep, and kill it, or sell it; 176
22: 1 steal an ox, or a sheep, and kill it, o sell it; 176
22: 4 whether it be ox, o ass, or sheep; 5704
22: 4 whether it be ox, or ass, o sheep; 5704
22: 5 shall cause a field o vineyard to be eaten, 176
22: 6 of corn, o the standing corn, or the field, 176
22: 6 of corn, or the standing corn, o the field, 176
22: 7 unto his neighbour money o stuff to keep, 176
22: 9 o for any manner of lost *thing,* which NIH
22:10 o an ox, or a sheep, or any beast, to keep; 176
22:10 or an ox, o a sheep, or any beast, to keep; 176
22:10 or an ox, or a sheep, o any beast, to keep; 2050.1
22:10 it die, o be hurt, or driven away, no man 176
22:10 it die, or be hurt, o driven away, no man 176
22:14 it be hurt, o die, the owner thereof *being* not 176
22:22 not afflict any widow, o fatherless child. 2050.1
23: 4 thine enemy's ox o his ass going astray, 176
28:43 o when they come near unto the altar to 176
29:34 o of the bread, remain unto the morning, 2050.1
30:20 o when they come near to the altar to 176
30:33 o whosoever putteth *any* of it upon a 2050.1
34:19 *whether* ox o sheep, *that* is male. 2050.1
Lev 1:10 o of the goats, for a burnt sacrifice; 176
1:14 offering of turtledoves, o of young pigeons. 176
2: 4 o unleavened wafers anointed with oil. 2050.1
3: 1 whether *it be* a male o female, he shall offer 518
3: 6 male o female, he shall offer it without 176
4:23 O if his sin, wherein he hath sinned, come to 176
4:28 O if his sin, which he hath sinned, come to 176
5: 1 whether he hath seen o known *of it;* if he do 176
5: 2 O if a soul touch any unclean thing, 176
5: 2 o a carcase of unclean cattle, or the carcase 176
5: 2 o the carcase of unclean creeping things, and 176
5: 3 O if he touch the uncleanness of man, 176
5: 4 O if a soul swear, pronouncing with *his* lips 176
5: 4 with *his* lips to do evil, o to do good, 176
5: 6 a lamb o a kid of the goats, for a sin 176
5: 7 two turtledoves, o two young pigeons, 176
5:11 o two young pigeons, then he that sinned 176
6: 2 o in fellowship, or in a thing taken away by 176
6: 2 o in a thing taken away by violence, or 176
6: 2 by violence, o hath deceived his neighbour; 176
6: 3 O have found that which was lost, and 176
6: 4 o the thing which he hath deceitfully gotten, 176
6: 4 o that which was delivered him to keep, or 176
Lev 6: 4 him to keep, o the lost *thing* which he found, 176
6: 5 O all *that* about which he hath sworn falsely; 176
7:16 his offering *be* a vow, o a voluntary offering, 176
7:21 o *any* unclean beast, or any abominable 176
7:21 o any abominable unclean *thing,* and eat of 176
7:23 *manner* fat, of ox, o of sheep, or of goat. 2050.1
7:23 *manner* fat, of ox, or of sheep, o of goat. 2050.1
7:26 *whether it be* of fowl o of beast, in any of 2050.1
11: 4 the cud, o of them that divide the hoof: 2050.1
11:32 vessel of wood, o raiment, or skin, or sack, 176
11:32 vessel of wood, or raiment, o skin, or sack, 176
11:32 vessel of wood, or raiment, or skin, o sack, 176
11:35 *whether it be* oven, o ranges for pots, 2050.1
11:36 Nevertheless a fountain o pit, 2050.1
11:42 o whatsoever hath more feet among all 5704
12: 6 are fulfilled, for a son, o for a daughter, 176
12: 6 a young pigeon, o a turtledove, for a sin 176
12: 7 law for her that hath born a male o a female. 176
12: 8 shall bring two turtles, o two young pigeons; 176
13: 2 o bright spot, and it be in the skin of his 176
13: 2 the priest, o unto one of his sons the priests: 176
13:16 O if the raw flesh turn again, and be changed 176
13:19 o a bright spot, white, *and* 176
13:24 O if there be *any* flesh, in the skin whereof 176
13:24 bright spot, somewhat reddish, o white; 176
13:29 If a man o woman hath a plague upon 176
13:29 hath a plague upon the head o the beard; 176
13:30 *even* a leprosy upon the head o beard. 176
13:38 If a man also o a woman have in the skin of 176
13:42 o bald forehead, a white reddish sore; 176
13:42 up in his bald head, o his bald forehead. 176
13:43 o in his bald forehead, as the leprosy 176
13:47 *it be* a woollen garment, o a linen garment; 176
13:48 Whether *it be* in the warp, o woof; of linen, 176
13:48 the warp, or woof; of linen, o of woollen; 2050.1
13:48 in a skin, o in any thing made of skin; 176
13:49 plague be greenish o reddish in the garment, 176
13:49 o in the skin, either in the warp, or in 176
13:49 o in the woof, or in any thing of skin; 176
13:49 or in the woof, o in any thing of skin; 176
13:51 o in the woof, or in a skin, *or* in any work 176
13:51 o in a skin, *or* in any work that is made of 176
13:51 in a skin, *o* in any work that is made of skin; NIH
13:52 whether warp o woof, in woollen or in linen, 176
13:52 in woollen o in linen, or any thing of skin, 176
13:52 in woollen or in linen, o any thing of skin, 176
13:53 o in the woof, or in any thing of skin; 176
13:53 or in the woof, o in any thing of skin; 176
13:55 *whether* it *be* bare within o without. 176
13:56 o out of the skin, or out of the warp, or 176
13:56 o out of the warp, or out of the woof: 176
13:56 or out of the warp, o out of the woof: 176
13:57 o in the woof, or in any thing of skin; 176
13:57 or in the woof, o in any thing of skin; 176
13:58 o woof, or whatsoever thing of skin *it be,* 176
13:58 o whatsoever thing of skin *it be,* which thou 176
13:59 of leprosy in a garment of woollen o linen, 176
13:59 *in* the warp, o woof, or any thing of skins, 176
13:59 *in* the warp, or woof, o any thing of skins, 176
13:59 it clean, o to pronounce it unclean. 176
14:22 two turtledoves, o two young pigeons, 176
14:30 o of the young pigeons, such as he can get; 176
14:37 greenish o reddish, which in sight *are* lower 176
15: 3 o his flesh be stopped from his issue, it *is* his 176
15:14 o two young pigeons, and come before 176
15:23 o on *any* thing whereon she sitteth, when he 176
15:25 o if it run beyond the time of her separation; 176
15:29 o two young pigeons, and bring them unto 176
16:29 o a stranger that sojourneth among you: 2050.1
17: 3 o lamb, or goat, in the camp, or that killeth *it* 176
17: 3 or lamb, o goat, in the camp, or that killeth *it* 176
17: 3 in the camp, o that killeth *it* out of the camp, 176
17: 8 o of the strangers which sojourn among 2050.1
17: 8 that offereth a burnt offering o sacrifice, 176
17:10 o of the strangers that sojourn among 2050.1
17:13 o of the strangers that sojourn among 2050.1
17:13 which hunteth and catcheth *any* beast o 176
17:15 o that which was torn *with beasts,* 2050.1
17:15 o a stranger, he shall both wash his 2050.1
18: 7 o the nakedness of thy mother, shalt thou 2050.1
18: 9 of thy father, o daughter of thy mother, 176
18: 9 *whether she be* born at home, o born abroad, 176
18:10 son's daughter, o of thy daughter's daughter, 176
18:17 o her daughter's daughter, to uncover her 2050.1
19:35 in meteyard, in weight, o in measure. 2050.1
20: 2 o of the strangers that sojourn in Israel, 2050.1
20: 9 For every one that curseth his father o his 2050.1
20: 9 he hath cursed his father o his mother; 2050.1
20:17 o his mother's daughter, and see her 176
20:25 o by fowl, or by any *manner of living* 2050.1
20:25 o by any *manner of living thing* that 2050.1
20:27 A man also o woman that hath a familiar 176
20:27 o that is a wizard, shall surely be put to 176
21: 7 not take a wife *that is* a whore, o profane; 2050.1
21:11 himself for his father, o for his mother; 2050.1
21:14 o a divorced *woman,* or profane, *or* 2050.1
21:14 or a divorced *woman,* o profane, *or* 2050.1
21:14 or a divorced *woman,* or profane, *o* a harlot, NIH
21:18 o a lame, or he that hath a flat nose, or 176
21:18 o he that hath a flat nose, or any thing 176
21:18 that hath a flat nose, o any thing superfluous, 176
21:19 O a man that is brokenfooted, 176
21:19 a man that is brokenfooted, o brokenhanded, 176
21:20 O crookbackt, or a dwarf, or that hath a 176
21:20 o a dwarf, or that hath a blemish in his eye, 176
21:20 o that hath a blemish in his eye, or 176
21:20 o be scurvy, or scabbed, or hath his stones 176
21:20 o scabbed, or hath his stones broken; 176
21:20 or scabbed, o hath his stones broken; 176
22: 4 of Aaron *is* a leper, o hath a running issue; 176
22: 4 o a man whose seed goeth from him; 176
22: 5 O whosoever toucheth any creeping thing, 176
22: 5 o a man of whom he may take uncleanness, 176
22: 8 o is torn *with beasts,* he shall not eat to 2050.1
22:10 o a hired servant, shall not eat *of* the holy 2050.1
Lev 22:13 o divorced, and have no child, and 2050.1
22:16 O suffer them to bear the iniquity of 2050.1
22:18 of Israel, o of the strangers in Israel, 2050.1
22:19 of the beeves, of the sheep, o of the goats. 2050.1
22:21 o a freewill offering in beeves or sheep, 176
22:21 or a freewill offering in beeves o sheep, 176
22:22 o broken, or maimed, or having a wen, or 176
22:22 o maimed, or having a wen, or scurvy, or 176
22:22 o having a wen, or scurvy, or scabbed, 176
22:22 or having a wen, o scurvy, or scabbed, 176
22:22 or having a wen, or scurvy, o scabbed, 176
22:23 Either a bullock o a lamb that hath any 2050.1
22:23 thing superfluous o lacking in his parts, 2050.1
22:24 is bruised, o crushed, or broken, or cut; 2050.1
22:24 is bruised, or crushed, o broken, or cut; 2050.1
22:24 is bruised, or crushed, or broken, o cut; 2050.1
22:27 o a sheep, or a goat, is brought forth, then 176
22:27 or a sheep, o a goat, is brought forth, then 176
22:28 *whether it be* cow o ewe, ye shall not kill it 176
25:14 o buyest *ought* of thy neighbour's hand, 176
25:35 *yea, though he be* a stranger, o 2050.1
25:36 Take thou no usury of him, o increase: 2050.1
25:47 if a sojourner o stranger wax rich by thee, 2050.1
25:47 unto the stranger *o* sojourner by thee, NIH
25:47 o to the stock of the stranger's family: 176
25:49 Either his uncle, o his uncle's son, 176
25:49 o *any* that is nigh of kin unto him of his 176
25:49 o if he be able, he may redeem himself. 176
26:15 o if your soul abhor my judgments, so 2050.1
27:10 a good for a bad, o a bad for a good: 176
27:12 shall value it, whether it be good o bad: 2050.1
27:14 estimate it, whether it be good o bad: 2050.1
27:20 o if he have sold the field to another man, 2050.1
27:26 shall sanctify it; whether *it be* ox, o sheep: 518
27:27 o if it be not redeemed, then it shall be 2050.1
27:28 his possession, shall be sold o redeemed: 2050.1
27:30 *o* of the fruit of the tree, *is* the LORD'S: NIH
27:32 the tithe of the herd, o of the flock, 2050.1
27:33 shall not search whether it be good o bad, NIH
Nu 5: 6 When a man o woman shall commit any sin 176
5:14 o if the spirit of jealousy come upon him, 176
5:30 O when the spirit of jealousy cometh upon 176
6: 2 When either man o woman shall separate 176
6: 3 of wine, o vinegar of strong drink, 2050.1
6: 3 of grapes, nor eat moist grapes, o dried. 2050.1
6: 7 o for his mother, for his brother, or for his 2050.1
6: 7 o for his sister, when they die: 2050.1
6:10 o two young pigeons, to the priest, 176
9:10 If any man of you o of your posterity shall 176
9:10 o *be* in a journey afar off, yet he shall keep 176
9:21 whether *it was* by day o by night that 2050.1
9:22 O *whether it were* two days, or a month, or 176
9:22 *it were* two days, o a month, or a year, 176
9:22 *it were* two days, or a month, o a year, 176
11: 8 o beat *it* in a mortar, and baked *it* in pans, 176
11:22 o shall all the fish of the sea be gathered 518
11:23 my word shall come to pass unto thee o not. 518
13:18 whether they *be* strong o weak, few 1886.2
13:18 whether they *be* strong or weak, few o many; 518
13:19 that they dwell in, whether it *be* good o bad; 518
13:19 dwell in, whether in tents, o in strong holds; 518
13:20 what the land *is,* whether it *be* fat o lean, 518
13:20 lean, whether there be wood therein, o not. 518
14: 2 o would God we had died in this wilderness! 176
15: 3 o a sacrifice in performing a vow, or in a 176
15: 3 o in a freewill offering, or in your solemn 176
15: 3 a freewill offering, o in your solemn feasts, 176
15: 3 unto the LORD, of the herd, o of the flock: 176
15: 5 prepare with the burnt offering o sacrifice, 176
15: 6 O for a ram, thou shalt prepare *for* a meat 176
15: 8 o *for* a sacrifice in performing a vow, or 176
15: 8 a vow, o peace offerings unto the LORD: 176
15:11 o for one ram, or for a lamb, or a kid. 176
15:11 or for one ram, o for a lamb, or a kid. 176
15:11 or for one ram, or for a lamb, o a kid. 176
15:14 o whosoever *be* among you in your 176
15:30 *he be* born in the land, o a stranger, 2050.1
16:14 o given us inheritance of fields and 2050.1
16:29 o if they be visited after the visitation of 2050.1
18:15 *whether it be* of men o beasts, shall be 2050.1
18:17 o the firstling of a sheep, or the firstling of a 176
18:17 o the firstling of a goat, thou shalt not 176
19:16 o a dead *body,* or a bone of a man, or a 176
19:16 or a dead *body,* o a bone of a man, or a 176
19:16 a dead *body,* or a bone of a man, o a grave, 176
19:18 a bone, o one slain, or one dead, or a grave: 176
19:18 a bone, or one slain, o one dead, or a grave: 176
19:18 a bone, or one slain, or one dead, o a grave: 176
20: 5 o of figs, or vines, or of pomegranates; 2050.1
20: 5 or of figs, o vines, or of pomegranates; 2050.1
20: 5 or of figs, or vines, o of pomegranates; 2050.1
20:17 the fields, o through the vineyards, 2050.1
21:22 turn into the fields, o into the vineyards; 2050.1
22:18 of the LORD my God, to do less o more. 176
22:26 turn *either to* the right hand o *to* the left. 2050.1
23: 8 o how shall I defy, *whom* the LORD 2050.1
23:19 shall he not do *it?* o hath he spoken, and 2050.1
24:13 to do *either* good o bad of mine own mind; 176
30: 2 o swear an oath to bind his soul with a bond; 176
30: 5 o of her bonds wherewith she hath bound 2050.1
30: 6 she vowed, o uttered ought out of her lips, 176
30:10 o bound her soul by a bond with an oath; 176
30:12 o concerning the bond of her soul, 2050.1
30:13 o her husband may make it void. 2050.1
30:14 o all her bonds, which *are* upon her: 176
32:19 them on *yonder* side Jordan, o forward; 2050.1
35:18 O *if* he smite him with a hand weapon of 176
35:20 o hurl at him by laying of wait, that he die; 176
35:21 O in enmity smite him with his hand, that he 176
35:22 o have cast upon him any thing without 176
35:23 O with any stone, wherewith *a man* may die, 176
Dt 3:24 for what God *is there* in heaven o 2050.1
4:16 of any figure, the likeness of male o female, 176
4:23 *o* the likeness of any *thing,* which NIH
4:25 *o* the likeness of any *thing,* and shall do evil NIH

Dt 4:32 this great thing is, o hath been heard like it? 176
4:34 O hath God assayed to go and take him a 176
5: 8 o any likeness of any thing that is in heaven NIH
5: 8 o that is in the earth beneath, or that is in 2050.1
5: 8 o that is in the waters beneath the earth: 2050.1
5:21 o his manservant, or his maidservant, 2050.1
5:21 o his maidservant, his ox, or his ass, or 2050.1
5:21 o his ass, or any thing that is thy 2050.1
5:21 o any thing that is thy neighbour's. 2050.1
5:32 turn aside to the right hand o to the left. 2050.1
7:14 there shall not be male o female barren 2050.1
7:14 barren among you, o among your cattle. 2050.1
7:25 desire the silver o gold that is on them, 2050.1
8: 2 wouldest keep his commandments, o no. 518
9: 5 o for the uprightness of thine heart, 2050.1
12:17 o of thy wine, or of thy oil, or 2050.1
12:17 o of thy oil, or the firstlings of thy herds 2050.1
12:17 o the firstlings of thy herds or of thy 2050.1
12:17 the firstlings of thy herds o of thy flock, 2050.1
12:17 o heave offering of thine hand: 2050.1
13: 1 o a dreamer of dreams, and giveth thee a 176
13: 1 and giveth thee a sign o a wonder, 176
13: 2 the sign o the wonder come to pass, 2050.1
13: 3 of that prophet, o that dreamer of dreams: 176
13: 5 And that prophet, o that dreamer of dreams, 176
13: 6 o thy son, or thy daughter, or the wife of thy 176
13: 6 o thy daughter, or the wife of thy bosom, or 176
13: 6 o the wife of thy bosom, or thy friend, 176
13: 6 or the wife of thy bosom, o thy friend, 176
13: 7 nigh unto thee, o far off from thee, 176
14: 7 o of them that divide the cloven hoof; 2050.1
14:21 eat it; o thou mayest sell it unto an alien: 176
14:24 o if the place be too far from thee, which NIH
14:26 o for sheep, or for wine, or for strong 2050.1
14:26 o for wine, or for strong drink, 2050.1
14:26 o for strong drink, or for whatsoever thy 2050.1
14:26 o for whatsoever thy soul desireth: 2050.1
15: 2 exact it of his neighbour, o of his brother; 2050.1
15:12 a Hebrew man, o a Hebrew woman, be sold 176
15:21 if it be lame, o blind, or have any ill blemish, 176
15:21 it be lame, or blind, o have any ill blemish, NIH
17: 1 o sheep, wherein is blemish, or any evil 2050.1
17: 1 wherein is blemish, o any evil favouredness: NIH
17: 2 LORD thy God giveth thee, man o woman, 176
17: 3 o moon, or any of the host of heaven, 176
17: 3 or moon, o any of the host of heaven, 176
17: 5 thou bring forth that man o that woman, 176
17: 5 even that man o that woman, and shalt stone 176
17: 6 mouth of two witnesses, o three witnesses, 176
17:12 o unto the judge, even that man shall die: 176
17:20 to the right hand, o to the left: 2050.1
18: 3 offer a sacrifice, whether it be ox o sheep; 518
18:10 o his daughter to pass through the fire, 2050.1
18:10 o that useth divination, or an observer of NIH
18:10 o an observer of times, or an enchanter, or NIH
18:10 of times, o an enchanter, or a witch, 2050.1
18:10 of times, or an enchanter, o a witch, 2050.1
18:11 O a charmer, or a consulter with familiar 2050.1
18:11 o a consulter with familiar spirits, or 2050.1
18:11 o a wizard, or a necromancer. 2050.1
18:11 or a wizard, o a necromancer. 2050.1
18:20 o that shall speak in the name of other 2050.1
19:15 o for any sin, in any sin that he sinneth: 2050.1
19:15 o at the mouth of three witnesses, shall 176
21:18 o the voice of his mother, and that, when 2050.1
22: 1 see thy brother's ox o his sheep go astray, 176
22: 2 o if thou know him not, then thou shalt 2050.1
22: 4 brother's ass o his ox fall down by the way, 176
22: 6 o on the ground, whether they be young 176
22: 6 o eggs, and the dam sitting upon the young, 176
22: 6 dam sitting upon the young, o upon the eggs, 176
23: 1 o hath his privy member cut off, 2050.1
23: 3 An Ammonite o Moabite shall not enter 2050.1
23:18 the hire of a whore, o the price of a dog, 2050.1
24: 3 o if the latter husband die, which took her to 176
24: 6 No man shall take the nether o the upper 2050.1
24: 7 merchandise of him, o selleth him; 2050.1
24:14 o of thy strangers that are in thy land within 176
27:15 that maketh any graven o molten image, 2050.1
27:16 setteth light by his father o his mother. 2050.1
27:22 of his father, o the daughter of his mother. 176
28:14 to the right hand, o to the left, to go after 2050.1
28:51 o oil, or the increase of thy kine, or 2050.1
28:51 o the increase of thy kine, or flocks of thy NIH
28:51 of thy kine, o flocks of thy sheep, 2050.1
29: 6 have you drunk wine o strong drink: 2050.1
29:18 you man, o woman, or family, or tribe, 176
29:18 you man, or woman, o family, or tribe, 176
29:18 you man, or woman, or family, o tribe, 176
32:36 is gone, and there is none shut up, o left. 2050.1
Jos 1: 7 not from it to the right hand o to the left, 2050.1
5:13 Art thou for us, o for our adversaries? 518
7: 3 but let about two o three thousand men go up 176
8:17 there was not a man left in Ai o Beth-el, 2050.1
8:20 had no power to flee this way o that way: 2050.1
8:22 they let none of them remain o escape. 2050.1
10:14 was no day like that before it o after it, 2050.1
19: 2 o Sheba, and Moladah, 2050.1
22:22 o if in transgression against the LORD, 2050.1
22:23 o if to offer thereon burnt offering or 2050.1
22:23 thereon burnt offering o meat offering, 2050.1
22:23 o if to offer peace offerings thereon, 2050.1
22:28 when they should so say to us o to our 2050.1
22:29 for meat offerings, o for sacrifices, 2050.1
23: 6 therefrom to the right hand o to the left; 2050.1
24:15 o the gods of the Amorites, in whose 518+2050.1
Jdg 2:22 as their fathers did keep it, o not. 518
5: 8 was there a shield o spear seen among 2050.1
5:30 the prey; to every man a damsel o two; NIH
9: 2 reign over you, o that one reign over you? 2050.1
11:25 o did he ever fight against them, 518
13:14 neither let her drink wine o strong drink, 2050.1
14: 3 of thy brethren, o among all my people, 2050.1
14: 6 he told not his father o his mother what 2050.1
18:19 o that thou be a priest unto a tribe and 176

Jdg 19:13 to lodge all night, in Gibeah, o in Ramah. 176
20:28 of Benjamin my brother, o shall I cease? 518
21:22 when their fathers o their brethren come unto 176
Ru 1:16 o to return from following after thee: NIH
3:10 not young men, whether poor o rich. 518+2050.1
1Sa 2:14 it into the pan, o kettle, or caldron, or pot; 176
2:14 it into the pan, or kettle, o caldron, or pot; 176
2:14 it into the pan, or kettle, or caldron, o pot; 176
6:12 not aside to the right hand o to the left; 2050.1
12: 3 o whose ass have I taken? or whom have 2050.1
12: 3 o whom have I defrauded? whom have I 2050.1
12: 3 o of whose hand have I received any 2050.1
13:19 the Hebrews make them swords o spears: 176
14: 6 to the LORD to save by many o by few. 176
14:52 o any valiant man, he took him unto him. 2050.1
16: 7 o on the height of his stature; 2050.1
18:18 is my life, o my father's family in Israel, NIH
20: 2 father will do nothing either great o small, 176
20:10 o what if thy father answer thee roughly? 176
20:12 o the third day, and behold, if there be good NIH
21: 3 bread in mine hand, o what there is present. 176
21: 8 not here under thine hand spear o sword? 176
22: 8 o sheweth unto me that my son hath 2050.1
22:15 servant knew nothing of all this, less o more. 176
25:31 o that my lord hath avenged himself: 2050.1
25:36 o more, until the morning light. 2050.1
26:10 o his day shall come to die; or he shall 176
26:10 o he shall descend into battle, and perish. 176
26:18 have I done? o what evil is in mine hand? 2050.1
29: 3 o these years, and I have found no fault in 176
30: 2 either great o small, but 5704+2050.1
2Sa 2:21 thee aside to thy right hand o to thy left, 176
3:29 o that is a leper, or that leaneth on a staff, 2050.1
3:29 o that leaneth on a staff, or that falleth on 2050.1
3:29 o that falleth on the sword, or that lacketh 2050.1
3:29 falleth on the sword, o that lacketh bread. 2050.1
3:35 and more also, if I taste bread, o ought else, 176
14:19 none can turn to the right hand o to 2050.1
15: 4 any suit o cause might come unto me, 2050.1
15:21 whether in death o life, even there also will 518
17: 9 hid now in some pit, o in some other place: 176
19:35 servant taste what I eat o what I drink? 2050.1
19:42 the king's cost? o hath he given us any gift? 518
20:20 that I should swallow up o destroy. 518+2050.1
24:13 o wilt thou flee three months before thine 518
24:13 o that there be three days' pestilence in 2050.1
1Ki 3: 7 I know not how to go out o come in. 2050.1
8:23 in heaven above, o on earth beneath, 2050.1
8:37 mildew, locust, o if there be caterpillar; NIH
8:38 made by any man, o by all thy people Israel, NIH
8:46 unto the land of the enemy, far o near; 176
9: 6 you o your children, and will not keep my 2050.1
15:17 to go out o come in to Asa king of Judah. 2050.1
18:10 God liveth, there is no nation o kingdom, 2050.1
18:27 either he is talking, o he is 3588+2050.1
18:27 or he is pursuing, o he is in a 3588+2050.1
18:27 o peradventure he sleepeth, and must be NIH
20:18 o whether they be come out for war, 2050.1
20:39 o else thou shalt pay a talent of silver. 176
21: 2 o, if it seem good to thee, I will give thee NIH
21: 6 o else, if it please thee, I will give thee 176
22: 6 Ramoth-gilead to battle, o shall I forbear? 518
22:15 Ramoth-gilead to battle, o shall we forbear? 518
2Ki 2:16 upon some mountain, o into some valley. 176
2:21 thence any more death o barren land. 2050.1
4:13 for to the king, o to the captain of the host? 176
6:27 out of the barnfloor, o out of the winepress? 176
9:32 looked out to him two o three eunuchs. NIH
12:13 any vessels of gold, o vessels of silver, 2050.1
13:19 shouldest have smitten five o six times; 176
17:34 o after their ordinances, or after the law 2050.1
17:34 o after the law and commandment which 2050.1
20: 9 forward ten degrees, o go back ten degrees? 518
22: 2 not aside to the right hand o to the left. 2050.1
23:10 that no man might make his son o his 2050.1
1Ch 21:12 o three months to be destroyed 518+2050.1
21:12 o else three days the sword of 518+2050.1
2Ch 1:11 hast not asked riches, wealth, o honour, 2050.1
6:28 o mildew, locusts, or caterpillars; 2050.1
6:28 or mildew, locusts, o caterpillars; 2050.1
6:28 whatsoever sore o whatsoever sickness 2050.1
6:29 Then what prayer o what supplication NIH
6:29 o of all thy people Israel, when every one 2050.1
6:36 away captives unto a land far off o near; 176
7:13 o if I command the locusts to devour 2050.1
7:13 o if I send pestilence among my people; 2050.1
8:15 any matter, o concerning the treasures. 2050.1
14:11 with many, o with them that have no power: NIH
15:13 whether small o great, 5704+2050.1
15:13 or great, whether man o woman. 5704+2050.1
16: 1 go out o come in to Asa king of Judah. 2050.1
18: 5 to Ramoth-gilead to battle, o shall I forbear? 518
18:14 to Ramoth-gilead to battle, o shall I forbear? 518
18:30 saying, Fight ye not with small o great, NIH
20: 9 judgment, o pestilence, or famine, 2050.1
20: 9 judgment, or pestilence, o famine, 2050.1
32:15 for no god of any nation o kingdom was 2050.1
36:17 compassion upon young man o maiden, 2050.1
36:17 old man, o him that stooped for age: 2050.1
Ezr 7:24 o ministers of this house of God, 2050.3
7:24 impose toll, tribute, o custom, upon them. 2050.3
7:26 o to banishment, or to confiscation of 2006
7:26 o to confiscation of goods, or 2006
7:26 confiscation of goods, o to imprisonment. 2050.3
9:12 seek their peace o their wealth for ever: 2050.1
10:13 neither is this a work of one day o two: 2050.1
Ne 2:16 knew not whither I went, o what I did; 2050.1
5: 8 o shall they be sold unto us? Then held 2050.1
10:31 o any victuals on the sabbath day to sell, 2050.1
10:31 of them on the sabbath, o on the holy day: 2050.1
13:20 lodged without Jerusalem once o twice. 2050.1
13:25 unto your sons, o for yourselves. 2050.1
Est 4:11 that whosoever, whether man o woman, 2050.1
4:16 eat nor drink three days, night o day; 2050.1
8: 6 o how can I endure to see the destruction 2050.1

Est 9:12 o what is thy request further? and it shall 2050.1
Job 3:12 o why the breasts that I should suck? 2050.1
3:15 O with princes that had gold, who filled their 176
3:16 O as a hidden untimely birth I had not been; 176
4: 7 o where were the righteous cut off? 2050.1
6: 5 hath grass? o loweth the ox over his fodder? 518
6: 6 o is there any taste in the white of an egg? 518
6:12 strength of stones? o is my flesh of brass? 518
6:22 o, Give a reward for me of your 2050.1
6:23 O, Deliver me from the enemy's hand? 2050.1
6:23 o, Redeem me from the hand of 2050.1
7:12 Am I a sea, o a whale, that thou settest a 518
8: 3 o doth the Almighty pervert justice? 518+2050.1
10: 4 eyes of flesh? o seest thou as man seeth? 518
11:10 o gather together, then who can hinder 2050.1
12: 8 O speak to the earth, and it shall teach thee: 176
13: 9 o as one man mocketh another, do ye so 518
13:22 o let me speak, and answer thou me. 176
15: 3 o with speeches wherewith he can do no 2050.1
15: 7 o wast thou made before the hills? 2050.1
16: 3 o what emboldeneth thee that thou 176
22: 3 o is it gain to him, that thou makest thy 2050.1
22:11 O darkness, that thou canst not see; and 176
25: 4 o how can he be clean that is born of a 2050.1
28:16 with the precious onyx, o the sapphire. 2050.1
28:18 shall be made of coral, o of pearls: 2050.1
31: 5 o if my foot hath hasted to deceit; 2050.1
31: 9 o if I have laid wait at my neighbour's 2050.1
31:13 of my manservant o of my maidservant, 2050.1
31:16 o have caused the eyes of the widow to 2050.1
31:17 O have eaten my morsel myself alone, 2050.1
31:19 of clothing, o any poor without covering; 2050.1
31:24 o have said to the fine gold, Thou art my 2050.1
31:26 o the moon walking in brightness; 2050.1
31:27 o my mouth hath kissed my hand: 2050.1
31:29 o lift up myself when evil found him: 2050.1
31:34 o did the contempt of families terrify me, 2050.1
31:38 o that the furrows likewise thereof 2050.1
31:39 o have caused the owners thereof to lose 2050.1
32:12 convinced Job, o that answered his words: NIH
34:13 o who hath disposed the whole world? 2050.1
34:29 against a nation, o against a man only: 2050.1
34:33 whether thou refuse, o whether thou choose; NIH
35: 6 o if thy transgressions be multiplied, 2050.1
35: 7 thou him? o what receiveth he of thine hand? 176
36:23 o who can say, Thou hast wrought 2050.1
36:29 of the clouds, o the noise of his tabernacle? NIH
37:13 for correction, o for his land, or for mercy. 518
37:13 for correction, or for his land, o for mercy. 518
38: 5 o who hath stretched the line upon it? 176
38: 6 o who laid the corner stone thereof; 176
38: 8 O who shut up the sea with doors, 2050.1
38:16 o hast thou walked in the search of 2050.1
38:17 o hast thou seen the doors of the shadow 2050.1
38:21 o because the number of thy days is 2050.1
38:22 o hast thou seen the treasures of the hail, 2050.1
38:25 o a way for the lightning of thunder; 2050.1
38:28 o who hath begotten the drops of dew? 176
38:31 of Pleiades, o loose the bands of Orion? 176
38:32 o canst thou guide Arcturus with his 2050.1
38:36 o who hath given understanding to the heart? 176
38:37 o who can stay the bottles of heaven, 2050.1
38:39 o fill the appetite of the young lions, 2050.1
39: 1 o canst thou mark when the hinds do calve? NIH
39: 2 o knowest thou the time when they bring 2050.1
39: 5 o who hath loosed the bands of the wild 2050.1
39: 9 be willing to serve thee, o abide by thy crib? 518
39:10 o will he harrow the valleys after thee? 518
39:11 o wilt thou leave thy labour to him? 2050.1
39:13 o wings and feathers unto the ostrich? 518
39:15 o that the wild beast may break them. 2050.1
40: 9 o, canst thou thunder with a voice like 2050.1
41: 1 o his tongue with a cord which thou 2050.1
41: 2 o bore his jaw through with a thorn? 2050.1
41: 5 o wilt thou bind him for thy maidens? 2050.1
41: 7 barbed irons? o his head with fish spears? 2050.1
41:13 o who can come to him with his double NIH
41:20 as out of a seething pot o caldron. 2050.1
Ps 18:31 o who is a rock save our God? 2050.1
32: 9 Be ye not as the horse, o as the mule, NIH
35:14 as though he had been my friend o brother. NIH
44:20 o stretched out our hands to a strange 2050.1
50: 8 for thy sacrifices o thy burnt offerings, 2050.1
50:13 flesh of bulls, o drink the blood of goats? 2050.1
50:16 o that thou shouldest take my covenant in 2050.1
66: T To the chief Musician, A Song o Psalm. NIH
67: T Musician on Neginoth, A Psalm o Song. NIH
68: T chief Musician, A Psalm o Song of David. NIH
69:31 an ox o bullock that hath horns and hoofs. NIH
75: T Al-taschith, A Psalm o Song of Asaph. NIH
76: T on Neginoth, A Psalm o Song of Asaph. NIH
83: T A Song o Psalm of Asaph. NIH
87: T A Psalm o Song for the sons of Korah. NIH
88: T A Song o Psalm for the sons of Korah. NIH
88:11 the grave? o thy faithfulness in destruction? NIH
89: 8 o to thy faithfulness round about thee? 2050.1
90: 2 o ever thou hadst formed the earth and 2050.1
92: T A Psalm o Song for the sabbath day. NIH
94:16 o who will stand up for me against NIH
108: T A Song o Psalm of David. NIH
120: 3 o what shall be done unto thee, thou false 2050.1
131: 1 great matters, o in things too high for me. 2050.1
132: 4 to mine eyes, o slumber to mine eyelids, NIH
139: 7 o whither shall I flee from thy presence? 2050.1
144: 3 o the son of man, that thou makest account NIH
Pr 6: 7 Which having no guide, overseer, o ruler, 2050.1
7:22 o as a fool to the correction of the stocks; 2050.1
8: 8 is nothing froward o perverse in them. 2050.1
8:23 the beginning, o ever the earth was. 4480+6924
20:20 Whoso curseth his father o his mother, 2050.1
22:26 o of them that are sureties for debts. NIH
23:34 o as he that lieth upon the top of a mast. 2050.1
28:24 Whoso robbeth his father o his mother, 2050.1
29: 9 whether he rage o laugh, there is no rest. 2050.1
30: 4 ascended up into heaven, o descended? 2050.1

O

Pr 30: 9 o lest I be poor, and steal, and take 2050.1
30:32 o if thou hast thought evil, *lay thine* hand 2050.1
Ecc 2:19 whether he shall be a wise *man* o a fool? 176
2:25 o who else can hasten *hereunto,* more 2050.1
5:12 *is* sweet, whether he eat little o much: 2050.1
9: 1 no man knoweth either love o hatred *by* all 1571
11: 3 fall toward the south, o toward the north, 2050.1
11: 6 either this o that, or whether they both *shall* 176
11: 6 o whether they both *shall be* alike good. 2050.1
12: 2 o the light, or the moon, or the stars, 2050.1
12: 2 or the light, o the moon, or the stars, 2050.1
12: 2 or the light, or the moon, o the stars, 2050.1
12: 6 **O ever** the silver cord be 834+3808+5704
12: 6 o the golden bowl be broken, or 2050.1
12: 6 o the pitcher be broken at the fountain, or 2050.1
12: 6 o the wheel broken at the cistern. 2050.1
12:14 whether *it be* good, o whether *it be* evil. 2050.1
SS 2: 9 My beloved *is* like a roe o a young hart: 176
2:17 be thou like a roe o a young hart upon 176
6:12 **O ever** I was aware, my soul made me *like* 3808
8:14 be thou like to a roe o to a young hart upon 176
Isa 1:11 of bullocks, o of lambs, or of he goats. 2050.1
1:11 of bullocks, or of lambs, o of he goats. 2050.1
7:11 it either in the depth, o in the height above. 176
10:14 the wing, o opened the mouth, or peeped. 2050.1
10:14 the wing, or opened the mouth, o peeped. 2050.1
10:15 o shall the saw magnify itself against him NIH
10:15 o as if the staff should lift up *itself, as if it* NIH
17: 6 two o three berries in the top of NIH
17: 6 four o five in the outmost fruitful branches NIH
17: 8 either the groves, o the images. 2050.1
19:15 which the head o tail, branch or rush, 2050.1
19:15 which the head or tail, branch o rush, 2050.1
27: 5 O let him take hold of my strength, *that* he 176
27: 7 o is he slain according to the slaughter of NIH
29: 8 o as when a thirsty *man* dreameth, and 2050.1
29:16 o shall the thing framed say of him that 2050.1
30:14 o to take water *withal* out of the pit. 2050.1
38:14 Like a crane o a swallow, so did I chatter: NIH
40:13 o *being* his counseller hath taught him? 2050.1
40:18 o what likeness will ye compare unto 2050.1
40:25 then will ye liken me, o shall I be equal? 2050.1
41:22 end of them; o declare us *things* for to come. 176
41:23 yea, do good, o do evil, that we may be 2050.1
42:19 o deaf, as my messenger *that* I sent? 2050.1
43: 9 o let them hear, and say, *It is* truth. 2050.1
44:10 o molten a graven image *that* is profitable 2050.1
45: 9 o thy work, He hath no hands? 2050.1
45:10 o to the woman, What hast thou brought 2050.1
49:24 o the lawful captive delivered? 518+2050.1
50: 1 o which of my creditors *is it* to whom I have 176
50: 2 o have I no power to deliver? 518+2050.1
57:11 of whom hast thou been afraid o feared, 2050.1
66: 8 o shall a nation be born at once? for as soon NIH
Jer 2:18 o what hast thou to do in the way of 2050.1
2:32 forget her ornaments, o a bride her attire? NIH
7:22 concerning burnt offerings o sacrifices: 2050.1
11:14 neither lift up a cry o prayer for them: 2050.1
11:19 I *was* like a lamb o an ox *that* is brought to NIH
13:23 change his skin, o the leopard his spots? 2050.1
14:22 o can the heavens give showers? *art* not 2050.1
15: 5 o who shall bemoan thee? or who shall go 2050.1
15: 5 o who shall go aside to ask how thou 2050.1
16: 7 to drink for their father o for their mother. 2050.1
16:10 o what *is* our iniquity? or what *is* our sin 2050.1
16:10 o what *is* our sin that we have committed 2050.1
18:14 o shall the cold flowing waters that come NIH
20:17 o that my mother might have been my 2050.1
21:13 o who shall enter into our habitations? 2050.1
22:18 o, Ah sister! they shall not lament for 2050.1
22:18 for him, *saying,* Ah lord! o, Ah his glory. 2050.1
23:33 o the prophet, or a priest, shall ask thee, 176
23:33 or the prophet, o a priest, shall ask thee, 176
32:43 ye say, *It is* desolate without man o beast; 2050.1
34: 9 *being* a Hebrew o a Hebrewess, go free; 2050.1
36:23 when Jehudi had read three o four leaves, 2050.1
37:18 o against thy servants, or against this 2050.1
37:18 against thy servants, o against this people, 2050.1
40: 5 o go wheresoever it seemeth convenient unto 176
42: 6 Whether *it be* good, o whether *it be* evil, 2050.1
42:17 none of them shall remain o escape from 2050.1
44:14 shall escape o remain, that *they* should 2050.1
44:28 whose words shall stand, mine, o theirs. 2050.1
48:24 the cities of the land of Moab, far o near. 2050.1
Eze 2: 5 will hear, o whether they will forbear, 2050.1
2: 7 will hear, o whether they will forbear: 2050.1
3:11 will hear, o whether they will forbear. 2050.1
4:14 which dieth of itself, o is torn in pieces; 2050.1
14: 7 o of the stranger that sojourneth in Israel, 2050.1
14:17 O *if* I bring a sword upon that land, and say, 176
14:19 O *if* I send a pestilence into that land, 176
15: 2 o *than* a branch which is among the trees of NIH
15: 3 o will *men* take a pin of it to hang any vessel 518
17: 9 even without great power o many people 2050.1
17:15 o shall he break the covenant, 2050.1
21:16 **Go thee one way o other**, *either* on the right 258
21:16 other, *either* on the right hand, o on the left, NIH
22:14 heart endure, o can thine hands be strong, 518
34: 6 and none did search o seek *after them.* 2050.1
44:22 o a widow that had a priest before. 2050.1
44:25 o for mother, or for son, or for daughter, 2050.1
44:25 or for mother, o for son, or for daughter, 2050.1
44:25 or for mother, or for son, o for daughter, 2050.1
44:25 o for sister that hath had no husband, 2050.1
44:31 o torn, whether it be fowl or beast. 2050.1
44:31 or torn, whether it be fowl o beast. 2050.1
46:12 o peace offerings voluntarily unto 176
Da 2:10 any magician, o astrologer, or Chaldean. 2050.3
2:10 any magician, or astrologer, o Chaldean. 2050.3
4:19 o the interpretation thereof, trouble thee. 2050.3
4:35 o say unto him, What doest thou? 2050.3
6: 4 was there any error o fault found in him. 2050.3
6: 7 petition of any God o man for thirty days, 2050.3
6:12 of any God o man within thirty days, 2050.3
6:24 brake all their bones in pieces o ever they 5705

Da 11:29 shall not be as the former, o as the latter. 2050.1
Joel 1: 2 o even in the days of your fathers? 2050.1
Am 3:12 of the lion two legs, o a piece of an ear; 176
4: 8 So two o three cities wandered unto one NIH
5:19 o went *into* the house, and leaned his 2050.1
6: 2 o their border greater than your border? 518
Mic 6: 7 o with ten thousands of rivers of oil? NIH
Hag 2:12 o pottage, or wine, or oil, or any meat, 2050.1
2:12 or pottage, o wine, or oil, or any meat, 2050.1
2:12 or pottage, or wine, o oil, or any meat, 2050.1
2:12 or pottage, or wine, or oil, o any meat, 2050.1
Zec 8:10 o came in because of the affliction: 2050.1
Mal 1: 8 he be pleased with thee, o accept thy person? 176
2:13 o receiveth *it with* good will at your hand. 2050.1
2:17 in them; o, Where *is* the God of judgment? 176
Mt 5:17 am come to destroy the law, o the prophets: 2228
5:18 one jot o one tittle shall in no wise pass 2228
5:36 thou canst not make one hair white o black. 2228
6:24 **o else** he will hold to the one, and 2228
6:25 what ye shall eat, o what ye shall drink; 2532
6:31 o, What shall we drink? or, 2228
6:31 o, Wherewithal shall we be clothed? 2228
7: 4 O how wilt thou say to thy brother, Let me 2228
7: 9 O what man is there of you, whom if his 2228
7:10 O if he ask a fish, will he give him a 2532
7:16 gather grapes of thorns, o figs of thistles? 2228
9: 5 be forgiven thee; o to say, Arise, and walk? 2228
10:11 into whatsoever city o town ye shall enter, 2228
10:14 when ye depart out of that house o city, 2228
10:19 take no thought how o what ye shall speak: 2228
10:37 He that loveth father o mother more than 2228
10:37 and he that loveth son o daughter more than 2228
11: 3 should come, o do we look for another? 2228
12: 5 O have ye not read in the law, how that on 2228
12:25 and every city o house divided against itself 2228
12:29 **O else** how can one enter into a strong 2228
12:33 **o else** make the tree corrupt, and his fruit 2228
13:21 o persecution ariseth because of the word, 2228
15: 4 and, He that curseth father o mother, 2228
15: 5 shall say to *his* father o *his* mother, 2228
15: 6 And honour not his father o his mother, 2228
16:14 and others, Jeremias, o one of the prophets. 2228
16:26 o what shall a man give in exchange for his 2228
17:25 the kings of the earth take custom o tribute? 2228
17:25 of their own children, o of strangers? 2228
18: 8 if thy hand o thy foot offend thee, 2228
18: 8 for thee to enter into life halt o maimed, 2228
18: 8 rather than having two hands o two feet to 2228
18:16 *then* take with thee one o two more, 2228
18:16 that in the mouth of two o three witnesses 2228
18:20 For where two o three are gathered together 2228
19:29 o brethren, or sisters, or father, or mother, 2228
19:29 o sisters, or father, or mother, or wife, or 2228
19:29 o father, or mother, or wife, or children, or 2228
19:29 o mother, or wife, or children, or lands, 2228
19:29 or mother, o wife, or children, or lands, 2228
19:29 or mother, or wife, o children, or lands, 2228
19:29 or mother, or wife, or children, o lands, 2228
21:25 from heaven, o of men? And they reasoned 2228
22:17 it lawful to give tribute unto Cesar, o not? 2228
23:17 o the temple that sanctifieth the gold? 2228
23:19 the gift, o the altar that sanctifieth the gift? 2228
24:23 say unto you, Lo, here *is* Christ, o there; 2228
25:37 and fed *thee?* o thirsty, and gave *thee* 2228
25:38 took *thee* in? o naked, and clothed *thee?* 2228
25:39 O when saw we thee sick, 1161
25:39 thee sick, o in prison, and came unto thee? 2228
25:44 o athirst, or a stranger, or naked, or sick, or 2228
25:44 o a stranger, or naked, or sick, or in prison, 2228
25:44 o naked, or sick, or in prison, and did not 2228
25:44 o sick, or in prison, and did not minister 2228
25:44 o in prison, and did not minister unto thee? 2228
27:17 Barabbas, o Jesus which is called Christ? 2228
Mk 2: 9 o to say, Arise, and take up thy bed, and 2228
3: 4 do good on the sabbath days, o to do evil? 2228
3: 4 to save life, o to kill? But they held their 2228
3:33 saying, Who is my mother, o my brethren? 2228
4:17 when affliction o persecution ariseth for 2228
4:21 to be put under a bushel, o under a bed? 2228
4:30 o with what comparison shall we compare 2228
6:15 it is a prophet, o as one of the prophets. 2228
6:56 into villages, o cities, or country, 2228
6:56 into villages, or cities, o country, 2228
7:10 and, Whoso curseth father o mother, 2228
7:11 If a man shall say to *his* father o mother, 2228
7:12 to do ought for his father o his mother; 2228
8:37 O what shall a man give in exchange for 2228
10:29 o brethren, or sisters, or father, or mother, 2228
10:29 o sisters, or father, or mother, or wife, or 2228
10:29 o father, or mother, or wife, or children, or 2228
10:29 o mother, or wife, or children, or lands, 2228
10:29 or mother, o wife, or children, or lands, 2228
10:29 or mother, or wife, o children, or lands, 2228
10:29 or mother, or wife, or children, o lands, 2228
11:30 of John, was *it* from heaven, o of men? 2228
12:14 Is it lawful to give tribute to Cesar, o not? 2228
12:15 Shall we give, o shall we not give? But he, 2228
13:21 to you, Lo, here *is* Christ; o lo, *he is* there; 2228
13:35 o at midnight, or at the cockcrowing, or 2228
13:35 o at the cockcrowing, or in the morning: 2228
13:35 or at the cockcrowing, o in the morning: 2228
Lk 2:24 A pair of turtledoves, o two young pigeons. 2228
3:15 of John, **whether** he were the Christ, **o not**; 3379
5:23 forgiven thee; o to say, Rise up and walk? 2228
6: 9 the sabbath days to do good, o to do evil? 2228
6: 9 or to do evil? to save life, o to destroy *it?* 2228
7:19 that should come? o look we for another? 2228
7:20 that should come? o look we for another? 2228
8:16 it with a vessel, o putteth *it* under a bed; 2228
9:25 and lose himself, o be cast away? 2228
11:11 o if *he ask* a fish, will he for a fish give him 2532
11:12 O if he shall ask an egg, will he offer him a 2228
12:11 take ye no thought how o what *thing* ye 2228
12:11 *thing* ye shall answer, o what ye shall say: 2228
12:14 made me a judge o a divider over you? 2228

Lk 12:29 o what ye shall drink, neither be ye of 2228
12:38 o come in the third watch, and find *them* 2532
12:41 thou this parable unto us, o even to all? 2228
13: 4 O those eighteen, upon whom the tower in 2228
13:15 sabbath loose his ox o *his* ass from the stall, 2228
14: 5 shall have an ass o an ox fallen into a pit, 2228
14:12 When thou makest a dinner o a supper, 2228
14:31 O what king, going to make war against 2228
14:32 **O else**, while the other is yet a great way 1490
16:13 **o else** he will hold to the one, and 2228
17: 7 having a servant plowing o feeding cattle, 2228
17:21 o, lo there: for behold, the kingdom of God 2228
17:23 they shall say to you, See here; o, see there: 2228
18:11 unjust, adulterers, o even as this publican. 2228
18:29 o parents, or brethren, or wife, or children, 2228
18:29 or parents, o brethren, or wife, or children, 2228
18:29 or parents, or brethren, o wife, or children, 2228
18:29 or parents, or brethren, or wife, o children, 2228
20: 2 o who is he that gave thee this authority? 2228
20: 4 of John, was it from heaven, o of men? 2228
20:22 for us to give tribute unto Cesar, o no? 2228
22:27 he that sitteth at meat, o he that serveth? 2228
Jn 2: 6 containing two o three firkins apiece. 2228
4:27 seekest thou? o, Why talkest thou with her? 2228
6:19 about five and twenty o thirty furlongs, 2228
7:17 it be of God, o *whether* I speak of myself. 2228
7:48 Have any of the rulers o of the Pharisees 2228
9: 2 who did sin, this *man,* o his parents, 2228
9:21 o who hath opened his eyes, we know not: 2228
9:25 Whether he be a sinner o *no,* I know not: NIG
13:29 o that he should give something to the poor. 2228
14:11 **o else** believe me for the very works' sake. 1490
18:34 of thyself, o did others tell *it* thee of me? 2228
Ac 1: 7 for you to know *the* times o *the* seasons, 2228
3:12 o why look ye *so* earnestly on us, as though 2228
3:12 as though by our own power o holiness we 2228
4: 7 By what power, o by what name, 2228
4:34 possessors of lands o houses sold them, 2228
5:38 for if this counsel o this work be of men, 2228
7:49 the Lord: o what *is* the place of my rest? 2228
8:34 of himself, o of some other *man?* 2228
9: 2 *this* way, whether they were men o women, 2532
10:14 eaten any *thing that is* common o unclean. 2228
10:28 o come unto one of another nation; 2228
10:28 not call any man common o unclean. 2228
11: 8 for nothing common o unclean hath at any 2228
17:21 but *either* to tell, o to hear some new *thing.*) 2532
17:29 o silver, or stone, graven by art and 2228
17:29 or silver, o stone, graven by art and 2228
18:14 were a matter of wrong o wicked lewdness, 2228
19:12 unto the sick handkerchiefs o aprons, 2228
20:33 coveted no *man's* silver, o gold, or apparel. 2228
20:33 coveted no *man's* silver, or gold, o apparel. 2228
23: 9 but if a spirit o an angel hath spoken to 2228
23:15 and we, o ever he come near, are ready to NIG
23:29 to his charge worthy of death o of bonds. 2228
24:20 **O else** let these same *here* say, if they have 2228
24:23 acquaintance to minister o come unto him. 2228
25:11 o have committed any *thing* worthy of 2532
26:31 doeth nothing worthy of death o of bonds. 2228
28: 6 have swollen, o fallen down dead suddenly: 2228
28:17 the people, o customs of our fathers, 2228
28:21 came shewed o spake any harm of thee. 2228
Ro 2: 4 O despisest thou the riches of his goodness 2228
2:15 o else excusing one another;) 2228
3: 1 o what profit *is there* of circumcision? 2228
4: 9 then upon the circumcision *only,* o 2228
4:10 was in circumcision, o in uncircumcision? 2228
4:13 o to his seed, through the law, but 2228
6:16 o of obedience unto righteousness? 2228
8:35 o distress, or persecution, or famine, or 2228
8:35 o persecution, or famine, or nakedness, or 2228
8:35 o famine, or nakedness, or peril, or sword? 2228
8:35 or famine, o nakedness, or peril, or sword? 2228
8:35 or famine, or nakedness, o peril, or sword? 2228
8:35 or famine, or nakedness, or peril, o sword? 2228
9:11 neither having done any good o evil, 2228
10: 7 O, Who shall descend into the deep? 2228
11:34 the Lord? o who hath been his counseller? 2228
11:35 O who hath first given to him, and it shall 2228
12: 7 O ministry, *let us wait* on *our* ministering: 1535
12: 7 o he that teacheth, on teaching; 1535
12: 8 O he that exhorteth, on exhortation: he that 1535
14: 4 to his own master he standeth o falleth. 2228
14: 8 o die, we are the Lord's. 1437+5037
14:10 o why dost thou set at nought thy brother? 2228
14:13 that no *man* put a stumblingblock o 2228
14:21 o is offended, or is *made* weak. 2228
14:21 or is offended, o is *made* weak. 2228
1Co 1:13 o were ye baptized in the name of Paul? 2228
2: 1 not with excellency of speech o of wisdom, 2228
3:22 o Apollos, or Cephas, or the world, or life, 1535
3:22 o Cephas, or the world, or life, or death, or 1535
3:22 o the world, or life, or death, or 1535
3:22 o life, or death, or *things* present, or 1535
3:22 o death, or *things* present, or *things* to 1535
3:22 death, o *things* present, or *things* to come; 1535
3:22 death, or *things* present, o *things* to come; 1535
4: 3 be judged of you, o of man's judgment: 2228
4:21 o in love, and *in* the spirit of meekness? 2228
5:10 o with the covetous, or extortioners, or 2228
5:10 o extortioners, or with idolaters; 2228
5:10 or extortioners, o with idolaters; 2228
5:11 o covetous, or an idolater, or a railer, or 2228
5:11 o an idolater, or a railer, or a drunkard, or 2228
5:11 o a railer, or a drunkard, or an extortioner; 2228
5:11 or a railer, o a drunkard, or an extortioner; 2228
5:11 or a railer, or a drunkard, o an extortioner; 2228
7:11 o be reconciled to *her* husband: 2228
7:15 A brother o a sister is not under bondage in 2228
7:16 o how knowest thou, O man, whether thou 2228
8: 5 whether in heaven o in earth, (as there be 1535
9: 6 O I only and Barnabas, have not we power 2228
9: 7 o who feedeth a flock, and eateth not of 2228
9: 8 a man? o saith not the law the same also? 2228

1Co 9:10 O saith he *it* altogether for our sakes? 2228
10:19 that the idol is any *thing,* o that which is 2228
10:31 ye eat, o drink, or whatsoever ye do, 1535
10:31 ye eat, or drink, o whatsoever ye do, 1535
11: 4 Every man praying o prophesying, 2228
11: 5 But every woman that prayeth o 2228
11: 6 a shame for a woman to be shorn o shaven, 2228
11:22 have ye not houses to eat and to drink *in?* o 2228
12:13 whether *we be* Jews o Gentiles, whether *we* 1535
12:13 or Gentiles, whether *we be* bond o free; 1535
12:26 suffer with *it;* o one member be honoured, 1535
13: 1 *as* sounding brass, o a tinkling cymbal. 2228
14: 6 o by knowledge, or by prophesying, or 2228
14: 6 o by prophesying, o by doctrine? 2228
14: 6 or by prophesying, o by doctrine? 2228
14: 7 life giving sound, whether pipe o harp, 1535
14: 7 shall it be known what is piped o harped? 2228
14:23 o unbelievers, will they not say that ye are 2228
14:24 o *one* unlearned, he is convinced of all, 2228
14:27 o at the most *by* three, and *that* by course; 2228
14:29 Let the prophets speak two o three, and 2228
14:36 out from you? o came it unto you only? 2228
14:37 think himself to be a prophet, o spiritual, 2228
15:11 Therefore whether *it were* I o they, so 1535
15:37 chance of wheat, o of some other *grain:* 2228
2Co 1: 6 o **whether** we be comforted, *it is* for your 1535
1:13 than what you read o acknowledge; 2228
1:17 o *the things* that I purpose, do I purpose 2228
3: 1 o need we, as some *others,* epistles of 2228
3: 1 o *letters* of commendation from you? 2228
5: 9 we labour, that, whether present o absent, 1535
5:10 that he hath done, whether *it be* good o bad. 1535
5:13 o **whether** we be sober, *it is* for your cause. 1535
6:15 o what part hath he that believeth with an 2228
8:23 o our brethren *be inquired of, they are* 1535
9: 7 *him give;* not grudgingly, o of necessity: 2228
10:12 o compare ourselves with some that 2228
11: 4 o *if* ye receive another spirit, which ye have 2228
11: 4 ye have not received, o another gospel, 2228
12: 2 o **whether** out of the body, I cannot tell: 1535
12: 3 in the body, o out of the body, I cannot tell: 1535
12: 6 he seeth me *to be,* o that he heareth of me. 2228
13: 1 In the mouth of two o three witnesses shall 2532
Gal 1: 8 But though we, o an angel from heaven, 2228
1:10 For do I now persuade men, o God? or do I 2228
1:10 o do I seek to please men? for if I yet 2228
2: 2 any means I should run, o had run, in vain. 2228
3: 2 works of the law, o by the hearing of faith? 2228
3: 5 works of the law, o by the hearing of faith? 2228
3:15 no *man* disannulleth, o added thereto. 2228
4: 9 o rather are known of God, how turn ye 1161
Eph 3:20 abundantly above all that we ask o think, 2228
5: 3 and all uncleanness, o covetousness, 2228
5:27 o wrinkle, or any such *thing;* but that it 2228
5:27 o any such *thing;* but that it should be holy 2228
6: 8 of the Lord, whether *he be* bond o free. 1535
Php 1:18 in pretence, o in truth, Christ is preached; 1535
1:20 my body, whether *it be* by life, o by death. 1535
1:27 I come and see you, o *else* be absent, 1535
2: 3 nothing *be done* through strife o vainglory; 2228
Col 1:16 o dominions, or principalities, or powers: 1535
1:16 or dominions, o principalities, or powers: 1535
1:16 or dominions, or principalities, o powers: 1535
1:20 *they be things* in earth, o *things* in heaven. 1535
2:16 o in drink, or in respect of a holyday, or 2228
2:16 o in respect of a holyday, or of the new 2228
2:16 o of the new moon, or of the sabbath days: 2228
2:16 or of the new moon, o of the sabbath days: 2228
3:17 And whatsoever ye do in word o deed, 2228
1Th 2:19 *is* our hope, o joy, or crown of rejoicing? 2228
2:19 *is* our hope, or joy, o crown of rejoicing? 2228
5:10 died for us, that, whether we wake o sleep, 1535
2Th 2: 2 o be troubled, neither by spirit, nor by 3366
2: 4 all that is called God, o that is worshipped; 2228
2:15 whether by word, o by our epistle. 1535
1Ti 2: 9 o gold, or pearls, or costly array; 2532
2: 9 or gold, o pearls, or costly array; 2228
2: 9 or gold, or pearls, o costly array; 2228
5: 4 But if any widow have children o nephews, 2228
5:16 If any man o woman that believeth have 2228
5:19 but before two o three witnesses. 2228
Tit 1: 6 children not accused of riot o unruly. 2228
3:12 I shall send Artemas unto thee, o Tychicus, 2228
Phm 1:18 he hath wronged thee, o oweth *thee* ought, 2228
Heb 2: 6 o the son of man, that thou visitest him? 2228
10:28 without mercy under two o three witnesses: 2228
12:16 any fornicator, o profane *person,* as Esau, 2228
12:20 be stoned, o thrust through with a dart: 2228
Jas 2: 3 thou there, o sit here under my footstool: 2228
2:15 If a brother o sister be naked, and 2228
4:13 To day o to morrow we will go into such a 2532
4:15 Lord will, we shall live, and do this, o that. 2228
1Pe 1:11 o what manner of time the Spirit of Christ 2228
2:14 O unto governors, as unto them that are 1535
3: 3 wearing of gold, o of putting on of apparel; 2228
3: 9 rendering evil for evil, o railing for railing: 2228
4:15 o *as* a thief, or *as* an evildoer, or as a 2228
4:15 o *as* an evildoer, or as a busybody in other 2228
4:15 o as a busybody in other men's matters. 2228
Rev 2: 5 o **else** I *will* come unto thee quickly, and 1490
2:16 o **else** I *will* come unto thee quickly, and 1490
3:15 cold nor hot: I would thou wert cold o hot. 2228
13:16 in their right hand, o in their foreheads: 2228
13:17 And that no *man* might buy o sell, save he 2228
13:17 o the name of the beast, or the number of 2228
13:17 of the beast, o the number of his name. 2228
14: 9 *his* mark in his forehead, o in his hand, 2228
20: 4 mark upon their foreheads, o in their hands; 2532
21:27 worketh abomination, o *maketh* a lie: 2532

ORACLE (17) [ORACLES]

2Sa 16:23 *was* as if a man had inquired at the o of 1697
1Ki 6: 5 *both* of the temple and of the o: 1687
6:16 *even* for the o, *even* for the most holy 1687
6:19 the o he prepared in the house within, to set 1687
6:20 the o in the forepart *was* twenty cubits in 1687
6:21 partition by the chains of gold before the o; 1687
6:22 also the whole altar that *was* by the o he 1687
6:23 within the o he made two cherubims *of* 1687
6:31 for the entering of the o he made doors of 1687
7:49 five on the left, before the o, with 1687
8: 6 into the o of the house, to the most holy 1687
8: 8 seen out in the holy *place* before the o, 1687
2Ch 3:16 *as* in the o, and put *them* on the heads of 1687
4:20 should burn after the manner before the o, 1687
5: 7 to the o of the house, into the most holy 1687
5: 9 staves were seen from the ark before the o; 1687
Ps 28: 2 when I lift up my hands toward thy holy o. 1687

ORACLES (4) [ORACLE]

Ac 7:38 who received *the* lively o to give unto us: 3051
Ro 3: 2 that unto them were committed the o of 3051
Heb 5:12 *be* the first principles of the o of God; 3051
1Pe 4:11 *man* speak, *let him speak* as the o of God; 3051

ORATION (1) [ORATOR]

Ac 12:21 upon his throne, and **made an o** unto them. 1215

ORATOR (2) [ORATION]

Isa 3: 3 the cunning artificer, and the eloquent o. 3908
Ac 24: 1 and *with* a certain o *named* Tertullus, 4489

ORCHARD (1) [ORCHARDS]

SS 4:13 Thy plants *are* an o of pomegranates, 6508

ORCHARDS (1) [ORCHARD]

Ecc 2: 5 I made me gardens and o, and I planted 6508

ORDAIN (5) [FOREORDAINED, ORDAINED, ORDAINETH]

1Ch 9:22 Samuel the seer did o in their set office. 3245
17: 9 Also I will o a place for my people Israel, 7760
Isa 26:12 LORD, thou wilt o peace for us: for thou 8239
1Co 7:17 so let him walk. And so o I in all churches. 1299
Tit 1: 5 and o elders in every city, as I had 2525

ORDAINED (37) [ORDAIN]

Nu 28: 6 which was o in mount Sinai for a sweet 6213
1Ki 12:32 Jeroboam o a feast in the eighth month, 6213
12:33 and o a feast unto the children of Israel: 6213
2Ki 23: 5 whom the kings of Judah had o to burn 5414
2Ch 11:15 he o him priests for the high places, and 5975
23:18 with singing, **as** it was o **by** David. 3027+5921
29:27 with the instruments o **by** David king 3027+5921
Est 9:27 The Jews o, and took upon them, and 6965
Ps 8: 2 sucklings hast thou o strength because 3245
8: 3 the moon and the stars, which thou hast o; 3559
81: 5 This he o in Joseph *for* a testimony, 7760
132:17 to bud: I have o a lamp for mine anointed. 6186
Isa 30:33 For Tophet *is* o of old; yea, for the king it is 6186
Jer 1: 5 *and* I o thee a prophet unto the nations. 5414
Da 2:24 whom the king had o to destroy the wise 4483
Hab 1:12 O LORD, thou hast o them for judgment; 7760
Mk 3:14 And he o twelve, that they should be with 4160
Jn 15:16 and o you, that you should go and 5087
Ac 1:22 must one be o *to be* a witness with us of his 1096
10:42 to testify that it is he which was o of God *to* 3724
13:48 as many as were o to eternal life believed. 5021
14:23 And when they had o them elders in every 5500
16: 4 that were o of the apostles and elders which 2919
17:31 righteousness by *that* man whom he hath o; 3724
Ro 7:10 And the commandment, which was *o* to life, NIG
13: 1 of God: the powers that be are o of God. 5021
1Co 2: 7 *even* the hidden *wisdom,* which God o 4309
9:14 hath the Lord o that they which preach 1299
Gal 3:19 *it was* o by angels in the hand of a 1299
Eph 2:10 which God hath **before** o that we should 4282
1Ti 2: 7 Whereunto I am o a preacher, and 5087
2Ti 4: S o the first bishop of the church of 5500
Tit 3: S o the first bishop of the church of 5500
Heb 5: 1 is o for men *in things* pertaining to God, 2525
8: 3 For every high priest is o to offer gifts and 2525
9: 6 Now when these *things* were thus o, 2680
Jude 1: 4 who were **before** of old o to this 4270

ORDAINETH (1) [ORDAIN]

Ps 7:13 he o his arrows against the persecutors. 6466

ORDER (61) [ORDERED, ORDERETH, ORDERINGS, ORDERLY]

Ge 22: 9 **laid** the wood **in** o, and bound Isaac his 6186
Ex 26:17 in one board, **set in** o one against another: 7947
27:21 his sons shall o it from evening to morning 6186
39:37 *even with* the lamps to be **set in** o, and all 4634
40: 4 **set in** o the things that are to be set in order 6186
40: 4 set in order the things that are to be **set in** o 6187
40:23 he **set** the bread **in** o upon it before 6186+6187
Lev 1: 7 and **lay** the wood **in** o upon the fire: 6186
1: 8 **lay** the parts, the head, and the fat, **in** o 6186
1:12 the priest shall **lay** them **in** o on the wood 6186
6:12 **lay** the burnt offering **in** o upon it; 6186
24: 3 shall Aaron o it from the evening unto 6186
24: 4 He shall o the lamps upon the pure 6186
24: 8 Every sabbath he shall **set** it **in** o before 6186
Jos 2: 6 which she had **laid in** o upon the roof. 6186
Jdg 13:12 How shall we o the child, and 1961+4941
2Sa 17:23 **put** his household **in** o, and 6680
1Ki 18:33 he **put** the wood **in** o, and cut the bullock in 6186
20:14 he said, Who shall o the battle? And he 631
2Ki 20: 1 saith the LORD, **Set** thine house **in** o; 6680
23: 4 high priest, and the priests of the **second** o; 4932
1Ch 6:32 waited on their office according to their o. 4941
15:13 for that we sought him not after the **due** o. 4941
23:31 according to the o **commanded** unto them, 4941
25: 2 which prophesied according to the o of 3027
25: 6 according to the king's o *to* Asaph, 3027
2Ch 8:14 according to the o of David his father, 4941
13:11 the *shew*bread also *set they* **in** o upon 4635
29:35 of the house of the LORD was **set in** o. 3559
Job 10:22 without any o, and *where* the light is as 5468
23: 4 I would o *my* cause before him, and fill my 6186
33: 5 **set** *thy words* **in** o before me, stand up. 6186
37:19 *for* we cannot o *our speech* by reason of 6186
Ps 40: 5 they cannot be **reckoned up in** o unto thee: 6186
50:21 and **set** *them* **in** o before thine eyes. 6186
110: 4 Thou *art* a priest for ever after the o of 1700
119:133 O my steps in thy word: and let not any 3559
Ecc 12: 9 and sought out, *and* **set in** o many proverbs. 8626
Isa 9: 7 to o it, and to stablish it with judgment and 3559
38: 1 saith the LORD, **Set** thine house **in** o: 6680
44: 7 and shall declare it, and **set** it **in** o for me, 6186
Jer 46: 3 O ye the buckler and shield, and draw near 6186
Eze 41: 6 one over another, and thirty *in* o; 6471
Lk 1: 1 **set forth in** o a declaration of those things 392
1: 3 to write unto thee **in** o, most excellent 2517
1: 8 office before God in the o of his course, 5010
Ac 11: 4 *and* expounded *it* **by** o unto them, saying, 2517
18:23 *all* the country of Galatia and Phrygia **in** o, 2517
1Co 11:34 And the rest will I **set in** o when I come. 1299
14:40 Let all *things* be done decently and in o. 5010
15:23 But every man in his own o: Christ 5001
16: 1 as I have **given** o to the churches of 1299
Col 2: 5 joying and beholding your o, and 5010
Tit 1: 5 that thou shouldest **set in** o the *things* that 1930
Heb 5: 6 a priest for ever after the o of Melchisedec. 5010
5:10 Called of God a high priest after the o of 5010
6:20 made a high priest for ever after the o of 5010
7:11 should rise after the o of Melchisedec, 5010
7:11 and not be called after the o of Aaron? 5010
7:17 Thou *art* a priest for ever after the o of 5010
7:21 Thou *art* a priest for ever after the o of 5010

ORDERED (4) [ORDER]

Jdg 6:26 in the o **place**, and take the second bullock, 4634
2Sa 23: 5 o in all *things,* and sure: 6186
Job 13:18 Behold now, I have o *my* cause; I know 6186
Ps 37:23 The steps of a *good* man are o by 3559

ORDERETH (1) [ORDER]

Ps 50:23 to him that o *his* conversation *aright* will I 7760

ORDERINGS (1) [ORDER]

1Ch 24:19 These *were* the o of them in their service to 6486

ORDERLY (1) [ORDER]

Ac 21:24 but *that* thou thyself also **walkest** o, and 4748

ORDINANCE (30) [ORDINANCES]

Ex 12:14 you shall keep it a feast by an o for ever. 2708
12:17 day in your generations by an o for ever. 2708
12:24 ye shall observe this thing for an o to thee 2706
12:43 and Aaron, This *is* the o of the passover: 2708
13:10 keep this o in his season from year to year. 2708
15:25 there he made for them a statute and an o, 4941
Lev 18:30 Therefore ye shall keep mine o, that *ye* 4931
22: 9 They shall therefore keep mine o, lest they 4931
Nu 9:14 according to the o of the passover, and 2708
9:14 ye shall have one o, both for the stranger, 2708
10: 8 they shall be to you for an o for ever 2708
15:15 One o *shall be both* for you *of* 2708
15:15 *with you,* an o for ever in your generations: 2708
18: 8 and to thy sons, by an o for ever. 2706
19: 2 This *is* the o of the law which the LORD 2708
31:21 This *is* the o of the law which the LORD 2708
Jos 24:25 and set them a statute and an o in Shechem. 4941
1Sa 30:25 it a statute and an o for Israel unto this day. 4941
2Ch 2: 4 our God. This *is an* o for ever to Israel. NIH
35:13 the passover with fire according to the o: 4941
35:25 to *this* day, and made them an o in Israel: 2706
Ezr 3:10 after the o of David king of Israel. 3027
Ps 99: 7 and the o *that* he gave them. 2706
Isa 24: 5 have transgressed the laws, changed the o, 2706
58: 2 and forsook not the o of their God: 4941
Eze 45:14 Concerning the o of oil, the bath *of* oil, 2706
46:14 a meat offering continually *by* a perpetual o 2708
Mal 3:14 and what profit *is it* that we have kept his o, 4931
Ro 13: 2 resisteth the power, resisteth the o of God: 1296
1Pe 2:13 Submit yourselves to every o of man for 2937

ORDINANCES (27) [ORDINANCE]

Ex 18:20 thou shalt teach them o and laws, and 2706
Lev 18: 3 ye not do: neither shall ye walk in their o. 2708
18: 4 and keep mine o, to walk therein: 2708
Nu 9:12 according to all the o of the passover they 2708
2Ki 17:34 or after their o, or after the law and 4941
17:37 the o, and the law, and the commandment, 4941
2Ch 33: 8 the statutes and the o by the hand of Moses. 4941
Ne 10:32 Also we made o for us, to charge ourselves 4687
Job 38:33 Knowest thou the o of heaven? canst thou 2708
Ps 119:91 continue *this* day according to thine o: 4941
Isa 58: 2 they ask of me the o of justice; they take 4941
Jer 31:35 *and* the o of the moon and of the stars for a 2708
31:36 If those o depart from before me, saith 2706
33:25 *if* I have not appointed the o of heaven and 2708
Eze 11:20 my statutes, and keep mine o, and do them: 4941
43:11 all the o thereof, and all the forms thereof, 2708
43:11 and all the o thereof, and do them. 2708
43:18 These *are* the o of the altar in the day when 2708
44: 5 all the o of the house of the LORD, 2708
Mal 3: 7 your fathers ye are gone away from mine o, 2706
Lk 1: 6 and o of the Lord blameless. 1345
1Co 11: 2 remember me in all *things,* and keep the o, 3862
Eph 2:15 the law of commandments *contained* in o; 1378
Col 2:14 Blotting out the handwriting of o that was 1378
2:20 living in the world, are ye **subject to** o, 1379
Heb 9: 1 Then verily the first *covenant* had also o of 1345
9:10 drinks, and divers washings, and carnal o, 1345

ORDINARY (1)

Eze 16:27 have diminished thine o *food,* and 2706

OREB (7)
Jdg 7:25 two princes of the Midianites, O and Zeeb; 6159
7:25 they slew O upon the rock Oreb, and Zeeb 6159
7:25 they slew Oreb upon the rock O, and Zeeb 6159
7:25 brought the heads of O and Zeeb to Gideon 6159
8: 3 hands the princes of Midian, O and Zeeb: 6159
Ps 83:11 Make their nobles like O, and like Zeeb: 6159
Isa 10:26 to the slaughter of Midian at the rock O: 6159

OREN (1)
1Ch 2:25 and Bunah, and O, and Ozem, *and* Ahijah. 767

ORGAN (3) [ORGANS]
Ge 4:21 father of all such as handle the harp and o. 5748
Job 21:12 and harp, and rejoice at the sound of the o. 5748
30:31 and my o into the voice of them that weep. 5748

ORGANS (1) [ORGAN]
Ps 150: 4 praise him with stringed instruments and o. 5748

ORION (3)
Job 9: 9 O, and Pleiades, and the chambers of 3685
38:31 of Pleiades, or loose the bands of O? 3685
Am 5: 8 *him* that maketh the seven stars and O, 3685

ORNAMENT (7) [ORNAMENTS]
Pr 1: 9 For they *shall be* an o of grace unto thy 3880
4: 9 She shall give to thine head an o of grace: 3880
25:12 an o of fine gold, *so is* a wise reprover upon 2481
Isa 30:22 and the o of thy molten images of gold: 642
49:18 as with an o, and bind them *on thee,* as a 5716
Eze 7:20 As for the beauty of his o, he set it in 5716
1Pe 3: 4 *even the* o of a meek and quiet spirit, NIG

ORNAMENTS (14) [ORNAMENT]
Ex 33: 4 and no man did put on him his o. 5716
33: 5 therefore now put off thy o from thee, that I 5716
33: 6 themselves of their o by the mount Horeb. 5716
Jdg 8:21 took away the o that *were* on their camels' 7720
8:26 beside o, and collars, and purple raiment 7720
2Sa 1:24 who put on o of gold upon your apparel. 5716
Isa 3:18 bravery of *their* **tinkling** o *about their feet,* 5914
3:20 the o **of the legs**, and the headbands, and 6807
61:10 as a bridegroom decketh *himself* with o, 6287
Jer 2:32 Can a maid forget her o, *or* a bride her 5716
4:30 though thou deckest thee with o of gold, 5716
Eze 16: 7 and thou art come to **excellent** o: 5716+5716
16:11 I decked thee also *with* o, and I put 5716
23:40 and **deckedst** thyself **with** o, 5710+5716

ORNAN (12) [ARAUNAH]
1Ch 21:15 by the threshingfloor of O the Jebusite. 771
21:18 in the threshingfloor of O the Jebusite. 771
21:20 O turned back, and saw the angel; and 771
21:20 Now O was threshing wheat. 771
21:21 And as David came to O, Ornan looked and 771
21:21 O looked and saw David, and went out of 771
21:22 David said to O, Grant me the place of *this* 771
21:23 And O said unto David, Take *it* to thee, and 771
21:24 king David said to O, Nay; but I will verily 771
21:25 So David gave to O for the place six 771
21:28 him in the threshingfloor of O the Jebusite, 771
2Ch 3: 1 in the threshingfloor of O the Jebusite. 771

O

ORPAH (2)
Ru 1: 4 the name of the one *was* O, and the name 6204
1:14 O kissed her mother in law; but Ruth clave 6204

ORPHANS (1)
La 5: 3 We are o and fatherless, our mothers *are* as 3490

OSEE (1) [HOSEA]
Ro 9:25 As he saith also in O, I will call *them* my *5617*

OSHEA (2) [JOSHUA]
Nu 13: 8 Of the tribe of Ephraim, O the son of Nun. 1954
13:16 Moses called O the son of Nun, Jehoshua. 1954

OSPRAY (2)
Lev 11:13 the eagle, and the ossifrage, and the o, 5822
Dt 14:12 the eagle, and the ossifrage, and the o, 5822

OSPREY See GIER

OSSIFRAGE (2)
Lev 11:13 the eagle, and the o, and the ospray, 6538
Dt 14:12 not eat: the eagle, and the o, and the ospray, 6538

OSTRICH (1) [OSTRICHES]
Job 39:13 or wings and feathers *unto* the o? 2624

OSTRICHES (1) [OSTRICH]
La 4: 3 become cruel, like the o in the wilderness. 3283

OTHER (465) [OTHER'S, OTHERS, OTHERWISE]
Ge 4:19 *was* Adah, and the name of the o Zillah. 8145
8:10 he stayed yet o seven days; and again he sent 312
8:12 he stayed yet o seven days; and sent forth 312
13:11 separated themselves the one from the o^S. 251
20:16 and with all o: thus she was reproved. NIH
25:23 *the one* people shall be stronger than *the* o NIH
28:17 this *is* **none** o but the house of God, and 369
29:27 thou shalt serve with me yet seven o years. 312
29:30 and served with him yet seven o years. 312
31:50 if thou shalt take o wives beside my NIH
32: 8 the o company which is left shall escape. NIH
41: 3 seven o kine came up after them out of 312
41: 3 stood by the o kine upon the brink of NIH
41:19 seven o kine came up after them, poor and 312
43:14 that he may send away your o brother, and 312
43:22 o money have we brought down in our hands 312
47:21 borders of Egypt even to the o end thereof. NIH
Ex 1:15 *was* Shiphrah, and the name of the o Puah: 8145
4: 7 behold, it was turned again as his o flesh. NIH
14:20 that the one came not near the o all 2088
17:12 on the one side, and the o on the other side; 259
17:12 the one side, and the other on the o **side**; 2088
18: 4 the name of the o *was* Eliezer; for the God 259
18: 7 and they asked each o^S of *their* welfare; and 7453
20: 3 Thou shalt have no o gods before me. 312
23:13 and make no mention of the name of o gods, 312
25:12 side of it, and two rings in the o side of it. 8145
25:19 one end, and the o cherub on the other end: 259
25:19 and the other cherub on the o end: 2088
25:32 of the candlestick out of the o side: 8145
25:33 three bowls made like almonds in the o 259
26: 3 o five curtains *shall be* coupled one to NIH
26:13 a cubit on the o **side** of that which 2088
26:27 five bars for the boards of the o side of 8145
27:15 on the o side *shall be* hangings, 8145
28:10 the o six names of the rest on the other NIH
28:10 the *other* six names of the rest on the o 8145
28:25 *the* o two ends of the two wreathen *chains* NIH
28:27 two o rings of gold thou shalt make, and NIH
28:27 over against *the* o coupling thereof, NIH
29:19 thou shalt take the o ram; and Aaron and 8145
29:39 and the o lamb thou shalt offer at even: 8145
29:41 the o lamb thou shalt offer at even, *and* 8145
30:32 neither shall ye make *any* o like it, after NIH
32:15 the one side and on **the** o *were* they written. 2088
34:14 For thou shalt worship no o god: for 312
36:10 *the* o five curtains he coupled one unto NIH
36:25 for the o side of the tabernacle, *which is* 8145
36:32 five bars for the boards of the o side of 8145
36:33 the boards from the one end to the o^S. 7097
37: 3 of it, and two rings upon the o side of it. 8145
37: 8 another cherub on the o end on that side: NIH
37:18 of the candlestick out of the o side thereof: 8145
38:15 for the o side of the court gate, on this hand 8145
39:20 they made two o golden rings, and put them NIH
39:20 of it, over against the o coupling thereof, NIH
Lev 5: 7 a sin offering, and the o for a burnt offering. 259
6:11 put on o garments, and carry forth the ashes 312
7:24 torn *with beasts,* may be used in any o use: NIH
8:22 he brought the o ram, the ram of 8145
11:23 all o flying creeping things, which have four NIH
12: 8 burnt offering, and the o for a sin offering: 259
13:26 it *be* no lower than the o skin, but *be* NIH
14:22 be a sin offering, and the o a burnt offering. 259
14:31 the o *for* a burnt offering, with the meat 259
14:42 they shall take o stones, and put *them* in 312
14:42 he shall take o morter, and shall plaister 312
15:15 sin offering, and the o *for* a burnt offering; 259
15:30 sin offering, and the o *for* a burnt offering; 259
16: 8 the LORD, and the o lot for the scapegoat. 259
18:18 besides **the** o in her life *time.* 1886.3
20:24 which have separated you from o people. NIH
20:26 have severed you from o people, that *ye* NIH
25:53 *the* o shall not rule with rigour over him in NIH
Nu 6:11 the o for a burnt offering, and make an 259
8:12 the o *for* a burnt offering, unto the LORD, 259
10:21 *the* o did set up the tabernacle against they NIH
11:26 *was* Eldad, and the name of the o Medad: 8145
11:31 as it were a day's journey **on the** o **side**, 3541
21:13 and pitched on the o side of Arnon, NIH
24: 1 he went not, as **at** o **times**, to 6471+6471+871.1
28: 4 and the o lamb shalt thou offer at even; 8145
28: 8 the o lamb shalt thou offer at even: as 8145
32:38 gave o **names** unto the cities which 8034+8034
36: 3 *if* they be married to any of the sons of the o NIH
Dt 4:32 the one side of heaven unto the o^S, 7097+8064
5: 7 Thou shalt have none o gods before me. 312
6:14 Ye shall not go after o gods, of the gods of 312
7: 4 following me, that they may serve o gods: 312
8:19 walk after o gods, and serve them, and 312
11:16 and serve o gods, and worship them; 312
11:28 to go after o gods, which ye have not known. 312
11:30 *Are* they not on the o side Jordan, by NIH
13: 2 saying, Let us go after o gods, which thou 312
13: 6 saying, Let us go and serve o gods, 312
13: 7 of the earth even unto the o end of the earth; NIH
13:13 saying, Let us go and serve o gods, which ye 312
17: 3 hath gone and served o gods, and 312
18:20 or that shall speak in the name of o gods, 312
28:14 *to* the left, to go after o gods to serve them. 312
28:36 and there shalt thou serve o gods, wood and 312
28:64 the *one* end of the earth even unto the o^S; 7097
28:64 there thou shalt serve o gods, which neither 312
29:26 For they went and served o gods, and 312
30:17 and worship o gods, and serve them; 312
31:18 in that they are turned unto o gods. 312
31:20 will they turn unto o gods, and serve them, 312
Jos 2:10 that *were* on the o side Jordan, Sihon and NIH
7: 7 and dwelt on the o side Jordan! NIH
8:22 the o issued out of the city against them; 428
11:19 of Gibeon: all o they took in battle. NIH
12: 1 possessed their land on the o side Jordan NIH
13:27 of Cinnereth on the o side Jordan eastward. NIH
13:32 on the o side Jordan, *by* Jericho, eastward. NIH
14: 3 and a half tribe on the o side Jordan: NIH
17: 5 which *were* on the o side Jordan; NIH
20: 8 on the o side Jordan *by* Jericho eastward, NIH
21:27 out of the o half tribe of Manasseh *they* NIH
22: 4 the LORD gave you on the o side Jordan. NIH
22: 7 unto the o half thereof gave Joshua among NIH
23:16 have gone and served o gods, and 312
24: 2 Your fathers dwelt on the o side of the flood NIH
24: 2 the father of Nachor: and they served o gods. 312
24: 3 I took your father Abraham from the o side NIH
24: 8 which dwelt on the o side Jordan; NIH
24:14 fathers served on the o side of the flood, NIH
24:15 served that *were* on the o side of the flood, NIH
24:16 should forsake the LORD, to serve o gods; 312
Jdg 2:12 of the land of Egypt, and followed o gods, 312
2:17 they went a whoring after o gods, and 312
2:19 in following o gods to serve them, and 312
7: 7 let all the o people go every man unto his NIH
7:25 and Zeeb to Gideon on the o side Jordan. NIH
Jdg 9:44 the two o companies ran upon all *the people* NIH
10: 8 all the children of Israel that *were* on the o NIH
10:13 Yet ye have forsaken me, and served o gods: 312
11:18 pitched on the o side of Arnon, but NIH
13:10 unto me, that came unto me the o day. NIH
16:17 I shall become weak, and be like any o man. NIH
16:20 I will go out as **at** o **times** 6471+6471+871.1
16:29 his right hand, and of the o with his left. 259
20:30 against Gibeah, as **at** o **times**. 6471+6471+871.1
20:31 **at** o **times**, in the highways, 6471+6471+871.1
20:31 the o to Gibeah in the field, about thirty 259
Ru 1: 4 *was* Orpah, and the name of the o Ruth: 8145
2:22 that they meet thee not in *any* o field. 312
1Sa 1: 2 and the name of the o Peninnah: 8145
3:10 and called as **at** o **times**, 6471+6471+871.1
8: 8 and served o gods, so do they also unto thee. 312
14: 1 Philistines' garrison, that *is* on the o side. 1975
14: 4 the one side, and a sharp rock on the o side: 2088
14: 4 *was* Bozez, and the name of the o Seneh. 259
14: 5 and the o southward over against Gibeah. 259
14:40 I and Jonathan my son will be on the o side. 259
17: 3 Israel stood on a mountain on the o **side**: 2088
18:10 with his hand, as **at** o **times**: 3117+3117+871.1
19:21 he sent o messengers, and they prophesied 312
20:25 **at** o **times**, *even* upon a seat 6471+6471+871.1
21: 9 take *it:* for *there is* no o save that here. 312
26:13 David went over *to* the o side, and stood on NIH
26:19 of the LORD, saying, Go, serve o gods. 312
28: 8 put on o raiment, and he went, and two men 312
30:20 *which* they drave before those o cattle, and NIH
31: 7 when the men of Israel that *were* on the o NIH
31: 7 *they* that *were* on the o side Jordan, saw that NIH
2Sa 1:24 who clothed you in scarlet, with o delights, NIH
2:13 and the o on the other side of the pool. 428
2:13 the other on the o **side** of the pool. 2088+4480
4: 2 *was* Baanah, and the name of the o Rechab, 8145
12: 1 men in one city; the one rich, and the o poor. 259
13:16 *is* greater than the o that thou didst unto me. 312
14: 6 but the one smote the o, and slew him. 259
17: 9 is hid now in some pit, or in some o place: NIH
24:22 and o instruments of the oxen for wood. NIH
1Ki 3:22 the o woman said, Nay; but the living *is* my 312
3:23 **the** o saith, Nay; but thy son *is* the dead, 2063
3:25 and give half to the one, and half to the o. 259
3:26 **the** o said, Let it be neither mine nor thine, 2088
6:24 and five cubits the o wing of the cherub: 8145
6:24 the uttermost part of the o^S *were* ten cubits. 3671
6:25 the o cherub *was* ten cubits: both 8145
6:26 ten cubits, and so *was it* of the o cherub. 8145
6:27 the wing of the o cherub touched the other 8145
6:27 the wing of the other cherub touched the o 8145
6:34 the two leaves of the o door *were* folding. 8145
7: 6 *the* o pillars and the thick beam *were* before NIH
7: 7 cedar from one side of the floor to the o^S. 7172
7:16 the height of the o chapiter *was* five cubits: 8145
7:17 one chapiter, and seven for the o chapiter. 8145
7:18 and so did he for the o chapiter. 8145
7:20 *in* rows round about upon the o chapiter. 8145
7:23 ten cubits from the one brim to the o: 8193
9: 6 but go and serve o gods, and worship them: 312
9: 9 have taken hold upon o gods, and 312
10:20 one side and on **the** o upon the six steps: 2088
11: 4 *that* his wives turned away his heart after o 312
11:10 this thing, that *he* should not go after o gods: 312
12:29 the one in Beth-el, and the o put he in Dan. 259
14: 9 for thou hast gone and made thee o gods, 312
18:23 no fire *under:* and I will dress the o bullock, 259
20:29 they pitched one over against the o seven 428
2Ki 3:22 water **on the** o **side** *as* red as blood: 4480+5048
5:17 burnt offering nor sacrifice unto o gods, 312
12: 7 the o priests, and said unto them, NIH
17: 7 king of Egypt, and had feared o gods, 312
17:35 saying, Ye shall not fear o gods, 312
17:37 for evermore; and ye shall not fear o gods. 312
17:38 shall not forget; neither shall ye fear o gods. 312
22:17 and have burnt incense unto o gods, 312
1Ch 6:78 on the o side Jordan *by* Jericho, on the east NIH
9:32 o of their brethren, of the sons of NIH
12:37 on the o side of Jordan, of the Reubenites, NIH
23:17 Eliezer had none o sons; but the sons of 312
2Ch 3:11 the o wing *was likewise* five cubits, 312
3:11 reaching to the wing of the o cherub. 312
3:12 *one* wing of the o cherub *was* five cubits, 259
3:12 the o wing *was* five cubits *also,* joining to 312
3:12 *also,* joining to the wing of the o cherub. 312
3:17 one on the right hand, and the o on the left; 259
7:19 shall go and serve o gods, and worship them; 312
7:22 laid hold on o gods, and worshipped them, 312
9:19 one side and on **the** o upon the six steps. 2088
13: 9 after the manner of the nations of o lands? NIH
20: 1 and with them o beside the Ammonites, NIH
25:12 o ten thousand *left* alive did the children of NIH
28:25 high places to burn incense unto o gods, 312
29:34 until the o priests had sanctified themselves: NIH
30:23 the whole assembly took counsel to keep o 312
30:23 and they kept o seven days *with* gladness. NIH
32:13 have done unto all the people of o lands? NIH
32:17 As the gods of the nations of o lands have NIH
32:22 from the hand of all o, and guided them on NIH
34:12 o *of* the Levites, all that could skill of NIH
34:25 and have burned incense unto o gods, 312
35:13 the o holy *offerings* sod they in pots, and NIH
Ezr 1:10 and ten, *and* o vessels a thousand. 312
2:31 The children of the o Elam, a thousand two 312
Ne 3:11 repaired the o piece, and the tower of 8145
3:20 of Zabbai earnestly repaired the o piece, 8145
4:16 the o half of them held both the spears, NIH
4:17 and with the o *hand* held a weapon. 259
5: 5 *to redeem them;* for o **men** have our lands 312
7:33 The men of the o Nebo, fifty and two. 312
7:34 The children of the o Elam, a thousand two 312
11: 1 holy city, and nine parts *to dwell* in o cities. NIH
12:38 the o *company of them that gave* thanks 8145
Est 2:12 with o things for the purifying of NIH
9:16 the o Jews that *were* in the king's provinces 7605

Job 8:12 cut down, it withereth before any o herb. NIH
24:24 they are taken out of the way as all o, and NIH
Ps 73: 5 They are not in trouble as o men; neither are NIH
73: 5 neither are they plagued like o men. NIH
85:10 and peace have kissed each o. NIH
Ecc 3:19 as the one dieth, so dieth the o; yea, 2088
6: 5 any thing: this hath more rest than the o. 2088
7:14 also hath set the one over against the o, 2088
Isa 26:13 o lords besides thee have had dominion over NIH
49:20 after thou hast lost the o, shall say again in NIH
Jer 1:16 have burnt incense unto o gods, and 312
7: 6 neither walk after o gods to your hurt: 312
7: 9 and walk after o gods whom ye know not; 312
7:18 to pour out drink offerings unto o gods, that 312
11:10 and they went after o gods to serve them: 312
12:12 of the land even to the o end of the land: NIH
13:10 walk after o gods, to serve them, and 312
16:11 have walked after o gods, and have served 312
16:13 there shall ye serve o gods day and night; 312
19: 4 and have burnt incense in it unto o gods, 312
19:13 have poured out drink offerings unto o gods. 312
22: 9 and worshipped o gods, and served them. 312
24: 2 the o basket had very naughty figs, 259
25: 6 go not after o gods to serve them, and 312
25:33 of the earth even unto the o end of the earth: NIH
32:20 this day, and in Israel, and amongst o men; NIH
32:29 poured out drink offerings unto o gods, 312
35:15 go not after o gods to serve them, and 312
36:16 they were afraid both one and o[S], and 7453
44: 3 and to serve o gods, whom they knew not, 312
44: 5 to burn no incense unto o gods. 312
44: 8 burning incense unto o gods in the land of 312
44:15 their wives had burnt incense unto o gods, 312
Eze 1:23 their wings straight, the one toward the o[S]: 269
16:34 the contrary is in thee from o women in thy NIH
21:16 **Go thee one way or o**, *either* on the right 258
40: 6 the o threshold *of the gate, which was* one 259
40:40 on the o side, which *was* at the porch of 312
41: 1 one side, and six cubits broad on the **o side**, 6311
41: 2 the one side, and five cubits on the **o side**: 6311
41:15 thereof on the one side and on the **o side**, 6311
41:19 lion toward the palm tree on the **o side**: 6311
41:21 *of the one* as the appearance *of the* o. NIH
41:24 the one door, and two leaves for the o *door*. 312
41:26 trees on the one side and on the **o side**, 6311
42:14 shall put on o garments, and shall approach 312
44:19 and they shall put on o garments; 312
45: 7 on the **o side** of the oblation of the holy 2088
47: 7 many trees on the one side and on **the o**. 2088
48: 8 and *in* length as one of the o parts, NIH
48:21 one side and on **the o** of the holy oblation, 2088
Da 2:11 there is none o that can shew it before 321
2:44 the kingdom shall not be left to o people, 321
3:21 their o garments, and were cast into NIH
3:29 there is no o God that can deliver after this 321
7:20 *of* the o which came up, and before whom 317
8: 3 one *was* higher than the o, and the higher 8145
12: 5 and behold, there stood o two, 312
12: 5 the o on that side of the bank of the river. 259
Hos 3: 1 who look to o gods, and love flagons of 312
9: 1 Rejoice not, O Israel, for joy, as o people. NIH
13:10 where *is any* o that may save thee in all thy NIH
Ob 1:11 In the day that thou stoodest on the **o side**, 5048
Zec 4: 3 and the o upon the left *side* thereof. 259
11: 7 I called Beauty, and the o I called Bands; 259
11:14 I cut asunder mine o staff, *even* Bands, 8145
Mt 4:21 he saw o two brethren, James the *son* of 243
5:39 on thy right cheek, turn to him the o also. 243
6:24 either he will hate the one, and love the o; 2087
6:24 he will hold to the one, and despise the o. 2087
8:18 commandment to depart unto the **o side**. 4008
8:28 And when he was come to the **o side** into 4008
12:13 and it was restored whole, *like* as the o. 243
12:45 taketh with himself seven o spirits more 2087
13: 8 But o fell into good ground, and 243
14:22 and to go before him unto the **o side**, 4008
16: 5 when his disciples were come to the **o side**, 4008
20:21 and **the o[S]** on the left, in thy kingdom. 1520
21:36 Again, he sent o servants moe than the first: 243
21:41 will let out *his* vineyard unto o husbandmen, 243
22: 4 Again, he sent forth o servants, saying, 243
23:23 have done, **and** not to leave **the o** undone. 2548
24:31 from one end of heaven to the o[S]. 206
24:40 the one shall be taken, and **the o[S]** left. 1520
24:41 *the* one shall be taken, and *the* o[S] left. 1520
25:11 Afterward came also the o virgins, saying, 3062
25:16 with the same, and made *them* o five talents. 243
25:17 that *had received* two, he also gained o two. 243
25:20 five talents came and brought o five talents, 243
25:22 I have gained two o talents besides them. 243
27:61 there was Mary Magdalene, and the o Mary, 243
28: 1 and the o Mary to see the sepulchre. 243
Mk 3: 5 and his hand was restored whole as the o. 243
4: 8 And o fell on good ground, and did yield 243
4:19 and the lusts of o *things* entering in, 3062
4:35 unto them, Let us pass over unto the **o side**. 4008
4:36 And there were also with him o little ships. 243
5: 1 And they came over unto the **o side** of 4008
5:21 passed over again by ship unto the **o side**, 4008
6:45 to go to the **o side** before unto Bethsaida, 4008
7: 4 And many o *things* there be, which they 243
7: 8 and cups: and many o such like *things* ye do. 243
8:13 into the ship again departed to the **o side**. 4008
10:37 and **the o[S]** on thy left hand, in thy glory. 1520
12:31 There is none o commandment greater than 243
12:32 there is one God; and there is none o but he: 243
15:27 on *his* right hand, and **the o[S]** on his left. 1520
15:41 many o *women* which came up with him 243
Lk 3:18 And many o *things* in his exhortation 2087
4:43 I must preach the kingdom of God to o 2087
5: 7 which were in the o ship, that *they* should 2087
6:10 and his hand was restored whole as the o. 243
6:29 thee on the *one* cheek offer also the o; 243
7:41 ought five hundred pence, and the o fifty. 2087
8: 8 And o fell on good ground, and sprang up, 2087
Lk 8:22 Let us go over unto the **o side** of the lake. 4008
10: 1 After these *things* the Lord appointed o 2087
10:31 he saw him, he **passed by on the o side**. 492
10:32 looked *on him*, and **passed by on the o side**. 492
11:16 And o, tempting *him*, sought of him a sign 2087
11:26 taketh to *him* seven o spirits more wicked 2087
11:42 have done, **and** not to leave **the o** undone. 2548
14:32 Or else, while **the o[S]** is yet a great way off, 846
16:13 either he will hate the one, and love the o; 2087
16:13 he will hold to the one, and despise the o. 2087
17:24 shineth unto **the o** *part* under heaven; 3588
17:34 one shall be taken, and the o shall be left. 2087
17:35 the one shall be taken, and the o left. 2087
17:36 the one shall be taken, and the o left. 2087
18: 9 that they were righteous, and despised o: 3062
18:10 the one a Pharisee, and the o a publican. 2087
18:11 that I am not as o men *are*, extortioners, 3062
18:14 to his house justified *rather* than **the o[S]**: 1565
22:65 And many o *things* blasphemously spake 2087
23:32 And there were also two o, malefactors, 2087
23:33 on the right hand, and the o on the left. 3739
23:40 But the o answering rebuked him, saying, 2087
24:10 and o *women that were* with them, 3062
Jn 4:38 o *men* laboured, and ye are entered into their 243
6:22 when the people which stood **on the o side** 4008
6:22 the sea saw that there was none o boat there, 243
6:23 (Howbeit there came o boats from Tiberias 243
6:25 had found him **on the o side** of the sea, 4008
10: 1 but climbeth up **some o way**, the same is a 237
10:16 And o sheep I have, which are not of this 243
15:24 them the works which none o *man* did, 243
18:16 Then went out *that* o disciple, which was 243
19:18 and two o with him, on either side one, 243
19:32 and of the o which was crucified with him. 243
20: 2 and to the o disciple, whom Jesus loved, and 243
20: 3 and *that* o disciple, and came to 243
20: 4 and the o disciple did outrun Peter, and 243
20: 8 Then went in also *that* o disciple, 243
20:12 the one at the head, and **the o[S]** at the feet, 1520
20:25 The o disciples therefore said unto him, 243
20:30 And many o signs truly did Jesus in 243
21: 2 *sons* of Zebedee, and two o of his disciples. 243
21: 8 And the o disciples came in a little ship; 243
21:25 And there are also many o *things* which 243
Ac 2: 4 and began to speak with o tongues, as 2087
2:40 And with many o words did he testify and 2087
4:12 Neither is there salvation in any o: for there 243
4:12 for there is none o name under heaven 2087
5:29 and the o apostles answered and said, NIG
8:34 of himself, or of some o *man?* 2087
15: 2 and Barnabas, and certain o of them, 243
15:39 that they departed asunder **one** from **the o**: 240
17: 9 of Jason, and *of* the o, they let them go. 3062
17:18 o *some*, He seemeth to be a setter 1161+3588
19:39 But if ye inquire any *thing* concerning o 2087
23: 6 and the o Pharisees, he cried out in 2087
26:22 saying none o *things* **than** those which 1622
27: 1 certain o prisoners unto *one* named Julius, 2087
Ro 1:13 among you also, even as among o Gentiles. 3062
8:39 Nor height, nor depth, nor any o creature, 2087
13: 9 and if *there be* any o commandment, it is 2087
1Co 1:16 I know not whether I baptized any o. 243
3:11 For o foundation can no *man* lay than that is 243
7: 5 Defraud you not **one the o**, except *it be* with 240
8: 4 and that *there is* none o God but one. 2087
9: 5 as well as o apostles, and *as* the brethren of 3062
11:21 For in eating every one taketh before o his NIG
14:17 givest thanks well, but the o is not edified. 2087
14:21 With *men* of **o tongues** and other lips will I 2084
14:21 and o lips will I speak unto this people; 2087
14:29 speak two or three, and let the o judge. 243
15:37 may chance of wheat, or of some o *grain:* 3062
2Co 1:13 For we write none o *things* unto you, 243
2:16 and to the o the savour of life unto life. 3739
8:13 For *I mean* not that o *men* be eased, and 243
10:15 *our* measure, *that is*, of o *men's* labours; 245
11: 8 I robbed o churches, taking wages *of them*, 243
12:13 For what is it wherein ye were inferior to o 3062
13: 2 and to all o, that, if I come again, I will not 3062
Gal 1: 8 preach **any** o gospel unto you **than** *that* 3844
1: 9 **any** o gospel unto you **than** that ye have 3844
1:19 But o of the apostles saw I none, 2087
2:13 And the o Jews dissembled likewise with 3062
4:22 by a bondmaid, **the o[S]** by a freewoman. 1520
5:17 and these are contrary **the one to the o**: so 240
Eph 3: 5 Which in o ages was not made known unto 2087
4:17 that ye henceforth walk not as o Gentiles 3062
Php 1:13 in all the palace, and *in* all o *places;* 3062
1:17 But **the o** of love, knowing that I am set for 3588
2: 3 in lowliness of mind *let* **each** esteem o better 240
3: 4 If any o *man* thinketh that *he hath whereof* 243
4: 3 and *with* o my fellowlabourers, 3062
2Th 1: 3 one of you all towards **each** o aboundeth; 240
1Ti 1: 3 charge some that *they* **teach** no **o doctrine**, 2085
1:10 if *there be* any o *thing that* is contrary to 2087
5:22 no *man*, neither be partaker of o *men's* sins: 245
Jas 5:12 neither by the earth, neither by any o oath: 243
1Pe 4:15 or as a **busybody** in **o men's matters**. 244
2Pe 3:16 as *they do* also the o scriptures, 3062
Rev 2:24 I will put upon you none o burden. 243
8:13 o voices of the trumpet of the three angels, 3062
17:10 and one is, *and* the o is not yet come; 243

OTHER'S (1) [OTHER]

1Co 10:29 I say, not thine own, but of the o: 2087

OTHERS (67) [OTHER]

Job 8:19 of his way, and out of the earth shall o grow. 312
31:10 unto another, and let o bow down upon her. 312
34:24 *men* without number, and set o in their stead. 312
34:26 them as wicked *men* in the open sight of o; NIH
Ps 49:10 person perish, and leave their wealth to o. 312
Pr 5: 9 Lest thou give thine honour unto o, and 312
Ecc 7:22 that thou thyself likewise hast cursed o. 312
Isa 56: 8 Yet will I gather o to him, besides those that NIH
Jer 6:12 their houses shall be turned unto o, *with their* 312
8:10 Therefore will I give their wives unto o, *and* 312
Eze 9: 5 to the o he said in mine hearing, Go ye after 428
13: 6 they have made o to hope that *they* would NIH
13:10 lo, o daubed it *with* untempered *morter:* 3963.1
Da 7:19 which was diverse from all **the o**, 2006.2
11: 4 shall be pluckt up, even for o besides those. 312
Mt 5:47 what do ye more *than* o? do not even NIG
15:30 and many o, and cast them *down* at Jesus' 2087
16:14 and o, Jeremias, or one of the prophets. 2087
20: 3 and saw o standing idle in the marketplace, 243
20: 6 and found o standing idle, and saith unto 243
21: 8 o cut down branches from the trees, and 243
26:67 o smote *him* with the palms of their hands, 3588
27:42 He saved o; himself he cannot save. If he be 243
Mk 6:15 O said, That it is Elias. And others said, 243
6:15 And o said, That it is a prophet, or as one of 243
8:28 some *say*, Elias; and o, One of the prophets. 243
11: 8 and o cut down branches off the trees, 243
12: 5 and him they killed, and many o; 243
12: 9 and will give the vineyard unto o. 243
15:31 themselves with the scribes, He saved o; 243
Lk 5:29 and of o that sat down with them. 243
8: 3 and Susanna, and many o, 2087
8:10 but to o in parables; that seeing they might 3062
9: 8 and *of* o, that one of the old prophets was 243
9:19 o *say*, that one of the old prophets is risen 243
20:16 and shall give the vineyard to o. 243
23:35 with them derided *him*, saying, He saved o; 243
24: 1 they had prepared, and certain o with them. NIG
Jn 7:12 some said, He is a good *man:* o said, Nay; 243
7:41 O said, This is the Christ. But some said, 243
9: 9 o *said*, He is like him: *but* he said, I am *he*. 243
9:16 O said, How can a man *that is* a sinner do 243
10:21 O said, These are not the words of him that 243
12:29 it thundered: o said, An angel spake to him. 243
18:34 *thing* of thyself, or did o tell *it* thee of me? 243
Ac 2:13 O mocking said, *These men* are full of new 2087
15:35 the word of the Lord, with many o also. 2087
17:32 and o said, We will hear thee again of this 3588
17:34 a woman named Damaris, and o with them. 2087
28: 9 So when this was done, o also, which had 3062
1Co 9: 2 If I be not an apostle unto o, yet doubtless I 243
9:12 If o be partakers of *this* power over you, 243
9:27 by any means, when I have preached to o, 243
14:19 that *by my voice* I might teach o also, 243
2Co 3: 1 as some o, epistles of commendation to you, NIG
8: 8 but by occasion of the forwardness of o, 2087
Eph 2: 3 by nature the children of wrath, even as o. 3062
Php 2: 4 but every man also on the *things* of o. 2087
1Th 2: 6 sought we glory, neither of you, nor *yet* of o, 243
4:13 sorrow not, even as o which have no hope. 3062
5: 6 Therefore let us not sleep, as *do* o; but 3062
1Ti 5:20 sin rebuke before all, that o also may fear. 3062
2Ti 2: 2 who shall be able to teach o also. 2087
Heb 9:25 the holy *place* every year with blood of o; 245
11:35 and o were tortured, not accepting 243
11:36 And o had trial of *cruel* mockings and 2087
Jude 1:23 And o save with fear, pulling *them* out of 3739

OTHERWISE (15) [OTHER]

2Sa 18:13 O I should have wrought falsehood against 176
1Ki 1:21 O it shall come to pass, when my lord 2050.1
2Ch 30:18 **o than** it was written. 3808+871.1+3509.1
Ps 38:16 *Hear me*, lest o they should rejoice over me: NIH
Mt 6: 1 o ye have no reward of your Father which 1490
Lk 5:36 **if o**, *then* both the new maketh a rent, and 1490
Ro 11: 6 o grace is no more grace. But if *it be* of 1893
11: 6 it no more grace: o work is no more work. 1893
11:22 in *his* goodness: o thou also shalt be cut off. 1893
2Co 11:16 **if o**, yet as a fool receive me, that I may 1490
Gal 5:10 the Lord, that you will be none o minded: 243
Php 3:15 and if in any *thing* ye be o minded, 2088
1Ti 5:25 and they that are o cannot be hid. 247
6: 3 If any *man* **teach o**, and consent not to 2085
Heb 9:17 o it is of no strength at all whilst 1893

OTHNI (1)

1Ch 26: 7 O, and Rephael, and Obed, Elzabad, 6273

OTHNIEL (7)

Jos 15:17 O the son of Kenaz, the brother of Caleb, 6274
Jdg 1:13 O the son of Kenaz, Caleb's younger 6274
3: 9 delivered them, *even* O the son of Kenaz, 6274
3:11 forty years. And O the son of Kenaz died. 6274
1Ch 4:13 And the sons of Kenaz; O, and Seraiah: and 6274
4:13 and Seraiah: and the sons of O; Hathath. 6274
27:15 month *was* Heldai the Netophathite, of O: 6274

OUCHES (8)

Ex 28:11 thou shalt make them to be set *in* o *of* gold. 4865
28:13 And thou shalt make o *of* gold; 4865
28:14 and fasten the wreathen chains to the o. 4865
28:25 *chains* thou shalt fasten in the two o, 4865
39: 6 they wrought onyx stones inclosed *in* o *of* 4865
39:13 *they were* inclosed *in* o *of* gold in their 4865
39:16 they made two o *of* gold, and two gold 4865
39:18 wreathen *chains* they fastened in the two o, 4865

OUGHT (100) [OUGHTEST]

Ge 20: 9 thou hast done deeds unto me that o not to NIH
34: 7 which thing o not to be done. NIH
39: 6 he knew not o he had, save the bread which 3972
47:18 there is not o left in the sight of my lord, but NIH
Ex 5: 8 upon them; you shall not diminish o thereof: NIH
5:11 yet not o of your work *shall be* diminished. 1697
5:19 Ye shall not minish o from your bricks of NIH
12:46 thou shalt not carry forth o of the flesh NIH
22:14 if a man borrow o of his neighbour, and NIH
29:34 And if o of the flesh of the consecrations, or NIH
Lev 4: 2 (*concerning things* which o not to be done), NIH
4:27 *concerning things* which o not to be done, NIH
11:25 whosoever beareth o of the carcase of them NIH
19: 6 if o remain until the third day, it shall be NIH

Lev 25:14 if thou sell o unto thy neighbour, or 4376+4465
25:14 or buyest o of thy neighbour's hand, NIH
27:31 if a man will at all redeem o of his tithes, NIH
Nu 15:24 if o be committed by ignorance without NIH
15:30 the soul that doeth o presumptuously, NIH
30: 6 she vowed, or uttered o out of her lips, 4008
Dt 4: 2 neither shall you diminish o from it, NIH
15: 2 Every creditor that lendeth o unto his NIH
26:14 neither have I taken away o thereof for *any* NIH
26:14 *use,* nor given o thereof for the dead: NIH
Jos 21:45 There failed not o of any good thing which 1697
Ru 1:17 more also, *if* o but death part thee and me. NIH
1Sa 12: 4 neither hast thou taken o of any man's 3972
12: 5 that ye have not found o in my hand. 3972
25: 7 neither was there o missing unto them, 3972
30:22 we will not give them o of the spoil that we NIH
2Sa 3:35 more also, if I taste bread, or o else, 3605+3972
13:12 for no such thing o to be done in Israel: NIH
14:10 Whosoever saith o unto thee, bring him to NIH
14:19 to the left from o that my lord the king hath 3605
1Ch 12:32 of the times, to know what Israel o to do; NIH
15: 2 None o to carry the ark of God but NIH
2Ch 13: 5 O you not to know that the LORD God of NIH
Ne 5: 9 o ye not to walk in the fear of our God NIH
Ps 76:11 bring presents unto him that o to be feared. NIH
Mt 5:23 there rememberest that thy brother hath o *5100*
18:24 unto him, which o him ten thousand talents. *3781*
18:28 which o him an hundred pence: *3784*
21: 3 And if any *man* say o unto you, ye shall *5100*
23:23 these o *ye* to have done, and not to leave *1163*
Mk 7:12 And ye suffer him no more to do o for his *3762*
8:23 hands upon him, he asked him if he saw o. *5100*
11:25 forgive, if ye have o against any: *5100*
13:14 Daniel the prophet, standing where it o not, *1163*
Lk 7:41 the one o five hundred pence, and the other *3784*
11:42 these o *ye* to have done, and not to leave *1163*
12:12 you in the same hour what ye o to say. *1163*
13:14 There are six days in which *men* o to work: *1163*
13:16 And o not this *woman,* being a daughter of *1163*
18: 1 them *to this end,* that *men* o always to pray, *1163*
24:26 O not Christ to have suffered these *things,* *1163*
Jn 4:20 is the place where *men* o to worship. *1163*
4:33 Hath any *man* brought him o to eat? NIG
13:14 ye also o to wash one another's feet. *3784*
19: 7 and by our law he o to die, because *3784*
Ac 4:32 neither said any *of them* that o of the *things* *5100*
5:29 said, We o to obey God rather than men. *1163*
17:29 we o not to think that the Godhead is like *3784*
19:36 ye o to be quiet, and to do nothing rashly. *1163*
20:35 so labouring *ye* o to support the weak, *1163*
21:21 saying that they o not to circumcise *their* NIG
24:19 Who o to have been here before thee, and *1163*
24:19 and object, if they had o against me. *1536*
25:10 judgment seat, where I o to be judged: *1163*
25:24 crying that he o not to live any longer. *1163*
26: 9 that *I* o to do many *things* contrary to *1163*
28:19 not that I had o to accuse my nation of. *5100*
Ro 8:26 know not what we should pray for as we o: *1163*
12: 3 *of himself* more highly than he o to think; *1163*
15: 1 that are strong o to bear the infirmities of *3784*
1Co 8: 2 he knoweth nothing yet as he o to know. *1163*
11: 7 For a man indeed o not to cover *his* head, *3784*
11:10 For this cause o the woman to have power *3784*
2Co 2: 3 sorrow from *them of* whom I o to rejoice; *1163*
2: 7 So that contrariwise ye o rather to forgive NIG
12:11 for I o to have been commended of you: *3784*
12:14 for the children o not to lay up for *3784*
Eph 5:28 So o men to love their wives as their own *3784*
6:20 therein I may speak boldly, as I o to speak. *1163*
Col 4: 4 I may make it manifest, as I o to speak. *1163*
4: 6 that *you* may know how ye o to answer *1163*
1Th 4: 1 that as ye have received of us how ye o to *1163*
2Th 3: 7 For yourselves know how *ye* o to follow *1163*
1Ti 5:13 speaking *things* which they o not. *1163*
Tit 1:11 teaching *things* which *they* o not, for filthy *1163*
Phm 1:18 If he hath wronged thee, or oweth *thee* o, *5100*
Heb 2: 1 Therefore we o to give the more earnest *1163*
5: 3 And by reason hereof he o, as for *3784*
5:12 For when for the time ye o to be teachers, *3784*
Jas 3:10 My brethren, these *things* o not so to be. *5534*
4:15 For that ye *o* to say, If the Lord will, NIG
2Pe 3:11 what manner of *persons* o ye to be in all *1163*
1Jn 2: 6 He that saith *he* abideth in him o himself *3784*
3:16 we o to lay down *our* lives for the brethren. *3784*
4:11 so loved us, we o also to love one another. *3784*
3Jn 1: 8 We therefore o to receive such, that we *3784*

OUGHTEST (4) [OUGHT]

1Ki 2: 9 and knowest what thou o to do unto him; NIH
Mt 25:27 Thou o therefore to have put my money to *1163*
Ac 10: 6 he shall tell thee what thou o to do. *1163*
1Ti 3:15 that thou mayest know how *thou* o to *1163*

OUR (1165) [WE] See Index of Articles, Etc.

OURS (12) [WE]

Ge 26:20 saying, The water *is* o: 3807.1+5105.1
31:16 that *is* o, and our children's: 3807.1+5105.1
34:23 and every beast of theirs *be* o? 3807.1+5105.1
Nu 32:32 inheritance on *this* side Jordan *may be* o. 5105.1
1Ki 22: 3 ye that Ramoth in Gilead *is* o, 3807.1+5105.1
Eze 36: 2 even the ancient high places are o 3807.1+5105.1
Mk 12: 7 us kill him, and the inheritance shall be o. *1473*
Lk 20:14 us kill him, that the inheritance may be o. *1473*
1Co 1: 2 of Jesus Christ our Lord, both theirs and o: *1473*
2Co 1:14 even as ye also *are* o in the day of the Lord *1473*
Tit 3:14 And let o also learn to maintain good works *2251*
1Jn 2: 2 and not for o only, but also for *the sins of* *2251*

OURSELVES (51) [WE]

Ge 37:10 thy brethren indeed come to bow down o to NIH
44:16 or how shall we clear o? God hath found out NIH
Nu 32:17 we o will go ready armed before the children 587
Dt 2:35 Only the cattle we took for a prey unto o, 5105.1
3: 7 spoil of the cities, we took for a prey to o. 5105.1
1Sa 14: 8 and we will discover o unto them. NIH
1Ch 19:13 and let us behave o valiantly for our people, NIH
Ezr 4: 3 we o together will build unto the LORD 587
8:21 that *we* might afflict o before our God, NIH
Ne 10:32 to charge o yearly with the third *part* of a 5105.1
Job 34: 4 let us know among o what *is* good. NIH
Ps 83:12 Let us take to o the houses of God in 5105.1
100: 3 *it is* he *that* hath made us, and not we o; 587
Pr 7:18 until the morning: let us solace o with loves. NIH
Isa 28:15 and under falsehood have we hid o: NIH
56:12 and we will fill o with strong drink; NIH
Jer 50: 5 let us join o to the LORD *in* a perpetual NIH
Lk 22:71 for we o have heard of his own mouth. *846*
Jn 4:42 for we have heard *him* o, and know that this *846*
Ac 6: 4 But we will give o continually to prayer, NIG
23:14 said, We have bound o under a great curse, *1438*
Ro 8:23 And not only *they,* but o also, which have *846*
8:23 even we o groan within ourselves, *846*
8:23 even we ourselves groan within o, *1438*
15: 1 infirmities of the weak, and not to please o. *1438*
1Co 11:31 For if we would judge o, we should not be *1438*
2Co 1: 4 by the comfort wherewith we o are *846*
1: 9 But we had the sentence of death in o, *1438*
1: 9 that we should not trust in o, but in God *1438*
3: 1 Do we begin again to commend o? or need *1438*
3: 5 Not that we are sufficient of o to think any *1438*
3: 5 of ourselves to think any *thing* as of o; *1438*
4: 2 manifestation of the truth commending o *1438*
4: 5 For we preach not o, but Christ Jesus *1438*
4: 5 and o your servants for Jesus' sake. *1438*
5:12 For we commend not o again unto you, but *1438*
5:13 For whether we be besides o, *it is* to God: *1839*
6: 4 But in all *things* approving o as *1438*
7: 1 let us cleanse o from all filthiness of *1438*
10:12 For we dare not make o of the number, or NIG
10:12 compare o with some that commend *1438*
10:14 For we stretch not o beyond *our measure,* *1438*
12:19 Again, think you that we excuse o unto you? *626*
Gal 2:17 we o also are found sinners, *is* therefore *846*
1Th 2:10 unblameably we behaved o among you that NIG
2Th 1: 4 So that we o glory in you in the churches of *846*
3: 7 for we behaved not o disorderly among you; NIG
3: 9 to make o an ensample unto you to follow *1438*
Tit 3: 3 For we o also were sometimes foolish, *1473*
Heb 10:25 Not forsaking the assembling of o together, *1438*
1Jn 1: 8 we deceive o, and the truth is not in us. *1438*

OUT (2777) [OUTER, OUTMOST, THEREOUT, WITHOUT] See Index of Articles, Etc.

OUTCAST (1) [CAST, OUTCASTS]

Jer 30:17 because they called thee an O, *saying,* This 5080

OUTCASTS (7) [CAST, OUTCAST]

Ps 147: 2 he gathereth together the o of Israel. 1760
Isa 11:12 shall assemble the o of Israel, and 1760
16: 3 hide the o; bewray not him that wandereth. 5080
16: 4 Let mine o dwell with thee, Moab; be thou 5080
27:13 the o in the land of Egypt, and 5080
56: 8 The Lord GOD which gathereth the o of 1760
Jer 49:36 there shall be no nation whither the o of 5080

OUTER (3) [OUT]

Mt 8:12 kingdom shall be cast out into o darkness: *1857*
22:13 him away, and cast *him* into o darkness; *1857*
25:30 And cast ye the unprofitable servant into o *1857*

OUTGOINGS (8) [GO]

Jos 17: 9 of the river, and the o of it were at the sea: 8444
17:18 the o of it shall be thine: for thou shalt 8444
18:19 the o of the border were at the north bay of 8444
19:14 the o thereof are *in* the valley of 8444
19:22 and the o of their border were *at* Jordan: 8444
19:29 the o thereof are at the sea from the coast to 8444
19:33 and the o thereof were *at* Jordan: 8444
Ps 65: 8 thou makest the o of the morning and 4161

OUTLANDISH (1)

Ne 13:26 *nevertheless* even him did o women cause 5237

OUTLIVED (1) [LIVE]

Jdg 2: 7 all the days of the elders that o 310+748+3117

OUTMOST (4) [OUT]

Ex 26:10 of the one curtain *that is* o in the coupling, 7020
Nu 34: 3 the o coast of the salt sea eastward: 4480+7097
Dt 30: 4 be driven out unto the o parts of heaven, 7097
Isa 17: 6 *or* five in the o fruitful branches thereof, 871.1

OUTRAGEOUS (1)

Pr 27: 4 Wrath *is* cruel, and anger *is* o; but who is 7858

OUTRUN (1) [RUN]

Jn 20: 4 and the other disciple did o Peter, *4390+5030*

OUTSIDE (8)

Jdg 7:11 o of the armed *men* that *were* in the host. 7097
7:17 behold, when I come to the o of the camp, 7097
7:19 came unto the o of the camp *in* 7097
1Ki 7: 9 and *so* on the o toward the great court. 2351
Eze 40: 5 behold a wall on the o of the house round 2351
Mt 23:25 for ye make clean the o of the cup and *1855*
23:26 that the o of them may be clean also. *1622*
Lk 11:39 Now do ye Pharisees make clean the o of *1855*

OUTSTRETCHED (3) [STRETCH]

Dt 26: 8 with an o arm, and with great terribleness, 5186
Jer 21: 5 I myself will fight against you with an o 5186
27: 5 by my great power and by my o arm, and 5186

OUTWARD (14) [OUTWARDLY]

Nu 35: 4 o a thousand cubits round about. 2351+1886.5
1Sa 16: 7 for man looketh on the o appearance, but 5869
1Ch 26:29 his sons *were* for the o business over Israel, 2435
Ne 11:16 had the oversight of the o business of 2435
Est 6: 4 Now Haman was come into the o court of 2435
Eze 40:17 brought he me into the o court, and lo, 2435
40:20 the gate of the o court that looked toward 2435
40:34 the arches thereof *were* toward the o court; 2435
44: 1 o sanctuary which looketh *toward* the east; 2435
Mt 23:27 which indeed appear beautiful o, but *1855*
Ro 2:28 which is o in the flesh: *1722+3588+5318*
2Co 4:16 but though our o man perish, yet the inward *1854*
10: 7 ye look on *things* after the o appearance? *4383*
1Pe 3: 3 Whose adorning let it not be that o *1855*

OUTWARDLY (2) [OUTWARD]

Mt 23:28 so ye also o appear righteous unto men, *1855*
Ro 2:28 is not a Jew, which is one o; *1722+3588+5318*

OUTWENT (1) [GO]

Mk 6:33 and o them, and came together unto him. *4281*

OVEN (12) [OVENS]

Lev 2: 4 oblation of a meat offering baken in the o, 8574
7: 9 all the meat offering that is baken in the o, 8574
11:35 *whether it be* o, or ranges for pots, 8574
26:26 ten women shall bake your bread in one o, 8574
Ps 21: 9 Thou shalt make them as a fiery o in 8574
La 5:10 Our skin was black like an o because of 8574
Hos 7: 4 all adulterers, as an o heated by the baker, 8574
7: 6 they have made ready their heart like an o, 8574
7: 7 They are all hot as an o, and have devoured 8574
Mal 4: 1 the day cometh, that *shall* burn as an o; 8574
Mt 6:30 to day is, and to morrow is cast into the o, *2823*
Lk 12:28 the field, and to morrow is cast into the o; *2823*

OVENS (1) [OVEN]

Ex 8: 3 into thine o, and into thy kneadingtroughs: 8574

OVER (1009)

Ge 1:18 to rule o the day and over the night, and 871.1
1:18 to rule over the day and o the night, and 871.1
1:26 let them have dominion o the fish of 871.1
1:26 o the fowl of the air, and over the cattle, 871.1
1:26 o the cattle, and over all the earth, and 871.1
1:26 o all the earth, and over every creeping 871.1
1:26 o every creeping thing that creepeth upon 871.1
1:28 have dominion o the fish of the sea, and 871.1
1:28 o the fowl of the air, and over every living 871.1
1:28 o every living thing that moveth upon 871.1
3:16 *be* to thy husband, and he shall rule o thee. 871.1
4: 7 *be* his desire, and thou shalt rule o him. 871.1
8: 1 God made a wind to pass o the earth, and 5921
9:14 to pass, when I bring a cloud o the earth, 5921
21:16 sat her down o against *him* a good way off, 4480
21:16 she sat o against *him,* and lift up her voice, 4480
24: 2 of his house that ruled o all that he had, 871.1
25:25 came out red, all o like a hairy garment; 3605
27:29 be lord o thy brethren, and let thy 3807.1
31:21 passed o the river, and set his face *toward* 5674
31:52 that I will not pass o this heap to thee, and 5674
31:52 that thou shalt not pass o this heap and 5674
32:10 for with my staff I passed o this Jordan; 5674
32:16 Pass o before me, and put a space betwixt 5674
32:21 So went the present o before him: and 5674
32:22 eleven sons, and passed o the ford Jabbok. 5674
32:23 sent them o the brook, and sent over that he 5674
32:23 over the brook, and sent o that he had. 5674
32:31 as he passed o Penuel the sun rose upon 5674
33: 3 he passed o before them, and 5674
33:14 I pray thee, pass o before his servant: 5674
36:31 before there reigned *any* king o 3807.1
37: 8 said to him, Shalt thou indeed reign o us? 5921
37: 8 or shalt thou indeed have dominion o us? 871.1
39: 4 he made him overseer o his house, and 5921
39: 5 o all that he had, that the LORD blessed 5921
41:33 and wise, and set him o the land of Egypt. 5921
41:34 and let him appoint officers o the land, 5921
41:40 Thou shalt be o my house, and 5921
41:41 See, I have set thee o all the land of Egypt. 5921
41:43 he made him *ruler* o all the land of Egypt. 5921
41:45 Joseph went out o *all* the land of Egypt. 5921
41:56 the famine was o all the face of the earth: 5921
42: 6 Joseph *was* the governor o the land, *and* 5921
45:26 and he *is* governor o all the land of Egypt. 871.1
47: 6 then make them rulers o my cattle. 5921
47:20 because the famine prevailed o them: 5921
47:26 Joseph made it a law o the land of Egypt 5921
49:22 by a well; *whose* branches run o the wall. 5921
Ex 1: 8 Now there arose up a new king o Egypt, 5921
1:11 Therefore they did set o them taskmasters 5921
2:14 Who made thee a prince and a judge o us? 5921
5:14 which Pharaoh's taskmasters had set o 5921
8: 5 Stretch forth thine hand with thy rod o 5921
8: 5 o the rivers, and over the ponds, and 5921
8: 5 o the ponds, and cause frogs to come up 5921
8: 6 Aaron stretched out his hand o the waters 5921
8: 9 Moses said unto Pharaoh, Glory o me: 5921
10:12 Stretch out thine hand o the land of Egypt 5921
10:13 Moses stretched forth his rod o the land of 5921
10:14 the locusts went up o all the land of Egypt, 5921
10:21 that there may be darkness o the land of 5921
12:13 I will pass o you, and the plague shall not 6452
12:23 the LORD will pass o the door, and 6452
12:27 who passed o the houses of the children of 6452
14: 2 and the sea, o against Baal-zephon: 6440
14: 7 of Egypt, and captains o every one of them. 5921
14:16 stretch out thine hand o the sea, and 5921
14:21 Moses stretched out his hand o the sea; 5921
14:26 Stretch out thine hand o the sea, 5921
14:27 Moses stretched forth his hand o the sea, 5921
15:16 till thy people pass o, O LORD, till 5674
15:16 pass over, O LORD, till the people pass o, 5674
16:18 he that gathered much had nothing o, 5736
16:23 that which remaineth o lay up for you to 5736

Ex 18:21 place *such* **o** them, *to be* rulers of 5921
18:25 made them heads **o** the people, rulers of 5921
25:27 **O** against the border shall the rings be for 3807.1
25:37 that they may give light **o** against it. 5921
26:12 shall hang **o** the backside of the tabernacle. 5921
26:13 it shall hang **o** the sides of the tabernacle on 5921
26:35 the candlestick **o against** the table on 5227
28:27 the forepart thereof, **o against** 5980+3807.1
30: 6 before the mercy seat that *is* **o** 5921
36:14 *of* goats' *hair* for the tent **o** the tabernacle: 5921
37: 9 covered with their wings **o** the mercy seat, 5921
37:14 **O against** the border were 5980+3807.1
39:20 of it, **o** against the *other* coupling thereof, 3807.1
40:19 he spread abroad the tent **o** the tabernacle, 5921
40:24 **o against** the table, on the side of 5227
40:36 when the cloud was taken up from **o** 5921
Lev 14: 5 killed in an earthen vessel **o** running water: 5921
14: 6 the bird *that was* killed **o** the running water: 5921
14:50 birds in an earthen vessel **o** running water: 5921
16:21 confess **o** him all the iniquities of 5921
25:43 Thou shalt not rule **o** him with rigour; but 871.1
25:46 **o** your brethren the children of Israel, 871.1
25:46 ye shall not rule one **o** another with rigour. 871.1
25:53 *the other* shall not **rule** with rigour **o** him in 7287
26:16 I will even appoint **o** you terror, 5921
26:17 they that hate you shall reign **o** you; and 871.1
Nu 1:50 thou shalt appoint the Levites **o** 5921
1:50 **o** all the vessels thereof, and over all *things* 5921
1:50 and **o** all *things* that *belong* to it: 5921
3:32 *shall be* **chief o** the chief of the Levites, 5387
3:49 of them that were **o and above** 5736+5921
4: 6 shall spread **o** *it* a 4480+4605+1886.5+3807.1
5:30 he be jealous **o** his wife, and shall set NIH
7: 2 were **o** them that were numbered, 5921+5975
8: 2 light **o against** the candlestick. 413+4136+6440
8: 3 **o against** the candlestick, 413+4136+6440
10:10 ye shall blow with the trumpets **o** your 5921
10:10 and **o** the sacrifices of your peace offerings; 5921
10:14 **o** his host *was* Nahshon the son of 5921
10:15 **o** the host of the tribe of the children of 5921
10:16 **o** the host of the tribe of the children of 5921
10:18 **o** his host *was* Elizur the son of Shedeur. 5921
10:19 **o** the host of the tribe of the children of 5921
10:20 **o** the host of the tribe of the children of 5921
10:22 **o** his host *was* Elishama the son of 5921
10:23 **o** the host of the tribe of the children of 5921
10:24 **o** the host of the tribe of the children of 5921
10:25 **o** his host *was* Ahiezer the son of 5921
10:26 **o** the host of the tribe of the children of 5921
10:27 **o** the host of the tribe of the children of 5921
11:16 elders of the people, and officers **o** them; NIH
14:14 *that* thy cloud standeth **o** them, and 5921
16:13 thou make thyself altogether a prince **o** us? 5921
22: 5 and they abide **o against** me: 4136+4480
25:15 he *was* head **o** a people, *and* of a chief house NIH
27:16 of all flesh, set a man **o** the congregation, 5921
31:14 *with* the captains **o** thousands, and NIH
31:14 captains **o** hundreds, which came from NIH
31:48 the officers which *were* **o** thousands of 3807.1
32: 5 for a possession, *and* **bring** us not **o** Jordan. 5674
32: 7 **going o** into the land which the LORD 5674
32:21 will **go** all of you armed **o** Jordan before 5674
32:27 thy servants will **pass o**, every man armed 5674
32:29 the children of Reuben will **pass** with you **o** 5674
32:30 if they will not **pass o** with you armed, 5674
32:32 We will **pass o** armed before the LORD 5674
33:51 When ye are **passed o** Jordan into the land 5674
35:10 When ye be **come o** Jordan into the land of 5674
Dt 1: 1 in the plain **o against** the Red *sea,* between 4136
1:13 and I will make them rulers **o** you. 871.1
1:15 and known, and made them heads **o** you, 5921
1:15 captains **o** thousands, and captains over NIH
1:15 captains **o** hundreds, and captains over NIH
1:15 captains **o** fifties, and captains over tens, NIH
1:15 captains **o** tens, and officers among your NIH
2:13 *said I,* and **get** you **o** the brook Zered. 5674
2:13 And we **went o** the brook Zered. 5674
2:14 until we were **come o** the brook Zered, 5674
2:18 Thou art to **pass o** *through* Ar, the coast of 5674
2:19 *when* thou comest nigh **o against** 4136
2:24 your journey, and **pass o** the river Arnon: 5674
2:29 until I shall **pass o** Jordan into the land 5674
3:18 ye shall **pass o** armed before your brethren 5674
3:25 let me **go o**, and see the good land that *is* 5674
3:27 for thou shalt not **go o** this Jordan. 5674
3:28 for he shall **go o** before this people, and 5674
3:29 So we abode in the valley **o against** 4136
4:14 in the land whither ye **go o** to possess it. 5674
4:21 sware that I should not **go o** Jordan, and 5674
4:22 die in this land, I *must* not **go o** Jordan: 5674
4:22 ye *shall* **go o**, and possess that good land. 5674
4:26 whereunto you **go o** Jordan to possess it; 5674
4:46 in the valley **o against** Beth-peor, 4136
9: 1 Thou art to **pass o** Jordan *this* day, to go in 5674
9: 3 thy God *is* he which **goeth o** before thee; 5674
11:30 which dwell in the champaign **o against** 4136
11:31 For ye shall **pass o** Jordan to go in to 5674
12:10 *when* ye **go o** Jordan and dwell in the land 5674
15: 6 thou shalt reign **o** many nations, but 871.1
15: 6 but they shall not reign **o** thee. 871.1
17:14 shalt say, I will set a king **o** me, 5921
17:15 Thou shalt in any wise set *him* king **o** thee, 5921
17:15 thy brethren shalt thou set king **o** thee: 5921
17:15 thou mayest not set a stranger **o** thee, 5921
21: 6 **o** the heifer that is beheaded in the valley: 5921
24:20 thou shalt not **go o the boughs** again: 6286
27: 2 it shall be on the day when you shall **pass o** 5674
27: 3 words of this law, when thou art **passed o**, 5674
27: 4 Therefore it shall be when ye be **gone o** 5674
27:12 the people, when ye are **come o** Jordan; 5674
28:23 thy heaven that *is* **o** thy head shall be brass, 5921
28:36 and thy king which thou shalt set **o** thee, 5921
28:63 *that* as the LORD rejoiced **o** you to do you 5921
28:63 the LORD will rejoice **o** you to destroy 5921
30: 9 for the LORD will again rejoice **o** thee for 5921
Dt 30: 9 thee for good, as he rejoiced **o** thy fathers: 5921
30:13 Who shall go **o** the sea for us, and bring it 5676
30:18 whither thou **passest o** Jordan to go to 5674
31: 2 unto me, Thou shalt not **go o** this Jordan. 5674
31: 3 he will **go o** before thee, *and* he will 5674
31: 3 *and* Joshua, he shall **go o** before thee, as 5674
31:13 long as ye live in the land whither ye **go o** 5674
31:15 the pillar of the cloud stood **o** the door of 5921
32:11 fluttereth **o** her young, spreadeth abroad her 5921
32:47 whither ye **go o** Jordan to possess it. 5674
32:49 of Moab, that *is* **o against** Jericho; 5921+6440
34: 1 of Pisgah, that *is* **o against** Jericho. 5921+6440
34: 4 thine eyes, but thou shalt not **go o** thither. 5674
34: 6 in the land of Moab, **o against** Beth-peor: 4136
Jos 1: 2 **go o** this Jordan, thou, and all this people, 5674
1:11 for within three days ye shall **pass o** this 5674
2:23 **passed o**, and came to Joshua the son of 5674
3: 1 and lodged there before they **passed o**. 5674
3: 6 the covenant, and **pass o** before the people. 5674
3:11 *even* the Lord of all the earth **passeth o** 5674
3:14 to **pass o** Jordan, and the priests bearing 5674
3:16 the people **passed o** right against Jericho. 5674
3:17 all the Israelites **passed o** on dry *ground,* 5674
3:17 all the people were **passed** clean **o** Jordan. 5674
4: 1 when all the people were clean **passed o** 5674
4: 3 ye shall **carry** them **o** with you, and 5674
4: 5 **Pass o** before the ark of the LORD your 5674
4: 7 when it **passed o** Jordan, the waters of 5674
4: 8 **carried** them **o** with them unto the place 5674
4:10 and the people hasted and **passed o**. 5674
4:11 when all the people were clean **passed o**, 5674
4:11 that the ark of the LORD **passed o**, and 5674
4:12 **passed o** armed before the children of 5674
4:13 **passed o** before the LORD unto battle, 5674
4:18 flowed **o** all his banks, as *they did* before. 5921
4:22 Israel **came o** this Jordan on dry *land.* 5674
4:23 until ye were **passed o**, as the LORD your 5674
4:23 up from before us, until we were **gone o**: 5674
5: 1 until we were **passed o**, that their heart 5674
5:13 there stood a man **o against** him 5048+3807.1
7: 7 **at all brought** this people **o** Jordan, 5674+5674
7:26 they raised **o** him a great heap of stones 5921
8:31 **o** which no *man* hath lift up *any* iron: 5921
8:33 half of them **o against** mount 413+4136
8:33 and half of them **o** against mount Ebal; 413
9: 1 in all the coasts of the great sea **o** against 413
18:13 the border **went o** from thence toward Luz, 5674
18:17 which *is* **o against** the going up of 5227
18:18 passed along toward the side **o against** 4136
22:11 built an altar **o** against the land of Canaan, 413
22:19 **pass** ye **o** unto the land of the possession of 5674
24:11 ye **went o** Jordan, and came unto Jericho: 5674
Jdg 3:28 and suffered not a man to **pass o**. 5674
5:13 **made** him that remaineth **have dominion o** 7287
5:13 the LORD **made** me **have dominion o** 7287
6:33 **went o**, and pitched in the valley of Jezreel. 5674
8: 4 *and* **passed o**, he, and the three hundred 5674
8:22 Rule thou **o** us, both thou, and thy son, and 871.1
8:23 said unto them, I will not rule **o** you, 871.1
8:23 over you, neither shall my son rule **o** you: 871.1
8:23 rule over you: the LORD shall rule **o** you. 871.1
9: 2 reign **o** you, or that one reign over you? 871.1
9: 2 reign over you, or that one reign **o** you? 871.1
9: 8 forth on a time to anoint a king **o** them; 5921
9: 8 said unto the olive tree, Reign thou **o** us. 5921
9: 9 man, and go to be promoted **o** the trees? 5921
9:10 to the fig tree, Come thou, *and* reign **o** us. 5921
9:11 and go to be promoted **o** the trees? 5921
9:12 unto the vine, Come thou, *and* reign **o** us. 5921
9:13 man, and go to be promoted **o** the trees? 5921
9:14 the bramble, Come thou, *and* reign **o** us. 5921
9:15 If in truth ye anoint me king **o** you, *then* 5921
9:18 king **o** the men of Shechem, because he *is* 5921
9:22 When Abimelech had reigned three years **o** 5921
9:26 with his brethren, and **went o** to Shechem: 5674
10: 9 Moreover the children of Ammon **passed o** 5674
10:18 he shall be head **o** all the inhabitants of 3807.1
11: 8 our head **o** all the inhabitants of Gilead. 3807.1
11:11 people made him head and captain **o** them: 5921
11:29 he **passed o** Gilead and Manasseh, and 5674
11:29 **passed o** Mizpeh of Gilead, and 5674
11:29 from Mizpeh of Gilead he **passed o** *unto* 5674
11:32 So Jephthah **passed o** unto the children of 5674
12: 1 Wherefore **passedst** thou **o** to fight against 5674
12: 3 **passed o** against the children of Ammon, 5674
12: 5 which were escaped said, Let me **go o**; 5674
14: 4 time the Philistines had dominion **o** Israel. 871.1
15:11 thou not that the Philistines *are* rulers **o** us? 871.1
19:10 and departed, and came **o** against Jebus, 5704
19:12 children of Israel; we will **pass o** to Gibeah. 5674
20:43 trode them down with ease **o** against 5704
Ru 2: 5 said Boaz unto his servant that was set **o** 5921
2: 6 the servant that was set **o** the reapers 5921
3: 9 spread therefore thy skirt **o** thine handmaid; 5921
1Sa 2: 1 my mouth is enlarged **o** mine enemies; 5921
8: 1 that he made his sons judges **o** Israel. 3807.1
8: 7 rejected me, that *I* should not reign **o** them. 5921
8: 9 manner of the king that shall reign **o** them. 5921
8:11 manner of the king that shall reign **o** you: 5921
8:12 he will appoint him captains **o** thousands, NIH
8:12 over thousands, and captains **o** fifties, NIH
8:19 Nay, but we will have a king **o** us; 5921
9:16 thou shalt anoint him to be captain **o** my 5921
9:17 thee of: this *same* shall reign **o** my people. 871.1
10: 1 thee to be captain **o** his inheritance? 5921
10:19 said unto him, *Nay,* but set a king **o** us. 5921
11:12 Who *is* he that said, Shall Saul reign **o** us? 5921
12: 1 said unto me, and have made a king **o** you. 5921
12:12 unto me, Nay; but a king shall reign **o** us: 5921
12:13 behold, the LORD hath set a king **o** you. 5921
12:14 also the king that reigneth **o** you continue 5921
13: 1 and when he had reigned two years **o** Israel, 5921
13: 7 *some of the* Hebrews **went o** Jordan *to* 5674
13:14 commanded him to be captain **o** his people, 5921
14: 1 and let us **go o** to the Philistines' garrison, 5674
1Sa 14: 4 *by* which Jonathan sought to **go o** unto 5674
14: 5 *was* situate northward **o against** Michmash, 4136
14: 5 and the other southward **o against** Gibeah. 4136
14: 6 let us **go o** unto the garrison of these 5674
14: 8 we will **pass o** unto *these* men, and we will 5674
14:23 the battle **passed o** *unto* Beth-aven. 5674
14:47 So Saul took the kingdom **o** Israel, and 5921
15: 1 me to anoint thee to be king **o** his people, 5921
15: 1 thee to be king over his people, **o** Israel: 5921
15: 7 *to* Shur, that *is* **o against** Egypt. 5921+6440
15:17 the LORD anointed thee king **o** Israel? 5921
15:26 hath rejected thee from being king **o** Israel. 5921
15:35 that he had made Saul king **o** Israel. 5921
16: 1 seeing I have rejected him from reigning **o** 5921
17:50 So David prevailed **o** the Philistine with a 4480
18: 5 Saul set him **o** the men of war, and he was 5921
18:13 and made him his captain **o** a thousand; NIH
19:20 Samuel standing *as* appointed **o** them, 5921
22: 2 unto him; and he became a captain **o** them: 5921
22: 9 which *was* set **o** the servants of Saul, and 5921
23:17 thou shalt be king **o** Israel, and I shall be 5921
25:30 and shall have appointed thee ruler **o** Israel; 5921
26:13 David **went o** *to* the *other* side, and 5674
26:22 let one of the young men **come o** and 5674
27: 2 he **passed o** with the six hundred men that 5674
30:10 faint that they could not **go o** the brook 5674
2Sa 1:17 David lamented with this lamentation **o** 5921
1:17 over Saul and **o** Jonathan his son: 5921
1:24 Ye daughters of Israel, weep **o** Saul, 413
2: 4 there they anointed David king **o** the house 5921
2: 7 of Judah have anointed me king **o** them. 5921
2: 8 of Saul, and **brought** him **o** *to* Mahanaim; 5674
2: 9 he made him king **o** Gilead, and over 413
2: 9 **o** the Ashurites, and over Jezreel, and 413
2: 9 **o** Jezreel, and over Ephraim, and 413
2: 9 **o** Ephraim, and over Benjamin, and over all 5921
2: 9 and **o** Benjamin, and over all Israel. 5921
2: 9 and over Benjamin, and **o** all Israel. 5921
2:10 years old when he *began* to reign **o** Israel, 5921
2:11 the time that David was king in Hebron **o** 5921
2:15 and **went o** by number twelve of Benjamin, 5674
2:29 **passed o** Jordan, and went *through* all 5674
3:10 to set up the throne of David **o** Israel and 5921
3:10 the throne of David over Israel and **o** Judah, 5921
3:17 for David in times past to be king **o** you: 5921
3:21 that thou mayest reign **o** all that thine heart 871.1
3:33 the king lamented **o** Abner, and said, Died 413
3:34 And all the people wept again **o** him. 5921
4:12 and hanged *them* up **o** the pool in Hebron. 5921
5: 2 Also in time past, when Saul was king **o** us, 5921
5: 2 and thou shalt be a captain **o** Israel. 5921
5: 3 and they anointed David king **o** Israel. 5921
5: 5 In Hebron he reigned **o** Judah seven years 5921
5: 5 and three years **o** all Israel and Judah. 5921
5:12 LORD had established him king **o** Israel, 5921
5:17 that they had anointed David king **o** Israel, 5921
5:23 come upon them **o against** 4136+4480
6:21 to appoint me ruler **o** the people of 5921
6:21 over the people of the LORD, **o** Israel: 5921
7: 8 to be ruler **o** my people, over Israel: 5921
7: 8 to be ruler over my people, **o** Israel: 5921
7:11 judges *to be* **o** my people Israel, 5921
7:26 The LORD of hosts *is* the God **o** Israel: 5921
8:15 David reigned **o** all Israel; and David 5921
8:16 And Joab the son of Zeruiah *was* **o** the host; 5921
8:18 Benaiah the son of Jehoiada *was* **o** both NIH
10:17 and **passed o** Jordan, and came to Helam. 5674
12: 7 I anointed thee king **o** Israel, and 5921
15:22 David said to Ittai, Go and **pass o**. And Ittai 5674
15:22 Ittai the Gittite **passed o**, and all his men, 5674
15:23 a loud voice, and all the people **passed o**: 5674
15:23 the king also *himself* **passed o** the brook 5674
15:23 all the people **passed o**, toward the way of 5674
16: 9 let me **go o**, I pray thee, and take off his 5674
16:13 Shimei went along on the hill's side **o** 3807.1
17:16 the wilderness, but **speedily pass o**; 5674+5674
17:19 and spread a covering **o** the well's mouth, 5921
17:20 They be **gone o** the brook of water. 5674
17:21 Arise, and pass quickly **o** the water: 5674
17:22 *were* with him, and they **passed o** Jordan: 5674
17:22 not one *of them* that was not **gone o** Jordan. 5674
17:24 Absalom **passed o** Jordan, he and all 5674
18: 1 and captains of hundreds **o** them. 5921
18: 8 For the battle was there scattered **o** the face 5921
18:24 the watchman went *up* to the roof **o** the gate NIH
18:33 went up to the chamber **o** the gate, and NIH
19:10 Absalom, whom we anointed **o** us, is dead 5921
19:15 the king, to **conduct** the king **o** Jordan. 5674
19:17 and they **went o** Jordan before the king. 6743
19:18 there **went o** a ferry boat to carry over 5674
19:18 there went over a ferry boat to **carry o** 5674
19:18 before the king, as he was **come o** Jordan; 5674
19:22 for do not I know that I *am this* day king **o** 5921
19:31 **went o** Jordan with the king, to conduct 5674
19:31 with the king, to conduct him *o* Jordan. NIH
19:33 **Come** thou **o** with me, and I will feed thee 5674
19:36 Thy servant will **go** a little *way* **o** Jordan 5674
19:37 let him **go o** with my lord the king; and 5674
19:38 Chimham shall **go o** with me, and I will do 5674
19:39 all the people **went o** Jordan. And when 5674
19:39 when the king was **come o**, the king kissed 5674
19:41 **brought** the king, and his household, and all David's men with him, **o** 5674
20:21 his head *shall be* thrown to thee **o** the wall. 1157
20:23 Now Joab *was* **o** all the host of Israel: and 413
20:23 Benaiah the son of Jehoiada *was* **o** 5921
20:23 over the Cherethites and **o** the Pelethites: 5921
20:24 Adoram *was* **o** the tribute: and 5921
22:30 a troop: by my God have I **leaped o** a wall. 1801
23: 3 He that ruleth **o** men *must be* just, ruling *in* 871.1
23:23 *first* three. And David set him **o** his guard. 413
24: 5 they **passed o** Jordan, and pitched in Aroer, 5674
1Ki 1:34 Nathan the prophet anoint him there king **o** 5921
1:35 I have appointed him to be ruler **o** Israel 5921
1:35 him to be ruler over Israel and **o** Judah. 5921

O

1Ki 2:11 the days that David reigned **o** Israel *were* 5921
2:35 the son of Jehoiada in his room **o** the host: 5921
2:37 goest out, and **passest o** the brook Kidron, 5674
4: 1 So king Solomon was king **o** all Israel. 5921
4: 4 Benaiah the son of Jehoiada *was* **o** the host: 5921
4: 5 Azariah the son of Nathan *was* **o** 5921
4: 6 Ahishar *was* **o** the household: and 5921
4: 6 Adoniram the son of Abda *was* **o** 5921
4: 7 Solomon had twelve officers **o** all Israel, 5921
4:21 Solomon reigned **o** all kingdoms from 871.1
4:24 For he had dominion **o** all *the region* on 871.1
4:24 **o** all the kings on *this* side the river: 871.1
5: 7 which hath given unto David a wise son **o** 5921
5:14 at home: and Adoniram *was* **o** the levy. 5921
5:16 Solomon's officers which *were* **o** the work, 5921
5:16 which ruled **o** the people that wrought in 871.1
6: 1 in the fourth year of Solomon's reign **o** 5921
7:20 **o** against the belly which *was* by 4480
7:39 of the house eastward **o** against the south. 4480
8: 7 forth *their* two wings **o** the place of the ark, 413
8:16 but I chose David to be **o** my people Israel. 5921
9:23 of the officers that *were* **o** Solomon's work, 5921
9:23 which bare rule **o** the people that wrought 871.1
11:24 unto him, and became captain **o** a band, NIH
11:25 and he abhorred Israel, and reigned **o** Syria. 5921
11:28 he made him ruler **o** all the charge of 3807.1
11:37 thy soul desireth, and shalt be king **o** Israel. 5921
11:42 in Jerusalem **o** all Israel *was* forty years. 5921
12:17 cities of Judah, Rehoboam reigned **o** them. 5921
12:18 sent Adoram, who *was* **o** the tribute; 5921
12:20 and made him king **o** all Israel: 5921
13:30 they mourned **o** him, *saying,* Alas, 5921
14: 2 which told me that I should be king **o** this 5921
14: 7 and made thee prince **o** my people Israel, 5921
14:14 LORD shall raise him up a king **o** Israel, 5921
15: 1 the son of Nebat reigned Abijam **o** Judah. 5921
15: 9 king of Israel **reigned** Asa **o** Judah. 4427+4428
15:25 **o** Israel in the second year of Asa king of 5921
15:25 of Judah, and reigned **o** Israel two years. 5921
15:33 son of Ahijah to reign **o** all Israel in Tirzah, 5921
16: 2 and made thee prince **o** my people Israel; 5921
16: 8 son of Baasha to reign **o** Israel in Tirzah, 5921
16:16 the host, king **o** Israel that day in the camp. 5921
16:18 burnt the king's house **o** him with fire, and 5921
16:23 king of Judah *began* Omri to reign **o** Israel, 5921
16:29 Ahab the son of Omri to reign **o** Israel: 5921
16:29 Ahab the son of Omri reigned **o** Israel in 5921
19:15 anoint Hazael to be king **o** Syria: 5921
19:16 shalt thou anoint to be king **o** Israel: 5921
20:29 they pitched one **o against** the other seven 5227
22:31 and two captains that had rule **o** *his* chariots, NIH
22:41 **o** Judah in the fourth year of Ahab king of 5921
22:51 Ahaziah the son of Ahab *began* to reign **o** 5921
22:51 of Judah, and reigned two years **o** Israel. 5921
2Ki 2: 8 so that they two **went o** on dry *ground.* 5674
2: 9 it came to pass, when they were **gone o**, 5674
2:14 and thither: and Elisha **went o**. 5674
3: 1 **o** Israel in Samaria the eighteenth year of 5921
5:11 strike his hand **o** the place, and recover 413
8:13 shewed me *that* thou *shalt be* king **o** Syria. 5921
8:20 of Judah, and made a king **o** themselves. 5921
8:21 So Joram **went o** to Zair, and all 5674
9: 3 I have anointed thee king **o** Israel. 413
9: 6 I have anointed thee king **o** the people of 413
9: 6 over the people of the LORD, *even* **o** Israel. 413
9:12 I have anointed thee king **o** Israel. 413
9:29 of Ahab *began* Ahaziah to reign **o** Judah. 5921
10: 5 *he* that *was* **o** the house, and *he* that *was* 5921
10: 5 *he* that *was* **o** the city, the elders also, and 5921
10:22 he said unto *him* that *was* **o** the vestry, 5921
10:36 the time that Jehu reigned **o** Israel in 5921
11: 3 And Athaliah *did* reign **o** the land. 5921
11: 4 Jehoiada sent and fet the rulers **o** hundreds, NIH
11: 9 the captains **o** the hundreds did according to NIH
11:10 to the captains **o** hundreds did the priest NIH
11:18 the priest appointed officers **o** the house of 5921
11:19 he took the rulers **o** hundreds, and NIH
13: 1 of Jehu *began* to reign **o** Israel in Samaria, 5921
13:10 of Jehoahaz to reign **o** Israel in Samaria, 5921
13:14 wept **o** his face, and said, O my father, 5921
15: 5 And Jotham the king's son *was* **o** the house, 5921
15: 8 reign **o** Israel in Samaria six months. 5921
15:17 Menahem the son of Gadi to reign **o** Israel, 5921
15:23 *began* to reign **o** Israel in Samaria, 5921
15:27 *began* to reign **o** Israel in Samaria, 5921
17: 1 Elah to reign in Samaria **o** Israel nine years. 5921
18:18 which *was* **o** the household, and Shebna 5921
18:37 which *was* **o** the household, and Shebna 5921
19: 2 which *was* **o** the household, and Shebna 5921
21:13 I will stretch **o** Jerusalem the line of 5921
25:19 an officer that was set **o** the men of war, 5921
25:22 even **o** them he made Gedaliah the son of 5921
1Ch 1:43 *any* king reigned **o** the children of Israel; 3807.1
5:11 the children of Gad dwelt **o** against them, 3807.1
6:31 these *are they* whom David set **o** 5921
8:32 their brethren in Jerusalem, **o against** them. 5048
9:19 *were* **o** the work of the service, 5921
9:19 *being* **o** the host of the LORD, 5921
9:20 Phinehas the son of Eleazar was the ruler **o** 5921
9:26 were **o** the chambers and treasuries of 5921
9:31 had the set office **o** the things that were 5921
9:32 *were* **o** the shewbread, to prepare *it* every 5921
9:38 at Jerusalem, **o** against their brethren. 5048
11: 2 and thou shalt be ruler **o** my people Israel. 5921
11: 3 they anointed David king **o** Israel, 5921
11:25 *first* three: and David set him **o** his guard. 5921
12: 4 *man* among the thirty, and **o** the thirty; 5921
12:14 one of the least *was* **o** an hundred, and 3807.1
12:14 an hundred, and the greatest **o** a thousand. 3807.1
12:15 These *are* they that **went o** Jordan in 5674
12:38 to Hebron, to make David king **o** all Israel: 5921
14: 2 LORD had confirmed him king **o** Israel, 5921
14: 8 that David was anointed king **o** all Israel, 5921
14:14 come upon them **o against** 4136+4480
15:25 of Israel, and the captains **o** thousands, NIH

1Ch 17: 7 that *thou* shouldest be ruler **o** my people 5921
17:10 judges *to be* **o** my people Israel. 5921
18:14 So David reigned **o** all Israel, and executed 5921
18:15 And Joab the son of Zeruiah *was* **o** the host; 5921
18:17 Benaiah the son of Jehoiada *was* **o** 5921
19:17 **passed o** Jordan, and came upon them, and 5674
21:16 in his hand stretched out **o** Jerusalem. 5921
22:10 I will establish the throne of his kingdom **o** 5921
23: 1 he made Solomon his son king **o** Israel. 5921
24:31 These likewise cast lots **o** against their 3807.1
24:31 *even* the principal fathers **o** against their 3807.1
26:20 Ahijah *was* **o** the treasures of the house of 5921
26:20 and **o** the treasures of the dedicate *things.* 3807.1
26:22 *which were* **o** the treasures of the house of 5921
26:26 his brethren *were* **o** all the treasures of 5921
26:26 the captains **o** thousands and hundreds, and NIH
26:29 his sons *were* for the outward business **o** 5921
26:32 whom king David made rulers **o** 5921
27: 2 **O** the first course for the first month *was* 5921
27: 4 **o** the course of the second month *was* 5921
27:16 Furthermore **o** the tribes of Israel: the ruler 5921
27:25 **o** the king's treasures *was* Azmaveth 5921
27:25 **o** the storehouses in the fields, in the cities, 5921
27:26 **o** them that did the work of the field for 5921
27:27 **o** the vineyards *was* Shimei the Ramathite: 5921
27:27 **o** the increase of the vineyards for the wine 5921
27:28 **o** the olive trees and the sycomore trees that 5921
27:28 and **o** the cellars of oil *was* Joash: 5921
27:29 **o** the herds that fed in Sharon *was* Shitrai 5921
27:29 **o** the herds *that were* in the valleys *was* 5921
27:30 **O** the camels also *was* Obil the Ishmaelite: 5921
27:30 **o** the asses *was* Jehdeiah the Meronothite: 5921
27:31 **o** the flocks *was* Jaziz the Hagerite. 5921
28: 1 the captains **o** the thousands, and NIH
28: 1 captains **o** the hundreds, and the stewards NIH
28: 1 the stewards **o** all the substance and NIH
28: 4 of my father to be king **o** Israel for ever: 5921
28: 4 he liked me to make *me* king **o** all Israel: 5921
28: 5 of the kingdom of the LORD **o** Israel. 5921
29: 3 **o and above** 4480+4605+1886.5+3807.1
29: 6 with the rulers **o** the king's work, NIH
29:12 *come* of thee, and thou reignest **o** all; 871.1
29:26 Thus David the son of Jesse reigned **o** all 5921
29:27 the time that he reigned **o** Israel *was* forty 5921
29:30 the times that went **o** him, and over Israel, 5921
29:30 **o** Israel, and over all the kingdoms of 5921
29:30 and **o** all the kingdoms of the countries. 5921
2Ch 1: 9 for thou hast made me king **o** a people like 5921
1:11 my people, **o** whom I have made thee king: 5921
1:13 of the congregation, and reigned **o** Israel. 5921
2:11 his people, he hath made thee king **o** them. 5921
4:10 side of the east end, **o** against the south. 4480
5: 8 forth *their* wings **o** the place of the ark, 5921
6: 5 neither chose I any man to be a ruler **o** my 5921
6: 6 have chosen David to be **o** my people 5921
6:36 deliver them **o** before *their* enemies, and NIH
8:10 and fifty, that bare rule **o** the people. 871.1
9: 8 therefore made he thee king **o** them, to do 5921
9:26 he reigned **o** all the kings from the river 871.1
9:30 Solomon reigned in Jerusalem **o** all Israel 5921
10:17 cities of Judah, Rehoboam reigned **o** them. 5921
10:18 king Rehoboam sent Hadoram that *was* **o** 5921
13: 1 Jeroboam *began* Abijah to reign **o** Judah. 5921
13: 5 the kingdom **o** Israel to David for ever, 5921
19:11 Amariah the chief priest *is* **o** you in all 5921
20: 6 rulest *not* thou **o** all the kingdoms of 871.1
20:27 for the LORD had made them to rejoice **o** 4480
20:31 Jehoshaphat reigned **o** Judah: *he was* thirty 5921
22:12 six years: and Athaliah reigned **o** the land. 5921
23:14 of hundreds that were **set o** the host, 6485
25: 5 made them captains **o** thousands, and NIH
25: 5 over thousands, and captains **o** hundreds, NIH
26:21 Jotham his son *was* **o** the king's house, 5921
31:12 **o** which Cononiah the Levite *was* ruler, and 5921
31:14 *was* **o** the freewill offerings of God, 5921
32: 6 he set captains of war **o** the people, and 5921
32:11 Doth not Hezekiah persuade you to **give o** 5414
34:13 Also *they were* **o** the bearers of burdens, 5921
36: 4 made Eliakim his brother king **o** Judah 5921
36:10 made Zedekiah his brother king **o** Judah 5921
Ezr 4:10 the great and noble Asnappar **brought o**, 1541
4:20 There have been mighty kings also **o** 5922
4:20 which have ruled **o** all *countries* beyond 871.2
9: 6 iniquities are increased **o** 4605+1886.5+3807.1
Ne 2: 7 that they may **convey** me **o** till I come into 5674
3:10 of Harumaph, even **o against** his house. 5048
3:16 unto *the place* **o against** the sepulchres of 5048
3:19 another piece **o against** the going up 4480+5048
3:23 and Hashub **o against** their house. 5048
3:25 Palal the son of Uzai, **o against** 4480+5048
3:26 unto *the place* **o against** the water gate 5048
3:27 **o against** the great tower that lieth 4480+5048
3:28 every one **o against** his house. 5048+3807.1
3:29 the son of Immer **o against** his house. 5048
3:30 son of Berechiah **o against** his chamber. 5048
3:31 **o against** the gate Miphkad, and to 5048
5:15 *yea,* even their servants bare rule **o** 5921
7: 2 the ruler of the palace, charge **o** Jerusalem: 5921
7: 3 and every one *to be* **o against** his house. 5048
9:28 so that they had the dominion **o** them: 871.1
9:37 unto the kings whom thou hast set **o** us 5921
9:37 also they have dominion **o** our bodies, and 5921
9:37 **o** our cattle, at their pleasure, and we *are* in 871.1
11: 9 Judah the son of Senuah *was* second **o** 5921
11:21 and Ziha and Gispa *were* **o** the Nethinims. 5921
11:22 the singers *were* **o** the business of 5048+3807.1
12: 8 *which was* **o** the thanksgiving, he and 5921
12: 9 their brethren, *were* **o against** them 5048+3807.1
12:24 with their brethren **o against** them, 5048+3807.1
12:24 man of God, ward **o against** ward, 5980+3807.1
12:37 fountain gate, which *was* **o against** them, 5048
12:38 *them that gave* thanks went **o against** *them,* 4136
12:44 at that time were some appointed **o** 5921
13:13 I made treasurers **o** the treasuries, 5921
13:26 and God made him king **o** all Israel: 5921

Est 1: 1 ***o*** an hundred and seven and NIH
3:12 to the governors that *were* **o** every 5921
5: 1 king's house, **o against** the king's house: 5227
5: 1 **o against** the gate of the house. 5227
8: 2 Esther set Mordecai **o** the house of Haman. 5921
9: 1 of the Jews hoped to have power **o** them, 871.1
9: 1 the Jews had rule **o** them that hated them;) 871.1
Job 6: 5 hath grass? or loweth the ox **o** his fodder? 5921
7:12 or a whale, that thou settest a watch **o** me? 5921
14:16 my steps: dost thou not watch **o** my sin? 5921
16:11 **turned** me **o** into the hands of the wicked. 3399
26: 7 He stretcheth out the north **o** the empty 5921
34:13 Who hath given him a charge **o** the earth? 5921
41:34 He beholdeth all high *things:* he *is* a king **o** 5921
42:11 comforted him **o** all the evil that 5921
Ps 8: 6 Thou madest him to have dominion **o** 871.1
12: 4 our lips *are* our own: who *is* lord **o** us? 3807.1
13: 2 how long shall mine enemy be exalted **o** 5921
18:29 and by my God have I **leaped o** a wall. 1801
19:13 *sins;* let them not have dominion **o** me: 871.1
23: 5 my head with oil; my cup **runneth o**. 7310
25: 2 let not mine enemies triumph **o** me. 3807.1
27:12 **Deliver** me not **o** unto the will of mine 5414
30: 1 hast not made my foes to rejoice **o** me. 3807.1
35:19 mine enemies wrongfully rejoice **o** me: 3807.1
35:24 and let them not rejoice **o** me. 3807.1
38: 4 For mine iniquities are gone ***o*** mine head: NIH
38:16 lest *otherwise* they should rejoice **o** me: 3807.1
41:11 mine enemy doth not triumph **o** me. 5921
42: 7 thy waves and thy billows are gone **o** me. 5921
47: 2 *is* terrible; *he is* a great King **o** all the earth. 5921
47: 8 God reigneth **o** the heathen: God sitteth 5921
49:14 the upright shall have dominion **o** them in 871.1
60: 8 **o** Edom will I cast out my shoe: 5921
65:13 the valleys also are **covered o** with corn; 5848
66:12 Thou hast caused men to ride **o** our 3807.1
68:34 his excellency *is* **o** Israel, and his strength *is* 5921
78:50 but **gave** their life **o** to the pestilence; 5462
78:62 He **gave** his people **o** also unto the sword; 5462
83:18 *art* the most High **o** all the earth. 5921
88:16 Thy fierce wrath goeth **o** me; thy terrors 5921
91:11 For he shall give his angels charge **o** thee, 3807.1
103:16 For the wind passeth **o** it, and it is gone; 871.1
103:19 the heavens; and his kingdom ruleth **o** all. 871.1
104: 9 hast set a bound *that* they may not **pass o**; 5674
106:41 and they that hated them ruled **o** them. 871.1
108: 9 **o** Edom will I cast out my shoe; 5921
108: 9 cast out my shoe; **o** Philistia will I triumph. 5921
109: 6 Set thou a wicked *man* **o** him: and let Satan 5921
110: 6 he shall wound the heads **o** many countries. 5921
118:18 he hath not **given** me **o** unto death. 5414
119:133 let not any iniquity have dominion **o** me. 871.1
124: 4 the stream had **gone o** our soul: 5674
124: 5 Then the proud waters had **gone o** our soul. 5674
145: 9 and his tender mercies *are* **o** all his works. 5921
Pr 17: 2 A wise servant shall have rule **o** a son that 871.1
19:10 much less for a servant to have rule **o** 871.1
19:11 and *it is* his glory to pass **o** a transgression. 5921
20:26 the wicked, and bringeth the wheel **o** them. 5921
22: 7 The rich ruleth **o** the poor, and 871.1
24:31 it was all **grown o** *with* thorns, *and* 5927
25:28 He that *hath* no rule **o** his own spirit *is* 3807.1
28:15 *so is* a wicked ruler **o** the poor people. 5921
Ecc 1:12 I the Preacher was king **o** Israel in 5921
2:19 yet shall he have rule **o** all my labour 871.1
7:14 God also hath set the one **o against** 5980+3807.1
7:16 Be not righteous **o much**; neither make 7235
7:16 over much; neither make thyself **o** wise: 3148
7:17 Be not **o much** wicked, neither be thou 7235
8: 8 *There is* no man that hath power **o** 871.1
8: 9 *there is* a time wherein one man ruleth **o** 871.1
SS 2: 4 and his banner **o** me *was* love. 5921
2:11 the winter is past, the rain is **o** *and* gone; 2498
Isa 3: 4 their princes, and babes shall rule **o** them. 871.1
3:12 their oppressors, and women rule **o** them. 871.1
8: 7 and he shall come up **o** all his channels, and 5921
8: 7 all his channels, and go **o** all his banks: 5921
8: 8 he shall overflow and **go o**, he shall reach 5674
10:29 They are **gone o** the passage: they have 5674
11:15 wind shall he shake his hand **o** the river, 5921
11:15 and **make** *men* **go o** dryshod. 1869
14: 2 and they shall rule **o** their oppressors. 871.1
15: 2 Moab shall howl **o** Nebo, and 5921
15: 2 shall howl over Nebo, and **o** Medeba: 5921
16: 8 are stretched out, they are **gone o** the sea. 5674
19: 4 the Egyptians will I **give o** into the hand of 5534
19: 4 a fierce king shall rule **o** them, saith 871.1
19:16 the LORD of hosts, which he shaketh **o** it. 5921
22:15 which *is* **o** the house, *and say,* 5921
23: 2 that **pass o** the sea, have replenished. 5674
23: 6 **Pass** ye **o** to Tarshish; howl, ye inhabitants 5674
23:11 He stretched out his hand **o** the sea, 5921
23:12 arise, **pass o** *to* Chittim; there also shalt 5674
25: 7 the face of the covering cast **o** all people, 5921
25: 7 and the vail that is spread **o** all nations. 5921
26:13 lords besides thee have **had dominion o** us: 1166
28:19 for morning by morning shall it **pass o**, 5674
31: 5 and **passing o** he will preserve *it.* 6452
31: 9 he shall **pass o** *to* his strong hold for fear, 5674
35: 8 the unclean shall not **pass o** it; but it *shall* 5674
36: 3 which *was* **o** the house, and Shebna 5921
36:22 that *was* **o** the household, and Shebna 5921
37: 2 who *was* **o** the household, and Shebna 5921
40:19 and the goldsmith **spreadeth** it **o** with gold, 7554
40:27 my judgment is **passed o** from my God? 5674
41: 2 before him, and **made** *him* **rule o** kings? 7287
45:14 shall **come o** unto thee, and they shall be 5674
45:14 in chains they shall **come o**, and they shall 5674
47: 2 the leg, uncover the thigh, **pass o** the rivers. 5674
51:10 the sea a way for the ransomed to **pass o**? 5674
51:23 to thy soul, Bow down, that we may **go o**: 5674
51:23 and as the street, to them that **went o**. 5674
52: 5 they that **rule o** them make *them* to howl, 4910
54: 9 of Noah should no more go **o** the earth; 5921
62: 5 *as* the bridegroom rejoiceth **o** the bride, *so* 5921

Isa 62: 5 the bride, so shall thy God rejoice o thee. 5921
63:19 We are thine: thou never barest rule o 871.1
Jer 1:10 I have this day set thee o the nations and 5921
1:10 thee over the nations and o the kingdoms, 5921
2:10 For pass o the isles of Chittim, and see; and 5674
5: 6 a leopard shall watch o their cities: 5921
5:22 though they roar, yet can they not pass o it? 5674
6:17 Also I set watchmen o you, 5921
13:21 them to be captains, and as chief o thee: 5921
15: 3 I will appoint o them four kinds, saith 5921
23: 4 I will set up shepherds o them which shall 5921
31:28 that like as I have watched o them, to pluck 5921
31:28 so will I watch o them, to build, and 5921
31:39 go forth o against it upon the hill Gareb, 5048
32:41 I will rejoice o them to do them good, and 5921
33:26 his seed to be rulers o the seed of Abraham, 413
40: 5 hath made governor o the cities of Judah, 871.1
40:11 that he had set o them Gedaliah the son of 5921
41: 2 of Babylon had made governor o the land. 871.1
41:10 and departed to go o to the Ammonites. 5674
43:10 he shall spread his royal pavilion o them. 5921
44:27 I will watch o them for evil, and not for 5921
48:32 thy plants are gone o the sea, they reach 5674
48:40 an eagle, and shall spread his wings o Moab. 413
49:19 who is a chosen man, that I may appoint o 413
49:22 the eagle, and spread his wings o Bozrah: 5921
50:44 who is a chosen man, that I may appoint o 413
La 2:17 he hath caused thine enemy to rejoice o 5921
3:54 Waters flowed o mine head; then I said, 5921
5: 8 Servants have ruled o us: there is none that 871.1
Eze 1:20 were lifted up o against them: 5980+3807.1
1:21 were lifted up o against them: 5980+3807.1
1:22 stretched forth o their heads above. 5921
1:25 from the firmament that was o their heads, 5921
1:26 above the firmament that was o their heads 5921
3:13 the noise of the wheels o against 5980+3807.1
9: 1 Cause them that have charge o the city to 6486
10: 1 o them as it were a sapphire stone, 5921
10: 2 the cherubims, and scatter them o the city. 5921
10: 4 and stood o the threshold of the house; 5921
10:18 of the house, and stood o the cherubims. 5921
10:19 the glory of the God of Israel was o them 5921
11:22 the glory of the God of Israel was o them 5921
16: 8 I spread my skirt o thee, and covered thy 5921
16:27 I have stretched out my hand o thee, and 5921
19: 8 the provinces, and spread their net o him: 5921
20:33 and with fury poured out, will I rule o you: 5921
27:32 lament o thee, saying, What city is like 5921
29:15 that they shall no more rule o the nations. 871.1
32: 3 spread out my net o thee with a company of 5921
32: 8 lights of heaven will I make dark o thee, 5921
32:31 shall be comforted o all his multitude, 5921
34:23 I will set up one shepherd o them, and 5921
37:24 David my servant shall be king o them; 5921
40:18 o against the length of the gates 5980+3807.1
40:23 the gate of the inner court was o against 5048
41: 6 one o another, and thirty in order; 413
41:15 o against the separate place which 413+6440
41:16 on their three stories, o against the door, 5048
42: 1 that was o against the separate place, 5048
42: 3 O against the twenty cubits which were for 5048
42: 3 o against the pavement which was for 5048
42: 7 the wall that was without o against 5980+3807.1
42:10 o against the separate place, and over 413+6440
42:10 and o against the building. 413+6440
45: 6 o against the oblation of the holy 5980+3807.1
45: 7 the length shall be o against 5980+3807.1
46: 9 he came in, but shall go forth o against it. 5226
47: 5 and it was a river that I could not pass o: 5674
47: 5 swim in, a river that could not be passed o. 5674
47:20 till a man come o against Hamath. 5227
48:13 o against the border of the priests, 5980+3807.1
48:15 that are left in the breadth o against 5921+6440
48:18 the residue in length o against 5980+3807.1
48:18 it shall be o against the oblation of 5980+3807.1
48:21 o against the five and 413+6440
48:21 westward o against the five and 5921+6440
48:21 o against the portions for 5980+3807.1
Da 1:11 whom the prince of the eunuchs had set o 5921
2:38 and hath made thee ruler o them all 871.2
2:39 which shall bear rule o all the earth. 871.2
2:48 made him ruler o the whole province of 5922
2:48 chief of the governors o all the wise men of 5922
2:49 o the affairs of the province of Babylon: 5922
3:12 set o the affairs of the province of Babylon, 5922
4:16 unto him; and let seven times pass o him. 5922
4:17 and setteth up o it the basest of men. 5922
4:23 of the field, till seven times pass o him; 5922
4:25 and seven times shall pass o thee, 5922
4:32 as oxen, and seven times shall pass o thee, 5922
5: 5 wrote o against the candlestick upon 3807.2
5:21 that he appointeth o it whomsoever he will. 5922
6: 1 It pleased Darius to set o the kingdom an 5922
6: 1 which should be o the whole kingdom; 871.2
6: 2 o these three presidents; of whom 4481+5924
6: 3 the king thought to set him o the whole 5922
9: 1 which was made king o the realm of 5921
11:39 he shall cause them to rule o many, and 4910
11:40 and shall overflow and pass o. 5674
11:43 he shall have power o the treasures of gold 871.1
11:43 and o all the precious things of Egypt: 871.1
Hos 10: 5 for the people thereof shall mourn o it, and 5921
10:11 the corn: but I passed o upon her fair neck: 5674
12: 4 he had power o the angel, and prevailed: 413
Joel 2:17 that the heathen should rule o them: 4910
Ob 1:12 neither shouldest thou have rejoiced o 3807.1
Jnh 2: 3 all thy billows and thy waves passed o me. 5921
4: 6 and made it to come up o Jonah, 4480+5921
4: 6 that it might be a shadow o his head, 5921
Mic 3: 6 the sun shall go down o the prophets, and 5921
3: 6 and the day shall be dark o them. 5921
4: 7 the LORD shall reign o them in mount 5921
Na 3:19 the bruit of thee shall clap the hands o thee: 5921
Hab 1:11 and he shall pass o, and offend, 5674
1:14 creeping things, that have no ruler o them? 871.1
2:19 it is laid o with gold and silver, and there is 8610
Zep 3:17 he will save, he will rejoice o thee with joy; 5921
3:17 in his love, he will joy o thee with singing. 5921
Hag 1:10 Therefore the heaven o you is stayed from 5921
Zec 1:21 which lift up their horn o the land of Judah 413
5: 3 This is the curse that goeth forth o the face 5921
9:14 the LORD shall be seen o them, and 5921
14: 9 the LORD shall be king o all the earth: 5921
Mt 2: 9 and stood o where the young child was. 1883
9: 1 and passed o, and came into his own city. 1276
10:23 Ye shall not have gone o the cities of 5055
14:34 And when they were gone o, they came 1276
20:25 of the Gentiles exercise dominion o them, 2634
21: 2 Go into the village o against you, and 561
24:45 whom his lord hath made ruler o his 1909
24:47 That he shall make him ruler o all his 1909
25:21 thou hast been faithful o a few things, I will 1909
25:21 o many things: enter thou into the joy of 1909
25:23 thou hast been faithful o a few things, I will 1909
25:23 o many things: enter thou into the joy of 1909
27:37 And set up o his head his accusation 1883
27:45 darkness o all the land unto the ninth hour. 1909
27:61 other Mary, sitting o against the sepulchre. 561
Mk 4:35 Let us pass o unto the other side. 1330
5: 1 And they came o unto the other side of NIG
5:21 And when Jesus was passed o again by 1276
6: 7 and gave them power o unclean spirits; 1849
6:53 And when they had passed o, they came 1276
10:42 rule o the Gentiles exercise lordship over 757
10:42 over the Gentiles exercise lordship o them; 2634
11: 2 Go your way into the village o against you: 2713
12:41 And Jesus sat o against the treasury, and 2713
13: 3 the mount of Olives o against the temple, 2713
15:26 of his accusation was written o, 1924
15:33 there was darkness o the whole land until 1909
15:39 which stood o against him, saw that 1537+1727
Lk 1:33 And he shall reign o the house of Jacob for 1909
2: 8 keeping watch o their flock by night. 1909
4:10 He shall give his angels charge o thee, to 4012
4:39 And he stood o her, and rebuked the fever; 1883
6:38 and shaken together, and running o, 5240
8:22 Let us go o unto the other side of the lake. 1330
8:26 of the Gadarenes, which is o against Galilee. 495
9: 1 gave them power and authority o all devils, 1909
10:19 and o all the power of the enemy: 1909
11:42 and pass o judgment and the love of God: 3928
11:44 the men that walk o them are not aware of 1883
12:14 who made me a judge or a divider o you? 1909
12:42 whom his lord shall make ruler o his 1909
12:44 that he will make him ruler o all that he 1909
15: 7 that likewise joy shall be in heaven o one 1909
15: 7 more than o ninety and nine just persons 1909
15:10 angels of God o one sinner that repenteth. 1909
19:14 We will not have this man to reign o us. 1909
19:17 very little, have thou authority o ten cities. 1883
19:19 likewise to him, Be thou also o five cities. 1883
19:27 which would not that I should reign o them, 1909
19:30 Go ye into the village o against you; in 2713
19:41 he beheld the city, and wept o it, 1909
22:25 of the Gentiles exercise lordship o them; 2961
23:38 And a superscription also was written o 1909
23:44 there was a darkness o all the earth until 1909
Jn 6: 1 After these things Jesus went o the sea of 4008
6:13 which remained o and above unto them 4052
6:17 and went o the sea towards Capernaum. 4008
17: 2 As thou hast given him power o all flesh, 1849
18: 1 forth with his disciples o the brook Cedron, 4008
Ac 6: 3 whom we may appoint o this business. 1909
7:10 and he made him governor o Egypt and 1909
7:11 Now there came a dearth o all the land of 1909
7:16 And were carried o into Sychem, and 3346
7:27 Who made thee a ruler and a judge o us? 1909
8: 2 and made great lamentation o him. 1909
16: 9 Come o into Macedonia, and help us. 1224
18:23 and went o all the country of Galatia and 1330
19:13 took upon them to call o them which had 1909
20: 2 And when he had gone o those parts, and 1330
20:15 and came the next day o against Chios; 481
20:28 o the which the Holy Ghost hath made you 1722
21: 2 And finding a ship sailing o unto Phenicia, 1276
27: 5 And when we had sailed o the sea of 1277
27: 7 and scarce were come o against Cnidus, 2596
27: 7 we sailed under Crete, o against Salmone; 2596
Ro 1:28 God gave them o to a reprobate mind, to do 3860
5:14 even o them that had not sinned after 1909
6: 9 death hath no more dominion o him. 2961
6:14 For sin shall not have dominion o you: 2961
7: 1 how that the law hath dominion o a man, 2961
9: 5 the flesh Christ came, who is o all, 1909
9:21 Hath not the potter power o the clay, of 1849
10:12 for the same Lord o all is rich unto all that NIG
15:12 and he that shall rise to reign o the Gentiles; 757
1Co 7:37 but hath power o his own will, and hath so 4012
9:12 If others be partakers of this power o you, 1849
2Co 1:24 Not for that we have dominion o your 2961
3:13 not as Moses, which put a vail o his face, 1909
8:15 He that had gathered much had nothing o; 4121
11: 2 For I am jealous o you with godly jealousy: NIG
Eph 1:22 gave him to be the head o all things to 5228
4:19 given themselves o unto lasciviousness, 3860
Col 2:15 of them openly, triumphing o them in it. 2358
1Th 3: 7 we were comforted o you in all our 1909
5:12 and are o you in the Lord, and 4291
1Ti 2:12 nor to usurp authority o the man, but to be 831
Heb 2: 7 and didst set him o the works of thy hands: 1909
3: 6 But Christ as a Son o his own house; 1909
9: 5 And o it the cherubims of glory shadowing 5231
10:21 And having a high priest o the house of 1909
13: 7 Remember them which have the rule o 2233
13:17 Obey them that have the rule o you, and 2233
13:24 Salute all them that have the rule o you, 2233
Jas 5:14 and let them pray o him, anointing him 1909
1Pe 3:12 For the eyes of the Lord are o the righteous, 1909
5: 3 Neither as being lords o God's heritage, 2634
Jude 1: 7 giving themselves o to fornication, 1608
Rev 2:26 to him will I give power o the nations: 1909
6: 8 And power was given unto them o 1909
9:11 And they had a king o them, which is 1909
11: 6 have power o waters to turn them to blood, 1909
11:10 dwell upon the earth shall rejoice o them, 1909
13: 7 and power was given him o all kindreds, 1909
14:18 out from the altar, which had power o fire; 1909
15: 2 them that had gotten the victory o the beast, 1537
15: 2 and o his image, and over his mark, 1537
15: 2 and over his image, and o his mark, 1537
15: 2 his mark, and o the number of his name, 1537
16: 9 of God, which hath power o these plagues: 1909
17:18 which reigneth o the kings of the earth. 1909
18:11 of the earth shall weep and mourn o her; 1909
18:20 Rejoice o her, thou heaven, and ye holy 1909

OVERCAME (3) [OVERCOME]
Ac 19:16 and o them, and prevailed against them, so 2634
Rev 3:21 even as I also o, and am set down with my 3528
12:11 And they o him by the blood of the Lamb, 3528

OVERCAST See LOWRING

OVERCHARGE (1) [CHARGE, OVERCHARGED]
2Co 2: 5 but in part: that I may not o you all. 1912

OVERCHARGED (1) [OVERCHARGE]
Lk 21:34 lest at any time your hearts be o with 925

OVERCOME (22) [OVERCAME, OVERCOMETH]
Ge 49:19 Gad, a troop shall o him: but he shall 1464
49:19 overcome him: but he shall o at the last. 1464
Ex 32:18 is it the voice of them that cry for being o: 2476
Nu 13:30 for we are well able to o it. 3201+3201
22:11 peradventure I shall be able to o them, and 3898
2Ki 16: 5 they besieged Ahaz, but could not o him. 3898
SS 6: 5 thine eyes from me, for they have o me: 7292
Isa 28: 1 the fat valleys of them that are o with wine. 1986
Jer 23: 9 like a man whom wine hath o, because of 5674
Lk 11:22 than he shall come upon him, and o him, 3528
Jn 16:33 but be of good cheer; I have o the world. 3528
Ro 3: 4 and mightest o when thou art judged. 3528
12:21 Be not o of evil, but overcome evil with 3528
12:21 not overcome of evil, but o evil with good. 3528
2Pe 2:19 for of whom a man is o, of the same is he 2274
2:20 they are again entangled therein, and o, 2274
1Jn 2:13 because ye have o the wicked one. 3528
2:14 in you, and ye have o the wicked one. 3528
4: 4 are of God, little children, and have o them: 3528
Rev 11: 7 and shall o them, and kill them. 3528
13: 7 to make war with the saints, and to o them: 3528
17:14 with the Lamb, and the Lamb shall o them: 3528

OVERCOMETH (11) [OVERCOME]
1Jn 5: 4 For whatsoever is born of God o the world: 3528
5: 4 and this is the victory that o the world, 3528
5: 5 Who is he that o the world, but he that 3528
Rev 2: 7 To him that o will I give to eat of the tree 3528
2:11 He that o shall not be hurt of the second 3528
2:17 To him that o will I give to eat of 3528
2:26 And he that o, and keepeth my works unto 3528
3: 5 He that o, the same shall be clothed in 3528
3:12 Him that o will I make a pillar in 3528
3:21 To him that o will I grant to sit with me in 3528
21: 7 He that o shall inherit all things; and I will 3528

OVERDRIVE (1) [DRIVE]
Ge 33:13 if men should o them one day, all the flock 1849

OVERFLOW (13) [FLOW, OVERFLOWED, OVERFLOWETH, OVERFLOWING, OVERFLOWN]
Dt 11: 4 how he made the water of the Red sea to o 6687
Ps 69: 2 into deep waters, where the floods o me. 7857
69:15 Let not the waterflood o me, neither let 7857
Isa 8: 8 he shall o and go over, he shall reach even 7857
10:22 the consumption decreed shall o with 7857
28:17 and the waters shall o the hiding place. 7857
43: 2 through the rivers, they shall not o thee: 7857
Jer 47: 2 and shall o the land, and all that is therein; 7857
Da 11:10 certainly come, and o, and pass through: 7857
11:26 shall destroy him, and his army shall o: 7857
11:40 the countries, and shall o and pass over. 7857
Joel 2:24 and the fats shall o with wine and oil. 7783
3:13 you down; for the press is full, the fats o; 7783

OVERFLOWED (2) [OVERFLOW]
Ps 78:20 the waters gushed out, and the streams o; 7857
2Pe 3: 6 the world that then was, being o with water, 2626

OVERFLOWETH (1) [OVERFLOW]
Jos 3:15 (for Jordan o all his banks all 4390+5921

OVERFLOWING (11) [OVERFLOW]
Job 28:11 He bindeth the floods from o; and the thing 1065
38:25 divided a watercourse for the o of waters, 7858
Isa 28: 2 as a flood of mighty waters o, 7857
28:15 when the o scourge shall pass through, 7857
28:18 when the o scourge shall pass through, then 7857
30:28 his breath, as an o stream, shall reach to 7857
Jer 47: 2 shall be an o flood, and shall overflow 7857
Eze 13:11 there shall be an o shower; and ye, O great 7857
13:13 there shall be an o shower in mine anger, 7857
38:22 an o rain, and great hailstones, fire, and 7857
Hab 3:10 the o of the water passed by: the deep 2230

OVERFLOWN (3) [OVERFLOW]
1Ch 12:15 when it had o all his banks; 4390+5921
Job 22:16 whose foundation was o with a flood: 3332
Da 11:22 with the arms of a flood shall they be o 7857

OVERLAID (35) [OVERLAY]
Ex 26:32 four pillars of shittim wood o with gold: 6823
36:34 he o the boards with gold, and made their 6823

Ex 36:34 for the bars, and o the bars with gold. 6823
36:36 of shittim *wood*, and o them with gold: 6823
36:38 he o their chapiters and their fillets with 6823
37: 2 he o it with pure gold within and without, 6823
37: 4 of shittim wood, and o them with gold. 6823
37:11 he o it with pure gold, and made thereunto 6823
37:15 and o them with gold, to bear the table. 6823
37:26 he o it with pure gold, *both* the top of it, 6823
37:28 *of* shittim wood, and o them with gold. 6823
38: 2 were of the same: and he o it with brass. 6823
38: 6 *of* shittim wood, and o them with brass. 6823
38:28 and o their chapiters, and filleted them. 6823
1Ki 3:19 died in the night; because she o it. 5921+7901
6:20 he o it with pure gold; and *so* covered 6823
6:21 So Solomon o the house within with pure 6823
6:21 before the oracle; and he o it with gold. 6823
6:22 the whole house he o with gold, until *he* 6823
6:22 altar that *was* by the oracle he o with gold. 6823
6:28 And he o the cherubims with gold. 6823
6:30 the floor of the house he o with gold, 6823
6:32 o *them* with gold, and spread gold upon 6823
10:18 throne of ivory, and o it with the best gold. 6823
2Ki 18:16 which Hezekiah king of Judah had o, 6823
2Ch 3: 4 twenty: and he o it within with pure gold. 6823
3: 5 which he o with fine gold, and set thereon 2645
3: 7 He o also the house, the beams, the posts, 2645
3: 8 he o it with fine gold, *amounting* to six 2645
3: 9 And he o the upper chambers with gold. 2645
3:10 of image work, and o them with gold. 6823
4: 9 and o the doors of them with brass. 6823
9:17 throne of ivory, and o it with pure gold. 6823
SS 5:14 his belly *is as* bright ivory o *with* sapphires. 5968
Heb 9: 4 the ark of the covenant o round about with *4028*

OVERLAY (13) [LAY, OVERLAID, OVERLAYING]
Ex 25:11 thou shalt o it with pure gold, within and 6823
25:11 within and without shalt thou o it, and 6823
25:13 of shittim wood, and o them with gold. 6823
25:24 thou shalt o it with pure gold, and 6823
25:28 o them with gold, that the table may be 6823
26:29 thou shalt o the boards with gold, and make 6823
26:29 and thou shalt o the bars with gold. 6823
26:37 of shittim *wood*, and o them with gold, 6823
27: 2 of the same: and thou shalt o it with brass. 6823
27: 6 of shittim wood, and o them with brass. 6823
30: 3 thou shalt o it with pure gold, the top 6823
30: 5 *of* shittim wood, and o them with gold. 6823
1Ch 29: 4 to o the walls of the houses *withal:* 2902

OVERLAYING (2) [OVERLAY]
Ex 38:17 the o of their chapiters *of* silver; and all 6826
38:19 the o of their chapiters and their fillets *of* 6826

OVERLIVED (1) [LIVE]
Jos 24:31 all the days of the elders that o 310+748+3117

OVERMUCH (1) [MUCH]
2Co 2: 7 one should be swallowed up with o sorrow. *4055*

OVERPASS (1) [OVERPAST]
Jer 5:28 yea, they o the deeds of the wicked: 5674

OVERPAST (2) [OVERPASS]
Ps 57: 1 my refuge, until *these* calamities be o. 5674
Isa 26:20 a little moment, until the indignation be o. 5674

OVERPLUS (1)
Lev 25:27 restore the o unto the man to whom he sold 5736

OVERRAN (1) [OVERRUNNING]
2Sa 18:23 ran *by* the way of the plain, and o Cushi. 5674

OVERRUNNING (1) [OVERRAN, RUN]
Na 1: 8 with an o flood he will make an utter end of 5674

OVERSEE (2) [OVERSEER, OVERSEERS, OVERSIGHT, SEE]
1Ch 9:29 *Some* of them also *were* appointed to o 5921
2Ch 2: 2 and six hundred to o them. 5329+5921

OVERSEER (7) [OVERSEE]
Ge 39: 4 he **made** him o over his house, and all *that* 6485
39: 5 time *that* he had **made** him o in his house, 6485
Ne 11: 9 Joel the son of Zichri *was* their o: 6496
11:14 their o *was* Zabdiel, the son of *one of* 6496
11:22 The o also of the Levites at Jerusalem *was* 6496
12:42 singers sang loud, with Jezrahiah *their* o. 6496
Pr 6: 7 Which having no guide, o, or ruler, 7860

OVERSEERS (6) [OVERSEE]
2Ch 2:18 and six hundred o to set the people a work. 5329
31:13 *were* o under the hand of Cononiah and 6496
34:12 and the o of them *were* Jahath and Obadiah, 6485
34:13 *were* o of all that wrought the work in any 5329
34:17 have delivered it into the hand of the o, and 6485
Ac 20:28 the which the Holy Ghost hath made you o, *1985*

OVERSHADOW (2) [OVERSHADOWED, SHADOW]
Lk 1:35 and the power of the Highest shall o thee: *1982*
Ac 5:15 of Peter passing by might o some of them. *1982*

OVERSHADOWED (3) [OVERSHADOW]
Mt 17: 5 he yet spake, behold, a bright cloud o them: *1982*
Mk 9: 7 And there was a cloud that o them: and *1982*
Lk 9:34 thus spake, there came a cloud, and o them: *1982*

OVERSIGHT (11) [OVERSEE]
Ge 43:12 in your hand; peradventure it *was* an o: 4870
Nu 3:32 *have* the o of them that keep the charge of 6486
4:16 *and* the o of all the tabernacle, and of all 6486
2Ki 12:11 that **had** the o *of* the house of the LORD: 6485
22: 5 that have the o of the house of the LORD: 6485
2Ki 22: 9 that **have** the o *of* the house of the LORD. 6485
1Ch 9:23 their children had the o **of** the gates of 5921
2Ch 34:10 that had the o of the house of the LORD, 6485
Ne 11:16 **had the** o of the outward business of 5921
13: 4 **having the** o of the chamber of 5414+871.1
1Pe 5: 2 **taking the** o *thereof,* not by constraint, but *1983*

OVERSPREAD (1) [SPREAD, OVERSPREADING]
Ge 9:19 and of them was the whole earth o. 5310

OVERSPREADING (1) [OVERSPREAD]
Da 9:27 for the o of abominations he *shall* make *it* 3671

OVERTAKE (17) [OVERTAKEN, OVERTAKETH, OVERTOOK, TAKE]
Ge 44: 4 when thou dost o them, say unto them, 5381
Ex 15: 9 The enemy said, I will pursue, I will o, 5381
Dt 19: 6 o him, because the way is long, and 5381
28: 2 blessings shall come on thee, and o thee, 5381
28:15 curses shall come upon thee, and o thee: 5381
28:45 shall pursue thee, and o thee, till thou be 5381
Jos 2: 5 after them quickly; for ye shall o them. 5381
1Sa 30: 8 shall I o them? And he answered him, 5381
30: 8 for thou shalt **surely** o *them,* and 5381+5381
2Sa 15:14 lest he o us suddenly, and bring evil upon 5381
Isa 59: 9 far from us, neither doth justice o us: 5381
Jer 42:16 shall o you there in the land of Egypt, and 5381
Hos 2: 7 after her lovers, but she shall not o them; 5381
10: 9 the children of iniquity did not o them. 5381
Am 9:10 The evil shall not o nor prevent us. 5066
9:13 that the plowman shall o the reaper, and 5066
1Th 5: 4 that *that* day should o you as a thief. *2638*

OVERTAKEN (2) [OVERTAKE]
Ps 18:37 I have pursued mine enemies, and o them: 5381
Gal 6: 1 Brethren, if a man be o in a fault, ye which *4301*

OVERTAKETH (1) [OVERTAKE]
1Ch 21:12 while that the sword of thine enemies o 5381

OVERTHREW (12) [OVERTHROW]
Ge 19:25 he o those cities, and all the plain, and all 2015
19:29 when he o the cities in the which Lot dwelt. 2015
Ex 14:27 the LORD o the Egyptians in the midst of 5287
Dt 29:23 which the LORD o in his anger, and in his 2015
Ps 136:15 o Pharaoh and his host in the Red sea: 5287
Isa 13:19 shall be as when God o Sodom and 4114
Jer 20:16 man be as the cities which the LORD o, 2015
50:40 As God o Sodom and Gomorrah and 4114
Am 4:11 as God o Sodom and Gomorrah, and 4114
Mt 21:12 and o the tables of the moneychangers, and *2690*
Mk 11:15 and o the tables of the money-changers, *2690*
Jn 2:15 out the changers' money, and o the tables; *390*

OVERTHROW (19) [OVERTHREW, OVERTHROWETH, OVERTHROWN, THROW]
Ge 19:21 that I will not o *this* city, for the which thou 2015
19:29 and sent Lot out of the midst of the o, 2018
Ex 23:24 thou shalt **utterly** o them, and 2040+2040
Dt 12: 3 you shall o their altars, and break their 5422
29:23 like the o of Sodom, and Gomorrah, 4114
2Sa 10: 3 the city, and to spy it out, and to o it? 2015
11:25 battle *more* strong against the city, and o it: 2040
1Ch 19: 3 to search, and to o, and to spy out the land? 2015
Ps 106:26 against them, to o them in the wilderness: 5307
106:27 To o their seed also among the nations, and 5307
140: 4 who have purposed to o my goings. 1760
140:11 evil shall hunt the violent man to o *him.* 4073
Pr 18: 5 the wicked, to o the righteous in judgment. 5186
Jer 49:18 As *in* the o of Sodom and Gomorrah and 4114
Hag 2:22 I will o the throne of kingdoms, and I will 2015
2:22 I will o the chariots, and those that ride in 2015
Ac 5:39 But if it be of God, ye cannot o it; *2647*
2Ti 2:18 is past already; and o the faith of some. *396*
2Pe 2: 6 into ashes condemned *them* with an o, *2692*

OVERTHROWETH (5) [OVERTHROW]
Job 12:19 princes away spoiled, and o the mighty. 5557
Pr 13: 6 in the way: but wickedness o the sinner. 5557
21:12 *but God* o the wicked for *their* wickedness. 5557
22:12 and he o the words of the transgressor. 5557
29: 4 the land: but he that receiveth gifts o it. 2040

OVERTHROWN (16) [OVERTHROW]
Ex 15: 7 thou hast o them that rose up against thee: 2040
Jdg 9:40 before him, and many were o *and* wounded, 5307
2Sa 17: 9 when *some* of them be o at the first, 5307
2Ch 14:13 the Ethiopians were o, that they could not 5307
Job 19: 6 Know now that God hath o me, and 5791
Ps 141: 6 When their judges are o in stony places, 8058
Pr 11:11 but it is o by the mouth of the wicked. 2040
12: 7 The wicked *are* o, and *are* not: but 2015
14:11 The house of the wicked shall be o: but 8045
Isa 1: 7 and *it is* desolate, as o by strangers. 4114
Jer 18:23 thy sight, but let them be o before thee; 3782
La 4: 6 that was o as in a moment, and no hands 2015
Da 11:41 and many *countries* shall be o: 3782
Am 4:11 I have o *some* of you, as God overthrew 2015
Jnh 3: 4 Yet forty days, and Nineveh *shall be* o. 2015
1Co 10: 5 for they were o in the wilderness. *2693*

OVERTOOK (10) [OVERTAKE]
Ge 31:23 and they o him in the mount Gilead. 1692
31:25 Laban o Jacob. Now Jacob had pitched his 5381
44: 6 he o them, and he spake unto them these 5381
Ex 14: 9 o them encamping by the sea, 5381
Jdg 18:22 and o the children of Dan. 1692
20:42 the battle o them; and them which *came* out 1692
2Ki 25: 5 the king, and o him in the plains of Jericho: 5381
Jer 39: 5 and o Zedekiah in the plains of Jericho: 5381
52: 8 and o Zedekiah in the plains of Jericho; 5381
La 1: 3 all her persecutors o her between the straits. 5381

OVERTURN (4) [OVERTURNED, OVERTURNETH, TURN]
Job 12:15 he sendeth them out, and they o the earth. 2015
Eze 21:27 I will o, overturn, overturn it: and it shall be 5754
21:27 I will overturn, o, overturn it: and it shall be 5754
21:27 I will overturn, overturn, o it: and it shall be 5754

OVERTURNED (1) [OVERTURN]
Jdg 7:13 that it fell, and o it, 2015+4605+1886.5+3807.1

OVERTURNETH (3) [OVERTURN]
Job 9: 5 they know not: which o them in his anger. 2015
28: 9 the rock; he o the mountains by the roots. 2015
34:25 he o *them* in the night, so that they are 2015

OVERWHELM (1) [OVERWHELMED]
Job 6:27 Yea, ye o the fatherless, and you dig 5307+5921

OVERWHELMED (8) [OVERWHELM]
Ps 55: 5 are come upon me, and horror hath o me. 3680
61: 2 will I cry unto thee, when my heart is o: 5848
77: 3 I complained, and my spirit was o. Selah. 5848
78:53 they feared not: but the sea o their enemies. 3680
102: T when he is o, and poureth out his complaint 5848
124: 4 the waters had o us, the stream had gone 7857
142: 3 When my spirit was o within me, then 5848
143: 4 Therefore is my spirit o within me; 5848

OWE (1) [OWEST, OWETH]
Ro 13: 8 O no *man* any *thing,* but to love one *3784*

OWEST (4) [OWE]
Mt 18:28 by the throat, saying, Pay me that thou o. *3784*
Lk 16: 5 the first, How much o thou unto my lord? *3784*
16: 7 said he to another, And how much o thou? *3784*
Phm 1:19 o unto me even thine own self **besides**. *4359*

OWETH (2) [OWE]
Ac 21:11 at Jerusalem bind the man that o this girdle, *1510*
Phm 1:18 If he hath wronged thee, or o *thee* ought, *3784*

OWL (10) [OWLS]
Lev 11:16 the o, and the night hawk, and 1323+3284
11:17 the **little** o, and the cormorant, and 3563
11:17 and the cormorant, and the **great** o, 3244
Dt 14:15 the o, and the night hawk, and 1323+3284
14:16 The **little** o, and the great owl, and 3563
14:16 little owl, and the **great** o, and the swan, 3244
Ps 102: 6 the wilderness: I am like an o of the desert. 3563
Isa 34:11 the o also and the raven shall dwell in it: 3244
34:14 the **shrich** o also shall rest there, and 3917
34:15 There shall the **great** o make her nest, and 7091

OWLS (6) [OWL]
Job 30:29 to dragons, and a companion to o. 1323+3284
Isa 13:21 o shall dwell there, and satyrs shall 1323+3284
34:13 of dragons, *and* a court for o. 1323+3284
43:20 honour me, the dragons and the o: 1323+3284
Jer 50:39 and the o shall dwell therein: 1323+3284
Mic 1: 8 the dragons, and mourning as the o. 1323+3284

OWN (596) [OWNER, OWNERS, OWNETH]
Ge 1:27 So God created man in **his** o image, in 2050.2
5: 3 and begat *a son* in **his** o likeness, 2050.2
14:14 his trained *servants,* born in **his** o house, 2050.2
15: 4 he that shall come forth out of **thine** o 3509.2
30:25 that I may go unto **mine** o place, and 2967.1
30:30 now when shall I provide for **mine** o 2967.1
30:40 he put **his** o flocks by 2050.2+3807.1
47:24 four parts shall be **your** o, for seed of 3641.1
Ex 5:16 but the fault *is* in **thine** o people. 3509.2
18:27 and he went his way into **his** o land. 2050.2
21:36 and the dead shall be **his** o. 2050.2+3807.1
22: 5 of the best of **his** o field, and of the best 1930.2
22: 5 of the best of **his** o vineyard, shall he 2050.2
32:13 to whom thou swarest by **thine** o **self**, 3509.2
Lev 1: 3 he shall offer it of **his** o voluntary will at 2050.2
7:30 **His** o hands shall bring the offerings of 2050.2
14:15 *it* into the palm of **his** o left hand: 3548+1886.1
14:26 oil into the palm of **his** o left hand: 3548+1886.1
16:29 *at all, whether it be* one of **your** o **country**, 249
17:15 *beasts, whether it be* one of **your** o **country**, 249
18:10 for theirs *is* **thine** o nakedness. 3509.2
18:26 *neither* any of **your** o **nation**, nor any 249
19: 5 ye shall offer it at **your** o will. 3641.1
21:14 he shall take a virgin of **his** o people to 2050.2
22:19 *Ye shall offer* at **your** o will a male 3641.1
22:29 unto the LORD, offer *it* at **your** o will. 3641.1
24:22 the stranger, as for **one of** your o **country**: 249
25: 5 **That which groweth of it o accord** of thy 5599
25:41 shall return unto **his** o family, and 2050.2
Nu 1:52 every man by **his** o camp, and every man 1930.2
1:52 every man by **his** o standard, 2050.2
2: 2 of Israel shall pitch by **his** o standard, 2050.2
10:30 I will depart to **mine** o land, and to my 2967.1
13:33 we were in **our** o sight as grasshoppers, 5105.1
15:39 that ye seek not after **your** o heart and 3641.1
15:39 not after your own heart and **your** o eyes, 3641.1
16:28 for *I have* not *done them* of **mine** o mind. 2967.1
16:38 of these sinners against **their** o souls, 3963.1
24:13 to do *either* good or bad of **mine** o mind; 2967.1
27: 3 but died in **his** o sin, and had no sons. 2050.2
32:42 and called it Nobah, after **his** o name. 2050.2
36: 9 shall keep himself to **his** o inheritance. 2050.2
Dt 3:14 called them after **his** o name, 2050.2
12: 8 every man whatsoever *is* right in **his** o 2050.2
13: 6 or thy friend, which *is* as **thine** o soul, 3509.2
22: 2 thou shalt bring it unto **thine** o house, and 3509.2
23:24 thou mayest eat grapes thy fill at **thine** o 3509.2
24:13 that he may sleep in **his** o raiment, and 2050.2
24:16 every man shall be put to death for **his** o 2050.2
28:53 thou shalt eat the fruit of thine o body, 3509.2
33: 9 his brethren, nor knew **his** o children: 2050.2

Jos 7:11 have put *it* even amongst **their o** stuff. 1992.1
20: 6 come unto **his o** city, and unto his own 2050.2
20: 6 unto his own city, and unto **his o** house, 2050.2
Jdg 2:19 they ceased not from **their o** doings, 1992.1
7: 2 saying, **Mine o** hand hath saved me. 2967.1
8:29 of Joash went and dwelt in **his o** house. 2050.2
17: 6 did *that* which *was* right in **his o** eyes. 2050.2
21:25 did *that* which *was* right in **his o** eyes. 2050.2
Ru 4: 6 for myself, lest I mar **mine o** inheritance: 2967.1
1Sa 2:20 And they went unto **their o** home. 2050.2
5:11 let it go again to **his o** place, that it slay 2050.2
6: 9 if it goeth up *by* the way of **his o** coast *to* 2050.2
13:14 hath sought him a man after **his o** heart, 2050.2
14:46 and the Philistines went to **their o** place. 3963.1
15:17 When thou *wast* little in **thine o** sight, 3509.2
18: 1 and Jonathan loved him as **his o** soul. 2050.2
18: 3 because he loved him as **his o** soul. 2050.2
20:17 for he loved him as he loved **his o** soul. 2050.2
20:30 the son of Jesse to **thine o** confusion, 3509.2
25:26 *from* avenging thyself with **thine o** hand, 3509.2
25:33 *from* avenging myself with **mine o** hand. 2967.1
25:39 the wickedness of Nabal upon **his o** head. 2050.2
28: 3 buried him in Ramah, even in **his o** city. 2050.2
2Sa 4:11 person in **his o** house upon his bed? 2050.2
6:22 and will be base in **mine o** sight: 2967.1
7:10 that they may dwell in a place of **their o**, 2050.2
7:21 and according to **thine o** heart, 3509.2
12: 3 it did eat of **his o** meat, and drank of his 2050.2
12: 3 drank of **his o** cup, and lay in his bosom, 2050.2
12: 4 he spared to take of **his o** flock and of his 2050.2
12: 4 to take of his own flock and of **his o** herd, 2050.2
12:11 up evil against thee out of **thine o** house, 3509.2
12:20 he came to **his o** house; and when he 2050.2
14:24 Let him turn to **his o** house, and let him 2050.2
14:24 So Absalom returned to **his o** house, and 2050.2
17:11 *that* thou go to battle in **thine o** person. 3509.2
18:13 wrought falsehood against **mine o** life: 2967.1
18:18 he called the pillar after **his o** name: and 2050.2
19:28 among them that did eat at **thine o** table. 3509.2
19:30 is come *again* in peace unto **his o** house. 2050.2
19:37 that I may die in **mine o** city, *and* 2967.1
19:39 and he returned unto **his o** place. 2050.2
23:21 and slew him with **his o** spear. 2050.2
1Ki 1:12 that thou mayest save **thine o** life, and 3509.3
1:33 son to ride upon **mine o** mule, 2967.1+3807.1
2:23 not spoken this word against **his o** life. 2050.2
2:26 Get thee *to* Anathoth, unto **thine o** fields; 3509.2
2:32 shall return his blood upon **his o** head, 2050.2
2:34 he was buried in **his o** house in 2050.2
2:37 thy blood shall be upon **thine o** head. 3509.2
2:44 return thy wickedness upon **thine o** head; 3509.2
3: 1 had made an end of building **his o** house, 2050.2
7: 1 Solomon was building **his o** house 2050.2
8:38 every man the plague of **his o** heart, 2050.2
9:15 **his o** house, and Millo, and the wall of 2050.2
10: 6 It was a true report that I heard in **mine o** 2967.1
10:13 So she turned and went to **her o** country, 1886.3
11:19 that he gave him *to* wife the sister of **his o** 2050.2
11:21 that I may go to **mine o** country. 2967.1
11:22 thou seekest to go to **thine o** country? 3509.2
12:16 now see to **thine o** house, David. 3509.2
12:33 which he had devised of **his o** heart; 2050.2
13:30 he laid his carcase in **his o** grave; and 2050.2
14:12 thou therefore, get thee to **thine o** house: 3509.3
17:19 he abode, and laid him upon **his o** bed. 2050.2
22:36 his city, and every man to **his o** country. 2050.2
2Ki 2:12 he took hold of **his o** clothes, and 2050.2
3:27 from him, and returned to *their o* land. NIH
4:13 I dwell among **mine o** people. 2967.1
12:18 **his o** hallowed *things*, and all the gold 2050.2
14: 6 every man shall be put to death for **his o** 2050.2
17:23 So was Israel carried away out of **their o** 2050.2
17:29 every nation made gods of **their o**, 2050.2
17:33 the LORD, and served **their o** gods, 1992.1
18:27 that *they* may eat **their o** dung, and drink 3963.1
18:27 and drink **their o** piss with you? 1992.1
18:31 *then* eat ye every man of **his o** vine, and 2050.2
18:32 take you away to a land like **your o** land, 3641.1
19: 7 a rumour, and shall return to **his o** land; 2050.2
19: 7 him to fall by the sword in **his o** land. 2050.2
19:34 for **mine o** sake, and for my servant 2967.1
20: 6 I will defend this city for **mine o** sake, 2967.1
21:18 was buried in the garden of **his o** house, 2050.2
21:23 and slew the king in **his o** house. 2050.2
23:30 and buried him in **his o** sepulchre. 2050.2
1Ch 11:23 and slew him with **his o** spear. 2050.2
17:19 and according to **thine o** heart, 3509.2
17:21 to redeem *to be* **his o** people, 2050.2+3807.1
17:22 make **thine o** people for ever; 3509.2+3807.1
29: 3 I have of **mine o** proper good, 2967.1+3807.1
29:14 of thee, and of thine o have we given thee. 3027
29:16 *cometh* of thine hand, and *is* all **thine o**. 3509.2
2Ch 6:23 recompensing his way upon **his o** head; 2050.2
6:29 when every one shall know **his o** sore and 2050.2
6:29 shall know his own sore and **his o** grief, 2050.2
7:11 in **his o** house, he prosperously effected. 2050.2
8: 1 the house of the LORD, and **his o** house, 2050.2
9: 5 I heard in **mine o** land of thine acts, 2967.1
9:12 went away to **her o** land, she and 1886.3
10:16 *and* now, David, see to **thine o** house. 3509.2
16:14 they buried him in **his o** sepulchres, 2050.2
24:25 **his o** servants conspired against him for 2050.2
25: 4 but every man shall die for **his o** sin. 2050.2
25:15 which could not deliver **their o** people 3963.1
31: 1 man to his possession, into **their o** cities. 1992.1
32:21 returned with shame of face to **his o** land. 2050.2
32:21 they that came forth of **his o** bowels slew 2050.2
33:20 and they buried him *in* **his o** house: 2050.2
33:24 against him, and slew him in **his o** house. 2050.2
Ezr 7:13 *which are* **minded** of their o **freewill** to go 5069
Ne 4: 4 turn their reproach upon **their o** head, and 3963.1
6: 8 thou feignest them out of **thine o** heart. 3509.2
6:16 were much cast down in **their o** eyes: 1992.1
Est 1:22 that every man should bear rule in **his o** 2050.2
2: 7 were dead, took for **his o** daughter. 2050.2
Est 9:25 should return upon **his o** head, and that he 2050.2
Job 2:11 they came every one from **his o** place; 2050.2
5:13 He taketh the wise in **their o** craftiness: 3963.1
9:20 **mine o** mouth shall condemn me: 2967.1
9:31 and **mine o** clothes shall abhor me. 2967.1
13:15 I will maintain **mine o** ways before him. 2967.1
15: 6 **Thine o** mouth condemneth thee, and 3509.2
15: 6 yea, **thine o** lips testify against thee. 3509.2
18: 7 and **his o** counsel shall cast him down. 1930.2
18: 8 For he is cast into a net by **his o** feet, and 2050.2
19:17 for the children's *sake* of mine *o* body. NIH
20: 7 *Yet* he shall perish for ever like **his o** 2050.2
32: 1 because he *was* righteous in **his o** eyes. 2050.2
40:14 will I also confess unto thee that **thine o** 3509.2
Ps 4: 4 commune with **your o** heart upon your 3641.1
5:10 O God; let them fall by **their o** counsels; 1992.1
7:16 His mischief shall return upon **his o** head, 2050.2
7:16 dealing shall come down upon **his o** pate. 2050.2
9:15 in the net which they hid is **their o** foot 3963.1
9:16 the wicked is snared in the work of **his o** 2050.2
12: 4 tongue will we prevail; our lips *are* our **o**: 854
15: 4 *He that* sweareth to *his o* hurt, and NIH
17:10 They are inclosed *in* **their o** fat: 4123.1
20: 4 Grant thee according to **thine o** heart, and 3509.2
21:13 thou exalted, LORD, in **thine o** strength: 3509.2
22:29 and none can keep alive **his o** soul. 2050.2
33:12 the people *whom* he hath chosen for **his o** 2050.2
35:13 my prayer returned into **mine o** bosom. 2967.1
36: 2 For he flattereth himself in **his o** eyes, 2050.2
37:15 Their sword shall enter into **their o** heart, 3963.1
41: 9 Yea, **mine o** familiar friend, in whom I 2967.1
44: 3 the land in possession by **their o** sword, 3963.1
44: 3 neither did **their o** arm save them: 3963.1
45:10 forget also **thine o** people, and 3509.3
49:11 they call *their* lands after **their o** names. 3963.1
50:20 thou slanderest **thine o** mother's son. 3509.2
64: 8 So they shall make **their o** tongue to fall 3963.1
67: 6 *and* God, *even* **our o** God, shall bless us. 5105.1
74:22 Arise, O God, plead **thine o** cause: 3509.2
77: 6 I commune with **mine o** heart: and 2967.1
78:29 for he gave them **their o** desire; 3963.1
78:52 made **his o** people to go forth like sheep, 2050.2
81:12 So I gave them up unto **their o** heart's 3963.1
81:12 *and* they walked in **their o** counsels. 1992.1
94:23 he shall bring upon them **their o** iniquity, 3963.1
94:23 shall cut them off in **their o** wickedness; 3963.1
106:39 Thus were they defiled with **their o** 1992.1
106:39 went a whoring with **their o** inventions. 1992.1
106:40 insomuch that he abhorred **his o** 2050.2
109:29 let them cover *themselves with* **their o** 3963.1
138: 8 forsake not the works of **thine o** hands. 3509.2
140: 9 the mischief of **their o** lips cover them. 4123.1
141:10 Let the wicked fall into **their o** nets, 2050.2
Pr 1:18 they lay wait for **their o** blood; they lurk 3963.1
1:18 they lurk privily for **their o** lives. 3963.1
1:31 shall they eat of the fruit of **their o** way, 3963.1
1:31 and be filled with **their o** devices. 1992.1
3: 5 and lean not unto **thine o** understanding. 3509.2
3: 7 Be not wise in **thine o** eyes: fear 3509.2
5:15 Drink waters out of **thine o** cistern, and 3509.2
5:15 and running waters out of **thine o** well. 3509.2
5:17 Let them be only **thine o**, and 3509.2+3807.1
5:22 **His o** iniquities shall take the wicked 2050.2
6:32 he *that* doeth it destroyeth **his o** soul. 1931
8:36 he that sinneth *against* me wrongeth **his o** 2050.2
11: 5 the wicked shall fall by **his o** wickedness. 2050.2
11: 6 transgressors shall be taken in their o NIH
11:17 The merciful man doeth good to **his o** 2050.2
11:17 but *he that is* cruel troubleth **his o** flesh. 2050.2
11:19 he that pursueth evil *pursueth it* to **his o** 2050.2
11:29 He that troubleth **his o** house shall inherit 2050.2
12:15 The way of a fool *is* right in **his o** eyes: 2050.2
14:10 The heart knoweth **his o** bitterness; 5315+2050.2
14:14 in heart shall be filled with **his o** ways: 2050.2
14:20 The poor is hated even of **his o** 1930.2
15:27 He that is greedy of gain troubleth **his o** 2050.2
15:32 refuseth instruction despiseth **his o** soul: 2050.2
16: 2 All the ways of a man *are* clean in **his o** 2050.2
18:11 and as a high wall in **his o** conceit. 2050.2
18:17 *He that is* first in **his o** cause *seemeth* 2050.2
19: 8 He that getteth wisdom loveth **his o** soul: 2050.2
19:16 the commandment keepeth **his o** soul; 2050.2
20: 2 him to anger sinneth *against* **his o** soul. 2050.2
20: 6 Most men will proclaim every one **his o** 2050.2
20:24 can a man then understand **his o** way? 2050.2
21: 2 Every way of a man *is* right in **his o** eyes: 2050.2
23: 4 to be rich: cease from **thine o** wisdom. 3509.2
25:27 *men* to search **their o** glory *is not* glory. 3963.1
25:28 He that *hath* no rule over **his o** spirit *is* 2050.2
26: 5 his folly, lest he be wise in **his o** conceit. 2050.2
26:12 Seest thou a man wise in **his o** conceit? 2050.2
26:16 The sluggard *is* wiser in **his o** conceit 2050.2
27: 2 *man* praise thee, and not **thine o** mouth; 3509.2
27: 2 a stranger, and not **thine o** lips. 3509.2
27:10 **Thine o** friend, and thy father's friend, 3509.2
28:10 he shall fall himself into **his o** pit: 2050.2
28:11 The rich man *is* wise in **his o** conceit; but 2050.2
28:26 He that trusteth in **his o** heart *is* a fool: 2050.2
29:24 Whoso is partner with a thief hateth **his o** 2050.2
30:12 a generation *that are* pure in **their o** eyes, 2050.2
31:31 let **her o** works praise her in the gates. 1886.3
Ecc 1:16 I communed with **mine o** heart, saying, 2967.1
3:22 than that a man should rejoice in **his o** 2050.2
4: 5 his hands together, and eateth **his o** flesh. 2050.2
7:22 For oftentimes also **thine o** heart knoweth 3509.2
8: 9 ruleth over another to **his o** hurt. 2050.2+3807.1
SS 1: 6 *but* **mine o** vineyard have I not kept. 2967.1
Isa 2: 8 they worship the work of **their o** hands, 2050.2
2: 8 *that* which **their o** fingers have made: 2050.2
4: 1 We will eat **our o** bread, and wear our 5105.1
4: 1 our own bread, and wear **our o** apparel: 5105.1
5:21 Woe unto *them that are* wise in **their o** 1992.1
5:21 own eyes, and prudent in **their o** sight! 1992.1
9:20 they shall eat every man the flesh of **his o** 2050.2
13:14 they shall every man turn to **his o** people, 2050.2
Isa 13:14 and flee every one into **his o** land. 2050.2
14: 1 and set them in **their o** land: 3963.1
14:18 lie in glory, every one in **his o** house. 2050.2
23: 7 **her o** feet shall carry her afar off to 1886.3
31: 7 which **your o** hands have made unto you 3641.1
36:12 that *they* may eat **their o** dung, and drink 3963.1
36:12 and drink **their o** piss with you? 1992.1
36:16 drink ye every one the waters of **his o** 2050.2
36:17 take you away to a land like **your o** land, 3641.1
37: 7 hear a rumour, and return to **his o** land; 2050.2
37: 7 him to fall by the sword in **his o** land. 2050.2
37:35 defend this city to save it for **mine o** sake, 2967.1
43:25 out thy transgressions for **mine o** sake, 2967.1
44: 9 they *are* **their o** witnesses; they see not, 1992.1
48:11 For **mine o** sake, *even* for mine own sake, 2967.1
48:11 For mine own sake, *even* for **mine o** sake, 2967.1
49:26 them that oppress thee with **their o** flesh; 3963.1
49:26 they shall be drunken with **their o** blood, 3963.1
53: 6 we have turned every one to **his o** way; 2050.2
56:11 they all look to **their o** way, every one for 3963.1
58: 7 that thou hide not thyself from **thine o** 3509.2
58:13 shalt honour him, not doing **thine o** ways, 3509.2
58:13 own ways, nor finding **thine o** pleasure, 3509.2
58:13 own pleasure, nor speaking *thine o* words: NIH
63: 5 **mine o** arm brought salvation unto me; 2967.1
65: 2 *that was* not good, after **their o** thoughts; 1992.1
66: 3 they have chosen **their o** ways, and 1992.1
Jer 1:16 worshipped the works of **their o** hands. 1992.1
2:19 **Thine o** wickedness shall correct thee, 3509.3
2:30 **your o** sword hath devoured your 3641.1
7:19 to the confusion of **their o** faces? 1992.1
9:14 after the imagination of **their o** heart, 3963.1
18:12 we will walk after **our o** devices, and 5105.1
23: 8 and they shall dwell in **their o** land. 3963.1
23:16 they speak a vision of **their o** heart, *and* 3963.1
23:17 after the imagination of **his o** heart, 2050.2
23:26 *they are* prophets of the deceit of **their o** 3963.1
25: 7 the works of your hands to **your o** hurt. 3641.1
25:14 according to the works of **their o** hands. 1992.1
27:11 those will I let remain still in **their o** land, 2050.2
30:18 the city shall be builded upon **her o** heap, 1886.3
31:17 shall come again to **their o** border. 3963.1
31:30 every one shall die for **his o** iniquity: 2050.2
37: 7 shall return *to* Egypt into **their o** land. 2050.2
42:12 and cause you to return to **your o** land. 3641.1
44: 9 **your o** wickedness, and the wickedness 3641.1
44:17 thing goeth forth out of **our o** mouth, 5105.1
46:16 let us go again to **our o** people, and to 5105.1
50:16 they shall flee every one to **his o** land. 2050.2
51: 9 let us go every one into **his o** country: 2050.2
52:27 carried away captive out of **his o** land. 2050.2
La 4:10 women have sodden **their o** children: 2006.1
Eze 11:21 I will recompense their way upon **their o** 3963.1
13: 2 them that prophesy out of **their o** hearts, 3963.1
13: 3 that follow **their o** spirit, and have seen 3963.1
13:17 which prophesy out of **their o** heart; 2006.1
14: 5 take the house of Israel in **their o** heart, 3963.1
14:14 *but* **their o** souls by their righteousness, 3963.1
14:20 **their o** souls by their righteousness. 3963.1
16: 6 and saw thee polluted in **thine o** blood, 3509.3
16:15 thou didst trust in **thine o** beauty, and 3509.3
16:52 bear **thine o** shame for thy sins that thou 3509.3
16:54 That thou mayest bear **thine o** shame, and 3509.3
17:19 it will I recompense upon **his o** head. 2050.2
20:26 I polluted them in **their o** gifts, in that 3963.1
20:43 ye shall lothe yourselves in **your o** sight 3641.1
22:31 **their o** way have I recompensed upon 3963.1
23:34 and pluck off **thine o** breasts: 3509.3
29: 3 My river *is* **mine o**, and I have 2967.1+3807.1
32:10 every man for **his o** life, in the day of thy 2050.2
33: 4 his blood shall be upon **his o** head. 2050.2
33:13 if he trust to **his o** righteousness, and 2050.2
34:13 will bring them to **their o** land, and 3963.1
36:17 when the house of Israel dwelt in **their o** 3963.1
36:17 they defiled it by **their o** way and by their 3963.1
36:24 and will bring you into **your o** land. 3641.1
36:31 shall ye remember **your o** evil ways, and 3641.1
36:31 shall lothe yourselves in **your o** sight for 3641.1
36:32 and confounded for **your o** ways, 3641.1
37:14 and I shall place you in **your o** land: 3641.1
37:21 and bring them into **their o** land: 3963.1
39:28 I have gathered them unto **their o** land, 3963.1
46:18 sons inheritance out of **his o** possession: 2050.2
Da 3:28 nor worship any god, except **their o** God. 1952.1
6:17 the king sealed it with **his o** signet, and 1886.8
8:24 shall be mighty, but not by **his o** power: 2050.2
9:19 defer not, for **thine o** sake, O my God: 3509.2
11: 9 and shall return into **his o** land. 2050.2
11:16 him shall do according to **his o** will, 2050.2
11:18 a prince for **his o** behalf shall cause 2050.2
11:18 without **his o** reproach he shall cause *it* to 2050.2
11:19 his face towards the fort of **his o** land: 2050.2
11:28 shall do *exploits*, and return to **his o** land. 2050.2
Hos 7: 2 now **their o** doings have beset them 1992.1
10: 6 Israel shall be ashamed of **his o** counsel. 2050.2
11: 6 devour *them*, because of **their o** counsels. 1992.1
13: 2 idols according to **their o** understanding, 3963.1
Joel 3: 4 your recompence upon **your o** head; 3641.1
3: 7 will return your recompence upon **your o** 3641.1
Am 6:13 Have we not taken to us horns by **our o** 5105.1
7:11 be led away captive out of **their o** land. 2050.2
Ob 1:15 reward shall return upon **thine o** head. 3509.2
Jnh 2: 8 lying vanities forsake **their o** mercy. 3963.1
Mic 7: 6 a man's enemies *are* the men of **his o** 2050.2
Hag 1: 9 and ye run every man unto **his o** house. 2050.2
Zec 5:11 and set there upon **her o** base. 1886.3
11: 5 and **their o** shepherds pity them not. 1992.1
12: 6 shall be inhabited again in **her o** place, 1886.3
Mal 3:17 a man spareth **his o** son that serveth him. 2050.2
Mt 2:12 they departed into **their o** country another *846*
7: 3 considerest not the beam that is in **thine o** *4674*
7: 4 and behold, a beam *is* in **thine o** eye? *4771*
7: 5 first cast out the beam out of **thine o** eye; *4771*
9: 1 and passed over, and came into **his o** city. *2398*
10:36 And a man's foes *shall be* they of **his o** *846*

O

Mt 13:54 And when he was come into his o country, 846
13:57 save in his o country, and in his own house. 846
13:57 save in his own country, and in his o house. 846
16:26 gain the whole world, and lose his o soul? 846
17:25 tribute? of their o children, or of strangers? 846
20:15 for me to do what I will with mine o? 1699
25:14 who called his o servants, and 2398
25:27 I should have received mine o with usury. 1699
27:31 and put his o raiment on him, and led him 846
27:60 And laid it in his o new tomb, which he had 846
Mk 6: 1 from thence, and came into his o country; 846
6: 4 but in his o country, and among his own kin, 846
6: 4 and among his o kin, and in his own house. 846
6: 4 and among his own kin, and in his o house. 846
7: 9 of God, that ye may keep your o tradition. 4771
8: 3 And if I send them away fasting to their o 846
8:36 gain the whole world, and lose his o soul? 846
15:20 and put his o clothes on him, and led him 2398
Lk 1:23 he departed to his o house. 846
1:56 three months, and returned to her o house. 846
2: 3 went to be taxed, every one into his o city. 2398
2:35 a sword shall pierce through thy o soul also,) 846
2:39 into Galilee, to their o city Nazareth. 846
4:24 No prophet is accepted in his o country. 846
5:25 and departed to his o house, glorifying God. 846
5:29 And Levi made him a great feast in his o 846
6:41 perceivest not the beam that is in thine o 2398
6:42 not the beam that is in thine o eye? 4771
6:42 cast out first the beam out of thine o eye, 4771
6:44 For every tree is known by his o fruit. 2398
8:39 Return to thine o house, and shew how 4771
9:26 when he shall come in his o glory, and in his 846
10:34 and set him on his o beast, and brought him 2398
14:26 and sisters, yea, and his o life also, 1438
16:12 who shall give you that which is your o? 5212
18: 7 And shall not God avenge his o elect, 846
19:22 Out of thine o mouth will I judge thee, 4771
19:23 I might have required mine o with usury? NIG
21:30 know of your o selves that summer is now 1438
22:71 for we ourselves have heard of his o mouth. 846
Jn 1:11 He came unto his o, and his own received 2398
1:11 unto his own, and his o received him not. 2398
1:41 He first findeth his o brother Simon, and 2398
4:41 many moe believed because of his o word; NIG
4:44 that a prophet hath no honour in his o 2398
5:30 I can of mine o self do nothing: as I hear, 1683
5:30 is just; because I seek not mine o will, 1699
5:43 if another shall come in his o name, him ye 2398
6:38 not to do mine o will, but the will of him 1699
7:18 He that speaketh of himself seeketh his o 2398
7:53 And every man went unto his o house. 846
8: 9 it, being convicted by their o conscience, NIG
8:44 he speaketh a lie, he speaketh of his o: 2398
8:50 And I seek not mine o glory: there is one 1473
10: 3 and he calleth his o sheep by name, and 2398
10: 4 And when he putteth forth his o sheep, he 2398
10:12 the shepherd, whose o the sheep are not, 2398
13: 1 having loved his o which were in 2398
15:19 of the world, the world would love his o: 2398
16:32 every man to his o, and shall leave me 2398
17: 5 glorify thou me with thine o self with 4572
17:11 keep through thine o name those whom 4771
18:35 Thine o nation and the chief priests have 4674
19:27 that disciple took her unto his o home. 2398
20:10 went away again unto their o home. 1438
Ac 1: 7 which the Father hath put in his o power. 2398
1:25 that he might go to his o place. 2398
2: 6 that every man heard them speak in his o 2398
2: 8 And how hear we every man in our o 2398
3:12 as though by our o power or holiness we 2398
4:23 they went to their o company, and 2398
4:32 of the things which he possessed was his o; 2398
5: 4 Whiles it remained, was it not thine o? and 4771
5: 4 it was sold, was it not in thine o power? 4674
7:21 him up, and nourished him for her o son. 1438
7:41 and rejoiced in the works of their o hands. 846
12:10 which opened to them of his o accord: 844
13:22 a man after mine o heart, which shall fulfil 1473
13:36 after he had served his o generation by 2398
14:16 suffered all nations to walk in their o ways. 846
15:22 to send chosen men of their o company to 846
17:28 as certain also of your o poets have 2596+4771
18: 6 Your blood be upon your o heads; 4771
20:28 which he hath purchased with his o blood. 2398
20:30 Also of your o selves shall men arise, 846
21:11 and bound his o hands and feet, and said, NIG
25:19 against him of their o superstition, 2398
26: 4 which was at the first among mine o nation 1473
27:19 with our o hands the tackling of the ship. 849
28:30 And Paul dwelt two whole years in his o 2398
Ro 1:24 through the lusts of their o hearts, 846
1:24 to dishonour their o bodies between 846
4:19 he considered not his o body now dead, 1438
8: 3 God sending his o Son in the likeness of 1438
8:32 He that spared not his o Son, but 2398
10: 3 going about to establish their o 2398
11:24 branches, be graffed into their o olive tree? 2398
11:25 lest ye should be wise in your o conceits; 1438
12:16 low estate. Be not wise in your o conceits. 1438
14: 4 to his o master he standeth or falleth. Yea, 2398
14: 5 man be fully persuaded in his o mind. 2398
16: 4 Who have for my life laid down their o 1438
16:18 not our Lord Jesus Christ, but their o belly; 1438
1Co 1:15 say that I had baptized in mine o name. 1699
3: 8 every man shall receive his o reward 2398
3: 8 his own reward according to his o labour. 2398
3:19 He taketh the wise in their o craftiness. 846
4: 3 yea, I judge not mine o self. 1683
4:12 And labour, working with our o hands: 2398
6:14 and will also raise up us by his o power. 846
6:18 fornication sinneth against his o body. 2398
6:19 ye have of God, and ye are not your o? 1438
7: 2 let every man have his o wife, and let every 1438
7: 2 and let every woman have her o husband. 2398
7: 4 The wife hath not power of her o body, but 2398

1Co 7: 4 the husband hath not power of his o body, 2398
7:35 And this I speak for your o profit; not that I 846
7:37 but hath power over his o will, and hath so 2398
9: 7 Who goeth a warfare any time at his o 2398
10:24 Let no man seek his o, but every man 1438
10:29 I say, not thine o, but of the other's: 1438
10:33 in all things, not seeking mine o profit, 1683
11:21 every one taketh before other his o supper: 2398
13: 5 seeketh not her o, is not easily provoked, 1438
15:23 But every man in his o order: Christ 2398
15:38 pleased him, and to every seed his o body. 2398
16:21 The salutation of me Paul with mine o 1699
2Co 6:12 but ye are straitened in your o bowels. 4771
8: 5 but first gave their o selves to the Lord, 1438
8:17 of his o accord he went unto you. 830
11:26 of robbers, in perils by my o countrymen, NIG
13: 5 ye be in the faith; prove your o selves. 1438
13: 5 Know ye not your o selves, how that Jesus 1438
Gal 1:14 above many my equals in mine o nation, 1473
4:15 ye would have plucked out your o eyes, 4771
6: 4 But let every man prove his o work, and 1438
6: 5 For every man shall bear his o burden. 2398
6:11 I have written unto you with mine o hand. 1699
Eph 1:11 all things after the counsel of his o will: 846
1:20 set him at his o right hand in the heavenly 846
5:22 submit yourselves unto your o husbands, 2398
5:24 let the wives be to their o husbands in 2398
5:28 So ought men to love their wives as their o 1438
5:29 For no man ever yet hated his o flesh; but 1438
Php 2: 4 Look not every man on his o things, but 1438
2:12 work out your o salvation with fear and 1438
2:21 For all seek their o, not the things which 1438
3: 9 not having mine o righteousness, which is 1699
Col 3:18 submit yourselves unto your o husbands, 2398
1Th 2: 8 but also our o souls, because ye were dear 1438
2:14 suffered like things of your o countrymen, 2398
2:15 and their o prophets, and have persecuted 2398
4:11 and to do your o business, and to work 2398
4:11 and to work with your o hands, 2398
2Th 3:12 quietness they work, and eat their o bread. 1438
3:17 The salutation of Paul with mine o hand, 1699
1Ti 1: 2 Unto Timothy, my o son in the faith: 1103
3: 4 One that ruleth well his o house, having his 2398
3: 5 (For if a man know not how to rule his o 2398
3:12 their children and their o houses well. 2398
5: 8 But if any provide not for his o, and 2398
5: 8 and specially for those of his o house, NIG
6: 1 count their o masters worthy of all honour, 2398
2Ti 1: 9 but according to his o purpose and grace, 2398
3: 2 For men shall be lovers of their o selves, 5367
4: 3 after their o lusts shall they heap to 2398
Tit 1: 4 mine o son after the common faith: 1103
1:12 even a prophet of their o, said, 2398
2: 5 good, obedient to their o husbands, 2398
2: 9 Exhort servants to be obedient unto their o 2398
Phm 1:12 receive him, that is, mine o bowels: 1699
1:19 I Paul have written it with mine o hand, 1699
1:19 owest unto me even thine o self besides. 4572
Heb 2: 4 of the Holy Ghost, according to his o will? 846
3: 6 But Christ as a Son over his o house; 846
4:10 he also hath ceased from his o works, 846
7:27 first for his o sins, and then for 2398
9:12 by his o blood he entered in once into 2398
12:10 few days chastened us after their o pleasure; 846
13:12 that he might sanctify the people with his o 2398
Jas 1:14 when he is drawn away of his o lust, and 2398
1:18 Of his o will begat he us with the word of 1014
1:22 not hearers only, deceiving your o selves. 1438
1:26 not his tongue, but deceiveth his o heart, 846
1Pe 2:24 Who his o self bare our sins in his own body 846
2:24 Who his own self bare our sins in his o body 846
3: 1 be in subjection to your o husbands; 2398
3: 5 being in subjection unto their o husbands: 2398
2Pe 2:12 and shall utterly perish in their o corruption; 846
2:13 sporting themselves with their o deceivings 846
2:22 The dog is turned to his o vomit again; 2398
3: 3 days scoffers, walking after their o lusts, 2398
3:16 other scriptures, unto their o destruction. 2398
3:17 the wicked, fall from your o stedfastness. 2398
1Jn 3:12 Because his o works were evil, and his 846
Jude 1: 6 their first estate, but left their o habitation, 2398
1:13 of the sea, foaming out their o shame; 1438
1:16 complainers, walking after their o lusts; 846
1:18 who should walk after their o ungodly 1438
Rev 1: 5 and washed us from our sins in his o blood, 846

OWNER (13) [OWN]

Ex 21:28 be eaten; but the o of the ox shall be quit. 1167
21:29 it hath been testified to his o, and he hath 1167
21:29 and his o also shall be put to death. 1167
21:34 The o of the pit shall make it good, and 1167
21:34 it good, and give money unto the o of them; 1167
21:36 in time past, and his o hath not kept him in; 1167
22:11 the o of it shall accept thereof, and he shall 1167
22:12 he shall make restitution unto the o thereof. 1167
22:14 or die, the o thereof being not with it, 1167
22:15 But if the o thereof be with it, he shall not 1167
1Ki 16:24 the name of Shemer, o of the hill, Samaria. 113
Isa 1: 3 The ox knoweth his o, and the ass his 7069
Ac 27:11 believed the master and the o of the ship, 3490

OWNERS (5) [OWN]

Job 31:39 have caused the o thereof to lose their life: 1167
Pr 1:19 which taketh away the life of the o thereof. 1167
Ecc 5:11 what good is there to the o thereof, 1167
5:13 namely, riches kept for the o thereof to 1167
Lk 19:33 the o thereof said unto them, Why loose ye 2962

OWNETH (1) [OWN]

Lev 14:35 he that o the house shall come and tell 3807.1

OX (64) [OXEN]

Ex 20:17 nor his maidservant, nor his o, nor his ass, 7794
21:28 If an o gore a man or a woman, that they 7794

Ex 21:28 the o shall be surely stoned, and his flesh 7794
21:28 but the owner of the o shall be quit. 7794
21:29 if the o were wont to push with his horn in 7794
21:29 the o shall be stoned, and his owner also 7794
21:32 If the o shall push a manservant or 7794
21:32 shekels of silver, and the o shall be stoned. 7794
21:33 not cover it, and an o or an ass fall therein; 7794
21:35 if one man's o hurt another's, that he die; 7794
21:35 they shall sell the live o, and divide 7794
21:35 of it; and the dead o also they shall divide. NIH
21:36 Or if it be known that the o hath used to 7794
21:36 he shall surely pay o for ox; and the dead 7794
21:36 he shall surely pay ox for o; and the dead 7794
22: 1 If a man shall steal an o, or a sheep, and 7794
22: 1 he shall restore five oxen for an o, and 7794
22: 4 hand alive, whether it be o, or ass, or sheep; 7794
22: 9 whether it be for o, for ass, for sheep, 7794
22:10 or an o, or a sheep, or any beast, to keep; 7794
23: 4 If thou meet thine enemy's o or his ass 7794
23:12 that thine o and thine ass may rest, and 7794
34:19 thy cattle, whether o or sheep, that is male. 7794
Lev 7:23 no manner fat, of o, or of sheep, or of goat. 7794
17: 3 that killeth an o, or lamb, or goat, in 7794
27:26 shall sanctify it; whether it be o, or sheep: 7794
Nu 7: 3 two of the princes, and for each one an o: 7794
22: 4 as the o licketh up the grass of the field. 7794
Dt 5:14 thy maidservant, nor thine o, nor thine ass, 7794
5:21 his o, or his ass, or any thing that is thy 7794
14: 4 ye shall eat: the o, the sheep, and the goat, 7794
14: 5 and the wild o, and the chamois. 8377
18: 3 offer a sacrifice, whether it be o or sheep; 7794
22: 1 Thou shalt not see thy brother's o or his 7794
22: 4 brother's ass or his o fall down by the way, 7794
22:10 Thou shalt not plow with an o and an ass 7794
25: 4 Thou shalt not muzzle the o when he 7794
28:31 Thine o shall be slain before thine eyes, and 7794
Jos 6:21 and old, and o, and sheep, and ass, 7794
Jdg 3:31 Philistines six hundred men with an o goad: 1241
6: 4 for Israel, neither sheep, nor o, nor ass. 7794
1Sa 12: 3 whose o have I taken? or whose ass have I 7794
14:34 Bring me hither every man his o, and 7794
14:34 all the people brought every man his o with 7794
15: 3 and suckling, o and sheep, camel and ass. 7794
Ne 5:18 which was prepared for me daily was one o 7794
Job 6: 5 hath grass? or loweth the o over his fodder? 7794
24: 3 they take the widow's o for a pledge. 7794
40:15 I made with thee; he eateth grass as an o. 1241
Ps 69:31 shall please the LORD better than an o 7794
106:20 into the similitude of an o that eateth grass. 7794
Pr 7:22 as an o goeth to the slaughter, or as a fool 7794
14: 4 much increase is by the strength of the o. 7794
15:17 than a stalled o and hatred therewith. 7794
Isa 1: 3 The o knoweth his owner, and the ass his 7794
11: 7 and the lion shall eat straw like the o. 1241
32:20 that send forth thither the feet of the o and 7794
66: 3 He that killeth an o is as if he slew a man; 7794
Jer 11:19 or an o that is brought to the slaughter; 441
Eze 1:10 they four had the face of an o on the left 7794
Lk 13:15 each one of you on the sabbath loose his o 1016
14: 5 shall have an ass or an o fallen into a pit, 1016
1Co 9: 9 Thou shalt not muzzle the mouth of the o 1016
1Ti 5:18 Thou shalt not muzzle the o that treadeth 1016

OXEN (102) [OX]

Ge 12:16 o, and he asses, and menservants, and 1241
20:14 o, and menservants, and womenservants, 1241
21:27 Abraham took sheep and o, and gave them 1241
32: 5 I have o, and asses, flocks, and 7794
34:28 their o, and their asses, and that which was 1241
Ex 9: 3 the camels, upon the o, and upon the sheep: 1241
20:24 thy peace offerings, thy sheep, and thine o: 1241
22: 1 he shall restore five o for an ox, and 1241
22:30 Likewise shalt thou do with thine o, and 7794
24: 5 sacrificed peace offerings of o unto 6499
Nu 7: 3 six covered wagons, and twelve o; 1241
7: 6 Moses took the wagons and the o, and 1241
7: 7 four o he gave unto the sons of Gershon, 1241
7: 8 eight o he gave unto the sons of Merari, 1241
7:17 two o, five rams, five he goats, five lambs 1241
7:23 two o, five rams, five he goats, five lambs 1241
7:29 two o, five rams, five he goats, five lambs 1241
7:35 two o, five rams, five he goats, five lambs 1241
7:41 two o, five rams, five he goats, five lambs 1241
7:47 two o, five rams, five he goats, five lambs 1241
7:53 two o, five rams, five he goats, five lambs 1241
7:59 two o, five rams, five he goats, five lambs 1241
7:65 two o, five rams, five he goats, five lambs 1241
7:71 two o, five rams, five he goats, five lambs 1241
7:77 two o, five rams, five he goats, five lambs 1241
7:83 two o, five rams, five he goats, five lambs 1241
7:87 All the o for the burnt offering were twelve 1241
7:88 all the o for the sacrifice of the peace 1241
22:40 Balak offered o and sheep, and sent to 1241
23: 1 prepare me here seven o and seven rams. 6499
Dt 14:26 for o, or for sheep, or for wine, or 1241
Jos 7:24 his o, and his asses, and his sheep, and his 7794
1Sa 11: 7 he took a yoke of o, and hewed them in 1241
11: 7 after Samuel, so shall it be done unto his o. 1241
14:14 acre of land, which a yoke of o might plow. NIH
14:32 o, and calves, and slew them on the ground: 1241
15: 9 of the o, and of the fatlings, and the lambs, 1241
15:14 and the lowing of the o which I hear? 1241
15:15 spared the best of the sheep and of the o, 1241
15:21 the people took of the spoil, sheep and o, 1241
22:19 and sucklings, and o, and asses, and sheep, 7794
27: 9 the o, and the asses, and the camels, and 1241
2Sa 6: 6 and took hold of it; for the o shook it. 1241
6:13 gone six paces, he sacrificed o and fatlings. 7794
24:22 here be o for burnt sacrifice, and threshing 1241
24:22 and other instruments of the o for wood. 1241
24:24 and the o for fifty shekels of silver. 1241
1Ki 1: 9 Adonijah slew sheep and o and fat cattle by 1241
1:19 he hath slain o and fat cattle and sheep in 7794
1:25 hath slain o and fat cattle and sheep in 7794
4:23 Ten fat o, and twenty oxen out of 1241

O

1Ki 4:23 twenty **o** out of the pastures, and 1241
7:25 It stood upon twelve **o**, three looking 1241
7:29 the ledges *were* lions, **o**, and cherubims: 1241
7:29 **o** *were certain* additions made of thin work. 1241
7:44 And one sea, and twelve **o** under the sea; 1241
8: 5 him before the ark, sacrificing sheep and **o**, 1241
8:63 two and twenty thousand **o**, and an hundred 1241
19:19 who *was* plowing *with* twelve yoke *of* **o** NIH
19:20 he left the **o**, and ran after Elijah, and said, 1241
19:21 took a yoke of **o**, and slew them, and boiled 1241
19:21 their flesh with the instruments of the **o**, 1241
2Ki 5:26 and **o**, and menservants, and maidservants? 1241
16:17 took down the sea from off the brasen **o** 1241
1Ch 12:40 and on mules, and on **o**, *and* meat, meal, 1241
12:40 wine, and oil, and **o**, and sheep abundantly: 1241
13: 9 his hand to hold the ark; for the **o** stumbled. 1241
21:23 lo, I give *thee* the **o** *also* for burnt offerings, 1241
2Ch 4: 3 under it *was* the similitude of **o**, which did 1241
4: 3 Two rows *of* **o** *were* cast, when it was cast. 1241
4: 4 It stood upon twelve **o**, three looking 1241
4:15 One sea, and twelve **o** under it. 1241
5: 6 sacrificed sheep and **o**, which could not be 1241
7: 5 a sacrifice of twenty and two thousand **o**, 1241
15:11 seven hundred **o** and seven thousand sheep. 1241
18: 2 killed sheep and **o** for him in abundance, 1241
29:33 the consecrated *things were* six hundred **o** 1241
31: 6 they also brought in the tithe of **o** and 1241
35: 8 hundred *small cattle*, and three hundred **o**. 1241
35: 9 thousand *small cattle*, and five hundred **o**. 1241
35:12 book of Moses. And so *did they* with the **o**. 1241
Job 1: 3 five hundred yoke of **o**, and five hundred 1241
1:14 The **o** were plowing, and the asses feeding 1241
42:12 a thousand yoke of **o**, and a thousand she 1241
Ps 8: 7 All sheep and **o**, yea, and the beasts of 504
144:14 *That* our **o** *may be* strong to labour; 441
Pr 14: 4 Where no **o** *are*, the crib *is* clean: but 504
Isa 7:25 it shall be for the sending forth of **o**, and 7794
22:13 and gladness, slaying **o**, and killing sheep, 1241
30:24 The **o** likewise and the young asses that ear 504
Jer 51:23 pieces the husbandman and his **yoke of o**; 6776
Da 4:25 they shall make thee to eat grass as **o**, 8450
4:32 they shall make thee to eat grass as **o**, and 8450
4:33 did eat grass as **o**, and his body was wet 8450
5:21 they fed him with grass like **o**, and his body 8450
Am 6:12 will *one* plow *there* with **o**? for ye have 1241
Mt 22: 4 my **o** and *my* fatlings *are* killed, and *5022*
Lk 14:19 I have bought five yoke of **o**, and I go to *1016*
Jn 2:14 And found in the temple those that sold **o** *1016*
2:15 out of the temple, and the sheep and the **o**; *1016*
Ac 14:13 brought **o** and garlands unto the gates, and *5022*
1Co 9: 9 out the corn. Doth God take care for **o**? *1016*

OXGOAD See GOAD

OZEM (2)
1Ch 2:15 **O** the sixth, David the seventh: 684
2:25 and Bunah, and Oren, and **O**, *and* Ahijah. 684

OZIAS (2) [AHAZIAH]
Mt 1: 8 Josaphat begat Joram; and Joram begat **O**; *3604*
1: 9 And **O** begat Joatham; and Joatham begat *3604*

OZNI (1) [OZNITES]
Nu 26:16 Of **O**, the family of the Oznites: of Eri, 244

OZNITES (1) [OZNI]
Nu 26:16 Of Ozni, the family of the **O**: of Eri, 244

P

PAARAI (1)
2Sa 23:35 Hezrai the Carmelite, **P** the Arbite, 6474

PACATIANA (1)
1Ti 6: S which is the chiefest city of Phrygia **P**. *3818*

PACES (1)
2Sa 6:13 ark of the LORD had **gone** six **p**, 6805+6806

PACIFIED (2) [PACIFY]
Est 7:10 for Mordecai. Then was the king's wrath **p**. 7918
Eze 16:63 when I am **p** toward thee for all that thou 3722

PACIFIETH (2) [PACIFY]
Pr 21:14 A gift in secret **p** anger: and a reward in 3711
Ecc 10: 4 not thy place; for yielding **p** great offences. 3240

PACIFY (1) [PACIFIED, PACIFIETH]
Pr 16:14 of death: but a wise man will **p** it. 3722

PADAN (1) [PADAN-ARAM]
Ge 48: 7 as for me, when I came from **P**, 6307

PADAN-ARAM (10) [ARAM, PADAN]
Ge 25:20 the daughter of Bethuel the Syrian of **P**, 6307
28: 2 Arise, go to **P**, to the house of Bethuel thy 6307
28: 5 he went to **P** unto Laban, son of Bethuel 6307
28: 6 sent him away to **P**, to take him a wife from 6307
28: 7 and his mother, and was gone to **P**; 6307
31:18 of his getting, which he had gotten in **P**, 6307
33:18 the land of Canaan, when he came from **P**; 6307
35: 9 when he came out of **P**, and blessed him. 6307
35:26 sons of Jacob, which were born to him in **P**. 6307
Ge 46:15 which she bare unto Jacob in **P**, with his 6307

PADDAN See PADAN

PADDAN ARAM See PADAN-ARAM

PADDLE (1)
Dt 23:13 thou shalt have a **p** upon thy weapon; and 3489

PADON (2)
Ezr 2:44 the children of Siaha, the children of **P**, 6303
Ne 7:47 the children of Sia, the children of **P**, 6303

PAGAN See CHEMARIMS

PAGANS See PUBLICAN

PAGIEL (5)
Nu 1:13 Of Asher; **P** the son of Ocran. 6295
2:27 of Asher *shall be* **P** the son of Ocran. 6295
7:72 On the eleventh day **P** the son of Ocran, 6295
7:77 this *was* the offering of **P** the son of Ocran. 6295
10:26 children of Asher *was* **P** the son of Ocran. 6295

PAHATH-MOAB (6)
Ezr 2: 6 The children of **P**, of the children of Jeshua 6355
8: 4 Of the sons of **P**; Elihoenai the son of 6355
10:30 of the sons of **P**; Adna, and Chelal, 6355
Ne 3:11 Hashub the son of **P**, repaired the other 6355
7:11 The children of **P**, of the children of Jeshua 6355
10:14 the people; Parosh, **P**, Elam, Zatthu, Bani, 6355

PAI (1)
1Ch 1:50 the name of his city *was* **P**; and his wife's 6464

PAID (4) [PAY]
Ezr 4:20 toll, tribute, and custom, *was* **p** unto them. 3052
Jnh 1: 3 so he **p** the fare thereof, and went down 5414
Mt 5:26 till thou hast **p** the uttermost farthing. *591*
Lk 12:59 till thou hast **p** the very last mite. *591*

PAIN (25) [PAINED, PAINFUL, PAINFULNESS, PAINS]
Job 14:22 his flesh upon him shall **have p**, and 3510
15:20 The wicked *man* **travaileth with p** all his 2342
33:19 He is chastened also with **p** upon his bed, 4341
33:19 the multitude of his bones *with* strong *p*: NIH
Ps 25:18 Look upon mine affliction and my **p**; and 5999
48: 6 them there, *and* **p**, as of a woman in travail. 2427
Isa 13: 8 shall be **in p** as a woman that travaileth: 2342
21: 3 Therefore are my loins filled *with* **p**: 2479
26:17 is **in p**, *and* crieth out in her pangs; 2342
26:18 have been with child, we have been **in p**, 2342
66: 7 before her **p** came, she was delivered of a 2256
Jer 6:24 hold of us, *and* **p**, as of a woman in travail. 2427
12:13 they have **put** themselves **to p**, *but* shall not 2470
15:18 Why is my **p** perpetual, and my wound 3511
22:23 upon thee, the **p** as of a woman in travail. 2427
30:23 it shall **fall with p** upon the head of 2342
51: 8 take balm for her **p**, if so be she may be 4341
Eze 30: 4 **great p** shall be in Ethiopia, when the slain 2479
30: 9 **great p** shall come upon them, as *in* 2479
30:16 Sin shall **have great p**, and No shall 2342+2342
Mic 4:10 Be **in p**, and labour to bring forth, 2342
Na 2:10 **much p** *is* in all loins, and the faces of them 2479
Ro 8:22 and **travaileth in p together** until now. *4944*
Rev 16:10 and they gnawed their tongues for **p**, *4192*
21: 4 neither shall there be any more **p**: *4192*

PAINED (5) [PAIN]
Ps 55: 4 My heart is **sore p** within me: and 2342
Isa 23: 5 shall they be **sorely p** *at* the report of Tyre. 2342
Jer 4:19 I am **p** *at* my very heart; my heart maketh a 2342
Joel 2: 6 their face *the* people shall be **much p**: 2342
Rev 12: 2 travailing in birth, and **p** to be delivered. *928*

PAINFUL (1) [PAIN]
Ps 73:16 I thought to know this, it *was* too **p** for me; 5999

PAINFULNESS (1) [PAIN]
2Co 11:27 In weariness and **p**, in watchings often, *3449*

PAINS (4) [PAIN]
1Sa 4:19 and travailed; for her **p** came upon her. 6735
Ps 116: 3 and the **p** of hell gat hold upon me: 4712
Ac 2:24 raised up, having loosed the **p** of death: *5604*
Rev 16:11 because of their **p** and their sores, *4192*

PAINTED (2) [PAINTEDST, PAINTING]
2Ki 9:30 heard *of it*; and she **p** 7760+7760+871.1+1886.1
Jer 22:14 *is* cieled with cedar, and **p** with vermilion. 4886

PAINTEDST (1) [PAINTED]
Eze 23:40 for whom thou didst wash *thyself*, **p** thy 3583

PAINTING (1) [PAINTED]
Jer 4:30 though thou rentest thy face with **p**, in vain 6320

PAIR (4)
Am 2: 6 for silver, and the poor for a **p** of shoes; NIH
8: 6 for silver, and the needy for a **p** of shoes; NIH
Lk 2:24 A **p** of turtledoves, or two young pigeons. *2201*
Rev 6: 5 he that sat on him had a **p of balances** in *2218*

PALACE (48) [PALACES]
1Ki 16:18 that he went into the **p** of the king's house, 759
21: 1 hard by the **p** of Ahab king of Samaria. 1964
2Ki 15:25 in the **p** of the king's house, with Argob and 759
20:18 they shall be eunuchs in the **p** of the king of 1964
1Ch 29: 1 for the **p** *is* not for man, but for the LORD 1002
29:19 to do all *these things*, and to build the **p**, 1002
2Ch 9:11 to the king's **p**, and harps and psalteries for 1004
Ezr 4:14 we have maintenance from *the king's* **p**, 1965
Ezr 6: 2 in the **p** that *is* in the province of 1001
Ne 1: 1 twentieth year, as I was in Shushan the **p**, 1002
2: 8 of the **p** which *appertained* to the house, 1002
7: 2 Hananiah the ruler of the **p**, charge over 1002
Est 1: 2 his kingdom, which *was* in Shushan the **p**, 1002
1: 5 people that were present in Shushan the **p**, 1002
1: 5 in the court of the garden of the king's **p**; 1055
2: 3 the fair young virgins unto Shushan the **p**, 1002
2: 5 *Now* in Shushan the **p** there was a certain 1002
2: 8 were gathered together unto Shushan the **p**, 1002
3:15 and the decree was given in Shushan the **p**. 1002
7: 7 of wine in his wrath *went* into the **p** garden: 1055
7: 8 the king returned out of the **p** garden into 1055
8:14 and the decree was given at Shushan the **p**. 1002
9: 6 in Shushan the **p** the Jews slew and 1002
9:11 Shushan the **p** was brought before the king. 1002
9:12 five hundred men in Shushan the **p**, 1002
Ps 45:15 they shall enter into the king's **p**. 1964
144:12 polished *after* the similitude of a **p**: 1964
SS 8: 9 a wall, we will build upon her a **p** of silver: 2918
Isa 25: 2 a **p** of strangers to be no city; it shall never 759
39: 7 they shall be eunuchs in the **p** of the king of 1964
Jer 30:18 the **p** shall remain after the manner thereof. 759
Da 1: 4 *had* ability in them to stand in the king's **p**, 1964
4: 4 rest in mine house, and flourishing in my **p**: 1965
4:29 walked in the **p** of the kingdom of Babylon. 1965
5: 5 upon the plaister of the wall of the king's **p**: 1965
6:18 the king went to his **p**, and passed the night 1965
8: 2 when I saw, that I *was* at Shushan *in* the **p**, 1002
11:45 he shall plant the tabernacles of his **p** 643
Am 4: 3 ye shall cast *them* into the **p**, saith 2038
Na 2: 6 be opened, and the **p** shall be dissolved. 1964
Mt 26: 3 of the people, unto the **p** of the high priest, *833*
26:58 him afar off unto the high priest's **p**, *833*
26:69 Now Peter sat without in the **p**: and a damsel *833*
Mk 14:54 afar off, even into the **p** of the high priest: *833*
14:66 And as Peter was beneath in the **p**, *833*
Lk 11:21 When a strong *man* armed keepeth his **p**, his *833*
Jn 18:15 went in with Jesus into the **p** of the high *833*
Php 1:13 bonds in Christ are manifest in all the **p**, *4232*

PALACES (33) [PALACE]
2Ch 36:19 burnt all the **p** thereof with fire, and 759
Ps 45: 8 and aloes, *and* cassia, out of the ivory **p**, 1964
48: 3 God is known in her **p** for a refuge. 759
48:13 Mark ye well her bulwarks, consider her **p**; 759
78:69 he built his sanctuary like high *p*, like NIH
122: 7 within thy walls, *and* prosperity within thy **p**. 759
Pr 30:28 hold with her hands, and *is* in kings' **p**. 1964
Isa 13:22 and dragons in *their* pleasant **p**: 1964
23:13 towers thereof, they raised up the **p** thereof; 759
32:14 Because the **p** shall be forsaken; 759
34:13 thorns shall come up *in* her **p**, nettles and 759
Jer 6: 5 let us go by night, and let us destroy her **p**. 759
9:21 *and* is entered into our **p**, to cut off 759
17:27 it shall devour the **p** of Jerusalem, and 759
49:27 and it shall consume the **p** of Ben-hadad. 759
La 2: 5 up Israel, he hath swallowed up all her **p**: 759
2: 7 the hand of the enemy the walls of her **p**; 759
Eze 19: 7 he knew their **desolate p**, and he laid waste 490
25: 4 they shall set their **p** in thee, and make their 2918
Hos 8:14 his cities, and it shall devour the **p** thereof. 759
Am 1: 4 which shall devour the **p** of Ben-hadad. 759
1: 7 of Gaza, which shall devour the **p** thereof: 759
1:10 of Tyrus, which shall devour the **p** thereof. 759
1:12 which shall devour the **p** of Bozrah. 759
1:14 it shall devour the **p** thereof, with shouting in 759
2: 2 and it shall devour the **p** of Kerioth: 759
2: 5 and it shall devour the **p** of Jerusalem. 759
3: 9 Publish in the **p** at Ashdod, and in 759
3: 9 and in the **p** in the land of Egypt, and say, 759
3:10 who store up violence and robbery in their **p**. 759
3:11 from thee, and thy **p** shall be spoiled. 759
6: 8 the excellency of Jacob, and hate his **p**: 759
Mic 5: 5 when he shall tread in our **p**, then shall we 759

PALAL (1)
Ne 3:25 **P** the son of Uzai, over against the turning 6420

PALE (2) [PALENESS]
Isa 29:22 neither shall his face now **wax p**. 2357
Rev 6: 8 And I looked, and behold a **p** horse: and *5515*

PALENESS (1) [PALE]
Jer 30: 6 in travail, and all faces are turned into **p**? 3420

PALESTINA (3) [PALESTINE]
Ex 15:14 shall take hold on the inhabitants of **P**. 6429
Isa 14:29 whole **P**, because the rod of him that smote 6429
14:31 cry, O city; thou, whole **P**, *art* dissolved: 6429

PALESTINE (1) [PALESTINA]
Joel 3: 4 O Tyre, and Zidon, and all the coasts of **P**? 6429

PALLU (4) [PALLUITES]
Ex 6:14 Hanoch, and **P**, Hezron, and Carmi: 6396
Nu 26: 5 of **P**, the family of the Palluites: 6396
26: 8 And the sons of **P**; Eliab. 6396
1Ch 5: 3 *were*, Hanoch, and **P**, Hezron, and Carmi. 6396

PALLUITES (1) [PALLU]
Nu 26: 5 of Pallu, the family of the **P**: 6384

PALM (37) [PALMS]
Ex 15:27 of water, and threescore and ten **p trees**: 8558
Lev 14:15 and pour *it* into the **p of** his own left **hand**: 3709
14:26 of the oil into the **p of** his own left **hand**: 3709
23:40 branches of **p trees**, and the boughs of 8558
Nu 33: 9 of water, and threescore and ten **p trees**; 8558
Dt 34: 3 of Jericho, the city of **p trees**, unto Zoar. 8558
Jdg 1:16 went up out of the city of **p trees** with 8558
3:13 and possessed the city of **p trees**. 8558
4: 5 she dwelt under the **p tree** of Deborah 8560
1Ki 6:29 of cherubims and **p trees** and open flowers, 8561

1Ki 6:32 of cherubims and **p trees** and open flowers, 8561
6:32 upon the cherubims, and upon the **p trees**. 8561
6:35 and **p trees** and open flowers: 8561
7:36 he graved cherubims, lions, and **p trees**, 8561
2Ch 3: 5 and set thereon **p trees** and chains. 8561
28:15 the city of **p trees**, to their brethren: 8558
Ne 8:15 and **p** branches, and branches of thick trees, 8558
Ps 92:12 The righteous shall flourish like the **p tree**: 8558
SS 7: 7 This thy stature is like to a **p tree**, and 8558
7: 8 I said, I will go up to the **p tree**, I will take 8558
Jer 10: 5 They *are* upright as the **p tree**, but 8560
Eze 40:16 and upon *each* post *were* **p trees**. 8561
40:22 and their arches, and their **p trees**, 8561
40:26 it had **p trees**, one on this side, and 8561
40:31 and **p trees** *were* upon the posts thereof: 8561
40:34 **p trees** *were* upon the posts thereof, on this 8561
40:37 **p trees** *were* upon the posts thereof, on this 8561
41:18 *it was* made *with* cherubims and **p trees**, 8561
41:18 so that a **p tree** *was* between a cherub and a 8561
41:19 man *was* toward the **p tree** on the one side, 8561
41:19 the face of a young lion toward the **p tree** 8561
41:20 the door *were* cherubims and **p trees** made, 8561
41:25 doors of the temple, cherubims and **p trees**, 8561
41:26 **p trees** on the one side and on the other 8561
Joel 1:12 the **p tree** also, and the apple tree, 8558
Jn 12:13 Took branches of **p trees**, and went forth to *5404*
18:22 **stroke** Jesus **with the p of** his **hand**, *1325+4475*

PALMERWORM (3) [WORM]
Joel 1: 4 That which the **p** hath left hath the locust 1501
2:25 and the caterpillar, and the **p**, 1501
Am 4: 9 the **p** devoured *them:* yet have ye not 1501

PALMS (7) [PALM]
1Sa 5: 4 both the **p** of his hands *were* cut off upon 3709
2Ki 9:35 and the feet, and the **p** of *her* hands. 3709
Isa 49:16 I have graven thee upon the **p of** *my* **hands**; 3709
Da 10:10 my knees and *upon* the **p** of my hands. 3709
Mt 26:67 **smote** *him* **with the p of** their **hands**, *4474*
Mk 14:65 **strike** him **with the p of** their **hands**. *906+4475*
Rev 7: 9 with white robes, and **p** in their hands; *5404*

PALSIES (1) [PALSY]
Ac 8: 7 *with them:* and many **taken with p**, *3886*

PALSY (13) [PALSIES]
Mt 4:24 were lunatick, and those that **had the p**; *3885*
8: 6 my servant lieth at home **sick of the p**, *3885*
9: 2 they brought to him a **man sick of the p**, *3885*
9: 2 their faith said unto the **sick of the p**; *3885*
9: 6 (then saith he to the **sick of the p**,) *3885*
Mk 2: 3 bringing **one sick of the p**, *which was* *3885*
2: 4 down the bed wherein the **sick of the p** lay. *3885*
2: 5 he said unto the **sick of the p**, Son, thy sins *3885*
2: 9 is it easier to say to the **sick of the p**, *3885*
2:10 forgive sins, (he saith to the **sick of the p**,) *3885*
Lk 5:18 in a bed a man which was **taken with a p**: *3886*
5:24 (he said unto the **sick of the p**,) *3886*
Ac 9:33 his bed eight years, and was **sick of the p**. *3886*

PALTI (1)
Nu 13: 9 the tribe of Benjamin, **P** the son of Raphu. 6406

PALTIEL (1)
Nu 34:26 children of Issachar, **P** the son of Azzan. 6409

PALTITE (1)
2Sa 23:26 Helez the **P**, Ira the son of Ikkesh 6407

PAMPHYLIA (5)
Ac 2:10 Phrygia, and **P**, in Egypt, and in the parts of *3828*
13:13 from Paphos, they came to Perga in **P**: *3828*
14:24 passed throughout Pisidia, they came to **P**. *3828*
15:38 *them,* who departed from them from **P**, *3828*
27: 5 we had sailed over the sea of Cilicia and **P**, *3828*

PAN (7) [FIREPANS, FRYINGPAN, PANS]
Lev 2: 5 oblation *be* a meat offering *baken* in a **p**, 4227
6:21 In a **p** it shall be made with oil; *and when it* 4227
7: 9 is dressed in the fryingpan, and in the **p**, 4227
1Sa 2:14 he strooke *it* into the **p**, or kettle, or 3595
2Sa 13: 9 she took a **p**, and poured *them* out before 4958
1Ch 23:29 for *that which is baked in* the **p**, and for that 4227
Eze 4: 3 Moreover take thou unto thee an iron **p**, 4227

PANELED See CIELED

PANELS See CIELED

PANGS (9)
Isa 13: 8 **p** and sorrows shall take hold of *them;* they 6735
21: 3 **p** have taken hold upon me, as the pangs of 6735
21: 3 as the **p** of a woman that travaileth: 6735
26:17 is in pain, *and* crieth out in her **p**; 2256
Jer 22:23 how gracious shalt thou be when **p** come 2256
48:41 shall be as the heart of a woman **in** her **p**. 6887
49:22 Edom be as the heart of a woman **in** her **p**. 6887
50:43 hold of him, *and* **p** as of a woman in travail. 2427
Mic 4: 9 for **p** have taken thee as a woman in travail. 2427

PANIC See DISCOMFITED; DISCOMFITURE

PANNAG (1)
Eze 27:17 and **P**, and honey, and oil, and balm. 6436

PANS (4) [PAN]
Ex 27: 3 thou shalt make his **p** to receive his ashes, 5518
Nu 11: 8 and baked *it* in **p**, and made cakes *of* it: 6517
1Ch 9:31 over the things that were made in the **p**. 2281
2Ch 35:13 in **p**, and divided *them* speedily among all 6745

PANT (1) [PANTED, PANTETH]
Am 2: 7 That **p** after the dust of the earth on 7602

PANTED (2) [PANT]
Ps 119:131 I opened my mouth, and **p**: for I longed for 7602
Isa 21: 4 My heart **p**, fearfulness affrighted me: 8582

PANTETH (3) [PANT]
Ps 38:10 My heart **p**, my strength faileth me: as for 5503
42: 1 As the hart **p** after the water brooks, so 6165
42: 1 so **p** my soul after thee, O God. 6165

PAPER (2)
Isa 19: 7 The **p reeds** by the brooks, by the mouth of 6169
2Jn 1:12 unto you, I would not *write* with **p** and ink: *5489*

PAPHOS (2)
Ac 13: 6 they had gone through the isle unto **P**, *3974*
13:13 when Paul and his company loosed from **P**, *3974*

PAPS (4)
Eze 23:21 by the Egyptians for the **p** of thy youth. 7699
Lk 11:27 and the **p** which thou hast sucked. *3149*
23:29 and the **p** which never gave suck. *3149*
Rev 1:13 and girt about the **p** with a golden girdle. *3149*

PAPYRUS See BULRUSH; BULRUSHES

PARABLE (49) [PARABLES]
Nu 23: 7 he took up his **p**, and said, Balak the king 4912
23:18 he took up his **p**, and said, Rise up, Balak, 4912
24: 3 he took up his **p**, and said, Balaam the son 4912
24:15 he took up his **p**, and said, Balaam the son 4912
24:20 on Amalek, he took up his **p**, and said, 4912
24:21 took up his **p**, and said, Strong *is* thy 4912
24:23 he took up his **p**, and said, Alas, who shall 4912
Job 27: 1 Moreover Job continued his **p**, and said, 4912
29: 1 Moreover Job continued his **p**, and said, 4912
Ps 49: 4 I will incline mine ear to a **p**: I will open 4912
78: 2 I will open my mouth in a **p**: I will utter 4912
Pr 26: 7 not equal: so *is* a **p** in the mouth of fools. 4912
26: 9 a drunkard, so *is* a **p** in the mouth of fools. 4912
Eze 17: 2 **speak a p** unto the house of Israel; 4911+4912
24: 3 And utter a **p** unto the rebellious house, and 4912
Mic 2: 4 In that day shall *one* take up a **p** against 4912
Hab 2: 6 Shall not all these take up a **p** against him, 4912
Mt 13:18 Hear ye therefore the **p** of the sower. *3850*
13:24 Another **p** put he forth unto them, saying, *3850*
13:31 Another **p** put he forth unto them, saying, *3850*
13:33 Another **p** spake he unto them; *3850*
13:34 and without a **p** spake he not unto them: *3850*
13:36 Declare unto us the **p** of the tares of *3850*
15:15 and said unto him, Declare unto us this **p**. *3850*
21:33 Hear another **p**: There was a certain *3850*
24:32 Now learn a **p** of the fig tree; When his *3850*
Mk 4:10 him with the twelve asked of him the **p**. *3850*
4:13 he said unto them, Know ye not this **p**? *3850*
4:34 But without a **p** spake he not unto them: *3850*
7:17 his disciples asked him concerning the **p**. *3850*
12:12 for they knew that he had spoken the **p** *3850*
13:28 Now learn a **p** of the fig tree; When her *3850*
Lk 5:36 And he spake also a **p** unto them; No *man* *3850*
6:39 And he spake a **p** unto them, Can the blind *3850*
8: 4 to him out of every city, he spake by a **p**: *3850*
8: 9 asked him, saying, What might this **p** be? *3850*
8:11 Now the **p** is this: The seed is the word of *3850*
12:16 And he spake a **p** unto them, saying, *3850*
12:41 speakest thou this **p** unto us, or even to all? *3850*
13: 6 He spake also this **p**; A certain *man* had a *3850*
14: 7 And he put forth a **p** to those which were *3850*
15: 3 And he spake this **p** unto them, saying, *3850*
18: 1 And he spake a **p** unto them *to this end,* *3850*
18: 9 And he spake this **p** unto certain which *3850*
19:11 heard these *things,* he added and spake a **p**, *3850*
20: 9 began he to speak to the people this **p**; *3850*
20:19 for they perceived that he had spoken this **p** *3850*
21:29 And he spake to them a **p**; Behold the fig *3850*
Jn 10: 6 This **p** spake Jesus unto them: but *3942*

PARABLES (16) [PARABLE]
Eze 20:49 they say of me, Doth he not speak **p**? 4912
Mt 13: 3 And he spake many *things* unto them in **p**, *3850*
13:10 Why speakest thou unto them in **p**? *3850*
13:13 Therefore speak I to them in **p**: because *3850*
13:34 *things* spake Jesus unto the multitude in **p**; *3850*
13:35 saying, I will open my mouth in **p**; *3850*
13:53 *that* when Jesus had finished these **p**, *3850*
21:45 chief priests and Pharisees had heard his **p**, *3850*
22: 1 and spake unto them again by **p**, *3850*
Mk 3:23 them unto *him,* and said unto them in **p**, *3850*
4: 2 And he taught them many *things* by **p**, and *3850*
4:11 are without, all *these things* are done in **p**: *3850*
4:13 and how *then* will ye know all **p**? *3850*
4:33 And with many such **p** spake he the word *3850*
12: 1 And he began to speak unto them by **p**. *3850*
Lk 8:10 but to others in **p**; that seeing they might *3850*

PARADISE (3)
Lk 23:43 To day shalt thou be with me in **p**. *3857*
2Co 12: 4 How that he was caught up into **p**, and *3857*
Rev 2: 7 which is in the midst of the **p** of God. *3857*

PARAH (1)
Jos 18:23 And Avim, and **P**, and Ophrah, 6511

PARALYTIC See PALSY

PARALYZED See PALSY

PARAMOURS (1)
Eze 23:20 For she doted upon their **p**, whose flesh *is* 6370

PARAN (11) [EL-PARAN]
Ge 21:21 he dwelt in the wilderness of **P**: and 6290
Nu 10:12 and the cloud rested in the wilderness of **P**. 6290
12:16 and pitched in the wilderness of **P**. 6290
Nu 13: 3 sent them from the wilderness of **P**: 6290
13:26 unto the wilderness of **P**, to Kadesh; 6290
Dt 1: 1 plain over against the Red *sea,* between **P**, 6290
33: 2 he shined forth from mount **P**, and he came 6290
1Sa 25: 1 and went down to the wilderness of **P**. 6290
1Ki 11:18 they arose out of Midian, and came *to* **P**: 6290
11:18 they took men with them out of **P**, and 6290
Hab 3: 3 and the Holy One from mount **P**. 6290

PARAPET See BATTLEMENT

PARBAR (2)
1Ch 26:18 At **P** westward, four at the causeway, *and* 6503
26:18 four at the causeway, *and* two at **P**. 6503

PARCEL (6)
Ge 33:19 he bought a **p** of a field, where he had 2513
Jos 24:32 in a **p** of ground which Jacob bought of 2513
Ru 4: 3 selleth a **p** of land, which *was* our brother 2513
1Ch 11:13 where was a **p** of ground full *of* barley; 2513
11:14 they set themselves in the midst of *that* **p**, 2513
Jn 4: 5 near to the **p of ground** that Jacob gave to *5564*

PARCHED (9)
Lev 23:14 neither bread, nor **p** *corn,* nor green ears, 7039
Jos 5:11 and **p** *corn* in the selfsame day. 7033
Ru 2:14 he reached her **p** *corn,* and she did eat, and 7039
1Sa 17:17 for thy brethren an ephah of this **p** *corn,* 7039
25:18 five measures of **p** *corn,* and an hundred 7039
2Sa 17:28 **p** *corn,* and beans, and lentiles, and 7039
17:28 and beans, and lentiles, and **p** *pulse,* 7039
Isa 35: 7 And the **p ground** shall become a pool, and 8273
Jer 17: 6 shall inhabit the **p places** in the wilderness, 2788

PARCHMENTS (1)
2Ti 4:13 and the books, *but* especially the **p**. *3200*

PARDON (16) [PARDONED, PARDONETH]
Ex 23:21 for he will not **p** your transgressions: 5375
34: 9 **p** our iniquity and our sin, and take us for 5545
Nu 14:19 **P**, I beseech thee, the iniquity of this people 5545
1Sa 15:25 **p** my sin, and turn again with me, 5375
2Ki 5:18 In this thing the LORD **p** thy servant, 5545
5:18 the LORD **p** thy servant in this thing. 5545
24: 4 which the LORD would not **p**. 5545
2Ch 30:18 The good LORD **p** every one 3722
Ne 9:17 thou *art* a God **ready to p**, gracious and 5547
Job 7:21 why dost thou not **p** my transgression, and 5375
Ps 25:11 name's sake, O LORD, **p** mine iniquity; 5545
Isa 55: 7 and to our God, for he will abundantly **p**. 5545
Jer 5: 1 that seeketh the truth; and I will **p** it. 5545
5: 7 How shall I **p** thee for this? thy children 5545
33: 8 I will **p** all their iniquities, whereby they 5545
50:20 be found: for I will **p** them whom I reserve. 5545

PARDONED (3) [PARDON]
Nu 14:20 I have **p** according to thy word: 5545
Isa 40: 2 is accomplished, that her iniquity is **p**: 7521
La 3:42 and have rebelled: thou hast not **p**. 5545

PARDONETH (1) [PARDON]
Mic 7:18 that **p** iniquity, and passeth by 5375

PARE (1)
Dt 21:12 she shall shave her head, and **p** her nails; 6213

PARENTS (21)
Mt 10:21 the children shall rise up against *their* **p**, *1118*
Mk 13:12 and children shall rise up against *their* **p**, *1118*
Lk 2:27 and when the **p** brought in the child Jesus, *1118*
2:41 Now his **p** went to Jerusalem every year at *1118*
8:56 And her **p** were astonished: but he charged *1118*
18:29 or **p**, or brethren, or wife, or children, *1118*
21:16 And ye shall be betrayed both by **p**, and *1118*
Jn 9: 2 Master, who did sin, this *man,* or his **p**, *1118*
9: 3 Neither hath this *man* sinned, nor his **p**: *1118*
9:18 until they called the **p** of him that had *1118*
9:20 His **p** answered them and said, We know *1118*
9:22 These *words* spake his **p**, because *1118*
9:23 Therefore said his **p**, He is of age; ask him. *1118*
Ro 1:30 inventors of evil *things,* disobedient to **p**, *1118*
2Co 12:14 the children ought not to lay up for the **p**, *1118*
12:14 for the parents, but the **p** for the children. *1118*
Eph 6: 1 Children, obey your **p** in the Lord: for this *1118*
Col 3:20 obey *your* **p** in all *things:* for this is well *1118*
1Ti 5: 4 shew piety at home, and to requite *their* **p**: *4269*
2Ti 3: 2 disobedient to **p**, unthankful, unholy, *1118*
Heb 11:23 was hid three months of his **p**, because *3962*

PARLOUR (5) [PARLOURS]
Jdg 3:20 he was sitting in a summer **p**, which he had 5944
3:23 shut the doors of the **p** upon him, and 5944
3:24 the doors of the **p** *were* locked, they said, 5944
3:25 behold, he opened not the doors of the **p**; 5944
1Sa 9:22 brought them into the **p**, and made them sit 3957

PARLOURS (1) [PARLOUR]
1Ch 28:11 of the inner **p** thereof, and of the place of 2315

PARMASHTA (1)
Est 9: 9 **P**, and Arisai, and Aridai, and Vajezatha, 6534

PARMENAS (1)
Ac 6: 5 and **P**, and Nicolas a proselyte of Antioch: *3937*

PARNACH (1)
Nu 34:25 of Zebulun, Elizaphan the son of **P**. 6535

PAROSH (5)
Ezr 2: 3 The children of **P**, two thousand an 6551
10:25 of the sons of **P**; Ramiah, and Jeziah, and 6551
Ne 3:25 the prison. After him Pedaiah the son of **P**. 6551
7: 8 The children of **P**, two thousand an 6551

Ne 10:14 P, Pahath-moab, Elam, Zatthu, Bani, 6551

PARSHANDATHA (1)

Est 9: 7 And P, and Dalphon, and Aspatha, 6577

PARSIN See UPHARSIN

PART (214) [APART, FOREPART, PARTED, PARTETH, PARTING, PARTITION, PARTLY, PARTS]

Ge 41:34 take up the fifth p of the land of Egypt in NIH
47:24 that you shall give the fifth p unto Pharaoh, NIH
47:26 that Pharaoh should have the fifth p; except NIH
Ex 16:36 Now an omer is the tenth p of an ephah. NIH
19:17 they stood at the nether p of the mount. 8482
29:26 before the LORD: and it shall be thy p. 4490
29:40 with the fourth p of a hin of beaten oil; 7253
29:40 the fourth p of a hin of wine for a drink NIH
Lev 1:16 cast it beside the altar on the east p, by 6924
2: 6 Thou shalt p it in pieces, and 6595+6626
2:16 p of the beaten corn thereof, and part of NIH
2:16 beaten corn thereof, and p of the oil thereof, NIH
5:11 p of an ephah of fine flour for a sin NIH
5:16 holy thing, and shall add the fifth p thereto, NIH
6: 5 shall add the fifth p more thereto, and NIH
6:20 the tenth p of an ephah of fine flour for a NIH
7:33 shall have the right shoulder for his p. 4490
8:29 of the ram of consecration it was Moses' p; 4490
11:35 every thing whereupon any p of their NIH
11:37 if any p of their carcase fall upon any NIH
11:38 any p of their carcase fall thereon, it shall NIH
13:41 he that hath his hair fallen off from the p of 6285
22:14 he shall put the fifth p thereof unto it, and NIH
23:13 shall be of wine, the fourth p of a hin. NIH
27:13 he shall add a fifth p thereof unto thy NIH
27:15 he shall add the fifth p of the money of thy NIH
27:16 LORD some p of a field of his possession, NIH
27:19 he shall add the fifth p of the money of thy NIH
27:27 and shall add a fifth p of it thereto: NIH
27:31 he shall add thereto the fifth p thereof. NIH
Nu 5: 7 add unto it the fifth p thereof, and give it NIH
5:15 the tenth p of an ephah of barley meal; NIH
15: 4 mingled with the fourth p of a hin of oil. NIH
15: 5 the fourth p of a hin of wine for a drink NIH
15: 6 mingled with the third p of a hin of oil. NIH
15: 7 thou shalt offer the third p of a hin of wine, NIH
18:20 neither shalt thou have any p among them: 2506
18:20 I am thy p and thine inheritance among 2506
18:26 for the LORD, even a tenth p of the tithe. NIH
18:29 even the hallowed p thereof out of it. NIH
22:41 that thence he might see the utmost p of 7097
23:10 and the number of the fourth p of Israel? 7255
23:13 thou shalt see but the utmost p of them, 7097
28: 5 a tenth p of an ephah of flour for a meat NIH
28: 5 mingled with the fourth p of a hin of beaten NIH
28: 7 be the fourth p of a hin for the one lamb: NIH
28:14 the third p of a hin unto a ram, and a fourth NIH
28:14 a ram, and a fourth p of a hin unto a lamb: NIH
Dt 10: 9 Wherefore Levi hath no p nor inheritance 2506
12:12 forasmuch as he hath no p nor inheritance 2506
14:27 for he hath no p nor inheritance with thee. 2506
14:29 he hath no p nor inheritance with thee,) 2506
18: 1 shall have no p nor inheritance with Israel: 2506
33:21 he provided the first p for himself, because NIH
Jos 14: 4 they gave no p unto the Levites in the land, 2506
15: 1 the uttermost p of the south coast. 4480+7097
15: 5 bay of the sea at the uttermost p of Jordan: 7097
15:13 he gave a p among the children of Judah, 2506
18: 7 the Levites have no p among you; for 2506
19: 9 for the p of the children of Judah was too 2506
22:25 of Gad; ye have no p in the LORD: 2506
22:27 time to come, Ye have no p in the LORD. 2506
Ru 1:17 if ought but death p thee and me. 6504
2: 3 her hap was to light on a p of the field 2513
3:13 perform unto thee the p of a kinsman, 1350
3:13 well; let him do the kinsman's p: 1350
3:13 if he will not do the p of a kinsman to 1350
3:13 will I do the p of a kinsman to thee, as 1350
1Sa 9: 8 I have here at hand the fourth p of a shekel 7253
14: 2 Saul tarried in the uttermost p of Gibeah 7097
23:20 our p shall be to deliver him into the king's NIH
30:24 as his p is that goeth down to the battle, so 2506
30:24 so shall his p be that tarrieth by the stuff: 2506
30:24 that tarrieth by the stuff: they shall p alike. 2505
2Sa 14: 6 there was none to p them, but the one 996+5337
18: 2 David sent forth a third p of the people 7992
18: 2 a third p under the hand of Abishai the son 7992
18: 2 a third p under the hand of Ittai the Gittite. 7992
20: 1 and said, We have no p in David, 2506
1Ki 6:24 from the uttermost p of the one wing unto 7098
6:24 uttermost p of the other were ten cubits. 7098
6:31 and side posts were a fifth p of the wall. NIH
6:33 posts of olive tree, a fourth p of the wall. NIH
2Ki 6:25 the fourth p of a kab of dove's dung for 7255
7: 5 when they were come to the uttermost p of 7097
7: 8 when these lepers came to the uttermost p 7097
11: 5 A third p of you that enter in on the sabbath NIH
11: 6 And a third p shall be at the gate of Sur; and NIH
11: 6 and a third p at the gate behind the guard: NIH
18:23 if thou be able on thy p to set riders upon 3807.1
1Ch 12:29 for hitherto the greatest p of them had kept 4768
2Ch 23: 4 A third p of you entering on the sabbath, NIH
23: 5 a third p shall be at the king's house, and NIH
23: 5 and a third p at the gate of the foundation: NIH
29:16 the priests went into the inner p of 6441
Ne 1: 9 out unto the uttermost p of the heaven, 7097
3: 9 of Hur, the ruler of the half p of Jerusalem. 6418
3:12 the ruler of the half p of Jerusalem, he and 6418
3:14 of Rechab, the ruler of p of Beth-haccerem; 6418
3:15 son of Col-hozeh, the ruler of p of Mizpah; 6418
3:16 the ruler of the half p of Beth-zur, 6418
3:17 the ruler of the half p of Keilah, in his part. 6418
3:17 the ruler of the half part of Keilah, in his p. 6418
3:18 the ruler of the half p of Keilah. 6418
Ne 5:11 also the hundredth p of the money, and NIH
9: 3 LORD their God one fourth p of the day; NIH
9: 3 another fourth p they confessed, and NIH
10:32 to charge ourselves yearly with the third p NIH
Job 32:17 I said, I will answer also my p, I also will 2506
41: 6 shall they p him among the merchants? 2673
Ps 5: 9 their inward p is very wickedness; NIH
22:18 They p my garments among them, and 2505
51: 6 in the hidden p thou shalt make me to know NIH
118: 7 The LORD taketh my p with them that 3807.1
Pr 8:26 nor the highest p of the dust of the world. 7218
8:31 Rejoicing in the habitable p of his earth; 8398
17: 2 shall have p of the inheritance among 2505
Isa 7:18 is in the uttermost p of the rivers of Egypt, 7097
24:16 From the uttermost p of the earth have we 3671
36: 8 if thou be able on thy p to set riders upon 3807.1
44:16 He burneth p thereof in the fire; with part 2677
44:16 with p thereof he eateth flesh; he roasteth 2677
44:19 to say, I have burnt p of it in the fire; 2677
Eze 4:11 also water by measure, the sixth p of a hin: NIH
5: 2 Thou shalt burn with fire a third p in NIH
5: 2 thou shalt take a third p, and smite about it NIH
5: 2 a third p thou shalt scatter in the wind; and NIH
5:12 A third p of thee shall die with NIH
5:12 a third p shall fall by the sword round about NIH
5:12 and I will scatter a third p into all the winds, NIH
39: 2 leave but the sixth p of thee, and 8338
45:11 that the bath may contain the tenth p of a 4643
45:11 and the ephah the tenth p of a homer: NIH
45:13 the sixth p of an ephah of a homer of wheat, NIH
45:13 ye shall give the sixth p of an ephah of a 8341
45:14 ye shall offer the tenth p of a bath out of 4643
45:17 it shall be the prince's p to give burnt 5921
46:14 the sixth p of an ephah, and the third part of NIH
46:14 of an ephah, and the third p of a hin of oil, NIH
Da 1: 2 p of the vessels of the house of God: 4480+7117
2:33 of iron, his feet p of iron and part of clay. 4481
2:33 of iron, his feet part of iron and p of clay. 4481
2:41 toes, p of potter's clay, and part of iron, 4481
2:41 toes, part of potter's clay, and p of iron, 4481
2:42 as the toes of the feet were p of iron, and 4481
2:42 p of clay, so the kingdom shall be partly 4481
5: 5 the king saw the p of the hand that wrote. 6447
5:24 was the p of the hand sent from him; and 6447
11:31 arms shall stand on his p, and they shall 4480
Joel 2:20 his hinder p towards the utmost sea, and 5490
Am 7: 4 devoured the great deep, and did eat up a p. 2506
Zec 13: 9 And I will bring the third p through the fire, NIH
Mk 4:38 And he was in the hinder p of the ship, 4403
9:40 For he that is not against us is on our p. 5228
13:27 from the uttermost p of the earth to 206
13:27 of the earth to the uttermost p of heaven. 206
Lk 10:42 and Mary hath chosen that good p, 3310
11:36 therefore be full of light, having no p dark, 3313
11:39 but your inward p is full of ravening and 2081
17:24 that lighteneth out of the one p under NIG
17:24 shineth unto the other p under heaven; NIG
Jn 13: 8 If I wash thee not, thou hast no p with me. 3313
19:23 and made four parts, to every soldier a p; 3313
Ac 1: 8 and unto the uttermost p of the earth. 2078
1:17 and had obtained p of this ministry. 2819
1:25 That he may take p of this ministry and 2819
5: 2 And kept back p of the price, his wife also NIG
5: 2 being privy to it, and brought a certain p, 3313
5: 3 and to keep back p of the price of the land? NIG
8:21 Thou hast neither p nor lot in this matter: 3310
14: 4 and p held with the Jews, and part 3303+3588
14: 4 the Jews, and p with the apostles. 1161+3588
16:12 which is the chief city of that p of 3310
19:32 the more p knew not wherefore they were 4183
23: 6 But when Paul perceived that the one p 3313
23: 9 the scribes that were of the Pharisees' p 3313
27:12 the more p advised to depart thence also, 4183
27:41 the hinder p was broken with the violence 4403
Ro 11:25 that blindness in p is happened to Israel, 3313
1Co 12:24 abundant honour to that p which lacked: NIG
13: 9 For we know in p, and we prophesy in part. 3313
13: 9 For we know in part, and we prophesy in p. 3313
13:10 then that which is in p shall be done away. 3313
13:12 now I know in p; but then shall I know 3313
15: 6 of whom the greater p remain unto this 4183
16:17 for that which was lacking on your p they 4771
2Co 1:14 As also you have acknowledged us in p, 3313
2: 5 he hath not grieved me, but in p: 3313
6:15 what p hath he that believeth with an 3310
Eph 4:16 working in the measure of every p, 3313
Tit 2: 8 that he that is of the contrary p may be NIG
Heb 2:14 he also himself likewise took p of 3348
7: 2 To whom also Abraham gave a tenth p of NIG
1Pe 4:14 on their p he is evil spoken of, but on your 2596
4:14 spoken of, but on your p he is glorified. 2596
Rev 6: 8 unto them over the fourth p of the earth, NIG
8: 7 and the third p of trees was burnt up, and all NIG
8: 8 and the third p of the sea became blood; NIG
8: 9 And the third p of the creatures which were NIG
8: 9 and the third p of the ships were destroyed. NIG
8:10 and it fell upon the third p of the rivers, and NIG
8:11 the third p of the waters became NIG
8:12 and the third p of the sun was smitten, and NIG
8:12 and the third p of the moon, and the third NIG
8:12 of the moon, and the third p of the stars; NIG
8:12 so as the third p of them was darkened and NIG
8:12 and the day shone not for a third p of it, NIG
9:15 and a year, for to slay the third p of men. NIG
9:18 By these three was the third p of men killed, NIG
11:13 and the tenth p of the city fell, and in NIG
12: 4 And his tail drew the third p of the stars of NIG
20: 6 holy is he that hath p in the first 3313
21: 8 shall have their p in the lake which burneth 3313
22:19 God shall take away his p out of the book 3313

PARTAKER (9) [PARTAKERS, PARTAKEST]

Ps 50:18 with him, and hast been p with adulterers. 2506
1Co 9:10 that he that thresheth in hope should be p of 3348
9:23 that I might be p thereof with you. 4791
10:30 For if I by grace be a p, why am I evil 3348
1Ti 5:22 no man, neither be p of other men's sins: 2841
2Ti 1: 8 be thou p of the afflictions of the gospel 4777
2: 6 that laboureth must be first p of the fruits. 3335
1Pe 5: 1 also a p of the glory that shall be revealed: 2844
2Jn 1:11 For he that biddeth him God speed is p of 2841

PARTAKERS (22) [PARTAKER]

Mt 23:30 we would not have been p with them in 2844
Ro 15:27 For if the Gentiles have been made p of 2841
1Co 9:12 If others be p of this power over you, 3348
9:13 they which wait at the altar are p with 4829
10:17 one body: for we are all p of that one bread. 3348
10:18 are not they which eat of the sacrifices p of 2844
10:21 ye cannot be p of the Lord's table, and 3348
2Co 1: 7 that as you are p of the sufferings, so 2844
Eph 3: 6 p of his promise in Christ by the gospel: 4830
5: 7 Be not ye therefore p with them. 4830
Php 1: 7 of the gospel, ye all are p of my grace. 4791
Col 1:12 which hath made us meet to be p of 3310
1Ti 6: 2 are faithful and beloved, p of the benefit. 482
Heb 2:14 then as the children are p of flesh and 2841
3: 1 holy brethren, p of the heavenly calling, 3353
3:14 For we are made p of Christ, if we hold 3353
6: 4 and were made p of the Holy Ghost, 3353
12: 8 whereof all are p, then are ye bastards, and 3353
12:10 that we might be p of his holiness. 3335
1Pe 4:13 inasmuch as ye are p of Christ's sufferings; 2841
2Pe 1: 4 that by these you might be p of the divine 2844
Rev 18: 4 that ye be not p of her sins, and that ye 4790

PARTAKEST (1) [PARTAKER]

Ro 11:17 and with them p of the root and 1096+4791

PARTED (12) [PART]

Ge 2:10 from thence it was p, and became into four 6504
2Ki 2:11 horses of fire, and p them both asunder; 6504
2:14 the waters, they p hither and thither: 2673
Job 38:24 By what way is the light p, which scattereth 2505
Joel 3: 2 among the nations, and p my land. 2505
Mt 27:35 and p his garments, casting lots: 1266
27:35 They p my garments among them, and 1266
Mk 15:24 they p his garments, casting lots upon 1266
Lk 23:34 And they p his raiment, and cast lots. 1266
24:51 he was p from them, and carried up into 1339
Jn 19:24 They p my raiment among them, and 1266
Ac 2:45 p them to all men, as every man had need. 1266

PARTETH (3) [PART]

Lev 11: 3 Whatsoever p the hoof, and 6536
Dt 14: 6 every beast that p the hoof, and 6536
Pr 18:18 to cease, and p between the mighty. 6504

PARTHIANS (1)

Ac 2: 9 P, and Medes, and Elamites, and 3934

PARTIAL (2) [PARTIALITY]

Mal 2: 9 kept my ways, but have been p in the law. 6440
Jas 2: 4 Are ye not then p in yourselves, and 1252

PARTIALITY (2) [PARTIAL]

1Ti 5:21 one before another, doing nothing by p. 4346
Jas 3:17 without p, and without hypocrisy. 87

PARTICIPATION See COMMUNION

PARTICULAR (2) [PARTICULARLY]

1Co 12:27 are the body of Christ, and members in p. 3313
Eph 5:33 Nevertheless let every one of you in p so 2596

PARTICULARLY (2) [PARTICULAR]

Ac 21:19 he declared p what things God 1520+1538+2596
Heb 9: 5 of which we cannot now speak p. 2596+3313

PARTIES (1)

Ex 22: 9 the cause of both p[s] shall come before 1992.1

PARTING (1) [PART]

Eze 21:21 For the king of Babylon stood at the p of 517

PARTITION (2) [PART]

1Ki 6:21 he made a p by the chains of gold before 5674
Eph 2:14 hath broken down the middle wall of p 5418

PARTLY (5) [PART]

Da 2:42 so the kingdom shall be p strong, and 4481+7118
2:42 shall be partly strong, and p broken. 4481
1Co 11:18 among you; and I p believe it. 3313+5100
Heb 10:33 P, whilst ye were made a 3303+3778
10:33 and p, whilst ye became companions 1161+3778

PARTNER (3) [PARTNERS]

Pr 29:24 Whoso is p with a thief hateth his own 2505
2Co 8:23 he is my p and fellowhelper concerning 2844
Phm 1:17 If thou count me therefore a p, receive him 2844

PARTNERS (2) [PARTNER]

Lk 5: 7 And they beckoned unto their p, 3353
5:10 sons of Zebedee, which were p with Simon. 2844

PARTRIDGE (2)

1Sa 26:20 as when one doth hunt a p in 7124
Jer 17:11 As the p sitteth on eggs, and hatcheth them 7124

PARTS (64) [PART]

Ge 47:24 four p shall be your own, for seed of 3027
Ex 33:23 mine hand, and thou shalt see my back p: 268
Lev 1: 8 shall lay the p, the head, and the fat, 5409
22:23 any thing superfluous or lacking in his p, 7038
Nu 10: 5 the camps that lie on the east p shall go 6924
11: 1 that were in the uttermost p of the camp. 7097
31:27 divide the prey into two p; between them 2673

Dt 19: 3 **divide** the coasts of thy land, which the LORD
thy God giveth thee to inherit, **into three p**, 8027
30: 4 driven out unto the **outmost p** of heaven, 7097
Jos 18: 5 they shall divide it into seven **p**: Judah shall 2506
18: 6 therefore describe the land *into* seven **p**, 2506
18: 9 described it by cities into seven **p** in a 2506
1Sa 5: 9 and they had emerods in their **secret p**. 8368
2Sa 19:43 We have ten **p** in the king, and we have 3027
1Ki 6:38 was the house finished throughout all the **p** 1697
7:25 and all their **hinder p** *were* inward. 268
16:21 the people of Israel divided into **two p**: 2677
2Ki 11: 7 two **p** of all you that go forth on 3027
2Ch 4: 4 and all their **hinder p** *were* inward. 268
Ne 11: 1 and nine **p** *to dwell* in *other* cities. 3027
Job 26:14 Lo, these *are* **p** of his ways: but how little a 7098
38:36 Who hath put wisdom in the **inward p**? or 2910
41:12 I will not conceal his **p**, nor *his* power, 907
Ps 2: 8 the **uttermost p** of the earth *for* thy 657
51: 6 Behold, thou desirest truth in the **inward p**: 2910
63: 9 to destroy *it*, shall go into the **lower p** of 8482
65: 8 They also that dwell in the **uttermost p** are 7099
78:66 he smote his enemies in the **hinder p**: he put 268
136:13 To him which divided the Red sea into **p**: 1506
139: 9 *and* dwell in the **uttermost p** of the sea; 319
139:15 curiously wrought in the **lowest p** of 8482
Pr 18: 8 they go down *into* the **innermost p** of 2315
20:27 searching all the **inward p** of the belly. 2315
20:30 so *do* stripes the **inward p** of the belly. 2315
26:22 they go down *into* the **innermost p** of 2315
Isa 3:17 the LORD will discover their **secret p**. 6596
16:11 and mine **inward p** for Kir-haresh. 7130
44:23 hath done *it*: shout, ye **lower p** of the earth: 8482
Jer 31:33 I will put my law in their **inward p**, and 7130
34:18 in twain, and passed between the **p** thereof, 1335
34:19 which passed between the **p** of the calf; 1335
Eze 26:20 shall set thee **in the low p** of the earth, 8482
31:14 to the **nether p** of the earth, in the midst of 8482
31:16 shall be comforted in the **nether p** of 8482
31:18 of Eden unto the **nether p** of the earth: 8482
32:18 unto the **nether p** of the earth, with them 8482
32:24 into the **nether p** of the earth, 8482
37:11 our hope is lost: we are cut off **for** our **p**. 3807.1
38:15 come from thy place out of the north **p**, 3411
39: 2 cause thee to come up from the north **p**, 3411
48: 8 and *in* length as one of the *other* **p**, 2506
Zec 13: 8 two **p** therein shall be cut off *and* die; 6310
Mt 2:22 he turned aside into the **p** of Galilee: *3313*
12:42 for she came from the **uttermost p** of *4009*
Mk 8:10 and came into the **p** of Dalmanutha. *3313*
Lk 11:31 for she came from the **utmost p** of the earth *4009*
Jn 19:23 took his garments, and made four **p**, *3313*
Ac 2:10 and in the **p** of Libya about Cyrene, and *3313*
20: 2 And when he had gone over those **p**, and *3313*
Ro 15:23 But now having no more place in these **p**, *2824*
1Co 12:23 our uncomely *p* have more abundant NIG
12:24 For our comely *p* have no need: NIG
Eph 4: 9 that he also descended first into the lower **p** *3313*
Rev 16:19 And the great city was *divided* into three **p**, *3313*

PARUAH (1)

1Ki 4:17 Jehoshaphat the son of **P**, in Issachar: 6515

PARVAIM (1)

2Ch 3: 6 for beauty: and the gold *was* gold of **P**. 6516

PASACH (1)

1Ch 7:33 of Japhlet; **P**, and Bimhal, and Ashvath. 6457

PAS-DAMMIM (1)

1Ch 11:13 He was with David at **P**, and there 6450

PASEAH (3) [PHASEAH]

1Ch 4:12 and **P**, and Tehinnah the father of Irnahash. 6454
Ezr 2:49 the children of **P**, the children of Besai, 6454
Ne 3: 6 the old gate repaired Jehoiada the son of **P**, 6454

PASHHUR See PASHUR

PASHUR (14)

1Ch 9:12 the son of **P**, the son of Malchijah, and 6583
Ezr 2:38 The children of **P**, a thousand two hundred 6583
10:22 of the sons of **P**; Elioenai, Maaseiah, 6583
Ne 7:41 The children of **P**, a thousand two hundred 6583
10: 3 **P**, Amariah, Malchijah, 6583
11:12 the son of **P**, the son of Malchiah, 6583
Jer 20: 1 Now **P** the son of Immer the priest, 6583
20: 2 **P** smote Jeremiah the prophet, and put him 6583
20: 3 that **P** brought forth Jeremiah out of 6583
20: 3 The LORD hath not called thy name **P**, 6583
20: 6 **P**, and all that dwell in thine house shall go 6583
21: 1 when king Zedekiah sent unto him **P** 6583
38: 1 Gedaliah the son of **P**, and Jucal the son of 6583
38: 1 of Shelemiah, and **P** the son of Malchiah, 6583

PASS (830) [OVERPASS, PASSAGE, PASSAGES, PASSED, PASSEDST, PASSENGERS, PASSEST, PASSETH, PASSING, PAST]

Ge 4: 3 in process of time it **came to p**, that Cain 1961
4: 8 it **came to p**, when they were in the field, 1961
4:14 it shall **come to p**, *that* every one that 1961
6: 1 it **came to p**, when men began to multiply 1961
7:10 it **came to p** after seven days, that 1961
8: 1 God **made** a wind **to p** over the earth, and 5674
8: 6 it **came to p** at the end of forty days, 1961
8:13 it **came to p** in the six hundredth and 1961
9:14 it shall **come to p**, when I bring a cloud 1961
11: 2 it **came to p**, as they journeyed from 1961
12:11 it **came to p**, when he was come near to 1961
12:12 Therefore it shall **come to p**, when 1961
12:14 it **came to p**, that, when Abram was come 1961
14: 1 it **came to p** in the days of Amraphel king 1961
15:17 it **came to p**, that, when the sun went 1961
18: 3 **p** not **away**, I pray thee, from thy servant: 5674
18: 5 ye your hearts; after *that* you shall **p on**: 5674
Ge 19:17 it **came to p**, when they had brought them 1961
19:29 it **came to p**, when God destroyed the cities 1961
19:34 it **came to p** on the morrow, that 1961
20:13 it **came to p**, when God caused me to 1961
21:22 it **came to p** at that time, that Abimelech 1961
22: 1 it **came to p** after these things, that God did 1961
22:20 it **came to p** after these things, that it was 1961
24:14 let it **come to p**, *that* the damsel to whom I 1961
24:15 it **came to p**, before he had done speaking, 1961
24:22 it **came to p**, as the camels had done 1961
24:30 it **came to p**, when he saw the earring and 1961
24:43 it shall **come to p**, *that when* the virgin 1961
24:52 it **came to p**, that, when Abraham's servant 1961
25:11 it **came to p** after the death of Abraham, 1961
26: 8 it **came to p**, when he had been there a long 1961
26:32 it **came to p** the same day, that Isaac's 1961
27: 1 it **came to p**, that when Isaac was old, and 1961
27:30 it **came to p**, as soon as Isaac had made an 1961
27:40 it shall **come to p** when thou shalt have 1961
29:10 it **came to p**, when Jacob saw Rachel 1961
29:13 it **came to p**, when Laban heard the tidings 1961
29:23 it **came to p** in the evening, that he took 1961
29:25 it **came to p**, that in the morning, behold, 1961
30:25 it **came to p**, when Rachel had born 1961
30:32 I will **p** through all thy flock to day, 5674
30:41 it **came to p**, whensoever the stronger 1961
31:10 it **came to p** at the time that the cattle 1961
31:52 that I will not **p over** this heap to thee, and 5674
31:52 that thou shalt not **p over** this heap and 5674
32:16 **P over** before me, and put a space betwixt 5674
33:14 I pray thee, **p over** before his servant: 5674
34:25 it **came to p** on the third day, when they 1961
35:17 it **came to p**, when she was in hard labour, 1961
35:18 it **came to p**, as her soul was in departing 1961
35:22 it **came to p**, when Israel dwelt in that land, 1961
37:23 it **came to p**, when Joseph was come unto 1961
38: 1 it **came to p** at that time, that Judah went 1961
38: 9 it **came to p**, when he went in unto his 1961
38:24 it **came to p** about three months after, 1961
38:27 it **came to p** in the time of her travail, that, 1961
38:28 it **came to p**, when she travailed, that 1961
38:29 it **came to p**, as he drew back his hand, 1961
39: 5 it **came to p** from the time *that* he had 1961
39: 7 it **came to p** after these things, that his 1961
39:10 it **came to p**, as she spake to Joseph day by 1961
39:11 it **came to p** about this time, that *Joseph* 1961
39:13 it **came to p**, when she saw that he had left 1961
39:15 it **came to p**, when he heard that I lifted up 1961
39:18 it **came to p**, as I lift up my voice and 1961
39:19 it **came to p**, when his master heard 1961
40: 1 it **came to p** after these things, *that* 1961
40:20 it **came to p** the third day, *which was* 1961
41: 1 it **came to p** at the end of two full years, 1961
41: 8 it **came to p** in the morning that his spirit 1961
41:13 And it **came to p**, as he interpreted to us, so 1961
41:32 by God, and God will shortly **bring** it **to p**. 6213
42:35 it **came to p** as they emptied their sacks, 1961
43: 2 it **came to p**, when they had eaten up 1961
43:21 it **came to p**, when we came to the inn, 1961
44:24 it **came to p** when we came up unto thy 1961
44:31 It shall **come to p**, when he seeth that 1961
46:33 it shall **come to p**, when Pharaoh shall call 1961
47:24 it shall **come to p** in the increase, that you 1961
48: 1 it **came to p** after these things, that *one* told 1961
50:20 it unto good, to **bring to p**, as *it is* this day, 6213
Ex 1:10 lest they multiply, and it **come to p**, that, 1961
1:21 it **came to p**, because the midwives feared 1961
2:11 it **came to p** in those days, when Moses 1961
2:23 it **came to p** in process of time, that 1961
3:21 it shall **come to p**, that, when ye go, 1961
4: 8 it shall **come to p**, if they will not believe 1961
4: 9 it shall **come to p**, if they will not believe 1961
4:24 it **came to p** by the way in the inn, that 1961
6:28 it **came to p** on the day *when* the LORD 1961
12:12 For I will **p** through the land of Egypt this 5674
12:13 I will **p over** you, and the plague shall not 6452
12:23 For the LORD will **p through** to smite 5674
12:23 the LORD will **p over** the door, and 6452
12:25 it shall **come to p**, when ye be come to 1961
12:26 it shall **come to p**, when your children shall 1961
12:29 it **came to p**, that at midnight the LORD 1961
12:41 it **came to p** at the end of the four hundred 1961
12:41 even the selfsame day it **came to p**, 1961
12:51 it **came to p** the selfsame day, *that* 1961
13:15 it **came to p**, when Pharaoh would hardly 1961
13:17 it **came to p**, when Pharaoh had let 1961
14:24 it **came to p**, that in the morning watch 1961
15:16 till thy people **p over**, O LORD, till 5674
15:16 O LORD, till the people **p over**, 5674
16: 5 it shall **come to p**, that on the sixth day 1961
16:10 it **came to p**, as Aaron spake unto 1961
16:13 it **came to p**, that at even the quails came 1961
16:22 it **came to p**, *that* on the sixth day they 1961
16:27 it **came to p**, *that* there went out *some* of 1961
17:11 it **came to p**, when Moses held up his hand, 1961
18:13 it **came to p** on the morrow, that Moses sat 1961
19:16 it **came to p** on the third day in 1961
22:27 it shall **come to p**, when he crieth unto me, 1961
32:19 it **came to p**, as soon as he came nigh unto 1961
32:30 it **came to p** on the morrow, that Moses 1961
33: 7 it **came to p**, *that* every one which sought 1961
33: 8 it **came to p**, when Moses went out unto 1961
33: 9 it **came to p**, as Moses entered into 1961
33:19 I will **make** all my goodness **p** before thee, 5674
33:22 it shall **come to p**, while my glory passeth 1961
33:22 will cover thee with my hand while I **p by**: 5674
34:29 it **came to p**, when Moses came down from 1961
40:17 it **came to p** in the first month in 1961
Lev 9: 1 it **came to p** on the eighth day, *that* Moses 1961
18:21 thou shalt not let *any* of thy seed **p through** 5674
Nu 5:27 it shall **come to p**, *that*, if she be defiled, 1961
7: 1 it **came to p** on the day that Moses had 1961
10:11 it **came to p** on the twentieth *day* of 1961
10:35 And it **came to p**, when the ark set forward, 1961
11:23 whether my word shall **come to p** unto thee 7136
Nu 11:25 it **came to p**, that when the spirit rested 1961
16:31 it **came to p**, as he had made an end of 1961
16:42 it **came to p**, when the congregation was 1961
17: 5 it shall **come to p**, *that* the man's rod, 1961
17: 8 it **came to p**, that on the morrow Moses 1961
20:17 Let us **p**, I pray thee, through thy country: 5674
20:17 we will not **p** through the fields, or 5674
20:18 said unto him, Thou shalt not **p** by me, 5674
21: 8 it shall **come to p**, that every one that is 1961
21: 9 put it upon a pole, and it **came to p**, that if 1961
21:22 Let me **p** through thy land: we will not turn 5674
21:23 Sihon would not suffer Israel to **p** through 5674
22:41 it **came to p** on the morrow, that Balak 1961
26: 1 it **came to p** after the plague, that 1961
27: 7 **cause** the inheritance of their father **to p** 5674
27: 8 ye shall **cause** his inheritance **to p** unto his 5674
32:27 thy servants will **p over**, every man armed 5674
32:29 of Reuben will **p** with you **over** Jordan, 5674
32:30 if they will not **p over** with you armed, 5674
32:32 We will **p over** armed before the LORD 5674
33:55 it shall come to **p**, *that those* which ye let 1961
33:56 Moreover it shall **come to p**, *that* I shall do 1961
34: 4 to the ascent of Akrabbim, and **p on** to Zin: 5674
34: 4 go on *to* Hazar-addar, and **p on** to Azmon: 5674
Dt 1: 3 it **came to p** in the fortieth year, in 1961
2: 4 Ye are to **p** through the coast of your 5674
2:16 So it **came to p**, when all the men of war 1961
2:18 Thou art to **p over** *through* Ar, the coast of 5674
2:24 your journey, and **p over** the river Arnon: 5674
2:27 Let me **p** through thy land: I will go along 5674
2:28 only I will **p through** on my feet; 5674
2:29 until I shall **p over** Jordan into the land 5674
2:30 Sihon king of Heshbon would not let us **p** 5674
3:18 ye shall **p over** armed before your brethren 5674
5:23 it **came to p**, when ye heard the voice out 1961
7:12 Wherefore it shall **come to p**, if ye hearken 1961
9: 1 Thou art to **p over** Jordan *this* day, to go in 5674
9:11 it **came to p** at the end of forty days and 1961
11:13 it shall **come to p**, if you shall hearken 1961
11:29 it shall **come to p**, when the LORD thy 1961
11:31 For ye shall **p over** Jordan to go in to 5674
13: 2 the sign or the wonder **come to p**, 935
18:10 **maketh** his son or his daughter **to p through** 5674
18:19 it shall **come to p**, *that* whosoever will not 1961
18:22 if the thing follow not, nor **come to p**, that *is* 935
24: 1 it **come to p** that she find no favour in his 1961
27: 2 it shall be on the day when you shall **p over** 5674
28: 1 it shall **come to p**, if thou shalt hearken 1961
28:15 it shall **come to p**, if thou wilt not hearken 1961
28:63 it shall **come to p**, *that* as the LORD 1961
29:19 it **come to p**, when he heareth the words of 1961
30: 1 it shall **come to p**, when all these things are 1961
31:21 it shall **come to p**, when many evils and 1961
31:24 it **came to p**, when Moses had made an end 1961
Jos 1: 1 the servant of the LORD it **came to p**, 1961
1:11 **P** through the host, and command 5674
1:11 for within three days ye shall **p over** this 5674
1:14 ye shall **p** before your brethren armed, 5674
2: 5 it **came to p** *about the time* of shutting of 1961
3: 2 it **came to p** after three days, that 1961
3: 6 the covenant, and **p over** before the people. 5674
3:13 it shall **come to p**, as soon as the soles of 1961
3:14 it **came to p**, when the people removed 1961
3:14 to **p over** Jordan, and the priests bearing 5674
4: 1 it **came to p**, when all the people were 1961
4: 5 **P over** before the ark of the LORD your 5674
4:11 it **came to p**, when all the people were 1961
4:18 it **came to p**, when the priests that bare 1961
5: 1 it **came to p**, when all the kings of 1961
5: 8 it **came to p**, when they had done 1961
5:13 it **came to p**, when Joshua was by Jericho, 1961
6: 5 it shall **come to p**, *that* when *they* make a 1961
6: 7 **P on**, and compass the city, and let him that 5674
6: 7 let him that is armed **p on** before the ark of 5674
6: 8 it **came to p**, when Joshua had spoken unto 1961
6:15 it **came to p** on the seventh day, that they 1961
6:16 it **came to p** at the seventh time, when 1961
6:20 it **came to p**, when the people heard 1961
8: 5 it shall **come to p**, when they come out 1961
8:14 it **came to p**, when the king of Ai saw *it*, 1961
8:24 it **came to p**, when Israel had made an end 1961
9: 1 it **came to p**, when all the kings which 1961
9:16 it **came to p** at the end of three days after 1961
10: 1 Now it **came to p**, when Adoni-zedek king 1961
10:11 it **came to p**, as they fled from before 1961
10:20 it **came to p**, when Joshua and the children 1961
10:24 it **came to p**, when they brought out those 1961
10:27 it **came to p** at the time of the going down 1961
11: 1 it **came to p**, when Jabin king of Hazor had 1961
15:18 it **came to p**, as she came *unto him*, that 1961
17:13 Yet it **came to p**, when the children of 1961
21:45 unto the house of Israel; all **came to p**. 935
22:19 **p** ye **over** unto the land of the possession of 5674
23: 1 it **came to p** a long time after that 1961
23:14 all are **come to p** unto you, *and* not one thing 935
23:15 Therefore it shall **come to p**, *that* as all 1961
24:29 it **came to p** after these things, that Joshua 1961
Jdg 1: 1 Now after the death of Joshua it **came to p**, 1961
1:14 it **came to p**, when she came *to him*, that 1961
1:28 it **came to p**, when Israel was strong, 1961
2: 4 it **came to p**, when the angel of the LORD 1961
2:19 it **came to p**, when the judge was dead, 1961
3:27 it **came to p**, when he was come, that he 1961
3:28 and suffered not a man to **p over**. 5674
6: 7 it **came to p**, when the children of Israel 1961
6:25 it **came to p** the same night, that 1961
7: 9 it **came to p** the same night, that 1961
8:33 it **came to p**, as soon as Gideon was dead, 1961
9:42 it **came to p** on the morrow, that the people 1961
11: 4 it **came to p** in process of time, that 1961
11:17 Let me, I pray thee, **p** through thy land: 5674
11:19 Israel said unto him, Let us **p**, we pray thee, 5674
11:20 Sihon trusted not Israel to **p** through his 5674
11:35 it **came to p**, when he saw her, that he rent 1961
11:39 it **came to p** at the end of two months, 1961

Jdg 13:12 Manoah said, Now let thy words **come to p**. 935
13:17 that when thy sayings **come to p** we may do 935
13:20 For it **came to p**, when the flame went up 1961
14:11 it **came to p**, when they saw him, that they 1961
14:15 it **came to p** on the seventh day, that they 1961
14:17 it **came to p** on the seventh day, that he 1961
15: 1 it **came to p** within a while after, in 1961
15:17 it **came to p**, when he had made an end of 1961
16: 4 it **came to p** afterward, that he loved a 1961
16:16 it **came to p**, when she pressed him daily 1961
16:25 it **came to p**, when their hearts were merry, 1961
19: 1 it **came to p** in those days, when *there was* 1961
19: 5 it **came to p** on the fourth day, when they 1961
19:12 of Israel; we will **p over** to Gibeah. 5674
21: 3 of Israel, why is this **come to p** in Israel, 1961
21: 4 it **came to p** on the morrow, that the people 1961
Ru 1: 1 Now it **came to p** in the days when 1961
1:19 it **came to p**, when they were come *to* 1961
3: 8 it **came to p** at midnight, that the man was 1961
1Sa 1:12 it **came to p**, as she continued praying 1961
1:20 Wherefore it **came to p**, when the time was 1961
2:36 it shall **come to p**, *that* every one that is left 1961
3: 2 it **came to p** at that time, when Eli *was* laid 1961
4:18 it **came to p**, when he made mention of 1961
5:10 it **came to p**, as the ark of God came *to* 1961
7: 2 it **came to p**, while the ark abode in 1961
8: 1 it **came to p**, when Samuel was old, that he 1961
9: 6 all that he saith **cometh surely to p**: 935+935
9:26 it **came to p** about the spring of the day, 1961
9:27 Bid the servant **p on** before us, (and 5674
10: 5 it shall **come to p**, when thou art come 1961
10: 9 and all those signs **came to p** that day. 935
10:11 it **came to p**, when all that knew him 1961
11:11 it **came to p**, that they which remained 1961
13:10 it **came to p**, that as soon as he had made 1961
13:22 So it **came to p** in the day of battle, 1961
14: 1 Now it **came to p** upon a day, that Jonathan 1961
14: 8 we will **p over** unto *these* men, and we will 5674
14:19 it **came to p**, while Saul talked unto 1961
16: 6 it **came to p**, when they were come, that he 1961
16: 8 and **made** him **p** before Samuel. 5674
16: 9 Jesse **made** Shammah **to p by**. And he 5674
16:10 Jesse **made** seven of his sons **to p** before 5674
16:16 it shall **come to p**, when the evil spirit from 1961
16:23 it **came to p**, when the *evil* spirit from God 1961
17:48 it **came to p**, when the Philistine arose, 1961
18: 1 it **came to p**, when he made an end of 1961
18: 6 it **came to p** as they came, when David was 1961
18:10 it **came to p** on the morrow, that the evil 1961
18:19 it **came to p** at the time when Merab Saul's 1961
18:30 it **came to p**, after they went forth, 1961
20:27 it **came to p** on the morrow, *which was* 1961
20:35 it **came to p** in the morning, that Jonathan 1961
23: 6 it **came to p**, when Abiathar the son of 1961
23:23 it shall **come to p**, if he be in the land, 1961
24: 1 it **came to p**, when Saul was returned from 1961
24: 5 it **came to p** afterward, that David's heart 1961
24:16 it **came to p**, when David had made an end 1961
25:30 it shall **come to p**, when the LORD shall 1961
25:37 it **came to p** in the morning, when the wine 1961
25:38 it **came to p** about ten days *after*, that 1961
28: 1 it **came to p** in those days, that 1961
30: 1 it **came to p**, when David and his men were 1961
31: 8 it **came to p** on the morrow, when 1961
2Sa 1: 1 Now it **came to p** after the death of Saul, 1961
1: 2 It **came** even **to p** on the third day, that 1961
2: 1 it **came to p** after this, that David inquired 1961
2:23 it **came to p**, that as many as came to 1961
3: 6 it **came to p**, while there was war between 1961
4: 4 it **came to p**, as she made haste to flee, 1961
7: 1 it **came to p**, when the king sat in his 1961
7: 4 it **came to p** that night, that the word of 1961
8: 1 after this it **came to p**, that David smote 1961
10: 1 it **came to p** after this, that the king of 1961
11: 1 it **came to p**, after the year was expired, 1961
11: 2 it **came to p** in an eveningtide, that David 1961
11:14 it **came to p** in the morning, that David 1961
11:16 it **came to p**, when Joab observed the city, 1961
12:18 it **came to p** on the seventh day, that 1961
12:31 and **made** them **p** through the brickkiln: 5674
13: 1 it **came to p** after this, that Absalom 1961
13:23 it **came to p** after two full years, 1961
13:30 it **came to p**, while they *were* in the way, 1961
13:36 it **came to p**, as soon as he had made an 1961
15: 1 it **came to p** after this, that Absalom 1961
15: 7 it **came to p** after forty years, that Absalom 1961
15:22 David said to Ittai, Go and **p over**. 5674
15:32 it **came to p**, that *when* David was come to 1961
16:16 it **came to p**, when Hushai the Archite, 1961
17: 9 it will **come to p**, when *some* of them be 1961
17:16 the wilderness, but **speedily p over**; 5674+5674
17:21 it **came to p**, after they were departed, 1961
17:21 Arise, and **p quickly** over the water: 4120
17:27 it **came to p**, when David was come to 1961
19:25 it **came to p**, when he was come *to* 1961
21:18 it **came to p** after this, that there was again 1961
1Ki 1:21 Otherwise it shall **come to p**, when my lord 1961
2:39 it **came to p** at the end of three years, 1961
3:18 it **came to p** the third day after that I was 1961
5: 7 it **came to p**, when Hiram heard the words 1961
6: 1 it **came to p** in the four hundred and 1961
8:10 it **came to p**, when the priests were come 1961
9: 1 it **came to p**, when Solomon had finished 1961
9:10 it **came to p** at the end of twenty years, 1961
11: 4 For it **came to p**, when Solomon was old, 1961
11:15 For it **came to p**, when David was in 1961
11:29 it **came to p** at that time when Jeroboam 1961
12: 2 it **came to p**, when Jeroboam the son of 1961
12:20 it **came to p**, when all Israel heard that 1961
13: 4 it **came to p**, when king Jeroboam heard 1961
13:20 it **came to p**, as they sat at the table, 1961
13:23 it **came to p**, after he had eaten bread, and 1961
13:31 it **came to p**, after he had buried him, that 1961
13:32 of Samaria, shall **surely come to p**. 1961+1961
14:25 it **came to p** in the fifth year of king 1961
1Ki 15:21 it **came to p**, when Baasha heard *thereof*, 1961
15:29 it **came to p**, when he reigned, *that* he 1961
16:11 it **came to p**, when he *began* to reign, 1961
16:18 it **came to p**, when Zimri saw that the city 1961
16:31 it **came to p**, as if it had been a light thing 1961
17: 7 it **came to p** after a while, that the brook 1961
17:17 it **came to p** after these things, *that* the son 1961
18: 1 it **came to p** *after* many days, that the word 1961
18: 6 So they divided the land between them to **p** 5674
18:12 it shall **come to p**, *as soon as* I am gone 1961
18:17 it **came to p**, when Ahab saw Elijah, 1961
18:27 it **came to p** at noon, that Elijah mocked 1961
18:29 it **came to p**, when midday was past, and 1961
18:36 it **came to p** at *the time of* the offering of 1961
18:44 it **came to p** at the seventh *time*, that he 1961
18:45 it **came to p** in the mean while, that 1961
19:17 it shall **come to p**, *that* him that escapeth 1961
20:12 it **came to p**, when *Ben-hadad* heard this 1961
20:26 it **came to p** at the return of the year, 1961
21: 1 it **came to p** after these things, *that* Naboth 1961
21:15 it **came to p**, when Jezebel heard that 1961
21:16 it **came to p**, when Ahab heard that Naboth 1961
21:27 it **came to p**, when Ahab heard those 1961
22: 2 it **came to p** on the third year, that 1961
22:32 it **came to p**, when the captains of 1961
22:33 it **came to p**, when the captains of 1961
2Ki 2: 1 it **came to p**, when the LORD would take 1961
2: 9 it **came to p**, when they were gone over, 1961
2:11 it **came to p**, *as* they still went on, 1961
3: 5 it **came to p**, when Ahab was dead, that 1961
3:15 it **came to p**, when the minstrel played, 1961
3:20 it **came to p** in the morning, when the meat 1961
4: 6 it **came to p**, when the vessels were full, 1961
4:25 it **came to p**, when the man of God saw her 1961
4:40 it **came to p**, as they were eating of 1961
5: 7 it **came to p**, when the king of Israel had 1961
6: 9 Beware that *thou* **p** not such a place; 5674
6:20 it **came to p**, when they were come *into* 1961
6:24 it **came to p** after this, that Ben-hadad king 1961
6:30 it **came to p**, when the king heard 1961
7:18 it **came to p** as the man of God had spoken 1961
8: 3 it **came to p** at the seven years' end, 1961
8: 5 it **came to p**, *as* he was telling the king how 1961
8:15 it **came to p** on the morrow, that he took a 1961
9:22 it **came to p**, when Joram saw Jehu, that he 1961
10: 7 it **came to p**, when the letter came to them, 1961
10: 9 it **came to p** in the morning, that he went 1961
10:25 it **came to p**, as soon as he had made an 1961
13:21 it **came to p**, as they were burying a man, 1961
14: 5 it **came to p**, as soon as the kingdom was 1961
15:12 the fourth *generation*. And so it **came to p**. 1961
16: 3 yea, and **made** his son **to p** through the fire, 5674
17:17 **caused** their sons and their daughters **to p** 5674
18: 1 Now it **came to p** in the third year of 1961
18: 9 it **came to p** in the fourth year of king 1961
19: 1 it **came to p**, when king Hezekiah heard *it*, 1961
19:25 now have I **brought** it **to p**, that thou 935
19:35 it **came to p** that night, that the angel of 1961
19:37 it **came to p**, as he was worshipping *in* 1961
20: 4 it **came to p**, afore Isaiah was gone out *into* 1961
21: 6 he **made** his son **p** through the fire, and 5674
22: 3 it **came to p** in the eighteenth year of king 1961
22:11 it **came to p**, when the king had heard 1961
23:10 might **make** his son or his daughter **to p** 5674
24:20 of the LORD it **came to p** in Jerusalem 1961
25: 1 it **came to p** in the ninth year of his reign, 1961
25:25 it **came to p** in the seventh month, 1961
25:27 it **came to p** in the seven and thirtieth year 1961
1Ch 10: 8 it **came to p** on the morrow, when 1961
15:26 it **came to p**, when God helped the Levites 1961
15:29 it **came to p**, *as* the ark of the covenant of 1961
17: 1 Now it **came to p**, as David sat in his 1961
17: 3 it **came to p** the same night, that the word 1961
17:11 it shall **come to p**, when thy days be 1961
18: 1 Now after this it **came to p**, that David 1961
19: 1 Now it **came to p** after this, that Nahash 1961
20: 1 it **came to p**, that after the year was 1961
20: 4 it **came to p** after this, that there arose war 1961
2Ch 5:11 it **came to p**, when the priests were come 1961
5:13 It **came** even **to p**, as the trumpeters and 1961
8: 1 it **came to p** at the end of twenty years, 1961
10: 2 it **came to p**, when Jeroboam the son of 1961
12: 1 it **came to p**, when Rehoboam had 1961
12: 2 it **came to p**, *that* in the fifth year of king 1961
13:15 it **came to p**, that God smote Jeroboam and 1961
16: 5 it **came to p**, when Baasha heard *it*, that he 1961
18:31 it **came to p**, when the captains of 1961
18:32 For it **came to p**, that when the captains of 1961
20: 1 It **came to p** after this also, *that* 1961
21:19 it **came to p**, that in process of time, after 1961
22: 8 it **came to p**, that when Jehu was executing 1961
24: 4 it **came to p** after this, *that* Joash was 1961
24:11 Now it **came to p**, that at *what* time 1961
24:23 it **came to p** at the end of the year, *that* 1961
25: 3 Now it **came to p**, when the kingdom was 1961
25:14 Now it **came to p**, after that Amaziah was 1961
25:16 it **came to p**, as he talked with him, that 1961
33: 6 he **caused** his children **to p** through the fire 5674
34:19 it **came to p**, when the king had heard 1961
Ne 1: 1 it **came to p** in the month Chisleu, *in* 1961
1: 4 it **came to p**, when I heard these words, 1961
2: 1 it **came to p** in the month Nisan, *in* 1961
2:14 place for the beast *that was* under me to **p**. 5674
4: 1 it **came to p**, that when Sanballat heard that 1961
4: 7 it **came to p**, *that* when Sanballat, and 1961
4:12 it **came to p**, that when the Jews which 1961
4:15 it **came to p**, when our enemies heard that 1961
4:16 it **came to p** from that time forth, *that* 1961
6: 1 Now it **came to p**, when Sanballat, and 1961
6:16 it **came to p**, that when all our enemies 1961
7: 1 Now it **came to p**, when the wall was built, 1961
13: 3 Now it **came to p**, when they had heard 1961
13:19 it **came to p**, that when the gates of 1961
Est 1: 1 Now it **came to p** in the days of Ahasuerus, 1961
2: 8 So it **came to p**, when the king's 1961
Est 3: 4 Now it **came to p**, when they spake daily 1961
5: 1 Now it **came to p** on the third day, 1961
Job 6:15 *and* as the stream of brooks they **p away**; 5674
11:16 *and* remember *it* as waters *that* **p away**: 5674
14: 5 hast appointed his bounds that he cannot **p**; 5674
19: 8 He hath fenced up my way that I cannot **p**, 5674
34:20 shall be troubled at midnight, and **p away**: 5674
Ps 37: 5 trust also in him; and he shall **bring** *it* **to p**. 6213
37: 7 man who **bringeth** wicked devices **to p**. 6213
58: 8 let *every one of them* **p away**: 1980
78:13 the sea, and **caused** them **to p through**; 5674
80:12 that all they which **p by** the way do pluck 5674
89:41 All that **p by** the way spoil him: he is a 5674
104: 9 hast set a bound *that* they may not **p over**; 5674
136:14 **made** Israel **to p through** the midst of it: 5674
148: 6 he hath made a decree which shall not **p**. 5674
Pr 4:15 Avoid it, **p** not by it, turn from it, and 5674
4:15 pass not by it, turn from it, and **p away**. 5674
8:29 that the waters should not **p** his 5674
16:30 moving his lips he **bringeth** evil **to p**. 3615
19:11 and *it is* his glory to **p** over a transgression. 5674
22: 3 but the simple **p on**, and are punished. 5674
27:12 *but* the simple **p on**, *and* are punished. 5674
Isa 2: 2 it shall **come to p** in the last days, *that* 1961
3:24 it shall **come to p**, *that* instead of sweet 1961
4: 3 it shall **come to p**, *that* he that is left in 1961
7: 1 it **came to p** in the days of Ahaz the son of 1961
7: 7 It shall not stand, neither shall it **come to p**. 1961
7:18 it shall **come to p** in that day, *that* 1961
7:21 it shall **come to p** in that day, *that* a man 1961
7:22 it shall **come to p**, for the abundance of 1961
7:23 it shall **come to p** in that day, *that* every 1961
8: 8 he shall **p** through Judah; he shall overflow 2498
8:21 they shall **p** through it, hardly bestead and 5674
8:21 it shall **come to p**, that when they shall be 1961
10:12 Wherefore it shall **come to p**, *that* when 1961
10:20 it shall **come to p** in that day, *that* 1961
10:27 it shall **come to p** in that day, *that* his 1961
11:11 it shall **come to p** in that day, *that* the Lord 1961
14: 3 it shall **come to p** in the day that 1961
14:24 as I have thought, so shall it **come to p**; 1961
16:12 it shall **come to p**, when it is seen that 1961
17: 4 in that day it shall **come to p**, *that* the glory 1961
21: 1 As whirlwinds in the south **p through**; *so* 2498
22: 7 it shall **come to p**, *that* thy choicest valleys 1961
22:20 it shall **come to p** in that day, that I will 1961
23: 2 that **p over** the sea, have replenished. 5674
23: 6 **P** ye **over** to Tarshish; howl, ye inhabitants 5674
23:10 **P through** thy land as a river, O daughter 5674
23:12 arise, **p over** *to* Chittim; there also shalt 5674
23:15 it shall **come to p** in that day, that Tyre 1961
23:17 it shall **come to p** after the end of seventy 1961
24:18 it shall **come to p**, *that* he who fleeth from 1961
24:21 it shall **come to p** in that day, *that* 1961
27:12 it shall **come to p** in that day, *that* 1961
27:13 it shall **come to p** in that day, *that* the great 1961
28:15 the overflowing scourge shall **p through**, 5674
28:18 the overflowing scourge shall **p through**, 5674
28:19 for morning by morning shall it **p over**, 5674
28:21 and **bring to p** his act, his strange act. 5647
30:32 *place* where the grounded staff shall **p**, 4569
31: 9 he shall **p over** *to* his strong hold for fear, 5674
33:21 neither shall gallant ship **p** thereby. 5674
34:10 none shall **p** through it for ever and ever. 5674
35: 8 the unclean shall not **p over** it; but it *shall* 5674
36: 1 Now it **came to p** in the fourteenth year of 1961
37: 1 it **came to p**, when king Hezekiah heard *it*, 1961
37:26 now have I **brought** it **to p**, that thou 935
37:38 it **came to p**, as he was worshipping *in* 1961
42: 9 the former *things* are **come to p**, and 935
46:11 I have spoken *it*, I will also **bring** it **to p**; 935
47: 2 uncover the thigh, **p over** the rivers. 5674
48: 3 I did *them* suddenly, and they **came to p**. 935
48: 5 to thee; before it **came to p** I shewed *it* thee: 935
51:10 the sea a way for the ransomed to **p over**? 5674
65:24 it shall **come to p**, that before they call, 1961
66:23 it shall **come to p**, *that* from one new moon 1961
Jer 2:10 For **p over** the isles of Chittim, and see; 5674
3: 9 it **came to p** through the lightness of her 1961
3:16 it shall **come to p**, when ye be multiplied 1961
4: 9 it shall **come to p** at that day, saith 1961
5:19 it shall **come to p**, when ye shall say, 1961
5:22 *by* a perpetual decree, that it cannot **p** it: 5674
5:22 they roar, yet can they not **p over** it? 5674
8:13 I have given them shall **p away from** them. 5674
9:10 that none can **p through** *them*; neither can 5674
12:15 it shall **come to p**, after that I have plucked 1961
12:16 it shall **come to p**, if they will diligently 1961
13: 6 it **came to p** after many days, that 1961
15: 2 it shall **come to p**, if they say unto thee, 1961
15:14 I will **make** *thee* **to p** with thine enemies 5674
16:10 it shall **come to p**, when thou shalt shew 1961
17:24 it shall **come to p**, if ye diligently hearken 1961
20: 3 it **came to p** on the morrow, that Pashur 1961
22: 8 many nations shall **p** by this city, and 5674
25:12 it shall **come to p**, when seventy years are 1961
26: 8 Now it **came to p**, when Jeremiah had 1961
27: 8 it shall **come to p**, *that* the nation and 1961
28: 1 it **came to p** the same year, in 1961
28: 9 the word of the prophet shall **come to p**, 935
30: 8 For it shall **come to p** in that day, saith 1961
31:28 it shall **come to p**, *that* like as I have 1961
32:24 what thou hast spoken is **come to p**; and 1961
32:35 **cause** their sons and their daughters
to p through 5674
33:13 shall the flocks **p** again under the hands of 5674
35:11 it **came to p**, when Nebuchadrezzar king of 1961
36: 1 it **came to p** in the fourth year of Jehoiakim 1961
36: 9 it **came to p** in the fifth year of Jehoiakim 1961
36:16 Now it **came to p** when they had heard all 1961
36:23 it **came to p**, *that* when Jehudi had read 1961
37:11 it **came to p**, *that* when the army of 1961
39: 4 it **came to p**, *that* when Zedekiah the king 1961
41: 1 Now it **came to p** in the seventh month, 1961
41: 4 it **came to p** the second day after *he* had 1961

Jer 41: 6 it **came to p**, as he met them, he said unto 1961
41:13 Now it **came to p**, *that* when all the people 1961
42: 4 it shall **come to p**, *that* whatsoever thing 1961
42: 7 it **came to p** after ten days, that the word of 1961
42:16 it shall **come to p**, *that* the sword, which ye 1961
43: 1 it **came to p**, *that* when Jeremiah had made 1961
49:39 it shall **come to p** in the latter days, *that* I 1961
51:43 neither doth *any* son of man **p** thereby. 5674
52: 3 of the LORD it **came to p** in Jerusalem 1961
52: 4 it **came to p** in the ninth year of his reign, 1961
52:31 it **came to p** in the seven and thirtieth year 1961
La 1:12 *Is it* nothing to you, all ye that **p by**? 1870+5674
2:15 All that **p** by clap *their* hands at thee; 5674
3:37 Who *is* he *that* saith, and it **cometh to p**, 1961
3:44 that *our* prayer should not **p through**. 5674
4:21 the cup also shall **p through** unto thee: 5674
Eze 1: 1 Now it **came to p** in the thirtieth year, 1961
3:16 it **came to p** at the end of seven days, 1961
5: 1 **cause** *it* **to p** upon thine head and upon thy 5674
5:14 about thee, in the sight of all that **p by**. 5674
5:17 pestilence and blood shall **p** through thee; 5674
8: 1 it **came to p** in the sixth year, in the sixth 1961
9: 8 it **came to p**, while they were slaying them, 1961
10: 6 it **came to p**, *that* when he had commanded 1961
11:13 it **came to p**, when I prophesied, 1961
12:25 the word that I shall speak shall **come to p**; 6213
14:15 If I **cause** noisome beasts **to p** through 5674
14:15 that no man may **p through** because of 5674
16:21 delivered them to **cause** them **to p through** 5674
16:23 it **came to p** after all thy wickedness, (woe, 1961
20: 1 it **came to p** in the seventh year, in the fifth 1961
20:26 in that they **caused to p through** *the fire* all 5674
20:31 when *ye* **make** your sons **to p** through 5674
20:37 I will **cause** you **to p** under the rod, and 5674
21: 7 it cometh, and shall be **brought to p**, 1961
23:37 **caused** their sons, whom they bare unto me,
to p for them **through** 5674
24:14 LORD have spoken *it*: it shall **come to p**, 935
26: 1 it **came to p** in the eleventh year, in 1961
29:11 No foot of man shall **p** through it, nor foot 5674
29:11 nor foot of beast shall **p** through it, 5674
29:17 it **came to p** in the seven and 1961
30:20 it **came to p** in the eleventh year, in 1961
31: 1 it **came to p** in the eleventh year, in 1961
32: 1 it **came to p** in the twelfth year, in 1961
32:17 It **came to p** also in the twelfth year, in 1961
32:19 Whom dost thou **p** in beauty? go down, and 4480
33:21 it **came to p** in the twelfth year of our 1961
33:28 be desolate, that none shall **p through**. 5674
33:33 when this **cometh to p**, (lo, it will come) 935
37: 2 **caused** me **to p** by them round about: 5674
38:10 It shall also **come to p**, *that* at the same 1961
38:18 it shall **come to p** at the same time when 1961
39:11 it shall **come to p** in that day, *that* I will 1961
39:15 the passengers *that* **p through** the land, 5674
44:17 it shall **come to p**, *that* when they enter in 1961
46:21 **caused** me **to p** by the four corners of 5674
47: 5 *and it was* a river that I could not **p over**: 5674
47: 9 it shall **come to p**, *that* every thing that 1961
47:10 it shall **come to p**, *that* the fishers shall 1961
47:22 it shall **come to p**, *that* ye shall divide it *by* 1961
47:23 it shall **come to p**, *that* in what tribe 1961
Da 2:29 thy bed, what should **come to p** hereafter: 1934
2:29 known to thee what shall **come to p**. 1934
2:45 to the king what shall **come to p** hereafter: 1934
4:16 unto him; and let seven times **p** over him. 2499
4:23 of the field, till seven times **p** over him; 2499
4:25 and seven times shall **p** over thee, 2499
4:32 as oxen, and seven times shall **p** over thee, 2499
7:14 which shall not **p away**, and his kingdom 5709
8: 2 it **came to p**, when I saw, that I *was* at 1961
8:15 it **came to p**, when I, *even* I Daniel, had 1961
11:10 and overflow, and **p through**: 5674
11:40 and shall overflow and **p over**. 5674
Hos 1: 5 it shall **come to p** at that day, that I will 1961
1:10 it shall **come to p**, *that* in the place where it 1961
2:21 it shall **come to p** in that day, I will hear, 1961
Joel 2:28 it shall **come to p** afterward, that I will 1961
2:32 it shall **come to p**, *that* whosoever shall call 1961
3:17 there shall no strangers **p** through her any 5674
3:18 it shall **come to p** in that day, *that* 1961
Am 5: 5 enter *into* Gilgal, and **p** not *to* Beer-sheba: 5674
5:17 for I will **p** through thee, saith the LORD. 5674
6: 2 **P** ye *unto* Calneh, and see; and from thence 5674
6: 9 it shall **come to p**, if there remain ten men 1961
7: 2 it **came to p**, *that* when they had made an 1961
7: 8 I will not again **p** by them any more: 5674
8: 2 I will not again **p** by them any more. 5674
8: 9 it shall **come to p** in that day, saith the Lord 1961
Jnh 4: 8 it **came to p**, when the sun did arise, 1961
Mic 1:11 **P** ye **away**, thou inhabitant of Saphir, 5674
2: 8 that **p by** securely *as men* averse from war. 5674
2:13 their king shall **p** before them, and 5674
4: 1 in the last days it shall **come to p**, *that* 1961
5:10 it shall **come to p** in that day, saith 1961
Na 1:12 be cut down, when he shall **p through**. 5674
1:15 for the wicked shall no more **p** through 5674
3: 7 it shall **come to p**, *that* all they that look 1961
Hab 1:11 and he shall **p over**, and offend, 5674
Zep 1: 8 it shall **come to p** in the day of 1961
1:10 it shall **come to p** in that day, saith 1961
1:12 it shall **come to p** at that time, *that* I will 1961
2: 2 bring forth, *before* the day **p** as the chaff, 5674
Zec 3: 4 I have **caused** thine iniquity **to p** from thee, 5674
6:15 *this* shall **come to p**, if ye will diligently 1961
7: 1 it **came to p** in the fourth year of king 1961
7:13 Therefore it is **come to p**, *that* as he cried, 1961
8:13 it shall **come to p**, *that* as ye were a curse 1961
8:20 *It shall* yet *come to* **p**, that there shall come NIH
8:23 In those days *it shall come to* **p**, that ten NIH
9: 8 no oppressor shall **p** through them any 5674
10:11 he shall **p** through the sea *with* affliction, 5674
12: 9 it shall **come to p** in that day, *that* I will 1961
13: 2 it shall **come to p** in that day, saith 1961
13: 2 **cause** the prophets and the unclean spirit **to p** 5674

Zec 13: 3 it shall **come to p**, *that* when any shall yet 1961
13: 4 it shall **come to p** in that day, *that* 1961
13: 8 it shall **come to p**, *that* in all the land, 1961
14: 6 it shall **come to p** in that day, *that* the light 1961
14: 7 it shall **come to p**, *that* at evening time it 1961
14:13 it shall **come to p** in that day, *that* a great 1961
14:16 it shall **come to p**, *that* every one that is left 1961
Mt 5:18 Till heaven and earth **p**, one jot or one tittle *3928*
5:18 or one tittle shall in no wise **p** from the law, *3928*
7:28 And it **came to p**, when Jesus had ended *1096*
8:28 so that no *man* might **p** by that way. *3928*
9:10 And it **came to p**, as Jesus sat at meat in *1096*
11: 1 And it **came to p**, when Jesus had made an *1096*
13:53 And it **came to p**, *that* when Jesus had *1096*
19: 1 And it **came to p**, *that* when Jesus had *1096*
24: 6 for all *these things* must **come to p**, but *1096*
24:34 I say unto you, This generation shall not **p**, *3928*
24:35 Heaven and earth shall **p away**, but *3928*
24:35 pass away, but my words shall not **p away**. *3928*
26: 1 And it **came to p**, when Jesus had finished *1096*
26:39 if it be possible, let this cup **p** from me: *3928*
26:42 if this cup may not **p away** from me, *3928*
Mk 1: 9 And it **came to p** in those days, *that* Jesus *1096*
2:15 And it **came to p**, that, as *Jesus* sat at meat *1096*
2:23 And it **came to p**, that he went through *1096*
4: 4 And it **came to p**, as *he* sowed, some fell *1096*
4:35 Let us **p over** unto the other side. *1330*
11:23 *things* which he saith shall **come to p**; *1096*
13:29 when ye shall see these *things* **come to p**, *1096*
13:30 unto you, that this generation shall not **p**, *3928*
13:31 Heaven and earth shall **p away**: but *3928*
13:31 pass away: but my words shall not **p away**. *3928*
14:35 were possible, the hour might **p** from him. *3928*
Lk 1: 8 And it **came to p**, *that* while he executed *1096*
1:23 And it **came to p** *that*, as soon as the days *1096*
1:41 And it **came to p** *that*, when Elisabeth *1096*
1:59 And it **came to p**, *that* on the eighth day *1096*
2: 1 And it **came to p** in those days, *that* there *1096*
2:15 And it **came to p**, as the angels were gone *1096*
2:15 and see this thing which is **come to p**, *1096*
2:46 And it **came to p**, *that* after three days they *1096*
3:21 it **came to p**, *that* Jesus also being baptized, *1096*
5: 1 And it **came to p** that, as the people *1096*
5:12 And it **came to p**, when he was in a certain *1096*
5:17 And it **came to p** on a certain day, as he *1096*
6: 1 And it **came to p** on the second sabbath *1096*
6: 6 And it **came to p** also on another sabbath, *1096*
6:12 And it **came to p** in those days, *that* he *1096*
7:11 And it **came to p** the *day* after, *that* he went *1096*
8: 1 And it **came to p** afterward, that he went *1096*
8:22 Now it **came to p** on a certain day, that he *1096*
8:40 And it **came to p** that, when Jesus was *1096*
9:18 And it **came to p**, as he was alone praying, *1096*
9:28 And it **came to p** about an eight days after *1096*
9:33 And it **came to p**, as they departed from *1096*
9:37 And it **came to p**, *that* on the next day, *1096*
9:51 And it **came to p**, when the time was come *1096*
9:57 And it **came to p** *that*, as they went in *1096*
10:38 Now it **came to p**, as they went, that he *1096*
11: 1 And it **came to p** *that*, as he was praying in *1096*
11:14 And it **came to p**, when the devil was gone *1096*
11:27 And it **came to p**, as he spake these *things*, *1096*
11:42 and **p over** judgment and the love of God: *3928*
12:55 There will be heat; and it **cometh to p**. *1096*
14: 1 And it **came to p**, as he went into the house *1096*
16:17 And it is easier for heaven and earth to **p**, *3928*
16:22 And it **came to p** that the beggar died, and *1096*
16:26 that they which would **p** from hence to you *1224*
16:26 neither can they **p** to us, that *would come* *1276*
17:11 And it **came to p**, as he went to Jerusalem, *1096*
17:14 And it **came to p** *that*, as they went, *1096*
18:35 And it **came to p**, *that* as he was come nigh *1096*
18:36 And hearing the multitude **p by**, he asked *1279*
19: 4 tree to see him: for he was to **p** that *way*. *1330*
19:15 And it **came to p**, that when he was *1096*
19:29 And it **came to p**, when he was come nigh *1096*
20: 1 And it **came to p**, *that* on one of those *1096*
21: 7 *there be* when these *things* shall **come to p**? *1096*
21: 9 for these *things* must first **come to p**; but *1096*
21:28 And when these *things* begin to **come to p**, *1096*
21:31 when ye see these *things* **come to p**, *1096*
21:32 This generation shall not **p away**, till all be *3928*
21:33 Heaven and earth shall **p away**: but *3928*
21:33 pass away: but my words shall not **p away**. *3928*
21:36 escape all these *things* that shall **come to p**, *1096*
24: 4 And it **came to p**, as they were *much* *1096*
24:12 in himself at that which was **come to p**. *1096*
24:15 And it **came to p**, that while they *1096*
24:18 which are **come to p** there in these days? *1096*
24:30 And it **came to p**, as he sat at meat with *1096*
24:51 And it **came to p**, while he blessed them, *1096*
Jn 13:19 that, when it is **come to p**, ye may believe *1096*
14:29 now I have told you before it **come to p**, *1096*
14:29 that, when it is **come to p**, ye might *1096*
15:25 But *this cometh to* **p**, that the word might be NIG
Ac 2:17 And it shall **come to p** in the last days, *1510*
2:21 And it shall **come to p**, *that* whosoever *1510*
3:23 And it shall **come to p**, *that* every soul, *1510*
4: 5 And it **came to p** on the morrow, that their *1096*
9:32 And it **came to p**, as Peter passed *1096*
9:37 And it **came to p** in those days, that she *1096*
9:43 And it **came to p**, that he tarried many days *1096*
11:26 And it **came to p**, that a whole year they *1096*
11:28 which **came to p** in the days of Claudius *1096*
14: 1 And it **came to p** in Iconium, that they *1096*
16:16 And it **came to p**, as we went to prayer, *1096*
18:27 And when he was disposed to **p** into *1330*
19: 1 And it **came to p** that, while Apollos was at *1096*
21: 1 And it **came to p**, that after we were gotten *1096*
22: 6 And it **came to p**, that, as I made my *1096*
22:17 And it **came to p**, that, when I was come *1096*
27:44 And so it **came to p**, that *they* escaped all *1096*
28: 8 And it **came to p**, that the father of Publius *1096*
28:17 And it **came to p**, that after three days Paul *1096*
Ro 9:26 And it shall **come to p**, *that* in the place *1510*

1Co 7:36 if she **p the flower of** *her* **age**, *1510+5230*
15:54 shall be **brought to p** the saying that is *1096*
16: 5 when I shall **p through** Macedonia: *1330*
16: 5 for I do **p through** Macedonia. *1330*
2Co 1:16 And to **p** by you into Macedonia, and *1330*
1Th 3: 4 even as it **came to p**, and ye know. *1096*
Jas 1:10 as the flower of the grass he shall **p away**. *3928*
1Pe 1:17 **p** the time of your sojourning *here* in fear: *390*
2Pe 3:10 in the which the heavens shall **p away** with *3928*
Rev 1: 1 *things* which must shortly **come to p**; *1096*

PASSAGE (4) [PASS]

Nu 20:21 Thus Edom refused to give Israel **p** through 5674
Jos 22:11 of Jordan, at the **p** of the children of Israel. 5676
1Sa 13:23 Philistines went out to the **p** of Michmash. 4569
Isa 10:29 They are gone over the **p**: they have taken 4569

PASSAGES (5) [PASS]

Jdg 12: 5 the Gileadites took the **p** of Jordan before 4569
12: 6 took him, and slew him at the **p** of Jordan: 4569
1Sa 14: 4 between the **p**, *by* which Jonathan sought to 4569
Jer 22:20 up thy voice in Bashan, and cry from the **p**: 5676
51:32 *that* the **p** are stopped, and the reeds they 4569

PASSED (161) [PASS]

Ge 12: 6 Abram **p** through the land unto the place of 5674
15:17 a burning lamp that **p** between those pieces. 5674
31:21 **p over** the river, and set his face *toward* 5674
32:10 for with my staff I **p over** this Jordan; 5674
32:22 eleven sons, and **p over** the ford Jabbok. 5674
32:31 as he **p over** Penuel the sun rose upon him, 5674
33: 3 he **p over** before them, and bowed himself 5674
37:28 there **p by** Midianites merchantmen; and 5674
Ex 12:27 who **p over** the houses of the children of 6452
34: 6 the LORD **p by** before him, and 5674
Nu 14: 7 The land, which we **p** through to search it, 5674
20:17 nor *to* the left, until we have **p** thy borders. 5674
33: 8 **p through** the midst of the sea into 5674
33:51 When ye are **p over** Jordan into the land of 5674
Dt 2: 8 when we **p by** from our brethren 5674
2: 8 **p** *by* the way of the wilderness of Moab. 5674
27: 3 the words of this law, when thou art **p over**, 5674
29:16 came through the nations which ye **p by**; 5674
Jos 2:23 **p over**, and came to Joshua the son of Nun, 5674
3: 1 and lodged there before they **p over**. 5674
3: 4 for ye have not **p** *this* way heretofore. 5674
3:16 and the people **p over** right against Jericho. 5674
3:17 all the Israelites **p over** on dry *ground*, until 5674
3:17 all the people were **p** clean **over** Jordan. 5674
4: 1 when all the people were clean **p over** 5674
4: 7 when it **p over** Jordan, the waters of Jordan 5674
4:10 and the people hasted and **p over**. 5674
4:11 when all the people were clean **p over**, 5674
4:11 that the ark of the LORD **p over**, and 5674
4:12 **p over** armed before the children of Israel; 5674
4:13 war **p over** before the LORD unto battle, 5674
4:23 until ye were **p over**, as the LORD your 5674
5: 1 until we were **p over**, that their heart 5674
6: 8 of rams' horns **p on** before the LORD, 5674
10:29 Joshua **p** from Makkedah, and all Israel 5674
10:31 Joshua **p** from Libnah, and all Israel with 5674
10:34 from Lachish Joshua **p** unto Eglon, and 5674
15: 3 **p along** to Zin, and ascended up on 5674
15: 3 **p along** *to* Hezron, and went up to Adar, 5674
15: 4 *From thence* it **p** toward Azmon, and 5674
15: 6 and **p along** by the north of Beth-arabah; 5674
15: 7 the border **p** towards the waters of 5674
15:10 **p along** unto the side of mount Jearim, 5674
15:10 *to* Beth-shemesh, and **p on** *to* Timnah: 5674
15:11 **p along** *to* mount Baalah, and went out 5674
16: 6 and **p by** it on the east *to* Janohah; 5674
18: 9 the men went and **p through** the land, and 5674
18:18 **p along** toward the side over against 5674
18:19 the border **p along** to the side of 5674
24:17 among all the people through whom we **p**: 5674
Jdg 3:26 **p beyond** the quarries, and escaped unto 5674
8: 4 *and* **p over**, he, and the three hundred men 5674
10: 9 Moreover the children of Ammon **p over** 5674
11:29 he **p over** Gilead and Manasseh, and 5674
11:29 **p over** Mizpeh of Gilead, and from Mizpeh 5674
11:29 from Mizpeh of Gilead he **p over** *unto* 5674
11:32 So Jephthah **p over** unto the children of 5674
12: 3 **p over** against the children of Ammon, and 5674
18:13 they **p** thence *unto* mount Ephraim, and 5674
19:14 they **p on** and went *their way*; and the sun 5674
1Sa 9: 4 he **p** through mount Ephraim, and 5674
9: 4 **p** through the land of Shalisha, but 5674
9: 4 they **p** through the land of Shalim, and 5674
9: 4 he **p** through the land of the Benjamites, 5674
9:27 servant pass on before us, (and he **p on**,) 5674
14:23 and the battle **p over** *unto* Beth-aven. 5674
15:12 and **p on**, and gone down *to* Gilgal. 5674
27: 2 he **p over** with the six hundred men that 5674
29: 2 the lords of the Philistines **p on** by 5674
29: 2 his men **p on** in the rereward with Achish. 5674
2Sa 2:29 **p over** Jordan, and went *through* all 5674
10:17 and **p over** Jordan, and came to Helam. 5674
15:18 all his servants **p on** beside him; and all 5674
15:18 after him from Gath, **p on** before the king. 5674
15:22 Ittai the Gittite **p over**, and all his men, 5674
15:23 a loud voice, and all the people **p over**: 5674
15:23 the king also *himself* **p over** the brook 5674
15:23 all the people **p over**, toward the way of 5674
17:22 that *were* with him, and they **p over** Jordan: 5674
17:24 Absalom **p over** Jordan, he and all the men 5674
24: 5 they **p over** Jordan, and pitched in Aroer, 5674
1Ki 13:25 men **p by**, and saw the carcase cast in 5674
19:11 the LORD **p by**, and a great and 5674
19:19 Elijah **p by** him, and cast his mantle upon 5674
20:39 as the king **p by**, he cried unto the king: 5674
2Ki 4: 8 it fell on a day, that Elisha **p** to Shunem, 5674
4: 8 *so* it was, *that* as oft as he **p by**, he turned 5674
4:31 Gehazi **p on** before them, and laid the staff 5674
6:30 he **p by** upon the wall, and the people 5674

2Ki 14: 9 there p by a wild beast that *was* in 5674
1Ch 19:17 p over Jordan, and came upon them, and 5674
2Ch 9:22 king Solomon p all the kings of 1431+4480
25:18 there p by a wild beast that *was* in 5674
30:10 So the posts p from city to city through 5674
Job 4:15 a spirit p before my face; the hair of my 2498
9:26 They are p away as the swift ships: as 2498
15:19 was given, and no stranger p among them. 5674
28: 8 not trodden it, nor the fierce lion p by it. 5710
Ps 18:12 *that was* before him his thick clouds p, 5674
37:36 Yet he p away, and lo, he *was* not: yea, 5674
48: 4 kings were assembled, they p by together. 5674
90: 9 For all our days are p away in thy wrath: 6437
SS 3: 4 *It was* but a little that I p from them, but I 5674
Isa 10:28 He is come to Aiath, he is p to Migron; 5674
40:27 and my judgment is p over from my God? 5674
41: 3 He pursued them, *and* p safely; *even by* 5674
Jer 2: 6 through a land that no man p through, 5674
11:15 and the holy flesh is p from thee? 5674
34:18 in twain, and p between the parts thereof, 5674
34:19 which p between the parts of the calf; 5674
46:17 *but* a noise; he hath p the time appointed. 5674
Eze 16: 6 when I p by thee, and saw thee polluted in 5674
16: 8 Now when I p by thee, and looked upon 5674
16:15 out thy fornications on every one that p by; 5674
16:25 hast opened thy feet to every one that p by, 5674
36:34 it lay desolate in the sight of all that p by. 5674
47: 5 to swim in, a river that could not be p over. 5674
Da 3:27 nor the smell of fire had p on them. 5709
6:18 went to his palace, and p the night fasting: 956
Hos 10:11 *the corn;* but I p over upon her fair neck: 5674
Jnh 2: 3 all thy billows and thy waves p over me. 5674
Mic 2:13 have p through the gate, and are gone out 5674
Na 3:19 for upon whom hath not thy wickedness p 5674
Hab 3:10 the overflowing of the water p by: the deep 5674
Zec 7:14 that no man p through nor returned: 5674
Mt 9: 1 and p over, and came into his own city. *1276*
9: 9 And as Jesus p forth from thence, he saw a *3855*
20:30 when they heard that Jesus p by, cried out, *3855*
27:39 And they that p by, reviled him, *3899*
Mk 2:14 And as he p by, he saw Levi the *son* of *3855*
5:21 And when Jesus was p over again by ship *1276*
6:35 is a desert place, and now the time *is* far p: *4183*
6:48 upon the sea, and would have p by them. *3928*
6:53 And when they had p over, they came into *1276*
9:30 departed thence, and p through Galilee; *3899*
11:20 And in the morning, as they p by, they saw *3899*
15:21 who p by, coming out of the country, *3855*
15:29 And they that p by railed on him, *3899*
Lk 10:31 he saw him, he p by on the other side. *492*
10:32 looked *on him,* and p by on the other side. *492*
17:11 that he p through the midst of *1330*
19: 1 And *Jesus* entered and p through Jericho. *1330*
Jn 5:24 but is p from death unto life. *3327*
8:59 through the midst of them, and so p by. *3855*
9: 1 And as *Jesus* p by, he saw a man *which* *3855*
Ac 9:32 as Peter p throughout all *quarters,* he came *1330*
12:10 they went out, and p on through one street; *4281*
14:24 And after they had p throughout Pisidia, *1330*
15: 3 they p through Phenice and Samaria, *1330*
17: 1 Now when they had p through Amphipolis *1353*
17:23 For as I p by, and beheld your devotions, *1330*
19: 1 Paul having p through the upper coasts *1330*
19:21 when he had p through Macedonia and *1330*
Ro 5:12 and so death p upon all men, for that all *1330*
1Co 10: 1 under the cloud, and all p through the sea; *1330*
Eph 2:11 that ye *being* in time p Gentiles in *4218*
Heb 4:14 that is p into the heavens, Jesus the Son of *1330*
11:29 By faith they p through the Red sea as by *1224*
1Jn 3:14 We know that we have p from death unto *3327*
Rev 21: 1 and the first earth were p away; *3928*
21: 4 more pain: for the former *things* are p away. *565*

PASSEDST (1) [PASS]

Jdg 12: 1 Wherefore p thou over to fight against 5674

PASSENGERS (5) [PASS]

Pr 9:15 To call p who go right *on* their ways: 1870+5674
Eze 39:11 the valley of the p *on* the east of the sea: 5674
39:11 it *shall* stop the *noses of the* p: and 5674
39:14 passing through the land to bury with the p 5674
39:15 the p *that* pass through the land, when *any* 5674

PASSEST (5) [PASS]

Dt 3:21 do unto all the kingdoms whither thou p. 5674
30:18 whither thou p over Jordan to go to possess 5674
2Sa 15:33 If thou p on with me, then thou shalt be a 5674
1Ki 2:37 goest out, and p over the brook Kidron, 5674
Isa 43: 2 When thou p through the waters, I *will be* 5674

PASSETH (38) [PASS]

Ex 30:13 every one that p among them that are 5674
30:14 Every one that p among them that are 5674
33:22 it shall come to pass, while my glory p by, 5674
Lev 27:32 *even of* whatsoever p under the rod, 5674
Jos 3:11 *even* the Lord of all the earth p over before 5674
16: 2 p along unto the borders of Archi *to* 5674
19:13 from thence p on along on the east to 5674
1Ki 9: 8 every one that p by it shall be astonished, 5674
2Ki 4: 9 man of God, which p by us continually. 5674
12: 4 *even* the money of every one that p 5674
2Ch 7:21 shall be an astonishment to every one that p 5674
Job 9:11 he p on also, but I perceive him not. 2498
14:20 prevailest for ever against him, and he p: 1980
30:15 and my welfare p away as a cloud. 5674
37:21 but the wind p, and cleanseth them. 5674
Ps 8: 8 *whatsoever* p *through* the paths of the seas. 5674
78:39 a wind that p away, and cometh not again. 1980
103:16 For the wind p over it, and it is gone; and 5674
144: 4 his days *are* as a shadow that p away. 5674
Pr 10:25 As the whirlwind p, so *is* the wicked no 5674
26:17 He that p by, *and* meddleth with strife 5674
Ecc 1: 4 *One* generation p away, and 1980
Isa 29: 5 terrible ones *shall be* as chaff that p away: 5674

Jer 9:12 up like a wilderness, that none p through? 5674
13:24 that p away by the wind of the wilderness. 5674
18:16 every one that p thereby shall be 5674
19: 8 every one that p thereby shall be astonished 5674
Eze 35: 7 cut off from it him that p out and him that 5674
Hos 13: 3 and as the early dew that p away, 1980
Mic 7:18 p by the transgression of the remnant of his 5674
Zep 2:15 every one that p by her shall hiss, *and* 5674
3: 6 I made their streets waste, that none p by: 5674
Zec 9: 8 because of him that p by, and because 5674
Lk 18:37 they told him, that Jesus of Nazareth p by. *3928*
1Co 7:31 *it:* for the fashion of this world p away. *3855*
Eph 3:19 the love of Christ, which p knowledge, *5235*
Php 4: 7 which p all understanding, shall keep your *5242*
1Jn 2:17 And the world p away, and the lust thereof: *3855*

PASSING (13) [PASS]

Jdg 19:18 We are p from Beth-lehem-judah toward 5674
2Sa 1:26 to me was wonderful, p the love of women. 4480
15:24 until all the people had done p out of 5674
2Ki 6:26 as the king of Israel was p by upon 5674
Ps 84: 6 *Who* p through the valley of Baca make it a 5674
Pr 7: 8 P through the street near her corner; and 5674
Isa 31: 5 deliver *it;* and p over he will preserve *it.* 6452
Eze 39:14 p through the land to bury with 5674
Lk 4:30 But he p through the midst of them *1330*
Ac 5:15 that at the least the shadow of Peter p by *2064*
8:40 and p through he preached in all the cities, *1330*
16: 8 And they p by Mysia came down to Troas. *3928*
27: 8 And hardly p it, came unto a place *which is* *3881*

PASSION (1) [PASSIONS]

Ac 1: 3 alive after his p by many infallible proofs, *3958*

PASSIONS (2) [PASSION]

Ac 14:15 We also are men of like p with you, *3663*
Jas 5:17 Elias was a man subject to like p as we *3663*

PASSOVER (76) [PASSOVERS]

Ex 12:11 ye shall eat it in haste: it *is* the LORD'S p. 6453
12:21 according to your families, and kill the p. 6453
12:27 It *is* the sacrifice of the LORD'S p, 6453
12:43 and Aaron, This *is* the ordinance of the p: 6453
12:48 will keep the p to the LORD, let all his 6453
34:25 the feast of the p be left unto the morning. 6453
Lev 23: 5 the first month at even *is* the LORD'S p. 6453
Nu 9: 2 Let the children of Israel also keep the p at 6453
9: 4 of Israel, that they should keep the p. 6453
9: 5 they kept the p on the fourteenth day of 6453
9: 6 that they could not keep the p on that day: 6453
9:10 yet he shall keep the p unto the LORD. 6453
9:12 according to all the ordinances of the p 6453
9:13 in a journey, and forbeareth to keep the p, 6453
9:14 and will keep the p unto the LORD; 6453
9:14 according to the ordinance of the p, and 6453
28:16 of the first month *is* the p of the LORD. 6453
33: 3 on the morrow after the p the children of 6453
Dt 16: 1 and keep the p unto the LORD thy God: 6453
16: 2 sacrifice the p unto the LORD thy God, 6453
16: 5 Thou mayest not sacrifice the p within any 6453
16: 6 *in,* there thou shalt sacrifice the p at even, 6453
Jos 5:10 kept the p on the fourteenth day of 6453
5:11 corn of the land on the morrow after the p, 6453
2Ki 23:21 Keep the p unto the LORD your God, 6453
23:22 Surely there was not holden such a p from 6453
23:23 *wherein* this p was holden to the LORD in 6453
2Ch 30: 1 to keep the p unto the LORD God of 6453
30: 2 to keep the p in the second month. 6453
30: 5 that *they* should come to keep the p unto 6453
30:15 they killed the p on the fourteenth *day* of 6453
30:18 yet did they eat the p otherwise than it was 6453
35: 1 Moreover Josiah kept a p unto the LORD 6453
35: 1 they killed the p on the fourteenth *day* of 6453
35: 6 So kill the p, and sanctify yourselves, and 6453
35: 7 all for the p *offerings,* for all that were 6453
35: 8 gave unto the priests for the p *offerings* two 6453
35: 9 gave unto the Levites for p *offerings* five 6453
35:11 they killed the p, and the priests sprinkled 6453
35:13 they roasted the p with fire according to 6453
35:16 to keep the p, and to offer burnt offerings 6453
35:17 that were present kept the p at that time, 6453
35:18 there was no p like to that, kept in Israel 6453
35:18 kings of Israel keep such a p as Josiah kept, 6453
35:19 year of the reign of Josiah was this p kept. 6453
Ezr 6:19 the children of the captivity kept the p upon 6453
6:20 killed the p for all the children of 6453
Eze 45:21 ye shall have the p, a feast of seven days; 6453
Mt 26: 2 that after two days is *the feast of the* p, *3957*
26:17 thou *that* we prepare for thee to eat the p? *3957*
26:18 I will keep the p at thy house with my *3957*
26:19 appointed them; and they made ready the p. *3957*
Mk 14: 1 After two days was *the feast of* the p, and *3957*
14:12 when they killed the p, his disciples said *3957*
14:12 and prepare that thou mayest eat the p? *3957*
14:14 where I shall eat the p with my disciples? *3957*
14:16 said unto them: and they made ready the p. *3957*
Lk 2:41 Jerusalem every year at the feast of the p. *3957*
22: 1 bread drew nigh, which is called the P. *3957*
22: 7 when the p must be killed. *3957*
22: 8 and John, saying, Go and prepare us the p, *3957*
22:11 where I shall eat the p with my disciples? *3957*
22:13 said unto them: and they made ready the p. *3957*
22:15 With desire I have desired to eat this p with *3957*
Jn 2:13 And the Jews' p was at hand, and *3957*
2:23 Now when he was in Jerusalem at the p, *3957*
6: 4 And the p, a feast of the Jews, was nigh. *3957*
11:55 And the Jews' p was nigh at hand: and *3957*
11:55 of the country up to Jerusalem before the p, *3957*
12: 1 Then Jesus six days before the p came to *3957*
13: 1 Now before the feast of the p, when Jesus *3957*
18:28 be defiled; but that they might eat the p. *3957*
18:39 that I should release unto you one at the p: *3957*
19:14 And it was the preparation of the p, and *3957*
1Co 5: 7 For even Christ our p is sacrificed for us: *3957*

Heb 11:28 Through faith he kept the p, and *3957*

PASSOVERS (1) [PASSOVER]

2Ch 30:17 of the p for every one *that was* not clean, 6453

PAST (51) [PASS]

Ge 50: 4 And when the days of his mourning were p, 5674
Ex 21:29 push with his horn in time p, 4480+8032+8543
21:36 *hath* used to push in time p, 4480+8032+8543
Nu 21:22 king's *high* way, until we be p thy borders. 5674
Dt 2:10 Emims dwelt therein in times p, 6440+3807.1
4:32 For ask now of the days that are p, 7223
4:42 hated him not in times p; 4480+8032+8543
19: 4 whom he hated not in time p; 4480+8032+8543
19: 6 as he hated him not in time p. 4480+8032+8543
1Sa 15:32 Surely the bitterness of death is p. 5493
19: 7 he was in his presence, as in times p. 865+8032
2Sa 3:17 in times p to be king 1571+1571+8032+8543
5: 2 Also in time p, when Saul was 865+1571+8032
11:27 when the mourning was p, David sent and 5674
16: 1 when David was a little p the top *of* 5674
1Ki 18:29 when midday was p, and they prophesied 5674
1Ch 9:20 was the ruler over them in time p, 6440+3807.1
11: 2 *And* moreover in time p, even when 8032+8543
Job 9:10 Which doeth great *things* p finding 369+5704
14:13 keep me secret, until thy wrath be p, 7725
17:11 My days are p, my purposes are broken off, 5674
29: 2 O that I were as *in* months p, as *in* the days 6924
Ps 90: 4 thy sight *are but* as yesterday when it is p, 5674
Ecc 3:15 and God requireth that which is p. 7291
SS 2:11 For lo, the winter is p, the rain is over *and* 5674
Jer 8:20 The harvest is p, the summer is ended, and 5674
Mt 14:15 is a desert place, and the time is now p; *3928*
Mk 16: 1 And when the sabbath was p, *1230*
Lk 9:36 And when the voice was p, Jesus was *1096*
Ac 12:10 When they were p the first and the second *1330*
14:16 Who in times p suffered all nations to walk *3944*
27: 9 because the fast was now already p, Paul *3928*
Ro 3:25 for the remission of sins that are p, *4266*
11:30 For as ye in times p have not believed *4218*
11:33 his judgments, and his ways p finding out! *421*
2Co 5:17 old *things* are p away; behold, all *things* *3928*
Gal 1:13 in time p in the Jews' religion, *4218*
1:23 That he which persecuted us in times p *4218*
5:21 as I have also told *you* in time p, *4302*
Eph 2: 2 Wherein in time p ye walked according to *4218*
2: 3 in times p in the lusts of our flesh, *4218*
4:19 Who being p feeling have given themselves *524*
2Ti 2:18 saying that the resurrection is p already; *1096*
Phm 1:11 Which in time p was to thee unprofitable, *4218*
Heb 1: 1 in divers manners spake in time p unto *3819*
11:11 was delivered of a child when *she* was p *3844*
1Pe 2:10 Which in time p *were* not a people, but *4218*
4: 3 For the time p of *our* life may suffice us to *3928*
1Jn 2: 8 because the darkness is p, and the true light *3855*
Rev 9:12 One woe is p; *and* behold, there come two *565*
11:14 The second woe is p; *and* behold, the third *565*

PASTOR (1) [PASTORS]

Jer 17:16 I have not hastened from *being* a p to 7462

PASTORS (8) [PASTOR]

Jer 2: 8 the p also transgressed against me, and 7462
3:15 I will give you p according to mine heart, 7462
10:21 For the p are become brutish, and have not 7462
12:10 Many p have destroyed my vineyard, 7462
22:22 The wind shall eat up all thy p, and 7462
23: 1 Woe be unto *the* p that destroy and 7462
23: 2 of Israel against the p that feed my people; 7462
Eph 4:11 evangelists; and some, p and teachers; *4166*

PASTURE (20) [PASTURES]

Ge 47: 4 for thy servants have no p for their flocks; 4829
1Ch 4:39 *side* of the valley, to seek p for their flocks. 4829
4:40 they found fat p and good, and the land *was* 4829
4:41 because *there was* p there for their flocks. 4829
Job 39: 8 The range of the mountains *is* his p, and 4829
Ps 74: 1 anger smoke against the sheep of thy p? 4830
79:13 sheep of thy p will give thee thanks for 4830
95: 7 we *are* the people of his p, and the sheep of 4830
100: 3 *we are* his people, and the sheep of his p. 4830
Isa 32:14 for ever, a joy of wild asses, a p of flocks; 4829
Jer 23: 1 that destroy and scatter the sheep of my p! 4830
25:36 *heard:* for the LORD *hath* spoiled their p. 4830
La 1: 6 princes are become like harts *that* find no p, 4829
Eze 34:14 I will feed them in a good p, and upon 4829
34:14 *in* a fat p shall they feed upon 4829
34:18 thing unto you to have eaten up the good p, 4829
34:31 the flock of my p, *are* men, *and* I *am* your 4830
Hos 13: 6 According to their p, so were they filled; 4830
Joel 1:18 are perplexed, because they have no p; 4829
Jn 10: 9 and shall go in and out, and find p. *3542*

PASTURELAND See SUBURBS

PASTURES (11) [PASTURE]

1Ki 4:23 twenty oxen out of the p, and an hundred 7471
Ps 23: 2 He maketh me to lie down in green p: 4999
65:12 They drop *upon* the p of the wilderness: 4999
65:13 The p are clothed with flocks; the valleys 3733
Isa 30:23 in that day shall thy cattle feed *in* large p. 3733
49: 9 and their p *shall be* in all high places. 4830
Eze 34:18 down with your feet the residue of your p? 4829
45:15 of two hundred, out of the fat p of Israel; 4945
Joel 1:19 for the fire hath devoured the p of 4999
1:20 the fire hath devoured the p of 4999
2:22 for the p of the wilderness do spring, 4999

PATARA (1)

Ac 21: 1 unto Rhodes, and from thence unto P: *3959*

PATE (1)

Ps 7:16 dealing shall come down upon his own p. 6936

PATH (23) [PATHS, PATHWAY]

Ge 49:17 an adder in the p, that biteth the horse heels, 734
Nu 22:24 the angel of the LORD stood in a p of 4934
Job 28: 7 There is a p which no fowl knoweth, and 5410
30:13 They mar my p, they set forward my 5410
41:32 He maketh a p to shine after him; 5410
Ps 16:11 Thou wilt shew me the p of life: in thy 734
27:11 lead me in a plain p, because of mine 734
77:19 thy p in the great waters, and thy footsteps 7635
119:35 Make me to go in the p of thy 5410
119:105 a lamp unto my feet, and a light unto my p. 5410
139: 3 Thou compassest my p and my lying down, 734
142: 3 within me, then thou knewest my p. 5410
Pr 1:15 with them; refrain thy foot from their p: 5410
2: 9 judgment, and equity; yea, every good p. 4570
4:14 Enter not into the p of the wicked, and 734
4:18 the p of the just is as the shining light, 734
4:26 Ponder the p of thy feet, and let all thy 4570
5: 6 Lest thou shouldest ponder the p of life, 734
Isa 26: 7 most upright, dost weigh the p of the just. 4570
30:11 ye out of the way, turn aside out of the p, 734
40:14 taught him in the p of judgment, and 734
43:16 in the sea, and a p in the mighty waters; 5410
Joel 2: 8 they shall walk every one in his p: 4546

PATHROS (5)

Isa 11:11 from P, and from Cush, and from Elam, 6624
Jer 44: 1 at Noph, and in the country of P, saying, 6624
44:15 of Egypt, in P, answered Jeremiah, saying, 6624
Eze 29:14 will cause them to return into the land of P, 6624
30:14 I will make P desolate, and will set fire in 6624

PATHRUSIM (2)

Ge 10:14 P, and Casluhim, (out of whom came 6625
1Ch 1:12 P, and Casluhim, (of whom came 6625

PATHRUSITES See PATHRUSIM

PATHS (42) [PATH]

Job 6:18 The p of their way are turned aside; they go 734
8:13 So are the p of all that forget God; and 734
13:27 and lookest narrowly unto all my p; 734
19: 8 and he hath set darkness in my p. 5410
24:13 the ways thereof, nor abide in the p thereof. 5410
33:11 my feet in the stocks, he marketh all my p. 734
38:20 that thou shouldest know the p to the house 5410
Ps 8: 8 whatsoever passeth through the p of 734
17: 4 I have kept me from the p of the destroyer. 734
17: 5 Hold up my goings in thy p, that my 4570
23: 3 he leadeth me in the p of righteousness for 4570
25: 4 me thy ways, O LORD; teach me thy p. 734
25:10 All the p of the LORD are mercy and 734
65:11 with thy goodness; and thy p drop fatness. 4570
Pr 2: 8 He keepeth the p of judgment, and 734
2:13 Who leave the p of uprightness, to walk in 734
2:15 are crooked, and they froward in their p: 4570
2:18 unto death, and her p unto the dead. 4570
2:19 again, neither take they hold of the p of life. 734
2:20 good men, and keep the p of the righteous. 734
3: 6 acknowledge him, and he shall direct thy p. 734
3:17 of pleasantness, and all her p are peace. 5410
4:11 way of wisdom; I have led thee in right p. 4570
7:25 decline to her ways, go not astray in her p. 5410
8: 2 places by the way, in the places of the p. 5410
8:20 in the midst of the p of judgment: 5410
Isa 2: 3 us of his ways, and we will walk in his p: 734
3:12 thee to err, and destroy the way of thy p. 734
42:16 I will lead them in p that they have not 5410
58:12 of the breach, The restorer of p to dwell in. 5410
59: 7 wasting and destruction are in their p. 4546
59: 8 they have made them crooked p: 5410
Jer 6:16 in the ways, and see, and ask for the old p, 5410
18:15 to stumble in their ways from the ancient p, 7635
18:15 to walk in p, in a way not cast up; 5410
La 3: 9 hewn stone, he hath made my p crooked. 5410
Hos 2: 6 make a wall, that she shall not find her p. 5410
Mic 4: 2 us of his ways, and we will walk in his p: 734
Mt 3: 3 ye the way of the Lord, make his p straight. 5147
Mk 1: 3 ye the way of the Lord, make his p straight. 5147
Lk 3: 4 ye the way of the Lord, make his p straight. 5147
Heb 12:13 And make straight p for your feet, lest that 5163

PATHWAY (1) [PATH]

Pr 12:28 and in the p thereof there is no death. 1870+5410

PATIENCE (34) [PATIENT, PATIENTLY]

Mt 18:26 have p with me, and I will pay thee all. 3114
18:29 Have p with me, and I will pay thee all. 3114
Lk 8:15 keep it, and bring forth fruit with p. 5281
21:19 In your p possess ye your souls. 5281
Ro 5: 3 knowing that tribulation worketh p; 5281
5: 4 And p, experience; and experience, hope: 5281
8:25 we see not, then do we with p wait for it. 5281
15: 4 that we through p and comfort of 5281
15: 5 Now the God of p and consolation grant 5281
2Co 6: 4 in much p, in afflictions, in necessities, 5281
12:12 apostle were wrought among you in all p, 5281
Col 1:11 unto all p and longsuffering with 5281
1Th 1: 3 and p of hope in our Lord Jesus Christ, 5281
2Th 1: 4 in you in the churches of God for your p 5281
1Ti 6:11 godliness, faith, love, p, meekness. 5281
2Ti 3:10 faith, longsuffering, charity, p, 5281
Tit 2: 2 temperate, sound in faith, in charity, in p. 5281
Heb 6:12 through faith and p inherit the promises. 3115
10:36 For ye have need of p, that, after ye have 5281
12: 1 let us run with p the race that is set before 5281
Jas 1: 3 this, that the trying of your faith worketh p. 5281
1: 4 But let p have her perfect work, that ye 5281
5: 7 and hath long p for it, until he receive 3114
5:10 an example of suffering affliction, and of p. 3115
5:11 Ye have heard of the p of Job, and 5281
2Pe 1: 6 and to temperance p; and to patience 5281
1: 6 to temperance patience; and to p godliness; 5281
Rev 1: 9 and in the kingdom and p of Jesus Christ, 5281
2: 2 and thy p, and how thou canst not bear 5281
2: 3 and hast p, and for my name's sake hast 5281
2:19 and faith, and thy p, and thy works; 5281
3:10 Because thou hast kept the word of my p, 5281
13:10 Here is the p and the faith of the saints. 5281
14:12 Here is the p of the saints: here are they 5281

PATIENT (9) [PATIENCE]

Ecc 7: 8 the p in spirit is better than the proud in 750
Ro 2: 7 To them who by p continuance in well 5281
12:12 Rejoicing in hope; p in tribulation; 5278
1Th 5:14 support the weak, be p toward all men. 3114
2Th 3: 5 of God, and into the p waiting for Christ. 5281
1Ti 3: 3 but p, not a brawler, not covetous; 1933
2Ti 2:24 but be gentle unto all men, apt to teach, p, 420
Jas 5: 7 Be p therefore, brethren, unto the coming 3114
5: 8 Be ye also p; stablish your hearts: for 3114

PATIENTLY (6) [PATIENCE]

Ps 37: 7 Rest in the LORD, and wait p for him: 2342
40: 1 I waited p for the LORD; and 6960+6960
Ac 26: 3 wherefore I beseech thee to hear me p. 3116
Heb 6:15 And so, after he had p endured, 3114
1Pe 2:20 buffeted for your faults, ye shall take it p? 5278
2:20 ye do well, and suffer for it, ye take it p, 5278

PATMOS (1)

Rev 1: 9 was in the isle that is called P, for the word 3963

PATRIARCH (2) [PATRIARCHS]

Ac 2:29 let me freely speak unto you of the p 3966
Heb 7: 4 the p Abraham gave the tenth of the spoils. 3966

PATRIARCHS (2) [PATRIARCH]

Ac 7: 8 begat Jacob; and Jacob begat the twelve p. 3966
7: 9 And the p, moved with envy, sold Joseph 3966

PATRIMONY (1)

Dt 18: 8 beside that which cometh of the sale of his p. 1

PATROBAS (1)

Ro 16:14 P, Hermes, and the brethren which are with 3969

PATTERN (14) [PATTERNS]

Ex 25: 9 after the p of the tabernacle, and the pattern 8403
25: 9 the p of all the instruments thereof, even 8403
25:40 look that thou make them after their p, 8403
Nu 8: 4 according unto the p which the LORD had 4758
Jos 22:28 that we may say again, Behold the p of 8403
2Ki 16:10 the p of it, according to all 8403
1Ch 28:11 David gave to Solomon his son the p of 8403
28:12 the p of all that he had by the spirit, of 8403
28:18 gold for the p of the chariot of 8403
28:19 hand upon me, even all the works of this p. 8403
Eze 43:10 their iniquities: and let them measure the p. 8508
1Ti 1:16 for a p to them which should hereafter 5296
Tit 2: 7 In all things shewing thyself a p of good 5179
Heb 8: 5 to the p shewed to thee in the mount. 5179

PATTERNS (1) [PATTERN]

Heb 9:23 necessary that the p of things in 5262

PAU (1)

Ge 36:39 the name of his city was P; and his wife's 6464

PAUL (157) [PAUL'S, SAUL]

Ac 13: 9 Then Saul, (who also is called P,) 3972
13:13 Now when P and his company loosed from 3972
13:16 Then P stood up, and beckoning with his 3972
13:43 and religious proselytes followed P and 3972
13:45 those things which were spoken by P, 3972
13:46 Then P and Barnabas waxed bold, and said, 3972
13:50 and raised persecution against P and 3972
14: 9 The same heard P speak: who stedfastly 3972
14:11 And when the people saw what P had done, 3972
14:12 and P, Mercurius, because he was the chief 3972
14:14 Which when the apostles, Barnabas and P, 3972
14:19 and, having stoned P, drew him out of 3972
15: 2 When therefore P and Barnabas had no 3972
15: 2 they determined that P and Barnabas, and 3972
15:12 and gave audience to Barnabas and P, 3972
15:22 of their own company to Antioch with P 3972
15:25 unto you with our beloved Barnabas and P, 3972
15:35 P also and Barnabas continued in Antioch, 3972
15:36 And some days after P said unto Barnabas, 3972
15:38 But P thought not good to take him with 3972
15:40 And P chose Silas, and departed, 3972
16: 3 Him would P have to go forth with him; 3972
16: 9 And a vision appeared to P in the night; 3972
16:14 unto the things which were spoken of P. 3972
16:17 The same followed P and us, and cried, 3972
16:18 But P, being grieved, turned and said to 3972
16:19 they caught P and Silas, and drew them 3972
16:25 And at midnight P and Silas prayed, and 3972
16:28 But P cried with a loud voice, saying, 3972
16:29 and fell down before P and Silas, 3972
16:36 keeper of the prison told this saying to P, 3972
16:37 But P said unto them, They have beaten us 3972
17: 2 And P, as his manner was, went in unto 3972
17: 4 and consorted with P and Silas; 3972
17:10 And the brethren immediately sent away P 3972
17:13 word of God was preached of P at Berea, 3972
17:14 immediately the brethren sent away P to go 3972
17:15 And they that conducted P brought him 3972
17:16 Now while P waited for them at Athens, his 3972
17:22 Then P stood in the midst of Mars' hill, and 3972
17:33 So P departed from among them. 3972
18: 1 After these things P departed from Athens, 3972
18: 5 P was pressed in spirit, and testified to 3972
18: 9 Then spake the Lord to P in the night by a 3972
18:12 insurrection with one accord against P, 3972
18:14 And when P was now about to open his 3972
18:18 And P after this tarried there yet a good 3972
19: 1 P having passed through the upper coasts 3972
19: 4 Then said P, John verily baptized with 3972
19: 6 And when P had laid his hands upon them, 3972
19:11 wrought special miracles by the hands of P: 3972
19:13 We adjure you by Jesus whom P preacheth. 3972
19:15 and said, Jesus I know, and P I know; 3972
19:21 things were ended, P purposed in the spirit, 3972
19:26 this P hath persuaded and turned away 3972
19:30 And when P would have entered in unto 3972
20: 1 P called unto him the disciples, and 3972
20: 7 P preached unto them, ready to depart on 3972
20: 9 and as P was long preaching, he sunk down 3972
20:10 And P went down, and fell on him, and 3972
20:13 unto Assos, there intending to take in P: 3972
20:16 For P had determined to sail by Ephesus, 3972
21: 4 who said to P through the Spirit, that he 3972
21:13 Then P answered, What mean ye to weep 3972
21:18 And the day following P went in with us 3972
21:26 Then P took the men, and the next day 3972
21:29 whom they supposed that P had brought 3972
21:30 and they took P, and drew him out of 3972
21:32 and the soldiers, they left beating of P. 3972
21:37 And as P was to be led into the castle, 3972
21:39 But P said, I am a man which am a Jew of 3972
21:40 P stood on the stairs, and beckoned with 3972
22:25 P said unto the centurion that stood by, Is it 3972
22:28 And P said, But I was free born. 3972
22:30 and brought P down, and set him before 3972
23: 1 And P, earnestly beholding the council, 3972
23: 3 Then said P unto him, God shall smite thee, 3972
23: 5 Then said P, I wist not, brethren, that he 3972
23: 6 But when P perceived that the one part 3972
23:10 fearing lest P should have been pulled in 3972
23:11 by him, and said, Be of good cheer, P: 3972
23:12 neither eat nor drink till they had killed P. 3972
23:14 we will eat nothing until we have slain P. 3972
23:16 and entered into the castle, and told P. 3972
23:17 Then P called one of the centurions unto 3972
23:18 P the prisoner called me unto him, and 3972
23:20 bring down P to morrow into the council, 3972
23:24 that they may set P on, and bring him safe 3972
23:31 took P, and brought him by night to 3972
23:33 the governor, presented P also before him. 3972
24: 1 who informed the governor against P. 3972
24:10 Then P, after that the governor had 3972
24:23 And he commanded a centurion to keep P, 3972
24:24 he sent for P, and heard him concerning 3972
24:26 money should have been given him of P, 3972
24:27 to shew the Jews a pleasure, left P bound. 3972
25: 2 chief of the Jews informed him against P, 3972
25: 4 that P should be kept at Cesarea, and 3972
25: 6 commanded P to be brought. 3972
25: 7 and grievous complaints against P, 3972
25: 9 answered P, and said, Wilt thou go up to 3972
25:10 Then said P, I stand at Cesar's judgment 3972
25:19 was dead, whom P affirmed to be alive. 3972
25:21 But when P had appealed to be reserved 3972
25:23 at Festus' commandment P was brought 3972
26: 1 Then Agrippa said unto P, Thou art 3972
26: 1 Then P stretched forth the hand, and 3972
26:24 a loud voice, P, thou art beside thyself; 3972
26:28 Then Agrippa said unto P, Almost thou 3972
26:29 And P said, I would to God, that not only 3972
27: 1 they delivered P and certain other prisoners 3972
27: 3 And Julius courteously entreated P, and 3972
27: 9 was now already past, P admonished them, 3972
27:11 than those things which were spoken by P. 3972
27:21 But after long abstinence P stood forth in 3972
27:24 Saying, Fear not, P; thou must be brought 3972
27:31 P said to the centurion and to the soldiers, 3972
27:33 P besought them all to take meat, saying, 3972
27:43 But the centurion, willing to save P, 3972
28: 3 And when P had gathered a bundle of 3972
28: 8 to whom P entered in, and prayed, and 3972
28:15 whom when P saw, he thanked God, and 3972
28:16 P was suffered to dwell by himself with a 3972
28:17 that after three days P called the chief of 3972
28:25 after that P had spoken one word, 3972
28:30 And P dwelt two whole years in his own 3972
Ro 1: 1 P, a servant of Jesus Christ, called to be an 3972
1Co 1: 1 P, called to be an apostle of Jesus Christ 3972
1:12 I say, that every one of you saith, I am of P; 3972
1:13 was P crucified for you? or were ye 3972
1:13 or were ye baptized in the name of P? 3972
3: 4 For while one saith, I am of P; and another, 3972
3: 5 Who then is P, and who is Apollos, but 3972
3:22 Whether P, or Apollos, or Cephas, or 3972
16:21 The salutation of me P with mine own 3972
2Co 1: 1 P, an apostle of Jesus Christ by the will of 3972
10: 1 Now I P myself beseech you by 3972
Gal 1: 1 P, an apostle, (not of men, neither by man, 3972
5: 2 Behold, I P say unto you, that if ye be 3972
Eph 1: 1 P, an apostle of Jesus Christ by the will of 3972
3: 1 For this cause I P, the prisoner of Jesus 3972
Php 1: 1 P and Timotheus, the servants of Jesus 3972
Col 1: 1 P, an apostle of Jesus Christ by the will of 3972
1:23 whereof I P am made a minister; 3972
4:18 The salutation by the hand of me P. 3972
1Th 1: 1 P, and Silvanus, and Timotheus, unto 3972
2:18 come unto you, even I P, once and again; 3972
2Th 1: 1 P, and Silvanus, and Timotheus, unto 3972
3:17 The salutation of P with mine own hand, 3972
1Ti 1: 1 P, an apostle of Jesus Christ by 3972
2Ti 1: 1 P, an apostle of Jesus Christ by the will of 3972
4: S when P was brought before Nero 3972
Tit 1: 1 P, a servant of God, and an apostle of Jesus 3972
Phm 1: 1 P, a prisoner of Jesus Christ, and 3972
1: 9 thee, being such a one as P the aged, 3972
1:19 I P have written it with mine own hand, 3972
2Pe 3:15 even as our beloved brother P also 3972

PAUL'S (6) [PAUL]

Ac 19:29 men of Macedonia, P companions in travel, 3972
20:37 and fell on P neck, and kissed him, 3972
21: 8 And the next day we that were of P 3972
21:11 he took P girdle, and bound his own hands 3972

Ac 23:16 And when **P** sister's son heard of *their* 3972
25:14 Festus declared **P** cause unto the king, 3972

PAULUS (1)
Ac 13: 7 with the deputy *of the country,* Sergius **P**, 3972

PAVED (2) [PAVEMENT]
Ex 24:10 *there was* under his feet as it were a **p** work 3840
SS 3:10 the midst thereof being **p** *with* love, 7528

PAVEMENT (9) [PAVED]
2Ki 16:17 *were* under it, and put it upon a **p** of stones. 4837
2Ch 7: 3 *with their* faces to the ground upon the **p**, 7531
Est 1: 6 upon a **p** of red, and blue, and white, and 7531
Eze 40:17 and a **p** made for the court round about: 7531
40:17 thirty chambers *were* upon the **p**. 7531
40:18 the **p** by the side of the gates over against 7531
40:18 the length of the gates *was* the lower **p**. 7531
42: 3 over against the **p** which *was* for the utter 7531
Jn 19:13 judgment seat in a place *that is* called the **P**, 3038

PAVILION (4) [PAVILIONS]
Ps 18:11 his **p** round about him *were* dark waters 5521
27: 5 time of trouble he shall hide me in his **p**: 5520
31:20 thou shalt keep them secretly in a **p** from 5521
Jer 43:10 and he shall spread his **royal p** over them. 8237

PAVILIONS (3) [PAVILION]
2Sa 22:12 he made darkness **p** round about him, 5521
1Ki 20:12 he *was* drinking, he and the kings in the **p**, 5521
20:16 *was* drinking *himself* drunk in the **p**, 5521

PAW (2) [PAWETH, PAWS]
1Sa 17:37 The LORD that delivered me out of the **p** 3027
17:37 out of the **p** of the bear, he will deliver me 3027

PAWETH (1) [PAW]
Job 39:21 He **p** in the valley, and rejoiceth in *his* 2658

PAWS (1) [PAW]
Lev 11:27 whatsoever goeth upon his **p**, among all 3709

PAY (39) [PAID, PAYED, PAYETH, PAYMENT]
Ex 21:19 only he shall **p** *for* the loss of his time, and 5414
21:22 and he shall **p** as the judges determine. 5414
21:36 he shall **surely p** ox for ox; and 7999+7999
22: 7 if the thief be found, let him **p** double. 7999
22: 9 he shall **p** double unto his neighbour. 7999
22:17 he shall **p** money according to the dowry of 8254
Nu 20:19 *of* thy water, then I will **p** for it: 4377+5414
Dt 23:21 thy God, thou shalt not slack to **p** it: 7999
2Sa 15: 7 I pray thee, let me go and **p** my vow, 7999
1Ki 20:39 or else thou shalt **p** a talent of silver. 8254
2Ki 4: 7 **p** thy debt, and live thou and thy children 7999
2Ch 8: 8 them did Solomon **make to p** tribute until 5927
27: 5 So much did the children of Ammon **p** unto 7725
Ezr 4:13 walls set up *again, then* will they not **p** toll, 5415
Est 3: 9 I will **p** ten thousand talents of silver to 8254
4: 7 to **p** to the king's treasuries for the Jews, 8254
Job 22:27 shalt hear thee, and thou shalt **p** thy vows. 7999
Ps 22:25 I will **p** my vows before them that fear him. 7999
50:14 and **p** thy vows unto the most High: 7999
66:13 with burnt offerings: I will **p** thee my vows, 7999
76:11 Vow, and **p** unto the LORD your God: 7999
116:14 I will **p** my vows unto the LORD now in 7999
116:18 I will **p** my vows unto the LORD now in 7999
Pr 19:17 which he hath given will he **p** him **again**. 7999
22:27 If thou hast nothing to **p**, why should he 7999
Ecc 5: 4 vowest a vow unto God, defer not to **p** it; 7999
5: 4 in fools: **p** that which thou hast vowed. 7999
5: 5 than that thou shouldest vow and not **p**. 7999
Jnh 2: 9 I will **p** *that* that I have vowed. 7999
Mt 17:24 and said, Doth not your master **p** tribute? *5055*
18:25 But forasmuch as he had not to **p**, his lord *591*
18:26 have patience with me, and I will **p** thee all. *591*
18:28 by the throat, saying, **P** me that thou owest. *591*
18:29 Have patience with me, and I will **p** thee all. *591*
18:30 him into prison, till he should **p** the debt. *591*
18:34 till he should **p** all that was due unto him. *591*
23:23 for ye **p tithe of** mint and anise and cummin, *586*
Lk 7:42 And when they had nothing to **p**, he frankly *591*
Ro 13: 6 For for this cause **p** you tribute also: *5055*

PAYED (2) [PAY]
Pr 7:14 with me; *this* day have I **p** my vows. 7999
Heb 7: 9 who receiveth tithes, **p tithes** in Abraham. *1183*

PAYETH (1) [PAY]
Ps 37:21 The wicked borroweth, and **p** not **again**: 7999

PAYMENT (1) [PAY]
Mt 18:25 and all that he had, and **p** to be **made**. *591*

PEACE (429) [PEACEABLE, PEACEABLY, PEACEMAKERS]
Ge 15:15 thou shalt go to thy fathers in **p**; thou shalt 7965
24:21 the man wondering at her **held** his **p**, to wit 2790
26:29 but good, and have sent thee away in **p**: 7965
26:31 and they departed from him in **p**. 7965
28:21 that I come again to my father's house in **p**; 7965
34: 5 and Jacob **held** his **p** until they were come. 2790
41:16 God shall give Pharaoh an answer of **p**. 7965
43:23 he said, **P** *be* to you, fear not: your God, 7965
44:17 as for you, get you up in **p** unto your father. 7965
Ex 4:18 And Jethro said to Moses, Go in **p**. 7965
14:14 fight for you, and ye shall **hold** your **p**. 2790
18:23 this people shall also go to their place in **p**. 7965
20:24 thy **p offerings**, thy sheep, and thine oxen: 8002
24: 5 sacrificed **p** offerings *of* oxen unto 8002
29:28 Israel of the sacrifice of their **p offerings**, 8002
32: 6 burnt offerings, and brought **p offerings**; 8002
Lev 3: 1 if his oblation *be* a sacrifice of **p offering**, 8002
3: 3 **p offering** an offering made by fire unto 8002
Lev 3: 6 if his offering for a sacrifice of **p offering** 8002
3: 9 **p offering** an offering made by fire unto 8002
4:10 the bullock of the sacrifice of **p offerings**: 8002
4:26 as the fat of the sacrifice of **p offerings**: 8002
4:31 away from off the sacrifice of **p offerings**; 8002
4:35 away from the sacrifice of the **p offerings**; 8002
6:12 burn thereon the fat of the **p offerings**. 8002
7:11 *is* the law of the sacrifice of **p offerings**, 8002
7:13 sacrifice of thanksgiving of his **p offerings**. 8002
7:14 that sprinkleth the blood of the **p offerings**. 8002
7:15 the flesh of the sacrifice of his **p offerings** 8002
7:18 **p offerings** be eaten at all on the third day, 8002
7:20 *of* the flesh of the sacrifice of **p offerings**, 8002
7:21 of the flesh of the sacrifice of **p offerings**, 8002
7:29 **p offerings** unto the LORD shall bring his 8002
7:29 LORD of the sacrifice of his **p offerings**. 8002
7:32 of the sacrifices of your **p offerings**. 8002
7:33 that offereth the blood of the **p offerings**, 8002
7:34 from off the sacrifices of their **p offerings**, 8002
7:37 and of the sacrifice of the **p offerings**; 8002
9: 4 Also a bullock and a ram for **p offerings**, 8002
9:18 and the ram *for* a sacrifice of **p offerings**, 8002
9:22 and the burnt offering, and **p offerings**. 8002
10: 3 I will be glorified. And Aaron **held** his **p**. 1826
10:14 of **p offerings** of the children of Israel. 8002
17: 5 offer them *for* **p** offerings unto the LORD. 8002
19: 5 if ye offer a sacrifice of **p offerings** unto 8002
22:21 **p offerings** unto the LORD to accomplish 8002
23:19 the first year for a sacrifice of **p offerings**. 8002
26: 6 I will give **p** in the land, and ye shall lie 7965
Nu 6:14 one ram without blemish for **p offerings**, 8002
6:17 a sacrifice of **p offerings** unto the LORD, 8002
6:18 *is* under the sacrifice of the **p offerings**. 8002
6:26 his countenance upon thee, and give thee **p**. 7965
7:17 for a sacrifice of **p offerings**, two oxen, 8002
7:23 for a sacrifice of **p offerings**, two oxen, 8002
7:29 for a sacrifice of **p offerings**, two oxen, 8002
7:35 for a sacrifice of **p offerings**, two oxen, 8002
7:41 for a sacrifice of **p offerings**, two oxen, 8002
7:47 for a sacrifice of **p offerings**, two oxen, 8002
7:53 for a sacrifice of **p offerings**, two oxen, 8002
7:59 for a sacrifice of **p offerings**, two oxen, 8002
7:65 for a sacrifice of **p offerings**, two oxen, 8002
7:71 for a sacrifice of **p offerings**, two oxen, 8002
7:77 for a sacrifice of **p offerings**, two oxen, 8002
7:83 for a sacrifice of **p offerings**, two oxen, 8002
7:88 the sacrifice of the **p offerings** *were* twenty 8002
10:10 and over the sacrifices of your **p offerings**; 8002
15: 8 a vow, or **p offerings** unto the LORD: 8002
25:12 Behold, I give unto him my covenant of **p**: 7965
29:39 drink offerings, and for your **p offerings**. 8002
30: 4 and her father shall **hold** his **p** at her: 2790
30: 7 **held** his **p** at her in the day that he heard *it*: 2790
30:11 her husband heard *it*, and **held** his **p** at her, 2790
30:14 if her husband **altogether hold** his **p** 2790+2790
30:14 he **held** his **p** at her in the day that he 2790
Dt 2:26 Sihon king of Heshbon *with* words of **p**, 7965
20:10 to fight against it, then proclaim **p** unto it. 7965
20:11 if it make thee answer of **p**, and open unto 7965
20:12 if it will **make** no **p** with thee, but 7999
23: 6 Thou shalt not seek their **p** nor their 7965
27: 7 thou shalt offer **p offerings**, and shalt eat 8002
29:19 himself in his heart, saying, I shall have **p**, 7965
Jos 8:31 the LORD, and sacrificed **p offerings**. 8002
9:15 Joshua made **p** with them, and made a 7965
10: 1 how the inhabitants of Gibeon had **made p** 7999
10: 4 for it hath **made p** with Joshua and with 7999
10:21 to the camp to Joshua *at* Makkedah in **p**: 7965
11:19 There was not a city that **made p** with 7999
22:23 or if to offer **p** offerings thereon, 8002
22:27 our sacrifices, and with our **p offerings**; 8002
Jdg 4:17 for *there was* **p** between Jabin the king of 7965
6:23 the LORD said unto him, **P** *be* unto thee; 7965
8: 9 saying, When I come again in **p**, I will 7965
11:31 when I return in **p** from the children of 7965
18: 6 the priest said unto them, Go in **p**: 7965
18:19 they said unto him, **Hold** thy **p**, lay thine 2790
19:20 the old man said, **P** *be* with thee; 7965
20:26 and **p offerings** before the LORD. 8002
21: 4 and offered burnt offerings and **p offerings**. 8002
1Sa 1:17 Eli answered and said, Go in **p**: and 7965
7:14 there was **p** between Israel and 7965
10: 8 *and* to sacrifice sacrifices of **p offerings**: 8002
10:27 him no presents. But he **held** his **p**. 2790+3509.1
11:15 *of* **p offerings** before the LORD; 8002
13: 9 a burnt offering to me, and **p offerings**. 8002
20: 7 say thus, *It is* well; thy servant shall have **p**: 7965
20:13 send thee away, that thou mayest go in **p**: 7965
20:21 for *there is* **p** to thee, and no hurt; *as* 7965
20:42 Jonathan said to David, Go in **p**, 7965
25: 6 that liveth *in prosperity,* **P** *be* both *to* thee, 7965
25: 6 **p** *be to* thine house, and peace *be unto* all 7965
25: 6 and **p** *be unto* all that thou hast. 7965
25:35 said unto her, Go up in **p** to thine house; 7965
29: 7 Wherefore now return, and go in **p**, 7965
2Sa 3:21 David sent Abner away; and he went in **p**. 7965
3:22 had sent him away, and he was gone in **p**. 7965
3:23 he hath sent him away, and he is gone in **p**. 7965
6:17 and **p offerings** before the LORD. 8002
6:18 of offering burnt offerings and **p offerings**, 8002
10:19 they **made p** with Israel, and served them. 7999
13:20 **hold** now thy **p**, my sister: he *is* thy 2790
15: 9 the king said unto him, Go in **p**. So he 7965
15:27 return *into* the city in **p**, and your two sons 7965
17: 3 all returned: *so* all the people shall be *in* **p**. 7965
19:24 departed until the day he came *again* in **p**. 7965
19:30 is come *again* in **p** unto his own house. 7965
24:25 and offered burnt offerings and **p offerings**. 8002
1Ki 2: 5 shed the blood of war in **p**, and put 7965
2: 6 his hoar head go down *to* the grave in **p**. 7965
2:33 shall there be **p** for ever from the LORD. 7965
3:15 offered **p offerings**, and made a feast to all 8002
4:24 and he had **p** on all sides round about him. 7965
5:12 there was **p** between Hiram and Solomon; 7965
8:63 Solomon offered a sacrifice of **p offerings**, 8002
1Ki 8:64 and the fat of the **p offerings**: 8002
8:64 and the fat of the **p offerings**. 8002
9:25 **p offerings** upon the altar which he built 8002
20:18 he said, Whether they be come out for **p**, 7965
22:17 let them return every man to his house in **p**. 7965
22:27 with water of affliction, until I come in **p**. 7965
22:28 Micaiah said, If thou return at all in **p**, 7965
22:44 Jehoshaphat **made p** with the king of 7999
2Ki 2: 3 he said, Yea, I know *it;* **hold** you your **p**. 2814
2: 5 Yea, I know *it;* **hold** you your **p**. 2814
5:19 he said unto him, Go in **p**. So he departed 7965
7: 9 *is* a day of good tidings, and we **hold** our **p**: 2814
9:17 send to meet them, and let him say, *Is it* **p**? 7965
9:18 and said, Thus saith the king, *Is it* **p**? 7965
9:18 Jehu said, What hast thou to do with **p**? 7965
9:19 and said, Thus saith the king, *Is it* **p**? 7965
9:19 What hast thou to do with **p**? 7965
9:22 Joram saw Jehu, that he said, *Is it* **p**, Jehu? 7965
9:22 What **p**, so long as the whoredoms of thy 7965
9:31 she said, *Had* Zimri **p**, who slew his 7965
16:13 sprinkled the blood of his **p offerings**. 8002
18:36 the people **held** their **p**, and answered him 2790
20:19 *Is it* not *good,* if **p** and truth be in my days? 7965
22:20 thou shalt be gathered into thy grave in **p**; 7965
1Ch 12:18 **p**, peace *be* unto thee, and peace *be* to thine 7965
12:18 **p** *be* unto thee, and peace *be* to thine 7965
12:18 *be* unto thee, and **p** *be* to thine helpers; 7965
16: 1 and **p offerings** before God. 8002
16: 2 the burnt offerings and the **p offerings**, 8002
19:19 they **made p** with David, and became his 7999
21:26 and offered burnt offerings and **p offerings**, 8002
22: 9 I will give **p** and quietness unto Israel in his 7965
2Ch 7: 7 the fat of the **p offerings**, because 8002
15: 5 in those times *there was* no **p** to him that 7965
18:16 *therefore* every man to his house in **p**. 7965
18:26 with water of affliction, until I return in **p**. 7965
18:27 If thou certainly return in **p**, *then* hath not 7965
19: 1 returned to his house in **p** to Jerusalem. 7965
29:35 with the fat of the **p offerings**, and 8002
30:22 offering **p** offerings, and 8002
31: 2 for burnt offerings and for **p offerings**, 8002
33:16 sacrificed thereon **p** offerings and 8002
34:28 thou shalt be gathered to thy grave in **p**, 7965
Ezr 4:17 rest beyond the river: **P**, and at such a time. 8001
5: 7 written thus: Unto Darius the king, all **p**. 8001
7:12 of heaven, perfect *p*, and at such a time. NIH
9:12 nor seek their **p** or their wealth for ever: 7965
Ne 5: 8 **held** they their **p**, and found nothing *to* 2790
8:11 **Hold** your **p**, for the day *is* holy; 2013
Est 4:14 For if thou **altogether holdest** thy **p** 2790+2790
9:30 of Ahasuerus, *with* words of **p** and truth, 7965
10: 3 his people, and speaking **p** to all his seed. 7965
Job 5:23 the beasts of the field shall be **at p** with 7999
5:24 shalt know that thy tabernacle *shall be in* **p**; 7965
11: 3 Should thy lies **make** men **hold** their **p**? 2790
13: 5 you would **altogether hold** your **p**, 2790+2790
13:13 **Hold** your **p**, let me alone, that I may 2790
22:21 now thyself with him, and be **at p**: 7999
25: 2 with him, he maketh **p** in his high places. 7965
29:10 The nobles **held** their **p**, and 2244+6963
33:31 unto me: **hold** thy **p**, and I will speak. 2790
33:33 **hold** thy **p**, and I shall teach thee wisdom. 2790
Ps 4: 8 I will both lay me down in **p**, and sleep: 7965
7: 4 evil *unto* him that was **at p** with me; 7999
28: 3 which speak **p** to their neighbours, but 7965
29:11 the LORD will bless his people with **p**. 7965
34:14 and do good; seek **p**, and pursue it. 7965
35:20 For they speak not **p**: but they devise 7965
37:11 delight themselves in the abundance of **p**. 7965
37:37 the upright: for the end of *that* man *is* **p**. 7965
39: 2 *with* silence, I **held** my **p**, *even* from good; 2814
39:12 ear unto my cry; **hold** not thy **p** at my tears: 2790
55:18 He hath delivered my soul in **p** from 7965
55:20 his hands against such as be **at p** with him: 7999
72: 3 The mountains shall bring **p** to the people, 7965
72: 7 abundance of **p** so long as the moon 7965
83: 1 **hold** not thy **p**, and be not still, O God. 2790
85: 8 for he will speak **p** unto his people, and 7965
85:10 and **p** have kissed *each other.* 7965
109: 1 **Hold** not thy **p**, O God of my praise; 2790
119:165 Great **p** have they which love thy law: and 7965
120: 6 soul hath long dwelt with him that hateth **p**. 7965
120: 7 *I am for* **p**: but when I speak, they *are* for 7965
122: 6 Pray for the **p** of Jerusalem: they shall 7965
122: 7 **P** be within thy walls, *and* prosperity within 7965
122: 8 I will now say, **P** *be* within thee. 7965
125: 5 of iniquity: *but* **p** *shall be* upon Israel. 7965
128: 6 thy children's children, *and* **p** upon Israel. 7965
147:14 He maketh **p** *in* thy borders, *and* filleth thee 7965
Pr 3: 2 For length of days, and long life, and **p**, 7965
3:17 of pleasantness, and all her paths *are* **p**. 7965
7:14 *I have* **p** offerings with me; *this* day have I 8002
11:12 but a man of understanding **holdeth** his **p**. 2790
12:20 but to the counsellers of **p** *is* joy. 7965
16: 7 he **maketh** even his enemies **to be at p** 7999
17:28 Even a fool, when he **holdeth** his **p**, 2790
Ecc 3: 8 time to hate; a time of war, and a time of **p**. 7965
Isa 9: 6 The everlasting Father, The Prince of **P**. 7965
9: 7 *his* government and **p** *there shall be* no end, 7965
26: 3 Thou wilt keep *him in* **perfect p**, 7965+7965
26:12 LORD, thou wilt ordain **p** for us: for thou 7965
27: 5 my strength, *that* he may make **p** with me; 7965
27: 5 with me; *and* he shall make **p** with me. 7965
32:17 the work of righteousness shall be **p**; and 7965
33: 7 the ambassadors of **p** shall weep bitterly. 7965
36:21 they **held** their **p**, and answered him not a 2790
38:17 Behold, for **p** I had great bitterness: 7965
39: 8 For there shall be **p** and truth in my days. 7965
42:14 I have long time **holden** my **p**; I have been 2814
45: 7 I make **p**, and create evil: I the LORD do 7965
48:18 had thy **p** been as a river, and 7965
48:22 *There is* no **p**, saith the LORD, unto 7965
52: 7 bringeth good tidings, that publisheth **p**; 7965
53: 5 the chastisement of our **p** *was* upon him; 7965
54:10 neither shall the covenant of my **p** be 7965

P

Isa 54:13 and great *shall be* the **p** of thy children. 7965
55:12 go out with joy, and be led forth with **p**: 7965
57: 2 He shall enter *into* **p**: they shall rest in their 7965
57:11 have not I **held** my **p** even of old, and thou 2814
57:19 **P**, peace to *him that is* far off, and to *him* 7965
57:19 **p** to *him that is* far off, and to *him that is* 7965
57:21 *There is* no **p**, saith my God, to the wicked. 7965
59: 8 The way of **p** they know not; and *there is* 7965
59: 8 whosoever goeth therein shall not know **p**. 7965
60:17 I will also make thy officers **p**, and 7965
62: 1 For Zion's sake will I not **hold my p**, and 2814
62: 6 *which* shall never **hold** their **p** day nor 2814
64:12 wilt thou **hold** thy **p**, and afflict us very 2814
66:12 I will extend **p** to her like a river, and 7965
Jer 4:10 Jerusalem, saying, Ye shall have **p**; 7965
4:19 I cannot **hold** my **p**, because thou hast 2790
6:14 *of* my people slightly, saying, **P**, peace; 7965
6:14 *of* my people slightly, saying, Peace, **p**; 7965
6:14 Peace, peace; when *there is* no **p**. 7965
8:11 of my people slightly, saying, **P**, peace; 7965
8:11 of my people slightly, saying, Peace, **p**; 7965
8:11 Peace, peace; when *there is* no **p**. 7965
8:15 *We* looked for **p**, but no good *came; and* 7965
12: 5 *if* in the land of **p**, *wherein* thou trustedst, 7965
12:12 *other* end of the land: no flesh *shall* have **p**. 7965
14:13 but I will give you assured **p** in this place. 7965
14:19 *we* looked for **p**, and *there is* no good; and 7965
16: 5 for I have taken away my **p** from this 7965
23:17 The LORD hath said, Ye shall have **p**; 7965
28: 9 The prophet which prophesieth of **p**, 7965
29: 7 seek the **p** of the city whither I have caused 7965
29: 7 for in the **p** thereof shall ye have peace. 7965
29: 7 for in the peace thereof shall ye have **p**. 7965
29:11 the LORD, thoughts of **p**, and not of evil, 7965
30: 5 a voice of trembling, of fear, and not of **p**. 7965
33: 6 will reveal unto them the abundance of **p** 7965
34: 5 *But* thou shalt die in **p**: and with 7965
43:12 and he shall go forth from thence in **p**. 7965
La 3:17 thou hast removed my soul far off from **p**: 7965
Eze 7:25 they shall seek **p**, and *there shall be* none. 7965
13:10 they have seduced my people, saying, **P**; 7965
13:10 *there was* no **p**; and one built up a wall, and 7965
13:16 which see visions of **p** for her, and *there is* 7965
13:16 and *there is* no **p**, saith the Lord GOD. 7965
34:25 And I will make with them a covenant of **p**, 7965
37:26 Moreover I will make a covenant of **p** with 7965
43:27 upon the altar, and your **p offerings**; 8002
45:15 for a burnt offering, and for **p offerings**, 8002
45:17 and the burnt offering, and the **p offerings**, 8002
46: 2 his burnt offering and his **p offerings**, 8002
46:12 or **p offerings** voluntarily unto the LORD, 8002
46:12 his burnt offering and his **p offerings**, 8002
Da 4: 1 in all the earth; **P** be multiplied unto you. 8001
6:25 in all the earth; **P** be multiplied unto you. 8001
8:25 in his heart, and by **p** shall destroy many: 7962
10:19 **p** *be* unto thee, be strong, yea, be strong. 7965
Am 5:22 I regard the **p offerings** of your fat beasts. 8002
Ob 1: 7 the men that were at **p** with thee have 7965
Mic 3: 5 that bite with their teeth, and cry, **P**; 7965
5: 5 this *man* shall be *the* **p**, when the Assyrian 7965
Na 1:15 bringeth good tidings, that publisheth **p**. 7965
Zep 1: 7 **Hold** thy **p** at the presence of the Lord 2013
Hag 2: 9 in this place will I give **p**, saith the LORD 7965
Zec 6:13 the counsel of **p** shall be between them 7965
8:10 neither *was there any* **p** to him that went 7965
8:16 the judgment of truth and **p** in your gates: 7965
8:19 therefore love the truth and **p**. 7965
9:10 he shall speak **p** unto the heathen: and 7965
Mal 2: 5 My covenant was with him of life and **p**; 7965
2: 6 he walked with me in **p** and equity, and 7965
Mt 10:13 house be worthy, let your **p** come upon it: *1515*
10:13 if it be not worthy, let your **p** return to you. *1515*
10:34 Think not that I am come to send **p** on *1515*
10:34 on earth: I came not to send **p**, but a sword. *1515*
20:31 because they should **hold** their **p**: *4623*
26:63 But Jesus **held** his **p**. And the high priest *4623*
Mk 1:25 saying, **Hold** thy **p**, and come out of him. *5392*
3: 4 save life, or to kill? But they **held** their **p**. *4623*
4:39 the wind, and said unto the sea, **P**, be still. *4623*
5:34 go in **p**, and be whole of thy plague. *1515*
9:34 But they **held** their **p**: for by the way they *4623*
9:50 in yourselves, and **have p** one with another. *1514*
10:48 charged him that he should **hold** his **p**: *4623*
14:61 But he **held** his **p**, and answered nothing. *4623*
Lk 1:79 to guide our feet into the way of **p**. *1515*
2:14 and on earth **p**, good will towards men. *1515*
2:29 now lettest thou thy servant depart in **p**, *1515*
4:35 saying, **Hold** thy **p**, and come out of him. *5392*
7:50 Thy faith hath saved thee; go in **p**. *1515*
8:48 thy faith hath made thee whole; go in **p**.) *1515*
10: 5 house ye enter, first say, **P** *be* to this house. *1515*
10: 6 And if the son of **p** be there, your peace *1515*
10: 6 of peace be there, your **p** shall rest upon it: *1515*
11:21 keepeth his palace, his goods are in **p**: *1515*
12:51 Suppose ye that I am come to give **p** on *1515*
14: 4 And they **held** their **p**. And he took *him*, *2270*
14:32 an ambassage, and desireth conditions of **p**. *1515*
18:39 rebuked him, that he should **hold** his **p**: *4623*
19:38 **p** in heaven, and glory in the highest. *1515*
19:40 I tell you that, if these should **hold** their **p**, *4623*
19:42 the *things* which belong unto thy **p**! *1515*
20:26 marvelled at his answer, and **held** their **p**. *4601*
24:36 and saith unto them, **P** *be* unto you. *1515*
Jn 14:27 **P** I leave with you, my peace I give unto *1515*
14:27 I leave with you, my **p** I give unto you: *1515*
16:33 unto you, that in me ye might have **p**. *1515*
20:19 and saith unto them, **P** *be* unto you. *1515*
20:21 said Jesus to them again, **P** *be* unto you: *1515*
20:26 stood in the midst, and said, **P** *be* unto you. *1515*
Ac 10:36 of Israel, preaching **p** by Jesus Christ: *1515*
11:18 they heard these *things*, they **held** their **p**, *2270*
12:17 unto them with the hand to **hold** their **p**, *4601*
12:20 king's chamberlain their friend, desired **p**; *1515*
15:13 And after they had **held** their **p**, *4601*
15:33 they were let go in **p** from the brethren unto *1515*
Ac 16:36 you go: now therefore depart, and go in **p**. *1515*
18: 9 not afraid, but speak, and **hold** not thy **p**: *4623*
Ro 1: 7 Grace to you and **p** from God our Father, *1515*
2:10 But glory, honour, and **p**, to every *man* that *1515*
3:17 And the way of **p** have they not known: *1515*
5: 1 we have **p** with God through our Lord *1515*
8: 6 but to be spiritually minded *is* life and **p**. *1515*
10:15 the feet of them that preach the gospel of **p**, *1515*
14:17 and **p**, and joy in the Holy Ghost. *1515*
14:19 follow *after the things* which make for **p**, *1515*
15:13 fill you with all joy and **p** in believing, *1515*
15:33 Now the God of **p** *be* with you all. Amen. *1515*
16:20 And the God of **p** shall bruise Satan under *1515*
1Co 1: 3 Grace *be* unto you, and **p**, from God our *1515*
7:15 in such *cases*: but God hath called us to **p**. *1515*
14:30 that sitteth *by*, let the first **hold** his **p**. *4601*
14:33 but of **p**, as in all churches of the saints. *1515*
16:11 but conduct him forth in **p**, that he may *1515*
2Co 1: 2 *be* to you and **p** from God our Father, *1515*
13:11 of good comfort, be of one mind, **live in p**; *1514*
13:11 the God of love and **p** shall be with you. *1515*
Gal 1: 3 Grace *be* to you and **p** from God the Father, *1515*
5:22 joy, **p**, longsuffering, gentleness, goodness, *1515*
6:16 to this rule, **p** *be* on them, and mercy, *1515*
Eph 1: 2 Grace *be* to you, and **p**, from God our *1515*
2:14 For he is our **p**, who hath made both one, *1515*
2:15 of twain one new man, *so* making **p**; *1515*
2:17 and preached **p** to you which were afar off, *1515*
4: 3 keep the unity of the Spirit in the bond of **p**. *1515*
6:15 with the preparation of the gospel of **p**; *1515*
6:23 **P** *be* to the brethren, and love with faith, *1515*
Php 1: 2 Grace *be* unto you, and **p**, from God our *1515*
4: 7 And the **p** of God, which passeth all *1515*
4: 9 do: and the God of **p** shall be with you. *1515*
Col 1: 2 Grace *be* unto you, and **p**, from God our *1515*
1:20 having **made p** through the blood of his *1517*
3:15 And let the **p** of God rule in your hearts, *1515*
1Th 1: 1 Grace *be* unto you, and **p**, from God our *1515*
5: 3 For when they shall say, **P** and safety; then *1515*
5:13 *And* be at **p** among yourselves. *1514*
5:23 And the very God of **p** sanctify you wholly; *1515*
2Th 1: 2 Grace unto you, and **p**, from God our *1515*
3:16 Now the Lord of **p** himself give you peace *1515*
3:16 Now the Lord of peace himself give you **p** *1515*
1Ti 1: 2 Grace, mercy, *and* **p**, from God our Father *1515*
2Ti 1: 2 Grace, mercy, *and* **p**, from God the Father *1515*
2:22 but follow righteousness, faith, charity, **p**, *1515*
Tit 1: 4 Grace, mercy, *and* **p**, from God the Father *1515*
Phm 1: 3 Grace to you, and **p**, from God our Father *1515*
Heb 7: 2 also King of Salem, which is, King of **p**; *1515*
11:31 when she had received the spies with **p**. *1515*
12:14 Follow **p** with all *men*, and holiness, *1515*
13:20 Now the God of **p**, that brought again from *1515*
Jas 2:16 Depart in **p**, be you warmed and filled; *1515*
3:18 And the fruit of righteousness is sown in **p** *1515*
3:18 is sown in peace of them that make **p**. *1515*
1Pe 1: 2 Grace unto you, and **p**, be multiplied. *1515*
3:11 and do good; let him seek **p**, and ensue it. *1515*
5:14 **P** *be* with you all that are in Christ Jesus. *1515*
2Pe 1: 2 **p** be multiplied unto you through *1515*
3:14 diligent that ye may be found of him in **p**, *1515*
2Jn 1: 3 Grace be with you, mercy, *and* **p**, from God *1515*
3Jn 1:14 **P** *be* to thee. *Our* friends salute thee. *1515*
Jude 1: 2 unto you, and **p**, and love, be multiplied. *1515*
Rev 1: 4 Grace *be* unto you, and **p**, from him which *1515*
6: 4 that sat thereon to take **p** from the earth, *1515*

PEACEABLE (8) [PEACE]

Ge 34:21 These men *are* **p** with us; therefore let them 8003
2Sa 20:19 I *am one of them that are* **p** *and* faithful in 7999
1Ch 4:40 and the land *was* wide, and quiet, and **p**; 7961
Isa 32:18 my people shall dwell in a **p** habitation, 7965
Jer 25:37 the **p** habitations are cut down because of 7965
1Ti 2: 2 and **p** life in all godliness and honesty. *2272*
Heb 12:11 nevertheless afterward it yieldeth the **p** fruit *1516*
Jas 3:17 then **p**, gentle, *and* easy to be intreated, *1516*

PEACEABLY (12) [PEACE]

Ge 37: 4 hated him, and could not speak **p** unto him. 7965
Jdg 11:13 restore those *lands* again **p**. 7965+871.1
21:13 the rock Rimmon, and to call **p** unto them. 7965
1Sa 16: 4 at his coming, and said, Comest thou **p**? 7965
16: 5 he said, **P**: I am come to sacrifice unto 7965
1Ki 2:13 she said, Comest thou **p**? And he said, 7965
2:13 Comest thou peaceably? And he said, **P**. 7965
1Ch 12:17 ye be come **p** unto me to help me, 7965+3807.1
Jer 9: 8 *one* speaketh **p** to his neighbour with his 7965
Da 11:21 he shall come in **p**, and obtain the kingdom 7962
11:24 He shall enter **p** even upon 7962+871.1
Ro 12:18 as much as lieth in you, **live p** with all men. *1514*

PEACEMAKERS (1) [PEACE]

Mt 5: 9 Blessed *are* the **p**: for they shall be called *1518*

PEACOCKS (3)

1Ki 10:22 and silver, ivory, and apes, and **p**. 8500
2Ch 9:21 and silver, ivory, and apes, and **p**. 8500
Job 39:13 *Gavest thou* the goodly wings unto the **p**? 5965

PEARL (2) [PEARLS]

Mt 13:46 when he had found one **p** of great price, *3135*
Rev 21:21 every several gate was of one **p**: *3135*

PEARLS (8) [PEARL]

Job 28:18 No mention shall be made of coral, or of **p**: 1378
Mt 7: 6 neither cast ye your **p** before swine, *3135*
13:45 unto a merchant man, seeking goodly **p**: *3135*
1Ti 2: 9 broided hair, or gold, or **p**, or costly array; *3135*
Rev 17: 4 decked with gold and precious stone and **p**, *3135*
18:12 and of **p**, and fine linen, and purple, and *3135*
18:16 with gold, and precious stones, and **p**: *3135*
21:21 And the twelve gates *were* twelve **p**; *3135*

PECULIAR (7)

Ex 19: 5 ye shall be a **p treasure** unto me above all 5459
Dt 14: 2 the LORD hath chosen thee to be a **p** 5459
26:18 avouched thee *this* day to be his **p** people, 5459
Ps 135: 4 unto himself, *and* Israel for his **p treasure**. 5459
Ecc 2: 8 the **p treasure** of kings and of 5459
Tit 2:14 and purify unto himself a **p** people, *4041*
1Pe 2: 9 a holy nation, a **p** people; *1519+4047*

PEDAHEL (1)

Nu 34:28 of Naphtali, **P** the son of Ammihud. 6300

PEDAHZUR (5)

Nu 1:10 of Manasseh; Gamaliel the son of **P**. 6301
2:20 Manasseh *shall be* Gamaliel the son of **P**. 6301
7:54 eighth day *offered* Gamaliel the son of **P**, 6301
7:59 *was* the offering of Gamaliel the son of **P**. 6301
10:23 of Manasseh *was* Gamaliel the son of **P**. 6301

PEDAIAH (8)

2Ki 23:36 *was* Zebudah, the daughter of **P** of Rumah. 6305
1Ch 3:18 **P**, and Shenazar, Jecamiah, Hoshama, and 6305
3:19 the sons of **P** *were*, Zerubbabel, and 6305
27:20 half tribe of Manasseh, Joel the son of **P**: 6305
Ne 3:25 the prison. After him **P** the son of Parosh. 6305
8: 4 **P**, and Mishael, and Malchiah, and 6305
11: 7 the son of Joed, the son of **P**, the son of 6305
13:13 and Zadok the scribe, and of the Levites, **P**: 6305

PEDIGREES (1)

Nu 1:18 they **declared** their **p** after their families, 3205

PEELED (3)

Isa 18: 2 to a nation scattered and **p**, 4178
18: 7 of hosts *of* a people scattered and **p**, 4178
Eze 29:18 *was* made bald, and every shoulder *was* **p**: 4803

PEEP (1) [PEEPED]

Isa 8:19 and unto wizards that **p**, and that mutter: 6850

PEEPED (1) [PEEP]

Isa 10:14 moved the wing, or opened the mouth, or **p**. 6850

PEKAH (11)

2Ki 15:25 **P** the son of Remaliah, a captain of his, 6492
15:27 fiftieth year of Azariah king of Judah **P** 6492
15:29 In the days of **P** king of Israel came 6492
15:30 a conspiracy against **P** the son of Remaliah, 6492
15:31 the rest of the acts of **P**, and all that he did, 6492
15:32 In the second year of **P** the son of Remaliah 6492
15:37 king of Syria, and **P** the son of Remaliah. 6492
16: 1 In the seventeenth year of **P** the son of 6492
16: 5 **P** son of Remaliah king of Israel came up 6492
2Ch 28: 6 For **P** the son of Remaliah slew in Judah an 6492
Isa 7: 1 and **P** the son of Remaliah, king of Israel, 6492

PEKAHIAH (3)

2Ki 15:22 and **P** his son reigned in his stead. 6494
15:23 **P** the son of Menahem *began* to reign over 6494
15:26 the rest of the acts of **P**, and all that he did, 6494

PEKOD (2)

Jer 50:21 against it, and against the inhabitants of **P**: 6489
Eze 23:23 all the Chaldeans, **P**, and Shoa, and Koa, 6489

PELAIAH (3)

1Ch 3:24 **P**, and Akkub, and Johanan, and Dalaiah, 6411
Ne 8: 7 Jozabad, Hanan, **P**, and the Levites, 6411
10:10 Shebaniah, Hodijah, Kelita, **P**, Hanan, 6411

PELALIAH (1)

Ne 11:12 the son of **P**, the son of Amzi, the son of 6421

PELATIAH (5)

1Ch 3:21 the sons of Hananiah; **P**, and Jesaiah: 6410
4:42 having for their captains **P**, and Neariah, 6410
Ne 10:22 **P**, Hanan, Anaiah, 6410
Eze 11: 1 **P** the son of Benaiah, princes of the people. 6410
11:13 that **P** the son of Benaiah died. 6410

PELEG (7) [PHALEC]

Ge 10:25 the name of one *was* **P**; for in his days was 6389
11:16 lived four and thirty years, and begat **P**: 6389
11:17 Eber lived after he begat **P** four hundred 6389
11:18 And **P** lived thirty years, and begat Reu: 6389
11:19 **P** lived after he begat Reu two hundred 6389
1Ch 1:19 the name of the one *was* **P**; because in his 6389
1:25 Eber, **P**, Rehu, 6389

PELET (2)

1Ch 2:47 Geshan, and **P**, and Ephah, and Shaaph. 6404
12: 3 Jeziel, and **P**, the sons of Azmaveth; and 6404

PELETH (2) [PELETHITES]

Nu 16: 1 On, the son of **P**, sons of Reuben, 6431
1Ch 2:33 the sons of Jonathan; **P**, and Zaza. 6431

PELETHITES (7) [PELETH]

2Sa 8:18 *was over* both the Cherethites and the **P**; 6432
15:18 and all the **P**, and all the Gittites, 6432
20: 7 the **P**, and all the mighty *men*: and 6432
20:23 *was* over the Cherethites and over the **P**: 6432
1Ki 1:38 the **P**, went down, and caused Solomon to 6432
1:44 the **P**, and they have caused him to ride 6432
1Ch 18:17 *was* over the Cherethites and the **P**; 6432

PELICAN (3)

Lev 11:18 And the swan, and the **p**, and the gier eagle, 6893
Dt 14:17 the **p**, and the gier eagle, and 6893
Ps 102: 6 I am like a **p** of the wilderness: I am like an 6893

PELONITE (3)
1Ch 11:27 Shammoth the Harorite, Helez the **P**, 6397
11:36 Hepher the Mecherathite, Ahijah the **P**, 6397
27:10 for the seventh month *was* Helez the **P**, 6397

PEN (7)
Jdg 5:14 out of Zebulun they that handle the **p** of 7626
Job 19:24 That they were graven with an iron **p** and 5842
Ps 45: 1 my tongue *is* the **p** of a ready writer. 5842
Isa 8: 1 write in it with a man's **p** concerning 2747
Jer 8: 8 certainly in vain made he *it;* the **p** of 5842
17: 1 The sin of Judah *is* written with a **p** of iron, 5842
3Jn 1:13 I will not with ink and **p** write unto thee: *2563*

PENCE (5)
Mt 18:28 which ought him an hundred **p**: *1220*
Mk 14: 5 been sold for more than three hundred **p**, *1220*
Lk 7:41 the one ought five hundred **p**, and the other *1220*
10:35 he took out two **p**, and gave *them* to *1220*
Jn 12: 5 not this ointment sold for three hundred **p**, *1220*

PENIEL (1) [PENUEL]
Ge 32:30 Jacob called the name of the place **P**: for I 6439

PENINNAH (3)
1Sa 1: 2 *was* Hannah, and the name of the other **P**: 6444
1: 2 **P** had children, but Hannah had no 6444
1: 4 he gave to **P** his wife, and to all her sons 6444

PENKNIFE (1)
Jer 36:23 he cut it with the **p**, and 5608+8593+1886.1

PENNY (9) [PENNYWORTH]
Mt 20: 2 had agreed with the labourers for a **p** a day, *1220*
20: 9 eleventh hour, they received every man a **p**. *1220*
20:10 and they likewise received every man a **p**. *1220*
20:13 didst not thou agree with me for a **p**? *1220*
22:19 And they brought unto him a **p**. *1220*
Mk 12:15 ye me? bring me a **p**, that I may see *it*. *1220*
Lk 20:24 Shew me a **p**. Whose image and *1220*
Rev 6: 6 A measure of wheat for a **p**, and *1220*
6: 6 and three measures of barley for a **p**; *1220*

PENNYWORTH (2) [PENNY]
Mk 6:37 we go and buy two hundred **p** of bread, *1220*
Jn 6: 7 Two hundred **p** of bread is not sufficient *1220*

PENTECOST (3)
Ac 2: 1 And when the day of **P** was fully come, *4005*
20:16 for him, to be at Jerusalem the day of **P**. *4005*
1Co 16: 8 But I will tarry at Ephesus until **P**. *4005*

PENUEL (8) [PENIEL]
Ge 32:31 as he passed over **P** the sun rose upon him, 6439
Jdg 8: 8 he went up thence *to* **P**, and spake unto 6439
8: 8 the men of **P** answered him as the men of 6439
8: 9 he spake also unto the men of **P**, saying, 6439
8:17 he beat down the tower of **P**, and slew 6439
1Ki 12:25 went out from thence, and built **P**. 6439
1Ch 4: 4 **P** the father of Gedor, and Ezer the father 6439
8:25 And Iphedeiah, and **P**, the sons of Shashak; 6439

PENURY (2)
Pr 14:23 but the talk of the lips *tendeth* only to **p**. 4270
Lk 21: 4 she of her **p** hath cast in all the living that *5303*

PEOPLE (2139) [PEOPLE'S, PEOPLES]
Ge 11: 6 the **p** *is* one, and they have all one 5971
14:16 his goods, and the women also, and the **p**. 5971
17:14 that soul shall be cut off from his **p**; 5971
17:16 of nations; kings of **p** shall be of her. 5971
19: 4 and young, all the **p** from every quarter: 5971
23: 7 and bowed himself to the **p** of the land, 5971
23:11 in the presence of the sons of my **p** give I it 5971
23:12 Abraham bowed down himself before the **p** 5971
23:13 Ephron in the audience of the **p** of the land, 5971
25: 8 and full *of years;* and was gathered to his **p**. 5971
25:17 and died; and was gathered unto his **p**. 5971
25:23 two manner of **p** shall be separated from 3816
25:23 *the one* **p** shall be stronger than *the other* 3816
25:23 people shall be stronger than *the other* **p**; 3816
26:10 one of the **p** might lightly have lien with 5971
26:11 Abimelech charged all *his* **p**, saying, 5971
27:29 Let **p** serve thee, and nations bow down to 5971
28: 3 that thou mayest be a multitude of **p**; 5971
29: 1 came into the land of the **p** of the east. 1121
32: 7 and he divided the **p** that *was* with him, and 5971
34:16 dwell with you, and we will become one **p**. 5971
34:22 to be one **p**, if every male among us be 5971
35: 6 he and all the **p** that *were* with him. 5971
35:29 died, and was gathered unto his **p**, 5971
41:40 according unto thy word shall all my **p** be 5971
41:55 the **p** cried to Pharaoh for bread: 5971
42: 6 he *it was* that sold to all the **p** of the land: 5971
47:21 as for the **p**, he removed them to cities from 5971
47:23 Joseph said unto the **p**, Behold, I have 5971
48: 4 and I will make of thee a multitude of **p**, 5971
48:19 I know *it:* he also shall become a **p**, and 5971
49:10 unto him *shall* the gathering of the **p** *be*. 5971
49:16 Dan shall judge his **p**, as one of the tribes 5971
49:29 unto them, I *am to be* gathered unto my **p**: 5971
49:33 up the ghost, and was gathered unto his **p**. 5971
50:20 as *it is* this day, to save much **p** alive. 5971
Ex 1: 9 he said unto his **p**, Behold, the people of 5971
1: 9 the **p** of the children of Israel *are* more and 5971
1:20 the **p** multiplied, and waxed very mighty. 5971
1:22 Pharaoh charged all his **p**, saying, 5971
3: 7 I have surely seen the affliction of my **p** 5971
3:10 that thou mayest bring forth my **p** 5971
3:12 When thou hast brought forth the **p** out of 5971
3:21 I will give this **p** favour in the sight of 5971
4:16 he shall be thy spokesman unto the **p**: and 5971
4:21 his heart, that he shall not let the **p** go. 5971
Ex 4:30 and did the signs in the sight of the **p**. 5971
4:31 the **p** believed: and when they heard that 5971
5: 1 the LORD God of Israel, Let my **p** go, 5971
5: 4 and Aaron, let the **p** from their works? 5971
5: 5 the **p** of the land now *are* many, and 5971
5: 6 the same day the taskmasters of the **p**, 5971
5: 7 Ye shall no more give the **p** straw to make 5971
5:10 the taskmasters of the **p** went out, and 5971
5:10 and they spake to the **p**, saying, 5971
5:12 So the **p** were scattered abroad throughout 5971
5:16 *are* beaten; but the fault *is* in thine own **p**. 5971
5:22 hast thou *so* evil entreated this **p**? 5971
5:23 in thy name, he hath done evil to this **p**; 5971
5:23 neither hast thou delivered thy **p** at all. 5971
6: 7 I will take you to me for a **p**, and I will be 5971
7: 4 *and* my **p** the children of Israel, 5971
7:14 *is* hardened, he refuseth to let the **p** go. 5971
7:16 saying, Let my **p** go, that they may serve 5971
8: 1 Thus saith the LORD, Let my **p** go, 5971
8: 3 upon thy **p**, and into thine ovens, and 5971
8: 4 and upon thy **p**, and upon all thy servants. 5971
8: 8 away the frogs from me, and from my **p**; 5971
8: 8 I will let the **p** go, that they may do 5971
8: 9 for thee, and for thy servants, and for thy **p**, 5971
8:11 and from thy servants, and from thy **p**; 5971
8:20 Thus saith the LORD, Let my **p** go, 5971
8:21 Else, if thou wilt not let my **p** go, behold, 5971
8:21 and upon thy **p**, and into thy houses: 5971
8:22 in which my **p** dwell, that no swarms *of* 5971
8:23 I will put a division between my **p** and thy 5971
8:23 a division between my people and thy **p**: 5971
8:29 his servants, and from his **p**, to morrow: 5971
8:29 letting the **p** go to sacrifice to the LORD. 5971
8:31 from his servants, and from his **p**; 5971
8:32 this time also, neither would he let the **p** go. 5971
9: 1 Let my **p** go, that they may serve me. 5971
9: 7 was hardened, and he did not let the **p** go. 5971
9:13 Let my **p** go, that they may serve me. 5971
9:14 and upon thy servants, and upon thy **p**; 5971
9:15 I may smite thee and thy **p** with pestilence; 5971
9:17 As yet exaltest thou thyself against my **p**, 5971
9:27 *is* righteous, and I and my **p** *are* wicked. 5971
10: 3 let my **p** go, that they may serve me. 5971
10: 4 Else, if thou refuse to let my **p** go, behold, 5971
11: 2 Speak now in the ears of the **p**, and 5971
11: 3 the LORD gave the **p** favour in the sight 5971
11: 3 and in the sight of the **p**.) 5971
11: 8 Get thee out, and all the **p** that follow thee: 5971
12:27 And the **p** bowed the head and worshipped. 5971
12:31 *and* get you forth from amongst my **p**, 5971
12:33 the Egyptians were urgent upon the **p**, that 5971
12:34 the **p** took their dough before it was 5971
12:36 the LORD gave the **p** favour in the sight 5971
13: 3 Moses said unto the **p**, Remember this day, 5971
13:17 to pass, when Pharaoh had let the **p** go, 5971
13:17 Lest peradventure the **p** repent when they 5971
13:18 God led the **p** about, *through* the way of 5971
13:22 pillar of fire by night, *from* before the **p**. 5971
14: 5 it was told the king of Egypt that the **p** fled: 5971
14: 5 of his servants was turned against the **p**, 5971
14: 6 ready his chariot, and took his **p** with him: 5971
14:13 Moses said unto the **p**, Fear ye not, 5971
14:31 the **p** feared the LORD, and believed 5971
15:13 Thou in thy mercy hast led forth the **p** 5971
15:14 The **p** shall hear, *and* be afraid: 5971
15:16 till thy **p** pass over, O LORD, till 5971
15:16 pass over, O LORD, till the **p** pass over, 5971
15:24 the **p** murmured against Moses, saying, 5971
16: 4 the **p** shall go out and gather a certain rate 5971
16:27 *that* there went out *some* of the **p** on 5971
16:30 So the **p** rested on the seventh day. 5971
17: 1 and *there was* no water for the **p** to drink. 5971
17: 2 Wherefore the **p** did chide with Moses, and 5971
17: 3 the **p** thirsted there for water; and 5971
17: 3 the **p** murmured against Moses, and said, 5971
17: 4 What shall I do unto this **p**? 5971
17: 5 Go on before the **p**, and take with thee of 5971
17: 6 come water out of it, that the **p** may drink. 5971
17:13 and his **p** with the edge of the sword. 5971
18: 1 for Israel his **p**, *and* that the LORD had 5971
18:10 who hath delivered the **p** from under 5971
18:13 the morrow, that Moses sat to judge the **p**: 5971
18:13 the **p** stood by Moses from the morning 5971
18:14 father in law saw all that he did to the **p**, 5971
18:14 What *is* this thing that thou doest to the **p**? 5971
18:14 all the **p** stand by thee from morning unto 5971
18:15 Because the **p** come unto me to inquire of 5971
18:18 both thou, and this **p** that *is* with thee: 5971
18:19 be thou for the **p** to God-ward, that thou 5971
18:21 Moreover thou shalt provide out of all the **p** 5971
18:22 let them judge the **p** at all seasons: and 5971
18:23 all this **p** shall also go to their place in 5971
18:25 made them heads over the **p**, rulers of 5971
18:26 they judged the **p** at all seasons: the hard 5971
19: 5 be a peculiar treasure unto me above all **p**: 5971
19: 7 and called for the elders of the **p**, 5971
19: 8 all the **p** answered together, and said, 5971
19: 8 Moses returned the words of the **p** unto 5971
19: 9 that the **p** may hear when I speak with thee, 5971
19: 9 Moses told the words of the **p** unto 5971
19:10 Go unto the **p**, and sanctify them to day and 5971
19:11 in the sight of all the **p** upon mount Sinai. 5971
19:12 thou shalt set bounds unto the **p** round 5971
19:14 went down from the mount unto the **p**, 5971
19:14 unto the people, and sanctified the **p**; 5971
19:15 he said unto the **p**, Be ready against 5971
19:16 that all the **p** that *was* in the camp trembled. 5971
19:17 Moses brought forth the **p** out of the camp 5971
19:21 said unto Moses, Go down, charge the **p**, 5971
19:23 The **p** cannot come up to mount Sinai: 5971
19:24 the **p** break through to come up unto 5971
19:25 So Moses went down unto the **p**, and 5971
20:18 all the **p** saw the thunderings, and 5971
20:18 when the **p** saw *it*, they removed, and 5971
20:20 Moses said unto the **p**, Fear not: for God is 5971
Ex 20:21 the **p** stood afar off, and Moses drew near 5971
22:25 If thou lend money to *any of* my **p** *that is* 5971
22:28 revile the gods, nor curse the ruler of thy **p**. 5971
23:11 and lie still; that the poor of thy **p** may eat: 5971
23:27 will destroy all the **p** to whom thou shalt 5971
24: 2 neither shall the **p** go up with him. 5971
24: 3 and told the **p** all the words of the LORD, 5971
24: 3 all the **p** answered *with* one voice, and said, 5971
24: 7 and read in the audience of the **p**: 5971
24: 8 and sprinkled *it* on the **p**, and said, 5971
30:33 a stranger, shall even be cut off from his **p**. 5971
30:38 shall even be cut off from his **p**. 5971
31:14 soul shall be cut off from amongst his **p**. 5971
32: 1 when the **p** saw that Moses delayed to 5971
32: 1 the **p** gathered themselves together unto 5971
32: 3 all the **p** brake off the golden earrings 5971
32: 6 the **p** sat down to eat and to drink, and 5971
32: 7 for thy **p**, which thou broughtest out of 5971
32: 9 I have seen this **p**, and behold, it *is* a 5971
32: 9 and behold, it *is* a stiffnecked **p**: 5971
32:11 why doth thy wrath wax hot against thy **p**, 5971
32:12 and repent of *this* evil against thy **p**. 5971
32:14 the evil which he thought to do unto his **p**. 5971
32:17 when Joshua heard the noise of the **p** as 5971
32:21 What did this **p** unto thee, that thou hast 5971
32:22 thou knowest the **p**, that they *are set* on 5971
32:25 when Moses saw that the **p** *were* naked; 5971
32:28 there fell of the **p** that day about three 5971
32:30 that Moses said unto the **p**, Ye have sinned 5971
32:31 this **p** have sinned a great sin, and 5971
32:34 lead the **p** unto *the place* of which I have 5971
32:35 the LORD plagued the **p**, because they 5971
33: 1 the **p** which thou hast brought up out of 5971
33: 3 midst of thee; for thou *art* a stiffnecked **p**: 5971
33: 4 when the **p** heard these evil tidings, they 5971
33: 5 children of Israel, Ye *are* a stiffnecked **p**: 5971
33: 8 *that* all the **p** rose up, and stood every man 5971
33:10 all the **p** saw the cloudy pillar stand *at* 5971
33:10 all the **p** rose up and worshipped, 5971
33:12 See, thou sayest unto me, Bring up this **p**: 5971
33:13 and consider that this nation *is* thy **p**. 5971
33:16 and thy **p** have found grace in thy sight? 5971
33:16 so shall we be separated, I and thy **p**, 5971
33:16 from all the **p** that *are* upon the face of 5971
34: 9 for it *is* a stiffnecked **p**; and pardon our 5971
34:10 before all thy **p** I will do marvels, such as 5971
34:10 all the **p** among which thou *art* shall see 5971
36: 5 The **p** bring much more than enough for 5971
36: 6 So the **p** were restrained from bringing. 5971
Lev 4: 3 do sin according to the sin of the **p**; 5971
4:27 if any one of the common **p** sin through 5971
7:20 even that soul shall be cut off from his **p**. 5971
7:21 even that soul shall be cut off from his **p**. 5971
7:25 that eateth *it* shall be cut off from his **p**. 5971
7:27 even that soul shall be cut off from his **p**. 5971
9: 7 an atonement for thyself, and for the **p**: 5971
9: 7 offer the offering of the **p**, and make an 5971
9:15 which *was* the sin offering for the **p**, and 5971
9:18 of peace offerings, which *was* for the **p**: 5971
9:22 Aaron lift up his hand toward the **p**, and 5971
9:23 and came out, and blessed the **p**: 5971
9:23 of the LORD appeared unto all the **p**. 5971
9:24 *which* when all the **p** saw, they shouted, 5971
10: 3 and before all the **p** I will be glorified. 5971
10: 6 you die, and lest wrath come upon all the **p**: 5712
16:15 that *is* for the **p**, and bring his blood within 5971
16:24 the burnt offering of the **p**, and make an 5971
16:24 an atonement for himself, and for the **p**. 5971
16:33 and for all the **p** of the congregation. 5971
17: 4 that man shall be cut off from among his **p**: 5971
17: 9 that man shall be cut off from among his **p**. 5971
17:10 and will cut him off from among his **p**. 5971
18:29 *them* shall be cut off from among their **p**. 5971
19: 8 that soul shall be cut off from among his **p**. 5971
19:16 and down *as* a talebearer among thy **p**: 5971
19:18 any grudge against the children of thy **p**, 5971
20: 2 the **p** of the land shall stone him with 5971
20: 3 and will cut him off from among his **p**; 5971
20: 4 if the **p** of the land do any ways hide their 5971
20: 5 with Molech, from among their **p**. 5971
20: 6 and will cut him off from among his **p**. 5971
20:17 shall be cut off in the sight of their **p**: 1121+5971
20:18 them shall be cut off from among their **p**. 5971
20:24 which have separated you from *other* **p**. 5971
20:26 have severed you from *other* **p**, that *ye* 5971
21: 1 none be defiled for the dead among his **p**: 5971
21: 4 *being* a chief man among his **p**, to profane 5971
21:14 he shall take a virgin of his own **p** to wife. 5971
21:15 shall he profane his seed among his **p**: 5971
23:29 he shall be cut off from among his **p**. 5971
23:30 same soul will I destroy from among his **p**. 5971
26:12 and will be your God, and ye shall be my **p**. 5971
Nu 5:21 make thee a curse and an oath among thy **p**, 5971
5:27 the woman shall be a curse among her **p**. 5971
9:13 soul shall be cut off from among his **p**: 5971
11: 1 *when* the **p** complained, it displeased 5971
11: 2 the **p** cried unto Moses; and when Moses 5971
11: 8 *And* the **p** went about, and gathered *it*, and 5971
11:10 Moses heard the **p** weep throughout their 5971
11:11 that *thou* layest the burden of all this **p** 5971
11:12 Have I conceived all this **p**? have I 5971
11:13 should I have flesh to give unto all this **p**? 5971
11:14 I am not able to bear all this **p** alone, 5971
11:16 thou knowest to be the elders of the **p**, 5971
11:17 they shall bear the burden of the **p** with 5971
11:18 say thou unto the **p**, Sanctify yourselves 5971
11:21 Moses said, The **p**, amongst whom I *am*, 5971
11:24 told the **p** the words of the LORD, and 5971
11:24 the seventy men of the elders of the **p**, 5971
11:29 would God that all the LORD'S **p** were 5971
11:32 the **p** stood up all that day, and all *that* 5971
11:33 of the LORD was kindled against the **p**, 5971
11:33 the LORD smote the **p** *with* a very great 5971
11:34 because there they buried the **p** that lusted. 5971
11:35 *And* the **p** journeyed from 5971

P

Nu 12:15 the **p** journeyed not till Miriam was 5971
12:16 afterward the **p** removed from Hazeroth, 5971
13:18 what it *is;* and the **p** that dwelleth therein, 5971
13:28 Nevertheless the **p** *be* strong that dwell in 5971
13:30 Caleb stilled the **p** before Moses, and said, 5971
13:31 We be not able to go up against the **p**; 5971
13:32 all the **p** that we saw in it *are* men of a great 5971
14: 1 and cried; and the **p** wept that night. 5971
14: 9 neither fear ye the **p** of the land; 5971
14:11 How long will this **p** provoke me? 5971
14:13 up this **p** in thy might from among them;) 5971
14:14 heard that thou LORD *art* among this **p**, 5971
14:15 Now *if* thou shalt kill *all* this **p** as one man, 5971
14:16 **p** into the land which he sware unto them, 5971
14:19 the iniquity of this **p** according unto 5971
14:19 as thou hast forgiven this **p**, from Egypt 5971
14:39 of Israel: and the **p** mourned greatly. 5971
15:26 seeing all the **p** were in ignorance. 5971
15:30 that soul shall be cut off from among his **p**. 5971
16:41 saying, Ye have killed the **p** of the LORD. 5971
16:47 behold, the plague was begun among the **p**: 5971
16:47 and made an atonement for the **p**. 5971
20: 1 the **p** abode in Kadesh; and Miriam died 5971
20: 3 the **p** chode with Moses, and spake, saying, 5971
20:20 Edom came out against him with much **p**, 5971
20:24 Aaron shall be gathered unto his **p**: for he 5971
20:26 Aaron shall be gathered *unto his p,* and NIH
21: 2 If thou wilt indeed deliver this **p** into my 5971
21: 4 and the soul of the **p** was much discouraged 5971
21: 5 the **p** spake against God, and 5971
21: 6 LORD sent fiery serpents among the **p**, 5971
21: 6 among the people, and they bit the **p**; 5971
21: 6 bit the people; and much **p** of Israel died. 5971
21: 7 Therefore the **p** came to Moses, and said, 5971
21: 7 from us. And Moses prayed for the **p**. 5971
21:16 Gather the **p** together, and I will give them 5971
21:18 the well, the nobles of the **p** digged it, 5971
21:23 Sihon gathered all his **p** together, and 5971
21:29 thou art undone, O **p** of Chemosh: he hath 5971
21:33 he, and all his **p**, to the battle *at* Edrei. 5971
21:34 into thy hand, and all his **p**, and his land; 5971
21:35 they smote him, and his sons, and all his **p**, 5971
22: 3 Moab was sore afraid of the **p**, because 5971
22: 5 the river *of* the land of the children of his **p**, 5971
22: 5 Behold, there is a **p** come out from Egypt: 5971
22: 6 now therefore, I pray thee, curse me this **p**; 5971
22:11 Behold, *there is* a **p** come out of Egypt, 5971
22:12 go with them; thou shalt not curse the **p**: 5971
22:17 I pray thee, curse me this **p**. 5971
22:41 he might see the utmost part of the **p**. 5971
23: 9 lo, the **p** shall dwell alone, and shall not be 5971
23:24 the **p** shall rise up as a great lion, and lift up 5971
24:14 now behold, I go unto my **p**: come 5971
24:14 I will advertise thee what this **p** shall do to 5971
24:14 people shall do to thy **p** in the latter days. 5971
25: 1 the **p** begun to commit whoredom with 5971
25: 2 they called the **p** unto the sacrifices of their 5971
25: 2 the **p** did eat, and bowed down to their 5971
25: 4 Take all the heads of the **p**, and hang them 5971
25:15 he *was* head over a **p**, *and* of a chief house in 523
26: 4 *Take the sum of the* **p**, from twenty years NIH
27:13 thou also shalt be gathered unto thy **p**, 5971
31: 2 afterward shalt thou be gathered unto thy **p**. 5971
31: 3 Moses spake unto the **p**, saying, Arm some 5971
32:15 and ye shall destroy all this **p**. 5971
33:14 where was no water for the **p** to drink. 5971
Dt 1:28 The **p** *is* greater and taller than we; 5971
2: 4 command thou the **p**, saying, Ye are to pass 5971
2:10 a **p** great, and many, and tall, as 5971
2:16 and dead from among the **p**, 5971
2:21 A **p** great, and many, and tall, as 5971
2:32 he and all his **p**, to fight *at* Jahaz. 5971
2:33 we smote him, and his sons, and all his **p**. 5971
3: 1 he and all his **p**, to battle *at* Edrei. 5971
3: 2 and all his **p**, and his land, into thy hand; 5971
3: 3 Og also, the king of Bashan, and all his **p**: 5971
3:28 for he shall go over before this **p**, and 5971
4: 6 great nation *is* a wise and understanding **p**. 5971
4:10 Gather me the **p** together, and I will make 5971
4:20 to be unto him a **p** of inheritance, as *ye are* 5971
4:33 Did *ever* **p** hear the voice of God speaking 5971
5:28 have heard the voice of the words of this **p**, 5971
6:14 of the gods of the **p** which *are* round about 5971
7: 6 For thou *art* a holy **p** unto the LORD thy 5971
7: 6 chosen thee to be a special **p** unto himself, 5971
7: 6 above all **p** that *are* upon the face of 5971
7: 7 ye were moe in number than any **p**; 5971
7: 7 any people; for ye *were* the fewest of all **p**: 5971
7:14 Thou shalt be blessed above all **p**: 5971
7:16 thou shalt consume all the **p** which 5971
7:19 shall the LORD thy God do unto all the **p** 5971
9: 2 A **p** great and tall, the children of 5971
9: 6 for thou *art* a stiffnecked **p**. 5971
9:12 for thy **p** which thou hast brought forth out 5971
9:13 saying, I have seen this **p**, and behold, it *is* 5971
9:13 and behold, it *is* a stiffnecked **p**: 5971
9:26 destroy not thy **p** and thine inheritance, 5971
9:27 look not unto the stubbornness of this **p**, 5971
9:29 Yet they *are* thy **p** and thine inheritance, 5971
10:11 Arise, take thy journey before the **p**, 5971
10:15 *even* you above all **p**, as *it is* this day. 5971
13: 7 *Namely,* of the gods of the **p** which *are* 5971
13: 9 and afterwards the hand of all the **p**. 5971
14: 2 For thou *art* a holy **p** unto the LORD thy 5971
14: 2 chosen thee to be a peculiar **p** unto himself, 5971
14:21 for thou *art* a holy **p** unto the LORD thy 5971
16:18 they shall judge the **p** *with* just judgment. 5971
17: 7 and afterward the hands of all the **p**. 5971
17:13 all the **p** shall hear, and fear, and do no 5971
17:16 nor cause the **p** to return to Egypt, to 5971
18: 3 this shall be the priest's due from the **p**, 5971
20: 1 and chariots, *and* a **p** more than thou, 5971
20: 2 priest shall approach and speak unto the **p**, 5971
20: 5 the officers shall speak unto the **p**, saying, 5971
20: 8 the officers shall speak further unto the **p**, 5971

Dt 20: 9 have made an end of speaking unto the **p**, 5971
20: 9 make captains of the armies to lead the **p**. 5971
20:11 *that* all the **p** that is found therein shall be 5971
20:16 of the cities of these **p**, which the LORD 5971
21: 8 Be merciful, O LORD, unto thy **p** Israel, 5971
21: 8 lay not innocent blood unto thy **p** of 5971
26:15 bless thy **p** Israel, and the land which thou 5971
26:18 avouched thee *this* day to be his peculiar **p**, 5971
26:19 that thou mayest be a holy **p** unto 5971
27: 1 with the elders of Israel commanded the **p**, 5971
27: 9 this day thou art become the **p** of 5971
27:11 Moses charged the **p** the same day, saying, 5971
27:12 stand upon mount Gerizzim to bless the **p**, 5971
27:15 putteth *it* in *a* secret *place.* And all the **p** 5971
27:16 his mother. And all the **p** shall say, Amen. 5971
27:17 And all the **p** shall say, Amen. 5971
27:18 of the way. And all the **p** shall say, Amen. 5971
27:19 and widow. And all the **p** shall say, Amen. 5971
27:20 And all the **p** shall say, Amen. 5971
27:21 *of* beast. And all the **p** shall say, Amen. 5971
27:22 his mother. And all the **p** shall say, Amen. 5971
27:23 in law. And all the **p** shall say, Amen. 5971
27:24 And all the **p** shall say, Amen. 5971
27:25 And all the **p** shall say, Amen. 5971
27:26 to do them. And all the **p** shall say, Amen. 5971
28: 9 The LORD shall establish thee a holy **p** 5971
28:10 all **p** of the earth shall see that thou art 5971
28:32 thy daughters *shall be* given unto another **p**, 5971
28:64 the LORD shall scatter thee among all **p**, 5971
29:13 That he may establish thee to day for a **p** 5971
31: 7 for thou must go with this **p** unto the land 5971
31:12 Gather the **p** together, men, and women, 5971
31:16 this **p** will rise up, and go a whoring after 5971
32: 6 the LORD, O foolish **p** and unwise? 5971
32: 8 he set the bounds of the **p** according to 5971
32: 9 For the LORD'S portion *is* his **p**; Jacob *is* 5971
32:21 to jealousy with *those which are* not a **p**; 5971
32:36 For the LORD shall judge his **p**, and 5971
32:43 Rejoice, O ye nations, *with* his **p**: for he 5971
32:43 will be merciful *unto* his land, *and to* his **p**. 5971
32:44 the words of this song in the ears of the **p**, 5971
32:50 thou goest up, and be gathered unto thy **p**; 5971
32:50 in mount Hor, and was gathered unto his **p**: 5971
33: 3 Yea, he loved the **p**; all his saints *are* in thy 5971
33: 5 when the heads of the **p** *and* the tribes of 5971
33: 7 voice of Judah, and bring him unto his **p**: 5971
33:17 with them he shall push the **p** together *to* 5971
33:19 They shall call the **p** *unto* the mountain; 5971
33:21 he came *with* the heads of the **p**, 5971
33:29 *is* like unto thee, O **p** saved by the LORD, 5971
Jos 1: 2 go over this Jordan, thou, and all this **p**, 5971
1: 6 for unto this **p** shalt thou divide for an 5971
1:10 Joshua commanded the officers of the **p**, 5971
1:11 command the **p**, saying, Prepare you 5971
3: 3 they commanded the **p**, saying, When ye 5971
3: 5 Joshua said unto the **p**, Sanctify yourselves: 5971
3: 6 of the covenant, and pass over before the **p**. 5971
3: 6 ark of the covenant, and went before the **p**. 5971
3:14 when the **p** removed from their tents, 5971
3:14 the ark *of* the covenant before the **p**; 5971
3:16 and the **p** passed over right against Jericho. 5971
3:17 all the **p** were passed clean over Jordan. 1471
4: 1 when all the **p** were clean passed over 1471
4: 2 Take you twelve men out of the **p**, out of 5971
4:10 commanded Joshua to speak unto the **p**, 5971
4:10 and the **p** hasted and passed over. 5971
4:11 when all the **p** were clean passed over, 5971
4:11 and the priests, in the presence of the **p**. 5971
4:19 the **p** came up out of Jordan on the tenth 5971
4:24 That all the **p** of the earth might know 5971
5: 4 All the **p** that came out of Egypt, *that were* 5971
5: 5 Now all the **p** that came out were 5971
5: 5 all the **p** *that were* born in the wilderness by 5971
5: 6 till all the **p** *that were* men of war, 1471
5: 8 when they had done circumcising all the **p**, 1471
6: 5 all the **p** shall shout *with* a great shout; 5971
6: 5 the **p** shall ascend up every man straight 5971
6: 7 he said unto the **p**, Pass on, and 5971
6: 8 when Joshua had spoken unto the **p**, 5971
6:10 Joshua had commanded the **p**, saying, 5971
6:16 the trumpets, Joshua said unto the **p**, Shout; 5971
6:20 So the **p** shouted when *the priests* blew 5971
6:20 when the **p** heard the sound of the trumpet, 5971
6:20 the **p** shouted *with* a great shout, that 5971
6:20 so that the **p** went up into the city, 5971
7: 3 and said unto him, Let not all the **p** go up; 5971
7: 3 *and* make not all the **p** to labour thither; 5971
7: 4 So there went up thither of the **p** about 5971
7: 5 wherefore the hearts of the **p** melted, and 5971
7: 7 wherefore hast thou at all brought this **p** 5971
7:13 Up, sanctify the **p**, and say, 5971
8: 1 take all the **p** of war with thee, and arise, 5971
8: 1 of Ai, and his **p**, and his city, and his land: 5971
8: 3 So Joshua arose, and all the **p** of war, to go 5971
8: 5 I, and all the **p** that *are* with me, 5971
8: 9 but Joshua lodged that night among the **p**. 5971
8:10 numbered the **p**, and went up, he and 5971
8:10 and the elders of Israel, before the **p** *to* Ai. 5971
8:11 all the **p**, *even the people* of war that *were* 5971
8:11 *even the* **p** of war that *were* with him, NIH
8:13 when they had set the **p**, *even* all the host 5971
8:14 he and all his **p**, at a time appointed, before 5971
8:16 all the **p** that *were* in Ai were called 5971
8:20 the **p** that fled *to* the wilderness turned back 5971
8:33 that they should bless the **p** of Israel. 5971
10: 7 he, and all the **p** of war with him, and 5971
10:13 until the **p** had avenged themselves upon 1471
10:21 all the **p** returned to the camp to Joshua *at* 5971
10:33 Joshua smote him and his **p**, until *he* had 5971
11: 4 they and all their hosts with them, much **p**, 5971
11: 7 Joshua came, and all the **p** of war with him, 5971
14: 8 up with me made the heart of the **p** melt: 5971
17:14 one portion to inherit, seeing I *am* a great **p**, 5971
17:15 If thou *be* a great **p**, *then* get thee up to 5971
17:17 Thou *art* a great **p**, and hast great power: 5971

Jos 24: 2 Joshua said unto all the **p**, Thus saith 5971
24:16 the **p** answered and said, God forbid that 5971
24:17 among all the **p** through whom we passed: 5971
24:18 LORD drave out from before us all the **p**, 5971
24:19 Joshua said unto the **p**, Ye cannot serve 5971
24:21 the **p** said unto Joshua, Nay; but we will 5971
24:22 Joshua said unto the **p**, Ye *are* witnesses 5971
24:24 the **p** said unto Joshua, The LORD our 5971
24:25 So Joshua made a covenant with the **p** that 5971
24:27 Joshua said unto all the **p**, Behold, this 5971
24:28 So Joshua let the **p** depart, every man unto 5971
Jdg 1:16 and they went and dwelt among the **p**. 5971
2: 4 that the **p** lift up their voice, and wept. 5971
2: 6 when Joshua had let the **p** go, the children 5971
2: 7 the **p** served the LORD all the days of 5971
2:12 of the gods of the **p** that *were* round about 5971
2:20 Because that this **p** hath transgressed my 1471
3:18 he sent away the **p** that bare the present. 5971
4:13 of iron, and all the **p** that *were* with him, 5971
5: 2 when the **p** willingly offered themselves. 5971
5: 9 offered themselves willingly among the **p**. 5971
5:11 shall the **p** of the LORD go down to 5971
5:13 dominion over the nobles *among* the **p**: 5971
5:14 after thee, Benjamin, among thy **p**; out of 5971
5:18 Naphtali *were* a **p** *that* jeoparded their lives 5971
7: 1 all the **p** that *were* with him, rose up early, 5971
7: 2 The **p** that *are* with thee *are* too many for 5971
7: 3 go to, proclaim in the ears of the **p**, 5971
7: 3 there returned of the **p** twenty and 5971
7: 4 said unto Gideon, The **p** *are* yet *too* many; 5971
7: 5 So he brought down the **p** unto the water: 5971
7: 6 all the rest of the **p** bowed down upon their 5971
7: 7 let all the *other* **p** go every man unto his 5971
7: 8 So the **p** took victuals in their hand, and 5971
8: 5 loaves of bread unto the **p** that follow me; 5971
9:29 would to God this **p** were under my hand; 5971
9:32 thou and the **p** that *is* with thee, *and* lie in 5971
9:33 the **p** that *is* with him come out against 5971
9:34 all the **p** that *were* with him, by night, and 5971
9:35 the **p** that *were* with him, from lying in 5971
9:36 And when Gaal saw the **p**, he said to Zebul, 5971
9:36 there come **p** down from the top of 5971
9:37 See there come **p** down by the middle of 5971
9:38 *is* not this the **p** that thou hast despised? go 5971
9:42 that the **p** went out *into* the field; 5971
9:43 he took the **p**, and divided them into three 5971
9:43 the **p** *were* come forth out of the city; 5971
9:44 the two *other* companies ran upon all *the* **p** NIH
9:45 slew the **p** that *was* therein, and beat down 5971
9:48 he and all the **p** that *were* with him; 5971
9:48 and said unto the **p** that *were* with him, 5971
9:49 all the **p** likewise cut down every man his 5971
10:18 the **p** *and* princes of Gilead said one to 5971
11:11 the **p** made him head and captain over 5971
11:20 Sihon gathered all his **p** together, and 5971
11:21 and all his **p** into the hand of Israel, 5971
11:23 the Amorites from before his **p** Israel, 5971
12: 2 my **p** were at great strife with the children 5971
14: 3 of thy brethren, or among all my **p**, 5971
14:16 put forth a riddle unto the children of my **p**, 5971
14:17 she told the riddle to the children of her **p**. 5971
16:24 when the **p** saw him, they praised their god: 5971
16:30 and upon all the **p** that *were* therein. 5971
18: 7 to Laish, and saw the **p** that *were* therein, 5971
18:10 ye shall come unto a **p** secure, and to a 5971
18:20 and went in the midst of the **p**. 5971
18:27 unto a **p** *that were* at quiet and secure: 5971
20: 2 the chief of all the **p**, *even* of all the tribes 5971
20: 2 themselves in the assembly of the **p** of God, 5971
20: 8 all the **p** arose as one man, saying, We will 5971
20:10 to fetch victual for the **p**, that *they* may do, 5971
20:16 Among all this **p** *there were* seven hundred 5971
20:22 the **p** the men of Israel encouraged 5971
20:26 all the **p**, went up, and came *unto* the house 5971
20:31 of Benjamin went out against the **p**, 5971
20:31 they began to smite of the **p**, *and* kill, as at 5971
21: 2 the **p** came *to* the house of God, and 5971
21: 4 that the **p** rose early, and built there an 5971
21: 9 For the **p** were numbered, and behold, 5971
21:15 the **p** repented them for Benjamin, because 5971
Ru 1: 6 had visited his **p** in giving them bread. 5971
1:10 Surely we will return with thee unto thy **p**. 5971
1:15 thy sister in law is gone back unto her **p**, 5971
1:16 thy **p** *shall be* my people, and thy God my 5971
1:16 thy people *shall be* my **p**, and thy God my 5971
2:11 art come unto a **p** which thou knewest not 5971
3:11 for all the city of my **p** doth know that thou 5971
4: 4 and before the elders of my **p**. 5971
4: 9 *unto* all the **p**, Ye *are* witnesses *this* day, 5971
4:11 all the **p** that *were* in the gate, and 5971
1Sa 2:13 the priests' custom with the **p** *was, that* 5971
2:23 for I hear of your evil dealings by all this **p**. 5971
2:24 *ye* make the LORD'S **p** to transgress. 5971
2:29 chiefest of all the offerings of Israel my **p**? 5971
4: 3 when the **p** were come into the camp, 5971
4: 4 So the **p** sent *to* Shiloh, that they might 5971
4:17 been also a great slaughter among the **p**, 5971
5:10 the God of Israel to us, to slay us and our **p**. 5971
5:11 his own place, that it slay us not, and our **p**: 5971
6: 6 did they not let **the p** go, and 3963.1
6:19 even he smote of the **p** fifty thousand 5971
6:19 the **p** lamented, because the LORD had 5971
6:19 the LORD had smitten *many* of the **p** *with* 5971
8: 7 Hearken unto the voice of the **p** in all that 5971
8:10 unto the **p** that asked of him a king. 5971
8:19 Nevertheless the **p** refused to obey 5971
8:21 Samuel heard all the words of the **p**, and 5971
9: 2 upward *he was* higher than any of the **p**. 5971
9:12 for *there is* a sacrifice of the **p** to day in 5971
9:13 for the **p** will not eat until he come, because 5971
9:16 anoint him to be captain over my **p** Israel, 5971
9:16 that *he* may save my **p** out of the hand of 5971
9:16 for I have looked upon my **p**, because 5971
9:17 to thee of: this *same* shall reign over my **p**. 5971
9:24 for thee since *I* said, I have invited the **p**. 5971

1Sa 10:11 the prophets, then the **p** said one to another, 5971
10:17 Samuel called the **p** together unto 5971
10:23 when he stood among the **p**, he was higher 5971
10:23 he was higher than any of the **p** from his 5971
10:24 Samuel said to all the **p**, See ye him whom 5971
10:24 that *there is* none like him among all the **p**? 5971
10:24 all the **p** shouted, and said, God save 5971
10:25 Samuel told the **p** the manner of 5971
10:25 Samuel sent all the **p** away, every man to 5971
11: 4 and told the tidings in the ears of the **p**: 5971
11: 4 and all the **p** lift up their voices, and wept. 5971
11: 5 Saul said, What aileth the **p** that they weep? 5971
11: 7 the fear of the LORD fell on the **p**, and 5971
11:11 that Saul put the **p** *in* three companies; 5971
11:12 the **p** said unto Samuel, Who *is* he that said, 5971
11:14 said Samuel to the **p**, Come, and let us go 5971
11:15 all the **p** went *to* Gilgal; and there they 5971
12: 6 Samuel said unto the **p**, *It is* the LORD 5971
12:18 all the **p** greatly feared the LORD and 5971
12:19 all the **p** said unto Samuel, Pray for thy 5971
12:20 Samuel said unto the **p**, Fear not: ye have 5971
12:22 For the LORD will not forsake his **p** for 5971
12:22 hath pleased the LORD to make you his **p**. 5971
13: 2 the rest of the **p** he sent every man to his 5971
13: 4 the **p** were called together after Saul *to* 5971
13: 5 **p** as the sand which *is* on the sea shore in 5971
13: 6 were in a strait, (for the **p** were distressed,) 5971
13: 6 the **p** did hide themselves in caves, and 5971
13: 7 and all the **p** followed him trembling. 5971
13: 8 and the **p** were scattered from him. 5971
13:11 Because I saw that the **p** were scattered 5971
13:14 commanded him to be captain over his **p**, 5971
13:15 Saul numbered the **p** that were present with 5971
13:16 and the **p** that were present with them, 5971
13:22 the hand of any of the **p** that *were* with Saul 5971
14: 2 the **p** that *were* with him *were* about six 5971
14: 3 the **p** knew not that Jonathan was gone. 5971
14:15 the host, in the field, and among all the **p**: 5971
14:17 said Saul unto the **p** that *were* with him, 5971
14:20 all the **p** that *were* with him assembled 5971
14:24 for Saul had adjured the **p**, saying, 5971
14:24 So none of the **p** tasted *any* food. 5971
14:26 when the **p** were come into the wood, 5971
14:26 to his mouth: for the **p** feared the oath. 5971
14:27 his father charged the **p** with the oath: 5971
14:28 answered one of the **p**, and said, Thy father 5971
14:28 Thy father straitly charged the **p** with an 5971
14:28 *any* food *this* day. And the **p** were faint. 5971
14:30 if haply the **p** had eaten freely to day of 5971
14:31 to Aijalon: and the **p** were very faint. 5971
14:32 the **p** flew upon the spoil, and took sheep, 5971
14:32 and the **p** did eat *them* with the blood. 5971
14:33 Behold, the **p** sin against the LORD, 5971
14:34 Disperse yourselves among the **p**, and 5971
14:34 all the **p** brought every man his ox with him 5971
14:38 Draw ye near hither, all the chief of the **p**: 5971
14:39 *there was* not a *man* among all the **p** *that* 5971
14:40 the **p** said unto Saul, Do what seemeth 5971
14:41 Jonathan were taken: but the **p** escaped. 5971
14:45 the **p** said unto Saul, Shall Jonathan die, 5971
14:45 So the **p** rescued Jonathan, that he died not. 5971
15: 1 sent me to anoint thee to be king over his **p**, 5971
15: 4 Saul gathered the **p** together, and 5971
15: 8 utterly destroyed all the **p** with the edge of 5971
15: 9 Saul and the **p** spared Agag, and the best of 5971
15:15 for the **p** spared the best of the sheep and 5971
15:21 the **p** took of the spoil, sheep and oxen, 5971
15:24 because I feared the **p**, and obeyed their 5971
15:30 before the elders of my **p**, and before Israel, 5971
17:27 the **p** answered him after this manner, 5971
17:30 the **p** answered him again after the former 5971
18: 5 he was accepted in the sight of all the **p**, 5971
18:13 and he went out and came in before the **p**. 5971
23: 8 Saul called all the **p** together to war, to go 5971
26: 5 and the **p** pitched round about him. 5971
26: 7 and Abishai came to the **p** by night: 5971
26: 7 but Abner and the **p** lay round about him. 5971
26:14 David cried to the **p**, and to Abner the son 5971
26:15 for there came one of the **p** in to destroy 5971
27:12 He hath made his **p** Israel utterly to abhor 5971
30: 4 the **p** that *were* with him lift up their voice 5971
30: 6 for the **p** spake of stoning him, because 5971
30: 6 because the soul of all the **p** was grieved, 5971
30:21 and to meet the **p** that *were* with him: 5971
30:21 when David came near to the **p**, he saluted 5971
31: 9 the house of their idols, and among the **p**. 5971
2Sa 1: 4 That the **p** are fled from the battle, and 5971
1: 4 and many of the **p** also are fallen and dead; 5971
1:12 for the **p** of the LORD, and for the house 5971
2:26 ere thou bid the **p** return from following 5971
2:27 in the morning the **p** had gone up every one 5971
2:28 all the **p** stood still, and pursued after Israel 5971
2:30 when he had gathered all the **p** together, 5971
3:18 **p** Israel out of the hand of the Philistines, 5971
3:31 to all the **p** that *were* with him, Rent your 5971
3:32 at the grave of Abner; and all the **p** wept. 5971
3:34 And all the **p** wept again over him. 5971
3:35 when all the **p** came to cause David to eat 5971
3:36 all the **p** took notice *of it*, and it pleased 5971
3:36 whatsoever the king did, pleased all the **p**. 5971
3:37 For all the **p** and all Israel understood that 5971
5: 2 Thou shalt feed my **p** Israel, and thou shalt 5971
5:12 that he had exalted his kingdom for his **p** 5971
6: 2 went with all the **p** that *were* with him from 5971
6:18 he blessed the **p** in the name of the LORD 5971
6:19 he dealt among all the **p**, *even* among 5971
6:19 a flagon *of wine*. So all the **p** departed 5971
6:21 to appoint me ruler over the **p** of 5971
7: 7 whom I commanded to feed my **p** Israel, 5971
7: 8 to be ruler over my **p**, over Israel: 5971
7:10 Moreover I will appoint a place for my **p** 5971
7:11 commanded judges *to be* over my **p** Israel, 5971
7:23 what one nation in the earth *is* like thy **p**, 5971
7:23 whom God went to redeem for a **p** to 5971
7:23 and terrible, for thy land, before thy **p**, 5971

2Sa 7:24 For thou hast confirmed to thyself thy **p** 5971
7:24 people Israel to be a **p** unto thee for ever; 5971
8:15 and justice unto all his **p**. 5971
10:10 the rest of the **p** he delivered into the hand 5971
10:12 let us play the men for our **p**, and for 5971
10:13 drew nigh, and the **p** that *were* with him, 5971
11: 7 how the **p** did, and how the war prospered. 5971
11:17 there fell *some* of the **p** of the servants of 5971
12:28 therefore gather the rest of the **p** together, 5971
12:29 David gathered all the **p** together, and 5971
12:31 he brought forth the **p** that *were* therein, 5971
12:31 and all the **p** returned *unto* Jerusalem. 5971
13:34 there came much **p** by the way of the hill 5971
14:13 hast thou thought such a thing against the **p** 5971
14:15 *it is* because the **p** have made me afraid: 5971
15:12 for the **p** increased continually with 5971
15:17 all the **p** after him, and tarried *in* a place 5971
15:23 a loud voice, and all the **p** passed over: 5971
15:23 all the **p** passed over, toward the way of 5971
15:24 until all the **p** had done passing out of 5971
15:30 all the **p** that *was* with him covered every 5971
16: 6 all the **p** and all the mighty *men were* on 5971
16:14 all the **p** that *were* with him, came weary, 5971
16:15 and all the **p** the men of Israel, 5971
16:18 this **p**, and all the men of Israel, choose, 5971
17: 2 all the **p** that *are* with him shall flee; and 5971
17: 3 I will bring back all the **p** unto thee: 5971
17: 3 if all returned: *so* all the **p** shall be *in* peace. 5971
17: 8 a man of war, and will not lodge with the **p**. 5971
17: 9 There is a slaughter among the **p** that 5971
17:16 and all the **p** that *are* with him. 5971
17:22 all the **p** that *were* with him, and 5971
17:29 and for the **p** that *were* with him, to eat: 5971
17:29 The **p** *is* hungry, and weary, and thirsty, 5971
18: 1 David numbered the **p** that *were* with him, 5971
18: 2 David sent forth a third part of the **p** under 5971
18: 2 the king said unto the **p**, I will surely go 5971
18: 3 the **p** answered, Thou shalt not go forth: 5971
18: 4 all the **p** came out by hundreds and 5971
18: 5 all the **p** heard when the king gave all 5971
18: 6 So the **p** went out *into* the field against 5971
18: 7 Where the **p** of Israel were slain before 5971
18: 8 the wood devoured more **p** that day than 5971
18:16 the **p** returned from pursuing after Israel: 5971
18:16 after Israel: for Joab held back the **p**. 5971
19: 2 was *turned* into mourning unto all the **p**: 5971
19: 2 for the **p** heard say that day *how* the king 5971
19: 3 the **p** gat them by stealth that day *into* 5971
19: 3 as **p** being ashamed steal away when they 5971
19: 8 they told unto all the **p**, saying, Behold, 5971
19: 8 all the **p** came before the king: for Israel 5971
19: 9 all the **p** were at strife throughout all 5971
19:39 all the **p** went over Jordan. And when 5971
19:40 all the **p** of Judah conducted the king, and 5971
19:40 the king, and also half the **p** of Israel. 5971
20:12 when the man saw that all the **p** stood still, 5971
20:13 all the **p** went on after Joab, to pursue after 376
20:15 all the **p** that *were* with Joab battered 5971
20:22 the woman went unto all the **p** in her 5971
22:28 the afflicted **p** thou wilt save: but thine eyes 5971
22:44 delivered me from the strivings of my **p**, 5971
22:44 a **p** *which* I knew not shall serve me. 5971
22:48 and that bringeth down the **p** under me, 5971
23:10 the **p** returned after him only to spoil. 5971
23:11 and the **p** fled from the Philistines. 5971
24: 2 even to Beer-sheba, and number ye the **p**, 5971
24: 2 that I may know the number of the **p**. 5971
24: 3 Now the LORD thy God add unto the **p**, 5971
24: 4 of the king, to number the **p** *of* Israel. 5971
24: 9 sum of the number of the **p** unto the king: 5971
24:10 him after that he had numbered the **p**. 5971
24:15 there died of the **p** from Dan even to 5971
24:16 said to the angel that destroyed the **p**, *It is* 5971
24:17 when he saw the angel that smote the **p**, 5971
24:21 that the plague may be stayed from the **p**. 5971
1Ki 1:39 and all the **p** said, God save king Solomon. 5971
1:40 all the **p** came up after him, and the people 5971
1:40 the **p** piped with pipes, and rejoiced *with* 5971
3: 2 Only the **p** sacrificed in high places, 5971
3: 8 thy servant *is* in the midst of thy **p** which 5971
3: 8 a great **p**, that cannot be numbered nor 5971
3: 9 an understanding heart to judge thy **p**, 5971
3: 9 who is able to judge this thy *so* great a **p**? 5971
4:34 there came of all **p** to hear the wisdom of 5971
5: 7 unto David a wise son over this great **p**. 5971
5:16 which ruled over the **p** that wrought in 5971
6:13 of Israel, and will not forsake my **p** Israel. 5971
8:16 Since the day that I brought forth my **p** 5971
8:16 but I chose David to be over my **p** Israel. 5971
8:30 of thy **p** Israel, when they shall pray 5971
8:33 When thy **p** Israel be smitten down before 5971
8:34 forgive the sin of thy **p** Israel, and 5971
8:36 the sin of thy servants, and of thy **p** Israel, 5971
8:36 which thou hast given to thy **p** for an 5971
8:38 be *made* by any man, *or* by all thy **p** Israel, 5971
8:41 that *is* not of thy **p** Israel, but cometh out of 5971
8:43 that all **p** of the earth may know thy name, 5971
8:43 thy name, to fear thee, as *do* thy **p** Israel; 5971
8:44 If thy **p** go out to battle against their 5971
8:50 forgive thy **p** that have sinned against thee, 5971
8:51 For they *be* thy **p**, and thine inheritance, 5971
8:52 unto the supplication of thy **p** Israel, 5971
8:53 them from among all the **p** of the earth, 5971
8:56 that hath given rest unto his **p** Israel, 5971
8:59 the cause of his **p** Israel at all times, as 5971
8:60 That all the **p** of the earth may know that 5971
8:66 On the eighth day he sent the **p** away: and 5971
8:66 for David his servant, and for Israel his **p**. 5971
9: 7 be a proverb and a byword among all **p**: 5971
9:20 *And* all the **p** that were left of the Amorites, 5971
9:23 which bare rule over the **p** that wrought in 5971
12: 5 then come again to me. And the **p** departed. 5971
12: 6 do you advise that *I* may answer this **p**? 5971
12: 7 If thou wilt be a servant unto this **p** *this* 5971
12: 9 counsel give ye that we may answer this **p**, 5971

1Ki 12:10 Thus shalt thou speak unto this **p** that spake 5971
12:12 all the **p** came to Rehoboam the third day, 5971
12:13 the king answered the **p** roughly, and 5971
12:15 the king hearkened not unto the **p**; 5971
12:16 the **p** answered the king, saying, 5971
12:23 and *to* the remnant of the **p**, saying, 5971
12:27 If this **p** go up to do sacrifice in the house 5971
12:27 shall the heart of this **p** turn again unto their 5971
12:30 for the **p** went *to worship* before the one, 5971
12:31 made priests of the lowest of the **p**, 5971
13:33 made again of the lowest of the **p** priests of 5971
14: 2 told me that I should be king over this **p**. 5971
14: 7 as I exalted thee from among the **p**, 5971
14: 7 and made thee prince over my **p** Israel, 5971
16: 2 and made thee prince over my **p** Israel; 5971
16: 2 hast made my **p** Israel to sin, to provoke me 5971
16:15 the **p** *were* encamped against Gibbethon, 5971
16:16 the **p** that *were* encamped heard say, 5971
16:21 were the **p** of Israel divided into two parts: 5971
16:21 half of the **p** followed Tibni the son of 5971
16:22 the **p** that followed Omri prevailed against 5971
16:22 the **p** that followed Tibni the son of Ginath: 5971
18:21 Elijah came unto all the **p**, and said, How 5971
18:21 And the **p** answered him not a word. 5971
18:22 said Elijah unto the **p**, I, *even* I only, 5971
18:24 all the **p** answered and said, It is well 5971
18:30 Elijah said unto all the **p**, Come near unto 5971
18:30 all the **p** came near unto him. And he 5971
18:37 that this **p** may know that thou *art* 5971
18:39 when all the **p** saw *it*, they fell on their 5971
19:21 and gave unto the **p**, and they did eat. 5971
20: 8 all the elders and all the **p** said unto him, 5971
20:10 for handfuls for all the **p** that follow me. 5971
20:15 after them he numbered all the **p**, *even* all 5971
20:42 go for his life, and thy **p** for his people. 5971
20:42 go for his life, and thy people for his **p**. 5971
21: 9 a fast, and set Naboth on high among the **p**: 5971
21:12 a fast, and set Naboth on high among the **p**. 5971
21:13 in the presence of the **p**, saying, 5971
22: 4 I *am* as thou *art*, my **p** as thy people, my 5971
22: 4 I *am* as thou *art*, my people as thy **p**, my 5971
22:28 he said, Hearken, O **p**, every one of you. 5971
22:43 *for* the **p** offered and burnt incense yet in 5971
2Ki 3: 7 I *am* as thou *art*, my **p** as thy people, *and* 5971
3: 7 I *am* as thou *art*, my people as thy **p**, *and* 5971
4:13 she answered, I dwell among mine own **p**. 5971
4:41 he said, Pour out for the **p**, that they may 5971
4:42 he said, Give unto the **p**, that they may eat. 5971
4:43 He said again, Give the **p**, that they may 5971
6:18 said, Smite this **p**, I pray thee, 1471
6:30 the wall, and the **p** looked, and behold, 5971
7:16 the **p** went out, and spoiled the tents of 5971
7:17 the **p** trode upon him in the gate, and 5971
7:20 for the **p** trode upon him in the gate, and 5971
8:21 the chariots: and the **p** fled into their tents. 5971
9: 6 I have anointed thee king over the **p** of 5971
10: 9 stood, and said to all the **p**, Ye *be* 5971
10:18 Jehu gathered all the **p** together, and 5971
11:13 heard the noise of the guard *and* of the **p**, 5971
11:13 she came to the **p** *into* the temple of 5971
11:14 all the **p** of the land rejoiced, and blew with 5971
11:17 the LORD and the king and the **p**, 5971
11:17 that *they* should be the LORD'S **p**; 5971
11:17 between the king also and the **p**. 5971
11:18 all the **p** of the land went *into* the house of 5971
11:19 and the guard, and all the **p** of the land; 5971
11:20 all the **p** of the land rejoiced, and the city 5971
12: 3 the **p** still sacrificed and burnt incense in 5971
12: 8 to receive no *more* money of the **p**, 5971
13: 7 Neither did he leave *of* the **p** to Jehoahaz 5971
14: 4 as yet the **p** did sacrifice and burnt incense 5971
14:21 all the **p** of Judah took Azariah, which *was* 5971
15: 4 the **p** sacrificed and burnt incense still on 5971
15: 5 over the house, judging the **p** of the land. 5971
15:10 smote him before the **p**, and slew him, and 5971
15:35 the **p** sacrificed and burnt incense still in 5971
16: 9 carried *the* **p** *of* it captive to Kir, and slew NIH
16:15 with the burnt offering of all the **p** of 5971
18:26 in the ears of the **p** that *are* on the wall. 5971
18:36 the **p** held their peace, and answered him 5971
20: 5 and tell Hezekiah the captain of my **p**, 5971
21:24 the **p** of the land slew all them that had 5971
21:24 the **p** of the land made Josiah his son king 5971
22: 4 keepers of the door have gathered of the **p**: 5971
22:13 for me, and for the **p**, and for all Judah, 5971
23: 2 and all the **p**, both small and great: 5971
23: 3 And all the **p** stood to the covenant. 5971
23: 6 upon the graves of the children of the **p**. 5971
23:21 the king commanded all the **p**, saying, 5971
23:30 the **p** of the land took Jehoahaz the son of 5971
23:35 the silver and the gold of the **p** of the land, 5971
24:14 save the poorest sort of the **p** of the land. 5971
25: 3 there was no bread for the **p** of the land. 5971
25:11 Now the rest of the **p** that were left in 5971
25:19 which mustered the **p** of the land, and 5971
25:19 threescore men of the **p** of the land that 5971
25:22 *as for* the **p** that remained in the land of 5971
25:26 all the **p**, both small and great, and 5971
1Ch 5:25 went a whoring after the gods of the **p** of 5971
10: 9 carry tidings unto their idols, and to the **p**. 5971
11: 2 Thou shalt feed my **p** Israel, and thou shalt 5971
11: 2 and thou shalt be ruler over my **p** Israel. 5971
11:13 and the **p** fled from before the Philistines. 5971
13: 4 the thing was right in the eyes of all the **p**. 5971
14: 2 *was* lift up on high, because of his **p** Israel. 5971
16: 2 he blessed the **p** in the name of 5971
16: 8 make known his deeds among the **p**. 5971
16:20 and from *one* kingdom to another **p**; 5971
16:26 For all the gods of the **p** *are* idols: but 5971
16:28 unto the LORD, ye kindreds of the **p**, 5971
16:36 all the **p** said, Amen, and praised 5971
16:43 all the **p** departed every man to his house: 5971
17: 6 whom I commanded to feed my **p**, saying, 5971
17: 7 that *thou* shouldest be ruler over my **p** 5971
17: 9 Also I will ordain a place for my **p** Israel, 5971

1Ch 17:10 commanded judges *to be* over my **p** Israel. 5971
17:21 what one nation in the earth *is* like thy **p** 5971
17:21 whom God went to redeem *to be* his own **p**, 5971
17:21 by driving out nations from before thy **p**, 5971
17:22 For thy **p** Israel didst thou make thine own 5971
17:22 Israel didst thou make thine own **p** for ever; 5971
18:14 and justice among all his **p**. 5971
19: 7 and the king of Maachah and his **p**; 5971
19:11 the rest of the **p** he delivered unto the hand 5971
19:13 let us behave ourselves valiantly for our **p**, 5971
19:14 the **p** that *were* with him drew nigh before 5971
20: 3 he brought out the **p** that *were* in it, and 5971
20: 3 and all the **p** returned *to* Jerusalem. 5971
21: 2 said to Joab and to the rulers of the **p**, 5971
21: 3 The LORD make his **p** an hundred times 5971
21: 5 Joab gave the sum of the number of the **p** 5971
21:17 *Is it* not I *that* commanded the **p** to be 5971
21:17 not on thy **p**, that *they* should be plagued. 5971
21:22 that the plague may be stayed from the **p**. 5971
22:18 before the LORD, and before his **p**. 5971
23:25 God of Israel hath given rest unto his **p**, 5971
28: 2 and said, Hear me, my brethren, and my **p**: 5971
28:21 all the **p** *will be* wholly at thy 5971
29: 9 the **p** rejoiced, for that they offered 5971
29:14 who *am* I, and what *is* my **p**, that we should 5971
29:17 and now have I seen with joy thy **p**, 5971
29:18 of the thoughts of the heart of thy **p**, 5971
2Ch 1: 9 for thou hast made me king over a **p** like 5971
1:10 that I may go out and come in before this **p**: 5971
1:10 for who can judge this thy **p**, *that is so* 5971
1:11 for thyself, that thou mayest judge my **p**, 5971
2:11 Because the LORD hath loved his **p**, 5971
2:18 six hundred overseers to set the **p** a work. 5971
6: 5 Since the day that I brought forth my **p** out 5971
6: 5 I any man to be a ruler over my **p** Israel: 5971
6: 6 have chosen David to be over my **p** Israel. 5971
6:21 of thy servant, and of thy **p** Israel, 5971
6:24 if thy **p** Israel be put to the worse before 5971
6:25 forgive the sin of thy **p** Israel, and 5971
6:27 the sin of thy servants, and of thy **p** Israel, 5971
6:27 which thou hast given unto thy **p** for an 5971
6:29 or of all thy **p** Israel, when every one shall 5971
6:32 which *is* not of thy **p** Israel, but is come 5971
6:33 that all **p** of the earth may know thy name, 5971
6:33 as *doth* thy **p** Israel, and may know that this 5971
6:34 If thy **p** go out to war against their enemies 5971
6:39 forgive thy **p** which have sinned against 5971
7: 4 all the **p** offered sacrifices before 5971
7: 5 and all the **p** dedicated the house of God. 5971
7:10 month he sent the **p** away into their tents, 5971
7:10 and to Solomon, and to Israel his **p**. 5971
7:13 or if I send pestilence among my **p**; 5971
7:14 If my **p**, which are called by my name, 5971
8: 7 *As for* all the **p** that were left of the Hittites, 5971
8:10 and fifty, that bare rule over the **p**. 5971
10: 5 me after three days. And the **p** departed. 5971
10: 6 give ye *me* to return answer to this **p**? 5971
10: 7 If thou be kind to this **p**, and please them, 5971
10: 9 give ye that we may return answer to this **p**, 5971
10:10 Thus shalt thou answer the **p** that spake 5971
10:12 all the **p** came to Rehoboam on the third 5971
10:15 So the king hearkened not unto the **p**: 5971
10:16 the **p** answered the king, saying, 5971
12: 3 the **p** *were* without number that came with 5971
13:17 and his **p** slew them *with* a great slaughter: 5971
14:13 the **p** that *were* with him pursued them unto 5971
16:10 Asa oppressed *some* of the **p** the same time. 5971
17: 9 all the cities of Judah, and taught the **p**. 5971
18: 2 for the **p** that *he had* with him, and 5971
18: 3 I *am* as thou *art*, and my **p** as thy people; 5971
18: 3 I *am* as thou *art*, and my people as thy **p**; 5971
18:27 by me. And he said, Hearken, all ye **p**. 5971
19: 4 he went out again through the **p** from 5971
20: 7 inhabitants of this land before thy **p** Israel, 5971
20:21 when he had consulted with the **p**, he 5971
20:25 his **p** came to take away the spoil of them, 5971
20:33 for as yet the **p** had not prepared their 5971
21:14 a great plague will the LORD smite thy **p**, 5971
21:19 his **p** made no burning for him, like 5971
23: 5 all the **p** *shall be* in the courts of the house 5971
23: 6 all the **p** shall keep the watch of 5971
23:10 he set all the **p**, every man having his 5971
23:12 when Athaliah heard the noise of the **p** 5971
23:12 she came to the **p** *into* the house of 5971
23:13 all the **p** of the land rejoiced, and 5971
23:16 between all the **p**, and between the king, 5971
23:16 that *they* should be the LORD'S **p**. 5971
23:17 all the **p** went *to* the house of Baal, and 5971
23:20 the governors of the **p**, and all the people of 5971
23:20 all the **p** of the land, and brought down 5971
23:21 all the **p** of the land rejoiced: and the city 5971
24:10 all the princes and all the **p** rejoiced, and 5971
24:20 which stood above the **p**, and said unto 5971
24:23 destroyed all the princes of the **p** from 5971
24:23 the princes of the people from among the **p**, 5971
25:11 led forth his **p**, and went *to* the valley of 5971
25:15 hast thou sought after the gods of the **p**, 5971
25:15 which could not deliver their own **p** out of 5971
26: 1 all the **p** of Judah took Uzziah, who *was* 5971
26:21 the king's house, judging the **p** of the land. 5971
27: 2 of the LORD. And the **p** did yet corruptly. 5971
29:36 Hezekiah rejoiced, and all the **p**, that God 5971
29:36 all the people, that God had prepared the **p**: 5971
30: 3 neither had the **p** gathered themselves 5971
30:13 there assembled *at* Jerusalem much **p** to 5971
30:18 For a multitude of the **p**, *even* many of 5971
30:20 hearkened to Hezekiah, and healed the **p**. 5971
30:27 priests the Levites arose and blessed the **p**: 5971
31: 4 Moreover he commanded the **p** that dwelt 5971
31: 8 they blessed the LORD, and his **p** Israel. 5971
31:10 Since the **p** began to bring the offerings *into* NIH
31:10 for the LORD hath blessed his **p**; and 5971
32: 4 So there was gathered much **p** together, 5971
32: 6 he set captains of war over the **p**, and 5971
32: 8 the **p** rested themselves upon the words of 5971
2Ch 32:13 my fathers have done unto all the **p** of *other* 5971
32:14 that could deliver his **p** out of mine hand, 5971
32:15 kingdom was able to deliver his **p** out of 5971
32:17 have not delivered their **p** out of mine hand, 5971
32:17 shall not the God of Hezekiah deliver his **p** 5971
32:18 the **p** of Jerusalem that *were* on the wall, 5971
32:19 as against the gods of the **p** of the earth, 5971
33:10 LORD spake to Manasseh, and to his **p**: 5971
33:17 Nevertheless the **p** did sacrifice still in 5971
33:25 the **p** of the land slew all them that had 5971
33:25 the **p** of the land made Josiah his son king 5971
34:30 the Levites, and all the **p**, great and small: 5971
35: 3 the LORD your God, and his **p** Israel, 5971
35: 5 of the fathers of your brethren the **p**, 1121+5971
35: 7 Josiah gave to the **p**, *of* the flock, 1121+5971
35: 8 his princes gave willingly unto the **p**, to 5971
35:12 the divisions of the families of the **p**, 1121+5971
35:13 *them* speedily among all the **p**. 1121+5971
36: 1 the **p** of the land took Jehoahaz the son of 5971
36:14 all the chief of the priests, and the **p**, 5971
36:15 because he had compassion on his **p**, and 5971
36:16 wrath of the LORD arose against his **p**, 5971
36:23 Who *is there* among you of all his **p**? 5971
Ezr 1: 3 Who *is there* among you of all his **p**? 5971
2: 2 The number of the men of the **p** of Israel: 5971
2:70 *some* of the **p**, and the singers, and 5971
3: 1 the **p** gathered themselves together as one 5971
3: 3 because of the **p** of *those* countries: 5971
3:11 all the **p** shouted *with* a great shout, 5971
3:13 So that the **p** could not discern the noise of 5971
3:13 joy from the noise of the weeping of the **p**: 5971
3:13 for the **p** shouted *with* a loud shout, and 5971
4: 4 the **p** of the land weakened the hands of 5971
4: 4 land weakened the hands of the **p** of Judah, 5971
5:12 carried the **p** away into Babylon. 5972
6:12 name to dwell there destroy all kings and **p**, 5972
7:13 that all they of the **p** of Israel, and *of* his 5972
7:16 with the freewill offering of the **p**, and 5972
7:25 which may judge all the **p** that *are* beyond 5972
8:15 I viewed the **p**, and the priests, and 5971
8:36 they furthered the **p**, and the house of God. 5971
9: 1 The **p** of Israel, and the priests, and 5971
9: 1 have not separated themselves from the **p** 5971
9: 2 themselves with the **p** of *those* lands: 5971
9:11 with the filthiness of the **p** of the lands, 5971
9:14 join in affinity with the **p** of these 5971
10: 1 and children: for the **p** wept very sore. 5971
10: 2 have taken strange wives of the **p** of 5971
10: 9 all the **p** sat in the street of the house of 5971
10:11 separate yourselves from the **p** of the land, 5971
10:13 the **p** *are* many, and *it is* a time of much 5971
Ne 1:10 Now these *are* thy servants and thy **p**, 5971
4: 6 half thereof: for the **p** had a mind to work. 5971
4:13 I even set the **p** after *their* families with 5971
4:14 and to the rulers, and to the rest of the **p**, 5971
4:19 to the rulers, and to the rest of the **p**, 5971
4:22 Likewise at the same time said I unto the **p**, 5971
5: 1 there was a great cry of the **p** and of their 5971
5:13 And the **p** did according to this promise. 5971
5:15 *been* before me were chargeable unto the **p**, 5971
5:15 even their servants bare rule over the **p**: 5971
5:18 the bondage was heavy upon this **p**. 5971
5:19 *according to* all that I have done for this **p**. 5971
7: 4 the **p** *were* few therein, and the houses *were* 5971
7: 5 the rulers, and the **p**, that *they* might be 5971
7: 7 *I say*, of the men of the **p** of Israel *was* 5971
7:72 *that* which the rest of the **p** gave *was* 5971
7:73 *some* of the **p**, and the Nethinims, and 5971
8: 1 all the **p** gathered themselves together as 5971
8: 3 the ears of all the **p** *were attentive* unto 5971
8: 5 opened the book in the sight of all the **p**; 5971
8: 5 (for he was above all the **p**;) and when he 5971
8: 5 and when he opened *it*, all the **p** stood *up*: 5971
8: 6 all the **p** answered, Amen, Amen, 5971
8: 7 caused the **p** to understand the law: 5971
8: 7 the law: and the **p** *stood* in their place. 5971
8: 9 the Levites that taught the **p**, said unto all 5971
8: 9 that taught the people, said unto all the **p**, 5971
8: 9 For all the **p** wept, when they heard 5971
8:11 So the Levites stilled all the **p**, saying, 5971
8:12 all the **p** went *their way* to eat, and to drink, 5971
8:13 together the chief of the fathers of all the **p**, 5971
8:16 So the **p** went forth, and brought *them*, and 5971
9:10 all his servants, and on all the **p** of his land: 5971
9:24 with their kings, and the **p** of the land, 5971
9:30 gavest thou them into the hand of the **p** of 5971
9:32 and on our fathers, and on all thy **p**, 5971
10:14 The chief of the **p**; Parosh, Pahath-moab, 5971
10:28 the rest of the **p**, the priests, the Levites, 5971
10:28 the **p** of the lands unto the law of God, 5971
10:30 give our daughters unto the **p** of the land, 5971
10:31 *if* the **p** of the land bring ware or 5971
10:34 the Levites, and the **p**, for the wood 5971
11: 1 the rulers of the **p** dwelt at Jerusalem: 5971
11: 1 the rest of the **p** also cast lots, to bring one 5971
11: 2 the **p** blessed all the men, that willingly 5971
11:24 king's hand in all matters concerning the **p**. 5971
12:30 purified the **p**, and the gates, and the wall. 5971
12:38 and the half of the **p** upon the wall, 5971
13: 1 the book of Moses in the audience of the **p**; 5971
13:24 to the language of **each p**. 5971+5971+2050.1
Est 1: 5 the king made a feast unto all the **p** that 5971
1:11 to shew the **p** and the princes her beauty: 5971
1:16 to all the **p** that *are* in all the provinces of 5971
1:22 to **every p** after their 5971+5971+2050.1
1:22 according to the language of every **p**. 5971
2:10 Esther had not shewed her **p** nor her 5971
2:20 had not *yet* shewed her kindred nor her **p**; 5971
3: 6 for they had shewed him the **p** of 5971
3: 6 of Ahasuerus, *even* the **p** of Mordecai. 5971
3: 8 There is a certain **p** scattered abroad and 5971
3: 8 dispersed among the **p** in all the provinces 5971
3: 8 their laws *are* diverse from all **p**; 5971
3:11 The silver *is* given to thee, the **p** also, 5971
3:12 to the rulers of **every p** of 5971+5971+2050.1
Est 3:12 **every p** after their language; 5971+5971+2050.1
3:14 in every province *was* published unto all **p**, 5971
4: 8 and to make request before him for her **p**. 5971
4:11 the **p** of the king's provinces, do know, 5971
7: 3 me at my petition, and my **p** at my request: 5971
7: 4 I and my **p**, to be destroyed, to be slain, and 5971
8: 6 to see the evil that shall come unto my **p**? 5971
8: 9 *unto* **every p** after their 5971+5971+2050.1
8:11 all the power of the **p** and province that 5971
8:13 in every province *was* published unto all **p**, 5971
8:17 many of the **p** of the land became Jews; 5971
9: 2 for the fear of them fell upon all **p**. 5971
10: 3 seeking the wealth of his **p**, and 5971
Job 12: 2 No doubt but ye *are* the **p**, and 5971
12:24 the heart of the chief of the **p** of the earth, 5971
17: 6 He hath made me also a byword of the **p**; 5971
18:19 neither have son nor nephew among his **p**, 5971
34:20 the **p** shall be troubled at midnight, 5971
34:30 hypocrite reign not, lest the **p** be ensnared. 5971
36:20 the night, when **p** are cut off in their place. 5971
36:31 For by them judgeth he the **p**; he giveth 5971
Ps 2: 1 and the **p** imagine a vain *thing?* 3816
3: 6 I will not be afraid of ten thousands of **p**, 5971
3: 8 thy blessing *is* upon thy **p**. Selah. 5971
7: 7 So shall the congregation of the **p** compass 3816
7: 8 The LORD shall judge the **p**: judge me, 5971
9: 8 he shall minister judgment to the **p** in 3816
9:11 in Zion: declare among the **p** his doings. 5971
14: 4 who eat up my **p** *as* they eat bread, *and* 5971
14: 7 bringeth back the captivity of his **p**, 5971
18:27 For thou wilt save the afflicted **p**; but 5971
18:43 delivered me from the strivings of the **p**; 5971
18:43 a **p** *whom* I have not known shall serve me. 5971
18:47 avengeth me, and subdueth the **p** under me. 5971
22: 6 a reproach of men, and despised of the **p**. 5971
22:31 shall declare his righteousness unto a **p** that 5971
28: 9 Save thy **p**, and bless thine inheritance: 5971
29:11 The LORD will give strength unto his **p**; 5971
29:11 the LORD will bless his **p** with peace. 5971
33:10 he maketh the devices of the **p** of none 5971
33:12 the **p** *whom* he hath chosen for his own 5971
35:18 I will praise thee among much **p**. 5971
44: 2 *how* thou didst afflict the **p**, and cast them 3816
44:12 Thou sellest thy **p** for nought, and dost not 5971
44:14 a shaking of the head among the **p**. 3816
45: 5 *whereby* the **p** fall under thee. 5971
45:10 forget also thine own **p**, and thy father's 5971
45:12 *even* the rich among the **p** shall intreat thy 5971
45:17 shall the **p** praise thee for ever and ever. 5971
47: 1 O clap *your* hands, all ye **p**; shout unto God 5971
47: 3 He shall subdue the **p** under us, and 5971
47: 9 The princes of the **p** are gathered together, 5971
47: 9 *even* the **p** of the God of Abraham: 5971
49: 1 Hear this, all ye **p**; give ear, all ye 5971
50: 4 and to the earth, that *he* may judge his **p**. 5971
50: 7 Hear, O my **p**, and I will speak; O Israel, 5971
53: 4 who eat up my **p** *as* they eat bread: 5971
53: 6 God bringeth back the captivity of his **p**, 5971
56: 7 in *thine* anger cast down the **p**, O God. 5971
57: 9 I will praise thee, O Lord, among the **p**: 5971
59:11 Slay them not, lest my **p** forget: 5971
60: 3 Thou hast shewed thy **p** hard *things*: thou 5971
62: 8 ye **p**, pour out your heart before him: 5971
65: 7 of their waves, and the tumult of the **p**. 3816
66: 8 ye **p**, and make the voice of his praise to be 5971
67: 3 Let the **p** praise thee, O God; let all 5971
67: 3 praise thee, O God; let all the **p** praise thee. 5971
67: 4 for thou shalt judge the **p** righteously, and 5971
67: 5 Let the **p** praise thee, O God; let all 5971
67: 5 praise thee, O God; let all the **p** praise thee. 5971
68: 7 when thou wentest forth before thy **p**, 5971
68:22 I will bring *my* **p** again from the depths of NIH
68:30 of the bulls, with the calves of the **p**, 5971
68:30 scatter thou the **p** *that* delight in war. 5971
68:35 that giveth strength and power unto *his* **p**. 5971
72: 2 He shall judge thy **p** with righteousness, 5971
72: 3 The mountains shall bring peace to the **p**, 5971
72: 4 He shall judge the poor of the **p**, he shall 5971
73:10 Therefore his **p** return hither: and waters of 5971
74:14 gavest him *to be* meat to the **p** inhabiting 5971
74:18 *that* the foolish **p** have blasphemed thy 5971
77:14 hast declared thy strength among the **p**. 5971
77:15 Thou hast with *thine* arm redeemed thy **p**, 5971
77:20 Thou leddest thy **p** like a flock by the hand 5971
78: 1 Give ear, O my **p**, to my law: incline your 5971
78:20 bread also? can he provide flesh for his **p**? 5971
78:52 made his own **p** to go forth like sheep, and 5971
78:62 He gave his **p** over also unto the sword; and 5971
78:71 young he brought him to feed Jacob his **p**, 5971
79:13 So we thy **p** and sheep of thy pasture will 5971
80: 4 thou be angry against the prayer of thy **p**? 5971
81: 8 Hear, O my **p**, and I will testify unto thee: 5971
81:11 my **p** would not hearken to my voice; and 5971
81:13 O that my **p** had hearkened unto me, *and* 5971
83: 3 have taken crafty counsel against thy **p**, 5971
85: 2 Thou hast forgiven the iniquity of thy **p**, 5971
85: 6 us again: that thy **p** may rejoice in thee? 5971
85: 8 for he will speak peace unto his **p**, and 5971
87: 6 shall count, when he writeth *up* the **p**, 5971
89:15 Blessed *is* the **p** that know the joyful sound: 5971
89:19 I have exalted *one* chosen out of the **p**. 5971
89:50 my bosom *the reproach of* all the mighty **p**; 5971
94: 5 They break in pieces thy **p**, O LORD, and 5971
94: 8 Understand, ye brutish among the **p**: and 5971
94:14 For the LORD will not cast off his **p**, 5971
95: 7 we *are* the **p** of his pasture, and the sheep of 5971
95:10 It *is* a **p** that do err in *their* heart, and 5971
96: 3 the heathen, his wonders among all **p**. 5971
96: 7 unto the LORD, O ye kindreds of the **p**, 5971
96:10 be moved: he shall judge the **p** righteously. 5971
96:13 with righteousness, and the **p** with his truth. 5971
97: 6 and all the **p** see his glory. 5971
98: 9 he judge the world, and the **p** with equity. 5971
99: 1 The LORD reigneth; let the **p** tremble: 5971
99: 2 in Zion; and he *is* high above all the **p**. 5971

P

Ps 100: 3 *we are* his **p**, and the sheep of his pasture. 5971
102:18 the **p** which *shall be* created shall praise 5971
102:22 When the **p** are gathered together, and 5971
105: 1 make known his deeds among the **p**. 5971
105:13 to another, from *one* kingdom to another **p**; 5971
105:20 *even* the ruler of the **p**, and let him go free. 5971
105:24 He increased his **p** greatly; and made them 5971
105:25 He turned their heart to hate his **p**, to deal 5971
105:40 *The* **p** asked, and he brought quails, and NIH
105:43 he brought forth his **p** with joy, *and* 5971
105:44 and they inherited the labour of the **p**; 3816
106: 4 the favour *that thou bearest* unto thy **p**: 5971
106:40 wrath of the LORD kindled against his **p**, 5971
106:48 let all the **p** say, Amen. Praise ye 5971
107:32 exalt him also in the congregation of the **p**, 5971
108: 3 I will praise thee, O LORD, among the **p**: 5971
110: 3 Thy **p** *shall be* willing in the day of thy 5971
111: 6 He hath shewed his **p** the power of his 5971
111: 9 He sent redemption unto his **p**: he hath 5971
113: 8 with princes, *even* with the princes of his **p**. 5971
114: 1 the house of Jacob from a **p** of strange 5971
116:14 LORD now in the presence of all his **p**. 5971
116:18 LORD now in the presence of all his **p**, 5971
117: 1 all ye nations: praise him, all ye **p**. 523
125: 2 the LORD *is* round about his **p** from 5971
135:12 an heritage, an heritage unto Israel his **p**. 5971
135:14 For the LORD will judge his **p**, and 5971
136:16 To him which led his **p** through 5971
144: 2 I trust; who subdueth my **p** under me. 5971
144:15 Happy *is that* **p**, that is in such a case: *yea,* 5971
144:15 *yea,* happy *is that* **p**, whose God *is* 5971
148:11 Kings of the earth, and all **p**; princes, and 3816
148:14 He also exalteth the horn of his **p**, 5971
148:14 of the children of Israel, a **p** near unto him. 5971
149: 4 For the LORD taketh pleasure in his **p**: 5971
149: 7 the heathen, *and* punishments upon the **p**; 3816
Pr 11:14 Where no counsel *is,* the **p** fall: but in 5971
11:26 withholdeth corn, the **p** shall curse him: 3816
14:28 In the multitude of **p** *is* the king's honour: 5971
14:28 in the want of **p** *is* the destruction of 3816
14:34 a nation: but sin *is* a reproach to any **p**. 3816
24:24 him shall the **p** curse, nations shall abhor 5971
28:15 *so is* a wicked ruler over the poor **p**. 5971
29: 2 the righteous are in authority, the **p** rejoice: 5971
29: 2 when the wicked beareth rule, the **p** mourn. 5971
29:18 Where *there is* no vision, the **p** perish: but 5971
30:25 The ants *are* a **p** not strong, yet they 5971
Ecc 4:16 *There is* no end of all the **p**, *even* of all that 5971
12: 9 was wise, he still taught the **p** knowledge; 5971
Isa 1: 3 doth not know, my **p** doth not consider. 5971
1: 4 Ah sinful nation, a **p** laden with iniquity, 5971
1:10 unto the law of our God, ye **p** of Gomorrah. 5971
2: 3 many **p** shall go and say, Come ye, and 5971
2: 4 the nations, and shall rebuke many **p**: 5971
2: 6 Therefore thou hast forsaken thy **p** 5971
3: 5 the **p** shall be oppressed, every one by 5971
3: 7 nor clothing: make me not a ruler of the **p**. 5971
3:12 *As for* my **p**, children *are* their oppressors, 5971
3:12 O my **p**, they which lead thee cause *thee* to 5971
3:13 *up* to plead, and standeth to judge the **p**. 5971
3:14 Into judgment with the ancients of his **p**, 5971
3:15 What mean ye *that* ye beat my **p** to pieces, 5971
5:13 Therefore my **p** are gone into captivity, 5971
5:25 anger of the LORD kindled against his **p**, 5971
6: 5 I dwell in the midst of a **p** of unclean lips: 5971
6: 9 he said, Go, and tell this **p**, Hear ye indeed, 5971
6:10 Make the heart of this **p** fat, and make their 5971
7: 2 his heart was moved, and the heart of his **p**, 5971
7: 8 shall Ephraim be broken, that *it be* not a **p**. 5971
7:17 upon thy **p**, and upon thy father's house, 5971
8: 6 Forsomuch as this **p** refuseth the waters of 5971
8: 9 O ye **p**, and ye shall be broken in pieces; 5971
8:11 that *I* should not walk in the way of this **p**, 5971
8:12 to all *them to* whom this **p** shall say, 5971
8:19 should not a **p** seek unto their God? for 5971
9: 2 The **p** that walked in darkness have seen a 5971
9: 9 all the **p** shall know, *even* Ephraim and 5971
9:13 For the **p** turneth not unto him that smiteth 5971
9:16 For the leaders of this **p** cause *them* to err; 5971
9:19 and the **p** shall be as the fuel of the fire: 5971
10: 2 take away the right from the poor of my **p**, 5971
10: 6 against the **p** of my wrath will I give him a 5971
10:13 I have removed the bounds of the **p**, and 5971
10:14 hath found as a nest the riches of the **p**: 5971
10:22 For though thy **p** Israel be as the sand of 5971
10:24 O my **p** that dwellest in Zion, be not afraid 5971
11:10 which shall stand for an ensign of the **p**; 5971
11:11 time to recover the remnant of his **p**, 5971
11:16 shall be a highway for the remnant of his **p**, 5971
12: 4 his name, declare his doings among the **p**, 5971
13: 4 in the mountains, like as of a great **p**; 5971
13:14 they shall every man turn to his own **p**, and 5971
14: 2 the **p** shall take them, and bring them to 5971
14: 6 He who smote the **p** in wrath *with* a 5971
14:20 hast destroyed thy land, *and* slain thy **p**: 5971
14:32 and the poor of his **p** shall trust in it. 5971
17:12 Woe to the multitude of many **p**, 5971
18: 2 to a **p** terrible from their beginning hitherto; 5971
18: 7 unto the LORD of hosts *of* a **p** scattered 5971
18: 7 from a **p** terrible from their beginning 5971
19:25 Blessed *be* Egypt my **p**, and Assyria 5971
22: 4 of the spoiling of the daughter of my **p**. 5971
23:13 this **p** was not, *till* the Assyrian founded it 5971
24: 2 it shall be, as *with* the **p**, so *with* the priest; 5971
24: 4 the haughty **p** of the earth do languish. 5971
24:13 be in the midst of the land among the **p**, 5971
25: 3 Therefore shall the strong **p** glorify thee, 5971
25: 6 hosts make unto all **p** a feast of fat things, 5971
25: 7 the face of the covering cast over all **p**, 5971
25: 8 the rebuke of his **p** shall he take away from 5971
26:11 and be ashamed for *their* envy at the **p**; 5971
26:20 Come, my **p**, enter thou into thy chambers, 5971
27:11 for it *is* a **p** of no understanding: therefore 5971
28: 5 diadem of beauty, unto the residue of his **p**, 5971
28:11 and another tongue will he speak to this **p**. 5971

Isa 28:14 that rule this **p** which *is* in Jerusalem. 5971
29:13 Forasmuch as this **p** draw near *me* with 5971
29:14 to do a marvellous work amongst this **p**, 5971
30: 5 They were all ashamed of a **p** *that* could not 5971
30: 6 of camels, to a **p** *that* shall not profit *them.* 5971
30: 9 That this *is* a rebellious **p**, lying children, 5971
30:19 For the **p** shall dwell in Zion at Jerusalem: 5971
30:26 the LORD bindeth up the breach of his **p**, 5971
30:28 *there shall be* a bridle in the jaws of the **p**, 5971
32:13 Upon the land of my **p** shall come up 5971
32:18 my **p** shall dwell in a peaceable habitation, 5971
33: 3 At the noise of the tumult the **p** fled; at 5971
33:12 the **p** shall be *as* the burnings of lime: 5971
33:19 Thou shalt not see a fierce **p**, a people of a 5971
33:19 a **p** of a deeper speech than *thou* canst 5971
33:24 the **p** that dwell therein *shall be* forgiven 5971
34: 1 ye nations, to hear; and hearken, ye **p**: 3816
34: 5 and upon the **p** of my curse, to judgment. 5971
36:11 in the ears of the **p** that *are* on the wall. 5971
40: 1 Comfort ye, comfort ye my **p**, saith your 5971
40: 7 bloweth upon it: surely the **p** *is* grass. 5971
41: 1 and let the **p** renew *their* strength: 3816
42: 5 he that giveth breath unto the **p** upon it, and 5971
42: 6 and give thee for a covenant of the **p**, 5971
42:22 this *is* a **p** robbed and spoiled; *they are* all 5971
43: 4 will I give men for thee, and **p** for thy life. 3816
43: 8 Bring forth the blind **p** that have eyes, and 5971
43: 9 and let the **p** be assembled: 3816
43:20 to give drink to my **p**, my chosen. 5971
43:21 This **p** have I formed for myself; they shall 5971
44: 7 for me, since I appointed the ancient **p**? 5971
47: 6 I was wroth with my **p**, I have polluted 5971
49: 1 unto me; and hearken, ye **p**, from afar; 3816
49: 8 and give thee for a covenant of the **p**, 5971
49:13 for the LORD hath comforted his **p**, and 5971
49:22 and set up my standard to the **p**: 5971
51: 4 Hearken unto me, my **p**; and give ear unto 5971
51: 4 my judgment to rest for a light of the **p**. 5971
51: 5 and mine arms shall judge the **p**; 5971
51: 7 the **p** in whose heart *is* my law; 5971
51:16 and say unto Zion, Thou *art* my **p**. 5971
51:22 thy God *that* pleadeth the cause of his **p**, 5971
52: 4 My **p** went down aforetime *into* Egypt to 5971
52: 5 that my **p** is taken away for nought? 5971
52: 6 Therefore my **p** shall know my name: 5971
52: 9 for the LORD hath comforted his **p**, 5971
53: 8 for the transgression of my **p** was he 5971
55: 4 I have given him *for* a witness to the **p**, 3816
55: 4 a leader and commander to the **p**. 3816
56: 3 hath utterly separated me from his **p**: 5971
56: 7 shall be called a house of prayer for all **p**. 5971
57:14 the stumblingblock out of the way of my **p**. 5971
58: 1 shew my **p** their transgression, and 5971
60: 2 cover the earth, and gross darkness the **p**: 3816
60:21 Thy **p** also *shall be* all righteous: they shall 5971
61: 9 and their offspring among the **p**: 5971
62:10 prepare you the way of the **p**; cast up, 5971
62:10 out the stones; lift up a standard for the **p**. 5971
62:12 they shall call them, The holy **p**, 5971
63: 3 and of the **p** *there was* none with me: 5971
63: 6 I will tread down the **p** in mine anger, and 5971
63: 8 For he said, Surely they *are* my **p**, 5971
63:11 the days of old, Moses, *and* his **p**, 5971
63:14 so didst thou lead thy **p**, to make thyself a 5971
63:18 The **p** of thy holiness have possessed *it* but 5971
64: 9 see, we beseech thee, we *are* all thy **p**. 5971
65: 2 mine hands all the day unto a rebellious **p**, 5971
65: 3 A **p** that provoketh me to anger continually 5971
65:10 lie down in, for my **p** that have sought me. 5971
65:18 Jerusalem a rejoicing, and her **p** a joy. 5971
65:19 I will rejoice in Jerusalem, and joy in my **p**: 5971
65:22 as the days of a tree *are* the days of my **p**, 5971
Jer 1:18 and against the **p** of the land. 5971
2:11 my **p** have changed their glory for *that* 5971
2:13 For my **p** have committed two evils; 5971
2:31 wherefore say my **p**, We are lords; we will 5971
2:32 yet my **p** have forgotten me days without 5971
4:10 surely thou hast greatly deceived this **p** 5971
4:11 At that time shall it be said to this **p** and 5971
4:11 wilderness toward the daughter of my **p**, 5971
4:22 For my **p** *is* foolish, they have not known 5971
5:14 and this **p** wood, and it shall devour them. 5971
5:21 O foolish **p**, and without understanding; 5971
5:23 this **p** hath a revolting and a rebellious 5971
5:26 For among my **p** are found wicked *men:* 5971
5:31 by their means; and my **p** love *to have it* so: 5971
6:14 the hurt of *the daughter of* my **p** slightly, 5971
6:19 behold, I will bring evil upon this **p**, 5971
6:21 I will lay stumblingblocks before this **p**, 5971
6:22 a **p** cometh from the north country, and 5971
6:26 O daughter of my **p**, gird *thee* with 5971
6:27 thee *for* a tower *and* a fortress among my **p**, 5971
7:12 I did to it for the wickedness of my **p** Israel. 5971
7:16 Therefore pray not thou for this **p**, neither 5971
7:23 I will be your God, and ye shall be my **p**: 5971
7:33 the carcases of this **p** shall be meat for 5971
8: 5 is this **p** of Jerusalem slidden back *by* a 5971
8: 7 my **p** know not the judgment of 5971
8:11 the hurt of the daughter of my **p** slightly, 5971
8:19 the voice of the cry of the daughter of my **p** 5971
8:21 For the hurt of the daughter of my **p** am I 5971
8:22 is not the health of the daughter of my **p** 5971
9: 1 night for the slain of the daughter of my **p**! 5971
9: 2 that I might leave my **p**, and go from them! 5971
9: 7 how shall I do for the daughter of my **p**? 5971
9:15 Behold, I *will* feed them, *even* this **p**, with 5971
10: 3 For the customs of the **p** *are* vain: for *one* 5971
11: 4 so shall ye be my **p**, and I will be your 5971
11:14 Therefore pray not thou for this **p**, neither 5971
12:14 which I have caused my **p** Israel to inherit; 5971
12:16 they will diligently learn the ways of my **p**, 5971
12:16 as they taught my **p** to swear by Baal; then 5971
12:16 shall they be built in the midst of my **p**. 5971
13:10 This evil **p**, which refuse to hear my words, 5971
13:11 that *they* might be unto me for a **p**, and 5971

Jer 14:10 Thus saith the LORD unto this **p**, Thus 5971
14:11 unto me, Pray not for this **p** for *their* good. 5971
14:16 the **p** to whom they prophesy shall be cast 5971
14:17 for the virgin daughter of my **p** is broken 5971
15: 1 *yet* my mind *could* not *be* toward this **p**: 5971
15: 7 *them* of children, I will destroy my **p**, 5971
15:20 I will make thee unto this **p** a fenced brasen 5971
16: 5 I have taken away my peace from this **p**, 5971
16:10 when thou shalt shew this **p** all these 5971
17:19 stand in the gate of the children of the **p**, 5971
18:15 Because my **p** hath forgotten me, they have 5971
19: 1 *take* of the ancients of the **p**, and of 5971
19:11 Even so will I break this **p** and this city, as 5971
19:14 the LORD'S house; and said to all the **p**, 5971
21: 7 the **p**, and such as are left in this city from 5971
21: 8 unto this **p** thou shalt say, Thus saith 5971
22: 2 and thy **p** that enter in by these gates: 5971
22: 4 on horses, he, and his servants, and his **p**. 5971
23: 2 of Israel against the pastors that feed my **p**; 5971
23:13 in Baal, and caused my **p** Israel to err. 5971
23:22 had caused my **p** to hear my words, then 5971
23:27 Which think to cause my **p** to forget my 5971
23:32 cause my **p** to err by their lies, and by their 5971
23:32 therefore they shall not profit this **p** at all, 5971
23:33 And when this **p**, or the prophet, or a priest, 5971
23:34 and the priest, and the **p**, that shall say, 5971
24: 7 they shall be my **p**, and I will be their God: 5971
25: 1 **p** of Judah in the fourth year of Jehoiakim 5971
25: 2 the prophet spake unto all the **p** of Judah, 5971
25:19 his servants, and his princes, and all his **p**; 5971
25:20 all the **mingled p**, and all the kings of 6153
25:24 all the kings of the **mingled p** that dwell in 6153
26: 7 all the **p** heard Jeremiah speaking these 5971
26: 8 commanded *him* to speak unto all the **p**, 5971
26: 8 and the prophets and all the **p** took him, 5971
26: 9 all the **p** were gathered against Jeremiah in 5971
26:11 prophets unto the princes and to all the **p**, 5971
26:12 unto all the princes and to all the **p**, 5971
26:16 all the **p** unto the priests and to 5971
26:17 spake to all the assembly of the **p**, saying, 5971
26:18 spake to all the **p** of Judah, saying, 5971
26:23 body into the graves of the common **p**. 5971
26:24 into the hand of the **p** to put him to death. 5971
27:12 and serve him and his **p**, and live. 5971
27:13 thou and thy **p**, by the sword, by 5971
27:16 Also I spake to the priests and to all this **p**, 5971
28: 1 the presence of the priests and of all the **p**, 5971
28: 5 in the presence of all the **p** that stood in 5971
28: 7 in thine ears, and in the ears of all the **p**. 5971
28:11 Hananiah spake in the presence of all the **p**, 5971
28:15 but thou makest this **p** to trust in a lie. 5971
29: 1 to all the **p** whom Nebuchadnezzar had 5971
29:16 of all the **p** that dwelleth in this city, 5971
29:25 name unto all the **p** that *are* at Jerusalem, 5971
29:32 shall not have a man to dwell among this **p**; 5971
29:32 he behold the good that I will do for my **p**, 5971
30: 3 that I will bring again the captivity of my **p** 5971
30:22 ye shall be my **p**, and I will be your God. 5971
31: 1 families of Israel, and they shall be my **p**. 5971
31: 2 The **p** which were left of the sword found 5971
31: 7 praise ye, and say, O LORD, save thy **p**, 5971
31:14 my **p** shall be satisfied with my goodness, 5971
31:33 will be their God, and they shall be my **p**. 5971
32:21 hast brought forth thy **p** Israel out of 5971
32:38 they shall be my **p**, and I will be their God: 5971
32:42 have brought all this great evil upon this **p**, 5971
33:24 Considerest thou not what this **p** have 5971
33:24 thus they have despised my **p**, that *they* 5971
34: 1 all the **p**, fought against Jerusalem, and 5971
34: 8 with all the **p** which *were* at Jerusalem, 5971
34:10 *Now* when all the princes, and all the **p**, 5971
34:19 and the priests, and all the **p** of the land, 5971
35:16 but this **p** hath not hearkened unto me: 5971
36: 6 **p** *in* the LORD'S house upon the fasting 5971
36: 7 the LORD hath pronounced against this **p**. 5971
36: 9 before the LORD *to* all the **p** in Jerusalem, 5971
36: 9 *to* all the **p** that came from the cities of 5971
36:10 LORD'S house, in the ears of all the **p**. 5971
36:13 Baruch read the book in the ears of the **p**. 5971
36:14 wherein thou hast read in the ears of the **p**, 5971
37: 2 nor his servants, nor the **p** of the land, 5971
37: 4 came in and went out among the **p**: 5971
37:12 himself thence in the midst of the **p**. 5971
37:18 or against thy servants, or against this **p**, 5971
38: 1 that Jeremiah had spoken unto all the **p**, 5971
38: 4 the hands of all the **p**, in speaking such 5971
38: 4 this man seeketh not the welfare of this **p**, 5971
39: 8 the houses of the **p**, with fire, and brake 5971
39: 9 remnant of the **p** that remained in the city, 5971
39: 9 to him, with the rest of the **p** that remained. 5971
39:10 of the guard left of the poor of the **p**, 5971
39:14 carry him home: so he dwelt among the **p**. 5971
40: 5 of Judah, and dwell with him among the **p**: 5971
40: 6 dwelt with him among the **p** that were left 5971
41:10 all the residue of the **p** that *were* in Mizpah, 5971
41:10 and all the **p** that remained in Mizpah, 5971
41:13 *that* when all the **p** which *were* with 5971
41:14 So all the **p** that Ishmael had carried away 5971
41:16 all the remnant of the **p** whom he had 5971
42: 1 all the **p** from the least even unto 5971
42: 8 all the **p** from the least even to the greatest, 5971
43: 1 **p** all the words of the LORD their God, 5971
43: 4 all the captains of the forces, and all the **p**, 5971
44:15 even all the **p** that dwelt in the land of 5971
44:20 Jeremiah said unto all the **p**, to the men, 5971
44:20 to all the **p** which had given him *that* 5971
44:21 and your princes, and the **p** of the land, 5971
44:24 Moreover Jeremiah said unto all the **p**, and 5971
46:16 let us go again to our own **p**, and to 5971
46:24 she shall be delivered into the hand of the **p** 5971
48:42 Moab shall be destroyed from *being* a **p**, 5971
48:46 the **p** of Chemosh perisheth: for thy sons 5971
49: 1 inherit Gad, and his **p** dwell in his cities? 5971
50: 6 My **p** hath been lost sheep: their shepherds 5971
50:16 sword they shall turn every one to his **p**, 5971

Jer 50:37 upon all the mingled **p** that *are* in the midst 6153
50:41 a **p** shall come from the north, and a great 5971
51:45 My **p**, go ye out of the midst of her, and 5971
51:58 the **p** shall labour in vain, and the folk in 5971
52: 6 that there was no bread for the **p** of 5971
52:15 away captive *certain* of the poor of the **p**, 5971
52:15 the residue of the **p** that remained in 5971
52:25 of the host, who mustered the **p** of the land; 5971
52:25 threescore men of the **p** of the land, 5971
52:28 This *is* the **p** whom Nebuchadrezzar carried 5971
La 1: 1 doth the city sit solitary, *that was* full of **p**! 5971
1: 7 when her **p** fell into the hand of the enemy, 5971
1:11 All her **p** sigh, they seek bread; they have 5971
1:18 I pray you, all **p**, and behold my sorrow: 5971
2:11 for the destruction of the daughter of my **p**; 5971
3:14 I was a derision to all my **p**; *and* their song 5971
3:45 and refuse in the midst of the **p**. 5971
3:48 for the destruction of the daughter of my **p**. 5971
4: 3 the daughter of my **p** *is* become cruel, 5971
4: 6 **p** is greater than the punishment of the sin 5971
4:10 in the destruction of the daughter of my **p**. 5971
Eze 3: 5 For thou *art* not sent to a **p** of a strange 5971
3: 6 Not to many **p** of a strange speech and of a 5971
3:11 unto the children of thy **p**, and speak unto 5971
7:27 the hands of the **p** of the land shall be 5971
11: 1 the son of Benaiah, princes of the **p**. 5971
11:17 I will even gather you from the **p**, and 5971
11:20 they shall be my **p**, and I will be their God. 5971
12:19 say unto the **p** of the land, Thus saith 5971
13: 9 they shall not be in the assembly of my **p**, 5971
13:10 even because they have seduced my **p**, 5971
13:17 set thy face against the daughters of thy **p**, 5971
13:18 Will ye hunt the souls of my **p**, and will ye 5971
13:19 will ye pollute me among my **p** for 5971
13:19 by your lying to my **p** that hear *your* lies? 5971
13:21 deliver my **p** out of your hand, and 5971
13:23 for I will deliver my **p** out of your hand: 5971
14: 8 I will cut him off from the midst of my **p**; 5971
14: 9 will destroy him from the midst of my **p** 5971
14:11 that they may be my **p**, and I may be their 5971
17: 9 many **p** to pluck it up by the roots thereof. 5971
17:15 *they* might give him horses and much **p**. 5971
18:18 and did *that* which *is* not good among his **p**, 5971
20:34 I will bring you out from the **p**, and 5971
20:35 will bring you into the wilderness of the **p**, 5971
20:41 when I bring you out from the **p**, and 5971
21:12 for it shall be upon my **p**, it *shall be* upon 5971
21:12 by reason of the sword shall be upon my **p**: 5971
22:29 The **p** of the land have used oppression, 5971
23:24 and wheels, and with an assembly of **p**, 5971
24:18 So I spake unto the **p** in the morning: and 5971
24:19 the **p** said unto me, Wilt thou not tell us 5971
25: 7 I will cut thee off from the **p**, and I will 5971
25:14 upon Edom by the hand of my **p** Israel: 5971
26: 2 she is broken *that was* the gates of the **p**: 5971
26: 7 and companies, and much **p**. 5971
26:11 he shall slay thy **p** by the sword, and 5971
26:20 with the **p** of old time, and shall set thee in 5971
27: 3 *which art* a merchant of the **p** for many 5971
27:33 forth out of the seas, thou filledst many **p**; 5971
27:36 The merchants among the **p** shall hiss at 5971
28:19 All they that know thee among the **p** shall 5971
28:25 from the **p** among whom they are scattered, 5971
29:13 from the **p** whither they were scattered: 5971
30: 5 all the **mingled** **p**, and Chub, and the men 6153
30:11 He and his **p** with him, the terrible of 5971
31:12 all the **p** of the earth are gone down from 5971
32: 3 net over thee with a company of many **p**; 5971
32: 9 I will also vex the hearts of many **p**, when I 5971
32:10 I will make many **p** amazed at thee, and 5971
33: 2 speak to the children of thy **p**, and say unto 5971
33: 2 if the **p** of the land take a man of their 5971
33: 3 he blow the trumpet, and warn the **p**; 5971
33: 6 not the trumpet, and the **p** be not warned; 5971
33:12 son of man, say unto the children of thy **p**, 5971
33:17 Yet the children of thy **p** say, The way of 5971
33:30 the children of thy **p** still are talking against 5971
33:31 they come unto thee as the **p** cometh, and 5971
33:31 they sit before thee *as* my **p**, and they hear 5971
34:13 I will bring them out from the **p**, and 5971
34:30 of Israel, *are* my **p**, saith the Lord GOD. 5971
36: 3 lips of talkers, and *are* an infamy of the **p**: 5971
36: 8 and yield your fruit to my **p** of Israel; 5971
36:12 men to walk upon you, *even* my **p** Israel; 5971
36:15 neither shalt thou bear the reproach of the **p** 5971
36:20 These *are* the **p** of the LORD, and 5971
36:28 ye shall be my **p**, and I will be your God. 5971
37:12 Behold, O my **p**, I *will* open your graves, 5971
37:13 O my **p**, and brought you up out of your 5971
37:18 when the children of thy **p** shall speak unto 5971
37:23 so shall they be my **p**, and I will be their 5971
37:27 I will be their God, and they shall be my **p**. 5971
38: 6 and all his bands: *and* many **p** with thee. 5971
38: 8 *and is* gathered out of many **p**, against 5971
38: 9 and all thy bands, and many **p** with thee. 5971
38:12 upon the **p** *that are* gathered out of 5971
38:14 In that day when my **p** of Israel dwelleth 5971
38:15 thou, and many **p** with thee, all of them 5971
38:16 thou shalt come up against my **p** of Israel, 5971
38:22 and upon the many **p** that *are* with him, 5971
39: 4 all thy bands, and the **p** that *is* with thee: 5971
39: 7 name known in the midst of my **p** Israel; 5971
39:13 all the **p** of the land shall bury *them;* and 5971
39:27 I have brought them again from the **p**, 5971
42:14 to *those things* which *are* for the **p**. 5971
44:11 burnt offering and the sacrifice for the **p**, 5971
44:19 *even* into the utter court to the **p**, 5971
44:19 they shall not sanctify the **p** with their 5971
44:23 they shall teach my **p** *the difference* 5971
45: 8 my princes shall no more oppress my **p**; 5971
45: 9 take away your exactions from my **p**, 5971
45:16 All the **p** of the land shall give this oblation 5971
45:22 for all the **p** of the land a bullock *for* a sin 5971
46: 3 Likewise the **p** of the land shall worship *at* 5971
46: 9 when the **p** of the land shall come before 5971
Eze 46:18 that my **p** be not scattered every man from 5971
46:20 out into the utter court, to sanctify the **p**. 5971
46:24 of the house shall boil the sacrifice of the **p**. 5971
Da 2:44 and the kingdom shall not be left to other **p**, 5972
3: 4 O **p**, nations, and languages, 5972
3: 7 when all the **p** heard the sound of 5972
3: 7 all the **p**, the nations, and the languages, 5972
3:29 That every **p**, nation, and language, 5972
4: 1 unto all **p**, nations, and languages, that 5972
5:19 all **p**, nations, and languages, trembled 5972
6:25 king Darius wrote unto all **p**, nations, 5972
7:14 that all **p**, nations, and languages, 5972
7:27 *shall be* given to the **p** of the saints of 5972
8:24 and shall destroy the mighty and the holy **p**. 5971
9: 6 and our fathers, and to all the **p** of the land. 5971
9:15 that hast brought thy **p** forth out of the land 5971
9:16 thy **p** *are become* a reproach to all *that are* 5971
9:19 thy city and thy **p** are called by thy name. 5971
9:20 my sin and the sin of my **p** Israel, 5971
9:24 Seventy weeks are determined upon thy **p** 5971
9:26 the **p** of the prince that *shall* come shall 5971
10:14 what shall befall thy **p** in the latter days: 5971
11:14 also the robbers of thy **p** shall exalt 5971
11:15 shall not withstand, neither his chosen **p**, 5971
11:23 and shall become strong with a small **p**. 1471
11:32 the **p** that do know their God shall be 5971
11:33 they that understand among the **p** shall 5971
12: 1 which standeth for the children of thy **p**: 5971
12: 1 at that time thy **p** shall be delivered, 5971
12: 7 to scatter the power of the holy **p**, 5971
Hos 1: 9 for ye *are* not my **p**, and I will not be your 5971
1:10 Ye *are* not my **p**, *there* it shall be said unto 5971
2:23 I will say to *them which were* not my **p**, 5971
2:23 *which were* not my people, Thou *art* my **p**; 5971
4: 4 for thy **p** *are* as they that strive with 5971
4: 6 My **p** are destroyed for lack of knowledge, 5971
4: 8 They eat *up* the sin of my **p**, and they set 5971
4: 9 there shall be, like **p**, like priest: and I will 5971
4:12 My **p** ask *counsel* at their stocks, and 5971
4:14 the **p** *that* doth not understand shall fall. 5971
6:11 when I returned the captivity of my **p**. 5971
7: 8 he hath mixed himself among the **p**; 5971
9: 1 Rejoice not, O Israel, for joy, as *other* **p**: 5971
10: 5 for the **p** thereof shall mourn over it, and 5971
10:10 *the* **p** shall be gathered against them, 5971
10:14 Therefore shall a tumult arise among thy **p**, 5971
11: 7 my **p** are bent to backsliding from me: 5971
Joel 2: 2 a great **p** and a strong; there hath not been 5971
2: 5 the stubble, as a strong **p** set in battle array. 5971
2: 6 Before their face *the* **p** shall be much 5971
2:16 Gather the **p**, sanctify the congregation, 5971
2:17 Spare thy **p**, O LORD, and give not thine 5971
2:17 wherefore should they say among the **p**, 5971
2:18 be jealous for his land, and pity his **p**. 5971
2:19 the LORD will answer and say unto his **p**, 5971
2:26 and my **p** shall never be ashamed. 5971
2:27 and my **p** shall never be ashamed. 5971
3: 2 will plead with them there for my **p** and 5971
3: 3 they have cast lots for my **p**; and 5971
3: 8 sell them to the Sabeans, to a **p** far off: 1471
3:16 the LORD *will be* the hope of his **p**, and 5971
Am 1: 5 the **p** of Syria shall go into captivity unto 5971
3: 6 blown in the city, and the **p** not be afraid? 5971
7: 8 I *will* set a plumbline in the midst of my **p** 5971
7:15 unto me, Go, prophesy unto my **p** Israel. 5971
8: 2 The end is come upon my **p** *of* Israel; 5971
9:10 All the sinners of my **p** shall die by 5971
9:14 I will bring again the captivity of my **p** of 5971
Ob 1:13 gate of my **p** in the day of their calamity: 5971
Jnh 1: 8 *is* thy country? and of what **p** *art* thou? 5971
3: 5 So the **p** of Nineveh believed God, and 376
Mic 1: 2 Hear, all ye **p**; hearken, O earth, and all that 5971
1: 9 he is come unto the gate of my **p**, *even* to 5971
2: 4 he hath changed the portion of my **p**: 5971
2: 8 Even of late my **p** is risen up as an enemy: 5971
2: 9 The women of my **p** have ye cast out from 5971
2:11 he shall even be the prophet of this **p**. 5971
3: 3 Who also eat the flesh of my **p**, and 5971
3: 5 the prophets that make my **p** err, 5971
4: 1 above the hills; and **p** shall flow unto it. 5971
4: 3 he shall judge among many **p**, and 5971
4: 5 For all **p** will walk every one in the name 5971
4:13 thou shalt beat in pieces many **p**: and I will 5971
5: 7 of many **p** as a dew from the LORD, 5971
5: 8 **p** as a lion among the beasts of the forest, 5971
6: 2 the LORD hath a controversy with his **p**, 5971
6: 3 O my **p**, what have I done unto thee? and 5971
6: 5 O my **p**, remember now what Balak king of 5971
6:16 ye shall bear the reproach of my **p**. 5971
7:14 Feed thy **p** with thy rod, the flock of thine 5971
Na 3:13 thy **p** in the midst of thee *are* women: 5971
3:18 thy nobles shall dwell *in the dust:* thy **p** is 5971
Hab 2: 5 him all nations, and heapeth unto him all **p**: 5971
2: 8 all the remnant of the **p** shall spoil thee; 5971
2:10 shame to thy house by cutting off many **p**, 5971
2:13 *is it* not of the LORD of hosts that the **p** 5971
2:13 the **p** shall weary themselves for very 3816
3:13 wentest forth for the salvation of thy **p**, 5971
3:16 when *he* cometh up unto the **p**, he will 5971
Zep 1:11 for all the merchant **p** are cut down; 5971
2: 8 whereby they have reproached my **p**, and 5971
2: 9 the residue of my **p** shall spoil them, and 5971
2: 9 the remnant of my **p** shall possess them. 1471
2:10 magnified *themselves* against the **p** of 5971
3: 9 then will I turn to the **p** a pure language, 5971
3:12 in the midst of thee an afflicted and poor **p**, 5971
3:20 and a praise among all **p** of the earth, 5971
Hag 1: 2 This **p** say, The time is not come, 5971
1:12 high priest, with all the remnant of the **p**, 5971
1:12 and the **p** did fear before the LORD. 5971
1:13 in the LORD'S message unto the **p**, 5971
1:14 and the spirit of all the remnant of the **p**; 5971
2: 2 the high priest and to the residue of the **p**, 5971
2: 4 be strong, all ye **p** of the land, saith 5971
2:14 So *is* this **p**, and so *is* this nation before me, 5971
Zec 2:11 the LORD in that day, and shall be my **p**: 5971
7: 5 Speak unto all the **p** of the land, and to 5971
8: 6 eyes of the remnant of this **p** in these days, 5971
8: 7 I *will* save my **p** from the east country, and 5971
8: 8 they shall be my **p**, and I will be their God, 5971
8:11 now I *will* not *be* unto the residue of this **p** 5971
8:12 I will cause the remnant of this **p** to 5971
8:20 yet *come to pass,* that there shall come **p**, 5971
8:22 many **p** and strong nations shall come to 5971
9:16 save them in that day as the flock of his **p**: 5971
10: 9 I will sow them among the **p**: and they shall 5971
11:10 covenant which I had made with all the **p**. 5971
12: 2 cup of trembling unto all the **p** round about, 5971
12: 3 Jerusalem a burdensome stone for all **p**: 5971
12: 3 though all the **p** of the earth be gathered 1471
12: 4 will smite every horse of the **p** with 5971
12: 6 they shall devour all the **p** round about, 5971
13: 9 I will say, It *is* my **p**: and they shall say, 5971
14: 2 the residue of the **p** shall not be cut off 5971
14:12 the **p** that have fought against Jerusalem; 5971
Mal 1: 4 The **p** *against* whom the LORD hath 5971
2: 9 you contemptible and base before all the **p**, 5971
Mt 1:21 for he shall save his **p** from their sins. *2992*
2: 4 chief priests and scribes of the **p** together, *2992*
2: 6 a Governor, that shall rule my **p** Israel. *2992*
4:16 The **p** which sat in darkness saw great *2992*
4:23 and all *manner of* disease among the **p**. *2992*
4:24 they brought unto him all **sick** **p** that *2192+2560*
4:25 him great multitudes *of* **p** from Galilee, NIG
7:28 the **p** were astonished at his doctrine: *3793*
9:23 saw the minstrels and the **p** making a noise, *3793*
9:25 But when the **p** were put forth, he went in, *3793*
9:35 and every disease among the **p**. *2992*
12:23 And all the **p** were amazed, and said, Is this *3793*
12:46 While he yet talked to the **p**, behold, *3793*
14:13 when the **p** had heard *thereof,* they *3793*
15: 8 This **p** draweth nigh unto me with their *2992*
21:23 the elders of the **p** came unto him as he was *2992*
21:26 But if we shall say, Of men; we fear the **p**; *3793*
26: 3 and the scribes, and the elders of the **p**, *2992*
26: 5 *day,* lest there be an uproar among the **p**. *2992*
26:47 from the chief priests and elders of the **p**. *2992*
27: 1 elders of the **p** took counsel against Jesus to *2992*
27:15 was wont to release unto the **p** a prisoner, *3793*
27:25 Then answered all the **p**, and said, *2992*
27:64 and steal him *away,* and say unto the **p**, *2992*
Mk 5:21 the other side, much **p** gathered unto him: *3793*
5:24 and much **p** followed him, and *3793*
6:33 And the **p** saw them departing, and *3793*
6:34 saw much **p**, and was moved with *3793*
6:45 unto Bethsaida, while he sent away the **p**. *3793*
7: 6 This **p** honoureth me with *their* lips, but *2992*
7:14 And when he had called all the **p** unto *him,* *3793*
7:17 he was entered into *the* house from the **p**, *3793*
8: 6 And he commanded the **p** to sit down on *3793*
8: 6 and they did set *them* before the **p**. *3793*
8:34 And when he had called the **p** unto *him* *3793*
9:15 And straightway all the **p**, when they *3793*
9:25 When Jesus saw that the **p** came running *3793*
10: 1 and the **p** resort unto him again; and, as he *3793*
10:46 with his disciples and a great number of **p**, *3793*
11:18 all the **p** was astonished at his doctrine. *3793*
11:32 if we shall say, Of men; they feared the **p**: *2992*
12:12 sought to lay hold on him, but feared the **p**: *3793*
12:37 And the common **p** heard him gladly. *3793*
12:41 beheld how the **p** cast money into *3793*
14: 2 feast *day,* lest there be an uproar of the **p**. *2992*
15:11 But the chief priests moved the **p**, that he *3793*
15:15 And *so* Pilate, willing to content the **p**, *3793*
Lk 1:10 And the whole multitude of the **p** were *2992*
1:17 to make ready a **p** prepared for the Lord. *2992*
1:21 And the **p** waited for Zacharias, and *2992*
1:68 for he hath visited and redeemed his **p**, *2992*
1:77 To give knowledge of salvation unto his **p** *2992*
2:10 tidings of great joy, which shall be to all **p**. *2992*
2:31 thou hast prepared before the face of all **p**; *2992*
2:32 the Gentiles, and the glory of thy **p** Israel. *2992*
3:10 And the **p** asked him, saying, What shall *3793*
3:15 And as the **p** were in expectation, and *2992*
3:18 in his exhortation preached he unto the **p**. *2992*
3:21 Now when all the **p** were baptized, it came *2992*
4:42 and the **p** sought him, and came unto him, *3793*
5: 1 as the **p** pressed upon him to hear the word *3793*
5: 3 sat down, and taught the **p** out of the ship. *3793*
6:17 a great multitude of **p** out of all Judea and *2992*
7: 1 all his sayings in the audience of the **p**, *2992*
7: 9 and said unto the **p** that followed him, *3793*
7:11 of his disciples went with him, and much **p**. *3793*
7:12 and much **p** of the city was with her. *3793*
7:16 among us; and, That God hath visited his **p**. *2992*
7:24 he began to speak unto the **p** concerning *3793*
7:29 And all the **p** that heard *him,* and *2992*
8: 4 And when much **p** were gathered together, *3793*
8:40 was returned, the **p** gladly received him: *3793*
8:42 (But as he went the **p** thronged him. *3793*
8:47 she declared unto him before all the **p** for *2992*
9:11 And the **p**, when they knew *it,* followed *3793*
9:13 we should go and buy meat for all this **p**. *2992*
9:18 saying, Whom say the **p** that I am? *3793*
9:37 come down from the hill, much **p** met him. *3793*
11:14 the dumb spake; and the **p** wondered. *3793*
11:29 And when the **p** were gathered thick *3793*
12: 1 together an innumerable multitude of **p**, *3793*
12:54 And he said also to the **p**, When ye see a *3793*
13:14 on the sabbath day, and said unto the **p**, *3793*
13:17 all the **p** rejoiced for all the glorious *things* *3793*
18:43 and all the **p**, when they saw *it,* gave praise *2992*
19:47 the chief of the **p** sought to destroy him, *2992*
19:48 for all the **p** were very attentive to hear *2992*
20: 1 as he taught the **p** in the temple, and *2992*
20: 6 if we say, Of men; all the **p** will stone us: *2992*
20: 9 Then began he to speak to the **p** this *2992*
20:19 to lay hands on him; and they feared the **p**: *2992*
20:26 not take hold of his words before the **p**: *2992*
20:45 Then in the audience of all the **p** he said *2992*

Lk 21:23 distress in the land, and wrath upon this **p**. 2992
21:38 And all the **p** came early in the morning to 2992
22: 2 they might kill him; for they feared the **p**. 2992
22:66 the elders of the **p** and the chief priests and 2992
23: 4 said Pilate to the chief priests and *to* the **p**, 3793
23: 5 saying, He stirreth up the **p**, 2992
23:13 the chief priests and the rulers and the **p**, 2992
23:14 man unto me, as one that perverteth the **p**: 2992
23:27 there followed him a great company of **p**, 2992
23:35 And the **p** stood beholding. And the rulers 2992
23:48 And all the **p** that came together to that 3793
24:19 in deed and word before God and all the **p**: 2992
Jn 6:22 when the **p** which stood on the other side of 3793
6:24 When the **p** therefore saw that Jesus was 3793
7:12 murmuring among the **p** concerning him: 3793
7:12 others said, Nay; but he deceiveth the **p**. 3793
7:20 The **p** answered and said, Thou hast a 3793
7:31 And many of the **p** believed on him, and 3793
7:32 The Pharisees heard that the **p** murmured 3793
7:40 Many of the **p** therefore, when they heard 3793
7:43 So there was a division among the **p** 3793
7:49 But this **p** who knoweth not the law are 3793
8: 2 the temple, and all the **p** came unto him; 2992
11:42 of the **p** which stand by I said *it*, that they 3793
11:50 that one man should die for the **p**, and 2992
12: 9 Much **p** of the Jews therefore knew that he 3793
12:12 On the next day much **p** that were come to 3793
12:17 The **p** therefore that was with him when he 3793
12:18 For this cause the **p** also met him, for that 3793
12:29 The **p** therefore, that stood *by*, and heard *it*, 3793
12:34 The **p** answered him, We have heard out of 3793
18:14 that one man should die for the **p**. 2992
Ac 2:47 and having favour with all the **p**. 2992
3: 9 And all the **p** saw him walking and 2992
3:11 all the **p** ran together unto them in 2992
3:12 when Peter saw *it*, he answered unto the **p**, 2992
3:23 shall be destroyed from among the **p**. 2992
4: 1 And as they spake unto the **p**, the priests, 2992
4: 2 Being grieved that they taught the **p**, and 2992
4: 8 Ye rulers of the **p**, and elders of Israel, 2992
4:10 unto you all, and to all the **p** of Israel, 2992
4:17 But that it spread no further among the **p**, 2992
4:21 they might punish them, because of the **p**: 2992
4:25 and the **p** imagine vain *things?* 2992
4:27 with the Gentiles, and the **p** of Israel, 2992
5:12 and wonders wrought among the **p**; 2992
5:13 himself to them: but the **p** magnified them. 2992
5:20 speak in the temple to the **p** all the words of 2992
5:25 standing in the temple, and teaching the **p**. 2992
5:26 for they feared the **p**, lest they should have 2992
5:34 had in reputation among all the **p**, and 2992
5:37 and drew away much **p** after him: 2992
6: 8 great wonders and miracles among the **p**. 2992
6:12 And they stirred up the **p**, and the elders, 2992
7:17 the **p** grew and multiplied in Egypt, 2992
7:34 I have seen the affliction of my **p** which is 2992
8: 6 And the **p** with one accord gave heed unto 3793
8: 9 and bewitched the **p** of Samaria, giving out 1484
10: 2 which gave much alms to the **p**, and 2992
10:41 Not to all the **p**, but unto witnesses chosen 2992
10:42 he commanded us to preach unto the **p**, 2992
11:24 and much **p** was added unto the Lord. 3793
11:26 and taught much **p**, and the disciples were 3793
12: 4 after Easter to bring him forth to the **p**. 2992
12:11 *from* all the expectation of the **p** of 2992
12:22 And the **p** gave a shout, *saying, It is* 1218
13:15 ye have *any* word of exhortation for the **p**, 2992
13:17 The God of this **p** of Israel chose our 2992
13:17 exalted the **p** when *they* dwelt as strangers 2992
13:24 baptism of repentance to all the **p** of Israel. 2992
13:31 who are his witnesses unto the **p**. 2992
14:11 And when the **p** saw what Paul had done, 3793
14:13 and would have done sacrifice with the **p**. 3793
14:14 and ran in among the **p**, crying out, 3793
14:18 these sayings scarce restrained they the **p**, 3793
14:19 and Iconium, who persuaded the **p**, and, 3793
15:14 to take out of them a **p** for his name. 2992
17: 5 and sought to bring them out to the **p**. 1218
17: 8 And they troubled the **p** and the rulers of 3793
17:13 they came thither also, and stirred up the **p**. 3793
18:10 to hurt thee: for I have much **p** in this city. 2992
19: 4 baptism of repentance, saying unto the **p**, 2992
19:26 hath persuaded and turned away much **p**, 3793
19:30 Paul would have entered in unto the **p**, 1218
19:33 would have made *his* defence unto the **p**. 1218
19:35 when the townclerk had appeased the **p**, 3793
21:27 stirred up all the **p**, and laid hands on him, 3793
21:28 teacheth all *men* every where against the **p**, 2992
21:30 the city was moved, and the **p** ran together: 2992
21:35 of the soldiers for the violence of the **p**. 3793
21:36 For the multitude of the **p** followed *after*, 2992
21:39 beseech thee, suffer me to speak unto the **p**. 2992
21:40 and beckoned with the hand unto the **p**. 2992
23: 5 shalt not speak evil of the ruler of thy **p**. 2992
24:12 with any *man*, neither raising up the **p**, 3793
26:17 Delivering thee from the **p**, and *from* 2992
26:23 and should shew light unto the **p**, and to 2992
28: 2 And the **barbarous p** shewed us no little 915
28:17 I have committed nothing against the **p**, 2992
28:26 Saying, Go unto this **p**, and say, Hearing ye 2992
28:27 For the heart of this **p** is waxed gross, and 2992
Ro 9:25 he saith also in Osee, I will call *them* my **p**, 2992
9:25 call *them* my people, which were not my **p**; 2992
9:26 it was said unto them, Ye *are* not my **p**; 2992
10:19 you to jealousy by *them that are* no **p**, 1484
10:21 hands unto a disobedient and gainsaying **p**. 2992
11: 1 I say then, Hath God cast away his **p**? 2992
11: 2 God hath not cast away his **p** which he 2992
15:10 *he* saith, Rejoice, *ye* Gentiles, with his **p**. 2992
15:11 all ye Gentiles; and laud him, all ye **p**. 2992
1Co 10: 7 The **p** sat down to eat and drink, and 2992
14:21 and other lips will I speak unto this **p**; 2992
2Co 6:16 I will be their God, and they shall be my **p**. 2992
Tit 2:14 and purify unto himself a peculiar **p**, 2992
Heb 2:17 to make reconciliation for the sins of the **p**. 2992
4: 9 therefore a rest to the **p** of God. 2992
5: 3 as for the **p**, so also for himself, to offer for 2992
7: 5 to take tithes of the **p** according to the law, 2992
7:11 (for under it the **p** received the law,) 2992
8:10 to them a God, and they shall be to me a **p**: 2992
9: 7 for himself, and *for* the errors of the **p**: 2992
9:19 precept to all the **p** according to the law, 2992
9:19 and sprinkled both the book, and all the **p**, 2992
10:30 And again, The Lord shall judge his **p**. 2992
11:25 rather to suffer affliction with the **p** of God, 2992
13:12 that he might sanctify the **p** with his own 2992
1Pe 2: 9 a holy nation, a peculiar **p**; 2992
2:10 Which in time past *were* not a **p**, but 2992
2:10 not a people, but *are* now the **p** of God: 2992
2Pe 2: 1 there were false prophets also among the **p**, 2992
Jude 1: 5 having saved the **p** out of the land of Egypt, 2992
Rev 5: 9 and tongue, and **p**, and nation; 2992
7: 9 and kindreds, and **p**, and tongues, 2992
11: 9 And *they* of the **p** and kindreds and tongues 2992
14: 6 and kindred, and tongue, and **p**, 2992
18: 4 saying, Come out of her, my **p**, that ye be 2992
19: 1 I heard a great voice of much **p** in heaven, 3793
21: 3 and they shall be his **p**, and God himself 2992

PEOPLE'S (4) [PEOPLE]

Lev 9:15 he brought the **p** offering, and took 5971
Eze 46:18 Moreover the prince shall not take of the **p** 5971
Mt 13:15 For this **p** heart is waxed gross, and *their* 2992
Heb 7:27 first for his own sins, *and* then for the **p**: 2992

PEOPLES (2) [PEOPLE]

Rev 10:11 Thou must prophesy again before many **p**, 2992
17:15 are **p**, and multitudes, and nations, and 2992

PEOR (4) [BAAL-PEOR, BETH-PEOR, PEOR'S, PERADVENTURE]

Nu 23:28 Balak brought Balaam *unto* the top of **P**, 6465
25:18 they have beguiled you in the matter of **P**, 6465
31:16 against the LORD in the matter of **P**, 6465
Jos 22:17 *Is* the iniquity of **P** *too* little for us, from 6465

PEOR'S (1) [PEOR]

Nu 25:18 slain in the day of the plague for **P** sake. 6465

PERADVENTURE (32) [PEOR]

Ge 18:24 **P** there be fifty righteous within the city: 194
18:28 **P** there shall lack five of the fifty righteous: 194
18:29 said, **P** there shall be forty found there. 194
18:30 **P** there shall thirty be found there. And he 194
18:31 **P** there shall be twenty found there. And he 194
18:32 **P** ten shall be found there. And he said, 194
24: 5 **P** the woman will not be willing to follow 194
24:39 my master, **P** the woman will not follow me. 194
27:12 My father **p** will feel me, and I shall seem to 194
31:31 **P** thou wouldest take by force thy 6435
32:20 I will see his face; **p** he will accept of me. 194
38:11 for he said, **Lest p** he die also, as his 6435
42: 4 for he said, **Lest p** mischief befall him. 6435
43:12 *it* again in your hand; **p** it *was* an oversight: 194
44:34 **lest p** I see the evil that shall come on my 6435
50:15 Joseph will **p** hate us, and will certainly 3863
Ex 13:17 **Lest p** the people repent when they see 6435
32:30 **p** I shall make an atonement for your sin. 194
Nu 22: 6 **p** I shall prevail, *that* we may smite them, 194
22:11 **p** I shall be able to overcome them, and 194
23: 3 **p** the LORD will come to meet me: and 194
23:27 **p** it will please God that thou mayest curse 194
Jos 9: 7 said unto the Hivites, **P** ye dwell among us; 194
1Sa 6: 5 **p** he will lighten his hand from off you, and 194
9: 6 **p** he can shew us our way that we should go. 194
1Ki 18: 5 **p** we may find grass to save the horses and 194
18:27 *or* **p** he sleepeth, and must be awaked. 194
20:31 to the king of Israel: **p** he will save thy life. 194
2Ki 2:16 **lest p** the spirit of the LORD hath taken 6435
Jer 20:10 *saying*, **P** he will be enticed, and we shall 194
Ro 5: 7 yet **p** for a good *man* some would even dare 5029
2Ti 2:25 **if** God **p** will give them repentance to 3379

PERAZIM (1) [BAAL-PERAZIM]

Isa 28:21 For the LORD shall rise up as *in* mount **P**, 6559

PERCEIVE (25) [PERCEIVED, PERCEIVEST, PERCEIVETH, PERCEIVING]

Dt 29: 4 the LORD hath not given you a heart to **p**, 3045
Jos 22:31 *This* day we **p** that the LORD *is* among 3045
1Sa 12:17 that ye may **p** and see that your wickedness 3045
2Sa 19: 6 for *this* day I **p**, that if Absalom had lived, 3045
2Ki 4: 9 I **p** that this *is* a holy man of God, 3045
Job 9:11 *him* not: he passeth on also, but I **p** him not. 995
23: 8 not *there;* and backward, but I cannot **p** him: 995
Pr 1: 2 instruction; to **p** the words of understanding; 995
Ecc 3:22 Wherefore I **p** that *there is* nothing better, 7200
Isa 6: 9 and see ye indeed, but **p** not. 3045
33:19 of a deeper speech than *thou* canst **p**; 8085
Mt 13:14 and seeing ye shall see, and shall not **p**: 1492
Mk 4:12 That seeing they may see, and not **p**; and 1492
7:18 Do ye not **p**, that whatsoever *thing* from 3539
8:17 **p** ye not yet, neither understand? have ye 3539
Lk 8:46 for I **p** that virtue is gone out of me. 1097
Jn 4:19 unto him, Sir, I **p** that thou art a prophet. 2334
12:19 **P** ye how ye prevail nothing? 2334
Ac 8:23 For I **p** that thou art in the gall of bitterness, 3708
10:34 Of a truth I **p** that God is no respecter of 2638
17:22 I **p** that in all *things* ye are too 2334
27:10 I **p** that *this* voyage will be with hurt and 2334
28:26 and seeing ye shall see, and not **p**: 1492
2Co 7: 8 for I **p** that the same epistle hath made you 991
1Jn 3:16 Hereby **p** we the love *of God*, because 1097

PERCEIVED (35) [PERCEIVE]

Ge 19:33 he **p** not when she lay down, nor when she 3045
19:35 he **p** not when she lay down, nor when she 3045
Jdg 6:22 when Gideon **p** that he *was* an angel of 7200
1Sa 3: 8 Eli **p** that the LORD had called the child. 995
28:14 Saul **p** that it *was* Samuel, and he stooped 3045
2Sa 5:12 David **p** that the LORD had established 3045
12:19 David **p** that the child was dead: 995
14: 1 Now Joab the son of Zeruiah **p** that 3045
1Ki 22:33 when the captains of the chariots **p** that it 7200
1Ch 14: 2 David **p** that the LORD had confirmed 3045
2Ch 18:32 that when the captains of the chariots **p** that 7200
Ne 6:12 lo, I **p** that God had not sent him; but 5234
6:16 for they **p** that this work was wrought of 3045
13:10 I **p** that the portions of the Levites had not 3045
Est 4: 1 When Mordecai **p** all that was done, 3045
Job 38:18 Hast thou **p** the breadth of the earth? 995
Ecc 1:17 folly: I **p** that this also *is* vexation of spirit. 3045
2:14 I myself **p** also that one event happeneth to 3045
Isa 64: 4 nor **p by the ear**, neither hath the eye seen, 238
Jer 23:18 and hath **p** and heard his word? 7200
38:27 with him; for the matter was not **p**. 8085
Mt 16: 8 *Which* when Jesus **p**, he said unto them, 1097
21:45 his parables, they **p** that he spake of them. 1097
22:18 But Jesus **p** their wickedness, and said, 1097
Mk 2: 8 when Jesus **p** in his spirit that they so 1921
Lk 1:22 they **p** that he had seen a vision in 1921
5:22 But when Jesus **p** their thoughts, 1921
9:45 and it was hid from them, that they **p** it not: 143
20:19 for they **p** that he had spoken this parable 1097
20:23 But he **p** their craftiness, and said unto 2657
Jn 6:15 therefore **p** that they would come and 1097
Ac 4:13 and **p** that they were unlearned and 2638
23: 6 But when Paul **p** that the one part were 1097
23:29 Whom I **p** to be accused of questions of 2147
Gal 2: 9 **p** the grace that was given unto me, 1097

PERCEIVEST (2) [PERCEIVE]

Pr 14: 7 when thou **p** not *in him* the lips of 3045
Lk 6:41 but **p** not the beam that is in thine own eye? 2657

PERCEIVETH (3) [PERCEIVE]

Job 14:21 they are brought low, but he **p** *it* not of them. 995
33:14 speaketh once, yea twice, *yet man* **p** it not. 7789
Pr 31:18 She **p** that her merchandise *is* good: 2938

PERCEIVING (3) [PERCEIVE]

Mk 12:28 and **p** that he had answered them well, 1492
Lk 9:47 And Jesus, **p** the thought of their heart, 1492
Ac 14: 9 and **p** that he had faith to be healed, 1492

PERDITION (8)

Jn 17:12 and none of them is lost, but the son of **p**; 684
Php 1:28 which is to them an evident token of **p**, but 684
2Th 2: 3 and *that* man of sin be revealed, the son of **p**; 684
1Ti 6: 9 which drown men in destruction and **p**. 684
Heb 10:39 we are not of *them* who draw back unto **p**; 684
2Pe 3: 7 the day of judgment and **p** of ungodly men. 684
Rev 17: 8 out of the bottomless *pit*, and go into **p**: 684
17:11 and is of the seven, and goeth into **p**. 684

PERES (1)

Da 5:28 **P**; Thy kingdom is divided, and given to 6537

PERESH (1)

1Ch 7:16 bare a son, and she called his name **P**; 6570

PEREZ (3)

1Ch 27: 3 Of the children of **P** *was* the chief of all 6557
Ne 11: 4 the son of Mahalaleel, of the children of **P**; 6557
11: 6 All the sons of **P** that dwelt at Jerusalem 6557

PEREZITE See PHARZITES

PEREZ-UZZA (1) [PEREZ-UZZAH, UZZAH]

1Ch 13:11 wherefore that place is called **P** to this day. 6560

PEREZ-UZZAH (1) [PEREZ-UZZA, UZZAH]

2Sa 6: 8 he called *the name* of the place **P** to this 6560

PERFECT (99) [PERFECTED, PERFECTING, PERFECTION, PERFECTLY, PERFECTNESS, UNPERFECT]

Ge 6: 9 was a just man *and* **p** in his generations, 8549
17: 1 walk before me, and be thou **p**. 8549
Lev 22:21 or sheep, it shall be **p** to be accepted; 8549
Dt 18:13 Thou shalt be **p** with the LORD thy God. 8549
25:15 *But* thou shalt have a **p** and just weight, 8003
25:15 a **p** and just measure shalt thou have: 8003
32: 4 *He is* the Rock, his work *is* **p**: for all his 8549
1Sa 14:41 Give a **p** *lot*. And Saul and Jonathan were 8549
2Sa 22:31 *As for* God, his way *is* **p**; the word of 8549
22:33 *and* power: and he maketh my way **p**. 8549
1Ki 8:61 therefore be **p** with the LORD our God, 8003
11: 4 his heart was not **p** with the LORD his 8003
15: 3 his heart was not **p** with the LORD his 8003
15:14 nevertheless Asa's heart was **p** with 8003
2Ki 20: 3 before thee in truth and with a **p** heart, 8003
1Ch 12:38 keep rank, came with a **p** heart to Hebron, 8003
28: 9 serve him with a **p** heart and with a willing 8003
29: 9 with **p** heart they offered willingly to 8003
29:19 give unto Solomon my son a **p** heart, 8003
2Ch 4:21 the tongs, *made he of* gold, *and* that **p** gold; 4357
15:17 nevertheless the heart of Asa was **p** all his 8003
16: 9 of *them* whose heart *is* **p** towards him. 8003
19: 9 the LORD, faithfully, and with a **p** heart. 8003
25: 2 sight of the LORD, but not with a **p** heart. 8003
Ezr 7:12 God of heaven, **p** *peace*, and at such a time. 1585
Job 1: 1 that man was **p** and upright, and one that 8535
1: 8 a **p** and an upright man, one that feareth 8535
2: 3 a **p** and an upright man, one that feareth 8535
8:20 God will not cast away a **p** *man*, neither 8535
9:20 *if I say*, I *am* **p**, it shall also prove me 8535
9:21 *Though* I *were* **p**, *yet* would I not know my 8535
9:22 therefore I said *it*, He destroyeth the **p** and 8535
22: 3 gain *to him*, that thou **makest** thy ways **p**? 8552
36: 4 *he that is* **p** in knowledge *is* with thee. 8549
37:16 the wondrous works of *him which is* **p** in 8549

P

Ps 18:30 As for God, his way is p: the word of 8549
18:32 me with strength, and maketh my way p. 8549
19: 7 The law of the LORD is p, converting 8549
37:37 Mark the p man, and behold the upright: 8535
64: 4 That they may shoot in secret at the p: 8535
101: 2 I will behave myself wisely in a p way. 8549
101: 2 I will walk within my house with a p heart. 8537
101: 6 he that walketh in a p way, he shall serve 8549
138: 8 The LORD will p that which concerneth 1584
139:22 I hate them with p hatred: I count them 8503
Pr 2:21 in the land, and the p shall remain in it. 8549
4:18 that shineth more and more unto the p day. 3559
11: 5 The righteousness of the p shall direct his 8549
Isa 18: 5 when the bud is p, and the sour grape is 8552
26: 3 Thou wilt keep him in p peace, 7965+7965
38: 3 before thee in truth and with a p heart, 8003
42:19 who is blind as he that is p, and blind as 7999
Eze 16:14 for it was p through my comeliness, 3632
27: 3 O Tyrus, thou hast said, I am of p beauty. 3632
27:11 round about; they have made thy beauty p. 3634
28:12 the sum, full of wisdom, and p in beauty. 3632
28:15 Thou wast p in thy ways from the day that 8549
Mt 5:48 Be ye therefore p, even as your Father 5046
5:48 even as your Father which is in heaven is p. 5046
19:21 If thou wilt be p, go and sell that thou hast, 5046
Lk 1: 3 having had p understanding of all things 199
6:40 every one that is p shall be as his master. 2675
Jn 17:23 in me, that they may be made p in one; 5048
Ac 3:16 this p soundness in the presence of you all. 3647
22: 3 taught according to the p manner of the law 195
24:22 having more p knowledge of that way, 197
Ro 12: 2 and acceptable, and p, will of God. 5046
1Co 2: 6 we speak wisdom among them that are p: 5046
13:10 But when that which is p is come, then 5046
2Co 12: 9 for my strength is made p in weakness. 5048
13:11 Be p, be of good comfort, be of one mind, 2675
Gal 3: 3 the Spirit, are ye now made p by the flesh? 2005
Eph 4:13 of the Son of God, unto a p man, 5046
Php 3:12 had already attained, either were already p: 5048
3:15 as many as be p, be thus minded: 5046
Col 1:28 that we may present every man p in Christ 5046
4:12 that ye may stand p and complete in all 5046
1Th 3:10 might p that which is lacking in your faith? 2675
2Ti 3:17 That the man of God may be p, 739
Heb 2:10 to make the captain of their salvation p 5048
5: 9 And being made p, he became the author 5048
7:19 For the law made nothing p, but 5048
9: 9 could not make him that did the service p, 5048
9:11 by a greater and more p tabernacle, 5046
10: 1 continually make the comers thereunto p. 5048
11:40 that they without us should not be made p. 5048
12:23 and to the spirits of just men made p, 5048
13:21 Make you p in every good work to do his 2675
Jas 1: 4 But let patience have her p work, that ye 5046
1: 4 that ye may be p and entire, 5046
1:17 good gift and every p gift is from above, 5046
1:25 But whoso looketh into the p law of liberty, 5046
2:22 his works, and by works was faith made p? 5048
3: 2 the same is a p man, and able also to bridle 5046
1Pe 5:10 make you p, stablish, strengthen, 2675
1Jn 4:17 Herein is our love made p, that we may 5048
4:18 no fear in love; but p love casteth out fear: 5046
4:18 He that feareth is not made p in love. 5048
Rev 3: 2 for I have not found thy works p before 4137

PERFECTED (8) [PERFECT]
2Ch 8:16 So the house of the LORD was p. 8003
24:13 the work was p by them, and they set 724+5927
Eze 27: 4 of the seas, thy builders have p thy beauty. 3634
Mt 21:16 of babes and sucklings thou hast p praise? 2675
Lk 13:32 to morrow, and the third day I shall be p. 5048
Heb 10:14 For by one offering he hath p for ever them 5048
1Jn 2: 5 in him verily is the love of God p: 5048
4:12 God dwelleth in us, and his love is p in us. 5048

PERFECTING (2) [PERFECT]
2Co 7: 1 and spirit, p holiness in the fear of God. 2005
Eph 4:12 For the p of the saints for the work of 2677

PERFECTION (11) [PERFECT]
Job 11: 7 canst thou find out the Almighty unto p? 8503
15:29 neither shall he prolong the p thereof upon 4512
28: 3 searcheth out all p, the stones of darkness, 8503
Ps 50: 2 Out of Zion, the p of beauty, God hath 4359
119:96 I have seen an end of all p: but 8502
Isa 47: 9 they shall come upon thee in their p for 8537
La 2:15 saying, Is this the city that men call The p 3632
Lk 8:14 of this life, and bring no fruit to p. 5052
2Co 13: 9 and this also we wish, even your p. 2676
Heb 6: 1 the doctrine of Christ, let us go on unto p; 5047
7:11 p were by the Levitical priesthood, 5050

PERFECTLY (7) [PERFECT]
Jer 23:20 in the latter days ye shall consider it p. 995+998
Mt 14:36 as many as touched were made p whole. 1295
Ac 18:26 unto him the way of God more p. 197
23:15 inquire something more p concerning him: 197
23:20 would inquire somewhat of him more p. 197
1Co 1:10 that ye be p joined together in the same 2675
1Th 5: 2 For yourselves know p that the day of 199

PERFECTNESS (1) [PERFECT]
Col 3:14 put on charity, which is the bond of p. 5047

PERFORM (42) [PERFORMANCE, PERFORMED, PERFORMETH, PERFORMING]
Ge 26: 3 I will p the oath which I sware unto 6965
Ex 18:18 thou art not able to p it thyself alone. 6213
Nu 4:23 all that enter in to p the service, to 6633+6635
Dt 4:13 which he commanded you to p, even ten 6213
9: 5 that he may p the word which the LORD 6965
23:23 gone out of thy lips thou shalt keep and p; 6213
25: 5 p the duty of a husband's brother unto 2992
25: 7 not p the duty of my husband's brother. 2992
Ru 3:13 he will p unto thee the part of a kinsman, 1350
1Sa 3:12 In that day I will p against Eli all things 6965
2Sa 14:15 it may be that the king will p the request of 6213
1Ki 6:12 will I p my word with thee, which I spake 6965
12:15 the LORD, that he might p his saying, 6965
2Ki 23: 3 to p the words of this covenant that were 6965
23:24 that he might p the words of the law which 6965
2Ch 10:15 of God, that the LORD might p his word, 6965
34:31 to p the words of the covenant which are 6213
Est 5: 8 to p my request, let the king and 6213
Job 5:12 so that their hands cannot p their enterprise. 6213
Ps 21:11 which they are not able to p. NIH
61: 8 name for ever, that I may daily p my vows. 7999
119:106 I will p it, that I will keep thy righteous 6965
119:112 I have inclined mine heart to p thy statutes 6213
Isa 9: 7 The zeal of the LORD of hosts will p this. 6213
19:21 shall vow a vow unto the LORD, and p it. 7999
44:28 is my shepherd, and shall p all my pleasure: 7999
Jer 1:12 well seen: for I will hasten my word to p it. 6213
11: 5 That I may p the oath which I have sworn 6965
28: 6 the LORD p thy words which thou hast 6965
29:10 p my good word towards you, in causing 6965
33:14 that I will p that good thing which I have 6965
44:25 We will surely p our vows that we have 6213
44:25 your vows, and surely p your vows. 6213+6213
Eze 12:25 will I say the word, and will p it, 6213
Mic 7:20 Thou wilt p the truth to Jacob, and 5414
Na 1:15 keep thy solemn feasts, p thy vows: 7999
Mt 5:33 but shalt p unto the Lord thine oaths: 591
Lk 1:72 To p the mercy promised to our fathers, 4160
Ro 4:21 he had promised, he was able also to p. 4160
7:18 but how to p that which is good I find not. 2716
2Co 8:11 p the doing of it; that as there was a 2005
Php 1: 6 you will p it until the day of Jesus Christ: 2005

PERFORMANCE (2) [PERFORM]
Lk 1:45 for there shall be a p of those things which 5050
2Co 8:11 there may be a p also out of that which you 2005

PERFORMED (21) [PERFORM]
1Sa 15:11 and hath not p my commandments. 6965
15:13 I have p the commandment of the LORD. 6965
2Sa 21:14 they p all that the king commanded. 6213
1Ki 8:20 the LORD hath p his word that he spake, 6965
2Ch 6:10 hath p his word that he hath spoken: 6965
Ne 9: 8 it, I say, to his seed, and hast p thy words; 6965
Est 1:15 she hath not p the commandment of 6213
5: 6 to the half of the kingdom it shall be p. 6213
7: 2 it shall be p, even to the half of 6213
Ps 65: 1 in Zion: and unto thee shall the vow be p. 7999
Isa 10:12 that when the Lord hath p his whole work 1214
Jer 23:20 and till he have p the thoughts of his heart: 6965
30:24 and until he have p the intents of his heart: 6965
34:18 which have not p the words of the covenant 6965
35:14 his sons not to drink wine, are p; 6965
35:16 have p the commandment of their father, 6965
51:29 for every purpose of the LORD shall be p 6965
Eze 37:14 have spoken it, and p it, saith the LORD. 6213
Lk 1:20 until the day that these things shall be p, 1096
2:39 And when they had p all things according 5055
Ro 15:28 When therefore I have p this, and 2005

PERFORMETH (4) [PERFORM]
Ne 5:13 from his labour, that p not this promise, 6965
Job 23:14 For he p the thing that is appointed for me: 7999
Ps 57: 2 unto God that p all things for me. 1584
Isa 44:26 and p the counsel of his messengers; 7999

PERFORMING (2) [PERFORM]
Nu 15: 3 or a sacrifice in p a vow, or in a freewill 6381
15: 8 or for a sacrifice in p a vow, or 6381

PERFUME (3) [PERFUMED, PERFUMES]
Ex 30:35 thou shalt make it a p, a confection after 7004
30:37 as for the p which thou shalt make, 7004
Pr 27: 9 Ointment and p rejoice the heart: so 7004

PERFUME-MAKERS See APOTHECARIES

PERFUMED (2) [PERFUME]
Pr 7:17 I have p my bed with myrrh, aloes, and 5130
SS 3: 6 p with myrrh and frankincense, with all 6999

PERFUMER See APOTHECARY

PERFUMERS See CONFECTIONARIES

PERFUMES (1) [PERFUME]
Isa 57: 9 didst increase thy p, and didst send thy 7547

PERGA (3)
Ac 13:13 from Paphos, they came to P in Pamphylia: 4011
13:14 But when they departed from P, they came 4011
14:25 And when they had preached the word in P, 4011

PERGAMOS (2)
Rev 1:11 and unto P, and unto Thyatira, and 4010
2:12 And to the angel of the church in P write; 4010

PERGAMUM See PERGAMOS

PERHAPS (3)
Ac 8:22 if p the thought of thine heart may be 686
2Co 2: 7 comfort him, lest p such a one should be 3381
Phm 1:15 For p he therefore departed for a season, 5029

PERIDA (1) [PERUDA]
Ne 7:57 the children of Sophereth, the children of P, 6514

PERIL (2) [PERILOUS, PERILS]
La 5: 9 We gat our bread with the p of our lives NIH
Ro 8:35 or famine, or nakedness, or p, or sword? 2794

PERILOUS (1) [PERIL]
2Ti 3: 1 that in the last days p times shall come. 5467

PERILS (8) [PERIL]
2Co 11:26 in p of waters, in perils of robbers, 2794
11:26 in perils of waters, in p of robbers, 2794
11:26 of robbers, in p by my own countrymen, 2794
11:26 in p by the heathen, in perils in the city, 2794
11:26 in perils by the heathen, in p in the city, 2794
11:26 in p in the wilderness, in perils in the sea, 2794
11:26 in perils in the wilderness, in p in the sea, 2794
11:26 perils in the sea, in p among false brethren; 2794

PERISH (120) [PERISHED, PERISHETH, PERISHING]
Ge 41:36 that the land p not through the famine. 3772
Ex 19:21 the LORD to gaze, and many of them p. 5307
21:26 his servant, or the eye of his maid, that it p; 7843
Lev 26:38 ye shall p among the heathen, and the land of 6
Nu 17:12 Behold, we die, we p, we all perish. 6
17:12 Behold, we die, we perish, we all p. 6
24:20 but his latter end shall be that he p for ever. 8
24:24 shall afflict Eber, and he also shall p for ever. 8
Dt 4:26 that ye shall soon utterly p from off the land 6+6
8:19 against you this day that ye shall surely p. 6+6
8:20 destroyeth before your face, so shall ye p; 6
11:17 lest ye p quickly from off the good land which 6
26: 5 A Syrian ready to p was my father, and 6
28:20 thou be destroyed, and until thou p quickly; 6
28:22 and they shall pursue thee until thou p. 6
30:18 that ye shall surely p, and that ye shall not 6+6
Jos 23:13 until ye p from off this good land which 6
23:16 ye shall p quickly from off the good land 6
Jdg 5:31 So let all thine enemies p, O LORD: but 6
1Sa 26:10 or he shall descend into battle, and p. 5595
27: 1 I shall now p one day by the hand of Saul: 5595
2Ki 9: 8 For the whole house of Ahab shall p: and I will 6
Est 3:13 to destroy, to kill, and to cause to p, all Jews, 6
4:16 is not according to the law: and if I p, I perish. 6
4:16 is not according to the law: and if I perish, I p. 6
7: 4 to be destroyed, to be slain, and to p. 6
8:11 their life, to destroy, to slay, and to cause to p, 6
9:28 nor the memorial of them p from their seed. 5486
Job 3: 3 Let the day p wherein I was born, and the night 6
4: 9 By the blast of God they p, and by the breath 6
4:20 they p for ever without any regarding it. 6
6:18 way are turned aside; they go to nothing, and p. 6
8:13 forget God; and the hypocrite's hope shall p: 6
18:17 His remembrance shall p from the earth, and 6
20: 7 Yet he shall p for ever like his own dung: 6
29:13 The blessing of him that was ready to p came 6
31:19 If I have seen any p for want of clothing, or 6
34:15 All flesh shall p together, and man shall 1478
36:12 they shall p by the sword, and they shall 5674
Ps 1: 6 but the way of the ungodly shall p. 6
2:12 lest he be angry, and ye p from the way, 6
9: 3 they shall fall and p at thy presence. 6
9:18 the expectation of the poor shall not p for ever. 6
37:20 the wicked shall p, and the enemies of 6
41: 5 evil of me, When shall he die, and his name p? 6
49:10 likewise the fool and the brutish person p, and 6
49:12 abideth not: he is like the beasts that p. 1820
49:20 understandeth not, is like the beasts that p. 1820
68: 2 so let the wicked p at the presence of God. 6
73:27 For lo, they that are far from thee shall p: 6
80:16 they p at the rebuke of thy countenance. 6
83:17 for ever; yea, let them be put to shame, and p: 6
92: 9 O LORD, for lo, thine enemies shall p; 6
102:26 They shall p, but thou shalt endure: yea, all of 6
112:10 melt away: the desire of the wicked shall p. 6
146: 4 to his earth; in that very day his thoughts p. 6
Pr 10:28 but the expectation of the wicked shall p. 6
11: 7 a wicked man dieth, his expectation shall p: 6
11:10 and when the wicked p, there is shouting. 6
19: 9 and he that speaketh lies shall p. 6
21:28 A false witness shall p: but the man that 6
28:28 but when they p, the righteous increase. 6
29:18 Where there is no vision, the people p: but 6544
31: 6 Give strong drink unto him that is ready to p, 6
Ecc 5:14 those riches p by evil travail: and he begetteth 6
Isa 26:14 and made all their memory to p. 6
27:13 they shall come which were ready to p in 6
29:14 for the wisdom of their wise men shall p, and 6
41:11 and they that strive with thee shall p. 6
60:12 and kingdom that will not serve thee shall p; 6
Jer 4: 9 that the heart of the king shall p, and the heart 6
6:21 the neighbour and his friend shall p. 6
10:11 even they shall p from the earth, and 7
10:15 in the time of their visitation they shall p. 6
18:18 for the law shall not p from the priest, 6
27:10 that I should drive you out, and ye should p. 6
27:15 that ye might p, ye, and the prophets that 6
40:15 be scattered, and the remnant in Judah p? 6
48: 8 the valley also shall p, and the plain shall be 6
51:18 in the time of their visitation they shall p. 6
Eze 7:26 the law shall p from the priest, and 6
25: 7 and I will cause thee to p out of the countries: 6
Da 2:18 his fellows should not p with the rest of 7
Am 1: 8 the remnant of the Philistines shall p, saith 6
2:14 Therefore the flight shall p from the swift, and 6
3:15 the houses of ivory shall p, and the great 6
Jnh 1: 6 be that God will think upon us, that we p not. 6
1:14 let us not p for this man's life, and lay not upon 6
3: 9 turn away from his fierce anger, that we p not? 6
Zec 9: 5 the king shall p from Gaza, and Ashkelon shall 6
Mt 5:29 for thee that one of thy members should p, 622
5:30 for thee that one of thy members should p, 622
8:25 and awoke him, saying, Lord, save us: we p. 622
9:17 and the wine runneth out, and the bottles p: 622
18:14 that one of these little ones should p. 622
26:52 for all they that take the sword shall p with 622
Mk 4:38 unto him, Master, carest thou not that we p? 622
Lk 5:37 and be spilled, and the bottles shall p. 622
8:24 awoke him, saying, Master, master, we p. 622
13: 3 but, except ye repent, ye shall all likewise p. 622

Lk 13: 5 but except ye repent, ye shall all likewise p. 622
13:33 for it cannot be that a prophet p out of 622
15:17 and to spare, and I p with hunger? 622
21:18 But there shall not a hair of your head p. 622
Jn 3:15 whosoever believeth in him should not p, 622
3:16 whosoever believeth in him should not p, 622
10:28 and they shall never p, neither shall any *man* 622
11:50 the people, and *that* the whole nation p not. 622
Ac 8:20 Thy money p with thee, 684+1510+1519
13:41 Behold *ye* despisers, and wonder, and p: 853
Ro 2:12 sinned without law shall also p without law: 622
1Co 1:18 of the cross is to them that p foolishness; 622
8:11 thy knowledge shall the weak brother p, 622
2Co 2:15 in them that are saved, and in them that p: 622
4:16 but though our outward man p, yet 1311
Col 2:22 Which all are to p with the using;) after 5356
2Th 2:10 of unrighteousness in them that p; 622
Heb 1:11 They shall p; but thou remainest; and 622
2Pe 2:12 and shall utterly p in their own corruption; 2704
3: 9 not willing that any should p, but that all 622

PERISHED (26) [PERISH]

Nu 16:33 and they p from among the congregation. 6
21:30 Heshbon is p even unto Dibon, and we have 6
Jos 22:20 and that man p not alone in his iniquity. 1478
2Sa 1:27 the mighty fallen, and the weapons of war p! 6
Job 4: 7 Remember, I pray thee, who *ever* p, 6
30: 2 their hands profit me, in whom old age was p? 6
Ps 9: 6 destroyed cities; their memorial is p *with* them. 6
10:16 and ever: the heathen are p out of his land. 6
83:10 *Which* p at En-dor: they became *as* dung 8045
119:92 I should then have p in mine affliction. 6
Ecc 9: 6 and their hatred, and their envy, is now p; 6
Jer 7:28 truth is p, and is cut off from their mouth. 6
48:36 because the riches *that* he hath gotten are p. 6
49: 7 is counsel p from the prudent? is their wisdom 6
La 3:18 and my hope is p from the LORD: 6
Joel 1:11 the barley; because the harvest of the field is p. 6
Jnh 4:10 which came up in a night, and p in a night: 6
Mic 4: 9 is thy counseller p? for pangs have taken thee 6
7: 2 The good *man* is p out of the earth: and *there is* 6
Mt 8:32 steep place into the sea, and p in the waters. 599
Lk 11:51 which p between the altar and the temple: 622
Ac 5:37 he also p; and all, *even* as many as obeyed 622
1Co 15:18 also which are fallen asleep in Christ are p. 622
Heb 11:31 By faith the harlot Rahab p not with them 4881
2Pe 3: 6 then was, being overflowed with water, p: 622
Jude 1:11 for reward, and p in the gainsaying of Core. 622

PERISHETH (9) [PERISH]

Job 4:11 The old lion p for lack of prey, and the stout 6
Pr 11: 7 shall perish: and the hope of unjust *men* p. 6
Ecc 7:15 there is a just *man* that p in his righteousness, 6
Isa 57: 1 The righteous p, and no man layeth *it* to heart: 6
Jer 9:12 for what the land p *and* is burnt up like a 6
48:46 the people of Chemosh p: for thy sons are 6
Jn 6:27 Labour not for the meat which p, but for *that* 622
Jas 1:11 and the grace of the fashion of it p: 622
1Pe 1: 7 much more precious than of gold that p, 622

PERISHING (1) [PERISH]

Job 33:18 the pit, and his life from p by the sword. 5674

PERIZZITE (5) [PERIZZITES]

Ge 13: 7 and the P dwelled then in the land. 6522
Ex 33: 2 and the P, and the Hivite, and the Jebusite: 6522
34:11 and the P, and the Hivite, and the Jebusite. 6522
Jos 9: 1 the P, the Hivite, and the Jebusite, 6522
11: 3 the P, and the Jebusite in the mountains, 6522

PERIZZITES (18) [PERIZZITE]

Ge 15:20 the Hittites, and the P, and the Rephaims, 6522
34:30 the land, amongst the Canaanites and the P: 6522
Ex 3: 8 the P, and the Hivites, and the Jebusites. 6522
3:17 the P, and the Hivites, and the Jebusites, 6522
23:23 the P, and the Canaanites, the Hivites, and 6522
Dt 7: 1 the P, and the Hivites, and the Jebusites, 6522
20:17 and the P, the Hivites, and the Jebusites; 6522
Jos 3:10 the P, and the Girgashites, and 6522
12: 8 the P, the Hivites, and the Jebusites: 6522
17:15 down for thyself there in the land of the P 6522
24:11 the P, and the Canaanites, and the Hittites, 6522
Jdg 1: 4 the Canaanites and the P into their hand: 6522
1: 5 and they slew the Canaanites and the P. 6522
3: 5 and P, and Hivites, and Jebusites: 6522
1Ki 9:20 Hittites, P, Hivites, and Jebusites, 6522
2Ch 8: 7 the P, and the Hivites, and the Jebusites, 6522
Ezr 9: 1 the Hittites, the P, the Jebusites, 6522
Ne 9: 8 the P, and the Jebusites, and 6522

PERJURED (1)

1Ti 1:10 for p *persons*, and if *there be* any other 1965

PERMISSION (1) [PERMIT]

1Co 7: 6 But I speak this by p, *and* not of 4774

PERMIT (2) [PERMISSION, PERMITTED]

1Co 16: 7 to tarry a while with you, if the Lord p. 2010
Heb 6: 3 And this will we do, if God p. 2010

PERMITTED (2) [PERMIT]

Ac 26: 1 unto Paul, Thou art p to speak for thyself. 2010
1Co 14:34 for it is not p unto them to speak; but 2010

PERNICIOUS (1)

2Pe 2: 2 And many shall follow their p ways; 684

PERPETUAL (28) [PERPETUALLY]

Ge 9:12 creature that *is* with you, for p generations: 5769
Ex 29: 9 the priest's office shall be theirs for a p 5769
30: 8 a p incense before the LORD throughout 8548
31:16 their generations, *for* a p covenant. 5769
Lev 3:17 *It shall be* a p statute for your generations 5769
6:20 an ephah of fine flour *for* a meat offering p, 8548
Lev 24: 9 of the LORD made by fire, *by* a p statute. 5769
25:34 may not be sold; for it *is* their p possession. 5769
Nu 19:21 it shall be a p statute unto them, that he that 5769
Ps 9: 6 destructions are come to a p end: 5331+3807.1
74: 3 Lift up thy feet unto the p desolations; 5331
78:66 hinder parts: he put them to a p reproach. 5769
Jer 5:22 sand *for* the bound of the sea *by* a p decree, 5769
8: 5 Jerusalem slidden back *by* a p backsliding? 5329
15:18 Why is my pain p, and my wound 5331
18:16 make their land desolate, *and* a p hissing; 5769
23:40 a p shame, which shall not be forgotten. 5769
25: 9 and a hissing, and p desolations. 5769
25:12 and will make it p desolations. 5769
49:13 and all the cities thereof shall be p wastes. 5769
50: 5 let us join ourselves to the LORD *in* a p 5769
51:39 sleep a p sleep, and not wake, saith 5769
51:57 mighty *men:* and they shall sleep a p sleep, 5769
Eze 35: 5 Because thou hast had a p hatred, and 5769
35: 9 I will make thee p desolations, and 5769
46:14 a meat offering continually *by* a p 5769
Hab 3: 6 were scattered, the p hills did bow: 5769
Zep 2: 9 and saltpits, and a p desolation: 5704+5769

PERPETUALLY (3) [PERPETUAL]

1Ki 9: 3 mine heart shall be there p. 3117+3605+1886.1
2Ch 7:16 mine heart shall be there p. 3117+3605+1886.1
Am 1:11 his anger did tear p, and he kept his 5703+3807.1

PERPLEXED (5) [PERPLEXITY]

Est 3:15 down to drink; but the city Shushan was p. 943
Joel 1:18 the herds of cattle are p, because they have 943
Lk 9: 7 and he was p, because that it was said of 1280
24: 4 as they were *much* p thereabout, behold, 1280
2Co 4: 8 not distressed; *we are* p, but not in despair; 639

PERPLEXITY (3) [PERPLEXED]

Isa 22: 5 of p by the Lord GOD of hosts in 3998
Mic 7: 4 thy visitation cometh; now shall be their p. 3998
Lk 21:25 upon the earth distress of nations, with p; 640

PERSECUTE (25) [PERSECUTED, PERSECUTEST, PERSECUTING, PERSECUTION, PERSECUTIONS, PERSECUTOR, PERSECUTORS]

Job 19:22 Why do ye p me as God, and are not 7291
19:28 ye should say, Why p we him? seeing 7291
Ps 7: 1 save me from all them that p me, and 7291
7: 5 Let the enemy p my soul, and take *it;* yea, 7291
10: 2 The wicked in *his* pride doth p the poor: 1814
31:15 of mine enemies, and from them that p me. 7291
35: 3 and stop *the way* against them that p me: 7291
35: 6 and let the angel of the LORD p them. 7291
69:26 For they p *him* whom thou hast smitten; 7291
71:11 p and take him; for *there is* none to deliver 7291
83:15 So p them with thy tempest, and 7291
119:84 thou execute judgment on them that p me? 7291
119:86 they p me wrongfully; help thou me. 7291
Jer 17:18 Let them be confounded that p me, but 7291
29:18 I will p them with the sword, with 7291
La 3:66 P and destroy them in anger from under 7291
Mt 5:11 and p *you,* and shall say all manner of evil 1377
5:44 which despitefully use you, and p you; 1377
10:23 But when they p you in this city, flee ye 1377
23:34 and p *them* from city to city: 1377
Lk 11:49 and *some* of them they shall slay and p: 1559
21:12 p *you,* delivering *you* up to *the* synagogues, 1377
Jn 5:16 And therefore did the Jews p Jesus, and 1377
15:20 have persecuted me, they will also p you; 1377
Ro 12:14 Bless them which p you: bless, and 1377

PERSECUTED (20) [PERSECUTE]

Dt 30: 7 and on them that hate thee, which p thee. 7291
Ps 109:16 p the poor and needy man, that *he* might 7291
119:161 Princes have p me without a cause: but 7291
143: 3 For the enemy hath p my soul; he hath 7291
Isa 14: 6 nations in anger, *is* p, *and* none hindereth. 4783
La 3:43 Thou hast covered with anger, and p us: 7291
Mt 5:10 Blessed *are* they which are p for 1377
5:12 p they the prophets which were before you. 1377
Jn 15:20 If they have p me, they will also persecute 1377
Ac 7:52 of the prophets have not your fathers p? 1377
22: 4 And I p this way unto the death, binding 1377
26:11 I p *them* even unto strange cities. 1377
1Co 4:12 we bless; being p, we suffer *it:* 1377
15: 9 an apostle, because I p the church of God. 1377
2Co 4: 9 P, but not forsaken; cast down, but 1377
Gal 1:13 how that beyond measure I p the church of 1377
1:23 That he which p us in times past now 1377
4:29 he that was born after the flesh p him that 1377
1Th 2:15 and their own prophets, and have p us; 1559
Rev 12:13 he p the woman which brought forth 1377

PERSECUTEST (6) [PERSECUTE]

Ac 9: 4 unto him, Saul, Saul, why p thou me? 1377
9: 5 the Lord said, I am Jesus whom thou p: 1377
22: 7 unto me, Saul, Saul, why p thou me? 1377
22: 8 I am Jesus of Nazareth, whom thou p. 1377
26:14 Saul, Saul, why p thou me? 1377
26:15 And he said, I am Jesus whom thou p. 1377

PERSECUTING (1) [PERSECUTE]

Php 3: 6 Concerning zeal, p the church; touching 1377

PERSECUTION (10) [PERSECUTE]

La 5: 5 Our necks *are* under p: we labour, *and* 7291
Mt 13:21 or p ariseth because of the word, 1375
Mk 4:17 or p ariseth for the word's sake, 1375
Ac 8: 1 And at that time there was a great p against 1375
11:19 p that arose about Stephen travelled as far 2347
13:50 and raised p against Paul and Barnabas, 1375
Ro 8:35 or p, or famine, or nakedness, or peril, or 1375
Gal 5:11 why do I yet suffer p? 1377
6:12 only lest they should suffer p for the cross 1377
2Ti 3:12 live godly in Christ Jesus shall suffer p. 1377

PERSECUTIONS (5) [PERSECUTE]

Mk 10:30 mothers, and children, and lands, with p; 1375
2Co 12:10 in reproaches, in necessities, in p, 1375
2Th 1: 4 and faith in all your p and tribulations that 1375
2Ti 3:11 P, afflictions, which came unto me at 1375
3:11 at Iconium, at Lystra; what p I endured: 1375

PERSECUTOR (1) [PERSECUTE]

1Ti 1:13 before a blasphemer, and a p, and injurious: 1376

PERSECUTORS (8) [PERSECUTE]

Ne 9:11 and their p thou threwest into the deeps, 7291
Ps 7:13 he ordaineth his arrows against the p. 1814
119:157 Many *are* my p and mine enemies; *yet* do I 7291
142: 6 deliver me from my p; for they are stronger 7291
Jer 15:15 and visit me, and revenge me of my p; 7291
20:11 therefore my p shall stumble, and they shall 7291
La 1: 3 all her p overtook her between the straits. 7291
4:19 Our p are swifter than the eagles of 7291

PERSEVERANCE (1)

Eph 6:18 and watching thereunto with all p and 4343

PERSIA (29) [PERSIAN, PERSIANS]

2Ch 36:20 sons until the reign of the kingdom of P: 6539
36:22 Now in the first year of Cyrus king of P, 6539
36:22 stirred up the spirit of Cyrus king of P, 6539
36:23 Thus saith Cyrus king of P, All 6539
Ezr 1: 1 Now in the first year of Cyrus king of P, 6539
1: 1 stirred up the spirit of Cyrus king of P, 6539
1: 2 Thus saith Cyrus king of P, The LORD 6539
1: 8 Even those did Cyrus king of P bring forth 6539
3: 7 the grant that they had of Cyrus king of P. 6539
4: 3 as king Cyrus the king of P hath 6539
4: 5 all the days of Cyrus king of P, 6539
4: 5 even until the reign of Darius king of P. 6539
4: 7 unto Artaxerxes king of P; 6539
4:24 year of the reign of Darius king of P. 6540
6:14 and Darius, and Artaxerxes king of P. 6540
7: 1 in the reign of Artaxerxes king of P, 6539
9: 9 mercy unto us in the sight of the kings of P, 6539
Est 1: 3 the power of P and Media, the nobles and 6539
1:14 the seven princes of P and Media, 6539
1:18 Likewise shall the ladies of P and 6539
10: 2 the chronicles of the kings of Media and P? 6539
Eze 27:10 They of P and of Lud and of Phut were in 6539
38: 5 P, Ethiopia, and Libya with them; all of 6539
Da 8:20 two horns *are* the kings of Media and P. 6539
10: 1 In the third year of Cyrus king of P a thing 6539
10:13 the prince of the kingdom of P withstood 6539
10:13 and I remained there with the kings of P. 6539
10:20 will I return to fight with the prince of P: 6539
11: 2 there *shall* stand up yet three kings in P; 6539

PERSIAN (2) [PERSIA]

Ne 12:22 also the priests, to the reign of Darius the P. 6542
Da 6:28 of Darius, and in the reign of Cyrus the P. 6543

PERSIANS (5) [PERSIA]

Est 1:19 let it be written among the laws of the P 6539
Da 5:28 is divided, and given to the Medes and P. 6540
6: 8 according to the law of the Medes and P, 6540
6:12 according to the law of the Medes and P, 6540
6:15 P *is,* That no decree nor statute which 6540

PERSIS (1)

Ro 16:12 Salute the beloved P, which laboured much 4069

PERSON (56) [PERSONS]

Ge 39: 6 Joseph was *a* goodly p, and well favoured. NIH
Ex 12:48 for no uncircumcised p shall eat thereof. 6189
Lev 19:15 thou shalt not respect the p of the poor, 6440
19:15 of the poor, nor honour the p of the mighty: 6440
Nu 5: 6 against the LORD, and that p be guilty; 5315
19:17 for an unclean *p* they shall take of the ashes NIH
19:18 a clean p shall take hyssop, and dip *it* in 376
19:19 the clean *p* shall sprinkle upon the unclean NIH
19:22 whatsoever the unclean *p* toucheth shall be NIH
31:19 whosoever hath killed *any* p, and 5315
35:11 which killeth *any* p at unawares. 5315
35:15 that every one that killeth *any* p unawares 5315
35:30 Whoso killeth *any* p, the murderer shall be 5315
35:30 one witness shall not testify against *any* p 5315
Dt 15:22 the unclean and the clean *p shall eat it* alike, NIH
27:25 that taketh reward to slay an innocent p[S]. 1818
28:50 which shall not regard the p of the old, 6440
Jos 20: 3 That the slayer that killeth *any* p unawares 5315
20: 9 that whosoever killeth *any* p at unawares 5315
1Sa 9: 2 the children of Israel a goodlier p than he: 376
16:18 and a comely p, and the LORD *is* with him. 376
25:35 to thy voice, and have accepted thy p. 6440
2Sa 4:11 when wicked men have slain a righteous p in 376
14:14 up *again;* neither doth God respect *any* p: 5315
17:11 and *that* thou go to battle in thine own p. 6440
Job 13: 8 Will ye accept his p? will ye contend for 6440
22:29 and he shall save the humble p. 5869+7807
32:21 Let me not, I pray you, accept *any* man's p, 6440
Ps 15: 4 In whose eyes a vile *p* is contemned; but he NIH
49:10 likewise the fool and the brutish p perish, 1198
101: 4 from me: I will not know a wicked *p.* NIH
105:37 *there was* not *one* feeble *p* among their NIH
Pr 6:12 A naughty p, a wicked man, walketh *with* a 120
18: 5 *It is* not good to accept the p of the wicked, 6440
24: 8 to do evil shall be called a mischievous p. 1167
28:17 to the blood of *any* p shall flee to the pit; 5315
Isa 32: 5 The vile p shall be no more called liberal, 5036
32: 6 For the vile p will speak villany, and 5036
Jer 43: 6 every p that Nebuzar-adan the captain of 5315
52:25 men of them that were near the king's p, 6440
Eze 16: 5 to the lothing of thy p, in the day that thou 5315
33: 6 and take *any* p from among them, 5315
44:25 they shall come at no dead p to defile 120
Da 11:21 in his estate shall stand up a vile p, to whom 959

P

Mal 1: 8 he be pleased with thee, or accept thy **p**? 6440
Mt 22:16 *man:* for thou regardest not the **p** of men. *4383*
27:24 I am innocent of the blood of this just *p*: NIG
Mk 12:14 *man:* for thou regardest not the **p** of men, *4383*
Lk 20:21 neither acceptest thou the **p** *of any,* but *4383*
1Co 5:13 from among yourselves *that* wicked **p**. NIG
2Co 2:10 your sakes *forgave I it* in the **p** of Christ; *4383*
Gal 2: 6 God accepteth no man's **p**:) for they who *4383*
Eph 5: 5 nor unclean *p*, nor covetous man who is an NIG
Heb 1: 3 and the express image of his **p**, and *5287*
12:16 *be* any fornicator, or profane *p*, as Esau, NIG
2Pe 2: 5 saved Noah the eighth *p*, a preacher of NIG

PERSONS (56) [PERSON]

Ge 14:21 Give me the **p**, and take the goods to 5315
36: 6 all the **p** of his house, and his cattle, and 5315
Ex 16:16 *according to* the number of your **p**; 5315
Lev 27: 2 the **p** *shall be* for the LORD by thy 5315
Nu 19:18 upon the **p** that were there, and upon him 5315
31:28 *both* of the **p**, and of the beeves, and of 120
31:30 of the **p**, of the beeves, of the asses, and 120
31:35 thirty and two thousand **p** in all, 120+5315
31:40 the **p** *were* sixteen thousand; of which 120+5315
31:40 the LORD'S tribute *was* thirty and two **p**. 5315
31:46 And sixteen thousand **p**;) 120+5315
Dt 1:17 Ye shall not respect **p** in judgment; *but* 6440
10:17 and a terrible, which regardeth not **p**, 6440
10:22 down into Egypt with threescore and ten **p**; 5315
16:19 thou shalt not respect **p**, neither take a gift: 6440
Jdg 9: 2 *which are* threescore and ten **p**, reign over 376
9: 4 wherewith Abimelech hired vain and light **p**, 376
9: 5 *being* threescore and ten **p**, upon one stone: 376
9:18 threescore and ten **p**, upon one stone, and 376
20:39 *and* kill of the men of Israel about thirty **p**: 376
1Sa 9:22 that were bidden, which *were* about thirty **p**. 376
22:18 and five **p** that did wear a linen ephod. 376
22:22 I have occasioned *the death* of all the **p** of 5315
2Ki 10: 6 Now the king's sons, *being* seventy **p**, 376
10: 7 slew seventy **p**, and put their heads in 376
2Ch 19: 7 nor respect of **p**, nor taking of gifts. 6440
Job 13:10 reprove you, if ye do secretly accept **p**. 6440
34:19 *to him* that accepteth not the **p** of princes, 6440
Ps 26: 4 I have not sat with vain **p**, neither will I go 4962
82: 2 and accept the **p** of the wicked? 6440
Pr 12:11 he that followeth vain *p is* void of NIH
24:23 *It is* not good to have respect of **p** in 6440
28:19 he that followeth after vain *p* shall have NIH
28:21 To have respect of **p** *is* not good: for for a 6440
Jer 52:29 Jerusalem eight hundred thirty and two **p**: 5315
52:30 *of* the Jews seven hundred forty and five **p**: 5315
52:30 all the **p** *were* four thousand and 5315
La 4:16 they respected not the **p** of the priests, 6440
Eze 17:17 and building forts, to cut off many **p**: 5315
27:13 they traded the **p** of men and vessels of 5315
Jnh 4:11 wherein are more than sixscore thousand **p** 120
Zep 3: 4 Her prophets *are* light *and* treacherous **p**: 376
Mal 1: 9 will he **regard** your **p**? 4480+5375+6440
Lk 15: 7 and nine just *p* which need no repentance. NIG
Ac 10:34 I perceive that God is no **respecter of p**: *4381*
17:17 and with the devout *p*, and in the market NIG
Ro 2:11 For there is no **respect of p** with God. *4382*
2Co 1:11 **p** thanks may be given by many on our *4383*
Eph 6: 9 neither is there **respect of p** with him. *4382*
Col 3:25 he hath done: and there is no **respect of p**. *4382*
1Ti 1:10 for perjured **p**, and if *there be* any other NIG
Jas 2: 1 *the Lord* of glory, with **respect of p**. *4382*
2: 9 But if ye **have respect to p**, ye commit sin, *4380*
1Pe 1:17 who **without respect of p** judgeth according *678*
2Pe 3:11 what manner *of p* ought ye to be in all holy NIG
Jude 1:16 *words,* having *men's* **p** in admiration NIG

PERSUADE (9) [PERSUADED, PERSUADEST, PERSUADETH, PERSUADING, PERSUASION]

1Ki 22:20 Who shall **p** Ahab, that he may go up and 6601
22:21 before the LORD, and said, I will **p** him. 6601
22:22 he said, Thou shalt **p** *him,* and prevail also: 6601
2Ch 32:11 Doth not Hezekiah **p** you to give over 5496
32:15 nor **p** you on this *manner,* neither yet 5496
Isa 36:18 *Beware* lest Hezekiah **p** you, saying, 5496
Mt 28:14 we will **p** him, and secure you. *3982*
2Co 5:11 therefore the terror of the Lord, we **p** men; *3982*
Gal 1:10 For do I now **p** men, or God? or do I seek *3982*

PERSUADED (20) [PERSUADE]

2Ch 18: 2 **p** him to go up *with him* to Ramoth-gilead. 5496
Pr 25:15 By long forbearing is a prince **p**, and a soft 6601
Mt 27:20 elders **p** the multitude that they should ask *3982*
Lk 16:31 and the prophets, neither will they be **p**, *3982*
20: 6 for they be **p** that John was a prophet. *3982*
Ac 13:43 **p** them to continue in the grace of God. *3982*
14:19 and Iconium, who **p** the people, and, *3982*
18: 4 and **p** *the* Jews and *the* Greeks. *3982*
19:26 this Paul hath **p** and turned away much *3982*
21:14 And when he would not be **p**, we ceased, *3982*
26:26 for I am **p** that none of these *things* are *3982*
Ro 4:21 And being **fully p** that, what he had *4135*
8:38 For I am **p**, that neither death, nor life, *3982*
14: 5 Let every man be **fully p** in his own mind. *4135*
14:14 I know, and am **p** by the Lord Jesus, *3982*
15:14 And I myself also am **p** of you, *3982*
2Ti 1: 5 mother Eunice; and I am **p** that in thee also. *3982*
1:12 I am **p** that he is able to keep that which I *3982*
Heb 6: 9 we are **p** better *things* of you, and *3982*
11:13 and were **p** of *them,* and embraced *them,* *3982*

PERSUADEST (1) [PERSUADE]

Ac 26:28 Almost thou **p** me to be a Christian. *3982*

PERSUADETH (2) [PERSUADE]

2Ki 18:32 not unto Hezekiah, when he **p** you, saying, 5496
Ac 18:13 This *fellow* **p** men to worship God contrary *374*

PERSUADING (2) [PERSUADE]

Ac 19: 8 **p** the *things* concerning the kingdom of *3982*
28:23 **p** them concerning Jesus, both out of *3982*

PERSUASION (1) [PERSUADE]

Gal 5: 8 *This* **p** *cometh* not of him that calleth you. *3988*

PERTAIN (6) [PERTAINED, PERTAINETH, PERTAINING]

Lev 7:20 that *p* unto the LORD, having his NIH
7:21 which *p* unto the LORD, even that soul NIH
1Sa 25:22 if I leave of all that *p* to him by the morning NIH
Ro 15:17 Christ *in those things* which **p** to God. *4314*
1Co 6: 3 how much more *things* **that p to** *this* **life**? *982*
2Pe 1: 3 hath given unto us all *things* that *p* unto life NIG

PERTAINED (17) [PERTAIN]

Nu 31:43 (Now the half that **p** unto the congregation NIH
Jos 24:33 they buried him in a hill that **p** to Phinehas NIH
Jdg 6:11 in Ophrah, that *p* unto Joash the Abi-ezrite: NIH
1Sa 25:21 that nothing was missed of all that *p* unto NIH
2Sa 2:15 which *p* to Ish-bosheth the son of Saul, and NIH
9: 9 I have given unto thy master's son all that **p** 1961
16: 4 thine *are* all that *p* unto Mephibosheth. NIH
1Ki 4:10 to him *p* Sochoh, and all the land of NIH
4:12 *to him p* Taanach and Megiddo, and NIH
4:13 to him *p* the towns of Jair the son of NIH
4:13 to him *also p* the region of Argob, which *is* NIH
7:48 Solomon made all the vessels that *p unto* NIH
2Ki 24: 7 Euphrates all that **p** to the king of Egypt. 1961
1Ch 9:27 the opening *thereof* every morning **p to** 5921
11:31 that **p** to the children of Benjamin, NIH
2Ch 12: 4 he took the fenced cities which *p* to Judah, NIH
34:33 the countries that **p** to the children of Israel, NIH

PERTAINETH (8) [PERTAIN]

Lev 14:32 whose hand is not able to get *that which p* NIH
Nu 4:16 of Aaron the priest *p* the oil for the light, NIH
Dt 22: 5 The woman shall not wear **that which p** 3627
1Sa 27: 6 wherefore Ziklag **p** unto the kings of Judah 1961
2Sa 6:12 all that *p* unto him, because of the ark of NIH
2Ch 26:18 said unto him, *It p* not unto thee, Uzziah, NIH
Ro 9: 4 to whom **p** the adoption, and the glory, and NIG
Heb 7:13 these *things* are spoken **p to** another tribe, *3348*

PERTAINING (8) [PERTAIN]

Jos 13:31 *were* **p** unto the children of Machir the son NIH
1Ch 26:32 for every matter **p** to God, and affairs of NIH
Ac 1: 3 speaking of the *things* **p** to the kingdom of *4012*
Ro 4: 1 our father, **as p to** the flesh, hath found? *2596*
1Co 6: 4 ye have judgments *of things* **p to** *this* **life**, *982*
Heb 2:17 and faithful high priest *in things* **p** to God, *4314*
5: 1 is ordained for men *in things* **p** to God, *4314*
9: 9 the service perfect, **as p to** the conscience; *2596*

PERUDA (1) [PERIDA]

Ezr 2:55 the children of Sophereth, the children of **P**, 6514

PERVERSE (20) [PERVERT]

Nu 22:32 because *thy* way is **p** before me: 3399
Dt 32: 5 *they are* a **p** and crooked generation. 6141
1Sa 20:30 Thou son of the **p** rebellious *woman,* do not 5753
Job 6:30 cannot my taste discern **p things**? 1942
9:20 *I say,* I *am* perfect, it shall also **prove** me **p**. 6140
Pr 4:24 and **p** lips put far from thee. 3891
8: 8 *there is* nothing froward or **p** in them. 6141
12: 8 but he that is of a **p** heart shall be despised. 5753
14: 2 but he that is **p** in his ways despiseth him. 3868
17:20 he that hath a **p** tongue falleth into 2015
19: 1 than *he that is* **p** in his lips, and *is* a fool. 6141
23:33 and thine heart shall utter **p things**. 8419
28: 6 than *he that is* **p** in *his* ways, though he *be* 6141
28:18 *he that is* **p** in *his* ways shall fall at once. 6140
Isa 19:14 The LORD hath mingled a **p** spirit in 5773
Mt 17:17 and said, O faithless and **p** generation, *1294*
Lk 9:41 O faithless and **p** generation, *1294*
Ac 20:30 speaking **p** *things,* to draw away disciples *1294*
Php 2:15 in the midst of a crooked and **p** nation, *1294*
1Ti 6: 5 **P disputings** of men of corrupt minds, and *3859*

PERVERSELY (3) [PERVERT]

2Sa 19:19 **did p** the day that my lord the king went 5753
1Ki 8:47 saying, We have sinned, and have **done p**, 5753
Ps 119:78 for they **dealt p with** me without a cause: 5791

PERVERSENESS (6) [PERVERT]

Nu 23:21 in Jacob, neither hath he seen **p** in Israel: 5999
Pr 11: 3 the **p** of transgressors shall destroy them. 5558
15: 4 but **p** therein *is* a breach in the spirit. 5558
Isa 30:12 trust in oppression and **p**, and stay thereon: 3868
59: 3 spoken lies, your tongue hath muttered **p**. 5766
Eze 9: 9 land is full *of* blood, and the city full *of* **p**: 4297

PERVERT (10) [PERVERSE, PERVERSELY, PERVERSENESS, PERVERTED, PERVERTETH, PERVERTING]

Dt 16:19 the wise, and **p** the words of the righteous. 5557
24:17 Thou shalt not **p** the judgment of 5186
Job 8: 3 Doth God **p** judgment? or doth 5791
8: 3 or doth the Almighty **p** justice? 5791
34:12 neither will the Almighty **p** judgment. 5791
Pr 17:23 of the bosom to **p** the ways of judgment. 5186
31: 5 and **p** the judgment of any of the afflicted. 8138
Mic 3: 9 that abhor judgment, and **p** all equity. 6140
Ac 13:10 wilt thou not cease to **p** the right ways of *1294*
Gal 1: 7 and would **p** the gospel of Christ. *3344*

PERVERTED (5) [PERVERT]

1Sa 8: 3 and took bribes, and **p** judgment. 5186
Job 33:27 **p** *that which was* right, and it profited me 5753
Isa 47:10 and thy knowledge, it hath **p** thee; 7725
Jer 3:21 for they have **p** their way, *and* they have 5753
23:36 for ye have **p** the words of the living God, 2015

PERVERTETH (5) [PERVERT]

Ex 23: 8 the wise, and **p** the words of the righteous. 5557
Dt 27:19 Cursed *be* he that **p** the judgment of 5186
Pr 10: 9 but he that **p** his ways shall be known. 6140
19: 3 The foolishness of man **p** his way: and 5557
Lk 23:14 this man unto me, as one that **p** the people: *654*

PERVERTING (2) [PERVERT]

Ecc 5: 8 **violent p** of judgment and justice in a 1499
Lk 23: 2 We found this *fellow* **p** the nation, and *1294*

PESTILENCE (47) [PESTILENCES, PESTILENT]

Ex 5: 3 lest he fall upon us with **p**, or with 1698
9:15 I may smite thee and thy people with **p**; 1698
Lev 26:25 your cities, I will send the **p** among you; 1698
Nu 14:12 I will smite them with the **p**, and 1698
Dt 28:21 The LORD shall make the **p** cleave unto 1698
2Sa 24:13 or that there be three days' **p** in thy land? 1698
24:15 So the LORD sent a **p** upon Israel from 1698
1Ki 8:37 if there be **p**, blasting, mildew, locust, *or* 1698
1Ch 21:12 even the **p**, in the land, and the angel of 1698
21:14 So the LORD sent **p** upon Israel: and 1698
2Ch 6:28 if there be **p**, if there be blasting, or 1698
7:13 the land, or if I send **p** among my people; 1698
20: 9 *as* the sword, judgment, or **p**, or famine, 1698
Ps 78:50 from death, but gave their life over to the **p**; 1698
91: 3 of the fowler, *and* from the noisome **p**. 1698
91: 6 *Nor* for the **p** *that* walketh in darkness; 1698
Jer 14:12 the sword, and by the famine, and by the **p**. 1698
21: 6 and beast: they shall die of a great **p**. 1698
21: 7 and such as are left in this city from the **p**, 1698
21: 9 the sword, and by the famine, and by the **p**: 1698
24:10 the famine, and the **p**, among them, 1698
27: 8 and with the famine, and with the **p**, 1698
27:13 by the sword, by the famine, and by the **p**, 1698
28: 8 of war, and of evil, and of **p**. 1698
29:17 the **p**, and will make them like vile figs, 1698
29:18 with the **p**, and will deliver them to be 1698
32:24 the sword, and *of* the famine, and *of* the **p**: 1698
32:36 the sword, and by the famine, and by the **p**; 1698
34:17 to the sword, to the **p**, and to the famine; 1698
38: 2 by the sword, by the famine, and by the **p**: 1698
42:17 by the sword, by the famine, and by the **p**: 1698
42:22 by the famine, and by the **p**, in the place 1698
44:13 by the sword, by the famine, and by the **p**: 1698
Eze 5:12 A third *part* of thee shall die with the **p**, and 1698
5:17 **p** and blood shall pass through thee; and 1698
6:11 by the sword, by the famine, and by the **p**. 1698
6:12 *He* that *is* far off shall die of the **p**; and 1698
7:15 *is* without, and the **p** and the famine within: 1698
7:15 in the city, famine and **p** shall devour him. 1698
12:16 the sword, from the famine, and from the **p**; 1698
14:19 Or *if* I send a **p** into that land, and pour out 1698
14:21 and the noisome beast, and the **p**, 1698
28:23 For I will send into her **p**, and blood into 1698
33:27 the forts and in the caves shall die of the **p**. 1698
38:22 I will plead against him with **p** and 1698
Am 4:10 I have sent among you the **p** after 1698
Hab 3: 5 Before him went the **p**, and burning coals 1698

PESTILENCES (2) [PESTILENCE]

Mt 24: 7 and **p**, and earthquakes in divers places. *3061*
Lk 21:11 be in divers places, and famines, and **p**; *3061*

PESTILENT (1) [PESTILENCE]

Ac 24: 5 For we have found this man a **p** *fellow,* and *3061*

PESTLE (1)

Pr 27:22 a fool in a mortar among wheat with a **p**, 5940

PETER (158) [CEPHAS, PETER'S, SIMON]

Mt 4:18 Simon called **P**, and Andrew his brother, *4074*
10: 2 who is called **P**, and Andrew his brother; *4074*
14:28 And **P** answered him and said, Lord, if it be *4074*
14:29 And when **P** was come down out of *4074*
15:15 Then answered **P** and said unto him, *4074*
16:16 And Simon **P** answered and said, Thou art *4074*
16:18 That thou art **P**, and upon this rock I will *4074*
16:22 Then **P** took him, and began to rebuke him, *4074*
16:23 But he turned, and said unto **P**, Get thee *4074*
17: 1 And after six days Jesus taketh **P**, James, *4074*
17: 4 Then answered **P**, and said unto Jesus, *4074*
17:24 they that received tribute money came to **P**, *4074*
17:26 **P** saith unto him, Of strangers. Jesus saith *4074*
18:21 Then came **P** to him, and said, Lord, *4074*
19:27 Then answered **P** and said unto him, *4074*
26:33 **P** answered and said unto him, Though all *4074*
26:35 **P** said unto him, Though I should die with *4074*
26:37 And he took with *him* **P** and the two sons *4074*
26:40 them asleep, and saith unto **P**, What, *4074*
26:58 But **P** followed him afar off unto the high *4074*
26:69 Now **P** sat without in the palace: and *4074*
26:73 unto *him* they that stood *by,* and said to **P**, *4074*
26:75 And **P** remembered the word of Jesus, *4074*
Mk 3:16 And Simon he surnamed **P**; *4074*
5:37 save **P**, and James, and John the brother of *4074*
8:29 And **P** answereth and saith unto him, *4074*
8:32 And **P** took him, and began to rebuke him. *4074*
8:33 he rebuked **P**, saying, Get thee behind me, *4074*
9: 2 And after six days Jesus taketh *with him* **P**, *4074*
9: 5 And **P** answered and said to Jesus, Master, *4074*
10:28 Then **P** began to say unto him, Lo, we have *4074*
11:21 And **P** calling to remembrance saith unto *4074*
13: 3 **P** and James and John and Andrew asked *4074*
14:29 But **P** said unto him, Although all shall be *4074*
14:33 And he taketh with him **P** and James and *4074*
14:37 and saith unto **P**, Simon, sleepest thou? *4074*
14:54 And **P** followed him afar off, even into *4074*
14:66 And as **P** was beneath in the palace, *4074*
14:67 And when she saw **P** warming himself, *4074*
14:70 they that stood by said again to **P**, *4074*
14:72 And **P** called to mind the word that Jesus *4074*
16: 7 and **P** that he goeth before you into Galilee: *4074*
Lk 5: 8 When Simon **P** saw *it,* he fell down at *4074*

Lk 6:14 Simon, (whom he also named P,) and 4074
8:45 P and they that were with him said, Master, 4074
8:51 he suffered no *man* to go in, save P, 4074
9:20 I am? P answering said, The Christ of God. 4074
9:28 he took P and John and James, and went up 4074
9:32 But P and they that were with him were 4074
9:33 from him, P said unto Jesus, Master, 4074
12:41 Then P said unto him, Lord, speakest thou 4074
18:28 Then P said, Lo, we have left all, 4074
22: 8 And he sent P and John, saying, Go and 4074
22:34 And he said, I tell thee, P, *the* cock shall 4074
22:54 priest's house. And P followed afar off. 4074
22:55 set down together, P sat down among them. 4074
22:58 also of them. And P said, Man, I am not. 4074
22:60 And P said, Man, I know not what thou 4074
22:61 And the Lord turned, and looked upon P. 4074
22:61 And P remembered the word of the Lord, 4074
22:62 And P went out, 4074
24:12 Then arose P, and ran unto the sepulchre; 4074
Jn 1:44 of Bethsaida, the city of Andrew and P. 4074
6:68 Then Simon P answered him, Lord, 4074
13: 6 Then cometh he to Simon P: and 4074
13: 6 and *P* saith unto him, Lord, dost thou wash NIG
13: 8 P saith unto him, Thou shalt never wash 4074
13: 9 Simon P saith unto him, Lord, not my feet 4074
13:24 Simon P therefore beckoned to him, that *he* 4074
13:36 Simon P said unto him, Lord, whither goest 4074
13:37 P said unto him, Lord, why cannot I follow 4074
18:10 Then Simon P having a sword drew it, and 4074
18:11 Then said Jesus unto P, Put up thy sword 4074
18:15 And Simon P followed Jesus, and *so* 4074
18:16 But P stood at the door without. Then went 4074
18:16 her that kept the door, and brought in P. 4074
18:17 saith the damsel that kept the door unto P, 4074
18:18 and P stood with them, and 4074
18:25 And Simon P stood and warmed himself. 4074
18:26 being *his* kinsman whose ear P cut off, 4074
18:27 P then denied again: and immediately 4074
20: 2 and cometh to Simon P, and to the other 4074
20: 3 P therefore went forth, and *that* other 4074
20: 4 and the other disciple did outrun P, and 4074
20: 6 Then cometh Simon P following him, and 4074
21: 2 There were together Simon P, and 4074
21: 3 Simon P saith unto them, I go a fishing. 4074
21: 7 disciple whom Jesus loved saith unto P, 4074
21: 7 Now when Simon P heard that it was 4074
21:11 Simon P went up, and drew the net to land 4074
21:15 Jesus saith to Simon P, Simon, *son* of 4074
21:17 P was grieved because he said unto him 4074
21:20 Then P, turning about, seeth the disciple 4074
21:21 P seeing him saith to Jesus, Lord, and 4074
Ac 1:13 where abode both P, and James, and John, 4074
1:15 And in those days P stood up in the midst 4074
2:14 But P, standing up with the eleven, lift up 4074
2:37 and said unto P and *to* the rest of 4074
2:38 Then P said unto them, Repent, and 4074
3: 1 Now P and John went up together into 4074
3: 3 Who seeing P and John about to go into 4074
3: 4 And P, fastening his eyes upon him with 4074
3: 6 Then P said, Silver and gold have I none; 4074
3:11 as the lame *man* which was healed held P 4074
3:12 And when P saw *it,* he answered unto 4074
4: 8 Then P, filled with the Holy Ghost, 4074
4:13 Now when they saw the boldness of P and 4074
4:19 But P and John answered and said unto 4074
5: 3 But P said, Ananias, why hath Satan filled 4074
5: 8 And P answered unto her, Tell me whether 4074
5: 9 Then P said unto her, How *is it* that ye have 4074
5:15 that at the least the shadow of P passing by 4074
5:29 Then P and the *other* apostles answered and 4074
8:14 of God, they sent unto them P and John: 4074
8:20 But P said unto him, Thy money perish 4074
9:32 as P passed throughout all *quarters,* he 4074
9:34 And P said unto him, Aeneas, Jesus Christ 4074
9:38 the disciples had heard that P was there, 4074
9:39 Then P arose and went with them. When he 4074
9:40 But P put *them* all forth, 4074
9:40 her eyes: and when she saw P, she sat up. 4074
10: 5 call for *one* Simon, whose surname is P: 4074
10: 9 P went up upon the house to pray about 4074
10:13 And there came a voice to him, Rise, P; 4074
10:14 But P said, Not so, Lord; for I have never 4074
10:17 Now while P doubted in himself what *this* 4074
10:18 which was surnamed P, were lodged there. 4074
10:19 While P thought on the vision, the Spirit 4074
10:21 Then P went down to the men which were 4074
10:23 lodged *them.* And on the morrow P went 4074
10:25 And as P was coming in, Cornelius met 4074
10:26 But P took him up, saying, Stand up; 4074
10:32 and call hither Simon, whose surname is P; 4074
10:34 Then P opened *his* mouth, and said, Of a 4074
10:44 While P yet spake these words, the Holy 4074
10:45 as many as came with P, because that on 4074
10:46 and magnify God. Then answered P, 4074
11: 2 And when P was come up to Jerusalem, 4074
11: 4 But P *rehearsed the matter* from 4074
11: 7 I heard a voice saying unto me, Arise, P; 4074
11:13 and call for Simon, whose surname is P; 4074
12: 3 he proceeded further to take P also. 4074
12: 5 P therefore was kept in prison: but 4074
12: 6 the same night P was sleeping between two 4074
12: 7 and he smote P on the side, and raised him 4074
12:11 And when P was come to himself, he said, 4074
12:13 And as P knocked at the door of the gate, 4074
12:14 and told how P stood before the gate. 4074
12:16 But P continued knocking: and when they 4074
12:18 among the soldiers, what was become of P. 4074
15: 7 P rose up, and said unto them, Men *and* 4074
Gal 1:18 three years I went up to Jerusalem to see P, 4074
2: 7 *the gospel* of the circumcision *was* unto P; 4074
2: 8 (For he that wrought effectually in P to 4074
2:11 But when P was come to Antioch, 4074
2:14 I said unto P before *them* all, If thou, 4074
1Pe 1: 1 P, an apostle of Jesus Christ, to 4074
2Pe 1: 1 Simon P, a servant and an apostle of Jesus 4074

PETER'S (4) [PETER]
Mt 8:14 And when Jesus was come into P house, 4074
Jn 1:40 was Andrew, Simon P brother. 4074
6: 8 Andrew, Simon P brother, saith unto him, 4074
Ac 12:14 And when she knew P voice, she opened 4074

PETHAHIAH (4)
1Ch 24:16 The nineteenth to P, the twentieth to 6611
Ezr 10:23 (the same *is* Kelita,) P, Judah, and Eliezer. 6611
Ne 9: 5 *and* P, said, Stand up *and* bless the LORD 6611
11:24 P the son of Meshezabeel, of the children 6611

PETHOR (2)
Nu 22: 5 therefore unto Balaam the son of Beor to P, 6604
Dt 23: 4 the son of Beor of P of Mesopotamia, 6604

PETHUEL (1)
Joel 1: 1 the LORD that came to Joel the son of P. 6602

PETITION (13) [PETITIONS]
1Sa 1:17 the God of Israel grant *thee* thy p that thou 7596
1:27 the LORD hath given me my p which I 7596
1Ki 2:16 now I **ask** one p of thee, deny me 7592+7596
2:20 she said, I desire one small p of thee; *I pray* 7596
Est 5: 6 at the banquet of wine, What *is* thy p? 7596
5: 7 and said, My p and my request *is;* 7596
5: 8 if it please the king to grant my p, and 7596
7: 2 of wine, What *is* thy p, queen Esther? 7596
7: 3 let my life be given me at my p, and 7596
9:12 now what *is* thy p? and it shall be granted 7596
Da 6: 7 that whosoever shall ask a p of any God or 1159
6:12 that every man that shall ask *a p* of any God NIH
6:13 but **maketh** his p three times a day. 1156+1159

PETITIONS (2) [PETITION]
Ps 20: 5 up *our* banners: the LORD fulfil all thy p. 4862
1Jn 5:15 we know that we have the p that we desired *155*

PEULLETHAI See PEULTHAI

PEULTHAI (1)
1Ch 26: 5 the sixth, Issachar the seventh, P the eighth: 6469

PHALEC (1) [PELEG]
Lk 3:35 which was *the son* of P, which was *the son* *5317*

PHALLU (1)
Ge 46: 9 Hanoch, and P, and Hezron, and Carmi. 6396

PHALTI (1) [PHALTIEL]
1Sa 25:44 David's wife, to P the son of Laish, 6406

PHALTIEL (1) [PHALTI]
2Sa 3:15 *her* husband, *even* from P the son of Laish. 6409

PHANUEL (1)
Lk 2:36 a prophetess, the daughter of P, of the tribe *5323*

PHARAOH (225) [PHARAOH'S, PHARAOH-HOPHRA, PHARAOH-NECHO, PHARAOH-NECHOH]
Ge 12:15 The princes also of P saw her, and 6547
12:15 saw her, and commended her before P: 6547
12:17 the LORD plagued P and his house with 6547
12:18 P called Abram, and said, What *is* this *that* 6547
12:20 P commanded *his* men concerning him: 6547
39: 1 Potiphar, an officer of P, captain of 6547
40: 2 P was wroth against two *of* his officers, 6547
40:13 Yet within three days shall P lift up thine 6547
40:14 make mention of me unto P, and bring me 6547
40:17 *there was* of all *manner of* bakemeats for P; 6547
40:19 Yet within three days shall P lift up thy 6547
41: 1 at the end of two full years, that P dreamed: 6547
41: 4 well favoured and fat kine. So P awoke. 6547
41: 7 And P awoke, and behold, *it was* a dream. 6547
41: 8 P told them his dream; but *there was* none 6547
41: 8 *was* none that could interpret them unto P. 6547
41: 9 spake the chief butler unto P, saying, I do 6547
41:10 P was wroth with his servants, and put me 6547
41:14 P sent and called Joseph, and they brought 6547
41:14 changed his raiment, and came in unto P. 6547
41:15 P said unto Joseph, I have dreamed a 6547
41:16 Joseph answered P, saying, *It is* not in me: 6547
41:16 God shall give P an answer of peace. 6547
41:17 P said unto Joseph, In my dream, behold, 6547
41:25 Joseph said unto P, The dream of Pharaoh 6547
41:25 said unto Pharaoh, The dream of P *is* one: 6547
41:25 God hath shewed P what he *is* about to do. 6547
41:28 *is* the thing which I have spoken unto P: 6547
41:28 God *is* about to do he sheweth unto P. 6547
41:32 for that the dream was doubled unto P 6547
41:33 let P look out a man discreet and wise, 6547
41:34 Let P do *this,* and let him appoint officers 6547
41:35 lay up corn under the hand of P, and 6547
41:37 the thing was good in the eyes of P, and 6547
41:38 P said unto his servants, Can we find *such* 6547
41:39 P said unto Joseph, Forasmuch as God hath 6547
41:41 P said unto Joseph, See, I have set thee 6547
41:42 P took off his ring from his hand, and put it 6547
41:44 P said unto Joseph, I *am* Pharaoh, and 6547
41:44 I *am* P, and without thee shall no man lift 6547
41:45 P called Joseph's name Zaphnath-paaneah; 6547
41:46 old when he stood before P king of Egypt. 6547
41:46 Joseph went out from the presence of P, 6547
41:55 the people cried to P for bread: 6547
41:55 P said unto all the Egyptians, Go unto 6547
42:15 By the life of P ye shall not go forth hence, 6547
42:16 or else by the life of P surely ye *are* spies. 6547
44:18 against thy servant: for thou *art* even as P. 6547
45: 2 and the Egyptians and the house of P heard. 6547
45: 8 he hath made me a father to P, and lord of 6547
45:16 and it pleased P well, and his servants. 6547
45:17 P said unto Joseph, Say unto thy brethren, 6547
Ge 45:21 according to the commandment of P, and 6547
46: 5 in the wagons which P had sent to carry 6547
46:31 I will go up, and shew P, and say unto him, 6547
46:33 when P shall call you, and shall say, 6547
47: 1 Joseph came and told P, and said, 6547
47: 2 *even* five men, and presented them unto P. 6547
47: 3 P said unto his brethren, What *is* your 6547
47: 3 they said unto P, Thy servants *are* 6547
47: 4 They said moreover unto P, For to sojourn 6547
47: 5 P spake unto Joseph, saying, Thy father 6547
47: 7 in Jacob his father, and set him before P: 6547
47: 7 him before Pharaoh: and Jacob blessed P. 6547
47: 8 And P said unto Jacob, How old *art* thou? 6547
47: 9 Jacob said unto P, The days of the years of 6547
47:10 Jacob blessed P, and went out from before 6547
47:10 and went out from before P. 6547
47:11 the land of Rameses, as P had commanded. 6547
47:19 we and our land will be servants unto P: 6547
47:20 Joseph bought all the land of Egypt for P; 6547
47:22 priests had a portion assigned them of P, 6547
47:22 did eat their portion which P gave them: 6547
47:23 bought you *this* day and your land for P: 6547
47:24 that you shall give the fifth *part* unto P, and 6547
47:26 *that* P should have the fifth *part;* except 6547
50: 4 Joseph spake unto the house of P, saying, 6547
50: 4 speak, I pray you, in the ears of P, saying, 6547
50: 6 P said, Go up, and bury thy father, 6547
50: 7 with him went up all the servants of P, 6547
Ex 1:11 they built for P treasure cities, Pithom and 6547
1:19 the midwives said unto P, Because 6547
1:22 P charged all his people, saying, Every son 6547
2: 5 the daughter of P came down to wash 6547
2:15 Now when P heard this thing, he sought to 6547
2:15 Moses fled from the face of P, and dwelt in 6547
3:10 now therefore, and I will send thee unto P, 6547
3:11 that I should go unto P, and that I should 6547
4:21 see that thou do all *those* wonders before P, 6547
4:22 thou shalt say unto P, Thus saith 6547
5: 1 and Aaron went in, and told P, 6547
5: 2 P said, Who *is* the LORD, that I should 6547
5: 5 P said, Behold, the people of the land now 6547
5: 6 P commanded the same day 6547
5:10 spake to the people, saying, Thus saith P, 6547
5:15 children of Israel came and cried unto P, 6547
5:20 in the way, as they came forth from P: 6547
5:21 our savour to be abhorred in the eyes of P, 6547
5:23 For since I came to P to speak in thy name, 6547
6: 1 Now shalt thou see what I will do to P: 6547
6:11 Go in, speak unto P king of Egypt, that he 6547
6:12 how then shall P hear me, who *am* of 6547
6:13 of Israel, and unto P king of Egypt, 6547
6:27 *These are* they which spake to P king of 6547
6:29 speak thou unto P king of Egypt all that I 6547
6:30 and how shall P hearken unto me? 6547
7: 1 See, I have made thee a god to P: 6547
7: 2 Aaron thy brother shall speak unto P, 6547
7: 4 P shall not hearken unto you, that I may lay 6547
7: 7 three years old, when they spake unto P. 6547
7: 9 When P shall speak unto you, saying, 6547
7: 9 cast *it* before P, *and* it shall become a 6547
7:10 Moses and Aaron went in unto P, and 6547
7:10 Aaron cast down his rod before P, and 6547
7:11 P also called the wise men and 6547
7:15 Get thee unto P in the morning; lo, 6547
7:20 in the sight of P, and in the sight of his 6547
7:23 P turned and went into his house, 6547
8: 1 Go unto P, and say unto him, Thus saith 6547
8: 8 P called for Moses and Aaron, and said, 6547
8: 9 Moses said unto P, Glory over me: when 6547
8:12 Moses and Aaron went out from P: and 6547
8:12 the frogs which he had brought against P. 6547
8:15 when P saw that there was respite, he 6547
8:19 the magicians said unto P, This *is* the finger 6547
8:20 early in the morning, and stand before P; 6547
8:24 grievous swarm *of flies* into the house of P, 6547
8:25 P called for Moses and for Aaron, and said, 6547
8:28 P said, I will let you go, that ye may 6547
8:29 that the swarms *of flies* may depart from P, 6547
8:29 let not P deal deceitfully any more in not 6547
8:30 Moses went out from P, and intreated 6547
8:31 and he removed the swarms *of flies* from P, 6547
8:32 P hardened his heart at this time also, 6547
9: 1 unto Moses, Go in unto P, and tell him, 6547
9: 7 P sent, and behold, there was not one of 6547
9: 7 the heart of P was hardened, and he did not 6547
9: 8 it towards the heaven in the sight of P. 6547
9:10 ashes of the furnace, and stood before P; 6547
9:12 the LORD hardened the heart of P, and 6547
9:13 and stand before P, and say unto him, 6547
9:20 the servants of P made his servants 6547
9:27 P sent, and called for Moses and Aaron, 6547
9:33 Moses went out of the city from P, 6547
9:34 when P saw that the rain and the hail and 6547
9:35 the heart of P was hardened, neither would 6547
10: 1 the LORD said unto Moses, Go in unto P: 6547
10: 3 Moses and Aaron came in unto P, and 6547
10: 6 he turned himself, and went out from P. 6547
10: 8 and Aaron were brought again unto P: 6547
10:16 P called for Moses and Aaron in haste; 6547
10:18 he went out from P, and intreated 6547
10:24 P called unto Moses, and said, Go ye, 6547
10:28 P said unto him, Get thee from me, 6547
11: 1 Yet will I bring one plague *more* upon P, 6547
11: 5 from the firstborn of P that sitteth upon his 6547
11: 8 And he went out from P in a great anger. 6547
11: 9 unto Moses, P shall not hearken unto you; 6547
11:10 and Aaron did all these wonders before P: 6547
12:29 from the firstborn of P that sat on his 6547
12:30 P rose up in the night, he, and all his 6547
13:15 to pass, when P would hardly let us go, 6547
13:17 came to pass, when P had let the people go, 6547
14: 3 For P will say of the children of Israel, 6547
14: 4 I will be honoured upon P, and upon all his 6547
14: 5 the heart of P and of his servants was 6547
14: 8 the LORD hardened the heart of P king of 6547

Ex 14: 9 after them (all the horses *and* chariots of **P**, 6547
14:10 when **P** drew nigh, the children of Israel lift 6547
14:17 I will get me honour upon **P**, and upon all 6547
14:18 when I have gotten me honour upon **P**, 6547
14:28 all the host of **P** that came into the sea after 6547
15:19 For the horse of **P** went in with his chariots 6547
18: 4 and delivered me from the sword of **P**: 6547
18: 8 in law all that the LORD had done unto **P** 6547
18:10 of the Egyptians, and out of the hand of **P**, 6547
Dt 6:22 upon **P**, and upon all his household, 6547
7: 8 from the hand of **P** king of Egypt. 6547
7:18 what the LORD thy God did unto **P**, 6547
11: 3 which he did in the midst of Egypt unto **P** 6547
29: 2 your eyes in the land of Egypt unto **P**, 6547
34:11 sent him to do in the land of Egypt to **P**, 6547
1Sa 6: 6 the Egyptians and **P** hardened their hearts? 6547
1Ki 3: 1 Solomon made affinity with **P** king of 6547
9:16 *For* **P** king of Egypt had gone up, and 6547
11: 1 together with the daughter of **P**, *women of* 6547
11:18 they came *to* Egypt, unto **P** king of Egypt; 6547
11:19 Hadad found great favour in the sight of **P**, 6547
11:20 Pharaoh's household among the sons of **P**. 6547
11:21 Hadad said to **P**, Let me depart, that I may 6547
11:22 **P** said unto him, But what *hast* thou lacked 6547
2Ki 17: 7 from under the hand of **P** king of Egypt, 6547
18:21 *is* **P** king of Egypt unto all that trust on 6547
23:35 Jehoiakim gave the silver and the gold to **P**; 6547
23:35 according to the commandment of **P**: 6547
1Ch 4:18 *are* the sons of Bithiah the daughter of **P**, 6547
2Ch 8:11 Solomon brought up the daughter of **P** out 6547
Ne 9:10 shewedst signs and wonders upon **P**, and 6547
Ps 135: 9 O Egypt, upon **P**, and upon all his servants. 6547
136:15 overthrew **P** and his host in the Red sea: 6547
Isa 19:11 the counsel of the wise counsellers of **P** is 6547
19:11 how say ye unto **P**, I *am* the son of 6547
30: 2 strengthen themselves in the strength of **P**, 6547
30: 3 Therefore shall the strength of **P** be your 6547
36: 6 so *is* **P** king of Egypt to all that trust in him. 6547
Jer 25:19 **P** king of Egypt, and his servants, and his 6547
46:17 cry there, **P** king of Egypt *is but* a noise; 6547
46:25 **P**, and Egypt, with their gods, and their 6547
46:25 even **P**, and *all* them that trust in him: 6547
47: 1 the Philistines, before that **P** smote Gaza. 6547
Eze 17:17 Neither shall **P** with *his* mighty army and 6547
29: 2 set thy face against **P** king of Egypt, and 6547
29: 3 Behold, I *am* against thee, **P** king of Egypt, 6547
30:21 I have broken the arm of **P** king of Egypt; 6547
30:22 I *am* against **P** king of Egypt, and 6547
30:25 and the arms of **P** shall fall down; 6547
31: 2 speak unto **P** king of Egypt, and to his 6547
31:18 This *is* **P** and all his multitude, saith 6547
32: 2 take up a lamentation for **P** king of Egypt, 6547
32:31 **P** shall see them, and shall be comforted 6547
32:31 *even* **P** and all his army slain by the sword, 6547
32:32 *even* **P** and all his multitude, saith the Lord 6547
Ac 7:10 and wisdom in the sight of **P** king of Egypt; *5328*
7:13 Joseph's kindred was made known unto **P**. *5328*
Ro 9:17 For the scripture saith unto **P**, Even for this *5328*

PHARAOH'S (48) [PHARAOH]

Ge 12:15 and the woman was taken into **P** house. 6547
37:36 an officer of **P**, *and* captain of the guard. 6547
40: 7 he asked **P** officers that *were* with him in 6547
40:11 **P** cup *was* in my hand: and I took 6547
40:11 pressed them into **P** cup, and I gave the cup 6547
40:11 and I gave the cup into **P** hand. 6547
40:13 thou shalt deliver **P** cup into his hand, 6547
40:20 to pass the third day, *which was* **P** birthday, 6547
40:21 and he gave the cup into **P** hand: 6547
45:16 And the fame *thereof* was heard *in* **P** house, 6547
47:14 Joseph brought the money into **P** house. 6547
47:20 over them: so the land became **P**. 6547+3807.1
47:25 my lord, and we will be **P** servants. 6547+3807.1
47:26 priests only, *which* became not **P**. 6547+3807.1
Ex 2: 7 said his sister to **P** daughter, Shall I go 6547
2: 8 **P** daughter said to her, Go. And the maid 6547
2: 9 **P** daughter said unto her, Take this child 6547
2:10 she brought him unto **P** daughter, and 6547
5:14 which **P** taskmasters had set over them, 6547
7: 3 I will harden **P** heart, and multiply my 6547
7:13 he hardened **P** heart, that he hearkened not 6547
7:14 **P** heart *is* hardened, he refuseth to let 6547
7:22 **P** heart was hardened, neither did he 6547
8:19 **P** heart was hardened, and he hearkened 6547
10: 7 **P** servants said unto him, How long shall 6547
10:11 And they were driven out from **P** presence. 6547
10:20 the LORD hardened **P** heart, so that he 6547
10:27 the LORD hardened **P** heart, and 6547
11: 3 in the sight of **P** servants, and in the sight 6547
11:10 the LORD hardened **P** heart, so that he 6547
14: 4 I will harden **P** heart, that he shall follow 6547
14:23 *even* all **P** horses, his chariots, and 6547
15: 4 **P** chariots and his host hath he cast into 6547
Dt 6:21 thy son, We were **P** bondmen in Egypt; 6547
1Sa 2:27 when they were in Egypt in **P** house? 6547
1Ki 3: 1 took **P** daughter, and brought her into 6547
7: 8 Solomon made also a house for **P** daughter, 6547
9:24 **P** daughter came up out of the city of David 6547
11:20 whom Tahpenes weaned in **P** house: 6547
11:20 Genubath was *in* **P** household among 6547
SS 1: 9 to a company of horses in **P** chariots. 6547
Jer 37: 5 **P** army was come forth out of Egypt: and 6547
37: 7 Behold, **P** army, which is come forth to 6547
37:11 up from Jerusalem for fear of **P** army, 6547
43: 9 which *is* at the entry of **P** house in 6547
Eze 30:24 I will break **P** arms, and he shall groan 6547
Ac 7:21 **P** daughter took him up, and nourished him *5328*
Heb 11:24 refused to be called the son of **P** daughter; *5328*

PHARAOH-HOPHRA (1) [PHARAOH]

Jer 44:30 I *will* give **P** king of Egypt into the hand of 6548

PHARAOH-NECHO (1) [PHARAOH]

Jer 46: 2 against the army of **P** king of Egypt, 6549

PHARAOH-NECHOH (4) [PHARAOH]

2Ki 23:29 In his days **P** king of Egypt went up against 6549
23:33 **P** put him in bands at Riblah in the land of 6549
23:34 **P** made Eliakim the son of Josiah king in 6549
23:35 according to his taxation, to give *it* unto **P**. 6549

PHARES (3) [PHAREZ]

Mt 1: 3 And Judas begat **P** and Zara of Thamar; *5329*
1: 3 and **P** begat Esrom; and Esrom begat *5329*
Lk 3:33 which was *the son* of **P**, which was *the son* *5329*

PHAREZ (12) [PHARES, PHARZITES]

Ge 38:29 upon thee: therefore his name was called **P**. 6557
46:12 and Onan, and Shelah, and **P**, and Zerah: 6557
46:12 And the sons of **P** were Hezron and Hamul. 6557
Nu 26:20 of **P**, the family of the Pharzites: of Zerah, 6557
26:21 the sons of **P** were; of Hezron, the family 6557
Ru 4:12 let thy house be like the house of **P**, 6557
4:18 Now these *are* the generations of **P**: 6557
4:18 the generations of Pharez: **P** begat Hezron, 6557
1Ch 2: 4 Tamar his daughter in law bare him **P** and 6557
2: 5 The sons of **P**; Hezron, and Hamul. 6557
4: 1 **P**, Hezron, and Carmi, and Hur, and 6557
9: 4 of the children of **P** the son of Judah. 6557

PHARISEE (11) [PHARISEE'S, PHARISEES, PHARISEES']

Mt 23:26 *Thou* blind **P**, cleanse first that *which is* *5330*
Lk 7:39 Now when the **P** which had bidden him *5330*
11:37 a certain **P** besought him to dine with him: *5330*
11:38 And when the **P** saw *it*, he marvelled that *5330*
18:10 the one a **P**, and the other a publican. *5330*
18:11 The **P** stood and prayed thus with himself, *5330*
Ac 5:34 a **P**, named Gamaliel, a doctor of law, *5330*
23: 6 Men *and* brethren, I am a **P**, the son of a *5330*
23: 6 brethren, I am a Pharisee, the son of a **P**: *5330*
26: 5 straitest sect of our religion I lived a **P**. *5330*
Php 3: 5 of the Hebrews; as touching the law, a **P**; *5330*

PHARISEE'S (2) [PHARISEE]

Lk 7:36 eat with him. And he went into the **P** house, *5330*
7:37 knew that *Jesus* sat at meat in the **P** house, *5330*

PHARISEES (86) [PHARISEE]

Mt 3: 7 But when he saw many of the **P** and *5330*
5:20 *the righteousness* of the scribes and **P**, *5330*
9:11 And when the **P** saw *it*, they said unto his *5330*
9:14 Why do we and the **P** fast oft, but *5330*
9:34 But the **P** said, He casteth out the devils *5330*
12: 2 But when the **P** saw *it*, they said unto him, *5330*
12:14 Then the **P** went out, and held a council *5330*
12:24 But when the **P** heard *it*, they said, *5330*
12:38 of the scribes and of the **P** answered, *5330*
15: 1 Then came to Jesus scribes and **P**, *5330*
15:12 Knowest thou that the **P** were offended, *5330*
16: 1 The **P** also with the Sadducees came, and *5330*
16: 6 and beware of the leaven of the **P** and *5330*
16:11 that *ye* should beware of the leaven of the **P** *5330*
16:12 but of the doctrine of the **P** and *of* *5330*
19: 3 The **P** also came unto him, tempting him, *5330*
21:45 chief priests and **P** had heard his parables, *5330*
22:15 Then went the **P**, and took counsel how *5330*
22:34 But when the **P** had heard that he had put *5330*
22:41 While the **P** were gathered together, Jesus *5330*
23: 2 The scribes and the **P** sit in Moses' seat: *5330*
23:13 woe unto you, scribes and **P**, hypocrites! *5330*
23:14 Woe unto you, scribes and **P**, hypocrites! *5330*
23:15 Woe unto you, scribes and **P**, hypocrites! *5330*
23:23 Woe unto you, scribes and **P**, hypocrites! *5330*
23:25 Woe unto you, scribes and **P**, hypocrites! *5330*
23:27 Woe unto you, scribes and **P**, hypocrites! *5330*
23:29 Woe unto you, scribes and **P**, hypocrites! *5330*
27:62 and **P** came together unto Pilate, *5330*
Mk 2:16 and **P** saw him eat with publicans and *5330*
2:18 disciples of John and of the **P** used to fast: *5330*
2:18 do the disciples of John and of the **P** fast, *5330*
2:24 And the **P** said unto him, Behold, why do *5330*
3: 6 And the **P** went forth, and straightway took *5330*
7: 1 Then came together unto him the **P**, and *5330*
7: 3 For the **P**, and all the Jews, except they *5330*
7: 5 Then the **P** and scribes asked him, *5330*
8:11 And the **P** came forth, and began to *5330*
8:15 beware of the leaven of the **P**, and *of* *5330*
10: 2 And the **P** came to *him*, and asked him, Is it *5330*
12:13 And they send unto him certain of the **P** *5330*
Lk 5:17 that there were **P** and doctors of the law *5330*
5:21 And the scribes and the **P** began to reason, *5330*
5:30 and **P** murmured against his disciples, *5330*
5:33 and likewise the *disciples* of the **P**; *5330*
6: 2 And certain of the **P** said unto them, *5330*
6: 7 And the scribes and **P** watched him, *5330*
7:30 But the **P** and lawyers rejected the counsel *5330*
7:36 And one of the **P** desired him that he would *5330*
11:39 Now do ye **P** make clean the outside of *5330*
11:42 But woe unto you, **P**! for ye tithe mint and *5330*
11:43 Woe unto you, **P**! for ye love *5330*
11:44 Woe unto you, scribes and **P**, hypocrites! *5330*
11:53 and the **P** began to urge *him* vehemently, *5330*
12: 1 *of all*, Beware ye of the leaven of the **P**, *5330*
13:31 The same day there came certain *of the* **P**, *5330*
14: 1 the chief **P** to eat bread on the sabbath day, *5330*
14: 3 answering spake unto the lawyers and **P**, *5330*
15: 2 And the **P** and scribes murmured, saying, *5330*
16:14 And the **P** also, who were covetous, *5330*
17:20 And when he was demanded of the **P**, *5330*
19:39 And some of the **P** from among *5330*
Jn 1:24 And they which were sent were of the **P**. *5330*
3: 1 There was a man of the **P**, *5330*
4: 1 the Lord knew how the **P** had heard that *5330*
7:32 The **P** heard that the people murmured such *5330*
7:32 and the **P** and the chief priests sent officers *5330*
7:45 came the officers to the chief priests and **P**; *5330*
7:47 Then answered them the **P**, Are ye also *5330*
7:48 of the rulers or of the **P** believed on him? *5330*
Jn 8: 3 **P** brought unto him a woman taken in *5330*
8:13 The **P** therefore said unto him, *5330*
9:13 They brought to the **P** him that aforetime *5330*
9:15 Then again the **P** also asked him how he *5330*
9:16 Therefore said some of the **P**, This man is *5330*
9:40 And *some* of the **P** which were with him *5330*
11:46 But some of them went their ways to the **P**, *5330*
11:47 the chief priests and the **P** a council, *5330*
11:57 and the **P** had given a commandment, *5330*
12:19 The **P** therefore said among themselves, *5330*
12:42 of the **P** they did not confess *him*, lest they *5330*
18: 3 and officers from the chief priests and **P**, *5330*
Ac 15: 5 certain of the sect of the **P** which believed, *5330*
23: 6 and the other **P**, he cried out in the council, *5330*
23: 7 there arose a dissension between the **P** and *5330*
23: 8 angel nor spirit: but the **P** confess both. *5330*

PHARISEES' (1) [PHARISEE]

Ac 23: 9 the scribes *that were* of the **P** part arose, *5330*

PHAROSH (1)

Ezr 8: 3 Of the sons of Shechaniah, of the sons of **P**; 6551

PHARPAR (1)

2Ki 5:12 *Are* not Abana and **P**, rivers of Damascus, 6554

PHARZITES (1) [PHAREZ]

Nu 26:20 of Pharez, the family of the **P**: of Zerah, 6558

PHASEAH (1) [PASEAH]

Ne 7:51 the children of Uzza, the children of **P**, 6454

PHEBE (2)

Ro 16: 1 I commend unto you **P** our sister, which is *5402*
16: S *sent* by **P** servant of the church at *5402*

PHENICE (3) [PHENICIA]

Ac 11:19 arose about Stephen travelled as far as **P**, *5403*
15: 3 they passed through **P** and Samaria, *5403*
27:12 if by any means they might attain to **P**, *and* *5405*

PHENICIA (1) [PHENICE, SYROPHENICIAN]

Ac 21: 2 And finding a ship sailing over unto **P**, *5403*

PHI-BESETH (1)

Eze 30:17 of Aven and of **P** shall fall by the sword: 6364

PHICHOL (3)

Ge 21:22 **P** the chief captain of his host spake unto 6369
21:32 **P** the chief captain of his host, and 6369
26:26 and **P** the chief captain of his army. 6369

PHICOL See PHICHOL

PHILADELPHIA (2)

Rev 1:11 unto Sardis, and unto **P**, and unto Laodicea. *5359*
3: 7 And to the angel of the church in **P** write; *5359*

PHILEMON (2)

Phm 1: 1 unto **P** *our* dearly beloved, and *5371*
1: S Written from Rome to **P**, by Onesimus a *5371*

PHILETUS (1)

2Ti 2:17 a canker: of whom is Hymeneus and **P**; *5372*

PHILIP (33) [PHILIP'S]

Mt 10: 3 **P**, and Bartholomew; Thomas, and *5376*
Mk 3:18 and **P**, and Bartholomew, and Matthew, *5376*
Lk 3: 1 and his brother **P** tetrarch of Iturea and *5376*
6:14 and John, **P** and Bartholomew, *5376*
Jn 1:43 and findeth **P**, and saith unto him, *5376*
1:44 Now **P** was of Bethsaida, the city of *5376*
1:45 **P** findeth Nathanael, and saith unto him, *5376*
1:46 **P** saith unto him, Come and see. *5376*
1:48 said unto him, Before that **P** called thee, *5376*
6: 5 he saith unto **P**, Whence shall we buy *5376*
6: 7 **P** answered him, Two hundred pennyworth *5376*
12:21 The same came therefore to **P**, which was *5376*
12:22 **P** cometh and telleth Andrew: and *5376*
12:22 and again Andrew and **P** tell Jesus. *5376*
14: 8 **P** saith unto him, Lord, shew us the Father, *5376*
14: 9 and *yet* hast thou not known me, **P**? *5376*
Ac 1:13 and John, and Andrew, **P**, and Thomas, *5376*
6: 5 and **P**, and Prochorus, and Nicanor, and *5376*
8: 5 Then **P** went down to the city of Samaria, *5376*
8: 6 gave heed unto those *things* which **P** spake, *5376*
8:12 But when they believed **P** preaching *5376*
8:13 he continued with **P**, and wondered, *5376*
8:26 And *the* angel of the Lord spake unto **P**, *5376*
8:29 Then the Spirit said unto **P**, Go near, and *5376*
8:30 And **P** ran *thither* to *him*, and heard him *5376*
8:31 And he desired **P** that *he* would come up *5376*
8:34 And the eunuch answered **P**, and said, *5376*
8:35 Then **P** opened his mouth, *5376*
8:37 And **P** said, If thou believest with all *thine* *5376*
8:38 both into the water, both **P** and the eunuch; *5376*
8:39 the Spirit of the Lord caught away **P**, *5376*
8:40 But **P** was found at Azotus: and *5376*
21: 8 we entered into the house of **P** *5376*

PHILIP'S (3) [PHILIP]

Mt 14: 3 for Herodias' sake, his brother **P** wife. *5376*
Mk 6:17 for Herodias' sake, his brother **P** wife: *5376*
Lk 3:19 by him for Herodias his brother **P** wife, *5376*

PHILIPPI (8) [PHILIPPIANS]

Mt 16:13 Jesus came into the coasts of Cesarea **P**, *5376*
Mk 8:27 his disciples, into the towns of Cesarea **P**: *5376*
Ac 16:12 And from thence to **P**, which is the chief *5375*
20: 6 And we sailed away from **P** after the days *5375*
1Co 16: S was written from **P** by Stephanas, *5375*
2Co 13: S to the Corinthians was written from **P**, *5375*
Php 1: 1 all the saints in Christ Jesus which are at **P**, *5375*

1Th 2: 2 shamefully entreated, as ye know, at P, 5375

PHILIPPIANS (2) [PHILIPPI]
Php 4:15 Now ye P know also, that in the beginning 5374
4: S It was written to the P from Rome by 5374

PHILISTIA (3) [PHILISTIM, PHILISTIMS, PHILISTINE, PHILISTINES, PHILISTINES']
Ps 60: 8 my shoe: P, triumph thou because of me. 6429
87: 4 behold P, and Tyre, with Ethiopia; this *man* 6429
108: 9 I cast out my shoe; over P will I triumph. 6429

PHILISTIM (1) [PHILISTIA]
Ge 10:14 and Casluhim, (out of whom came P) 6430

PHILISTIMS (5) [PHILISTIA]
Ge 26: 1 Isaac went unto Abimelech king of the P 6430
26: 8 that Abimelech king of the P looked out at 6430
26:14 store of servants: and the P envied him. 6430
26:15 the P had stopped them, and filled them 6430
26:18 for the P had stopped them after the death 6430

PHILISTINE (33) [PHILISTIA]
1Sa 17: 8 *am* not I a P, and you servants to Saul? 6430
17:10 the P said, I defy the armies of Israel this 6430
17:11 and all Israel heard those words of the P, 6430
17:16 the P drew near morning and evening, and 6430
17:23 the P of Gath, Goliath by name, 6430
17:26 shall be done to the man that killeth this P, 6430
17:26 for who *is* this uncircumcised P, that he 6430
17:32 thy servant will go and fight with this P. 6430
17:33 Thou art not able to go against this P to 6430
17:36 this uncircumcised P shall be as one of 6430
17:37 he will deliver me out of the hand of this P. 6430
17:40 *was* in his hand: and he drew near to the P. 6430
17:41 the P came on and drew near unto David; 6430
17:42 when the P looked about, and saw David, 6430
17:43 the P said unto David, *Am* I a dog, 6430
17:43 And the P cursed David by his gods. 6430
17:44 the P said to David, Come to me, and I will 6430
17:45 said David to the P, Thou comest to me 6430
17:48 when the P arose, and came and drew nigh 6430
17:48 and ran *toward* the army to meet the P. 6430
17:49 slang *it*, and smote the P in his forehead, 6430
17:50 So David prevailed over the P with a sling 6430
17:50 a stone, and smote the P, and slew him; 6430
17:51 stood upon the P, and took his sword, and 6430
17:54 David took the head of the P, and 6430
17:55 Saul saw David go forth against the P, 6430
17:57 David returned from the slaughter of the P, 6430
17:57 Saul with the head of the P in his hand. 6430
18: 6 was returned from the slaughter of the P, 6430
19: 5 slew the P, and the LORD wrought a great 6430
21: 9 the priest said, The sword of Goliath the P, 6430
22:10 and gave him the sword of Goliath the P. 6430
2Sa 21:17 and smote the P, and killed him. 6430

PHILISTINES (246) [PHILISTIA]
Ge 21:32 and they returned into the land of the P. 6430
Ex 13:17 not *through* the way of the land of the P, 6430
23:31 the Red sea even unto the sea of the P, 6430
Jos 13: 2 all the borders of the P, and all Geshuri, 6430
13: 3 five lords of the P; the Gazathites, and 6430
Jdg 3: 3 *Namely,* five lords of the P, and all 6430
3:31 which slew *of* the P six hundred men with 6430
10: 6 the gods of the P, and forsook the LORD, 6430
10: 7 he sold them into the hands of the P, and 6430
10:11 the children of Ammon, and from the P? 6430
13: 1 them into the hand of the P forty years. 6430
13: 5 to deliver Israel out of the hand of the P. 6430
14: 1 in Timnath of the daughters of the P. 6430
14: 2 in Timnath of the daughters of the P: 6430
14: 3 to take a wife of the uncircumcised P? 6430
14: 4 that he sought an occasion against the P: 6430
14: 4 for at that time the P had dominion over 6430
15: 3 Now shall I be more blameless than the P, 6430
15: 5 let *them* go into the standing corn of the P, 6430
15: 6 the P said, Who hath done this? And they 6430
15: 6 the P came up, and burnt her and her father 6430
15: 9 the P went up, and pitched in Judah, and 6430
15:11 Knowest thou not that the P *are* rulers over 6430
15:12 we may deliver thee into the hand of the P. 6430
15:14 came unto Lehi, the P shouted against him: 6430
15:20 he judged Israel in the days of the P twenty 6430
16: 5 the lords of the P came up unto her, and 6430
16: 8 the lords of the P brought up to her seven 6430
16: 9 unto him, The P *be* upon thee, Samson. 6430
16:12 unto him, The P *be* upon thee, Samson. 6430
16:14 unto him, The P *be* upon thee, Samson. 6430
16:18 she sent and called for the lords of the P, 6430
16:18 the lords of the P came up unto her, and 6430
16:20 she said, The P *be* upon thee, Samson. 6430
16:21 the P took him, and put out his eyes, and 6430
16:23 the lords of the P gathered them together 6430
16:27 all the lords of the P *were* there; and 6430
16:28 that I may be at once avenged of the P for 6430
16:30 Samson said, Let me die with the P. And he 6430
1Sa 4: 1 Now Israel went out against the P to battle, 6430
4: 1 and the P pitched in Aphek. 6430
4: 2 the P put *themselves* in array against Israel: 6430
4: 2 Israel was smitten before the P: 6430
4: 3 the LORD smitten us to day before the P? 6430
4: 6 when the P heard the noise of the shout, 6430
4: 7 the P were afraid, for they said, God is 6430
4: 9 and quit yourselves like men, O ye P, 6430
4:10 the P fought, and Israel was smitten, and 6430
4:17 Israel is fled before the P, and there hath 6430
5: 1 the P took the ark of God, and brought it 6430
5: 2 When the P took the ark of God, they 6430
5: 8 gathered all the lords of the P unto them, 6430
5:11 and gathered together all the lords of the P, 6430
6: 1 was in the country of the P seven months. 6430
6: 2 the P called for the priests and the diviners, 6430
6: 4 *to* the number of the lords of the P: 6430
1Sa 6:12 the lords of the P went after them unto 6430
6:16 when the five lords of the P had seen *it*, 6430
6:17 these *are* the golden emerods which the P 6430
6:18 cities of the P *belonging* to the five lords, 6430
6:21 The P have brought again the ark of 6430
7: 3 he will deliver you out of the hand of the P. 6430
7: 7 when the P heard that the children of Israel 6430
7: 7 the lords of the P went up against Israel. 6430
7: 7 of Israel heard *it*, they were afraid of the P. 6430
7: 8 he will save us out of the hand of the P. 6430
7:10 the P drew near to battle against Israel: 6430
7:10 with a great thunder on that day upon the P, 6430
7:11 pursued the P, and smote them, until *they* 6430
7:13 So the P were subdued, and they came no 6430
7:13 the hand of the LORD was against the P 6430
7:14 the cities which the P had taken from Israel 6430
7:14 did Israel deliver out of the hands of the P. 6430
9:16 save my people out of the hand of the P: 6430
10: 5 hill of God, where *is* the garrison of the P: 6430
12: 9 into the hand of the P, and into the hand of 6430
13: 3 Jonathan smote the garrison of the P that 6430
13: 3 the P heard *of it*. And Saul blew 6430
13: 4 *that* Saul had smitten a garrison of the P, 6430
13: 4 also was had in abomination with the P. 6430
13: 5 the P gathered themselves together to fight 6430
13:11 *that* the P gathered themselves together *at* 6430
13:12 The P will come down now upon me *to* 6430
13:16 but the P encamped in Michmash. 6430
13:17 the spoilers came out of the camp of the P 6430
13:19 for the P said, Lest the Hebrews make *them* 6430
13:20 all the Israelites went down *to* the P, 6430
13:23 the garrison of the P went out to 6430
14: 1 themselves unto the garrison of the P: 6430
14:11 the P said, Behold, the Hebrews come forth 6430
14:19 that the noise that *was* in the host of the P 6430
14:21 Moreover the Hebrews *that* were with the P 6430
14:22 *when* they heard that the P fled, even they 6430
14:30 now a much greater slaughter among the P? 6430
14:31 they smote the P that day from Michmash 6430
14:36 Let us go down after the P by night, and 6430
14:37 of God, Shall I go down after the P? 6430
14:46 Saul went up from following the P: and 6430
14:46 and the P went to their own place. 6430
14:47 the kings of Zobah, and against the P: 6430
14:52 there was sore war against the P all 6430
17: 1 Now the P gathered together their armies to 6430
17: 2 and set the battle in array against the P. 6430
17: 3 the P stood on a mountain on the one side, 6430
17: 4 out a champion out of the camp of the P, 6430
17:19 in the valley of Elah, fighting with the P. 6430
17:21 and the P had put *the battle* in array, 6430
17:23 out of the armies of the P, and 6430
17:46 I will give the carcases of the host of the P 6430
17:51 when the P saw their champion was dead, 6430
17:52 and shouted, and pursued the P, 6430
17:52 the wounded of the P fell down by the way 6430
17:53 of Israel returned from chasing after the P, 6430
18:17 but let the hand of the P be upon him. 6430
18:21 that the hand of the P may be against him. 6430
18:25 but an hundred foreskins of the P, 6430
18:25 to make David fall by the hand of the P. 6430
18:27 and slew of the P two hundred men; 6430
18:30 the princes of the P went forth: and it came 6430
19: 8 fought with the P, and slew them with a 6430
23: 1 the P fight against Keilah, and they rob 6430
23: 2 Shall I go and smite these P? 6430
23: 2 Go, and smite the P, and save Keilah. 6430
23: 3 come *to* Keilah against the armies of the P? 6430
23: 4 for I will deliver the P into thine hand. 6430
23: 5 fought with the P, and brought away their 6430
23:27 and come; for the P have invaded the land. 6430
23:28 after David, and went against the P: 6430
24: 1 Saul was returned from following the P, 6430
27: 1 speedily escape into the land of the P; 6430
27: 7 dwelt in the country of the P was a full year 6430
27:11 while he dwelleth in the country of the P. 6430
28: 1 that the P gathered their armies together for 6430
28: 4 the P gathered themselves together, and 6430
28: 5 when Saul saw the host of the P, he was 6430
28:15 for the P make war against me, and God is 6430
28:19 Israel with thee into the hand of the P: 6430
28:19 the host of Israel into the hand of the P. 6430
29: 1 Now the P gathered together all their 6430
29: 2 the lords of the P passed on by hundreds, 6430
29: 3 said the princes of the P, What *do* these 6430
29: 3 And Achish said unto the princes of the P, 6430
29: 4 the princes of the P were wroth with him; 6430
29: 4 the princes of the P said unto him, 6430
29: 7 that thou displease not the lords of the P. 6430
29: 9 notwithstanding the princes of the P have 6430
29:11 to return into the land of the P. 6430
29:11 And the P went up *to* Jezreel. 6430
30:16 that they had taken out of the land of the P, 6430
31: 1 Now the P fought against Israel: and 6430
31: 1 the men of Israel fled from before the P, 6430
31: 2 the P followed hard upon Saul and upon his 6430
31: 2 the P slew Jonathan, and Abinadab, and 6430
31: 7 fled; and the P came and dwelt in them. 6430
31: 8 when the P came to strip the slain, that they 6430
31: 9 and sent into the land of the P round about, 6430
31:11 heard of that which the P had done to Saul, 6430
2Sa 1:20 lest the daughters of the P rejoice, lest 6430
3:14 to me for an hundred foreskins of the P. 6430
3:18 my people Israel out of the hand of the P, 6430
5:17 when the P heard that they had anointed 6430
5:17 all the P came up to seek David; 6430
5:18 The P also came and spread themselves in 6430
5:19 the LORD, saying, Shall I go up to the P? 6430
5:19 for I will doubtless deliver the P into thine 6430
5:22 the P came up yet again, and 6430
5:24 out before thee, to smite the host of the P. 6430
5:25 smote the P from Geba until thou come *to* 6430
8: 1 that David smote the P, and subdued them: 6430
8: 1 Metheg-ammah out of the hand of the P. 6430
8:12 of the P, and of Amalek, and of the spoil of 6430
2Sa 19: 9 he delivered us out of the hand of the P; 6430
21:12 where the P had hanged them, when 6430
21:12 when the P had slain Saul in Gilboa: 6430
21:15 Moreover the P had yet war again with 6430
21:15 with him, and fought against the P: 6430
21:18 that there was again a battle with the P at 6430
21:19 there was again a battle in Gob with the P, 6430
23: 9 when they defied the P *that* were there 6430
23:10 smote the P until his hand was weary, and 6430
23:11 the P were gathered together into a troop, 6430
23:11 *of* lentiles: and the people fled from the P. 6430
23:12 and defended it, and slew the P: 6430
23:13 the troop of the P pitched in the valley of 6430
23:14 the garrison of the P *was* then 6430
23:16 *men* brake through the host of the P, 6430
1Ki 4:21 from the river *unto* the land of the P, 6430
15:27 at Gibbethon, which *belongeth* to the P; 6430
16:15 which *belonged* to the P. 6430
2Ki 8: 2 sojourned in the land of the P seven years. 6430
8: 3 woman returned out of the land of the P: 6430
18: 8 He smote the P, *even* unto Gaza, and 6430
1Ch 1:12 and Casluhim, (of whom came the P,) 6430
10: 1 Now the P fought against Israel; and 6430
10: 1 the men of Israel fled from before the P, 6430
10: 2 the P followed hard after Saul, and after his 6430
10: 2 the P slew Jonathan, and Abinadab, and 6430
10: 7 fled: and the P came and dwelt in them. 6430
10: 8 when the P came to strip the slain, that they 6430
10: 9 and sent into the land of the P round about, 6430
10:11 when all Jabesh-gilead heard all that the P 6430
11:13 there the P were gathered together to battle, 6430
11:13 and the people fled from before the P. 6430
11:14 *that* parcel, and delivered it, and slew the P; 6430
11:15 the host of the P encamped in the valley of 6430
11:18 the three brake through the host of the P, 6430
12:19 when he came with the P against Saul to 6430
12:19 for the lords of the P upon advisement sent 6430
14: 8 when the P heard that David was anointed 6430
14: 8 all Israel, all the P went up to seek David. 6430
14: 9 the P came and spread themselves in 6430
14:10 of God, saying, Shall I go up against the P? 6430
14:13 the P yet again spread themselves abroad in 6430
14:15 forth before thee to smite the host of the P. 6430
14:16 they smote the host of the P from Gibeon 6430
18: 1 that David smote the P, and subdued them, 6430
18: 1 and her towns out of the hand of the P. 6430
18:11 and from the P, and from Amalek. 6430
20: 4 that there arose war at Gezer with the P; 6430
20: 5 there was war again with the P; and 6430
2Ch 9:26 from the river even unto the land of the P, 6430
17:11 Also *some* of the P brought Jehoshaphat 6430
21:16 up against Jehoram the spirit of the P, 6430
26: 6 he went forth and warred against the P, 6430
26: 6 built cities about Ashdod, and among the P. 6430
26: 7 God helped him against the P, and 6430
28:18 The P also had invaded the cities of the low 6430
Ps 56: T of David, when the P took him in Gath. 6430
83: 7 Amalek; the P with the inhabitants of Tyre; 6429
Isa 2: 6 *are* soothsayers like the P, and they please 6430
9:12 The Syrians before, and the P behind; 6430
11:14 they shall fly upon the shoulders of the P 6430
Jer 25:20 all the kings of the land of the P, and 6430
47: 1 came to Jeremiah the prophet against the P, 6430
47: 4 of the day that cometh to spoil all the P, 6430
47: 4 for the LORD *will* spoil the P, 6430
Eze 16:27 the daughters of the P, which are ashamed 6430
16:57 *are* round about her, the daughters of the P, 6430
25:15 Because the P have dealt by revenge, and 6430
25:16 I *will* stretch out mine hand upon the P, and 6430
Am 1: 8 the remnant of the P shall perish, saith 6430
6: 2 go down *to* Gath of the P: *be they* better 6430
9: 7 the P from Caphtor, and the Syrians from 6430
Ob 1:19 mount of Esau; and *they of* the plain the P: 6430
Zep 2: 5 O Canaan, the land of the P, I will even 6430
Zec 9: 6 and I will cut off the pride of the P. 6430

PHILISTINES' (4) [PHILISTIA]
Ge 21:34 Abraham sojourned in the P land many 6430
1Sa 14: 1 Come, and let us go over to the P garrison, 6430
14: 4 sought to go over unto the P garrison, 6430
1Ch 11:16 and the P garrison *was* then at Beth-lehem. 6430

PHILOLOGUS (1)
Ro 16:15 Salute P, and Julia, Nereus, and his sister, 5378

PHILOSOPHERS (1) [PHILOSOPHY]
Ac 17:18 Then certain p of the Epicureans, and of 5386

PHILOSOPHY (1) [PHILOSOPHERS]
Col 2: 8 Beware lest any *man* spoil you through p 5385

PHINEHAS (24) [PHINEHAS']
Ex 6:25 of Putiel to wife; and she bare him P: 6372
Nu 25: 7 when P, the son of Eleazar, the son of 6372
25:11 P, the son of Eleazar, the son of Aaron 6372
31: 6 them and P the son of Eleazar the priest, 6372
Jos 22:13 of Gilead, P the son of Eleazar the priest, 6372
22:30 when P the priest, and the princes of 6372
22:31 P the son of Eleazar the priest said unto 6372
22:32 P the son of Eleazar the priest, and 6372
24:33 they buried him in a hill that pertained to P 6372
Jdg 20:28 P, the son of Eleazar, the son of Aaron, 6372
1Sa 1: 3 the two sons of Eli, Hophni and P, 6372
2:34 come upon thy two sons, on Hophni and P; 6372
4: 4 the two sons of Eli, Hophni and P, 6372
4:11 two sons of Eli, Hophni and P, were slain. 6372
4:17 Hophni and P, are dead, and the ark of God 6372
14: 3 the son of P, the son of Eli, 6372
1Ch 6: 4 Eleazar begat P, Phinehas begat Abishua, 6372
6: 4 Eleazar begat Phinehas, P begat Abishua, 6372
6:50 Eleazar his son, P his son, Abishua his son, 6372
9:20 P the son of Eleazar was the ruler over 6372
Ezr 7: 5 the son of P, the son of Eleazar, 6372
8: 2 Of the sons of P; Gershom: of the sons of 6372

Ezr 8:33 with him *was* Eleazar the son of P; and 6372
Ps 106:30 stood up P, and executed judgment: and 6372

PHINEHAS' (1) [PHINEHAS]
1Sa 4:19 P wife, was with child, *near* to be 6372

PHLEGON (1)
Ro 16:14 P, Hermas, Patrobas, Hermes, and *5393*

PHOEBE See PHEBE

PHOENICIA See PHENICE; PHENICIA

PHOENIX See PHENICE

PHRYGIA (4)
Ac 2:10 P, and Pamphylia, in Egypt, and in *5435*
16: 6 Now when they had gone throughout P and *5435*
18:23 *all* the country of Galatia and P in order, *5435*
1Ti 6: S which is the chiefest city of P Pacatiana. *5435*

PHURAH (2)
Jdg 7:10 go thou with P thy servant down to 6513
7:11 went he down with P his servant unto 6513

PHUT (2)
Ge 10: 6 Cush, and Mizraim, and P, and Canaan. 6316
Eze 27:10 and of Lud and of P were in thine army, 6316

PHUVAH (1) [PUAH]
Ge 46:13 Tola, and P, and Job, and Shimron. 6312

PHYGELLUS (1)
2Ti 1:15 from me; of whom are P and Hermogenes. *5436*

PHYGELUS See PHYGELLUS

PHYLACTERIES (1)
Mt 23: 5 they make broad their **p**, and enlarge *5440*

PHYSICIAN (6) [PHYSICIANS]
Jer 8:22 no balm in Gilead; *is there* no **p** there? 7495
Mt 9:12 They that be whole need not a **p**, but *2395*
Mk 2:17 They that are whole have no need of *the* **p**, *2395*
Lk 4:23 say unto me this proverb, P, heal thyself: *2395*
5:31 They that are whole need not a **p**; *2395*
Col 4:14 Luke, the beloved **p**, and Demas, greet you. *2395*

PHYSICIANS (6) [PHYSICIAN]
Ge 50: 2 Joseph commanded his servants the **p** to 7495
50: 2 his father: and the **p** embalmed Israel. 7495
2Ch 16:12 he sought not *to* the LORD, but to the **p**. 7495
Job 13: 4 *are* forgers of lies, ye *are* all **p** of no value. 7495
Mk 5:26 And had suffered many *things* of many **p**, *2395*
Lk 8:43 which had spent all *her* living upon **p**, *2395*

PICK (1)
Pr 30:17 the ravens of the valley shall **p** it **out**, and 5365

PICKED TROOPS See WORTHIES

PICTURES (3)
Nu 33:52 destroy all their **p**, and destroy all their 4906
Pr 25:11 spoken *is like* apples of gold in **p** of silver. 4906
Isa 2:16 ships of Tarshish, and upon all pleasant **p**. 7914

PIECE (43) [PIECES, SHOULDERPIECES]
Ge 15:10 and laid each **p** one against another: 1335
Ex 37: 7 **beaten out of one p** made he them, on 4749
Nu 10: 2 of a **whole p** thou shalt make them: 4749
Jdg 9:53 a certain woman cast a **p** of a millstone 6400
1Sa 2:36 crouch to him for a **p** of silver and a morsel of 95
2:36 priests' offices, that *I* may eat a **p** of bread. 6595
30:12 they gave him a **p** of a cake *of figs*, and 6400
2Sa 6:19 a **good p** *of flesh*, and a flagon *of wine*. So 829
11:21 did not a woman cast a **p** of a millstone 6400
23:11 where was a **p** of ground full *of* lentiles: 2513
2Ki 3:19 and mar every good **p of land** with stones. 2513
3:25 *on* every good **p of land** cast every man his 2513
1Ch 16: 3 and a **good p** *of flesh*, and a flagon *of wine*. 829
Ne 3:11 repaired the other **p**, and the tower of 4060
3:19 another **p** over against the going up to 4060
3:20 of Zabbai earnestly repaired the other **p**, 4060
3:21 the son of Urijah the son of Koz another **p**, 4060
3:24 Binnui the son of Henadad another **p**, 4060
3:27 After them the Tekoites repaired another **p**, 4060
3:30 Hanun the sixth son of Zalaph, another **p**. 4060
Job 41:24 yea, as hard as a **p** of the nether *millstone*. 6400
42:11 every man also gave him a **p of money**, 7192
Pr 6:26 woman *a man is brought* to a **p** of bread: 3603
28:21 for for a **p** of bread *that* man will 6595
SS 4: 3 thy temples *are* like a **p** of a pomegranate 6400
6: 7 As a **p** of a pomegranate *are* thy temples 6400
Jer 37:21 that *they* should give him daily a **p** of bread 3603
Eze 24: 4 *even* every good **p**, the thigh, and 5409
24: 6 bring it out **p** by piece; let no lot fall upon 5409
24: 6 bring it out piece by **p**; let no lot fall upon 5409
Am 3:12 mouth of the lion two legs, or a **p** of an ear; 915
4: 7 one **p** was rained upon, and the piece 2513
4: 7 and the **p** whereupon it rained not withered. 2513
Mt 9:16 No *man* putteth a **p** of new cloth unto an *1915*
17:27 his mouth, thou shalt find a **p of money**: *4715*
Mk 2:21 No *man* also seweth a **p** of new cloth on an *1915*
2:21 else the new **p that filled it up** taketh away *4138*
Lk 5:36 No *man* putteth a **p** of a new garment upon *1915*
5:36 the **p** that was *taken* out of the new agreeth *1915*
14:18 I have bought a **p of ground**, and I must *68*
15: 8 if she lose one **p**, doth not light a candle, *1406*
15: 9 for I have found the **p** which I had lost. *1406*
24:42 And they gave him a **p** of a broiled fish, *3313*

PIECES (121) [PIECE]
Ge 15:17 burning lamp that passed between those **p**. 1506
20:16 I have given thy brother a thousand *p* of NIH
33:19 for an hundred **p of money**. 7192
37:28 sold Joseph to the Ishmeelites for twenty *p* NIH
37:33 Joseph is **without doubt rent in p**. 2963+2963
44:28 and I said, Surely he is **torn in p**; 2963+2963
45:22 to Benjamin he gave three hundred *p* of NIH
Ex 15: 6 O LORD, hath **dashed in p** the enemy. 7492
22:13 If it be **torn in p**, *then* let him bring 2963+2963
29:17 thou shalt cut the ram in **p**, and wash 5409
29:17 and put *them* unto his **p**, and unto his head. 5409
Lev 1: 6 flay the burnt offering, and cut it into his **p**. 5409
1:12 he shall cut it into his **p**, with his head and 5409
2: 6 Thou shalt **part** it **in p**, and pour oil 6595+6626
6:21 the baken **p** of the meat offering shalt thou 6595
8:20 he cut the ram into **p**; and Moses burnt 5409
8:20 burnt the head, and the **p**, and the fat. 5409
9:13 unto him, with the **p** thereof, and the head: 5409
Jos 24:32 of Shechem for an hundred **p of silver**: 7192
Jdg 9: 4 ten *p* of silver out of the house of NIH
16: 5 every one *of us* eleven hundred *p* of silver. NIH
19:29 into twelve **p**, and sent her into all 5409
20: 6 **cut** her **in p**, and sent her throughout all 5408
1Sa 2:10 of the LORD shall be **broken to p**; 2865
11: 7 **hewed** them **in p**, and sent *them* throughout 5408
15:33 Samuel **hewed** Agag **in p** before 8158
1Ki 11:30 that *was* on him, and rent it *in* twelve **p**: 7168
11:31 he said to Jeroboam, Take thee ten **p**: 7168
18:23 **cut** it **in p**, and lay *it* on wood, and put no 5408
18:33 **cut** the bullock **in p**, and laid *him* on 5408
19:11 **brake in p** the rocks before the LORD; 7665
2Ki 2:12 own clothes, and **rent** them **in** two **p**. 7167+7168
5: 5 six thousand *p* of gold, and ten changes of NIH
6:25 until an ass's head was *sold* for fourscore *p* NIH
6:25 of a kab of dove's dung for five *p* of silver. NIH
11:18 and his images **brake** they **in p** throughly, 7665
18: 4 **brake in p** the brasen serpent that Moses 3807
23:14 he **brake in p** the images, and cut down 7665
24:13 **cut in p** all the vessels of gold which 7112
25:13 did the Chaldees break *in p*, and carried NIH
2Ch 23:17 **brake** his altars and his images **in p**, and 7665
25:12 of the rock, that they all were **broken in p**. 1234
28:24 **cut in p** the vessels of the house of God, 7112
31: 1 brake the images *in p*, and cut down NIH
34: 4 he brake *in p*, and made dust *of them*, and NIH
Job 16:12 **shaken** me **to p**, and set me up for his 6327
19: 2 my soul, and **break** me **in p** with words? 1792
34:24 He shall **break in p** mighty *men* without 7489
40:18 His bones *are as* **strong p** of brass; his bones 650
Ps 2: 9 thou shalt **dash** them **in p** like a potter's 5310
7: 2 **rending** *it* **in p**, while *there is* none to 6561
50:22 lest I **tear** *you* **in p**, and *there be* none to 2963
58: 7 *to shoot* his arrows, let them be as **cut in p**. 4135
68:30 *till every one* submit himself with **p** of 7518
72: 4 and shall **break in p** the oppressor. 1792
74:14 Thou **brakest** the heads of leviathan **in p**, 7533
89:10 Thou hast **broken** Rahab **in p**, as one that 1792
94: 5 They **break in p** thy people, O LORD, 1792
SS 8:11 thereof was to bring a thousand *p* of silver. NIH
Isa 3:15 What mean ye *that* ye **beat** my people **to p**, 1792
8: 9 O ye people, and ye shall be **broken in p**; 2865
8: 9 and ye shall be **broken in p**; 2865
8: 9 and ye shall be **broken in p**. 2865
13:16 Their children also shall be **dashed to p** 7376
13:18 bows also shall **dash** the young men **to p**; 7376
30:14 of the potters' vessel that is **broken in p**; 3807
45: 2 I will **break in p** the gates of brass, and 7665
Jer 5: 6 that goeth out thence shall be **torn in p**: 2963
23:29 like a hammer *that* **breaketh** the rock **in p**? 6327
50: 2 is confounded, Merodach is **broken in p**; 2865
50: 2 her images are **broken in p**. 2865
51:20 for with thee will I **break in p** the nations, 5310
51:21 with thee will I **break in p** the horse and 5310
51:21 with thee will I **break in p** the chariot and 5310
51:22 With thee also will I **break in p** man and 5310
51:22 with thee will I **break in p** old and young; 5310
51:22 with thee will I **break in p** the young man 5310
51:23 I will also **break in p** with thee 5310
51:23 with thee will I **break in p** the husbandman 5310
51:23 with thee will I **break in p** captains and 5310
La 3:11 turned aside my ways, and **pulled** me **in p**: 6582
Eze 4:14 *of* that which dieth of itself, or is **torn in p**; 2966
13:19 for handfuls of barley and for **p** of bread, 6595
24: 4 Gather the **p** thereof into it, *even* every 5409
Da 2: 5 ye shall be cut in **p**, and your houses shall 1917
2:34 *were* of iron and clay, and **brake** them **in p**. 1855
2:35 **broken to p** together, and became like 1855
2:40 forasmuch as iron **breaketh in p** and 1855
2:40 all these, shall it **break in p** and bruise. 1855
2:44 *but* it shall **break in p** and consume all 1855
2:45 *that* it **brake in p** the iron, the brass, 1855
3:29 shall be cut in **p**, and their houses shall be 1917
6:24 **brake** all their bones **in p** or ever they 1855
7: 7 it devoured and **brake in p**, and 1855
7:19 **brake in p**, and stamped the residue with 1855
7:23 and shall tread it down, and **break** it **in p**. 1855
Hos 3: 2 So I bought her to me for fifteen *p* of silver, NIH
8: 6 the calf of Samaria shall be **broken in p**. 7616
10:14 the mother was **dashed in p** upon *her* 7376
13:16 their infants shall be **dashed in p**, and 7376
Mic 1: 7 graven images thereof shall be **beaten to p**, 3807
3: 3 **chop** *them* **in p**, as for the pot, and as flesh 6566
4:13 thou shalt **beat in p** many people: and 1854
5: 8 and **teareth in p**, and none can deliver. 2963
Na 2: 1 He that **dasheth in p** is come up before thy 6327
2:12 The lion did **tear in p** enough for his 2963
3:10 her young children also were **dashed in p** 7376
Zec 11:12 So they weighed *for* my price thirty *p* of NIH
11:13 I took the thirty *p* of silver, and cast them to NIH
11:16 flesh of the fat, and **tear** their claws **in p**. 6561
12: 3 themselves with it shall be **cut in p**, 8295+8295
Mt 26:15 And they covenanted with him for thirty **p** NIG
27: 3 brought again the thirty **p** of silver to NIG
27: 5 And he cast down the **p** of silver in NIG
27: 6 And the chief priests took the silver **p**, and NIG
27: 9 saying, And they took the thirty **p** of silver, NIG
Mk 5: 4 by him, and the fetters **broken in p**: *4937*
Lk 15: 8 Either what woman having ten **p** of silver, NIG
Ac 19:19 and found *it* fifty thousand *p* of silver. NIG
23:10 Paul should have been **pulled in p** of them, *1288*
27:44 and some on **broken** *p* of the ship. *5100*

PIERCE (4) [PIERCED, PIERCETH, PIERCING, PIERCINGS]
Nu 24: 8 and **p** *them* **through** *with* his arrows. 4272
2Ki 18:21 man lean, it will go into his hand, and **p** it: 5344
Isa 36: 6 man lean, it will go into his hand, and **p** it: 5344
Lk 2:35 a sword shall **p through** thy own soul *1330*

PIERCED (8) [PIERCE]
Jdg 5:26 when she had **p** and stricken through his 4272
Job 30:17 My bones are **p** in me in the night season: 5365
Ps 22:16 inclosed me: they **p** my hands and my feet. 3738
Zec 12:10 they shall look upon me whom they have **p**, 1856
Jn 19:34 But one of the soldiers with a spear **p** his *3572*
19:37 They shall look on *him* whom they **p**. *1574*
1Ti 6:10 **p** themselves **through** with many sorrows. *4044*
Rev 1: 7 shall see him, and they *also* which **p** him: *1574*

PIERCETH (1) [PIERCE]
Job 40:24 it with his eyes: *his* nose **p** through snares. 5344

PIERCING (2) [PIERCE]
Isa 27: 1 strong sword shall punish leviathan the **p** 1281
Heb 4:12 **p** even to the dividing asunder of soul and *1338*

PIERCINGS (1) [PIERCE]
Pr 12:18 There is that speaketh like the **p** of a sword: 4094

PIETY (1)
1Ti 5: 4 let them learn first to **shew p** at home, and *2151*

PIG See SWINE

PIGEON (2) [PIGEONS]
Ge 15: 9 years old, and a turtle-dove, and a **young p**. 1469
Lev 12: 6 a young **p**, or a turtledove, for a sin 3123

PIGEONS (10) [PIGEON]
Lev 1:14 his offering of turtledoves, or of young **p**. 3123
5: 7 two turtledoves, or two young **p**, unto 3123
5:11 or two young **p**, then he that sinned shall 3123
12: 8 she shall bring two turtles, or two young **p**; 3123
14:22 two turtledoves, or two young **p**, such as he 3123
14:30 or of the young **p**, such as he can get; 3123
15:14 or two young **p**, and come before 3123
15:29 or two young **p**, and bring them unto 3123
Nu 6:10 two turtles, or two young **p**, to the priest, 3123
Lk 2:24 A pair of turtledoves, or two young **p**. *4058*

PI-HAHIROTH (4)
Ex 14: 2 that they turn and encamp before **P**, 6367
14: 9 by the sea, beside **P**, before Baal-zephon. 6367
Nu 33: 7 turned again unto **P**, which *is* before 6367
33: 8 they departed from before *P*ahiroth, and 6367

PILATE (56)
Mt 27: 2 delivered him to Pontius **P** the governor. *4091*
27:13 Then said **P** unto him, Hearest thou not *4091*
27:17 **P** said unto them, Whom will ye *that* I *4091*
27:22 **P** saith unto them, What shall I do then *4091*
27:24 When **P** saw that he could prevail nothing, *4091*
27:58 He went to **P**, and begged the body of *4091*
27:58 Then **P** commanded the body to be *4091*
27:62 and Pharisees came together unto **P**, *4091*
27:65 **P** said unto them, Ye have a watch: go your *4091*
Mk 15: 1 carried *him* away, and delivered *him* to **P**. *4091*
15: 2 And **P** asked him, Art thou the King of *4091*
15: 4 And **P** asked him again, saying, *4091*
15: 5 yet answered nothing; so that **P** marvelled. *4091*
15: 9 But **P** answered them, saying, Will ye *that* I *4091*
15:12 And **P** answered and said again unto them, *4091*
15:14 Then **P** said unto them, Why, what evil *4091*
15:15 And *so* **P**, willing to content the people, *4091*
15:43 and went in boldly unto **P**, and craved *4091*
15:44 And **P** marvelled if he were already dead: *4091*
Lk 3: 1 Pontius **P** being governor of Judea, and *4091*
13: 1 whose blood **P** had mingled with their *4091*
23: 1 of them arose, and led him unto **P**. *4091*
23: 3 And **P** asked him, saying, Art thou *4091*
23: 4 Then said **P** to the chief priests and *to* *4091*
23: 6 When **P** heard of Galilee, he asked whether *4091*
23:11 in a gorgeous robe, and sent him again to **P**. *4091*
23:12 And the same day **P** and Herod were made *4091*
23:13 And **P**, when he had called together *4091*
23:20 **P** therefore, willing to release Jesus, spake *4091*
23:24 And **P** gave sentence that it should be as *4091*
23:52 This *man* went unto **P**, and begged *4091*
Jn 18:29 **P** then went out unto them, and said, What *4091*
18:31 Then said **P** unto them, Take ye him, and *4091*
18:33 Then **P** entered into the judgment hall *4091*
18:35 **P** answered, Am I a Jew? Thine own *4091*
18:37 **P** therefore said unto him, Art thou a king *4091*
18:38 **P** saith unto him, What is truth? And when *4091*
19: 1 Then **P** therefore took Jesus, and *4091*
19: 4 **P** therefore went forth again, and *4091*
19: 5 And *P* saith unto them, Behold the man. NIG
19: 6 Crucify *him*, crucify *him*. **P** saith unto *4091*
19: 8 When **P** therefore heard that saying, he was *4091*
19:10 Then saith **P** unto him, Speakest thou not *4091*
19:12 *And* from thenceforth **P** sought to release *4091*
19:13 When **P** therefore heard that saying, *4091*
19:15 **P** saith unto them, Shall I crucify your *4091*
19:19 And **P** wrote a title, and put *it* on the cross. *4091*
19:21 Then said the chief priests of the Jews to **P**, *4091*
19:22 **P** answered, What I have written I have *4091*
19:31 besought **P** that their legs might be broken, *4091*
19:38 besought **P** that he might take away *4091*
19:38 and **P** gave *him* leave. He came therefore, *4091*
Ac 3:13 and denied him in the presence of **P**, *4091*

Ac 4:27 both Herod, and Pontius **P**, with *4091*
13:28 *yet* desired they **P** that he should be slain. *4091*
1Ti 6:13 who before Pontius **P** witnessed a good *4091*

PILDASH (1)
Ge 22:22 and Hazo, and **P**, and Jidlaph, and Bethuel. 6394

PILE (2)
Isa 30:33 the **p** thereof *is* fire and much wood; 4071
Eze 24: 9 I will even make the **p for fire** great. 4071

PILE OF RUBBLE See DUNGHILL

PILEHA (1)
Ne 10:24 Hallohesh, **P**, Shobek, 6401

PILGRIMAGE (4) [PILGRIMS]
Ge 47: 9 The days of the years of my **p** *are* an 4033
47: 9 the life of my fathers in the days of their **p**. 4033
Ex 6: 4 the land of their **p**, wherein they were 4033
Ps 119:54 have been my songs in the house of my **p**. 4033

PILGRIMS (2) [PILGRIMAGE]
Heb 11:13 that they were strangers and **p** on the earth. *3927*
1Pe 2:11 I beseech *you* as strangers and **p**, *3927*

PILHA See PILEHA

PILLAR (47) [PILLARS]
Ge 19:26 behind him, and she became a **p** of salt. 5333
28:18 set it up *for* a **p**, and poured oil upon 4676
28:22 this stone, which I have set *for* a **p**, shall be 4676
31:13 where thou anointedst the **p**, *and* 4676
31:45 Jacob took a stone, and set it up *for* a **p**. 4676
31:51 Behold this heap, and behold *this* **p**, 4676
31:52 This heap *be* witness, and *this* **p** *be* witness, 4676
31:52 not pass over this heap and this **p** unto me, 4676
35:14 Jacob set up a **p** in the place where he 4678
35:14 he talked with him, *even* a **p** of stone: 4678
35:20 Jacob set a **p** upon her grave: that *is* 4676
35:20 that *is* the **p** of Rachel's grave unto *this* 4678
Ex 13:21 the LORD went before them by day in a **p** 5982
13:21 by night in a **p** of fire, to give them light; 5982
13:22 He took not away the **p** of the cloud by day, 5982
13:22 nor the **p** of fire by night, *from* before 5982
14:19 the **p** of the cloud went from before their 5982
14:24 host of the Egyptians through the **p** of fire 5982
33: 9 the cloudy **p** descended, and stood *at* 5982
33:10 all the people saw the cloudy **p** stand *at* 5982
Nu 12: 5 the LORD came down in the **p** of 5982
14:14 by day time in a **p** of a cloud, and in a pillar 5982
14:14 pillar of a cloud, and in a **p** of fire by night. 5982
Dt 31:15 appeared in the tabernacle in a **p** of a cloud: 5982
31:15 the **p** of the cloud stood over the door of 5982
Jdg 9: 6 by the plain of the **p** that *was* in Shechem. 5324
20:40 arise up out of the city *with* a **p** of smoke, 5982
2Sa 18:18 had taken and reared up for himself a **p**, 4678
18:18 he called the **p** after his own name: and it is 4678
1Ki 7:21 he set up the right **p**, and called the name 5982
7:21 he set up the left **p**, and called the name 5982
2Ki 11:14 behold, the king stood by a **p**, as 5982
23: 3 the king stood by a **p**, and made a covenant 5982
25:17 The height of the one **p** *was* eighteen 5982
25:17 like unto these had the second **p** with 5982
2Ch 23:13 the king stood at his **p** at the entering in, 5982
Ne 9:12 thou leddest them in the day by a cloudy **p**; 5982
9:12 in the night by a **p** of fire, to give them 5982
9:19 the **p** of the cloud departed not from them 5982
9:19 neither the **p** of fire by night, to shew them 5982
Ps 99: 7 He spake unto them in the cloudy **p**: 5982
Isa 19:19 and a **p** at the border thereof to the LORD. 4676
Jer 1:18 an iron **p**, and brasen walls against 5982
52:21 the height of one **p** *was* eighteen cubits; 5982
52:22 The second **p** also and the pomegranates 5982
1Ti 3:15 living God, the **p** and ground of the truth. *4769*
Rev 3:12 Him that overcometh will I make a **p** in *4769*

PILLARS (89) [PILLAR]
Ex 24: 4 an altar under the hill, and twelve **p**, 4676
26:32 thou shalt hang it upon four **p** of shittim 5982
26:37 thou shalt make for the hanging five **p** of 5982
27:10 the twenty **p** thereof and their twenty 5982
27:10 the hooks of the **p** and their fillets *shall be* 5982
27:11 his twenty **p** and their twenty sockets *of* 5982
27:11 the hooks of the **p** and their fillets *of* silver. 5982
27:12 their **p** ten, and their sockets ten. 5982
27:14 their **p** three, and their sockets three. 5982
27:15 fifteen *cubits:* their **p** three, and 5982
27:16 *and* their **p** *shall be* four, and their sockets 5982
27:17 All the **p** round about the court *shall be* 5982
35:11 his boards, his bars, his **p**, and his sockets, 5982
35:17 his **p**, and their sockets, and the hanging for 5982
36:36 he made thereunto four **p** of shittim *wood,* 5982
36:38 the five **p** of it with their hooks: and 5982
38:10 Their **p** *were* twenty, and their brasen 5982
38:10 the hooks of the **p** and their fillets *were of* 5982
38:11 their **p** *were* twenty, and their sockets *of* 5982
38:11 the hooks of the **p** and their fillets *of* silver. 5982
38:12 their **p** ten, and their sockets ten; 5982
38:12 the hooks of the **p** and their fillets *of* silver. 5982
38:14 their **p** three, and their sockets three. 5982
38:15 their **p** three, and their sockets three. 5982
38:17 the sockets for the **p** *were of* brass; 5982
38:17 the hooks of the **p** and their fillets *of* silver; 5982
38:17 all the **p** of the court *were* filleted *with* 5982
38:19 their **p** *were* four, and their sockets *of* brass 5982
38:28 and five *shekels* he made hooks for the **p**, 5982
39:33 his bars, and his **p**, and his sockets, 5982
39:40 his **p**, and his sockets, and the hanging for 5982
40:18 put in the bars thereof, and reared up his **p**. 5982
Nu 3:36 the **p** thereof, and the sockets thereof, and 5982
3:37 the **p** of the court round about, and 5982
4:31 and the **p** thereof, and sockets thereof, 5982
4:32 the **p** of the court round about, and 5982

Dt 12: 3 break their **p**, and burn their groves with 4676
Jdg 16:25 them sport: and they set him between the **p**. 5982
16:26 Suffer me that I may feel the **p** whereupon 5982
16:29 Samson took hold of the two middle **p** 5982
1Sa 2: 8 for the **p** of the earth *are* the LORD'S, and 4690
1Ki 7: 2 thirty cubits, upon four rows of cedar **p**, 5982
7: 2 cedar pillars, with cedar beams upon the **p**. 5982
7: 3 that *lay* on forty five **p**, fifteen *in* a row. 5982
7: 6 he made a porch of **p**; the length thereof 5982
7: 6 *the other* **p** and the thick beam *were* before 5982
7:15 For he cast two **p** *of* brass, of eighteen 5982
7:16 molten brass, to set upon the tops of the **p**; 5982
7:17 chapiters which *were* upon the top of the **p**; 5982
7:18 he made the **p**, and two rows round about 5982
7:19 top of the **p** *were* of lily work in the porch, 5982
7:20 the chapiters upon the two **p** *had* 5982
7:21 he set up the **p** in the porch of the temple: 5982
7:22 upon the top of the **p** *was* lily work: so 5982
7:22 so was the work of the **p** finished. 5982
7:41 The two **p**, and the two bowls of 5982
7:41 chapiters that *were* on the top of the *two* **p**; 5982
7:41 chapiters which *were* upon the top of the **p**; 5982
7:42 bowls of the chapiters that *were* upon the **p**; 5982
10:12 the king made *of* the almug trees **p** for 4552
2Ki 18:16 *from* the **p** which Hezekiah king of Judah 547
25:13 the **p** of brass that *were in* the house of 5982
25:16 The two **p**, one sea, and the bases which 5982
1Ch 18: 8 and the **p**, and the vessels of brass. 5982
2Ch 3:15 Also he made before the house two **p** of 5982
3:16 and put *them* on the heads of the **p**; 5982
3:17 he reared up the **p** before the temple, 5982
4:12 *To wit,* the two **p**, and the pommels, and 5982
4:12 *which were* on the top of the two **p**, 5982
4:12 chapiters which *were* on the top of the **p**; 5982
4:13 of the chapiters which *were* upon the **p**. 5982
Est 1: 6 and purple to silver rings and **p** of marble: 5982
Job 9: 6 out of her place, and the **p** thereof tremble. 5982
26:11 The **p** of heaven tremble and are astonished 5982
Ps 75: 3 *are* dissolved: I bear up the **p** of it. Selah. 5982
Pr 9: 1 her house, she hath hewn out her seven **p**: 5982
SS 3: 6 out of the wilderness like **p** of smoke, 8490
3:10 He made the **p** thereof *of* silver, the bottom 5982
5:15 His legs *are as* **p** of marble, set upon 5982
Jer 27:19 saith the LORD of hosts concerning the **p**, 5982
52:17 Also the **p** of brass that *were* in the house 5982
52:20 The two **p**, one sea, and twelve brasen bulls 5982
52:21 *concerning* the **p**, the height of one pillar 5982
Eze 40:49 *there were* **p** by the posts, one on this side, 5982
42: 6 but had not **p** as the pillars of the courts: 5982
42: 6 but had not pillars as the **p** of the courts: 5982
Joel 2:30 the earth, blood, and fire, and **p** of smoke. 8490
Gal 2: 9 Cephas, and John, who seemed to be **p**, *4769*
Rev 10: 1 as *it were* the sun, and his feet as **p** of fire: *4769*

PILLED (2)
Ge 30:37 **p** white strakes in them, and made 6478
30:38 he set the rods which he had **p** before 6478

PILLOW (3) [PILLOWS]
1Sa 19:13 put a **p** of goats' *hair for* his bolster, and 3523
19:16 with a **p** of goats' *hair for* his bolster. 3523
Mk 4:38 in the hinder part of the ship, asleep on a **p**: *4344*

PILLOWS (4) [PILLOW]
Ge 28:11 put *them for* his **p**, and lay down in that 4763
28:18 took the stone that he had put *for* his **p**, and 4763
Eze 13:18 Woe to *the women* that sew **p** to all 3704
13:20 Behold, I *am* against your **p**, where*with* ye 3704

PILOTS (4)
Eze 27: 8 O Tyrus, *that* were in thee, *were* thy **p**. 2259
27:27 thy **p**, thy calkers, and the occupiers of thy 2259
27:28 shall shake at the sound of the cry of thy **p**. 2259
27:29 the mariners, *and* all the **p** of the sea, 2259

PILTAI (1)
Ne 12:17 Zichri; of Miniamin, of Moadiah, **P**; 6408

PIN (3) [PINS]
Jdg 16:14 she fastened *it* with the **p**, and said unto 3489
16:14 went away with the **p** of the beam, and 3489
Eze 15: 3 will *men* take a **p** of it to hang any vessel 3489

PINE (8) [PINETH, PINING]
Lev 26:39 they that are left of you shall **p away** in 4743
26:39 their fathers shall they **p away** with them. 4743
Ne 8:15 **p** branches, and myrtle branches, and 8081
Isa 41:19 *and* the **p**, and the box tree together: 8410
60:13 the fir tree, the **p tree**, and the box together, 8410
La 4: 9 for these **p away**, stricken through for *want* 2100
Eze 24:23 ye shall **p away** for your iniquities, and 4743
33:10 we **p away** in them, how should we then 4743

PINETH (1) [PINE]
Mk 9:18 and gnasheth with his teeth, and **p away**: *3583*

PINING (1) [PINE]
Isa 38:12 he will cut me off with **p sickness**: 1803

PINNACLE (2)
Mt 4: 5 and setteth him on a **p** of the temple, *4419*
Lk 4: 9 and set him on a **p** of the temple, and *4419*

PINON (2)
Ge 36:41 Duke Aholibamah, duke Elah, duke **P**, 6373
1Ch 1:52 Duke Aholibamah, duke Elah, duke **P**, 6373

PINS (11) [PIN]
Ex 27:19 all the **p** thereof, and all the pins of 3489
27:19 and all the **p** of the court, *shall be of* brass. 3489
35:18 The **p** of the tabernacle, and the pins of 3489
35:18 and the **p** of the court, and their cords, 3489
38:20 all the **p** of the tabernacle, and of the court 3489

Ex 38:31 all the **p** of the tabernacle, and all the pins 3489
38:31 and all the **p** of the court round about. 3489
39:40 his **p**, and all the vessels of the service of 3489
Nu 3:37 their sockets, and their **p**, and their cords. 3489
4:32 their sockets, and their **p**, and their cords, 3489
Isa 3:22 and the wimples, and the **crisping p**, 2754

PIPE (4) [PIPED, PIPERS, PIPES]
1Sa 10: 5 a tabret, and a **p**, and a harp, before them; 2485
Isa 5:12 and the viol, the tabret, and **p**, and wine, 2485
30:29 as when one goeth with a **p** to come into 2485
1Co 14: 7 without life giving sound, whether **p** or harp, *836*

PIPED (4) [PIPE]
1Ki 1:40 the people **p** with pipes, and rejoiced *with* 2490
Mt 11:17 We have **p** unto you, and ye have not *832*
Lk 7:32 We have **p** unto you, and ye have not *832*
1Co 14: 7 how shall it be known what is **p** or harped? *832*

PIPERS (1) [PIPE]
Rev 18:22 and musicians, and of **p**, and trumpeters, *834*

PIPES (6) [PIPE]
1Ki 1:40 the people piped with **p**, and rejoiced *with* 2485
Jer 48:36 mine heart shall sound for Moab like **p**, 2485
48:36 mine heart shall sound like **p** for the men of 2485
Eze 28:13 of thy **p** was prepared in thee in the day 5345
Zec 4: 2 and seven **p** to the seven lamps, 4166
4:12 **p** empty the golden *oil* out of themselves? 6804

PIRAM (1)
Jos 10: 3 unto **P** king of Jarmuth, and unto Japhia 6502

PIRATHON (1) [PIRATHONITE]
Jdg 12:15 was buried in **P** in the land of Ephraim, 6552

PIRATHONITE (5) [PIRATHON]
Jdg 12:13 Abdon the son of Hillel, a **P**, judged Israel. 6553
12:15 Abdon the son of Hillel the **P** died, and 6553
2Sa 23:30 Benaiah the **P**, Hiddai of the brooks of 6553
1Ch 11:31 to the children of Benjamin, Benaiah the **P**, 6553
27:14 for the eleventh month *was* Benaiah the **P**, 6553

PISGAH (5)
Nu 21:20 *is* in the country of Moab, *to* the top of **P**, 6449
23:14 to the top of **P**, and built seven altars, and 6449
Dt 3:27 Get thee up *into* the top of **P**, and lift up 6449
4:49 the sea of the plain, under the springs of **P**. 6449
34: 1 *to* the top of **P**, that *is* over against Jericho. 6449

PISHON See PISON

PISIDIA (2)
Ac 13:14 they came to Antioch in **P**, and went into *4099*
14:24 And after they had passed throughout **P**, *4099*

PISON (1)
Ge 2:11 The name of the first *is* **P**: that *is it* which 6376

PISPAH (1)
1Ch 7:38 sons of Jether; Jephunneh, and **P**, and Ara. 6462

PISS (2) [PISSETH]
2Ki 18:27 and drink their own **p** with you? 4325+7272
Isa 36:12 and drink their own **p** with you? 4325+7272

PISSETH (6) [PISS]
1Sa 25:22 morning light *any that* **p** against the wall. 8366
25:34 morning light *any that* **p** against the wall. 8366
1Ki 14:10 will cut off from Jeroboam *him that* **p** 8366
16:11 he left him not *one that* **p** against a wall, 8366
21:21 will cut off from Ahab *him that* **p** against 8366
2Ki 9: 8 I will cut off from Ahab *him that* **p** against 8366

P

PIT (88) [PITS, SALTPITS, SLIMEPITS]
Ge 37:20 and cast him into some **p**, and we will say, 953
37:22 cast him into this **p** that *is* in the wilderness, 953
37:24 they took him, and cast him into a **p**: and 953
37:24 the **p** *was* empty, *there was* no water in it. 953
37:28 they drew and lift up Joseph out of the **p**, 953
37:29 Reuben returned unto the **p**; and behold, 953
37:29 behold, Joseph *was* not in the **p**; and he rent 953
Ex 21:33 if a man shall open a **p**, or if a man shall dig 953
21:33 or if a man shall dig a **p**, and not cover it, 953
21:34 The owner of the **p** shall make *it* good, *and* 953
Lev 11:36 Nevertheless a fountain or **p**, *wherein there* 953
Nu 16:30 and they go down quick into the **p**; 7585
16:33 went down alive into the **p**, and the earth 7585
2Sa 17: 9 he is hid now in some **p**, or in some *other* 6354
18:17 and cast him into a great **p** in the wood, and 6354
23:20 slew a lion in the midst of a **p** in time of 953
2Ki 10:14 and slew them at the **p** of the shearing house, 953
1Ch 11:22 and slew a lion in a **p** in a snowy day. 953
Job 6:27 and you dig *a* **p** for your friend. NIH
17:16 They shall go down *to* the bars of the **p**, 7585
33:18 He keepeth back his soul from the **p**, and 7845
33:24 Deliver him from going down *to* the **p**: 7845
33:28 will deliver his soul from going into the **p**, 7845
33:30 To bring back his soul from the **p**, to be 7845
Ps 7:15 He made a **p**, and digged it, and is fallen into 953
9:15 The heathen are sunk down in the **p** *that* 7845
28: 1 I become like them that go down into the **p**. 953
30: 3 me alive, that I should not go down *to* the **p**. 953
30: 9 in my blood, when I go down to the **p**? 7845
35: 7 cause have they hid for me their net *in* a **p**, 7845
40: 2 He brought me up also out of a horrible **p**, 953
55:23 shalt bring them down into the **p** of 875
57: 6 they have digged a **p** before me, into 7882
69:15 and let not the **p** shut her mouth upon me. 875
88: 4 counted with them that go down into the **p**: 953
88: 6 Thou hast laid me in the lowest **p**, 953
94:13 until the **p** be digged for the wicked. 7845
143: 7 I be like unto them that go down into the **p**. 953

Pr 1:12 and whole, as those that go down into the **p**: 953
22:14 The mouth of strange *women is* a deep **p**: 7745
23:27 and a strange *woman is* a narrow **p**. 875
26:27 Whoso diggeth a **p** shall fall therein: and 7845
28:10 he shall fall himself into his own **p**: 7816
28:17 to the blood of *any* person shall flee to the **p**; 953
Ecc 10: 8 He that diggeth a **p** shall fall into it; and 1475
Isa 14:15 brought down to hell, to the sides of the **p**. 953
14:19 a sword, that go down to the stones of the **p**; 953
24:17 Fear, and the **p**, and the snare, *are* upon 6354
24:18 the noise of the fear shall fall into the **p**; 6354
24:18 he that cometh up out of the midst of the **p** 6354
24:22 *as* prisoners are gathered in the **p**, and 953
30:14 or to take water *withal* out of the **p**. 1360
38:17 soul *delivered it* from the **p** of corruption: 7845
38:18 they that go down into the **p** cannot hope for 953
51: 1 to the hole of the **p** *whence* ye are digged. 953
51:14 that he should not die in the **p**, nor that his 7845
Jer 18:20 for they have digged a **p** for my soul. 7745
18:22 for they have digged a **p** to take me, and 7745
41: 7 *and cast them* into the midst of the **p**, he, and 953
41: 9 Now the **p** wherein Ishmael had cast all 953
48:43 Fear, and the **p**, and the snare, *shall be* 6354
48:44 that fleeth from the fear shall fall into the **p**; 6354
48:44 he that getteth up out of the **p** shall be taken 6354
Eze 19: 4 he was taken in their **p**, and they brought 7845
19: 8 their net over him: he was taken in their **p**. 7845
26:20 thee down with them that descend into the **p**, 953
26:20 of old, with them that go down to the **p**, 953
28: 8 They shall bring thee down to the **p**, and 7845
31:14 of men, with them that go down to the **p**. 953
31:16 to hell with them that descend into the **p**: 953
32:18 the earth, with them that go down into the **p**. 953
32:23 Whose graves are set in the sides of the **p**, 953
32:24 their shame with them that go down to the **p**. 953
32:25 their shame with them that go down to the **p**: 953
32:29 and with them that go down to the **p**. 953
32:30 their shame with them that go down to the **p**. 953
Zec 9:11 prisoners out of the **p** wherein *is* no water. 953
Mt 12:11 and if it fall into a **p** on the sabbath day, *999*
Lk 14: 5 shall have an ass or an ox fallen into a **p**, *5421*
Rev 9: 1 him was given the key of the bottomless **p**. *5421*
9: 2 And he opened the bottomless **p**; and *5421*
9: 2 and there arose a smoke out of the **p**, as *5421*
9: 2 darkened by reason of the smoke of the **p**. *5421*
9:11 *which is* the angel of the bottomless ***p***, NIG
11: 7 bottomless ***p*** shall make war against them, NIG
17: 8 shall ascend out of the bottomless ***p***, and NIG
20: 1 having the key of the bottomless ***p*** and NIG
20: 3 And cast him into the bottomless ***p***, and NIG

PITCH (19) [PITCHED]

Ge 6:14 and shalt **p** it within and without with pitch. 3722
6:14 and shalt pitch it within and without with **p**. 3724
Ex 2: 3 daubed it with slime and with **p**, and 2203
Nu 1:52 the children of Israel shall **p** their **tents**, 2583
1:53 the Levites shall **p** round about 2583
2: 2 Every man of the children of Israel shall **p** 2583
2: 2 tabernacle of the congregation shall they **p**. 2583
2: 3 camp of Judah **p** throughout their armies: 2583
2: 5 those that do **p** next unto him *shall be* 2583
2:12 those which **p** by him *shall be* the tribe of 2583
3:23 The families of the Gershonites shall **p** 2583
3:29 The families of the sons of Kohath shall **p** 2583
3:35 *these* shall **p** on the side of the tabernacle 2583
Dt 1:33 to search you out a place to **p** your **tents** *in,* 2583
Jos 4:20 took out of Jordan, did Joshua **p** in Gilgal. 6965
Isa 13:20 neither shall the Arabian **p tent** there; 167
34: 9 the streams thereof shall be turned into **p**, 2203
34: 9 the land thereof shall become burning **p**. 2203
Jer 6: 3 they shall **p** *their* tents against her round 8628

PITCHED (82) [PITCH]

Ge 12: 8 **p** his tent, *having* Beth-el on the west, and 5186
13:12 of the plain, and **p** his **tent** toward Sodom. 167
26:17 **p** his **tent** in the valley of Gerar, and 2583
26:25 name of the LORD, and **p** his tent there: 5186
31:25 Now Jacob had **p** his tent in the mount: and 8628
31:25 Laban with his brethren **p** in the mount of 8628
33:18 and **p** his **tent** before the city. 2583
Ex 17: 1 of the LORD, and **p** in Rephidim: 2583
19: 2 desert of Sinai, and had **p** in the wilderness; 2583
33: 7 **p** it without the camp, afar off from 5186
Nu 1:51 when the tabernacle is to be **p**, the Levites 2583
2:34 so they **p** by their standards, and so they set 2583
9:17 there the children of Israel **p** their **tents**. 2583
9:18 at the commandment of the LORD they **p**: 2583
12:16 and **p** in the wilderness of Paran. 2583
21:10 of Israel set forward, and **p** in Oboth. 2583
21:11 journeyed from Oboth, and **p** at Ije-abarim, 2583
21:12 they removed, and **p** in the valley of Zared. 2583
21:13 and **p** on the *other* side of Arnon, 2583
22: 1 **p** in the plains of Moab on *this* side Jordan 2583
33: 5 removed from Rameses, and **p** in Succoth. 2583
33: 6 departed from Succoth, and **p** in Etham, 2583
33: 7 and they **p** before Migdol. 2583
33: 8 the wilderness of Etham, and **p** in Marah. 2583
33: 9 and ten palm trees; and they **p** there. 2583
33:15 and **p** in the wilderness of Sinai. 2583
33:16 desert of Sinai, and **p** at Kibroth-hattaavah. 2583
33:18 departed from Hazeroth, and **p** in Rithmah. 2583
33:19 from Rithmah, and **p** at Rimmon-parez. 2583
33:20 from Rimmon-parez, and **p** in Libnah. 2583
33:21 removed from Libnah, and **p** at Rissah. 2583
33:22 from Rissah, and **p** in Kehelathah. 2583
33:23 from Kehelathah, and **p** in mount Shapher. 2583
33:25 from Haradah, and **p** in Makheloth. 2583
33:27 they departed from Tahath, and **p** at Tarah. 2583
33:28 removed from Tarah, and **p** in Mithcah. 2583
33:29 went from Mithcah, and **p** in Hashmonah. 2583
33:31 from Moseroth, and **p** in Bene-jaakan. 2583
33:33 from Hor-hagidgad, and **p** in Jotbathah. 2583
33:36 **p** in the wilderness of Zin, which *is* 2583
33:37 **p** in mount Hor, in the edge of the land of 2583
33:41 from mount Hor, and **p** in Zalmonah. 2583
Nu 33:42 departed from Zalmonah, and **p** in Punon. 2583
33:43 they departed from Punon, and **p** in Oboth. 2583
33:44 and **p** in Ije-abarim, in the border of Moab. 2583
33:45 departed from Iim, and **p** in Dibon-gad. 2583
33:47 **p** in the mountains of Abarim, before Nebo. 2583
33:48 **p** in the plains of Moab by Jordan *near* 2583
33:49 they **p** by Jordan, from Beth-jesimoth *even* 2583
Jos 8:11 the city, and **p** on the north side of Ai: 2583
11: 5 and **p** together at the waters of Merom, 2583
Jdg 4:11 **p** his tent unto the plain of Zaanaim, 5186
6:33 went over, and **p** in the valley of Jezreel. 2583
7: 1 up early, and **p** beside the well of Harod: 2583
11:18 **p** on the *other* side of Arnon, but came not 2583
11:20 and **p** in Jahaz, and fought against Israel. 2583
15: 9 **p** in Judah, and spread themselves in Lehi. 2583
18:12 went up, and **p** in Kirjath-jearim, in Judah: 2583
1Sa 4: 1 to battle, and **p** beside Eben-ezer: 2583
4: 1 and the Philistines **p** in Aphek. 2583
13: 5 they came up, and **p** in Michmash, 2583
17: 1 **p** between Shochoh and Azekah, 2583
17: 2 **p** by the valley of Elah, and set the battle in 2583
26: 3 Saul **p** in the hill of Hachilah, which *is* 2583
26: 5 and came to the place where Saul had **p**: 2583
26: 5 and the people **p** round about him. 2583
28: 4 and came and **p** in Shunem: 2583
28: 4 all Israel together, and they **p** in Gilboa. 2583
29: 1 the Israelites **p** by a fountain which *is* in 2583
2Sa 6:17 of the tabernacle that David had **p** for it: 5186
17:26 and Absalom **p** *in* the land of Gilead. 2583
23:13 the troop of the Philistines **p** in the valley 2583
24: 5 they passed over Jordan, and **p** in Aroer, 2583
1Ki 20:27 the children of Israel **p** before them like 2583
20:29 they **p** one over against the other seven 2583
2Ki 25: 1 his host, against Jerusalem, and **p** against it; 2583
1Ch 15: 1 place for the ark of God, and **p** for it a tent. 5186
16: 1 the midst of the tent that David had **p** for it: 5186
19: 7 who came and **p** before Medeba. 2583
2Ch 1: 4 for it: for he had **p** a tent for it at Jerusalem. 5186
Jer 52: 4 **p** against it, and built forts against it round 2583
Heb 8: 2 which the Lord **p**, and not man. *4078*

PITCHER (12) [PITCHERS]

Ge 24:14 Let down thy **p**, I pray thee, that I may 3537
24:15 with her **p** upon her shoulder. 3537
24:16 to the well, and filled her **p**, and came up. 3537
24:17 I pray thee, drink a little water of thy **p**. 3537
24:18 let down her **p** upon her hand, and 3537
24:20 emptied her **p** into the trough, and ran again 3537
24:43 I pray thee, a little water of thy **p** to drink; 3537
24:45 Rebekah came forth with her **p** on her 3537
24:46 let down her **p** from her *shoulder,* and said, 3537
Ecc 12: 6 or the **p** be broken at the fountain, or 3537
Mk 14:13 there shall meet you a man bearing a **p** of *2765*
Lk 22:10 shall a man meet you, bearing a **p** of water; *2765*

PITCHERS (5) [PITCHER]

Jdg 7:16 with empty **p**, and lamps within 3537
7:16 empty pitchers, and lamps within the **p**. 3537
7:19 and brake the **p** that *were* in their hands. 3537
7:20 brake the **p**, and held the lamps in their left 3537
La 4: 2 how are they esteemed as earthen **p**, 5035

PITHOM (1)

Ex 1:11 for Pharaoh treasure cities, **P** and Raamses. 6619

PITHON (2)

1Ch 8:35 the sons of Micah *were,* **P**, and Melech, 6377
9:41 the sons of Micah *were,* **P**, and Melech, 6377

PITIED (6) [PITY]

Ps 106:46 He made them also to be **p** of all those that 7356
La 2: 2 all the habitations of Jacob, and hath not **p**: 2550
2:17 he hath thrown down, and hath not **p**: and 2550
2:21 of thine anger; thou hast killed, *and* not **p**. 2550
3:43 thou hast slain, thou hast not **p**. 2550
Eze 16: 5 None eye **p** thee, to do any of these unto 2347

PITIETH (3) [PITY]

Ps 103:13 Like as a father **p** *his* children, *so* 7355
103:13 *so* the LORD **p** them that fear him. 7355
Eze 24:21 of your eyes, and that which your soul **p**; 4263

PITIFUL (3) [PITY]

La 4:10 The hands of the **p** women have sodden 7362
Jas 5:11 that the Lord is **very p**, and of tender *4184*
1Pe 3: 8 love as brethren, *be* **p**, *be* courteous: *2155*

PITS (6) [PIT]

1Sa 13: 6 and in rocks, and in high places, and in **p**. 953
Ps 119:85 The proud have digged **p** for me, which *are* 7882
140:10 into **deep p**, *that* they rise not up again. 4113
Jer 2: 6 through a land of deserts and of **p**, 7745
14: 3 they came to the **p**, *and* found no water; 1356
La 4:20 was taken in their **p**, *of* whom we said, 7825

PITTANCE See NOUGHT

PITY (30) [PITIED, PITIETH, PITIFUL]

Dt 7:16 thine eye shall have no **p** upon them: 2347
13: 8 neither shall thine eye **p** him, neither shalt 2347
19:13 Thine eye shall not **p** him, but thou shalt 2347
19:21 thine eye shall not **p**; *but* life *shall go* for 2347
25:12 cut off her hand, thine eye shall not **p** *her.* 2347
2Sa 12: 6 he did this thing, and because he **had** no **p**. 2550
Job 6:14 To him that is afflicted **p** *should be shewed* 2617
19:21 **Have p** upon me, have pity upon me, O ye 2603
19:21 **have p** upon me, O ye my friends; 2603
Ps 69:20 I looked *for some* to **take p**, but *there was* 5110
Pr 19:17 He that **hath p** upon the poor lendeth unto 2603
28: 8 he shall gather it for him that will **p** 2603
Isa 13:18 they shall **have** no **p** on the fruit of 7355
63: 9 in his love and in his **p** he redeemed them; 2551
Jer 13:14 I will not **p**, nor spare, nor have mercy, but 2550
15: 5 For who shall **have p** upon thee, 2550
Jer 21: 7 neither **have p**, nor have mercy. 2550
Eze 5:11 mine eye spare, neither will I **have** any **p**. 2550
7: 4 shall not spare thee, neither will I **have p**: 2550
7: 9 eye shall not spare, neither will I **have p**: 2550
8:18 eye shall not spare, neither will I **have p**: 2550
9: 5 let not your eye spare, neither **have** ye **p**: 2550
9:10 neither will I **have p**, *but* I will recompense 2550
36:21 I **had p** for mine holy name, which 2550
Joel 2:18 be jealous for his land, and **p** his people. 2550
Am 1:11 did cast off all **p**, and his anger did tear 7356
Jnh 4:10 the LORD, Thou hast **had p** on the gourd, 2347
Zec 11: 5 and their own shepherds **p** them not. 2550
11: 6 For I will no more **p** the inhabitants of 2550
Mt 18:33 thy fellowservant, even as I **had p** on thee? *1653*

PLACE (721) [BURYINGPLACE, PLACED, PLACES, THRESHINGPLACE]

Ge 1: 9 the heaven be gathered together unto one **p**, 4725
12: 6 Abram passed through the land unto the **p** 4725
13: 3 unto the **p** where his tent had been at 4725
13: 4 Unto the **p** of the altar, which he had made 4725
13:14 look from the **p** where thou *art* northward, 4725
18:24 not spare the **p** for the fifty righteous that 4725
18:26 then I will spare all the **p** for their sakes. 4725
18:33 and Abraham returned unto his **p**. 4725
19:12 hast in the city, bring *them* out of *this* **p**: 4725
19:13 For we will destroy this **p**, because the cry 4725
19:14 and said, Up, get ye out of this **p**; 4725
19:27 to the **p** where he stood before the LORD: 4725
20:11 Surely the fear of God *is* not in this **p**; 4725
20:13 at every **p** whither we shall come, say of 4725
21:31 Wherefore he called that **p** Beer-sheba; 4725
22: 3 went unto the **p** of which God had told him. 4725
22: 4 lift up his eyes, and saw the **p** afar off. 4725
22: 9 they came to the **p** which God had told him 4725
22:14 Abraham called the name of that **p** 4725
26: 7 the men of the **p** asked *him* of his wife; 4725
26: 7 *said he,* the men of the **p** should kill me for 4725
28:11 he lighted upon a *certain* **p**, and 4725
28:11 he took of the stones of *that* **p**, and 4725
28:11 his pillows, and lay down in that **p** to sleep. 4725
28:16 and he said, Surely the LORD is in this **p**; 4725
28:17 and said, How dreadful *is* this **p**! 4725
28:19 he called the name of that **p** Beth-el: but 4725
29: 3 stone again upon the well's mouth in his **p**. 4725
29:22 gathered together all the men of the **p**, 4725
30:25 that I may go unto mine own **p**, and to my 4725
31:55 Laban departed, and returned unto his **p**. 4725
32: 2 and he called the name of that **p** Mahanaim. 4725
32:30 Jacob called the name of the **p** Peniel: for I 4725
33:17 the name of the **p** is called Succoth. 4725
35: 7 there an altar, and called the **p** El-beth-el: 4725
35:13 God went up from him in the **p** where he 4725
35:14 Jacob set up a pillar in the **p** where he 4725
35:15 Jacob called the name of the **p** where God 4725
38:14 and sat in an **open p**, 5869+6607
38:21 he asked the men of that **p**, saying, 4725
38:21 they said, There was no harlot in this ***p***. NIH
38:22 also the men of the **p** said, *that* there was 4725
38:22 *that* there was no harlot in this ***p***. NIH
39:20 a **p** where the king's prisoners *were* bound: 4725
40: 3 the prison, the **p** where Joseph *was* bound. 4725
40:13 up thine head, and restore thee unto thy **p**: 3653
48: 9 whom God hath given me in this ***p***. And he NIH
50:19 Fear not: for *am* I **in the p** of God? 8478
Ex 3: 5 for the **p** whereon thou standest *is* holy 4725
3: 8 unto the **p** of the Canaanites, and 4725
10:23 neither rose any from his **p** for three days: 8478
13: 3 ***p***: there shall no leavened bread be eaten. NIH
15:17 *in* the **p**, O LORD, *which* thou hast made 4349
16:29 abide ye every man **in** his **p**, let no man go 8478
16:29 let no man go out of his **p** on the seventh 4725
17: 7 he called the name of the **p** Massah, and 4725
18:21 **p** *such* over them, *to be* rulers of thousands, 7760
18:23 all this people shall also go to their **p** in 4725
21:13 I will appoint thee a **p** whither he shall flee. 4725
23:20 to bring thee into the **p** which I have 4725
26:33 shall divide unto you between the holy ***p*** NIH
26:34 ark of the Testimony in the most holy ***p***. NIH
28:29 when he goeth in unto the holy ***p***, for a NIH
28:35 goeth in unto the holy ***p*** before the LORD, NIH
28:43 in the holy ***p***; that they bear not iniquity, NIH
29:30 the congregation to minister in the holy ***p***. NIH
29:31 and seethe his flesh in the holy **p**. 4725
31:11 sweet incense for the holy ***p***: according to NIH
32:34 lead the people unto *the* ***p*** of which I have NIH
33:21 *there is* a **p** by me, and thou shalt stand 4725
35:19 to do service in the holy ***p***, the holy NIH
38:24 of the holy ***p***, even the gold of the offering, NIH
39: 1 to do service in the holy ***p***, and made NIH
39:41 of service to do service in the holy ***p***, NIH
Lev 1:16 altar on the east part, by the **p** of the ashes: 4725
4:12 carry forth without the camp unto a clean **p**, 4725
4:24 kill it in the **p** where they kill the burnt 4725
4:29 slay the sin offering in the **p** of the burnt 4725
4:33 slay it for a sin offering in the **p** where they 4725
6:11 the ashes without the camp unto a clean **p**. 4725
6:16 bread shall it be eaten in the holy **p**; 4725
6:25 In the **p** where the burnt offering is killed 4725
6:26 in the holy **p** shall it be eaten, in the court 4725
6:27 that whereon it was sprinkled in the holy **p**. 4725
6:30 *withal* in the holy ***p***, shall be eaten: NIH
7: 2 In the **p** where they kill the burnt offering 4725
7: 6 it shall be eaten in the holy **p**: it *is* most 4725
10:13 ye shall eat it in the holy **p**, because it *is* thy 4725
10:14 heave shoulder shall ye eat in a clean **p**; 4725
10:17 ye not eaten the sin offering in the holy **p**, 4725
10:18 ***p***: ye should indeed have eaten it in the holy NIH
10:18 have eaten it in the holy ***p***, as I commanded. NIH
13:19 in the **p** of the boil there be a white rising, 4725
13:23 if the bright spot stay **in** his **p**, *and* 8478
13:28 if the bright spot stay **in** his **p**, *and* 8478
14:13 he shall slay the lamb in the **p** where he 4725
14:13 and the burnt offering, in the holy **p**: 4725
14:28 upon the **p** of the blood of the trespass 4725

Lev 14:40 they shall cast them into an unclean **p** 4725
14:41 off without the city into an unclean **p**: 4725
14:42 and put *them* in the **p** of *those* stones; 8478
14:45 *them* forth out of the city into an unclean **p**. 4725
16: 2 that he come not at all times into the holy ***p*** NIH
16: 3 Thus shall Aaron come into the holy ***p***: with NIH
16:16 he shall make an atonement for the holy ***p***, NIH
16:17 atonement in the holy ***p***, until he come out, NIH
16:20 hath made an end of reconciling the holy ***p***, NIH
16:23 he put on when he went into the holy ***p***, NIH
16:24 wash his flesh with water in the holy **p**, 4725
16:27 ***p***, shall *one* carry forth without the camp; NIH
24: 9 his sons'; and they shall eat it in the holy **p**: 4725
Nu 2:17 every man in his **p** by their standards. 3027
9:17 in the **p** where the cloud abode, there 4725
10:14 In the first ***p*** went the standard of the camp NIH
10:29 We *are* journeying unto the **p** of which 4725
10:33 to search out a **resting p** for them. 4496
11: 3 he called the name of the **p** Taberah: 4725
11:34 he called the name of that **p** 4725
13:24 The **p** was called the brook Eshcol, because 4725
14:40 will go up unto the **p** which the LORD 4725
18:10 In the most holy ***p*** shalt thou eat it; NIH
18:31 ye shall eat it in every **p**, ye and 4725
19: 9 lay *them* up without the camp in a clean **p**, 4725
20: 5 out of Egypt, to bring us in unto this evil **p**? 4725
20: 5 it *is* no **p** of seed, or of figs, or vines, or 4725
21: 3 and he called the name of the **p** Hormah. 4725
22:26 went further, and stood in a narrow **p**, 4725
23: 3 me I will tell thee. And he went to a **high p**. 8205
23:13 Come, I pray thee, with me unto another **p**, 4725
23:27 I pray thee, I will bring thee unto another **p**; 4725
24:11 Therefore now flee thou to thy **p**: I thought 4725
24:21 Strong *is* thy **dwelling p**, and thou puttest 4186
24:25 rose up, and went and returned to his **p**: 4725
28: 7 in the holy ***p*** shalt thou cause the strong NIH
32: 1 that behold, the **p** *was* a place for cattle; 4725
32: 1 that behold, the place *was* a **p** for cattle; 4725
32:17 until we have brought them unto their **p**: 4725
33:54 shall be in the **p where** his lot falleth; 8033
Dt 1:31 way that ye went, until ye came into this **p**. 4725
1:33 to search you out a **p** to pitch your tents *in*, 4725
2:37 *nor unto* any **p** of the river Jabbok, nor *unto* 3027
9: 7 until ye came unto this **p**, ye have been 4725
11: 5 in the wilderness, until ye came into this **p**; 4725
11:24 Every **p** whereon the soles of your feet 4725
12: 3 destroy the names of them out of that **p**. 4725
12: 5 unto the **p** which the LORD your God 4725
12:11 there shall be a **p** which the LORD your 4725
12:13 burnt offerings in every **p** that thou seest: 4725
12:14 in the **p** which the LORD shall choose in 4725
12:18 **p** which the LORD thy God shall choose, 4725
12:21 If the **p** which the LORD thy God hath 4725
12:26 go unto the **p** which the LORD shall 4725
14:23 in the **p** which he shall choose to place his 4725
14:23 in the place which he shall choose to **p** his 7931
14:24 *or* if the **p** be too far from thee, which 4725
14:25 shalt go unto the **p** which the LORD thy 4725
15:20 in the **p** which the LORD shall choose, 4725
16: 2 in the **p** which the LORD shall choose to 4725
16: 2 LORD shall choose to **p** his name there. 7931
16: 6 at the **p** which the LORD thy God shall 4725
16: 6 **p** his name *in*, there thou shalt sacrifice 7931
16: 7 eat *it* in the **p** which the LORD thy God 4725
16:11 in the **p** which the LORD thy God hath 4725
16:11 thy God hath chosen to **p** his name there. 7931
16:15 in the **p** which the LORD shall choose: 4725
16:16 thy God in the **p** which he shall choose; 4725
17: 8 get thee up into the **p** which the LORD 4725
17:10 which *they* of that **p** which the LORD 4725
18: 6 unto the **p** which the LORD shall choose; 4725
21:19 elders of his city, and unto the gate of his **p**; 4725
23:12 Thou shalt have a **p** also without the camp, 3027
23:16 in *that* **p** which he shall choose in one of 4725
26: 2 shalt go unto the **p** which the LORD thy 4725
26: 2 thy God shall choose to **p** his name there. 7931
26: 9 he hath brought us into this **p**, and 4725
27:15 putteth *it* in *a* secret ***p***. And all the people NIH
29: 7 when ye came unto this **p**, Sihon the king 4725
31:11 thy God in the **p** which he shall choose, 4725
Jos 1: 3 Every **p** that the sole of your foot shall 4725
3: 3 ye shall remove from your **p**, and go after 4725
4: 3 out of the **p** where the priests' feet stood 2088
4: 3 leave them in the **lodging p**, where you 4411
4: 8 with them unto the **p where** they **lodged**, 4411
4: 9 **in the p** where the feet of the priests which 8478
4:18 the waters of Jordan returned unto their **p**, 4725
5: 9 Wherefore the name of the **p** is called 4725
5:15 for the **p** whereon thou standest *is* holy. 4725
7:26 Wherefore the name of that **p** was called, 4725
8:19 the ambush arose quickly out of their **p**, 4725
9:27 this day, in the **p** which he should choose. 4725
20: 4 give him a **p**, that he may dwell among 4725
Jdg 2: 5 And they called the name of that **p** Bochim: 4725
6:26 in the **ordered p**, and take the second 4634
7: 7 the *other* people go every man unto his **p**. 4725
7:21 they stood every man **in** his **p** round about 8478
9:55 they departed every man unto his **p**. 4725
11:19 we pray thee, through thy land into my **p**. 4725
15:17 of his hand, and called that **p** Ramath-lehi. 4725
15:19 God clave a **hollow p** that *was* in the jaw, 4388
17: 8 to sojourn where he could find *a* ***p***: NIH
17: 9 I go to sojourn where I may find *a* ***p***. NIH
18: 3 what makest thou in this ***p***? and what hast NIH
18:10 a **p** where *there is* no want of any thing that 4725
18:12 wherefore they called that **p** Mahaneh-dan 4725
19:16 but the men of the **p** *were* Benjamites. 4725
19:28 the man rose up, and gat him unto his **p**. 4725
20:22 set *their* battle again in array in the **p** where 4725
20:33 all the men of Israel rose up out of their **p**, 4725
20:36 for the men of Israel gave **p** to 4725
21:19 *in a* **p** which *is* on the north side of Beth-el, NIH
Ru 1: 7 Wherefore she went forth out of the **p** 4725
3: 4 that thou shalt mark the **p** where he shall 4725
4:10 his brethren, and from the gate of his **p**: 4725
1Sa 3: 2 when Eli *was* laid down in his **p**, and 4725
3: 9 So Samuel went and lay down in his **p**. 4725
5: 3 took Dagon, and set him in his **p** again. 4725
5:11 let it go again to his own **p**, that it slay us 4725
6: 2 tell us wherewith we shall send it to his **p**. 4725
9:12 sacrifice of the people to day in the **high p**: 1116
9:13 before he go up to the **high p** to eat: 1116
9:14 out against them, for to go up *to* the **high p**. 1116
9:19 go up before me *unto* the **high p**; for ye 1116
9:22 made them sit in the chiefest **p** among them 4725
9:25 come down from the **high p** *into* the city, 1116
10: 5 down from the **high p** with a psaltery, 1116
10:12 one of **the same p** answered and said, 8033
10:13 end of prophesying, he came *to* the **high p**. 1116
12: 8 of Egypt, and made them dwell in this **p**. 4725
14: 9 we will stand still **in** our **p**, and will not go 8478
14:46 and the Philistines went to their own **p**. 4725
15:12 he set him up a **p**, and is gone about, and 3027
19: 2 and abide in a **secret p**, and hide thyself: 5643
20:19 come to the **p** where thou didst hide thyself 4725
20:25 by Saul's side, and David's **p** was empty. 4725
20:27 of the month, that David's **p** was empty: 4725
20:37 when the lad was come to the **p** of 4725
20:41 David arose out of *a* ***p*** toward the south, and NIH
21: 2 *my* servants to such and such a **p**. 4725
23:22 know and see his **p** where his haunt is, *and* 4725
23:28 they called that **p** Sela-hammahlekoth. 4725
26: 5 and came to the **p** where Saul had pitched: 4725
26: 5 David beheld the **p** where Saul lay, and 4725
26:25 went on his way, and Saul returned to his **p**. 4725
27: 5 let them give me a **p** in some town in 4725
29: 4 fellow return, that he may go again to his **p**, 4725
2Sa 2:16 wherefore that **p** was called 4725
2:23 he fell down there, and died **in the same p**: 8478
2:23 that as many as came to the **p** where Asahel 4725
5:20 Therefore he called the name of that **p** 4725
6: 8 he called *the name* of the **p** Perez-uzzah to 4725
6:17 in the ark of the LORD, and set it in his **p**, 4725
7:10 Moreover I will appoint a **p** for my people 4725
7:10 that they may dwell **in a p** of their own, 8478
11:16 that he assigned Uriah unto a **p** where he 4725
15:17 after him, and tarried *in* a **p** that *was* far off. 1004
15:19 return to thy **p**, and abide with the king: 4725
15:21 surely in what **p** my lord the king shall be, 4725
17: 9 is hid now in some pit, or in some *other* **p**: 4725
17:12 So shall we come upon him in some **p** 4725
18:18 and it is called unto this day, Absalom's **p**. 3027
19:39 and he returned unto his own **p**. 4725
22:20 He brought me forth also into a **large p**: he 4800
23: 7 be utterly burnt with fire in the same **p**. 7675
1Ki 3: 4 for that *was* the great **high p**: 1116
4:12 *even* unto *the* ***p*** *that is* beyond Jokneam: NIH
4:28 dromedaries brought they unto the **p** where 4725
5: 9 flotes unto the **p** that thou shalt appoint me, 4725
6:16 for the oracle, *even* for the most holy ***p***. NIH
7:50 the most holy ***p***, *and* for the doors of NIH
8: 6 of the covenant of the LORD unto his **p**, 4725
8: 6 to the most holy ***p***, even under the wings of NIH
8: 7 forth *their* two wings over the **p** of the ark, 4725
8: 8 seen out in the holy ***p*** before the oracle, NIH
8:10 ***p***, that the cloud filled the house of NIH
8:13 a **settled p** for thee to abide in for ever. 4349
8:21 I have set there a **p** for the ark, wherein *is* 4725
8:29 *even* toward the **p** of which thou hast said, 4725
8:29 thy servant shall make towards this **p**. 4725
8:30 when they shall pray towards this **p**: 4725
8:30 hear thou in heaven thy dwelling **p**: and 4725
8:35 if they pray towards this **p**, and confess thy 4725
8:39 hear thou *in* heaven thy dwelling **p**, and 4349
8:43 Hear thou *in* heaven thy dwelling **p**, and 4349
8:49 their supplication *in* heaven thy dwelling **p**, 4349
10:19 *there were* stays on either side on the **p** of 4725
11: 7 did Solomon build a **high p** for Chemosh, 1116
13: 8 will I eat bread nor drink water in this **p**: 4725
13:16 bread nor drink water with thee in this **p**: 4725
13:22 hast eaten bread and drunk water in the **p**, 4725
20:24 every man out of his **p**, and put captains in 4725
21:19 In the **p** where dogs licked the blood of 4725
22:10 in a **void p** *in* the entrance of the gate of 1637
2Ki 5:11 strike his hand over the **p**, and recover 4725
6: 1 the **p** where we dwell with thee is too strait 4725
6: 2 let us make us a **p** there, where we may 4725
6: 6 he shewed him the **p**. And he cut down a 4725
6: 8 In such and such a **p** *shall be* my camp. 4725
6: 9 Beware that *thou* pass not such a **p**; 4725
6:10 the king of Israel sent to the **p** which 4725
18:25 the LORD against this **p** to destroy it? 4725
22:16 I will bring evil upon this **p**, and upon 4725
22:17 my wrath shall be kindled against this **p**, 4725
22:19 thou heardest what I spake against this **p**, 4725
22:20 all the evil which I will bring upon this **p**. 4725
23:15 the **high p** which Jeroboam the son of 1116
23:15 that altar and the **high p** he brake down, 1116
23:15 burnt the **high p**, *and* stamped *it* small to 1116
1Ch 6:32 they ministered before the **dwelling p** of 4908
6:49 *were appointed* for all the work of the ***p*** NIH
13:11 wherefore that **p** is called Perez-uzza to this 4725
14:11 they called the name of that **p** 4725
15: 1 prepared a **p** for the ark of God, and 4725
15: 3 bring up the ark of the LORD unto his **p**, 4725
15:12 Israel unto *the* ***p*** *that* I have prepared for it. NIH
16:27 strength and gladness *are* in his **p**. 4725
16:39 LORD in the **high p** that *was* at Gibeon, 1116
17: 9 Also I will ordain a **p** for my people Israel, 4725
17: 9 they shall dwell **in** their **p**, and shall be 8478
21:22 Grant me the **p** of *this* threshingfloor, 4725
21:25 So David gave to Ornan for the **p** six 4725
21:29 *were* at that season in the **high p** at Gibeon. 1116
23:32 the charge of the holy ***p***, and the charge of NIH
28:11 and of the **p** of the mercy seat, 1004
2Ch 1: 3 went to the **high p** that *was* at Gibeon; 1116
1: 4 to *the* ***p*** *which* David had prepared for it: NIH
1:13 the **high p** that *was* at Gibeon *to* Jerusalem, 1116
3: 1 in the **p** that David had prepared in 4725
4:22 the inner doors thereof for the most holy ***p***, NIH
5: 7 of the covenant of the LORD unto his **p**, 4725
5: 7 into the most holy ***p***, even under the wings NIH
5: 8 forth *their* wings over the **p** of the ark, 4725
5:11 ***p***: (for all the priests that were present were NIH
6: 2 for thee, and a **p** for thy dwelling for ever. 4349
6:20 upon the **p** whereof thou hast said that *thou* 4725
6:20 which thy servant prayeth towards this **p**. 4725
6:21 which they shall make towards this **p**: 4725
6:21 hear thou from thy dwelling **p**, *even* from 4725
6:26 *yet* if they pray towards this **p**, and 4725
6:30 hear thou from heaven thy dwelling **p**, 4349
6:33 *even* from thy dwelling **p**, and do according 4349
6:39 *even* from thy dwelling **p**, their prayer and 4349
6:40 attent unto the prayer *that is made* in this **p**. 4725
6:41 into thy **resting p**, thou, and the ark of thy 5118
7:12 have chosen this **p** to myself for a house of 4725
7:15 attent unto the prayer *that is made* in this **p**. 4725
9:18 stays on each side of the sitting **p**, and 4725
18: 9 they sat in a **void p** *at* the entering in of 1637
20:26 the name of the same **p** was called, 4725
24:11 and took it, and carried it to his **p** again. 4725
29: 5 carry forth the filthiness out of the holy ***p***. NIH
29: 7 in the holy ***p*** unto the God of Israel. NIH
30:16 they stood in their **p** after their manner, 5977
30:27 their prayer came *up* to his holy dwelling **p**, 4583
34:24 I will bring evil upon this **p**, and upon 4725
34:25 my wrath shall be poured out upon this **p**, 4725
34:27 thou heardest his words against this **p**, 4725
34:28 see all the evil that I will bring upon this **p**, 4725
34:31 the king stood in his **p**, and made a 5977
35: 5 stand in the holy ***p*** according to NIH
35:10 the priests stood in their **p**, and the Levites 5977
35:15 singers the sons of Asaph *were* in their **p**, 4612
36:15 on his people, and on his **dwelling p**: 4583
Ezr 1: 4 whosoever remaineth in any **p** where he 4725
1: 4 let the men of his **p** help him with silver, 4725
2:68 for the house of God to set it up in his **p**: 4349
5:15 and let the house of God be builded in his **p**. 870
6: 3 the **p** where they offered sacrifices, and 870
6: 5 *every one* to his **p**, and place *them* in 870
6: 5 his place, and **p** *them* in the house of God. 5182
6: 7 of the Jews build this house of God in his **p**. 870
8:17 unto Iddo the chief at the **p** Casiphia, 4725
8:17 brethren the Nethinims, at the **p** Casiphia, 4725
9: 8 and to give us a nail in his holy **p**, 4725
Ne 1: 9 will bring them unto the **p** that I have 4725
2: 3 the **p** of my fathers' sepulchres, *lieth* waste, 1004
2:14 *there was* no **p** for the beast *that was* under 4725
3:16 unto *the* ***p*** over against the sepulchres of NIH
3:26 unto *the* ***p*** over against the water gate NIH
3:31 son unto the **p** of the Nethinims, 1004
4:20 In what **p** *therefore* ye hear the sound of 4725
8: 7 the law: and the people *stood* in their **p**. 5977
9: 3 they stood up in their **p**, and read in 5977
13:11 them together, and set them in their **p**. 5977
Est 2: 9 her maids unto the best ***p*** of the house of NIH
4:14 arise to the Jews from another **p**; 4725
7: 8 garden into the **p** of the banquet of wine; 1004
Job 2:11 they came every one from his own **p**; 4725
6:17 it is hot, they are consumed out of their **p**. 4725
7:10 neither shall his **p** know him any more. 4725
8:17 about the heap, *and* seeth the **p** of stones. 1004
8:18 If he destroy him from his **p**, then *it* shall 4725
8:22 the **dwelling p** of the wicked shall come to 168
9: 6 Which shaketh the earth out of her **p**, and 4725
14:18 and the rock is removed out of his **p**. 4725
16:18 thou my blood, and let my cry have no **p**. 4725
18: 4 and shall the rock be removed out of his **p**? 4725
18:21 this *is* the **p** *of him that* knoweth not God. 4725
20: 9 neither shall his **p** any more behold him. 4725
26: 7 stretcheth out the north over the **empty p**, 8414
27:21 and as a storm hurleth him out of his **p**. 4725
27:23 at him, and shall hiss him out of his **p**. 4725
28: 1 and a **p** for gold *where* they fine *it*. 4725
28: 6 The stones of it *are* the **p** of sapphires: and 4725
28:12 and where *is* the **p** of understanding? 4725
28:20 and where *is* the **p** of understanding? 4725
28:23 way thereof, and he knoweth the **p** thereof. 4725
36:16 thee out of the strait *into* a **broad p**, 7338
36:20 when people are cut off **in** their **p**. 8478
37: 1 heart trembleth, and is moved out of his **p**. 4725
38:10 brake up for it my decreed ***p***, and set bars NIH
38:12 *and* caused the dayspring to know his **p**; 4725
38:19 and *as for* darkness, where *is* the **p** thereof, 4725
39:28 upon the crag of the rock, and the **strong p**. 4686
40:12 and tread down the wicked **in** their **p**. 8478
Ps 18:11 He made darkness his **secret p**; his pavilion 5643
18:19 He brought me forth also into a **large p**; 4800
24: 3 and who shall stand in his holy **p**? 4725
26: 8 and the **p** where thine honour dwelleth. 4725
26:12 My foot standeth in an **even p**: in 4334
32: 7 Thou *art* my **hiding p**; thou shalt preserve 5643
33:14 From the **p** of his habitation he looketh 4349
37:10 thou shalt diligently consider his **p**, and 4725
44:19 Though thou hast sore broken us in the **p** of 4725
46: 4 the holy ***p*** of the tabernacles of the most NIH
52: 5 pluck thee out of *thy* **dwelling p**, and 168
66:12 but thou broughtest us out into a wealthy ***p***. NIH
68:17 *is* among them, *as in* Sinai, in the holy ***p***. NIH
74: 7 the **dwelling p** of thy name to the ground. 4908
76: 2 his tabernacle, and his **dwelling p** in Zion. 4585
79: 7 and laid waste his **dwelling p**. 5116
81: 7 I answered thee in the **secret p** of thunder: 5643
90: 1 thou hast been our **dwelling p** in all 4583
91: 1 He that dwelleth in the **secret p** of the most 5643
103:16 and the **p** thereof shall know it no more. 4725
104: 8 they go down *by* the valleys unto the **p** 4725
118: 5 answered me, *and set me* in a **large p**. 4800
119:114 Thou *art* my **hiding p** and my shield: 5643
132: 5 Until I find out a **p** for the LORD, 4725
Pr 1:21 She crieth in the **chief p** of concourse, 7218
14:26 and his children shall have a **p of refuge**. 4268
15: 3 The eyes of the LORD *are* in every **p**, 4725
24:15 of the righteous; spoil not his **resting p**: 7258
25: 6 and stand not in the **p** of great *men*: 4725

Pr 27: 8 so *is* a man that wandereth from his **p**. 4725
Ecc 1: 5 and hasteth to his **p** where he arose. 4725
1: 7 unto the **p** from whence the rivers come, 4725
3:16 moreover I saw under the sun the **p** of 4725
3:16 the **p** of righteousness, *that* iniquity *was* 4725
3:20 All go unto one **p**; all are of the dust, and 4725
6: 6 he seen no good: do not all go to one **p**? 4725
8:10 had come and gone from the **p** of the holy, 4725
10: 4 ruler rise up against thee, leave not thy **p**; 4725
10: 6 in great dignity, and the rich sit in **low p**. 8216
11: 3 *in* the **p** where the tree falleth, there it shall 4725
Isa 4: 5 upon every **dwelling p** of mount Zion, 4349
4: 6 for a **p of refuge**, and for a covert from 4268
5: 8 *that* lay field to field, till *there be* no **p**, 4725
7:23 to pass in that day, *that* every **p** shall be, 4725
13:13 and the earth shall remove out of her **p**, 4725
14: 2 shall take them, and bring them to their **p**: 4725
16:12 it is seen that Moab is weary on the **high p**, 1116
18: 4 I will consider in my **dwelling p** like a 4349
18: 7 to the **p** of the name of the LORD of 4725
22:23 I will fasten him *as* a nail in a sure **p**; and 4725
22:25 shall the nail that is fastened in the sure **p** 4725
25: 5 noise of strangers, as the heat in a **dry p**; 6724
26:21 the LORD cometh out of his **p** to punish 4725
28: 8 *and* filthiness, *so that there is* no **p** *clean*. 4725
28:17 and the waters shall overflow the **hiding p**. 5643
28:25 the appointed barley and the rye *in* their **p**? 1367
30:32 *in* every **p** where the grounded staff shall NIH
32: 2 a man shall be as a **hiding p** from the wind, 4224
32: 2 as rivers of water in a **dry p**, as the shadow 6724
32:19 and the city shall be low in a **low p**. 8218
33:16 his **p of defence** *shall be* the munitions of 4869
33:21 LORD *will be* unto us a **p** of broad rivers 4725
34:14 rest there, and find for herself a **p of rest**. 4494
35: 1 and the **solitary p** shall be glad *for* them; 6723
45:19 spoken in secret, in a dark **p** of the earth: 4725
46: 7 and set him in his **p**, and he standeth; 8478
46: 7 from his **p** shall he not remove: 4725
46:13 I will **p** salvation in Zion for Israel my 5414
49:20 in thine ears, The **p** *is* too strait for me: 4725
49:20 strait for me: **give p** to me that I may dwell. 5066
54: 2 Enlarge the **p** of thy tent, and let them 4725
56: 5 within my walls a **p** and a name better than 3027
57:15 holy **p**, with him also *that is* of a contrite NIH
60:13 to beautify the **p** of my sanctuary; 4725
60:13 and I will make the **p** of my feet glorious. 4725
65:10 of Achor a **p** for the herds **to lie down in**, 7258
66: 1 unto me? and where *is* the **p** of my rest? 4725
Jer 4: 7 he is gone forth from his **p** to make thy 4725
4:26 lo, the **fruitful p** *was* a wilderness, and 3759
6: 3 they shall feed every one *in* his **p**. 3027
7: 3 and I will cause you to dwell in this **p**. 4725
7: 6 and shed not innocent blood in this **p**, 4725
7: 7 will I cause you to dwell in this **p**, in 4725
7:12 go ye now unto my **p** which *was* in Shiloh, 4725
7:14 unto the **p** which I gave to you and to your 4725
7:20 my fury *shall be* poured out upon this **p**, 4725
7:32 they shall bury in Tophet, till there be no **p**. 4725
9: 2 O that I had in the wilderness a **lodging p** 4411
13: 7 took the girdle from the **p** where I had hid 4725
14:13 but I will give you assured peace in this **p**. 4725
16: 2 shalt thou have sons nor daughters in this **p**. 4725
16: 3 the daughters that are born in this **p**, 4725
16: 9 I will cause to cease out of this **p** in your 4725
17:12 the beginning *is* the **p** of our sanctuary. 4725
18:14 that come from **another p** be forsaken? 2114
19: 3 Behold, I *will* bring evil upon this **p**, 4725
19: 4 have estranged this **p**, and have burnt 4725
19: 4 have filled this **p** *with* the blood of 4725
19: 6 that this **p** shall no more be called Tophet, 4725
19: 7 counsel of Judah and Jerusalem in this **p**; 4725
19:11 *them* in Tophet, till *there be* no **p** to bury. 4725
19:12 Thus will I do unto this **p**, saith 4725
19:13 shall be defiled as the **p** of Tophet, because 4725
22: 3 neither shed innocent blood in this **p**. 4725
22:11 his father, which went forth out of this **p**; 4725
22:12 he shall die in the **p** whither they have led 4725
24: 5 whom I have sent out of this **p** *into* the land 4725
27:22 I bring them up, and restore them to this **p**. 4725
28: 3 **p** all the vessels of the LORD'S house, 4725
28: 3 king of Babylon took away from this **p**, 4725
28: 4 I *will* bring again to this **p** Jeconiah the son 4725
28: 6 away captive, from Babylon into this **p**. 4725
29:10 in causing you to return to this **p**. 4725
29:14 I will bring you again into the **p** whence I 4725
32:37 I will bring them again unto this **p**, and 4725
33:10 Again there shall be heard in this **p**, which 4725
33:12 Again in this **p**, *which is* desolate without 4725
38: 9 he is like to die for hunger **in the p where** 8478
40: 2 God hath pronounced this evil upon this **p**. 4725
42:18 a reproach; and ye shall see this **p** no more. 4725
42:22 in the **p** whither ye desire to go *and* 4725
44:29 the LORD, that I will punish you in this **p**, 4725
50: 6 to hill, they have forgotten their **resting p**. 7258
51:37 a **dwelling p** for dragons, an astonishment, 4583
51:62 O LORD, thou hast spoken against this **p**, 4725
Eze 3:12 *be* the glory of the LORD from his **p**. 4725
6:13 the **p** where they did offer sweet savour to 4725
7:22 they shall pollute my secret **p**: for NIH
10:11 *to* the **p** whither the head looked they 4725
12: 3 thou shalt remove from thy **p** to another 4725
12: 3 from thy place to another **p** in their sight: 4725
16:24 thou hast also built unto thee an **eminent p**, 1354
16:24 and hast made thee a **high p** in every street. 7413
16:25 Thou hast built thy **high p** at every head of 7413
16:31 In that thou buildest thine **eminent p** in 1354
16:31 and makest thine **high p** in every street; 7413
16:39 they shall throw down thine **eminent p**, 1354
17:16 surely in the **p** *where* the king *dwelleth* that 4725
20:29 What *is* the **high p** whereunto ye go? 1116
21:19 choose thou a **p**, choose *it*, at the head of 3027
21:30 I will judge thee in the **p** where thou wast 4725
25: 5 the Ammonites a **couching p** for flocks: 4769
26: 5 It shall be *a* **p** *for* the spreading of nets in NIH
26:14 thou shalt be *a* **p** to spread nets upon; NIH
Eze 37:14 and I shall **p** you in your own land: 3240
37:26 I will **p** them, and multiply them, and 5414
38:15 thou shalt come from thy **p** out of the north 4725
39:11 *that* I will give unto Gog a **p** there of graves 4725
41: 4 he said unto me, This *is* the most holy **p**. NIH
41: 9 *that* which *was* left *was* the **p** of the side 1004
41:11 chambers *were* toward *the* **p** that *was* left, NIH
41:11 the breadth of the **p** that was left *was* five 4725
41:12 **separate p** *at* the end toward the west *was* 1508
41:13 the **separate p**, and the building, with 1508
41:14 of the **separate p** toward the east, 1508
41:15 against the **separate p** which *was* behind it, 1508
42: 1 that *was* over against the **separate p**, 1508
42:10 over against the **separate p**, and over 1508
42:13 which *are* before the **separate p**, 1508
42:13 and the trespass offering; for the **p** *is* holy. 4725
42:14 shall they not go out of the holy **p** into NIH
42:20 between the sanctuary and the profane **p**. NIH
43: 7 the **p** of my throne, and the place of 4725
43: 7 and the **p** of the soles of my feet, 4725
43:13 and this *shall be* the **higher p** of the altar. 1354
43:21 he shall burn it in the **appointed p** of 4662
44:13 any of my holy *things*, in the most holy **p**: NIH
45: 3 shall be the sanctuary *and* the most holy **p**. NIH
45: 4 it shall be a **p** for their houses, and a holy 4725
45: 4 their houses, and a **holy p** for the sanctuary. 4720
46:19 there *was* a **p** on the two sides westward. 4725
46:20 This *is* the **p** where the priests shall boil 4725
47:10 they shall be a **p to spread forth** nets; 4894
48:15 *shall be* a profane **p** for the city, NIH
Da 2:35 them away, that no **p** was found for them: 870
8:11 and the **p** of his sanctuary was cast down. 4349
11:31 they shall **p** the abomination that maketh 5414
Hos 1:10 *that* in the **p** where it was said unto them, 4725
4:16 will feed them as a lamb in a **large p**. 4800
5:15 I will go *and* return to my **p**, till they 4725
9:13 as I saw Tyrus, *is* planted in a **pleasant p**: 5116
11:11 I will **p** them in their houses, saith 3427
13:13 for he should not stay long in *the* **p** *of* NIH
Joel 3: 7 I *will* raise them out of the **p** whither ye 4725
Am 8: 3 *there shall be* many dead bodies in every **p**; 4725
Mic 1: 3 the LORD cometh forth out of his **p**, and 4725
1: 4 the waters *that are* poured down a **steep p**. 4174
Na 1: 8 he will make an utter end of the **p** thereof, 4725
2:11 the **feeding p** of the young lions, where 4829
3:17 and their **p** is not known where they *are*. 4725
Zep 1: 4 will cut off the remnant of Baal from this **p**, 4725
2:11 shall worship him, every one from his **p**, 4725
2:15 a desolation, a **p** for beasts **to lie down in**! 4769
Hag 2: 9 in this **p** will I give peace, saith the LORD 4725
Zec 6:12 he shall grow up out of his **p**, and he shall 8478
10: 6 and I will **bring** them *again* **to p** them; 3427
10:10 Lebanon; and **p** shall not be found for them. NIH
12: 6 shall be inhabited again in her own **p**, 8478
14:10 it shall be lifted up, and inhabited **in** her **p**, 8478
14:10 from Benjamin's gate unto the **p** of the first 4725
Mal 1:11 in every **p** incense *shall be* offered unto my 4725
Mt 8:32 ran violently down a **steep p** into the sea, *2911*
9:24 He said unto them, **Give p**: for the maid is *402*
12: 6 That **in this p** is *one* greater than *5602*
14:13 thence by ship into a desert **p** apart: *5117*
14:15 *This* is a desert **p**, and the time is now past; *5117*
14:35 And when the men of that **p** had knowledge *5117*
17:20 this mountain, Remove hence **to yonder p**; *1563*
24:15 stand in the holy **p**, (whoso readeth, let him *5117*
26:36 Then cometh Jesus with them unto a **p** *5564*
26:52 Put up again thy sword into his **p**: *5117*
27:33 And when they were come unto a **p** called *5117*
27:33 that is to say, a **p** of a skull, *5117*
28: 6 Come, see the **p** where the Lord lay. *5117*
Mk 1:35 and departed into a solitary **p**, and *5117*
5:13 the herd ran violently down a **steep p** into *2911*
6:10 **In what p soever** ye enter into a *1437+3699*
6:10 there abide till ye depart **from that p**. *1564*
6:31 Come ye yourselves apart into a desert **p**, *5117*
6:32 And they departed into a desert **p** by ship *5117*
6:35 *This* is a desert **p**, and now the time *is* far *5117*
11: 4 door without in a **p** where two ways met; NIG
12: 1 about *it*, and digged *a* **p** *for* the winefat, NIG
14:32 And they came to a **p** which was named *5564*
15:22 And they bring him unto the **p** Golgotha, *5117*
15:22 being interpreted, The **p** of a skull. *5117*
16: 6 not here: behold the **p** where they laid him. *5117*
Lk 4:17 he found the **p** where it was written, *5117*
4:37 And the fame of him went out into every **p** *5117*
4:42 he departed and went into a desert **p**: *5117*
8:33 the herd ran violently down a **steep p** into *2911*
9:10 went aside privately into a desert **p** *5117*
9:12 get victuals: for we are here in a desert **p**. *5117*
10: 1 two before his face into every city and **p**, *5117*
10:32 when he was at the **p**, came and looked *on* *5117*
11: 1 pass *that*, as he was praying in a certain **p**, *5117*
11:33 putteth *it* in a **secret p**, neither under a *2927*
14: 9 him come and say to thee, Give this *man* **p**; *5117*
16:28 lest they also come into this **p** of torment. *5117*
19: 5 And when Jesus came to the **p**, he looked *5117*
22:40 And when he was at the **p**, he said unto *5117*
23: 5 all Jewry, beginning from Galilee to **this p**. *5602*
23:33 And when they were come to the **p**, *5117*
Jn 4:20 that in Jerusalem is the **p** where *men* ought *5117*
5:13 himself away, a multitude being in *that* **p**. *5117*
6:10 Now there was much grass in the **p**. So *5117*
6:23 nigh unto the **p** where they did eat bread, *5117*
8:37 kill me, because my word **hath** no **p** in you. *5562*
10:40 into the **p** where John at first baptized; *5117*
11: 6 he abode two days *still* in the *same* **p** where *5117*
11:30 but was in *that* **p** where Martha met him. *5117*
11:41 Then they took away the stone *from the* **p** NIG
11:48 and take away both our **p** and nation. *5117*
14: 2 have told you. I go to prepare a **p** for you. *5117*
14: 3 And if I go and prepare a **p** for you, I will *5117*
18: 2 which betrayed him, knew the **p**: *5117*
19:13 sat down in the judgment seat in a **p** *that is* *5117*
19:17 And he bearing his cross went forth into a **p** *5117*
19:17 forth into a place called *the* **p** of a skull, NIG
Jn 19:20 for the **p** where Jesus was crucified was *5117*
19:41 Now in the **p** where he was crucified there *5117*
20: 7 but wrapped together in a **p** by itself. *5117*
Ac 1:25 that *he* might go to his own **p**. *5117*
2: 1 all with one accord **in one p**. *846+1909+3588*
4:31 the **p** was shaken where they were *5117*
6:13 blasphemous words against this holy **p**, *5117*
6:14 this Jesus of Nazareth shall destroy this **p**, *5117*
7: 7 they come forth, and serve me in this **p**. *5117*
7:33 for the **p** where thou standest is holy *5117*
7:49 saith the Lord: or what *is* the **p** of my rest? *5117*
8:32 The **p** of the scripture which he read was *4042*
12:17 And he departed, and went into another **p**. *5117*
21:12 and they of that **p**, besought him not to go *1786*
21:28 against the people, and the law, and this **p**: *5117*
21:28 the temple, and hath polluted this holy **p**. *5117*
25:23 and were entered into the **p of hearing**, *201*
27: 8 came unto a **p** *which is* called The fair *5117*
27:41 And falling into a **p** where two seas met, *5117*
Ro 9:26 *that* in the **p** where it was said unto them, *5117*
12:19 but *rather* give **p** unto wrath: *5117*
15:23 But now having no more **p** in these parts, *5117*
1Co 1: 2 with all that in every **p** call upon the name *5117*
4:11 and **have no certain dwelling p**; *790*
11:20 therefore **into one p**, *846+1909+3588*
14:23 be come together **into one p**, *846+1909+3588*
2Co 2:14 savour of his knowledge by us in every **p**. *5117*
Gal 2: 5 To whom we **gave p** by subjection, no, *1502*
Eph 4:27 Neither give **p** to the devil. *5117*
1Th 1: 8 also in every **p** your faith to God-ward is *5117*
Heb 2: 6 But one in **a certain p** testified, saying, *4225*
4: 4 For *he* spake in **a certain p** of the seventh *4225*
4: 5 And in this **p** again, If they shall enter into NIG
5: 6 As he saith also in another **p**, Thou *art* a NIG
8: 7 should no **p** have been sought for *5117*
9:12 **p**, having obtained eternal redemption *for* NIG
9:25 as the high priest entereth into the holy **p** NIG
11: 8 when he was called to go out into a **p** *5117*
12:17 for he found no **p** of repentance, though he *5117*
Jas 2: 3 say unto him, Sit thou **here in a** good **p**; *5602*
3:11 Doth a fountain send forth at the same **p** *3692*
2Pe 1:19 as unto a light that shineth in a dark **p**, *5117*
Rev 2: 5 will remove thy candlestick out of his **p**, *5117*
12: 6 where she hath a **p** prepared of God, *5117*
12: 8 neither was their **p** found any more in *5117*
12:14 into her **p**, where she is nourished for a *5117*
16:16 And he gathered them together into a **p** *5117*
20:11 and there was found no **p** for them. *5117*

PLACED (14) [PLACE]

Ge 3:24 he **p** at the east of the garden of Eden 7931
47:11 Joseph **p** his father and his brethren, and 3427
1Ki 12:32 he **p** in Beth-el the priests of the high 5975
2Ki 17: 6 **p** them in Halah and in Habor *by* the river 3427
17:24 **p** *them* in the cities of Samaria instead of 3427
17:26 and **p** in the cities of Samaria, 3427
2Ch 1:14 which he **p** in the chariot cities, and 3240
4: 8 **p** *them* in the temple, five on the right side, 3240
17: 2 he **p** forces in all the fenced cities of Judah, 5414
Job 20: 4 *not* this of old, since man was **p** upon earth, 7760
Ps 78:60 of Shiloh, the tent *which* he **p** among men; 7931
Isa 5: 8 that they may be **p** alone in the midst of 3427
Jer 5:22 which have **p** the sand *for* the bound of 7760
Eze 17: 5 he **p** *it* by great waters, *and* set it *as* a 3947

PLACES (220) [PLACE]

Ge 28:15 will keep thee in all **p** whither thou goest, NIH
36:40 their families, after their **p**, by their names; 4725
Ex 20:24 in all **p** where I record my name I will 4725
25:27 rings be for **p** of the staves to bear the table. 1004
26:29 make their rings *of* gold *for* **p** for the bars: 1004
30: 4 they shall be for **p** for the staves to bear it 1004
36:34 made their rings *of* gold *to be* **p** for 1004
37:14 the **p** for the staves to bear the table. 1004
37:27 to be **p** for the staves to bear it withal. 1004
38: 5 of the grate of brass, *to be* **p** for the staves. 1004
Lev 26:30 I will destroy your **high p**, and cut down 1116
Nu 21:28 *and* the lords of the **high p** of Arnon. 1116
22:41 and brought him up *into* the **high p** of Baal, 1116
33:52 and quite pluck down all their **high p**: 1116
Dt 1: 7 unto all *the* **p** nigh thereunto, in the plain, NIH
12: 2 Ye shall utterly destroy all the **p**, 4725
32:13 He made him ride on the **high p** of 1116
33:29 and thou shalt tread upon their **high p**. 1116
Jos 5: 8 that they abode **in** their **p** in the camp, 8478
Jdg 5:11 **p of drawing** *water*, there shall they 4857
5:18 unto the death in the **high p** of the field. 4791
19:13 let us draw near to one of *these* **p** to lodge 4725
20:33 in wait of Israel came forth out of their **p**, 4725
1Sa 7:16 and judged Israel in all those **p**. 4725
13: 6 and in rocks, and in **high p**, and in pits. 6877
23:23 take knowledge of all the **lurking p** where 4224
30:31 to all the **p** where David himself and 4725
2Sa 1:19 beauty of Israel *is* slain upon thy **high p**: 1116
1:25 O Jonathan, *thou wast* slain in thine **high p**. 1116
7: 7 In all *the* **p** wherein I have walked with all NIH
22:34 hinds' *feet*: and setteth me upon my **high p**. 1116
22:46 and they shall be afraid out of their **close p**. 4526
1Ki 3: 2 Only the people sacrificed in **high p**, 1116
3: 3 he sacrificed and burnt incense in **high p**. 1116
12:31 he made a house of **high p**, and 1116
12:32 priests of the **high p** which he had made. 1116
13: 2 of the **high p** that burn incense upon thee, 1116
13:32 against all the houses of the **high p** which 1116
13:33 lowest of the people priests of the **high p**: 1116
13:33 he became *one of* the priests of the **high p**. 1116
14:23 For they also built them **high p**, and 1116
15:14 the **high p** were not removed: 1116
22:43 the **high p** were not taken away; 1116
22:43 and burnt incense yet in the **high p**. 1116
2Ki 12: 3 the **high p** were not taken away: the people 1116
12: 3 and burnt incense in the **high p**. 1116
14: 4 Howbeit the **high p** were not taken away: 1116
14: 4 and burnt incense on the **high p**. 1116
15: 4 Save that the **high p** were not removed: 1116

2Ki 15: 4 and burnt incense still on the **high p**. 1116
15:35 Howbeit the **high p** were not removed: 1116
15:35 and burnt incense still in the **high p**. 1116
16: 4 and burnt incense in the **high p**, 1116
17: 9 they built them **high p** in all their cities, 1116
17:11 there they burnt incense in all the **high p**, 1116
17:29 put *them* in the houses of the **high p** which 1116
17:32 of the lowest of them priests of the **high p**, 1116
17:32 for them in the houses of the **high p**. 1116
18: 4 He removed the **high p**, and brake 1116
18:22 whose **high p** and whose altars Hezekiah 1116
19:24 have I dried up all the rivers of besieged *p*. NIH
21: 3 For he built *up* again the **high p** which 1116
23: 5 incense in the **high p** in the cities of Judah, 1116
23: 5 and in the **p round about** Jerusalem; 4524
23: 8 defiled the **high p** where the priests had 1116
23: 8 brake down the **high p** of the gates that 1116
23: 9 Nevertheless the priests of the **high p** came 1116
23:13 the **high p** that *were* before Jerusalem, 1116
23:14 and filled their **p** *with* the bones of men. 4725
23:19 all the houses also of the **high p** that *were* 1116
23:20 he slew all the priests of the **high p** that 1116
1Ch 6:54 Now these *are* their **dwelling p** throughout 4186
2Ch 8:11 because *the p are* holy, whereunto the ark of NIH
11:15 he ordained him priests for the **high p**, and 1116
14: 3 altars of the strange *gods*, and the **high p**, 1116
14: 5 out of all the cities of Judah the **high p** 1116
15:17 the **high p** were not taken away out of 1116
17: 6 moreover he took away the **high p** and 1116
20:33 Howbeit the **high p** were not taken away: 1116
21:11 Moreover he made **high p** in the mountains 1116
28: 4 and burnt incense in the **high p**, 1116
28:25 **high p** to burn incense unto other gods, 1116
31: 1 threw down the **high p** and the altars out of 1116
32:12 the same Hezekiah taken away his **high p** 1116
33: 3 For he built again the **high p** which 1116
33:17 the people did sacrifice still in the **high p**, 1116
33:19 the **p** wherein he built high places, and 4725
33:19 the places wherein he built **high p**, and 1116
34: 3 and Jerusalem from the **high p**, 1116
Ne 4:12 From all **p** whence ye shall return unto us 4725
4:13 Therefore set I in the lower **p** behind 4725
4:13 behind the wall, *and* on the **higher p**, 6706
12:27 they sought the Levites out of all their **p**, 4725
Job 3:14 which built **desolate p** for themselves; 2723
20:26 All darkness *shall be* hid in his **secret p**: 6845
21:28 and where *are* the dwelling **p** of the wicked? 168
25: 2 with him, he maketh peace in his **high p**. 4791
37: 8 beasts go into dens, and remain in their **p**. 4585
Ps 10: 8 He sitteth in the **lurking p** of the villages: 3993
10: 8 in the **secret p** doth he murder 4565
16: 6 The lines are fallen unto me in pleasant *p*; NIH
17:12 as it were a young lion lurking in **secret p**. 4565
18:33 hinds' *feet*, and setteth me upon my **high p**. 1116
18:45 and be afraid out of their **close p**. 4526
49:11 *and* their **dwelling p** to all generations; 4908
68:35 O God, *thou art* terrible out of thy **holy p**: 4720
73:18 Surely thou didst set them in slippery *p*: NIH
74:20 for the **dark p** of the earth are full *of* 4285
78:58 provoked him to anger with their **high p**, 1116
95: 4 In his hand *are* the **deep p** of the earth: 4278
103:22 all his works in all **p** of his dominion: 4725
105:41 they ran in the dry *p like* a river. NIH
109:10 *their bread* also out of their **desolate p**. 2723
110: 6 he shall fill *the p with* the dead bodies; NIH
135: 6 and in earth, in the seas, and all **deep p**. 8415
141: 6 their judges are overthrown in stony **p**, 3027
Pr 8: 2 She standeth in the top of **high p** by 4791
8: 2 places by the way, *in* the **p** of the paths. 1004
9: 3 crieth upon the **highest p** of the city, 1610+4791
9:14 on a seat in the **high p** of the city, 4791
SS 2:14 in the **secret p** of the stairs, let me see thy 5643
Isa 5:17 the **waste p** of the fat ones shall strangers 2723
15: 2 and *to* Dibon, the **high p**, to weep: 1116
32:18 in sure dwellings, and in quiet **resting p**; 4496
36: 7 whose **high p** and whose altars Hezekiah 1116
37:25 I dried up all the rivers of the besieged *p*. NIH
40: 4 be made straight, and the **rough p** plain: 7406
41:18 I will open rivers in **high p**, and 8205
44:26 and I will raise up the **decayed p** thereof: 2723
45: 2 and make the **crooked p** straight: 1921
45: 3 hidden riches of **secret p**, that thou mayest 4565
49: 9 and their pastures *shall be* in all **high p**. 8205
49:19 For thy waste and thy **desolate p**, and 8074
51: 3 he will comfort all her **waste p**; and he will 2723
52: 9 sing together, ye **waste p** of Jerusalem: 2723
58:12 *shall be* of thee shall build the old **waste p**: 2723
58:14 I will cause thee to ride upon the **high p** of 1116
59:10 the night; *we are* in **desolate p** as dead *men*. 820
Jer 3: 2 Lift up thine eyes unto the **high p**, and 8205
3:21 A voice was heard upon the **high p**, 8205
4:11 A dry wind of the **high p** in the wilderness 8205
4:12 *Even* a full wind from those *p* shall come NIH
5: 1 and know, and seek in the **broad p** thereof, 7339
7:29 and take up a lamentation on **high p**; 8205
7:31 they have built the **high p** of Tophet, 1116
8: 3 which remain in all the **p** whither I have 4725
12:12 The spoilers are come upon all **high p** 8205
13:17 my soul shall weep in **secret p** for *your* 4565
14: 6 the wild asses did stand in the **high p**, 8205
17: 3 *and* thy **high p** for sin, throughout all thy 1116
17: 6 shall inhabit the **parched p** in 2788
17:26 from the **p** about Jerusalem, and from NIH
19: 5 They have built also the **high p** of Baal, 1116
23:10 the **pleasant p** of the wilderness are dried 4999
23:24 Can any hide himself in **secret p** that I shall 4565
24: 9 a curse, in all **p** whither I shall drive them. 4725
26:18 the mountain of the house as the **high p** of 1116
29:14 from all the **p** whither I have driven you, 4725
30:18 and have mercy on his **dwelling p**; 4908
32:35 they built the **high p** of Baal, which *are* in 1116
32:44 in the **p** about Jerusalem, and in the cities of NIH
33:13 in the **p** about Jerusalem, and in the cities of NIH
40:12 Even all the Jews returned out of all **p** 4725
45: 5 thee for a prey in all **p** whither thou goest. 4725
Jer 48:35 him that offereth *in* the **high p**, and 1116
49:10 I have uncovered his **secret p**, and he shall 4565
51:30 they have burnt her **dwelling p**; her bars 4908
La 2: 6 he hath destroyed his **p of** the **assembly**: 4150
3: 6 He hath set me in **dark p**, as they that be 4285
3:10 bear lying in wait, *and as* a lion in **secret p**. 4565
Eze 6: 3 upon you, and I will destroy your **high p**. 1116
6: 6 In all your **dwelling p** the cities shall be 4186
6: 6 laid waste, and the **high p** shall be desolate; 1116
7:24 to cease; and their **holy p** shall be defiled. 6942
16:16 deckedst thy **high p** with divers colours, 1116
16:39 and shall break down thy **high p**: 7413
21: 2 drop *thy word* toward the **holy p**, and 4720
26:20 in **p desolate** of old, with them that go 2723
34:12 will deliver them out of all **p** where they 4725
34:13 and in all the **inhabited p** of the country. 4186
34:26 and the **p round about** my hill a blessing; 5439
36: 2 even the ancient **high p** are ours in 1116
36:36 know that I the LORD build the ruined *p*, NIH
37:23 I will save them out of all their **dwelling p**, 4186
38:12 to turn thine hand upon the **desolate p** *that* 2723
38:20 the **steep p** shall fall, and every wall shall 4095
43: 7 the carcases of their kings *in* their **high p**. 1116
46:23 *it was* made *with* **boiling p** under the rows 4018
46:24 unto me, These *are* the **p** of them that boil, 1004
47:11 the **miry p** thereof and the marishes thereof 1207
Da 11:24 even upon the **fattest p** of the province; 4924
Hos 9: 6 the pleasant *p* for their silver, nettles shall NIH
10: 8 The **high p** also of Aven, the sin of Israel, 1116
Am 4: 6 your cities, and want of bread in all your **p**: 4725
4:13 treadeth upon the **high p** of the earth, 1116
7: 9 the **high p** of Isaac shall be desolate, and 1116
Mic 1: 3 and tread upon the **high p** of the earth. 1116
1: 5 what *are* the **high p** of Judah? *are they* not 1116
3:12 the mountain of the house as the **high p** of 1116
Hab 1: 6 to possess the **dwelling p** *that are* not 4908
3:19 he will make me to walk upon mine **high p**. 1116
Zec 3: 7 I will give thee **p to walk** among these that 4108
Mal 1: 4 but we will return and build the **desolate p**; 2723
Mt 12:43 he walketh through dry **p**, seeking rest, and *5117*
13: 5 Some fell upon stony *p*, where they had not NIG
13:20 But he that received the seed into stony *p*, NIG
24: 7 pestilences, and earthquakes in divers **p**. *5117*
Mk 1:45 into the city, but was without in desert **p**: *5117*
13: 8 and there shall be earthquakes in divers **p**, *5117*
Lk 11:24 he walketh through dry **p**, seeking rest; *5117*
21:11 And great earthquakes shall be in divers **p**, *5117*
Ac 24: 3 *it* always, and **in all p**, most noble Felix, *3837*
Eph 1: 3 spiritual blessings in heavenly *p* in Christ: NIG
1:20 at his own right hand in the heavenly *p*, NIG
2: 6 made *us* sit together in heavenly *p* in Christ NIG
3:10 powers in heavenly *p* might be known by NIG
6:12 against spiritual wickedness in high *p*. NIG
Php 1:13 in all the palace, and *in* all other *p*; NIG
Heb 9:24 For Christ is not entered into the holy *p* NIG
Rev 6:14 and island were moved out of their **p**. *5117*

PLAGUE (98) [PLAGUED, PLAGUES]

Ex 11: 1 Yet will I bring one **p** *more* upon Pharaoh, 5061
12:13 the **p** shall not be upon you to destroy *you*, 5063
30:12 that there be no **p** amongst them, when *thou* 5063
Lev 13: 2 it be in the skin of his flesh like the **p** of 5061
13: 3 the priest shall look on the **p** in the skin of 5061
13: 3 *when* the hair in the **p** is turned white, and 5061
13: 3 the **p** in sight *be* deeper than the skin of his 5061
13: 3 the skin of his flesh, it *is* a **p** of leprosy: 5061
13: 4 the priest shall shut up *him that hath* the **p** 5061
13: 5 *if* the **p** in his sight be at a stay, *and* 5061
13: 5 at a stay, *and* the **p** spread not in the skin; 5061
13: 6 *if* the **p** *be* somewhat dark, and the plague 5061
13: 6 and the **p** spread not in the skin, 5061
13: 9 When the **p** of leprosy is in a man, then 5061
13:12 *hath* the **p** from his head even to his foot, 5061
13:13 shall pronounce *him* clean *that hath* the **p**: 5061
13:17 behold, *if* the **p** be turned into white; then 5061
13:17 shall pronounce *him* clean *that hath* the **p**: 5061
13:20 it *is* a **p** of leprosy broken out of the boil. 5061
13:22 shall pronounce him unclean: it *is* a **p**. 5061
13:25 him unclean: it *is* the **p** of leprosy. 5061
13:27 him unclean: it *is* the **p** of leprosy. 5061
13:29 a man or woman hath a **p** upon the head or 5061
13:30 the priest shall see the **p**: and behold, *if* it 5061
13:31 if the priest look on the **p** of the scall, and 5061
13:31 the priest shall shut up *him that hath* the **p** 5061
13:32 seventh day the priest shall look on the **p**: 5061
13:44 him utterly unclean, his **p** *is* in his head. 5061
13:45 the leper in whom the **p** *is*, his clothes shall 5061
13:46 All the days wherein the **p** *shall be* in him 5061
13:47 The garment also that the **p** of leprosy is in, 5061
13:49 *if* the **p** be greenish or reddish in 5061
13:49 it *is* a **p** of leprosy, and shall be shewed 5061
13:50 the priest shall look upon the **p**, and shut up 5061
13:50 and shut up *it that hath* the **p** seven days: 5061
13:51 he shall look on the **p** on the seventh day: 5061
13:51 if the **p** be spread in the garment, either in 5061
13:51 the **p** *is* a fretting leprosy; it *is* unclean. 5061
13:52 or any thing of skin, wherein the **p** is: 5061
13:53 behold, the **p** be not spread in the garment, 5061
13:54 that they wash *the thing* wherein the **p** *is*, 5061
13:55 the priest shall look on the **p**, after *that* it is 5061
13:55 *if* the **p** have not changed his colour, and 5061
13:55 his colour, and the **p** be not spread; 5061
13:56 the **p** *be* somewhat dark after the washing 5061
13:57 it *is* a spreading *p*: thou shalt burn that NIH
13:57 shalt burn that wherein the **p** *is* with fire. 5061
13:58 if the **p** be departed from them, then it shall 5061
13:59 This *is* the law of the **p** of leprosy in a 5061
14: 3 *if* the **p** of leprosy be healed in the leper; 5061
14:32 This *is* the law *of him* in whom *is* the **p** of 5061
14:34 I put the **p** of leprosy in a house of the land 5061
14:35 It seemeth to me *there is* as it were a **p** in 5061
14:36 before the priest go *into it* to see the **p**, 5061
14:37 he shall look on the **p**, and behold, *if* 5061
14:37 *if* the **p** *be* in the walls of the house with 5061
14:39 *if* the **p** be spread in the walls of the house; 5061
Lev 14:40 they take away the stones in which the **p** *is*, 5061
14:43 if the **p** come again, and break out in 5061
14:44 and behold, *if* the **p** be spread in the house, 5061
14:48 behold, the **p** hath not spread in the house, 5061
14:48 the house clean, because the **p** is healed. 5061
14:54 This *is* the law for all *manner of* **p** of 5061
Nu 8:19 that there be no **p** among the children of 5063
11:33 smote the people *with* a very great **p**. 4347
14:37 the land, died by the **p** before the LORD. 4046
16:46 gone out from the LORD; the **p** is begun. 5063
16:47 behold, the **p** was begun among the people: 5063
16:48 and the living; and the **p** was stayed. 4046
16:49 Now they that died in the **p** were fourteen 4046
16:50 of the congregation: and the **p** was stayed. 4046
25: 8 So the **p** was stayed from the children of 4046
25: 9 those that died in the **p** were twenty and 4046
25:18 which was slain in the day of the **p** for 4046
26: 1 it came to pass after the **p**, that the LORD 4046
31:16 there was a **p** among the congregation of 4046
Dt 24: 8 Take heed in the **p** of leprosy, that *thou* 5061
28:61 Also every sickness, and every **p**, which *is* 4347
Jos 22:17 although there was a **p** in the congregation 5063
1Sa 6: 4 for one **p** *was* on you all, and on your lords. 4046
2Sa 24:21 that the **p** may be stayed from the people. 4046
24:25 the land, and the **p** was stayed from Israel. 4046
1Ki 8:37 whatsoever **p**, whatsoever sickness *there* 5061
8:38 which shall know every man the **p** of his 5061
1Ch 21:22 that the **p** may be stayed from the people. 4046
2Ch 21:14 *with* a great **p** will the LORD smite thy 4046
Ps 89:23 before his face, and **p** them that hate him. 5062
91:10 neither shall *any* **p** come nigh thy dwelling. 5061
106:29 and the **p** brake in upon them. 4046
106:30 and *so* the **p** was stayed. 4046
Zec 14:12 this shall be the **p** where*with* the LORD 4046
14:15 so shall be the **p** of the horse, of the mule, 4046
14:15 beasts that shall be in these tents, as this **p**. 4046
14:18 that *have* no *rain*; there shall be the **p**, 4046
Mk 5:29 in *her* body that she was healed of *that* **p**. *3148*
5:34 go in peace, and be whole of thy **p**. *3148*
Rev 16:21 because of the **p** of the hail; *4127*
16:21 for the **p** thereof was exceeding great. *4127*

PLAGUED (6) [PLAGUE]

Ge 12:17 the LORD **p** Pharaoh and his house with 5060
Ex 32:35 the LORD **p** the people, because they 5062
Jos 24: 5 I sent Moses also and Aaron, and I **p** Egypt, 5062
1Ch 21:17 not on thy people, that *they* should be **p**. 4046
Ps 73: 5 neither are they **p** like *other* men. 5060
73:14 For all the day long have I been **p**, and 5060

PLAGUES (24) [PLAGUE]

Ge 12:17 his house with great **p** because of Sarai 5061
Ex 9:14 For I will at this time send all my **p** upon 4046
Lev 26:21 I will bring seven *times* moe **p** upon you 4347
Dt 28:59 the LORD will make thy **p** wonderful, 4347
28:59 the **p** of thy seed, *even* great plagues, and 4347
28:59 *even* great **p**, and of long continuance, and 4347
29:22 when they see the **p** of that land, and 4347
1Sa 4: 8 Egyptians with all the **p** in the wilderness. 4347
Jer 19: 8 and hiss because of all the **p** thereof. 4347
49:17 and shall hiss at all the **p** thereof. 4347
50:13 shall be astonished, and hiss at all her **p**. 4347
Hos 13:14 O death, I will be thy **p**; O grave, I will be 1698
Mk 3:10 him for to touch him, as many as had **p**. *3148*
Lk 7:21 he cured many of *their* infirmities and **p**, *3148*
Rev 9:20 **p** *yet* repented not of the works of their *4127*
11: 6 and to smite the earth with all **p**, as often as *4127*
15: 1 seven angels having the seven last **p**; *4127*
15: 6 having the seven **p**, clothed in pure and *4127*
15: 8 till the seven **p** of the seven angels were *4127*
16: 9 of God, which hath power over these **p**: *4127*
18: 4 of her sins, and that ye receive not of her **p**. *4127*
18: 8 Therefore shall her **p** come in one day, *4127*
21: 9 had the seven vials full of the seven last **p**, *4127*
22:18 unto him the **p** that are written in this book: *4127*

PLAIN (75) [PLAINLY, PLAINNESS, PLAINS]

Ge 11: 2 that they found a **p** in the land of Shinar; 1237
12: 6 the place of Sichem, unto the **p** of Moreh. 436
13:10 up his eyes, and beheld all the **p** of Jordan, 3603
13:11 Then Lot chose him all the **p** of Jordan; and 3603
13:12 Lot dwelled in the cities of the **p**, and 3603
13:18 came and dwelt in the **p** of Mamre, which *is* 436
14:13 for he dwelt in the **p** of Mamre the Amorite, 436
19:17 behind thee, neither stay thou in all the **p**; 3603
19:25 all the **p**, and all the inhabitants of 3603
19:28 toward all the land of the **p**, and beheld, 3603
19:29 when God destroyed the cities of the **p**, 3603
25:27 and Jacob *was* a **p** man, dwelling in tents. 8535
Dt 1: 1 in the **p** over against the Red *sea*, between 6160
1: 7 in the **p**, in the hills, and in the vale, and 6160
2: 8 through the way of the **p** from Elath, and 6160
3:10 All the cities of the **p**, and all Gilead, and 4334
3:17 The **p** also, and Jordan, and the coast 6160
3:17 from Chinnereth even unto the sea of the **p**, 6160
4:43 in the **p** country, of the Reubenites; 4334
4:49 all the **p** on *this* side Jordan eastward, even 6160
4:49 even unto the sea of the **p**, under 6160
34: 3 the south, and the **p** of the valley of Jericho, 3603
Jos 3:16 that came down toward the sea of the **p**, 6160
8:14 at a time appointed, before the **p**; 6160
11:16 the **p**, and the mountain of Israel, and 6160
12: 1 mount Hermon, and all the **p** on the east: 6160
12: 3 *from* the **p** to the sea of Cinneroth on 6160
12: 3 unto the sea of the **p**, *even* the salt sea on 6160
13: 9 and all the **p** of Medeba unto Dibon; 4334
13:16 midst of the river, and all the **p** by Medeba; 4334
13:17 Heshbon, and all her cities that *are* in the **p**; 4334
13:21 all the cities of the **p**, and all the kingdom 4334
20: 8 upon the **p** out of the tribe of Reuben, 4334
Jdg 4:11 pitched his tent unto the **p** of Zaanaim, 436
9: 6 by the **p** of the pillar that *was* in Shechem. 436
9:37 another company come along by the **p** of 436
11:33 twenty cities, and unto the **p** of the vineyards, 58

P

1Sa 10: 3 thou shalt come to the **p** of Tabor, and 436
23:24 of Maon, in the **p** on the south of Jeshimon. 6160
2Sa 2:29 his men walked all that night through the **p**, 6160
4: 7 and gat them away through the **p** all night. 6160
15:28 See, I will tarry in the **p** of the wilderness, 6160
18:23 Ahimaaz ran *by* the way of the **p**, and 3603
1Ki 7:46 In the **p** of Jordan did the king cast them, 3603
20:23 let us fight against them in the **p**, and 4334
20:25 we will fight against them in the **p**, *and* 4334
2Ki 14:25 entering of Hamath unto the sea of the **p**, 6160
25: 4 and *the king* went the way toward the **p**. 6160
2Ch 4:17 In the **p** of Jordan did the king cast them, 3603
Ne 3:22 him repaired the priests, the men of the **p**. 3603
6: 2 in *some one of* the villages in the **p** of Ono. 1237
12:28 both out of the **p country** round about 3603
Ps 27:11 lead me in a **p** path, because of mine 4334
Pr 8: 9 They *are* all **p** to him that understandeth, 5228
15:19 but the way of the righteous *is* **made p**. 5549
Isa 28:25 When he hath **made p** the face thereof, 7737
40: 4 be made straight, and the rough places **p**: 1237
Jer 17:26 from the **p**, and from the mountains, and 8219
21:13 *and* rock of the **p**, saith the LORD; 4334
39: 4 and he went out the way of the **p**. 6160
48: 8 shall perish, and the **p** shall be destroyed, 4334
48:21 judgment is come upon the **p** country; 4334
52: 7 and they went *by* the way of the **p**. 6160
Eze 3:22 go forth into the **p**, and I will there talk 1237
3:23 I arose, and went forth into the **p**: and 1237
8: 4 according to the vision that I saw in the **p**. 1237
Da 3: 1 he set it up in the **p** of Dura, in the province 1236
Am 1: 5 cut off the inhabitant from the **p** of Aven, 1237
Ob 1:19 of Esau; and *they of* the **p** the Philistines: 8219
Hab 2: 2 Write the vision, and **make** *it* **p** upon tables, 874
Zec 4: 7 before Zerubbabel *thou shalt* become a **p**: 4334
7: 7 when *men* inhabited the south and the **p**? 8219
14:10 All the land shall be turned as a **p** from 6160
Mk 7:35 of his tongue was loosed, and he spake **p**. *3723*
Lk 6:17 and stood in the **p**, and the company *3977+5117*

PLAINLY (11) [PLAIN]
Ex 21: 5 if the servant shall **p say**, I love my 559+559
Dt 27: 8 the stones all the words of this law very **p**. 874
1Sa 2:27 Did I **p appear** unto the house of thy 1540+1540
10:16 **told** us **p** that the asses were found. 5046+5046
Ezr 4:18 ye sent unto us *hath been* **p** read before me. 6568
Isa 32: 4 of the stammerers shall be ready to speak **p**. 6703
Jn 10:24 us to doubt? If thou be the Christ, tell us **p**. *3954*
11:14 Then said Jesus unto them **p**, Lazarus is *3954*
16:25 but I shall shew you **p** of the Father. *3954*
16:29 Lo, now speakest thou **p**, and *1722+3954*
Heb 11:14 For they that say such *things* **declare p** that *1718*

PLAINNESS (1) [PLAIN]
2Co 3:12 have such hope, we use great **p of speech**: *3954*

PLAINS (25) [PLAIN]
Ge 18: 1 the LORD appeared unto him in the **p** of 436
Nu 22: 1 pitched in the **p** of Moab on *this* side 6160
26: 3 Eleazar the priest spake with them in the **p** 6160
26:63 in the **p** of Moab by Jordan *near* Jericho. 6160
31:12 unto the camp at the **p** of Moab, which *are* 6160
33:48 pitched in the **p** of Moab by Jordan *near* 6160
33:49 *even* unto Abel-shittim in the **p** of Moab. 6160
33:50 the LORD spake unto Moses in the **p** of 6160
35: 1 the LORD spake unto Moses in the **p** of 6160
36:13 in the **p** of Moab by Jordan *near* Jericho. 6160
Dt 11:30 over against Gilgal, beside the **p** of Moreh? 436
34: 1 Moses went up from the **p** of Moab unto 6160
34: 8 for Moses in the **p** of Moab thirty days: 6160
Jos 4:13 the LORD unto battle, to the **p** of Jericho. 6160
5:10 of the month at even in the **p** of Jericho. 6160
11: 2 of the **p** south of Cinneroth, and in 6160
12: 8 in the **p**, and in the springs, and in 6160
13:32 distribute for inheritance in the **p** of Moab, 6160
2Sa 17:16 Lodge not *this* night in the **p** of 6160
2Ki 25: 5 and overtook him in the **p** of Jericho: 6160
1Ch 27:28 the sycomore trees that *were* in the **low p** 8219
2Ch 9:27 trees that *are* in the **low p** in abundance. 8219
26:10 both in the low country, and in the **p**: 4334
Jer 39: 5 and overtook Zedekiah in the **p** of Jericho: 6160
52: 8 and overtook Zedekiah in the **p** of Jericho; 6160

PLAISTER (7) [PLAISTERED]
Lev 14:42 take other morter, and shall **p** the house. 2902
Dt 27: 2 up great stones, and **p** them with plaister: 7874
27: 2 up great stones, and plaister them with **p**: 7875
27: 4 and thou shalt **p** them with plaister. 7874
27: 4 and thou shalt plaister them with **p**. 7875
Isa 38:21 **lay** *it* **for a p** upon the boil, and he shall 4799
Da 5: 5 upon the **p** of the wall of the king's palace: 1528

PLAISTERED (2) [PLAISTER]
Lev 14:43 he hath scraped the house, and after it is **p**; 2902
14:48 spread in the house, after the house was **p**: 2902

PLAITING (1) [PLATTED]
1Pe 3: 3 not be that outward *adorning* of **p** the hair, *1708*

PLANE See CHESNUT

PLANES (1)
Isa 44:13 he fitteth it with **p**, and he marketh it out 4741

PLANETS (1)
2Ki 23: 5 and to the **p**, and to all the host of heaven. 4208

PLANKS (3)
1Ki 6:15 covered the floor of the house with **p** of fir. 6763
Eze 41:25 *there were* thick **p** upon the face of 6086
41:26 side chambers of the house, and **thick p**. 5646

PLANT (42) [PLANTATION, PLANTED, PLANTEDST, PLANTERS, PLANTETH, PLANTING, PLANTINGS, PLANTS]
Ge 2: 5 every **p** of the field before it was in 7880
Ex 15:17 **p** them in the mountain of thine 5193
Dt 16:21 Thou shalt not **p** thee a grove *of* any trees 5193
28:30 thou shalt **p** a vineyard, and shalt not gather 5193
28:39 Thou shalt **p** vineyards, and dress *them*, but 5193
2Sa 7:10 will **p** them, that they may dwell in a place 5193
2Ki 19:29 and **p** vineyards, and eat the fruits thereof. 5193
1Ch 17: 9 will **p** them, and they shall dwell in their 5193
Job 14: 9 it will bud, and bring forth boughs like a **p**. 5194
Ps 107:37 sow the fields, and **p** vineyards, which may 5193
Ecc 3: 2 a time to **p**, and a time to pluck up *that* 5193
Isa 5: 7 and the men of Judah his pleasant **p**: 5194
17:10 therefore shalt thou **p** pleasant plants, and 5193
17:11 In the day shalt thou make thy **p** to grow, 5194
37:30 and **p** vineyards, and eat the fruit thereof. 5193
41:19 I will **p** in the wilderness the cedar, 5414
51:16 that I may **p** the heavens, and lay 5193
53: 2 he shall grow up before him as a **tender p**, 3126
65:21 inhabit *them;* and they shall **p** vineyards, 5193
65:22 they shall not **p**, and another eat: 5193
Jer 1:10 and to throw down, to build, and to **p**. 5193
2:21 the degenerate **p of** a strange **vine** unto me? 1612
18: 9 concerning a kingdom, to build and to **p** *it;* 5193
24: 6 and I will **p** them, and not pluck *them* up. 5193
29: 5 dwell *in them;* and **p** gardens, and eat 5193
29:28 dwell *in them;* and **p** gardens, and eat 5193
31: 5 Thou shalt yet **p** vines upon the mountains 5193
31: 5 the planters shall **p**, and shall eat *them* as 5193
31:28 to build, and to **p**, saith the LORD. 5193
32:41 I will **p** them in this land assuredly with my 5193
35: 7 nor **p** vineyard, nor have *any:* but all your 5193
42:10 and I will **p** you, and not pluck *you* up: 5193
Eze 17:22 will **p** *it* upon a high mountain and 8362
17:23 mountain of the height of Israel will I **p** it: 8362
28:26 shall build houses, and **p** vineyards; 5193
34:29 I will raise up for them a **p** of renown, and 4302
36:36 ruined *places, and* **p** that that was desolate: 5193
Da 11:45 he shall **p** the tabernacles of his palace 5193
Am 9:14 inhabit *them;* and they shall **p** vineyards, 5193
9:15 I will **p** them upon their land, and they shall 5193
Zep 1:13 inhabit *them;* and they shall **p** vineyards, 5193
Mt 15:13 But he answered and said, Every **p**, *5451*

PLANTATION (1) [PLANT]
Eze 17: 7 *he* might water it by the furrows of her **p**. 4302

PLANTED (39) [PLANT]
Ge 2: 8 the LORD God **p** a garden eastward in 5193
9:20 *to be* a husbandman, and he **p** a vineyard: 5193
21:33 *Abraham* **p** a grove in Beer-sheba, and 5193
Lev 19:23 shall have **p** all *manner of* trees for food, 5193
Nu 24: 6 of lign aloes *which* the LORD hath **p**, 5193
Dt 20: 6 what man *is he* that hath **p** a vineyard, and 5193
Jos 24:13 and oliveyards which ye **p** not do ye eat. 5193
Ps 1: 3 he shall be like a tree **p** by the rivers of 8362
80: 8 thou hast cast out the heathen, and **p** it. 5193
80:15 the vineyard which thy right hand hath **p**, 5193
92:13 Those that be **p** in the house of the LORD 8362
94: 9 He that **p** the ear, shall he not hear? he that 5193
104:16 the cedars of Lebanon, which he hath **p**; 5193
Ecc 2: 4 I builded me houses; I **p** me vineyards: 5193
2: 5 and I **p** trees in them of all *kind of* fruits: 5193
3: 2 and a time to pluck up *that which is* **p**; 5193
Isa 5: 2 **p** it *with* the choicest vine, and built a 5193
40:24 Yea, they shall not be **p**; yea, they shall not 5193
Jer 2:21 Yet I had **p** thee a noble vine, wholly a 5193
11:17 For the LORD of hosts, that **p** thee, 5193
12: 2 Thou hast **p** them, yea, they have taken 5193
17: 8 For he shall be as a tree **p** by the waters, 8362
45: 4 *that* which I have **p** I *will* pluck up, 5193
Eze 17: 5 seed of the land, and **p** it in a fruitful field; 5414
17: 8 It *was* **p** in a good soil by great waters, 8362
17:10 Yea behold, *being* **p**, shall it prosper? shall 8362
19:10 *is* like a vine in thy blood, **p** by the waters: 8362
19:13 And now she *is* **p** in the wilderness, in a dry 8362
Hos 9:13 as I saw Tyrus, *is* **p** in a pleasant place: 8362
Am 5:11 ye have **p** pleasant vineyards, but ye shall 5193
Mt 15:13 which my heavenly Father hath not **p**, *5452*
21:33 which **p** a vineyard, and hedged it round *5452*
Mk 12: 1 A *certain* man **p** a vineyard, and set a hedge *5452*
Lk 13: 6 A certain *man* had a fig tree **p** in his *5452*
17: 6 up by the root, and be thou **p** in the sea; *5452*
17:28 they drank, they bought, they sold, they **p**, *5452*
20: 9 A certain man **p** a vineyard, and let it forth *5452*
Ro 6: 5 For if we have been **p together** in *4854*
1Co 3: 6 I have **p**, Apollos watered; but God gave *5452*

PLANTEDST (2) [PLANT]
Dt 6:11 vineyards and olive trees, which thou **p** not; 5193
Ps 44: 2 out the heathen *with* thy hand, and **p** them; 5193

PLANTERS (1) [PLANT]
Jer 31: 5 the **p** shall plant, and shall eat *them* as 5193

PLANTETH (5) [PLANT]
Pr 31:16 with the fruit of her hands she **p** a vineyard. 5193
Isa 44:14 he **p** an ash, and the rain doth nourish *it*. 5193
1Co 3: 7 neither is he that **p** any *thing*, neither he *5452*
3: 8 Now he that **p** and he that watereth are one: *5452*
9: 7 who **p** a vineyard, and eateth not of *5452*

PLANTING (2) [PLANT]
Isa 60:21 the branch of my **p**, the work of my hands, 4302
61: 3 the **p** of the LORD, that *he* might be 4302

PLANTINGS (1) [PLANT]
Mic 1: 6 a heap of the field, *and* as **p** of a vineyard: 4302

PLANTS (8) [PLANT]
1Ch 4:23 and those that dwelt amongst **p** and hedges: 5196
Ps 128: 3 thy children like olive **p** round about thy 8363
144:12 That our sons *may be* as **p** grown up in 5195
SS 4:13 Thy **p** *are* an orchard of pomegranates, 7973
Isa 16: 8 have broken down the **principal p** thereof, 8291
17:10 therefore shalt thou plant pleasant **p**, and 5194
Jer 48:32 thy **p** are gone over the sea, they reach *even* 5189
Eze 31: 4 with her rivers running round about his **p**, 4302

PLASTER See MORTER

PLAT (2)
2Ki 9:26 I will requite thee in this **p**, saith 2513
9:26 cast him into the **p** *of ground*, according to 2513

PLATE (3) [BREASTPLATE, BREASTPLATES, PLATES]
Ex 28:36 thou shalt make a **p** *of* pure gold, and 6731
39:30 they made the **p** of the holy crown *of* pure 6731
Lev 8: 9 did he put the golden **p**, the holy crown; 6731

PLATES (6) [PLATE]
Ex 39: 3 they did beat the gold into **thin p**, and cut *it* 6341
Nu 16:38 let them make them broad **p** *for* a covering 6341
16:39 they were made broad **p** *for* a covering of NIH
1Ki 7:30 had four brasen wheels, and **p** of brass: 5633
7:36 For on the **p** of the ledges thereof, and 3871
Jer 10: 9 Silver **spread into p** is brought from 7554

PLATFORM See SCAFFOLD

PLATTED (3) [PLAITING]
Mt 27:29 And when they had **p** a crown of thorns, *4120*
Mk 15:17 and **p** a crown of thorns, and put *it* about *4120*
Jn 19: 2 And the soldiers **p** a crown of thorns, and *4120*

PLATTER (3)
Mt 23:25 clean the outside of the cup and of the **p**, *3953*
23:26 first that *which is* within the cup and **p**, *3953*
Lk 11:39 clean the outside of the cup and the **p**; *4094*

PLAY (17) [PLAYED, PLAYEDST, PLAYER, PLAYERS, PLAYETH, PLAYING]
Ex 32: 6 down to eat and to drink, and rose up to **p**. 6711
Dt 22:21 to **p the whore** *in* her father's house: 2181
1Sa 16:16 that he shall **p** with his hand, and thou shalt 5059
16:17 Provide me now a man that can **p** well, and 5059
21:15 *fellow* to **p the mad man** in my presence? 7696
2Sa 2:14 the young men now arise, and **p** before us. 7832
6:21 therefore will I **p** before the LORD. 7832
10:12 let us **p the men** for our people, and for 2388
Job 40:20 where all the beasts of the field **p**. 7832
41: 5 Wilt thou **p** with him as *with* a bird? or 7832
Ps 33: 3 a new song; **p** skilfully with a loud noise. 5059
104:26 *whom* thou hast made to **p** therein. 7832
Isa 11: 8 the sucking child shall **p** on the hole of 8173
Eze 33:32 and can **p** well **on an instrument**: 5059
Hos 3: 3 thou shalt not **p the harlot**, and thou shalt 2181
4:15 Though thou, Israel, **p the harlot**, *yet* let 2181
1Co 10: 7 sat down to eat and drink, and rose up to **p**. *3815*

PLAYED (18) [PLAY]
Ge 38:24 thy daughter in law hath **p the harlot**; 2181
Jdg 19: 2 his concubine **p the whore** against him, 2181
1Sa 16:23 David took a harp, and **p** with his hand: 5059
18: 7 the women answered' *one another* as they **p**, 7832
18:10 David **p** with his hand, as at other times: 5059
19: 9 in his hand: and David **p** with *his* hand. 5059
26:21 I have **p the fool**, and have erred 5528
2Sa 6: 5 all the house of Israel **p** before the LORD 7832
2Ki 3:15 it came to pass, when the minstrel **p**, 5059
1Ch 13: 8 all Israel **p** before God with all *their* might, 7832
Jer 3: 1 thou hast **p the harlot** with many lovers; 2181
3: 6 green tree, and there hath **p the harlot**. 2181
3: 8 feared not, but went and **p the harlot** also. 2181
Eze 16:28 Thou hast **p the whore** also with 2181
16:28 thou hast **p the harlot** with them, and 2181
23: 5 Aholah **p the harlot** when she was mine; 2181
23:19 wherein she had **p the harlot** in the land of 2181
Hos 2: 5 For their mother hath **p the harlot**: she that 2181

PLAYEDST (2) [PLAY]
Eze 16:15 **p the harlot** because of thy renown, and 2181
16:16 divers colours, and **p the harlot** thereupon: 2181

PLAYER (1) [PLAY]
1Sa 16:16 out a man, *who is* a cunning **p** on a harp: 5059

PLAYERS (2) [PLAY]
Ps 68:25 the **p on instruments** *followed* after; 5059
87: 7 **p on instruments** *shall be there:* all my 2490

PLAYETH (1) [PLAY]
Eze 23:44 *they* go in unto a woman that **p the harlot**: 2181

PLAYING (7) [PLAY]
Lev 21: 9 if she profane herself by **p the whore**, she 2181
1Sa 16:18 *that is* cunning in **p**, and a mighty valiant 5059
1Ch 15:29 a window saw king David dancing and **p**: 7832
Ps 68:25 *them were* the damsels **p** with **timbrels**. 8608
Jer 2:20 green tree thou wanderest, **p the harlot**. 2181
Eze 16:41 will cause thee to cease from **p the harlot**, 2181
Zec 8: 5 *of* boys and girls **p** in the streets thereof. 7832

PLEA (2) [PLEAD]
Dt 17: 8 between **p** and plea, and between stroke 1779
17: 8 between plea and **p**, and between stroke 1779

PLEAD (39) [PLEA, PLEADED, PLEADETH, PLEADINGS]
Jdg 6:31 that stood against him, Will ye **p** for Baal? 7378
6:31 he that will **p** for him, let him be put to 7378
6:31 let him **p** for himself, because *one* hath cast 7378
6:32 saying, Let Baal **p** against him, because 7378
1Sa 24:15 **p** my cause, and deliver me out of thine 7378

Job 9:19 of judgment, who shall set me a time to p? NIH
13:19 Who is he that will p with me? for now, if I 7378
16:21 O that one might p for a man with God, 3198
19: 5 against me, and p against me my reproach: 3198
23: 6 Will he p against me with his great power? 7378
Ps 35: 1 P my cause, O LORD, with them that 7378
43: 1 and p my cause against an ungodly nation: 7378
74:22 Arise, O God, p thine own cause: 7378
119:154 P my cause, and deliver me: quicken me 7378
Pr 22:23 For the LORD will p their cause, and 7378
23:11 is mighty; he shall p their cause with thee. 7378
31: 9 and p the cause of the poor and needy. 1777
Isa 1:17 judge the fatherless, p for the widow. 7378
3:13 The LORD standeth up to p, and 7378
43:26 let us p together: declare thou, that thou 8199
66:16 by his sword will the LORD p with all 8199
Jer 2: 9 Wherefore I will yet p with you, saith 7378
2: 9 and with your children's children will I p. 7378
2:29 Wherefore will ye p with me? ye all have 7378
2:35 Behold, I will p with thee, because 8199
12: 1 art thou, O LORD, when I p with thee: 7378
25:31 with the nations, he will p with all flesh; 8199
30:13 There is none to p thy cause, that thou 1777
50:34 he shall throughly p their cause, that 7378+7378
51:36 I will p thy cause, and take vengeance for 7378
Eze 17:20 will p with him there for his trespass that 8199
20:35 and there will I p with you face to face. 8199
20:36 so will I p with you, saith the Lord GOD. 8199
38:22 I will p against him with pestilence and 8199
Hos 2: 2 P with your mother, plead: for she is not 7378
2: 2 Plead with your mother, p: for she is not 7378
Joel 3: 2 will p with them there for my people and 8199
Mic 6: 2 with his people, and he will p with Israel. 3198
7: 9 until he p my cause, and execute judgment 7378

PLEADED (3) [PLEAD]

1Sa 25:39 that hath p the cause of my reproach from 7378
La 3:58 O Lord, thou hast p the causes of my soul; 7378
Eze 20:36 Like as I p with your fathers in 8199

PLEADETH (3) [PLEAD]

Job 16:21 with God, as a man p for his neighbour. NIH
Isa 51:22 thy God that p the cause of his people, 7378
59: 4 None calleth for justice, nor any p for truth: 8199

PLEADINGS (1) [PLEAD]

Job 13: 6 and hearken to the p of my lips. 7379

PLEASANT (57) [PLEASE]

Ge 2: 9 to grow every tree that is p to the sight, 2530
3: 6 that it was p to the eyes, and a tree to be 8378
49:15 rest was good, and the land that it was p; 5276
2Sa 1:23 Jonathan were lovely and p in their lives, 5273
1:26 very p hast thou been unto me: thy love to 5276
1Ki 20: 6 shall be, that whatsoever is p in thine eyes, 4261
2Ki 2:19 I pray thee, the situation of this city is p, 2896
2Ch 32:27 for shields, and for all manner of p jewels; 2532
Ps 16: 6 The lines are fallen unto me in p places; 5273
81: 2 the timbrel, the p harp with the psaltery. 5273
106:24 Yea, they despised the p land, 2532
133: 1 how p it is for brethren to dwell together in 5273
135: 3 sing praises unto his name; for it is p. 5273
147: 1 our God; for it is p; and praise is comely. 5273
Pr 2:10 and knowledge is p unto thy soul; 5276
5:19 Let her be as the loving hind and p roe; 2580
9:17 are sweet, and bread eaten in secret is p. 5276
15:26 but the words of the pure are p words. 5278
16:24 P words are as a honeycomb, sweet to 5278
22:18 For it is a p thing if thou keep them within 5273
24: 4 be filled with all precious and p riches. 5273
Ecc 11: 7 a p thing it is for the eyes to behold the sun: 2896
SS 1:16 Behold, thou art fair, my beloved, yea, p: 5273
4:13 an orchard of pomegranates, with p fruits; 4022
4:16 come into his garden, and eat his p fruits. 4022
7: 6 How fair and how p art thou, O love, 5276
7:13 at our gates are all manner of p fruits, new 4022
Isa 2:16 ships of Tarshish, and upon all p pictures. 2532
5: 7 of Israel, and the men of Judah his p plant: 8191
13:22 and dragons in their p palaces: 6027
17:10 therefore shalt thou plant p plants, and 5282
32:12 for the p fields, for the fruitful vine. 2531
54:12 and all thy borders of p stones. 2656
64:11 and all our p things are laid waste. 4261
Jer 3:19 among the children, and give thee a p land, 2532
12:10 they have made my p portion a desolate 2532
23:10 the p places of the wilderness are dried up, 4999
25:34 And ye shall fall like a p vessel. 2532
31:20 is he a p child? for since I spake against 8191
La 1: 7 of her miseries all her p things that she had 4262
1:10 spread out his hand upon all her p things: 4261
1:11 they have given their p things for meat to 4261
2: 4 slew all that were p to the eye, in 4261
Eze 26:12 down thy walls, and destroy thy p houses: 2532
33:32 very lovely song of one that hath a p voice, 3303
Da 8: 9 and toward the east, and toward the p land. 6643
10: 3 I ate no p bread, neither came flesh nor 2532
11:38 and with precious stones, and p things. 2532
Hos 9: 6 the p places for their silver, nettles shall 4261
9:13 as I saw Tyrus, is planted in a p place: 5116
13:15 he shall spoil the treasure of all p vessels. 2532
Joel 3: 5 into your temples my goodly p things: 4261
Am 5:11 ye have planted p vineyards, but ye shall 2531
Mic 2: 9 have ye cast out from their p houses; 8588
Na 2: 9 and glory out of all the p furniture. 2532
Zec 7:14 for they laid the p land desolate. 2532
Mal 3: 4 and Jerusalem be p unto the LORD, 6149

PLEASANTNESS (1) [PLEASE]

Pr 3:17 Her ways are ways of p, and all her paths 5278

PLEASE (39) [MENPLEASERS, PLEASANT, PLEASANTNESS, PLEASED, PLEASETH, PLEASING, PLEASURE, PLEASURES]

Ex 21: 8 If she p not her master, 5869+7451+871.1
Nu 23:27 peradventure it will p God 3474+5869+871.1
1Sa 20:13 but if it p my father to do thee evil, 413+3190
2Sa 7:29 Therefore now let it p thee to bless 2974
1Ki 21: 6 or else, if it p thee, I will give thee another 2655
1Ch 17:27 let it p thee to bless the house of thy 2974
2Ch 10: 7 and p them, and speak good words to them, 7521
Ne 2: 5 If it p the king, and if thy servant 2895+5921
2: 7 I said unto the king, If it p the king, 2895+5921
Est 1:19 If it p the king, let there go a royal 2895
3: 9 If it p the king, let it be written that they 2895
5: 8 and if it p the king to grant my petition, and 2895
7: 3 in thy sight, O king, and if it p the king, 2895
8: 5 If it p the king, and if I have found favour 2896
9:13 said Esther, If it p the king, let it be granted 2896
Job 6: 9 Even that it would p God to destroy me: 2974
20:10 His children shall seek to p the poor, and 7521
Ps 69:31 This also shall p the LORD better than an 3190
Pr 16: 7 When a man's ways p the LORD, 7521
SS 2: 7 ye stir not up, nor awake my love, till he p. 2654
3: 5 ye stir not up, nor awake my love, till he p. 2654
8: 4 stir not up, nor awake my love, until he p. 2654
Isa 2: 6 they p themselves in the children of 5606
55:11 it shall accomplish that which I p, and 2654
56: 4 choose the things that p me, and take hold 2654
Jn 8:29 for I do always those things that p him. 701
Ro 8: 8 then they that are in the flesh cannot p God. 700
15: 1 of the weak, and not to p ourselves. 700
15: 2 Let every one of us p his neighbour for his 700
1Co 7:32 belong to the Lord, how he may p the Lord: 700
7:33 that are of the world, how he may p his wife. 700
7:34 of the world, how she may p her husband. 700
10:33 Even as I p all men in all things, not seeking 700
Gal 1:10 or do I seek to p men? for if I yet pleased 700
1Th 2:15 and they p not God, and are contrary to all 700
4: 1 of us how ye ought to walk and to p God, 700
2Ti 2: 4 that he may p him who hath chosen him to 700
Tit 2: 9 to p them well in all things; not 1510+2101
Heb 11: 6 But without faith it is impossible to p him: 2100

PLEASED (62) [PLEASE]

Ge 28: 8 daughters of Canaan p not Isaac 5869+7451+871.1
33:10 the face of God, and thou wast p with me. 7521
34:18 their words p Hamor, and 3190+5869+871.1
45:16 p Pharaoh well, and his 3190+5869+871.1
Nu 24: 1 when Balaam saw that it p 2896+5869+871.1
Dt 1:23 the saying p me well: and 3190+5869+871.1
Jos 22:30 of Manasseh spake, it p them. 3190+5869+871.1
22:33 the thing p the children of 3190+5869+871.1
Jdg 13:23 unto him, If the LORD were p to kill us, 2654
14: 7 and she p Samson well. 3474+5869+871.1
1Sa 12:22 it hath p the LORD to make you his 2974
18:20 told Saul, and the thing p him. 3474+5869+871.1
18:26 p David well to be the king's 3474+5869+871.1
2Sa 3:36 notice of it, and it p them: 3190+5869+871.1
3:36 the king did, p all the people. 2896+5869+871.1
17: 4 the saying p Absalom well, 3474+5869+871.1
19: 6 then it had p thee well. 3477+5869+871.1
1Ki 3:10 the speech p the Lord, 3190+5869+871.1
9: 1 all Solomon's desire which he was p to do, 2654
9:12 and they p him not. 3474+5869+871.1
2Ch 30: 4 the thing p the king and all 3474+5869+871.1
Ne 2: 6 So it p the king to send me; 3190+6440+3807.1
Est 1:21 the saying p the king and 3190+5869+871.1
2: 4 p the king; and he did so. 3190+5869+871.1
2: 9 the maiden p him, and 3190+5869+871.1
5:14 the thing p Haman; and he caused 3190
Ps 40:13 Be p, O LORD, to deliver me: O LORD, 7521
51:19 shalt thou be p with the sacrifices of 2654
115: 3 the heavens: he hath done whatsoever he p. 2654
135: 6 Whatsoever the LORD p, that did he in 2654
Isa 42:21 The LORD is well p for his righteousness' 2654
53:10 Yet it p the LORD to bruise him; he hath 2654
Da 6: 1 It p Darius to set over the kingdom an 8232
Jnh 1:14 for thou, O LORD, hast done as it p thee. 2654
Mic 6: 7 Will the LORD be p with thousands of 7521
Mal 1: 8 will he be p with thee, or accept thy 7521
Mt 3:17 is my beloved Son, in whom I am well p. 2106
12:18 my beloved, in whom my soul is well p: 2106
14: 6 Herodias danced before them, and p Herod. 700
17: 5 is my beloved Son, in whom I am well p; 2106
Mk 1:11 art my beloved Son, in whom I am well p. 2106
6:22 and p Herod and them that sat with him, 700
Lk 3:22 art my beloved Son; in thee I am well p. 2106
Ac 6: 5 And the saying p the whole multitude: and 700
12: 3 And because he saw it p the Jews, 701+1510
15:22 Then p it the apostles and elders, with 1380
15:34 Notwithstanding it p Silas to abide there 1380
Ro 15: 3 For even Christ p not himself; but, as it is 700
15:26 For it hath p them of Macedonia and 2106
15:27 It hath p them verily; and their debtors they 2106
1Co 1:21 it p God by the foolishness of preaching to 2106
7:12 and she be p to dwell with him, let him not 4909
7:13 and if he be p to dwell with her, let her not 4909
10: 5 with many of them God was not well p: 2106
12:18 one of them in the body, as it hath p him. 2309
15:38 But God giveth it a body as it hath p him, 2309
Gal 1:10 for if I yet p men, I should not be the servant 700
1:15 But when it p God, who separated me from 2106
Col 1:19 For it p the Father that in him should all 2106
Heb 11: 5 he had this testimony, that he p God. 2100
13:16 for with such sacrifices God is well p. 2100
2Pe 1:17 is my beloved Son, in whom I am well p. 2106

PLEASETH (6) [PLEASE]

Ge 16: 6 do to her as it p thee. 2896+5869+871.1
20:15 dwell where it p thee. 2896+5869+871.1
Jdg 14: 3 Get her for me; for she p me well. 3474+5869
Est 2: 4 let the maiden which p 3190+5869+871.1
Ecc 7:26 whoso p God shall escape 2896+6440+3807.1
8: 3 evil thing; for he doeth whatsoever p him. 2654

PLEASING (8) [PLEASE]

Est 8: 5 right before the king, and I be p in his eyes, 2896
Hos 9: 4 neither shall they be p unto him: 6149
Php 4:18 a sacrifice acceptable, well p to God. 2101
Col 1:10 ye might walk worthy of the Lord unto all p, 699
3:20 all things: for this is well p unto the Lord. 2101
1Th 2: 4 not as p men, but God, which trieth our 700
Heb 13:21 working in you that which is well p in his 2101
1Jn 3:22 and do those things that are p in his sight. 701

PLEASURE (61) [PLEASE]

Ge 18:12 saying, After I am waxed old shall I have p, 5730
Dt 23:24 mayest eat grapes thy fill at thine own p; 5315
1Ch 29:17 triest the heart, and hast p in uprightness. 7521
Ezr 5:17 let the king send his p to us concerning 7470
10:11 LORD God of your fathers, and do his p: 7522
Ne 9:37 at their p, and we are in great distress. 7522
Est 1: 8 they should do according to every man's p. 7522
Job 21:21 For what p hath he in his house after him, 2656
21:25 of his soul, and never eateth with p. 2896
22: 3 Is it any p to the Almighty, that thou art 2656
Ps 5: 4 For thou art not a God that hath p in 2655
35:27 which hath p in the prosperity of his 2655
51:18 Do good in thy good p unto Zion: 7522
102:14 For thy servants take p in her stones, and 7521
103:21 his hosts; ye ministers of his, that do his p. 7522
105:22 To bind his princes at his p; and teach his 5315
111: 2 sought out of all them that have p therein. 2656
147:10 he taketh not p in the legs of a man. 7521
147:11 The LORD taketh p in them that fear 7521
149: 4 For the LORD taketh p in his people: 7521
Pr 21:17 He that loveth p shall be a poor man: 8057
Ecc 2: 1 prove thee with mirth, therefore enjoy p: 2896
5: 4 defer not to pay it; for he hath no p in fools: 2656
12: 1 when thou shalt say, I have no p in them; 2656
Isa 21: 4 the night of my p hath he turned into fear 2837
44:28 is my shepherd, and shall perform all my p: 2656
46:10 counsel shall stand, and I will do all my p: 2656
48:14 he will do his p on Babylon, and his arm 2656
53:10 the p of the LORD shall prosper in his 2656
58: 3 in the day of your fast ye find p, and 2656
58:13 from doing thy p on my holy day; 2656
58:13 thine own ways, nor finding thine own p, 2656
Jer 2:24 that snuffeth up the wind at her p; 185
22:28 is he a vessel wherein is no p? 2656
34:16 whom ye had set at liberty at their p, 5315
48:38 broken Moab like a vessel wherein is no p, 2656
Eze 16:37 with whom thou hast taken p, and all them 6149
18:23 Have I any p at all that the wicked 2654+2654
18:32 For I have no p in the death of him that 2654
33:11 I have no p in the death of the wicked; 2654
Hos 8: 8 the Gentiles as a vessel wherein is no p. 2656
Hag 1: 8 I will take p in it, and I will be glorified, 7521
Mal 1:10 I have no p in you, saith the LORD of 2656
Lk 12:32 for it is your Father's good p to give you 2106
Ac 24:27 and Felix, willing to shew the Jews a p, 5485
25: 9 But Festus, willing to do the Jews a p, 5485
Ro 1:32 the same, but have p in them that do them. 4909
2Co 12:10 Therefore I take p in infirmities, 2106
Eph 1: 5 according to the good p of his will, 2107
1: 9 according to his good p which he had 2107
Php 2:13 in you both to will and to do of his good p. 2107
2Th 1:11 and fulfil all the good p of his goodness, 2107
2:12 not the truth, but had p in unrighteousness. 2106
1Ti 5: 6 But she that liveth in p is dead while she 4684
Heb 10: 6 and sacrifices for sin thou hast had no p. 2106
10: 8 neither hadst p therein: which are offered 2106
10:38 draw back, my soul shall have no p in him. 2106
12:10 a few days chastened us after their own p; 1380
Jas 5: 5 Ye have lived in p on the earth, and 5171
2Pe 2:13 as they that count it p to riot in the day 2237
Rev 4:11 and for thy p they are and were created. 2307

PLEASURES (8) [PLEASE]

Job 36:11 days in prosperity, and their years in p. 5273
Ps 16:11 at thy right hand there are p for evermore. 5273
36: 8 shalt make them drink of the river of thy p. 5730
Isa 47: 8 thou that art given to p, that dwellest 5719
Lk 8:14 with cares and riches and p of this life, 2237
2Ti 3: 4 lovers of p more than lovers of God; 5369
Tit 3: 3 deceived, serving divers lusts and p, 2237
Heb 11:25 than to enjoy the p of sin for a season; 619

PLEDGE (22) [PLEDGES]

Ge 38:17 she said, Wilt thou give me a p, till thou 6162
38:18 he said, What p shall I give thee? And she 6162
38:20 to receive his p from the woman's hand: 6162
Ex 22:26 at all take thy neighbour's raiment to p, 2254+2254
Dt 24: 6 take the nether or the upper millstone to p: 2254
24: 6 to pledge: for he taketh a man's life to p. 2254
24:10 shalt not go into his house to fetch his p. 5667
24:11 lend shall bring out the p abroad unto thee. 5667
24:12 be poor, thou shalt not sleep with his p: 5667
24:13 In any case thou shalt deliver him the p 5667
24:17 nor take a widow's raiment to p: 2254
1Sa 17:18 how thy brethren fare, and take their p. 6161
Job 22: 6 For thou hast taken a p from thy brother 2254
24: 3 they take the widow's ox for a p. 2254
24: 9 from the breast, and take a p of the poor. 2254
Pr 20:16 and take a p of him for a strange woman. 2254
27:13 and take a p of him for a strange woman. 2254
Eze 18: 7 but hath restored to the debtor his p, 2258
18:12 hath not restored the p, and hath lift up his 2258
18:16 hath not withholden the p, 2254+2258
33:15 If the wicked restore the p, give again that 2258
Am 2: 8 down upon clothes laid to p by every altar, 2254

PLEDGES (2) [PLEDGE]

2Ki 18:23 give p to my lord the king of Assyria, and 6148
Isa 36: 8 Now therefore give p, I pray thee, to my 6148

PLEIADES (2)

Job 9: 9 and P, and the chambers of the south. 3598
38:31 Canst thou bind the sweet influences of P, 3598

PLENTEOUS (12) [PLENTY]
Ge 41:34 of the land of Egypt in the seven p years. 7647
41:47 in the seven p years the earth brought forth 7647
Dt 28:11 the LORD shall make thee p in goods, 3498
30: 9 the LORD thy God will make thee p in 3498
2Ch 1:15 and gold at Jerusalem *as* p as stones, NIH
Ps 86: 5 p in mercy unto all them that call upon 7227
86:15 longsuffering, and p in mercy and truth. 7227
103: 8 gracious, slow to anger, and p in mercy. 7227
130: 7 *is* mercy, and with him *is* p redemption. 7235
Isa 30:23 of the earth, and it shall be fat and p: 8082
Hab 1:16 them their portion *is* fat, and their meat p. 1277
Mt 9:37 The harvest truly is p, but the labourers *are* *4183*

PLENTEOUSNESS (2) [PLENTY]
Ge 41:53 the seven years of p, that was in the land of 7647
Pr 21: 5 The thoughts of the diligent *tend* only to p; 4195

PLENTIFUL (4) [PLENTY]
Ps 68: 9 Thou, O God, didst send a p rain, 5071
Isa 16:10 is taken away, and joy out of the p field; 3759
Jer 2: 7 I brought you into a p country, to eat 3759
48:33 and gladness is taken from the p field, 3759

PLENTIFULLY (3) [PLENTY]
Job 26: 3 thou p declared the thing as it is? 7230+3807.1
Ps 31:23 and p rewardeth the proud doer. 3499
Lk 12:16 of a certain rich man brought forth p: *2164*

PLENTY (13) [PLENTEOUS, PLENTEOUSNESS, PLENTIFUL, PLENTIFULLY]
Ge 27:28 of the earth, and p of corn and wine: 7230
41:29 there come seven years of great p 7647
41:30 all the p shall be forgotten in the land of 7647
41:31 the p shall not be known in the land by 7647
Lev 11:36 or pit, *wherein there is* p of water, 4723
1Ki 10:11 brought in from Ophir great p of almug 7235
2Ch 31:10 had enough to eat, and have left p: 7230+3807.1
Job 22:25 thy defence, and thou shalt have p of silver. 8443
37:23 and *in* judgment, and *in* p of justice: 7230
Pr 3:10 So shall thy barns be filled *with* p, and 7647
28:19 He that tilleth his land shall have p *of* 7646
Jer 44:17 for *then* had we p of victuals, and 7646
Joel 2:26 ye shall eat in p, and be satisfied, and 398+398

PLOT See FORECAST

PLOTTETH (1)
Ps 37:12 The wicked p against the just, and 2161

PLOUGH (1) [PLOW]
Lk 9:62 No *man* having put his hand to the p, and *723*

PLOW (8) [PLOUGH, PLOWED, PLOWERS, PLOWETH, PLOWING, PLOWMAN, PLOWMEN, PLOWSHARES]
Dt 22:10 Thou shalt not p with an ox and an ass 2790
1Sa 14:14 acre of land, *which* a yoke *of oxen might* p. NIH
Job 4: 8 they that p iniquity, and sow wickedness, 2790
Pr 20: 4 The sluggard will not p by reason of 2790
Isa 28:24 Doth the plowman p all day to sow? 2790
Hos 10:11 Judah shall p, *and* Jacob shall break his 2790
Am 6:12 will *one* p *there* with oxen? for ye have 2790
1Co 9:10 that he that ploweth should p in hope; and *722*

PLOWED (5) [PLOW]
Jdg 14:18 unto them, If ye had not p with my heifer, 2790
Ps 129: 3 The plowers p upon my back: they made 2790
Jer 26:18 Zion shall be p *like* a field, and 2790
Hos 10:13 Ye have p wickedness, ye have reaped 2790
Mic 3:12 Therefore shall Zion for your sake be p *as* a 2790

PLOWERS (1) [PLOW]
Ps 129: 3 The p plowed upon my back: they made 2790

PLOWETH (1) [PLOW]
1Co 9:10 that he that p should plow in hope; and *722*

PLOWING (4) [PLOW]
1Ki 19:19 who *was* p *with* twelve yoke *of oxen* before 2790
Job 1:14 The oxen were p, and the asses feeding 2790
Pr 21: 4 proud heart, *and* the p of the wicked, *is* sin. 5215
Lk 17: 7 of you, having a servant p or feeding cattle, *722*

PLOWMAN (2) [MAN, PLOW]
Isa 28:24 Doth the p plow all day to sow? doth he 2790
Am 9:13 that the p shall overtake the reaper, and 2790

PLOWMEN (2) [MAN, PLOW]
Isa 61: 5 and the sons of the alien *shall be* your p and 406
Jer 14: 4 the p were ashamed, they covered their 406

PLOWSHARES (3) [PLOW]
Isa 2: 4 they shall beat their swords into p, and 855
Joel 3:10 Beat your p into swords, and 855
Mic 4: 3 they shall beat their swords into p, and 855

PLUCK (30) [PLUCKED, PLUCKETH, PLUCKT]
Lev 1:16 he shall p away his crop with his feathers, 5493
Nu 33:52 and quite p down all their high places: 8045
Dt 23:25 thou mayest p the ears with thine hand; 6998
2Ch 7:20 will I p them up by the roots out of my 5428
Job 24: 9 They p the fatherless from the breast, and 1497
Ps 25:15 for he shall p my feet out of the net. 3318
52: 5 p thee out of *thy* dwelling place, and 5255
74:11 even thy right hand? p *it* out of thy bosom. 3615
80:12 that all they which pass by the way do p her? 717
Ecc 3: 2 and a time to p up *that which is* planted; 6131
Jer 12:14 I will p them out of their land, and pluck 5428
12:14 p out the house of Judah from among them. 5428
12:17 I will utterly p up and destroy that 5428+5428
18: 7 to p up, and to pull down, and to destroy 5428
22:24 my right hand, yet would I p thee thence; 5423
24: 6 and I will plant them, and not p *them* up. 5428
31:28 to p up, and to break down, and to throw 5428
42:10 and I will plant you, and not p *you* up: 5428
45: 4 *that* which I have planted I *will* p up, 5428
Eze 17: 9 many people to p it up by the roots thereof. 5375
23:34 and p off thine own breasts: 5423
Mic 3: 2 who p off their skin from off them, and 1497
5:14 I will p up thy groves out of the midst of 5428
Mt 5:29 offend thee, p it out, and cast *it* from thee: *1807*
12: 1 and began to p the ears of corn, and to eat. *5089*
18: 9 offend thee, p it out, and cast *it* from thee: *1807*
Mk 2:23 as they went, to p the ears of corn. *5089*
9:47 And if thine eye offend thee, p it out: it is *1544*
Jn 10:28 neither shall any *man* p them out of my *726*
10:29 no *man* is able to p *them* out of my Father's *726*

PLUCKED (14) [PLUCK]
Ex 4: 7 p it out of his bosom, and behold, it was 3318
Dt 28:63 ye shall be p from off the land whither thou 5255
Ru 4: 7 a man p off his shoe, and gave *it* to his 8025
2Sa 23:21 p the spear out of the Egyptian's hand, and 1497
Isa 50: 6 and my cheeks to them that p off the hair: 4803
Jer 6:29 in vain: for the wicked are not p away. 5423
12:15 after that I have p them out, I will return, 5428
31:40 it shall not be p up, nor thrown down any 5428
Eze 19:12 she was p up in fury, she was cast down to 5428
Mk 5: 4 and the chains had been p asunder by him, *1288*
Lk 6: 1 and his disciples p the ears of corn, and *5089*
17: 6 Be thou p up by the root, and be thou *1610*
Gal 4:15 ye would have p out your own eyes, and *1846*
Jude 1:12 twice dead, p up by the roots; *1610*

PLUCKETH (1) [PLUCK]
Pr 14: 1 but the foolish p it down with her hands. 2040

PLUCKT (10) [PLUCK]
Ge 8:11 and lo, in her mouth *was* an olive leaf p off: 2965
1Ch 11:23 p the spear out of the Egyptian's hand, and 1497
Ezr 9: 3 p off the hair of my head and of my beard, 4803
Ne 13:25 p off their hair, and made them swear by 4803
Job 29:17 the wicked, and p the spoil out of his teeth. 7993
Da 7: 4 I beheld till the wings thereof were p, and 4804
7: 8 three of the first horns p up by the roots: 6132
11: 4 for his kingdom shall be p up, even for 5428
Am 4:11 ye were as a firebrand p out of the burning: 5337
Zec 3: 2 *is* not this a brand p out of the fire? 5337

PLUMBLINE (4) [LINE]
Am 7: 7 the Lord stood upon a wall made by a p, 594
7: 7 made by a plumbline, with a p in his hand. 594
7: 8 And I said, A p. Then said the Lord, Behold, 594
7: 8 I *will* set a p in the midst of my people 594

PLUMMET (3)
2Ki 21:13 of Samaria, and the p of the house of Ahab: 4949
Isa 28:17 I lay to the line, and righteousness to the p: 4949
Zec 4:10 shall see the p in the hand of Zerubbabel 68+913

PLUNDER See BOOTY; PREY; SPOIL

PLUNGE (1)
Job 9:31 Yet shalt thou p me in the ditch, and 2881

POCHERETH OF ZEBAIM (1) [POCHERETH ZEBAIM]
Ezr 2:57 the children of P, the children 6380

POCHERETH ZEBAIM (1) [POCHERETH OF ZEBAIM]
Ne 7:59 of Hattil, the children of P, 6380

POETS (1)
Ac 17:28 as certain also of your own p have said, *4163*

POINT (9) [POINTED, POINTS]
Ge 25:32 Esau said, Behold, I *am* at the p to die: 1980
Nu 34: 7 from the great sea you shall p out for you 8376
34: 8 From mount Hor ye shall p out *your border* 8376
34:10 ye shall p out your east border from 184
Jer 17: 1 a pen of iron, *and* with the p of a diamond: 6856
Eze 21:15 I have set the p of the sword against all their 19
Mk 5:23 daughter lieth at the p of death: *2079+2192*
Jn 4:47 heal his son: for he was at the p of death. *3195*
Jas 2:10 and *yet* offend in one *p*, he is guilty of all. NIG

POINTED (1) [POINT]
Job 41:30 he spreadeth sharp p *things* upon the mire. 2742

POINTING See SIGNIFY

POINTS (2) [POINT]
Ecc 5:16 *that* in all p as he came, so shall he go: 5980
Heb 4:15 was in all *p* tempted like as *we are*, *yet* NIG

POISON (9)
Dt 32:24 with the p of serpents of the dust. 2534
32:33 Their wine *is* the p of dragons, and 2534
Job 6: 4 the p whereof drinketh up my spirit: 2534
20:16 He shall suck the p of asps: the viper's 7219
Ps 58: 4 Their p *is* like the poison of a serpent: 2534
58: 4 Their poison *is* like the p of a serpent: 2534
140: 3 like a serpent; adder's p *is* under their lips. 2534
Ro 3:13 used deceit; the p of asps *is* under their lips: *2447*
Jas 3: 8 *it is* an unruly evil, full of deadly p. *2447*

POISONOUS See HEMLOCK

POKERETH HAZZEBAIM See POCHERETH [OF] ZEBAIM

POLE (2)
Nu 21: 8 thee a fiery *serpent*, and set it upon a p: 5251
21: 9 put it upon a p, and it came to pass, that if a 5251

POLES See STAVES

POLICY (1)
Da 8:25 through his p also he shall cause craft to 7922

POLISHED (3) [POLISHING]
Ps 144:12 p *after* the similitude of a palace: 2404
Isa 49: 2 hath he hid me, and made me a p shaft; 1305
Da 10: 6 and his feet like in colour to p brass, 7044

POLISHING (1) [POLISHED]
La 4: 7 body than rubies, their p *was of* sapphire: 1508

POLL (3) [POLLED, POLLS]
Nu 3:47 shalt even take five shekels apiece by the p, 1538
Eze 44:20 they shall only p their heads. 3697+3697
Mic 1:16 and p thee for thy delicate children; 1494

POLLED (3) [POLL]
2Sa 14:26 when he p his head, (for it was at every 1548
14:26 (for it was at every year's end that he p *it:* 1548
14:26 *hair* was heavy on him, therefore he p it:) 1548

POLLS (6) [POLL]
Nu 1: 2 of *their* names, every male by their p; 1538
1:18 twenty years old and upward, by their p. 1538
1:20 by their p, every male from twenty years 1538
1:22 by their p, every male from twenty years 1538
1Ch 23: 3 their number by their p, man by man, 1538
23:24 counted by number of names by their p, 1538

POLLUTE (11) [POLLUTED, POLLUTING, POLLUTION, POLLUTIONS]
Nu 18:32 neither shall ye p the holy *things* of 2490
35:33 So ye shall not p the land wherein ye *are:* 2610
Jer 7:30 house which is called by my name, to p it. 2930
Eze 7:21 of the earth for a spoil; and they shall p it. 2490
7:22 they shall p my secret *place:* for the robbers 2490
13:19 will ye p me among my people for handfuls 2490
20:31 ye p yourselves with all your idols, 2930
20:39 p ye my holy name no more with your 2490
39: 7 I will not let *them* p my holy name any 2490
44: 7 be in my sanctuary, to p it, *even* my house, 2490
Da 11:31 they shall p the sanctuary *of* strength, and 2490

POLLUTED (40) [POLLUTE]
Ex 20:25 thou lift up thy tool upon it, thou hast p it. 2490
2Ki 23:16 and burnt *them* upon the altar, and p it, 2930
2Ch 36:14 p the house of the LORD which he had 2930
Ezr 2:62 therefore were they, as p, put from 1351
Ne 7:64 therefore were they, as p, put from 1351
Ps 106:38 of Canaan: and the land was p with blood. 2610
Isa 47: 6 I have p mine inheritance, and given them 2490
48:11 will I do *it:* for how should *my name* be p? 2490
Jer 2:23 How canst thou say, I am not p, I have not 2930
3: 1 shall not that land be greatly p? 2610+2610
3: 2 thou hast p the land with thy whoredoms 2610
34:16 ye turned and p my name, and caused every 2490
La 2: 2 he hath p the kingdom and the princes 2490
4:14 they have p themselves with blood, so 1351
Eze 4:14 behold, my soul *hath* not *been* p: 2930
14:11 neither be p any more with all their 2930
16: 6 by thee, and saw thee p in thine own blood, 947
16:22 and bare, *and* wast p in thy blood. 947
20: 9 that *it* should not be p before the heathen, 2490
20:13 in them; and my sabbaths they greatly p: 2490
20:14 that *it* should not be p before the heathen, 2490
20:16 not in my statutes, but p my sabbaths: 2490
20:21 even live in them; they p my sabbaths: 2490
20:22 that *it* should not be p in the sight of 2490
20:24 had p my sabbaths, and their eyes were 2490
20:26 I p them in their own gifts, in that they 2930
20:30 Are ye p after the manner of your fathers? 2930
23:17 she was p with them, and her mind was 2930
23:30 *and* because thou art p with their idols. 2930
36:18 and for their idols *wherewith* they had p it: 2930
Hos 6: 8 that work iniquity, *and is* p with blood. 6121
9: 4 of mourners; all that eat thereof shall be p: 2930
Am 7:17 by line; and thou shalt die in a p land: 2931
Mic 2:10 because it is p, it shall destroy *you*, even 2930
Zep 3: 1 Woe to her that is filthy and p, to 1351
3: 4 her priests have p the sanctuary, they have 2490
Mal 1: 7 *Ye* offer p bread upon mine altar; and 1351
1: 7 and ye say, Wherein have we p thee? 1351
1:12 in that ye say, The table of the LORD *is* p; 1351
Ac 21:28 into the temple, and hath p this holy place. *2840*

POLLUTING (2) [POLLUTE]
Isa 56: 2 that keepeth the sabbath from p it, and 2490
56: 6 every one that keepeth the sabbath from p 2490

POLLUTION (1) [POLLUTE]
Eze 22:10 they humbled her that was set apart for p. 2931

POLLUTIONS (2) [POLLUTE]
Ac 15:20 that *they* abstain from p of idols, and *234*
2Pe 2:20 For if after they have escaped the p of *3393*

POLLUX (1)
Ac 28:11 in the isle, *whose* sign *was* Castor and P. *1359*

POMEGRANATE (10) [POMEGRANATES]
Ex 28:34 A golden bell and a p, a golden bell and 7416
28:34 and a pomegranate, a golden bell and a p, 7416
39:26 A bell and a p, a bell and a pomegranate, 7416
39:26 A bell and a pomegranate, a bell and a p, 7416
1Sa 14: 2 Gibeah under a p tree which *is* in Migron: 7416
SS 4: 3 thy temples *are* like a piece of a p within 7416
6: 7 As a piece of a p *are* thy temples within thy 7416
8: 2 drink of spiced wine, of the juice of my p. 7416
Joel 1:12 the p tree, the palm tree also, and the apple 7416

Hag 2:19 the fig tree, and the p, and the olive tree, 7416

POMEGRANATES (23) [POMEGRANATE]

Ex 28:33 the hem of it thou shalt make p of blue, 7416
39:24 they made upon the hems of the robe p of 7416
39:25 put the bells between the p upon the hem of 7416
39:25 of the robe, round about between the p; 7416
Nu 13:23 and *they brought* of the p, and of the figs. 7416
20: 5 place of seed, or of figs, or vines, or of p; 7416
Dt 8: 8 and barley, and vines, and fig trees, and p; 7416
1Ki 7:18 chapiters that *were* upon the top, *with* p: 7416
7:20 the chapiters upon the two pillars *had* p also NIH
7:20 the p *were* two hundred *in* rows round 7416
7:42 four hundred p for the two networks, 7416
7:42 *even* two rows *of* p for one network, 7416
2Ki 25:17 p upon the chapiter round about, all *of* 7416
2Ch 3:16 made an hundred p, and put *them* on 7416
4:13 four hundred p on the two wreaths; 7416
4:13 two rows *of* p on each wreath, to cover 7416
SS 4:13 Thy plants *are* an orchard of p, 7416
6:11 the vine flourished, *and* the p budded. 7416
7:12 tender grape appear, *and* the p bud forth: 7416
Jer 52:22 and p upon the chapiters round about, 7416
52:22 pillar also and the p *were* like unto these. 7416
52:23 there were ninety and six p on a side; *and* 7416
52:23 all the p upon the network *were* an hundred 7416

POMMELS (3)

2Ch 4:12 the p, and the chapiters *which were* on 1543
4:12 the two wreaths to cover the two p of 1543
4:13 to cover the two p of the chapiters which 1543

POMP (7)

Isa 5:14 and their p, and he that rejoiceth, 7588
14:11 Thy p is brought down *to* the grave, *and* 1347
Eze 7:24 I will also make the p of the strong to 1347
30:18 the p of her strength shall cease in her: 1347
32:12 they shall spoil the p of Egypt, and all 1347
33:28 the p of her strength shall cease; 1347
Ac 25:23 with great p, and were entered into *5325*

PONDER (2) [PONDERED, PONDERETH]

Pr 4:26 P the path of thy feet, and let all thy ways 6424
5: 6 Lest thou shouldest p the path of life, 6424

PONDERED (1) [PONDER]

Lk 2:19 all these things, and p *them* in her heart. *4820*

PONDERETH (3) [PONDER]

Pr 5:21 eyes of the LORD, and he p all his goings. 6424
21: 2 his own eyes: but the LORD p the hearts. 8505
24:12 doth not he that p the heart consider *it?* and 8505

PONDS (3)

Ex 7:19 upon their p, and upon all their pools of 98
8: 5 over the p, and cause frogs to come up upon 98
Isa 19:10 all that make sluces *and* p for fish. 99

PONTIUS (4)

Mt 27: 2 and delivered him to P Pilate the governor. *4194*
Lk 3: 1 P Pilate being governor of Judea, and *4194*
Ac 4:27 both Herod, and P Pilate, with the Gentiles, *4194*
1Ti 6:13 who before P Pilate witnessed a good *4194*

PONTUS (3)

Ac 2: 9 in Judea, and Cappadocia, in P, and Asia, *4195*
18: 2 born in P, lately come from Italy, with his *4193*
1Pe 1: 1 to the strangers scattered throughout P, *4195*

POOL (22) [FISHPOOLS, POOLS]

2Sa 2:13 and met together by the p of Gibeon: 1295
2:13 the one on the one side of the p, and 1295
2:13 and the other on the other side of the p. 1295
4:12 and hanged *them* up over the p in Hebron. 1295
1Ki 22:38 *one* washed the chariot in the p of Samaria; 1295
2Ki 18:17 and stood by the conduit of the upper p, 1295
20:20 how he made a p, and a conduit, and 1295
Ne 2:14 the gate of the fountain, and to the king's p: 1295
3:15 the wall of the p of Siloah by the king's 1295
3:16 to the p that was made, and unto the house 1295
Isa 7: 3 at the end of the conduit of the upper p in 1295
22: 9 gathered together the waters of the lower p. 1295
22:11 the two walls for the water of the old p: 1295
35: 7 the parched ground shall become a p, and 98
36: 2 he stood by the conduit of the upper p in 1295
41:18 I will make the wilderness a p of water, and 98
Na 2: 8 Nineveh *is* of old like a p of water: yet they 1295
Jn 5: 2 is at Jerusalem by the sheep *market* a p, *2861*
5: 4 went down at a *certain* season into the p, *2861*
5: 7 the water is troubled, to put me into the p: *2861*
9: 7 said unto him, Go, wash in the p of Siloam, *2861*
9:11 unto me, Go to the p of Siloam, and wash: *2861*

POOLS (5) [POOL]

Ex 7:19 their ponds, and upon all their p of water, 4723
Ps 84: 6 make it a well; the rain also filleth the p. 1295
Ecc 2: 6 I made me p of water, to water therewith 1295
Isa 14:23 it a possession for the bittern, and p of water: 98
42:15 the rivers islands, and I will dry up the p. 98

POOR (205) [POVERTY]

Ge 41:19 p and very ill favoured and leanfleshed, 1803
Ex 22:25 to *any of* my people *that is* p by thee, 6041
23: 3 Neither shalt thou countenance a p *man* in 1800
23: 6 Thou shalt not wrest the judgment of thy p in 34
23:11 and lie still; that the p of thy people may eat: 34
30:15 the p shall not give less than half a shekel, 1800
Lev 14:21 if he *be* p, and cannot get *so much;* then 1800
19:10 thou shalt leave them for the p and 6041
19:15 thou shalt not respect the person of the p, 1800
23:22 thou shalt leave them unto the p, and to 6041
25:25 If thy brother be waxen p, and hath sold 4134
25:35 if thy brother be waxen p, and fallen in 4134
Lev 25:39 brother *that dwelleth* by thee be waxen p, 4134
25:47 thy brother *that dwelleth* by him wax p, 4134
Dt 15: 4 Save when there shall be no p among you; 34
15: 7 If there be among you a p man of one of thy 34
15: 7 nor shut thine hand from thy p brother: 34
15: 9 thine eye be evil against thy p brother, and 34
15:11 For the p shall never cease out of the land: 34
15:11 to thy p, and to thy needy, in thy land. 6041
24:12 if the man *be* p, thou shalt not sleep with 6041
24:14 shalt not oppress a hired servant *that is* p 6041
24:15 for he *is* p, and setteth his heart upon it: 6041
Jdg 6:15 my family *is* p in Manasseh, and I *am* 1800
Ru 3:10 not young men, whether p or rich. 1800
1Sa 2: 7 The LORD maketh p, and maketh rich: 3423
2: 8 He raiseth up the p out of the dust, *and* 1800
18:23 seeing that I *am* a p man, and 7326
2Sa 12: 1 in one city; the one rich, and the other p. 7326
12: 3 the p *man* had nothing, save one little ewe 7326
12: 4 took the p man's lamb, and dressed it for 7326
2Ki 25:12 the captain of the guard left of the p of 1803
Est 9:22 portions one to another, and gifts to the p. 34
Job 5:15 he saveth the p from the sword, from their 34
5:16 So the p hath hope, and iniquity stoppeth 1800
20:10 His children shall *seek to* please the p, and 1800
20:19 he hath oppressed *and* hath forsaken the p; 1800
24: 4 the p of the earth hide themselves together. 6041
24: 9 from the breast, and take a pledge of the p. 6041
24:14 murderer rising with the light killeth the p 6041
29:12 Because I delivered the p that cried, and 6041
29:16 I *was* a father to the p: and the cause *which* I 34
30:25 in trouble? was *not* my soul grieved for the p? 34
31:16 If I have withheld the p from *their* desire, 1800
31:19 want of clothing, or *any* p without covering; 34
34:19 nor regardeth the rich more than the p? 1800
34:28 So that *they* cause the cry of the p to come 1800
36: 6 life of the wicked: but giveth right to the p. 6041
36:15 He delivereth the p in his affliction, and 6041
Ps 9:18 the expectation of the p shall *not* perish for 6041
10: 2 wicked in *his* pride doth persecute the p: 6041
10: 8 his eyes are privily set against the p. 2489
10: 9 he lieth in wait to catch the p: he doth catch 6041
10: 9 he doth catch the p, when he draweth him 6041
10:10 that the p may fall by his strong *ones.* 2489
10:14 the p committeth *himself* unto thee; 2489
12: 5 For the oppression of the p, for the sighing 6041
14: 6 You have shamed the counsel of the p, 6041
34: 6 This p *man* cried, and the LORD heard 6041
35:10 which deliverest the p from him that is too 6041
35:10 the p and the needy from him that spoileth 6041
37:14 to cast down the p and needy, *and* to slay 6041
40:17 I *am* p and needy; *yet* the Lord thinketh 6041
41: 1 Blessed *is* he that considereth the p: 1800
49: 2 Both low and high, rich and p, together. 34
68:10 hast prepared of thy goodness for the p. 6041
69:29 I *am* p and sorrowful: let thy salvation, 6041
69:33 For the LORD heareth the p, and despiseth 34
70: 5 I *am* p and needy: make haste unto me, 6041
72: 2 and thy p with judgment. 6041
72: 4 He shall judge the p of the people, he shall 6041
72:12 the p also, and *him* that hath no helper. 6041
72:13 He shall spare the p and needy, and 1800
74:19 not the congregation of thy p for ever. 6041
74:21 let the p and needy praise thy name. 6041
82: 3 Defend the p and fatherless: do justice to 1800
82: 4 Deliver the p and needy: rid *them* out of 1800
86: 1 O LORD, hear me: for I *am* p and needy. 6041
107:41 Yet setteth he the p on high from affliction, 34
109:16 persecuted the p and needy man, that *he* 6041
109:22 For I *am* p and needy, and my heart is 6041
109:31 For he shall stand at the right hand of the p, 34
112: 9 He hath dispersed, he hath given to the p; 34
113: 7 He raiseth up the p out of the dust, *and* 1800
132:15 her provision: I will satisfy her p *with* bread. 34
140:12 cause of the afflicted, *and* the right of the p. 34
Pr 10: 4 *He becometh* p that dealeth *with* a slack 7326
10:15 the destruction of the p *is* their poverty. 1800
13: 7 *there is* that maketh himself p, yet *hath* 7326
13: 8 *are* his riches: but the p heareth not rebuke. 7326
13:23 Much food *is in* the tillage of the p: but 7326
14:20 The p is hated even of his own neighbour: 7326
14:21 he that hath mercy on the p, happy *is* he. 6035
14:31 He that oppresseth the p reproacheth his 1800
14:31 he that honoureth him hath mercy on the p. 34
17: 5 Whoso mocketh the p reproacheth his 7326
18:23 The p useth intreaties; but the rich 7326
19: 1 Better *is* the p that walketh in his integrity, 7326
19: 4 but the p is separated from his neighbour. 1800
19: 7 All the brethren of the p do hate him: 7326
19:17 He that hath pity upon the p lendeth unto 1800
19:22 and a p *man is* better than a liar. 7326
21:13 Whoso stoppeth his ears at the cry of the p, 1800
21:17 He that loveth pleasure *shall be* a p man: 4270
22: 2 The rich and p meet together: the LORD 7326
22: 7 The rich ruleth over the p, and the borrower 7326
22: 9 for he giveth of his bread to the p. 1800
22:16 He that oppresseth the p to increase his 1800
22:22 Rob not the p, because he *is* poor: 1800
22:22 Rob not the poor, because he *is* p: 1800
28: 3 A p man that oppresseth the poor *is like* a 7326
28: 3 A poor man that oppresseth the p *is like* a 1800
28: 6 Better *is* the p that walketh in his 7326
28: 8 shall gather it for him that will pity the p. 1800
28:11 the p that hath understanding searcheth him 1800
28:15 *so is* a wicked ruler over the p people. 1800
28:27 He that giveth unto the p *shall* not lack: but 7326
29: 7 righteous considereth the cause of the p: 1800
29:13 The p and the deceitful man meet together: 7326
29:14 The king that faithfully judgeth the p, 1800
30: 9 or lest I be p, and steal, and take the name 3423
30:14 to devour the p from off the earth, and 6041
31: 9 and plead the cause of the p and needy. 6041
31:20 She stretcheth out her hand to the p; yea, 6041
Ecc 4:13 Better *is* a p and a wise child than an old 4542
4:14 *he that is* born in his kingdom becometh p. 7326
5: 8 If thou seest the oppression of the p, and 7326
Ecc 6: 8 what hath the p, that knoweth to walk 6041
9:15 Now there was found in it a p wise man, 4542
9:15 yet no man remembered that *same* p man. 4542
9:16 nevertheless the p *man's* wisdom *is* 4542
Isa 3:14 the spoil of the p *is* in your houses. 6041
3:15 to pieces, and grind the faces of the p? 6041
10: 2 to take away the right from the p of my 6041
10:30 *it* to be heard unto Laish, O p Anathoth. 6041
11: 4 But with righteousness shall he judge the p, 1800
14:30 the firstborn of the p shall feed, and 1800
14:32 and the p of his people shall trust in it. 6041
25: 4 For thou hast been a strength to the p, 1800
26: 6 *even* the feet of the p, *and* the steps of 6041
29:19 the p among men shall rejoice in the Holy 34
32: 7 he deviseth wicked devices to destroy the p 6041
41:17 *When* the p and needy seek water, and 6041
58: 7 that thou bring the p that are cast out *to thy* 6041
66: 2 *even to him that is* p and of a contrite spirit, 6041
Jer 2:34 the blood of the souls of the p innocents: 34
5: 4 Therefore I said, Surely these *are* p; 1800
20:13 for he hath delivered the soul of the p from 34
22:16 He judged the cause of the p and needy; 6041
39:10 of the guard left of the p of the people, 1800
40: 7 and children, and of the p of the land, 1803
52:15 away captive *certain* of the p of the people, 1803
52:16 *certain* of the p of the land for vinedressers 1803
Eze 16:49 neither did she strengthen the hand of the p 6041
18:12 Hath oppressed the p and needy, 6041
18:17 *That* hath taken off his hand from the p, 6041
22:29 and have vexed the p and needy: 6041
Da 4:27 thine iniquities by shewing mercy to the p; 6033
Am 2: 6 for silver, and the p for a pair of shoes; 34
2: 7 the dust of the earth on the head of the p, 1800
4: 1 which oppress the p, which crush 1800
5:11 as your treading *is* upon the p, 1800
5:12 they turn aside the p in the gate *from their* 34
8: 4 even to make the p of the land to fail, 6041
8: 6 That *we* may buy the p for silver, and 1800
Hab 3:14 their rejoicing *was* as to devour the p 6041
Zep 3:12 the midst of thee an afflicted and p people, 1800
Zec 7:10 nor the fatherless, the stranger, nor the p; 6041
11: 7 of slaughter, *even* you, O p of the flock. 6041
11:11 the p of the flock that waited upon me 6041
Mt 5: 3 Blessed *are* the p in spirit: for theirs is *4434*
11: 5 and the p have the gospel preached to them. *4434*
19:21 and give to the p, and thou shalt have *4434*
26: 9 been sold for much, and given to the p. *4434*
26:11 For ye have the p always with you; but *4434*
Mk 10:21 and give to the p, and thou shalt have *4434*
12:42 And there came a certain p widow, and *4434*
12:43 That this p widow hath cast more in, *4434*
14: 5 and have been given to the p. *4434*
14: 7 For ye have the p with you always, and *4434*
Lk 4:18 anointed me to preach the gospel to the p; *4434*
6:20 on his disciples, and said, Blessed *be ye* p: *4434*
7:22 are raised, to the p the gospel is preached. *4434*
14:13 call the p, the maimed, the lame, the blind: *4434*
14:21 and bring in hither the p, and the maimed, *4434*
18:22 and distribute unto the p, and thou shalt *4434*
19: 8 Lord, the half of my goods I give to the p; *4434*
21: 2 And he saw also a certain p widow casting *3998*
21: 3 that this p widow hath cast in more than *4434*
Jn 12: 5 three hundred pence, and given to the p? *4434*
12: 6 This he said, not that he cared for the p; but *4434*
12: 8 For the p always ye have with you; but *4434*
13:29 or that he should give something to the p. *4434*
Ro 15:26 for the p saints which are at Jerusalem. *4434*
1Co 13: 3 though I bestow all my goods to feed *the* p, NIG
2Co 6:10 as p, yet making many rich; as having *4434*
8: 9 was rich, *yet* for your sakes he became p, *4433*
9: 9 dispersed abroad; he hath given to the p: *3993*
Gal 2:10 *they would* that we should remember the p; *4434*
Jas 2: 2 there come in also a p *man* in vile raiment; *4434*
2: 3 and say to the p, Stand thou there, or *4434*
2: 5 Hath not God chosen the p of this world *4434*
2: 6 But ye have despised the p. Do not rich *4434*
Rev 3:17 and miserable, and p, and blind, and naked: *4434*
13:16 and great, rich and p, free and bond, *4434*

POORER (1) [POVERTY]

Lev 27: 8 if he be p than thy estimation, then he shall 4134

POOREST (1) [POVERTY]

2Ki 24:14 save the p sort of the people of the land. 1803

POPLAR (1) [POPLARS]

Ge 30:37 Jacob took him rods of green p, and of 3839

POPLARS (1) [POPLAR]

Hos 4:13 under oaks and p and elms, because 3839

POPULOUS (2)

Dt 26: 5 there a nation, great, mighty, and p: 7227
Na 3: 8 Art thou better than p No, that was situate 527

PORATHA (1)

Est 9: 8 And P, and Adalia, and Aridatha, 6334

PORCH (39) [PORCHES]

Jdg 3:23 Ehud went forth through the p, and shut 4528
1Ki 6: 3 the p before the temple of the house, 197
7: 6 he made a p of pillars; the length thereof *was* 197
7: 6 the p *was* before them: and the *other* pillars 197
7: 7 he made a p for the throne where he might 197
7: 7 he might judge, *even* the p of judgment: 197
7: 8 he dwelt *had* another court within the p, 197
7: 8 whom he had taken *to wife,* like unto this p. 197
7:12 of the LORD, and for the p of the house. 197
7:19 top of the pillars *were* of lily work in the p, 197
7:21 he set up the pillars in the p of the temple: 197
1Ch 28:11 gave to Solomon his son the pattern of the p, 197
2Ch 3: 4 the p that *was* in the front *of the house,* 197
8:12 the LORD, which he had built before the p, 197
15: 8 that *was* before the p of the LORD. 197

2Ch 29: 7 Also they have shut up the doors of the **p**, 197
29:17 the month came they to the **p** of the LORD: 197
Eze 8:16 between the **p** and the altar, *were* about five 197
40: 7 the threshold of the gate by the **p** of the gate 197
40: 8 He measured also the **p** of the gate within, 197
40: 9 measured he the **p** of the gate, eight cubits; 197
40: 9 two cubits; and the **p** of the gate *was* inward. 197
40:15 of the **p** of the inner gate *were* fifty cubits. 197
40:39 in the **p** of the gate *were* two tables on this 197
40:40 which *was* at the **p** of the gate, *were* two 197
40:48 he brought me to the **p** of the house, and 197
40:48 measured *each* post of the **p**, five cubits on 197
40:49 The length of the **p** *was* twenty cubits, and 197
41:25 thick planks upon the face of the **p** without. 197
41:26 on the sides of the **p**, and *upon* the side 197
44: 3 he shall enter by the way of the **p** of *that* 197
46: 2 the prince shall enter by the way of the **p** of 197
46: 8 he shall go in *by* the way of the **p** of *that* 197
Joel 2:17 weep between the **p** and the altar, and 197
Mt 26:71 And when he was gone out into the **p**, *4440*
Mk 14:68 And he went out into the **p**; and *the* cock *4259*
Jn 10:23 Jesus walked in the temple in Solomon's **p**. *4745*
Ac 3:11 unto them in the **p** that is called Solomon's, *4745*
5:12 were all with one accord in Solomon's **p**. *4745*

PORCHES (2) [PORCH]

Eze 41:15 with the inner temple, and the **p** of the court; 197
Jn 5: 2 Hebrew tongue Bethesda, having five **p**. *4745*

PORCIUS (1)

Ac 24:27 But after two years **P** Festus came into *4201*

PORT (1)

Ne 2:13 to the dung **p**, and viewed the walls of 8179

PORTER (6) [PORTERS]

2Sa 18:26 the watchman called unto the **p**, and said, 7778
2Ki 7:10 they came and called unto the **p** of the city: 7778
1Ch 9:21 **p** of the door of the tabernacle of 7778
2Ch 31:14 of Imnah the Levite, the **p** toward the east, 7778
Mk 13:34 his work, and commanded the **p** to watch. *2377*
Jn 10: 3 To him the **p** openeth; and the sheep hear *2377*

PORTERS (33) [PORTER]

2Ki 7:11 he called the **p**; and they told *it to* 7778
1Ch 9:17 the **p** *were,* Shallum, and Akkub, and 7778
9:18 they *were* **p** in the companies of 7778
9:22 All these which were chosen to be **p** in 7778
9:24 In four quarters were the **p**, toward the east, 7778
9:26 For these Levites, the four chief **p**, *were* in 7778
15:18 Mikneiah, and Obed-edom, and Jeiel, the **p**. 7778
16:38 also the son of Jeduthun and Hosah to be **p**: 7778
16:42 of God. And the sons of Jeduthun *were* **p**. 8179
23: 5 Moreover four thousand *were* **p**; and 7778
26: 1 Concerning the divisions of the **p**: Of 7778
26:12 Among these *were* the divisions of the **p**, 7778
26:19 These *are* the divisions of the **p** among 7778
2Ch 8:14 the **p** also by their courses at every gate: for 7778
23: 4 and of the Levites, *shall be* **p** of the doors; 7778
23:19 he set the **p** at the gates of the house of 7778
34:13 *there were* scribes, and officers, and **p**. 7778
35:15 king's seer; and the **p** *waited* at every gate; 7778
Ezr 2:42 The children of the **p**: the children of 7778
2:70 the singers, and the **p**, and the Nethinims, 7778
7: 7 the singers, and the **p**, and the Nethinims, 7778
7:24 any of the priests and Levites, singers, **p**, 8652
10:24 and of the **p**; Shallum, and Telem, and Uri. 7778
Ne 7: 1 the **p** and the singers and the Levites were 7778
7:45 The **p**: the children of Shallum, the children 7778
7:73 the **p**, and the singers, and *some* of 7778
10:28 the priests, the Levites, the **p**, the singers, 7778
10:39 that minister, and the **p**, and the singers: 7778
11:19 Moreover the **p**, Akkub, Talmon, and 7778
12:25 *were* **p** keeping the ward at the thresholds 7778
12:45 and the **p** kept the ward of their God, 7778
12:47 gave the portions of the singers and the **p**, 7778
13: 5 to the Levites, and the singers, and the **p**; 7778

PORTICO See ARCHES

PORTION (100) [PORTIONS]

Ge 14:24 the **p** of the men which went with me, 2506
14:24 Eshcol, and Mamre; let them take their **p**. 2506
31:14 *Is there* yet any **p** or inheritance for us in 2506
47:22 for the priests had a **p** assigned them of 2706
47:22 did eat their **p** which Pharaoh gave them: 2706
48:22 Moreover I have given to thee one **p** above 7926
Lev 6:17 I have given it *unto them for* their **p** of my 2506
7:35 This *is the* **p** of the anointing of Aaron, and NIH
Nu 31:30 thou shalt take one **p** of fifty, of the persons, 270
31:36 *which was* the **p** of them that went out to 2506
31:47 Moses took one **p** of fifty, *both* of man and 270
Dt 21:17 by giving him a double **p** of all that he 6310
32: 9 For the LORD'S **p** *is* his people; Jacob *is* 2506
33:21 because there, *in* a **p** of the lawgiver, 2513
Jos 17:14 given me *but* one lot and one **p** to inherit, 2256
19: 9 Out of the **p** of the children of Judah *was* 2256
1Sa 1: 5 unto Hannah he gave a worthy **p**; for he 4490
9:23 Bring the **p** which I gave thee, of which I 4490
1Ki 12:16 the king, saying, What **p** have we in David? 2506
2Ki 2: 9 let a double **p** of thy spirit be upon me. 6310
9:10 the dogs shall eat Jezebel in the **p** of 2506
9:21 met him in the **p** of Naboth the Jezreelite. 2513
9:25 cast him in the **p** of the field of Naboth 2513
9:36 In the **p** of Jezreel shall dogs eat the flesh 2506
9:37 the face of the field in the **p** of Jezreel; 2506
2Ch 10:16 the king, saying, What **p** have we in David? 2506
28:21 For Ahaz **took away a p** *out* of the house 2505
31: 3 *He appointed* also the king's **p** of his 4521
31: 4 in Jerusalem to give the **p** of the priests 4521
31:16 *his* daily **p** for their service in their charges 1697
Ezr 4:16 by this means thou shalt have no **p** on *this* 2508
Ne 2:20 you have no **p**, nor right, nor memorial, 2506
11:23 that a **certain p** *should be* for the singers, 548
12:47 the singers and the porters, every day his **p**: 1697
Job 20:29 This *is* the **p** of a wicked man from God, 2506
24:18 as the waters; their **p** is cursed in the earth: 2513
26:14 how little a **p** is heard of him? but 1697
27:13 This *is* the **p** of a wicked man with God, 2506
31: 2 For what **p** of God *is there* from above? and 2506
Ps 11: 6 *this shall be* the **p** of their cup. 4521
16: 5 The LORD *is* the **p** of mine inheritance 4490
17:14 *which have* their **p** in *this* life, and 2506
63:10 by the sword: they shall be a **p** for foxes. 4521
73:26 the strength of my heart, and my **p** for ever. 2506
119:57 *Thou art* my **p**, O LORD: I have said that 2506
142: 5 *and* my **p** in the land of the living. 2506
Pr 31:15 to her household, and a **p** to her maidens. 2706
Ecc 2:10 and this was my **p** of all my labour. 2506
2:21 laboured therein shall he leave it *for* his **p**. 2506
3:22 rejoice in his own works; for that *is* his **p**: 2506
5:18 which God giveth him: for it *is* his **p**. 2506
5:19 to take his **p**, and to rejoice in his labour; 2506
9: 6 neither have they any more a **p** for ever in 2506
9: 9 for that *is* thy **p** in *this* life, and in thy 2506
11: 2 Give a **p** to seven, and also to eight; 2506
Isa 17:14 This *is* the **p** of them that spoil us, and 2506
53:12 Therefore will I divide him *a* **p** with NIH
57: 6 the smooth *stones* of the stream *is* thy **p**; 2506
61: 7 *for* confusion they shall rejoice in their **p**: 2506
Jer 10:16 The **p** of Jacob *is* not like them: for he *is* 2506
12:10 they have trodden my **p** under foot, 2513
12:10 they have made my pleasant **p** a desolate 2513
13:25 *is* thy lot, the **p** of thy measures from me, 4490
51:19 The **p** of Jacob *is* not like them; for he *is* 2506
52:34 every day a **p** until the day of his death, 1697
La 3:24 The LORD *is* my **p**, saith my soul; 2506
Eze 45: 1 unto the LORD, a holy **p** of the land: NIH
45: 4 The holy ***p*** of the land shall be for NIH
45: 6 over against the oblation of the holy ***p***: it NIH
45: 7 *a* ***p*** *shall be* for the prince on the one side NIH
45: 7 the other side of the oblation of the holy ***p***, NIH
45: 7 before the oblation of the holy ***p***, and NIH
48: 1 are his sides east *and* west; a ***p*** *for* Dan. NIH
48: 2 east side unto the west side, a ***p*** *for* Asher. NIH
48: 3 even unto the west side, a ***p*** *for* Naphtali. NIH
48: 4 side unto the west side, a ***p*** *for* Manasseh. NIH
48: 5 side unto the west side, a ***p*** *for* Ephraim. NIH
48: 6 even unto the west side, a ***p*** *for* Reuben. NIH
48: 7 east side unto the west side, a ***p*** *for* Judah. NIH
48:18 the holy ***p*** *shall be* ten thousand eastward, NIH
48:18 be over against the oblation of the holy ***p***; NIH
48:23 the west side, Benjamin *shall have* a ***p***. NIH
48:24 unto the west side, Simeon *shall have* a ***p***. NIH
48:25 east side unto the west side, Issachar a ***p***. NIH
48:26 east side unto the west side, Zebulun a ***p***. NIH
48:27 the east side unto the west side, Gad a ***p***. NIH
Da 1: 8 himself with the **p of** the king's **meat**, 6598
1:13 that eat *of* the **p of** the king's **meat**: 6598
1:15 which did eat the **p of** the king's **meat**. 6598
1:16 Thus Melzar took away the **p of** their **meat**, 6598
4:15 *let* his **p** *be* with the beasts in the grass of 2508
4:23 *let* his **p** *be* with the beasts of the field, 2508
11:26 they that feed of the **p of** his **meat** shall 6598
Mic 2: 4 he hath changed the **p** of my people: 2506
Hab 1:16 because by them their **p** *is* fat, and 2506
Zec 2:12 the LORD shall inherit Judah his **p** in 2506
Mt 24:51 and appoint *him* his **p** with the hypocrites: *3313*
Lk 12:42 to give *them their* **p of meat** in due season? *4620*
12:46 will appoint *him* his **p** with the unbelievers. *3313*
15:12 give me the **p** of goods that falleth to *me*. *3313*

PORTIONS (16) [PORTION]

Dt 18: 8 They shall have like **p** to eat, beside that 2506
Jos 17: 5 there fell ten **p** to Manasseh, beside 2256
1Sa 1: 4 and to all her sons and her daughters, **p**: 4490
2Ch 31:19 to give **p** to all the males among the priests, 4490
Ne 8:10 send **p** unto *them* for whom nothing is 4490
8:12 to send **p**, and to make great mirth, because 4490
12:44 of the cities the **p** of the law for the priests 4521
12:47 gave the **p** of the singers and the porters, 4521
13:10 I perceived that the **p** of the Levites had not 4521
Est 9:19 good day, and *of* sending **p** one to another. 4490
9:22 of sending **p** one to another, and gifts to 4490
Eze 45: 7 length *shall be* over against one of the **p**, 2506
47:13 tribes of Israel: Joseph *shall have two* **p**. 2256
48:21 over against the **p** for the prince: 2506
48:29 and these *are* their **p**, saith the Lord GOD. 4256
Hos 5: 7 shall a month devour them with their **p**. 2506

POSSESS (106) [POSSESSED, POSSESSEST, POSSESSETH, POSSESSING, POSSESSION, POSSESSIONS, POSSESSOR, POSSESSORS]

Ge 22:17 thy seed shall **p** the gate of his enemies; 3423
24:60 let thy seed **p** the gate of those which hate 3423
Lev 20:24 their land, and I will give it unto you to **p** it, 3423
Nu 13:30 and said, Let us go up at once, and **p** it; 3423
14:24 whereinto he went; and his seed shall **p** it. 3423
27:11 next to him of his family, and he shall **p** it: 3423
33:53 for I have given you the land to **p** it. 3423
Dt 1: 8 **p** the land which the LORD sware unto 3423
1:21 **p** *it,* as the LORD God of thy fathers hath 3423
1:39 unto them will I give it, and they shall **p** it. 3423
2:24 begin to **p** *it,* and contend with him *in* 3423
2:31 begin to **p**, that *thou* mayest inherit his 3423
3:18 your God hath given you this land to **p** it: 3423
3:20 *until* they also **p** the land which the LORD 3423
4: 1 **p** the land which the LORD God of your 3423
4: 5 so in the land whither ye go to **p** it. 3423
4:14 them in the land whither ye go over to **p** it. 3423
4:22 but ye *shall* go over, and **p** that good land. 3423
4:26 land whereunto you go over Jordan to **p** it; 3423
5:31 *them* in the land which I give them to **p** it. 3423
5:33 *your* days in the land which ye shall **p**. 3423
6: 1 do *them* in the land whither ye go to **p** it: 3423
6:18 **p** the good land which the LORD sware 3423
7: 1 thee into the land whither thou goest to **p** it, 3423
8: 1 **p** the land which the LORD sware unto 3423
Dt 9: 1 to go in to **p** nations greater and 3423
9: 4 LORD hath brought me in to **p** this land: 3423
9: 5 of thine heart, dost thou go to **p** their land: 3423
9: 6 this good land to **p** it for thy righteousness; 3423
9:23 and **p** the land which I have given you; 3423
10:11 that they may go in and **p** the land, 3423
11: 8 ye may be strong, and go in and **p** the land, 3423
11: 8 and possess the land, whither ye go to **p** it; 3423
11:10 For the land, whither thou goest in to **p** it, 3423
11:11 the land, whither ye go to **p** it, *is* a land of 3423
11:23 ye shall **p** greater nations and mightier than 3423
11:29 in unto the land whither thou goest to **p** it, 3423
11:31 For ye shall pass over Jordan to go in to **p** 3423
11:31 and ye shall **p** it, and dwell therein. 3423
12: 1 God of thy fathers giveth thee to **p** it, 3423
12: 2 wherein the nations which ye shall **p** served 3423
12:29 whither thou goest to **p** them, and 3423
15: 4 God giveth thee *for* an inheritance to **p** it: 3423
17:14 shalt **p** it, and shalt dwell therein, and 3423
18:14 For these nations, which thou shalt **p**, 3423
19: 2 which the LORD thy God giveth thee to **p** it. 3423
19:14 that the LORD thy God giveth thee to **p** it. 3423
21: 1 the LORD thy God giveth thee to **p** it, 3423
23:20 to in the land whither thou goest to **p** it. 3423
25:19 God giveth thee *for* an inheritance to **p** it, 3423
28:21 off the land, whither thou goest to **p** it. 3423
28:63 from off the land whither thou goest to **p** it. 3423
30: 5 thy fathers possessed, and thou shalt **p** it; 3423
30:16 thee in the land whither thou goest to **p** it. 3423
30:18 whither thou passest over Jordan to go to **p** 3423
31: 3 from before thee, and thou shalt **p** them: 3423
31:13 the land whither ye go over Jordan to **p** it. 3423
32:47 the land, whither ye go over Jordan to **p** it. 3423
33:23 the LORD: **p** thou the west and the south. 3423
Jos 1:11 pass over this Jordan, to go in to **p** the land, 3423
1:11 the LORD your God giveth you to **p** it. 3423
18: 3 How long *are* you slack to go to **p** the land, 3423
23: 5 ye shall **p** their land, as the LORD your 3423
24: 4 I gave unto Esau mount Seir, to **p** it; 3423
24: 8 into your hand, that ye might **p** their land; 3423
Jdg 2: 6 man unto his inheritance to **p** the land. 3423
11:23 his people Israel, and shouldest thou **p** it? 3423
11:24 Wilt not thou **p** that which Chemosh thy 3423
11:24 which Chemosh thy god **giveth** thee **to p**? 3423
11:24 drive out from before us, them will we **p**. 3423
18: 9 slothful to go, *and* to enter to **p** the land. 3423
1Ki 21:18 of Naboth, whither he is gone down to **p** it. 3423
1Ch 28: 8 that ye may **p** *this* good land, and leave *it* 3423
Ezr 9:11 The land, *unto* which ye go to **p** it, 3423
Ne 9:15 promisedst them that *they* should go in to **p** 3423
9:23 their fathers, that *they* should go in to **p** *it.* 3423
Job 7: 3 So am I **made to p** months of vanity, and 5157
13:26 **makest** me **to p** the iniquities of my youth. 3423
Isa 14: 2 the house of Israel shall **p** them in the land 5157
14:21 *that* they do not rise, nor **p** the land, nor fill 3423
34:11 the cormorant and the bittern shall **p** it; 3423
34:17 they shall **p** it for ever, from generation to 3423
57:13 he that putteth his trust in me shall **p** 5157
61: 7 in their land they shall **p** the double: 3423
Jer 30: 3 I gave to their fathers, and they shall **p** it. 3423
Eze 7:24 the heathen, and they shall **p** their houses: 3423
33:25 and shed blood: and shall ye **p** the land? 3423
33:26 neighbour's wife: and shall ye **p** the land? 3423
35:10 countries shall be mine, and we will **p** it; 3423
36:12 they shall **p** thee, and thou shalt be their 3423
Da 7:18 **p** the kingdom for ever, even for ever and 2631
Hos 9: 6 *places* for their silver, nettles shall **p** them: 3423
Am 2:10 to **p** the land of the Amorite. 3423
9:12 That they may **p** the remnant of Edom, and 3423
Ob 1:17 the house of Jacob shall **p** their 3423
1:19 *they of* the south shall **p** the mount of Esau; 3423
1:19 they shall **p** the fields of Ephraim, and 3423
1:19 of Samaria: and Benjamin *shall* **p** Gilead. NIH
1:20 of Israel *shall* **p** that of the Canaanites, NIH
1:20 in Sepharad, shall **p** the cities of the south. 3423
Hab 1: 6 to **p** the dwelling places *that are* not theirs. 3423
Zep 2: 9 and the remnant of my people shall **p** them. 5157
Zec 8:12 I will **cause** the remnant of this people to **p** 5157
Lk 18:12 in the week, I give tithes of all that I **p**. *2932*
21:19 In your patience **p** ye your souls. *2932*
1Th 4: 4 know how to **p** his vessel in sanctification *2932*

POSSESSED (39) [POSSESS]

Nu 21:24 **p** his land from Arnon unto Jabbok, 3423
21:35 none left him alive: and they **p** his land. 3423
Dt 3:12 *which* we **p** at that time, from Aroer, 3423
4:47 they **p** his land, and the land of Og king of 3423
30: 5 bring thee into the land which thy fathers **p**, 3423
Jos 1:15 they also have **p** the land which 3423
12: 1 **p** their land on the *other* side Jordan toward 3423
13: 1 there remaineth *yet* very much land to be **p**. 3423
19:47 **p** it, and dwelt therein, and called Leshem, 3423
21:43 and they **p** it, and dwelt therein. 3423
22: 9 of their possession, whereof they were **p**, 270
Jdg 3:13 smote Israel, and **p** the city of palm trees. 3423
11:21 so Israel **p** all the land of the Amorites, 3423
11:22 they **p** all the coasts of the Amorites, 3423
2Ki 17:24 they **p** Samaria, and dwelt in the cities 3423
Ne 9:22 so they **p** the land of Sihon, and the land of 3423
9:24 So the children went in and **p** the land, and 3423
9:25 a fat land, and **p** houses full *of* all goods, 3423
Ps 139:13 For thou hast **p** my reins: thou hast covered 7069
Pr 8:22 The LORD **p** me *in* the beginning of his 7069
Isa 63:18 The people of thy holiness have **p** *it* but 3423
Jer 32:15 and vineyards shall be **p** again in this land. 7069
32:23 they came in, and **p** it; but they obeyed not 3423
Da 7:22 the time came that the saints **p** 2631
Mt 4:24 and those which were **p with devils**, and *1139*
8:16 unto him many *that were* **p with devils**: *1139*
8:28 there met him two **p with devils**, *1139*
8:33 what was befallen to the **p of the devils**. *1139*
9:32 brought to him a dumb man **p with a devil**. *1139*
12:22 was brought unto him **one p with a devil**, *1139*
Mk 1:32 and them that were **p with devils**. *1139*
5:15 and see him that was **p with the devil**, and *1139*

Mk 5:16 it befell to him that was **p with the devil**, *1139*
5:18 he that had been **p with the devil** prayed *1139*
Lk 8:36 he that was **p of the devils** was healed. *1139*
Ac 4:32 of the *things* which he **p** was his own; *5225*
8: 7 came out of many that were **p** *with them:* *2192*
16:16 a certain damsel **p with** a spirit of *2192*
1Co 7:30 and they that buy, as though they **p** not; *2722*

POSSESSEST (1) [POSSESS]
Dt 26: 1 and **p** it, and dwellest therein; 3423

POSSESSETH (2) [POSSESS]
Nu 36: 8 that **p** an inheritance in any tribe of 3423
Lk 12:15 in the abundance of the *things* which he **p**. *5225*

POSSESSING (1) [POSSESS]
2Co 6:10 as having nothing, and *yet* **p** all *things.* *2722*

POSSESSION (105) [POSSESS]
Ge 17: 8 all the land of Canaan, for an everlasting **p**; 272
23: 4 give me a **p** of a buryingplace with you, 272
23: 9 it me for a **p** of a buryingplace amongst you. 272
23:18 Unto Abraham for a **p** in the presence of 4736
23:20 were made sure unto Abraham for a **p** of a 272
26:14 For he had **p** of flocks, and possession of 4735
26:14 and **p** of herds, and great store of servants: 4735
36:43 to their habitations in the land of their **p**: 272
47:11 and gave them a **p** in the land of Egypt, 272
47:27 they **had p** therein, and grew, and 270
48: 4 to thy seed after thee *for* an everlasting **p**. 272
49:30 Ephron the Hittite for a **p** of a buryingplace. 272
50:13 which Abraham bought with the field for a **p** 272
Lev 14:34 which I give to you for a **p**, and I put 272
14:34 of leprosy in a house of the land of your **p**; 272
25:10 and ye shall return every man unto his **p**, and 272
25:13 jubile ye shall return every man unto his **p**. 272
25:24 in all the land of your **p** ye shall grant a 272
25:25 hath sold away *some* of his **p**, and *if any of* 272
25:27 he sold it; that he may return unto his **p**. 272
25:28 it shall go out, and he shall return unto his **p**. 272
25:32 *and* the houses of the cities of their **p**, 272
25:33 the house that was sold, and the city of his **p**, 272
25:33 *are* their **p** among the children of Israel. 272
25:34 may not be sold; for it *is* their perpetual **p**. 272
25:41 and unto the **p** of his fathers shall he return. 272
25:45 begat in your land: and they shall be your **p**. 272
25:46 children after you, to inherit *them for* a **p**; 272
27:16 the LORD *some part* of a field of his **p**, 272
27:21 the **p** thereof shall be the priest's. 272
27:22 which *is* not of the fields of his **p**; 272
27:24 *even* to him to whom the **p** of the land *did* 272
27:28 of man and beast, and of the field of his **p**, 272
Nu 24:18 Edom shall be a **p**, Seir also shall be a 3424
24:18 Seir also shall be a **p** for his enemies; 3424
26:56 According to the lot shall the **p** thereof be 5159
27: 4 a **p** among the brethren of our father. 272
27: 7 thou shalt surely give them a **p** of an 272
32: 5 this land be given unto thy servants for a **p**, 272
32:22 this land shall be your **p** before the LORD. 272
32:29 ye shall give them the land of Gilead for a **p**: 272
32:32 that the **p** of our inheritance on *this* side 272
35: 2 the inheritance of their **p** cities to dwell in; 272
35: 8 *shall be* of the **p** of the children of Israel: 272
35:28 the slayer shall return into the land of his **p**. 272
Dt 2: 5 I have given mount Seir unto Esau *for* a **p**. 3425
2: 9 for I will not give thee of their land *for* a **p**; 3425
2: 9 given Ar unto the children of Lot *for* a **p**. 3425
2:12 as Israel did unto the land of his **p**, 3425
2:19 the land of the children of Ammon *any* **p**; 3425
2:19 given it unto the children of Lot *for* a **p**. 3425
3:20 *then* shall ye return every man unto his **p**, 3425
11: 6 and all the substance that *was* in their **p**, 7272
32:49 I give unto the children of Israel for a **p**: 272
Jos 1:15 ye shall return unto the land of your **p**, and 3425
12: 6 LORD gave it *for* a **p** unto the Reubenites, 3425
12: 7 Israel *for* a **p** according to their divisions; 3425
13:29 *this* was *the* **p** of the half tribe of NIH
21:12 they to Caleb the son of Jephunneh for his **p**. 272
21:41 All the cities of the Levites within the **p** of 272
22: 4 unto your tents, *and* unto the land of your **p**, 272
22: 7 of Manasseh Moses had given **p** in Bashan: NIH
22: 9 to the land of their **p**, whereof they were 272
22:19 if the land of your **p** *be* unclean, *then* pass ye 272
22:19 pass ye over unto the land of the **p** of 272
22:19 tabernacle dwelleth, and **take p** among us: 270
1Ki 21:15 **take p** of the vineyard of Naboth 3423
21:16 of Naboth the Jezreelite, to **take p** of it. 3423
21:19 Hast thou killed, and also **taken p**? 3423
1Ch 28: 1 over all the substance and **p** of the king, 4735
2Ch 11:14 For the Levites left their suburbs and their **p**, 272
20:11 reward us, to come to cast us out of thy **p**, 3425
31: 1 every man to his **p**, into their own cities. 272
Ne 11: 3 Judah dwelt every one in his **p** in their cities, 272
Ps 2: 8 and the uttermost parts of the earth *for* thy **p**. 272
44: 3 For they **got** not the land **in p** by their own 3423
69:35 that they may dwell there, and **have** it **in p**. 3423
83:12 **take** to ourselves the houses of God **in p**. 3423
Pr 28:10 but the upright shall have good *things* in **p**. 5157
Isa 14:23 I will also make it a **p** for the bittern, and 4180
Eze 11:15 the LORD: unto us is this land given in **p**. 4181
25: 4 deliver thee to the men of the east for a **p**, 4181
25:10 the Ammonites, and will give them in **p**, 4181
36: 2 even the ancient high places are ours in **p**: 4181
36: 3 that ye might be a **p** unto the residue of 4181
36: 5 which have appointed my land into their **p** 4181
44:28 ye shall give them no **p** in Israel: I *am* their 272
44:28 them no possession in Israel: I *am* their **p**. 272
45: 5 for themselves, for a **p** *for* twenty chambers. 272
45: 6 ye shall appoint the **p** of the city five 272
45: 7 of the holy *portion*, and of the **p** of the city, 272
45: 7 the holy *portion*, and before the **p** of the city, 272
45: 8 In the land shall be his **p** in Israel: and 272
46:16 his sons'; it *shall be* their **p** by inheritance. 272
46:18 by oppression to thrust them out of their **p**; 272
Eze 46:18 give his sons inheritance out of his own **p**: 272
46:18 be not scattered every man from his **p**. 272
48:20 oblation foursquare, with the **p** of the city. 272
48:21 and of the **p** of the city, over against the five 272
48:22 Moreover from the **p** of the Levites, *and* 272
48:22 of the Levites, *and* from the **p** of the city, 272
Ac 5: 1 with Sapphira his wife, sold a **p**, *2933*
7: 5 that *he* would give it to him for a **p**, *2697*
7:45 in with Jesus into the **p** of the Gentiles, *2697*
Eph 1:14 until the redemption of the **purchased p**, *4047*

POSSESSIONS (12) [POSSESS]
Ge 34:10 and trade you therein, and **get** you **p** therein. 270
Nu 32:30 they shall **have p** among you in the land of 270
1Sa 25: 2 a man in Maon, whose **p** *were* in Carmel; 4639
1Ch 7:28 their **p** and habitations *were*, Beth-el and 272
9: 2 Now the first inhabitants that *dwelt* in their **p** 272
2Ch 32:29 and **p** of flocks and herds in abundance: 4735
Ecc 2: 7 also I had great **p** of great and small cattle 4735
Ob 1:17 the house of Jacob shall possess their **p**. 4180
Mt 19:22 he went away sorrowful: for he had great **p**. *2933*
Mk 10:22 and went away grieved: for he had great **p**. *2933*
Ac 2:45 And sold their **p** and goods, and *2933*
28: 7 In the same quarters were **p** of the chief *5564*

POSSESSOR (2) [POSSESS]
Ge 14:19 the most high God, **p** of heaven and earth: 7069
14:22 most high God, the **p** of heaven and earth, 7069

POSSESSORS (2) [POSSESS]
Zec 11: 5 Whose **p** slay them, and hold themselves 7069
Ac 4:34 for as many as were **p** of lands or *2935*

POSSIBLE (15) [IMPOSSIBLE, UNPOSSIBLE]
Mt 19:26 is unpossible; but with God all *things* are **p**. *1415*
24:24 insomuch that, if *it were* **p**, *they shall* *1415*
26:39 and prayed, saying, O my Father, if it be **p**, *1415*
Mk 9:23 all *things are* **p** to him that believeth. *1415*
10:27 not with God: for with God all *things* are **p**. *1415*
13:22 and wonders, to seduce, if *it were* **p**, *1415*
14:35 on the ground, and prayed that, if it were **p**, *1415*
14:36 Abba, Father, all *things are* **p** unto thee; *1415*
Lk 18:27 *are* unpossible with men are **p** with God. *1415*
Ac 2:24 it was not **p** that he should be holden of it. *1415*
20:16 for he hasted, if it were **p** for him, to be at *1415*
27:39 if it were **p**, to thrust in the ship. *1410*
Ro 12:18 If *it be* **p**, as much as lieth in you, *1415*
Gal 4:15 for I bear you record, that if *it had been* **p**, *1415*
Heb 10: 4 For *it is* **not p** that the blood of bulls and *102*

POST (11) [POSTS]
Ex 12: 7 and on the **upper door p** of the houses, 4947
21: 6 bring him to the door, or unto the **door p**; 4201
1Sa 1: 9 Now Eli the priest sat upon a seat by a **p** of 4201
Job 9:25 Now my days are swifter than a **p**: they flee 7323
Jer 51:31 One **p** shall run to meet another, and 7323
Eze 40:14 even unto the **p** of the court round about 352
40:16 and upon *each* **p** *were* palm trees. 352
40:48 measured *each* **p** of the porch, five cubits on 352
41: 3 measured the **p** of the door, two cubits; 352
43: 8 their **p** by my posts, and the wall between 4201
46: 2 shall stand by the **p** of the gate, and 4201

POSTERITY (9)
Ge 45: 7 God sent me before you to preserve you a **p** 7611
Nu 9:10 of your **p** shall be unclean by reason of a 1755
1Ki 16: 3 I will take away the **p** of Baasha, and 310
16: 3 posterity of Baasha, and the **p** of his house; 310
21:21 will take away thy **p**, and will cut off from 310
Ps 49:13 yet their **p** approve their sayings. Selah. 310
109:13 Let his **p** be cut off; *and* in the generation 319
Da 11: 4 not to his **p**, nor according to his dominion 319
Am 4: 2 away with hooks, and your **p** with fishhooks. 319

POSTS (42) [POST]
Ex 12: 7 strike *it* on the two **side p** and on the upper 4201
12:22 the two **side p** with the blood that *is* in 4201
12:23 on the two **side p**, the LORD will pass 4201
Dt 6: 9 thou shalt write them upon the **p** of thy 4201
11:20 thou shalt write them upon the **door p** of 4201
Jdg 16: 3 the two **p**, and went away with them, bar 4201
1Ki 6:31 *and* **side p** *were* a fifth *part of the wall.* 4201
6:33 he for the door of the temple **p** of olive tree, 4201
7: 5 all the doors and **p** *were* square, *with* 4201
2Ch 3: 7 the **p**, and the walls thereof, and the doors 5592
30: 6 So the **p** went with the letters from the king 7323
30:10 So the **p** passed from city to city through 7323
Est 3:13 the letters were sent by **p** into all the king's 7323
3:15 The **p** went out, being hastened by 7323
8:10 sent letters by **p** on horseback, *and* 7323
8:14 *So* the **p** that rode upon mules *and* 7323
Pr 8:34 at my gates, waiting at the **p** of my doors. 4201
Isa 6: 4 the **p** of the door moved at the voice of him 520
57: 8 the **p** hast thou set up thy remembrance: 4201
Eze 40: 9 the **p** thereof, two cubits; and the porch of 352
40:10 the **p** had one measure on this side and 352
40:14 He made also **p** *of* threescore cubits, 352
40:16 to their **p** within the gate round about, 352
40:21 the **p** thereof and the arches thereof were 352
40:24 he measured the **p** thereof and the arches 352
40:26 and another on that side, upon the **p** thereof. 352
40:29 the **p** thereof, and the arches thereof, 352
40:31 and palm trees *were* upon the **p** thereof: 352
40:33 and the **p** thereof, and the arches thereof, 352
40:34 palm trees *were* upon the **p** thereof, on this 352
40:36 the **p** thereof, and the arches thereof, and 352
40:37 the **p** thereof *were* toward the utter court; 352
40:37 palm trees *were* upon the **p** thereof, on this 352
40:38 the entries thereof *were* by the **p** of the gates, 352
40:49 *there were* pillars by the **p**, one on this side, 352
41: 1 measured the **p**, six cubits broad on the one 352
41:16 The **door p**, and the narrow windows, and 5592
41:21 The **p** of the temple *were* squared, *and* 4201
43: 8 their post by my **p**, and the wall between 4201
Eze 45:19 put *it* upon the **p** of the house, and upon 4201
45:19 upon the **p** of the gate of the inner court. 4201
Am 9: 1 the lintel of the door, that the **p** may shake: 5592

POT (22) [POTS, POTSHERD, POTSHERDS, POTTER, POTTER'S, POTTERS, POTTERS', WASHPOT, WATERPOT, WATERPOTS]
Ex 16:33 Take a **p**, and put an omer full of manna 6803
Lev 6:28 if it be sodden in a brasen **p**, it shall be both 3627
Jdg 6:19 he put the broth in a **p**, and brought *it* out 6517
1Sa 2:14 *it* into the pan, or kettle, or caldron, or **p**; 6517
2Ki 4: 2 not any thing in the house, save a **p** of oil. 610
4:38 Set on the great **p**, and seethe pottage for 5518
4:39 came and shred *them* into the **p** of pottage: 5518
4:40 O thou man of God, *there is* death in the **p**. 5518
4:41 he cast *it* into the **p**; and he said, Pour out 5518
4:41 may eat. And there was no harm in the **p**. 5518
Job 41:20 as *out of* a seething **p** or caldron. 1731
41:31 He maketh the deep to boil like a **p**: 5518
41:31 he maketh the sea like a **p of ointment**. 4841
Pr 17: 3 The **fining p** *is* for silver, and the furnace 4715
27:21 *As* the **fining p** for silver, and the furnace 4715
Ecc 7: 6 For as the crackling of thorns under a **p**, so 5518
Jer 1:13 I said, I see a seething **p**; and the face 5518
Eze 24: 3 Set on a **p**, set *it* on, and also pour water 5518
24: 6 to the **p** whose scum *is* therein, and 5518
Mic 3: 3 as for the **p**, and as flesh within the caldron. 5518
Zec 14:21 every **p** in Jerusalem and in Judah shall be 5518
Heb 9: 4 wherein *was* the golden **p** that had manna, *4713*

POTENTATE (1)
1Ti 6:15 *who is* the blessed and only **P**, the King of *1413*

POTIPHAR (2)
Ge 37:36 the Medanites sold him into Egypt unto **P**, 6318
39: 1 **P**, an officer of Pharaoh, captain of 6318

POTI-PHERAH (3)
Ge 41:45 Asenath the daughter of **P** priest of On. 6319
41:50 which Asenath the daughter of **P** priest of 6319
46:20 which Asenath the daughter of **P** priest of 6319

POTS (15) [POT]
Ex 16: 3 when we sat by the flesh **p**, *and* when we 5518
38: 3 the **p**, and the shovels, and the basons, 5518
Lev 11:35 *whether it be* oven, or **ranges for p**, 3600
1Ki 7:45 the **p**, and the shovels, and the basons: and 5518
2Ki 25:14 the **p**, and the shovels, and the snuffers, 5518
2Ch 4:11 Huram made the **p**, and the shovels, and 5518
4:16 The **p** also, and the shovels, and 5518
35:13 the *other* holy *offerings* sod they in **p**, and 5518
Ps 58: 9 Before your **p** can feel the thorns, he shall 5518
68:13 Though ye have lien among the **p**, *yet shall* 8240
81: 6 his hands were delivered from the **p**. 1731
Jer 35: 5 the house of the Rechabites **p** full *of* wine, 1375
Zec 14:20 the **p** in the LORD'S house shall be like 5518
Mk 7: 4 and **p**, brasen vessels, and of tables. *3582*
7: 8 of men, *as* the washing of **p** and cups: *3582*

POTSHERD (4) [POT]
Job 2: 8 he took him a **p** to scrape himself withal; 2789
Ps 22:15 My strength is dried up like a **p**; and 2789
Pr 26:23 a wicked heart *are like* a **p** covered with 2789
Isa 45: 9 *Let* the **p** *strive* with the potsherds of 2789

POTSHERDS (1) [POT]
Isa 45: 9 *Let* the potsherd *strive* with the **p** of 2789

POTTAGE (7)
Ge 25:29 Jacob sod **p**: and Esau came from the field, 5138
25:30 with that same red **p**; for I *am* faint: NIH
25:34 Jacob gave Esau bread and **p** of lentiles; 5138
2Ki 4:38 and seethe **p** for the sons of the prophets. 5138
4:39 and came and shred *them* into the pot of **p**: 5138
4:40 as they were eating of the **p**, that they cried 5138
Hag 2:12 or **p**, or wine, or oil, or any meat, shall it be 5138

POTTER (10) [POT]
Isa 41:25 as *upon* morter, and as the **p** treadeth clay. 3335
64: 8 we *are* the clay, and thou our **p**; and we all 3335
Jer 18: 4 of clay was marred in the hand of the **p**: 3335
18: 4 as seemed good to the **p** to make *it*. 3335
18: 6 of Israel, cannot I do with you as this **p**? 3335
La 4: 2 the work of the hands of the **p**! 3335
Zec 11:13 LORD said unto me, Cast it unto the **p**: 3335
11:13 cast them to the **p** *in* the house of 3335
Ro 9:21 Hath not the **p** power over the clay, of *2763*
Rev 2:27 as the vessels of a **p** *shall* they be broken to *2764*

POTTER'S (10) [POT]
Ps 2: 9 thou shalt dash them in pieces like a **p** 3335
Isa 29:16 down shall be esteemed as the **p** clay: 3335
Jer 18: 2 go down *to* the **p** house, and there I will 3335
18: 3 I went down *to* the **p** house, and behold, 3335
18: 6 as the clay *is* in the **p** hand, so *are* ye in 3335
19: 1 Go and get a **p** earthen bottle, and *take* of 3335
19:11 this city, as *one* breaketh a **p** vessel, 3335
Da 2:41 and toes, part of **p** clay, and part of iron, 6353
Mt 27: 7 and bought with them the **p** field, to bury *2763*
27:10 And gave them for the **p** field, as the Lord *2763*

POTTERS (1) [POT]
1Ch 4:23 These *were* the **p**, and those that dwelt 3335

POTTERS' (1) [POT]
Isa 30:14 he shall break it as the breaking of the **p** 3335

POUND (10) [POUNDS]
1Ki 10:17 three **p** *of* gold went to one shield: 4488
Ezr 2:69 five thousand **p** *of* silver, and one hundred 4488
Ne 7:71 two thousand and two hundred **p** *of* silver. 4488
7:72 two thousand **p** *of* silver, and threescore 4488
Lk 19:16 saying, Lord, thy **p** hath gained ten pounds. *3414*

Lk 19:18 Lord, thy **p** hath gained five pounds. 3414
19:20 saying, Lord, behold, *here is* thy **p**, 3414
19:24 Take from him the **p**, and give *it* to him that 3414
Jn 12: 3 Then took Mary a **p** of ointment of 3046
19:39 and aloes, about an hundred **p** *weight*. 3046

POUNDS (5) [POUND]
Lk 19:13 and delivered them ten **p**, and said unto 3414
19:16 saying, Lord, thy pound hath gained ten **p**. 3414
19:18 saying, Lord, thy pound hath gained five **p**. 3414
19:24 and give *it* to him that hath ten **p**. 3414
19:25 they said unto him, Lord, he hath ten **p**.) 3414

POUR (63) [POURED, POUREDST, POURETH, POURING]
Ex 4: 9 **p** *it upon* the dry *land*: and the water which 8210
29: 7 and **p** *it* upon his head, and anoint him. 3332
29:12 **p** all the blood beside the bottom of 8210
30: 9 neither shall ye **p** drink offering thereon. 5258
Lev 2: 1 he shall **p** oil upon it, and put frankincense 3332
2: 6 shalt part it in pieces, and **p** oil thereon: 3332
4: 7 shall **p** all the blood of the bullock at 8210
4:18 shall **p out** all the blood at the bottom of 8210
4:25 shall **p out** his blood at the bottom of 8210
4:30 shall **p out** all the blood thereof at 8210
4:34 shall **p out** all the blood thereof at 8210
14:15 and **p** *it* into the palm of his own left hand: 3332
14:18 **p** upon the head of him that is to be 5414
14:26 the priest shall **p** of the oil into the palm of 3332
14:41 they shall **p out** the dust that they scrape 8210
17:13 he shall even **p out** the blood thereof, and 8210
Nu 5:15 he shall **p** no oil upon it, nor put 3332
24: 7 He shall **p** the water out of his buckets, and 5140
Dt 12:16 ye shall **p** it upon the earth as water. 8210
12:24 thou shalt **p** it upon the earth as water. 8210
15:23 thou shalt **p** it upon the ground as water. 8210
Jdg 6:20 *them* upon this rock, and **p out** the broth. 8210
1Ki 18:33 **p** *it* on the burnt sacrifice, and on the wood. 3332
2Ki 4: 4 shalt **p out** into all those vessels, and 3332
4:41 he said, **P out** for the people, that they may 3332
9: 3 **p** *it* on his head, and say, Thus saith 3332
Job 36:27 they **p down** rain according to the vapour 2212
Ps 42: 4 When I remember these *things*, I **p out** my 8210
62: 8 ye people, **p out** your heart before him: 8210
69:24 **P out** thine indignation upon them, and 8210
79: 6 **P out** thy wrath upon the heathen that have 8210
Pr 1:23 behold, I will **p out** my spirit unto you, 5042
Isa 44: 3 For I will **p** water upon *him that is* thirsty, 3332
44: 3 floods upon the dry *ground*: I will **p** my 3332
45: 8 and let the skies **p down** righteousness: 5140
Jer 6:11 I *will* **p** *it* **out** upon the children abroad, and 8210
7:18 to **p out** drink offerings unto other gods, 5258
10:25 **P out** thy fury upon the heathen that know 8210
14:16 for I will **p** their wickedness upon them. 8210
18:21 **p out** their *blood* by the force of the sword; 5064
44:17 to **p out** drink offerings unto her, as we 5258
44:18 to **p out** drink offerings unto her, we have 5258
44:19 **p out** drink offerings unto her, without our 5258
44:25 and to **p out** drink offerings unto her: 5258
La 2:19 **p out** thine heart like water before the face 8210
Eze 7: 8 Now will I shortly **p out** my fury upon 8210
14:19 **p out** my fury upon it in blood, to cut off 8210
20: 8 I said, *I* will **p out** my fury upon them, 8210
20:13 *I* would **p out** my fury upon them in 8210
20:21 I said, *I* would **p out** my fury upon them, 8210
21:31 I will **p out** mine indignation upon thee, 8210
24: 3 on a pot, set *it* on, and also **p** water into it: 3332
30:15 I will **p** my fury upon Sin, the strength of 8210
Hos 5:10 I will **p out** my wrath upon them like 8210
Joel 2:28 that I will **p out** my spirit upon all flesh; 8210
2:29 in those days will I **p out** my spirit. 8210
Mic 1: 6 I will **p down** the stones thereof into 5064
Zep 3: 8 to **p** upon them mine indignation, *even* all 8210
Zec 12:10 I will **p** upon the house of David, and 8210
Mal 3:10 and **p** you **out** a blessing, 7324
Ac 2:17 I will **p out** of my Spirit upon all flesh: 1632
2:18 on my handmaidens I will **p out** in those 1632
Rev 16: 1 **p out** the vials of the wrath of God upon 1632

POURED (84) [POUR]
Ge 28:18 up *for* a pillar, and **p** oil upon the top of it. 3332
35:14 he **p** a drink offering thereon, and 5258
35:14 drink offering thereon, and he **p** oil thereon. 3332
Ex 9:33 and the rain was not **p** upon the earth. 5413
30:32 Upon man's flesh shall it not be **p**, 3251
Lev 4:12 where the ashes are **p out**, and burn him on 8211
4:12 where the ashes are **p out** shall he be burnt. 8211
8:12 he **p** of the anointing oil upon Aaron's 3332
8:15 **p** the blood at the bottom of the altar, and 3332
9: 9 **p out** the blood at the bottom of the altar: 3332
21:10 upon whose head the anointing oil was **p**, 3332
Nu 28: 7 **cause** the strong wine **to be p** unto 5258
Dt 12:27 the blood of thy sacrifices shall be **p out** 8210
1Sa 1:15 but have **p out** my soul before the LORD. 8210
7: 6 **p** *it* **out** before the LORD, and fasted on 8210
10: 1 **p** *it* upon his head, and kissed him, and 3332
2Sa 13: 9 she took a pan, and **p** *them* **out** before him; 3332
23:16 drink thereof, but **p** it **out** unto the LORD. 5258
1Ki 13: 3 the ashes that *are* upon it shall be **p out**. 8210
13: 5 *was* rent, and the ashes **p out** from the altar, 8210
2Ki 3:11 which **p** water on the hands of Elijah. 3332
4: 5 brought *the vessels* to her; and she **p out**. 3332
4:40 So they **p out** for the men to eat. And it 3332
9: 6 he **p** the oil on his head, and said unto him, 3332
16:13 **p** his drink offering, and sprinkled 5258
1Ch 11:18 not drink *of* it, but **p** it **out** to the LORD, 5258
2Ch 12: 7 my wrath shall not be **p out** upon 5413
34:21 wrath of the LORD that is **p out** upon us, 5413
34:25 my wrath shall be **p out** upon this place, 5413
Job 3:24 and my roarings are **p out** like the waters. 5413
10:10 Hast thou not **p** me **out** as milk, and 5413
29: 6 and the rock **p** me **out** rivers of oil; 6694
30:16 now my soul is **p out** upon me; the days of 8210
Ps 22:14 I am **p out** like water, and all my bones are 8210
Ps 45: 2 grace is **p** into thy lips: therefore God hath 3332
77:17 The clouds **p out** water: the skies sent out a 2229
142: 2 I **p out** my complaint before him; I shewed 8210
SS 1: 3 ointments thy name *is as* ointment **p forth**, 7324
Isa 26:16 they **p out** a prayer *when* thy chastening 6694
29:10 For the LORD hath **p out** upon you 5258
32:15 Until the spirit be **p** upon us from on high, 6168
42:25 Therefore he hath **p** upon him the fury of 8210
53:12 because he hath **p out** his soul unto death: 6168
57: 6 even to them hast thou **p** a drink offering, 8210
Jer 7:20 and my fury *shall be* **p out** upon this place, 5413
19:13 have **p out** drink offerings unto other gods. 5258
32:29 **p out** drink offerings unto other gods, 5258
42:18 my fury hath been **p forth** upon 5413
42:18 so shall my fury be **p forth** upon you, 5413
44: 6 my fury and mine anger was **p forth**, 5413
44:19 **p out** drink offerings unto her, did we make 5258
La 2: 4 of Zion: he **p out** his fury like fire. 8210
2:11 are troubled, my liver is **p** upon the earth, 8210
2:12 when their soul was **p out** into their 8210
4: 1 the stones of the sanctuary are **p out** in 8210
4:11 he hath **p out** his fierce anger, and 8210
Eze 16:36 Because thy filthiness was **p out**, and 8210
20:28 and **p out** there their drink offerings. 5258
20:33 and with fury **p out**, will I rule over you: 8210
20:34 a stretched out arm, and with fury **p out**. 8210
22:22 ye shall know that I the LORD have **p out** 8210
22:31 Therefore have I **p out** mine indignation 8210
23: 8 and **p** their whoredom upon her. 8210
24: 7 she **p** it not upon the ground, to cover it 8210
36:18 Wherefore I **p** my fury upon them for 8210
39:29 for I have **p out** my spirit upon the house of 8210
Da 9:11 therefore the curse is **p** upon us, and 5413
9:27 that determined shall be **p** upon 5413
Mic 1: 4 as the waters *that are* **p** down a steep place. 5064
Na 1: 6 his fury is **p out** like fire, and the rocks are 5413
Zep 1:17 their blood shall be **p out** as dust, and 8210
Mt 26: 7 and **p** *it* on his head, as he sat at meat. 2708
26:12 For in that she hath **p** this ointment on my 906
Mk 14: 3 and she brake the box, and **p** *it* on his head. 2708
Jn 2:15 and **p out** the changers' money, and 1632
Ac 10:45 that on the Gentiles also was **p out** the gift 1632
Rev 14:10 which is **p out** without mixture into the cup 2767
16: 2 and **p out** his vial upon the earth; 1632
16: 3 And the second angel **p out** his vial upon 1632
16: 4 And the third angel **p out** his vial upon 1632
16: 8 And the fourth angel **p out** his vial upon 1632
16:10 And the fifth angel **p out** his vial upon 1632
16:12 And the sixth angel **p out** his vial upon 1632
16:17 And the seventh angel **p out** his vial into 1632

POUREDST (1) [POUR]
Eze 16:15 **p out** thy fornications on every one that 8210

POURETH (11) [POUR]
Job 12:21 He **p** contempt upon princes, and 8210
16:13 he **p out** my gall upon the ground. 8210
16:20 *but* mine eye **p out** *tears* unto God. 1811
Ps 75: 8 is full *of* mixture; and he **p out** of the same: 5064
102: T and **p out** his complaint before the LORD. 8210
107:40 He **p** contempt upon princes, and 8210
Pr 15: 2 but the mouth of fools **p out** foolishness. 5042
15:28 the mouth of the wicked **p out** evil *things*. 5042
Am 5: 8 and **p** them **out** upon the face of the earth: 8210
9: 6 and **p** them **out** upon the face of the earth: 8210
Jn 13: 5 he **p** water into a bason, and began to wash 906

POURING (2) [POUR]
Eze 9: 8 in thy **p out** of thy fury upon Jerusalem? 8210
Lk 10:34 **p in** oil and wine, and set him on his own 2022

POURTRAY (1) [POURTRAYED]
Eze 4: 1 and **p** upon it *the* city, *even* Jerusalem: 2710

POURTRAYED (3) [POURTRAY]
Eze 8:10 of Israel, **p** upon the wall round about. 2707
23:14 for when she saw men **p** upon the wall, 2707
23:14 the images of the Chaldeans **p** with 2710

POVERTY (15) [IMPOVERISH, IMPOVERISHED, POOR, POORER, POOREST]
Ge 45:11 and all that thou hast, **come to p**. 3423
Pr 6:11 So shall thy **p** come as one that travelleth, 7389
10:15 the destruction of the poor *is* their **p**. 7389
11:24 more than is meet, but *it tendeth* to **p**. 4270
13:18 **P** and shame *shall be to* him that refuseth 7389
20:13 Love not sleep, lest thou **come to p**; 3423
23:21 and the glutton shall **come to p**: 3423
24:34 So shall thy **p** come *as* one that travelleth; 7389
28:19 after vain *persons* shall have **p** enough. 7389
28:22 considereth not that **p** shall come *upon* him. 2639
30: 8 give me neither **p** nor riches; feed me with 7389
31: 7 forget his **p**, and remember his misery no 7389
2Co 8: 2 their deep **p** abounded unto the riches of 4432
8: 9 that ye through his **p** might be rich. 4432
Rev 2: 9 and tribulation, and **p**, (but thou art rich) 4432

POWDER (8) [POWDERS]
Ex 32:20 ground *it* to **p**, and strawed *it* upon 1854
Dt 28:24 The LORD shall make the rain of thy land **p** 80
2Ki 23: 6 stampt *it* small to **p**, and cast the powder 6083
23: 6 cast the **p** thereof upon the graves of 6083
23:15 *and* stampt *it* small to **p**, and burnt 6083
2Ch 34: 7 had beaten the graven images into **p**, and 1854
Mt 21:44 it shall fall, it will **grind** him **to p**. 3039
Lk 20:18 it shall fall, it will **grind** him **to p**. 3039

POWDERS (1) [POWDER]
SS 3: 6 and frankincense, with all **p** of the merchant? 81

POWER (272) [POWERFUL, POWERS]
Ge 31: 6 ye know that with all my **p** I have served 3581
31:29 It is in the **p** of my hand to do you hurt: but 410
32:28 for **as a prince hast** thou **p** with God and 8280
Ge 49: 3 of dignity, and the excellency of **p**: 5794
Ex 9:16 I raised thee up, for to shew *in* thee my **p**; 3581
15: 6 O LORD, is become glorious in **p**: 3581
21: 8 unto a strange nation he shall **have** no **p**, 4910
32:11 forth out of the land of Egypt with great **p**, 3581
Lev 26:19 I will break the pride of your **p**; and I will 5797
26:37 ye shall have no **p to stand** before your 8617
Nu 14:17 beseech thee, let the **p** of my Lord be great, 3581
22:38 have I now **any p at all** to say any 3201+3201
Dt 4:37 in his sight with his mighty **p** out of Egypt; 3581
8:17 My **p** and the might of mine hand hath 3581
8:18 for *it is* he that giveth thee **p** to get wealth, 3581
9:29 which thou broughtest out by thy mighty **p** 3581
32:36 when he seeth that *their* **p** is gone, and 3027
Jos 8:20 they had no **p** to flee this way or 3027+871.1
17:17 Thou *art* a great people, and hast great **p**: 3581
1Sa 9: 1 of Aphiah, a Benjamite, a mighty *man* of **p**. 2428
30: 4 wept, until they had no more **p** to weep. 3581
2Sa 22:33 God *is* my strength *and* **p**: and he maketh 2428
2Ki 17:36 up out of the land of Egypt with great **p** 3581
19:26 Therefore their inhabitants *were* of small **p**, 3027
1Ch 20: 1 *to battle*, Joab led forth the **p** of the army, 2428
29:11 the **p**, and the glory, and the victory, and 1369
29:12 in thine hand *is* **p** and might; and in thine 3581
2Ch 14:11 with many, *or* with *them that have* no **p**: 3581
20: 6 in thine hand *is there not* **p** and might, so 3581
22: 9 So the house of Ahaziah had no **p** to keep 3581
25: 8 for God hath **p** to help, and to cast down. 3581
26:13 five hundred, that made war with mighty **p**, 3581
32: 9 against Lachish, and all his **p** with him,) 4475
Ezr 4:23 and made them to cease by force and **p**. 2429
8:22 his **p** and his wrath *is* against all them that 5797
Ne 1:10 whom thou hast redeemed by thy great **p**, 3581
5: 5 **p** *to redeem them*; for other men have 410+3027
Est 1: 3 the **p** of Persia and Media, the nobles and 2428
8:11 all the **p** of the people and province that 2428
9: 1 of the Jews hoped to **have p** over them, 7980
10: 2 all the acts of his **p** and of his might, and 8633
Job 1:12 Behold, all that he hath *is* in thy **p**; 3027
5:20 and in war from the **p** of the sword. 3027
21: 7 become old, yea, are mighty *in* **p**? 2428
23: 6 Will he plead against me with *his* great **p**? 3581
24:22 He draweth also the mighty with his **p**: 3581
26: 2 hast thou helped *him that is* without **p**? 3581
26:12 He divideth the sea with his **p**, and by his 3581
26:14 the thunder of his **p** who can understand? 1369
36:22 Behold, God exalteth by his **p**: 3581
37:23 *he is* excellent in **p**, and *in* judgment, and 3581
41:12 nor *his* **p**, nor his comely proportion. 1369
Ps 21:13 *so* will we sing and praise thy **p**. 1369
22:20 my darling from the **p** of the dog. 3027
37:35 I have seen the wicked in **great p**, and 6184
49:15 God will redeem my soul from the **p** of 3027
59:11 scatter them by thy **p**; and bring them 2428
59:16 I will sing of thy **p**; yea, I will sing aloud of 5797
62:11 I heard this; that **p** *belongeth* unto God. 5797
63: 2 To see thy **p** and thy glory, so *as* I have 5797
65: 6 fast the mountains; *being* girded with **p**: 1369
66: 3 through the greatness of thy **p** shall thine 5797
66: 7 He ruleth by his **p** for ever; his eyes behold 1369
68:35 that giveth strength and **p** unto *his* people. 8592
71:18 *and* thy **p** to every one *that* is to come. 1369
78:26 and by his **p** he brought in the south wind. 5797
79:11 according to the greatness of thy **p**; 2220
90:11 Who knoweth the **p** of thine anger? 5797
106: 8 that *he* might make his **mighty p** to be 1369
110: 3 people *shall be* willing in the day of thy **p**, 2428
111: 6 He hath shewed his people the **p** of his 3581
145:11 the glory of thy kingdom, and talk of thy **p**; 1369
147: 5 Great *is* our Lord, and of great **p**: 3581
150: 1 praise him in the firmament of his **p**. 5797
Pr 3:27 when it is in the **p** of thine hand to do *it*. 410
18:21 Death and life *are* in the **p** of the tongue: 3027
Ecc 4: 1 on the side of their oppressors *there was* **p**; 3581
5:19 hath **given** him **p** to eat thereof, and to take 7980
6: 2 yet God **giveth** him not **p** to eat thereof, but 7980
8: 4 Where the word of a king *is*, *there is* **p**: and 7983
8: 8 *There is* no man that hath **p** over the spirit 7989
8: 8 neither *hath he* **p** in the day of death: 7983
Isa 37:27 Therefore their inhabitants *were* of small **p**, 3027
40:26 of *his* might, for that *he is* strong in **p**; 3581
40:29 He giveth **p** to the faint; and to *them that* 3581
43:17 the chariot and horse, the army and the **p**; 5808
47:14 they shall not deliver themselves from the **p** 3027
50: 2 or have I no **p** to deliver? behold, at my 3581
Jer 10:12 He hath made the earth by his **p**, he hath 3581
27: 5 by my great **p** and by my outstretched arm, 3581
32:17 the earth by thy great **p** and stretched out 3581
51:15 He hath made the earth by his **p**, he hath 3581
Eze 17: 9 even without great **p** or many people to 2220
22: 6 every one were in thee to their **p** to shed 2220
30: 6 and the pride of her **p** shall come down: 5797
Da 2:37 thee a kingdom, **p**, and strength, and glory. 2632
3:27 upon whose bodies the fire had no **p**, 7981
4:30 of the kingdom by the might of my **p**, 2632
6:27 who hath delivered Daniel from the **p** of 3028
8: 6 and ran unto him in the fury of his **p**. 3581
8: 7 there was no **p** in the ram to stand before 3581
8:22 stand up out of the nation, but not in his **p**. 3581
8:24 his **p** shall be mighty, but not by his own 3581
8:24 shall be mighty, but not by his own **p**: 3581
11: 6 she shall not retain the **p** of the arm; 3581
11:25 he shall stir up his **p** and his courage 3581
11:43 he shall **have p** over the treasures of gold 4910
12: 7 to scatter the **p** of the holy people, 3027
Hos 12: 3 and by his strength he **had p** with God: 8280
12: 4 he **had p** over *the* angel, and prevailed: 7786
13:14 I will ransom them from the **p** of the grave; 3027
Mic 2: 1 because it is in the **p** of their hand. 410
3: 8 truly I am full *of* **p** by the spirit of 3581
Na 1: 3 great in **p**, and will not at all acquit 3581
2: 1 *thy* loins strong, fortify *thy* **p** mightily. 3581
Hab 1:11 offend, *imputing* this his **p** unto his god. 3581
2: 9 that *he* may be delivered from the **p** of evil! 3709
3: 4 his hand: and there *was* the hiding of his **p**. 5797

Zec 4: 6 Not by might, nor by **p**, but by my spirit, 3581
9: 4 her out, and he will smite her **p** in the sea; 2428
Mt 6:13 and the **p**, and the glory, for ever. 1411
9: 6 Son of man hath **p** on earth to forgive sins, 1849
9: 8 which had given such **p** unto men. 1849
10: 1 he gave them **p** against unclean spirits, 1849
22:29 knowing the scriptures, nor the **p** of God. 1411
24:30 man coming in the clouds of heaven with **p** 1411
26:64 Son of man sitting on the right hand of **p**, 1411
28:18 All **p** is given unto me in heaven and 1849
Mk 2:10 Son of man hath **p** on earth to forgive sins, 1849
3:15 And to have **p** to heal sicknesses, and to 1849
6: 7 two; and gave them **p over** unclean spirits; 1849
9: 1 seen the kingdom of God come with **p**. 1411
12:24 not the scriptures, neither the **p** of God? 1411
13:26 of man coming in *the* clouds with great **p** 1411
14:62 Son of man sitting on the right hand of **p**, 1411
Lk 1:17 go before him in the spirit and **p** of Elias, 1411
1:35 the **p** of the Highest shall overshadow thee: 1411
4: 6 All this **p** will I give thee, and the glory of 1849
4:14 And Jesus returned in the **p** of the Spirit 1411
4:32 at his doctrine: for his word was with **p**. 1849
4:36 and **p** he commandeth the unclean spirits, 1411
5:17 the **p** of the Lord was *present* to heal them. 1411
5:24 of man hath **p** upon earth to forgive sins, 1849
9: 1 and gave them **p** and authority over all 1849
9:43 And they were all amazed at the **mighty p** 3168
10:19 I give unto you **p** to tread on serpents and 1849
10:19 scorpions, and over all the **p** of the enemy: 1411
12: 5 which after *he* hath killed hath **p** to cast 1849
20:20 *so they* might deliver him unto the **p** and 746
21:27 the Son of man coming in a cloud with **p** 1411
22:53 but this is your hour, and the **p** of darkness. 1849
22:69 man sit on the right hand of the **p** of God. 1411
24:49 until ye be endued with **p** from on high. 1411
Jn 1:12 to them gave he **p** to become the sons of 1849
10:18 I have **p** to lay it down, and I have power to 1849
10:18 to lay it down, and I have **p** to take it again. 1849
17: 2 As thou hast given him **p over** all flesh, 1849
19:10 knowest thou not that I have **p** to crucify 1849
19:10 to crucify thee, and have **p** to release thee? 1849
19:11 Thou couldest have no **p** *at all* against me, 1849
Ac 1: 7 which the Father hath put in his own **p**. 1849
1: 8 But ye shall receive **p**, after that the Holy 1411
3:12 as though by our own **p** or holiness we had 1411
4: 7 they asked, By what **p**, or by what name, 1411
4:33 And with great **p** gave the apostles witness 1411
5: 4 after it was sold, was it not in thine own **p**? 1849
6: 8 And Stephen, full of faith and **p**, did great 1411
8:10 saying, This *man* is the great **p** of God. 1411
8:19 Saying, Give me also this **p**, that on 1849
10:38 Nazareth with the Holy Ghost and with **p**: 1411
26:18 to light, and *from* the **p** of Satan unto God, 1849
Ro 1: 4 *And* declared *to be* the Son of God with **p**, 1411
1:16 for it is the **p** of God unto salvation to 1411
1:20 are made, *even* his eternal **p** and Godhead; 1411
9:17 that I might shew my **p** in thee, and that my 1411
9:21 Hath not the potter **p over** the clay, of 1849
9:22 shew *his* wrath, and to make his **p** known, 1415
13: 1 For there is no **p** but of God: the powers 1849
13: 2 Whosoever therefore resisteth the **p**, 1849
13: 3 Wilt thou then not be afraid of the **p**? 1849
15:13 in hope, through the **p** of the Holy Ghost. 1411
15:19 and wonders, by the **p** of the Spirit of God; 1411
16:25 Now to him that is of **p** to stablish you 1410
1Co 1:18 unto us which are saved it is the **p** of God. 1411
1:24 Christ the **p** of God, and the wisdom of 1411
2: 4 but in demonstration of the Spirit and of **p**: 1411
2: 5 in the wisdom of men, but in the **p** of God. 1411
4:19 of them which are puffed up, but the **p**. 1411
4:20 kingdom of God *is* not in word, but in **p**. 1411
5: 4 with the **p** of our Lord Jesus Christ, 1411
6:12 I will not be **brought under** the **p** of any. 1850
6:14 and will *also* raise up us by his own **p**. 1411
7: 4 The wife **hath** not **p** of her own body, but 1850
7: 4 likewise also the husband **hath** not **p** of his 1850
7:37 but hath **p** over his own will, and hath so 1849
9: 4 Have we not **p** to eat and to drink? 1849
9: 5 Have we not **p** to lead about a sister, a wife, 1849
9: 6 have not we **p** to forbear working? 1849
9:12 If others be partakers of *this* **p over** you, 1849
9:12 Nevertheless we have not used this **p**; but 1849
9:18 that *I* abuse not my **p** in the gospel. 1849
11:10 For this cause ought the woman to have **p** 1849
15:24 put down all rule and all authority and **p**. 1411
15:43 it is sown in weakness; it is raised in **p**: 1411
2Co 4: 7 that the excellency of the **p** may be of God, 1411
6: 7 By the word of truth, by the **p** of God, 1411
8: 3 For to *their* **p**, I bear record, *yea*, and 1411
8: 3 beyond *their* **p** *they were* willing of 1411
12: 9 that the **p** of Christ may rest upon me. 1411
13: 4 yet he liveth by the **p** of God. 1411
13: 4 we shall live with him by the **p** of God 1411
13:10 according to the **p** which the Lord hath 1849
Eph 1:19 greatness of his **p** to us-ward who believe, 1411
1:19 according to the working of his mighty **p**, 2479
1:21 and **p**, and might, and dominion, and 1849
2: 2 according to the prince of the **p** of the air, 1849
3: 7 unto me by the effectual working of his **p**. 1411
3:20 think, according to the **p** that worketh in us, 1411
6:10 in the Lord, and in the **p** of his might. 2904
Php 3:10 and the **p** of his resurrection, and 1411
Col 1:11 according to his glorious **p**, unto all 2904
1:13 Who hath delivered us from the **p** of 1849
2:10 which is the head of all principality and **p**: 1849
1Th 1: 5 but also in **p**, and in the Holy Ghost, and 1411
2Th 1: 9 of the Lord, and from the glory of his **p**; 2479
1:11 *his* goodness, and the work of faith with **p**: 1411
2: 9 is after the working of Satan with all **p** 1411
3: 9 Not because we have not **p**, but to make 1849
1Ti 6:16 to whom *be* honour and **p** everlasting. 2904
2Ti 1: 7 but of **p**, and of love, and of a sound mind. 1411
1: 8 of the gospel according to the **p** of God; 1411
3: 5 of godliness, but denying the **p** thereof: 1411
Heb 1: 3 upholding all *things* by the word of his **p**, 1411
Heb 2:14 might destroy him that had the **p** of death, 2904
7:16 but after the **p** of an endless life. 1411
1Pe 1: 5 Who are kept by the **p** of God through faith 1411
2Pe 1: 3 According as his divine **p** hath given unto 1411
1:16 when we made known unto you the **p** and 1411
2:11 which are greater in **p** and might, 2479
Jude 1:25 *be* glory and majesty, dominion and **p**, 1849
Rev 2:26 to him will I give **p** over the nations: 1849
4:11 O Lord, to receive glory and honour and **p**: 1411
5:12 is the Lamb that was slain to receive **p**, 1411
5:13 Blessing, and honour, and glory, and **p**, 2904
6: 4 ***p*** was given to him that sat thereon to take NIG
6: 8 And **p** was given unto them over the fourth 1849
7:12 and honour, and **p**, and might, 1411
9: 3 and unto them was given **p**, as 1849
9: 3 as the scorpions of the earth have **p**. 1849
9:10 and their **p** *was* to hurt men five months. 1849
9:19 For their **p** is in their mouth, and in their 1849
11: 3 And I will give ***p*** unto my two witnesses, NIG
11: 6 These have **p** to shut heaven, that it rain not 1849
11: 6 have **p** over waters to turn them to blood, 1849
11:17 because thou hast taken *to thee* thy great **p**, 1411
12:10 of our God, and the **p** of his Christ: 1849
13: 2 and the dragon gave him his **p**, and his seat, 1411
13: 4 the dragon which gave **p** unto the beast: 1849
13: 5 **p** was given unto him to continue forty *and* 1849
13: 7 and **p** was given him over all kindreds, and 1849
13:12 And he exerciseth all the **p** of the first beast 1849
13:14 he **had p** to do in the sight of the beast; 1325
13:15 And he **had p** to give life unto the image of 1325
14:18 out from the altar, which had **p** over fire; 1849
15: 8 from the glory of God, and from his **p**; 1411
16: 8 ***p*** was given unto him to scorch men with NIG
16: 9 of God, which hath **p** over these plagues: 1849
17:12 receive **p** as kings one hour with the beast. 1849
17:13 and shall give their **p** and strength unto 1411
18: 1 come down from heaven, having great **p**; 1849
19: 1 Salvation, and glory, and honour, and **p**, 1411
20: 6 on such the second death hath no **p**, but 1849

POWERFUL (3) [POWER]

Ps 29: 4 The voice of the LORD *is* **p**; the voice of 3581
2Co 10:10 For *his* letters, say they, *are* weighty and **p**; 2478
Heb 4:12 and **p**, and sharper than any twoedged 1756

POWERS (14) [POWER]

Mt 24:29 and the **p** of the heavens shall be shaken: 1411
Mk 13:25 the **p** that are in heaven shall be shaken. 1411
Lk 12:11 and *unto* magistrates, and **p**, take ye no 1849
21:26 for the **p** of heaven shall be shaken. 1411
Ro 8:38 nor angels, nor principalities, nor **p**, 1411
13: 1 Let every soul be subject unto the higher **p**. 1849
13: 1 of God: the **p** that be are ordained of God. 1849
Eph 3:10 **p** in heavenly *places* might be known by 1849
6:12 blood, but against principalities, against **p**, 1849
Col 1:16 or dominions, or principalities, or **p**: 1849
2:15 *And* having spoiled principalities and **p**, 1849
Tit 3: 1 mind to be subject to principalities and **p**, 1849
Heb 6: 5 of God, and the **p** of the world to come, 1411
1Pe 3:22 and **p** being made subject unto him. 1411

PRACTICES (1) [PRACTISE]

2Pe 2:14 heart they have exercised with **covetous p**; 4124

PRACTISE (4) [PRACTICES, PRACTISED]

Ps 141: 4 to **p** wicked works with men that work 5953
Isa 32: 6 to **p** hypocrisy, and to utter error against 6213
Da 8:24 **p**, and shall destroy the mighty and the holy 6213
Mic 2: 1 they **p** it, because it is in the power of their 6213

PRACTISED (2) [PRACTISE]

1Sa 23: 9 David knew that Saul **secretly p** mischief 2790
Da 8:12 truth to the ground; and it **p**, and prospered. 6213

PRAISE (248) [PRAISED, PRAISES, PRAISETH, PRAISING]

Ge 29:35 she said, Now will I **p** the LORD: 3034
49: 8 thou *art he* whom thy brethren shall **p**: 3034
Lev 19:24 shall be holy to **p** the LORD *withal*. 1974
Dt 10:21 He *is* thy **p**, and he *is* thy God, that hath 8416
26:19 in **p**, and in name, and in honour; 8416
Jdg 5: 2 **P** ye the LORD for the avenging of Israel, 1288
5: 3 I will sing ***p*** to the LORD God of Israel. NIH
1Ch 16: 4 to thank and **p** the LORD God of Israel: 1984
16:35 thanks to thy holy name, *and* glory in thy **p**. 8416
23: 5 which I made, *said David*, to **p** *therewith*. 1984
23:30 every morning to thank and **p** the LORD, 1984
25: 3 a harp, to give thanks and to **p** the LORD. 1984
29:13 we thank thee, and **p** thy glorious name. 1984
2Ch 7: 6 which David the king had made to **p** 3034
8:14 to **p** and minister before the priests, 1984
20:19 stood up to **p** the LORD God of Israel 1984
20:21 that should **p** the beauty of holiness, as *they* 1984
20:21 before the army, and to say, **P** the LORD; 3034
20:22 when they began to sing and to **p**, 8416
23:13 of musick, and such as taught to *sing* **p**. 1984
29:30 **p** unto the LORD with the words of 1984
31: 2 to **p** in the gates of the tents of the LORD. 1984
Ezr 3:10 to **p** the LORD, after the ordinance of 1984
Ne 9: 5 which *is* exalted above all blessing and **p**. 8416
12:24 over against them, to **p** *and* to give thanks, 1984
12:46 and songs of **p** and thanksgiving unto God. 8416
Ps 7:17 I will **p** the LORD according to his 3034
7:17 will sing ***p*** to the name of the LORD most NIH
9: 1 I will **p** *thee*, O LORD, with my whole 3034
9: 2 I will sing ***p*** to thy name, O thou most High. NIH
9:14 That I may shew forth all thy **p** in the gates 8416
21:13 *so* will we sing and **p** thy power. 2167
22:22 in the midst of the congregation will I **p** 1984
22:23 Ye that fear the LORD, **p** him; all ye 1984
22:25 My **p** *shall be* of thee in the great 8416
22:26 they shall **p** the LORD that seek him: 1984
28: 7 and with my song will I **p** him. 3034
30: 9 Shall the dust **p** thee? shall it declare thy 3034
Ps 30:12 To the end that *my* glory may sing ***p*** to thee, NIH
33: 1 *for* **p** is comely for the upright. 8416
33: 2 **P** the LORD with harp: sing unto him 3034
34: 1 his **p** *shall* continually *be* in my mouth. 8416
35:18 I will **p** thee among much people. 1984
35:28 *and* of thy **p** all the day long. 8416
40: 3 song in my mouth, *even* **p** unto our God: 8416
42: 4 with the voice of joy and **p**, *with* a 8426
42: 5 for I shall yet **p** him *for* the help of his 3034
42:11 for I shall yet **p** him, *who is* the health of 3034
43: 4 yea, upon the harp will I **p** thee, O God my 3034
43: 5 for I shall yet **p** him, *who is* the health of 3034
44: 8 all the day long, and **p** thy name for ever. 3034
45:17 shall the people **p** thee for ever and ever. 3034
48:10 so *is* thy **p** unto the ends of the earth: 8416
49:18 *men* will **p** thee, when thou doest well to 3034
50:23 Whoso offereth **p** glorifieth me: and to him 8426
51:15 and my mouth shall shew forth thy **p**. 8416
52: 9 I will **p** thee for ever, because thou hast 3034
54: 6 I will **p** thy name, O LORD; for *it is* good. 3034
56: 4 In God I will **p** his word, in God I have put 1984
56:10 In God will I **p** *his* word: in the LORD 1984
56:10 *his* word: in the LORD will I **p** *his* word. 1984
57: 7 my heart is fixed: I will sing and **give p**. 2167
57: 9 I will **p** thee, O Lord, among the people: 3034
61: 8 So will I sing ***p*** unto thy name for ever, NIH
63: 3 *is* better than life, my lips shall **p** thee. 7623
63: 5 and my mouth shall **p** *thee with* joyful lips: 1984
65: 1 **P** waiteth for thee, O God, in Zion: and 8416
66: 2 honour of his name: make his **p** glorious. 8416
66: 8 and make the voice of his **p** to be heard: 8416
67: 3 Let the people **p** thee, O God; let all 3034
67: 3 O God; let all the people **p** thee. 3034
67: 5 Let the people **p** thee, O God; let all 3034
67: 5 O God; let all the people **p** thee. 3034
69:30 I will **p** the name of God with a song; and 1984
69:34 Let the heaven and earth **p** him, the seas, 1984
71: 6 my **p** *shall be* continually of thee. 8416
71: 8 Let my mouth be filled *with* thy **p** *and* 8416
71:14 and will yet **p** thee more and more. 8416
71:22 I will also **p** thee with the psaltery, *even* thy 3034
74:21 let the poor and needy **p** thy name. 1984
76:10 Surely the wrath of man shall **p** thee: 3034
79:13 we will shew forth thy **p** to all generations. 8416
86:12 I will **p** thee, O Lord my God, with all my 3034
88:10 shall the dead arise *and* **p** thee? Selah. 3034
89: 5 the heavens shall **p** thy wonders, 3034
98: 4 make a loud noise, and rejoice, and sing ***p***. NIH
99: 3 Let them **p** thy great and terrible name; 3034
100: T A Psalm of **p**. 8426
100: 4 *and* into his courts with **p**: 8416
102:18 the people which *shall be* created shall **p** 1984
102:21 the LORD in Zion, and his **p** in Jerusalem; 8416
104:33 I will sing ***p*** to my God while I have my NIH
104:35 the LORD, O my soul. **P** ye the LORD. 1984
105:45 and keep his laws. **P** ye the LORD. 1984
106: 1 **P** ye the LORD. O give thanks unto 1984
106: 2 the LORD? *who* can shew forth all his **p**? 8416
106:12 believed they his words; they sang his **p**. 8416
106:47 thy holy name, *and* to triumph in thy **p**. 8416
106:48 all the people say, Amen. **P** ye the LORD. 1984
107: 8 Oh that *men* would **p** the LORD *for* his 3034
107:15 Oh that *men* would **p** the LORD *for* his 3034
107:21 Oh that *men* would **p** the LORD *for* his 3034
107:31 Oh that *men* would **p** the LORD *for* his 3034
107:32 and **p** him in the assembly of the elders. 1984
108: 1 I will sing and **give p**, even *with* my glory. 2167
108: 3 I will **p** thee, O LORD, among the people: 3034
109: 1 Hold not thy peace, O God of my **p**; 8416
109:30 I will greatly **p** the LORD with my mouth; 3034
109:30 yea, I will **p** him among the multitude. 1984
111: 1 **P** ye the LORD. I will praise the LORD 1984
111: 1 I will **p** the LORD with *my* whole heart, 3034
111:10 *commandments:* his **p** endureth for ever. 8416
112: 1 **P** ye the LORD. Blessed *is* the man *that* 1984
113: 1 **P** ye the LORD. Praise, O ye servants of 1984
113: 1 **P**, O ye servants of the LORD, praise 1984
113: 1 of the LORD, **p** the name of the LORD. 1984
113: 9 joyful mother of children. **P** ye the LORD. 1984
115:17 The dead **p** not the LORD, neither any 1984
115:18 time forth and for evermore. **P** the LORD. 1984
116:19 of thee, O Jerusalem. **P** ye the LORD. 1984
117: 1 O **p** the LORD, all ye nations: praise him, 1984
117: 1 all ye nations: **p** him, all ye people. 7623
117: 2 *endureth* for ever. **P** ye the LORD. 1984
118:19 will go into them, *and* I will **p** the LORD: 3034
118:21 I will **p** thee: for thou hast heard me, and 3034
118:28 Thou *art* my God, and I will **p** thee: *thou art* 3034
119: 7 I will **p** thee with uprightness of heart, 3034
119:164 Seven *times* a day do I **p** thee because 1984
119:171 My lips shall utter **p**, when thou hast taught 8416
119:175 Let my soul live, and it shall **p** thee; and 1984
135: 1 **P** ye the LORD. Praise ye the name of 1984
135: 1 **P** ye the name of the LORD; praise *him*, 1984
135: 1 **p** *him*, O ye servants of the LORD. 1984
135: 3 **P** the LORD; for the LORD *is* good: 1984
135:21 dwelleth at Jerusalem. **P** ye the LORD. 1984
138: 1 I will **p** thee with my whole heart: 3034
138: 1 before the gods will I sing ***p*** unto thee. NIH
138: 2 **p** thy name for thy lovingkindness and 3034
138: 4 All the kings of the earth shall **p** thee, 3034
139:14 I will **p** thee; for I am fearfully and 3034
142: 7 soul out of prison, that *I* may **p** thy name: 3034
145: T David's *Psalm of* **p**. 8416
145: 2 and I will **p** thy name for ever and ever. 1984
145: 4 One generation shall **p** thy works to 7623
145:10 All thy works shall **p** thee, O LORD; and 3034
145:21 My mouth shall speak the **p** of the LORD: 8416
146: 1 **P** ye the LORD. Praise the LORD, O my 1984
146: 1 ye the LORD. **P** the LORD, O my soul. 1984
146: 2 While I live will I **p** the LORD: I will sing 1984
146:10 unto all generations. **P** ye the LORD. 1984
147: 1 **P** ye the LORD: for *it is* good to sing 1984
147: 1 our God; for *it is* pleasant; *and* **p** is comely. 8416
147: 7 sing ***p*** upon the harp unto our God: NIH

Ps 147:12 **P** the LORD, O Jerusalem; praise thy 7623
147:12 O Jerusalem; **p** thy God, O Zion. 1984
147:20 have not known them. **P** ye the LORD. 1984
148: 1 **P** ye the LORD. Praise ye the LORD 1984
148: 1 **P** ye the LORD from the heavens: 1984
148: 1 from the heavens: **p** him in the heights. 1984
148: 2 **P** ye him, all his angels: praise ye him, 1984
148: 2 all his angels: **p** ye him, all his hosts. 1984
148: 3 **P** ye him, sun and moon: praise him, all ye 1984
148: 3 sun and moon: **p** him, all ye stars of light. 1984
148: 4 **P** him, ye heavens of heavens, and 1984
148: 5 Let them **p** the name of the LORD: for he 1984
148: 7 **P** the LORD from the earth, ye dragons, 1984
148:13 Let them **p** the name of the LORD: for his 1984
148:14 horn of his people, the **p** of all his saints; 8416
148:14 a people near unto him. **P** ye the LORD. 1984
149: 1 **P** ye the LORD. Sing unto the LORD a 1984
149: 1 *and* his **p** in the congregation of saints. 8416
149: 3 Let them **p** his name in the dance: let them 1984
149: 9 have all his saints. **P** ye the LORD. 1984
150: 1 **P** ye the LORD. Praise God in his 1984
150: 1 **P** God in his sanctuary: praise him in 1984
150: 1 **p** him in the firmament of his power. 1984
150: 2 **P** him for his mighty acts: praise him 1984
150: 2 **p** him according to his excellent greatness. 1984
150: 3 **P** him with the sound of the trumpet: 1984
150: 3 **p** him with the psaltery and harp. 1984
150: 4 **P** him with the timbrel and dance: 1984
150: 4 **p** him with stringed instruments and 1984
150: 5 **P** him upon the loud cymbals: praise him 1984
150: 5 **p** him upon the high sounding cymbals. 1984
150: 6 Let every *thing that hath* breath **p** 1984
150: 6 breath praise the LORD. **P** ye the LORD. 1984
Pr 27: 2 Let another *man* **p** thee, and not thine own 1984
27:21 the furnace for gold; so *is* a man to his **p**. 4110
28: 4 They that forsake the law **p** the wicked: but 1984
31:31 and let her own works **p** her in the gates. 1984
Isa 12: 1 day thou shalt say, O LORD, I will **p** thee: 3034
12: 4 ye say, **P** the LORD, call upon his name, 3034
25: 1 I will exalt thee, I will **p** thy name; 3034
38:18 For the grave cannot **p** thee, death can *not* 3034
38:19 The living, the living, he shall **p** thee, as I 3034
42: 8 to another, neither my **p** to graven images. 8416
42:10 *and* his **p** from the end of the earth, ye that 8416
42:12 and declare his **p** in the islands. 8416
43:21 for myself; they shall shew forth my **p**. 8416
48: 9 *for* my **p** will I refrain for thee, that *I* cut 8416
60:18 call thy walls Salvation, and thy gates **P**. 8416
61: 3 the garment of **p** for the spirit of heaviness; 8416
61:11 and **p** to spring forth before all the nations. 8416
62: 7 and till he make Jerusalem a **p** in the earth. 8416
62: 9 gathered it shall eat it, and **p** the LORD; 1984
Jer 13:11 and for a name, and for a **p**, and for a glory: 8416
17:14 and I shall be saved: for thou *art* my **p**. 8416
17:26 and incense, and bringing *sacrifices of* **p**, 8426
20:13 Sing unto the LORD, **p** ye the LORD: 1984
31: 7 publish ye, **p** ye, and say, O LORD, save 1984
33: 9 a **p** and an honour before all the nations of 8416
33:11 them that shall say, **P** the LORD of hosts: 3034
33:11 of them that shall bring the **sacrifice of p** 8426
48: 2 *There shall be* no more **p** of Moab: 8416
49:25 How is the city of **p** not left, the city of my 8416
51:41 *how* is the **p** of the whole earth surprised! 8416
Da 2:23 I thank thee, and **p** thee, O thou God of my 7624
4:37 Now I Nebuchadnezzar **p** and extol and 7624
Joel 2:26 and **p** the name of the LORD your God, 1984
Hab 3: 3 the heavens, and the earth was full *of* his **p**. 8416
Zep 3:19 I will get them **p** and fame in every land 8416
3:20 and a **p** among all people of the earth, 8416
Mt 21:16 and sucklings thou hast perfected **p**? *136*
Lk 18:43 when they saw *it*, gave **p** unto God. *136*
19:37 **p** God with a loud voice for all the mighty *134*
Jn 9:24 and said unto him, Give God the **p**: *1391*
12:43 For they loved the **p** of men more than *1391*
12:43 the praise of men more than the **p** of God. *1391*
Ro 2:29 whose **p** *is* not of men, but of God. *1868*
13: 3 *is* good, and thou shalt have **p** of the same: *1868*
15:11 And again, **P** the Lord, all ye Gentiles; and *134*
1Co 4: 5 and then shall every man have **p** of God. *1868*
11: 2 Now I **p** you, brethren, that you remember *1867*
11:17 Now in this that I declare *unto you* I **p** *you* *1867*
11:22 shall I **p** you in this? I praise *you* not. *1867*
11:22 shall I praise you in this? I **p** *you* not. *1867*
2Co 8:18 whose **p** *is* in the gospel throughout all *1868*
Eph 1: 6 To the **p** of the glory of his grace, *1868*
1:12 That we should be to the **p** of his glory, *1868*
1:14 unto the **p** of his glory. *1868*
Php 1:11 Jesus Christ unto the glory and **p** of God. *1868*
4: 8 if *there be* any virtue, and if *there be* any **p**, *1868*
Heb 2:12 in the midst of the church will I **sing p** unto *5214*
13:15 let us offer the sacrifice of **p** to God *133*
1Pe 1: 7 might be found unto **p** and honour and *1868*
2:14 and *for* the **p** of them that do well. *1868*
4:11 to whom be **p** and dominion for ever and *1391*
Rev 19: 5 saying, **P** our God, all ye his servants, and *134*

PRAISED (26) [PRAISE]

Jdg 16:24 when the people saw him, they **p** their god: 1984
2Sa 14:25 to be so much **p** as Absalom for his beauty: 1984
22: 4 call on the LORD, who is *worthy* to be **p**: 1984
1Ch 16:25 great *is* the LORD, and greatly to be **p**: 1984
16:36 the people said, Amen, and **p** the LORD. 1984
23: 5 four thousand **p** the LORD with 1984
2Ch 5:13 and **p** the LORD, *saying*, For *he is* good; 1984
7: 3 worshipped, and **p** the LORD, *saying*, For 3034
7: 6 for ever, when David **p** by their ministry; 1984
30:21 and the priests **p** the LORD day by day, 1984
Ezr 3:11 when they **p** the LORD, because 1984
Ne 5:13 Amen, and **p** the LORD. 1984
Ps 18: 3 upon the LORD, who is *worthy* to be **p**: 1984
48: 1 and greatly to be **p** in the city of our God, 1984
72:15 for him continually; *and* daily shall he be **p**. 1288
96: 4 the LORD *is* great, and greatly to be **p**: 1984
113: 3 of the same the LORD'S name *is* to be **p**. 1984
145: 3 Great *is* the LORD, and greatly to be **p**; 1984

Pr 31:30 that feareth the LORD, she shall be **p**. 1984
Ecc 4: 2 Wherefore I **p** the dead which are already 7623
SS 6: 9 and the concubines, and they **p** her. 1984
Isa 64:11 beautiful house, where our fathers **p** thee, 1984
Da 4:34 I **p** and honoured him that liveth for ever, 7624
5: 4 **p** the gods of gold, and of silver, of brass, 7624
5:23 and thou hast **p** the gods of silver, and gold, 7624
Lk 1:64 tongue *loosed*, and he spake, and **p** God. *2127*

PRAISES (29) [PRAISE]

Ex 15:11 in holiness, fearful *in* **p**, doing wonders? 8416
2Sa 22:50 and I will **sing p** unto thy name. 2167
2Ch 29:30 they *sang* **p** with gladness, and they bowed 1984
Ps 9:11 Sing ***p*** to the LORD, which dwelleth in NIH
18:49 the heathen, and sing ***p*** unto thy name. NIH
22: 3 O thou that inhabitest the **p** of Israel. 8416
27: 6 yea, I will sing ***p*** unto the LORD. NIH
47: 6 Sing ***p*** to God, sing *praises:* sing *praises* NIH
47: 6 sing ***p***: sing *praises* unto our King, NIH
47: 6 sing *praises:* sing ***p*** unto our King, NIH
47: 6 *praises:* sing *praises* unto our King, sing ***p***. NIH
47: 7 all the earth: sing ye ***p*** with understanding. NIH
56:12 upon me, O God: I will render **p** unto thee. 8426
68: 4 Sing unto God, sing ***p*** *to* his name: NIH
68:32 of the earth; O sing ***p*** *unto* the Lord; Selah. NIH
75: 9 for ever; I will sing ***p*** to the God of Jacob. NIH
78: 4 shewing to the generation to come the **p** of 8416
92: 1 and to sing ***p*** unto thy name, O most High: NIH
108: 3 I will sing ***p*** unto thee among the nations. NIH
135: 3 sing ***p*** unto his name; for *it is* pleasant. NIH
144: 9 an instrument of ten strings will I sing ***p*** NIH
146: 2 I will sing ***p*** unto my God while I have *any* NIH
147: 1 for *it is* good to sing ***p*** unto our God; for *it* NIH
149: 3 let them sing ***p*** unto him with the timbrel NIH
149: 6 *Let* the high ***p*** of God *be* in their mouth, and NIH
Isa 60: 6 they shall shew forth the **p** of the LORD. 8416
63: 7 of the LORD, *and* the **p** of the LORD, 8416
Ac 16:25 and Silas prayed, and **sang p** unto God: *5214*
1Pe 2: 9 that ye should shew forth the **p** of him who *703*

PRAISETH (1) [PRAISE]

Pr 31:28 her blessed; her husband *also*, and he **p** her. 1984

PRAISING (10) [PRAISE]

2Ch 5:13 to make one sound to be heard in **p** and 1984
23:12 noise of the people running and **p** the king, 1984
Ezr 3:11 they sung together by course in **p** and 1984
Ps 84: 4 in thy house: they will be still **p** thee. Selah. 1984
Lk 2:13 a multitude of the heavenly host **p** God, *134*
2:20 **p** God for all *the things* that they had heard *134*
24:53 in the temple, **p** and blessing God. *134*
Ac 2:47 **P** God, and having favour with all *134*
3: 8 the temple, walking, and leaping, and **p** God. *134*
3: 9 all the people saw him walking and **p** God: *134*

PRANSING (1) [PRANSINGS]

Na 3: 2 of the **p** horses, and of the jumping 1725

PRANSINGS (2) [PRANSING]

Jdg 5:22 horsehoofs broken by the means of the **p**, 1726
5:22 the pransings, the **p** of their mighty *ones*. 1726

PRATING (3)

Pr 10: 8 but a **p** fool shall fall. 8193
10:10 eye causeth sorrow: but a **p** fool shall fall. 8193
3Jn 1:10 **p against** us with malicious words: *5396*

PRAY (313) [PRAYED, PRAYER, PRAYERS, PRAYEST, PRAYETH, PRAYING]

Ge 12:13 Say, **I p thee**, thou *art* my sister: that it may 4994
13: 8 **I p thee**, between me and thee, and 4994
13: 9 separate thyself, **I p thee**, from me: if *thou* 4994
16: 2 **I p thee**, go in unto my maid; it may be that 4994
18: 3 pass not away, **I p thee**, from thy servant: 4994
18: 4 **I p you**, be fetched, and wash your feet, 4994
19: 2 Behold now, my lords, turn in, **I p you**, 4994
19: 7 **I p you**, brethren, do not *so* wickedly. 4994
19: 8 let me, **I p you**, bring them out unto you, 4994
20: 7 and he shall **p** for thee, and thou shalt live: 6419
23:13 saying, But if thou *wilt give it*, **I p thee**, 3863
24: 2 Put, **I p thee**, thy hand under my thigh: 4994
24:12 **I p thee**, send me good speed *this* day, and 4994
24:14 thy pitcher, **I p thee**, that I may drink; 4994
24:17 ran to meet her, and said, Let me, **I p thee**, 4994
24:23 tell me, **I p thee**: is there room *in* thy 4994
24:43 and I say to her, Give me, **I p thee**, 4994
24:45 and I said unto her, Let me drink, **I p thee**. 4994
25:30 Esau said to Jacob, Feed me, **I p thee**, 4994
27: 3 Now therefore take, **I p thee**, thy weapons, 4994
27:19 arise, **I p thee**, sit and eat of my venison, 4994
27:21 Come near, **I p thee**, that I may feel thee, 4994
30:14 Give me, **I p thee**, of thy son's mandrakes. 4994
30:27 Laban said unto him, **I p thee**, if I have 4994
32:11 Deliver me, **I p thee**, from the hand of my 4994
32:29 asked *him*, and said, Tell *me*, **I p thee**, 4994
33:10 Jacob said, Nay, **I p thee**, if now I have 4994
33:11 Take, **I p thee**, my blessing that is brought 4994
33:14 Let my lord, **I p thee**, pass over before his 4994
34: 8 **I p you** give her him to wife. 4994
37: 6 he said unto them, Hear, **I p you**, this 4994
37:14 he said to him, Go, **I p thee**, see whether it 4994
37:16 tell me, **I p thee**, where they feed *their* 4994
38:16 said, Go to, **I p thee**, let me come in unto 4994
38:25 she said, Discern, **I p thee**, whose *are* 4994
40: 8 *belong* to God? tell me *them*, **I p you**. 4994
40:14 **I p thee**, unto me, and make mention of me 4994
44:18 said, O my lord, let thy servant, **I p thee**, 4994
44:33 Now therefore, **I p thee**, let thy servant 4994
45: 4 his brethren, Come near to me, **I p you**. 4994
47: 4 now therefore, **we p thee**, let thy servants 4994
47:29 put, **I p thee**, thy hand under my thigh, and 4994
47:29 with me; bury me not, **I p thee**, in Egypt: 4994
48: 9 **I p thee**, unto me, and I will bless them. 4994
50: 4 speak, **I p you**, in the ears of Pharaoh, 4994

Ge 50: 5 **I p thee**, and bury my father, and I will 4994
50:17 Forgive, I **p** thee now, the trespass of thy 577
50:17 now, **we p thee**, forgive the trespass of 4994
Ex 4:13 he said, O my Lord, send, **I p thee**, by 4994
4:18 **I p thee**, and return unto my brethren 4994
5: 3 let us go, **we p thee**, three days' journey 4994
10:17 Now therefore forgive, **I p thee**, my sin 4994
32:32 if not, blot me, **I p thee**, out of thy book 4994
33:13 Now therefore, **I p thee**, if I have found 4994
34: 9 O Lord, let my Lord, **I p thee**, go amongst 4994
Nu 10:31 he said, Leave us not, **I p thee**; 4994
11:15 thus with me, kill me, **I p thee**, out of hand, 4994
16: 8 unto Korah, Hear, **I p you**, ye sons of Levi: 4994
16:26 saying, Depart, **I p you**, from the tents of 4994
20:17 Let us pass, **I p thee**, through thy country: 4994
21: 7 **p** unto the LORD, that he take away 6419
22: 6 Come now therefore, **I p thee**, curse me 4994
22:16 Let nothing, **I p thee**, hinder thee from 4994
22:17 come therefore, **I p thee**, curse me this 4994
22:19 Now therefore, **I p you**, tarry ye also here 4994
23:13 Balak said unto him, Come, **I p thee**, 4994
23:27 Balak said unto Balaam, Come, **I p thee**, 4994
Dt 3:25 **I p thee**, let me go over, and see the good 4994
Jos 2:12 Now therefore, **I p you**, swear unto me by 4994
7:19 said unto Achan, My son, give, **I p thee**, 4994
Jdg 1:24 they said unto him, Shew us, **we p thee**, 4994
4:19 he said unto her, Give me, **I p thee**, a little 4994
6:18 Depart not hence, **I p thee**, until I come 4994
6:39 **I p thee**, but *this* once with the fleece; 4994
8: 5 unto the men of Succoth, Give, **I p you**, 4994
9: 2 Speak, **I p you**, in the ears of all the men of 4994
9:38 go out, **I p** now, and fight with them. 4994
10:15 deliver us only, **we p thee**, this day. 4994
11:17 saying, Let me, **I p thee**, pass through thy 4994
11:19 said unto him, Let us pass, **we p thee**, 4994
13: 4 **I p thee**, and drink not wine nor strong 4994
13:15 **I p thee**, let us detain thee, until we shall 4994
15: 2 than she? take her, **I p** thee, instead of her. 4994
16: 6 Delilah said to Samson, Tell me, **I p thee**, 4994
16:10 now tell me, **I p thee**, wherewith thou 4994
16:28 **I p thee**, and strengthen me, I pray thee, 4994
16:28 **I p thee**, only this once, O God, 4994
18: 5 unto him, Ask *counsel*, **we p thee**, of God, 4994
19: 6 **I p thee**, and tarry all night, and let thine 4994
19: 8 father said, Comfort thine heart, **I p thee**. 4994
19: 9 towards evening, **I p you** tarry all night: 4994
19:11 **I p thee**, and let us turn in into this city of 4994
19:23 *nay*, **I p you**, do not *so* wickedly; 4994
Ru 2: 7 **I p you**, let me glean and gather after 4994
1Sa 2:36 of bread, and shall say, Put me, **I p thee**, 4994
3:17 **I p thee** hide *it* not from me: God do so 4994
7: 5 and I will **p** for you unto the LORD. 6419
9:18 said, Tell me, **I p thee**, where the seer's 4994
10:15 Saul's uncle said, Tell me, **I p thee**, 4994
12:19 **P** for thy servants unto the LORD thy 6419
12:23 against the LORD in ceasing to **p** for you: 6419
14:29 see, **I p you**, how mine eyes have been 4994
15:25 **I p thee**, pardon my sin, and turn again 4994
15:30 *yet* honour me now, **I p thee**, 4994
16:22 saying, Let David, **I p thee**, stand before 4994
19: 2 now therefore, **I p thee**, take heed to 4994
20:29 he said, Let me go, **I p thee**; for our family 4994
20:29 get away, **I p thee**, and see my brethren. 4994
22: 3 **I p thee**, come forth, *and be* with you, 4994
23:22 Go, **I p you**, prepare yet, and know and 4994
25: 8 give, **I p thee**, whatsoever cometh to thine 4994
25:24 and let thine handmaid, **I p thee**, 4994
25:25 Let not my lord, **I p thee**, regard this man 4994
25:28 **I p thee**, forgive the trespass of thine 4994
26: 8 now therefore let me smite him, **I p thee**, 4994
26:11 but, **I p thee**, take thou now the spear that 6258
26:19 Now therefore, **I p thee**, let my lord 4994
28: 8 he said, **I p thee**, divine unto me by 4994
28:22 Now therefore, **I p thee**, hearken thou also 4994
30: 7 Ahimelech's son, **I p thee**, bring me hither 4994
2Sa 1: 4 **I p thee**, tell me. And he answered, 4994
1: 9 Stand, **I p thee**, upon me, and slay me: 4994
7:27 hath thy servant found in his heart to **p** this 6419
13: 5 say unto him, **I p thee**, let my sister Tamar 4994
13: 6 **I p thee**, let Tamar my sister come, and 4994
13:13 Now therefore, **I p thee**, speak unto 4994
13:26 said Absalom, If not, **I p thee**, let my 4994
14: 2 a wise woman, and said unto her, **I p thee**, 4994
14:11 said she, **I p thee**, let the king remember 4994
14:12 woman said, Let thine handmaid, **I p thee**, 4994
14:18 the woman, Hide not from me, **I p thee**, 4994
15: 7 **I p thee**, let me go and pay my vow, 4994
15:31 David said, O LORD, **I p thee**, turn 4994
16: 9 me go over, **I p thee**, and take off his head. 4994
18:22 howsoever, let me, **I p thee**, also run after 4994
19:37 Let thy servant, **I p thee**, turn back again, 4994
20:16 say, **I p you**, unto Joab, Come near hither, 4994
24:17 let thine hand, **I p thee**, be against me, and 4994
1Ki 1:12 Now therefore come, let me, **I p thee**, 4994
2:17 he said, Speak, **I p thee**, unto Solomon 4994
2:20 petition of thee; ***I p*** *thee*, say me not nay. NIH
8:26 of Israel, let thy word, **I p thee**, be verified, 4994
8:30 when they shall **p** towards this place: 6419
8:33 **p**, and make supplication unto thee in this 6419
8:35 if they **p** towards this place, and confess thy 6419
8:42 he shall come and **p** towards this house; 6419
8:44 shall **p** unto the LORD toward the city 6419
8:48 and **p** unto thee toward their land, 6419
13: 6 **p** for me, that my hand may be restored me 6419
14: 2 Arise, **I p thee**, and disguise thyself, 4994
17:10 called to her, and said, Fetch me, **I p thee**, 4994
17:11 said, Bring me, **I p thee**, a morsel of bread 4994
17:21 and said, O LORD my God, **I p thee**, 4994
19:20 said, Let me, **I p thee**, kiss my father and 4994
20: 7 **I p you**, and see how this *man* seeketh 4994
20:31 let us, **I p thee**, put sackcloth on our loins, 4994
20:32 Ben-hadad saith, **I p thee**, let me live. 4994
20:35 word of the LORD, Smite me, **I p thee**. 4994
20:37 another man, and said, Smite me, **I p thee**. 4994
22: 5 Inquire, **I p thee**, at the word of 4994

1Ki 22:13 let thy word, **I p thee**, be like the word of 4994
2Ki 1:13 **I p thee**, let my life, and the life of these 4994
2:2 said unto Elisha, Tarry here, **I p thee**; 4994
2:4 said unto him, Elisha, tarry here, **I p thee**; 4994
2:6 Elijah said unto him, Tarry, **I p thee**, here; 4994
2:9 Elisha said, **I p thee**, let a double portion of 4994
2:16 them go, **we p thee**, and seek thy master: 4994
2:19 Behold, **I p thee**, the situation of *this* city *is* 4994
4:10 make a little chamber, **I p thee**, on the wall; 4994
4:22 said, Send me, **I p thee**, one of the young 4994
4:26 Run now, **I p thee**, to meet her, and 4994
5:7 **I p you**, and see how he seeketh a quarrel 4994
5:15 now therefore, **I p thee**, take a blessing of 4994
5:17 Naaman said, Shall there not then, **I p thee**, 4994
5:22 give them, **I p thee**, a talent of silver, and 4994
6:2 Let us go, **we p thee**, unto Jordan, and 4994
6:3 **I p thee**, and go with thy servants. 4994
6:17 said, LORD, **I p thee**, open his eyes, 4994
6:18 Smite this people, **I p thee**, with blindness. 4994
7:13 and said, Let *some* take, **I p thee**, 4994
8:4 saying, Tell me, **I p thee**, all the great 4994
18:23 Now therefore, **I p thee**, give pledges to 4994
18:26 Joah, unto Rab-shakeh, Speak, **I p thee**, 4994
1Ch 17:25 thy servant hath found *in his heart* to **p** 6419
21:17 let thine hand, **I p thee**, O LORD my 4994
2Ch 6:24 **p** and make supplication before thee in this 6419
6:26 *yet* if they **p** towards this place, and 6419
6:32 out arm; if they come and **p** in this house; 6419
6:34 they **p** unto thee toward this city which 6419
6:37 **p** unto thee in the land of their captivity, 2603
6:38 **p** toward their land, which thou gavest unto 6419
7:14 **p**, and seek my face, and turn from their 6419
18:4 Inquire, **I p thee**, at the word of 4994
18:12 **I p thee**, be like one of theirs, and 4994
Ezr 6:10 **p** for the life of the king, and of his sons. 6739
Ne 1:6 which **I p** before thee now, day and night, 6419
1:11 prosper, **I p thee**, thy servant *this* day, and 4994
5:10 corn: **I p you**, let us leave off this usury. 4994
5:11 Restore, **I p you**, to them, even *this* day, 4994
Job 4:7 Remember, **I p thee**, who *ever* perished, 4994
6:29 Return, **I p you**, let it not be iniquity; yea, 4994
8:8 For inquire, **I p thee**, of the former age, and 4994
21:15 profit should we have, if we **p** unto him? 6293
22:22 Receive, **I p thee**, the law from his mouth, 4994
32:21 Let me not, **I p you**, accept *any* man's 4994
33:1 Wherefore, Job, **I p thee**, hear my 4994
33:26 He shall **p** unto God, and he will be 6279
42:8 and my servant Job shall **p** for you: 6419
Ps 5:2 and my God: for unto thee will **I p**. 6419
32:6 For this shall every one *that is* godly **p** unto 6419
55:17 and at noon, will **I p**, and cry aloud: 7878
119:76 Let, **I p thee**, thy merciful kindness be for 4994
122:6 **P** for the peace of Jerusalem: they shall 7592
Isa 5:3 judge, **I p you**, betwixt me and my 4994
16:12 that he shall come to his sanctuary to **p**; 6419
29:11 that is learned, saying, Read this, **I p thee**: 4994
29:12 is not learned, saying, Read this, **I p thee**: 4994
36:8 Now therefore give pledges, **I p thee**, 4994
36:11 and Joah unto Rabshakeh, Speak, **I p thee**, 4994
45:20 and **p** unto a god *that* cannot save. 6419
Jer 7:16 Therefore **p** not thou for this people, 6419
11:14 Therefore **p** not thou for this people, 6419
14:11 **P** not for this people for *their* good. 6419
21:2 Inquire, **I p thee**, of the LORD for us; for 4994
29:7 and **p** unto the LORD for it: 6419
29:12 ye shall go and **p** unto me, and I will 6419
32:8 said unto me, Buy my field, **I p thee**, that *is* 4994
37:3 **P** now unto the LORD our God for us. 6419
37:20 hear now, **I p thee**, O my lord the king: 4994
37:20 let my supplication, **I p thee**, be accepted 4994
40:15 **I p thee**, and I will slay Ishmael the son of 4994
42:2 **p** for us unto the LORD thy God, *even* for 6419
42:4 I *will* **p** unto the LORD your God 6419
42:20 **P** for us unto the LORD our God; 6419
La 1:18 hear, **I p you**, all people, and behold my 4994
Eze 33:30 **I p you**, and hear what *is* the word that 4994
Jnh 1:8 said they unto him, Tell us, **we p thee**, 4994
4:2 said, **I p thee**, O LORD, *was* not this my 577
Mic 3:1 I said, Hear, **I p you**, O heads of Jacob, 4994
3:9 Hear this, **I p you**, ye heads of the house of 4994
Hag 2:15 now, **I p you**, consider from this day and 4994
Zec 7:2 and their men, to **p** before the LORD, 2470
8:21 Let us go speedily to **p** before the LORD, 2470
8:22 in Jerusalem, and to **p** before the LORD. 2470
Mal 1:9 now, **I p you**, beseech God that he will be 4994
Mt 5:44 and **p** for them which despitefully use you, *4336*
6:5 they love to **p** standing in the synagogues *4336*
6:6 thy door, **p** to thy Father which is in secret; *4336*
6:7 But when ye **p**, use not vain repetitions, *4336*
6:9 After this manner therefore **p** ye: *4336*
9:38 **P** ye therefore the Lord of the harvest, *1189*
14:23 he went up into a mountain apart to **p**: *4336*
19:13 he should put *his* hands on them, and **p**: *4336*
24:20 But **p** ye that your flight be not in *4336*
26:36 Sit ye here, while I go and **p** yonder. *4336*
26:41 Watch and **p**, that ye enter not into *4336*
26:53 Thinkest thou that I cannot now **p** to my *3870*
Mk 5:17 And they began to **p** him to depart out of *3870*
5:23 *I p thee,* come and lay *thy* hands on her, NIG
6:46 he departed into a mountain to **p**. *4336*
11:24 when ye **p**, believe that ye receive *them,* *4336*
13:18 And **p** ye that your flight be not in *4336*
13:33 Take ye heed, watch and **p**: for ye know *4336*
14:32 to his disciples, Sit ye here, while I shall **p**. *4336*
14:38 Watch ye and **p**, lest ye enter into *4336*
Lk 6:12 *that* he went out into a mountain to **p**, and *4336*
6:28 and **p** for them which despitefully use you. *4336*
9:28 James, and went up into a mountain to **p**. *4336*
10:2 **p** ye therefore the Lord of the harvest, *1189*
11:1 Lord, teach us to **p**, as John also taught his *4336*
11:2 And he said unto them, When ye **p**, say, *4336*
14:18 and see it: I **p** thee have me excused. *2065*
14:19 to prove them: I **p** thee have me excused. *2065*
16:27 Then he said, I **p** thee therefore, father, *2065*
18:1 *to this end,* that *men* ought always to **p**, *4336*

Lk 18:10 Two men went up into the temple to **p**; *4336*
21:36 Watch ye therefore, and **p** always, that ye *1189*
22:40 **P** that *ye* enter not into temptation. *4336*
22:46 rise and **p**, lest ye enter into temptation. *4336*
Jn 14:16 And I will **p** the Father, and he shall give *2065*
16:26 unto you, that I will **p** the Father for you: *2065*
17:9 I **p** for them: I pray not for the world, but *2065*
17:9 I **p** not for the world, but for *them* which *2065*
17:15 I **p** not that thou shouldest take them out of *2065*
17:20 Neither **p** I for these alone, but for them *2065*
Ac 8:22 of this thy wickedness, and **p** God, *1189*
8:24 and said, **P** ye to the Lord for me, *1189*
8:34 eunuch answered Philip, and said, I **p** thee, *1189*
10:9 Peter went up upon the house to **p** about *4336*
24:4 I **p** *thee* that thou wouldest hear us of thy *3870*
27:34 Wherefore I **p** you to take *some* meat: *3870*
Ro 8:26 for we know not what we should **p** for as *4336*
1Co 11:13 is it comely that a woman **p** unto God *4336*
14:13 an *unknown* tongue **p** that he may interpret. *4336*
14:14 For if I **p** in an *unknown* tongue, my spirit *4336*
14:15 I will **p** with the spirit, and will pray with *4336*
14:15 and will **p** with the understanding also: *4336*
2Co 5:20 we **p** *you* in Christ's stead, be ye reconciled *1189*
13:7 Now I **p** to God that ye do no evil; not that *2172*
Php 1:9 And this I **p**, that your love may abound yet *4336*
Col 1:9 since the day we heard *it,* do not cease to **p** *4336*
1Th 5:17 **P** without ceasing. *4336*
5:23 and *I p God* your whole spirit and soul and NIG
5:25 Brethren, **p** for us. *4336*
2Th 1:11 Wherefore also we **p** always for you, *4336*
3:1 Finally, brethren, **p** for us, that the word of *4336*
1Ti 2:8 I will therefore that men **p** every where, *4336*
2Ti 4:16 *I p God* that it may not be laid to their NIG
Heb 13:18 **P** for us: for we trust we have a good *4336*
Jas 5:13 let him **p**. Is any merry? let him sing *4336*
5:14 and let them **p** over him, anointing him *4336*
5:16 and **p** one for another, that ye may be *2172*
1Jn 5:16 I do not say that he shall **p** for it. *2065*

PRAYED (65) [PRAY]

Ge 20:17 So Abraham **p** unto God: and God healed 6419
Nu 11:2 when Moses **p** unto the LORD, the fire 6419
21:7 from us. And Moses **p** for the people. 6419
Dt 9:20 and I **p** for Aaron also the same time. 6419
9:26 I **p** therefore unto the LORD, and said, 6419
1Sa 1:10 and **p** unto the LORD, and wept sore. 6419
1:27 For this child I **p**; and the LORD hath 6419
2:1 Hannah **p**, and said, My heart rejoiceth in 6419
8:6 judge us. And Samuel **p** unto the LORD. 6419
2Ki 4:33 upon them twain, and **p** unto the LORD. 6419
6:17 Elisha **p**, and said, LORD, I pray thee, 6419
6:18 Elisha **p** unto the LORD, and said, 6419
19:15 Hezekiah **p** before the LORD, and said, 6419
19:20 *That* which thou hast **p** to me against 6419
20:2 to the wall, and **p** unto the LORD, saying, 6419
2Ch 30:18 Hezekiah **p** for them, saying, The good 6419
32:20 the son of Amoz, **p** and cried *to* heaven. 6419
32:24 sick to the death, and **p** unto the LORD: 6419
33:13 **p** unto him: and he was intreated of him, 6419
Ezr 10:1 Now when Ezra had **p**, and when he had 6419
Ne 1:4 and fasted, and **p** before the God of heaven, 6419
2:4 make request? So I **p** to the God of heaven. 6419
Job 42:10 captivity of Job, when he **p** for his friends: 6419
Isa 37:15 And Hezekiah **p** unto the LORD, saying, 6419
37:21 Whereas thou hast **p** to me against 6419
38:2 toward the wall, and **p** unto the LORD, 6419
Jer 32:16 son of Neriah, I **p** unto the LORD, saying, 6419
Da 6:10 **p**, and gave thanks before his God, as he 6739
9:4 I **p** unto the LORD my God, and made my 6419
Jnh 2:1 Jonah **p** unto the LORD his God out of 6419
4:2 he **p** unto the LORD, and said, I pray thee, 6419
Mt 26:39 fell on his face, and **p**, saying, O my Father, *4336*
26:42 second time, and **p**, saying, O my Father, *4336*
26:44 and went away again, and **p** the third time, *4336*
Mk 1:35 departed into a solitary place, and there **p**. *4336*
5:18 he that had been possessed with the devil **p** *3870*
14:35 the ground, and **p** that, if it were possible, *4336*
14:39 and **p**, and spake the same words. *4336*
Lk 5:3 **p** him that *he* would thrust out a little from *2065*
5:16 himself into the wilderness, and **p**. *4336*
9:29 And as he **p**, the fashion of his countenance *4336*
18:11 The Pharisee stood and **p** thus with himself, *4336*
22:32 But I have **p** for thee, that thy faith fail not: *1189*
22:41 a stone's cast, and kneeled down, and **p**, *4336*
22:44 And being in an agony he **p** more earnestly: *4336*
Jn 4:31 In the mean while *his* disciples **p** him, *2065*
Ac 1:24 And they **p**, and said, Thou, Lord, *4336*
4:31 And when they had **p**, the place was shaken *1189*
6:6 and when they had **p**, they laid *their* hands *4336*
8:15 when they were come down, **p** for them, *4336*
9:40 *them* all forth, and kneeled down, and **p**; *4336*
10:2 alms to the people, and **p** to God alway. *1189*
10:30 and at the ninth hour I **p** in my house, and *4336*
10:48 Then **p** they him to tarry certain days. *2065*
13:3 And when they had fasted and **p**, and *4336*
14:23 and had **p** with fasting, they commended *4336*
16:9 and **p** him, saying, Come over into *3870*
16:25 And at midnight Paul and Silas **p**, and *4336*
20:36 he kneeled down, and **p** with them all. *4336*
21:5 and we kneeled down on the shore, and **p**. *4336*
22:17 even while I **p** in the temple, I was in a *4336*
23:18 **p** *me* to bring this young man unto thee, *2065*
28:8 and **p**, and laid *his* hands on him, and *4336*
Jas 5:17 he **p earnestly** that it might not rain: *4335+4336*
5:18 And he **p** again, and the heaven gave rain, *4336*

PRAYER (114) [PRAY]

2Sa 7:27 found in his heart to pray this **p** unto thee. 8605
1Ki 8:28 Yet have thou respect unto the **p** of thy 8605
8:28 to hearken unto the cry and to the **p**, 8605
8:29 **p** which thy servant shall **make** 6419+8605
8:38 What **p** and supplication soever be *made* by 8605
8:45 hear thou *in* heaven their **p** and their 8605
8:49 hear thou their **p** and their supplication *in* 8605
8:54 had made an end of praying all this **p** 8605
1Ki 9:3 I have heard thy **p** and thy supplication, 8605
2Ki 19:4 wherefore lift up *thy* **p** for the remnant that 8605
20:5 I have heard thy **p**, I have seen thy tears: 8605
2Ch 6:19 therefore to the **p** of thy servant, 8605
6:19 the **p** which thy servant prayeth before 8605
6:20 to hearken unto the **p** which thy servant 8605
6:29 *Then* what **p** *or* what supplication soever 8605
6:35 hear thou from the heavens their **p** and 8605
6:39 their **p** and their supplications, and 8605
6:40 *let* thine ears *be* attent unto the **p** *that is* 8605
7:12 I have heard thy **p**, and have chosen this 8605
7:15 mine ears attent unto the **p** *that is made* in 8605
30:27 their **p** came *up* to his holy dwelling place, 8605
33:18 his **p** unto his God, and the words of 8605
33:19 His **p** also, and *how God* was intreated of 8605
Ne 1:6 that *thou* mayest hear the **p** of thy servant, 8605
1:11 let now thine ear be attentive to the **p** of thy 8605
1:11 to the **p** of thy servants, who desire to fear 8605
4:9 Nevertheless we **made** our **p** unto our God, 6419
11:17 the principal to begin the thanksgiving in **p**: 8605
Job 15:4 off fear, and restrainest **p** before God. 7881
16:17 injustice in mine hands: also my **p** is pure. 8605
22:27 Thou shalt **make** thy **p** unto him, and 6279
Ps 4:1 have mercy upon me, and hear my **p**. 8605
5:3 *in* the morning will I direct *my* **p** unto thee, NIH
6:9 the LORD will receive my **p**. 8605
17:T A **P** of David. 8605
17:1 attend unto my cry, give ear unto my **p**, 8605
35:13 and my **p** returned into mine own bosom. 8605
39:12 Hear my **p**, O LORD, and give ear unto 8605
42:8 with me, *and my* **p** unto the God of my life. 8605
54:2 Hear my **p**, O God; give ear to the words of 8605
55:1 Give ear to my **p**, O God; and hide not 8605
61:1 Hear my cry, O God; attend unto my **p**. 8605
64:1 Hear my voice, O God, in my **p**: 7879
65:2 O thou that hearest **p**, unto thee shall all 8605
66:19 *me;* he hath attended to the voice of my **p**. 8605
66:20 *be* God, which hath not turned away my **p**, 8605
69:13 *as for* me, my **p** *is* unto thee, O LORD, 8605
72:15 **p** also shall be **made** for him continually; 6419
80:4 how long wilt thou be angry against the **p** 8605
84:8 O LORD God *of* hosts, hear my **p**: 8605
86:T A **P** of David. 8605
86:6 Give ear, O LORD, unto my **p**; and 8605
88:2 Let my **p** come before thee: incline thine 8605
88:13 and in the morning shall my **p** prevent thee. 8605
90:T A **P** of Moses the man of God. 8605
102:T A **P** of the afflicted, when he is 8605
102:1 Hear my **p**, O LORD, and let my cry 8605
102:17 He will regard the **p** of the destitute, and 8605
102:17 of the destitute, and not despise their **p**. 8605
109:4 my adversaries: but I *give myself unto* **p**. 8605
109:7 be condemned: and let his **p** become sin. 8605
141:2 Let my **p** be set forth before thee *as* 8605
141:5 for yet my **p** also *shall be* in their 8605
142:T of David; A **P** when he was in the cave. 8605
143:1 Hear my **p**, O LORD, give ear to my 8605
Pr 15:8 but the **p** of the upright *is* his delight. 8605
15:29 but he heareth the **p** of the righteous. 8605
28:9 the law, even his **p** *shall be* abomination. 8605
Isa 26:16 they poured out a **p** *when* thy chastening 3908
37:4 wherefore lift up *thy* **p** for the remnant that 8605
38:5 I have heard thy **p**, I have seen thy tears: 8605
56:7 and make them joyful in my house of **p**: 8605
56:7 for mine house shall be called a house of **p** 8605
Jer 7:16 neither lift up cry nor **p** for them, 8605
11:14 neither lift up a cry or **p** for them: 8605
La 3:8 when I cry and shout, he shutteth out my **p**. 8605
3:44 a cloud, that *our* **p** should not pass through. 8605
Da 9:3 to seek *by* **p** and supplications, with fasting, 8605
9:13 yet **made** we not our **p** before the LORD 2470
9:17 hear the **p** of thy servant, and 8605
9:21 Yea, whiles I *was* speaking in **p**, even 8605
Jnh 2:7 my **p** came in unto thee, into thine holy 8605
Hab 3:1 A **p** of Habakkuk the prophet upon 8605
Mt 17:21 this kind goeth not out but by **p** and fasting. *4335*
21:13 My house shall be called the house of **p**; *4335*
21:22 all *things,* whatsoever ye shall ask in **p**, *4335*
23:14 and for a pretence **make** long **p**: *4336*
Mk 9:29 forth by nothing, but by **p** and fasting. *4335*
11:17 shall be called of all nations the house of **p**? *4335*
Lk 1:13 for thy **p** is heard; and thy wife Elisabeth *1162*
6:12 to pray, and continued all night in **p** to God. *4335*
19:46 It is written, My house is the house of **p**: *4335*
22:45 And when he rose up from **p**, and *4335*
Ac 1:14 These all continued with one accord in **p** *4335*
3:1 up together into the temple at the hour of **p**, *4335*
6:4 But we will give ourselves continually to **p**, *4335*
10:31 thy **p** is heard, and thine alms are had in *4335*
12:5 **p** was made without ceasing of the church *4335*
16:13 a river side, where **p** was wont to be made; *4335*
16:16 And it came to pass, as we went to **p**, *4335*
Ro 10:1 my heart's desire and **p** to God for Israel is, *1162*
12:12 in tribulation; continuing instant in **p**; *4335*
1Co 7:5 ye may give yourselves to fasting and **p**, *4335*
2Co 1:11 You also helping together by **p** for us, *1162*
9:14 And by their **p** for you, which long after *1162*
Eph 6:18 Praying always with all **p** and *4335*
Php 1:4 Always in every **p** of mine for you all *1162*
1:19 shall turn to my salvation through your **p**, *1162*
4:6 but in every *thing* by **p** and supplication *4335*
Col 4:2 Continue in **p**, and watch in the same with *4335*
1Ti 4:5 it is sanctified by the word of God and **p**. *1783*
Jas 5:15 And the **p** of faith shall save the sick, and *2171*
5:16 The effectual fervent **p** of a righteous *man* *1162*
1Pe 4:7 be ye therefore sober, and watch unto **p**. *4335*

PRAYERS (24) [PRAY]

Ps 72:20 The **p** of David the son of Jesse are ended. 8605
Isa 1:15 yea, when ye make many **p**, I will not hear: 8605
Mk 12:40 and for a pretence **make** long **p**: *4336*
Lk 2:37 *God* with fastings and **p** night and day. *1162*
5:33 and make **p**, and likewise the *disciples* of *1162*
20:47 and for a shew **make** long **p**: *4336*
Ac 2:42 and in breaking of bread, and in **p**. *4335*

Ac 10: 4 Thy p and thine alms are come up for a 4335
Ro 1: 9 I make mention of you, always in my p, 4335
15:30 that ye strive together with me in your p to 4335
Eph 1:16 for you, making mention of you in my p; 4335
Col 4:12 always labouring fervently for you in p, 4335
1Th 1: 2 you all, making mention of you in our p; 4335
1Ti 2: 1 p, intercessions, and giving of thanks, 4335
5: 5 in supplications and p night and day. 4335
2Ti 1: 3 I have remembrance of thee in my p night 1162
Phm 1: 4 making mention of thee always in my p, 4335
1:22 for I trust that through your p I shall be 4335
Heb 5: 7 when he had offered up p and 1162
1Pe 3: 7 grace of life; that your p be not hindered. 4335
3:12 and his ears are open unto their p: 1162
Rev 5: 8 full of odours, which are the p of saints. 4335
8: 3 that he should offer it with the p of all 4335
8: 4 which came with the p of the saints, 4335

PRAYEST (2) [PRAY]

Mt 6: 5 And when thou p, thou shalt not be as 4336
6: 6 But thou, when thou p, enter into thy 4336

PRAYETH (7) [PRAY]

1Ki 8:28 which thy servant p before thee to day: 6419
2Ch 6:19 the prayer which thy servant p before thee: 6419
6:20 which thy servant p towards this place. 6419
Isa 44:17 worshippeth it, and p unto it, and saith, 6419
Ac 9:11 one called Saul, of Tarsus: for behold, he p, 4336
1Co 11: 5 But every woman that p or 4336
14:14 my spirit p, but my understanding is 4336

PRAYING (20) [PRAY]

1Sa 1:12 as she continued p before the LORD, 6419
1:26 that stood by thee here, p unto the LORD. 6419
1Ki 8:54 that when Solomon had made an end of p 6419
2Ch 7: 1 Now when Solomon had made an end of p, 6419
Da 6:11 found Daniel p and making supplication 1156
9:20 p, and confessing my sin and the sin of my 6419
Mk 11:25 And when ye stand p, forgive, if ye have 4336
Lk 1:10 were p without at the time of incense. 4336
3:21 and p, the heaven was opened, 4336
9:18 And it came to pass, as he was alone p, 4336
11: 1 And it came to pass that, as he was p in a 4336
Ac 11: 5 I was in the city of Joppa p: and in a trance 4336
12:12 where many were gathered together p. 4336
1Co 11: 4 Every man p or prophesying, having his 4336
2Co 8: 4 P us with much intreaty that we would 1189
Eph 6:18 P always with all prayer and supplication in 4336
Col 1: 3 of our Lord Jesus Christ, p always for you, 4336
4: 3 Withal p also for us, that God would open 4336
1Th 3:10 day p exceedingly that we might see your 1189
Jude 1:20 your most holy faith, p in the Holy Ghost, 4336

PREACH (50) [PREACHED, PREACHER, PREACHEST, PREACHETH, PREACHING]

Ne 6: 7 thou hast also appointed prophets to p of 7121
Isa 61: 1 me to p good tidings unto the meek; 1319
Jnh 3: 2 and p unto it the preaching that I bid thee. 7121
Mt 4:17 From that time Jesus began to p, and to say, 2784
10: 7 And as ye go, p, saying, The kingdom of 2784
10:27 in the ear, that p ye upon the housetops. 2784
11: 1 thence to teach and to p in their cities. 2784
Mk 1: 4 p the baptism of repentance for 2784
1:38 into the next towns, that I may p there also: 2784
3:14 and that he might send them forth to p, 2784
16:15 and p the gospel to every creature. 2784
Lk 4:18 he hath anointed me to p the gospel to 2097
4:18 to p deliverance to the captives, and 2784
4:19 To p the acceptable year of the Lord. 2784
4:43 I must p the kingdom of God to other cities 2097
9: 2 And he sent them to p the kingdom of God, 2784
9:60 but go thou and p the kingdom of God. 1229
Ac 5:42 they ceased not to teach and p Jesus Christ. 2097
10:42 And he commanded us to p unto 2784
14:15 p unto you that ye should turn from these 2097
15:21 old time hath in every city them that p him, 2784
16: 6 were forbidden of the Holy Ghost to p 2980
16:10 had called us for to p the gospel unto them. 2097
17: 3 this Jesus, whom I p unto you, is Christ. 2605
Ro 1:15 I am ready to p the gospel to you that are at 2097
10: 8 that is, the word of faith, which we p; 2784
10:15 And how shall they p, except they be sent? 2784
10:15 the feet of them that p the gospel of peace, 2097
15:20 Yea, so have I strived to p the gospel, 2097
1Co 1:17 sent me not to baptize, but to p the gospel: 2097
1:23 But we p Christ crucified, unto the Jews a 2784
9:14 hath the Lord ordained that they which p 2605
9:16 For though I p the gospel, I have nothing 2097
9:16 yea, woe is unto me, if I p not the gospel! 2097
9:18 Verily that, when I p the gospel, I may 2097
15:11 were I or they, so we p, and so ye believed. 2784
2Co 2:12 when I came to Troas to p Christ's gospel, NIG
4: 5 For we p not ourselves, but Christ Jesus 2784
10:16 To p the gospel in the regions beyond you, 2097
Gal 1: 8 p any other gospel unto you than that 2097
1: 9 If any man p any other gospel unto you 2097
1:16 that I might p him among the heathen; 2097
2: 2 that gospel which I p among the Gentiles, 2784
5:11 And I, brethren, if I yet p circumcision, 2784
Eph 3: 8 that I should p among the Gentiles 2097
Php 1:15 Some indeed p Christ even of envy and 2784
1:16 The one p Christ of contention, 2605
Col 1:28 Whom we p, warning every man, and 2605
2Ti 4: 2 P the word; be instant in season, out of 2784
Rev 14: 6 having the everlasting gospel to p unto 2097

PREACHED (61) [PREACH]

Ps 40: 9 I have p righteousness in the great 1319
Mt 11: 5 and the poor have the gospel p to them. 2097
24:14 And this gospel of the kingdom shall be p 2784
26:13 Wheresoever this gospel shall be p in 2784
Mk 1: 7 And p, saying, There cometh one mightier 2784
1:39 And he p in their synagogues throughout 2784
2: 2 the door: and he p the word unto them. 2980
6:12 went out, and p that men should repent. 2784
14: 9 Wheresoever this gospel shall be p 2784
16:20 And they went forth, and p every where, 2784
Lk 3:18 And many other things in his exhortation p 2097
4:44 And he p in the synagogues of Galilee. 2784
7:22 dead are raised, to the poor the gospel is p. 2097
16:16 since that time the kingdom of God is p, 2097
20: 1 and p the gospel, the chief priests and 2097
24:47 remission of sins should be p in his name 2784
Ac 3:20 Jesus Christ, which before was p unto you: 4296
4: 2 p through Jesus the resurrection from 2605
8: 5 the city of Samaria, and p Christ unto them. 2784
8:25 had testified and p the word of the Lord, 2980
8:25 p the gospel in many villages of 2097
8:35 at the same scripture, and p unto him Jesus. 2097
8:40 and passing through he p in all the cities, 2097
9:20 And straightway he p Christ in 2784
9:27 how he had p boldly at Damascus in 3955
10:37 after the baptism which John p; 2784
13: 5 they p the word of God in the synagogues 2605
13:24 When John had first p before his coming 4296
13:38 that through this man is p unto you 2605
13:42 words might be p to them the next sabbath. 2980
14: 7 And there they p the gospel. 2097
14:21 And when they had p the gospel to that 2097
14:25 And when they had p the word in Perga, 2980
15:36 city where we have p the word of the Lord, 2605
17:13 the word of God was p of Paul at Berea, 2605
17:18 because he p unto them Jesus, and 2097
20: 7 Paul p unto them, ready to depart on 1256
Ro 15:19 I have fully p the gospel of Christ. NIG
1Co 9:27 that by any means, when I have p to others, 2784
15: 1 I declare unto you the gospel which I p 2097
15: 2 if ye keep in memory what I p unto you, 2097
15:12 Now if Christ be p that he rose from 2784
2Co 1:19 who was p among you by us, even by me 2784
11: 4 whom we have not p, or if ye receive 2784
11: 7 I have p to you the gospel of God freely? 2097
Gal 1: 8 you than that which we have p unto you, 2097
1:11 that the gospel which was p of me is not 2097
3: 8 p before the gospel unto Abraham, 4283
4:13 flesh I p the gospel unto you at the first. 2097
Eph 2:17 and p peace to you which were afar off, 2097
Php 1:18 whether in pretence, or in truth, Christ is p; 2605
Col 1:23 which was p to every creature which is 2784
1Th 2: 9 of you, we p unto you the gospel of God. 2784
1Ti 3:16 seen of angels, p unto the Gentiles, 2784
Heb 4: 2 For unto us was the gospel p, as well as 2097
4: 2 but the word p did not profit them, 189
4: 6 they to whom it was first p entered not in 2097
1Pe 1:12 p the gospel unto you with the Holy Ghost 2097
1:25 word which by the gospel is p unto you. 2097
3:19 he went and p unto the spirits in prison; 2784
4: 6 For for this cause was the gospel p also to 2097

PREACHER (11) [PREACH]

Ecc 1: 1 The words of the P, the son of David, 6953
1: 2 of vanities, saith the P, vanity of vanities; 6953
1:12 I the P was king over Israel in Jerusalem. 6953
7:27 Behold, this have I found, saith the P, 6953
12: 8 Vanity of vanities, saith the P; all is vanity. 6953
12: 9 moreover, because the P was wise, he still 6953
12:10 The P sought to find out acceptable words: 6953
Ro 10:14 and how shall they hear without a p? 2784
1Ti 2: 7 Whereunto I am ordained a p, and 2783
2Ti 1:11 Whereunto I am appointed a p, and 2783
2Pe 2: 5 saved Noah the eighth person, a p of 2783

PREACHEST (1) [PREACH]

Ro 2:21 thou that p a man should not steal, 2784

PREACHETH (3) [PREACH]

Ac 19:13 We adjure you by Jesus whom Paul p. 2784
2Co 11: 4 For if he that cometh p another Jesus, 2784
Gal 1:23 now p the faith which once he destroyed. 2097

PREACHING (27) [PREACH]

Jnh 3: 2 and preach unto it the p that I bid thee. 7150
Mt 3: 1 the Baptist, p in the wilderness of Judea, 2784
4:23 and p the gospel of the kingdom, 2784
9:35 and p the gospel of the kingdom, and 2784
12:41 because they repented at the p of Jonas; 2782
Mk 1:14 p the gospel of the kingdom of God, 2784
Lk 3: 3 p the baptism of repentance for 2784
8: 1 p and shewing the glad tidings of 2784
9: 6 p the gospel, and healing every where. 2097
11:32 for they repented at the p of Jonas; and 2782
Ac 8: 4 abroad went every where p the word. 2097
8:12 But when they believed Philip p the things 2097
10:36 children of Israel, p peace by Jesus Christ: 2097
11:19 p the word to none but unto the Jews only. 2980
11:20 spake unto the Grecians, p the Lord Jesus. 2097
15:35 teaching and p the word of the Lord, 2097
20: 9 and as Paul was long p, he sunk down with 1256
20:25 among whom I have gone p the kingdom of 2784
28:31 P the kingdom of God, and teaching those 2784
Ro 16:25 and the p of Jesus Christ, according to 2782
1Co 1:18 For the p of the cross is to them that perish 3056
1:21 it pleased God by the foolishness of p to 2782
2: 4 my p was not with enticing words of man's 2782
15:14 then is our p vain, and your faith is also 2782
2Co 10:14 for we are come as far as to you also in p NIG
2Ti 4:17 that by me the p might be fully known, and 2782
Tit 1: 3 due times manifested his word through p, 2782

PRECEPT (11) [PRECEPTS]

Isa 28:10 For p must be upon precept, precept upon 6673
28:10 For precept must be upon p, precept upon 6673
28:10 must be upon precept, p upon precept; 6673
28:10 must be upon precept, precept upon p; 6673
28:13 the word of the LORD was unto them p 6673
28:13 the LORD was unto them precept upon p, 6673
28:13 them precept upon precept, p upon precept; 6673
28:13 them precept upon precept, precept upon p; 6673
Isa 29:13 their fear towards me is taught by the p of 4687
Mk 10: 5 hardness of your heart he wrote you this p. 1785
Heb 9:19 For when Moses had spoken every p to all 1785

PRECEPTS (24) [PRECEPT]

Ne 9:14 commandedst them p, statutes, and laws, 4687
Ps 119: 4 Thou hast commanded us to keep thy p 6490
119:15 I will meditate in thy p, and have respect 6490
119:27 Make me to understand the way of thy p: 6490
119:40 Behold, I have longed after thy p: 6490
119:45 And I will walk at liberty: for I seek thy p. 6490
119:56 This I had, because I kept thy p. 6490
119:63 that fear thee, and of them that keep thy p. 6490
119:69 but I will keep thy p with my whole heart. 6490
119:78 a cause: but I will meditate in thy p. 6490
119:87 me upon earth; but I forsook not thy p. 6490
119:93 I will never forget thy p: for with them thou 6490
119:94 am thine, save me; for I have sought thy p. 6490
119:100 than the ancients, because I keep thy p. 6490
119:104 Through thy p I get understanding: 6490
119:110 a snare for me: yet I erred not from thy p. 6490
119:128 Therefore I esteem all thy p concerning all 6490
119:134 the oppression of man: so will I keep thy p. 6490
119:141 and despised: yet do not I forget thy p. 6490
119:159 Consider how I love thy p: quicken me, 6490
119:168 I have kept thy p and thy testimonies: 6490
119:173 hand help me; for I have chosen thy p. 6490
Jer 35:18 kept all his p, and done according unto all 4687
Da 9: 5 even by departing from thy p and from thy 4687

PRECIOUS (76)

Ge 24:53 to her brother and to her mother p things. 4030
Dt 33:13 for the p things of heaven, for the dew, and 4022
33:14 for the p fruits brought forth by the sun, 4022
33:14 and for the p things put forth by the moon, 4022
33:15 and for the p things of the lasting hills, 4022
33:16 for the p things of the earth and 4022
1Sa 3: 1 the word of the LORD was p in those 3368
26:21 my soul was p in thine eyes this day: 3365
2Sa 12:30 was a talent of gold with the p stones: 3368
1Ki 10: 2 and very much gold, and p stones: 3368
10:10 and of spices very great store, and p stones: 3368
10:11 great plenty of almug trees, and p stones. 3368
2Ki 1:13 of these fifty thy servants, be p in thy sight. 3365
1:14 therefore let my life now be p in thy sight. 3365
20:13 shewed them all the house of his p things, 5238
20:13 the p ointment, and all the house of his 2896
1Ch 20: 2 talent of gold, and there were p stones in it; 3368
29: 2 all manner of p stones, and marble stones 3368
29: 8 they with whom p stones were found gave NIH
2Ch 3: 6 he garnished the house with p stones for 3368
9: 1 and gold in abundance, and p stones: 3368
9: 9 of spices great abundance, and p stones: 3368
9:10 brought algum trees and p stones. 3368
20:25 p jewels, which they stript off for 2532
21: 3 of gold, and of p things, with fenced cities 4030
32:27 for p stones, and for spices, and for shields, 3368
Ezr 1: 6 and with beasts, and with p things, 4030
8:27 and two vessels of fine copper, p as gold. 2532
Job 28:10 the rocks; and his eye seeth every p thing. 3366
28:16 of Ophir, with the p onyx, or the sapphire. 3368
Ps 49: 8 (For the redemption of their soul is p, and 3365
72:14 and p shall their blood be in his sight. 3365
116:15 P in the sight of the LORD is the death of 3368
126: 6 goeth forth and weepeth, bearing p seed, 4901
133: 2 It is like the p ointment upon the head, 2896
139:17 How p also are thy thoughts unto me, 3365
Pr 1:13 We shall find all p substance, we shall fill 3368
3:15 She is more p than rubies: and all the things 3368
6:26 and the adulteress will hunt for the p life. 3368
12:27 but the substance of a diligent man is p. 3368
17: 8 A gift is as a p stone in the eyes of him that 2580
20:15 but the lips of knowledge are a p jewel. 3366
24: 4 shall the chambers be filled with all p 3368
Ecc 7: 1 A good name is better than p ointment; and 2896
Isa 13:12 I will make a man more p than fine gold; 3365
28:16 a p corner stone, a sure foundation: 3368
39: 2 shewed them the house of his p things, 5238
39: 2 the p ointment, and all the house of his 2896
43: 4 Since thou wast p in my sight, thou hast 3365
Jer 15:19 if thou take forth the p from the vile, 3368
20: 5 all the p things thereof, and all 3366
La 4: 2 The p sons of Zion, comparable to fine 3368
Eze 22:25 they have taken the treasure and p things; 3366
27:20 Dedan was thy merchant in p clothes for 2667
27:22 all spices, and with all p stones, and gold. 3368
28:13 every p stone was thy covering, the sardius, 3368
Da 11: 8 and with their p vessels of silver and 2532
11:38 and with p stones, and pleasant things. 3368
11:43 of silver, and over all the p things of Egypt: 2532
Mt 26: 7 having an alabaster box of very p ointment, 927
Mk 14: 3 box of ointment of spikenard very p; 4185
1Co 3:12 silver, p stones, wood, hay, stubble; 5093
Jas 5: 7 the husbandman waiteth for the p fruit of 5093
1Pe 1: 7 being much more p than of gold that 5093
1:19 But with the p blood of Christ, as of a lamb 5093
2: 4 indeed of men, but chosen of God, and p, 1784
2: 6 I lay in Sion a chief corner stone, elect, p: 1784
2: 7 Unto you therefore which believe he is p: 5092
2Pe 1: 1 to them that have obtained like p faith with 2472
1: 4 unto us exceeding great and p promises: 5093
Rev 17: 4 decked with gold and p stone and pearls, 5093
18:12 and p stones, and of pearls, and fine linen, 5093
18:12 and all manner vessels of most p wood, 5093
18:16 decked with gold, and p stones, and pearls! 5093
21:11 and her light was like unto a stone most p, 5093
21:19 were garnished with all manner of p stones. 5093

PREDESTINATE (2) [PREDESTINATED]

Ro 8:29 he also did p to be conformed to the image 4309
8:30 Moreover whom he did p, them he also 4309

PREDESTINATED (2) [PREDESTINATE]

Eph 1: 5 Having p us unto the adoption of children 4309

Eph 1:11 being p according to the purpose of him 4309

PREDESTINED See PREDESTINATE; PREDESTINATED

PREEMINENCE (3) [EMINENT]
Ecc 3:19 so that a man hath no p above a beast: 4195
Col 1:18 that in all *things* he might have the p. *4409*
3Jn 1:9 who loveth to have the p among them, *5383*

PREFER (1) [PREFERRED, PREFERRING]
Ps 137:6 if I p not Jerusalem above my chief joy. 5927

PREFERRED (5) [PREFER]
Est 2:9 he p her and her maids unto the best *place* 8138
Da 6:3 this Daniel was p above the presidents 5330
Jn 1:15 that cometh after me is p before me: *1096+1715*
1:27 it is, who coming after me is p before me, *1096*
1:30 cometh a man which is p before me: *1096+1715*

PREFERRING (2) [PREFER]
Ro 12:10 brotherly love; in honour p one another; *4285*
1Ti 5:21 that thou observe these *things* without p *4299*

PREMEDITATE (1)
Mk 13:11 what ye shall speak, neither do ye p: *3191*

PREPARATION (9) [PREPARE]
1Ch 22:5 I will *therefore* now make p for it. 3559
Na 2:3 *be* with flaming torches in the day of his p, 3559
Mt 27:62 that followed the *day of the* p, the chief *3904*
Mk 15:42 because it was the p, that is, the day before *3904*
Lk 23:54 And *that* day was the p, and the sabbath *3904*
Jn 19:14 And it was the p of the passover, and *3904*
19:31 The Jews therefore, because it was the p, *3904*
19:42 of the Jews' p *day;* for the sepulchre was *3904*
Eph 6:15 And *your* feet shod with the p of the gospel *2091*

PREPARATIONS (1) [PREPARE]
Pr 16:1 The p of the heart in man, and the answer 4633

PREPARE (81) [PREPARATION, PREPARATIONS, PREPARED, PREPAREDST, PREPAREST, PREPARETH, PREPARING, UNPREPARED]
Ex 15:2 *is* my God, and I will p him a habitation; 5115
16:5 that on the sixth day they shall p *that* which 3559
Nu 15:5 offering shalt thou p with the burnt offering 6213
15:6 thou shalt p *for* a meat offering two tenth 6213
15:12 According to the number that ye shall p, so 6213
23:1 and p me here seven oxen and seven rams. 3559
23:29 p me here seven bullocks and seven rams. 3559
Dt 19:3 Thou shalt p thee a way, and divide 3559
Jos 1:11 the people, saying, P you victuals; 3559
22:26 we said, Let us now p to build us an altar, 6213
1Sa 7:3 p your hearts unto the LORD, and 3559
23:22 p yet, and know and see his place where his 3559
1Ki 18:44 unto Ahab, P *thy chariot,* and get thee down, 631
1Ch 9:32 over the shewbread, to p *it* every sabbath. 3559
29:18 of thy people, and p their heart unto thee: 3559
2Ch 2:9 Even to p me timber in abundance: for 3559
31:11 Hezekiah commanded to p chambers in 3559
35:4 p *yourselves* by the houses of your fathers, 3559
35:6 sanctify yourselves, and p your brethren, 3559
Est 5:8 Haman come to the banquet that I shall p 6213
Job 8:8 and p *thyself* to the search of their fathers: 3559
11:13 If thou p thine heart, and stretch out thine 3559
27:16 silver as the dust, and p raiment as the clay; 3559
27:17 He may p *it,* but the just shall put *it* on, and 3559
Ps 10:17 thou wilt p their heart, thou wilt cause thine 3559
59:4 and p themselves without *my* fault: 3559
61:7 O p mercy and truth, *which* may preserve 4487
107:36 that they may p a city for habitation; 3559
Pr 24:27 P thy work without, and make it fit for 3559
30:25 yet they p their meat in the summer; 3559
Isa 14:21 P slaughter for his children for the iniquity 3559
21:5 P the table, watch *in* the watchtower, eat, 6186
40:3 P ye the way of the LORD, 6437
40:20 a cunning workman to p a graven image, 3559
57:14 shall say, Cast ye up, cast ye up, p the way, 6437
62:10 p you the way of the people; cast up, 6437
65:11 that p a table for *that* troop, and that furnish 6186
Jer 6:4 P ye war against her; arise, and let us go up 6942
12:3 and p them for the day of slaughter. 6942
22:7 I will p destroyers against thee, every one 6942
46:14 say ye, Stand fast, and p thee; for the sword 3559
51:12 set up the watchmen, p the ambushes: 3559
51:27 the nations, p the nations against her, 6942
51:28 P against her the nations with the kings of 6942
Eze 4:15 and thou shalt p thy bread therewith. 6213
12:3 p thee stuff for removing, and remove by 6213
35:6 I will p thee unto blood, and blood shall 6213
38:7 p for thyself, thou, and all thy company 3559
43:25 Seven days shalt thou p every day a goat 6213
43:25 they shall also p a young bullock, and 6213
45:17 he shall p the sin offering, and the meat 6213
45:22 upon that day shall the prince p for himself 6213
45:23 seven days of the feast he shall p a burnt 6213
45:24 he shall p a meat offering *of* an ephah for a 6213
46:2 the priests shall p his burnt offering and 6213
46:7 he shall p a meat offering, an ephah for a 6213
46:12 Now when the prince shall p a voluntary 6213
46:12 he shall p his burnt offering and his peace 6213
46:13 Thou shalt daily p a burnt offering unto 6213
46:13 thou shalt p it every morning. 6213
46:14 thou shalt p a meat offering for it every 6213
46:15 Thus shall they p the lamb, and the meat 6213
Joel 3:9 P war, wake up the mighty *men,* let all 6942
Am 4:12 this unto thee, p to meet thy God, O Israel. 3559
Mic 3:5 their mouths, they even p war against him. 6942
Mal 3:1 and he shall p the way before me: 6437
Mt 3:3 P ye the way of the Lord, make his paths *2090*
11:10 thy face, which shall p thy way before thee. *2680*
26:17 Where wilt thou *that* we p for thee to eat *2090*
Mk 1:2 thy face, which shall p thy way before thee. *2680*
1:3 P ye the way of the Lord, make his paths *2090*
14:12 and p that thou mayest eat the passover? *2090*
Lk 1:76 before the face of the Lord to p his ways; *2090*
3:4 P ye the way of the Lord, make his paths *2090*
7:27 thy face, which shall p thy way before thee. *2680*
22:8 and John, saying, Go and p us the passover, *2090*
22:9 said unto him, Where wilt thou *that* we p? *2090*
Jn 14:2 have told you. I go to p a place for you. *2090*
14:3 And if I go and p a place for you, I will *2090*
1Co 14:8 who shall p himself to the battle? *3903*
Phm 1:22 But withal p me also a lodging: for I trust *2090*

PREPARED (101) [PREPARE]
Ge 24:31 for I have p the house, and room for 6437
27:17 and the bread, which she had p, 6213
Ex 12:39 neither had they p for themselves any 6213
23:20 to bring thee into the place which I have p. 3559
Nu 21:27 let the city of Sihon be built and p: 3559
23:4 I have p seven altars, and I have offered 6186
Jos 4:4 whom he had p of the children of Israel, 3559
4:13 About forty thousand p for war passed over 2502
2Sa 15:1 that Absalom p him chariots and horses, 6213
1Ki 1:5 he p him chariots and horsemen, and 6213
5:18 so they p timber and stones to build 3559
6:19 the oracle he p in the house within, to set 3559
2Ki 6:23 he p great provision for them: and 3739
1Ch 12:39 drinking: for their brethren had p for them. 3559
15:1 p a place for the ark of God, and 3559
15:3 unto his place, which he had p for it. 3559
15:12 of Israel unto *the place that* I have p for it. 3559
22:3 David p iron in abundance for the nails for 3559
22:5 So David p abundantly before his death. 3559
22:14 in my trouble I have p for the house of 3559
22:14 timber also and stone have I p; and 3559
29:2 Now I have p with all my might for 3559
29:3 above all *that* I have p for the holy house, 3559
29:16 all this store that we have p to build thee a 3559
2Ch 1:4 to *the place which* David had p for it: 3559
3:1 in the place that David had p in 3559
8:16 Now all the work of Solomon was p unto 3559
12:14 he p not his heart to seek the LORD. 3559
16:14 divers kinds *of spices* p by 7543
17:18 fourscore thousand ready p for the war. 2502
19:3 the land, and hast p thine heart to seek God. 3559
20:33 for as yet the people had not p their hearts 3559
26:14 Uzziah p for them throughout all the host 3559
27:6 he p his ways before the LORD his God. 3559
29:19 have we p and sanctified, and, behold, 3559
29:36 all the people, that God had p the people: 3559
31:11 the house of the LORD; and they p *them,* 3559
35:10 So the service was p, and the priests stood 3559
35:14 therefore the Levites p for themselves, and 3559
35:15 for their brethren the Levites p for them. 3559
35:16 So all the service of the LORD was p 3559
35:20 all this, when Josiah had p the temple, 3559
Ezr 7:10 For Ezra had p his heart to seek the law of 3559
Ne 5:18 Now *that* which was p *for me* daily *was* 6213
5:18 also fowls were p for me, and once in ten 6213
8:10 portions unto *them* for whom nothing is p: 3559
13:5 he had p for him a great chamber, where 6213
Est 5:4 day unto the banquet that I have p for him. 6213
5:5 came to the banquet that Esther had p. 6213
5:12 the king unto the banquet that she had p 6213
6:4 on the gallows that he had p for him. 3559
6:14 Haman unto the banquet that Esther had p. 6213
7:10 on the gallows that he had p for Mordecai. 3559
Job 28:27 declare it; he p it, yea, and searched it out. 3559
29:7 the city, *when* I p my seat in the street; 3559
Ps 7:13 He hath also p for him the instruments of 3559
9:7 for ever: he hath p his throne for judgment. 3559
57:6 They have p a net for my steps; my soul is 3559
68:10 O God, hast p of thy goodness for the poor. 3559
74:16 *is* thine: thou hast p the light and the sun. 3559
103:19 The LORD hath p his throne in 3559
Pr 8:27 When he p the heavens, I *was* there: 3559
19:29 Judgments are p for scorners, and 3559
21:31 The horse *is* p against the day of battle: but 3559
Isa 30:33 yea, for the king it is p; he hath made *it* 3559
64:4 *what* he hath p for him that waiteth for him. 6213
Eze 23:41 upon a stately bed, and a table p before it, 6186
28:13 of thy pipes was p in thee in the day that 3559
38:7 Be thou p, and prepare for thyself, thou, 3559
Da 2:9 for ye have p lying and corrupt words to 2164
Hos 2:8 her silver and gold, *which* they p for Baal. 6213
6:3 his going forth *is* p as the morning; and 3559
Jnh 1:17 Now the LORD had p a great fish to 4487
4:6 the LORD God p a gourd, and made *it* to 4487
4:7 God p a worm when the morning rose 4487
4:8 did arise, that God p a vehement east wind; 4487
Na 2:5 the wall thereof, and the defence shall be p. 3559
Zep 1:7 for the LORD hath p a sacrifice, he hath 3559
Mt 20:23 *it shall be given to them* for whom it is p of *2090*
22:4 are bidden, Behold, I have p my dinner: *2090*
25:34 inherit the kingdom p for you from *2090*
25:41 p for the devil and his angels: *2090*
Mk 10:40 *it shall be given to them* for whom it is p. *2090*
14:15 you a large upper room furnished *and* p: *2092*
Lk 1:17 to make ready a people p for the Lord. *2680*
2:31 Which thou hast p before the face of all *2090*
12:47 p not *himself,* neither did according to his *2090*
23:56 they returned, and p spices and ointments; *2090*
24:1 bringing the spices which they had p, and *2090*
Ro 9:23 of mercy, which he had afore p unto glory, *4282*
1Co 2:9 *the things* which God hath p for them that *2090*
2Ti 2:21 master's use, *and* p unto every good work. *2090*
Heb 10:5 wouldest not, but a body hast thou p me: *2675*
11:7 p an ark to the saving of his house; *2680*
11:16 their God: for he hath p for them a city. *2090*
Rev 8:6 the seven trumpets p themselves to sound. *2090*
9:7 locusts *were* like unto horses p unto battle; *2090*
9:15 which were p for an hour, and a day, and *2090*
12:6 where she hath a place p of God, *2090*
16:12 the way of the kings of the east might be p. *2090*
21:2 p as a bride adorned for her husband. *2090*

PREPAREDST (1) [PREPARE]
Ps 80:9 Thou p *room* before it, and didst cause it to 6437

PREPAREST (3) [PREPARE]
Nu 15:8 when thou p a bullock *for* a burnt offering, 6213
Ps 23:5 Thou p a table before me in the presence of 6186
65:9 thou p them corn, when thou hast so 3559

PREPARETH (3) [PREPARE]
2Ch 30:19 *That* p his heart to seek God, the LORD 3559
Job 15:35 bring forth vanity, and their belly p deceit. 3559
Ps 147:8 with clouds, who p rain for the earth, 3559

PREPARING (2) [PREPARE]
Ne 13:7 in p him a chamber in the courts of 6213
1Pe 3:20 while the ark was a p, wherein few, that is, *2680*

PRESBYTERY (1)
1Ti 4:14 with the laying on of the hands of the p. *4244*

PRESCRIBED (1) [PRESCRIBING]
Isa 10:1 that write grievousness *which* they have p; 3789

PRESCRIBING (1) [PRESCRIBED]
Ezr 7:22 baths *of* oil, and salt without p *how much.* 3792

PRESENCE (116) [PRESENT]
Ge 3:8 his wife hid themselves from the p of 6440
4:16 Cain went out from the p of 6440+3807.1
16:12 he shall dwell in the p of all his brethren. 6440
23:11 in the p of the sons of my people give I it 5869
23:18 Unto Abraham for a possession in the p of 5869
25:18 *and* he died in the p of all his brethren. 6440
27:30 Jacob was yet scarce gone out from the p of 6440
41:46 Joseph went out from the p of Pharaoh, 6440
45:3 answer him; for they were troubled at his p. 6440
47:15 for why should we die in thy p? for 5048
Ex 10:11 they were driven out from Pharaoh's p. 6440
33:14 My p shall go *with thee,* and I will give 6440
33:15 If thy p go not *with me,* carry us not up 6440
35:20 of Israel departed from the p of Moses. 6440
Lev 22:3 that soul shall be cut off from my p: 6440
Nu 20:6 Aaron went from the p of the assembly 6440
Dt 25:9 wife come unto him in the p of the elders, 5869
Jos 4:11 and the priests, in the p of the people. 6440
8:32 which he wrote in the p of the children of 6440
1Sa 18:11 *it.* And David avoided out of his p twice. 6440
19:7 and he was in his p, as in times past. 6440
19:10 he slipt away out of Saul's p, and he smote 6440
21:15 this *fellow* to play the mad man in my p? 5921
2Sa 16:19 *should* I not *serve* in the p of his son? as I 6440
16:19 as I have served in thy father's p, so will I 6440
16:19 thy father's presence, so will I be in thy p. 6440
24:4 the captains of the host went out from the p 6440
1Ki 1:28 she came into the king's p, and 6440
8:22 in the p of all the congregation of Israel, 5048
12:2 heard *of it,* (for he was fled from the p of 6440
21:13 in the p of the people, saying, 5048
2Ki 3:14 were it not that I regard the p of 6440
5:27 he went out from his p a leper *as white* as 6440
13:23 neither cast he them from his p as yet. 6440
24:20 until he had cast them out from his p, 6440
25:19 of them that were in the king's p, 6440+7200
1Ch 16:27 Glory and honour *are* in his p; strength and 6440
16:33 shall the trees of the wood sing out at the p 6440
24:31 sons of Aaron in the p of David the king, 6440
2Ch 6:12 in the p of all the congregation of Israel, 5048
9:23 all the kings of the earth sought the p of 6440
10:2 whither he had fled from the p of Solomon 6440
20:9 we stand before this house, and in thy p, 6440
34:4 brake down the altars of Baalim in his p; 6440
Ne 2:1 Now I had not been *beforetime* sad in his p. 6440
Est 1:10 the seven chamberlains that served in the p 6440
8:15 Mordecai went out from the p of the king 6440
Job 1:12 So Satan went forth from the p of 6440
2:7 So went Satan forth from the p of 6440
23:15 Therefore am I troubled at his p: when I 6440
Ps 9:3 they shall fall and perish at thy p. 6440
16:11 in thy p *is* fulness of joy; at thy right hand 6440
17:2 Let my sentence come forth from thy p, 6440
23:5 Thou preparest a table before me in the p 5048
31:20 Thou shalt hide them in the secret of thy p 6440
51:11 Cast me not away from thy p; and take not 6440
68:2 *so* let the wicked perish at the p of God. 6440
68:8 the heavens also dropped at the p of God: 6440
68:8 *even* Sinai itself *was moved* at the p of 6440
95:2 Let us come before his p with 6440
97:5 The hills melted like wax at the p of 6440
97:5 at the p of the Lord of the whole earth. 6440
100:2 come before his p with singing. 6440
114:7 Tremble, thou earth, at the p of the Lord, 6440
114:7 at the p of the God of Jacob; 6440+3807.1
116:14 the LORD now in the p of all his people. 5048
116:18 the LORD now in the p of all his people, 5048
139:7 or whither shall I flee from thy p? 6440
140:13 thy name: the upright shall dwell in thy p. 6440
Pr 14:7 Go from the p of a foolish man, when thou 5048
17:18 *and* becometh surety in the p of his friend. 6440
25:6 Put not forth thyself in the p of the king, 6440
25:7 p of the prince whom thine eyes have seen. 6440
Isa 1:7 strangers devour it in your p, and *it is* 5048
19:1 the idols of Egypt shall be moved at his p, 6440
63:9 and the angel of his p saved them: 6440
64:1 the mountains might flow down at thy p, 6440
64:2 *that* the nations may tremble at thy p. 6440
64:3 the mountains flowed down at thy p. 6440
Jer 4:26 were broken down at the p of the LORD, 6440
5:22 will ye not tremble at my p, which have 6440
23:39 and your fathers, *and cast you* out of my p: 6440
28:1 in the p of the priests and of all the people, 5869
28:5 the prophet Hananiah in the p of the priests, 5869
28:5 in the p of all the people that stood in 5869
28:11 Hananiah spake in the p of all the people, 5869
32:12 in the p of the witnesses that subscribed 5869

P

Jer 52: 3 Judah, till he had cast them out from his **p**, 6440
Eze 38:20 shall shake at my **p**, and the mountains 6440
Da 2:27 Daniel answered **in the p** of the king, and 6925
Jnh 1: 3 Tarshish from the **p** of the LORD, 6440+3807.1
1: 3 Tarshish from the **p** of the LORD. 6440+3807.1
1:10 For the men knew that he fled from the **p** of 6440
Na 1: 5 the earth is burnt at his **p**, yea, the world, 6440
Zep 1: 7 Hold thy peace at the **p** of the Lord GOD: 6440
Lk 1:19 I am Gabriel, that stand **in the p** of God; *1799*
13:26 We have eaten and drunk **in** thy **p**, and *1799*
14:10 shalt thou have worship **in the p** of them *1799*
15:10 there is joy **in the p** of the angels of God *1799*
Jn 20:30 truly did Jesus **in the p** of his disciples, *1799*
Ac 3:13 and denied him **in the p** of Pilate, *2596+4383*
3:16 this perfect soundness **in the p** of you all. *561*
3:19 shall come from the **p** of the Lord; *4383*
5:41 And they departed from the **p** of *4383*
27:35 and gave thanks to God **in p** of *them* all: *1799*
1Co 1:29 That no flesh should glory in his **p**. *1799*
2Co 10: 1 who in **p** *am* base among you, but *4383*
10:10 but *his* bodily **p** *is* weak, and *his* speech *3952*
Php 2:12 not as in my **p** only, but now much more in *3952*
1Th 2:17 being taken from you for a short time **in p**, *4383*
2:19 *Are* not even ye **in the p** of our Lord Jesus *1715*
2Th 1: 9 destruction from the **p** of the Lord, *4383*
Heb 9:24 now to appear in the **p** of God for us: *4383*
Jude 1:24 to present *you* faultless **before the p** of his *2714*
Rev 14:10 and brimstone **in the p** of the holy angels, *1799*
14:10 the holy angels, and **in the p** of the Lamb: *1799*

PRESENT (106) [PRESENCE, PRESENTED, PRESENTING, PRESENTLY, PRESENTS]

Ge 32:13 took of that which came to his hand a **p** for 4503
32:18 it *is* a **p** sent unto my lord Esau: 4503
32:20 I will appease him with the **p** that goeth 4503
32:21 So went the **p** over before him: and 4503
33:10 in thy sight, then receive my **p** at my hand: 4503
43:11 carry down the man a **p**, a little balm, and 4503
43:15 the men took that **p**, and they took double 4503
43:25 they made ready the **p** against Joseph came 4503
43:26 they brought him the **p** which *was* in their 4503
Ex 34: 2 **p** thyself there to me in the top of 5324
Lev 14:11 the priest that maketh *him* clean shall **p** 5975
16: 7 **p** them before the LORD *at* the door of 5975
27: 8 he shall **p** himself before the priest, and 5975
27:11 then he shall **p** the beast before the priest: 5975
Nu 3: 6 and **p** them before Aaron the priest, 5975
Dt 31:14 **p** yourselves in the tabernacle of 3320
Jdg 3:15 by him the children of Israel sent a **p** unto 4503
3:17 he brought the **p** unto Eglon king of Moab: 4503
3:18 when he had made an end to offer the **p**, 4503
3:18 he sent away the people that bare the **p**. 4503
6:18 and bring forth my **p**, and set *it* before thee. 4503
1Sa 9: 7 *there is* not a **p** to bring to the man of God: 8670
10:19 **p** yourselves before the LORD by your 3320
13:15 Saul numbered the people that were **p** with 4672
13:16 and the people that were **p** with them, 4672
21: 3 *of* bread in mine hand, or what there is **p**. 4672
30:26 Behold a **p** for you of the spoil of 1293
2Sa 20: 4 *within* three days, and be thou here **p**. 5975
1Ki 9:16 given it *for* a **p** unto his daughter, 7964
10:25 they brought every man his **p**, vessels of 4503
15:19 I have sent unto thee a **p** of silver and gold; 7810
20:27 and were all **p**, and went against them: 3557
2Ki 8: 8 Take a **p** in thine hand, and go, meet 4503
8: 9 went to meet him, and took a **p** with him, 4503
16: 8 and sent *it for* a **p** to the king of Assyria. 7810
17: 4 brought no **p** to the king of Assyria, as *he* 4503
18:31 Make *an agreement* with me *by* a **p**, and 1293
20:12 sent letters and a **p** unto Hezekiah: 4503
1Ch 29:17 which are **p** here, to offer willingly unto 4672
2Ch 5:11 all the priests that were **p** were sanctified, 4672
9:24 they brought every man his **p**, vessels of 4503
29:29 all that were **p** with him bowed themselves, 4672
30:21 the children of Israel that were **p** at 4672
31: 1 all Israel that were **p** went out to the cities 4672
34:32 he caused all that were **p** in Jerusalem and 4672
34:33 made all that were **p** in Israel to serve, 4672
35: 7 the passover *offerings*, for all that were **p**, 4672
35:17 the children of Israel that were **p** kept 4672
35:18 all Judah and Israel that were **p**, and 4672
Ezr 8:25 his lords, and all Israel *there* **p**, had offered: 4672
Est 1: 5 people that were **p** in Shushan the palace, 4672
4:16 gather together all the Jews that are **p** in 4672
Job 1: 6 came to **p** themselves before the LORD, 3320
2: 1 came to **p** themselves before the LORD, 3320
2: 1 Satan came also among them to **p** himself 3320
Ps 46: 1 and strength, a very **p** help in trouble. 4672
Isa 18: 7 In that time shall the **p** be brought unto 7862
36:16 Make *an agreement* with me *by* a **p**, and 1293
39: 1 sent letters and a **p** to Hezekiah: 4503
Jer 36: 7 It may be they will **p** their supplication 5307
42: 9 unto whom ye sent me to **p** your 5307
Eze 27:15 they brought thee *for* a **p** horns of ivory and 814
Da 9:18 for we do not **p** our supplications before 5307
Hos 10: 6 It shall be also carried unto Assyria *for* a **p** 4503
Lk 2:22 him to Jerusalem, to **p** *him* to the Lord; *3936*
5:17 the power of the Lord was **p** to heal them. NIG
13: 1 There were **p** at that season some that told *3918*
18:30 not receive manifold more in this **p** time, NIG
Jn 14:25 I spoken unto you, being *yet* **p** with you. *3306*
Ac 10:33 therefore are we all **here p** before God, *3918*
21:18 us unto James; and all the elders were **p**. *3854*
25:24 and all men which are **here p with** us, *4840*
28: 2 because of the **p** rain, and because of *2186*
Ro 7:18 dwelleth no good *thing:* for to will is **p** with *3873*
7:21 when I would do good, evil is **p** with me. *3873*
8:18 For I reckon that the sufferings of *this* **p** *3568*
8:38 nor principalities, nor powers, nor *things* **p**, *1764*
11: 5 at *this* **p** time also there is a remnant *3568*
12: 1 that *ye* **p** your bodies a living sacrifice, *3936*
1Co 3:22 or death, or *things* **p**, or *things* to come; *1764*
4:11 Even unto this **p** hour we both hunger, and *737*
5: 3 I verily, as absent in body, but **p** in spirit, *3918*
5: 3 have judged already, as though I were **p**, *3918*
7:26 therefore that this is good for the **p** distress, *1764*
15: 6 of whom the greater part remain unto **this p**, *737*
2Co 4:14 us also by Jesus, and shall **p** *us* with you. *3936*
5: 8 from the body, and to be **p** with the Lord. *1736*
5: 9 we labour, that, whether **p** or absent, *1736*
10: 2 be bold when I am **p** with *that* confidence, *3918*
10:11 *will we be* also in deed when we are **p**. *3918*
11: 2 that *I* may **p** *you as* a chaste virgin to *3936*
11: 9 And when I was **p** with you, and wanted, *3918*
13: 2 foretell *you,* as if I were **p** the second *time;* *3918*
13:10 lest being **p** I should use sharpness, *3918*
Gal 1: 4 that he might deliver us from *this* **p** evil *1764*
4:18 and not only when I am **p** with you. *3918*
4:20 I desire to be **p** with you now, and *3918*
Eph 5:27 That he might **p** it to himself a glorious *3936*
Col 1:22 to **p** you holy and unblameable and *3936*
1:28 that we may **p** every man perfect in Christ *3936*
2Ti 4:10 having loved *this* **p** world, and is departed *3568*
Tit 2:12 and godly, in *this* **p** world; *3568*
Heb 9: 9 Which *was* a figure for the time *then* **p**, *1764*
12:11 Now no chastening for the **p** seemeth to be *3918*
2Pe 1:12 know *them,* and be stablished in the **p** truth. *3918*
Jude 1:24 to **p** *you* faultless before the presence of his *2476*

PRESENTED (18) [PRESENT]

Ge 46:29 to Goshen, and **p** himself unto him; 7200
47: 2 *even* five men, and **p** them unto Pharaoh. 3322
Lev 2: 8 when it is **p** unto the priest, he shall bring it 7126
7:35 in the day *when* he **p** them to minister unto 7126
9:12 Aaron's sons **p** unto him the blood, 4672
9:13 they **p** the burnt offering unto him, with 4672
9:18 Aaron's sons **p** unto him the blood, 4672
16:10 shall be **p** alive before the LORD, to make 5975
Dt 31:14 **p** themselves in the tabernacle of 3320
Jos 24: 1 and they **p** themselves before God. 3320
Jdg 6:19 *it* out unto him under the oak, and **p** *it.* 5066
20: 2 **p** themselves in the assembly of the people 3320
1Sa 17:16 and evening, and **p** himself forty days. 3320
Jer 38:26 I **p** my supplication before the king, 5307
Eze 20:28 there they **p** the provocation of their 5414
Mt 2:11 their treasures, they **p** unto him gifts; *4374*
Ac 9:41 called the saints and widows, **p** her alive. *3936*
23:33 to the governor, **p** Paul also **before** him. *3936*

PRESENTING (1) [PRESENT]

Da 9:20 **p** my supplication before the LORD my 5307

PRESENTLY (5) [PRESENT]

1Sa 2:16 not fail to burn the fat **p**, 3117+1886.1+3509.1
Pr 12:16 A fool's wrath is **p** known: 3117+871.1+1886.1
Mt 21:19 for ever. And **p** the fig tree withered away. *3916*
26:53 he shall **p** give me more than twelve legions *737*
Php 2:23 Him therefore I hope to send **p**, so soon as *1824*

PRESENTS (10) [PRESENT]

1Sa 10:27 they despised him, and brought him no **p**. 4503
1Ki 4:21 they brought **p**, and served Solomon all 4503
2Ki 17: 3 became his servant, and gave him **p**. 4503
2Ch 17: 5 and all Judah brought to Jehoshaphat **p**; and 4503
17:11 of the Philistines brought Jehoshaphat **p**, 4503
32:23 and **p** to Hezekiah king of Judah: 4030
Ps 68:29 at Jerusalem shall kings bring **p** unto thee. 7862
72:10 of Tarshish and *of* the isles shall bring **p**: 4503
76:11 let all that be round about him bring **p** unto 7862
Mic 1:14 Therefore shalt thou give **p** to 7964

PRESERVE (30) [PRESERVED, PRESERVER, PRESERVEST, PRESERVETH]

Ge 19:32 with him, that we may **p** seed of our father. 2421
19:34 with him, that we may **p** seed of our father. 2421
45: 5 for God did send me before you to **p life**. 4241
45: 7 God sent me before you to **p** you a 7760
Dt 6:24 that he might **p** us **alive**, as *it is at* this day. 2421
Ps 12: 7 thou shalt **p** them from this generation for 5341
16: 1 **P** me, O God: for in thee do I put my trust. 8104
25:21 Let integrity and uprightness **p** me; for I 5341
32: 7 hiding place; thou shalt **p** me from trouble; 5341
40:11 and thy truth continually **p** me. 5341
41: 2 The LORD will **p** him, and keep him 8104
61: 7 prepare mercy and truth, *which* may **p** him. 5341
64: 1 **p** my life from fear of the enemy. 5341
79:11 **p** thou those that are appointed to die; 3498
86: 2 **P** my soul; for I *am* holy: O thou my God, 8104
121: 7 The LORD shall **p** thee from all evil: 8104
121: 7 thee from all evil: he shall **p** thy soul. 8104
121: 8 The LORD shall **p** thy going out and 8104
140: 1 the evil man: **p** me from the violent man; 5341
140: 4 of the wicked; **p** me from the violent man; 5341
Pr 2:11 Discretion shall **p** thee, understanding shall 8104
4: 6 Forsake her not, and she shall **p** thee: 8104
14: 3 but the lips of the wise shall **p** them. 8104
20:28 Mercy and truth **p** the king: and his throne 5341
22:12 The eyes of the LORD **p** knowledge, and 5341
Isa 31: 5 deliver *it;* and passing over he will **p** *it.* 4422
49: 8 I will **p** thee, and give thee for a covenant 5341
Jer 49:11 thy fatherless children, I will **p** *them* **alive**; 2421
Lk 17:33 and whosoever shall lose *his life* shall **p** it. *2225*
2Ti 4:18 and will **p** *me* unto his heavenly kingdom: *4982*

PRESERVED (16) [PRESERVE]

Ge 32:30 seen God face to face, and my life is **p**. 5337
Jos 24:17 **p** us in all the way wherein we went, and 8104
1Sa 30:23 who hath **p** us, and delivered the company 8104
2Sa 8: 6 the LORD **p** David whithersoever he 3467
8:14 the LORD **p** David whithersoever he 3467
1Ch 18: 6 Thus the LORD **p** David whithersoever he 3467
18:13 Thus the LORD **p** David whithersoever he 3467
Job 10:12 favour, and thy visitation hath **p** my spirit. 8104
29: 2 as *in* the days *when* God **p** me; 8104
Ps 37:28 forsaketh not his saints; they are **p** for ever: 8104
Isa 49: 6 of Jacob, and to restore the **p** of Israel: 5341
Hos 12:13 out of Egypt, and by a prophet was he **p**. 8104
Mt 9:17 new wine into new bottles, and both are **p**. *4933*
Lk 5:38 be put into new bottles; and both are **p**. *4933*
1Th 5:23 body be **p** blameless unto the coming of *5083*
Jude 1: 1 and **p** *in* Jesus Christ, *and* called: *5083*

PRESERVER (1) [PRESERVE]

Job 7:20 what shall I do unto thee, O thou **p** of men? 5341

PRESERVEST (2) [PRESERVE]

Ne 9: 6 and all that *is* therein, and thou **p** them all; 2421
Ps 36: 6 O LORD, thou **p** man and beast. 3467

PRESERVETH (8) [PRESERVE]

Job 36: 6 He **p** not the **life** of the wicked: but 2421
Ps 31:23 *for* the LORD **p** the faithful, and 5341
97:10 he **p** the souls of his saints; he delivereth 8104
116: 6 The LORD **p** the simple: I was brought 8104
145:20 The LORD **p** all them that love him: but 8104
146: 9 The LORD **p** the strangers; he relieveth 8104
Pr 2: 8 of judgment, and **p** the way of his saints. 8104
16:17 he that keepeth his way **p** his soul. 8104

PRESIDENTS (5)

Da 6: 2 over these three **p**; of whom Daniel *was* 5632
6: 3 this Daniel was preferred above the **p** and 5632
6: 4 the **p** and princes sought to find occasion 5632
6: 6 these **p** and princes assembled *together* to 5632
6: 7 All the **p** of the kingdom, the governors, 5632

PRESS (9) [PRESSED, PRESSES, PRESSETH, PRESSFAT, WINEPRESS, WINEPRESSES]

Joel 3:13 for the **p** is full, the fats overflow; 1660
Hag 2:16 for to draw out fifty *vessels out of* the **p**, 6333
Mk 2: 4 could not come nigh unto him for the **p**, *3793*
5:27 came in the **p** behind, and touched his *3793*
5:30 turned him about in the **p**, and said, *3793*
Lk 8:19 and could not come at him for the **p**. *3793*
8:45 throng thee and **p** *thee,* and sayest thou, *598*
19: 3 and could not for the **p**, because he was *3793*
Php 3:14 I **p** toward the mark for the prize of *1377*

PRESS CHARGES See ACCUSE; IMPLEAD

PRESSED (15) [PRESS]

Ge 19: 3 he **p** upon them greatly; and they turned in 6484
19: 9 they **p** sore upon the man, *even* Lot, and 6484
40:11 **p** them into Pharaoh's cup, and I gave 7818
Jdg 16:16 when she **p** him daily with her words, and 6693
2Sa 13:25 he **p** him: howbeit he would not go, but 6555
13:27 Absalom **p** him, that he let Amnon and all 6555
Est 8:14 and **p on** by the king's commandment, 1765
Eze 23: 3 there were their breasts **p**, and there they 4600
Am 2:13 Behold, I am **p** under you, as a cart is 5781
2:13 as a cart is **p** *that is* full *of* sheaves. 5781
Mk 3:10 insomuch that *they* **p upon** him for to touch *1968*
Lk 5: 1 as the people **p upon** him to hear the word *1945*
6:38 **p down**, and shaken *together*, and *4085*
Ac 18: 5 Paul was **p** in spirit, and testified to *4912*
2Co 1: 8 that we were **p** out of measure, above *916*

PRESSES (4) [PRESS]

Ne 13:15 Judah *some* treading **wine p** on the sabbath, 1660
Pr 3:10 and thy **p** shall burst out with new wine. 3342
Isa 16:10 treaders shall tread out no wine in *their* **p**; 3342
Jer 48:33 I have caused wine to fail from the **wine p**: 3342

PRESSETH (2) [PRESS]

Ps 38: 2 fast in me, and thy hand **p** me **sore**. 5181+5921
Lk 16:16 of God is preached, and every *man* **p** into it. *971*

PRESSFAT (1) [PRESS]

Hag 2:16 when *one* came to the **p** for to draw out 3342

PRESUME (2) [PRESUMED, PRESUMPTUOUS, PRESUMPTUOUSLY]

Dt 18:20 which shall **p** to speak a word in my name, 2102
Est 7: 5 *is* he, that **durst p** in his heart to do so? 4390

PRESUMED (1) [PRESUME]

Nu 14:44 they **p** to go up unto the hill top: 6075

PRESUMPTUOUS (2) [PRESUME]

Ps 19:13 Keep back thy servant also from **p** *sins;* let 2086
2Pe 2:10 **P** *are they,* selfwilled, they are not afraid to *5113*

PRESUMPTUOUSLY (6) [PRESUME]

Ex 21:14 if a man **come p** upon his neighbour, 2102
Nu 15:30 the soul that doeth *ought* **p**, 3027+7311+871.1
Dt 1:43 of the LORD, and went **p** up into the hill. 2102
17:12 the man that will do **p**, and will not 2087+871.1
17:13 shall hear, and fear, and do no more **p**. 2102
18:22 the prophet hath spoken it **p**: 2087+871.1

PRETENCE (3)

Mt 23:14 and for a **p** make long prayer: *4392*
Mk 12:40 and for a **p** make long prayers: *4392*
Php 1:18 every way, whether in **p**, or in truth, *4392*

PRETORIUM (1)

Mk 15:16 led him away into the hall, called **P**; *4232*

PREVAIL (29) [PREVAILED, PREVAILEST, PREVAILETH]

Ge 7:20 Fifteen cubits upward did the waters **p**; and 1396
Nu 22: 6 peradventure I shall **p**, *that* we may smite 3201
Jdg 16: 5 and by what *means* we may **p** against him, 3201
1Sa 2: 9 in darkness; for by strength shall no man **p**. 1396
17: 9 if I **p** against him, and kill him, then 3201
26:25 do great things, and also shalt **still p**. 3201+3201
1Ki 22:22 Thou shalt persuade *him,* and **p** also: 3201
2Ch 14:11 *art* our God; let not man **p** against thee. 6113
18:21 shalt entice *him,* and thou shalt also **p**: 3201
Est 6:13 thou shalt not **p** against him, but 3201
Job 15:24 *they* shall **p against** him, as a king ready to 8630
18: 9 the heel, *and* the robber shall **p** against him. 2388

P

Ps 9:19 Arise, O LORD; let not man **p**: let 5810
12: 4 Who have said, With our tongue will we **p**; 1396
65: 3 Iniquities **p** against me: *as for* our 1396
Ecc 4:12 if one **p** **against** him, two shall withstand 8630
Isa 7: 1 to war against it, but could not **p** against it. 3898
16:12 to his sanctuary to pray; but he shall not **p**. 3201
42:13 yea, roar; he shall **p** against his enemies. 1396
47:12 be able to profit, if so be thou mayest **p**. 6206
Jer 1:19 they shall not **p** against thee; for I *am* with 3201
5:22 thereof toss themselves, yet can they not **p**; 3201
15:20 but they shall not **p** against thee: 3201
20:10 we shall **p** against him, and we shall take 3201
20:11 shall stumble, and they shall not **p**: 3201
Da 11: 7 and shall deal against them, and shall **p**: 2388
Mt 16:18 and the gates of hell shall not **p** **against** it. *2729*
27:24 When Pilate saw that he could **p** nothing, *5623*
Jn 12:19 Perceive ye how ye **p** nothing? *5623*

PREVAILED (37) [PREVAIL]

Ge 7:18 the waters **p**, and were increased greatly 1396
7:19 the waters **p** exceedingly upon the earth; 1396
7:24 And the waters **p** upon the earth an hundred 1396
30: 8 I wrestled with my sister, and I have **p**: 3201
32:25 And when he saw that he **p** not against him, 3201
32:28 power with God and with men, and hast **p**. 3201
47:20 his field, because the famine **p** over them: 2388
49:26 The blessings of thy father have **p** above 1396
Ex 17:11 when Moses held up his hand, that Israel **p**: 1396
17:11 and when he let down his hand, Amalek **p**. 1396
Jdg 1:35 yet the hand of the house of Joseph **p**, so 3513
3:10 and his hand **p** against Chushan-rishathaim. 5810
4:24 **p** against Jabin the king of Canaan, 7186
6: 2 the hand of Midian **p** against Israel: *and* 5810
1Sa 17:50 So David **p** over the Philistine with a sling 2388
2Sa 11:23 Surely the men **p** against us, and came out 1396
24: 4 Notwithstanding the king's word **p** against 2388
1Ki 16:22 the people that followed Omri **p** against 2388
2Ki 25: 3 the *fourth* month the famine **p** in the city, 2388
1Ch 5: 2 For Judah **p** above his brethren, and of him 1396
21: 4 Nevertheless the king's word **p** against 2388
2Ch 8: 3 went *to* Hamath-zobah, and **p** against it. 2388
13:18 the children of Judah **p**, because they relied 553
27: 5 king of the Ammonites, and **p** against them. 2388
Ps 13: 4 mine enemy say, I have **p** **against** him; 3201
129: 2 my youth: yet they have not **p** against me. 3201
Jer 20: 7 thou art stronger than I, and hast **p**: I am in 3201
38:22 have set thee on, and have **p** against thee: 3201
La 1:16 children are desolate, because the enemy **p**. 1396
Da 7:21 war with the saints, and **p** against them; 3202
Hos 12: 4 Yea, he had power over *the* angel, and **p**: 3201
Ob 1: 7 thee have deceived thee, *and* **p** against thee; 3201
Lk 23:23 voices of them and of the chief priests **p**. *2729*
Ac 19:16 and **p** against them, so that *they* fled out of *2480*
19:20 So mightily grew the word of God and **p**. *2480*
Rev 5: 5 hath **p** to open the book, and to loose *3528*
12: 8 And **p** not; neither was their place found *2480*

PREVAILEST (1) [PREVAIL]

Job 14:20 Thou **p** for ever **against** him, and 8630

PREVAILETH (1) [PREVAIL]

La 1:13 fire into my bones, and it **p** against them: 7287

PREVALENT See SUPERFLUITY; SUPERFLUOUS

PREVENT (7) [PREVENTED, PREVENTEST]

Job 3:12 Why did the knees **p** me? or why 6923
Ps 59:10 The God of my mercy shall **p** me: 6923
79: 8 let thy tender mercies speedily **p** us: for we 6923
88:13 and in the morning shall my prayer **p** thee. 6923
119:148 Mine eyes **p** the *night* watches, that *I* might 6923
Am 9:10 The evil shall not overtake nor **p** us. 6923
1Th 4:15 the Lord shall not **p** them which are asleep. *5348*

PREVENTED (9) [PREVENT]

2Sa 22: 6 me about; the snares of death **p** me: 6923
22:19 They **p** me in the day of my calamity: but 6923
Job 30:27 and rested not: the days of affliction **p** me. 6923
41:11 Who hath **p** me, that I should repay *him?* 6923
Ps 18: 5 me about: the snares of death **p** me. 6923
18:18 They **p** me in the day of my calamity: but 6923
119:147 I **p** the dawning of the morning, and cried: 6923
Isa 21:14 they **p** with their bread him that fled. 6923
Mt 17:25 Jesus **p** him, saying, What thinkest thou, *4399*

PREVENTEST (1) [PREVENT]

Ps 21: 3 For thou **p** him *with* the blessings of 6923

PREY (73)

Ge 49: 9 from the **p**, my son, thou art gone up: 2964
49:27 in the morning he shall devour the **p**, and 5706
Nu 14: 3 our wives and our children should be a **p**? 957
14:31 your little ones, which ye said should be a **p**, 957
23:24 he shall not lie down until he eat *of* the **p**, 2964
31:11 and all the **p**, *both* of men and of beasts. 4455
31:12 the **p**, and the spoil, unto Moses, and 4455
31:26 Take the sum of the **p** that was taken, *both* 4455
31:27 divide the **p** into two parts; between them 4455
31:32 *being* the rest of the **p** which the men of war 957
Dt 1:39 which ye said should be a **p**, and 957
2:35 Only the cattle we **took for a p** unto 962
3: 7 of the cities, we **took for a p** to ourselves. 962
Jos 8: 2 shall ye **take for a p** unto yourselves: 962
8:27 the spoil of that city Israel **took for a p** unto 962
11:14 the children of Israel **took for a p** unto 962
Jdg 5:30 have they *not* divided the **p**; to every man a 7998
5:30 to Sisera a **p** of divers colours, a prey of 7998
5:30 a **p** of divers colours of needlework, 7998
8:24 give me every man the earrings of his **p**. 7998
8:25 cast therein every man the earrings of his **p**. 7998
2Ki 21:14 they shall become a **p** and a spoil to all their 957
Ne 4: 4 give them for a **p** in the land of captivity: 961
Est 3:13 and *to take* the spoil of them for a **p**. 962
Est 8:11 women, and *to take* the spoil of them for a **p**, 962
9:15 but on the **p** they laid not their hand. 961
9:16 but they laid not their hands on the **p**, 961
Job 4:11 The old lion perisheth for lack of **p**, and 2964
9:26 swift ships: as the eagle *that* hasteth to the **p**. 400
24: 5 forth to their work; rising betimes for a **p**: 2964
38:39 Wilt thou hunt the **p** for the lion? or fill 2964
39:29 From thence she seeketh the **p**, *and* her eyes 400
Ps 17:12 Like as a lion *that* is greedy of his **p**, and 2963
76: 4 *and* excellent than the mountains of **p**. 2964
104:21 The young lions roar after *their* **p**, and seek 2964
124: 6 who hath not given us *as* a **p** to their teeth. 2964
Pr 23:28 She also lieth in wait as *for* a **p**, and 2863
Isa 5:29 lay hold of the **p**, and shall carry *it* away 2964
10: 2 that widows may be their **p**, and *that* they 7998
10: 6 to take the **p**, and to tread them down like 957
31: 4 and the young lion roaring on his **p**, 2964
33:23 is the **p** of a great spoil divided; the lame 5706
33:23 of a great spoil divided; the lame take the **p**. 957
42:22 they are for a **p**, and none delivereth; *for* a 957
49:24 Shall the **p** be taken from the mighty, or 4455
49:25 and the **p** of the terrible shall be delivered: 4455
59:15 departeth from evil **maketh** himself a **p**: 7997
Jer 21: 9 and his life shall be unto him for a **p**. 7998
30:16 all that **p** **upon** thee will I give for a prey. 962
30:16 all that prey upon thee will I give for a **p**. 957
38: 2 for he shall have his life for a **p**, and 7998
39:18 but thy life shall be for a **p** unto thee: 7998
45: 5 thy life will I give unto thee for a **p** in all 7998
Eze 7:21 give it into the hands of the strangers for a **p**, 957
19: 3 a young lion, and it learned to catch the **p**; 2964
19: 6 learned to catch the **p**, *and* devoured men. 2964
22:25 like a roaring lion ravening the **p**; 2964
22:27 thereof *are* like wolves ravening the **p**, 2964
26:12 and **make a p** of thy merchandise: 962
29:19 and take her spoil, and **take** her **p**; 957+962
34: 8 surely because my flock became a **p**, and 957
34:22 my flock, and they shall no more be a **p**; 957
34:28 they shall no more be a **p** to the heathen, 957
36: 4 which became a **p** and derision to the residue 957
36: 5 with despiteful minds, to cast it out for a **p**. 957
38:12 To take a spoil, and to **take a p**; to turn 957+962
38:13 gathered thy company to **take a p**? 957+962
Da 11:24 he shall scatter among them the **p**, and spoil, 961
Am 3: 4 a lion roar in the forest, when he hath no **p**? 2964
Na 2:12 filled his holes *with* **p**, and his dens *with* 2964
2:13 I will cut off thy **p** from the earth, and 2964
3: 1 full *of* lies *and* robbery; the **p** departeth not; 2964
Zep 3: 8 until the day that I rise up to the **p**: 5706

PRICE (33) [PRICES, PRISED]

Lev 25:16 of years thou shalt increase the **p** thereof, 4736
25:16 of years thou shalt diminish the **p** of it: 4736
25:50 the **p** of his sale shall be according unto 3701
25:51 **p** **of** his **redemption** out of the money that 1353
25:52 he give *him* again the **p** **of** his **redemption**. 1353
Dt 23:18 bring the hire of a whore, or the **p** of a dog, 4242
2Sa 24:24 Nay; but I will surely buy *it* of thee at a **p**: 4242
1Ki 10:28 merchants received the linen yarn at a **p**. 4242
1Ch 21:22 thou shalt grant it me for the full **p**: that 3701
21:24 Nay; but I will verily buy *it* for the full **p**: 3701
2Ch 1:16 merchants received the linen yarn at a **p**. 4242
Job 28:13 Man knoweth not the **p** thereof; neither is it 6187
28:15 neither shall silver be weighed *for* the **p** 4242
28:18 for the **p** of wisdom *is* above rubies. 4901
Ps 44:12 and dost not increase *thy wealth* by their **p**. 4242
Pr 17:16 Wherefore *is there* a **p** in the hand of a fool 4242
27:26 and the goats *are* the **p** of the field. 4242
31:10 for her **p** *is* far above rubies. 4377
Isa 45:13 not for **p** nor reward, saith the LORD of 4242
55: 1 and milk without money and without **p**. 4242
Jer 15:13 treasures will I give to the spoil without **p**, 4242
Zec 11:12 unto them, If ye think good, give *me* my **p**; 7939
11:12 So they weighed *for* my **p** thirty *pieces* of 7939
11:13 a goodly **p** that I was prised at of them. 3366
Mt 13:46 when he had found one pearl of **great p**, *4186*
27: 6 the treasury, because it is the **p** of blood. *5092*
27: 9 of silver, the **p** of him that was valued, *5092*
Ac 5: 2 And kept back *part* of the **p**, his wife also *5092*
5: 3 and to keep back *part* of the **p** of the land? *5092*
19:19 all *men:* and they counted the **p** of them, *5092*
1Co 6:20 For ye are bought with a **p**: therefore *5092*
7:23 Ye are bought with a **p**; be not ye *5092*
1Pe 3: 4 which is in the sight of God of **great p**. *4185*

PRICES (1) [PRICE]

Ac 4:34 brought the **p** of the *things* that were sold, *5092*

PRICKED (2) [PRICKING]

Ps 73:21 heart was grieved, and I was **p** *in* my reins. 8150
Ac 2:37 Now when they heard *this*, they were **p** in *2660*

PRICKING (1) [PRICKED, PRICKS]

Eze 28:24 there shall be no more a **p** brier unto 3992

PRICKS (3) [PRICKING]

Nu 33:55 let remain of them *shall be* **p** in your eyes, 7899
Ac 9: 5 *it is* hard for thee to kick against the **p**. *2759*
26:14 *it is* hard for thee to kick against the **p**. *2759*

PRIDE (49) [PROUD, PROUDLY]

Lev 26:19 I will break the **p** of your power; and I will 1347
1Sa 17:28 I know thy **p**, and the naughtiness of thine 2087
2Ch 32:26 humbled himself for the **p** of his heart, 1363
Job 33:17 *from his* purpose, and hide **p** from man. 1466
35:12 because of the **p** of evil men. 1347
41:15 *His* scales *are his* **p**, shut up *together as* 1346
41:34 he *is* a king over all the children of **p**. 7830
Ps 10: 2 The wicked in *his* **p** doth persecute 1346
10: 4 through the **p** of his countenance, 1363
31:20 secret of thy presence from the **p** of man: 7407
36:11 Let not the foot of **p** come against me, and 1346
59:12 their lips let them even be taken in their **p**: 1347
73: 6 Therefore **p** compasseth them about as a 1346
Pr 8:13 **p**, and arrogancy, and the evil way, and 1344
11: 2 *When* **p** cometh, then cometh shame: but 2087
13:10 Only by **p** cometh contention: but with 2087
14: 3 In the mouth of the foolish *is* a rod of **p**: but 1346
16:18 **P** *goeth* before destruction, and a haughty 1347
29:23 A man's **p** shall bring him low: but 1346
Isa 9: 9 that say in the **p** and stoutness of heart, 1346
16: 6 We have heard of the **p** of Moab; *he is* very 1347
16: 6 of his haughtiness, and his **p**, and his wrath: 1347
23: 9 to stain the **p** of all glory, *and* to bring into 1347
25:11 he shall bring down their **p** together with 1346
28: 1 Woe to the crown of **p**, to the drunkards of 1348
28: 3 The crown of **p**, the drunkards of Ephraim, 1348
Jer 13: 9 After this manner will I mar the **p** of Judah, 1347
13: 9 of Judah, and the great **p** of Jerusalem. 1347
13:17 soul shall weep in secret places for *your* **p**; 1466
48:29 We have heard the **p** of Moab; *he is* 1347
48:29 and his **p**, and the haughtiness of his heart. 1346
49:16 hath deceived thee, *and* the **p** of thine heart, 2087
Eze 7:10 the rod hath blossomed, **p** hath budded. 2087
16:49 **p**, fulness of bread, and abundance of 1347
16:56 by thy mouth in the day of thy **p**, 1347
30: 6 and the **p** of her power shall come down: 1347
Da 4:37 and those that walk in **p** he *is* able to abase. 1467
5:20 was lifted up, and his mind hardened in **p**, 2103
Hos 5: 5 the **p** of Israel doth testify to his face: 1347
7:10 the **p** of Israel testifieth to his face: and 1347
Ob 1: 3 The **p** of thine heart hath deceived thee, 2087
Zep 2:10 This shall they have for their **p**, because 1347
3:11 the midst of thee them that rejoice in thy **p**, 1346
Zec 9: 6 and I will cut off the **p** of the Philistines. 1347
10:11 and the **p** of Assyria shall be brought down, 1347
11: 3 young lions; for the **p** of Jordan is spoiled. 1347
Mk 7:22 an evil eye, blasphemy, **p**, foolishness: *5243*
1Ti 3: 6 lest being **lifted up with p** he fall into *5187*
1Jn 2:16 and the lust of the eyes, and the **p** of life, *212*

PRIEST (496) [PRIEST'S, PRIESTHOOD, PRIESTS, PRIESTS']

Ge 14:18 and he *was* the **p** of the most high God. 3548
41:45 the daughter of Poti-pherah **p** of On. 3548
41:50 of Poti-pherah **p** of On bare unto him. 3548
46:20 of Poti-pherah **p** of On bare unto him. 3548
Ex 2:16 Now the **p** of Midian had seven daughters: 3548
3: 1 of Jethro his father in law, the **p** of Midian: 3548
18: 1 When Jethro, the **p** of Midian, 3548
29:30 *And* that son that is **p** in his stead shall put 3548
31:10 the holy garments for Aaron the **p**, and 3548
35:19 *place*, the holy garments for Aaron the **p**, 3548
38:21 by the hand of Ithamar, son to Aaron the **p**. 3548
39:41 and the holy garments for Aaron the **p**, 3548
Lev 1: 7 the sons of Aaron the **p** shall put fire upon 3548
1: 9 the **p** shall burn all on the altar, *to be* a 3548
1:12 the **p** shall lay them in order on the wood 3548
1:13 the **p** shall bring *it* all, and burn *it* upon 3548
1:15 the **p** shall bring it unto the altar, and 3548
1:17 the **p** shall burn it upon the altar, upon 3548
2: 2 the **p** shall burn the memorial of it upon 3548
2: 8 when it is presented unto the **p**, he shall 3548
2: 9 the **p** shall take from the meat offering a 3548
2:16 the **p** shall burn the memorial of it, *part* of 3548
3:11 the **p** shall burn it upon the altar: *it is* 3548
3:16 the **p** shall burn them upon the altar: *it is* 3548
4: 3 If the **p** that is anointed do sin according to 3548
4: 5 the **p** that is anointed shall take of 3548
4: 6 the **p** shall dip his finger in the blood, and 3548
4: 7 the **p** shall put *some* of the blood upon 3548
4:10 the **p** shall burn them upon the altar of 3548
4:16 the **p** that is anointed shall bring of 3548
4:17 the **p** shall dip his finger *in some* of 3548
4:20 the **p** shall make an atonement for them, 3548
4:25 the **p** shall take of the blood of the sin 3548
4:26 the **p** shall make an atonement for him as 3548
4:30 the **p** shall take of the blood thereof with 3548
4:31 the **p** shall burn *it* upon the altar for a sweet 3548
4:31 the **p** shall make an atonement for him, and 3548
4:34 the **p** shall take of the blood of the sin 3548
4:35 the **p** shall burn them upon the altar, 3548
4:35 the **p** shall make an atonement for his sin 3548
5: 6 the **p** shall make an atonement for him 3548
5: 8 he shall bring them unto the **p**, who shall 3548
5:10 the **p** shall make an atonement for him for 3548
5:12 shall he bring it to the **p**, and the priest shall 3548
5:12 the **p** shall take his handful of it, *even* a 3548
5:13 the **p** shall make an atonement for him as 3548
5:16 the fifth *part* thereto, and give it unto the **p**: 3548
5:16 the **p** shall make an atonement for him with 3548
5:18 for a trespass offering, unto the **p**: 3548
5:18 the **p** shall make an atonement for him 3548
6: 6 for a trespass offering, unto the **p**: 3548
6: 7 the **p** shall make an atonement for him 3548
6:10 the **p** shall put on his linen garment, and 3548
6:12 the **p** shall burn wood on it every morning, 3548
6:22 the **p** of his sons that is anointed in his 3548
6:23 For every meat offering for the **p** shall be 3548
6:26 The **p** that offereth it for sin shall eat it: 3548
7: 5 the **p** shall burn them upon the altar *for* an 3548
7: 7 the **p** that maketh atonement therewith 3548
7: 8 the **p** that offereth *any* man's burnt 3548
7: 8 *even* the **p** shall have to himself the skin of 3548
7:31 the **p** shall burn the fat upon the altar: but 3548
7:32 the right shoulder shall ye give unto the **p** 3548
7:34 have given them unto Aaron the **p** and 3548
12: 6 tabernacle of the congregation, unto the **p**: 3548
12: 8 the **p** shall make an atonement for her, and 3548
13: 2 he shall be brought unto Aaron the **p**, or 3548
13: 3 the **p** shall look on the plague in the skin of 3548
13: 3 the **p** shall look on him, and pronounce him 3548
13: 4 the **p** shall shut up *him that hath* the plague 3548
13: 5 the **p** shall look on him the seventh day: 3548
13: 5 the **p** shall shut him up seven days more: 3548
13: 6 the **p** shall look on him again the seventh 3548
13: 6 the skin, the **p** shall pronounce him clean: 3548
13: 7 after that he hath been seen of the **p** for his 3548
13: 7 he shall be seen of the **p** again: 3548

P

Lev 13: 8 *if* the **p** see that behold, the scab spreadeth 3548
13: 8 then the **p** shall pronounce him unclean: 3548
13: 9 a man, then he shall be brought unto the **p**; 3548
13:10 the **p** shall see *him:* and behold, *if* the rising 3548
13:11 the **p** shall pronounce him unclean, *and* 3548
13:12 even to his foot, wheresoever the **p** looketh; 3548
13:13 the **p** shall consider: and behold, *if* 3548
13:15 the **p** shall see the raw flesh, and 3548
13:16 unto white, he shall come unto the **p**; 3548
13:17 the **p** shall see him: and behold, *if* 3548
13:17 the **p** shall pronounce *him* clean *that hath* 3548
13:19 and it be shewed to the **p**; 3548
13:20 if, when the **p** seeth it, behold, it *be* in sight 3548
13:20 the **p** shall pronounce him unclean: 3548
13:21 if the **p** look on it, and behold, *there be* no 3548
13:21 then the **p** shall shut him up seven days: 3548
13:22 then the **p** shall pronounce him unclean: 3548
13:23 and the **p** shall pronounce him clean. 3548
13:25 the **p** shall look upon it: and behold, *if* 3548
13:25 wherefore the **p** shall pronounce him 3548
13:26 if the **p** look on it, and behold, *there be* no 3548
13:26 then the **p** shall shut him up seven days: 3548
13:27 the **p** shall look upon him the seventh day: 3548
13:27 then the **p** shall pronounce him unclean: 3548
13:28 and the **p** shall pronounce him clean: 3548
13:30 Then the **p** shall see the plague: and behold, 3548
13:30 then the **p** shall pronounce him unclean: 3548
13:31 if the **p** look on the plague of the scall, and 3548
13:31 the **p** shall shut up *him that hath* the plague 3548
13:32 in the seventh day the **p** shall look on 3548
13:33 the **p** shall shut up *him that hath* the scall 3548
13:34 in the seventh day the **p** shall look on 3548
13:34 then the **p** shall pronounce him clean: 3548
13:36 the **p** shall look on him: and behold, *if* 3548
13:36 the **p** shall not seek for yellow hair: 3548
13:37 and the **p** shall pronounce him clean. 3548
13:39 the **p** shall look: and behold, *if* the bright 3548
13:43 the **p** shall look upon it: and behold, *if* 3548
13:44 the **p** shall pronounce him utterly unclean, 3548
13:49 of leprosy, and shall be shewed unto the **p**: 3548
13:50 the **p** shall look upon the plague, and 3548
13:53 if the **p** shall look, and behold, the plague 3548
13:54 the **p** shall command that they wash 3548
13:55 the **p** shall look on the plague, after *that* it 3548
13:56 if the **p** look, and behold, the plague *be* 3548
14: 2 He shall be brought unto the **p**: 3548
14: 3 the **p** shall go forth out of the camp; and 3548
14: 3 the **p** shall look, and behold, *if* the plague 3548
14: 4 shall the **p** command to take for him that is 3548
14: 5 the **p** shall command that one of the birds 3548
14:11 the **p** that maketh *him* clean shall present 3548
14:12 the **p** shall take one he lamb, and offer him 3548
14:14 the **p** shall take *some* of the blood of 3548
14:14 the **p** shall put *it* upon the tip of the right 3548
14:15 the **p** shall take *some* of the log of oil, and 3548
14:16 the **p** shall dip his right finger in the oil that 3548
14:17 **p** put upon the tip of the right ear of him 3548
14:18 the **p** shall make an atonement for him 3548
14:19 the **p** shall offer the sin offering, and 3548
14:20 the **p** shall offer the burnt offering and 3548
14:20 the **p** shall make an atonement for him, and 3548
14:23 the eighth day for his cleansing unto the **p**, 3548
14:24 the **p** shall take the lamb of the trespass 3548
14:24 the **p** shall wave them *for* a wave offering 3548
14:25 the **p** shall take *some* of the blood of 3548
14:26 the **p** shall pour of the oil into the palm of 3548
14:27 the **p** shall sprinkle with his right finger 3548
14:28 the **p** shall put of the oil that *is* in his hand 3548
14:31 the **p** shall make an atonement for him that 3548
14:35 owneth the house shall come and tell the **p**, 3548
14:36 the **p** shall command that they empty 3548
14:36 before the **p** go *into it* to see the plague, 3548
14:36 afterward the **p** shall go in to see the house: 3548
14:38 the **p** shall go out of the house to the door 3548
14:39 the **p** shall come again the seventh day, 3548
14:40 the **p** shall command that they take away 3548
14:44 the **p** shall come and look, and behold, 3548
14:48 if the **p** shall come in, and look *upon it,* 3548
14:48 the **p** shall pronounce the house clean, 3548
15:14 the congregation, and give them unto the **p**: 3548
15:15 the **p** shall offer them, the one *for* a sin 3548
15:15 the **p** shall make an atonement for him 3548
15:29 young pigeons, and bring them unto the **p**, 3548
15:30 the **p** shall offer the one *for* a sin offering, 3548
15:30 the **p** shall make an atonement for her 3548
16:30 For on that day shall *the p* make an NIH
16:32 the **p**, whom he shall anoint, and whom he 3548
17: 5 unto the **p**, and offer them *for* peace 3548
17: 6 the **p** shall sprinkle the blood upon the altar 3548
19:22 the **p** shall make an atonement for him with 3548
21: 9 the daughter of any **p**, if she profane herself 3548
21:10 *he that is* the high **p** among his brethren, 3548
21:21 hath a blemish, of the seed of Aaron the **p**, 3548
22:11 if the **p** buy *any* soul with his money, 3548
22:14 shall give *it* unto the **p** with the holy *thing.* 3548
23:10 of the firstfruits of your harvest unto the **p**: 3548
23:11 on the morrow after the sabbath the **p** shall 3548
23:20 the **p** shall wave them with the bread of 3548
23:20 they shall be holy to the LORD for the **p**. 3548
27: 8 he shall present himself before the **p**, and 3548
27: 8 before the priest, and the **p** shall value him; 3548
27: 8 his ability that vowed shall the **p** value him. 3548
27:11 then he shall present the beast before the **p**: 3548
27:12 the **p** shall value it, whether it be good or 3548
27:12 thou valuest it, *who art* the **p**, so shall it be. 3548
27:14 the **p** shall estimate it, whether it be good 3548
27:14 as the **p** shall estimate it, so shall it stand. 3548
27:18 the **p** shall reckon unto him the money 3548
27:23 the **p** shall reckon unto him the worth of 3548
Nu 3: 6 and present them before Aaron the **p**, 3548
3:32 Eleazar the son of Aaron the **p** *shall be* 3548
4:16 Aaron the **p** *pertaineth* the oil for the light, 3548
4:28 the hand of Ithamar the son of Aaron the **p**. 3548
4:33 the hand of Ithamar the son of Aaron the **p**. 3548
5: 8 unto the LORD, *even* to the **p**; 3548
Nu 5: 9 which they bring unto the **p**, shall be his. 3548
5:10 whatsoever any man giveth the **p**, it shall 3548
5:15 shall the man bring his wife unto the **p**, 3548
5:16 the **p** shall bring her near, and set her 3548
5:17 the **p** shall take holy water in an earthen 3548
5:17 the floor of the tabernacle the **p** shall take, 3548
5:18 the **p** shall set the woman before 3548
5:18 the **p** shall have in his hand the bitter water 3548
5:19 the **p** shall charge her by an oath, and 3548
5:21 the **p** shall charge the woman with an oath 3548
5:21 the **p** shall say unto the woman, 3548
5:23 the **p** shall write these curses in a book, 3548
5:25 the **p** shall take the jealousy offering out of 3548
5:26 the **p** shall take a handful of the offering, 3548
5:30 the **p** shall execute upon her all this law. 3548
6:10 two turtles, or two young pigeons, to the **p**, 3548
6:11 the **p** shall offer the one for a sin offering, 3548
6:16 the **p** shall bring *them* before the LORD, 3548
6:17 the **p** shall offer also his meat offering, and 3548
6:19 the **p** shall take the sodden shoulder of 3548
6:20 the **p** shall wave them *for* a wave offering 3548
6:20 this *is* holy for the **p**, with the wave breast 3548
7: 8 the hand of Ithamar the son of Aaron the **p**. 3548
15:25 the **p** shall make an atonement for all 3548
15:28 the **p** shall make an atonement for the soul 3548
16:37 Speak unto Eleazar the son of Aaron the **p**, 3548
16:39 Eleazar the **p** took the brasen censers, 3548
18:28 LORD'S heave offering to Aaron the **p**. 3548
19: 3 ye shall give her unto Eleazar the **p**, that he 3548
19: 4 Eleazar the **p** shall take of her blood with 3548
19: 6 the **p** shall take cedar wood, and hyssop, 3548
19: 7 the **p** shall wash his clothes, and he shall 3548
19: 7 and the **p** shall be unclean until the even. 3548
25: 7 the son of Eleazar, the son of Aaron the **p**, 3548
25:11 the son of Eleazar, the son of Aaron the **p**, 3548
26: 1 and unto Eleazar the son of Aaron the **p**, 3548
26: 3 Eleazar the **p** spake with them in the plains 3548
26:63 numbered by Moses and Eleazar the **p**, 3548
26:64 whom Moses and Aaron the **p** numbered, 3548
27: 2 before Eleazar the **p**, and before the princes 3548
27:19 set him before Eleazar the **p**, and before all 3548
27:21 he shall stand before Eleazar the **p**, 3548
27:22 set him before Eleazar the **p**, and before all 3548
31: 6 them and Phinehas the son of Eleazar the **p**, 3548
31:12 Eleazar the **p**, and unto the congregation of 3548
31:13 Eleazar the **p**, and all the princes of 3548
31:21 Eleazar the **p** said unto the men of war 3548
31:26 Eleazar the **p**, and the chief fathers of 3548
31:29 of their half, and give *it* unto Eleazar the **p**, 3548
31:31 Eleazar the **p** did as the LORD 3548
31:41 unto Eleazar the **p**, as the LORD 3548
31:51 and Eleazar the **p** took the gold of them, 3548
31:54 Eleazar the **p** took the gold of the captains 3548
32: 2 to Eleazar the **p**, and unto the princes of 3548
32:28 them Moses commanded Eleazar the **p**, 3548
33:38 Aaron the **p** went up into mount Hor at 3548
34:17 Eleazar the **p**, and Joshua the son of Nun. 3548
35:25 abide in it unto the death of the high **p**, 3548
35:28 of his refuge until the death of the high **p**: 3548
35:28 after the death of the high **p** the slayer shall 3548
35:32 to dwell in the land, until the death of the **p**. 3548
Dt 17:12 will not hearken unto the **p** that standeth to 3548
18: 3 they shall give unto the **p** the shoulder, and 3548
20: 2 that the **p** shall approach and speak unto 3548
26: 3 thou shalt go unto the **p** that shall be in 3548
26: 4 the **p** shall take the basket out of thine 3548
Jos 14: 1 which Eleazar the **p**, and Joshua the son of 3548
17: 4 they came near before Eleazar the **p**, and 3548
19:51 which Eleazar the **p**, and Joshua the son of 3548
20: 6 until the death of the high **p** that shall be in 3548
21: 1 fathers of the Levites unto Eleazar the **p**, 3548
21: 4 the children of Aaron the **p**, *which were* of 3548
21:13 of Aaron the **p** Hebron with her suburbs, 3548
22:13 Phinehas the son of Eleazar the **p**, 3548
22:30 when Phinehas the **p**, and the princes of 3548
22:31 Phinehas the son of Eleazar the **p** said unto 3548
22:32 Phinehas the son of Eleazar the **p**, and 3548
Jdg 17: 5 one of his sons, who became his **p**. 3548
17:10 be unto me a father and a **p**, and I will give 3548
17:12 the young man became his **p**, and was in 3548
17:13 me good, seeing I have a Levite to *my* **p** 3548
18: 4 with me, and hath hired me, and I am his **p**. 3548
18: 6 the **p** said unto them, Go in peace: 3548
18:17 the **p** stood *in* the entering of the gate with 3548
18:18 Then said the **p** unto them, What do ye? 3548
18:19 go with us, and be to us a father and a **p**: 3548
18:19 *is it* better for thee to be a **p** unto the house 3548
18:19 or that thou be a **p** unto a tribe and a family 3548
18:24 I made, and the **p**, and ye are gone away: 3548
18:27 the **p** which he had, and came unto Laish, 3548
1Sa 1: 9 Now Eli the **p** sat upon a seat by a post of 3548
2:11 minister unto the LORD before Eli the **p**. 3548
2:14 all that the fleshhook brought up the **p** took 3548
2:15 that sacrificed, Give flesh to roast for the **p**; 3548
2:28 out of all the tribes of Israel to be my **p**, 3548
2:35 I will raise me up a faithful **p**, *that* shall do 3548
14: 3 the son of Eli, the LORD'S **p** in Shiloh, 3548
14:19 came to pass, while Saul talked unto the **p**, 3548
14:19 Saul said unto the **p**, Withdraw thine hand. 3548
14:36 said the **p**, Let us draw near hither unto 3548
21: 1 came David to Nob to Ahimelech the **p**: 3548
21: 2 David said unto Ahimelech the **p**, The king 3548
21: 4 the **p** answered David, and said, *There is* no 3548
21: 5 David answered the **p**, and said unto him, 3548
21: 6 So the **p** gave him hallowed *bread:* for 3548
21: 9 the **p** said, The sword of Goliath 3548
22:11 the king sent to call Ahimelech the **p**, 3548
23: 9 he said to Abiathar the **p**, Bring hither 3548
30: 7 David said to Abiathar the **p**, 3548
2Sa 15:27 The king said also unto Zadok the **p**, *Art* 3548
1Ki 1: 7 the son of Zeruiah, and with Abiathar the **p**: 3548
1: 8 Zadok the **p**, and Benaiah the son of 3548
1:19 Abiathar the **p**, and Joab the captain of 3548
1:25 the captains of the host, and Abiathar the **p**; 3548
1:26 Zadok the **p**, and Benaiah the son of 3548
1Ki 1:32 Call me Zadok the **p**, and Nathan 3548
1:34 let Zadok the **p** and Nathan the prophet 3548
1:38 So Zadok the **p**, and Nathan the prophet, 3548
1:39 Zadok the **p** took a horn of oil out of 3548
1:42 Jonathan the son of Abiathar the **p** came: 3548
1:44 the king hath sent with him Zadok the **p**, 3548
1:45 Zadok the **p** and Nathan the prophet have 3548
2:22 for Abiathar the **p**, and for Joab the son of 3548
2:26 unto Abiathar the **p** said the king, Get thee 3548
2:27 Abiathar from being **p** unto the LORD; 3548
2:35 Zadok the **p** did the king put in the room of 3548
4: 2 he had; Azariah the son of Zadok the **p**, 3548
2Ki 11: 9 all *things* that Jehoiada the **p** commanded: 3548
11: 9 on the sabbath, and came to Jehoiada the **p**. 3548
11:10 to the captains over hundreds did the **p** give 3548
11:15 Jehoiada the **p** commanded the captains of 3548
11:15 For the **p** had said, Let her not be slain *in* 3548
11:18 slew Mattan the **p** of Baal before the altars. 3548
11:18 the **p** appointed officers over the house of 3548
12: 2 days where*in* Jehoiada the **p** instructed him. 3548
12: 7 king Jehoash called for Jehoiada the **p**, 3548
12: 9 Jehoiada the **p** took a chest, and bored a 3548
12:10 the king's scribe and the high **p** came up, 3548
16:10 king Ahaz sent to Urijah the **p** the fashion 3548
16:11 Urijah the **p** built an altar according to all 3548
16:11 Urijah the **p** made *it* against king Ahaz 3548
16:15 king Ahaz commanded Urijah the **p**, 3548
16:16 Thus did Urijah the **p**, according to all that 3548
22: 4 Go up to Hilkiah the high **p**, that he may 3548
22: 8 Hilkiah the high **p** said unto Shaphan 3548
22:10 Hilkiah the **p** hath delivered me a book. 3548
22:12 the king commanded Hilkiah the **p**, and 3548
22:14 So Hilkiah the **p**, and Ahikam, and Achbor, 3548
23: 4 the king commanded Hilkiah the high **p**, 3548
23:24 the **p** found *in* the house of the LORD. 3548
25:18 of the guard took Seraiah the chief **p**, 3548
25:18 Zephaniah the second **p**, and the three 3548
1Ch 16:39 Zadok the **p**, and his brethren the priests, 3548
24: 6 Zadok the **p**, and Ahimelech the son of 3548
27: 5 *was* Benaiah the son of Jehoiada, a chief **p**: 3548
29:22 to be the chief governor, and Zadok to be **p**. 3548
2Ch 13: 9 *the same* may be a **p** of *them that are* no 3548
15: 3 and without a teaching **p**, and without law. 3548
19:11 Amariah the chief **p** *is* over you in all 3548
22:11 king Jehoram, the wife of Jehoiada the **p**, 3548
23: 8 *things* that Jehoiada the **p** had commanded, 3548
23: 8 for Jehoiada the **p** dismissed not 3548
23: 9 Moreover Jehoiada the **p** delivered to 3548
23:14 Jehoiada the **p** brought out the captains of 3548
23:14 For the **p** said, Slay her not *in* the house of 3548
23:17 slew Mattan the **p** of Baal before the altars. 3548
24: 2 the LORD all the days of Jehoiada the **p**. 3548
24:20 upon Zechariah the son of Jehoiada the **p**, 3548
24:25 for the blood of the sons of Jehoiada the **p**, 3548
26:17 Azariah the **p** went in after him, and 3548
26:20 Azariah the chief **p**, and all the priests, 3548
31:10 Azariah the chief **p** of the house of Zadok 3548
34: 9 when they came to Hilkiah the high **p**, 3548
34:14 Hilkiah the **p** found a book of the law of 3548
34:18 saying, Hilkiah the **p** hath given me a book. 3548
Ezr 2:63 *things* till there stood *up* a **p** with Urim 3548
7: 5 of Eleazar, the son of Aaron the chief **p**: 3548
7:11 the king Artaxerxes gave unto Ezra the **p**, 3548
7:12 Artaxerxes, king of kings, unto Ezra the **p**, 3549
7:21 that whatsoever Ezra the **p**, the scribe of 3549
8:33 hand of Meremoth the son of Uriah the **p**; 3548
10:10 Ezra the **p** stood up, and said unto them, 3548
10:16 Ezra the **p**, *with* certain chief of the fathers, 3548
Ne 3: 1 Eliashib the high **p** rose up with his 3548
3:20 door of the house of Eliashib the high **p**. 3548
7:65 *things,* till there stood *up* a **p** with Urim 3548
8: 2 Ezra the **p** brought the law before 3548
8: 9 Ezra the **p** the scribe, and the Levites that 3548
10:38 the **p** the son of Aaron shall be with 3548
12:26 the governor, and of Ezra the **p**, the scribe. 3548
13: 4 before this, Eliashib the **p**, having 3548
13:13 Shelemiah the **p**, and Zadok the scribe, and 3548
13:28 of Joiada, the son of Eliashib the high **p**, 3548
Ps 110: 4 Thou *art* a **p** for ever after the order of 3548
Isa 8: 2 Uriah the **p**, and Zechariah the son of 3548
24: 2 shall be, as *with* the people, so *with* the **p**; 3548
28: 7 the **p** and the prophet have erred through 3548
Jer 6:13 from the prophet even unto the **p** every one 3548
8:10 from the prophet even unto the **p** every one 3548
14:18 the **p** go about into a land that they know 3548
18:18 for the law shall not perish from the **p**, 3548
20: 1 Now Pashur the son of Immer the **p**, 3548
21: 1 Zephaniah the son of Maaseiah the **p**, 3548
23:11 For both prophet and **p** are profane; yea, 3548
23:33 or the prophet, or a **p**, shall ask thee, 3548
23:34 and the **p**, and the people, that shall say, 3548
29:25 to Zephaniah the son of Maaseiah the **p**, 3548
29:26 The LORD hath made thee **p** in the stead 3548
29:26 thee priest in the stead of Jehoiada the **p**, 3548
29:29 Zephaniah the **p** read this letter in the ears 3548
37: 3 Zephaniah the son of Maaseiah the **p** to 3548
52:24 of the guard took Seraiah the chief **p**, 3548
52:24 Zephaniah the second **p**, and the three 3548
La 2: 6 indignation of his anger the king and the **p**. 3548
2:20 shall the **p** and the prophet be slain in 3548
Eze 1: 3 LORD came expressly unto Ezekiel the **p**, 3548
7:26 the law shall perish from the **p**, and 3548
44:13 unto me, to **do the office of a p** unto me, 3547
44:21 Neither shall any **p** drink wine, when they 3548
44:22 of Israel, or a widow that had a **p** before. 3548
44:30 ye shall also give unto the **p** the first of 3548
45:19 the **p** shall take of the blood of the sin 3548
Hos 4: 4 thy people *are* as they that strive with the **p**. 3548
4: 6 reject thee, that *thou* shalt be no **p** to me: 3547
4: 9 there shall be, like people, like **p**: and I will 3548
Am 7:10 Amaziah *the* **p** of Beth-el sent to Jeroboam 3548
Hag 1: 1 to Joshua the son of Josedech the high **p**, 3548
1:12 Joshua the son of Josedech the high **p**, 3548
1:14 of Joshua the son of Josedech the high **p**, 3548
2: 2 to Joshua the son of Josedech the high **p** 3548

Hag 2: 4 O Joshua, son of Josedech, the high **p**; 3548
Zec 3: 1 he shewed me Joshua the high **p** standing 3548
3: 8 O Joshua the high **p**, thou, and thy fellows 3548
6:11 of Joshua the son of Josedech the high **p**; 3548
6:13 he shall be a **p** upon his throne: and 3548
Mt 8: 4 shew thyself to the **p**, and offer the gift that *2409*
26: 3 of the people, unto the palace of the **high p**, *749*
26:57 Jesus led *him* away to Caiaphas the **high p**, *749*
26:62 And the **high p** arose, and said unto him, *749*
26:63 And the **high p** answered and said unto him, *749*
26:65 Then the **high p** rent his clothes, saying, *749*
Mk 1:44 shew thyself to the **p**, and offer for thy *2409*
2:26 of God in the days of Abiathar the **high p**, *749*
14:47 and smote a servant of the **high p**, and *749*
14:53 And they led Jesus away to the **high p**: and *749*
14:54 afar off, even into the palace of the **high p**: *749*
14:60 And the **high p** stood up in the midst, and *749*
14:61 Again the **high p** asked him, and said unto *749*
14:63 Then the **high p** rent his clothes, and saith, *749*
14:66 there cometh one of the maids of the **high p**: *749*
Lk 1: 5 king of Judea, a certain **p** named Zacharias, *2409*
5:14 no *man:* but go, and shew thyself to the **p**, *2409*
10:31 And by chance there came down a certain **p** *2409*
22:50 one of them smote the servant of the **high p**, *749*
Jn 11:49 being the **high p** that *same* year, said unto *749*
11:51 but being **high p** that year, he prophesied *749*
18:13 which was the **high p** that *same* year. *749*
18:15 that disciple was known unto the **high p**, and *749*
18:15 in with Jesus into the palace of the **high p**. *749*
18:16 which was known unto the **high p**, and *749*
18:19 The **high p** then asked Jesus of his disciples, *749*
18:22 saying, Answerest thou the **high p** so? *749*
18:24 sent him bound unto Caiaphas the **high p**. *749*
18:26 One of the servants of the **high p**, being *his* *749*
Ac 4: 6 And Annas the **high p**, and Caiaphas, and *749*
4: 6 many as were of the kindred of the **high p**, *748*
5:17 Then the **high p** rose up, and all they that *749*
5:21 But the **high p** came, and they that were *749*
5:24 Now when the *high* **p** and the captain of *2409*
5:27 the council: and the **high p** asked them, *749*
7: 1 Then said the **high p**, Are these *things* so? *749*
9: 1 disciples of the Lord, went unto the **high p**, *749*
14:13 Then the **p** of Jupiter, which was before *2409*
22: 5 As also the **high p** doth bear me witness, and *749*
23: 2 And the **high p** Ananias commanded them *749*
23: 4 stood by said, Revilest thou God's **high p**? *749*
23: 5 I wist not, brethren, that he was the **high p**: *749*
24: 1 And after five days Ananias the **high p** *749*
25: 2 Then the **high p** and the chief of the Jews *749*
Heb 2:17 faithful **high p** *in things* pertaining to God, *749*
3: 1 the Apostle and **High P** of our profession, *749*
4:14 Seeing then that we have a great **high p**, *749*
4:15 For we have not a **high p** which cannot be *749*
5: 1 For every **high p** taken from among men is *749*
5: 5 glorified not himself to be made a **high p**; *749*
5: 6 a **p** for ever after the order of Melchisedec. *2409*
5:10 Called of God a **high p** after the order of *749*
6:20 made a **high p** for ever after the order of *749*
7: 1 king of Salem, **p** of the most high God, *2409*
7: 3 the Son of God; abideth a **p** continually. *2409*
7:11 what further need *was there* that another **p** *2409*
7:15 of Melchisedec there ariseth another **p**, *2409*
7:17 Thou *art* a **p** for ever after the order of *2409*
7:20 as not without an oath *he was made* **p**: NIG
7:21 Thou *art* a **p** for ever after the order of *2409*
7:26 For such a **high p** became us, *who is* holy, *749*
8: 1 We have such a **high p**, who is set on *749*
8: 3 For every **high p** is ordained to offer gifts *749*
8: 4 if he were on earth, he should not be a **p**, *2409*
9: 7 But into the second *went* the **high p** alone *749*
9:11 But Christ being come a **high p** of good *749*
9:25 as the **high p** entereth into the holy *place* *749*
10:11 And every **p** standeth daily ministering and *2409*
10:21 And *having* a high **p** over the house of *2409*
13:11 into the sanctuary by the **high p** for sin, *749*

PRIEST'S (46) [PRIEST]

Ex 28: 1 he may **minister** unto me **in the p office**, 3547
28: 3 he may **minister** unto me **in the p office**. 3547
28: 4 he may **minister** unto me **in the p office**. 3547
28:41 they may **minister** unto me **in the p office**. 3547
29: 1 to **minister** unto me **in the p office**: 3547
29: 9 the **p office** shall be theirs for a perpetual 3550
29:44 his sons, to **minister** to me **in the p office**. 3547
30:30 *they* may **minister** unto me **in the p office**. 3547
31:10 of his sons, to **minister in the p office**, 3547
35:19 of his sons, to **minister in the p office**. 3547
39:41 sons' garments, to **minister in the p office**. 3547
40:13 he may **minister** unto me **in the p office**. 3547
40:15 they may **minister** unto me **in the p office**: 3547
Lev 5:13 *the remnant* shall be the **p**, as a 3548+3807.1
7: 9 in the pan, shall be the **p** that offereth it. 3548
7:14 it shall be the **p** that sprinkleth 3548+3807.1
7:35 **minister** unto the LORD **in the p office**; 3547
14:13 for as the sin offering *is* the **p**, *so is* 3548
14:18 the remnant of the oil that *is* in the **p** hand 3548
14:29 the rest of the oil that *is* in the **p** hand he 3548
16:32 **minister in the p office** in his father's 3547
22:10 eat *of* the holy *thing:* a sojourner of the **p**, 3548
22:12 If the **p** daughter also be *married* unto a 3548
22:13 if the **p** daughter be a widow, or divorced, 3548
27:21 the possession thereof shall be the **p**. 3548
Nu 3: 3 he consecrated to **minister in the p office**. 3547
3: 4 Ithamar **ministered in the p office** in 3547
3:10 and they shall wait on their **p office**: 3550
18: 7 thy sons with thee shall keep your **p office** 3550
18: 7 I have given your **p office** *unto you as* a 3550
Dt 10: 6 Eleazar his son **ministered in the p office** 3547
18: 3 And this shall be the **p** due from the people, 3548
Jdg 18:20 the **p** heart was glad, and he took 3548
1Sa 2:13 the **p** servant came, while the flesh was in 3548
2:15 the **p** servant came, and said to the man that 3548
1Ch 6:10 (he *it is* that **executed the p office** in 3547
24: 2 Eleazar and Ithamar **executed the p office**. 3547
2Ch 11:14 **executing the p office** unto the LORD: 3547
24:11 and the high **p** officer came and 3548
Mal 2: 7 For the **p** lips should keep knowledge, and 3548
Mt 26:51 and stroke a servant of the **high p**, and *749*
26:58 followed him afar off unto the **high p** palace, *749*
Lk 1: 8 *that* while he **executed the p office** before *2407*
1: 9 According to the custom of the **p office**, *2405*
22:54 and brought him into the **high p** house. *749*
Jn 18:10 and smote the **high p** servant, and cut off his *749*

PRIESTHOOD (16) [PRIEST]

Ex 40:15 everlasting **p** throughout their generations. 3550
Nu 16:10 of Levi with thee: and seek ye the **p** also? 3550
18: 1 with thee shall bear the iniquity of your **p**. 3550
25:13 *even* the covenant of an everlasting **p**; 3550
Jos 18: 7 for the **p** of the LORD *is* their inheritance: 3550
Ezr 2:62 were they, as polluted, put from the **p**. 3550
Ne 7:64 were they, as polluted, put from the **p**. 3550
13:29 because they have defiled the **p**, and 3550
13:29 the covenant of the **p**, and of the Levites. 3550
Heb 7: 5 **office of the p** have a commandment to *2405*
7:11 perfection were by the Levitical **p**, *2420*
7:12 For the **p** being changed, there is made of *2420*
7:14 tribe Moses spake nothing concerning **p**. *2420*
7:24 continueth ever, hath an unchangeable **p**. *2420*
1Pe 2: 5 are built *up* a spiritual house, a holy **p**, *2406*
2: 9 a royal **p**, a holy nation, a peculiar people; *2406*

PRIESTS (392) [PRIEST]

Ge 47:22 Only the land of the **p** bought he not; 3548
47:22 for the **p** had a portion assigned them of 3548
47:26 the fifth *part;* except the land of the **p** only, 3548
Ex 19: 6 ye shall be unto me a kingdom of **p**, and 3548
19:22 let the **p** also, which come near to 3548
19:24 let not the **p** and the people break through 3548
Lev 1: 5 the **p**, Aaron's sons, shall bring the blood, 3548
1: 8 And the **p**, Aaron's sons, shall lay the parts, 3548
1:11 the **p**, Aaron's sons, shall sprinkle his blood 3548
2: 2 he shall bring it to Aaron's sons the **p**: and 3548
3: 2 Aaron's sons the **p** shall sprinkle the blood 3548
6:29 All the males among the **p** shall eat thereof: 3548
7: 6 Every male among the **p** shall eat thereof: 3548
13: 2 the priest, or unto one of his sons the **p**: 3548
16:33 he shall make an atonement for the **p**, and 3548
21: 1 Speak unto the **p** the sons of Aaron, and 3548
Nu 3: 3 sons of Aaron, the **p** which were anointed, 3548
10: 8 the sons of Aaron, the **p**, shall blow with 3548
Dt 17: 9 And thou shalt come unto the **p** the Levites, 3548
17:18 of *that which is* before the **p** the Levites: 3548
18: 1 The **p** the Levites, *and* all the tribe of Levi, 3548
19:17 before the **p** and the judges, which shall be 3548
21: 5 the **p** the sons of Levi shall come near; 3548
24: 8 do according to all that the **p** the Levites 3548
27: 9 and the **p** the Levites spake unto all Israel, 3548
31: 9 delivered it unto the **p** the sons of Levi, 3548
Jos 3: 3 the **p** the Levites bearing it, then ye shall 3548
3: 6 Joshua spake unto the **p**, saying, Take up 3548
3: 8 thou shalt command the **p** that bear the ark 3548
3:13 as soon as the soles of the feet of the **p** that 3548
3:14 the **p** bearing the ark *of* the covenant before 3548
3:15 the feet of the **p** that bare the ark were 3548
3:17 the **p** that bare the ark *of* the covenant of 3548
4: 9 in the place where the feet of the **p** which 3548
4:10 For the **p** which bare the ark stood in 3548
4:11 and the **p**, in the presence of the people. 3548
4:16 Command the **p** that bear the ark of 3548
4:17 Joshua therefore commanded the **p**, saying, 3548
4:18 when the **p** that bare the ark of the covenant 3548
6: 4 seven **p** shall bear before the ark seven 3548
6: 4 and the **p** shall blow with the trumpets. 3548
6: 6 Joshua the son of Nun called the **p**, and 3548
6: 6 let seven **p** bear seven trumpets of rams' 3548
6: 8 that the seven **p** bearing the seven trumpets 3548
6: 9 the armed men went before the **p** that blew 3548
6: 9 *the* **p** going on, and blowing with NIH
6:12 and the **p** took up the ark of the LORD. 3548
6:13 seven **p** bearing seven trumpets of rams' 3548
6:13 *the* **p** going on, and blowing with NIH
6:16 when the **p** blew with the trumpets, Joshua 3548
6:20 So the people shouted when *the* **p** blew with NIH
8:33 and on that side before the **p** the Levites, 3548
21:19 the cities of the children of Aaron, the **p**, 3548
Jdg 18:30 his sons were **p** to the tribe of Dan until 3548
1Sa 1: 3 Hophni and Phinehas, the **p** of the LORD, 3548
5: 5 Therefore neither the **p** of Dagon, nor any 3548
6: 2 the Philistines called for the **p** and 3548
22:11 his father's house, the **p** that *were* in Nob: 3548
22:17 Turn, and slay the **p** of the LORD; 3548
22:17 their hand to fall upon the **p** of the LORD. 3548
22:18 to Doeg, Turn thou, and fall upon the **p**. 3548
22:18 he fell upon the **p**, and slew on that day 3548
22:19 Nob, the city of the **p**, smote he with 3548
22:21 David that Saul had slain the LORD'S **p**. 3548
2Sa 8:17 Ahimelech the son of Abiathar, *were* the **p**; 3548
15:35 there with thee Zadok and Abiathar the **p**? 3548
15:35 shalt tell *it* to Zadok and Abiathar the **p**. 3548
17:15 Hushai unto Zadok and to Abiathar the **p**, 3548
19:11 David sent to Zadok and to Abiathar the **p**, 3548
20:25 and Zadok and Abiathar *were* the **p**: 3548
1Ki 4: 4 and Zadok and Abiathar *were* the **p**: 3548
8: 3 of Israel came, and the **p** took up the ark. 3548
8: 4 even those did the **p** and the Levites bring 3548
8: 6 the **p** brought in the ark of the covenant of 3548
8:10 when the **p** were come out of the holy 3548
8:11 So that the **p** could not stand to minister 3548
12:31 made **p** of the lowest of the people, 3548
12:32 he placed in Beth-el the **p** of the high 3548
13: 2 upon thee shall he offer the **p** of the high 3548
13:33 made again of the lowest of the people **p** of 3548
13:33 he became *one of* the **p** of the high places. 3548
2Ki 10:11 his great *men,* and his kinsfolks, and his **p**, 3548
10:19 of Baal, all his servants, and all his **p**; 3548
12: 4 Jehoash said to the **p**, All the money of 3548
12: 5 Let the **p** take *it* to them, every man of his 3548
12: 6 twentieth year of king Jehoash the **p** had 3548
12: 7 the *other* **p**, and said unto them, Why repair 3548
12: 8 the **p** consented to receive no *more* money 3548
12: 9 the **p** that kept the door put therein all 3548
17:27 Carry thither one of the **p** whom ye brought 3548
17:28 one of the **p** whom they had carried away 3548
17:32 of the lowest of them **p** of the high places, 3548
19: 2 Shebna the scribe, and the elders of the **p**, 3548
23: 2 the **p**, and the prophets, and all the people, 3548
23: 4 high priest, and the **p** of the second order; 3548
23: 5 he put down the **idolatrous p**, whom 3649
23: 8 he brought all the **p** out of the cities of 3548
23: 8 defiled the high places where the **p** had 3548
23: 9 Nevertheless the **p** of the high places came 3548
23:20 he slew all the **p** of the high places that 3548
1Ch 9: 2 the **p**, Levites, and the Nethinims. 3548
9:10 of the **p**; Jedaiah, and Jehoiarib, and Jachin, 3548
9:30 *some* of the sons of the **p** made 3548
13: 2 with them *also to* the **p** and Levites *which* 3548
15:11 David called for Zadok and Abiathar the **p**, 3548
15:14 So the **p** and the Levites sanctified 3548
15:24 Zechariah, and Benaiah, and Eliezer, the **p**, 3548
16: 6 Jahaziel the **p** with trumpets continually 3548
16:39 Zadok the priest, and his brethren the **p**, 3548
18:16 Abimelech the son of Abiathar, *were* the **p**; 3548
23: 2 of Israel, with the **p** and the Levites. 3548
24: 6 *before* the chief of the fathers of the **p** and 3548
24:31 the chief of the fathers of the **p** and Levites, 3548
28:13 Also for the courses of the **p** and 3548
28:21 the courses of the **p** and the Levites, 3548
2Ch 4: 6 but the sea *was* for the **p** to wash in. 3548
4: 9 Furthermore he made the court of the **p**, 3548
5: 5 these did the **p** *and* the Levites bring up. 3548
5: 7 the **p** brought in the ark of the covenant of 3548
5:11 when the **p** were come out of the holy 3548
5:11 all the **p** that were present were sanctified, 3548
5:12 and twenty **p** sounding with trumpets:) 3548
5:14 So that the **p** could not stand to minister by 3548
6:41 let thy **p**, O LORD God, be clothed *with* 3548
7: 2 the **p** could not enter into the house of 3548
7: 6 the **p** waited on their offices: the Levites 3548
7: 6 the **p** sounded trumpets before them, and 3548
8:14 the courses of the **p** to their service, and 3548
8:14 to praise and minister before the **p**, 3548
8:15 the commandment of the king unto the **p** 3548
11:13 the **p** and the Levites that *were* in all Israel 3548
11:15 he ordained him **p** for the high places, and 3548
13: 9 Have ye not cast out the **p** of the LORD, 3548
13: 9 have made you **p** after the manner of 3548
13:10 the **p**, which minister unto the LORD, 3548
13:12 his **p** with sounding trumpets to cry alarm 3548
13:14 and the **p** sounded with the trumpets. 3548
17: 8 and with them Elishama and Jehoram, **p**. 3548
19: 8 *of* the **p**, and of the chief of the fathers of 3548
23: 4 of the **p** and of the Levites, *shall be* porters 3548
23: 6 save the **p**, and they that minister of 3548
23:18 LORD by the hand of the **p** the Levites, 3548
24: 5 he gathered together the **p** and the Levites, 3548
26:17 with him fourscore **p** of the LORD, 3548
26:18 the LORD, but to the **p** the sons of Aaron, 3548
26:19 while he was wroth with the **p**, the leprosy 3548
26:19 before the **p** in the house of the LORD, 3548
26:20 and all the **p**, looked upon him, and behold, 3548
29: 4 he brought in the **p** and the Levites, and 3548
29:16 the **p** went into the inner part *of* the house 3548
29:21 he commanded the **p** the sons of Aaron to 3548
29:22 the **p** received the blood, and sprinkled *it* 3548
29:24 the **p** killed them, and they made 3548
29:26 of David, and the **p** with the trumpets. 3548
29:34 the **p** were *too* few, so that they could not 3548
29:34 until the *other* **p** had sanctified themselves: 3548
29:34 in heart to sanctify themselves than the **p**. 3548
30: 3 the **p** had not sanctified themselves 3548
30:15 the **p** and the Levites were ashamed, and 3548
30:16 the **p** sprinkled the blood, *which they* 3548
30:21 and the **p** praised the LORD day by day, 3548
30:24 a great number of **p** sanctified themselves. 3548
30:25 with the **p** and the Levites, and all 3548
30:27 the **p** the Levites arose and blessed 3548
31: 2 Hezekiah appointed the courses of the **p** 3548
31: 2 the **p** and Levites for burnt offerings and 3548
31: 4 in Jerusalem to give the portion of the **p** 3548
31: 9 Hezekiah questioned with the **p** and 3548
31:15 and Shecaniah, in the cities of the **p**, 3548
31:17 Both *to* the genealogy of the **p** by the house 3548
31:19 Also of the sons of Aaron the **p**, 3548
31:19 give portions to all the males among the **p**, 3548
34: 5 he burnt the bones of the **p** upon their 3548
34:30 the **p**, and the Levites, and all the people, 3548
35: 2 he set the **p** in their charges, and 3548
35: 8 the people, to the **p**, and to the Levites: 3548
35: 8 gave unto the **p** for the passover *offerings* 3548
35:10 the **p** stood in their place, and the Levites in 3548
35:11 the **p** sprinkled *the blood* from their hands, 3548
35:14 made ready for themselves, and for the **p**: 3548
35:14 the **p** the sons of Aaron *were busied* in 3548
35:14 and for the **p** the sons of Aaron. 3548
35:18 the **p**, and the Levites, and all Judah and 3548
36:14 Moreover all the chief of the **p**, and 3548
Ezr 1: 5 and Benjamin, and the **p**, and the Levites, 3548
2:36 The **p**: the children of Jedaiah, of the house 3548
2:61 of the children of the **p**: the children of 3548
2:70 So the **p**, and the Levites, and *some* of 3548
3: 2 his brethren the **p**, and Zerubbabel the son 3548
3: 8 the remnant of their brethren the **p** and 3548
3:10 they set the **p** in their apparel with 3548
3:12 many of the **p** and Levites and chief of 3548
6: 9 according to the appointment of the **p** 3549
6:16 the **p**, and the Levites, and the rest of 3549
6:18 they set the **p** in their divisions, and 3549
6:20 For the **p** and the Levites were purified 3548
6:20 for their brethren the **p**, and for themselves. 3548
7: 7 of the **p**, and the Levites, and the singers, 3548
7:13 and *of* his **p** and Levites, in my realm, 3549
7:16 offering of the people, and of the **p**, 3549
7:24 that *touching* any of the **p** and Levites, 3549
8:15 the **p**, and found there none of the sons of 3548

P

Ezr 8:24 I separated twelve of the chief of the **p**, 3548
8:29 ye weigh *them* before the chief of the **p** 3548
8:30 So took the **p** and the Levites the weight of 3548
9: 1 people of Israel, and the **p**, and the Levites, 3548
9: 7 iniquities have we, our kings, *and* our **p**, 3548
10: 5 made the chief **p**, the Levites, and all Israel, 3548
10:18 among the sons of the **p** there were found 3548
Ne 2:16 nor to the **p**, nor to the nobles, nor to 3548
3: 1 high priest rose up with his brethren the **p**, 3548
3:22 after him repaired the **p**, the men of 3548
3:28 From above the horse gate repaired the **p**, 3548
5:12 I called the **p**, and took an oath of them, 3548
7:39 The **p**: the children of Jedaiah, of the house 3548
7:63 of the **p**: the children of Habaiah, 3548
7:73 So the **p**, and the Levites, and the porters, 3548
8:13 the **p**, and the Levites, unto Ezra the scribe, 3548
9:32 on our **p**, and on our prophets, and on our 3548
9:34 our princes, our **p**, nor our fathers, kept thy 3548
9:38 write *it;* and our princes, Levites, *and* **p**, 3548
10: 8 Bilgai, Shemaiah: these *were* the **p**. 3548
10:28 the **p**, the Levites, the porters, the singers, 3548
10:34 we cast the lots *among* the **p**, the Levites, 3548
10:36 unto the **p** that minister in the house of our 3548
10:37 *of* trees, of wine and of oil, unto the **p**, 3548
10:39 the **p** that minister, and the porters, and 3548
11: 3 the **p**, and the Levites, and the Nethinims, 3548
11:10 Of the **p**: Jedaiah the son of Joiarib, Jachin, 3548
11:20 residue of Israel, of the **p**, *and* the Levites, 3548
12: 1 Now these *are* the **p** and the Levites that 3548
12: 7 These *were* the chief of the **p** and of their 3548
12:12 in the days of Joiakim were **p**, the chief of 3548
12:22 also the **p**, to the reign of Darius 3548
12:30 the **p** and the Levites purified themselves, 3548
12:41 the **p**; Eliakim, Maaseiah, Miniamin, 3548
12:44 the cities the portions of the law for the **p** 3548
12:44 for Judah rejoiced for the **p** and for 3548
13: 5 and the porters; and the offerings of the **p**. 3548
13:30 appointed the wards of the **p** and 3548
Ps 78:64 Their **p** fell by the sword; and their widows 3548
99: 6 Moses and Aaron among his **p**, and 3548
132: 9 Let thy **p** be clothed *with* righteousness; 3548
132:16 I will also clothe her **p** with salvation: and 3548
Isa 37: 2 the elders of the **p** covered with sackcloth, 3548
61: 6 But ye shall be named the **P** of the LORD: 3548
66:21 I will also take of them for **p** *and* 3548
Jer 1: 1 of the **p** that *were* in Anathoth in the land 3548
1:18 against the **p** thereof, and against 3548
2: 8 The **p** said not, Where *is* the LORD? and 3548
2:26 and their **p**, and their prophets, 3548
4: 9 the **p** shall be astonished, and the prophets 3548
5:31 and the **p** bear rule by their means; 3548
8: 1 the bones of the **p**, and the bones of 3548
13:13 the **p**, and the prophets, and all 3548
19: 1 of the people, and of the ancients of the **p**; 3548
26: 7 So the **p** and the prophets and all the people 3548
26: 8 that the **p** and the prophets and all 3548
26:11 spake the **p** and the prophets unto 3548
26:16 all the people unto the **p** and to 3548
27:16 Also I spake to the **p** and to all this people, 3548
28: 1 in the presence of the **p** and of all 3548
28: 5 prophet Hananiah in the presence of the **p**, 3548
29: 1 to the **p**, and to the prophets, and to all 3548
29:25 the priest, and to all the **p**, saying, 3548
31:14 I will satiate the soul of the **p** with fatness, 3548
32:32 their **p**, and their prophets, and the men of 3548
33:18 Neither shall the **p** the Levites want a man 3548
33:21 and with the Levites the **p**, my ministers. 3548
34:19 and the **p**, and all the people of the land, 3548
48: 7 shall go forth into captivity *with* his **p** 3548
49: 3 *and* his **p** and his princes together. 3548
La 1: 4 her **p** sigh: her virgins *are* afflicted, and 3548
1:19 my **p** and mine elders gave up the ghost in 3548
4:13 of her prophets, *and* the iniquities of her **p**, 3548
4:16 they respected not the persons of the **p**, 3548
Eze 22:26 Her **p** have violated my law, and 3548
40:45 prospect *is* toward the south, *is* for the **p**, 3548
40:46 prospect *is* toward the north *is* for the **p**, 3548
42:13 where the **p** that approach unto the LORD 3548
42:14 When the **p** enter *therein*, then shall they 3548
43:19 thou shalt give to the **p** the Levites that *be* 3548
43:24 the **p** shall cast salt upon them, and 3548
43:27 the **p** shall make your burnt offerings upon 3548
44:15 the **p** the Levites, the sons of Zadok, 3548
44:31 The **p** shall not eat *of* any thing that is dead 3548
45: 4 be for the **p** the ministers of the sanctuary, 3548
46: 2 the **p** shall prepare his burnt offering and 3548
46:19 into the holy chambers of the **p**, 3548
46:20 This *is* the place where the **p** shall boil 3548
48:10 for them, *even* for the **p**, shall be *this* holy 3548
48:11 *It shall be* for the **p** that are sanctified of 3548
48:13 over against the border of the **p**, the Levites 3548
Hos 5: 1 Hear ye this, O **p**; and hearken, ye house of 3548
6: 9 the company of **p** murder *in* the way by 3548
10: 5 the **p** thereof *that* rejoiced on it, for 3649
Joel 1: 9 the **p**, the LORD'S ministers, mourn. 3548
1:13 Gird yourselves, and lament, ye **p**: howl, 3548
2:17 Let the **p**, the ministers of the LORD, 3548
Mic 3:11 the **p** thereof teach for hire, and 3548
Zep 1: 4 *and* the name of the Chemarims with the **p**; 3548
3: 4 her **p** have polluted the sanctuary, 3548
Hag 2:11 Ask now the **p** *concerning* the law, saying, 3548
2:12 be holy? And the **p** answered and said, No. 3548
2:13 the **p** answered and said, It shall be 3548
Zec 7: 3 *And* to speak unto the **p** which *were* in 3548
7: 5 to the **p**, saying, When ye fasted and 3548
Mal 1: 6 hosts unto you, O **p**, that despise my name. 3548
2: 1 now, O ye **p**, this commandment *is* for you. 3548
Mt 2: 4 And when he had gathered all the **chief p** *749*
12: 4 which were with him, but only for the **p**? *2409*
12: 5 how that on the sabbath days the **p** in *2409*
16:21 *things* of the elders and **chief p** and scribes, *749*
20:18 of man shall be betrayed unto the **chief p** *749*
21:15 And when the **chief p** and scribes saw *749*
21:23 the **chief p** and the elders of the people came *749*
21:45 And when the **chief p** and Pharisees had *749*
Mt 26: 3 Then assembled together the **chief p**, and *749*
26:14 called Judas Iscariot, went unto the **chief p**, *749*
26:47 from the **chief p** and elders of the people. *749*
26:59 Now the **chief p**, and elders, and all *749*
27: 1 all the **chief p** and elders of the people took *749*
27: 3 again the thirty pieces of silver to the **chief p** *749*
27: 6 And the **chief p** took the silver pieces, and *749*
27:12 And when he was accused of the **chief p** and *749*
27:20 But the **chief p** and elders persuaded *749*
27:41 Likewise also the **chief p** mocking *him*, with *749*
27:62 the **chief p** and Pharisees came together unto *749*
28:11 shewed unto the **chief p** all the *things* that *749*
Mk 2:26 which is not lawful to eat but for the **p**, and *2409*
8:31 of the elders, and *of* the **chief p**, and scribes, *749*
10:33 of man shall be delivered unto the **chief p**, *749*
11:18 And the scribes and **chief p** heard *it*, and *749*
11:27 there come to him the **chief p**, and *749*
14: 1 and the **chief p** and the scribes sought how *749*
14:10 one of the twelve, went unto the **chief p**, *749*
14:43 from the **chief p** and the scribes and *749*
14:53 with him were assembled all the **chief p** and *749*
14:55 And the **chief p** and all the council sought *749*
15: 1 And straightway in the morning the **chief p** *749*
15: 3 And the **chief p** accused him of many *things:* *749*
15:10 For he knew that the **chief p** had delivered *749*
15:11 But the **chief p** moved the people, that he *749*
15:31 Likewise also the **chief p** mocking said *749*
Lk 3: 2 Annas and Caiaphas being the **high p**, *749*
6: 4 it is not lawful to eat but for the **p** alone? *2409*
9:22 of the elders and **chief p** and scribes, *749*
17:14 unto them, Go shew yourselves unto the **p**. *2409*
19:47 But the **chief p** and the scribes and the chief *749*
20: 1 the **chief p** and the scribes came upon *him* *749*
20:19 And the **chief p** and the scribes the same *749*
22: 2 And the **chief p** and scribes sought how they *749*
22: 4 and communed with the **chief p** and *749*
22:52 Then Jesus said unto the **chief p**, and *749*
22:66 the elders of the people and the **chief p** and *749*
23: 4 Then said Pilate to the **chief p** and *to* *749*
23:10 And the **chief p** and scribes stood and *749*
23:13 when he had called together the **chief p** and *749*
23:23 voices of them and of the **chief p** prevailed. *749*
24:20 And how the **chief p** and our rulers delivered *749*
Jn 1:19 when the Jews sent **p** and Levites from *2409*
7:32 and the **chief p** sent officers to take him. *749*
7:45 Then came the officers to the **chief p** and *749*
11:47 Then gathered the **chief p** and the Pharisees *749*
11:57 Now both the chief **p** and the Pharisees had *749*
12:10 But the **chief p** consulted that they might put *749*
18: 3 and officers from the **chief p** and Pharisees, *749*
18:35 and the **chief p** have delivered thee unto me: *749*
19: 6 When the **chief p** therefore and officers saw *749*
19:15 The **chief p** answered, We have no king but *749*
19:21 Then said the **chief p** of the Jews to Pilate, *749*
Ac 4: 1 the **p**, and the captain of the temple, and *2409*
4:23 and reported all that the **chief p** and elders *749*
5:24 and the **chief p** heard these things, *749*
6: 7 a great company of the **p** were obedient to *2409*
9:14 And here he hath authority from the **chief p** *749*
9:21 he might bring them bound unto the **chief p**? *749*
19:14 a Jew, *and* **chief of the p**, which did so. *749*
22:30 and commanded the **chief p** and all their *749*
23:14 And they came to the **chief p** and elders, and *749*
25:15 the **chief p** and the elders of the Jews *749*
26:10 having received authority from the **chief p**; *749*
26:12 and commission from the **chief p**, *749*
Heb 7:21 (For those **p** were made without an oath; *2409*
7:23 And they truly were many **p**, because *2409*
7:27 as *those* **high p**, to offer up sacrifice, first for *749*
7:28 For the law maketh men **high p** which have *749*
8: 4 seeing that there are **p** that offer gifts *2409*
9: 6 the **p** went always into the first tabernacle, *2409*
Rev 1: 6 us kings and **p** unto God and his Father; *2409*
5:10 hast made us unto our God kings and **p**: *2409*
20: 6 but they shall be **p** of God and of Christ, *2409*

PRIESTS' (10) [PRIEST]

Jos 4: 3 out of the place where the **p** feet stood firm, 3548
4:18 the soles of the **p** feet were lift up unto 3548
1Sa 2:13 the **p** custom with the people *was, that* 3548
2:36 I pray thee, into one of the **p offices**, 3550
2Ki 12:16 *into* the house of the LORD: it was the **p**. 3548
Ezr 2:69 *of* silver, and one hundred **p** garments. 3548
Ne 7:70 five hundred and thirty **p** garments. 3548
7:72 and threescore and seven **p** garments. 3548
12:35 *certain* of the **p** sons with trumpets; 3548
Eze 44:30 of your oblations, shall be the **p**: 3548+3807.1

PRINCE (102) [PRINCE'S, PRINCES, PRINCESS, PRINCESSES]

Ge 23: 6 thou *art* a mighty **p** among us: in the choice 5387
32:28 for **as a p hast** thou **power** with God and 8280
34: 2 **p** of the country, saw her, he took her, and 5387
Ex 2:14 Who made thee a **p** and a judge over us? 8269
Nu 7:11 each **p** on *his* day, for the dedicating of 5387
7:18 the son of Zuar, **p** of Issachar, did offer: 5387
7:24 **p** of the children of Zebulun, *did offer:* 5387
7:30 **p** of the children of Reuben, *did offer:* 5387
7:36 **p** of the children of Simeon, *did offer:* 5387
7:42 of Deuel, **p** of the children of Gad, *offered:* 5387
7:48 **p** of the children of Ephraim, *offered:* 5387
7:54 of Pedahzur, **p** of the children of Manasseh: 5387
7:60 **p** of the children of Benjamin, *offered:* 5387
7:66 **p** of the children of Dan, *offered:* 5387
7:72 **p** of the children of Asher, *offered:* 5387
7:78 **p** of the children of Naphtali, *offered:* 5387
16:13 **make** thyself **altogether a p** over 8323+8323
17: 6 for each **p** one, according to their fathers' 5387
25:14 a **p** of a chief house among the Simeonites. 5387
25:18 the daughter of a **p** of Midian, their sister, 5387
34:18 ye shall take one **p** of every tribe, to divide 5387
34:22 the **p** of the tribe of the children of Dan, 5387
34:23 The **p** of the children of Joseph, for 5387
34:24 the **p** of the tribe of the children of 5387
Nu 34:25 the **p** of the tribe of the children of 5387
34:26 the **p** of the tribe of the children of 5387
34:27 the **p** of the tribe of the children of Asher, 5387
34:28 the **p** of the tribe of the children of 5387
Jos 22:14 of each chief house a **p** throughout all the tribes 1
2Sa 3:38 Know ye not that there is a **p** and a great 8269
1Ki 11:34 I will make him **p** all the days of his life for 5387
14: 7 and made thee **p** over my people Israel, 5057
16: 2 and made thee **p** over my people Israel; 5057
1Ch 2:10 begat Nahshon, **p** of the children of Judah; 5387
5: 6 away captive: he *was* **p** of the Reubenites. 5387
Ezr 1: 8 them unto Sheshbazzar, the **p** of Judah. 5387
Job 21:28 For ye say, Where *is* the house of the **p**? 5081
31:37 my steps; as a **p** would I go near unto him. 5057
Pr 14:28 want of people *is* the destruction of the **p**. 7333
17: 7 not a fool: much less do lying lips a **p**. 5081
19: 6 Many will intreat the favour of the **p**: and 5081
25: 7 of the **p** whom thine eyes have seen. 5081
25:15 By long forbearing is a **p** persuaded, and 7101
28:16 The **p** that wanteth understanding *is* also a 5057
Isa 9: 6 The everlasting Father, The **P** of Peace. 8269
Jer 51:59 of his reign. And *this* Seraiah *was* a quiet **p**. 8269
Eze 7:27 the **p** shall be clothed with desolation, and 5387
12:10 This burden *concerneth* the **p** in Jerusalem, 5387
12:12 the **p** that *is* among them shall bear upon 5387
21:25 thou, profane wicked **p** of Israel, whose day 5387
28: 2 Son of man, say unto the **p** of Tyrus, 5057
30:13 there shall be no more a **p** of the land of 5387
34:24 and my servant David a **p** among them; 5387
37:25 my servant David *shall be* their **p** for ever. 5387
38: 2 the chief **p** of Meshech and Tubal, and 5387
38: 3 O Gog, the chief **p** of Meshech and Tubal: 5387
39: 1 O Gog, the chief **p** of Meshech and Tubal: 5387
44: 3 *It is* for the **p**; the prince, he shall sit in it to 5387
44: 3 the **p**, he shall sit in it to eat bread before 5387
45: 7 *a portion shall be* for the **p** on the one side 5387
45:16 shall give this oblation for the **p** in Israel. 5387
45:22 upon that day shall the **p** prepare for 5387
46: 2 the **p** shall enter by the way of the porch of 5387
46: 4 the burnt offering that the **p** shall offer unto 5387
46: 8 when the **p** shall enter, he shall go in *by* 5387
46:10 the **p** in the midst of them, when they go in, 5387
46:12 Now when the **p** shall prepare a voluntary 5387
46:16 If the **p** give a gift unto any of his sons, 5387
46:17 year of liberty; after, it shall return to the **p**: 5387
46:18 Moreover the **p** shall not take of 5387
48:21 the residue *shall be* for the **p**, on the one 5387
48:21 over against the portions for the **p**: 5387
48:22 the border of Benjamin, shall be for the **p**. 5387
Da 1: 7 Unto whom the **p** of the eunuchs gave 8269
1: 8 he requested of the **p** of the eunuchs that he 8269
1: 9 and tender love with the **p** of the eunuchs. 8269
1:10 the **p** of the eunuchs said unto Daniel, I fear 8269
1:11 whom the **p** of the eunuchs had set over 8269
1:18 the **p** of the eunuchs brought them in before 8269
8:11 he magnified *himself even* to the **p** of 8269
8:25 he shall also stand up against the **P** of 8269
9:25 to build Jerusalem unto the Messiah the **P** 5057
9:26 the people of the **p** that *shall* come shall 5057
10:13 the **p** of the kingdom of Persia withstood 8269
10:20 now will I return to fight with the **p** of 8269
10:20 gone forth, lo, the **p** of Grecia shall come. 8269
10:21 me in these *things*, but Michael your **p**. 8269
11:18 a **p** for his own behalf shall cause 7101
11:22 be broken; yea also, the **p** of the covenant. 5057
12: 1 the great **p** which standeth for the children 8269
Hos 3: 4 without a **p**, and without a sacrifice, and 8269
Mic 7: 3 the **p** asketh, and the judge *asketh* for a 8269
Mt 9:34 He casteth out the devils through the **p** of *758*
12:24 but by Beelzebub the **p** of the devils. *758*
Mk 3:22 by the **p** of the devils casteth he out devils. *758*
Jn 12:31 now shall the **p** of this world be cast out. *758*
14:30 for the **p** of this world cometh, and *758*
16:11 because the **p** of this world is judged. *758*
Ac 3:15 And killed the **P** of life, whom God hath *747*
5:31 God exalted with his right hand *to be* a **P** *747*
Eph 2: 2 according to the **p** of the power of the air, *758*
Rev 1: 5 the dead, and the **p** of the kings of the earth. *758*

PRINCE'S (3) [PRINCE]

SS 7: 1 are thy feet with shoes, O **p** daughter! 5081
Eze 45:17 it shall be the **p** part *to give* burnt offerings, 5387
48:22 in the midst *of that* which is the **p**, 5387+3807.1

PRINCES (273) [PRINCE]

Ge 12:15 The **p** also of Pharaoh saw her, and 8269
17:20 twelve **p** shall he beget, and I will make 5387
25:16 twelve **p** according to their nations. 5387
Nu 1:16 **p** of the tribes of their fathers, heads of 5387
1:44 and Aaron numbered, and the **p** of Israel, 5387
7: 2 That the **p** of Israel, heads of the house of 5387
7: 2 who *were* the **p** of the tribes, and were over 5387
7: 3 a wagon for two of the **p**, and for *each* one 5387
7:10 the **p** offered *for* dedicating of the altar in 5387
7:10 even the **p** offered their offering before 5387
7:84 when it was anointed, by the **p** of Israel: 5387
10: 4 they blow *but* with one *trumpet*, then the **p**, 5387
16: 2 two hundred and fifty **p** of the assembly, 5387
17: 2 of all their **p** according to the house of their 5387
17: 6 every one of their **p** gave him a rod apiece, 5387
21:18 The **p** digged the well, the nobles of 8269
22: 8 and the **p** of Moab abode with Balaam. 8269
22:13 said unto the **p** of Balak, Get you into your 8269
22:14 the **p** of Moab rose up, and they went unto 8269
22:15 Balak sent yet again **p**, more, and 8269
22:21 his ass, and went with the **p** of Moab. 8269
22:35 So Balaam went with the **p** of Balak. 8269
22:40 to Balaam, and to the **p** that *were* with him. 8269
23: 6 burnt sacrifice, he, and all the **p** of Moab. 8269
23:17 burnt offering, and the **p** of Moab with him. 8269
27: 2 and before the **p** and all the congregation, 5387
31:13 the priest, and all the **p** of the congregation, 5387
32: 2 and unto the **p** of the congregation, saying, 5387
36: 1 and spake before Moses, and before the **p**, 5387
Jos 9:15 the **p** of the congregation sware unto them. 5387

Jos 9:18 the p of the congregation had sworn unto 5387
9:18 the congregation murmured against the p. 5387
9:19 all the p said unto all the congregation, 5387
9:21 the p said unto them, Let them live; but 5387
9:21 as the p had promised them. 5387
13:21 whom Moses smote with the p of Midian, 5387
17: 4 the son of Nun, and before the p, saying, 5387
22:14 with him ten p, of each chief house a prince 5387
22:30 the p of the congregation and heads of 5387
22:32 the p, returned from the children of 5387
Jdg 5: 3 give ear, O ye p; I, *even* I, will sing unto 7336
5:15 the p of Issachar *were* with Deborah; 8269
7:25 they took two p of the Midianites, Oreb 8269
8: 3 God hath delivered into your hands the p of 8269
8: 6 the p of Succoth said, *Are* the hands of 8269
8:14 he described unto him the p of Succoth, 8269
10:18 *and* p of Gilead said one to another, 8269
1Sa 2: 8 to set *them* among p, and to make them 5081
18:30 the p of the Philistines went forth: and 8269
29: 3 said the p of the Philistines, What *do* these 8269
29: 3 Achish said unto the p of the Philistines, 8269
29: 4 the p of the Philistines were wroth with 8269
29: 4 the p of the Philistines said unto him, 8269
29: 9 notwithstanding the p of the Philistines 8269
2Sa 10: 3 the p of the children of Ammon said unto 8269
19: 6 that thou regardest neither p nor servants: 8269
1Ki 4: 2 these *were* the p which he had; Azariah 8269
9:22 his p, and his captains, and rulers of his 8269
20:14 *Even* by the young men of the p of 8269
20:15 he numbered the young men of the p of 8269
20:17 the young men of the p of the provinces 8269
20:19 So these young men of the p of 8269
2Ki 11:14 as the manner *was*, and the p and 8269
24:12 and his servants, and his p, and his officers: 8269
24:14 all the p, and all the mighty *men* of valour, 8269
1Ch 4:38 These mentioned by *their* names *were* p in 5387
7:40 *and* mighty *men* of valour, chief of the p. 5387
19: 3 the p of the children of Ammon said to 8269
22:17 David also commanded all the p of Israel to 8269
23: 2 he gathered together all the p of Israel, 8269
24: 6 the p, and Zadok the priest, and 8269
27:22 These *were* the p of the tribes of Israel. 8269
28: 1 David assembled all the p of Israel, 8269
28: 1 the p of the tribes, and the captains of 8269
28:21 also the p and all the people *will be* wholly 8269
29: 6 of the fathers and p of the tribes of Israel, 8269
29:24 all the p, and the mighty *men*, and all 8269
2Ch 12: 5 *to* the p of Judah, that were gathered 8269
12: 6 Whereupon the p of Israel and the king 8269
17: 7 the third year of his reign he sent to his p, 8269
21: 4 the sword, and *divers* also of the p of Israel. 8269
21: 9 Jehoram went forth with his p, and all *his* 8269
22: 8 found the p of Judah, and the sons of 8269
23:13 and the p and the trumpets by the king: 8269
24:10 all the p and all the people rejoiced, and 8269
24:17 Now after the death of Jehoiada came the p 8269
24:23 destroyed all the p of the people from 8269
28:14 the spoil before the p and all 8269
28:21 of the p, and gave *it* unto the king of 8269
29:30 the p commanded the Levites to *sing* praise 8269
30: 2 his p, and all the congregation in 8269
30: 6 and his p throughout all Israel and Judah, 8269
30:12 the commandment of the king and of the p, 8269
30:24 the p gave to the congregation a thousand 8269
31: 8 and the p came and saw the heaps, 8269
32: 3 He took counsel with his p and his mighty 8269
32:31 *of* the ambassadors of the p of Babylon, 8269
35: 8 his p gave willingly unto the people, to 8269
36:18 and the treasures of the king, and of his p; 8269
Ezr 7:28 and before all the king's mighty p. 8269
8:20 the p had appointed for the service of 8269
9: 1 the p came to me, saying, The people of 8269
9: 2 the hand of the p and rulers hath been chief 8269
10: 8 according to the counsel of the p and 8269
Ne 9:32 on our p, and on our priests, and on our 8269
9:34 our p, our priests, nor our fathers, kept thy 8269
9:38 write *it*; and our p, Levites, *and* priests, 8269
12:31 I brought up the p of Judah upon the wall, 8269
12:32 went Hoshaiah, and half of the p of Judah, 8269
Est 1: 3 he made a feast unto all his p and 8269
1: 3 Media, the nobles and p of the provinces, 8269
1:11 to shew the people and the p her beauty: 8269
1:14 Memucan, the seven p of Persia and Media, 8269
1:16 answered before the king and the p, 8269
1:16 *also* to all the p, and to all the people that 8269
1:18 Media say this day unto all the king's p, 8269
1:21 the saying pleased the king and the p; and 8269
2:18 the king made a great feast unto all his p 8269
3: 1 set his seat above all the p that *were* with 8269
5:11 how he had advanced him above the p and 8269
6: 9 the hand of one of the king's most noble p, 8269
Job 3:15 Or with p that had gold, who filled their 8269
12:19 He leadeth p away spoiled, and 3548
12:21 He poureth contempt upon p, and 5081
29: 9 The p refrained talking, and laid *their* hand 8269
34:18 *art* wicked? *and* to p, *Ye are* ungodly? 5081
34:19 *to him* that accepteth not the persons of p, 8269
Ps 45:16 whom thou mayest make p in all the earth. 8269
47: 9 The p of the people are gathered together, 5081
68:27 the p of Judah *and* their council, the princes 8269
68:27 the p of Zebulun, *and* the princes of 8269
68:27 princes of Zebulun, *and* the p of Naphtali. 8269
68:31 P shall come out of Egypt; Ethiopia shall 2831
76:12 He shall cut off the spirit of p: *he is* terrible 5057
82: 7 die like men, and fall like one of the p 8269
83:11 yea, all their p as Zebah, and as Zalmunna: 5257
105:22 To bind his p at his pleasure; and teach his 8269
107:40 He poureth contempt upon p, and 5081
113: 8 That *he* may set *him* with p, *even* with 5081
113: 8 with princes, *even* with the p of his people. 5081
118: 9 in the LORD than to put confidence in p. 5081
119:23 P also did sit *and* speak against me: *but* 8269
119:161 P have persecuted me without a cause: but 8269
146: 3 Put not your trust in p, *nor* in the son of 5081
148:11 all people; p, and all judges of the earth: 8269
Pr 8:15 By me kings reign, and p decree justice. 7336
8:16 By me p rule, and nobles, *even* all 8269
17:26 just *is* not good, *nor* to strike p for equity. 5081
19:10 much less for a servant to have rule over p. 8269
28: 2 of a land many *are* the p thereof: 8269
31: 4 kings to drink wine; nor for p strong drink: 7336
Ecc 10: 7 and p walking as servants upon the earth. 8269
10:16 *is* a child, and thy p eat in the morning. 8269
10:17 thy p eat in due season, for strength, and 8269
Isa 1:23 Thy p *are* rebellious, and companions of 8269
3: 4 I will give children *to be* their p, and 8269
3:14 ancients of his people, and the p thereof: 8269
10: 8 he saith, *Are* not my p altogether kings? 8269
19:11 Surely the p of Zoan *are* fools, the counsel 8269
19:13 The p of Zoan are become fools, 8269
19:13 become fools, the p of Noph are deceived; 8269
21: 5 eat, drink: arise, ye p, *and* anoint the shield. 8269
23: 8 the crowning *city*, whose merchants *are* p, 8269
30: 4 For his p were at Zoan, and 8269
31: 9 his p shall be afraid of the ensign, saith 8269
32: 1 and p shall rule in judgment. 8269
34:12 *be* there, and all her p shall be nothing. 8269
40:23 That bringeth the p to nothing; he maketh 7336
41:25 he shall come *upon* p as *upon* morter, and 5461
43:28 Therefore I have profaned the p of 8269
49: 7 shall see and arise, p also shall worship, 8269
Jer 1:18 against the p thereof, against the priests 8269
2:26 their p, and their priests, and their prophets, 8269
4: 9 the king shall perish, and the heart of the p; 8269
8: 1 the bones of his p, and the bones of 8269
17:25 and p sitting upon the throne of David, 8269
17:25 in chariots and on horses, they, and their p, 8269
24: 1 the p of Judah, with the carpenters and 8269
24: 8 his p, and the residue of Jerusalem, 8269
25:18 and the kings thereof, *and* the p thereof, 8269
25:19 his servants, and his p, and all his people; 8269
26:10 When the p of Judah heard these things, 8269
26:11 the prophets unto the p and to all 8269
26:12 spake Jeremiah unto all the p and to all 8269
26:16 said the p and all the people unto the priests 8269
26:21 with all his mighty *men*, and all the p, 8269
29: 2 the p of Judah and Jerusalem, and 8269
32:32 they, their kings, their p, their priests, and 8269
34:10 *Now* when all the p, and all the people, 8269
34:19 The p of Judah, and the princes of 8269
34:19 the p of Jerusalem, the eunuchs, and 8269
34:21 his p will I give into the hand of their 8269
35: 4 of God, which *was* by the chamber of the p, 8269
36:12 lo, all the p sat there, *even* Elishama 8269
36:12 the son of Hananiah, and all the p. 8269
36:14 Therefore all the p sent Jehudi the son of 8269
36:19 said the p unto Baruch, Go, hide thee, thou 8269
36:21 in the ears of all the p which stood beside 8269
37:14 took Jeremiah, and brought him to the p. 8269
37:15 Wherefore the p were wroth with Jeremiah, 8269
38: 4 Therefore the p said unto the king, 8269
38:17 go forth unto the king of Babylon's p, 8269
38:18 wilt not go forth to the king of Babylon's p, 8269
38:22 *be* brought forth to the king of Babylon's p, 8269
38:25 if the p hear that I have talked with thee, 8269
38:27 came all the p unto Jeremiah, and 8269
39: 3 all the p of the king of Babylon came in, 8269
39: 3 with all the residue of the p of the king of 8269
39:13 Rab-mag, and all the king of Babylon's p; 7227
41: 1 of the seed royal, and the p of the king, 7227
44:17 we, and our fathers, our kings, and our p, 8269
44:21 and your p, and the people of the land, 8269
48: 7 captivity *with* his priests and his p together. 8269
49: 3 *and* his priests and his p together. 8269
49:38 will destroy from thence the king and the p, 8269
50:35 and upon her p, and upon her wise *men*. 8269
51:57 I will make drunk her p, and her wise *men*, 8269
52:10 he slew also all the p of Judah in Riblah. 8269
La 1: 6 her p are become like harts *that* find no 8269
2: 2 polluted the kingdom and the p thereof. 8269
2: 9 her king and her p *are* among the Gentiles: 8269
5:12 P are hanged up by their hand: the faces of 8269
Eze 11: 1 the son of Benaiah, p of the people. 8269
17:12 the p thereof, and led them with him to 8269
19: 1 thou up a lamentation for the p of Israel, 5387
21:12 it *shall be* upon all the p of Israel: 5387
22: 6 Behold, the p of Israel, every one were in 5387
22:27 Her p in the midst thereof *are* like wolves 8269
23:15 upon their heads, all of them p to look to, 7991
26:16 all the p of the sea shall come down from 5387
27:21 Arabia, and all the p of Kedar, 5387
32:29 There *is* Edom, her kings, and all her p, 5387
32:30 There *be* the p of the north, all of them, and 5257
39:18 drink the blood of the p of the earth, 5387
45: 8 and my p shall no more oppress my people; 5387
45: 9 Let it suffice you, O p of Israel: 5387
Da 1: 3 and of the king's seed, and of the p; 6579
3: 2 the king sent to gather together the p, 324
3: 3 the p, the governors and captains, the judges, 324
3:27 the p, governors, and captains, and 324
5: 2 and his p, his wives, and his concubines, 7261
5: 3 the king, and his p, his wives, and 7261
6: 1 over the kingdom an hundred and twenty p, 324
6: 2 that the p might give accounts unto them, 324
6: 3 was preferred above the presidents and p, 324
6: 4 p sought to find occasion against Daniel 324
6: 6 p assembled *together* to the king, 324
6: 7 the governors, and the p, the counsellers and 324
8:25 shall also stand up against the Prince of p; 8269
9: 6 our p, and our fathers, and to all the people 8269
9: 8 to our p, and to our fathers, because 8269
10:13 lo, Michael, one of the chief p, came to 8269
11: 5 the south shall be strong, and *one* of his p; 8269
11: 8 with their p, *and* with their precious vessels 5257
Hos 5:10 The p of Judah were like them that remove 8269
7: 3 their wickedness, and the p with their lies. 8269
7: 5 *In* the day of our king the p have made *him* 8269
7:16 their p shall fall by the sword for the rage 8269
8: 4 they have **made** p, and I knew *it* not: 7786
8:10 a little for the burden of the king of p. 8269
Hos 9:15 love them no more: all their p *are* revolters. 8269
13:10 whom thou saidst, Give me a king and p? 8269
Am 1:15 he and his p together, saith the LORD. 8269
2: 3 will slay all the p thereof with him, 8269
Mic 3: 1 of Jacob, and ye p of the house of Israel; 7101
3: 9 p of the house of Israel, that abhor 7101
Hab 1:10 and the p *shall be* a scorn unto them: 7336
Zep 1: 8 that I will punish the p, and the king's 8269
3: 3 Her p within her *are* roaring lions; 8269
Mt 2: 6 art not the least among the p of Juda: *2232*
20:25 Ye know that the p of the Gentiles exercise *758*
1Co 2: 6 nor of the p of this world, that come to *758*
2: 8 Which none of the p of this world knew: *758*

PRINCESS (1) [PRINCE]

La 1: 1 *and* p among the provinces, *how* is she 8282

PRINCESSES (1) [PRINCE]

1Ki 11: 3 p, and three hundred concubines: 8282

PRINCIPAL (17) [PRINCIPALITIES, PRINCIPALITY]

Ex 30:23 Take thou also unto thee p spices, of pure 7218
Lev 6: 5 he shall even restore it in the p, and 7218
Nu 5: 7 he shall recompense his trespass with the p 7218
1Ki 4: 5 Zabud the son of Nathan *was* **p officer**, *and* 3548
2Ki 25:19 in the city, and the p scribe of the host, 8269
1Ch 24: 6 one p household being taken for Eleazar, and 1
24:31 *even* the p fathers over against their 7218
Ne 11:17 *was* the p to begin the thanksgiving in 7218
Pr 4: 7 Wisdom *is* the **p thing**; *therefore* 7225
Isa 16: 8 have broken down the **p plants** thereof, 8291
28:25 cast in the p wheat and the appointed 7795
Jer 25:34 wallow yourselves *in the ashes*, ye p of 117
25:35 way to flee, nor the p of the flock to escape. 117
25:36 and a howling of the p of the flock, 117
52:25 the p scribe of the host, who mustered 8269
Mic 5: 5 him seven shepherds, and eight p men. 5257
Ac 25:23 the chief captains, and p men of the city, *1851*

PRINCIPALITIES (7) [PRINCIPAL]

Jer 13:18 for your p shall come down, *even* 4761
Ro 8:38 nor life, nor angels, nor p, nor powers, *746*
Eph 3:10 To the intent that now unto the p and *746*
6:12 not against flesh and blood, but against p, *746*
Col 1:16 *be* thrones, or dominions, or p, or powers: *746*
2:15 *And* having spoiled p and powers, he made a *746*
Tit 3: 1 Put them in mind to be subject to p and *746*

PRINCIPALITY (2) [PRINCIPAL]

Eph 1:21 Far above all p, and power, and might, and *746*
Col 2:10 in him, which is the head of all p and power: *746*

PRINCIPLES (2)

Heb 5:12 which *be* the first p of the oracles of God; *4747*
6: 1 Therefore leaving the p of the doctrine of *746*

PRINT (4) [PRINTED]

Lev 19:28 for the dead, nor p any marks upon you: 5414
Job 13:27 thou **settest a p** upon the heels of my feet. 2707
Jn 20:25 Except I shall see in his hands the p of *5179*
20:25 and put my finger into the p of the nails, *5179*

PRINTED (1) [PRINT]

Job 19:23 now written! O that they were p in a book! 2710

PRISCA (1) [PRISCILLA]

2Ti 4:19 Salute P and Aquila, and the household of *4251*

PRISCILLA (5) [PRISCA]

Ac 18: 2 lately come from Italy, with his wife P; *4252*
18:18 into Syria, and with him P and Aquila: *4252*
18:26 whom when Aquila and P had heard, *4252*
Ro 16: 3 Greet P and Aquila my helpers in Christ *4252*
1Co 16:19 Aquila and P salute you much in the Lord, *4252*

PRISED (1) [PRICE]

Zec 11:13 a goodly price that I was p at of them. 3365

PRISON (90) [FELLOWPRISONER, FELLOWPRISONERS, IMPRISONED, IMPRISONMENT, IMPRISONMENTS, PRISONER, PRISONERS, PRISONS]

Ge 39:20 and put him into the p, 1004+5470+1886.1
39:20 and he was there in the p. 1004+5470+1886.1
39:21 sight of the keeper of the p. 1004+5470+1886.1
39:22 the keeper of the p 1004+5470+1886.1
39:22 prisoners that *were* in the p; 1004+5470+1886.1
39:23 The keeper of the p looked 1004+5470+1886.1
40: 3 into the p, the place where 1004+5470+1886.1
40: 5 which *were* bound in the p. 1004+5470+1886.1
42:16 fetch your brother, and ye shall be **kept in p**, 631
42:19 brethren be bound in the house of your p: 4929
Jdg 16:21 of brass; and he did grind in the p house. 631
16:25 they called for Samson out of the p house; 631
1Ki 22:27 Put this *fellow* in the p, 1004+3608+1886.1
2Ki 17: 4 shut him up, and bound him *in* p. 1004+3608
25:27 of Jehoiachin king of Judah out of p; 1004+3608
25:29 changed his p garments: and he did eat 3608
2Ch 16:10 with the seer, and put him *in* a p house; 4115
18:26 Put this *fellow* in the p, 1004+3608+1886.1
Ne 3:25 high house, that *was* by the court of the p. 4307
12:39 and they stood still in the p gate. 4307
Ps 142: 7 Bring my soul out of p, that I may praise 4525
Ecc 4:14 For out of p he cometh to 631+1004+1886.1
Isa 24:22 shall be shut up in the p, and after many 4525
42: 7 to bring out the prisoners from the p, *and* 4525
42: 7 them that sit in darkness out of the p house. 3608
42:22 in holes, and they are hid in p houses: 3608
53: 8 He was taken from p and from judgment: 6115
61: 1 the **opening of the p** to *them that are* 6495
Jer 29:26 that thou shouldest put him in p, and in 4115
32: 2 prophet was shut up in the court of the p, 4307
32: 8 the p according to the word of the LORD, 4307

P

Jer 32:12 all the Jews that sat in the court of the p. 4307
33: 1 he was yet shut up in the court of the p, 4307
37: 4 they had not put him *into* p. 1004+3628+1886.1
37:15 put him *in* p *in* the house of 612+1004+1886.1
37:15 for they had made that the p. 1004+3608+1886.1
37:18 that ye have put me in p? 1004+3608+1886.1
37:21 commit Jeremiah into the court of the p, 4307
37:21 Jeremiah remained in the court of the p. 4307
38: 6 that *was* in the court of the p: 4307
38:13 Jeremiah remained in the court of the p. 4307
38:28 So Jeremiah abode in the court of the p 4307
39:14 took Jeremiah out of the court of the p, and 4307
39:15 while he was shut up in the court of the p, 4307
52:11 in p till the day of his death. 1004+6486+1886.1
52:31 brought him forth out of p; 1004+3628+1886.1
52:33 changed his p garments: and he did 3608
Mt 4:12 Jesus had heard that John was **cast into** p, *3860*
5:25 thee to the officer, and thou be cast into p. *5438*
11: 2 Now when John had heard in the p *1201*
14: 3 and put *him* in p for Herodias' sake, *5438*
14:10 And he sent, and beheaded John in the p. *5438*
18:30 but went and cast him into p, till he should *5438*
25:36 I was in p, and ye came unto me. *5438*
25:39 we thee sick, or in p, and came unto thee? *5438*
25:43 sick, and in p, and ye visited me not. *5438*
25:44 or in p, and did not minister unto thee? *5438*
Mk 1:14 Now after that John was **put in** p, Jesus *3860*
6:17 and bound him in p for Herodias' sake, *5438*
6:27 and he went and beheaded him in the p, *5438*
Lk 3:20 yet this above all, that he shut up John in p. *5438*
12:58 the officer, and the officer cast thee into p. *5438*
22:33 to go with thee, both into p, and to death. *5438*
23:19 in the city, and *for* murder, was cast into p.) *5438*
23:25 for sedition and murder was cast into p, *5438*
Jn 3:24 For John was not yet cast into p. *5438*
Ac 5:18 and put them in the common p. *5084*
5:19 of the Lord by night opened the p doors, *5438*
5:21 and sent to the p to have them brought. *1201*
5:22 and found them not in the p, they returned, *5438*
5:23 The p truly found we shut with all safety, *1201*
5:25 the men whom ye put in p are standing in *5438*
8: 3 and women committed *them* to p. *5438*
12: 4 he put *him* in p, and delivered *him* to four *5438*
12: 5 Peter therefore was kept in p: but *5438*
12: 6 and *the* keepers before the door kept the p. *5438*
12: 7 came upon *him*, and a light shined in the p: *3612*
12:17 how the Lord had brought him out of the p. *5438*
16:23 they cast *them* into p, charging the jailor to *5438*
16:24 thrust them into the inner p, and made their *5438*
16:26 that the foundations of the p were shaken: *1201*
16:27 And the **keeper of the** p awaking out of his *1200*
16:27 and seeing the p doors open, he drew out *5438*
16:36 And the **keeper of the** p told this saying to *1200*
16:37 being Romans, and have cast *us* into p; *5438*
16:40 And they went out of the p, and *5438*
26:10 and many of the saints did I shut up in p, *5438*
1Pe 3:19 he went and preached unto the spirits in p; *5438*
Rev 2:10 the devil shall cast *some* of you into p, *5438*
20: 7 Satan shall be loosed out of his p, *5438*

PRISONER (13) [PRISON]
Ps 79:11 Let the sighing of the p come before thee, 615
102:20 To hear the groaning of the p; to loose those 615
Mt 27:15 was wont to release unto the people a p, *1198*
27:16 And they had then a notable p, *1198*
Mk 15: 6 at *that* feast he released unto them one p, *1198*
Ac 23:18 Paul the p called me unto *him*, and *1198*
25:27 it seemeth to me unreasonable to send a p, *1198*
28:17 *yet* was I delivered p from Jerusalem into *1198*
Eph 3: 1 the p of Jesus Christ for you Gentiles, *1198*
4: 1 I therefore, the p of the Lord, beseech you *1198*
2Ti 1: 8 the testimony of our Lord, nor of me his p: *1198*
Phm 1: 1 a p of Jesus Christ, and Timothy *our* *1198*
1: 9 the aged, and now also a p of Jesus Christ. *1198*

PRISONERS (20) [PRISON]
Ge 39:20 a place where the king's p *were* bound: 615
39:22 hand all the p that *were* in the prison; 615
Nu 21: 1 and **took** *some* of them p. 7617+7628
Job 3:18 *There* the p rest together; they hear not 615
Ps 69:33 heareth the poor, and despiseth not his p. 615
146: 7 to the hungry. The LORD looseth the p: 631
Isa 10: 4 me they shall bow down under the p, 616
14:17 *that* opened not the house of his p? 615
20: 4 king of Assyria lead away the Egyptians p, 7628
24:22 *as* p are gathered in the pit, and shall be shut 616
42: 7 to bring out the p from the prison, *and* 616
49: 9 That *thou* mayest say to the p, Go forth; 631
La 3:34 To crush under his feet all the p of the earth, 615
Zec 9:11 forth thy p out of the pit wherein *is* no water. 615
9:12 Turn ye to the strong hold, ye p of hope: 615
Ac 16:25 praises unto God: and the p heard them. *1198*
16:27 supposing that the p had been fled. *1198*
27: 1 and certain other p unto *one* named Julius, *1202*
27:42 And the soldiers' counsel was to kill the p, *1202*
28:16 the centurion delivered the p to the captain *1198*

PRISONS (3) [PRISON]
Lk 21:12 and into p, being brought before kings and *5438*
Ac 22: 4 binding and delivering into p both men and *5438*
2Co 11:23 in p more frequent, in deaths oft. *5438*

PRIVATE (1) [PRIVATELY, PRIVILY, PRIVY]
2Pe 1:20 that no prophecy of the scripture is of *any* p *2398*

PRIVATELY (8) [PRIVATE]
Mt 24: 3 the disciples came unto him p, *2398+2596*
Mk 6:32 into a desert place by ship p. *2398+2596*
9:28 his disciples asked him p, Why could *2398+2596*
13: 3 and John and Andrew asked him p, *2398+2596*
Lk 9:10 went aside p into a desert place *2398+2596*
10:23 him unto *his* disciples, and said p, *2398+2596*
Ac 23:19 the hand, and went *with him* aside p, *2398+2596*
Gal 2: 2 but p to them which were of *2398+2596*

PRIVILY (15) [PRIVATE]
Jdg 9:31 sent messengers unto Abimelech p, 8649+871.1
1Sa 24: 4 the skirt of Saul's robe p. 3909+871.1+1886.1
Ps 10: 8 his eyes are p **set** against the poor. 6845
11: 2 that *they* may p shoot at the upright in 652+1119
31: 4 Pull me out of the net that they have **laid** p 2934
64: 5 they commune of **laying** snares p; they say, 2934
101: 5 Whoso p slandereth his neighbour, him will 5643
142: 3 I walked have they p **laid** a snare for me. 2934
Pr 1:11 let us **lurk** p for the innocent without 6845
1:18 own blood; they **lurk** p for their own lives. 6845
Mt 1:19 was minded to put her away p. *2977*
2: 7 when he had p called the wise men, *2977*
Ac 16:37 and now do they thrust us out p? *2977*
Gal 2: 4 who **came in** p to spy out our liberty which *3922*
2Pe 2: 1 who p shall **bring in** damnable heresies, *3919*

PRIVY (4) [PRIVATE]
Dt 23: 1 in the stones, or hath *his* p **member** cut off, 8212
1Ki 2:44 all the wickedness which thine heart is p to, 3045
Eze 21:14 which **entereth into** their p **chambers**. 2314
Ac 5: 2 his wife also being p *to it*, and brought a *4894*

PRIZE (2)
1Co 9:24 in a race run all, but one receiveth the p? *1017*
Php 3:14 I press toward the mark for the p of *1017*

PROCEED (15) [PROCEEDED, PROCEEDETH, PROCEEDING]
Ex 25:35 according to the six branches that p **out** of 3318
Jos 6:10 neither shall *any* word p out of your mouth, 3318
2Sa 7:12 which shall p out of thy bowels, and I will 3318
Job 40: 5 yea, twice; but I will p no **further**. 3254
Isa 29:14 I will p to do a marvellous work amongst 3254
51: 4 for a law shall p from me, and I will make 3318
Jer 9: 3 for they p from evil to evil, and they know 3318
30:19 out of them shall p thanksgiving and 3318
30:21 their governor shall p from the midst of 3318
Hab 1: 7 and their dignity shall p of themselves. 3318
Mt 15:18 But those *things* which p out of the mouth *1607*
15:19 For out of the heart p evil thoughts, *1831*
Mk 7:21 p evil thoughts, adulteries, fornications, *1607*
Eph 4:29 Let no corrupt communication p **out** of *1607*
2Ti 3: 9 But they shall p no further: for their folly *4298*

PROCEEDED (9) [PROCEED]
Nu 30:12 whatsoever p **out** of her lips concerning her 4161
32:24 do that which hath p out of your mouth. 3318
Jdg 11:36 do to me according to that which hath p out 3318
Job 36: 1 Elihu also p, and said, 3254
Lk 4:22 gracious words which p **out** of his mouth. *1607*
Jn 8:42 for I p **forth** and came from God; *1831*
Ac 12: 3 the Jews, he p **further** to take Peter also. *4369*
Rev 4: 5 And out of the throne p lightnings and *1607*
19:21 the horse, which *sword* p out of his mouth: *1607*

PROCEEDETH (11) [PROCEED]
Ge 24:50 and said, The thing p from the LORD: 3318
Nu 30: 2 he shall do according to all that p out of his 3318
Dt 8: 3 by every *word* **that** p **out** of the mouth of 4161
1Sa 24:13 Wickedness p from the wicked: 3318
Ecc 10: 5 the sun, as an error *which* p from the ruler: 3318
La 3:38 Out of the mouth of the most High p not 3318
Hab 1: 4 the righteous; therefore wrong judgment p. 3318
Mt 4: 4 by every word that p out of the mouth of *1607*
Jn 15:26 which p from the Father, he shall testify of *1607*
Jas 3:10 Out of the same mouth p blessing and *1831*
Rev 11: 5 fire p **out** of their mouth, and *1607*

PROCEEDING (1) [PROCEED]
Rev 22: 1 p **out** of the throne of God and of *1607*

PROCESS (5)
Ge 4: 3 in p of time it came to pass, that Cain 7093
38:12 **in** p **of time** the daughter of 3117+7235+1886.1
Ex 2:23 to pass in p **of time**, 3117+7227+1886.1+1886.1
Jdg 11: 4 it came to pass **in** p **of time**, that 3117+4480
2Ch 21:19 that **in** p **of time**, 3117+3117+4480+3807.1

PROCHORUS (1)
Ac 6: 5 and P, and Nicanor, and Timon, and *4402*

PROCLAIM (23) [PROCLAIMED, PROCLAIMETH, PROCLAIMING, PROCLAMATION]
Ex 33:19 I will p the name of the LORD 7121+871.1
Lev 23: 2 which ye shall p *to be* holy convocations, 7121
23: 4 which ye shall p in their seasons. 7121
23:21 ye shall p on the selfsame day, *that* it may 7121
23:37 which ye shall p *to be* holy convocations, 7121
25:10 p liberty throughout *all* the land unto all 7121
Dt 20:10 city to fight against it, then p peace unto it. 7121
Jdg 7: 3 therefore go to, p in the ears of the people, 7121
1Ki 21: 9 P a fast, and set Naboth on high among 7121
2Ki 10:20 Jehu said, P a solemn assembly for Baal. 6942
Ne 8:15 and p in all their cities, 5674+6963
Est 6: 9 the street of the city, and p before him, 7121
Pr 20: 6 Most men will p every one his own 7121
Isa 61: 1 to p liberty to the captives, and the opening 7121
61: 2 To p the acceptable year of the LORD, 7121
Jer 3:12 Go and p these words toward the north, and 7121
7: 2 p there this word, and say, Hear the word 7121
11: 6 P all these words in the cities of Judah, and 7121
19: 2 and p there the words that I shall tell thee, 7121
34: 8 *were* at Jerusalem, to p liberty unto them; 7121
34:17 behold, I p a liberty for you, saith 7121
Joel 3: 9 P ye this among the Gentiles; Prepare war, 7121
Am 4: 5 and p *and* publish the free offerings: 7121

PROCLAIMED (16) [PROCLAIM]
Ex 34: 5 and p the name of the LORD. 7121+871.1
34: 6 p, The LORD, The LORD God, merciful 7121
36: 6 they **caused** it **to be** p throughout 5674+6963
1Ki 21:12 They p a fast, and set Naboth on high 7121
2Ki 10:20 a solemn assembly for Baal. And they p *it*. 7121
23:16 of the LORD which the man of God p, 7121
23:16 of God proclaimed, who p these words. 7121
23:17 p these things that thou hast done against 7121
2Ch 20: 3 and p a fast throughout all Judah. 7121
Ezr 8:21 I p a fast there, at the river Ahava, that *we* 7121
Est 6:11 the street of the city, and p before him, 7121
Isa 62:11 the LORD hath p unto the end of 8085
Jer 36: 9 *that* they p a fast before the LORD *to* all 7121
Jnh 3: 5 and p a fast, and put on sackcloth, 7121
3: 7 he **caused** *it* **to be** p and published through 2199
Lk 12: 3 ear in closets shall be p upon the housetops. *2784*

PROCLAIMETH (1) [PROCLAIM]
Pr 12:23 but the heart of fools p foolishness. 7121

PROCLAIMING (3) [PROCLAIM]
Jer 34:15 in p liberty every man to his neighbour; 7121
34:17 in p liberty, every one to his brother, and 7121
Rev 5: 2 And I saw a strong angel p with a loud *2784*

PROCLAMATION (9) [PROCLAIM]
Ex 32: 5 Aaron **made** p, and said, To morrow *is* a 7121
1Ki 15:22 king Asa **made** a p throughout all Judah; 8085
22:36 there went a p throughout the host about 7440
2Ch 24: 9 they made a p through Judah and 6963
30: 5 to **make** p throughout all Israel, 5674+6963
36:22 that he **made a** p throughout all his 5674+6963
Ezr 1: 1 that he **made a** p throughout all his 5674+6963
10: 7 they **made** p throughout Judah and 5674+6963
Da 5:29 his neck, and **made a** p concerning him, 3745

PROCORUS See PROCHORUS

PROCURE (2) [PROCURED, PROCURETH]
Jer 26:19 Thus *might* we p great evil against our 6213
33: 9 and for all the prosperity that I p unto it. 6213

PROCURED (2) [PROCURE]
Jer 2:17 Hast thou not p this unto thyself, in that 6213
4:18 thy doings have p these *things* unto thee; 6213

PROCURETH (1) [PROCURE]
Pr 11:27 He that diligently seeketh good p favour: 1245

PRODUCE (1)
Isa 41:21 P your cause, saith the LORD; bring forth 7126

PROFANE (33) [PROFANED, PROFANENESS, PROFANETH, PROFANING]
Lev 18:21 neither shalt thou p the name of thy God: 2490
19:12 neither shalt thou p the name of thy God: 2490
20: 3 my sanctuary, and to p my holy name. 2490
21: 4 a chief man among his people, to p himself. 2490
21: 6 their God, and not p the name of their God: 2490
21: 7 shall not take a wife *that is* a whore, or p; 2491
21: 9 if she p herself by playing the whore, she 2490
21:12 nor p the sanctuary of his God; 2490
21:14 or a divorced *woman*, or p, *or* a harlot, 2491
21:15 Neither shall he p his seed among his 2490
21:23 a blemish; that he p not my sanctuaries: 2490
22: 2 that they p not my holy name *in those* 2490
22: 9 sin for it, and die therefore, if they p it: 2490
22:15 they shall not p the holy *things* of 2490
22:32 Neither shall ye p my holy name; but I will 2490
Ne 13:17 *is* this that ye do, and p the sabbath day? 2490
Jer 23:11 For both prophet and priest are p; yea, 2610
Eze 21:25 thou, p wicked prince of Israel, whose day 2491
22:26 put no difference between the holy and p, 2455
23:39 the same day into my sanctuary to p it; 2490
24:21 Behold, I *will* p my sanctuary, 2490
28:16 I will **cast** thee **as** p out of the mountain of 2490
42:20 between the sanctuary and the p *place*. 2455
44:23 *the difference* between the holy and p, 2455
48:15 *shall be* a p *place* for the city, for dwelling, 2455
Am 2: 7 in unto the *same* maid, to p my holy name: 2490
Mt 12: 5 days the priests in the temple p the sabbath, *953*
Ac 24: 6 Who also hath gone about to p the temple: *953*
1Ti 1: 9 and for sinners, for unholy and p, *952*
4: 7 But refuse p and old wives' fables, and *952*
6:20 avoiding p *and* vain babblings, and *952*
2Ti 2:16 But shun p *and* vain babblings: for they will *952*
Heb 12:16 there *be* any fornicator, or p *person*, as Esau, *952*

PROFANED (15) [PROFANE]
Lev 19: 8 he hath p the hallowed *thing* of 2490
Ps 89:39 thou hast p his crown *by casting it* to 2490
Isa 43:28 Therefore I have p the princes of 2490
Eze 22: 8 mine holy *things*, and hast p my sabbaths. 2490
22:26 have p mine holy *things*: they have put no 2490
22:26 from my sabbaths, and I am p among them. 2490
23:38 in the same day, and have p my sabbaths. 2490
25: 3 Aha, against my sanctuary, when it was p; 2490
36:20 whither they went, they p my holy name, 2490
36:21 which the house of Israel had p among 2490
36:22 which ye have p among the heathen, 2490
36:23 which was p among the heathen, 2490
36:23 which ye have p in the midst of them; 2490
Mal 1:12 ye *have* p it, in that ye say, The table of 2490
2:11 for Judah hath p the holiness of the LORD 2490

PROFANENESS (1) [PROFANE]
Jer 23:15 for from the prophets of Jerusalem is p 2613

PROFANETH (1) [PROFANE]
Lev 21: 9 by playing the whore, she p her father: 2490

PROFANING (2) [PROFANE]
Ne 13:18 yet ye bring more wrath upon Israel by p 2490
Mal 2:10 by p the covenant of our fathers? 2490

PROFESS (3) [PROFESSED, PROFESSING, PROFESSION]
Dt 26: 3 I p this day unto the LORD thy God, 5046
Mt 7:23 And then will I p unto them, I never knew 3670
Tit 1:16 They p that they know God; but in works 3670

PROFESSED (2) [PROFESS]
2Co 9:13 your p subjection unto the gospel of Christ, 3671
1Ti 6:12 hast p a good profession before many 3670

PROFESSING (3) [PROFESS]
Ro 1:22 P themselves to be wise, they became 5335
1Ti 2:10 But (which becometh women p godliness) 1861
6:21 Which some p have erred concerning 1861

PROFESSION (4) [PROFESS]
1Ti 6:12 hast professed a good p before many 3671
Heb 3: 1 the Apostle and High Priest of our p, 3671
4:14 Jesus the Son of God, let us hold fast our p. 3671
10:23 Let us hold fast the p of our hope without 3671

PROFIT (45) [PROFITABLE, PROFITED, PROFITETH, PROFITING, UNPROFITABLE]
Ge 25:32 what p shall this birthright do to 4100+3807.1
37:26 What p is it if we slay our brother, and 1215
1Sa 12:21 vain things, which cannot p nor deliver; 3276
Est 3: 8 it is not for the king's p to suffer them. 7737
Job 21:15 what p should we have, if we pray unto 3276
30: 2 might the strength of their hands p me, 3807.1
35: 3 and, What p shall I have, if I be cleansed, 3276
35: 8 thy righteousness may p the son of man. NIH
Ps 30: 9 What p is there in my blood, when I go 1215
Pr 10: 2 Treasures of wickedness p nothing: but 3276
11: 4 Riches p not in the day of wrath: but 3276
14:23 In all labour there is p: but the talk of 4195
Ecc 1: 3 What p hath a man of all his labour which 3504
2:11 of spirit, and there was no p under the sun. 3504
3: 9 What p hath he that worketh in that 3504
5: 9 Moreover the p of the earth is for all: 3504
5:16 what p hath he that hath laboured for 3504
7:11 and by it there is p to them that see the sun. 3148
Isa 30: 5 ashamed of a people that could not p them, 3276
30: 5 nor be a help nor p, but a shame, and also a 3276
30: 6 to a people that shall not p them. 3276
44: 9 their delectable things shall not p; and 3276
47:12 if so be thou shalt be able to p, if so be thou 3276
48:17 LORD thy God which teacheth thee to p, 3276
57:12 and thy works; for they shall not p thee. 3276
Jer 2: 8 and walked after things that do not p. 3276
2:11 their glory for that which doth not p. 3276
7: 8 ye trust in lying words, that cannot p. 3276
12:13 put themselves to pain, but shall not p: 3276
16:19 vanity, and things wherein there is no p. 3276
23:32 they shall not p this people at all, 3276+3276
Mal 3:14 what p is it that we have kept his 1215
Mk 8:36 For what shall it p a man, if he shall gain 5623
Ro 3: 1 or what p is there of circumcision? 5622
1Co 7:35 And this I speak for your own p; not that I 4851
10:33 men in all things, not seeking mine own p, 4851
10:33 but the p of many, that they may be saved. NIG
12: 7 the Spirit is given to every man to p withal. 4851
14: 6 speaking with tongues, what shall I p you, 5623
Gal 5: 2 be circumcised, Christ shall p you nothing. 5623
2Ti 2:14 that they strive not about words to no p, 5539
Heb 4: 2 but the word preached did not p them, 5623
12:10 but he for our p, that we might be partakers 4851
Jas 2:14 What doth it p, my brethren, though a man 3786
2:16 are needful to the body; what doth it p? 3786

PROFITABLE (13) [PROFIT]
Job 22: 2 Can a man be p unto God, as he that is wise 5532
22: 2 as he that is wise may be p unto himself? 5532
Ecc 10:10 to more strength: but wisdom is p to direct. 3504
Isa 44:10 molten a graven image that is p for 3276
Jer 13: 7 the girdle was marred, it was p for nothing. 6743
Mt 5:29 for it is p for thee that one of thy members 4851
5:30 for it is p for thee that one of thy members 4851
Ac 20:20 And how I kept back nothing that was p 4851
1Ti 4: 8 godliness is p unto all things, having 5624
2Ti 3:16 and is p for doctrine, for reproof, 5624
4:11 with thee: for he is p to me for the ministry. 2173
Tit 3: 8 These things are good and p unto men. 5624
Phm 1:11 but now p to thee and to me: 2173

PROFITED (6) [PROFIT]
Job 33:27 that which was right, and it p me not; 7737
Mt 15: 5 by whatsoever thou mightest be p by me; 5623
16:26 For what is a man p, if he shall gain 5623
Mk 7:11 by whatsoever thou mightest be p by me; 5623
Gal 1:14 And p in the Jews' religion above many my 4298
Heb 13: 9 which have not p them that have been 5623

PROFITETH (6) [PROFIT]
Job 34: 9 It p a man nothing that he should delight 5532
Hab 2:18 What p the graven image that the maker 3276
Jn 6:63 spirit that quickeneth; the flesh p nothing: 5623
Ro 2:25 For circumcision verily p, if thou keep 5623
1Co 13: 3 and have not charity, it p me nothing. 5623
1Ti 4: 8 For bodily exercise p little: 1510+5624

PROFITING (1) [PROFIT]
1Ti 4:15 to them; that thy p may appear to all. 4297

PROFOUND (1)
Hos 5: 2 the revolters are p to make slaughter, 6009

PROGENITORS (1)
Ge 49:26 p unto the utmost bound of the everlasting 2029

PROGNOSTICATORS (1)
Isa 47:13 the monthly p, stand up, and save thee from 3045

PROJECTIONS See TENONS

PROLONG (14) [PROLONGED, PROLONGETH]
Dt 4:26 ye shall not p your days upon it, but 748
4:40 that thou mayest p thy days upon the earth, 748
5:33 that ye may p your days in the land which ye 748
11: 9 that ye may p your days in the land, 748
17:20 to the end that he may p his days in his 748
22: 7 with thee, and that thou mayest p thy days. 748
30:18 that ye shall not p your days upon the land, 748
32:47 through this thing ye shall p your days in 748
Job 6:11 what is mine end, that I should p my life? 748
15:29 neither shall he p the perfection thereof 5186
Ps 61: 6 Thou wilt p the king's life: 3117+3117+5921
Pr 28:16 he that hateth covetousness shall p his days. 748
Ecc 8:13 neither shall he p his days, which are as a 748
Isa 53:10 he shall p his days, and the pleasure of 748

PROLONGED (9) [PROLONG]
Dt 5:16 that thy days may be p, and that it may go 748
6: 2 days of thy life; and that thy days may be p. 748
Pr 28: 2 and knowledge the state thereof shall be p. 748
Ecc 8:12 do evil an hundred times, and his days be p, 748
Isa 13:22 is near to come, and her days shall not be p. 4900
Eze 12:22 The days are p, and every vision faileth? 748
12:25 shall come to pass; it shall be no more p: 4900
12:28 There shall none of my words be p any 4900
Da 7:12 yet their lives were p for a season and time. 754

PROLONGETH (2) [PROLONG]
Pr 10:27 The fear of the LORD p days: but 3254
Ecc 7:15 there is a wicked man that p his life in his 748

PROMISCUOUS See WHORE; WHORE'S; WHORES

PROMISE (53) [PROMISED, PROMISEDST, PROMISES, PROMISING]
Nu 14:34 and ye shall know my breach of p. 8569
1Ki 8:56 hath not failed one word of all his good p, 1697
2Ch 1: 9 let thy p unto David my father be 1697
Ne 5:12 that they should do according to this p. 1697
5:13 from his labour, that performeth not this p, 1697
5:13 And the people did according to this p. 1697
Ps 77: 8 gone for ever? doth his p fail for evermore? 562
105:42 For he remembered his holy p, 1697
Lk 24:49 I send the p of my Father upon you: 1860
Ac 1: 4 but wait for the p of the Father, which, 1860
2:33 having received of the Father the p of 1860
2:39 For the p is unto you, and to your children, 1860
7:17 But when the time of the p drew nigh, 1860
13:23 to his p raised unto Israel a Saviour, 1860
13:32 how that the p which was made unto 1860
23:21 are they ready, looking for a p from thee. 1860
26: 6 am judged for the hope of the p made of 1860
26: 7 Unto which p our twelve tribes, NIG
Ro 4:13 For the p, that he should be the heir of 1860
4:14 made void, and the p made of none effect: 1860
4:16 to the end the p might be sure to all 1860
4:20 He staggered not at the p of God through 1860
9: 8 the children of the p are counted for 1860
9: 9 For this is the word of p, At this time will I 1860
Gal 3:14 that we might receive the p of the Spirit 1860
3:17 that it should make the p of none effect. 1860
3:18 inheritance be of the law, it is no more of p: 1860
3:18 but God gave it to Abraham by p. 1860
3:19 should come to whom the p was made; 1861
3:22 that the p by faith of Jesus Christ might be 1860
3:29 and heirs according to the p. 1860
4:23 but he of the freewoman was by p. 1860
4:28 as Isaac was, are the children of p. 1860
Eph 1:13 ye were sealed with that holy Spirit of p, 1860
2:12 and strangers from the covenants of p, 1860
3: 6 partakers of his p in Christ by the gospel: 1860
6: 2 (which is the first commandment with p;) 1860
1Ti 4: 8 all things, having p of the life that now is, 1860
2Ti 1: 1 according to the p of life which is in Christ 1860
Heb 4: 1 a p being left us of entering into his rest, 1860
6:13 For when God made p to Abraham, 1861
6:15 he had patiently endured, he obtained the p. 1860
6:17 heirs of p the immutability of his counsel, 1860
9:15 they which are called might receive the p 1860
10:36 the will of God, ye might receive the p. 1860
11: 9 By faith he sojourned in the land of p, as in 1860
11: 9 Jacob, the heirs with him of the same p: 1860
11:39 report through faith, received not the p: 1860
2Pe 2:19 While they p them liberty, they themselves 1861
3: 4 And saying, Where is the p of his coming? 1860
3: 9 The Lord is not slack concerning his p, 1860
3:13 Nevertheless we, according to his p, 1862
1Jn 2:25 And this is the p that he hath promised us, 1860

PROMISED (48) [PROMISE]
Ex 12:25 according as he hath p, that ye shall keep 1696
Nu 14:40 up unto the place which the LORD hath p: 559
Dt 1:11 as ye are, and bless you, as he hath p you!) 1696
6: 3 as the LORD God of thy fathers hath p 1696
9:28 bring them into the land which he p them, 1696
10: 9 according as the LORD thy God p him. 1696
12:20 as he hath p thee, and thou shalt say, I will 1696
15: 6 thy God blesseth thee, as he p thee: 1696
19: 8 give thee all the land which he p to give 1696
23:23 thy God, which thou hast p with thy mouth. 1696
26:18 as he hath p thee, and that thou shouldest 1696
27: 3 as the LORD God of thy fathers hath p 1696
Jos 9:21 as the princes had p them. 1696
22: 4 given rest unto your brethren, as he p them: 1696
23: 5 as the LORD your God hath p unto you. 1696
23:10 it is that fighteth for you, as he hath p you. 1696
23:15 which the LORD your God p you; 1696
2Sa 7:28 thou hast p this goodness unto thy servant: 1696
1Ki 2:24 who hath made me a house, as he p, 1696
5:12 gave Solomon wisdom, as he p him: 1696
8:20 as the LORD p, and have built a house for 1696
8:56 his people Israel, according to all that he p: 1696
1Ki 8:56 which he p by the hand of Moses his 1696
9: 5 as I p to David thy father, saying, 1696
2Ki 8:19 as he p him to give to him alway a light, and 559
1Ch 17:26 and hast p this goodness unto thy servant: 1696
2Ch 6:10 as the LORD p, and have built the house 1696
6:15 my father that which thou hast p him; 1696
6:16 my father that which thou hast p him, 1696
21: 7 as he p to give a light to him and to his sons 559
Ne 9:23 concerning which thou hadst p to their 559
Est 4: 7 of the sum of the money that Haman had p 559
Jer 32:42 upon them all the good that I have p them. 1696
33:14 which I have p unto the house of Israel 1696
Mt 14: 7 Whereupon he p with an oath to give her 3670
Mk 14:11 they were glad, and p to give him money. 1861
Lk 1:72 To perform the mercy p to our fathers, and NIG
22: 6 And he p, and sought opportunity to betray 1843
Ac 7: 5 yet he p that he would give it to him for a 1861
Ro 1: 2 (Which he had p afore by his prophets in 4279
4:21 what he had p, he was able also to perform. 1861
Tit 1: 2 that cannot lie, p before the world began; 1861
Heb 10:23 without wavering; (for he is faithful that p;) 1861
11:11 she judged him faithful who had p. 1861
12:26 but now he hath p, saying, Yet once more I 1861
Jas 1:12 which the Lord hath p to them that love 1861
2: 5 heirs of the kingdom which he hath p to 1861
1Jn 2:25 And this is the promise that he hath p us, 1861

PROMISEDST (3) [PROMISE]
1Ki 8:24 servant David my father that thou p him: 1696
8:25 servant David my father that thou p him, 1696
Ne 9:15 p them that they should go in to possess 559

PROMISES (13) [PROMISE]
Ro 9: 4 the law, and the service of God, and the p; 1860
15: 8 to confirm the p made unto the fathers: 1860
2Co 1:20 For all the p of God in him are yea, and 1860
7: 1 Having therefore these p, dearly beloved, 1860
Gal 3:16 to Abraham and his seed were the p made. 1860
3:21 Is the law then against the p of God? 1860
Heb 6:12 through faith and patience inherit the p. 1860
7: 6 and blessed him that had the p. 1860
8: 6 which was established upon better p. 1860
11:13 not having received the p, but having seen 1860
11:17 he that had received the p offered up his 1860
11:33 wrought righteousness, obtained p, 1860
2Pe 1: 4 unto us exceeding great and precious p: 1862

PROMISING (1) [PROMISE]
Eze 13:22 return from his wicked way, by p him life: 2421

PROMOTE (5) [PROMOTED, PROMOTION]
Nu 22:17 I will p thee unto very great honour, 3513+3513
22:37 am I not able indeed to p thee to honour? 3513
24:11 to p thee unto great honour; 3513+3513
Est 3: 1 After these things did king Ahasuerus p 1431
Pr 4: 8 Exalt her, and she shall p thee: she shall 7311

PROMOTED (5) [PROMOTE]
Jdg 9: 9 and man, and go to be p over the trees? 5128
9:11 good fruit, and go to be p over the trees? 5128
9:13 and man, and go to be p over the trees? 5128
Est 5:11 all the things wherein the king had p him, 1431
Da 3:30 the king p Shadrach, Meshach, and 6744

PROMOTION (2) [PROMOTE]
Ps 75: 6 For p cometh neither from the east, 7311
Pr 3:35 but shame shall be the p of fools. 7311

PRONOUNCE (23) [PRONOUNCED, PRONOUNCING]
Lev 5: 4 whatsoever it be that a man shall p with an 981
13: 3 shall look on him, and p him unclean. 2930
13: 6 not in the skin, the priest shall p him clean: 2891
13: 8 then the priest shall p him unclean: 2930
13:11 the priest shall p him unclean, and 2930
13:13 he shall p him clean that hath the plague: 2891
13:15 see the raw flesh, and p him to be unclean: 2930
13:17 the priest shall p him clean that hath 2891
13:20 the priest shall p him unclean: 2930
13:22 then the priest shall p him unclean: 2930
13:23 and the priest shall p him clean. 2891
13:25 wherefore the priest shall p him unclean: it 2930
13:27 then the priest shall p him unclean: 2930
13:28 and the priest shall p him clean: 2891
13:30 then the priest shall p him unclean: 2930
13:34 the skin; then the priest shall p him clean: 2891
13:37 is clean: and the priest shall p him clean. 2891
13:44 priest shall p him utterly unclean, 2930+2930
13:59 to p it clean, or to pronounce it unclean. 2891
13:59 to pronounce it clean, or to p it unclean. 2930
14: 7 shall p him clean, and shall let the living 2891
14:48 the priest shall p the house clean, because 2891
Jdg 12: 6 for he could not frame to p it right. 1696

PRONOUNCED (14) [PRONOUNCE]
Ne 6:12 but that he p this prophecy against me: 1696
Jer 11:17 that planted thee, hath p evil against thee, 1696
16:10 Wherefore hath the LORD p all this great 1696
18: 8 If that nation, against whom I have p, turn 1696
19:15 upon all her towns all the evil that I have p 1696
25:13 land all my words which I have p against it, 1696
26:13 him of the evil that he hath p against you. 1696
26:19 of the evil which he had p against them? 1696
34: 5 for I have p the word, saith the LORD. 1696
35:17 all the evil that I have p against them: 1696
36: 7 the fury that the LORD hath p against this 1696
36:18 He p all these words unto me with his 7121
36:31 all the evil that I have p against them; 1696
40: 2 The LORD thy God hath p this evil upon 1696

PRONOUNCING (1) [PRONOUNCE]
Lev 5: 4 p with his lips to do evil, or to do good, 981

P

PROOF (5) [PROVE]
2Co 2: 9 did I write, that I might know the **p** of you, 1382
8:24 the **p** of your love, and of our boasting on 1732
13: 3 Since ye seek a **p** of Christ speaking in me, 1382
Php 2:22 But ye know the **p** of him, that, as a son 1382
2Ti 4: 5 an evangelist, **make full p** of thy ministry. 4135

PROOFS (1) [PROVE]
Ac 1: 3 alive after his passion by many **infallible p**, 5039

PROPER (4)
1Ch 29: 3 I have of mine own **p good**, *of* gold and 5459
Ac 1:19 insomuch as that field is called in their **p** 2398
1Co 7: 7 But every man hath **his p** gift of God, 2398
Heb 11:23 because they saw *he was* a **p** child; 791

PROPERTY See HABITATION

PROPHECIES (2) [PROPHESY]
1Co 13: 8 but whether *there be* **p**, they shall fail; 4394
1Ti 1:18 according to the **p** which went before on 4394

PROPHECY (21) [PROPHESY]
2Ch 9:29 in the **p** of Ahijah the Shilonite, and in 5016
15: 8 the **p** *of* Oded the prophet, he took courage, 5016
Ne 6:12 but *that* he pronounced *this* **p** against me: 5016
Pr 30: 1 words of Agur the son of Jakeh, *even* the **p**: 4853
31: 1 the **p** that his mother taught him. 4853
Da 9:24 to seal up the vision and **p**, and to anoint 5030
Mt 13:14 And in them is fulfilled the **p** of Esaias, 4394
Ro 12: 6 whether **p**, *let us prophesy* according to 4394
1Co 12:10 to another **p**; to another discerning of 4394
13: 2 And though I have *the gift of* **p**, and 4394
1Ti 4:14 that is in thee, which was given thee by **p**, 4394
2Pe 1:19 We have also a more sure word **of p**; 4397
1:20 that no **p** of the scripture is of *any* private 4394
1:21 For the **p** came not in old time by the will 4394
Rev 1: 3 and they that hear the words of *this* **p**, and 4394
11: 6 that it rain not in the days of their **p**: 4394
19:10 for the testimony of Jesus is the spirit of **p**. 4394
22: 7 keepeth the sayings of the **p** of this book. 4394
22:10 Seal not the sayings of the **p** of this book: 4394
22:18 that heareth the words of the **p** of this book, 4394
22:19 away from the words of the book of this **p**, 4394

PROPHESIED (50) [PROPHESY]
Nu 11:25 rested upon them, they **p**, and did not cease. 5012
11:26 unto the tabernacle: and they **p** in the camp. 5012
1Sa 10:10 God came upon him, and he **p** among them. 5012
10:11 he **p** among the prophets, then the people 5012
18:10 and he **p** in the midst of the house: 5012
19:20 the messengers of Saul, and they also **p**. 5012
19:21 sent other messengers, and they **p** likewise. 5012
19:21 again the third time, and they **p** also. 5012
19:23 he went on, and **p**, until he came to Naioth 5012
19:24 **p** before Samuel in like manner, and 5012
1Ki 18:29 they **p** until *the time* of the offering of 5012
22:10 and all the prophets **p** before them. 5012
22:12 all the prophets **p** so, saying, Go up *to* 5012
1Ch 25: 2 which **p** according to the order of the king. 5012
25: 3 who **p** with a harp, to give thanks and 5012
2Ch 18: 7 for he never **p** good unto me, but 5012
18: 9 and all the prophets **p** before them. 5012
18:11 all the prophets **p** so, saying, Go up *to* 5012
20:37 Eliezer the son of Dodavah of Mareshah **p** 5012
Ezr 5: 1 **p** unto the Jews that *were* in Judah and 5013
Jer 2: 8 the prophets **p** by Baal, and walked after 5012
20: 1 heard *that* Jeremiah **p** these things. 5012
20: 6 all thy friends, to whom thou hast **p** lies. 5012
23:13 they **p** in Baal, and caused my people Israel 5012
23:21 I have not spoken to them, yet they **p**. 5012
25:13 which Jeremiah hath **p** against all 5012
26: 9 Why hast thou **p** in the name of 5012
26:11 for he hath **p** against this city, as ye have 5012
26:18 Micah the Morasthite **p** in the days of 5012
26:20 there was also a man that **p** in the name of 5012
26:20 who **p** against this city and against this land 5012
28: 6 perform thy words which thou hast **p**, 5012
28: 8 before thee of old **p** both against many 5012
29:31 Because that Shemaiah hath **p** unto you, 5012
37:19 Where *are* now your prophets which **p** unto 5012
Eze 11:13 it came to pass, when I **p**, that Pelatiah 5012
37: 7 So I **p** as I was commanded: and as I 5012
37: 7 as I **p**, there was a noise, and behold a 5012
37:10 So I **p** as he commanded me, and the breath 5012
38:17 which **p** in those days *many* years, that *I* 5012
Zec 13: 4 every one of his vision, when he hath **p**; 5012
Mt 7:22 Lord, Lord, have we not **p** in thy name? 4395
11:13 all the prophets and the law **p** until John. 4395
Mk 7: 6 Well hath Esaias **p** of you hypocrites, as it 4395
Lk 1:67 filled with the Holy Ghost, and **p**, saying, 4395
Jn 11:51 he **p** that Jesus should die for *that* nation; 4395
Ac 19: 6 and they spake with tongues, and **p**. 4395
1Co 14: 5 all spake with tongues, but rather that ye **p**: 4395
1Pe 1:10 who **p** of the grace *that should come* unto 4395
Jude 1:14 from Adam, **p** of these, saying, Behold, 4395

PROPHESIETH (7) [PROPHESY]
Jer 28: 9 The prophet which **p** of peace, when 5012
Eze 12:27 and he **p** of the times *that are* far off. 5012
Zec 13: 3 him shall thrust him through when he **p**. 5012
1Co 11: 5 **p** with *her* head uncovered dishonoureth 4395
14: 3 But he that **p** speaketh unto men *to* 4395
14: 4 but he that **p** edifieth *the* church. 4395
14: 5 for greater *is* he that **p** than he that speaketh 4395

PROPHESY (90) [PROPHECIES, PROPHECY, PROPHESIED, PROPHESIETH, PROPHESYING, PROPHESYINGS, PROPHET, PROPHET'S, PROPHETESS, PROPHETS]
Nu 11:27 said, Eldad and Medad do **p** in the camp. 5012
1Sa 10: 5 and a harp, before them; and they shall **p**: 5012
10: 6 thou shalt **p** with them, and shalt be turned 5012
1Ki 22: 8 for he doth not **p** good concerning me, but 5012
22:18 Did I not tell thee that he would **p** no good 5012
1Ch 25: 1 and of Jeduthun, who should **p** with harps, 5012
2Ch 18:17 Did I not tell thee *that* he would not **p** good 5012
Isa 30:10 **P** not unto us right *things*, speak unto us 2372
30:10 speak unto us smooth *things*, **p** deceits: 2372
Jer 5:31 The prophets **p** falsely, and the priests bear 5012
11:21 **P** not in the name of the LORD, 5012
14:14 unto me, The prophets **p** lies in my name: 5012
14:14 they **p** unto you a false vision and 5012
14:15 concerning the prophets that **p** in my name, 5012
14:16 the people to whom they **p** shall be cast out 5012
19:14 whither the LORD had sent him to **p**; 5012
23:16 the words of the prophets that **p** unto you: 5012
23:25 that **p** lies in my name, saying, I have 5012
23:26 be in the heart of the prophets that **p** lies? 5012
23:32 I *am* against them that **p** false dreams, 5012
25:30 Therefore **p** thou against them all these 5012
26:12 The LORD sent me to **p** against this house 5012
27:10 For they **p** a lie unto you, to remove you far 5012
27:14 king of Babylon: for they **p** a lie unto you. 5012
27:15 the LORD, yet they **p** a lie in my name; 5012
27:15 ye, and the prophets that **p** unto you. 5012
27:16 the words of your prophets that **p** unto you, 5012
27:16 from Babylon: for they **p** a lie unto you. 5012
29: 9 For they **p** falsely unto you in my name: 5012
29:21 which **p** a lie unto you in my name; 5012
32: 3 saying, Wherefore dost thou **p**, and say, 5012
Eze 4: 7 *be* uncovered, and thou shalt **p** against it. 5012
6: 2 the mountains of Israel, and **p** against them, 5012
11: 4 Therefore **p** against them, prophesy, O son 5012
11: 4 prophesy against them, **p**, O son of man. 5012
13: 2 **p** against the prophets of Israel that 5012
13: 2 against the prophets of Israel that **p**, 5012
13: 2 say thou unto them that **p** out of their own 5030
13:16 *To wit,* the prophets of Israel which **p** 5012
13:17 thy people, which **p** out of their own heart; 5012
13:17 of their own heart; and **p** thou against them, 5012
20:46 and **p** against the forest of the south field; 5012
21: 2 and **p** against the land of Israel, 5012
21: 9 Son of man, **p**, and say, Thus saith 5012
21:14 **p**, and smite *thine* hands together, and 5012
21:28 thou, son of man, **p** and say, Thus saith 5012
25: 2 against the Ammonites, and **p** against them; 5012
28:21 set thy face against Zidon, and **p** against it, 5012
29: 2 and **p** against him, and against all Egypt: 5012
30: 2 Son of man, **p** and say, Thus saith the Lord 5012
34: 2 **p** against the shepherds of Israel, prophesy, 5012
34: 2 shepherds of Israel, **p**, and say unto them, 5012
35: 2 face against mount Seir, and **p** against it, 5012
36: 1 **p** unto the mountains of Israel, and say, 5012
36: 3 Therefore **p** and say, Thus saith the Lord 5012
36: 6 **P** therefore concerning the land of Israel, 5012
37: 4 **P** upon these bones, and say unto them, 5012
37: 9 **P** unto the wind, prophesy, son of man, and 5012
37: 9 **p**, son of man, and say to the wind, 5012
37:12 Therefore **p** and say unto them, Thus saith 5012
38: 2 of Meshech and Tubal, and **p** against him, 5012
38:14 Therefore, son of man, **p** and say unto Gog, 5012
39: 1 thou son of man, **p** against Gog, and say, 5012
Joel 2:28 your sons and your daughters shall **p**, 5012
Am 2:12 commanded the prophets, saying, **P** not. 5012
3: 8 Lord GOD hath spoken, who can but **p**? 5012
7:12 of Judah, and there eat bread, and **p** there: 5012
7:13 **p** not again any more *at* Beth-el: for it *is* 5012
7:15 said unto me, Go, **p** unto my people Israel. 5012
7:16 **P** not against Israel, and drop not *thy word* 5012
Mic 2: 6 **P** ye not, *say they to them that* prophesy: 5197
2: 6 Prophesy ye not, *say they to them that* **p**: 5197
2: 6 they shall not **p** to them, *that* they shall not 5197
2:11 *saying,* I will **p** unto thee of wine and 5197
Zec 13: 3 *that* when any shall yet **p**, then his father 5012
Mt 15: 7 well did Esaias **p** of you, saying, 4395
26:68 Saying, **P** unto us, *thou* Christ, Who is he 4395
Mk 14:65 and to buffet him, and to say unto him, **P**: 4395
Lk 22:64 and asked him, saying, **P**, who is it that 4395
Ac 2:17 and your sons and your daughters shall **p**, 4395
2:18 in those days of my Spirit; and they shall **p**: 4395
21: 9 had four daughters, virgins, which did **p**. 4395
Ro 12: 6 *let us* **p** according to the proportion of faith; NIG
1Co 13: 9 For we know in part, and we **p** in part. 4395
14: 1 spiritual *gifts*, but rather that ye may **p**. 4395
14:24 But if all **p**, and there come in one that 4395
14:31 For ye may all **p** one by one, that all may 4395
14:39 covet to **p**, and forbid not to speak with 4395
Rev 10:11 Thou must **p** again before many peoples, 4395
11: 3 they shall **p** a thousand two hundred *and* 4395

PROPHESYING (6) [PROPHESY]
1Sa 10:13 when he had made an end of **p**, he came *to* 5012
19:20 they saw the company of the prophets **p**, 5012
Ezr 6:14 they prospered through the **p** of Haggai 5017
1Co 11: 4 Every man praying or **p**, having *his* head 4395
14: 6 or by knowledge, or by **p**, or by doctrine? 4394
14:22 but **p** *serveth* not for them that believe not, 4394

PROPHESYINGS (1) [PROPHESY]
1Th 5:20 Despise not **p**. 4394

PROPHET (242) [PROPHESY]
Ge 20: 7 for he *is* a **p**, and he shall pray for thee, and 5030
Ex 7: 1 and Aaron thy brother shall be thy **p**. 5030
Nu 12: 6 If there be a **p** among you, *I* the LORD 5030
Dt 13: 1 If there arise among you a **p**, or a dreamer 5030
13: 3 shalt not hearken unto the words of that **p**, 5030
13: 5 that **p**, or that dreamer of dreams, shall be 5030
18:15 up unto thee a **P** from the midst of thee, 5030
18:18 I will raise them up a **P** from among their 5030
18:20 the **p**, which shall presume to speak a word 5030
18:20 name of other gods, even that **p** shall die. 5030
18:22 When a **p** speaketh in the name of 5030
18:22 the **p** hath spoken it presumptuously: 5030
Dt 34:10 there arose not a **p** since in Israel like unto 5030
Jdg 6: 8 That the LORD sent a **p** unto the children 5030
1Sa 3:20 *was* established to be a **p** of the LORD. 5030
9: 9 for *he that is* now *called* a **P** was beforetime 5030
22: 5 the **p** Gad said unto David, Abide not in 5030
2Sa 7: 2 That the king said unto Nathan the **p**, 5030
12:25 he sent by the hand of Nathan the **p**; and 5030
24:11 the word of the LORD came unto the **p** 5030
1Ki 1: 8 Nathan the **p**, and Shimei, and Rei, and 5030
1:10 Nathan the **p**, and Benaiah, and the mighty 5030
1:22 with the king, Nathan the **p** also came in. 5030
1:23 told the king, saying, Behold Nathan the **p**. 5030
1:32 Nathan the **p**, and Benaiah the son of 5030
1:34 Nathan the **p** anoint him there king over 5030
1:38 Nathan the **p**, and Benaiah the son of 5030
1:44 Nathan the **p**, and Benaiah the son of 5030
1:45 Nathan the **p** have anointed him king in 5030
11:29 that the **p** Ahijah the Shilonite found him in 5030
13:11 Now there dwelt an old **p** in Beth-el; and 5030
13:18 I *am* a **p** also as thou *art;* and an angel 5030
13:20 came unto the **p** that brought him back: 5030
13:23 *to wit,* for the **p** whom he had brought 5030
13:25 and told *it* in the city where the old **p** dwelt. 5030
13:26 when the **p** that brought him back from 5030
13:29 the **p** took up the carcase of the man of 5030
13:29 the old **p** came to the city, to mourn and 5030
14: 2 behold, there *is* Ahijah the **p**, which told 5030
14:18 by the hand of his servant Ahijah the **p**. 5030
16: 7 also by the hand of the **p** Jehu the son of 5030
16:12 he spake against Baasha by Jehu the **p**, 5030
18:22 I, *even* I only, remain a **p** of the LORD; 5030
18:36 that Elijah the **p** came near, and said, 5030
19:16 shalt thou anoint to be **p** in thy room. 5030
20:13 there came a **p** unto Ahab king of Israel, 5030
20:22 the **p** came to the king of Israel, and 5030
20:38 So the **p** departed, and waited for the king 5030
22: 7 *Is there* not here a **p** of the LORD besides, 5030
2Ki 3:11 *Is there* not here a **p** of the LORD, 5030
5: 3 Would God my lord *were* with the **p** that *is* 5030
5: 8 and he shall know that there is a **p** in Israel. 5030
5:13 *if* the **p** had bid thee *do some* great thing, 5030
6:12 Elisha, the **p** that *is* in Israel, telleth 5030
9: 1 Elisha the **p** called one of the children of 5030
9: 4 the young man, *even* the young man the **p**, 5030
14:25 the son of Amittai, the **p**, which *was* of 5030
19: 2 to Esai the **p** the son of Amoz. 5030
20: 1 the **p** Isaiah the son of Amoz came to him, 5030
20:11 Isaiah the **p** cried unto the LORD: and 5030
20:14 came Isaiah the **p** unto king Hezekiah, 5030
23:18 with the bones of the **p** that came out of 5030
1Ch 17: 1 that David said to Nathan the **p**, Lo, 5030
29:29 in the book of Nathan the **p**, and in 5030
2Ch 9:29 not written in the book of Nathan the **p**, 5030
12: 5 came Shemaiah the **p** to Rehoboam, and 5030
12:15 not written in the book of Shemaiah the **p**, 5030
13:22 *are* written in the story of the **p** Iddo. 5030
15: 8 the prophecy *of* Oded the **p**, he took 5030
18: 6 *Is there* not here a **p** of the LORD besides, 5030
21:12 came a writing to him from Elijah the **p**, 5030
25:15 he sent unto him a **p**, which said unto him, 5030
25:16 the **p** forbare, and said, I know that God 5030
26:22 first and last, did Isaiah the **p**, the son of 5030
28: 9 a **p** of the LORD was there, whose name 5030
29:25 of Gad the king's seer, and Nathan the **p**: 5030
32:20 the **p** Isaiah the son of Amoz, prayed and 5030
32:32 *are* written in the vision of Isaiah the **p**, 5030
35:18 in Israel from the days of Samuel the **p**; 5030
36:12 humbled not himself before Jeremiah the **p** 5030
Ezr 5: 1 Haggai the **p**, and Zechariah the son of 5029
6:14 through the prophesying of Haggai the **p** 5029
Ps 51: T when Nathan the **p** came unto him, 5030
74: 9 *there is* no more any **p**: neither *is there* 5030
Isa 3: 2 and the **p**, and the prudent, and the ancient, 5030
9:15 and the **p** that teacheth lies, he *is* the tail. 5030
28: 7 and the **p** have erred through strong drink, 5030
37: 2 unto Isaiah the **p** the son of Amoz. 5030
38: 1 Isaiah the **p** the son of Amoz came unto 5030
39: 3 came Isaiah the **p** unto king Hezekiah, 5030
Jer 1: 5 *and* I ordained thee a **p** unto the nations. 5030
6:13 from the **p** even unto the priest every one 5030
8:10 from the **p** even unto the priest every one 5030
14:18 both the **p** and the priest go about into a 5030
18:18 from the wise, nor the word from the **p**. 5030
20: 2 Pashur smote Jeremiah the **p**, and put him 5030
23:11 For both **p** and priest are profane; yea, 5030
23:28 The **p** that hath a dream, let him tell a 5030
23:33 or the **p**, or a priest, shall ask thee, saying, 5030
23:34 *as for* the **p**, and the priest, and the people, 5030
23:37 Thus shalt thou say to the **p**, What hath 5030
25: 2 The which Jeremiah the **p** spake unto all 5030
28: 1 *that* Hananiah the son of Azur the **p**, 5030
28: 5 the **p** Jeremiah said unto the prophet 5030
28: 5 the prophet Jeremiah said unto the **p** 5030
28: 6 Even the **p** Jeremiah said, Amen: 5030
28: 9 The **p** which prophesieth of peace, 5030
28: 9 when the word of the **p** shall come to pass, 5030
28: 9 *then* shall the **p** be known, that the LORD 5030
28:10 Hananiah the **p** took the yoke from off 5030
28:10 the yoke from off the **p** Jeremiah's neck, 5030
28:11 And the **p** Jeremiah went his way. 5030
28:12 **p**, after that Hananiah the prophet had NIH
28:12 **p** had broken the yoke from off the neck of 5030
28:12 yoke from off the neck of the **p** Jeremiah, 5030
28:15 said the **p** Jeremiah unto Hananiah 5030
28:15 the prophet Jeremiah unto Hananiah the **p**, 5030
28:17 So Hananiah the **p** died the same year in 5030
29: 1 **p** sent from Jerusalem unto the residue of 5030
29:26 man *that is* mad, and **maketh** himself **a p**, 5012
29:27 which **maketh** himself **a p** to you? 5012
29:29 read this letter in the ears of Jeremiah the **p**. 5030
32: 2 Jeremiah the **p** was shut up in the court of 5030
34: 6 Jeremiah the **p** spake all these words unto 5030
36: 8 to all that Jeremiah the **p** commanded him, 5030
36:26 take Baruch the scribe and Jeremiah the **p**: 5030
37: 2 which he spake by the **p** Jeremiah. 5030

Jer 37: 3 of Maaseiah the priest to the **p** Jeremiah, 5030
37: 6 came the word of the LORD unto the **p** 5030
37:13 he took Jeremiah the **p**, saying, Thou fallest 5030
38: 9 in all that they have done to Jeremiah the **p**, 5030
38:10 take up Jeremiah the **p** out of the dungeon, 5030
38:14 took Jeremiah the **p** unto him into the third 5030
42: 2 said unto Jeremiah the **p**, Let, we beseech 5030
42: 4 Jeremiah the **p** said unto them, I have heard 5030
43: 6 Jeremiah the **p**, and Baruch the son of 5030
45: 1 The word that Jeremiah the **p** spake unto 5030
46: 1 to Jeremiah the **p** against the Gentiles; 5030
46:13 that the LORD spake to Jeremiah the **p**, 5030
47: 1 to Jeremiah the **p** against the Philistines, 5030
49:34 **p** against Elam in the beginning of 5030
50: 1 land of the Chaldeans by Jeremiah the **p**. 5030
51:59 The word which Jeremiah the **p** 5030
La 2:20 the **p** be slain in the sanctuary of the Lord? 5030
Eze 2: 5 yet shall know that there hath been a **p** 5030
7:26 shall they seek a vision of the **p**; but 5030
14: 4 before his face, and cometh to the **p**; 5030
14: 7 cometh to a **p** to inquire of him concerning 5030
14: 9 if the **p** be deceived when he hath spoken a 5030
14: 9 I the LORD have deceived that **p**, and 5030
14:10 the punishment of the **p** shall be even as 5030
33:33 shall they know that a **p** hath been among 5030
Da 9: 2 of the LORD came to Jeremiah the **p**, 5030
Hos 4: 5 the **p** also shall fall with thee *in* the night, 5030
9: 7 Israel shall know *it:* the **p** *is* a fool, 5030
9: 8 the **p** *is* a snare of a fowler in all his ways, 5030
12:13 by a **p** the LORD brought Israel out of 5030
12:13 out of Egypt, and by a **p** was he preserved. 5030
Am 7:14 and said to Amaziah, I *was* no **p**, 5030
Mic 2:11 he shall even be the **p** of this people. 5197
Hab 1: 1 The burden which Habakkuk the **p** did see. 5030
3: 1 A prayer of Habakkuk the **p** upon 5030
Hag 1: 1 the **p** unto Zerubbabel the son of Shealtiel, 5030
1: 3 the word of the LORD by Haggai the **p**, 5030
1:12 the words of Haggai the **p**, as the LORD 5030
2: 1 came the word of the LORD by the **p** 5030
2:10 the word of the LORD by Haggai the **p**, 5030
Zec 1: 1 of Berechiah, the son of Iddo the **p**, saying, 5030
1: 7 of Berechiah, the son of Iddo the **p**, saying, 5030
13: 5 he shall say, I *am* no **p**, I *am* a 5030
Mal 4: 5 I *will* send you Elijah the **p** before 5030
Mt 1:22 which was spoken of the Lord by the **p**, *4396*
2: 5 of Judea: for thus it is written by the **p**, *4396*
2:15 spoken of the Lord by the **p**, saying, *4396*
2:17 that which was spoken by Jeremie the **p**, *4396*
3: 3 For this is he that was spoken of by the **p** *4396*
4:14 fulfilled which was spoken by Esaias the **p**, *4396*
8:17 fulfilled which was spoken by Esaias the **p**, *4396*
10:41 He that receiveth a **p** in the name of a *4396*
10:41 of a **p** shall receive a prophet's reward; *4396*
11: 9 A **p**? yea, I say unto you, and more than a *4396*
11: 9 yea, I say unto you, and more than a **p**. *4396*
12:17 fulfilled which was spoken by Esaias the **p**, *4396*
12:39 be given to it, but the sign of the **p** Jonas: *4396*
13:35 be fulfilled which was spoken by the **p**, *4396*
13:57 A **p** is not without honour, save in his own *4396*
14: 5 because they counted him as a **p**. *4396*
16: 4 be given unto it, but the sign of the **p** Jonas. *4396*
21: 4 be fulfilled which was spoken by the **p**, *4396*
21:11 This is Jesus the **p** of Nazareth of Galilee. *4396*
21:26 we fear the people; for all hold John as a **p**. *4396*
21:46 because they took him for a **p**. *4396*
24:15 spoken of by Daniel the **p**, stand in the holy *4396*
27: 9 that which was spoken by Jeremie the **p**, *4396*
27:35 be fulfilled which was spoken by the **p**, *4396*
Mk 6: 4 A **p** is not without honour, but in his own *4396*
6:15 That it is a **p**, or as one of the prophets. *4396*
11:32 *men* counted John, that he was a **p** indeed. *4396*
13:14 spoken of by Daniel the **p**, standing where *4396*
Lk 1:76 child, shalt be called the **p** of the Highest: *4396*
3: 4 in the book of the words of Esaias the **p**, *4396*
4:17 unto him the book of the **p** Esaias. *4396*
4:24 No **p** is accepted in his own country. *4396*
4:27 were in Israel in the time of Eliseus the **p**; *4396*
7:16 saying, That a great **p** is risen up among us; *4396*
7:26 A **p**? Yea, I say unto you, and much more *4396*
7:26 I say unto you, and much more than a **p**. *4396*
7:28 is not a greater **p** than John the Baptist: *4396*
7:39 saying, This *man*, if he were a **p**, *4396*
11:29 sign be given it, but the sign of Jonas the **p**. *4396*
13:33 for it cannot be that a **p** perish out of *4396*
20: 6 for they be persuaded that John was a **p**. *4396*
24:19 which was a **p** mighty in deed and *4396*
Jn 1:21 Art thou *that* **p**? And he answered, No. *4396*
1:23 the way of the Lord, as said the **p** Esaias. *4396*
1:25 be not *that* Christ, nor Elias, neither *that* **p**? *4396*
4:19 unto him, Sir, I perceive that thou art a **p**. *4396*
4:44 that a **p** hath no honour in his own country. *4396*
6:14 This is of a truth *that* **p** that should come *4396*
7:40 *this* saying, said, Of a truth this is the **P**. *4396*
7:52 and look: for out of Galilee ariseth no **p**. *4396*
9:17 hath opened thine eyes? He said, He is a **p**. *4396*
12:38 That the saying of Esaias the **p** might be *4396*
Ac 2:16 But this is that which was spoken by the **p** *4396*
2:30 Therefore being a **p**, and knowing that God *4396*
3:22 A **p** shall the Lord your God raise up unto *4396*
3:23 *that* every soul, which will not hear that **p**, *4396*
7:37 A **p** shall the Lord your God raise up unto *4396*
7:48 in temples made with hands; as saith the **p**, *4396*
8:28 and sitting in his chariot read Esaias the **p**. *4396*
8:30 to *him*, and heard him read the **p** Esaias, *4396*
8:34 I pray thee, of whom speaketh the **p** this? *4396*
13: 6 a **false p**, a Jew, whose name *was* *5578*
13:20 and fifty years, until Samuel the **p**. *4396*
21:10 there came down from Judea a certain **p**, *4396*
28:25 Well spake the Holy Ghost by Esaias the **p** *4396*
1Co 14:37 If any *man* think himself to be a **p**, or *4396*
Tit 1:12 of themselves, *even* a **p** of their own, said, *4396*
2Pe 2:16 man's voice forbad the madness of the **p**. *4396*
Rev 16:13 and out of the mouth of the **false p**. *5578*
19:20 with him the **false p** that wrought miracles *5578*
20:10 where the beast and the **false p** *are*, and *5578*

PROPHET'S (2) [PROPHESY]

Am 7:14 I *was* no prophet, neither *was* I a **p** son; 5030
Mt 10:41 name of a prophet shall receive a **p** reward; *4396*

PROPHETESS (8) [PROPHESY]

Ex 15:20 Miriam the **p**, the sister of Aaron, took a 5031
Jdg 4: 4 Deborah, a **p**, the wife of Lapidoth, 5031
2Ki 22:14 and Asahiah, went unto Huldah the **p**, 5031
2Ch 34:22 king *had appointed*, went to Huldah the **p**, 5031
Ne 6:14 on the **p** Noadiah, and the rest of 5031
Isa 8: 3 I went unto the **p**; and she conceived, and 5031
Lk 2:36 a **p**, the daughter of Phanuel, of the tribe of *4398*
Rev 2:20 which calleth herself a **p**, to teach and *4398*

PROPHETS (239) [PROPHESY]

Nu 11:29 God that all the LORD'S people were **p**, 5030
1Sa 10: 5 that thou shalt meet a company of **p** 5030
10:10 the hill, behold, a company of **p** met him; 5030
10:11 he prophesied among the **p**, then the people 5030
10:11 the son of Kish? *Is* Saul also among the **p**? 5030
10:12 a proverb, *Is* Saul also among the **p**? 5030
19:20 when they saw the company of the **p** 5030
19:24 they say, *Is* Saul also among the **p**? 5030
28: 6 neither by dreams, nor by Urim, nor by **p**. 5030
28:15 me no more, neither by **p**, nor by dreams: 5030
1Ki 18: 4 when Jezebel cut off the **p** of the LORD, 5030
18: 4 that Obadiah took an hundred **p**, and 5030
18:13 did when Jezebel slew the **p** of the LORD, 5030
18:13 men of the LORD'S **p** by fifty in a cave, 5030
18:19 the **p** of Baal four hundred and fifty, and 5030
18:19 fifty, and the **p** of the groves four hundred, 5030
18:20 gathered the **p** together unto mount Carmel. 5030
18:22 Baal's **p** *are* four hundred and fifty men. 5030
18:25 Elijah said unto the **p** of Baal, Choose you 5030
18:40 Elijah said unto them, Take the **p** of Baal; 5030
19: 1 withal how he had slain all the **p** with 5030
19:10 thine altars, and slain thy **p** with the sword; 5030
19:14 thine altars, and slain thy **p** with the sword; 5030
20:35 a certain man of the sons of the **p** said unto 5030
20:41 of Israel discerned him that he *was* of the **p**. 5030
22: 6 the king of Israel gathered the **p** together, 5030
22:10 and all the **p** prophesied before them. 5030
22:12 all the **p** prophesied so, saying, Go up *to* 5030
22:13 the words of the **p** *declare* good unto 5030
22:22 be a lying spirit in the mouth of all his **p**. 5030
22:23 a lying spirit in the mouth of all these thy **p**, 5030
2Ki 2: 3 the sons of the **p** that *were at* Beth-el came 5030
2: 5 the sons of the **p** that *were* at Jericho came 5030
2: 7 fifty men of the sons of the **p** went, and 5030
2:15 when the sons of the **p** which *were* to view 5030
3:13 get thee to the **p** of thy father, and to 5030
3:13 of thy father, and to the **p** of thy mother. 5030
4: 1 the wives of the sons of the **p** unto Elisha, 5030
4:38 the sons of the **p** *were* sitting before him: 5030
4:38 and seethe pottage for the sons of the **p**. 5030
5:22 two young men of the sons of the **p**: 5030
6: 1 the sons of the **p** said unto Elisha, 5030
9: 1 prophet called one of the children of the **p**, 5030
9: 7 may avenge the blood of my servants the **p**, 5030
10:19 therefore call unto me all the **p** of Baal, 5030
17:13 by all the **p**, *and by* all the seers, saying, 5030
17:13 which I sent to you by my servants the **p**. 5030
17:23 as he had said by all his servants the **p**. 5030
21:10 the LORD spake by his servants the **p**, 5030
23: 2 the **p**, and all the people, both small and 5030
24: 2 which he spake by his servants the **p**. 5030
1Ch 16:22 not mine anointed, and do my **p** no harm. 5030
2Ch 18: 5 gathered together *of* **p** four hundred men, 5030
18: 9 and all the **p** prophesied before them. 5030
18:11 all the **p** prophesied so, saying, Go up *to* 5030
18:12 the words of the **p** *declare* good to the king 5030
18:21 be a lying spirit in the mouth of all his **p**. 5030
18:22 a lying spirit in the mouth of these thy **p**, 5030
20:20 believe his **p**, so shall ye prosper. 5030
24:19 Yet he sent **p** to them, to bring them again 5030
29:25 the commandment of the LORD by his **p**. 5030
36:16 and despised his words, and misused his **p**, 5030
Ezr 5: 1 the **p**, Haggai the prophet, and 5029
5: 2 with them *were* the **p** of God helping them. 5029
9:11 hast commanded by thy servants the **p**, 5030
Ne 6: 7 thou hast also appointed **p** to preach of thee 5030
6:14 prophetess Noadiah, and the rest of the **p** 5030
9:26 slew thy **p** which testified against them to 5030
9:30 against them by thy spirit in thy **p**: 5030
9:32 on our **p**, and on our fathers, and on all thy 5030
Ps 105:15 not mine anointed, and do my **p** no harm. 5030
Isa 29:10 the **p** and your rulers, the seers hath he 5030
30:10 to the **p**, Prophesy not unto us right *things*, 2374
Jer 2: 8 the **p** prophesied by Baal, and walked after 5030
2:26 their princes, and their priests, and their **p**, 5030
2:30 your own sword hath devoured your **p**, 5030
4: 9 shall be astonished, and the **p** shall wonder. 5030
5:13 the **p** shall become wind, and the word *is* 5030
5:31 The **p** prophesy falsely, and the priests bear 5030
7:25 even sent unto you all my servants the **p**, 5030
8: 1 the bones of the **p**, and the bones of 5030
13:13 the **p**, and all the inhabitants of Jerusalem, 5030
14:13 behold, the **p** say unto them, Ye shall not 5030
14:14 unto me, The **p** prophesy lies in my name: 5030
14:15 the **p** that prophesy in my name, 5030
14:15 and famine shall those **p** be consumed. 5030
23: 9 heart within me is broken because of the **p**; 5030
23:13 I have seen folly in the **p** of Samaria; 5030
23:14 I have seen also in the **p** of Jerusalem a 5030
23:15 saith the LORD of hosts concerning the **p**; 5030
23:15 for from the **p** of Jerusalem is profaneness 5030
23:16 Hearken not unto the words of the **p** that 5030
23:21 I have not sent *these* **p**, yet they ran: I have 5030
23:25 I have heard what the **p** said, that prophesy 5030
23:26 How long shall *this* be in the heart of the **p** 5030
23:26 *they are* **p** of the deceit of their own heart; 5030
23:30 I *am* against the **p**, saith the LORD, 5030
23:31 Behold, I *am* against the **p**, saith 5030
25: 4 hath sent unto you all his servants the **p**, 5030

Jer 26: 5 hearken to the words of my servants the **p**, 5030
26: 7 So the priests and the **p** and all the people 5030
26: 8 that the priests and the **p** and all the people 5030
26:11 the **p** unto the princes and to all the people, 5030
26:16 all the people unto the priests and to the **p**; 5030
27: 9 Therefore hearken not ye to your **p**, nor to 5030
27:14 the words of the **p** that speak unto you, 5030
27:15 ye, and the **p** that prophesy unto you. 5030
27:16 Hearken not to the words of your **p** that 5030
27:18 if they *be* **p**, and if the word of the LORD 5030
28: 8 The **p** that have been before me and before 5030
29: 1 to the **p**, and to all the people whom 5030
29: 8 Let not your **p** and your diviners, that *be* in 5030
29:15 The LORD hath raised us up **p** in 5030
29:19 I sent unto them by my servants the **p**, 5030
32:32 their **p**, and the men of Judah, and 5030
35:15 sent also unto you all my servants the **p**, 5030
37:19 Where *are* now your **p** which prophesied 5030
44: 4 I sent unto you all my servants the **p**, 5030
La 2: 9 the law *is* no *more;* her **p** also find no 5030
2:14 Thy **p** have seen vain and foolish things for 5030
4:13 For the sins of her **p**, *and* the iniquities of 5030
Eze 13: 2 prophesy against the **p** of Israel that 5030
13: 3 Woe unto the foolish **p**, that follow their 5030
13: 4 thy **p** are like the foxes in the deserts. 5030
13: 9 mine hand shall be upon the **p** that see 5030
13:16 *To wit,* the **p** of Israel which prophesy 5030
22:25 *There is* a conspiracy of her **p** in the midst 5030
22:28 her **p** have daubed them *with* untempered 5030
38:17 in old time by my servants the **p** of Israel, 5030
Da 9: 6 have we hearkened unto thy servants the **p**, 5030
9:10 he set before us by his servants the **p**. 5030
Hos 6: 5 Therefore have I hewed *them* by the **p**; 5030
12:10 I have also spoken by the **p**, and I have 5030
12:10 used similitudes by the ministry of the **p**. 5030
Am 2:11 I raised up of your sons for **p**, and of your 5030
2:12 commanded the **p**, saying, Prophesy not. 5030
3: 7 revealeth his secret unto his servants the **p**. 5030
Mic 3: 5 Thus saith the LORD concerning the **p** 5030
3: 6 the sun shall go down over the **p**, and 5030
3:11 and the **p** thereof divine for money: 5030
Zep 3: 4 Her **p** *are* light *and* treacherous persons: 5030
Zec 1: 4 unto whom the former **p** have cried, saying, 5030
1: 5 *are* they? and the **p**, do they live for ever? 5030
1: 6 which I commanded my servants the **p**, 5030
7: 3 to the **p**, saying, Should I weep in the fifth 5030
7: 7 the LORD hath cried by the former **p**, 5030
7:12 hosts hath sent in his spirit by the former **p**: 5030
8: 9 days these words by the mouth of the **p**, 5030
13: 2 also I will cause the **p** and the unclean spirit 5030
13: 4 *that* the **p** shall be ashamed every one of his 5030
Mt 2:23 be fulfilled which was spoken by the **p**, *4396*
5:12 persecuted they the **p** which were before *4396*
5:17 that I am come to destroy the law, or the **p**: *4396*
7:12 so to them: for this is the law and the **p**. *4396*
7:15 Beware of **false p**, which come to you in *5578*
11:13 For all the **p** and the law prophesied until *4396*
13:17 That many **p** and righteous *men* have *4396*
16:14 Elias; and others, Jeremias, or one of the **p**. *4396*
22:40 commandments hang all the law and the **p** *4396*
23:29 because ye build the tombs of the **p**, and *4396*
23:30 partakers with them in the blood of the **p**. *4396*
23:31 are the children of them which killed the **p**. *4396*
23:34 I send unto you **p**, and wise *men*, and *4396*
23:37 *thou* that killest the **p**, and stonest them *4396*
24:11 And many **false p** shall rise, and *5578*
24:24 and **false p**, and shall shew great signs and *5578*
26:56 that the scriptures of the **p** might be *4396*
Mk 1: 2 As it is written in the **p**, Behold, I send my *4396*
6:15 That it is a prophet, or as one of the **p**. *4396*
8:28 some *say,* Elias; and others, One of the **p**. *4396*
13:22 For false Christs and **false p** shall rise, and *5578*
Lk 1:70 (As he spake by the mouth of his holy **p**, *4396*
6:23 the like manner did their fathers unto the **p**. *4396*
6:26 for so did their fathers to the **false p**. *5578*
9: 8 that one of the old **p** was risen again. *4396*
9:19 others *say,* that one of the old **p** is risen *4396*
10:24 that many **p** and kings have desired to see *4396*
11:47 for ye build the sepulchres of the **p**, and *4396*
11:49 I will send them **p** and apostles, and *4396*
11:50 That the blood of all the **p**, which was shed *4396*
13:28 and Isaac, and Jacob, and all the **p**, in *4396*
13:34 which killest the **p**, and stonest them that *4396*
16:16 The law and the **p** *were* until John: *4396*
16:29 saith unto him, They have Moses and the **p**; *4396*
16:31 unto him, If they hear not Moses and the **p**, *4396*
18:31 all *things* that are written by the **p** *4396*
24:25 slow of heart to believe all that the **p** have *4396*
24:27 And beginning at Moses and all the **p**, *4396*
24:44 and *in* the **p**, and *in* the psalms, *4396*
Jn 1:45 and the **p**, did write, Jesus of Nazareth, *4396*
6:45 It is written in the **p**, And they shall be all *4396*
8:52 Abraham is dead, and the **p**; and *4396*
8:53 and the **p** are dead: whom makest thou *4396*
Ac 3:18 had shewed by the mouth of all his **p**, *4396*
3:21 of all his holy **p** since the world began. *4396*
3:24 and all the **p** from Samuel and those that *4396*
3:25 Ye are the children of the **p**, and of *4396*
7:42 as it is written in the book of the **p**, O *ye* *4396*
7:52 Which of the **p** have not your fathers *4396*
10:43 To him give all the **p** witness, that through *4396*
11:27 And in these days came **p** from Jerusalem *4396*
13: 1 in the church that was at Antioch certain **p** *4396*
13:15 the **p** the rulers of the synagogue sent unto *4396*
13:27 nor *yet* the voices of the **p** which are read *4396*
13:40 upon you, which is spoken of in the **p**; *4396*
15:15 And to this agree the words of the **p**; as it is *4396*
15:32 and Silas, being **p** also themselves, *4396*
24:14 which are written in the law and the **p**: *4396*
26:22 none other *things* than those which the **p** *4396*
26:27 King Agrippa, believest thou the **p**? I know *4396*
28:23 and *out of* the **p**, from morning till evening. *4396*
Ro 1: 2 (Which he had promised afore by his **p** in *4396*
3:21 being witnessed by the law and the **p**; *4396*
11: 3 they have killed thy **p**, and digged down *4396*

P

Ro 16:26 and by the scriptures of the **p**, *4397*
1Co 12:28 first apostles, secondarily **p**, *4396*
12:29 *are* all **p**? *are* all teachers? *are* all workers *4396*
14:29 Let the **p** speak two or three, and let *4396*
14:32 And the spirits of the **p** are subject to *4396*
14:32 spirits of the prophets are subject to the **p**: *4396*
Eph 2:20 upon the foundation of the apostles and **p**, *4396*
3: 5 unto his holy apostles and **p** by the Spirit; *4396*
4:11 and some, **p**; and some, evangelists; and *4396*
1Th 2:15 and their own **p**, and have persecuted us; *4396*
Heb 1: 1 spake in time past unto the fathers by the **p**, *4396*
11:32 *of* David also, and Samuel, and *of* the **p**: *4396*
Jas 5:10 Take, my brethren, the **p**, who have spoken *4396*
1Pe 1:10 Of which salvation the **p** have inquired and *4396*
2Pe 2: 1 But there were **false p** also among *5578*
3: 2 which were spoken before by the holy **p**, *4396*
1Jn 4: 1 many **false p** are gone out into the world. *5578*
Rev 10: 7 as he hath declared to his servants the **p**. *4396*
11:10 these two **p** tormented them that dwelt on *4396*
11:18 give reward unto thy servants the **p**, *4396*
16: 6 they have shed the blood of saints and **p**, *4396*
18:20 *thou* heaven, and ye holy apostles and **p**; *4396*
18:24 And in her was found the blood of **p**, and *4396*
22: 6 the Lord God of the holy **p** sent his angel to *4396*
22: 9 and of thy brethren the **p**, and of them *4396*

PROPITIATION (3)
Ro 3:25 Whom God hath set forth *to be* a **p** through *2435*
1Jn 2: 2 And he is the **p** for our sins: and not for *2434*
4:10 and sent his Son *to be* the **p** for our sins. *2434*

PROPORTION (3)
1Ki 7:36 according to the **p** of every one, and 4626
Job 41:12 his parts, nor his power, nor his comely **p**. 6187
Ro 12: 6 *let us prophesy* according to the **p** of faith; *356*

PROPRIETY See SOBRIETY

PROSELYTE (2) [PROSELYTES]
Mt 23:15 ye compass sea and land to make one **p**, *4339*
Ac 6: 5 and Parmenas, and Nicolas a **p** of Antioch: *4339*

PROSELYTES (2) [PROSELYTE]
Ac 2:10 and strangers of Rome, Jews and **p**, *4339*
13:43 and religious **p** followed Paul and *4339*

PROSPECT (6)
Eze 40:44 and their **p** *was* toward the south: 6440
40:44 one at the side of the east gate *having* the **p** 6440
40:45 This chamber, whose **p** *is* toward the south, 6440
40:46 the chamber whose **p** *is* toward the north *is* 6440
42:15 toward the gate whose **p** *is* toward the east, 6440
43: 4 way of the gate whose **p** *is* toward the east. 6440

PROSPER (49) [PROSPERED, PROSPERETH, PROSPERITY, PROSPEROUS, PROSPEROUSLY]
Ge 24:40 send his angel with thee, and **p** thy way; 6743
24:42 if now thou do **p** my way which I go: 6743
39: 3 *that* the LORD **made** all that he did **to p** 6743
39:23 which he did, the LORD **made** *it* **to p**. 6743
Nu 14:41 of the LORD? but it shall not **p**. 6743
Dt 28:29 and thou shalt not **p** in thy ways: 6743
29: 9 do them, that ye may **p** *in* all that ye do. 7919
Jos 1: 7 that thou mayest **p** whithersoever thou 7919
1Ki 2: 3 that thou mayest **p** *in* all that thou doest, 7919
22:12 saying, Go up *to* Ramoth-gilead, and **p**: 6743
22:15 he answered him, Go, and **p**: for 6743
1Ch 22:11 **p** thou, and build the house of the LORD 6743
22:13 shalt thou **p**, if thou takest heed to fulfil 6743
2Ch 13:12 God of your fathers; for you shall not **p**. 6743
18:11 saying, Go up *to* Ramoth-gilead, and **p**: 6743
18:14 **p**, and they shall be delivered into your 6743
20:20 believe his prophets, so shall ye **p**. 6743
24:20 of the LORD, that ye cannot **p**? 6743
26: 5 he sought the LORD, God **made** him **to p**. 6743
Ne 1:11 **p**, I pray thee, thy servant *this* day, and 6743
2:20 The God of heaven, he will **p** us; 6743
Job 12: 6 The tabernacles of robbers **p**, and they that 7951
Ps 1: 3 and whatsoever he doeth shall **p**. 6743
73:12 these *are* the ungodly, who **p** in the world; 7961
122: 6 of Jerusalem: they shall **p** that love thee. 7951
Pr 28:13 He that covereth his sins shall not **p**: but 6743
Ecc 11: 6 for thou knowest not whether shall **p**, 3787
Isa 53:10 the pleasure of the LORD shall **p** in his 6743
54:17 weapon *that* is formed against thee shall **p**; 6743
55:11 and it shall **p** *in the thing* whereto I sent it. 6743
Jer 2:37 and thou shalt not **p** in them. 6743
5:28 the cause of the fatherless, yet they **p**; 6743
10:21 therefore they shall not **p**; and all their 7919
12: 1 Wherefore doth the way of the wicked **p**? 6743
20:11 for they shall not **p**: *their* everlasting 7919
22:30 a man *that* shall not **p** in his days: 6743
22:30 for no man of his seed shall **p**, sitting upon 6743
23: 5 a King shall reign and **p**, and shall execute 7919
32: 5 ye fight with the Chaldeans, ye shall not **p**. 6743
La 1: 5 adversaries are the chief, her enemies **p**; 7951
Eze 16:13 and thou didst **p** into a kingdom. 6743
17: 9 Thus saith the Lord GOD; Shall it **p**? 6743
17:10 Yea behold, *being* planted, shall it **p**? shall 6743
17:15 Shall he **p**? shall he escape that doeth such 6743
Da 8:24 shall **p**, and practise, and shall destroy 6743
8:25 also he shall **cause** craft **to p** in his hand; 6743
11:27 speak lies at one table; but it shall not **p**: 6743
11:36 shall **p** till the indignation be accomplished: 6743
3Jn 1: 2 I wish above all *things* that thou mayest **p** *2137*

PROSPERED (13) [PROSPER]
Ge 24:56 me not, seeing the LORD hath **p** my way; 6743
Jdg 4:24 the hand of the children of Israel **p**, 1980
2Sa 11: 7 the people did, and **how** the war **p**. 7965+3807.1
2Ki 18: 7 *and* he **p** whithersoever he went forth: 7919
1Ch 29:23 as king instead of David his father, and **p**; 6743
2Ch 14: 7 us rest on every side. So they built and **p**. 6743
31:21 his God, he did *it* with all his heart, and **p**. 6743
32:30 of David. And Hezekiah **p** in all his works. 6743
Ezr 6:14 they **p** through the prophesying of Haggai 6744
Job 9: 4 hardened *himself* against him, and hath **p**? 7999
Da 6:28 So this Daniel **p** in the reign of Darius, and 6744
8:12 truth to the ground; and it practised, and **p**. 6743
1Co 16: 2 as *God* hath **p** him, that there be no *2137*

PROSPERETH (4) [PROSPER]
Ezr 5: 8 work goeth fast on, and **p** in their hands. 6744
Ps 37: 7 because of him who **p** *in* his way, 6743
Pr 17: 8 that hath it: whithersoever it turneth, it **p**. 7919
3Jn 1: 2 and be in health, even as thy soul **p**. *2137*

PROSPERITY (17) [PROSPER]
Dt 23: 6 Thou shalt not seek their peace nor their **p** 2896
1Sa 25: 6 thus shall ye say to him that liveth *in p*, NIH
1Ki 10: 7 and **p** exceedeth the fame which I heard. 2896
Job 15:21 in **p** the destroyer shall come *upon* him. 7965
36:11 serve *him*, they shall spend their days in **p**, 2896
Ps 30: 6 And in my **p** I said, I shall never be moved. 7959
35:27 which hath pleasure in the **p** of his servant. 7965
73: 3 the foolish, *when* I saw the **p** of the wicked. 7965
118:25 O LORD, I beseech thee, **send** now **p**. 6743
122: 7 within thy walls, *and* **p** within thy palaces. 7962
Pr 1:32 and the **p** of fools shall destroy them. 7962
Ecc 7:14 In the day of **p** be joyful, but in the day of 2896
Jer 22:21 I spake unto thee in thy **p**; *but* thou saidst, 7962
33: 9 and for all the **p** that I procure unto it. 7965
La 3:17 my soul far off from peace: I forgat **p**. 2896
Zec 1:17 My cities through **p** shall yet be spread 2896
7: 7 when Jerusalem was inhabited and in **p**, 7961

PROSPEROUS (8) [PROSPER]
Ge 24:21 the LORD had **made** his journey **p** 6743
39: 2 was with Joseph, and he was a **p** man; 6743
Jos 1: 8 for then thou shalt **make** thy way **p**, and 6743
Jdg 18: 5 whether our way which we go shall be **p**. 6743
Job 8: 6 **make** the habitation of thy righteousness **p**. 7999
Isa 48:15 brought him, and he shall **make** his way **p**. 6743
Zec 8:12 For the seed *shall be* **p**; the vine shall give 7965
Ro 1:10 **have a p journey** by the will of God to *2137*

PROSPEROUSLY (2) [PROSPER]
2Ch 7:11 and in his own house, he **p effected**. 6743
Ps 45: 4 *in* thy majesty ride **p** because of truth and 6743

PROSTITUTE (1)
Lev 19:29 Do not **p** thy daughter, to cause her to be a 2490

PROSTITUTES See HARLOTS; SODOMITES; WHORE; WHORE'S; WHORES

PROSTITUTION See WHORE; WHORE'S; WHORES; WHOREDOM

PROTECTION (1)
Dt 32:38 them rise up and help you, *and* be your **p**. 5643

PROTEST (3) [PROTESTED, PROTESTING]
Ge 43: 3 man did **solemnly p** unto us, saying, 5749+5749
1Sa 8: 9 howbeit yet **p solemnly** unto them, 5749+5749
1Co 15:31 **I p** by your rejoicing which I have in Christ *3513*

PROTESTED (3) [PROTEST]
1Ki 2:42 and **p** unto thee, saying, Know for a certain, 5749
Jer 11: 7 For I **earnestly p** unto your fathers 5749+5749
Zec 3: 6 the angel of the LORD **p** unto Joshua, 5749

PROTESTING (1) [PROTEST]
Jer 11: 7 rising early and **p**, saying, Obey my voice. 5749

PROUD (48) [PRIDE]
Job 9:13 his anger, the **p** helpers do stoop under him. 7293
26:12 his understanding he smiteth through the **p**. 7293
38:11 and here shall thy **p** waves be stayed? 1347
40:11 behold every one *that is* **p**, and abase him. 1343
40:12 Look on every one *that is* **p**, *and* bring him 1343
Ps 12: 3 *and* the tongue that speaketh **p** *things*: 1419
31:23 and plentifully rewardeth the **p** doer. 1346
40: 4 respecteth not the **p**, nor such as turn aside 7295
86:14 the **p** are risen against me, and 2086
94: 2 judge of the earth: render a reward to the **p**. 1343
101: 5 a high look and a **p** heart will not I suffer. 7342
119:21 Thou hast rebuked the **p** *that are* cursed, 2086
119:51 The **p** have had me greatly in derision: 2086
119:69 The **p** have forged a lie against me: *but* 2086
119:78 Let the **p** be ashamed; for they dealt 2086
119:85 The **p** have digged pits for me, which *are* 2086
119:122 servant for good: let not the **p** oppress me. 2086
123: 4 are at ease, *and with* the contempt of the **p**. 1349
124: 5 Then the **p** waters had gone over our soul. 2121
138: 6 the lowly: but the **p** he knoweth afar off. 1364
140: 5 The **p** have hid a snare for me, and cords; 1343
Pr 6:17 A **p** look, a lying tongue, and hands that 7311
15:25 LORD will destroy the house of the **p**: 1343
16: 5 Every one *that is* **p** in heart *is* an 1362
16:19 than to divide the spoil with the **p**. 1343
21: 4 a **p** heart, *and* the plowing of the wicked, 7342
21:24 **P** *and* haughty scorner *is* his name, 2086
21:24 *is* his name, who dealeth in **p** wrath. 2087
28:25 He that is of a **p** heart stirreth up strife: but 7342
Ecc 7: 8 the patient in spirit *is* better than the **p** in 1362
Isa 2:12 of hosts *shall be* upon every one *that is* **p** 1343
13:11 I will cause the arrogancy of the **p** to cease, 2086
16: 6 heard of the pride of Moab; *he is* very **p**: 1341
Jer 13:15 Hear ye, and give ear; be not **p**: for 1361
43: 2 all the **p** men, saying unto Jeremiah, 2086
48:29 heard the pride of Moab; *he is* exceeding **p**: 1343
50:29 for she hath been **p** against the LORD, 2102
50:31 Behold, I *am* against thee, *O thou* most **p**, 2087
50:32 the **most p** shall stumble and fall, and 2087
Hab 2: 5 *he is* a **p** man, neither keepeth at home, 3093
Mal 3:15 now we call the **p** happy; yea, they that 2086
4: 1 all the **p**, yea, and all that do wickedly, 2086
Lk 1:51 he hath scattered the **p** in the imagination *5244*
Ro 1:30 haters of God, despiteful, **p**, boasters, *5244*
1Ti 6: 4 He is **p**, knowing nothing, but doting about *5187*
2Ti 3: 2 covetous, boasters, **p**, blasphemers, *5244*
Jas 4: 6 God resisteth the **p**, but giveth grace unto *5244*
1Pe 5: 5 for God resisteth the **p**, and giveth grace to *5244*

PROUDLY (9) [PRIDE]
Ex 18:11 for in the thing wherein they **dealt p** *he was* 2102
1Sa 2: 3 Talk no more *so* **exceeding p**; let *not* 1364+1364
Ne 9:10 for thou knewest that they **dealt p** against 2102
9:16 they and our fathers **dealt p**, and 2102
9:29 yet they **dealt p**, and hearkened not unto 2102
Ps 17:10 *with* their mouth they speak **p**. 1348+871.1
31:18 which speak grievous things **p** and 1346+871.1
Isa 3: 5 the child shall **behave** himself **p** against 7292
Ob 1:12 neither shouldest thou have spoken **p** in 1431

PROVE (25) [PROOF, PROOFS, PROVED, PROVETH, PROVING]
Ex 16: 4 a certain rate every day, that I may **p** them, 5254
20:20 for God is come to **p** you, and that his fear 5254
Dt 8: 2 to humble thee, *and* to **p** thee, to know what 5254
8:16 humble thee, and that he might **p** thee, 5254
33: 8 whom thou didst **p** at Massah, *and* 5254
Jdg 2:22 That through them I may **p** Israel, 5254
3: 1 which the LORD left, to **p** Israel by them, 5254
3: 4 they were to **p** Israel by them, to know 5254
6:39 let me **p**, I pray thee, but *this* once with 5254
1Ki 10: 1 she came to **p** him with hard questions. 5254
2Ch 9: 1 she came to **p** Solomon with hard questions 5254
Job 9:20 I *am* perfect, it shall also **p** me **perverse**. 6140
Ps 26: 2 Examine me, O LORD, and **p** me; try my 5254
Ecc 2: 1 I will **p** thee with mirth, therefore 5254
Da 1:12 **P** thy servants, I beseech thee, ten days; 5254
Mal 3:10 **p** me now herewith, saith the LORD of 974
Lk 14:19 five yoke of oxen, and I go to **p** them: *1381*
Jn 6: 6 And this he said to **p** him: for he himself *3985*
Ac 24:13 Neither can they **p** *the things* whereof they *3936*
25: 7 against Paul, which they could not **p**. *584*
Ro 12: 2 that ye may **p** what *is that* good, and *1381*
2Co 8: 8 and to **p** the sincerity of your love. *1381*
13: 5 ye be in the faith; **p** your own selves. *1381*
Gal 6: 4 But let every man **p** his own work, and then *1381*
1Th 5:21 **P** all *things*; hold fast *that which is* good. *1381*

PROVED (15) [PROVE]
Ge 42:15 Hereby ye shall be **p**: By the life of Pharaoh 974
42:16 be kept in prison, that your words may be **p**, 974
Ex 15:25 and an ordinance, and there he **p** them, 5254
1Sa 17:39 for he had not **p** *it*. And David said unto 5254
17:39 for I have not **p** *them*. And David put them 5254
Ps 17: 3 Thou hast **p** mine heart; thou hast visited *me* 974
66:10 For thou, O God, hast **p** us: thou hast tried 974
81: 7 I **p** thee at the waters of Meribah. Selah. 974
95: 9 fathers tempted me, **p** me, and saw my work. 974
Ecc 7:23 All this have I **p** by wisdom: I said, I will 5254
Da 1:14 to them in this matter, and **p** them ten days. 5254
Ro 3: 9 for we have **before p** both Jews and *4256*
2Co 8:22 whom we have oftentimes **p** diligent in *1381*
1Ti 3:10 And let these also first be **p**; then let them *1381*
Heb 3: 9 **p** me, and saw my works forty years. *1381*

PROVENDER (7)
Ge 24:25 We have both straw and **p** enough, and 4554
24:32 gave straw and **p** for the camels, and 4554
42:27 opened his sack to give his ass **p** in the inn, 4554
43:24 washed their feet; and he gave their asses **p**. 4554
Jdg 19:19 Yet there is both straw and **p** for our asses; 4554
19:21 into his house, and **gave p** unto the asses: 1101
Isa 30:24 asses that ear the ground shall eat clean **p**, 1098

PROVERB (20) [PROVERBS]
Dt 28:37 an astonishment, a **p**, and a byword, 4912
1Sa 10:12 Therefore it became a **p**, *Is* Saul also 4912
24:13 As saith the **p** of the ancients, 4912
1Ki 9: 7 Israel shall be a **p** and a byword among all 4912
2Ch 7:20 will make it to be a **p** and a byword among 4912
Ps 69:11 also my garment; and I became a **p** to them. 4912
Pr 1: 6 To understand a **p**, and the interpretation; 4912
Isa 14: 4 That thou shalt take up this **p** against 4912
Jer 24: 9 to be a reproach and a **p**, a taunt and a 4912
Eze 12:22 what *is* that **p** *that* ye have in the land of 4912
12:23 I will make this **p** to cease, and they shall 4912
12:23 they shall no more **use** it **as a p** in Israel; 4911
14: 8 will make him a sign and a **p**, and I will cut 4912
16:44 useth proverbs shall **use** *this* **p** against thee, 4911
18: 2 that ye **use** this **p** concerning the land 4911+4912
18: 3 any more to **use** this **p** in Israel. 4911+4912
Hab 2: 6 and a taunting **p** against him, and say, 2420
Lk 4:23 Ye will surely say unto me this **p**, *3850*
Jn 16:29 speakest thou plainly, and speakest no **p**. *3942*
2Pe 2:22 unto them according to the true **p**, *3942*

PROVERBS (9) [PROVERB]
Nu 21:27 Wherefore they that **speak in p** say, 4911
1Ki 4:32 he spake three thousand **p**: and his songs 4912
Pr 1: 1 The **p** of Solomon the son of David, king of 4912
10: 1 The **p** of Solomon. A wise son maketh a 4912
25: 1 These *are* also **p** of Solomon, which 4912
Ecc 12: 9 and sought out, *and* set in order many **p**. 4912
Eze 16:44 every one that **useth p** shall use *this* 4911
Jn 16:25 These *things* have I spoken unto you in **p**: *3942*
16:25 when I shall no more speak unto you in **p**, *3942*

PROVETH (1) [PROVE]
Dt 13: 3 for the LORD your God **p** you, to know 5254

PROVIDE (11) [PROVIDED, PROVIDENCE, PROVIDETH, PROVIDING, PROVISION]
Ge 22: 8 God will **p** himself a lamb for a burnt 7200
30:30 now when shall I **p** for mine own house 6213
Ex 18:21 Moreover thou shalt **p** out of all the people 2372

1Sa 16:17 P me now a man that can play well, and 7200
2Ch 2: 7 in Jerusalem, whom David my father did p. 3559
Ps 78:20 bread also? can he p flesh for his people? 3559
Mt 10: 9 P neither gold, nor silver, nor brass in your 2932
Lk 12:33 p yourselves bags which wax not old, 4160
Ac 23:24 And p *them* beasts, that they may set Paul 3936
Ro 12:17 P *things* honest in the sight of all men. 4306
1Ti 5: 8 But if any p not for his own, and 4306

PROVIDED (9) [PROVIDE]
Dt 33:21 he p the first *part* for himself, because 7200
1Sa 16: 1 for I have p me a king among his sons. 7200
2Sa 19:32 he had p the king of sustenance while he 3557
1Ki 4: 7 which p victuals for the king and his 3557
4:27 those officers p victual for king Solomon, 3557
2Ch 32:29 Moreover he p him cities, and 6213
Ps 65: 9 them corn, when thou hast so p for it. 3559
Lk 12:20 shall *those things* be, which thou hast p? 2090
Heb 11:40 God having p some better *thing* for us, 4265

PROVIDENCE (1) [PROVIDE]
Ac 24: 2 deeds are done unto this nation by thy p, 4307

PROVIDETH (2) [PROVIDE]
Job 38:41 Who p for the raven his food? when his 3559
Pr 6: 8 P her meat in the summer, *and* 3559

PROVIDING (1) [PROVIDE]
2Co 8:21 P *for* honest *things,* not only in the sight of 4306

PROVINCE (27) [PROVINCES]
Ezr 2: 1 Now these *are* the children of the p that 4082
5: 8 the king, that we went into the p of Judea, 4083
6: 2 in the palace that *is* in the p of the Medes, 4083
7:16 gold that thou canst find in all the p of 4083
Ne 1: 3 there in the p *are* in great affliction 4082
7: 6 These *are* the children of the p, that went 4082
11: 3 Now these *are* the chief of the p that dwelt 4082
Est 1:22 into every p according to 4082+4082+2050.1
3:12 that *were* over every p, 4082+4082+2050.1
3:12 every p according to 4082+4082+2050.1
3:14 every p *was* published 3605+4082+4082+2050.1
4: 3 in every p, 3605+4082+4082+2050.1
8: 9 *unto* every p according to 4082+4082+2050.1
8:11 the people and p that would assault them, 4082
8:13 every p *was* published 3605+4082+4082+2050.1
8:17 in every p, and 3605+4082+4082+2050.1
9:28 every p, and every city; 4082+4082+2050.1
Ecc 5: 8 perverting of judgment and justice in a p, 4082
Da 2:48 made him ruler over the whole p of 4083
2:49 over the affairs of the p of Babylon: 4083
3: 1 in the plain of Dura, in the p of Babylon. 4083
3:12 set over the affairs of the p of Babylon, 4083
3:30 and Abed-nego, in the p of Babylon. 4083
8: 2 *in* the palace, which *is* in the p of Elam; 4082
11:24 even upon the fattest places of the p; 4082
Ac 23:34 read *the letter,* he asked of what p he was: 1885
25: 1 Now when Festus was come into the p, 1885

PROVINCES (30) [PROVINCE]
1Ki 20:14 by the young men of the princes of the p. 4082
20:15 the young men of the princes of the p, 4082
20:17 the young men of the princes of the p went 4082
20:19 So these young men of the princes of the p 4082
Ezr 4:15 hurtful unto kings and p, and that they have 4083
Est 1: 1 *over* an hundred and seven and twenty p:) 4082
1: 3 and Media, the nobles and princes of the p, 4082
1:16 to all the people that *are* in all the p of 4082
1:22 For he sent letters into all the king's p, 4082
2: 3 let the king appoint officers in all the p of 4082
2:18 he made a release to the p, and gave gifts, 4082
3: 8 dispersed among the people in all the p of 4082
3:13 were sent by posts into all the king's p, 4082
4:11 the people of the king's p, do know, 4082
8: 5 the Jews which *are* in all the king's p: 4082
8: 9 rulers of the p which *are* from India unto 4082
8: 9 an hundred twenty and seven p, *unto* every 4082
8:12 Upon one day in all the p of king 4082
9: 2 throughout all the p of the king Ahasuerus, 4082
9: 3 all the rulers of the p, and the lieutenants, 4082
9: 4 and his fame went out throughout all the p: 4082
9:12 have they done in the rest of the king's p? 4082
9:16 the other Jews that *were* in the king's p 4082
9:20 that *were* in all the p of the king Ahasuerus, 4082
9:30 and seven p of the kingdom of Ahasuerus, 4082
Ecc 2: 8 the peculiar treasure of kings and of the p: 4082
La 1: 1 *and* princess among the p, *how* is she 4082
Eze 19: 8 set against him on every side from the p, 4082
Da 3: 2 the sheriffs, and all the rulers of the p, 4083
3: 3 the sheriffs, and all the rulers of the p, 4083

PROVING (2) [PROVE]
Ac 9:22 at Damascus, p that this is *very* Christ. 4822
Eph 5:10 P what is acceptable unto the Lord. 1381

PROVISION (11) [PROVIDE]
Ge 42:25 his sack, and to give them p for the way: 6720
45:21 of Pharaoh, and gave them p for the way. 6720
Jos 9: 5 all the bread of their p was dry *and* mouldy. 6718
9:12 This our bread we took hot for our p out of 6679
1Ki 4: 7 each man *his* month in a year made p. 3557
4:22 Solomon's p for one day was thirty 3899
2Ki 6:23 he prepared great p for them: and 3740
1Ch 29:19 the palace, *for* the which I have made p. 3559
Ps 132:15 I will abundantly bless her p: I will satisfy 6718
Da 1: 5 the king appointed them a daily p of 1697
Ro 13:14 and make not p for the flesh, to *fulfil* 4307

PROVOCATION (8) [PROVOKE]
1Ki 15:30 by his p where*with* he provoked 3708
21:22 for the p wherewith thou hast provoked *me* 3708
Job 17: 2 and *doth not* mine eye continue in their p? 4784
Ps 95: 8 as *in* the p, *and* as *in* the day of temptation 4808
Jer 32:31 city hath been to me *as* a p of mine anger 639
Eze 20:28 there they presented the p of their offering: 3708
Heb 3: 8 Harden not your hearts, as in the p, in 3894
3:15 harden not your hearts, as in the p. 3894

PROVOCATIONS (3) [PROVOKE]
2Ki 23:26 of all the p that Manasseh had provoked 3708
Ne 9:18 up out of Egypt, and had wrought great p; 5007
9:26 them to thee, and they wrought great p. 5007

PROVOKE (42) [PROVOCATION, PROVOCATIONS, PROVOKED, PROVOKEDST, PROVOKETH, PROVOKING]
Ex 23:21 of him, and obey his voice, p him not; 4843
Nu 14:11 How long will this people p me? 5006
Dt 4:25 of the LORD thy God, to p him to anger: 3707
9:18 the sight of the LORD, to p him to anger. 3707
31:20 and p me, and break my covenant. 5006
31:29 to p him to anger through the work of your 3707
32:21 I will p them to anger with a foolish 3707
1Ki 14: 9 to p me to anger, and hast cast me behind 3707
16: 2 to sin, to p me to anger with their sins; 3707
16:26 to p the LORD God of Israel to anger 3707
16:33 p the LORD God of Israel to anger than 3707
2Ki 17:11 wicked things to p the LORD to anger: 3707
17:17 the sight of the LORD, to p him to anger. 3707
21: 6 the sight of the LORD, to p *him* to anger. 3707
22:17 that they might p me to anger with all 3707
23:19 Israel had made to p *the LORD* to anger, 3707
2Ch 33: 6 the sight of the LORD, to p him to anger. 3707
34:25 that *they* might p me to anger with all 3707
Job 12: 6 and they that p God are secure; 7264
Ps 78:40 How oft did they p him in the wilderness, 4784
Isa 3: 8 the LORD, to p the eyes of his glory. 4784
Jer 7:18 other gods, that *they* may p me to anger. 3707
7:19 Do they p me to anger? saith the LORD: 3707
7:19 *do they* not p themselves to the confusion of NIH
11:17 p me to anger in offering incense unto 3707
25: 6 p me not to anger with the works of your 3707
25: 7 that *ye* might p me to anger with the works 3707
32:29 unto other gods, to p me to anger. 3707
32:32 which they have done to p me to anger, 3707
44: 3 they have committed to p me to anger, 3707
44: 8 In that *ye* p me unto wrath with the works 3707
Eze 8:17 *with* violence, and have returned to p me 3707
16:26 thy whoredoms, to p me to anger. 3707
Lk 11:53 and to p him to speak of many *things:* 653
Ro 10:19 I will p you to jealousy by *them that are* no 3863
11:11 the Gentiles, for to p them to jealousy. 3863
11:14 If by any means I may p to emulation 3863
1Co 10:22 Do we p the Lord to jealousy? are we 3863
Eph 6: 4 ye fathers, p not your children to wrath: 3949
Col 3:21 p not your children *to anger,* lest they be 2042
Heb 3:16 For some, when they had heard, did p: 3893
10:24 And let us consider one another to p unto 3948

PROVOKED (33) [PROVOKE]
Nu 14:23 neither shall any of them that p me see it: 5006
16:30 ye shall understand that these men have p 5006
Dt 9: 8 Also in Horeb ye p the LORD to wrath, 7107
9:22 ye p the LORD to wrath. 7107
32:16 They p him to jealousy with strange *gods,* 7065
32:16 with abominations p they him to anger. 3707
32:21 they have p me to anger with their 3707
Jdg 2:12 unto them, and p the LORD to anger. 3707
1Sa 1: 6 her adversary also p her sore, for to 3707+3708
1: 7 to the house of the LORD, so she p her; 3707
1Ki 14:22 they p him to jealousy with their sins 7065
15:30 he p the LORD God of Israel to anger. 3707
21:22 wherewith thou hast p *me* to anger, 3707
22:53 and p to anger the LORD God of Israel, 3707
2Ki 21:15 have p me to anger, since the day their 3707
23:26 of all the provocations that Manasseh had p 3707
1Ch 21: 1 and p David to number Israel. 5496
2Ch 28:25 p to anger the LORD God of his fathers. 3707
Ezr 5:12 had p the God of heaven unto wrath, 7265
Ne 4: 5 for they have p *thee* to anger before 3707
Ps 78:56 Yet they tempted and p the most high God, 4784
78:58 For they p him to anger with their high 3707
106: 7 but p *him* at the sea, *even* at the Red sea. 4784
106:29 Thus they p *him* to anger with their 3707
106:33 Because they p his spirit, so that he spake 4784
106:43 they p *him* with their counsel, and 4784
Isa 1: 4 have p the Holy One of Israel unto anger, 5006
Jer 8:19 Why have they p me to anger with their 3707
32:30 p me to anger with the work of their 3707
Hos 12:14 Ephraim p *him* to anger most bitterly: 3707
Zec 8:14 when your fathers p me to wrath, saith 7107
1Co 13: 5 her own, is not easily p, thinketh no evil; 3947
2Co 9: 2 a year ago; and your zeal hath p very many. 2042

PROVOKEDST (1) [PROVOKE]
Dt 9: 7 how thou p the LORD thy God to wrath 7107

PROVOKETH (3) [PROVOKE]
Pr 20: 2 whoso p him to anger sinneth *against* his 5674
Isa 65: 3 A people that p me to anger continually to 3707
Eze 8: 3 the image of jealousy, which p to jealousy. 7069

PROVOKING (6) [PROVOKE]
Dt 32:19 because of the p of his sons, 3708
1Ki 14:15 made their groves, p the LORD to anger. 3707
16: 7 in p him to anger with the work of his 3707
16:13 in p the LORD God of Israel to anger 3707
Ps 78:17 they sinned yet more against him by p 4784
Gal 5:26 p one another, envying one another. 4292

PRUDENCE (3) [PRUDENT, PRUDENTLY]
2Ch 2:12 endued with p and understanding, 7922
Pr 8:12 I wisdom dwell *with* p, and find out 6195
Eph 1: 8 abounded toward us in all wisdom and p; 5428

PRUDENT (24) [PRUDENCE]
1Sa 16:18 p in matters, and a comely person, and 995
Pr 12:16 but a p *man* covereth shame. 6175
12:23 A p man concealeth knowledge: but 6175
13:16 Every p *man* dealeth with knowledge: but 6175
14: 8 The wisdom of the p *is* to understand his 6175
14:15 but the p *man* looketh well to his going. 6175
14:18 but the p are crowned *with* knowledge. 6175
15: 5 but he that regardeth reproof is p. 6191
16:21 The wise in heart shall be called p: and 995
18:15 The heart of the p getteth knowledge; and 995
19:14 and a p wife *is* from the LORD. 7919
22: 3 A p *man* foreseeth the evil, and 6175
27:12 A p *man* foreseeth the evil, *and* 6175
Isa 3: 2 and the prophet, and the p, and the ancient, 7080
5:21 in their own eyes, and p in their own sight! 995
10:13 have done *it,* and by my wisdom; for I am p: 995
29:14 the understanding of their p *men* shall be 995
Jer 49: 7 is counsel perished from the p? is their 995
Hos 14: 9 and he shall understand these *things?* p, and 995
Am 5:13 Therefore the p shall keep silence in that 7919
Mt 11:25 hast hid these *things* from the wise and p, 4908
Lk 10:21 hast hid these *things* from the wise and p, 4908
Ac 13: 7 *of the country,* Sergius Paulus, a p man; 4908
1Co 1:19 bring to nothing the understanding of the p. 4908

PRUDENTLY (1) [PRUDENCE]
Isa 52:13 Behold, my servant shall deal p, he shall be 7919

PRUNE (2) [PRUNED, PRUNING, PRUNINGHOOKS]
Lev 25: 3 six years thou shalt p thy vineyard, and 2168
25: 4 neither sow thy field, nor p thy vineyard. 2168

PRUNED (1) [PRUNE]
Isa 5: 6 it shall not be p, nor digged; but there shall 2168

PRUNING (1) [PRUNE]
Isa 18: 5 shall both cut off the sprigs with p hooks, 4211

PRUNINGHOOKS (3) [HOOK, PRUNE]
Isa 2: 4 into plowshares, and their spears into p: 4211
Joel 3:10 into swords, and your p into spears: 4211
Mic 4: 3 into plowshares, and their spears into p: 4211

PSALM (88) [PSALMIST, PSALMS]
1Ch 16: 7 on that day David delivered first *this* p to NIH
Ps 3: T A P of David, when he fled from Absalom 4210
4: T chief Musician on Neginoth, A P of David. 4210
5: T Musician upon Nehiloth, A P of David. 4210
6: T Neginoth upon Sheminith, A P of David. 4210
8: T chief Musician upon Gittith, A P of David. 4210
9: T Musician upon Muth-labben, A P of David. 4210
11: T To the chief Musician, *A P* of David. NIH
12: T Musician upon Sheminith, A P of David. 4210
13: T To the chief Musician, A P of David. 4210
14: T To the chief Musician, *A P* of David. NIH
15: T A P of David. 4210
18: T To the chief Musician, *A P* of David, NIH
19: T To the chief Musician, A P of David. 4210
20: T To the chief Musician, A P of David. 4210
21: T To the chief Musician, A P of David. 4210
22: T upon Aijeleth Shahar, A P of David. 4210
23: T A P of David. 4210
24: T A P of David. 4210
25: T *A P* of David. NIH
26: T *A P* of David. NIH
27: T *A P* of David. NIH
28: T *A P* of David. NIH
29: T A P of David. 4210
30: T A P *and* Song *at* the dedication of the house 4210
31: T To the chief Musician, A P of David. 4210
32: T *A P* of David, Maschil. NIH
34: T *A P* of David, when he changed his NIH
35: T *A P* of David. NIH
36: T *A P* of David the servant of the LORD. NIH
37: T *A P* of David. NIH
38: T A P of David, to bring to remembrance. 4210
39: T *even* to Jeduthun, A P of David. 4210
40: T To the chief Musician, A P of David. 4210
41: T To the chief Musician, A P of David. 4210
47: T chief Musician, A P for the sons of Korah 4210
48: T A Song *and* P for the sons of Korah. 4210
49: T chief Musician, A P for the sons of Korah. 4210
50: T A P of Asaph. 4210
51: T To the chief Musician, A P of David, 4210
52: T the chief Musician, Maschil, *A P* of David, NIH
53: T upon Mahalath, Maschil, *A P* of David. NIH
54: T Maschil, *A P* of David, when the Ziphims NIH
55: T on Neginoth, Maschil, *A P* of David. NIH
61: T Musician upon Neginah, *A P* of David. NIH
62: T chief Musician, to Jeduthun, A P of David. 4210
63: T A P of David, when he was in 4210
64: T To the chief Musician, A P of David. 4210
65: T the chief Musician, A P *and* Song of David. 4210
66: T To the chief Musician, A Song *or* P. 4210
67: T chief Musician on Neginoth, A P *or* Song. 4210
68: T the chief Musician, A P *or* Song of David. 4210
69: T Musician upon Shoshannim, *A P* of David. NIH
70: T To the chief Musician, *A P* of David, NIH
72: T *A P* for Solomon. NIH
73: T A P of Asaph. 4210
75: T Al-taschith, A P *or* Song of Asaph. 4210
76: T on Neginoth, A P *or* Song of Asaph. 4210
77: T chief Musician, to Jeduthun, A P of Asaph. 4210
79: T A P of Asaph. 4210
80: T upon Shoshannim-Eduth, A P of Asaph. 4210
81: T chief Musician upon Gittith, *A P* of Asaph. NIH
81: 2 Take a p, and bring hither the timbrel, 2172
82: T A P of Asaph. 4210
83: T A Song *or* P of Asaph. 4210
84: T upon Gittith, A P for the sons of Korah. 4210
85: T chief Musician, A P for the sons of Korah. 4210
87: T A P *or* Song for the sons of Korah. 4210
88: T A Song *or* P for the sons of Korah. To 4210
92: T A P *or* Song for the sabbath day. 4210
98: T A P. 4210

P

Ps 98: 5 with the harp, and the voice of a **p**. 2172
100: T A **P** of praise. 4210
101: T A **P** of David. 4210
103: T *A* **P** of David. NIH
108: T A Song *or* **P** of David. 4210
109: T To the chief Musician, A **P** of David. 4210
110: T A **P** of David. 4210
138: T *A* **P** of David. NIH
139: T To the chief Musician, A **P** of David. 4210
140: T To the chief Musician, A **P** of David. 4210
141: T A **P** of David. 4210
143: T A **P** of David. 4210
144: T *A* **P** of David. NIH
145: T David's **P** *of* praise. NIH
Ac 13:33 as it is also written in the second **p**, *5568*
13:35 Wherefore he saith also in another **p**, Thou NIG
1Co 14:26 every one of you hath a **p**, hath a doctrine, *5568*

PSALMIST (1) [PSALM]
2Sa 23: 1 of Jacob, and the sweet **p** of Israel, said, 2158

PSALMS (9) [PSALM]
1Ch 16: 9 Sing unto him, **sing p** unto him, talk you of 2167
Ps 95: 2 *and* make a joyful noise unto him with **p**. 2158
105: 2 Sing unto him, **sing p** unto him: talk ye of 2167
Lk 20:42 And David himself saith in the book of **P**, *5568*
24:44 the prophets, and *in* the **p**, concerning me. *5568*
Ac 1:20 For it is written in the book of **P**, Let his *5568*
Eph 5:19 Speaking to yourselves in **p** and hymns and *5568*
Col 3:16 and admonishing one another in **p** and *5568*
Jas 5:13 let him pray. Is any merry? let him **sing p**. *5567*

PSALTERIES (14) [PSALTERY]
2Sa 6: 5 on **p**, and on timbrels, and on cornets, and 5035
1Ki 10:12 king's house, harps also and **p** for singers: 5035
1Ch 13: 8 with **p**, and with timbrels, and 5035
15:16 **p** and harps and cymbals, sounding, 5035
15:20 and Benaiah, with **p** on Alamoth; 5035
15:28 making a noise with **p** and harps. 5035
16: 5 Jeiel with **p** and with harps; but 5035
25: 1 with harps, with **p**, and with cymbals: 5035
25: 6 with cymbals, **p**, and harps, for the service 5035
2Ch 5:12 having cymbals and **p** and harps, 5035
9:11 king's palace, and harps and **p** for singers: 5035
20:28 they came *to* Jerusalem with **p** and harps 5035
29:25 with **p**, and with harps, according to 5035
Ne 12:27 *with* cymbals, **p**, and with harps. 5035

PSALTERY (13) [PSALTERIES]
1Sa 10: 5 coming down from the high place with a **p**, 5035
Ps 33: 2 sing unto him with the **p** *and* an instrument 5035
57: 8 Awake up, my glory; awake, **p** and harp: 5035
71:22 I will also praise thee with the **p**, 3627+5035
81: 2 the timbrel, the pleasant harp with the **p**. 5035
92: 3 instrument of ten strings, and upon the **p**; 5035
108: 2 Awake, **p** and harp: I *myself* will awake 5035
144: 9 upon a **p** *and* an instrument of ten strings 5035
150: 3 the trumpet: praise him with the **p** and harp. 5035
Da 3: 5 flute, harp, sackbut, **p**, dulcimer, and 6460
3: 7 sackbut, **p**, and all kinds of musick, 6460
3:10 **p**, and dulcimer, and all kinds of musick, 6460
3:15 **p**, and dulcimer, and all kinds of musick, 6460

PTOLEMAIS (1)
Ac 21: 7 we came to **P**, and saluted the brethren, and *4424*

PUA (1) [PUAH]
Nu 26:23 the Tolaites: of **P**, the family of the Punites: 6312

PUAH (3) [PHUVAH, PUA, PUNITES]
Ex 1:15 *was* Shiphrah, and the name of the other **P**: 6326
Jdg 10: 1 arose to defend Israel Tola the son of **P**, 6312
1Ch 7: 1 and **P**, Jashub, and Shimron, four. 6312

PUBLIC See OPEN; OPENLY; PUBLICK; PUBLICKLY

PUBLICAN (6) [PUBLICANS]
Mt 10: 3 Bartholomew; Thomas, and Matthew the **p**; *5057*
18:17 him be unto thee as a heathen *man* and a **p**. *5057*
Lk 5:27 and saw a **p**, named Levi, sitting at *5057*
18:10 the one a Pharisee, and the other a **p**. *5057*
18:11 unjust, adulterers, or even as this **p**. *5057*
18:13 And the **p**, standing afar off, would not lift *5057*

PUBLICANS (17) [PUBLICAN]
Mt 5:46 have ye? do not even the **p** the same? *5057*
5:47 ye more *than others?* do not even the **p** so? *5057*
9:10 many **p** and sinners came and sat down *5057*
9:11 Why eateth your Master with **p** and *5057*
11:19 and a winebibber, a friend of **p** and sinners. *5057*
21:31 That the **p** and the harlots go into *5057*
21:32 but the **p** and the harlots believed him: and *5057*
Mk 2:15 many **p** and sinners sat also together with *5057*
2:16 and Pharisees saw him eat with **p** and *5057*
2:16 he eateth and drinketh with **p** and sinners? *5057*
Lk 3:12 Then came also **p** to be baptized, and *5057*
5:29 and there was a great company of **p** and *5057*
5:30 do ye eat and drink with **p** and sinners? *5057*
7:29 all the people that heard *him,* and the **p**, *5057*
7:34 and a winebibber, a friend of **p** and sinners. *5057*
15: 1 Then drew near unto him all the **p** and *5057*
19: 2 which was *the* **chief among** the **p**, and *754*

PUBLICK (1) [PUBLICKLY]
Mt 1:19 and not willing to **make** her **a p example**, *3856*

PUBLICKLY (2) [PUBLICK]
Ac 18:28 he mightily convinced the Jews, *and that* **p**, *1219*
20:20 and have taught you **p**, and from house to *1219*

PUBLISH (17) [PUBLISHED, PUBLISHETH]
Dt 32: 3 Because I will **p** the name of the LORD: 7121
1Sa 31: 9 to **p** *it in* the house of their idols, and 1319
2Sa 1:20 in Gath, **p** *it* not in the streets of Askelon; 1319
Ne 8:15 that they should **p** and proclaim in all their 8085
Ps 26: 7 That *I* may **p** with the voice of 8085
Jer 4: 5 Declare ye in Judah, and **p** in Jerusalem; 8085
4:16 behold, **p** against Jerusalem, *that* watchers 8085
5:20 house of Jacob, and **p** it in Judah, saying, 8085
31: 7 **p** ye, praise ye, and say, O LORD, save 8085
46:14 **p** in Migdol, and publish in Noph and 8085
46:14 and **p** in Noph and in Tahpanhes: 8085
50: 2 the nations, and **p**, and set up a standard; 8085
50: 2 and set up a standard; **p**, *and* conceal not: 8085
Am 3: 9 **P** in the palaces at Ashdod, and in 8085
4: 5 and proclaim *and* **p** the free offerings: 8085
Mk 1:45 and began to **p** *it* much, and to blaze abroad *2784*
5:20 began to **p** in Decapolis how great *things* *2784*

PUBLISHED (11) [PUBLISH]
Est 1:20 make shall be **p** throughout all his empire, 8085
1:22 that it should be **p** according to 1696
3:14 in every province *was* **p** unto all people, 1540
8:13 in every province *was* **p** unto all people, 1540
Ps 68:11 great *was* the company of those that **p** *it.* 1319
Jnh 3: 7 **p** through Nineveh by the decree of the king 559
Mk 7:36 *so* much the more a great deal they **p** *it;* *2784*
13:10 And the gospel must first be **p** among all *2784*
Lk 8:39 **p** throughout the whole city how great *2784*
Ac 10:37 which was **p** throughout all Judea, and *1096*
13:49 And the word of the Lord was **p** throughout *1308*

PUBLISHETH (4) [PUBLISH]
Isa 52: 7 that bringeth good tidings, that **p** peace; 8085
52: 7 good tidings of good, that **p** salvation; 8085
Jer 4:15 and **p** affliction from mount Ephraim. 8085
Na 1:15 that bringeth good tidings, that **p** peace. 8085

PUBLIUS (2)
Ac 28: 7 chief *man* of the island, whose name was **P**; *4196*
28: 8 that the father of **P** lay sick of a fever and *4196*

PUDENS (1)
2Ti 4:21 and **P**, and Linus, and Claudia, and all *4227*

PUFFED (5) [PUFFETH]
1Co 4: 6 that no one of you be **p up** for one against *5448*
4:18 Now some are **p up**, as though I would not *5448*
4:19 not the speech of them which are **p up**, but *5448*
5: 2 And ye are **p up**, and have not rather *5448*
13: 4 charity vaunteth not itself, is not **p up**, *5448*

PUFFETH (3) [PUFFED, PUFT]
Ps 10: 5 *as for* all his enemies, he **p** at them. 6315
12: 5 I will set *him* in safety *from him that* **p** at 6315
1Co 8: 1 Knowledge **p up**, but charity edifieth. *5448*

PUFT (1) [PUFFETH]
Col 2:18 not seen, vainly **p up** by his fleshly mind, *5448*

PUHITES (1)
1Ch 2:53 the **P**, and the Shumathites, and 6336

PUITES See PUNITES

PUL (4) [TIGLATH-PILESER]
2Ki 15:19 *And* **P** the king of Assyria came against 6322
15:19 Menahem gave **P** a thousand talents of 6322
1Ch 5:26 the God of Israel stirred up the spirit of **P** 6322
Isa 66:19 *to* Tarshish, **P**, and Lud, that draw the bow, 6322

PULL (15) [PULLED, PULLING]
1Ki 13: 4 so that he could not **p** it **in again** to him. 7725
Ps 31: 4 **P** me **out** of the net that they have laid 3318
Isa 22:19 and from thy state shall he **p** thee **down**. 2040
Jer 1:10 to **p down**, and to destroy, and to throw 5422
12: 3 **p** them **out** like sheep for the slaughter, and 5423
18: 7 pluck up, and to **p down**, and to destroy *it;* 5422
24: 6 I will build them, and not **p** *them* **down**; 2040
42:10 not **p** *you* **down**, and I will plant you, and 2040
Eze 17: 9 shall he not **p up** the roots thereof, and cut 5423
Mic 2: 8 ye **p** off the robe with the garment from 6584
Mt 7: 4 Let me **p out** the mote out of thine eye; *1544*
Lk 6:42 let me **p out** the mote that is in thine eye, *1544*
6:42 shalt thou see clearly to **p out** the mote that *1544*
12:18 I will **p down** my barns, and build greater; *2507*
14: 5 will not straightway **p** him **out** on *385*

PULLED (7) [PULL]
Ge 8: 9 took her, and **p** her **in** unto him into the ark. 935
19:10 **p** Lot into the house to them, and shut to 935
Ezr 6:11 let timber be **p down** from his house, and 5256
La 3:11 turned aside my ways, and **p** me **in pieces**: 6582
Am 9:15 they shall no more be **p up** out of their land 5428
Zec 7:11 **p** away the shoulder, and stopped their ears, 5414
Ac 23:10 Paul should have been **p in pieces** of them, *1288*

PULLING (2) [PULL]
2Co 10: 4 mighty through God to the **p down** of *2506*
Jude 1:23 others save with fear, **p** *them* out of the fire; *726*

PULPIT (1)
Ne 8: 4 Ezra the scribe stood upon a **p** of wood, 4026

PULSE (3)
2Sa 17:28 and beans, and lentiles, and parched **p**, NIH
Da 1:12 let them give us **p** to eat, and water to 2235
1:16 that they should drink; and gave them **p**. 2235

PUNISH (32) [PUNISHED, PUNISHMENT, PUNISHMENTS, UNPUNISHED]
Lev 26:18 I will **p** you seven *times* more for your sins. 3256
26:24 will **p** you yet seven *times* for your sins. 5221
Pr 17:26 Also to **p** the just *is* not good, *nor* to strike 6064
Isa 10:12 I will **p** the fruit of the stout heart of 6485
Isa 13:11 I will **p** the world for *their* evil, and 6485
24:21 *that* the LORD shall **p** the host of the high 6485
26:21 the LORD cometh out of his place to **p** 6485
27: 1 strong sword shall **p** leviathan the piercing 6485
Jer 9:25 that I will **p** all *them which are* circumcised 6485
11:22 the LORD of hosts, Behold, I will **p** them: 6485
13:21 What wilt thou say when he shall **p** thee? 6485
21:14 I will **p** you according to the fruit of your 6485
23:34 I will even **p** that man and his house. 6485
25:12 *that* I will **p** the king of Babylon, and that 6485
27: 8 that nation will I **p**, saith the LORD, 6485
29:32 I will **p** Shemaiah the Nehelamite, and his 6485
30:20 and I will **p** all that oppress them. 6485
36:31 I will **p** him and his seed and his servants 6485
44:13 For I will **p** them that dwell in the land of 6485
44:29 the LORD, that I will **p** you in this place, 6485
46:25 I will **p** the multitude of No, and Pharaoh, 6485
50:18 I *will* **p** the king of Babylon and his land, 6485
51:44 I will **p** Bel in Babylon, and I will bring 6485
Hos 4: 9 I will **p** them for their ways, and 6485
4:14 I will not **p** your daughters when they 6485
12: 2 and *will* **p** Jacob according to his ways; 6485
Am 3: 2 therefore I will **p** you for all your iniquities. 6485
Zep 1: 8 that I will **p** the princes, and the king's 6485
1: 9 In the same day also will I **p** all those that 6485
1:12 and **p** the men that are settled on their lees: 6485
Zec 8:14 As I thought to **p** you, when your fathers 7489
Ac 4:21 finding nothing how they might **p** them, *2849*

PUNISHED (17) [PUNISH]
Ex 21:20 under his hand; he shall be **surely p**. 5358+5358
21:21 he continue a day or two, he shall not be **p**: 5358
21:22 he shall be **surely p**, according as 6064+6064
Ezr 9:13 seeing that thou our God hast **p** us less than 2820
Job 31:11 yea, it *is* an iniquity *to be* **p** *by* the judges. NIH
31:28 This also *were* an iniquity *to be* **p** *by* NIH
Pr 21:11 When the scorner is **p**, the simple is made 6064
22: 3 but the simple pass on, and are **p**. 6064
27:12 *but* the simple pass on, *and* are **p**. 6064
Jer 44:13 as I have **p** Jerusalem, by the sword, by 6485
50:18 his land, as I have **p** the king of Assyria. 6485
Zep 3: 7 should not be cut off, howsoever I **p** them: 6485
Zec 10: 3 against the shepherds, and I **p** the goats: 6485
Ac 22: 5 bound unto Jerusalem, for to be **p**. *5097*
26:11 And I **p** them oft in every synagogue, and *5097*
2Th 1: 9 Who shall be **p** *with* everlasting *1349+5099*
2Pe 2: 9 the unjust unto the day of judgment *to be* **p**: *2849*

PUNISHMENT (27) [PUNISH]
Ge 4:13 My **p** *is* greater than *I* can bear. 5771
Lev 26:41 they then accept of the **p of** their **iniquity**: 5771
26:43 they shall accept of the **p of** their **iniquity**: 5771
1Sa 28:10 there shall no **p** happen to thee for this 5771
Job 31: 3 and a **strange p** to the workers of iniquity? 5235
Pr 19:19 *A man* of great wrath *shall* suffer **p**: for if 6066
La 3:39 man complain, a man for the **p** of his **sins**? 2399
4: 6 For the **p of** the **iniquity** of the daughter of 5771
4: 6 is greater than the **p of** the **sin** of Sodom, 2403
4:22 The **p of** thine **iniquity** is accomplished, 5771
Eze 14:10 they shall bear the **p of** their **iniquity**: 5771
14:10 the **p** of the prophet shall be even as 5771
14:10 even as the **p** of him that seeketh *unto him;* 5771
Am 1: 3 for four, I will not turn away *the* **p** thereof; NIH
1: 6 for four, I will not turn away *the* **p** thereof; NIH
1: 9 for four, I will not turn away *the* **p** thereof; NIH
1:11 for four, I will not turn away *the* **p** thereof; NIH
1:13 for four, I will not turn away *the* **p** thereof; NIH
2: 1 for four, I will not turn away *the* **p** thereof; NIH
2: 4 for four, I will not turn away *the* **p** thereof; NIH
2: 6 for four, I will not turn away *the* **p** thereof; NIH
Zec 14:19 This shall be the **p** of Egypt, and 2403
14:19 the **p** of all nations that come not up to 2403
Mt 25:46 And these shall go away into everlasting **p**: *2851*
2Co 2: 6 Sufficient to such *a man is* this **p**, *2009*
Heb 10:29 Of how much sorer **p**, suppose ye, shall he *5098*
1Pe 2:14 as unto them that are sent by him for the **p** *1557*

PUNISHMENTS (2) [PUNISH]
Job 19:29 for wrath *bringeth* the **p** of the sword, 5771
Ps 149: 7 upon the heathen, *and* **p** upon the people; 8433

PUNITES (1) [PUAH]
Nu 26:23 of the Tolaites: of Pua, the family of the **P**: 6324

PUNON (2)
Nu 33:42 departed from Zalmonah, and pitched in **P**. 6325
33:43 they departed from **P**, and pitched in 6325

PUR (3) [PURIM]
Est 3: 7 they cast **P**, that *is,* the lot, before Haman 6332
9:24 had cast **P**, that *is,* the lot, to consume 6332
9:26 these days Purim after the name of **P**. 6332

PURAH See PHURAH

PURCHASE (8) [PURCHASED]
Ge 49:32 The **p** of the field and of the cave that *is* 4735
Lev 25:33 if a man **p** of the Levites, then the house 1350
Jer 32:11 So I took the evidence of the **p**, *both* that 4736
32:12 I gave the evidence of the **p** unto Baruch 4736
32:12 witnesses that subscribed the book of the **p**, 4736
32:14 this evidence of the **p**, both which is sealed, 4736
32:16 of the **p** unto Baruch the son of Neriah, 4736
1Ti 3:13 deacon well **p** to themselves a good degree, *4046*

PURCHASED (9) [PURCHASE]
Ge 25:10 The field which Abraham **p** of the sons of 7069
Ex 15:16 till the people pass over, *which* thou hast **p**. 7069
Ru 4:10 the wife of Mahlon, have I **p** to be my wife, 7069
Ps 74: 2 thy congregation, *which* thou hast **p** of old; 7069
78:54 this mountain, *which* his right hand had **p**. 7069
Ac 1:18 Now this *man* **p** a field with the reward of *2932*
8:20 that the gift of God may be **p** with money. *2932*
20:28 which he hath **p** with his own blood. *4046*

Eph 1:14 until the redemption of the **p possession**, *4047*

PURE (97) [PURIFY]

Ex 25:11 thou shalt overlay it with **p** gold, within 2889
25:17 thou shalt make a mercy seat *of* **p** gold: 2889
25:24 thou shalt overlay it with **p** gold, and 2889
25:29 *of* **p** gold shalt thou make them. 2889
25:31 thou shalt make a candlestick of **p** gold: 2889
25:36 all it *shall be* one beaten work *of* **p** gold. 2889
25:38 the snuffdishes thereof, *shall be of* **p** gold. 2889
25:39 *Of* a talent of **p** gold shall he make it, 2889
27:20 that they bring thee **p** oil olive beaten for 2134
28:14 two chains *of* **p** gold at the ends; 2889
28:22 at the ends *of* wreathen work *of* **p** gold. 2889
28:36 thou shalt make a plate *of* **p** gold, and 2889
30: 3 thou shalt overlay it with **p** gold, the top 2889
30:23 of **p** myrrh five hundred *shekels*, and 1865
30:34 *these* sweet spices with **p** frankincense: 2134
30:35 tempered together, **p** *and* holy: 2889
31: 8 the **p** candlestick with all his furniture, and 2889
37: 2 he overlaid it with **p** gold within 2889
37: 6 he made the mercy seat *of* **p** gold: 2889
37:11 he overlaid it with **p** gold, and 2889
37:16 and *his* covers to cover withal, *of* **p** gold. 2889
37:17 he made the candlestick *of* **p** gold: 2889
37:22 all of it *was* one beaten work *of* **p** gold. 2889
37:23 his snuffers, and his snuffdishes, *of* **p** gold. 2889
37:24 *Of* a talent of **p** gold made he it, and all 2889
37:26 he overlaid it with **p** gold, *both* the top of it, 2889
37:29 and the **p** incense of sweet spices, 2889
39:15 at the ends, *of* wreathen work *of* **p** gold. 2889
39:25 they made bells of **p** gold, and put the bells 2889
39:30 they made the plate of the holy crown *of* **p** 2889
39:37 The **p** candlestick, *with* the lamps thereof, 2889
Lev 24: 2 that they bring unto thee **p** oil olive beaten 2134
24: 4 He shall order the lamps upon the **p** 2889
24: 6 a row, upon the **p** table before the LORD. 2889
24: 7 thou shalt put **p** frankincense upon *each* 2134
Dt 32:14 thou didst drink the **p** blood of the grape. 2561
2Sa 22:27 With the **p** thou wilt shew thyself pure; and 1305
22:27 With the pure thou wilt **shew** thyself **p**; and 1305
1Ki 5:11 and twenty measures of **p** oil: 3795
6:20 he overlaid it with **p** gold; and *so* 5462
6:21 overlaid the house within with **p** gold: 5462
7:49 the candlesticks *of* **p** gold, five on the right 5462
7:50 and the spoons, and the censers *of* **p** gold; 5462
10:21 of the forest of Lebanon *were of* **p** gold: 5462
1Ch 28:17 Also **p** gold *for* the fleshhooks, and 2889
2Ch 3: 4 and he overlaid it within with **p** gold. 2889
4:20 the manner before the oracle, *of* **p** gold; 5462
4:22 and the spoons, and the censers, of **p** gold: 5462
9:17 throne of ivory, and overlaid it with **p** gold. 2889
9:20 of the forest of Lebanon *were of* **p** gold: 5462
13:11 also *set they* in order upon the **p** table; 2889
Ezr 6:20 all of them *were* **p**, and killed the passover 2889
Job 4:17 shall a man be more **p** than his Maker? 2891
8: 6 If thou *wert* **p** and upright; surely now he 2134
11: 4 My doctrine *is* **p**, and I am clean in thine 2134
16:17 in mine hands: also my prayer is **p**. 2134
25: 5 yea, the stars are not **p** in his sight. 2141
28:19 neither shall it be valued with **p** gold. 2889
Ps 12: 6 The words of the LORD *are* **p** words: 2889
18:26 With the **p** thou wilt shew thyself pure; and 1305
18:26 With the pure thou wilt **shew** thyself **p**; and 1305
19: 8 the commandment of the LORD *is* **p**, 1249
21: 3 thou settest a crown of **p gold** on his head. 6337
24: 4 He that hath clean hands, and a **p** heart; 1249
119:140 Thy word *is* very **p**: therefore thy servant 6884
Pr 15:26 but *the words of* the **p** *are* pleasant words. 2889
20: 9 made my heart clean, I am **p** from my sin? 2891
20:11 whether his work *be* **p**, and whether *it be* 2134
21: 8 strange: but *as for* the **p**, his work *is* right. 2134
30: 5 Every word of God *is* **p**: he *is* a shield unto 6884
30:12 *There is* a generation *that are* **p** in their own 2889
Da 7: 9 and the hair of his head like the **p** wool: 5343
Mic 6:11 Shall I **count** *them* **p** with the wicked 2135
Zep 3: 9 then will I turn to the people a **p** language, 1305
Mal 1:11 *be* offered unto my name, and a **p** offering: 2889
Mt 5: 8 Blessed *are* the **p** in heart: for they shall see *2513*
Ac 20:26 that I *am* **p** from the blood of all *men*. *2513*
Ro 14:20 All *things* indeed *are* **p**; but *it is* evil for *2513*
Php 4: 8 *things are* just, whatsoever *things are* **p**, *53*
1Ti 1: 5 commandment is charity out of a **p** heart, *2513*
3: 9 Holding the mystery of the faith in a **p** *2513*
5:22 partaker of other *men's* sins: keep thyself **p**. *53*
2Ti 1: 3 whom I serve from *my* forefathers with **p** *2513*
2:22 with them that call on the Lord out of a **p** *2513*
Tit 1:15 Unto the **p** all *things are* pure: but *2513*
1:15 Unto the pure all *things are* **p**: but *2513*
1:15 are defiled and unbelieving *is* nothing **p**; *2513*
Heb 10:22 and *our* bodies washed with **p** water. *2513*
Jas 1:27 **P** religion and undefiled before God and *2513*
3:17 But the wisdom that is from above is first **p**, *53*
1Pe 1:22 *see that ye* love one another with a **p** heart *2513*
2Pe 3: 1 in both which I stir up your **p** minds by *1506*
1Jn 3: 3 hope in him purifieth himself, even as he is **p**. *53*
Rev 15: 6 clothed in **p** and white linen, and *2513*
21:18 and the city *was* **p** gold, like unto clear *2513*
21:21 and the street of the city *was* **p** gold, as *it* *2513*
22: 1 And he shewed me a **p** river of water of *2513*

PURELY (1) [PURIFY]

Isa 1:25 **p** purge away thy dross, 1253+1886.1+3509.1

PURENESS (3) [PURIFY]

Job 22:30 and it is delivered by the **p** of thine hands. 1252
Pr 22:11 He that loveth **p** of heart, *for* the grace of 2889
2Co 6: 6 By **p**, by knowledge, by longsuffering, *54*

PURER (2) [PURIFY]

La 4: 7 Her Nazarites were **p** than snow, they were 2141
Hab 1:13 *Thou art* of **p** eyes than to behold evil, and 2889

PURGE (15) [PURGED, PURGETH, PURGING]

2Ch 34: 3 in the twelfth year he began to **p** Judah and 2891
Ps 51: 7 **P** me with hyssop, and I shall be clean: 2398
65: 3 our transgressions, thou shalt **p** them **away**. 3722
79: 9 deliver us, and **p away** our sins, for thy 3722
Isa 1:25 purely **p away** thy dross, and take away all 6884
Eze 20:38 I will **p out** from among you the rebels, 1305
43:20 thus shalt thou cleanse and **p** it. 3722
43:26 Seven days shall they **p** the altar and 3722
Da 11:35 try them, and to **p**, and to make *them* white, 1305
Mal 3: 3 sons of Levi, and **p** them as gold and silver, 2212
Mt 3:12 and he will **throughly p** his floor, and *1245*
Lk 3:17 and he will **throughly p** his floor, and *1245*
1Co 5: 7 **P out** therefore the old leaven, that ye may *1571*
2Ti 2:21 If a man therefore **p** himself from these, *1571*
Heb 9:14 **p** your conscience from dead works to *2511*

PURGED (14) [PURGE]

1Sa 3:14 the iniquity of Eli's house shall not be **p** 3722
2Ch 34: 8 when he had **p** the land, and the house, 2891
Pr 16: 6 By mercy and truth iniquity is **p**: and by 3722
Isa 4: 4 shall have **p** the blood of Jerusalem from 1740
6: 7 thine iniquity is taken away, and thy sin **p**. 3722
22:14 Surely this iniquity shall not be **p** from you 3722
27: 9 shall the iniquity of Jacob be **p**; 3722
Eze 24:13 because I have **p** thee, and thou wast not 2891
24:13 I have purged thee, and thou wast not **p**, 2891
24:13 thou shalt not be **p** from thy filthiness any 2891
Heb 1: 3 when he had by himself **p** our sins, *2512+4160*
9:22 And almost all *things* are by the law **p** with *2511*
10: 2 that the worshippers once **p** should have *2508*
2Pe 1: 9 hath forgotten that *he* was **p** from his old *2512*

PURGETH (1) [PURGE]

Jn 15: 2 and every *branch* that beareth fruit, he **p** it, *2508*

PURGING (1) [PURGE]

Mk 7:19 goeth out into the draught, **p** all meats? *2511*

PURIFICATION (8) [PURIFY]

Nu 19: 9 for a water of separation: it *is* a **p for sin**. 2403
19:17 of the ashes of the burnt *heifer* of **p for sin**, 2403
2Ch 30:19 according to the **p** of the sanctuary. 2893
Ne 12:45 ward of their God, and the ward of the **p**, 2893
Est 2: 3 and let their **things for p** be given *them*: 8562
2: 9 he speedily gave her her **things for p**, 8562
Lk 2:22 And when the days of her **p** according to *2512*
Ac 21:26 signify the accomplishment of the days of **p**, *49*

PURIFICATIONS (1) [PURIFY]

Est 2:12 so were the days of their **p** accomplished, 4795

PURIFIED (12) [PURIFY]

Lev 8:15 **p** the altar, and poured the blood at 2398
Nu 8:21 the Levites were **p**, and they washed their 2398
31:23 nevertheless it shall be **p** with the water of 2398
2Sa 11: 4 for she was **p** from her uncleanness: 6942
Ezr 6:20 the priests and the Levites were **p** together, 2891
Ne 12:30 the priests and the Levites **p** themselves, 2891
12:30 **p** the people, and the gates, and the wall. 2891
Ps 12: 6 tried in a furnace of earth, **p** seven times. 2212
Da 12:10 Many shall be **p**, and made white, and 1305
Ac 24:18 Jews from Asia found me **p** in the temple, *48*
Heb 9:23 in the heavens should be **p** with these; *2511*
1Pe 1:22 Seeing ye have **p** your souls in obeying *48*

PURIFIER (1) [PURIFY]

Mal 3: 3 he shall sit *as* a refiner and **p** of silver: and 2891

PURIFIETH (2) [PURIFY]

Nu 19:13 **p** not himself, defileth the tabernacle of 2398
1Jn 3: 3 And every *man* that hath this hope in him **p** *48*

PURIFY (14) [PURE, PURELY, PURENESS, PURER, PURIFICATION, PURIFICATIONS, PURIFIED, PURIFIER, PURIFIETH, PURIFYING, PURITY]

Nu 19:12 He shall **p** himself with it on the third day, 2398
19:12 if he **p** not himself the third day, then 2398
19:19 on the seventh day he shall **p** him*self*, and 2398
19:20 shall be unclean, and shall not **p** himself, 2398
31:19 **p** *both* yourselves and your captives on 2398
31:20 **p** all *your* raiment, and all that is made of 2398
Job 41:25 by reason of breakings they **p** themselves. 2398
Isa 66:17 **p** themselves in the gardens behind one *tree* 2891
Eze 43:26 days shall they purge the altar and **p** it; 2891
Mal 3: 3 he shall **p** the sons of Levi, and purge them 2891
Jn 11:55 before the passover, to **p** themselves. *48*
Ac 21:24 and **p** thyself with them, and be at charges *48*
Tit 2:14 and **p** unto himself a peculiar people, *2511*
Jas 4: 8 and **p** *your* hearts, *ye* double minded. *48*

PURIFYING (12) [PURIFY]

Lev 12: 4 continue in the blood of her **p** three and 2893
12: 4 until the days of her **p** be fulfilled. 2892
12: 5 she shall continue in the blood of her **p** 2893
12: 6 when the days of her **p** are fulfilled, for a 2892
Nu 8: 7 Sprinkle water of **p** upon them, and 2403
1Ch 23:28 in the **p** of all holy *things*, and the work of 2893
Est 2:12 with *other* **things for the p** of the women;) 8562
Jn 2: 6 after the manner of the **p** of the Jews, *2512*
3:25 of John's disciples and the Jews about **p**. *2512*
Ac 15: 9 and them, **p** their hearts by faith. *2511*
21:26 the next day **p** himself with them entered into *48*
Heb 9:13 the unclean, sanctifieth to the **p** of the flesh: *2514*

PURIM (5) [PUR]

Est 9:26 Wherefore they called these days **P** after 6332
9:28 *that* these days of **P** should not fail from 6332
9:29 to confirm this second letter of **P**. 6332
9:31 To confirm these days of **P** in their times 6332
9:32 of Esther confirmed these matters of **P**; 6332

PURITY (2) [PURIFY]

1Ti 4:12 in charity, in spirit, in faith, in **p**. *47*
5: 2 as mothers; the younger as sisters, with all **p**. *47*

PURLOINING (1)

Tit 2:10 Not **p**, but shewing all good fidelity; *3557*

PURPLE (48)

Ex 25: 4 **p**, and scarlet, and fine linen, and 713
26: 1 twined linen, and blue, and **p**, and scarlet: 713
26:31 **p**, and scarlet, and fine twined linen *of* 713
26:36 and **p**, and scarlet, and fine twined linen, 713
27:16 and **p**, and scarlet, and fine twined linen, 713
28: 5 and blue, and **p**, and scarlet, and fine linen. 713
28: 6 *of* blue, and *of* **p**, *of* scarlet, and fine twined 713
28: 8 and **p**, and scarlet, and fine twined linen. 713
28:15 *of* **p**, and *of* scarlet, and *of* fine twined linen, 713
28:33 of **p**, and of scarlet, round about the hem 713
35: 6 **p**, and scarlet, and fine linen, and 713
35:23 **p**, and scarlet, and fine linen, and goats' *hair*, 713
35:25 and of **p**, *and* of scarlet, and of fine linen. 713
35:35 in blue, and in **p**, in scarlet, and in fine linen, 713
36: 8 twined linen, and blue, and **p**, and scarlet: 713
36:35 and **p**, and scarlet, and fine twined linen: 713
36:37 **p**, and scarlet, and fine twined linen, 713
38:18 and **p**, and scarlet, and fine twined linen: 713
38:23 and in **p**, and in scarlet, and fine linen. 713
39: 1 of the blue, and **p**, and scarlet, they made 713
39: 2 and **p**, and scarlet, and fine twined linen. 713
39: 3 in the **p**, and in the scarlet, and in the fine 713
39: 5 and **p**, and scarlet, and fine twined linen; 713
39: 8 and **p**, and scarlet, and fine twined linen. 713
39:24 of blue, and **p**, and scarlet, *and* twined *linen*. 713
39:29 and blue, and **p**, and scarlet, *of* needlework; 713
Nu 4:13 from the altar, and spread a **p** cloth thereon: 713
Jdg 8:26 **p** raiment that *was* on the kings of Midian, 713
2Ch 2: 7 in **p**, and crimson, and blue, and that can 710
2:14 in **p**, in blue, and in fine linen, and 713
3:14 **p**, and crimson, and fine linen, and 713
Est 1: 6 and **p** to silver rings and pillars of marble: 713
8:15 and *with* a garment of fine linen and **p**: 713
Pr 31:22 of tapestry; her clothing *is* silk and **p**. 713
SS 3:10 thereof *of* gold, the covering of it *of* **p**, 713
7: 5 and the hair of thine head like **p**; 713
Jer 10: 9 blue and **p** *is* their clothing: they *are* all 713
Eze 27: 7 **p** from the isles of Elishah was that which 713
27:16 **p**, and broidered work, and fine linen, and 713
Mk 15:17 And they clothed him with **p**, and platted a *4209*
15:20 they took off the **p** from him, and put his *4209*
Lk 16:19 which was clothed in **p** and fine linen, and *4209*
Jn 19: 2 on his head, and they put on him a **p** robe, *4210*
19: 5 the crown of thorns, and the **p** robe. *4210*
Ac 16:14 a **seller of p**, of the city of Thyatira, *4211*
Rev 17: 4 And the woman was arrayed in **p** and *4209*
18:12 and **p**, and silk, and scarlet, and all thyine *4209*
18:16 and **p**, and scarlet, and decked with gold, *4210*

PURPOSE (36) [PURPOSED, PURPOSES, PURPOSETH, PURPOSING]

Ru 2:16 **let fall** also *some* of the handfuls **of p** 7997+7997
1Ki 5: 5 I **p** to build a house unto the name of 559
2Ch 28:10 now ye **p** to keep under the children of Judah 559
Ezr 4: 5 to frustrate their **p**, all the days of Cyrus 6098
Ne 8: 4 of wood, which they had made for the **p**; 1697
Job 33:17 That *he* may withdraw man *from his* **p**, and 4639
Pr 20:18 Every **p** is established by counsel: and 4284
Ecc 3: 1 and a time to every **p** under the heaven: 2656
3:17 for *there is* a time there for every **p** and 2656
8: 6 Because to every **p** there is time and 2656
Isa 1:11 **To what p** *is* the multitude of your 3807.1
14:26 This *is* the **p** that is purposed upon 6098
30: 7 Egyptians shall help in vain, and to **no p**: 7385
Jer 6:20 To what **p** cometh there to me incense 2088
26: 3 which I **p** to do unto them because of 2803
36: 3 hear all the evil which I **p** to do unto them; 2803
49:30 and hath conceived a **p** against you. 4284
51:29 for every **p** of the LORD shall be 4284
Da 6:17 that the **p** might not be changed concerning 6640
Mt 26: 8 saying, To **what p** *is* this waste? *5101*
Ac 11:23 that with **p** of heart *they* would cleave unto *4286*
26:16 for I have appeared unto thee for this **p**, to NIG
27:13 supposing that *they* had obtained *their* **p**, *4286*
27:43 to save Paul, kept them from *their* **p**; *1013*
Ro 8:28 them who are *the* called according to *his* **p**. *4286*
9:11 that the **p** of God according to election *4286*
9:17 Even for this same **p** have I raised thee up, NIG
2Co 1:17 or *the things* that I **p**, do I purpose *1011*
1:17 that I purpose, do I **p** according to the flesh, *1011*
Eph 1:11 being predestinated according to the **p** of *4286*
3:11 According to the eternal **p** which he *4286*
6:22 Whom I have sent unto you **for** the same **p**, *1519*
Col 4: 8 Whom I have sent unto you **for** the same **p**, *1519*
2Ti 1: 9 but according to his own **p** and grace, *4286*
3:10 **p**, faith, longsuffering, charity, patience, *4286*
1Jn 3: 8 For this **p** the Son of God was manifested, NIG

PURPOSED (19) [PURPOSE]

2Ch 32: 2 that he was **p** to fight against Jerusalem, 6440
Ps 17: 3 I am **p** *that* my mouth shall not transgress. 2161
140: 4 who have **p** to overthrow my goings. 2803
Isa 14:24 to pass; and as I have **p**, *so* shall it stand: 3289
14:26 This *is* the purpose that is **p** upon the whole 3289
14:27 For the LORD of hosts hath **p**, and 3289
19:12 the LORD of hosts hath **p** upon Egypt. 3289
23: 9 The LORD of hosts hath **p** it, to stain 3289
46:11 bring it to pass; I have **p** *it*, I will also do it. 3335
Jer 4:28 because I have spoken *it*, I have **p** *it*, and 2161
49:20 that he hath **p** against the inhabitants of 2803
50:45 that he hath **p** against the land of 2803
La 2: 8 The LORD hath **p** to destroy the wall of 2803
Da 1: 8 Daniel **p** in his heart that he would not 7760
Ac 19:21 *things* were ended, Paul **p** in the spirit, *5087*
20: 3 he **p** to return through Macedonia. *1096+1106*
Ro 1:13 that oftentimes I **p** to come unto you, (but *4388*

P

Eph 1: 9 good pleasure which he had **p** in himself: *4388*
3:11 to the eternal purpose which he **p** *4160*

PURPOSES (5) [PURPOSE]

Job 17:11 My days are past, my **p** are broken off, 2154
Pr 15:22 Without counsel **p** *are* disappointed: but 4284
Isa 19:10 they shall be broken *in* the **p** thereof, 8356
Jer 49:20 his **p**, that he hath purposed against 4284
50:45 his **p**, that he hath purposed against the land 4284

PURPOSETH (1) [PURPOSE]

2Co 9: 7 Every man according as he **p** in *his* heart, *4255*

PURPOSING (1) [PURPOSE]

Ge 27:42 doth comfort himself, ***p*** to kill thee. NIH

PURSE (5) [PURSES]

Pr 1:14 in thy lot among us; let us all have one **p**: 3599
Mk 6: 8 no scrip, no bread, no money in *their* **p**: *2223*
Lk 10: 4 Carry neither **p**, nor scrip, nor shoes: and *905*
22:35 When I sent you without **p**, and scrip, and *905*
22:36 But now, he that hath a **p**, let him take *it*, and *905*

PURSES (1) [PURSE]

Mt 10: 9 neither gold, nor silver, nor brass in your **p**; *2223*

PURSUE (29) [PURSUED, PURSUER, PURSUERS, PURSUETH, PURSUING]

Ge 35: 5 and they did not **p** after the sons of Jacob. 7291
Ex 15: 9 The enemy said, I will **p**, I will overtake, 7291
Dt 19: 6 Lest the avenger of the blood **p** the slayer, 7291
28:22 and they shall **p** thee until thou perish. 7291
28:45 shall **p** thee, and overtake thee, till thou be 7291
Jos 2: 5 **p** after them quickly; for ye shall overtake 7291
8:16 in Ai were called *together* to **p** after them: 7291
10:19 *but* **p** after your enemies, and smite 7291
20: 5 if the avenger of blood **p** after him, then 7291
1Sa 24:14 after whom dost thou **p**? after a dead dog, 7291
25:29 Yet a man is risen to **p** thee, and to seek thy 7291
26:18 Wherefore doth my lord thus **p** after his 7291
30: 8 saying, Shall I **p** after this troop? 7291
30: 8 he answered him, **P**: for thou shalt surely 7291
2Sa 17: 1 and I will arise and **p** after David *this* night: 7291
20: 6 **p** after him, lest he get him fenced cities, 7291
20: 7 to **p** after Sheba the son of Bichri. 7291
20:13 to **p** after Sheba the son of Bichri. 7291
24:13 before thine enemies, while they **p** thee? 7291
Job 13:25 and fro? and wilt thou **p** the dry stubble? 7291
30:15 they **p** my soul as the wind: and my welfare 7291
Ps 34:14 and do good; seek peace, and **p** it. 7291
Isa 30:16 therefore shall they that **p** you be swift. 7291
Jer 48: 2 O Madmen; the sword shall **p** thee. 310+1980
Eze 35: 6 thee unto blood, and blood shall **p** thee: 7291
35: 6 not hated blood, even blood shall **p** thee. 7291
Hos 8: 3 *thing that is* good: the enemy shall **p** him. 7291
Am 1:11 he did **p** his brother with the sword, 7291
Na 1: 8 and darkness shall **p** his enemies. 7291

PURSUED (38) [PURSUE]

Ge 14:14 and eighteen, and **p** *them* unto Dan. 7291
14:15 and smote them, and **p** them unto Hobah, 7291
31:23 and **p** after him seven days' journey; 7291
31:36 my sin, that thou hast *so* **hotly p** after me? 1814
Ex 14: 8 and he **p** after the children of Israel: 7291
14: 9 the Egyptians **p** after them (all the horses 7291
14:23 the Egyptians **p**, and went in after them to 7291
Dt 11: 4 sea to overflow them as they **p** after you, 7291
Jos 2: 7 the men **p** after them the way to Jordan 7291
2: 7 as soon as they which **p** after them were 7291
8:16 they **p** after Joshua, and were drawn away 7291
8:17 they left the city open, and **p** after Israel. 7291
24: 6 the Egyptians **p** after your fathers with 7291
Jdg 1: 6 they **p** after him, and caught him, and 7291
4:16 Barak **p** after the chariots, and after 7291
4:22 behold, as Barak **p** Sisera, Jael came out to 7291
7:23 of all Manasseh, and **p** after the Midianites. 7291
7:25 **p** Midian, and brought the heads of Oreb 7291
8:12 he **p** after them, and took the two kings of 7291
20:45 **p hard** after them unto Gidom, and 1692
1Sa 7:11 **p** the Philistines, and smote them, 7291
17:52 and shouted, and **p** the Philistines, 7291
23:25 when Saul heard *that*, he **p** after David *in* 7291
30:10 David **p**, he and four hundred men: for two 7291
2Sa 2:19 Asahel **p** after Abner; and in going he 7291
2:24 Joab also and Abishai **p** after Abner: and 7291
2:28 stood still, and **p** after Israel no more, 7291
20:10 Abishai his brother **p** after Sheba the son of 7291
22:38 I have **p** mine enemies, and 7291
1Ki 20:20 the Syrians fled; and Israel **p** them: and 7291
2Ki 25: 5 the army of the Chaldees **p** after the king, 7291
2Ch 13:19 Abijah **p** after Jeroboam, and took cities 7291
14:13 the people that *were* with him **p** them unto 7291
Ps 18:37 I have **p** mine enemies, and 7291
Isa 41: 3 He **p** them, *and* passed safely; *even by* 7291
Jer 39: 5 the Chaldeans' army **p** after them, and 7291
52: 8 the army of the Chaldeans **p** after the king, 7291
La 4:19 they **p** us upon the mountains, they laid 1814

PURSUER (1) [PURSUE]

La 1: 6 they are gone without strength before the **p**. 7291

PURSUERS (5) [PURSUE]

Jos 2:16 you to the mountain, lest the **p** meet you; 7291
2:16 there three days, until the **p** be returned: 7291
2:22 there three days, until the **p** were returned: 7291
2:22 the **p** sought *them* throughout all the way, 7291
8:20 *to* the wilderness turned back upon the **p**. 7291

PURSUETH (8) [PURSUE]

Lev 26:17 and ye shall flee when none **p** you. 7291
26:36 a sword; and they shall fall when none **p**. 7291
26:37 as it were before a sword, when none **p**: 7291
Pr 11:19 he that **p** evil *pursueth it* to his own death. 7291
11:19 he that pursueth evil ***p*** *it* to his own death. NIH

Pr 13:21 Evil **p** sinners: but to the righteous good 7291
19: 7 he **p** *them with* words, *yet* they *are* 7291
28: 1 The wicked flee when no man **p**: but 7291

PURSUING (8) [PURSUE]

Jdg 8: 4 men that *were* with him, faint, yet **p** *them*. 7291
8: 5 I am **p** after Zebah and Zalmunna, kings of 7291
1Sa 23:28 Wherefore Saul returned from **p** after 7291
2Sa 3:22 of David and Joab came from ***p*** a troop, NIH
18:16 and the people returned from **p** after Israel: 7291
1Ki 18:27 or he is **p**, or he is in a journey, *or* 7873
22:33 of Israel, that they turned back from **p** him. 310
2Ch 18:32 of Israel, they turned back *again* from **p** him. 310

PURTENANCE (1)

Ex 12: 9 head with his legs, and with the **p** thereof. 7130

PUSH (9) [PUSHING, PUSHT]

Ex 21:29 if the ox *were* **wont to p with his horn** in 5056
21:32 If the ox shall **p** a manservant or 5055
21:36 Or *if* it be known that the ox *hath* **used to p** 5056
Dt 33:17 with them he shall **p** the people together *to* 5055
1Ki 22:11 With these shalt thou **p** the Syrians, 5055
2Ch 18:10 With these thou shalt **p** Syria until they be 5055
Job 30:12 they **p away** my feet, and they raise up 7971
Ps 44: 5 Through thee will we **p down** our enemies: 5055
Da 11:40 the end shall the king of the south **p** at him: 5055

PUSHING (1) [PUSH]

Da 8: 4 I saw the ram **p** westward, and northward, 5055

PUSHT (1) [PUSH]

Eze 34:21 and **p** all the diseased with your horns, 5055

PUT (911) [PUTTEST, PUTTETH, PUTTING]

Ge 2: 8 there he **p** the man whom he had formed. 7760
2:15 **p** him into the garden of Eden to dress it 3240
3:15 I will **p** enmity between thee and 7896
3:22 lest he **p forth** his hand, and take also of 7971
8: 9 he **p forth** his hand, and took her, and 7971
19:10 the men **p forth** their hand, and pulled Lot 7971
24: 2 **P**, I pray thee, thy hand under my thigh: 7760
24: 9 the servant **p** his hand under the thigh of 7760
24:47 I **p** the earring upon her face, and 7760
26:11 his wife shall **surely be p to death**. 4191+4191
27:15 and **p** them **upon** Jacob her younger son: 3847
27:16 she **p** the skins of the kids of the goats upon 3847
28:11 **p** *them for* his pillows, and lay down in that 7760
28:18 took the stone that he had **p** *for* his pillows, 7760
28:20 give me bread to eat, and raiment to **p on**, 3847
29: 3 **p** the stone **again** upon the well's mouth in 7725
30:40 he **p** his own flocks by themselves, and 7896
30:40 **p** them not unto Laban's cattle. 7896
30:42 the cattle were feeble, he **p** *them* not **in**: 7760
31:34 **p** them in the camel's furniture, and 7760
32:16 and **p** a space betwixt drove and drove. 7760
33: 2 he **p** the handmaids and their children 7760
35: 2 **P away** the strange gods that *are* among 5493
37:34 **p** sackcloth upon his loins, and 7760
38:14 she **p** her widow's garments **off** from her, 5493
38:19 and **p on** the garments of her widowhood. 3847
38:28 she travailed, that *the one* **p out** *his* hand: 5414
39: 4 and all *that* he had he **p** into his hand. 5414
39:20 master took him, and **p** him into the prison, 5414
40: 3 he **p** them in ward *in* the house of 5414
40:15 that they should **p** me into the dungeon. 7760
41:10 **p** me in ward *in* the captain of the guard's 5414
41:42 **p** it upon Joseph's hand, and arrayed him in 5414
41:42 and **p** a gold chain about his neck; 7760
42:17 he **p** them **all together** into ward three days. 622
43:22 we cannot tell who **p** our money in our 7760
44: 1 **p** every man's money in his sack's mouth. 7760
44: 2 **p** my cup, the silver cup, in the sack's 7760
46: 4 Joseph shall **p** his hand upon thine eyes. 7896
47:29 **p**, I pray thee, thy hand under my thigh, 7760
48:18 **p** thy right hand upon his head. 7760
50:26 and he was **p** in a coffin in Egypt. 3455
Ex 2: 3 and with pitch, and **p** the child therein; 7760
3: 5 **p off** thy shoes from off thy feet, for 5394
3:22 ye shall **p** *them* upon your sons, and 7760
4: 4 **P forth** thine hand, and take it by the tail. 7971
4: 4 he **p forth** his hand, and caught it, and 7971
4: 6 unto him, **P** now thine hand into thy bosom. 935
4: 6 he **p** his hand into his bosom: and when he 935
4: 7 he said, **P** thine hand into thy bosom **again**. 7725
4: 7 he **p** his hand into his bosom **again**; and 7725
4:15 speak unto him, and **p** words in his mouth: 7760
4:21 which I have **p** in thine hand: 7760
5:21 to **p** a sword in their hand to slay us. 5414
8:23 I will **p** a division between my people and 7760
11: 7 doth **p a difference** between the Egyptians 6395
12:15 even the first day ye shall **p away** leaven 7673
15:26 I will **p** none of *these* diseases upon thee, 7760
16:33 **p** an omer full of manna therein, and lay it 5414
17:12 and **p** *it* under him, and he sat thereon; 7760
17:14 for I will **utterly p out** 4229+4229
19:12 mount shall be **surely p to death**: 4191+4191
21:12 he die, shall be **surely p to death**. 4191+4191
21:15 shall be **surely p to death**. 4191+4191
21:16 he shall **surely** be **p to death**. 4191+4191
21:17 shall **surely** be **p to death**. 4191+4191
21:29 and his owner also shall be **p to death**. 4191
22: 5 shall **p in** his beast, and shall feed in 7971
22: 8 *to see* whether he have **p** his hand unto his 7971
22:11 that he hath not **p** his hand unto his 7971
22:19 a beast shall **surely be p to death**. 4191+4191
23: 1 **p** not thine hand with the wicked to be an 7896
24: 6 took half of the blood, and **p** *it* in basons; 7760
25:12 and **p** *them* in the four corners thereof; 5414
25:14 thou shalt **p** the staves into the rings by 935
25:16 thou shalt **p** into the ark the Testimony 5414
25:21 thou shalt **p** the mercy seat above upon 5414
25:21 in the ark thou shalt **p** the Testimony that I 5414
25:26 **p** the rings in the four corners that *are* on 5414

Ex 26:11 **p** the taches into the loops, and couple 935
26:34 thou shalt **p** the mercy seat upon the ark of 5414
26:35 and thou shalt **p** the table on the north side. 5414
27: 5 thou shalt **p** it under the compass of 5414
27: 7 And the staves shall be **p** into the rings, and 935
28:12 thou shalt **p** the two stones upon 7760
28:23 shalt **p** the two rings on the two ends of 5414
28:24 thou shalt **p** the two wreathen *chains of* 5414
28:25 **p** *them* on the shoulderpieces of the ephod 5414
28:26 thou shalt **p** them upon the two ends of 7760
28:27 shalt **p** them on the two sides of the ephod 5414
28:30 thou shalt **p** in the breastplate of judgment 5414
28:37 thou shalt **p** it on a blue lace, that it may be 7760
28:41 thou shalt **p** them **upon** Aaron thy brother, 3847
29: 3 thou shalt **p** them into one basket, and 5414
29: 5 **p upon** Aaron the coat, and the robe of 3847
29: 6 thou shalt **p** the mitre upon his head, and 7760
29: 6 and **p** the holy crown upon the mitre. 5414
29: 8 bring his sons, and **p** coats **upon** them. 3847
29: 9 and his sons, and **p** the bonnets on them: 2280
29:10 his sons shall **p** their hands upon the head 5564
29:12 **p** *it* upon the horns of the altar with thy 5414
29:15 his sons shall **p** their hands upon the head 5564
29:17 **p** *them* unto his pieces, and unto his head. 5414
29:19 his sons shall **p** their hands upon the head 5564
29:20 **p** *it* upon the tip of the *right* ear of Aaron, 5414
29:24 thou shalt **p** all in the hands of Aaron, and 7760
29:30 in his stead shall **p** them **on** seven days, 3847
30: 6 thou shalt **p** it before the vail that *is* by 5414
30:18 thou shalt **p** it between the tabernacle of 5414
30:18 the altar, and thou shalt **p** water therein. 5414
30:36 **p** of it before the Testimony in 5414
31: 6 all that are wise hearted I have **p** wisdom, 5414
31:14 defileth it shall **surely** be **p to death**: 4191+4191
31:15 he shall **surely** be **p to death**. 4191+4191
32:27 **P** every man his sword by his side, *and* 7760
33: 4 and no man did **p** on him his ornaments. 7896
33: 5 now **p off** thy ornaments from thee, 3381
33:22 that I will **p** thee in a clift of the rock, and 7760
34:33 speaking with them, he **p** a vail on his face. 5414
34:35 Moses **p** the vail upon his face **again**, 7725
35: 2 doeth work therein shall be **p to death**. 4191
35:34 he hath **p** in his heart that *he* may teach, 5414
36: 1 in whom the LORD **p** wisdom and 5414
36: 2 in whose heart the LORD had **p** wisdom, 5414
37: 5 he **p** the staves into the rings by the sides of 935
37:13 **p** the rings upon the four corners that *were* 5414
38: 7 he **p** the staves into the rings on the sides of 935
39: 7 he **p** them on the shoulders of the ephod, 7760
39:16 **p** the two rings in the two ends of 5414
39:17 they **p** the two wreathen *chains of* gold in 5414
39:18 **p** them on the shoulderpieces of the ephod, 5414
39:19 **p** *them* on the two ends of the breastplate, 7760
39:20 **p** them on the two sides of the ephod 5414
39:25 **p** the bells between the pomegranates upon 5414
40: 3 thou shalt **p** therein the ark of 7760
40: 5 **p** the hanging of the door to the tabernacle. 7760
40: 7 and the altar, and shalt **p** water therein. 5414
40:13 thou shalt **p upon** Aaron the holy garments, 3847
40:18 **p in** the bars thereof, and reared up his 5414
40:19 **p** the covering of the tent above upon it; 7760
40:20 he took and **p** the Testimony into the ark, 5414
40:20 and **p** the mercy seat above upon the ark: 5414
40:22 he **p** the table in the tent of 5414
40:24 he **p** the candlestick in the tent of 7760
40:26 he **p** the golden altar in the tent of 7760
40:29 he **p** the altar of burnt offering *by* the door 7760
40:30 and the altar, and **p** water there, 5414
Lev 1: 4 he shall **p** his hand upon the head of 5564
1: 7 the sons of Aaron the priest shall **p** fire 5414
2: 1 oil upon it, and **p** frankincense thereon: 5414
2:15 thou shalt **p** oil upon it, and 5414
4: 7 the priest shall **p** *some* of the blood upon 5414
4:18 he shall **p** *some* of the blood upon the horns 5414
4:25 **p** *it* upon the horns of the altar of burnt 5414
4:30 **p** *it* upon the horns of the altar of burnt 5414
4:34 **p** *it* upon the horns of the altar of burnt 5414
5:11 he shall **p** no oil upon it, neither shall he 7760
5:11 neither shall he **p** *any* frankincense thereon: 5414
6:10 the priest shall **p on** his linen garment, and 3847
6:10 *his* linen breeches shall he **p** upon his flesh, 3847
6:10 and he shall **p** them besides the altar. 7760
6:11 he shall **p off** his garments, and put on 6584
6:11 **p on** other garments, and carry forth 3847
6:12 shall be burning in it; it shall not be **p out**: 3518
8: 7 he **p** upon him the coat, and girded him 5414
8: 7 **p** the ephod upon him, and he girded him 5414
8: 8 he **p** the breastplate upon him: also he put 7760
8: 8 also he **p** in the breastplate the Urim and 5414
8: 9 he **p** the mitre upon his head; also upon 7760
8: 9 did he **p** the golden plate, the holy crown; 7760
8:13 **p** coats **upon** them, and girded them *with* 3847
8:13 *with* girdles, and **p** bonnets upon them; 2280
8:15 **p** *it* upon the horns of the altar round about 5414
8:23 **p** *it* upon the tip of Aaron's right ear, and 5414
8:24 Moses **p** of the blood upon the tip of their 5414
8:26 **p** *them* on the fat, and upon the right 7760
8:27 he **p** all upon Aaron's hands, and upon his 5414
9: 9 **p** *it* upon the horns of the altar, and poured 5414
9:20 they **p** the fat upon the breasts, and he burnt 7760
10: 1 **p** fire therein, and put incense thereon, 5414
10: 1 **p** incense thereon, and offered strange fire 7760
10:10 And that *ye* may **p difference** between holy 914
11:32 it must be **p** into water, and it shall be 935
11:38 if *any* water be **p** upon the seed, and 5414
13:45 he shall **p a covering** upon *his* upper lip, 5844
14:14 the priest shall **p** *it* upon the tip of the right 5414
14:17 **p** upon the tip of the right ear of him that is 5414
14:25 **p** *it* upon the tip of the right ear of him that 5414
14:28 the priest shall **p** of the oil that *is* in his 5414
14:29 **p** upon the head of him that is to be 5414
14:34 I **p** the plague of leprosy in a house of 5414
14:42 and **p** *them* in the place of *those* stones; 935
15:19 be blood, she shall be **p apart** seven days: 5079
16: 4 He shall **p on** the holy linen coat, and 3847

Lev 16: 4 wash his flesh in water, and *so* **p** them **on.** 3847
16:13 he shall **p** the incense upon the fire before 5414
16:18 **p** *it* upon the horns of the altar round about. 5414
16:23 shall **p off** the linen garments, which he put 6584
16:23 which he **p** on when he went into the holy 3847
16:24 **p on** his garments, and come forth, and 3847
16:32 shall **p on** the linen clothes, *even* the holy 3847
18:19 as long as she is **p apart** for her 5079
19:14 nor **p** a stumblingblock before the blind, 5414
19:20 they shall not be **p to death**, because 4191
20: 2 he shall **surely** be **p to death**: 4191+4191
20: 9 mother shall be **surely p to death**: 4191+4191
20:10 adulteress shall **surely** be **p to death**. 4191+4191
20:11 of them shall **surely** be **p to death**; 4191+4191
20:12 of them shall **surely** be **p to death**: 4191+4191
20:13 they shall **surely** be **p to death**; their 4191+4191
20:15 he shall **surely** be **p to death**: 4191+4191
20:16 they shall **surely** be **p to death**; their 4191+4191
20:25 **p difference** between clean beasts 914
20:27 a wizard, shall **surely** be **p to death**: 4191+4191
21: 7 neither shall they take a woman **p away** 1644
21:10 that is consecrated to **p on** the garments, 3847
22:14 he shall **p** the fifth *part* thereof unto it, and 3254
24: 7 thou shalt **p** pure frankincense upon *each* 5414
24:12 they **p** him in ward, that the mind of 3240
24:16 he shall **surely** be **p to death**, *and* 4191+4191
24:16 name *of the LORD*, shall be **p to death**. 4191
24:17 any man shall **surely** be **p to death**. 4191+4191
24:21 that killeth a man, he shall be **p to death**. 4191
26: 8 of you shall **p** ten thousand **to flight**: 7291
27:29 *but* shall **surely** be **p to death**. 4191+4191
Nu 1:51 that cometh nigh shall be **p to death**. 4191
3:10 that cometh nigh shall be **p to death**. 4191
3:38 that cometh nigh shall be **p to death**. 4191
4: 6 shall **p** thereon the covering of badgers' 5414
4: 6 of blue, and shall **p in** the staves thereof. 7760
4: 7 **p** thereon the dishes, and the spoons, and 5414
4: 8 and shall **p in** the staves thereof. 7760
4:10 they shall **p** it and all the vessels thereof 5414
4:10 of badgers' skins, and shall **p** *it* upon a bar. 5414
4:11 and shall **p to** the staves thereof: 7760
4:12 **p** *them* in a cloth of blue, and cover them 5414
4:12 badgers' skins, and shall **p** *them* on a bar: 5414
4:14 they shall **p** upon it all the vessels thereof, 5414
4:14 of badgers' skins, and **p to** the staves of it. 7760
5: 2 that they **p out** of the camp every leper, and 7971
5: 3 Both male and female shall ye **p out**, 7971
5: 3 put out, without the camp shall ye **p** them; 7971
5: 4 did so, and **p** them **out** without the camp: 7971
5:15 no oil upon it, nor **p** frankincense thereon; 5414
5:17 the priest shall take, and **p** *it* into the water: 5414
5:18 **p** the offering of memorial in her hands, 5414
6:18 **p** *it* in the fire which *is* under the sacrifice 5414
6:19 shall **p** *them* upon the hands of 5414
6:27 they shall **p** my name upon the children of 7760
8:10 the children of Israel shall **p** their hands 5564
11:17 *is* upon thee, and will **p** *it* upon them; 7760
11:29 that the LORD would **p** his spirit upon 5414
15:34 they **p** him in ward, because it was not 3240
15:35 The man shall be **surely p to death**: 4191+4191
15:38 that they **p** upon the fringe of the borders a 5414
16: 7 **p** fire therein, and put incense in them 5414
16: 7 **p** incense in them before the LORD to 7760
16:14 wilt thou **p out** the eyes of these men? 5365
16:17 **p** incense in them, and bring ye before 5414
16:18 **p** fire in them, and laid incense thereon, 5414
16:46 **p** fire therein from off the altar, and put on 5414
16:46 **p on** incense, and go quickly unto 7760
16:47 he **p on** incense, and made an atonement 5414
18: 7 that cometh nigh shall be **p to death**. 4191
19:17 running water shall be **p** thereto in a vessel: 5414
20:26 and **p** them **upon** Eleazar his son: 3847
20:28 and **p** them **upon** Eleazar his son; 3847
21: 9 **p** it upon a pole, and it came to pass, that if 7760
23: 5 the LORD **p** a word in Balaam's mouth, 7760
23:12 which the LORD hath **p** in my mouth? 7760
23:16 **p** a word in his mouth, and said, Go again 7760
27:20 thou shalt **p** *some* of thine honour upon 5414
35:16 murderer shall **surely** be **p to death**. 4191+4191
35:17 murderer shall **surely** be **p to death**. 4191+4191
35:18 murderer shall **surely** be **p to death**. 4191+4191
35:21 *him* shall **surely** be **p to death**; 4191+4191
35:30 the murderer shall be **p to death** by 7523
35:31 but he shall be **surely p to death**. 4191+4191
36: 3 shall be **p** to the inheritance of the tribe 3254
36: 4 shall their inheritance be **p** unto 3254
Dt 2:25 This day will I begin to **p** the dread of thee 5414
7:15 will **p** none of the evil diseases of Egypt, 7760
7:22 the LORD thy God will **p out** those 5394
10: 2 and thou shalt **p** them in the ark. 7760
10: 5 **p** the tables in the ark which I had made; 7760
11:29 that thou shalt **p** the blessing upon mount 5414
12: 5 out of all your tribes to **p** his name there, 7760
12: 7 rejoice in all that you **p** your hand **unto**, 4916
12:21 to **p** his name there be too far from thee, 7760
13: 5 dreamer of dreams, shall be **p to death**; 4191
13: 5 So shalt thou **p** the evil **away** from 1197
13: 9 shall be first upon him to **p** him **to death**, 4191
16: 9 *as thou* beginnest *to* **p** the sickle to the corn. NIH
17: 6 he that is *worthy* of death be **p to death**; 4191
17: 6 of one witness he shall not be **p to death**. 4191
17: 7 shall be first upon him to **p** him **to death**, 4191
17: 7 So thou shalt **p** the evil **away** from among 1197
17:12 and thou shalt **p away** the evil from Israel. 1197
18:18 and will **p** my words in his mouth; 5414
19:13 thou shalt **p away** *the guilt of* innocent 1197
19:19 shalt thou **p** the evil **away** from among you. 1197
21: 9 So shalt thou **p away** the *guilt of* innocent 1197
21:13 she shall **p** the raiment of her captivity 5493
21:21 so shalt thou **p** evil **away** from among you; 1197
21:22 he be *to be* **p to death**, and thou hang him 4191
22: 5 neither shall a man **p on** a woman's 3847
22:19 he may not **p** her **away** all his days. 7971
22:21 so shalt thou **p** evil **away** from among you. 1197
22:22 so shalt thou **p away** evil from Israel. 1197
Dt 22:24 so thou shalt **p away** evil from among you. 1197
22:29 he may not **p** her **away** all his days. 7971
23:24 but thou shalt not **p** *any* in thy vessel. 5414
24: 7 thou shalt **p** evil **away** from among you. 1197
24:16 The fathers shall not be **p to death** for 4191
24:16 neither shall the children be **p to death** for 4191
24:16 every man shall be **p to death** for his own 4191
25: 6 that his name be not **p out** of Israel. 4229
26: 2 shalt **p** *it* in a basket, and shalt go unto 7760
28:48 and he shall **p** a yoke of iron upon thy neck, 5414
30: 7 the LORD thy God will **p** all these curses 5414
31:19 **p** it in their mouths, that this song may be a 7760
31:26 **p** it in the side of the ark of the covenant of 7760
32:30 two **p** ten thousand **to flight**, except their 5127
33:10 they shall **p** incense before thee, and 7760
33:14 for the precious things **p forth** by 1645
Jos 1:18 commandest him, he shall be **p to death**: 4191
6:24 they **p** *into* the treasury of the house of 5414
7: 6 of Israel, and **p** dust upon their heads. 5927
7:11 they have **p** *it* even amongst their own 7760
10:24 **p** your feet upon the necks of these kings. 7760
10:24 and **p** their feet upon the necks of them. 7760
17:13 that they **p** the Canaanites to tribute; 5414
24: 7 he **p** darkness between you and 7760
24:14 **p away** the gods which your fathers served 5493
24:23 Now therefore **p away**, *said he*, the strange 5493
Jdg 1:28 that they **p** the Canaanites to tribute, and 7760
3:21 Ehud **p forth** his left hand, and took 7971
5:26 She **p** her hand to the nail, and her right 7971
6:19 the flesh he **p** in a basket, and he put 7760
6:19 he **p** the broth in a pot, and brought *it* out 7760
6:21 the angel of the LORD **p forth** the end of 7971
6:31 let him be **p to death** whilst *it is yet* 4191
6:37 I will **p** a fleece of wool in the floor; 3322
7:16 he **p** a trumpet in every man's hand, 5414
8:27 and **p** it in his city, *even* in Ophrah: 3322
9:15 *then* come *and* **p** your **trust** in my shadow: 2620
9:26 the men of Shechem **p** their **confidence** in 982
9:49 **p** *them* to the hold, and set the hold on fire 7760
10:16 they **p away** the strange gods from among 5493
12: 3 I **p** my life in my hands, and passed over 7760
14:12 I will now **p forth** a riddle unto you: 2330
14:13 **P forth** thy riddle, that we may hear it. 2330
14:16 thou hast **p forth** a riddle unto the children 2330
15: 4 **p** a firebrand in the midst between two 7760
15:15 **p forth** his hand, and took it, and slew a 7971
16: 3 bar and all, and **p** *them* upon his shoulders, 7760
16:21 **p out** his eyes, and brought him down to 5365
18: 7 that might **p** *them* **to shame** in *any* thing; 3637
18:21 **p** the little ones and the cattle and 7760
20:13 that we may **p** them **to death**, and put away 4191
20:13 them to death, and **p away** evil from Israel. 1197
20:20 the men of Israel **p** *themselves* **in array** to 6186
20:22 they **p** *themselves* **in array** the first day. 6186
20:30 **p** *themselves* **in array** against Gibeah, as at 6186
20:33 and **p** *themselves* **in array** at Baal-tamar: 6186
21: 5 He shall **surely** be **p to death**. 4191+4191
Ru 3: 3 **p** thy raiment upon thee, and get thee down 7760
1Sa 1:14 be drunken? **p away** thy wine from thee. 5493
2:36 of bread, and shall say, **P** me, I pray thee, 5596
4: 2 the Philistines **p** *themselves* **in array** 6186
6: 8 **p** the jewels of gold, which ye return him 7760
6:15 gold *were*, and **p** *them* on the great stone: 7760
7: 3 *then* **p away** the strange gods and 5493
7: 4 the children of Israel did **p away** Baalim 5493
8:16 and your asses, and **p** *them* to his work. 6213
11:11 that Saul **p** the people *in* three companies; 7760
11:12 the men, that we may **p** them **to death**. 4191
11:13 There shall not a man be **p to death** this 4191
14:26 but no man **p** his hand to his mouth: 5381
14:27 wherefore he **p forth** the end of the rod that 7971
14:27 a honeycomb, and **p** his hand to his mouth; 7725
17:21 the Philistines had **p** *the battle* **in array**, 6186
17:38 and he **p** a helmet of brass upon his head; 5414
17:39 proved *them*. And David **p** them **off** him. 5493
17:40 **p** them in a shepherd's bag which he had, 7760
17:49 David **p** his hand in *his* bag, and 7971
17:54 but he **p** his armour in his tent. 7760
19: 5 For he did **p** his life in his hand, and 7760
19:13 **p** a pillow of goats' *hair* for his bolster, and 7760
21: 6 to **p** hot bread in the day when it was taken 7760
22:17 the servants of the king would not **p forth** 7971
24:10 I will not **p forth** mine hand against my 7971
28: 3 Saul had **p away** those that had familiar 5493
28: 8 **p on** other raiment, and he went, and 3847
28:21 I have **p** my life in my hand, and 7760
31:10 they **p** his armour *in* the house of 7760
2Sa 1:24 who **p on** ornaments of gold upon your 5927
3:34 *were* not bound, nor thy feet **p** into fetters: 5066
6: 6 Uzzah **p forth** *his hand* to the ark of God, 7971
7:15 whom I **p away** before thee. 4480+5493
8: 2 *with* two lines measured he to **p to death**, 4191
8: 6 David **p** garrisons in Syria of Damascus: 7760
8:14 he **p** garrisons in Edom; throughout all 7760
8:14 throughout all Edom **p** he garrisons, and 7760
10: 8 **p** the battle **in array** *at* the entering in of 6186
10: 9 and **p** *them* **in array** against the Syrians: 6186
10:10 that he might **p** *them* **in array** against 6186
12:13 The LORD also hath **p away** thy sin; 5674
12:31 **p** *them* under saws, and under harrows of 7760
13:17 **P** now this *woman* out from me, and 7971
13:19 Tamar **p** ashes on her head, and rent her 3947
14: 2 **p on** now mourning apparel, and anoint not 3847
14: 3 So Joab **p** the words in her mouth. 7760
14:19 he **p** all these words in the mouth of thine 7760
15: 5 he **p forth** his hand, and took him, and 7971
17:23 **p** his household **in order**, and 6680
18:12 *yet* would I not **p forth** mine hand against 7971
19:21 Shall not Shimei be **p to death** for this, 4191
19:22 shall there any man be **p to death** *this* day 4191
20: 3 **p** them *in* ward, and fed them, but went not 5414
20: 8 Joab's garment that he had **p on** *was* girded 3830
21: 9 and were **p to death** in the days of harvest, 4191
1Ki 2: 5 **p** the blood of war upon his girdle that *was* 5414
2: 8 I will not **p** thee **to death** with the sword. 4191
1Ki 2:24 Adonijah shall be **p to death** *this* day. 4191
2:26 I will not at this time **p** thee **to death**, 4191
2:35 the king **p** Benaiah the son of Jehoiada in 5414
2:35 Zadok the priest did the king **p** in the room 5414
5: 3 until the LORD **p** them under the soles of 5414
7:39 he **p** five bases on the right side of 5414
7:51 did he **p** among the treasures of the house 5414
8: 9 of stone, which Moses **p** there at Horeb, 3240
9: 3 hast built, to **p** my name there for ever; 7760
10:17 the king **p** them *in* the house of the forest of 5414
10:24 his wisdom, which God had **p** in his heart. 5414
11:36 the city which I have chosen me to **p** my 7760
12: 4 his heavy yoke which he **p** upon us, lighter, 5414
12: 9 Make the yoke which thy father did **p** upon 5414
12:29 one in Beth-el, and the other **p** he in Dan. 5414
13: 4 that he **p forth** his hand from the altar, 7971
13: 4 which he **p forth** against him, dried up, so 7971
14:21 all the tribes of Israel, to **p** his name there. 7760
18:23 **p** no fire *under:* and I will dress the other 7760
18:23 and lay *it* on wood, and **p** no fire *under:* 7760
18:25 the name of your gods, but **p** no fire *under.* 7760
18:33 he **p** the wood **in order**, and cut the bullock 6186
18:42 the earth, and **p** his face between his knees, 7760
20: 6 they shall **p** *it* in their hand, and take *it* 7760
20:24 of his place, and **p** captains in their rooms: 7760
20:31 **p** sackcloth on our loins, and ropes upon 7760
20:32 *p* ropes on their heads, and came to the king NIH
21:27 **p** sackcloth upon his flesh, and fasted, and 7760
22:10 each on his throne, having **p on** *their* robes, 3847
22:23 the LORD hath **p** a lying spirit in 5414
22:27 **P** this *fellow in* the prison, and feed him 7760
22:30 into the battle; but **p** thou **on** thy robes. 3847
2Ki 2:20 Bring me a new cruse, and **p** salt therein. 7760
3: 2 for he **p away** the image of Baal that his 5493
3:21 all that *were able to* **p on armour**, 2290+2296
4:34 **p** his mouth upon his mouth, and his eyes 7760
6: 7 to thee. And he **p out** his hand, and took it. 7971
9:13 **p** *it* under him on the top of the stairs, and 7760
10: 7 **p** their heads in baskets, and sent him *them* 7760
11:12 **p** the crown upon him, and *gave him* 5414
12: 9 the priests that kept the door **p** therein all 5414
12:10 they **p up** *in bags*, and told the money that 6696
13:16 king of Israel, **P** thine hand upon the bow. 7392
13:16 he **p** his hand *upon it:* and Elisha put his 7392
13:16 Elisha **p** his hands upon the king's hands. 7760
14: 6 The fathers shall not be **p to death** for 4191
14: 6 nor the children be **p to death** for 4191
14: 6 every man shall be **p to death** for his own 4191
14:12 Judah was **p to the worse** before Israel; 5062
16:14 and **p** it on the north side of the altar. 5414
16:17 and **p** it upon a pavement of stones. 5414
17:29 **p** *them* in the houses of the high places 3240
18:11 **p** them in Halah and in Habor *by* the river 5148
18:24 **p** thy **trust** on Egypt for chariots and 982
19:28 therefore I will **p** my hook in thy nose, and 7760
21: 4 In Jerusalem will I **p** my name. 7760
21: 7 tribes of Israel, will I **p** my name for ever: 7760
23: 5 he **p down** the idolatrous priests, whom 7673
23:24 and in Jerusalem, did Josiah **p away**, 1197
23:33 Pharaoh-nechoh **p** him **in bands** at Riblah in 631
23:33 **p** the land to a tribute of an hundred talents 5414
25: 7 **p out** the eyes of Zedekiah, and bound him 5786
1Ch 1: 8 Cush, and Mizraim, **P**, and Canaan. 6316
5:20 of them; because they **p** their **trust** in him. 982
10:10 they **p** his armour *in* the house of their 7760
11:19 men that **have p** their lives **in jeopardy**? 871.1
12:15 they **p to flight** all *them of* the valleys, 1272
13: 9 Uzza **p forth** his hand to hold the ark; 7971
13:10 because he **p** his hand to the ark: 7971
18: 6 David **p** *garrisons* in Syria-damascus; 7760
18:13 he **p** garrisons in Edom; and all 7760
19: 9 **p** the battle **in array** *before* the gate of 6186
19:10 and **p** *them* **in array** against the Syrians. 6186
19:16 that they were **p to the worse** before Israel, 5062
19:17 So when David had **p** the battle **in array** 6186
19:19 that they were **p to the worse** before Israel, 5062
21:27 he **p up** his sword **again** into the sheath 7725
27:24 neither was the number **p** in the account of 5927
2Ch 1: 5 he **p** before the tabernacle of the LORD: 7760
2:14 to find out every device which shall be **p** to 5414
3:16 and **p** *them* on the heads of the pillars; 5414
3:16 and **p** *them* on the chains. 5414
4: 6 **p** five on the right hand, and five on 5414
5: 1 **p** he among the treasures of the house of 5414
5:10 two tables which Moses **p** *therein* at Horeb, 5414
6:11 in it have I **p** the ark, wherein *is* 7760
6:20 said that *thou* wouldest **p** thy name there; 7760
6:24 if thy people Israel be **p to the worse** 5062
9:16 the king **p** them in the house of the forest of 5414
9:23 his wisdom, that God had **p** in his heart. 5414
10: 4 his heavy yoke that he **p** upon us, and 5414
10: 9 the yoke that thy father did **p** upon us? 5414
10:11 For whereas my father **p** a heavy yoke 6006
10:11 yoke upon you, I will **p more** to your yoke: 3254
11:11 and **p** captains in them, and store of victual, 5414
11:12 in every several city *he* **p** shields and spears, NIH
12:13 all the tribes of Israel, to **p** his name there. 7760
15: 8 **p away** the abominable idols out of all 5674
15:13 God of Israel should be **p to death**, 4191
16:10 with the seer, and **p** him *in* a prison house; 5414
17:19 besides *those* whom the king **p** in 5414
18:22 the LORD hath **p** a lying spirit in 5414
18:26 **P** this *fellow* in the prison, and feed him 7760
18:29 go to the battle; but **p** thou **on** thy robes. 3847
22:11 and **p** him and his nurse in a bedchamber. 5414
23: 7 into the house, he shall be **p to death**: 4191
23:11 **p** upon him the crown, and *gave him* 5414
25:22 Judah was **p to the worse** before Israel, 5062
29: 7 **p out** the lamps, and have not burnt incense 3518
33: 7 tribes of Israel, will I **p** my name for ever: 7760
33:14 **p** captains of war in all the fenced cities of 7760
34:10 they **p** *it* in the hand of the workmen that 5414
35: 3 **P** the holy ark in the house which Solomon 5414
35:24 and **p** him in the second chariot that he had; 7392
36: 3 the king of Egypt **p** him **down** at 5493

2Ch 36: 7 and **p** them in his temple at Babylon. 5414
36:22 and **p** *it* also in writing, saying, NIH
Ezr 1: 1 and **p** *it* also in writing, saying, NIH
1: 7 and had **p** them in the house of his gods; 5414
2:62 as polluted, **p from** the priesthood. 4480
6:12 that shall **p** to their hand to alter *and* 7972
7:27 which hath **p** *such a thing* as this in 5414
10: 3 with our God to **p away** all the wives, 3318
10:19 hands that *they* would **p away** their wives; 3318
Ne 2:12 neither told I *any* man what my God had **p** 5414
3: 5 their nobles **p** not their necks to the work of 935
4:23 followed me, none of us **p off** our clothes, 6584
4:23 *saving that* every one **p** them **off** *for* 7973
6:14 the prophets, that would have **p** me **in fear**. 3372
6:19 *And* Tobiah sent letters to **p** me **in fear**. 3372
7: 5 my God **p** into mine heart to gather 5414
7:64 as polluted, **p from** the priesthood. 4480
Est 4: 1 **p on** sackcloth with ashes, and went out 3847
4:11 *there is* one law of his to **p** *him* **to death**, 4191
5: 1 that Esther **p on** *her* royal *apparel*, and 3847
8: 3 besought him with tears to **p away** 5674
9: 1 his decree drew near to be **p in execution**, 6213
Job 1:11 **p forth** thine hand now, and touch all that 7971
1:12 only upon himself **p** not **forth** thine hand. 7971
2: 5 **p forth** thine hand now, and touch his bone 7971
4:18 Behold, he **p** no **trust** in his servants; and his 539
11:14 **p** it **far away**, and let not wickedness dwell 7368
13:14 in my teeth, and **p** my life in mine hand? 7760
17: 3 Lay down now, **p** me **in a surety** with thee; 6148
18: 5 the light of the wicked shall be **p out**, and 1846
18: 6 and his candle shall be **p out** with him. 1846
19:13 He hath **p** my brethren **far** from me, and 7368
21:17 How oft is the candle of the wicked **p out**! 1846
22:23 **p away** iniquity **far** from thy tabernacles. 7368
23: 6 No; but he would **p** *strength* in me. 7760
27:17 He may prepare *it*, but the just shall **p** *it* **on**, 3847
29:14 I **p on** righteousness, and it clothed me: 3847
38:36 Who hath **p** wisdom in the inward parts? or 7896
41: 2 Canst thou **p** a hook into his nose? or 7760
Ps 2:12 blessed *are* all they that **p** their **trust** in 2620
4: 5 and **p** your **trust** in the LORD. 982
4: 7 Thou hast **p** gladness in my heart, 5414
5:11 let all those that **p** their **trust** in thee 2620
7: 1 LORD my God, in thee do I **p** my **trust**: 2620
8: 6 thou hast **p** all *things* under his feet: 7896
9: 5 thou hast **p out** their name for ever and 4229
9:10 they that know thy name will **p** their **trust** in 982
9:20 **P** them in fear, O LORD: *that* the nations 7896
11: 1 In the LORD **p** I my **trust**: how say ye to 2620
16: 1 O God: for in thee do I **p** my **trust**. 2620
17: 7 **p** their **trust** *in thee* from those that rise up 2620
18:22 and I did not **p away** his statutes from me. 5493
25:20 not be ashamed; for I **p** my **trust** in thee. 2620
27: 9 from me; **p** not thy servant **away** in anger: 5186
30:11 thou hast **p off** my sackcloth, and 6605
31: 1 In thee, O LORD, do I **p** my **trust**; let me 2620
31:18 Let the lying lips be **p to silence**; 481
35: 4 and **p to shame** that seek after my soul: 3637
36: 7 the children of men **p** their **trust** under 2620
40: 3 he hath **p** a new song in my mouth, 5414
40:14 and **p to shame** that wish me evil. 3637
44: 7 and hast **p** them **to shame** that hated us. 954
44: 9 thou hast cast off, and **p** us **to shame**; and 3637
53: 5 thou hast **p** *them* **to shame**, because 954
55:20 He hath **p forth** his hands against such as 7971
56: 4 praise his word, in God I have **p** my **trust**; 982
56: 8 **p** thou my tears into thy bottle: *are they* not 7760
56:11 In God have I **p** my **trust**: I will not be 982
70: 2 and **p to confusion**, that desire my hurt. 3637
71: 1 In thee, O LORD, do I **p** my **trust**: let me 2620
71: 1 put my trust: let me never be **p to confusion**. 954
73:28 I have **p** my trust in the Lord GOD, that *I* 7896
78:66 he **p** them to a perpetual reproach. 5414
83:17 yea, let them be **p** to shame, and perish: NIH
88: 8 Thou hast **p away** mine acquaintance **far** 7368
88:18 Lover and friend hast thou **p far** from me, 7368
118: 8 in the LORD than to **p confidence** in man. 982
118: 9 the LORD than to **p confidence** in princes. 982
119:31 O LORD, **p** me not **to shame**. 954
125: 3 lest the righteous **p forth** their hands unto 7971
146: 3 **P** not your **trust** in princes, *nor* in the son of 982
Pr 4:24 **P away** from thee a froward mouth, and 5493
4:24 and perverse lips **p far** from thee. 7368
8: 1 and understanding **p forth** her voice? 5414
13: 9 but the lamp of the wicked shall be **p out**. 1846
20:20 his lamp shall be **p out** in obscure darkness. 1846
23: 2 **p** a knife to thy throat, if thou *be* a man 7760
24:20 the candle of the wicked shall be **p out**. 1846
25: 6 **P** not **forth** thyself in the presence of 1921
25: 7 than that thou shouldest be **p lower** in 8213
25: 8 when thy neighbour hath **p** thee **to shame**. 3637
25:10 Lest he that heareth *it* **p** thee **to shame**, and 2616
30: 5 he *is* a shield unto them that **p** their **trust** in 2620
Ecc 3:14 nothing can be **p** to it, nor any thing taken 3254
10:10 the edge, then must he **p to more** strength: 1396
11:10 thy heart, and **p away** evil from thy flesh: 5674
SS 5: 3 I have **p off** my coat; how shall I put it on? 6584
5: 3 I have put off my coat; how shall I **p** it **on**? 3847
5: 4 My beloved **p in** his hand by the hole *of* 7971
Isa 1:16 **p away** the evil of your doings from before 5493
5:20 that **p** darkness for light, and light for 7760
5:20 that **p** bitter for sweet, and sweet for bitter! 7760
10:13 I have **p down** the inhabitants like a 3381
11: 8 the weaned child shall **p** his hand on 1911
20: 2 thy loins, and **p off** thy shoe from thy foot. 2502
36: 9 **p** thy **trust** on Egypt for chariots and 982
37:29 therefore will I **p** my hook in thy nose, and 7760
42: 1 I have **p** my spirit upon him: 5414
43:26 **P** me **in remembrance**: let us plead 2142
47:11 upon thee; thou shalt not be able to **p** it **off**: 3722
50: 1 whom I have **p away**? 7971
50: 1 your transgressions *is* your mother **p away**. 7971
51: 9 Awake, awake, **p on** strength, O arm of 3847
51:16 I have **p** my words in thy mouth, and 7760
51:23 I will **p** it into the hand of them that afflict 7760

Isa 52: 1 Awake, awake; **p on** thy strength, O Zion; 3847
52: 1 **p on** thy beautiful garments, O Jerusalem, 3847
53:10 to bruise him; he hath **p** *him* **to grief**: 2470
54: 4 for thou shalt not be **p to shame**: 2659
59:17 For he **p on** righteousness as a breastplate, 3847
59:17 **p on** the garments of vengeance
for **clothing**, 3847+8516
59:21 and my words which I have **p** in thy mouth, 7760
63:11 where *is* he that **p** his holy Spirit within 7760
Jer 1: 9 the LORD **p forth** his hand, and 7971
1: 9 Behold, I have **p** my words in thy mouth. 5414
3: 1 If a man **p away** his wife, and she go from 7971
3: 8 committed adultery I had **p** her **away**, 7971
3:19 How shall I **p** thee among the children, and 7896
4: 1 if thou wilt **p away** thine abominations out 5493
7:21 **P** your burnt offerings unto your sacrifices, 5595
8:14 the LORD our God hath **p** us **to silence**, 1826
12:13 they have **p** themselves **to pain**, *but* 2470
13: 1 **p** it upon thy loins, and put it not in water. 7760
13: 1 put it upon thy loins, and **p** it not in water. 935
13: 2 word of the LORD, and **p** *it* on my loins. 7760
18:21 and let their men be **p to death**; 2026+4194
20: 2 **p** him in the stocks that *were* in the high 5414
26:15 ye for certain, that if ye **p** me **to death**, 4191
26:19 and all Judah **p** him **at all to death**? 4191+4191
26:21 the king sought to **p** him **to death**: 4191
26:24 the hand of the people to **p** him **to death**. 4191
27: 2 and yokes, and **p** them upon thy neck, 5414
27: 8 that will not **p** their neck under the yoke of 5414
28:14 I have **p** a yoke of iron upon the neck of all 5414
29:26 that thou shouldest **p** him in prison, and 5414
31:33 I will **p** my law in their inward parts, and 5414
32:14 **p** them in an earthen vessel, that they may 5414
32:40 I will **p** my fear in their hearts, that *they* 5414
37: 4 for they had not **p** him *into* prison. 5414
37:15 **p** him *in* prison *in* the house of Jonathan 5414
37:18 this people, that ye have **p** me in prison? 5414
38: 4 beseech thee, let this man be **p to death**: 4191
38: 7 heard that they had **p** Jeremiah in 5414
38:12 **P** now *these* old cast clouts and rotten rags 7760
38:15 wilt thou not **surely p** me **to death**? 4191+4191
38:16 us this soul, I will not **p** thee **to death**, 4191
38:25 from us, and we will not **p** thee **to death**; 4191
39: 7 Moreover he **p out** Zedekiah's eyes, and 5786
39:18 because thou hast **p** thy **trust** in me, saith 982
40:10 oil, and **p** *them* in your vessels, and 7760
43: 3 that *they* might **p** us **to death**, and carry us 4191
46: 4 the spears, *and* **p on** the brigandines. 3847
47: 6 **p up** thyself into thy scabbard, rest, and 622
50:14 **P** *yourselves* **in array** against Babylon 6186
50:42 *every one* **p in array**, like a man to 6186
52:11 he **p out** the eyes of Zedekiah; and the king 5786
52:11 and **p** him in prison till the day of his death. 5414
52:27 **p** them **to death** in Riblah in the land of 4191
Eze 3:25 they shall **p** bands upon thee, and shall bind 5414
4: 9 **p** them in one vessel, and make thee bread 5414
8: 3 he **p forth** the form of a hand, and took me 7971
8:17 and lo, they **p** the branch to their nose. 7971
10: 7 **p** *it* into the hands of *him that was* clothed 5414
11:19 and I will **p** a new spirit within you; 5414
14: 3 **p** the stumblingblock of their iniquity 5414
16:11 I **p** bracelets upon thine hands, and a chain 5414
16:12 I **p** a jewel on thy forehead, and earrings in 5414
16:14 which I had **p** upon thee, saith the Lord 7760
17: 2 **p forth a riddle**, and speak a parable 2330+2420
19: 9 they **p** him in ward in chains, and 5414
22:26 they have **p** no **difference** between the holy 914
23:42 which **p** bracelets upon their hands, and 5414
24:17 **p on** thy shoes upon thy feet, and cover not 7760
26:16 and **p off** their broidered garments: 6584
29: 4 I will **p** hooks in thy jaws, and I will cause 5414
30:13 and I will **p** a fear in the land of Egypt. 5414
30:21 to **p** a roller to bind it, to make it strong to 7760
30:24 of Babylon, and **p** my sword in his hand: 5414
30:25 when I shall **p** my sword into the hand of 5414
32: 7 when *I* shall **p** thee **out**, I will cover 3518
32:25 he is **p** in the midst of *them that be* slain. 5414
36:26 and a new spirit will I **p** within you: 5414
36:27 I will **p** my spirit within you, and cause you 5414
37: 6 and **p** breath in you, and ye shall live; 5414
37:14 shall **p** my spirit in you, and ye shall live, 5414
37:19 will **p** them with him, *even* with the stick of 5414
38: 4 **p** hooks into thy jaws, and I will bring thee 5414
42:14 shall **p on** other garments, and 3847
43: 9 **p away** their whoredom, and the carcases of
their kings, **far** 7368
43:20 **p** *it* on the four horns of it, and on the four 5414
44:19 they shall **p off** their garments wherein they 6584
44:19 and they shall **p on** other garments; 3847
44:22 wives a widow, nor her that is **p away**: 1644
45:19 **p** *it* upon the posts of the house, and 5414
Da 5:19 he set up; and whom he would he **p down**. 8214
5:29 *p* a chain of gold about his neck, and NIH
Hos 2: 2 **p away** her whoredoms out of her sight, 5493
Joel 3:13 **P** ye in the sickle, for the harvest is ripe: 7971
Am 6: 3 Ye that **p far away** the evil day, and 5077
Jnh 3: 5 and proclaimed a fast, and **p on** sackcloth, 3847
Mic 2:12 I will **p** them together as the sheep of 7760
7: 5 in a friend, **p** ye not **confidence** in a guide: 982
Na 3: 9 *was* infinite; P and Lubim were thy helpers. 6316
Zep 3:19 fame in every land where they have been **p** NIH
Hag 1: 6 he that earneth wages earneth wages *to* **p** *it* NIH
Mt 1:19 was minded to **p** her **away** privily. *630*
5:15 and **p** it under a bushel, but on a *5087*
5:31 been said, Whosoever shall **p away** his wife, *630*
5:32 That whosoever shall **p away** his wife, *630*
6:25 nor yet for your body, what ye shall **p on**. *1746*
8: 3 And Jesus **p forth** *his* hand, and *1614*
9:16 for that which is **p in to fill it up** taketh *4138*
9:17 Neither do *men* **p** new wine into old bottles: *906*
9:17 but they **p** new wine into new bottles, and *906*
9:25 But when the people were **p forth**, he went *1544*
10:21 and cause them to be **p to death**. *2289*
12:18 I will **p** my spirit upon him, and he shall *5087*
13:24 Another parable **p** he **forth** unto them, *3908*

Mt 13:31 Another parable **p** he **forth** unto them, *3908*
14: 3 and **p** *him* in prison for Herodias' sake, *5087*
14: 5 And when he would have **p** him **to death**, *615*
19: 3 Is it lawful for a man to **p away** his wife for *630*
19: 6 joined together, let not man **p asunder**. *5563*
19: 7 writing of divorcement, and to **p** her **away**? *630*
19: 8 hearts suffered you to **p away** your wives: *630*
19: 9 unto you, Whosoever shall **p away** his wife, *630*
19: 9 whoso marrieth her *which is* **p away** doth *630*
19:13 that he should **p** *his* hands on them, and *2007*
21: 7 and the colt, and **p** on them their clothes, *2007*
22:34 that he had **p** the Sadducees **to silence**, *5392*
25:27 to have **p** my money to the exchangers, *906*
26:52 **P up again** thy sword into his place: *654*
26:59 witness against Jesus, to **p** him **to death**; *2289*
27: 1 counsel against Jesus to **p** him **to death**: *2289*
27: 6 It is not lawful for to **p** them into *906*
27:28 stripped him, and **p on** him a scarlet robe. *4060*
27:29 they **p** *it* **upon** his head, and a reed in *2007*
27:31 and **p** his own raiment **on** him, and led him *1746*
27:48 and **p** *it* **on** a reed, and gave him to drink. *4060*
Mk 1:14 Now after that John was **p in prison**, Jesus *3860*
1:41 **p forth** *his* hand, and touched him, and *1614*
2:22 but new wine must be **p** into new bottles. *992*
4:21 Is a candle brought to be **p** under a bushel, *5087*
5:40 But when he had **p** *them* all **out**, he taketh *1544*
6: 9 shod with sandals; and not **p on** two coats. *1746*
7:32 they beseech him to **p** *his* hand upon him. *2007*
7:33 and **p** his fingers into his ears, and he spit, *906*
8:23 spit on his eyes, and **p** *his* hands **upon** him, *2007*
8:25 After that he **p** *his* hands again upon his *2007*
10: 2 Is it lawful for a man to **p away** *his* wife? *630*
10: 4 a bill of divorcement, and to **p** *her* **away**. *630*
10: 9 joined together, let not man **p asunder**. *5563*
10:11 Whosoever shall **p away** his wife, and *630*
10:12 And if a woman shall **p away** her husband, *630*
10:16 **p** *his* hands upon them, and blessed them. *5087*
13:12 and shall cause them to be **p to death**. *2289*
14: 1 might take him by craft, and **p** *him* **to death**. *615*
14:55 for witness against Jesus to **p** him **to death**; *2289*
15:17 a crown of thorns, and **p** *it* **about** his *head*, *4060*
15:20 and **p** his own clothes **on** him, and led him *1746*
15:36 and **p** *it* **on** a reed, and gave him to drink, *4060*
Lk 1:52 He hath **p down** the mighty from *their* *2507*
5:13 And he **p forth** *his* hand, and touched him, *1614*
5:38 But new wine **must be p** into new bottles; *992*
8:54 And he **p** *them* all out, and took her by *1544*
9:62 No *man* having **p** his hand **to** *1911*
12:22 neither for the body, what ye shall **p on**. *1746*
14: 7 And he **p forth** a parable to those which *3004*
15:22 Bring forth the best robe, and **p** *it* **on** him; *1746*
15:22 and put *it* on him; and **p** a ring on his hand, *1325*
16: 4 that, when I am **p out** of the stewardship, *3179*
16:18 whosoever marrieth her that is **p away** from *630*
18:33 they shall scourge *him*, and **p** him **to death**: *615*
21:16 of you shall they cause to be **p to death**. *2289*
23:32 malefactors, led with him to be **p to death**. *337*
Jn 5: 7 the water is troubled, to **p** me into the pool: *906*
9:15 He **p** clay upon mine eyes, and I washed, *2007*
9:22 he should be **p out of the synagogue**. *656*
11:53 took counsel together for to **p** him **to death**. *615*
12: 6 had the bag, and bare what was **p** *therein*. *906*
12:10 that they might **p** Lazarus also **to death**; *615*
12:42 lest they should be **p out of the synagogue**: *656*
13: 2 the devil having now **p** into the heart of *906*
16: 2 They shall **p** you out of the synagogues: *4160*
18:11 unto Peter, **P up** thy sword into the sheath: *906*
18:31 It is not lawful for us to **p** any *man* **to death**: *615*
19: 2 and **p** *it* **on** his head, and they put on him a *2007*
19: 2 his head, and they **p on** him a purple robe, *4016*
19:19 Pilate wrote a title, and **p** *it* on the cross. *5087*
19:29 and **p** *it* **upon** hyssop, and put *it* to his *4060*
19:29 put *it* upon hyssop, and **p** *it* to his mouth. *4374*
20:25 and **p** my finger into the print of the nails, *906*
Ac 1: 7 which the Father hath **p** in his own power. *5087*
4: 3 and **p** *them* in hold unto the next day: *5087*
5:18 and **p** them in the common prison. *5087*
5:25 the men whom ye **p** in prison are standing *5087*
5:34 commanded to **p** the apostles forth a little *4160*
7:33 Lord to him, **P off** *thy* shoes **from** thy feet: *3089*
9:40 But Peter **p** *them* all **forth**, *1544*
12: 4 he **p** *him* in prison, and delivered *him* to *5087*
12:19 commanded that *they* should be **p to death**. *520*
13:46 but seeing ye **p** it **from** *you*, and *683*
15: 9 And **p** no **difference** between us and them, *1252*
15:10 **p** a yoke **upon** the neck of *2007*
26:10 and when they were **p to death**, I gave my *337*
27: 6 sailing into Italy; and he **p** us therein. *1688*
Ro 13:12 and let us **p on** the armour of light. *1746*
13:14 But **p** ye **on** the Lord Jesus Christ, and *1746*
14:13 **p** a stumblingblock or an occasion to fall
in *his* brother's **way**. *5087*
1Co 5:13 Therefore **p away** from among yourselves *1808*
7:11 and let not the husband **p away** *his* wife. *863*
7:12 to dwell with him, let him not **p** her **away**. *863*
13:11 I became a man, I **p away** childish *things*. *2673*
15:24 when he shall have **p down** all rule and *2673*
15:25 till he hath **p** all enemies under his feet. *5087*
15:27 For he hath **p** all *things* under his feet. *5293*
15:27 all *things* are **p under** *him*, *it is* manifest *5293*
15:27 which did **p** all *things* **under** him. *5293*
15:28 unto him that **p** all *things* **under** him, *5293*
15:53 For this corruptible must **p on** incorruption, *1746*
15:53 and this mortal *must* **p on** immortality. *1746*
15:54 So when this corruptible shall have **p on** *1746*
15:54 this mortal shall have **p on** immortality, *1746*
2Co 3:13 not as Moses, *which* **p** a vail over his face, *5087*
8:16 which **p** the same earnest care into the heart *1325*
Gal 3:27 been baptized into Christ have **p on** Christ. *1746*
Eph 1:22 And hath **p** all *things* under his feet, and *5293*
4:22 That ye **p off** concerning the former *659*
4:24 And that *ye* **p on** the new man, which after *1746*
4:31 and evil speaking, be **p away** from you, *142*
6:11 **P on** the whole armour of God, that ye may *1746*
Col 3: 8 But now you also **p off** all *these;* anger, *659*

P

Col 3: 9 seeing that ye have **p off** the old man with *554*
3:10 And have **p on** the new *man,* which is *1746*
3:12 **P on** therefore, as the elect of God, holy *1746*
3:14 And above all these *things* **p** *on* charity, NIG
1Th 2: 4 of God to be **p in trust** with the gospel, *4100*
1Ti 1:19 which some having **p away**, concerning faith *683*
4: 6 If thou **p** the brethren **in remembrance** of *5294*
2Ti 1: 6 Wherefore I **p** thee **in remembrance** that *363*
2:14 Of these *things* **p** *them* **in remembrance**, *5279*
Tit 3: 1 **P** them **in mind** to be subject to *5279*
Phm 1:18 oweth *thee* ought, **p** that **on** mine **account**; *1677*
Heb 2: 5 he not **p in subjection** the world to come, *5293*
2: 8 Thou hast **p** all *things* **in subjection** under *5293*
2: 8 For in that *he* **p** all **in subjection under** *5293*
2: 8 he left nothing *that is* **not p under** him. *506*
2: 8 But now we see not yet all *things* **p under** *5293*
2:13 And again, I will **p** my **trust** in him. *3982*
6: 6 God afresh, and **p** *him* **to an open shame**. *3856*
8:10 I will **p** my laws into their mind, and *1325*
9:26 to **p away** sin by the sacrifice of himself. *115*
10:16 I will **p** my laws into their hearts, and *1325*
Jas 3: 3 Behold, we **p** bits in the horses' mouths, *906*
1Pe 2:15 that with well doing *ye* may **p to silence** *5392*
3:18 being **p to death** in the flesh, but *2289*
2Pe 1:12 **p** you always **in remembrance** of these *5279*
1:14 Knowing that shortly *I* must **p off** *this* my *595*
Jude 1: 5 I will therefore **p** you **in remembrance**, *5279*
Rev 2:24 I will **p** upon you none other burden. *906*
11: 9 shall not suffer their dead bodies to be **p** in *5087*
17:17 For God hath **p** in their hearts to fulfil his *1325*

PUTEOLI (1)
Ac 28:13 wind blew, and we came the next day to **P**: *4223*

PUTHITES See PUHITES

PUTIEL (1)
Ex 6:25 took him *one* of the daughters of **P** to wife; 6317

PUTRIFYING (1)
Isa 1: 6 in it; *but* wounds, and bruises, and **p** sores: 2961

PUTTEST (7) [PUT]
Nu 24:21 and thou **p** thy nest in a rock. 7760
Dt 12:18 thy God in all that thou **p** thine hands **unto**. 4916
15:10 and in all that thou **p** thine hand **unto**. 4916
2Ki 18:14 *that* which thou **p** on me will I bear. 5414
Job 13:27 Thou **p** my feet also in the stocks, and 7760
Ps 119:119 Thou **p away** all the wicked of the earth 7673
Hab 2:15 that **p** thy bottle to *him,* and makest *him* 5596

PUTTETH (30) [PUT]
Ex 30:33 or whosoever **p** *any* of it upon a stranger, 5414
Nu 22:38 the word that God **p** in my mouth, that shall 7760
Dt 25:11 **p forth** her hand, and taketh him by 7971
27:15 **p** *it* in *a* secret *place.* And all the people 7760
1Ki 20:11 *his harness* boast himself as he that **p** *it* **off**. 6605
Job 15:15 Behold, he **p** no **trust** in his saints; yea, 539
28: 9 He **p forth** his hand upon the rock; 7971
33:11 He **p** my feet in the stocks, he marketh all 7760
Ps 15: 5 *He that* **p** not **out** his money to usury, 5414
75: 7 he **p down** one, and setteth up another. 8213
Pr 28:25 he that **p** his **trust** in the LORD shall be 982
29:25 whoso **p** his **trust** in the LORD shall be 982
SS 2:13 The fig tree **p forth** her green figs, and 2590
Isa 57:13 he that **p** his **trust** in me shall possess 2620
Jer 43:12 of Egypt, as a shepherd **p on** his garment; 5844
La 3:29 He **p** his mouth in the dust; if so be there 5414
Eze 14: 4 **p** the stumblingblock of his iniquity before 7760
14: 7 **p** the stumblingblock of his iniquity before 7760
Mic 3: 5 he that **p** not into their mouths, they even 5414
Mt 9:16 No *man* **p** a piece of new cloth unto an old *1911*
24:32 and **p forth** leaves, ye know that summer *is* *1631*
Mk 2:22 And no *man* **p** new wine into old bottles: *906*
4:29 immediately he **p in** the sickle, because *649*
13:28 and **p forth** leaves, ye know that summer is *1631*
Lk 5:36 No *man* **p** a piece of a new garment upon *1911*
5:37 And no *man* **p** new wine into old bottles; *906*
8:16 it with a vessel, or **p** *it* under a bed; *5087*
11:33 **p** *it* in a secret place, neither under a *5087*
16:18 Whosoever **p away** his wife, and *630*
Jn 10: 4 And when he **p forth** his own sheep, he *1544*

PUTTING (17) [PUT]
Ge 21:14 **p** *it* on her shoulder, and the child, and 7760
Lev 16:21 **p** them upon the head of the goat, and 5414
Jdg 7: 6 **p** their hand to their mouth, were three NIH
Isa 58: 9 the **p forth** of the finger, and 7971
Mal 2:16 God of Israel, saith that he hateth **p away**: 7971
Ac 9:12 and **p** *his* hand **on** him, that he might *2007*
9:17 and **p** his hands **on** him said, *2007*
19:33 of the multitude, the Jews **p** him **forward**. *4261*
Ro 15:15 as **p** you **in mind**, because of the grace that *1878*
Eph 4:25 Wherefore **p away** lying, speak every man *659*
Col 2:11 in **p off** the body of the sins of the flesh, *555*
1Th 5: 8 **p on** the breastplate of faith and love; *1746*
1Ti 1:12 counted me faithful, **p** *me* into the ministry; *5087*
2Ti 1: 6 which is in thee by the **p on** of my hands. *1936*
1Pe 3: 3 of wearing of gold, or of **p on** of apparel; *1745*
3:21 us (not the **p away** of the filth of the flesh, *595*
2Pe 1:13 to stir you up by **p** *you* **in remembrance**; *5280*

PYGARG (1)
Dt 14: 5 the **p**, and the wild ox, and the chamois. 1788

Q

QUAILS (4)
Ex 16:13 that at even the **q** came up, and covered 7958
Nu 11:31 brought **q** from the sea, and let *them* fall by 7958
11:32 all the next day, and they gathered the **q**: 7958
Ps 105:40 he brought **q**, and satisfied them *with* 7958

QUAKE (4) [EARTHQUAKE, EARTHQUAKES, QUAKED, QUAKING]
Joel 2:10 The earth shall **q** before them; the heavens 7264
Na 1: 5 The mountains **q** at him, and the hills melt, 7493
Mt 27:51 and the earth did **q**, and the rocks rent; *4579*
Heb 12:21 *that* Moses said, I exceedingly fear and **q**;) *1790*

QUAKED (2) [QUAKE]
Ex 19:18 a furnace, and the whole mount **q** greatly. 2729
1Sa 14:15 they also trembled, and the earth **q**: 7264

QUAKING (2) [QUAKE]
Eze 12:18 eat thy bread with **q**, and drink thy water 7494
Da 10: 7 a great **q** fell upon them, so that they fled to 2731

QUANTITY (1)
Isa 22:24 and the issue, all vessels of **small q**, 6996

QUARREL (4)
Lev 26:25 shall **avenge the q** of *my* covenant: 5358+5359
2Ki 5: 7 and see how he **seeketh a q** against me. 579
Mk 6:19 Therefore Herodias **had a q against** him, *1758*
Col 3:13 if any *man* have a **q** against any: *3437*

QUARRIES (2)
Jdg 3:19 he himself turned again from the **q** that 6456
3:26 passed beyond the **q**, and escaped unto 6456

QUARTER (8) [QUARTERS]
Ge 19: 4 and young, all the people from **every q**: 7097
Nu 34: 3 your south **q** shall be from the wilderness 6285
Jos 15: 5 *their* border in the north **q** *was* 6285+3807.1
18:14 the children of Judah: this *was* the west **q**. 6285
18:15 the south **q** *was* from the end of 6285
Isa 47:15 they shall wander every one to his **q**; 5676
56:11 every one for his gain, from his **q**. 7097
Mk 1:45 and they came to him **from every q**. *3836*

QUARTERS (9) [QUARTER]
Ex 13: 7 there be leaven seen with thee in all thy **q**. 1366
Dt 22:12 thee fringes upon the four **q** of thy vesture, 3671
1Ch 9:24 In four **q** were the porters, toward the east, 7307
Jer 49:36 the four winds from the four **q** of heaven, 7098
Eze 38: 6 the house of Togarmah *of* the north **q**, and 3411
Ac 9:32 as Peter passed throughout all *q*, he came NIG
16: 3 because of the Jews which were in those **q**: *5117*
28: 7 In the same **q** were possessions of the chief *5117*
Rev 20: 8 nations which are in the four **q** of the earth, *1137*

QUARTUS (1)
Ro 16:23 of the city saluteth you, and **Q** a brother. *2890*

QUATERNIONS (1)
Ac 12: 4 delivered *him* to four **q** of soldiers to keep *5069*

QUEEN (54) [QUEENS]
1Ki 10: 1 when the **q** of Sheba heard of the fame of 4436
10: 4 when the **q** of Sheba had seen all 4436
10:10 the **q** of Sheba gave to king Solomon. 4436
10:13 king Solomon gave unto the **q** of Sheba all 4436
11:19 his own wife, the sister of Tahpenes the **q**. 1377
15:13 even her he removed from *being* **q**, because 1377
2Ki 10:13 of the king and the children of the **q**. 1377
2Ch 9: 1 when the **q** of Sheba heard of the fame of 4436
9: 3 when the **q** of Sheba had seen the wisdom 4436
9: 9 neither was there any such spice as the **q** of 4436
9:12 king Solomon gave to the **q** of Sheba all 4436
15:16 he removed her from *being* **q**, because 1377
Ne 2: 6 said unto me, (the **q** also sitting by him,) 7694
Est 1: 9 Also Vashti the **q** made a feast for 4436
1:11 To bring Vashti the **q** before the king with 4436
1:12 the **q** Vashti refused to come at the king's 4436
1:15 What shall *we* do unto the **q** Vashti 4436
1:16 Vashti the **q** hath not done wrong to 4436
1:17 For *this* deed of the **q** shall come abroad 4436
1:17 Vashti the **q** to be brought in before him, 4436
1:18 which have heard of the deed of the **q**. 4436
2: 4 let the maiden which pleaseth the king be **q** 4427
2:17 her head, and **made** her **q** instead of Vashti. 4427
2:22 to Mordecai, who told *it* unto Esther the **q**; 4436
4: 4 was the **q** exceedingly grieved; and she sent 4436
5: 2 when the king saw Esther the **q** standing in 4436
5: 3 king unto her, What wilt thou, **q** Esther? 4436
5:12 Esther the **q** did let no *man* come in with 4436
7: 1 Haman came to banquet with Esther the **q**. 4436
7: 2 of wine, What *is* thy petition, **q** Esther? 4436
7: 3 Esther the **q** answered and said, If I have 4436
7: 5 and said unto Esther the **q**, 4436
7: 6 was afraid before the king and the **q**. 4436
7: 7 to make request for his life to Esther the **q**; 4436
7: 8 Will he force the **q** also before me in 4436
8: 1 Haman the Jews' enemy unto Esther the **q**. 4436
8: 7 the king Ahasuerus said unto Esther the **q** 4436
9:12 the king said unto Esther the **q**, The Jews 4436
9:29 Esther the **q**, the daughter of Abihail, and 4436
9:31 and Esther the **q** had enjoined them, 4436
Ps 45: 9 right hand did stand the **q** in gold of Ophir. 7694

Jer 7:18 to make cakes to the **q** of heaven, and 4446
13:18 Say unto the king and to the **q**, 1377
29: 2 the **q**, and the eunuchs, the princes of Judah 1377
44:17 to burn incense unto the **q** of heaven, and 4446
44:18 since we left off to burn incense to the **q** of 4446
44:19 when we burnt incense to the **q** of heaven, 4446
44:25 to burn incense to the **q** of heaven, and 4446
Da 5:10 *Now* the **q**, by reason of the words of 4433
5:10 *and* the **q** spake and said, O king, live for 4433
Mt 12:42 *The* **q** of the south shall rise up in *938*
Lk 11:31 *The* **q** of the south shall rise up in *938*
Ac 8:27 authority under Candace **q** of the Ethiopians, *938*
Rev 18: 7 I sit a **q**, and am no widow, and shall see no *938*

QUEENS (3) [QUEEN]
SS 6: 8 There *are* threescore **q**, and 4436
6: 9 *yea,* the **q** and the concubines, and 4436
Isa 49:23 and their **q** thy nursing mothers: 8282

QUENCH (12) [QUENCHED, UNQUENCHABLE]
2Sa 14: 7 *so* they shall **q** my coal which is left, and 3518
21:17 to battle, that thou **q** not the light of Israel. 3518
Ps 104:11 of the field: the wild asses **q** their thirst. 7665
SS 8: 7 Many waters cannot **q** love, neither can 3518
Isa 1:31 both burn together, and none shall **q** *them.* 3518
42: 3 and the smoking flax shall he not **q**: 3518
Jer 4: 4 burn that none can **q** *it,* because of the evil 3518
21:12 burn that none can **q** *it,* because of the evil 3518
Am 5: 6 and *there be* none to **q** *it* in Beth-el. 3518
Mt 12:20 not break, and smoking flax shall he not **q**, *4570*
Eph 6:16 wherewith ye shall be able to **q** all the fiery *4570*
1Th 5:19 **Q** not the Spirit. *4570*

QUENCHED (17) [QUENCH]
Nu 11: 2 prayed unto the LORD, the fire was **q**. 8257
2Ki 22:17 against this place, and shall not be **q**. 3518
2Ch 34:25 out upon this place, and shall not be **q**. 3518
Ps 118:12 like bees; they are **q** as the fire of thorns: 1846
Isa 34:10 It shall not be **q** night nor day; the smoke 3518
43:17 not rise: they are extinct, they are **q** as tow. 3518
66:24 shall not die, neither shall their fire be **q**; 3518
Jer 7:20 and it shall burn, and shall not be **q**. 3518
17:27 palaces of Jerusalem, and it shall not be **q**. 3518
Eze 20:47 the flaming flame shall not be **q**, and 3518
20:48 LORD have kindled it: it shall not be **q**. 3518
Mk 9:43 into hell, into the fire that **never** shall **be q**: *762*
9:44 their worm dieth not, and the fire is not **q**. *4570*
9:45 into hell, into the fire that **never** shall **be q**: *762*
9:46 their worm dieth not, and the fire is not **q**. *4570*
9:48 their worm dieth not, and the fire is not **q**. *4570*
Heb 11:34 **Q** the violence of fire, escaped the edge of *4570*

QUESTION (14) [QUESTIONED, QUESTIONING, QUESTIONS]
Mt 22:35 asked *him a* **q**, tempting him, and saying, NIG
Mk 8:11 came forth, and began to **q with** him, *4802*
9:16 he asked the scribes, What **q** ye with them? *4802*
11:29 I will also ask of you one **q**, and *3056*
12:34 And no *man* after that durst ask him *any q*. NIG
Lk 20:40 And after that they durst not ask him any *q* NIG
Jn 3:25 Then there arose a **q** between *some* of *2214*
Ac 15: 2 unto the apostles and elders about this **q**. *2213*
18:15 But if it be a **q** of words and names, and *2213*
19:40 For we are in danger to be **called in q** for *1458*
23: 6 resurrection of the dead I am **called in q**. *2919*
24:21 the dead I am **called in q** by you this day. *2919*
1Co 10:25 *that* eat, **asking** no **q** for conscience sake: *350*
10:27 eat, **asking** no **q** for conscience sake. *350*

QUESTIONED (3) [QUESTION]
2Ch 31: 9 Hezekiah **q** with the priests and the Levites 1875
Mk 1:27 insomuch that *they* **q** among themselves, *4802*
Lk 23: 9 Then he **q** *with* him in many words; but *1905*

QUESTIONING (2) [QUESTION]
Mk 9:10 **q** *one* **with** *another* what the rising from *4802*
9:14 about them, and *the* scribes **q** with them. *4802*

QUESTIONS (14) [QUESTION]
1Ki 10: 1 she came to prove him with **hard q**. 2420
10: 3 Solomon told her all her **q**: there was not 1697
2Ch 9: 1 she came to prove Solomon with **hard q** at 2420
9: 2 Solomon told her all her **q**: and there was 1697
Mt 22:46 from that day forth ask him any moe *q*. NIG
Lk 2:46 both hearing them, and asking them *q*. NIG
Ac 23:29 Whom I perceived to be accused of **q** of *2213*
25:19 But had certain **q** against him of their own *2213*
25:20 because I doubted of such *manner of* **q**, *2214*
26: 3 customs and **q** which are among the Jews: *2213*
1Ti 1: 4 and endless genealogies, which minister **q**, *2214*
6: 4 but doting about **q** and strifes of words, *2214*
2Ti 2:23 But foolish and unlearned **q** avoid, *2214*
Tit 3: 9 But avoid foolish **q**, and genealogies, and *2214*

QUICK (10) [QUICKEN, QUICKENED, QUICKENETH, QUICKENING, QUICKLY, QUICKSANDS]
Lev 13:10 *there be* **q raw** flesh in the rising; 2416+4241
13:24 the **q** *flesh* that burneth have a white bright 4241
Nu 16:30 unto them, and they go down **q** into the pit; 2416
Ps 55:15 *and* let them go down **q** *into* hell: 2416
124: 3 they had swallowed us up **q**, when their 2416
Isa 11: 3 shall **make him of q understanding** in 7306
Ac 10:42 was ordained of God *to be* the Judge of **q** *2198*
2Ti 4: 1 who shall judge the **q** and the dead at his *2198*
Heb 4:12 For the word of God *is* **q**, and powerful, *2198*
1Pe 4: 5 account to him that is ready to judge the **q** *2198*

QUICKEN (13) [QUICK]
Ps 71:20 shalt **q** me again, and shalt bring me up 2421
80:18 **q** us, and we will call upon thy name. 2421
119:25 the dust: **q** thou me according to thy word. 2421
119:37 *and* **q** thou me in thy way. 2421

Ps 119:40 thy precepts: **q** me in thy righteousness. 2421
119:88 **Q** me after thy lovingkindness; so shall I 2421
119:107 **q** me, O LORD, according unto thy word. 2421
119:149 **q** me according to thy judgment. 2421
119:154 deliver me: **q** me according to thy word. 2421
119:156 **q** me according to thy judgments. 2421
119:159 **q** me, O LORD, according to thy 2421
143:11 **Q** me, O LORD, for thy name's sake: 2421
Ro 8:11 **q** your mortal bodies by his Spirit that *2227*

QUICKENED (7) [QUICK]
Ps 119:50 in my affliction: for thy word hath **q** me. 2421
119:93 thy precepts: for with them thou hast **q** me. 2421
1Co 15:36 *Thou* fool, *that* which thou sowest is not **q**, *2227*
Eph 2: 1 And you *hath he* **q**, who were dead in NIG
2: 5 hath **q** *us* **together with** Christ, (by grace *4806*
Col 2:13 of your flesh, hath he **q together** with him, *4806*
1Pe 3:18 put to death in the flesh, but **q** by the Spirit: *2227*

QUICKENETH (5) [QUICK]
Jn 5:21 and **q** *them;* even so the Son quickeneth *2227*
5:21 *them;* even so the Son **q** whom he will. *2227*
6:63 It is the spirit that **q**; the flesh profiteth *2227*
Ro 4:17 who **q** the dead, and calleth those *things* *2227*
1Ti 6:13 who **q** all *things,* and *before* Christ Jesus, *2227*

QUICKENING (1) [QUICK]
1Co 15:45 the last Adam *was made* a **q** spirit. *2227*

QUICKLY (39) [QUICK]
Ge 18: 6 **Make ready q** three measures of fine meal, 4116
27:20 How *is* it *that* thou hast found *it so* **q**, my 4116
Ex 32: 8 They have turned aside **q** out of the way 4118
Nu 16:46 go **q** unto the congregation, and make an 4120
Dt 9: 3 thou drive them out, and destroy them **q**, 4118
9:12 Arise, get thee down **q** from hence; 4118
9:12 **q** turned aside out of the way which I 4118
9:16 ye had turned aside **q** out of the way which 4118
11:17 *lest* ye perish **q** from off the good land 4120
28:20 thou be destroyed, and until thou perish **q**; 4118
Jos 2: 5 pursue after them **q**; for ye shall overtake 4118
8:19 the ambush arose **q** out of their place, and 4120
10: 6 come up to us **q**, and save us, and help us: 4120
23:16 ye shall perish **q** from off the good land 4120
Jdg 2:17 they turned **q** out of the way which their 4118
1Sa 20:19 *then* thou shalt go down **q**, and come to 3966
2Sa 17:16 Now therefore send **q**, and tell David, 4120
17:18 they went both of them away **q**, and 4120
17:21 Arise, and **pass q** over the water: 4120
2Ki 1:11 thus hath the king said, Come down **q**. 4120
2Ch 18: 8 and said, **Fetch q** Micaiah the son of Imla. 4116
Ecc 4:12 and a threefold cord is not **q** broken. 4120+871.1
Mt 5:25 Agree with thine adversary **q**, whiles thou *5036*
28: 7 And go **q**, and tell his disciples that he is *5036*
28: 8 And they departed **q** from the sepulchre *5036*
Mk 16: 8 And they went out **q**, and fled from *5036*
Lk 14:21 Go out **q** into the streets and lanes of *5030*
16: 6 thy bill, and sit down **q**, and write fifty. *5030*
Jn 11:29 As soon as she heard *that,* she arose **q**, and *5036*
13:27 said Jesus unto him, That thou doest, do **q**. *5030*
Ac 12: 7 raised him up, saying, Arise up **q**. *1722+5034*
22:18 and get *thee* **q** out of Jerusalem: *1722+5034*
Rev 2: 5 or else I *will* come unto thee **q**, and *5034*
2:16 or else I *will* come unto thee **q**, and *5036*
3:11 Behold, I come **q**: hold *that* fast which thou *5036*
11:14 is past; *and* behold, the third woe cometh **q**. *5036*
22: 7 Behold, I come **q**: blessed *is* he that *5036*
22:12 And behold, I come **q**; and my reward *is* *5036*
22:20 these *things* saith, Surely I come **q**. *5036*

QUICKSANDS (1) [QUICK, SAND]
Ac 27:17 and fearing lest they should fall into the **q**, *4950*

QUIET (31) [QUIETED, QUIETETH, QUIETLY, QUIETNESS]
Jdg 16: 2 were **q** all the night, saying, In the morning, 2790
18: 7 the manner of the Zidonians, **q** and secure; 8252
18:27 unto a people *that were* at **q** and secure: 8252
2Ki 11:20 of the land rejoiced, and the city was **in q**: 8252
1Ch 4:40 the land *was* wide, and **q**, and peaceable; 8252
2Ch 14: 1 In his days the land was **q** ten years. 8252
14: 5 and the kingdom was **q** before him. 8252
20:30 So the realm of Jehoshaphat was **q**: for his 8252
23:21 the city was **q**, after that they had slain 8252
Job 3:13 For now should I have lien *still* and been **q**, 8252
3:26 in safety, neither had I rest, neither was I **q**; 5117
21:23 full strength, *being* wholly at ease and **q**. 7961
Ps 35:20 matters against *them that are* **q** in the land. 7282
107:30 are they glad because they be **q**; so 8367
Pr 1:33 and shall be **q** from fear of evil. 7599
Ecc 9:17 The words of wise *men are* heard in **q**, 5183
Isa 7: 4 say unto him, Take heed, and be **q**; 8252
14: 7 The whole earth is at rest, *and* is **q**: 8252
32:18 in sure dwellings, and in **q** resting places; 7600
33:20 thine eyes shall see Jerusalem a **q** 7600
Jer 30:10 and be **q**, and none shall make *him* afraid. 7599
47: 6 how long *will it be* ere thou be **q**? 8252
47: 7 How can it be **q**, seeing the LORD hath 8252
49:23 *there is* sorrow on the sea; it cannot be **q**. 8252
51:59 his reign. And *this* Seraiah *was* a **q** prince. 4496
Eze 16:42 and I will be **q**, and will be no more angry. 8252
Na 1:12 Though *they be* **q**, and likewise many, 8003
Ac 19:36 ye ought to be **q**, and to do nothing rashly. *2687*
1Th 4:11 And that *ye* study to be **q**, and to do your *2270*
1Ti 2: 2 that we may lead a **q** and peaceable life in *2263*
1Pe 3: 4 *even the ornament* of a meek and **q** spirit, *2272*

QUIETED (2) [QUIET]
Ps 131: 2 Surely I have behaved and **q** myself, as a 1826
Zec 6: 8 have **q** my spirit in the north country. 5117

QUIETETH (1) [QUIET]
Job 37:17 when he **q** the earth by the south *wind?* 8252

QUIETLY (2) [QUIET]
2Sa 3:27 gate to speak with him **q**, 7987+871.1+1886.1
La 3:26 and **q wait** for the salvation of the LORD. 1748

QUIETNESS (10) [QUIET]
Jdg 8:28 the country was **in q** forty years in the days 8252
1Ch 22: 9 give peace and **q** unto Israel in his days. 8253
Job 20:20 Surely he shall not feel **q** in his belly, 7961
34:29 When he **giveth q**, who then can make 8252
Pr 17: 1 Better *is* a dry morsel, and **q** therewith, 7962
Ecc 4: 6 Better *is* a handful *with* **q**, than both 5183
Isa 30:15 in **q** and in confidence shall be your 8252
32:17 the effect of righteousness **q** and 8252
Ac 24: 2 Seeing that by thee we enjoy great **q**, and *1515*
2Th 3:12 that with **q** they work, and eat their own *2271*

QUIRINIUS See CYRENIUS

QUIT (6)
Ex 21:19 his staff, then shall he that smote *him* be **q**: 5352
21:28 be eaten; but the owner of the ox *shall be* **q**. 5355
Jos 2:20 we will be **q** of thine oath which thou hast 5355
1Sa 4: 9 Be strong, and **q** yourselves like men, O ye 1961
4: 9 to you: **q** yourselves like men, and fight. 1961
1Co 16:13 fast in the faith, **q** you **like men**, be strong. *407*

QUITE (7)
Ge 31:15 and hath **q devoured** also our money. 398+398
Ex 23:24 and **q break down** their images. 7665+7665
Nu 17:10 thou shalt **q take away** their murmurings 3615
33:52 and **q pluck down** all their high places: 8045
2Sa 3:24 sent him away, and he is **q gone**? 1980+1980
Job 6:13 in me? and is wisdom driven **q** from me? NIH
Hab 3: 9 Thy bow was **made q naked**, 5783+6181

QUIVER (7)
Ge 27: 3 thy **q** and thy bow, and go out to the field, 8522
Job 39:23 The **q** rattleth against him, the glittering 827
Ps 127: 5 Happy *is* the man that hath his **q** full of 827
Isa 22: 6 Elam bare the **q** with chariots of men *and* 827
49: 2 me a polished shaft; in his **q** hath he hid me; 827
Jer 5:16 Their **q** *is* as an open sepulchre, they *are* all 827
La 3:13 He hath caused the arrows of his **q** to enter 827

QUIVERED (1)
Hab 3:16 my belly trembled; my lips **q** at the voice: 6750

R

RAAMAH (5)
Ge 10: 7 Havilah, and Sabtah, and **R**, and Sabtecha: 7484
10: 7 and the sons of **R**; Sheba, and Dedan. 7484
1Ch 1: 9 Havilah, and Sabta, and **R**, and Sabtecha. 7484
1: 9 And the sons of **R**; Sheba, and Dedan. 7484
Eze 27:22 The merchants of Sheba and **R**, they *were* 7484

RAAMIAH (1)
Ne 7: 7 Azariah, **R**, Nahamani, Mordecai, Bilshan, 7485

RAAMSES (1) [RAMESES]
Ex 1:11 for Pharaoh treasure cities, Pithom and **R**. 7486

RABBAH (13) [RABBATH]
Jos 13:25 of Ammon, unto Aroer that *is* before **R**; 7237
15:60 which *is* Kirjath-jearim, and **R**; 7237
2Sa 11: 1 the children of Ammon, and besieged **R**. 7237
12:26 Joab fought against **R** of the children of 7237
12:27 I have fought against **R**, and have taken 7237
12:29 went to **R**, and fought against it, and 7237
17:27 that Shobi the son of Nahash of **R** of 7237
1Ch 20: 1 of Ammon, and came and besieged **R**. 7237
20: 1 And Joab smote **R**, and destroyed it. 7237
Jer 49: 2 of war to be heard in **R** of the Ammonites; 7237
49: 3 cry, ye daughters of **R**, gird ye with 7237
Eze 25: 5 I will make **R** a stable for camels, and 7237
Am 1:14 I will kindle a fire in the wall of **R**, and 7237

RABBATH (2) [RABBAH]
Dt 3:11 *is* it not in **R** of the children of Ammon? 7237
Eze 21:20 that the sword may come to **R** of 7237

RABBI (8) [RABBONI]
Mt 23: 7 and to be called of men, **R**, Rabbi. *4461*
23: 7 and to be called of men, Rabbi, **R**. *4461*
23: 8 But be not ye called **R**: for one is your *4461*
Jn 1:38 **R**, (which is to say, being interpreted, *4461*
1:49 Nathanael answered and saith unto him, **R**, *4461*
3: 2 to Jesus by night, and said unto him, **R**, *4461*
3:26 they came unto John, and said unto him, **R**, *4461*
6:25 they said unto him, **R**, when camest thou *4461*

RABBIT See HARE

RABBITH (1)
Jos 19:20 And **R**, and Kishion, and Abez, 7245

RABBONI (1) [RABBI]
Jn 20:16 She turned herself, and saith unto him, **R**; *4462*

RAB-MAG (2)
Jer 39: 3 Sarsechim, Rab-saris, Nergal-sharezer, **R**, 7248
39:13 **R**, and all the king of Babylon's princes; 7248

RABSARIS, RAB-SARIS (3) [RABSARIS]
2Ki 18:17 the king of Assyria sent Tartan and **R** and 7249
Jer 39: 3 Samgar-nebo, Sarsechim, **R**, 7249
39:13 **R**, and Nergal-sharezer, Rab-mag, and 7249

RABSHAKEH, RAB-SHAKEH (16) [RAB-SHAKEH]
2Ki 18:17 **R** from Lachish to king Hezekiah with a 7262
18:19 **R** said unto them, Speak ye now to 7262
18:26 Shebna, and Joah, unto **R**, Speak, I pray 7262
18:27 **R** said unto them, Hath my master sent me 7262
18:28 **R** stood and cried with a loud voice in 7262
18:37 clothes rent, and told him the words of **R**. 7262
19: 4 thy God will hear all the words of **R**, 7262
19: 8 So **R** returned, and found the king of 7262
Isa 36: 2 the king of Assyria sent **R** from Lachish to 7262
36: 4 **R** said unto them, Say ye now to Hezekiah, 7262
36:11 said Eliakim and Shebna and Joah unto **R**, 7262
36:12 **R** said, Hath my master sent me to thy 7262
36:13 **R** stood, and cried with a loud voice in 7262
36:22 clothes rent, and told him the words of **R**. 7262
37: 4 LORD thy God will hear the words of **R**, 7262
37: 8 So **R** returned, and found the king of 7262

RACA (1)
Mt 5:22 **R**, shall be in danger of the council: *4469*

RACAL See RACHAL

RACE (4)
Ps 19: 5 *and* rejoiceth as a strong *man* to run a **r**. 734
Ecc 9:11 under the sun, that the **r** *is* not to the swift, 4793
1Co 9:24 Know ye not that they which run in a **r** run *4712*
Heb 12: 1 let us run with patience the **r** that is set before *73*

RACHAB (1) [RAHAB]
Mt 1: 5 And Salmon begat Booz of **R**; and *4477*

RACHAL (1)
1Sa 30:29 to *them* which *were* in **R**, and to *them* 7403

RACHEL (42) [RACHEL'S, RAHEL]
Ge 29: 6 **R** his daughter cometh with the sheep. 7354
29: 9 with them, **R** came with her father's sheep: 7354
29:10 when Jacob saw **R** the daughter of Laban 7354
29:11 Jacob kissed **R**, and lifted up his voice, 7354
29:12 Jacob told **R** that he *was* her father's 7354
29:16 and the name of the younger *was* **R**. 7354
29:17 but **R** was beautiful and well favoured. 7354
29:18 Jacob loved **R**; and said, I will serve thee 7354
29:18 I will serve thee seven years for **R** thy 7354
29:20 Jacob served seven years for **R**; and 7354
29:25 did not I serve with thee for **R**? wherefore 7354
29:28 he gave him **R** his daughter to wife *also.* 7354
29:29 Laban gave to **R** his daughter Bilhah his 7354
29:30 he went in also unto **R**, and he loved also 7354
29:30 he loved also **R** more than Leah, and 7354
29:31 he opened her womb: but **R** *was* barren. 7354
30: 1 when **R** saw that she bare Jacob no 7354
30: 1 bare Jacob no *children,* **R** envied her sister; 7354
30: 2 Jacob's anger was kindled against **R**: and 7354
30: 6 **R** said, God hath judged me, and hath also 7354
30: 8 **R** said, With great wrestlings have I 7354
30:14 **R** said to Leah, Give me, I pray thee, of thy 7354
30:15 **R** said, Therefore he shall lie with thee to 7354
30:22 God remembered **R**, and God hearkened to 7354
30:25 it came to pass, when **R** had born Joseph, 7354
31: 4 Jacob sent and called **R** and Leah to 7354
31:14 **R** and Leah answered and said unto him, 7354
31:19 **R** had stolen the images that *were* her 7354
31:32 For Jacob knew not that **R** had stolen them. 7354
31:34 Now **R** had taken the images, and put them 7354
33: 1 and unto **R**, and unto the two handmaids. 7354
33: 2 and **R** and Joseph hindermost. 7354
33: 7 after came Joseph near and **R**, and 7354
35:16 and **R** travailed, and she had hard labour. 7354
35:19 **R** died, and was buried in the way to 7354
35:24 The sons of **R**; Joseph, and Benjamin: 7354
46:19 The sons of **R** Jacob's wife; Joseph, and 7354
46:22 These *are* the sons of **R**, which were born 7354
46:25 which Laban gave unto **R** his daughter, and 7354
48: 7 **R** died by me in the land of Canaan in 7354
Ru 4:11 woman that is come into thine house like **R** 7354
Mt 2:18 **R** weeping for her children, and would not *4478*

RACHEL'S (5) [RACHEL]
Ge 30: 7 Bilhah **R** maid conceived again, and 7354
31:33 out of Leah's tent, and entered into **R** tent. 7354
35:20 that *is* the pillar of **R** grave unto *this* day. 7354
35:25 the sons of Bilhah, **R** handmaid; Dan, and 7354
1Sa 10: 2 thou shalt find two men by **R** sepulchre in 7354

RADDAI (1)
1Ch 2:14 Nethaneel the fourth, **R** the fifth, 7288

RAFTERS (1)
SS 1:17 of our house *are* cedar, *and* our **r** of fir. 7351

RAGAU (1)
Lk 3:35 which was *the son* of **R**, which was *the son* *4466*

RAGE (18) [RAGED, RAGETH, RAGING]
2Ki 5:12 So he turned and went away in a **r**. 2534
19:27 and thy coming in, and thy **r** against me. 7264
19:28 Because thy **r** against me and thy tumult is 7264
2Ch 16:10 for *he was* in a **r** with him because of this 2197
28: 9 ye have slain them in a **r** *that* reacheth up 2197
Job 39:24 the ground with fierceness and **r**: 7267
40:11 Cast abroad the **r** of thy wrath: and 5678
Ps 2: 1 Why do the heathen **r**, and the people 7283
7: 6 because of the **r** of mine enemies: 5678
Pr 6:34 For jealousy *is* the **r** of a man: therefore 2534
29: 9 whether he **r** or laugh, *there is* no rest. 7264
Isa 37:28 and thy coming in, and thy **r** against me. 7264

Isa 37:29 Because thy r against me, and thy tumult, 7264
Jer 46: 9 r, ye chariots; and let the mighty men come 1984
Da 3:13 Nebuchadnezzar in his r and 7266
Hos 7:16 fall by the sword for the r of their tongue: 2195
Na 2: 4 The chariots shall r in the streets, they shall 1984
Ac 4:25 Why did the heathen r, and the people 5433

RAGED (1) [RAGE]
Ps 46: 6 The heathen r, the kingdoms were moved: 1993

RAGETH (1) [RAGE]
Pr 14:16 from evil: but the fool r, and is confident. 5674

RAGGED (1)
Isa 2:21 into the tops of the r rocks, for fear of 5553

RAGING (5) [RAGE]
Ps 89: 9 Thou rulest the r of the sea: when 1348
Pr 20: 1 Wine is a mocker, strong drink is r: and 1993
Jnh 1:15 into the sea: and the sea ceased from her r. 2197
Lk 8:24 rebuked the wind and the r of the water: 2830
Jude 1:13 R waves of the sea, foaming out their own 66

RAGS (4)
Pr 23:21 and drowsiness shall clothe a man with r. 7168
Isa 64: 6 and all our righteousnesses are as filthy r; 899
Jer 38:11 thence old cast clouts and old rotten r, 4418
38:12 rotten r under thine armholes under 4418

RAGUEL (1)
Nu 10:29 the son of R the Midianite, Moses' father in 7467

RAHAB (10) [RACHAB]
Jos 2: 1 harlot's house, named R, and lodged there. 7343
2: 3 the king of Jericho sent unto R, saying, 7343
6:17 only R the harlot shall live, she and all that 7343
6:23 brought out R, and her father, and 7343
6:25 Joshua saved R the harlot alive, and her 7343
Ps 87: 4 I will make mention of R and Babylon to 7294
89:10 Thou hast broken R in pieces, as one that is 7294
Isa 51: 9 Art thou not it that hath cut R, and 7294
Heb 11:31 By faith the harlot R perished not with 4460
Jas 2:25 Likewise also was not R the harlot justified 4460

RAHAM (1)
1Ch 2:44 Shema begat R, the father of Jorkoam: and 7357

RAHEL (1) [RACHEL]
Jer 31:15 R weeping for her children refused to be 7354

RAIDING See ROVERS

RAIL (1) [RAILED, RAILER, RAILING, RAILINGS]
2Ch 32:17 He wrote also letters to r on the LORD 2778

RAILED (3) [RAIL]
1Sa 25:14 to salute our master; and he r on them. 5860
Mk 15:29 And they that passed by r on him, 987
Lk 23:39 malefactors which were hanged r on him, 987

RAILER (1) [RAIL]
1Co 5:11 or a r, or a drunkard, or an extortioner; 3060

RAILING (4) [RAIL]
1Pe 3: 9 Not rendering evil for evil, or r for railing: 3059
3: 9 Not rendering evil for evil, or railing for r: 3059
2Pe 2:11 bring not r accusation against them before 989
Jude 1: 9 durst not bring against him a r accusation, 988

RAILINGS (1) [RAIL]
1Ti 6: 4 cometh envy, strife, r, evil surmisings, 988

RAIMENT (57)
Ge 24:53 of gold, and r, and gave them to Rebekah: 899
27:15 Rebekah took goodly r of her eldest son 899
27:27 he smelled the smell of his r, and 899
28:20 will give me bread to eat, and r to put on, 899
41:14 he shaved himself, and changed his r, and 8071
45:22 all of them he gave each man changes of r; 8071
45:22 pieces of silver, and five changes of r. 8071
Ex 3:22 jewels of silver, and jewels of gold, and r: 8071
12:35 jewels of silver, and jewels of gold, and r: 8071
21:10 her r, and her duty of marriage, shall he not 3682
22: 9 for r, or for any manner of lost thing, which 8008
22:26 If thou at all take thy neighbour's r to 8008
22:27 is his covering only, it is his r for his skin: 8071
Lev 11:32 be any vessel of wood, or r, or skin, or sack, 899
Nu 31:20 purify all your r, and all that is made of 899
Dt 8: 4 Thy r waxed not old upon thee, neither did 8071
10:18 the stranger, in giving him food and r. 8071
21:13 she shall put the r of her captivity from off 8071
22: 3 so shalt thou do with his r; and with all lost 8071
24:13 that he may sleep in his own r, and 8008
24:17 nor take a widow's r to pledge: 899
Jos 22: 8 and with iron, and with very much r: 8008
Jdg 3:16 he did gird it under his r upon his right 4055
8:26 purple r that was on the kings of Midian, 899
Ru 3: 3 put thy r upon thee, and get thee down to 8071
1Sa 28: 8 put on other r, and he went, and two men 899
2Ki 5: 5 pieces of gold, and ten changes of r. 899
7: 8 r, and went and hid it; and came again, and 899
2Ch 9:24 r, harness, and spices, horses, and mules, 8008
Est 4: 4 she sent r to clothe Mordecai, and to take 899
Job 27:16 silver as the dust, and prepare r as the clay; 4403
Ps 45:14 brought unto the king in r of needlework: 7553
Isa 14:19 and as the r of those that are slain, 3830
63: 3 my garments, and I will stain all my r. 4403
Eze 16:13 thy r was of fine linen, and silk, and 4403
Zec 3: 4 and I will clothe thee with change of r. 4254
Mt 3: 4 And the same John had his r of camel's 1742
6:25 life more than meat, and the body than r? 1742
6:28 And why take ye thought for r? 1742
11: 8 A man clothed in soft r? behold, they that 2440
Mt 17: 2 as the sun, and his r was white as the light. 2440
27:31 and put his own r on him, and led him 2440
28: 3 was like lightning, and his r white as snow: 1742
Mk 9: 3 And his r became shining, exceeding white 2440
Lk 7:25 A man clothed in soft r? Behold, 2440
9:29 and his r was white and glistering. 2441
10:30 which stripped him of his r, and 1562
12:23 than meat, and the body is more than r. 1742
23:34 And they parted his r, and cast lots. 2440
Jn 19:24 They parted my r among them, and for my 2440
Ac 18: 6 he shook his r, and said unto them, 2440
22:20 and kept the r of them that slew him. 2440
1Ti 6: 8 and r let us be therewith content. 4629
Jas 2: 2 and there come in also a poor man in vile r; 2066
Rev 3: 5 the same shall be clothed in white r; 2440
3:18 and white r, that thou mayest be clothed, 2440
4: 4 twenty elders sitting, clothed in white r; 2440

RAIN (102) [RAINBOW, RAINED, RAINY]
Ge 2: 5 for the LORD God had not caused it to r 4305
7: 4 I will cause it to r upon the earth forty days 4305
7:12 the r was upon the earth forty days and 1653
8: 2 and the r from heaven was restrained; 1653
Ex 9:18 I will cause it to r a very grievous hail, 4305
9:33 and the r was not poured upon the earth. 4306
9:34 when Pharaoh saw that the r and the hail 4306
16: 4 Behold, I will r bread from heaven for you; 4305
Lev 26: 4 I will give you r in due season, and the land 1653
Dt 11:11 and drinketh water of the r of heaven: 4306
11:14 That I will give you the r of your land in 4306
11:14 the first r and the latter rain, that thou 3138
11:14 the first rain and the latter r, that thou 4456
11:17 that there be no r, and that the land yield 4306
28:12 the heaven to give the r unto thy land in his 4306
28:24 The LORD shall make the r of thy land 4306
32: 2 My doctrine shall drop as the r, my speech 4306
32: 2 as the small r upon the tender herb, and 8164
1Sa 12:17 and he shall send thunder and r; 4306
12:18 the LORD sent thunder and r that day: 4306
2Sa 1:21 be no dew, neither let there be r upon you, 4306
23: 4 out of the earth by clear shining after r. 4306
1Ki 8:35 there is no r, because they have sinned 4306
8:36 give r upon thy land, which thou hast given 4306
17: 1 there shall not be dew nor r these years, but 4306
17: 7 because there had been no r in the land. 1653
17:14 until the day that the LORD sendeth r 1653
18: 1 unto Ahab; and I will send r upon the earth. 4306
18:41 for there is a sound of abundance of r. 1653
18:44 and get thee down, that the r stop thee not. 1653
18:45 and wind, and there was a great r. 1653
2Ki 3:17 shall not see wind, neither shall ye see r; 1653
2Ch 6:26 there is no r, because they have sinned 4306
6:27 send r upon thy land, which thou hast given 4306
7:13 If I shut up heaven that there be no r, or if I 4306
Ezr 10: 9 because of this matter, and for the great r. 1653
10:13 it is a time of much r, and we are not able 1653
Job 5:10 Who giveth r upon the earth, and 4306
20:23 and shall r it upon him while he is eating. 4305
28:26 When he made a decree for the r, and 4306
29:23 they waited for me as for the r; and 4306
29:23 opened their mouth wide as for the latter r. 4456
36:27 they pour down r according to the vapour 4306
37: 6 likewise to the small r, and to the great rain 1653
37: 6 small rain, and to the great r of his strength. 1653
38:26 To cause it to r on the earth, where no man 4305
38:28 Hath the r a father? or who hath begotten 4306
Ps 11: 6 Upon the wicked he shall r snares, fire and 4305
68: 9 Thou, O God, didst send a plentiful r, 1653
72: 6 He shall come down like r upon the mown 4306
84: 6 make it a well; the r also filleth the pools. 4175
105:32 He gave them hail for r, and flaming fire in 1653
135: 7 he maketh lightnings for the r; he bringeth 4306
147: 8 with clouds, who prepareth r for the earth, 4306
Pr 16:15 and his favour is as a cloud of the latter r. 4456
25:14 false gift is like clouds and wind without r. 1653
25:23 The north wind driveth away r: so doth an 1653
26: 1 as r in harvest, so honour is not seemly for 4306
28: 3 is like a sweeping r which leaveth no food. 4306
Ecc 11: 3 If the clouds be full of r, they empty 1653
12: 2 nor the clouds return after the r: 1653
SS 2:11 the winter is past, the r is over and gone; 1653
Isa 4: 6 and for a covert from storm and from r. 4306
5: 6 I will also command the clouds that they r 4305
5: 6 the clouds that they rain no r upon it. 4306
30:23 shall he give the r of thy seed, that thou 4306
44:14 planteth an ash, and the r doth nourish it. 1653
55:10 For as the r cometh down, and the snow 1653
Jer 3: 3 and there hath been no latter r; 4456
5:24 that giveth r, both the former and the latter, 1653
10:13 he maketh lightnings with r, and 4306
14: 4 for there was no r in the earth, 1653
14:22 vanities of the Gentiles that can cause r? 1652
51:16 he maketh lightnings with r, and 4306
Eze 1:28 the bow that is in the cloud in the day of r, 1653
38:22 I will r upon him, and upon his bands, and 4305
38:22 an overflowing r, and great hailstones, fire, 1653
Hos 6: 3 he shall come unto us as the r, as the latter 1653
6: 3 as the latter and former r unto the earth. 3384
10:12 till he come and r righteousness upon you. 3384
Joel 2:23 for he hath given you the former r 4175
2:23 he will cause to come down for you the r, 1653
2:23 the former r, and the latter rain in the first 4175
2:23 and the latter r in the first month. 4456
Am 4: 7 also I have withholden the r from you, 1653
4: 7 I caused it to r upon one city, and caused it 4305
4: 7 and caused it not to r upon another city: 4305
Zec 10: 1 Ask ye of the LORD r in the time of 4306
10: 1 the LORD rain in the time of the latter r; 4456
10: 1 give them showers of r, to every one grass 1653
14:17 of hosts, even upon them shall be no r. 1653
14:18 that have no r; there shall be the plague, NIH
Mt 5:45 and sendeth r on the just and on the unjust. 1026
7:25 And the r descended, and the floods came, 1028
7:27 And the r descended, and the floods came, 1028
Ac 14:17 and gave us r from heaven, and 5205
Ac 28: 2 because of the present r, and because of 5205
Heb 6: 7 For the earth which drinketh in the r that 5205
Jas 5: 7 for it, until he receive the early and latter r. 5205
5:17 and he prayed earnestly that it might not r: 1026
5:18 and the heaven gave r, and the earth 5205
Rev 11: 6 it r not in the days of their prophecy: 1026+5205

RAINBOW (2) [BOW, RAIN]
Rev 4: 3 and there was a r round about the throne, 2463
10: 1 and a r was upon his head, and his face was 2463

RAINED (9) [RAIN]
Ge 19:24 the LORD r upon Sodom and 4305
Ex 9:23 the LORD r hail upon the land of Egypt. 4305
Ps 78:24 had r down manna upon them to eat, and 4305
78:27 He r flesh also upon them as dust, and 4305
Eze 22:24 nor r upon in the day of indignation. 1656
Am 4: 7 one piece was r upon, and the piece 4305
4: 7 and the piece whereupon it r not withered. 4305
Lk 17:29 day that Lot went out of Sodom it r fire 1026
Jas 5:17 it r not on the earth by the space of three 1026

RAINY (1) [RAIN]
Pr 27:15 A continual dropping in a very r day and 5464

RAISE (59) [RAISED, RAISER, RAISETH, RAISING]
Ge 38: 8 and marry her, and r up seed to thy brother. 6965
Ex 23: 1 Thou shalt not r a false report: put not thine 5375
Dt 18:15 The LORD thy God will r up unto thee a 6965
18:18 I will r them up a Prophet from among 6965
25: 7 My husband's brother refuseth to r up unto 6965
Jos 8:29 r thereon a great heap of stones, 6965
Ru 4: 5 to r up the name of the dead upon his 6965
4:10 to r up the name of the dead upon his 6965
1Sa 2:35 I will r me up a faithful priest, that shall do 6965
2Sa 12:11 I will r up evil against thee out of thine 6965
12:17 went to him, to r him up from the earth: 6965
1Ki 14:14 Moreover the LORD shall r him up a 6965
1Ch 17:11 that I will r up thy seed after thee, 6965
Job 3: 8 who are ready to r up their mourning. 5782
19:12 r up their way against me, and 5549
30:12 they r up against me the ways of their 5549
Ps 41:10 be merciful unto me, and r me up, 6965
Isa 15: 5 for in the way of Horonaim they shall r up 5782
29: 3 a mount, and I will r forts against thee. 6965
44:26 and I will r up the decayed places thereof: 6965
49: 6 be my servant to r up the tribes of Jacob, 6965
58:12 thou shalt r up the foundations of many 6965
61: 4 they shall r up the former desolations, and 6965
Jer 23: 5 that I will r unto David a righteous Branch, 6965
30: 9 their king, whom I will r up unto them. 6965
50: 9 I will r and cause to come up against 5782
50:32 and fall, and none shall r him up: 6965
51: 1 I will r up against Babylon, and 5782
Eze 23:22 Behold, I will r up thy lovers against thee, 5782
34:29 I will r up for them a plant of renown, and 6965
Hos 6: 2 in the third day he will r us up, and 6965
Joel 3: 7 I will r them out of the place whither ye 5782
Am 5: 2 upon her land; there is none to r her up. 6965
6:14 I will r up against you a nation, 6965
9:11 In that day will I r up the tabernacle of 6965
9:11 I will r up his ruins, and I will build it as in 6965
Mic 5: 5 shall we r up against him seven shepherds, 6965
Hab 1: 3 there are that r up strife and contention. 5375
1: 6 For lo, I r up the Chaldeans, that bitter and 6965
Zec 11:16 For lo, I will r up a shepherd in the land, 6965
Mt 3: 9 that God is able of these stones to r up 1453
10: 8 the lepers, r the dead, cast out devils: 1453
22:24 his wife, and r up seed unto his brother. 450
Mk 12:19 his wife, and r up seed unto his brother. 1817
Lk 3: 8 That God is able of these stones to r up 1453
20:28 his wife, and r up seed unto his brother. 1817
Jn 2:19 this temple, and in three days I will r it up. 1453
6:39 but should r it up again at the last day. 450
6:40 and I will r him up at the last day. 450
6:44 draw him: and I will r him up at the last day. 450
6:54 and I will r him up at the last day. 450
Ac 2:30 he would r up Christ to sit on his throne; 450
3:22 A prophet shall the Lord your God r up unto 450
7:37 A prophet shall the Lord your God r up unto 450
26: 8 with you, that God should r the dead? 1453
1Co 6:14 and will also r up us by his own power. 1825
2Co 4:14 the Lord Jesus shall r up us also by Jesus, 1453
Heb 11:19 Accounting that God was able to r him up, 1453
Jas 5:15 save the sick, and the Lord shall r him up; 1453

RAISED (85) [RAISE]
Ex 9:16 in very deed for this cause have I r thee up, 5975
Jos 5: 7 their children, whom he r up in their stead, 6965
7:26 they r over him a great heap of stones unto 6965
Jdg 2:16 Nevertheless the LORD r up judges, 6965
2:18 when the LORD r them up judges, then 6965
3: 9 the LORD r up a deliverer to the children 6965
3:15 the LORD r them up a deliverer, Ehud 6965
2Sa 23: 1 and the man who was r up on high, 6965
1Ki 5:13 And king Solomon r a levy out of all Israel; 5927
9:15 reason of the levy which king Solomon r; 5927
2Ch 32: 5 r it up to the towers, and another wall 5927
33:14 r it up a very great height, and 1361
Ezr 1: 5 with all them whose spirit God had r, 5782
Job 14:12 shall not awake, nor be r out of their sleep. 5782
SS 8: 5 I r thee up under the apple tree: there thy 5782
Isa 14: 9 it hath r up from their thrones all the kings 6965
23:13 they r up the palaces thereof; 6209
41: 2 Who r up the righteous man from the east, 5782
41:25 I have r up one from the north, and he shall 5782
45:13 I have r him up in righteousness, and I will 5782
Jer 6:22 a great nation shall be r from the sides of 5782
25:32 a great whirlwind shall be r up from 5782
29:15 The LORD hath r us up prophets in 6965
50:41 many kings shall be r up from the coasts of 5782
51:11 the LORD hath r up the spirit of the kings 5782
Da 7: 5 it r up itself on one side, and it had three 6966
Am 2:11 I r up of your sons for prophets, and 6965

Zec 2:13 for he is **r up** out of his holy habitation. 5782
9:13 and **r up** thy sons, O Zion, against thy sons, 5782
Mt 1:24 Then Joseph being **r** from sleep did as *1326*
11: 5 the dead are **r up**, and the poor have *1453*
16:21 and be killed, and be **r** *again* the third day. *1453*
17:23 the third day he shall be **r** *again*. And they *1453*
Lk 1:69 And hath **r up** a horn of salvation for us in *1453*
7:22 are cleansed, the deaf hear, the dead are **r**, *1453*
9:22 scribes, and be slain, and be **r** the third day. *1453*
20:37 Now that the dead are **r**, even Moses *1453*
Jn 12: 1 had been dead, whom he **r** from the dead. *1453*
12: 9 whom he had **r** from the dead. *1453*
12:17 and **r** him from the dead, bare record. *1453*
Ac 2:24 Whom God hath **r up**, having loosed *450*
2:32 This Jesus hath God **r up**, whereof we all are *450*
3:15 of life, whom God hath **r** from the dead; *1453*
3:26 you first God, having **r up** his Son Jesus, *450*
4:10 ye crucified, whom God **r** from the dead, *1453*
5:30 The God of our fathers **r up** Jesus, *1453*
10:40 Him God **r up** the third day, and *1453*
12: 7 and **r** him **up**, saying, Arise up quickly. *1453*
13:22 he **r up** unto them David to be their king; *1453*
13:23 to *his* promise **r** unto Israel a Saviour, *1453*
13:30 But God **r** him from the dead: *1453*
13:33 in that he hath **r up** Jesus **again**; *450*
13:34 And as concerning that he **r** him **up** from *450*
13:37 whom God **r** *again*, saw no corruption. *1453*
13:50 and **r** persecution against Paul and *1892*
17:31 all *men*, in that he hath **r** him from the dead. *450*
Ro 4:24 if we believe on him that **r up** Jesus our *1453*
4:25 and was **r** *again* for our justification. *1453*
6: 4 that like as Christ was **r up** from the dead *1453*
6: 9 Knowing that Christ being **r** from the dead *1453*
7: 4 *even* to him who is **r** from the dead, *1453*
8:11 But if the Spirit of him that **r up** Jesus from *1453*
8:11 he that **r up** Christ from the dead shall also *1453*
9:17 for this same *purpose* have I **r** thee **up**, *1825*
10: 9 shalt believe in thine heart that God hath **r** *1453*
1Co 6:14 And God hath both **r up** the Lord, and *1453*
15:15 we have testified of God that he **r up** *1453*
15:15 whom he **r** not **up**, if so be that the dead *1453*
15:16 For if the dead rise not, then is not Christ **r**: *1453*
15:17 And if Christ be not **r**, your faith *is* vain; *1453*
15:35 some *man* will say, How are the dead **r up**? *1453*
15:42 sown in corruption; it is **r** in incorruption: *1453*
15:43 It is sown in dishonour; it is **r** in glory: it is *1453*
15:43 it is sown in weakness; it is **r** in power: *1453*
15:44 sown a natural body; it is **r** a spiritual body. *1453*
15:52 and the dead shall be **r** incorruptible, and *1453*
2Co 4:14 Knowing that he which **r up** the Lord Jesus *1453*
Gal 1: 1 God the Father, who **r** him from the dead;) *1453*
Eph 1:20 when he **r** him from the dead, and set *him* *1453*
2: 6 And hath **r** *us* **up together**, and made *us* sit *4891*
Col 2:12 of God, who hath **r** him from the dead. *1453*
1Th 1:10 whom he **r** from the dead, *even* Jesus, *1453*
2Ti 2: 8 **r** from the dead according to my gospel: *1453*
Heb 11:35 received their dead **r to life again**: *386+1537*
1Pe 1:21 that **r** him **up** from the dead, and gave him *1453*

RAISER (1) [RAISE]

Da 11:20 shall stand up in his estate a **r** of taxes *in* 5674

RAISETH (8) [RAISE]

1Sa 2: 8 He **r up** the poor out of the dust, *and* 6965
Job 41:25 When he **r up** *himself*, the mighty are 7613
Ps 107:25 he commandeth, and **r** the stormy wind, 5975
113: 7 He **r up** the poor out of the dust, *and* 6965
145:14 and **r up** all those that be bowed down. 2210
146: 8 the LORD **r** them that are bowed down: 2210
Jn 5:21 For as the Father **r up** the dead, and *1453*
2Co 1: 9 in ourselves, but in God which **r** the dead: *1453*

RAISING (2) [RAISE]

Hos 7: 4 *who* ceaseth from **r** after *he* hath kneaded 5782
Ac 24:12 any *man*, neither **r up** the people, *1999+4160*

RAISINS (4)

1Sa 25:18 parched *corn*, and an hundred **clusters of r**, 6778
30:12 of a cake *of figs*, and two **clusters of r**: 6778
2Sa 16: 1 an hundred **bunches of r**, and an hundred 6778
1Ch 12:40 cakes *of figs*, and **bunches of r**, and wine, 6778

RAKEM (1)

1Ch 7:16 and his sons *were* Ulam and **R**. 7552

RAKKATH (1)

Jos 19:35 Zer, and Hammath, **R**, and Chinnereth, 7557

RAKKON (1)

Jos 19:46 Me-jarkon, and **R**, with the border before 7542

RAM (97) [RAM'S, RAMS, RAMS']

Ge 15: 9 and a **r** of three years old, and a turtle-dove, 352
22:13 behold behind *him* a **r** caught in a thicket by 352
22:13 Abraham went and took the **r**, and 352
Ex 29:15 Thou shalt also take one **r**; and Aaron and 352
29:15 shall put their hands upon the head of the **r**. 352
29:16 thou shalt slay the **r**, and thou shalt take his 352
29:17 thou shalt cut the **r** in pieces, and wash 352
29:18 thou shalt burn the whole **r** upon the altar: 352
29:19 thou shalt take the other **r**; and Aaron and 352
29:19 shall put their hands upon the head of the **r**. 352
29:20 shalt thou kill the **r**, and take of his blood, 352
29:22 Also thou shalt take of the **r** the fat and 352
29:22 right shoulder; for it *is* a **r** of consecration: 352
29:26 thou shalt take the breast of the **r** of Aaron's 352
29:27 is heaved up, of the **r** of the consecration, 352
29:31 And thou shalt take the **r** of the consecration, 352
29:32 and his sons shall eat the flesh of the **r**, 352
Lev 5:15 a **r** without blemish out of the flocks, 352
5:16 for him with the **r** of the trespass offering, 352
5:18 he shall bring a **r** without blemish out of 352
6: 6 a **r** without blemish out of the flock, with thy 352
8:18 he brought the **r** for the burnt offering: and 352
Lev 8:18 sons laid their hands upon the head of the **r**. 352
8:20 he cut the **r** into pieces; and Moses burnt 352
8:21 and Moses burnt the whole **r** upon the altar: 352
8:22 he brought the other **r**, the ram of 352
8:22 brought the other ram, the **r** of consecration: 352
8:22 sons laid their hands upon the head of the **r**. 352
8:29 *for* of the **r** of consecration it was Moses' 352
9: 2 and a **r** for a burnt offering, without blemish, 352
9: 4 Also a bullock and a **r** for peace offerings, 352
9:18 and the **r** *for* a sacrifice of peace offerings, 352
9:19 the fat of the bullock and of the **r**, the rump, 352
16: 3 a sin offering, and a **r** for a burnt offering. 352
16: 5 a sin offering, and one **r** for a burnt offering. 352
19:21 *even* a **r** for a trespass offering. 352
19:22 **r** of the trespass offering before the LORD 352
Nu 5: 8 beside the **r** of the atonement, whereby an 352
6:14 one **r** without blemish for peace offerings, 352
6:17 he shall offer the **r** *for* a sacrifice of peace 352
6:19 priest shall take the sodden shoulder of the **r**, 352
7:15 One young bullock, one **r**, one lamb of 352
7:21 One young bullock, one **r**, one lamb of 352
7:27 One young bullock, one **r**, one lamb of 352
7:33 One young bullock, one **r**, one lamb of 352
7:39 One young bullock, one **r**, one lamb of 352
7:45 One young bullock, one **r**, one lamb of 352
7:51 One young bullock, one **r**, one lamb of 352
7:57 One young bullock, one **r**, one lamb of 352
7:63 One young bullock, one **r**, one lamb of 352
7:69 One young bullock, one **r**, one lamb of 352
7:75 One young bullock, one **r**, one lamb of 352
7:81 One young bullock, one **r**, one lamb of 352
15: 6 Or for a **r**, thou shalt prepare *for* a meat 352
15:11 or for one **r**, or for a lamb, or a kid. 352
23: 2 offered on *every* altar a bullock and a **r**. 352
23: 4 offered upon *every* altar a bullock and a **r**. 352
23:14 and offered a bullock and a **r** on *every* altar. 352
23:30 and offered a bullock and a **r** on *every* altar. 352
28:11 two young bullocks, and one **r**, seven lambs 352
28:12 a meat offering, mingled with oil, for one **r**; 352
28:14 the third *part* of a hin unto a **r**, and a fourth 352
28:19 and one **r**, and seven lambs of the first year: 352
28:20 for a bullock, and two tenth deals for a **r**; 352
28:27 two young bullocks, one **r**, seven lambs of 352
28:28 unto one bullock, two tenth deals unto one **r**, 352
29: 2 one **r**, *and* seven lambs of the first year 352
29: 3 for a bullock, *and* two tenth deals for a **r**, 352
29: 8 one **r**, *and* seven lambs of the first year; 352
29: 9 to a bullock, *and* two tenth deals to one **r**, 352
29:14 two tenth deals to each **r** of the two rams, 352
29:36 one bullock, one **r**, seven lambs of the first 352
29:37 for the **r**, and for the lambs, *shall be* 352
Ru 4:19 Hezron begat **R**, and Ram begat 7410
4:19 begat Ram, and **R** begat Amminadab, 7410
1Ch 2: 9 unto him; Jerahmeel, and **R**, and Chelubai. 7410
2:10 **R** begat Amminadab; and 7410
2:25 **R** the firstborn, and Bunah, and Oren, and 7410
2:27 the sons of **R** the firstborn of Jerahmeel 7410
Ezr 10:19 *they offered* a **r** of the flock for their 352
Job 32: 2 of Barachel the Buzite, of the kindred of **R**: 7410
Eze 43:23 and a **r** out of the flock without blemish. 352
43:25 and a **r** out of the flock, without blemish. 352
45:24 an ephah for a **r**, and a hin of oil for an 352
46: 4 without blemish, and a **r** without blemish. 352
46: 5 the meat offering *shall be* an ephah for a **r**, 352
46: 6 without blemish, and six lambs, and a **r**: 352
46: 7 an ephah for a **r**, and for the lambs according 352
46:11 an ephah to a **r**, and to the lambs as he is 352
Da 8: 3 there stood before the river a **r** which had 352
8: 4 I saw the **r** pushing westward, 352
8: 6 he came to the **r** that had two horns, which I 352
8: 7 I saw him come close unto the **r**, and he was 352
8: 7 and smote the **r**, and brake his two horns: 352
8: 7 there was no power in the **r** to stand before 352
8: 7 there was none that could deliver the **r** out of 352
8:20 The **r** which thou sawest having two horns 352

RAM'S (1) [RAM]

Jos 6: 5 *that* when *they* make a long blast with the **r** 3104

RAMA (1) [RAMAH]

Mt 2:18 In **R** was there a voice heard, lamentation, *4471*

RAMAH (36) [RAMA, RAMATHITE]

Jos 18:25 Gibeon, and **R**, and Beeroth, 7414
19:29 *then* the coast turneth *to* **R**, and to 7414
19:36 And Adamah, and **R**, and Hazor, 7414
Jdg 4: 5 under the palm tree of Deborah between **R** 7414
19:13 places to lodge all night, in Gibeah, or in **R**. 7414
1Sa 1:19 and returned, and came to their house to **R**: 7414
2:11 Elkanah went to **R** to his house. And 7414
7:17 his return *was* to **R**; for there *was* his 7414
8: 4 and came to Samuel unto **R**, 7414
15:34 Samuel went to **R**; and Saul went up to his 7414
16:13 So Samuel rose up, and went to **R**. 7414
19:18 came to Samuel to **R**, and told him all that 7414
19:19 Behold, David *is* at Naioth in **R**. 7414
19:22 went he also to **R**, and came to a great well 7414
19:22 *one* said, Behold, *they be* at Naioth in **R**. 7414
19:23 he went thither to Naioth in **R**: and 7414
19:23 prophesied, until he came to Naioth in **R**. 7414
20: 1 David fled from Naioth in **R**, and came 7414
22: 6 Saul abode in Gibeah under a tree in **R**, 7414
25: 1 and buried him in his house at **R**. 7414
28: 3 and buried him in **R**, even in his own city. 7414
1Ki 15:17 built **R**, that *he* might not suffer *any* to go 7414
15:21 heard *thereof*, that he left off building of **R**, 7414
15:22 they took away the stones of **R**, and 7414
2Ki 8:29 which the Syrians had given him at **R**, 7414
2Ch 16: 1 built **R**, to the intent that *he* might let none 7414
16: 5 heard *it*, that he left off building of **R**, 7414
16: 6 they carried away the stones of **R**, and 7414
22: 6 of the wounds which were given him at **R**, 7414
Ezr 2:26 The children of **R** and Gaba, six hundred 7414
Ne 7:30 The men of **R** and Geba, six hundred 7414
Ne 11:33 Hazor, **R**, Gittaim, 7414
Isa 10:29 at Geba; **R** is afraid; Gibeah of Saul is fled. 7414
Jer 31:15 A voice was heard in **R**, lamentation, *and* 7414
40: 1 captain of the guard had let him go from **R**, 7414
Hos 5: 8 the cornet in Gibeah, *and* the trumpet in **R**: 7414

RAMATH (1)

Jos 19: 8 these cities to Baalath-beer, **R** of the south. 7414

RAMATH MIZPAH See RAMATH-MIZPEH

RAMATHAIM See RAMATHAIM-ZOPHIM

RAMATHAIM-ZOPHIM (1) [ZOPHIM]

1Sa 1: 1 Now there was a certain man of **R**, 7436

RAMATHITE (1) [RAMAH]

1Ch 27:27 over the vineyards *was* Shimei the **R**: over 7435

RAMATH-LEHI (1) [LEHI]

Jdg 15:17 out of his hand, and called that place **R**. 7437

RAMATH-MIZPEH (1) [MIZPEH]

Jos 13:26 from Heshbon unto **R**, and Betonim; and 7434

RAMESES (4) [RAAMSES]

Ge 47:11 in the best of the land, in the land of **R**, 7486
Ex 12:37 the children of Israel journeyed from **R** to 7486
Nu 33: 3 they departed from **R** in the first month, 7486
33: 5 the children of Israel removed from **R**, and 7486

RAMIAH (1)

Ezr 10:25 **R**, and Jeziah, and Malchiah, and Miamin, 7422

RAMOTH (8) [RAMOTH-GILEAD]

Dt 4:43 **R** in Gilead, of the Gadites; and Golan in 7216
Jos 20: 8 **R** in Gilead out of the tribe of Gad, and 7216
21:38 tribe of Gad, **R** in Gilead with her suburbs, 7433
1Sa 30:27 to *them* which *were* in south **R**, and to *them* 7418
1Ki 22: 3 Know ye that **R** in Gilead *is* ours, and 7433
1Ch 6:73 **R** with her suburbs, and Anem with her 7216
6:80 **R** in Gilead with her suburbs, and 7216
Ezr 10:29 and Adaiah, Jashub, and Sheal, and **R**. 7433

RAMOTH-GILEAD (19) [GILEAD, RAMOTH]

1Ki 4:13 The son of Geber, in **R**; to him *pertained* 1568
22: 4 Wilt thou go with me to battle *to* **R**? 7433
22: 6 Shall I go against **R** to battle, or shall I 7433
22:12 saying, Go up *to* **R**, and prosper: 7433
22:15 shall we go against **R** to battle, or shall we 7433
22:20 that he may go up and fall at **R**? 7433
22:29 the king of Judah went up *to* **R**. 7433
2Ki 8:28 the war against Hazael king of Syria in **R**; 7433
9: 1 this box of oil in thine hand, and go to **R**: 7433
9: 4 *even* the young man the prophet, went *to* **R**. 7433
9:14 (Now Joram had kept **R**, he and all Israel, 7433
2Ch 18: 2 and persuaded him to go up *with him* to **R**. 7433
18: 3 king of Judah, Wilt thou go with me *to* **R**? 7433
18: 5 Shall we go to **R** to battle, or shall I 7433
18:11 saying, Go up *to* **R**, and prosper: 7433
18:14 shall we go to **R** to battle, or shall I 7433
18:19 of Israel, that he may go up and fall at **R**? 7433
18:28 the king of Judah went up to **R**. 7433
22: 5 to war against Hazael king of Syria at **R**: 7433

RAMPART (2)

La 2: 8 therefore he made the **r** and the wall to 2426
Na 3: 8 whose **r** *was* the sea, *and* her wall *was* from 2426

RAMS (68) [RAM]

Ge 31:10 the **r** which leaped upon the cattle *were* 6260
31:12 all the **r** which leap upon the cattle *are* 6260
31:38 and the **r** of thy flock have I not eaten. 352
32:14 he goats, two hundred ewes, and twenty **r**, 352
Ex 29: 1 young bullock, and two **r** without blemish, 352
29: 3 in the basket, with the bullock and the two **r**. 352
35:23 goats' *hair*, and red skins of **r**, and 352
Lev 8: 2 and two **r**, and a basket of unleavened bread; 352
23:18 first year, and one young bullock, and two **r**: 352
Nu 7:17 two oxen, five **r**, five he goats, five lambs of 352
7:23 two oxen, five **r**, five he goats, five lambs of 352
7:29 two oxen, five **r**, five he goats, five lambs of 352
7:35 two oxen, five **r**, five he goats, five lambs of 352
7:41 two oxen, five **r**, five he goats, five lambs of 352
7:47 two oxen, five **r**, five he goats, five lambs of 352
7:53 two oxen, five **r**, five he goats, five lambs of 352
7:59 two oxen, five **r**, five he goats, five lambs of 352
7:65 two oxen, five **r**, five he goats, five lambs of 352
7:71 two oxen, five **r**, five he goats, five lambs of 352
7:77 two oxen, five **r**, five he goats, five lambs of 352
7:83 two oxen, five **r**, five he goats, five lambs of 352
7:87 the **r** twelve, the lambs of the first year 352
7:88 *were* twenty and four bullocks, the **r** sixty, 352
23: 1 and prepare me here seven oxen and seven **r**. 352
23:29 prepare me here seven bullocks and seven **r**. 352
29:13 two **r**, *and* fourteen lambs of the first year; 352
29:14 two tenth deals to each ram of the two **r**, 352
29:17 two **r**, fourteen lambs of the first year 352
29:18 for the **r**, and for the lambs, *shall be* 352
29:20 And on the third day eleven bullocks, two **r**, 352
29:21 for the **r**, and for the lambs, *shall be* 352
29:23 two **r**, *and* fourteen lambs of the first year 352
29:24 for the **r**, and for the lambs, *shall be* 352
29:26 two **r**, *and* fourteen lambs of the first year 352
29:27 for the **r**, and for the lambs, *shall be* 352
29:29 two **r**, *and* fourteen lambs of the first year 352
29:30 for the **r**, and for the lambs, *shall be* 352
29:32 two **r**, *and* fourteen lambs of the first year 352
29:33 for the **r**, and for the lambs, *shall be* 352
Dt 32:14 and **r** of the breed of Bashan, and goats, 352
1Sa 15:22 *and* to hearken than the fat of **r**. 352
2Ki 3: 4 and an hundred thousand **r**, *with* the wool. 352
1Ch 15:26 that they offered seven bullocks and seven **r**. 352
29:21 a thousand **r**, *and* a thousand lambs, 352

R

2Ch 13: 9 himself with a young bullock and seven **r**, 352
17:11 seven thousand and seven hundred **r**, and 352
29:21 seven **r**, and seven lambs, and seven he 352
29:22 likewise, when they had killed the **r**, they 352
29:32 an hundred **r**, *and* two hundred lambs: 352
Ezr 6: 9 both young bullocks, and **r**, and lambs, 1798
6:17 two hundred **r**, four hundred lambs; 1798
7:17 **r**, lambs, with their meat offerings and 1798
8:35 ninety and six **r**, seventy and seven lambs, 352
Job 42: 8 unto you now seven bullocks and seven **r**, 352
Ps 66:15 sacrifices of fatlings, with the incense of **r**; 352
114: 4 The mountains skipped like **r**, *and* the little 352
114: 6 Ye mountains, *that* ye skipped like **r**; *and* 352
Isa 1:11 I am full *of* the burnt offerings of **r**, and 352
34: 6 and goats, with the fat of the kidneys of **r**: 352
60: 7 the **r** of Nebajoth shall minister unto thee: 352
Jer 51:40 lambs to the slaughter, like **r** with he goats. 352
Eze 4: 2 and set *battering* **r** against it round about. 3733
21:22 to appoint *battering* **r** against the gates, 3733
27:21 with thee in lambs, and **r**, and goats: 352
34:17 and cattle, between the **r** and the he goats. 352
39:18 of **r**, of lambs, and of goats, of bullocks, 352
45:23 seven **r** without blemish daily the seven 352
Mic 6: 7 the LORD be pleased with thousands of **r**, 352

RAMS' (9) [RAM]
Ex 25: 5 **r** skins dyed red, and badgers' skins, and 352
26:14 thou shalt make a covering for the tent *of* **r** 352
35: 7 **r** skins dyed red, and badgers' skins, and 352
36:19 he made a covering for the tent *of* **r** skins 352
39:34 the covering of **r** skins dyed red, and 352
Jos 6: 4 before the ark seven trumpets of **r horns**: 3104
6: 6 of **r horns** before the ark of the LORD. 3104
6: 8 of **r horns** passed on before the LORD, 3104
6:13 **r horns** before the ark of the LORD went 3104

RAN (61) [RUN]
Ge 18: 2 when he saw *them*, he **r** to meet them from 7323
18: 7 Abraham **r** unto the herd, and fetcht a calf 7323
24:17 the servant **r** to meet her, and said, Let me, 7323
24:20 **r** again unto the well to draw *water*, and 7323
24:28 the damsel **r**, and told *them of* her mother's 7323
24:29 Laban **r** out unto the man, unto the well. 7323
29:12 and she **r** and told her father. 7323
29:13 that he **r** to meet him, and embraced him, 7323
33: 4 Esau **r** to meet him, and embraced him, 7323
Ex 9:23 hail, and the fire **r along** upon the ground; 1980
Nu 11:27 there **r** a young man, and told Moses, and 7323
16:47 and **r** into the midst of the congregation; 7323
Jos 7:22 sent messengers, and they **r** unto the tent; 7323
8:19 they **r** as soon as *he* had stretched out his 7323
Jdg 7:21 and all the host **r**, and cried, and fled. 7323
9:21 Jotham **r away**, and fled, and went to Beer, 5127
9:44 the two *other* companies **r** upon all 6584
13:10 **r**, and shewed her husband, and said unto 7323
1Sa 3: 5 he **r** unto Eli, and said, Here *am* I; for thou 7323
4:12 there **r** a man of Benjamin out of the army, 7323
10:23 they **r** and fetched him thence: and when he 7323
17:22 **r** *into* the army, and came and saluted his 7323
17:48 **r** *toward* the army to meet the Philistine. 7323
17:51 Therefore David **r**, and stood upon 7323
20:36 *And* as the lad **r**, he shot an arrow beyond 7323
2Sa 18:21 And Cushi bowed himself unto Joab, and **r**. 7323
18:23 Ahimaaz **r** *by* the way of the plain, and 7323
1Ki 2:39 that two of the servants of Shimei **r away** 1272
18:35 the water **r** round about the altar; and 1980
18:46 **r** before Ahab to the entrance of Jezreel. 7323
19:20 **r** after Elijah, and said, Let me, I pray thee, 7323
22:35 the blood **r out** of the wound into the midst 3332
2Ch 32: 4 the brook that **r** through the midst of 7857
Ps 77: 2 my sore **r** in the night, and ceased not: 5064
105:41 they **r** in the dry *places like* a river. 1980
133: 2 that **r down** upon the beard, *even* Aaron's 3381
Jer 23:21 I have not sent *these* prophets, yet they **r**: 7323
Eze 1:14 the living creatures **r** and returned as 7519
47: 2 behold, there **r out** waters on the right side. 6379
Da 8: 6 and **r** unto him in the fury of his power. 7323
Mt 8:32 the whole herd of swine **r violently** down a *3729*
27:48 And straightway one of them **r**, and took a *5143*
Mk 5: 6 Jesus afar off, he **r** and worshipped him, *5143*
5:13 the herd **r violently** down a steep place into *3729*
6:33 and **r** afoot thither out of all cities, and *4936*
6:55 And **r through** that whole region round *4063*
15:36 And one **r** and filled a spunge *full* of *5143*
Lk 8:33 the herd **r violently** down a steep place into *3729*
15:20 and **r**, and fell on his neck, and kissed him. *5143*
19: 4 And he **r before**, *4390*
24:12 Then arose Peter, and **r** unto the sepulchre; *5143*
Jn 20: 4 So they **r** both together: and the other *5143*
Ac 3:11 all the people **r together** unto them in *4936*
7:57 their ears, and **r** upon him with one accord, *3729*
8:30 And Philip **r** *thither* **to** *him*, and heard him *4370*
12:14 but **r in**, and told how Peter stood before *1532*
14:14 and **r in** among the people, crying out, *1530*
21:30 and the people **r together**: *1096+4890*
21:32 and centurions, and **r down** unto them: *2701*
27:41 two seas met, they **r** the ship **aground**; *2027*
Jude 1:11 **r greedily after** the error of Balaam for *1632*

RANG (2) [RING]
1Sa 4: 5 *with* a great shout, so that the earth **r again**. 1949
1Ki 1:45 thence rejoicing, so that the city **r again**. 1949

RANGE (1) [RANGES, RANGING]
Job 39: 8 The **r** of the mountains *is* his pasture, and 3491

RANGES (4) [RANGE]
Lev 11:35 *whether it be* oven, or **r for pots**, they shall 3600
2Ki 11: 8 he that cometh within the **r**, let him be 7713
11:15 unto them, Have her forth without the **r**: 7713
2Ch 23:14 and said unto them, Have her forth of the **r**: 7713

RANGING (1) [RANGE]
Pr 28:15 *As* a roaring lion, and a **r** bear; *so is* a 8264

RANK (6) [RANKS]
Ge 41: 5 corn came up upon one stalk, **r** and good. 1277
41: 7 the seven thin ears devoured the seven **r** 1277
Nu 2:16 And they shall set forth in the **second r**. 8145
2:24 And they shall go forward in the **third r**. 7992
1Ch 12:33 of war, fifty thousand, which could **keep r**: 5737
12:38 All these men of war, that could keep **r**, 4634

RANKS (4) [RANK]
1Ki 7: 4 and light *was* against light *in* three **r**. 6471
7: 5 and light *was* against light *in* three **r**. 6471
Joel 2: 7 on his ways, and they shall not break their **r**: 734
Mk 6:40 And they sat down **in r**, by hundreds, *4237+4237*

RANSACKED See RIFLED

RANSOM (13) [RANSOMED]
Ex 21:30 he shall give *for* the **r** of his life whatsoever 6306
30:12 shall they give every man a **r** for his soul 3724
Job 33:24 going down *to* the pit: I have found a **r**. 3724
36:18 then a great **r** cannot deliver thee. 3724
Ps 49: 7 *his* brother, nor give to God a **r** for him: 3724
Pr 6:35 He will not regard any **r**; neither will he 3724
13: 8 The **r** of a man's life *are* his riches: but 3724
21:18 The wicked *shall be* a **r** for the righteous, 3724
Isa 43: 3 I gave Egypt *for* thy **r**, Ethiopia and 3724
Hos 13:14 I will **r** them from the power of the grave; 6299
Mt 20:28 and to give his life a **r** for many. *3083*
Mk 10:45 and to give his life a **r** for many. *3083*
1Ti 2: 6 Who gave himself a **r** for all, to be testified *487*

RANSOMED (3) [RANSOM]
Isa 35:10 the **r** of the LORD shall return, and 6299
51:10 of the sea a way for the **r** to pass over? 1350
Jer 31:11 **r** him from the hand of *him that was* 1350

RAPHA (2) [BETH-RAPHA]
1Ch 8: 2 Nohah the fourth, and **R** the fifth. 7498
8:37 **R** *was* his son, Eleasah his son, Azel his 7498

RAPHU (1)
Nu 13: 9 Of the tribe of Benjamin, Palti the son of **R**. 7505

RARE (1)
Da 2:11 *it is* a **r** thing that the king requireth, and 3358

RASE (2)
Ps 137: 7 **R** *it*, rase *it*, *even* to the foundation thereof. 6168
137: 7 Rase *it*, **r** *it*, *even* to the foundation thereof. 6168

RASH (2) [RASHLY]
Ecc 5: 2 Be not **r** with thy mouth, and let not thine 926
Isa 32: 4 The heart also of the **r** shall understand 4116

RASHLY (1) [RASH]
Ac 19:36 ye ought to be quiet, and to do nothing **r**. *4312*

RASOR (7)
Nu 6: 5 there shall no **r** come upon his head: 8593
Jdg 13: 5 a son; and no **r** shall come on his head: 4177
16:17 There hath not come a **r** upon mine head; 4177
1Sa 1:11 and there shall no **r** come upon his head. 4177
Ps 52: 2 like a sharp **r**, working deceitfully. 8593
Isa 7:20 shall the Lord shave with a **r** that is hired, 8593
Eze 5: 1 take thee a barber's **r**, and cause *it* to pass 8593

RAT See MOUSE

RATE (5)
Ex 16: 4 go out and gather a **certain r** every day, 1697
1Ki 10:25 spices, horses, and mules, a **r** year by year. 1697
2Ki 25:30 a daily **r** for every day, all the days of his 1697
2Ch 8:13 Even after a **certain r** every day, offering 1697
9:24 spices, horses, and mules, a **r** year by year. 1697

RATHER (62)
Jos 22:24 if we have not **r** done it for fear of *this* NIH
2Sa 10: 3 hath not David **r** sent his servants unto thee, NIH
2Ki 5:13 thou not have done *it*? **how much r** then, 637
Job 7:15 *and* death **r than** my life. 4480
32: 2 because he justified himself **r than** God. 4480
36:21 for this hast thou chosen **r than** affliction. 4480
Ps 52: 3 *and* lying **r than** to speak righteousness. 4480
84:10 I had **r** be a doorkeeper in the house of my 977
Pr 8:10 and knowledge **r than** choice gold. 4480
16:16 to get understanding **r** to be chosen **than** 4480
17:12 meet a man, **r** than a fool in his folly. 2050.1
22: 1 A *good* name *is* **r** to be chosen **than** great 4480
22: 1 *and* loving favour **r** than silver and gold. 4480
Jer 8: 3 death shall be chosen **r than** life by all 4480
Mt 10: 6 But go **r** to the lost sheep of the house of *3123*
10:28 **r** fear him which is able to destroy both *3123*
18: 8 **r than** having two hands or two feet to be *2228*
18: 9 **r than** having two eyes to be cast into hell *2228*
25: 9 but go ye **r** to them that sell, and buy for *3123*
27:24 but *that* **r** a tumult was made, he took *3123*
Mk 5:26 was nothing bettered, but **r** grew worse, *3123*
15:11 that he should **r** release Barabbas unto *3123*
Lk 10:20 but **r** rejoice, because your names are *3123*
11:28 But he said, **Yea r**, blessed *are* they that *3304*
11:41 **But r** give alms *of* such *things* as *you* have; *4133*
12:31 **But r** seek ye the kingdom of God; *4133*
12:51 on earth? I tell you, Nay; but **r** division: *2228*
17: 8 And will not **r** say unto him, Make ready NIG
18:14 this man went down to his house justified **r** NIG
Jn 3:19 and men loved darkness **r** than light, *3123*
Ac 5:29 said, We ought to obey God **r** than men. *3123*
Ro 3: 8 And not **r**, (as we be slanderously reported, NIG
8:34 *It is* Christ that died, yea **r**, that is risen *3123*
11:11 **r** through their fall salvation *is come* unto NIG
12:19 not yourselves, but **r** give place unto wrath: NIG
14:13 but judge this **r**, that no *man* put a *3123*
1Co 5: 2 ye are puffed up, and have not **r** mourned, *3123*
6: 7 Why do ye not **r** take wrong? why do ye *3123*
6: 7 why do ye not **r** *suffer yourselves to* be *3123*
7:21 but if thou mayest be made free, use *it* **r**. *3123*
9:12 of *this* power over you, *are* not we **r**? *3123*
14: 1 spiritual *gifts*, but **r** that ye may prophesy. *3123*
14: 5 with tongues, but **r** that ye prophesied: *3123*
14:19 Yet in the church I **had r** speak five words *2309*
2Co 2: 7 So that contrariwise ye *ought* **r** to forgive *3123*
3: 8 the ministration of the spirit be **r** glorious? *3123*
5: 8 and willing **r** to be absent from the body, *3123*
12: 9 therefore will I **r** glory in my infirmities, *3123*
Gal 4: 9 or **r** are known of God, how turn ye again *3123*
Eph 4:28 but **r** let him labour, working with *his* *3123*
5: 4 are not convenient: but **r** giving of thanks. *3123*
5:11 works of darkness, but **r** reprove *them*. *3123*
Php 1:12 out **r** unto the furtherance of the gospel; *3123*
1Ti 1: 4 **r** than godly edifying which is in faith: *3123*
4: 7 and exercise thyself **r** unto godliness. NIG
6: 2 but **r** do *them* service, because they are *3123*
Phm 1: 9 *Yet* for love's sake I **r** beseech *thee*, being *3123*
Heb 11:25 Choosing **r** to suffer affliction with *3123*
12: 9 shall we not much **r** be in subjection unto *3123*
12:13 turned out of the way; but let it **r** be healed. *3123*
13:19 But I beseech *you* the **r** to do this, that I *4056*
2Pe 1:10 Wherefore the **r**, brethren, give diligence to *3123*

RATS See MICE

RATTLETH (1) [RATTLING]
Job 39:23 The quiver **r** against him, the glittering 7439

RATTLING (1) [RATTLETH]
Na 3: 2 the noise of the **r** of the wheels, and of 7494

RAVEN (6) [RAVENS]
Ge 8: 7 he sent forth a **r**, which went forth to and 6158
Lev 11:15 Every **r** after his kind; 6158
Dt 14:14 And every **r** after his kind, 6158
Job 38:41 Who provideth for the **r** his food? when his 6158
SS 5:11 his locks *are* bushy, *and* black as a **r**. 6158
Isa 34:11 the owl also and the **r** shall dwell in it: 6158

RAVENING (5) [RAVENOUS]
Ps 22:13 *with* their mouths, *as* a **r** and a roaring lion. 2963
Eze 22:25 midst thereof, like a roaring lion **r** the prey; 2963
22:27 the midst thereof *are* like wolves **r** the prey, 2963
Mt 7:15 but inwardly they are **r** wolves. *727*
Lk 11:39 but your inward part is full of **r** and *724*

RAVENOUS (3) [RAVENING]
Isa 35: 9 nor *any* **r** beast shall go up thereon, 6530
46:11 Calling a **r bird** from the east, the man that 5861
Eze 39: 4 I will give thee unto the **r** birds of every 5861

RAVENS (5) [RAVEN]
1Ki 17: 4 I have commanded the **r** to feed thee there. 6158
17: 6 the **r** brought him bread and flesh in 6158
Ps 147: 9 his food, *and* to the young **r** which cry. 6158
Pr 30:17 the **r** of the valley shall pick it out, and 6158
Lk 12:24 Consider the **r**: for they neither sow nor *2876*

RAVIN (2)
Ge 49:27 Benjamin shall **r** *as* a wolf: in the morning 2963
Na 2:12 his holes *with* prey, and his dens *with* **r**. 2966

RAVINES See BROOKS

RAVISHED (5) [RAVISHT]
SS 4: 9 Thou hast **r** my **heart**, my sister, 3823
4: 9 thou hast **r** my **heart** with one of thine 3823
Isa 13:16 houses shall be spoiled, and their wives **r**. 7901
La 5:11 They **r** the women in Zion, *and* the maids 6031
Zec 14: 2 and the houses rifled, and the women **r**; 7901

RAVISHT (2) [RAVISHED]
Pr 5:19 and be thou **r** always with her love. 7686
5:20 be **r** with a strange *woman*, and 7686

RAW (7)
Ex 12: 9 Eat not of it **r**, nor sodden at all with water, 4995
Lev 13:10 *there be* **quick r** flesh in the rising; 2416+4241
13:14 when **r** flesh appeareth in him, he shall be 2416
13:15 the priest shall see the **r** flesh, 2416
13:15 *for* the **r** flesh *is* unclean: it *is* a leprosy. 2416
13:16 Or if the **r** flesh turn again, and be changed 2416
1Sa 2:15 he will not have sodden flesh of thee, but **r**. 2416

RAZOR See RASOR

REACH (15) [REACHED, REACHETH, REACHING]
Ge 11: 4 and a tower, whose top *may* **r** unto heaven; NIH
Ex 26:28 midst of the boards shall **r** from end to end. 1272
28:42 the loins even unto the thighs they shall **r**: 1961
Lev 26: 5 your threshing shall **r unto** the vintage, 5381
26: 5 the vintage shall **r unto** the sowing time: 5381
Nu 34:11 shall **r** unto the side of the sea of 4229
35: 4 *shall* **r** from the wall of the city and NIH
Job 20: 6 the heavens, and his head **r** unto the clouds; 5060
Isa 8: 8 and go over, he shall **r** *even* to the neck; 5060
30:28 shall **r to** the midst of the neck, 5704
Jer 48:32 over the sea, they **r** *even* to the sea of Jazer: 5060
Zec 14: 5 for the valley of the mountains shall **r** unto 5060
Jn 20:27 **R** hither thy finger, and behold my hands; *5342*
20:27 and **r** *hither* thy hand, and thrust *it* into my *5342*
2Co 10:13 to us, a measure to **r** even unto you. *2185*

REACHED (8) [REACH]
Ge 28:12 on the earth, and the top of it **r** to heaven: 5060
Jos 19:11 **r** to Dabbasheth, and reached to the river 6293
19:11 and **r** to the river that *is* before Jokneam; 6293
Ru 2:14 he **r** her parched *corn*, and she did eat, and 6642
Da 4:11 the height thereof **r** unto heaven, and 4291
4:20 whose height **r** unto the heaven, and 4291
2Co 10:14 *our measure*, as though we **r** not unto you: *2185*

R

Rev 18: 5 For her sins have **r** unto heaven, and God *190*

REACHETH (14) [REACH]

Nu 21:30 even unto Nophah, which *r* unto Medeba. NIH
Jos 19:22 the coast **r** to Tabor, and Shahazimah, and 6293
19:26 **r** to Carmel westward, and 6293
19:27 **r** to Zebulun, and to the valley of 6293
19:34 **r** to Zebulun on the south side, and 6293
19:34 **r** to Asher on the west side, and to Judah 6293
2Ch 28: 9 ye have slain them in a rage *that* **r** up unto 5060
Ps 36: 5 *and* thy faithfulness *r* unto the clouds. NIH
108: 4 the heavens: and thy truth *r* unto the clouds. NIH
Pr 31:20 yea, she **r forth** her hands to the needy. 7971
Jer 4:10 whereas the sword **r** unto the soul). 5060
4:18 *it is* bitter, because it **r** unto thine heart. 5060
51: 9 for her judgment **r** unto heaven, and 5060
Da 4:22 **r** unto heaven, and thy dominion to the end 4291

REACHING (4) [REACH]

2Ch 3:11 *was* five cubits, **r** to the wall of the house: 5060
3:11 **r** to the wing of the other cherub. 5060
3:12 *was* five cubits, **r** to the wall of the house: 5060
Php 3:13 **r forth** unto those *things which are* before, *1901*

READ (70) [READEST, READETH, READING]

Ex 24: 7 and **r** in the audience of the people: 7121
Dt 17:19 he shall **r** therein all the days of his life: 7121
31:11 thou shalt **r** this law before all Israel in 7121
Jos 8:34 afterward he **r** all the words of the law, 7121
8:35 which Joshua **r** not before all 7121
2Ki 5: 7 when the king of Israel had **r** the letter, 7121
19:14 of the hand of the messengers, and **r** it: 7121
22: 8 gave the book to Shaphan, and he **r** it. 7121
22:10 a book. And Shaphan **r** it before the king. 7121
22:16 of the book which the king of Judah hath **r**: 7121
23: 2 he **r** in their ears all the words of the book 7121
2Ch 34:18 a book. And Shaphan **r** it before the king. 7121
34:24 which they have **r** before the king of Judah: 7121
34:30 he **r** in their ears all the words of the book 7121
Ezr 4:18 sent unto us *hath been* plainly **r** before me. 7123
4:23 Artaxerxes' letter *was* **r** before Rehum, 7123
Ne 8: 3 he **r** therein before the street that *was* 7121
8: 8 So they **r** in the book in the law of God 7121
8:18 last day, he **r** in the book of the law of God. 7121
9: 3 **r** in the book of the law of the LORD their 7121
13: 1 On that day they **r** in the book of Moses in 7121
Est 6: 1 and they were **r** before the king. 7121
Isa 29:11 that is learned, saying, **R** this, I pray thee: 7121
29:12 is not learned, saying, **R** this, I pray thee: 7121
34:16 ye out of the book of the LORD, and **r**: 7121
37:14 from the hand of the messengers, and **r** it: 7121
Jer 29:29 Zephaniah the priest **r** this letter in the ears 7121
36: 6 Therefore go thou, and **r** in the roll, 7121
36: 6 also thou shalt **r** them in the ears of all 7121
36:10 **r** Baruch in the book the words of Jeremiah 7121
36:13 when Baruch **r** the book in the ears of 7121
36:14 thou hast **r** in the ears of the people, 7121
36:15 Sit down now, and **r** it in our ears. 7121
36:15 it in our ears. So Baruch **r** *it* in their ears. 7121
36:21 Jehudi **r** it in the ears of the king, and in 7121
36:23 *that* when Jehudi had **r** three or four leaves, 7121
51:61 and shalt see, and shalt **r** all these words; 7121
Da 5: 7 Whosoever shall **r** this writing, and 7123
5: 8 wise *men:* but they could not **r** the writing, 7123
5:15 that they should **r** this writing, and 7123
5:16 now if thou canst **r** the writing, and 7123
5:17 yet I will **r** the writing unto the king, and 7123
Mt 12: 3 unto them, Have ye not **r** what David did, *314*
12: 5 Or have ye not **r** in the law, how that on *314*
19: 4 and said unto them, Have ye not **r**, *314*
21:16 have ye never **r**, Out of the mouth of babes *314*
21:42 unto them, Did ye never **r** in the scriptures, *314*
22:31 have ye not **r** that which was spoken unto *314*
Mk 2:25 Have ye never **r** what David did, when he *314*
12:10 And have ye not **r** this scripture; The stone *314*
12:26 have ye not **r** in the book of Moses, how in *314*
Lk 4:16 on the sabbath day, and stood up for to **r**. *314*
6: 3 Have ye not **r** so much as this, what David *314*
Jn 19:20 This title then **r** many of the Jews: for *314*
Ac 8:28 sitting in his chariot **r** Esaias the prophet. *314*
8:30 to *him,* and heard him **r** the prophet Esaias, *314*
8:32 The place of the scripture which he **r** was *314*
13:27 *yet* the voices of the prophets which are **r** *314*
15:21 being **r** in the synagogues every sabbath day. *314*
15:31 *Which* when they had **r**, they rejoiced for *314*
23:34 And when the governor had **r** *the letter,* he *314*
2Co 1:13 unto you, than what you **r** or acknowledge; *314*
3: 2 in our hearts, known and **r** of all men: *314*
3:15 But *even* unto this day, when Moses is **r**, *314*
Eph 3: 4 Whereby, when ye **r**, ye may understand my *314*
Col 4:16 And when *this* epistle is **r** amongst you, *314*
4:16 cause that it be **r** also in the church of *314*
4:16 that ye likewise **r** the *epistle* from Laodicea. *314*
1Th 5:27 *this* epistle be **r** unto all the holy brethren. *314*
Rev 5: 4 was found worthy to open and to **r** the book, *314*

READEST (2) [READ]

Lk 10:26 What is written in the law? how **r** thou? *314*
Ac 8:30 and said, Understandest thou what thou **r**? *314*

READETH (4) [READ]

Hab 2: 2 plain upon tables, that he may run that **r** it. 7121
Mt 24:15 holy place, (whoso **r**, let him understand:) *314*
Mk 13:14 it ought not, (let him that **r** understand,) *314*
Rev 1: 3 Blessed *is* he that **r**, and they that hear *314*

READINESS (3) [READY]

Ac 17:11 they received the word with all **r of mind**, *4288*
2Co 8:11 the doing *of it;* that as *there was* a **r** *4288*
10: 6 And having in a **r** to revenge all *2092*

READING (6) [READ]

Ne 8: 8 and caused *them* to understand the **r**. 4744
Jer 36: 8 **r** in the book the words of the LORD *in* 7121
51:63 when thou hast made an end of **r** this book, 7121
Ac 13:15 And after the **r** of the law and the prophets *320*
2Co 3:14 untaken away in the **r** of the old testament; *320*
1Ti 4:13 Till I come, give attendance to **r**, *320*

READY (100) [ALREADY, READINESS]

Ge 18: 6 **Make r quickly** three measures of fine 4116
43:16 *these* men home, and slay, and **make r**; 3559
43:25 they **made r** the present against Joseph 3559
46:29 Joseph **made r** his chariot, and went up to 631
Ex 14: 6 he **made r** his chariot, and took his people 631
17: 4 this people? they be almost **r** to stone me. NIH
19:11 be **r** against the third day: for the third day 3559
19:15 unto the people, Be **r** against the third day: 3559
34: 2 be **r** in the morning, and come up in 3559
Nu 32:17 we ourselves will go **r** armed before 2363
Dt 1:41 of war, ye were **r** to go up into the hill. 1951
26: 5 A Syrian **r to perish** *was* my father, and 6
Jos 8: 4 not very far from the city, but be ye all **r**: 3559
Jdg 6:19 **made r** a kid, and unleavened *cakes of* an 6213
13:15 until we shall have **made r** a kid for thee. 6213
1Sa 25:18 five sheep **r dressed**, and five measures of 6213
2Sa 15:15 thy servants *are* **r** *to do* whatsoever my lord NIH
18:22 my son, seeing that thou hast no tidings **r**? 4672
1Ki 6: 7 was built *of* stone **made r** *before it was* 8003
2Ki 9:21 Joram said, **Make r**. And his chariot was 631
9:21 his chariot was **made r**. And Joram king of 631
1Ch 12:23 of the bands that were **r armed** to the war, 2502
12:24 and eight hundred, **r armed** to the war. 2502
28: 2 our God, and had **made r** for the building: 3559
2Ch 17:18 fourscore thousand **r prepared for** the war. 2502
35:14 afterward they **made r** for themselves, and 3559
Ezr 7: 6 he *was* a **r** scribe in the law of Moses, 4106
Ne 9:17 thou *art* a God **r to pardon**, gracious and 5547
Est 3:14 that *they* should be **r** against that day. 6264
8:13 that the Jews should be **r** against that day to 6264
Job 3: 8 who are **r** to raise up their mourning. 6264
12: 5 He that is **r** to slip with *his* feet *is as* a lamp 3559
15:23 that the day of darkness is **r** at his hand. 3559
15:24 against him, as a king **r** to the battle. 6264
15:28 which are **r to become** heaps. 6257
17: 1 my days are extinct, the graves *are* **r** for me. NIH
18:12 and destruction *shall be* **r** at his side. 3559
29:13 The blessing of him that was **r to perish** came 6
32:19 no vent; it is **r to burst** like new bottles. 1234
Ps 7:12 he hath bent his bow, and **made** it **r**. 3559
11: 2 they **make r** their arrow upon the string, 3559
21:12 *when* thou shalt **make r** *thine arrows* upon 3559
38:17 For I *am* **r** to halt, and my sorrow *is* 3559
45: 1 *the* king: my tongue *is* the pen of a **r** writer. 4106
86: 5 For thou, Lord, *art* good, and **r to forgive**; 5546
88:15 **r to die** from *my* youth *up: while* I suffer 1478
Pr 24:11 unto death, and *those that are* **r** to be slain; 4131
31: 6 Give strong drink unto him that is **r to perish**, 6
Ecc 5: 1 *be* more **r** to hear, than to give the sacrifice 7138
Isa 27:13 they shall come which were **r** to perish in NIH
30:13 iniquity shall be to you as a breach **r** to fall, NIH
32: 4 the tongue of the stammerers shall be **r** to 4116
38:20 The LORD *was* **r** to save me: therefore NIH
41: 7 the anvil, saying, It *is* **r** for the sodering: 2896
51:13 of the oppressor, as if he were **r** to destroy? 3559
Eze 7:14 blown the trumpet, even to **make** all **r**; 3559
Da 3:15 Now if ye be **r** that at what time ye hear 6263
Hos 7: 6 For they have **made r** their heart like an 7126
Mt 22: 4 *my* fatlings *are* killed, and all *things are* **r**: *2092*
22: 8 The wedding is **r**, but they which were *2092*
24:44 Therefore be ye also **r**: for in such an hour *2092*
25:10 they *that were* **r** went in with him to *2092*
26:19 and they **made r** the passover. *2090*
Mk 14:15 *and* prepared: there **make r** for us. *2090*
14:16 unto them: and they **made r** the passover. *2090*
14:38 The spirit truly *is* **r**, but the flesh *is* weak. *4289*
Lk 1:17 to **make r** a people prepared for the Lord. *2090*
7: 2 was dear unto him, was sick, and **r** to die. *3195*
9:52 of the Samaritans, to **make r** for him. *2090*
12:40 Be ye therefore **r** also: for the Son of man *2092*
14:17 Come; for all *things* are now **r**. *2092*
17: 8 **Make r** wherewith I may sup, and *2090*
22:12 large upper room furnished: there **make r**. *2090*
22:13 unto them: and they **made r** the passover. *2090*
22:33 Lord, I am **r** to go with thee, both into *2092*
Jn 7: 6 is not yet come: but your time is alway **r**. *2092*
Ac 10:10 but while they **made r**, he fell into a trance, *3903*
20: 7 unto them, **r** to depart on the morrow; *3195*
21:13 for I am **r** not to be bound only, but also to *2093*
23:15 we, or ever he come near, are **r** to kill him. *2092*
23:21 and now are they **r**, looking for a promise *2092*
23:23 **Make r** two hundred soldiers to go to *2090*
Ro 1:15 I am **r** to preach the gospel to you that are *4289*
2Co 8:19 same Lord, and *declaration of* your **r mind**: *4288*
9: 2 that Achaia was **r** a year ago; *3903*
9: 3 in this behalf; that, as I said, ye may be **r**: *3903*
9: 5 that the same might be **r**, as *a matter of* *2092*
10:16 line of *things* **made r** to our **hand**. *1519+2092*
12:14 the third *time* I am **r** to come to you; *2093*
1Ti 6:18 **r to distribute**, willing to communicate; *2130*
2Ti 4: 6 For I am **now r** to be offered, and the time *2235*
Tit 3: 1 to be **r** to every good work, *2092*
Heb 8:13 and waxeth old *is* **r** to vanish away. *1451*
1Pe 1: 5 salvation **r** to be revealed in the last time. *2092*
3:15 *be* **r** always to *give* an answer to every *man* *2092*
4: 5 Who shall give account to him that is **r** to *2093*
5: 2 not for filthy lucre, but **of a r mind**; *4290*
Rev 3: 2 the *things* which remain, that are **r to** die: *3195*
12: 4 the woman which was **r to** be delivered, *3195*
19: 7 is come, and his wife hath **made** herself **r**. *2090*

REAIA (1)

1Ch 5: 5 Micah his son, **R** his son, Baal his son, 7211

REAIAH (3)

1Ch 4: 2 **R** the son of Shobal begat Jahath; and 7211
Ezr 2:47 the children of Gahar, the children of **R**, 7211
Ne 7:50 The children of **R**, the children of Rezin, 7211

REALIZE See WIST

REALLY See SURETY; THROUGHLY

REALM (7)

2Ch 20:30 So the **r** of Jehoshaphat was quiet: for his 4438
Ezr 7:13 and *of* his priests and Levites, in my **r**, 4437
7:23 for why should there be wrath against the **r** 4437
Da 1:20 *and* astrologers that *were* in all his **r**. 4438
6: 3 king thought to set him over the whole **r**. 4437
9: 1 which was made king over the **r** of 4438
11: 2 he shall stir up all against the **r** of Grecia. 4438

REAP (32) [REAPED, REAPER, REAPERS, REAPEST, REAPETH, REAPING]

Lev 19: 9 when ye **r** the harvest of your land, 7114
19: 9 thou shalt not **wholly r** the corners 3615+3807.1
23:10 shall **r** the harvest thereof, then ye shall 7114
23:22 when ye **r** the harvest of your land, 7114
25: 5 own accord of thy harvest thou shalt not **r**, 7114
25:11 neither **r** that which groweth of itself in it, 7114
Ru 2: 9 *Let* thine eyes *be* on the field that they do **r**, 7114
1Sa 8:12 to **r** his harvest, and to make his 7114
2Ki 19:29 **r**, and plant vineyards, and eat the fruits 7114
Job 4: 8 and sow wickedness, **r** the same. 7114
24: 6 They **r** *every one* his corn in the field: and 7114
Ps 126: 5 They that sow in tears shall **r** in joy. 7114
Pr 22: 8 He that soweth iniquity shall **r** vanity: and 7114
Ecc 11: 4 and he that regardeth the clouds shall not **r**. 7114
Isa 37:30 **r**, and plant vineyards, and eat the fruit 7114
Jer 12:13 They have sown wheat, but shall **r** thorns: 7114
Hos 8: 7 the wind, and they shall **r** the whirlwind: 7114
10:12 to yourselves in righteousness, **r** in mercy; 7114
Mic 6:15 Thou shalt sow, but thou shalt not **r**; 7114
Mt 6:26 for they sow not, neither do they **r**, *2325*
25:26 thou knewest that I **r** where I sowed not, *2325*
Lk 12:24 for they neither sow nor **r**; which neither *2325*
Jn 4:38 I sent you to **r** *that* whereon ye bestowed no *2325*
1Co 9:11 great *thing* if we shall **r** your carnal *things?* *2325*
2Co 9: 6 soweth sparingly shall **r** also sparingly; *2325*
9: 6 he which soweth bountifully shall **r** also *2325*
Gal 6: 7 a man soweth, that shall he also **r**. *2325*
6: 8 to his flesh shall of the flesh **r** corruption; *2325*
6: 8 Spirit shall of the Spirit **r** life everlasting. *2325*
6: 9 for in due season we shall **r**, if we faint not. *2325*
Rev 14:15 sat on the cloud, Thrust in thy sickle, and **r**: *2325*
14:15 for the time is come for thee to **r**; for *2325*

REAPED (4) [REAP]

Hos 10:13 plowed wickedness, ye have **r** iniquity; 7114
Jas 5: 4 the hire of the labourers which have **r** *down* *270*
5: 4 the cries of them which have **r** are entered *2325*
Rev 14:16 his sickle on the earth; and the earth was **r**. *2325*

REAPER (1) [REAP]

Am 9:13 that the plowman shall overtake the **r**, and 7114

REAPERS (9) [REAP]

Ru 2: 3 came, and gleaned in the field after the **r**: 7114
2: 4 said unto the **r**, The LORD *be* with you. 7114
2: 5 unto his servant that was set over the **r**, 7114
2: 6 the servant that was set over the **r** answered 7114
2: 7 and gather after the **r** amongst the sheaves: 7114
2:14 she sat beside the **r**: and he reached her 7114
2Ki 4:18 a day, that he went out to his father to the **r**. 7114
Mt 13:30 in the time of harvest I will say to the **r**, *2327*
13:39 end of the world; and the **r** are *the* angels. *2327*

REAPEST (2) [REAP]

Lev 23:22 of the corners of thy field when thou **r**, 7114
Lk 19:21 not down, and **r** that thou didst not sow. *2325*

REAPETH (4) [REAP]

Isa 17: 5 the corn, and **r** the ears *with* his arm; 7114
Jn 4:36 And he that **r** receiveth wages, and *2325*
4:36 and he that **r** may rejoice together. *2325*
4:37 saying true, One soweth, and another **r**. *2325*

REAPING (3) [REAP]

1Sa 6:13 *they of* Beth-shemesh *were* **r** *their* wheat 7114
Mt 25:24 **r** where thou hast not sown, and *2325*
Lk 19:22 I laid not down, and **r** that I did not sow: *2325*

REAR (4) [REARED]

Ex 26:30 thou shalt **r up** the tabernacle according to 6965
Lev 26: 1 neither **r** you **up** a standing image, 6965
2Sa 24:18 **r** an altar unto the LORD in 6965
Jn 2:20 and wilt thou **r** it **up** in three days? *1453*

REAR GUARD See REREWARD

REARED (10) [REAR]

Ex 40:17 of the month, *that* the tabernacle was **r up**. 6965
40:18 Moses **r up** the tabernacle, and fastened his 6965
40:18 put in the bars thereof, and **r up** his pillars. 6965
40:33 he **r up** the court round about 6965
Nu 9:15 on the day that the tabernacle was **r up**, 6965
2Sa 18:18 had taken and **r up** for himself a pillar, 5324
1Ki 16:32 he **r up** an altar for Baal *in* the house of 6965
2Ki 21: 3 he **r up** altars for Baal, and made a grove, 6965
2Ch 3:17 he **r up** the pillars before the temple, 6965
33: 3 he **r up** altars for Baalim, and made groves, 6965

REASON (71) [REASONABLE, REASONED, REASONING, REASONS, UNREASONABLE]

Ge 41:31 land **by r** of that famine following; 4480+6440
47:13 *all* the land of Canaan fainted **by r of** 4480+6440
Ex 2:23 the children of Israel sighed **by r of** 4480
2:23 their cry came up unto God **by r of** 4480
3: 7 have heard their cry **by r of** their 4480+6440
8:24 the land was corrupted **by r of** 4480+6440
Nu 9:10 of your posterity shall be unclean **by r of** 3807.1
18: 8 unto thee have I given them **by r of** 3807.1

Nu 18:32 ye shall bear no sin by r of it, when ye 5921
Dt 5: 5 for ye were afraid by r of the fire, 4480+6440
23:10 that is not clean by r of uncleanness that 4480
Jos 9:13 our shoes are become old by r of the very 4480
Jdg 2:18 of their groanings by r of them that 4480
1Sa 12: 7 that I may r with you before the LORD of 8199
1Ki 9:15 this is the r of the levy which king 1697
14: 4 for his eyes were set by r of his age. 4480
2Ch 5:14 stand to minister by r of the cloud: 4480+6440
20:15 Be not afraid nor dismayed by r of 4480+6440
21:15 until thy bowels fall out by r of 4480
21:19 his bowels fell out by r of his sickness: 5973
Job 6:16 Which are blackish by r of the ice, and 4480
9:14 and choose out my words to r with him? NIH
13: 3 to the Almighty, and I desire to r with God. 3198
15: 3 Should he r with unprofitable talk? or 3198
17: 7 Mine eye also is dim by r of sorrow, and 4480
31:23 and by r of his highness I could not endure. 4480
35: 9 By r of the multitude of oppressions they 4480
35: 9 they cry out by r of the arm of the mighty. 4480
37:19 order our speech by r of darkness. 4480+6440
41:25 by r of breakings they purify themselves. 4480
Ps 38: 8 I have roared by r of the disquietness of my 4480
44:16 blasphemeth; by r of the enemy and 4480+6440
78:65 like a mighty man that shouteth by r of 4480
88: 9 Mine eye mourneth by r of affliction: 4480
90:10 if by r of strength they be fourscore years, 871.1
102: 5 By r of the voice of my groaning my bones 4480
Pr 20: 4 The sluggard will not plow by r of 4480
26:16 conceit than seven men that can render a r. 2940
Ecc 7:25 the r of things, and to know the wickedness 2808
Isa 1:18 Come now, and let us r together, saith 3198
49:19 shall even now be too narrow by r of 4480
Eze 19:10 and full of branches by r of many waters. 4480
21:12 terrors by r of the sword shall be upon my 413
26:10 By r of the abundance of his horses their 4480
27:12 Tarshish was thy merchant by r of 4480
27:16 Syria was thy merchant by r of 4480
28:17 thou hast corrupted thy wisdom by r of thy 5921
Da 4:36 At the same time my r returned unto me; 4486
5:10 by r of the words of the king and his lords, 6903
8:12 the daily sacrifice by r of transgression, 871.1
Jnh 2: 2 I cried by r of mine affliction unto 4480
Mic 2:12 they shall make great noise by r of 4480
Mt 16: 8 why r ye among yourselves, because 1260
Mk 2: 8 Why r ye these things in your hearts? 1260
8:17 Why r ye, because ye have no bread? 1260
Lk 5:21 the scribes and the Pharisees began to r, 1260
5:22 said unto them, What r ye in your hearts? 1260
Jn 6:18 And the sea arose by r of a great wind that NIG
12:11 Because that by r of him many of the Jews 1223
Ac 6: 2 It is not r that we should leave the word of 701
18:14 r would that I should bear with you: 2596+3056
Ro 8:20 by r of him who hath subjected the same, 1223
2Co 3:10 this respect, by r of the glory that excelleth. 1752
Heb 5: 3 And by r hereof he ought, as for 1223+3778
5:14 even those who by r of use have their 1223
7:23 suffered to continue by r of death: 1223+3588
1Pe 3:15 a r of the hope that is in you with meekness 3056
2Pe 2: 2 by r of whom the way of truth shall be evil 1223
Rev 8:13 to the inhabiters of the earth by r of 1537
9: 2 the air were darkened by r of the smoke of 1537
18:19 had ships in the sea by r of her costliness: 1537

REASONABLE (1) [REASON]
Ro 12: 1 unto God, which is your r service. 3050

REASONED (12) [REASON]
Mt 16: 7 And they r among themselves, saying, It is 1260
21:25 And they r with themselves, saying, If we 1260
Mk 2: 8 his spirit that they so r within themselves, 1260
8:16 And they r among themselves, saying, It is 1260
11:31 And they r with themselves, saying, If we 3049
Lk 20: 5 And they r with themselves, saying, If we 4817
20:14 they r among themselves, saying, This is 1260
24:15 that while they communed together and r, 4802
Ac 17: 2 three sabbath days r with them out of 1256
18: 4 And he r in the synagogue every sabbath, 1256
18:19 into the synagogue, and r with the Jews. 1256
24:25 And as he r of righteousness, temperance, 1256

REASONING (5) [REASON]
Job 13: 6 Hear now my r, and hearken to 8433
Mk 2: 6 scribes sitting there, and r in their hearts, 1260
12:28 and having heard them r together, and 4802
Lk 9:46 Then there arose a r among them, which of 1261
Ac 28:29 and had great r among themselves. 4803

REASONS (2) [REASON]
Job 32:11 I gave ear to your r, whilst you searched 8394
Isa 41:21 bring forth your strong r, saith the King of NIH

REBA (2)
Nu 31: 8 and Rekem, and Zur, and Hur, and R, 7254
Jos 13:21 Evi, and Rekem, and Zur, and Hur, and R, 7254

REBECCA (1) [REBEKAH]
Ro 9:10 but when R also had conceived by one, 4479

REBEKAH (28) [REBECCA, REBEKAH'S]
Ge 22:23 Bethuel begat R: these eight Milcah did 7259
24:15 that behold, R came out, who was born to 7259
24:29 R had a brother, and his name was Laban: 7259
24:30 when he heard the words of R his sister, 7259
24:45 R came forth with her pitcher on her 7259
24:51 Behold, R is before thee, take her, and go, 7259
24:53 of gold, and raiment, and gave them to R: 7259
24:58 they called R, and said unto her, Wilt thou 7259
24:59 they sent away R their sister, and her nurse, 7259
24:60 they blessed R, and said unto her, Thou art 7259
24:61 R arose, and her damsels, and they rode 7259
24:61 and the servant took R, and went his way. 7259
24:64 R lift up her eyes, and when she saw Isaac, 7259
24:67 and took R, and she became his wife; 7259
Ge 25:20 Isaac was forty years old when he took R to 7259
25:21 intreated of him, and R his wife conceived. 7259
25:28 did eat of his venison: but R loved Jacob. 7259
26: 7 the men of the place should kill me for R; 7259
26: 8 behold, Isaac was sporting with R his wife. 7259
26:35 were a grief of mind unto Isaac and to R. 7259
27: 5 R heard when Isaac spake to Esau his son. 7259
27: 6 R spake unto Jacob her son, saying, 7259
27:11 Jacob said to R his mother, Behold, 7259
27:15 R took goodly raiment of her eldest son 7259
27:42 words of Esau her elder son were told to R: 7259
27:46 R said to Isaac, I am weary of my life 7259
28: 5 the brother of R, Jacob's and 7259
49:31 there they buried Isaac and R his wife; and 7259

REBEKAH'S (2) [REBEKAH]
Ge 29:12 her father's brother, and that he was R son: 7259
35: 8 Deborah R nurse died, and she was buried 7259

REBEL (14) [REBELLED, REBELLEST, REBELLION, REBELLIOUS, REBELS]
Nu 14: 9 Only r not ye against the LORD, 4775
Jos 1:18 Whosoever he be that doth r against thy 4784
22:16 that ye might r this day against 4775
22:18 seeing ye r to day against the LORD, 4775
22:19 r not against the LORD, nor rebel against 4775
22:19 not against the LORD, nor r against us, 4775
22:29 God forbid that we should r against 4775
1Sa 12:14 not r against the commandment of 4784
12:15 r against the commandment of the LORD, 4784
Ne 2:19 thing that ye do? will ye r against the king? 4775
6: 6 saith it, that thou and the Jews think to r: 4775
Job 24:13 They are of those that r against the light; 4775
Isa 1:20 if ye refuse and r, ye shall be devoured 4784
Hos 7:14 for corn and wine, and they r against me. 5493

REBELLED (34) [REBEL]
Ge 14: 4 and in the thirteenth year they r. 4775
Nu 20:24 ye r against my word at the water of 4784
27:14 For ye r against my commandment in 4784
Dt 1:26 r against the commandment of the LORD 4784
1:43 r against the commandment of the LORD, 4784
9:23 you r against the commandment of 4784
1Ki 12:19 So Israel r against the house of David unto 6586
2Ki 1: 1 Moab r against Israel after the death of 6586
3: 5 that the king of Moab r against the king of 6586
3: 7 The king of Moab hath r against me: 6586
18: 7 he r against the king of Assyria, and 4775
24: 1 then he turned and r against him. 4775
24:20 that Zedekiah r against the king of 4775
2Ch 10:19 Israel r against the house of David unto this 6586
13: 6 is risen up, and hath r against his lord. 4775
36:13 he also r against king Nebuchadnezzar, 4775
Ne 9:26 r against thee, and cast thy law behind their 4775
Ps 5:10 for they have r against thee. 4784
105:28 it dark; and they r not against his word. 4784
107:11 Because they r against the words of God, 4784
Isa 1: 2 up children, and they have r against me. 6586
63:10 they r, and vexed his holy Spirit: therefore 4784
Jer 52: 3 that Zedekiah r against the king of 4775
La 1:18 for I have r against his commandment: 4784
1:20 within me; for I have grievously r: 4784+4784
3:42 We have transgressed and have r: thou hast 4784
Eze 2: 3 to a rebellious nation that hath r against 4775
17:15 he r against him in sending his 4775
20: 8 they r against me, and would not hearken 4784
20:13 the house of Israel r against me in 4784
20:21 Notwithstanding the children r against me: 4784
Da 9: 5 and have done wickedly, and have r, 4775
9: 9 though we have r against him; 4775
Hos 13:16 for she hath r against her God: 4784

REBELLEST (2) [REBEL]
2Ki 18:20 dost thou trust, that thou r against me? 4775
Isa 36: 5 dost thou trust, that thou r against me? 4775

REBELLION (9) [REBEL]
Dt 31:27 For I know thy r, and thy stiff neck: 4805
Jos 22:22 if it be in r, or if in transgression against 4777
1Sa 15:23 For r is as the sin of witchcraft, and 4805
Ezr 4:19 that r and sedition have been made therein. 4776
Ne 9:17 in their r appointed a captain to return to 4805
Job 34:37 For he addeth r unto his sin, he clappeth his 6588
Pr 17:11 An evil man seeketh only r: therefore 4805
Jer 28:16 thou hast taught r against the LORD. 5627
29:32 he hath taught r against the LORD. 5627

REBELLIOUS (36) [REBEL]
Dt 9: 7 ye have been r against the LORD. 4784
9:24 You have been r against the LORD from 4784
21:18 If a man have a stubborn and r son, 4784
21:20 This our son is stubborn and r, he will not 4784
31:27 ye have been r against the LORD; 4784
1Sa 20:30 Thou son of the perverse r woman, do not I 4780
Ezr 4:12 building the r and the bad city, and have set 4779
4:15 know that this city is a r city, and 4779
Ps 66: 7 let not the r exalt themselves. Selah. 5637
68: 6 with chains: but the r dwell in a dry land. 5637
68:18 yea, for the r also, that the LORD God 5637
78: 8 their fathers, a stubborn and r generation; 4784
Isa 1:23 Thy princes are r, and companions of 5637
30: 1 Woe to the r children, saith the LORD, 5637
30: 9 That this is a r people, lying children, 4805
50: 5 and I was not r, neither turned away back. 4784
65: 2 out mine hands all the day unto a r people, 5637
Jer 4:17 because she hath been r against me, 4784
5:23 this people hath a revolting and a r heart; 4784
Eze 2: 3 to a r nation that hath rebelled against me: 4775
2: 5 they will forbear, (for they are a r house,) 4805
2: 6 at their looks, though they be a r house. 4805
2: 7 they will forbear: for they are most r. 4805
2: 8 Be not thou r like that rebellious house: 4805
2: 8 Be not thou rebellious like that r house: 4805
3: 9 at their looks, though they be a r house. 4805
Eze 3:26 to them a reprover: for they are a r house. 4805
3:27 let him forbear: for they are a r house. 4805
12: 2 thou dwellest in the midst of a r house, 4805
12: 2 to hear, and hear not: for they are a r house. 4805
12: 3 will consider, though they be a r house. 4805
12: 9 the r house, said unto thee, What doest 4805
12:25 for in your days, O r house, will I say 4805
17:12 Say now to the r house, Know ye not what 4805
24: 3 utter a parable unto the r house, and 4805
44: 6 thou shalt say to the r, even to the house of 4805

REBELS (3) [REBEL]
Nu 17:10 to be kept for a token against the r; 1121+4805
20:10 and he said unto them, Hear now, ye r; 4784
Eze 20:38 And I will purge out from among you the r, 4775

REBIRTH See REGENERATION

REBUKE (46) [REBUKED, REBUKER, REBUKES, REBUKETH, REBUKING, UNREBUKEABLE]
Lev 19:17 thou shalt in any wise r thy 3198+3198
Dt 28:20 send upon thee cursing, vexation, and r, 4045
Ru 2:16 that she may glean them, and r her not. 1605
2Ki 19: 3 a day of trouble, and of r, and blasphemy: 8433
1Ch 12:17 God of our fathers look thereon, and r it. 3198
Ps 6: 1 O LORD, r me not in thine anger, 3198
18:15 of the world were discovered at thy r, 1606
38: 1 O LORD, r me not in thy wrath: 3198
68:30 R the company of spearmen, the multitude 1605
76: 6 At thy r, O God of Jacob, both the chariot 1606
80:16 they perish at the r of thy countenance. 1606
104: 7 At thy r they fled; at the voice of thy 1606
Pr 9: 8 r a wise man, and he will love thee. 3198
13: 1 but a scorner heareth not r. 1606
13: 8 are his riches: but the poor heareth not r. 1606
24:25 to them that r him shall be delight, and 3198
27: 5 Open r is better than secret love. 8433
Ecc 7: 5 It is better to hear the r of the wise, than for 1606
Isa 2: 4 the nations, and shall r many people: 3198
17:13 God shall r them, and they shall flee far 1605
25: 8 the r of his people shall he take away from 2781
30:17 One thousand shall flee at the r of one; 1606
30:17 rebuke of one; at the r of five shall ye flee: 1606
37: 3 day of trouble, and of r, and of blasphemy: 8433
50: 2 behold, at my r I dry up the sea, I make 1606
51:20 of the fury of the LORD, the r of thy God. 1606
54: 9 I would not be wroth with thee, nor r thee. 1605
66:15 with fury, and his r with flames of fire. 1606
Jer 15:15 know that for thy sake I have suffered r. 2781
Hos 5: 9 Ephraim shall be desolate in the day of r: 8433
Mic 4: 3 many people, and r strong nations afar off; 3198
Zec 3: 2 unto Satan, The LORD r thee, O Satan; 1605
3: 2 LORD that hath chosen Jerusalem r thee: 1605
Mal 3:11 I will r the devourer for your sakes, and 1605
Mt 16:22 and began to r him, saying, Be it far from 2008
Mk 8:32 And Peter took him, and began to r him. 2008
Lk 17: 3 If thy brother trespass against thee, r him; 2008
19:39 said unto him, Master, r thy disciples. 2008
Php 2:15 and harmless, the sons of God without r, 298
1Ti 5: 1 R not an elder, but intreat him as a father; 1969
5:20 Them that sin r before all, that others also 1651
2Ti 4: 2 reprove, r, exhort with all longsuffering 2008
Tit 1:13 Wherefore r them sharply, that they may be 1651
2:15 and exhort, and r with all authority. 1651
Jude 1: 9 but said, The Lord r thee. 2008
Rev 3:19 As many as I love, I r and chasten: 1651

REBUKED (25) [REBUKE]
Ge 31:42 labour of my hands, and r thee yesternight. 3198
37:10 his father r him, and said unto him, What is 1605
Ne 5: 7 I r the nobles, and the rulers, and said unto 7378
Ps 9: 5 Thou hast r the heathen, thou hast 1605
106: 9 He r the Red sea also, and it was dried up: 1605
119:21 Thou hast r the proud that are cursed, 1605
Mt 8:26 Then he arose, and r the winds and the sea; 2008
17:18 And Jesus r the devil; and he departed out 2008
19:13 and pray: and the disciples r them. 2008
20:31 And the multitude r them, because 2008
Mk 1:25 And Jesus r him, saying, Hold thy peace, 2008
4:39 and r the wind, and said unto the sea, 2008
8:33 he r Peter, saying, Get thee behind me, 2008
9:25 he r the foul spirit, saying unto him, 2008
10:13 and his disciples r those that brought them. 2008
Lk 4:35 And Jesus r him, saying, Hold thy peace, 2008
4:39 And he stood over her, and r the fever; and 2008
8:24 and r the wind and the raging of the water: 2008
9:42 tare him. And Jesus r the unclean spirit, 2008
9:55 But he turned, and r them, and said, 2008
18:15 but when his disciples saw it, they r them. 2008
18:39 And they which went before r him, that he 2008
23:40 But the other answering r him, saying, Dost 2008
Heb 12: 5 the Lord, nor faint when thou art r of him: 1651
2Pe 2:16 But was r for his iniquity: the dumb ass 1649

REBUKER (1) [REBUKE]
Hos 5: 2 though I have been a r of them all. 4148

REBUKES (3) [REBUKE]
Ps 39:11 When thou with r dost correct man for 8433
Eze 5:15 in thee in anger and in fury and in furious r. 8433
25:17 great vengeance upon them with furious r. 8433

REBUKETH (4) [REBUKE]
Pr 9: 7 he that r a wicked man getteth himself a 3198
28:23 He that r a man, afterwards shall find more 3198
Am 5:10 They hate him that r in the gate, and 3198
Na 1: 4 He r the sea, and maketh it dry, and 1605

REBUKING (2) [REBUKE]
2Sa 22:16 at the r of the LORD, at the blast of 1606
Lk 4:41 And he r them suffered them not to speak: 2008

RECAB See RECHAB

RECABITE See RECHABITES

RECAH See RECHAH

RECALL (1)
La 3:21 This I r to my mind, therefore have I hope. 7725

RECEDED See ABATED

RECEIPT (3) [RECEIVE]
Mt 9: 9 named Matthew, sitting at the r of custom: *5058*
Mk 2:14 *son* of Alpheus sitting at the r of custom, *5058*
Lk 5:27 named Levi, sitting at the r of custom: *5058*

RECEIVE (176) [RECEIPT, RECEIVED, RECEIVEDST, RECEIVER, RECEIVETH, RECEIVING]
Ge 4:11 which hath opened her mouth to r thy 3947
33:10 in thy sight, then r my present at my hand: 3947
38:20 to r *his* pledge from the woman's hand: 3947
Ex 27: 3 thou shalt make his pans to r his ashes, 1878
29:25 thou shalt r them of their hands, and 3947
Nu 18:28 which ye r of the children of Israel; 3947
Dt 9: 9 When I was gone up into the mount to r 3947
33: 3 at thy feet; *every one* shall r of thy words. 5375
1Sa 10: 4 of bread; which thou shalt r of their hands. 3947
2Sa 18:12 Though I should r a thousand *shekels of* 8254
1Ki 5: 9 thou shalt r *them:* and thou shalt 5375
8:64 *was* too little to r the burnt offerings, 3557
2Ki 5:16 before whom I stand, I will r none. 3947
5:26 *Is it* a time to r money, and to receive 3947
5:26 to r garments, and oliveyards, and 3947
12: 7 r no *more* money of your acquaintance, 3947
12: 8 the priests consented to r no *more* money 3947
2Ch 7: 7 made was not able to r the burnt offerings, 3557
Job 2:10 shall we r good at the hand of God, and 6901
2:10 at the hand of God, and shall we not r evil? 6901
22:22 R, I pray thee, the law from his mouth, and 3947
27:13 *which* they shall r of the Almighty. 3947
Ps 6: 9 the LORD will r my prayer. 3947
24: 5 He shall r the blessing from the LORD, 5375
49:15 of the grave: for he shall r me. Selah. 3947
73:24 thy counsel, and afterward r me *to* glory. 3947
75: 2 When I shall r the congregation I will 3947
Pr 1: 3 To r the instruction of wisdom, justice, and 3947
2: 1 if thou wilt r my words, and hide my 3947
4:10 Hear, O my son, and r my sayings; and 3947
8:10 R my instruction, and not silver; and 3947
10: 8 The wise in heart will r commandments: 3947
19:20 Hear counsel, and r instruction, that thou 6901
Isa 57: 6 meat offering. Should I r comfort in these? 5162
Jer 5: 3 *but* they have refused to r correction: 3947
9:20 let your ear r the word of his mouth, and 3947
17:23 that *they* might not hear, nor r instruction. 3947
32:33 they have not hearkened to r instruction. 3947
35:13 Will ye not r instruction to hearken to my 3947
Eze 3:10 all my words that I shall speak unto thee r 3947
16:61 when thou shalt r thy sisters, thine elder 3947
36:30 that ye shall r no more reproach of famine 3947
Da 2: 6 ye shall r of me gifts and rewards and 6902
Hos 10: 6 Ephraim shall r shame, and Israel shall be 3947
14: 2 Take away all iniquity, and r *us* graciously: 3947
Mic 1:11 of Beth-ezel; he shall r of you his standing. 3947
Zep 3: 7 thou wilt fear me, thou wilt r instruction; 3947
Mal 3:10 that *there shall* not *be room* enough *to r it.* NIH
Mt 10:14 And whosoever shall not r you, nor hear *1209*
10:41 of a prophet shall r a prophet's reward; *2983*
10:41 *man* shall r a righteous *man's* reward. *2983*
11: 5 The blind r their sight, and the lame walk, *308*
11:14 And if ye will r *it,* this is Elias, which was *1209*
18: 5 And whoso shall r one such little child in *1209*
19:11 unto them, All *men* cannot r this saying, *5562*
19:12 He that is able to r *it,* let him receive *it.* *5562*
19:12 He that is able to receive *it,* let him r *it.* *5562*
19:29 shall r an hundredfold, and shall inherit *2983*
20: 7 and whatsoever is right, *that* shall ye r. *2983*
21:22 ye shall ask in prayer, believing, ye shall r. *2983*
21:34 that *they* might r the fruits of it. *2983*
23:14 therefore ye shall r the greater damnation. *2983*
Mk 2: 2 insomuch that there was no room to r *them,* NIG
4:16 the word, immediately r it with gladness; *2983*
4:20 the word, and r *it,* and bring forth fruit, *3858*
6:11 And whosoever shall not r you, nor hear *1209*
9:37 Whosoever shall r one of such children in *1209*
9:37 and whosoever shall r me, receiveth not *1209*
10:15 Whosoever shall not r the kingdom of God *1209*
10:30 But he shall r an hundredfold now in this *2983*
10:51 said unto him, Lord, that I might r my sight. *308*
11:24 believe that ye r *them,* and ye shall have *2983*
12: 2 that he might r from the husbandmen of *2983*
12:40 these shall r greater damnation. *2983*
Lk 6:34 if ye lend *to them* of whom ye hope to r, *618*
6:34 also lend to sinners, to r as much again. *618*
8:13 when they hear, r the word with joy; *1209*
9: 5 And whosoever will not r you, when ye go *1209*
9:48 Whosoever shall r this child in my name *1209*
9:48 whosoever shall r me receiveth him that *1209*
9:53 And they did not r him, because his face *1209*
10: 8 whatsoever city ye enter, and they r you, *1209*
10:10 city ye enter, and they r you not, *1209*
16: 4 they may r me into their houses. *1209*
16: 9 they may r you into everlasting habitations. *1209*
18:17 Whosoever shall not r the kingdom of God *1209*
18:30 Who shall not r manifold more in this *618*
18:41 And he said, Lord, that I may r my sight. *308*
18:42 And Jesus said unto him, R thy sight: *308*
19:12 a far country to r for himself a kingdom, *2983*
20:47 the same shall r greater damnation. *2983*
23:41 for we r the due reward of our deeds: *618*
Jn 3:11 that we have seen; and ye r not our witness. *2983*
3:27 and said, A man can r nothing, *2983*
5:34 But I r not testimony from man: *2983*
5:41 I r not honour from men. *2983*
5:43 in my Father's name, and ye r me not: *2983*
5:43 shall come in his own name, him ye will r. *2983*
Jn 5:44 which r honour one of another, and *2983*
7:23 If a man on the sabbath day r circumcision, *2983*
7:39 which they that believe on him should r: *2983*
14: 3 I will come again, and r you unto myself; *3880*
14:17 whom the world cannot r, because it seeth *2983*
16:14 for he shall r of mine, and shall shew *it* *2983*
16:24 ask, and ye shall r, that your joy may be *2983*
20:22 and saith unto them, R ye the Holy Ghost: *2983*
Ac 1: 8 But ye shall r power, after that the Holy *2983*
2:38 and ye shall r the gift of the Holy Ghost. *2983*
3: 5 expecting to r something of them. *2983*
3:21 Whom the heaven must r until the times of *1209*
7:59 and saying, Lord Jesus, r my spirit. *1209*
8:15 for them, that they might r the Holy Ghost: *2983*
8:19 I lay hands, he may r the Holy Ghost. *2983*
9:12 *his* hand on him, that he might r his sight. *308*
9:17 that thou mightest r thy sight, and be filled *308*
10:43 believeth in him shall r remission of sins. *2983*
16:21 which are not lawful for us to r, neither to *3858*
18:27 exhorting the disciples to r him: *588*
20:35 he said, It is more blessed to give than to r. *2983*
22:13 and said unto me, Brother Saul, r thy sight. *308*
22:18 for they will not r thy testimony concerning *3858*
26:18 that they may r forgiveness of sins, and *2983*
Ro 5:17 much more they which r abundance of *2983*
13: 2 they that resist shall r to themselves *2983*
14: 1 Him that is weak in the faith r you, *but* *4355*
15: 7 Wherefore r ye one another, as Christ also *4355*
16: 2 That ye r her in the Lord, as becometh *4327*
1Co 3: 8 every man shall r his own reward *2983*
3:14 he hath built thereupon, he shall r a reward. *2983*
4: 7 and what hast thou that thou didst not r? *2983*
4: 7 now if thou didst r *it,* why dost thou glory, *2983*
14: 5 he interpret, that the church may r edifying. *2983*
2Co 5:10 that every one may r the *things done* in *his* *2865*
6: 1 also that ye r not the grace of God in vain. *1209*
6:17 not the unclean *thing;* and I will r you, *1523*
7: 2 R us; we have wronged no *man,* we have *5562*
7: 9 that ye might r damage by us in nothing. *2210*
8: 4 with much intreaty that we would r the gift, *1209*
11: 4 or *if* ye r another spirit, which ye have not *2983*
11:16 if otherwise, yet as a fool r me, that I may *1209*
Gal 3:14 that we might r the promise of the Spirit *2983*
4: 5 that we might r the adoption of sons. *618*
Eph 6: 8 the same shall he r of the Lord, whether *he* *2865*
Php 2:29 R him therefore in the Lord with all *4327*
Col 3:24 Knowing that of the Lord ye shall r *618*
3:25 But he that doeth wrong shall r *for* *2865*
4:10 if he come unto you, r him;) *1209*
1Ti 5:19 Against an elder r not an accusation, but *3858*
Phm 1:12 thou therefore r him, that is, mine own *4355*
1:15 a season, that thou shouldest r him for ever; *568*
1:17 therefore a partner, r him as myself. *4355*
Heb 7: 5 r the office of the priesthood have a *2983*
7: 8 And here men that die r tithes; but there he *2983*
9:15 they which are called might r the promise *2983*
10:36 the will of God, ye might r the promise. *2865*
11: 8 which he should after r for an inheritance, *2983*
Jas 1: 7 For let not that man think that he shall r *2983*
1:12 he is tried, he shall r the crown of life, *2983*
1:21 and r with meekness the engrafted word, *1209*
3: 1 knowing that we shall r the greater *2983*
4: 3 Ye ask, and r not, because ye ask amiss, *2983*
5: 7 for it, until he r the early and latter rain. *2983*
1Pe 5: 4 ye shall r a crown of glory that fadeth not *2865*
2Pe 2:13 And shall r the reward of unrighteousness, *2865*
1Jn 3:22 we r of him, because we keep his *2983*
5: 9 If we r the witness of men, the witness of *2983*
2Jn 1: 8 have wrought, but *that* we r a full reward. *618*
1:10 not this doctrine, r him not into *your* house, *2983*
3Jn 1: 8 We therefore ought to r such, that we might *618*
1:10 neither doth he himself r the brethren, and *1926*
Rev 4:11 O Lord, to r glory and honour and power: *2983*
5:12 Worthy is the Lamb that was slain to r *2983*
13:16 to r a mark in their right hand, or in their *1325*
14: 9 and r *his* mark in his forehead, or in his *2983*
17:12 r power as kings one hour with the beast. *2983*
18: 4 of her sins, and that ye r not of her plagues. *2983*

RECEIVED (160) [RECEIVE]
Ge 26:12 r in the same year an hundredfold: 4672
Ex 32: 4 he r *them* at their hand, and fashioned it 3947
36: 3 they r of Moses all the offering, which 3947
Nu 12:14 and after *that* let her be r in *again.* 622
23:20 Behold, I have r *commandment* to bless: 3947
34:14 have r *their inheritance;* and half the tribe 3947
34:14 half the tribe of Manasseh have r their 3947
34:15 the half tribe have r their inheritance on 3947
36: 3 of the tribe whereunto they are r: 1961+3807.1
36: 4 of the tribe whereunto they are r: 1961+3807.1
Jos 13: 8 and the Gadites have r their inheritance, 3947
18: 2 which had not *yet* r their inheritance. 2505
18: 7 have r their inheritance beyond Jordan on 3947
Jdg 13:23 he would not have r a burnt offering and 3947
1Sa 12: 3 of whose hand have I r *any* bribe to blind 3947
25:35 So David r of her hand *that* which she had 3947
1Ki 10:28 the king's merchants r the linen yarn at a 3947
2Ki 19:14 Hezekiah r the letter of the hand of 3947
1Ch 12:18 David r them, and made them captains of 6901
2Ch 1:16 the king's merchants r the linen yarn at a 3947
4: 5 *and* it r and held three thousand baths. 2388
29:22 the priests r the blood, and sprinkled *it* on 6901
30:16 *which they* r of the hand of the Levites. NIH
Est 4: 4 his sackcloth from him: but he r *it* not. 6901
Job 4:12 to me, and mine ear r a little thereof. 3947
Ps 68:18 thou hast r gifts for men; yea, *for* 3947
Pr 24:32 *it* well: I looked upon *it, and* r instruction. 3947
Isa 37:14 Hezekiah r the letter from the hand of 3947
40: 2 for she hath r of the LORD'S hand double 3947
Jer 2:30 smitten your children; they r no correction: 3947
Eze 18:17 *that* hath not r usury nor increase, 3947
Zep 3: 2 obeyed not the voice; she r not correction; 3947
Mt 10: 8 out devils: freely ye have r, freely give. *2983*
13:19 This is he which r seed by the way side. *4687*
13:20 But he that r the seed into stony *places,* *4687*
Mt 13:22 He also that r seed among the thorns is he *4687*
13:23 But he that r seed into the good ground is *4687*
17:24 they that r tribute money came to Peter, *2983*
20: 9 eleventh hour, they r every man a penny. *2983*
20:10 they supposed that they should have r *2983*
20:10 and they likewise r every man a penny. *2983*
20:11 And when they had r *it,* they murmured *2983*
20:34 and immediately their eyes r sight, and *308*
25:16 Then he that had r the five talents went *2983*
25:17 And likewise he that *had* r two, he also NIG
25:18 But he that had r one went and digged in *2983*
25:20 And *so* he that had r five talents came and *2983*
25:22 He also that had r two talents came and *2983*
25:24 Then he which had r the one talent came *2983*
25:27 at my coming I should have r mine own *2865*
Mk 7: 4 which they have r to hold, *as* the washing *3880*
10:52 And immediately he r his sight, and *308*
15:23 wine mingled with myrrh: but he r *it* not. *2983*
16:19 he was r up into heaven, and sat on the right *353*
Lk 6:24 that are rich: for ye have r your consolation. *568*
8:40 Jesus was returned, the people gladly r him: *588*
9:11 and he r them, and spake unto them of *1209*
9:51 the time was come that he should be r up, *354*
10:38 a certain woman named Martha r him into *5264*
15:27 because he hath r him *safe and* sound. *618*
18:43 And immediately he r his sight, and *308*
19: 6 and came down, and r him joyfully. *5264*
19:15 having r the kingdom, then he commanded *2983*
Jn 1:11 came unto his own, and his own r him not. *3880*
1:12 But as many as r him, to them gave he *2983*
1:16 And of his fulness have all we r, and *2983*
3:33 He that hath r his testimony hath set to *his* *2983*
4:45 was come into Galilee, the Galileans r him, *1209*
6:21 Then they willingly r him into the ship: and *2983*
9:11 wash: and I went and washed, and I r sight. *308*
9:15 also asked him how he had r his sight. *308*
9:18 that he had been blind, and r his sight, *308*
9:18 called the parents of him that had r his sight. *308*
10:18 This commandment have I r of my Father. *2983*
13:30 having r the sop went immediately out: *2983*
17: 8 and they have r *them,* and have known *2983*
18: 3 having r a band *of men,* and officers from *2983*
19:30 When Jesus therefore had r the vinegar, *2983*
Ac 1: 9 and a cloud r him out of their sight. *5274*
2:33 having r of the Father the promise of *2983*
2:41 Then they that gladly r his word were *588*
3: 7 his feet and ankle bones r strength, *4732*
7:38 who r *the* lively oracles to give unto us: *1209*
7:53 Who have r the law by the disposition of *2983*
8:14 heard that Samaria had r the word of God, *1209*
8:17 hands on them, and they r the Holy Ghost. *2983*
9:18 and he r sight forthwith, and arose, and *308*
9:19 And when he had r meat, he was *2983*
10:16 and the vessel was r up again into heaven. *353*
10:47 which have r the Holy Ghost as well as *2983*
11: 1 the Gentiles had also r the word of God. *1209*
15: 4 they were r of the church, and *of* *588*
16:24 Who, having r such a charge, thrust them *2983*
17: 7 Whom Jason hath r: and these all do *5264*
17:11 in that they r the word with all readiness of *1209*
19: 2 Have ye r the Holy Ghost since ye *2983*
20:24 which I have r of the Lord Jesus, *2983*
21:17 come to Jerusalem, the brethren r us gladly. *1209*
22: 5 from whom also I r letters unto *1209*
26:10 having r authority from the chief priests; *2983*
28: 2 and r us every one, because of the present *4355*
28: 7 who r us, and lodged *us* three days *324*
28:21 We neither r letters out of Judea *1209*
28:30 hired house, and r all that came in unto him, *588*
Ro 1: 5 By whom we have r grace and apostleship, *2983*
4:11 And he r the sign of circumcision, a seal of *2983*
5:11 by whom we have now r the atonement. *2983*
8:15 For ye have not r the spirit of bondage *2983*
8:15 but ye have r the Spirit of adoption, *2983*
14: 3 judge him that eateth: for God hath r him. *4355*
15: 7 as Christ also r us, to the glory of God. *4355*
1Co 2:12 Now we have r, not the spirit of the world, *2983*
4: 7 dost thou glory, as if thou hadst not r *it?* *2983*
11:23 For I have r of the Lord *that* which also I *3880*
15: 1 which also you have r, and wherein ye *3880*
15: 3 unto you first *of all* that which I also r, *3880*
2Co 4: 1 as we have r mercy, we faint not; *1653*
7:15 how with fear and trembling you r him. *1209*
11: 4 which ye have not r, or another gospel, *2983*
11:24 Of the Jews five times r I forty *stripes* save *2983*
Gal 1: 9 other gospel unto you than that ye have r, *3880*
1:12 For I neither r it of man, neither was I *3880*
3: 2 R ye the Spirit by the works of the law, or *2983*
4:14 but r me as an angel of God, *even* as *1209*
Php 4: 9 and r, and heard, and seen in me, do: *3880*
4:18 having r of Epaphroditus the *things which* *1209*
Col 2: 6 ye have therefore r Christ Jesus the Lord, *3880*
4:10 (touching whom ye r commandments: *2983*
4:17 Take heed to the ministry which thou hast r *3880*
1Th 1: 6 having r the word in much affliction, *1209*
2:13 when ye r the word of God which *ye* heard *3880*
2:13 ye r *it* not as the word of men, but as it is in *1209*
4: 1 that as ye have r of us how ye ought to *3880*
2Th 2:10 because they r not the love of the truth, *1209*
3: 6 and not after the tradition which he r of us. *3880*
1Ti 3:16 believed on in the world, r up into glory. *353*
4: 3 which God hath created to be r with *3336*
4: 4 to be refused, if it be r with thanksgiving: *2983*
Heb 2: 2 disobedience r a just recompence of *2983*
7: 6 counted from them r tithes of Abraham, *1183*
7:11 (for under it the people r the law,) *3549*
10:26 For if we sin wilfully after that *we* have r *2983*
11:11 Through faith also Sara herself r strength to *2983*
11:13 not having r the promises, but having seen *2983*
11:17 he that had r the promises offered up *his* *324*
11:19 from whence also he r him in a figure. *2865*
11:31 when she had r the spies with peace. *1209*
11:35 Women r their dead raised to life again: *2983*
11:39 report through faith, r not the promise: *2865*
Jas 2:25 when she had r the messengers, and *5264*

R

1Pe 1:18 **r by tradition from** your **fathers**; *3970*
4:10 As every man hath **r** *the* gift, *even so* *2983*
2Pe 1:17 For he **r** from God the Father honour and *2983*
1Jn 2:27 But the anointing which ye have **r** of him *2983*
2Jn 1: 4 as we have **r** a commandment from *2983*
Rev 2:27 broken to shivers: even as I **r** of my Father. *2983*
3: 3 therefore how thou hast **r** and heard, *2983*
17:12 ten kings, which have **r** no kingdom as yet; *2983*
19:20 with which he deceived them that had **r** *2983*
20: 4 neither had **r** *his* mark upon their *2983*

RECEIVEDST (1) [RECEIVE]
Lk 16:25 remember that thou in thy lifetime **r** thy *618*

RECEIVER (1) [RECEIVE]
Isa 33:18 where *is* the **r**? where *is* he that counted 8254

RECEIVETH (37) [RECEIVE]
Jdg 19:18 and there *is* no man that **r** me to house. 622
Job 35: 7 thou him? or what **r** he of thine hand? 3947
Pr 21:11 the wise is instructed, he **r** knowledge. 3947
29: 4 the land: but he that **r** gifts overthroweth it. NIH
Jer 7:28 of the LORD their God, nor **r** correction: 3947
Mal 2:13 or **r** *it with* good will at your hand. 3947
Mt 7: 8 For every one that asketh **r**; and he that *2983*
10:40 He that **r** you receiveth me, and he that *1209*
10:40 He that receiveth you **r** me, and he that *1209*
10:40 he that **r** me receiveth him that sent me. *1209*
10:40 he that receiveth me **r** him that sent me. *1209*
10:41 He that **r** a prophet in the name of a *1209*
10:41 he that **r** a righteous *man* in the name of a *2983*
13:20 heareth the word, and anon with joy **r** it; *2983*
18: 5 one such little child in my name **r** me. *1209*
Mk 9:37 one of such children in my name, **r** me: *1209*
9:37 receive me, **r** not me, but him that sent me. *1209*
Lk 9:48 shall receive this child in my name **r** me: *1209*
9:48 whosoever shall receive me **r** him that sent *1209*
11:10 For every one that asketh **r**; and he that *2983*
15: 2 This *man* **r** sinners, and eateth with them. *4327*
Jn 3:32 he testifieth; and no *man* **r** his testimony. *2983*
4:36 And he that reapeth **r** wages, and *2983*
12:48 He that rejecteth me, and **r** not my words, *2983*
13:20 He that **r** whomsoever I send receiveth me; *2983*
13:20 He that receiveth whomsoever I send **r** me; *2983*
13:20 he that **r** me receiveth him that sent me. *2983*
13:20 he that receiveth me **r** him that sent me. *2983*
1Co 2:14 But the natural man **r** not the *things* of *1209*
9:24 run in a race run all, but one **r** the prize? *2983*
Heb 6: 7 whom it is dressed, **r** blessing from God: *3335*
7: 8 there he **r** *them,* of whom it is witnessed NIG
7: 9 as *I* may so say, Levi also, who **r** tithes, *2983*
12: 6 and scourgeth every son whom he **r**. *3858*
3Jn 1: 9 the preeminence among them, **r** us not. *1926*
Rev 2:17 which no *man* knoweth saving he that **r** *it.* *2983*
14:11 and whosoever **r** the mark of his name. *2983*

RECEIVING (7) [RECEIVE]
2Ki 5:20 in not **r** at his hands *that* which he brought: 3947
Ac 17:15 and **r** a commandment unto Silas and *2983*
Ro 1:27 **r** in themselves *that* recompence of their *618*
11:15 what *shall* the **r** *of them be,* but life from *4356*
Php 4:15 with me as concerning giving and **r**, *3028*
Heb 12:28 Wherefore we **r** a kingdom which cannot *3880*
1Pe 1: 9 **R** the end of your faith, *even* the salvation *2865*

RECENT CONVERT See NOVICE

RECHAB (13) [RECHABITES]
2Sa 4: 2 *was* Baanah, and the name of the other **R**, 7394
4: 5 **R** and Baanah, went, and came about 7394
4: 6 and **R** and Baanah his brother escaped. 7394
4: 9 David answered **R** and Baanah his brother, 7394
2Ki 10:15 he lighted on Jehonadab the son of **R** 7394
10:23 Jehu went, and Jehonadab the son of **R**, 7394
1Ch 2:55 of Hemath, the father of the house of **R**. 7394
Ne 3:14 dung gate repaired Malchiah the son of **R**, 7394
Jer 35: 6 for Jonadab the son of **R** our father 7394
35: 8 **R** our father in all that he hath charged us, 7394
35:14 The words of Jonadab the son of **R**, that he 7394
35:16 Because the sons of Jonadab the son of **R** 7394
35:19 Jonadab the son of **R** shall not want a man 7394

RECHABITES (4) [RECHAB]
Jer 35: 2 Go unto the house of the **R**, and speak unto 7397
35: 3 all his sons, and the whole house of the **R**; 7397
35: 5 I set before the sons of the house of the **R** 7397
35:18 Jeremiah said unto the house of the **R**, 7397

RECHAH (1)
1Ch 4:12 father of Irnahash. These *are* the men of **R**. 7397

RECITE See REHEARSE

RECKON (8) [RECKONED, RECKONETH, RECKONING]
Lev 25:50 he shall **r** with him that bought him from 2803
27:18 the priest shall **r** unto him the money 2803
27:23 the priest shall **r** unto him the worth of thy 2803
Nu 4:32 by name ye shall **r** the instruments of 6485
Eze 44:26 they shall **r** unto him seven days. 5608
Mt 18:24 And when he had begun to **r**, one was *4868*
Ro 6:11 Likewise **r** ye also yourselves to be dead *3049*
8:18 For I **r** that the sufferings of *this* present *3049*

RECKONED (22) [RECKON]
Nu 18:27 *this* your heave offering shall be **r** unto 2803
23: 9 and shall not be **r** among the nations. 2803
2Sa 4: 2 (for Beeroth also was **r** to Benjamin: 2803
2Ki 12:15 Moreover they **r** not with the men, 2803
1Ch 5: 1 the **genealogy** is not to be **r** after 3187
5: 7 the **genealogy** of their generations was **r**, 3187
5:17 All these were **r by genealogies** in the days 3187
7: 5 **r** in all **by** their **genealogies** fourscore and 3187
7: 7 were **r by** their **genealogies** twenty and 3187
1Ch 9: 1 So all Israel were **r by genealogies**; and 3187
9:22 These were **r by** their **genealogy** in their 3187
2Ch 31:19 to all that were **r by genealogies** among 3187
Ezr 2:62 *among* those that were **r by genealogy**, 3187
8: 3 with him were **r by genealogy** of the males 3187
Ne 7: 5 that *they* might be **r by genealogy**. 3187
7:64 *among* those that were **r by genealogy**, 3187
Ps 40: 5 they cannot be **r up in order** unto thee: *if* I 6186
Isa 38:13 I **r** till morning, *that,* as a lion, so will he 7737
Lk 22:37 And he was **r** among the transgressors: *3049*
Ro 4: 4 that worketh is the reward not **r** of grace, *3049*
4: 9 for we say that faith was **r** to Abraham for *3049*
4:10 How was it then **r**? when he was in *3049*

RECKONETH (1) [RECKON]
Mt 25:19 servants cometh, and **r** with them. *3056+4868*

RECKONING (2) [RECKON]
2Ki 22: 7 Howbeit there was no **r made** with them of 2803
1Ch 23:11 therefore they were in one **r**, according to 6486

RECOMMENDED (2)
Ac 14:26 from whence they had been **r** to the grace *3860*
15:40 being **r** by the brethren unto the grace of *3860*

RECOMPENCE (20) [RECOMPENSE]
Dt 32:35 To me *belongeth* vengeance, and **r**; 8005
Job 15:31 trust in vanity: for vanity shall be his **r**. 8545
Pr 12:14 the **r** of a man's hands shall be rendered 1576
Isa 35: 4 come *with* vengeance, *even* God *with* a **r**; 1576
59:18 fury to his adversaries, **r** to his enemies; 1576
59:18 his enemies; to the islands he will repay **r**. 1576
66: 6 a voice of the LORD that rendereth **r** to 1576
Jer 51: 6 he *will* render unto her a **r**. 1576
La 3:64 Render unto them a **r**, O LORD, 1576
Hos 9: 7 visitation are come, the days of **r** are come; 7966
Joel 3: 4 will ye render me a **r**? and if ye 1576
3: 4 speedily will I return your **r** upon your own 1576
3: 7 and will return your **r** upon your own head: 1576
Lk 14:12 also bid thee again, and a **r** be made thee. *468*
Ro 1:27 receiving in themselves *that* **r** of their error *489*
11: 9 and a stumblingblock, and a **r** unto them: *468*
2Co 6:13 Now for a **r** in the same, (I speak as unto *my* *489*
Heb 2: 2 disobedience received a **just r** of reward; *1738*
10:35 which hath great **r of reward**. *3405*
11:26 for he had respect unto the **r of** the **reward**. *3405*

RECOMPENCES (2) [RECOMPENSE]
Isa 34: 8 the year of **r** for the controversy of Zion. 7966
Jer 51:56 for the LORD God of **r** shall surely 1578

RECOMPENSE (26) [RECOMPENCE, RECOMPENCES, RECOMPENSED, RECOMPENSEST, RECOMPENSING]
Nu 5: 7 he shall **r** his trespass with the principal 7725
5: 8 if the man have no kinsman to **r** 7725
Ru 2:12 The LORD **r** thy work, and a full reward 7999
2Sa 19:36 why should the king **r** *it* me *with* such a 1580
Job 34:33 he will **r** it, whether thou refuse, or 7999
Pr 20:22 Say not thou, I will **r** evil; *but* wait on 7999
Isa 65: 6 I will not keep silence, but will **r**, 7999
65: 6 will recompense, even **r** into their bosom, 7999
Jer 16:18 first I will **r** their iniquity and their sin 7999
25:14 I will **r** them according to their deeds, and 7999
50:29 **r** her according to her work; according to 7999
Eze 7: 3 and will **r** upon thee all thine abominations. 5414
7: 4 I will **r** thy ways upon thee, and 5414
7: 8 and will **r** thee for all thine abominations. 5414
7: 9 I will **r** thee according to thy ways and 5414
9:10 *but* I will **r** their way upon their head. 5414
11:21 I will **r** their way upon their own heads, 5414
16:43 I also will **r** thy way upon *thine* head, 5414
17:19 even it will I **r** upon his own head. 5414
23:49 they shall **r** your lewdness upon you, and 5414
Hos 12: 2 according to his doings will he **r** him. 7725
Joel 3: 4 if ye **r** me, swiftly *and* speedily will I return 1580
Lk 14:14 thou shalt be blessed; for they cannot **r** thee: *467*
Ro 12:17 **R** to no *man* evil for evil. Provide *things* *591*
2Th 1: 6 Seeing *it is* a righteous *thing* with God to **r** *467*
Heb 10:30 *belongeth* unto me, I will **r**, saith the Lord. *467*

RECOMPENSED (10) [RECOMPENSE]
Nu 5: 8 *let* the trespass *be* **r** unto the LORD, 7725
2Sa 22:21 to the cleanness of my hands hath he **r** me. 7725
22:25 Therefore the LORD hath **r** me according 7725
Ps 18:20 to the cleanness of my hands hath he **r** me. 7725
18:24 Therefore hath the LORD **r** me according 7725
Pr 11:31 the righteous shall be **r** in the earth: 7999
Jer 18:20 Shall evil be **r** for good? for they have 7999
Eze 22:31 their own way have I **r** upon their heads, 5414
Lk 14:14 for thou shalt be **r** at the resurrection of *467*
Ro 11:35 to him, and it shall be **r** unto him *again?* *467*

RECOMPENSEST (1) [RECOMPENSE]
Jer 32:18 **r** the iniquity of the fathers into the bosom 7999

RECOMPENSING (1) [RECOMPENSE]
2Ch 6:23 by **r** his way upon his own head; 5414

RECONCILE (5) [RECONCILED, RECONCILIATION, RECONCILING]
Lev 6:30 to **r** *withal* in the holy *place,* shall be eaten: 3722
1Sa 29: 4 for wherewith should he **r** himself unto his 7521
Eze 45:20 *him that is* simple: so shall ye **r** the house. 3722
Eph 2:16 And *that* he might **r** both unto God in one *604*
Col 1:20 his cross, by him to **r** all *things* unto himself; *604*

RECONCILED (7) [RECONCILE]
Mt 5:24 first be **r** to thy brother, and then come and *1259*
Ro 5:10 we were **r** to God by the death of his Son, *2644*
5:10 much more, being **r**, we shall be saved by *2644*
1Co 7:11 remain unmarried, or be **r** to *her* husband: *2644*
2Co 5:18 who hath **r** us to himself by Jesus Christ, *2644*
2Co 5:20 pray *you* in Christ's stead, be ye **r** to God. *2644*
Col 1:21 mind by wicked works, yet now hath he **r** *604*

RECONCILIATION (8) [RECONCILE]
Lev 8:15 and sanctified it, to **make r** upon it. 3722
2Ch 29:24 they **made r** with their blood upon 2398
Eze 45:15 for peace offerings, to **make r** for them, 3722
45:17 to **make r** for the house of Israel. 3722
Da 9:24 to **make r** for iniquity, and to bring in 3722
2Co 5:18 and hath given to us the ministry of **r**; *2643*
5:19 and hath committed unto us the word of **r**. *2643*
Heb 2:17 to **make r** for the sins of the people. *2433*

RECONCILING (3) [RECONCILE]
Lev 16:20 when he hath made an end of **r** the holy 3722
Ro 11:15 For if the casting away of them *be* the **r** of *2643*
2Co 5:19 that God was in Christ **r** the world unto *2644*

RECORD (30) [RECORDED, RECORDER, RECORDS]
Ex 20:24 in all places where I **r** my name I will come 2142
Dt 30:19 I **call** heaven and earth **to r** *this* day against 5749
31:28 and **call** heaven and earth **to r** against them. 5749
1Ch 16: 4 to **r**, and to thank and praise the LORD 2142
Ezr 6: 2 a roll, and therein *was* a **r** thus written: 1799
Job 16:19 witness *is* in heaven, and my **r** *is* on high. 7717
Isa 8: 2 I **took** unto me faithful witnesses **to r**, 5749
Jn 1:19 And this is the **r** of John, when the Jews *3141*
1:32 And John **bare r**, saying, I saw the Spirit *3140*
1:34 and **bare r** that this is the Son of God. *3140*
8:13 said unto him, Thou **bearest r** of thyself; *3140*
8:13 bearest record of thyself; thy **r** is not true. *3141*
8:14 said unto them, Though I **bear r** of myself, *3140*
8:14 I bear record of myself, *yet* my **r** is true: *3141*
12:17 and raised him from the dead, **bare r**. *3140*
19:35 And he that saw *it* **bare r**, and his record is *3140*
19:35 he that saw *it* bare record, and his **r** is true: *3141*
Ac 20:26 Wherefore I **take** you **to r** this day, that I *3143*
Ro 10: 2 For I **bear** them **r** that they have a zeal of *3140*
2Co 1:23 Moreover I call God for a **r** upon my soul, *3144*
8: 3 I **bear r**, *yea,* and beyond *their* power *they* *3140*
Gal 4:15 for I **bear** you **r**, that if *it had been* *3140*
Php 1: 8 For God is my **r**, how *greatly* I long after *3144*
Col 4:13 For I **bear** him **r**, that he hath a great zeal *3140*
1Jn 5: 7 For there are three that **bear r** in heaven, *3140*
5:10 he believeth not the **r** that God gave of his *3141*
5:11 And this is the **r**, that God hath given to us *3141*
3Jn 1:12 yea, and we also **bear r**; and ye know that *3140*
1:12 bear record; and ye know that our **r** is true. *3141*
Rev 1: 2 Who **bare r** of the word of God, and of *3140*

RECORDED (1) [RECORD]
Ne 12:22 and Jaddua, *were* **r** chief of the fathers: 3789

RECORDER (9) [RECORD]
2Sa 8:16 and Jehoshaphat the son of Ahilud *was* **r**; 2142
20:24 and Jehoshaphat the son of Ahilud *was* **r**: 2142
1Ki 4: 3 Jehoshaphat the son of Ahilud, the **r**. 2142
2Ki 18:18 the scribe, and Joah the son of Asaph the **r**. 2142
18:37 the scribe, and Joah the son of Asaph the **r**, 2142
1Ch 18:15 and Jehoshaphat the son of Ahilud, **r**. 2142
2Ch 34: 8 the city, and Joah the son of Joahaz the **r**, 2142
Isa 36: 3 the scribe, and Joah, Asaph's son, the **r**. 2142
36:22 and Joah, the son of Asaph, the **r**, 2142

RECORDS (3) [RECORD]
Ezr 4:15 be made in the book of the **r** of thy fathers: 1799
4:15 so shalt thou find in the book of the **r**, and 1799
Est 6: 1 he commanded to bring the book of **r** of 2146

RECOUNT (1)
Na 2: 5 He shall **r** his worthies: they shall stumble 2142

RECOVER (21) [RECOVERED, RECOVERING]
Jdg 11:26 did ye not **r** *them* within that time? 5337
1Sa 30: 8 and **without fail r** *all.* 5337+5337
2Sa 8: 3 as he went to **r** his border at the river 7725
2Ki 1: 2 of Ekron whether I shall **r** of this disease. 2421
5: 3 for he would **r** him of his leprosy. 622
5: 6 that thou mayest **r** him of his leprosy. 622
5: 7 that this *man* doth send unto me to **r** a man 622
5:11 his hand over the place, and **r** the leper. 622
8: 8 by him, saying, Shall I **r** of this disease? 2421
8: 9 me to thee, saying, Shall I **r** of this disease? 2421
8:10 unto him, Thou mayest **certainly r**: 2421+2421
8:14 told me *that* thou shouldest **surely r**. 2421+2421
2Ch 13:20 Neither did Jeroboam **r** strength again in 6113
14:13 that they could not **r** themselves; 4241
Ps 39:13 O spare me, that I may **r strength**, before I 1082
Isa 11:11 second time to **r** the remnant of his people, 7069
38:16 so wilt thou **r** me, and make me to live. 2492
38:21 for a plaister upon the boil, and he shall **r**. 2421
Hos 2: 9 will **r** my wool and my flax *given* to cover 5337
Mk 16:18 hands on the sick, and they shall **r**. *2192+2573*
2Ti 2:26 And *that* they may **r** themselves out of *366*

RECOVERED (11) [RECOVER]
1Sa 30:18 David **r** all that the Amalekites had carried 5337
30:19 that they had taken to them: David **r** all. 7725
30:22 give them *ought* of the spoil that we have **r**, 5337
2Ki 13:25 Joash beat him, and **r** the cities of Israel. 7725
14:28 and how he **r** Damascus, and Hamath, 7725
16: 6 At that time Rezin king of Syria **r** Elath to 7725
20: 7 they took and laid *it* on the boil, and he **r**. 2421
Isa 38: 9 he had been sick, and was **r** of his sickness: 2421
39: 1 had heard that he had been sick, and was **r**. 2388
Jer 8:22 the health of the daughter of my people **r**? 5927
41:16 the remnant of the people whom he had **r** 7725

RECOVERING (1) [RECOVER]
Lk 4:18 to the captives, and **r of sight** to the blind, *309*

RED (53) [REDDISH, REDNESS]
Ge 25:25 the first came out r, all over like a hairy 132
25:30 with that same r *pottage;* for I *am* faint: 122
49:12 *His* eyes *shall be* r with wine, and *his* teeth 2447
Ex 10:19 the locusts, and cast them into the R sea; 5488
13:18 *through* the way of the wilderness of the R 5488
15: 4 captains also are drowned in the R sea. 5488
15:22 So Moses brought Israel from the R sea, 5488
23:31 I will set thy bounds from the R sea even 5488
25: 5 And rams' skins dyed r, and badgers' skins, 119
26:14 a covering for the tent *of* rams' skins dyed r, 119
35: 7 And rams' skins dyed r, and badgers' skins, 119
35:23 goats' *hair,* and r skins of rams, and 119
36:19 a covering for the tent *of* rams' skins dyed r, 119
39:34 And the covering of rams' skins dyed r, and 119
Nu 14:25 *into* the wilderness *by* the way of the R sea. 5488
19: 2 that they bring thee a r heifer without spot, 122
21: 4 from mount Hor *by* the way of the R sea, 5488
21:14 What he did in the R sea, and *in* the brooks 5492
33:10 from Elim, and encamped by the R sea. 5488
33:11 they removed from the R sea, and 5488
Dt 1: 1 in the plain over against the R *sea,* between 5489
1:40 into the wilderness *by* the way of the R sea. 5488
2: 1 into the wilderness *by* the way of the R sea, 5488
11: 4 how he made the water of the R sea to 5488
Jos 2:10 dried up the water of the R sea for you, 5488
4:23 as the LORD your God did to the R sea, 5488
24: 6 with chariots and horsemen *unto* the R sea. 5488
Jdg 11:16 walked through the wilderness unto the R 5488
1Ki 9:26 on the shore of the R sea, in the land of 5488
2Ki 3:22 saw the water on the other side *as* r as blood: 122
Ne 9: 9 and heardest their cry by the R sea; 5488
Est 1: 6 upon a pavement of r, and blue, and white, 923
Ps 75: 8 LORD *there is* a cup, and the wine is r; 2560
106: 7 provoked *him* at the sea, *even* at the R sea. 5488
106: 9 He rebuked the R sea also, and it was dried 5488
106:22 of Ham, *and* terrible *things* by the R sea. 5488
136:13 To him which divided the R sea into parts: 5488
136:15 and his host in the R sea: 5488
Pr 23:31 Look not thou upon the wine when it is r, 119
Isa 1:18 though they be r like crimson, they shall be 119
27: 2 day sing ye unto her, A vineyard of r wine. 2561
63: 2 Wherefore *art thou* r in thine apparel, and 122
Jer 49:21 the noise thereof was heard in the R sea. 5488
Na 2: 3 The shield of his mighty *men is* made r, 119
Zec 1: 8 and behold a man riding upon a r horse, and 122
1: 8 behind him *were there* r horses, speckled, 122
6: 2 In the first chariot *were* r horses; and in 122
Mt 16: 2 *It will be* fair weather: for the sky is r. *4449*
16: 3 for the sky is r and lowring. O *ye* *4449*
Ac 7:36 and in the R sea, and in the wilderness *2063*
Heb 11:29 By faith they passed through the R sea as *2063*
Rev 6: 4 there went out another horse *that was* r: *4450*
12: 3 and behold a great r dragon, having seven *4450*

REDDISH (6) [RED]
Lev 13:19 *and* somewhat r, and it be shewed to 125
13:24 a white bright spot, somewhat r, or white; 125
13:42 bald head, or bald forehead, a white r sore; 125
13:43 *if* the rising of the sore *be* white r in his bald 125
13:49 *if* the plague be greenish or r in the garment, 125
14:37 greenish or r, which in sight *are* lower than 125

REDEEM (56) [REDEEMED, REDEEMEDST, REDEEMER, REDEEMETH, REDEEMING, REDEMPTION]
Ex 6: 6 I will r you with a stretched out arm, and 1350
13:13 every firstling of an ass thou shalt r with a 6299
13:13 if thou wilt not r *it,* then thou shalt break 6299
13:13 of man amongst thy children shalt thou r. 6299
13:15 but all the firstborn of my children I r. 6299
34:20 the firstling of an ass thou shalt r with a 6299
34:20 if thou r *him* not, then shalt thou break his 6299
34:20 All the firstborn of thy sons thou shalt r. 6299
Lev 25:25 *if any of* his kin come to r it, then shall he 1350
25:25 then shall he r that which his brother sold. 1350
25:26 if the man have none to r *it,* and himself be 1350
25:26 redeem *it,* and himself be able to r it; 1353+4672
25:29 he may r it within a whole year after 1353+1961
25:29 is sold; *within* a full year may he r it. 1353+1961
25:32 may the Levites r at any time. 1353
25:48 one of his brethren may r him: 1350
25:49 may r him, or *any* that is nigh of kin unto 1350
25:49 of kin unto him of his family may r him; 1350
25:49 or if he be able, he may r himself. 1350
27:13 if he will at all r it, then he shall add 1350+1350
27:15 if he that sanctified *it* will r his house, then 1350
27:19 the field will in any wise r it, 1350+1350
27:20 if he will not r the field, or if he have sold 1350
27:27 he shall r *it* according to thine estimation, 6299
27:31 if a man will at all r *ought* of his 1350+1350
Nu 18:15 firstborn of man shalt thou surely r, 6299+6299
18:15 the firstling of unclean beasts shalt thou r. 6299
18:16 *be* redeemed from a month old shalt thou r, 6299
18:17 or the firstling of a goat, thou shalt not r; 6299
Ru 4: 4 If thou wilt r *it,* redeem *it:* but if thou wilt 1350
4: 4 If thou wilt redeem *it,* r *it:* but if thou wilt 1350
4: 4 but if thou wilt not r *it, then* tell me, 1350
4: 4 for *there is* none to r *it* besides thee; and 1350
4: 4 and I *am* after thee. And he said, I will r *it.* 1350
4: 6 the kinsman said, I cannot r *it* for myself, 1350
4: 6 r thou my right to thyself; for I cannot 1350
4: 6 thou my right to thyself; for I cannot r *it.* 1350
2Sa 7:23 whom God went to r for a people to 6299
1Ch 17:21 whom God went to r *to be* his own people, 6299
Ne 5: 5 *to* r *them;* for other men have our lands NIH
Job 5:20 In famine he shall r thee from death: and 6299
6:23 or, R me from the hand of the mighty? 6299
Ps 25:22 R Israel, O God, out of all his troubles. 6299
26:11 r me, and be merciful unto me. 6299
44:26 for our help, and r us for thy mercy's sake. 6299
49: 7 None *of them* can by any means r 6299+6299
49:15 God will r my soul from the power of 6299
69:18 Draw nigh unto my soul, *and* r it: 1350
72:14 He shall r their soul from deceit and 1350
130: 8 And he shall r Israel from all his iniquities. 6299
Isa 50: 2 my hand shortened at all, that *it* cannot r? 6304
Jer 15:21 I will r thee out of the hand of the terrible. 6299
Hos 13:14 of the grave; I will r them from death: 1350
Mic 4:10 there the LORD shall r thee from the hand 1350
Gal 4: 5 To r them that were under the law, that we *1805*
Tit 2:14 that he might r us from all iniquity, and *3084*

REDEEMED (62) [REDEEM]
Ge 48:16 The Angel which r me from all evil, 1350
Ex 15:13 hast led forth the people *which* thou hast r: 1350
21: 8 her to himself, then shall he let her be r: 6299
Lev 19:20 not at all r, nor freedom given her; 6299+6299
25:30 if it be not r within the space of a full year, 1350
25:31 they may be r, and they shall go out 1353+1961
25:48 After *that* he is sold he may be r again; 1353
25:54 if he be not r in these *years,* then he shall 1350
27:20 to another man, it shall not be r any more. 1350
27:27 or if it be not r, then it shall be sold 1350
27:28 field of his possession, shall be sold or r: 1350
27:29 which shall be devoted of men, shall be r; 6299
27:33 thereof shall be holy; it shall not be r. 1350
Nu 3:46 for those that are *to be* r of the two 6302
3:48 the odd number of them is *to be* r, 6302
3:49 and above them that were r by the Levites: 6302
3:51 the money of them that were r unto Aaron 6302
18:16 those that are *to be* r from a month old 6299
Dt 7: 8 r you out of the house of bondmen, 6299
9:26 which thou hast r through thy greatness, 6299
13: 5 and r you out of the house of bondage, 6299
15:15 of Egypt, and the LORD thy God r thee: 6299
21: 8 whom thou hast r, and lay not innocent 6299
24:18 and the LORD thy God r thee thence: 6299
2Sa 4: 9 who hath r my soul out of all adversity, 6299
1Ki 1:29 that hath r my soul out of all distress, 6299
1Ch 17:21 thy people, whom thou hast r out of Egypt? 6299
Ne 1:10 whom thou hast r by thy great power, and 6299
5: 8 We after our ability have r our brethren 7069
Ps 31: 5 thou hast r me, O LORD God of truth. 6299
71:23 unto thee; and my soul, which thou hast r. 6299
74: 2 rod of thine inheritance, *which* thou hast r; 1350
77:15 Thou hast with *thine* arm r thy people, 1350
106:10 and r them from the hand of the enemy. 1350
107: 2 Let the r of the LORD say *so,* whom he 1350
107: 2 whom he hath r from the hand of 1350
136:24 hath r us from our enemies: for his mercy 6561
Isa 1:27 Zion shall be r with judgment, and 6299
29:22 who r Abraham, concerning the house of 6299
35: 9 be found there; but the r shall walk *there:* 1350
43: 1 for I have r thee, I have called *thee* by thy 1350
44:22 thy sins: return unto me; for I have r thee. 1350
44:23 for the LORD hath r Jacob, and 1350
48:20 The LORD hath r his servant Jacob. 1350
51:11 Therefore the r of the LORD shall return, 6299
52: 3 and ye shall be r without money. 1350
52: 9 comforted his people, he hath r Jerusalem. 1350
62:12 The holy people, The r of the LORD: 1350
63: 4 in mine heart, and the year of my r is come. 1350
63: 9 in his love and in his pity he r them; and 1350
Jer 31:11 For the LORD hath r Jacob, and 6299
La 3:58 the causes of my soul; thou hast r my life. 1350
Hos 7:13 though I have r them, yet they have spoken 6299
Mic 6: 4 and r thee out of the house of servants; 6299
Zec 10: 8 and gather them; for I have r them: 6299
Lk 1:68 for he hath visited and r his people, 3085+4160
24:21 it had been he which should have r Israel: *3084*
Gal 3:13 Christ hath r us from the curse of the law, *1805*
1Pe 1:18 Forasmuch as ye know that ye were not r *3084*
Rev 5: 9 hast r us to God by thy blood out of every *59*
14: 3 four thousand, which were r from the earth. *59*
14: 4 These were r from among men, *being* *59*

REDEEMEDST (1) [REDEEM]
2Sa 7:23 which thou r to thee from Egypt, *from* 6299

REDEEMER (18) [REDEEM]
Job 19:25 For I know *that* my R liveth, and *that* he 1350
Ps 19:14 O LORD, my strength, and my r. 1350
78:35 *was* their rock, and the high God their r. 1350
Pr 23:11 For their R *is* mighty; he shall plead their 1350
Isa 41:14 will help thee, saith the LORD, and thy r, 1350
43:14 the LORD, your r, the Holy One of Israel; 1350
44: 6 of Israel, and his r the LORD of hosts; 1350
44:24 thy r, and he that formed thee from 1350
47: 4 *As for* our r, the LORD of hosts *is* his 1350
48:17 the LORD, thy r, the Holy One of Israel; 1350
49: 7 the r of Israel, *and* his Holy One, 1350
49:26 that I the LORD *am* thy Saviour and thy r, 1350
54: 5 his name; and thy r the Holy One of Israel; 1350
54: 8 mercy on thee, saith the LORD thy r. 1350
59:20 the r shall come to Zion, and unto them 1350
60:16 that I the LORD *am* thy Saviour and thy r, 1350
63:16 thou, O LORD, *art* our father, our r; 1350
Jer 50:34 Their r *is* strong; the LORD of hosts *is* his 1350

REDEEMETH (2) [REDEEM]
Ps 34:22 The LORD r the soul of his servants: and 6299
103: 4 Who r thy life from destruction; 1350

REDEEMING (3) [REDEEM]
Ru 4: 7 in former time in Israel concerning r 1353
Eph 5:16 R the time, because the days are evil. *1805*
Col 4: 5 toward them that are without, r the time. *1805*

REDEMPTION (20) [REDEEM]
Lev 25:24 possession ye shall grant a r for the land. 1353
25:51 price of his r out of the money that he was 1353
25:52 shall he give *him* again the price of his r. 1353
Nu 3:49 Moses took the r money of them that were 6306
Ps 49: 8 (For the r of their soul is precious, and 6306
111: 9 He sent r unto his people: he hath 6304
130: 7 *there is* mercy, and with him *is* plenteous r. 6304
Jer 32: 7 for the right of r *is* thine to buy *it.* 1353
32: 8 of inheritance *is* thine, and the r *is* thine; 1353
Lk 2:38 spake of him to all them that looked for r in *3085*
21:28 lift up your heads; for your r draweth nigh. *629*
Ro 3:24 grace through the r that is in Christ Jesus: *629*
8:23 for the adoption, *to wit,* the r of our body. *629*
1Co 1:30 and righteousness, and sanctification, and r: *629*
Eph 1: 7 In whom we have r through his blood, *629*
1:14 until the r of the purchased possession, *629*
4:30 whereby ye are sealed unto the day of r. *629*
Col 1:14 In whom we have r through his blood, *629*
Heb 9:12 *place,* having obtained eternal r *for us.* *3085*
9:15 for the r of the transgressions that were *629*

REDNESS (1) [RED]
Pr 23:29 wounds without cause? who hath r of eyes? 2448

REDOUND (1)
2Co 4:15 thanksgiving of many r to the glory of God. *4052*

REDUCE See MINISH; MINISHED

REED (33) [REEDS]
1Ki 14:15 as a r is shaken in the water, and he shall 7070
2Ki 18:21 thou trustest upon the staff of this bruised r, 7070
Job 40:21 shady trees, in the covert of the r, and fens. 7070
Isa 36: 6 thou trustest in the staff of this broken r, 7070
42: 3 A bruised r shall he not break, and 7070
Eze 29: 6 they have been a staff of r to the house of 7070
40: 3 line of flax in his hand, and a measuring r; 7070
40: 5 in the man's hand a measuring r of six 7070
40: 5 the breadth of the building, one r; 7070
40: 5 one reed; and the height, one r. 7070
40: 6 of the gate, *which was* one r broad; 7070
40: 6 *of the gate, which was* one r broad. 7070
40: 7 *every* little chamber *was* one r long, and 7070
40: 7 *was* one reed long, and one r broad; 7070
40: 7 by the porch of the gate within *was* one r. 7070
40: 8 also the porch of the gate within, one r. 7070
41: 8 chambers *were* a full r of six great cubits. 7070
42:16 the east side with the measuring r, 7070
42:16 with the measuring r round about. 7070
42:17 with the measuring r round about. 7070
42:18 five hundred reeds, with the measuring r. 7070
42:19 five hundred reeds with the measuring r. 7070
Mt 11: 7 to see? A r shaken with the wind? *2563*
12:20 A bruised r shall he not break, and *2563*
27:29 *it* upon his head, and a r in his right hand: *2563*
27:30 and took the r, and smote him on the head. *2563*
27:48 and put *it* on a r, and gave him to drink. *2563*
Mk 15:19 And they smote him on the head with a r, *2563*
15:36 and put *it* on a r, and gave him to drink, *2563*
Lk 7:24 for to see? A r shaken with the wind? *2563*
Rev 11: 1 And there was given me a r like unto a rod: *2563*
21:15 And he that talked with me had a golden r *2563*
21:16 and he measured the city with the r, *2563*

REEDS (11) [REED]
Isa 19: 6 and dried up: the r and flags shall wither. 7070
19: 7 The paper r by the brooks, by the mouth of 6169
35: 7 each lay, *shall be* grass with r and rushes. 7070
Jer 51:32 the r they have burnt with fire, and the men of 98
Eze 42:16 five hundred r, with the measuring reed 7070
42:17 He measured the north side, five hundred r, 7070
42:18 five hundred r, with the measuring reed. 7070
42:19 measured five hundred r with 7070
42:20 five hundred *r* long, and five hundred NIH
45: 1 twenty thousand *r,* and the breadth *shall be* NIH
48: 8 *of* five and twenty thousand *r in* breadth, NIH

REEL (2)
Ps 107:27 They r to and fro, and stagger like a 2287
Isa 24:20 The earth shall r to and fro like a 5128+5128

REELAIAH (1)
Ezr 2: 2 Seraiah, R, Mordecai, Bilshan, Mizpar, 7480

REFINE (1) [REFINED, REFINER, REFINER'S]
Zec 13: 9 will r them as silver is refined, and will try 6884

REFINED (5) [REFINE]
1Ch 28:18 for the altar of incense r gold by weight; 2212
29: 4 and seven thousand talents of r silver, 2212
Isa 25: 6 full of marrow, of wines on the lees well r. 2212
48:10 Behold, I have r thee, but not with silver; 6884
Zec 13: 9 will refine them as silver is r, and will try 6884

REFINER (1) [REFINE]
Mal 3: 3 And he shall sit *as* a r and purifier of silver: 6884

REFINER'S (1) [REFINE]
Mal 3: 2 for he *is* like a r fire, and like fullers' sope: 6884

REFORMATION (1) [REFORMED]
Heb 9:10 imposed *on them* until the time of r. *1357*

REFORMED (1) [REFORMATION]
Lev 26:23 if ye will not be r by me by these *things,* 3256

REFRAIN (9) [REFRAINED, REFRAINETH]
Ge 45: 1 Joseph could not r himself before all them 662
Job 7:11 Therefore I will not r my mouth; I will 2820
Pr 1:15 way with them; r thy foot from their path: 4513
Ecc 3: 5 and a time to r from embracing; 7368
Isa 48: 9 *for* my praise will I r for thee, that *I* cut 2413
64:12 Wilt thou r thyself for these *things,* O 662
Jer 31:16 R thy voice from weeping, and thine eyes 4513
Ac 5:38 R from these men, and let them alone: *868*
1Pe 3:10 let him r his tongue from evil, and his lips *3973*

REFRAINED (7) [REFRAIN]
Ge 43:31 went out, and r himself, and said, Set on 662
Est 5:10 Nevertheless Haman r himself: and when he 662
Job 29: 9 The princes r talking, and laid *their* hand 6113

Ps 40: 9 lo, I have not **r** my lips, O LORD, 3607
119:101 I have **r** my feet from every evil way, that I 3607
Isa 42:14 my peace; I have been still, *and* **r** myself: 662
Jer 14:10 they have not **r** their feet, therefore 2820

REFRAINETH (1) [REFRAIN]

Pr 10:19 not sin: but he that **r** his lips *is* wise. 2820

REFRESH (3) [REFRESHED, REFRESHETH, REFRESHING]

1Ki 13: 7 and **r** *thyself,* and I will give thee a reward. 5582
Ac 27: 3 to go unto *his* friends to **r** himself. *1958+5177*
Phm 1:20 of thee in the Lord: **r** my bowels in the Lord. *373*

REFRESHED (10) [REFRESH]

Ex 23:12 thy handmaid, and the stranger, may be **r**. 5314
31:17 on the seventh day he rested, and was **r**. 5314
1Sa 16:23 so Saul was **r**, and was well, and the evil 7304
2Sa 16:14 came weary, and **r** themselves there. 5314
Job 32:20 I will speak, that I may be **r**: I will open my 7304
Ro 15:32 by the will of God, and may **with** you be **r**. *4875*
1Co 16:18 For they have **r** my spirit and yours: *373*
2Co 7:13 of Titus, because his spirit was **r** by you all. *373*
2Ti 1:16 for he oft **r** me, and was not ashamed of my *404*
Phm 1: 7 the bowels of the saints are **r** by thee, *373*

REFRESHETH (1) [REFRESH]

Pr 25:13 send him: for he **r** the soul of his masters. 7725

REFRESHING (2) [REFRESH]

Isa 28:12 cause the weary to rest; and this *is* the **r**: 4774
Ac 3:19 when *the* times of **r** shall come from *403*

REFUGE (47)

Nu 35: 6 the Levites *there shall be* six cities for **r**, 4733
35:11 ye shall appoint you cities to be cities of **r** 4733
35:12 they shall be unto you cities for **r** from 4733
35:13 ye shall give six cities shall ye have for **r**. 4733
35:14 land of Canaan, *which* shall be cities of **r**. 4733
35:15 These six cities shall be a **r**, *both* for 4733
35:25 shall restore him to the city of his **r**, 4733
35:26 come *without* the border of the city of his **r**, 4733
35:27 him without the borders of the city of his **r**, 4733
35:28 of his **r** until the death of the high priest: 4733
35:32 for him that is fled to the city of his **r**, 4733
Dt 33:27 The eternal God *is thy* **r**, and underneath 4585
Jos 20: 2 Appoint out for you cities of **r**, 4733
20: 3 they shall be your **r** from the avenger of 4733
21:13 her suburbs, *to be* a city of **r** for the slayer; 4733
21:21 *to be* a city of **r** for the slayer; 4733
21:27 her suburbs, *to be* a city of **r** for the slayer; 4733
21:32 her suburbs, *to be* a city of **r** for the slayer; 4733
21:38 her suburbs, *to be* a city of **r** for the slayer; 4733
2Sa 22: 3 my high tower, and my **r**, my saviour; 4498
1Ch 6:57 *the city* of **r**, and Libnah with her suburbs, 4733
6:67 they gave unto them, *of* the cities of **r**, 4733
Ps 9: 9 The LORD also will be a **r** for 4869
9: 9 for the oppressed, a **r** in times of trouble. 4869
14: 6 of the poor, because the LORD *is* his **r**. 4268
46: 1 God *is* our **r** and strength, a very present 4268
46: 7 hosts *is* with us; the God of Jacob *is* our **r**. 4869
46:11 hosts *is* with us; the God of Jacob *is* our **r**. 4869
48: 3 God is known in her palaces for a **r**. 4869
57: 1 the shadow of thy wings will I **make** my **r**, 2620
59:16 my defence and **r** in the day of my trouble. 4498
62: 7 rock of my strength, *and* my **r**, *is* in God. 4268
62: 8 heart before him: God *is* a **r** for us. Selah. 4268
71: 7 unto many; but thou *art* my strong **r**. 4268
91: 2 of the LORD, *He is* my **r** and my fortress: 4268
91: 9 *which is* my **r**, *even* the most High, 4268
94:22 and my God *is* the rock of my **r**. 4268
104:18 The high hills *are* a **r** for the wild goats; 4268
142: 4 **r** failed me; no man cared for my soul. 4498
142: 5 Thou *art* my **r** *and* my portion in the land of 4268
Pr 14:26 and his children shall have a **place of r**. 4268
Isa 4: 6 for a **place of r**, and for a covert from 4268
25: 4 a **r** from the storm, a shadow from the heat, 4268
28:15 for we have made lies our **r**, and 4268
28:17 the hail shall sweep away the **r** of lies, and 4268
Jer 16:19 and my **r** in the day of affliction, 4498
Heb 6:18 who have **fled for r** to lay hold upon *2703*

REFUSE (26) [REFUSED, REFUSEDST, REFUSETH]

Ex 4:23 *if* thou **r** to let him go, behold, I will slay 3985
8: 2 if thou **r** to let *them* go, behold, I will smite 3986
9: 2 For if thou **r** to let *them* go, and wilt hold 3986
10: 3 How long wilt thou **r** to humble thyself 3985
10: 4 Else, if thou **r** to let my people go, behold, 3986
16:28 How long **r** ye to keep my commandments 3985
22:17 If her father **utterly r** to give her 3985+3985
1Sa 15: 9 every thing *that was* vile and **r**, that they 4549
Job 34:33 whether thou **r**, or whether thou choose; 3988
Pr 8:33 Hear instruction, and be wise, and **r** *it* not. 6544
21: 7 because they **r** to do judgment. 3985
21:25 killeth him; for his hands **r** to labour. 3985
Isa 1:20 if ye **r** and rebel, ye shall be devoured *with* 3985
7:15 that he may know to **r** the evil, and 3988
7:16 For before the child shall know to **r** 3988
Jer 8: 5 they hold fast deceit, they **r** to return. 3985
9: 6 through deceit they **r** to know me, saith 3985
13:10 This evil people, which **r** to hear my words, 3987
25:28 if they **r** to take the cup at thine hand to 3985
38:21 if thou **r** to go forth, this *is* the word that 3986
La 3:45 and **r** in the midst of the people. 3973
Am 8: 6 of shoes; *yea,* and sell the **r** of the wheat? 4651
Ac 25:11 any *thing* worthy of death, I **r** not to die: *3868*
1Ti 4: 7 But **r** profane and old wives' fables, and *3868*
5:11 But the younger widows **r**: for when they *3868*
Heb 12:25 See *that* ye **r** not him that speaketh: for if *3868*

REFUSED (33) [REFUSE]

Ge 37:35 he **r** to be comforted; and he said, For I will 3985
39: 8 he **r**, and said unto his master's wife, 3985
48:19 his father **r**, and said, I know *it,* my son, 3985
Nu 20:21 Thus Edom **r** to give Israel passage through 3985
1Sa 8:19 Nevertheless the people **r** to obey the voice 3985
16: 7 height of his stature; because I have **r** him: 3988
28:23 he **r**, and said, I will not eat. But his 3985
2Sa 2:23 Howbeit he **r** to turn aside: 3985
13: 9 poured *them* out before him; but he **r** to eat. 3985
1Ki 20:35 I pray thee. And the man **r** to smite him. 3985
21:15 which he **r** to give thee for money: 3985
2Ki 5:16 And he urged him to take *it;* but he **r**. 3985
Ne 9:17 **r** to obey, neither were mindful of thy 3985
Est 1:12 the queen Vashti **r** to come at the king's 3985
Job 6: 7 The things *that* my soul **r** to touch *are* as 3985
Ps 77: 2 and ceased not: my soul **r** to be comforted. 3985
78:10 covenant of God, and **r** to walk in his law; 3985
78:67 Moreover he **r** the tabernacle of Joseph, 3988
118:22 The stone *which* the builders **r** is become 3988
Pr 1:24 Because I have called, and ye **r**; I have 3985
Isa 54: 6 of youth, when thou wast **r**, saith thy God. 3988
Jer 5: 3 *but* they have **r** to receive correction: 3985
5: 3 harder than a rock; they have **r** to return. 3985
11:10 their forefathers, which **r** to hear my words; 3985
31:15 Rahel weeping for her children **r** to be 3985
50:33 held them fast; they **r** to let them go. 3985
Eze 5: 6 for they have **r** my judgments, and 3988
Hos 11: 5 shall be his king, because they **r** to return. 3985
Zec 7:11 they **r** to hearken, and pulled away 3985
Ac 7:35 This Moses whom they **r**, saying, Who made *720*
1Ti 4: 4 creature of God *is* good, and nothing to be **r**, *579*
Heb 11:24 **r** to be called the son of Pharaoh's daughter; *720*
12:25 for if they escaped not who **r** him that *3868*

REFUSEDST (1) [REFUSE]

Jer 3: 3 a whore's forehead, thou **r** to be ashamed. 3985

REFUSETH (9) [REFUSE]

Ex 7:14 heart *is* hardened, he **r** to let the people go. 3985
Nu 22:13 for the LORD **r** to give me leave to go 3985
22:14 and said, Balaam **r** to come with us. 3985
Dt 25: 7 My husband's brother **r** to raise up unto his 3985
Pr 10:17 but he that **r** reproof erreth. 5800
13:18 shame *shall be to* him that **r** instruction: 6544
15:32 He that **r** instruction despiseth his own 6544
Isa 8: 6 Forsomuch as this people **r** the waters of 3988
Jer 15:18 my wound incurable, *which* **r** to be healed? 3985

REGARD (30) [REGARDED, REGARDEST, REGARDETH, REGARDING]

Ge 45:20 Also **r** not your stuff; for the good of 2347+5869
Ex 5: 9 and let them not **r** vain words. 8159
Lev 19:31 **R** not them that have familiar spirits, 413+6437
Dt 28:50 which shall not **r** the person of the old, 5375
1Sa 4:20 answered not, neither did she **r** *it.* 3820+7896
25:25 I pray thee, **r** this man of Belial, 3820+7760
2Sa 13:20 he *is* thy brother; **r** not this thing. So 3820+7896
2Ki 3:14 were it not that I **r** the presence of 5375
Job 3: 4 let not God **r** it from above, neither let 1875
35:13 hear vanity, neither will the Almighty **r** it. 7789
36:21 Take heed, **r** not iniquity: for this hast 413+6437
Ps 28: 5 Because they **r** not the works of the LORD, 995
31: 6 I have hated them that **r** lying vanities: but 8104
66:18 If I **r** iniquity in my heart, the Lord will 7200
94: 7 not see, neither shall the God of Jacob **r** *it.* 995
102:17 He will **r** the prayer of the destitute, and 6437
Pr 5: 2 That *thou* mayest **r** discretion, and *that* thy 8104
6:35 He will not **r** any ransom; 5375+6440
Ecc 8: 2 and *that* in **r** of the oath of God. 1700
Isa 5:12 they **r** not the work of the LORD, 5027
13:17 against them, which shall not **r** silver; 2803
La 4:16 hath divided them; he will no more **r** them: 5027
Da 11:37 Neither shall he **r** the God of his fathers, 995
11:37 nor the desire of women, nor **r** any god: 995
Am 5:22 I will not accept *them:* neither will I **r** 5027
Hab 1: 5 and **r**, and wonder marvellously: 5027
Mal 1: 9 will he **r** your **persons**? 4480+5375+6440
Lk 18: 4 Though I fear not God, nor **r** man; *1788*
Ac 8:11 And to him they **had r**, because that of *4337*
Ro 14: 6 to the Lord he doth not **r** *it.* He that eateth, *5426*

REGARDED (9) [REGARD]

Ex 9:21 he that **r** not the word of the LORD 3820+7760
1Ki 18:29 nor any to answer, nor any that **r**. 7182
1Ch 17:17 hast **r** me according to the estate of a man 7200
Ps 106:44 Nevertheless he **r** their affliction, when he 7200
Pr 1:24 have stretched out my hand, and no man **r**; 7181
Da 3:12 these men, O king, have not **r** thee: 2942+7761
Lk 1:48 For he hath **r** the low estate of his *1914*
18: 2 which feared not God, neither **r** man: *1788*
Heb 8: 9 and I **r** them **not**, saith the Lord. *272*

REGARDEST (4) [REGARD]

2Sa 19: 6 that thou **r** neither princes nor servants: 3807.1
Job 30:20 not hear me: I stand *up,* and thou **r** me *not.* 995
Mt 22:16 neither carest thou for any *man:* for thou **r** *991*
Mk 12:14 carest for no *man:* for thou **r** not *991+1519*

REGARDETH (15) [REGARD]

Dt 10:17 and a terrible, which **r** not persons, 5375
Job 34:19 nor **r** the rich more than the poor? 5234
39: 7 neither **r** he the crying of the driver. 8085
Pr 12:10 A righteous *man* **r** the life of his beast: but 3045
13:18 but he that **r** reproof shall be honoured. 8104
15: 5 but he that **r** reproof is prudent. 8104
29: 7 of the poor: *but* the wicked **r** not to know *it.* 995
Ecc 5: 8 for *he that is* higher than the highest **r**; and 8104
11: 4 and he that **r** the clouds shall not reap. 7200
Isa 33: 8 he hath despised the cities, he **r** no man. 2803
Da 6:13 **r** not thee, O king, nor the decree that thou 7761
Mal 2:13 insomuch that *he* **r** not the offering 413+6437
Ro 14: 6 He that **r** the day, regardeth *it* unto *5426*
14: 6 that regardeth the day, **r** *it* unto the Lord; *5426*
14: 6 and he that **r** not the day, to the Lord he *5426*

REGARDING (2) [REGARD]

Job 4:20 they perish for ever without *any* **r** *it.* 7760
Php 2:30 **not r** *his* life, to supply your lack of service *3851*

REGEM (1)

1Ch 2:47 **R**, and Jotham, and Geshan, and Pelet, and 7276

REGEMMELECH (1)

Zec 7: 2 sent *unto* the house of God Sherezer and **R**, 7278

REGENERATION (2)

Mt 19:28 That ye which have followed me, in the **r**, *3824*
Tit 3: 5 by the washing of **r**, and renewing of *3824*

REGION (15) [REGIONS]

Dt 3: 4 threescore cities, all the **r** of Argob, 2256
3:13 all the **r** of Argob, with all Bashan, which 2256
1Ki 4:11 The son of Abinadab, *in* all the **r** of Dor; 5299
4:13 to him *also pertained* the **r** of Argob, 2256
4:24 For he had dominion over all *the* **r** on *this* NIH
Mt 3: 5 and all the **r round about** Jordan, *4066*
4:16 and to them which sat in the **r** and *5561*
Mk 1:28 throughout all the **r round about** Galilee. *4066*
6:55 And ran through that whole **r round about**, *4066*
Lk 3: 1 of Iturea and of the **r** of Trachonitis, *5561*
4:14 fame of him through all the **r round about**. *4066*
7:17 and throughout all the **r round about**. *4066*
Ac 13:49 Lord was published throughout all the **r**. *5561*
14: 6 and *unto* the **r that lieth round about**: *4066*
16: 6 throughout Phrygia and the **r** of Galatia, *5561*

REGIONS (4) [REGION]

Ac 8: 1 scattered abroad throughout the **r** of Judea *5561*
2Co 10:16 To preach the gospel in the **r** beyond you, NIG
11:10 stop me of this boasting in the **r** of Achaia. *2824*
Gal 1:21 Afterwards I came into the **r** of Syria and *2824*

REGISTER (3)

Ezr 2:62 These sought their **r** *among* those that were 3791
Ne 7: 5 I found a **r** of the genealogy of them which 5612
7:64 These sought their **r** *among* those that were 3791

REGULAR See SERVILE

REHABIAH (5)

1Ch 23:17 the sons of Eliezer *were,* **R** the chief. 7345
23:17 but the sons of **R** were very many. 7345
24:21 Concerning **R**: of the sons of Rehabiah, 7345
24:21 of the sons of **R**, the first *was* Isshiah. 7345
26:25 **R** his son, and Jeshaiah his son, and 7345

REHEARSE (2) [REHEARSED]

Ex 17:14 in a book, and **r** *it* in the ears of Joshua: 7760
Jdg 5:11 they **r** the righteous acts of the LORD, 8567

REHEARSED (4) [REHEARSE]

1Sa 8:21 and he **r** them in the ears of the LORD. 1696
17:31 David spake, they **r** *them* before Saul: 5046
Ac 11: 4 But Peter *r the matter* from the beginning, NIG
14:27 they **r** all that God had done with them, and *312*

REHOB (10) [BETH REHOB]

Nu 13:21 the land from the wilderness of Zin unto **R**, 7340
Jos 19:28 and **R**, and Hammon, and Kanah, 7340
19:30 Ummah also, and Aphek, and **R**: twenty 7340
21:31 with her suburbs, and **R** with her suburbs; 7340
Jdg 1:31 nor of Helbah, nor of Aphik, nor of **R**: 7340
2Sa 8: 3 the son of **R**, king of Zobah, 7340
8:12 of Hadadezer, son of **R**, king of Zobah. 7340
10: 8 and of **R**, and Ish-tob, and Maacah, 7340
1Ch 6:75 with her suburbs, and **R** with her suburbs: 7340
Ne 10:11 Micha, **R**, Hashabiah, 7340

REHOBOAM (50) [ROBOAM]

1Ki 11:43 and **R** his son reigned in his stead. 7346
12: 1 **R** went *to* Shechem: for all Israel were 7346
12: 3 of Israel came, and spake unto **R**, saying, 7346
12: 6 king **R** consulted with the old men, 7346
12:12 and all the people came to **R** the third day, 7346
12:17 in the cities of Judah, **R** reigned over them. 7346
12:18 king **R** sent Adoram, who *was* over 7346
12:18 Therefore king **R** made speed to get *him* up 7346
12:21 when **R** was come *to* Jerusalem, he 7346
12:21 to bring the kingdom again to **R** the son of 7346
12:23 Speak unto **R**, the son of Solomon, king of 7346
12:27 *even* unto **R** king of Judah, and they shall 7346
12:27 kill me, and go again to **R** king of Judah. 7346
14:21 **R** the son of Solomon reigned in Judah. 7346
14:21 **R** *was* forty and one years old when he 7346
14:25 it came to pass in the fifth year of king **R**, 7346
14:27 king **R** made in their stead brasen shields, 7346
14:29 Now the rest of the acts of **R**, and all that 7346
14:30 there was war between **R** and Jeroboam all 7346
14:31 **R** slept with his fathers, and was buried 7346
15: 6 there was war between **R** and Jeroboam all 7346
1Ch 3:10 Solomon's son *was* **R**, Abia his son, 7346
2Ch 9:31 and **R** his son reigned in his stead. 7346
10: 1 **R** went to Shechem: for *to* Shechem were 7346
10: 3 and all Israel came and spake to **R**, 7346
10: 6 king **R** took counsel with the old men that 7346
10:12 all the people came to **R** on the third day, 7346
10:13 king **R** forsook the counsel of the old men, 7346
10:17 in the cities of Judah, **R** reigned over them. 7346
10:18 king **R** sent Hadoram that *was* over 7346
10:18 king **R** made speed to get *him* up to *his* 7346
11: 1 when **R** was come *to* Jerusalem, he 7346
11: 1 that *he* might bring the kingdom again to **R**. 7346
11: 3 Speak unto **R** the son of Solomon, king of 7346
11: 5 **R** dwelt in Jerusalem, and built cities for 7346
11:17 made **R** the son of Solomon strong, 7346
11:18 **R** took him Mahalath the daughter of 7346
11:21 **R** loved Maachah the daughter of Absalom 7346
11:22 **R** made Abijah the son of Maachah 7346
12: 1 when **R** had established the kingdom, and 7346
12: 2 *that* in the fifth year of king **R** Shishak king 7346
12: 5 came Shemaiah the prophet to **R**, and *to* 7346

2Ch 12:10 Instead of which king R made shields of 7346
12:13 So king R strengthened himself in 7346
12:13 for R *was* one and forty years old when he 7346
12:15 Now the acts of R, first and last, *are* they 7346
12:15 *there were* wars between R and 7346
12:16 R slept with his fathers, and was buried in 7346
13: 7 have strengthened themselves against R 7346
13: 7 when R was young and tender hearted, and 7346

REHOBOTH (4)

Ge 10:11 builded Nineveh, and the city R, and Calah, 7344
26:22 he called the name of it R; and he said, 7344
36:37 Saul of R *by* the river reigned in his stead. 7344
1Ch 1:48 Shaul of R *by* the river reigned in his stead. 7344

REHU (1)

1Ch 1:25 Eber, Peleg, R, 7466

REHUM (8)

Ezr 2: 2 Bilshan, Mizpar, Bigvai, R, Baanah. 7348
4: 8 R the chancellor and Shimshai the scribe 7348
4: 9 *wrote* R the chancellor, and Shimshai 7348
4:17 *Then* sent the king an answer unto R 7348
4:23 king Artaxerxes' letter *was* read before R, 7348
Ne 3:17 him repaired the Levites, R the son of Bani. 7348
10:25 R, Hashabnah, Maaseiah, 7348
12: 3 Shechaniah, R, Meremoth, 7348

REI (1)

1Ki 1: 8 R, and the mighty *men* which *belonged* to 7472

REIGN (168) [REIGNED, REIGNEST, REIGNETH, REIGNING]

Ge 37: 8 to him, Shalt thou **indeed** r over us? 4427+4427
Ex 15:18 The LORD shall r for ever and ever. 4427
Lev 26:17 they that hate you shall r over you; and 7287
Dt 15: 6 thou shalt r over many nations, but 4910
15: 6 but they shall not r over thee. 4910
Jdg 9: 2 r over you, or that one reign over you? 4910
9: 2 reign over you, or that one r over you? 4910
9: 8 said unto the olive tree, R thou over us. 4427
9:10 to the fig tree, Come thou, *and* r over us. 4427
9:12 unto the vine, Come thou, *and* r over us. 4427
9:14 the bramble, Come thou, *and* r over us. 4427
1Sa 8: 7 rejected me, that *I* should not r over them. 4427
8: 9 manner of the king that shall r over them. 4427
8:11 manner of the king that shall r over you: 4427
9:17 thee of: this *same* shall r over my people. 6113
11:12 Who *is* he that said, Shall Saul r over us? 4427
12:12 unto me, Nay; but a king shall r over us: 4427
2Sa 2:10 years old when he *began* to r over Israel, 4427
3:21 that thou mayest r over all that thine heart 4427
5: 4 *was* thirty years old when he *began* to r, 4427
1Ki 1:11 that Adonijah the son of Haggith doth r, 4427
1:13 Assuredly Solomon thy son shall r after 4427
1:13 my throne? why then doth Adonijah r? 4427
1:17 *saying,* Assuredly Solomon thy son shall r 4427
1:24 Adonijah shall r after me, and he shall sit 4427
1:30 Assuredly Solomon thy son shall r after 4427
2:15 Israel set their faces on me, that *I* should r: 4427
6: 1 in the fourth year of Solomon's r over 4427
11:37 thou shalt r according to all that thy soul 4427
14:21 and one years old when he *began* to r, 4427
15:25 Nadab the son of Jeroboam *began* to r over 4427
15:33 son of Ahijah to r over all Israel in Tirzah, 4427
16: 8 the son of Baasha to r over Israel in Tirzah, 4427
16:11 it came to pass, when he *began* to r, 4427
16:15 of Judah did Zimri r seven days in Tirzah. 4427
16:23 king of Judah *began* Omri to r over Israel, 4427
16:29 Ahab the son of Omri to r over Israel: 4427
22:41 Jehoshaphat the son of Asa *began* to r over 4427
22:42 and five years old when he *began* to r; 4427
22:51 Ahaziah the son of Ahab *began* to r over 4427
2Ki 3: 1 Now Jehoram the son of Ahab *began* to r 4427
8:16 of Jehoshaphat king of Judah *began* to r. 4427
8:17 two years old was he when he *began* to r; 4427
8:25 son of Jehoram king of Judah *begin* to r. 4427
8:26 years old *was* Ahaziah when he *began* to r; 4427
9:29 of Ahab *began* Ahaziah to r over Judah. 4427
11: 3 six years. And Athaliah *did* r over the land. 4427
11:21 years old *was* Jehoash when he *began* to r. 4427
12: 1 seventh year of Jehu Jehoash *began* to r; 4427
13: 1 of Jehu *began* to r over Israel in Samaria, 4427
13:10 son of Jehoahaz to r over Israel in Samaria, 4427
14: 2 and five years old when he *began* to r, 4427
14:23 Joash king of Israel *began* to r in Samaria, 4427
15: 1 Azariah son of Amaziah king of Judah to r. 4427
15: 2 years old was he when he *began* to r, 4427
15: 8 r over Israel in Samaria six months. 4427
15:13 Shallum the son of Jabesh *began* to r in 4427
15:17 Menahem the son of Gadi to r over Israel, 4427
15:23 *began* to r over Israel in Samaria, 4427
15:27 Remaliah *began* to r over Israel in Samaria, 4427
15:32 the son of Uzziah king of Judah to r. 4427
15:33 years old was he when he *began* to r, 4427
16: 1 the son of Jotham king of Judah *began* to r. 4427
16: 2 years old *was* Ahaz when he *began* to r, 4427
17: 1 Elah to r in Samaria over Israel nine years. 4427
18: 1 the son of Ahaz king of Judah *began* to r. 4427
18: 2 five years old was he when he *began* to r; 4427
21: 1 *was* twelve years old when he *began* to r, 4427
21:19 and two years old when he *began* to r, 4427
22: 1 *was* eight years old when he *began* to r, 4427
23:31 and three years old when he *began* to r; 4427
23:33 that *he* might not r in Jerusalem; 4427
23:36 and five year old when he *began* to r; 4427
24: 8 *was* eighteen years old when he *began* to r, 4427
24:12 took him in the eighth year of his r. 4427
24:18 and one years old when he *began* to r, 4427
25: 1 it came to pass in the ninth year of his r, 4427
25:27 of Babylon, in the year that he *began* to r, 4427
1Ch 4:31 These *were* their cities unto the r of David. 4427
26:31 In the fortieth year of the r of David they 4438
29:30 With all his r and his might, and the times 4438
2Ch 1: 8 and hast **made** me **to** r in his stead. 4427
3: 2 second month, in the fourth year of his r. 4438
12:13 and forty years old when he *began* to r, 4427
13: 1 Jeroboam *began* Abijah to r over Judah. 4427
15:10 in the fifteenth year of the r of Asa. 4438
15:19 the five and thirtieth year of the r of Asa. 4438
16: 1 thirtieth year of the r of Asa Baasha king of 4438
16:12 ninth year of his r was diseased in his feet, 4438
16:13 died in the one and fortieth year of his r. 4427
17: 7 Also in the third year of his r he sent to his 4427
20:31 and five years old when he *began* to r, 4427
21: 5 and two years old when he *began* to r, 4427
21:20 two *years* old was he when he *began* to r, 4427
22: 2 years old *was* Ahaziah when he *began* to r, 4427
23: 3 unto them, Behold, the king's son shall r, 4427
24: 1 *was* seven years old when he *began* to r, 4427
25: 1 and five years old *when* he *began* to r, 4427
26: 3 years old *was* Uzziah when he *began* to r, 4427
27: 1 and five years old when he *began* to r, 4427
27: 8 and twenty years old when he *began* to r, 4427
28: 1 *was* twenty years old when he *began* to r, 4427
29: 1 Hezekiah *began* to r *when he was* five and 4427
29: 3 He in the first year of his r, in the first 4427
29:19 which king Ahaz in his r did cast away in 4438
33: 1 *was* twelve years old when he *began* to r, 4427
33:21 and twenty years old when he *began* to r, 4427
34: 1 *was* eight years old when he *began* to r, 4427
34: 3 For in the eighth year of his r, while he was 4427
34: 8 Now in the eighteenth year of his r, 4427
35:19 In the eighteenth year of the r of Josiah was 4438
36: 2 and three years old when he *began* to r, 4427
36: 5 and five years old when he *began* to r, 4427
36: 9 *was* eight years old when he *began* to r, 4427
36:11 and twenty years old when he *began* to r, 4427
36:20 his sons until the r of the kingdom of 4427
Ezr 4: 5 even until the r of Darius king of Persia. 4438
4: 6 in the r of Ahasuerus, in the beginning of 4438
4: 6 of Ahasuerus, in the beginning of his r, 4438
4:24 So it ceased unto the second year of the r 4437
6:15 which *was in* the sixth year of the r of 4437
7: 1 in the r of Artaxerxes king of Persia, 4438
8: 1 in the r of Artaxerxes the king. 4438
Ne 12:22 the priests, to the r of Darius the Persian. 4438
Est 1: 3 In the third year of his r, he made a feast 4427
2:16 month Tebeth, in the seventh year of his r. 4438
Job 34:30 That the hypocrite r not, lest the people be 4427
Ps 146:10 The LORD shall r for ever, *even* thy God, 4427
Pr 8:15 By me kings r, and princes decree justice. 4427
Ecc 4:14 For out of prison he cometh to r; 4427
Isa 24:23 when the LORD of hosts shall r in mount 4427
32: 1 a king shall r in righteousness, and princes 4427
Jer 1: 2 of Judah, in the thirteenth year of his r. 4427
22:15 Shalt thou r, because thou closest *thyself* in 4427
23: 5 a King shall r and prosper, and 4427
26: 1 In the beginning of the r of Jehoiakim 4468
27: 1 In the beginning of the r of Jehoiakim 4467
28: 1 in the beginning of the r of Zedekiah king 4467
33:21 that he should not have a son to r upon his 4427
49:34 of the r of Zedekiah king of Judah, 4438
51:59 *into* Babylon in the fourth year of his r. 4427
52: 1 and twenty year old when he *began* to r, 4427
52: 4 it came to pass in the ninth year of his r, 4427
52:31 r lifted up the head of Jehoiachin king of 4438
Da 1: 1 In the third year of the r of Jehoiakim king 4438
2: 1 in the second year of the r of 4438
6:28 So this Daniel prospered in the r of Darius, 4437
6:28 of Darius, and in the r of Cyrus the Persian. 4437
8: 1 In the third year of the r of king Belshazzar 4438
9: 2 In the first year of his r I Daniel understood 4427
Mic 4: 7 the LORD shall r over them in mount 4427
Mt 2:22 But when he heard that Archelaus did r in 936
Lk 1:33 And he shall r over the house of Jacob for 936
3: 1 Now in the fifteenth year of the r of 2231
19:14 We will not have this *man* to r over us. 936
19:27 which would not that I should r over them, 936
Ro 5:17 of the gift of righteousness shall r in life by 936
5:21 might grace r through righteousness unto 936
6:12 Let not sin therefore r in your mortal body, 936
15:12 and he that *shall* rise to r **over** the Gentiles; 757
1Co 4: 8 and I would *to God* ye did r, that we also 936
4: 8 ye did reign, that we also might r **with** you. 4821
15:25 For he must r, till he hath put all enemies 936
2Ti 2:12 we shall also r **with** *him:* if we deny *him,* 4821
Rev 5:10 and priests: and we shall r on the earth. 936
11:15 his Christ; and he shall r for ever and ever. 936
20: 6 and shall r with him a thousand years. 936
22: 5 and they shall r for ever and ever. 936

REIGNED (176) [REIGN]

Ge 36:31 these *are* the kings that r in the land of 4427
36:31 before there r *any* king over the children of 4427
36:32 Bela the son of Beor r in Edom: and 4427
36:33 Jobab the son of Zerah of Bozrah r in his 4427
36:34 Husham of the land of Temani r in his 4427
36:35 Midian in the field of Moab, r in his stead: 4427
36:36 and Samlah of Masrekah r in his stead. 4427
36:37 Saul of Rehoboth *by* the river r in his stead. 4427
36:38 Baal-hanan the son of Achbor r in his 4427
36:39 of Achbor died, and Hadar r in his stead: 4427
Jos 12: 5 r in mount Hermon, and in Salcah, and 4910
13:10 which r in Heshbon, unto the border of 4427
13:12 which r in Ashtaroth and in Edrei, 4427
13:21 king of the Amorites, which r in Heshbon, 4427
Jdg 4: 2 of Jabin king of Canaan, that r in Hazor; 4427
9:22 When Abimelech had r three years over 7786
1Sa 13: 1 Saul r one year; and when he had reigned 4427
13: 1 and when he had r two years over Israel, 4427
2Sa 2:10 *began* to reign over Israel, and r two years. 4427
5: 4 he *began* to reign, *and* he r forty years. 4427
5: 5 In Hebron he r over Judah seven years and 4427
5: 5 in Jerusalem he r thirty and three years 4427
8:15 David r over all Israel; and David executed 4427
10: 1 and Hanun his son r in his stead. 4427
16: 8 house of Saul, in whose stead thou hast r; 4427
1Ki 2:11 the days that David r over Israel *were* forty 4427
1Ki 2:11 seven years r he in Hebron, and thirty and 4427
2:11 and thirty and three years r he in Jerusalem. 4427
4:21 Solomon r over all kingdoms from the river 4910
11:24 and dwelt therein, and r in Damascus. 4427
11:25 and he abhorred Israel, and r over Syria. 4427
11:42 the time that Solomon r in Jerusalem over 4427
11:43 and Rehoboam his son r in his stead. 4427
12:17 the cities of Judah, Rehoboam r over them. 4427
14:19 of Jeroboam, how he warred, and how he r, 4427
14:20 the days which Jeroboam r *were* two and 4427
14:20 and Nadab his son r in his stead. 4427
14:21 Rehoboam the son of Solomon r in Judah. 4427
14:21 and he r seventeen years in Jerusalem, 4427
14:31 And Abijam his son r in his stead. 4427
15: 1 the son of Nebat r Abijam over Judah. 4427
15: 2 Three years r he in Jerusalem. And his 4427
15: 8 of David: and Asa his son r in his stead. 4427
15: 9 king of Israel r Asa **over** Judah. 4427+4428
15:10 forty and one years r he in Jerusalem. 4427
15:24 and Jehoshaphat his son r in his stead. 4427
15:25 king of Judah, and r over Israel two years. 4427
15:28 did Baasha slay him, and r in his stead. 4427
15:29 it came to pass, when he r, *that* he smote all 4427
16: 6 in Tirzah: and Elah his son r in his stead. 4427
16:10 of Asa king of Judah, and r in his stead. 4427
16:22 son of Ginath: so Tibni died, and Omri r. 4427
16:23 twelve years: six years r he in Tirzah. 4427
16:28 in Samaria: and Ahab his son r in his stead. 4427
16:29 Ahab the son of Omri r over Israel in 4427
22:40 and Ahaziah his son r in his stead. 4427
22:42 he r twenty and five years in Jerusalem. 4427
22:50 and Jehoram his son r in his stead. 4427
22:51 king of Judah, and r two years over Israel. 4427
2Ki 1:17 Jehoram r in his stead in the second year of 4427
3: 1 king of Judah, and r twelve years. 4427
3:27 he took his eldest son that should have r in 4427
8:15 so that he died: and Hazael r in his stead. 4427
8:17 to reign; and he r eight years in Jerusalem. 4427
8:24 and Ahaziah his son r in his stead. 4427
8:26 to reign; and he r one year in Jerusalem. 4427
10:35 And Jehoahaz his son r in his stead. 4427
10:36 the time that Jehu r over Israel in Samaria 4427
12: 1 to reign; and forty years r he in Jerusalem. 4427
12:21 and Amaziah his son r in his stead. 4427
13: 1 Israel in Samaria, *and r* seventeen years. NIH
13: 9 in Samaria: and Joash his son r in his stead. 4427
13:10 over Israel in Samaria, *and r* sixteen years. NIH
13:24 and Ben-hadad his son r in his stead. 4427
14: 1 r Amaziah the son of Joash king of Judah. 4427
14: 2 and r twenty and nine years in Jerusalem. 4427
14:16 and Jeroboam his son r in his stead. 4427
14:23 reign in Samaria, *and r* forty and one years. NIH
14:29 and Zachariah his son r in his stead. 4427
15: 2 and he r two and fifty years in Jerusalem. 4427
15: 7 of David: and Jotham his son r in his stead. 4427
15:10 and slew him, and r in his stead. 4427
15:13 of Judah; and he r a full month in Samaria. 4427
15:14 and slew him, and r in his stead. 4427
15:17 over Israel, *and r* ten years in Samaria. NIH
15:22 and Pekahiah his son r in his stead. 4427
15:23 over Israel in Samaria, *and r* two years. NIH
15:25 he killed him, and r in his room. 4427
15:27 over Israel in Samaria, *and r* twenty years. NIH
15:30 and slew him, and r in his stead, 4427
15:33 and he r sixteen years in Jerusalem. 4427
15:38 his father: and Ahaz his son r in his stead. 4427
16: 2 r sixteen years in Jerusalem, and did not 4427
16:20 and Hezekiah his son r in his stead. 4427
18: 2 he r twenty and nine years in Jerusalem. 4427
19:37 And Esarhaddon his son r in his stead. 4427
20:21 and Manasseh his son r in his stead. 4427
21: 1 and r fifty and five years in Jerusalem. 4427
21:18 of Uzza: and Amon his son r in his stead. 4427
21:19 to reign, and he r two years in Jerusalem. 4427
21:26 of Uzza: and Josiah his son r in his stead. 4427
22: 1 and he r thirty and one years in Jerusalem. 4427
23:31 and he r three months in Jerusalem. 4427
23:36 and he r eleven years in Jerusalem. 4427
24: 6 and Jehoiachin his son r in his stead. 4427
24: 8 and he r in Jerusalem three months. 4427
24:18 and he r eleven years in Jerusalem. 4427
1Ch 1:43 Now these *are* the kings that r in the land 4427
1:43 *any* king r over the children of Israel; 4427
1:44 Jobab the son of Zerah of Bozrah r in his 4427
1:45 Husham of the land of the Temanites r in 4427
1:46 Midian in the field of Moab, r in his stead: 4427
1:47 Samlah of Masrekah r in his stead. 4427
1:48 Shaul of Rehoboth *by* the river r in his 4427
1:49 Baal-hanan the son of Achbor r in his 4427
1:50 Baal-hanan was dead, Hadad r in his stead: 4427
3: 4 and there he r seven years and six months: 4427
3: 4 and in Jerusalem he r thirty and three years. 4427
18:14 So David r over all Israel, and executed 4427
19: 1 of Ammon died, and his son r in his stead. 4427
29:26 Thus David the son of Jesse r over all 4427
29:27 the time that he r over Israel *was* forty 4427
29:27 seven years r he in Hebron, and thirty and 4427
29:27 and thirty and three *years* r he in Jerusalem. 4427
29:28 honour: and Solomon his son r in his stead. 4427
2Ch 1:13 of the congregation, and r over Israel. 4427
9:26 he r over all the kings from the river even 4910
9:30 Solomon r in Jerusalem over all Israel forty 4427
9:31 and Rehoboam his son r in his stead. 4427
10:17 the cities of Judah, Rehoboam r over them. 4427
12:13 strengthened himself in Jerusalem, and r: 4427
12:13 and he r seventeen years in Jerusalem, 4427
12:16 of David: and Abijah his son r in his stead. 4427
13: 2 He r three years in Jerusalem. His mother's 4427
14: 1 Asa his son r in his stead. In his days 4427
17: 1 Jehoshaphat his son r in his stead, and 4427
20:31 Jehoshaphat r over Judah: *he was* thirty 4427
20:31 he r twenty and five years in Jerusalem. 4427
21: 1 And Jehoram his son r in his stead. 4427
21: 5 to reign, and he r eight years in Jerusalem. 4427
21:20 he r in Jerusalem eight years, and 4427

2Ch 22: 1 the son of Jehoram king of Judah **r**. 4427
22: 2 to reign, and he **r** one year in Jerusalem. 4427
22:12 God six years: and Athaliah **r** over the land. 4427
24: 1 to reign, and he **r** forty years in Jerusalem. 4427
24:27 And Amaziah his son **r** in his stead. 4427
25: 1 he **r** twenty and nine years in Jerusalem. 4427
26: 3 and he **r** fifty and two years in Jerusalem. 4427
26:23 *is* a leper: and Jotham his son **r** in his stead. 4427
27: 1 and he **r** sixteen years in Jerusalem. 4427
27: 8 to reign, and **r** sixteen years in Jerusalem. 4427
27: 9 of David: and Ahaz his son **r** in his stead. 4427
28: 1 and he **r** sixteen years in Jerusalem: 4427
28:27 and Hezekiah his son **r** in his stead. 4427
29: 1 he **r** nine and twenty years in Jerusalem. 4427
32:33 And Manasseh his son **r** in his stead. 4427
33: 1 and he **r** fifty and five years in Jerusalem: 4427
33:20 and Amon his son **r** in his stead. 4427
33:21 to reign, and **r** two years in Jerusalem. 4427
34: 1 and he **r** in Jerusalem one and thirty years. 4427
36: 2 and he **r** three months in Jerusalem. 4427
36: 5 and he **r** eleven years in Jerusalem: 4427
36: 8 Judah: and Jehoiachin his son **r** in his stead. 4427
36: 9 he **r** three months and ten days in 4427
36:11 to reign, and **r** eleven years in Jerusalem. 4427
Est 1: 1 (this *is* Ahasuerus which **r**, from India even 4427
Isa 37:38 and Esar-haddon his son **r** in his stead. 4427
Jer 22:11 which **r** instead of Josiah his father, 4427
37: 1 king Zedekiah the son of Josiah **r** instead of 4427
52: 1 and he **r** eleven years in Jerusalem. 4427
Ro 5:14 Nevertheless death **r** from Adam to Moses, *936*
5:17 For if by one man's offence death **r** by one; *936*
5:21 That as sin hath **r** unto death, even so might *936*
1Co 4: 8 ye are rich, ye have **r as kings** without us: *936*
Rev 11:17 taken *to thee* thy great power, and hast **r**. *936*
20: 4 and **r** with Christ a thousand years. *936*

REIGNEST (1) [REIGN]

1Ch 29:12 honour *come* of thee, and thou **r** over all; 4910

REIGNETH (13) [REIGN]

1Sa 12:14 also the king that **r** over you continue 4427
2Sa 15:10 then ye shall say, Absalom **r** in Hebron. 4427
1Ki 1:18 now behold, Adonijah **r**; and now, my lord 4427
1Ch 16:31 *men* say among the nations, The LORD **r**. 4427
Ps 47: 8 God **r** over the heathen: God sitteth upon 4427
93: 1 The LORD **r**, he is clothed with majesty; 4427
96:10 Say among the heathen *that* the LORD **r**: 4427
97: 1 The LORD **r**; let the earth rejoice; let 4427
99: 1 The LORD **r**; let the people tremble: 4427
Pr 30:22 For a servant when he **r**; and a fool when 4427
Isa 52: 7 that saith unto Zion, Thy God **r**! 4427
Rev 17:18 which **r** over the kings of the earth. *932+2192*
19: 6 Alleluia: for the Lord God Omnipotent **r**. *936*

REIGNING (1) [REIGN]

1Sa 16: 1 seeing I have rejected him from **r** over 4427

REINS (15)

Job 16:13 he cleaveth my **r** asunder, and doth not 3629
19:27 *though* my **r** be consumed within me. 3629
Ps 7: 9 the righteous God trieth the hearts and **r**. 3629
16: 7 my **r** also instruct me *in* the night seasons. 3629
26: 2 and prove me; try my **r** and my heart. 3629
73:21 was grieved, and I was pricked *in* my **r**. 3629
139:13 For thou hast possessed my **r**: thou hast 3629
Pr 23:16 Yea, my **r** shall rejoice, when thy lips 3629
Isa 11: 5 and faithfulness the girdle of his **r**. 2504
Jer 11:20 that triest the **r** and the heart, 3629
12: 2 *art* near in their mouth, and far from their **r**. 3629
17:10 I the LORD search the heart, *I* try the **r**, 3629
20:12 the righteous, *and* seest the **r** and the heart, 3629
La 3:13 the arrows of his quiver to enter into my **r**. 3629
Rev 2:23 know that I am he which searcheth the **r** *3510*

REJECT (4) [REJECTED, REJECTETH]

Hos 4: 6 hast rejected knowledge, I will also **r** thee, 3988
Mk 6:26 which sat with *him,* he would not **r** her. *114*
7: 9 Full well ye **r** the commandment of God, *114*
Tit 3:10 after the first and second admonition, **r**; *3868*

REJECTED (29) [REJECT]

1Sa 8: 7 for they have not **r** thee, but they have 3988
8: 7 have not rejected thee, but they have **r** me, 3988
10:19 ye have *this* day **r** your God, who himself 3988
15:23 Because thou hast **r** the word of 3988
15:23 he hath also **r** thee from *being* king. 3988
15:26 for thou hast **r** the word of the LORD, and 3988
15:26 the LORD hath **r** thee from being king 3988
16: 1 seeing I have **r** him from reigning over 3988
2Ki 17:15 they **r** his statutes, and his covenant that he 3988
17:20 the LORD **r** all the seed of Israel, and 3988
Isa 53: 3 He is despised and **r** of men; a man of 2310
Jer 2:37 for the LORD hath **r** thy confidences, and 3988
6:19 unto my words, nor *to* my law, but **r** it. 3988
6:30 call them, because the LORD hath **r** them. 3988
7:29 for the LORD hath **r** and forsaken 3988
8: 9 lo, they have **r** the word of the LORD; 3988
14:19 Hast thou **utterly r** Judah? hath thy 3988+3988
La 5:22 thou hast **utterly r** us; thou art very 3988+3988
Hos 4: 6 because thou hast **r** knowledge, I will also 3988
Mt 21:42 The stone which the builders **r**, *593*
Mk 8:31 suffer many *things,* and be **r** of the elders, *593*
12:10 The stone which the builders **r** is become *593*
Lk 7:30 lawyers **r** the counsel of God against *114*
9:22 and be **r** of the elders and chief priests and *593*
17:25 many *things,* and be **r** of this generation. *593*
20:17 is written, The stone which the builders **r**, *593*
Gal 4:14 was in my flesh ye despised not, nor **r**; *1609*
Heb 6: 8 But that which beareth thorns and briers *is* **r**, *96*
12:17 would have inherited the blessing, he was **r**: *593*

REJECTETH (1) [REJECT]

Jn 12:48 He that **r** me, and receiveth not my words, *114*

REJOICE (192) [REJOICED, REJOICEST, REJOICETH, REJOICING]

Lev 23:40 ye shall **r** before the LORD your God 8055
Dt 12: 7 ye shall **r** in all that you put your hand 8055
12:12 ye shall **r** before the LORD your God, 8055
12:18 thou shalt **r** before the LORD thy God in 8055
14:26 and thou shalt **r**, thou and thine household, 8055
16:11 thou shalt **r** before the LORD thy God, 8055
16:14 thou shalt **r** in thy feast, thou, and thy son, 8055
16:15 therefore thou shalt surely **r**. 1961+8056
26:11 thou shalt **r** in every good *thing* which 8055
27: 7 eat there, and **r** before the LORD thy God. 8055
28:63 the LORD will **r** over you to destroy you, 7797
30: 9 for the LORD will again **r** over thee for 7797
32:43 **R**, O ye nations, *with* his people: for he will 7442
33:18 he said, **R**, Zebulun, in thy going out; 8055
Jdg 9:19 *then* **r** ye in Abimelech, and let him also 8055
9:19 ye in Abimelech, and let him also **r** in you: 8055
16:23 sacrifice unto Dagon their god, and to **r**: 8057
1Sa 2: 1 mine enemies; because I **r** in thy salvation. 8055
19: 5 thou sawest *it,* and didst **r**: wherefore then 8055
2Sa 1:20 lest the daughters of the Philistines **r**, 8055
1Ch 16:10 let the heart of them **r** that seek 8055
16:31 Let the heavens be glad, and let the earth **r**: 1523
16:32 let the fields **r**, and all that *is* therein. 5970
2Ch 6:41 and let thy saints **r** in goodness. 8055
20:27 for the LORD had **made** them **to r** over 8055
Ne 12:43 for God had **made** them **r** *with* great joy: 8055
Job 3:22 Which **r exceedingly**, *and* 413+1524+8056
20:18 restitution *be,* and he shall not **r** *therein.* 5965
21:12 and harp, and **r** at the sound of the organ. 8055
Ps 2:11 the LORD with fear, and **r** with trembling. 1523
5:11 let all those that put their trust in thee **r**: 8055
9: 2 I will be glad and **r** in thee: I will sing 5970
9:14 daughter of Zion: I will **r** in thy salvation. 1523
13: 4 those that trouble me **r** when I am moved. 1523
13: 5 thy mercy; my heart shall **r** in thy salvation. 1523
14: 7 Jacob shall **r**, *and* Israel shall be glad. 1523
20: 5 We will **r** in thy salvation, and in the name 7442
21: 1 and in thy salvation how greatly shall he **r**! 1523
30: 1 and hast not **made** my foes **to r** over me. 8055
31: 7 I will be glad and **r** in thy mercy: for thou 8055
32:11 Be glad in the LORD, and **r**, ye righteous: 1523
33: 1 **R** in the LORD, O ye righteous: *for* praise 7442
33:21 For our heart shall **r** in him, because 8055
35: 9 in the LORD: it shall **r** in his salvation. 7797
35:19 are mine enemies wrongfully **r** over me: 8055
35:24 and let them not **r** over me. 8055
35:26 brought to confusion together that **r** at mine 8056
38:16 *Hear me,* lest *otherwise* they should **r** over 8055
40:16 Let all those that seek thee **r** and be glad in 7797
48:11 Let mount Zion **r**, let the daughters of 8055
51: 8 the bones *which* thou hast broken may **r**. 1523
53: 6 Jacob shall **r**, *and* Israel shall be glad. 1523
58:10 The righteous shall **r** when he seeth 8055
60: 6 I will **r**, I will divide Shechem, and 5937
63: 7 in the shadow of thy wings will I **r**. 7442
63:11 the king shall **r** in God; every one that 8055
65: 8 **makest** the outgoings of the morning and evening **to r**. 7442
65:12 and the little hills **r** on every side. 1524
66: 6 the flood on foot: there did we **r** in him. 8055
68: 3 righteous be glad; let them **r** before God: 5970
68: 3 yea, let them **exceedingly r**. 7797+8057+871.1
68: 4 by his name JAH, and **r** before him. 5937
70: 4 Let all those that seek thee **r** and be glad in 7797
71:23 My lips shall **greatly r** when I sing unto 7442
85: 6 us again: that thy people may **r** in thee? 8055
86: 4 **R** the soul of thy servant: for unto thee, 8055
89:12 Tabor and Hermon shall **r** in thy name. 7442
89:16 In thy name shall they **r** all the day: and 1523
89:42 thou hast **made** all his enemies **to r**. 8055
90:14 that we may **r** and be glad all our days. 7442
96:11 Let the heavens **r**, and let the earth be glad; 8055
96:12 shall all the trees of the wood **r** 7442
97: 1 The LORD reigneth; let the earth **r**; 1523
97:12 **R** in the LORD, ye righteous; and 8055
98: 4 make a loud noise, and **r**, and sing *praise.* 7442
104:31 for ever: the LORD shall **r** in his works. 8055
105: 3 let the heart of them **r** that seek 8055
106: 5 that *I* may **r** in the gladness of thy nation, 8055
107:42 The righteous shall see *it,* and **r**: and 8055
108: 7 I will **r**, I will divide Shechem, and 5937
109:28 let them be ashamed; but let thy servant **r**. 8055
118:24 hath made; we will **r** and be glad in it. 1523
119:162 I **r** at thy word, as one that findeth great 7797
149: 2 Let Israel **r** in him that made him: let 8055
Pr 2:14 Who **r** to do evil, *and* delight in 8056
5:18 and **r** with the wife of thy youth. 8055
23:15 heart be wise, my heart shall **r**, even mine. 8055
23:16 Yea, my reins shall **r**, when thy lips speak 5937
23:24 of the righteous shall **greatly r**: 1523+1524
23:25 shall be glad, and she that bare thee shall **r**. 1523
24:17 **R** not when thine enemy falleth, and let not 8055
27: 9 Ointment and perfume **r** the heart: so 8055
28:12 When righteous *men* do **r**, *there is* great 5970
29: 2 the righteous are in authority, the people **r**: 8055
29: 6 *is* a snare: but the righteous doth sing and **r**. 8056
31:25 and she shall **r** in time to come. 7832
Ecc 3:12 for *a man* to **r**, and to do good in his life. 8055
3:22 than that a man should **r** in his own works; 8055
4:16 they also that come after shall not **r** in him. 8055
5:19 to take his portion, and to **r** in his labour; 8055
11: 8 if a man live many years, *and* **r** in them all; 8055
11: 9 **R**, O young man, in thy youth; and let thy 8055
SS 1: 4 we will be glad and **r** in thee, we will 8055
Isa 8: 6 and **r** in Rezin and Remaliah's son; 4885
9: 3 *and* as *men* **r** when they divide the spoil. 1523
13: 3 *even* them that **r** in my highness. 5947
14: 8 the fir trees **r** at thee, *and* the cedars of 8055
14:29 **R** not thou, whole Palestina, because 8055
23:12 he said, Thou shalt no more **r**, O thou 5937
24: 8 the noise of them that **r** endeth, the joy of 5947
25: 9 we will be glad and **r** in his salvation. 8055
29:19 the poor among men shall **r** in the Holy 1523
35: 1 the desert shall **r**, and blossom as the rose. 1523
35: 2 **r** even *with* joy and singing: 1523
41:16 thou shalt **r** in the LORD, *and* shalt glory 1523
61: 7 *for* confusion they shall **r** in their portion: 7442
61:10 I will **greatly r** in the LORD, 7797+7797
62: 5 over the bride, *so* shall thy God **r** over thee. 7797
65:13 my servants shall **r**, but ye shall be 8055
65:18 and **r** for ever *in that* which I create: 1523
65:19 I will **r** in Jerusalem, and joy in my people: 1523
66:10 **R** ye with Jerusalem, and be glad with her, 8055
66:10 **r** for joy with her, all ye that mourn for her: 7797
66:14 when ye see *this,* your heart shall **r**, and 7797
Jer 31:13 shall the virgin **r** in the dance, both young 8055
31:13 and **make** them **r** from their sorrow. 8055
32:41 I will **r** over them to do them good, and 7797
51:39 that they may **r**, and sleep a perpetual 5937
La 2:17 he hath **caused** *thine* enemy **to r** over thee, 8055
4:21 **R** and be glad, O daughter of Edom, 7797
Eze 7:12 let not the buyer **r**, nor the seller mourn: 8055
35:15 As thou didst **r** at the inheritance of 8057
Hos 9: 1 **R** not, O Israel, for joy, as *other* people: 8055
Joel 2:21 Fear not, O land; be glad and **r**: for 8055
2:23 of Zion, and **r** in the LORD your God: 8055
Am 6:13 *Ye* which **r** in a thing of nought, which say, 8056
Mic 7: 8 **R** not against me, O mine enemy: when I 8055
Hab 1:15 in their drag: therefore they **r** and are glad. 8055
3:18 Yet I will **r** in the LORD, I will joy in 5937
Zep 3:11 of the midst of thee them that **r** in thy pride, 5947
3:14 be glad and **r** with all the heart, O daughter 5937
3:17 he will save, he will **r** over thee with joy; 7797
Zec 2:10 Sing and **r**, O daughter of Zion: for lo, 8055
4:10 the day of small *things?* for they shall **r**, 8055
9: 9 **R** greatly, O daughter of Zion; shout, 1523
10: 7 and their heart shall **r** as *through* wine: 8055
10: 7 be glad; their heart shall **r** in the LORD. 1523
Mt 5:12 **R**, and be exceeding glad: for great *is* your *5463*
Lk 1:14 and gladness; and many shall **r** at his birth. *5463*
6:23 **R** ye in that day, and leap *for joy:* for *5463*
10:20 Notwithstanding in this **r** not, that *5463*
10:20 but rather **r**, because your names are *5463*
15: 6 saying unto them, **R with** me; *4796*
15: 9 neighbours together, saying, **R with** me; *4796*
19:37 whole multitude of the disciples began to **r** *5463*
Jn 4:36 and he that reapeth may **r** together. *5463*
5:35 ye were willing for a season to **r** in his light. *21*
14:28 If ye loved me, ye would **r**, because I said, *5463*
16:20 and lament, but the world shall **r**: *5463*
16:22 and your heart shall **r**, and your joy no *man* *5463*
Ac 2:26 Therefore did my heart **r**, and my tongue *2165*
Ro 5: 2 and **r** in hope of the glory of God. *2744*
12:15 **R** with them that do rejoice, and weep with *5463*
12:15 Rejoice with them that do **r**, and weep with *5463*
15:10 *he* saith, **R**, *ye* Gentiles, with his people. *2165*
1Co 7:30 and they that **r**, as though they rejoiced not; *5463*
12:26 be honoured, all the members **r with** *it.* *4796*
2Co 2: 3 sorrow from *them of* whom I ought to **r**; *5463*
7: 9 Now I **r**, not that ye were made sorry, but *5463*
7:16 I **r** therefore that I have confidence in you *5463*
Gal 4:27 For it is written, **R**, *thou* barren that bearest *2165*
Php 1:18 and I therein do **r**, yea, and will rejoice. *5463*
1:18 and I therein do rejoice, yea, and will **r**. *5463*
2:16 that I may **r** in the day of Christ, that I have *2745*
2:17 of your faith, I joy, and **r with** you all. *4796*
2:18 same *cause* also do ye joy, and **r with** me. *4796*
2:28 ye may **r**, and *that* I may be the less *5463*
3: 1 Finally, my brethren, **r** in the Lord. *5463*
3: 3 and **r** in Christ Jesus, and have no *2744*
4: 4 **R** in the Lord alway: *and* again I say, *5463*
4: 4 in the Lord alway: *and* again I say, **R**. *5463*
Col 1:24 Who now **r** in my sufferings for you, and *5463*
1Th 5:16 **R** evermore. *5463*
Jas 1: 9 Let the brother of low degree **r** in that he is *2744*
4:16 But now ye **r** in your boastings: all such *2744*
1Pe 1: 6 Wherein ye **greatly r**, though now for a *21*
1: 8 ye **r** with joy unspeakable and full of glory: *21*
4:13 But **r**, inasmuch as ye are partakers of *5463*
Rev 11:10 And they that dwell upon the earth shall **r** *5463*
12:12 Therefore **r**, ye heavens, and ye that dwell *2165*
18:20 **R** over her, *thou* heaven, and ye holy *2165*
19: 7 Let us be glad and **r**, and give honour to him: *21*

REJOICED (47) [REJOICE]

Ex 18: 9 Jethro **r** for all the goodness which 2302
Dt 28:63 *that* as the LORD **r** over you to do you 7797
30: 9 over thee for good, as he **r** over thy fathers: 7797
Jdg 19: 3 of the damsel saw him, he **r** to meet him. 8055
1Sa 6:13 their eyes, and saw the ark, and **r** to see *it.* 8055
11:15 and all the men of Israel **r** greatly. 8055
1Ki 1:40 **r** *with* great joy, so that the earth rent with 8056
5: 7 that he **r** greatly, and said, Blessed *be* 8055
2Ki 11:14 all the people of the land **r**, and blew with 8056
11:20 all the people of the land **r**, and the city was 8055
1Ch 29: 9 the people **r**, for that they offered willingly, 8055
29: 9 and David the king also **r** *with* great joy. 8055
2Ch 15:15 all Judah **r** at the oath: for they had sworn 8055
23:13 all the people of the land **r**, and 8056
23:21 all the people of the land **r**: and the city 8055
24:10 And all the princes and all the people **r**, and 8055
29:36 Hezekiah **r**, and all the people, that God 8055
30:25 land of Israel, and that dwelt in Judah, **r**. 8055
Ne 12:43 that day they offered great sacrifices, and **r**: 8055
12:43 the wives also and the children **r**: so 8055
12:44 for Judah **r** for the priests and for 8057
Est 8:15 and the city of Shushan **r** and was glad. 6670
Job 31:25 If I **r** because my wealth *was* great, and 8055
31:29 If I **r** at the destruction of him that hated 8055
Ps 35:15 in mine adversity they **r**, and 8055
97: 8 the daughters of Judah **r**, because of thy 1523
119:14 I have **r** in the way of thy testimonies, 7797
Ecc 2:10 any joy; for my heart **r** in all my labour: 8056
Jer 15:17 not in the assembly of the mockers, nor **r**; 5937
50:11 Because ye were glad, because ye **r**, O ye 5937
Eze 25: 6 **r** in heart with all thy despite against 8055
Hos 10: 5 the priests thereof *that* **r** on it, for the glory 1523

R

Ob 1:12 neither shouldest thou have r over 8055
Mt 2:10 the star, they r *with* exceeding great joy. *5463*
Lk 1:47 And my spirit hath r in God my Saviour. *21*
1:58 great mercy upon her; and they r **with** her. *4796*
10:21 In that hour Jesus r in spirit, and said, I thank *21*
13:17 all the people r for all the glorious *things* *5463*
Jn 8:56 Your father Abraham r to see my day: and *21*
Ac 7:41 and r in the works of their own hands. *2165*
15:31 they had read, they r for the consolation. *5463*
16:34 he set meat before *them,* and r, believing in *21*
1Co 7:30 and they that rejoice, as though they r not; *5463*
2Co 7: 7 mind toward me; so that I r the more. *5463*
Php 4:10 But I r in the Lord greatly, that now at *5463*
2Jn 1: 4 I r greatly that I found of thy children *5463*
3Jn 1: 3 For I r greatly, when *the* brethren came and *5463*

REJOICEST (1) [REJOICE]
Jer 11:15 when thou doest evil, then thou r. 5937

REJOICETH (18) [REJOICE]
1Sa 2: 1 and said, My heart r in the LORD, 5970
Job 39:21 paweth in the valley, and r in *his* strength. 7797
Ps 16: 9 Therefore my heart is glad, and my glory r: 1523
19: 5 *and* r as a strong *man* to run a race. 7797
28: 7 therefore my heart **greatly** r; and with my 5937
Pr 11:10 it goeth well with the righteous, the city r: 5970
13: 9 The light of the righteous r: but the lamp of 8055
15:30 The light of the eyes r the heart: *and* a good 8055
29: 3 Whoso loveth wisdom r his father: but 8055
Isa 5:14 and their pomp, and he that r, 5938
62: 5 *as* the bridegroom r over the bride, *so* 4885
64: 5 Thou meetest him that r and 7797
Eze 35:14 When the whole earth r, I will make thee 8055
Mt 18:13 he r more of that *sheep,* than of the ninety *5463*
Jn 3:29 r **greatly** because of *5463+5479*
1Co 13: 6 R not in iniquity, but rejoiceth in the truth; *5463*
13: 6 Rejoiceth not in iniquity, but r **in** the truth; *4796*
Jas 2:13 no mercy; and mercy r **against** judgment. *2620*

REJOICING (28) [REJOICE]
1Ki 1:45 they are come up from thence r, so that 8056
2Ch 23:18 with r and with singing, as it was ordained 8057
Job 8:21 mouth *with* laughing, and thy lips *with* r. 8643
Ps 19: 8 statutes of the LORD *are* right, r the heart: 8055
45:15 With gladness and r shall they be brought: 1524
107:22 and declare his works with r. 7440
118:15 The voice of r and salvation *is* in 7440
119:111 for ever: for they *are* the r of my heart. 8342
126: 6 shall doubtless come again with r, 7440
Pr 8:30 was daily *his* delight, r always before him; 7832
8:31 R in the habitable part of his earth; and 7832
Isa 65:18 I create Jerusalem a r, and her people a joy. 1525
Jer 15:16 was unto me the joy and r of mine heart: 8057
Hab 3:14 their r *was* as to devour the poor secretly. 5951
Zep 2:15 This *is* the r city that dwelt carelessly, 5947
Lk 15: 5 found *it,* he layeth *it* on his shoulders, r. *5463*
Ac 5:41 r that they were counted worthy to suffer *5463*
8:39 him no more: and he went *on* his way r. *5463*
Ro 12:12 R in hope; patient in tribulation; *5463*
1Co 15:31 I protest by your r which I have in Christ *2746*
2Co 1:12 For our r is this, the testimony of our *2746*
1:14 us in part, that we are your r, *2745*
6:10 As sorrowful, yet alway r; as poor, *5463*
Gal 6: 4 and then shall he have r in himself alone, *2745*
Php 1:26 That your r may be *more* abundant in Jesus *2745*
1Th 2:19 For what *is* our hope, or joy, or crown of r? *2746*
Heb 3: 6 and the r of the hope firm unto the end. *2745*
Jas 4:16 rejoice in your boastings: all such r is evil. *2746*

REKEM (5)
Nu 31: 8 and R, and Zur, and Hur, and Reba, 7552
Jos 13:21 Evi, and R, and Zur, and Hur, and Reba, 7552
18:27 And R, and Irpeel, and Taralah, 7552
1Ch 2:43 Korah, and Tappuah, and R, and Shema. 7552
2:44 father of Jorkoam: and R begat Shammai. 7552

RELATIVES See KINDRED; KINDREDS

RELEASE (21) [RELEASED]
Dt 15: 1 of *every* seven years thou shalt make a r. 8059
15: 2 this *is* the manner of the r: Every creditor 8059
15: 2 r *it;* he shall not exact *it* of his neighbour, 8058
15: 2 because it is called the LORD'S r. 8059
15: 3 is thine with thy brother thine hand shall r; 8058
15: 9 The seventh year, the year of r, is at hand; 8059
31:10 in the solemnity of the year of r, in 8059
Est 2:18 he made a r to the provinces, and 2010
Mt 27:15 Now at *that* feast the governor was wont to r *630*
27:17 unto them, Whom will ye *that* I r unto you? *630*
27:21 Whether of the twain will ye *that* I r unto *630*
Mk 15: 9 Will ye *that* I r unto you the King of *630*
15:11 that he should rather r Barabbas unto them. *630*
Lk 23:16 I will therefore chastise him, and r *him.* *630*
23:17 (For of necessity he must r one unto them at *630*
23:18 with this *man,* and r unto us Barabbas: *630*
23:20 Pilate therefore, willing to r Jesus, spake *630*
Jn 18:39 that I should r unto you one at the passover: *630*
18:39 *that* I r unto you the King of the Jews? *630*
19:10 to crucify thee, and have power to r thee? *630*
19:12 *And* from thenceforth Pilate sought to r him: *630*

RELEASED (4) [RELEASE]
Mt 27:26 Then r he Barabbas unto them: *630*
Mk 15: 6 Now at *that* feast he r unto them one *630*
15:15 r Barabbas unto them, and delivered Jesus, *630*
Lk 23:25 And he r unto them him that for sedition and *630*

RELIED (3) [RELY]
2Ch 13:18 they r upon the LORD God of their 8172
16: 7 Because thou hast r on the king of Syria, 8172
16: 7 not r on the LORD thy God, therefore is 8172

RELIEF (1) [RELIEVE, RELIEVED, RELIEVETH]
Ac 11:29 determined to send r unto *1248+1519*

RELIEVE (7) [RELIEF]
Lev 25:35 in decay with thee; then thou shalt r him: 2388
Isa 1:17 seek judgment, r the oppressed, judge 833
La 1:11 their pleasant things for meat to r the soul: 7725
1:16 the comforter that *should* r my soul is far 7725
1:19 they sought their meat, to r their souls. 7725
1Ti 5:16 let them r them, and let not the church be *1884*
5:16 that it may r them that are widows indeed. *1884*

RELIEVED (1) [RELIEF]
1Ti 5:10 the saints' feet, if she have r the afflicted, *1884*

RELIEVETH (1) [RELIEF]
Ps 146: 9 he r the fatherless and widow: 5749

RELIGION (5) [RELIGIOUS]
Ac 26: 5 that after the most straitest sect of our r I *2356*
Gal 1:13 conversation in time past in the **Jews'** r, *2454*
1:14 And profited in the **Jews'** r above many *2454*
Jas 1:26 his own heart, this *man's* r *is* vain. *2356*
1:27 Pure r and undefiled before God and *2356*

RELIGIOUS (2) [RELIGION]
Ac 13:43 and r proselytes followed Paul and *4576*
Jas 1:26 If any *man* among you seem to be r, and *2357*

RELY (1) [RELIED]
2Ch 16: 8 yet, because thou didst r on the LORD, 8172

REMAIN (79) [REMAINDER, REMAINED, REMAINEST, REMAINETH, REMAINING, REMNANT]
Ge 38:11 R a widow *at* thy father's house, till Shelah 3427
Ex 8: 9 *that* they may r in the river only? 7604
8:11 thy people; they shall r in the river only. 7604
12:10 ye shall let nothing of it r until 3498
23:18 neither shall the fat of my sacrifice r until 3885
29:34 r unto the morning, then thou shalt burn 3498
Lev 19: 6 if ought r until the third day, it shall be 3498
25:28 that which is sold shall r in the hand of him 1961
25:52 if there r but few years unto the year of 7604
27:18 the money according to the years that r, 3498
Nu 33:55 **come to** pass, *that those* which ye let r 3498
Dt 2:34 little ones, of every city, we left none to r: 8300
16: 4 day at even, r **all night** until the morning. 3885
19:20 those which r shall hear, and fear, and 7604
21:13 shall r in thine house, and bewail her father 3427
21:23 His body shall not r **all night** upon the tree, 3885
Jos 1:14 shall r in the land which Moses gave you 3427
2:11 neither did there r any more courage in any 6965
8:22 so that *they* let none of them r or escape. 8300
10:27 cave's mouth, *which* r until this very day. NIH
10:28 the souls that *were* therein; he let none r: 8300
10:30 he let none r in it; but did unto the king 8300
23: 4 divided unto you *by lot* these nations that r, 7604
23: 7 these nations, these that r amongst you; 7604
23:12 *even* these that r among you, and 7604
Jdg 5:17 why did Dan r *in* ships? Asher continued 1481
21: 7 How shall we do for wives for them that r, 3498
21:16 How shall we do for wives for them that r, 3498
1Sa 20:19 was *in hand,* and shalt r by the stone Ezel. 3427
1Ki 11:16 (For six months did Joab r there with all 3427
18:22 I, *even* I only, r a prophet of the LORD; 3498
2Ki 7:13 I pray thee, five of the horses that r, 7604
Ezr 9:15 for we r *yet* escaped, as *it is* this day: 7604
Job 21:32 to the grave, and shall r in the tomb. 8245
27:15 Those that r of him shall be buried in 8300
37: 8 beasts go into dens, and r in their places. 7931
Ps 55: 7 I wander far off, *and* r in the wilderness. 3885
Pr 2:21 *in* the land, and the perfect shall r in it. 3498
21:16 shall r in the congregation of the dead. 5117
Isa 10:32 As yet shall *he* r at Nob *that* day: he shall 5975
32:16 and righteousness r in the fruitful field. 3427
44:13 beauty of a man; that it may r *in* the house. 3427
65: 4 Which r among the graves, and lodge in 3427
66:22 *shall* r before me, saith the LORD, so 5975
66:22 so shall your seed and your name r. 5975
Jer 8: 3 residue of them that r of this evil family, 7604
8: 3 which r in all the places whither I have 7604
17:25 of Jerusalem: and this city shall r for ever. 3427
24: 8 that r in this land, and them that dwell in 7604
27:11 those will I let r **still** in their own land, 3240
27:19 concerning the residue of the vessels that r 3498
27:21 concerning the vessels that r *in* the house 3498
30:18 the palace shall r after the manner thereof. 3427
38: 4 hands of the men of war that r in this city, 7604
42:17 none of them shall r or escape from the evil 8300
44: 7 out of Judah, to leave you none to r; 7611
44:14 shall escape or r, that *they* should return 8300
51:62 to cut it off, that none shall r in it, 3427
Eze 7:11 none of them *shall* r, nor of their multitude, NIH
17:21 they that r shall be scattered towards all 7604
31:13 his ruin shall all the fowls of the heaven r, 7931
32: 4 will **cause** all the fowls of the heaven **to** r 7931
39:14 those that r upon the face of the earth, 3498
Am 6: 9 if there r ten men in one house, that they 3498
Ob 1:14 those of his that did r in the day of distress. 8300
Zec 5: 4 it shall r in the midst of his house, and 3885
12:14 All the families that r, every family apart, 7604
Lk 10: 7 And in the same house r, eating and *3306*
Jn 6:12 Gather up the fragments that r, that nothing *4052*
15:11 that my joy might r in you, and *that* your *3306*
15:16 forth fruit, and *that* your fruit should r: *3306*
19:31 that the bodies should not r upon the cross *3306*
1Co 7:11 let her r unmarried, or be reconciled to *her* *3306*
15: 6 of whom the greater part r unto this *3306*
1Th 4:15 r unto the coming of the Lord shall not *4035*
4:17 r shall be caught up together with them in *4035*
Heb 12:27 those *things* which cannot be shaken may r. *3306*
1Jn 2:24 heard from the beginning shall r in you, *3306*
Rev 3: 2 and strengthen the *things* which r, *3062*

REMAINDER (6) [REMAIN]
Ex 29:34 then thou shalt burn the r with fire: 3498
Lev 6:16 the r thereof shall Aaron and his sons eat: 3498
7:16 on the morrow also the r of it shall be 3498
7:17 the r of the flesh of the sacrifice on 3498
2Sa 14: 7 husband *neither* name nor r upon the earth. 7611
Ps 76:10 the r of wrath shalt thou restrain. 7611

REMAINED (53) [REMAIN]
Ge 7:23 Noah only r *alive,* and *they* that *were* with 7604
14:10 and they that r fled to the mountain. 7604
Ex 8:31 and from his people; there r not one. 7604
10:15 there r not any green thing in the trees, or 3498
10:19 there r not one locust in all the coasts of 7604
14:28 there r not so much as one of them. 7604
Nu 11:26 there r two *of the* men in the camp, 7604
35:28 Because he should have r in the city of his 3427
36:12 their inheritance r in the tribe of the family 1961
Dt 3:11 For only Og king of Bashan r of 7604
4:25 ye shall have r **long** in the land, and 3462
Jos 10:20 that the rest *which* r of them entered into 8277
11:22 in Gaza, in Gath, and in Ashdod, there r. 7604
13:12 who r of the remnant of the giants: 7604
18: 2 there r among the children of Israel seven 3498
21:20 the Levites which r of the children of 3498
21:26 families of the children of Kohath that r. 3498
Jdg 7: 3 and two thousand; and there r ten thousand. 7604
1Sa 11:11 that they which r were scattered, so 7604
23:14 r in a mountain in the wilderness of Ziph. 3427
24: 3 and his men r in the sides of the cave. 3427
2Sa 13:20 So Tamar r desolate *in* her brother 3427
1Ki 22:46 which r in the days of his father Asa, 7604
2Ki 10:11 So Jehu slew all that r of the house of Ahab 7604
10:17 he slew all that r unto Ahab in Samaria, 7604
13: 6 there r the grove also in Samaria.) 5975
24:14 none r, save the poorest sort of the people 7604
25:22 *as for* the people that r in the land of Judah, 7604
1Ch 13:14 the ark of God r with the family of 3427
Ecc 2: 9 in Jerusalem: also my wisdom r with me. 5975
Jer 34: 7 for these defenced cities r of the cities of 7604
37:10 there r *but* wounded men among them, 7604
37:16 and Jeremiah had r there many days; 3427
37:21 Thus Jeremiah r in the court of the prison. 3427
38:13 and Jeremiah r in the court of the prison. 3427
39: 9 the remnant of the people that r in the city, 7604
39: 9 to him, with the rest of the people that r. 7604
41:10 and all the people that r in Mizpah, 7604
48:11 therefore his taste r in him, and his sent is 5975
51:30 forborn to fight, they have r in *their* holds: 3427
52:15 the residue of the people that r in the city, 7604
La 2:22 of the LORD'S anger none escaped nor r: 8300
Eze 3:15 r there astonished among them seven days. 3427
Da 10: 8 great vision, and there r no strength in me: 7604
10:13 and I r there with the kings of Persia. 3498
10:17 straightway there r no strength in me, 5975
Mt 11:23 in Sodom, it would have r until this day. *3306*
14:20 they took up of the fragments that r twelve *4052*
Lk 1:22 he beckoned unto them, and r speechless. *1265*
9:17 there was taken up of fragments that r to *4052*
Jn 6:13 which r **over and above** unto them that *4052*
Ac 5: 4 Whiles it r, was it not thine own? and *3306*
27:41 and r unmoveable, but the hinder part was *3306*

REMAINEST (2) [REMAIN]
La 5:19 Thou, O LORD, r for ever; thy throne 3427
Heb 1:11 but thou r; and they all shall wax old as *1265*

REMAINETH (37) [REMAIN]
Ge 8:22 While the earth r, seedtime and harvest, 3117
Ex 10: 5 is escaped which r unto you from the hail, 7604
12:10 that which r of it until the morning ye shall 3498
16:23 that which r **over** lay up for you to be kept 5736
26:12 the remnant that r of the curtains of 5736
26:12 the half curtain that r, shall hang over 5736
26:13 a cubit on the other side of that which r in 5736
Lev 8:32 that which r of the flesh and of the bread 3498
10:12 Take the meat offering that r of 3498
16:16 that r among them in the midst of their 7931
Nu 24:19 and shall destroy him that r of the city. 8300
Jos 8:29 a great heap of stones, *that* r unto this day. NIH
13: 1 there r *yet* very much land to be possessed. 7604
13: 2 This is the land that *yet* r: all the borders of 7604
Jdg 5:13 he made him that r have dominion over 8300
1Sa 6:18 *which stone* r unto this day in the field of NIH
16:11 There r yet the youngest, and behold, 7604
1Ch 17: 1 the ark of the covenant of the LORD r NIH
Ezr 1: 4 whosoever r in any place where he 7604
Job 19: 4 *that* I have erred, mine error r with myself. 3885
21:34 seeing *in* your answers there r falsehood? 7604
41:22 In his neck r strength, and sorrow is turned 3885
Isa 4: 3 he that r in Jerusalem, shall be called holy, 3498
Jer 38: 2 He that r in this city shall die by the sword, 3427
47: 4 from Tyrus and Zidon every helper that r: 8300
Eze 6:12 he that r and is besieged shall die by 7604
Hag 2: 5 out of Egypt, so my spirit r among you: 5975
Zec 9: 7 he that r, even he, *shall be* for our God, and 7604
Jn 9:41 now ye say, We see; therefore your sin r. *3306*
1Co 7:29 it r, that both they that have *1510+3062+3588*
2Co 3:11 much more that which r *is* glorious. *3306*
3:14 for until this day r the same vail untaken *3306*
9: 9 to the poor: his righteousness r for ever. *3306*
Heb 4: 6 therefore it r that some *must* enter therein, *620*
4: 9 There r therefore a rest to the people of God. *620*
10:26 the truth, there r no more sacrifice for sins, *620*
1Jn 3: 9 doth not commit sin; for his seed r in him: *3306*

REMAINING (14) [REMAIN]
Nu 9:22 r thereon, the children of Israel abode in 7931
Dt 3: 3 we smote him until none was left to him r. 8300
Jos 10:33 and his people, until *he* had left him none r. 8300
10:37 he left none r, according to all that he had 8300
10:39 the souls that *were* therein; he left none r: 8300
10:40 he left none r, but utterly destroyed all that 8300
11: 8 smote them, until *they* left them none r. 8300

Jos 21:40 which were r of the families of the Levites, 3498
2Sa 21: 5 from r in any of the coasts of Israel, 3320
2Ki 10:11 and his priests, until *he* left him none r. 8300
1Ch 9:33 *who* r in the chambers *were* free: NIH
Job 18:19 his people, nor *any* r in his dwellings. 8300
Ob 1:18 there shall not be *any* r of the house of 8300
Jn 1:33 see the Spirit descending, and r on him, *3306*

REMALIAH (11) [REMALIAH'S]

2Ki 15:25 Pekah the son of R, a captain of his, 7425
15:27 of R *began* to reign over Israel in Samaria, 7425
15:30 a conspiracy against Pekah the son of R, 7425
15:32 In the second year of Pekah the son of R 7425
15:37 the king of Syria, and Pekah the son of R. 7425
16: 1 R Ahaz the son of Jotham king of Judah 7425
16: 5 Pekah son of R king of Israel came up *to* 7425
2Ch 28: 6 For Pekah the son of R slew in Judah an 7425
Isa 7: 1 and Pekah the son of R, king of Israel, 7425
7: 4 of Rezin with Syria, and of the son of R. 7425
7: 5 Because Syria, Ephraim, and the son of R, 7425

REMALIAH'S (2) [REMALIAH]

Isa 7: 9 and the head of Samaria *is* R son. 7425
8: 6 go softly, and rejoice in Rezin and R son; 7425

REMEDY (3)

2Ch 36:16 arose against his people, till *there was* no r. 4832
Pr 6:15 suddenly shall he be broken without r. 4832
29: 1 suddenly be destroyed, and that without r. 4832

REMEMBER (148) [REMEMBERED, REMEMBEREST, REMEMBERETH, REMEMBERING, REMEMBRANCE, REMEMBRANCES]

Ge 9:15 I will r my covenant, which *is* between me 2142
9:16 that I may r the everlasting covenant 2142
40:23 Yet did not the chief butler r Joseph, but 2142
41: 9 saying, I do r my faults *this* day: 2142
Ex 13: 3 Moses said unto the people, R this day, 2142
20: 8 R the sabbath day, to keep it holy. 2142
32:13 R Abraham, Isaac, and Israel, thy servants, 2142
Lev 26:42 will I r my covenant with Jacob, and 2142
26:42 also my covenant with Abraham will I r; 2142
26:42 will I remember; and I will r the land. 2142
26:45 I will for their sakes r the covenant of their 2142
Nu 11: 5 We r the fish, which we did eat in Egypt 2142
15:39 r all the commandments of the LORD, 2142
15:40 That ye may r, and do all my 2142
Dt 5:15 r that thou wast a servant in the land of 2142
7:18 shalt **well** r what the LORD thy 2142+2142
8: 2 thou shalt r all the way which the LORD 2142
8:18 thou shalt r the LORD thy God: for *it is* 2142
9: 7 R, *and* forget not, how thou provokedst 2142
9:27 R thy servants, Abraham, Isaac, and Jacob; 2142
15:15 thou shalt r that thou wast a bondman in 2142
16: 3 that thou mayest r the day when thou 2142
16:12 thou shalt r that thou wast a bondman in 2142
24: 9 R what the LORD thy God did unto 2142
24:18 thou shalt r that thou wast a bondman in 2142
24:22 thou shalt r that thou wast a bondman in 2142
25:17 R what Amalek did unto thee by the way, 2142
32: 7 R the days of old, consider the years of 2142
Jos 1:13 R the word which Moses the servant of 2142
Jdg 9: 2 r also that I *am* your bone and your flesh. 2142
16:28 r me, I pray thee, and strengthen me, I pray 2142
1Sa 1:11 r me, and not forget thine handmaid, but 2142
15: 2 I r *that* which Amalek did to Israel, 6485
25:31 well with my lord, then r thine handmaid. 2142
2Sa 14:11 let the king r the LORD thy God, 2142
19:19 neither do thou r *that* which thy servant did 2142
2Ki 9:25 for r how that, when I and thou rode 2142
20: 3 r now how I have walked before thee in 2142
1Ch 16:12 R his marvellous works that he hath done, 2142
2Ch 6:42 r the mercies of David thy servant. 2142
Ne 1: 8 R, I beseech thee, the word that thou 2142
4:14 r the Lord, *which is* great and terrible, and 2142
13:14 R me, O my God, concerning this, and 2142
13:22 R me, O my God, *concerning* this also, and 2142
13:29 R them, O my God, because they have 2142
13:31 the firstfruits. R me, O my God, for good. 2142
Job 4: 7 R, I pray thee, who *ever* perished, 2142
7: 7 O r that my life *is* wind: mine eye shall no 2142
10: 9 R, I beseech thee, that thou hast made me 2142
11:16 *and* r *it* as waters *that* pass away: 2142
14:13 wouldest appoint me a set time, and r me. 2142
21: 6 Even when I r I am afraid, and 2142
36:24 R that thou magnify his work, which men 2142
41: 8 hand upon him, r the battle, do no more. 2142
Ps 20: 3 R all thy offerings, and accept thy burnt 2142
20: 7 we will r the name of the LORD our God. 2142
22:27 All the ends of the world shall r and 2142
25: 6 R, O LORD, thy tender mercies and 2142
25: 7 R not the sins of my youth, nor my 2142
25: 7 according to thy mercy r thou me for thy 2142
42: 4 When I r these *things,* I pour out my soul in 2142
42: 6 will I r thee from the land of Jordan, 2142
63: 6 When I r thee upon my bed, *and* 2142
74: 2 R thy congregation, *which* thou hast 2142
74:18 R this, *that* the enemy hath reproached, 2142
74:22 r how the foolish *man* reproacheth thee 2142
77:10 *I will* r the years of the right hand of NIH
77:11 I will r the works of the LORD: surely I 2142
77:11 surely I will r thy wonders of old. 2142
79: 8 O r not against us former iniquities: let thy 2142
89:47 R how short my time is: wherefore hast 2142
89:50 R, Lord, the reproach of thy servants; 2142
103:18 to those that r his commandments to do 2142
105: 5 R his marvellous works that he hath done; 2142
106: 4 R me, O LORD, with the favour *that thou* 2142
119:49 R the word unto thy servant, upon which 2142
132: 1 LORD, r David, *and* all his afflictions: 2142
137: 6 If I do not r thee, let my tongue cleave to 2142
137: 7 R, O LORD, the children of Edom *in* 2142
143: 5 I r the days of old; I meditate on all thy 2142
Pr 31: 7 his poverty, and r his misery no more. 2142
Ecc 5:20 For he shall not much r the days of his life; 2142
11: 8 them all; yet let him r the days of darkness; 2142
12: 1 R now thy Creator in the days of thy youth, 2142
SS 1: 4 in thee, we will r thy love more than wine: 2142
Isa 38: 3 said, R now, O LORD, I beseech thee, 2142
43:18 R ye not the former *things,* neither consider 2142
43:25 for mine own sake, and will not r thy sins. 2142
44:21 R these, O Jacob and Israel; for thou *art* my 2142
46: 8 R this, and shew yourselves men: bring *it* 2142
46: 9 R the former *things* of old: for I *am* God, 2142
47: 7 thy heart, neither didst r the latter end of it. 2142
54: 4 shalt not r the reproach of thy widowhood 2142
64: 5 *those that* r thee in thy ways: 2142
64: 9 O LORD, neither r iniquity for ever: 2142
Jer 2: 2 I r thee, the kindness of thy youth, the love 2142
3:16 neither shall they r it; neither shall they 2142
14:10 he will now r their iniquity, and visit their 2142
14:21 r, break not thy covenant with us. 2142
15:15 r me, and visit me, and revenge me of my 2142
17: 2 Whilst their children r their altars and 2142
18:20 R that I stood before thee to speak good for 2142
31:20 I do **earnestly** r him still: 2142+2142
31:34 their iniquity, and I will r their sin no more. 2142
44:21 did not the LORD r them, and came it *not* 2142
51:50 r the LORD afar off, and let Jerusalem 2142
La 5: 1 R, O LORD, what is come upon us: 2142
Eze 6: 9 they that escape of you shall r me among 2142
16:60 Nevertheless I will r my covenant with thee 2142
16:61 thou shalt r thy ways, and be ashamed, 2142
16:63 That thou mayest r, and be confounded, 2142
20:43 there shall ye r your ways, and all your 2142
23:27 eyes unto them, nor r Egypt any more. 2142
36:31 shall ye r your own evil ways, and 2142
Hos 7: 2 they consider not in their hearts *that* I r all 2142
8:13 now will he r their iniquity, and visit their 2142
9: 9 *therefore* he will r their iniquity, he will 2142
Mic 6: 5 r now what Balak king of Moab consulted, 2142
Hab 3: 2 of the years make known; in wrath r mercy. 2142
Zec 10: 9 they shall r me in far countries; and 2142
Mal 4: 4 R ye the law of Moses my servant, which I 2142
Mt 16: 9 neither r the five loaves of the five *3421*
27:63 Saying, Sir, we r that that deceiver said, *3415*
Mk 8:18 having ears, hear ye not? and do ye not r? *3421*
Lk 1:72 to our fathers, and to r his holy covenant; *3415*
16:25 r that thou in thy lifetime receivedst thy *3415*
17:32 R Lot's wife. *3421*
23:42 r me when thou comest into thy kingdom. *3415*
24: 6 r how he spake unto you when he was yet *3415*
Jn 15:20 R the word that I said unto you, *3421*
16: 4 ye may r that I told you of them. *3421*
Ac 20:31 Therefore watch, and r, that *by the space of* *3421*
20:35 and to r the words of the Lord Jesus, *3421*
1Co 11: 2 that you r me in all *things,* and keep *3415*
Gal 2:10 Only *they would* that we should r the poor; *3421*
Eph 2:11 Wherefore r, that ye *being* in time passed *3421*
Col 4:18 R my bonds. Grace *be* with you. Amen. *3421*
1Th 2: 9 For ye r, brethren, our labour and travail: *3421*
2Th 2: 5 R ye not, that, when I was yet with you, *3421*
2Ti 2: 8 R that Jesus Christ of the seed of David *3421*
Heb 8:12 and their iniquities will I r no more. *3415*
10:17 their sins and iniquities will I r no more. *3415*
13: 3 R *them that are* in bonds, as bound with *3403*
13: 7 R them which have the rule over you, *3421*
3Jn 1:10 if I come, I will r his deeds which he doeth, *5279*
Jude 1:17 r ye the words which were spoken before *3415*
Rev 2: 5 R therefore from whence thou art fallen, *3421*
3: 3 R therefore how thou hast received and *3421*

REMEMBERED (57) [REMEMBER]

Ge 8: 1 God r Noah, and every living thing, and 2142
19:29 that God r Abraham, and sent Lot out of 2142
30:22 God r Rachel, and God hearkened to her, 2142
42: 9 Joseph r the dreams which he dreamed of 2142
Ex 2:24 God r his covenant with Abraham, 2142
6: 5 keep in bondage; and I have r my covenant. 2142
Nu 10: 9 ye shall be r before the LORD your God, 2142
Jdg 8:34 the children of Israel r not the LORD their 2142
1Sa 1:19 Hannah his wife; and the LORD r her. 2142
2Ch 24:22 Thus Joash the king r not the kindness 2142
Est 2: 1 he r Vashti, and what she had done, and 2142
9:28 *that* these days *should be* r and 2142
Job 24:20 he shall be no more r; and wickedness shall 2142
Ps 45:17 I will **make** thy name **to be** r in all 2142
77: 3 I r God, and was troubled: I complained, 2142
78:35 they r that God *was* their rock, and the high 2142
78:39 For he r that they *were but* flesh; a wind 2142
78:42 They r not his hand: *nor* the day when he 2142
98: 3 He hath r his mercy and his truth toward 2142
105: 8 He hath r his covenant for ever, the word 2142
105:42 For he r his holy promise, *and* Abraham his 2142
106: 7 they r not the multitude of thy mercies; but 2142
106:45 he r for them his covenant, and 2142
109:14 Let the iniquity of his fathers be r with 2142
109:16 Because that he r not to shew mercy, but 2142
111: 4 He hath made his wonderful works to be r: 2143
119:52 I r thy judgments of old, O LORD; and 2142
119:55 I have r thy name, O LORD, in the night, 2142
136:23 Who r us in our low estate: for his mercy 2142
137: 1 sat down, yea, we wept, when we r Zion. 2142
Ecc 9:15 the city; yet no man r that *same* poor man. 2142
Isa 23:16 sing many songs, that thou mayest be r. 2142
57:11 that thou hast lied, and hast not r me, 2142
63:11 he r the days of old, Moses, *and* his people, 2142
65:17 the former shall not be r, nor come into 2142
Jer 11:19 the living, that his name may be no more r. 2142
La 1: 7 Jerusalem r in the days of her affliction and 2142
2: 1 r not his footstool in the day of his anger! 2142
Eze 3:20 which he hath done shall not be r; 2142
16:22 thy whoredoms thou hast not r the days of 2142
16:43 Because thou hast not r the days of thy 2142
21:24 ye have **made** your iniquity **to be** r, 2142
21:32 midst of the land; thou shalt be no *more* r: 2142
25:10 that the Ammonites may not be r among 2142
33:13 all his righteousnesses shall not be r; 2142
Hos 2:17 and they shall no more be r by their name. 2142
Am 1: 9 to Edom, and r not the brotherly covenant: 2142
Jnh 2: 7 When my soul fainted within me I r 2142
Zec 13: 2 out of the land, and they shall no more be r: 2142
Mt 26:75 And Peter r the word of Jesus, which said *3415*
Lk 22:61 And Peter r the word of the Lord, how he *5279*
24: 8 And they r his words, *3415*
Jn 2:17 And his disciples r that it was written, *3415*
2:22 his disciples r that he had said this unto *3415*
12:16 r they that these *things* were written of him, *3415*
Ac 11:16 Then r I the word of the Lord, how that he *3415*
Rev 18: 5 unto heaven, and God hath r her iniquities. *3421*

REMEMBEREST (2) [REMEMBER]

Ps 88: 5 that lie in the grave, whom thou r no more: 2142
Mt 5:23 there r that thy brother hath ought against *3415*

REMEMBERETH (5) [REMEMBER]

Ps 9:12 he maketh inquisition for blood, he r them: 2142
103:14 knoweth our frame; he r that we *are* dust. 2142
La 1: 9 she r not her last end; therefore she came 2142
Jn 16:21 of the child, she r no more the anguish, *3421*
2Co 7:15 whilst he r the obedience of you all, *363*

REMEMBERING (2) [REMEMBER]

La 3:19 R mine affliction and my misery, 2142
1Th 1: 3 R without ceasing your work of faith, and *3421*

REMEMBRANCE (53) [REMEMBER]

Ex 17:14 for I will utterly put out the r of Amalek 2143
Nu 5:15 of memorial, **bringing** iniquity **to** r. 2142
Dt 25:19 *that* thou shalt blot out the r of Amalek 2143
32:26 I would make the r of them to cease from 2143
2Sa 18:18 I have no son to **keep** my name **in** r: 2142
1Ki 17:18 art thou come unto me to **call** my sin **to** r, 2142
Job 18:17 His r shall perish from the earth, and 2143
Ps 6: 5 For in death *there is* no r of thee: in 2143
30: 4 and give thanks at the r of his holiness. 2143
34:16 to cut off the r of them from the earth. 2143
38: T A Psalm of David, to **bring to** r. 2142
70: T *A Psalm* of David, to **bring to** r. 2142
77: 6 I **call to** r my song in the night: I commune 2142
83: 4 the name of Israel may be no more **in** r. 2142
97:12 and give thanks at the r of his holiness. 2143
102:12 for ever; and thy r unto all generations. 2143
112: 6 the righteous shall be in everlasting r. 2143
Ecc 1:11 *There is* no r of former *things;* neither shall 2146
1:11 r of *things* that are to come with *those* that 2146
2:16 For *there is* no r of the wise more than of 2146
Isa 26: 8 *our* soul *is* to thy name, and to the r of thee. 2143
43:26 **Put** me **in** r: let us plead together: 2142
57: 8 and the posts hast thou set up thy r: 2146
La 3:20 My soul hath *them* **still in** r, and 2142+2142
Eze 21:23 he will **call to** r the iniquity, that *they* may 2142
21:24 because, *I say,* that ye are **come to** r, 2142
23:19 in **calling to** r the days of her youth, 2142
23:21 Thus thou **calledst to** r the lewdness of thy 6485
29:16 which **bringeth** *their* iniquity **to** r, 2142
Mal 3:16 a book of r was written before him for 2146
Mk 11:21 And Peter **calling to** r saith unto him, *363*
Lk 1:54 holpen his servant Israel, in r of *his* mercy, *3415*
22:19 which is given for you: this do in r of me. *364*
Jn 14:26 all *things,* and **bring** all *things* **to** your r, *5279*
Ac 10:31 thine alms are had in r in the sight of God. *3415*
1Co 4:17 who shall **bring** you **into** r of my ways *363*
11:24 which is broken for you: this do in r of me. *364*
11:25 this do ye, as oft as ye drink *it,* in r of me. *364*
Php 1: 3 I thank my God upon every r of you, *3417*
1Th 3: 6 and that ye have good r of us always, *3417*
1Ti 4: 6 If thou **put** the brethren **in** r of these *things,* *5294*
2Ti 1: 3 that without ceasing I have r of thee in my *3417*
1: 5 When I call to r the unfeigned faith that is *5280*
1: 6 Wherefore I **put** thee **in** r that *thou* stir up *363*
2:14 Of these *things* **put** *them* **in** r, *5279*
Heb 10: 3 But in those *sacrifices there is* a r *again* *364*
10:32 But **call to** r the former days, in which, *363*
2Pe 1:12 **put** you always **in** r of these *things,* though *5279*
1:13 to stir you up by **putting** *you* **in** r; *5280*
1:15 decease to have these *things* always in r. *3420*
3: 1 I stir up your pure minds by way of r: *5280*
Jude 1: 5 I will therefore **put** you **in** r, though ye *5279*
Rev 16:19 and great Babylon **came in** r before God, *3415*

REMEMBRANCES (1) [REMEMBER]

Job 13:12 Your r *are* like unto ashes, your bodies to 2146

REMETH (1)

Jos 19:21 R, and En-gannim, and En-haddah, and 7432

REMISSION (10) [REMIT]

Mt 26:28 which is shed for many for the r of sins. *859*
Mk 1: 4 preach the baptism of repentance for the r of *859*
Lk 1:77 unto his people by the r of their sins, *859*
3: 3 preaching the baptism of repentance for the r *859*
24:47 r of sins should be preached in his name *859*
Ac 2:38 in the name of Jesus Christ for the r of sins, *859*
10:43 believeth in him shall receive r of sins. *859*
Ro 3:25 to declare his righteousness for the r of sins *3929*
Heb 9:22 and without shedding of blood is no r. *859*
10:18 Now where r of these *is, there is* no more *859*

REMIT (1) [REMISSION, REMITTED]

Jn 20:23 Whose soever sins ye r, they are remitted *863*

REMITTED (1) [REMIT]

Jn 20:23 soever sins ye remit, they are r unto them; *863*

REMMON (1)

Jos 19: 7 Ain, R, and Ether, and Ashan; four cities 7417

REMMON-METHOAR (1)

Jos 19:13 and goeth out *to* R *to* Neah; 7417+8388+1886.1

R

REMNANT (92) [REMAIN]

Ex 26:12 the **r** that remaineth of the curtains of 5629
Lev 2: 3 the **r** of the meat offering *shall be* Aaron's 3498
5:13 *the* **r** shall be the priest's, as a meat NIH
14:18 the **r** of the oil that *is* in the priest's hand he 3498
Dt 3:11 king of Bashan remained of the **r** of giants; 3499
28:54 towards the **r** of his children which he shall 3499
Jos 12: 4 *which was* of the **r** of the giants, that dwelt 3499
13:12 who remained of the **r** of the giants: 3499
23:12 cleave unto the **r** of these nations, 3499
2Sa 21: 2 of Israel, but of the **r** of the Amorites; 3499
1Ki 12:23 and *to* the **r** of the people, saying, 3499
14:10 will take away the **r** of the house of 310
22:46 the **r** of the sodomites, which remained in 3499
2Ki 19: 4 wherefore lift up *thy* prayer for the **r** that 7611
19:30 the **r** that is escaped of the house of Judah 7604
19:31 For out of Jerusalem shall go forth a **r**, and 7611
21:14 I will forsake the **r** of mine inheritance, 7611
25:11 of Babylon, with the **r** of the multitude, 3499
1Ch 6:70 for the family of the **r** of the sons of 3498
2Ch 30: 6 Israel, and he will return to the **r** of you, 7604
34: 9 of all the **r** of Israel, and of all Judah and 7611
Ezr 3: 8 the **r** of their brethren the priests and 7605
9: 8 to leave us a **r to escape**, and to give us a 6413
9:14 so that *there should be* no **r** nor escaping? 7611
Ne 1: 3 The **r** that are left of the captivity there in 7604
Job 22:20 but the **r** of them the fire consumeth. 3499
Isa 1: 9 of hosts had left unto us a very small **r**, 8300
10:20 *that* the **r** of Israel, and such as are escaped 7605
10:21 The **r** shall return, *even* the remnant of 7605
10:21 *even* the **r** of Jacob, unto the mighty God. 7605
10:22 sand of the sea, *yet* a **r** of them shall return: 7605
11:11 second time to recover the **r** of his people, 7605
11:16 there shall be a highway for the **r** of his 7605
14:22 **r**, and son, and nephew, saith the LORD. 7605
14:30 root with famine, and he shall slay thy **r**. 7611
15: 9 of Moab, and upon the **r** of the land. 7611
16:14 the **r** *shall be* very small *and* feeble. 7605
17: 3 from Damascus, and the **r** of Syria: 7605
37: 4 wherefore lift up *thy* prayer for the **r** that is 7611
37:31 the **r** that is escaped of the house of Judah 7604
37:32 For out of Jerusalem shall go forth a **r**, and 7611
46: 3 and all the **r** of the house of Israel, 7611
Jer 6: 9 They shall throughly glean the **r** of Israel as 7611
11:23 there shall be no **r** of them: for I will bring 7611
15:11 Verily it shall be well with thy **r**; 8281
23: 3 I will gather the **r** of my flock out of all 7611
25:20 and Ekron, and the **r** of Ashdod: 7611
31: 7 O LORD, save thy people, the **r** of Israel. 7611
39: 9 **r** of the people that remained in the city, 3499
40:11 heard that the king of Babylon had left a **r** 7611
40:15 be scattered, and the **r** in Judah perish? 7611
41:16 all the **r** of the people whom he had 7611
42: 2 the LORD thy God, *even* for all this **r**; 7611
42:15 the word of the LORD, ye **r** of Judah; 7611
42:19 hath said concerning you, O ye **r** of Judah; 7611
43: 5 of the forces, took all the **r** of Judah, 7611
44:12 I will take the **r** of Judah, that have set their 7611
44:14 So that none of the **r** of Judah, which are 7611
44:28 all the **r** of Judah, that are gone into 7611
47: 4 the **r** of the country of Caphtor. 7611
47: 5 Ashkelon is cut off *with* the **r** of their 7611
Eze 5:10 the whole **r** of thee will I scatter into all 7611
6: 8 Yet will I **leave a r**, that ye may have *some* 3498
11:13 *wilt* thou make a full end of the **r** of Israel? 7611
14:22 therein shall be left a **r** that shall be brought 6413
23:25 thine ears; and thy **r** shall fall by the sword: 319
25:16 and destroy the **r** of the sea coast. 7611
Joel 2:32 and in the **r** whom the LORD *shall* call. 8300
Am 1: 8 the **r** of the Philistines shall perish, saith 7611
5:15 hosts will be gracious unto the **r** of Joseph. 7611
9:12 That they may possess the **r** of Edom, and 7611
Mic 2:12 of thee; I will surely gather the **r** of Israel; 7611
4: 7 I will make her that halted a **r**, and her that 7611
5: 3 the **r** of his brethren shall return unto 3499
5: 7 the **r** of Jacob shall be in the midst of many 7611
5: 8 the **r** of Jacob shall be among the Gentiles 7611
7:18 passeth by the transgression of the **r** of his 7611
Hab 2: 8 all the **r** of the people shall spoil thee; 3499
Zep 1: 4 I will cut off the **r** of Baal from this place, 7605
2: 7 the coast shall be for the **r** of the house of 7611
2: 9 and the **r** of my people shall possess them. 3499
3:13 The **r** of Israel shall not do iniquity, 7611
Hag 1:12 the high priest, with all the **r** of the people, 7611
1:14 and the spirit of all the **r** of the people; 7611
Zec 8: 6 If it be marvellous in the eyes of the **r** of 7611
8:12 I will cause the **r** of this people to possess 7611
Mt 22: 6 And the **r** took his servants, and *3062*
Ro 9:27 be as the sand of the sea, a **r** shall be saved: *2640*
11: 5 at *this* present time also there is a **r** *3005*
Rev 11:13 and the **r** were affrighted, and gave glory to *3062*
12:17 went to make war with the **r** of her seed, *3062*
19:21 And the **r** were slain with the sword of him *3062*

REMOVE (45) [REMOVED, REMOVETH, REMOVING]

Ge 48:17 to **r** it from Ephraim's head unto 5493
Nu 36: 7 the children of Israel **r** from tribe to tribe: 5437
36: 9 Neither shall the inheritance **r** from *one* 5437
Dt 19:14 Thou shalt not **r** thy neighbour's landmark, 5253
Jos 3: 3 ye shall **r** from your place, and go after it. 5265
Jdg 9:29 under my hand; then would I **r** Abimelech. 5493
2Sa 6:10 So David would not **r** the ark of 5493
2Ki 23:27 I will **r** Judah also out of my sight, 5493
24: 3 to **r** *them* out of his sight, for the sins of 5493
2Ch 33: 8 Neither will I any more **r** the foot of Israel 5493
Job 24: 2 *Some* **r** the landmarks; they violently take 5381
27: 5 till I die I will not **r** my integrity from me. 5493
Ps 36:11 and let not the hand of the wicked **r** me. 5110
39:10 **R** thy stroke away from me: I am 5493
119:22 **R** from me reproach and contempt; for I 1556
119:29 **R** from me the way of lying: and grant me 5493
Pr 4:27 hand nor *to* the left: **r** thy foot from evil. 5493
5: 8 **R** thy way **far** from her, and come not nigh 7368
22:28 **R** not the ancient landmark, which thy 5253
23:10 **R** not the old landmark; and enter not into 5253
30: 8 **R far** from me vanity and lies: give me 7368
Ecc 11:10 Therefore **r** sorrow from thy heart, and 5493
Isa 13:13 and the earth shall **r** out of her place, 7493
46: 7 he standeth; from his place shall he not **r**: 4185
Jer 4: 1 out of my sight, then shalt thou not **r**. 5110
27:10 a lie unto you, to **r** you **far** from your land; 7368
32:31 that *I* should **r** it from before my face, 5493
50: 3 they shall **r**, they shall depart, both man 5110
50: 8 **R** out of the midst of Babylon, and go forth 5110
Eze 12: 3 for removing, and **r** by day in their sight; 1540
12: 3 thou shalt **r** from thy place to another place 1540
12:11 they shall **r** *and* go into captivity. 1473
21:26 **R** the diadem, and take off the crown: 5493
45: 9 **r** violence and spoil, and execute judgment 5493
Hos 5:10 The princes of Judah were like them that **r** 5253
Joel 2:20 I will **r far off** from you the northern *army,* 7368
3: 6 that *ye* might **r** them **far** from their border. 7368
Mic 2: 3 from which ye shall not **r** your necks; 4185
Zec 3: 9 I will **r** the iniquity of that land in one day. 4185
14: 4 half of the mountain shall **r** toward 4185
Mt 17:20 this mountain, **R** hence to yonder place; *3327*
17:20 and it shall **r**; and nothing shall be *3327*
Lk 22:42 if thou be willing, **r** this cup from me: *3911*
1Co 13: 2 so that *I* could **r** mountains, and have no *3179*
Rev 2: 5 and will **r** thy candlestick out of his place, *2795*

REMOVED (91) [REMOVE]

Ge 8:13 Noah **r** the covering of the ark, and looked, 5493
12: 8 he **r** from thence unto a mountain on 6275
13:18 Abram **r** his **tent**, and came and dwelt in 167
26:22 he **r** from thence, and digged another well; 6275
30:35 he **r** that day the he goats that were 5493
47:21 he **r** them to cities from *one* end of 5674
Ex 8:31 he **r** the swarms *of flies* from Pharaoh, 5493
14:19 the camp of Israel, **r** and went behind them; 5265
20:18 when the people saw *it,* they **r**, and 5128
Nu 12:16 afterward the people **r** from Hazeroth, and 5265
21:12 From thence they **r**, and pitched in 5265
21:13 From thence they **r**, and pitched on 5265
33: 5 the children of Israel **r** from Rameses, and 5265
33: 7 they **r** from Etham, and turned again unto 5265
33: 9 they **r** from Marah, and came unto Elim: 5265
33:10 they **r** from Elim, and encamped by 5265
33:11 they **r** from the Red sea, and encamped in 5265
33:14 they **r** from Alush, and encamped at 5265
33:16 they **r** from the desert of Sinai, and 5265
33:21 they **r** from Libnah, and pitched at Rissah. 5265
33:24 they **r** from mount Shapher, and 5265
33:25 they **r** from Haradah, and pitched in 5265
33:26 they **r** from Makheloth, and encamped at 5265
33:28 they **r** from Tarah, and pitched in Mithcah. 5265
33:32 they **r** from Bene-jaakan, and encamped at 5265
33:34 they **r** from Jotbathah, and encamped at 5265
33:36 they **r** from Ezion-gaber, and pitched in 5265
33:37 they **r** from Kadesh, and pitched in mount 5265
33:46 they **r** from Dibon-gad, and encamped in 5265
33:47 they **r** from Almon-diblathaim, and 5265
Dt 28:25 shalt be **r** into all the kingdoms of the earth. 2189
Jos 3: 1 they **r** from Shittim, and came to Jordan, 5265
3:14 when the people **r** from their tents, to pass 5265
1Sa 6: 3 to you why his hand is not **r** from you. 5493
18:13 Therefore Saul **r** him from him, and 5493
2Sa 20:12 he **r** Amasa out of the highway *into* 5437
20:13 When he was **r** out of the highway, all 3014
1Ki 15:12 and **r** all the idols that his fathers had made. 5493
15:13 even her he **r** from *being* queen, because 5493
15:14 the high places were not **r**: 5493
2Ki 15: 4 Save that the high places were not **r**: 5493
15:35 Howbeit the high places were not **r**: 5493
16:17 of the bases, and **r** the laver from off them; 5493
17:18 with Israel, and **r** them out of his sight: 5493
17:23 Until the LORD **r** Israel out of his sight, 5493
17:26 The nations which thou hast **r**, and 1540
18: 4 He **r** the high places, and brake the images, 5493
23:27 as I have **r** Israel, and will cast off this city 5493
1Ch 8: 6 of Geba, and they **r** them to Manahath: 1540
8: 7 he **r** them, and begat Uzza, and Ahihud. 1540
2Ch 15:16 he **r** her from *being* queen, because she had 5493
35:12 they **r** the burnt offerings, that they might 5493
Job 14:18 to nought, and the rock is **r** out of his place. 6275
18: 4 and shall the rock be **r** out of his place? 6275
19:10 and mine hope hath he **r** like a tree. 5265
36:16 would he have **r** thee out of the strait *into* a 5496
Ps 46: 2 though the earth be **r**, and though 4171
81: 6 I **r** his shoulder from the burden: his hands 5493
103:12 *so* **far** hath he **r** our transgressions from us. 7368
104: 5 of the earth, *that* it should not be **r** for ever. 4131
125: 1 *which* cannot be **r**, *but* abideth for ever. 4131
Pr 10:30 The righteous shall never be **r**: but 4131
Isa 6:12 the LORD have **r** men **far away**, and 7368
10:13 I have **r** the bounds of the people, and 5493
10:31 Madmenah is **r**; the inhabitants of Gebim 5074
22:25 nail that is fastened in the sure place be **r**, 4185
24:20 a drunkard, and shall be **r** like a cottage; 5110
26:15 thou hadst **r** *it* **far** *unto* all the ends of 7368
29:13 have **r** their heart **far** from me, and 7368
30:20 yet shall not thy teachers be **r into a corner** 3670
33:20 not one of the stakes thereof shall ever be **r**, 5265
38:12 and is **r** from me as a shepherd's tent: 1540
54:10 mountains shall depart, and the hills be **r**; 4131
54:10 neither shall the covenant of my peace be **r**, 4131
Jer 15: 4 I will cause them to be **r** into all kingdoms 2189
24: 9 I will deliver them to be **r** into all 2189
29:18 will deliver them to be **r** to all 2189
34:17 I will make you to be **r** into all 2189
La 1: 8 hath grievously sinned; therefore she is **r**: 5206
3:17 thou hast **r** my soul **far off** from peace: 2186
Eze 7:19 in the streets, and their gold shall be **r**: 5079
23:46 and *will* give them to be **r** and spoiled. 2189
36:17 me as the uncleanness of a **r woman**. 5079
Am 6: 7 them that stretched themselves shall be **r**. 5493
Mic 2: 4 how hath he **r** it from me! turning away he 4185
7:11 *in* that day shall the decree be **far r**. 7368
Mt 21:21 Be thou **r**, and be thou cast into the sea; *142*
Mk 11:23 Be thou **r**, and be thou cast into the sea; *142*
Ac 7: 4 he **r** him into this land, wherein ye now *3351*
13:22 And when he had **r** him, he raised up unto *3179*
Gal 1: 6 soon **r** from him that called you into *3346*

REMOVETH (5) [REMOVE]

Dt 27:17 Cursed *be* he that **r** his neighbour's 5253
Job 9: 5 Which **r** the mountains, and they know not: 6275
12:20 He **r away** the speech of the trusty, and 5493
Ecc 10: 9 Whoso **r** stones shall be hurt therewith; 5265
Da 2:21 he **r** kings, and setteth up kings: he giveth 5709

REMOVING (5) [REMOVE]

Ge 30:32 **r** from thence all the speckled and 5493
Isa 49:21 *am* desolate, a captive, and **r to and fro**? 5493
Eze 12: 3 prepare thee stuff for **r**, and remove by day 1473
12: 4 thy stuff by day in their sight, as stuff for **r**: 1473
Heb 12:27 the **r** of those *things* that are shaken, *3331*

REMPHAN (1)

Ac 7:43 of Moloch, and the star of your god **R**, *4481*

REND (9) [RENDER, RENDERED, RENDEREST, RENDERETH, RENDERING, RENDING, RENT, RENTEST]

Ex 39:23 round about the hole, *that* it should not **r**. 7167
Lev 10: 6 not your heads, neither **r** your clothes; 6533
13:56 he shall **r** it out of the garment, or out of 7167
21:10 not uncover his head, nor **r** his clothes; 6533
1Ki 11:11 I will **surely r** the kingdom from 7167+7167
11:12 *but* I will **r** it out of the hand of thy son. 7167
11:13 Howbeit I will not **r away** all the kingdom; 7167
2Ch 34:27 didst **r** thy clothes, and weep before me; 7167
Isa 64: 1 O that thou wouldest **r** the heavens, 7167

RENDER (33) [REND]

Nu 18: 9 which they shall **r** unto me, *shall be* most 7725
Dt 32:41 I will **r** vengeance to mine enemies, and 7725
32:43 and will **r** vengeance to his adversaries, and 7725
Jdg 9:57 of Shechem did God **r** upon their heads: 7725
1Sa 26:23 The LORD **r** to every man his 7725
2Ch 6:30 **r** unto every man according unto all his 5414
Job 33:26 for he will **r** unto man his righteousness. 7725
34:11 For the work of a man shall he **r** unto him, 7999
Ps 28: 4 work of their hands; **r** to them their desert. 7725
38:20 They also that **r** evil for good are mine 7999
56:12 upon me, O God: I will **r** praises unto thee. 7999
79:12 **r** unto our neighbours sevenfold into their 7725
94: 2 judge of the earth: **r** a reward to the proud. 7725
116:12 What shall I **r** unto the LORD *for* all his 7725
Pr 24:12 shall *not* he **r** to *every* man according to his 7725
24:29 I will **r** to the man according to his work. 7725
26:16 conceit than seven *men* that can **r** a reason. 7725
Isa 66:15 to **r** his anger with fury, and his rebuke 7725
Jer 51: 6 he *will* **r** unto her a recompence. 7999
51:24 I will **r** unto Babylon and to all 7999
La 3:64 **R** unto them a recompence, O LORD, 7725
Hos 14: 2 so will we **r** the calves of our lips. 7999
Joel 3: 4 will ye **r** me a recompence? and if ye 7999
Zec 9:12 even to day do I declare *that* I will **r** double 7725
Mt 21:41 which shall **r** him the fruits in their seasons. *591*
22:21 **R** therefore unto Cesar the *things* which are *591*
Mk 12:17 **R** to Cesar the *things* that are Cesar's, and *591*
Lk 20:25 **R** therefore unto Cesar the *things* which be *591*
Ro 2: 6 Who will **r** to every *man* according to his *591*
13: 7 **R** therefore to all *their* dues: tribute to whom *591*
1Co 7: 3 Let the husband **r** unto the wife due *591*
1Th 3: 9 For what thanks can we **r** to God **again** for *467*
5:15 See that none **r** evil for evil unto any *man;* *591*

RENDERED (4) [REND]

Jdg 9:56 Thus God **r** the wickedness of Abimelech, 7725
2Ki 3: 4 **r** unto the king of Israel an hundred 7725
2Ch 32:25 Hezekiah **r** not **again** according to 7725
Pr 12:14 the recompence of a man's hands shall be **r** 7725

RENDEREST (1) [REND]

Ps 62:12 for thou **r** to *every* man according to his 7999

RENDERETH (1) [REND]

Isa 66: 6 a voice of the LORD that **r** recompence to 7999

RENDERING (1) [REND]

1Pe 3: 9 Not **r** evil for evil, or railing for railing: but *591*

RENDING (1) [REND]

Ps 7: 2 **r** *it* **in pieces**, while *there is* none to deliver. 6561

RENEW (6) [RENEWED, RENEWEST, RENEWING]

1Sa 11:14 let us go *to* Gilgal, and **r** the kingdom there. 2318
Ps 51:10 O God; and **r** a right spirit within me. 2318
Isa 40:31 they that wait upon the LORD shall **r** *their* 2498
41: 1 and let the people **r** *their* strength: 2498
La 5:21 and we shall be turned; **r** our days as of old. 2318
Heb 6: 6 fall away, to **r** *them* again unto repentance; *340*

RENEWED (6) [RENEW]

2Ch 15: 8 **r** the altar of the LORD, that *was* before 2318
Job 29:20 fresh in me, and my bow was **r** in my hand. 2498
Ps 103: 5 *so that* thy youth is **r** like the eagle's. 2318
2Co 4:16 yet the inward *man* is **r** day by day. *341*
Eph 4:23 And be **r** in the spirit of your mind; *365*
Col 3:10 And have put on the new *man,* which is **r** in *341*

RENEWEST (2) [RENEW]

Job 10:17 Thou **r** thy witnesses against me, and 2318
Ps 104:30 are created: and thou **r** the face of the earth. 2318

RENEWING (2) [RENEW]

Ro 12: 2 but be ye transformed by the **r** of your mind, *342*
Tit 3: 5 of regeneration, and **r** of the Holy Ghost; *342*

R

RENOUNCED (1)
2Co 4: 2 But have r the hidden things of dishonesty, 550

RENOWN (7) [RENOWNED]
Ge 6: 4 mighty men which were of old, men of r. 8034
Nu 16: 2 famous in the congregation, men of r: 8034
Eze 16:14 thy r went forth among the heathen for thy 8034
16:15 playedst the harlot because of thy r, and 8034
34:29 I will raise up for them a plant of r, and 8034
39:13 it shall be to them a r the day that I shall be 8034
Da 9:15 and hast gotten thee r, as at this day; 8034

RENOWNED (4) [RENOWN]
Nu 1:16 These were the r of the congregation, 7121
Isa 14:20 the seed of evildoers shall never be r. 7121
Eze 23:23 captains and rulers, great lords and r, all of 7121
26:17 the r city, which wast strong in the sea, she 1984

RENT (76) [REND]
Ge 37:29 was not in the pit; and he r his clothes. 7167
37:33 Joseph is without doubt r in pieces. 2963+2963
37:34 Jacob r his clothes, and put sackcloth upon 7167
44:13 they r their clothes, and laded every man 7167
Ex 28:32 the hole of an habergeon, that it be not r. 7167
Lev 13:45 whom the plague is, his clothes shall be r, 6533
Nu 14: 6 them that searched the land, r their clothes: 7167
Jos 7: 6 Joshua r his clothes, and fell to the earth 7167
9: 4 and wine bottles, old, and r, and bound up; 1234
9:13 we filled, were new; and behold, they be r: 1234
Jdg 11:35 that he r his clothes, and said, Alas, 7167
14: 6 he r him as he would have rent a kid, and 8156
14: 6 he rent him as he would have r a kid, and 8156
1Sa 4:12 to Shiloh the same day with his clothes r, 7167
15:27 hold upon the skirt of his mantle, and it r. 7167
15:28 The LORD hath r the kingdom of Israel 7167
28:17 for the LORD hath r the kingdom out of 7167
2Sa 1: 2 of the camp from Saul with his clothes r, 7167
1:11 David took hold on his clothes, and r them; 7167
3:31 R your clothes, and gird you with 7167
13:19 r her garment of divers colours that was on 7167
13:31 his servants stood by with their clothes r. 7167
15:32 Archite came to meet him with his coat r, 7167
1Ki 1:40 so that the earth r with the sound of them. 1234
11:30 that was on him, and r it in twelve pieces: 7167
11:31 I will r the kingdom out of the hand of 7167
13: 3 the altar shall be r, and the ashes that are 7167
13: 5 The altar also was r, and the ashes poured 7167
14: 8 r the kingdom away from the house of 7167
19:11 a great and strong wind r the mountains, 6561
21:27 that he r his clothes, and put sackcloth 7167
2Ki 2:12 and r them in two pieces. 7167+7168
5: 7 that he r his clothes, and said, Am I God, 7167
5: 8 that the king of Israel had r his clothes, 7167
5: 8 Wherefore hast thou r thy clothes? 7167
6:30 words of the woman, that he r his clothes; 7167
11:14 Athaliah r her clothes, and cried, Treason, 7167
17:21 For he r Israel from the house of David; 7167
18:37 to Hezekiah with their clothes r, and 7167
19: 1 when king Hezekiah heard it, that he r his 7167
22:11 of the book of the law, that he r his clothes. 7167
22:19 and hast r thy clothes, and wept before me; 7167
2Ch 23:13 Athaliah r her clothes, and said, Treason, 7167
34:19 the words of the law, that he r his clothes. 7167
Ezr 9: 3 I r my garment and my mantle, and 7167
9: 5 having r my garment and my mantle, I fell 7167
Est 4: 1 Mordecai r his clothes, and put on 7167
Job 1:20 r his mantle, and shaved his head, and 7167
2:12 they r every one his mantle, and 7167
26: 8 and the cloud is not r under them. 1234
Ecc 3: 7 A time to r, and a time to sew; a time to 7167
Isa 3:24 instead of a girdle a r; and instead of well 5364
36:22 to Hezekiah with their clothes r, and 7167
37: 1 when king Hezekiah heard it, that he r his 7167
Jer 36:24 nor r their garments, neither the king, 7167
41: 5 their clothes r, and having cut themselves, 7167
Eze 13:11 shall fall; and a stormy wind shall r it. 1234
13:13 I will even r it with a stormy wind in my 1234
29: 7 thou didst break, and r all their shoulder: 1234
30:16 No shall be r asunder, and Noph shall 1234
Hos 13: 8 will r the caul of their heart, and there will 7167
Joel 2:13 r your heart, and not your garments, and 7167
Mt 7: 6 under their feet, and turn again and r you. 4486
9:16 from the garment, and the r is made worse. 4978
26:65 Then the high priest r his clothes, saying, 1284
27:51 the vail of the temple was r in twain from 4977
27:51 and the earth did quake, and the rocks r; 4977
Mk 2:21 from the old, and the r is made worse. 4978
9:26 and r him sore, and came out of him: and 4682
14:63 Then the high priest r his clothes, and saith, 1284
15:38 And the vail of the temple was r in twain 4977
Lk 5:36 then both the new maketh a r, and 4977
23:45 the vail of the temple was r in the midst. 4977
Jn 19:24 Let us not r it, but cast lots for it, whose it 4977
Ac 14:14 heard of, they r their clothes, and ran in 1284
16:22 and the magistrates r off their clothes, and 4048

RENTEST (1) [REND]
Jer 4:30 though thou r thy face with painting, 7167

REPAIR (14) [REPAIRED, REPAIRER, REPAIRING]
2Ki 12: 5 let them r the breaches of the house, 2388
12: 7 Why r ye not the breaches of the house? 2388
12: 8 neither to r the breaches of the house. 2388
12:12 hewed stone to r the breaches of the house 2388
12:12 for all that was laid out for the house to r 2394
22: 5 the LORD, to r the breaches of the house, 2388
22: 6 buy timber and hewn stone to r the house. 2388
2Ch 24: 4 that Joash was minded to r the house of 2318
24: 5 gather of all Israel money to r the house of 2388
24:12 carpenters to r the house of the LORD, 2318
34: 8 to r the house of the LORD his God. 2388
34:10 of the LORD, to r and mend the house: 918
Ezr 9: 9 to r the desolations thereof, and to give us a 5975
Isa 61: 4 they shall r the waste cities, the desolations 2318

REPAIRED (44) [REPAIR]
Jdg 21:23 and r the cities, and dwelt in them. 1129
1Ki 11:27 r the breaches of the city of David his 5462
18:30 he r the altar of the LORD that was 7495
2Ki 12: 6 priests had not r the breaches of the house. 2388
12:14 r therewith the house of the LORD. 2388
1Ch 11: 8 round about: and Joab r the rest of the city. 2421
2Ch 29: 3 of the house of the LORD, and r them. 2388
32: 5 r Millo in the city of David, and made darts 2388
33:16 he r the altar of the LORD, and 1129
Ne 3: 4 next unto them r Meremoth the son of 2388
3: 4 next unto them r Meshullam the son of 2388
3: 4 next unto them r Zadok the son of Baana. 2388
3: 5 next unto them the Tekoites r; but 2388
3: 6 Moreover the old gate r Jehoiada the son of 2388
3: 7 next unto them r Melatiah the Gibeonite, 2388
3: 8 Next unto him r Uzziel the son of 2388
3: 8 Next unto him also r Hananiah the son of 2388
3: 9 next unto them r Rephaiah the son of Hur, 2388
3:10 next unto them r Jedaiah the son of 2388
3:10 next unto him r Hattush the son of 2388
3:11 r the other piece, and the tower of 2388
3:12 next unto him r Shallum the son of 2388
3:13 The valley gate r Hanun, and 2388
3:14 the dung gate r Malchiah the son of 2388
3:15 the gate of the fountain r Shallun the son of 2388
3:16 After him r Nehemiah the son of Azbuk, 2388
3:17 After him r the Levites, Rehum the son of 2388
3:17 Next unto him r Hashabiah, the ruler of 2388
3:18 After him r their brethren, Bavai the son of 2388
3:19 next to him r Ezer the son of Jeshua, 2388
3:20 son of Zabbai earnestly r the other piece, 2388
3:21 After him r Meremoth the son of Urijah 2388
3:22 after him r the priests, the men of the plain. 2388
3:23 After him r Benjamin and Hashub over 2388
3:23 After him r Azariah the son of Maaseiah 2388
3:24 After him r Binnui the son of Henadad 2388
3:27 After them the Tekoites r another piece, 2388
3:28 From above the horse gate r the priests, 2388
3:29 After them r Zadok the son of Immer over 2388
3:29 After him r also Shemaiah the son of 2388
3:30 After him r Hananiah the son of 2388
3:30 After him r Meshullam the son of 2388
3:31 After him r Malchiah the goldsmith's son 2388
3:32 corner unto the sheep gate r the goldsmiths 2388

REPAIRER (1) [REPAIR]
Isa 58:12 thou shalt be called, The r of the breach, 1443

REPAIRING (1) [REPAIR]
2Ch 24:27 upon him, and the r of the house of God, 3247

REPAY (8) [REPAYED, REPAYETH]
Dt 7:10 that hateth him, he will r him to his face. 7999
Job 21:31 and who shall r him what he hath done? 7999
41:11 that I should r him? whatsoever is under 7999
Isa 59:18 accordingly he will r, fury to his 7999
59:18 to the islands he will r recompence. 7999
Lk 10:35 when I come again, I will r thee. 591
Ro 12:19 Vengeance is mine; I will r, saith the Lord. 467
Phm 1:19 I will r it: albeit I do not say to thee how 661

REPAYED (1) [REPAY]
Pr 13:21 but to the righteous good shall be r. 7999

REPAYETH (1) [REPAY]
Dt 7:10 r them that hate him to their face, 7999

REPAYING See REQUITE; REQUITED; REQUITING

REPEATETH (1) [REPETITIONS]
Pr 17: 9 he that r a matter separateth very friends. 8138

REPENT (46) [REPENTANCE, REPENTED, REPENTEST, REPENTETH, REPENTING, REPENTINGS]
Ex 13:17 Lest peradventure the people r when they 5162
32:12 and r of this evil against thy people. 5162
Nu 23:19 neither the son of man, that he should r: 5162
Dt 32:36 his people, and r himself for his servants, 5162
1Sa 15:29 also the Strength of Israel will not lie nor r: 5162
15:29 for he is not a man, that he should r. 5162
1Ki 8:47 r, and make supplication unto thee in 7725
Job 42: 6 I abhor myself, and r in dust and ashes. 5162
Ps 90:13 and let it r thee concerning thy servants. 5162
110: 4 The LORD hath sworn, and will not r, 5162
135:14 he will r himself concerning his servants. 5162
Jer 4:28 spoken it, I have purposed it, and will not r, 5162
18: 8 I will r of the evil that I thought to do unto 5162
18:10 not my voice, then I will r of the good, 5162
26: 3 that I may r me of the evil, which I purpose 5162
26:13 the LORD will r him of the evil that he 5162
42:10 for I r me of the evil that I have done unto 5162
Eze 14: 6 R, and turn yourselves from your idols; and 7725
18:30 R, and turn yourselves from all your 7725
24:14 neither will I spare, neither will I r; 5162
Joel 2:14 Who knoweth if he will return and r, and 5162
Jnh 3: 9 Who can tell if God will turn and r, and 5162
Mt 3: 2 And saying, R ye: for the kingdom of 3340
4:17 time Jesus began to preach, and to say, R: 3340
Mk 1:15 is at hand: r ye, and believe the gospel. 3340
6:12 went out, and preached that men should r. 3340
Lk 13: 3 but, except ye r, ye shall all likewise 3340
13: 5 but, except ye r, ye shall all likewise perish. 3340
16:30 went unto them from the dead, they will r. 3340
17: 3 rebuke him; and if he r, forgive him. 3340
17: 4 in a day turn again to thee, saying, I r; 3340
Ac 2:38 R, and be baptized every one of you in 3340
3:19 R ye therefore, and be converted, that your 3340
8:22 R therefore of this thy wickedness, and 3340
17:30 now commandeth all men every where to r: 3340
26:20 that they should r and turn to God, and 3340
2Co 7: 8 with a letter, I do not r, though I did repent: 3338
7: 8 with a letter, I do not repent, though I did r: 3338
Heb 7:21 unto him, The Lord sware and will not r, 3338
Rev 2: 5 art fallen, and r, and do the first works; 3340
2: 5 candlestick out of his place, except thou r. 3340
2:16 R; or else I will come unto thee quickly, and will fight against them with the sword of my mouth. 3340
2:21 And I gave her space to r of her 3340
2:22 except they r of their deeds. 3340
3: 3 and heard, and hold fast, and r. 3340
3:19 and chasten: be zealous therefore, and r. 3340

REPENTANCE (26) [REPENT]
Hos 13:14 r shall be hid from mine eyes. 5164
Mt 3: 8 Bring forth therefore fruits meet for r: 3341
3:11 I indeed baptize you with water unto r: but 3341
9:13 come to call the righteous, but sinners to r. 3341
Mk 1: 4 preach the baptism of r for the remission of 3341
2:17 not to call the righteous, but sinners to r. 3341
Lk 3: 3 preaching the baptism of r for 3341
3: 8 Bring forth therefore fruits worthy of r, and 3341
5:32 not to call the righteous, but sinners to r. 3341
15: 7 and nine just persons which need no r. 3341
24:47 And that r and remission of sins should be 3341
Ac 5:31 for to give r to Israel, and forgiveness of 3341
11:18 God also to the Gentiles granted r unto life. 3341
13:24 the baptism of r to all the people of Israel. 3341
19: 4 John verily baptized with the baptism of r, 3341
20:21 r toward God, and faith toward our Lord 3341
26:20 and turn to God, and do works meet for r. 3341
Ro 2: 4 that the goodness of God leadeth thee to r? 3341
11:29 the gifts and calling of God are without r. 278
2Co 7: 9 were made sorry, but that ye sorrowed to r: 3341
7:10 For godly sorrow worketh r to salvation not 3341
2Ti 2:25 if God peradventure will give them r to 3341
Heb 6: 1 not laying again the foundation of r from 3341
6: 6 shall fall away, to renew them again unto r; 3341
12:17 for he found no place of r, though he 3341
2Pe 3: 9 should perish, but that all should come to r. 3341

REPENTED (32) [REPENT]
Ge 6: 6 it r the LORD that he had made man on 5162
Ex 32:14 the LORD r of the evil which he thought 5162
Jdg 2:18 for it r the LORD because of their 5162
21: 6 the children of Israel r them for Benjamin 5162
21:15 the people r them for Benjamin, because 5162
1Sa 15:35 the LORD r that he had made Saul king 5162
2Sa 24:16 the LORD r him of the evil, and said to 5162
1Ch 21:15 he r him of the evil, and said to the angel 5162
Ps 106:45 r according to the multitude of his mercies. 5162
Jer 8: 6 no man r him of his wickedness, saying, 5162
20:16 which the LORD overthrew, and r not: 5162
26:19 the LORD r him of the evil which he had 5162
31:19 Surely after that I was turned, I r; and 5162
Am 7: 3 The LORD r for this: It shall not be, 5162
7: 6 The LORD r for this: This also shall not 5162
Jnh 3:10 God r of the evil, that he had said that he 5162
Zec 8:14 saith the LORD of hosts, and I r not: 5162
Mt 11:20 works were done, because they r not. 3340
11:21 Sidon they would have r long ago in 3340
12:41 because they r at the preaching of Jonas; 3340
21:29 I will not: but afterward he r, and went. 3338
21:32 ye, when ye had seen it, r not afterward, 3338
27: 3 r himself, and brought again the thirty 3338
Lk 10:13 they had a great while ago r, sitting in 3340
11:32 for they r at the preaching of Jonas; and 3340
2Co 7:10 repentance to salvation not to be r of: 278
12:21 and have not r of the uncleanness and 3340
Rev 2:21 to repent of her fornication; and she r not. 3340
9:20 yet r not of the works of their hands, 3340
9:21 Neither r they of their murders, nor of their 3340
16: 9 and they r not to give him glory. 3340
16:11 and their sores, and r not of their deeds. 3340

REPENTEST (1) [REPENT]
Jnh 4: 2 of great kindness, and r thee of the evil. 5162

REPENTETH (5) [REPENT]
Ge 6: 7 the air; for it r me that I have made them. 5162
1Sa 15:11 It r me that I have set up Saul to be king: 5162
Joel 2:13 and of great kindness, and r him of the evil. 5162
Lk 15: 7 shall be in heaven over one sinner that r, 3340
15:10 of the angels of God over one sinner that r. 3340

REPENTING (1) [REPENT]
Jer 15: 6 and destroy thee; I am weary with r. 5162

REPENTINGS (1) [REPENT]
Hos 11: 8 within me, my r are kindled together. 5150

REPETITIONS (1) [REPEATETH]
Mt 6: 7 But when ye pray, use not vain r, as 945

REPHAEL (1)
1Ch 26: 7 Othni, and R, and Obed, Elzabad, 7501

REPHAH (1)
1Ch 7:25 R was his son, also Resheph, and Telah his 7506

REPHAIAH (5)
1Ch 3:21 the sons of R, the sons of Arnan, the sons 7509
4:42 Neariah, and R, and Uzziel, the sons of 7509
7: 2 R, and Jeriel, and Jahmai, and Jibsam, and 7509
9:43 R his son, Eleasah his son, Azel his son. 7509
Ne 3: 9 next unto them repaired R the son of Hur, 7509

REPHAIM (6) [REPHAIMS]
2Sa 5:18 and spread themselves in the valley of R. 7497
5:22 and spread themselves in the valley of R. 7497
23:13 of the Philistines pitched in the valley of R. 7497
1Ch 11:15 the Philistines encamped in the valley of R. 7497
14: 9 and spread themselves in the valley of R. 7497
Isa 17: 5 as he that gathereth ears in the valley of R. 7497

R

REPHAIMS (2) [REPHAIM]
Ge 14: 5 smote the **R** in Ashteroth Karnaim, and 7497
15:20 the Hittites, and the Perizzites, and the **R**, 7497

REPHAITES See GIANT; REPHAIMS

REPHAN See REMPHAN

REPHIDIM (5)
Ex 17: 1 of the LORD, and pitched in **R**: 7508
17: 8 came Amalek, and fought with Israel in **R**. 7508
19: 2 For they were departed from **R**, and 7508
Nu 33:14 removed from Alush, and encamped at **R**, 7508
33:15 they departed from **R**, and pitched in 7508

REPLENISH (2) [REPLENISHED]
Ge 1:28 and multiply, and **r** the earth, and subdue it: 4390
9: 1 Be fruitful, and multiply, and **r** the earth. 4390

REPLENISHED (5) [REPLENISH]
Isa 2: 6 because they be **r** from the east, and 4390
23: 2 of Zidon, that pass over the sea, have **r**. 4390
Jer 31:25 and I have **r** every sorrowful soul. 4390
Eze 26: 2 unto me: I shall be **r**, *now* she is laid waste: 4390
27:25 thou wast **r**, and made very glorious in 4390

REPLIEST (1)
Ro 9:20 O man, who art thou that **r against** God? *470*

REPORT (30) [REPORTED]
Ge 37: 2 Joseph brought unto his father their evil **r**. 1681
Ex 23: 1 Thou shalt not raise a false **r**: put not thine 8088
Nu 13:32 they brought up an **evil r** of the land which 1681
14:37 Even *those* men that did bring up the evil **r** 1681
Dt 2:25 who shall hear **r** of thee, and shall tremble, 8088
1Sa 2:24 my sons; for *it is* no good **r** that I hear: 8052
1Ki 10: 6 It was a true **r** that I heard in mine own 1697
2Ch 9: 5 *It was* a true **r** which I heard in mine own 1697
Ne 6:13 *that* they might have *matter* for an evil **r**, 8034
Pr 15:30 *and* a good **r** maketh the bones fat. 8052
Isa 23: 5 As *at* the **r** concerning Egypt, so shall they 8088
23: 5 shall they be sorely pained *at* the **r** of Tyre. 8088
28:19 shall be a vexation only *to* understand the **r**. 8052
53: 1 Who hath believed our **r**? and to whom is 8052
Jer 20:10 **R**, *say they,* and we will report it. All my 5046
20:10 Report, *say they,* and we will **r** it. All my 5046
50:43 The king of Babylon hath heard the **r** of 8088
Jn 12:38 he spake, Lord, who hath believed our **r**? *189*
Ac 6: 3 ye out among you seven men **of honest r**, *3140*
10:22 of **good r** among all the nation of the Jews, *3140*
22:12 **having a good r** of all the Jews which *3140*
Ro 10:16 Esaias saith, Lord, who hath believed our **r**? *189*
1Co 14:25 and **r** that God is in you of a truth. *518*
2Co 6: 8 and dishonour, by **evil r** and good report: *1426*
6: 8 and dishonour, by evil report and **good r**: *2162*
Php 4: 8 *are* lovely, whatsoever *things are* of **good r**; *2163*
1Ti 3: 7 Moreover he must have a good **r** of them *3141*
Heb 11: 2 For by it the elders **obtained a good r**. *3140*
11:39 having **obtained a good r** through faith, *3140*
3Jn 1:12 Demetrius **hath good r** of all *men,* and *3140*

REPORTED (12) [REPORT]
Ne 6: 6 *It is* **r** among the heathen, and 8085
6: 7 now shall it be **r** to the king according to 8085
6:19 Also they **r** his good deeds before me, and 559
Est 1:17 husbands in their eyes, when it shall be **r**, 559
Eze 9:11 inkhorn by his side, **r** the matter, saying, 7725
Mt 28:15 this saying is **commonly r** among the Jews *1310*
Ac 4:23 and **r** all that the chief priests and elders had *518*
16: 2 Which was **well r of** by the brethren that *3140*
Ro 3: 8 And not *rather,* (as we be **slanderously r**, *987*
1Co 5: 1 It is **r** commonly *that there is* fornication *191*
1Ti 5:10 **Well r** of for good works; if she have *3140*
1Pe 1:12 which are now **r** unto you by them that have *312*

REPRESENTATIVE See DEPUTED

REPROACH (88) [REPROACHED, REPROACHES, REPROACHEST, REPROACHETH, REPROACHFULLY]
Ge 30:23 a son; and said, God hath taken away my **r**: 2781
34:14 is uncircumcised; for that *were* a **r** unto us: 2781
Jos 5: 9 *This* day have I rolled away the **r** of Egypt 2781
Ru 2:15 even among the sheaves, and **r** her not: 3637
1Sa 11: 2 right eyes, and lay it *for* a **r** upon all Israel. 2781
17:26 and taketh away the **r** from Israel? 2781
25:39 that hath pleaded the cause of my **r** from 2781
2Ki 19: 4 his master hath sent to **r** the living God; 2778
19:16 which hath sent him to **r** the living God. 2778
Ne 1: 3 in the province *are* in great affliction and **r**: 2781
2:17 wall of Jerusalem, that we be no more a **r**. 2781
4: 4 turn their **r** upon their own head, and 2781
5: 9 of the **r** of the heathen our enemies? 2781
6:13 for an evil report, that they might **r** me. 2778
Job 19: 5 against me, and plead against me my **r**: 2781
20: 3 I have heard the check of my **r**, and 3639
27: 6 my heart shall not **r** *me* so long as I live. 2778
Ps 15: 3 nor taketh up a **r** against his neighbour. 2781
22: 6 a **r** of men, and despised of the people. 2781
31:11 I was a **r** among all mine enemies, but 2781
39: 8 make me not the **r** of the foolish. 2781
42:10 a sword in my bones, mine enemies **r** me; 2778
44:13 Thou makest us a **r** to our neighbours, 2781
57: 3 save me *from* the **r** of him that would 2778
69: 7 Because for thy sake I have borne **r**; 2781
69:10 my soul with fasting, that was to my **r**. 2781
69:19 Thou hast known my **r**, and my shame, and 2781
69:20 **R** hath broken my heart; and I am full of 2781
71:13 let them be covered *with* **r** and 2781
74:10 O God, how long shall the adversary **r**? 2778
78:66 hinder parts: he put them to a perpetual **r**. 2781
79: 4 We are become a **r** to our neighbours, 2781
79:12 sevenfold into their bosom their **r**, 2781
89:41 way spoil him: he is a **r** to his neighbours. 2781
89:50 Remember, Lord, the **r** of thy servants; 2781
89:50 *how* I do bear in my bosom *the* **r** *of* all NIH
102: 8 Mine enemies **r** me all the day; *and* 2778
109:25 I became also a **r** unto them: *when* they 2781
119:22 Remove from me **r** and contempt; for I 2781
119:39 Turn away my **r** which I fear: for thy 2781
Pr 6:33 he get; and his **r** shall not be wiped away. 2781
14:34 a nation: but sin *is* a **r** to any people. 2617
18: 3 also contempt, and with ignominy **r**. 2781
19:26 a son that causeth shame, and **bringeth r**. 2659
22:10 shall go out; yea, strife and **r** shall cease. 7036
Isa 4: 1 be called by thy name, to take away our **r**. 2781
30: 5 a help nor profit, but a shame, and also a **r**. 2781
37: 4 his master hath sent to **r** the living God, 2778
37:17 which hath sent to **r** the living God. 2778
51: 7 fear ye not the **r** of men, neither be ye 2781
54: 4 shalt not remember the **r** of thy widowhood 2781
Jer 6:10 the word of the LORD is unto them a **r**; 2781
20: 8 the word of the LORD was made a **r** unto 2781
23:40 I will bring an everlasting **r** upon you, and 2781
24: 9 to be a **r** and a proverb, a taunt and a curse, 2781
29:18 and an astonishment, and a hissing, and a **r**, 2781
31:19 because I did bear the **r** of my youth. 2781
42:18 and an astonishment, and a curse, and a **r**; 2781
44: 8 and a **r** among all the nations of the earth? 2781
44:12 an astonishment, and a curse, and a **r**. 2781
49:13 a desolation, a **r**, a waste, and a curse; 2781
51:51 are confounded, because we have heard **r**: 2781
La 3:30 that smiteth him: he is filled full with **r**. 2781
3:61 Thou hast heard their **r**, O LORD, *and* 2781
5: 1 come upon us: consider, and behold our **r**. 2781
Eze 5:14 a **r** among the nations that *are* round about 2781
5:15 So it shall be a **r** and a taunt, an instruction 2781
16:57 as *at* the time of *thy* **r** of the daughters of 2781
21:28 the Ammonites, and concerning their **r**; 2781
22: 4 have I made thee a **r** unto the heathen, 2781
36:15 neither shalt thou bear the **r** of the people 2781
36:30 that ye shall receive no more **r** of famine 2781
Da 9:16 thy people *are become* a **r** to all *that are* 2781
11:18 a prince for his own behalf shall cause the **r** 2781
11:18 without his own **r** he shall cause *it* to turn 2781
Hos 12:14 and his **r** shall his Lord return unto him. 2781
Joel 2:17 O LORD, and give not thine heritage to **r**, 2781
2:19 I will no more make you a **r** among 2781
Mic 6:16 therefore ye shall bear the **r** of my people. 2781
Zep 2: 8 I have heard the **r** of Moab, and 2781
3:18 of thee, *to whom* the **r** of it *was* a burden. 2781
Lk 1:25 on *me,* to take away my **r** among men. *3681*
6:22 and shall **r** *you,* and cast out your name as *3679*
2Co 11:21 I speak as concerning **r**, as though we had *819*
1Ti 3: 7 lest he fall into **r** and the snare of the devil. *3680*
4:10 For therefore we both labour and **suffer r**, *3679*
Heb 11:26 Esteeming the **r** of Christ greater riches *3680*
13:13 unto him without the camp, bearing his **r**. *3680*

REPROACHED (15) [REPROACH]
2Ki 19:22 Whom hast thou **r** and blasphemed? and 2778
19:23 By thy messengers thou hast **r** the Lord, 2778
Job 19: 3 These ten times have ye **r** me: you are not 3637
Ps 55:12 For *it was* not an enemy *that* **r** me; then 2778
69: 9 the reproaches of them that **r** thee are fallen 2778
74:18 *that* the enemy hath **r**, O LORD, and 2778
79:12 wherewith they have **r** thee, O Lord. 2778
89:51 Wherewith thine enemies have **r**, 2778
89:51 wherewith they have **r** the footsteps of 2778
Isa 37:23 Whom hast thou **r** and blasphemed? and 2778
37:24 By thy servants hast thou **r** the Lord, and 2778
Zep 2: 8 whereby they have **r** my people, and 2778
2:10 because they have **r** and 2778
Ro 15: 3 The reproaches of them that **r** thee fell on *3679*
1Pe 4:14 If ye be **r** for the name of Christ, happy *are* *3679*

REPROACHES (5) [REPROACH]
Ps 69: 9 the **r** of them that reproached thee are 2781
Isa 43:28 given Jacob to the curse, and Israel to **r**. 1421
Ro 15: 3 The **r** of them that reproached thee fell on *3680*
2Co 12:10 in **r**, in necessities, in persecutions, *5196*
Heb 10:33 ye were made a gazingstock both by **r** *3680*

REPROACHEST (1) [REPROACH]
Lk 11:45 Master, thus saying thou **r** us also. *5195*

REPROACHETH (7) [REPROACH]
Nu 15:30 or a stranger, the same **r** the LORD; 1442
Ps 44:16 For the voice of him that **r** and 2778
74:22 remember how the foolish *man* **r** thee 2781
119:42 I have wherewith to answer him that **r** me: 2778
Pr 14:31 He that oppresseth the poor **r** his Maker: 2778
17: 5 Whoso mocketh the poor **r** his Maker: *and* 2778
27:11 heart glad, that I may answer him that **r** me. 2778

REPROACHFULLY (2) [REPROACH]
Job 16:10 have smitten me upon the cheek **r**; 2781+871.1
1Ti 5:14 none occasion to the adversary to **speak r**. *3059*

REPROBATE (4) [REPROBATES]
Jer 6:30 **R** silver shall *men* call them, because 3988
Ro 1:28 God gave them over to a **r** mind, to do those *96*
2Ti 3: 8 men of corrupt minds, **r** concerning the faith. *96*
Tit 1:16 and disobedient, and unto every good work **r**. *96*

REPROBATES (3) [REPROBATE]
2Co 13: 5 that Jesus Christ is in you, except ye be **r**? *96*
13: 6 I trust that ye shall know that we are not **r**. *96*
13: 7 do *that which is* honest, though we be as **r**. *96*

REPROOF (15) [REPROVE]
Job 26:11 heaven tremble and are astonished at his **r**. 1606
Pr 1:23 Turn you at my **r**: behold, I will pour out 8433
1:25 all my counsel, and would none of my **r**: 8433
1:30 none of my counsel: they despised all my **r**. 8433
5:12 hated instruction, and my heart despised **r**; 8433
10:17 but he that refuseth **r** erreth. 8433
12: 1 but he that hateth **r** *is* brutish. 8433
13:18 but he that regardeth **r** shall be honoured. 8433
15: 5 but he that regardeth **r** is prudent. 8433
15:10 the way: *and* he that hateth **r** shall die. 8433
15:31 The ear that heareth the **r** of life abideth 8433
15:32 but he that heareth **r** getteth understanding. 8433
17:10 A **r** entereth more into a wise *man* than an 1606
29:15 The rod and **r** give wisdom: but a child left 8433
2Ti 3:16 profitable for doctrine, for **r**, for correction, *1650*

REPROOFS (2) [REPROVE]
Ps 38:14 heareth not, and in whose mouth *are* no **r**. 8433
Pr 6:23 and **r** of instruction *are* the way of life: 8433

REPROVE (19) [REPROOF, REPROOFS, REPROVED, REPROVER, REPROVETH, UNREPROVEABLE]
2Ki 19: 4 will **r** the words which the LORD thy God 3198
Job 6:25 right words! but what doth your arguing **r**? 3198
6:26 Do ye imagine to **r** words, and the speeches 3198
13:10 He will **surely r** you, if ye do 3198+3198
22: 4 Will he **r** thee for fear of thee? will he enter 3198
Ps 50: 8 I will not **r** thee for thy sacrifices or 3198
50:21 *but* I will **r** thee, and set *them* in order 3198
141: 5 let him **r** me; *it shall be* an excellent oil, 3198
Pr 9: 8 **R** not a scorner, lest he hate thee: rebuke a 3198
19:25 **r** one that hath understanding, *and* he will 3198
30: 6 lest he **r** thee, and thou be found a liar. 3198
Isa 11: 3 neither **r** after the hearing of his ears: 3198
11: 4 and **r** with equity for the meek of the earth: 3198
37: 4 will **r** the words which the LORD thy God 3198
Jer 2:19 and thy backslidings shall **r** thee: 3198
Hos 4: 4 Yet let no man strive, nor **r** another: for thy 3198
Jn 16: 8 he will **r** the world of sin, and *1651*
Eph 5:11 works of darkness, but rather **r** *them.* *1651*
2Ti 4: 2 **r**, rebuke, exhort with all longsuffering and *1651*

REPROVED (10) [REPROVE]
Ge 20:16 and with all *other:* thus she was **r**. 3198
21:25 Abraham **r** Abimelech because of a well of 3198
1Ch 16:21 them wrong: yea, he **r** kings for their sakes, 3198
Ps 105:14 them wrong: yea, he **r** kings for their sakes; 3198
Pr 29: 1 He, that being often **r** hardeneth *his* neck, 8433
Jer 29:27 why hast thou not **r** Jeremiah of Anathoth, 1605
Hab 2: 1 and what I shall answer when I am **r**. 8433
Lk 3:19 being **r** by him for Herodias his brother *1651*
Jn 3:20 to the light, lest his deeds should be **r**. *1651*
Eph 5:13 But all *things* that are **r** are made manifest *1651*

REPROVER (2) [REPROVE]
Pr 25:12 *so is* a wise **r** upon an obedient ear. 3198
Eze 3:26 shalt be dumb, and shalt not be to them a **r**: 376

REPROVETH (4) [REPROVE]
Job 40: 2 the Almighty instruct *him?* he that **r** God, 3198
Pr 9: 7 He that **r** a scorner getteth to himself 3256
15:12 A scorner loveth not one that **r** him: 3198
Isa 29:21 lay a snare for him that **r** in the gate, and 3198

REPUTATION (5) [REPUTED]
Ecc 10: 1 *doth* a little folly *him that is* in **r** for 3368
Ac 5:34 had in **r** among all the people, and *5093*
Gal 2: 2 but privately to them which were **of r**, *1380*
Php 2: 7 But **made** himself **of no r**, and took *upon* *2758*
2:29 Lord with all gladness; and hold such in **r**: *1784*

REPUTED (2) [REPUTATION]
Job 18: 3 counted as beasts, *and* **r vile** in your sight? 2933
Da 4:35 all the inhabitants of the earth *are* **r** as 2804

REQUEST (19) [REQUESTED, REQUESTS]
Jdg 8:24 unto them, I would **desire a r** of you, 7592+7596
2Sa 14:15 it may be that the king will perform the **r** of 1697
14:22 in that the king hath fulfilled the **r** of his 1697
Ezr 7: 6 the king granted him all his **r**, according to 1246
Ne 2: 4 said unto me, For what dost thou **make r**? 1245
Est 4: 8 and to **make r** before him for her people. 1245
5: 3 what *is* thy **r**? it shall be even given thee to 1246
5: 6 what *is* thy **r**? even to the half of 1246
5: 7 and said, My petition and my **r** *is;* 1246
5: 8 to perform my **r**, let the king and 1246
7: 2 what *is* thy **r**? and it shall be performed, 1246
7: 3 me at my petition, and my people at my **r**: 1246
7: 7 Haman stood *up* to **make r** for his life to 1245
9:12 or what *is* thy **r** further? and it shall be 1246
Job 6: 8 O that I might have my **r**; and *that* God 7596
Ps 21: 2 and hast not withholden the **r** of his lips. 782
106:15 he gave them their **r**; but sent leanness into 7596
Ro 1:10 **Making r**, if by any means now at length I *1189*
Php 1: 4 of mine for you all making **r** with joy, *1162*

REQUESTED (5) [REQUEST]
Jdg 8:26 the weight of the golden earrings that he **r** 7592
1Ki 19: 4 he **r** for himself that he might die; and said, 7592
1Ch 4:10 And God granted *him that* which he **r**. 7592
Da 1: 8 he **r** of the prince of the eunuchs that he 1245
2:49 Daniel **r** of the king, and he set Shadrach, 1156

REQUESTS (1) [REQUEST]
Php 4: 6 supplication with thanksgiving let your **r** be *155*

REQUIRE (29) [REQUIRED, REQUIREST, REQUIRETH, REQUIRING]
Ge 9: 5 surely your blood of your lives will I **r**; 1875
9: 5 at the hand of every beast will I **r** it, and 1875
9: 5 at the hand of every man's brother will I **r** 1875
31:39 of my hand didst thou **r** it, *whether* stolen 1245
43: 9 for him; of my hand shalt thou **r** him: 1245
Dt 10:12 what doth the LORD thy God **r** of thee, 7592
18:19 shall speak in my name, I will **r** *it* of him. 1875
23:21 for the LORD thy God will **surely r** 1875+1875
Jos 22:23 let the LORD himself **r** *it;* 1245
1Sa 20:16 *saying,* Let the LORD even **r** *it* at 1245

2Sa 3:13 one thing I **r** of thee, that is, Thou shalt not 7592
4:11 therefore now **r** his blood of your hand, 1245
19:38 whatsoever thou shalt **r** of me, *that* will I do 977
1Ki 8:59 Israel at all times, **as the matter** shall **r**: 1697
1Ch 21: 3 doth my lord **r** this *thing?* why will he be a 1245
2Ch 24:22 he said, The LORD look upon *it*, and **r** *it.* 1875
Ezr 7:21 shall **r** of you, *it* be done speedily, 7593
8:22 For I was ashamed to **r** of the king a band 7592
Ne 5:12 restore *them*, and will **r** nothing of them; 1245
Ps 10:13 he hath said in his heart, Thou wilt not **r** *it.* 1875
Eze 3:18 but his blood will I **r** at thine hand. 1245
3:20 but his blood will I **r** at thine hand. 1245
20:40 there will I **r** your offerings, and 1875
33: 6 his blood will I **r** at the watchman's hand. 1875
33: 8 but his blood will I **r** at thine hand. 1245
34:10 I will **r** my flock at their hand, and 1875
Mic 6: 8 what doth the LORD **r** of thee, but to do 1875
1Co 1:22 For the Jews **r** a sign, and the Greeks seek *154*
7:36 and need so **r**, let him do what he will, *1096*

REQUIRED (22) [REQUIRE]
Ge 42:22 therefore, behold, also his blood is **r**. 1875
Ex 12:36 *as they* **r**. And they spoiled the Egyptians. NIH
1Sa 21: 8 because the king's business **r** haste. 1961
2Sa 12:20 when he **r**, they set bread before him, and 7592
1Ch 16:37 the ark continually, as every day's **work** **r**: 1697
2Ch 8:14 the priests, as the **duty** of every day **r**: 1697
24: 6 Why hast thou not **r** of the Levites to bring 1875
Ezr 3: 4 to the custom, **as** the duty of every day **r**; 4941
Ne 5:18 yet for *all* this **r** not I the bread of 1245
Est 2:15 she **r** nothing but what Hegai the king's 1245
Ps 40: 6 and sin offering hast thou not **r**. 7592
137: 3 that carried us away captive **r** of us a song; 7592
137: 3 they that wasted us **r** *of us* mirth, NIH
Pr 30: 7 Two *things* have I **r** of thee; deny me *them* 7592
Isa 1:12 who hath **r** this at your hand, to tread my 1245
Lk 11:50 of the world, may be **r** of this generation; *1567*
11:51 unto you, It shall be **r** of this generation. *1567*
12:20 this night thy soul shall be **r** of thee: *523*
12:48 much is given, of him shall be much **r**: *2212*
19:23 that at my coming I might have **r** *mine own* *4238*
23:24 gave sentence that it should be as they **r**. *155*
1Co 4: 2 Moreover it is **r** in stewards, that a man be *2212*

REQUIREST (1) [REQUIRE]
Ru 3:11 fear not; I will do to thee all that thou **r**: 559

REQUIRETH (2) [REQUIRE]
Ecc 3:15 already been; and God **r** that which is past. 1245
Da 2:11 *it is* a rare thing that the king **r**, and there is 7593

REQUIRING (1) [REQUIRE]
Lk 23:23 loud voices, **r** that he might be crucified. *154*

REQUITE (9) [REQUITED, REQUITING]
Ge 50:15 will **certainly** **r** us all the evil which 7725+7725
Dt 32: 6 Do ye thus **r** the LORD, O foolish people 1580
2Sa 2: 6 I also will **r** you this kindness, 854+6213
16:12 that the LORD will **r** me good for his 7725
2Ki 9:26 I will **r** thee in this plat, saith the LORD. 7999
Ps 10:14 and spite, to **r** *it* with thy hand: 5414
41:10 and raise me up, that I may **r** them. 7999
Jer 51:56 God of recompences shall **surely** **r**. 7999+7999
1Ti 5: 4 piety at home, and to **r** *their* parents: *287+591*

REQUITED (2) [REQUITE]
Jdg 1: 7 as I have done, so God hath **r** me. And they 7999
1Sa 25:21 unto him: and he hath **r** me evil for good. 7725

REQUITING (1) [REQUITE]
2Ch 6:23 do, and judge thy servants, by **r** the wicked, 7725

REREWARD (6)
Nu 10:25 *which was* the **r** of all the camps throughout 622
Jos 6: 9 the **r** came after the ark, *the priests* going on, 622
6:13 the **r** came after the ark of the LORD, 622
1Sa 29: 2 and his men passed on in the **r** with Achish. 314
Isa 52:12 and the God of Israel *will be* your **r**. 622
58: 8 the glory of the LORD shall be thy **r**. 622

RESCUE (3) [RESCUED, RESCUETH]
Dt 28:31 and thou shalt have none to **r** *them.* 3467
Ps 35:17 **r** my soul from their destructions, 7725
Hos 5:14 I will take away, and none shall **r** *him.* 5337

RESCUED (3) [RESCUE]
1Sa 14:45 So the people **r** Jonathan, that he died not. 6299
30:18 carried away: and David **r** his two wives. 5337
Ac 23:27 then came I with an army, and **r** him, *1807*

RESCUETH (1) [RESCUE]
Da 6:27 He delivereth and **r**, and he worketh signs 5338

RESEMBLANCE (1) [RESEMBLE]
Zec 5: 6 This *is* their **r** through all the earth. 5869

RESEMBLE (1) [RESEMBLANCE, RESEMBLED]
Lk 13:18 of God like? and whereunto shall I **r** it? *3666*

RESEMBLED (1) [RESEMBLE]
Jdg 8:18 *each* one **r** the children of a king. 8389+3509.1

RESEN (1)
Ge 10:12 **R** between Nineveh and Calah: the same *is* 7449

RESERVE (3) [RESERVED, RESERVETH]
Jer 3: 5 Will he **r** *his anger* for ever? will he keep *it* 5201
50:20 be found: for I will pardon them whom I **r**. 7604
2Pe 2: 9 to **r** the unjust unto the day of judgment *to* *5083*

RESERVED (16) [RESERVE]
Ge 27:36 he said, Hast thou not **r** a blessing for me? 680
Nu 18: 9 This shall be thine of the most holy *things*, **r** NIH
Jdg 21:22 we **r** not to each man his wife in the war: 3947
Ru 2:18 gave to her that she **had r** after she was 3498
2Sa 8: 4 but **r** of them *for* an hundred chariots. 3498
1Ch 18: 4 but **r** of them an hundred chariots. 3498
Job 21:30 That the wicked is **r** to the day of 2820
38:23 Which I have **r** against the time of trouble, 2820
Ac 25:21 But when Paul had appealed to be **r** unto *5083*
Ro 11: 4 I have **r** to myself seven thousand men, *2641*
1Pe 1: 4 that fadeth not away, **r** in heaven for you, *5083*
2Pe 2: 4 chains of darkness, *to be* **r** unto judgment; *5083*
2:17 to whom the mist of darkness is **r** for ever. *5083*
3: 7 **r** unto fire against the day of judgment and *5083*
Jude 1: 6 he hath **r** in everlasting chains under *5083*
1:13 to whom is **r** the blackness of darkness for *5083*

RESERVETH (2) [RESERVE]
Jer 5:24 he **r** unto us the appointed weeks of 8104
Na 1: 2 and he **r** *wrath* for his enemies. 5201

RESHEPH (1)
1Ch 7:25 also **R**, and Telah his son, and Tahan his 7566

RESIDUE (34)
Ex 10: 5 they shall eat the **r** of that which is escaped 3499
1Ch 6:66 *the* **r** of the families of the sons of Kohath NIH
Ne 11:20 the **r** of Israel, of the priests, *and* 7605
Isa 21:17 the **r** of the number of archers, the mighty 7605
28: 5 diadem of beauty, unto the **r** of his people, 7605
38:10 I am deprived of the **r** of my years. 3499
44:17 the **r** thereof he maketh a god, *even* his 7611
44:19 shall I make the **r** thereof an abomination? 3499
Jer 8: 3 **r** of them that remain of this evil family, 7611
15: 9 the **r** of them will I deliver to the sword 7611
24: 8 his princes, and the **r** of Jerusalem, 7611
27:19 concerning the **r** of the vessels that remain 3499
29: 1 **r** of the elders which were carried away 3499
39: 3 with all the **r** of the princes of the king of 7611
41:10 Ishmael carried away captive all the **r** of 7611
52:15 the **r** of the people that remained in 3499
Eze 9: 8 *wilt* thou destroy all the **r** of Israel in thy 7611
23:25 and thy **r** shall be devoured by the fire. 319
34:18 ye must tread down with your feet the **r** of 3499
34:18 but ye must foul the **r** with your feet? 3498
36: 3 that ye might be a possession unto the **r** of 7611
36: 4 derision to the **r** of the heathen that *are* 7611
36: 5 have I spoken against the **r** of the heathen, 7611
48:18 the **r** in length over against the oblation of 3498
48:21 the **r** *shall be* for the prince, on the one side 3498
Da 7: 7 and stamped the **r** with the feet of it: 7606
7:19 in pieces, and stamped the **r** with his feet; 7606
Zep 2: 9 the **r** of my people shall spoil them, and 7611
Hag 2: 2 the high priest and to the **r** of the people, 7611
Zec 8:11 now I *will* not *be* unto the **r** of this people 7611
14: 2 the **r** of the people shall not be cut off from 3499
Mal 2:15 Yet had he the **r** of the spirit. And 7605
Mk 16:13 And they went and told *it* unto the **r**: *3062*
Ac 15:17 That the **r** of men might seek after *2645*

RESIN See BDELLIUM

RESIST (10) [RESISTED, RESISTETH]
Zec 3: 1 Satan standing at his right hand to **r** him. 7853
Mt 5:39 But I say unto you, That *ye* **r** not evil: but *436*
Lk 21:15 shall not be able to gainsay nor **r**. *436*
Ac 6:10 And they were not able to **r** the wisdom and *436*
7:51 and ears, ye do always **r** the Holy Ghost: *496*
Ro 13: 2 they that **r** shall receive to themselves *436*
2Ti 3: 8 so do these also **r** the truth: *436*
Jas 4: 7 **R** the devil, and he will flee from you. *436*
5: 6 *and* killed the just; *and* he doth not **r** you. *498*
1Pe 5: 9 Whom **r** stedfast in the faith, knowing that *436*

RESISTED (2) [RESIST]
Ro 9:19 he yet find fault? For who hath **r** his will? *436*
Heb 12: 4 Ye have not yet **r** unto blood, *478*

RESISTETH (4) [RESIST]
Ro 13: 2 Whosoever therefore **r** the power, *498*
13: 2 resisteth the power, **r** the ordinance of God: *436*
Jas 4: 6 God **r** the proud, but giveth grace unto *498*
1Pe 5: 5 for God **r** the proud, and giveth grace to *498*

RESOLVED (1)
Lk 16: 4 I am **r** what to do, that, when I am put out *1097*

RESORT (4) [RESORTED]
Ne 4:20 sound of the trumpet, **r** ye thither unto us: 6908
Ps 71: 3 whereunto *I* may continually **r**: 935
Mk 10: 1 and the people **r** unto him again; and, as he *4848*
Jn 18:20 in the temple, whither the Jews always **r**; *4905*

RESORTED (5) [RESORT]
2Ch 11:13 the Levites that *were* in all Israel **r** to him 3320
Mk 2:13 and all the multitude **r** unto him, and *2064*
Jn 10:41 And many **r** unto him, and said, John did *2064*
18: 2 for Jesus ofttimes **r** thither with his *4863*
Ac 16:13 and spake unto the women which **r** *thither.* *4905*

RESPECT (34) [RESPECTED, RESPECTER, RESPECTETH]
Ge 4: 4 the LORD had **r** unto Abel and to his 8159
4: 5 unto Cain and to his offering he had not **r**. 8159
Ex 2:25 of Israel, and God **had r unto** *them.* 3045
Lev 19:15 thou shalt not **r** the person of the poor, 5375
26: 9 For I will have **r** unto you, and make you 6437
Nu 16:15 unto the LORD, **R** not thou their offering: 6437
Dt 1:17 Ye shall not **r** persons in judgment; *but* 5234
16:19 thou shalt not **r** persons, neither take a gift: 5234
2Sa 14:14 up *again;* neither doth God **r** *any* person: 5375
1Ki 8:28 Yet **have** thou **r** unto the prayer of thy 6437
2Ki 13:23 had **r** unto them, because of his covenant 6437
2Ch 6:19 **Have r** therefore to the prayer of thy 6437
19: 7 nor **r** of persons, nor taking of gifts. 4856
Ps 74:20 **Have r** unto the covenant: for the dark 5027
119: 6 when I have **r** unto all thy commandments. 5027
119:15 in thy precepts, and **have r** unto thy ways. 5027
119:117 I will **have r** unto thy statutes continually. 8159
138: 6 *be* high, yet **hath** he **r** unto the lowly: 7200
Pr 24:23 *It is* not good to have **r** of persons in 5234
28:21 To have **r** of persons *is* not good: for for a 5234
Isa 17: 7 his eyes shall have **r** to the Holy One of 7200
17: 8 neither shall **r** *that* which his fingers have 7200
22:11 neither had **r** unto him that fashioned it 7200
Ro 2:11 For there is no **r of persons** with God. *4382*
2Co 3:10 was made glorious had no glory in this **r**, *3313*
Eph 6: 9 neither is there **r of persons** with him. *4382*
Php 4:11 Not that I speak **in r of** want: for I have *2596*
Col 2:16 or in **r** of a holyday, or of the new moon, or *3313*
3:25 he hath done: and there is no **r of persons.** *4382*
Heb 11:26 for he had **r** unto the recompence of *578*
Jas 2: 1 *the Lord* of glory, with **r of persons.** *4382*
2: 3 And ye have **r** to him that weareth the gay *1914*
2: 9 But if ye **have r to persons**, ye commit sin, *4380*
1Pe 1:17 who **without r of persons** judgeth according *678*

RESPECTED (1) [RESPECT]
La 4:16 they **r** not the persons of the priests, 5375

RESPECTER (1) [RESPECT]
Ac 10:34 truth I perceive that God is no **r of persons**: *4381*

RESPECTETH (2) [RESPECT]
Job 37:24 he **r** not any *that are* wise of heart. 7200
Ps 40: 4 **r** not the proud, nor such as turn aside 413+6437

RESPITE (2)
Ex 8:15 when Pharaoh saw that there was **r**, he 7309
1Sa 11: 3 said unto him, **Give** us seven days' **r**, 7503

RESPONSIBLE See OCCASIONED

REST (275) [RESTED, RESTEST, RESTETH, RESTING, RESTS]
Ge 8: 9 the dove found no **r** for the sole of her foot, 4494
18: 4 your feet, and **r** yourselves under the tree: 8172
30:36 and Jacob fed the **r** of Laban's flocks. 3498
49:15 he saw that **r** *was* good, and the land that *it* 4496
Ex 5: 5 and you **make** them **r** from their burdens. 7673
16:23 To morrow *is* the **r** of the holy sabbath unto 7677
23:11 the seventh *year* thou shalt let it **r** and 8058
23:12 and on the seventh day thou shalt **r**: 7673
23:12 that thine ox and thine ass may **r**, and 5117
28:10 the *other* six names of the **r** on the other 3498
31:15 in the seventh *is* the sabbath of **r**, holy to 7677
33:14 shall go *with thee,* and I will **give** thee **r**. 5117
34:21 but on the seventh day thou shalt **r**: 7673
34:21 in earing time and in harvest thou shalt **r**. 7673
35: 2 a holy *day,* a sabbath of **r** to the LORD: 7677
Lev 5: 9 the **r** of the blood shall be wrung out at 7604
14:17 of the **r** of the oil that *is* in his hand shall 3499
14:29 the **r** of the oil that *is* in the priest's hand he 3498
16:31 It *shall be* a sabbath of **r** unto you, and 7677
23: 3 the seventh day *is* the sabbath of **r**, a holy 7677
23:32 It *shall be* unto you a sabbath of **r**, and 7677
25: 4 in the seventh year shall be a sabbath of **r** 7677
25: 5 *for* it is a year of **r** unto the land. 7677
26:34 *even* then shall the land **r**, and enjoy her 7673
26:35 As long as it lieth desolate it shall **r**; 7673
26:35 because it did not **r** in your sabbaths, 7673
Nu 31: 8 beside *the* **r** *of* them that were slain; NIH
31:32 *being* the **r** of the prey which the men of 3499
Dt 3:13 the **r** of Gilead, and all Bashan, *being* 3499
3:20 Until the LORD have **given** **r** unto your 5117
5:14 and thy maidservant may **r** as well as thou. 5117
12: 9 For ye are not as yet come to the **r** and 4496
12:10 *when* he **giveth** you **r** from all your 5117
25:19 the LORD thy God hath **given** thee **r** 5117
28:65 neither shall the sole of thy foot have **r**: 4494
Jos 1:13 The LORD your God hath **given** you **r**, 5117
1:15 the LORD have **given** your brethren **r**, 5117
3:13 all the earth, shall **r** in the waters of Jordan, 5117
10:20 that the **r** *which* remained of them entered 8300
13:27 the **r** of the kingdom of Sihon king of 3499
14:15 the Anakims. And the land **had r** from war. 8252
17: 2 There was also *a lot* for the **r** of 3498
17: 6 the **r** of Manasseh's sons had the land of 3498
21: 5 the **r** of the children of Kohath had by lot 3498
21:34 the **r** of the Levites, out of the tribe of 3498
21:44 the LORD **gave** them **r** round about, 5117
22: 4 now the LORD your God hath **given r** 5117
23: 1 **given r** unto Israel from all their enemies 5117
Jdg 3:11 the land **had r** forty years. And Othniel 8252
3:30 And the land **had r** fourscore years. 8252
5:31 his might. And the land **had r** forty years. 8252
7: 6 all the **r** of the people bowed down upon 3499
7: 8 he sent all *the* **r** *of* Israel every man unto his NIH
Ru 1: 9 The LORD grant you that ye may find **r**, 4496
3: 1 My daughter, shall I not seek **r** for thee, 4494
3:18 for the man will not be in **r**, until he have 8252
1Sa 13: 2 the **r** of the people he sent every man to his 3499
15:15 and the **r** we have utterly destroyed. 3498
2Sa 3:29 Let it **r** on the head of Joab, and on all his 2342
7: 1 the LORD had **given** him **r** round about 5117
7:11 have **caused** thee **to r** from all thine 5117
10:10 the **r** of the people he delivered into 3499
12:28 gather the **r** of the people together, 3499
21:10 suffered neither the birds of the air to **r** on 5117
1Ki 5: 4 now the LORD my God hath **given** me **r** 5117
8:56 that hath given **r** unto his people Israel, 4496
11:41 the **r** of the acts of Solomon, and all that he 3499
14:19 the **r** of the acts of Jeroboam, how he 3499
14:29 Now the **r** of the acts of Rehoboam, and 3499
15: 7 Now the **r** of the acts of Abijam, and 3499
15:23 The **r** of all the acts of Asa, and all his 3499
15:31 Now the **r** of the acts of Nadab, and all that 3499
16: 5 Now the **r** of the acts of Baasha, and 3499
16:14 Now the **r** of the acts of Elah, and all that 3499
16:20 Now the **r** of the acts of Zimri, and 3499

R

1Ki 16:27 Now the **r** of the acts of Omri which he did, 3499
20:30 the **r** fled to Aphek, into the city; and 3498
22:39 Now the **r** of the acts of Ahab, and all that 3499
22:45 Now the **r** of the acts of Jehoshaphat, and 3499
2Ki 1:18 Now the **r** of the acts of Ahaziah which he 3499
2:15 The spirit of Elijah doth **r** on Elisha. 5117
4: 7 and live thou and thy children of the **r**. 3498
8:23 the **r** of the acts of Joram, and all that he 3499
10:34 Now the **r** of the acts of Jehu, and all that 3499
12:19 the **r** of the acts of Joash, and all that he 3499
13: 8 Now the **r** of the acts of Jehoahaz, and 3499
13:12 the **r** of the acts of Joash, and all that he 3499
14:15 Now the **r** of the acts of Jehoash which he 3499
14:18 the **r** of the acts of Amaziah, *are* they not 3499
14:28 Now the **r** of the acts of Jeroboam, and 3499
15: 6 the **r** of the acts of Azariah, and all that he 3499
15:11 the **r** of the acts of Zachariah, behold, 3499
15:15 the **r** of the acts of Shallum, and 3499
15:21 the **r** of the acts of Menahem, and all that 3499
15:26 the **r** of the acts of Pekahiah, and all that he 3499
15:31 the **r** of the acts of Pekah, and all that he 3499
15:36 Now the **r** of the acts of Jotham, and 3499
16:19 Now the **r** of the acts of Ahaz which he did, 3499
20:20 the **r** of the acts of Hezekiah, and all his 3499
21:17 Now the **r** of the acts of Manasseh, and 3499
21:25 Now the **r** of the acts of Amon which he 3499
23:28 Now the **r** of the acts of Josiah, and all that 3499
24: 5 Now the **r** of the acts of Jehoiakim, and 3499
25:11 Now the **r** of the people that were left in 3499
1Ch 4:43 they smote the **r** of the Amalekites that 7611
6:31 of the LORD, after that the ark had **r**. 4494
6:77 Unto the **r** of the children of Merari *were* 3498
11: 8 and Joab repaired the **r** of the city. 7605
12:38 all the **r** also of Israel *were of* one heart to 7611
16:41 and Jeduthun, and the **r** that were chosen, 7605
19:11 the **r** of the people he delivered unto 3499
22: 9 *be* born to thee, who shall be a man of **r**; 4496
22: 9 I will **give** him **r** from all his enemies round 5117
22:18 hath he *not* **given** you **r** on every side? 5117
23:25 The LORD God of Israel hath **given r** 5117
24:20 the **r** of the sons of Levi *were these:* Of 3498
28: 2 **r** for the ark of the covenant of the LORD, 4496
2Ch 9:29 Now the **r** of the acts of Solomon, first and 7605
13:22 the **r** of the acts of Abijah, and his ways, 3499
14: 6 for the land had **r**, and he had no war in 8252
14: 6 because the LORD had **given** him **r**. 5117
14: 7 and he hath **given** us **r** on every side. 5117
14:11 for we **r** on thee, and in thy name we go 8172
15:15 and the LORD **gave** them **r** round about. 5117
20:30 for his God **gave** him **r** round about. 5117
20:34 Now the **r** of the acts of Jehoshaphat, first 3499
24:14 they had finished *it*, they brought the **r** 7605
25:26 Now the **r** of the acts of Amaziah, first and 3499
26:22 Now the **r** of the acts of Uzziah, first and 3499
27: 7 Now the **r** of the acts of Jotham, and all his 3499
28:26 Now the **r** of his acts and of all his ways, 3499
32:32 Now the **r** of the acts of Hezekiah, and 3499
33:18 Now the **r** of the acts of Manasseh, and 3499
35:26 Now the **r** of the acts of Josiah, and 3499
36: 8 Now the **r** of the acts of Jehoiakim, and 3499
Ezr 4: 3 the **r** of the chief of the fathers of Israel, 7605
4: 7 Tabeel, and the **r** of their companions, 7605
4: 9 the scribe, and the **r** of their companions; 7606
4:10 the **r** of the nations whom the great and 7606
4:10 the **r** *that are on this* side the river, and 7606
4:17 *to* the **r** of their companions that dwell in 7606
4:17 in Samaria, and *unto* the **r** beyond the river: 7606
6:16 and the **r** of the children of the captivity, 7606
7:18 to do with the **r** of the silver and gold, 7606
Ne 2:16 to the rulers, nor to the **r** that did the work. 3499
4:14 and to the rulers, and to the **r** of the people, 3499
4:19 to the rulers, and to the **r** of the people, 3499
6: 1 the Arabian, and the **r** of our enemies, 3499
6:14 and the **r** of the prophets, 3499
7:72 *that* which the **r** of the people gave *was* 7611
9:28 after they had **r**, they did evil again before 5117
10:28 the **r** of the people, the priests, the Levites, 7605
11: 1 the **r** of the people also cast lots, to bring 7605
Est 9:12 what have they done in the **r** of the king's 7605
9:16 had **r** from their enemies, and slew of their 5118
Job 3:13 I should have slept: then had I been **at r**, 5117
3:17 *from* troubling; and there the weary be **at r**. 5117
3:18 *There* the prisoners **r** together; they hear 7599
3:26 I was not in safety, neither had I **r**, 8252
11:18 *and* thou shalt **take** thy **r** in safety. 7901
14: 6 Turn from him, that he may **r**, till he shall 2308
17:16 the pit, when *our* **r** together *is* in the dust. 5183
30:17 the night season: and my sinews **take** no **r**. 7901
Ps 16: 9 my flesh also shall **r** in hope. 7931
17:14 leave the **r** of their *substance* to their babes. 3499
37: 7 **R** in the LORD, and wait patiently for 1826
38: 3 neither *is there any* **r** in my bones because 7965
55: 6 *for then* would I fly away, and be **at r**. 7931
94:13 That *thou* mayest **give** him **r** from the days 8252
95:11 wrath that they should not enter into my **r**. 4496
116: 7 Return unto thy **r**, O my soul; for 4494
125: 3 For the rod of the wicked shall not **r** upon 5117
132: 8 Arise, O LORD, into thy **r**; thou, and 4496
132:14 This *is* my **r** for ever: here will I dwell; 4496
Pr 6:35 neither will he **r content**, though thou givest 14
29: 9 whether he rage or laugh, *there is* no **r**. 5183
29:17 Correct thy son, and he shall **give** thee **r**; 5117
Ecc 2:23 yea, his heart **taketh** not **r** in the night. 7901
6: 5 nor known *any thing:* this hath more **r** than 5183
SS 1: 7 where thou **makest** *thy flock* **to r** at noon: 7257
Isa 7:19 shall **r** all of them in the desolate valleys, 5117
10:19 the **r** of the trees of his forest shall be few, 7605
11: 2 the Spirit of the LORD shall **r** upon him, 5117
11:10 Gentiles seek: and his **r** shall be glorious. 4496
14: 3 LORD shall **give** thee **r** from thy sorrow, 5117
14: 7 The whole earth is **at r**, *and* is quiet: 5117
18: 4 I will **take** my **r**, and I will consider in my 8252
23:12 *to* Chittim; there also shalt thou have no **r**. 5117
25:10 mountain shall the hand of the LORD **r**, 5117
28:12 This *is* the **r** *wherewith* ye may cause 4496
Isa 28:12 *wherewith* ye may **cause** the weary **to r**; 5117
30:15 In returning and **r** shall ye be saved; 5183
34:14 the shrich owl also shall **r** there, and 7280
34:14 rest there, and find for herself a **place of r**. 4494
51: 4 I will **make** my judgment **to r** for a light of 7280
57: 2 they shall **r** in their beds, *each one* walking 5117
57:20 when it cannot **r**, whose waters cast up 8252
62: 1 and for Jerusalem's sake I will not **r**, 8252
62: 7 give him no **r**, till he establish, and till he 1824
63:14 the Spirit of the LORD **caused** him **to r**: 5117
66: 1 unto me? and where *is* the place of my **r**? 4496
Jer 6:16 and ye shall find **r** for your souls. 4771
30:10 shall be **in r**, and be quiet, and none shall 8252
31: 2 *even* Israel when *I* went to **cause** him **to r**. 7280
39: 9 with the **r** of the people that remained. 3499
45: 3 I fainted in my sighing, and I find no **r**. 4496
46:27 be **in r** and at ease, and none shall make 8252
47: 6 up thyself into thy scabbard, **r**, and be still. 7280
50:34 that he may **give r** to the land, and 7280
52:15 king of Babylon, and the **r** of the multitude. 3499
La 1: 3 among the heathen, she findeth no **r**: 4494
2:18 give thyself no **r**; let not the apple of thine 6314
5: 5 we labour, *and* have no **r**. 5117
Eze 5:13 I will **cause** my fury **to r** upon them, and 5117
16:42 So will I **make** my fury towards thee **to r**, 5117
21:17 and I will **cause** my fury **to r**: 5117
24:13 till I have **caused** my fury **to r** upon thee. 5117
38:11 I will go *to* them that are **at r**, that dwell 8252
44:30 that he may **cause** the blessing **to r** in thine 5117
45: 8 *the r of* the land shall they give to the house NIH
48:23 As for the **r** of the tribes, from the east side 3499
Da 2:18 his fellows should not perish with the **r** of 7606
4: 4 I Nebuchadnezzar was at **r** in mine house, 7954
7:12 As concerning the **r** of the beasts, they had 7606
12:13 thy way till the end *be:* for thou shalt **r**, 5117
Mic 2:10 Arise ye, and depart; for this *is* not *your* **r**: 4496
Hab 3:16 that I might **r** in the day of trouble: 5117
Zep 3:17 he will **r** in his love, he will joy over thee 2790
Zec 1:11 behold, all the earth sitteth still, and is **at r**. 8252
9: 1 and Damascus *shall be* the **r** thereof: 4496
11: 9 let the **r** eat every one the flesh of another. 7604
Mt 11:28 and are heavy laden, and I will **give** you **r**. *373*
11:29 in heart: and ye shall find **r** unto your souls. *372*
12:43 dry places, seeking **r**, and findeth none. *372*
26:45 unto them, Sleep on now, and **take** your **r**: *373*
27:49 The **r** said, Let be, let us see whether Elias *3062*
Mk 6:31 apart into a desert place, and **r** a while: *373*
14:41 unto them, Sleep on now, and **take** your **r**: *373*
Lk 10: 6 peace be there, your peace shall **r** upon it: *1879*
11:24 he walketh through dry places, seeking **r**; *372*
12:26 *is* least, why take ye thought for the **r**? *3062*
24: 9 *things* unto the eleven, and *to* all the **r**. *3062*
Jn 11:13 that he had spoken of **taking of r** in sleep. *2838*
Ac 2:26 moreover also my flesh shall **r** in hope: *2681*
2:37 said unto Peter and *to* the **r** of the apostles, *3062*
5:13 And of the **r** durst no *man* join himself to *3062*
7:49 the Lord: or what *is* the place of my **r**? *2663*
9:31 Then had the churches **r** throughout all *1515*
27:44 And the **r**, some on boards, and some on *3062*
Ro 11: 7 hath obtained *it*, and the **r** were blinded, *3062*
1Co 7:12 But to the **r** speak I, not the Lord: If any *3062*
11:34 And the **r** will I set in order when I come. *3062*
2Co 2:13 I had no **r** in my spirit, because I found not *425*
7: 5 our flesh had no **r**, but *we were* troubled on *425*
12: 9 that the power of Christ may **r** upon me. *1981*
2Th 1: 7 And to you who are troubled **r** with us, *425*
Heb 3:11 in my wrath, They shall not enter into my **r**. *2663*
3:18 he that *they* should not enter into his **r**, *2663*
4: 1 promise being left *us* of entering into his **r**, *2663*
4: 3 For we which have believed do enter into **r**, *2663*
4: 3 in my wrath, if they shall enter into my **r**: *2663*
4: 4 And God did **r** the seventh day from all his *2664*
4: 5 *place* again, If they shall enter into my **r**. *2663*
4: 8 For if Jesus had **given** them **r**, *then* *2664*
4: 9 therefore a **r** to the people of God. *4520*
4:10 For he that is entered into his **r**, he also *2663*
4:11 Let us labour therefore to enter into that **r**, *2663*
1Pe 4: 2 That *he* no longer should live the **r** of *his* *1954*
Rev 2:24 unto you I say, and unto the **r** in Thyatira, *3062*
4: 8 and they **r** not day and night, saying, *372+2192*
6:11 that they should **r** yet for a little season, *373*
9:20 And the **r** of the men which were not killed *3062*
14:11 and they have no **r** day nor night, *372*
14:13 the Spirit, that they may **r** from their labours; *373*
20: 5 But the **r** of the dead lived not again until *3062*

RESTED (21) [REST]

Ge 2: 2 he **r** on the seventh day from all his work 7673
2: 3 that in it he had **r** from all his work which 7673
8: 4 the ark **r** in the seventh month, on 5117
Ex 10:14 of Egypt, and **r** in all the coasts of Egypt: 5117
16:30 So the people **r** on the seventh day. 7673
20:11 all that in them *is*, and **r** the seventh day: 5117
31:17 on the seventh day he **r**, and was refreshed. 7673
Nu 9:18 upon the tabernacle they **r in** the **tents**. 2583
9:23 of the LORD they **r in** the **tents**, 2583
10:12 and the cloud **r** in the wilderness of Paran. 7931
10:36 when it **r**, he said, Return, O LORD, 5117
11:25 to pass, that when the spirit **r** upon them, 5117
11:26 the spirit **r** upon them; and they *were* of 5117
Jos 11:23 by their tribes. And the land **r** from war. 8252
1Ki 6:10 and they **r** on the house with timber of cedar. 270
2Ch 32: 8 the people **r** themselves upon the words of 5564
Est 9:17 on the fourteenth day of the same **r** they, 5118
9:18 on the fifteenth *day* of the same they **r**, and 5118
9:22 As the days wherein the Jews **r** from their 5117
Job 30:27 My bowels boiled, and **r** not: the days of 1826
Lk 23:56 **r** the sabbath day according to *2270*

RESTEST (1) [REST]

Ro 2:17 and **r** in the law, and makest thy boast of *1879*

RESTETH (4) [REST]

Job 24:23 be given him *to be* in safety, whereon he **r**; 8172
Pr 14:33 Wisdom **r** in the heart of him that hath 5117
Ecc 7: 9 be angry: for anger **r** in the bosom of fools. 5117
1Pe 4:14 the spirit of glory and of God **r** upon you: *373*

RESTING (5) [REST]

Nu 10:33 to search out a **r place** for them. 4496
2Ch 6:41 into thy **r place**, thou, and the ark of thy 5118
Pr 24:15 of the righteous; spoil not his **r place**: 7258
Isa 32:18 and in sure dwellings, and in quiet **r places**; 4496
Jer 50: 6 to hill, they have forgotten their **r place**. 7258

RESTITUTION (6)

Ex 22: 3 *for* he should **make full r**; if he have 7999+7999
22: 5 best of his own vineyard, shall he **make r**. 7999
22: 6 kindled the fire shall **surely make r**. 7999+7999
22:12 he shall **make r** unto the owner thereof. 7999
Job 20:18 according to *his* substance *shall* the **r** *be*, 8545
Ac 3:21 **r** of all *things*, which God hath spoken by *605*

RESTORE (40) [RESTORED, RESTORER, RESTORETH]

Ge 20: 7 Now therefore **r** the man *his* wife; for he *is* 7725
20: 7 if thou **r** *her* not, know thou that thou shalt 7725
40:13 lift up thine head, and **r** thee unto thy place: 7725
42:25 to **r** every man's money into his sack, and 7725
Ex 22: 1 he shall **r** five oxen for an ox, and 7999
22: 4 it be ox, or ass, or sheep; he shall **r** double. 7999
Lev 6: 4 that he shall **r** that which he took violently 7725
6: 5 he shall even **r** it in the principal, and 7999
24:21 And he that killeth a beast, he shall **r** it: and 7999
25:27 **r** the overplus unto the man to whom he 7725
25:28 if he be not able to **r** *it* to him, then 7725
Nu 35:25 the congregation shall **r** him to the city of 7725
Dt 22: 2 after it, and thou shalt **r** it to him **again**. 7725
Jdg 11:13 therefore **r** those *lands* **again** peaceably. 7725
17: 3 now therefore I will **r** it unto thee. 7725
1Sa 12: 3 mine eyes therewith? and I will **r** *it* you. 7725
2Sa 9: 7 will **r** thee all the land of Saul thy father; 7725
12: 6 he shall **r** the lamb fourfold, because he did 7999
16: 3 To day shall the house of Israel **r** me 7725
1Ki 20:34 my father took from thy father, I will **r**; 7725
2Ki 8: 6 **R** all that *was* hers, and all the fruits of 7725
Ne 5:11 **R**, I pray you, to them, even *this* day, 7725
5:12 We will **r** *them*, and will require nothing of 7725
Job 20:10 the poor, and his hands shall **r** their goods. 7725
20:18 That which he laboured for shall he **r**, and 7725
Ps 51:12 **R** unto me the joy of thy salvation; and 7725
Pr 6:31 *if* he be found, he shall **r** sevenfold; he 7999
Isa 1:26 I will **r** thy judges as at the first, and 7725
42:22 *for* a spoil, and none saith, **R**. 7725
49: 6 of Jacob, and to **r** the preserved of Israel: 7725
57:18 **r** comforts unto him and to his mourners. 7999
Jer 27:22 I bring them up, and **r** them to this place. 7725
30:17 For I will **r** health unto thee, and I will heal 5927
Eze 33:15 *If* the wicked **r** the pledge, give again that 7725
Da 9:25 the going forth of the commandment to **r** 7725
Joel 2:25 I will **r** to you the years that the locust hath 7999
Mt 17:11 Elias truly shall first come, and **r** all *things*. *600*
Lk 19: 8 *man* by false accusation, I **r** *him* fourfold. *591*
Ac 1: 6 wilt thou at this time **r again** the kingdom to *600*
Gal 6: 1 **r** such a one in the spirit of meekness; *2675*

RESTORED (27) [RESTORE]

Ge 20:14 unto Abraham, and **r** him Sarah his wife. 7725
40:21 **r** the chief butler unto his butlership **again**; 7725
41:13 me he **r** unto mine office, and him he 7725
42:28 he said unto his brethren, My money is **r**; 7725
Dt 28:31 before thy face, and shall not be **r** to thee: 7725
Jdg 17: 3 when he had **r** the eleven hundred *shekels* 7725
17: 4 Yet he **r** the money unto his mother; and 7725
1Sa 7:14 had taken from Israel were **r** to Israel, 7725
1Ki 13: 6 for me, that my hand may be **r** me **again**. 7725
13: 6 the king's hand was **r** him **again**, and 7725
2Ki 8: 1 whose son he had **r to life**, saying, Arise, 2421
8: 5 the king how he had **r** a dead *body* **to life**, 2421
8: 5 the woman, whose son he had **r to life**, 2421
8: 5 and this *is* her son, whom Elisha **r to life**. 2421
14:22 He built Elath, and **r** it to Judah, after that 7725
14:25 He **r** the coast of Israel from the entering of 7725
2Ch 8: 2 That the cities which Huram had **r** to 5414
26: 2 He built Eloth, and **r** it to Judah, after that 7725
Ezr 6: 5 be **r**, and brought *again* unto the temple 8421
Ps 69: 4 then I **r** *that* which I took not away. 7725
Eze 18: 7 *but* hath **r** *to* the debtor his pledge, 7725
18:12 hath not **r** the pledge, and hath lift up his 7725
Mt 12:13 *it* forth; and it was **r** whole, *like* as the other. *600*
Mk 3: 5 *it* out: and his hand was **r** whole as the other. *600*
8:25 and he was **r**, and saw every *man* clearly. *600*
Lk 6:10 and his hand was **r** whole as the other. *600*
Heb 13:19 to do this, that I may be **r** to you the sooner. *600*

RESTORER (2) [RESTORE]

Ru 4:15 he shall be unto thee a **r** of *thy* life, and 7725
Isa 58:12 of the breach, The **r** of paths to dwell in. 7725

RESTORETH (2) [RESTORE]

Ps 23: 3 He **r** my soul: he leadeth me in the paths of 7725
Mk 9:12 and **r** all *things;* and how it is written of *600*

RESTRAIN (2) [RESTRAINED, RESTRAINEST, RESTRAINT]

Job 15: 8 of God? and dost thou **r** wisdom to thyself? 1639
Ps 76:10 the remainder of wrath shalt thou **r**. 2296

RESTRAINED (8) [RESTRAIN]

Ge 8: 2 and the rain from heaven was **r**; 3607
11: 6 now nothing will be **r** from them, 1219
16: 2 the LORD hath **r** me from bearing: 6113
Ex 36: 6 So the people were **r** from bringing. 3607
1Sa 3:13 made themselves vile, and he **r** them not. 3543
Isa 63:15 and of thy mercies towards me? are they **r**? 662
Eze 31:15 I **r** the floods thereof, and the great waters 4513
Ac 14:18 And with these sayings scarce **r** they *2664*

RESTRAINEST (1) [RESTRAIN]
Job 15: 4 castest off fear, and **r** prayer before God. 1639

RESTRAINT (1) [RESTRAIN]
1Sa 14: 6 for *there is* no **r** to the LORD to save by 4622

RESTS (1) [REST]
1Ki 6: 6 house he made **narrowed r** round about, 4052

RESURRECTION (41)
Mt 22:23 which say that there is no **r**, and asked him, *386*
22:28 Therefore in the **r** whose wife shall she be of *386*
22:30 For in the **r** they neither marry, nor are given *386*
22:31 But as touching the **r** of the dead, have ye *386*
27:53 And came out of the graves after his **r**, and *1454*
Mk 12:18 him *the* Sadducees, which say there is no **r**; *386*
12:23 In the **r** therefore, when they shall rise, *386*
Lk 14:14 for thou shalt be recompensed at the **r** of *386*
20:27 which deny that there is any **r**; *386*
20:33 Therefore in the **r** whose wife of them is *386*
20:35 and the **r** from the dead, neither marry, *386*
20:36 children of God, being the children of the **r**. *386*
Jn 5:29 they that have done good, unto the **r** of life; *386*
5:29 that have done evil, unto the **r** of damnation. *386*
11:24 I know that he shall rise again in the **r** at *386*
11:25 Jesus said unto her, I am the **r**, and the life: *386*
Ac 1:22 be ordained *to be* a witness with us of his **r**. *386*
2:31 seeing *this* before, spake of the **r** of Christ, *386*
4: 2 preached through Jesus the **r** from the dead. *386*
4:33 apostles witness of the **r** of the Lord Jesus: *386*
17:18 he preached unto them Jesus, and the **r**. *386*
17:32 And when they heard of the **r** of the dead, *386*
23: 6 and **r** of the dead I am called in question. *386*
23: 8 For the Sadducees say that there is no **r**, *386*
24:15 that there shall be a **r** of the dead, both of *386*
24:21 Touching the **r** of the dead I am called in *386*
Ro 1: 4 the Spirit of holiness, by the **r** from the dead: *386*
6: 5 we shall be also *in the likeness* of *his* **r**: *386*
1Co 15:12 how say some among you that there is no **r** *386*
15:13 But if there be no **r** of the dead, then *386*
15:21 by man *came* also the **r** of the dead. *386*
15:42 So also *is* the **r** of the dead. It is sown in *386*
Php 3:10 and the power of his **r**, and the fellowship of *386*
3:11 If by any means I might attain unto the **r** of *1815*
2Ti 2:18 have erred, saying that the **r** is past already; *386*
Heb 6: 2 and of **r** of the dead, and of eternal *386*
11:35 that they might obtain a better **r**: *386*
1Pe 1: 3 hope by the **r** of Jesus Christ from the dead, *386*
3:21 toward God,) by the **r** of Jesus Christ: *386*
Rev 20: 5 years were finished. This *is* the first **r**. *386*
20: 6 and holy *is* he that hath part in the first **r**: *386*

RETAIN (7) [RETAINED, RETAINETH]
Job 2: 9 unto him, Dost thou still **r** thine integrity? 2388
Pr 4: 4 said unto me, Let thine heart **r** my words: 8551
11:16 retaineth honour: and strong *men* **r** riches. 8551
Ecc 8: 8 hath power over the spirit to **r** the spirit; 3607
Da 11: 6 she shall not **r** the power of the arm; 6113
Jn 20:23 *and* whose soever *sins* ye **r**, they are *2902*
Ro 1:28 And even as they did not like to **r** God in *2192*

RETAINED (6) [RETAIN]
Jdg 7: 8 his tent, and **r** *those* three hundred men: 2388
19: 4 in law, the damsel's father, **r** him; 2388+871.1
Da 10: 8 in me into corruption, and I **r** no strength. 6113
10:16 turned upon me, and I have **r** no strength. 6113
Jn 20:23 *and* whose soever *sins* ye retain, they are **r**. *2902*
Phm 1:13 Whom I would have **r** with me, that in thy *2722*

RETAINETH (3) [RETAIN]
Pr 3:18 upon her: and happy *is* every one that **r** her. 8551
11:16 A gracious woman **r** honour: and 8551
Mic 7:18 he **r** not his anger for ever, because 2388

RETIRE (2) [RETIRED]
2Sa 11:15 **r** ye from him, that he may be smitten, and 7725
Jer 4: 6 **r**, stay not: for I will bring evil from 5756

RETIRED (2) [RETIRE]
Jdg 20:39 when the men of Israel **r** in the battle, 2015
2Sa 20:22 they **r** from the city, every man to his tent. 6327

RETURN (263) [RETURNED, RETURNETH, RETURNING]
Ge 3:19 thou eat bread, till thou **r** unto the ground; 7725
3:19 for dust thou *art*, and unto dust shalt thou **r**. 7725
14:17 his **r** from the slaughter of Chedorlaomer, 7725
16: 9 **R** to thy mistress, and submit thyself under 7725
18:10 I will **certainly r** unto thee according 7725+7725
18:14 At the time appointed I will **r** unto thee, 7725
31: 3 **R** unto the land of thy fathers, and to thy 7725
31:13 and **r** unto the land of thy kindred. 7725
32: 9 **R** unto thy country, and to thy kindred, and 7725
Ex 4:18 **r** unto my brethren which *are* in Egypt, and 7725
4:19 unto Moses in Midian, Go, **r** *into* Egypt: 7725
4:21 When thou goest to **r** into Egypt, 7725
13:17 when they see war, and they **r** to Egypt: 7725
Lev 25:10 ye shall **r** every man unto his possession, 7725
25:10 and ye shall **r** every man unto his family. 7725
25:13 In the year of this jubile ye shall **r** every 7725
25:27 sold it; that he may **r** unto his possession. 7725
25:28 go out, and he shall **r** unto his possession. 7725
25:41 shall **r** unto his own family, and unto 7725
25:41 unto the possession of his fathers shall he **r**. 7725
27:24 In the year of the jubile the field shall **r** 7725
Nu 10:36 when it rested, he said, **R**, O LORD, 7725
14: 3 were it not better for us to **r** into Egypt? 7725
14: 4 us make a captain, and let us **r** into Egypt. 7725
23: 5 **R** unto Balak, and thus thou shalt speak. 7725
32:18 We will not **r** unto our houses, until 7725
32:22 afterward ye shall **r**, and be guiltless before 7725
35:28 shall **r** into the land of his possession. 7725
Dt 3:20 shall ye **r** every man unto his possession, 7725
17:16 nor **cause** the people **to r** to Egypt, to 7725
17:16 Ye shall henceforth **r** no more that way. 7725
20: 5 let him go and **r** to his house, lest he die in 7725
20: 6 let him *also* go and **r** unto his house, lest he 7725
20: 7 let him go and **r** unto his house, lest he die 7725
20: 8 let him go and **r** unto his house, lest his 7725
30: 2 shalt **r** unto the LORD thy God, and 7725
30: 3 will **r** and gather thee from all the nations, 7725
30: 8 thou shalt **r** and obey the voice of 7725
Jos 1:15 ye shall **r** unto the land of your possession, 7725
20: 6 shall the slayer **r**, and come unto his own 7725
22: 4 therefore now **r** ye, and get ye unto your 6437
22: 8 **R** with much riches unto your tents, and 7725
Jdg 7: 3 let him **r** and depart early from mount 7725
11:31 when I **r** in peace from the children of 7725
Ru 1: 6 that she might **r** from the country of Moab: 7725
1: 7 they went on the way to **r** unto the land of 7725
1: 8 in law, Go, **r** each to her mother's house: 7725
1:10 Surely we will **r** with thee unto thy people. 7725
1:15 unto her gods: **r** thou after thy sister in law. 7725
1:16 *or* to **r** from following after thee: 7725
1Sa 6: 3 **in any wise r** him a trespass 7725+7725
6: 4 trespass offering which we shall **r** to him? 7725
6: 8 which ye **r** him *for* a trespass offering, 7725
7: 3 If ye do **r** unto the LORD with all your 7725
7:17 his **r** *was* to Ramah; for there *was* his 8666
9: 5 that *was* with him, Come, and let us **r**; 7725
15:26 said unto Saul, I will not **r** with thee: 7725
26:21 **r**, my son David: for I will no more do thee 7725
29: 4 **Make** *this* fellow **r**, that he may go again to 7725
29: 7 Wherefore now **r**, and go in peace, 7725
29:11 to **r** into the land of the Philistines. 7725
2Sa 2:26 ere thou bid the people **r** from following 7725
3:16 said Abner unto him, Go, **r**. And he 7725
10: 5 until your beards be grown, and *then* **r**. 7725
12:23 I shall go to him, but he shall not **r** to me. 7725
15:19 **r** to thy place, and abide with the king: 7725
15:20 I may, **r** thou, and take back thy brethren: 7725
15:27 **r** *into* the city in peace, and your two sons 7725
15:34 if thou **r** *to* the city, and say unto Absalom, 7725
19:14 unto the king, **R** thou, and all thy servants. 7725
24:13 see what answer I shall **r** *to* him that sent 7725
1Ki 2:32 the LORD shall **r** his blood upon his own 7725
2:33 therefore **r** upon the head of Joab, 7725
2:44 the LORD shall **r** thy wickedness upon 7725
8:48 *so* **r** unto thee with all their heart, and 7725
12:24 **r** every man to his house; for this thing is 7725
12:26 Now shall the kingdom **r** to the house of 7725
13:16 he said, I may not **r** with thee, nor go in 7725
19:15 **r** on thy way to the wilderness of 7725
20:22 for at the **r** of the year the king of Syria will 8666
20:26 it came to pass at the **r** of the year, 8666
22:17 let them **r** every man to his house in peace. 7725
22:28 Micaiah said, If thou **r at all** in 7725+7725
2Ki 18:14 I have offended; **r** from me: 7725
19: 7 hear a rumour, and shall **r** to his own land; 7725
19:33 *by the same* shall he **r**, and shall not come 7725
20:10 but let the shadow **r** backward ten degrees. 7725
1Ch 19: 5 until your beards be grown, and *then* **r**. 7725
2Ch 6:24 shall **r** and confess thy name, and pray and 7725
6:38 If they **r** to thee with all their heart and 7725
10: 6 What counsel give ye *me* to **r** answer to 7725
10: 9 What advice give ye that we may **r** answer 7725
11: 4 **r** every man to his house, for this thing is 7725
18:16 let them **r** *therefore* every man to his house 7725
18:26 with water of affliction, until I **r** in peace. 7725
18:27 If thou **certainly r** in peace, *then* 7725+7725
30: 6 Israel, and he will **r** to the remnant of you, 7725
30: 9 away *his* face from you, if ye **r** unto him. 7725
Ne 2: 6 when wilt thou **r**? So it pleased the king to 7725
4:12 From all places whence ye shall **r** unto us 7725
9:17 in their rebellion appointed a captain to **r** to 7725
Est 4:15 Esther bade *them* **r** Mordecai *this answer:* 7725
9:25 should **r** upon his own head, and that he 7725
Job 1:21 mother's womb, and naked shall I **r** thither: 7725
6:29 **R**, I pray you, let it not be iniquity; yea, 7725
6:29 yea, **r** again, my righteousness *is* in it. 7725
7:10 He shall **r** no more to his house, 7725
10:21 Before I go whence I shall not **r**, *even* to 7725
15:22 He believeth not that *he* shall **r** out of 7725
16:22 then I shall go the way *whence* I shall not **r**. 7725
17:10 But *as for* you all, do you **r**, and come now: 7725
22:23 If thou **r** to the Almighty, thou shalt be 7725
33:25 he shall **r** to the days of his youth: 7725
36:10 and commandeth that they **r** from iniquity. 7725
39: 4 they go forth, and **r** not unto them. 7725
Ps 6: 4 **R**, O LORD, deliver my soul: O save me 7725
6:10 let them **r** *and* be ashamed suddenly. 7725
7: 7 for their sakes therefore **r** thou on high. 7725
7:16 His mischief shall **r** upon his own head, 7725
59: 6 They **r** at evening: they make a noise like a 7725
59:14 at evening let them **r**; *and* let them make a 7725
73:10 Therefore his people **r** hither: and waters of 7725
74:21 O let not the oppressed **r** ashamed: let 7725
80:14 **R**, we beseech thee, O God *of* hosts: 7725
90: 3 and sayest, **R**, ye children of men. 7725
90:13 **R**, O LORD, how long? and let it repent 7725
94:15 judgment shall **r** unto righteousness: and 7725
104:29 their breath, they die, and **r** to their dust. 7725
116: 7 **R** unto thy rest, O my soul; for the LORD 7725
Pr 2:19 None that go *unto* her **r** *again*, neither take 7725
26:27 he that rolleth a stone, it will **r** upon him. 7725
Ecc 1: 7 the rivers come, thither they **r again**. 1980+7725
5:15 naked shall he **r** to go as he came, and 7725
12: 2 nor the clouds **r** after the rain: 7725
12: 7 shall the dust **r** to the earth as it was: and 7725
12: 7 and the spirit shall **r** unto God who gave it. 7725
SS 6:13 **R**, return, O Shulamite; return, return, 7725
6:13 Return, **r**, O Shulamite; return, return, 7725
6:13 **r**, return, that we may look upon thee. 7725
6:13 return, **r**, that we may look upon thee. 7725
Isa 6:13 *be* a tenth, and *it* shall **r**, and shall be eaten: 7725
10:21 The remnant shall **r**, *even* the remnant of 7725
10:22 of the sea, *yet* a remnant of them shall **r**: 7725
19:22 and they shall **r** *even* to the LORD, 7725
21:12 if ye will inquire, inquire ye: **r**, come. 7725
35:10 the ransomed of the LORD shall **r**, and 7725
37: 7 shall hear a rumour, and **r** to his own land; 7725
37:34 *by the same* shall he **r**, and shall not come 7725
44:22 **r** unto me; for I have redeemed thee. 7725
45:23 shall not **r**, That unto me every knee shall 7725
51:11 the redeemed of the LORD shall **r**, 7725
55: 7 let him **r** unto the LORD, and he will have 7725
55:11 it shall not **r** unto me void, but it shall 7725
63:17 **R** for thy servants' sake, the tribes of thine 7725
Jer 3: 1 another man's, shall he **r** unto her again? 7725
3: 1 yet **r again** to me, saith the LORD. 7725
3:12 say, **R**, thou backsliding Israel, saith 7725
3:22 **R**, ye backsliding children, *and* I will heal 7725
4: 1 If thou wilt **r**, O Israel, saith the LORD, 7725
4: 1 O Israel, saith the LORD, **r** unto me: 7725
5: 3 harder than a rock; they have refused to **r**. 7725
8: 4 not arise? shall he turn away, and not **r**? 7725
8: 5 they hold fast deceit, they refuse to **r**. 7725
12:15 I will **r**, and have compassion on them, and 7725
15: 7 my people, *sith* they **r** not from their ways. 7725
15:19 If thou **r**, then will I bring thee again, *and* 7725
15:19 let them **r** unto thee; but return not thou 7725
15:19 return unto thee; but **r** not thou unto them. 7725
18:11 **r** ye now every one from his evil way, and 7725
22:10 for he shall **r** no more, nor see his native 7725
22:11 this place; He shall not **r** thither any more: 7725
22:27 to the land whereunto they desire to **r**, 7725
22:27 desire to return, thither shall they not **r**. 7725
23:14 that none doth **r** from his wickedness: 7725
23:20 The anger of the LORD shall not **r**, 7725
24: 7 for they shall **r** unto me with their whole 7725
29:10 in **causing** you **to r** to this place. 7725
30: 3 I will **cause** them **to r** to the land that I 7725
30:10 Jacob shall **r**, and shall be in rest, and 7725
30:24 The fierce anger of the LORD shall not **r**, 7725
31: 8 a great company shall **r** thither. 7725
32:44 for I will **cause** their captivity **to r**, 7725
33: 7 **cause** the captivity of Judah and the captivity of Israel **to r**, 7725
33:11 For I will **cause to r** the captivity of 7725
33:26 for I will **cause** their captivity **to r**, 7725
34:11 **caused** the servants and the handmaids, whom they had let go free, **to r**, 7725
34:16 **caused** every man his servant, . . . **to r**, 7725
34:22 and **cause** them **to r** to this city; 7725
35:15 **R** ye now every man from his evil way, and 7725
36: 3 that they may **r** every man from his evil 7725
36: 7 and will **r** every one from his evil way: 7725
37: 7 shall **r** *to* Egypt into their own land. 7725
37:20 that thou **cause** me not **to r** to the house of 7725
38:26 that *he* would not **cause** me **to r** *to* 7725
42:12 and **cause** you **to r** to your own land. 7725
44:14 that *they* should **r** *into* the land of Judah, 7725
44:14 to the which they have a desire to **r** to 7725
44:14 for none shall **r** but such as shall escape. 7725
44:28 **r** out of the land of Egypt *into* the land of 7725
46:27 and Jacob shall **r**, and be in rest and at ease, 7725
50: 9 a mighty expert *man*; none shall **r** in vain. 7725
Eze 7:13 For the seller shall not **r** to that which is 7725
7:13 whole multitude thereof, *which* shall not **r**; 7725
13:22 that *he* should not **r** from his wicked way, 7725
16:55 shall **r** to their former estate, and Samaria 7725
16:55 her daughters shall **r** to their former estate, 7725
16:55 thy daughters shall **r** to your former estate. 7725
18:23 *and* not that he should **r** from his ways, and 7725
21: 5 out of his sheath: it shall not **r** any more. 7725
21:30 Shall I **cause** *it* **to r** into his sheath? I will 7725
29:14 will **cause** them **to r** *into* the land of 7725
35: 9 and thy cities shall not **r**: 7725
46: 9 he shall not **r** *by* the way of the gate 7725
46:17 year of liberty; after, it shall **r** to the prince: 7725
47: 6 **caused** me **to r** to the brink of the river. 7725
Da 10:20 now will I **r** to fight with the prince of 7725
11: 9 *his* kingdom, and shall **r** into his own land. 7725
11:10 shall he **r**, and be stirred up, *even* to his 7725
11:13 For the king of the north shall **r**, and 7725
11:28 shall he **r** *into* his land with great riches; 7725
11:28 he shall do *exploits*, and **r** to his own land. 7725
11:29 At the time appointed he shall **r**, and 7725
11:30 **r**, and have indignation against the holy 7725
11:30 he shall even **r**, and have intelligence with 7725
Hos 2: 7 she say, I will go and **r** to my first husband; 7725
2: 9 Therefore will I **r**, and take *away* my corn 7725
3: 5 Afterward shall the children of Israel **r**, and 7725
5:15 I will go *and* **r** to my place, till they 7725
6: 1 Come and let us **r** unto the LORD: for he 7725
7:10 they do not **r** to the LORD their God, 7725
7:16 They **r**, *but* not *to* the most High: they are 7725
8:13 and visit their sins: they shall **r** *to* Egypt. 7725
9: 3 Ephraim shall **r** *to* Egypt, and they shall eat 7725
11: 5 He shall not **r** into the land of Egypt, but 7725
11: 5 shall be his king, because they refused to **r**. 7725
11: 9 mine anger, I will not **r** to destroy Ephraim: 7725
12:14 and his reproach shall his Lord **r** unto him. 7725
14: 1 O Israel, **r** unto the LORD thy God; 7725
14: 7 They that dwell under his shadow shall **r**; 7725
Joel 2:14 Who knoweth *if* he will **r** and repent, and 7725
3: 4 speedily will I **r** your recompence upon 7725
3: 7 will **r** your recompence upon your own 7725
Ob 1:15 thy reward shall **r** upon thine own head. 7725
Mic 1: 7 and they shall **r** to the hire of a harlot. 7725
5: 3 the remnant of his brethren shall **r** unto 7725
Mal 1: 4 but we will **r** and build the desolate places; 7725
3: 7 have not kept *them*. **R** unto me, and I will 7725
3: 7 I will **r** unto you, saith the LORD of hosts. 7725
3: 7 of hosts. But ye said, Wherein shall we **r**? 7725
3:18 shall ye **r**, and discern between 7725
Mt 2:12 in a dream that *they* should not **r** to Herod, *344*
10:13 if it be not worthy, let your peace **r** to you. *1994*
12:44 I will **r** into my house from whence I came *1994*
24:18 Neither let him which is in the field **r** back *1994*
Lk 8:39 **R** to thine own house, and shew how great *5290*
11:24 I will **r** unto my house whence I came out. *5290*
12:36 their lord, when he will **r** from the wedding; *360*

R

Lk 17:31 is in the field, let him likewise not r back. 1994
19:12 to receive for himself a kingdom, and to r. 5290
Ac 13:34 *now* no more to r to corruption, he said on 5290
15:16 After this I will r, and will build again 390
18:21 but I will r again unto you, if God will. 344
20: 3 he purposed to r through Macedonia. 5290

RETURNED (185) [RETURN]
Ge 8: 3 the waters r from off the earth continually: 7725
8: 9 she r unto him into the ark, for the waters 7725
8:12 which r not again unto him any more. 7725
14: 7 they r, and came to En-mishpat, which *is* 7725
18:33 and Abraham r unto his place. 7725
21:32 and they r into the land of the Philistines. 7725
22:19 So Abraham r unto his young men, and 7725
31:55 and Laban departed, and r unto his place. 7725
32: 6 the messengers r to Jacob, saying, 7725
33:16 So Esau r that day on his way unto Seir. 7725
37:29 Reuben r unto the pit; and behold, 7725
37:30 he r unto his brethren, and said, The child 7725
38:22 he r to Judah, and said, I cannot find her; 7725
42:24 r to them *again*, and communed with them, 7725
43:10 surely now we had r this second time. 7725
43:18 Because of the money that was r in our 7725
44:13 laded every man his ass, and r to the city. 7725
50:14 Joseph r into Egypt, he, and his brethren, 7725
Ex 4:18 and r to Jethro his father in law, 7725
4:20 upon an ass, and he r to the land of Egypt: 7725
5:22 Moses r unto the LORD, and said, Lord, 7725
14:27 the sea r to his strength when the morning 7725
14:28 the waters r, and covered the chariots, and 7725
19: 8 Moses r the words of the people unto 7725
32:31 Moses r unto the LORD, and said, Oh, 7725
34:31 all the rulers of the congregation r unto 7725
Lev 22:13 no child, and is r unto her father's house, 7725
Nu 13:25 they r from searching of the land after forty 7725
14:36 who r, and made all the congregation to 7725
16:50 Aaron r unto Moses unto the door of 7725
23: 6 he r unto him, and lo, *he* stood by his burnt 7725
24:25 rose up, and went and r to his place: 7725
Dt 1:45 ye r and wept before the LORD; but 7725
Jos 2:16 there three days, until the pursuers be r: 7725
2:22 there three days, until the pursuers were r: 7725
2:23 So the two men r, and descended from 7725
4:18 that the waters of Jordan r unto their place, 7725
6:14 the city once, and r *into* the camp: 7725
7: 3 they r to Joshua, and said unto him, Let not 7725
8:24 that all the Israelites r *unto* Ai, and smote it 7725
10:15 Joshua r, and all Israel with him, unto 7725
10:21 all the people r to the camp to Joshua *at* 7725
10:38 Joshua r, and all Israel with him, to Debir; 7725
10:43 Joshua r, and all Israel with him, unto 7725
22: 9 of Gad and the half tribe of Manasseh r, 7725
22:32 r from the children of Reuben, and 7725
Jdg 2:19 *that* they r, and corrupted *themselves* more 7725
5:29 answered *her*, yea, she r answer to herself, 7725
7: 3 there r of the people twenty and 7725
7:15 r into the host of Israel, and said, Arise; 7725
8:13 Gideon the son of Joash r from battle 7725
11:39 of two months, that she r unto her father, 7725
14: 8 after a time he r to take her, and he turned 7725
21:23 they went and r unto their inheritance, and 7725
Ru 1:22 So Naomi r, and Ruth the Moabitess, 7725
1:22 which r out of the country of Moab: 7725
1Sa 1:19 and r, and came to their house to Ramah: 7725
6:16 had seen *it*, they r *to* Ekron the same day. 7725
6:17 r *for* a trespass offering unto the LORD; 7725
17:15 r from Saul to feed his father's sheep *at* 7725
17:53 the children of Israel r from chasing after 7725
17:57 as David r from the slaughter of 7725
18: 6 when David was r from the slaughter of the 7725
23:28 Wherefore Saul r from pursuing after 7725
24: 1 when Saul was r from following 7725
25:39 for the LORD hath r the wickedness of 7725
26:25 went on his way, and Saul r to his place. 7725
27: 9 and the apparel, and r, and came to Achish. 7725
2Sa 1: 1 when David was r from the slaughter of 7725
1:22 and the sword of Saul r not empty. 7725
2:30 Joab r from following Abner: and when he 7725
3:16 said Abner unto him, Go, return. And he r. 7725
3:27 when Abner was r *to* Hebron, Joab took 7725
6:20 David r to bless his household. And Michal 7725
8:13 David gat *him* a name when he r from 7725
10:14 So Joab r from the children of Ammon, and 7725
11: 4 her uncleanness: and she r unto her house. 7725
12:31 and all the people r unto Jerusalem. 7725
14:24 So Absalom r to his own house, and 5437
16: 8 The LORD hath r upon thee all the blood 7725
17: 3 the man whom thou seekest *is* as if all r: *so* 7725
17:20 could not find *them*, they r *to* Jerusalem. 7725
18:16 and the people r from pursuing after Israel: 7725
19:15 So the king r, and came to Jordan. 7725
19:39 blessed him; and he r unto his own place. 7725
20:22 And Joab r *to* Jerusalem unto the king. 7725
23:10 the people r after him only to spoil. 7725
1Ki 12:24 to the word of the LORD, and r to depart, 7725
13:10 r not by the way that he came to Beth-el. 7725
13:33 After this thing Jeroboam r not from his 7725
19:21 he r **back** from him, and took a yoke of 7725
2Ki 2:25 and from thence he r *to* Samaria. 7725
3:27 departed from him, and r to *their own* land. 7725
4:35 he r, and walked in the house to and fro; 7725
5:15 he r to the man of God, he and all his 7725
7:15 And the messengers r, and told the king. 7725
8: 3 that the woman r out of the land of 7725
9:15 king Joram was r to be healed in Jezreel of 7725
14:14 and hostages, and r to Samaria. 7725
19: 8 So Rab-shakeh r, and found the king of 7725
19:36 and went and r, and dwelt at Nineveh. 7725
23:20 bones upon them, and r *to* Jerusalem. 7725
1Ch 16:43 his house: and David r to bless his house. 5437
20: 3 and all the people r *to* Jerusalem. 7725
2Ch 10: 2 heard *it*, that Jeroboam r out of Egypt. 7725
11: 4 and r from going against Jeroboam. 7725
14:15 camels in abundance, and r *to* Jerusalem. 7725
2Ch 19: 1 Jehoshaphat the king of Judah r to his 7725
19: 8 when they r *to* Jerusalem. 7725
20:27 they r, every man of Judah and Jerusalem, 7725
22: 6 he r to be healed in Jezreel because of 7725
25:10 and they r home in great anger. 7725
25:24 the hostages also, and r *to* Samaria. 7725
28:15 to their brethren: then they r *to* Samaria. 7725
31: 1 *them all.* Then all the children of Israel r, 7725
32:21 So he r with shame of face to his own land. 7725
34: 7 all the land of Israel, he r to Jerusalem. 7725
34: 9 and Benjamin; and they r *to* Jerusalem. 7725
Ezr 5: 5 they r **answer** by letter concerning this 8421
5:11 thus they r us answer, saying, We are 8421
Ne 2:15 entered by the gate of the valley, and *so* r. 7725
4:15 that we r all of us to the wall, every one 7725
9:28 yet when they r, and cried unto thee, thou 7725
Est 2:14 on the morrow she r into the second house 7725
7: 8 the king r out of the palace garden into 7725
Ps 35:13 and my prayer r into mine own bosom. 7725
60: T when Joab r, and smote of Edom in 7725
78:34 and they r and inquired early after God. 7725
Ecc 4: 1 So I r, and considered all the oppressions 7725
4: 7 Then I r, and I saw vanity under the sun. 7725
9:11 I r, and saw under the sun, that the race *is* 7725
Isa 37: 8 So Rabshakeh r, and found the king of 7725
37:37 and went and r, and dwelt at Nineveh. 7725
38: 8 So the sun r ten degrees, by which degrees 7725
Jer 3: 7 she r not. And her treacherous sister Judah 7725
14: 3 no water; they r *with* their vessels empty; 7725
40:12 Even all the Jews r out of all places whither 7725
41:14 captive from Mizpah cast about and r, 7725
43: 5 that were r from all nations, whither they 7725
Eze 1:14 r as the appearance of a flash of lightning. 7725
8:17 and have r to provoke me to anger: 7725
47: 7 Now when I had r, behold, at the bank of 7725
Da 4:34 mine understanding r unto me, and 8421
4:36 At the same time my reason r unto me; and 8421
4:36 mine honour and brightness r unto me; 8421
Hos 6:11 when I r the captivity of my people. 7725
Am 4: 6 yet have ye not r unto me, saith 7725
4: 8 yet have ye not r unto me, saith 7725
4: 9 devoured *them:* yet have ye not r unto me, 7725
4:10 yet have ye not r unto me, saith 7725
4:11 yet have ye not r unto me, saith 7725
Zec 1: 6 they r and said, Like as the LORD of 7725
1:16 I am r to Jerusalem with mercies: 7725
7:14 that no man passed through nor r: 7725
8: 3 I am r unto Zion, and will dwell in 7725
Mt 21:18 Now in the morning as he r into the city, 1877
Mk 14:40 And when he r, he found them asleep 5290
Lk 1:56 three months, and r to her own house. 5290
2:20 And the shepherds r, glorifying and 1994
2:39 they r into Galilee, to their own city 5290
2:43 when they had fulfilled the days, as they r, 5290
4: 1 And Jesus being full of the Holy Ghost r 5290
4:14 And Jesus r in the power of the Spirit into 5290
8:37 he went *up* into the ship, and r *back again.* 5290
8:40 And it came to pass that, when Jesus was r, 5290
9:10 And the apostles, when they were r, 5290
10:17 And the seventy r *again* with joy, saying, 5290
17:18 There are not found that r to give glory to 5290
19:15 And it came to pass, that when he was r, 1880
23:48 were done, smote their breasts, and r. 5290
23:56 And they r, and prepared spices and 5290
24: 9 And r from the sepulchre, and told all these 5290
24:33 and r to Jerusalem, and found the eleven 5290
24:52 and r to Jerusalem with great joy: 5290
Ac 1:12 Then r they unto Jerusalem from the mount 5290
5:22 them not in the prison, they r, and told, 390
8:25 r to Jerusalem, and preached the gospel in 5290
12:25 And Barnabas and Saul r from Jerusalem, 5290
13:13 John departing from them r to Jerusalem. 5290
14:21 they r *again* to Lystra, and *to* Iconium, and 5290
21: 6 we took ship; and they r home *again.* 5290
23:32 to go with him, and r to the castle: 5290
Gal 1:17 into Arabia, and r again unto Damascus. 5290
Heb 11:15 they might have had opportunity to have r. 344
1Pe 2:25 but are now r unto the Shepherd and 1994

RETURNETH (7) [RETURN]
Ps 146: 4 His breath goeth forth, he r to his earth; 7725
Pr 26:11 As a dog r to his vomit, *so* a fool returneth 7725
26:11 to his vomit, *so* a fool r to his folly. 8138
Ecc 1: 6 the wind r *again* according to his circuits. 7725
Isa 55:10 r not thither, but watereth the earth, and 7725
Eze 35: 7 from it him that passeth out and him that r. 7725
Zec 9: 8 that passeth by, and because of him that r: 7725

RETURNING (4) [RETURN]
Isa 30:15 In r and rest shall ye be saved; in quietness 7729
Lk 7:10 And they that were sent, r to the house, 5290
Ac 8:28 Was r, and sitting in his chariot read Esaias 5290
Heb 7: 1 who met Abraham r from the slaughter of 5290

REU (4)
Ge 11:18 And Peleg lived thirty years, and begat R: 7466
11:19 Peleg lived after he begat R two hundred 7466
11:20 R lived two and thirty years, and 7466
11:21 R lived after he begat Serug two hundred 7466

REUBEN (74) [REUBENITE, REUBENITES]
Ge 29:32 and bare a son, and she called his name R: 7205
30:14 R went in the days of wheat harvest, and 7205
35:22 that R went and lay with Bilhah his father's 7205
35:23 R, Jacob's firstborn, and Simeon, and Levi, 7205
37:21 R heard *it*, and he delivered him out of 7205
37:22 R said unto them, Shed no blood, *but* 7205
37:29 R returned unto the pit; and behold, 7205
42:22 R answered them, saying, Spake I not unto 7205
42:37 R spake unto his father, saying, Slay my 7205
46: 8 Jacob and his sons: R, Jacob's firstborn. 7205
46: 9 the sons of R; Hanoch, and Phallu, and 7205
48: 5 as R and Simeon, they shall be mine. 7205
49: 3 R, thou *art* my firstborn, my might, and 7205
Ex 1: 2 R, Simeon, Levi, and Judah, 7205
6:14 The sons of R the firstborn of Israel; 7205
6:14 and Carmi: these *be* the families of R. 7205
Nu 1: 5 of *the tribe of* R; Elizur the son of Shedeur. 7205
1:20 the children of R, Israel's eldest son, 7205
1:21 *even* of the tribe of R, *were* forty and 7205
2:10 of the camp of R according to their armies: 7205
2:10 the captain of the children of R *shall be* 7205
2:16 All that were numbered in the camp of R 7205
7:30 prince of the children of R, *did offer:* 7205
10:18 the standard of the camp of R set forward 7205
13: 4 of the tribe of R, Shammua the son of 7205
16: 1 On, the son of Peleth, sons of R, took *men:* 7205
26: 5 R, the eldest son of Israel: the children of 7205
26: 5 the children of R; Hanoch, *of whom* 7205
32: 1 Now the children of R and the children of 7205
32: 2 the children of R came and spake unto 7205
32: 6 children of Gad and to the children of R, 7205
32:25 and the children of R spake unto Moses, 7205
32:29 the children of R will pass with you over 7205
32:31 of Gad and the children of R answered, 7205
32:33 to the children of R, and unto half the tribe 7205
32:37 the children of R built Heshbon, and 7205
34:14 For the tribe of the children of R according 7206
Dt 11: 6 the sons of Eliab, the son of R: 7205
27:13 R, Gad, and Asher, and Zebulun, Dan, and 7205
33: 6 Let R live, and not die; and let *not* his men 7205
Jos 4:12 the children of R, and the children of Gad, 7205
13:15 of R *inheritance* according to their families. 7205
13:23 the border of the children of R was Jordan, 7205
13:23 of the children of R after their families, 7205
15: 6 went up *to* the stone of Bohan the son of R: 7205
18: 7 Gad, and R, and half the tribe of Manasseh, 7205
18:17 *to* the stone of Bohan the son of R, 7205
20: 8 upon the plain out of the tribe of R, 7205
21: 7 by their families *had* out of the tribe of R, 7205
21:36 out of the tribe of R, Bezer with her 7205
22: 9 the children of R and the children of Gad 7205
22:10 the children of R and the children of Gad 7205
22:11 the children of R and the children of Gad 7205
22:13 of Israel sent unto the children of R, 7205
22:15 they came unto the children of R, and 7205
22:21 the children of R and the children of Gad 7205
22:25 ye children of R and children of Gad; 7205
22:30 heard the words that the children of R and 7205
22:31 the priest said unto the children of R, 7205
22:32 returned from the children of R, and 7205
22:33 destroy the land wherein the children of R 7205
22:34 the children of R and the children of Gad 7205
Jdg 5:15 For the divisions of R *there were* great 7205
5:16 For the divisions of R *there were* great 7205
1Ch 2: 1 R, Simeon, Levi, and Judah, Issachar, and 7205
5: 1 Now the sons of R the firstborn of Israel, 7205
5: 3 *I say,* of R the firstborn of Israel *were,* 7205
5:18 The sons of R, and the Gadites, and half 7205
6:63 out of the tribe of R, and out of the tribe of 7205
6:78 *were given them* out of the tribe of R, 7205
Eze 48: 6 even unto the west side, a *portion for* R. 7205
48: 7 by the border of R, from the east side unto 7205
48:31 one gate of R, one gate of Judah, one gate 7205
Rev 7: 5 Of the tribe of R *were* sealed twelve 4502

REUBENITE (1) [REUBEN]
1Ch 11:42 Adina the son of Shiza the R, a captain of 7206

REUBENITES (16) [REUBEN]
Nu 26: 7 These *are* the families of the R: and 7206
Dt 3:12 gave I unto the R and to the Gadites. 7206
3:16 unto the R and unto the Gadites I gave 7206
4:43 in the plain country, of the R; 7206
29: 8 gave it for an inheritance unto the R, and 7206
Jos 1:12 to the R, and to the Gadites, and to half 7206
12: 6 LORD gave it *for* a possession unto the R, 7206
13: 8 With whom the R and the Gadites have 7206
22: 1 Joshua called the R, and the Gadites, and 7206
2Ki 10:33 and the R, and the Manassites, from Aroer, 7206
1Ch 5: 6 away captive: he *was* prince of the R. 7206
5:26 even the R, and the Gadites, and the half 7206
11:42 a captain of the R, and thirty with him, 7206
12:37 of the R, and the Gadites, and of the half 7206
26:32 whom king David made rulers over the R, 7206
27:16 the ruler of the R *was* Eliezer the son of 7206

REUEL (10) [DEUEL]
Ge 36: 4 to Esau Eliphaz; and Bashemath bare R; 7467
36:10 R the son of Bashemath the wife of Esau. 7467
36:13 these *are* the sons of R; Nahath, and Zerah, 7467
36:17 these *are* the sons of R Esau's son; 7467
36:17 these *are* the dukes *that came* of R in 7467
Ex 2:18 when they came to R their father, he said, 7467
Nu 2:14 sons of Gad *shall be* Eliasaph the son of R. 7467
1Ch 1:35 R, and Jeush, and Jaalam, and Korah. 7467
1:37 The sons of R; Nahath, Zerah, Shammah, 7467
9: 8 the son of R, the son of Ibnijah; 7467

REUMAH (1)
Ge 22:24 his concubine, whose name *was* R, she bare 7208

REVEAL (7) [REVEALED, REVEALER, REVEALETH, REVELATION, REVELATIONS]
Job 20:27 The heaven shall r his iniquity; and 1540
Jer 33: 6 will r unto them the abundance of peace 1540
Da 2:47 seeing thou couldest r this secret. 1541
Mt 11:27 and *he* to whomsoever the Son will r *him.* 601
Lk 10:22 the Son, and *he* to whom the Son will r *him.* 601
Gal 1:16 To r his Son in me, that I might preach him 601
Php 3:15 God shall r even this unto you. 601

REVEALED (38) [REVEAL]
Dt 29:29 *those things* which are r *belong* unto us and 1540
1Sa 3: 7 neither was the word of the LORD yet r 1540
3:21 for the LORD r himself to Samuel in 1540
2Sa 7:27 of Israel, hast r to thy servant, saying, 241+1540
Isa 22:14 it was r in mine ears *by* the LORD of 1540

R

Isa 23: 1 from the land of Chittim it is r to them. 1540
40: 5 And the glory of the LORD shall be r, and 1540
53: 1 and to whom is the arm of the LORD r? 1540
56: 1 near to come, and my righteousness to be r. 1540
Jer 11:20 on them: for unto thee have I r my cause. 1540
Da 2:19 *was* the secret r unto Daniel in a night 1541
2:30 this secret *is* not r to me for *any* wisdom 1541
10: 1 king of Persia a thing was r unto Daniel, 1540
Mt 10:26 there is nothing covered, that shall not be r; *601*
11:25 and prudent, and hast r them unto babes. *601*
16:17 for flesh and blood hath not r *it* unto thee, *601*
Lk 2:26 And it was r unto him by the Holy Ghost, *5537*
2:35 that the thoughts of many hearts may be r. *601*
10:21 and prudent, and hast r them unto babes: *601*
12: 2 there is nothing covered, that shall not be r; *601*
17:30 it be in the day when the Son of man is r. *601*
Jn 12:38 to whom hath the arm of the Lord been r? *601*
Ro 1:17 For therein is the righteousness of God r *601*
1:18 For the wrath of God is r from heaven *601*
8:18 with the glory which shall be r in us. *601*
1Co 2:10 But God hath r *them* unto us by his Spirit: *601*
3:13 shall declare *it,* because it shall be r by fire; *601*
14:30 If *any thing* be r to another that sitteth *by,* let *601*
Gal 3:23 unto the faith which should afterwards be r. *601*
Eph 3: 5 as it is now r unto his holy apostles and *601*
2Th 1: 7 when the Lord Jesus shall be r from heaven *602*
2: 3 and *that* man of sin be r, the son of *601*
2: 6 withholdeth that he might be r in his time. *601*
2: 8 And then shall *that* Wicked be r, whom *601*
1Pe 1: 5 unto salvation ready to be r in the last time. *601*
1:12 Unto whom it was r, that not unto *601*
4:13 that, when his glory shall be r, ye may be *602*
5: 1 also a partaker of the glory that shall be r: *601*

REVEALER (1) [REVEAL]

Da 2:47 a Lord of kings, and a r of secrets, 1541

REVEALETH (6) [REVEAL]

Pr 11:13 A talebearer r secrets: but he that is of a 1540
20:19 He that goeth about *as* a talebearer r 1540
Da 2:22 He r the deep and secret *things:* he 1541
2:28 there is a God in heaven that r secrets, and 1541
2:29 he that r secrets maketh known to thee 1541
Am 3: 7 he r his secret unto his servants 1540

REVELATION (10) [REVEAL]

Ro 2: 5 and r of the righteous judgment of God; *602*
16:25 according to the r of the mystery, *602*
1Co 14: 6 except I shall speak to you either by r, or *602*
14:26 hath a doctrine, hath a tongue, hath a r, *602*
Gal 1:12 was I taught *it,* but by the r of Jesus Christ. *602*
2: 2 And I went up by r, and communicated unto *602*
Eph 1:17 of wisdom and r in the knowledge of him: *602*
3: 3 How that by r he made known unto me *602*
1Pe 1:13 *be* brought unto you at the r of Jesus Christ; *602*
Rev 1: 1 The R of Jesus Christ, which God gave unto *602*

REVELATIONS (2) [REVEAL]

2Co 12: 1 I will come to visions and r of the Lord. *602*
12: 7 measure through the abundance of the r, *602*

REVELING See SPORTING

REVELLINGS (2)

Gal 5:21 murders, drunkenness, r, and such like: *2970*
1Pe 4: 3 r, banquetings, and abominable idolatries: *2970*

REVENGE (5) [VENGEANCE]

Jer 15:15 and visit me, and r me of my persecutors; 5358
20:10 and we shall take our r on him. 5360
Eze 25:15 Because the Philistines have dealt by r, and 5360
2Co 7:11 yea, *what* zeal, yea, *what* r! *1557*
10: 6 And having in a readiness to r all *1556*

REVENGED (1) [VENGEANCE]

Eze 25:12 greatly offended, and r himself upon them; 5358

REVENGER (7) [VENGEANCE]

Nu 35:19 The r of blood himself shall slay 1350
35:21 the r of blood shall slay the murderer, 1350
35:24 the r of blood according to these 1350
35:25 the slayer out of the hand of the r of blood, 1350
35:27 the r of blood find him without the borders 1350
35:27 the r of blood kill the slayer; 1350
Ro 13: 4 a r to *execute* wrath upon him that doeth *1558*

REVENGERS (1) [VENGEANCE]

2Sa 14:11 that thou wouldest not suffer the r of blood 1350

REVENGES (1) [VENGEANCE]

Dt 32:42 from the beginning of r upon the enemy. 6546

REVENGETH (2) [VENGEANCE]

Na 1: 2 God *is* jealous, and the LORD r; 5358
1: 2 the LORD r, and *is* furious; 5358

REVENGING (1) [VENGEANCE]

Ps 79:10 r of the blood of thy servants which is 5360

REVENUE (3) [REVENUES]

Ezr 4:13 *so* thou shalt endamage the r of the kings. 674
Pr 8:19 than fine gold; and my r than choice silver. 8393
Isa 23: 3 of Sihor, the harvest of the river, *is* her r; 8393

REVENUES (3) [REVENUE]

Pr 15: 6 but in the r of the wicked *is* trouble. 8393
16: 8 righteousness than great r without right. 8393
Jer 12:13 they shall be ashamed of your r because 8393

REVERENCE (13) [REVERENCED, REVEREND]

Lev 19:30 keep my sabbaths, and r my sanctuary: 3372
26: 2 keep my sabbaths, and r my sanctuary: 3372
2Sa 9: 6 unto David, he fell on his face, and did r. 7812
1Ki 1:31 did r to the king, and said, Let my lord 7812
Est 3: 2 But Mordecai bowed not, nor did *him* r. 7812
3: 5 nor did him r, *then* was Haman full *of* 7812
Ps 89: 7 to be had in r of all them that are about 3372
Mt 21:37 them his son, saying, They will r my son. *1788*
Mk 12: 6 last unto them, saying, They will r my son. *1788*
Lk 20:13 it may be they will r *him* when they see *1788*
Eph 5:33 and the wife *see* that she r *her* husband. *5399*
Heb 12: 9 which corrected *us,* and we gave *them* r: *1788*
12:28 we may serve God acceptably with r *127*

REVERENCED (1) [REVERENCE]

Est 3: 2 in the king's gate, bowed, and r Haman: 7812

REVEREND (1) [REVERENCE]

Ps 111: 9 covenant for ever: holy and r *is* his name. 3372

REVERSE (3)

Nu 23:20 and he hath blessed; and I cannot r it. 7725
Est 8: 5 let it be written to r the letters devised by 7725
8: 8 sealed with the king's ring, may no man r. 7725

REVILE (2) [REVILED, REVILERS, REVILEST, REVILINGS]

Ex 22:28 Thou shalt not r the gods, nor curse 7043
Mt 5:11 when *men* shall r you, and persecute *you,* *3679*

REVILED (6) [REVILE]

Mt 27:39 that passed by, r him, wagging their heads, *987*
Mk 15:32 And they that were crucified with him r *3679*
Jn 9:28 Then they r him, and said, Thou art his *3058*
1Co 4:12 being r, we bless; being persecuted, *3058*
1Pe 2:23 Who, when he was r, reviled not again; *3058*
2:23 Who, when he was reviled, r not again; *486*

REVILERS (1) [REVILE]

1Co 6:10 nor covetous, nor drunkards, nor r, *3060*

REVILEST (1) [REVILE]

Ac 23: 4 stood by said, R thou God's high priest? *3058*

REVILINGS (2) [REVILE]

Isa 51: 7 of men, neither be ye afraid of their r. 1421
Zep 2: 8 and the r of the children of Ammon, 1421

REVIVE (8) [REVIVED, REVIVING]

Ne 4: 2 will they r the stones out of the heaps of 2421
Ps 85: 6 Wilt thou not r us again: that thy people 2421
138: 7 in the midst of trouble, thou wilt r me: 2421
Isa 57:15 to r the spirit of the humble, and to revive 2421
57:15 and to r the heart of the contrite ones. 2421
Hos 6: 2 After two days will he r us: in the third day 2421
14: 7 they shall r *as* the corn, and grow as 2421
Hab 3: 2 r thy work in the midst of the years, 2421

REVIVED (6) [REVIVE]

Ge 45:27 carry him, the spirit of Jacob their father r: 2421
Jdg 15:19 had drunk, his spirit came again, and he r: 2421
1Ki 17:22 of the child came into him again, and he r. 2421
2Ki 13:21 of Elisha, he r, and stood up on his feet. 2421
Ro 7: 9 the commandment came, sin r, and I died. *326*
14: 9 to this end Christ both died, and rose, and r, *326*

REVIVING (2) [REVIVE]

Ezr 9: 8 and give us a little r in our bondage. 4241
9: 9 to give us a r, to set up the house of our 4241

REVOLT (3) [REVOLTED, REVOLTERS, REVOLTING]

2Ch 21:10 The same time also did Libnah r from 6586
Isa 1: 5 ye will r more and more: the whole head *is* 5627
59:13 speaking oppression and r, conceiving and 5627

REVOLTED (7) [REVOLT]

2Ki 8:20 In his days Edom r from under the hand of 6586
8:22 Yet Edom r from under the hand of Judah 6586
8:22 this day. Then Libnah r at the same time. 6586
2Ch 21: 8 In his days the Edomites r from under 6586
21:10 So the Edomites r from under the hand of 6586
Isa 31: 6 whom the children of Israel have deeply r. 5627
Jer 5:23 and a rebellious heart; they are r and gone. 5493

REVOLTERS (3) [REVOLT]

Jer 6:28 They *are* all grievous r, walking with 5637
Hos 5: 2 the r are profound to make slaughter, 7846
9:15 love them no more: all their princes *are* r. 5637

REVOLTING (1) [REVOLT]

Jer 5:23 this people hath a r and a rebellious heart; 5637

REWARD (80) [REWARDED, REWARDER, REWARDETH, REWARDS]

Ge 15: 1 I *am* thy shield, *and* thy exceeding great r. 7939
Nu 18:31 for it *is* your r for your service in 7939
Dt 10:17 which regardeth not persons, nor taketh r: 7810
27:25 Cursed *be* he that taketh r to slay an 7810
32:41 and will r them that hate me. 7999
Ru 2:12 a full r be given thee of the LORD God of 4909
1Sa 24:19 wherefore the LORD r thee good for that 7999
2Sa 3:39 the LORD shall r the doer of evil 7999
4:10 I would have given him a r for *his* tidings: 1309
19:36 the king recompense *it* me *with* such a r? 1578
1Ki 13: 7 and refresh *thyself,* and I will give thee a r. 4991
2Ch 20:11 Behold, I say, *how* they r us, to come to 1580
Job 6:22 or, Give a r for me of your substance? 7809
7: 2 as a hireling looketh for the r of his work: 6467
Ps 15: 5 to usury, nor taketh r against the innocent. 7810
19:11 *and* in keeping of them *there is* great r. 6118
40:15 Let them be desolate for a r of their shame 6118
54: 5 He shall r evil unto mine enemies: cut them 7725
58:11 Verily *there is* a r for the righteous: 6529
70: 3 Let them be turned back for a r of their 6118
91: 8 thou behold and see the r of the wicked. 8011
94: 2 judge of the earth: render a r to the proud. 1576
Ps 109:20 *Let* this *be* the r of mine adversaries from 6468
127: 3 *and* the fruit of the womb *is his* r. 7939
Pr 11:18 that soweth righteousness *shall be* a sure r. 7938
21:14 and a r in the bosom strong wrath. 7810
24:14 thou hast found *it,* then there shall be a r, 319
24:20 For there shall be no r to the evil *man;* 319
25:22 upon his head, and the LORD shall r thee. 7999
Ecc 4: 9 because they have a good r for their labour. 7939
9: 5 any thing, neither have they any more a r; 7939
Isa 3:11 *it shall be* ill *with him:* for the r of his 1576
5:23 Which justify the wicked for r, and 7810
40:10 his r *is* with him, and his work before him. 7939
45:13 not for price nor r, saith the LORD of 7810
62:11 his r *is* with him, and his work before him. 7939
Jer 40: 5 of the guard gave him victuals and a r, 4864
Eze 16:34 in that thou givest a r, and no reward is 868
16:34 no r is given unto thee, therefore thou art 868
Hos 4: 9 for their ways, and r them their doings. 7725
9: 1 thou hast loved a r upon every cornfloor. 868
Ob 1:15 thy r shall return upon thine own head. 1576
Mic 3:11 The heads thereof judge for r, and 7810
7: 3 prince asketh, and the judge *asketh* for a r; 7966
Mt 5:12 for great *is* your r in heaven: for so *3408*
5:46 love them which love you, what r have ye? *3408*
6: 1 otherwise ye have no r of your Father *3408*
6: 2 Verily I say unto you, They have their r. *3408*
6: 4 seeth in secret himself shall r thee openly. *591*
6: 5 Verily I say unto you, They have their r. *3408*
6: 6 thy Father which seeth in secret shall r thee *591*
6:16 Verily I say unto you, They have their r. *3408*
6:18 which seeth in secret, shall r thee openly. *591*
10:41 of a prophet shall receive a prophet's r; *3408*
10:41 *man* shall receive a righteous *man's* r. *3408*
10:42 say unto you, he shall in no wise lose his r. *3408*
16:27 he shall r every man according to his works. *591*
Mk 9:41 I say unto you, he shall not lose his r. *3408*
Lk 6:23 *joy:* for behold, your r *is* great in heaven: *3408*
6:35 and your r shall be great, and ye shall be *3408*
23:41 for we receive the due r of our deeds: *514*
Ac 1:18 Now this *man* purchased a field with the r *3408*
Ro 4: 4 Now to him that worketh is the r not *3408*
1Co 3: 8 every man shall receive his own r *3408*
3:14 hath built thereupon, he shall receive a r. *3408*
9:17 For if I do this *thing* willingly, I have a r: *3408*
9:18 What is my r then? *Verily* that, when I *3408*
Col 2:18 Let no *man* beguile you of your r in a *2603*
3:24 ye shall receive the r of the inheritance: *469*
1Ti 5:18 And, The labourer *is* worthy of his r. *3408*
2Ti 4:14 the Lord r him according to his works: *591*
Heb 2: 2 received a just recompence of r; *3405*
10:35 which hath great recompence of r. *3405*
11:26 had respect unto the recompence of the r. *3405*
2Pe 2:13 And shall receive the r of unrighteousness, *3408*
2Jn 1: 8 have wrought, but *that* we receive a full r. *3408*
Jude 1:11 ran greedily after the error of Balaam for r, *3408*
Rev 11:18 that *thou* shouldest give r unto thy servants *3408*
18: 6 R her even as she rewarded you, and *591*
22:12 and my r *is* with me, to give every man *3408*

REWARDED (14) [REWARD]

Ge 44: 4 Wherefore have ye r evil for good? 7999
1Sa 24:17 for thou hast r me good, whereas I have 1580
24:17 me good, whereas I have r thee evil. 1580
2Sa 22:21 The LORD r me according to my 1580
2Ch 15: 7 hands be weak: for your work shall be r. 7939
Ps 7: 4 If I have r evil *unto* him that was at peace 1580
18:20 The LORD r me according to my 1580
35:12 They r me evil for good *to* the spoiling of 7999
103:10 nor r us according to our iniquities. 1580
109: 5 they have r me evil for good, and hatred for 7760
Pr 13:13 that feareth the commandment shall be r. 7999
Isa 3: 9 for they have r evil unto themselves. 1580
Jer 31:16 for thy work shall be r, saith the LORD; 7939
Rev 18: 6 Reward her even as she r you, and *591*

REWARDER (1) [REWARD]

Heb 11: 6 *that* he is a r of them that diligently seek *3406*

REWARDETH (6) [REWARD]

Job 21:19 he r him, and he shall know *it.* 7999
Ps 31:23 and plentifully r the proud doer. 7999
137: 8 happy *shall he be,* that r thee as thou hast 7999
Pr 17:13 Whoso r evil for good, evil shall not depart 7725
26:10 The great *God* that formed all *things* both r 7936
26:10 rewardeth the fool, and r transgressors. 7936

REWARDS (5) [REWARD]

Nu 22: 7 with the r of divination in their hand; 7081
Isa 1:23 one loveth gifts, and followeth after r: 8021
Da 2: 6 receive of me gifts and r and great honour: 5023
5:17 be to thyself, and give thy r to another; 5023
Hos 2:12 These *are* my r that my lovers have given 866

REZEPH (2)

2Ki 19:12 R, and the children of Eden which *were* in 7530
Isa 37:12 R, and the children of Eden which *were* in 7530

REZIA (1)

1Ch 7:39 the sons of Ulla; Arah, and Haniel, and R. 7525

REZIN (11)

2Ki 15:37 to send against Judah R the king of Syria, 7526
16: 5 R king of Syria and Pekah son of Remaliah 7526
16: 6 At that time R king of Syria recovered 7526
16: 9 *the people of* it captive to Kir, and slew R. 7526
Ezr 2:48 The children of R, the children of Nekoda, 7526
Ne 7:50 the children of R, the children of Nekoda, 7526
Isa 7: 1 *that* R the king of Syria, and Pekah the son 7526
7: 4 for the fierce anger of R with Syria, and 7526
7: 8 and the head of Damascus *is* R; 7526
8: 6 and rejoice in R and Remaliah's son; 7526
9:11 set up the adversaries of R against him, 7526

R

REZON (1)
1Ki 11:23 up *another* adversary, **R** the son of Eliadah, 7331

RHEGIUM (1)
Ac 28:13 thence we fet a compass, and came to **R**: *4484*

RHESA (1)
Lk 3:27 *the son* of Joanna, which was *the son* of **R**, *4488*

RHODA (1)
Ac 12:13 a damsel came to hearken, named **R**. *4498*

RHODES (1)
Ac 21: 1 and the *day* following unto **R**, and from *4499*

RIB (5) [RIBS]
Ge 2:22 the **r**, which the LORD God had taken 6763
2Sa 2:23 fifth *r*, that the spear came out behind him; NIH
3:27 smote him there *under* the fifth *r*, that he NIH
4: 6 they smote him under the fifth *r*: and NIH
20:10 so he smote him therewith in the fifth *r*, and NIH

RIBAI (2)
2Sa 23:29 Ittai the son of **R** out of Gibeah of 7380
1Ch 11:31 Ithai the son of **R** of Gibeah, that pertained 7380

RIBBAND (1)
Nu 15:38 upon the fringe of the borders a **r** of blue: 6616

RIBLAH (11)
Nu 34:11 coast shall go down from Shepham *to* **R**, 7247
2Ki 23:33 Pharaoh-nechoh put him in bands at **R** in 7247
25: 6 him up to the king of Babylon to **R**; 7247
25:20 brought them to the king of Babylon to **R**: 7247
25:21 and slew them at **R** in the land of Hamath. 7247
Jer 39: 5 of Babylon to **R** in the land of Hamath, 7247
39: 6 the sons of Zedekiah in **R** before his eyes: 7247
52: 9 of Babylon to **R** in the land of Hamath; 7247
52:10 he slew also all the princes of Judah in **R**. 7247
52:26 brought them to the king of Babylon to **R**. 7247
52:27 put them to death in **R** in the land of 7247

RIBS (2) [RIB]
Ge 2:21 he took one of his **r**, and closed up the flesh 6763
Da 7: 5 *it had* three **r** in the mouth of it between 5967

RICH (81) [ENRICH, ENRICHED, ENRICHEST, RICHER, RICHES, RICHLY]
Ge 13: 2 Abram *was* very **r** in cattle, in silver, and 3513
14:23 thou shouldest say, I have **made** Abram **r**: 6238
Ex 30:15 The **r** shall not give more, and the poor 6223
Lev 25:47 or stranger **wax r** by thee, 3027+5381
Ru 3:10 not young men, whether poor or **r**. 6223
1Sa 2: 7 The LORD maketh poor, and **maketh r**: 6238
2Sa 12: 1 in one city; the one **r**, and the other poor. 6223
12: 2 The **r** *man* had exceeding many flocks and 6223
12: 4 there came a traveller unto the **r** man, and 6223
Job 15:29 He shall not be **r**, neither shall his 6238
27:19 The **r** *man* shall lie down, but he shall not 6223
34:19 nor regardeth the **r** more than the poor? 7771
Ps 45:12 *even* the **r** among the people shall intreat 6223
49: 2 Both low and high, **r** and poor, together. 6223
49:16 Be not thou afraid when one is **made r**, 6238
Pr 10: 4 but the hand of the diligent **maketh r**. 6238
10:15 The **r** *man's* wealth *is* his strong city: 6223
10:22 it **maketh r**, and he addeth no sorrow with 6238
13: 7 There is that maketh himself **r**, yet *hath* 6238
14:20 but the **r** *hath* many friends. 6223
18:11 The **r** *man's* wealth *is* his strong city, and 6223
18:23 but the **r** answereth roughly. 6223
21:17 he that loveth wine and oil shall not be **r**. 6238
22: 2 The **r** and poor meet together: the LORD 6223
22: 7 The **r** ruleth over the poor, and 6223
22:16 his *riches, and* he that giveth to the **r**, 6223
23: 4 Labour not to be **r**: cease from thine own 6238
28: 6 *that is* perverse in *his* ways, though he *be* **r**. 6223
28:11 The **r** man *is* wise in his own conceit; but 6223
28:20 he that maketh haste to be **r** shall not be 6238
28:22 He that hasteth to be **r** *hath* an evil eye, and 1952
Ecc 5:12 the abundance of the **r** will not suffer him 6223
10: 6 in great dignity, and the **r** sit in low place. 6223
10:20 and curse not the **r** in thy bedchamber: 6223
Isa 53: 9 the wicked, and with the **r** in his death; 6223
Jer 5:27 they are become great, and **waxen r**. 6238
9:23 let not the **r** *man* glory in his riches: 6223
Eze 27:24 broidered work, and in chests of **r apparel**, 1264
Hos 12: 8 Ephraim said, Yet I am **become r**, I have 6238
Mic 6:12 For the **r** *men* thereof are full *of* violence, 6223
Zec 11: 5 Blessed *be* the LORD; for I am **r**: 6238
Mt 19:23 That a **r** *man* shall hardly enter into *4145*
19:24 than for a **r** *man* to enter into the kingdom *4145*
27:57 there came a **r** man of Arimathea, *4145*
Mk 10:25 than for a **r** *man* to enter into the kingdom *4145*
12:41 and many *that were* **r** cast in much. *4145*
Lk 1:53 and the **r** he hath sent empty away. *4147*
6:24 But woe unto you that are **r**: for ye have *4145*
12:16 The ground of a certain **r** man brought *4145*
12:21 for himself, and is not **r** towards God. *4147*
14:12 neither thy kinsmen, nor *thy* **r** neighbours; *4145*
16: 1 There was a certain **r** man, which had a *4145*
16:19 There was a certain **r** man, which was *4145*
16:21 crumbs which fell from the **r** *man's* table: *4145*
16:22 the **r** *man* also died, and was buried; *4145*
18:23 he was very sorrowful: for he was very **r**. *4145*
18:25 than for a **r** *man* to enter into the kingdom *4145*
19: 2 chief among the publicans, and he was **r**. *4145*
21: 1 saw the **r** *men* casting their gifts into *4145*
Ro 10:12 for the same Lord over all *is* **r** unto all that *4147*
1Co 4: 8 Now ye are full, now ye are **r**, ye have *4147*
2Co 6:10 as poor, yet **making** many **r**; as having *4148*
8: 9 that, though he was **r**, *yet* for your sakes he *4145*
8: 9 that ye through his poverty might be **r**. *4147*
Eph 2: 4 But God, who is **r** in mercy, for his great *4145*
1Ti 6: 9 But they that will be **r** fall into temptation *4147*
6:17 Charge *them that are* **r** in this world, *4145*
6:18 that *they* be **r** in good works, ready to *4147*
Jas 1:10 But the **r**, in that he is made low: because *4145*
1:11 also shall the **r** *man* fade away in his ways. *4145*
2: 5 chosen the poor of this world **r** in faith, *4145*
2: 6 Do not **r** *men* oppress you, and draw you *4145*
5: 1 ye **r** *men*, weep and howl for your miseries *4145*
Rev 2: 9 and tribulation, and poverty, (but thou art **r**) *4145*
3:17 I am **r**, and increased with goods, and *4145*
3:18 gold tried in the fire, that thou mayest be **r**; *4147*
6:15 and the **r** *men*, and the chief captains, and *4145*
13:16 and great, **r** and poor, free and bond, *4145*
18: 3 the merchants of the earth are **waxed r** *4147*
18:15 of these *things*, which were **made r** by her, *4147*
18:19 wherein were **made r** all that had ships in *4147*

RICHER (1) [RICH]
Da 11: 2 the fourth shall be far **r** than *they* all: 6238+6239

RICHES (98) [RICH]
Ge 31:16 For all the **r** which God hath taken from 6239
36: 7 For their **r** were more than that they might 7399
Jos 22: 8 Return with much **r** unto your tents, and 5233
1Sa 17:25 the king will enrich him *with* great **r**, and 6239
1Ki 3:11 neither hast asked **r** for thyself, nor hast 6239
3:13 thou hast not asked, both **r**, and honour: 6239
10:23 exceeded all the kings of the earth for **r** 6239
1Ch 29:12 Both **r** and honour *come* of thee, and 6239
29:28 a good old age, full of days, **r**, and honour: 6239
2Ch 1:11 thou hast not asked **r**, wealth, or honour, 6239
1:12 I will give thee **r**, and wealth, and honour, 6239
9:22 passed all the kings of the earth in **r** 6239
17: 5 and he had **r** and honour in abundance. 6239
18: 1 Now Jehoshaphat had **r** and honour in 6239
20:25 in abundance both **r** with the dead bodies, 7399
32:27 Hezekiah had exceeding much **r** and 6239
Est 1: 4 When he shewed the **r** of his glorious 6239
5:11 Haman told them of the glory of his **r**, and 6239
Job 20:15 He hath swallowed down **r**, and he shall 2428
36:19 Will he esteem thy **r**? *no*, not gold, nor all 7769
Ps 37:16 hath *is* better than the **r** of many wicked. 1995
39: 6 he heapeth up *r*, and knoweth not who shall NIH
49: 6 boast themselves in the multitude of their **r**; 6239
52: 7 trusted in the abundance of his **r**, *and* 6239
62:10 if **r** increase, set not *your* heart *upon them*. 2428
73:12 prosper in the world; they increase *in* **r**. 2428
104:24 made them all: the earth is full *of* thy **r**. 7075
112: 3 Wealth and **r** *shall be* in his house: and 6239
119:14 way of thy testimonies, as *much as* in all **r**. 1952
Pr 3:16 and in her left hand **r** and honour. 6239
8:18 **R** and honour *are* with me; *yea*, durable 6239
8:18 with me; *yea*, durable **r** and righteousness. 1952
11: 4 **R** profit not in the day of wrath: but 1952
11:16 retaineth honour: and strong *men* retain **r**. 6239
11:28 He that trusteth in his **r** shall fall: but 6239
13: 7 that maketh himself poor, yet *hath* great **r**. 1952
13: 8 The ransom of a man's life *are* his **r**: but 6239
14:24 The crown of the wise *is* their **r**: *but* 6239
19:14 House and **r** *are* the inheritance of fathers: 1952
22: 1 name *is* rather to be chosen than great **r**, 6239
22: 4 *and* the fear of the LORD *are* **r**, 6239
22:16 that oppresseth the poor to increase his *r*, NIH
23: 5 for *r* certainly make themselves wings; NIH
24: 4 be filled *with* all precious and pleasant **r**. 1952
27:24 For **r** *are* not for ever: and doth the crown 2633
30: 8 give me neither poverty nor **r**; feed me with 6239
Ecc 4: 8 neither is his eye satisfied *with* **r**; 6239
5:13 *namely*, **r** kept for the owners thereof to 6239
5:14 those **r** perish by evil travail: and 6239
5:19 Every man also to whom God hath given **r** 6239
6: 2 A man to whom God hath given **r**, wealth, 6239
9:11 the wise, nor yet **r** to men of understanding, 6239
Isa 8: 4 the **r** of Damascus and the spoil of Samaria 2428
10:14 my hand hath found as a nest the **r** of 2428
30: 6 they will carry their **r** upon the shoulders of 2428
45: 3 **hidden r** of secret places, that thou mayest 4301
61: 6 ye shall eat the **r** of the Gentiles, and 2428
Jer 9:23 let not the rich *man* glory in his **r**: 6239
17:11 *so* he that getteth **r**, and not by right, 6239
48:36 the **r** *that* he hath gotten are perished. 3502
Eze 26:12 they shall make a spoil of thy **r**, and make a 2428
27:12 by reason of the multitude of all *kind of* **r**; 1952
27:18 of thy making, for the multitude of all **r**; 1952
27:27 Thy **r**, and thy fairs, thy merchandise, 1952
27:33 of the earth with the multitude of thy **r** 1952
28: 4 thine understanding thou hast gotten thee **r**, 2428
28: 5 by thy traffick hast thou increased thy **r**, 2428
28: 5 and thine heart is lifted up because of thy **r**: 2428
Da 11: 2 by his strength through his **r** he shall stir up 6239
11:13 years with a great army and with much **r**. 7399
11:24 among them the prey, and spoil, and **r**: 7399
11:28 shall he return *into* his land with great **r**; 7399
Mt 13:22 and the deceitfulness of **r**, choke the word, *4149*
Mk 4:19 and the deceitfulness of **r**, and the lusts of *4149*
10:23 How hardly shall they that have **r** enter into *5536*
10:24 how hard is it for them that trust in **r** to *5536*
Lk 8:14 with cares and **r** and pleasures of *this* life, *4149*
16:11 who will commit to your trust the true *r*? *NIG*
18:24 How hardly shall they that have **r** enter into *5536*
Ro 2: 4 Or despisest thou the **r** of his goodness and *4149*
9:23 And that he might make known the **r** of his *4149*
11:12 Now if the fall of them *be* the **r** of *4149*
11:12 the diminishing of them the **r** of *4149*
11:33 O the depth of the **r** both of the wisdom *4149*
2Co 8: 2 their deep poverty abounded unto the **r** of *4149*
Eph 1: 7 of sins, according to the **r** of his grace; *4149*
1:18 what the **r** of the glory of his inheritance in *4149*
2: 7 **r** of his grace in *his* kindness towards us *4149*
3: 8 the Gentiles the unsearchable **r** of Christ; *4149*
3:16 grant you, according to the **r** of his glory, *4149*
Php 4:19 according to his **r** in glory by Christ Jesus. *4149*
Col 1:27 **r** of the glory of this mystery among *4149*
2: 2 unto all **r** of the full assurance of *4149*
1Ti 6:17 nor trust in uncertain **r**, but in the living *4149*
Heb 11:26 Esteeming the reproach of Christ greater **r** *4149*
Jas 5: 2 Your **r** are corrupted, and your garments *4149*
Rev 5:12 and **r**, and wisdom, and strength, and *4149*
18:17 in one hour so great **r** is come to nought. *4149*

RICHLY (2) [RICH]
Col 3:16 Let the word of Christ dwell in you **r** in all *4146*
1Ti 6:17 who giveth us **r** all *things* to enjoy; *4146*

RICHLY ORNAMENTED ROBE See COAT OF MANY COLOURS; DIVERS; DIVERSE

RID (6) [RIDDANCE]
Ge 37:22 that he might **r** him out of their hands, 5337
Ex 6: 6 I will **r** you out of their bondage, and I will 5337
Lev 26: 6 I will **r** evil beasts out of the land, 7673
Ps 82: 4 **r** *them* out of the hand of the wicked. 5337
144: 7 **r** me, and deliver me out of great waters, 6475
144:11 **R** me, and deliver me from the hand of 6475

RIDDANCE (2) [RID]
Lev 23:22 thou shalt not **make clean r** of the corners 3615
Zep 1:18 for he shall make even a speedy **r** of all 3617

RIDDEN (1) [RIDE]
Nu 22:30 upon which thou hast **r** ever since *I was* 7392

RIDDLE (9)
Jdg 14:12 I will now put forth a **r** unto you: 2420
14:13 Put forth thy **r**, that we may hear it. 2420
14:14 they could not *in* three days expound the **r**. 2420
14:15 that he may declare unto us the **r**, lest we 2420
14:16 thou hast put forth a **r** unto the children of 2420
14:17 she told the **r** to the children of her people. 2420
14:18 with my heifer, ye had not found out my **r**. 2420
14:19 unto them which expounded the **r**. 2420
Eze 17: 2 **put forth a r**, and speak a parable 2330+2420

RIDDLES See DARK SAYINGS; DARK SPEECHES; HARD SENTENCES

RIDE (20) [RIDDEN, RIDER, RIDERS, RIDETH, RIDING, RODE]
Ge 41:43 he **made** him **to r** in the second chariot 7392
Dt 32:13 He **made** him **r** on the high places of 7392
Jdg 5:10 Speak, ye that **r on** white asses, ye that sit 7392
2Sa 16: 2 asses *be* for the king's household to **r on**; 7392
19:26 that I may **r** thereon, and go to the king; 7392
1Ki 1:33 **cause** Solomon my son **to r** upon mine 7392
1:38 **caused** Solomon **to r** upon king David's 7392
1:44 they have **caused** him **to r** upon the king's 7392
2Ki 10:16 So they **made** him **r** in his chariot. 7392
Job 30:22 thou **causest** me **to r** *upon it*, and 7392
Ps 45: 4 *in* thy majesty **r** prosperously because 7392
66:12 Thou hast **caused** men **to r** over our heads; 7392
Isa 30:16 and, We will **r** upon the swift; therefore 7392
58:14 I will **cause** thee **to r** upon the high places 7392
Jer 6:23 they **r** upon horses, set in array as men for 7392
50:42 they shall **r** upon horses, *every one* put in 7392
Hos 10:11 I will **make** Ephraim **to r**; Judah shall 7392
14: 3 we will not **r** upon horses: neither will we 7392
Hab 3: 8 that thou didst **r** upon thine horses *and* 7392
Hag 2:22 the chariots, and those that **r** in them; 7392

RIDER (7) [RIDE]
Ge 49:17 so that his **r** shall fall backward. 7392
Ex 15: 1 and his **r** hath he thrown into the sea. 7392
15:21 and his **r** hath he thrown into the sea. 7392
Job 39:18 on high, she scorneth the horse and his **r**. 7392
Jer 51:21 will I break in pieces the horse and his **r**; 7392
51:21 will I break in pieces the chariot and his **r**; 7392
Zec 12: 4 with astonishment, and his **r** with madness: 7392

RIDERS (5) [RIDE]
2Ki 18:23 if thou be able on thy part to set **r** upon 7392
Est 8:10 *and* **r** on mules, camels, *and* 7392
Isa 36: 8 if thou be able on thy part to set **r** upon 7392
Hag 2:22 the horses and their **r** shall come down, 7392
Zec 10: 5 and the **r** on horses shall be confounded. 7392

RIDETH (7) [RIDE]
Lev 15: 9 what saddle soever he **r** upon that hath 7392
Dt 33:26 *who* **r** *upon* the heaven in thy help, and 7392
Est 6: 8 the horse that the king **r** upon, and 7392
Ps 68: 4 extol him that **r** upon the heavens by his 7392
68:33 To him that **r** upon the heavens of heavens, 7392
Isa 19: 1 the LORD **r** upon a swift cloud, and 7392
Am 2:15 shall he that **r** the horse deliver himself. 7392

RIDGES (1)
Ps 65:10 *Thou* waterest the **r** thereof abundantly: 8525

RIDING (10) [RIDE]
Nu 22:22 Now he was **r** upon his ass, and his two 7392
2Ki 4:24 and go *forward;* slack not *thy* **r** for me, 7392
Jer 17:25 **r** in chariots and on horses, they, and 7392
22: 4 **r** in chariots and on horses, he, and 7392
Eze 23: 6 young men, horsemen **r** upon horses. 7392
23:12 most gorgeously, horsemen **r** upon horses, 7392
23:23 and renowned, all of them **r** upon horses. 7392
38:15 all of them **r** upon horses, a great company, 7392
Zec 1: 8 behold a man **r** upon a red horse, and 7392
9: 9 **r** upon an ass, and upon a colt the foal of an 7392

RIFLED (1)
Zec 14: 2 and the houses **r**, and the women ravished; 8155

RIGHT (359) [ARIGHT, BIRTHRIGHT, RIGHTEOUS, RIGHTEOUSLY, RIGHTEOUSNESS, RIGHTEOUSNESS', RIGHTEOUSNESSES, RIGHTLY, UNRIGHTEOUS]
Ge 13: 9 *take* the left hand, then I will **go to the r**; 3231

R

Ge 13: 9 or if *thou depart to* the **r hand**, then I will 3225
18:25 Shall not the Judge of all the earth do **r**? 4941
24:48 which had led me in the **r** way to take my 571
24:49 that I may turn to the **r hand**, or to the left. 3225
48:13 Ephraim in his **r hand** toward Israel's left 3225
48:13 in his left hand towards Israel's **r hand**, 3225
48:14 Israel stretched out his **r hand**, and laid *it* 3225
48:17 when Joseph saw that his father laid his **r** 3225
48:18 the firstborn; put thy **r hand** upon his head. 3225
Ex 14:22 *were* a wall unto them on their **r hand**, 3225
14:29 *were* a wall unto them on their **r hand**, 3225
15: 6 Thy **r hand**, O LORD, is become glorious 3225
15: 6 thy **r hand**, O LORD, hath dashed in 3225
15:12 Thou stretchedst out thy **r hand**, the earth 3225
15:26 wilt do that which is **r** in his sight, and 3477
29:20 and put *it* upon the tip of the *r* ear of Aaron, NIH
29:20 upon the tip of the **r** ear of his sons, and 3233
29:20 upon the thumb of their **r** hand, and 3233
29:20 upon the great toe of their **r** foot, and 3233
29:22 fat that *is* upon them, and the **r** shoulder; 3233
Lev 7:32 the **r** shoulder shall ye give unto the priest 3225
7:33 shall have the **r** shoulder for *his* part. 3225
8:23 put *it* upon the tip of Aaron's **r** ear, and 3233
8:23 upon the thumb of his **r** hand, and upon 3233
8:23 and upon the great toe of his **r** foot. 3233
8:24 put of the blood upon the tip of their **r** ear, 3233
8:24 upon the thumbs of their **r** hands, and 3233
8:24 and upon the great toes of their **r** feet: 3233
8:25 and their fat, and the **r** shoulder: 3225
8:26 *them* on the fat, and upon the **r** shoulder: 3225
9:21 the **r** shoulder Aaron waved *for* a wave 3225
14:14 the priest shall put *it* upon the tip of the **r** 3233
14:14 upon the thumb of his **r** hand, and upon 3233
14:14 and upon the great toe of his **r** foot: 3233
14:16 the priest shall dip his **r** finger in the oil 3233
14:17 tip of the **r** ear of him that is to be cleansed, 3233
14:17 upon the thumb of his **r** hand, and upon 3233
14:17 and upon the great toe of his **r** foot, 3233
14:25 put *it* upon the tip of the **r** ear of him that is 3233
14:25 upon the thumb of his **r** hand, and upon 3233
14:25 and upon the great toe of his **r** foot: 3233
14:27 the priest shall sprinkle with his **r** finger 3233
14:28 tip of the **r** ear of him that is to be cleansed, 3233
14:28 upon the thumb of his **r** hand, and upon 3233
14:28 and upon the great toe of his **r** foot, 3233
Nu 18:18 wave breast and as the **r** shoulder are thine. 3225
20:17 we will not turn *to* the **r hand** nor *to* 3225
22:26 *was* no way to turn *either to* the **r hand** 3225
27: 7 The daughters of Zelophehad speak **r**: 3651
Dt 2:27 I will neither turn *unto* the **r hand** nor *to* 3225
5:32 ye shall not turn aside *to* the **r hand** or 3225
6:18 thou shalt do *that which is* **r** and good in 3477
12: 8 every man whatsoever *is* **r** in his own eyes. 3477
12:25 when thou shalt do *that which is* **r** in 3477
12:28 and **r** in the sight of the LORD thy God. 3477
13:18 to do *that which is* **r** in the eyes of 3477
17:11 shew thee, *to* the **r hand**, nor *to* the left. 3225
17:20 *to* the **r hand**, or *to* the left: 3225
21: 9 when thou shalt do *that which is* **r** in 3477
21:17 of his strength; the **r** of the firstborn *is* his. 4941
28:14 *to* the **r hand**, or *to* the left, to go after 3225
32: 4 and without iniquity, just and **r** *is* he. 3477
33: 2 from his **r hand** *went* a fiery law for them. 3225
Jos 1: 7 turn not from it *to* the **r hand** or *to* the left, 3225
3:16 the people passed over **r against** Jericho. 5048
9:25 seemeth good and **r** unto thee to do unto us, 3477
17: 7 the border went *along* on the **r hand** unto 3225
23: 6 *ye* turn not aside therefrom *to* the **r hand** 3225
Jdg 3:16 he did gird it under his raiment upon his **r** 3225
3:21 took the dagger from his **r** thigh, and 3225
5:26 and her **r hand** to the workmen's hammer; 3225
7:20 the trumpets in their **r** hands to blow 3225
12: 6 for he could not frame to pronounce *it* **r**. 3651
16:29 of the one with his **r hand**, and of the other 3225
17: 6 every man did *that* which *was* **r** in his own 3477
21:25 every man did *that* which *was* **r** in his own 3477
Ru 4: 6 redeem thou my **r** to thyself; for I cannot 1353
1Sa 6:12 turned not aside *to* the **r hand** or *to* the left; 3225
11: 2 that *I* may thrust out all your **r** eyes, and 3225
12:23 but I will teach you the good and the **r** way: 3477
2Sa 2:19 in going he turned not to the **r hand** nor to 3225
2:21 Turn thee aside to thy **r hand** or to thy left, 3225
14:19 none can **turn to the r hand** or to the left 3231
15: 3 unto him, See, thy matters *are* good and **r**; 5228
16: 6 all the mighty *men were* on his **r hand** and 3225
19:28 What **r** therefore have I yet to cry any more 6666
19:43 and we have also more *r* in David than ye: NIH
20: 9 Joab took Amasa by the beard with the **r** 3225
24: 5 *on* the **r side** of the city that *lieth* in 3225
1Ki 2:19 king's mother; and she sat on his **r hand**. 3225
6: 8 chamber *was* in the **r** side of the house: 3233
7:21 he set up the **r** pillar, and called the name 3233
7:39 he put five bases on the **r** side of the house, 3225
7:39 he set the sea on the **r** side of the house 3233
7:49 five on the **r side**, and five on the left, 3225
11:33 to do *that* which *is* **r** in mine eyes, and 3477
11:38 do that *is* **r** in my sight, to keep my statutes 3477
14: 8 to do *that* only which *was* **r** in mine eyes; 3477
15: 5 Because David did *that* which *was* **r** in 3477
15:11 Asa did *that* which *was* **r** in the eyes of 3477
22:19 of heaven standing by him on his **r hand** 3225
22:43 doing *that* which *was* **r** in the eyes of 3477
2Ki 10:15 and said to him, Is thine heart **r**, 3477
10:30 in executing *that* which *is* **r** in mine eyes, 3477
11:11 from the **r** corner of the temple to the left 3233
12: 2 Jehoash did *that* which *was* **r** in the sight of 3477
12: 9 on the **r side** as one cometh *into* the house 3225
14: 3 he did *that* which *was* **r** in the sight of 3477
15: 3 he did *that* which *was* **r** in the sight of 3477
15:34 he did *that* which *was* **r** in the sight of 3477
16: 2 did not *that* which *was* **r** in the sight of 3477
17: 9 *were* not **r** against the LORD their God, 3651
18: 3 he did *that* which *was* **r** in the sight of 3477
22: 2 he did *that* which *was* **r** in the sight of 3477
22: 2 turned not aside *to* the **r hand** or *to* the left. 3225
2Ki 23:13 which *were* on the **r hand** of the mount of 3225
1Ch 6:39 brother Asaph, who stood on his **r hand**, 3225
12: 2 could **use** both **the r hand** and the left in 3231
13: 4 for the thing was **r** in the eyes of all 3474
2Ch 3:17 one on the **r hand**, and the other on the left; 3225
3:17 called the name of *that on* the **r hand** 3233
4: 6 put five on the **r hand**, and five on the left, 3225
4: 7 five on the **r hand**, and five on the left. 3225
4: 8 five on the **r side**, and five on the left. 3225
4:10 he set the sea on the **r** side of the east end, 3233
14: 2 and **r** in the eyes of the LORD his God: 3477
18:18 the host of heaven standing on his **r hand** 3225
20:32 doing *that* which *was* **r** in the sight of 3477
23:10 from the **r** side of the temple to the left side 3233
24: 2 Joash did *that* which *was* **r** in the sight of 3477
25: 2 he did *that* which *was* **r** in the sight of 3477
26: 4 he did *that* which *was* **r** in the sight of 3477
27: 2 he did *that* which *was* **r** in the sight of 3477
28: 1 he did not *that* which *was* **r** in the sight of 3477
29: 2 he did *that* which *was* **r** in the sight of 3477
31:20 wrought *that* which *was* good and **r** and 3477
34: 2 he did *that* which *was* **r** in the sight of 3477
34: 2 declined neither *to* the **r hand**, nor *to* 3225
Ezr 8:21 to seek of him a **r** way for us, and for our 3477
Ne 2:20 nor **r**, nor memorial, in Jerusalem. 6666
8: 4 and Hilkiah, and Maaseiah, on his **r hand**; 3225
9:13 gavest them **r** judgments, and true laws, 3477
9:33 for thou hast done **r**, but we have done 571
12:31 whereof *one* went on the **r hand** upon 3225
Est 8: 5 the thing **seem r** before the king, and I *be* 3787
Job 6:25 How forcible are **r** words! but what doth 3476
23: 9 *him:* he hideth *himself* on the **r hand**, 3225
30:12 Upon *my* **r hand** rise the youth; they push 3225
33:27 perverted *that which was* **r**, and it profited 3477
34: 6 Should I lie against my **r**? my wound *is* 4941
34:17 Shall even he that hateth **r** govern? and wilt 4941
34:23 For he will not lay upon man more *than r*; NIH
35: 2 Thinkest thou this to be **r**, *that* thou saidst, 4941
36: 6 life of the wicked: but giveth **r** to the poor. 4941
40:14 thee that thine own **r hand** can save thee. 3225
42: 7 have not spoken of me *the thing that is* **r**, 3559
42: 8 have not spoken of me *the thing which is* **r**, 3559
Ps 9: 4 For thou hast maintained my **r** and 4941
9: 4 thou satest in the throne judging **r**. 6664
16: 8 because *he is* at my **r hand**, I shall not be 3225
16:11 at thy **r hand** *there are* pleasures for 3225
17: 1 Hear the **r**, O LORD, attend unto my cry, 6664
17: 7 O thou that savest by thy **r hand** them 3225
18:35 thy **r hand** hath holden me up, and 3225
19: 8 The statutes of the LORD *are* **r**, 3477
20: 6 with the saving strength of his **r hand**. 3225
21: 8 thy **r hand** shall find out those that hate 3225
26:10 and their **r hand** is full *of* bribes. 3225
33: 4 For the word of the LORD *is* **r**; and all his 3477
44: 3 thy **r hand**, and thine arm, and the light of 3225
45: 4 thy **r hand** shall teach thee terrible *things*. 3225
45: 6 the sceptre of thy kingdom *is* a **r** sceptre. 4334
45: 9 **r hand** did stand the queen in gold of 3225
46: 5 God shall help her, *and that* **r** early. 6437
48:10 thy **r hand** is full *of* righteousness. 3225
51:10 O God; and renew a **r** spirit within me. 3559
60: 5 save *with* thy **r hand**, and hear me. 3225
63: 8 hard after thee: thy **r hand** upholdeth me. 3225
73:23 thou hast holden *me* by my **r** hand. 3225
74:11 thou thy hand, even thy **r hand**? 3225
77:10 *I will remember* the years of the **r hand** of 3225
78:37 For their heart was not **r** with him, 3559
78:54 *which* his **r hand** had purchased. 3225
80:15 the vineyard which thy **r hand** hath 3225
80:17 thy hand be upon the man of thy **r hand**, 3225
89:13 strong is thy hand, *and* high is thy **r hand**. 3225
89:25 also in the sea, and his **r hand** in the rivers. 3225
89:42 Thou hast set up the **r hand** of his 3225
91: 7 at thy side, and ten thousand at thy **r hand**; 3225
98: 1 he hath done marvellous *things:* his **r hand**, 3225
107: 7 he led them forth by the **r** way, that *they* 3477
108: 6 save *with* thy **r hand**, and answer me. 3225
109: 6 over him: and let Satan stand at his **r hand**. 3225
109:31 For he shall stand at the **r hand** of the poor, 3225
110: 1 said unto my Lord, Sit thou at my **r hand**, 3225
110: 5 The Lord at thy **r hand** shall strike through 3225
118:15 the **r hand** of the LORD doeth valiantly. 3225
118:16 The **r hand** of the LORD is exalted: 3225
118:16 the **r hand** of the LORD doeth valiantly. 3225
119:75 that thy judgments *are* **r**, and *that* thou *in* 6664
119:128 **esteem** all *thy* precepts concerning all *things*
to be r; 3474
121: 5 the LORD *is* thy shade upon thy **r** hand. 3225
137: 5 let my **r hand** forget *her cunning*. 3225
138: 7 and thy **r hand** shall save me. 3225
139:10 lead me, and thy **r hand** shall hold me. 3225
139:14 and *that* my soul knoweth **r well**. 3966
140:12 cause of the afflicted, *and the* **r** of the poor. 4941
142: 4 I looked *on my* **r hand**, and beheld, but 3225
144: 8 their **r hand** *is* a right hand of falsehood. 3225
144: 8 their right hand *is* a **r hand** of falsehood. 3225
144:11 their **r hand** *is* a right hand of falsehood: 3225
144:11 their right hand *is* a **r hand** of falsehood: 3225
Pr 3:16 Length of days *is* in her **r hand**; and in her 3225
4:11 way of wisdom; I have led thee in **r** paths. 3476
4:25 Let thine eyes look **r on**, and 5227+3807.1
4:27 Turn not *to* the **r hand** nor *to* the left: 3225
8: 6 the opening of my lips *shall be* **r things**. 4339
8: 9 and **r** to them that find knowledge. 3477
9:15 To call passengers who **go r** *on* their ways: 3474
12: 5 The thoughts of the righteous *are* **r**: *but* 4941
12:15 The way of a fool *is* **r** in his own eyes: but 3477
14:12 There is a way which seemeth **r** unto a 3477
16: 8 than great revenues without **r**. 4941
16:13 of kings; and *they* love him that speaketh **r**. 3477
16:25 There is a way that seemeth **r** unto a man, 3477
20:11 his work *be* pure, and whether *it be* **r**. 3477
21: 2 Every way of a man *is* **r** in his own eyes: 3477
21: 8 strange: but *as for* the pure, his work *is* **r**. 3477
23:16 shall rejoice, when thy lips speak **r things**. 4339
Pr 24:26 *Every man* shall kiss *his* lips that giveth a **r** 5228
27:16 the wind, and the ointment of his **r hand**, 3225
Ecc 4: 4 I considered all travail, and every **r** work, 3788
10: 2 A wise *man's* heart *is* at his **r hand**; but 3225
SS 2: 6 my head, and his **r hand** doth embrace me. 3225
8: 3 and his **r hand** should embrace me. 3225
Isa 9:20 he shall snatch on the **r hand**, and 3225
10: 2 to take away the **r** from the poor of my 4941
30:10 Prophesy not unto us **r** *things*, speak unto 5229
30:21 when ye **turn to the r hand**, and when ye 541
32: 7 even when the needy speaketh **r**. 4941
41:10 I will uphold thee with the **r hand** of my 3225
41:13 I the LORD thy God will hold thy **r hand**, 3225
44:20 nor say, *Is there* not a lie in my **r hand**? 3225
45: 1 to Cyrus, whose **r hand** I have holden, to 3225
45:19 I declare **things that are r**. 4339
48:13 and my **r hand** hath spanned the heavens: 3225
54: 3 For thou shalt break forth *on* the **r hand** 3225
62: 8 The LORD hath sworn by his **r hand**, and 3225
63:12 That led *them* by the **r hand** of Moses *with* 3225
Jer 2:21 planted thee a noble vine, wholly a **r** seed: 571
5:28 and the **r** of the needy do they not judge. 4941
17:11 *so* he that getteth riches, and not by **r**, 4941
17:16 out of my lips was **r before** thee. 5227+6440
22:24 of Judah were the signet upon my **r** hand, 3225
23:10 their course is evil, and their force *is* not **r**. 3651
32: 7 for the **r** of redemption *is* thine to buy *it*. 4941
32: 8 for the **r** of inheritance *is* thine, and 4941
34:15 now turned, and had done **r** in my sight, 3477
49: 5 be driven out every man **r forth**; 6440+3807.1
La 2: 3 he hath drawn back his **r hand** from before 3225
2: 4 *he* stood *with* his **r hand** as an adversary, 3225
3:35 To turn aside the **r** of a man before the face 4941
Eze 1:10 a man, and the face of a lion, on the **r side**: 3225
4: 6 lie again on thy **r** side, and thou shalt bear 3233
10: 3 Now the cherubims stood on the **r side** of 3225
16:46 that dwelleth at thy **r hand**, *is* Sodom and 3225
18: 5 be just, and do that which is lawful and **r**, 6666
18:19 son hath done that which is lawful and **r**, 6666
18:21 do that which is lawful and **r**, he shall 6666
18:27 doeth that which is lawful and **r**, he shall 6666
21:16 other, *either* **on the r hand**, *or* on the left, 3231
21:22 At his **r hand** was the divination for 3225
21:27 it shall be no *more*, until he come whose **r** 4941
33:14 his sin, and do that which is lawful and **r**; 6666
33:16 he hath done that which is lawful and **r**; 6666
33:19 do that which is lawful and **r**, he shall live 6666
39: 3 will cause thine arrows to fall out of thy **r** 3225
47: 1 from under from the **r** side of the house, 3233
47: 2 behold, there ran out waters on the **r** side. 3233
Da 12: 7 when he held up his **r hand** and his left 3225
Hos 14: 9 for the ways of the LORD *are* **r**, and 3477
Am 3:10 For they know not to do **r**, saith 5229
5:12 turn aside the poor in the gate *from their r*. NIH
Jnh 4:11 that cannot discern between their **r hand** 3225
Hab 2:16 the cup of the LORD'S **r hand** shall be 3225
Zec 3: 1 Satan standing at his **r hand** to resist him. 3225
4: 3 one upon the **r** *side* of the bowl, and 3225
4:11 What *are* these two olive trees upon the **r** 3225
11:17 *shall be* upon his arm, and upon his **r** eye: 3225
11:17 and his **r** eye shall be utterly darkened. 3225
12: 6 round about, on the **r hand** and on the left: 3225
Mal 3: 5 that turn aside the stranger *from his r*, and NIH
Mt 5:29 And if thy **r** eye offend thee, pluck it out, *1188*
5:30 And if thy **r** hand offend thee, cut it off, *1188*
5:39 whosoever shall smite thee on thy **r** cheek, *1188*
6: 3 let not thy left hand know what thy **r hand** *1188*
20: 4 and whatsoever is **r** I will give you. *1342*
20: 7 and whatsoever is **r**, *that* shall ye receive. *1342*
20:21 the one on thy **r hand**, and the other on *1188*
20:23 am baptized *with:* but to sit on my **r hand**, *1188*
22:44 said unto my Lord, Sit thou on my **r hand**, *1188*
25:33 And he shall set the sheep on his **r hand**, *1188*
25:34 shall the King say unto them on his **r hand**, *1188*
26:64 Son of man sitting on the **r hand** of power, *1188*
27:29 *it* upon his head, and a reed in his **r hand**: *1188*
27:38 one on the **r hand**, and another on the left. *1188*
Mk 5:15 sitting, and clothed, and **in his r mind**: *4993*
10:37 one on thy **r hand**, and the other on thy left *1188*
10:40 But to sit on my **r hand** and on my left *1188*
12:36 said to my Lord, Sit thou on my **r hand**, *1188*
14:62 Son of man sitting on the **r hand** of power, *1188*
15:27 the one on *his* **r hand**, and the other on his *1188*
16: 5 they saw a young man sitting on the **r side**, *1188*
16:19 into heaven, and sat on the **r hand** of God. *1188*
Lk 1:11 on the **r side** of the altar of incense. *1188*
6: 6 there was a man whose **r** hand was *1188*
8:35 feet of Jesus, clothed, and **in his r mind**: *4993*
10:28 he said unto him, Thou hast answered **r**: *3723*
12:57 even of yourselves judge ye not what *is* **r**? *1342*
20:42 said to my Lord, Sit thou on my **r hand**, *1188*
22:50 of the high priest, and cut off his **r** ear. *1188*
22:69 man sit on the **r hand** of the power of God. *1188*
23:33 one on the **r hand**, and the other on the left. *1188*
Jn 18:10 high priest's servant, and cut off his **r** ear. *1188*
21: 6 Cast the net on the **r** side of the ship, and *1188*
Ac 2:25 for he is on my **r hand**, that I should not be *1188*
2:33 Therefore being by the **r hand** of God *1188*
2:34 said unto my Lord, Sit thou on my **r hand**, *1188*
3: 7 And he took him by the **r** hand, and lift *him* *1188*
4:19 Whether it be **r** in the sight of God to *1342*
5:31 Him hath God exalted with his **r hand** *to* *1188*
7:55 and Jesus standing on the **r hand** of God, *1188*
7:56 the Son of man standing on the **r hand** of *1188*
8:21 for thy heart is not **r** in the sight of God. *2117*
13:10 wilt thou not cease to pervert the **r** ways of *2117*
Ro 8:34 *again*, who is even at the **r hand** of God, *1188*
2Co 6: 7 the armour of righteousness on the **r hand** *1188*
Gal 2: 9 and Barnabas the **r hands** of fellowship; *1188*
Eph 1:20 set *him* at his own **r hand** in the heavenly *1188*
6: 1 obey your parents in the Lord: for this is **r**. *1342*
Col 3: 1 where Christ sitteth on the **r hand** of God. *1188*
Heb 1: 3 sat down on the **r hand** of the Majesty on *1188*
1:13 Sit on my **r hand**, until I make thine *1188*
8: 1 who is set on the **r hand** of the throne of *1188*

Heb 10:12 for ever, sat down on the **r hand** of God; *1188*
12: 2 is set down at the **r hand** of the throne of *1188*
13:10 whereof they have no **r** to eat which serve *1849*
1Pe 3:22 into heaven, and is on the **r hand** of God; *1188*
2Pe 2:15 Which have forsaken the **r** way, and *2117*
Rev 1:16 And he had in his **r** hand seven stars: and *1188*
1:17 And he laid his **r** hand upon me, *1188*
1:20 stars which thou sawest in my **r hand**, *1188*
2: 1 that holdeth the seven stars in his **r hand**, *1188*
5: 1 And I saw in the **r hand** of him that sat on *1188*
5: 7 took the book out of the **r hand** of him that *1188*
10: 2 and he set his **r** foot upon the sea, and *1188*
13:16 to receive a mark in their **r** hand, or in their *1188*
22:14 that they may have **r** to the tree of life, and *1849*

RIGHTEOUS (238) [RIGHT]

Ge 7: 1 for thee have I seen **r** before me in this 6662
18:23 Wilt thou also destroy the **r** with 6662
18:24 Peradventure there be fifty **r** within 6662
18:24 not spare the place for the fifty **r** that *are* 6662
18:25 this manner, to slay the **r** with the wicked: 6662
18:25 that the **r** should be as the wicked, that be 6662
18:26 If I find in Sodom fifty **r** within the city, 6662
18:28 there shall lack five of the fifty **r**: 6662
20: 4 Lord, wilt thou slay also a **r** nation? 6662
38:26 and said, She hath been more **r** than I; 6663
Ex 9:27 the LORD *is* **r**, and I and my people *are* 6662
23: 7 and the innocent and **r** slay thou not: 6662
23: 8 the wise, and perverteth the words of the **r**. 6662
Nu 23:10 Let me die the death of the **r**, and let my 3477
Dt 4: 8 and judgments *so* **r** as all this law, 6662
16:19 of the wise, and pervert the words of the **r**. 6662
25: 1 they shall justify the **r**, and condemn 6662
Jdg 5:11 they rehearse the **r acts** of the LORD, 6666
5:11 *even* the **r acts** *towards the inhabitants* of 6666
1Sa 12: 7 the LORD of all the **r acts** of the LORD, 6666
24:17 he said to David, Thou *art* more **r** than I: 6662
2Sa 4:11 when wicked men have slain a **r** person in 6662
1Ki 2:32 who fell upon two men more **r** and 6662
8:32 justifying the **r**, to give him according to 6662
2Ki 10: 9 stood, and said to all the people, Ye *be* **r**: 6662
2Ch 6:23 by justifying the **r**, by giving him according 6662
12: 6 and they said, The LORD *is* **r**. 6662
Ezr 9:15 O LORD God of Israel, thou *art* **r**: for we 6662
Ne 9: 8 hast performed thy words; for thou *art* **r**: 6662
Job 4: 7 or where were the **r** cut off? 3477
9:15 Whom, though I were **r**, *yet* would I not 6663
10:15 and *if* I be **r**, *yet* will I not lift up my head. 6663
15:14 *is* born of a woman, that he should be **r**? 6663
17: 9 The **r** also shall hold on his way, and 6662
22: 3 pleasure to the Almighty, that thou art **r**? 6663
22:19 The **r** see *it*, and are glad: and the innocent 6662
23: 7 There the **r** *might* dispute with him; so 3477
32: 1 because he *was* **r** in his own eyes. 6662
34: 5 For Job hath said, I am **r**: and God hath 6663
35: 7 If thou be **r**, what givest thou him? or 6663
36: 7 He withdraweth not his eyes from the **r**: but 6662
40: 8 thou condemn me, that thou mayest be **r**? 6663
Ps 1: 5 nor sinners in the congregation of the **r**. 6662
1: 6 For the LORD knoweth the way of the **r**: 6662
5:12 For thou, LORD, wilt bless the **r**; 6662
7: 9 for the **r** God trieth the hearts and reins. 6662
7:11 God judgeth the **r**, and God is angry *with* 6662
11: 3 be destroyed, what can the **r** do? 6662
11: 5 The LORD trieth the **r**: but the wicked 6662
11: 7 For the **r** LORD loveth righteousness; 6662
14: 5 for God *is* in the generation of the **r**. 6662
19: 9 of the LORD *are* true *and* **r** altogether. 6663
31:18 and contemptuously against the **r**. 6662
32:11 Be glad in the LORD, and rejoice, ye **r**: 6662
33: 1 Rejoice in the LORD, O ye **r**: *for* praise is 6662
34:15 The eyes of the LORD *are* upon the **r**, and 6662
34:17 *The* **r** cry, and the LORD heareth, and NIH
34:19 Many *are* the afflictions of the **r**: but 6662
34:21 and they that hate the **r** shall be desolate. 6662
35:27 and be glad, that favour my **r cause**: 6664
37:16 A little that a **r** *man* hath *is* better than 6662
37:17 be broken: but the LORD upholdeth the **r**. 6662
37:21 but the **r** sheweth mercy, and giveth. 6662
37:25 yet have I not seen the **r** forsaken, nor his 6662
37:29 The **r** shall inherit the land, and 6662
37:30 The mouth of the **r** speaketh wisdom, and 6662
37:32 The wicked watcheth the **r**, and seeketh to 6662
37:39 the salvation of the **r** *is* of the LORD: 6662
52: 6 The **r** also shall see, and fear, and 6662
55:22 he shall never suffer the **r** to be moved. 6662
58:10 The **r** shall rejoice when he seeth 6662
58:11 shall say, Verily *there is* a reward for the **r**: 6662
64:10 The **r** shall be glad in the LORD, and 6662
68: 3 let the **r** be glad; let them rejoice before 6662
69:28 of the living, and not be written with the **r**. 6662
72: 7 In his days shall the **r** flourish; and 6662
75:10 *but* the horns of the **r** shall be exalted. 6662
92:12 The **r** shall flourish like the palm tree: 6662
94:21 together against the soul of the **r**, 6662
97:11 Light is sown for the **r**, and gladness for 6662
97:12 Rejoice in the LORD, ye **r**; and 6662
107:42 The **r** shall see *it*, and rejoice: and 3477
112: 4 *is* gracious, and full of compassion, and **r**. 6662
112: 6 the **r** shall be in everlasting remembrance. 6662
116: 5 Gracious *is* the LORD, and **r**; yea, 6662
118:15 and salvation *is* in the tabernacles of the **r**: 6662
118:20 of the LORD, into which the **r** shall enter. 6662
119: 7 when I shall have learned thy **r** judgments. 6664
119:62 unto thee because of thy **r** judgments. 6664
119:106 I will perform *it*, that *I* will keep thy **r** 6664
119:137 **R** *art* thou, O LORD, and upright *are* thy 6662
119:138 testimonies *that* thou hast commanded *are* **r** 6664
119:160 every one of thy **r** judgments *endureth* for 6664
119:164 do I praise thee because of thy **r** judgments. 6664
125: 3 wicked shall not rest upon the lot of the **r**; 6662
125: 3 lest the **r** put forth their hands unto iniquity. 6662
Ps 129: 4 The LORD *is* **r**: he hath cut asunder 6662
140:13 Surely the **r** shall give thanks unto thy 6662
141: 5 Let the **r** smite me; *it shall be* a kindness: 6662
142: 7 the **r** shall compass me about; for thou shalt 6662
145:17 The LORD *is* **r** in all his ways, and 6662
146: 8 are bowed down: the LORD loveth the **r**: 6662
Pr 2: 7 He layeth up sound wisdom for the **r**: *he is* 3477
2:20 of good *men*, and keep the paths of the **r**. 6662
3:32 to the LORD: but his secret *is* with the **r**. 3477
10: 3 The LORD will not suffer the soul of the **r** 6662
10:11 The mouth of a **r** *man is* a well of life: but 6662
10:16 The labour of the **r** *tendeth* to life: the fruit 6662
10:21 The lips of the **r** feed many: but fools die 6662
10:24 but the desire of the **r** shall be granted. 6662
10:25 but the **r** *is* an everlasting foundation. 6662
10:28 The hope of the **r** *shall be* gladness: but 6662
10:30 The **r** shall never be removed: but 6662
10:32 The lips of the **r** know what is acceptable: 6662
11: 8 The **r** is delivered out of trouble, and 6662
11:10 When it goeth well with the **r**, the city 6662
11:21 but the seed of the **r** shall be delivered. 6662
11:23 The desire of the **r** *is* only good: *but* 6662
11:28 but the **r** shall flourish as a branch. 6662
11:30 The fruit of the **r** *is* a tree of life; and 6662
11:31 the **r** shall be recompensed in the earth: 6662
12: 3 but the root of the **r** shall not be moved. 6662
12: 5 The thoughts of the **r** *are* right: *but* 6662
12: 7 *are* not: but the house of the **r** shall stand. 6662
12:10 A **r** *man* regardeth the life of his beast: but 6662
12:12 but the root of the **r** yieldeth *fruit*. 6662
12:26 The **r** *is* more excellent than his neighbour: 6662
13: 5 A **r** *man* hateth lying: but a wicked *man* is 6662
13: 9 The light of the **r** rejoiceth: but the lamp of 6662
13:21 but to the **r** good shall be repayed. 6662
13:25 The **r** eateth to the satisfying of his soul: 6662
14: 9 at sin: but among the **r** *there is* favour. 3477
14:19 and the wicked at the gates of the **r**. 6662
14:32 but the **r** hath hope in his death. 6662
15: 6 *In* the house of the **r** *is* much treasure: but 6662
15:19 but the way of the **r** *is* made plain. 3477
15:28 The heart of the **r** studieth to answer: but 6662
15:29 but he heareth the prayer of the **r**. 6662
16:13 **R** lips *are* the delight of kings; and 6664
18: 5 the wicked, to overthrow the **r** in judgment. 6662
18:10 the **r** runneth into it, and is safe. 6662
21:12 The **r** *man* wisely considereth the house of 6662
21:18 The wicked *shall be* a ransom for the **r**, and 6662
21:26 day long: but the **r** giveth and spareth not. 6662
23:24 The father of the **r** shall greatly rejoice: 6662
24:15 wicked *man*, against the dwelling of the **r**; 6662
24:24 He that saith unto the wicked, Thou *art* **r**; 6662
25:26 A **r** *man* falling down before the wicked *is* 6662
28: 1 man pursueth: but the **r** are bold as a lion. 6662
28:10 Whoso causeth the **r** to go astray in an evil 3477
28:12 When **r** *men* do rejoice, *there is* great glory: 6662
28:28 but when they perish, the **r** increase. 6662
29: 2 When the **r** are in authority, the people 6662
29: 6 *is* a snare: but the **r** doth sing and rejoice. 6662
29: 7 The **r** considereth the cause of the poor: *but* 6662
29:16 but the **r** shall see their fall. 6662
Ecc 3:17 God shall judge the **r** and the wicked: 6662
7:16 Be not **r** over much; neither make thyself 6662
8:14 it happeneth according to the work of the **r**: 6662
9: 1 that the **r**, and the wise, and their works, 6662
9: 2 *there is* one event to the **r**, and to 6662
Isa 3:10 Say ye *to* the **r**, that *it shall be* well *with* 6662
5:23 take away the righteousness of the **r** from 6662
24:16 have we heard songs, *even* glory to the **r**. 6662
26: 2 that the **r** nation which keepeth the truth 6662
41: 2 Who raised up the **r** *man* from the east, 6664
41:26 beforetime, that we may say, *He is* **r**? yea, 6662
53:11 by his knowledge shall my **r** servant justify 6662
57: 1 The **r** perisheth, and no man layeth *it* to 6662
57: 1 none considering that the **r** is taken away 6662
60:21 Thy people also *shall be* all **r**: they shall 6662
Jer 12: 1 **R** *art* thou, O LORD, when I plead with 6662
20:12 that triest the **r**, *and* seest the reins and 6662
23: 5 that I will raise unto David a **r** Branch, and 6662
La 1:18 The LORD *is* **r**; for I have rebelled 6662
Eze 3:20 When a **r** *man* doth turn from his 6662
3:21 Nevertheless if thou warn the **r** *man*, that 6662
3:21 warn the righteous *man*, that the **r** sin not, 6662
13:22 lies *ye* have made the heart of the **r** sad, 6662
16:52 they are more **r** than thou: yea, be thou 6663
18:20 the righteousness of the **r** shall be upon 6662
18:24 when the **r** turneth away from his 6662
18:26 When a **r** *man* turneth away from his 6662
21: 3 will cut off from thee the **r** and the wicked. 6662
21: 4 then that I will cut off from thee the **r** and 6662
23:45 *the* **r** men, they shall judge them after 6662
33:12 The righteousness of the **r** shall not deliver 6662
33:12 neither shall the **r** be able to live for his 6662
33:13 When I shall say to the **r**, *that* he shall 6662
33:18 When the **r** turneth from his righteousness, 6662
Da 9:14 for the LORD our God *is* **r** in all his 6662
Am 2: 6 because they sold the **r** for silver, and 6662
Hab 1: 4 for the wicked doth compass about the **r**; 6662
1:13 devoureth *the man that is* more **r** than he? 6662
Mal 3:18 and discern between the **r** and the wicked, 6662
Mt 9:13 for I am not come to call *the* **r**, but *1342*
10:41 he that receiveth a **r** *man* in the name of a *1342*
10:41 **r** *man* shall receive a righteous *man's* *1342*
10:41 *man* shall receive a **r** *man's* reward. *1342*
13:17 **r** *men* have desired to see *those things* *1342*
13:43 Then shall the **r** shine forth as the sun in *1342*
23:28 so ye also outwardly appear **r** unto men, *1342*
23:29 and garnish the sepulchres of the **r**, *1342*
23:35 That upon you may come all the **r** blood *1342*
23:35 from the blood of **r** Abel unto the blood of *1342*
25:37 Then shall the **r** answer him, saying, Lord, *1342*
25:46 but the **r** into life eternal. *1342*
Mk 2:17 I came not to call *the* **r**, but sinners to *1342*
Lk 1: 6 And they were both **r** before God, *1342*
5:32 I came not to call *the* **r**, but sinners to *1342*
18: 9 trusted in themselves that they were **r**, *1342*
Lk 23:47 saying, Certainly this was a **r** man. *1342*
Jn 7:24 to the appearance, but judge **r** judgment. *1342*
17:25 O **r** Father, the world hath not known thee: *1342*
Ro 2: 5 and revelation of the **r judgment** of God; *1341*
3:10 it is written, There is none **r**, no, not one: *1342*
5: 7 For scarcely for a **r** *man* will one die: *1342*
5:19 the obedience of one shall many be made **r**. *1342*
2Th 1: 5 *Which is* a manifest token of the **r** *1342*
1: 6 Seeing *it is* a **r** *thing* with God to *1342*
1Ti 1: 9 that the law is not made for a **r** *man*, but *1342*
2Ti 4: 8 which the Lord, the **r** judge, shall give me *1342*
Heb 11: 4 by which he obtained witness that he was **r**, *1342*
Jas 5:16 The effectual fervent prayer of a **r** *man* *1342*
1Pe 3:12 For the eyes of the Lord *are* over the **r**, and *1342*
4:18 And if the **r** scarcely be saved, where shall *1342*
2Pe 2: 8 (For *that* **r** *man* dwelling among them, *1342*
2: 8 vexed *his* **r** soul from day to day with *their* *1342*
1Jn 2: 1 with the Father, Jesus Christ *the* **r**: *1342*
2:29 If ye know that he is **r**, ye know that every *1342*
3: 7 he that doeth righteousness is **r**, even as he *1342*
3: 7 righteousness is righteous, even as he is **r**. *1342*
3:12 own works were evil, and his brother's **r**. *1342*
Rev 16: 5 Thou art **r**, O Lord, which art, and wast, *1342*
16: 7 true and **r** *are* thy judgments. *1342*
19: 2 For true and **r** *are* his judgments: for he *1342*
22:11 and *he that is* **r**, let him be righteous still: *1342*
22:11 and *he that is* righteous, let him be **r** still: *1344*

RIGHTEOUSLY (8) [RIGHT]

Dt 1:16 judge **r** between every man and his brother, 6664
Ps 67: 4 for thou shalt judge the people **r**, and 4334
96:10 he shall judge the people **r**. 4339+871.1
Pr 31: 9 judge **r**, and plead the cause of the poor and 6664
Isa 33:15 He that walketh **r**, and speaketh uprightly; 6666
Jer 11:20 that judgest **r**, that triest the reins and 6664
Tit 2:12 **r**, and godly, in *this* present world; *1346*
1Pe 2:23 committed *himself* to him that judgeth **r**: *1346*

RIGHTEOUSNESS (302) [RIGHT]

Ge 15: 6 the LORD; and he counted it to him *for* **r**. 6666
30:33 So shall my **r** answer for me in time to 6666
Lev 19:15 *but* in **r** shalt thou judge thy neighbour. 6664
Dt 6:25 it shall be our **r**, if we observe to do all 6666
9: 4 For my **r** the LORD hath brought me in to 6666
9: 5 Not for thy **r**, or for the uprightness of thine 6666
9: 6 not this good land to possess it for thy **r**; 6666
24:13 it shall be **r** unto thee before the LORD 6666
33:19 there they shall offer sacrifices of **r**: 6664
1Sa 26:23 The LORD render to every man his **r** and 6666
2Sa 22:21 LORD rewarded me according to my **r**: 6666
22:25 hath recompensed me according to my **r**; 6666
1Ki 3: 6 in **r**, and in uprightness of heart with thee; 6666
8:32 to give him according to his **r**. 6666
2Ch 6:23 by giving him according to his **r**. 6666
Job 6:29 be iniquity; yea, return again, my **r** *is* in it. 6664
8: 6 make the habitation of thy **r** prosperous. 6664
27: 6 My **r** I hold fast, and will not let it go: 6666
29:14 I put on **r**, and it clothed me: my judgment 6664
33:26 with joy: for he will render unto man his **r**. 6666
35: 2 *that* thou saidst, My **r** *is* more than God's? 6664
35: 8 and thy **r** *may profit* the son of man. 6666
36: 3 from afar, and will ascribe **r** to my Maker. 6664
Ps 4: 1 Hear me when I call, O God of my **r**: 6664
4: 5 Offer the sacrifices of **r**, and put your trust 6664
5: 8 in thy **r** because of mine enemies; 6666
7: 8 according to my **r**, and according to mine 6664
7:17 I will praise the LORD according to his **r**: 6664
9: 8 he shall judge the world in **r**, he shall 6664
11: 7 For the righteous LORD loveth **r**; 6666
15: 2 worketh **r**, and speaketh the truth in his 6664
17:15 *As for* me, I will behold thy face in **r**: 6664
18:20 LORD rewarded me according to my **r**; 6664
18:24 recompensed me according to my **r**, 6664
22:31 shall declare his **r** unto a people that *shall* 6666
23: 3 he leadeth me in the paths of **r** for his 6664
24: 5 and **r** from the God of his salvation. 6666
31: 1 me never be ashamed: deliver me in thy **r**. 6666
33: 5 He loveth **r** and judgment: the earth is full 6666
35:24 O LORD my God, according to thy **r**; 6664
35:28 my tongue shall speak of thy **r** *and* of thy 6664
36: 6 Thy **r** *is* like the great mountains; 6666
36:10 know thee; and thy **r** to the upright in heart. 6666
37: 6 he shall bring forth thy **r** as the light, and 6664
40: 9 I have preached **r** in the great congregation: 6664
40:10 I have not hid thy **r** within my heart; I have 6666
45: 4 of truth and meekness *and* **r**; 6664
45: 7 Thou lovest **r**, and hatest wickedness: 6664
48:10 ends of the earth: thy right hand is full *of* **r**. 6664
50: 6 the heavens shall declare his **r**: for God *is* 6664
51:14 *and* my tongue shall sing aloud of thy **r**. 6666
51:19 thou be pleased with the sacrifices of **r**, 6664
52: 3 than good; *and* lying rather than to speak **r**. 6664
58: 1 Do ye indeed speak **r**, O congregation? 6664
65: 5 *By* terrible *things* in **r** wilt thou answer us, 6664
69:27 and let them not come into thy **r**. 6666
71: 2 Deliver me in thy **r**, and cause me to 6666
71:15 My mouth shall shew forth thy **r** *and* 6666
71:16 I will make mention of thy **r**, *even* of thine 6666
71:19 Thy **r** also, O God, *is* very high, who hast 6666
71:24 My tongue also shall talk of thy **r** all 6666
72: 1 O God, and thy **r** unto the king's son. 6666
72: 2 He shall judge thy people with **r**, and 6664
72: 3 to the people, and the little hills, by **r**. 6666
85:10 **r** and peace have kissed *each other*. 6664
85:11 and **r** shall look down from heaven. 6664
85:13 **R** shall go before him; and shall set *us* in 6664
88:12 and thy **r** in the land of forgetfulness? 6666
89:16 the day: and in thy **r** shall they be exalted. 6666
94:15 judgment shall return unto **r**: and all 6664
96:13 he shall judge the world with **r**, and 6664
97: 2 **r** and judgment *are* the habitation of his 6664

R

Ps 97: 6 The heavens declare his **r**, and all 6664
98: 2 his **r** hath he openly shewed in the sight of 6666
98: 9 with **r** shall he judge the world, and 6664
99: 4 thou executest judgment and **r** in Jacob. 6666
103: 6 The LORD executeth **r** and judgment for 6666
103:17 fear him, and his **r** unto children's children; 6666
106: 3 *and* he that doeth **r** at all times. 6666
106:31 *that* was counted unto him for **r** unto all 6666
111: 3 and glorious: and his **r** endureth for ever. 6666
112: 3 *be* in his house: and his **r** endureth for ever. 6666
112: 9 given to the poor; his **r** endureth for ever; 6666
118:19 Open to me the gates of **r**: I will go into 6664
119:40 after thy precepts: quicken me in thy **r**. 6666
119:123 for thy salvation, and for the word of thy **r**. 6664
119:142 Thy **r** *is* an everlasting righteousness, and 6666
119:142 Thy righteousness *is* an everlasting **r**, and 6664
119:144 The **r** of thy testimonies *is* everlasting: give 6664
119:172 thy word: for all thy commandments *are* **r**. 6664
132: 9 Let thy priests be clothed *with* **r**; and let thy 6664
143: 1 in thy faithfulness answer me, *and* in thy **r**. 6666
145: 7 thy great goodness, and shall sing of thy **r**. 6666
Pr 2: 9 shalt thou understand **r**, and judgment, 6664
8: 8 All the words of my mouth *are* in **r**; *there is* 6664
8:18 *are* with me; *yea*, durable riches and **r**. 6666
8:20 I lead in the way of **r**, in the midst of 6666
10: 2 profit nothing: but **r** delivereth from death. 6666
11: 4 day of wrath: but **r** delivereth from death. 6666
11: 5 The **r** of the perfect shall direct his way: 6666
11: 6 The **r** of the upright shall deliver them: but 6666
11:18 *to* him that soweth **r** *shall be* a sure reward. 6666
11:19 As **r** *tendeth* to life: so he that pursueth evil 6666
12:17 *He that* speaketh truth sheweth forth **r**: but 6664
12:28 In the way of **r** *is* life; and *in* the pathway 6666
13: 6 **R** keepeth *him that is* upright in the way: 6666
14:34 **R** exalteth a nation: but sin *is* a reproach to 6666
15: 9 but he loveth him that followeth after **r**. 6666
16: 8 Better *is* a little with **r** than great revenues 6666
16:12 for the throne is established by **r**. 6666
16:31 of glory, *if* it be found in the way of **r**. 6666
21:21 He that followeth after **r** and mercy findeth 6666
21:21 and mercy findeth life, **r**, and honour. 6666
25: 5 and his throne shall be established in **r**. 6664
Ecc 3:16 the place of **r**, *that* iniquity *was* there. 6664
7:15 there is a just *man* that perisheth in his **r**, 6664
Isa 1:21 **r** lodged in it; but now murderers. 6664
1:26 be called, The city of **r**, the faithful city. 6664
1:27 with judgment, and her converts with **r**. 6666
5: 7 behold oppression; for **r**, but behold a cry. 6666
5:16 and God that is holy shall be sanctified in **r**. 6666
5:23 take away the **r** of the righteous from him. 6666
10:22 consumption decreed shall overflow *with* **r**. 6666
11: 4 with **r** shall he judge the poor, and 6664
11: 5 **r** shall be the girdle of his loins, and 6664
16: 5 and seeking judgment, and hasting **r**. 6664
26: 9 the inhabitants of the world will learn **r**. 6664
26:10 to the wicked, *yet* will he not learn **r**: 6664
28:17 will I lay to the line, and **r** to the plummet: 6666
32: 1 a king shall reign in **r**, and princes shall 6664
32:16 and **r** remain in the fruitful field. 6666
32:17 the work of **r** shall be peace; and the effect 6666
32:17 the effect of **r** quietness and assurance for 6666
33: 5 he hath filled Zion *with* judgment and **r**. 6666
41:10 uphold thee with the right hand of my **r**. 6664
42: 6 I the LORD have called thee in **r**, and 6664
45: 8 from above, and let the skies pour down **r**: 6664
45: 8 forth salvation, and let **r** spring up together; 6666
45:13 I have raised him up in **r**, and I will direct 6664
45:19 I the LORD speak **r**, I declare things that 6664
45:23 the word is gone out of my mouth *in* **r**, and 6666
45:24 in the LORD have I **r** and strength: 6666
46:12 ye stouthearted, that *are* far from **r**: 6666
46:13 I bring near my **r**; it shall not be far off, and 6666
48: 1 the God of Israel, *but* not in truth, nor in **r**. 6666
48:18 as a river, and thy **r** as the waves of the sea: 6666
51: 1 Hearken to me, ye that follow after **r**, 6664
51: 5 My **r** *is* near; my salvation is gone forth, 6664
51: 6 for ever, and my **r** shall not be abolished. 6666
51: 7 Hearken unto me, ye that know **r**, 6664
51: 8 my **r** shall be for ever, and my salvation 6666
54:14 In **r** shalt thou be established: thou shalt be 6666
54:17 and their **r** *is* of me, saith the LORD. 6666
56: 1 *is* near to come, and my **r** to be revealed. 6666
57:12 I will declare thy **r**, and thy works; for they 6666
58: 2 as a nation that did **r**, and forsook not 6666
58: 8 thy **r** shall go before thee; the glory of 6664
59:16 unto him; and his **r**, it sustained him. 6666
59:17 For he put on **r** as a breastplate, and 6666
60:17 thy officers peace, and thine exactors **r**. 6666
61: 3 that they might be called trees of **r**, 6664
61:10 he hath covered me with the robe of **r**, as a 6666
61:11 so the Lord GOD will cause **r** and 6666
62: 1 until the **r** thereof go forth as brightness, 6664
62: 2 the Gentiles shall see thy **r**, and all kings 6664
63: 1 I that speak in **r**, mighty to save. 6666
64: 5 meetest him that rejoiceth and worketh **r**, 6664
Jer 4: 2 in truth, in judgment, and in **r**; 6666
9:24 judgment, and **r**, in the earth: 6666
22: 3 Execute ye judgment and **r**, and deliver 6666
23: 6 he shall be called, THE LORD OUR **R**. 6664
33:15 will I cause the Branch of **r** to grow up 6666
33:15 he shall execute judgment and **r** in the land. 6666
33:16 she shall be called, The LORD our **r**. 6664
51:10 The LORD hath brought forth our **r**: 6666
Eze 3:20 When a righteous *man* doth turn from his **r**, 6664
3:20 his **r** which he hath done shall not be 6666
14:14 *but* their own souls by their **r**, 6666
14:20 *but* deliver their own souls by their **r**. 6666
18:20 the **r** of the righteous shall be upon him, 6666
18:22 in his **r** that he hath done he shall live. 6666
18:24 the righteous turneth away from his **r**, 6666
18:24 All his **r** that he hath done shall not be 6666
18:26 a righteous *man* turneth away from his **r**, 6666
33:12 The **r** of the righteous shall not deliver him 6666
33:12 to live for his **r** in the day that he sinneth. NIH
33:13 if he trust to his own **r**, and 6666

Eze 33:18 When the righteous turneth from his **r**, and 6666
Da 4:27 break off thy sins by **r**, and thine iniquities 6665
9: 7 **r** *belongeth* unto thee, but unto us 6666
9:16 O Lord, according to all thy **r**, I beseech 6666
9:24 to bring in everlasting **r**, and to seal up 6664
12: 3 they that **turn** many **to r** as the stars for 6663
Hos 2:19 I will betroth thee unto me in **r**, and 6664
10:12 Sow to yourselves in **r**, reap in mercy; 6666
10:12 till he come and rain **r** upon you. 6664
Am 5: 7 to wormwood, and leave off **r** in the earth, 6666
5:24 down as waters, and **r** as a mighty stream. 6666
6:12 into gall, and the fruit of **r** into hemlock: 6666
Mic 6: 5 that *ye* may know the **r** of the LORD. 6666
7: 9 forth to the light, *and* I shall behold his **r**. 6666
Zep 2: 3 his judgment; seek **r**, seek meekness: 6664
Zec 8: 8 and I will be their God, in truth and in **r**. 6666
Mal 3: 3 may offer unto the LORD an offering in **r**. 6666
4: 2 the Sun of **r** arise with healing in his wings; 6666
Mt 3:15 for thus it becometh us to fulfil all **r**. *1343*
5: 6 *are* they which do hunger and thirst after **r**: *1343*
5:20 That except your **r** shall exceed *1343*
5:20 shall exceed *the* **r** of the scribes NIG
6:33 seek ye first the kingdom of God, and his **r**; *1343*
21:32 For John came unto you in the way of **r**, *1343*
Lk 1:75 In holiness and **r** before him, all the days of *1343*
Jn 16: 8 the world of sin, and of **r**, and of judgment: *1343*
16:10 Of **r**, because I go to my Father, and ye see *1343*
Ac 10:35 and worketh **r**, is accepted with him. *1343*
13:10 *thou* child of the devil, *thou* enemy of all **r**, *1343*
17:31 in the which he will judge the world in **r** by *1343*
24:25 And as he reasoned of **r**, temperance, and *1343*
Ro 1:17 For therein is the **r** of God revealed from *1343*
2:26 Therefore if the uncircumcision keep the **r** *1345*
3: 5 But if our unrighteousness commend the **r** *1343*
3:21 But now the **r** of God without the law is *1343*
3:22 Even the **r** of God *which is* by faith of *1343*
3:25 to declare his **r** for the remission of sins *1343*
3:26 To declare, *I say*, at this time his **r**: that he *1343*
4: 3 and it was counted unto him for **r**. *1343*
4: 5 the ungodly, his faith is counted for **r**. *1343*
4: 6 unto whom God imputeth **r** without works, *1343*
4: 9 that faith was reckoned to Abraham for **r**. *1343*
4:11 a seal of the **r** of the faith which he had *yet* *1343*
4:11 that **r** might be imputed unto them also: *1343*
4:13 through the law, but through the **r** of faith. *1343*
4:22 And therefore it was imputed to him for **r**. *1343*
5:17 of the gift of **r** shall reign in life by one, *1343*
5:18 by the **r** of one *the free gift came* upon all *1345*
5:21 might grace reign through **r** unto eternal *1343*
6:13 your members *as* instruments of **r** unto *1343*
6:16 of sin unto death, or of obedience unto **r**? *1343*
6:18 free from sin, ye became the servants of **r**. *1343*
6:19 now yield your members servants to **r** unto *1343*
6:20 the servants of sin, ye were free from **r**. *1343*
8: 4 That the **r** of the law might be fulfilled in *1345*
8:10 of sin; but the Spirit *is* life because of **r**. *1343*
9:28 he will finish the work, and cut *it* short in **r**: *1343*
9:30 the Gentiles, which followed not *after* **r**, *1343*
9:30 not *after* righteousness, have attained to **r**, *1343*
9:30 even the **r** which is of faith. *1343*
9:31 which followed *after* the law of **r**, *1343*
9:31 hath not attained to the law of **r**. *1343*
10: 3 For they being ignorant of God's **r**, and *1343*
10: 3 and going about to establish their own **r**, *1343*
10: 3 have not submitted themselves unto the **r** of *1343*
10: 4 For Christ *is* the end of the law for **r** to *1343*
10: 5 For Moses describeth the **r** which is of *1343*
10: 6 But the **r** which is of faith speaketh on this *1343*
10:10 For with the heart *man* believeth unto **r**; *1343*
14:17 but **r**, and peace, and joy in the Holy Ghost. *1343*
1Co 1:30 and **r**, and sanctification, and redemption: *1343*
15:34 Awake to **r**, and sin not: for some have not *1346*
2Co 3: 9 much more doth the ministration of **r** *1343*
5:21 that we might be made the **r** of God in him. *1343*
6: 7 by the armour of **r** on the right hand and *1343*
6:14 for what fellowship hath **r** with *1343*
9: 9 given to the poor: his **r** remaineth for ever. *1343*
9:10 and increase the fruits of your **r**;) *1343*
11:15 also be transformed as the ministers of **r**; *1343*
Gal 2:21 for if **r** *come* by the law, then Christ is dead *1343*
3: 6 and it was accounted to him for **r**. *1343*
3:21 verily **r** should have been by the law. *1343*
5: 5 the Spirit wait for the hope of **r** by faith. *1343*
Eph 4:24 which after God is created in **r** and *1343*
5: 9 Spirit *is* in all goodness and **r** and truth;) *1343*
6:14 and having on the breastplate of **r**; *1343*
Php 1:11 Being filled with the fruits of **r**, which are *1343*
3: 6 touching the **r** which is in the law, *1343*
3: 9 not having mine own **r**, which is of the law, *1343*
3: 9 of Christ, the **r** which is of God by faith: *1343*
1Ti 6:11 flee these *things*; and follow *after* **r**, *1343*
2Ti 2:22 but follow **r**, faith, charity, peace, *1343*
3:16 for correction, for instruction in **r**: *1343*
4: 8 there is laid up for me a crown of **r**, *1343*
Tit 3: 5 Not by works of **r** which we have done, but *1343*
Heb 1: 8 a sceptre of **r** *is* the sceptre of thy kingdom. *2118*
1: 9 Thou hast loved **r**, and hated iniquity; *1343*
5:13 that useth milk *is* unskilful in the word of **r**: *1343*
7: 2 first being by interpretation King of **r**, and *1343*
11: 7 and became heir of the **r** which is by faith. *1343*
11:33 wrought **r**, obtained promises, stopped *1343*
12:11 of **r** unto them which are exercised thereby. *1343*
Jas 1:20 For the wrath of man worketh not the **r** of *1343*
2:23 and it was imputed unto him for **r**: *1343*
3:18 And the fruit of **r** is sown in peace of them *1343*
1Pe 2:24 being dead to sins, should live unto **r**: *1343*
2Pe 1: 1 precious faith with us through the **r** of God *1343*
2: 5 Noah the eighth *person*, a preacher of **r**, *1343*
2:21 for them not to have known the way of **r**, *1343*
3:13 and a new earth, wherein dwelleth **r**. *1343*
1Jn 2:29 ye know that every one which doeth **r** is *1343*
3: 7 he that doeth **r** is righteous, even as he is *1343*
3:10 whosoever doeth not **r** is not of God, *1343*
Rev 19: 8 white: for the fine linen is the **r** of saints. *1345*
19:11 True, and in **r** he doth judge and make war. *1343*

RIGHTEOUSNESS' (4) [RIGHT]

Ps 143:11 for thy **r** sake bring my soul out of trouble. 6666
Isa 42:21 The LORD is well pleased for his **r** sake; 6664
Mt 5:10 Blessed *are* they which are persecuted for **r** *1343*
1Pe 3:14 But and if ye suffer for **r** sake, happy *are* *1343*

RIGHTEOUSNESSES (3) [RIGHT]

Isa 64: 6 and all our **r** *are* as filthy rags; 6666
Eze 33:13 all his **r** shall not be remembered; 6666
Da 9:18 our supplications before thee for our **r**, 6666

RIGHTLY (4) [RIGHT]

Ge 27:36 he said, Is not he **r** named Jacob? for he 3588
Lk 7:43 And he said unto him, Thou hast **r** judged. *3723*
20:21 we know that thou sayest and teachest **r**, *3723*
2Ti 2:15 be ashamed, **r dividing** the word of truth. *3718*

RIGOUR (5)

Ex 1:13 made the children of Israel to serve with **r**: 6531
1:14 wherein they made them serve, *was* with **r**. 6531
Lev 25:43 Thou shalt not rule over him with **r**; but 6531
25:46 ye shall not rule one over another with **r**. 6531
25:53 *the other* shall not rule with **r** over him in 6531

RIMMON (14) [GATH-RIMMON, HADADRIMMON, RIMMON-PAREZ]

Jos 15:32 And Lebaoth, and Shilhim, and Ain, and **R**: 7417
Jdg 20:45 toward the wilderness unto the rock of **R**: 7417
20:47 and fled to the wilderness unto the rock **R**, 7417
20:47 and abode in the rock **R** four months. 7417
21:13 of Benjamin that *were* in the rock **R**, 7417
2Sa 4: 2 the sons of **R** a Beerothite, of the children 7417
4: 5 the sons of **R** the Beerothite, Rechab and 7417
4: 9 the sons of **R** the Beerothite, and said unto 7417
2Ki 5:18 goeth *into* the house of **R** to worship there, 7417
5:18 and I bow myself *in* the house of **R**: 7417
5:18 when I bow down myself *in* the house of **R**, 7417
1Ch 4:32 Ain, **R**, and Tochen, and Ashan, five cities: 7417
6:77 **R** with her suburbs, Tabor with her 7417
Zec 14:10 a plain from Geba to **R** south of Jerusalem: 7417

RIMMON PEREZ See RIMMON-PAREZ

RIMMON-PAREZ (2) [RIMMON]

Nu 33:19 departed from Rithmah, and pitched at **R**. 7428
33:20 they departed from **R**, and pitched in 7428

RING (11) [EARRING, EARRINGS, RANG, RINGLEADER, RINGS, RINGSTRAKED]

Ge 41:42 Pharaoh took off his **r** from his hand, and 2885
Ex 26:24 together above the head of it unto one **r**: 2885
36:29 together at the head thereof, to one **r**: 2885
Est 3:10 the king took his **r** from his hand, and 2885
3:12 was it written, and sealed with the king's **r**. 2885
8: 2 the king took off his **r**, which he had taken 2885
8: 8 king's name, and seal *it* with the king's **r**: 2885
8: 8 sealed with the king's **r**, may no man 2885
8:10 sealed *it* with the king's **r**, and sent letters 2885
Lk 15:22 and put *it* on him; and put a **r** on his hand, *1146*
Jas 2: 2 unto your assembly a man **with a gold r**, *5554*

RINGLEADER (1) [LEAD, RING]

Ac 24: 5 and a **r** of the sect of the Nazarenes: *4414*

RINGS (44) [RING]

Ex 25:12 And thou shalt cast four **r** of gold for it, and 2885
25:12 two **r** *shall be* in the one side of it, and 2885
25:12 side of it, and two **r** in the other side of it. 2885
25:14 thou shalt put the staves into the **r** by 2885
25:15 The staves shall be in the **r** of the ark: 2885
25:26 thou shalt make for it four **r** of gold, and 2885
25:26 put the **r** in the four corners that *are* on 2885
25:27 Over against the border shall the **r** be for 2885
26:29 make their **r** *of* gold *for* places for the bars: 2885
27: 4 upon the net shalt thou make four brasen **r** 2885
27: 7 the staves shall be put into the **r**, and 2885
28:23 thou shalt make upon the breastplate two **r** 2885
28:23 shalt put the two **r** on the two ends of 2885
28:24 **r** *which are* on the ends of the breastplate. 2885
28:26 thou shalt make two **r** of gold, and 2885
28:27 two *other* **r** of gold thou shalt make, and 2885
28:28 they shall bind the breastplate by the **r** 2885
28:28 unto the **r** of the ephod with a lace of blue, 2885
30: 4 two golden **r** shalt thou make to it under 2885
35:22 and earrings, and **r**, and tablets, 2885
36:34 made their **r** *of* gold *to be* places for 2885
37: 3 he cast for it four **r** of gold, *to be set* by 2885
37: 3 even two **r** upon the one side of it, and 2885
37: 3 of it, and two **r** upon the other side of it. 2885
37: 5 he put the staves into the **r** by the sides of 2885
37:13 he cast for it four **r** of gold, and put 2885
37:13 put the **r** upon the four corners that *were* in 2885
37:14 Over against the border were the **r**, 2885
37:27 he made two **r** of gold for it under 2885
38: 5 he cast four **r** for the four ends of the grate 2885
38: 7 he put the staves into the **r** on the sides of 2885
39:16 made two ouches *of* gold, and two gold **r**; 2885
39:16 put the two **r** in the two ends of 2885
39:17 in the two **r** on the ends of the breastplate. 2885
39:19 they made two **r** of gold, and put *them* on 2885
39:20 they made two *other* golden **r**, and put them 2885
39:21 they did bind the breastplate by his **r** unto 2885
39:21 unto the **r** of the ephod with a lace of blue, 2885
Nu 31:50 and bracelets, **r**, earrings, and tablets, 2885
Est 1: 6 and purple to silver **r** and pillars of marble: 1550
SS 5:14 His hands *are as* gold **r** set with the beryl: 1550
Isa 3:21 The **r**, and nose jewels, 2885
Eze 1:18 As for their **r**, they were so high that they 1354
1:18 their **r** *were* full *of* eyes round about them 1354

RINGSTRAKED (7) [RING]

Ge 30:35 removed that day the he goats that were **r** 6124
30:39 brought forth cattle **r**, speckled, and 6124

R

Ge 30:40 set the faces of the flocks toward the **r**, and 6124
31: 8 if he said thus, The **r** shall be thy hire; then 6124
31: 8 shall be thy hire; then bare all the cattle **r**. 6124
31:10 rams which leaped upon the cattle *were* **r**, 6124
31:12 the rams which leap upon the cattle *are* **r**, 6124

RINNAH (1)
1Ch 4:20 and **R**, Ben-hanan, and Tilon. 7441

RINSED (3)
Lev 6:28 it shall be both scoured, and **r** in water. 7857
15:11 hath not **r** his hands in water, he shall wash 7857
15:12 every vessel of wood shall be **r** in water. 7857

RIOT (3) [RIOTING, RIOTOUS]
Tit 1: 6 having faithful children not accused of **r** or *810*
1Pe 4: 4 run not with *them* to the same excess of **r**, *810*
2Pe 2:13 *as* they that count it pleasure to **r** in the day *5172*

RIOTING (1) [RIOT]
Ro 13:13 not in **r** and drunkenness, not in *2970*

RIOTOUS (3) [RIOT]
Pr 23:20 amongst **r eaters** of flesh: 2151
28: 7 he that is a companion of **r** *men* shameth 2151
Lk 15:13 and there wasted his substance with **r** living. *811*

RIP (1) [RIPT]
2Ki 8:12 and **r up** their women with child. 1234

RIPE (8) [FIRSTRIPE, RIPENING, UNRIPE]
Ge 40:10 the clusters thereof **brought forth r** grapes: 1310
Ex 22:29 not delay *to offer the first of* thy **r fruits**, 4395
Nu 13:20 Now the time *was* the time of the **first r** 1061
18:13 *And* whatsoever is **first r** in the land, 1061
Jer 24: 2 good figs, *even* like the figs *that are* **first r**: 1073
Joel 3:13 Put ye in the sickle, for the harvest is **r**: 1310
Rev 14:15 to reap; for the harvest of the earth is **r**. *3583*
14:18 vine of the earth; for her grapes are **fully r**. *187*

RIPENING (1) [RIPE]
Isa 18: 5 and the sour grape is **r** in the flower, 1580

RIPHATH (2)
Ge 10: 3 Ashkenaz, and **R**, and Togarmah. 7384
1Ch 1: 6 Ashchenaz, and **R**, and Togarmah. 7384

RIPT (3) [RIP]
2Ki 15:16 therein that were with child he **r up**. 1234
Hos 13:16 and their women with child shall be **r up**. 1234
Am 1:13 they have **r up** the women with child at 1234

RISE (142) [ARISE, ARISETH, ARISING, AROSE, RISEN, RISEST, RISETH, RISING, ROSE, SUNRISING]
Ge 19: 2 ye shall **r up early**, and go on your ways. 7925
31:35 my lord that I cannot **r up** before thee; 6965
Ex 8:20 **R up early** in the morning, and 7925
9:13 **R up early** in the morning, and 7925
12:31 **R up**, *and* get you forth from amongst my 6965
21:19 If he **r again**, and walk abroad upon his 6965
Lev 19:32 Thou shalt **r up** before the hoary head, and 6965
Nu 10:35 **R up**, LORD, and let thine enemies be 6965
22:20 come to call thee, **r up**, *and* go with them; 6965
23:18 and said, **R up**, Balak, and hear; 6965
23:24 the people shall **r up** as a great lion, and 6965
24:17 a Sceptre shall **r** out of Israel, and 6965
Dt 2:13 Now **r up**, *said I*, and get you over 6965
2:24 **R** ye **up**, take your journey, and pass over 6965
19:11 **r up** against him, and smite him mortally 6965
19:15 One witness shall not **r up** against a man 6965
19:16 If a false witness **r up** against any man to 6965
28: 7 **r up** against thee *to be* smitten before thy 6965
29:22 of your children that shall **r up** after you, 6965
31:16 this people will **r up**, and go a whoring 6965
32:38 let them **r up** and help you, *and* be your 6965
33:11 smite through the loins of them that **r** 6965
33:11 of them that hate him, that they **r** not again. 6965
Jos 8: 7 ye shall **r up** from the ambush, and 6965
18: 4 they shall **r**, and go through the land, and 6965
Jdg 8:21 Zalmunna said, **R** thou, and fall upon us: 6965
9:33 thou shalt **r early**, and set upon the city: 7925
20:38 **make** a great flame with smoke **r up** out of 5927
1Sa 22:13 that *he* should **r** against me, to lie in wait, 6965
24: 7 and suffered them not to **r** against Saul. 6965
29:10 Wherefore now **r up early** in the morning 7925
2Sa 12:21 child was dead, thou didst **r** and eat bread. 6965
18:32 all that **r** against thee to do *thee* hurt, be as 6965
2Ki 16: 7 the king of Israel, which **r up** against me. 6965
Ne 2:18 they said, Let us **r up** and build. So they 6965
Job 20:27 and the earth shall **r up** against him. 6965
30:12 Upon *my* right hand **r** the youth; they push 6965
Ps 3: 1 many *are* they that **r up** against me. 6965
17: 7 *in thee* from those that **r up** *against them*. 6965
18:38 wounded them that they were not able to **r**: 6965
18:48 thou liftest me up above those that **r up** 6965
27: 3 though war should **r** against me, in this *will* 6965
35:11 False witnesses did **r up**; they laid to my 6965
36:12 are cast down, and shall not be able to **r**. 6965
41: 8 and *now* that he lieth he shall **r up** no more. 6965
44: 5 we tread them under that **r up** against us. 6965
59: 1 defend me from them that **r up** against me. 6965
74:23 the tumult of those that **r up** against thee 6965
92:11 *desire* of the wicked that **r up** against me. 6965
94:16 Who will **r up** for me against 6965
119:62 At midnight I will **r** to give thanks unto 6965
127: 2 *It is* vain for you to **r up** early, to sit up 6965
139:21 am not I grieved with those that **r up** 8618
140:10 into deep pits, *that* they **r** not **up again**. 6965
Pr 24:22 For their calamity shall **r** suddenly; and 6965
28:12 but when the wicked **r**, a man is hidden. 6965
28:28 When the wicked **r**, men hide themselves: 6965
Ecc 10: 4 If the spirit of the ruler **r up** against thee, 5927
Ecc 12: 4 he shall **r up** at the voice of the bird, and 6965
SS 2:10 **R up**, my love, my fair one, and 6965
3: 2 I will **r** now, and go about the city in 6965
Isa 5:11 Woe unto them that **r up early** in 7925
14:21 *that* they do not **r**, nor possess the land, 6965
14:22 For I will **r up** against them, saith 6965
24:20 upon it; and it shall fall, and not **r** again. 6965
26:14 not live; *they are* deceased, they shall not **r**: 6965
28:21 For the LORD shall **r up** as *in* mount 6965
32: 9 **R up**, ye women that are at ease, hear my 6965
33:10 Now will I **r**, saith the LORD; now will I 6965
43:17 shall lie down together, they shall not **r**: 6965
54:17 every tongue *that* shall **r** against thee in 6965
58:10 shall thy light **r** in obscurity, and 2224
Jer 25:27 spue, and fall, and **r** no more, because 6965
37:10 *yet* should they **r up** every man in his tent, 6965
47: 2 waters **r up** out of the north, and shall be an 5927
49:14 come against her, and **r up** to the battle. 6965
51: 1 in the midst of them that **r up** against me, 6965
51:64 shall not **r** from the evil that I *will* bring 6965
La 1:14 *from whom* I am not able to **r up**. 6965
Da 7:24 another shall **r** after them; and he shall be 6966
Am 5: 2 of Israel is fallen; she shall no more **r**: 6965
7: 9 I will **r** against the house of Jeroboam with 6965
8: 8 it shall **r up** wholly as a flood; and it shall 5927
8:14 even they shall fall, and never **r up** again. 6965
9: 5 it shall **r up** wholly like a flood; and 5927
Ob 1: 1 and let us **r up** against her in battle. 6965
Na 1: 9 affliction shall not **r up** the second time. 6965
Hab 2: 7 Shall they not **r up** suddenly that *shall* bite 6965
Zep 3: 8 until the day that I **r up** to the prey: 6965
Zec 14:13 his hand shall **r up** against the hand of his 5927
Mt 5:45 for he **maketh** his sun **to r** on the evil and *393*
10:21 the children shall **r up against** *their* *1881*
12:41 *The* men of Nineveh shall **r** in judgment *450*
12:42 *The* queen of the south shall **r up** in *1453*
20:19 and the third day he shall **r again**. *450*
24: 7 For nation shall **r** against nation, and *1453*
24:11 And many false prophets shall **r**, and *1453*
26:46 **R**, let us be going: behold, he is at hand *1453*
27:63 yet alive, After three days I will **r** *again*. *1453*
Mk 3:26 And if Satan **r up** against himself, and *450*
4:27 and **r** night and day, and the seed should *1453*
8:31 and be killed, and after three days **r again**. *450*
9:31 after that he is killed, he shall **r** the third day. *450*
10:34 kill him: and the third day he shall **r again**. *450*
10:49 saying unto him, Be of good comfort, **r**; *1453*
12:23 the resurrection therefore, when they shall **r**, *450*
12:25 For when they shall **r** from the dead, *450*
12:26 And as touching the dead, that they **r**: *1453*
13: 8 For nation shall **r** against nation, and *1453*
13:12 children shall **r up** against *their* parents, *1881*
13:22 For false Christs and false prophets shall **r**, *1453*
14:42 **R up**, let us go; lo, he that betrayeth me is *1453*
Lk 5:23 be forgiven thee; or to say, **R up** and walk? *1453*
6: 8 **R up**, and stand *forth* in the midst. *1453*
11: 7 are with me in bed; I cannot **r** and give thee? *450*
11: 8 Though he will not **r** and give him, because *450*
11: 8 yet because of his importunity he will **r** and *450*
11:31 *The* queen of the south shall **r up** in *1453*
11:32 *The* men of Nineveh shall **r up** in *450*
12:54 When ye see a cloud **r out** of the west, *393*
18:33 to death: and the third day he shall **r again**. *450*
21:10 Nation shall **r** against nation, and *1453*
22:46 **r** and pray, lest ye enter into temptation. *450*
24: 7 and be crucified, and the third day **r again**. *450*
24:46 and to **r** from the dead the third day: *450*
Jn 5: 8 unto him, **R**, take up thy bed, and walk. *1453*
11:23 saith unto her, Thy brother shall **r again**. *450*
11:24 I know that he shall **r again** in *450*
20: 9 that he must **r again** from the dead. *450*
Ac 3: 6 the name of Jesus Christ of Nazareth **r up** *1453*
10:13 And there came a voice to him, **R**, Peter; *450*
26:16 But **r**, and stand upon thy feet: for I have *450*
26:23 that he *should be* the first *that* should **r** from *386*
Ro 15:12 and he that *shall* **r** to reign over the Gentiles; *450*
1Co 15:15 raised not up, if so be that the dead **r** not. *1453*
15:16 For if the dead **r** not, then is not Christ *1453*
15:29 for the dead, if the dead **r** not at all? *1453*
15:32 what advantageth it me, if the dead **r** not? *1453*
1Th 4:16 of God: and the dead in Christ shall **r** first: *450*
Heb 7:11 should **r** after the order of Melchisedec, *450*
Rev 11: 1 **R**, and measure the temple of God, and *1453*
13: 1 and saw a beast **r up** out of the sea, *305*

RISEN (51) [RISE]
Ge 19:23 The sun was **r** upon the earth when Lot 3318
Ex 22: 3 If the sun be **r** upon him, *there shall be* 2224
Nu 32:14 ye are **r up** in your fathers' stead, 6965
Jdg 9:18 ye are **r up** against my father's house *this* 6965
Ru 2:15 when she was **r up** to glean, Boaz 6965
1Sa 25:29 Yet a man is **r** to pursue thee, and to seek 6965
2Sa 14: 7 the whole family is **r** against thine 6965
1Ki 8:20 I am **r up** in the room of David my father, 6965
2Ki 6:15 when the servant of the man of God was **r** 6965
2Ch 6:10 for I am **r up** in the room of David my 6965
13: 6 is **r up**, and hath rebelled against his lord. 6965
21: 4 Now when Jehoram was **r up** to 6965
Ps 20: 8 and fallen: but we are **r**, and stand upright. 6965
27:12 for false witnesses are **r up** against me, and 6965
54: 3 For strangers are **r up** against me, and 6965
86:14 the proud are **r** against me, and 6965
Isa 60: 1 and the glory of the LORD is **r** upon thee. 2224
Eze 7:11 Violence is **r up** into a rod of wickedness: 6965
47: 5 for the waters were **r**, waters to swim in, 1342
Mic 2: 8 Even of late my people is **r up** as an 6965
Mt 11:11 hath not **r** a greater than John the Baptist: *1453*
14: 2 he is **r** from the dead; and therefore mighty *1453*
17: 9 the Son of man be **r again** from the dead. *450*
26:32 But after I am **r** *again*, I will go before you *1453*
27:64 say unto the people, He is **r** from the dead: *1453*
28: 6 for he is **r**, as he said. Come, see the place *1453*
28: 7 tell his disciples that he is **r** from the dead; *1453*
Mk 6:14 That John the Baptist was **r** from the dead, *1453*
6:16 whom I beheaded: he is **r** from the dead. *1453*
Mk 9: 9 till the Son of man were **r** from the dead. *450*
14:28 But after that I am **r**, I will go before you *1453*
16: 6 he is **r**; he is not here: behold the place *1453*
16: 9 Now when *Jesus* was **r** early the first *day* of *450*
16:14 them which had seen him after he was **r**. *1453*
Lk 7:16 That a great prophet is **r up** among us; *1453*
9: 7 of some, that John was **r** from the dead; *1453*
9: 8 that one of the old prophets was **r again**. *450*
9:19 *say*, that one of the old prophets is **r again**. *450*
13:25 When once the master of the house is **r up**, *1453*
24: 6 He is not here, but is **r**: remember how he *1453*
24:34 The Lord is **r** indeed, and hath appeared to *1453*
Jn 2:22 When therefore he was **r** from the dead, *1453*
21:14 after that he was **r** from the dead. *1453*
Ac 17: 3 have suffered, and **r again** from the dead; *450*
Ro 8:34 that is **r** *again*, who is even at the right hand *1453*
1Co 15:13 of the dead, then is Christ not **r**: *1453*
15:14 And if Christ be not **r**, then *is* our *1453*
15:20 But now is Christ **r** from the dead, *and* *1453*
Col 2:12 wherein also ye are **r with** *him* through *4891*
3: 1 If ye then be **r with** Christ, seek those *4891*
Jas 1:11 For the sun is no sooner **r** with a burning *393*

RISEST (2) [RISE]
Dt 6: 7 when thou liest down, and when thou **r up**. 6965
11:19 when thou liest down, and when thou **r up**. 6965

RISETH (14) [RISE]
Dt 22:26 for as when a man **r** against his neighbour, 6965
Jos 6:26 that **r up** and buildeth this city Jericho: 6965
2Sa 23: 4 *when* the sun **r**, *even* a morning without 2224
Job 9: 7 Which commandeth the sun, and it **r** not; 2224
14:12 So man lieth down, and **r** not: till 6965
24:22 he **r up**, and no *man* is sure of life. 6965
27: 7 he that **r up** against me as the unrighteous. 6965
31:14 What then shall I do when God **r up**? and 6965
Pr 24:16 falleth seven *times*, and **r up** *again*: but 6965
31:15 She **r** also while *it is* yet night, and 6965
Isa 47:11 thou shalt not know from whence it **r**: 7837
Jer 46: 8 Egypt **r up** like a flood, and *his* waters are 5927
Mic 7: 6 the daughter **r up** against her mother, 6965
Jn 13: 4 He **r** from supper, and laid aside *his* *1453*

RISING (39) [RISE]
Lev 13: 2 a man shall have in the skin of his flesh a **r**, 7613
13:10 *if* the **r** *be* white in the skin, and it have 7613
13:10 and *there be* quick raw flesh in the **r**; 7613
13:19 in the place of the boil there be a white **r**, 7613
13:28 it *is* a **r** of the burning, and the priest shall 7613
13:43 *if* the **r** of the sore *be* white reddish in his 7613
14:56 for a **r**, and for a scab, and for a bright spot: 7613
Nu 2: 3 on the east side toward the **r of the sun** 4217
Jos 12: 1 *other* side Jordan toward the **r** of the sun, 4217
2Ch 36:15 his messengers, **r up betimes**, and sending; 7925
Ne 4:21 half of them held the spears from the **r** of 5927
Job 16: 8 my leanness **r up** in me beareth witness to 6965
24: 5 forth to their work; **r betimes** for a prey: 7836
24:14 The murderer **r** with the light killeth 6965
Ps 50: 1 called the earth from the **r** of the sun unto 4217
113: 3 From the **r** of the sun unto the going down 4217
Pr 27:14 **r early** in the morning, it shall be counted a 7925
30:31 and a king, against whom *there is* **no r up**. 510
Isa 41:25 from the **r** of the sun shall he call upon my 4217
45: 6 That they may know from the **r** of the sun, 4217
59:19 and his glory from the **r** of the sun. 4217
60: 3 and kings to the brightness of thy **r**. 2225
Jer 7:13 **r up early** and speaking, but ye heard not; 7925
7:25 daily **r up early** and sending *them*: 7925
11: 7 **r early** and protesting, saying, Obey my 7925
25: 3 spoken unto you, **r early** and speaking; 7925
25: 4 **r early** and sending *them*; but ye have not 7925
26: 5 both **r up early**, and sending *them*, but 7925
29:19 **r up early** and sending *them*; but ye would 7925
32:33 **r up early** and teaching *them*, yet they 7925
35:14 spoken unto you, **r early** and speaking; 7925
35:15 **r up early** and sending *them*, saying, 7925
44: 4 **r early** and sending *them*, saying, Oh, 7925
La 3:63 Behold their sitting down, and their **r up**; 7012
Mal 1:11 For from the **r** of the sun even unto 4217
Mk 1:35 **r up** a great while before day, he went out, *450*
9:10 questioning *one* with *another* what the **r** *450*
16: 2 they came unto the sepulchre at the **r** of *393*
Lk 2:34 set for the fall and **r again** of many in Israel; *386*

RISKED See HAZARDED; JEOPARDED

RISSAH (2)
Nu 33:21 removed from Libnah, and pitched at **R**. 7446
33:22 they journeyed from **R**, and pitched in 7446

RITES (1)
Nu 9: 3 according to all the **r** of it, and according to 2708

RITHMAH (2)
Nu 33:18 departed from Hazeroth, and pitched in **R**. 7575
33:19 they departed from **R**, and pitched at 7575

RIVAL See VEX; VEXATION; VEXED

RIVER (176) [RIVER'S, RIVERS]
Ge 2:10 a **r** went out of Eden to water the garden; 5104
2:13 the name of the second **r** *is* Gihon: 5104
2:14 the name of the third **r** *is* Hiddekel: that *is* 5104
2:14 of Assyria. And the fourth **r** *is* Euphrates. 5104
15:18 from the **r** of Egypt unto the great river, 5104
15:18 from the river of Egypt unto the great **r**, 5104
15:18 Egypt unto the great river, the **r** Euphrates: 5104
31:21 passed over the **r**, and set his face *toward* 5104
36:37 Saul of Rehoboth *by* the **r** reigned in his 5104
41: 1 and behold, he stood by the **r**. 2975
41: 2 there came up out of the **r** seven well 2975
41: 3 other kine came up after them out of the **r**, 2975
41: 3 by the *other* kine upon the brink of the **r**. 2975
41:17 behold, I stood upon the bank of the **r**: 2975

R

Ge 41:18 there came up out of the r seven kine, 2975
Ex 1:22 son that is born ye shall cast into the r, 2975
2: 5 came down to wash herself at the r; 2975
4: 9 that thou shalt take of the water of the r, 2975
4: 9 the water which thou takest out of the r 2975
7:17 hand upon the waters which are in the r, 2975
7:18 the fish that is in the r shall die, and 2975
7:18 in the river shall die, and the r shall stink; 2975
7:18 shall lothe to drink of the water of the r. 2975
7:20 and smote the waters that were in the r, 2975
7:20 all the waters that were in the r were turned 2975
7:21 the fish that was in the r died; and the river 2975
7:21 the r stunk, and the Egyptians could not 2975
7:21 could not drink of the water of the r; 2975
7:24 all the Egyptians digged round about the r 2975
7:24 they could not drink of the water of the r. 2975
7:25 after that the LORD had smitten the r. 2975
8: 3 the r shall bring forth frogs abundantly, 2975
8: 9 that they may remain in the r only? 2975
8:11 thy people; they shall remain in the r only. 2975
17: 5 thy rod, wherewith thou smotest the r, 2975
23:31 and from the desert unto the r: 5104
Nu 22: 5 which is by the r of the land of the children 5104
24: 6 they spread forth, as gardens by the r side, 5104
34: 5 compass from Azmon unto the r of Egypt, 5158
Dt 1: 7 unto Lebanon, unto the great r, the river 5104
1: 7 unto the great river, the r Euphrates. 5104
2:24 your journey, and pass over the r Arnon: 5158
2:36 which is by the brink of the r of Arnon, and 5158
2:36 from the city that is by the r, even unto 5158
2:37 nor unto any place of the r Jabbok, 5158
3: 8 from the r of Arnon unto mount Hermon; 5158
3:12 which is by the r Arnon, and half mount 5158
3:16 I gave from Gilead even unto the r Arnon, 5158
3:16 and the border, even unto the r Jabbok, 5158
4:48 which is by the bank of the r Arnon, 5158
11:24 the wilderness and Lebanon, from the r, 5104
11:24 from the river, the r Euphrates, 5104
Jos 1: 4 and this Lebanon even unto the great r, 5104
1: 4 the r Euphrates, all the land of the Hittites, 5104
12: 1 from the r Arnon unto mount Hermon, and 5158
12: 2 which is upon the bank of the r of Arnon, 5158
12: 2 from the middle of the r, and from half 5158
12: 2 from half Gilead, even unto the r Jabbok, 5158
13: 9 that is upon the bank of the r Arnon, and 5158
13: 9 and the city that is in the midst of the r, and 5158
13:16 that is on the bank of the r Arnon, and 5158
13:16 and the city that is in the midst of the r, and 5158
15: 4 and went out unto the r of Egypt; 5158
15: 7 which is on the south side of the r: 5158
15:47 unto the r of Egypt, and the great sea, and 5158
16: 8 from Tappuah westward unto the r Kanah; 5158
17: 9 the coast descended unto the r Kanah, 5158
17: 9 unto the river Kanah, southward of the r: 5158
17: 9 also was on the north side of the r, 5158
19:11 and reached to the r that is before Jokneam; 5158
Jdg 4: 7 I will draw unto thee to the r Kishon 5158
4:13 from Harosheth of the Gentiles unto the r 5158
5:21 The r of Kishon swept them away, 5158
5:21 them away, that ancient r, the river Kishon. 5158
5:21 them away, that ancient river, the r Kishon. 5158
2Sa 8: 3 as he went to recover his border at the r 5104
10:16 out the Syrians that were beyond the r: 5104
17:13 to that city, and we will draw it into the r, 5158
24: 5 city that lieth in the midst of the r of Gad, 5158
1Ki 4:21 from the r unto the land of the Philistines, 5104
4:24 over all the region on this side the r, 5104
4:24 over all the kings on this side the r: 5104
8:65 from the entering in of Hamath unto the r 5158
14:15 shall scatter them beyond the r, because 5104
2Ki 10:33 from Aroer, which is by the r Arnon, 5158
17: 6 in Halah and in Habor by the r of Gozan, 5104
18:11 in Halah and in Habor by the r of Gozan, 5104
23:29 the king of Assyria to the r Euphrates: 5104
24: 7 r of Egypt unto the river Euphrates all that 5158
24: 7 r Euphrates all that pertained to the king of 5104
1Ch 1:48 Shaul of Rehoboth by the r reigned in his 5104
5: 9 in of the wilderness from the r Euphrates: 5104
5:26 Habor, and Hara, and to the r Gozan, 5104
18: 3 as he went to stablish his dominion by the r 5104
19:16 forth the Syrians that were beyond the r: 5104
2Ch 7: 8 from the entering in of Hamath unto the r 5158
9:26 he reigned over all the kings from the r 5104
Ezr 4:10 the rest that are on this side the r, and 5103
4:11 Thy servants the men on this side the r, and 5103
4:16 shalt have no portion on this side the r. 5103
4:17 in Samaria, and unto the rest beyond the r: 5103
4:20 have ruled over all countries beyond the r; 5103
5: 3 governor on this side the r, and 5103
5: 6 governor on this side the r, and 5103
5: 6 which were on this side the r, sent unto 5103
6: 6 therefore, Tatnai, governor beyond the r, 5103
6: 6 which are beyond the r, be ye far from 5103
6: 8 even of the tribute beyond the r, 5103
6:13 Tatnai, governor on this side the r, 5103
7:21 to all the treasurers which are beyond the r, 5103
7:25 judge all the people that are beyond the r, 5103
8:15 I gathered them together to the r that 5104
8:21 I proclaimed a fast there, at the r Ahava, 5104
8:31 we departed from the r of Ahava on 5104
8:36 and to the governors on this side the r: 5104
Ne 2: 7 be given me to the governors beyond the r, 5104
2: 9 I came to the governors beyond the r, and 5104
3: 7 throne of the governor on this side the r. 5104
Job 40:23 Behold, he drinketh up a r, and hasteth not: 5104
Ps 36: 8 thou shalt make them drink of the r of thy 5158
46: 4 There is a r, the streams whereof shall 5104
65: 9 thou greatly enrichest it with the r of God, 6388
72: 8 and from the r unto the ends of the earth. 5104
80:11 unto the sea, and her branches unto the r. 5104
105:41 they ran in the dry places like a r. 5104
Isa 7:20 namely, by them beyond the r, by the king 5104
8: 7 bringeth up upon them the waters of the r, 5104
11:15 wind shall he shake his hand over the r, 5104
19: 5 and the r shall be wasted and dried up. 5104
Isa 23: 3 the harvest of the r, is her revenue; 2975
23:10 Pass through thy land as a r, O daughter of 2975
27:12 channel of the r unto the stream of Egypt, 5104
48:18 had thy peace been as a r, and 5104
66:12 I will extend peace to her like a r, and 5104
Jer 2:18 of Assyria, to drink the waters of the r? 5104
17: 8 that spreadeth out her roots by the r, and 3105
46: 2 which was by the r Euphrates in 5104
46: 6 fall toward the north by the r Euphrates. 5104
46:10 in the north country by the r Euphrates. 5104
La 2:18 let tears run down like a r day and night: 5158
Eze 1: 1 as I was among the captives by the r of 5104
1: 3 in the land of the Chaldeans by the r 5104
3:15 that dwelt by the r of Chebar, and I sat 5104
3:23 as the glory which I saw by the r of 5104
10:15 creature that I saw by the r of Chebar. 5104
10:20 under the God of Israel by the r of Chebar; 5104
10:22 same faces which I saw by the r of Chebar, 5104
29: 3 My r is mine own, and I have made it for 2975
29: 9 The r is mine, and I have made it. 2975
43: 3 like the vision that I saw by the r Chebar; 5104
47: 5 and it was a r that I could not pass over: 5158
47: 5 swim in, a r that could not be passed over. 5158
47: 6 caused me to return to the brink of the r. 5158
47: 7 at the bank of the r were very many trees 5158
47: 9 every thing shall live whither the r cometh. 5158
47:12 by the r upon the bank thereof, on this side 5158
47:19 of strife in Kadesh, the r to the great sea. 5159
48:28 and to the r toward the great sea. 5159
Da 8: 2 I saw in a vision, and I was by the r of Ulai. 180
8: 3 there stood before the r a ram which had two 180
8: 6 which I had seen standing before the r, and 180
10: 4 as I was by the side of the great r, which is 5104
12: 5 the one on this side of the bank of the r, 2975
12: 5 the other on that side of the bank of the r. 2975
12: 6 which was upon the waters of the r, 2975
12: 7 which was upon the waters of the r, 2975
Am 6:14 in of Hemath unto the r of the wilderness. 5158
Mic 7:12 from the fortress even to the r, and 5104
Zec 9:10 and from the r even to the ends of the earth. 5104
10:11 and all the deeps of the r shall dry up: 2975
Mk 1: 5 were all baptized of him in the r of Jordan, 4215
Ac 16:13 sabbath we went out of the city by a r side, 4215
Rev 9:14 which are bound in the great r Euphrates. 4215
16:12 out his vial upon the great r Euphrates; 4215
22: 1 And he shewed me a pure r of water of life, 4215
22: 2 and of either side of the r, was there 4215

RIVER'S (3) [RIVER]

Ex 2: 3 she laid it in the flags by the r brink. 2975
2: 5 her maidens walked along by the r side; 2975
7:15 thou shalt stand by the r brink against he 2975

RIVERS (77) [RIVER]

Ex 7:19 upon their r, and upon their ponds, and 2975
8: 5 over the r, and over the ponds, and 2975
Lev 11: 9 in the seas, and in the r, them shall ye eat. 5158
11:10 in the r, of all that move in the waters, and 5158
Dt 10: 7 Gudgodah to Jotbath, a land of r of waters. 5158
2Ki 5:12 Are not Abana and Pharpar, r of Damascus, 5104
19:24 have I dried up all the r of besieged places. 2975
Job 20:17 He shall not see the r, the floods, 6390
28:10 He cutteth out r among the rocks; and 2975
29: 6 and the rock poured me out r of oil; 6388
Ps 1: 3 he shall be like a tree planted by the r of 6388
74:15 and the flood: thou driedst up mighty r. 5104
78:16 and caused waters to run down like r. 5104
78:44 had turned their r into blood; and 2975
89:25 also in the sea, and his right hand in the r. 5104
107:33 He turneth r into a wilderness, and 5104
119:136 R of waters run down mine eyes, because 6388
137: 1 By the r of Babylon, there we sat down, 5104
Pr 5:16 and r of waters in the streets. 6388
21: 1 the hand of the LORD, as the r of water: 6388
Ecc 1: 7 All the r run into the sea; yet the sea is not 5158
1: 7 unto the place from whence the r come, 5158
SS 5:12 His eyes are as the eyes of doves by the r of 650
Isa 7:18 is in the uttermost part of the r of Egypt, 2975
18: 1 which is beyond the r of Ethiopia: 5104
18: 2 whose land the r have spoiled. 5104
18: 7 under foot, whose land the r have spoiled, 5104
19: 6 they shall turn the r far away; and 5104
30:25 r and streams of waters in the day of 6388
32: 2 as r of water in a dry place, as the shadow 6388
33:21 LORD will be unto us a place of broad r 5104
37:25 I dried up all the r of the besieged places. 2975
41:18 I will open r in high places, and 5104
42:15 I will make the r islands, and I will dry up 5104
43: 2 through the r, they shall not overflow thee: 5104
43:19 a way in the wilderness, and r in the desert. 5104
43:20 and r in the desert, to give drink to my 5104
44:27 to the deep, Be dry, and I will dry up thy r: 5104
47: 2 the leg, uncover the thigh, pass over the r. 5104
50: 2 I dry up the sea, I make the r a wilderness: 5104
Jer 31: 9 I will cause them to walk by the r of waters 5158
46: 7 a flood, whose waters are moved as the r? 5104
46: 8 and his waters are moved like the r; 5104
La 3:48 Mine eye runneth down with r of water for 6388
Eze 6: 3 and to the hills, to the r, and to the valleys; 650
29: 3 great dragon that lieth in the midst of his r, 2975
29: 4 I will cause the fish of thy r to stick unto 2975
29: 4 will bring thee up out of the midst of thy r, 2975
29: 4 all the fish of thy r shall stick unto thy 2975
29: 5 thee and all the fish of thy r: 2975
29:10 against thy r, and I will make the land of 2975
30:12 I will make the r dry, and sell the land into 2975
31: 4 the deep set him up on high with her r 5104
31: 4 sent out her little r unto all the trees of 8585
31:12 his boughs are broken by all the r of 650
32: 2 thou camest forth with thy r, and 5104
32: 2 waters with thy feet, and fouledst their r. 5104
32: 6 the mountains; and the r shall be full of thee. 650
32:14 cause their r to run like oil, saith the Lord 5104
34:13 them upon the mountains of Israel by the r, 650
35: 8 in thy valleys, and in all thy r, shall they fall 650
Eze 36: 4 to the hills, to the r, and to the valleys, to 650
36: 6 and to the hills, to the r, and to the valleys, 650
47: 9 whithersoever the r shall come, shall live: 5158
Joel 1:20 for the r of waters are dried up, and the fire 650
3:18 and all the r of Judah shall flow with waters, 650
Mic 6: 7 of rams, or with ten thousands of r of oil? 5158
Na 1: 4 and maketh it dry, and drieth up all the r: 5104
2: 6 The gates of the r shall be opened, and 5104
3: 8 populous No, that was situate among the r, 2975
Hab 3: 8 Was the LORD displeased against the r? 5104
3: 8 was thine anger against the r? was thy 5104
3: 9 Selah. Thou didst cleave the earth with r. 5104
Zep 3:10 From beyond the r of Ethiopia my 5104
Jn 7:38 out of his belly shall flow r of living water. 4215
Rev 8:10 and it fell upon the third part of the r, and 4215
16: 4 third angel poured out his vial upon the r 4215

RIZIA See REZIA

RIZPAH (4)

2Sa 3: 7 whose name was R, the daughter of Aiah: 7532
21: 8 the king took the two sons of R 7532
21:10 And R the daughter of Aiah took sackcloth, 7532
21:11 it was told David what R the daughter of 7532

ROAD (1)

1Sa 27:10 Whither have ye made a r to day? 6584

ROAR (23) [ROARED, ROARETH, ROARING, ROARINGS]

1Ch 16:32 Let the sea r, and the fulness thereof: 7481
Ps 46: 3 Though the waters thereof r and 1993
74: 4 Thine enemies r in the midst of thy 7580
96:11 let the sea r, and the fulness thereof. 7481
98: 7 Let the sea r, and the fulness thereof; 7481
104:21 The young lions r after their prey, and seek 7580
Isa 5:29 be like a lion, they shall r like young lions: 7580
5:29 they shall r, and lay hold of the prey, and 5098
5:30 in that day they shall r against them like 5098
42:13 he shall cry, yea, r; he shall prevail against 6873
59:11 We r all like bears, and mourn sore like 1993
Jer 5:22 though they r, yet can they not pass over it? 1993
25:30 The LORD shall r from on high, and 7580
25:30 he shall mightily r upon his 7580+7580
31:35 divideth the sea when the waves thereof r; 1993
50:42 their voice shall r like the sea, and 1993
51:38 They shall r together like lions: they shall 7580
51:55 when her waves do r like great waters, 1993
Hos 11:10 he shall r like a lion: when he shall roar, 7580
11:10 when he shall r, then the children shall 7580
Joel 3:16 The LORD also shall r out of Zion, and 7580
Am 1: 2 The LORD will r from Zion, and utter his 7580
3: 4 Will a lion r in the forest, when he hath no 7580

ROARED (5) [ROAR]

Jdg 14: 5 behold, a young lion r against him. 7580
Ps 38: 8 I have r by reason of the disquietness of my 7580
Isa 51:15 that divided the sea, whose waves r: 1993
Jer 2:15 The young lions r upon him, and yelled, 7580
Am 3: 8 The lion hath r, who will not fear? the Lord 7580

ROARETH (3) [ROAR]

Job 37: 4 After it a voice r: he thundereth with 7580
Jer 6:23 their voice r like the sea; and they ride 1993
Rev 10: 3 cried with a loud voice, as when a lion r: 3455

ROARING (16) [ROAR]

Job 4:10 The r of the lion, and the voice of the fierce 7581
Ps 22: 1 helping me, and from the words of my r? 7581
22:13 their mouths, as a ravening and a r lion. 7580
32: 3 my bones waxed old through my r all 7581
Pr 19:12 The king's wrath is as the r of a lion; but 5099
20: 2 The fear of a king is as the r of a lion: 5099
28:15 As a r lion, and a ranging bear; so is a 5098
Isa 5:29 Their r shall be like a lion, they shall roar 7581
5:30 shall roar against them like the r of the sea: 5100
31: 4 as the lion and the young lion r on his prey, 1897
Eze 19: 7 the fulness thereof, by the noise of his r. 7581
22:25 like a r lion ravening the prey; 7580
Zep 3: 3 Her princes within her are r lions; 7580
Zec 11: 3 a voice of the r of young lions; for 7581
Lk 21:25 with perplexity; the sea and the waves r; 2278
1Pe 5: 8 the devil, as a r lion, walketh about, 5612

ROARINGS (1) [ROAR]

Job 3:24 and my r are poured out like the waters. 7581

ROAST (5) [ROASTED, ROASTETH]

Ex 12: 8 r with fire, and unleavened bread; 6748
12: 9 nor sodden at all with water, but r with fire; 6748
Dt 16: 7 thou shalt r and eat it in the place which 1310
1Sa 2:15 Give flesh to r for the priest; 6740
Isa 44:16 eateth flesh; he roasteth r, and is satisfied: 6748

ROASTED (3) [ROAST]

2Ch 35:13 they r the passover with fire according to 1310
Isa 44:19 I have r flesh, and eaten it: and shall I make 6740
Jer 29:22 whom the king of Babylon r in the fire; 7033

ROASTETH (2) [ROAST]

Pr 12:27 The slothful man r not that which he took 2760
Isa 44:16 he eateth flesh; he r roast, and is satisfied: 6740

ROB (8) [ROBBED, ROBBER, ROBBERS, ROBBERY, ROBBETH]

Lev 19:13 neither r him: the wages of him that is 1497
26:22 which shall r you of your children, and 7921
1Sa 23: 1 and they r the threshingfloors. 8154
Pr 22:22 R not the poor, because he is poor: 1497
Isa 10: 2 their prey, and that they may r the fatherless. 962
17:14 that spoil us, and the lot of them that r us. 962
Eze 39:10 r those that robbed them, saith the Lord 962
Mal 3: 8 Will a man r God? Yet ye have robbed me. 6906

ROBBED (13) [ROB]

Jdg 9:25 they **r** all that came along *that* way by 1497
2Sa 17: 8 as a bear **r of** her **whelps** in the field: 7909
Ps 119:61 The bands of the wicked have **r** me: *but* 5749
Pr 17:12 *Let* a bear **r** of her whelps meet a man, 7909
Isa 10:13 have **r** their treasures, and I have put down 8154
42:22 this *is* a people **r** and spoiled; *they are* all of 962
Jer 50:37 *is* upon her treasures; and they shall be **r**. 962
Eze 33:15 give again that he had **r**, walk in 1500
39:10 rob those that **r** them, saith the Lord GOD. 962
Mal 3: 8 Yet ye *have* **r** me. But ye say, Wherein 6906
3: 8 ye say, Wherein have we **r** thee? *In* tithes 6906
3: 9 for ye *have* **r** me, *even* this whole nation. 6906
2Co 11: 8 I **r** other churches, taking wages *of them,* to *4813*

ROBBER (5) [ROB]

Job 5: 5 and the **r** swalloweth up their substance. 6782
18: 9 the heel, *and* the **r** shall prevail against him. 6782
Eze 18:10 If he beget a son *that is* a **r**, a shedder of 6530
Jn 10: 1 some other way, the same is a thief and a **r**. *3027*
18:40 but Barabbas. Now Barabbas was a **r**. *3027*

ROBBERS (11) [ROB]

Job 12: 6 The tabernacles of **r** prosper, and they that 7703
Isa 42:24 gave Jacob for a spoil, and Israel to the **r**? 962
Jer 7:11 my name, become a den of **r** in your eyes? 6530
Eze 7:22 they shall pollute my secret *place:* for the **r** 6530
Da 11:14 also the **r** of thy people shall exalt 1121+6530
Hos 6: 9 as troops *of* **r** wait for a man, *so* NIH
7: 1 *and* the troop *of* **r** spoileth without. NIH
Ob 1: 5 to thee, if **r** by night, (how art thou cut off!) 7703
Jn 10: 8 that ever came before me are thieves and **r**: *3027*
Ac 19:37 *which are* neither **r of churches**, nor yet *2417*
2Co 11:26 *in* perils of waters, *in* perils of **r**, *3027*

ROBBERY (7) [ROB]

Ps 62:10 in oppression, and become not vain in **r**: 1498
Pr 21: 7 The **r** of the wicked shall destroy them; 7701
Isa 61: 8 love judgment, I hate **r** for burnt offering; 1498
Eze 22:29 **exercised r**, and have vexed the poor 1497+1498
Am 3:10 store up violence and **r** in their palaces. 7701
Na 3: 1 it *is* all full *of* lies *and* **r**; the prey departeth 6563
Php 2: 6 thought it not **r** to be equal with God: *725*

ROBBETH (1) [ROB]

Pr 28:24 Whoso **r** his father or his mother, and saith, 1497

ROBE (26) [ROBES]

Ex 28: 4 a **r**, and a broidered coat, a mitre, and 4598
28:31 thou shalt make the **r** of the ephod all of 4598
28:34 upon the hem of the **r** round about. 4598
29: 5 the **r** of the ephod, and the ephod, and 4598
39:22 he made the **r** of the ephod *of* woven work, 4598
39:23 *there was* a hole in the midst of the **r**, as 4598
39:24 they made upon the hems of the **r** 4598
39:25 the pomegranates upon the hem of the **r**, 4598
39:26 round about the hem of the **r** to minister *in;* 4598
Lev 8: 7 clothed him with the **r**, and put the ephod 4598
1Sa 18: 4 Jonathan stript himself of the **r** that *was* 4598
24: 4 and cut off the skirt of Saul's **r** privily. 4598
24:11 see, yea see the skirt of thy **r** in my hand: 4598
24:11 for in that I cut off the skirt of thy **r**, and 4598
1Ch 15:27 David *was* clothed with a **r** of fine linen, 4598
Job 29:14 my judgment *was* as a **r** and a diadem. 4598
Isa 22:21 I will clothe him with thy **r**, and 3801
61:10 he hath covered me with the **r** of 4598
Jnh 3: 6 he laid his **r** from him, and covered *him* with 155
Mic 2: 8 ye pull off the **r** with the garment from them 145
Mt 27:28 stripped him, and put on him a scarlet **r**. *5511*
27:31 they took the **r** off from him, and put his *5511*
Lk 15:22 Bring forth the best **r**, and put *it* on him; *4749*
23:11 and arrayed him in a gorgeous **r**, *2066*
Jn 19: 2 on his head, and they put on him a purple **r**, *2440*
19: 5 the crown of thorns, and the purple **r**. *2440*

ROBES (11) [ROBE]

2Sa 13:18 for with such **r** were the king's daughters 4598
1Ki 22:10 sat each on his throne, having put on *their* **r**, 899
22:30 enter into the battle; but put thou on thy **r**. 899
2Ch 18: 9 clothed in *their* **r**, and they sat in a void 899
18:29 will go to the battle; but put thou on thy **r**. 899
Eze 26:16 lay away their **r**, and put off their broidered 4598
Lk 20:46 which desire to walk in **long r**, and *4749*
Rev 6:11 And white **r** were given unto every one of *4749*
7: 9 clothed with white **r**, and palms in their *4749*
7:13 are these which are arrayed in white **r**? *4749*
7:14 and have washed their **r**, and made them *4749*

ROBOAM (2) [REHOBOAM]

Mt 1: 7 And Solomon begat **R**; and Roboam begat *4497*
1: 7 and **R** begat Abia; and Abia begat Asa; *4497*

ROCK (119) [ROCKS]

Ex 17: 6 I will stand before thee there upon the **r** in 6697
17: 6 thou shalt smite the **r**, and there shall come 6697
33:21 place by me, and thou shalt stand upon a **r**: 6697
33:22 that I will put thee in a clift of the **r**, and 6697
Nu 20: 8 and speak ye unto the **r** before their eyes; 5553
20: 8 shalt bring forth to them water out of the **r**: 5553
20:10 the congregation together before the **r**, 5553
20:10 must we fetch you water out of this **r**? 5553
20:11 and with his rod he smote the **r** twice: 5553
24:21 and thou puttest thy nest in a **r**. 5553
Dt 8:15 who brought thee forth water out of the **r** of 6697
32: 4 *He is* the **R**, his work *is* perfect: for all his 6697
32:13 he made him to suck honey out of the **r**, 5553
32:13 out of the rock, and oil out of the flinty **r**; 6697
32:15 and lightly esteemed the **R** of his salvation. 6697
32:18 Of the **R** *that* begat thee thou art unmindful, 6697
32:30 except their **R** had sold them, and 6697
32:31 For their **r** *is* not as our Rock, even our 6697
32:31 For their rock *is* not as our **R**, even our 6697
32:37 *are* their gods, *their* **r** in whom they trusted, 6697
Jdg 1:36 up to Akrabbim, from the **r**, and upward. 5553
6:20 unleavened *cakes,* and lay *them* upon this **r**, 5553
6:21 and there rose up fire out of the **r**, 6697
6:26 the LORD thy God upon the top of this **r**, 4581
7:25 they slew Oreb upon the **r** Oreb, and Zeeb 6697
13:19 and offered *it* upon a **r** unto the LORD: 6697
15: 8 and dwelt in the top of the **r** Etam. 5553
15:11 men of Judah went to the top of the **r** Etam, 5553
15:13 new cords, and brought him up from the **r**. 5553
20:45 fled toward the wilderness unto the **r** of 5553
20:47 fled to the wilderness unto the **r** Rimmon, 5553
20:47 and abode in the **r** Rimmon four months. 5553
21:13 of Benjamin that *were* in the **r** Rimmon, 5553
1Sa 2: 2 neither *is there* any **r** like our God. 6697
14: 4 *there was* a sharp **r** on the one side, and 5553
14: 4 one side, and a sharp **r** on the other side: 5553
23:25 wherefore he came down *into* a **r**, and 5553
2Sa 21:10 and spread it for her upon the **r**, 6697
22: 2 The LORD *is* my **r**, and my fortress, and 5553
22: 3 The God of my **r**; in him will I trust: *he is* 6697
22:32 the LORD? and who *is* a **r**, save our God? 6697
22:47 blessed *be* my **r**; and exalted be the God of 6697
22:47 exalted be the God of the **r** of my salvation. 6697
23: 3 of Israel said, the **R** of Israel spake to me, 6697
1Ch 11:15 thirty captains went down to the **r** to David, 6697
2Ch 25:12 brought them unto the top of the **r**, and 5553
25:12 cast them down from the top of the **r**, 5553
Ne 9:15 broughtest forth water for them out of the **r** 5553
Job 14:18 and the **r** is removed out of his place. 6697
18: 4 and shall the **r** be removed out of his place? 6697
19:24 with an iron pen and lead in the **r** for ever! 6697
24: 8 and embrace the **r** for want of a shelter. 6697
28: 9 He putteth forth his hand upon the **r**; 2496
29: 6 and the **r** poured me out rivers of oil; 6697
39: 1 when the wild goats of the **r** bring forth? 5553
39:28 She dwelleth and abideth on the **r**, upon 5553
39:28 upon the crag of the **r**, and the strong place. 5553
Ps 18: 2 The LORD *is* my **r**, and my fortress, and 5553
18:31 the LORD? or who *is* a **r** save our God? 6697
18:46 blessed *be* my **r**; and let the God of my 6697
27: 5 he hide me; he shall set me up upon a **r**. 6697
28: 1 Unto thee will I cry, O LORD, my **r**; 6697
31: 2 be thou my strong **r**, for a house of defence 6697
31: 3 For thou *art* my **r** and my fortress; therefore 5553
40: 2 set my feet upon a **r**, *and* established my 5553
42: 9 I will say unto God my **r**, Why hast thou 5553
61: 2 lead me to the **r** *that* is higher than I. 6697
62: 2 He only *is* my **r** and my salvation; *he is* my 6697
62: 6 He only *is* my **r** and my salvation: *he is* my 6697
62: 7 the **r** of my strength, *and* my refuge, *is* in 6697
71: 3 save me; for thou *art* my **r** and my fortress. 5553
78:16 He brought streams also out of the **r**, and 5553
78:20 Behold, he smote the **r**, that the waters 6697
78:35 And they remembered that God *was* their **r**, 6697
81:16 *with* honey out of the **r** should I have 6697
89:26 my God, and the **r** of my salvation. 6697
92:15 *he is* my **r**, and *there is* no unrighteousness 6697
94:22 and my God *is* the **r** of my refuge. 6697
95: 1 let us make a joyful noise to the **r** of our 6697
105:41 He opened the **r**, and the waters gushed 6697
114: 8 Which turned the **r** *into* a standing water, 6697
Pr 30:19 in the air; the way of a serpent upon a **r**; 6697
SS 2:14 O my dove, *that art* in the clefts of the **r**, 5553
Isa 2:10 Enter into the **r**, and hide thee in the dust, 6697
8:14 for a **r** of offence to both the houses of 6697
10:26 to the slaughter of Midian at the **r** Oreb: 6697
17:10 hast not been mindful of the **r** of thy 6697
22:16 that graveth a habitation for himself in a **r**? 5553
32: 2 as the shadow of a great **r** in a weary land. 5553
42:11 let the inhabitants of the **r** sing, let them 5553
48:21 he caused the waters to flow out of the **r** for 6697
48:21 he clave the **r** also, and the waters gushed 6697
51: 1 look unto the **r** *whence* ye are hewn, and 6697
Jer 5: 3 they have made their faces harder than a **r**; 5553
13: 4 and hide it there in a hole of the **r**. 5553
18:14 *which cometh* from the **r** of the field? 6697
21:13 *and* **r** of the plain, saith the LORD; 6697
23:29 like a hammer *that* breaketh the **r** in pieces? 5553
48:28 dwell in the **r**, and be like the dove *that* 5553
49:16 O thou that dwellest in the clefts of the **r**, 5553
Eze 24: 7 she set it upon the top of a **r**; she poured it 5553
24: 8 I have set her blood upon the top of a **r**, 5553
26: 4 from her, and make her like the top of a **r**. 5553
26:14 I will make thee like the top of a **r**: 5553
Am 6:12 Shall horses run upon the **r**? will *one* plow 5553
Ob 1: 3 thou that dwellest in the clefts of the **r**, 5553
Mt 7:24 a wise man, which built his house upon a **r**: *4073*
7:25 and it fell not: for it was founded upon a **r**. *4073*
16:18 and upon this **r** I will build my church; *4073*
27:60 new tomb, which he had hewn out in the **r**: *4073*
Mk 15:46 in a sepulchre which was hewn out of a **r**, *4073*
Lk 6:48 digged deep, and laid the foundation on a **r**: *4073*
6:48 not shake it: for it was founded upon a **r**. *4073*
8: 6 And some fell upon a **r**; and as soon as it *4073*
8:13 They on the **r** *are they,* which, when they *4073*
Ro 9:33 in Sion a stumblingstone and **r** of offence: *4073*
1Co 10: 4 for they drank of *that* spiritual **R** that *4073*
10: 4 that followed *them:* and *that* **R** was Christ. *4073*
1Pe 2: 8 a stone of stumbling, and a **r** of offence, *4073*

ROCKS (23) [ROCK]

Nu 23: 9 For from the top of the **r** I see him, and 6697
1Sa 13: 6 and in **r**, and in high places, and in pits. 5553
24: 2 and his men upon the **r** of the wild goats. 6697
1Ki 19:11 brake in pieces the **r** before the LORD; 5553
Job 28:10 He cutteth out rivers among the **r**; and 6697
30: 6 *in* caves of the earth, and *in* the **r**. 3710
Ps 78:15 He clave the **r** in the wilderness, and 6697
104:18 for the wild goats; *and* the **r** for the conies. 5553
Pr 30:26 yet make they their houses in the **r**; 5553
Isa 2:19 they shall go into the holes of the **r**, and 6697
2:21 To go into the clifts of the **r**, and into 6697
2:21 into the tops of the **ragged r**, for fear of 5553
7:19 in the holes of the **r**, and upon all thorns, 5553
33:16 of defence *shall be* the munitions of **r**: 5553
Isa 57: 5 in the valleys under the clifts of the **r**? 5553
Jer 4:29 go into thickets, and climb up upon the **r**: 3710
16:16 every hill, and out of the holes of the **r**. 5553
51:25 roll thee down from the **r**, and will make 5553
Na 1: 6 like fire, and the **r** are thrown down by him. 6697
Mt 27:51 and the earth did quake, and the **r** rent; *4073*
Ac 27:29 lest we should have fallen upon **r**, *5117+5138*
Rev 6:15 in the dens and in the **r** of the mountains; *4073*
6:16 And said to the mountains and **r**, Fall on us, *4073*

ROD (86) [RODS]

Ex 4: 2 *is* that in thine hand? And he said, A **r**. 4294
4: 4 and caught it, and it became a **r** in his hand: 4294
4:17 thou shalt take this **r** in thine hand, 4294
4:20 and Moses took the **r** of God in his hand. 4294
7: 9 Take thy **r**, and cast *it* before Pharaoh, *and* 4294
7:10 Aaron cast down his **r** before Pharaoh, and 4294
7:12 For they cast down every man his **r**, and 4294
7:12 but Aaron's **r** swallowed up their rods. 4294
7:15 the **r** which was turned to a serpent shalt 4294
7:17 I will smite with the **r** that *is* in mine hand 4294
7:19 Take thy **r**, and stretch out thine hand upon 4294
7:20 he lift up the **r**, and smote the waters that 4294
8: 5 Stretch forth thine hand with thy **r** over 4294
8:16 Stretch out thy **r**, and smite the dust of 4294
8:17 for Aaron stretched out his hand with his **r**, 4294
9:23 Moses stretched forth his **r** toward heaven: 4294
10:13 Moses stretched forth his **r** over the land of 4294
14:16 lift thou up thy **r**, and stretch out thine hand 4294
17: 5 and thy **r**, wherewith thou smotest the river, 4294
17: 9 of the hill with the **r** of God in mine hand. 4294
21:20 with a **r**, and he die under his hand; 7626
Lev 27:32 *even of* whatsoever passeth under the **r**, 7626
Nu 17: 2 take of every one of them a **r** according to 4294
17: 2 write thou every man's name upon his **r**. 4294
17: 3 thou shalt write Aaron's name upon the **r** 4294
17: 3 for one **r** *shall be* for the head of the house 4294
17: 5 *that* the man's **r**, whom I shall choose, shall 4294
17: 6 every one of their princes gave him a **r** 4294
17: 6 and the **r** of Aaron *was* among their rods. 4294
17: 8 the **r** of Aaron for the house of Levi was 4294
17: 9 and they looked, and took every man his **r**. 4294
17:10 Bring Aaron's **r** again before 4294
20: 8 Take the **r**, and gather thou the assembly 4294
20: 9 Moses took the **r** from before the LORD, 4294
20:11 and with his **r** he smote the rock twice: 4294
1Sa 14:27 wherefore he put forth the end of the **r** that 4294
14:43 taste a little honey with the end of the **r** that 4294
2Sa 7:14 I will chasten him with the **r** of men, and 7626
Job 9:34 Let him take his **r** away from me, and 7626
21: 9 neither *is* the **r** of God upon them. 7626
Ps 2: 9 Thou shalt break them with a **r** of iron; 7626
23: 4 thy **r** and thy staff they comfort me. 7626
74: 2 the **r** of thine inheritance, *which* thou hast 7626
89:32 will I visit their transgression with the **r**, 7626
110: 2 The LORD shall send the **r** of thy strength 4294
125: 3 For the **r** of the wicked shall not rest upon 7626
Pr 10:13 a **r** *is* for the back of him that is void of 7626
13:24 He that spareth his **r** hateth his son: but 7626
14: 3 In the mouth of the foolish *is* a **r** of pride: 2415
22: 8 reap vanity: and the **r** of his anger shall fail. 7626
22:15 the **r** of correction shall drive it far from 7626
23:13 for *if* thou beatest him with the **r**, he shall 7626
23:14 Thou shalt beat him with the **r**, and 7626
26: 3 for the ass, and a **r** for the fools' back. 7626
29:15 The **r** and reproof give wisdom: but a child 7626
Isa 9: 4 the **r** of his oppressor, as *in* the day of 7626
10: 5 the **r** of mine anger, and the staff in their 7626
10:15 as if the **r** should shake *itself against* them 7626
10:24 he shall smite thee with a **r**, and shall lift up 7626
10:26 *as* his **r** *was* upon the sea, so shall he lift it 4294
11: 1 there shall come forth a **r** out of the stem of 2415
11: 4 he shall smite the earth with the **r** of his 7626
14:29 the **r** of him that smote thee is broken: 7626
28:27 out with a staff, and the cummin with a **r**. 7626
30:31 be beaten down, *which* smote with a **r**. 7626
Jer 1:11 And I said, I see a **r** of an almond tree. 4731
10:16 and Israel *is* the **r** of his inheritance: 7626
48:17 the strong staff broken, *and* the beautiful **r**! 4731
51:19 and *Israel is* the **r** of his inheritance: 7626
La 3: 1 hath seen affliction by the **r** of his wrath. 7626
Eze 7:10 the **r** hath blossomed, pride hath budded. 4294
7:11 Violence is risen up into a **r** of wickedness: 4294
19:14 fire is gone out of a **r** of her branches, 4294
19:14 that she hath no strong **r** *to be* a sceptre to 4294
20:37 I will cause you to pass under the **r**, and 7626
21:10 it contemneth the **r** of my son, *as* every 7626
21:13 and what if *the sword* contemn even the **r**? 7626
Mic 5: 1 they shall smite the judge of Israel with a **r** 7626
6: 9 hear ye the **r**, and who hath appointed it. 4294
7:14 Feed thy people with thy **r**, the flock of 7626
1Co 4:21 shall I come unto you with a **r**, or in love, *4464*
Heb 9: 4 and Aaron's **r** that budded, and the tables *4464*
Rev 2:27 And he shall rule them with a **r** of iron; *4464*
11: 1 there was given me a reed like unto a **r**: *4464*
12: 5 who was to rule all nations with a **r** of iron: *4464*
19:15 and he shall rule them with a **r** of iron: and *4464*

RODE (15) [RIDE]

Ge 24:61 they **r** upon the camels, and followed 7392
Jdg 10: 4 he had thirty sons that **r** on thirty ass colts, 7392
12:14 that **r** on threescore and ten ass colts: 7392
1Sa 25:20 it was *so, as* she **r** on the ass, that she came 7392
25:42 Abigail hasted, and rose, and **r** upon an ass, 7392
30:17 young men, which **r** upon camels, and fled. 7392
2Sa 18: 9 Absalom **r** upon a mule, and the mule went 7392
22:11 he **r** upon a cherub, and did fly: and he was 7392
1Ki 13:13 they saddled him the ass: and he **r** thereon, 7392
18:45 great rain. And Ahab **r**, and went to Jezreel. 7392
2Ki 9:16 So Jehu **r** *in a chariot,* and went to Jezreel; 7392
9:25 and thou **r** together after Ahab his father, 7392
Ne 2:12 beast with me, save the beast that I **r** upon. 7392
Est 8:14 *So* the posts that **r** upon mules *and* 7392
Ps 18:10 he **r** upon a cherub, and did fly: yea, he did 7392

R

RODENTS See MOLE; MOLES

RODS (15) [ROD]

Ge 30:37 Jacob took him **r** of green poplar, and 4731
30:37 made the white appear which *was* in the **r**. 4731
30:38 he set the **r** which he had pilled before 4731
30:39 the flocks conceived before the **r**, and 4731
30:41 that Jacob laid the **r** before the eyes of 4731
30:41 that they might conceive among the **r**. 4731
Ex 7:12 but Aaron's rod swallowed up their **r**. 4294
Nu 17: 2 to the house of their fathers twelve **r**: 4294
17: 6 to their fathers' houses, *even* twelve **r**: 4294
17: 6 and the rod of Aaron *was* among their **r**. 4294
17: 7 Moses laid up the **r** before the LORD in 4294
17: 9 Moses brought out all the **r** from before 4294
Eze 19:11 she had strong **r** for the sceptres of them 4294
19:12 her strong **r** were broken and withered; 4294
2Co 11:25 Thrice was I **beaten with r**, once was I *4463*

ROE (7) [ROEBUCK, ROEBUCKS, ROES]

2Sa 2:18 and Asahel *was as* light of foot as a wild **r**. 6643
Pr 5:19 *her be as* the loving hind and pleasant **r**; 3280
6: 5 Deliver thyself as a **r** from the hand *of* 6643
SS 2: 9 My beloved *is* like a **r** or a young hart: 6643
2:17 be thou like a **r** or a young hart upon 6643
8:14 be thou like to a **r** or to a young hart upon 6643
Isa 13:14 it shall be as the chased **r**, and as a sheep 6643

ROEBUCK (4) [ROE]

Dt 12:15 eat thereof, as of the **r**, and as of the hart. 6643
12:22 Even as the **r** and the hart is eaten, so 6643
14: 5 the **r**, and the fallow deer, and the wild 6643
15:22 *shall eat it* alike, as the **r**, and as the hart. 6643

ROEBUCKS (1) [ROE]

1Ki 4:23 and **r**, and fallowdeer, and fatted fowl. 6643

ROES (5) [ROE]

1Ch 12: 8 *were* as swift as the **r** upon the mountains: 6643
SS 2: 7 by the **r**, and by the hinds of the field, 6643
3: 5 by the **r**, and by the hinds of the field, 6643
4: 5 Thy two breasts *are* like two young **r** *that* 6646
7: 3 Thy two breasts *are* like two young **r** *that* 6646

ROGELIM (2)

2Sa 17:27 and Barzillai the Gileadite of **R**, 7274
19:31 Barzillai the Gileadite came down from **R**, 7274

ROHGAH (1)

1Ch 7:34 Ahi, and **R**, Jehubbah, and Aram. 7303

ROLL (28) [ROLLED, ROLLER, ROLLETH, ROLLING, ROLLS]

Ge 29: 8 *till* they **r** the stone from the well's mouth; 1556
Jos 10:18 **R** great stones upon the mouth of the cave, 1556
1Sa 14:33 **r** a great stone unto me *this* day. 1556
Ezr 6: 2 a **r**, and therein *was* a record thus written: 4040
Isa 8: 1 Take thee a great **r**, and write in it with a 1549
Jer 36: 2 Take thee a **r** of a book, and write therein 4039
36: 4 had spoken unto him, upon a **r** of a book. 4039
36: 6 Therefore go thou, and read in the **r**, 4039
36:14 Take in thine hand the **r** wherein thou hast 4039
36:14 So Baruch the son of Neriah took the **r** in 4039
36:20 they laid up the **r** in the chamber of 4039
36:21 So the king sent Jehudi to fet the **r**: and 4039
36:23 until all the **r** was consumed in the fire that 4039
36:25 to the king that *he* would not burn the **r**: 4039
36:27 after that the king had burnt the **r**, and 4039
36:28 Take thee again another **r**, and write in it 4039
36:28 all the former words that were in the first **r**, 4039
36:29 Thou hast burnt this **r**, saying, Why hast 4039
36:32 took Jeremiah another **r**, and gave it to 4039
51:25 **r** thee **down** from the rocks, and will make 1556
Eze 2: 9 unto me; and lo, a **r** of a book *was* therein; 4039
3: 1 eat this **r**, and go speak unto the house of 4039
3: 2 my mouth, and he caused me to eat that **r**. 4039
3: 3 fill thy bowels with this **r** that I give thee. 4039
Mic 1:10 in the house of Aphrah **r** thyself *in* the dust. 6428
Zec 5: 1 and looked, and behold, a flying **r**. 4039
5: 2 I answered, I see a flying **r**; the length 4039
Mk 16: 3 Who shall **r** us **away** the stone from the door *617*

ROLLED (12) [ROLL]

Ge 29: 3 they **r** the stone from the well's mouth, and 1556
29:10 **r** the stone from the well's mouth, and 1556
Jos 5: 9 *This* day have I **r away** the reproach of 1556
Job 30:14 the desolation they **r** themselves *upon me.* 1556
Isa 9: 5 confused noise, and garments **r** in blood; 1556
34: 4 the heavens shall be **r together** as a scrole: 1556
Mt 27:60 he **r** a great stone to the door of *4351*
28: 2 came and **r back** the stone from the door, *617*
Mk 15:46 **r** a stone unto the door of the sepulchre. *4351*
16: 4 they saw that the stone was **r away**: *617*
Lk 24: 2 And they found the stone **r away** from *617*
Rev 6:14 departed as a scrole when it is **r together**; *1507*

ROLLER (1) [ROLL]

Eze 30:21 to put a **r** to bind it, to make it strong to 2848

ROLLETH (1) [ROLL]

Pr 26:27 he that **r** a stone, it will return upon him. 1556

ROLLING (1) [ROLL]

Isa 17:13 and like a **r thing** before the whirlwind. 1534

ROLLS (1) [ROLL]

Ezr 6: 1 and search was made in the house of the **r**, 5609

ROMAMTI-EZER (2)

1Ch 25: 4 Hanani, Eliathah, Giddalti, and **R**, 7320
25:31 The four and twentieth to **R**, *he,* his sons, 7320

ROMAN (5) [ROME]

Ac 22:25 lawful for you to scourge a man *that is* a **R**, *4514*
22:26 heed what thou doest: for this man is a **R**. *4514*
22:27 and said unto him, Tell me, art thou a **R**? *4514*
22:29 after he knew that he was a **R**, and because *4514*
23:27 having understood that he was a **R**. *4514*

ROMANS (7) [ROME]

Jn 11:48 and the **R** shall come and take away both *4514*
Ac 16:21 us to receive, neither to observe, being **R**. *4514*
16:37 being **R**, and have cast *us* into prison; *444+4514*
16:38 when they heard that they were **R**, *4514*
25:16 It is not the manner of the **R** to deliver any *4514*
28:17 from Jerusalem into the hands of the **R**. *4514*
Ro 16: S Written to the **R** from Corinthus, *and* *4514*

ROME (15) [ROMAN, ROMANS]

Ac 2:10 and strangers **of R**, Jews and proselytes, *4514*
18: 2 had commanded all Jews to depart from **R**:) *4516*
19:21 After I have been there, I must also see **R**. *4516*
23:11 so must thou bear witness also at **R**. *4516*
28:14 them seven days: and so we went toward **R**. *4516*
28:16 And when we came to **R**, the centurion *4516*
Ro 1: 7 To all that be in **R**, beloved of God, *4516*
1:15 preach the gospel to you that are at **R** also. *4516*
Gal 6: S Unto the Galatians written from **R**. *4516*
Eph 6: S Written from **R** unto the Ephesians by *4516*
Php 4: S It was written to the Philippians from **R** by *4516*
Col 4: S Written from **R** to the Colossians by *4516*
2Ti 1:17 But, when he was in **R**, he sought me out *4516*
4: S was written from **R**, when Paul was *4516*
Phm 1: S Written from **R** to Philemon, by Onesimus *4516*

ROOF (20) [ROOFS]

Ge 19: 8 came they under the shadow of my **r**. 6982
Dt 22: 8 then thou shalt make a battlement for thy **r**, 1406
Jos 2: 6 had brought them up to the **r of** the **house**, 1406
2: 6 which she had laid in order upon the **r**. 1406
2: 8 she came up unto them upon the **r**; 1406
Jdg 16:27 *there were* upon the **r** about three thousand 1406
2Sa 11: 2 and walked upon the **r** of the king's house: 1406
11: 2 from the **r** he saw a woman washing 1406
18:24 the watchman went *up* to the **r** over 1406
Ne 8:16 every one upon the **r of** his **house**, and 1406
Job 29:10 tongue cleaved to the **r of** their **mouth**. 2441
Ps 137: 6 let my tongue cleave to the **r of** my **mouth**; 2441
SS 7: 9 the **r of** thy **mouth** like the best wine, 2441
La 4: 4 cleaveth to the **r of** his **mouth** for thirst: 2441
Eze 3:26 thy tongue cleave to the **r of** thy **mouth**, 2441
40:13 the gate from the **r** of *one* little chamber to 1406
40:13 of *one* little chamber to the **r** of another: 1406
Mt 8: 8 that thou shouldest come under my **r**: *4721*
Mk 2: 4 they uncovered the **r** where he was: *4721*
Lk 7: 6 that thou shouldest enter under my **r**: *4721*

ROOFS (2) [ROOF]

Jer 19:13 of all the houses upon whose **r** they have 1406
32:29 upon whose **r** they have offered incense 1406

ROOM (32) [ROOMS]

Ge 24:23 is there **r** *in* thy father's house for us to 4725
24:25 and provender enough, and **r** to lodge in. 4725
24:31 prepared the house, and **r** for the camels. 4725
26:22 For now the LORD hath **made r** for us, 7337
2Sa 19:13 host before me continually in the **r** of Joab. 8478
1Ki 2:35 the son of Jehoiada **in** his **r** over the host: 8478
2:35 Zadok the priest did the king put **in** the **r** of 8478
5: 1 anointed him king **in the r of** his father: 8478
5: 5 whom I will set upon thy throne **in** thy **r**, 8478
8:20 I am risen up **in the r of** David my father, 8478
19:16 shalt thou anoint to be prophet **in** thy **r**. 8478
2Ki 15:25 he killed him, and reigned **in** his **r**. 8478
23:34 of Josiah king **in the r of** Josiah his father, 8478
2Ch 6:10 for I am risen up **in the r of** David my 8478
26: 1 made him king **in the r of** his father 8478
Ps 31: 8 thou hast set my feet in a **large r**. 4800
80: 9 Thou preparedst *r* before it, and didst cause NIH
Pr 18:16 A man's gift **maketh r** for him, and 7337
Mal 3:10 that *there shall* not *be r* enough *to receive* NIH
Mt 2:22 reign in Judea **in the r of** his father Herod, *473*
Mk 2: 2 insomuch that there was no **r** to receive *5562*
14:15 And he will shew you a large **upper r** *508*
Lk 2: 7 because there was no **r** for them in the inn. *5117*
12:17 I have no **r** where to bestow my fruits? NIG
14: 8 to a wedding, sit not down in the **highest r**; *4411*
14: 9 thou begin with shame to take the lowest **r**. *5117*
14:10 art bidden, go and sit down in the lowest **r**; *5117*
14:22 as thou hast commanded, and yet there is **r**. *5117*
22:12 And he shall shew you a large **upper r** *508*
Ac 1:13 they went up into an **upper r**, where abode *5253*
24:27 Porcius Festus **came into** Felix' **r**: *1240+2983*
1Co 14:16 how shall he that occupieth the **r** of *5117*

ROOMS (7) [ROOM]

Ge 6:14 **r** shalt thou make *in* the ark, and shalt pitch 7064
1Ki 20:24 out of his place, and put captains **in** their **r**: 8478
1Ch 4:41 utterly unto this day, and dwelt **in** their **r**: 8478
Mt 23: 6 And love the **uppermost r** at feasts, and *4411*
Mk 12:39 and the **uppermost r** at feasts: *4411*
Lk 14: 7 he marked how they chose out the **chief r**; *4411*
20:46 in the synagogues, and the **chief r** at feasts; *4411*

ROOSTER See COCK; COCKCROWING; GREYHOUND

ROOT (44) [ROOTED, ROOTS]

Dt 29:18 lest there should be among you a **r** that 8328
Jdg 5:14 Out of Ephraim *was there* a **r** of them 8328
1Ki 14:15 he shall **r up** Israel out of this good land, 5428
2Ki 19:30 of Judah shall *yet* again **take r** downward, 8328
Job 5: 3 I have seen the foolish **taking r**: but 8327
14: 8 Though the **r** thereof wax old in the earth, 8328
19:28 seeing the **r** of the matter is found in me; 8328
29:19 My **r** *was* spread out by the waters, and 8328
31:12 and would **r out** all mine increase. 8327
Ps 52: 5 and **r** thee **out** of the land of the living. 8327
80: 9 didst **cause** it **to take deep r**, and 8327+8328
Pr 12: 3 the **r** of the righteous shall not be moved. 8328
12:12 but the **r** of the righteous yieldeth *fruit.* 8328
Isa 5:24 *so* their **r** shall be as rottenness, and 8328
11:10 in that day there shall be a **r** of Jesse, 8328
14:29 for out of the serpent's **r** shall come forth a 8328
14:30 I will kill thy **r** with famine, and he shall 8328
27: 6 **cause** them that come of Jacob **to take r**: 8327
37:31 of Judah shall again take **r** downward, 8328
40:24 yea, their stock shall not **take r** in the earth: 8327
53: 2 tender plant, and as a **r** out of a dry ground: 8328
Jer 1:10 to **r out**, and to pull down, and to destroy, 5428
12: 2 hast planted them, yea, they have **taken r**: 8327
Eze 31: 7 his branches: for his **r** was by great waters. 8328
Hos 9:16 Ephraim is smitten, their **r** is dried up, 8328
Mal 4: 1 that it shall leave them neither **r** nor branch. 8328
Mt 3:10 And now also the axe is laid unto the **r** of *4491*
13: 6 and because *they* had not **r**, they withered *4491*
13:21 Yet hath he not **r** in himself, but dureth for *4491*
13:29 the tares, ye **r up** also the wheat with them. *1610*
Mk 4: 6 and because *it* had no **r**, it withered away. *4491*
4:17 And have no **r** in themselves, and so endure *4491*
Lk 3: 9 And now also the axe is laid unto the **r** of *4491*
8:13 and these have no **r**, which for a while *4491*
17: 6 Be thou **plucked up by the r**, and be thou *1610*
Ro 11:16 the lump *is* also *holy:* and if the **r** *be* holy, *4491*
11:17 and with *them* partakest of the **r** and *4491*
11:18 thou bearest not the **r**, but the root thee. *4491*
11:18 thou bearest not the root, but the **r** thee. *4491*
15:12 There shall be a **r** of Jesse, and he that *shall* *4491*
1Ti 6:10 For the love of money is the **r** of all evil: *4491*
Heb 12:15 lest any **r** of bitterness springing up trouble *4491*
Rev 5: 5 Lion of the tribe of Juda, the **r** of David, *4491*
22:16 I am the **r** and the offspring of David, *and* *4491*

ROOTED (8) [ROOT]

Dt 29:28 the LORD **r** them **out** of their land in 5428
Job 18:14 His confidence shall be **r out** of his 5423
31: 8 another eat; yea, let my offspring be **r out**. 8327
Pr 2:22 and the transgressors shall be **r** out of it. 5255
Zep 2: 4 at the noon day, and Ekron shall be **r up**. 6131
Mt 15:13 Father hath not planted, shall be **r up**. *1610*
Eph 3:17 that ye, being **r** and grounded in love, *4492*
Col 2: 7 **R** and built up in him, and stablished in *4492*

ROOTS (20) [ROOT]

2Ch 7:20 will I **pluck** them **up by the r** out of my 5428
Job 8:17 His **r** are wrapped about the heap, *and* 8328
18:16 His **r** shall be dried up beneath, and 8328
28: 9 he overturneth the mountains by the **r**. 8328
30: 4 by the bushes, and juniper **r** *for* their meat. 8328
Isa 11: 1 and a Branch shall grow out of his **r**: 8328
Jer 17: 8 *that* spreadeth out her **r** by the river, and 8328
Eze 17: 6 and the **r** thereof were under him: 8328
17: 7 this vine did bend her **r** toward him, and 8328
17: 9 shall he not pull up the **r** thereof, and cut 8328
17: 9 many people to pluck it up by the **r** thereof. 8328
Da 4:15 Nevertheless leave the stump of his **r** in 8330
4:23 yet leave the stump of the **r** thereof in 8330
4:26 to leave the stump of the tree **r**; 8330
7: 8 three of the first horns **pluckt up by** the **r**: 6132
11: 7 out of a branch of her **r** shall *one* stand up 8328
Hos 14: 5 as the lily, and cast forth his **r** as Lebanon. 8328
Am 2: 9 fruit from above, and his **r** from beneath. 8328
Mk 11:20 they saw the fig tree dried up from the **r**. *4491*
Jude 1:12 twice dead, **plucked up by the r**; *1610*

ROPE (1) [ROPES]

Isa 5:18 of vanity, and sin as it were with a cart **r**: 5688

ROPES (6) [ROPE]

Jdg 16:11 If they bind me fast with new **r** that never 5688
16:12 Delilah therefore took new **r**, and 5688
2Sa 17:13 shall all Israel bring **r** to that city, and 2256
1Ki 20:31 **r** upon our heads, and go out to the king of 2256
20:32 *put* **r** on their heads, and came to the king 2256
Ac 27:32 Then the soldiers cut off the **r** of the boat, *4979*

ROSE (136) [RISE]

Ge 4: 8 that Cain **r up** against Abel his brother, and 6965
18:16 the men **r up** from thence, and 6965
19: 1 Lot seeing *them* **r up** to meet them; and 6965
20: 8 Therefore Abimelech **r early** in 7925
21:14 Abraham **r up early** in the morning, and 7925
21:32 Abimelech **r up**, and Phichol the chief 6965
22: 3 Abraham **r up early** in the morning, and 7925
22: 3 **r up**, and went unto the place of which God 6965
22:19 they **r up** and went together to Beer-sheba; 6965
24:54 they **r up** in the morning, and he said, 6965
25:34 and drink, and **r up**, and went his way: 6965
26:31 they **r up betimes** in the morning, and 7925
28:18 Jacob **r up early** in the morning, and 7925
31:17 Jacob **r up**, and set his sons and his wives 6965
31:21 he **r up**, and passed over the river, and 6965
31:55 **early** in the morning Laban **r up**, and 7925
32:22 he **r up** that night, and took his two wives, 6965
32:31 as he passed over Penuel the sun **r** upon 2224
37:35 and all his daughters **r up** to comfort him; 6965
43:15 **r up**, and went down *to* Egypt, and 6965
46: 5 Jacob **r up** from Beer-sheba: and the sons 6965
Ex 10:23 neither **r** any from his place for three days: 6965
12:30 Pharaoh **r up** in the night, he, and all his 6965
15: 7 overthrown them that **r up against** thee: 6965
24: 4 **r up early** in the morning, and builded an 7925
24:13 Moses **r up**, and his minister Joshua: and 6965
32: 6 they **r up early** on the morrow, and 7925
32: 6 down to eat and to drink, and **r up** to play. 6965
33: 8 *that* all the people **r up**, and stood every 6965
33:10 all the people **r up** and worshipped, 6965
34: 4 Moses **r up early** in the morning, and 7925
Nu 14:40 they **r up early** in the morning, and 7925

Nu 16: 2 they **r up** before Moses, with certain of 6965
16:25 Moses **r up** and went unto Dathan and 6965
22:13 Balaam **r up** in the morning, and said unto 6965
22:14 the princes of Moab **r up**, and they went 6965
22:21 Balaam **r up** in the morning, and 6965
24:25 Balaam **r up**, and went and returned to his 6965
25: 7 saw *it*, he **r up** from amongst 6965
Dt 33: 2 from Sinai, and **r up** from Seir unto them; 2224
Jos 3: 1 Joshua **r early** in the morning; and 7925
3:16 above stood *and* **r up** *upon* a heap very far, 6965
6:12 Joshua **r early** in the morning, and 7925
6:15 that they **r early** about the dawning of 7925
7:16 So Joshua **r up early** in the morning, and 7925
8:10 Joshua **r up early** in the morning, and 7925
8:14 Ai saw *it*, that they hasted and **r up early**, 7925
Jdg 6:21 and there **r up** fire out of the rock, 5927
6:38 for he **r up early** on the morrow, and 7925
7: 1 **r up early**, and pitched beside the well of 7925
9:34 Abimelech **r up**, and all the people that 6965
9:35 Abimelech **r up**, and the people that *were* 6965
9:43 and he **r up** against them, and smote them. 6965
19: 5 early in the morning, that he **r up** to depart: 6965
19: 7 when the man **r up** to depart, his father in 6965
19: 9 when the man **r up** to depart, he, and 6965
19:10 he **r up** and departed, and came over 6965
19:27 her lord **r up** in the morning, and 6965
19:28 the man **r up**, and gat him unto his place. 6965
20: 5 the men of Gibeah **r** against me, and 6965
20:19 the children of Israel **r up** in the morning, 6965
20:33 all the men of Israel **r up** out of their place, 6965
21: 4 that the people **r early**, and built there an 7925
Ru 3:14 she **r up** before one could know another. 6965
1Sa 1: 9 So Hannah **r up** after *they* had eaten in 6965
1:19 they **r up** in the morning **early**, and 7925
15:12 when Samuel **r early** to meet Saul in 7925
16:13 So Samuel **r up**, and went to Ramah. 6965
17:20 David **r up early** in the morning, and 7925
24: 7 Saul **r up** out of the cave, and went on *his* 6965
24: 8 David also **r** afterward, and went out of 6965
25:42 Abigail hasted, and **r**, and rode upon an ass, 6965
29:11 his men **r up early** to depart in 7925
2Sa 15: 2 Absalom **r up early**, and stood beside 7925
18:31 *this* day of all them that **r up** against thee. 6965
19: 8 the king **r**, and sat in the gate. And they 6965
22:40 them that **r up** against me hast thou 6965
22:49 on high above them that **r up** against me: 6965
1Ki 1:49 and **r up**, and went every man his way. 6965
2:19 the king **r up** to meet her, and 6965
3:20 she **r** at midnight, and took my son from 6965
3:21 when I **r** in the morning to give my child 6965
21:16 that Ahab **r up** to go down to the vineyard 6965
2Ki 3:22 they **r up early** in the morning, and the sun 7925
3:24 the Israelites **r up** and smote the Moabites, 6965
7: 5 they **r up** in the twilight, to go unto 6965
8:21 he **r** by night, and smote the Edomites 6965
2Ch 20:20 they **r early** in the morning, and went forth 7925
21: 9 he **r up** by night, and smote the Edomites 6965
26:19 the leprosy even **r up** in his forehead 2224
28:15 men which were expressed by name **r up**, 6965
29:20 Hezekiah the king **r early**, and gathered 7925
Ezr 1: 5 **r up** the chief of the fathers of Judah and 6965
5: 2 **r up** Zerubbabel the son of Shealtiel, and 6966
10: 6 Ezra **r up** from before the house of God, 6965
Ne 3: 1 Eliashib the high priest **r up** with his 6965
4:14 **r up**, and said unto the nobles, and to 6965
Job 1: 5 **r up early** in the morning, and 7925
Ps 18:39 under me those that **r up against** me. 6965
124: 2 was on our side, when men **r up** against us: 6965
SS 2: 1 I am the **r** of Sharon, *and* the lily of 2261
5: 5 I **r up** to open to my beloved; and 6965
Isa 35: 1 desert shall rejoice, and blossom as the **r**. 2261
Jer 26:17 **r up** certain of the elders of the land, and 6965
La 3:62 The lips of those that **r up** against me, and 6965
Da 3:24 **r up** in haste, *and* spake, and said unto his 6966
8:27 afterward I **r up**, and did the king's 6965
Jnh 1: 3 Jonah **r up** to flee unto Tarshish from 6965
4: 7 God prepared a worm when the morning **r** 5927
Zep 3: 7 they **r early**, *and* corrupted all their doings. 7925
Mk 10: 1 And he **r** from thence, *450*
10:50 away his garment, **r**, and came to Jesus. *450*
Lk 4:29 And **r up**, and thrust him out of the city, and *450*
5:25 And immediately he **r up** before them, and *450*
5:28 And he left all, **r up**, and followed him. *450*
8:24 Master, master, we perish. Then he **r**, *1453*
16:31 be persuaded, though one **r** from the dead. *450*
22:45 And when he **r up** from prayer, and *450*
24:33 And they **r up** the same hour, and *450*
Jn 11:31 that she **r up** hastily and went out, *450*
Ac 5:17 Then the high priest **r up**, and all they that *450*
5:36 For before these days **r up** Theudas, *450*
5:37 After this *man* **r up** Judas of Galilee in *450*
10:41 and drink with him after he **r** from the dead. *450*
14:20 about him, he **r up**, and came into the city: *450*
15: 5 But there **r up** certain of the sect of *1817*
15: 7 Peter **r up**, and said unto them, Men *and* *450*
16:22 And the multitude **r up together** against *4911*
26:30 thus spoken, the king **r up**, and the governor, *450*
Ro 14: 9 For to this end Christ both died, and **r**, *450*
1Co 10: 7 sat down to eat and drink, and **r up** to play. *450*
15: 4 that he **r** *again* the third day according to *1453*
15:12 Now if Christ be preached that he **r** from *1453*
2Co 5:15 unto him which died for them, and **r** *again*. *1453*
1Th 4:14 if we believe that Jesus died and **r again**, *450*
Rev 19: 3 And her smoke **r up** for ever and ever. *305*

ROSH (1)

Ge 46:21 and Ashbel, Gera, and Naaman, Ehi, and **R**, 7220

ROT (5) [ROTTEN, ROTTENNESS]

Nu 5:21 when the LORD doth make thy thigh to **r**, 5307
5:22 make *thy* belly to swell, and *thy* thigh to **r**: 5307
5:27 her belly shall swell, and her thigh shall **r**: 5307
Pr 10: 7 but the name of the wicked shall **r**. 7537
Isa 40:20 no oblation chooseth a tree *that* will not **r**; 7537

ROTTEN (5) [ROT]

Job 13:28 he, as a **r thing**, consumeth, as a garment 7538
41:27 iron as straw, *and* brass as **r** wood. 7539
Jer 38:11 took thence old cast clouts and old **r rags**, 4418
38:12 **r rags** under thine armholes under 4418
Joel 1:17 The seed is **r** under their clods, the garners 5685

ROTTENNESS (5) [ROT]

Pr 12: 4 she that maketh ashamed *is* as **r** in his 7538
14:30 of the flesh: but envy the **r** of the bones. 7538
Isa 5:24 *so* their root shall be as **r**, and their blossom 4716
Hos 5:12 as a moth, and to the house of Judah as **r**. 7538
Hab 3:16 **r** entered into my bones, and I trembled in 7538

ROUGH (7) [ROUGHLY]

Dt 21: 4 shall bring down the heifer unto a **r** valley, 386
Isa 27: 8 he stayeth his **r** wind in the day of the east 7186
40: 4 be made straight, and the **r places** plain: 7406
Jer 51:27 cause the horses to come up as the **r** 5569
Da 8:21 the **r** goat *is* the king of Grecia: and 8163
Zec 13: 4 neither shall they wear a **r** garment to 8181
Lk 3: 5 and the **r** ways *shall be* made smooth; *5138*

ROUGHLY (6) [ROUGH]

Ge 42: 7 strange unto them, and spake **r** unto them; 7186
42:30 spake **r** to us, and took us for spies of 7186
1Sa 20:10 tell me? or what *if* thy father answer thee **r**? 7186
1Ki 12:13 the king answered the people **r**, and 7186
2Ch 10:13 the king answered them **r**; and king 7186
Pr 18:23 useth intreaties; but the rich answereth **r**. 5794

ROUND (320)

Ge 19: 4 **compassed** the house **r**, both old and 5437
23:17 that *were* in all the borders **r about**, 5439
35: 5 was upon the cities that *were* **r about** them, 5439
37: 7 your sheaves **stood r about**, and 5437
41:48 of the field, which *was* **r about** every city, 5439
Ex 7:24 all the Egyptians digged **r about** the river 5439
16:13 in the morning the dew lay **r about** 5439
16:14 of the wilderness *there lay* a small **r thing**, 2636
19:12 shalt set bounds unto the people **r about**, 5439
25:11 shalt make upon it a crown *of* gold **r about**. 5439
25:24 and make thereto a crown *of* gold **r about**. 5439
25:25 unto it a border of a handbreadth **r about**, 5439
25:25 golden crown to the border thereof **r about**. 5439
27:17 All the pillars **r about** the court *shall be* 5439
28:32 of woven work **r about** the hole of it, 5439
28:33 and of scarlet, **r about** the hem thereof; 5439
28:33 and bells of gold between them **r about**: 5439
28:34 upon the hem of the robe **r about**. 5439
29:16 and sprinkle *it* **r about** upon the altar. 5439
29:20 sprinkle the blood upon the altar **r about**. 5439
30: 3 the sides thereof **r about**, and the horns 5439
30: 3 shalt make unto it a crown *of* gold **r about**. 5439
37: 2 and made a crown *of* gold to it **r about**. 5439
37:11 made thereunto a crown *of* gold **r about**. 5439
37:12 a border of a handbreadth **r about**; 5439
37:12 of gold for the border thereof **r about**. 5439
37:26 the sides thereof **r about**, and the horns of 5439
37:26 he made unto it a crown *of* gold **r about**. 5439
38:16 All the hangings of the court **r about** *were* 5439
38:20 and of the court **r about**, *were of* brass. 5439
38:31 the sockets of the court **r about**, and 5439
38:31 and all the pins of the court **r about**. 5439
39:23 *with* a band **r about** the hole, *that* it should 5439
39:25 **r about** between the pomegranates; 5439
39:26 **r about** the hem of the robe to minister *in;* 5439
40: 8 thou shalt set up the court **r about**, and 5439
40:33 he reared up the court **r about** 5439
Lev 1: 5 sprinkle the blood **r about** upon the altar 5439
1:11 shall sprinkle his blood **r about** upon 5439
3: 2 sprinkle the blood upon the altar **r about**. 5439
3: 8 the blood thereof **r about** upon the altar. 5439
3:13 the blood thereof upon the altar **r about**. 5439
7: 2 the blood thereof shall he sprinkle **r about** 5439
8:15 put *it* upon the horns of the altar **r about** 5439
8:19 sprinkled the blood upon the altar **r about**. 5439
8:24 sprinkled the blood upon the altar **r about**. 5439
9:12 which he sprinkled **r about** upon the altar. 5439
9:18 which he sprinkled upon the altar **r about**, 5439
14:41 the house to be scraped within **r about**, 5439
16:18 put *it* upon the horns of the altar **r about**. 5439
19:27 Ye shall not **r** the corners of your heads, 5362
25:31 **r about** them shall be counted as the fields 5439
25:44 *shall be* of the heathen that *are* **r about** 5439
Nu 1:50 and shall encamp **r about** the tabernacle. 5439
1:53 the Levites shall pitch **r about** 5439
3:26 by the altar **r about**, and the cords of it for 5439
3:37 the pillars of the court **r about**, and 5439
4:26 by the tabernacle and by the altar **r about**, 5439
4:32 the pillars of the court **r about**, and 5439
11:24 and set them **r about** the tabernacle. 5439
11:31 **r about** the camp, and as it were two cubits 5439
11:32 abroad for themselves **r about** the camp. 5439
16:34 all Israel that *were* **r about** them fled at 5439
22: 4 company lick up all *that are* **r about** us, 5439
32:33 *even* the cities of the country **r about**. 5439
34:12 your land with the coasts thereof **r about**. 5439
35: 2 Levites suburbs for the cities **r about** them. 5439
35: 4 and outward a thousand cubits **r about**. 5439
Dt 6:14 of the gods of the people which *are* **r about** 5439
12:10 rest from all your enemies **r about**, 4480+5439
13: 7 gods of the people which *are* **r about** you, 5439
21: 2 cities which *are* **r about** him that is slain: 5439
25:19 rest from all thine enemies **r about**, 4480+5439
Jos 6: 3 men of war, *and* **go r about** the city once. 5362
7: 9 land shall hear *of it*, and shall **environ** us **r**, 5437
15:12 Judah **r about** according to their families. 5439
18:20 by the coasts thereof **r about**, according to 5439
19: 8 all the villages that *were* **r about** these 5439
21:11 with the suburbs thereof **r about** it. 5439
21:42 every one with their suburbs **r about** them: 5439
21:44 the LORD gave them rest **r about**, 5439
23: 1 Israel from all their enemies **r about**, 4480+5439
Jdg 2:12 of the gods of the people that *were* **r about** 5439
2:14 the hands of their enemies **r about**, 4480+5439
7:21 they stood every man in his place **r about** 5439
19:22 **beset** the house **r about**, *and* beat at 5437
20: 5 **beset** the house **r about** upon me by night, 5437
20:29 And Israel set liers in wait **r about** Gibeah. 5439
20:43 *Thus* they **inclosed** the Benjamites **r about**, 3803
1Sa 14:21 into the camp *from the country* **r about**, 5439
23:26 **compassed** David and his men **r about** 5849
26: 5 and the people pitched **r about** him. 5439
26: 7 but Abner and the people lay **r about** him. 5439
31: 9 sent into the land of the Philistines **r about**, 5439
2Sa 5: 9 David built **r about** from Millo and inward. 5439
7: 1 rest **r about** from all his enemies; 4480+5439
22:12 he made darkness pavilions **r about** him, 5439
1Ki 3: 1 and the wall of Jerusalem **r about**. 5439
4:24 had peace on all sides **r about** him. 4480+5439
4:31 and his fame was in all nations **r about**. 5439
6: 5 of the house he built chambers **r about**, 5439
6: 5 *against* the walls of the house **r about**, 5439
6: 5 the oracle: and he made chambers **r about**: 5439
6: 6 the house he made narrowed rests **r about**, 5439
6:29 he carved all the walls of the house **r about** 4524
7:12 the great court **r about** *was with* three rows 5439
7:18 two rows **r about** upon the one network, 5439
7:20 *in* rows **r about** upon the other chapiter. 5439
7:23 *it was* **r** all about, and his height *was* five 5696
7:23 thirty cubits did **compass** it **r about**. 5437+5439
7:24 **r about** *there were* knops **compassing** 5437+5439
7:24 ten in a cubit, compassing the sea **r about**: 5439
7:31 the mouth thereof *was* **r** *after* the work of 5696
7:31 with their borders, foursquare, not **r**. 5696
7:35 in the top of the base *was there* a **r** compass 5696
7:36 of every one, and additions **r about**. 5439
10:19 and the top of the throne *was* **r** behind: 5696
18:35 the water ran **r about** the altar; and 5439
2Ki 6:17 and chariots of fire **r about** Elisha. 5439
11: 8 ye shall compass the king **r about**, 5439
11:11 his weapons in his hand, **r about** the king, 5439
17:15 *went* after the heathen that *were* **r about** 5439
23: 5 and in the **places r about** Jerusalem; 4524
25: 1 and they built forts against it **r about**. 5439
25: 4 Chaldees *were* against the city **r about**:) 5439
25:10 brake down the walls of Jerusalem **r about**. 5439
25:17 pomegranates upon the chapiter **r about**, 5439
1Ch 4:33 all their villages that *were* **r about** the same 5439
6:55 and the suburbs thereof **r about** it. 5439
9:27 they lodged **r about** the house of God, 5439
10: 9 sent into the land of the Philistines **r about**, 5439
11: 8 he built the city **r about**, even from Millo 5439
11: 8 city round about, even from Millo **r about**: 5439
22: 9 rest from all his enemies **r about**: 4480+5439
28:12 of all the chambers **r about**, of 5439
2Ch 4: 2 **r** in compass, and five cubits the height 5696
4: 2 line of thirty cubits did compass it **r about**. 5439
4: 3 which did compass it **r about**: 5439+5439
4: 3 ten in a cubit, compassing the sea **r about**. 5439
14:14 they smote all the cities **r about** Gerar; 5439
15:15 the LORD gave them rest **r about**. 4480+5439
17:10 of the lands that *were* **r about** Judah, 5439
20:30 for his God gave him rest **r about**. 4480+5439
23: 7 the Levites shall compass the king **r about**, 5439
23:10 and the temple, by the king **r about**. 5439
34: 6 unto Naphtali, with their mattocks **r about**. 5439
Ne 12:28 both out of the plain country **r about** 5439
12:29 builded them villages **r about** Jerusalem. 5439
Job 10: 8 and fashioned me together **r about**; 5439
16:13 His archers **compass** me **r about**, he 5437
19:12 and encamp **r about** my tabernacle. 5439
22:10 Therefore snares *are* **r about** thee, and 5439
37:12 it is turned **r about** by his counsels: 4524
41:14 of his face? his teeth *are* terrible **r about**. 5439
Ps 3: 6 have set *themselves* against me **r about**. 5439
18:11 his pavilion **r about** him *were* dark waters 5439
22:12 strong *bulls* of Bashan have **beset** me **r**. 3803
27: 6 lifted up above mine enemies **r about** me: 5439
34: 7 encampeth **r about** them that fear him, 5439
44:13 and a derision to them that are **r about** us. 5439
48:12 Walk about Zion, and **go r about** her: 5362
50: 3 it shall be very tempestuous **r about** him. 5439
59: 6 a noise like a dog, and **go r about** the city. 5437
59:14 a noise like a dog, and **go r about** the city. 5437
76:11 let all that be **r about** him bring presents 5439
78:28 of their camp, **r about** their habitations. 5439
79: 3 they shed like water **r about** Jerusalem; 5439
79: 4 and derision to them that are **r about** us. 5439
88:17 They **came r about** me daily like water; 5437
89: 8 or *to* thy faithfulness **r about** thee? 5439
97: 2 Clouds and darkness *are* **r about** him: 5439
97: 3 and burneth up his enemies **r about**. 5439
125: 2 *As* the mountains *are* **r about** Jerusalem, so 5439
125: 2 the LORD *is* **r about** his people from 5439
128: 3 thy children like olive plants **r about** thy 5439
SS 7: 2 Thy navel *is like* a **r** goblet, *which* wanteth 5469
Isa 3:18 *their* cauls, and *their* **r tires like the moon**, 7720
15: 8 For the cry is **gone r about** the borders of 5362
29: 3 camp against thee **r about**, 1754+1886.1+3509.1
42:25 it hath set him on fire **r about**, yet he 4480+5439
49:18 Lift up thine eyes **r about**, and behold: 5439
60: 4 Lift up thine eyes **r about**, and see: all they 5439
Jer 1:15 against all the walls thereof **r about**, and 5439
4:17 a field, are they against her **r about**; 4480+5439
6: 3 shall pitch *their* tents against her **r about**; 5439
12: 9 the birds **r about** *are* against her; 5439
21:14 and it shall devour all things **r about** it. 5439
25: 9 against all these nations **r about**, and 5439
46: 5 fear *was* **r about**, saith the LORD. 4480+5439
46:14 for the sword shall devour **r about** thee. 5439
50:14 in array against Babylon **r about**: 5439
50:15 Shout against her **r about**: she hath given 5439
50:29 that bend the bow, camp against it **r about**; 5439
50:32 and it shall devour all **r about** him. 5439
51: 2 they shall be against her **r about**. 4480+5439
52: 4 against it, and built forts against it **r about**. 5439
52: 7 the Chaldeans *were* by the city **r about**:) 5439

Jer 52:14 down all the walls of Jerusalem **r about.** 5439
52:22 pomegranates upon the chapiters **r about,** 5439
52:23 upon the network *were* an hundred **r about.** 5439
La 1:17 *that* his adversaries *should be* **r about** him: 5439
2: 3 a flaming fire, *which* devoureth **r about.** 5439
2:22 *in* a solemn day my terrors **r about,** 4480+5439
Eze 1:18 their rings *were* full *of* eyes **r about** them 5439
1:27 as the appearance of fire **r about** within it, 5439
1:27 of fire, and it had brightness **r about.** 5439
1:28 the appearance of the brightness **r about.** 5439
4: 2 and set *battering* rams against it **r about.** 5439
5: 5 and countries *that are* **r about** her. 5439
5: 6 than the countries that *are* **r about** her: 5439
5: 7 more than the nations that *are* **r about** you, 5439
5: 7 of the nations that *are* **r about** you; 5439
5:12 a third *part* shall fall by the sword **r about** 5439
5:14 among the nations that *are* **r about** thee, 5439
5:15 unto the nations that *are* **r about** thee, 5439
6: 5 I will scatter your bones **r about** your 5439
6:13 be among their idols **r about** their altars, 5439
8:10 pourtrayed upon the wall **r about.** 5439+5439
10:12 and the wheels, *were* full *of* eyes **r about,** 5439
11:12 of the heathen that *are* **r about** you. 5439
16:37 I will even gather them **r about** 4480+5439
16:57 all *that are* **r about** her, the daughters of 5439
16:57 which despise thee **r about.** 4480+5439
23:24 thee buckler and shield and helmet **r about:** 5439
27:11 thine army *were* upon thy walls **r about,** 5439
27:11 their shields upon thy walls **r about;** 5439
28:24 grieving thorn of all *that are* **r about** them, 5439
28:26 that despise them **r about** them; 4480+5439
31: 4 with her rivers running **r about** his plants, 5439
32:23 and her company is **r about** her grave: 5439
32:24 and all her multitude **r about** her grave, 5439
32:25 her graves *are* **r about** him: all of them 5439
32:26 her graves *are* **r about** him: all of them 5439
34:26 and the **places r about** my hill a blessing; 5439
36: 4 of the heathen that *are* **r about;** 4480+5439
36:36 the heathen that are left **r about** you shall 5439
37: 2 caused me to pass by them **r about:** 5439+5439
40: 5 on the outside of the house **r about,** 5439+5439
40:14 post of the court **r about** the gate. 5439+5439
40:16 to their posts within the gate **r about,** 5439+5439
40:16 windows *were* **r about** inward: 5439+5439
40:17 made for the court **r about:** 5439+5439
40:25 and in the arches thereof **r about,** 5439+5439
40:29 and in the arches thereof **r about:** 5439+5439
40:30 the arches **r about** *were* five and 5439+5439
40:33 in the arches thereof **r about:** 5439+5439
40:36 and the windows to it **r about:** 5439+5439
40:43 a hand broad, fastened **r about:** 5439+5439
41: 5 **r about** the house on every side. 5439+5439
41: 6 house for the side chambers **r about,** 5439+5439
41: 7 *went* still upward **r about** the house: 5439+5439
41: 8 also the height of the house **r about:** 5439+5439
41:10 cubits **r about** the house on every side. 5439
41:11 that was left *was* five cubits **r about.** 5439+5439
41:12 *was* five cubits thick **r about,** 5439+5439
41:16 the galleries **r about** on their three *stories,* 5439
41:16 cieled with wood **r about,** and 5439+5439
41:17 by all the wall **r about** within 5439+5439
41:19 made through all the house **r about.** 5439+5439
42:15 the east, and measured it **r about.** 5439+5439
42:16 with the measuring reed **r about.** 5439
42:17 with the measuring reed **r about.** 5439
42:20 it had a wall **r about,** five hundred 5439+5439
43:12 thereof **r about** *shall be* most holy. 5439+5439
43:13 by the edge thereof **r about** *shall be* a span: 5439
43:20 of the settle, and upon the border **r about:** 5439
45: 1 *be* holy in all the borders thereof **r about.** 5439
45: 2 five hundred *in breadth,* square **r about;** 5439
45: 2 fifty cubits **r about** *for* the suburbs thereof. 5439
46:23 *there was* a row *of building* **r about** in 5439
46:23 **r about** them four, and *it was* made *with* 5439
46:23 *with* boiling places under the rows **r about.** 5439
48:35 *It was* **r about** eighteen thousand *measures:* 5439
Joel 3:11 gather yourselves together **r about:** 4480+5439
3:12 I sit to judge all the heathen **r about.** 4480+5439
Am 3:11 An adversary *there shall be* even **r about** 5439
Jnh 2: 5 the depth **closed** me **r about,** the weeds 5437
Na 3: 8 *that had* the waters **r about** it, 5439
Zec 2: 5 will be unto her a wall of fire **r about,** and 5439
7: 7 and the cities thereof **r about** her, 5439
12: 2 of trembling unto all the people **r about,** 5439
12: 6 they shall devour all the people **r about,** 5439
14:14 the wealth of all the heathen **r about** shall 5439
Mt 3: 5 and all the **region r about** Jordan, 4066
14:35 they sent out into all that **country r about,** 4066
21:33 and hedged it **r about,** and digged a 4060
Mk 1:28 throughout all the **region r about** Galilee. 4066
3: 5 And when he had **looked r about** on them 4017
3:34 And he looked **r about** on them which sat 2945
5:32 And he **looked r about** to see her that had 4017
6: 6 And he went **r about** the villages, teaching. 2945
6:36 that they may go into the country **r about,** 2945
6:55 ran through that whole **region r about,** 4066
9: 8 when they had **looked r about,** 4017
10:23 And Jesus **looked r about,** and saith unto 4017
11:11 when he had **looked r about** upon all 4017
Lk 1:65 And fear came on all that **dwelt r about** 4039
2: 9 the glory of the Lord **shone r about** them: 4034
4:14 fame of him through all the **region r about.** 4066
4:37 into every place of the **country r about.** 4066
6:10 And **looking r about** upon them all, he said 4017
7:17 and throughout all the **region r about.** 4066
8:37 **country** of the Gadarenes **r about** 4066
9:12 may go into the towns and country **r about,** 2945
19:43 and **compass** thee **r,** and keep thee in on 4033
Jn 10:24 Then **came** the Jews **r about** him, and 2944
Ac 5:16 *out* of the cities **r about** unto Jerusalem, 4038
9: 3 suddenly there **shined r about** him a light 4015
14: 6 and *unto* the **region that lieth r about:** 4066
14:20 as the disciples **stood r about** him, 2944
22: 6 from heaven a great light **r about** me. 4012
25: 7 came down from Jerusalem **stood r about,** 4026
Ac 26:13 **shining r about** me and them which 4034
Ro 15:19 and **r about** unto Illyricum, 2945
Heb 9: 4 the ark of the covenant overlaid **r about** 3840
Rev 4: 3 *there was* a rainbow **r about** the throne, 2943
4: 4 And **r about** the throne *were* four and 2943
4: 6 midst of the throne, and **r about** the throne, 2945
5:11 I heard the voice of many angels **r about** 2943
7:11 And all the angels stood **r about** the throne, 2945

ROUSE (1)
Ge 49: 9 and as an old lion; who shall **r** him **up?** 6965

ROUTED See DISCOMFITED; DISCOMFITURE

ROUTING See DISCOMFITED; DISCOMFITURE

ROVERS (1)
1Ch 12:21 they helped David against the band *of the* **r.** NIH

ROW (17) [ROWED, ROWERS, ROWING, ROWS]
Ex 28:17 *the first* **r** *shall be* a sardius, a topaz, and 2905
28:17 and a carbuncle: this *shall be* the first **r.** 2905
28:18 the second **r** *shall be* an emerald, 2905
28:19 the third **r** a ligure, an agate, and 2905
28:20 the fourth **r** a beryl, and an onyx, and 2905
39:10 *the first* **r** *was* a sardius, a topaz, and 2905
39:10 and a carbuncle: *this was* the first **r.** 2905
39:11 the second **r,** an emerald, a sapphire, and 2905
39:12 the third **r,** a ligure, an agate, and 2905
39:13 the fourth **r,** a beryl, an onyx, and a jasper: 2905
Lev 24: 6 thou shalt set them *in* two rows, six on a **r,** 4635
24: 7 shalt put pure frankincense upon *each* **r,** 4635
1Ki 6:36 of hewed stone, and a **r** of cedar beams. 2905
7: 3 that *lay* on forty five pillars, fifteen *in* a **r.** 2905
7:12 a **r** of cedar beams, both for the inner court 2905
Ezr 6: 4 rows of great stones, and a **r** of new timber: 5073
Eze 46:23 *there was* a **r** *of building* round about in 2905

ROWED (2) [ROW]
Jnh 1:13 Nevertheless the men **r hard** to bring *it* to 2864
Jn 6:19 So when they had **r** about five and twenty 1643

ROWERS (1) [ROW]
Eze 27:26 Thy **r** have brought thee into great waters: 7751

ROWING (1) [ROW]
Mk 6:48 And he saw them toiling in **r;** for the wind 1643

ROWS (16) [ROW]
Ex 28:17 it settings of stones, *even* four **r** of stones: 2905
39:10 they set in it four **r** of stones: *the first* row 2905
Lev 24: 6 thou shalt set them *in* two **r,** six on a row, 4634
1Ki 6:36 he built the inner court *with* three **r** of 2905
7: 2 thirty cubits, upon four **r** of cedar pillars, 2905
7: 4 *there were* windows *in* three **r,** and 2905
7:12 about *was with* three **r** *of* hewed stones, 2905
7:18 two **r** round about upon the one network, 2905
7:20 the pomegranates *were* two hundred *in* **r** 2905
7:24 the knops *were* cast *in* two **r,** when it was 2905
7:42 *even* two **r** *of* pomegranates for one 2905
2Ch 4: 3 Two **r** *of* oxen *were* cast, when it was cast. 2905
4:13 two **r** *of* pomegranates on each wreath, to 2905
Ezr 6: 4 *With* three **r** of great stones, and a row of 5073
SS 1:10 Thy cheeks are comely with **r** *of jewels,* 8447
Eze 46:23 *it was* made *with* boiling places under the **r** 2918

ROYAL (29)
Ge 49:20 *shall be* fat, and he shall yield **r** dainties. 4428
Jos 10: 2 as one of the **r** cities, and because it *was* 4467
1Sa 27: 5 for why should thy servant dwell in the **r** 4467
2Sa 12:26 the children of Ammon, and took the **r** city. 4410
1Ki 10:13 which Solomon gave her of his **r** bounty. 4428
2Ki 11: 1 she arose and destroyed all the seed **r.** 4467
25:25 of the seed **r,** came, and ten men with him, 4410
1Ch 29:25 bestowed upon him *such* **r** majesty as had 4438
2Ch 22:10 destroyed all the seed **r** of the house of 4467
Est 1: 7 **r** wine in abundance, according to the state 4438
1: 9 **r** house which *belonged* to king Ahasuerus. 4438
1:11 the queen before the king with the crown **r,** 4438
1:19 let there go a **r** commandment from him, 4438
1:19 let the king give her **r estate** unto another 4438
2:16 into his house **r** in the tenth month, 4438
2:17 so that he set the **r** crown upon her head, 4438
5: 1 that Esther put on *her* **r** *apparel,* and 4438
5: 1 the king sat upon his **r** throne in the royal 4438
5: 1 the king sat upon his royal throne in the **r** 4438
6: 8 Let the **r** apparel be brought which the king 4438
6: 8 the crown **r** which is set upon his head: 4438
8:15 the presence of the king in **r** apparel *of* blue 4438
Isa 62: 3 and a **r** diadem in the hand of thy God. 4410
Jer 41: 1 of the seed **r,** and the princes of the king, 4410
43:10 he shall spread his **r pavilion** over them. 8237
Da 6: 7 have consulted together to establish a **r** 4430
Ac 12:21 arrayed in **r** apparel, sat upon his throne, and 937
Jas 2: 8 If ye fulfil the **r** law according to 937
1Pe 2: 9 a **r** priesthood, a holy nation, a peculiar 934

RUBBING (1)
Lk 6: 1 of corn, and did eat, **r** *them* in *their* hands. 5597

RUBBISH (2)
Ne 4: 2 out of the heaps of the **r** which are burnt? 6083
4:10 of burdens is decayed, and *there is* much **r;** 6083

RUBIES (6)
Job 28:18 for the price of wisdom *is* above **r.** 6443
Pr 3:15 She *is* more precious than **r:** and all 6443
8:11 For wisdom *is* better than **r;** and all 6443
20:15 There is gold, and a multitude of **r:** but 6443
31:10 for her price *is* far above **r.** 6443
La 4: 7 they were more ruddy *in* body than **r,** 6443

RUBY See AGATES; SARDIUS

RUDDER (1)
Ac 27:40 and loosed the **r** bands, and hoised up 4079

RUDDY (4)
1Sa 16:12 Now he *was* **r,** *and* withal of a beautiful 132
17:42 *but* a youth, and **r,** and of a fair countenance. 132
SS 5:10 My beloved *is* white and **r,** the chiefest 122
La 4: 7 they were more **r** *in* body than rubies, 119

RUDE (1)
2Co 11: 6 But though *I be* **r** in speech, yet not in 2399

RUDIMENTS (2)
Col 2: 8 after the **r** of the world, and not after 4747
2:20 be dead with Christ from the **r** of the world, 4747

RUE (1)
Lk 11:42 for ye tithe mint and **r** and all *manner of* 4076

RUFUS (2)
Mk 15:21 the father of Alexander and **R,** to bear his 4504
Ro 16:13 Salute **R** chosen in the Lord, and 4504

RUHAMAH (1) [LO-RUHAMAH]
Hos 2: 1 Ammi; and to your sisters, **R.** 7355

RUIN (11) [RUINED, RUINOUS, RUINS]
2Ch 28:23 they were the **r** of him, and of all Israel. 3782
Ps 89:40 thou hast brought his strong holds to **r.** 4288
Pr 24:22 and who knoweth the **r** of them both? 6365
26:28 by it; and a flattering mouth worketh **r.** 4072
Isa 3: 6 our ruler, and *let* this **r** *be* under thy hand: 4384
23:13 the palaces thereof; *and* he brought it to **r.** 4654
25: 2 of a city a heap; *of* a defenced city a **r:** 4654
Eze 18:30 so iniquity shall not be your **r.** 4383
27:27 the midst of the seas in the day of thy **r.** 4658
31:13 Upon his **r** shall all the fowls of the heaven 4658
Lk 6:49 it fell; and the **r** of that house was great. 4485

RUINED (3) [RUIN]
Isa 3: 8 For Jerusalem is **r,** and Judah is fallen: 3782
Eze 36:35 and **r** cities *are become* fenced, 2040
36:36 know that I the LORD build the **r** *places,* 2040

RUINOUS (3) [RUIN]
2Ki 19:25 be to lay waste fenced cities *into* **r** heaps. 5327
Isa 17: 1 from *being* a city, and it shall be a **r** heap. 4654
37:26 be to lay waste defenced cities *into* **r** heaps. 5327

RUINS (3) [RUIN]
Eze 21:15 heart may faint, and *their* **r** be multiplied: 4383
Am 9:11 I will raise up his **r,** and I will build it as *in* 2034
Ac 15:16 and I will build again the **r** thereof, and 2679

RULE (66) [RULED, RULER, RULER'S, RULERS, RULEST, RULETH, RULING]
Ge 1:16 the greater light to **r** the day, and the lesser 4475
1:16 the day, and the lesser light to **r** the night: 4475
1:18 to **r** over the day and over the night, and 4910
3:16 *be* to thy husband, and he shall **r** over thee. 4910
4: 7 *be* his desire, and thou shalt **r** over him. 4910
Lev 25:43 Thou shalt not **r** over him with rigour; but 7287
25:46 ye shall not **r** one over another with rigour. 7287
25:53 *the other* shall not **r** with rigour **over** him in 7287
Jdg 8:22 **R** thou over us, both thou, and thy son, and 4910
8:23 said unto them, I will not **r** over you, 4910
8:23 over you, neither shall my son **r** over you: 4910
8:23 rule over you: the LORD shall **r** over you. 4910
1Ki 9:23 which **bare r** over the people that wrought 7287
22:31 two captains that had **r** over *his* chariots, NIH
2Ch 8:10 and fifty, that **bare r** over the people. 7287
Ne 5:15 *yea,* even their servants **bare r** over 7980
Est 1:22 that every man should **bear r** in his own 8323
9: 1 the Jews had **r** over them that hated them;) 7980
Ps 110: 2 **r** thou in the midst of thine enemies. 7287
136: 8 The sun to **r** by day: for his mercy *endureth* 4475
136: 9 The moon and stars to **r** by night: for his 4475
Pr 8:16 By me princes **r,** and nobles, *even* all 8323
12:24 The hand of the diligent shall **bear r:** but 4910
17: 2 A wise servant shall **have r** over a son that 4910
19:10 much less for a servant to **have r** over 4910
25:28 He that *hath* no **r** over his own spirit *is like* 4623
29: 2 when the wicked **beareth r,** the people 4910
Ecc 2:19 yet shall he **have r** over all my labour 7980
Isa 3: 4 their princes, and babes shall **r** over them. 4910
3:12 their oppressors, and women **r** over them. 4910
14: 2 and they shall **r** over their oppressors. 7287
19: 4 a fierce king shall **r** over them, saith 4910
28:14 that **r** this people which *is* in Jerusalem. 4910
32: 1 and princes shall **r** in judgment. 8323
40:10 strong *hand,* and his arm *shall* **r** for him: 4910
41: 2 before him, and **made** *him* **r over** kings? 7287
44:13 The carpenter stretcheth out *his* **r;** 6957
52: 5 they that **r over** them make *them* to howl, 4910
63:19 We are *thine:* thou never **barest r** over 4910
Jer 5:31 and the priests **bear r** by their means; 7287
Eze 19:11 rods for the sceptres of them that **bare r,** 4910
19:14 she hath no strong rod *to be* a sceptre to **r.** 4910
20:33 and with fury poured out, will I **r** over you: 4427
29:15 that *they* shall no more **r** over the nations. 7287
Da 2:39 which shall **bear r** over all the earth. 7981
4:26 shalt have known that the heavens do **r.** 7990
11: 3 that shall **r** *with* great dominion, and 4910
11:39 he shall **cause** them to **r over** many, and 4910
Joel 2:17 that the heathen should **r over** them: 4910
Zec 6:13 and shall sit and **r** upon his throne: 4910
Mt 2: 6 a Governor, that shall **r** my people Israel. 4165
Mk 10:42 **r over** the Gentiles exercise lordship over 757
1Co 15:24 when he shall have put down all **r** and 746
2Co 10:13 according to the measure of the **r** which 2583
10:15 by you according to our **r** abundantly, 2583

R

Gal 6:16 And as many as walk according to this **r**, *2583*
Php 3:16 *let us* walk by the same **r**, *let us* mind *2583*
Col 3:15 And let the peace of God **r** in your hearts, *1018*
1Ti 3: 5 (For if a man know not how to **r** his own *4291*
5:17 Let the elders that **r** well be counted worthy *4291*
Heb 13: 7 Remember them which **have the r over** *2233*
13:17 Obey them that **have the r over** you, and *2233*
13:24 Salute all them that **have the r over** you, *2233*
Rev 2:27 And he shall **r** them with a rod of iron; *4165*
12: 5 who was to **r** all nations with a rod of iron: *4165*
19:15 and he shall **r** them with a rod of iron: and *4165*

RULED (13) [RULE]

Ge 24: 2 of his house that **r** over all that he had, 4910
41:40 unto thy word shall all my people be **r**: 5401
Jos 12: 2 who dwelt in Heshbon, *and* **r** from Aroer, 4910
Ru 1: 1 came to pass in the days when the judges **r**, 8199
1Ki 5:16 which **r** over the people that wrought in 7287
1Ch 26: 6 that **r** throughout the house of their father: 4474
Ezr 4:20 which have **r** over all *countries* beyond 7990
Ps 106:41 and they that hated them **r** over them. 4910
Isa 14: 6 he that **r** the nations in anger, *is* persecuted, 7287
La 5: 8 Servants have **r** over us: *there is* none that 4910
Eze 34: 4 with force and with cruelty have ye **r** them. 7287
Da 5:21 till he knew that the most high God **r** in 7990
11: 4 nor according to his dominion which he **r**: 4910

RULER (84) [RULE]

Ge 41:43 he made him **r** over all the land of Egypt. NIH
43:16 he said to **the r** of his house, 834+5921
45: 8 and a **r** throughout all the land of Egypt. 4910
Ex 22:28 the gods, nor curse the **r** of thy people. 5387
Lev 4:22 When a **r** hath sinned, and done somewhat 5387
Nu 13: 2 ye send a man, every one a **r** among them. 5387
Jdg 9:30 when Zebul the **r** of the city heard 8269
1Sa 25:30 and shall have appointed thee **r** over Israel; 5057
2Sa 6:21 to appoint me **r** over the people of 5057
7: 8 to be **r** over my people, over Israel: 5057
20:26 Ira also the Jairite was a **chief r** about 3548
1Ki 1:35 I have appointed him to be **r** over Israel and 5057
11:28 he **made** him **r** over all the charge of 6485
2Ki 25:22 **made** Gedaliah the son of Ahikam, the son of Shaphan, **r**. 6485
1Ch 5: 2 his brethren, and of him *came* the **chief r**; 5057
9:11 son of Ahitub, the **r** of the house of God; 5057
9:20 Phinehas the son of Eleazar was the **r** over 5057
11: 2 and thou shalt be **r** over my people Israel. 5057
17: 7 that *thou* shouldest be **r** over my people 5057
26:24 the son of Moses, *was* **r** of the treasures. 5057
27: 4 and *of* his course *was* Mikloth also the **r**: 5057
27:16 the **r** of the Reubenites *was* Eliezer the son 5057
28: 4 for he hath chosen Judah to be the **r**; and 5057
2Ch 6: 5 neither chose I any man to be a **r** over my 5057
7:18 There shall not fail thee a man *to be* **r** in 4910
11:22 the chief, to be **r** among his brethren: 5057
19:11 the **r** of the house of Judah, for all 5057
26:11 hand of Jeiel the scribe and Maaseiah the **r**, 7860
31:12 over which Cononiah the Levite *was* **r**, and 5057
31:13 and Azariah the **r** of the house of God. 5057
Ne 3: 9 of Hur, the **r** of the half part of Jerusalem. 8269
3:12 the **r** of the half part of Jerusalem, he and 8269
3:14 of Rechab, the **r** of part of Beth-haccerem; 8269
3:15 son of Col-hozeh, the **r** of part of Mizpah; 8269
3:16 of Azbuk, the **r** of the half part of Beth-zur, 8269
3:17 the **r** of the half part of Keilah, in his part. 8269
3:18 of Henadad, the **r** of the half part of Keilah. 8269
3:19 Ezer the son of Jeshua, the **r** of Mizpah, 8269
7: 2 Hananiah the **r** of the palace, charge over 8269
11:11 of Ahitub, *was* the **r** of the house of God. 5057
Ps 68:27 There *is* little Benjamin *with* their **r**, 7287
105:20 *even* the **r** of the people, and let him go 4910
105:21 lord of his house, and **r** of all his substance: 4910
Pr 6: 7 Which having no guide, overseer, or **r**, 4910
23: 1 When thou sittest to eat with a **r**, 4910
28:15 *so is* a wicked **r** over the poor people. 4910
29:12 If a **r** hearken to lies, all his servants *are* 4910
Ecc 10: 4 If the spirit of the **r** rise up against thee, 4910
10: 5 as an error *which* proceedeth from the **r**: 7989
Isa 3: 6 be thou our **r**, and *let* this ruin *be* under thy 7101
3: 7 make me not a **r** of the people. 7101
16: 1 Send ye the lamb *to* the **r** of the land from 4910
Jer 51:46 and violence in the land, **r** against ruler. 4910
51:46 and violence in the land, ruler against **r**. 4910
Da 2:10 therefore *there is* no king, lord, nor **r**, 7990
2:38 and hath **made** thee **r** over them all. 7981
2:48 **made** him **r** over the whole province of 7981
5: 7 and shall be the third **r** in the kingdom. 7981
5:16 and shalt be the third **r** in the kingdom. 7981
5:29 that he should be the third **r** in it 7990
Mic 5: 2 come forth unto me *that is* to be **r** in Israel; 4910
Hab 1:14 creeping things, *that have* no **r** over them? 4910
Mt 9:18 there came a *certain* **r**, and worshipped him, *758*
24:45 whom his lord hath **made r** over his *2525*
24:47 That he shall **make** him **r** over all his *2525*
25:21 **make** thee **r** over many *things:* enter thou *2525*
25:23 **make** thee **r** over many *things:* enter thou *2525*
Mk 5:35 there came from the **r of the synagogue's** *752*
5:36 he saith unto the **r of the synagogue**, Be not *752*
5:38 to the house of the **r of the synagogue**, *752*
Lk 8:41 and he was a **r** of the synagogue: *758*
8:49 **r of the synagogue's** *house,* saying to him, *752*
12:42 whom *his* lord shall **make r** over his *2525*
12:44 that he will **make** him **r** over all that he *2525*
13:14 And the **r of the synagogue** answered with *752*
18:18 And a certain **r** asked him, saying, *758*
Jn 2: 9 When the **r of the feast** had tasted the water *755*
3: 1 named Nicodemus, a **r** of the Jews: *758*
Ac 7:27 Who made thee a **r** and a judge over us? *758*
7:35 saying, Who made thee a **r** and a judge? *758*
7:35 the same did God send *to be* a **r** and *758*
18: 8 And Crispus, the *chief* **r of the synagogue**, *752*
18:17 the *chief* **r of the synagogue**, and beat *him* *752*
23: 5 Thou shalt not speak evil of the **r** of thy *758*

RULER'S (2) [RULE]

Pr 29:26 Many seek the **r** favour; but *every* man's 4910
Mt 9:23 And when Jesus came into the **r** house, and *758*

RULERS (78) [RULE]

Ge 47: 6 then make them **r** over my cattle. 8269
Ex 16:22 all the **r** of the congregation came and 5387
18:21 *to be* **r** of thousands, *and* rulers of 8269
18:21 *and* **r** of hundreds, rulers of fifties, and 8269
18:21 of hundreds, **r** of fifties, and rulers of tens: 8269
18:21 of hundreds, rulers of fifties, and **r** of tens: 8269
18:25 **r** of thousands, rulers of hundreds, rulers of 8269
18:25 **r** of hundreds, rulers of fifties, and rulers of 8269
18:25 of hundreds, **r** of fifties, and rulers of tens. 8269
18:25 of hundreds, rulers of fifties, and **r** of tens. 8269
34:31 all the **r** of the congregation returned unto 5387
35:27 the **r** brought onyx stones, and stones to be 5387
Dt 1:13 and I will make them **r** over you. 7218
Jdg 15:11 Knowest thou not that the Philistines *are* **r** 4910
2Sa 8:18 and David's sons were **chief r**. 3548
1Ki 9:22 and **r** of his chariots, and his horsemen. 8269
2Ki 10: 1 unto the **r** of Jezreel, to the elders, and 8269
11: 4 Jehoiada sent and fet the **r** over hundreds, 8269
11:19 he took the **r** over hundreds, and 8269
1Ch 21: 2 said to Joab and to the **r** of the people, 8269
26:32 whom king David **made r** over 6485
27:31 All these *were* the **r** of the substance which 8269
29: 6 with the **r** over the king's work, 8269
2Ch 29:20 gathered the **r** of the city, and went up *to* 8269
35: 8 and Jehiel, **r** of the house of God, 5057
Ezr 9: 2 and **r** hath been chief in this trespass. 5461
10:14 Let now our **r** of all the congregation stand, 8269
Ne 2:16 the **r** knew not whither I went, or what I 5461
2:16 to the priests, nor to the nobles, nor to the **r**, 5461
4:14 and to the **r**, and to the rest of the people, 5461
4:16 the **r** *were* behind all the house of Judah. 8269
4:19 to the **r**, and to the rest of the people, 5461
5: 7 the **r**, and said unto them, You exact usury, 5461
5:17 an hundred and fifty of the Jews and **r**, 5461
7: 5 the **r**, and the people, that *they* might be 5461
11: 1 the **r** of the people dwelt at Jerusalem: 8269
12:40 of God, and I, and the half of the **r** with me: 5461
13:11 contended I with the **r**, and said, Why is 5461
Est 3:12 to the **r** of every people of every province 8269
8: 9 **r** of the provinces which *are* from India 8269
9: 3 all the **r** of the provinces, and 8269
Ps 2: 2 the **r** take counsel together, against 7336
Isa 1:10 the word of the LORD, ye **r** of Sodom; 7101
14: 5 staff of the wicked, *and* the sceptre of the **r**. 4910
22: 3 All thy **r** are fled together, they are bound 7101
29:10 the prophets and your **r**, the seers hath he 7218
49: 7 to a servant of **r**, Kings shall see and arise, 4910
Jer 33:26 that *I* will not take *any* of his seed *to be* **r** 4910
51:23 thee will I break in pieces captains and **r**. 5461
51:28 all the **r** thereof, and all the land of his 5461
51:57 her **r**, and her mighty *men:* and they shall 5461
Eze 23: 6 *were* clothed with blue, captains and **r**, 5461
23:12 captains and **r** clothed most gorgeously, 5461
23:23 captains and **r**, great lords and renowned, 5461
Da 3: 2 the sheriffs, and all the **r** of the provinces, 7984
3: 3 the sheriffs, and all the **r** of the provinces, 7984
Hos 4:18 her **r** *with* shame do love, Give ye. 4043
Mk 5:22 there cometh one of the **r of the synagogue**, *752*
13: 9 and ye shall be brought before **r** and *2232*
Lk 21:12 before kings and **r** for my name's sake. *2232*
23:13 the chief priests and the **r** and the people, *758*
23:35 And the **r** also with them derided *him,* *758*
24:20 our **r** delivered him to be condemned to *758*
Jn 7:26 Do the **r** know indeed that this is the very *758*
7:48 Have any of the **r** or of the Pharisees *758*
12:42 Nevertheless among the *chief* **r** also many *758*
Ac 3:17 ignorance ye did *it,* as *did* also your **r**. *758*
4: 5 that their **r**, and elders, and scribes, *758*
4: 8 Ye **r** of the people, and elders of Israel, *758*
4:26 the **r** were gathered together against *758*
13:15 the prophets the **r of the synagogue** sent *752*
13:27 and their **r**, because they knew him not, *758*
14: 5 and *also* of the Jews with their **r**, to use *them* *758*
16:19 drew *them* into the market-place unto the **r**, *758*
17: 6 and certain brethren unto the **r of the city**, *4173*
17: 8 troubled the people and the **r of the city**, *4173*
Ro 13: 3 For **r** are not a terror to good works, but *758*
Eph 6:12 against the **r** of the darkness of this world, *2888*

RULEST (2) [RULE]

2Ch 20: 6 **r** *not* thou over all the kingdoms of 4910
Ps 89: 9 Thou **r** the raging of the sea: when 4910

RULETH (14) [RULE]

2Sa 23: 3 He that **r** over men *must be* just, ruling *in* 4910
Ps 59:13 let them know that God **r** in Jacob unto 4910
66: 7 He **r** by his power for ever; his eyes behold 4910
103:19 in the heavens; and his kingdom **r** over all. 4910
Pr 16:32 he that **r** his spirit than he that taketh a city. 4910
22: 7 The rich **r** over the poor, and the borrower 4910
Ecc 8: 9 *there is* a time wherein one man **r** over 7980
9:17 more than the cry of him that **r** among 4910
Da 4:17 the most High **r** in the kingdom of men, 7990
4:25 till thou know that the most High **r** in 7990
4:32 until thou know that the most High **r** in 7990
Hos 11:12 Judah yet **r** with God, and is faithful with 7300
Ro 12: 8 he that **r**, with diligence; he that sheweth *4291*
1Ti 3: 4 One that **r** well his own house, having *his* *4291*

RULING (3) [RULE]

2Sa 23: 3 over men *must be* just, **r** *in* the fear of God. 4910
Jer 22:30 throne of David, and **r** any more in Judah. 4910
1Ti 3:12 **r** *their* children and their own houses well. *4291*

RUMAH (1)

2Ki 23:36 *was* Zebudah, the daughter of Pedaiah of **R**. 7316

RUMBLING (1)

Jer 47: 3 *and at* the **r** of his wheels, the fathers shall 1995

RUMOUR (10) [RUMOURS]

2Ki 19: 7 he shall hear a **r**, and shall return to his own 8052
Isa 37: 7 he shall hear a **r**, and return to his own 8052
Jer 49:14 I have heard a **r** from the LORD, and 8052
51:46 ye fear for the **r** that shall be heard in 8052
51:46 a **r** shall both come *one* year, and after that 8052
51:46 after that in *another* year *shall come* a **r**, 8052
Eze 7:26 upon mischief, and **r** shall be upon rumour; 8052
7:26 upon mischief, and rumour shall be upon **r**; 8052
Ob 1: 1 We have heard a **r** from the LORD, and 8052
Lk 7:17 And this **r** of him went forth throughout all *3056*

RUMOURS (2) [RUMOUR]

Mt 24: 6 And ye shall hear of wars and **r** of wars: *189*
Mk 13: 7 when ye shall hear of wars and **r** of wars, *189*

RUMP (5)

Ex 29:22 thou shalt take of the ram the fat and the **r**, 451
Lev 3: 9 the fat thereof, *and* the whole **r**, it shall he 451
7: 3 the **r**, and the fat that covereth the inwards, 451
8:25 the **r**, and all the fat that *was* upon 451
9:19 the **r**, and that which covereth *the inwards,* 451

RUN (71) [FORERUNNER, OUTRUN, OVERRUNNING, RAN, RUNNEST, RUNNETH, RUNNING]

Ge 49:22 by a well; *whose* branches **r** over the wall. 6805
Lev 15: 3 *whether* his flesh **r** with his issue, or 7325
15:25 or if it **r** beyond the time of her separation; 2100
Jdg 18:25 lest angry fellows **r** upon thee, and 6293
1Sa 8:11 and *some* shall **r** before his chariots. 7323
17:17 and **r** *to* the camp to thy brethren; 7323
20: 6 me that *he* might **r** *to* Beth-lehem his city: 7323
20:36 he said unto his lad, **R**, find out now 7323
2Sa 15: 1 and horses, and fifty men to **r** before him. 7323
18:19 Let me now **r**, and bear the king tidings, 7323
18:22 let me, I pray thee, also **r** after Cushi. 7323
18:22 Joab said, Wherefore wilt thou **r**, my son, 7323
18:23 howsoever, *said he,* let me **r**. And he said 7323
18:23 he said unto him, **R**. Then Ahimaaz ran *by* 7323
22:30 For by thee I have **r** *through* a troop: by my 7323
1Ki 1: 5 horsemen, and fifty men to **r** before him. 7323
2Ki 4:22 that I may **r** to the man of God, and 7323
4:26 **R** now, I pray thee, to meet her, and 7323
5:20 I will **r** after him, and take somewhat of 7323
2Ch 16: 9 For the eyes of the LORD **r to and fro** 7751
Ps 18:29 For by thee I have **r** *through* a troop; and 7323
19: 5 *and* rejoiceth as a strong *man* to **r** a race. 7323
58: 7 melt away as waters *which* **r continually**: 1980
59: 4 They **r** and prepare themselves without *my* 7323
78:16 and **caused** waters **to r down** like rivers. 3381
104:10 into the valleys, *which* **r** among the hills. 1980
119:32 I will **r** the way of thy commandments, 7323
119:136 Rivers of waters **r down** mine eyes, 3381
Pr 1:16 For their feet **r** to evil, and make haste to 7323
Ecc 1: 7 All the rivers **r** into the sea; yet the sea *is* 1980
SS 1: 4 Draw me, we will **r** after thee: the king 7323
Isa 33: 4 and fro of locusts shall he **r** upon them. 8264
40:31 they shall **r**, and not be weary; *and* 7323
55: 5 nations *that* knew not thee shall **r** unto thee 7323
59: 7 Their feet **r** to evil, and they make haste to 7323
Jer 5: 1 **R** ye **to and fro** through the streets of 7751
9:18 that our eyes may **r down** *with* tears, and 3381
12: 5 If thou hast **r** with the footmen, and 7323
13:17 **r down** *with* tears, because the LORD'S 3381
14:17 Let mine eyes **r down** *with* tears night and 3381
49: 3 lament, and **r to and fro** by the hedges; 7751
49:19 I will suddenly **make** him **r** away from her: 7323
50:44 I will **make** them suddenly **r** away from 7323
51:31 One post shall **r** to meet another, and 7323
La 2:18 let tears **r down** like a river day and night: 3381
Eze 24:16 nor weep, neither shall thy tears **r down**. 935
32:14 **cause** their rivers **to r** like oil, saith 1980
Da 12: 4 many shall **r to and fro**, and knowledge 7751
Joel 2: 4 of horses; and as horsemen, so shall they **r**. 7323
2: 7 They shall **r** like mighty *men;* they shall 7323
2: 9 They shall **r to and fro** in the city; 8264
2: 9 they shall **r** upon the wall, they shall climb 7323
Am 5:24 let judgment **r down** as waters, and 1556
6:12 Shall horses **r** upon the rock? will *one* plow 7323
8:12 they shall **r to and fro** to seek the word of 7751
Na 2: 4 like torches, they shall **r** like the lightnings. 7323
Hab 2: 2 upon tables, that he may **r** that readeth it. 7323
Hag 1: 9 and ye **r** every man unto his own house. 7323
Zec 2: 4 said unto him, **R**, speak to this young man, 7323
4:10 which **r to and fro** through the whole 7751
Mt 28: 8 and did **r** to bring his disciples word. *5143*
1Co 9:24 Know ye not that they which **r** in a race run *5143*
9:24 Know ye not that they which run in a race **r** *5143*
9:24 the prize? So **r**, that ye may obtain. *5143*
9:26 I therefore so **r**, not as uncertainly; so *5143*
Gal 2: 2 lest by any means I should **r**, or had run, *5143*
2: 2 any means I should run, or had **r**, in vain. *5143*
5: 7 Ye did **r** well; who did hinder you that *ye* *5143*
Php 2:16 that I have not **r** in vain, neither laboured in *5143*
Heb 12: 1 let us **r** with patience the race that is set *5143*
1Pe 4: 4 **r** not **with** *them* to the same excess of riot, *4936*

RUNNEST (1) [RUN]

Pr 4:12 and when thou **r**, thou shalt not stumble. 7323

RUNNETH (11) [RUN]

Ezr 8:15 I gathered them together to the river that **r** to 935
Job 15:26 He **r** upon him, *even* on *his* neck, upon 7323
16:14 upon breach, he **r** upon me like a giant. 7323
Ps 23: 5 anointest my head with oil; my cup **r over**. 7310
147:15 *upon* earth: his word **r** very swiftly. 7323
Pr 18:10 the righteous **r** into it, and is safe. 7323
La 1:16 mine eye **r down** *with* water, because 3381
3:48 Mine eye **r down** *with* rivers of water for 3381
Mt 9:17 and the wine **r out**, and the bottles perish: *1632*
Jn 20: 2 Then she **r**, and cometh to Simon Peter, *5143*
Ro 9:16 nor of him that **r**, but of God that sheweth *5143*

RUNNING (26) [RUN]
Lev 14: 5 be killed in an earthen vessel over **r** water: 2416
14: 6 of the bird *that was* killed over the **r** water: 2416
14:50 the birds in an earthen vessel over **r** water: 2416
14:51 in the **r** water, and sprinkle the house seven 2416
14:52 with the **r** water, and with the living bird, 2416
15: 2 When any man hath a **r issue** out of his 2100
15:13 bathe his flesh in **r** water, and shall be 2416
22: 4 seed of Aaron *is* a leper, or hath a **r issue**; 2100
Nu 19:17 and **r** water shall be put thereto in a vessel: 2416
2Sa 18:24 and looked, and behold a man **r** alone. 7323
18:26 the watchman saw another man **r**: and 7323
18:26 and said, Behold *another* man **r** alone. 7323
18:27 Me thinketh the **r** of the foremost *is* like 4794
18:27 *is* like the **r** of Ahimaaz the son of Zadok. 4794
2Ki 5:21 when Naaman saw *him* **r** after him, he 7323
2Ch 23:12 Athaliah heard the noise of the people **r** 7323
Pr 5:15 and **r waters** out of thine own well. 5140
6:18 feet that be swift in **r** to mischief, 7323
Isa 33: 4 as the **r to and fro** of locusts shall he run 4944
Eze 31: 4 with her rivers **r** round about his plants, 1980
Mk 9:15 greatly amazed, and **r** to *him* saluted him. *4370*
9:25 Jesus saw that the people **came r together**, *1998*
10:17 there **came** one **r**, and kneeled to him, and *4370*
Lk 6:38 and shaken *together*, and **r over**, *5240*
Ac 27:16 And **r under** a certain island *which is* *5295*
Rev 9: 9 of chariots of many horses **r** to battle. *5143*

RUSE See WILILY

RUSH (4) [BULRUSH, BULRUSHES, RUSHED, RUSHES, RUSHETH, RUSHING]
Job 8:11 Can the **r** grow up without mire? can 1573
Isa 9:14 off from Israel head and tail, branch and **r**, 100
17:13 The nations shall **r** like the rushing of many 7582
19:15 which the head or tail, branch or **r**, may do. 100

RUSHED (3) [RUSH]
Jdg 9:44 **r forward**, and stood *in* the entering of 6584
20:37 the liers in wait hasted, and **r** upon Gibeah; 6584
Ac 19:29 they **r** with one accord into the theatre. *3729*

RUSHES (1) [RUSH]
Isa 35: 7 each lay, *shall be* grass with reeds and **r**. 1573

RUSHETH (1) [RUSH]
Jer 8: 6 to his course, as the horse **r** into the battle. 7857

RUSHING (8) [RUSH]
Isa 17:12 to the **r** of nations, *that* make a rushing like 7588
17:12 *that* **make a r** like the rushing of mighty 7582
17:12 *that* make a rushing like the **r** of mighty 7588
17:13 The nations shall rush like the **r** of many 7588
Jer 47: 3 of his strong *horses*, at the **r** of his chariots, 7494
Eze 3:12 and I heard behind me a voice of a great **r**, 7494
3:13 over against them, and a noise of a great **r**. 7494
Ac 2: 2 a sound from heaven as of a **r** mighty wind, *5342*

RUST (3)
Mt 6:19 where moth and **r** doth corrupt, and *1035*
6:20 where neither moth nor **r** doth corrupt, and *1035*
Jas 5: 3 the **r** of them shall be a witness against *2447*

RUTH (13)
Ru 1: 4 *was* Orpah, and the name of the other **R**: 7327
1:14 her mother in law; but **R** clave unto her. 7327
1:16 **R** said, Intreat me not to leave thee, *or* 7327
1:22 So Naomi returned, and **R** the Moabitess, 7327
2: 2 **R** the Moabitess said unto Naomi, Let me 7327
2: 8 said Boaz unto **R**, Hearest thou not, 7327
2:21 **R** the Moabitess said, He said unto me also, 7327
2:22 Naomi said unto **R** her daughter in law, 7327
3: 9 she answered, I *am* **R** thine handmaid: 7327
4: 5 thou must buy *it* also of **R** the Moabitess, 7327
4:10 Moreover **R** the Moabitess, the wife of 7327
4:13 So Boaz took **R**, and she was his wife: and 7327
Mt 1: 5 and Booz begat Obed of **R**; and Obed begat *4503*

RUTHLESS See IMPLACABLE

RUTHLESSLY See RIGOUR

RYE (2)
Ex 9:32 the wheat and the **r** were not smitten: 3698
Isa 28:25 appointed barley and the **r** *in* their place? 3698

S

SABACHTHANI (2)
Mt 27:46 a loud voice, saying, ELI, ELI, LAMA **S**? *4518*
Mk 15:34 loud voice, saying, ELOI, ELOI, LAMA **S**? *4518*

SABAOTH (2)
Ro 9:29 Except the Lord of **s** had left us a seed, *4519*
Jas 5: 4 are entered into the ears of the Lord of **s**. *4519*

SABBATH (137) [SABBATHS]
Ex 16:23 To morrow *is* the rest of the holy **s** unto 7676
16:25 to day; for to day *is* a **s** unto the LORD: 7676
16:26 on the seventh day, *which is* the **s**, in it 7676
16:29 for that the LORD hath given you the **s**, 7676
20: 8 Remember the **s** day, to keep it holy. 7676
20:10 the seventh day *is* the **s** of the LORD thy 7676
20:11 wherefore the LORD blessed the **s** day, 7676
31:14 Ye shall keep the **s** therefore; for it *is* holy 7676
31:15 in the seventh *is* the **s** of rest, holy to 7676
31:15 whosoever doeth *any* work in the **s** day, 7676
31:16 the children of Israel shall keep the **s**, 7676
31:16 to observe the **s** throughout their 7676
35: 2 to you a holy *day*, a **s** of rest to the LORD: 7676
35: 3 throughout your habitations upon the **s** day. 7676
Lev 16:31 It *shall be* a **s** of rest unto you, and ye shall 7676
23: 3 the seventh day *is* the **s** of rest, a holy 7676
23: 3 ye shall do no work *therein*: it *is* the **s** of 7676
23:11 on the morrow after the **s** the priest shall 7676
23:15 count unto you from the morrow after the **s**, 7676
23:16 Even unto the morrow after the seventh **s** 7676
23:24 the first *day* of the month, shall ye have a **s**, 7677
23:32 It *shall be* unto you a **s** of rest, and ye shall 7676
23:32 unto even, shall ye **celebrate** your **s**. 7673+7676
23:39 on the first day *shall be* a **s**, and on 7677
23:39 and on the eighth day *shall be* a **s**. 7677
24: 8 **Every s** he shall set it in order 3117+3117+7676+7676 +871.1+871.1+1886.1+1886.1
25: 2 the land **keep a s** unto the LORD. 7673+7676
25: 4 in the seventh year shall be a **s** of rest unto 7676
25: 4 of rest unto the land, a **s** for the LORD: 7676
25: 6 the **s** of the land shall be meat for you; 7676
Nu 15:32 a man that gathered sticks upon the **s** day. 7676
28: 9 on the **s** day two lambs of the first year 7676
28:10 the burnt offering of **every s**, 7676+7676+871.1
Dt 5:12 Keep the **s** day to sanctify it, as the LORD 7676
5:14 the seventh day *is* the **s** of the LORD thy 7676
5:15 thy God commanded thee to keep the **s** day. 7676
2Ki 4:23 *it is* neither new moon, nor **s**. And she said, 7676
11: 5 A third *part* of you that enter in on the **s** 7676
11: 7 two parts of all you that go forth on the **s**, 7676
11: 9 man his men that were to come in on the **s**, 7676
11: 9 with them that should go out on the **s**, and 7676
16:18 the covert for the **s** that they had built in 7676
1Ch 9:32 the shewbread, to prepare *it* **every s**. 7676+7676
2Ch 23: 4 A third *part* of you entering on the **s**, of 7676
23: 8 man his men that were to come in on the **s**, 7676
23: 8 with them that were to go out on the **s**: 7676
36:21 *for* as long as *she* lay desolate she **kept s**, 7673
Ne 9:14 madest known unto them thy holy **s**, and 7676
10:31 or any victuals on the **s** day to sell, 7676
10:31 *that* we would not buy *it* of them on the **s**, 7676
13:15 Judah *some* treading wine presses on the **s**, 7676
13:15 which they brought *into* Jerusalem on the **s** 7676
13:16 sold on the **s** unto the children of Judah, 7676
13:17 *is* this that ye do, and profane the **s** day? 7676
13:18 more wrath upon Israel by profaning the **s**. 7676
13:19 of Jerusalem began to be dark before the **s**, 7676
13:19 they should not be opened till after the **s**: 7676
13:19 no burden be brought in on the **s** day. 7676
13:21 that time forth came they no *more* on the **s**. 7676
13:22 *and* keep the gates, to sanctify the **s** day. 7676
Ps 92: T A Psalm *or* Song for the **s** day. 7676
Isa 56: 2 that keepeth the **s** from polluting it, and 7676
56: 6 every one that keepeth the **s** from polluting 7676
58:13 If thou turn away thy foot from the **s**, 7676
58:13 call the **s** a delight, the holy of the LORD, 7676
66:23 moon to another, and from one **s** to another, 7676
Jer 17:21 bear no burden on the **s** day, 7676
17:22 a burden out of your houses on the **s** day, 7676
17:22 do ye any work, but hallow ye the **s** day, 7676
17:24 through the gates of this city on the **s** day, 7676
17:24 but hallow the **s** day, to do no work therein; 7676
17:27 not hearken unto me to hallow the **s** day, 7676
17:27 in at the gates of Jerusalem on the **s** day; 7676
Eze 46: 1 on the **s** it shall be opened, and in 3117+7676
46: 4 **s** day *shall be* six lambs without blemish, 7676
46:12 his peace offerings, as he did on the **s** day: 7676
Am 8: 5 the **s**, that we may set forth wheat, 7676
Mt 12: 1 At that time Jesus went on the **s** day *4521*
12: 2 which is not lawful to do upon the **s** day. *4521*
12: 5 how that on the **s** days the priests in *4521*
12: 5 days the priests in the temple profane the **s**, *4521*
12: 8 For the Son of man is Lord even of the **s** *4521*
12:10 saying, Is it lawful to heal on the **s** days? *4521*
12:11 and if it fall into a pit on the **s** day, will he *4521*
12:12 Wherefore it is lawful to do well on the **s** *4521*
24:20 be not in the winter, neither on the **s** day: *4521*
28: 1 In the end of the **s**, as it began to dawn *4521*
Mk 1:21 straightway on the **s** day he entered into *4521*
2:23 that he went through the corn fields on the **s** *4521*
2:24 why do they on the **s** day *that* which is not *4521*
2:27 The **s** was made for man, *and* not man for *4521*
2:27 was made for man, *and* not man for the **s**: *4521*
2:28 the Son of man is Lord also of the **s**. *4521*
3: 2 whether he would heal him on the **s** day; *4521*
3: 4 Is it lawful to do good on the **s** days, or *4521*
6: 2 And when the **s** day was come, he began to *4521*
15:42 that is, the **day before the s**, *4315*
16: 1 And when the **s** was past, Mary Magdalene, *4521*
Lk 4:16 he went into the synagogue on the **s** day, *4521*
4:31 of Galilee, and taught them on the **s** days. *4521*
6: 1 And it came to pass on the second **s** after *4521*
6: 2 which is not lawful to do on the **s** days? *4521*
6: 5 That the Son of man is Lord also of the **s**. *4521*
6: 6 And it came to pass also on another **s**, *4521*
6: 7 whether he would heal on the **s** day; *4521*
6: 9 *thing;* Is it lawful on the **s** days to do good, *4521*
13:10 teaching in one of the synagogues on the **s**. *4521*
13:14 because that Jesus had healed on the **s** day, *4521*
13:14 come and be healed, and not on the **s** day. *4521*
13:15 doth not each one of you on the **s** loose his *4521*
13:16 be loosed from this bond on the **s** day? *4521*
14: 1 chief Pharisees to eat bread on the **s** day, *4521*
14: 3 saying, Is it lawful to heal on the **s** day? *4521*
14: 5 will not straightway pull him out on the **s** *4521*
23:54 day was the preparation, and the **s** drew on. *4521*
23:56 rested the **s** day according to *4521*
Jn 5: 9 and walked: and on the same day was the **s**. *4521*
5:10 said unto him that was cured, It is the **s** day: *4521*
5:16 he had done these *things* on the **s** day. *4521*
5:18 because he not only had broken the **s**, but *4521*
7:22 and ye on the **s** day circumcise a man. *4521*
7:23 If a man on the **s** day receive circumcision, *4521*
7:23 made a man every whit whole on the **s** day? *4521*
9:14 And it was the **s** day when Jesus made *4521*
9:16 of God, because he keepeth not the **s** day. *4521*
19:31 not remain upon the cross on the **s** day, *4521*
19:31 (for that **s** day was a high day,) *4521*
Ac 1:12 Jerusalem a **s day's journey**. *2192+3598+4521*
13:14 and went into the synagogue on the **s** day, *4521*
13:27 of the prophets which are read every **s** day, *4521*
13:42 might be preached to them the next **s**. *4521*
13:44 And the next **s** day came almost the whole *4521*
15:21 being read in the synagogues every **s** day. *4521*
16:13 And on the **s** we went out of the city by a *4521*
17: 2 three **s** days reasoned with them out of *4521*
18: 4 And he reasoned in the synagogue every **s**, *4521*
Col 2:16 or of the new moon, or of the **s days**: *4521*

SABBATHS (35) [SABBATH]
Ex 31:13 of Israel, saying, Verily my **s** ye shall keep: 7676
Lev 19: 3 his mother, and his father, and keep my **s**: 7676
19:30 Ye shall keep my **s**, and reverence my 7676
23:15 wave offering; seven **s** shall be complete: 7676
23:38 Beside the **s** of the LORD, and 7676
25: 8 thou shalt number seven **s** of years unto 7676
25: 8 the space of the seven **s** of years shall be 7676
26: 2 Ye shall keep my **s**, and reverence my 7676
26:34 shall the land enjoy her **s**, as long as it lieth 7676
26:34 then shall the land rest, and enjoy her **s**. 7676
26:35 because it did not rest in your **s**, when ye 7676
26:43 shall be left of them, and shall enjoy her **s**, 7676
1Ch 23:31 burnt sacrifices unto the LORD in the **s**, 7676
2Ch 2: 4 on the **s**, and on the new moons, and on 7676
8:13 on the **s**, and on the new moons, and on 7676
31: 3 the burnt offerings for the **s**, and for 7676
36:21 until the land had enjoyed her **s**: 7676
Ne 10:33 of the **s**, of the new moons, for the set 7676
Isa 1:13 the new moons and **s**, the calling of 7676
56: 4 LORD unto the eunuchs that keep my **s**, 7676
La 1: 7 adversaries saw her, *and* did mock at her **s**. 4868
2: 6 solemn feasts and **s** to be forgotten in Zion, 7676
Eze 20:12 Moreover also I gave them my **s**, to be a 7676
20:13 in them; and my **s** they greatly polluted: 7676
20:16 not in my statutes, but polluted my **s**: 7676
20:20 hallow my **s**; and they shall be a sign 7676
20:21 shall even live in them; they polluted my **s**: 7676
20:24 had polluted my **s**, and their eyes were after 7676
22: 8 mine holy *things*, and hast profaned my **s**. 7676
22:26 have hid their eyes from my **s**, and I am 7676
23:38 in the same day, and have profaned my **s**. 7676
44:24 and they shall hallow my **s**. 7676
45:17 in the **s** in all solemnities of the house of 7676
46: 3 door of this gate before the LORD in the **s** 7676
Hos 2:11 and her **s**, and all her solemn feasts. 7676

SABEANS (4)
Job 1:15 the **S** fell *upon them*, and took them away; 7614
Isa 45:14 merchandise of Ethiopia and of the **S**, 5436
Eze 23:42 sort *were* brought **S** from the wilderness, 5436
Joel 3: 8 they shall sell them to the **S**, to a people far 7615

SABTA (1) [SABTAH]
1Ch 1: 9 Havilah, and **S**, and Raamah, and Sabtecha. 5454

SABTAH (1) [SABTA]
Ge 10: 7 Havilah, and **S**, and Raamah, and Sabtecha: 5454

SABTECA See SABTECHA

SABTECHA (2)
Ge 10: 7 Havilah, and Sabtah, and Raamah, and **S**: 5455
1Ch 1: 9 Havilah, and Sabta, and Raamah, and **S**. 5455

SACAR (2)
1Ch 11:35 Ahiam the son of **S** the Hararite, Eliphal 7940
26: 4 and **S** the fourth, and Nethaneel the fifth, 7940

SACK (9) [SACK'S, SACKBUT, SACKCLOTH, SACKCLOTHES, SACKS, SACKS']
Ge 42:25 to restore every man's money into his **s**, 8242
42:27 as one *of them* opened his **s** to give his ass 8242
42:28 money is restored; and lo, *it is* even in my **s**: 572
42:35 every man's bundle of money *was* in his **s**: 8242
43:21 man's money *was* in the mouth of his **s**, 572
44:11 they speedily took down every man his **s** to 572
44:11 to the ground, and opened every man his **s**. 572
44:12 and the cup was found in Benjamin's **s**. 572
Lev 11:32 vessel of wood, or raiment, or skin, or **s**, 8242

SACK'S (3) [SACK]
Ge 42:27 his money; for behold, it *was* in his **s** mouth. 572
44: 1 and put every man's money in his **s** mouth. 572
44: 2 in the **s** mouth of the youngest, and his corn 572

SACKBUT (4) [SACK]
Da 3: 5 flute, harp, **s**, psaltery, dulcimer, and 5443
3: 7 flute, harp, **s**, psaltery, and all kinds of 5443
3:10 flute, harp, **s**, psaltery, and dulcimer, and 5443
3:15 flute, harp, **s**, psaltery, and dulcimer, and 5443

SACKCLOTH (46) [CLOTH, SACK]
Ge 37:34 put **s** upon his loins, and mourned for his 8242
2Sa 3:31 gird you with **s**, and mourn before Abner. 8242
21:10 Rizpah the daughter of Aiah took **s**, and 8242
1Ki 20:31 put **s** on our loins, and ropes upon our 8242
20:32 So they girded **s** on their loins, and 8242
21:27 put **s** upon his flesh, and fasted, and lay in 8242
21:27 and fasted, and lay in **s**, and went softly. 8242
2Ki 6:30 and behold, *he had* **s** within upon his flesh. 8242
19: 1 covered himself with **s**, and went *into* 8242
19: 2 and the elders of the priests, covered with **s**, 8242
1Ch 21:16 the elders *of Israel, who were* clothed in **s**, 8242

S

Est 4: 1 put on s with ashes, and went out into 8242
4: 2 enter into the king's gate clothed with s. 8242
4: 3 and wailing; *and* many lay in s and ashes. 8242
4: 4 and to take away his s from him: 8242
Job 16:15 I have sewed s upon my skin, and 8242
Ps 30:11 thou hast put off my s, and girded me *with* 8242
35:13 when they were sick, my clothing *was* s: 8242
69:11 I made s also my garment; and I became a 8242
Isa 3:24 instead of a stomacher a girding of s; *and* 8242
15: 3 streets they shall gird themselves with s: 8242
20: 2 Go and loose the s from off thy loins, and 8242
22:12 and to baldness, and to girding with s: 8242
32:11 make ye bare, and gird *s* upon *your* loins. NIH
37: 1 covered himself with s, and went *into* 8242
37: 2 and the elders of the priests covered with s, 8242
50: 3 with blackness, and I make s their covering. 8242
58: 5 to spread s and ashes *under him?* wilt thou 8242
Jer 4: 8 For this gird you with s, lament and howl: 8242
6:26 gird *thee* with s, and wallow thyself in 8242
48:37 *shall be* cuttings, and upon the loins s. 8242
49: 3 cry, ye daughters of Rabbah, gird ye with s; 8242
La 2:10 they have girded themselves with s: 8242
Eze 7:18 They shall also gird *themselves* with s, and 8242
27:31 gird them with s, and they shall weep for 8242
Da 9: 3 with fasting, and s, and ashes: 8242
Joel 1: 8 Lament like a virgin girded with s for 8242
1:13 come, lie all night in s, ye ministers of my 8242
Am 8:10 I will bring up s upon all loins, and 8242
Jnh 3: 5 and proclaimed a fast, and put on s, 8242
3: 6 and covered *him* with s, and sat in ashes. 8242
3: 8 let man and beast be covered with s, and 8242
Mt 11:21 they would have repented long ago in s *4526*
Lk 10:13 while ago repented, sitting in s and ashes. *4526*
Rev 6:12 and the sun became black as s of hair, and *4526*
11: 3 *and* threescore days, clothed in s. *4526*

SACKCLOTHES (1) [CLOTH, SACK]

Ne 9: 1 and with s, and earth upon them. 8242

SACKS (9) [SACK]

Ge 42:25 Joseph commanded to fill their s *with* corn, 3627
42:35 it came to pass as they emptied their s, 8242
43:12 was brought again in the mouth of your s, 572
43:18 in our s at the first time *are* we brought in; 572
43:21 to the inn, that we opened our s, and behold, 572
43:22 we cannot tell who put our money in our s. 572
43:23 hath given you treasure in your s: 572
44: 1 saying, Fill the men's s *with* food, as much 572
Jos 9: 4 took old s upon their asses, and 8242

SACKS' (1) [SACK]

Ge 44: 8 the money, which we found in our s mouths, 572

SACRED See HALLOW; HALLOWED

SACRIFICE (218) [SACRIFICED, SACRIFICEDST, SACRIFICES, SACRIFICETH, SACRIFICING]

Ge 31:54 Jacob offered s upon the mount, and 2077
Ex 3:18 that we may s to the LORD our God. 2076
5: 3 the desert, and s unto the LORD our God; 2076
5: 8 saying, Let us go *and* s to our God. 2076
5:17 ye say, Let us go *and* do s to the LORD. 2076
8: 8 that they may do s unto the LORD. 2076
8:25 and said, Go ye, s to your God in the land. 2076
8:26 for we shall s the abomination of 2076
8:26 shall we s the abomination of the Egyptians 2076
8:27 s to the LORD our God, as he shall 2076
8:28 that ye may s to the LORD your God in 2076
8:29 letting the people go to s to the LORD. 2076
10:25 that we may s unto the LORD our God. 6213
12:27 It *is* the s of the LORD'S passover, 2077
13:15 I s to the LORD all that openeth 2076
20:24 shalt s thereon thy burnt offerings, and thy 2076
23:18 Thou shalt not offer the blood of my s with 2077
23:18 neither shall the fat of my s remain until 2282
29:28 of Israel of the s of their peace offerings, 2077
30: 9 nor burnt s, nor meat offering; 5930
34:15 do s unto their gods, and *one* call thee, and 2076
34:15 and *one* call thee, and thou eat of his s; 2077
34:25 Thou shalt not offer the blood of my s with 2077
34:25 neither shall the s of the feast of 2077
Lev 1: 3 If his offering *be* a burnt s of the herd, 5930
1: 9 *to be* a burnt s, an offering made by fire, 5930
1:10 of the sheep, or of the goats, for a burnt s; 5930
1:13 it *is* a burnt s, an offering made by fire, 5930
1:14 if the burnt s for his offering to 5930
1:17 it *is* a burnt s, an offering made by fire, 5930
3: 1 if his oblation *be* a s of peace offering, if he 2077
3: 3 he shall offer of the s of the peace offering 2077
3: 5 shall burn it on the altar upon the burnt s, 5930
3: 6 if his offering for a s of peace offering unto 2077
3: 9 he shall offer of the s of the peace offering 2077
4:10 the bullock of the s of peace offerings: 2077
4:26 as the fat of the s of peace offerings: 2077
4:31 as the fat is taken away from off the s of 2077
4:35 away from the s of the peace offerings; 2077
7:11 this *is* the law of the s of peace offerings, 2077
7:12 he shall offer with the s of thanksgiving 2077
7:13 the s of thanksgiving of his peace offerings. 2077
7:15 the flesh of the s of his peace offerings for 2077
7:16 if the s of his offering *be* a vow, or 2077
7:16 be eaten the *same* day that he offereth his s: 2077
7:17 the remainder of the flesh of the s on 2077
7:18 if *any* of the flesh of the s of his peace 2077
7:20 the soul that eateth *of* the flesh of the s of 2077
7:21 eat of the flesh of the s of peace offerings, 2077
7:29 He that offereth the s of his peace offerings 2077
7:29 the LORD of the s of his peace offerings. 2077
7:37 and of the s of the peace offerings; 2077
8:21 it *was* a burnt s for a sweet savour, *and* 5930
9: 4 for peace offerings, to s before the LORD; 2076
9:17 the altar, beside the burnt s of the morning. 5930
9:18 and the ram *for* a s of peace offerings, 2077
17: 8 that offereth a burnt offering or s, 2077

Lev 19: 5 if ye offer a s of peace offerings unto 2076+2077
22:21 whosoever offereth a s of peace offerings 2077
22:29 when ye will offer a s of thanksgiving unto 2077
23:19 ye shall s one kid of the goats for a sin 6213
23:19 two lambs of the first year for a s of peace 2077
23:37 a meat offering, a s, and drink offerings, 2077
27:11 of which they do not offer a s unto 7133
Nu 6:17 he shall offer the ram *for* a s of peace 2077
6:18 put *it* in the fire which *is* under the s of 2077
7:17 for a s of peace offerings, two oxen, 2077
7:23 for a s of peace offerings, two oxen, 2077
7:29 for a s of peace offerings, two oxen, 2077
7:35 for a s of peace offerings, two oxen, 2077
7:41 for a s of peace offerings, two oxen, 2077
7:47 for a s of peace offerings, two oxen, 2077
7:53 for a s of peace offerings, two oxen, 2077
7:59 for a s of peace offerings, two oxen, 2077
7:65 for a s of peace offerings, two oxen, 2077
7:71 for a s of peace offerings, two oxen, 2077
7:77 for a s of peace offerings, two oxen, 2077
7:83 for a s of peace offerings, two oxen, 2077
7:88 all the oxen for the s of the peace offerings 2077
15: 3 or a s in performing a vow, or in a freewill 2077
15: 5 thou prepare with the burnt offering or s, 2077
15: 8 or *for* a s in performing a vow, or 2077
15:25 a s made by fire unto the LORD, and 801
23: 6 lo, *he* stood by his burnt s, he, and all 5930
28: 6 a s made by fire unto the LORD. 801
28: 8 thou shalt offer *it*, a s made by fire, 801
28:13 a s made by fire unto the LORD. 801
28:19 ye shall offer a s made by fire *for* a burnt 801
28:24 seven days, the meat of the s made by fire, 801
29: 6 a s made by fire unto the LORD. 801
29:13 shall offer a burnt offering, a s made by fire, 801
29:36 shall offer a burnt offering, a s made by fire, 801
Dt 15:21 thou shalt not s it unto the LORD thy 2076
16: 2 s the passover unto the LORD thy God, 2076
16: 5 Thou mayest not s the passover within any 2076
16: 6 *in*, there thou shalt s the passover at even, 2076
17: 1 Thou shalt not s unto the LORD thy God 2076
18: 3 from them that offer a s, whether *it be* ox or 2077
33:10 and whole *burnt s* upon thine altar. NIH
Jos 22:26 us an altar, not for burnt offering, nor for s: 2077
Jdg 6:26 offer a burnt s with the wood of the grove 5930
16:23 for to offer a great s unto Dagon their god, 2077
1Sa 1: 3 to s unto the LORD of hosts in Shiloh. 2076
1:21 up to offer unto the LORD the yearly s, 2077
2:13 people *was, that* when any man offered s, 2077
2:19 up with her husband to offer the yearly s. 2077
2:29 Wherefore kick ye at my s and at mine 2077
3:14 not be purged with s nor offering for ever. 2077
9:12 for *there is* a s of the people to day in 2077
9:13 until he come, because he doth bless the s; 2077
10: 8 *and* to s sacrifices of peace offerings: 2076
15:15 of the oxen, to s unto the LORD thy God; 2076
15:21 to s unto the LORD thy God in Gilgal. 2076
15:22 to obey *is* better than s, *and* to hearken than 2077
16: 2 say, I am come to s to the LORD. 2076
16: 3 call Jesse to the s, and I will shew thee 2077
16: 5 I am come to s unto the LORD: 2076
16: 5 and come with me to the s. 2077
16: 5 and his sons, and called them to the s. 2077
20: 6 for *there is* a yearly s there for all 2077
20:29 for our family hath a s in the city; and 2077
2Sa 24:22 *here be* oxen for burnt s, and threshing 5930
1Ki 3: 4 the king went to Gibeon to s there; for that 2076
8:62 with him, offered s before the LORD. 2077
8:63 Solomon offered a s of peace offerings, 2077
12:27 If this people go up to do s in the house of 2077
18:29 *the time* of the offering of the *evening* s, 4503
18:33 pour *it* on the burnt s, and on the wood. 5930
18:36 at *the time of* the offering of the *evening* s, 4503
18:38 consumed the burnt s, and the wood, and 5930
2Ki 5:17 neither burnt offering nor s unto other gods, 2077
10:19 for I have a great s *to do* to Baal; 2077
14: 4 as yet the people did s and burnt incense on 2076
16:15 the king's burnt s, and his meat offering, 5930
16:15 burnt offering, and all the blood of the s: 2077
17:35 to them, nor serve them, nor s to them: 2076
17:36 shall ye worship, and to him shall ye do s. 2076
2Ch 2: 6 a house, save only to burn s before him? 6999
7: 5 king Solomon offered a s of twenty and 2077
7:12 chosen this place to myself for a house of s. 2077
11:16 to s unto the LORD God of their fathers. 2076
28:23 *therefore* will I s to them, that they may 2076
33:17 Nevertheless the people did s still in 2076
Ezr 4: 2 we do s unto him since the days of 2076
9: 4 and I sat astonied until the evening s. 4503
9: 5 at the evening s I arose up from my 4503
Ne 4: 2 will they s? will they make an end in a day? 2076
Ps 20: 3 all thy offerings, and accept thy burnt s. 5930
40: 6 S and offering thou didst not desire; mine 2077
50: 5 that have made a covenant with me by s. 2077
51:16 For thou desirest not s; else would I give *it*: 2077
54: 6 I will freely s unto thee: I will praise thy 2076
107:22 let them s the sacrifices of thanksgiving, 2076
116:17 I will offer to thee the s of thanksgiving, 2077
118:27 bind the s with cords, *even* unto the horns 2282
141: 2 the lifting up of my hands *as* the evening s. 4503
Pr 15: 8 The s of the wicked *is* an abomination to 2077
21: 3 *is* more acceptable to the LORD than s. 2077
21:27 The s of the wicked *is* abomination: 2077
Ecc 5: 1 ready to hear, than to give the s of fools: 2077
Isa 19:21 in that day, and shall do s and oblation; 2077
34: 6 for the LORD hath a s in Bozrah, and 2077
57: 7 even thither wentest thou up to offer s. 2077
Jer 33:11 of them that shall bring the s of praise *into* 8426
33:18 meat offerings, and to do s continually. 2077
46:10 for the Lord GOD of hosts hath a s in 2077
Eze 39:17 gather yourselves on every side to my s that 2077
39:17 side to my sacrifice that I do s for you, 2076
39:17 *even* a great s upon the mountains of Israel, 2077
39:19 of my s which I have sacrificed for you. 2077
40:42 they slew the burnt offering and the s. 2077
44:11 the burnt offering and the s for the people, 2077

Eze 46:24 of the house shall boil the s of the people. 2077
Da 8:11 by him the daily *s* was taken away, and NIH
8:12 a host was given *him* against the daily *s* by NIH
8:13 *shall be* the vision *concerning* the daily *s*, NIH
9:27 *in* the midst of the week he shall cause the s 2077
11:31 shall take away the daily *s*, and they shall NIH
12:11 from the time *that* the daily *s* shall be taken NIH
Hos 3: 4 without a s, and without an image, and 2077
4:13 They s upon the tops of the mountains, and 2076
4:14 with whores, and they s with harlots: 2076
6: 6 For I desired mercy, and not s; and 2077
8:13 They s flesh *for* the sacrifices of mine 2076
12:11 they s bullocks in Gilgal; yea, their altars 2076
13: 2 of them, Let the men that s kiss the calves. 2076
Am 4: 5 offer a s of thanksgiving with leaven, and 8426
Jnh 1:16 offered a s unto the LORD, and 2077
2: 9 I will s unto thee with the voice of 2076
Hab 1:16 Therefore they s unto their net, and 2076
Zep 1: 7 for the LORD hath prepared a s, he hath 2077
1: 8 come to pass in the day of the LORD'S s, 2077
Zec 14:21 all they that s shall come and take of them, 2076
Mal 1: 8 And if ye offer the blind for s, *is it* not evil? 2076
Mt 9:13 *that* meaneth, I will have mercy, and not s: *2378*
12: 7 *this* meaneth, I will have mercy, and not s, *2378*
Mk 9:49 and every s shall be salted with salt. *2378*
Lk 2:24 And to offer a s according to that which is *2378*
Ac 7:41 and offered s unto the idol, and rejoiced in *2378*
14:13 and would have done s with the people. *2380*
14:18 that *they* had not done s unto them. *2380*
Ro 12: 1 that *ye* present your bodies a living s, holy, *2378*
1Co 8: 4 things that are offered in s unto idols, *1494*
10:19 that which is offered in s to idols is any *1494*
10:20 *I say*, that *the things* which the Gentiles s, *2380*
10:20 they s to devils, and not to God: *2380*
10:28 unto you, This is offered in s unto idols, *1494*
Eph 5: 2 and a s to God for a sweetsmelling savour. *2378*
Php 2:17 and if I be offered upon the s and service of *2378*
4:18 a s acceptable, well pleasing to God. *2378*
Heb 7:27 as *those* high priests, to offer up s, first for *2378*
9:26 to put away sin by the s of himself. *2378*
10: 5 S and offering thou wouldest not, but *2378*
10: 8 S and offering and burnt offerings and *2378*
10:12 But this *man*, after he had offered one s for *2378*
10:26 there remaineth no more s for sins, *2378*
11: 4 unto God a more excellent s than Cain, *2378*
13:15 let us offer the s of praise to God *2378*

SACRIFICED (33) [SACRIFICE]

Ex 24: 5 s peace offerings *of* oxen unto the LORD. 2076
32: 8 have s thereunto, and said, These *be* thy 2076
Dt 32:17 They s unto devils, not *to* God; *to* gods 2076
Jos 8:31 unto the LORD, and s peace offerings. 2076
Jdg 2: 5 and they s there unto the LORD. 2076
1Sa 2:15 servant came, and said to the man that s, 2076
6:15 s sacrifices the same day unto the LORD. 2076
11:15 there they s sacrifices *of* peace offerings 2076
2Sa 6:13 had gone six paces, he s oxen and fatlings. 2076
1Ki 3: 2 Only the people s in high places, because 2076
3: 3 only he s and burnt incense in high places. 2076
11: 8 which burnt incense and s unto their gods. 2076
2Ki 12: 3 the people still s and burnt incense in 2076
15: 4 the people s and burnt incense still on 2076
15:35 the people s and burnt incense still in 2076
16: 4 he s and burnt incense in the high places, 2076
17:32 which s for them in the houses of the high 6213
1Ch 21:28 of Ornan the Jebusite, then he s there. 2076
29:21 they s sacrifices unto the LORD, and 2076
2Ch 5: 6 s sheep and oxen, which could not be told 2076
28: 4 He s also and burnt incense in the high 2076
28:23 For he s unto the gods of Damascus, 2076
33:16 s thereon peace offerings and 2076
33:22 for Amon s unto all the carved images 2076
34: 4 the graves of them that had s unto them. 2076
Ps 106:37 they s their sons and their daughters unto 2076
106:38 whom they s unto the idols of Canaan: 2076
Eze 16:20 these hast thou s unto them to be devoured. 2076
39:19 of my sacrifice which I have s for you. 2076
Hos 11: 2 they s unto Baalim, and burned incense to 2076
1Co 5: 7 For even Christ our passover is s for us: *2380*
Rev 2:14 to eat things s unto idols, and to commit *1494*
2:20 and to eat things s unto idols. *1494*

SACRIFICEDST (1) [SACRIFICE]

Dt 16: 4 which thou s the first day at even, 2076

SACRIFICES (79) [SACRIFICE]

Ge 46: 1 offered s unto the God of his father Isaac. 2077
Ex 10:25 Thou must give us also s and 2077
18:12 in law, took a burnt offering and s for God: 2077
Lev 7:32 offering of the s of your peace offerings. 2077
7:34 from off the s of their peace offerings, 2077
10:13 of the s of the LORD made by fire: 801
10:14 *which* are given out of the s of peace 2077
17: 5 that the children of Israel may bring their s, 2077
17: 7 they shall no more offer their s unto devils, 2077
Nu 10:10 and over the s of your peace offerings; 2077
25: 2 they called the people unto the s of their 2077
28: 2 *and* my bread for my s made by fire, 801
Dt 12: 6 your s, and your tithes, and heave offerings 2077
12:11 your s, your tithes, and the heave offering 2077
12:27 the blood of thy s shall be poured out upon 2077
32:38 Which did eat the fat of their s, *and* 2077
33:19 there they shall offer s of righteousness: 2077
Jos 13:14 s of the LORD God of Israel made by fire 801
22:27 with our s, and with our peace offerings; 2077
22:28 not for burnt offerings, nor for s; 2077
22:29 burnt offerings, for meat offerings, or for s, 2077
1Sa 6:15 sacrificed s the same day unto the LORD. 2077
10: 8 *and* to sacrifice s of peace offerings: 2077
11:15 there they sacrificed s *of* peace offerings 2077
15:22 *as great* delight in burnt offerings and s, 2077
2Sa 15:12 *even* from Giloh, while he offered s. 2077
2Ki 10:24 when they went in to offer s and 2077
1Ch 16: 1 they offered burnt s and peace offerings 5930

1Ch 23:31 to offer all **burnt s** unto the LORD in 5930
29:21 they sacrificed **s** unto the LORD, and 2077
29:21 and **s** in abundance for all Israel: 2077
2Ch 7: 1 and consumed the burnt offering and the **s**; 2077
7: 4 all the people offered **s** before the LORD. 2077
13:11 every evening **burnt s** and sweet incense: 5930
29:31 come near and bring **s** and thank offerings 2077
29:31 the congregation brought in **s** and 2077
Ezr 6: 3 the place where they offered **s**, and *let* 1685
6:10 That they may offer **s** of sweet savours unto 7127
Ne 12:43 Also that day they offered great **s**, and 2077
Ps 4: 5 Offer the **s** of righteousness, and put your 2077
27: 6 will I offer in his tabernacle **s** of joy; 2077
50: 8 I will not reprove thee for thy **s** or thy burnt 2077
51:17 The **s** of God *are* a broken spirit: a broken 2077
51:19 shalt thou be pleased with the **s** of 2077
66:15 I will offer unto thee **burnt s** of fatlings, 5930
106:28 unto Baal-peor, and ate the **s** of the dead. 2077
107:22 let them sacrifice the **s** of thanksgiving, 2077
Pr 17: 1 than a house full *of* **s** with strife. 2077
Isa 1:11 To what purpose *is* the multitude of your **s** 2077
29: 1 add ye year to year; let them kill **s**. 2282
43:23 neither hast thou honoured me *with* thy **s**. 2077
43:24 hast thou filled me *with* the fat of thy **s**: 2077
56: 7 their **s** *shall be* accepted upon mine altar; 2077
Jer 6:20 not acceptable, nor your **s** sweet unto me. 2077
7:21 Put your burnt offerings unto your **s**, and 2077
7:22 of Egypt, concerning burnt offerings or **s**: 2077
17:26 **s**, and meat offerings, and incense, and 2077
17:26 and incense, and bringing **s** *of* praise, NIH
Eze 20:28 they offered there their **s**, and there they 2077
40:41 eight tables, whereupon they slew *their* **s**. NIH
Hos 4:19 they shall be ashamed because of their **s**. 2077
8:13 They sacrifice flesh *for* the **s** of mine 2077
9: 4 their **s** *shall be* unto them as the bread of 2077
Am 4: 4 bring your **s** *every* morning, *and* your tithes 2077
5:25 Have ye offered unto me **s** and offerings in 2077
Mk 12:33 more than all whole burnt offerings and **s**. *2378*
Lk 13: 1 blood Pilate had mingled with their **s**. *2378*
Ac 7:42 **s** *by the space of* forty years in *2378*
1Co 10:18 are not they which eat *of* the **s** partakers of *2378*
Heb 5: 1 that he may offer both gifts and **s** for sins: *2378*
8: 3 high priest is ordained to offer gifts and **s**: *2378*
9: 9 in which were offered both gifts and **s**, *2378*
9:23 *things* themselves with better **s** than these. *2378*
10: 1 can never with those **s** which they offered *2378*
10: 3 But in those **s** *there is* a remembrance *again* NIG
10: 6 and **s** for sin thou hast had no pleasure. NIG
10:11 and offering oftentimes the same **s**, *2378*
13:16 for with such **s** God is well pleased. *2378*
1Pe 2: 5 a holy priesthood, to offer up spiritual **s**, *2378*

SACRIFICETH (6) [SACRIFICE]
Ex 22:20 He that **s** unto *any* god, save unto 2076
Ecc 9: 2 to him that **s**, and to him that sacrificeth 2076
9: 2 him that sacrificeth, and to him that **s** not: 2076
Isa 65: 3 that **s** in gardens, and burneth incense upon 2076
66: 3 he that **s** a lamb, *as if* he cut off a dog's 2076
Mal 1:14 **s** unto the Lord a corrupt *thing*: for I *am* a 2076

SACRIFICING (2) [SACRIFICE]
1Ki 8: 5 with him before the ark, **s** sheep and oxen, 2076
12:32 **s** unto the calves that he had made: 2076

SACRILEGE (1)
Ro 2:22 that abhorrest idols, dost thou **commit s**? *2416*

SAD (11) [SADLY, SADNESS]
Ge 40: 6 looked upon them, and behold, they *were* **s**. 2196
1Sa 1:18 and her countenance was no more **s**. NIH
1Ki 21: 5 said unto him, Why is thy spirit **so s**, 5620
Ne 2: 1 Now I had not been *beforetime* **s** in his 7451
2: 2 Why *is* thy countenance **s**, seeing thou *art* 7451
2: 3 why should not my countenance be **s**, 3415
Eze 13:22 *ye* have **made** the heart of the righteous **s**, 3512
13:22 the righteous sad, whom I have not **made s**; 3510
Mt 6:16 not as the hypocrites, of a **s countenance**: *4659*
Mk 10:22 And he was **s** at *that* saying, and went away *4768*
Lk 24:17 have one to another, as ye walk, and are **s**? *4659*

SADDLE (4) [SADDLED]
Lev 15: 9 what **s** soever he rideth upon that hath 4817
2Sa 19:26 for thy servant said, I will **s** me an ass, 2280
1Ki 13:13 he said unto his sons, **S** me the ass. So they 2280
13:27 he spake to his sons, saying, **S** me the ass. 2280

SADDLED (10) [SADDLE]
Ge 22: 3 **s** his ass, and took two of his young men 2280
Nu 22:21 **s** his ass, and went with the princes of 2280
Jdg 19:10 *there were* with him two asses **s**, 2280
2Sa 16: 1 with a couple of asses **s**, and upon them 2280
17:23 he **s** *his* ass, and arose, and gat him *home* to 2280
1Ki 2:40 **s** his ass, and went to Gath to Achish to 2280
13:13 So they **s** him the ass: and he rode thereon, 2280
13:23 after he had drunk, that he **s** for him the ass, 2280
13:27 Saddle me the ass. And they **s** *him*. 2280
2Ki 4:24 she **s** an ass, and said to her servant, Drive, 2280

SADDLES See FURNITURE

SADDUCEES (14)
Mt 3: 7 of the Pharisees and **S** come to his baptism, *4523*
16: 1 The Pharisees also with the **S** came, and *4523*
16: 6 of the leaven of the Pharisees and *of the* **S**. *4523*
16:11 of the leaven of the Pharisees and *of the* **S**? *4523*
16:12 the doctrine of the Pharisees and *of the* **S**. *4523*
22:23 The same day came to him *the* **S**, which say *4523*
22:34 had heard that he had put the **S** to silence, *4523*
Mk 12:18 Then come unto him *the* **S**, which say there *4523*
Lk 20:27 Then came to *him* certain of the **S**, *4523*
Ac 4: 1 of the temple, and the **S**, came upon them, *4523*
5:17 were with him, (which is the sect of the **S**,) *4523*
23: 6 Paul perceived that the one part were **S**, *4523*
23: 7 dissension between the Pharisees and the **S**: *4523*
Ac 23: 8 For the **S** say that there is no resurrection, *4523*

SADLY (1) [SAD]
Ge 40: 7 Wherefore look ye *so* **s** to day? 7451

SADNESS (1) [SAD]
Ecc 7: 3 for by the **s** of the countenance the heart is 7455

SADOC (2)
Mt 1:14 And Azor begat **S**; and Sadoc begat Achim; *4524*
1:14 and **S** begat Achim; and Achim begat *4524*

SAFE (13) [SAVE]
1Sa 12:11 enemies on every side, and ye dwelled **s**. 983
2Sa 18:29 the king said, *Is* the young man Absalom **s**? 7965
18:32 unto Cushi, *Is* the young man Absalom **s**? 7965
Job 21: 9 Their houses *are* **s** from fear, neither *is* 7965
Ps 119:117 Hold thou me up, and I shall be **s**: and 3467
Pr 18:10 the righteous runneth into it, and is **s**. 7682
29:25 putteth his trust in the LORD shall be **s**. 7682
Isa 5:29 shall **carry** *it* **away s**, and none shall 6403
Eze 34:27 they shall be **s** in their land, and shall know 983
Lk 15:27 because he hath received him **s** *and* sound. NIG
Ac 23:24 and **bring** *him* **s** unto Felix the governor. *1295*
27:44 to pass, that *they* **escaped** all **s** to land. *1295*
Php 3: 1 me indeed *is* not grievous, but for you *it is* **s**. *804*

SAFEGUARD (1) [GUARD, SAVE]
1Sa 22:23 thy life: but with me thou *shalt be* **in s**. 4931

SAFELY (21) [SAVE]
Lev 26: 5 to the full, and dwell in your land **s**. 983+3807.1
1Ki 4:25 Judah and Israel dwelt **s**, every man 983+3807.1
Ps 78:53 he led them on **s**, so that they feared 983+3807.1
Pr 1:33 But whoso hearkeneth unto me shall dwell **s**, 983
3:23 shalt thou walk *in* thy way **s**, and 983+3807.1
31:11 The heart of her husband doth **s** trust in her, NIH
Isa 41: 3 He pursued them, *and* passed **s**; *even by* 7965
Jer 23: 6 be saved, and Israel shall dwell **s**: 983+3807.1
32:37 I will cause them to dwell **s**: 983+3807.1
33:16 and Jerusalem shall dwell **s**: 983+3807.1
Eze 28:26 they shall dwell **s** therein, and 983+3807.1
34:25 they shall dwell **s** in the wilderness, 983+3807.1
34:28 they shall dwell **s**, and none shall 983+3807.1
38: 8 and they shall dwell **s** all of them. 983+3807.1
38:11 *to* them that are at rest, that dwell **s**, 983+3807.1
38:14 when my people of Israel dwelleth **s**, 983+3807.1
39:26 when they dwelt **s** in their land, and 983+3807.1
Hos 2:18 the earth, and will make them to lie down **s**. 983
Zec 14:11 but Jerusalem shall be **s** inhabited. 983
Mk 14:44 same is he; take him, and lead *him* away **s**. *806*
Ac 16:23 charging the jailor to keep them **s**: *806*

SAFETY (19) [SAVE]
Lev 25:18 do them; and ye shall dwell in the land in **s**. 983
25:19 ye shall eat *your* fill, and dwell therein in **s**. 983
Dt 12:10 enemies round about, so that ye dwell **in s**; 983
33:12 The beloved of the LORD shall dwell in **s** 983
33:28 Israel then shall dwell *in* **s** alone: 983
Job 3:26 I was not **in s**, neither had I rest, 7951
5: 4 His children are far from **s**, and they are 3468
5:11 those which mourn may be exalted *to* **s**. 3468
11:18 *about thee, and* thou shalt take thy rest in **s**. 983
24:23 *Though* it be given him *to be* in **s**, 983
Ps 4: 8 LORD, only makest me dwell in **s**. 983
12: 5 I will set *him* in **s** *from him that* puffeth at 3468
33:17 A horse *is* a vain thing for **s**: neither shall 8668
Pr 11:14 in the multitude of counsellers *there is* **s**. 8668
21:31 the day of battle: but **s** *is* of the LORD. 8668
24: 6 and in multitude of counsellers *there is* **s**. 8668
Isa 14:30 shall feed, and the needy shall lie down in **s**: 983
Ac 5:23 The prison truly found we shut with all **s**, *803*
1Th 5: 3 For when they shall say, Peace and **s**; then *803*

SAFFRON (1)
SS 4:14 Spikenard and **s**; calamus and cinnamon, 3750

SAID (4001) [SAY]
Ge 1: 3 God **s**, Let there be light: and there was light. 559
1: 6 God **s**, Let there be a firmament in the midst 559
1: 9 God **s**, Let the waters under the heaven be 559
1:11 God **s**, Let the earth bring forth grass, 559
1:14 God **s**, Let there be lights in the firmament 559
1:20 God **s**, Let the waters bring forth abundantly 559
1:24 God **s**, Let the earth bring forth the living 559
1:26 God **s**, Let us make man in our image, 559
1:28 God **s** unto them, Be fruitful, and multiply, 559
1:29 God **s**, Behold, I have given you every herb 559
2:18 the LORD God **s**, *It is* not good that 559
2:23 And Adam **s**, This *is* now bone of my bones, 559
3: 1 he **s** unto the woman, Yea, hath God said, 559
3: 1 he said unto the woman, Yea, hath God **s**, 559
3: 2 the woman **s** unto the serpent, We may eat of 559
3: 3 God hath **s**, Ye shall not eat of it, 559
3: 4 the serpent **s** unto the woman, Ye shall not 559
3: 9 unto Adam, and **s** unto him, Where *art* thou? 559
3:10 he **s**, I heard thy voice in the garden, and 559
3:11 he **s**, Who told thee that thou *wast* naked? 559
3:12 the man **s**, The woman whom thou gavest *to* 559
3:13 the LORD God **s** unto the woman, What *is* 559
3:13 And the woman **s**, The serpent beguiled me, 559
3:14 the LORD God **s** unto the serpent, 559
3:16 Unto the woman he **s**, I will greatly multiply 559
3:17 unto Adam he **s**, Because thou hast 559
3:22 the LORD God **s**, Behold, the man is 559
4: 1 she conceived, and bare Cain, and **s**, I have 559
4: 6 the LORD **s** unto Cain, Why art thou 559
4: 9 the LORD **s** unto Cain, Where *is* Abel thy 559
4: 9 he **s**, I know not: *Am* I my brother's keeper? 559
4:10 he **s**, What hast thou done? the voice of thy 559
4:13 Cain **s** unto the LORD, My punishment *is* 559
4:15 the LORD **s** unto him, Therefore 559
4:23 Lamech **s** unto his wives, Adah and Zillah, 559
4:25 **s** *she*, hath appointed me another seed NIH
Ge 6: 3 the LORD **s**, My spirit shall not always 559
6: 7 the LORD **s**, I will destroy man whom I 559
6:13 God **s** unto Noah, The end of all flesh is 559
7: 1 the LORD **s** unto Noah, Come thou and 559
8:21 the LORD **s** in his heart, I will not again 559
9: 1 blessed Noah and his sons, and **s** unto them, 559
9:12 God **s**, This *is* the token of the covenant 559
9:17 God **s** unto Noah, This *is* the token of 559
9:25 he **s**, Cursed *be* Canaan; a servant of servants 559
9:26 he **s**, Blessed *be* the LORD God of Shem; 559
10: 9 wherefore it is **s**, *Even* as Nimrod the mighty 559
11: 3 they **s** one to another, Go to, let us make 559
11: 4 they **s**, Go to, let us build us a city and 559
11: 6 the LORD **s**, Behold, the people *is* one, 559
12: 1 Now the LORD had **s** unto Abram, 559
12: 7 and **s**, Unto thy seed will I give this land: 559
12:11 that he **s** unto Sarai his wife, Behold now, 559
12:18 Pharaoh called Abram, and **s**, What *is* this 559
13: 8 Abram **s** unto Lot, Let there be no strife, 559
13:14 the LORD **s** unto Abram, after that Lot was 559
14:19 he blessed him, and **s**, Blessed *be* Abram of 559
14:21 the king of Sodom **s** unto Abram, Give me 559
14:22 Abram **s** to the king of Sodom, I have lift up 559
15: 2 Abram **s**, Lord GOD, what wilt thou give 559
15: 3 Abram **s**, Behold, to me thou hast given no 559
15: 5 **s**, Look now towards heaven, and tell 559
15: 5 and he **s** unto him, So shall thy seed be. 559
15: 7 he **s** unto him, I *am* the LORD that brought 559
15: 8 he **s**, Lord GOD, whereby shall I know that 559
15: 9 he **s** unto him, Take me a heifer of three 559
15:13 he **s** unto Abram, Know of a surety that thy 559
16: 2 Sarai **s** unto Abram, Behold now, 559
16: 5 Sarai **s** unto Abram, My wrong *be* upon thee: 559
16: 6 Abram **s** unto Sarai, Behold, thy maid *is* in 559
16: 8 he **s**, Hagar, Sarai's maid, whence camest 559
16: 8 she **s**, I flee from the face of my mistress 559
16: 9 the angel of the LORD **s** unto her, 559
16:10 the angel of the LORD **s** unto her, I will 559
16:11 the angel of the LORD **s** unto her, Behold, 559
16:13 for she **s**, Have I also here looked after him 559
17: 1 and **s** unto him, I *am* the Almighty God; 559
17: 9 God **s** unto Abraham, Thou shalt keep my 559
17:15 God **s** unto Abraham, *As for* Sarai thy wife, 559
17:17 his face, and laughed, and **s** in his heart, 559
17:18 Abraham **s** unto God, O that Ishmael might 559
17:19 God **s**, Sarah thy wife shall bear thee a son 559
17:23 in the selfsame day, as God had **s** unto him. 1696
18: 3 **s**, My Lord, if now I have found favour in 559
18: 5 And they **s**, So do, as thou hast said. 559
18: 5 And they said, So do, as thou hast **s**. 1696
18: 6 hastened into the tent unto Sarah, and **s**, 559
18: 9 they **s** unto him, Where *is* Sarah thy wife? 559
18: 9 thy wife? And he **s**, Behold, in the tent. 559
18:10 he **s**, I will certainly return unto thee 559
18:13 the LORD **s** unto Abraham, Wherefore did 559
18:15 And he **s**, Nay; but thou didst laugh. 559
18:17 the LORD **s**, Shall I hide from Abraham 559
18:20 the LORD **s**, Because the cry of Sodom 559
18:23 Abraham drew near, and **s**, Wilt thou also 559
18:26 the LORD **s**, If I find in Sodom fifty 559
18:27 And Abraham answered and **s**, Behold now, 559
18:28 he **s**, If I find there forty and five, I will not 559
18:29 he spake unto him yet again, and **s**, 559
18:29 And he **s**, I will not do *it* for forty's sake. 559
18:30 he **s** *unto him*, Oh let not the Lord be angry, 559
18:30 he **s**, I will not do *it*, if I find thirty there. 559
18:31 he **s**, Behold now, I have taken upon me to 559
18:31 he **s**, I will not destroy *it* for twenty's sake. 559
18:32 he **s**, Oh let not the Lord be angry, and I will 559
18:32 And he **s**, I will not destroy *it* for ten's sake. 559
19: 2 he **s**, Behold now, my lords, turn in, I pray 559
19: 2 they **s**, Nay; but we will abide in the street 559
19: 5 they called unto Lot, and **s** unto him, 559
19: 7 **s**, I pray you, brethren, do not *so* wickedly. 559
19: 9 they **s**, Stand back. And they said *again*, *This* 559
19: 9 they **s** *again*, *This* one *fellow* came in to 559
19:12 the men **s** unto Lot, Hast thou here any 559
19:14 and **s**, Up, get ye out of this place; 559
19:17 forth abroad, that he **s**, Escape for thy life; 559
19:18 And Lot **s** unto them, Oh, not so, my Lord: 559
19:21 he **s** unto him, See, I have accepted thee 559
19:31 the firstborn **s** unto the younger, Our father 559
19:34 that the firstborn **s** unto the younger, Behold, 559
20: 2 Abraham **s** of Sarah his wife, She *is* my 559
20: 3 **s** to him, Behold, thou *art but* a dead man, 559
20: 4 he **s**, Lord, wilt thou slay also a righteous 559
20: 5 **S** he not unto me, She *is* my sister? and she, 559
20: 5 she, even she herself **s**, He *is* my brother: 559
20: 6 God **s** unto him in a dream, Yea, I know that 559
20: 9 **s** unto him, What hast thou done unto us? 559
20:10 Abimelech **s** unto Abraham, What sawest 559
20:11 Abraham **s**, Because I thought, Surely 559
20:13 that I **s** unto her, This *is* thy kindness which 559
20:15 Abimelech **s**, Behold, my land *is* before thee: 559
20:16 unto Sarah he **s**, Behold, I have given thy 559
21: 1 the LORD visited Sarah as he had **s**, and 559
21: 6 And Sarah **s**, God hath made me to laugh, *so* 559
21: 7 she **s**, Who would have said unto Abraham, 559
21: 7 she said, Who would have **s** unto Abraham, 4448
21:10 Wherefore she **s** unto Abraham, Cast out this 559
21:12 God **s** unto Abraham, Let it not be grievous 559
21:12 in all that Sarah hath **s** unto thee, 559
21:16 for she **s**, Let me not see the death of 559
21:17 and **s** unto her, What aileth thee, Hagar? 559
21:24 And Abraham **s**, I will swear. 559
21:26 Abimelech **s**, I wot not who hath done this 559
21:29 Abimelech **s** unto Abraham, What *mean* 559
21:30 he **s**, For *these* seven ewe lambs shalt thou 559
22: 1 tempt Abraham, and **s** unto him, Abraham: 559
22: 1 Abraham: and he **s**, Behold, *here* I *am*. 559
22: 2 he **s**, Take now thy son, thine only *son* Isaac, 559
22: 5 Abraham **s** unto his young men, Abide you 559
22: 7 unto Abraham his father, and **s**, My father: 559
22: 7 he **s**, Here *am* I, my son. And he said, 559
22: 7 And he **s**, Behold the fire and the wood: but 559

Ge 22: 8 Abraham **s**, My son, God will provide 559
22:11 out of heaven, and **s**, Abraham, Abraham: 559
22:11 Abraham, Abraham: and he **s**, Here *am* I. 559
22:12 he **s**, Lay not thine hand upon the lad, 559
22:14 as it is **s** *to this* day, In the mount of 559
22:16 **s**, By myself have I sworn, saith the LORD, 559
24: 2 Abraham **s** unto his eldest servant of his 559
24: 5 the servant **s** unto him, Peradventure 559
24: 6 Abraham **s** unto him, Beware thou that thou 559
24:12 he **s**, O LORD God of my master Abraham, 559
24:17 ran to meet her, and **s**, Let me, I pray thee, 559
24:18 she **s**, Drink, my lord: and she hasted, and 559
24:19 she **s**, I will draw *water* for thy camels also, 559
24:23 **s**, Whose daughter *art* thou? tell me, I pray 559
24:24 she **s** unto him, I *am* the daughter of Bethuel 559
24:25 She **s** moreover unto him, We have both 559
24:27 he **s**, Blessed *be* the LORD God of my 559
24:31 he **s**, Come in, thou blessed of the LORD; 559
24:33 he **s**, I will not eat, until I have told mine 559
24:33 I have told mine errand. And he **s**, Speak on. 559
24:34 And he **s**, I *am* Abraham's servant. 559
24:39 I **s** unto my master, Peradventure the woman 559
24:40 he **s** unto me, The LORD, before whom I 559
24:42 I came this day unto the well, and **s**, 559
24:45 drew *water:* and I **s** unto her, Let me drink, 559
24:46 down her pitcher from her *shoulder,* and **s**, 559
24:47 I asked her, and **s**, Whose daughter *art* thou? 559
24:47 she **s**, The daughter of Bethuel, Nahor's son, 559
24:50 Laban and Bethuel answered and **s**, 559
24:54 they rose up in the morning, and he **s**, 559
24:55 her brother and her mother **s**, Let the damsel 559
24:56 he **s** unto them, Hinder me not, seeing 559
24:57 they **s**, We will call the damsel, and 559
24:58 they called Rebekah, and **s** unto her, Wilt 559
24:58 thou go with this man? And she **s**, I will go. 559
24:60 and **s** unto her, Thou *art* our sister, 559
24:65 For she had **s** unto the servant, What man *is* 559
24:65 the servant had **s**, It *is* my master: therefore 559
25:22 and she **s**, If *it be* so, why *am* I thus? 559
25:23 the LORD **s** unto her, Two nations *are* in 559
25:30 Esau **s** to Jacob, Feed me, I pray thee, 559
25:31 And Jacob **s**, Sell me *this* day thy birthright. 559
25:32 And Esau **s**, Behold, I *am* at the point to die: 559
25:33 Jacob **s**, Swear to me *this* day; and he sware 559
26: 2 unto him, and **s**, Go not down into Egypt; 559
26: 7 *him* of his wife; and he **s**, She *is* my sister: 559
26: 7 ***s he,*** the men of the place should kill me for NIH
26: 9 and **s**, Behold, of a surety she *is* thy wife: 559
26: 9 Isaac **s** unto him, Because I said, Lest I die 559
26: 9 said unto him, Because I **s**, Lest I die for her. 559
26:10 Abimelech **s**, What *is* this thou hast done 559
26:16 Abimelech **s** unto Isaac, Go from us; 559
26:22 he **s**, For now the LORD hath made room 559
26:24 **s**, I *am* the God of Abraham thy father: 559
26:27 Isaac **s** unto them, Wherefore come ye to 559
26:28 they **s**, We saw certainly that the LORD 559
26:28 we **s**, Let there be now an oath betwixt us, 559
26:32 and **s** unto him, We have found water. 559
27: 1 Esau his eldest son, and **s** unto him, My son: 559
27: 1 and he **s** unto him, Behold, *here am* I. 559
27: 2 he **s**, Behold now, I am old, I know not 559
27:11 And Jacob **s** to Rebekah his mother, Behold, 559
27:13 his mother **s** unto him, Upon me *be* thy 559
27:18 he came unto his father, and **s**, My father: 559
27:18 and he **s**, Here *am* I; who *art* thou, my son? 559
27:19 Jacob **s** unto his father, I *am* Esau thy 559
27:20 Isaac **s** unto his son, How *is it that* thou hast 559
27:20 he **s**, Because the LORD thy God brought *it* 559
27:21 Isaac **s** unto Jacob, Come near, I pray thee, 559
27:22 he felt him, and **s**, The voice *is* Jacob's 559
27:24 he **s**, *Art* thou my very son Esau? And he 559
27:24 *Art* thou my very son Esau? And he **s**, I *am.* 559
27:25 he **s**, Bring *it* near to me, and I will eat of my 559
27:26 his father Isaac **s** unto him, Come near now, 559
27:27 of his raiment, and blessed him, and **s**, See, 559
27:31 **s** unto his father, Let my father arise, and 559
27:32 Isaac his father **s** unto him, Who *art* thou? 559
27:32 And he **s**, I *am* thy son, thy firstborn Esau. 559
27:33 trembled very exceedingly, and **s**, Who? 559
27:34 **s** unto his father, Bless me, *even* me also, 559
27:35 he **s**, Thy brother came with subtilty, and 559
27:36 he **s**, Is not he rightly named Jacob? for he 559
27:36 he **s**, Hast thou not reserved a blessing for 559
27:37 Isaac answered and **s** unto Esau, Behold, 559
27:38 Esau **s** unto his father, Hast thou but one 559
27:39 Isaac his father answered and **s** unto him, 559
27:41 Esau **s** in his heart, The days of mourning for 559
27:42 **s** unto him, Behold, thy brother Esau, 559
27:46 Rebekah **s** to Isaac, I am weary of my life 559
28: 1 and charged him, and **s** unto him, 559
28:13 the LORD stood above it, and **s**, 559
28:16 and he **s**, Surely the LORD is in this place; 559
28:17 he was afraid, and **s**, How dreadful *is* this 559
29: 4 Jacob **s** unto them, My brethren, whence *be* 559
29: 4 whence *be* ye? And they **s**, Of Haran *are* we. 559
29: 5 he **s** unto them, Know ye Laban the son of 559
29: 5 son of Nahor? And they **s**, We know *him.* 559
29: 6 he **s** unto them, *Is* he well? And they said, 559
29: 6 they **s**, *He is* well: and behold, Rachel his 559
29: 7 he **s**, Lo, *it is* yet high day, neither *is it* time 559
29: 8 they **s**, We cannot, until all the flocks be 559
29:14 Laban **s** to him, Surely thou *art* my bone 559
29:15 Laban **s** unto Jacob, Because thou *art* my 559
29:18 **s**, I will serve thee seven years for Rachel 559
29:19 Laban **s**, *It is* better that I give her to thee, 559
29:21 Jacob **s** unto Laban, Give *me* my wife, 559
29:25 he **s** to Laban, What *is* this thou hast done 559
29:26 Laban **s**, It must not be so done in our 559
29:32 for she **s**, Surely the LORD hath looked 559
29:33 **s**, Because the LORD hath heard that I *was* 559
29:34 **s**, Now *this* time will my husband be joined 559
29:35 she **s**, Now will I praise the LORD: 559
30: 1 **s** unto Jacob, Give me children, or else I die. 559
30: 2 he **s**, *Am* I in God's stead, who hath 559
30: 3 she **s**, Behold my maid Bilhah, go in unto 559

Ge 30: 6 Rachel **s**, God hath judged me, and hath also 559
30: 8 Rachel **s**, With great wrestlings have I 559
30:11 Leah **s**, A troop cometh: and she called his 559
30:13 Leah **s**, Happy am I, for the daughters will 559
30:14 Then Rachel **s** to Leah, Give me, I pray thee, 559
30:15 she **s** unto her, *Is it* a small matter that thou 559
30:15 Rachel **s**, Therefore he shall lie with thee to 559
30:16 Leah went out to meet him, and **s**, 559
30:18 Leah **s**, God hath given *me* my hire, because 559
30:20 Leah **s**, God hath endued me with a good 559
30:23 and **s**, God hath taken away my reproach: 559
30:24 **s**, The LORD shall add to me another son. 559
30:25 that Jacob **s** unto Laban, Send me away, 559
30:27 Laban **s** unto him, I pray thee, if I have 559
30:28 he **s**, Appoint me thy wages, and I will give 559
30:29 he **s** unto him, Thou knowest how I have 559
30:31 he **s**, What shall I give thee? And Jacob said, 559
30:31 Jacob **s**, Thou shalt not give me any thing: 559
30:34 Laban **s**, Behold, I would it might be 559
31: 3 the LORD **s** unto Jacob, Return unto 559
31: 5 **s** unto them, I see your father's countenance, 559
31: 8 If he **s** thus, The speckled shall be thy 559
31: 8 if he **s** thus, The ringstraked shall be thy 559
31:11 a dream, *saying,* Jacob: And I **s**, Here *am* I. 559
31:12 he **s**, Lift up now thine eyes, and see, all 559
31:14 and Leah answered and **s** unto him, 559
31:16 whatsoever God hath **s** unto thee, do. 559
31:24 **s** unto him, Take heed that thou speak not to 559
31:26 And Laban **s** to Jacob, What hast thou done, 559
31:31 Jacob answered and **s** to Laban, Because I 559
31:31 for I **s**, Peradventure thou wouldest take by 559
31:35 she **s** to her father, Let it not displease my 559
31:36 Jacob answered and **s** to Laban, What *is* my 559
31:43 Laban answered and **s** unto Jacob, *These* 559
31:46 Jacob **s** unto his brethren, Gather stones; 559
31:48 Laban **s**, This heap *is* a witness between me 559
31:49 for he **s**, The LORD watch between me and 559
31:51 And Laban **s** to Jacob, Behold this heap, and 559
32: 2 Jacob saw them, he **s**, This *is* God's host: 559
32: 8 **s**, If Esau come to the one company, and 559
32: 9 And Jacob **s**, O God of my father Abraham, 559
32:16 and **s** unto his servants, Pass over before me, 559
32:20 For he **s**, I will appease him with the present 559
32:26 he **s**, Let me go, for the day breaketh. And he 559
32:26 he **s**, I will not let thee go, except thou bless 559
32:27 he **s** unto him, What *is* thy name? And he 559
32:27 What *is* thy name? And he **s**, Jacob. 559
32:28 he **s**, Thy name shall be called no more 559
32:29 Jacob asked *him,* and **s**, Tell *me,* I pray thee, 559
32:29 he **s**, Wherefore *is* it *that* thou dost ask after 559
33: 5 the children; and **s**, Who *are* those with thee? 559
33: 5 he **s**, The children which God hath 559
33: 8 he **s**, What meanest thou by all this drove 559
33: 8 he **s**, *These are* to find grace in the sight of 559
33: 9 Esau **s**, I have enough, my brother; keep that 559
33:10 Jacob **s**, Nay, I pray thee, if now I have 559
33:12 he **s**, Let us take our journey, and let us go, 559
33:13 he **s** unto him, My lord knoweth that 559
33:15 Esau **s**, Let me now leave with thee *some* of 559
33:15 he **s**, What needeth it? let me find grace in 559
34:11 Shechem **s** unto her father and unto her 559
34:13 **s**, because he had defiled Dinah their sister: 1696
34:14 they **s** unto them, We cannot do this thing, 559
34:30 Jacob **s** to Simeon and Levi, Ye have 559
34:31 they **s**, Should he deal with our sister as with 559
35: 1 God **s** unto Jacob, Arise, go up to Beth-el, 559
35: 2 Jacob **s** unto his household, and to all that 559
35:10 God **s** unto him, Thy name *is* Jacob: 559
35:11 God **s** unto him, I *am* God Almighty: 559
35:17 that the midwife **s** unto her, Fear not; 559
37: 6 he **s** unto them, Hear, I pray you, this dream 559
37: 8 his brethren **s** to him, Shalt thou indeed reign 559
37: 9 told it his brethren, and **s**, Behold, I have 559
37:10 his father rebuked him, and **s** unto him, 559
37:13 Israel **s** unto Joseph, Do not thy brethren 559
37:13 thee unto them. And he **s** to him, Here *am* I. 559
37:14 he **s** to him, Go, I pray thee, see whether it 559
37:16 he **s**, I seek my brethren: tell me, I pray thee, 559
37:17 the man **s**, They are departed hence; for I 559
37:19 they **s** one to another, Behold, this dreamer 559
37:21 out of their hands; and **s**, Let us not kill him. 559
37:22 And Reuben **s** unto them, Shed no blood, *but* 559
37:26 Judah **s** unto his brethren, What profit *is it* if 559
37:30 unto his brethren, and **s**, The child *is* not; 559
37:32 *it* to their father; and **s**, This have we found: 559
37:33 he knew it, and **s**, *It is* my son's coat; an evil 559
37:35 he **s**, For I will go down into the grave unto 559
38: 8 Judah **s** unto Onan, Go in unto thy brother's 559
38:11 **s** Judah to Tamar his daughter in law, 559
38:11 for he **s**, Lest peradventure he die also, as his 559
38:16 **s**, Go to, I pray thee, let me come in unto 559
38:16 she **s**, What wilt thou give me, that thou 559
38:17 he **s**, I will send *thee* a kid from the flock. 559
38:17 she **s**, Wilt thou give *me* a pledge, till thou 559
38:18 he **s**, What pledge shall I give thee? And she 559
38:18 And she **s**, Thy signet, and thy bracelets, and 559
38:21 they **s**, There was no harlot in this *place.* 559
38:22 returned to Judah, and **s**, I cannot find her; 559
38:22 also the men of the place **s**, *that* there was 559
38:23 Judah **s**, Let her take *it* to her, lest we be 559
38:24 Judah **s**, Bring her forth, and let her be burnt. 559
38:25 she **s**, Discern, I pray thee, whose *are* these, 559
38:26 Judah acknowledged *them,* and **s**, She hath 559
38:29 she **s**, How hast thou broken forth? 559
39: 7 eyes upon Joseph; and she **s**, Lie with me. 559
39: 8 and **s** unto his master's wife, Behold, 559
40: 8 they **s** unto him, We have dreamed a dream, 559
40: 8 Joseph **s** unto them, *Do* not interpretations 559
40: 9 **s** to him, In my dream, behold, a vine *was* 559
40:12 Joseph **s** unto him, This *is* the interpretation 559
40:16 he **s** unto Joseph, I also *was* in my dream, 559
40:18 Joseph answered and **s**, This *is* 559
41:15 Pharaoh **s** unto Joseph, I have dreamed a 559
41:17 Pharaoh **s** unto Joseph, In my dream, 1696
41:25 Joseph **s** unto Pharaoh, The dream of 559

Ge 41:38 Pharaoh **s** unto his servants, Can we find 559
41:39 Pharaoh **s** unto Joseph, Forasmuch as God 559
41:41 Pharaoh **s** unto Joseph, See, I have set thee 559
41:44 Pharaoh **s** unto Joseph, I *am* Pharaoh, and 559
41:51 ***s he,*** hath made me forget all my toil, and NIH
41:54 began to come, according as Joseph had **s**: 559
41:55 Pharaoh **s** unto all the Egyptians, Go unto 559
42: 1 Jacob **s** unto his sons, Why do ye look one 559
42: 2 he **s**, Behold, I have heard that there is corn 559
42: 4 for he **s**, Lest peradventure mischief befall 559
42: 7 and he **s** unto them, Whence come ye? 559
42: 7 they **s**, From the land of Canaan to buy food. 559
42: 9 of them, and **s** unto them, Ye *are* spies; 559
42:10 they **s** unto him, Nay, my lord, but to buy 559
42:12 he **s** unto them, Nay, but to see 559
42:13 they **s**, Thy servants *are* twelve brethren, 559
42:14 Joseph **s** unto them, That *is it* that I spake 559
42:18 Joseph **s** unto them the third day, This do, 559
42:21 they **s** one to another, We *are* verily guilty 559
42:28 he **s** unto his brethren, My money is 559
42:31 we **s** unto him, We *are* true *men;* we are no 559
42:33 the man, the lord of the country, **s** unto us, 559
42:36 Jacob their father **s** unto them, Me have ye 559
42:38 he **s**, My son shall not go down with you; 559
43: 2 their father **s** unto them, Go again, buy us a 559
43: 5 for the man **s** unto us, Ye shall not see my 559
43: 6 Israel **s**, Wherefore dealt ye *so* ill with me, 559
43: 7 they **s**, The man asked us straitly of our state, 559
43: 8 Judah **s** unto Israel his father, Send the lad 559
43:11 their father Israel **s** unto them, If *it must be* 559
43:16 he **s** to the ruler of his house, Bring *these* 559
43:18 they **s**, Because of the money that was 559
43:20 **s**, O sir, we came indeed down at the first 559
43:23 he **s**, Peace *be* to you, fear not: your God, 559
43:27 **s**, *Is* your father well, the old man of whom 559
43:29 brother Benjamin, his mother's son, and **s**, 559
43:29 he **s**, God be gracious unto thee, my son. 559
43:31 and refrained himself, and **s**, Set on bread. 559
44: 4 *yet* far off, Joseph **s** unto his steward, Up, 559
44: 7 they **s** unto him, Wherefore saith my lord 559
44:10 he **s**, Now also *let it be* according unto your 559
44:15 Joseph **s** unto them, What deed *is* this that ye 559
44:16 Judah **s**, What shall we say unto my lord? 559
44:17 And he **s**, God forbid that I should do so: *but* 559
44:18 and **s**, O my lord, let thy servant, I pray thee, 559
44:20 we **s** unto my lord, We have a father, an old 559
44:22 we **s** unto my lord, The lad cannot leave his 559
44:25 our father **s**, Go again, *and* buy us a little 559
44:26 we **s**, We cannot go down: if our youngest 559
44:27 thy servant my father **s** unto us, Ye know 559
44:28 from me, and I **s**, Surely he is torn in pieces; 559
45: 3 And Joseph **s** unto his brethren, I *am* Joseph; 559
45: 4 Joseph **s** unto his brethren, Come near to me, 559
45: 4 he **s**, I *am* Joseph your brother, whom ye 559
45:17 Pharaoh **s** unto Joseph, Say unto thy 559
45:24 he **s** unto them, See that ye fall not out by 559
45:27 words of Joseph, which he had **s** unto them: 1696
45:28 Israel **s**, *It is* enough; Joseph my son *is* yet 559
46: 2 the visions of the night, and **s**, Jacob, Jacob. 559
46: 2 and said, Jacob, Jacob. And he **s**, Here *am* I. 559
46: 3 he **s**, I *am* God, the God of thy father: 559
46:30 Israel **s** unto Joseph, Now let me die, since I 559
46:31 Joseph **s** unto his brethren, and unto his 559
47: 1 **s**, My father and my brethren, and 559
47: 3 Pharaoh **s** unto his brethren, What *is* your 559
47: 3 they **s** unto Pharaoh, Thy servants *are* 559
47: 4 They **s** moreover unto Pharaoh, For to 559
47: 8 Pharaoh **s** unto Jacob, How old *art* thou? 559
47: 9 Jacob **s** unto Pharaoh, The days of the years 559
47:15 came unto Joseph, and **s**, Give us bread: 559
47:16 Joseph **s**, Give your cattle; and I will give 559
47:18 **s** unto him, We will not hide *it* from my lord, 559
47:23 Joseph **s** unto the people, Behold, I have 559
47:25 they **s**, Thou hast saved our lives: let us find 559
47:29 and he called his son Joseph, and **s** unto him, 559
47:30 And he **s**, I will do as thou hast said. 559
47:30 And he said, I will do as thou hast **s**. 1697
47:31 he **s**, Swear unto me. And he sware unto 559
48: 2 *one* told Jacob, and **s**, Behold, thy son 559
48: 3 Jacob **s** unto Joseph, God Almighty appeared 559
48: 4 **s** unto me, Behold, I will make thee fruitful, 559
48: 8 beheld Joseph's sons, and **s**, Who *are* these? 559
48: 9 Joseph **s** unto his father, They *are* my sons, 559
48: 9 God hath given me in this *place.* And he **s**, 559
48:11 Israel **s** unto Joseph, I had not thought to see 559
48:15 he blessed Joseph, and **s**, God, before whom 559
48:18 Joseph **s** unto his father, Not so, my father: 559
48:19 his father refused, and **s**, I know *it,* my son, 559
48:21 Israel **s** unto Joseph, Behold, I die: but 559
49: 1 his sons, and **s**, Gather yourselves together, 559
49:29 he charged them, and **s** unto them, I *am to be* 559
50: 6 Pharaoh **s**, Go up, and bury thy father, 559
50:11 the mourning in the floor of Atad, they **s**, 559
50:15 they **s**, Joseph will peradventure hate us, and 559
50:18 and they **s**, Behold, we *be* thy servants. 559
50:19 Joseph **s** unto them, Fear not: for *am* I in 559
50:24 Joseph **s** unto his brethren, I die: and 559
Ex 1: 9 he **s** unto his people, Behold, the people of 559
1:16 he **s**, When ye do the office of a midwife to 559
1:18 **s** unto them, Why have ye done this thing, 559
1:19 the midwives **s** unto Pharaoh, Because 559
2: 6 she had compassion on him, and **s**, This *is* 559
2: 7 **s** his sister to Pharaoh's daughter, Shall I go 559
2: 8 Pharaoh's daughter **s** to her, Go. And 559
2: 9 Pharaoh's daughter **s** unto her, Take this 559
2:10 she **s**, Because I drew him out of the water. 559
2:13 he **s** to him that did the wrong, Wherefore 559
2:14 he **s**, Who made thee a prince and a judge 559
2:14 Moses feared, and **s**, Surely *this* thing is 559
2:18 he **s**, How *is it that* you are come so soon to 559
2:19 they **s**, An Egyptian delivered us out of 559
2:20 he **s** unto his daughters, And where *is* he? 559
2:22 for he **s**, I have been a stranger in a strange 559
3: 3 Moses **s**, I will now turn aside, and see this 559
3: 4 the midst of the bush, and **s**, Moses, Moses. 559

Ex 3: 4 said, Moses, Moses. And he **s**, Here *am* I. 559
3: 5 he **s**, Draw not nigh hither: put off thy shoes 559
3: 6 Moreover he **s**, I *am* the God of thy father, 559
3: 7 the LORD **s**, I have surely seen 559
3:11 Moses **s** unto God, Who *am* I, that I should 559
3:12 he **s**, Certainly I will be with thee; and 559
3:13 Moses **s** unto God, Behold, *when* I come 559
3:14 And God **s** unto Moses, I AM THAT I AM: 559
3:14 he **s**, Thus shalt thou say unto the children of 559
3:15 God **s** moreover unto Moses, Thus shalt thou 559
3:17 I have **s**, I will bring you up out of 559
4: 1 Moses answered and **s**, But behold, they will 559
4: 2 the LORD **s** unto him, What *is* that in thine 559
4: 2 What *is* that in thine hand? And he **s**, A rod. 559
4: 3 he **s**, Cast it on the ground. And he cast it on 559
4: 4 the LORD **s** unto Moses, Put forth thine 559
4: 6 the LORD **s** furthermore unto him, Put now 559
4: 7 he **s**, Put thine hand into thy bosom again. 559
4:10 Moses **s** unto the LORD, O my Lord, I *am* 559
4:11 the LORD **s** unto him, Who hath made 559
4:13 he **s**, O my Lord, send, I pray thee, by 559
4:14 he **s**, Is not Aaron the Levite thy brother? 559
4:18 **s** unto him, Let me go, I pray thee, and 559
4:18 And Jethro **s** to Moses, Go in peace. 559
4:19 the LORD **s** unto Moses in Midian, Go, 559
4:21 the LORD **s** unto Moses, When thou goest 559
4:25 of her son, and cast *it* at his feet, and **s**, 559
4:26 she **s**, A bloody husband *thou art*, because 559
4:27 the LORD **s** to Aaron, Go into 559
5: 2 Pharaoh **s**, Who *is* the LORD, that I should 559
5: 3 they **s**, The God of the Hebrews hath met 559
5: 4 the king of Egypt **s** unto them, Wherefore do 559
5: 5 Pharaoh **s**, Behold, the people of the land 559
5:17 he **s**, Ye *are* idle, *ye are* idle: therefore 559
5:19 see *that* they *were* in evil *case*, after it was **s**, 559
5:21 they **s** unto them, The LORD look upon 559
5:22 **s**, Lord, wherefore hast thou *so* evil entreated 559
6: 1 the LORD **s** unto Moses, Now shalt thou 559
6: 2 and **s** unto him, I *am* the LORD: 559
6:26 and Moses, to whom the LORD **s**, 559
6:30 Moses **s** before the LORD, Behold, I *am* of 559
7: 1 the LORD **s** unto Moses, See, I have made 559
7:13 not unto them; as the LORD had **s**. 1696
7:14 the LORD **s** unto Moses, Pharaoh's heart *is* 559
7:22 he hearken unto them; as the LORD had **s**. 1696
8: 8 Pharaoh called for Moses and Aaron, and **s**, 559
8: 9 Moses **s** unto Pharaoh, Glory over me: when 559
8:10 he **s**, To morrow. And he said, *Be it* 559
8:10 he **s**, *Be it* according to thy word: that thou 559
8:15 not unto them; as the LORD had **s**. 1696
8:16 the LORD **s** unto Moses, Say unto Aaron, 559
8:19 the magicians **s** unto Pharaoh, This *is* 559
8:19 not unto them; as the LORD had **s**. 1696
8:20 the LORD **s** unto Moses, Rise up early in 559
8:25 for Moses and for Aaron, and **s**, Go ye, 559
8:26 Moses **s**, It is not meet so to do; for we shall 559
8:28 Pharaoh **s**, I will let you go, that ye may 559
8:29 Moses **s**, Behold, I go out from thee, and 559
9: 1 the LORD **s** unto Moses, Go in unto 559
9: 8 the LORD **s** unto Moses and unto Aaron, 559
9:13 the LORD **s** unto Moses, Rise up early in 559
9:22 the LORD **s** unto Moses, Stretch forth thine 559
9:27 for Moses and Aaron, and **s** unto them, 559
9:29 Moses **s** unto him, As soon as I am gone out 559
10: 1 the LORD **s** unto Moses, Go in unto 559
10: 3 came in unto Pharaoh, and **s** unto him, 559
10: 7 Pharaoh's servants **s** unto him, How long 559
10: 8 he **s** unto them, Go, serve the LORD your 559
10: 9 Moses **s**, We will go with our young and 559
10:10 he **s** unto them, Let the LORD be so 559
10:12 the LORD **s** unto Moses, Stretch out thine 559
10:16 he **s**, I have sinned against the LORD your 559
10:21 the LORD **s** unto Moses, Stretch out thine 559
10:24 unto Moses, and **s**, Go ye, serve the LORD; 559
10:25 Moses **s**, Thou must give us also sacrifices 559
10:28 And Pharaoh **s** unto him, Get thee from me, 559
10:29 Moses **s**, Thou hast spoken well, I will see 559
11: 1 (And the LORD **s** unto Moses, Yet will I 559
11: 4 Moses **s**, Thus saith the LORD, 559
11: 9 the LORD **s** unto Moses, Pharaoh shall not 559
12:21 **s** unto them, Draw out and take you a lamb 559
12:31 **s**, Rise up, *and* get you forth from amongst 559
12:31 and go, serve the LORD, as ye have **s**. 1696
12:32 and your herds, as ye have **s**, and be gone; 1696
12:33 in haste; for they **s**, We *be* all dead *men*. 559
12:43 the LORD **s** unto Moses and Aaron, This *is* 559
13: 3 Moses **s** unto the people, Remember this 559
13:17 for God **s**, Lest peradventure the people 559
14: 5 they **s**, Why have we done this, that we have 559
14:11 they **s** unto Moses, Because *there were* no 559
14:13 Moses **s** unto the people, Fear ye not, 559
14:15 the LORD **s** unto Moses, Wherefore criest 559
14:25 so that the Egyptians **s**, Let us flee from 559
14:26 the LORD **s** unto Moses, Stretch out thine 559
15: 9 The enemy **s**, I will pursue, I will overtake, 559
15:26 **s**, If thou wilt diligently hearken to the voice 559
16: 3 the children of Israel **s** unto them, Would to 559
16: 4 **s** the LORD unto Moses, Behold, I will rain 559
16: 6 and Aaron **s** unto all the children of Israel, 559
16: 8 Moses **s**, *This shall be*, when the LORD 559
16:15 when the children of Israel saw *it*, they **s** one 559
16:15 for they wist not what it *was*. And Moses **s** 559
16:19 Moses **s**, Let no man leave of it till 559
16:23 he **s** unto them, This *is that* which 559
16:23 This *is that* which the LORD hath **s**, 1696
16:25 Moses **s**, Eat that to day; for to day *is* a 559
16:28 the LORD **s** unto Moses, How long refuse 559
16:32 Moses **s**, This *is* the thing which the LORD 559
16:33 Moses **s** unto Aaron, Take a pot, and put an 559
17: 2 and **s**, Give us water that we may drink. 559
17: 2 Moses **s** unto them, Why chide ye with me? 559
17: 3 the people murmured against Moses, and **s**, 559
17: 5 the LORD **s** unto Moses, Go on before 559
17: 9 Moses **s** unto Joshua, Choose us out men, 559
17:10 So Joshua did as Moses had **s** to him, and 559

Ex 17:14 the LORD **s** unto Moses, Write this *for* a 559
17:16 For he **s**, Because the LORD hath sworn 559
18: 3 for he **s**, I have been an alien in a strange 559
18: 4 *s he, was* mine help, and delivered me from NIH
18: 6 he **s** unto Moses, I thy father in law Jethro 559
18:10 Jethro **s**, Blessed *be* the LORD, who hath 559
18:14 he **s**, What *is* this thing that thou doest to 559
18:15 Moses **s** unto his father in law, Because 559
18:17 Moses' father in law **s** unto him, The thing 559
18:24 of his father in law, and did all that he had **s**. 559
19: 8 And all the people answered together, and **s**, 559
19: 9 the LORD **s** unto Moses, Lo, I come unto 559
19:10 the LORD **s** unto Moses, Go unto 559
19:15 he **s** unto the people, Be ready against 559
19:21 the LORD **s** unto Moses, Go down, 559
19:23 Moses **s** unto the LORD, The people 559
19:24 the LORD **s** unto him, Away, get thee 559
20:19 And they **s** unto Moses, Speak thou with us, 559
20:20 Moses **s** unto the people, Fear not: for God is 559
20:22 the LORD **s** unto Moses, Thus thou shalt 559
23:13 in all *things* that I have **s** unto you be 559
24: 1 he **s** unto Moses, Come up unto the LORD, 559
24: 3 the people answered *with* one voice, and **s**, 559
24: 3 All the words which the LORD hath **s** will 1696
24: 7 they **s**, All that the LORD hath said will we 559
24: 7 All that the LORD hath **s** will we do, and 1696
24: 8 and sprinkled *it* on the people, and **s**, 559
24:12 the LORD **s** unto Moses, Come up to me 559
24:14 he **s** unto the elders, Tarry ye here for us, 559
30:34 the LORD **s** unto Moses, Take unto thee 559
32: 1 **s** unto him, Up, make us gods, which shall 559
32: 2 Aaron **s** unto them, Break off the golden 559
32: 4 they **s**, These *be* thy gods, O Israel, 559
32: 5 Aaron made proclamation, and **s**, To morrow 559
32: 7 the LORD **s** unto Moses, Go, get thee 1696
32: 8 and **s**, These *be* thy gods, O Israel, 559
32: 9 the LORD **s** unto Moses, I have seen this 559
32:11 the LORD his God, and **s**, LORD, 559
32:17 he **s** unto Moses, *There is* a noise of war in 559
32:18 he **s**, *It is* not the voice of *them that* shout for 559
32:21 Moses **s** unto Aaron, What did this people 559
32:22 Aaron **s**, Let not the anger of my lord wax 559
32:23 For they **s** unto me, Make us gods, 559
32:24 I **s** unto them, Whosoever hath *any* gold, 559
32:26 and **s**, Who *is* on the LORD'S side? 559
32:27 he **s** unto them, Thus saith the LORD God 559
32:29 For Moses had **s**, Consecrate yourselves to 559
32:30 that Moses **s** unto the people, Ye have sinned 559
32:31 **s**, Oh, this people have sinned a great sin, 559
32:33 the LORD **s** unto Moses, Whosoever hath 559
33: 1 the LORD **s** unto Moses, Depart, *and* 1696
33: 5 For the LORD had **s** unto Moses, Say unto 559
33:12 Moses **s** unto the LORD, See, thou sayest 559
33:12 Yet thou hast **s**, I know thee by name, and 559
33:14 he **s**, My presence shall go *with thee*, and 559
33:15 he **s** unto him, If thy presence go not *with* 559
33:17 the LORD **s** unto Moses, I will do this 559
33:18 And he **s**, I beseech thee, shew me thy glory. 559
33:19 he **s**, I will make all my goodness pass 559
33:20 he **s**, Thou canst not see my face: for there 559
33:21 the LORD **s**, Behold, *there is* a place by 559
34: 1 the LORD **s** unto Moses, Hew thee two 559
34: 9 he **s**, If now I have found grace in thy sight, 559
34:10 he **s**, Behold, I make a covenant: before all 559
34:27 the LORD **s** unto Moses, Write thou these 559
35: 1 **s** unto them, These *are* the words which 559
35:30 And Moses **s** unto the children of Israel, See, 559
Lev 8: 5 Moses **s** unto the congregation, This *is* 559
8:31 Moses **s** unto Aaron and to his sons, Boil 559
9: 2 he **s** unto Aaron, Take thee a young calf for a 559
9: 6 Moses **s**, This *is* the thing which the LORD 559
9: 7 And Moses **s** unto Aaron, Go unto the altar, 559
10: 3 Moses **s** unto Aaron, This *is it* that 559
10: 4 uncle of Aaron, and **s** unto them, Come near, 559
10: 5 their coats out of the camp; as Moses had **s**. 1696
10: 6 Moses **s** unto Aaron, and unto Eleazar and 559
10:19 Aaron **s** unto Moses, Behold, *this* day have 1696
16: 2 the LORD **s** unto Moses, Speak unto Aaron 559
17:12 Therefore I **s** unto the children of Israel, No 559
17:14 therefore I **s** unto the children of Israel, 559
20:24 I have **s** unto you, Ye shall inherit their land, 559
21: 1 the LORD **s** unto Moses, Speak unto 559
Nu 3:40 the LORD **s** unto Moses, Number all 559
7:11 the LORD **s** unto Moses, They shall offer 559
9: 7 those men **s** unto him, We *are* defiled by 559
9: 8 Moses **s** unto them, Stand still, and I will 559
10:29 Moses **s** unto Hobab, the son of Raguel 559
10:29 unto the place of which the LORD **s**, 559
10:30 he **s** unto him, I will not go; but I will depart 559
10:31 he **s**, Leave us not, I pray thee; forasmuch as 559
10:35 that Moses **s**, Rise up, LORD, and let thine 559
10:36 And when it rested, he **s**, Return, O LORD, 559
11: 4 and **s**, Who shall give us flesh to eat? 559
11:11 Moses **s** unto the LORD, Wherefore hast 559
11:16 the LORD **s** unto Moses, Gather unto me 559
11:21 Moses **s**, The people, amongst whom I *am*, 559
11:21 thou hast **s**, I will give them flesh, that they 559
11:23 the LORD **s** unto Moses, Is the LORD'S 559
11:27 **s**, Eldad and Medad do prophesy in 559
11:28 answered and **s**, My lord Moses, 559
11:29 Moses **s** unto him, Enviest thou for my sake? 559
12: 2 they **s**, Hath the LORD indeed spoken only 559
12: 6 he **s**, Hear now my words: If there be a 559
12:11 Aaron **s** unto Moses, Alas, my lord, 559
12:14 the LORD **s** unto Moses, If her father had 559
13:17 **s** unto them, Get you up this *way* southward, 559
13:27 they told him, and **s**, We came unto the land 559
13:30 and **s**, Let us go up at once, and possess it; 559
13:31 the men that went up with him **s**, We be not 559
14: 2 the whole congregation **s** unto them, 559
14: 4 they **s** one to another, Let us make a captain, 559
14:11 the LORD **s** unto Moses, How long will 559
14:13 Moses **s** unto the LORD, Then 559
14:20 the LORD **s**, I have pardoned according to 559
14:31 your little ones, which ye **s** should be a prey, 559

Nu 14:35 I the LORD have **s**, I will surely do it unto 1696
14:41 Moses **s**, Wherefore now do ye transgress 559
15:35 the LORD **s** unto Moses, The man shall be 559
16: 3 and against Aaron, and **s** unto them, 559
16: 8 Moses **s** unto Korah, Hear, I pray you, 559
16:12 sons of Eliab: which **s**, We will not come up: 559
16:15 was very wroth, and **s** unto the LORD, 559
16:16 Moses **s** unto Korah, Be thou and all thy 559
16:22 And they fell upon their faces, and **s**, O God, 559
16:28 Moses **s**, Hereby ye shall know that 559
16:34 for they **s**, Lest the earth swallow us up *also*. 559
16:40 as the LORD **s** to him by the hand of 1696
16:46 And Moses **s** unto Aaron, Take a censer, and 559
17:10 the LORD **s** unto Moses, Bring Aaron's rod 559
18: 1 the LORD **s** unto Aaron, Thou and thy sons 559
18:24 therefore I have **s** unto them, Among 559
20:10 and he **s** unto them, Hear now, ye rebels; 559
20:18 Edom **s** unto him, Thou shalt not pass by me, 559
20:19 the children of Israel **s** unto him, We will go 559
20:20 he **s**, Thou shalt not go through. And Edom 559
21: 2 Israel vowed a vow unto the LORD, and **s**, 559
21: 7 came to Moses, and **s**, We have sinned, 559
21: 8 the LORD **s** unto Moses, Make thee a fiery 559
21:14 Wherefore it is **s** in the book of the wars of 559
21:34 And the LORD **s** unto Moses, Fear him not: 559
22: 4 Moab **s** unto the elders of Midian, Now shall 559
22: 8 he **s** unto them, Lodge here *this* night, and 559
22: 9 God came unto Balaam, and **s**, What men 559
22:10 Balaam **s** unto God, Balak the son of Zippor, 559
22:12 God **s** unto Balaam, Thou shalt not go with 559
22:13 **s** unto the princes of Balak, Get you into 559
22:14 they went unto Balak, and **s**, 559
22:16 they came to Balaam, and **s** to him, 559
22:18 and **s** unto the servants of Balak, 559
22:20 and **s** unto him, If the men come to call thee, 559
22:28 she **s** unto Balaam, What have I done unto 559
22:29 Balaam **s** unto the ass, Because thou hast 559
22:30 the ass **s** unto Balaam, *Am* not I thine ass, 559
22:30 ever wont to do so unto thee? And he **s**, Nay. 559
22:32 the angel of the LORD **s** unto him, 559
22:34 And Balaam **s** unto the angel of the LORD, 559
22:35 And the angel of the LORD **s** unto Balaam, 559
22:37 Balak **s** unto Balaam, Did I not earnestly 559
22:38 Balaam **s** unto Balak, Lo, I am come unto 559
23: 1 Balaam **s** unto Balak, Build me here seven 559
23: 3 Balaam **s** unto Balak, Stand by thy burnt 559
23: 4 he **s** unto him, I have prepared seven altars, 559
23: 5 **s**, Return unto Balak, and thus thou shalt 559
23: 7 he took up his parable, and **s**, Balak the king 559
23:11 Balak **s** unto Balaam, What hast thou done 559
23:12 he answered and **s**, Must I not take heed to 559
23:13 Balak **s** unto him, Come, I pray thee, 559
23:15 he **s** unto Balak, Stand here by thy burnt 559
23:16 and **s**, Go again unto Balak, and say thus. 559
23:17 Balak **s** unto him, What hath the LORD 559
23:18 his parable, and **s**, Rise up, Balak, and hear; 559
23:19 hath he **s**, and shall he not do *it?* or hath he 559
23:23 according to *this* time it shall be **s** of Jacob 559
23:25 Balak **s** unto Balaam, Neither curse them at 559
23:26 Balaam answered and **s** unto Balak, Told not 559
23:27 Balak **s** unto Balaam, Come, I pray thee, 559
23:29 Balaam **s** unto Balak, Build me here seven 559
23:30 Balak did as Balaam had **s**, and offered a 559
24: 3 he took up his parable, and **s**, Balaam the son 559
24: 3 Balaam the son of Beor hath **s**, and the man 5002
24: 3 and the man whose eyes are open hath **s**: 5002
24: 4 He hath **s**, which heard the words of God, 5002
24:10 Balak **s** unto Balaam, I called thee to curse 559
24:12 Balaam **s** unto Balak, Spake I not also to thy 559
24:15 he took up his parable, and **s**, Balaam the son 559
24:15 Balaam the son of Beor hath **s**, and the man 5002
24:15 and the man whose eyes are open hath **s**: 5002
24:16 He hath **s**, which heard the words of God, 5002
24:20 on Amalek, he took up his parable, and **s**, 559
24:21 took up his parable, and **s**, Strong *is* thy 559
24:23 he took up his parable, and **s**, Alas, 559
25: 4 the LORD **s** unto Moses, Take all the heads 559
25: 5 Moses **s** unto the judges of Israel, Slay ye 559
26:65 For the LORD had **s** of them, They shall 559
27:12 the LORD **s** unto Moses, Get thee up into 559
27:18 the LORD **s** unto Moses, Take thee Joshua 559
31:15 Moses **s** unto them, Have ye saved all 559
31:21 Eleazar the priest **s** unto the men of war 559
31:49 they **s** unto Moses, Thy servants have taken 559
32: 5 Wherefore, **s** they, if we have found grace in 559
32: 6 Moses **s** unto the children of Gad and to 559
32:16 they came near unto him, and **s**, We will 559
32:20 Moses **s** unto them, If ye will do this thing, 559
32:29 Moses **s** unto them, If the children of Gad 559
32:31 As the LORD hath **s** unto thy servants, so 1696
36: 2 they **s**, The LORD commanded my lord to 559
36: 5 The tribe of the sons of Joseph hath **s** well. 1696
Dt 1:14 ye answered me, and **s**, The thing which 559
1:20 I **s** unto you, Ye are come unto the mountain 559
1:21 God of thy fathers hath **s** unto thee; 1696
1:22 **s**, We will send men before us, and 559
1:25 unto us, and brought us word again, and **s**, 559
1:27 and **s**, Because the LORD hated us, 559
1:29 I **s** unto you, Dread not, neither be afraid of 559
1:39 which ye **s** should be a prey, and 559
1:41 ye answered and **s** unto me, We have sinned 559
1:42 the LORD **s** unto me, Say unto them, 559
2: 9 the LORD **s** unto me, Distress not 559
2:13 *s I*, and get you over the brook Zered. NIH
2:31 the LORD **s** unto me, Behold, I have begun 559
3: 2 the LORD **s** unto me, Fear him not: for I 559
3:26 the LORD **s** unto me, Let it suffice thee; 559
4:10 when the LORD **s** unto me, Gather me 559
5: 1 **s** unto them, Hear, O Israel, the statutes and 559
5:24 ye **s**, Behold, the LORD our God hath 559
5:28 the LORD **s** unto me, I have heard 559
5:28 they have well *s* all that they have spoken. NIH
9: 3 as the LORD hath **s** unto thee. 1696
9:12 the LORD **s** unto me, Arise, get thee down 559
9:25 the LORD had **s** he would destroy you. 559

S

Dt 9:26 unto the LORD, and **s**, O Lord GOD, 559
10: 1 At that time the LORD **s** unto me, 559
10:11 the LORD **s** unto me, Arise, take thy 559
11:25 ye shall tread upon, as he hath **s** unto you. 1696
17:16 forasmuch as the LORD hath **s** unto you, 559
18: 2 *is* their inheritance, as he hath **s** unto them. 1696
18:17 the LORD **s** unto me, They have well 559
29: 2 called unto all Israel, and **s** unto them, 559
29:13 as he hath **s** unto thee, and as he hath sworn 1696
31: 2 he **s** unto them, I *am* an hundred and 559
31: 2 also the LORD hath **s** unto me, Thou shalt 559
31: 3 go over before thee, as the LORD hath **s**. 1696
31: 7 **s** unto him in the sight of all Israel, Be strong 559
31:14 the LORD **s** unto Moses, Behold, thy days 559
31:16 the LORD **s** unto Moses, Behold, thou shalt 559
31:23 **s**, Be strong and of a good courage: 559
32:20 he **s**, I will hide my face from them, I will 559
32:26 I **s**, I would scatter them into corners, 559
32:46 he **s** unto them, Set your hearts unto all 559
33: 2 And he **s**, The LORD came from Sinai, and 559
33: 7 and he **s**, Hear, LORD, the voice of Judah, 559
33: 8 of Levi he **s**, *Let* thy Thummim and 559
33: 9 Who **s** unto his father and to his mother, 559
33:12 *And* of Benjamin he **s**, The beloved of 559
33:13 of Joseph he **s**, Blessed of the LORD *be* his 559
33:18 of Zebulun he **s**, Rejoice, Zebulun, in thy 559
33:20 of Gad he **s**, Blessed *be* he that enlargeth 559
33:22 of Dan he **s**, Dan *is* a lion's whelp: he shall 559
33:23 of Naphtali he **s**, O Naphtali, satisfied with 559
33:24 of Asher he **s**, *Let* Asher *be* blessed with 559
34: 4 the LORD **s** unto him, This *is* the land 559
Jos 1: 3 have I given unto you, as I **s** unto Moses. 1696
2: 4 hid them, and **s** thus, There came men unto 559
2: 9 she **s** unto the men, I know that the LORD 559
2:16 she **s** unto them, Get you to the mountain, 559
2:17 the men **s** unto her, We *will be* blameless of 559
2:21 she **s**, According unto your words, so *be* it. 559
2:24 they **s** unto Joshua, Truly the LORD hath 559
3: 5 Joshua **s** unto the people, 559
3: 7 the LORD **s** unto Joshua, This day will I 559
3: 9 Joshua **s** unto the children of Israel, 559
3:10 Joshua **s**, Hereby ye shall know that 559
4: 5 Joshua **s** unto them, Pass over before the ark 559
5: 2 At that time the LORD **s** unto Joshua, 559
5: 9 the LORD **s** unto Joshua, *This* day have I 559
5:13 **s** unto him, *Art* thou for us, or for our 559
5:14 he **s**, Nay; but *as* captain of the host of 559
5:14 did worship, and **s** unto him, What saith my 559
5:15 the captain of the LORD'S host **s** unto 559
6: 2 the LORD **s** unto Joshua, See, I have given 559
6: 6 **s** unto them, Take up the ark of the covenant, 559
6: 7 he **s** unto the people, Pass on, and 559
6:16 Joshua **s** unto the people, Shout; 559
6:22 Joshua had **s** unto the two men that had spied 559
7: 3 and **s** unto him, Let not all the people go up; 559
7: 7 Joshua **s**, Alas, O Lord GOD, 559
7:10 And the LORD **s** unto Joshua, Get thee up; 559
7:19 Joshua **s** unto Achan, My son, give, I pray 559
7:20 Achan answered Joshua, and **s**, Indeed I 559
7:25 Joshua **s**, Why hast thou troubled us? 559
8: 1 the LORD **s** unto Joshua, Fear not, 559
8:18 the LORD **s** unto Joshua, Stretch out 559
9: 6 **s** unto him, and to the men of Israel, We be 559
9: 7 the men of Israel **s** unto the Hivites, 559
9: 8 And they **s** unto Joshua, We *are* thy servants. 559
9: 8 Joshua **s** unto them, Who *are* ye? and 559
9: 9 they **s** unto him, From a very far country thy 559
9:19 all the princes **s** unto all the congregation, 559
9:21 the princes **s** unto them, Let them live; but 559
9:24 they answered Joshua, and **s**, Because it was 559
10: 8 the LORD **s** unto Joshua, Fear them not: 559
10:12 he **s** in the sight of Israel, Sun, stand thou 559
10:18 Joshua **s**, Roll great stones upon the mouth 559
10:22 Then **s** Joshua, Open the mouth of the cave, 559
10:24 **s** unto the captains of the men of war which 559
10:25 Joshua **s** unto them, Fear not, nor be 559
11: 6 And the LORD **s** unto Joshua, Be not afraid 559
11:23 according to all that the LORD **s** unto 1696
13: 1 and the LORD **s** unto him, Thou art old *and* 559
13:14 fire *are* their inheritance, as he **s** unto them. 1696
13:33 *was* their inheritance, as he **s** unto them. 1696
14: 6 Caleb the son of Jephunneh the Kenezite **s** 559
14: 6 Thou knowest the thing that the LORD **s** 1696
14:10 me alive, as he **s**, these forty and five years, 1696
14:12 *be able to* drive them out, as the LORD **s**. 1696
15:16 And Caleb **s**, He that smiteth Kirjath-sepher, 559
15:18 and Caleb **s** unto her, What wouldest thou? 559
17:16 the children of Joseph **s**, The hill is not 559
18: 3 Joshua **s** unto the children of Israel, How 559
22: 2 **s** unto them, Ye have kept all that Moses 559
22:21 **s** unto the heads of the thousands of Israel, 1696
22:26 Therefore we **s**, Let us now prepare to build 559
22:28 Therefore **s** we, that it shall be, when they 559
22:31 Phinehas the son of Eleazar the priest **s** unto 559
23: 2 **s** unto them, I am old *and* stricken in age: 559
24: 2 Joshua **s** unto all the people, Thus saith 559
24:16 the people answered and **s**, God forbid that 559
24:19 Joshua **s** unto the people, Ye cannot serve 559
24:21 the people **s** unto Joshua, Nay; but we will 559
24:22 Joshua **s** unto the people, Ye *are* witnesses 559
24:22 to serve him. And they **s**, *We are* witnesses. 559
24:23 ***s** he,* the strange gods which *are* among you, NIH
24:24 the people **s** unto Joshua, The LORD our 559
24:27 Joshua **s** unto all the people, Behold, this 559
Jdg 1: 2 the LORD **s**, Judah shall go up: behold, 559
1: 3 Judah **s** unto Simeon his brother, Come up 559
1: 7 Adoni-bezek **s**, Threescore and ten kings, 559
1:12 And Caleb **s**, He that smiteth Kirjath-sepher, 559
1:14 and Caleb **s** unto her, What wilt thou? 559
1:15 she **s** unto him, Give me a blessing: for thou 559
1:20 they gave Hebron unto Caleb, as Moses **s**: 1696
1:24 and they **s** unto him, Shew us, we pray thee, 559
2: 1 and **s**, I made you to go up out of Egypt, and 559
2: 1 I **s**, I will never break my covenant with you. 559
2: 3 Wherefore I also **s**, I will not drive them out 559
Jdg 2:15 as the LORD had **s**, and as the LORD 1696
2:20 he **s**, Because that this people hath 559
3:19 **s**, I have a secret errand unto thee, O king: 559
3:19 who **s**, Keep silence. And all that stood by 559
3:20 Ehud **s**, I have a message from God unto 559
3:24 the doors of the parlour *were* locked, they **s**, 559
3:28 he **s** unto them, Follow after me: for 559
4: 6 **s** unto him, Hath not the LORD God of 559
4: 8 Barak **s** unto her, If thou wilt go with me, 559
4: 9 she **s**, I will surely go with thee: 559
4:14 Deborah **s** unto Barak, Up; for this *is* the day 559
4:18 **s** unto him, Turn in, my lord, turn in to me; 559
4:19 he **s** unto her, Give me, I pray thee, a little 559
4:20 Again he **s** unto her, Stand *in* the door of 559
4:22 **s** unto him, Come, and I will shew thee 559
5:23 Curse ye Meroz, **s** the angel of the LORD, 559
6: 8 which **s** unto them, Thus saith the LORD 559
6:10 I **s** unto you, I *am* the LORD your God; 559
6:12 **s** unto him, The LORD *is* with thee, 559
6:13 Gideon **s** unto him, O my lord, if the LORD 559
6:14 **s**, Go in this thy might, and thou shalt save 559
6:15 he **s** unto him, O my Lord, wherewith shall I 559
6:16 the LORD **s** unto him, Surely I will be with 559
6:17 he **s** unto him, If now I have found grace in 559
6:18 And he **s**, I will tarry until thou come again. 559
6:20 the angel of God **s** unto him, Take the flesh 559
6:22 the LORD, Gideon **s**, Alas, O Lord GOD! 559
6:23 the LORD **s** unto him, Peace *be* unto thee; 559
6:25 that the LORD **s** unto him, Take thy 559
6:27 and did as the LORD had **s** unto him: 1696
6:29 they **s** one to another, Who hath done this 559
6:29 when they inquired and asked, they **s**, 559
6:30 the men of the city **s** unto Joash, Bring out 559
6:31 Joash **s** unto all that stood against him, Will 559
6:36 Gideon **s** unto God, If thou wilt save Israel 559
6:36 save Israel by mine hand, as thou hast **s**, 1696
6:37 save Israel by mine hand, as thou hast **s**. 1696
6:39 Gideon **s** unto God, Let not thine anger be 559
7: 2 the LORD **s** unto Gideon, The people that 559
7: 4 the LORD **s** unto Gideon, The people *are* 559
7: 5 the LORD **s** unto Gideon, Every one that 559
7: 7 the LORD **s** unto Gideon, By the three 559
7: 9 that the LORD **s** unto him, Arise, get thee 559
7:13 and **s**, Behold, I dreamed a dream, and lo, 559
7:14 his fellow answered and **s**, This *is* nothing 559
7:15 returned into the host of Israel, and **s**, Arise; 559
7:17 he **s** unto them, Look on me, and 559
8: 1 the men of Ephraim **s** unto him, Why hast 559
8: 2 he **s** unto them, What have I done now in 559
8: 3 was abated toward him, when he had **s** that. 1696
8: 5 he **s** unto the men of Succoth, Give, I pray 559
8: 6 the princes of Succoth **s**, *Are* the hands of 559
8: 7 Gideon **s**, Therefore when the LORD hath 559
8:15 **s**, Behold Zebah and Zalmunna, with whom 559
8:18 **s** he unto Zebah and Zalmunna, 559
8:19 he **s**, They *were* my brethren, *even* the sons 559
8:20 he **s** unto Jether his firstborn, Up, *and* 559
8:21 Then Zebah and Zalmunna **s**, Rise thou, and 559
8:22 the men of Israel **s** unto Gideon, Rule thou 559
8:23 Gideon **s** unto them, I will not rule over you, 559
8:24 Gideon **s** unto them, I would desire a request 559
9: 3 for they **s**, He *is* our brother. 559
9: 7 lift up his voice, and cried, and **s** unto them, 559
9: 8 they **s** unto the olive tree, Reign thou over 559
9: 9 the olive tree **s** unto them, Should I leave my 559
9:10 the trees **s** to the fig tree, Come thou, *and* 559
9:11 the fig tree **s** unto them, Should I forsake my 559
9:12 **s** the trees unto the vine, Come thou, *and* 559
9:13 the vine **s** unto them, Should I leave my 559
9:14 **s** all the trees unto the bramble, Come thou, 559
9:15 the bramble **s** unto the trees, If in truth ye 559
9:28 Gaal the son of Ebed **s**, Who *is* Abimelech, 559
9:29 And he **s** to Abimelech, Increase thine army, 559
9:36 Gaal saw the people, he **s** to Zebul, Behold, 559
9:36 Zebul **s** unto him, Thou seest the shadow of 559
9:37 Gaal spake again and **s**, See there come 559
9:38 **s** Zebul unto him, Where *is* now thy mouth, 559
9:48 and **s** unto the people that *were* with him, 559
9:54 **s** unto him, Draw thy sword, and slay me, 559
10:11 the LORD **s** unto the children of Israel, 559
10:15 the children of Israel **s** unto the LORD, 559
10:18 *and* princes of Gilead **s** one to another, 559
11: 2 and they thrust out Jephthah, and **s** unto him, 559
11: 6 they **s** unto Jephthah, Come, and be our 559
11: 7 Jephthah **s** unto the elders of Gilead, Did not 559
11: 8 the elders of Gilead **s** unto Jephthah, 559
11: 9 Jephthah **s** unto the elders of Gilead, If ye 559
11:10 the elders of Gilead **s** unto Jephthah, 559
11:15 **s** unto him, Thus saith Jephthah, Israel took 559
11:19 Israel **s** unto him, Let us pass, we pray thee, 559
11:30 vowed a vow unto the LORD, and **s**, 559
11:35 he rent his clothes, and **s**, Alas, my daughter, 559
11:36 she **s** unto him, My father, *if* thou hast 559
11:37 she **s** unto her father, Let this thing be done 559
11:38 he **s**, Go. And he sent her away *for* two 559
12: 1 and went northward, and **s** unto Jephthah, 559
12: 2 Jephthah **s** unto them, I and my people were 559
12: 4 of Gilead smote Ephraim, because they **s**, 559
12: 5 those Ephraimites which were escaped **s**, 559
12: 5 that the men of Gilead **s** unto him, *Art* thou 559
12: 5 *Art* thou an Ephraimite? If he **s**, Nay; 559
12: 6 **s** they unto him, Say now Shibboleth: and 559
12: 6 he **s** Sibboleth: for he could not frame to 559
13: 3 and **s** unto her, Behold now, thou *art* barren, 559
13: 7 he **s** unto me, Behold, thou *shalt* conceive, 559
13: 8 intreated the LORD, and **s**, O my Lord, 559
13:10 her husband, and **s** unto him, Behold, 559
13:11 and came to the man, and **s** unto him, 559
13:11 spakest unto the woman? And he **s**, I *am*. 559
13:12 Manoah **s**, Now let thy words come to pass. 559
13:13 And the angel of the LORD **s** unto Manoah, 559
13:13 Of all that I **s** unto the woman let her 559
13:15 And Manoah **s** unto the angel of the LORD, 559
13:16 And the angel of the LORD **s** unto Manoah, 559
13:17 And Manoah **s** unto the angel of the LORD, 559
Jdg 13:18 the angel of the LORD **s** unto him, Why 559
13:22 Manoah **s** unto his wife, We shall surely die, 559
13:23 his wife **s** unto him, If the LORD were 559
14: 2 and told his father and his mother, and **s**, 559
14: 3 his father and his mother **s** unto him, *Is there* 559
14: 3 Samson **s** unto his father, Get her for me; 559
14:12 Samson **s** unto them, I will now put forth a 559
14:13 they **s** unto him, Put forth thy riddle, that we 559
14:14 he **s** unto them, Out of the eater came forth 559
14:15 that they **s** unto Samson's wife, Entice thy 559
14:16 **s**, Thou dost but hate me, and lovest me not: 559
14:16 he **s** unto her, Behold, I have not told *it* my 559
14:18 the men of the city **s** unto him on the seventh 559
14:18 he **s** unto them, If ye had not plowed with 559
15: 1 he **s**, I will go in to my wife into 559
15: 2 her father **s**, I verily thought that thou hadst 559
15: 3 Samson **s** concerning them, Now shall I be 559
15: 6 the Philistines **s**, Who hath done this? 559
15: 7 Samson **s** unto them, Though ye have done 559
15:10 the men of Judah **s**, Why are ye come up 559
15:11 **s** to Samson, Knowest thou not that 559
15:11 And he **s** unto them, As they did unto me, so 559
15:12 they **s** unto him, We are come down to bind 559
15:12 Samson **s** unto them, Swear unto me, that ye 559
15:16 Samson **s**, With the jawbone of an ass, 559
15:18 sore athirst, and called on the LORD, and **s**, 559
16: 5 **s** unto her, Entice him, and see wherein his 559
16: 6 Delilah **s** to Samson, Tell me, I pray thee, 559
16: 7 Samson **s** unto her, If they bind me with 559
16: 9 she **s** unto him, The Philistines *be* upon thee, 559
16:10 Delilah **s** unto Samson, Behold, thou hast 559
16:11 he **s** unto her, If they bind me fast with new 559
16:12 and bound him therewith, and **s** unto him, 559
16:13 Delilah **s** unto Samson, Hitherto thou hast 559
16:13 he **s** unto her, If thou weavest the seven 559
16:14 and **s** unto him, The Philistines *be* upon thee, 559
16:15 she **s** unto him, How canst thou say, I love 559
16:17 That he told her all his heart, and **s** unto her, 559
16:20 she **s**, The Philistines *be* upon thee, Samson. 559
16:20 he awoke out of his sleep, and **s**, I will go 559
16:23 for they **s**, Our god hath delivered Samson 559
16:24 for they **s**, Our god hath delivered into our 559
16:25 that they **s**, Call for Samson, that he may 559
16:26 Samson **s** unto the lad that held him by 559
16:28 **s**, O Lord GOD, remember me, I pray thee, 559
16:30 Samson **s**, Let me die with the Philistines. 559
17: 2 he **s** unto his mother, The eleven hundred 559
17: 2 his mother **s**, Blessed *be thou* of the LORD, 559
17: 3 his mother **s**, I had wholly dedicated 559
17: 9 Micah **s** unto him, Whence comest thou? 559
17: 9 he **s** unto him, I *am* a Levite of 559
17:10 Micah **s** unto him, Dwell with me, and 559
17:13 **s** Micah, Now know I that the LORD will 559
18: 2 and they **s** unto them, Go, search the land: 559
18: 3 they turned in thither, and **s** unto him, 559
18: 4 he **s** unto them, Thus and thus dealeth Micah 559
18: 5 they **s** unto him, Ask *counsel*, we pray thee, 559
18: 6 the priest **s** unto them, Go in peace: 559
18: 8 and their brethren **s** unto them, What *say* ye? 559
18: 9 they **s**, Arise, that we may go up against 559
18:14 **s** unto their brethren, Do ye know that there 559
18:18 Then **s** the priest unto them, What do ye? 559
18:19 they **s** unto him, Hold thy peace, lay thine 559
18:23 and **s** unto Micah, What aileth thee, 559
18:24 he **s**, Ye have taken away my gods which I 559
18:25 the children of Dan **s** unto him, Let not thy 559
19: 5 and the damsel's father **s** unto his son in law, 559
19: 6 for the damsel's father had **s** unto the man, 559
19: 8 the damsel's father **s**, Comfort thine heart, 559
19: 9 the damsel's father, **s** unto him, Behold now, 559
19:11 the servant **s** unto his master, Come, I pray 559
19:12 his master **s** unto him, We will not turn aside 559
19:13 he **s** unto his servant, Come, and let us draw 559
19:17 the old man **s**, Whither goest thou? and 559
19:18 he **s** unto him, We are passing from 559
19:20 the old man **s**, Peace *be* with thee; 559
19:23 **s** unto them, Nay, my brethren, *nay*, I pray 559
19:28 he **s** unto her, Up, and let us be going. 559
19:30 it was so, that all that saw it **s**, There was no 559
20: 3 **s** the children of Israel, Tell *us*, how was this 559
20: 4 of the woman that was slain, answered and **s**, 559
20:18 of God, and asked *counsel* of God, and **s**, 559
20:18 And the LORD **s**, Judah *shall go up* first. 559
20:23 And the LORD **s**, Go up against him.) 559
20:28 the LORD **s**, Go up; for to morrow I will 559
20:32 the children of Benjamin **s**, They *are* smitten 559
20:32 the children of Israel **s**, Let us flee, and 559
20:39 for they **s**, Surely they are smitten down 559
21: 3 **s**, O LORD God of Israel, why is this come 559
21: 5 the children of Israel **s**, Who *is there* among 559
21: 6 **s**, There is one tribe cut off from Israel *this* 559
21: 8 they **s**, What one *is there* of the tribes of 559
21:16 the elders of the congregation **s**, How shall 559
21:17 they **s**, *There must be* an inheritance for 559
21:19 they **s**, Behold, *there is* a feast of the LORD 559
Ru 1: 8 And Naomi **s** unto her two daughters in law, 559
1:10 they **s** unto her, Surely we will return with 559
1:11 Naomi **s**, Turn again, my daughters: why 559
1:15 she **s**, Behold, thy sister in law is gone back 559
1:16 Ruth **s**, Intreat me not to leave thee, *or* 559
1:19 about them, and they **s**, *Is* this Naomi? 559
1:20 she **s** unto them, Call me not Naomi, call me 559
2: 2 Ruth the Moabitess **s** unto Naomi, Let me 559
2: 2 And she **s** unto her, Go, my daughter. 559
2: 4 **s** unto the reapers, The LORD *be* with you. 559
2: 5 **s** Boaz unto his servant that was set over 559
2: 6 that was set over the reapers answered and **s**, 559
2: 7 she **s**, I pray you, let me glean and 559
2: 8 **s** Boaz unto Ruth, Hearest thou not, 559
2:10 bowed herself to the ground, and **s** unto him, 559
2:11 Boaz answered and **s** unto her, It hath fully 559
2:13 she **s**, Let me find favour in thy sight, 559
2:14 Boaz **s** unto her, At mealtime come thou 559
2:19 her mother in law **s** unto her, Where hast 559
2:19 **s**, The man's name with whom I wrought to 559

Ru 2:20 Naomi **s** unto her daughter in law, 559
2:20 Naomi **s** unto her, The man *is* near of kin 559
2:21 Ruth the Moabitess **s**, He said unto me also, 559
2:21 Ruth the Moabitess said, He **s** unto me also, 559
2:22 And Naomi **s** unto Ruth her daughter in law, 559
3: 1 Naomi her mother in law **s** unto her, 559
3: 5 she **s** unto her, All that thou sayest unto me I 559
3: 9 And he **s**, Who *art* thou? And she answered, 559
3:10 he **s**, Blessed *be* thou of the LORD, 559
3:14 he **s**, Let it not be known that a woman came 559
3:15 Also he **s**, Bring the vail that *thou hast* upon 559
3:16 in law, she **s**, Who *art* thou, my daughter? 559
3:17 she **s**, These six *measures* of barley gave he 559
3:17 for he **s** to me, Go not empty unto thy 559
3:18 **s** she, Sit still, my daughter, until thou know 559
4: 1 unto whom he **s**, *Ho*, such a one, turn aside, 559
4: 2 elders of the city, and **s**, Sit ye down here. 559
4: 3 he **s** unto the kinsman, Naomi, that is come 559
4: 4 I *am* after thee. And he **s**, I will redeem *it*. 559
4: 5 **s** Boaz, What day thou buyest the field of 559
4: 6 the kinsman **s**, I cannot redeem *it* for myself, 559
4: 8 Therefore the kinsman **s** unto Boaz, Buy *it* 559
4: 9 Boaz **s** unto the elders, and *unto* all 559
4:11 the gate, and the elders, **s**, *We are* witnesses. 559
4:14 the women **s** unto Naomi, Blessed *be* 559
1Sa 1: 8 Then **s** Elkanah her husband to her, Hannah, 559
1:11 she vowed a vow, and **s**, O LORD of hosts, 559
1:14 Eli **s** unto her, How long wilt thou be 559
1:15 Hannah answered and **s**, No, my lord, I *am* a 559
1:17 Eli answered and **s**, Go in peace: and 559
1:18 she **s**, Let thine handmaid find grace in thy 559
1:22 for she **s** unto her husband, *I will not go up* 559
1:23 Elkanah her husband **s** unto her, Do what 559
1:26 she **s**, O my lord, *as* thy soul liveth, my lord, 559
2: 1 Hannah prayed, and **s**, My heart rejoiceth in 559
2:15 and **s** to the man that sacrificed, 559
2:16 *if any* man **s** unto him, Let them not fail to 559
2:20 And Eli blessed Elkanah and his wife, and **s**, 559
2:23 And he **s** unto them, Why do ye such things? 559
2:27 and **s** unto him, Thus saith the LORD, 559
2:30 I **s indeed** *that* thy house, and the house 559+559
3: 5 he ran unto Eli, and **s**, Here *am* I; for thou 559
3: 5 he **s**, I called not; lie down again. And he 559
3: 6 and went to Eli, and **s**, Here *am* I; 559
3: 8 he arose and went to Eli, and **s**, Here *am* I; 559
3: 9 Therefore Eli **s** unto Samuel, Go, lie down: 559
3:11 the LORD **s** to Samuel, Behold, I will do a 559
3:16 Eli called Samuel, and **s**, Samuel, my son. 559
3:17 he **s**, What *is* the thing that *the LORD* hath 559
3:17 What *is* the thing that *the LORD* hath **s** 1696
3:17 me of all the things that he **s** unto thee. 1696
3:18 he **s**, It *is* the LORD: let him do what 559
4: 3 come into the camp, the elders of Israel **s**, 559
4: 6 heard the noise of the shout, they **s**, 559
4: 7 for they **s**, God is come into the camp. 559
4: 7 they **s**, Woe unto us: for there hath not been 559
4:14 he **s**, What *meaneth* the noise of this tumult? 559
4:16 the man **s** unto Eli, I *am* he that came out of 559
4:16 And he **s**, What is there done, my son? 559
4:17 the messenger answered and **s**, Israel is fled 559
4:20 that stood by her **s** *unto her*, Fear not; 1696
4:22 And she **s**, The glory is departed from Israel: 559
5: 7 the men of Ashdod saw that *it was* so, they **s**, 559
5: 8 the lords of the Philistines unto them, and **s**, 559
5:11 **s**, Send away the ark of the God of Israel, 559
6: 3 they **s**, If ye send away the ark of the God of 559
6: 4 **s** they, What *shall be* the trespass offering 559
6:20 the men of Beth-shemesh **s**, Who is able to 559
7: 5 Samuel **s**, Gather all Israel to Mizpeh, and 559
7: 6 and fasted on that day, and **s** there, 559
7: 8 the children of Israel **s** to Samuel, Cease not 559
8: 5 **s** unto him, Behold, thou art old, and 559
8: 6 when they **s**, Give us a king to judge us. 559
8: 7 the LORD **s** unto Samuel, Hearken unto 559
8:11 he **s**, This will be the manner of the king that 559
8:19 they **s**, Nay, but we will have a king over us; 559
8:22 the LORD **s** to Samuel, Hearken unto their 559
8:22 Samuel **s** unto the men of Israel, Go ye every 559
9: 3 Kish **s** to Saul his son, Take now one of 559
9: 5 Saul **s** to his servant that *was* with him, 559
9: 6 he **s** unto him, Behold now, *there is* in this 559
9: 7 **s** Saul to his servant, But behold, *if* we go, 559
9: 8 servant answered Saul again, and **s**, Behold, 559
9:10 Then **s** Saul to his servant, Well said; come, 559
9:10 Then said Saul to his servant, Well **s**; come, 1697
9:11 and **s** unto them, Is the seer here? 559
9:12 they answered them, and **s**, He is; behold, 559
9:17 Samuel saw Saul, the LORD **s** unto him, 6030
9:18 **s**, Tell me, I pray thee, where the seer's 559
9:19 Samuel answered Saul, and **s**, I *am* the seer: 559
9:21 Saul answered and **s**, *Am* not I a Benjamite, 559
9:23 Samuel **s** unto the cook, Bring the portion 559
9:23 of which I **s** unto thee, Set it by thee. 559
9:24 *Samuel* **s**, Behold that which is left; set *it* 559
9:24 *this* time *hath it* been kept for thee since *I* **s**, 559
9:27 Samuel **s** to Saul, Bid the servant pass on 559
10: 1 **s**, *Is it* not because the LORD hath anointed 559
10:11 then the people **s** one to another, 559
10:12 one of the same place answered and **s**, 559
10:14 Saul's uncle **s** unto him and to his servant, 559
10:14 he **s**, To seek the asses: and when we saw 559
10:15 Saul's uncle **s**, Tell me, I pray thee, 559
10:15 I pray thee, what Samuel **s** unto you. 559
10:16 Saul **s** unto his uncle, He told us plainly that 559
10:18 **s** unto the children of Israel, Thus saith 559
10:19 ye have **s** unto him, *Nay*, but set a king over 559
10:24 Samuel **s** to all the people, See ye him whom 559
10:24 the people shouted, and **s**, God save the king. 559
10:27 the children of Belial **s**, How shall this *man* 559
11: 1 all the men of Jabesh **s** unto Nahash, Make a 559
11: 3 the elders of Jabesh **s** unto him, Give us 559
11: 5 Saul **s**, What aileth the people that they 559
11: 9 they **s** unto the messengers that came, 559
11:10 Therefore the men of Jabesh **s**, To morrow 559
11:12 the people **s** unto Samuel, Who *is* he that 559

1Sa 11:12 Who *is* he that **s**, Shall Saul reign over us? 559
11:13 Saul **s**, There shall not a man be put to death 559
11:14 **s** Samuel to the people, Come, and let us go 559
12: 1 Samuel **s** unto all Israel, Behold, I have 559
12: 1 unto your voice in all that ye **s** unto me, 559
12: 4 they **s**, Thou hast not defrauded us, 559
12: 5 he **s** unto them, The LORD *is* witness 559
12: 6 Samuel **s** unto the people, *It is* the LORD 559
12:10 **s**, We have sinned, because we have 559
12:12 came against you, ye **s** unto me, Nay; 559
12:19 all the people **s** unto Samuel, Pray for thy 559
12:20 Samuel **s** unto the people, Fear not: ye have 559
13: 9 Saul **s**, Bring hither a burnt offering to me, 559
13:11 Samuel **s**, What hast thou done? And Saul 559
13:11 Saul **s**, Because I saw that the people were 559
13:12 Therefore **s** I, The Philistines will come 559
13:13 Samuel **s** to Saul, Thou hast done foolishly: 559
13:19 for the Philistines **s**, Lest the Hebrews make 559
14: 1 that Jonathan the son of Saul **s** unto 559
14: 6 Jonathan **s** to the young man that bare his 559
14: 7 his armourbearer **s** unto him, Do all that *is* in 559
14: 8 **s** Jonathan, Behold, we will pass over unto 559
14:11 the Philistines **s**, Behold, the Hebrews come 559
14:12 **s**, Come up to us, and we will shew you a 559
14:12 Jonathan **s** unto his armourbearer, Come up 559
14:17 **s** Saul unto the people that *were* with him, 559
14:18 Saul **s** unto Ahiah, Bring hither the ark of 559
14:19 Saul **s** unto the priest, Withdraw thine hand. 559
14:28 answered one of the people, and **s**, 559
14:29 **s** Jonathan, My father hath troubled the land: 559
14:33 he **s**, Ye have transgressed: roll a great stone 559
14:34 Saul **s**, Disperse yourselves among 559
14:36 Saul **s**, Let us go down after the Philistines 559
14:36 they **s**, Do whatsoever seemeth good unto 559
14:36 **s** the priest, Let us draw near hither unto 559
14:38 Saul **s**, Draw ye near hither, all the chief of 559
14:40 Then **s** he unto all Israel, Be ye on one side, 559
14:40 the people **s** unto Saul, Do what seemeth 559
14:41 Therefore Saul **s** unto the LORD God of 559
14:42 Saul **s**, Cast *lots* between me and Jonathan 559
14:43 Saul **s** to Jonathan, Tell me what thou hast 559
14:43 **s**, I did but taste a little honey with the end 559
14:45 the people **s** unto Saul, Shall Jonathan die, 559
15: 1 Samuel also **s** unto Saul, The LORD sent 559
15: 6 Saul **s** unto the Kenites, Go, depart, get you 559
15:13 Saul **s** unto him, Blessed *be* thou of 559
15:14 Samuel **s**, What *meaneth* then this bleating 559
15:15 Saul **s**, They have brought them from 559
15:16 Samuel **s** unto Saul, Stay, and I will tell thee 559
15:16 I will tell thee what the LORD hath **s** to 1696
15:16 to me *this* night. And he **s** unto him, Say on. 559
15:17 Samuel **s**, When thou *wast* little in thine own 559
15:18 **s**, Go and utterly destroy the sinners 559
15:20 Saul **s** unto Samuel, Yea, I have obeyed 559
15:22 Samuel **s**, Hath the LORD *as great* delight 559
15:24 Saul **s** unto Samuel, I have sinned: for I have 559
15:26 Samuel **s** unto Saul, I will not return with 559
15:28 Samuel **s** unto him, The LORD hath rent 559
15:30 he **s**, I have sinned: *yet* honour me now, 559
15:32 **s** Samuel, Bring you hither to me Agag 559
15:32 Agag **s**, Surely the bitterness of death is past. 559
15:33 Samuel **s**, As thy sword hath made women 559
16: 1 the LORD **s** unto Samuel, How long wilt 559
16: 2 Samuel **s**, How can I go? if Saul hear *it*, he 559
16: 2 the LORD **s**, Take a heifer with thee, 559
16: 4 his coming, and **s**, Comest thou peaceably? 559
16: 5 he **s**, Peaceably: I am come to sacrifice unto 559
16: 6 were come, that he looked on Eliab, and **s**, 559
16: 7 the LORD **s** unto Samuel, Look not on his 559
16: 8 he **s**, Neither hath the LORD chosen this. 559
16: 9 he **s**, Neither hath the LORD chosen this. 559
16:10 Samuel **s** unto Jesse, The LORD hath not 559
16:11 Samuel **s** unto Jesse, Are here all *thy* 559
16:11 And he **s**, There remaineth yet the youngest, 559
16:11 Samuel **s** unto Jesse, Send and fetch him: 559
16:12 the LORD **s**, Arise, anoint him: for this *is* 559
16:15 And Saul's servants **s** unto him, Behold now, 559
16:17 Saul **s** unto his servants, Provide me now a 559
16:18 answered one of the servants, and **s**, Behold, 559
16:19 **s**, Send me David thy son, which *is* with 559
17: 8 unto the armies of Israel, and **s** unto them, 559
17:10 the Philistine **s**, I defy the armies of Israel 559
17:17 Jesse **s** unto David his son, Take now for thy 559
17:25 the men of Israel **s**, Have ye seen this man 559
17:28 and he **s**, Why camest thou down hither? 559
17:29 David **s**, What have I now done? *Is there* not 559
17:32 And David **s** to Saul, Let no man's heart fail 559
17:33 Saul **s** to David, Thou art not able to go 559
17:34 David **s** unto Saul, Thy servant kept his 559
17:37 David **s** moreover, The LORD that 559
17:37 Saul **s** unto David, Go, and the LORD be 559
17:39 for he had not proved *it*. And David **s** unto 559
17:43 And the Philistine **s** unto David, *Am* I a dog, 559
17:44 the Philistine **s** to David, Come to me, and 559
17:45 **s** David to the Philistine, Thou comest to me 559
17:55 he **s** unto Abner, the captain of the host, 559
17:55 Abner **s**, *As* thy soul liveth, O king, I cannot 559
17:56 the king **s**, Inquire thou whose son 559
17:58 Saul **s** to him, Whose son *art* thou, *thou* 559
18: 7 **s**, Saul hath slain his thousands, and 559
18: 8 he **s**, They have ascribed unto David ten 559
18:11 for he **s**, I will smite David even to the wall 559
18:17 Saul **s** to David, Behold my elder daughter 559
18:17 For Saul **s**, Let not mine hand be upon him, 559
18:18 David **s** unto Saul, Who *am* I? and what *is* 559
18:21 Saul **s**, I will give him her, that she may be a 559
18:21 Wherefore Saul **s** to David, Thou shalt *this* 559
18:23 David **s**, Seemeth it to you a light *thing* to be 559
18:25 Saul **s**, Thus shall ye say to David, The king 559
19: 4 **s** unto him, Let not the king sin against his 559
19:14 messengers to take David, she **s**, He *is* sick. 559
19:17 Saul **s** unto Michal, Why hast thou deceived 559
19:17 answered Saul, He **s** unto me, Let me go; 559
19:22 he asked and **s**, Where *are* Samuel and 559
19:22 *one* **s**, Behold, *they be* at Naioth in Ramah. 559

1Sa 20: 1 came and **s** before Jonathan, What have I 559
20: 2 he **s** unto him, God forbid; thou shalt not die: 559
20: 3 David sware moreover, and **s**, Thy father 559
20: 4 **s** Jonathan unto David, Whatsoever thy soul 559
20: 5 David **s** unto Jonathan, Behold, to morrow *is* 559
20: 9 Jonathan **s**, Far be it from thee: for if I knew 559
20:10 **s** David to Jonathan, Who shall tell me? 559
20:11 Jonathan **s** unto David, Come, and let us go 559
20:12 Jonathan **s** unto David, O LORD God of 559
20:18 Jonathan **s** to *David*, To morrow *is* the new 559
20:27 Saul **s** unto Jonathan his son, 559
20:29 he **s**, Let me go, I pray thee; for our family 559
20:30 kindled against Jonathan, and he **s** unto him, 559
20:32 and **s** unto him, Wherefore shall he be slain? 559
20:36 he **s** unto his lad, Run, find out now 559
20:37 Jonathan cried after the lad, and **s**, *Is* not 559
20:40 and **s** unto him, Go, carry *them to* the city. 559
20:42 Jonathan **s** to David, Go in peace, 559
21: 1 **s** unto him, Why *art* thou alone, and no man 559
21: 2 David **s** unto Ahimelech the priest, The king 559
21: 2 me a business, and hath **s** unto me, 559
21: 4 the priest answered David, and **s**, *There is* no 559
21: 5 David answered the priest, and **s** unto him, 559
21: 8 David **s** unto Ahimelech, And is there not 559
21: 9 the priest **s**, The sword of Goliath 559
21: 9 David **s**, *There is* none like that; give it me. 559
21:11 the servants of Achish **s** unto him, *Is* not this 559
21:14 **s** Achish unto his servants, Lo, you see 559
22: 3 he **s** unto the king of Moab, Let my father 559
22: 5 the prophet Gad **s** unto David, Abide not in 559
22: 7 Saul **s** unto his servants that stood about him, 559
22: 9 and **s**, I saw the son of Jesse coming to Nob, 559
22:12 Saul **s**, Hear now, thou son of Ahitub. 559
22:13 Saul **s** unto him, Why have ye conspired 559
22:14 **s**, And who *is so* faithful among all thy 559
22:16 the king **s**, Thou shalt surely die, Ahimelech, 559
22:17 the king **s** unto the footmen that stood about 559
22:18 the king **s** to Doeg, Turn thou, and fall upon 559
22:22 David **s** unto Abiathar, I knew *it* that day, 559
23: 2 the LORD **s** unto David, Go, and smite 559
23: 3 David's men **s** unto him, Behold, we *be* 559
23: 4 And the LORD answered him and **s**, Arise, 559
23: 7 Saul **s**, God hath delivered him into mine 559
23: 9 he **s** to Abiathar the priest, Bring hither 559
23:10 **s** David, O LORD God of Israel, 559
23:11 And the LORD **s**, He will come down. 559
23:12 **s** David, Will the men of Keilah deliver me 559
23:12 the LORD **s**, They will deliver *thee* up. 559
23:17 he **s** unto him, Fear not: for the hand of Saul 559
23:21 Saul **s**, Blessed *be* ye of the LORD; for ye 559
24: 4 the men of David **s** unto him, Behold the day 559
24: 4 Behold the day of which the LORD **s** unto 559
24: 6 he **s** unto his men, The LORD forbid that I 559
24: 9 David **s** to Saul, Wherefore hearest thou 559
24:10 I **s**, I will not put forth mine hand against my 559
24:16 that Saul **s**, *Is* this thy voice, my son David? 559
24:17 he **s** to David, Thou *art* more righteous than 559
25: 5 David **s** unto the young men, Get you up to 559
25:10 David's servants, and **s**, Who *is* David? 559
25:13 David **s** unto his men, Gird you on every 559
25:19 she **s** unto her servants, Go on before me; 559
25:21 Now David had **s**, Surely in vain have I kept 559
25:24 fell at his feet, and **s**, Upon me, my lord, 559
25:32 David **s** to Abigail, Blessed *be* the LORD 559
25:35 **s** unto her, Go up in peace to thine house; 559
25:39 was dead, he **s**, Blessed *be* the LORD, 559
25:41 *on her* face to the earth, and **s**, Behold, 559
26: 6 and **s** to Ahimelech the Hittite, 559
26: 6 And Abishai **s**, I will go down with thee. 559
26: 8 **s** Abishai to David, God hath delivered thine 559
26: 9 David **s** to Abishai, Destroy him not: 559
26:10 David **s** furthermore, *As* the LORD liveth, 559
26:14 Abner answered and **s**, Who *art* thou *that* 559
26:15 David **s** to Abner, *Art* not thou a *valiant* 559
26:17 and **s**, *Is* this thy voice, my son David? 559
26:17 David **s**, *It is* my voice, my lord, O king. 559
26:18 he **s**, Wherefore doth my lord thus pursue 559
26:21 **s** Saul, I have sinned: return, my son David: 559
26:22 David answered and **s**, Behold, the king's 559
26:25 Saul **s** to David, Blessed *be* thou, my son 559
27: 1 David **s** in his heart, I shall now perish one 559
27: 5 David **s** unto Achish, If I have now found 559
27:10 Achish **s**, Whither have ye made a road to 559
27:10 David **s**, Against the south of Judah, and 559
28: 1 Achish **s** unto David, Know thou assuredly, 559
28: 2 David **s** to Achish, Surely thou shalt know 559
28: 2 Achish **s** to David, Therefore will I make 559
28: 7 **s** Saul unto his servants, Seek me a woman 559
28: 7 his servants **s** to him, Behold, *there is* a 559
28: 8 he **s**, I pray thee, divine unto me by 559
28: 9 the woman **s** unto him, Behold, 559
28:11 **s** the woman, Whom shall I bring up unto 559
28:11 unto thee? And he **s**, Bring me up Samuel. 559
28:13 the king **s** unto her, Be not afraid: for what 559
28:13 the woman **s** unto Saul, I saw gods 559
28:14 he **s** unto her, What form is he of? And she 559
28:14 she **s**, An old man cometh up; and he *is* 559
28:15 Samuel **s** to Saul, Why hast thou disquieted 559
28:16 **s** Samuel, Wherefore then dost thou ask of 559
28:21 was sore troubled, and **s** unto him, Behold, 559
28:23 he refused, and **s**, I will not eat. But his 559
29: 3 **s** the princes of the Philistines, What *do* 559
29: 3 What *do* these Hebrews *here?* And Achish **s** 559
29: 4 and the princes of the Philistines **s** unto him, 559
29: 6 and **s** unto him, Surely, *as* the LORD liveth, 559
29: 8 David **s** unto Achish, But what have I done? 559
29: 9 Achish answered and **s** to David, I know that 559
29: 9 the princes of the Philistines have **s**, 559
30: 7 David **s** to Abiathar the priest, 559
30:13 David **s** unto him, To whom *belongest* thou? 559
30:13 he **s**, I *am* a young man of Egypt, servant to 559
30:15 David **s** to him, Canst thou bring me down to 559
30:15 he **s**, Swear unto me by God, that thou wilt 559
30:20 *other* cattle, and **s**, This *is* David's spoil. 559
30:22 of those that went with David, and **s**, 559

1Sa 30:23 **s** David, Ye shall not do so, my brethren, 559
31: 4 **s** Saul unto his armourbearer, Draw thy 559
2Sa 1: 3 David **s** unto him, From whence comest 559
1: 3 he **s** unto him, Out of the camp of Israel am I 559
1: 4 David **s** unto him, How went the matter? 559
1: 5 David **s** unto the young man that told him, 559
1: 6 the young man that told him **s**, As I 559
1: 8 he **s** unto me, Who *art* thou? And I answered 559
1: 9 He **s** unto me again, Stand, I pray thee, 559
1:13 David **s** unto the young man that told him, 559
1:14 David **s** unto him, How wast thou not afraid 559
1:15 and **s**, Go near, *and* fall upon him. 559
1:16 David **s** unto him, Thy blood *be* upon thy 559
2: 1 the LORD **s** unto him, Go up. And David 559
2: 1 David **s**, Whither shall I go up? And he said, 559
2: 1 shall I go up? And he **s**, Unto Hebron. 559
2: 5 **s** unto them, Blessed *be* ye of the LORD, 559
2:14 Abner **s** to Joab, Let the young men now 559
2:14 play before us. And Joab **s**, Let them arise. 559
2:20 looked behind him, and **s**, *Art* thou Asahel? 559
2:21 Abner **s** to him, Turn thee aside to thy right 559
2:22 Abner **s** again to Asahel, Turn thee aside 559
2:26 Abner called to Joab, and **s**, Shall the sword 559
2:27 Joab **s**, *As* God liveth, unless thou hadst 559
3: 7 *Ish-bosheth* **s** to Abner, Wherefore hast thou 559
3: 8 of Ish-bosheth, and **s**, *Am* I a dog's head, 559
3:13 he **s**, Well; I will make a league with thee: 559
3:16 **s** Abner unto him, Go, return. And he 559
3:21 And Abner **s** unto David, I will arise and go, 559
3:24 to the king, and **s**, What hast thou done? 559
3:28 afterward when David heard *it*, he **s**, I and 559
3:31 David **s** to Joab, and to all the people that 559
3:33 and **s**, Died Abner as a fool dieth? 559
3:38 the king **s** unto his servants, Know ye not 559
4: 8 **s** to the king, Behold the head of Ish-bosheth 559
4: 9 and **s** unto them, *As* the LORD liveth, 559
5: 2 the LORD **s** to thee, Thou shalt feed my 559
5: 8 David **s** on that day, Whosoever getteth up to 559
5: 8 *shall be chief and captain.* Wherefore they **s**, 559
5:19 the LORD **s** unto David, Go up: for I will 559
5:20 and David smote them there, and **s**, 559
5:23 of the LORD, he **s**, Thou shalt not go up; 559
6: 9 **s**, How shall the ark of the LORD come to 559
6:20 **s**, How glorious was the king of Israel to 559
6:21 David **s** unto Michal, *It was* before 559
7: 2 That the king **s** unto Nathan the prophet, 559
7: 3 Nathan **s** to the king, Go, do all that *is* in 559
7:18 and he **s**, Who *am* I, O Lord GOD? 559
7:25 establish *it* for ever, and do as thou hast **s**. 1696
9: 1 David **s**, Is there yet *any* that is left of 559
9: 2 the king **s** unto him, *Art* thou Ziba? 559
9: 2 *Art* thou Ziba? And he **s**, Thy servant *is he.* 559
9: 3 the king **s**, *Is there* not yet any of the house 559
9: 3 Ziba **s** unto the king, Jonathan hath yet a son, 559
9: 4 the king **s** unto him, Where *is* he? And Ziba 559
9: 4 Ziba **s** unto the king, Behold, he *is in* 559
9: 6 David **s**, Mephibosheth. And he answered, 559
9: 7 David **s** unto him, Fear not: for I will surely 559
9: 8 bowed himself, and **s**, What *is* thy servant, 559
9: 9 to Ziba, Saul's servant, and **s** unto him, 559
9:11 **s** Ziba unto the king, According to all that 559
9:11 **s** *the king*, he shall eat at my table, NIH
10: 2 **s** David, I will shew kindness unto Hanun 559
10: 3 the princes of the children of Ammon **s** unto 559
10: 5 the king **s**, Tarry at Jericho until your beards 559
10:11 And he **s**, If the Syrians be too strong for me, 559
11: 3 *one* **s**, *Is* not this Bath-sheba, the daughter of 559
11: 5 sent and told David, and **s**, I *am* with child. 559
11: 8 David **s** to Uriah, Go down to thy house, 559
11:10 David **s** unto Uriah, Camest thou not from 559
11:11 And Uriah **s** unto David, The ark, and Israel, 559
11:12 David **s** to Uriah, Tarry here to day also, 559
11:23 the messenger **s** unto David, Surely the men 559
11:25 David **s** unto the messenger, Thus shalt thou 559
12: 1 he came unto him, and **s** unto him, 559
12: 5 he **s** to Nathan, *As* the LORD liveth, 559
12: 7 Nathan **s** to David, Thou *art* the man. 559
12:13 David **s** unto Nathan, I have sinned against 559
12:13 Nathan **s** unto David, The LORD also hath 559
12:18 for they **s**, Behold, while the child was *yet* 559
12:19 therefore David **s** unto his servants, Is 559
12:19 Is the child dead? And they **s**, He is dead. 559
12:21 **s** his servants unto him, What thing *is* this 559
12:22 he **s**, While the child *was* yet alive, I fasted 559
12:22 for I **s**, Who can tell *whether* GOD will be 559
12:27 **s**, I have fought against Rabbah, and 559
13: 4 he **s** unto him, Why *art* thou, *being* 559
13: 4 Amnon **s** unto him, I love Tamar, my brother 559
13: 5 Jonadab **s** unto him, Lay *thee* down on thy 559
13: 6 Amnon **s** unto the king, I pray thee, 559
13: 9 Amnon **s**, Have out all men from me. 559
13:10 Amnon **s** unto Tamar, Bring the meat *into* 559
13:11 and **s** unto her, Come lie with me, my sister. 559
13:15 And Amnon **s** unto her, Arise, be gone. 559
13:16 she **s** unto him, *There is* no cause: this evil in 559
13:17 and **s**, Put now this *woman* out from me, and 559
13:20 Absalom her brother **s** unto her, Hath 559
13:24 **s**, Behold now, thy servant hath 559
13:25 the king **s** to Absalom, Nay, my son, let us 559
13:26 **s** Absalom, If not, I pray thee, let my brother 559
13:26 the king **s** unto him, Why should he go with 559
13:32 of Shimeah David's brother, answered and **s**, 559
13:35 Jonadab **s** unto the king, Behold, the king's 559
13:35 king's sons come: as thy servant **s**, so it is. 1697
14: 2 a wise woman, and **s** unto her, I pray thee, 559
14: 4 and did obeisance, and **s**, Help, O king. 559
14: 5 the king **s** unto her, What aileth thee? 559
14: 7 they **s**, Deliver him that smote his brother, 559
14: 8 the king **s** unto the woman, Go to thine 559
14: 9 the woman of Tekoah **s** unto the king, 559
14:10 the king **s**, Whosoever saith *ought* unto thee, 559
14:11 **s** she, I pray thee, let the king remember 559
14:11 he **s**, *As* the LORD liveth, there shall not 559
14:12 the woman **s**, Let thine handmaid, I pray 559
14:12 unto my lord the king. And he **s**, Say on. 559
2Sa 14:13 the woman **s**, Wherefore then hast thou 559
14:15 thy handmaid **s**, I will now speak unto 559
14:17 thine handmaid **s**, The word of my lord 559
14:18 the king answered and **s** unto the woman, 559
14:18 the woman **s**, Let my lord the king now 559
14:19 the king **s**, *Is not* the hand of Joab with thee 559
14:19 the woman answered and **s**, *As* thy soul 559
14:21 the king **s** unto Joab, Behold now, I have 559
14:22 Joab **s**, To day thy servant knoweth that I 559
14:24 the king **s**, Let him turn to his own house, 559
14:30 Therefore he **s** unto his servants, See, 559
14:31 to Absalom unto *his* house, and **s** unto him, 559
15: 2 called unto him, and **s**, Of what city *art* thou? 559
15: 2 he **s**, Thy servant *is* of one of the tribes of 559
15: 3 Absalom **s** unto him, See, thy matters *are* 559
15: 4 Absalom **s** moreover, Oh that I were made 559
15: 7 that Absalom **s** unto the king, I pray thee, 559
15: 9 the king **s** unto him, Go in peace. So he 559
15:14 David **s** unto all his servants that *were* with 559
15:15 the king's servants **s** unto the king, Behold, 559
15:19 **s** the king to Ittai the Gittite, Wherefore 559
15:21 **s**, *As* the LORD liveth, and *as* my lord 559
15:22 David **s** to Ittai, Go and pass over. And Ittai 559
15:25 the king **s** unto Zadok, Carry back the ark of 559
15:27 The king **s** also unto Zadok the priest, *Art* 559
15:31 David **s**, O LORD, I pray thee, turn 559
15:33 Unto whom David **s**, If thou passest on with 559
16: 2 the king **s** unto Ziba, What meanest thou by 559
16: 2 Ziba **s**, The asses *be* for the king's household 559
16: 3 the king **s**, And where *is* thy master's son? 559
16: 3 Ziba **s** unto the king, Behold, he abideth at 559
16: 3 for he **s**, To day shall the house of Israel 559
16: 4 **s** the king to Ziba, Behold, thine *are* all that 559
16: 4 Ziba **s**, I humbly beseech thee *that* I may 559
16: 7 thus **s** Shimei when he cursed, Come out, 559
16: 9 **s** Abishai the son of Zeruiah unto the king, 559
16:10 And the king **s**, What have I to do with you, 559
16:10 because the LORD hath **s** unto him, 559
16:11 David **s** to Abishai, and to all his servants, 559
16:16 that Hushai **s** unto Absalom, God save 559
16:17 Absalom **s** to Hushai, *Is* this thy kindness to 559
16:18 Hushai **s** unto Absalom, Nay; but whom 559
16:20 **s** Absalom to Ahithophel, Give counsel 559
16:21 Ahithophel **s** unto Absalom, Go in unto thy 559
17: 1 Moreover Ahithophel **s** unto Absalom, 559
17: 5 **s** Absalom, Call now Hushai the Archite 559
17: 7 Hushai **s** unto Absalom, The counsel that 559
17: 8 For, (**s** Hushai,) thou knowest thy father and 559
17:14 Absalom and all the men of Israel **s**, 559
17:15 **s** Hushai unto Zadok and to Abiathar 559
17:20 they **s**, Where *is* Ahimaaz and Jonathan? 559
17:20 the woman **s** unto them, They be gone over 559
17:21 **s** unto David, Arise, and pass quickly over 559
17:29 for they **s**, The people *is* hungry, and weary, 559
18: 2 the king **s** unto the people, I will surely go 559
18: 4 the king **s** unto them, What seemeth you best 559
18:10 man saw *it*, and told Joab, and **s**, Behold, 559
18:11 Joab **s** unto the man that told him, 559
18:12 the man **s** unto Joab, Though I should 559
18:14 **s** Joab, I may not tarry thus with thee. 559
18:18 for he **s**, I have no son to keep my name in 559
18:19 **s** Ahimaaz the son of Zadok, Let me now 559
18:20 Joab **s** unto him, Thou *shalt* not bear tidings 559
18:21 **s** Joab to Cushi, Go tell the king what thou 559
18:22 **s** Ahimaaz the son of Zadok yet again to 559
18:22 Joab **s**, Wherefore wilt thou run, my son, 559
18:23 howsoever, **s** *he*, let me run. And he said NIH
18:23 he **s** unto him, Run. Then Ahimaaz ran *by* 559
18:25 the king **s**, If he *be* alone, *there is* tidings in 559
18:26 and **s**, Behold *another* man running alone. 559
18:26 And the king **s**, He also bringeth tidings. 559
18:27 the watchman **s**, Me thinketh the running of 559
18:27 the king **s**, He *is* a good man, and 559
18:28 and **s** unto the king, All is well. 559
18:28 and **s**, Blessed *be* the LORD thy God, 559
18:29 the king **s**, *Is* the young man Absalom safe? 559
18:30 the king **s** *unto him*, Turn aside, *and* 559
18:31 and Cushi **s**, Tidings, my lord the king: 559
18:32 the king **s** unto Cushi, *Is* the young man 559
18:33 as he went, thus he **s**, O my son Absalom, 559
19: 5 Joab came *into* the house to the king, and **s**, 559
19:19 **s** unto the king, Let not my lord impute 559
19:21 Abishai the son of Zeruiah answered and **s**, 559
19:22 David **s**, What have I to do with you, ye sons 559
19:23 Therefore the king **s** unto Shimei, Thou shalt 559
19:25 that the king **s** unto him, Wherefore wentest 559
19:26 for thy servant **s**, I will saddle me an ass, 559
19:29 the king **s** unto him, Why speakest thou any 559
19:29 I have **s**, Thou and Ziba divide the land. 559
19:30 Mephibosheth **s** unto the king, Yea, let him 559
19:33 the king **s** unto Barzillai, Come thou over 559
19:34 Barzillai **s** unto the king, How long have I to 559
19:41 Israel came to the king, and **s** unto the king, 559
19:43 **s**, We have ten parts in the king, and 559
20: 1 he blew a trumpet, and **s**, We have no part in 559
20: 4 **s** the king to Amasa, Assemble me the men 559
20: 6 David **s** to Abishai, Now shall Sheba the son 559
20: 9 Joab **s** to Amasa, *Art* thou in health, 559
20:11 **s**, He that favoureth Joab, and he that *is* for 559
20:17 near unto her, the woman **s**, *Art* thou Joab? 559
20:17 he answered, I *am he.* Then she **s** unto him, 559
20:20 Joab answered and **s**, Far be it, far be it from 559
20:21 the woman **s** unto Joab, Behold, his head 559
21: 2 king called the Gibeonites, and **s** unto them; 559
21: 3 Wherefore David **s** unto the Gibeonites, 559
21: 4 the Gibeonites **s** unto him, We will have no 559
21: 4 he **s**, What you shall say, *that* will I do for 559
21: 6 did choose. And the king **s**, I will give *them.* 559
22: 2 he **s**, The LORD *is* my rock, and 559
23: 1 David the son of Jesse **s**, and the man *who* 5002
23: 1 of Jacob, and the sweet psalmist of Israel, **s**, 5002
23: 3 The God of Israel **s**, the Rock of Israel spake 559
23:15 David longed, and **s**, Oh that one would give 559
23:17 he **s**, Be it far from me, O LORD, that I 559
24: 2 For the king **s** to Joab the captain of the host, 559
2Sa 24: 3 Joab **s** unto the king, Now the LORD thy 559
24:10 David **s** unto the LORD, I have sinned 559
24:13 came to David, and told him, and **s** unto him, 559
24:14 And David **s** unto Gad, I am in a great strait: 559
24:16 and **s** to the angel that destroyed the people, 559
24:17 **s**, Lo, I have sinned, and I have done 559
24:18 that day to David, and **s** unto him, Go up, 559
24:21 Araunah **s**, Wherefore is my lord the king 559
24:21 David **s**, To buy the threshingfloor of thee, 559
24:22 Araunah **s** unto David, Let my lord the king 559
24:23 Araunah **s** unto the king, The LORD thy 559
24:24 the king **s** unto Araunah, Nay; but I will 559
1Ki 1: 2 Wherefore his servants **s** unto him, Let there 559
1:16 And the king **s**, What wouldest thou? 559
1:17 she **s** unto him, My lord, thou swarest by 559
1:24 Nathan **s**, My lord O king, hast thou said, 559
1:24 Nathan said, My lord O king, hast thou **s**, 559
1:28 king David answered and **s**, Call me 559
1:29 the king sware, and **s**, *As* the LORD liveth, 559
1:31 did reverence to the king, and **s**, Let my lord 559
1:32 And king David **s**, Call me Zadok the priest, 559
1:33 The king also **s** unto them, Take with you 559
1:36 of Jehoiada answered the king, and **s**, Amen: 559
1:39 all the people **s**, God save king Solomon. 559
1:41 Joab heard the sound of the trumpet, he **s**, 559
1:42 Adonijah **s** *unto him*, Come in; for thou *art* a 559
1:43 Jonathan answered and **s** to Adonijah, 559
1:48 also thus **s** the king, Blessed *be* the LORD 559
1:52 Solomon **s**, If he will shew himself a worthy 559
1:53 and Solomon **s** unto him, Go to thine house. 559
2: 4 all their soul, there shall not fail thee (**s** he) 559
2:13 she **s**, Comest thou peaceably? And he said, 559
2:13 thou peaceably? And he **s**, Peaceably. 559
2:14 He **s** moreover, I have somewhat to say unto 559
2:14 to say unto thee. And she **s**, Say on. 559
2:15 he **s**, Thou knowest that the kingdom was 559
2:16 deny me not. And she **s** unto him, Say on. 559
2:17 he **s**, Speak, I pray thee, unto Solomon 559
2:18 Bath-sheba **s**, Well; I will speak for thee 559
2:20 she **s**, I desire one small petition of thee; 559
2:20 And the king **s** unto her, Ask on, my mother: 559
2:21 she **s**, Let Abishag the Shunammite be given 559
2:22 Solomon answered and **s** unto his mother, 559
2:26 unto Abiathar the priest **s** the king, Get thee 559
2:30 **s** unto him, Thus saith the king, Come forth. 559
2:30 he **s**, Nay; but I will die here. And Benaiah 559
2:30 Thus **s** Joab, and thus he answered me. 1696
2:31 And the king **s** unto him, Do as he hath said, 559
2:31 Do as he hath **s**, and fall upon him, and 1696
2:36 and called for Shimei, and **s** unto him, 559
2:38 Shimei **s** unto the king, The saying *is* good: 559
2:38 as my lord the king hath **s**, so will thy 1696
2:42 and called for Shimei, and **s** unto him, 559
2:44 The king **s** moreover to Shimei, 559
3: 5 and God **s**, Ask what I shall give thee. 559
3: 6 Solomon **s**, Thou hast shewed unto thy 559
3:11 God **s** unto him, Because thou hast asked 559
3:17 the one woman **s**, O my lord, I and 559
3:22 the other woman **s**, Nay; but the living *is* my 559
3:22 this **s**, No; but the dead *is* thy son, and 559
3:23 **s** the king, The one saith, This *is* my son that 559
3:24 the king **s**, Bring me a sword. And they 559
3:25 the king **s**, Divide the living child in two, 559
3:26 she **s**, O my lord, give her the living child, 559
3:26 the other **s**, Let it be neither mine nor thine, 559
3:27 the king answered and **s**, Give her the living 559
5: 7 that he rejoiced greatly, and **s**, Blessed *be* 559
8:12 The LORD **s** that *he* would dwell in 559
8:15 he **s**, Blessed *be* the LORD God of Israel, 559
8:18 the LORD **s** unto David my father, 559
8:23 he **s**, LORD God of Israel, *there is* no God 559
8:29 *even* toward the place of which thou hast **s**, 559
9: 3 the LORD **s** unto him, I have heard thy 559
9:13 he **s**, What cities *are* these which thou hast 559
10: 6 she **s** to the king, It was a true report that I 559
11: 2 the LORD **s** unto the children of Israel, 559
11:11 Wherefore the LORD **s** unto Solomon, 559
11:21 Hadad **s** to Pharaoh, Let me depart, that I 559
11:22 Pharaoh **s** unto him, But what *hast* thou 559
11:31 And he **s** to Jeroboam, Take thee ten pieces: 559
12: 5 he **s** unto them, Depart yet *for* three days, 559
12: 6 **s**, How do you advise that *I* may answer this 559
12: 9 he **s** unto them, What counsel give ye that 559
12:26 Jeroboam **s** in his heart, Now shall 559
12:28 made two calves of gold, and **s** unto them, 559
13: 2 and **s**, O altar, altar, thus saith the LORD; 559
13: 6 king answered and **s** unto the man of God, 559
13: 7 the king **s** unto the man of God, 1696
13: 8 the man of God **s** unto the king, If thou wilt 559
13:12 their father **s** unto them, What way went 1696
13:13 he **s** unto his sons, Saddle me the ass. 559
13:14 he **s** unto him, *Art* thou the man of God that 559
13:14 that camest from Judah? And he **s**, I *am.* 559
13:15 he **s** unto him, Come home with me, 559
13:16 he **s**, I may not return with thee, nor go in 559
13:17 For it was **s** to me by the word of 1697
13:18 He **s** unto him, I *am* a prophet also as thou 559
13:26 him back from the way heard *thereof*, he **s**, 559
14: 2 Jeroboam **s** to his wife, Arise, I pray thee, 559
14: 5 the LORD **s** unto Ahijah, Behold, the wife 559
14: 6 that he **s**, Come in, thou wife of Jeroboam; 559
17: 1 **s** unto Ahab, *As* the LORD God of Israel 559
17:10 he called to her, and **s**, Fetch me, I pray thee, 559
17:11 **s**, Bring me, I pray thee, a morsel of bread in 559
17:12 she **s**, *As* the LORD thy God liveth, I have 559
17:13 Elijah **s** unto her, Fear not; go *and* do as thou 559
17:13 unto her, Fear not; go *and* do as thou hast **s**: 1697
17:18 she **s** unto Elijah, What have I to do with 559
17:19 he **s** unto her, Give me thy son. And he took 559
17:20 unto the LORD, and **s**, O LORD my God, 559
17:21 and **s**, O LORD my God, I pray thee, 559
17:23 his mother: and Elijah **s**, See, thy son liveth. 559
17:24 the woman **s** to Elijah, Now *by* this I know 559
18: 5 And Ahab **s** unto Obadiah, Go into the land, 559
18: 7 and he knew him, and fell on his face, and **s**, 559

1Ki 18: 9 he **s**, What have I sinned, that thou wouldest 559
18:10 when they **s**, *He is* not *there;* he took an oath 559
18:15 And Elijah **s**, *As* the LORD of hosts liveth, 559
18:17 Ahab saw Elijah, that Ahab **s** unto him, 559
18:21 Elijah came unto all the people, and **s**, How 559
18:22 Then **s** Elijah unto the people, I, *even* I only, 559
18:24 all the people answered and **s**, It is well 559
18:25 Elijah **s** unto the prophets of Baal, 559
18:27 that Elijah mocked them, and **s**, Cry aloud: 559
18:30 Elijah **s** unto all the people, Come near unto 559
18:33 in pieces, and laid *him* on the wood, and **s**, 559
18:34 he **s**, Do *it* the second time. And they did *it* 559
18:34 he **s**, Do *it* the third time. And they did *it* 559
18:36 **s**, LORD God of Abraham, Isaac, and 559
18:39 they **s**, The LORD, he *is* the God; 559
18:40 Elijah **s** unto them, Take the prophets of 559
18:41 And Elijah **s** unto Ahab, Get thee up, eat and 559
18:43 **s** to his servant, Go up now, look toward 559
18:43 he went up, and looked, and **s**, *There is* 559
18:43 *is* nothing. And he **s**, Go again seven times. 559
18:44 it came to pass at the seventh *time,* that he **s**, 559
18:44 he **s**, Go up, say unto Ahab, Prepare *thy* 559
19: 4 **s**, *It is* enough; now, O LORD, take away 559
19: 5 touched him, and **s** unto him, Arise *and* eat. 559
19: 7 and touched him, and **s**, Arise *and* eat; 559
19: 9 he **s** unto him, What doest thou here, Elijah? 559
19:10 he **s**, I have been very jealous for 559
19:11 he **s**, Go forth, and stand upon the mount 559
19:13 and **s**, What doest thou here, Elijah? 559
19:14 he **s**, I have been very jealous for 559
19:15 the LORD **s** unto him, Go, return on thy 559
19:20 and **s**, Let me, I pray thee, kiss my father and 559
19:20 he **s** unto him, Go back again: for what have 559
20: 2 and **s** unto him, Thus saith Ben-hadad, 559
20: 4 the king of Israel answered and **s**, My lord, 559
20: 5 **s**, Thus speaketh Ben-hadad, saying, 559
20: 7 **s**, Mark, I pray you, and see how this *man* 559
20: 8 all the elders and all the people **s** unto him, 559
20: 9 Wherefore he **s** unto the messengers of 559
20:10 **s**, The gods do so unto me, and more also, 559
20:11 the king of Israel answered and **s**, Tell *him,* 559
20:12 in the pavilions, that he **s** unto his servants, 559
20:14 Ahab **s**, By whom? And he said, Thus saith 559
20:14 he **s**, Thus saith the LORD, *Even* by 559
20:14 he **s**, Who shall order the battle? And he 559
20:18 he **s**, Whether they be come out for peace, 559
20:22 **s** unto him, Go, strengthen thyself, and mark, 559
20:23 the servants of the king of Syria **s** unto him, 559
20:28 king of Israel, and **s**, Thus saith the LORD, 559
20:28 the LORD, Because the Syrians have **s**, 559
20:31 his servants **s** unto him, Behold now, 559
20:32 and came to the king of Israel, and **s**, 559
20:32 And he **s**, *Is* he yet alive? he *is* my brother. 559
20:33 did hastily catch *it:* and they **s**, Thy brother 559
20:33 he **s**, Go ye, bring him. Then Ben-hadad 559
20:34 *Ben-hadad* **s** unto him, The cities, which my 559
20:34 ***s*** *Ahab,* I will send thee away with *this* NIH
20:35 a certain man of the sons of the prophets **s** 559
20:36 **s** he unto him, Because thou hast not obeyed 559
20:37 another man, and **s**, Smite me, I pray thee. 559
20:39 he **s**, Thy servant went out into the midst of 559
20:39 a man unto me, and **s**, Keep this man: 559
20:40 the king of Israel **s** unto him, So *shall* thy 559
20:42 he **s** unto him, Thus saith the LORD, 559
21: 3 Naboth **s** to Ahab, The LORD forbid it me, 559
21: 4 for he had **s**, I will not give thee 559
21: 5 **s** unto him, Why is thy spirit so sad, 1696
21: 6 he **s** unto her, Because I spake unto Naboth 1696
21: 6 **s** unto him, Give me thy vineyard for money; 559
21: 7 Jezebel his wife **s** unto him, Dost thou now 559
21:15 and was dead, that Jezebel **s** to Ahab, Arise, 559
21:20 Ahab **s** to Elijah, Hast thou found me, 559
22: 3 the king of Israel **s** unto his servants, Know 559
22: 4 he **s** unto Jehoshaphat, Wilt thou go with me 559
22: 4 Jehoshaphat **s** to the king of Israel, I *am* as 559
22: 5 Jehoshaphat **s** unto the king of Israel, 559
22: 6 about four hundred men, and **s** unto them, 559
22: 6 they **s**, Go up; for the Lord shall deliver *it* 559
22: 7 Jehoshaphat **s**, *Is there* not here a prophet of 559
22: 8 the king of Israel **s** unto Jehoshaphat, 559
22: 8 And Jehoshaphat **s**, Let not the king say so. 559
22: 9 **s**, Hasten *hither* Micaiah the son of Imlah. 559
22:11 he **s**, Thus saith the LORD, With these 559
22:14 Micaiah **s**, *As* the LORD liveth, what 559
22:15 the king **s** unto him, Micaiah, shall we go 559
22:16 the king **s** unto him, How many times shall I 559
22:17 he **s**, I saw all Israel scattered upon the hills, 559
22:17 the LORD **s**, These have no master: 559
22:18 the king of Israel **s** unto Jehoshaphat, Did I 559
22:19 he **s**, Hear thou therefore the word of 559
22:20 the LORD **s**, Who shall persuade Ahab, 559
22:20 one **s** on this manner, and another said on 559
22:20 this manner, and another **s** on that manner. 559
22:21 the LORD, and **s**, I will persuade him. 559
22:22 the LORD **s** unto him, Wherewith? And he 559
22:22 he **s**, I will go forth, and I will be a lying 559
22:22 he **s**, Thou shalt persuade *him,* and 559
22:24 and smote Micaiah on the cheek, and **s**, 559
22:25 Micaiah **s**, Behold, thou shalt see in that day, 559
22:26 the king of Israel **s**, Take Micaiah, and 559
22:28 And Micaiah **s**, If thou return at all in peace, 559
22:28 he **s**, Hearken, O people, every one of you. 559
22:30 the king of Israel **s** unto Jehoshaphat, I will 559
22:32 that they **s**, Surely it *is* the king of Israel. 559
22:34 wherefore he **s** unto the driver of his chariot, 559
22:49 **s** Ahaziah the son of Ahab unto Jehoshaphat, 559
2Ki 1: 2 he sent messengers, and **s** unto them, Go, 559
1: 3 the angel of the LORD **s** to Elijah 1696
1: 5 he **s** unto them, Why are ye now turned 559
1: 6 they **s** unto him, There came a man up to 559
1: 6 a man up to meet us, and **s** unto us, Go, 559
1: 7 he **s** unto them, What manner of man *was* 1696
1: 8 his loins. And he **s**, It *is* Elijah the Tishbite. 559
1: 9 man of God, the king hath **s**, Come down. 1696
1:10 and **s** to the captain of fifty, 1696

2Ki 1:11 he answered and **s** unto him, O man of 1696
1:11 O man of God, thus hath the king **s**, 559
1:12 Elijah answered and **s** unto them, If I *be* a 1696
1:13 besought him, and **s** unto him, O man of 1696
1:15 the angel of the LORD **s** unto Elijah, 1696
1:16 he **s** unto him, Thus saith the LORD, 1696
2: 2 Elijah **s** unto Elisha, Tarry here, I pray thee; 559
2: 2 Elisha **s** *unto him, As* the LORD liveth, 559
2: 3 Beth-el came forth to Elisha, and **s** unto him, 559
2: 3 he **s**, Yea, I know *it;* hold you your peace. 559
2: 4 Elijah **s** unto him, Elisha, tarry here, I pray 559
2: 4 he **s**, *As* the LORD liveth, and *as* thy soul 559
2: 5 at Jericho came to Elisha, and **s** unto him, 559
2: 6 Elijah **s** unto him, Tarry, I pray thee, here; 559
2: 6 he **s**, *As* the LORD liveth, and *as* thy soul 559
2: 9 were gone over, that Elijah **s** unto Elisha, 559
2: 9 Elisha **s**, I pray thee, let a double portion of 559
2:10 he **s**, Thou hast asked a hard thing: 559
2:14 smote the waters, and **s**, Where *is* 559
2:15 they **s**, The spirit of Elijah doth rest on 559
2:16 they **s** unto him, Behold now, there be with 559
2:16 some valley. And he **s**, Ye shall not send. 559
2:17 urged him till *he* was ashamed, he **s**, Send. 559
2:18 he **s** unto them, Did I not say unto you, 559
2:19 the men of the city **s** unto Elisha, Behold, 559
2:20 he **s**, Bring me a new cruse, and put salt 559
2:21 cast the salt in there, and **s**, Thus saith 559
2:23 mocked him, and **s** unto him, Go up, 559
3: 7 he **s**, I will go up: I *am* as thou *art,* my 559
3: 8 he **s**, Which way shall we go up? And he 559
3:10 the king of Israel **s**, Alas, that the LORD 559
3:11 Jehoshaphat **s**, *Is there* not here a prophet of 559
3:11 the king of Israel's servants answered and **s**, 559
3:12 Jehoshaphat **s**, The word of the LORD is 559
3:13 Elisha **s** unto the king of Israel, What have I 559
3:13 the king of Israel **s** unto him, Nay: for 559
3:14 And Elisha **s**, *As* the LORD of hosts liveth, 559
3:16 he **s**, Thus saith the LORD, Make this 559
3:23 they **s**, This *is* blood: the kings are surely 559
4: 2 Elisha **s** unto her, What shall I do for thee? 559
4: 2 she **s**, Thine handmaid hath not any thing in 559
4: 3 he **s**, Go, borrow thee vessels abroad of all 559
4: 6 that she **s** unto her son, Bring me yet a 559
4: 6 he **s** unto her, *There is* not a vessel more. 559
4: 7 he **s**, Go, sell the oil, and pay thy debt, and 559
4: 9 she **s** unto her husband, Behold now, 559
4:12 he **s** to Gehazi his servant, Call this 559
4:13 he **s** unto him, Say now unto her, Behold, 559
4:14 he **s**, What then *is* to be done for her? 559
4:15 he **s**, Call her. And when he had called her, 559
4:16 he **s**, About this season, according to 559
4:16 she **s**, Nay, my lord, thou man of God, 559
4:17 bare a son at that season that Elisha had **s** 1696
4:19 And he **s** unto his father, My head, my head. 559
4:19 And he **s** to a lad, Carry him to his mother. 559
4:22 **s**, Send me, I pray thee, one of the young 559
4:23 he **s**, Wherefore wilt thou go to him to day? 559
4:23 nor sabbath. And she **s**, *It shall be* well. 559
4:24 **s** to her servant, Drive, and go *forward;* slack 559
4:25 that he **s** to Gehazi his servant, Behold, 559
4:27 the man of God **s**, Let her alone; for her soul 559
4:28 she **s**, Did I desire a son of my lord? did I not 559
4:29 he **s** to Gehazi, Gird up thy loins, and 559
4:30 the mother of the child **s**, *As* the LORD 559
4:36 he called Gehazi, and **s**, Call this 559
4:36 was come in unto him, he **s**, Take up thy son. 559
4:38 he **s** unto his servant, Set on the great pot, 559
4:40 that they cried out, and **s**, O thou man of 559
4:41 he **s**, Then bring meal. And he cast *it* into 559
4:41 he **s**, Pour out for the people, that they may 559
4:42 he **s**, Give unto the people, that they may eat. 559
4:43 his servitor **s**, What, should I set this before 559
4:43 He **s** again, Give the people, that they may 559
5: 3 she **s** unto her mistress, Would God my lord 559
5: 4 thus **s** the maid that *is* of the land of Israel. 1696
5: 5 the king of Syria **s**, Go to, go, and I will send 559
5: 7 and **s**, *Am* I God, to kill and to make alive, 559
5:11 and went away, and **s**, Behold, I thought, 559
5:13 and spake unto him, and **s**, My father, 559
5:15 he **s**, Behold, now I know that *there is* no 559
5:16 he **s**, *As* the LORD liveth, before whom I 559
5:17 Naaman **s**, Shall there not then, I pray thee, 559
5:19 he **s** unto him, Go in peace. So he departed 559
5:20 servant of Elisha the man of God, **s**, Behold, 559
5:21 the chariot to meet him, and **s**, *Is all* well? 559
5:22 he **s**, *All is* well. My master hath sent me, 559
5:23 And Naaman **s**, Be content, take two talents. 559
5:25 Elisha **s** unto him, Whence *comest thou,* 559
5:25 And he **s**, Thy servant went no whither. 559
5:26 he **s** unto him, Went not mine heart *with* 559
6: 1 the sons of the prophets **s** unto Elisha, 559
6: 3 one **s**, Be content, I pray thee, and go with 559
6: 5 he cried, and **s**, Alas, master, for it *was* 559
6: 6 the man of God **s**, Where fell it? And he 559
6: 7 Therefore **s** he, Take *it* up to thee. And he 559
6:11 he called his servants, and **s** unto them, Will 559
6:12 one of his servants **s**, None, my lord, O king: 559
6:13 he **s**, Go and spy where he *is,* that I may send 559
6:15 And his servant **s** unto him, Alas, my master, 559
6:17 **s**, LORD, I pray thee, open his eyes, that he 559
6:18 **s**, Smite this people, I pray thee, 559
6:19 And Elisha **s** unto them, This *is* not the way, 559
6:20 come *into* Samaria, that Elisha **s**, LORD, 559
6:21 the king of Israel **s** unto Elisha, when he saw 559
6:27 he **s**, *If* the LORD do not help thee, whence 559
6:28 the king **s** unto her, What aileth thee? 559
6:28 This woman **s** unto me, Give thy son, 559
6:29 I **s** unto her on the next day, Give thy son, 559
6:31 he **s**, God do so and more also to me, if 559
6:32 messenger came to him, he **s** to the elders, 559
6:33 and he **s**, Behold, this evil *is* of the LORD; 559
7: 1 Elisha **s**, Hear ye the word of the LORD; 559
7: 2 **s**, Behold, *if* the LORD would make 559
7: 2 he **s**, Behold, thou shalt see *it* with thine 559
7: 3 they **s** one to another, Why sit we here until 559

2Ki 7: 6 they **s** one to another, Lo, the king of Israel 559
7: 9 Then they **s** one to another, We do not well: 559
7:12 arose in the night, and **s** unto his servants, 559
7:13 one of his servants answered and **s**, Let *some* 559
7:17 and he died, as the man of God had **s**, 1696
7:19 the man of God, and **s**, Now behold, 559
7:19 he **s**, Behold, thou shalt see *it* with thine 559
8: 5 Gehazi **s**, My lord, O king, this *is* 559
8: 8 the king **s** unto Hazael, Take a present in 559
8: 9 and came and stood before him, and **s**, 559
8:10 Elisha **s** unto him, Go, say unto him, 559
8:12 Hazael **s**, Why weepeth my lord? And he 559
8:13 And Hazael **s**, But what, *is* thy servant a dog, 559
8:14 who **s** to him, What said Elisha to thee? 559
8:14 who said to him, What **s** Elisha to thee? 559
9: 1 **s** unto him, Gird up thy loins, and take this 559
9: 5 and he **s**, I have an errand to thee, O captain. 559
9: 5 Jehu **s**, Unto which of all us? And he said, 559
9: 5 of all us? And he **s**, To thee, O captain. 559
9: 6 poured the oil on his head, and **s** unto him, 559
9:11 *one* **s** unto him, *Is all* well? wherefore came 559
9:11 he **s** unto them, Ye know the man, and his 559
9:12 they **s**, *It is* false; tell us now. And he said, 559
9:12 he **s**, Thus and thus spake he to me, saying, 559
9:15 Jehu **s**, If it be your minds, *then* let none go 559
9:17 of Jehu as he came, and **s**, I see a company. 559
9:17 Joram **s**, Take a horseman, and send to meet 559
9:18 and **s**, Thus saith the king, *Is it* peace? 559
9:18 Jehu **s**, What hast thou to do with peace? 559
9:19 and **s**, Thus saith the king, *Is it* peace? 559
9:21 Joram **s**, Make ready. And his chariot was 559
9:22 Joram saw Jehu, that he **s**, *Is it* peace, Jehu? 559
9:23 fled, and **s** to Ahaziah, *There is* treachery, 559
9:25 **s** *Jehu* to Bidkar his captain, Take up, *and* 559
9:27 Jehu followed after him, and **s**, Smite him 559
9:31 she **s**, *Had* Zimri peace, who slew his 559
9:32 to the window, and **s**, Who *is* on my side? 559
9:33 he **s**, Throw her down. So they threw her 559
9:34 was come in, he did eat and drink, and **s**, Go, 559
9:36 he **s**, This *is* the word of the LORD, 559
10: 4 **s**, Behold, two kings stood not before him: 559
10: 8 he **s**, Lay ye them *in* two heaps *at* 559
10: 9 stood, and **s** to all the people, Ye *be* 559
10:13 Ahaziah king of Judah, and **s**, Who *are* ye? 559
10:14 he **s**, Take them alive. And they took them 559
10:15 he saluted him, and **s** to him, Is thine heart 559
10:16 he **s**, Come with me, and see my zeal for 559
10:18 and **s** unto them, Ahab served Baal a little; 559
10:20 Jehu **s**, Proclaim a solemn assembly for 559
10:22 he **s** unto *him* that *was* over the vestry, 559
10:23 **s** unto the worshippers of Baal, Search, and 559
10:24 appointed fourscore men without, and **s**, 559
10:25 that Jehu **s** to the guard and to the captains, 559
10:30 the LORD **s** unto Jehu, Because thou hast 559
11:12 clapt their hands, and **s**, God save the king. 559
11:15 the officers of the host, and **s** unto them, 559
11:15 For the priest had **s**, Let her not be slain *in* 559
12: 4 Jehoash **s** to the priests, All the money of 559
12: 7 the *other* priests, and **s** unto them, 559
13:14 over his face, and **s**, O my father, my father, 559
13:15 Elisha **s** unto him, Take bow and arrows. 559
13:16 he **s** to the king of Israel, Put thine hand 559
13:17 he **s**, Open the window eastward. And he 559
13:17 he opened *it.* Then Elisha **s**, Shoot. And he 559
13:17 he **s**, The arrow of the LORD'S 559
13:18 he **s**, Take the arrows. And he took *them.* 559
13:18 he took *them.* And he **s** unto the king of 559
13:19 **s**, *Thou* shouldest have smitten five or 559
14:27 the LORD **s** not that *he* would blot out 1696
17:12 whereof the LORD had **s** unto them, 559
17:23 as he had **s** by all his servants the prophets. 1696
18:19 Rab-shakeh **s** unto them, Speak ye now to 559
18:22 and hath **s** to Judah and Jerusalem, 559
18:25 The LORD **s** to me, Go up against this 559
18:26 **s** Eliakim the son of Hilkiah, and Shebna, 559
18:27 Rab-shakeh **s** unto them, Hath my master 559
19: 3 they **s** unto him, Thus saith Hezekiah, 559
19: 6 Isaiah **s** unto them, Thus shall ye say to your 559
19:15 **s**, O LORD God of Israel, which dwellest 559
19:23 thou hast reproached the Lord, and hast **s**, 559
20: 1 **s** unto him, Thus saith the LORD, Set thine 559
20: 7 Isaiah **s**, Take a lump of figs. And they took 559
20: 8 Hezekiah **s** unto Isaiah, What *shall be* 559
20: 9 Isaiah **s**, This sign shalt thou have of 559
20:14 and **s** unto him, What said these men? 559
20:14 and said unto him, What **s** these men? 559
20:14 Hezekiah **s**, They are come from a far 559
20:15 he **s**, What have they seen in thine house? 559
20:16 Isaiah **s** unto Hezekiah, Hear the word of 559
20:19 **s** Hezekiah unto Isaiah, Good *is* the word of 559
20:19 he **s**, *Is it* not *good,* if peace and truth be in 559
21: 4 of which the LORD **s**, In Jerusalem will I 559
21: 7 of which the LORD **s** to David, and 559
22: 8 Hilkiah the high priest **s** unto Shaphan 559
22: 9 and brought the king word again, and **s**, 559
22:15 she **s** unto them, Thus saith the LORD God 559
23:17 he **s**, What title *is* that that I see? And 559
23:18 he **s**, Let him alone; let no man move his 559
23:27 the LORD **s**, I will remove Judah also out 559
23:27 the house of which I **s**, My name shall be 559
24:13 of the LORD, as the LORD had **s**. 1696
25:24 to them, and to their men, and **s** unto them, 559
1Ch 10: 4 **s** Saul to his armourbearer, Draw thy sword, 559
11: 2 the LORD thy God **s** unto thee, Thou shalt 559
11: 5 the inhabitants of Jebus **s** to David, 559
11: 6 David **s**, Whosoever smiteth the Jebusites 559
11:17 David longed, and **s**, Oh that one would give 559
11:19 **s**, My God forbid it me, that *I* should do this 559
12:17 to meet them, and answered and **s** unto them, 559
12:18 *and he* **s**, Thine *are we,* David, and on thy NIH
13: 2 David **s** unto all the congregation of Israel, 559
13: 4 all the congregation **s** that *they* would do so: 559
14:10 the LORD **s** unto him, Go up; for I will 559
14:11 David **s**, God hath broken in upon mine 559
14:14 God **s** unto him, Go not up after them; 559

1Ch 15: 2 David **s**, None ought to carry the ark of God 559
15:12 **s** unto them, Ye *are* the chief of the fathers 559
16:36 all the people **s**, Amen, and praised 559
17: 1 that David **s** to Nathan the prophet, Lo, 559
17: 2 Nathan **s** unto David, Do all that *is* in thine 559
17:16 **s**, Who *am* I, O LORD God, and what *is* 559
17:23 established for ever, and do as thou hast **s**. 1696
19: 2 David **s**, I will shew kindness unto Hanun 559
19: 3 the princes of the children of Ammon **s** to 559
19: 5 the king **s**, Tarry at Jericho until your beards 559
19:12 And he **s**, If the Syrians be too strong for me, 559
21: 2 David **s** to Joab and to the rulers of 559
21: 8 David **s** unto God, I have sinned greatly, 559
21:11 So Gad came to David, and **s** unto him, 559
21:13 And David **s** unto Gad, I am in a great strait: 559
21:15 **s** to the angel that destroyed, *It is* enough, 559
21:17 David **s** unto God, *Is it* not I *that* 559
21:22 David **s** to Ornan, Grant me the place of *this* 559
21:23 And Ornan **s** unto David, Take *it* to thee, and 559
21:24 king David **s** to Ornan, Nay; but I will verily 559
22: 1 David **s**, This *is* the house of the LORD 559
22: 5 And David **s**, Solomon my son *is* young and 559
22: 7 And David **s** to Solomon, My son, *as for* me, 559
22:11 the LORD thy God, as he hath **s** of thee. 1696
23: 5 which I made, ***s** David,* to praise *therewith.* NIH
23:25 For David **s**, The LORD God of Israel hath 559
27:23 the LORD had **s** *he* would increase Israel 559
28: 2 and **s**, Hear me, my brethren, and my people: 559
28: 3 God **s** unto me, Thou shalt not build a house 559
28: 6 he **s** unto me, Solomon thy son, he shall 559
28:19 All *this,* ***s** David,* the LORD made me NIH
28:20 David **s** to Solomon his son, Be strong and 559
29: 1 Furthermore David the king **s** unto all 559
29:10 David **s**, Blessed *be* thou, LORD God of 559
29:20 David **s** to all the congregation, Now bless 559
2Ch 1: 7 and **s** unto him, Ask what I shall give thee. 559
1: 8 Solomon **s** unto God, Thou hast shewed 559
1:11 God **s** to Solomon, Because this was in thine 559
2:12 Huram **s** moreover, Blessed *be* the LORD 559
6: 1 **s** Solomon, The LORD hath said that *he* 559
6: 1 The LORD hath **s** that *he* would dwell in 559
6: 4 he **s**, Blessed *be* the LORD God of Israel, 559
6: 8 the LORD **s** to David my father, 559
6:14 **s**, O LORD God of Israel, *there is* no God 559
6:20 upon the place whereof thou hast **s** that *thou* 559
7:12 and **s** unto him, I have heard thy prayer, and 559
8:11 for he **s**, My wife shall not dwell in 559
9: 5 she **s** to the king, *It was* a true report which I 559
10: 5 he **s** unto them, Come again unto me after 559
10: 9 he **s** unto them, What advice give ye that we 559
12: 5 of Shishak, and **s** unto them, 559
12: 6 and they **s**, The LORD *is* righteous. 559
13: 4 **s**, Hear me, *thou* Jeroboam, and all Israel; 559
14: 7 Therefore he **s** unto Judah, Let us build these 559
14:11 **s**, LORD, *it is* nothing with thee to help, 559
15: 2 **s** unto him, Hear ye me, Asa, and all Judah 559
16: 7 **s** unto him, Because thou hast relied on 559
18: 3 Ahab king of Israel **s** unto Jehoshaphat king 559
18: 4 Jehoshaphat **s** unto the king of Israel, 559
18: 5 **s** unto them, Shall we go to Ramoth-gilead 559
18: 5 they **s**, Go up; for God will deliver *it* into 559
18: 6 Jehoshaphat **s**, *Is there* not here a prophet of 559
18: 7 the king of Israel **s** unto Jehoshaphat, 559
18: 7 And Jehoshaphat **s**, Let not the king say so. 559
18: 8 **s**, Fetch quickly Micaiah the son of Imla. 559
18:10 **s**, Thus saith the LORD, With these thou 559
18:13 Micaiah **s**, *As* the LORD liveth, even what 559
18:14 to the king, the king **s** unto him, Micaiah, 559
18:14 he **s**, Go ye up, and prosper, and they shall 559
18:15 the king **s** to him, How many times shall I 559
18:16 he **s**, I did see all Israel scattered upon 559
18:16 the LORD **s**, These have no master; 559
18:17 the king of Israel **s** to Jehoshaphat, Did I not 559
18:18 Again he **s**, Therefore hear the word of 559
18:19 the LORD **s**, Who shall entice Ahab king of 559
18:20 before the LORD, and **s**, I will entice him. 559
18:20 And the LORD **s** unto him, Wherewith? 559
18:21 he **s**, I will go out, and be a lying spirit in 559
18:21 *the LORD* **s**, Thou shalt entice *him,* and 559
18:23 and smote Micaiah upon the cheek, and **s**, 559
18:24 Micaiah **s**, Behold, thou shalt see on that day 559
18:25 the king of Israel **s**, Take ye Micaiah, and 559
18:27 Micaiah **s**, If thou certainly return in peace, 559
18:27 by me. And he **s**, Hearken, all ye people. 559
18:29 the king of Israel **s** unto Jehoshaphat, I will 559
18:31 that they **s**, It *is* the king of Israel. 559
18:33 therefore he **s** to *his* chariot man, Turn thine 559
19: 2 **s** to king Jehoshaphat, Shouldest thou help 559
19: 6 **s** to the judges, Take heed what ye do: for ye 559
20: 6 **s**, O LORD God of our fathers, *art* not thou 559
20:15 he **s**, Hearken ye, all Judah, and 559
20:20 Jehoshaphat stood and **s**, Hear me, O Judah, 559
22: 9 Because, **s** they, he *is* the son of 559
23: 3 he **s** unto them, Behold, the king's son shall 559
23: 3 as the LORD hath **s** of the sons of David. 1696
23:11 sons anointed him, and **s**, God save the king. 559
23:13 rent her clothes, and **s**, Treason, Treason. 559
23:14 **s** unto them, Have her forth of the ranges: 559
23:14 For the priest **s**, Slay her not *in* the house of 559
24: 5 the priests and the Levites, and **s** to them, 559
24: 6 called for Jehoiada the chief, and **s** unto him, 559
24:20 the people, and **s** unto them, Thus saith God, 559
24:22 when he died, he **s**, The LORD look upon 559
25: 9 Amaziah **s** to the man of God, But what *shall* 559
25:15 sent unto him a prophet, which **s** unto him, 559
25:16 he talked with him, that *the king* **s** unto him, 559
25:16 the prophet forbare, and **s**, I know that God 559
26:18 **s** unto him, *It pertaineth* not unto thee, 559
26:23 to the kings; for they **s**, He *is* a leper: 559
28: 9 **s** unto them, Behold, because the LORD 559
28:13 **s** unto them, Ye shall not bring in 559
28:23 he **s**, Because the gods of the kings of Syria 559
29: 5 **s** unto them, Hear me, ye Levites, 559
29:18 they went in to Hezekiah the king, and **s**, 559
29:31 Hezekiah answered and **s**, Now ye have 559

2Ch 31:10 of the house of Zadok answered him, and **s**, 559
33: 4 whereof the LORD had **s**, In Jerusalem 559
33: 7 of which God had **s** to David and 559
34:15 and **s** to Shaphan the scribe, 559
35: 3 And **s** unto the Levites that taught all Israel, 559
35:23 the king **s** to his servants, Have me away; 559
Ezr 2:63 the Tirshatha **s** unto them, that they should 559
4: 2 and **s** unto them, Let us build with you: 559
4: 3 the chief of the fathers of Israel, **s** unto them, 559
5: 3 and their companions, and **s** thus unto them, 560
5: 4 **s** we unto them after this manner, What are 560
5: 9 asked we those elders, *and* **s** unto them thus, 560
5:15 **s** unto him, Take these vessels, go, 560
8:28 I **s** unto them, Ye *are* holy unto the LORD; 559
9: 6 **s**, O my God, I am ashamed and blush to lift 559
10: 2 the sons of Elam, answered and **s** unto Ezra, 559
10:10 **s** unto them, Ye have transgressed, and 559
10:12 and **s** *with* a loud voice, 559
10:12 a loud voice, As thou hast **s**, so must we do. 1697
Ne 1: 3 they **s** unto me, The remnant that are left of 559
1: 5 **s**, I beseech thee, O LORD God of heaven, 559
2: 2 Wherefore the king **s** unto me, Why *is* thy 559
2: 3 **s** unto the king, Let the king live for ever: 559
2: 4 the king **s** unto me, For what dost thou make 559
2: 5 I **s** unto the king, If it please the king, and 559
2: 6 the king **s** unto me, (the queen also sitting by 559
2: 7 Moreover I **s** unto the king, If it please 559
2:17 **s** I unto them, Ye see the distress that we *are* 559
2:18 they **s**, Let us rise up and build. So they 559
2:19 despised us, and **s**, What *is* this thing that ye 559
2:20 **s** unto them, The God of heaven, he will 559
4: 2 his brethren and the army of Samaria, and **s**, 559
4: 3 he **s**, Even *that* which they build, if a fox go 559
4:10 Judah **s**, The strength of the bearers of 559
4:11 And our adversaries **s**, They shall not know, 559
4:12 by them came, they **s** unto us ten times, 559
4:14 **s** unto the nobles, and to the rulers, and 559
4:19 I **s** unto the nobles, and to the rulers, and 559
4:22 Likewise at the same time **s** I unto 559
5: 2 For there were that **s**, We, our sons, and 559
5: 3 *Some* also there were that **s**, We *have* 559
5: 4 There were also that **s**, We have borrowed 559
5: 7 the rulers, and **s** unto them, You exact usury, 559
5: 8 I **s** unto them, We after our ability have 559
5: 9 Also I **s**, It *is* not good that ye do: ought ye 559
5:12 **s** they, We will restore *them,* and 559
5:13 Also I shook my lap, and **s**, So God shake 559
5:13 all the congregation **s**, Amen, and praised 559
6:10 he **s**, Let us meet together in the house of 559
6:11 I **s**, Should such a man as I flee? and who *is* 559
7: 3 I **s** unto them, Let not the gates of Jerusalem 559
7:65 the Tirshatha **s** unto them, that they should 559
8: 9 that taught the people, **s** unto all the people, 559
8:10 he **s** unto them, Go *your way,* eat the fat, 559
9: 5 **s**, Stand up *and* bless the LORD your God 559
9:18 they had made them a molten calf, and **s**, 559
13:11 contended I with the rulers, and **s**, Why is 559
13:17 **s** unto them, What evil thing *is* this that ye 559
13:21 I testified against them, and **s** unto them, 559
Est 1:13 the king **s** to the wise *men,* which knew 559
2: 2 **s** the king's servants that ministered unto 559
3: 3 *were* in the king's gate, **s** unto Mordecai, 559
3: 8 Haman **s** unto king Ahasuerus, There is a 559
3:11 the king **s** unto Haman, The silver *is* given to 559
5: 3 **s** the king unto her, What wilt thou, queen 559
5: 5 the king **s**, Cause Haman to make haste, 559
5: 5 that *he* may do as Esther hath **s**. 1697
5: 6 the king **s** unto Esther at the banquet of 559
5: 7 and **s**, My petition and my request *is;* 559
5: 8 and I will do to morrow as the king hath **s**. 1697
5:12 Haman **s** moreover, Yea, Esther the queen 559
5:14 **s** Zeresh his wife and all his friends unto 559
6: 3 the king **s**, What honour and dignity hath 559
6: 3 **s** the king's servants that ministered unto 559
6: 4 the king **s**, Who *is* in the court? Now Haman 559
6: 5 And the king's servants **s** unto him, Behold, 559
6: 5 the court. And the king **s**, Let him come in. 559
6: 6 the king **s** unto him, What shall be done unto 559
6:10 the king **s** to Haman, Make haste, *and* 559
6:10 as thou hast **s**, and do *even* so to Mordecai 1696
6:13 **s** his wise *men* and Zeresh his wife unto him, 559
7: 2 the king **s** again unto Esther on the second 559
7: 3 Esther the queen answered and **s**, If I have 559
7: 5 and **s** unto Esther the queen, 559
7: 6 Esther **s**, The adversary and enemy *is* this 559
7: 8 bed whereon Esther *was.* Then **s** the king, 559
7: 9 **s** before the king, Behold also, 559
7: 9 Then the king **s**, Hang him thereon. 559
8: 5 **s**, If it please the king, and if I have found 559
8: 7 the king Ahasuerus **s** unto Esther the queen 559
9:12 the king **s** unto Esther the queen, The Jews 559
9:13 **s** Esther, If it please the king, let it be 559
Job 1: 5 for Job **s**, It may be that my sons have 559
1: 7 the LORD **s** unto Satan, Whence comest 559
1: 7 **s**, From going to and fro in the earth, and 559
1: 8 the LORD **s** unto Satan, Hast thou 559
1: 9 and **s**, Doth Job fear God for nought? 559
1:12 the LORD **s** unto Satan, Behold, all that he 559
1:14 **s**, The oxen were plowing, and the asses 559
1:16 yet speaking, there came also another, and **s**, 559
1:17 yet speaking, there came also another, and **s**, 559
1:18 **s**, Thy sons and thy daughters *were* eating 559
1:21 **s**, Naked came I out of my mother's womb, 559
2: 2 the LORD **s** unto Satan, From whence 559
2: 2 **s**, From going to and fro in the earth, and 559
2: 3 the LORD **s** unto Satan, Hast thou 559
2: 4 the LORD, and **s**, Skin for skin, yea, 559
2: 6 the LORD **s** unto Satan, Behold, he *is* in 559
2: 9 **s** his wife unto him, Dost thou still retain 559
2:10 he **s** unto her, Thou speakest as one of 559
3: 2 And Job spake, and **s**, 559
3: 3 the night *in which it was* **s**, There is a man 559
4: 1 Then Eliphaz the Temanite answered and **s**, 559
6: 1 But Job answered and **s**, 559
8: 1 Then answered Bildad the Shuhite, and **s**, 559

Job 9: 1 Then Job answered and **s**, 559
9:22 therefore I **s** *it,* He destroyeth the perfect and 559
11: 1 answered Zophar the Naamathite, and **s**, 559
11: 4 For thou hast **s**, My doctrine *is* pure, and 559
12: 1 And Job answered and **s**, 559
15: 1 Then answered Eliphaz the Temanite, and **s**, 559
16: 1 Then Job answered and **s**, 559
17:14 I have **s** to corruption, Thou *art* my father: 7121
18: 1 Then answered Bildad the Shuhite, and **s**, 559
19: 1 Then Job answered and **s**, 559
20: 1 answered Zophar the Naamathite, and **s**, 559
21: 1 But Job answered and **s**, 559
22: 1 Then Eliphaz the Temanite answered and **s**, 559
22:17 Which **s** unto God, Depart from us: and 559
23: 1 Then Job answered and **s**, 559
25: 1 Then answered Bildad the Shuhite, and **s**, 559
26: 1 But Job answered and **s**, 559
27: 1 Moreover Job continued his parable, and **s**, 559
28:28 unto man he **s**, Behold, the fear of the Lord, 559
29: 1 Moreover Job continued his parable, and **s**, 559
29:18 I **s**, I shall die in my nest, and I shall 559
31:24 or have **s** to the fine gold, *Thou art* my 559
31:31 If the men of my tabernacle **s** not, O that we 559
32: 6 son of Barachel the Buzite answered and **s**, 559
32: 7 I **s**, Days should speak, and multitude of 559
32:10 Therefore I **s**, Hearken to me; I also will 559
32:17 *I* **s**, I will answer also my part, I also will NIH
34: 1 Furthermore Elihu answered and **s**, 559
34: 5 For Job hath **s**, I am righteous: and God hath 559
34: 9 For he hath **s**, It profiteth a man nothing that 559
34:31 Surely it is *meet to be* **s** unto God, I have 559
35: 1 Elihu spake moreover, and **s**, 559
36: 1 Elihu also proceeded, and **s**, 559
38: 1 answered Job out of the whirlwind, and **s**, 559
38:11 **s**, Hitherto shalt thou come, but no further: 559
40: 1 Moreover the LORD answered Job, and **s**, 559
40: 3 Then Job answered the LORD, and **s**, 559
40: 6 unto Job out of the whirlwind, and **s**, 559
42: 1 Then Job answered the LORD, and **s**, 559
42: 7 the LORD **s** to Eliphaz the Temanite, 559
Ps 2: 7 the LORD hath **s** unto me, Thou *art* my 559
10: 6 He hath **s** in his heart, I shall not be moved: 559
10:11 He hath **s** in his heart, God hath forgotten: 559
10:13 he hath **s** in his heart, Thou wilt not require 559
12: 4 Who have **s**, With our tongue will we 559
14: 1 The fool hath **s** in his heart, *There is* no God. 559
16: 2 *O my soul,* thou hast **s** unto the LORD, 559
18: T and from the hand of Saul: And he **s**, 559
27: 8 my heart **s** unto thee, Thy face, LORD, 559
30: 6 in my prosperity I **s**, I shall never be moved. 559
31:14 in thee, O LORD: I **s**, Thou *art* my God. 559
31:22 For I **s** in my haste, I am cut off from before 559
32: 5 I **s**, I will confess my transgressions unto 559
35:21 *and* **s**, Aha, aha, our eye hath seen *it.* 559
38:16 For I **s**, *Hear me,* lest *otherwise* they should 559
39: 1 I **s**, I will take heed to my ways, that *I* sin not 559
40: 7 **s** I, Lo, I come: in the volume of the book *it* 559
41: 4 I **s**, LORD, be merciful unto me: heal my 559
52: T Edomite came and told Saul, and **s** unto him, 559
53: 1 The fool hath **s** in his heart, *There is* no God. 559
54: T when the Ziphims came and **s** to Saul, 559
55: 6 I **s**, O that I had wings like a dove, *for then* 559
68:22 The Lord **s**, I will bring again from Bashan, 559
74: 8 They **s** in their hearts, Let us destroy them 559
75: 4 I **s** unto the fools, Deal not foolishly: and 559
77:10 I **s**, This *is* my infirmity: *but I will remember* 559
78:19 they **s**, Can God furnish a table in 559
82: 6 I have **s**, Ye *are* gods; and all of you *are* 559
83: 4 They have **s**, Come, and let us cut them off 559
83:12 Who **s**, Let us take to ourselves the houses of 559
87: 5 of Zion it shall be **s**, This and that man was 559
89: 2 For I have **s**, Mercy shall be built up for 559
94:18 When I **s**, My foot slippeth; thy mercy, 559
95:10 and **s**, It *is* a people that do err in *their* heart, 559
102:24 I **s**, O my God, take me not away in 559
106:23 Therefore he **s** that *he* would destroy them, 559
110: 1 The LORD **s** unto my Lord, Sit thou at my 5002
116:11 I **s** in my haste, All men *are* liars. 559
119:57 I have **s** that *I* would keep thy words. 559
122: 1 I was glad when they **s** unto me, Let us go 559
126: 2 **s** they among the heathen, The LORD hath 559
137: 7 who **s**, Rase *it,* rase *it, even* to the foundation 559
140: 6 I **s** unto the LORD, Thou *art* my God: 559
142: 5 I **s**, Thou *art* my refuge *and* my portion in 559
Pr 4: 4 He taught me also, and **s** unto me, Let thine 559
7:13 and with an impudent face **s** unto him, 559
25: 7 For better *it is* that it be **s** unto thee, 559
Ecc 1:10 Is there *any* thing whereof it may be **s**, See, 559
2: 1 I **s** in mine heart, Go to now, I will prove 559
2: 2 I **s** of laughter, *It is* mad: and of mirth, 559
2:15 **s** I in my heart, As it happeneth to the fool, 559
2:15 Then I **s** in my heart, that this also *is* vanity. 1696
3:17 I **s** in mine heart, God shall judge 559
3:18 I **s** in my heart concerning the estate of 559
7:23 I **s**, I will be wise; but it *was* far from me. 559
8:14 of the righteous: I **s** that this also *is* vanity. 559
9:16 **s** I, Wisdom *is* better than strength: 559
SS 2:10 **s** unto me, Rise up, my love, my fair one, 559
3: 3 *to whom I* **s**, Saw ye *him* whom my soul NIH
7: 8 I **s**, I will go up to the palm tree, I will take 559
Isa 5: 9 In mine ears ***s** the* LORD of hosts, Of a NIH
6: 3 **s**, Holy, holy, holy, *is* the LORD of hosts: 559
6: 5 **s** I, Woe *is* me! for I am undone; because 559
6: 7 and **s**, Lo, this hath touched thy lips; 559
6: 8 will go for us? Then I **s**, Here *am* I; send me. 559
6: 9 he **s**, Go, and tell this people, Hear ye 559
6:11 Then **s** I, Lord, how long? And he answered, 559
7: 3 **s** the LORD unto Isaiah, Go forth now to 559
7:12 Ahaz **s**, I will not ask, neither will I tempt 559
7:13 he **s**, Hear ye now, O house of David; *Is it* a 559
8: 1 Moreover the LORD **s** unto me, Take thee 559
8: 3 **s** the LORD to me, Call his name 559
14:13 For thou hast **s** in thine heart, I will ascend 559
18: 4 For so the LORD **s** unto me, I will take my 559
20: 3 the LORD **s**, Like as my servant Isaiah hath 559

S

Isa 21: 6 For thus hath the Lord **s** unto me, Go, set a 559
21: 9 he answered and **s**, Babylon is fallen, 559
21:12 The watchman **s**, The morning cometh, and 559
21:16 For thus hath the Lord **s** unto me, Within a 559
22: 4 Therefore **s** I, Look away from me; I will 559
23:12 he **s**, Thou shalt no more rejoice, O thou 559
24:16 I **s**, My leanness, my leanness, woe unto me! 559
25: 9 it **s** in that day, Lo, this *is* our God; 559
28:12 To whom he **s**, This *is* the rest *wherewith* ye 559
28:15 Because ye have **s**, We have made a 559
29:13 Wherefore the Lord **s**, Forasmuch as this 559
30:16 ye **s**, No; for we will flee upon horses; 559
32: 5 called liberal, nor the churl **s** *to be* bountiful. 559
36: 4 Rabshakeh **s** unto them, Say ye now to 559
36: 7 **s** to Judah and to Jerusalem, Ye shall 559
36:10 the LORD **s** unto me, Go up against this 559
36:11 **s** Eliakim and Shebna and Joah unto 559
36:12 Rabshakeh **s**, Hath my master sent me to thy 559
36:13 **s**, Hear ye the words of the great king, 559
37: 3 they **s** unto him, Thus saith Hezekiah, 559
37: 6 Isaiah **s** unto them, Thus shall ye say unto 559
37:24 hast thou reproached the Lord, and hast **s**, 559
38: 1 **s** unto him, Thus saith the LORD, Set thine 559
38: 3 **s**, Remember now, O LORD, I beseech 559
38:10 I **s**, in the cutting off of my days, I shall go 559
38:11 I **s**, I shall not see the LORD, *even* 559
38:21 For Isaiah had **s**, Let them take a lump of 559
38:22 Hezekiah also had **s**, What *is* the sign that I 559
39: 3 and **s** unto him, What said these men? 559
39: 3 and said unto him, What **s** these men? 559
39: 3 Hezekiah **s**, They are come from a far 559
39: 4 **s** he, What have they seen in thine house? 559
39: 5 **s** Isaiah to Hezekiah, Hear the word of 559
39: 8 **s** Hezekiah to Isaiah, Good *is* the word of 559
39: 8 He **s** moreover, For there shall be peace and 559
40: 6 The voice **s**, Cry. And he said, What shall I 559
40: 6 he **s**, What shall I cry? All flesh *is* grass, 559
41: 6 *every one* **s** to his brother, Be of good 559
41: 9 and **s** unto thee, Thou *art* my servant; 559
45:19 I **s** not unto the seed of Jacob, Seek ye me in 559
47:10 thou hast **s**, None seeth me. Thy wisdom and 559
47:10 thou hast **s** in thine heart, I *am*, and none else 559
49: 3 **s** unto me, Thou *art* my servant, O Israel, 559
49: 4 I **s**, I have laboured in vain, I have spent my 559
49: 6 he **s**, It is a light thing that thou shouldest be 559
49:14 Zion **s**, The LORD hath forsaken me, and 559
51:23 which have **s** to thy soul, Bow down, that we 559
63: 8 For he **s**, Surely they *are* my people, 559
65: 1 I **s**, Behold me, behold me, unto a nation *that* 559
66: 5 name's sake, **s**, Let the LORD be glorified: 559
Jer 1: 6 **s** I, Ah, Lord GOD, behold, I cannot speak: 559
1: 7 the LORD **s** unto me, Say not, I *am* a child: 559
1: 9 the LORD **s** unto me, Behold, I have put 559
1:11 And I **s**, I see a rod of an almond tree. 559
1:12 **s** the LORD unto me, Thou hast well seen: 559
1:13 I **s**, I see a seething pot; and the face thereof 559
1:14 the LORD **s** unto me, Out of the north an 559
2: 6 Neither **s** they, Where *is* the LORD that 559
2: 8 The priests **s** not, Where *is* the LORD? and 559
3: 6 The LORD **s** also unto me in the days of 559
3: 7 I **s** after she had done all these *things*, Turn 559
3:11 the LORD **s** unto me, The backsliding 559
3:19 I **s**, How shall I put thee among the children, 559
3:19 I **s**, Thou shalt call me, My father; and 559
4:10 Then **s** I, Ah, Lord GOD! surely thou hast 559
4:11 At that time shall it be **s** to this people and 559
4:27 For thus hath the LORD **s**, The whole land 559
5: 4 Therefore I **s**, Surely these *are* poor; they are 559
5:12 have belied the LORD, and **s**, *It is* not he; 559
6: 6 For thus hath the LORD of hosts **s**, Hew ye 559
6:16 But they **s**, We will not walk *therein*. 559
6:17 the trumpet. But they **s**, We will not hearken. 559
10:19 I **s**, Truly this *is* a grief, and I must bear it. 559
11: 5 Then answered I, and **s**, So be it, O LORD. 559
11: 6 the LORD **s** unto me, Proclaim all these 559
11: 9 the LORD **s** unto me, A conspiracy is 559
12: 4 because they **s**, He shall not see our last end. 559
13: 6 that the LORD **s** unto me, Arise, go to 559
14:11 **s** the LORD unto me, Pray not for this 559
14:13 **s** I, Ah, Lord GOD! behold, the prophets 559
14:14 the LORD **s** unto me, The prophets 559
15: 1 Then **s** the LORD unto me, Though Moses 559
15:11 The LORD **s**, Verily it shall be well with 559
16:14 saith the LORD, that it shall no more be **s**, 559
17:19 Thus **s** the LORD unto me; Go and stand in 559
18:10 wherewith I **s** *I* would benefit them. 559
18:12 they **s**, There is no hope: but we will walk 559
18:18 **s** they, Come, and let us devise devices 559
19:14 the LORD'S house; and **s** to all the people, 559
20: 3 **s** Jeremiah unto him, The LORD hath not 559
20: 9 I **s**, I will not make mention of him, 559
21: 3 **s** Jeremiah unto them, Thus shall ye say to 559
23:17 The LORD hath **s**, Ye shall have peace; 1696
23:25 I have heard what the prophets **s**, 559
24: 3 **s** the LORD unto me, What seest thou, 559
24: 3 I **s**, Figs; the good figs, very good; and 559
25: 5 *They* **s**, Turn ye again now every one from 559
26:16 **s** the princes and all the people unto 559
28: 5 the prophet Jeremiah **s** unto the prophet 559
28: 6 Even the prophet Jeremiah **s**, Amen: 559
28:15 **s** the prophet Jeremiah unto Hananiah 559
29:15 Because ye have **s**, The LORD hath raised 559
32: 6 Jeremiah **s**, The word of the LORD came 559
32: 8 **s** unto me, Buy my field, I pray thee, that *is* 559
32:25 thou hast **s** unto me, O Lord GOD, 559
35: 5 and cups, and I **s** unto them, Drink ye wine. 559
35: 6 they **s**, We will drink no wine: for Jonadab 559
35:11 that we **s**, Come, and let us go *to* Jerusalem 559
35:18 Jeremiah **s** unto the house of the Rechabites, 559
36:15 they **s** unto him, Sit down now, and read it in 559
36:16 afraid both one and other, and **s** unto Baruch, 559
36:19 **s** the princes unto Baruch, Go, hide thee, 559
37:14 **s** Jeremiah, *It is* false; I fall not away to 559
37:17 and **s**, Is there *any* word from the LORD? 559
37:17 Jeremiah **s**, There is: for, said he, thou shalt 559
37:17 for, **s** he, thou shalt be delivered into 559
37:18 Moreover Jeremiah **s** unto king Zedekiah, 559
38: 4 Therefore the princes **s** unto the king, 559
38: 5 Zedekiah the king **s**, Behold, he *is* in your 559
38:12 Ebed-melech the Ethiopian **s** unto Jeremiah, 559
38:14 the king **s** unto Jeremiah, I *will* ask thee a 559
38:15 Jeremiah **s** unto Zedekiah, If I declare *it* unto 559
38:17 **s** Jeremiah unto Zedekiah, Thus saith 559
38:19 Zedekiah the king **s** unto Jeremiah, I am 559
38:20 Jeremiah **s**, They shall not deliver *thee*. 559
38:24 **s** Zedekiah unto Jeremiah, Let no man know 559
38:25 Declare unto us now what thou hast **s** unto 1696
38:25 to death; also what the king **s** unto thee: 1696
40: 2 of the guard took Jeremiah, and **s** unto him, 559
40: 3 brought *it*, and done according as he hath **s**: 1696
40: 5 *he s*, Go back also to Gedaliah the son of NIH
40:14 **s** unto him, Dost thou certainly know that 559
40:16 Gedaliah the son of Ahikam **s** unto Johanan 559
41: 6 to pass, as he met them, he **s** unto them, 559
41: 8 ten men were found among them that **s** unto 559
42: 2 **s** unto Jeremiah the prophet, Let, we beseech 559
42: 4 Jeremiah the prophet **s** unto them, I have 559
42: 5 they **s** to Jeremiah, The LORD be a true 559
42: 9 **s** unto them, Thus saith the LORD, the God 559
42:19 The LORD hath **s** concerning you, O ye 1696
44:20 Jeremiah **s** unto all the people, to the men, 559
44:24 Moreover Jeremiah **s** unto all the people, and 559
46:16 they **s**, Arise, and let us go again to our own 559
50: 7 their adversaries **s**, We offend not, because 559
51:61 Jeremiah **s** to Seraiah, When thou comest *to* 559
La 3:18 I **s**, My strength and my hope is perished 559
3:54 over mine head; *then* I **s**, I am cut off. 559
4:15 they **s** among the heathen, They shall no 559
4:20 was taken in their pits, *of* whom we **s**, 559
Eze 2: 1 he **s** unto me, Son of man, stand upon thy 559
2: 3 he **s** unto me, Son of man, I send thee to 559
3: 1 Moreover he **s** unto me, Son of man, eat that 559
3: 3 he **s** unto me, Son of man, cause thy belly to 559
3: 4 he **s** unto me, Son of man, go, get thee unto 559
3:10 Moreover he **s** unto me, Son of man, all my 559
3:22 he **s** unto me, Arise, go forth into the plain, 559
3:24 and spake with me, and **s** unto me, Go, 559
4:13 the LORD **s**, Even thus shall the children of 559
4:14 **s** I, Ah Lord GOD, behold, my soul *hath* 559
4:15 he **s** unto me, Lo, I have given thee cow's 559
4:16 Moreover he **s** unto me, Son of man, behold, 559
6:10 *that* I have not **s** in vain that *I* would do this 1696
8: 5 **s** he unto me, Son of man, lift up thine eyes 559
8: 6 He **s** furthermore unto me, Son of man, seest 559
8: 8 **s** he unto me, Son of man, dig now in 559
8: 9 he **s** unto me, Go in, and behold the wicked 559
8:12 **s** he unto me, Son of man, hast thou seen 559
8:13 He **s** also unto me, Turn thee yet again, *and* 559
8:15 **s** he unto me, Hast thou seen *this*, O son of 559
8:17 he **s** unto me, Hast thou seen *this*, O son of 559
9: 4 the LORD **s** unto him, Go through 559
9: 5 to the others he **s** in mine hearing, Go ye 559
9: 7 he **s** unto them, Defile the house, and fill 559
9: 8 my face, and cried, and **s**, Ah Lord GOD, 559
9: 9 **s** he unto me, The iniquity of the house of 559
10: 2 **s**, Go in between the wheels, *even* under 559
11: 2 **s** he unto me, Son of man, these *are* the men 559
11: 5 LORD fell upon me, and **s** unto me, Speak; 559
11: 5 Thus have ye **s**, O house of Israel: 559
11:13 *with* a loud voice, and **s**, Ah Lord GOD, 559
11:15 whom the inhabitants of Jerusalem have **s**, 559
12: 9 **s** unto thee, What doest thou? 559
13:12 the wall is fallen, shall it not be **s** unto you, 559
16: 6 I **s** unto thee *when thou wast* in thy blood, 559
16: 6 I **s** unto thee *when thou wast* in thy blood, 559
20: 7 **s** I unto them, Cast ye away every man 559
20: 8 I **s**, *I* will pour out my fury upon them, 559
20:13 I **s**, *I* would pour out my fury upon them in 559
20:18 But I **s** unto their children in the wilderness, 559
20:21 I **s**, *I* would pour out my fury upon them, 559
20:29 I **s** unto them, What *is* the high place 559
20:49 **s** I, Ah Lord GOD, they say of me, Doth he 559
21:17 my fury to rest: I the LORD have **s** *it*. 1696
23:36 The LORD **s** moreover unto me; Son of 559
23:43 **s** I unto *her that was* old *in* adulteries, 559
24:19 the people **s** unto me, Wilt thou not tell us 559
26: 2 because that Tyrus hath **s** against Jerusalem, 559
27: 3 O Tyrus, thou hast **s**, I *am* of perfect beauty. 559
28: 2 thou hast **s**, I *am* a God, I sit *in* the seat of 559
29: 3 which hath **s**, My river *is* mine own, and 559
29: 9 because he hath **s**, The river *is* mine, and 559
35:10 Because thou hast **s**, These two nations and 559
36: 2 Because the enemy hath **s** against you, Aha, 559
36:20 my holy name, when *they* **s** to them, 559
37: 3 he **s** unto me, Son of man, can these bones 559
37: 4 Again he **s** unto me, Prophesy upon these 559
37: 9 Then **s** he unto me, Prophesy unto the wind, 559
37:11 he **s** unto me, Son of man, these bones *are* 559
40: 4 the man **s** unto me, Son of man, 1696
40:45 he **s** unto me, This chamber, 1696
41: 4 he **s** unto me, This *is* the most holy *place*. 559
41:22 he **s** unto me, This *is* the table that *is* before 1696
42:13 Then **s** he unto me, The north chambers *and* 559
43: 7 he **s** unto me, Son of man, the place of my 559
43:18 he **s** unto me, Son of man, thus saith 559
44: 2 **s** the LORD unto me; This gate shall be 559
44: 5 the LORD **s** unto me, Son of man, 559
46:20 **s** he unto me, This *is* the place where 559
46:24 **s** he unto me, These *are* the places of them 559
47: 6 he **s** unto me, Son of man, hast thou seen 559
47: 8 **s** he unto me, These waters issue out toward 559
Da 1:10 And the prince of the eunuchs **s** unto Daniel, 559
1:11 **s** Daniel to Melzar, whom the prince of 559
1:18 that the king had **s** *he* should bring them in, 559
2: 3 the king **s** unto them, I have dreamed a 559
2: 5 The king answered and **s** to the Chaldeans, 560
2: 7 They answered again and **s**, Let the king tell 560
2: 8 The king answered and **s**, I know of certainty 560
2:10 Chaldeans answered before the king, and **s**, 560
2:15 and **s** to Arioch the king's captain, 560
Da 2:20 Daniel answered and **s**, Blessed be the name 560
2:24 he went and **s** thus unto him; Destroy not 560
2:25 **s** thus unto him, I have found a man of 560
2:26 The king answered and **s** to Daniel, 560
2:27 answered in the presence of the king, and **s**, 560
2:47 The king answered unto Daniel, and **s**, Of a 560
3: 9 and **s** to the king Nebuchadnezzar, 560
3:14 Nebuchadnezzar spake and **s** unto them, *Is it* 560
3:16 and Abed-nego, answered and **s** to the king, 560
3:24 *and* spake, and **s** unto his counsellers, 560
3:24 They answered and **s** unto the king, True, O 560
3:25 He answered and **s**, Lo, I see four men loose, 560
3:26 *and* spake, and **s**, Shadrach, Meshach, and 560
3:28 *Then* Nebuchadnezzar spake, and **s**, 560
4:14 He cried aloud, and **s** thus, Hew down 560
4:19 The king spake, and **s**, Belteshazzar, let not 560
4:19 Belteshazzar answered and **s**, My lord, 560
4:30 The king spake, and **s**, *Is* not this great 560
5: 7 and **s** to the wise *men* of Babylon, 560
5:10 *and* the queen spake and **s**, O king, live for 560
5:13 *And* the king spake and **s** unto Daniel, 560
5:17 Then Daniel answered and **s** before the king, 560
6: 5 **s** these men, We shall not find any occasion 560
6: 6 **s** thus unto him, King Darius, live for ever. 560
6:12 The king answered and **s**, The thing *is* true, 560
6:13 answered they and **s** before the king, 560
6:15 **s** unto the king, Know, O king, that the law 560
6:16 *Now* the king spake and **s** unto Daniel, 560
6:20 *and* the king spake and **s** to Daniel, 560
6:21 **s** Daniel unto the king, O king, live for 4449
7: 2 Daniel spake and **s**, I saw in my vision by 560
7: 5 they **s** thus unto it, Arise, devour much flesh. 560
7:23 Thus he **s**, The fourth beast shall be 560
8:13 another saint **s** unto that certain *saint* which 559
8:14 he **s** unto me, Unto two thousand and 559
8:16 which called, and **s**, Gabriel, make this *man* 559
8:17 but he **s** unto me, Understand, O son of man: 559
8:19 he **s**, Behold, I *will* make thee know what 559
9: 4 and **s**, O Lord, the great and dreadful God, 559
9:22 and talked with me, and **s**, O Daniel, 559
10:11 he **s** unto me, O Daniel, a man greatly 559
10:12 **s** he unto me, Fear not, Daniel: for from 559
10:16 spake, and **s** unto him that stood before me, 559
10:19 **s**, O man greatly beloved, fear not: peace *be* 559
10:19 was strengthened, and **s**, Let my lord speak; 559
10:20 **s** he, Knowest thou wherefore I come unto 559
12: 6 *one* **s** to the man clothed in linen, which *was* 559
12: 8 **s** I, O my lord, what *shall be* the end of 559
12: 9 he **s**, Go thy way, Daniel: for the words *are* 559
Hos 1: 2 the LORD **s** to Hosea, Go, take unto thee a 559
1: 4 the LORD **s** unto him, Call his name 559
1: 6 *God* **s** unto him, Call her name Lo-ruhamah: 559
1: 9 **s** *God*, Call his name Lo-ammi: for ye *are* 559
1:10 *that* in the place where it was **s** unto them, 559
1:10 not my people, *there* it shall be **s** unto them, 559
2: 5 for she **s**, I will go after my lovers, that give 559
2:12 and her fig trees, where*of* she hath **s**, 559
3: 1 **s** the LORD unto me, Go yet, love a 559
3: 3 I **s** unto her, Thou shalt abide for me many 559
12: 8 Ephraim **s**, Yet I am become rich, I have 559
Joel 2:32 as the LORD hath **s**, and in the remnant 559
Am 1: 2 he **s**, The LORD will roar from Zion, and 559
7: 2 I **s**, O Lord GOD, forgive, I beseech thee: 559
7: 5 **s** I, O Lord GOD, cease, I beseech thee: 559
7: 8 the LORD **s** unto me, Amos, what seest 559
7: 8 I **s**, A plumbline. Then said the Lord, 559
7: 8 **s** the Lord, Behold, I *will* set a plumbline in 559
7:12 Also Amaziah **s** unto Amos, O thou seer, go, 559
7:14 and **s** to Amaziah, I *was* no prophet, 559
7:15 the LORD **s** unto me, Go, prophesy unto 559
8: 2 he **s**, Amos, what seest thou? And I said, 559
8: 2 I **s**, A basket of summer fruit. Then said 559
8: 2 **s** the LORD unto me, The end is come 559
9: 1 he **s**, Smite the lintel of the door, that 559
Jnh 1: 6 **s** unto him, What meanest thou, O sleeper? 559
1: 7 they **s** every one to his fellow, Come, and 559
1: 8 Then **s** they unto him, Tell us, we pray thee, 559
1: 9 he **s** unto them, I *am* a Hebrew; and I fear 559
1:10 **s** unto him, Why hast thou done this? 559
1:11 **s** they unto him, What shall we do unto thee, 559
1:12 he **s** unto them, Take me up, and cast me 559
1:14 **s**, We beseech thee, O LORD, we beseech 559
2: 2 **s**, I cried by reason of mine affliction unto 559
2: 4 I **s**, I am cast out of thy sight; yet I will look 559
3: 4 he cried, and **s**, Yet forty days, and 559
3:10 that he had **s** that he would do unto them; 1696
4: 2 **s**, I pray thee, O LORD, *was* not this my 559
4: 4 **s** the LORD, Doest thou well to be angry? 559
4: 8 and wished in himself to die, and **s**, 559
4: 9 God **s** to Jonah, Doest thou well to be angry 559
4: 9 he **s**, I do well to be angry, *even* unto death. 559
4:10 **s** the LORD, Thou hast had pity on 559
Mic 3: 1 And I **s**, Hear, I pray you, O heads of Jacob, 559
7:10 and shame shall cover her which **s** unto me, 559
Hab 2: 2 **s**, Write the vision, and make *it* plain upon 559
Zep 2:15 that **s** in her heart, I *am*, and *there is* none 559
3: 7 I **s**, Surely thou wilt fear me, thou wilt 559
3:16 In that day it shall be **s** to Jerusalem, 559
Hag 2:12 be holy? And the priests answered and **s**, No. 559
2:13 **s** Haggai, If *one that is* unclean *by* a dead 559
2:13 the priests answered and **s**, It shall be 559
2:14 **s**, So *is* this people, and so *is* this nation 559
Zec 1: 6 they returned and **s**, Like as the LORD of 559
1: 9 **s** I, O my lord, what *are* these? And 559
1: 9 And the angel that talked with me **s** unto me, 559
1:10 among the myrtle trees answered and **s**, 559
1:11 **s**, We have walked to and fro through 559
1:12 the angel of the LORD answered and **s**, 559
1:14 So the angel that communed with me **s** unto 559
1:19 I **s** unto the angel that talked with me, 559
1:21 **s** I, What come these to do? And he spake, 559
2: 2 **s** I, Whither goest thou? And he said unto 559
2: 2 he **s** unto me, To measure Jerusalem, to see 559
2: 4 **s** unto him, Run, speak to this young man, 559
3: 2 the LORD **s** unto Satan, The LORD 559

S

Zec 3: 4 unto him he **s**, Behold, I have caused thine 559
3: 5 I **s**, Let them set a fair mitre upon his head. 559
4: 2 And **s** unto me, What seest thou? And I said, 559
4: 2 I **s**, I have looked, and behold, a candlestick 559
4: 5 that talked with me answered and **s** unto me, 559
4: 5 Knowest thou not what these *be?* And I **s**, 559
4:11 answered I, and **s** unto him, What *are* these 559
4:12 I answered again, and **s** unto him, What *be* 559
4:13 he answered me and **s**, Knowest thou not 559
4:13 Knowest thou not what these *be?* And I **s**, 559
4:14 Then **s** he, These *are* the two anointed ones, 559
5: 2 he **s** unto me, What seest thou? And I 559
5: 3 **s** he unto me, This *is* the curse that goeth 559
5: 5 **s** unto me, Lift up now thine eyes, and 559
5: 6 I **s**, What *is* it? And he said, This *is* an ephah 559
5: 6 he **s**, This *is* an ephah that goeth forth. 559
5: 6 He **s** moreover, This *is* their resemblance 559
5: 8 he **s**, This *is* wickedness. And he cast it into 559
5:10 **s** I to the angel that talked with me, 559
5:11 he **s** unto me, To build it a house in the land 559
6: 4 and **s** unto the angel that talked with me, 559
6: 5 the angel answered and **s** unto me, These *are* 559
6: 7 he **s**, Get ye *hence,* walk to and fro through 559
11: 9 **s** I, I will not feed you: that that dieth, let it 559
11:12 I **s** unto them, If ye think good, give *me* my 559
11:13 the LORD **s** unto me, Cast it unto 559
11:15 the LORD **s** unto me, Take unto thee yet 559
Mal 1:13 Ye **s** also, Behold, what a weariness *is it!* 559
3: 7 of hosts. But ye **s**, Wherein shall we return? 559
3:14 Ye have **s**, It *is* vain to serve God: and 559
Mt 2: 5 And they **s** unto him, In Bethlehem of 3004
2: 8 and **s**, Go and search diligently for 3004
3: 7 he **s** unto them, O generation of vipers, 3004
3:15 And Jesus answering **s** unto him, Suffer *it* 3004
4: 3 to him, he **s**, If thou be the Son of God, 3004
4: 4 But he answered and **s**, It is written, Man 3004
4: 7 Jesus **s** unto him, It is written again, 5346
5:21 Ye have heard that it was **s** by them of old 3004
5:27 Ye have heard that it was **s** by them of old 3004
5:31 It hath been **s**, Whosoever shall put away 3004
5:33 ye have heard that it hath been **s** by them of 3004
5:38 Ye have heard that it hath been **s**, An eye 3004
5:43 Ye have heard that it hath been **s**, 3004
8: 8 The centurion answered and **s**, Lord, I am 5346
8:10 and **s** to them that followed, Verily I say 3004
8:13 And Jesus **s** unto the centurion, Go thy 3004
8:19 scribe came, and **s** unto him, Master, 3004
8:21 And another of his disciples **s** unto him, 3004
8:22 But Jesus **s** unto him, Follow me; and 3004
8:32 And he **s** unto them, Go. And when they 3004
9: 2 Jesus seeing their faith **s** unto the sick of 3004
9: 3 certain of the scribes **s** within themselves, 3004
9: 4 And Jesus knowing their thoughts **s**, 3004
9:11 And when the Pharisees saw *it,* they **s** unto 3004
9:12 But when Jesus heard *that,* he **s** unto them, 3004
9:15 And Jesus **s** unto them, Can the children of 3004
9:21 For she **s** within herself, If I may but 3004
9:22 and when he saw her, he **s**, Daughter, be of 3004
9:24 He **s** unto them, Give place: for the maid is 3004
9:28 to do this? They **s** unto him, Yea, Lord. 3004
9:34 But the Pharisees **s**, He casteth out 3004
11: 3 And **s** unto him, Art thou he that should 3004
11: 4 Jesus answered and **s** unto them, Go and 3004
11:25 At that time Jesus answered and **s**, I thank 3004
12: 2 But when the Pharisees saw *it,* they **s** unto 3004
12: 3 But he **s** unto them, Have ye not read what 3004
12:11 And he **s** unto them, What man shall there 3004
12:23 and **s**, Is this the son of David? 3004
12:24 But when the Pharisees heard *it,* they **s**, 3004
12:25 Jesus knew their thoughts, and **s** unto them, 3004
12:39 But he answered and **s** to them, An evil and 3004
12:47 Then one **s** unto him, Behold, thy mother 3004
12:48 he answered and **s** unto him that told him, 3004
12:49 and **s**, Behold my mother and my brethren. 3004
13:10 And the disciples came, and **s** unto him, 3004
13:11 He answered and **s** unto them, Because it is 3004
13:27 of the householder came and **s** unto him, 3004
13:28 He **s** unto them, An enemy hath done this. 5346
13:28 The servants **s** unto him, Wilt thou then 3004
13:29 But he **s**, Nay; lest while ye gather up 5346
13:37 He answered and **s** unto them, He that 3004
13:52 Then **s** he unto them, Therefore every 3004
13:54 and **s**, Whence hath this *man* this wisdom, 3004
13:57 But Jesus **s** unto them, A prophet is not 3004
14: 2 And **s** unto his servants, This is John 3004
14: 4 For John **s** unto him, It is not lawful for 3004
14: 8 being before instructed of her mother, **s**, 5346
14:16 But Jesus **s** unto them, They need not 3004
14:18 He **s**, Bring them hither to me. 3004
14:28 And Peter answered him and **s**, Lord, if it 3004
14:29 And he **s**, Come. And when Peter was 3004
14:31 and caught him, and **s** unto him, O thou of 3004
15: 3 But he answered and **s** unto them, Why do 3004
15:10 and **s** unto them, Hear, and understand: 3004
15:12 Then came his disciples, and **s** unto him, 3004
15:13 But he answered and **s**, Every plant, 3004
15:15 Then answered Peter and **s** unto him, 3004
15:16 And Jesus **s**, Are ye also yet without 3004
15:24 But he answered and **s**, I am not sent but 3004
15:26 But he answered and **s**, It is not meet to 3004
15:27 And she **s**, Truth, Lord: yet the dogs eat of 3004
15:28 Then Jesus answered and **s** unto her, 3004
15:32 Jesus called his disciples unto *him,* and **s**, 3004
15:34 And they **s**, Seven, and a few little fishes. 3004
16: 2 He answered and **s** unto them, When it is 3004
16: 6 Then Jesus **s** unto them, Take heed and 3004
16: 8 he **s** unto them, O ye of little faith, 3004
16:14 And they **s**, Some *say that thou art* John 3004
16:16 And Simon Peter answered and **s**, Thou art 3004
16:17 And Jesus answered and **s** unto him, 3004
16:23 But he turned, and **s** unto Peter, Get thee 3004
16:24 Then **s** Jesus unto his disciples, If any *man* 3004
17: 4 answered Peter, and **s** unto Jesus, Lord, 3004
17: 5 which **s**, This is my beloved Son, in whom 3004
17: 7 and **s**, Arise, and be not afraid. 3004

Mt 17:11 And Jesus answered and **s** unto them, 3004
17:17 Then Jesus answered and **s**, O faithless and 3004
17:19 and **s**, Why could not we cast him out? 3004
17:20 And Jesus **s** unto them, Because of your 3004
17:22 they abode in Galilee, Jesus **s** unto them, 3004
17:24 and **s**, Doth not your master pay tribute? 3004
18: 3 And **s**, Verily I say unto you, Except ye be 3004
18:21 Then came Peter to him, and **s**, Lord, 3004
18:32 **s** unto him, O *thou* wicked servant, 3004
19: 4 And he answered and **s** unto them, Have ye 3004
19: 5 And **s**, For this cause shall a man leave 3004
19:11 But he **s** unto them, All *men* cannot receive 3004
19:14 But Jesus **s**, Suffer little children, and 3004
19:16 And behold, one came and **s** unto him, 3004
19:17 And he **s** unto him, Why callest thou me 3004
19:18 Jesus **s**, Thou shalt do no murder, 3004
19:21 Jesus **s** unto him, If thou wilt be perfect, go 5346
19:23 Then **s** Jesus unto his disciples, Verily I say 3004
19:26 But Jesus beheld *them,* and **s** unto them, 3004
19:27 Then answered Peter and **s** unto him, 3004
19:28 And Jesus **s** unto them, Verily I say unto 3004
20: 4 And **s** unto them; Go ye also into 3004
20:13 of them, and **s**, Friend, I do thee no wrong: 3004
20:17 disciples apart in the way, and **s** unto them, 3004
20:21 And he **s** unto her, What wilt thou? 3004
20:22 But Jesus answered and **s**, Ye know not 3004
20:25 But Jesus called them unto *him,* and **s**, 3004
20:32 Jesus stood still, and called them, and **s**, 3004
21:11 And the multitude **s**, This is Jesus 3004
21:13 And **s** unto them, It is written, My house 3004
21:16 And **s** unto him, Hearest thou what these 3004
21:19 but leaves only, and **s** unto it, 3004
21:21 Jesus answered and **s** unto them, Verily I 3004
21:23 and **s**, By what authority doest thou these 3004
21:24 And Jesus answered and **s** unto them, I also 3004
21:27 they answered Jesus, and **s**, We cannot tell. 3004
21:27 And he **s** unto them, Neither tell I you by 5346
21:28 and he came to the first, and **s**, Son, 3004
21:29 He answered and **s**, I will not: but 3004
21:30 And he came to the second, and **s** likewise. 3004
21:30 And he answered and **s**, I *go,* sir: and 3004
21:38 they **s** among themselves, This is the heir; 3004
22: 1 spake unto them again by parables, and **s**, 3004
22:13 Then **s** the king to the servants, Bind him 3004
22:18 and **s**, Why tempt ye me, *ye* hypocrites? 3004
22:24 Saying, Master, Moses **s**, If a man die, 3004
22:29 Jesus answered and **s** unto them, Ye do err, 3004
22:37 Jesus **s** unto him, Thou shalt love the Lord 3004
22:44 The LORD **s** unto my Lord, Sit thou on my 3004
24: 2 And Jesus **s** unto them, See ye not all these 3004
24: 4 And Jesus answered and **s** unto them, 3004
25: 8 And the foolish **s** unto the wise, Give us of 3004
25:12 But he answered and **s**, Verily I say unto 3004
25:21 His lord **s** unto him, Well *done, thou* good 5346
25:22 that had received two talents came and **s**, 3004
25:23 His lord **s** unto him, Well *done,* good and 5346
25:24 had received the one talent came and **s**, 3004
25:26 His lord answered and **s** unto him, 3004
26: 1 all these sayings, he **s** unto his disciples, 3004
26: 5 But they **s**, Not on the feast *day,* lest there 3004
26:10 When Jesus understood *it,* he **s** unto them, 3004
26:15 And **s** *unto them,* What will ye give me, 3004
26:18 And he **s**, Go into the city to such a man, 3004
26:21 And as they did eat, he **s**, Verily I say unto 3004
26:23 And he answered and **s**, He that dippeth *his* 3004
26:25 answered and **s**, Master, is it I? 3004
26:25 is it I? He **s** unto him, Thou hast said. 3004
26:25 is it I? He said unto him, Thou hast **s**. 3004
26:26 gave *it* to the disciples, and **s**, Take, eat; 3004
26:33 Peter answered and **s** unto him, Though all 3004
26:34 Jesus **s** unto him, Verily I say unto thee, 5346
26:35 Peter **s** unto him, Though I should die with 3004
26:35 deny thee. Likewise also **s** all the disciples. 3004
26:49 he came to Jesus, and **s**, Hail, master; 3004
26:50 And Jesus **s** unto him, Friend, wherefore art 3004
26:52 Then **s** Jesus unto him, Put up again thy 3004
26:55 In that *same* hour **s** Jesus to the multitudes, 3004
26:61 And **s**, This *fellow* said, I am able to 3004
26:61 And said, This *fellow* **s**, I am able to 5346
26:62 and **s** unto him, Answerest thou nothing? 3004
26:63 the high priest answered and **s** unto him, 3004
26:64 Jesus saith unto him, Thou hast **s**: 3004
26:66 They answered and **s**, He is guilty of death. 3004
26:71 saw him, and **s** unto them that were there, 3004
26:73 unto *him* they that stood *by,* and **s** to Peter, 3004
26:75 which **s** unto him, Before the cock crow, 3004
27: 4 And they **s**, What *is that* to us? see thou *to* 3004
27: 6 chief priests took the silver pieces, and **s**, 3004
27:11 And Jesus **s** unto him, Thou sayest. 5346
27:13 Then **s** Pilate unto him, Hearest thou not 3004
27:17 Pilate **s** unto them, Whom will ye *that* I 3004
27:21 The governor answered and **s** unto them, 3004
27:21 *that* I release unto you? They **s**, Barabbas. 3004
27:23 And the governor **s**, Why, what evil hath he 5346
27:25 and **s**, His blood *be* on us, and on our 3004
27:41 mocking *him,* with the scribes and elders, **s**, 3004
27:43 have him: for he **s**, I am the Son of God. 3004
27:47 when they heard *that,* **s**, This *man* calleth 3004
27:49 The rest **s**, Let be, let us see whether Elias 3004
27:63 Sir, we remember that that deceiver **s**, 3004
27:65 Pilate **s** unto them, Ye have a watch: 5346
28: 5 the angel answered and **s** unto the women, 3004
28: 6 for he is risen, as he **s**. Come, see the place 3004
28:10 Then **s** Jesus unto them, Be not afraid: 3004
Mk 1:17 And Jesus **s** unto them, Come ye after me, 3004
1:37 they **s** unto him, All *men* seek for thee. 3004
1:38 And he **s** unto them, Let us go into the next 3004
2: 5 he **s** unto the sick of the palsy, Son, thy sins 3004
2: 8 within themselves, he **s** unto them, 3004
2:14 of custom, and **s** unto him, Follow me. 3004
2:16 and sinners, they **s** unto his disciples, 3004
2:19 And Jesus **s** unto them, Can the children of 3004
2:24 And the Pharisees **s** unto him, Behold, 3004
2:25 And he **s** unto them, Have ye never read 3004
2:27 And he **s** unto them, The sabbath was made 3004

Mk 3:21 on him: for they **s**, He is beside himself. 3004
3:22 which came down from Jerusalem **s**, 3004
3:23 them unto *him,* and **s** unto them in parables, 3004
3:30 Because they **s**, He hath an unclean spirit. 3004
3:32 and they **s** unto him, Behold, thy mother 3004
3:34 and **s**, Behold my mother and my brethren. 3004
4: 2 and **s** unto them in his doctrine, 3004
4: 9 And he **s** unto them, He that hath ears to 3004
4:11 And he **s** unto them, Unto you it is given to 3004
4:13 And he **s** unto them, Know ye not this 3004
4:21 And he **s** unto them, Is a candle brought to 3004
4:24 And he **s** unto them, Take heed what you 3004
4:26 And he **s**, So is the kingdom of God, as if a 3004
4:30 And he **s**, Whereunto shall we liken 3004
4:39 the wind, and **s** unto the sea, Peace, be still. 3004
4:40 And he **s** unto them, Why are ye so 3004
4:41 and **s** one to another, What *manner of* man 3004
5: 7 and **s**, What have I to do with thee, Jesus, 3004
5: 8 For he **s** unto him, Come out of the man, 3004
5:28 For she **s**, If I may touch but his clothes, 3004
5:30 the press, and **s**, Who touched my clothes? 3004
5:31 And his disciples **s** unto him, Thou seest 3004
5:34 And he **s** unto her, Daughter, thy faith hath 3004
5:35 of the synagogue's *house certain* which **s**, 3004
5:41 the hand, and **s** unto her, TALITHA CUMI; 3004
6: 4 But Jesus **s** unto them, A prophet is not 3004
6:10 And he **s** unto them, In what place soever 3004
6:14 and he **s**, That John the Baptist was risen 3004
6:15 Others **s**, That it is Elias. And others said, 3004
6:15 And others **s**, That it is a prophet, or as one 3004
6:16 But when Herod heard *thereof,* he **s**, It is 3004
6:18 For John had **s** unto Herod, It is not lawful 3004
6:22 And when the daughter of **the s** Herodias 846
6:22 them that sat with *him,* the king **s** unto 3004
6:24 and **s** unto her mother, What shall I ask? 3004
6:24 And she **s**, The head of John the Baptist. 3004
6:31 And he **s** unto them, Come ye yourselves 3004
6:35 and **s**, *This* is a desert place, and now 3004
6:37 He answered and **s** unto them, Give ye 3004
7: 6 He answered and **s** unto them, Well hath 3004
7: 9 And he **s** unto them, Full well ye reject 3004
7:10 For Moses **s**, Honour thy father and 3004
7:14 all the people unto *him,* he **s** unto them, 3004
7:20 And he **s**, That which cometh out of 3004
7:27 But Jesus **s** unto her, Let the children first 3004
7:28 And she answered and **s** unto him, Yes, 3004
7:29 And he **s** unto her, For this saying go thy 3004
8: 5 many loaves have ye? And they **s**, Seven. 3004
8:20 fragments took ye up? And they **s**, Seven. 3004
8:21 And he **s** unto them, How *is it that* ye do 3004
8:24 and **s**, I see men as trees, walking. 3004
8:34 he **s** unto them, Whosoever will come after 3004
9: 1 And he **s** unto them, Verily I say unto you, 3004
9: 5 And Peter answered and **s** to Jesus, Master, 3004
9:17 And one of the multitude answered and **s**, 3004
9:21 this came unto him? And he **s**, Of a child. 3004
9:23 Jesus **s** unto him, If thou canst believe, 3004
9:24 cried out, and **s** with tears, Lord, I believe; 3004
9:26 insomuch that many **s**, He is dead. 3004
9:29 And he **s** unto them, This kind can come 3004
9:31 he taught his disciples, and **s** unto them, 3004
9:36 had taken him in his arms, he **s** unto them, 3004
9:39 But Jesus **s**, Forbid him not: for there is no 3004
10: 3 And he answered and **s** unto them, 3004
10: 4 And they **s**, Moses suffered to write a bill 3004
10: 5 And Jesus answered and **s** unto them, 3004
10:14 and **s** unto them, Suffer the little children to 3004
10:18 And Jesus **s** unto him, Why callest thou me 3004
10:20 And he answered and **s** unto him, Master, 3004
10:21 and **s** unto him, One *thing* thou lackest: 3004
10:29 And Jesus answered and **s**, Verily I say 3004
10:36 And he **s** unto them, What would ye that I 3004
10:37 They **s** unto him, Grant unto us that we 3004
10:38 But Jesus **s** unto them, Ye know not what 3004
10:39 And they **s** unto him, We can. And Jesus 3004
10:39 And Jesus **s** unto them, Ye shall indeed 3004
10:51 And Jesus answered and **s** unto him, 3004
10:51 The blind man **s** unto him, Lord, that I 3004
10:52 And Jesus **s** unto him, Go thy way; 3004
11: 5 And certain of them that stood there **s** unto 3004
11: 6 And they **s** unto them even as Jesus had 3004
11:14 And Jesus answered and **s** unto it, No *man* 3004
11:29 And Jesus answered and **s** unto them, I will 3004
11:33 And they answered and **s** unto Jesus, 3004
12: 7 But those husbandmen **s** amongst 3004
12:15 **s** unto them, Why tempt ye me? 3004
12:16 And they **s** unto him, Cesar's. 3004
12:17 And Jesus answering **s** unto them, 3004
12:24 And Jesus answering **s** unto them, Do ye 3004
12:32 And the scribe **s** unto him, Well, Master, 3004
12:32 Well, Master, thou hast **s** the truth: 3004
12:34 he **s** unto him, Thou art not far from 3004
12:35 And Jesus answered and **s**, while he taught 3004
12:36 For David himself **s** by the Holy Ghost, 3004
12:36 The LORD **s** to my Lord, Sit thou on my 3004
12:38 And he **s** unto them in his doctrine, 3004
13: 2 And Jesus answering **s** unto him, Seest thou 3004
14: 2 But they **s**, Not on the feast *day,* lest there 3004
14: 4 and **s**, Why was this waste of the ointment 3004
14: 6 And Jesus **s**, Let her alone; why trouble you 3004
14:12 his disciples **s** unto him, Where wilt thou 3004
14:16 the city, and found as he had **s** unto them: 3004
14:18 And as they sat and did eat, Jesus **s**, 3004
14:19 one by one, *Is* it I? and another **s**, *Is* it I? NIG
14:20 And he answered and **s** unto them, *It is* one 3004
14:22 brake *it,* and gave to them, and **s**, Take, eat: 3004
14:24 And he **s** unto them, This is my blood of 3004
14:29 But Peter **s** unto him, Although all shall be 5346
14:31 thee in any wise. Likewise also **s** they all. 3004
14:36 And he **s**, Abba, Father, all *things are* 3004
14:48 And Jesus answered and **s** unto them, 3004
14:61 and **s** unto him, Art thou the Christ, the Son 3004
14:62 And Jesus **s**, I am: and ye shall see the Son 3004
14:67 she looked upon him, and **s**, 3004
14:70 they that stood by **s** again to Peter, 3004

S

Mk 14:72 to mind the word that Jesus s unto him, 3004
15: 2 And he answering s unto him, Thou sayest 3004
15:12 And Pilate answered and s again unto them, 3004
15:14 Then Pilate s unto them, Why, what evil 3004
15:31 Likewise also the chief priests mocking s 3004
15:35 when they heard *it*, s, Behold, he calleth 3004
15:39 so cried out, and gave up the ghost, he s, 3004
16: 3 And they s among themselves, Who shall 3004
16: 7 there shall ye see him, as he s unto you. 3004
16: 8 neither s they any *thing* to any *man*; for 3004
16:15 And he s unto them, Go ye into all 3004
Lk 1:13 But the angel s unto him, Fear not, 3004
1:18 And Zacharias s unto the angel, 3004
1:19 And the angel answering s unto him, I am 3004
1:28 and s, Hail, *thou that art* highly favoured, 3004
1:30 And the angel s unto her, Fear not, Mary: 3004
1:34 Then s Mary unto the angel, How shall this 3004
1:35 And the angel answered and s unto her, 3004
1:38 And Mary s, Behold the handmaid of 3004
1:42 and s, Blessed *art* thou among women, and 3004
1:46 And Mary s, My soul doth magnify 3004
1:60 And his mother answered and s, Not *so*; but 3004
1:61 And they s unto her, There is none of thy 3004
2:10 And the angel s unto them, Fear not: 3004
2:15 the shepherds s one to another, Let us now 3004
2:24 to that which is s in the law of the Lord, 3004
2:28 him *up* in his arms, and blessed God, and s, 3004
2:34 and s unto Mary his mother, Behold, 3004
2:48 and his mother s unto him, Son, why hast 3004
2:49 And he s unto them, How *is it* that ye 3004
3: 7 Then s he to the multitude that came forth 3004
3:12 and s unto him, Master, what shall we do? 3004
3:13 And he s unto them, Exact no more than 3004
3:14 And he s unto them, Do violence to no 3004
3:22 which s, Thou art my beloved Son; 3004
4: 3 And the devil s unto him, If thou be the Son 3004
4: 6 And the devil s unto him, All this power 3004
4: 8 And Jesus answered and s unto him, 3004
4: 9 and s unto him, If thou be the Son of God, 3004
4:12 And Jesus answering s unto him, It is said, 3004
4:12 And Jesus answering said unto him, It is s, 3004
4:22 And they s, Is not this Joseph's son? 3004
4:23 And he s unto them, Ye will surely say 3004
4:24 And he s, Verily I say unto you, No prophet 3004
4:43 And he s unto them, I must preach 3004
5: 4 he s unto Simon, Launch out into the deep, 3004
5: 5 And Simon answering s unto him, Master, 3004
5:10 And Jesus s unto Simon, Fear not; 3004
5:20 he s unto him, Man, thy sins are forgiven 3004
5:22 he answering s unto them, What reason ye 3004
5:24 (he s unto the sick of the palsy,) 3004
5:27 of custom: and he s unto him, Follow me. 3004
5:31 And Jesus answering s unto them, 3004
5:33 And they s unto him, Why do the disciples 3004
5:34 And he s unto them, Can ye make 3004
6: 2 And certain of the Pharisees s unto them, 3004
6: 3 And Jesus answering them s, Have ye not 3004
6: 5 And he s unto them, That the Son of man is 3004
6: 8 s to the man which had the withered hand, 3004
6: 9 Then s Jesus unto them, I will ask you one 3004
6:10 he s unto the man, Stretch forth thy hand. 3004
6:20 on his disciples, and s, Blessed *be ye* poor: 3004
7: 9 and s unto the people that followed him, 3004
7:13 on her, and s unto her, Weep not. 3004
7:14 And he s, Young man, I say unto thee, 3004
7:20 they s, John Baptist hath sent us unto thee, 3004
7:22 Then Jesus answering s unto them, Go *your* 3004
7:31 And the Lord s, Whereunto then shall I 3004
7:40 And Jesus answering s unto him, Simon, 3004
7:43 Simon answered and s, I suppose that *he*, to 3004
7:43 And he s unto him, Thou hast rightly 3004
7:44 and s unto Simon, Seest thou this woman? 5346
7:48 And he s unto her, Thy sins are forgiven. 3004
7:50 And he s to the woman, Thy faith hath 3004
8: 8 And when he s these *things*, he cried, 3004
8:10 And he s, Unto you it is given to know 3004
8:20 And it was told him *by certain* which s, 3004
8:21 And he answered and s unto them, 3004
8:22 and he s unto them, Let us go over unto 3004
8:25 And he s unto them, Where is your faith? 3004
8:28 down before him, and with a loud voice s, 3004
8:30 And he s, Legion: because many devils 3004
8:45 And Jesus s, Who touched me? When all 3004
8:45 Peter and they that were with him s, 3004
8:46 And Jesus s, Somebody hath touched me: 3004
8:48 And he s unto her, Daughter, be of good 3004
8:52 but he s, Weep not; she is not dead, but 3004
9: 3 And he s unto them, Take nothing for *your* 3004
9: 7 because that it was s of some, 3004
9: 9 And Herod s, John have I beheaded: but 3004
9:12 then came the twelve, and s unto him, 3004
9:13 But he s unto them, Give ye them to eat. 3004
9:13 And they s, We have no more but 3004
9:14 And he s to his disciples, Make them sit 3004
9:19 They answering s, John the Baptist; but 3004
9:20 He s unto them, But whom say ye that I 3004
9:20 Peter answering s, The Christ of God. 3004
9:23 And he s to *them* all, If any *man* will come 3004
9:33 from him, Peter s unto Jesus, Master, 3004
9:33 and one for Elias: not knowing what he s. 3004
9:41 And Jesus answering s, O faithless and 3004
9:43 which Jesus did, he s unto his disciples, 3004
9:48 And s unto them, Whosoever shall receive 3004
9:49 And John answered and s, Master, we saw 3004
9:50 And Jesus s unto him, Forbid *him* not: 3004
9:54 disciples James and John saw *this*, they s, 3004
9:55 But he turned, and rebuked them, and s, 3004
9:57 a certain *man* s unto him, Lord, I will 3004
9:58 And Jesus s unto him, Foxes have holes, 3004
9:59 And he s unto another, Follow me. But he 3004
9:59 But he s, Lord, suffer me first to go and 3004
9:60 Jesus s unto him, Let the dead bury their 3004
9:61 And another also s, Lord, I will follow 3004
9:62 And Jesus s unto him, No *man* having put 3004
10: 2 Therefore s he unto them, The harvest truly 3004

Lk 10:18 And he s unto them, I beheld Satan as 3004
10:21 and s, I thank thee, O Father, Lord of 3004
10:23 him unto *his* disciples, and s privately, 3004
10:26 He s unto him, What is written in the law? 3004
10:27 And he answering s, Thou shalt love 3004
10:28 And he s unto him, Thou hast answered 3004
10:29 willing to justify himself, s unto Jesus, 3004
10:30 And Jesus answering s, A certain man went 3004
10:35 the host, and s unto him, Take care of him; 3004
10:37 And he s, He that shewed mercy on him. 3004
10:37 Then s Jesus unto him, Go, and do thou 3004
10:40 and came to *him*, and s, Lord, 3004
10:41 And Jesus answered and s unto her, 3004
11: 1 one of his disciples s unto him, Lord, 3004
11: 2 And he s unto them, When ye pray, say, 3004
11: 5 And he s unto them, Which of you shall 3004
11:15 But some of them s, He casteth out devils 3004
11:17 knowing their thoughts, s unto them, 3004
11:27 and s unto him, Blessed *is* the womb that 3004
11:28 But he s, Yea rather, blessed *are* they that 3004
11:39 And the Lord s unto him, Now do ye 3004
11:45 one of the lawyers, and s unto him, Master, 3004
11:46 And he s, Woe unto you also, *ye* lawyers! 3004
11:49 Therefore also s the wisdom of God, I will 3004
11:53 And as he s these *things* unto them, 3004
12:13 And one of the company s unto him, 3004
12:14 And he s unto him, Man, who made me a 3004
12:15 And he s unto them, Take heed, and 3004
12:18 And he s, This will I do: I will pull down 3004
12:20 But God s unto him, *Thou* fool, this night 3004
12:22 And he s unto his disciples, Therefore I say 3004
12:41 Then Peter s unto him, Lord, speakest thou 3004
12:42 And the Lord s, Who then is *that* faithful 3004
12:54 And he s also to the people, When ye see a 3004
13: 2 And Jesus answering s unto them, 3004
13: 7 Then s he unto the dresser of his vineyard, 3004
13: 8 And he answering s unto him, Lord, let it 3004
13:12 he called *her* to *him*, and s unto her, 3004
13:14 on the sabbath day, and s unto the people, 3004
13:15 The Lord then answered him, and s, 3004
13:17 And when he had s these *things*, all his 3004
13:18 Then s he, Unto what is the kingdom of 3004
13:20 And again he s, Whereunto shall I liken 3004
13:23 Then s one unto him, Lord, are there few 3004
13:23 few that be saved? And he s unto them, 3004
13:32 And he s unto them, Go ye, and tell that 3004
14:12 Then s he also to him that bade him, 3004
14:15 with *him* heard these *things*, he s unto him, 3004
14:16 Then s he unto him, A certain man made a 3004
14:18 The first s unto him, I have bought a piece 3004
14:19 And another s, I have bought five yoke of 3004
14:20 And another s, I have married a wife, and 3004
14:21 of the house being angry s to his servant, 3004
14:22 And the servant s, Lord, it is done as thou 3004
14:23 And the lord s unto the servant, Go out into 3004
14:25 with him: and he turned, and s unto them, 3004
15:11 And he s, A certain man had two sons: 3004
15:12 And the younger of them s to *his* father, 3004
15:17 And when he came to himself, he s, How 3004
15:21 And the son s unto him, Father, I have 3004
15:22 But the father s to his servants, Bring forth 3004
15:27 And he s unto him, Thy brother is come; 3004
15:29 And he answering s to *his* father, Lo, 3004
15:31 And he s unto him, Son, thou art ever with 3004
16: 1 And he s also unto his disciples, There was 3004
16: 2 And he called him, and s unto him, How *is* 3004
16: 3 Then the steward s within himself, 3004
16: 5 lord's debtors unto *him*, and s unto the first, 3004
16: 6 And he s, An hundred measures of oil. 3004
16: 6 And he s unto him, Take thy bill, and 3004
16: 7 Then s he to another, And how much owest 3004
16: 7 And he s, An hundred measures of wheat. 3004
16: 7 And he s unto him, Take thy bill, and 3004
16:15 And he s unto them, Ye are they which 3004
16:24 And he cried and s, Father Abraham, 3004
16:25 But Abraham s, Son, remember that thou in 3004
16:27 Then he s, I pray thee therefore, father, 3004
16:30 And he s, Nay, father Abraham: but if one 3004
16:31 And he s unto him, If they hear not Moses 3004
17: 1 Then s he unto the disciples, It is 3004
17: 5 And the apostles s unto the Lord, 3004
17: 6 And the Lord s, If ye had faith as a grain of 3004
17:13 and s, Jesus, Master, have mercy on us. 3004
17:14 And when he saw *them*, he s unto them, 3004
17:17 And Jesus answering s, Were there not ten 3004
17:19 And he s unto him, Arise, go *thy way*: thy 3004
17:20 God should come, he answered them and s, 3004
17:22 And he s unto the disciples, The days will 3004
17:37 And they answered and s unto him, Where, 3004
17:37 And he s unto them, Wheresoever the body 3004
18: 4 but afterward he s within himself, Though I 3004
18: 6 And the Lord s, Hear what the unjust judge 3004
18:16 But Jesus called them unto *him*, and s, 3004
18:19 And Jesus s unto him, Why callest thou me 3004
18:21 And he s, All these have I kept from my 3004
18:22 Now when Jesus heard these *things*, he s 3004
18:24 Jesus saw that he was very sorrowful, he s, 3004
18:26 And they that heard *it* s, Who then can be 3004
18:27 And he s, The *things which are* impossible 3004
18:28 Then Peter s, Lo, we have left all, 3004
18:29 And he s unto them, Verily I say unto you, 3004
18:31 and s unto them, Behold, we go up to 3004
18:41 And he s, Lord, that I may receive my 3004
18:42 And Jesus s unto him, Receive thy sight: 3004
19: 5 and saw him, and s unto him, Zaccheus, 3004
19: 8 And Zaccheus stood, and s unto the Lord; 3004
19: 9 And Jesus s unto him, This day is salvation 3004
19:12 He s therefore, A certain nobleman went 3004
19:13 and s unto them, Occupy till I come. 3004
19:17 And he s unto him, Well, *thou* good 3004
19:19 And he s likewise to him, Be thou also over 3004
19:24 And he s unto them that stood by, 3004
19:25 (And they s unto him, Lord, he hath ten 3004
19:32 and found even as he had s unto them. 3004
19:33 the owners thereof s unto them, Why loose 3004

Lk 19:34 And they s, The Lord hath need of him. 3004
19:39 from among the multitude s unto him, 3004
19:40 And he answered and s unto them, I tell 3004
20: 3 And he answered and s unto them, I will 3004
20: 8 And Jesus s unto them, Neither tell I you 3004
20:13 Then s the lord of the vineyard, What shall 3004
20:16 And when they heard *it*, they s, God forbid. 3004
20:17 and s, What is this then that is written, 3004
20:23 and s unto them, Why tempt ye me? 3004
20:24 hath it? They answered and s, Cesar's. 3004
20:25 And he s unto them, Render therefore 3004
20:34 And Jesus answering s unto them, 3004
20:39 Then certain of the scribes answering s, 3004
20:39 answering said, Master, thou hast well s. 3004
20:41 And he s unto them, How say they that 3004
20:42 The LORD s to my Lord, Sit thou on my 3004
20:45 Then in the audience of all the people he s 3004
21: 3 And he s, Of a truth I say unto you, that this 3004
21: 5 adorned with goodly stones and gifts, he s, 3004
21: 8 And he s, Take heed that ye be not 3004
21:10 Then s he unto them, Nation shall rise 3004
22: 9 And they s unto him, Where wilt thou *that* 3004
22:10 And he s unto them, Behold, when ye are 3004
22:13 and found as he had s unto them: 3004
22:15 And he s unto them, With desire I have 3004
22:17 and s, Take this, and divide *it* among 3004
22:25 And he s unto them, The kings of 3004
22:31 And the Lord s, Simon, Simon, behold, 3004
22:33 And he s unto him, Lord, I am ready to go 3004
22:34 And he s, I tell thee, Peter, *the* cock shall 3004
22:35 And he s unto them, When I sent you 3004
22:35 and shoes, lacked ye any *thing*? And they s, 3004
22:36 Then s he unto them, But now, he that hath 3004
22:38 And they s, Lord, behold, here *are* two 3004
22:38 And he s unto them, It is enough. 3004
22:40 when he was at the place, he s unto them, 3004
22:46 And s unto them, Why sleep ye? rise and 3004
22:48 But Jesus s unto him, Judas, betrayest thou 3004
22:49 they s unto him, Lord, shall we smite with 3004
22:51 And Jesus answered and s, Suffer ye thus 3004
22:52 Then Jesus s unto the chief priests, and 3004
22:56 and earnestly looked upon him, and s, 3004
22:58 saw him, and s, Thou art also of them. 5346
22:58 also of them. And Peter s, Man, I am not. 3004
22:60 And Peter s, Man, I know not what thou 3004
22:61 how he had s unto him, Before *the* cock 3004
22:67 And he s unto them, If I tell you, you will 3004
22:70 Then s they all, Art thou then the Son of 3004
22:70 And he s unto them, Ye say that I am. 5346
22:71 And they s, What need we any further 3004
23: 3 And he answered him and s, Thou sayest 5346
23: 4 Then s Pilate to the chief priests and *to* 3004
23:14 S unto them, Ye have brought this man 3004
23:22 And he s unto them the third time, Why, 3004
23:28 s, Daughters of Jerusalem, weep not for 3004
23:34 Then s Jesus, Father, forgive them; for they 3004
23:42 And he s unto Jesus, Lord, remember me 3004
23:43 And Jesus s unto him, Verily I say unto 3004
23:46 he s, Father, into thy hands I commend my 3004
23:46 and having s thus, he gave up the ghost. 3004
24: 5 *their* faces to the earth, they s unto them, 3004
24:17 And he s unto them, What *manner of* 3004
24:18 answering s unto him, Art thou only a 3004
24:19 And he s unto them, What *things*? And they 3004
24:19 What *things*? And they s unto him, 3004
24:23 vision of angels, which s that he was alive. 3004
24:24 and found *it* even so as the women had s: 3004
24:25 Then he s unto them, O fools, and slow of 3004
24:32 And they s one to another, Did not our 3004
24:38 And he s unto them, Why are ye troubled? 3004
24:41 and wondered, he s unto them, Have ye 3004
24:44 And he s unto them, These *are* the words 3004
24:46 And s unto them, Thus it is written, and 3004
Jn 1:22 Then s they unto him, Who art thou? 3004
1:23 He s, I *am* the voice of one crying in 5346
1:23 way of the Lord, as s the prophet Esaias. 3004
1:25 And they asked him, and s unto him, 3004
1:30 This is he of whom I s, After me cometh a 3004
1:33 to baptize with water, the same s unto me, 3004
1:38 They s unto him, Rabbi, (which is to say, 3004
1:42 And when Jesus beheld him, he s, Thou art 3004
1:46 And Nathanael s unto him, Can there any 3004
1:48 Jesus answered and s unto him, Before that 3004
1:50 Jesus answered and s unto him, Because I 3004
1:50 and said unto him, Because I s unto thee, 3004
2:16 And s unto them that sold doves, 3004
2:18 Then answered the Jews and s unto him, 3004
2:19 Jesus answered and s unto them, 3004
2:20 Then s the Jews, Forty and six years was 3004
2:22 his disciples remembered that he had s this 3004
2:22 and the word which Jesus had s. 3004
3: 2 to Jesus by night, and s unto him, Rabbi, 3004
3: 3 Jesus answered and s unto him, Verily, 3004
3: 7 Marvel not that I s unto thee, Ye must be 3004
3: 9 Nicodemus answered and s unto him, 3004
3:10 Jesus answered and s unto him, Art thou a 3004
3:26 came unto John, and s unto him, Rabbi, 3004
3:27 John answered and s, A man can receive 3004
3:28 that I s, I am not the Christ, but that I am 3004
4:10 Jesus answered and s unto her, If thou 3004
4:13 Jesus answered and s unto her, 3004
4:17 The woman answered and s, I have no 3004
4:17 Jesus s unto her, Thou hast well said, I have 3004
4:17 Thou hast well s, I have no husband: 3004
4:27 yet no *man* s, What seekest thou? or, 3004
4:32 But he s unto them, I have meat to eat that 3004
4:33 Therefore s the disciples one to another, 3004
4:42 And s unto the woman, *Now* we believe, 3004
4:48 Then s Jesus unto him, Except ye see signs 3004
4:52 And they s unto him, Yesterday at 3004
4:53 in the which Jesus s unto him, Thy son 3004
5:10 therefore s unto him that was cured, 3004
5:11 the same s unto me, Take up thy bed, and 3004
5:12 What man is that which s unto thee, 3004
5:14 and s unto him, Behold, thou art made 3004

S

Jn 5:18 but s also that God was his Father, 3004
5:19 Then answered Jesus and s unto them, 3004
6: 6 And this he s to prove him: for he himself 3004
6:10 And Jesus s, Make the men sit down. 3004
6:12 they were filled, he s unto his disciples, 3004
6:14 they had seen the miracle that Jesus did, s, 3004
6:25 they s unto him, Rabbi, when camest thou 3004
6:26 Jesus answered them and s, Verily, verily, 3004
6:28 Then s they unto him, What shall we do, 3004
6:29 Jesus answered and s unto them, This is 3004
6:30 They s therefore unto him, What sign 3004
6:32 Then Jesus s unto them, Verily, verily, 3004
6:34 Then s they unto him, Lord, evermore give 3004
6:35 And Jesus s unto them, I am the bread of 3004
6:36 But I s unto you, That ye also have seen 3004
6:41 then murmured at him, because he s, 3004
6:42 And they s, Is not this Jesus, the son of 3004
6:43 Jesus therefore answered and s unto them, 3004
6:53 Then Jesus s unto them, Verily, verily, 3004
6:59 These *things* s he in the synagogue, as he 3004
6:60 his disciples, when they had heard *this,* s, 3004
6:61 at it, he s unto them, Doth this offend you? 3004
6:65 And he s, Therefore said I unto you, that no 3004
6:65 And he said, Therefore s I unto you, that no 3004
6:67 Then s Jesus unto the twelve, Will ye also 3004
7: 3 His brethren therefore s unto him, 3004
7: 6 Then Jesus s unto them, My time is not yet 3004
7: 9 When he had s these *words* unto them, 3004
7:11 sought him at the feast, and s, Where is he? 3004
7:12 *for* some s, He is a good *man:* others said, 3004
7:12 some said, He is a good *man:* others s, Nay; 3004
7:16 Jesus answered them, and s, My doctrine is 3004
7:20 The people answered and s, Thou hast a 3004
7:21 Jesus answered and s unto them, I have 3004
7:25 Then s some of them of Jerusalem, Is not 3004
7:31 on him, and s, When Christ cometh, 3004
7:33 Then s Jesus unto them, Yet a little while 3004
7:35 Then s the Jews among themselves, 3004
7:36 What *manner of* saying is this that he s, 3004
7:38 that believeth on me, as the scripture hath s, 3004
7:40 when they heard *this* saying, s, Of a truth 3004
7:41 Others s, This is the Christ. But some said, 3004
7:41 But some s, Shall Christ come out of 3004
7:42 Hath not the scripture s, That Christ cometh 3004
7:45 and they s unto them, Why have ye not 3004
7:52 They answered and s unto him, Art thou 3004
8: 6 This they s, tempting him, that they might 3004
8: 7 he lift up *himself,* and s unto them, He that 3004
8:10 but the woman, he s unto her, Woman, 3004
8:11 She s, No *man,* Lord. And Jesus said unto 3004
8:11 And Jesus s unto her, Neither do I condemn 3004
8:13 The Pharisees therefore s unto him, 3004
8:14 Jesus answered and s unto them, Though I 3004
8:19 Then s they unto him, Where is thy Father? 3004
8:21 Then s Jesus again unto them, I go my way, 3004
8:22 Then s the Jews, Will he kill himself? 3004
8:23 And he s unto them, Ye are from beneath; 3004
8:24 I s therefore unto you, that ye shall die in 3004
8:25 Then s they unto him, Who art thou? 3004
8:25 Even the same that I s unto you *from* 2980
8:28 Then s Jesus unto them, When ye have lift 3004
8:31 Then s Jesus to those Jews which believed 3004
8:39 They answered and s unto him, Abraham is 3004
8:41 Then s they to him, We be not born of 3004
8:42 Jesus s unto them, If God were your Father, 3004
8:48 Then answered the Jews, and s unto him, 3004
8:52 Then s the Jews unto him, Now we know 3004
8:57 Then s the Jews unto him, Thou art not yet 3004
8:58 Jesus s unto them, Verily, verily, I say unto 3004
9: 7 And s unto him, Go, wash in the pool of 3004
9: 8 s, Is not this he that sat and begged? 3004
9: 9 Some s, This is he: others *said,* He is like 3004
9: 9 others *s,* He is like him: *but* he said, I am NIG
9: 9 *said,* He is like him: *but* he s, I am *he.* 3004
9:10 Therefore s they unto him, How were thine 3004
9:11 He answered and s, A man *that is* called 3004
9:11 and anointed mine eyes, and s unto me, Go 3004
9:12 Then s they unto him, Where is he? 3004
9:12 unto him, Where is he? He s, I know not. 3004
9:15 He s unto them, He put clay upon mine 3004
9:16 Therefore s some of the Pharisees, 3004
9:16 Others s, How can a man *that is* a sinner do 3004
9:17 opened thine eyes? He s, He is a prophet. 3004
9:20 His parents answered them and s, We know 3004
9:23 Therefore s his parents, He is of age; 3004
9:24 and s unto him, Give God the praise: 3004
9:25 He answered and s, Whether he be a sinner 3004
9:26 Then s they to him again, What did he to 3004
9:28 reviled him, and s, Thou art his disciple; 3004
9:30 The man answered and s unto them, 3004
9:34 They answered and s unto him, Thou wast 3004
9:35 and when he had found him, he s unto him, 3004
9:36 He answered and s, Who is he, Lord, that I 3004
9:37 And Jesus s unto him, Thou hast both seen 3004
9:38 And he s, Lord, I believe. And he 5346
9:39 And Jesus s, For judgment I am come into 3004
9:40 him heard these *words,* and s unto him, 3004
9:41 Jesus s unto them, If ye were blind, 3004
10: 7 Then s Jesus unto them again, Verily, 3004
10:20 And many of them s, He hath a devil, and 3004
10:21 Others s, These are not the words of him 3004
10:24 the Jews round about him, and s unto him, 3004
10:26 ye are not of my sheep, as I s unto you. 3004
10:34 it not written in your law, I s, Ye are gods? 3004
10:36 because I s, I am the Son of God? 3004
10:41 unto him, and s, John did no miracle: 3004
11: 4 When Jesus heard *that,* he s, This sickness 3004
11:11 These *things* s he: and after that he saith 3004
11:12 Then s his disciples, Lord, if he sleep, 3004
11:14 Then s Jesus unto them plainly, Lazarus is 3004
11:16 Then s Thomas, which is called Didymus, 3004
11:21 Then s Martha unto Jesus, Lord, if thou 3004
11:25 Jesus s unto her, I am the resurrection, and 3004
11:28 And when she had so s, she went her way, 3004
11:34 And s, Where have ye laid him? They say 3004

Jn 11:36 Then s the Jews, Behold, how he loved 3004
11:37 And some of them s, Could not this *man,* 3004
11:39 Jesus s, Take ye away the stone. Martha, 3004
11:40 Jesus saith unto her, S I not unto thee, that, 3004
11:41 And Jesus lift up *his* eyes, and s, Father, 3004
11:42 of the people which stand by I s *it,* that they 3004
11:47 the Pharisees a council, and s, What do we? 3004
11:49 s unto them, Ye know nothing at all, 3004
12: 6 This he s, not that he cared for the poor; but 3004
12: 7 Then s Jesus, Let her alone: against the day 3004
12:19 therefore s among themselves, 3004
12:29 stood *by,* and heard *it,* s that it thundered: 3004
12:29 others s, An angel spake to him. 3004
12:30 Jesus answered and s, This voice came not 3004
12:33 This he s, signifying what death he should 3004
12:35 Then Jesus s unto them, Yet a little while is 3004
12:39 not believe, because that Esaias s again, 3004
12:41 These *things* s Esaias, when he saw his 3004
12:44 Jesus cried and s, He that believeth on me, 3004
12:50 even as the Father s unto me, so I speak. 3004
13: 7 Jesus answered and s unto him, What I do 3004
13:11 therefore s he, Ye are not all clean. 3004
13:12 and was set down again, he s unto them, 3004
13:21 When Jesus had thus s, he was troubled in 3004
13:21 and testified, and s, Verily, verily, I say 3004
13:27 Then s Jesus unto him, That thou doest, 3004
13:29 had the bag, that Jesus had s unto him, 3004
13:31 Therefore, when he was gone out, Jesus s, 3004
13:33 and as I s unto the Jews, Whither I go, 3004
13:36 Simon Peter s unto him, Lord, 3004
13:37 Peter s unto him, Lord, why cannot I follow 3004
14:23 Jesus answered and s unto him, If a man 3004
14:26 what*soever* I have s unto you. 3004
14:28 Ye have heard how I s unto you, I go away, 3004
14:28 ye loved me, ye would rejoice, because I s, 3004
15:20 Remember the word that I s unto you, 3004
16: 4 And these *things* I s not unto you at 3004
16: 6 But because I have s these *things* unto you, 2980
16:15 therefore s I, that he shall take of mine, and 3004
16:17 Then s *some* of his disciples among 3004
16:18 They s therefore, What is this that he saith, 3004
16:19 and s unto them, Do ye inquire among 3004
16:19 Do ye inquire among yourselves of that I s, 3004
16:29 His disciples s unto him, Lo, now speakest 3004
17: 1 to heaven, and s, Father, the hour is come; 3004
18: 4 went forth, and s unto them, Whom seek 3004
18: 6 As soon then as he had s unto them, I am 3004
18: 7 seek ye? And they s, Jesus of Nazareth. 3004
18:11 Then s Jesus unto Peter, Put up thy sword 3004
18:20 and in secret have I s nothing. 2980
18:21 ask them which heard *me,* what I have s 2980
18:21 said unto them: behold, they know what I s. 3004
18:25 They s therefore unto him, Art not thou 3004
18:25 his disciples? He denied *it,* and s, I am not. 3004
18:29 Pilate then went out unto them, and s, What 3004
18:30 They answered and s unto him, If he were 3004
18:31 Then s Pilate unto them, Take ye him, and 3004
18:31 The Jews therefore s unto him, It is not 3004
18:33 and called Jesus, and s unto him, Art thou 3004
18:37 Pilate therefore s unto him, Art thou a king 3004
18:38 And when he had s this, he went out again 3004
19: 3 And s, Hail, King of the Jews: and 3004
19:21 Then s the chief priests of the Jews to 3004
19:21 but that he s, I am King of the Jews. 3004
19:24 They s therefore among themselves, Let us 3004
19:30 received the vinegar, he s, It is finished: 3004
20:14 And when she had thus s, she turned herself 3004
20:20 And when he had so s, he shewed unto 3004
20:21 Then s Jesus to them again, Peace *be* unto 3004
20:22 And when he had s this, he breathed on 3004
20:25 The other disciples therefore s unto him, 3004
20:25 But he s unto them, Except I shall see in his 3004
20:26 and stood in the midst, and s, Peace *be* 3004
20:28 And Thomas answered and s unto him, 3004
21: 6 And he s unto them, Cast the net on 3004
21:17 because he s unto him the third time, 3004
21:17 And he s unto him, Lord, thou knowest all 3004
21:20 and s, Lord, which is he that betrayeth 3004
21:23 yet Jesus s not unto him, He shall not die; 3004
Ac 1: 7 And he s unto them, It is not for you to 3004
1:11 Which also s, Ye men of Galilee, 3004
1:15 and s, (the number of names together were 3004
1:24 And they prayed, and s, Thou, Lord, 3004
2:13 Others mocking s, *These men* are full of 3004
2:14 lift up his voice, and s unto them, Ye men of 669
2:34 saith himself, The LORD s unto my Lord, 3004
2:37 and s unto Peter and *to* the rest of 3004
2:38 Then Peter s unto them, Repent, and 5346
3: 4 his eyes upon him with John, s, Look on us. 3004
3: 6 Then Peter s, Silver and gold have I none; 3004
3:22 For Moses truly s unto the fathers, 3004
4: 8 s unto them, Ye rulers of the people, and 3004
4:19 and John answered and s unto them, 3004
4:23 the chief priests and elders had s unto them. 3004
4:24 and s, Lord, thou *art* God, which hast made 3004
4:25 by the mouth of thy servant David hast s, 3004
4:32 neither s any *of them* that ought of 3004
5: 3 But Peter s, Ananias, why hath Satan filled 3004
5: 8 so much? And she s, Yea, for so much. 3004
5: 9 Then Peter s unto her, How *is it* that ye 3004
5:19 prison doors, and brought them forth, and s, 3004
5:29 and the *other* apostles answered and s, 3004
5:35 And s unto them, Ye men of Israel, 3004
6: 2 multitude of the disciples unto *them,* and s, 3004
6:11 Then they suborned men, which s, We have 3004
6:13 And set up false witnesses, which s, 3004
7: 1 Then s the high priest, Are these *things* so? 3004
7: 2 And he s, Men, brethren, and fathers, 5346
7: 3 And s unto him, Get thee out of thy 3004
7: 7 shall be in bondage will I judge, s God: 3004
7:33 Then s the Lord to him, Put off *thy* shoes 3004
7:37 which s unto the children of Israel, 3004
7:56 And s, Behold, I see the heavens opened, 3004
7:60 And when he had s this, he fell asleep. 3004
8:20 But Peter s unto him, Thy money perish 3004

Ac 8:24 Then answered Simon, and s, Pray ye to 3004
8:29 Then the Spirit s unto Philip, Go near, and 3004
8:30 heard him read the prophet Esaias, and s, 3004
8:31 And he s, How can I, except some *man* 3004
8:34 eunuch answered Philip, and s, I pray thee, 3004
8:36 and the eunuch s, See, *here is* water; 5346
8:37 And Philip s, If thou believest with all *thine* 3004
8:37 And he answered and s, I believe that Jesus 3004
9: 5 And he s, Who art thou, Lord? And 3004
9: 5 And the Lord s, I am Jesus whom thou 3004
9: 6 And he trembling and astonished s, Lord, 3004
9: 6 And the Lord *s* unto him, Arise, and go into NIG
9:10 and to him s the Lord in a vision, Ananias. 3004
9:10 And he s, Behold, I *am here,* Lord. 3004
9:11 And the Lord *s* unto him, Arise, and go into NIG
9:15 But the Lord s unto him, Go *thy way:* for 3004
9:17 and putting his hands on him s, 3004
9:21 But all that heard *him* were amazed, and s; 3004
9:34 And Peter s unto him, Aeneas, Jesus Christ 3004
9:40 and turning *him* to the body s, Tabitha, 3004
10: 4 he was afraid, and s, What is it, Lord? 3004
10: 4 And he s unto him, Thy prayers and 3004
10:14 But Peter s, Not so, Lord; for I have never 3004
10:19 the Spirit s unto him, Behold, three men 3004
10:21 and s, Behold, I am he whom ye seek: 3004
10:22 And they s, Cornelius the centurion, a just 3004
10:28 And he s unto them, Ye know how that it is 5346
10:30 And Cornelius s, Four days ago I was 5346
10:31 And s, Cornelius, thy prayer is heard, and 5346
10:34 Then Peter opened *his* mouth, and s, Of a 3004
11: 8 But I s, Not so, Lord: for nothing common 3004
11:13 which stood and s unto him, Send men to 3004
11:16 how that he s, John indeed baptized with 3004
12: 8 And the angel s unto him, Gird thyself, and 3004
12:11 he s, Now I know of a surety, that the Lord 3004
12:15 And they s unto her, Thou art mad. But she 3004
12:15 it was *even* so. Then s they, It is his angel. 3004
12:17 And he s, *Go* shew these *things* unto James, 3004
13: 2 and fasted, the Holy Ghost s, Separate me 3004
13:10 And s, O full of all subtilty and 3004
13:16 and beckoning with *his* hand s, Men of 3004
13:22 to whom also he gave testimony, and s, 3004
13:25 *his* course, he s, Whom think ye that I am? 3004
13:34 to return to corruption, he s on this wise, 3004
13:46 Then Paul and Barnabas waxed bold, and s, 3004
14:10 S with a loud voice, Stand upright on thy 3004
15: 1 *s,* Except ye be circumcised after NIG
15: 7 and s unto them, Men *and* brethren, 3004
15:36 And some days after Paul s unto Barnabas, 3004
16:18 being grieved, turned and s to the spirit, 3004
16:30 And brought them out, and s, Sirs, 5346
16:31 And they s, Believe on the Lord Jesus 3004
16:37 But Paul s unto them, They have beaten us 5346
17:18 And some s, What will this babbler say? 3004
17:22 of Mars' hill, and s, *Ye* men of Athens, 5346
17:28 as certain also of your own poets have s, 3004
17:32 and others s, We will hear thee again of 3004
18: 6 he shook *his* raiment, and s unto them, 3004
18:14 Gallio s unto the Jews, If it were a matter of 3004
19: 2 He s unto them, Have ye received the Holy 3004
19: 2 And they s unto him, We have not so 3004
19: 3 And he s unto them, Unto what then 3004
19: 3 And they s, Unto John's baptism. 3004
19: 4 Then s Paul, John verily baptized *with* 3004
19:15 And the evil spirit answered and s, Jesus I 3004
19:25 and s, Sirs, ye know that by this craft we 3004
19:35 the people, he s, *Ye* men of Ephesus, 5346
20:10 and fell on him, and embracing *him* s, 3004
20:18 come to him, he s unto them, Ye know, 3004
20:35 how he s, It is more blessed to give than to 3004
21: 4 who s to Paul through the Spirit, that *he* 3004
21:11 and bound his *own* hands and feet, and s, 3004
21:20 and s unto him, Thou seest, brother, 3004
21:37 he s unto the chief captain, May I speak 3004
21:37 unto thee? Who s, Canst thou speak Greek? 5346
21:39 But Paul s, I am a man *which am* a Jew of 3004
22: 8 And he s unto me, I am Jesus of Nazareth, 3004
22:10 And I s, What shall I do, Lord? And 3004
22:10 And the Lord s unto me, Arise, and go into 3004
22:13 and stood, and s unto me, Brother Saul, 3004
22:14 And he s, The God of our fathers hath 3004
22:19 And I s, Lord, they know that I imprisoned 3004
22:21 And he s unto me, Depart: for I will send 3004
22:22 and *then* lift up their voices, and s, 3004
22:25 Paul s unto the centurion that stood *by,* Is it 3004
22:27 and s unto him, Tell me, art thou a Roman? 3004
22:27 Tell me, art thou a Roman? He s, Yea. 5346
22:28 And Paul s, But I was *free* born. 5346
23: 1 beholding the council, s, Men *and* brethren, 3004
23: 3 Then s Paul unto him, God shall smite thee, 3004
23: 4 And they that stood by s, Revilest thou 3004
23: 5 Then s Paul, I wist not, brethren, that he 5346
23: 7 And when he had so s, there arose a 2980
23:11 by him, and s, Be of good cheer, Paul: 3004
23:14 came to the chief priests and elders, and s, 3004
23:17 one of the centurions unto *him,* and s, 5346
23:18 and brought *him* to the chief captain, and s, 5346
23:20 And he s, The Jews have agreed to desire 3004
23:35 I will hear thee, s he, when thine accusers 5346
24:22 he deferred them, and s, When Lysias 3004
25: 5 Let them therefore, s he, which among you 5346
25: 9 answered Paul, and s, Wilt thou go up to 3004
25:10 Then s Paul, I stand at Cesar's judgment 3004
25:22 Then Agrippa s unto Festus, I would also 5346
25:22 To morrow, s he, thou shalt hear him. 5346
25:24 And Festus s, King Agrippa, and all men 5346
26: 1 Then Agrippa s unto Paul, Thou art 5346
26:15 And I s, Who art thou, Lord? And he said, 3004
26:15 And he s, I am Jesus whom thou 3004
26:24 Festus s with a loud voice, Paul, thou art 5346
26:25 But he s, I am not mad, most noble Festus; 5346
26:28 Then Agrippa s unto Paul, Almost thou 5346
26:29 And Paul s, I would to God, that not only 5346
26:32 Then s Agrippa unto Festus, This man 5346
27:10 And s unto them, Sirs, I perceive that *this* 3004

Ac 27:21 and **s**, Sirs, ye should have hearkened unto 3004
27:31 Paul **s** to the centurion and to the soldiers, 3004
28: 4 they **s** among themselves, No doubt this 3004
28: 6 their minds, and **s** that he was a god. 3004
28:17 he **s** unto them, Men and brethren, 3004
28:21 And they **s** unto him, We neither received 3004
28:29 And when he had **s** these words, the Jews 3004
Ro 7: 7 except the law had **s**, Thou shalt not covet. 3004
9:12 It was **s** unto her, The elder shall serve 3004
9:26 that in the place where it was **s** unto them, 3004
9:29 And as Esaias **s before**, Except the Lord of 4302
1Co 11:24 given thanks, he brake it, and **s**, Take, eat: 3004
2Co 6:16 as God hath **s**, I will dwell in them, and 3004
7: 3 this to condemn you: for I have **s before**, 4302
9: 3 in this behalf; that, as I **s**, ye may be ready: 3004
12: 9 And he **s** unto me, My grace is sufficient 3004
Gal 1: 9 As we **s before**, so say I now again, If any 4302
2:14 I **s** unto Peter before them all, If thou, 3004
Tit 1:12 even a prophet of their own, **s**, 3004
Heb 1: 5 For unto which of the angels **s** he at any 3004
1:13 But to which of the angels **s** he at any time, 3004
3:10 and **s**, They do alway err in their heart; 3004
3:15 Whilst it is **s**, To day if ye will hear his 3004
4: 3 as he **s**, As I have sworn in my wrath, 3004
4: 7 as it is **s**, To day if ye will hear his voice, 3004
5: 5 but he that **s** unto him, Thou art my Son, 2980
7:21 this with an oath by him that **s** unto him, 3004
10: 7 Then **s** I, Lo, I come (in the volume of 3004
10: 8 Above when he **s**, Sacrifice and offering 3004
10: 9 Then **s** he, Lo, I come to do thy will, 3004
10:15 witness to us: for after that he had **s before**, 4302
10:30 For we know him that hath **s**, 3004
11:18 Of whom it was **s**, That in Isaac shall thy 2980
12:21 that Moses **s**, I exceedingly fear and 3004
13: 5 for he hath **s**, I will never leave thee, 3004
Jas 2:11 For he that **s**, Do not commit adultery, 3004
2:11 Do not commit adultery, **s** also, Do not kill. 3004
Jude 1: 9 but **s**, The Lord rebuke thee. 3004
Rev 4: 1 which **s**, Come up hither, and I will shew 3004
5:14 And the four beasts **s**, Amen. And the four 3004
6:11 and it was **s** unto them, that they should rest 3004
6:16 And **s** to the mountains and rocks, Fall on 3004
7:14 And I **s** unto him, Sir, thou knowest. 3004
7:14 And he **s** to me, These are they which came 3004
10: 8 and **s**, Go and take the little book which is 3004
10: 9 and **s** unto him, Give me the little book. 3004
10: 9 And he **s** unto me, Take it, and eat it up; 3004
10:11 And he **s** unto me, Thou must prophesy 3004
17: 7 And the angel **s** unto me, Wherefore didst 3004
19: 3 And again they **s**, Alleluia. And her smoke 3004
19:10 And he **s** unto me, See thou do it not: I am 3004
21: 5 And he that sat upon the throne **s**, Behold, 3004
21: 5 And he **s** unto me, Write: for these words 3004
21: 6 And he **s** unto me, It is done. I am Alpha 3004
22: 6 And he **s** unto me, These sayings are 3004

SAIDST (22) [SAY]

Ge 12:19 Why **s** thou, She is my sister? so I might 559
26: 9 how **s** thou, She is my sister? And Isaac said 559
32: 9 father Isaac, the LORD which **s** unto me, 559
32:12 thou **s**, I will surely do thee good, and 559
44:21 thou **s** unto thy servants, Bring him down 559
44:23 thou **s** unto thy servants, Except your 559
Ex 32:13 swarest by thine own self, and **s** unto them, 1696
Jdg 9:38 wherewith thou **s**, Who is Abimelech, 559
1Ki 2:42 thou **s** unto me, The word that I have heard 559
Job 35: 2 Thinkest thou this to be right, that thou **s**, 559
35: 3 For thou **s**, What advantage will it be unto 559
Ps 27: 8 When thou **s**, Seek ye my face; my heart NIH
89:19 **s**, I have laid help upon one that is mighty; 559
Isa 47: 7 thou **s**, I shall be a lady for ever: so that thou 559
57:10 of thy way; yet **s** thou not, There is no hope: 559
Jer 2:20 thy bands; and thou **s**, I will not transgress; 559
2:25 thou **s**, There is no hope: no; for I have loved 559
22:21 in thy prosperity; but thou **s**, I will not hear. 559
La 3:57 day that I called upon thee: thou **s**, Fear not. 559
Eze 25: 3 Because thou **s**, Aha, against my sanctuary, 559
Hos 13:10 thy judges of whom thou **s**, Give me a king 559
Jn 4:18 hast is not thy husband: in that **s** thou truly. 3004

SAIL (8) [SAILED, SAILERS, SAILING]

Isa 33:23 their mast, they could not spread the **s**: 5251
Eze 27: 7 that which thou spreadest forth to be thy **s**; 5251
Ac 20: 3 wait for him, as he was about to **s** into Syria, 321
20:16 For Paul had determined to **s by** Ephesus, 3896
27: 1 when it was determined that we should **s** 636
27: 2 meaning to **s** by the coasts of Asia; 4126
27:17 strake **s**, and so were driven. 4632
27:24 God hath given thee all them that **s** with 4126

SAILED (15) [SAIL]

Lk 8:23 But as they **s** he fell asleep: and there came 4126
Ac 13: 4 and from thence they **s** to Cyprus. 636
14:26 And thence **s** to Antioch, from whence they 636
15:39 so Barnabas took Mark, and **s** unto Cyprus; 1602
18:18 and **s thence** into Syria, and with him 1602
18:21 if God will. And he **s** from Ephesus. 321
20: 6 And we **s away** from Philippi after the days 1602
20:13 we went before to ship, and **s** unto Assos, 321
20:15 And we **s** thence, and came the next day 636
21: 3 and **s** into Syria, and landed at Tyre: 4126
27: 4 we **s under** Cyprus, because the winds 5284
27: 5 And when we had **s over** the sea of Cilicia 1277
27: 7 And when we had **s slowly** many days, and 1020
27: 7 we **s under** Crete, over against Salmone; 5284
27:13 loosing thence, they **s** close by Crete. 3881

SAILERS (1) [SAIL]

Rev 18:17 and **s**, and as many as trade by sea, 3492

SAILING (3) [SAIL]

Ac 21: 2 And finding a ship **s over** unto Phenicia, 1276
27: 6 found a ship of Alexandria **s** into Italy; 4126
27: 9 and when **s** was now dangerous, because 4144

SAILORS See SHIPMEN

SAINT (5) [SAINTS, SAINTS']

Ps 106:16 the camp, and Aaron the **s** of the LORD. 6918
Da 8:13 I heard one **s** speaking, and another saint 6918
8:13 another **s** said unto that certain saint which 6918
8:13 another saint said unto that certain **s** which NIH
Php 4:21 Salute every **s** in Christ Jesus. The brethren 40

SAINTS (95) [SAINT]

Dt 33: 2 and he came with ten thousands of **s**: 6944
33: 3 loved the people; all his **s** are in thy hand: 6918
1Sa 2: 9 He will keep the feet of his **s**, and 2623
2Ch 6:41 and let thy **s** rejoice in goodness. 2623
Job 5: 1 and to which of the **s** wilt thou turn? 6918
15:15 Behold, he putteth no trust in his **s**; yea, 6918
Ps 16: 3 But to the **s** that are in the earth, and to 6918
30: 4 O ye **s** of his, and give thanks at 2623
31:23 O love the LORD, all ye his **s**: for 2623
34: 9 O fear the LORD, ye his **s**: for there is no 6918
37:28 loveth judgment, and forsaketh not his **s**; 2623
50: 5 Gather my **s** together unto me; those that 2623
52: 9 on thy name; for it is good before thy **s**. 2623
79: 2 the flesh of thy **s** unto the beasts of 2623
85: 8 speak peace unto his people, and to his **s**: 2623
89: 5 also in the congregation of the **s**. 6918
89: 7 to be feared in the assembly of the **s**, 6918
97:10 he preserveth the souls of his **s**; 2623
116:15 sight of the LORD is the death of his **s**. 2623
132: 9 and let thy **s** shout for joy. 2623
132:16 and her **s** shall shout aloud for joy. 2623
145:10 O LORD; and thy **s** shall bless thee. 2623
148:14 horn of his people, the praise of all his **s**; 2623
149: 1 and his praise in the congregation of **s**. 2623
149: 5 Let the **s** be joyful in glory: let them sing 2623
149: 9 this honour have all his **s**. Praise ye 2623
Pr 2: 8 and preserveth the way of his **s**. 2623
Da 7:18 the **s** of the most High shall take 6922
7:21 and the same horn made war with the **s**, and 6922
7:22 judgment was given to the **s** of the most 6922
7:22 the time came that the **s** possessed 6922
7:25 shall wear out the **s** of the most High, and 6922
7:27 shall be given to the people of the **s** of 6922
Hos 11:12 ruleth with God, and is faithful with the **s**. 6918
Zec 14: 5 my God shall come, and all the **s** with thee. 6918
Mt 27:52 and many bodies of **s** which slept arose, 40
Ac 9:13 how much evil he hath done to thy **s** at 40
9:32 down also to the **s** which dwelt at Lydda. 40
9:41 and when he had called the **s** and widows, 40
26:10 and many of the **s** did I shut up in prison, 40
Ro 1: 7 be in Rome, beloved of God, called to be **s**: 40
8:27 he maketh intercession for the **s** according to 40
12:13 Distributing to the necessity of **s**; given to 40
15:25 I go unto Jerusalem to minister unto the **s**. 40
15:26 for the poor **s** which are at Jerusalem. 40
15:31 I have for Jerusalem may be accepted of the **s**; 40
16: 2 as becometh **s**, and that ye assist her in 40
16:15 Olympas, and all the **s** which are with them. 40
1Co 1: 2 are sanctified in Christ Jesus, called to be **s**, 40
6: 1 to law before the unjust, and not before the **s**? 40
6: 2 Do ye not know that the **s** shall judge 40
14:33 but of peace, as in all churches of the **s**. 40
16: 1 Now concerning the collection for the **s**, as I 40
16:15 addicted themselves to the ministry of the **s**,) 40
2Co 1: 1 with all the **s** which are in all Achaia: 40
8: 4 us the fellowship of the ministering to the **s**. 40
9: 1 For as touching the ministering to the **s**, it is 40
9:12 service not only supplieth the want of the **s**, 40
13:13 All the **s** salute you. 40
Eph 1: 1 to the **s** which are at Ephesus, and to 40
1:15 faith in the Lord Jesus, and love unto all the **s**, 40
1:18 riches of the glory of his inheritance in the **s**, 40
2:19 but fellowcitizens with the **s**, and of 40
3: 8 Unto me, who am less than the least of all **s**, 40
3:18 May be able to comprehend with all **s** what is 40
4:12 For the perfecting of the **s** for the work of 40
5: 3 be once named amongst you, as becometh **s**; 40
6:18 all perseverance and supplication for all **s**; 40
Php 1: 1 to all the **s** in Christ Jesus which are at 40
4:22 All the **s** salute you, chiefly they that are of 40
Col 1: 2 To the **s** and faithful brethren in Christ which 40
1: 4 and of the love which ye have to all the **s**, 40
1:12 partakers of the inheritance of the **s** in light: 40
1:26 but now is made manifest to his **s**: 40
1Th 3:13 coming of our Lord Jesus Christ with all his **s**. 40
2Th 1:10 When he shall come to be glorified in his **s**, 40
Phm 1: 5 hast toward the Lord Jesus, and toward all **s**; 40
1: 7 the bowels of the **s** are refreshed by thee, 40
Heb 6:10 in that ye have ministered to the **s**, and 40
13:24 them that have the rule over you, and all the **s**. 40
Jude 1: 3 the faith which was once delivered unto the **s**. 40
1:14 the Lord cometh with ten thousands of his **s**, 40
Rev 5: 8 full of odours, which are the prayers of **s**. 40
8: 3 that he should offer it with the prayers of all **s** 40
8: 4 which came with the prayers of the **s**, 40
11:18 and to the **s**, and them that fear thy name, 40
13: 7 it was given unto him to make war with the **s**, 40
13:10 Here is the patience and the faith of the **s**. 40
14:12 Here is the patience of the **s**: here are they that 40
15: 3 just and true are thy ways, thou King of **s**. 40
16: 6 For they have shed the blood of **s** and 40
17: 6 the woman drunken with the blood of the **s**, 40
18:24 and of **s**, and of all that were slain upon 40
19: 8 for the fine linen is the righteousness of **s**. 40
20: 9 and compassed the camp of the **s** about, and 40

SAINTS' (1) [SAINT]

1Ti 5:10 if she have washed the **s** feet, 40

SAITH (1262) [SAY]

Ge 22:16 **s** the LORD, for because thou hast done 5002
32: 4 Thy servant Jacob **s** thus, I have sojourned 559
41:55 Go unto Joseph; what he **s** to you, do. 559
44: 7 Wherefore **s** my lord these words? 1696
45: 9 and say unto him, Thus **s** thy son Joseph, 559
Ex 4:22 Thus **s** the LORD, Israel is my son, 559
5: 1 Thus **s** the LORD God of Israel, 559
5:10 spake to the people, saying, Thus **s** Pharaoh, 559
7:17 Thus **s** the LORD, In this thou shalt know 559
8: 1 and say unto him, Thus **s** the LORD, 559
8:20 say unto him, Thus **s** the LORD, Let my 559
9: 1 Thus **s** the LORD God of the Hebrews, 559
9:13 Thus **s** the LORD God of the Hebrews, 559
10: 3 Thus **s** the LORD God of the Hebrews, 559
11: 4 Moses said, Thus **s** the LORD, 559
32:27 unto them, Thus **s** the LORD God of Israel, 559
Nu 14:28 unto them, As truly as I live, **s** the LORD, 5002
20:14 Thus **s** thy brother Israel, Thou knowest all 559
22:16 said to him, Thus **s** Balak the son of Zippor, 559
24:13 but what the LORD **s**, that will I speak? 1696
32:27 before the LORD to battle, as my lord **s**. 1696
Jos 5:14 unto him, What **s** my lord unto his servant? 1696
7:13 for thus **s** the LORD God of Israel, There is 559
22:16 Thus **s** the whole congregation of 559
24: 2 the people, Thus **s** the LORD God of Israel, 559
Jdg 6: 8 unto them, Thus **s** the LORD God of Israel, 559
11:15 said unto him, Thus **s** Jephthah, Israel took 559
1Sa 2:27 and said unto him, Thus **s** the LORD, 559
2:30 Wherefore the LORD God of Israel **s**, 5002
2:30 now the LORD **s**, Be it far from me; 5002
9: 6 all that he **s** cometh surely to pass: 1696
10:18 Thus **s** the LORD God of Israel, I brought 559
15: 2 Thus **s** the LORD of hosts, I remember that 559
20: 3 he **s**, Let not Jonathan know this, lest he be 559
24:13 As **s** the proverb of the ancients, 559
2Sa 7: 5 tell my servant David, Thus **s** the LORD, 559
7: 8 Thus **s** the LORD of hosts, I took thee from 559
12: 7 Thus **s** the LORD God of Israel, I anointed 559
12:11 Thus **s** the LORD, Behold, I will raise up 559
14:10 Whosoever **s** ought unto thee, bring him to 1696
17: 5 and let us hear likewise what he **s**. 6310+871.1
24:12 Go and say unto David, Thus **s** the LORD, 559
1Ki 2:30 said unto him, Thus **s** the king, Come forth. 559
3:23 said the king, The one **s**, This is my son that 559
3:23 and the other **s**, Nay; but thy son is the dead, 559
11:31 for thus **s** the LORD, the God of Israel, 559
12:24 Thus **s** the LORD, Ye shall not go up, 559
13: 2 and said, O altar, altar, thus **s** the LORD; 559
13:21 from Judah, saying, Thus **s** the LORD, 559
14: 7 Thus **s** the LORD God of Israel, 559
17:14 For thus **s** the LORD God of Israel, 559
20: 2 and said unto him, Thus **s** Ben-hadad, 559
20:13 saying, Thus **s** the LORD, Hast thou seen 559
20:14 he said, Thus **s** the LORD, Even by 559
20:28 king of Israel, and said, Thus **s** the LORD, 559
20:32 said, Thy servant Ben-hadad **s**, I pray thee, 559
20:42 he said unto him, Thus **s** the LORD, 559
21:19 saying, Thus **s** the LORD, Hast thou killed, 559
21:19 speak unto him, saying, Thus **s** the LORD, 559
22:11 he said, Thus **s** the LORD, With these shalt 559
22:14 what the LORD **s** unto me, that will I 559
22:27 say, Thus **s** the king, Put this fellow in 559
2Ki 1: 4 Now therefore thus **s** the LORD, Thou shalt 559
1: 6 Thus **s** the LORD, Is it not because there is 559
1:16 he said unto him, Thus **s** the LORD, 559
2:21 salt in there, and said, Thus **s** the LORD, 559
3:16 he said, Thus **s** the LORD, Make this valley 559
3:17 For thus **s** the LORD, Ye shall not see 559
4:43 for thus **s** the LORD, They shall eat, and 559
5:13 when he **s** to thee, Wash, and be clean? 559
7: 1 Thus **s** the LORD, To morrow about this 559
9: 3 it on his head, and say, Thus **s** the LORD, 559
9: 6 unto him, Thus **s** the LORD God of Israel, 559
9:12 spake he to me, saying, Thus **s** the LORD, 559
9:18 and said, Thus **s** the king, Is it peace? 559
9:19 and said, Thus **s** the king, Is it peace? 559
9:26 and the blood of his sons, **s** the LORD; 5002
9:26 will requite thee in this plat, **s** the LORD. 5002
18:19 Thus **s** the great king, the king of Assyria, 559
18:29 Thus **s** the king, Let not Hezekiah deceive 559
18:31 for thus **s** the king of Assyria, Make an 559
19: 3 they said unto him, Thus **s** Hezekiah, 559
19: 6 ye say to your master, Thus **s** the LORD, 559
19:20 Thus **s** the LORD God of Israel, 559
19:32 Therefore thus **s** the LORD concerning 559
19:33 shall not come into this city, **s** the LORD. 5002
20: 1 said unto him, Thus **s** the LORD, Set thine 559
20: 5 Thus **s** the LORD, the God of David thy 559
20:17 nothing shall be left, **s** the LORD. 559
21:12 Therefore thus **s** the LORD God of Israel, 559
22:15 unto them, Thus **s** the LORD God of Israel, 559
22:16 Thus **s** the LORD, Behold, I will bring evil 559
22:18 say to him, Thus **s** the LORD God of Israel, 559
22:19 I also have heard thee, **s** the LORD. 5002
1Ch 17: 4 tell David my servant, Thus **s** the LORD, 559
17: 7 Thus **s** the LORD of hosts, I took thee from 559
21:10 and tell David, saying, Thus **s** the LORD, 559
21:11 unto him, Thus **s** the LORD, Choose thee 559
2Ch 11: 4 Thus **s** the LORD, Ye shall not go up, 559
12: 5 and said unto them, Thus **s** the LORD, 559
18:10 said, Thus **s** the LORD, With these thou 559
18:13 even what my God **s**, that will I speak. 559
18:26 say, Thus **s** the king, Put this fellow in 559
20:15 Thus **s** the LORD unto you, 559
21:12 Thus **s** the LORD God of David thy father, 559
24:20 the people, and said unto them, Thus **s** God, 559
32:10 Thus **s** Sennacherib king of Assyria, 559
34:23 Thus **s** the LORD God of Israel, 559
34:24 Thus **s** the LORD, Behold, I will bring evil 559
34:26 Thus **s** the LORD God of Israel concerning 559
34:27 I have even heard thee also, **s** the LORD. 5002
36:23 Thus **s** Cyrus king of Persia, All 559
Ezr 1: 2 Thus **s** Cyrus king of Persia, The LORD 559
Ne 6: 6 Gashmu **s** it, that thou and the Jews think to 559
Job 28:14 The depth **s**, It is not in me: and the sea saith, 559
28:14 is not in me: and the sea **s**, It is not with me. 559
33:24 he is gracious unto him, and **s**, Deliver him 559
35:10 none **s**, Where is God my Maker, who giveth 559
37: 6 For he **s** to the snow, Be thou on the earth; 559

Job 39:25 He s among the trumpets, Ha, ha; and 559
Ps 12: 5 of the needy, now will I arise, s the LORD; 559
36: 1 The transgression of the wicked s within 5002
50:16 unto the wicked God s, What hast thou to do 559
Pr 9: 4 that wanteth understanding, she s to him, 559
9:16 that wanteth understanding, she s to him, 559
20:14 *It is* naught, *it is* naught, s the buyer: but 559
22:13 The slothful *man* s, *There is* a lion without, 559
23: 7 Eat and drink, s he to thee; but his heart *is* 559
24:24 He that s unto the wicked, Thou *art* 559
26:13 The slothful *man* s, *There is* a lion in 559
26:19 his neighbour, and s, Am not I in sport? 559
28:24 robbeth his father or his mother, and s, 559
30:16 and the fire *that* s not, *It is* enough. 559
30:20 she eateth, and wipeth her mouth, and s, 559
Ecc 1: 2 of vanities, s the Preacher, vanity of vanities; 559
4: 8 neither *s he*, For whom do I labour, and NIH
7:27 Behold, this have I found, s the Preacher, 559
10: 3 and he s to every one *that* he *is* a fool. 559
12: 8 Vanity of vanities, s the Preacher; all *is* 559
Isa 1:11 s the LORD: I am full *of* the burnt offerings 559
1:18 and let us reason together, s the LORD: 559
1:24 Therefore s the Lord, the LORD of hosts, 5002
3:15 of the poor? s the Lord GOD of hosts. 5002
3:16 Moreover the LORD s, Because 559
7: 7 Thus s the Lord GOD, It shall not stand, 559
10: 8 For he s, *Are* not my princes altogether 559
10:13 For he s, By the strength of my hand I have 559
10:24 Therefore thus s the Lord GOD of hosts, 559
14:22 s the LORD of hosts, and cut off from 5002
14:22 and son, and nephew, s the LORD. 5002
14:23 of destruction, s the LORD of hosts. 5002
17: 3 children of Israel, s the LORD of hosts. 5002
17: 6 s the LORD God of Israel. 5002
19: 4 over them, s the Lord, the LORD of hosts. 5002
22:14 you till ye die, s the Lord GOD of hosts. 559
22:15 Thus s the Lord GOD of hosts, Go, get thee 559
22:25 In that day, s the LORD of hosts, shall 5002
28:16 Therefore thus s the Lord GOD, Behold, 559
29:11 pray thee: and he s, I cannot; for it *is* sealed: 559
29:12 I pray thee: and he s, I am not learned. 559
29:22 Therefore thus s the LORD, who redeemed 559
30: 1 s the LORD, that take counsel, but not of 5002
30:12 Wherefore thus s the Holy One of Israel, 559
30:15 For thus s the Lord GOD, the Holy One of 559
31: 9 s the LORD, whose fire *is* in Zion, and his 5002
33:10 Now will I rise, s the LORD; now will I be 559
36: 4 Thus s the great king, the king of Assyria, 559
36:14 Thus s the king, Let not Hezekiah deceive 559
36:16 for thus s the king of Assyria, Make *an* 559
37: 3 they said unto him, Thus s Hezekiah, 559
37: 6 ye say unto your master, Thus s the LORD, 559
37:21 Thus s the LORD God of Israel, 559
37:33 Therefore thus s the LORD concerning 559
37:34 shall not come into this city, s the LORD. 5002
38: 1 said unto him, Thus s the LORD, Set thine 559
38: 5 Go and say to Hezekiah, Thus s the LORD, 559
39: 6 nothing shall be left, s the LORD. 559
40: 1 comfort ye my people, s your God. 559
40:25 or shall I be equal? s the Holy One. 559
41:14 help thee, s the LORD, and thy redeemer, 5002
41:21 Produce your cause, s the LORD; 559
41:21 bring forth your strong *reasons*, s the King of 559
42: 5 Thus s God the LORD, he that created 559
42:22 *for* a spoil, and none s, Restore. 559
43: 1 But now thus s the LORD that created thee, 559
43:10 s the LORD, and my servant whom I have 5002
43:12 my witnesses, s the LORD, that I *am* God. 5002
43:14 Thus s the LORD, your redeemer, the Holy 559
43:16 Thus s the LORD, which maketh a way in 559
44: 2 Thus s the LORD that made thee, and 559
44: 6 Thus s the LORD the King of Israel, and 559
44:16 and s, Aha, I am warm, I have seen the fire: 559
44:17 and prayeth unto it, and s, Deliver me; 559
44:24 Thus s the LORD, thy redeemer, and 559
44:26 that s to Jerusalem, Thou shalt be inhabited; 559
44:27 That s to the deep, Be dry, and I will dry up 559
44:28 That s of Cyrus, *He is* my shepherd, and 559
45: 1 Thus s the LORD to his anointed, to Cyrus, 559
45:10 Woe unto him that s unto *his* father, 559
45:11 Thus s the LORD, the Holy One of Israel, 559
45:13 for price nor reward, s the LORD of hosts. 559
45:14 Thus s the LORD, The labour of Egypt, 559
45:18 For thus s the LORD that created 559
48:17 Thus s the LORD, thy redeemer, the Holy 559
48:22 *is* no peace, s the LORD, unto the wicked. 559
49: 5 s the LORD that formed me from 559
49: 7 Thus s the LORD, the redeemer of Israel, 559
49: 8 Thus s the LORD, In an acceptable time 559
49:18 *As* I live, s the LORD, thou shalt surely 5002
49:22 Thus s the Lord GOD, Behold, I will lift up 559
49:25 thus s the LORD, Even the captives of 559
50: 1 Thus s the LORD, Where *is* the bill of your 559
51:22 Thus s thy Lord the LORD, and thy God 559
52: 3 For thus s the LORD, Ye have sold 559
52: 4 For thus s the Lord GOD, My people went 559
52: 5 what have I here, s the LORD, 5002
52: 5 them make *them* to howl, s the LORD; 5002
52: 7 that s unto Zion, Thy God reigneth! 559
54: 1 children of the married wife, s the LORD. 559
54: 6 of youth, when thou wast refused, s thy God. 559
54: 8 mercy on thee, s the LORD thy redeemer. 559
54:10 s the LORD that hath mercy on thee. 559
54:17 their righteousness *is* of me, s the LORD. 5002
55: 8 *are* your ways my ways, s the LORD. 5002
56: 1 Thus s the LORD, Keep ye judgment, and 559
56: 4 For thus s the LORD unto the eunuchs that 559
56: 8 which gathereth the outcasts of Israel s, 5002
57:15 For thus s the high and lofty One that 559
57:19 far off, and to *him that is* near, s the LORD; 559
57:21 *There is* no peace, s my God, to the wicked. 559
59:20 from transgression in Jacob, s the LORD. 5002
59:21 *is* my covenant with them, s the LORD; 559
59:21 s the LORD, from henceforth and for ever. 559
65: 7 of your fathers together, s the LORD, 559
Isa 65: 8 Thus s the LORD, As the new wine is 559
65: 8 in the cluster, and *one* s, Destroy it not; 559
65:13 Therefore thus s the Lord GOD, Behold, 559
65:25 in all my holy mountain, s the LORD. 559
66: 1 Thus s the LORD, The heaven *is* my 559
66: 2 all those *things* have been, s the LORD: 5002
66: 9 s the LORD: shall I cause to bring forth, 559
66: 9 bring forth, and shut *the womb?* s thy God. 559
66:12 For thus s the LORD, Behold, I will extend 559
66:17 shall be consumed together, s the LORD. 5002
66:20 my holy mountain Jerusalem, s the LORD, 559
66:21 for priests *and* for Levites, s the LORD. 559
66:22 s the LORD, so shall your seed and 5002
66:23 come to worship before me, s the LORD. 559
Jer 1: 8 *am* with thee to deliver thee, s the LORD. 5002
1:15 of the kingdoms of the north, s the LORD; 5002
1:19 *am* with thee, s the LORD, to deliver thee. 5002
2: 2 of Jerusalem, saying, Thus s the LORD; 559
2: 3 evil shall come upon them, s the LORD. 5002
2: 5 Thus s the LORD, What iniquity have your 559
2: 9 s the LORD, and with your children's 5002
2:12 be ye very desolate, s the LORD. 5002
2:19 *is* not in thee, s the Lord GOD of hosts. 5002
2:22 *is* marked before me, s the Lord GOD. 5002
2:29 transgressed against me, s the LORD. 5002
3: 1 yet return again to me, s the LORD. 5002
3:10 whole heart, but feignedly, s the LORD. 5002
3:12 thou backsliding Israel, s the LORD; 5002
3:12 s the LORD, *and* I will not keep *anger* for 5002
3:13 have not obeyed my voice, s the LORD. 5002
3:14 O backsliding children, s the LORD; 5002
3:16 in the land, in those days, s the LORD, 5002
3:20 with me, O house of Israel, s the LORD. 5002
4: 1 O Israel, s the LORD, return unto me: 5002
4: 3 For thus s the LORD to the men of Judah 559
4: 9 come to pass at that day, s the LORD, 5002
4:17 been rebellious against me, s the LORD. 5002
5: 9 Shall I not visit for these *things?* s 5002
5:11 treacherously against me, s the LORD. 5002
5:14 Wherefore thus s the LORD God of hosts, 559
5:15 from far, O house of Israel, s the LORD: 5002
5:18 Nevertheless in those days, s the LORD, 5002
5:22 s the LORD: will ye not tremble at my 5002
5:29 Shall I not visit for these *things?* s 5002
6: 9 Thus s the LORD of hosts, They shall 559
6:12 the inhabitants of the land, s the LORD. 5002
6:15 them they shall be cast down, s the LORD. 559
6:16 Thus s the LORD, Stand ye in the ways, 559
6:21 Therefore thus s the LORD, Behold, I will 559
6:22 Thus s the LORD, Behold, a people cometh 559
7: 3 Thus s the LORD of hosts, the God of 559
7:11 Behold, even I have seen *it*, s the LORD. 5002
7:13 s the LORD, and I spake unto you, 5002
7:19 s the LORD: *do they* not *provoke* 5002
7:20 Therefore thus s the Lord GOD; Behold, 559
7:21 Thus s the LORD of hosts, the God of 559
7:30 have done evil in my sight, s the LORD: 5002
7:32 the days come, s the LORD, 5002
8: 1 At that time, s the LORD, they shall bring 5002
8: 3 I have driven them, s the LORD of hosts. 5002
8: 4 shalt say unto them, Thus s the LORD; 559
8:12 they shall be cast down, s the LORD. 559
8:13 I will surely consume them, s the LORD: 5002
8:17 and they shall bite you, s the LORD. 5002
9: 3 and they know not me, s the LORD. 5002
9: 6 they refuse to know me, s the LORD. 5002
9: 7 Therefore thus s the LORD of hosts, 559
9: 9 Shall I not visit them for these *things?* s 5002
9:13 the LORD s, Because they have forsaken 559
9:15 Therefore thus s the LORD of hosts, 559
9:17 Thus s the LORD of hosts, Consider ye, 559
9:22 Speak, Thus s the LORD, Even 5002
9:23 Thus s the LORD, Let not the wise *man* 559
9:24 for in these *things* I delight, s the LORD. 5002
9:25 Behold, the days come, s the LORD, that I 5002
10: 2 Thus s the LORD, Learn not the way of 559
10:18 For thus s the LORD, Behold, I will sling 559
11: 3 unto them, Thus s the LORD God of Israel; 559
11:11 Therefore thus s the LORD, Behold, I *will* 559
11:21 Therefore thus s the LORD of the men of 559
11:22 Therefore thus s the LORD of hosts, 559
12:14 Thus s the LORD against all mine evil 559
12:17 and destroy that nation, s the LORD. 5002
13: 1 Thus s the LORD unto me, Go and get thee 559
13: 9 Thus s the LORD, After this manner will I 559
13:11 the whole house of Judah, s the LORD; 5002
13:12 Thus s the LORD God of Israel, 559
13:13 say unto them, Thus s the LORD, Behold, 559
13:14 and the sons together, s the LORD: 5002
13:25 of thy measures from me, s the LORD; 5002
14:10 Thus s the LORD unto this people, Thus 559
14:15 Therefore thus s the LORD concerning 559
15: 2 then thou shalt tell them, Thus s the LORD; 559
15: 3 over them four kinds, s the LORD: 5002
15: 6 Thou hast forsaken me, s the LORD, 5002
15: 9 sword before their enemies, s the LORD. 5002
15:19 Therefore thus s the LORD, If thou return, 559
15:20 save thee and to deliver thee, s the LORD. 5002
16: 3 For thus s the LORD concerning the sons 559
16: 5 For thus s the LORD, Enter not *into* 559
16: 5 s the LORD, *even* lovingkindness and 5002
16: 9 For thus s the LORD of hosts, the God of 559
16:11 s the LORD, and have walked after other 5002
16:14 the days come, s the LORD, 5002
16:16 s the LORD, and they shall fish them; 5002
17: 5 Thus s the LORD; Cursed *be* the man that 559
17:21 Thus s the LORD; Take heed to yourselves, 559
17:24 diligently hearken unto me, s the LORD, 5002
18: 6 s the LORD. Behold, as the clay *is* in 5002
18:11 of Jerusalem, saying, Thus s the LORD; 559
18:13 Therefore thus s the LORD; Ask ye now 559
19: 1 Thus s the LORD, Go and get a potter's 559
19: 3 Thus s the LORD of hosts, the God of 559
19: 6 the days come, s the LORD, 5002
19:11 say unto them, Thus s the LORD of hosts; 559
Jer 19:12 s the LORD, and to the inhabitants 5002
19:15 Thus s the LORD of hosts, the God of 559
20: 4 For thus s the LORD, Behold, I will make 559
21: 4 Thus s the LORD God of Israel; Behold, 559
21: 7 afterward, s the LORD, I will deliver 5002
21: 8 people thou shalt say, Thus s the LORD; 559
21:10 for evil, and not for good, s the LORD: 5002
21:12 O house of David, thus s the LORD; 559
21:13 *and* rock of the plain, s the LORD; 5002
21:14 to the fruit of your doings, s the LORD: 5002
22: 1 Thus s the LORD; Go down *to* the house of 559
22: 3 Thus s the LORD; Execute ye judgment 559
22: 5 I swear by myself, s the LORD, 5002
22: 6 For thus s the LORD unto the king's house 559
22:11 For thus s the LORD touching Shallum 559
22:14 That s, I will build me a wide house and 559
22:16 *was* not this to know me? s the LORD. 5002
22:18 Therefore thus s the LORD concerning 559
22:24 *As* I live, s the LORD, though Coniah 5002
22:30 Thus s the LORD, Write ye this man 559
23: 1 the sheep of my pasture! s the LORD. 5002
23: 2 Therefore thus s the LORD God of Israel 559
23: 2 you the evil of your doings, s the LORD. 5002
23: 4 neither shall they be lacking, s the LORD. 5002
23: 5 Behold, the days come, s the LORD, that I 5002
23: 7 the days come, s the LORD, 5002
23:11 I found their wickedness, s the LORD. 5002
23:12 the year of their visitation, s the LORD. 5002
23:15 Therefore thus s the LORD of hosts 559
23:16 Thus s the LORD of hosts, Hearken not 559
23:23 s the LORD, and not a God afar off? 5002
23:24 s the LORD. Do not I fill heaven and 5002
23:24 not I fill heaven and earth? s the LORD. 5002
23:28 *is* the chaff to the wheat? s the LORD. 5002
23:29 s the LORD; and like a hammer *that* 5002
23:30 I *am* against the prophets, s the LORD, 5002
23:31 s the LORD, that use their tongues, and 5002
23:31 that use their tongues, and say, He s. 5002
23:32 s the LORD, and do tell them, and 5002
23:32 not profit this people at all, s the LORD. 5002
23:33 I will even forsake you, s the LORD. 5002
23:38 of the LORD; therefore thus s the LORD; 559
24: 5 Thus s the LORD, the God of Israel; 559
24: 8 surely thus s the LORD, So will I give 559
25: 7 have not hearkened unto me, s the LORD; 5002
25: 8 Therefore thus s the LORD of hosts; 559
25: 9 s the LORD, and Nebuchadrezzar the king 5002
25:12 that nation, s the LORD, for their iniquity, 5002
25:15 For thus s the LORD God of Israel unto 559
25:27 Thus s the LORD of hosts, the God of 559
25:28 say unto them, Thus s the LORD of hosts; 559
25:29 of the earth, s the LORD of hosts. 5002
25:31 *that are* wicked to the sword, s the LORD. 5002
25:32 Thus s the LORD of hosts, Behold, 559
26: 2 Thus s the LORD; Stand in the court of 559
26: 4 shalt say unto them, Thus s the LORD; 559
26:18 saying, Thus s the LORD of hosts; 559
27: 2 Thus s the LORD to me; Make thee bonds 559
27: 4 Thus s the LORD of hosts, the God of 559
27: 8 s the LORD, with the sword, and with 5002
27:11 still in their own land, s the LORD; 5002
27:15 For I have not sent them, s the LORD, 5002
27:16 all this people, saying, Thus s the LORD; 559
27:19 For thus s the LORD of hosts concerning 559
27:21 Yea, thus s the LORD of hosts, the God of 559
27:22 the day that I visit them, s the LORD; 5002
28: 4 that went into Babylon, s the LORD: 5002
28:11 of all the people, saying, Thus s the LORD; 559
28:13 tell Hananiah, saying, Thus s the LORD; 559
28:14 For thus s the LORD of hosts, the God of 559
28:16 Therefore thus s the LORD; Behold, I will 559
29: 4 Thus s the LORD of hosts, the God of 559
29: 8 For thus s the LORD of hosts, the God of 559
29: 9 I have not sent them, s the LORD. 5002
29:10 For thus s the LORD, That after seventy 559
29:11 s the LORD, thoughts of peace, and not of 5002
29:14 I will be found of you, s the LORD: and 5002
29:14 whither I have driven you, s the LORD; 5002
29:16 *Know* that thus s the LORD of the king that 559
29:17 Thus s the LORD of hosts; Behold, I will 559
29:19 not hearkened to my words, s the LORD, 5002
29:19 but ye would not hear, s the LORD. 5002
29:21 Thus s the LORD of hosts, the God of 559
29:23 I know, and *am* a witness, s the LORD. 5002
29:31 Thus s the LORD concerning Shemaiah 559
29:32 Therefore thus s the LORD; Behold, I will 559
29:32 that I will do for my people, s the LORD; 5002
30: 3 For lo, the days come, s the LORD, that I 5002
30: 3 my people Israel and Judah, s the LORD: 559
30: 5 For thus s the LORD; We have heard a 559
30: 8 to pass in that day, s the LORD of hosts, 5002
30:10 O my servant Jacob, s the LORD; 5002
30:11 I *am* with thee, s the LORD, to save thee: 5002
30:12 For thus s the LORD, Thy bruise *is* 559
30:17 will heal thee of thy wounds, s the LORD; 5002
30:18 Thus s the LORD: Behold, I *will* bring 559
30:21 heart to approach unto me? s the LORD. 5002
31: 1 At the same time, s the LORD, will I be 5002
31: 2 Thus s the LORD, The people which were 559
31: 7 For thus s the LORD; Sing with gladness 559
31:14 satisfied with my goodness, s the LORD. 5002
31:15 Thus s the LORD; A voice was heard in 559
31:16 Thus s the LORD, Refrain thy voice from 559
31:16 thy work shall be rewarded, s the LORD; 5002
31:17 there is hope in thine end, s the LORD, 5002
31:20 surely have mercy upon him, s the LORD. 5002
31:23 Thus s the LORD of hosts, the God of 559
31:27 Behold, the days come, s the LORD, that I 5002
31:28 to build, and to plant, s the LORD. 5002
31:31 Behold, the days come, s the LORD, that I 5002
31:32 I was a husband unto them, s the LORD: 5002
31:33 After those days, s the LORD, I will put 5002
31:34 unto the greatest of them, s the LORD: 5002
31:35 Thus s the LORD, which giveth the sun for 559
31:36 s the LORD, *then* the seed of Israel also 5002

Jer 31:37 Thus **s** the LORD; If heaven above can be 559
31:37 for all that they have done, **s** the LORD. 5002
31:38 Behold, the days come, **s** the LORD, 5002
32: 3 and say, Thus **s** the LORD, Behold, 559
32: 5 shall he be until I visit him, **s** the LORD: 5002
32:14 Thus **s** the LORD of hosts, the God of 559
32:15 For thus **s** the LORD of hosts, the God of 559
32:28 Therefore thus **s** the LORD; Behold, I *will* 559
32:30 with the work of their hands, **s** the LORD. 5002
32:36 now therefore thus **s** the LORD, the God of 559
32:42 For thus **s** the LORD; Like as I have 559
32:44 their captivity to return, **s** the LORD. 5002
33: 2 Thus **s** the LORD the maker thereof, 559
33: 4 For thus **s** the LORD, the God of Israel, 559
33:10 Thus **s** the LORD; Again there shall be 559
33:11 of the land as at the first, **s** the LORD. 559
33:12 Thus **s** the LORD of hosts, Again in this 559
33:13 hands of him that telleth *them*, **s** the LORD. 559
33:14 Behold, the days come, **s** the LORD, that I 5002
33:17 For thus **s** the LORD; David shall never 559
33:20 Thus **s** the LORD; If you can break my 559
33:25 Thus **s** the LORD; If my covenant *be* not 559
34: 2 Thus **s** the LORD, the God of Israel; Go 559
34: 2 of Judah, and tell him, Thus **s** the LORD; 559
34: 4 Thus **s** the LORD of thee, Thou shalt not 559
34: 5 I have pronounced the word, **s** the LORD. 5002
34:13 Thus **s** the LORD, the God of Israel; 559
34:17 Therefore thus **s** the LORD; Ye have not 559
34:17 **s** the LORD, to the sword, to 5002
34:22 **s** the LORD, and cause them to return to 5002
35:13 Thus **s** the LORD of hosts, the God of 559
35:13 to hearken to my words? **s** the LORD. 5002
35:17 Therefore thus **s** the LORD God of hosts, 559
35:18 Thus **s** the LORD of hosts, the God of 559
35:19 Therefore thus **s** the LORD of hosts, 559
36:29 king of Judah, Thus **s** the LORD; 559
36:30 Therefore thus **s** the LORD of Jehoiakim 559
37: 7 Thus **s** the LORD, the God of Israel; 559
37: 9 Thus **s** the LORD; Deceive not yourselves, 559
38: 2 Thus **s** the LORD, He that remaineth in this 559
38: 3 Thus **s** the LORD, This city shall surely be 559
38:17 Thus **s** the LORD, the God of hosts, 559
39:16 saying, Thus **s** the LORD of hosts, the God 559
39:17 will deliver thee in that day, **s** the LORD: 5002
39:18 thou hast put thy trust in me, **s** the LORD. 5002
42: 9 Thus **s** the LORD, the God of Israel, 559
42:11 be not afraid of him, **s** the LORD: 5002
42:15 Thus **s** the LORD of hosts, the God of 559
42:18 For thus **s** the LORD of hosts, the God of 559
43:10 Thus **s** the LORD of hosts, the God of 559
44: 2 Thus **s** the LORD of hosts, the God of 559
44: 7 Therefore now thus **s** the LORD, the God 559
44:11 Therefore thus **s** the LORD of hosts, 559
44:25 Thus **s** the LORD of hosts, the God of 559
44:26 sworn by my great name, **s** the LORD, 559
44:29 this *shall be* a sign unto you, **s** the LORD, 5002
44:30 Thus **s** the LORD; Behold, I *will* give 559
45: 2 Thus **s** the LORD, the God of Israel, 559
45: 4 shalt thou say unto him, The LORD **s** thus; 559
45: 5 *will* bring evil upon all flesh, **s** the LORD: 5002
46: 5 *for* fear *was* round about, **s** the LORD. 5002
46: 8 he **s**, I will go up, *and* will cover the earth; 559
46:18 *As* I live, **s** the King, whose name *is* 5002
46:23 **s** the LORD, though it cannot be searched; 5002
46:25 The LORD of hosts, the God of Israel, **s**; 559
46:26 as *in* the days of old, **s** the LORD. 5002
46:28 O Jacob my servant, **s** the LORD: 5002
47: 2 Thus **s** the LORD; Behold, waters rise up 559
48: 1 Against Moab thus **s** the LORD of hosts, 559
48:12 the days come, **s** the LORD, 5002
48:15 **s** the King, whose name *is* the LORD of 5002
48:25 and his arm is broken, **s** the LORD. 5002
48:30 I know his wrath, **s** the LORD; but *it shall* 5002
48:35 **s** the LORD, him that offereth *in* the high 5002
48:38 wherein *is* no pleasure, **s** the LORD. 5002
48:40 For thus **s** the LORD; Behold, he shall fly 559
48:43 O inhabitant of Moab, **s** the LORD. 5002
48:44 the year of their visitation, **s** the LORD. 5002
48:47 of Moab in the latter days, **s** the LORD. 5002
49: 1 the Ammonites, thus **s** the LORD; 559
49: 2 the days come, **s** the LORD, 5002
49: 2 unto them that were his heirs, **s** the LORD. 559
49: 5 a fear upon thee, **s** the Lord GOD of hosts, 5002
49: 6 of the children of Ammon, **s** the LORD. 5002
49: 7 thus **s** the LORD of hosts; 559
49:12 For thus **s** the LORD; Behold, they whose 559
49:13 For I have sworn by myself, **s** the LORD, 5002
49:16 thee down from thence, **s** the LORD. 5002
49:18 **s** the LORD, no man shall abide there, 559
49:26 cut off in that day, **s** the LORD of hosts. 5002
49:28 of Babylon shall smite, thus **s** the LORD; 559
49:30 O ye inhabitants of Hazor, **s** the LORD; 5002
49:31 that dwelleth without care, **s** the LORD, 5002
49:32 from all sides thereof, **s** the LORD. 5002
49:35 Thus **s** the LORD of hosts; Behold, I *will* 559
49:37 *even* my fierce anger, **s** the LORD; 5002
49:38 the king and the princes, **s** the LORD. 5002
49:39 again the captivity of Elam, **s** the LORD. 5002
50: 4 those days, and in that time, **s** the LORD, 5002
50:10 spoil her shall be satisfied, **s** the LORD. 5002
50:18 Therefore thus **s** the LORD of hosts, 559
50:20 those days, and in that time, **s** the LORD, 5002
50:21 **s** the LORD, and do according to all that I 5002
50:30 shall be cut off in that day, **s** the LORD. 5002
50:31 most proud, **s** the Lord GOD of hosts: 5002
50:33 Thus **s** the LORD of hosts; The children of 559
50:35 **s** the LORD, and upon the inhabitants of 5002
50:40 the neighbour *cities* thereof, **s** the LORD; 5002
51: 1 Thus **s** the LORD; Behold, I *will* raise up 559
51:24 done in Zion in your sight, **s** the LORD. 5002
51:25 O destroying mountain, **s** the LORD, 5002
51:26 shalt be desolate for ever, **s** the LORD. 5002
51:33 For thus **s** the LORD of hosts, the God of 559
51:36 Therefore thus **s** the LORD; Behold, I *will* 559
51:39 and not wake, **s** the LORD. 5002

Jer 51:48 unto her from the north, **s** the LORD. 5002
51:52 the days come, **s** the LORD, 5002
51:53 shall spoilers come unto her, **s** the LORD. 5002
51:57 a perpetual sleep, and not wake, **s** the King, 5002
51:58 Thus **s** the LORD of hosts; The broad walls 559
La 3:24 The LORD *is* my portion, **s** my soul; 559
3:37 Who *is* he *that* **s**, and it cometh to pass, 559
Eze 2: 4 shalt say unto them, Thus **s** the Lord GOD. 559
3:11 and tell them, Thus **s** the Lord GOD; 559
3:27 shalt say unto them, Thus **s** the Lord GOD; 559
5: 5 Thus **s** the Lord GOD; This *is* Jerusalem: 559
5: 7 Therefore thus **s** the Lord GOD; 559
5: 8 Therefore thus **s** the Lord GOD; Behold, I, 559
5:11 Wherefore, *as* I live, **s** the Lord GOD; 5002
6: 3 Thus **s** the Lord GOD to the mountains, and 559
6:11 Thus **s** the Lord GOD; Smite with thine 559
7: 2 thus **s** the Lord GOD unto the land of 559
7: 5 Thus **s** the Lord GOD; An evil, an only 559
11: 5 said unto me, Speak; Thus **s** the LORD; 559
11: 7 Therefore thus **s** the Lord GOD; Your slain 559
11: 8 bring a sword upon you, **s** the Lord GOD. 5002
11:16 Therefore say, Thus **s** the Lord GOD; 559
11:17 Therefore say, Thus **s** the Lord GOD; I will 559
11:21 upon their own heads, **s** the Lord GOD. 5002
12:10 Say thou unto them, Thus **s** the Lord GOD; 559
12:19 Thus **s** the Lord GOD, of the inhabitants of 559
12:23 Tell them therefore, Thus **s** the Lord GOD; 559
12:25 and will perform it, **s** the Lord GOD. 5002
12:28 say unto them, Thus **s** the Lord GOD; 559
12:28 spoken shall be done, **s** the Lord GOD. 5002
13: 3 Thus **s** the Lord GOD; Woe unto 559
13: 6 lying divination, saying, The LORD **s**: 5002
13: 7 The LORD **s** *it;* albeit I have not spoken? 5002
13: 8 Therefore thus **s** the Lord GOD; 559
13: 8 behold, I *am* against you, **s** the Lord GOD. 5002
13:13 Therefore thus **s** the Lord GOD; I will even 559
13:16 and *there is* no peace, **s** the Lord GOD. 5002
13:18 say, Thus **s** the Lord GOD; Woe to 559
13:20 Wherefore thus **s** the Lord GOD; Behold, 559
14: 4 and say unto them, Thus **s** the Lord GOD; 559
14: 6 the house of Israel, Thus **s** the Lord GOD; 559
14:11 and I may be their God, **s** the Lord GOD. 5002
14:14 by their righteousness, **s** the Lord GOD. 5002
14:16 men *were* in it, *as* I live, **s** the Lord GOD, 5002
14:18 men *were* in it, *as* I live, **s** the Lord GOD, 5002
14:20 Job, *were* in it, *as* I live, **s** the Lord GOD, 5002
14:21 For thus **s** the Lord GOD; How much more 559
14:23 all that I have done in it, **s** the Lord GOD. 5002
15: 6 Therefore thus **s** the Lord GOD; As 559
15: 8 committed a trespass, **s** the Lord GOD. 5002
16: 3 Thus **s** the Lord GOD unto Jerusalem; 559
16: 8 **s** the Lord GOD, and thou becamest mine. 5002
16:14 I had put upon thee, **s** the Lord GOD. 5002
16:19 and *thus* it was, **s** the Lord GOD. 5002
16:23 (woe, woe unto thee! **s** the Lord GOD;) 5002
16:30 How weak is thine heart, **s** the Lord GOD, 5002
16:36 Thus **s** the Lord GOD; Because thy 559
16:43 thy way upon *thine* head, **s** the Lord GOD: 5002
16:48 *As* I live, **s** the Lord GOD, Sodom thy 5002
16:58 and thine abominations, **s** the LORD. 5002
16:59 For thus **s** the Lord GOD; I will even deal 559
16:63 all that thou hast done, **s** the Lord GOD. 5002
17: 3 say, Thus **s** the Lord GOD; A great eagle 559
17: 9 Say thou, Thus **s** the Lord GOD; Shall it 559
17:16 *As* I live, **s** the Lord GOD, surely in 5002
17:19 Therefore thus **s** the Lord GOD; *As* I live, 559
17:22 Thus **s** the Lord GOD; I will also take of 559
18: 3 *As* I live, **s** the Lord GOD, ye shall not 5002
18: 9 he shall surely live, **s** the Lord GOD. 5002
18:23 **s** the Lord GOD: *and* not that he should 5002
18:29 Yet **s** the house of Israel, The way of 559
18:30 according to his ways, **s** the Lord GOD. 5002
18:32 death of him that dieth, **s** the Lord GOD: 5002
20: 3 and say unto them, Thus **s** the Lord GOD; 559
20: 3 *As* I live, **s** the Lord GOD, I will not be 5002
20: 5 And say unto them, Thus **s** the Lord GOD; 559
20:27 and say unto them, Thus **s** the Lord GOD; 559
20:30 the house of Israel, Thus **s** the Lord GOD; 559
20:31 *As* I live, **s** the Lord GOD, I will not be 5002
20:33 *As* I live, **s** the Lord GOD, surely with a 5002
20:36 so will I plead with you, **s** the Lord GOD. 5002
20:39 O house of Israel, thus **s** the Lord GOD; 559
20:40 **s** the Lord GOD, there shall all the house 5002
20:44 O ye house of Israel, **s** the Lord GOD. 5002
20:47 Thus **s** the Lord GOD; Behold, I *will* kindle 559
21: 3 say to the land of Israel, Thus **s** the LORD; 559
21: 7 shall be brought to pass, **s** the Lord GOD. 5002
21: 9 prophesy, and say, Thus **s** the LORD; 559
21:13 it shall be no *more,* **s** the Lord GOD. 5002
21:24 Therefore thus **s** the Lord GOD; 559
21:26 Thus **s** the Lord GOD; Remove the diadem, 559
21:28 Thus **s** the Lord GOD concerning 559
22: 3 say thou, Thus **s** the Lord GOD, The city 559
22:12 and hast forgotten me, **s** the Lord GOD. 5002
22:19 Therefore thus **s** the Lord GOD; 559
22:28 unto them, saying, Thus **s** the Lord GOD, 559
22:31 upon their heads, **s** the Lord GOD. 5002
23:22 O Aholibah, thus **s** the Lord GOD; 559
23:28 For thus **s** the Lord GOD; Behold, I *will* 559
23:32 Thus **s** the Lord GOD; Thou shalt drink *of* 559
23:34 for I have spoken *it,* **s** the Lord GOD. 5002
23:35 Therefore thus **s** the Lord GOD; 559
23:46 For thus **s** the Lord GOD; *I will* bring up a 559
24: 3 and say unto them, Thus **s** the Lord GOD; 559
24: 6 Wherefore thus **s** the Lord GOD; Woe to 559
24: 9 Therefore thus **s** the Lord GOD; Woe to 559
24:14 shall they judge thee, **s** the Lord GOD. 5002
24:21 the house of Israel, Thus **s** the Lord GOD; 559
25: 3 Thus **s** the Lord GOD; Because thou saidst, 559
25: 6 For thus **s** the Lord GOD; Because thou 559
25: 8 Thus **s** the Lord GOD; Because that Moab 559
25:12 Thus **s** the Lord GOD; Because that Edom 559
25:13 Therefore thus **s** the Lord GOD; I will also 559
25:14 know my vengeance, **s** the Lord GOD. 5002
25:15 Thus **s** the Lord GOD; Because 559

Eze 25:16 Therefore thus **s** the Lord GOD; Behold, 559
26: 3 Therefore thus **s** the Lord GOD; Behold, 559
26: 5 for I have spoken *it,* **s** the Lord GOD: and 5002
26: 7 For thus **s** the Lord GOD; Behold, I *will* 559
26:14 for I the LORD have spoken *it,* **s** the Lord 5002
26:15 Thus **s** the Lord GOD to Tyrus; Shall not 559
26:19 For thus **s** the Lord GOD; When I shall 559
26:21 never be found again, **s** the Lord GOD. 5002
27: 3 for many isles, Thus **s** the Lord GOD; 559
28: 2 the prince of Tyrus, Thus **s** the Lord GOD; 559
28: 6 Therefore thus **s** the Lord GOD; 559
28:10 for I have spoken *it,* **s** the Lord GOD. 5002
28:12 and say unto him, Thus **s** the Lord GOD; 559
28:22 say, Thus **s** the Lord GOD; Behold, I *am* 559
28:25 Thus **s** the Lord GOD; When I shall have 559
29: 3 Speak, and say, Thus **s** the Lord GOD; 559
29: 8 Therefore thus **s** the Lord GOD; Behold, 559
29:13 Yet thus **s** the Lord GOD; At the end of 559
29:19 Therefore thus **s** the Lord GOD; Behold, 559
29:20 they wrought for me, **s** the Lord GOD. 5002
30: 2 prophesy and say, Thus **s** the Lord GOD; 559
30: 6 Thus **s** the LORD; They also that uphold 559
30: 6 fall in it by the sword, **s** the Lord GOD. 5002
30:10 Thus **s** the Lord GOD; I will also make 559
30:13 Thus **s** the Lord GOD; I will also destroy 559
30:22 Therefore thus **s** the Lord GOD; Behold, 559
31:10 Therefore thus **s** the Lord GOD; 559
31:15 Thus **s** the Lord GOD; In the day when he 559
31:18 and all his multitude, **s** the Lord GOD. 5002
32: 3 Thus **s** the Lord GOD; I will therefore 559
32: 8 darkness upon thy land, **s** the Lord GOD. 5002
32:11 For thus **s** the Lord GOD; The sword of 559
32:14 rivers to run like oil, **s** the Lord GOD. 5002
32:16 and for all her multitude, **s** the Lord GOD. 5002
32:31 army slain by the sword, **s** the Lord GOD. 5002
32:32 and all his multitude, **s** the Lord GOD. 5002
33:11 Say unto them, *As* I live, **s** the Lord GOD, 5002
33:25 say unto them, Thus **s** the Lord GOD; 559
33:27 thou thus unto them, Thus **s** the Lord GOD; 559
34: 2 Thus **s** the Lord GOD unto the shepherds; 559
34: 8 **s** the Lord GOD, surely because my flock 5002
34:10 Thus **s** the Lord GOD; Behold, I *am* against 559
34:11 For thus **s** the Lord GOD; Behold, I, *even* I, 559
34:15 cause them to lie down, **s** the Lord GOD. 5002
34:17 *for* you, O my flock, thus **s** the Lord GOD; 559
34:20 Therefore thus **s** the Lord GOD unto them; 559
34:30 of Israel, *are* my people, **s** the Lord GOD. 5002
34:31 *and* I *am* your God, **s** the Lord GOD. 5002
35: 3 say unto it, Thus **s** the Lord GOD; Behold, 559
35: 6 Therefore, *as* I live, **s** the Lord GOD, I 5002
35:11 Therefore, *as* I live, **s** the Lord GOD, 5002
35:14 Thus **s** the Lord GOD; When the whole 559
36: 2 Thus **s** the Lord GOD; Because the enemy 559
36: 3 and say, Thus **s** the Lord GOD; 559
36: 4 Thus **s** the Lord GOD to the mountains, and 559
36: 5 Therefore thus **s** the Lord GOD; Surely in 559
36: 6 and to the valleys, Thus **s** the Lord GOD; 559
36: 7 Therefore thus **s** the Lord GOD; I have 559
36:13 Thus **s** the Lord GOD; Because they say 559
36:14 thy nations any more, **s** the Lord GOD. 5002
36:15 nations to fall any more, **s** the Lord GOD. 5002
36:22 the house of Israel, Thus **s** the Lord GOD; 559
36:23 that I *am* the LORD, **s** the Lord GOD, 5002
36:32 Not for your sakes do I *this,* **s** the Lord 5002
36:33 Thus **s** the Lord GOD; In the day that I 559
36:37 Thus **s** the Lord GOD; I will yet *for* this be 559
37: 5 Thus **s** the Lord GOD unto these bones; 559
37: 9 and say to the wind, Thus **s** the Lord GOD; 559
37:12 and say unto them, Thus **s** the Lord GOD; 559
37:14 spoken *it,* and performed *it,* **s** the LORD. 5002
37:19 Say unto them, Thus **s** the Lord GOD; 559
37:21 And say unto them, Thus **s** the Lord GOD; 559
38: 3 say, Thus **s** the Lord GOD; Behold, I *am* 559
38:10 Thus **s** the Lord GOD; It shall also come to 559
38:14 and say unto Gog, Thus **s** the Lord GOD; 559
38:17 Thus **s** the Lord GOD; *Art* thou he of 559
38:18 **s** the Lord GOD, *that* my fury shall come 5002
38:21 all my mountains, **s** the Lord GOD: 5002
39: 1 and say, Thus **s** the Lord GOD; 559
39: 5 for I have spoken *it,* **s** the Lord GOD. 5002
39: 8 it is come, and it is done, **s** the Lord GOD; 5002
39:10 those that robbed them, **s** the Lord GOD. 5002
39:13 that I shall be glorified, **s** the Lord GOD. 5002
39:17 thou son of man, thus **s** the Lord GOD; 559
39:20 and *with* all men of war, **s** the Lord GOD. 5002
39:25 Therefore thus **s** the Lord GOD; Now will I 559
39:29 upon the house of Israel, **s** the Lord GOD. 5002
43:18 unto me, Son of man, thus **s** the Lord GOD; 559
43:19 to minister unto me, **s** the Lord GOD, 5002
43:27 and I will accept you, **s** the Lord GOD. 5002
44: 6 the house of Israel, Thus **s** the Lord GOD; 559
44: 9 Thus **s** the Lord GOD; No stranger, 559
44:12 **s** the Lord GOD, and they shall bear their 5002
44:15 me the fat and the blood, **s** the Lord GOD: 5002
44:27 offer his sin offering, **s** the Lord GOD. 5002
45: 9 Thus **s** the Lord GOD; Let it suffice you, 559
45: 9 from my people, **s** the Lord GOD. 5002
45:15 reconciliation for them, **s** the Lord GOD. 5002
45:18 Thus **s** the Lord GOD; In the first *month,* in 559
46: 1 Thus **s** the Lord GOD; The gate of the inner 559
46:16 Thus **s** the Lord GOD; If the prince give a 559
47:13 Thus **s** the Lord GOD; This *shall be* 559
47:23 give *him* his inheritance, **s** the Lord GOD. 5002
48:29 these *are* their portions, **s** the Lord GOD. 5002
Hos 2:13 her lovers, and forgat me, **s** the LORD. 5002
2:16 it shall be at that day, **s** the LORD, 5002
2:21 I will hear, **s** the LORD, I will hear 5002
11:11 place them in their houses, **s** the LORD. 5002
Joel 2:12 Therefore also now, **s** the LORD, turn ye 5002
Am 1: 3 Thus **s** the LORD; For three transgressions 559
1: 5 go into captivity unto Kir, **s** the LORD. 559
1: 6 Thus **s** the LORD; For three transgressions 559
1: 8 Philistines shall perish, **s** the Lord GOD. 559
1: 9 Thus **s** the LORD; For three transgressions 559
1:11 Thus **s** the LORD; For three transgressions 559

Am 1:13 Thus **s** the LORD; For three transgressions 559
1:15 he and his princes together, **s** the LORD. 559
2: 1 Thus **s** the LORD; For three transgressions 559
2: 3 the princes thereof with him, **s** the LORD. 559
2: 4 Thus **s** the LORD; For three transgressions 559
2: 6 Thus **s** the LORD; For three transgressions 559
2:11 O ye children of Israel? **s** the LORD. 5002
2:16 flee away naked in that day, **s** the LORD. 5002
3:10 **s** the LORD, who store up violence and 5002
3:11 Therefore thus **s** the Lord GOD; 559
3:12 Thus **s** the LORD; As the shepherd taketh 559
3:13 **s** the Lord GOD, the God of hosts, 5002
3:15 houses shall have an end, **s** the LORD. 5002
4: 3 cast *them* into the palace, **s** the LORD. 5002
4: 5 O ye children of Israel, **s** the Lord GOD. 5002
4: 6 ye not returned unto me, **s** the LORD. 5002
4: 8 ye not returned unto me, **s** the LORD. 5002
4: 9 ye not returned unto me, **s** the LORD. 5002
4:10 ye not returned unto me, **s** the LORD. 5002
4:11 ye not returned unto me, **s** the LORD. 5002
5: 3 For thus **s** the Lord GOD; The city that 559
5: 4 For thus **s** the LORD unto the house of 559
5:16 the God of hosts, the Lord, **s** thus; 559
5:17 for I will pass through thee, **s** the LORD. 559
5:27 **s** the LORD, whose name *is* The God of 559
6: 8 **s** the LORD the God of hosts, I abhor 5002
6:14 of Israel, **s** the LORD the God of hosts; 5002
7: 3 for this: It shall not be, **s** the LORD. 559
7: 6 This also shall not be, **s** the Lord GOD. 559
7:11 For thus Amos **s**, Jeroboam shall die by 559
7:17 Therefore thus **s** the LORD; Thy wife shall 559
8: 3 be howlings in that day, **s** the Lord GOD: 5002
8: 9 come to pass in that day, **s** the Lord GOD, 5002
8:11 Behold, the days come, **s** the Lord GOD, 5002
9: 7 **s** the LORD. Have not I brought up Israel 5002
9: 8 destroy the house of Jacob, **s** the LORD. 5002
9:12 by my name, **s** the LORD that doeth this. 5002
9:13 Behold, the days come, **s** the LORD, 5002
9:15 I have given them, **s** the LORD thy God. 559
Ob 1: 1 Thus **s** the Lord GOD concerning Edom; 559
1: 3 that **s** in his heart, Who shall bring me down 559
1: 4 will I bring thee down, **s** the LORD. 5002
1: 8 Shall I not in that day, **s** the LORD, 5002
Mic 2: 3 Therefore thus **s** the LORD; Behold, 559
3: 5 Thus **s** the LORD concerning the prophets 559
4: 6 In that day, **s** the LORD, will I assemble 5002
5:10 come to pass in that day, **s** the LORD, 5002
6: 1 Hear ye now what the LORD **s**; Arise, 559
Na 1:12 Thus **s** the LORD; Though *they be* quiet, 559
2:13 **s** the LORD of hosts, and I will burn her 5002
3: 5 I *am* against thee, **s** the LORD of hosts; 5002
Hab 2:19 Woe unto him that **s** to the wood, Awake; 559
Zep 1: 2 all *things* from off the land, **s** the LORD. 5002
1: 3 off man from off the land, **s** the LORD. 5002
1:10 come to pass in that day, **s** the LORD, 5002
2: 9 **s** the LORD of hosts, the God of Israel, 5002
3: 8 Therefore wait ye upon me, **s** the LORD, 5002
3:20 captivity before your eyes, **s** the LORD. 559
Hag 1: 5 Now therefore thus **s** the LORD of hosts; 559
1: 7 Thus **s** the LORD of hosts; Consider your 559
1: 8 in it, and I will be glorified, **s** the LORD. 559
1: 9 **s** the LORD of hosts. Because of mine 5002
1:13 I *am* with you, **s** the LORD. 5002
2: 4 be strong, O Zerubbabel, **s** the LORD; 5002
2: 4 people of the land, **s** the LORD, and work: 5002
2: 4 for I *am* with you, **s** the LORD of hosts: 5002
2: 6 For thus **s** the LORD of hosts; Yet once, 559
2: 7 this house *with* glory, **s** the LORD of hosts. 559
2: 8 and the gold *is* mine, **s** the LORD of hosts. 5002
2: 9 than of the former, **s** the LORD of hosts: 559
2: 9 will I give peace, **s** the LORD of hosts. 5002
2:11 Thus **s** the LORD of hosts; Ask now 559
2:14 so *is* this nation before me, **s** the LORD; 5002
2:17 yet ye *turned* not to me, **s** the LORD. 5002
2:23 In that day, **s** the LORD of hosts, will I 5002
2:23 **s** the LORD, and will make thee as a 5002
2:23 I have chosen thee, **s** the LORD of hosts. 5002
Zec 1: 3 thou unto them, Thus **s** the LORD of hosts; 559
1: 3 **s** the LORD of hosts, and I will turn unto 5002
1: 3 I will turn unto you, **s** the LORD of hosts. 559
1: 4 saying, Thus **s** the LORD of hosts; 559
1: 4 nor hearken unto me, **s** the LORD. 5002
1:14 saying, Thus **s** the LORD of hosts; 559
1:16 Therefore thus **s** the LORD; I am returned 559
1:16 **s** the LORD of hosts, and a line shall be 5002
1:17 Cry yet, saying, Thus **s** the LORD of hosts; 559
2: 5 For I, **s** the LORD, will be unto her a wall 5002
2: 6 from the land of the north, **s** the LORD: 5002
2: 6 the four winds of the heaven, **s** the LORD. 5002
2: 8 For thus **s** the LORD of hosts; After 559
2:10 dwell in the midst of thee, **s** the LORD. 5002
3: 7 Thus **s** the LORD of hosts; If thou wilt 559
3: 9 **s** the LORD of hosts, and I will remove 5002
3:10 In that day, **s** the LORD of hosts, shall ye 5002
4: 6 but by my spirit, **s** the LORD of hosts. 559
5: 4 **s** the LORD of hosts, and it shall enter 5002
7:13 and I would not hear, **s** the LORD of hosts: 559
8: 2 Thus **s** the LORD of hosts; I was jealous 559
8: 3 Thus **s** the LORD; I am returned unto Zion, 559
8: 4 Thus **s** the LORD of hosts; There shall yet 559
8: 6 Thus **s** the LORD of hosts; If it be 559
8: 6 in my eyes? **s** the LORD of hosts. 5002
8: 7 Thus **s** the LORD of hosts; Behold, I *will* 559
8: 9 Thus **s** the LORD of hosts; Let your hands 559
8:11 *in* the former days, **s** the LORD of hosts. 5002
8:14 For thus **s** the LORD of hosts; As I thought 559
8:14 **s** the LORD of hosts, and I repented not: 559
8:17 these *are things* that I hate, **s** the LORD. 5002
8:19 Thus **s** the LORD of hosts; The fast of 559
8:20 Thus **s** the LORD of hosts; *It shall* yet 559
8:23 Thus **s** the LORD of hosts; In those days *it* 559
10:12 and down in his name, **s** the LORD. 5002
11: 4 Thus **s** the LORD my God; Feed the flock 559
11: 6 the inhabitants of the land, **s** the LORD: 5002
12: 1 **s** the LORD, which stretcheth forth 5002
Zec 12: 4 In that day, **s** the LORD, I will smite 5002
13: 2 to pass in that day, **s** the LORD of hosts, 5002
13: 7 *that is* my fellow, **s** the LORD of hosts: 5002
13: 8 to pass, *that* in all the land, **s** the LORD, 5002
Mal 1: 2 I have loved you, **s** the LORD. Yet ye say, 559
1: 2 **s** the LORD: yet I loved Jacob, 5002
1: 4 Whereas Edom **s**, We are impoverished, but 559
1: 4 thus **s** the LORD of hosts, They shall build, 559
1: 6 **s** the LORD of hosts unto you, O priests, 559
1: 8 or accept thy person? **s** the LORD of hosts. 559
1: 9 regard your persons? **s** the LORD of hosts. 559
1:10 no pleasure in you, **s** the LORD of hosts, 559
1:11 among the heathen, **s** the LORD of hosts. 559
1:13 ye have snuffed at it, **s** the LORD of hosts; 559
1:13 I accept this of your hand? **s** the LORD. 559
1:14 **s** the LORD of hosts, and my name *is* 559
2: 2 glory unto my name, **s** the LORD of hosts, 559
2: 4 might be with Levi, **s** the LORD of hosts. 559
2: 8 the covenant of Levi, **s** the LORD of hosts. 559
2:16 God of Israel, **s** that he hateth putting away: 559
2:16 with his garment, **s** the LORD of hosts: 559
3: 1 he *shall* come, **s** the LORD of hosts. 559
3: 5 and fear not me, **s** the LORD of hosts. 559
3: 7 I will return unto you, **s** the LORD of hosts. 559
3:10 me now herewith, **s** the LORD of hosts, 559
3:11 the time in the field, **s** the LORD of hosts. 559
3:12 a delightsome land, **s** the LORD of hosts. 559
3:13 have been stout against me, **s** the LORD. 559
3:17 they shall be mine, **s** the LORD of hosts, 559
4: 1 shall burn them up, **s** the LORD of hosts, 559
4: 3 that I *shall* do *this*, **s** the LORD of hosts. 559
Mt 4: 6 And **s** unto him, If thou be the Son of God, *3004*
4: 9 And **s** unto him, All these *things* will I give *3004*
4:10 Then **s** Jesus unto him, Get thee hence, *3004*
4:19 And he **s** unto them, Follow me, and I will *3004*
7:21 Not every one that **s** unto me, Lord, Lord, *3004*
8: 4 And Jesus **s** unto him, See thou tell no *man; 3004*
8: 7 And Jesus **s** unto him, I will come and *3004*
8:20 And Jesus **s** unto him, The foxes have *3004*
8:26 And he **s** unto them, Why are ye fearful, *3004*
9: 6 (then **s** he to the sick of the palsy,) *3004*
9: 9 and he **s** unto him, Follow me. And he *3004*
9:28 and Jesus **s** unto them, Believe ye that I am *3004*
9:37 Then **s** he unto his disciples, The harvest *3004*
12:13 Then **s** he to the man, Stretch forth thine *3004*
12:44 Then he **s**, I will return into my house from *3004*
13:14 which **s**, By hearing ye shall hear, and *3004*
13:51 Jesus **s** unto them, Have ye understood all *3004*
15:34 And Jesus **s** unto them, How many loaves *3004*
16:15 He **s** unto them, But whom say ye that I *3004*
17:25 He **s**, Yes. And when he was come into *3004*
17:26 Peter **s** unto him, Of strangers. Jesus saith *3004*
17:26 Jesus **s** unto him, Then are the children *5346*
18:22 Jesus **s** unto him, I say not unto thee, *3004*
19: 8 He **s** unto them, Moses because of *3004*
19:18 He **s** unto him, Which? Jesus said, *3004*
19:20 The young man **s** unto him, All these *things 3004*
20: 6 found others standing idle, and **s** unto them, *3004*
20: 7 He **s** unto them, Go ye also into *3004*
20: 8 the lord of the vineyard **s** unto his steward, *3004*
20:21 She **s** unto him, Grant that these my two *3004*
20:23 And he **s** unto them, Ye shall drink indeed *3004*
21:16 And Jesus **s** unto them, Yea; have ye never *3004*
21:31 Jesus **s** unto them, Verily I say unto you, *3004*
21:42 Jesus **s** unto them, Did ye never read in *3004*
22: 8 Then **s** he to his servants, The wedding is *3004*
22:12 And he **s** unto him, Friend, how camest *3004*
22:20 And he **s** unto them, Whose *is* this image *3004*
22:21 Then **s** he unto them, Render therefore *3004*
22:43 He **s** unto them, How then doth David in *3004*
26:18 and say unto him, The Master **s**, My time is *3004*
26:31 Then **s** Jesus unto them, All ye shall be *3004*
26:36 and **s** unto the disciples, Sit ye here, while I *3004*
26:38 Then **s** he unto them, My soul is exceeding *3004*
26:40 them asleep, and **s** unto Peter, What, *3004*
26:45 and **s** unto them, Sleep on now, and *3004*
26:64 Jesus **s** unto him, Thou hast said: *3004*
27:22 Pilate **s** unto them, What shall I do then *3004*
Mk 1:41 and touched him, and **s** unto him, I will; *3004*
1:44 And **s** unto him, See thou say nothing to *3004*
2:10 forgive sins, (he **s** to the sick of the palsy,) *3004*
2:17 When Jesus heard *it*, he **s** unto them, They *3004*
3: 3 And he **s** unto the man which had *3004*
3: 4 And he **s** unto them, Is it lawful to do good *3004*
3: 5 he **s** unto the man, Stretch forth thine hand. *3004*
4:35 when the even was come, he **s** unto them, *3004*
5:19 but **s** unto him, Go home to thy *friends*, and *3004*
5:36 he **s** unto the ruler of the synagogue, Be not *3004*
5:39 he **s** unto them, Why make ye *this* ado, and *3004*
6:38 He **s** unto them, How many loaves have ye? *3004*
6:50 and **s** unto them, Be of good cheer: *3004*
7:18 And he **s** unto them, Are ye so *3004*
7:34 he sighed, and **s** unto him, EPHPHATHA, *3004*
8: 1 his disciples unto *him*, and **s** unto them, *3004*
8:12 And he sighed deeply in his spirit, and **s**, *3004*
8:17 And when Jesus knew *it*, he **s** unto them, *3004*
8:29 And he **s** unto them, But whom say ye that *3004*
8:29 And Peter answereth and **s** unto him, *3004*
9:19 He answereth him, and **s**, O faithless *3004*
9:35 and called the twelve, and **s** unto them, *3004*
10:11 And he **s** unto them, Whosoever shall put *3004*
10:23 round about, and **s** unto his disciples, *3004*
10:24 answereth again, and **s** unto them, Children, *3004*
10:27 And Jesus looking upon them **s**, With men *3004*
10:42 Jesus called them to *him*, and **s** unto them, *3004*
11: 2 And **s** unto them, Go your way into *3004*
11:21 And Peter calling to remembrance **s** unto *3004*
11:22 And Jesus answering **s** unto them, *3004*
11:23 shall believe that *those things* which he **s** *3004*
11:23 to pass; he shall have whatsoever he **s**. *3004*
11:33 And Jesus answering **s** unto them, *3004*
12:16 And they brought *it*. And he **s** unto them, *3004*
12:43 and **s** unto them, Verily I say unto you, *3004*
13: 1 one of his disciples **s** unto him, Master, *3004*
14:13 and **s** unto them, Go ye into the city, and *3004*
Mk 14:14 The Master **s**, Where is the guestchamber, *3004*
14:27 And Jesus **s** unto them, All ye shall be *3004*
14:30 And Jesus **s** unto him, Verily I say unto *3004*
14:32 and he **s** to his disciples, Sit ye here, while I *3004*
14:34 And **s** unto them, My soul is exceeding *3004*
14:37 and **s** unto Peter, Simon, sleepest thou? *3004*
14:41 and **s** unto them, Sleep on now, and *3004*
14:45 straightway to him, and **s**, Master, master; *3004*
14:63 Then the high priest rent his clothes, and **s**, *3004*
15:28 And the scripture was fulfilled, which **s**, *3004*
16: 6 And he **s** unto them, Be not affrighted: *3004*
Lk 3:11 He answereth and **s** unto them, He that hath *3004*
5:39 desireth new: for he **s**, The old is better. *3004*
7:40 to say unto thee. And he **s**, Master, say *on. 5346*
11:24 and finding none, he **s**, I will return unto *3004*
16:29 Abraham **s** unto him, They have Moses and *3004*
18: 6 the Lord said, Hear what the unjust judge **s**. *3004*
19:22 And he **s** unto him, Out of thine own mouth *3004*
20:42 And David himself **s** in the book of Psalms, *3004*
22:11 The Master **s** unto thee, Where is *3004*
24:36 and **s** unto them, Peace *be* unto you. *3004*
Jn 1:21 And he **s**, I am not. Art thou *that* prophet? *3004*
1:29 and **s**, Behold the Lamb of God, *3004*
1:36 he walked, he **s**, Behold the Lamb of God. *3004*
1:38 and **s** unto them, What seek ye? *3004*
1:39 He **s** unto them, Come and see. They came *3004*
1:41 and **s** unto him, We have found *3004*
1:43 findeth Philip, and **s** unto him, Follow me. *3004*
1:45 and **s** unto him, We have found him, *3004*
1:46 Philip **s** unto him, Come and see. *3004*
1:47 and **s** of him, Behold an Israelite indeed, *3004*
1:48 Nathanael **s** unto him, Whence knowest *3004*
1:49 Nathanael answered and **s** unto him, Rabbi, *3004*
1:51 And he **s** unto him, Verily, verily, I say *3004*
2: 3 the mother of Jesus **s** unto him, They have *3004*
2: 4 Jesus **s** unto her, Woman, what have I to do *3004*
2: 5 His mother **s** unto the servants, *3004*
2: 5 Whatsoever he **s** unto you, do *it*. *3004*
2: 7 Jesus **s** unto them, Fill the waterpots with *3004*
2: 8 And he **s** unto them, Draw out now, and *3004*
2:10 And **s** unto him, Every man at *3004*
3: 4 Nicodemus **s** unto him, How can a man be *3004*
4: 7 Jesus **s** unto her, Give me to drink. *3004*
4: 9 Then **s** the woman of Samaria unto him, *3004*
4:10 and who it is that **s** to thee, Give me to *3004*
4:11 The woman **s** unto him, Sir, thou hast *3004*
4:15 The woman **s** unto him, Sir, give me this *3004*
4:16 Jesus **s** unto her, Go, call thy husband, and *3004*
4:19 The woman **s** unto him, Sir, I perceive that *3004*
4:21 Jesus **s** unto her, Woman, believe me, *3004*
4:25 The woman **s** unto him, I know that *3004*
4:26 Jesus **s** unto her, I that speak unto thee am *3004*
4:28 her way into the city, and **s** to the men, *3004*
4:34 Jesus **s** unto them, My meat is to do the will *3004*
4:49 The nobleman **s** unto him, Sir, come down *3004*
4:50 Jesus **s** unto him, Go *thy way;* thy son *3004*
5: 6 now a long time *in that case*, he **s** unto him, *3004*
5: 8 Jesus **s** unto him, Rise, take up thy bed, and *3004*
6: 5 he **s** unto Philip, Whence shall we buy *3004*
6: 8 Andrew, Simon Peter's brother, **s** unto him, *3004*
6:20 But he **s** unto them, It is I; be not afraid. *3004*
6:42 how *is it* then *that* he **s**, I came down from *3004*
7:50 Nicodemus **s** unto them, (he that came to *3004*
8:22 because he **s**, Whither I go, ye cannot *3004*
8:25 And Jesus **s** unto them, Even the same that *3004*
8:39 Jesus **s** unto them, If ye were Abraham's *3004*
11: 7 Then after that **s** he to *his* disciples, Let us *3004*
11:11 and after that he **s** unto them, Our friend *3004*
11:23 Jesus **s** unto her, Thy brother shall rise *3004*
11:24 Martha **s** unto him, I know that he shall rise *3004*
11:27 She **s** unto him, Yea, Lord: I believe that *3004*
11:39 **s** unto him, Lord, by this time he stinketh: *3004*
11:40 Jesus **s** unto her, Said I not unto thee, that, *3004*
11:44 Jesus **s** unto them, Loose him, and let *him 3004*
12: 4 Then **s** one of his disciples, Judas Iscariot, *3004*
13: 6 and *Peter* **s** unto him, Lord, dost thou wash *3004*
13: 8 Peter **s** unto him, Thou shalt never wash my *3004*
13: 9 Simon Peter **s** unto him, Lord, not my feet *3004*
13:10 Jesus **s** to him, He that is washed needeth *3004*
13:25 He then lying on Jesus' breast **s** unto him, *3004*
14: 5 Thomas **s** unto him, Lord, we know not *3004*
14: 6 Jesus **s** unto him, I am the way, the truth, *3004*
14: 8 Philip **s** unto him, Lord, shew us the Father, *3004*
14: 9 Jesus **s** unto him, Have I been so long time *3004*
14:22 Judas **s** unto him, not Iscariot, Lord, how is *3004*
16:17 What is this that he **s** unto us, A little while, *3004*
16:18 What is this that he **s**, A little while? *3004*
16:18 A little while? we cannot tell what he **s**. *2980*
18: 5 Jesus **s** unto them, I am *he*. And Judas also, *3004*
18:17 Then **s** the damsel that kept the door unto *3004*
18:17 *one* of this man's disciples? He **s**, I am not. *3004*
18:26 **s**, Did not I see thee in the garden with *3004*
18:38 Pilate **s** unto him, What is truth? And when *3004*
18:38 and **s** unto them, I find in him no fault *at 3004*
19: 4 went forth again, and **s** unto them, Behold, *3004*
19: 5 And *Pilate* **s** unto them, Behold the man. *3004*
19: 6 Crucify *him*, crucify *him*. Pilate **s** unto *3004*
19: 9 and **s** unto Jesus, Whence art thou? *3004*
19:10 Then **s** Pilate unto him, Speakest thou not *3004*
19:14 and he **s** unto the Jews, Behold your King. *3004*
19:15 Pilate **s** unto them, Shall I crucify your *3004*
19:24 the scripture might be fulfilled, which **s**, *3004*
19:26 he **s** unto his mother, Woman, behold thy *3004*
19:27 Then **s** he to the disciple, Behold thy *3004*
19:28 the scripture might be fulfilled, **s**, I thirst. *3004*
19:35 and he knoweth that he **s** true, that ye might *3004*
19:37 And again another scripture **s**, They shall *3004*
20: 2 whom Jesus loved, and **s** unto them, *3004*
20:13 She **s** unto them, Because they have taken *3004*
20:15 Jesus **s** unto her, Woman, why weepest *3004*
20:15 him to be the gardener, **s** unto him, Sir, *3004*
20:16 Jesus **s** unto her, Mary. She turned herself, *3004*
20:16 turned herself, and **s** unto him, Rabboni; *3004*
20:17 Jesus **s** unto her, Touch me not; for I am *3004*
20:19 and stood in the midst, and **s** unto them, *3004*

S

Jn 20:22 he breathed on *them,* and s unto them, *3004*
20:27 Then s he to Thomas, Reach hither thy *3004*
20:29 Jesus s unto him, Thomas, because *3004*
21: 3 Simon Peter s unto them, I go a fishing. *3004*
21: 5 Then Jesus s unto them, Children, have ye *3004*
21: 7 Therefore that disciple whom Jesus loved s *3004*
21:10 Jesus s unto them, Bring of the fish which *3004*
21:12 Jesus s unto them, Come *and* dine. *3004*
21:15 Jesus s to Simon Peter, Simon, *son* of *3004*
21:15 He s unto him, Yea, Lord; thou knowest *3004*
21:15 I love thee. He s unto him, Feed my lambs. *3004*
21:16 He s to him again the second time, Simon, *3004*
21:16 He s unto him, Yea, Lord; thou knowest *3004*
21:16 I love thee. He s unto him, Feed my sheep. *3004*
21:17 He s unto him the third time, Simon, *son* of *3004*
21:17 love thee. Jesus s unto him, Feed my sheep. *3004*
21:19 had spoken this, he s unto him, Follow me. *3004*
21:21 Peter seeing him s to Jesus, Lord, and *3004*
21:22 Jesus s unto him, If I will that he tarry till I *3004*
Ac 1: 4 which, *s he,* ye have heard of me. NIG
2:17 it shall come to pass in the last days, s God, *3004*
2:34 but he s himself, The LORD said unto my *3004*
7:48 temples made with hands; as s the prophet, *3004*
7:49 s the Lord: or what *is* the place of my rest? *3004*
12: 8 And he s unto him, Cast thy garment about *3004*
13:35 Wherefore he s also in another *psalm,* Thou *3004*
15:17 s the Lord, who doeth all these *things.* *3004*
21:11 and feet, and said, Thus s the Holy Ghost, *3004*
22: 2 they kept the more silence: and he s,) *5346*
Ro 3:19 we know that what *things* soever the law s, *3004*
3:19 it s to them who are under the law: *2980*
4: 3 For what s the scripture? Abraham believed *3004*
9:15 For he s to Moses, I will have mercy on *3004*
9:17 For the scripture s unto Pharaoh, Even for *3004*
9:25 As he s also in Osee, I will call *them* my *3004*
10: 8 But what s it? The word is nigh thee, *3004*
10:11 For the scripture s, Whosoever believeth on *3004*
10:16 For Esaias s, Lord, who hath believed our *3004*
10:19 First Moses s, I will provoke you to *3004*
10:20 But Esaias is very bold, and s, I was found *3004*
10:21 But to Israel he s, All day long have I *3004*
11: 2 Wot ye not what the scripture s of Elias? *3004*
11: 4 But what s the answer of God unto him? *3004*
11: 9 And David s, Let their table be made a *3004*
12:19 Vengeance *is* mine; I will repay, s the Lord. *3004*
14:11 For it is written, *As* I live, s the Lord, every *3004*
15:10 And again *he* s, Rejoice, *ye* Gentiles, *3004*
15:12 And again Esaias s, There shall be a root of *3004*
1Co 1:12 I say, that every one of you s, I am of Paul; *3004*
3: 4 For while one s, I am of Paul; and another, *3004*
6:16 one body? for two, s *he,* shall be one flesh. *5346*
9: 8 as a man? or s not the law the same also? *3004*
9:10 Or s he *it* altogether for our sakes? For our *3004*
14:21 all that will they not hear me, s the Lord. *3004*
14:34 to be under obedience, as also s the law. *3004*
15:27 But when *he* s, all *things* are put under *him,* *3004*
2Co 6: 2 (For he s, I have heard thee in a time *3004*
6:17 s the Lord, and touch not the unclean *thing;* *3004*
6:18 and daughters, s the Lord Almighty. *3004*
Gal 3:16 *He* s not, And to seeds, as of many; but *3004*
4:30 Nevertheless what s the scripture? Cast out *3004*
Eph 4: 8 Wherefore *he* s, When he ascended up on *3004*
5:14 Wherefore *he* s, Awake thou that sleepest, *3004*
1Ti 5:18 For the scripture s, Thou shalt not muzzle *3004*
Heb 1: 6 he s, And let all the angels of God worship *3004*
1: 7 And of the angels he s, Who maketh his *3004*
1: 8 But unto the Son *he* s, Thy throne, O God, NIG
3: 7 Wherefore, as the Holy Ghost s, To day if *3004*
5: 6 As he s also in another *place,* Thou *art* a *3004*
8: 5 s *he, that* thou make all *things* according to *5346*
8: 8 *he* s, Behold, the days come, saith the Lord, *3004*
8: 8 *he* saith, Behold, the days come, s the Lord, *3004*
8: 9 and I regarded them not, s the Lord. *3004*
8:10 house of Israel after those days, s the Lord; *3004*
8:13 In that *he* s, A new *covenant,* he hath made *3004*
10: 5 he s, Sacrifice and offering thou wouldest *3004*
10:16 s the Lord, I will put my laws into their *3004*
10:30 unto me, I will recompense, s the Lord. *3004*
Jas 2:23 And the scripture was fulfilled which s, *3004*
4: 5 Do ye think that the scripture s in vain, *3004*
4: 6 Wherefore *he* s, God resisteth the proud, *3004*
1Jn 2: 4 He that s, I know him, and keepeth not his *3004*
2: 6 He that s *he* abideth in him ought himself *3004*
2: 9 He that s *he* is in the light, and hateth his *3004*
Rev 1: 8 s the Lord, which is, and which was, and *3004*
2: 1 These *things* s he that holdeth the seven *3004*
2: 7 let him hear what the Spirit s unto *3004*
2: 8 These *things* s the first and the last, *3004*
2:11 let him hear what the Spirit s unto *3004*
2:12 These *things* s he which hath the sharp *3004*
2:17 let him hear what the Spirit s unto *3004*
2:18 These *things* s the Son of God, who hath *3004*
2:29 let him hear what the Spirit s unto *3004*
3: 1 These *things* s he that hath the seven spirits *3004*
3: 6 let him hear what the Spirit s unto *3004*
3: 7 These *things* s he *that is* holy, he *that is* *3004*
3:13 let him hear what the Spirit s unto *3004*
3:14 These *things* s the Amen, the faithful and *3004*
3:22 let him hear what the Spirit s unto *3004*
5: 5 And one of the elders s unto me, Weep not: *3004*
14:13 Yea, s the Spirit, that they may rest from *3004*
17:15 And he s unto me, The waters which thou *3004*
18: 7 for she s in her heart, I sit a queen, and *3004*
19: 9 And he s unto me, Write, Blessed *are* they *3004*
19: 9 And he s unto me, These are the true *3004*
22: 9 Then s he unto me, See *thou do it* not: for I *3004*
22:10 And he s unto me, Seal not the sayings of *3004*
22:20 He which testifieth these *things* s, Surely I *3004*

SAKE (145) [SAKES]
Ge 3:17 cursed *is* the ground for thy s; in sorrow 5668
8:21 curse the ground any more for man's s; 5668
12:13 it may be well with me for thy s; 5668+871.1
12:16 he entreated Abram well for her s: 5668+871.1
18:29 he said, I will not do *it* for forty's s. 5668+871.1
Ge 18:31 I will not destroy *it* for twenty's s. 5668+871.1
18:32 I will not destroy *it* for ten's s. 5668+871.1
20:11 they will slay me for my wife's s. 1697+5921
26:24 seed for my servant Abraham's s. 5668+871.1
30:27 that the LORD hath blessed me for thy s. 1558
39: 5 the Egyptian's house for Joseph's s; 1558
Ex 18: 8 and to the Egyptians for Israel's s, 182
21:26 he shall let him go free for his eye's s. 8478
21:27 he shall let him go free for his tooth's s. 8478
Nu 11:29 said unto him, Enviest thou for my s? 3807.1
25:11 while he was zealous for my s among 2967.1
25:18 slain in the day of the plague for Peor's s. 1697
1Sa 12:22 his people for his great name's s: 5668+871.1
23:10 to destroy the city for my s. 5668+871.1
2Sa 5:12 kingdom for his people Israel's s. 5668+871.1
7:21 For thy word's s, and according to 5668+871.1
9: 1 shew him kindness for Jonathan's s? 5668+871.1
9: 7 kindness for Jonathan thy father's s, 5668+871.1
18: 5 *Deal* gently for my s with the young man, 3807.1
1Ki 8:41 of a far country for thy name's s; 4616+3807.1
11:12 not do it for David thy father's s: 4616+3807.1
11:13 thy son for David my servant's s, 4616+3807.1
11:13 for Jerusalem's s, which I have 4616+3807.1
11:32 one tribe for my servant David's s, 4616+3807.1
11:32 and for Jerusalem's s, 4616+3807.1
11:34 his life for David my servant's s, 4616+3807.1
15: 4 Nevertheless for David's s did 4616+3807.1
2Ki 8:19 Judah for David his servant's s, 4616+3807.1
19:34 to save it, for mine own s, and for 4616+3807.1
19:34 and for my servant David's s. 4616+3807.1
20: 6 defend this city for mine own s, 4616+3807.1
20: 6 and for my servant David's s. 4616+3807.1
1Ch 17:19 O LORD, for thy servant's s, and 5668+871.1
2Ch 6:32 far country for thy great name's s, 4616+3807.1
Ne 9:31 Nevertheless for thy great mercies' s thou 871.1
Job 19:17 though I intreated for the children's *s* of NIH
Ps 6: 4 O save me for thy mercy's s. 4616+3807.1
23: 3 of righteousness for his name's s. 4616+3807.1
25: 7 thou me for thy goodness' s, 4616+3807.1
25:11 For thy name's s, O LORD, 4616+3807.1
31: 3 therefore for thy name's s lead me, 4616+3807.1
31:16 thy servant: save me for thy mercy's s. 871.1
44:22 for thy s are we killed all the day long; 5921
44:26 and redeem us for thy mercy's s. 4616+3807.1
69: 6 GOD of hosts, be ashamed for my s: 871.1
69: 6 that seek thee be confounded for my s, 871.1
69: 7 Because for thy s I have borne reproach; 5921
79: 9 away our sins, for thy name's s. 4616+3807.1
106: 8 he saved them for his name's s, 4616+3807.1
109:21 GOD the Lord, for thy name's s: 4616+3807.1
115: 1 for thy mercy, *and* for thy truth's s. 5921
132:10 For thy servant David's s turn not 5668+871.1
143:11 O LORD, for thy name's s: 4616+3807.1
143:11 for thy righteousness' s bring my soul out 871.1
Isa 37:35 this city to save it for mine own s, 4616+3807.1
37:35 and for my servant David's s. 4616+3807.1
42:21 pleased for his righteousness' s; 4616+3807.1
43:14 the Holy One of Israel; For your s 4616+3807.1
43:25 thy transgressions for mine own s, 4616+3807.1
45: 4 For Jacob my servant's s, and 4616+3807.1
48: 9 For my name's s will I defer mine 4616+3807.1
48:11 For mine own s, *even* for mine 4616+3807.1
48:11 own sake, *even* for mine own s, 4616+3807.1
54:15 together against thee shall fall for thy s. 5921
62: 1 For Zion's s will I not hold my 4616+3807.1
62: 1 for Jerusalem's s I will not rest, 4616+3807.1
63:17 Return for thy servants' s, 4616+3807.1
66: 5 that cast you out for my name's s, 4616+3807.1
Jer 14: 7 do thou *it* for thy name's s: 4616+3807.1
14:21 Do not abhor *us,* for thy name's s, 4616+3807.1
15:15 know that for thy s I have suffered rebuke. 5921
Eze 20: 9 I wrought for my name's s, that *it* 4616+3807.1
20:14 I wrought for my name's s, that *it* 4616+3807.1
20:22 and wrought for my name's s, 4616+3807.1
20:44 wrought with you for my name's s, 4616+3807.1
36:22 of Israel, but for mine holy name's s, 3807.1
Da 9:17 that is desolate, for the Lord's s. 4616+3807.1
9:19 for thine own s, O my God: 4616+3807.1
Jnh 1:12 for I know that for my s this great 7945+871.1
Mic 3:12 Therefore shall Zion for your s be 1558+871.1
Mt 5:10 which are persecuted for righteousness' s: *1752*
5:11 of evil against you falsely, for my s. *1752*
10:18 before governors and kings for my s, *1752*
10:22 shall be hated of all *men* for my name's s: *1223*
10:39 he that loseth his life for my s shall find it. *1752*
14: 3 and put *him* in prison for Herodias' s, *1223*
14: 9 nevertheless for the oaths' s, and *1223*
16:25 whosoever will lose his life for my s shall *1752*
19:12 eunuchs for the kingdom of heaven's s. *1223*
19:29 or children, or lands, for my name's s, *1752*
24: 9 be hated of all nations for my name's s. *1223*
24:22 for the elect's s those days shall be *1223*
Mk 4:17 or persecution ariseth for the word's s, *1223*
6:17 and bound him in prison for Herodias' s, *1223*
6:26 *yet* for his oaths' s, and for their sakes *1223*
8:35 but whosoever shall lose his life for my s *1752*
10:29 or wife, or children, or lands, for my s, *1752*
13: 9 be brought before rulers and kings for my s, *1752*
13:13 shall be hated of all *men* for my name's s: *1223*
13:20 but for the elect's s, whom he hath chosen, *1223*
Lk 6:22 your name as evil, for the Son of man's s. *1752*
9:24 but whosoever will lose his life for my s, *1752*
18:29 or children, for the kingdom of God's s, *1752*
21:12 before kings and rulers for my name's s. *1752*
21:17 shall be hated of all *men* for my name's s. *1223*
Jn 12: 9 and they came not for Jesus' s only, *1223*
13:37 thee now? I will lay down my life for thy s. *5228*
13:38 Wilt thou lay down thy life for my s? *5228*
14:11 or else believe me for the very works' s. *1223*
15:21 will they do unto you for my name's s, *1223*
Ac 9:16 *things* he must suffer for my name's s. *5228*
26: 7 For which hope's s, king Agrippa, I am *4012*
Ro 4:23 Now it was not written for his s alone, *1223*
8:36 For thy s we are killed all the day long; *1752*
13: 5 only for wrath, but also for conscience s. *1223*
Ro 15:30 for the Lord Jesus Christ's s, and for *1223*
1Co 4:10 We *are* fools for Christ's s, but ye *are* wise *1223*
9:23 And this I do for the gospel's s, that I *1223*
10:25 asking no question for conscience s: *1223*
10:27 eat, asking no question for conscience s. *1223*
10:28 eat not for his s that shewed *it,* and *1223*
10:28 *for* conscience *s:* for the earth *is* the Lord's, NIG
2Co 4: 5 and ourselves your servants for Jesus' s. *1223*
4:11 are alway delivered unto death for Jesus' s, *1223*
12:10 in persecutions, in distresses for Christ's s: *5228*
Eph 4:32 even as God for Christ's s hath forgiven *1722*
Php 1:29 believe on him, but also to suffer for his s; *5228*
Col 1:24 of Christ in my flesh for his body's s, *5228*
3: 6 For which *things*' s the wrath of God *1223*
1Th 1: 5 of *men* we were among you for your s. *1223*
5:13 them very highly in love for their work's s. *1223*
1Ti 5:23 but use a little wine for thy stomach's s *1223*
Tit 1:11 which *they* ought not, for filthy lucre's s. *5484*
Phm 1: 9 *Yet* for love's s I rather beseech *thee,* being *1223*
1Pe 2:13 to every ordinance of man for the Lord's s: *1223*
3:14 But and if ye suffer for righteousness' s, *1223*
1Jn 2:12 *your* sins are forgiven you for his name's s. *1223*
2Jn 1: 2 For the truth's s, which dwelleth in us, and *1223*
3Jn 1: 7 Because that for his name's s they went *5228*
Rev 2: 3 and for my name's s hast laboured, and *1223*

SAKES (31) [SAKE]
Ge 18:26 I will spare all the place for their s. 5668+871.1
Lev 26:45 I will for their s remember the covenant 3807.1
Dt 1:37 the LORD was angry with me for your s, 1558
3:26 was wroth with me for your s, 4616+3807.1
4:21 the LORD was angry with me for your s, 1697
Jdg 21:22 Be favourable unto them for our s: NIH
Ru 1:13 for it grieveth me much for your s that 4480
1Ch 16:21 yea, he reproved kings for their s, 5921
Ps 7: 7 for their s therefore return thou on high. 5921
105:14 yea, he reproved kings for their s: 5921
106:32 it went ill with Moses for their s: 5668+871.1
122: 8 For my brethren and companions' s, 4616+3807.1
Isa 65: 8 so will I do for my servants' s, 4616+3807.1
Eze 36:22 I do not *this* for your s, O house of 4616+3807.1
36:32 Not for your s do I *this,* saith 4616+3807.1
Da 2:30 for *their* s that shall make known 1701
Mal 3:11 I will rebuke the devourer for your s, and 3807.1
Mk 6:26 for their s which sat with *him,* he would not NIG
Jn 11:15 And I am glad for your s that I was not *1223*
12:30 came not because of me, but for your s. *1223*
17:19 And for their s I sanctify myself, that they *5228*
Ro 11:28 the gospel, *they are* enemies for your s: *1223*
11:28 *they are* beloved for the fathers' s. *1223*
1Co 4: 6 to myself and *to* Apollos for your s; *1223*
9:10 Or saith he *it* altogether for our s? For our *1223*
9:10 For our s, no doubt, *this* is written: that he *1223*
2Co 2:10 for your s *forgave I it* in the person of *1223*
4:15 For all *things are* for your s, that *1223*
8: 9 he was rich, *yet* for your s he became poor, *1223*
1Th 3: 9 for all the joy wherewith we joy for your s *1223*
2Ti 2:10 I endure all *things* for the elect's s, *1223*

SAKIA See SHACHIA

SALA (1) [SALAH]
Lk 3:35 *the son* of Heber, which was *the son* of S, *4527*

SALAH (6) [SALA]
Ge 10:24 Arphaxad begat S; and Salah begat Eber. 7974
10:24 Arphaxad begat Salah; and S begat Eber. 7974
11:12 lived five and thirty years, and begat S: 7974
11:13 Arphaxad lived after he begat S four 7974
11:14 And S lived thirty years, and begat Eber: 7974
11:15 S lived after he begat Eber four hundred 7974

SALAMIS (1)
Ac 13: 5 And when they were at S, they preached *4529*

SALATHIEL (4)
1Ch 3:17 And the sons of Jeconiah; Assir, S his son, 7597
Mt 1:12 brought to Babylon, Jechonias begat S; *4528*
1:12 begat Salathiel; and S begat Zorobabel; *4528*
Lk 3:27 which was *the son* of S, which was *the son* *4528*

SALCAH (2) [SALCHAH]
Jos 12: 5 mount Hermon, and in S, and in all Bashan, 5548
13:11 all mount Hermon, and all Bashan unto S; 5548

SALCHAH (2) [SALCAH]
Dt 3:10 and all Bashan, unto S and Edrei, 5548
1Ch 5:11 against them, in the land of Bashan unto S: 5548

SALE (3) [SELL]
Lev 25:27 let him count the years of the s thereof, 4465
25:50 the price of his s shall be according unto 4465
Dt 18: 8 beside **that which cometh of** the s of his 4465

SALECAH See SALCAH; SALCHAH

SALEM (4) [JERUSALEM]
Ge 14:18 Melchizedek king of S brought forth bread 8004
Ps 76: 2 In S also is his tabernacle, and his dwelling 8004
Heb 7: 1 For this Melchisedec, king of S, priest of *4532*
7: 2 and after that also King of S, which is, *4532*

SALIM (1)
Jn 3:23 John also was baptizing in Aenon near to S, *4530*

SALLAI (2)
Ne 11: 8 S, nine hundred twenty and eight. 5543
12:20 Of S, Kallai; of Amok, Eber; 5543

SALLU (3)
1Ch 9: 7 S the son of Meshullam, the son of 5543
Ne 11: 7 S the son of Meshullam, the son of Joed, 5543
12: 7 S, Amok, Hilkiah, Jedaiah. These *were* 5543

SALMA (4)
1Ch 2:11 Nahshon begat **S**, and Salma begat Boaz, 8007
2:11 Nahshon begat Salma, and **S** begat Boaz, 8007
2:51 **S** the father of Beth-lehem, Hareph 8007
2:54 The sons of **S**; Beth-lehem, and 8007

SALMON (6)
Ru 4:20 begat Nahshon, and Nahshon begat **S**, 8009
4:21 And **S** begat Boaz, and Boaz begat Obed, 8012
Ps 68:14 kings in it, it was *white as* snow in **S**. 6756
Mt 1: 4 begat Naasson; and Naasson begat **S**; *4533*
1: 5 And **S** begat Booz of Rachab; and *4533*
Lk 3:32 *the son* of Booz, which was *the son* of **S**, *4533*

SALMONE (1)
Ac 27: 7 we sailed under Crete, over against **S**; *4534*

SALOME (2)
Mk 15:40 of James the less and of Joses, and **S**; *4539*
16: 1 and **S**, had bought *sweet* spices, that they *4539*

SALT (41) [SALTED, SALTNESS, SALTPITS]
Ge 14: 3 in the vale of Siddim, which *is* the **s** sea. 4417
19:26 behind him, and she became a pillar of **s**. 4417
Lev 2:13 thy meat offering shalt thou season with **s**; 4417
2:13 neither shalt thou suffer the **s** of 4417
2:13 with all thine offerings thou shalt offer **s**. 4417
Nu 18:19 it *is* a covenant of **s** for ever before 4417
34: 3 be the outmost coast of the **s** sea eastward: 4417
34:12 and the goings out of it shall be *at* the **s** sea: 4417
Dt 3:17 *even* the **s** sea, under Ashdoth-pisgah 4417
29:23 **s**, *and* burning, *that* it is not sown, 4417
Jos 3:16 *even* the **s** sea, failed, *and* were cut off: 4417
12: 3 sea of the plain, *even* the **s** sea on the east, 4417
15: 2 border was from the shore of the **s** sea, 4417
15: 5 the east border *was* the **s** sea, *even* unto 4417
15:62 and the city of **s**, and En-gedi; 4417
18:19 bay of the **s** sea at the south end of Jordan: 4417
Jdg 9:45 and beat down the city, and sowed it *with* **s**. 4417
2Sa 8:13 smiting of the Syrians in the valley of **s**, 4417
2Ki 2:20 Bring me a new cruse, and put **s** therein. 4417
2:21 cast the **s** in there, and said, Thus saith 4417
14: 7 He slew *of* Edom in the valley of **s** ten 4417
1Ch 18:12 in the valley of **s** eighteen thousand. 4417
2Ch 13: 5 to him and to his sons *by* a covenant of **s**? 4417
25:11 went *to* the valley of **s**, and smote *of* 4417
Ezr 6: 9 the God of heaven, wheat, **s**, wine, and oil, 4416
7:22 and **s** without prescribing *how much*. 4416
Job 6: 6 that which is unsavoury be eaten without **s**? 4417
Ps 60: T smote of Edom in the valley of **s** twelve 4417
Jer 17: 6 *in* a **s** land and not inhabited. 4420
Eze 43:24 the priests shall cast **s** upon them, and 4417
47:11 shall not be healed; they shall be given to **s**. 4417
Mt 5:13 Ye are the **s** of the earth: but if the salt have *217*
5:13 but if the **s** have lost his savour, *217*
Mk 9:49 and every sacrifice shall be salted with **s**. *251*
9:50 **S** *is* good: but if the salt have lost his *217*
9:50 but if the **s** have lost his saltness, *217*
9:50 Have **s** in yourselves, and have peace one *217*
Lk 14:34 **S** *is* good: but if the salt have lost his savour, *217*
14:34 but if the **s** have lost his savour, *217*
Col 4: 6 speech *be* alway with grace, seasoned with **s**, *217*
Jas 3:12 so *can* no fountain *both* yield **s** water and *252*

SALTED (4) [SALT]
Eze 16: 4 to supple *thee;* thou wast not **s at all**, 4414+4414
Mt 5:13 have lost his savour, wherewith shall it be **s**? *233*
Mk 9:49 For every one shall be **s** with fire, and *233*
9:49 and every sacrifice shall be **s** with salt. *233*

SALTNESS (1) [SALT]
Mk 9:50 but if the salt have **lost** his **s**, wherewith will *358*

SALTPITS (1) [PIT, SALT]
Zep 2: 9 and **s**, and a perpetual desolation: 4379+4417

SALU (1)
Nu 25:14 *was* Zimri, the son of **S**, a prince of a chief 5543

SALUTATION (6) [SALUTE]
Lk 1:29 cast in her mind what manner of **s** this *783*
1:41 *that,* when Elisabeth heard the **s** of Mary, *783*
1:44 as soon as the voice of thy **s** sounded in mine *783*
1Co 16:21 The **s** of *me* Paul with mine own hand. *783*
Col 4:18 The **s** by the hand of me Paul. *783*
2Th 3:17 The **s** of Paul with mine own hand, which is *783*

SALUTATIONS (1) [SALUTE]
Mk 12:38 and *love* **s** in the marketplaces, *783*

SALUTE (39) [SALUTATION, SALUTATIONS, SALUTED, SALUTETH]
1Sa 10: 4 they will **s** thee, and 7592+7965+3807.1
13:10 went out to meet him, that he might **s** him. 1288
25:14 out of the wilderness to **s** our master; 1288
2Sa 8:10 to **s** him, and to bless him, 7592+7965+3807.1
2Ki 4:29 *thy way:* if thou meet any man, **s** him not; 1288
4:29 if any **s** thee, answer him not *again:* and 1288
10:13 we go down to **s** the children of the king 7965
Mt 5:47 And if ye **s** your brethren only, what do ye *782*
10:12 And when ye come into a house **s** it. *782*
Mk 15:18 And began to **s** him, Hail, King of the Jews. *782*
Lk 10: 4 nor shoes: and **s** no *man* by the way. *782*
Ac 25:13 and Bernice came unto Cesarea to **s** Festus. *782*
Ro 16: 5 **S** my wellbeloved Epenetus, who is *782*
16: 7 **S** Andronicus and Junia, my kinsmen, and *782*
16: 9 **S** Urban our helper in Christ, and *782*
16:10 **S** Apelles approved in Christ. Salute them *782*
16:10 **S** them which are of Aristobulus' *782*
16:11 **S** Herodion my kinsman. Greet them that be *782*
16:12 **S** Tryphena and Tryphosa, who labour in *782*
16:12 **S** the beloved Persis, which laboured much *782*
16:13 **S** Rufus chosen in the Lord, and his mother *782*
Ro 16:14 **S** Asyncritus, Phlegon, Hermas, Patrobas, *782*
16:15 **S** Philologus, and Julia, Nereus, and *782*
16:16 **S** one another with a holy kiss. The churches *782*
16:16 a holy kiss. The churches of Christ **s** you. *782*
16:21 Jason, and Sosipater, my kinsmen, **s** you. *782*
16:22 who wrote *this* epistle, **s** you in the Lord. *782*
1Co 16:19 The churches of Asia **s** you. Aquila and *782*
16:19 Aquila and Priscilla **s** you much in the Lord, *782*
2Co 13:13 All the saints **s** you. *782*
Php 4:21 **S** every saint in Christ Jesus. The brethren *782*
4:22 All the saints **s** you, chiefly they that are of *782*
Col 4:15 **S** the brethren which are in Laodicea, and *782*
2Ti 4:19 **S** Prisca and Aquila, and the household of *782*
Tit 3:15 All that are with me **s** thee. Greet them that *782*
Phm 1:23 There **s** thee Epaphras, my fellowprisoner in *782*
Heb 13:24 **S** all them that have the rule over you, and *782*
13:24 and all the saints. They of Italy **s** you. *782*
3Jn 1:14 *Our* friends **s** thee. Greet the friends by *782*

SALUTED (9) [SALUTE]
Jdg 18:15 house of Micah, and **s** him. 7592+7965+3807.1
1Sa 17:22 and came and **s** his brethren. 7592+7965+3807.1
30:21 to the people, he **s** them. 7592+7965+3807.1
2Ki 10:15 he **s** him, and said to him, Is thine heart 1288
Mk 9:15 greatly amazed, and running to *him* **s** him. *782*
Lk 1:40 into the house of Zacharias, and **s** Elisabeth. *782*
Ac 18:22 and gone up, and **s** the church, he went down *782*
21: 7 and **s** the brethren, and abode with them one *782*
21:19 And when he had **s** them, he declared *782*

SALUTETH (5) [SALUTE]
Ro 16:23 mine host, and of the whole church, **s** you. *782*
16:23 Erastus the chamberlain of the city **s** you, *782*
Col 4:10 Aristarchus my fellowprisoner **s** you, and *782*
4:12 who is *one* of you, a servant of Christ, **s** you, *782*
1Pe 5:13 at Babylon, elected together with *you,* **s** you; *782*

SALVATION (164) [SAVE]
Ge 49:18 I have waited for thy **s**, O LORD. 3444
Ex 14:13 stand still, and see the **s** of the LORD, 3444
15: 2 and song, and he is become my **s**: 3444
Dt 32:15 and lightly esteemed the Rock of his **s**. 3444
1Sa 2: 1 mine enemies; because I rejoice in thy **s**. 3444
11:13 for to day the LORD hath wrought **s** in 8668
14:45 who hath wrought this great **s** in Israel? 3444
19: 5 the LORD wrought a great **s** for all Israel: 8668
2Sa 22: 3 the horn of my **s**, my high tower, and 3468
22:36 Thou hast also given me the shield of thy **s**: 3468
22:47 and exalted be the God of the rock of my **s**. 3468
22:51 *He is* the tower of **s** for his king: and 3444
23: 5 for *this is* all my **s**, and all *my* desire, 3468
1Ch 16:23 the earth; shew forth from day to day his **s**. 3444
16:35 O God of our **s**, and gather us together, and 3468
2Ch 6:41 be clothed *with* **s**, and let thy saints rejoice 8668
20:17 and see the **s** of the LORD with you, 3444
Job 13:16 He also *shall be* my **s**: for a hypocrite shall 3444
Ps 3: 8 **S** *belongeth* unto the LORD: thy blessing 3444
9:14 the daughter of Zion: I will rejoice in thy **s**. 3444
13: 5 thy mercy; my heart shall rejoice in thy **s**. 3444
14: 7 O that the **s** of Israel *were come* out of 3444
18: 2 and the horn of my **s**, *and* my high tower. 3468
18:35 Thou hast also given me the shield of thy **s**: 3468
18:46 and let the God of my **s** be exalted. 3468
20: 5 We will rejoice in thy **s**, and in the name of 3444
21: 1 and in thy **s** how greatly shall he rejoice! 3444
21: 5 His glory *is* great in thy **s**: honour and 3444
24: 5 and righteousness from the God of his **s**. 3468
25: 5 for thou *art* the God of my **s**; on thee do I 3468
27: 1 The LORD *is* my light and my **s**; whom 3468
27: 9 me not, neither forsake me, O God of my **s**. 3468
35: 3 persecute me: say unto my soul, I *am* thy **s**. 3444
35: 9 in the LORD: it shall rejoice in his **s**. 3444
37:39 the **s** of the righteous *is* of the LORD: 8668
38:22 Make haste to help me, O Lord my **s**. 8668
40:10 I have declared thy faithfulness and thy **s**: 8668
40:16 let such as love thy **s** say continually, 8668
50:23 *aright* will I shew the **s** of God. 3468
51:12 Restore unto me the joy of thy **s**; and 3468
51:14 O God, thou God of my **s**: 8668
53: 6 O that the **s** of Israel *were come* out of 3444
62: 1 waiteth upon God: from him *cometh* my **s**. 3444
62: 2 He only *is* my rock and my **s**; *he is* my 3444
62: 6 He only *is* my rock and my **s**: *he is* my 3444
62: 7 In God *is* my **s** and my glory: the rock of 3468
65: 5 wilt thou answer us, O God of our **s**; 3468
68:19 us *with benefits, even* the God of our **s**. 3444
68:20 *He that is* our God *is* the God of **s**; and 4190
69:13 of thy mercy hear me, in the truth of thy **s**. 3468
69:29 let thy **s**, O God, set me up on high. 3444
70: 4 let such as love thy **s** say continually, 3444
71:15 thy righteousness *and* thy **s** all the day; 8668
74:12 of old, working **s** in the midst of the earth. 3444
78:22 not in God, and trusted not in his **s**: 3444
79: 9 Help us, O God of our **s**, for the glory of 3468
85: 4 O God of our **s**, and cause thine anger 3468
85: 7 thy mercy, O LORD, and grant us thy **s**. 3468
85: 9 Surely his **s** *is* nigh them that fear him; 3468
88: 1 O LORD God of my **s**, I have cried day 3444
89:26 my Father, my God, and the rock of my **s**. 3444
91:16 life will I satisfy him, and shew him my **s**. 3444
95: 1 us make a joyful noise to the rock of our **s**. 3468
96: 2 his name; shew forth his **s** from day to day. 3444
98: 2 The LORD hath made known his **s**: 3444
98: 3 all the ends of the earth have seen the **s** of 3444
106: 4 unto thy people: O visit me with thy **s**; 3444
116:13 I will take the cup of **s**, and call upon 3444
118:14 my strength and song, and is become my **s**. 3444
118:15 and **s** *is* in the tabernacles of the righteous: 3444
118:21 thou hast heard me, and art become my **s**. 3444
119:41 O LORD, *even* thy **s**, according to thy 8668
119:81 My soul fainteth for thy **s**: *but* I hope in thy 8668
119:123 Mine eyes fail for thy **s**, and for the word of 3444
119:155 **S** *is* far from the wicked: for they seek not 3444
119:166 I have hoped for thy **s**, and done thy 3444
Ps 119:174 I have longed for thy **s**, O LORD; and 3444
132:16 I will also clothe her priests with **s**: and 3468
140: 7 O GOD the Lord, the strength of my **s**, 3444
144:10 *It is he* that giveth **s** unto kings: 8668
149: 4 he will beautify the meek with **s**. 3444
Isa 12: 2 Behold, God *is* my **s**; I will trust, and not be 3444
12: 2 and *my* song; he also is become my **s**. 3444
12: 3 shall ye draw water out of the wells of **s**. 3444
17:10 thou hast forgotten the God of thy **s**, 3468
25: 9 we will be glad and rejoice in his **s**. 3444
26: 1 **s** will *God* appoint *for* walls and bulwarks. 3444
33: 2 our **s** also in the time of trouble. 3444
33: 6 the stability of thy times, *and* strength of **s**: 3444
45: 8 let them bring forth **s**, and let righteousness 3468
45:17 saved in the LORD *with* an everlasting **s**: 8668
46:13 shall not be far off, and my **s** shall not tarry: 8668
46:13 I will place **s** in Zion for Israel my glory. 8668
49: 6 that *thou* mayest be my **s** unto the end of 3444
49: 8 and in a day of **s** have I helped thee: 3444
51: 5 my **s** is gone forth, and mine arms shall 3468
51: 6 my **s** shall be for ever, and 3444
51: 8 and my **s** from generation to generation. 3444
52: 7 good tidings of good, that publisheth **s**; 3444
52:10 all the ends of the earth shall see the **s** of 3444
56: 1 for my **s** *is* near to come, and 3444
59:11 *there is* none; for **s**, *but* it is far off from us. 3444
59:16 therefore his arm **brought s** unto him; and 3467
59:17 and a helmet of **s** upon his head; 3444
60:18 thou shalt call thy walls **S**, and thy gates 3444
61:10 he hath clothed me with the garments of **s**, 3468
62: 1 and the **s** thereof as a lamp *that* burneth. 3444
62:11 the daughter of Zion, Behold, thy **s** cometh; 3468
63: 5 mine own arm **brought s** unto me; 3467
Jer 3:23 Truly in vain *is* **s** *hoped for* from the hills, NIH
3:23 truly in the LORD our God *is* the **s** of 8668
La 3:26 and quietly wait for the **s** of the LORD. 8668
Jnh 2: 9 *that* that I have vowed. **S** *is* of the LORD. 3444
Mic 7: 7 I will wait for the God of my **s**: 3468
Hab 3: 8 upon thine horses *and* thy chariots of **s**? 3444
3:13 Thou wentest forth for the **s** of thy people, 3468
3:13 thy people, *even* for **s** with thine anointed; 3468
3:18 the LORD, I will joy in the God of my **s**. 3468
Zec 9: 9 he *is* just, and **having s**; lowly, and 3467
Lk 1:69 And hath raised up a horn of **s** for us in *4991*
1:77 To give knowledge of **s** unto his people by *4991*
2:30 For mine eyes have seen thy **s**, *4992*
3: 6 And all flesh shall see the **s** of God. *4992*
19: 9 unto him, This day is **s** come to this house, *4991*
Jn 4:22 know what we worship: for **s** is of the Jews. *4991*
Ac 4:12 Neither is there **s** in any other: for there is *4991*
13:26 to you is the word of this **s** sent. *4991*
13:47 that thou shouldest be for **s** unto the ends of *4991*
16:17 high God, which shew unto us the way of **s**. *4991*
28:28 that the **s** of God is sent unto the Gentiles, *4992*
Ro 1:16 for it is the power of God unto **s** to every *4991*
10:10 with the mouth confession is made unto **s**. *4991*
11:11 *rather* through their fall **s** *is come* unto *4991*
13:11 for now *is* our **s** nearer than when we *4991*
2Co 1: 6 be afflicted, *it is* for your consolation and **s**, *4991*
1: 6 *it is* for your consolation and **s**. *4991*
6: 2 and in the day of **s** have I succoured thee: *4991*
6: 2 accepted time; behold, now *is* the day of **s**.) *4991*
7:10 For godly sorrow worketh repentance to **s** *4991*
Eph 1:13 the word of truth, the gospel of your **s**: *4991*
6:17 And take the helmet of **s**, and the sword of *4992*
Php 1:19 For I know that this shall turn to my **s** *4991*
1:28 but to you of **s**, and that of God. *4991*
2:12 work out your own **s** with fear and *4991*
1Th 5: 8 and love; and for a helmet, the hope of **s**. *4991*
5: 9 but to obtain **s** by our Lord Jesus Christ, *4991*
2Th 2:13 you to **s** through sanctification of the Spirit *4991*
2Ti 2:10 that they may also obtain the **s** which is in *4991*
3:15 which are able to make thee wise unto **s** *4991*
Tit 2:11 For the grace of God that bringeth **s** hath *4992*
Heb 1:14 minister for them who shall be heirs of **s**? *4991*
2: 3 shall we escape, if we neglect so great **s**; *4991*
2:10 to make the captain of their **s** perfect *4991*
5: 9 he became the author of eternal **s** unto all *4991*
6: 9 and *things* that accompany **s**, though we *4991*
9:28 appear the second time without sin unto **s**. *4991*
1Pe 1: 5 unto **s** ready to be revealed in the last time. *4991*
1: 9 end of your faith, *even* the **s** of *your* souls. *4991*
1:10 Of which **s** the prophets have inquired and *4991*
2Pe 3:15 *that* the longsuffering of our Lord *is* **s**; *4991*
Jude 1: 3 to write unto you of the common **s**, *4991*
Rev 7:10 **S** to our God which sitteth upon the throne, *4991*
12:10 Now is come **s**, and strength, and *4991*
19: 1 saying, Alleluia; **S**, and glory, and honour, *4991*

SAMARIA (124) [SAMARITAN, SAMARITANS]
1Ki 13:32 the high places which *are* in the cities of **S**, 8111
16:24 he bought the hill **S** of Shemer for two 8111
16:24 the name of Shemer, owner of the hill, **S**. 8111
16:28 slept with his fathers, and was buried in **S**: 8111
16:29 son of Omri reigned over Israel in **S** twenty 8111
16:32 the house of Baal, which he had built in **S**. 8111
18: 2 And *there was* a sore famine in **S**. 8111
20: 1 he went up and besieged **S**, and 8111
20:10 if the dust of **S** shall suffice for handfuls for 8111
20:17 saying, There are men come out of **S**. 8111
20:34 thee in Damascus, as my father made in **S**. 8111
20:43 house heavy and displeased, and came to **S**. 8111
21: 1 hard by the palace of Ahab king of **S**. 8111
21:18 to meet Ahab king of Israel, which *is* in **S**: 8111
22:10 void place *in* the entrance of the gate of **S**; 8111
22:37 So the king died, and was brought *to* **S**; and 8111
22:37 *to* Samaria; and they buried the king in **S**. 8111
22:38 *one* washed the chariot in the pool of **S**; 8111
22:51 **S** the seventeenth year of Jehoshaphat king 8111
2Ki 1: 2 a lattice in his upper chamber that *was* in **S**, 8111
1: 3 up to meet the messengers of the king of **S**, 8111
2:25 and from thence he returned *to* **S**. 8111
3: 1 **S** the eighteenth year of Jehoshaphat king 8111
3: 6 king Jehoram went out of **S** the same time, 8111
5: 3 my lord *were* with the prophet that *is* in **S**; 8111

2Ki 6:19 man whom ye seek. But he led them to **S.** 8111
6:20 when they were come *into* **S**, that Elisha 8111
6:20 and behold, *they were* in the midst of **S.** 8111
6:24 all his host, and went up, and besieged **S.** 8111
6:25 there was a great famine in **S**: and behold, 8111
7:1 of barley for a shekel, in the gate of **S.** 8111
7:18 to morrow about *this* time in the gate of **S**: 8111
10:1 Ahab had seventy sons in **S.** And Jehu 8111
10:1 Jehu wrote letters, and sent *to* **S**, unto 8111
10:12 he arose and departed, and came *to* **S.** 8111
10:17 when he came *to* **S**, he slew all that 8111
10:17 he slew all that remained unto Ahab in **S**, 8111
10:35 they buried him in **S.** And Jehoahaz his son 8111
10:36 the time that Jehu reigned over Israel in **S** 8111
13:1 son of Jehu *began* to reign over Israel in **S**, 8111
13:6 there remained the grove also in **S.**) 8111
13:9 with his fathers; and they buried him in **S**: 8111
13:10 son of Jehoahaz to reign over Israel in **S**, 8111
13:13 Joash was buried in **S** with the kings of 8111
14:14 and hostages, and returned to **S.** 8111
14:16 was buried in **S** with the kings of Israel; 8111
14:23 of Joash king of Israel *began* to reign in **S**, 8111
15:8 Jeroboam reign over Israel in **S** six months. 8111
15:13 of Judah; and he reigned a full month in **S.** 8111
15:14 came *to* **S**, and smote Shallum the son of 8111
15:14 smote Shallum the son of Jabesh in **S**, and 8111
15:17 over Israel, *and reigned* ten years in **S.** 8111
15:23 Menahem *began* to reign over Israel in **S**, 8111
15:25 conspired against him, and smote him in **S**, 8111
15:27 of Remaliah *began* to reign over Israel in **S**, 8111
17:1 of Elah to reign in **S** over Israel nine years. 8111
17:5 went up *to* **S**, and besieged it three years. 8111
17:6 the king of Assyria took **S**, and 8111
17:24 placed *them* in the cities of **S** instead of 8111
17:24 they possessed **S**, and dwelt in the cities 8111
17:26 hast removed, and placed in the cities of **S**, 8111
17:28 whom they had carried away from **S** came 8111
18:9 king of Assyria came up against **S**, 8111
18:10 year of Hoshea king of Israel, **S** was taken. 8111
18:34 have they delivered **S** out of mine hand? 8111
21:13 I will stretch over Jerusalem the line of **S**, 8111
23:18 the bones of the prophet that came out of **S.** 8111
23:19 the high places that *were* in the cities of **S**, 8111
2Ch 18:2 *certain* years he went down to Ahab to **S.** 8111
18:9 place *at* the entering in of the gate of **S**; 8111
22:9 they caught him, (for he *was* hid in **S**,) and 8111
25:13 from **S** even unto Beth-horon, and 8111
25:24 the hostages also, and returned *to* **S.** 8111
28:8 spoil from them, and brought the spoil to **S.** 8111
28:9 he went out before the host that came to **S**, 8111
28:15 to their brethren: then they returned *to* **S.** 8111
Ezr 4:10 set in the cities of **S**, and the rest *that are on* 8115
4:17 the rest of their companions that dwell in **S**, 8115
Ne 4:2 before his brethren and the army of **S**, 8111
Isa 7:9 the head of Ephraim *is* **S**, and the head of 8111
7:9 and the head of **S** *is* Remaliah's son. 8111
8:4 the spoil of **S** shall be taken away before 8111
9:9 *even* Ephraim and the inhabitant of **S**, 8111
10:9 Hamath as Arpad? *is* not **S** as Damascus? 8111
10:10 did excel *them of* Jerusalem and *of* **S**; 8111
10:11 as I have done unto **S** and her idols, so 8111
36:19 and have they delivered **S** out of my hand? 8111
Jer 23:13 I have seen folly in the prophets of **S**; 8111
31:5 yet plant vines upon the mountains of **S**: 8111
41:5 from Shiloh, and from **S**, *even* fourscore 8111
Eze 16:46 thine elder sister *is* **S**, she and her daughters 8111
16:51 Neither hath **S** committed half of thy sins; 8111
16:53 the captivity of **S** and her daughters, then 8111
16:55 **S** and her daughters shall return to their 8111
23:4 **S** *is* Aholah, and Jerusalem Aholibah. 8111
23:33 and desolation, *with* the cup of thy sister **S.** 8111
Hos 7:1 was discovered, and the wickedness of **S**: 8111
8:5 Thy calf, O **S**, hath cast *thee* off; 8111
8:6 but the calf of **S** shall be broken in pieces. 8111
10:5 The inhabitants of **S** shall fear because 8111
10:7 *As for* **S**, her king is cut off as the foam 8111
13:16 **S** shall become desolate; for she hath 8111
Am 3:9 yourselves upon the mountains of **S**, 8111
3:12 out that dwell in **S** in the corner of a bed, 8111
4:1 of Bashan, that *are* in the mountain of **S**, 8111
6:1 ease in Zion, and trust in the mountain of **S**, 8111
8:14 They that swear by the sin of **S**, and say, 8111
Ob 1:19 the fields of Ephraim, and the fields of **S**: 8111
Mic 1:1 which he saw concerning **S** and Jerusalem. 8111
1:5 *is it* not **S**? and what *are* the high places of 8111
1:6 Therefore I will make **S** as a heap of 8111
Lk 17:11 that he passed through the midst of **S** and *4540*
Jn 4:4 And he must needs go through **S.** *4540*
4:5 Then cometh he to a city of **S**, which is *4540*
4:7 There cometh a woman of **S** to draw water: *4540*
4:9 Then saith the woman of **S** unto him, *4542*
4:9 drink of me, which am a woman of **S**? *4542*
Ac 1:8 and in **S**, and unto the uttermost part of *4540*
8:1 throughout the regions of Judea and **S**, *4540*
8:5 Then Philip went down to the city of **S**, and *4540*
8:9 and bewitched the people of **S**, giving out *4540*
8:14 heard that **S** had received the word of God, *4540*
9:31 rest throughout all Judea and Galilee and **S**, *4540*
15:3 they passed through Phenice and **S**, *4540*

SAMARITAN (3) [SAMARIA]

Lk 10:33 But a certain **S**, as he journeyed, *4541*
17:16 his feet, giving him thanks: and he was a **S.** *4541*
Jn 8:48 Say we not well that thou art a **S**, and hast a *4541*

SAMARITANS (7) [SAMARIA]

2Ki 17:29 of the high places which the **S** had made, 8118
Mt 10:5 and into *any* city of the **S** enter ye not: *4541*
Lk 9:52 and entered into a village of the **S**, *4541*
Jn 4:9 For the Jews have no dealings with the **S.** *4541*
4:39 And many of the **S** of that city believed on *4541*
4:40 So when the **S** were come unto him, *4541*
Ac 8:25 the gospel in many villages of the **S.** *4541*

SAME (332) [SELFSAME]

Ge 2:13 the **s** *is it* that compasseth the whole land of 1931
5:29 This *s* shall comfort us concerning our work NIH
6:4 the **s** *became* mighty *men* which *were* of 1992
7:11 the **s** day were all the fountains of the great 2088
10:12 and Calah: **the s** *is* a great city. 1931
14:8 and the king of Bela (**the s** *is* Zoar); 1931
15:18 In the **s** day the LORD made a covenant 1931
19:37 **the s** *is* the father of the Moabites unto *this* 1931
19:38 **the s** *is* the father of the children of 1931
21:8 Abraham made a great feast the *s* day that NIH
23:2 **the s** *is* Hebron in the land of Canaan: 1931
23:19 **the s** *is* Hebron in the land of Canaan. 1931
24:14 *let the s be* she *that* thou hast appointed for NIH
24:44 *let* **the s** *be* the woman whom the LORD 1931
25:30 with that s[S] red *pottage*; for I *am* faint: 122
26:12 received in the **s** year an hundredfold: 1931
26:24 the LORD appeared unto him **the s** night, 1931
26:32 it came to pass **the s** day, that Isaac's 1931
32:13 he lodged there that *s* night; and took of that NIH
41:48 about every city, laid he up in **the s.** 1886.3
44:6 and he spake unto them these *s* words. NIH
48:7 in the way of Ephrath; **the s** *is* Beth-lehem. 1931
Ex 5:6 Pharaoh commanded **the s** day 1931
12:6 *up* until the fourteenth day of **the s** month: 2088
19:1 the **s** day came they *into* the wilderness of 2088
25:31 and his flowers, shall be of **the s.** 5089.1
25:35 *be* a knop under two branches of **the s**, 5089.1
25:35 a knop under two branches of **the s**, and 5089.1
25:35 and a knop under two branches of **the s**, 5089.1
25:36 and their branches shall be of **the s**: 5089.1
27:2 his horns shall be of **the s**: and thou shalt 2050.2
28:8 which *is* upon it, shall be of **the s**, 5105.2
30:2 the horns thereof *shall be* of **the s.** 5105.2
37:17 his knops, and his flowers, were of **the s**: 5089.1
37:21 a knop under two branches of **the s**, and 5089.1
37:21 a knop under two branches of **the s**, and 5089.1
37:21 and a knop under two branches of **the s**, 5089.1
37:22 and their branches were of **the s**: 5089.1
37:25 of it; the horns thereof were of **the s.** 5105.2
38:2 of it; the horns thereof were of **the s**: 5105.2
39:5 that *was* upon it, *was* of **the s**, according to 1931
Lev 7:15 shall be eaten the **s** day that it is offered; NIH
7:16 it shall be eaten the *s* day that he offereth NIH
19:6 It shall be eaten the *s* day ye offer it, and NIH
22:30 On **the s** day it shall be eaten up; ye shall 1931
23:6 on the fifteenth day of the **s** month *is* 2088
23:28 ye shall do no work in that **s** day: for it *is* a 6106
23:29 *it be* that shall not be afflicted in that **s** day, 6106
23:30 soul *it be* that doeth any work in that **s** day, 6106
23:30 the **s** soul will I destroy from among his 1931
Nu 4:8 cover **the s** with a covering of badgers' 2050.2
6:11 and shall hallow his head that *s* day. NIH
9:13 even the **s** soul shall be cut off from among 1931
10:32 shall do unto us, the **s** will we do unto thee. NIH
15:30 a stranger, **the s** reproacheth the LORD; 1931
32:10 the LORD'S anger was kindled **the s** 1931
Dt 9:20 and I prayed for Aaron also **the s** time. 1931
14:28 all the tithe of thine increase **the s** year, 1931
27:11 Moses charged the people **the s** day, 1931
31:22 Moses therefore wrote this song **the s** day, 1931
Jos 6:15 compassed the city after the **s** manner seven 2088
11:16 of Israel, and the valley of the **s**; 1886.4
15:8 side of the Jebusite; the **s** *is* Jerusalem: 1931
Jdg 6:25 it came to pass the **s** night, that the LORD 1931
7:4 shall go with thee, **the s** shall go with thee; 1931
7:4 shall not go with thee, **the s** shall not go. 1931
7:9 it came to pass the **s** night, that the LORD 1931
1Sa 4:12 came *to* Shiloh **the s** day with his clothes 1931
6:15 sacrificed sacrifices **the s** day unto 1931
6:16 seen *it*, they returned *to* Ekron **the s** day. 1931
9:17 to thee of: this *s* shall reign over my people. NIH
10:12 one of **the s place** answered and said, 8033
14:35 **the s** was the first altar that he built unto 2050.2
17:23 and spake according to **the s** words: 428
17:30 and spake after **the s** manner: 2088
31:6 all his men, that *s* day together. NIH
2Sa 2:23 he fell down there, and died **in the s place**: 8478
5:7 hold of Zion: **the s** *is* the city of David. 1931
23:7 they shall be utterly burnt with fire in the **s** NIH
23:8 the captains; **the s** *was* Adino the Eznite: 1931
1Ki 7:35 and the borders thereof *were* of **the s.** 5089.1
8:64 **The s** day did the king hallow the middle of 1931
13:3 he gave a sign **the s** day, saying, This *is* 1931
13:9 nor turn again by the *s* way that thou NIH
2Ki 3:6 king Jehoram went out of Samaria **the s** 1931
8:22 Then Libnah revolted at **the s** time. 1931
19:29 second year **that which springeth of the s**; 7823
19:33 *by the s* shall he return, and shall not come NIH
1Ch 1:27 Abram; **the s** *is* Abraham. 1931
4:33 all their villages that *were* round about **the s** 428
16:17 hath confirmed **the s** to Jacob for a law, 1886.3
17:3 it came to pass **the s** night, that the word of 1931
2Ch 7:8 Also at **the s** time Solomon kept the feast 1931
13:9 *the s* may be a priest of *them that are* no NIH
15:11 they offered unto the LORD **the s** time, 1931
16:10 oppressed *some* of the people **the s** time. 1931
18:7 **the s** *is* Micaiah the son of Imla. 1931
20:26 the name of the **s** place was called, 1931
21:10 **The s** time also did Libnah revolt from 1931
27:5 the children of Ammon gave him **the s** year 1931
32:12 Hath not **the s** Hezekiah taken away his 1931
32:30 **This s** Hezekiah also stopped the upper 1931
34:28 and upon the inhabitants of **the s.** 2050.2
35:16 of the LORD was prepared **the s** day, 1931
Ezr 4:15 sedition within **the s** of old time: 1459+1886.9
5:3 At **the s** time came to them Tatnai, 0.2
5:13 *s* king Cyrus made a decree to build this NIH
5:16 came **the s** Sheshbazzar, *and* laid 1791
6:3 In the first year of Cyrus the king *the s* NIH
10:23 and Shimei, and Kelaiah, (the **s** *is* Kelita,) 1931
Ne 4:22 Likewise at the **s** time said I unto 1931
6:4 and I answered them after the **s** manner. 2088
10:37 that the **s** Levites *might* have the tithes in 1992
Est 9:1 on the thirteenth day of **the s**, 2050.2
9:17 on the fourteenth day of **the s** rested they, 2050.2
9:18 on the fifteenth *day* of **the s** they rested, 2050.2
9:21 and the fifteenth day of **the s**, yearly, 2050.2
Job 4:8 and sow wickedness, reap **the s.** 1930.2
13:2 What ye know, *the s* do I know also. I *am* NIH
Ps 68:23 *and* the tongue of thy dogs in **the s.** 1930.2
75:8 full *of* mixture; and he poureth out of **the s**: 2088
102:27 thou *art* **the s**, and thy years shall have no 1931
105:10 confirmed **the s** unto Jacob for a law, *and* 1886.3
113:3 **the s** the LORD'S name *is* to be praised. 2050.2
Pr 28:24 **the s** *is* the companion of a destroyer. 1931
Ecc 9:15 yet no man remembered that *s* poor man. NIH
Isa 7:20 In **the s** day shall the Lord shave with a 1931
20:2 At **the s** time spake the LORD by Isaiah 1931
37:30 second year **that which springeth of the s**: 7823
37:34 *by the s* shall he return, and shall not come NIH
Jer 27:8 kingdom which will not serve **the s** 2050.2
28:1 it came to pass **the s** year, in the beginning 1931
28:17 So Hananiah the prophet died **the s** year in 1931
31:1 At **the s** time, saith the LORD, will I be 1931
39:10 them vineyards and fields at **the s** time. 1931
Eze 3:18 **the s** wicked *man* shall die in his iniquity; 1931
10:16 the **s** wheels also turned not from beside 1992
10:22 the likeness of their faces *was* the **s** faces 1992
21:26 this *shall* not *be* **the s**: exalt *him that is* low, 2063
23:38 they have defiled my sanctuary in **the s** 1931
23:39 they came **the s** day into my sanctuary to 1931
24:2 thee the name of the day, *even* of this **s** day: 6106
24:2 set himself against Jerusalem this **s** day. 6106
38:10 *that* at **the s** time shall things come into thy 1931
38:18 it shall come to pass at **the s** time when 1931
44:3 and shall go out by the way of **the s.** 2050.2
Da 3:6 worshippeth shall **the s** hour be cast into 0.2
3:15 ye shall be cast the **s** hour into the midst 1886.9
4:33 The **s** hour was the thing fulfilled upon 1886.9
4:36 At **the s** time my reason returned unto me; 0.2
5:5 In the **s** hour came forth fingers of a 1886.9
5:12 of doubts, were found in the **s** Daniel, 1886.8
7:21 the **s** horn made war with the saints, and 1797
12:1 since there was a nation *even* to that **s** time: 1931
Am 2:7 and his father will go in unto the *s* maid, NIH
Zep 1:9 In the **s** day also will I punish all those that 1931
Zec 6:10 come thou the **s** day, and go *into* the house 1931
Mal 1:11 **the s** my name *shall be* great among 2050.2
Mt 3:4 And the **s** John had his raiment of camel's *846*
5:19 teach *them*, **the s** shall be called great in *3778*
5:46 have ye? do not even the publicans the **s**? *846*
10:19 for it shall be given you in that *s* hour what NIG
12:50 **the s** is my brother, and sister, and mother. *846*
13:1 **The s** day went Jesus out of the house, and *1565*
13:20 *places*, **the s** is he that heareth the word, *3778*
15:22 a woman of Canaan came out of **the s** *1565*
18:1 At **the s** time came the disciples unto Jesus, *1565*
18:4 **the s** is greatest in the kingdom of heaven. *3778*
18:28 But **the s** servant went out, and found one *1565*
21:42 **the s** is become the head of the corner: *3778*
22:23 **The s** day came to him *the* Sadducees, *1565*
24:13 endure unto the end, **the s** shall be saved. *3778*
25:16 the five talents went and traded with **the s**, *846*
26:23 with me in the dish, **the s** shall betray me. *3778*
26:44 prayed the third time, saying the **s** words. *846*
26:48 Whomsoever I shall kiss, that **s** is he: NIG
26:55 In that *s* hour said Jesus to the multitudes, NIG
27:44 crucified with him, cast the **s** in his teeth. *846*
Mk 3:35 **the s** is my brother, and my sister, and *3778*
4:35 And the **s** day, when the even was come, *1565*
8:35 and the gospel's, **the s** shall save it. *3778*
9:35 *the s* shall be last of all, and servant of all. NIG
10:10 disciples asked him again of the **s** *matter.* *846*
13:13 endure unto the end, **the s** shall be saved. *3778*
14:39 and prayed, and spake the **s** words. *846*
14:44 saying, Whomsoever I shall kiss, *that* **s** is he; *846*
Lk 2:8 And there were in the **s** country shepherds *846*
2:25 and the **s** man *was* just and devout, *3778*
6:33 have ye? for sinners also do *even* the **s.** *846*
6:38 For with the **s** measure that ye mete withal it *846*
7:21 And in that *s* hour he cured many of *their* NIG
7:47 to whom little is forgiven, *the s* loveth little. NIG
9:24 lose his life for my sake, **the s** shall save it. *3778*
9:48 is least among you all, **the s** shall be great. *3778*
10:7 And in **the s** house remain, eating and *846*
10:10 go *your ways* out into the streets of **the s**, *846*
12:12 For the Holy Ghost shall teach you in **the s** *846*
13:31 The **s** day there came certain *of* *846*
16:1 **the s** was accused unto him that he had *3778*
17:29 But the *s* day that Lot went out of Sodom it NIG
20:17 **the s** is become the head of the corner? *3778*
20:19 the scribes the **s** hour sought to lay hands on *846*
20:47 **the s** shall receive greater damnation. *3778*
23:12 And the **s** day Pilate and Herod were made *846*
23:40 seeing thou art in the **s** condemnation? *846*
23:51 (**The s** had not consented to the counsel *3778*
24:13 two of them went *that* **s** day to a village *846*
24:33 And they rose up the **s** hour, and returned to *846*
Jn 1:2 **The s** was in the beginning with God. *3778*
1:7 **The s** came for a witness, to bear witness *3778*
1:33 to baptize with water, **the s** said unto me, *1565*
1:33 **the s** is he which baptizeth with the Holy *3778*
3:2 **The s** came to Jesus by night, and said unto *3778*
3:26 **the s** baptizeth, and all *men* come to him. *3778*
4:53 So the father knew that *it was* at **the s** hour, *1565*
5:9 walked: and on the **s** day was the sabbath. *1565*
5:11 **the s** said unto me, Take up thy bed, and *1565*
5:36 **the s** works that I do, bear witness of me, *846*
7:18 **the s** is true, and no unrighteousness is in *3778*
8:25 Even the **s** that I said unto you *from* *5100*
10:1 other way, **the s** is a thief and a robber. *1565*
11:6 he abode two days *still* in the *s* place where NIG
11:49 being the high priest that *s* year, said unto NIG
12:21 **The s** came therefore to Philip, which was *3778*
12:48 **the s** shall judge him in the last day. *1565*
15:5 I in him, **the s** bringeth forth much fruit: *3778*
18:13 which was the high priest that *s* year. NIG
20:19 Then **the s** day at evening, being the first *1565*

Ac 1:11 this *s* Jesus, which is taken up from you into NIG
1:22 unto *that s* day that he was taken up from NIG
2:36 that God hath made **that** s Jesus, whom ye 3778
2:41 the s day there were added *unto them* about 1565
7:19 **The s** dealt subtilly with our kindred, and 3778
7:35 **the s** did God send *to be* a ruler and 3778
8: 9 which beforetime in the *s* city used sorcery, NIG
8:35 and began at the s scripture, and 3778
12: 6 the s night Peter was sleeping between two 1565
13:33 God hath fulfilled **the s** unto us their 3778
14: 9 **The s** heard Paul speak: who stedfastly 3778
15:27 who shall also tell *you* the s *things* by 846
16:17 **The s** followed Paul and us, and cried, 3778
16:18 come out of her. And he came out the s hour. 846
16:33 And he took them the s hour of the night, 1565
18: 3 And because *he* was of the s **craft**, 3673
19:23 And **the s** time there arose no small 1565+2596
21: 9 And **the s** *man* had four daughters, virgins, 3778
22:13 And the s hour I looked up upon him. 846
24:20 Or else let these s *here* say, if they have 846
28: 7 In the s quarters were possessions of 1565+4012
Ro 1:32 not only do the s, but have pleasure in them 846
2: 1 for thou that judgest doest the s *things*. 846
2: 3 them which do such *things*, and doest the s, 846
8:20 by reason of him who hath subjected *the s*, NIG
9:17 Even for this s *purpose* have I raised thee up, 846
9:21 of the s lump to make one vessel unto 846
10:12 for the s Lord over all *is* rich unto all that 846
12: 4 and all members have not the s office: 846
12:16 *Be* of the s mind one towards another. 846
13: 3 *is* good, and thou shalt have praise of the s: 846
1Co 1:10 that ye all speak the s thing, and *that* there be 846
1:10 *that* ye be perfectly joined together in the s 846
1:10 in the same mind and in the s judgment. 846
7:20 Let every man abide in **the s** calling 3588
8: 3 any *man* love God, **the s** is known of him. 3778
9: 8 as a man? or saith not the law the s also? 3778
10: 3 And did all eat the s spiritual meat; 846
10: 4 And did all drink the s spiritual drink: 846
11:23 That the Lord Jesus the *s* night in which he NIG
11:25 **After the s manner** also *he took* the cup, 5615
12: 4 there are diversities of gifts, but the s Spirit. 846
12: 5 of administrations, but the s Lord. 846
12: 6 but it is the s God which worketh all in all. 846
12: 8 to another the word of knowledge by the s 846
12: 9 To another faith by the s Spirit; to another 846
12: 9 to another the gifts of healing by the s Spirit; 846
12:25 *that* the members should have the s care one 846
15:39 All flesh *is* not the s flesh: but *there is* one 846
2Co 1: 6 which is effectual in the enduring of the s 846
2: 2 but *the s* which is made sorry by me? NIG
2: 3 And I wrote this s unto you, lest, when I 846
3:14 for until this day remaineth the s vail 846
3:18 are changed *into* the s image from glory to 846
4:13 We having the s spirit of faith, according as 846
6:13 Now for a recompence in the s, (I speak as 846
7: 8 for I perceive that the s epistle hath made 1565
8: 6 he would also finish in you **the s** grace 3778
8:16 which put the s earnest care into the heart of 846
8:19 administered by us to the glory of the s Lord, 846
9: 4 should be ashamed in this *s* confident NIG
9: 5 that **the s** might be ready, as *a matter of* 3778
12:18 walked we not in the s spirit? *walked we* not 846
12:18 same spirit? *walked we* not in the s steps? 846
Gal 2: 8 *the s* was mighty in me towards NIG
2:10 **the s** which I also was forward to do. 846+3778
3: 7 of faith, **the s** are the children of Abraham. 3778
Eph 3: 6 and **of the s body**, and partakers of his 4954
4:10 He that descended is **the s** also that ascended 846
6: 8 **the s** shall he receive of the Lord, 3778
6: 9 And, ye masters, do the s *things* unto them, 846
6:22 Whom I have sent unto you for the s 846
Php 1:30 Having the s conflict which ye saw in me, 846
2: 2 having the s love, *being* of one accord, 846
2:18 *For* the s *cause* also do ye joy, and 846
3: 1 To write the s *things* to you, to me indeed *is* 846
3:16 *let us* walk by the s rule, *let us* mind 846
3:16 by the same rule, *let us* mind the s *thing*. 846
4: 2 that *they* be of the s mind in the Lord. 846
Col 4: 2 and watch in the s with thanksgiving; 846
4: 8 Whom I have sent unto you for the s 846
2Ti 2: 2 the s commit thou to faithful men, 3778
Heb 1:12 but thou art **the s**, and thy years shall not 846
2:14 he also himself likewise took part of the s; 846
4:11 lest any *man* fall after the s example of 846
6:11 s diligence to the full assurance of hope unto 846
10:11 and offering oftentimes the s sacrifices, 846
11: 9 Jacob, the heirs with *him* of the s promise: 846
13: 8 Jesus Christ the s yesterday, and to day, and 846
Jas 3: 2 **the s** *is* a perfect man, *and* able also to 3778
3:10 Out of the s mouth proceedeth blessing and 846
3:11 Doth a fountain send forth at the s place 846
1Pe 2: 7 **the s** is made the head of the corner, 3778
4: 1 arm yourselves likewise with the s mind: 846
4: 4 you run not with *them* to the s excess of riot, 846
4:10 *even so* minister the s one to another, 846
5: 9 knowing that the s afflictions are 846
2Pe 2:19 of the s is he brought in bondage. 3778
3: 7 are now, by the s word are kept in store, 846
1Jn 2:23 denieth the Son, the s hath not the Father: NIG
2:27 as the s anointing teacheth you of all *things*, 846
Rev 3: 5 the s shall be clothed in white raiment; 3778
11:13 And **the s** hour was there a great 1565
14:10 **The s** shall drink of the wine of the wrath of 846

SAMGAR See SAMGAR-NEBO

SAMGAR-NEBO (1)

Jer 39: 3 S, Sarsechim, Rab-saris, Nergal-sharezer, 5562

SAMLAH (4)

Ge 36:36 and S of Masrekah reigned in his stead. 8072
36:37 S died, and Saul of Rehoboth *by* the river 8072
1Ch 1:47 S of Masrekah reigned in his stead. 8072
1:48 when S was dead, Shaul of Rehoboth *by* 8072

SAMOS (1)

Ac 20:15 and the next *day* we arrived at S, and 4544

SAMOTHRACE See SAMOTHRACIA

SAMOTHRACIA (1)

Ac 16:11 we came with a straight course to S, and 4543

SAMSON (36) [SAMSON'S]

Jdg 13:24 woman bare a son, and called his name S: 8123
14: 1 S went down *to* Timnath, and saw a woman 8123
14: 3 S said unto his father, Get her for me; 8123
14: 5 went S down, and his father and 8123
14: 7 with the woman; and she pleased S well. 8123
14:10 S made there a feast; for so used the young 8123
14:12 S said unto them, I will now put forth a 8123
15: 1 that S visited his wife with a kid; 8123
15: 3 S said concerning them, Now shall I be 8123
15: 4 S went and caught three hundred foxes, 8123
15: 6 they answered, S, the son in law of 8123
15: 7 S said unto them, Though ye have done 8123
15:10 they answered, To bind S are we come up, 8123
15:11 said to S, Knowest thou not that 8123
15:12 S said unto them, Swear unto me, that ye 8123
15:16 S said, With the jawbone of an ass, 8123
16: 1 went S to Gaza, and saw there a harlot, 8123
16: 2 *told* the Gazites, saying, S is come hither. 8123
16: 3 S lay till midnight, and arose at midnight, 8123
16: 6 Delilah said to S, Tell me, I pray thee, 8123
16: 7 S said unto her, If they bind me with seven 8123
16: 9 unto him, The Philistines *be* upon thee, S. 8123
16:10 Delilah said unto S, Behold, thou hast 8123
16:12 unto him, The Philistines *be* upon thee, S. 8123
16:13 Delilah said unto S, Hitherto thou hast 8123
16:14 unto him, The Philistines *be* upon thee, S. 8123
16:20 she said, The Philistines *be* upon thee, S. 8123
16:23 Our god hath delivered S our enemy into 8123
16:25 that they said, Call for S, that he may make 8123
16:25 they called for S out of the prison house; 8123
16:26 S said unto the lad that held him by 8123
16:27 women, that beheld while S made sport. 8123
16:28 S called unto the LORD, and said, O Lord 8123
16:29 S took hold of the two middle pillars upon 8123
16:30 S said, Let me die with the Philistines. 8123
Heb 11:32 and *of* Barak, and *of* S, and *of* Jephthae; 4546

SAMSON'S (3) [SAMSON]

Jdg 14:15 that they said unto S wife, Entice thy 8123
14:16 S wife wept before him, and said, 8123
14:20 S wife was *given* to his companion, 8123

SAMUEL (142)

1Sa 1:20 that she bare a son, and called his name S, 8050
2:18 S ministered before the LORD, *being* a 8050
2:21 And the child S grew before the LORD. 8050
2:26 the child S grew on, and was in favour both 8050
3: 1 the child S ministered unto the LORD 8050
3: 3 of God *was*, and S was laid down *to sleep*; 8050
3: 4 That the LORD called S: and 8050
3: 6 the LORD called yet again, S. 8050
3: 6 S arose and went to Eli, and said, Here *am* 8050
3: 7 Now S did not yet know the LORD, 8050
3: 8 the LORD called S again the third time. 8050
3: 9 Therefore Eli said unto S, Go, lie down: 8050
3: 9 So S went and lay down in his place. 8050
3:10 and called as at other times, S, Samuel. 8050
3:10 and called as at other times, Samuel, S. 8050
3:10 S answered, Speak; for thy servant heareth. 8050
3:11 the LORD said to S, Behold, I will do a 8050
3:15 S lay until the morning, and opened 8050
3:15 And S feared to shew Eli the vision. 8050
3:16 Eli called S, and said, Samuel, my son. 8050
3:16 Eli called Samuel, and said, S, my son. 8050
3:18 S told him every whit, and hid nothing 8050
3:19 And S grew, and the LORD was with him, 8050
3:20 S *was* established to be a prophet of 8050
3:21 for the LORD revealed himself to S in 8050
4: 1 the word of S came to all Israel. Now Israel 8050
7: 3 S spake unto all the house of Israel, saying, 8050
7: 5 S said, Gather all Israel to Mizpeh, and 8050
7: 6 S judged the children of Israel in Mizpeh. 8050
7: 8 the children of Israel said to S, Cease not to 8050
7: 9 S took a sucking lamb, and offered it *for* a 8050
7: 9 S cried unto the LORD for Israel; and 8050
7:10 as S was offering up the burnt offering, 8050
7:12 S took a stone, and set *it* between Mizpeh 8050
7:13 was against the Philistines all the days of S. 8050
7:15 And S judged Israel all the days of his life. 8050
8: 1 it came to pass, when S was old, that he 8050
8: 4 and came to S unto Ramah, 8050
8: 6 the thing displeased S, when they said, 8050
8: 6 judge us. And S prayed unto the LORD. 8050
8: 7 the LORD said unto S, Hearken unto 8050
8:10 S told all the words of the LORD unto 8050
8:19 the people refused to obey the voice of S; 8050
8:21 S heard all the words of the people, and 8050
8:22 the LORD said to S, Hearken unto their 8050
8:22 S said unto the men of Israel, Go ye every 8050
9:14 behold, S came out against them, for to go 8050
9:15 Now the LORD had told S in his ear a day 8050
9:17 when S saw Saul, the LORD said unto 8050
9:18 Saul drew near to S in the gate, and said, 8050
9:19 S answered Saul, and said, I *am* the seer: 8050
9:22 S took Saul and his servant, and 8050
9:23 S said unto the cook, Bring the portion 8050
9:24 *S* said, Behold that which is left; set *it* NIH
9:24 the people. So Saul did eat with S that day. 8050
9:25 *S* communed with Saul upon the top of NIH
9:26 that S called Saul to the top of the house, 8050
9:26 went out both of them, he and S, abroad. 8050
9:27 S said to Saul, Bid the servant pass on 8050
10: 1 S took a vial of oil, and poured *it* upon his 8050
10: 9 when he had turned his back to go from S, 8050
10:14 saw that *they were* no where, we came to S. 8050
1Sa 10:15 Tell me, I pray thee, what S said unto you. 8050
10:16 whereof S spake, he told him not. 8050
10:17 S called the people together unto 8050
10:20 when S had caused all the tribes of Israel to 8050
10:24 S said to all the people, See ye him whom 8050
10:25 S told the people the manner of 8050
10:25 S sent all the people away, every man to his 8050
11: 7 cometh not forth after Saul and after S, 8050
11:12 the people said unto S, Who *is* he that said, 8050
11:14 said S to the people, Come, and let us go *to* 8050
12: 1 S said unto all Israel, Behold, I have 8050
12: 6 S said unto the people, *It is* the LORD that 8050
12:11 S, and delivered you out of the hand of 8050
12:18 So S called unto the LORD; and 8050
12:18 people greatly feared the LORD and S. 8050
12:19 all the people said unto S, Pray for thy 8050
12:20 S said unto the people, Fear not: ye have 8050
13: 8 according to the set time that S *had* 8050
13: 8 *had appointed*: but S came not *to* Gilgal; 8050
13:10 offering the burnt offering, behold, S came; 8050
13:11 S said, What hast thou done? And Saul 8050
13:13 S said to Saul, Thou hast done foolishly: 8050
13:15 S arose, and gat him up from Gilgal *unto* 8050
15: 1 S also said unto Saul, The LORD sent me 8050
15:10 came the word of the LORD unto S, 8050
15:11 it grieved S; and he cried unto the LORD 8050
15:12 when S rose early to meet Saul in 8050
15:12 it was told S, saying, Saul came to Carmel, 8050
15:13 S came to Saul: and Saul said unto him, 8050
15:14 S said, What *meaneth* then this bleating of 8050
15:16 S said unto Saul, Stay, and I will tell thee 8050
15:17 S said, When thou *wast* little in thine own 8050
15:20 Saul said unto S, Yea, I have obeyed 8050
15:22 S said, Hath the LORD *as great* delight in 8050
15:24 Saul said unto S, I have sinned: for I have 8050
15:26 S said unto Saul, I will not return with thee: 8050
15:27 as S turned about to go away, he laid hold 8050
15:28 S said unto him, The LORD hath rent 8050
15:31 So S turned again after Saul; and 8050
15:32 said S, Bring you hither to me Agag 8050
15:33 S said, As thy sword hath made women 8050
15:33 S hewed Agag in pieces before the LORD 8050
15:34 S went to Ramah; and Saul went up to his 8050
15:35 S came no more to see Saul until the day of 8050
15:35 nevertheless S mourned for Saul: and 8050
16: 1 the LORD said unto S, How long wilt 8050
16: 2 S said, How can I go? if Saul hear *it*, he 8050
16: 4 S did *that* which the LORD spake, and 8050
16: 7 the LORD said unto S, Look not on his 8050
16: 8 and made him pass before S. 8050
16:10 made seven of his sons to pass before S. 8050
16:10 S said unto Jesse, The LORD hath not 8050
16:11 S said unto Jesse, Are here all *thy* children? 8050
16:11 S said unto Jesse, Send and fetch him: 8050
16:13 S took the horn of oil, and anointed him in 8050
16:13 So S rose up, and went to Ramah. 8050
19:18 came to S to Ramah, and told him all that 8050
19:18 And he and S went and dwelt in Naioth. 8050
19:20 S standing *as* appointed over them, 8050
19:22 he asked and said, Where *are* S and David? 8050
19:24 prophesied before S in like manner, and 8050
25: 1 S died; and all the Israelites were gathered 8050
28: 3 Now S was dead, and all Israel had 8050
28:11 up unto thee? And he said, Bring me up S. 8050
28:12 when the woman saw S, she cried with a 8050
28:14 Saul perceived that it *was* S, and he stooped 8050
28:15 S said to Saul, Why hast thou disquieted 8050
28:16 said S, Wherefore then dost thou ask of me, 8050
28:20 was sore afraid, because of the words of S: 8050
1Ch 6:28 And the sons of S; the firstborn Vashni, and 8050
9:22 and S the seer did ordain in their set office. 8050
11: 3 according to the word of the LORD by S. 8050
26:28 all that S the seer, and Saul the son of Kish, 8050
29:29 they *are* written in the book of S the seer, 8050
2Ch 35:18 kept in Israel from the days of S 8050
Ps 99: 6 and S among them that call upon his name; 8050
Jer 15: 1 Though Moses and S stood before me, 8050
Ac 3:24 and all the prophets from S and those that 4545
13:20 and fifty years, until S the prophet. 4545
Heb 11:32 *of* David also, and S, and *of* the prophets: 4545

SANBALLAT (10)

Ne 2:10 When S the Horonite, and Tobiah 5571
2:19 when S the Horonite, and Tobiah 5571
4: 1 that when S heard that we builded the wall, 5571
4: 7 *that* when S, and Tobiah, and the Arabians, 5571
6: 1 when S, and Tobiah, and Geshem 5571
6: 2 That S and Geshem sent unto me, saying, 5571
6: 5 sent S his servant unto me in like manner 5571
6:12 for Tobiah and S had hired him. 5571
6:14 and S according to these their works, 5571
13:28 *was* son in law to S the Horonite: 5571

SANCTIFICATION (5) [SANCTIFY]

1Co 1:30 and righteousness, and s, and redemption: 38
1Th 4: 3 For this is the will of God, *even* your s, 38
4: 4 should know how to possess his vessel in s 38
2Th 2:13 chosen you to salvation through s of the Spirit 38
1Pe 1: 2 through s of the Spirit, unto obedience and 38

SANCTIFIED (62) [SANCTIFY]

Ge 2: 3 God blessed the seventh day, and s it: 6942
Ex 19:14 mount unto the people, and s the people; 6942
29:43 and *the tabernacle* shall be s by my glory. 6942
Lev 8:10 and all that *was* therein, and s them. 6942
8:15 and s it, to make reconciliation upon it. 6942
8:30 s Aaron, *and* his garments, and his sons, 6942
10: 3 I will be s in them that come nigh me, and 6942
27:15 if he that s *it* will redeem his house, then 6942
27:19 if he that s the field will in any wise redeem 6942
Nu 7: 1 s it, and all the instruments thereof, 6942
7: 1 and had anointed them, and s them; 6942
8:17 in the land of Egypt, I s them for myself. 6942
20:13 with the LORD, and he was s in them. 6942

Dt 32:51 ye s me not in the midst of the children of 6942
1Sa 7: 1 s Eleazar his son to keep the ark of 6942
16: 5 he s Jesse and his sons, and called them to 6942
21: 5 yea, though it were s *this* day in the vessel. 6942
1Ch 15:14 the Levites s themselves to bring up the ark 6942
2Ch 5:11 (for all the priests that were present were s, 6942
7:16 For now have I chosen and s this house, 6942
7:20 this house, which I have s for my name, 6942
29:15 their brethren, and s themselves, and came, 6942
29:17 they s the house of the LORD in eight 6942
29:19 have we prepared and s, and behold, 6942
29:34 and until the *other* priests had s themselves: 6942
30: 3 the priests had not s themselves 6942
30: 8 into his sanctuary, which he hath s for ever: 6942
30:15 s themselves, and brought in the burnt 6942
30:17 many in the congregation that were not s: 6942
30:24 and a great number of priests s themselves. 6942
31:18 for in their set office they s themselves *in* 6942
Ne 3: 1 they s it, and set up the doors of it; 6942
3: 1 even unto the tower of Meah they s it, 6942
12:47 they s *holy things* unto the Levites; and 6942
12:47 the Levites s *them* unto the children of 6942
Job 1: 5 that Job sent and s them, and rose up early 6942
Isa 5:16 God that is holy shall be s in righteousness. 6942
13: 3 I have commanded my s ones, I have also 6942
Jer 1: 5 thou camest forth out of the womb I s thee, 6942
Eze 20:41 and I will be s in you before the heathen. 6942
28:22 judgments in her, and shall be s in her. 6942
28:25 shall be s in them in the sight of 6942
36:23 when I shall be s in you before their eyes. 6942
38:16 when I shall be s in thee, O Gog, 6942
39:27 am s in them in the sight of many nations; 6942
48:11 *It shall be* for the priests that are s of 6942
Jn 10:36 Say ye *of him,* whom the Father hath s, and *37*
17:19 that they also might be s through the truth. *37*
Ac 20:32 an inheritance among all them which are s. *37*
26:18 inheritance among them which are s by faith *37*
Ro 15:16 be acceptable, being s by the Holy Ghost. *37*
1Co 1: 2 to them that are s in Christ Jesus, called *to be* *37*
6:11 but ye are s, but ye are justified in the name of *37*
7:14 For the unbelieving husband is s by the wife, *37*
7:14 and the unbelieving wife is s by the husband: *37*
1Ti 4: 5 For it is s by the word of God and prayer. *37*
2Ti 2:21 s, and meet for the master's use, *and* *37*
Heb 2:11 and they who are s *are* all of one: *37*
10:10 By the which will we are s through *37*
10:14 he hath perfected for ever them that are s. *37*
10:29 wherewith he was s, an unholy *thing,* and *37*
Jude 1: 1 to them that are s by God the Father, and *37*

SANCTIFIETH (4) [SANCTIFY]

Mt 23:17 the gold, or the temple that s the gold? *37*
23:19 *is* greater, the gift, or the altar that s the gift? *37*
Heb 2:11 For both he that s and they who are sanctified *37*
9:13 the unclean, s to the purifying of the flesh: *37*

SANCTIFY (70) [SANCTIFICATION, SANCTIFIED, SANCTIFIETH]

Ex 13: 2 S unto me all the firstborn, 6942
19:10 s them to day and to morrow, and let them 6942
19:22 come near to the LORD, s themselves, 6942
19:23 Set bounds about the mount, and s it. 6942
28:41 and consecrate them, and s them, 6942
29:27 thou shalt s the breast of the wave offering, 6942
29:33 was made, to consecrate *and* to s them: 6942
29:36 for it, and thou shalt anoint it, to s it. 6942
29:37 make an atonement for the altar, and s it; 6942
29:44 I will s the tabernacle of the congregation, 6942
29:44 I will s also both Aaron and his sons, 6942
30:29 thou shalt s them, that they may be most 6942
31:13 know that I *am* the LORD that doth s you. 6942
40:10 and all his vessels, and s the altar: 6942
40:11 shalt anoint the laver and his foot, and s it. 6942
40:13 holy garments, and anoint him, and s him; 6942
Lev 8:11 both the laver and his foot, to s them. 6942
8:12 Aaron's head, and anointed him, to s him. 6942
11:44 ye shall therefore s yourselves, and ye shall 6942
20: 7 S yourselves therefore, and be ye holy: for I 6942
20: 8 and do them: I *am* the LORD which s you. 6942
21: 8 Thou shalt s him therefore; for he offereth 6942
21: 8 for I the LORD, which s you, *am* holy. 6942
21:15 his people: for I the LORD do s him. 6942
21:23 my sanctuaries: for I the LORD do s them. 6942
22: 9 if they profane it: I the LORD do s them. 6942
22:16 holy *things:* for I the LORD do s them. 6942
27:14 when a man shall s his house *to be* holy 6942
27:16 if a man shall s unto the LORD *some part* 6942
27:17 If he s his field from the year of jubile, 6942
27:18 if he s his field after the jubile, then 6942
27:22 if *a man* s unto the LORD a field which he 6942
27:26 be the LORD'S firstling, no man shall s it; 6942
Nu 11:18 S yourselves against to morrow, and 6942
20:12 to s me in the eyes of the children of Israel, 6942
27:14 to s me at the water before their eyes: 6942
Dt 5:12 Keep the sabbath day to s it, as the LORD 6942
15:19 of thy flock thou shalt s unto the LORD 6942
Jos 3: 5 Joshua said unto the people, S yourselves: 6942
7:13 Up, s the people, and say, 6942
7:13 and say, S yourselves against to morrow: 6942
1Sa 16: 5 s yourselves, and come with me to 6942
1Ch 15:12 s yourselves, *both* ye and your brethren, 6942
23:13 that he should s the most holy *things,* he 6942
2Ch 29: 5 s now yourselves, and sanctify the house of 6942
29: 5 s the house of the LORD God of your 6942
29:17 on the first *day* of the first month to s, 6942
29:34 in heart to s themselves than the priests. 6942
30:17 *was* not clean, to s *them* unto the LORD. 6942
35: 6 s yourselves, and prepare your brethren, 6942
Ne 13:22 *and* keep the gates, to s the sabbath day. 6942
Isa 8:13 S the LORD of hosts himself; and *let* him 6942
29:23 they shall s my name, and sanctify the Holy 6942
29:23 s the Holy One of Jacob, and shall fear 6942
66:17 They that s themselves, and purify 6942
Eze 20:12 know that I *am* the LORD that s them. 6942
36:23 I will s my great name, which was profaned 6942
37:28 shall know that I the LORD do s Israel, 6942
38:23 Thus will I magnify myself, and s myself; 6942
44:19 they shall not s the people with their 6942
46:20 not out into the utter court, to s the people. 6942
Joel 1:14 S ye a fast, call a solemn assembly, 6942
2:15 in Zion, s a fast, call a solemn assembly: 6942
2:16 Gather the people, s the congregation, 6942
Jn 17:17 S them through thy truth: thy word is truth. *37*
17:19 And for their sakes I s myself, that they also *37*
Eph 5:26 That he might s and cleanse *it* with *37*
1Th 5:23 And the very God of peace s you wholly; and *37*
Heb 13:12 that he might s the people with his own blood, *37*
1Pe 3:15 But s the Lord God in your hearts: and *37*

SANCTUARIES (5) [SANCTUARY]

Lev 21:23 he hath a blemish; that he profane not my s: 4720
26:31 bring your s unto desolation, and I will not 4720
Jer 51:51 for strangers are come into the s of 4720
Eze 28:18 Thou hast defiled thy s by the multitude of 4720
Am 7: 9 and the s of Israel shall be laid waste; 4720

SANCTUARY (137) [SANCTUARIES]

Ex 15:17 *in* the S, O Lord, *which* thy hands have 4720
25: 8 let them make me a s; that I may dwell 4720
30:13 half a shekel after the shekel of the s: 6944
30:24 hundred *shekels,* after the shekel of the s, 6944
36: 1 all *manner of* work for the service of the s, 6944
36: 3 brought for the work of the service of the s, 6944
36: 4 *men,* that wrought all the work of the s, 6944
36: 6 any more work for the offering of the s. 6944
38:24 and thirty shekels, after the shekel of the s. 6944
38:25 and fifteen shekels, after the shekel of the s: 6944
38:26 *is,* half a shekel, after the shekel of the s, 6944
38:27 of silver were cast the sockets of the s, 6944
Lev 4: 6 before the LORD, before the vail of the s. 6944
5:15 after the shekel of the s, for a trespass 6944
10: 4 carry your brethren from before the s out of 6944
12: 4 no hallowed *thing,* nor come into the s, 4720
16:33 he shall make an atonement for the holy s, 4720
19:30 keep my sabbaths, and reverence my s: 4720
20: 3 to defile my s, and to profane my holy 4720
21:12 Neither shall he go out of the s, nor profane 4720
21:12 the sanctuary, nor profane the s of his God; 4720
26: 2 keep my sabbaths, and reverence my s: 4720
27: 3 shekels of silver, after the shekel of the s. 6944
27:25 shall be according to the shekel of the s: 6944
Nu 3:28 six hundred, keeping the charge of the s. 6944
3:31 the vessels of the s wherewith they 6944
3:32 of them that keep the charge of the s. 6944
3:38 keeping the charge of the s for the charge 4720
3:47 after the shekel of the s shalt thou take 6944
3:50 and five *shekels,* after the shekel of the s: 6944
4:12 wherewith they minister in the s, and 6944
4:15 sons have made an end of covering the s, 6944
4:15 all the vessels of the s, as the camp is to set 6944
4:16 of all that therein *is,* in the s, and in 6944
7: 9 the service of the s belonging unto them 6944
7:13 of seventy shekels, after the shekel of the s; 6944
7:19 of seventy shekels, after the shekel of the s; 6944
7:25 of seventy shekels, after the shekel of the s; 6944
7:31 of seventy shekels, after the shekel of the s; 6944
7:37 of seventy shekels, after the shekel of the s; 6944
7:43 of seventy shekels, after the shekel of the s; 6944
7:49 of seventy shekels, after the shekel of the s; 6944
7:55 of seventy shekels, after the shekel of the s; 6944
7:61 of seventy shekels, after the shekel of the s; 6944
7:67 of seventy shekels, after the shekel of the s; 6944
7:73 of seventy shekels, after the shekel of the s; 6944
7:79 of seventy shekels, after the shekel of the s; 6944
7:85 hundred *shekels,* after the shekel of the s: 6944
7:86 ten *shekels* apiece, after the shekel of the s: 6944
8:19 the children of Israel come nigh unto the s. 6944
10:21 the Kohathites set forward, bearing the s: 4720
18: 1 with thee shall bear the iniquity of the s: 4720
18: 3 they shall not come nigh the vessels of the s 6944
18: 5 ye shall keep the charge of the s, and 6944
18:16 after the shekel of the s, which *is* twenty 6944
19:20 he hath defiled the s of the LORD: 4720
Jos 24:26 an oak, that *was* by the s of the LORD. 4720
1Ch 9:29 all the instruments of the s, and the fine 6944
22:19 and build ye the s of the LORD God, 4720
24: 5 for the governors of the s, and governors *of* 6944
28:10 hath chosen thee to build a house for the s: 4720
2Ch 20: 8 and have built thee a s therein for thy name, 4720
26:18 go out of the s; for thou hast trespassed; 4720
29:21 the kingdom, and for the s, and for Judah. 4720
30: 8 enter into his s, which he hath sanctified for 4720
30:19 according to the purification of the s. 6944
36:17 men with the sword in the house of their s, 4720
Ne 10:39 where *are* the vessels of the s, and 4720
Ps 20: 2 Send thee help from the s, and 6944
63: 2 thy glory, so *as* I have seen thee in the s. 6944
68:24 the goings of my God, my King, in the s. 6944
73:17 Until I went into the s of God; *then* 4720
74: 3 *that* the enemy hath done wickedly in the s. 6944
74: 7 They have cast fire into thy s, they have 4720
77:13 Thy way, O God, *is* in the s: who *is so* 6944
78:54 he brought them to the border of his s, 6944
78:69 he built his s like high *palaces,* like 4720
96: 6 before him: strength and beauty *are* in his s. 4720
102:19 hath looked down from the height of his s; 6944
114: 2 Judah was his s, *and* Israel his dominion. 6944
134: 2 Lift up your hands *in* the s, and bless 6944
150: 1 Praise God in his s: praise him in 6944
Isa 8:14 he shall be for a s; but for a stone of 4720
16:12 that he shall come to his s to pray; 4720
43:28 I have profaned the princes of the s, 6944
60:13 box together, to beautify the place of my s; 4720
63:18 our adversaries have trodden down thy s. 4720
Jer 17:12 from the beginning *is* the place of our s. 4720
La 1:10 seen *that* the heathen entered into her s, 4720
2: 7 cast off his altar, he hath abhorred his s, 4720
2:20 the prophet be slain in the s of the Lord? 4720
4: 1 the stones of the s are poured out in the top 6944
Eze 5:11 thou hast defiled my s with all thy 4720
8: 6 that *I* should go far off from my s? 4720
9: 6 upon whom *is* the mark; and begin at my s. 4720
11:16 yet will I be to them as a little s in 4720
23:38 they have defiled my s in the same day, and 4720
23:39 they came the same day into my s to 4720
24:21 Behold, I *will* profane my s, the excellency 4720
25: 3 Because thou saidst, Aha, against my s, 4720
37:26 will set my s in the midst of them for 4720
37:28 when my s shall be in the midst of them for 4720
41:21 temple *were* squared, *and* the face of the s; 6944
41:23 And the temple and the s had two doors. 6944
42:20 to make a separation between the s and 6944
43:21 appointed place of the house, without the s. 4720
44: 1 outward s which looketh *toward* the east; 4720
44: 5 the house, with every going forth of the s. 4720
44: 7 In that ye have brought *into my s* strangers, NIH
44: 7 to be in my s, to pollute it, *even* my house, 4720
44: 8 ye have set keepers of my charge in my s 4720
44: 9 in flesh, shall enter into my s, 4720
44:11 Yet they shall be ministers in my s, 4720
44:15 that kept the charge of my s when 4720
44:16 They shall enter into my s, and they shall 4720
44:27 in the day that he goeth into the s, unto 6944
44:27 unto the inner court, to minister in the s, 6944
45: 2 Of this there shall be for the s five hundred 6944
45: 3 in it shall be the s *and* the most holy *place.* 4720
45: 4 be for the priests the ministers of the s, 4720
45: 4 for their houses, and a holy place for the s. 4720
45:18 bullock without blemish, and cleanse the s: 4720
47:12 their waters they issued out of the s: 4720
48: 8 and the s shall be in the midst of it. 4720
48:10 the s of the LORD shall be in the midst 4720
48:21 the s of the house *shall be* in the midst 4720
Da 8:11 and the place of his s was cast down. 4720
8:13 to give both the s and the host to be trodden 6944
8:14 hundred days; then shall the s be cleansed. 6944
9:17 cause thy face to shine upon thy s that is 4720
9:26 *shall* come shall destroy the city and the s; 6944
11:31 they shall pollute the s *of* strength, and 4720
Zep 3: 4 her priests have polluted the s, they have 6944
Heb 8: 2 A minister of the s, and of the true tabernacle, *40*
9: 1 ordinances of divine service, and a worldly s. *40*
9: 2 and the shewbread; which is called the s. *40*
13:11 whose blood is brought into the s by the high *40*

SAND (28) [QUICKSANDS]

Ge 22:17 and as the s which *is* upon the sea shore; 2344
32:12 and make thy seed as the s of the sea, 2344
41:49 Joseph gathered corn as the s of the sea, 2344
Ex 2:12 he slew the Egyptian, and hid him in the s. 2344
Dt 33:19 of the seas, and *of* treasures hid in the s. 2344
Jos 11: 4 *even* as the s that *is* upon the sea shore in 2344
Jdg 7:12 as the s by the sea side for multitude. 2344
1Sa 13: 5 people as the s which *is* on the sea shore in 2344
2Sa 17:11 as the s that *is* by the sea for multitude; 2344
1Ki 4:20 as the s which *is* by the sea in multitude, 2344
4:29 *even* as the s that *is* on the sea shore. 2344
Job 6: 3 For now it would be heavier than the s of 2344
29:18 and I shall multiply *my* days as the s. 2344
Ps 78:27 and feathered fowls like as the s of the sea: 2344
139:18 they are more in number than the s: 2344
Pr 27: 3 A stone *is* heavy, and the s weighty; but 2344
Isa 10:22 For though thy people Israel be as the s of 2344
48:19 Thy seed also had been as the s, and 2344
Jer 5:22 which have placed the s *for* the bound of 2344
15: 8 are increased to me above the s of the seas: 2344
33:22 neither the s of the sea measured: 2344
Hos 1:10 of Israel shall be as the s of the sea, 2344
Hab 1: 9 and they shall gather the captivity as the s. 2344
Mt 7:26 which built his house upon the s: *285*
Ro 9:27 the children of Israel be as the s of the sea, *285*
Heb 11:12 as the s which is by the sea shore *285*
Rev 13: 1 And I stood upon the s of the sea, and saw a *285*
20: 8 the number of whom *is* as the s of the sea. *285*

SANDAL See SHOE; SHOE'S; SHOES

SANDALS (2)

Mk 6: 9 But *be* shod with s; and not put on two *4547*
Ac 12: 8 unto him, Gird thyself, and bind on thy s. *4547*

SANG (11) [SING]

Ex 15: 1 s Moses and the children of Israel this song 7891
Nu 21:17 Israel s this song, Spring up, O well; 7891
Jdg 5: 1 s Deborah and Barak the son of Abinoam 7891
1Sa 29: 5 of whom they s one to another in dances, 6030
2Ch 29:28 the singers s, and the trumpeters sounded: 7891
29:30 they *s* praises with gladness, and NIH
Ne 12:42 the singers s loud, with Jezrahiah *their* 8085
Job 38: 7 When the morning stars s together, and 7442
Ps 7: T of David, which he s unto the LORD, 7891
106:12 believed they his words; they s his praise. 7891
Ac 16:25 and Silas prayed, and s praises unto God: *5214*

SANK (2) [SINK]

Ex 15: 5 they s into the bottom as a stone. 3381
15:10 they s as lead in the mighty waters. 6749

SANSANNAH (1)

Jos 15:31 And Ziklag, and Madmannah, and S, 5578

SAP (1)

Ps 104:16 The trees of the LORD are full *of s;* NIH

SAPH (1)

2Sa 21:18 Sibbechai the Hushathite slew S, 5593

SAPHIR (1)

Mic 1:11 Pass ye away, thou inhabitant of S, 8208

SAPPHIRA (1)

Ac 5: 1 with S his wife, sold a possession, *4551*

S

SAPPHIRE (9) [SAPPHIRES]
Ex 24:10 feet as it were a paved work of a s stone, 5601
28:18 *shall be* an emerald, a s, and a diamond. 5601
39:11 an emerald, a s, and a diamond. 5601
Job 28:16 of Ophir, with the precious onyx, or the s. 5601
La 4: 7 body than rubies, their polishing *was of* s: 5601
Eze 1:26 of a throne, as the appearance of a s stone: 5601
10: 1 appeared over them as it were a s stone, 5601
28:13 the beryl, the onyx, and the jasper, the s, 5601
Rev 21:19 the second, s; the third, a chalcedony; *4552*

SAPPHIRES (3) [SAPPHIRE]
Job 28: 6 The stones of it *are* the place of s: and 5601
SS 5:14 his belly *is as* bright ivory overlaid *with* s. 5601
Isa 54:11 fair colours, and lay thy foundations with s. 5601

SARA (3) [SARAH]
Ro 9: 9 time will I come, and S shall have a son. *4564*
Heb 11:11 Through faith also S herself received *4564*
1Pe 3: 6 *Even* as S obeyed Abraham, calling him *4564*

SARA'S (1) [SARAH]
Ro 4:19 neither *yet* the deadness of S womb: *4564*

SARAH (37) [SARA, SARA'S, SARAH'S, SARAI, SARAI'S]
Ge 17:15 her name Sarai, but S *shall* her name *be.* 8283
17:17 and shall S, that is ninety years old, bear? 8283
17:19 S thy wife shall bear thee a son indeed; 8283
17:21 which S shall bear unto thee at this set time 8283
18: 6 And Abraham hastened into the tent unto S, 8283
18: 9 they said unto him, Where *is* S thy wife? 8283
18:10 of life; and lo, S thy wife shall have a son. 8283
18:10 S heard *it in* the tent door, which *was* 8283
18:11 Now Abraham and S *were* old *and* 8283
18:11 it ceased to be with S after the manner of 8283
18:12 Therefore S laughed within herself, saying, 8283
18:13 Wherefore did S laugh, saying, 8283
18:14 to the time of life, and S shall have a son. 8283
18:15 S denied, saying, I laughed not; for she was 8283
20: 2 Abraham said of S his wife, She *is* my 8283
20: 2 Abimelech king of Gerar sent, and took S. 8283
20:14 unto Abraham, and restored him S his wife. 8283
20:16 unto S he said, Behold, I have given thy 8283
20:18 because of S Abraham's wife. 8283
21: 1 the LORD visited S as he had said, and 8283
21: 1 the LORD did unto S as he had spoken. 8283
21: 2 For S conceived, and bare Abraham a son 8283
21: 3 born unto him, whom S bare to him, Isaac. 8283
21: 6 S said, God hath made me to laugh, *so* 8283
21: 7 that S should have given children suck? 8283
21: 9 S saw the son of Hagar the Egyptian, 8283
21:12 in all that S hath said unto thee, 8283
23: 1 S was an hundred and seven and 8283
23: 1 *these were* the years of the life of S. 8283
23: 2 S died in Kirjath-arba; the same *is* Hebron 8283
23: 2 Abraham came to mourn for S, and to weep 8283
23:19 Abraham buried S his wife in the cave of 8283
24:36 S my master's wife bare a son to my master 8283
25:10 there was Abraham buried, and S his wife. 8283
49:31 There they buried Abraham and S his wife; 8283
Nu 26:46 the name of the daughter of Asher *was* S. 8294
Isa 51: 2 your father, and unto S *that* bare you: 8283

SARAH'S (2) [SARAH]
Ge 24:67 Isaac brought her into his mother S tent, 8283
25:12 S handmaid, bare unto Abraham: 8283

SARAI (16) [SARAH]
Ge 11:29 the name of Abram's wife *was* S; and 8297
11:30 But S was barren; she had no child. 8297
11:31 S his daughter in law, his son Abram's 8297
12: 5 Abram took S his wife, and Lot his 8297
12:11 that he said unto S his wife, Behold now, 8297
12:17 great plagues because of S Abram's wife. 8297
16: 1 Now S Abram's wife bare him no *children:* 8297
16: 2 S said unto Abram, Behold now, 8297
16: 2 And Abram hearkened to the voice of S. 8297
16: 3 S Abram's wife took Hagar her maid 8297
16: 5 S said unto Abram, My wrong *be* upon 8297
16: 6 Abram said unto S, Behold, thy maid *is* in 8297
16: 6 when S dealt hardly with her, she fled from 8297
16: 8 I flee from the face of my mistress S. 8297
17:15 God said unto Abraham, *As for* S thy wife, 8297
17:15 thou shalt not call her name S, but 8297

S

SARAI'S (1) [SARAH]
Ge 16: 8 he said, Hagar, S maid, whence camest 8297

SARAPH (1)
1Ch 4:22 and the men of Chozeba, and Joash, and S, 8315

SARDINE (1)
Rev 4: 3 to look upon like a jasper and a s stone: *4555*

SARDIS (3)
Rev 1:11 and unto S, and unto Philadelphia, and *4554*
3: 1 And unto the angel of the church in S write; *4554*
3: 4 Thou hast a few names even in S, *4554*

SARDITES (1)
Nu 26:26 of Sered, the family of the S: of Elon, 5625

SARDIUS (4)
Ex 28:17 *the first* row *shall be* a s, a topaz, and 124
39:10 *the first* row *was* a s, a topaz, and 124
Eze 28:13 the s, topaz, and the diamond, the beryl, 124
Rev 21:20 The fifth, sardonyx; the sixth, s; *4556*

SARDONYX (1)
Rev 21:20 The fifth, s; the sixth, sardius; the seventh, *4557*

SAREPTA (1) [ZAREPHATH]
Lk 4:26 save unto S, *a city* of Sidon, unto a woman *4558*

SARGON (1)
Isa 20: 1 (when S the king of Assyria sent him,) 5623

SARID (2)
Jos 19:10 the border of their inheritance was unto S: 8301
19:12 turned from S eastward *toward* 8301

SARON (1)
Ac 9:35 And all that dwelt at Lydda and S saw him, *4565*

SARSECHIM (1)
Jer 39: 3 Samgar-nebo, S, Rab-saris, 8310

SARUCH (1)
Lk 3:35 Which was *the son* of S, which was *the son* *4562*

SAT (192) [SIT]
Ge 18: 1 he s *in* the tent door in the heat of the day; 3427
19: 1 at even; and Lot s in the gate of Sodom: 3427
21:16 s her **down** over against *him* a good way 3427
21:16 she s over against *him,* and lift up her 3427
31:34 in the camel's furniture, and s upon them. 3427
37:25 they s **down** to eat bread: and they lift up 3427
38:14 wrapped herself, and s in an open place, 3427
43:33 they s before him, the firstborn according 3427
48: 2 strengthened himself, and s upon the bed. 3427
Ex 2:15 land of Midian: and he s **down** by a well. 3427
12:29 from the firstborn of Pharaoh that s on his 3427
16: 3 when we s by the flesh pots, *and* when we 3427
17:12 and put *it* under him, and he s thereon; 3427
18:13 that Moses s to judge the people: 3427
32: 6 the people s **down** to eat and to drink, and 3427
Lev 15: 6 he that sitteth on *any* thing whereon he s 3427
15:22 whosoever toucheth any thing that she s 3427
Dt 33: 3 they s **down** at thy feet; *every one* shall 8497
Jdg 6:11 s under an oak which *was* in Ophrah, 3427
13: 9 again unto the woman as she s in the field: 3427
19: 6 they s **down,** and did eat and drink both of 3427
19:15 he s him **down** in a street of the city: 3427
20:26 s there before the LORD, and fasted that 3427
Ru 2:14 she s beside the reapers: and he reached her 3427
4: 1 Boaz up *to* the gate, and s him **down** there: 3427
4: 1 And he turned aside, and s **down.** 3427
4: 2 said, Sit ye down here. And they s **down.** 3427
1Sa 1: 9 Now Eli the priest s upon a seat by a post 3427
4:13 Eli s upon a seat *by* the wayside watching: 3427
19: 9 as he s in his house with his javelin in his 3427
20:24 the king s him **down** to eat meat. 3427
20:25 the king s upon his seat, as at other times, 3427
20:25 Abner s by Saul's side, and David's place 3427
28:23 he arose from the earth, and s upon the bed. 3427
2Sa 2:13 they s **down,** the one on the one side of 3427
7: 1 when the king s in his house, and 3427
7:18 s before the LORD, and he said, Who *am* 3427
18:24 David s between the two gates: and 3427
19: 8 the king rose, and s in the gate. And they 3427
23: 8 The Tachmonite that s in the seat, 3427
1Ki 2:12 s Solomon upon the throne of David his 3427
2:19 s **down** on his throne, and caused a seat to 3427
2:19 king's mother; and she s on his right hand. 3427
13:20 it came to pass, as they s at the table, 3427
16:11 to reign, as soon as he s on his throne, 3427
19: 4 and came and s **down** under a juniper tree: 3427
21:13 children of Belial, and s before him: 3427
22:10 Jehoshaphat the king of Judah s each on his 3427
2Ki 1: 9 behold, he s on the top of a hill. And he 3427
4:20 he s on her knees till noon, and *then* died. 3427
6:32 Elisha s in his house, and the elders sat 3427
6:32 sat in his house, and the elders s with him; 3427
11:19 And he s on the throne of the kings. 3427
13:13 and Jeroboam s upon his throne: 3427
1Ch 17: 1 it came to pass, as David s in his house, 3427
17:16 the king came and s before the LORD, 3427
29:23 Solomon s on the throne of the LORD as 3427
2Ch 18: 9 Jehoshaphat king of Judah s either of them 3427
18: 9 they s in a void place *at* the entering in of 3427
Ezr 9: 3 and of my beard, and s **down** astonied. 3427
9: 4 and I s astonied until the evening sacrifice. 3427
10: 9 all the people s in the street of the house of 3427
10:16 s **down** in the first day of the tenth month 3427
Ne 1: 4 *that* I s **down** and wept, and 3427
8:17 made booths, and s under the booths: 3427
Est 1: 2 when the king Ahasuerus s on the throne of 3427
1:14 *and* which s the first in the kingdom;) 3427
2:19 then Mordecai s in the king's gate. 3427
2:21 while Mordecai s in the king's gate, 3427
3:15 the king and Haman s **down** to drink; but 3427
5: 1 the king s upon his royal throne in the royal 3427
Job 2: 8 and he s **down** among the ashes. 3427
2:13 So they s **down** with him upon the ground 3427
29:25 s chief, and dwelt as a king in the army, 3427
Ps 26: 4 I have not s with vain persons, neither will 3427
137: 1 there we s **down,** yea, we wept, 3427
SS 2: 3 I s **down** under his shadow with great 3427
Jer 3: 2 In the ways hast thou s for them, as 3427
15:17 I s not in the assembly of the mockers, 3427
15:17 nor rejoiced; I s alone because of thy hand: 3427
26:10 s **down** in the entry of the new gate of 3427
32:12 before all the Jews that s in the court of 3427
36:12 lo, all the princes s there, *even* Elishama 3427
36:22 Now the king s *in* the winterhouse in 3427
39: 3 s in the middle gate, *even* Nergal-sharezer, 3427
Eze 3:15 I s where they sat, and remained there 3427
3:15 I sat where they s, and remained there 3427
8: 1 as I s in mine house, and the elders of 3427
8: 1 and the elders of Judah s before me, 3427
8:14 there s women weeping for Tammuz. 3427
14: 1 elders of Israel unto me, and s before me. 3427
20: 1 to inquire of the LORD, and s before me. 3427
Da 2:49 but Daniel *s* in the gate of the king. NIH
Jnh 3: 6 covered *him* with sackcloth, and s in ashes. 3427
Jnh 4: 5 s on the east side of the city, and 3427
4: 5 him a booth, and s under it in the shadow, 3427
Mt 4:16 The people which s in darkness saw great *2521*
4:16 and to them which s in the region and *2521*
9:10 as Jesus s **at meat** in the house, behold, *345*
9:10 and s **down with** him and his disciples. *4873*
13: 1 out of the house, and s by the sea side. *2521*
13: 2 unto him, so that he went into a ship, and s; *2521*
13:48 and s **down,** and gathered the good into *2523*
14: 9 and them which s **with** him **at meat,** *4873*
15:29 went up into a mountain, and s **down** there. *2521*
24: 3 And as he s upon the mount of Olives, *2521*
26: 7 and poured *it* on his head, as he s **at meat.** *345*
26:20 even was come, he s **down** with the twelve. *345*
26:55 I s daily with you teaching in the temple, *2516*
26:58 and went in, and s with the servants, to see *2521*
26:69 Now Peter s without in the palace: and *2521*
28: 2 back the stone from the door, and s upon it. *2521*
Mk 2:15 that as *Jesus* s **at meat** in his house, *2621*
2:15 and sinners s **also together with** Jesus and *4873*
3:32 And *the* multitude s about him, and they *2521*
3:34 round about on them which s about him, *2521*
4: 1 that he entered into a ship, and s in the sea; *2521*
6:22 them that s **with** him, the king said unto *4873*
6:26 for their sakes which s **with** *him,* he would *4873*
6:40 And they s **down** in ranks, by hundreds, and *377*
9:35 And he s **down,** and called the twelve, and *2523*
10:46 of Timeus, s by the *high*way side begging. *2521*
11: 2 shall find a colt tied, whereon never man s; *2523*
11: 7 their garments on him; and he s upon him. *2523*
12:41 And Jesus s over against the treasury, and *2523*
13: 3 And as he s upon the mount of Olives over *2521*
14: 3 house of Simon the leper, as he s **at meat,** *2621*
14:18 And as they s and did eat, Jesus said, *345*
14:54 and he s with the servants, and *4775*
16:14 appeared unto the eleven as they s **at meat,** *345*
16:19 into heaven, and s on the right hand of God. *2523*
Lk 4:20 gave *it* again to the minister, and s **down.** *2523*
5: 3 And he s **down,** and taught the people out *2523*
5:29 and of others that s down with them. *2621*
7:15 And he that was dead s **up,** and began to *339*
7:36 the Pharisee's house, and s **down to meat.** *347*
7:37 when she knew that *Jesus* s **at meat** in *345*
7:49 And they that s **at meat with** *him* began to *4873*
10:39 which also s at Jesus' feet, and heard his *3869*
11:37 and he went in, and s **down to meat.** *377*
14:15 And when one of them that s **at meat with** *4873*
18:35 a certain blind man s by the way side *2521*
19:30 find a colt tied, whereon yet never man s: *2523*
22:14 he s **down,** and the twelve apostles with him. *377*
22:55 down together, Peter s **down** among them. *2521*
22:56 But a certain maid beheld him as he s by *2521*
24:30 as he s **at meat** with them, he took bread, *2625*
Jn 4: 6 with *his* journey, s thus on the well: *2516*
6: 3 and there he s with his disciples. *2521*
6:10 So the men s **down,** *in* number about five *377*
8: 2 unto him; and he s **down,** and taught them. *2523*
9: 8 said, Is not this he that s and begged? *2521*
11:20 and met him: but Mary s *still* in the house. *2516*
12: 2 of them that s **at the table with** him. *4873*
12:14 when he had found a young ass, s thereon; *2523*
19:13 s **down** in the judgment seat in a place *that* *2523*
Ac 2: 3 like as of fire, and it s upon each of them. *2523*
3:10 And they knew that it was he which s for *2521*
6:15 And all that s in the council, *2516*
9:40 her eyes: and when she saw Peter, she s **up.** *339*
12:21 s upon his throne, and made an oration unto *2523*
13:14 synagogue on the sabbath day, and s **down.** *2523*
14: 8 And there s a certain man at Lystra, *2521*
16:13 and we s **down,** and spake unto the women *2523*
20: 9 And there s in a window a certain young *2521*
25:17 on the morrow I s on the judgment seat, *2523*
26:30 and Bernice, and they that s **with** them: *4775*
1Co 10: 7 The people s **down** to eat and drink, and *2523*
Heb 1: 3 s **down** on the right hand of the Majesty on *2523*
10:12 for ever, s **down** on the right hand of God; *2523*
Rev 4: 2 was set in heaven, and one s on the throne. *2521*
4: 3 And he that s was to look upon like a jasper *2521*
4: 9 and thanks to him that s on the throne, *2521*
4:10 twenty elders fall down before him that s *2521*
5: 1 And I saw in the right hand of him that s on *2521*
5: 7 right hand of him that s upon the throne. *2521*
6: 2 and he that s on him had a bow; and *2521*
6: 4 *power* was given to him that s thereon to *2521*
6: 5 he that s on him had a pair of balances in *2521*
6: 8 and his name that s on him *was* Death, and *2521*
9:17 and them that s on them, *2521*
11:16 which s before God on their seats, *2521*
14:14 upon the cloud one s like unto the Son of *2521*
14:15 crying with a loud voice to him that s on *2521*
14:16 And he that s on the cloud thrust in his *2521*
19: 4 and worshipped God that s on the throne, *2521*
19:11 he that s upon him *was* called Faithful and *2521*
19:19 make war against him that s on the horse, *2521*
19:21 the sword of him that s upon the horse, *2521*
20: 4 and they s upon them, and judgment was *2523*
20:11 and him that s on it, from whose face *2521*
21: 5 And he that s upon the throne said, Behold, *2521*

SATAN (55) [SATAN'S]
1Ch 21: 1 S stood *up* against Israel, and 7854
Job 1: 6 the LORD, and S came also among them. 7854
1: 7 the LORD said unto S, Whence comest 7854
1: 7 S answered the LORD, and said, 7854
1: 8 the LORD said unto S, Hast thou 7854
1: 9 S answered the LORD, and said, Doth Job 7854
1:12 the LORD said unto S, Behold, all that he 7854
1:12 So S went forth from the presence of 7854
2: 1 S came also among them to present himself 7854
2: 2 the LORD said unto S, From whence 7854
2: 2 S answered the LORD, and said, 7854
2: 3 the LORD said unto S, Hast thou 7854
2: 4 S answered the LORD, and said, Skin for 7854
2: 6 the LORD said unto S, Behold, he *is* in 7854
2: 7 So went S forth from the presence of 7854

Ps 109: 6 over him: and let S stand at his right hand. 7854
Zec 3: 1 S standing at his right hand to resist him. 7854
3: 2 the LORD said unto S, The LORD 7854
3: 2 unto Satan, The LORD rebuke thee, O S; 7854
Mt 4:10 saith Jesus unto him, Get thee hence, S: 4567
12:26 And if S cast out Satan, he is divided 4567
12:26 And if Satan cast out S, he is divided 4567
16:23 and said unto Peter, Get thee behind me, S: 4567
Mk 1:13 in the wilderness forty days, tempted of S; 4567
3:23 in parables, How can S cast out Satan? 4567
3:23 in parables, How can Satan cast out S? 4567
3:26 And if S rise up against himself, and 4567
4:15 S cometh immediately, and taketh away 4567
8:33 saying, Get thee behind me, S: 4567
Lk 4: 8 and said unto him, Get thee behind me, S: 4567
10:18 I beheld S as lightning fall from heaven. 4567
11:18 If S also be divided against himself, 4567
13:16 whom S hath bound, lo these eighteen 4567
22: 3 Then entered S into Judas surnamed 4567
22:31 Simon, behold, S hath desired to have you, 4567
Jn 13:27 And after the sop S entered into him. 4567
Ac 5: 3 why hath S filled thine heart to lie to 4567
26:18 to light, and from the power of S unto God, 4567
Ro 16:20 And the God of peace shall bruise S under 4567
1Co 5: 5 To deliver such a one unto S for 4567
7: 5 that S tempt you not for your incontinency. 4567
2Co 2:11 Lest S should get an advantage of us: 4567
11:14 for S himself is transformed into an angel 4567
12: 7 the messenger of S to buffet me, lest I 4566
1Th 2:18 I Paul, once and again; but S hindered us. 4567
2Th 2: 9 is after the working of S with all power 4567
1Ti 1:20 whom I have delivered unto S, that they 4567
5:15 For some are already turned aside after S. 4567
Rev 2: 9 and are not, but are the synagogue of S. 4567
2:13 was slain among you, where S dwelleth. 4567
2:24 and which have not known the depths of S, 4567
3: 9 I will make them of the synagogue of S, 4567
12: 9 called the devil, and S, which deceiveth 4567
20: 2 and S, and bound him a thousand years, 4567
20: 7 S shall be loosed out of his prison, 4567

SATAN'S (1) [SATAN]

Rev 2:13 even where S seat is: and thou holdest fast 4567

SATEST (2) [SIT]

Ps 9: 4 thou s in the throne judging right. 3427
Eze 23:41 s upon a stately bed, and a table prepared 3427

SATIATE (2) [SATIATED, UNSATIABLE]

Jer 31:14 I will s the soul of the priests with fatness, 7301
46:10 it shall be s and made drunk with their 7646

SATIATED (1) [SATIATE]

Jer 31:25 For I have s the weary soul, and I have 7301

SATISFACTION (2) [SATISFY]

Nu 35:31 Moreover ye shall take no s for the life of a 3724
35:32 ye shall take no s for him that is fled to 3724

SATISFIED (43) [SATISFY]

Ex 15: 9 the spoil; my lust shall be s upon them; 4390
Lev 26:26 by weight: and ye shall eat, and not be s. 7646
Dt 14:29 shall come, and shall eat and be s; 7646
33:23 s with favour, and full with the blessing of 7649
Job 19:22 me as God, and are not s with my flesh? 7646
27:14 and his offspring shall not be s with bread. 7646
31:31 O that we had of his flesh! we cannot be s. 7646
Ps 17:15 I shall be s, when I awake, with thy 7646
22:26 The meek shall eat and be s: they shall 7646
36: 8 They shall be **abundantly** s with 7301
37:19 and in the days of famine they shall be s. 7646
59:15 down for meat, and grudge if they be not s. 7646
63: 5 My soul shall be s as with marrow and 7646
65: 4 we shall be s with the goodness of thy 7646
81:16 with honey out of the rock should I have s 7646
104:13 the earth is s with the fruit of thy works. 7646
105:40 and s them with the bread of heaven. 7646
Pr 12:11 He that tilleth his land shall be s with 7646
12:14 A man shall be s with good by the fruit of 7646
14:14 and a good man shall be s from himself. NIH
18:20 A man's belly shall be s with the fruit of 7646
19:23 he that hath it shall abide s; he shall not be 7649
20:13 thine eyes, and thou shalt be s with bread. 7646
27:20 never full; so the eyes of man are never s. 7646
30:15 There are three things that are never s, 7646
Ecc 1: 8 man cannot utter it: the eye is not s with 7646
4: 8 his labour; neither is his eye s with riches; 7646
5:10 He that loveth silver shall not be s with 7646
Isa 9:20 eat on the left hand, and they shall not be s: 7646
44:16 he eateth flesh; he roasteth roast, and is s: 7646
53:11 see of the travail of his soul, and shall be s: 7646
66:11 be s with the breasts of her consolations; 7646
Jer 31:14 my people shall be s with my goodness, 7646
50:10 all that spoil her shall be s, saith 7646
50:19 his soul shall be s upon mount Ephraim and 7646
La 5: 6 and to the Assyrians, to be s with bread. 7646
Eze 16:28 harlot with them, and yet couldest not be s. 7646
16:29 and yet thou wast not s herewith. 7646
Joel 2:19 and oil, and ye shall be s therewith: 7646
2:26 be s, and praise the name of the LORD 7646
Am 4: 8 to drink water; but they were not s: 7646
Mic 6:14 Thou shalt eat, but not be s; and thy casting 7646
Hab 2: 5 cannot be s, but gathereth unto him all 7646

SATISFIEST (1) [SATISFY]

Ps 145:16 and s the desire of every living thing. 7646

SATISFIETH (3) [SATISFY]

Ps 103: 5 Who s thy mouth with good things; so 7646
107: 9 For he s the longing soul, and filleth 7646
Isa 55: 2 your labour for that which s not? hearken 7654

SATISFY (10) [SATISFACTION, SATISFIED, SATISFIEST, SATISFIETH, SATISFYING]

Job 38:27 To s the desolate and waste ground; and 7646
Ps 90:14 O s us early with thy mercy; that we may 7646
91:16 With long life will I s him, and shew him 7646
132:15 her provision: I will s her poor with bread. 7646
Pr 5:19 let her breasts s thee at all times; and 7301
6:30 if he steal to s his soul when he is hungry; 4390
Isa 58:10 soul to the hungry, and s the afflicted soul; 7646
58:11 s thy soul in drought, and make fat thy 7646
Eze 7:19 they shall not s their souls, neither fill their 7646
Mk 8: 4 From whence can a man s these men with 5526

SATISFYING (2) [SATISFY]

Pr 13:25 The righteous eateth to the s of his soul: but 7648
Col 2:23 not in any honour to the s of the flesh. 4140

SATRAP See LIEUTENANTS

SATYR (1) [SATYRS]

Isa 34:14 the island, and the s shall cry to his fellow; 8163

SATYRS (1) [SATYR]

Isa 13:21 shall dwell there, and s shall dance there. 8163

SAUL (394) [PAUL, SAUL'S]

Ge 36:37 S of Rehoboth by the river reigned in his 7586
36:38 S died, and Baal-hanan the son of Achbor 7586
1Sa 9: 2 he had a son, whose name was S, a choice 7586
9: 3 Kish said to S his son, Take now one of 7586
9: 5 S said to his servant that was with him, 7586
9: 7 said S to his servant, But behold, if we go, 7586
9: 8 the servant answered S again, and said, 7586
9:10 Then said S to his servant, Well said; come, 7586
9:15 told Samuel in his ear a day before S came, 7586
9:17 when Samuel saw S, the LORD said unto 7586
9:18 S drew near to Samuel in the gate, and 7586
9:19 Samuel answered S, and said, I am the seer: 7586
9:21 S answered and said, Am not I a Benjamite, 7586
9:22 Samuel took S and his servant, and 7586
9:24 that which was upon it, and set it before S. 7586
9:24 So S did eat with Samuel that day. 7586
9:25 Samuel communed with S upon the top of 7586
9:26 that Samuel called S to the top of 7586
9:26 S arose, and they went out both of them, 7586
9:27 Samuel said to S, Bid the servant pass on 7586
10:11 son of Kish? Is S also among the prophets? 7586
10:12 a proverb, Is S also among the prophets? 7586
10:16 S said unto his uncle, He told us plainly 7586
10:21 was taken, and S the son of Kish was taken: 7586
10:26 S also went home to Gibeah; and 7586
11: 4 came the messengers to Gibeah of S, and 7586
11: 5 S came after the herd out of the field; 7586
11: 5 S said, What aileth the people that they 7586
11: 6 the spirit of God came upon S when he 7586
11: 7 Whosoever cometh not forth after S and 7586
11:11 that S put the people in three companies; 7586
11:12 Who is he that said, Shall S reign over us? 7586
11:13 S said, There shall not a man be put to 7586
11:15 there they made S king before the LORD 7586
11:15 there S and all the men of Israel rejoiced 7586
13: 1 S reigned one year; and when he had 7586
13: 2 S chose him three thousand men of Israel; 7586
13: 2 whereof two thousand were with S in 7586
13: 3 the Philistines heard of it. And S blew 7586
13: 4 all Israel heard say that S had smitten a 7586
13: 4 the people were called together after S to 7586
13: 7 As for S, he was yet in Gilgal, and all 7586
13: 9 S said, Bring hither a burnt offering to me, 7586
13:10 S went out to meet him, that he might 7586
13:11 S said, Because I saw that the people were 7586
13:13 Samuel said to S, Thou hast done foolishly: 7586
13:15 S numbered the people that were present 7586
13:16 S, and Jonathan his son, and the people that 7586
13:22 hand of any of the people that were with S 7586
13:22 with S and with Jonathan his son was there 7586
14: 1 that Jonathan the son of S said unto 7586
14: 2 S tarried in the uttermost part of Gibeah 7586
14:16 the watchmen of S in Gibeah of Benjamin 7586
14:17 said S unto the people that were with him, 7586
14:18 S said unto Ahiah, Bring hither the ark of 7586
14:19 came to pass, while S talked unto the priest, 7586
14:19 S said unto the priest, Withdraw thine hand. 7586
14:20 S and all the people that were with him 7586
14:21 to be with the Israelites that were with S 7586
14:24 for S had adjured the people, saying, 7586
14:33 they told S, saying, Behold, the people sin 7586
14:34 S said, Disperse yourselves among 7586
14:35 S built an altar unto the LORD: the same 7586
14:36 S said, Let us go down after the Philistines 7586
14:37 S asked counsel of God, Shall I go down 7586
14:38 S said, Draw ye near hither, all the chief of 7586
14:40 the people said unto S, Do what seemeth 7586
14:41 Therefore S said unto the LORD God of 7586
14:41 Give a perfect lot. And S and 7586
14:42 S said, Cast lots between me and Jonathan 7586
14:43 S said to Jonathan, Tell me what thou hast 7586
14:44 S answered, God do so and more also: 7586
14:45 the people said unto S, Shall Jonathan die, 7586
14:46 S went up from following the Philistines: 7586
14:47 So S took the kingdom over Israel, and 7586
14:49 Now the sons of S were Jonathan, and 7586
14:51 Kish was the father of S; and Ner the father 7586
14:52 war against the Philistines all the days of S: 7586
14:52 when S saw any strong man, or any valiant 7586
15: 1 Samuel also said unto S, The LORD sent 7586
15: 4 S gathered the people together, and 7586
15: 5 S came to a city of Amalek, and laid wait in 7586
15: 6 S said unto the Kenites, Go, depart, get you 7586
15: 7 S smote the Amalekites from Havilah until 7586
15: 9 S and the people spared Agag, and the best 7586
15:11 It repenteth me that I have set up S to be 7586
15:12 when Samuel rose early to meet S in 7586
15:12 S came to Carmel, and behold, 7586
1Sa 15:13 Samuel came to S: and Saul said unto him, 7586
15:13 S said unto him, Blessed be thou of 7586
15:15 S said, They have brought them from 7586
15:16 Samuel said unto S, Stay, and I will tell 7586
15:20 S said unto Samuel, Yea, I have obeyed 7586
15:24 S said unto Samuel, I have sinned: for I 7586
15:26 Samuel said unto S, I will not return with 7586
15:31 So Samuel turned again after S; and 7586
15:31 after Saul; and S worshipped the LORD. 7586
15:34 S went up to his house to Gibeah of Saul. 7586
15:34 Saul went up to his house to Gibeah of S. 7586
15:35 Samuel came no more to see S until the day 7586
15:35 nevertheless Samuel mourned for S: and 7586
15:35 the LORD repented that he had made S 7586
16: 1 How long wilt thou mourn for S, 7586
16: 2 if S hear it, he will kill me. And 7586
16:14 the spirit of the LORD departed from S, 7586
16:17 S said unto his servants, Provide me now a 7586
16:19 Wherefore S sent messengers unto Jesse, 7586
16:20 and sent them by David his son unto S. 7586
16:21 David came to S, and stood before him: 7586
16:22 S sent to Jesse, saying, Let David, I pray 7586
16:23 when the evil spirit from God was upon S, 7586
16:23 so S was refreshed, and was well, and 7586
17: 2 S and the men of Israel were gathered 7586
17: 8 am not I a Philistine, and you servants to S? 7586
17:11 When S and all Israel heard those words of 7586
17:12 among men for an old man in the days of S. 7586
17:13 of Jesse went and followed S to the battle: 7586
17:14 and the three eldest followed S. 7586
17:15 returned from S to feed his father's sheep at 7586
17:19 Now S, and they, and all the men of Israel, 7586
17:31 David spake, they rehearsed them before S: 7586
17:32 David said to S, Let no man's heart fail 7586
17:33 S said to David, Thou art not able to go 7586
17:34 David said unto S, Thy servant kept his 7586
17:37 S said unto David, Go, and the LORD be 7586
17:38 S armed David with his armour, and he put 7586
17:39 had not proved it. And David said unto S, 7586
17:55 when S saw David go forth against 7586
17:57 brought him before S with the head of 7586
17:58 S said to him, Whose son art thou, thou 7586
18: 1 when he made an end of speaking unto S, 7586
18: 2 S took him that day, and would let him go 7586
18: 5 David went out whithersoever S sent him, 7586
18: 5 S set him over the men of war, and he was 7586
18: 6 singing and dancing, to meet king S, 7586
18: 7 S hath slain his thousands, and David his 7586
18: 8 S was very wroth, and the saying 7586
18: 9 S eyed David from that day and forward. 7586
18:10 that the evil spirit from God came upon S, 7586
18:11 S cast the javelin; for he said, I will smite 7586
18:12 S was afraid of David, because the LORD 7586
18:12 was with him, and was departed from S. 7586
18:13 Therefore S removed him from him, and 7586
18:15 Wherefore when S saw that he behaved 7586
18:17 S said to David, Behold my elder daughter 7586
18:17 For S said, Let not mine hand be upon him, 7586
18:18 David said unto S, Who am I? and what is 7586
18:20 and they told S, and the thing pleased him. 7586
18:21 S said, I will give him her, that she may be 7586
18:21 Wherefore S said to David, Thou shalt this 7586
18:22 S commanded his servants, 7586
18:24 the servants of S told him, saying, On this 7586
18:25 S said, Thus shall ye say to David, The 7586
18:25 S thought to make David fall by the hand of 7586
18:27 S gave him Michal his daughter to wife. 7586
18:28 S saw and knew that the LORD was with 7586
18:29 S was yet the more afraid of David; and 7586
18:29 and S became David's enemy continually. 7586
18:30 more wisely than all the servants of S; 7586
19: 1 S spake to Jonathan his son, and to all his 7586
19: 2 S my father seeketh to kill thee: 7586
19: 4 Jonathan spake good of David unto S his 7586
19: 6 S hearkened unto the voice of Jonathan: 7586
19: 6 S sware, As the LORD liveth, he shall not 7586
19: 7 Jonathan brought David to S, and he was in 7586
19: 9 the evil spirit from the LORD was upon S, 7586
19:10 S sought to smite David even to the wall 7586
19:11 S also sent messengers unto David's house, 7586
19:14 And when S sent messengers to take David, 7586
19:15 S sent the messengers again to see David, 7586
19:17 S said unto Michal, Why hast thou 7586
19:17 Michal answered S, He said unto me, 7586
19:18 and told him all that S had done to him. 7586
19:19 it was told S, saying, Behold, David is at 7586
19:20 S sent messengers to take David: and 7586
19:20 of God was upon the messengers of S, 7586
19:21 when it was told S, he sent other 7586
19:21 And S sent messengers again the third time, 7586
19:24 they say, Is S also among the prophets? 7586
20:26 Nevertheless S spake not any thing that 7586
20:27 S said unto Jonathan his son, 7586
20:28 Jonathan answered S, David earnestly 7586
20:32 Jonathan answered S his father, and 7586
20:33 S cast a javelin at him to smite him: 7586
21: 7 Now a certain man of the servants of S was 7586
21: 7 chiefest of the herdmen that belonged to S. 7586
21:10 fled that day for fear of S, and went to 7586
21:11 S hath slain his thousands, and David his 7586
22: 6 When S heard that David was discovered, 7586
22: 6 (now S abode in Gibeah under a tree in 7586
22: 7 S said unto his servants that stood about 7586
22: 9 which was set over the servants of S, and 7586
22:12 S said, Hear now, thou son of Ahitub. 7586
22:13 S said unto him, Why have ye conspired 7586
22:21 Abiathar shewed David that S had slain 7586
22:22 was there, that he would surely tell S: 7586
23: 7 it was told S that David was come to 7586
23: 7 S said, God hath delivered him into mine 7586
23: 8 S called all the people together to war, 7586
23: 9 David knew that S secretly practised 7586
23:10 thy servant hath certainly heard that S 7586
23:11 Will S come down, as thy servant hath 7586
23:12 deliver me and my men into the hand of S? 7586

S

1Sa 23:13 it was told **S** that David was escaped from 7586
23:14 **S** sought him every day, but God delivered 7586
23:15 David saw that **S** was come out to seek his 7586
23:17 for the hand of **S** my father shall not find 7586
23:17 and that also **S** my father knoweth. 7586
23:19 came up the Ziphites to **S** to Gibeah, 7586
23:21 **S** said, Blessed *be* ye of the LORD; for ye 7586
23:24 they arose, and went to Ziph before **S**: but 7586
23:25 **S** also and his men went to seek *him.* And 7586
23:25 when **S** heard *that,* he pursued after David 7586
23:26 **S** went on this side of the mountain, and 7586
23:26 David made haste to get away for fear of **S**; 7586
23:26 for **S** and his men compassed David and his 7586
23:27 there came a messenger unto **S**, saying, 7586
23:28 Wherefore **S** returned from pursuing after 7586
24: 1 when **S** was returned from following 7586
24: 2 **S** took three thousand chosen men out of all 7586
24: 3 *was* a cave; and **S** went in to cover his feet: 7586
24: 7 and suffered them not to rise against **S**. 7586
24: 7 **S** rose up out of the cave, and went on *his* 7586
24: 8 and cried after **S**, saying, My lord the king. 7586
24: 8 when **S** looked behind him, David stooped 7586
24: 9 David said to **S**, Wherefore hearest thou 7586
24:16 an end of speaking these words unto **S**, 7586
24:16 that **S** said, *Is* this thy voice, my son David? 7586
24:16 And **S** lift up his voice, and wept. 7586
24:22 David sware unto **S**. And Saul went home; 7586
24:22 **S** went home; but David and his men gat 7586
25:44 **S** had given Michal his daughter, 7586
26: 1 the Ziphites came unto **S** to Gibeah, saying, 7586
26: 2 **S** arose, and went down to the wilderness 7586
26: 3 **S** pitched in the hill of Hachilah, which *is* 7586
26: 3 he saw that **S** came after him into 7586
26: 4 understood that **S** was come in very deed. 7586
26: 5 and came to the place where **S** had pitched: 7586
26: 5 David beheld the place where **S** lay, and 7586
26: 5 **S** lay in the trench, and the people pitched 7586
26: 6 Who will go down with me to **S** to 7586
26: 7 **S** lay sleeping within the trench, and 7586
26:17 **S** knew David's voice, and said, *Is* this thy 7586
26:21 said **S**, I have sinned: return, my son David: 7586
26:25 **S** said to David, Blessed *be* thou, my son 7586
26:25 on his way, and **S** returned to his place. 7586
27: 1 shall now perish one day by the hand of **S**: 7586
27: 1 **S** shall despair of me, to seek me any more 7586
27: 4 it was told **S** that David was fled *to* Gath: 7586
28: 3 **S** had put away those that had familiar 7586
28: 4 **S** gathered all Israel together, and 7586
28: 5 when **S** saw the host of the Philistines, he 7586
28: 6 when **S** inquired of the LORD, 7586
28: 7 said **S** unto his servants, Seek me a woman 7586
28: 8 **S** disguised himself, and put on other 7586
28: 9 Behold, thou knowest what **S** hath done, 7586
28:10 **S** sware to her by the LORD, saying, 7586
28:12 the woman spake to **S**, saying, Why hast 7586
28:12 Why hast thou deceived me? for thou *art* **S**. 7586
28:13 the woman said unto **S**, I saw gods 7586
28:14 **S** perceived that it *was* Samuel, and 7586
28:15 Samuel said to **S**, Why hast thou disquieted 7586
28:15 **S** answered, I am sore distressed; for 7586
28:20 **S** fell straightway all along on the earth, 7586
28:21 the woman came unto **S**, and saw that he 7586
28:25 she brought *it* before **S**, and before his 7586
29: 3 the servant of **S** the king of Israel, 7586
29: 5 **S** slew his thousands, and David his ten 7586
31: 2 the Philistines followed hard upon **S** and 7586
31: 3 the battle went sore against **S**, and 7586
31: 4 said **S** unto his armourbearer, Draw thy 7586
31: 4 therefore **S** took a sword, and fell upon it. 7586
31: 5 when his armourbearer saw that **S** was 7586
31: 6 So **S** died, and his three sons, and 7586
31: 7 that **S** and his sons were dead, they forsook 7586
31: 8 that they found **S** and his three sons fallen 7586
31:11 of that which the Philistines had done to **S**, 7586
31:12 took the body of **S** and the bodies of his 7586
2Sa 1: 1 Now it came to pass after the death of **S**, 7586
1: 2 a man came out of the camp from **S** with 7586
1: 4 and **S** and Jonathan his son are dead also. 7586
1: 5 How knowest thou that **S** and Jonathan his 7586
1: 6 behold, **S** leaned upon his spear; 7586
1:12 for **S**, and for Jonathan his son, and for 7586
1:17 lamented with this lamentation over **S** 7586
1:21 the shield of **S**, *as though he had* not *been* 7586
1:22 and the sword of **S** returned not empty. 7586
1:23 **S** and Jonathan *were* lovely and pleasant in 7586
1:24 Ye daughters of Israel, weep over **S**, 7586
2: 4 of Jabesh-gilead *were they* that buried **S**. 7586
2: 5 *even* unto **S**, and have buried him. 7586
2: 7 for your master **S** is dead, and also 7586
2: 8 took Ish-bosheth the son of **S**, and 7586
2:12 the servants of Ish-bosheth the son of **S**, 7586
2:15 *pertained* to Ish-bosheth the son of **S**, 7586
3: 1 there was long war between the house of **S** 7586
3: 1 the house of **S** waxed weaker and weaker. 7586
3: 6 while there was war between the house of **S** 7586
3: 6 made himself strong for the house of **S**. 7586
3: 7 **S** had a concubine, whose name *was* 7586
3: 8 *this* day unto the house of **S** thy father, 7586
3:10 translate the kingdom from the house of **S**, 7586
4: 4 five years old when the tidings came of **S** 7586
4: 8 Behold the head of Ish-bosheth the son of **S** 7586
4: 8 avenged my lord the king this day of **S**, 7586
4:10 one told me, saying, Behold, **S** is dead, 7586
5: 2 Also in time past, when **S** was king over us, 7586
6:20 Michal the daughter of **S** came out to meet 7586
6:23 Therefore Michal the daughter of **S** had no 7586
7:15 as I took *it* from **S**, whom I put away before 7586
9: 1 there yet *any* that is left of the house of **S**, 7586
9: 2 *there was* of the house of **S** a servant whose 7586
9: 3 *Is there* not yet any of the house of **S**, 7586
9: 6 the son of Jonathan, the son of **S**, was come 7586
9: 7 will restore thee all the land of **S** thy father; 7586
9: 9 unto thy master's son all that pertained to **S** 7586
12: 7 and I delivered thee out of the hand of **S**; 7586
16: 5 out a man of the family of the house of **S**, 7586

2Sa 16: 8 upon thee all the blood of the house of **S**, 7586
19:17 Ziba the servant of the house of **S**, and 7586
19:24 Mephibosheth the son of **S** came down to 7586
21: 1 *It is* for **S**, and for *his* bloody house, 7586
21: 2 **S** sought to slay them in his zeal to 7586
21: 4 We will have no silver nor gold of **S**, nor of 7586
21: 6 them up unto the LORD in Gibeah of **S**, 7586
21: 7 the son of Jonathan the son of **S**, because 7586
21: 7 between David and Jonathan the son of **S**. 7586
21: 8 whom she bare unto **S**, Armoni and 7586
21: 8 the five sons of Michal the daughter of **S**, 7586
21:11 of Aiah, the concubine of **S**, had done. 7586
21:12 David went and took the bones of **S** and 7586
21:12 when the Philistines had slain **S** in Gilboa: 7586
21:13 he brought up from thence the bones of **S** 7586
21:14 the bones of **S** and Jonathan his son buried 7586
22: 1 of all his enemies, and out of the hand of **S**: 7586
1Ch 5:10 in the days of **S** they made war with 7586
8:33 Kish begat **S**, and Saul begat Jonathan, and 7586
8:33 **S** begat Jonathan, and Malchishua, and 7586
9:39 Kish begat **S**; and Saul begat Jonathan, and 7586
9:39 **S** begat Jonathan, and Malchishua, and 7586
10: 2 the Philistines followed hard after **S**, and 7586
10: 2 and Malchishua, the sons of **S**. 7586
10: 3 the battle went sore against **S**, and 7586
10: 4 said **S** to his armourbearer, Draw thy 7586
10: 4 So **S** took a sword, and fell upon it. 7586
10: 5 when his armourbearer saw that **S** was 7586
10: 6 So **S** died, and his three sons, and all his 7586
10: 7 that **S** and his sons were dead, then 7586
10: 8 that they found **S** and his sons fallen in 7586
10:11 heard all that the Philistines had done to **S**, 7586
10:12 took away the body of **S**, and the bodies of 7586
10:13 So **S** died for his transgression which he 7586
11: 2 in time past, even when **S** was king, 7586
12: 1 himself close because of **S** the son of Kish: 7586
12:19 when he came with the Philistines against **S** 7586
12:19 He will fall to his master **S** to *the jeopardy* 7586
12:23 to Hebron, to turn the kingdom of **S** to him, 7586
12:29 the kindred of **S**, three thousand: 7586
12:29 them had kept the ward of the house of **S**. 7586
13: 3 for we inquired not *at* it in the days of **S**. 7586
15:29 that Michal the daughter of **S** looking out at 7586
26:28 **S** the son of Kish, and Abner the son of 7586
Ps 18: T of all his enemies, and from the hand of **S**: 7586
52: T when Doeg the Edomite came and told **S**, 7586
54: T when the Ziphims came and said to **S**, 7586
57: T of David, when he fled from **S** in the cave. 7586
59: T when **S** sent, and they watcht the house to 7586
Isa 10:29 Ramah is afraid; Gibeah of **S** is fled. 7586
Ac 7:58 at a young man's feet, whose name was **S**. *4569*
8: 1 And **S** was consenting unto his death. *4569*
8: 3 As for **S**, he made havock of the church, *4569*
9: 1 And **S**, yet breathing out threatenings and *4569*
9: 4 **S**, Saul, why persecutest thou me? *4549*
9: 4 Saul, **S**, why persecutest thou me? *4549*
9: 8 And **S** arose from the earth; and when his *4569*
9:11 in the house of Judas for *one* called **S**, *4569*
9:17 him said, Brother **S**, the Lord, *even* Jesus, *4549*
9:19 Then was **S** certain days with the disciples *4569*
9:22 But **S** increased the more in strength, and *4569*
9:24 But their laying await was known of **S**. *4569*
9:26 And when **S** was come to Jerusalem, *4569*
11:25 departed Barnabas to Tarsus, for to seek **S**: *4569*
11:30 the elders by the hands of Barnabas and **S**. *4569*
12:25 and **S** returned from Jerusalem, *4569*
13: 1 brought up with Herod the tetrarch, and **S**. *4569*
13: 2 **S** for the work whereunto I have called *4569*
13: 7 who called for Barnabas and **S**, and *4569*
13: 9 Then **S**, (who also *is called* Paul,) *4569*
13:21 and God gave unto them **S** the son of Cis, *4549*
22: 7 unto me, **S**, Saul, why persecutest thou me? *4549*
22: 7 unto me, Saul, **S**, why persecutest thou me? *4549*
22:13 and stood, and said unto me, Brother **S**, *4549*
26:14 **S**, Saul, why persecutest thou me? *4549*
26:14 Saul, **S**, why persecutest thou me? *4549*

SAUL'S (31) [SAUL]

1Sa 9: 3 the asses of Kish **S** father were lost. 7586
10:14 **S** uncle said unto him and to his servant, 7586
10:15 **S** uncle said, Tell me, I pray thee, 7586
14:50 the name of **S** wife *was* Ahinoam, 7586
14:50 his host *was* Abner, the son of Ner, **S** uncle. 7586
16:15 **S** servants said unto him, Behold now, 7586
18: 5 and also in the sight of **S** servants. 7586
18:10 and *there was* a javelin in **S** hand. 7586
18:19 it came to pass at the time when Merab **S** 7586
18:20 Michal **S** daughter loved David: and 7586
18:23 **S** servants spake those words in the ears of 7586
18:28 and *that* Michal **S** daughter loved him. 7586
19: 2 Jonathan **S** son delighted much in David: 7586
19:10 he slipt away out of **S** presence, and 7586
20:25 Abner sat by **S** side, and David's place was 7586
20:30 Then **S** anger was kindled against Jonathan, 7586
23:16 Jonathan **S** son arose, and went to David 7586
24: 4 cut off the skirt of **S** robe privily. 7586+3807.1
24: 5 because he had cut off **S** skirt. 7586+3807.1
26:12 and the cruse of water from **S** bolster; 7586
31: 2 and Abinadab, and Malchishua, **S** sons. 7586
2Sa 2: 8 the son of Ner, captain of **S** host, 7586+3807.1
2:10 Ish-bosheth **S** son *was* forty years old when 7586
3:13 except thou first bring Michal **S** daughter, 7586
3:14 David sent messengers to Ish-bosheth **S** 7586
4: 1 when **S** son heard that Abner was dead in 7586
4: 2 **S** son had two men *that were* captains of 7586
4: 4 Jonathan, **S** son, had a son *that was* lame of 7586
6:16 Michal **S** daughter looked through a 7586
9: 9 called to Ziba, **S** servant, and said unto him, 7586
1Ch 12: 2 of a bow, *even* of **S** brethren of Benjamin. 7586

SAVE (233) [SAFE, SAFEGUARD, SAFELY, SAFETY, SALVATION, SAVED, SAVEST, SAVETH, SAVING, SAVIOUR, SAVIOURS]

Ge 12:12 they will kill me, but they will **s** thee **alive**. 2421
14:24 **S** only that which the young men have 1107
39: 6 he had, **s** the bread which he did eat. 518+3588
45: 7 and to **s** your **lives** by a great deliverance. 2421
50:20 as *it is* this day, to **s** much people **alive**. 2421
Ex 1:22 and every daughter ye shall **s** **alive**. 2421
12:16 **s** *that* which every man must eat, that only 389
22:20 **s** unto the LORD only, he shall be utterly 1115
Nu 14:30 **s** Caleb the son of Jephunneh, and 518+3588
26:65 **s** Caleb the son of Jephunneh, and 518+3588
32:12 **S** Caleb the son of Jephunneh the Kenezite, 1115
Dt 1:36 **S** Caleb the son of Jephunneh, he shall see 2108
15: 4 **S** when there shall be no poor among you; 657
20: 4 for you against your enemies, to **s** you. 3467
20:16 thou shalt **s** **alive** nothing that breatheth: 2421
22:27 damsel cried, and *there was* none to **s** her. 3467
28:29 spoiled evermore, and no man shall **s** *thee.* 3467
Jos 2:13 *that* ye will **s** **alive** my father, and 2421
10: 6 up to us quickly, and **s** us, and help us: 3467
11:13 Israel burned none of them, **s** Hazor only; 2108
11:19 **s** the Hivites the inhabitants of Gibeon: 1115
14: 4 **s** cities to dwell *in,* with their suburbs 518+3588
22:22 against the LORD, (**s** us not this day,) 3467
Jdg 6:14 thou shalt **s** Israel from the hand of 3467
6:15 O my Lord, wherewith shall I **s** Israel? 3467
6:31 will ye **s** him? he that will plead for him, 3467
6:36 If thou wilt **s** Israel by mine hand, as thou 3467
6:37 shall I know that thou wilt **s** Israel by mine 3467
7: 7 three hundred men that lapped will I **s** you, 3467
7:14 This *is* nothing else **s** the sword of Gideon 518
1Sa 4: 3 it may **s** us out of the hand of our enemies. 3467
7: 8 that he will **s** us out of the hand of 3467
9:16 that *he* may **s** my people out of the hand of 3467
10:24 people shouted, and said, **God** **s** the king. 2421
10:27 of Belial said, How shall this *man* **s** us? 3467
11: 3 then, if *there be* no man to **s** us, we will 3467
14: 6 for *there is* no restraint to the LORD to **s** 3467
19:11 saying, If thou **s** not thy life to night, 4422
21: 9 take *it:* for *there is* no other **s** that here. 2108
23: 2 Go, and smite the Philistines, and **s** Keilah. 3467
30:17 **s** four hundred young men, 518+3588
30:22 **s** *to* every man his wife and his 518+3588
2Sa 3:18 By the hand of my servant David I will **s** 3467
12: 3 **s** one little ewe lamb, which he had 518+3588
16:16 **God** **s** the king, God save the king. 2421
16:16 God save the king, **God** **s** the king. 2421
22:28 the afflicted people thou wilt **s**: but 3467
22:32 For who *is* God, **s** the LORD? and 1107+4480
22:32 And who *is* a rock, **s** our God? 1107+4480
22:42 They looked, but *there was* none to **s**; 3467
1Ki 1:12 that thou mayest **s** thine own life, and 4422
1:25 before him, and say, **God** **s** king Adonijah. 2421
1:34 the trumpet, and say, **God** **s** king Solomon. 2421
1:39 all the people said, **God** **s** king Solomon. 2421
3:18 with us in the house, **s** we two in the house. 2108
8: 9 *There was* nothing in the ark **s** the two 7535
15: 5 **s** **only** in the matter of Urijah the Hittite. 7535
18: 5 find grass to **s** the horses and mules **alive**, 2421
20:31 of Israel: peradventure he will **s** thy life. 2421
22:31 **s** only with the king of Israel. 518+3588
2Ki 4: 2 any thing in the house, **s** a pot of oil. 518+3588
7: 4 if they **s** us **alive**, we shall live; and if they 2421
11:12 clapt their hands, and said, **God** **s** the king. 2421
15: 4 **S** **that** the high places were not removed: 7535
16: 7 **s** me out of the hand of the king of Syria, 3467
19:19 I beseech thee, **s** *thou* us out of his hand, 3467
19:34 to **s** it, for mine own sake, and for my 3467
24:14 **s** the poorest sort of the people of the land. 2108
1Ch 16:35 say ye, **S** us, O God of our salvation, and 3467
2Ch 2: 6 **s** **only** to burn sacrifice before him? 518+3588
5:10 *There was* nothing in the ark **s** the two 7535
18:30 or great, **s** only with the king of Israel. 518+3588
21:17 **s** Jehoahaz, the youngest of his sons. 518+3588
23: 6 **s** the priests, and they that minister of 518+3588
23:11 anointed him, and said, **God** **s** the king. 2421
Ne 2:12 with me, **s** the beast that I rode upon. 518+3588
6:11 I *am,* would go in to the temple to **s** his **life**? 2421
Job 2: 6 Behold, he *is* in thine hand; but **s** his life. 8104
20:20 he shall not **s** of that which he desired. 4422
22:29 lifting up; and he shall **s** the humble person. 3467
40:14 thee that thine own right hand can **s** thee. 3467
Ps 3: 7 Arise, O LORD; **s** me, O my God: 3467
6: 4 my soul: O **s** me for thy mercy's sake. 3467
7: 1 **s** me from all them that persecute me, and 3467
18:27 For thou wilt **s** the afflicted people; but 3467
18:31 For who *is* God **s** the LORD? or 1107+4480
18:31 the LORD? or who *is* a rock **s** our God? 2108
18:41 *there was* none to **s** *them: even* unto 3467
20: 9 **S**, LORD: let the king hear us when we 3467
22:21 **S** me from the lion's mouth: for thou hast 3467
28: 9 **S** thy people, and bless thine inheritance: 3467
31: 2 strong rock, for a house of defence to **s** me. 3467
31:16 thy servant: **s** me for thy mercy's sake. 3467
37:40 and **s** them, because they trust in him. 3467
44: 3 neither did their own arm **s** them: 3467
44: 6 in my bow, neither shall my sword **s** me. 3467
54: 1 **S** me, O God, by thy name, and judge me 3467
55:16 call upon God; and the LORD shall **s** me. 3467
57: 3 **s** me *from* the reproach of him that would 3467
59: 2 of iniquity, and **s** me from bloody men. 3467
60: 5 **s** *with* thy right hand, and hear me. 3467
69: 1 **S** me, O God; for the waters are come in 3467
69:35 For God will **s** Zion, and will build 3467
71: 2 incline thine ear unto me, and **s** me. 3467
71: 3 thou hast given commandment to **s** me; 3467
72: 4 he shall **s** the children of the needy, and 3467
72:13 needy, and shall **s** the souls of the needy. 3467
76: 9 to judgment, to **s** all the meek of the earth. 3467
80: 2 stir up thy strength, and come and **s** us. 3444
86: 2 my God, **s** thy servant that trusteth in thee. 3467
86:16 and **s** the son of thine handmaid. 3467
106:47 **S** us, O LORD our God, and gather us 3467
108: 6 **s** *with* thy right hand, and answer me. 3467
109:26 my God: O **s** me according to thy mercy: 3467
109:31 to **s** *him* from those that condemn his soul. 3467
118:25 **S** now, I beseech thee, O LORD: 3467

S

Ps 119:94 I *am* thine, **s** me; for I have sought thy 3467
119:146 **s** me, and I shall keep thy testimonies. 3467
138: 7 and thy right hand shall **s** me. 3467
145:19 he also will hear their cry, and will **s** them. 3467
Pr 20:22 *but* wait on the LORD, and he shall **s** thee. 3467
Isa 25: 9 we have waited for him, and he will **s** us: 3467
33:22 the LORD *is* our king; he will **s** us. 3467
35: 4 *with* a recompence; he will come and **s** you. 3467
37:20 O LORD our God, **s** us from his hand, 3467
37:35 For I will defend this city to **s** it for mine 3467
38:20 The LORD *was ready* to **s** me: therefore 3467
45:20 and pray unto a god *that* cannot **s**. 3467
46: 7 he not answer, nor **s** him out of his trouble. 3467
47:13 **s** thee from *these things* that shall come 3467
47:15 every one to his quarter; none shall **s** thee. 3467
49:25 with thee, and I will **s** thy children. 3467
59: 1 hand is not shortened, that *it* cannot **s**; 3467
63: 1 I that speak in righteousness, mighty to **s**. 3467
Jer 2:27 their trouble they will say, Arise, and **s** us. 3467
2:28 if they can **s** thee in the time of thy trouble: 3467
11:12 they shall not **s** them **at all** in 3467+3467
14: 9 as a mighty *man that* cannot **s**? 3467
15:20 for I *am* with thee to **s** thee and to deliver 3467
17:14 I shall be healed; **s** me, and I shall be saved: 3467
30:10 I *will* **s** thee from afar, and thy seed from 3467
30:11 I *am* with thee, saith the LORD, to **s** thee: 3467
31: 7 praise ye, and say, O LORD, **s** thy people, 3467
42:11 for I *am* with you to **s** you, and to deliver 3467
46:27 I *will* **s** thee from afar off, and thy seed 3467
48: 6 **s** your lives, and be like the heath in 4422
La 4:17 watched for a nation *that* could not **s** *us*. 3467
Eze 3:18 wicked from his wicked way, to **s** his **life**; 2421
13:18 will ye **s** the souls **alive** *that come* unto 2421
13:19 and to **s** the souls **alive** that should not live, 2421
18:27 is lawful and right, he shall **s** his soul **alive**. 2421
34:22 Therefore will I **s** my flock, and they shall 3467
36:29 I will also **s** you from all your 3467
37:23 I will **s** them out of all their dwelling 3467
Da 6: 7 or man for thirty days, **s** of thee, O king, 3861
6:12 or man within thirty days, **s** of thee, O king, 3861
Hos 1: 7 will **s** them by the LORD their God, and 3467
1: 7 will not **s** them by bow, nor by sword, 3467
13:10 where *is any other* that may **s** thee in all thy 3467
14: 3 Asshur shall not **s** us: we will not ride upon 3467
Hab 1: 2 unto thee *of* violence, and thou wilt not **s**? 3467
Zep 3:17 he will **s**, he will rejoice over thee with joy; 3467
3:19 I will **s** her that halteth, and gather her that 3467
Zec 8: 7 I *will* **s** my people from the east country, 3467
8:13 so will I **s** you, and ye shall be a blessing: 3467
9:16 the LORD their God shall **s** them in that 3467
10: 6 I will **s** the house of Joseph, and I will bring 3467
12: 7 The LORD also shall **s** the tents of Judah 3467
Mt 1:21 for he shall **s** his people from their sins. *4982*
8:25 to *him*, and awoke him, saying, Lord, **s** us: *4982*
11:27 **s** the Son, and *he* to whomsoever the Son *1508*
13:57 **s** in his own country, and in his own house. *1508*
14:30 to sink, he cried, saying, Lord, **s** me. *4982*
16:25 For whosoever will **s** his life shall lose it: *4982*
17: 8 their eyes, they saw no *man*, **s** Jesus only. *1508*
18:11 For the Son of man is come to **s** that which *4982*
19:11 this saying, **s** *they* to whom it is given. *235*
27:40 and buildest *it* in three days, **s** thyself. *4982*
27:42 He saved others; himself he cannot **s**. If he *4982*
27:49 let us see whether Elias will come to **s** him. *4982*
Mk 3: 4 to **s** life, or to kill? But they held their *4982*
5:37 **s** Peter, and James, and John the brother of *1508*
6: 5 **s** that he laid *his* hands upon a few sick *1508*
6: 8 nothing for *their* journey, **s** a staff only; *1508*
8:35 For whosoever will **s** his life shall lose it; *4982*
8:35 and the gospel's, the same shall **s** it. *4982*
9: 8 *man* any more, **s** Jesus only with themselves. *235*
15:30 **S** thyself, and come down from the cross. *4982*
15:31 He saved others; himself he cannot **s**. *4982*
Lk 4:26 **s** unto Sarepta, *a city* of Sidon, unto a *1508*
6: 9 or to do evil? to **s** life, or to destroy *it*? *4982*
8:51 he suffered no *man* to go in, **s** Peter, *1508*
9:24 For whosoever will **s** his life shall lose it: *4982*
9:24 lose his life for my sake, the same shall **s** it. *4982*
9:56 to **s** *them*. And they went to another village. *4982*
17:18 to give glory to God, **s** this stranger *1508*
17:33 Whosoever shall seek to **s** his life shall lose *4982*
18:19 me good? none *is* good, **s** one, *that is*, God. *1508*
19:10 come to seek and to **s** that which was lost. *4982*
23:35 let him **s** himself, if he be Christ, *4982*
23:37 If thou be the King of the Jews, **s** thyself. *4982*
23:39 saying, If thou be Christ, **s** thyself and us. *4982*
Jn 6:22 **s** that one whereinto his disciples were *1508*
6:46 **s** he which is of God, he hath seen *1508*
12:27 Father, **s** me from this hour: but for this *4982*
12:47 not to judge the world, but to **s** the world. *4982*
13:10 He that is washed needeth not **s** to wash *his* *2228*
Ac 2:40 **S** yourselves from this untoward *4982*
20:23 **S** that the Holy Ghost witnesseth in every *4133*
21:25 **s only** that they keep themselves from *1508*
27:43 But the centurion, willing to **s** Paul, *1295*
Ro 11:14 *are* my flesh, and might **s** some of them. *4982*
1Co 1:21 of preaching to **s** them that believe. *4982*
2: 2 **s** Jesus Christ, and him crucified. *1508*
2:11 a man, **s** the spirit of man which is in him? *1508*
7:16 O wife, whether thou shalt **s** *thy* husband? *4982*
7:16 O man, whether thou shalt **s** *thy* wife? *4982*
9:22 all *men*, that I might by all means **s** some. *4982*
2Co 11:24 five times received I forty *stripes* **s** one. *3844*
Gal 1:19 saw I none, **s** James the Lord's brother. *1508*
6:14 **s** in the cross of our Lord Jesus Christ, *1508*
1Ti 1:15 that Christ Jesus came into the world to **s** *4982*
4:16 for in doing this thou shalt both **s** thyself, *4982*
Heb 5: 7 tears unto him that was able to **s** him from *4982*
7:25 Wherefore he is able also to **s** them to *4982*
Jas 1:21 which is able to **s** your souls. *4982*
2:14 and have not works? can faith **s** him? *4982*
4:12 who is able to **s** and to destroy: *4982*
5:15 And the prayer of faith shall **s** the sick, and *4982*
5:20 error of his way shall **s** a soul from death, *4982*
1Pe 3:21 **s** us (not the putting away of the filth of *4982*

Jude 1:23 And others **s** with fear, pulling *them* out of *4982*
Rev 13:17 **s** he that had the mark, or the name of *1508*

SAVED (104) [SAVE]

Ge 47:25 they said, Thou hast **s** our **lives**: let us find 2421
Ex 1:17 but **s** the men children **alive**. 2421
1:18 and have **s** the men children **alive**? 2421
14:30 Thus the LORD **s** Israel that day out of 3467
Nu 10: 9 and ye shall be **s** from your enemies. 3467
22:33 now also I had slain thee, and **s** her **alive**. 2421
31:15 unto them, Have ye **s** all the women **alive**? 2421
Dt 33:29 *is* like unto thee, O people **s** by the LORD, 3467
Jos 6:25 Joshua **s** Rahab the harlot **alive**, and her 2421
Jdg 7: 2 saying, Mine own hand hath **s** me. 3467
8:19 if ye had **s** them **alive**, I would not slay 2421
21:14 had **s** **alive** of the women of Jabesh-gilead: 2421
1Sa 10:19 who himself **s** you out of all your 3467
14:23 So the LORD **s** Israel that day: and 3467
23: 5 So David **s** the inhabitants of Keilah. 3467
27:11 David **s** neither man nor woman **alive**, 2421
2Sa 19: 5 which *this* day have **s** thy life, and the lives 4422
19: 9 The king **s** us out of the hand of our 5337
22: 4 so shall I be **s** from mine enemies. 3467
2Ki 6:10 and warned him of, and **s** himself there, 8104
14:27 he **s** them by the hand of Jeroboam the son 3467
1Ch 11:14 the LORD **s** *them by* a great deliverance. 3467
2Ch 32:22 Thus the LORD **s** Hezekiah and 3467
Ne 9:27 who **s** them out of the hand of their 3467
Ps 18: 3 so shall I be **s** from mine enemies. 3467
33:16 There is no king **s** by the multitude of a 3467
34: 6 heard *him*, and **s** him out of all his troubles. 3467
44: 7 thou hast **s** us from our enemies, and 3467
80: 3 cause thy face to shine; and we shall be **s**. 3467
80: 7 cause thy face to shine; and we shall be **s**. 3467
80:19 cause thy face to shine; and we shall be **s**. 3467
106: 8 Nevertheless he **s** them for his name's sake, 3467
106:10 he **s** them from the hand of him that hated 3467
107:13 *and* he **s** them out of their distresses. 3467
Pr 28:18 Whoso walketh uprightly shall be **s**: but 3467
Isa 30:15 In returning and rest shall ye be **s**; 3467
43:12 and have **s**, and I have shewed, 3467
45:17 *But* Israel shall be **s** in the LORD *with* an 3467
45:22 Look unto me, and be ye **s**, all the ends of 3467
63: 9 and the angel of his presence **s** them: 3467
64: 5 in those is continuance, and we shall be **s**. 3467
Jer 4:14 from wickedness, that thou mayest be **s**. 3467
8:20 the summer is ended, and we are not **s**. 3467
17:14 I shall be healed; save me, and I shall be **s**: 3467
23: 6 In his days Judah shall be **s**, and Israel shall 3467
30: 7 Jacob's trouble; but he shall be **s** out of it. 3467
33:16 In those days shall Judah be **s**, and 3467
Mt 10:22 but he that endureth to the end shall be **s**. *4982*
19:25 saying, Who then can be **s**? *4982*
24:13 endure unto the end, the same shall be **s**. *4982*
24:22 be shortened, there should no flesh be **s**: *4982*
27:42 He **s** others; himself he cannot save. If he *4982*
Mk 10:26 among themselves, Who then can be **s**? *4982*
13:13 endure unto the end, the same shall be **s**. *4982*
13:20 shortened *those* days, no flesh should be **s**: *4982*
15:31 themselves with the scribes, He **s** others; *4982*
16:16 He that believeth and is baptized shall be **s**; *4982*
Lk 1:71 That *we* should be **s** from our enemies, and *4991*
7:50 he said to the woman, Thy faith hath **s** thee; *4982*
8:12 lest they should believe and be **s**. *4982*
13:23 one unto him, Lord, are there few that be **s**? *4982*
18:26 they that heard *it* said, Who then can be **s**? *4982*
18:42 Receive thy sight: thy faith hath **s** thee. *4982*
23:35 with them derided *him*, saying, He **s** others; *4982*
Jn 3:17 but that the world through him might be **s**. *4982*
5:34 but these *things* I say, that ye might be **s**. *4982*
10: 9 he shall be **s**, and shall go in and out, and *4982*
Ac 2:21 call on the name of the Lord shall be **s**. *4982*
2:47 to the church daily such as should be **s**. *4982*
4:12 given among men, whereby we must be **s**. *4982*
11:14 whereby thou and all thy house shall be **s**. *4982*
15: 1 after the manner of Moses, ye cannot be **s**. *4982*
15:11 of the Lord Jesus Christ *we* shall be **s**, *4982*
16:30 and said, Sirs, what must I do to be **s**? *4982*
16:31 and thou shalt be **s**, and thy house. *4982*
27:20 lay on *us*, all hope that we should be **s** was *4982*
27:31 these abide in the ship, ye cannot be **s**. *4982*
Ro 5: 9 we shall be **s** from wrath through him. *4982*
5:10 being reconciled, we shall be **s** by his life. *4982*
8:24 For we are **s** by hope: but hope that is seen *4982*
9:27 as the sand of the sea, a remnant shall be **s**: *4982*
10: 1 to God for Israel is, that *they* might be **s**. *4991*
10: 9 raised him from the dead, thou shalt be **s**. *4982*
10:13 call upon the name of the Lord shall be **s**. *4982*
11:26 And so all Israel shall be **s**: as it is written, *4982*
1Co 1:18 unto us which are **s** it is the power of God. *4982*
3:15 but he himself shall be **s**; yet so as by fire. *4982*
5: 5 that the spirit may be **s** in the day of *4982*
10:33 but the *profit* of many, that they may be **s**. *4982*
15: 2 By which also ye are **s**, if ye keep in *4982*
2Co 2:15 in them that are **s**, and in them that perish: *4982*
Eph 2: 5 *us* together with Christ, (by grace ye are **s**;) *4982*
2: 8 For by grace are ye **s** through faith; and *4982*
1Th 2:16 speak to the Gentiles that they might be **s**, *4982*
2Th 2:10 the love of the truth, that they might be **s**. *4982*
1Ti 2: 4 Who will have all men to be **s**, and to come *4982*
2:15 Notwithstanding she shall be **s** in *4982*
2Ti 1: 9 Who hath **s** us, and called *us* with a holy *4982*
Tit 3: 5 but according to his mercy he **s** us, by *4982*
1Pe 3:20 that is, eight souls were **s** by water. *1295*
4:18 And if the righteous scarcely be **s**, *4982*
2Pe 2: 5 **s** Noah the eighth *person*, a preacher of *5442*
Jude 1: 5 having **s** the people out of the land of *4982*
Rev 21:24 And the nations of them which are **s** shall *4982*

SAVEST (3) [SAVE]

2Sa 22: 3 my saviour; thou **s** me from violence. 3467
Job 26: 2 *how* **s** thou the arm *that hath* no strength? 3467
Ps 17: 7 O thou that **s** by thy right hand them which 3467

SAVETH (7) [SAVE]

1Sa 14:39 For, *as* the LORD liveth, which **s** Israel, 3467
17:47 know that the LORD **s** not with sword 3467
Job 5:15 he **s** the poor from the sword, from their 3467
Ps 7:10 *is* of God, which **s** the upright in heart. 3467
20: 6 Now know I that the LORD **s** his 3467
34:18 and **s** such as be of a contrite spirit. 3467
107:19 he **s** them out of their distresses. 3467

SAVING (12) [SAVE]

Ge 19:19 which thou hast shewed unto me in **s** my 2421
Ne 4:23 *s that* every one put them off *for* washing. NIH
Ps 20: 6 heaven with the **s** strength of his right hand. 3468
28: 8 and he *is* the **s** strength of his anointed. 3444
67: 2 upon earth, thy **s** **health** among all nations. 3444
Ecc 5:11 **s** the beholding *of them* with their 518+3588
Am 9: 8 **s** that I will not utterly destroy the house of 657
Mt 5:32 **s for** the cause of fornication, causeth her *3924*
Lk 4:27 them was cleansed, **s** Naaman the Syrian. *1508*
Heb 10:39 but of *them* that believe to the **s** of the soul. *4047*
11: 7 prepared an ark to the **s** of his house; *4991*
Rev 2:17 which no *man* knoweth **s** he that receiveth *1508*

SAVIOUR (37) [SAVE]

2Sa 22: 3 my high tower, and my refuge, my **s**; 3467
2Ki 13: 5 (And the LORD gave Israel a **s**, so 3467
Ps 106:21 They forgat God their **s**, which had done 3467
Isa 19:20 he shall send them a **s**, and a great one, and 3467
43: 3 thy God, the Holy One of Israel, thy **S**: 3467
43:11 the LORD; and beside me *there is* no **s**. 3467
45:15 that hidest thyself, O God of Israel, the **s**. 3467
45:21 a just God and a **s**; *there is* none beside me. 3467
49:26 shall know that I the LORD *am* thy **S** 3467
60:16 thou shalt know that I the LORD *am* thy **S** 3467
63: 8 children *that* will not lie: so he was their **S**. 3467
Jer 14: 8 of Israel, the **s** thereof in time of trouble, 3467
Hos 13: 4 no god but me: for *there is* no **s** beside me. 3467
Lk 1:47 And my spirit hath rejoiced in God my **S**. *4990*
2:11 is born this day in the city of David a **S**, *4990*
Jn 4:42 this is indeed the Christ, the **S** of the world. *4990*
Ac 5:31 with his right hand *to be* a Prince and a **S**, *4990*
13:23 to *his* promise raised unto Israel a **S**, *4990*
Eph 5:23 of the church: and he is the **s** of the body. *4990*
Php 3:20 from whence also we look for the **S**, *4990*
1Ti 1: 1 Christ by the commandment of God our **S**, *4990*
2: 3 and acceptable in the sight of God our **S**; *4990*
4:10 in the living God, who is the **S** of all men, *4990*
2Ti 1:10 by the appearing of our **S** Jesus Christ, *4990*
Tit 1: 3 to the commandment of God our **S**; *4990*
1: 4 the Father and the Lord Jesus Christ our **S**. *4990*
2:10 the doctrine of God our **S** in all *things*. *4990*
2:13 of the great God and our **S** Jesus Christ; *4990*
3: 4 love of God our **S** toward man appeared, *4990*
3: 6 us abundantly through Jesus Christ our **S**; *4990*
2Pe 1: 1 of God and our **S** Jesus Christ: *4990*
1:11 kingdom of our Lord and **S** Jesus Christ. *4990*
2:20 knowledge of the Lord and **S** Jesus Christ, *4990*
3: 2 of us the apostles of the Lord and **S**: *4990*
3:18 knowledge of our Lord and **S** Jesus Christ. *4990*
1Jn 4:14 Father sent the Son *to be* the **S** of the world. *4990*
Jude 1:25 To the only wise God our **S**, *be* glory and *4990*

SAVIOURS (2) [SAVE]

Ne 9:27 to thy manifold mercies thou gavest them **s**, 3467
Ob 1:21 **s** shall come up on mount Zion to judge 3467

SAVOUR (54) [SAVOUREST, SAVOURS, SAVOURY, UNSAVOURY]

Ge 8:21 the LORD smelled a sweet **s**; and 7381
Ex 5:21 you have made our **s** to be abhorred in 7381
29:18 it *is* a sweet **s**, an offering made by fire unto 7381
29:25 for a sweet **s** before the LORD: 7381
29:41 to the drink offering thereof, for a sweet **s**, 7381
Lev 1: 9 made by fire, of a sweet **s** unto the LORD. 7381
1:13 made by fire, of a sweet **s** unto the LORD. 7381
1:17 made by fire, of a sweet **s** unto the LORD. 7381
2: 2 made by fire, of a sweet **s** unto the LORD: 7381
2: 9 made by fire, of a sweet **s** unto the LORD. 7381
2:12 shall not be burnt on the altar for a sweet **s**. 7381
3: 5 made by fire, of a sweet **s** unto the LORD. 7381
3:16 of the offering made by fire for a sweet **s**: 7381
4:31 the altar for a sweet **s** unto the LORD; 7381
6:15 shall burn *it upon* the altar *for* a sweet **s**, 7381
6:21 thou offer *for* a sweet **s** unto the LORD. 7381
8:21 it *was* a burnt sacrifice for a sweet **s**, *and* 7381
8:28 they *were* consecrations for a sweet **s**: it *is* 7381
17: 6 burn the fat for a sweet **s** unto the LORD. 7381
23:13 made by fire unto the LORD *for* a sweet **s**: 7381
23:18 made by fire, *of* a sweet **s** unto the LORD. 7381
26:31 I will not smell the **s** of your sweet odours. 7381
Nu 15: 3 to make a sweet **s** unto the LORD, of 7381
15: 7 hin *of* wine, *for* a sweet **s** unto the LORD. 7381
15:10 made by fire, of a sweet **s** unto the LORD. 7381
15:13 made by fire, of a sweet **s** unto the LORD. 7381
15:14 made by fire, of a sweet **s** unto the LORD; 7381
15:24 for a sweet **s** unto the LORD, with his 7381
18:17 by fire, for a sweet **s** unto the LORD. 7381
28: 2 made by fire, *for* a sweet **s** unto me, 7381
28: 6 was ordained in mount Sinai for a sweet **s**, 7381
28: 8 made by fire, *of* a sweet **s** unto the LORD. 7381
28:13 *for* a burnt offering *of* a sweet **s**, a sacrifice 7381
28:24 made by fire, *of* a sweet **s** unto the LORD: 7381
28:27 offering for a sweet **s** unto the LORD; 7381
29: 2 ye shall offer a burnt offering for a sweet **s** 7381
29: 6 according unto their manner, for a sweet **s**, 7381
29: 8 offering unto the LORD *for* a sweet **s**; 7381
29:13 made by fire, *of* a sweet **s** unto the LORD; 7381
29:36 made by fire, *of* a sweet **s** unto the LORD: 7381
Ecc 10: 1 of the apothecary to send forth a **stinking** **s**: 887
SS 1: 3 Because of the **s** of thy good ointments thy 7381
Eze 6:13 the place where they did offer sweet **s** to all 7381
16:19 hast even set it before them for a sweet **s**: 7381
20:28 there also they made their sweet **s**, and 7381
20:41 I will accept you with *your* sweet **s**, when I 7381

Joel 2:20 his **ill s** shall come up, because he hath 6709
Mt 5:13 but if the salt have **lost** his **s**, 3471
Lk 14:34 but if the salt have **lost** his **s**, 3471
2Co 2:14 maketh manifest the **s** of his knowledge by 3744
2:15 For we are unto God a **sweet s** of Christ, 2175
2:16 To the one *we are* the **s** of death unto death; 3744
2:16 and to the other the **s** of life unto life. 3744
Eph 5:2 a sacrifice to God for a sweetsmelling **s**. 3744

SAVOUREST (2) [SAVOUR]

Mt 16:23 for thou **s** not the *things* that be of God, but 5426
Mk 8:33 for thou **s** not the *things* that be of God, but 5426

SAVOURS (1) [SAVOUR]

Ezr 6:10 That they may offer sacrifices of **sweet s** 5208

SAVOURY (6) [SAVOUR]

Ge 27:4 make me **s meat**, such as I love, and 4303
27:7 make me **s meat**, that I may eat, and 4303
27:9 I will make them **s meat** for thy father, 4303
27:14 his mother made **s meat**, such as his father 4303
27:17 she gave the **s meat** and the bread, 4303
27:31 he also had made **s meat**, and brought *it* 4303

SAW (548) [SEE, SAWED, SAWN, SAWS]

Ge 1:4 God **s** the light, that *it was* good: and 7200
1:10 called he Seas: and God **s** that *it was* good. 7200
1:12 after his kind: and God **s** that *it was* good. 7200
1:18 the darkness: and God **s** that *it was* good. 7200
1:21 after his kind: and God **s** that *it was* good. 7200
1:25 after his kind: and God **s** that *it was* good. 7200
1:31 God **s** every thing that he had made, and 7200
3:6 when the woman **s** that the tree *was* good 7200
6:2 That the sons of God **s** the daughters of 7200
6:5 GOD **s** that the wickedness of man *was* 7200
9:22 **s** the nakedness of his father, and told his 7200
9:23 and they **s** not their father's nakedness. 7200
12:15 The princes also of Pharaoh **s** her, and 7200
16:4 when she **s** that she had conceived, her 7200
16:5 when she **s** that she had conceived, I was 7200
18:2 when he **s** *them,* he ran to meet them from 7200
21:9 Sarah **s** the son of Hagar the Egyptian, 7200
21:19 opened her eyes, and she **s** a well of water; 7200
22:4 lift up his eyes, and **s** the place afar off. 7200
24:30 when he **s** the earring and bracelets upon 7200
24:63 he lift up his eyes, and **s**, and behold, 7200
24:64 when she **s** Isaac, she lighted off the camel. 7200
26:8 **s**, and behold, Isaac *was* sporting with 7200
26:28 We **s certainly** that the LORD was 7200+7200
28:6 When Esau **s** that Isaac had blessed Jacob, 7200
29:10 when Jacob **s** Rachel the daughter of Laban 7200
29:31 when the LORD **s** that Leah *was* hated, 7200
30:1 when Rachel **s** that she bare Jacob no 7200
30:9 When Leah **s** that she had left bearing, she 7200
31:10 up mine eyes, and **s** in a dream, and behold, 7200
32:2 when Jacob **s** them, he said, This *is* God's 7200
32:25 when he **s** that he prevailed not against him, 7200
33:5 his eyes, and **s** the women and the children; 7200
34:2 **s** her, he took her, and lay with her, and 7200
37:4 when his brethren **s** that their father loved 7200
37:18 when they **s** him afar off, even before he 7200
38:2 Judah **s** there a daughter of a certain 7200
38:14 for she **s** that Shelah was grown, and 7200
38:15 When Judah **s** her, he thought her to be a 7200
39:3 his master **s** that the LORD *was* with him, 7200
39:13 when she **s** that he had left his garment in 7200
40:16 When the chief baker **s** that 7200
41:19 such as I never **s** in all the land of Egypt for 7200
41:22 I **s** in my dream, and behold, seven ears 7200
42:1 Now when Jacob **s** that there was corn in 7200
42:7 Joseph **s** his brethren, and he knew them, 7200
42:21 in that we **s** the anguish of his soul, 7200
42:35 and their father **s** the bundles of money, 7200
43:16 when Joseph **s** Benjamin with them, he said 7200
43:29 **s** his brother Benjamin, his mother's son, 7200
44:28 he is torn in pieces; and I **s** him not since: 7200
45:27 when he **s** the wagons which Joseph had 7200
48:17 when Joseph **s** that his father laid his right 7200
49:15 he **s** that rest *was* good, and the land that *it* 7200
50:11 **s** the mourning in the floor of Atad, they 7200
50:15 when Joseph's brethren **s** that their father 7200
50:23 Joseph **s** Ephraim's children of the third 7200
Ex 2:2 when she **s** him that he *was a* goodly *child,* 7200
2:5 when she **s** the ark among the flags, she 7200
2:6 when she had opened *it,* she **s** the child: 7200
2:12 and when he **s** that *there was* no man, 7200
3:4 when the LORD **s** that he turned aside to 7200
8:15 when Pharaoh **s** that there was respite, he 7200
9:34 when Pharaoh **s** that the rain and the hail 7200
10:23 They **s** not one another, neither rose any 7200
14:30 Israel **s** the Egyptians dead upon the sea 7200
14:31 Israel **s** *that* great work which the LORD 7200
16:15 when the children of Israel **s** *it,* they said 7200
18:14 when Moses' father in law **s** all that he did 7200
20:18 all the people **s** the thunderings, and 7200
20:18 when the people **s** *it,* they removed, and 7200
24:10 they **s** the God of Israel: and *there was* 7200
24:11 also they **s** God, and did eat and drink. 2372
32:1 when the people **s** that Moses delayed to 7200
32:5 when Aaron **s** *it,* he built an altar before it; 7200
32:19 that he **s** the calf, and the dancing: 7200
32:25 when Moses **s** that the people *were* naked; 7200
33:10 all the people **s** the cloudy pillar stand *at* 7200
34:30 and all the children of Israel **s** Moses, 7200
34:35 the children of Israel **s** the face of Moses, 7200
Lev 9:24 *which* when all the people **s**, they shouted, 7200
Nu 13:28 moreover we **s** the children of Anak there. 7200
13:32 all the people that we **s** in it *are* men of a 7200
13:33 there we **s** the giants, the sons of Anak, 7200
20:29 when all the congregation **s** that Aaron was 7200
22:2 Balak the son of Zippor **s** all that Israel had 7200
22:23 the ass **s** the angel of the LORD standing 7200
22:25 when the ass **s** the angel of the LORD, 7200
22:27 when the ass **s** the angel of the LORD, 7200
Nu 22:31 he **s** the angel of the LORD standing in 7200
22:33 the ass **s** me, and turned from me these 7200
24:1 when Balaam **s** that it pleased the LORD 7200
24:2 he **s** Israel abiding *in his tents* according to 7200
24:4 which **s** the vision of the Almighty, 2372
24:16 *which* **s** the vision of the Almighty, 2372
25:7 **s** *it,* he rose up from amongst 7200
32:1 when they **s** the land of Jazer, and the land 7200
32:9 up unto the valley of Eshcol, and **s** the land, 7200
Dt 1:19 which you **s** *by* the way of the mountain of 7200
4:12 the voice of the words, but **s** no similitude; 7200
4:15 for ye **s** no *manner of* similitude on the day 7200
7:19 The great temptations which thine eyes **s**, 7200
32:19 when the LORD **s** *it,* he abhorred *them,* 7200
Jos 7:21 When I **s** among the spoils a goodly 7200
8:14 when the king of Ai **s** *it,* that they hasted 7200
8:20 they **s**, and behold, the smoke of the city 7200
8:21 all Israel **s** that the ambush had taken 7200
Jdg 1:24 the spies **s** a man come forth out of the city, 7200
3:24 when they **s** that behold, the doors of 7200
9:36 when Gaal **s** the people, he said to Zebul, 7200
9:55 when the men of Israel **s** that Abimelech 7200
11:35 it came to pass, when he **s** her, that he rent 7200
12:3 when I **s** that ye delivered *me* not, I put my 7200
14:1 **s** a woman in Timnath of the daughters of 7200
14:11 it came to pass, when they **s** him, that they 7200
16:1 and **s** there a harlot, and went in unto her. 7200
16:18 when Delilah **s** that he had told her all his 7200
16:24 when the people **s** him, they praised their 7200
18:7 to Laish, and **s** the people that *were* therein, 7200
18:26 when Micah **s** that they *were* too strong for 7200
19:3 when the father of the damsel **s** him, 7200
19:17 he **s** a wayfaring man in the street of 7200
19:30 it was so, that all that **s** it said, There was 7200
20:36 So the children of Benjamin **s** that they 7200
20:41 for they **s** that evil was come upon them. 7200
Ru 1:18 When she **s** that she *was* stedfastly minded 7200
2:18 her mother in law **s** what she had gleaned: 7200
1Sa 5:7 when the men of Ashdod **s** that *it was* so, 7200
6:13 and **s** the ark, and rejoiced to see *it.* 7200
9:17 when Samuel **s** Saul, the LORD said unto 7200
10:11 when all that knew him beforetime **s** that 7200
10:14 when we **s** that *they were* no where, we 7200
12:12 when ye **s** that Nahash the king of 7200
13:6 When the men of Israel **s** that they were in 7200
13:11 Because I **s** that the people were scattered 7200
14:52 when Saul **s** any strong man, or any valiant 7200
17:24 when they **s** the man, fled from him, and 7200
17:42 and **s** David, he disdained him: 7200
17:51 when the Philistines **s** their champion was 7200
17:55 when Saul **s** David go forth against 7200
18:15 Wherefore when Saul **s** that he behaved 7200
18:28 Saul **s** and knew that the LORD *was* with 7200
19:20 when they **s** the company of the prophets 7200
22:9 said, I **s** the son of Jesse coming to Nob, 7200
23:15 David **s** that Saul was come out to seek his 7200
25:23 when Abigail **s** David, she hasted, and 7200
25:25 I thine handmaid **s** not the young men of 7200
26:3 he **s** that Saul came after him into 7200
26:12 no man **s** *it,* nor knew *it,* neither awaked: 7200
28:5 when Saul **s** the host of the Philistines, he 7200
28:12 when the woman **s** Samuel, she cried with a 7200
28:13 I **s** gods ascending out of the earth. 7200
28:21 **s** that he was sore troubled, and said unto 7200
31:5 when his armourbearer **s** that Saul was 7200
31:7 **s** that the men of Israel fled, and that Saul 7200
2Sa 1:7 behind him, he **s** me, and called unto me. 7200
6:16 **s** king David leaping and dancing before 7200
10:6 when the children of Ammon **s** that they 7200
10:9 When Joab **s** that the front of the battle was 7200
10:14 when the children of Ammon **s** that 7200
10:15 when the Syrians **s** that they were smitten 7200
10:19 **s** that they were smitten before Israel, 7200
11:2 from the roof he **s** a woman washing 7200
12:19 when David **s** that his servants whispered, 7200
14:24 to his own house, and **s** not the king's face. 7200
14:28 in Jerusalem, and **s** not the king's face. 7200
17:18 Nevertheless a lad **s** them, and 7200
17:23 when Ahithophel **s** that his counsel was not 7200
18:10 a certain man **s** *it,* and told Joab, and said, 7200
18:10 Behold, I **s** Absalom hanged in an oak. 7200
18:26 the watchman **s** another man running: and 7200
18:29 I **s** a great tumult, but I knew not what *it* 7200
20:12 when the man **s** that all the people stood 7200
20:12 when he **s** that every one that came by him 7200
24:17 David spake unto the LORD when he **s** 7200
24:20 **s** the king and his servants coming on 7200
1Ki 3:28 for they **s** that the wisdom of God *was* in 7200
12:16 So when all Israel **s** that the king hearkened 7200
13:25 **s** the carcase cast in the way, and the lion 7200
16:18 when Zimri **s** that the city was taken, 7200
18:17 it came to pass, when Ahab **s** Elijah, 7200
18:39 when all the people **s** *it,* they fell on their 7200
19:3 when he **s** *that,* he arose, and went for his 7200
22:17 I **s** all Israel scattered upon the hills, 7200
22:19 I **s** the LORD sitting on his throne, and 7200
22:32 when the captains of the chariots **s** 7200
2Ki 2:12 Elisha **s** *it,* and he cried, My father, 7200
2:12 he **s** him no more: and he took hold of his 7200
2:15 which *were* to view at Jericho **s** him, 7200
3:22 the Moabites **s** the water on the other side 7200
3:26 when the king of Moab **s** that the battle was 7200
4:25 to pass, when the man of God **s** her afar off, 7200
5:21 when Naaman **s** *him* running after him, 7200
6:17 the eyes of the young man; and he **s**: 7200
6:20 the LORD opened their eyes, and they **s**; 7200
6:21 unto Elisha, when he **s** them, My father, 7200
9:22 when Joram **s** Jehu, that he said, *Is it* peace, 7200
9:27 when Ahaziah the king of Judah **s** *this,* he 7200
11:1 when Athaliah the mother of Ahaziah **s** that 7200
12:10 when they **s** that *there was* much money in 7200
13:4 for he **s** the oppression of Israel, because 7200
14:26 For the LORD **s** the affliction of Israel, 7200
16:10 and **s** an altar that *was* at Damascus: 7200
16:12 come from Damascus, the king **s** the altar: 7200
1Ch 10:5 when his armourbearer **s** that Saul was 7200
10:7 that *were* in the valley **s** that they fled, 7200
15:29 out at a window **s** king David dancing 7200
19:6 when the children of Ammon **s** that they 7200
19:10 Now when Joab **s** that the battle was set 7200
19:15 when the children of Ammon **s** that 7200
19:16 when the Syrians **s** that they were put to 7200
19:19 when the servants of Hadarezer **s** that they 7200
21:16 **s** the angel of the LORD stand between 7200
21:20 Ornan turned back, and **s** the angel; and 7200
21:21 Ornan looked and **s** David, and went out of 7200
21:28 At that time when David **s** that the LORD 7200
2Ch 7:3 when all the children of Israel **s** how 7200
10:16 when all Israel **s** that the king would not 7200
12:7 when the LORD **s** that they humbled 7200
15:9 when they **s** that the LORD his God *was* 7200
18:18 I **s** the LORD sitting upon his throne, and 7200
18:31 when the captains of the chariots **s** 7200
22:10 when Athaliah the mother of Ahaziah **s** that 7200
24:11 when they **s** that *there was* much money, 7200
25:21 they **s** one another *in* the face, *both* he and 7200
31:8 and the princes came and **s** the heaps, 7200
32:2 when Hezekiah **s** that Sennacherib was 7200
Ne 6:16 all the heathen that *were* about us **s** *these* 7200
13:15 In those days **s** I in Judah *some* treading 7200
13:23 In those days also **s** I Jews *that* had married 7200
Est 1:14 which **s** the king's face, *and* which sat 7200
3:5 when Haman **s** that Mordecai bowed not, 7200
5:2 when the king **s** Esther the queen standing 7200
5:9 when Haman **s** Mordecai in the king's gate, 7200
7:7 for he **s** that there was evil determined 7200
Job 2:13 for they **s** that *his* grief was very great. 7200
3:16 had not been; as infants *which* never **s** light. 7200
20:9 The eye also *which* **s** him shall *see him* no 7805
29:8 The young men **s** me, and hid themselves: 7200
29:11 when the eye **s** *me,* it gave witness to me: 7200
31:21 the fatherless, when I **s** my help in the gate: 7200
32:5 When Elihu **s** that *there was* no answer in 7200
42:16 and **s** his sons, and his sons' sons, 7200
Ps 48:5 They **s** *it, and* so they marvelled; they were 7200
73:3 *when* I **s** the prosperity of the wicked. 7200
77:16 The waters **s** thee, O God, the waters saw 7200
77:16 waters saw thee, O God, the waters **s** thee; 7200
95:9 tempted me, proved me, and **s** my work. 7200
97:4 the world: the earth **s**, and trembled. 7200
114:3 The sea **s** *it,* and fled: Jordan was driven 7200
Pr 24:32 I **s**, *and* considered *it* well: I looked upon *it,* 2372
Ecc 2:13 I **s** that wisdom excelleth folly, as far as 7200
2:24 This also I **s**, that it *was* from the hand of 7200
3:16 moreover I **s** under the sun the place of 7200
4:7 I returned, and I **s** vanity under the sun. 7200
8:10 so I **s** the wicked buried, who had come 7200
9:11 I returned, and **s** under the sun, that the race 7200
SS 3:3 *to whom I said,* **S** ye *him* whom my soul 7200
6:9 The daughters **s** her, and blessed her; 7200
Isa 1:1 which he **s** concerning Judah and 2372
2:1 The word that Isaiah the son of Amoz **s** 2372
6:1 In the year that king Uzziah died I **s** also 7200
10:15 shall the **s** magnify itself against him that 4883
21:7 he **s** a chariot *with* a couple of horsemen, 7200
41:5 The isles **s** *it,* and feared; the ends of 7200
59:15 the LORD **s** *it,* and it displeased him that 7200
59:16 he **s** that *there was* no man, and 7200
Jer 3:7 And her treacherous sister Judah **s** *it.* 7200
3:8 I **s**, when for all the causes whereby 7200
39:4 *that* when Zedekiah the king of Judah **s** 7200
41:13 with Ishmael **s** Johanan the son of Kareah, 7200
44:17 of victuals, and were well, and **s** no evil. 7200
La 1:7 the adversaries **s** her, *and* did mock at her 7200
Eze 1:1 were opened, and I **s** visions of God. 7200
1:27 I **s** as the colour of amber, as 7200
1:27 I **s** as it were the appearance of fire, and 7200
1:28 when I **s** *it,* I fell upon my face, and I heard 7200
3:23 as the glory which I **s** by the river of 7200
8:4 according to the vision that I **s** in the plain. 7200
8:10 So I went in and **s**; and behold every form 7200
10:15 This *is* the living creature that I **s** by 7200
10:20 This *is* the living creature that I **s** under 7200
10:22 faces which I **s** by the river of Chebar, 7200
11:1 among whom I **s** Jaazaniah the son of Azur, 7200
16:6 and **s** thee polluted in thine own blood, 7200
16:50 therefore I took them away as I **s** *good.* 7200
19:5 Now when she **s** that she had waited, *and* 7200
20:28 they **s** every high hill, and all the thick 7200
23:11 when her sister Aholibah **s** *this,* she was 7200
23:13 I **s** that she was defiled, *that* they took both 7200
23:14 for when she **s** men pourtrayed upon 7200
23:16 as soon as she **s** them with her eyes, 4758
41:8 I **s** also the height of the house round about: 7200
43:3 to the appearance of the vision which I **s**, 7200
43:3 *even* according to the vision that I **s** when I 7200
43:3 the visions *were* like the vision that I **s** by 7200
Da 3:27 being gathered together, **s** these men, 2370
4:5 I **s** a dream which made me afraid, and 2370
4:10 I **s**, and behold, a tree in the midst of 2370
4:13 I **s** in the visions of my head upon my bed, 2370
4:23 whereas the king **s** a watcher and a holy 2370
5:5 the king **s** the part of the hand that wrote. 2370
7:2 said, I **s** in my vision by night, and behold, 2370
7:7 After this I **s** in the night visions, and 2370
7:13 I **s** in the night visions, and behold, *one* like 2370
8:2 I **s** in a vision; and it came to pass, when I 7200
8:2 it came to pass, when I **s**, that I *was* at 7200
8:2 I **s** in a vision, and I was by the river of 7200
8:3 I lifted up mine eyes, and **s**, and behold, 7200
8:4 I **s** the ram pushing westward, 7200
8:7 I **s** him come close unto the ram, and 7200
10:7 I Daniel alone **s** the vision: for the men that 7200
10:7 for the men that were with me **s** not 7200
10:8 **s** this great vision, and there remained no 7200
Hos 5:13 When Ephraim **s** his sickness, and 7200
5:13 Judah **s** his wound, then went Ephraim to NIH
9:10 I **s** your fathers as the firstripe in the fig 7200
9:13 Ephraim, as I **s** Tyrus, *is* planted in a 7200
Am 1:1 which he **s** concerning Israel in the days of 2372

Am 9: 1 I **s** the Lord standing upon the altar: and 7200
Jnh 3:10 God **s** their works, that they turned from 7200
Mic 1: 1 which he **s** concerning Samaria and 2372
Hab 3: 7 I **s** the tents of Cushan in affliction: *and* 7200
3:10 The mountains **s** thee, *and* they trembled: 7200
Hag 2: 3 Who *is* left among you that **s** this house in 7200
Zec 1: 8 I **s** by night, and behold a man riding upon 7200
1:18 up mine eyes, and **s**, and behold four horns. 7200
Mt 2: 9 and lo, the star, which they **s** in the east, *1492*
2:10 When they **s** the star, they rejoiced *with* *1492*
2:11 they **s** the young child with Mary his *1492*
2:16 when he **s** that he was mocked of the wise *1492*
3: 7 But when he **s** many of the Pharisees and *1492*
3:16 he **s** the Spirit of God descending like a *1492*
4:16 The people which sat in darkness **s** great *1492*
4:18 **s** two brethren, Simon called Peter, and *1492*
4:21 he **s** other two brethren, James the *son* of *1492*
8:14 he **s** his wife's mother laid, and sick of a *1492*
8:18 Now when Jesus **s** great multitudes about *1492*
8:34 and when they **s** him, they besought *him* *1492*
9: 8 But when the multitudes **s** *it,* they *1492*
9: 9 he **s** a man, named Matthew, sitting at *1492*
9:11 And when the Pharisees **s** *it,* they said unto *1492*
9:22 and when he **s** her, he said, Daughter, be of *1492*
9:23 and **s** the minstrels and the people making a *1492*
9:36 But when he **s** the multitudes, he was *1492*
12: 2 But when the Pharisees **s** *it,* they said unto *1492*
12:22 that the blind and dumb both spake and **s**. *991*
14:14 and **s** a great multitude, and was moved *1492*
14:26 And when the disciples **s** him walking on *1492*
14:30 But when he **s** the wind boisterous, he was *991*
15:31 when they **s** the dumb to speak, the maimed *991*
17: 8 their eyes, they **s** no *man,* save Jesus only. *1492*
18:31 So when his fellowservants **s** what was *1492*
20: 3 **s** others standing idle in the marketplace, *1492*
21:15 scribes **s** the wonderful *things* that he did, *1492*
21:19 And when he **s** a fig tree in the way, *1492*
21:20 And when the disciples **s** *it,* they marvelled, *1492*
21:38 But when the husbandmen **s** the son, *1492*
22:11 he **s** there a man which had not on a *1492*
25:37 when **s** we thee a hungred, and fed *thee?* or *1492*
25:38 When **s** we thee a stranger, and took *thee* *1492*
25:39 Or when **s** we thee sick, *1492*
25:44 when **s** we thee a hungred, or athirst, or *1492*
26: 8 But when his disciples **s** *it,* they had *1492*
26:71 another *maid* **s** him, and said unto them that *1492*
27: 3 when he **s** that he was condemned, *1492*
27:24 When Pilate **s** that he could prevail nothing, *1492*
27:54 **s** the earthquake, and *those things* that were *1492*
28:17 And when they **s** him, they worshipped *1492*
Mk 1:10 he **s** the heavens opened, and the Spirit like *1492*
1:16 he **s** Simon and Andrew his brother casting *1492*
1:19 he **s** James the *son* of Zebedee, and *1492*
2: 5 When Jesus **s** their faith, he said unto *1492*
2:12 saying, We never **s** *it* on this fashion. *1492*
2:14 he **s** Levi the *son* of Alpheus sitting at *1492*
2:16 and Pharisees **s** him eat with publicans and *1492*
3:11 And unclean spirits, when they **s** him, *2334*
5: 6 But when he **s** Jesus afar off, he ran and *1492*
5:16 And they that **s** *it* told them how it befell to *1492*
5:22 and when he **s** him, he fell at his feet, *1492*
6:33 And the people **s** them departing, and *1492*
6:34 **s** much people, and was moved with *1492*
6:48 And he **s** them toiling in rowing; for *1492*
6:49 But when they **s** him walking upon the sea, *1492*
6:50 For they all **s** him, and were troubled. *1492*
7: 2 And when they **s** some of his disciples eat *1492*
8:23 hands upon him, he asked him if he **s** ought. *991*
8:25 he was restored, and **s** every *man* clearly. *1689*
9: 8 they **s** no *man* any more, save Jesus only *1492*
9:14 he **s** a great multitude about them, and *1492*
9:20 and when he **s** him, straightway the spirit *1492*
9:25 When Jesus **s** that the people came running *1492*
9:38 we **s** one casting out devils in thy name, *1492*
10:14 But when Jesus **s** *it,* he was much *1492*
11:20 they **s** the fig tree dried up from the roots. *1492*
12:34 And when Jesus **s** that he answered *1492*
14:67 And when she **s** Peter warming himself, *1492*
14:69 And a maid **s** him again, and began to say *1492*
15:39 **s** that he so cried out, and gave up *1492*
16: 4 they **s** that the stone was rolled away: *2334*
16: 5 they **s** a young man sitting on the right side, *1492*
Lk 1:12 And when Zacharias **s** *him,* he was *1492*
1:29 And when she **s** *him,* she was troubled at *1492*
2:48 And when they **s** him, they were amazed: *1492*
5: 2 And **s** two ships standing by the lake: but *1492*
5: 8 When Simon Peter **s** *it,* he fell down at *1492*
5:20 And when he **s** their faith, he said unto him, *1492*
5:27 and **s** a publican, named Levi, sitting at *2300*
7:13 And when the Lord **s** her, he had *1492*
7:39 bidden him **s** *it,* he spake within himself, *1492*
8:28 When he **s** Jesus, he cried out, and *1492*
8:34 When they that fed *them* **s** what was done, *1492*
8:36 They also which **s** *it* told them by what *1492*
8:47 And when the woman **s** that she was not *1492*
9:32 they **s** his glory, and the two men that stood *1492*
9:49 we **s** one casting out devils in thy name; *1492*
9:54 disciples James and John **s** *this,* they said, *1492*
10:31 and when he **s** him, he passed by on *1492*
10:33 and when he **s** him, he had compassion *on* *1492*
11:38 And when the Pharisee **s** *it,* he marvelled *1492*
13:12 And when Jesus **s** her, he called *her* to *him,* *1492*
15:20 his father **s** him, and had compassion, and *1492*
17:14 And when he **s** *them,* he said unto them, *1492*
17:15 when he **s** that he was healed, turned back, *1492*
18:15 when *his* disciples **s** *it,* they rebuked them. *1492*
18:24 And when Jesus **s** that he was very *1492*
18:43 when they **s** *it,* gave praise unto God. *1492*
19: 5 and **s** him, and said unto him, Zaccheus, *1492*
19: 7 And when they **s** *it,* they all murmured, *1492*
20:14 But when the husbandmen **s** him, *1492*
21: 1 **s** the rich *men* casting their gifts into *1492*
21: 2 And he **s** also a certain poor widow casting *1492*
22:49 When they which were about him **s** what *1492*
22:58 And after a little while another **s** him, and *1492*
Lk 23: 8 And when Herod **s** Jesus, he was exceeding *1492*
23:47 Now when the centurion **s** what was done, *1492*
24:24 as the women had said: but him they **s** not. *1492*
Jn 1:32 I **s** the Spirit descending from heaven like a *2300*
1:34 And I **s**, and bare record that this is the Son *3708*
1:38 and **s** them following, and saith unto them, *2300*
1:39 They came and **s** where he dwelt, and *1492*
1:47 Jesus **s** Nathanael coming to him, and *1492*
1:48 when thou wast under the fig tree, I **s** thee. *1492*
1:50 I **s** thee under the fig tree, believest thou? *1492*
2:23 when they **s** the miracles which he did. *2334*
5: 6 When Jesus **s** him lie, and knew that he had *1492*
6: 2 they **s** his miracles which he did on them *3708*
6: 5 and **s** a great company come unto him, *2300*
6:22 sea **s** that there was none other boat there, *1492*
6:24 therefore **s** that Jesus was not there, *1492*
6:26 not because ye **s** *the* miracles, but because *1492*
8:10 lift up *himself,* and **s** none but the woman, *2300*
8:56 to see my day: and he **s** *it,* and was glad. *1492*
9: 1 he **s** a man *which was* blind from *his* birth. *1492*
11:31 and comforted her, when they **s** Mary, *1492*
11:32 and **s** him, she fell down at his feet, *1492*
11:33 When Jesus therefore **s** her weeping, and *1492*
12:41 when he **s** his glory, and spake of him. *1492*
19: 6 chief priests therefore and officers **s** him, *1492*
19:26 When Jesus therefore **s** *his* mother, and *1492*
19:33 and **s** that he was dead already, they brake *1492*
19:35 And he that **s** *it* bare record, and his record *3708*
20: 5 and looking in, **s** the linen clothes lying; *991*
20: 8 to the sepulchre, and he **s**, and believed. *1492*
20:14 and **s** Jesus standing, and knew not that it *2334*
20:20 the disciples glad, when they **s** the Lord. *1492*
21: 9 they **s** a fire of coals there, and fish laid *991*
Ac 3: 9 And all the people **s** him walking and *1492*
3:12 And when Peter **s** *it,* he answered unto *1492*
4:13 Now when they **s** the boldness of Peter and *2334*
6:15 **s** his face as it had been the face of an *1492*
7:31 When Moses **s** *it,* he wondered at the sight: *1492*
7:55 and **s** the glory of God, and Jesus standing *1492*
8:18 And when Simon **s** that through laying on *2300*
8:39 that the eunuch **s** him no more: *1492*
9: 8 he **s** no *man:* but they led him by the hand, *991*
9:35 all that dwelt at Lydda and Saron **s** him, *1492*
9:40 her eyes: and when she **s** Peter, she sat up. *1492*
10: 3 He **s** in a vision evidently, about the ninth *1492*
10:11 And **s** heaven opened, and a certain vessel *2334*
11: 5 and in a trance I **s** a vision, A certain vessel *1492*
11: 6 and **s** fourfooted beasts of the earth, and *1492*
12: 3 And because he **s** it pleased the Jews, *1492*
12: 9 done by the angel; but thought he **s** a vision. *991*
12:16 when they had opened *the door,* and **s** him, *1492*
13:12 when he **s** what was done, believed, *1492*
13:36 was laid unto his fathers, and **s** corruption: *1492*
13:37 whom God raised *again,* **s** no corruption. *1492*
13:45 But when the Jews **s** the multitudes, *1492*
14:11 And when the people **s** what Paul had done, *1492*
16:19 And when her masters **s** that the hope of *1492*
17:16 when he **s** the city wholly given to idolatry. *2334*
21:27 when they **s** him in the temple, stirred up *2300*
21:32 and when they **s** the chief captain and *1492*
22: 9 And they that were with me **s** indeed *2300*
22:18 And **s** him saying unto me, Make haste, and *1492*
26:13 O king, I **s** in the way a light from heaven, *1492*
28: 4 And when the barbarians **s** the *venomous* *1492*
28: 6 and **s** no harm come to him, they changed *2334*
28:15 whom when Paul **s**, he thanked God, and *1492*
Gal 1:19 But other of the apostles **s** I none, *3708*
2: 7 when they **s** that the gospel of *1492*
2:14 But when I **s** that they walked not uprightly *1492*
Php 1:30 Having the same conflict which ye **s** in me, *1492*
Heb 3: 9 proved me, and **s** my works forty years. *1492*
11:23 because they **s** *he was* a proper child; *1492*
Rev 1: 2 of Jesus Christ, and of all *things* that he **s**. *1492*
1:12 being turned, I **s** seven golden candlesticks; *1492*
1:17 And when I **s** him, I fell at his feet as dead. *1492*
4: 4 and upon the seats I **s** four and *1492*
5: 1 And I **s** in the right hand of him that sat on *1492*
5: 2 And I **s** a strong angel proclaiming with a *1492*
6: 1 And I **s** when the Lamb opened one of *1492*
6: 2 And I **s**, and behold a white horse: and *1492*
6: 9 I **s** under the altar the souls of them that *1492*
7: 1 And after these *things* I **s** four angels *1492*
7: 2 And I **s** another angel ascending from *1492*
8: 2 And I **s** the seven angels which stood *1492*
9: 1 I **s** a star fall from heaven unto the earth: *1492*
9:17 And thus I **s** the horses in the vision, and *1492*
10: 1 And I **s** another mighty angel come down *1492*
10: 5 And the angel which I **s** stand upon the sea *1492*
11:11 and great fear fell upon them which **s** them. *2334*
12:13 And when the dragon **s** that he was cast *1492*
13: 1 and **s** a beast rise up out of the sea, *1492*
13: 2 And the beast which I **s** was like unto a *1492*
13: 3 And I **s** one of his heads as *it were* *1492*
14: 6 And I **s** another angel fly in the midst of *1492*
15: 1 And I **s** another sign in heaven, great and *1492*
15: 2 And I **s** as *it were* a sea of glass mingled *1492*
16:13 And I **s** three unclean spirits like frogs *1492*
17: 3 I **s** a woman sit upon a scarlet coloured *1492*
17: 6 And I **s** the woman drunken with the blood *1492*
17: 6 and when I **s** her, I wondered *with* great *1492*
18: 1 And after these *things* I **s** another angel *1492*
18:18 And cried when they **s** the smoke of her *3708*
19:11 And I **s** heaven opened, and behold a white *1492*
19:17 And I **s** an angel standing in the sun; and *1492*
19:19 And I **s** the beast, and the kings of *1492*
20: 1 And I **s** an angel come down from heaven, *1492*
20: 4 And I **s** thrones, and they sat upon them, *1492*
20: 4 *I s* the souls of them that were beheaded for NIG
20:11 And I **s** a great white throne, and him that *1492*
20:12 And I **s** the dead, small and great, stand *1492*
21: 1 And I **s** a new heaven and a new earth: *1492*
21: 2 And I John **s** the holy city, new Jerusalem, *1492*
21:22 And I **s** no temple therein: for the Lord God *1492*
22: 8 And I John **s** these *things,* and heard *them.* *991*

SAWED (1) [SAW]

1Ki 7: 9 **s** with saws, within and without, even from 1641

SAWEST (21) [SEE]

Ge 20:10 What **s** thou, that thou hast done this thing? 7200
1Sa 19: 5 thou **s** *it,* and didst rejoice: wherefore then 7200
28:13 for what **s** thou? And the woman said unto 7200
2Sa 18:11 thou **s** *him,* and why didst thou not smite 7200
Ps 50:18 When thou **s** a thief, then thou consentedst 7200
Isa 57: 8 thou lovedst their bed where thou **s** *it.* 2372
Da 2:31 Thou, O king, **s**, and behold a great image. 2370
2:34 Thou **s** till that a stone was cut out without 2370
2:41 whereas thou **s** the feet and toes, part of 2370
2:41 forasmuch as thou **s** the iron mixed with 2370
2:43 whereas thou **s** iron mixt with miry clay, 2370
2:45 Forasmuch as thou **s** that the stone was cut 2370
4:20 The tree that thou **s**, which grew, and 2370
8:20 The ram which thou **s** having two horns *are* 7200
Rev 1:20 The mystery of the seven stars which thou **s** *1492*
1:20 the seven candlesticks which thou **s** are *1492*
17: 8 The beast that thou **s** was, and is not; and *1492*
17:12 And the ten horns which thou **s** are ten *1492*
17:15 he saith unto me, The waters which thou **s**, *1492*
17:16 And the ten horns which thou **s** upon *1492*
17:18 And the woman which thou **s** is *that* great *1492*

SAWN (1) [SAW]

Heb 11:37 they were **s asunder**, were tempted, *4249*

SAWS (3) [SAW]

2Sa 12:31 put *them* under **s**, and under harrows of 4050
1Ki 7: 9 sawed with **s**, within and without, even 4050
1Ch 20: 3 cut *them* with **s**, and with harrows of iron, 4050

SAY (1057) [GAINSAY, SAID, SAIDST, SAITH, SAYEST, SAYING, SAYINGS]

Ge 12:12 see thee, that they shall **s**, This *is* his wife: 559
12:13 **S**, I pray thee, thou *art* my sister: that it may 559
14:23 lest thou shouldest **s**, I have made Abram 559
20:13 we shall come, **s** of me, He *is* my brother. 559
24:14 *that* the damsel to whom I shall **s**, Let down 559
24:14 she shall **s**, Drink, and I will give thy camels 559
24:43 cometh forth to draw *water,* and I **s** to her, 559
24:44 she **s** to me, Both drink thou, and I will also 559
26: 7 for he feared to **s**, *She is* my wife; lest, 559
32:18 thou shalt **s**, *They be* thy servant Jacob's; 559
32:20 **s** ye moreover, Behold, thy servant Jacob *is* 559
34:11 and what ye shall **s** unto me I will give. 559
34:12 I will give according as ye shall **s** unto me: 559
37:17 for I heard *them* **s**, Let us go to Dothan. 559
37:20 and cast him into some pit, and we will **s**, 559
41:15 I have heard **s** of thee, *that* thou canst 559
43: 7 could we certainly know that he would **s**, 559
44: 4 when thou dost overtake them, **s** unto them, 559
44:16 Judah said, What shall we **s** unto my lord? 559
45: 9 and go up to my father, and **s** unto him, 559
45:17 unto Joseph, **S** unto thy brethren, This do ye; 559
46:31 **s** unto him, My brethren, and my father's 559
46:33 and shall **s**, What *is* your occupation? 559
46:34 That ye shall **s**, Thy servants' trade hath 559
50:17 So shall ye **s** unto Joseph, Forgive, I pray 559
Ex 3:13 the children of Israel, and shall **s** unto them, 559
3:13 and they shall **s** to me, What *is* his name? 559
3:13 What *is* his name? what shall I **s** unto them? 559
3:14 Thus shalt thou **s** unto the children of Israel, 559
3:15 Thus shalt thou **s** unto the children of Israel, 559
3:16 **s** unto them, The LORD God of your 559
3:18 the king of Egypt, and you shall **s** unto him, 559
4: 1 for they will **s**, The LORD hath not 559
4:12 thy mouth, and teach thee what thou shalt **s**. 1696
4:22 thou shalt **s** unto Pharaoh, Thus saith 559
4:23 I **s** unto thee, Let my son go, that he may 559
5:16 thy servants, and they **s** to us, Make brick: 559
5:17 therefore ye **s**, Let us go *and* do sacrifice to 559
6: 6 Wherefore **s** unto the children of Israel, I *am* 559
6:29 Pharaoh king of Egypt all that I **s** unto thee. 1696
7: 9 thou shalt **s** unto Aaron, Take thy rod, and 559
7:16 thou shalt **s** unto him, The LORD God of 559
7:19 **S** unto Aaron, Take thy rod, and stretch out 559
8: 1 Go unto Pharaoh, and **s** unto him, Thus saith 559
8: 5 LORD spake unto Moses, **S** unto Aaron, 559
8:16 **S** unto Aaron, Stretch out thy rod, and 559
8:20 **s** unto him, Thus saith the LORD, Let my 559
9:13 and stand before Pharaoh, and **s** unto him, 559
12:26 to pass, when your children shall **s** unto you, 559
12:27 That ye shall **s**, It *is* the sacrifice of 559
13:14 that thou shalt **s** unto him, By strength of 559
14: 3 For Pharaoh will **s** of the children of Israel, 559
16: 9 **S** unto all the congregation of the children of 559
19: 3 Thus shalt thou **s** to the house of Jacob, and 559
20:22 Thus thou shalt **s** unto the children of Israel, 559
21: 5 if the servant shall **plainly s**, I love my 559+559
32:12 **s**, For mischief did he bring them out, to slay 559
33: 5 **S** unto the children of Israel, Ye *are* a 559
Lev 1: 2 unto the children of Israel, and **s** unto them, 559
15: 2 unto the children of Israel, and **s** unto them, 559
17: 2 all the children of Israel, and **s** unto them; 559
17: 8 thou shalt **s** unto them, Whatsoever man 559
18: 2 and **s** unto them, I *am* the LORD your God. 559
19: 2 of Israel, and **s** unto them, Ye shall be holy: 559
20: 2 Again, thou shalt **s** to the children of Israel, 559
21: 1 priests the sons of Aaron, and **s** unto them, 559
22: 3 **S** unto them, Whosoever *he be* of all your 559
22:18 all the children of Israel, and **s** unto them, 559
23: 2 unto the children of Israel, and **s** unto them, 559
23:10 unto the children of Israel, and **s** unto them, 559
25: 2 unto the children of Israel, and **s** unto them, 559
25:20 if ye shall **s**, What shall we eat the seventh 559
27: 2 unto the children of Israel, and **s** unto them, 559
Nu 5:12 and **s** unto them, If any man's wife go aside, 559
5:19 **s** unto the woman, If no man have lain with 559
5:21 the priest shall **s** unto the woman, 559
5:22 to rot: And the woman shall **s**, Amen, amen. 559
6: 2 **s** unto them, When either man or 559

Nu 8: 2 Speak unto Aaron, and **s** unto him, 559
11:12 that thou shouldest **s** unto me, 559
11:18 **s** thou unto the people, Sanctify yourselves 559
14:28 **S** unto them, *As truly as* I live, saith 559
15: 2 unto the children of Israel, and **s** unto them, 559
15:18 unto the children of Israel, and **s** unto them, 559
18:26 speak unto the Levites, and **s** unto them, 559
18:30 Therefore thou shalt **s** unto them, When ye 559
21:27 Wherefore they that speak in proverbs **s**, 559
22:19 that I may know what the LORD will **s** 1696
22:20 yet the word which I shall **s** unto thee, 1696
22:38 have I now any power at all to **s** any thing? 1696
23:16 and said, Go again unto Balak, and **s** thus. 1696
25:12 Wherefore **s**, Behold, I give unto him my 559
28: 2 **s** unto them, My offering, *and* my bread for 559
28: 3 thou shalt **s** unto them, This *is* the offering 559
33:51 unto the children of Israel, and **s** unto them, 559
34: 2 the children of Israel, and **s** unto them, 559
35:10 unto the children of Israel, and **s** unto them, 559
Dt 1:42 **S** unto them, Go not up, neither fight; 559
4: 6 **s**, Surely this great nation *is* a wise and 559
5:27 and hear all that the LORD our God shall **s**: 559
5:30 Go **s** to them, Get you into your tents again. 559
6:21 thou shalt **s** unto thy son, We were Pharaoh's 559
7:17 If thou shalt **s** in thine heart, These nations 559
8:17 thou **s** in thine heart, My power and 559
9: 2 *of whom* thou hast heard *s*, Who can stand NIH
9:28 the land whence thou broughtest us out **s**, 559
12:20 thou shalt **s**, I will eat flesh, because thy soul 559
13:12 If thou shalt hear *s* in one of thy cities, NIH
15:16 it shall be, if he **s** unto thee, I will not go 559
17:14 and shalt dwell therein, and shalt **s**, 559
18:21 if thou **s** in thine heart, How shall we know 559
20: 3 shall **s** unto them, Hear, O Israel, 559
20: 8 they shall **s**, What man *is there that is* fearful 559
21: 7 they shall answer and **s**, Our hands have not 559
21:20 they shall **s** unto the elders of his city, 559
22:14 **s**, I took this woman, and when I came to 559
22:16 the damsel's father shall **s** unto the elders, 559
25: 7 wife go up to the gate unto the elders, and **s**, 559
25: 8 *if* he stand *to it*, and **s**, I like not to take her; 559
25: 9 and spit in his face, and shall answer and **s**, 559
26: 3 **s** unto him, I profess *this* day unto 559
26: 5 and **s** before the LORD thy God, 559
26:13 thou shalt **s** before the LORD thy God, 559
27:14 **s** unto all the men of Israel *with* a loud voice, 559
27:15 *place*. And all the people shall answer and **s**, 559
27:16 his mother. And all the people shall **s**, Amen. 559
27:17 And all the people shall **s**, Amen. 559
27:18 of the way. And all the people shall **s**, Amen. 559
27:19 widow. And all the people shall **s**, Amen. 559
27:20 And all the people shall **s**, Amen. 559
27:21 *of* beast. And all the people shall **s**, Amen. 559
27:22 his mother. And all the people shall **s**, Amen. 559
27:23 in law. And all the people shall **s**, Amen. 559
27:24 And all the people shall **s**, Amen. 559
27:25 And all the people shall **s**, Amen. 559
27:26 do them. And all the people shall **s**, Amen. 559
28:67 In the morning thou shalt **s**, Would God it 559
28:67 at even thou shalt **s**, Would God it were 559
29:22 shall **s**, when they see the plagues of that 559
29:24 Even all nations shall **s**, Wherefore hath 559
29:25 *men* shall **s**, Because they have forsaken 559
30:12 It *is* not in heaven, that *thou* shouldest **s**, 559
30:13 *is* it beyond the sea, that *thou* shouldest **s**, 559
31:17 so that they will **s** in that day, Are not these 559
32:27 *and* lest they should **s**, Our hand is high, and 559
32:37 he shall **s**, Where *are* their gods, *their* rock in 559
32:40 up my hand to heaven, and **s**, I live for ever. 559
33:27 from before thee; and shall **s**, Destroy *them*. 559
Jos 7: 8 O Lord, what shall I **s**, when Israel turneth 559
7:13 Up, sanctify the people, and **s**, 559
8: 6 for they will **s**, *They* flee before us, as at 559
9:11 go to meet them, and **s** unto them, We *are* 559
22:11 the children of Israel heard **s**, Behold, 559
22:27 that your children may not **s** to our children 559
22:28 when they should *so* **s** to us or to our 559
22:28 that we may **s** *again*, Behold the pattern of 559
Jdg 4:20 man doth come and inquire of thee, and **s**, 559
4:20 Is there any man here? that thou shalt **s**, No. 559
7: 4 it shall be, *that* of whom I **s** unto thee, 559
7: 4 of whomsoever I **s** unto thee, This shall not 559
7:11 thou shalt hear what they **s**; and 1696
7:18 **s**, *The sword* of the LORD, and of Gideon. 559
9:54 and slay me, that *men* **s** not of me, 559
12: 6 Then said they unto him, **S** now Shibboleth: 559
16:15 said unto him, How canst thou **s**, I love thee, 559
18: 8 their brethren said unto them, What *s* ye? NIH
18:24 what *is* this *that* ye **s** unto me, What aileth 559
21:22 that we will **s** unto them, Be favourable unto 559
Ru 1:12 If I should **s**, I have hope, *if* I should have a 559
1Sa 2:36 of bread, and shall **s**, Put me, I pray thee, 559
3: 9 call thee, that thou shalt **s**, Speak, LORD; 559
8: 7 of the people in all that they **s** unto thee: 559
10: 2 they will **s** unto thee, The asses which thou 559
11: 9 Thus shall ye **s** unto the men of 559
13: 4 all Israel heard **s** *that* Saul had smitten a 559
14: 9 If they **s** thus unto us, Tarry until we come to 559
14:10 if they **s** thus, Come up unto us; then we will 559
14:34 **s** unto them, Bring me hither every man his 559
15:16 me *this* night. And he said unto him, **S on**. 1696
16: 2 LORD said, Take a heifer with thee, and **s**, 559
18:22 **s**, Behold, the king hath delight in thee, and 559
18:25 Saul said, Thus shall ye **s** to David, The king 559
19:24 Wherefore they **s**, *Is* Saul also among 559
20: 6 If thy father at all miss me, then **s**, 559
20: 7 If he **s** thus, *It is* well; thy servant shall have 559
20:21 If I **expressly s** unto the lad, Behold, 559+559
20:22 If I **s** thus unto the young man, Behold, 559
25: 6 thus shall ye **s** to him that liveth *in* 559
2Sa 7: 8 so shalt thou **s** unto my servant David, 559
7:20 what can David **s** more unto thee? for thou, 1696
11:20 and he **s** unto thee, Wherefore approached ye 559
11:21 **s** thou, Thy servant Uriah the Hittite is dead 559
11:25 Thus shalt thou **s** unto Joab, Let not this 559
2Sa 13: 5 **s** unto him, I pray thee, let my sister Tamar 559
13:28 and when I **s** unto you, Smite Amnon; 559
14:12 unto my lord the king. And he said, **S on**. 1696
14:32 that I may send thee to the king, to **s**, 559
15:10 then ye shall **s**, Absalom reigneth in Hebron. 559
15:26 if he thus **s**, I have no delight in thee; behold, 559
15:34 **s** unto Absalom, I will be thy servant, 559
16:10 Who shall then **s**, Wherefore hast thou done 559
17: 9 at the first, that whosoever heareth *it* will **s**, 559
19: 2 for the people heard **s** that day *how* the king 559
19:13 And **s** ye to Amasa, *Art* thou not *of* my bone, 559
20:16 **s**, I pray you, unto Joab, Come near hither, 559
21: 4 he said, What you shall **s**, *that* will I do for 559
24: 1 he moved David against them to **s**, Go, 559
24:12 Go and **s** unto David, Thus saith 1696
1Ki 1:13 **s** unto him, Didst not thou, my lord O king, 559
1:25 behold, they eat and drink before him, and **s**, 559
1:34 the trumpet, and **s**, God save king Solomon. 559
1:36 the LORD God of my lord the king **s** so 559
2:14 I have **somewhat to s** unto thee. 1697
2:14 to say unto thee. And she said, **S on**. 1696
2:16 deny me not. And she said unto him, **S on**. 1696
2:17 the king, (for he will not **s** thee **nay**,) 6440+7725
2:20 of thee; *I pray thee*, **s** me not **nay**. 6440+7725
2:20 my mother: for I will not **s** thee **nay**. 6440+7725
9: 8 they shall **s**, Why hath the LORD done thus 559
12:10 thus shalt thou **s** unto them, My little *finger* 1696
13:22 of the which *the LORD* did **s** to thee, 1696
14: 5 thus and thus shalt thou **s** unto her: for it 1696
16:16 And the people that *were* encamped heard **s**, 559
18:44 he said, Go up, **s** unto Ahab, Prepare *thy* 559
22: 8 And Jehoshaphat said, Let not the king **s** so. 559
22:27 **s**, Thus saith the king, Put this *fellow in* 559
2Ki 1: 3 **s** unto them, *Is it* not because *there is* not a 1696
1: 6 **s** unto him, Thus saith the LORD, *Is it* not 1696
2:18 unto them, Did I not **s** unto you, Go not? 559
4:13 he said unto him, **S** now unto her, Behold, 559
4:26 I pray thee, to meet her, and **s** unto her, 559
4:28 of my lord? did I not **s**, Do not deceive me? 559
7: 4 If we **s**, We will enter *into* the city, then 559
7:13 *I s*, they *are even* as all the multitude of NIH
8:10 Elisha said unto him, Go, **s** unto him, 559
9: 3 pour *it* on his head, and **s**, Thus saith 559
9:17 send to meet them, and let him **s**, *Is it* peace? 559
9:37 *so* that they shall not **s**, This *is* Jezebel. 559
18:22 if ye **s** unto me, We trust in the LORD our 559
19: 6 Thus shall ye **s** to your master, Thus saith 559
19: 9 when he heard **s** of Tirhakah king of 559
22:18 thus shall ye **s** to him, Thus saith the LORD 559
1Ch 5: 3 *I s*, of Reuben the firstborn of Israel *were*, NIH
16:31 let *men* **s** among the nations, The LORD 559
16:35 **s** ye, Save us, O God of our salvation, and 559
17: 7 thus shalt thou **s** unto my servant David, 559
21:18 the LORD commanded Gad to **s** to David, 559
2Ch 7:21 so that he shall **s**, Why hath the LORD 559
10:10 thus shalt thou **s** unto them, My little *finger* 559
18: 7 And Jehoshaphat said, Let not the king **s** so. 559
18:15 times shall I adjure thee that thou **s** nothing 1696
18:26 **s**, Thus saith the king, Put this *fellow in* 559
20:11 Behold, I **s**, *how* they reward us, to come to NIH
20:21 the army, and to **s**, Praise the LORD; 559
34:26 of the LORD, so shall ye **s** unto him, 559
Ezr 8:17 I told them what they should **s** unto Iddo, 1696
9:10 O our God, what shall we **s** after this? 559
Ne 7: 7 *I s*, of the men of the people of Israel *was* NIH
9: 8 to give *it*, *I s*, to his seed, and NIH
Est 1:18 Media **s** this day unto all the king's princes, 559
Job 6:22 Did I **s**, Bring unto me? or, Give a reward 559
7: 4 When I lie down, I **s**, When shall I arise, and 559
7:13 When I **s**, My bed shall comfort me, 559
9:12 who will **s** unto him, What doest thou? 559
9:20 *if* I *s*, I *am* perfect, it shall also prove me NIH
9:27 If I **s**, I will forget my complaint, I will leave 559
10: 2 I will **s** unto God, Do not condemn me; 559
19:28 ye should **s**, Why persecute we him? 559
20: 7 they which have seen him shall **s**, Where *is* 559
21:14 Therefore they **s** unto God, Depart from us; 559
21:28 For ye **s**, Where *is* the house of the prince? 559
22:29 then thou shalt **s**, *There is* lifting up; 559
23: 5 and understand what he would **s** unto me. 559
28:22 Destruction and death **s**, We have heard 559
32:11 whilst you searched out **what to s**. 4405
32:13 Lest ye should **s**, We have found out 559
33:27 *if any* **s**, I have sinned, and perverted *that* 559
33:32 If *thou* hast **any thing to s**, answer me: 4405
34:18 *Is it fit* to **s** to a king, *Thou art* wicked? *and* 559
36:23 or who can **s**, Thou hast wrought iniquity? 559
37:19 Teach us what we shall **s** unto him; *for* we 559
38:35 they may go, and **s** unto thee, Here we *are*? 559
Ps 3: 2 Many *there be* which **s** of my soul, *There is* 559
4: 6 *There be* many that **s**, Who will shew us *any* 559
11: 1 how **s** ye to my soul, Flee *as* a bird *to* your 559
13: 4 Lest mine enemy **s**, I have prevailed against 559
27:14 thine heart: wait, I **s**, on the LORD. NIH
35: 3 **s** unto my soul, I *am* thy salvation. 559
35:10 All my bones shall **s**, LORD, who *is* like 559
35:25 Let them not **s** in their hearts, Ah, so 559
35:25 let them not **s**, We have swallowed him up. 559
35:27 yea, let them **s** continually, Let the LORD 559
40:15 for a reward of their shame that **s** unto me, 559
40:16 let such as love thy salvation **s** continually, 559
41: 8 evil disease, *s they*, cleaveth fast unto him: NIH
42: 3 and night, while *they* continually **s** unto me, 559
42: 9 I will **s** unto God my rock, Why hast thou 559
42:10 while they **s** daily unto me, Where *is* thy 559
58:11 So that a man shall **s**, Verily *there is* a 559
59: 7 *are* in their lips: for who, *s they*, doth hear? NIH
64: 5 snares privily; they **s**, Who shall see them? 559
66: 3 **S** unto God, How terrible *art thou in* thy 559
70: 3 back for a reward of their shame that **s**, 559
70: 4 let such as love thy salvation **s** continually, 559
73:11 they **s**, How doth God know? and is there 559
73:15 If I **s**, I will speak thus; behold, I should 559
79:10 Wherefore should the heathen **s**, Where *is* 559
91: 2 I will **s** of the LORD, *He is* my refuge and 559
Ps 94: 7 Yet they **s**, The LORD shall not see, 559
96:10 **S** among the heathen *that* the LORD 559
106:48 let all the people **s**, Amen. Praise ye 559
107: 2 Let the redeemed of the LORD **s** *so*, 559
115: 2 Wherefore should the heathen **s**, Where *is* 559
118: 2 Let Israel now **s**, that his mercy *endureth* for 559
118: 3 Let the house of Aaron now **s**, that his mercy 559
118: 4 Let them now that fear the LORD **s**, 559
122: 8 and companions' sakes, I will now **s**, 1696
124: 1 who was on our side, now may Israel **s**; 559
129: 1 me from my youth, may Israel now **s**: 559
129: 8 Neither do they which go by **s**, The blessing 559
130: 6 *I s*, *more than* they that watch for NIH
139:11 If I **s**, Surely the darkness shall cover me; 559
Pr 1:11 If they **s**, Come with us, let us lay wait for 559
3:28 **S** not unto thy neighbour, Go, and 559
5:12 **s**, How have I hated instruction, and 559
7: 4 **S** unto wisdom, Thou *art* my sister; and 559
20: 9 Who can **s**, I have made my heart clean, I am 559
20:22 **S** not thou, I will recompense evil; *but* 559
23:35 stricken me, *shalt thou s*, *and* I was not sick; NIH
24:29 **S** not, I will do so to him as he hath done to 559
30: 9 Lest I be full, and deny *thee*, and **s**, Who *is* 559
30:15 *yea*, four *things* **s** not, *It is* enough: 559
Ecc 5: 6 neither **s** thou before the angel, that it *was* an 559
6: 3 I **s**, *that* an untimely birth *is* better than he. 559
7:10 **S** not thou, What is *the cause* that the former 559
8: 4 and who may **s** unto him, What doest thou? 559
12: 1 nor the years draw nigh, when thou shalt **s**, 559
Isa 2: 3 many people shall go and **s**, Come ye, and 559
3:10 **S** ye *to* the righteous, that *it shall be* well 559
5:19 That **s**, Let him make speed, *and* hasten his 559
7: 4 **s** unto him, Take heed, and be quiet; 559
8:12 **S** ye not, A confederacy, to all *them to* 559
8:12 to all *them to* whom this people shall **s**, 559
8:19 when they shall **s** unto you, Seek unto them 559
9: 9 that **s** in the pride and stoutness of heart, 559
12: 1 in that day thou shalt **s**, O LORD, I will 559
12: 4 in that day shall ye **s**, Praise the LORD, 559
14: 4 and **s**, How hath the oppressor ceased! 559
14:10 All they shall speak and **s** unto thee, Art thou 559
19:11 how **s** ye unto Pharaoh, I *am* the son of 559
20: 6 the inhabitant of this isle shall **s** in that day, 559
22:15 which *is* over the house, *and s*, NIH
29:15 are in the dark, and they **s**, Who seeth us? 559
29:16 for shall the work **s** of him that made it, 559
29:16 shall the thing framed **s** of him that framed 559
30:10 Which **s** to the seers, See not; and to 559
30:22 thou shalt **s** unto it, Get thee hence. 559
33:24 the inhabitant shall not **s**, I am sick: 559
35: 4 **S** to them that are of a fearful heart, 559
36: 4 **S** ye now to Hezekiah, Thus saith the great 559
36: 5 I **s**, *sayest thou*, (but *they are but* vain words) 559
36: 7 if thou **s** to me, We trust in the LORD our 559
37: 6 Thus shall ye **s** unto your master, Thus saith 559
37: 9 he heard **s** concerning Tirhakah king of 559
38: 5 Go and **s** to Hezekiah, Thus saith 559
38:15 What shall I **s**? he hath both spoken unto 1696
40: 9 **s** unto the cities of Judah, Behold your God. 559
41:26 beforetime, that we may **s**, *He is* righteous? 559
41:27 The first *shall s* to Zion, Behold, NIH
42:17 that **s** to the molten images, Ye *are* our gods. 559
43: 6 I will **s** to the north, Give *up*; and to 559
43: 9 or let them hear, and **s**, *It is* truth. 559
44: 5 One shall **s**, I *am* the LORD'S; and 559
44:19 *is there* knowledge nor understanding to **s**, 559
44:20 that he cannot deliver his soul, nor **s**, *Is there* 559
45: 9 Shall the clay **s** to him that fashioneth it, 559
45:24 Surely, shall *one* **s**, in the LORD have I 559
48: 5 lest thou shouldest **s**, Mine idol hath done 559
48: 7 lest thou shouldest **s**, Behold, I knew them. 559
48:20 **s** ye, The LORD hath redeemed his servant 559
49: 9 That *thou* mayest **s** to the prisoners, 559
49:20 hast lost the other, shall **s** again in thine ears, 559
49:21 shalt thou **s** in thine heart, Who hath 559
51:16 and **s** unto Zion, Thou *art* my people. 559
56: 3 neither let the eunuch **s**, Behold, I *am* a dry 559
56:12 *s they*, I will fetch wine, and we will fill NIH
57:14 shall **s**, Cast ye up, cast ye up, prepare 559
58: 3 have we fasted, *s they*, and thou seest not? NIH
58: 9 thou shalt cry, and he shall **s**, Here I *am*. If 559
62:11 **S** ye to the daughter of Zion, Behold, 559
65: 5 Which **s**, Stand by thyself, come not near to 559
Jer 1: 7 LORD said unto me, **S** not, I *am* a child: 559
2:23 How canst thou **s**, I am not polluted, I have 559
2:27 in the time of their trouble they will **s**, Arise, 559
2:31 wherefore **s** my people, We are lords; 559
3: 1 They **s**, If a man put away his wife, and 559
3:12 **s**, Return, thou backsliding Israel, saith 559
3:16 saith the LORD, they shall **s** no more, 559
4: 5 and **s**, Blow ye the trumpet in the land: 559
4: 5 cry, gather together, and **s**, 559
5: 2 though they **s**, The LORD liveth; surely 559
5:15 neither understandest what they **s**. 1696
5:19 it shall come to pass, when ye shall **s**, 559
5:24 Neither **s** they in their heart, Let us now fear 559
7: 2 proclaim there this word, and **s**, Hear 559
7:10 which is called by my name, and **s**, 559
7:28 thou shalt **s** unto them, This *is* a nation that 559
8: 4 Moreover thou shalt **s** unto them, Thus saith 559
8: 8 How do ye **s**, We *are* wise, and the law of 559
10:11 Thus shall ye **s** unto them, The gods that 560
11: 3 **s** thou unto them, Thus saith the LORD 559
13:12 they shall **s** unto thee, Do we not certainly 559
13:13 shalt thou **s** unto them, Thus saith 559
13:18 **S** unto the king and to the queen, 559
13:21 What wilt thou **s** when he shall punish thee? 559
13:22 if thou **s** in thine heart, Wherefore come 559
14:13 behold, the prophets **s** unto them, Ye shall 559
14:15 yet they **s**, Sword and famine shall not be in 559
14:17 Therefore thou shalt **s** this word unto them; 559
15: 2 And it shall come to pass, if they **s** unto thee, 559
16:10 all these words, and they shall **s** unto thee, 559
16:11 shalt thou **s** unto them, Because your fathers 559
16:19 shall **s**, Surely our fathers have inherited lies, 559

S

Jer 17:15 Behold, they **s** unto me, Where *is* the word 559
17:20 **s** unto them, Hear ye the word of 559
19: 3 **s**, Hear ye the word of the LORD, O kings 559
19:11 shalt **s** unto them, Thus saith the LORD of 559
20:10 Report, *s they,* and we will report it. All my NIH
21: 3 unto them, Thus shall ye **s** to Zedekiah: 559
21: 8 unto this people thou shalt **s**, Thus saith 559
21:11 *s*, Hear ye the word of the LORD. NIH
21:13 which **s**, Who shall come down against us? 559
22: 2 **s**, Hear the word of the LORD, O king of 559
22: 8 and they shall **s** every man to his neighbour, 559
23: 7 saith the LORD, that they shall no more **s**, 559
23:17 They **s still** unto them that despise me, 559+559
23:17 they **s** *unto* every one that walketh after 559
23:31 that use their tongues, and **s**, He saith. 5001
23:33 thou shalt then **s** unto them, What burden? 559
23:34 and the priest, and the people, that shall **s**, 559
23:35 Thus shall ye **s** every one to his neighbour, 559
23:37 Thus shalt thou **s** to the prophet, What hath 559
23:38 sith ye **s**, The burden of the LORD; 559
23:38 Because you **s** this word, The burden of 559
23:38 I have sent unto you, saying, Ye shall not **s**, 559
25:27 Therefore thou shalt **s** unto them, Thus saith 559
25:28 shalt thou **s** unto them, Thus saith 559
25:30 **s** unto them, The LORD shall roar from on 559
26: 4 thou shalt **s** unto them, Thus saith 559
27: 4 And command them to **s** unto their masters, 559
27: 4 of Israel; Thus shall ye **s** unto your masters; 559
31: 7 publish ye, praise ye, and **s**, O LORD, save 559
31:10 and declare *it* in the isles afar off, and **s**, 559
31:29 In those days they shall **s** no more, 559
32: 3 and **s**, Thus saith the LORD, Behold, 559
32:36 of Israel, concerning this city, whereof ye **s**, 559
32:43 whereof ye **s**, *It is* desolate without man or 559
33:10 which ye **s** *shall be* desolate without man 559
33:11 of the bride, the voice of them that shall **s**, 559
36:29 And thou shalt **s** to Jehoiakim king of Judah, 559
37: 7 Thus shall ye **s** to the king of Judah, that sent 559
38:22 those *women shall* **s**, Thy friends have set 559
38:25 and they come unto thee, and **s** unto thee, 559
38:26 thou shalt **s** unto them, I presented my 559
39:12 do unto him even as he shall **s** unto thee. 1696
42:13 if ye **s**, We will not dwell in this land, 559
42:20 unto all that the LORD our God shall **s**, 559
43: 2 the LORD our God hath not sent thee to **s**, 559
43:10 **s** unto them, Thus saith the LORD of hosts, 559
45: 3 Thou didst **s**, Woe is me now! for 559
45: 4 Thus shalt thou **s** unto him, The LORD 559
46:14 **s** ye, Stand fast, and prepare thee; for 559
48:14 How **s** ye, We *are* mighty and strong men for 559
48:17 all ye that know his name, **s**, How is 559
48:19 and her that escapeth, *and* **s**, What is done? 559
50: 2 **s**, Babylon is taken, Bel is confounded, 559
51:35 upon Babylon, shall the inhabitant of Zion **s**; 559
51:35 the inhabitants of Chaldea, shall Jerusalem **s**. 559
51:62 shalt thou **s**, O LORD, thou hast spoken 559
51:64 thou shalt **s**, Thus shall Babylon sink, and 559
La 2:12 They **s** to their mothers, Where *is* corn and 559
2:16 they **s**, We have swallowed *her* up: 559
Eze 2: 4 thou shalt **s** unto them, Thus saith the Lord 559
2: 8 son of man, hear what I **s** unto thee; 1696
3:18 When I **s** unto the wicked, Thou shalt surely 559
3:27 open thy mouth, and thou shalt **s** unto them, 559
6: 3 **s**, Ye mountains of Israel, hear the word of 559
6:11 thine hand, and stamp with thy foot, and **s**, 559
8:12 for they **s**, The LORD seeth us not; 559
9: 9 for they **s**, The LORD hath forsaken 559
11: 3 Which **s**, *It is* not near; *let us* build houses: 559
11:16 Therefore **s**, Thus saith the Lord GOD; 559
11:17 Therefore **s**, Thus saith the Lord GOD; 559
12:10 **S** thou unto them, Thus saith the Lord 559
12:11 **S**, I *am* your sign: like as I have done, so 559
12:19 **s** unto the people of the land, Thus saith 559
12:23 **s** unto them, The days are at hand, and 1696
12:25 will I **s** the word, and will perform it, 1696
12:27 of man, behold, *they of* the house of Israel **s**, 559
12:28 Therefore **s** unto them, Thus saith the Lord 559
13: 2 **s** thou unto them that prophesy out of their 559
13: 7 not spoken a lying divination, whereas ye **s**, 559
13:11 **S** unto them which daub *it with* untempered 559
13:15 *with* untempered *morter,* and will **s** unto you, 559
13:18 **s**, Thus saith the Lord GOD; Woe to 559
14: 4 Therefore speak unto them, and **s** unto them, 559
14: 6 Therefore **s** unto the house of Israel, 559
14:17 that land, and **s**, Sword, go through the land; 559
16: 3 **s**, Thus saith the Lord GOD unto 559
17: 3 **s**, Thus saith the Lord GOD; A great eagle 559
17: 9 **S** thou, Thus saith the Lord GOD; Shall it 559
17:12 **S** now to the rebellious house, Know ye not 559
18:19 Yet **s** ye, Why? doth not the son bear 559
18:25 Yet ye **s**, The way of the Lord is not equal. 559
19: 2 **s**, What *is* thy mother? A lioness: she lay 559
20: 3 and **s** unto them, Thus saith the Lord GOD; 559
20: 5 **s** unto them, Thus saith the Lord GOD; 559
20:27 and **s** unto them, Thus saith the Lord GOD; 559
20:30 Wherefore **s** unto the house of Israel, 559
20:32 that ye **s**, We will be as the heathen, as 559
20:47 **s** to the forest of the south, Hear the word of 559
20:49 said I, Ah Lord GOD, they **s** of me, Doth 559
21: 3 **s** to the land of Israel, Thus saith 559
21: 7 it shall be, when they **s** unto thee, Wherefore 559
21: 9 Son of man, prophesy, and **s**, Thus saith 559
21: 9 **S**, A sword, a sword is sharpened, and 559
21:24 *I s,* that ye are come to remembrance, NIH
21:28 thou, son of man, prophesy and **s**, Thus saith 559
21:28 even **s** thou, The sword, the sword *is* drawn: 559
22: 3 **s** thou, Thus saith the Lord GOD, The city 559
22:24 Son of man, **s** unto her, Thou *art* the land 559
24: 3 and **s** unto them, Thus saith the Lord GOD; 559
25: 3 **s** unto the Ammonites, Hear the word of 559
25: 8 Because that Moab and Seir do **s**, Behold, 559
26:17 **s** to thee, How art thou destroyed, *that wast* 559
27: 3 **s** unto Tyrus, O thou that art situate at 559
28: 2 Son of man, **s** unto the prince of Tyrus, 559
28: 9 Wilt thou **yet s** before him that slayeth 559+559

Eze 28:12 and **s** unto him, Thus saith the Lord GOD; 559
28:22 **s**, Thus saith the Lord GOD; Behold, I *am* 559
29: 3 Speak, and **s**, Thus saith the Lord GOD; 559
30: 2 Son of man, prophesy and **s**, Thus saith 559
32: 2 **s** unto him, Thou art like a young lion of 559
33: 2 the children of thy people, and **s** unto them, 559
33: 8 When I **s** unto the wicked, O wicked *man,* 559
33:11 **S** unto them, *As* I live, saith the Lord GOD, 559
33:12 of man, **s** unto the children of thy people, 559
33:13 When I shall **s** to the righteous, *that* he shall 559
33:14 Again, when I **s** unto the wicked, Thou shalt 559
33:17 Yet the children of thy people **s**, The way of 559
33:20 Yet ye **s**, The way of the Lord is not equal. 559
33:25 Wherefore **s** unto them, Thus saith the Lord 559
33:27 **S** thou thus unto them, Thus saith the Lord 559
34: 2 of Israel, prophesy, and **s** unto them, 559
35: 3 **s** unto it, Thus saith the Lord GOD; 559
36: 1 **s**, Ye mountains of Israel, hear the word of 559
36: 3 Therefore prophesy and **s**, Thus saith 559
36: 6 **s** unto the mountains, and to the hills, to 559
36:13 Because they **s** unto you, Thou *land* 559
36:22 Therefore **s** unto the house of Israel, 559
36:35 they shall **s**, This land that was desolate is 559
37: 4 and **s** unto them, O ye dry bones, 559
37: 9 prophesy, son of man, and **s** to the wind, 559
37:11 behold, they **s**, Our bones are dried, and 559
37:12 Therefore prophesy and **s** unto them, 559
37:19 **S** unto them, Thus saith the Lord GOD; 1696
37:21 **s** unto them, Thus saith the Lord GOD; 1696
38: 3 **s**, Thus saith the Lord GOD; Behold, I *am* 559
38:11 thou shalt **s**, I will go up to the land of 559
38:13 shall **s** unto thee, Art thou come to take a 559
38:14 son of man, prophesy and **s** unto Gog, 559
39: 1 son of man, prophesy against Gog, and **s**, 559
44: 5 hear with thine ears all that I **s** unto thee 1696
44: 6 thou shalt **s** to the rebellious, *even* to 559
Da 4:35 his hand, or **s** unto him, What doest thou? 560
5:11 the king, *I s,* thy father, made master of NIH
Hos 2: 1 **S** ye unto your brethren, Ammi; and to your 559
2: 7 shall not find *them:* then shall she **s**, I will go 559
2:23 I will **s** to *them which were* not my people, 559
2:23 and they shall **s**, *Thou art* my God. 559
10: 3 For now they shall **s**, We have no king, 559
10: 8 they shall **s** to the mountains, Cover us; and 559
13: 2 they **s** of them, Let the men that sacrifice 559
14: 2 **s** unto him, Take away all iniquity, and 559
14: 3 neither will we **s** any more to the work of 559
14: 8 Ephraim *shall s,* What have I to do any NIH
Joel 2:17 the porch and the altar, and let them **s**, 559
2:17 wherefore should they **s** among the people, 559
2:19 LORD will answer and **s** unto his people, 559
3:10 into spears: let the weak **s**, I *am* strong. 559
Am 3: 9 in the palaces in the land of Egypt, and **s**, 559
4: 1 which **s** to their masters, Bring, and let us 559
5:16 and they shall **s** in all the highways, Alas! 559
6:10 shall **s** unto *him* that *is* by the sides of 559
6:10 he shall **s**, No. Then shall he say, Hold thy 559
6:10 shall he **s**, Hold thy tongue: for *we may* not 559
6:13 which rejoice in a thing of nought, which **s**, 559
8:14 of Samaria, and **s**, Thy god, O Dan, liveth; 559
9:10 which **s**, The evil shall not overtake nor 559
Mic 2: 4 *and* **s**, We be utterly spoiled: 559
2: 6 ye not, *s they to them that* prophesy: NIH
3:11 and **s**, *Is* not the LORD among us? 559
4: 2 **s**, Come, and let us go up to the mountain of 559
4:11 that **s**, Let her be defiled, and let our eye 559
Na 3: 7 flee from thee, and **s**, Nineveh is laid waste: 559
Hab 2: 1 will watch to see what he will **s** unto me, 1696
2: 6 and a taunting proverb against him, and **s**, 559
Zep 1:12 that **s** in their heart, The LORD will not do 559
Hag 1: 2 saying, This people **s**, The time is not come, 559
Zec 1: 3 Therefore **s** thou unto them, Thus saith 559
11: 5 they that sell them **s**, Blessed *be* the LORD; 559
12: 5 the governors of Judah shall **s** in their heart, 559
13: 3 his mother that begat him shall **s** unto him, 559
13: 5 he shall **s**, I *am* no prophet, I *am* a 559
13: 6 *one* shall **s** unto him, What *are* these wounds 559
13: 9 I will **s**, It *is* my people: and they shall say, 559
13: 9 and they shall **s**, The LORD *is* my God. 559
Mal 1: 2 Yet ye **s**, Wherein hast thou loved us? *was* 559
1: 5 your eyes shall see, and ye shall **s**, 559
1: 6 ye **s**, Wherein have we despised thy name? 559
1: 7 and ye **s**, Wherein have we polluted thee? 559
1: 7 In that ye **s**, The table of the LORD *is* 559
1:12 ye *have* profaned it, in that ye **s**, The table of 559
2:14 Yet ye **s**, Wherefore? Because the LORD 559
2:17 Yet ye **s**, Wherein have we wearied *him?* 559
2:17 Wherein have we wearied *him?* When ye **s**, 559
3: 8 ye **s**, Wherein have we robbed thee? *In* tithes 559
3:13 Yet ye **s**, What have we spoken so 559
Mt 3: 9 And think not to **s** within yourselves, *3004*
3: 9 for I **s** unto you, That God is able of these *3004*
4:17 Jesus began to preach, and to **s**, Repent: *3004*
5:11 shall **s** all manner of evil against you *3004*
5:18 For verily I **s** unto you, Till heaven and *3004*
5:20 For I **s** unto you, That except your *3004*
5:22 But I **s** unto you, That whosoever is angry *3004*
5:22 and whosoever shall **s** to his brother, Raca, *3004*
5:22 but whosoever shall **s**, *Thou* fool, shall be *3004*
5:26 Verily I **s** unto thee, Thou shalt by no *3004*
5:28 But I **s** unto you, That whosoever looketh *3004*
5:32 But I **s** unto you, That whosoever shall put *3004*
5:34 But I **s** unto you, Swear not at all; *3004*
5:39 But I **s** unto you, That *ye* resist not evil: but *3004*
5:44 But I **s** unto you, Love your enemies, *3004*
6: 2 Verily I **s** unto you, They have their *3004*
6: 5 Verily I **s** unto you, They have their *3004*
6:16 Verily I **s** unto you, They have their *3004*
6:25 Therefore I **s** unto you, Take no thought for *3004*
6:29 And yet I **s** unto you, That even Solomon in *3004*
7: 4 Or how wilt thou **s** to thy brother, Let me *3004*
7:22 Many will **s** to me in that day, Lord, Lord, *3004*
8: 9 and I **s** to this *man,* Go, and he goeth; and *3004*
8:10 Verily I **s** unto you, I have not found so *3004*
8:11 And I **s** unto you, That many shall come *3004*

Mt 9: 5 For whether is easier, to **s**, *Thy* sins be *3004*
9: 5 be forgiven thee; or to **s**, Arise, and walk? *3004*
10:15 Verily I **s** unto you, It shall be more *3004*
10:23 for verily I **s** unto you, Ye shall not have *3004*
10:42 verily I **s** unto you, he shall in no wise lose *3004*
11: 7 Jesus began to **s** unto the multitudes *3004*
11: 9 yea, I **s** unto you, and more than a prophet. *3004*
11:11 Verily I **s** unto you, Among *them that are* *3004*
11:18 nor drinking, and they **s**, He hath a devil. *3004*
11:19 man came eating and drinking, and they **s**, *3004*
11:22 But I **s** unto you, It shall be more tolerable *3004*
11:24 But I **s** unto you, that it shall be more *3004*
12: 6 But I **s** unto you, That in this place is *one* *3004*
12:31 Wherefore I **s** unto you, All *manner of* sin *3004*
12:36 But I **s** unto you, That every idle word that *3004*
13:17 For verily I **s** unto you, That many prophets *3004*
13:30 in the time of harvest I will **s** to the reapers, *3004*
13:51 all these *things?* They **s** unto him, *3004*
14:17 And they **s** unto him, We have here but five *3004*
15: 5 But ye **s**, Whosoever shall say to *his* father *3004*
15: 5 Whosoever shall **s** to *his* father or *3004*
15:33 And his disciples **s** unto him, *3004*
16: 2 said unto them, When it is evening, ye **s**, *3004*
16:13 Whom do men **s** that I the Son of man am? *3004*
16:14 Some *s that thou art* John the Baptist: NIG
16:15 saith unto them, But whom **s** ye that I am? *3004*
16:18 And I **s** also unto thee, That thou art Peter, *3004*
16:28 Verily I **s** unto you, There be some standing *3004*
17:10 **s** the scribes that Elias must first come? *3004*
17:12 But I **s** unto you, That Elias is come *3004*
17:20 for verily I **s** unto you, If ye have faith as a *3004*
17:20 ye shall **s** unto this mountain, *3004*
18: 3 And said, Verily I **s** unto you, Except ye be *3004*
18:10 for I **s** unto you, That in heaven their angels *3004*
18:13 so be that he find it, verily I **s** unto you, *3004*
18:18 Verily I **s** unto you, Whatsoever ye shall *3004*
18:19 Again I **s** unto you, That if two of you shall *3004*
18:22 I **s** not unto thee, Until seven times: *3004*
19: 7 They **s** unto him, Why did Moses then *3004*
19: 9 And I **s** unto you, Whosoever shall put *3004*
19:10 His disciples **s** unto him, If the case of *3004*
19:23 unto his disciples, Verily I **s** unto you, *3004*
19:24 And again I **s** unto you, It is easier for a *3004*
19:28 Jesus said unto them, Verily I **s** unto you, *3004*
20: 7 They **s** unto him, Because no *man* hath *3004*
20:22 that I am baptized *with?* They **s** unto him, *3004*
20:33 They **s** unto him, Lord, that our eyes may *3004*
21: 3 And if any *man* **s** ought unto you, ye shall *3004*
21: 3 ye shall **s**, The Lord hath need of them; *3004*
21:16 said unto him, Hearest thou what these **s**? *3004*
21:21 and said unto them, Verily I **s** unto you, *3004*
21:21 but also if ye shall **s** unto this mountain, *3004*
21:25 saying, If we shall **s**, From heaven; *3004*
21:25 he will **s** unto us, Why did ye not then *3004*
21:26 But if we shall **s**, Of men; we fear *3004*
21:31 They **s** unto him, The first. Jesus saith unto *3004*
21:31 Verily I **s** unto you, That the publicans and *3004*
21:41 They **s** unto him, He will miserably destroy *3004*
21:43 Therefore **s** I unto you, The kingdom of *3004*
22:21 They **s** unto him, Cesar's. Then saith he *3004*
22:23 which **s** that there is no resurrection, and *3004*
22:42 is he? They **s** unto him, *The Son* of David. *3004*
23: 3 ye after their works: for they **s**, and do not. *3004*
23:16 Woe unto you, *ye* blind guides, which **s**, *3004*
23:30 And **s**, If we had been in the days of our *3004*
23:36 Verily I **s** unto you, All these *things* shall *3004*
23:39 For I **s** unto you, Ye shall not see me *3004*
23:39 shall not see me henceforth, till ye shall **s**, *3004*
24: 2 See ye not all these *things?* verily I **s** unto *3004*
24:23 Then if any *man* shall **s** unto you, Lo, *3004*
24:26 Wherefore if they shall **s** unto you, Behold, *3004*
24:34 Verily I **s** unto you, This generation shall *3004*
24:47 Verily I **s** unto you, That he shall make him *3004*
24:48 *and* if that evil servant shall **s** in his heart, *3004*
25:12 he answered and said, Verily I **s** unto you, *3004*
25:34 Then shall the King **s** unto them on his *3004*
25:40 And the King shall answer and **s** unto them, *3004*
25:40 and say unto them, Verily I **s** unto you, *3004*
25:41 Then shall he **s** also unto them on the left *3004*
25:45 answer them, saying, Verily I **s** unto you, *3004*
26:13 Verily I **s** unto you, Wheresoever this *3004*
26:18 and **s** unto him, The Master saith, My time *3004*
26:21 as they did eat, he said, Verily I **s** unto you, *3004*
26:22 and began every one of them to **s** unto him, *3004*
26:29 But I **s** unto you, I will not drink henceforth *3004*
26:34 Verily I **s** unto thee, That this night, *3004*
26:64 nevertheless I **s** unto you, Hereafter shall ye *3004*
27:22 *They* all **s** unto him, Let him be crucified. *3004*
27:33 that is to **s**, a place of a skull, *3004*
27:46 that is to **s**, My God, my God, why hast thou NIG
27:64 and steal him *away,* and **s** unto the people, *3004*
28:13 Saying, **S** ye, His disciples came by night, *3004*
Mk 1:44 See thou **s** nothing to any *man:* but go thy *3004*
2: 9 Whether is it easier to **s** to the sick of *3004*
2: 9 or to **s**, Arise, and take up thy bed, and *3004*
2:11 I **s** unto thee, Arise, and take up thy bed, *3004*
2:18 and they come and **s** unto him, Why do *3004*
3:28 Verily I **s** unto you, All sins shall be *3004*
4:38 they awake him, and **s** unto him, Master, *3004*
5:41 being interpreted, Damsel (I **s** unto thee) *3004*
6:11 Verily I **s** unto you, It shall be more *3004*
6:37 And they **s** unto him, Shall we go and *3004*
6:38 they knew, they **s**, Five, and two fishes. *3004*
7: 2 that is to **s**, with unwashen, hands, NIG
7:11 But ye **s**, If a man shall say to *his* father or *3004*
7:11 If a man shall **s** to *his* father or mother, *3004*
7:11 or mother, *It is* Corban, that is to **s**, a gift, NIG
8:12 verily I **s** unto you, There shall no sign be *3004*
8:19 took ye up? They **s** unto him, Twelve. *3004*
8:27 unto them, Whom do men **s** that I am? *3004*
8:28 but some *s,* Elias; and others, One of NIG
8:29 saith unto them, But whom **s** ye that I am? *3004*
9: 1 And he said unto them, Verily I **s** unto you, *3004*
9: 6 For he wist not what to **s**; for they were *2980*
9:11 Why **s** the scribes that Elias must first *3004*

Mk 9:13 But I **s** unto you, That Elias is indeed come, *3004*
9:41 ye belong to Christ, verily I **s** unto you, *3004*
10:15 Verily I **s** unto you, Whosoever shall not *3004*
10:28 Then Peter began to **s** unto him, Lo, *3004*
10:29 and said, Verily I **s** unto you, *3004*
10:47 and **s**, Jesus, *thou* Son of David, *3004*
11: 3 And if any *man* **s** unto you, Why do ye *3004*
11: 3 **s** ye that the Lord hath need of him; and *3004*
11:23 For verily I **s** unto you, That whosoever *3004*
11:23 That whosoever shall **s** unto this mountain, *3004*
11:24 Therefore I **s** unto you, What *things* soever *3004*
11:28 And **s** unto him, By what authority doest *3004*
11:31 saying, If we shall **s**, From heaven; *3004*
11:31 he will **s**, Why then did ye not believe *3004*
11:32 But if we shall **s**, Of men; they feared *3004*
12:14 they **s** unto him, Master, we know that thou *3004*
12:18 which **s** there is no resurrection; *3004*
12:35 How **s** the scribes that Christ is the Son of *3004*
12:43 and saith unto them, Verily I **s** unto you, *3004*
13: 5 And Jesus answering them began to **s**, *3004*
13:21 And then if any *man* shall **s** to you, Lo, *3004*
13:30 Verily I **s** unto you, that this generation *3004*
13:37 And what I **s** unto you I say unto all, *3004*
13:37 And what I say unto you I **s** unto all, *3004*
14: 9 Verily I **s** unto you, Wheresoever this *3004*
14:14 **s** ye to the goodman of the house, The *3004*
14:18 and did eat, Jesus said, Verily I **s** unto you, *3004*
14:19 and to **s** unto him one by one, *Is* it I? *3004*
14:25 Verily I **s** unto you, I will drink no more of *3004*
14:30 Verily I **s** unto thee, That this day, *even* in *3004*
14:58 We heard him **s**, I will destroy this temple *3004*
14:65 to buffet him, and to **s** unto him, Prophesy: *3004*
14:69 and began to **s** to them that stood by, This *3004*
Lk 3: 8 and begin not to **s** within yourselves, *3004*
3: 8 for I **s** unto you, That God is able of these *3004*
4:21 And he began to **s** unto them, This day is *3004*
4:23 Ye will surely **s** unto me this proverb, *3004*
4:24 And he said, Verily I **s** unto you, *3004*
5:23 Whether is easier, to **s**, Thy sins be *3004*
5:23 be forgiven thee; or to **s**, Rise up and walk? *3004*
5:24 I **s** unto thee, Arise, and take up thy couch, *3004*
6:27 But I **s** unto you which hear, Love your *3004*
6:42 Either how canst thou **s** to thy brother, *3004*
6:46 Lord, and do not *the things* which I **s**? *3004*
7: 7 but **s** in a word, and my servant shall be *3004*
7: 8 and I **s** unto one, Go, and he goeth; *3004*
7: 9 I **s** unto you, I have not found so great faith, *3004*
7:14 he said, Young man, I **s** unto thee, Arise. *3004*
7:26 I **s** unto you, and much more than a *3004*
7:28 For I **s** unto you, Among *those that are* born *3004*
7:33 drinking wine; and ye **s**, He hath a devil. *3004*
7:34 and ye **s**, Behold a gluttonous man, and *3004*
7:40 Simon, I have somewhat to **s** unto thee. *3004*
7:40 say unto thee. And he saith, Master, **s** *on*. *3004*
7:47 Wherefore I **s** unto thee, Her sins, *3004*
7:49 with *him* began to **s** within themselves, *3004*
9:18 saying, Whom **s** the people that I am? *3004*
9:19 but some *s*, Elias; and others *say*, that one of NIG
9:19 others **s**, that one of the old prophets is risen NIG
9:20 said unto them, But whom **s** ye that I am? *3004*
10: 5 ye enter, first **s**, Peace *be* to this house. *3004*
10: 9 the sick that are therein, and **s** unto them, *3004*
10:10 *ways* out into the streets of the same, and **s**, *3004*
10:12 But I **s** unto you, that it shall be more *3004*
11: 2 And he said unto them, When ye pray, **s**, *3004*
11: 5 and **s** unto him, Friend, lend me three *3004*
11: 7 And he from within shall answer and **s**, *3004*
11: 8 I **s** unto you, Though he will not rise and *3004*
11: 9 And I **s** unto you, Ask, and it shall be given *3004*
11:18 ye **s** that I cast out devils through *3004*
11:29 he began to **s**, This is an evil generation: *3004*
11:51 verily I **s** unto you, It shall be required of *3004*
12: 1 he began to **s** unto his disciples first *of all*, *3004*
12: 4 And I **s** unto you my friends, Be not afraid *3004*
12: 5 cast into hell; yea, I **s** unto you, Fear him. *3004*
12: 8 Also I **s** unto you, Whosoever shall confess *3004*
12:11 *thing* ye shall answer, or what ye shall **s**: *3004*
12:12 you in the same hour what ye ought to **s**. *3004*
12:19 And I will **s** to my soul, Soul, thou hast *3004*
12:22 Therefore I **s** unto you, Take no thought for *3004*
12:27 and yet I **s** unto you, *that* Solomon in all his *3004*
12:37 verily I **s** unto you, that he shall gird *3004*
12:44 Of a truth I **s** unto you, that he will make *3004*
12:45 But and if that servant **s** in his heart, *3004*
12:54 straightway ye **s**, There cometh a shower; *3004*
12:55 south wind blow, ye **s**, There will be heat; *3004*
13:24 for many, I **s** unto you, will seek to enter in, *3004*
13:25 and he shall answer and **s** unto you, I know *3004*
13:26 Then shall ye begin to **s**, We have eaten *3004*
13:27 But he shall **s**, I tell you, I know you not *3004*
13:35 and verily I **s** unto you, Ye shall not see *3004*
13:35 until *the time* come when ye shall **s**, *3004*
14: 9 that bade thee and him come and **s** to thee, *3004*
14:10 he may **s** unto thee, Friend, go up higher: *3004*
14:17 And sent his servant at supper time to **s** to *3004*
14:24 For I **s** unto you, That none of those men *3004*
15: 7 I **s** unto you, that likewise joy shall be in *3004*
15:10 Likewise, I **s** unto you, there is joy in *3004*
15:18 to my father, and will **s** unto him, Father, *3004*
16: 9 And I **s** unto you, Make to yourselves *3004*
17: 6 ye might **s** unto this sycamine tree, Be thou *3004*
17: 7 or feeding cattle, will **s** *unto him* by and by, *3004*
17: 8 And will not *rather* **s** unto him, Make ready *3004*
17:10 **s**, We are unprofitable servants: *3004*
17:21 Neither shall they **s**, Lo here: or, lo there: *3004*
17:23 And they shall **s** to you, See here; or, *3004*
18:17 Verily I **s** unto you, Whosoever shall not *3004*
18:29 And he said unto them, Verily I **s** unto you, *3004*
19:26 For I **s** unto you, That unto every one *3004*
19:31 Why do ye loose *him?* thus shall ye **s** unto *3004*
20: 5 saying, If we shall **s**, From heaven; *3004*
20: 5 he will **s**, Why then believed ye him not? *3004*
20: 6 But *and* if we **s**, Of men; all the people will *3004*
20:41 How **s** they that Christ is David's son? *3004*
21: 3 And he said, Of a truth I **s** unto you, *3004*
Lk 21:32 Verily I **s** unto you, This generation shall *3004*
22:11 And ye shall **s** unto the goodman of the *3004*
22:16 For I **s** unto you, I will not any more eat *3004*
22:18 For I **s** unto you, I will not drink of the fruit *3004*
22:37 For I **s** unto you, that this that is written *3004*
22:70 And he said unto them, Ye **s** that I am. *3004*
23:29 days are coming, in the which they shall **s**, *3004*
23:30 Then shall they begin to **s** to the mountains, *3004*
23:43 Jesus said unto him, Verily I **s** unto thee, *3004*
Jn 1:38 Rabbi, (which is to **s**, being interpreted, *3004*
1:51 saith unto him, Verily, verily, I **s** unto you, *3004*
3: 3 said unto him, Verily, verily, I **s** unto thee, *3004*
3: 5 Verily, verily, I **s** unto thee, *3004*
3:11 Verily, verily, I **s** unto thee, We speak that *3004*
4:20 and ye **s**, that in Jerusalem is the place *3004*
4:35 **S** not ye, There are yet four months, and *3004*
4:35 behold, I **s** unto you, Lift up your eyes, and *3004*
5:19 said unto them, Verily, verily, I **s** unto you, *3004*
5:24 Verily, verily, I **s** unto you, He that heareth *3004*
5:25 Verily, verily, I **s** unto you, The hour is *3004*
5:34 but these *things* I **s**, that ye might be saved. *3004*
6:26 and said, Verily, verily, I **s** unto you, *3004*
6:32 said unto them, Verily, verily, I **s** unto you, *3004*
6:47 Verily, verily, I **s** unto you, He that *3004*
6:53 said unto them, Verily, verily, I **s** unto you, *3004*
7:26 and they **s** nothing unto him. *3004*
8: 4 They **s** unto him, Master, this woman was *3004*
8:26 I have many *things* to **s** and to judge of *2980*
8:34 answered them, Verily, verily, I **s** unto you, *3004*
8:46 And if I **s** the truth, why do ye not believe *3004*
8:48 **S** we not well that thou art a Samaritan, and *3004*
8:51 Verily, verily, I **s** unto you, If a man keep *3004*
8:54 of whom ye **s**, that he is your God: *3004*
8:55 and if I should **s**, I know him not, I shall be *3004*
8:58 said unto them, Verily, verily, I **s** unto you, *3004*
9:17 They **s** unto the blind man again, *3004*
9:19 Is this your son, who ye **s** was born blind? *3004*
9:41 but now ye **s**, We see; therefore your sin *3004*
10: 1 Verily, verily, I **s** unto you, He that entereth *3004*
10: 7 Verily, verily, I **s** unto you, I am the door of *3004*
10:36 **S** ye *of him*, whom the Father hath *3004*
11: 8 *His* disciples **s** unto him, Master, the Jews *3004*
11:34 They **s** unto him, Lord, come and see. *3004*
12:24 Verily, verily, I **s** unto you, Except a corn *3004*
12:27 is my soul troubled; and what shall I **s**? *3004*
12:49 what I should **s**, and what I should speak. *3004*
13:13 and Lord: and ye **s** well; for *so* I am. *3004*
13:16 Verily, verily, I **s** unto you, The servant is *3004*
13:20 Verily, verily, I **s** unto you, He that *3004*
13:21 and said, Verily, verily, I **s** unto you, *3004*
13:33 I go, ye cannot come; so now I **s** to you. *3004*
13:38 Verily, verily, I **s** unto thee, *The* cock shall *3004*
14:12 Verily, verily, I **s** unto you, He that *3004*
16:12 I have yet many *things* to **s** unto you, but *3004*
16:20 Verily, verily, I **s** unto you, That ye shall *3004*
16:23 Verily, verily, I **s** unto you, Whatsoever ye *3004*
16:26 and I **s** not unto you, that I will pray *3004*
20:13 And they **s** unto her, Woman, why weepest *3004*
20:16 unto him, Rabboni; which is to **s**, Master. *3004*
20:17 but go to my brethren, and **s** unto them, *3004*
21: 3 They **s** unto him, We also go with thee. *3004*
21:18 Verily, verily, I **s** unto thee, When thou *3004*
Ac 1:19 Aceldama, that is to **s**, The field of blood. NIG
3:22 in all *things* whatsoever he shall **s** unto you. *2980*
4:14 with them, they could **s** nothing **against** *it*. *471*
5:38 And now I **s** unto you, Refrain from these *3004*
6:14 For we have heard him **s**, that this Jesus of *3004*
10:37 *That* word, *I s*, you know, which was NIG
13:15 word of exhortation for the people, **s** *on*. *3004*
17:18 And some said, What will this babbler **s**? *3004*
21:23 Do therefore this that we **s** to thee: We have *3004*
23: 8 For the Sadducees **s** that there is no *3004*
23:18 who hath something to **s** unto thee. *2980*
23:30 to **s** before thee what *they had* against him. *3004*
24:20 Or else let these same *here* **s**, if they have *3004*
26:22 the prophets and Moses did **s** should come: *2980*
28:26 Saying, Go unto this people, and **s**, *3004*
Ro 3: 5 the righteousness of God, what shall we **s**? *3004*
3: 8 and as some affirm that we **s**,) *3004*
3:26 *I s*, at this time his righteousness: NIG
4: 1 What shall we **s** then that Abraham our *3004*
4: 9 for we **s** that faith was reckoned to *3004*
6: 1 What shall we **s** then? Shall we continue in *3004*
7: 7 What shall we **s** then? *Is* the law sin? *3004*
8:31 then **s** to these *things?* If God *be* for us, *3004*
9: 1 I **s** the truth in Christ, I lie not, *3004*
9:14 What shall we **s** then? *Is there* *3004*
9:19 Thou wilt **s** then unto me, Why doth he yet *3004*
9:20 Shall the thing formed **s** to him that formed *3004*
9:30 What shall we **s** then? That the Gentiles, *3004*
10: 6 **S** not in thine heart, Who shall ascend into *3004*
10:18 But I **s**, Have they not heard? Yes verily, *3004*
10:19 But I **s**, Did not Israel know? First Moses *3004*
11: 1 I **s** then, Hath God cast away his people? *3004*
11:11 I **s** then, Have they stumbled that they *3004*
11:19 Thou wilt **s** then, The branches were *3004*
12: 3 For I **s**, through the grace given unto me, *3004*
15: 8 Now I **s** that Jesus Christ was a minister of *3004*
1Co 1:12 Now this I **s**, that every one of you saith, I *3004*
1:15 Lest any should **s** that I had baptized in *3004*
7: 8 I **s** therefore to the unmarried and widows, *3004*
7:26 *I s*, that *it is* good for a man so to be. NIG
7:29 But this I **s**, brethren, the time *is* short: *5346*
9: 8 **S** I these *things* as a man? or saith not *2980*
10:15 I speak as to wise *men;* judge ye what I **s**. *5346*
10:19 What **s** I then? that the idol is any *thing*, or *5346*
10:20 But *I s*, that *the things* which the Gentiles NIG
10:28 But if any *man* **s** unto you, This is offered *3004*
10:29 Conscience, I **s**, not thine own, but of *3004*
11:22 What shall I **s** to you? shall I praise you in *3004*
12: 3 *that* no *man* can **s** that Jesus is the Lord, *3004*
12:15 If the foot shall **s**, Because I am not *3004*
12:16 And if the ear shall **s**, Because I am not *3004*
12:21 And the eye cannot **s** unto the hand, I have *3004*
14:16 unlearned **s** Amen at thy giving of thanks, *3004*
1Co 14:23 will they not **s** that ye are mad? *3004*
15:12 how **s** some among you that there is no *3004*
15:35 But some *man* will **s**, How are the dead *3004*
15:50 Now this I **s**, brethren, that flesh and *5346*
2Co 5: 8 I **s**, and willing rather to be absent from NIG
9: 4 you unprepared, we (that we **s** not, you) *3004*
9: 6 But this *I s*, He which soweth sparingly NIG
10:10 **s** they, *are* weighty and powerful; *5346*
11:16 I **s** again, Let no *man* think me a fool; *3004*
12: 6 I shall not be a fool; for I will **s** the truth: *3004*
Gal 1: 9 As we said before, so **s** I now again, If any *3004*
3:17 And this I **s**, *that* the covenant, that was *3004*
4: 1 Now I **s**, *That* the heir, as long as he is a *3004*
5: 2 Behold, I Paul **s** unto you, that if ye be *3004*
5:16 *This* I **s** then, Walk in the Spirit, and *3004*
Eph 4:17 This I **s** therefore, and testify in the Lord, *3004*
Php 4: 4 in the Lord alway: *and* again I **s**, Rejoice. *3004*
Col 1:20 *I s*, whether *they be things* in earth, or NIG
2: 4 And this I **s**, lest any *man* should beguile *3004*
4:17 And **s** to Archippus, Take heed to *3004*
1Th 4:15 For this we **s** unto you by the word of *3004*
5: 3 For when they shall **s**, Peace and safety; *3004*
1Ti 1: 7 understanding neither what they **s**, *3004*
2Ti 2: 7 Consider what I **s**; and the Lord give thee *3004*
Tit 2: 8 having no evil *thing* to **s** of you. *3004*
Phm 1:19 I will repay *it:* albeit I do not **s** to thee how *3004*
1:21 that thou wilt also do more than I **s**. *3004*
Heb 5:11 Of whom we have many things to **s**, and *3056*
7: 9 And as *I* may so **s**, Levi also, who receiveth *3004*
9:11 with hands, that is to **s**, not of this building, NIG
10:20 through the vail, that is to **s**, his flesh; NIG
11:14 For they that **s** such *things* declare plainly *3004*
11:32 And what shall I more **s**? for the time *3004*
13: 6 So that we may boldly **s**, The Lord *is* my *3004*
Jas 1:13 Let no *man* **s** when he is tempted, I am *3004*
2: 3 and **s** unto him, Sit thou here in a good *3004*
2: 3 and **s** to the poor, Stand thou there, or *3004*
2:14 though a man **s** *he* hath faith, and have not *3004*
2:16 And one of you **s** unto them, Depart in *3004*
2:18 Yea, a man may **s**, Thou hast faith, and I *3004*
4:13 ye that **s**, To day or to morrow we will go *3004*
4:15 For that ye *ought* to **s**, If the Lord will, *3004*
1Jn 1: 6 If we **s** that we have fellowship with him, *3004*
1: 8 If we **s** that we have no sin, we deceive *3004*
1:10 If we **s** that we have not sinned, we make *3004*
4:20 If a man **s**, I love God, and hateth his *3004*
5:16 I do not **s** that he shall pray for it. *3004*
Rev 2: 2 thou hast tried them which **s** *they* are *5335*
2: 9 *I know* the blasphemy of them which **s** they *3004*
2:24 But unto you I **s**, and unto the rest in *3004*
3: 9 which **s** they are Jews, and are not, but *3004*
6: 3 I heard the second beast **s**, Come and see. *3004*
6: 5 I heard the third beast **s**, Come and see. *3004*
6: 6 a voice in the midst of the four beasts **s**, *3004*
6: 7 I heard the voice of the fourth beast **s**, *3004*
16: 5 And I heard the angel of the waters **s**, *3004*
16: 7 And I heard another out of the altar **s**, *3004*
22:17 And the Spirit and the bride **s**, Come. *3004*
22:17 And let him that heareth **s**, Come. And let *3004*

SAYEST (40) [SAY]

Ex 33:12 See, thou **s** unto me, Bring up this people: 559
Nu 22:17 I will do whatsoever thou **s** unto me: 559
Ru 3: 5 unto her, All that thou **s** unto me I will do. 559
1Ki 18:11 now thou **s**, Go, tell thy lord, Behold, 559
18:14 now thou **s**, Go, tell thy lord, Behold, 559
2Ki 18:20 Thou **s**, (but *they are but* vain words,) *I have* 559
2Ch 25:19 Thou **s**, Lo, thou hast smitten the Edomites; 559
Ne 5:12 nothing of them; so will we do as thou **s**. 559
6: 8 There are no such things *done* as thou **s**, but 559
Job 22:13 thou **s**, How doth God know? can he judge 559
35:14 Although thou **s** thou shalt not see him, 559
Ps 90: 3 and **s**, Return, ye children of men. 559
Pr 24:12 If thou **s**, Behold, we knew it not; doth not 559
Isa 36: 5 I say, *s thou*, (but *they are but* vain words) NIH
40:27 Why **s** thou, O Jacob, and speakest, O Israel, 559
47: 8 that **s** in thine heart, I *am*, and none else 559
Jer 2:35 Yet thou **s**, Because I am innocent, surely his 559
2:35 with thee, because thou **s**, I have not sinned. 559
Am 7:16 Thou **s**, Prophesy not against Israel, and 559
Mt 26:70 *them* all, saying, I know not what thou **s**. *3004*
27:11 the Jews? And Jesus said unto him, Thou **s**. *3004*
Mk 5:31 and **s** thou, Who touched me? *3004*
14:68 know not, neither understand I what thou **s**. *3004*
15: 2 And he answering said unto him, Thou **s** *it*. *3004*
Lk 8:45 throng thee and press *thee*, and **s** thou, *3004*
20:21 we know that thou **s** and teachest rightly, *3004*
22:60 Peter said, Man, I know not what thou **s**. *3004*
23: 3 And he answered him and said, Thou **s** *it*. *3004*
Jn 1:22 them that sent us. What **s** thou of thyself? *3004*
8: 5 such should be stoned: but what **s** thou? *3004*
8:33 were never in bondage to any *man:* how **s** *3004*
8:52 and thou **s**, If a man keep my saying, *3004*
9:17 What **s** thou of him, that he hath opened *3004*
12:34 and how **s** thou, The Son of man must be *3004*
14: 9 and how **s** thou *then*, Shew us the Father? *3004*
18:34 answered him, **S** thou this *thing* of thyself, *3004*
18:37 Jesus answered, Thou **s** that I am a king. *3004*
Ro 2:22 Thou that **s** *a man* should not commit *3004*
1Co 14:16 seeing he understandeth not what thou **s**? *3004*
Rev 3:17 Because thou **s**, I am rich, and *3004*

SAYING (1445) [SAY]

Ge 1:22 **s**, Be fruitful, and multiply, and fill 559
2:16 the LORD God commanded the man, **s**, 559
3:17 commanded thee, **s**, Thou shalt not eat of it: 559
5:29 he called his name Noah, **s**, This *same* shall 559
8:15 And God spake unto Noah, **s**, 559
9: 8 unto Noah, and to his sons with him, **s**, 559
15: 1 unto Abram in a vision, **s**, Fear not, Abram: 559
15: 4 unto him, **s**, This shall not be thine heir; 559
15:18 **s**, Unto thy seed have I given this land, from 559
17: 3 fell on his face: and God talked with him, **s**, 559
18:12 Therefore Sarah laughed within herself, **s**, 559
18:13 Wherefore did Sarah laugh, **s**, 559

S

Ge 18:15 Sarah denied, **s**, I laughed not; for she was 559
19:15 **s**, Arise, take thy wife, and thy two 559
21:22 **s**, God *is* with thee in all that thou doest: 559
22:20 that it was told Abraham, **s**, Behold, Milcah, 559
23: 3 his dead, and spake unto the sons of Heth, **s**, 559
23: 5 of Heth answered Abraham, **s** unto him, 559
23: 8 he communed with them, **s**, If it be your 559
23:10 of all that went in *at* the gate of his city, **s**, 559
23:13 **s**, But if thou *wilt give it*, I pray thee, 559
23:14 And Ephron answered Abraham, **s** unto him, 559
24: 7 spake unto me, and that sware unto me, **s**, 559
24:30 his sister, **s**, Thus spake the man unto me; 559
24:37 my master made me swear, **s**, Thou shalt not 559
26:11 **s**, He that toucheth this man or his wife shall 559
26:20 with Isaac's herdmen, **s**, The water *is* ours: 559
27: 6 spake unto Jacob her son, **s**, Behold, 559
27: 6 thy father speak unto Esau thy brother, **s**, 559
28: 6 as he blessed him he gave him a charge, **s**, 559
28:20 **s**, If God will be with me, and will keep me 559
31: 1 he heard the words of Laban's sons, **s**, 559
31:11 of God spake unto me in a dream, *s*, Jacob: NIH
31:29 of your father spake unto me yesternight, **s**, 559
32: 4 he commanded them, **s**, Thus shall ye speak 559
32: 6 **s**, We came to thy brother Esau, and also he 559
32:17 he commanded the foremost, **s**, When Esau 559
32:17 and asketh thee, **s**, Whose *art* thou? 559
32:19 the third, and all that followed the droves, **s**, 559
34: 4 father Hamor, **s**, Get me this damsel to wife. 559
34: 8 Hamor communed with them, **s**, The soul of 559
34:20 and communed with the men of their city, **s**, 559
37:11 envied him; but his father observed the **s**. 1697
37:15 the man asked him, **s**, What seekest thou? 559
38:13 it was told Tamar, **s**, Behold thy father in 559
38:21 **s**, Where *is* the harlot, that *was* openly by 559
38:24 three months after, that it was told Judah, **s**, 559
38:25 she sent to her father in law, **s**, By the man, 559
38:28 hand a scarlet thread, **s**, This came out first. 559
39:12 caught him by his garment, **s**, Lie with me: 559
39:14 of her house, and spake unto them, **s**, See, 559
39:17 **s**, The Hebrew servant, which thou hast 559
39:19 which she spake unto him, **s**, After this 559
40: 7 **s**, Wherefore look ye *so* sadly to day? 559
41: 9 **s**, I do remember my faults *this* day: 559
41:16 Joseph answered Pharaoh, **s**, *It is* not in me: 559
42:14 *is it* that I spake unto you, **s**, Ye *are* spies: 559
42:22 **s**, Spake I not unto you, saying, Do not sin 559
42:22 saying, Spake I not unto you, **s**, Do not sin 559
42:28 and they were afraid, **s** one to another, 559
42:29 and told him all that befell unto them; **s**, 559
42:37 **s**, Slay my two sons, if I bring him not to 559
43: 3 Judah spake unto him, **s**, The man did 559
43: 3 **s**, Ye shall not see my face, except your 559
43: 7 of our kindred, **s**, *Is* your father yet alive? 559
44: 1 **s**, Fill the men's sacks *with* food, as much as 559
44:19 **s**, Have ye a father, or a brother? 559
44:32 **s**, If I bring him not unto thee, then I shall 559
45:16 **s**, Joseph's brethren are come: 559
45:26 told him, **s**, Joseph *is* yet alive, and he *is* 559
47: 5 **s**, Thy father and thy brethren are come unto 559
48:20 **s**, In thee shall Israel bless, saying, 559
48:20 saying, In thee shall Israel bless, **s**, 559
50: 4 **s**, If now I have found grace in your eyes, 559
50: 4 speak, I pray you, in the ears of Pharaoh, **s**, 559
50: 5 My father made me swear, **s**, Lo, I die: in my 559
50:16 they sent a messenger unto Joseph, **s**, 559
50:16 Thy father did command before he died, **s**, 559
50:25 **s**, God will surely visit you, and ye shall 559
Ex 1:22 Pharaoh charged all his people, **s**, Every son 559
3:16 of Isaac, and of Jacob, appeared unto me, **s**, 559
5: 6 of the people, and their officers, **s**, 559
5: 8 therefore they cry, **s**, Let us go *and* 559
5:10 spake to the people, **s**, Thus saith Pharaoh, 559
5:13 the taskmasters hasted *them*, **s**, Fulfil your 559
5:15 of Israel came and cried unto Pharaoh, **s**, 559
6:10 And the LORD spake unto Moses, **s**, 559
6:12 Moses spake before the LORD, **s**, Behold, 559
6:29 spake unto Moses, **s**, I *am* the LORD: 559
7: 8 spake unto Moses and unto Aaron, **s**, 559
7: 9 speak unto you, **s**, Shew a miracle for you: 559
7:16 **s**, Let my people go, that they may serve me 559
9: 5 the LORD appointed a set time, **s**, 559
11: 8 **s**, Get thee out, and all the people that follow 559
12: 1 and Aaron in the land of Egypt, **s**, 559
12: 3 ye unto all the congregation of Israel, **s**, 559
13: 1 And the LORD spake unto Moses, **s**, 559
13: 8 **s**, *This is done* because of that *which* 559
13:14 asketh thee in time to come, **s**, What *is* this? 559
13:19 of Israel, **s**, God will surely visit you; 559
14: 1 And the LORD spake unto Moses, **s**, 559
14:12 **s**, Let us alone, that we may serve 559
15: 1 spake, **s**, I will sing unto the LORD, for he 559
15:24 against Moses, **s**, What shall we drink? 559
16:11 And the LORD spake unto Moses, **s**, 559
16:12 speak unto them, **s**, At even ye shall eat 559
17: 4 **s**, What shall I do unto this people? 559
17: 7 because they tempted the LORD, **s**, Is 559
19: 3 **s**, Thus shalt thou say to the house of Jacob, 559
19:12 **s**, Take heed to yourselves, *that ye* go *not* up 559
19:23 for thou chargedst us, **s**, Set bounds about 559
20: 1 And God spake all these words, **s**, 559
25: 1 And the LORD spake unto Moses, **s**, 559
30:11 And the LORD spake unto Moses, **s**, 559
30:17 And the LORD spake unto Moses, **s**, 559
30:22 Moreover the LORD spake unto Moses, **s**, 559
30:31 shalt speak unto the children of Israel, **s**, 559
31: 1 And the LORD spake unto Moses, **s**, 559
31:12 And the LORD spake unto Moses, **s**, 559
31:13 **s**, Verily my sabbaths ye shall keep: 559
33: 1 to Isaac, and to Jacob, **s**, Unto thy seed will I 559
35: 4 **s**, This *is* the thing which the LORD 559
35: 4 the thing which the LORD commanded, **s**, 559
36: 5 they spake unto Moses, **s**, The people bring 559
36: 6 it to be proclaimed throughout the camp, **s**, 559
40: 1 And the LORD spake unto Moses, **s**, 559
Lev 1: 1 out of the tabernacle of the congregation, **s**, 559

Lev 4: 1 And the LORD spake unto Moses, **s**, 559
4: 2 Speak unto the children of Israel, **s**, If a soul 559
5:14 And the LORD spake unto Moses, **s**, 559
6: 1 And the LORD spake unto Moses, **s**, 559
6: 8 And the LORD spake unto Moses, **s**, 559
6: 9 Command Aaron and his sons, **s**, This *is* 559
6:19 And the LORD spake unto Moses, **s**, 559
6:24 And the LORD spake unto Moses, **s**, 559
6:25 Speak unto Aaron and to his sons, **s**, This *is* 559
7:22 And the LORD spake unto Moses, **s**, 559
7:23 **s**, Ye shall eat no *manner* fat, of ox, or 559
7:28 And the LORD spake unto Moses, **s**, 559
7:29 Speak unto the children of Israel, **s**, He that 559
8: 1 And the LORD spake unto Moses, **s**, 559
8:31 **s**, Aaron and his sons shall eat it. 559
9: 3 **s**, Take ye a kid of the goats for a sin 559
10: 3 This *is it* that the LORD spake, **s**, 559
10: 8 And the LORD spake unto Aaron, **s**, 559
10:16 the sons of Aaron which were left *alive*, **s**, 559
11: 1 spake unto Moses and to Aaron, **s** unto them, 559
11: 2 Speak unto the children of Israel, **s**, 559
12: 1 And the LORD spake unto Moses, **s**, 559
12: 2 **s**, If a woman have conceived seed, and 559
13: 1 the LORD spake unto Moses and Aaron, **s**, 559
14: 1 And the LORD spake unto Moses, **s**, 559
14:33 spake unto Moses and unto Aaron, **s**, 559
14:35 the house shall come and tell the priest, **s**, 559
15: 1 LORD spake unto Moses and to Aaron, **s**, 559
17: 1 And the LORD spake unto Moses, **s**, 559
17: 2 thing which the LORD hath commanded, **s**, 559
18: 1 And the LORD spake unto Moses, **s**, 559
19: 1 And the LORD spake unto Moses, **s**, 559
20: 1 And the LORD spake unto Moses, **s**, 559
21:16 And the LORD spake unto Moses, **s**, 559
21:17 Speak unto Aaron, **s**, Whosoever *he be* of 559
22: 1 And the LORD spake unto Moses, **s**, 559
22:17 And the LORD spake unto Moses, **s**, 559
22:26 And the LORD spake unto Moses, **s**, 559
23: 1 And the LORD spake unto Moses, **s**, 559
23: 9 And the LORD spake unto Moses, **s**, 559
23:23 And the LORD spake unto Moses, **s**, 559
23:24 **s**, In the seventh month, in the first *day* of 559
23:26 And the LORD spake unto Moses, **s**, 559
23:33 And the LORD spake unto Moses, **s**, 559
23:34 Speak unto the children of Israel, **s**, The 559
24: 1 And the LORD spake unto Moses, **s**, 559
24:13 And the LORD spake unto Moses, **s**, 559
24:15 **s**, Whosoever curseth his God shall bear his 559
25: 1 LORD spake unto Moses in mount Sinai, **s**, 559
27: 1 And the LORD spake unto Moses, **s**, 559
Nu 1: 1 they were come out of the land of Egypt, **s**, 559
1:48 For the LORD had spoken unto Moses, **s**, 559
2: 1 spake unto Moses and unto Aaron, **s**, 559
3: 5 And the LORD spake unto Moses, **s**, 559
3:11 And the LORD spake unto Moses, **s**, 559
3:14 unto Moses in the wilderness of Sinai, **s**, 559
3:44 And the LORD spake unto Moses, **s**, 559
4: 1 spake unto Moses and unto Aaron, **s**, 559
4:17 spake unto Moses and unto Aaron, **s**, 559
4:21 And the LORD spake unto Moses, **s**, 559
5: 1 And the LORD spake unto Moses, **s**, 559
5: 5 And the LORD spake unto Moses, **s**, 559
5:11 And the LORD spake unto Moses, **s**, 559
6: 1 And the LORD spake unto Moses, **s**, 559
6:22 And the LORD spake unto Moses, **s**, 559
6:23 Speak unto Aaron and unto his sons, **s**, 559
6:23 bless the children of Israel, **s** unto them, 559
7: 4 And the LORD spake unto Moses, **s**, 559
8: 1 And the LORD spake unto Moses, **s**, 559
8: 5 And the LORD spake unto Moses, **s**, 559
8:23 And the LORD spake unto Moses, **s**, 559
9: 1 they were come out of the land of Egypt, **s**, 559
9: 9 And the LORD spake unto Moses, **s**, 559
9:10 **s**, If any man of you or of your posterity 559
10: 1 And the LORD spake unto Moses, **s**, 559
11:13 unto me, **s**, Give us flesh, that we may eat. 559
11:18 **s**, Who shall give us flesh to eat? 559
11:20 have wept before him, **s**, Why came we forth 559
12:13 **s**, Heal her now, O God, I beseech thee. 559
13: 1 And the LORD spake unto Moses, **s**, 559
13:32 **s**, The land, through which we have gone to 559
14: 7 **s**, The land, which we passed through to 559
14:15 have heard the fame of thee will speak, **s**, 559
14:17 be great, according as thou hast spoken, **s**, 559
14:26 spake unto Moses and unto Aaron, **s**, 559
14:40 **s**, Lo, we *be here*, and will go up unto 559
15: 1 And the LORD spake unto Moses, **s**, 559
15:17 And the LORD spake unto Moses, **s**, 559
15:37 And the LORD spake unto Moses, **s**, 559
16: 5 unto Korah and unto all his company, **s**, 559
16:20 spake unto Moses and unto Aaron, **s**, 559
16:23 And the LORD spake unto Moses, **s**, 559
16:24 Speak unto the congregation, **s**, Get you up 559
16:26 **s**, Depart, I pray you, from the tents of these 559
16:36 And the LORD spake unto Moses, **s**, 559
16:41 against Moses and against Aaron, **s**, 559
16:44 And the LORD spake unto Moses, **s**, 559
17: 1 And the LORD spake unto Moses, **s**, 559
17:12 **s**, Behold, we die, we perish, we all perish. 559
18:25 And the LORD spake unto Moses, **s**, 559
19: 1 spake unto Moses and unto Aaron, **s**, 559
19: 2 **s**, Speak unto the children of Israel, that they 559
20: 3 the people chode with Moses, and spake, **s**, 559
20: 7 And the LORD spake unto Moses, **s**, 559
20:23 by the coast of the land of Edom, **s**, 559
21:21 unto Sihon king of the Amorites, **s**, 559
22: 5 to call him, **s**, Behold, there is a people come 559
22:10 king of Moab, hath sent unto me, *s*, NIH
23: 7 *s*, Come, curse me Jacob, and come, NIH
23:26 and said unto Balak, Told not I thee, **s**, 559
24:12 messengers which thou sentest unto me, **s**, 559
25:10 And the LORD spake unto Moses, **s**, 559
25:16 And the LORD spake unto Moses, **s**, 559
26: 1 unto Eleazar the son of Aaron the priest, **s**, 559
26: 3 the plains of Moab by Jordan *near* Jericho, **s**, 559

Nu 26:52 And the LORD spake unto Moses, **s**, 559
27: 2 door of the tabernacle of the congregation, **s**, 559
27: 6 And the LORD spake unto Moses, **s**, 559
27: 8 **s**, If a man die, and have no son, then 559
27:15 And Moses spake unto the LORD, **s**, 559
28: 1 And the LORD spake unto Moses, **s**, 559
30: 1 **s**, This *is* the thing which the LORD hath 559
31: 1 And the LORD spake unto Moses, **s**, 559
31: 3 Moses spake unto the people, **s**, Arm some 559
31:25 And the LORD spake unto Moses, **s**, 559
32: 2 and unto the princes of the congregation, **s**, 559
32:10 was kindled the same time, and he sware, **s**, 559
32:25 the children of Reuben spake unto Moses, **s**, 559
32:31 and the children of Reuben answered, **s**, 559
33:50 the plains of Moab by Jordan *near* Jericho, **s**, 559
34: 1 And the LORD spake unto Moses, **s**, 559
34:13 **s**, This *is* the land which ye shall inherit by 559
34:16 And the LORD spake unto Moses, **s**, 559
35: 1 the plains of Moab by Jordan *near* Jericho, **s**, 559
35: 9 And the LORD spake unto Moses, **s**, 559
36: 5 **s**, The tribe of the sons of Joseph hath said 559
36: 6 **s**, Let them marry to whom they think best; 559
Dt 1: 5 of Moab, began Moses to declare this law, **s**, 559
1: 6 **s**, Ye have dwelt long enough in this mount: 559
1: 9 I spake unto you at that time, **s**, I am not able 559
1:16 I charged your judges at that time, **s**, 559
1:23 the **s** pleased me well: and I took twelve 1697
1:28 **s**, The people *is* greater and taller than we; 559
1:34 of your words, and was wroth, and sware, **s**, 559
1:37 **s**, Thou also shalt not go in thither. 559
2: 2 And the LORD spake unto me, **s**, 559
2: 4 command thou the people, **s**, Ye are to pass 559
2:17 That the LORD spake unto me, **s**, 559
2:26 king of Heshbon *with* words of peace, **s**, 559
3:18 I commanded you at that time, **s**, 559
3:21 I commanded Joshua at that time, **s**, 559
3:23 And I besought the LORD at that time, **s**, 559
5: 5 the fire, and went not up into the mount;) **s**, 559
6:20 **s**, What *mean* the testimonies, and 559
9: 4 God hath cast them out from before thee, **s**, 559
9:13 **s**, I have seen this people, and behold, it *is* a 559
9:23 **s**, Go up and possess the land which I have 559
12:30 that thou inquire not after their gods, **s**, 559
13: 2 **s**, Let us go after other gods, which thou hast 559
13: 6 **s**, Let us go and serve other gods, 559
13:12 thy God hath given thee to dwell there, **s**, 559
13:13 **s**, Let us go and serve other gods, which ye 559
15: 9 **s**, The seventh year, the year of release, is at 559
15:11 therefore I command thee, **s**, Thou shalt 559
18:16 **s**, Let me not hear again the voice of 559
19: 7 Wherefore I command thee, **s**, Thou shalt 559
20: 5 the officers shall speak unto the people, **s**, 559
22:17 given occasions of speech *against her*, **s**, 559
27: 1 the elders of Israel commanded the people, **s**, 559
27: 9 **s**, Take heed, and hearken, O Israel; 559
27:11 Moses charged the people the same day, **s**, 559
29:19 himself in his heart, **s**, I shall have peace, 559
31:10 Moses commanded them, **s**, At the end of 559
31:25 the ark of the covenant of the LORD, **s**, 559
32:48 spake unto Moses that selfsame day, **s**, 559
34: 4 unto Isaac, and unto Jacob, **s**, I will give it 559
Jos 1: 1 Joshua the son of Nun, Moses' minister, **s**, 559
1:10 commanded the officers of the people, **s**, 559
1:11 the people, **s**, Prepare you victuals; 559
1:12 half the tribe of Manasseh, spake Joshua, **s**, 559
1:13 **s**, The LORD your God hath given you 559
1:16 they answered Joshua, **s**, All that thou 559
2: 1 **s**, Go view the land, even Jericho. 559
2: 2 it was told the king of Jericho, **s**, Behold, 559
2: 3 the king of Jericho sent unto Rahab, **s**, 559
3: 3 they commanded the people, **s**, When ye see 559
3: 6 **s**, Take up the ark of the covenant, and 559
3: 8 **s**, When ye are come to the brink of 559
4: 1 that the LORD spake unto Joshua, **s**, 559
4: 3 command you them, **s**, Take you hence out 559
4: 6 to come, **s**, What mean you by these stones? 559
4:15 And the LORD spake unto Joshua, **s**, 559
4:17 Joshua therefore commanded the priests, **s**, 559
4:21 he spake unto the children of Israel, **s**, 559
4:21 in time to come, **s**, What *mean* these stones? 559
4:22 ye shall let your children know, **s**, 559
6:10 **s**, Ye shall not shout, nor make any noise 559
6:26 Joshua adjured *them* at that time, **s**, 559
7: 2 unto them, **s**, Go up and view the country. 559
8: 4 he commanded them, **s**, Behold, ye shall lie 559
9:11 **s**, Take victuals with you for the journey, 559
9:22 called for them, and he spake unto them, **s**, 559
9:22 ye beguiled us, **s**, We *are* very far from you; 559
10: 3 of Lachish, and unto Debir king of Eglon, **s**, 559
10: 6 **s**, Slack not thy hand from thy servants; 559
10:17 it was told Joshua, **s**, The five kings are 559
14: 9 Moses sware on that day, **s**, Surely the land 559
17: 4 the son of Nun, and before the princes, **s**, 559
17:14 **s**, Why hast thou given me *but* one lot and 559
17:17 *even* to Ephraim and to Manasseh, **s**, 559
18: 8 **s**, Go and walk through the land, and 559
20: 1 The LORD also spake unto Joshua, **s**, 559
20: 2 Speak to the children of Israel, **s**, 559
21: 2 unto them at Shiloh in the land of Canaan, **s**, 559
22: 8 he spake unto them, **s**, Return with much 559
22:15 land of Gilead, and they spake with them, **s**, 559
22:24 not *rather* done it for fear of *this* thing, **s**, 559
22:24 **s**, What have you to do with the LORD 559
Jdg 1: 1 the children of Israel asked the LORD, **s**, 559
4: 6 *s*, Go and draw toward mount Tabor, and NIH
5: 1 and Barak the son of Abinoam on that day, **s**, 559
6:13 **s**, Did not the LORD bring us up from 559
6:32 **s**, Let Baal plead against him, because 559
7: 2 **s**, Mine own hand hath saved me. 559
7: 3 **s**, Whosoever *is* fearful and afraid, let him 559
7:24 **s**, Come down against the Midianites, and 559
8: 9 **s**, When I come again in peace, I will break 559
8:15 **s**, *Are* the hands of Zebah and 559
9: 1 family of the house of his mother's father, **s**, 559
9:31 **s**, Behold, Gaal the son of Ebed and 559

Jdg 10:10 s, We have sinned against thee, both because 559
11:12 s, What hast thou to do with me, that thou art 559
11:17 s, Let me, I pray thee, pass through thy land: 559
13: 6 the woman came and told her husband, s, 559
15:13 they spake unto him, s, No; but we will bind 559
16: 2 *told* the Gazites, s, Samson is come hither. 559
16: 2 s, In the morning, when it is day, we shall 559
16:18 s, Come up *this* once, for he hath shewed me 559
19:22 to the master of the house, the old man, s, 559
20: 8 s, We will not any *of us* go to his tent, 559
20:12 s, What wickedness *is* this that is done 559
20:23 and asked *counsel* of the LORD, s, 559
20:28 s, Shall I yet again go out to battle against 559
21: 1 the men of Israel had sworn in Mizpeh, s, 559
21: 5 *to* Mizpeh, s, He shall surely be put to death. 559
21:10 s, Go and smite the inhabitants of 559
21:18 for the children of Israel have sworn, s, 559
21:20 s, Go and lie in wait in the vineyards; 559
Ru 2:15 Boaz commanded his young men, s, 559
4: 4 s, Buy *it* before the inhabitants, and 559
4:17 it a name, s, There is a son born to Naomi; 559
1Sa 1:20 s, Because I have asked him of the LORD. NIH
4:21 s, The glory is departed from Israel: 559
5:10 *to* Ekron, that the Ekronites cried out, s, 559
6: 2 called for the priests and the diviners, s, 559
6:21 s, The Philistines have brought again the ark 559
7: 3 Samuel spake unto all the house of Israel, s, 559
7:12 Shen, and called the name of it Eben-ezer, s, 559
9:15 Samuel in his ear a day before Saul came, s, 559
9:26 the house, s, Up, that I may send thee away. 559
10: 2 sorroweth for you, s, What shall I do for my 559
11: 7 s, Whosoever cometh not forth after Saul 559
13: 3 all the land, s, Let the Hebrews hear. 559
14:24 for Saul had adjured the people, s, Cursed *be* 559
14:28 s, Cursed *be* the man that eateth *any* food 559
14:33 they told Saul, s, Behold, the people sin 559
15:10 the word of the LORD unto Samuel, s, 559
15:12 it was told Samuel, s, Saul came to Carmel, 559
16:22 s, Let David, I pray thee, stand before me; 559
17:26 David spake to the men that stood by him, s, 559
17:27 s, So shall it be done to the man that killeth 559
18: 8 was very wroth, and the s displeased him; 1697
18:22 *s*, Commune with David secretly, and say, NIH
18:24 told him, s, On this manner spake David. 559
19: 2 Jonathan told David, s, Saul my father 559
19:11 Michal David's wife told him, s, If thou save 559
19:15 s, Bring him up to me in the bed, that I may 559
19:19 it was told Saul, s, Behold, David *is* at 559
20:16 *s*, Let the LORD even require *it* at NIH
20:21 behold, I will send a lad, *s*, Go, find out NIH
20:42 s, The LORD be between me and thee, and 559
21:11 s, Saul hath slain his thousands, and 559
23: 1 they told David, s, Behold, the Philistines 559
23: 2 s, Shall I go and smite these Philistines? 559
23:19 came up the Ziphites to Saul to Gibeah, s, 559
23:27 unto Saul, s, Haste thee, and come; 559
24: 1 that it was told him, s, Behold, David *is* in 559
24: 8 and cried after Saul, s, My lord the king. 559
24: 9 s, Behold, David seeketh thy hurt? 559
25:14 men told Abigail, Nabal's wife, s, Behold, 559
25:40 they spake unto her, s, David sent us unto 559
26: 1 the Ziphites came unto Saul to Gibeah, s, 559
26: 6 the son of Zeruiah, brother to Joab, s, 559
26:14 son of Ner, s, Answerest thou not, Abner? 559
26:19 of the LORD, s, Go, serve other gods. 559
27:11 to bring *tidings to* Gath, s, Lest they should 559
27:11 s, So did David, and so *will be* his manner 559
27:12 Achish believed David, s, He hath made his 559
28:10 her by the LORD, s, *As* the LORD liveth, 559
28:12 the woman spake to Saul, s, Why hast thou 559
29: 5 s, Saul slew his thousands, and David his ten 559
30: 8 s, Shall I pursue after this troop? 559
30:26 the elders of Judah, *even* to his friends, s, 559
2Sa 1:16 s, I have slain the LORD'S anointed. 559
2: 1 that David inquired of the LORD, s, 559
2: 4 they told David, s, *That* the men of 559
3:12 to David on his behalf, s, Whose *is* the land? 559
3:12 s *also*, Make thy league with me, and behold, 559
3:14 Saul's son, s, Deliver *me* my wife Michal, 559
3:17 s, Ye sought for David in times past to be 559
3:18 *it*: for the LORD hath spoken of David, s, 559
3:23 they told Joab, s, Abner the son of Ner came 559
3:35 David sware, s, So do God to me, and more 559
4:10 When one told me, s, Behold, Saul is dead, 559
5: 1 spake, s, Behold, we *are* thy bone and 559
5: 6 which spake unto David, s, Except thou take 559
5:19 s, Shall I go up to the Philistines? 559
6:12 it was told king David, s, The LORD hath 559
7: 4 word of the LORD came unto Nathan, s, 559
7: 7 s, Why build ye not me a house of cedar? 559
7:26 let thy name be magnified for ever, s, 559
7:27 to thy servant, s, I will build thee a house: 559
11: 6 sent to Joab, *s*, Send me Uriah the Hittite. NIH
11:10 when they had told David, s, Uriah went not 559
11:15 he wrote in the letter, s, Set ye Uriah in 559
11:19 charged the messenger, s, When thou hast 559
13: 7 David sent home to Tamar, s, Go now *to* thy 559
13:28 Absalom had commanded his servants, s, 559
13:30 in the way, that tidings came to David, s, 559
14:32 Behold, I sent unto thee, s, Come hither, 559
15: 8 s, If the LORD shall bring me again indeed 559
15:10 s, As soon as ye hear the sound of 559
15:13 there came a messenger to David, s, 559
15:31 *one* told David, s, Ahithophel *is* among 559
17: 4 the s pleased Absalom well, and all 1697
17: 6 to Absalom, Absalom spake unto him, s, 559
17: 6 shall we do *after* his s? if not; speak thou. 1697
17:16 therefore send quickly, and tell David, s, 559
18: 5 commanded Joab and Abishai and Ittai, s, 559
18:12 king charged thee and Abishai and Ittai, s, 559
19: 8 s, Behold, the king doth sit in the gate. 559
19: 9 s, The king saved us out of the hand of our 559
19:11 sent to Zadok and to Abiathar the priests, s, 559
19:11 Speak unto the elders of Judah, s, 559
20:18 she spake, s, They were wont to speak in old 559
2Sa 20:18 They were wont to speak in old time, s, 559
21:17 the men of David sware unto him, s, 559
24:11 came unto the prophet Gad, David's seer, s, 559
24:19 David, according to the s of Gad, went up 1697
1Ki 1: 5 of Haggith exalted himself, s, I will be king: 559
1: 6 had not displeased him at any time in s, 559
1:11 s, Hast thou not heard that Adonijah the son 559
1:13 lord O king, swear unto thine handmaid, s, 559
1:17 *s*, Assuredly Solomon thy son shall reign NIH
1:23 they told the king, s, Behold Nathan 559
1:30 s, Assuredly Solomon thy son shall reign 559
1:47 s, God make the name of Solomon better 559
1:51 it was told Solomon, s, Behold, 559
1:51 hath caught hold on the horns of the altar, s, 559
2: 1 and he charged Solomon his son, s, 559
2: 4 s, If thy children take heed to their way, 559
2: 8 and I sware to him by the LORD, s, 559
2:23 s, God do so to me, and more also, 559
2:29 the son of Jehoiada, s, Go, fall upon him. 559
2:30 s, Thus said Joab, and thus he answered me. 559
2:38 Shimei said unto the king, The s *is* good: 1697
2:39 they told Shimei, s, Behold, thy servants *be* 559
2:42 protested unto thee, s, Know for a certain, 559
5: 2 And Solomon sent to Hiram, s, 559
5: 5 spake unto David my father, s, Thy son, 559
5: 8 Hiram sent to Solomon, s, I have considered 559
6:11 the word of the LORD came to Solomon, s, 559
8:15 and hath with his hand fulfilled *it*, s, 559
8:25 David my father that thou promisedst him, s, 559
8:47 s, We have sinned, and have done 559
8:55 congregation of Israel *with* a loud voice, s, 559
9: 5 as I promised to David thy father, s, 559
12: 3 of Israel came, and spake unto Rehoboam, s, 559
12: 7 they spake unto him, s, If thou wilt be a 559
12: 9 this people, who have spoken to me, s, 559
12:10 s, Thus shalt thou speak unto this people that 559
12:10 s, Thy father made our yoke heavy, but 559
12:12 as the king had appointed, s, Come to me 559
12:14 s, My father made your yoke heavy, and 559
12:15 the LORD, that *he* might perform his s, 1697
12:16 the people answered the king, s, 559
12:22 God came unto Shemaiah the man of God, s, 559
12:23 and *to* the remnant of the people, s, 559
13: 3 he gave a sign the same day, s, This *is* 559
13: 4 when king Jeroboam heard the s of the man 1697
13: 4 his hand from the altar, s, Lay hold on him. 559
13: 9 the LORD, s, Eat no bread, nor drink water, 559
13:18 s, Bring him back with thee into thine house, 559
13:21 came from Judah, s, Thus saith the LORD, 559
13:27 he spake to his sons, s, Saddle me the ass. 559
13:30 they mourned over him, *s*, Alas, my brother. NIH
13:31 s, When I am dead, then bury me in 559
13:32 For the s which he cried by the word of 1697
15:18 king of Syria, that dwelt at Damascus, s, 559
15:29 according unto the s of the LORD, 1697
16: 1 to Jehu the son of Hanani against Baasha, s, 559
17: 2 the word of the LORD came unto him, s, 559
17: 8 the word of the LORD came unto him, s, 559
17:15 and did according to the s of Elijah: 1697
18: 1 third year, s, Go, shew thyself unto Ahab; 559
18:26 morning even until noon, s, O Baal, hear us. 559
18:31 LORD came, s, Israel shall be thy name: 559
19: 2 s, So let the gods do *to me*, and more also, 559
20: 4 said, My lord, O king, according to thy s, 1697
20: 5 said, Thus speaketh Ben-hadad, s, 559
20: 5 Although I have sent unto thee, s, 559
20:13 s, Thus saith the LORD, Hast thou seen all 559
20:17 and Ben-hadad sent out, and they told him, s, 559
21: 2 spake unto Naboth, s, Give me thy vineyard, 559
21: 9 s, Proclaim a fast, and set Naboth on high 559
21:10 s, Thou didst blaspheme God and the king. 559
21:13 s, Naboth did blaspheme God and the king. 559
21:14 to Jezebel, s, Naboth is stoned, and is dead. 559
21:17 of the LORD came to Elijah the Tishbite, s, 559
21:19 s, Thus saith the LORD, Hast thou killed, 559
21:19 speak unto him, s, Thus saith the LORD, 559
21:23 of Jezebel also spake the LORD, s, 559
21:28 of the LORD came to Elijah the Tishbite, s, 559
22:12 s, Go up *to* Ramoth-gilead, and prosper: 559
22:13 call Micaiah spake unto him, s, Behold now, 559
22:31 s, Fight neither with small nor great, 559
22:36 s, Every man to his city, and every man to 559
2Ki 2:22 according to the s of Elisha which he spake. 1697
3: 7 and sent to Jehoshaphat the king of Judah, s, 559
4: 1 s, Thy servant my husband is dead; 559
4:31 and told him, s, The child is not awaked. 559
5: 4 s, Thus and thus said the maid that *is* of 559
5: 6 s, Now when this letter is come unto thee, 559
5: 8 that he sent to the king, s, Wherefore hast 559
5:10 s, Go and wash in Jordan seven times, and 559
5:14 according to the s of the man of God: 1697
5:22 My master hath sent me, s, Behold, 559
6: 8 s, In such and such a place *shall be* my 559
6: 9 s, Beware that *thou* pass not such a place; 559
6:13 it was told him, s, Behold, *he is* in Dothan. 559
6:26 a woman unto him, s, Help, my lord, O king. 559
7:10 they told them, s, We came to the camp of 559
7:12 s, When they come out of the city, we shall 559
7:14 after the host of the Syrians, s, Go and see. 559
7:18 s, Two measures of barley for a shekel, and 559
8: 1 s, Arise, and go thou and thine household, 559
8: 2 and did after the s of the man of God: 1697
8: 4 s, Tell me, I pray thee, all the great *things* 559
8: 6 s, Restore all that *was* hers, and all the fruits 559
8: 7 it was told him, s, The man of God is come 559
8: 8 of God, and inquire of the LORD by him, s, 559
8: 9 me to thee, s, Shall I recover of this disease? 559
9:12 he said, Thus and thus spake he to me, s, 559
9:13 and blew with trumpets, s, Jehu is king. 559
9:18 the watchman told, s, The messenger came 559
9:20 the watchman told, s, He came even unto 559
9:36 he spake by his servant Elijah the Tishbite, s, 559
10: 1 to them that brought up Ahab's *children*, s, 559
10: 5 s, We *are* thy servants, and will do all that 559
10: 6 s, If ye *be* mine, and *if* ye will hearken unto 559
2Ki 10: 8 there came a messenger, and told him, s, 559
10:17 according to the s of the LORD, which he 1697
11: 5 he commanded them, s, This *is* the thing that 559
14: 6 where*in* the LORD commanded, s, 559
14: 8 son of Jehu, king of Israel, s, Come, 559
14: 9 of Israel sent to Amaziah king of Judah, s, 559
14: 9 s, Give thy daughter to my son to wife: 559
15:12 of the LORD which he spake unto Jehu, s, 559
16: 7 of Assyria, s, I *am* thy servant and thy son: 559
16:15 king Ahaz commanded Urijah the priest, s, 559
17:13 by all the prophets, *and by* all the seers, s, 559
17:26 s, The nations which thou hast removed, and 559
17:27 the king of Assyria commanded, s, 559
17:35 charged them, s, Ye shall not fear other 559
18:14 of Assyria to Lachish, s, I have offended; 559
18:28 spake, s, Hear the word of the great king, 559
18:30 s, The LORD will surely deliver us, and 559
18:32 unto Hezekiah, when he persuadeth you, s, 559
18:36 commandment was, s, Answer him not. 559
19: 9 he sent messengers again unto Hezekiah, s, 559
19:10 shall ye speak to Hezekiah king of Judah, s, 559
19:10 God in whom thou trustest deceive thee, s, 559
19:20 s, Thus saith the LORD God of Israel, 559
20: 2 to the wall, and prayed unto the LORD, s, 559
20: 4 that the word of the LORD came to him, s, 559
21:10 spake by his servants the prophets, s, 559
22: 3 the scribe, *to* the house of the LORD, s, 559
22:10 Shaphan the scribe shewed the king, s, 559
22:12 and Asahiah a servant of the king's, s, 559
23:21 the king commanded all the people, s, 559
1Ch 4: 9 s, Because I bare *him* with sorrow. 559
4:10 Jabez called on the God of Israel, s, Oh that 559
11: 1 s, Behold, we *are* thy bone and thy flesh. 559
12:19 s, He will fall to his master Saul to 559
13:12 David was afraid of God that day, s, 559
14:10 David inquired of God, s, Shall I go up 559
16:18 S, Unto thee will I give the land of Canaan, 559
16:22 *S*, Touch not mine anointed, and do my NIH
17: 3 that the word of God came to Nathan, s, 559
17: 6 whom I commanded to feed my people, s, 559
17:24 that thy name may be magnified for ever, s, 559
21: 9 the LORD spake unto Gad, David's seer, s, 559
21:10 Go and tell David, s, Thus saith the LORD, 559
21:19 David went up at the s of Gad, which he 1697
22: 8 s, Thou hast shed blood abundantly, and 559
22:17 princes of Israel to help Solomon his son, *s*, NIH
2Ch 2: 3 s, As thou didst deal with David my father, 559
5:13 and praised the LORD, *s*, For *he is* good; NIH
6: 4 spake with his mouth to my father David, s, 559
6:16 s, There shall not fail thee a man in my sight 559
6:37 s, We have sinned, we have done amiss, and 559
7: 3 and praised the LORD, *s*, For *he is* good; NIH
7:18 s, There shall not fail thee a man *to be* ruler 559
10: 3 all Israel came and spake to Rehoboam, s, 559
10: 6 s, What counsel give ye *me* to return answer 559
10: 7 they spake unto him, s, If thou be kind to 559
10: 9 which have spoken to me, s, Ease somewhat 559
10:10 s, Thus shalt thou answer the people that 559
10:10 s, Thy father made our yoke heavy, but 559
10:12 as the king bade, s, Come again to me on 559
10:14 s, My father made your yoke heavy, but 559
10:16 the people answered the king, s, 559
11: 2 came to Shemaiah the man of God, s, 559
11: 3 and to all Israel in Judah and Benjamin, s, 559
12: 7 s, They have humbled themselves; 559
16: 2 king of Syria, that dwelt at Damascus, s, 559
18:11 s, Go up *to* Ramoth-gilead, and prosper: 559
18:12 went to call Micaiah spake to him, s, Behold, 559
18:19 one spake s after this manner, and 559
18:19 this manner, and another s after that manner. 559
18:30 s, Fight ye not with small or great, save only 559
19: 9 he charged them, s, Thus shall ye do in 559
20: 2 there came *some* that told Jehoshaphat, s, 559
20: 8 built thee a sanctuary therein for thy name, s, 559
20:37 s, Because thou hast joined thyself with 559
21:12 s, Thus saith the LORD God of David thy 559
25: 4 where the LORD commanded, s, 559
25: 7 there came a man of God to him, s, O king, 559
25:17 the son of Jehu, king of Israel, s, Come, 559
25:18 of Israel sent to Amaziah king of Judah, s, 559
25:18 s, Give thy daughter to my son to wife: 559
30: 6 of the king, s, Ye children of Israel, 559
30:18 Hezekiah prayed for them, s, The good 559
32: 4 s, Why should the kings of Assyria come, 559
32: 6 of the city, and spake comfortably to them, s, 559
32: 9 and unto all Judah that *were* at Jerusalem, s, 559
32:11 yourselves to die by famine and by thirst, s, 559
32:12 and commanded Judah and Jerusalem, s, 559
32:17 God of Israel, and to speak against him, s, 559
34:16 brought the king word back again, s, All that 559
34:18 Shaphan the scribe told the king, s, 559
34:20 and Asaiah a servant of the king's, s, 559
35:21 s, What have I to do with thee, thou king of 559
36:22 all his kingdom, and *put it* also in writing, s, 559
Ezr 1: 1 all his kingdom, and *put it* also in writing, s, 559
5:11 thus they returned us answer, s, We are 560
8:22 because we had spoken unto the king, s, 559
9: 1 s, The people of Israel, and the priests, and 559
9:11 s, The land, *unto* which ye go to possess it, 559
Ne 1: 8 s, *If* ye transgress, I will scatter you abroad 559
6: 2 and Geshem sent unto me, s, Come, 559
6: 3 s, I *am* doing a great work, so that I cannot 559
6: 7 at Jerusalem, s, *There is* a king in Judah: 559
6: 8 I sent unto him, s, There are no such things 559
6: 9 For they all made us afraid, s, Their hands 559
8:11 s, Hold your peace, for the day *is* holy; 559
8:15 and in Jerusalem, s, Go forth *unto* the mount, 559
13:25 *s*, Ye shall not give your daughters unto NIH
Est 1:21 the s pleased the king and the princes; and 1697
Job 4:16 *there was* silence, and I heard a voice, *s*, NIH
8:18 *it* shall deny him, *s*, I have not seen thee. NIH
15:23 *s*, Where *is it?* he knoweth that the day of NIH
24:15 for the twilight, s, No eye shall see me: 559
33: 8 and I have heard the voice of *thy* words, *s*, NIH
Ps 2: 2 the LORD, and against his anointed, *s*, NIH

S

Ps 22: 7 shoot out the lip, they shake the head, *s*, NIH
49: 4 I will open my **dark s** upon the harp. 2420
71:11 **S**, God hath forsaken him: persecute and 559
105:11 **S**, Unto thee will I give the land of Canaan, 559
105:15 *S*, Touch not mine anointed, and do my NIH
119:82 Mine eyes fail for thy word, **s**, When wilt 559
137: 3 *s*, Sing us *one* of the songs of Zion. NIH
Pr 1:21 in the city she uttereth her words, *s*, NIH
Ecc 1:16 **s**, Lo, I am come to great estate, and 559
SS 5: 2 of my beloved that knocketh *s*, Open to me, NIH
Isa 3: 6 *s*, Thou hast clothing, be thou our ruler, and NIH
3: 7 day shall he swear, **s**, I will not be a healer; 559
4: 1 **s**, We will eat our own bread, and wear our 559
6: 8 **s**, Whom shall I send, and who will go for 559
7: 2 **s**, Syria is confederate with Ephraim. 559
7: 5 have taken evil counsel against thee, **s**, 559
7:10 the LORD spake again unto Ahaz, **s**, 559
8: 5 The LORD spake also unto me again, **s**, 559
8:11 should not walk in the way of this people, **s**, 559
14: 8 of Lebanon, *s*, Since thou art laid down, NIH
14:16 *s*, *Is* this the man that made the earth to NIH
14:24 **s**, Surely as I have thought, so shall it come 559
16:14 **s**, Within three years, as the years of a 559
18: 2 *s*, Go, ye swift messengers, to a nation NIH
19:25 **s**, Blessed *be* Egypt my people, and 559
20: 2 **s**, Go and loose the sackcloth from off thy 559
23: 4 **s**, I travail not, nor bring forth children, 559
29:11 one that is learned, **s**, Read this, I pray thee: 559
29:12 that is not learned, **s**, Read this, I pray thee: 559
30:21 **s**, This *is* the way, walk ye in it, when ye 559
36:15 **s**, The LORD will surely deliver us: 559
36:18 persuade you, **s**, The LORD will deliver us. 559
36:21 commandment was, **s**, Answer him not. 559
37: 9 heard *it*, he sent messengers to Hezekiah, **s**, 559
37:10 **s**, Let not thy God, in whom thou trustest, 559
37:10 in whom thou trustest, deceive thee, **s**, 559
37:15 And Hezekiah prayed unto the LORD, **s**, 559
37:21 **s**, Thus saith the LORD God of Israel, 559
38: 4 came the word of the LORD to Isaiah, **s**, 559
41: 7 the anvil, **s**, It *is* ready for the sodering: 559
41:13 hold thy right hand, **s** unto thee, Fear not; 559
44:28 even **s** to Jerusalem, Thou shalt be built; and 559
45:14 unto thee, *s*, Surely God *is* in thee; NIH
46:10 **s**, My counsel shall stand, and I will do all 559
56: 3 hath joined himself to the LORD, speak, **s**, 559
63:11 *s*, Where *is* he that brought them up out of NIH
Jer 1: 4 the word of the LORD came unto me, **s**, 559
1:11 came unto me, **s**, Jeremiah, what seest thou? 559
1:13 unto me the second time, **s**, What seest thou? 559
2: 1 the word of the LORD came to me, **s**, 559
2: 2 ears of Jerusalem, **s**, Thus saith the LORD; 559
2:27 **S** to a stock, Thou *art* my father; and to a 559
4:10 deceived this people and Jerusalem, **s**, 559
4:31 *that* spreadeth her hands, *s*, Woe *is* me now! NIH
5:20 house of Jacob, and publish it in Judah, **s**, 559
6:14 *of* my people slightly, **s**, Peace, peace; 559
6:17 *S*, Hearken to the sound of the trumpet. NIH
7: 1 that came to Jeremiah from the LORD, **s**, 559
7: 4 **s**, The temple of the LORD, The temple of 559
7:23 **s**, Obey my voice, and I will be your God, 559
8: 6 him of his wickedness, **s**, What have I done? 559
8:11 of my people slightly, **s**, Peace, peace; 559
11: 1 that came to Jeremiah from the LORD, **s**, 559
11: 4 iron furnace, **s**, Obey my voice, and do them, 559
11: 6 in the streets of Jerusalem, **s**, Hear ye 559
11: 7 rising early and protesting, **s**, Obey my 559
11:19 *s*, Let us destroy the tree with the fruit NIH
11:21 that seek thy life, **s**, Prophesy not in 559
13: 3 LORD came unto me the second time, **s**, 559
13: 8 the word of the LORD came unto me, **s**, 559
16: 1 word of the LORD came also unto me, **s**, 559
18: 1 which came to Jeremiah from the LORD, **s**, 559
18: 5 Then the word of the LORD came to me, **s**, 559
18:11 of Jerusalem, **s**, Thus saith the LORD; 559
20:10 *s*, Peradventure he will be enticed, and NIH
20:15 my father, **s**, A man child is born unto thee; 559
21: 1 Zephaniah the son of Maaseiah the priest, **s**, 559
22:18 shall not lament for him, *s*, Ah my brother! NIH
22:18 they shall not lament for him, *s*, Ah lord! or, NIH
23:25 **s**, I have dreamed, I have dreamed. 559
23:33 or the prophet, or a priest, shall ask thee, **s**, 559
23:38 and I have sent unto you, **s**, Ye shall not say, 559
24: 4 the word of the LORD came unto me, **s**, 559
25: 2 and to all the inhabitants of Jerusalem, **s**, 559
26: 1 of Judah came this word from the LORD, **s**, 559
26: 8 the people took him, **s**, Thou shalt surely die. 559
26: 9 **s**, This house shall be like Shiloh, and this 559
26:11 unto the princes and to all the people, **s**, 559
26:12 unto all the princes and to all the people, **s**, 559
26:17 spake to all the assembly of the people, **s**, 559
26:18 of Judah, **s**, Thus saith the LORD of hosts; 559
27: 1 this word unto Jeremiah from the LORD, **s**, 559
27: 9 to your sorcerers, which speak unto you, **s**, 559
27:12 **s**, Bring your necks under the yoke of 559
27:14 **s**, Ye shall not serve the king of Babylon: 559
27:16 I spake to the priests and to all this people, **s**, 559
27:16 prophets that prophesy unto you, **s**, Behold, 559
28: 1 of the priests and of all the people, **s**, 559
28: 2 the LORD of hosts, the God of Israel, **s**, 559
28:11 of all the people, **s**, Thus saith the LORD; 559
28:12 from off the neck of the prophet Jeremiah, **s**, 559
28:13 Go and tell Hananiah, **s**, Thus saith 559
29: 3 to Nebuchadnezzar king of Babylon, **s**, 559
29:22 **s**, The LORD make thee like Zedekiah and 559
29:24 also speak to Shemaiah the Nehelamite, **s**, 559
29:25 the LORD of hosts, the God of Israel, **s**, 559
29:25 Maaseiah the priest, and to all the priests, **s**, 559
29:28 unto us *in* Babylon, **s**, This *captivity is* long: 559
29:30 the word of the LORD unto Jeremiah, **s**, 559
29:31 Send to all them of the captivity, **s**, 559
30: 1 that came to Jeremiah from the LORD, **s**, 559
30: 2 Thus speaketh the LORD God of Israel, **s**, 559
30:17 they called thee an Outcast, *s*, This *is* Zion, NIH
31: 3 *s*, Yea, I have loved thee *with* an everlasting NIH
31:34 every man his brother, **s**, Know the LORD: 559

Jer 32: 3 **s**, Wherefore dost thou prophesy, and say, 559
32: 6 The word of the LORD came unto me, **s**, 559
32: 7 **s**, Buy thee my field that *is* in Anathoth: 559
32:13 And I charged Baruch before them, **s**, 559
32:16 son of Neriah, I prayed unto the LORD, **s**, 559
32:26 the word of the LORD unto Jeremiah, **s**, 559
33: 1 was yet shut up in the court of the prison, **s**, 559
33:19 word of the LORD came unto Jeremiah, **s**, 559
33:23 the word of the LORD came to Jeremiah, **s**, 559
33:24 **s**, The two families which the LORD hath 559
34: 1 and against all the cities thereof, **s**, 559
34: 5 and they will lament thee, *s*, Ah lord! NIH
34:12 came to Jeremiah from the LORD, **s**, 559
34:13 of Egypt, out of the house of bondmen, **s**, 559
35: 1 Jehoiakim the son of Josiah king of Judah, **s**, 559
35: 6 **s**, Ye shall drink no wine, *neither* ye, 559
35:12 the word of the LORD unto Jeremiah, **s**, 559
35:15 rising up early and sending *them*, **s**, 559
36: 1 came unto Jeremiah from the LORD, **s**, 559
36: 5 commanded Baruch, **s**, I *am* shut up; 559
36:14 the son of Cushi, unto Baruch, **s**, 559
36:17 they asked Baruch, **s**, Tell us now, 559
36:27 Baruch wrote at the mouth of Jeremiah, **s**, 559
36:29 Thou hast burnt this roll, **s**, Why hast thou 559
36:29 saying, Why hast thou written therein, **s**, 559
37: 3 **s**, Pray now unto the LORD our God for us. 559
37: 6 of the LORD unto the prophet Jeremiah, **s**, 559
37: 9 Deceive not yourselves, **s**, The Chaldeans 559
37:13 he took Jeremiah the prophet, **s**, Thou fallest 559
37:19 **s**, The king of Babylon shall not come 559
38: 1 Jeremiah had spoken unto all the people, **s**, 559
38: 8 of the king's house, and spake to the king, **s**, 559
38:10 **s**, Take from hence thirty men with thee, and 559
38:16 **s**, *As* the LORD liveth, that made us this 559
39:11 to Nebuzar-adan the captain of the guard, **s**, 559
39:15 he was shut up in the court of the prison, **s**, 559
39:16 **s**, Thus saith the LORD of hosts, the God 559
40: 9 sware unto them and to their men, **s**, 559
40:15 **s**, Let me go, I pray thee, and I will slay 559
42:14 **S**, No; but we will go *into* the land of Egypt, 559
42:20 **s**, Pray for us unto the LORD our God; 559
43: 2 all the proud men, **s** unto Jeremiah, 559
43: 8 the LORD unto Jeremiah in Tahpanhes, **s**, 559
44: 1 at Noph, and in the country of Pathros, **s**, 559
44: 4 rising early and sending *them*, **s**, Oh, do not 559
44:15 of Egypt, in Pathros, answered Jeremiah, **s**, 559
44:20 people which had given him *that* answer, **s**, 559
44:25 the LORD of hosts, the God of Israel, **s**, 559
44:25 your mouths, and fulfilled with your hand, **s**, 559
44:26 the land of Egypt, **s**, The Lord GOD liveth. 559
45: 1 Jehoiakim the son of Josiah king of Judah, **s**, 559
48:39 They shall howl, *s*, How is it broken down! NIH
49: 4 her treasures, *s*, Who shall come unto me? NIH
49:14 *s*, Gather ye together, and come against her, NIH
49:34 of the reign of Zedekiah king of Judah, **s**, 559
50: 5 *s*, Come, and let us join ourselves to NIH
51:14 *s*, Surely I will fill thee *with* men, as *with* NIH
La 2:15 *s*, *Is* this the city that *men* call The NIH
Eze 3:12 *s*, Blessed *be* the glory of the LORD from NIH
3:16 the word of the LORD came unto me, **s**, 559
6: 1 the word of the LORD came unto me, **s**, 559
7: 1 the word of the LORD came unto me, **s**, 559
9: 1 cried also in mine ears *with* a loud voice, **s**, 559
9:11 inkhorn by his side, reported the matter, **s**, 559
10: 6 **s**, Take fire from between the wheels, 559
11:14 the word of the LORD came unto me, **s**, 559
12: 1 word of the LORD also came unto me, **s**, 559
12: 8 came the word of the LORD unto me, **s**, 559
12:17 the word of the LORD came to me, **s**, 559
12:21 the word of the LORD came unto me, **s**, 559
12:22 **s**, The days are prolonged, and every vision 559
12:26 the word of the LORD came to me, **s**, 559
13: 1 the word of the LORD came unto me, **s**, 559
13: 6 have seen vanity and lying divination, **s**, 559
13:10 they have seduced my people, **s**, Peace; 559
14: 2 the word of the LORD came unto me, **s**, 559
14:12 word of the LORD came again to me, **s**, 559
15: 1 the word of the LORD came unto me, **s**, 559
16: 1 the word of the LORD came unto me, **s**, 559
16:44 **s**, As *is* the mother, *so is* her daughter. 559
17: 1 the word of the LORD came unto me, **s**, 559
17:11 the word of the LORD came unto me, **s**, 559
18: 1 word of the LORD came unto me again, **s**, 559
18: 2 **s**, The fathers have eaten sour grapes, and 559
20: 2 came the word of the LORD unto me, **s**, 559
20: 5 unto them, **s**, I *am* the LORD your God; 559
20:45 the word of the LORD came unto me, **s**, 559
21: 1 the word of the LORD came unto me, **s**, 559
21: 8 the word of the LORD came unto me, **s**, 559
21:18 word of the LORD came unto me again, **s**, 559
22: 1 the word of the LORD came unto me, **s**, 559
22:17 the word of the LORD came unto me, **s**, 559
22:23 the word of the LORD came unto me, **s**, 559
22:28 divining lies unto them, **s**, Thus saith 559
23: 1 word of the LORD came again unto me, **s**, 559
24: 1 the word of the LORD came unto me, **s**, 559
24:15 the word of the LORD came unto me, **s**, 559
24:20 The word of the LORD came unto me, **s**, 559
25: 1 word of the LORD came again unto me, **s**, 559
26: 1 the word of the LORD came unto me, **s**, 559
27: 1 word of the LORD came again unto me, **s**, 559
27:32 lament over thee, *s*, What *city is* like Tyrus, NIH
28: 1 word of the LORD came again unto me, **s**, 559
28:11 the word of the LORD came unto me, **s**, 559
28:20 the word of the LORD came unto me, **s**, 559
29: 1 the word of the LORD came unto me, **s**, 559
29:17 the word of the LORD came unto me, **s**, 559
30: 1 word of the LORD came again unto me, **s**, 559
30:20 the word of the LORD came unto me, **s**, 559
31: 1 the word of the LORD came unto me, **s**, 559
32: 1 the word of the LORD came unto me, **s**, 559
32:17 the word of the LORD came unto me, **s**, 559
33: 1 the word of the LORD came unto me, **s**, 559
33:10 Thus ye speak, **s**, If our transgressions and 559
33:21 came unto me, **s**, The city is smitten. 559

Eze 33:23 the word of the LORD came unto me, **s**, 559
33:24 **s**, Abraham was one, and he inherited 559
33:30 **s**, Come, I pray you, and hear what *is* 559
34: 1 the word of the LORD came unto me, **s**, 559
35: 1 the word of the LORD came unto me, **s**, 559
35:12 **s**, They are laid desolate, they are given us to 559
36:16 the word of the LORD came unto me, **s**, 559
37:15 word of the LORD came again unto me, **s**, 559
37:18 **s**, Wilt thou not shew us what thou meanest 559
38: 1 the word of the LORD came unto me, **s**, 559
Da 4: 8 and before him I told the dream, *s*, NIH
4:23 **s**, Hew the tree down, and destroy it; 560
4:31 *s*, O king Nebuchadnezzar, to thee it is NIH
Am 2:12 commanded the prophets, **s**, Prophesy not. 559
3: 1 I brought up from the land of Egypt, **s**, 559
7:10 of Beth-el sent to Jeroboam king of Israel, **s**, 559
8: 5 **S**, When will the new moon be gone, that we 559
Jnh 1: 1 came unto Jonah the son of Amittai, **s**, 559
3: 1 LORD came unto Jonah the second time, **s**, 559
3: 7 by the decree of the king and his nobles, **s**, 559
4: 2 I pray thee, O LORD, *was* not this my **s**, 1697
Mic 2:11 *s*, I will prophesy unto thee of wine and NIH
Hag 1: 1 Joshua the son of Josedech the high priest, **s**, 559
1: 2 **s**, This people say, The time is not come, 559
1: 3 of the LORD by Haggai the prophet, **s**, 559
1:13 **s**, I *am* with you, saith the LORD. 559
2: 1 of the LORD by the prophet Haggai, **s**, 559
2: 2 and to the residue of the people, **s**, 559
2:10 of the LORD by Haggai the prophet, **s**, 559
2:11 Ask now the priests *concerning* the law, **s**, 559
2:20 in the four and twentieth *day* of the month, **s**, 559
2:21 Speak to Zerubbabel, governor of Judah, **s**, 559
Zec 1: 1 of Berechiah, the son of Iddo the prophet, **s**, 559
1: 4 **s**, Thus saith the LORD of hosts; 559
1: 7 of Berechiah, the son of Iddo the prophet, **s**, 559
1:14 Cry thou, **s**, Thus saith the LORD of hosts; 559
1:17 Cry yet, **s**, Thus saith the LORD of hosts; 559
1:21 he spake, **s**, These *are* the horns which have 559
2: 4 unto him, Run, speak to this young man, **s**, 559
3: 4 spake unto those that stood before him, **s**, 559
3: 6 of the LORD protested unto Joshua, **s**, 559
4: 4 talked with me, **s**, What *are* these, my lord? 559
4: 6 he answered and spake unto me, **s**, This *is* 559
4: 6 **s**, Not by might, nor by power, but by my 559
4: 8 the word of the LORD came unto me, **s**, 559
6: 8 he upon me, and spake unto me, **s**, Behold, 559
6: 9 the word of the LORD came unto me, **s**, 559
6:12 speak unto him, **s**, Thus speaketh 559
6:12 Thus speaketh the LORD of hosts, **s**, 559
7: 3 to the prophets, **s**, Should I weep in the fifth 559
7: 4 the word of the LORD of hosts unto me, **s**, 559
7: 5 to the priests, **s**, When ye fasted and 559
7: 8 word of the LORD came unto Zechariah, **s**, 559
7: 9 **s**, Execute true judgment, and shew mercy 559
8: 1 word of the LORD of hosts came *to me*, **s**, 559
8:18 of the LORD of hosts came unto me, **s**, 559
8:21 **s**, Let us go speedily to pray before 559
8:23 of him that is a Jew, **s**, We will go with you: 559
Mt 1:20 **s**, Joseph, *thou* son of David, fear not to *3004*
1:22 was spoken of the Lord by the prophet, **s**, *3004*
2: 2 **S**, Where is he that is born King of *3004*
2:13 **s**, Arise, and take the young child and *3004*
2:15 **s**, Out of Egypt have I called my son. *3004*
2:17 was spoken by Jeremie the prophet, **s**, *3004*
2:20 **S**, Arise, and take the young child and *3004*
3: 2 And **s**, Repent ye: for the kingdom of *3004*
3: 3 **s**, The voice of one crying in *3004*
3:14 But John forbad him, **s**, I have need to be *3004*
3:17 **s**, This is my beloved Son, in whom I am *3004*
4:14 which was spoken by Esaias the prophet, **s**, *3004*
5: 2 he opened his mouth, and taught them, **s**, *3004*
6:31 take no thought, **s**, What shall we eat? *3004*
8: 2 and worshipped him, **s**, Lord, if thou wilt, *3004*
8: 3 forth *his* hand, and touched him, **s**, I will; *3004*
8: 6 And **s**, Lord, my servant lieth at home sick *3004*
8:17 **s** Himself took our infirmities, and bare our *3004*
8:25 to *him*, and awoke him, **s**, Lord, save us: *3004*
8:27 But the men marvelled, **s**, What manner of *3004*
8:29 And behold, they cried out, **s**, What have *3004*
8:31 devils besought him, **s**, If thou cast us out, *3004*
9:14 **s**, Why do we and the Pharisees fast oft, but *3004*
9:18 a *certain* ruler, and worshipped him, **s**, *3004*
9:27 crying, and **s**, *Thou* Son of David, *3004*
9:29 Then touched he their eyes, **s**, According to *3004*
9:30 charged them, **s**, See *that* no *man* know *it*. *3004*
9:33 **s**, It was never so seen in Israel. *3004*
10: 5 Jesus sent forth, and commanded them, **s**, *3004*
10: 7 And as ye go, preach, **s**, The kingdom of *3004*
11:17 And **s**, We have piped unto you, and *3004*
12:10 And they asked him, **s**, Is it lawful to heal *3004*
12:17 which was spoken by Esaias the prophet, **s**, *3004*
12:38 and of the Pharisees answered, **s**, Master, *3004*
13: 3 **s**, Behold, a sower went forth to sow; *3004*
13:24 Another parable put he forth unto them, **s**, *3004*
13:31 Another parable put he forth unto them, **s**, *3004*
13:35 **s**, I will open my mouth in parables; *3004*
13:36 and his disciples came unto him, **s**, *3004*
14:15 **s**, *This* is a desert place, and the time is *3004*
14:26 the sea, they were troubled, **s**, It is a spirit; *3004*
14:27 Jesus spake unto them, **s**, Be of good cheer; *3004*
14:30 to sink, he cried, **s**, Lord, save me. *3004*
14:33 in the ship came and worshipped him, **s**, *3004*
15: 1 and Pharisees, which were of Jerusalem, **s**, *3004*
15: 4 **s**, Honour thy father and mother. *3004*
15: 7 well did Esaias prophesy of you, **s**, *3004*
15:12 were offended, after they heard *this* **s**? *3056*
15:22 and cried unto him, **s**, Have mercy on me, *3004*
15:23 his disciples came and besought him, **s**, *3004*
15:25 and worshipped him, **s**, Lord, help me. *3004*
16: 7 **s**, *It is* because we have taken no bread. *3004*
16:13 he asked his disciples, **s**, Whom do men say *3004*
16:22 to rebuke him, **s**, Be it far from thee, Lord: *3004*
17: 9 from the mountain, Jesus charged them, **s**, *3004*
17:10 **s**, Why then say the scribes that Elias must *3004*
17:14 a *certain* man, kneeling down to him, and **s**, *3004*

Mt 17:25 s, What thinkest thou, Simon? 3004
18: 1 s, Who is the greatest in the kingdom of 3004
18:26 fell down, and worshipped him, s, Lord, 3004
18:28 on him, and took him by the throat, s, 3004
18:29 and besought him, s, Have patience with 3004
19: 3 unto him, tempting him, and s unto him, 3004
19:11 unto them, All men cannot receive this s, 3056
19:22 But when the young man heard that s, 3056
19:25 s, Who then can be saved? 3004
20:12 S, These last have wrought but one hour, 3004
20:30 cried out, s, Have mercy on us, O Lord, 3004
20:31 s, Have mercy on us, O Lord, thou Son of 3004
21: 2 S unto them, Go into the village over 3004
21: 4 which was spoken by the prophet, s, 3004
21: 9 and that followed, cried, s, Hosanna to 3004
21:10 all the city was moved, s, Who is this? 3004
21:15 and s, Hosanna to the Son of David; 3004
21:20 s, How soon is the fig tree withered away! 3004
21:25 s, If we shall say, From heaven; 3004
21:37 his son, s, They will reverence my son. 3004
22: 4 Again, he sent forth other servants, s, 3004
22:16 s, Master, we know that thou art true, and 3004
22:24 S, Master, Moses said, If a man die, 3004
22:31 that which was spoken unto you by God, s, 3004
22:35 asked him a question, tempting him, and s, 3004
22:42 S, What think ye of Christ? whose son is 3004
22:43 then doth David in spirit call him Lord, s, 3004
23: 2 S, The scribes and the Pharisees sit in 3004
24: 3 s, Tell us, when shall these things be? 3004
24: 5 shall come in my name, s, I am Christ; 3004
25: 9 s, Not so; lest there be not enough for us 3004
25:11 the other virgins, s, Lord, Lord, open to us. 3004
25:20 and brought other five talents, s, Lord, 3004
25:37 s, Lord, when saw we thee a hungred, and 3004
25:44 s, Lord, when saw we thee a hungred, or 3004
25:45 he answer them, s, Verily I say unto you, 3004
26: 8 s, To what purpose is this waste? 3004
26:17 s unto him, Where wilt thou that we 3004
26:27 and gave thanks, and gave it to them, s, 3004
26:39 fell on his face, and prayed, s, O my Father, 3004
26:42 second time, and prayed, s, O my Father, 3004
26:44 prayed the third time, s the same words. 3004
26:48 s, Whomsoever I shall kiss, that same is he: 3004
26:65 his clothes, s, He hath spoken blasphemy; 3004
26:68 S, Prophesy unto us, thou Christ, Who is he 3004
26:69 and a damsel came unto him, s, Thou also 3004
26:70 them all, s, I know not what thou sayest. 3004
26:74 and to swear, s, I know not the man. NIG
27: 4 S, I have sinned in that I have betrayed 3004
27: 9 s, And they took the thirty pieces of silver, 3004
27:11 and the governor asked him, s, Art thou 3004
27:19 the judgment seat, his wife sent unto him, s, 3004
27:23 cried out the more, s, Let him be crucified. 3004
27:24 washed his hands before the multitude, s, 3004
27:29 and mocked him, s, Hail, King of the Jews! 3004
27:40 And s, Thou that destroyest the temple, and 3004
27:46 s, ELI, ELI, LAMA SABACHTHANI? 3004
27:54 that were done, they feared greatly, s, 3004
27:63 S, Sir, we remember that that deceiver said, 3004
28: 9 behold, Jesus met them, s, All hail. 3004
28:13 S, Say ye, His disciples came by night, and 3004
28:15 this s is commonly reported among 3056
28:18 And Jesus came and spake unto them, s, 3004
Mk 1: 7 And preached, s, There cometh one 3004
1:11 s, Thou art my beloved Son, in whom I am NIG
1:15 And s, The time is fulfilled, 3004
1:24 S, Let us alone; what have we to do with 3004
1:25 s, Hold thy peace, and come out of him. 3004
1:27 among themselves, s, What thing is this? 3004
1:40 down to him, and s unto him, If thou wilt, 3004
2:12 and glorified God, s, We never saw it on 3004
3:11 fell down before him, and cried, s, 3004
3:33 s, Who is my mother, or my brethren? 3004
5: 9 And he answered, s, My name is Legion: 3004
5:12 s, Send us into the swine, that we may enter 3004
5:23 And besought him greatly, s, My little 3004
6: 2 and many hearing him were astonished, s, 3004
6:25 and asked, s, I will that thou give me by 3004
7:29 And he said unto her, For this s go thy way; 3056
7:37 s, He hath done all things well: 3004
8:15 And he charged them, s, Take heed, 3004
8:16 s, It is because we have no bread. 3004
8:26 s, Neither go into the town, nor tell it to any 3004
8:27 s unto them, Whom do men say that I am? 3004
8:32 And he spake that s openly. And Peter took 3056
8:33 he rebuked Peter, s, Get thee behind me, 3004
9: 7 out of the cloud, s, This is my beloved Son: 3004
9:10 And they kept that s with themselves, 3056
9:11 And they asked him, s, Why say the scribes 3004
9:25 s unto him, Thou dumb and deaf spirit, 3004
9:32 But they understood not that s, and 4487
9:38 And John answered him, s, Master, we saw 3004
10:22 And he was sad at that s, and went away 3056
10:26 s among themselves, Who then can be 3004
10:33 S, Behold, we go up to Jerusalem; and NIG
10:35 sons of Zebedee, come unto him, s, Master, 3004
10:49 s unto him, Be of good comfort, rise; 3004
11: 9 and they that followed, cried, s, Hosanna; 3004
11:17 And he taught, s unto them, Is it not 3004
11:31 s, If we shall say, From heaven; 3004
12: 6 unto them, s, They will reverence my son. 3004
12:18 is no resurrection; and they asked him, s, 3004
12:26 s, I am the God of Abraham, and the God 3004
13: 6 s, I am Christ; and shall deceive many. 3004
14:44 s, Whomsoever I shall kiss, that same is he; 3004
14:57 and bare false witness against him, s, 3004
14:60 and asked Jesus, s, Answerest thou 3004
14:68 But he denied, s, I know not, neither 3004
14:71 s, I know not this man of whom ye speak. NIG
15: 4 him again, s, Answerest thou nothing? 3004
15: 9 But Pilate answered them, s, Will ye that I 3004
15:29 wagging their heads, and s, Ah, thou that 3004
15:34 s, ELOI, ELOI, LAMA SABACHTHANI? 3004
15:36 a reed, and gave him to drink, s, Let alone; 3004
Lk 1:24 and hid herself five months, s, 3004
1:29 she saw him, she was troubled at his s, 3056
1:63 and wrote, s, His name is John. 3004
1:66 s, What manner of child shall this be! 3004
1:67 with the Holy Ghost, and prophesied, s, 3004
2:13 of the heavenly host praising God, and s, 3004
2:17 s which was told them concerning this 4487
2:50 And they understood not the s which he 4487
3: 4 s, The voice of one crying in 3004
3:10 asked him, s, What shall we do then? 3004
3:14 demanded of him, s, And what shall we do? 3004
3:16 John answered, s unto them all, I indeed 3004
4: 4 And Jesus answered him, s, It is written, 3004
4:34 S, Let us alone; what have we to do with 3004
4:35 s, Hold thy peace, and come out of him. 3004
4:36 among themselves, s, What a word is this! 3004
4:41 crying out, and s, Thou art Christ the Son 3004
5: 8 down at Jesus' knees, s, Depart from me; 3004
5:12 and besought him, s, Lord, if thou wilt, 3004
5:13 forth his hand, and touched him, s, I will: 3004
5:21 and the Pharisees began to reason, s, 3004
5:26 glorified God, and were filled with fear, s, 3004
5:30 s, Why do ye eat and drink with publicans 3004
7: 4 to Jesus, they besought him instantly, s, 3004
7: 6 s unto him, Lord, trouble not thyself: 3004
7:16 and they glorified God, s, That a great 3004
7:19 to Jesus, s, Art thou he that should come? 3004
7:20 unto thee, s, Art thou he that should come? 3004
7:32 and calling one to another, and s, We have 3004
7:39 s, This man, if he were a prophet, 3004
8: 9 asked him, s, What might this parable be? 3004
8:24 awoke him, s, Master, master, we perish. 3004
8:25 s one to another, What manner of man is 3004
8:30 And Jesus asked him, s, What is thy name? 3004
8:38 be with him: but Jesus sent him away, s, 3004
8:49 ruler of the synagogue's house, s to him, 3004
8:50 heard it, he answered him, s, Fear not: 3004
8:54 her by the hand, and called, s, Maid, arise. 3004
9:18 and he asked them, s, Whom say the people 3004
9:22 S, The Son of man must suffer many 3004
9:35 out of the cloud, s, This is my beloved Son: 3004
9:38 s, Master, I beseech thee, look upon my 3004
9:45 But they understood not this s, and it was 4487
9:45 it not: and they feared to ask him of that s. 4487
10:17 seventy returned again with joy, s, Lord, 3004
10:25 stood up, and tempted him, s, Master, 3004
11:45 Master, thus s thou reproachest us also. 3004
12:16 And he spake a parable unto them, s, 3004
12:17 s, What shall I do, because I have no room 3004
13:25 at the door, s, Lord, Lord, open unto us; 3004
13:31 s unto him, Get thee out, and depart hence: 3004
14: 3 spake unto the lawyers and Pharisees, s, 3004
14: 5 And answered them, s, Which of you shall 3004
14: 7 chose out the chief rooms; s unto them, 3004
14:30 S, This man began to build, and was not 3004
15: 2 And the Pharisees and scribes murmured, s, 3004
15: 3 And he spake this parable unto them, s, 3004
15: 6 his friends and neighbours, s unto them, 3004
15: 9 neighbours together, s, Rejoice with me; 3004
17: 4 times in a day turn again to thee, s, I repent; 3004
18: 2 S, There was in a city a judge, which feared 3004
18: 3 and she came unto him, s, Avenge me of 3004
18:13 unto heaven, but smote upon his breast, s, 3004
18:18 a certain ruler asked him, s, Good Master, 3004
18:34 these things: and this s was hid from them, 4487
18:38 And he cried, s, Jesus, thou Son of David, 3004
18:41 S, What wilt thou that I shall do unto thee? 3004
19: 7 when they saw it, they all murmured, s, 3004
19:14 hated him, and sent a message after him, s, 3004
19:16 Then came the first, s, Lord, thy pound hath 3004
19:18 And the second came, s, Lord, thy pound 3004
19:20 s, Lord, behold, here is thy pound, 3004
19:30 S, Go ye into the village over against you; 3004
19:38 S, Blessed be the King that cometh in 3004
19:42 S, If thou hadst known, even thou, at least 3004
19:46 S unto them, It is written, My house is 3004
20: 2 And spake unto him, s, Tell us, by what 3004
20: 5 s, If we shall say, From heaven; 3004
20:14 among themselves, s, This is the heir: 3004
20:21 And they asked him, s, Master, we know 3004
20:28 S, Master, Moses wrote unto us, If any 3004
21: 7 And they asked him, s, Master, 3004
21: 8 s, I am Christ; and the time draweth near: 3004
22: 8 John, s, Go and prepare us the passover, 3004
22:19 and brake it, and gave unto them, s, 3004
22:20 Likewise also the cup after supper, s, 3004
22:42 S, Father, if thou be willing, remove this 3004
22:57 he denied him, s, Woman, I know him not. 3004
22:59 s, Of a truth this fellow also was with him: 3004
22:64 and asked him, s, Prophesy, who is it that 3004
22:66 and led him into their council, s, 3004
23: 2 And they began to accuse him, s, We found 3004
23: 2 to Cesar, s that he himself is Christ a King. 3004
23: 3 And Pilate asked him, s, Art thou the King 3004
23: 5 s, He stirreth up the people, 3004
23:18 s, Away with this man, and release unto us 3004
23:21 But they cried, s, Crucify him, crucify him. 3004
23:35 the rulers also with them derided him, s, 3004
23:37 And s, If thou be the King of the Jews, 3004
23:39 s, If thou be Christ, save thyself and us. 3004
23:40 rebuked him, s, Dost not thou fear God, 3004
23:47 he glorified God, s, Certainly this was a 3004
24: 7 S, The Son of man must be delivered into 3004
24:23 they found not his body, they came, s, 3004
24:29 But they constrained him, s, Abide with us: 3004
24:34 S, The Lord is risen indeed, and 3004
Jn 1:15 John bare witness of him, and cried, s, 3004
1:26 answered them, s, I baptize with water: 3004
1:32 And John bare record, s, I saw the Spirit 3004
4:31 his disciples prayed him, s, Master, eat. 3004
4:37 And herein is that s true, One soweth, 3056
4:39 believed on him for the s of the woman, 3056
4:42 Now we believe, not because of thy s: 2981
4:51 met him, and told him, s, Thy son liveth. 3004
6:52 therefore strove amongst themselves, s, 3004
6:60 they had heard this, said, This is a hard s; 3056
Jn 7:15 And the Jews marvelled, s, How knoweth 3004
7:28 s, Ye both know me, and ye know whence I 3004
7:36 What manner of s is this that he said, 3056
7:37 Jesus stood and cried, s, If any man thirst, 3004
7:40 when they heard this s, said, Of a truth this 3056
8:12 unto them, s, I am the light of the world: 3004
8:51 verily, I say unto you, If a man keep my s, 3056
8:52 and thou sayest, If a man keep my s, 3056
8:55 unto you: but I know him, and keep his s. 3056
9: 2 s, Master, who did sin, this man, or 3004
9:19 And they asked them, s, Is this your son, 3004
10:33 The Jews answered him, s, For a good 3004
11: 3 s, Lord, behold, he whom thou lovest is 3004
11:28 s, The Master is come, and calleth for thee. 3004
11:31 up hastily and went out, followed her, s, 3004
11:32 s unto him, Lord, if thou hadst been here, 3004
12:21 and desired him, s, Sir, we would see Jesus. 3004
12:23 Jesus answered them, s, The hour is come, 3004
12:28 s, I have both glorified it, and will glorify it NIG
12:38 That the s of Esaias the prophet might be 3056
15:20 if they have kept my s, they will keep yours 3056
18: 9 That the s might be fulfilled, which he 3056
18:22 s, Answerest thou the high priest so? 3004
18:32 That the s of Jesus might be fulfilled, 3056
18:40 all again, s, Not this man, but Barabbas. 3004
19: 6 and officers saw him, they cried out, s, 3004
19: 8 When Pilate therefore heard that s, he was 3056
19:12 but the Jews cried out, s, If thou let this 3004
19:13 When Pilate therefore heard that s, 3056
21:23 Then went this s abroad among 3056
Ac 1: 6 come together, they asked of him, s, Lord, 3004
2: 7 and marvelled, s one to another, Behold, 3004
2:12 and were in doubt, s one to another, 3004
2:40 other words did he testify and exhort, s, 3004
3:25 made with our fathers, s unto Abraham, 3004
4:16 S, What shall we do to these men? for that 3004
5:23 S, The prison truly found we shut with all 3004
5:25 Then came one and told them, s, Behold, 3004
5:28 S, Did not we straitly command you that 3004
6: 5 And the s pleased the whole multitude: and 3056
7:26 and would have set them at one again, s, 3004
7:27 s, Who made thee a ruler and a judge over 3004
7:29 Then fled Moses at this s, and was a 3056
7:32 S, I am the God of thy fathers, the God of NIG
7:35 s, Who made thee a ruler and a judge? 3004
7:40 S unto Aaron, Make us gods to go before 3004
7:59 calling upon God, and s, Lord Jesus, 3004
8:10 gave heed, from the least to the greatest, s, 3004
8:19 S, Give me also this power, that on 3004
8:26 s, Arise, and go toward the south unto 3004
9: 4 and heard a voice s unto him, Saul, Saul, 3004
10: 3 in to him, and s unto him, Cornelius. 3004
10:26 But Peter took him up, s, Stand up; I myself 3004
11: 3 S, Thou wentest in to men uncircumcised, 3004
11: 4 and expounded it by order unto them, s, 3004
11: 7 And I heard a voice s unto me, Arise, Peter; 3004
11:18 they held their peace, and glorified God, s, 3004
12: 7 and raised him up, s, Arise up quickly. 3004
12:22 s, It is the voice of a god, and not of a man. NIG
13:15 s, Ye men and brethren, if ye have any 3004
13:47 s, I have set thee to be a light of NIG
14:11 up their voices, s in the speech of Lycaonia, 3004
14:15 And s, Sirs, why do ye these things? We 3004
15: 5 s, That it was needful to circumcise them, 3004
15:13 James answered, s, Men and brethren, 3004
15:24 subverting your souls, s, Ye must be 3004
16: 9 and prayed him, s, Come over into 3004
16:15 and her household, she besought us, s, 3004
16:17 same followed Paul and us, and cried, s, 3004
16:20 s, These men, being Jews, do exceedingly 3004
16:28 with a loud voice, s, Do thyself no harm: 3004
16:35 sent the serjeants, s, Let those men go. 3004
16:36 And the keeper of the prison told this s to 3056
17: 7 s that there is another king, one Jesus. 3004
17:19 and brought him unto Areopagus, s, 3004
18:13 S, This fellow persuadeth men to worship 3004
18:21 But bade them farewell, s, I must by all 3004
19: 4 baptism of repentance, s unto the people, 3004
19:13 s, We adjure you by Jesus whom Paul 3004
19:21 and Achaia, to go to Jerusalem, s, 3004
19:26 away much people, s that they be no gods, 3004
19:28 and cried out, s, Great is Diana of 3004
20:23 s that bonds and afflictions abide me. 3004
21:14 we ceased, s, The will of the Lord be done. 3004
21:21 s that they ought not to circumcise their 3004
21:40 spake unto them in the Hebrew tongue, s, 3004
22: 7 and heard a voice s unto me, Saul, Saul, 3004
22:18 And saw him s unto me, Make haste, and 3004
22:26 that, he went and told the chief captain, s, 3004
23: 9 and strove, s, We find no evil in this man: 3004
23:12 s that they would neither eat nor drink till 3004
23:23 And he called unto him two centurions, s, 3004
24: 2 forth, Tertullus began to accuse him, s, 3004
24: 9 also assented, s that these things were so. 5335
25:14 declared Paul's cause unto the king, s, 3004
26:14 and s in the Hebrew tongue, Saul, Saul, 3004
26:22 s none other things than those which 3004
26:31 they talked between themselves, s, 3004
27:24 S, Fear not, Paul; thou must be brought 3004
27:33 Paul besought them all to take meat, s, 3004
28:26 S, Go unto this people, and say, Hearing ye 3004
Ro 4: 7 S, Blessed are they whose iniquities are NIG
11: 2 intercession to God against Israel, s, 3004
13: 9 it is briefly comprehended in this s, namely, 3056
1Co 11:25 when he had supped, s, This cup is the new 3004
15:54 shall be brought to pass the s that is written, 3056
Gal 3: 8 s, In thee shall all nations be blessed. NIG
1Ti 1:15 This is a faithful s, and worthy of all 3056
3: 1 This is a true s, If a man desire the office of 3056
4: 9 This is a faithful s and worthy of all 3056
2Ti 2:11 It is a faithful s: For if we be dead with 3056
2:18 s that the resurrection is past already; 3004
Tit 3: 8 This is a faithful s, and these things I will 3056
Heb 2: 6 s, What is man, that thou art mindful of 3004
2:12 S, I will declare thy name unto my 3004

Heb 4: 7 s in David, To day, after so long a time; *3004*
6:14 S, Surely blessing I will bless thee, and *3004*
8:11 every man his brother, s, Know the Lord: *3004*
9:20 S, This *is* the blood of the testament which *3004*
12:26 but now he hath promised, s, Yet once *3004*
2Pe 3: 4 And s, Where is the promise of his coming? *3004*
Jude 1:14 from Adam, prophesied of these, s, Behold, *3004*
Rev 1:11 S, I am Alpha and Omega, the first and *3004*
1:17 right hand upon me, s unto me, Fear not; *3004*
4: 8 rest not day and night, s, Holy, holy, holy, *3004*
4:10 and cast their crowns before the throne, s, *3004*
5: 9 And they sung a new song, s, Thou art *3004*
5:12 S with a loud voice, Worthy is the Lamb *3004*
5:13 heard I s, Blessing, and honour, and glory, *3004*
6: 1 one of the four beasts s, Come and see. *3004*
6:10 s, How long, O Lord, holy and true, *3004*
7: 3 S, Hurt not the earth, neither the sea, *3004*
7:10 And cried with a loud voice, s, Salvation to *3004*
7:12 S, Amen: Blessing, and glory, and wisdom, *3004*
7:13 And one of the elders answered, s unto me, *3004*
8:13 s with a loud voice, Woe, woe, woe, *3004*
9:14 S to the sixth angel which had the trumpet, *3004*
10: 4 and I heard a voice from heaven s unto me, *3004*
11: 1 s, Rise, and measure the temple of God, *3004*
11:12 And they heard a great voice from heaven s *3004*
11:15 and there were great voices in heaven, s, *3004*
11:17 S, We give thee thanks, O Lord God *3004*
12:10 And I heard a loud voice s in heaven, *3004*
13: 4 and they worshipped the beast, s, Who *is* *3004*
13:14 s to them that dwell on the earth, that *they* *3004*
14: 7 S with a loud voice, Fear God, and *3004*
14: 8 s, Babylon is fallen, is fallen, *that* great *3004*
14: 9 s with a loud voice, If any *man* worship *3004*
14:13 And I heard a voice from heaven s unto me, *3004*
14:18 s, Thrust in thy sharp sickle, and gather *3004*
15: 3 s, Great and marvellous *are* thy works, *3004*
16: 1 out of the temple s to the seven angels, *3004*
16:17 of heaven, from the throne, s, It is done. *3004*
17: 1 talked with me, s unto me, *Come* hither; *3004*
18: 2 s, Babylon the great is fallen, is fallen, and *3004*
18: 4 s, Come out of her, my people, that ye be *3004*
18:10 s, Alas, alas, *that* great city Babylon, *3004*
18:16 And s, Alas, alas, *that* great city, that was *3004*
18:18 s, What *city is* like unto *this* great city? *3004*
18:19 cried, weeping and wailing, s, Alas, alas, *3004*
18:21 a great millstone, and cast *it* into the sea, s, *3004*
19: 1 of much people in heaven, s, Alleluia; *3004*
19: 4 God that sat on the throne, s, Amen; *3004*
19: 5 s, Praise our God, all ye his servants, and *3004*
19: 6 voice of mighty thunderings, s, Alleluia: *3004*
19:17 s to all the fowls that fly in the midst of *3004*
21: 3 And I heard a great voice out of heaven s, *3004*
21: 9 and talked with me, s, *Come* hither, I will *3004*

SAYINGS (31) [SAY]

Nu 14:39 Moses told these s unto all the children of 1697
Jdg 13:17 that when thy s come to pass we may do 1697
1Sa 25:12 and came and told him all those s. 1697
2Ch 13:22 the acts of Abijah, and his ways, and his s, 1697
33:19 they *are* written among the s of the seers. 1697
Ps 49:13 yet their posterity approve their s. Selah. 6310
78: 2 in a parable: I will utter **dark** s of old: 2420
Pr 1: 6 the words of the wise, and their **dark** s. 2420
4:10 Hear, O my son, and receive my s; and 561
4:20 to my words; incline thine ear unto my s. 561
Mt 7:24 Therefore whosoever heareth these s of *3056*
7:26 And every one that heareth these s of mine, *3056*
7:28 to pass, when Jesus had ended these s, *3056*
19: 1 *that* when Jesus had finished these s, *3056*
26: 1 to pass, when Jesus had finished all these s, *3056*
Lk 1:65 all these s were noised abroad throughout *4487*
2:51 but his mother kept all these s in her heart. *4487*
6:47 to me, and heareth my s, and doeth them, *3056*
7: 1 Now when he had ended all his s in *4487*
9:28 to pass about an eight days after these s, *3056*
9:44 Let these s sink down into your ears: for *3056*
Jn 10:19 therefore again among the Jews for these s. *3056*
14:24 He that loveth me not keepeth not my s: *3056*
Ac 14:18 And with these s scarce restrained they *3004*
19:28 And when they heard *those* s, they were full NIG
Ro 3: 4 That thou mightest be justified in thy s, and *3056*
Rev 19: 9 saith unto me, These are the true s of God. *3056*
22: 6 said unto me, These s *are* faithful and true: *3056*
22: 7 blessed *is* he that keepeth the s of *3056*
22: 9 and of them which keep the s of this book: *3056*
22:10 Seal not the s of the prophecy of this book: *3056*

SCAB (7) [SCABBED]

Lev 13: 2 a s, or bright spot, and it be in the skin of 5597
13: 6 it *is but* a s: and he shall wash his clothes, 4556
13: 7 if the s spread much abroad in the skin, 4556
13: 8 the s spreadeth in the skin, then the priest 4556
14:56 a rising, and for a s, and for a bright spot: 5597
Dt 28:27 and with the s, and with the itch, 1618
Isa 3:17 Therefore the Lord will **smite with a s** 5596

SCABBARD (1)

Jer 47: 6 put up thyself into thy s, rest, and be still. 8593

SCABBED (2) [SCAB]

Lev 21:20 be scurvy, or s, or hath his stones broken; 3217
22:22 maimed, or having a wen, or scurvy, or s, 3217

SCAFFOLD (1)

2Ch 6:13 For Solomon had made a brasen s, of five 3595

SCALE ARMOR See MAIL

SCALES (10)

Lev 11: 9 whatsoever hath fins and s in the waters, 7193
11:10 all that have not fins nor s in the seas, and 7193
11:12 Whatsoever hath no fins nor s in the waters, 7193
Dt 14: 9 all that have fins and s shall ye eat: 7193
14:10 hath not fins and s ye may not eat; 7193
Job 41:15 *His* s *are his* pride, shut up *together as* 650+4043
Isa 40:12 weighed the mountains in s, and the hills in 6425
Eze 29: 4 the fish of thy rivers to stick unto thy s, 7193
29: 4 the fish of thy rivers shall stick unto thy s. 7193
Ac 9:18 there fell from his eyes as it had been s: *3013*

SCALETH (1)

Pr 21:22 A wise *man* s the city of the mighty, and 5927

SCALL (14)

Lev 13:30 it *is* a **dry** s, *even* a leprosy upon the head 5424
13:31 if the priest look on the plague of the s, 5424
13:31 *that hath* the plague of the s seven days: 5424
13:32 *if* the s spread not, and there be in it no 5424
13:32 the s *be* not in sight deeper than the skin; 5424
13:33 be shaven, but the s shall he not shave; 5424
13:33 the priest shall shut up *him that hath* the s 5424
13:34 seventh day the priest shall look on the s: 5424
13:34 behold, *if* the s be not spread in the skin, 5424
13:35 if the s spread much in the skin after his 5424
13:36 behold, *if* the s be spread in the skin, 5424
13:37 if the s be in his sight at a stay, and 5424
13:37 up therein; the s is healed, he *is* clean: 5424
14:54 for all *manner of* plague of leprosy, and s, 5424

SCALP (1)

Ps 68:21 the hairy s of such a one as goeth on still in 6936

SCANT (1)

Mic 6:10 and the s measure *that is* abominable? 7332

SCAPEGOAT (4) [GOAT]

Lev 16: 8 for the LORD, and the other lot for the s. 5799
16:10 the goat, on which the lot fell to be the s, 5799
16:10 *and* to let him go for a s into the wilderness. 5799
16:26 he that let go the goat for the s shall wash 5799

SCARCE (3) [SCARCELY, SCARCENESS, SCAREST]

Ge 27:30 Jacob was yet s **gone out** from 3318+3318
Ac 14:18 And with these sayings s restrained they *3433*
27: 7 and s were come over against Cnidus, *3433*

SCARCELY (2) [SCARCE]

Ro 5: 7 For s for a righteous *man* will one die: *3433*
1Pe 4:18 And if the righteous s be saved, where shall *3433*

SCARCENESS (1) [SCARCE]

Dt 8: 9 land wherein thou shalt eat bread without s, 4544

SCAREST (1) [SCARCE]

Job 7:14 thou s me with dreams, and terrifiest me 2865

SCARLET (52)

Ge 38:28 and bound upon his hand a s **thread**, 8144
38:30 that had the s **thread** upon his hand: 8144
Ex 25: 4 s, and fine linen, and goats' *hair,* 8144+8438
26: 1 and blue, and purple, and s: 8144+8438
26:31 s, and fine twined linen *of* cunning 8144+8438
26:36 purple, and s, and fine twined linen, 8144+8438
27:16 purple, and s, and fine twined linen, 8144+8438
28: 5 and purple, and s, and fine linen. 8144+8438
28: 6 *of* purple, *of* s, and fine twined linen, 8144+8438
28: 8 purple, and s, and fine twined linen. 8144+8438
28:15 and *of* s, and *of* fine twined linen, 8144+8438
28:33 of purple, and of s, round about 8144+8438
35: 6 s, and fine linen, and goats' *hair,* 8144+8438
35:23 s, and fine linen, and goats' *hair,* and 8144+8438
35:25 of purple, *and* of s, and of fine linen. 8144+8438
35:35 s, and in fine linen, and of 8144+8438
36: 8 and blue, and purple, and s: 8144+8438
36:35 purple, and s, and fine twined linen: 8144+8438
36:37 purple, and s, and fine twined linen, 8144+8438
38:18 purple, and s, and fine twined linen: 8144+8438
38:23 and in s, and fine linen. 8144+8438+1886.1
39: 1 the blue, and purple, and s, 8144+8438+1886.1
39: 2 purple, and s, and fine twined linen. 8144+8438
39: 3 and in the s, and in the fine linen, 8144+8438
39: 5 purple, and s, and fine twined linen; 8144+8438
39: 8 purple, and s, and fine twined linen. 8144+8438
39:24 and purple, and s, *and* twined *linen.* 8144+8438
39:29 and purple, and s, *of* needlework; 8144+8438
Lev 14: 4 and cedar wood, and s, and hyssop: 8144+8438
14: 6 the s, and the hyssop, and shall dip 8144+8438
14:49 and cedar wood, and s, and hyssop: 8144+8438
14:51 the s, and the living bird, and 8144+8438
14:52 and with the hyssop, and with the s: 8144+8438
Nu 4: 8 shall spread upon them a cloth of s, 8144+8438
19: 6 s, and cast *it* into the midst of 8144+8438
Jos 2:18 thou shalt bind this line of s thread in 8144
2:21 and she bound the s line in the window. 8144
2Sa 1:24 weep over Saul, who clothed you in s, 8144
Pr 31:21 for all her household *are* clothed with s. 8144
SS 4: 3 Thy lips *are* like a thread of s, and 8144
Isa 1:18 though your sins be as s, they shall be as 8144
La 4: 5 they that were brought up in s embrace 8438
Da 5: 7 shall be clothed with s, and *have* a chain of 711
5:16 thou shalt be clothed with s, and *have* a 711
5:29 they clothed Daniel with s, and *put* a chain 711
Na 2: 3 *men* is made red, the valiant men *are* in s: 8529
Mt 27:28 they stripped him, and put on him a s robe. *2847*
Heb 9:19 and s wool, and hyssop, and sprinkled both *2847*
Rev 17: 3 I saw a woman sit upon a s **coloured** beast, *2847*
17: 4 woman was arrayed in purple and s **colour**, *2847*
18:12 and s, and all thyine wood, and all *manner* *2847*
18:16 and s, and decked with gold, and *2847*

SCATTER (38) [SCATTERED, SCATTERETH, SCATTERING]

Ge 11: 9 from thence did the LORD s them **abroad** 6327
49: 7 divide them in Jacob, and s them in Israel. 6327
Lev 26:33 I will s you among the heathen, and 2219
Nu 16:37 of the burning, and s thou the fire yonder; 2219
Dt 4:27 the LORD shall s you among the nations, 6327
28:64 the LORD shall s thee among all people, 6327
32:26 I said, I would s them **into corners**, 6284
1Ki 14:15 shall s them beyond the river, because they 2219
Ne 1: 8 I will s you **abroad** among the nations: 6327
Ps 59:11 s them by thy power; and bring them down, 5128
68:30 s thou the people *that* delight in war. 967
106:27 the nations, and to s them in the lands. 2219
144: 6 Cast forth lightning, and s them: shoot out 6327
Isa 28:25 s the cummin, and cast in the principal 2236
41:16 them away, and the whirlwind shall s them: 6327
Jer 9:16 I will s them also among the heathen, 6327
13:24 Therefore will I s them as the stubble that 6327
18:17 I will s them as *with* an east wind before 6327
23: 1 that destroy and s the sheep of my pasture! 6327
49:32 I will s into all winds them *that are* in 2219
49:36 and will s them towards all those winds; 2219
Eze 5: 2 a third *part* thou shalt s in the wind; and 2219
5:10 the whole remnant of thee will I s into all 2219
5:12 I will s a third *part* into all the winds, and 2219
6: 5 I will s your bones round about your altars. 2219
10: 2 the cherubims, and s *them* over the city. 2236
12:14 I will s toward every wind all that *are* about 2219
12:15 when I shall s them among the nations, and 6327
20:23 that *I* would s them among the heathen, and 6327
22:15 I will s thee among the heathen, and 6327
29:12 I will s the Egyptians among the nations, 6327
30:23 I will s the Egyptians among the nations, 6327
30:26 I will s the Egyptians among the nations, 6327
Da 4:14 shake off his leaves, and s his fruit: 921
11:24 he shall s among them the prey, and spoil, 967
12: 7 when *he* shall have accomplished to s 5310
Hab 3:14 they came out as a whirlwind to s me: 6327
Zec 1:21 up *their* horn over the land of Judah to s it. 2219

SCATTERED (71) [SCATTER]

Ge 11: 4 lest we be s **abroad** upon the face of 6327
11: 8 So the LORD s them **abroad** from thence 6327
Ex 5:12 So the people were s **abroad** throughout all 6327
Nu 10:35 LORD, and let thine enemies be s; 6327
Dt 30: 3 whither the LORD thy God hath s thee. 6327
1Sa 11:11 that they which remained were s, so 6327
13: 8 *to* Gilgal; and the people were s from him. 6327
13:11 Because I saw that the people were s from 5310
2Sa 18: 8 For the battle was there s over the face of 6327
22:15 he sent out arrows, and s them; lightning, 6327
1Ki 22:17 he said, I saw all Israel s upon the hills, 6327
2Ki 25: 5 and all his army were s from him. 6327
2Ch 18:16 I did see all Israel s upon the mountains, 6327
Est 3: 8 There is a certain people s **abroad** and 6340
Job 4:11 and the stout lion's whelps are s **abroad.** 6504
18:15 brimstone shall be s upon his habitation. 2219
Ps 18:14 Yea, he sent out his arrows, and s them; 6327
44:11 for meat; and hast s us among the heathen. 2219
53: 5 for God hath s the bones of him that 6340
60: 1 O God, thou hast cast us off, thou hast s us, 6555
68: 1 Let God arise, let his enemies be s: let them 6327
68:14 When the Almighty s kings in it, it was 6566
89:10 thou hast s thine enemies with thy strong 6340
92: 9 all the workers of iniquity shall be s. 6504
141: 7 Our bones are s at the grave's mouth, 6340
Isa 18: 2 swift messengers, to a nation s and peeled, 4900
18: 7 unto the LORD of hosts *of* a people s 4900
33: 3 the lifting up of thyself the nations were s. 5310
Jer 3:13 hast s thy ways to the strangers under every 6340
10:21 not prosper; and all their flocks shall be s. 6327
23: 2 Ye have s my flock, and driven them away, 6327
30:11 full end of all nations whither I have s thee, 6327
31:10 He that s Israel will gather him, and 2219
40:15 which are gathered unto thee should be s, 6327
50:17 Israel *is* a s sheep; the lions have driven 6340
52: 8 and all his army was s from him. 6327
Eze 6: 8 when ye shall be s through the countries. 2219
11:16 although I have s them among 6327
11:17 out of the countries where ye have been s, 6327
17:21 they that remain shall be s towards all 6566
20:34 you out of the countries wherein ye are s, 6327
20:41 of the countries wherein ye have been s; 6327
28:25 from the people among whom they are s, 6327
29:13 from the people whither they were s: 6327
34: 5 they were s, because *there is* no shepherd: 6327
34: 5 all the beasts of the field, when they were s. 6327
34: 6 my flock was s upon all the face of 6327
34:12 day that he is among his sheep *that are* s; 6567
34:12 places where they have been s in the cloudy 6327
34:21 with your horns, till ye have s them abroad; 6327
36:19 I s them among the heathen, and they were 6327
46:18 that my people be not s every man from his 6327
Joel 3: 2 whom they have s among the nations, and 6340
Na 3:18 *dust:* thy people is s upon the mountains, 6335
Hab 3: 6 the everlasting mountains were s, 6327
Zec 1:19 These *are* the horns which have s Judah, 2219
1:21 These *are* the horns which have s Judah, so 2219
7:14 I s them **with a whirlwind** among all 5590
13: 7 the shepherd, and the sheep shall be s: 6327
Mt 9:36 because they fainted, and were s **abroad,** *4496*
26:31 the sheep of the flock shall be s **abroad.** *1287*
Mk 14:27 the shepherd, and the sheep shall be s. *1287*
Lk 1:51 he hath s the proud in the imagination of *1287*
Jn 11:52 the children of God that were s **abroad.** *1287*
16:32 yea, is now come, that ye shall be s, *4650*
Ac 5:36 obeyed him, were s, and brought to nought. *1262*
8: 1 they were all s **abroad** throughout *1289*
8: 4 Therefore they that were s **abroad** went *1289*
11:19 Now they which were s **abroad** upon *1289*
Jas 1: 1 tribes which are s **abroad,** *1290+1722+3588*
1Pe 1: 1 to the strangers s **throughout** Pontus, *1290*

SCATTERETH (10) [SCATTER]

Job 37:11 the thick cloud: he s his bright cloud: 6327
38:24 *which* s the east wind upon the earth? 6327
Ps 147:16 like wool: he s the hoarfrost like ashes. 6340
Pr 11:24 There is that s, and yet increaseth; and 6340
20: 8 of judgment s *away* all evil with his eyes. 2219
20:26 A wise king s the wicked, and bringeth 2219
Isa 24: 1 and s **abroad** the inhabitants thereof. 6327

S

Mt 12:30 and he that gathereth not with me s abroad. 4650
Lk 11:23 and he that gathereth not with me s. 4650
Jn 10:12 the wolf catcheth them, and s the sheep. 4650

SCATTERING (1) [SCATTER]
Isa 30:30 *with* s, and tempest, and hailstones. 5311

SCEPTRE (15) [SCEPTRES]
Ge 49:10 The s shall not depart from Judah, nor a 7626
Nu 24:17 a S shall rise out of Israel, and shall smite 7626
Est 4:11 whom the king shall hold out the golden s, 8275
5: 2 the king held out to Esther the golden s that 8275
5: 2 drew near, and touched the top of the s. 8275
8: 4 the king held out the golden s toward 8275
Ps 45: 6 the s of thy kingdom *is* a right sceptre. 7626
45: 6 the sceptre of thy kingdom *is* a right s. 7626
Isa 14: 5 staff of the wicked, *and* the s of the rulers. 7626
Eze 19:14 that she hath no strong rod *to be* a s to rule. 7626
Am 1: 5 him that holdeth the s from the house of 7626
1: 8 him that holdeth the s from Ashkelon, and 7626
Zec 10:11 and the s of Egypt shall depart away. 7626
Heb 1: 8 a s of righteousness *is* the sceptre of thy 4464
1: 8 a sceptre of righteousness *is* the s of thy 4464

SCEPTRES (1) [SCEPTRE]
Eze 19:11 she had strong rods for the s of them that 7626

SCEVA (1)
Ac 19:14 And there were seven sons of *one* S, a Jew, 4630

SCHEMES See MISCHIEF; MISCHIEFS

SCHEMING See SLEIGHT

SCHISM (1)
1Co 12:25 That there should be no s in the body; but 4978

SCHOLAR (2)
1Ch 25: 8 the small as the great, the teacher as the s. 8527
Mal 2:12 the master and the s, out of the tabernacles 6030

SCHOOL (1) [SCHOOLMASTER]
Ac 19: 9 disputing daily in the s of one Tyrannus. 4981

SCHOOLMASTER (2) [MASTER, SCHOOL]
Gal 3:24 Wherefore the law was our s *to bring us* 3807
3:25 faith is come, we are no longer under a s. 3807

SCIENCE (2)
Da 1: 4 understanding s, and such as *had* ability in 4093
1Ti 6:20 and oppositions of s falsely so called: 1108

SCOFF (1) [SCOFFERS]
Hab 1:10 they shall s at the kings, and the princes 7046

SCOFFERS (1) [SCOFF]
2Pe 3: 3 that there shall come in the last days s, 1703

SCORCH (1) [SCORCHED]
Rev 16: 8 *power* was given unto him to s men with 2739

SCORCHED (3) [SCORCH]
Mt 13: 6 And when the sun was up, they were s; and 2739
Mk 4: 6 But when the sun was up, it was s; and 2739
Rev 16: 9 And men were s *with* great heat, and 2739

SCORCHING See VEHEMENT

SCORN (16) [SCORNER, SCORNERS, SCORNEST, SCORNETH, SCORNFUL, SCORNING]
2Ki 19:21 hath despised thee, *and* **laughed** thee **to** s; 3932
2Ch 30:10 they **laughed** them **to** s, and mocked them. 7832
Ne 2:19 heard *it,* they **laughed** us **to** s, and 3932
Est 3: 6 he thought s to lay hands on Mordecai alone; 959
Job 12: 4 the just upright *man is* **laughed to** s. 7814
16:20 My friends s me: *but* mine eye poureth out 3887
22:19 are glad: and the innocent **laugh** them **to** s. 3932
Ps 22: 7 All they that see me **laugh** me **to** s: 3932
44:13 a s and a derision to them that are round 3933
79: 4 a s and derision to them that are round 3933
Isa 37:22 hath despised thee, *and* **laughed** thee **to** s; 3932
Eze 23:32 thou shalt be **laughed to** s and had in 6712
Hab 1:10 and the princes *shall be* a s unto them: 4890
Mt 9:24 but sleepeth. And they **laughed** him **to** s. 2606
Mk 5:40 And they **laughed** him **to** s. But when he 2606
Lk 8:53 And they **laughed** him **to** s, knowing that 2606

SCORNER (11) [SCORN]
Pr 9: 7 He that reproveth a s getteth to himself 3887
9: 8 Reprove not a s, lest he hate thee: rebuke a 3887
13: 1 but a s heareth not rebuke. 3887
14: 6 A s seeketh wisdom, and *findeth it* not: but 3887
15:12 A s loveth not one that reproveth him: 3887
19:25 Smite a s, and the simple will beware: and 3887
21:11 When the s is punished, the simple is made 3887
21:24 Proud *and* haughty s *is* his name, 3887
22:10 Cast out the s, and contention shall go out; 3887
24: 9 *is* sin: and the s *is* an abomination to men. 3887
Isa 29:20 the s is consumed, and all that watch for 3887

SCORNERS (4) [SCORN]
Pr 1:22 the s delight in their scorning, and 3887
3:34 Surely he scorneth the s: but he giveth 3887
19:29 Judgments are prepared for s, and 3887
Hos 7: 5 of wine; he stretched out his hand with s. 3945

SCORNEST (2) [SCORN]
Pr 9:12 but *if* thou s, thou alone shalt bear *it.* 3887
Eze 16:31 hast not been as a harlot, in that *thou* s hire; 7046

SCORNETH (4) [SCORN]
Job 39: 7 He s the multitude of the city, 7832
39:18 on high, she s the horse and his rider. 7832
Pr 3:34 Surely he s the scorners: but he giveth 3887
19:28 An ungodly witness s judgment: and 3887

SCORNFUL (3) [SCORN]
Ps 1: 1 of sinners, nor sitteth in the seat of the s. 3887
Pr 29: 8 S men bring a city into a snare: but 3944
Isa 28:14 hear the word of the LORD, ye s men, 3944

SCORNING (3) [SCORN]
Job 34: 7 *is* like Job, *who* drinketh up s like water? 3933
Ps 123: 4 Our soul is exceedingly filled *with* the s of 3933
Pr 1:22 the scorners delight in their s, and 3944

SCORPION (2) [SCORPIONS]
Lk 11:12 if he shall ask an egg, will he offer him a s? 4651
Rev 9: 5 and their torment *was* as the torment of a s, 4651

SCORPION PASS See MAALEH-ACRABBIM

SCORPIONS (9) [SCORPION]
Dt 8:15 s, and drought, where *there was* no water; 6137
1Ki 12:11 with whips, but I will chastise you with s. 6137
12:14 with whips, but I will chastise you with s. 6137
2Ch 10:11 with whips, but I *will chastise you* with s. 6137
10:14 with whips, but I *will chastise you* with s. 6137
Eze 2: 6 *be* with thee, and thou dost dwell among s: 6137
Lk 10:19 unto you power to tread on serpents and s, 4651
Rev 9: 3 as the s of the earth have power. 4651
9:10 And they had tails like unto s, and 4651

SCOUNDREL See NAUGHTINESS; NAUGHTY

SCOURED (1)
Lev 6:28 it shall be both s, and rinsed in water. 4838

SCOURGE (12) [SCOURGED, SCOURGES, SCOURGETH, SCOURGING, SCOURGINGS]
Job 5:21 Thou shalt be hid from the s of the tongue: 7752
9:23 If the s slay suddenly, he will laugh at 7752
Isa 10:26 the LORD of hosts shall stir up a s for him 7752
28:15 when the overflowing s shall pass through, 7752
28:18 when the overflowing s shall pass through, 7752
Mt 10:17 and they will s you in their synagogues; 3146
20:19 and to s, and to crucify *him: and* the third 3146
23:34 *some* of them shall ye s in your 3146
Mk 10:34 and shall s him, and shall spit upon him, 3146
Lk 18:33 And they shall s *him,* and put him to death: 3146
Jn 2:15 And when he had made a s of small cords, 5416
Ac 22:25 lawful for you to s a man *that is* a Roman, 3147

SCOURGED (4) [SCOURGE]
Lev 19:20 she shall be s; they shall not be put to 1244
Mt 27:26 and when he had s Jesus, he delivered *him* 5417
Mk 15:15 when he had s *him,* to be crucified. 5417
Jn 19: 1 therefore took Jesus, and s *him.* 3146

SCOURGES (1) [SCOURGE]
Jos 23:13 and s in your sides, and thorns in your eyes, 7850

SCOURGETH (1) [SCOURGE]
Heb 12: 6 and s every son whom he receiveth. 3146

SCOURGING (1) [SCOURGE]
Ac 22:24 and bade that he should be examined by s; 3148

SCOURGINGS (1) [SCOURGE]
Heb 11:36 others had trial of *cruel* mockings and s, 3148

SCRABLED (1)
1Sa 21:13 s on the doors of the gate, and let his spittle 8427

SCRAPE (3) [SCRAPED]
Lev 14:41 they shall pour out the dust that they s **off** 7096
Job 2: 8 he took him a potsherd to s himself withal; 1623
Eze 26: 4 I will also s her dust from her, and 5500

SCRAPED (2) [SCRAPE]
Lev 14:41 he shall **cause** the house **to be** s within 7106
14:43 after he hath s the house, and after it is 7096

SCRIBE (52) [SCRIBE'S, SCRIBES]
2Sa 8:17 *were* the priests; and Seraiah *was* the s; 5608
20:25 Sheva *was* s: and Zadok and Abiathar *were* 5608
2Ki 12:10 that the king's s and the high priest came 5608
18:18 Shebna the s, and Joah the son of Asaph 5608
18:37 Shebna the s, and Joah the son of Asaph 5608
19: 2 Shebna the s, and the elders of the priests, 5608
22: 3 the son of Meshullam, the s, *to* the house of 5608
22: 8 the high priest said unto Shaphan the s, 5608
22: 9 Shaphan the s came to the king, and 5608
22:10 Shaphan the s shewed the king, saying, 5608
22:12 Shaphan the s, and Asahiah a servant of 5608
25:19 in the city, and the principal s of the host, 5608
1Ch 18:16 *were* the priests; and Shavsha *was* s; 5608
24: 6 Shemaiah the son of Nethaneel the s, *one* of 5608
27:32 uncle *was* a counseller, a wise man, and a s: 5608
2Ch 24:11 the king's s and the high priest's officer 5608
26:11 of their account by the hand of Jeiel the s 5608
34:15 and said to Shaphan the s, 5608
34:18 Shaphan the s told the king, saying, 5608
34:20 Shaphan the s, and Asaiah a servant of 5608
Ezr 4: 8 Shimshai the s wrote a letter against 5613
4: 9 Shimshai the s, and the rest of their 5613
4:17 *to* Shimshai the s, and *to* the rest of their 5613
4:23 Shimshai the s, and their companions, 5613
7: 6 he *was* a ready s in the law of Moses, 5608
7:11 the s, *even* a scribe of the words of 5608
7:11 *even* a s of the words of 5608
7:12 a s of the law of the God of heaven, 5613
7:21 the s of the law of the God of heaven, 5613
Ne 8: 1 they spake unto Ezra the s to bring the book 5608
8: 4 Ezra the s stood upon a pulpit of wood, 5608
8: 9 Ezra the priest the s, and the Levites that 5608
8:13 the priests, and the Levites, unto Ezra the s, 5608
12:26 the governor, and of Ezra the priest, the s. 5608
12:36 man of God, and Ezra the s before them. 5608
13:13 Zadok the s, and of the Levites, Pedaiah: 5608
Isa 33:18 Where *is* the s? where *is* the receiver? 5608
36: 3 Shebna the s, and Joah, Asaph's son, 5608
36:22 Shebna the s, and Joah, the son of Asaph, 5608
37: 2 Shebna the s, and the elders of the priests 5608
Jer 36:10 of Gemariah the son of Shaphan the s, 5608
36:12 *even* Elishama the s, and Delaiah the son of 5608
36:20 the roll in the chamber of Elishama the s, 5608
36:26 to take Baruch the s and Jeremiah 5608
36:32 gave it to Baruch the s, the son of Neriah; 5608
37:15 *in* prison *in* the house of Jonathan the s: 5608
37:20 not to return *to* the house of Jonathan the s, 5608
52:25 the principal s of the host, who mustered 5608
Mt 8:19 And a certain s came, and said unto him, 1122
13:52 Therefore every s *which is* instructed unto 1122
Mk 12:32 And the s said unto him, Well, Master, 1122
1Co 1:20 where *is* the s? where *is* the disputer of this 1122

SCRIBE'S (2) [SCRIBE]
Jer 36:12 *into* the king's house, into the s chamber: 5608
36:21 he took it out of Elishama the s chamber. 5608

SCRIBES (68) [SCRIBE]
1Ki 4: 3 Elihoreph and Ahiah, the sons of Shisha, s; 5608
1Ch 2:55 the families of the s which dwelt at Jabez; 5608
2Ch 34:13 of the Levites *there were* s, and officers, 5608
Est 3:12 were the king's s called on the thirteenth 5608
8: 9 were the king's s called at that time in 5608
Jer 8: 8 certainly in vain made he *it;* the pen of the s 5608
Mt 2: 4 chief priests and s of the people together, 1122
5:20 shall exceed *the righteousness* of the s 1122
7:29 as *one* having authority, and not as the s. 1122
9: 3 certain of the s said within themselves, 1122
12:38 Then certain of the s and of the Pharisees 1122
15: 1 Then came to Jesus s and Pharisees, 1122
16:21 *things* of the elders and chief priests and s, 1122
17:10 then say the s that Elias must first come? 1122
20:18 unto the chief priests and *unto the* s, 1122
21:15 and s saw the wonderful *things* that he did, 1122
23: 2 The s and the Pharisees sit in Moses' seat: 1122
23:13 woe unto you, s and Pharisees, hypocrites! 1122
23:14 Woe unto you, s and Pharisees, hypocrites! 1122
23:15 Woe unto you, s and Pharisees, hypocrites! 1122
23:23 Woe unto you, s and Pharisees, hypocrites! 1122
23:25 Woe unto you, s and Pharisees, hypocrites! 1122
23:27 Woe unto you, s and Pharisees, hypocrites! 1122
23:29 Woe unto you, s and Pharisees, hypocrites! 1122
23:34 unto you prophets, and wise *men,* and s: 1122
26: 3 and the s, and the elders of the people, 1122
26:57 where the s and the elders were assembled. 1122
27:41 the chief priests mocking *him,* with the s 1122
Mk 1:22 as *one* that had authority, and not as the s. 1122
2: 6 But there were certain of the s sitting there, 1122
2:16 And when the s and Pharisees saw him eat 1122
3:22 And the s which came down from 1122
7: 1 and certain of the s, which came from 1122
7: 5 Then the Pharisees and s asked him, 1122
8:31 of the elders, and *of* the chief priests, and s, 1122
9:11 Why say the s that Elias must first come? 1122
9:14 and *the* s questioning with them. 1122
9:16 And he asked the s, What question ye with 1122
10:33 unto the chief priests, and unto the s; 1122
11:18 And the s and chief priests heard *it,* and 1122
11:27 the chief priests, and the s, and the elders, 1122
12:28 And one of the s came, and having heard 1122
12:35 How say the s that Christ is the Son of 1122
12:38 Beware of the s, which love to go in long 1122
14: 1 the s sought how they might take him by 1122
14:43 the chief priests and the s and the elders. 1122
14:53 all the chief priests and the elders and the s. 1122
15: 1 with the elders and s and the whole council, 1122
15:31 mocking said among themselves with the s, 1122
Lk 5:21 And the s and the Pharisees began to 1122
5:30 But their s and Pharisees murmured against 1122
6: 7 And the s and Pharisees watched him, 1122
9:22 of the elders and chief priests and s, 1122
11:44 Woe unto you, s and Pharisees, hypocrites! 1122
11:53 the s and the Pharisees began to urge *him* 1122
15: 2 And the Pharisees and s murmured, saying, 1122
19:47 But the chief priests and the s and the chief 1122
20: 1 and the s came upon *him* with the elders, 1122
20:19 the s the same hour sought to lay hands on 1122
20:39 Then certain of the s answering said, 1122
20:46 Beware of the s, which desire to walk in 1122
22: 2 and s sought how they might kill him; 1122
22:66 the chief priests and the s came together, 1122
23:10 And the chief priests and s stood and 1122
Jn 8: 3 And the s and Pharisees brought unto him a 1122
Ac 4: 5 that their rulers, and elders, and s, 1122
6:12 and the s, and came upon *him,* and 1122
23: 9 the s *that were* of the Pharisees' part arose, 1122

SCRIP (7)
1Sa 17:40 a shepherd's bag which he had, even in a s; 3219
Mt 10:10 Nor s for *your* journey, neither two coats, 4082
Mk 6: 8 no s, no bread, no money in *their* purse: 4082
Lk 9: 3 neither staves, nor s, neither bread, 4082
10: 4 Carry neither purse, nor s, nor shoes: and 4082
22:35 I sent you without purse, and s, and shoes, 4082
22:36 a purse, let him take *it,* and likewise *his* s: 4082

SCRIPTURE (32) [SCRIPTURES]
Da 10:21 I will shew thee that which is noted in the s 3791
Mk 12:10 And have ye not read this s; The stone 1124
15:28 And the s was fulfilled, which saith, 1124
Lk 4:21 This day is this s fulfilled in your ears. 1124
Jn 2:22 and they believed the s, and the word which 1124
7:38 He that believeth on me, as the s hath said, 1124
7:42 Hath not the s said, That Christ cometh of 1124
10:35 of God came, and the s cannot be broken; 1124
13:18 but that the s may be fulfilled, He that 1124

Jn 17:12 of perdition; that the s might be fulfilled. *1124*
19:24 that the s might be fulfilled, which saith, *1124*
19:28 that the s might be fulfilled, saith, I thirst. *1124*
19:36 were done, that the s should be fulfilled, *1124*
19:37 And again another s saith, They shall look *1124*
20: 9 For as yet they knew not the s, that he must *1124*
Ac 1:16 this s must needs have been fulfilled, *1124*
8:32 The place of the s which he read was this, *1124*
8:35 and began at the same s, and preached unto *1124*
Ro 4: 3 For what saith the s? Abraham believed *1124*
9:17 For the s saith unto Pharaoh, Even for this *1124*
10:11 For the s saith, Whosoever believeth on *1124*
11: 2 Wot ye not what the s saith of Elias? how *1124*
Gal 3: 8 And the s, foreseeing that God would *1124*
3:22 But the s hath concluded all under sin, *1124*
4:30 Nevertheless what saith the s? Cast out *1124*
1Ti 5:18 For the s saith, Thou shalt not muzzle *1124*
2Ti 3:16 All s *is* given by inspiration of God, and *1124*
Jas 2: 8 If ye fulfil the royal law according to the s, *1124*
2:23 And the s was fulfilled which saith, *1124*
4: 5 Do ye think that the s saith in vain, *1124*
1Pe 2: 6 Wherefore also it is contained in the s, *1124*
2Pe 1:20 that no prophecy of the s is of *any* private *1124*

SCRIPTURES (21) [SCRIPTURE]

Mt 21:42 saith unto them, Did ye never read in the s, *1124*
22:29 unto them, Ye do err, not knowing the s, *1124*
26:54 *But* how then shall the s be fulfilled, *1124*
26:56 that the s of the prophets might be fulfilled. *1124*
Mk 12:24 therefore err, because ye know not the s, *1124*
14:49 ye took me not: but the s must be fulfilled. *1124*
Lk 24:27 he expounded unto them in all the s *1124*
24:32 the way, and while he opened to us the s? *1124*
24:45 that *they* might understand the s, *1124*
Jn 5:39 Search the S; for in them ye think ye have *1124*
Ac 17: 2 days reasoned with them out of the s, *1124*
17:11 and searched the s daily, whether those *1124*
18:24 an eloquent man, *and* mighty in the s, *1124*
18:28 shewing by the s that Jesus was Christ. *1124*
Ro 1: 2 afore by his prophets in the holy s,) *1124*
15: 4 and comfort of the s might have hope. *1124*
16:26 and by the s of the prophets, *1124*
1Co 15: 3 Christ died for our sins according to the s; *1124*
15: 4 rose *again* the third day according to the s: *1124*
2Ti 3:15 from a child thou hast known the holy s, *1121*
2Pe 3:16 unstable wrest, as *they do* also the other s, *1124*

SCROLE (2)

Isa 34: 4 the heavens shall be rolled together as a s: 5612
Rev 6:14 And the heaven departed as a s when it is *975*

SCROLL See BOOK; SCROLE; VOLUME

SCUM (5)

Eze 24: 6 to the pot whose s *is* therein, and 2457
24: 6 *is* therein, and whose s is not gone out of it! 2457
24:11 in it, *that* the s of it may be consumed. 2457
24:12 and her great s went not forth out of her: 2457
24:12 forth out of her: her s *shall be* in the fire. 2457

SCURVY (2)

Lev 21:20 or be s, or scabbed, or hath his stones 1618
22:22 maimed, or having a wen, or s, or scabbed, 1618

SCYTHIAN (1)

Col 3:11 barbarian, S, bond *nor* free: *4658*

SEA (400) [SEAFARING, SEAS]

Ge 1:26 them have dominion over the fish of the s, 3220
1:28 have dominion over the fish of the s, and 3220
9: 2 the earth, and upon all the fishes of the s; 3220
14: 3 in the vale of Siddim, which *is* the salt s. 3220
22:17 and as the sand which *is* upon the s shore; 3220
32:12 make thy seed as the sand of the s, 3220
41:49 Joseph gathered corn as the sand of the s, 3220
49:13 Zebulun shall dwell at the haven of the s; 3220
Ex 10:19 the locusts, and cast them into the Red s; 3220
13:18 the way of the wilderness of the Red s: 3220
14: 2 between Migdol and the s, over against 3220
14: 2 before it shall ye encamp by the s. 3220
14: 9 overtook them encamping by the s, 3220
14:16 stretch out thine hand over the s, and 3220
14:16 on dry *ground* through the midst of the s. 3220
14:21 Moses stretched out his hand over the s; 3220
14:21 the LORD caused the s to go *back* by a 3220
14:21 made the s dry *land,* and the waters were 3220
14:22 into the midst of the s upon the dry *ground:* 3220
14:23 went in after them to the midst of the s, 3220
14:26 Stretch out thine hand over the s, 3220
14:27 Moses stretched forth his hand over the s, 3220
14:27 the s returned to his strength when 3220
14:27 the Egyptians in the midst of the s. 3220
14:28 all the host of Pharaoh that came into the s 3220
14:29 walked upon dry *land* in the midst of the s; 3220
14:30 Israel saw the Egyptians dead upon the s 3220
15: 1 and his rider hath he thrown into the s. 3220
15: 4 and his host hath he cast into the s: 3220
15: 4 captains also are drowned in the Red s. 3220
15: 8 depths were congealed in the heart of the s. 3220
15:10 blow with thy wind, the s covered them: 3220
15:19 and with his horsemen into the s, 3220
15:19 again the waters of the s upon them; 3220
15:19 went on dry *land* in the midst of the s. 3220
15:21 and his rider hath he thrown into the s. 3220
15:22 So Moses brought Israel from the Red s, 3220
20:11 the s, and all that in them *is,* and rested 3220
23:31 I will set thy bounds from the Red s even 3220
23:31 Red sea even unto the s of the Philistines, 3220
Nu 11:22 shall all the fish of the s be gathered 3220
11:31 brought quails from the s, and let *them* fall 3220
13:29 the Canaanites dwell by the s, and by 3220
14:25 *into* the wilderness *by* the way of the Red s. 3220
21: 4 from mount Hor *by* the way of the Red s, 3220
21:14 What he did in the Red s, and *in* the brooks 5492

Nu 33: 8 passed through the midst of the s into 3220
33:10 from Elim, and encamped by the Red s. 3220
33:11 they removed from the Red s, and 3220
34: 3 be the outmost coast of the salt s eastward: 3220
34: 5 and the goings out of it shall be at the s. 3220
34: 6 you shall even have the great s for a border: 3220
34: 7 from the great s you shall point out for you 3220
34:11 shall reach unto the side of the s of 3220
34:12 and the goings out of it shall be *at* the salt s: 3220
Dt 1: 1 in the plain over against the Red *s,* between NIH
1: 7 the vale, and in the south, and by the s side, 3220
1:40 into the wilderness *by* the way of the Red s. 3220
2: 1 into the wilderness *by* the way of the Red s, 3220
3:17 Chinnereth even unto the s of the plain, 3220
3:17 *even* the salt s, under Ashdoth-pisgah 3220
4:49 even unto the s of the plain, under 3220
11: 4 how he made the water of the Red s to 3220
11:24 even unto the uttermost s shall your coast 3220
30:13 Neither *is* it beyond the s, that *thou* 3220
30:13 Who shall go over the s for us, and bring it 3220
34: 2 and all the land of Judah, unto the utmost s, 3220
Jos 1: 4 unto the great s *toward* the going down of 3220
2:10 dried up the water of the Red s for you, 3220
3:16 those that came down toward the s of 3220
3:16 *even* the salt s, failed, *and* were cut off: 3220
4:23 as the LORD your God did to the Red s, 3220
5: 1 of the Canaanites, which *were* by the s, 3220
9: 1 in all the coasts of the great s over against 3220
11: 4 *even* as the sand that *is* upon the s shore in 3220
12: 3 *from* the plain to the s of Cinneroth on 3220
12: 3 unto the s of the plain, *even* the salt sea on 3220
12: 3 sea of the plain, *even* the salt s on the east, 3220
13:27 *even* unto the edge of the s of Cinnereth on 3220
15: 2 border was from the shore of the salt s, 3220
15: 4 the goings out of that coast were at the s: 3220
15: 5 the east border *was* the salt s, *even* unto 3220
15: 5 bay of the s at the uttermost part of Jordan: 3220
15:11 the goings out of the border were at the s. 3220
15:12 the west border *was* to the great s, and 3220
15:46 From Ekron even unto the s, all that *lay* 3220
15:47 and the great s, and the border *thereof.* 3220
16: 3 and the goings out thereof are at the s. 3220
16: 6 the border went out toward the s *to* 3220
16: 8 and the goings out thereof were at the s. 3220
17: 9 and the outgoings of it were at the s: 3220
17:10 *it was* Manasseh's, and the s is his border; 3220
18:14 compassed the corner of the s southward, 3220
18:19 bay of the salt s at the south end of Jordan: 3220
19:11 their border went up toward the s, and 3220
19:29 the outgoings thereof are at the s from 3220
23: 4 cut off, even *unto* the great s westward. 3220
24: 6 you came unto the s; and the Egyptians 3220
24: 6 with chariots and horsemen *unto* the Red s. 3220
24: 7 brought the s upon them, and 3220
Jdg 5:17 Asher continued on the s shore, and 3220
7:12 as the sand by the s side for multitude. 3220
11:16 through the wilderness unto the Red s, 3220
1Sa 13: 5 people as the sand which *is* on the s shore 3220
2Sa 17:11 as the sand that *is* by the s for multitude; 3220
22:16 the channels of the s appeared, 3220
1Ki 4:20 as the sand which *is* by the s in multitude, 3220
4:29 *even* as the sand that *is* on the s shore. 3220
5: 9 bring *them* down from Lebanon unto the s: 3220
5: 9 I will convey them by s *in* flotes unto 3220
7:23 he made a molten s, ten cubits from the one 3220
7:24 in a cubit, compassing the s round about: 3220
7:25 the s *was set* above upon them, and all their 3220
7:39 he set the s on the right side of the house 3220
7:44 And one s, and twelve oxen under the sea; 3220
7:44 And one sea, and twelve oxen under the s; 3220
9:26 on the shore of the Red s, in the land of 3220
9:27 shipmen that had knowledge of the s, 3220
10:22 For the king had at s a navy of Tharshish 3220
18:43 his servant, Go up now, look toward the s. 3220
18:44 there ariseth a little cloud out of the s, 3220
2Ki 14:25 entering of Hamath unto the s of the plain, 3220
16:17 took down the s from off the brasen oxen 3220
25:13 the brasen s that *was* in the house of 3220
25:16 one s, and the bases which Solomon had 3220
1Ch 16:32 Let the s roar, and the fulness thereof: 3220
18: 8 wherewith Solomon made the brasen s, and 3220
2Ch 2:16 we will bring it to thee *in* flotes by s *to* 3220
4: 2 Also he made a molten s of ten cubits from 3220
4: 3 in a cubit, compassing the s round about. 3220
4: 4 the s *was set* above upon them, and all their 3220
4: 6 but the s *was* for the priests to wash in. 3220
4:10 he set the s on the right side of the east end, 3220
4:15 One s, and twelve oxen under it. 3220
8:17 to Eloth, at the s side in the land of Edom. 3220
8:18 and servants that had knowledge of the s; 3220
20: 2 thee from beyond the s on this side Syria; 3220
Ezr 3: 7 to bring cedar trees from Lebanon to the s 3220
Ne 9: 9 and heardest their cry by the Red s; 3220
9:11 thou didst divide the s before them, so 3220
9:11 that they went through the midst of the s on 3220
Est 10: 1 upon the land, and *upon* the isles of the s. 3220
Job 6: 3 it would be heavier than the sand of the s: 3220
7:12 *Am* I a s, or a whale, that thou settest a 3220
9: 8 and treadeth upon the waves of the s. 3220
11: 9 than the earth, and broader than the s. 3220
12: 8 the fishes of the s shall declare unto thee. 3220
14:11 *As* the waters fail from the s, and the flood 3220
26:12 He divideth the s with his power, and 3220
28:14 not in me: and the s saith, *It is* not with me. 3220
36:30 upon it, and covereth the bottom of the s. 3220
38: 8 Or *who* shut up the s with doors, when it 3220
38:16 Hast thou entered into the springs of the s? 3220
41:31 he maketh the s like a pot of ointment. 3220
Ps 8: 8 the fish of the s, *and whatsoever* passeth 3220
33: 7 He gathereth the waters of the s together as 3220
46: 2 be carried into the midst of the s; 3220
65: 5 and of them that are afar off *upon* the s: 3220
66: 6 He turned the s into dry *land:* they went 3220
68:22 *my people* again from the depths of the s: 3220
72: 8 He shall have dominion also from s to sea, 3220

Ps 72: 8 He shall have dominion also from sea to s, 3220
74:13 Thou didst divide the s by thy strength: 3220
77:19 Thy way *is* in the s, and thy path in 3220
78:13 He divided the s, and caused them to pass 3220
78:27 feathered fowls like as the sand of the s: 3220
78:53 but the s overwhelmed their enemies. 3220
80:11 She sent out her boughs unto the s, and 3220
89: 9 Thou rulest the raging of the s: when 3220
89:25 I will set his hand also in the s, and 3220
93: 4 *yea, than* the mighty waves of the s. 3220
95: 5 The s *is* his, and he made it: and his hands 3220
96:11 let the s roar, and the fulness thereof. 3220
98: 7 Let the s roar, and the fulness thereof; 3220
104:25 *So is* this great and wide s, wherein *are* 3220
106: 7 provoked *him* at the s, *even* at the Red sea. 3220
106: 7 provoked *him* at the sea, *even* at the Red s. 3220
106: 9 He rebuked the Red s also, and it was dried 3220
106:22 of Ham, *and* terrible *things* by the Red s. 3220
107:23 They that go down to the s in ships, that do 3220
114: 3 The s saw *it,* and fled: Jordan was driven 3220
114: 5 What ailed thee, O thou s, that thou 3220
136:13 To him which divided the Red s into parts: 3220
136:15 and his host in the Red s: 3220
139: 9 *and* dwell in the uttermost parts of the s; 3220
146: 6 and earth, the s, and all that therein is: 3220
Pr 8:29 When he gave to the s his decree, that 3220
23:34 as he that lieth down in the midst of the s, 3220
30:19 the way of a ship in the midst of the s; and 3220
Ecc 1: 7 All the rivers run into the s; yet the sea *is* 3220
1: 7 rivers run into the sea; yet the s *is* not full; 3220
Isa 5:30 roar against them like the roaring of the s: 3220
9: 1 grievously afflict *her by* the way of the s, 3220
10:22 thy people Israel be as the sand of the s, 3220
10:26 *as* his rod *was* upon the s, so shall he lift it 3220
11: 9 of the LORD, as the waters cover the s. 3220
11:11 from Hamath, and from the islands of the s. 3220
11:15 utterly destroy the tongue of the Egyptian s; 3220
16: 8 are stretched out, they are gone over the s. 3220
18: 2 That sendeth ambassadors by the s, even in 3220
19: 5 the waters shall fail from the s, and 3220
21: 1 The burden of the desert of the s. 3220
23: 2 that pass over the s, have replenished. 3220
23: 4 for the s hath spoken, *even* the strength of 3220
23: 4 *even* the strength of the s, saying, I travail 3220
23:11 He stretched out his hand over the s, 3220
24:14 they shall cry aloud from the s. 3220
24:15 LORD God of Israel in the isles of the s. 3220
27: 1 and he shall slay the dragon that *is* in the s. 3220
42:10 ye that go down to the s, and all that is 3220
43:16 which maketh a way in the s, and a path in 3220
48:18 and thy righteousness as the waves of the s: 3220
50: 2 behold, at my rebuke I dry up the s, I make 3220
51:10 *Art* thou not it which hath dried the s, 3220
51:10 that hath made the depths of the s a way for 3220
51:15 that divided the s, whose waves roared: 3220
57:20 the wicked *are* like the troubled s, when it 3220
60: 5 the abundance of the s shall be converted 3220
63:11 out of the s with the shepherd of his flock? 3220
Jer 5:22 the bound of the s *by* a perpetual decree, 3220
6:23 their voice roareth like the s; and they ride 3220
25:22 kings of the isles which *are* beyond the s, 3220
27:19 concerning the s, and concerning the bases, 3220
31:35 which divideth the s when the waves 3220
33:22 neither the sand of the s measured: 3220
46:18 and as Carmel by the s, *so* shall he come. 3220
47: 7 against Ashkelon, and against the s shore? 3220
48:32 thy plants are gone over the s, they reach 3220
48:32 the sea, they reach *even* to the s of Jazer: 3220
49:21 the noise thereof was heard in the Red s. 3220
49:23 *there is* sorrow on the s; it cannot be quiet. 3220
50:42 their voice shall roar like the s, and 3220
51:36 I will dry up her s, and make her springs 3220
51:42 The s is come up upon Babylon: she is 3220
52:17 the brasen s that *was* in the house of 3220
52:20 one s, and twelve brasen bulls that *were* 3220
La 2:13 for thy breach *is* great like the s: who can 3220
4: 3 Even the s **monsters** draw out the breast, 8577
Eze 25:16 and destroy the remnant of the s coast. 3220
26: 3 as the s causeth his waves to come up. 3220
26: 5 the spreading of nets in the midst of the s: 3220
26:16 all the princes of the s shall come down 3220
26:17 which wast strong in the s, she and 3220
26:18 the isles that *are* in the s shall be troubled at 3220
27: 3 O thou that art situate at the entry of the s, 3220
27: 9 all the ships of the s with their mariners 3220
27:29 the mariners, *and* all the pilots of the s, 3220
27:32 like the destroyed in the midst of the s? 3220
38:20 So that the fishes of the s, and the fowls of 3220
39:11 valley of the passengers *on* the east of the s: 3220
47: 8 go down into the desert, and go into the s: 3220
47: 8 *which* being brought forth into the s, 3220
47:10 as the fish of the great s, exceeding many. 3220
47:15 from the great s, the way of Hethlon, as 3220
47:17 the border from the s shall be Hazar-enan, 3220
47:18 *by* Jordan, from the border unto the east s. 3220
47:19 of strife *in* Kadesh, *the* river to the great s. 3220
47:20 The west side also *shall be* the great s from 3220
48:28 *and to the* river toward the great s. 3220
Da 7: 2 winds of the heaven strove upon the great s. 3221
7: 3 four great beasts came up from the s, 3221
Hos 1:10 of Israel shall be as the sand of the s, 3220
4: 3 the fishes of the s also shall be taken away. 3220
Joel 2:20 with his face toward the east s, and 3220
2:20 his hinder part towards the utmost s, and 3220
Am 5: 8 that calleth for the waters of the s, and 3220
8:12 they shall wander from s to sea, and 3220
8:12 they shall wander from sea to s, and 3220
9: 3 be hid from my sight in the bottom of the s, 3220
9: 6 he that calleth for the waters of the s, and 3220
Jnh 1: 4 the LORD sent out a great wind into the s, 3220
1: 4 there was a mighty tempest in the s, so 3220
1: 5 the wares that *were* in the ship into the s, 3220
1: 9 which hath made the s and the dry *land.* 3220
1:11 unto thee, that the s may be calm unto us? 3220
1:11 for the s wrought, and was tempestuous. 3220

S

Jnh 1:12 Take me up, and cast me forth into the **s**; 3220
1:12 the sea; so shall the **s** be calm unto you: 3220
1:13 for the **s** wrought, and was tempestuous 3220
1:15 took up Jonah, and cast him forth into the **s**: 3220
1:15 the sea: and the **s** ceased from her raging. 3220
Mic 7:12 from **s** *to* sea, and *from* mountain *to* 3220
7:12 from sea *to* **s**, and *from* mountain *to* 3220
7:19 cast all their sins into the depths of the **s**. 3220
Na 1: 4 He rebuketh the **s**, and maketh it dry, and 3220
3: 8 whose rampart *was* the **s**, *and* her wall *was* 3220
3: 8 *was* the sea, *and* her wall *was* from the **s**? 3220
Hab 1:14 makest men as the fishes of the **s**, as 3220
2:14 of the LORD, as the waters cover the **s**. 3220
3: 8 *was* thy wrath against the **s**, that thou didst 3220
3:15 Thou didst walk through the **s** *with* thine 3220
Zep 1: 3 the fishes of the **s**, and the stumblingblocks 3220
2: 5 Woe unto the inhabitants of the **s** coast, 3220
2: 6 the **s** coast shall be dwellings *and* 3220
Hag 2: 6 and the earth, and the **s**, and the dry *land;* 3220
Zec 9: 4 and he will smite her power in the **s**; 3220
9:10 his dominion *shall be* from **s** *even* to sea, 3220
9:10 his dominion *shall be* from sea *even* to **s**, 3220
10:11 he shall pass through the **s** *with* affliction, 3220
10:11 shall smite the waves in the **s**, and all 3220
14: 8 half of them toward the former **s**, and 3220
14: 8 and half of them toward the hinder **s**: 3220
Mt 4:13 in Capernaum, which is **upon the s coast**, *3864*
4:15 *by* the way of the **s**, beyond Jordan, *2281*
4:18 And Jesus, walking by the **s** of Galilee, *2281*
4:18 Andrew his brother, casting a net into the **s**: *2281*
8:24 there arose a great tempest in the **s**, *2281*
8:26 he arose, and rebuked the winds and the **s**; *2281*
8:27 that even the winds and the **s** obey him? *2281*
8:32 ran violently down a steep place into the **s**, *2281*
13: 1 Jesus out of the house, and sat by the **s** side. *2281*
13:47 *that was* cast into the **s**, and gathered of *2281*
14:24 But the ship was now in the midst of the **s**, *2281*
14:25 Jesus went unto them, walking on the **s**. *2281*
14:26 the disciples saw him walking on the **s**, *2281*
15:29 and came nigh unto the **s** of Galilee; *2281*
17:27 go thou to the **s**, and cast a hook, and *2281*
18: 6 *that* he were drowned in the depth of the **s**. *2281*
21:21 thou removed, and be thou cast into the **s**; *2281*
23:15 for ye compass **s** and land to make one *2281*
Mk 1:16 Now as he walked by the **s** of Galilee, *2281*
1:16 Andrew his brother casting a net into the **s**: *2281*
2:13 And he went forth again by the **s** side; and *2281*
3: 7 himself with his disciples to the **s**: *2281*
4: 1 And he began again to teach by the **s** side: *2281*
4: 1 that he entered into a ship, and sat in the **s**; *2281*
4: 1 the whole multitude was by the **s** on *2281*
4:39 and said unto the **s**, Peace, be still. *2281*
4:41 that even the wind and the **s** obey him? *2281*
5: 1 they came over unto the other side of the **s**, *2281*
5:13 ran violently down a steep place into the **s**, *2281*
5:13 two thousand;) and were choked in the **s**. *2281*
5:21 unto him: and he was nigh unto the **s**. *2281*
6:47 the ship was in the midst of the **s**, and *2281*
6:48 walking upon the **s**, and would have passed *2281*
6:49 But when they saw him walking upon the **s**, *2281*
7:31 and Sidon, he came unto the **s** of Galilee, *2281*
9:42 about his neck, and he were cast into the **s**. *2281*
11:23 thou removed, and be thou cast into the **s**; *2281*
Lk 6:17 and *from* the **s coast** of Tyre and Sidon, *3882*
17: 2 and he cast into the **s**, than that he should *2281*
17: 6 up by the root, and be thou planted in the **s**; *2281*
21:25 the **s** and the waves roaring; *2281*
Jn 6: 1 After these *things* Jesus went over the **s** of *2281*
6: 1 the sea of Galilee, *which is* the **s** of Tiberias. NIG
6:16 his disciples went down unto the **s**, *2281*
6:17 and went over the **s** towards Capernaum. *2281*
6:18 And the **s** arose by reason of a great wind *2281*
6:19 they see Jesus walking on the **s**, and *2281*
6:22 **s** saw that there was none other boat there, *2281*
6:25 had found him on the other side of the **s**, *2281*
21: 1 again to the disciples at the **s** of Tiberias; *2281*
21: 7 was naked,) and did cast himself into the **s**. *2281*
Ac 4:24 and earth, and the **s**, and all that in them is: *2281*
7:36 and in the Red **s**, and in the wilderness *2281*
10: 6 a tanner, whose house is by the **s** side: *2281*
10:32 house of *one* Simon a tanner by the **s** side: *2281*
14:15 and the **s**, and all *things* that are therein: *2281*
17:14 sent away Paul to go as *it were* to the **s**: *2281*
27: 5 And when we had sailed over the **s** of *3989*
27:30 when they had let down the boat into the **s**, *2281*
27:38 the ship, and cast out the wheat into the **s**. *2281*
27:40 they committed *themselves* unto the **s**, and *2281*
27:43 swim should cast *themselves* first into *the* **s**, NIG
28: 4 whom, though he hath escaped the **s**, *2281*
Ro 9:27 the children of Israel be as the sand of the **s**, *2281*
1Co 10: 1 the cloud, and all passed through the **s**; *2281*
10: 2 unto Moses in the cloud and in the **s**; *2281*
2Co 11:26 *in* perils in the wilderness, *in* perils in the **s**, *2281*
Heb 11:12 as the sand which is by the **s** shore *2281*
11:29 By faith they passed through the Red **s** as *2281*
Jas 1: 6 for he that wavereth is like a wave of the **s** *2281*
3: 7 and of *things* **in the s**, is tamed, and *1724*
Jude 1:13 Raging waves of the **s**, foaming out their *2281*
Rev 4: 6 And before the throne *there was* a **s** of glass *2281*
5:13 and such as are in the **s**, and all that are in *2281*
7: 1 on the earth, nor on the **s**, nor on any tree. *2281*
7: 2 it was given to hurt the earth and the **s**, *2281*
7: 3 not the earth, neither the **s**, nor the trees, *2281*
8: 8 burning with fire was cast into the **s**: *2281*
8: 8 and the third *part* of the **s** became blood; *2281*
8: 9 *part* of the creatures which were in the **s**, *2281*
10: 2 and he set his right foot upon the **s**, and *2281*
10: 5 And the angel which I saw stand upon the **s** *2281*
10: 6 and the **s**, and the *things* which are therein, *2281*
10: 8 hand of the angel which standeth upon the **s** *2281*
12:12 to the inhabiters of the earth and of the **s**! *2281*
13: 1 And I stood upon the sand of the **s**, and *2281*
13: 1 and saw a beast rise up out of the **s**, *2281*
14: 7 and the **s**, and the fountains of waters. *2281*
15: 2 And I saw as *it were* a **s** of glass mingled *2281*
Rev 15: 2 stand on the **s** of glass, having *the* harps of *2281*
16: 3 second angel poured out his vial upon the **s**; *2281*
16: 3 and every living soul died in the **s**. *2281*
18:17 and sailers, and as many as trade by **s**, *2281*
18:19 ships in the **s** by reason of her costliness: *2281*
18:21 and cast *it* into the **s**, saying, *2281*
20: 8 the number of whom *is* as the sand of the **s**. *2281*
20:13 And the **s** gave up the dead which were in *2281*
21: 1 passed away; and there was no more **s**. *2281*

SEA COWS See BADGERS'

SEAFARING (1) [FARE, SEA]

Eze 26:17 *that wast* inhabited of **s** men, the renowned 3220

SEAL (26) [SEALED, SEALEST, SEALETH, SEALING, SEALS]

1Ki 21: 8 sealed *them* with his **s**, and sent the letters 2368
Ne 9:38 our princes, Levites, *and* priests, **s** *unto it.* 2856
Est 8: 8 king's name, and **s** *it* with the king's ring: 2856
Job 38:14 It is turned as clay *to* the **s**; and they stand 2368
41:15 *his* pride, shut up *together as with* a close **s**. 2368
SS 8: 6 Set me as a **s** upon thine heart, as a seal 2368
8: 6 seal upon thine heart, as a **s** upon thine arm: 2368
Isa 8:16 **s** the law among my disciples. 2856
Jer 32:44 **s** *them,* and take witnesses in the land of 2856
Da 9:24 to **s up** the vision and prophecy, and 2856
12: 4 shut up the words, and **s** the book, 2856
Jn 3:33 testimony hath **set to** *his* **s** that God is true. *4972*
Ro 4:11 a **s** of the righteousness of the faith which *4973*
1Co 9: 2 for the **s** of mine apostleship are ye in *4973*
2Ti 2:19 having this **s**, The Lord knoweth them that *4973*
Rev 6: 3 And when he had opened the second **s**, *4973*
6: 5 And when he had opened the third **s**, *4973*
6: 7 And when he had opened the fourth **s**, *4973*
6: 9 And when he had opened the fifth **s**, I saw *4973*
6:12 I beheld when he had opened the sixth **s**, *4973*
7: 2 the east, having the **s** of the living God: *4973*
8: 1 And when he had opened the seventh **s**, *4973*
9: 4 only *those* men which have not the **s** of *4973*
10: 4 **S** *up those things* which the seven thunders *4972*
20: 3 and shut him up, and **set a s** upon him, *4972*
22:10 **S** not the sayings of the prophecy of this *4972*

SEALED (36) [SEAL]

Dt 32:34 with me, *and* **s up** among my treasures? 2856
1Ki 21: 8 **s** *them* with his seal, and sent the letters 2856
Ne 10: 1 Now those that **s** *were,* Nehemiah, 2856
Est 3:12 was it written, and **s** with the king's ring. 2856
8: 8 **s** with the king's ring, may no man reverse. 2856
8:10 **s** *it* with the king's ring, and sent letters by 2856
Job 14:17 My transgression *is* **s up** in a bag, and 2856
SS 4:12 *my* spouse; a spring shut up, a fountain **s**. 2856
Isa 29:11 unto you as the words of a book that is **s**, 2856
29:11 pray thee: and he saith, I cannot; for it *is* **s**: 2856
Jer 32:10 **s** *it,* and took witnesses, and weighed *him* 2856
32:11 *both* that which was **s** *according to* the law 2856
32:14 both which is **s**, and this evidence which is 2856
Da 6:17 the king **s** it with his own signet, and 2857
12: 9 *are* closed up and **s** till the time of the end. 2856
Jn 6:27 unto you: for him hath God the Father **s**. *4972*
Ro 15:28 and have **s** to them this fruit, *4972*
2Co 1:22 Who hath also **s** us, and given the earnest *4972*
Eph 1:13 ye were **s** with *that* holy Spirit of promise, *4972*
4:30 whereby ye are **s** unto the day of *4972*
Rev 5: 1 and on the backside, **s** with seven seals. *2696*
7: 3 till we have **s** the servants of our God in *4972*
7: 4 I heard the number of them which were **s**: *4972*
7: 4 *and there were* **s** an hundred *and* forty *and* *4972*
7: 5 Of the tribe of Juda *were* **s** twelve *4972*
7: 5 Of the tribe of Reuben *were* **s** twelve *4972*
7: 5 Of the tribe of Gad *were* **s** twelve thousand. *4972*
7: 6 Of the tribe of Aser *were* **s** twelve *4972*
7: 6 Of the tribe of Nephthalim *were* **s** twelve *4972*
7: 6 Of the tribe of Manasses *were* **s** twelve *4972*
7: 7 Of the tribe of Simeon *were* **s** twelve *4972*
7: 7 Of the tribe of Levi *were* **s** twelve *4972*
7: 7 Of the tribe of Isachar *were* **s** twelve *4972*
7: 8 Of the tribe of Zabulon *were* **s** twelve *4972*
7: 8 Of the tribe of Joseph *were* **s** twelve *4972*
7: 8 Of the tribe of Benjamin *were* **s** twelve *4972*

SEALEST (1) [SEAL]

Eze 28:12 Thou **s up** the sum, full *of* wisdom, and 2856

SEALETH (3) [SEAL]

Job 9: 7 and it riseth not; and **s up** the stars. 1157+2856
33:16 the ears of men, and **s** their instruction. 2856
37: 7 He **s up** the hand of every man; that all 2856

SEALING (1) [SEAL]

Mt 27:66 **s** the stone, and setting a watch. *4972*

SEALS (5) [SEAL]

Rev 5: 1 and on the backside, sealed with seven **s**. *4973*
5: 2 open the book, and to loose the **s** thereof? *4973*
5: 5 the book, and to loose the seven **s** thereof. *4973*
5: 9 to take the book, and to open the **s** thereof: *4973*
6: 1 I saw when the Lamb opened one of the **s**, *4973*

SEAM (1)

Jn 19:23 now the coat was **without s**, woven from *729*

SEARCH (48) [SEARCHED, SEARCHEST, SEARCHETH, SEARCHING, SEARCHINGS, UNSEARCHABLE]

Lev 27:33 He shall not **s** whether it be good or bad, 1239
Nu 10:33 to **s out** a resting place for them. 8446
13: 2 that they may **s** the land of Canaan, 8446
13:32 through which we have gone to **s** it, 8446
14: 7 The land, which we passed through to **s** it, 8446
14:36 the men, which Moses sent to **s** the land, 8446
14:38 *which were* of the men that went to **s** 8446
Dt 1:22 they shall **s** us **out** the land, and bring us 2658
1:33 to **s** you **out** a place to pitch your tents *in,* 8446
13:14 and **make s**, and ask diligently; 2713
Jos 2: 2 the children of Israel to **s out** the country. 2658
2: 3 for they be come to **s out** all the country. 2658
Jdg 18: 2 to spy out the land, and to **s** it; 2713
18: 2 and they said unto them, Go, **s** the land: 2713
1Sa 23:23 that I will **s** him **out** throughout all 2664
2Sa 10: 3 to **s** the city, and to spy it out, and 2713
1Ki 20: 6 they shall **s** thine house, and the houses of 2664
2Ki 10:23 **S**, and look that there be here with you 2664
1Ch 19: 3 are not his servants come unto thee for to **s**, 2713
Ezr 4:15 That **s** may be **made** in the book of 1240
4:19 **s** hath been **made**, and it is found that this 1240
5:17 let there be **s made** in the king's treasure 1240
6: 1 and **s** was **made** in the house of the rolls, 1240
Job 8: 8 and prepare *thyself* to the **s** of their fathers: 2714
13: 9 *Is it* good that he should **s** you **out**? or 2713
38:16 or hast thou walked in the **s** of the depth? 2714
Ps 44:21 Shall not God **s** this **out**? for he knoweth 2713
64: 6 They **s out** iniquities; they accomplish a 2664
64: 6 out iniquities; they accomplish a diligent **s**: 2665
77: 6 own heart: and my spirit **made diligent s**. 2664
139:23 **S** me, O God, and know my heart: try me, 2713
Pr 25: 2 but the honour of kings *is* to **s out** a matter. 2713
25:27 so *for men* to **s** their own glory *is not* glory. 2714
Ecc 1:13 **s out** by wisdom concerning all *things* that 8446
7:25 to **s**, and to seek out wisdom, and 8446
Jer 2:34 I have not found it by **secret s**, but upon all 4290
17:10 I the LORD **s** the heart, *I* try the reins, 2713
29:13 find *me,* when ye shall **s for** me with all 1875
La 3:40 Let us **s** and try our ways, and turn again to 2664
Eze 34: 6 and none did **s** or seek *after them.* 1875
34: 8 neither did my shepherds **s** for my flock, 1875
34:11 will both **s** my sheep, and seek them out. 1875
39:14 after the end of seven months shall they **s**. 2713
Am 9: 3 I will **s** and take them out thence; 2664
Zep 1:12 *that* I will **s** Jerusalem with candles, and 2664
Mt 2: 8 Go and **s** diligently for the young child; *1833*
Jn 5:39 **S** the Scriptures; for in them ye think ye *2045*
7:52 **S**, and look: for out of Galilee ariseth no *2045*

SEARCHED (20) [SEARCH]

Ge 31:34 Laban **s** all the tent, but found *them* not. 4959
31:35 And he **s**, but found not the images. 2664
31:37 Whereas thou hast **s** all my stuff, what hast 4959
44:12 he **s**, *and* began at the eldest, and left at 2664
Nu 13:21 **s** the land from the wilderness of Zin unto 8446
13:32 which they had **s** unto the children of Israel, 8446
14: 6 *which were* of them that **s** the land, 8446
14:34 After the number of the days *in* which ye **s** 8446
Dt 1:24 unto the valley of Eshcol, and **s** it **out**. 7270
Job 5:27 we have **s** it, so it *is;* hear it, and know thou 2713
28:27 declare it; he prepared it, yea, and **s** it **out**. 2713
29:16 and the cause *which* I knew not I **s out**. 2713
32:11 your reasons, whilst you **s out** what to say. 2713
36:26 can the number of his years be **s out**. 2714
Ps 139: 1 O LORD, thou hast **s** me, and known *me.* 2713
Jer 31:37 the foundations of the earth **s out** beneath, 2713
46:23 saith the LORD, though it cannot be **s**; 2713
Ob 1: 6 How are *the things of* Esau **s out**! *how* are 2664
Ac 17:11 and **s** the scriptures daily, whether those *350*
1Pe 1:10 the prophets have inquired and **s diligently**, *1830*

SEARCHEST (2) [SEARCH]

Job 10: 6 after mine iniquity, and **s** after my sin? 1875
Pr 2: 4 as silver, and **s for** her as *for* hid treasures; 2664

SEARCHETH (8) [SEARCH]

1Ch 28: 9 for the LORD **s** all hearts, and 1875
Job 28: 3 **s out** all perfection, the stones of darkness, 2713
39: 8 and he **s** after every green thing. 1875
Pr 18:17 but his neighbour cometh and **s** him. 2713
28:11 the poor that hath understanding **s** him **out**. 2713
Ro 8:27 And he that **s** the hearts knoweth what *is* *2045*
1Co 2:10 for the Spirit **s** all *things,* yea, the deep *2045*
Rev 2:23 shall know that I am he which **s** the reins *2045*

SEARCHING (5) [SEARCH]

Nu 13:25 they returned from **s** of the land after forty 8446
Job 11: 7 Canst thou *by* **s** find out God? canst thou 2714
Pr 20:27 **s** all the inward parts of the belly. 2664
Isa 40:28 is weary? *there is* no **s** of his understanding. 2714
1Pe 1:11 **S** what, or what manner of time the Spirit *2045*

SEARCHINGS (1) [SEARCH]

Jdg 5:16 of Reuben *there were* great **s** of heart. 2714

SEARED (1)

1Ti 4: 2 having their conscience **s with a hot iron**; *2743*

SEAS (25) [SEA]

Ge 1:10 together of the waters called he **S**: 3220
1:22 fill the waters in the **s**, and let fowl multiply 3220
Lev 11: 9 in the **s**, and in the rivers, them shall ye eat. 3220
11:10 all that have not fins nor scales in the **s**, 3220
Dt 33:19 they shall suck *of* the abundance of the **s**, 3220
Ne 9: 6 the **s**, and all that *is* therein, and 3220
Ps 8: 8 passeth *through* the paths of the **s**. 3220
24: 2 For he hath founded it upon the **s**, and 3220
65: 7 Which stilleth the noise of the **s**, the noise 3220
69:34 the **s**, and every *thing* that moveth therein. 3220
135: 6 and in earth, in the **s**, and all deep places. 3220
Isa 17:12 *which* make a noise like the noise of the **s**; 3220
Jer 15: 8 are increased to me above the sand of the **s**: 3220
Eze 27: 4 Thy borders *are* in the midst of the **s**, 3220
27:25 made very glorious in the midst of the **s**. 3220
27:26 wind hath broken thee in the midst of the **s**. 3220
27:27 shall fall into the midst of the **s** in the day 3220
27:33 When thy wares went forth out of the **s**, 3220
27:34 broken by the **s** in the depths of the waters, 3220
28: 2 I sit *in* the seat of God, in the midst of the **s**; 3220
28: 8 of *them that are* slain in the midst of the **s**. 3220
32: 2 the nations, and thou *art* as a whale in the **s**: 3220

Da 11:45 the **s** in the glorious holy mountain; 3220
Jnh 2: 3 cast me *into* the deep, in the midst of the **s**; 3220
Ac 27:41 And falling into a place **where two s met**, *1337*

SEASON (56) [SEASONED, SEASONS]

Ge 40: 4 and they continued a **s** in ward. 3117
Ex 13:10 keep this ordinance in his **s** from year to 4150
Lev 2:13 of thy meat offering shalt thou **s** with salt; 4414
26: 4 I will give you rain in **due s**, and the land 6256
Nu 9: 2 also keep the passover at his **appointed s**. 4150
9: 3 at even, ye shall keep it in his **appointed s**: 4150
9: 7 **appointed s** among the children of Israel? 4150
9:13 offering of the LORD in his **appointed s**, 4150
28: 2 ye observe to offer unto me in their **due s**. 4150
Dt 11:14 give *you* the rain of your land in his **due s**, 6256
16: 6 *at* the **s** that thou camest forth out of Egypt. 4150
28:12 to give the rain unto thy land in his **s**, 6256
Jos 24: 7 and ye dwelt in the wilderness a long **s**. 3117
2Ki 4:16 he said, About this **s**, according to the time 4150
4:17 bare a son at that **s** that Elisha had said unto 4150
1Ch 21:29 *were* at that **s** in the high place at Gibeon. 6256
2Ch 15: 3 Now for a long **s** Israel *hath been* without 3117
Job 5:26 like as a shock of corn cometh in in his **s**. 6256
30:17 My bones are pierced in me in the **night s**: 3915
38:32 Canst thou bring forth Mazzaroth in his **s**? 6256
Ps 1: 3 that bringeth forth his fruit in his **s**; 6256
22: 2 and in the **night s**, and am not silent. 3915
104:27 *thou* mayest give *them* their meat in **due s**. 6256
145:15 and thou givest them their meat in **due s**. 6256
Pr 15:23 a word *spoken* in **due s**, how good 6256+2050.2
Ecc 3: 1 To every *thing there is* a **s**, and a time to 2165
10:17 thy princes eat in **due s**, for strength, and 6256
Isa 50: 4 to **speak** a word **in s** to *him that is* weary: 5790
Jer 5:24 both the former and the latter, in his **s**: 6256
33:20 there should not be day and night in their **s**; 6256
Eze 34:26 cause the shower to come down in his **s**; 6256
Da 7:12 yet their lives were prolonged for a **s** and 2166
Hos 2: 9 my wine in the **s** thereof, and will recover 4150
Mt 24:45 his household, to give them meat in **due s**? *2540*
Mk 9:50 lost his saltness, wherewith will you **s** it? *741*
12: 2 And at the **s** he sent to the husbandmen a *2540*
Lk 1:20 which shall be fulfilled in their **s**. *2540*
4:13 he departed from him for a **s**. *2540*
12:42 to give *them their* portion of meat in **due s**? *2540*
13: 1 There were present at that **s** some that told *2540*
20:10 And at the **s** he sent a servant to *2540*
23: 8 for he was desirous to see him of a long **s**, NIG
Jn 5: 4 For an angel went down at a *certain* **s** into *2540*
5:35 ye were willing for a **s** to rejoice in his *5610*
Ac 13:11 shalt be blind, not seeing the sun for a **s**. *2540*
19:22 but he himself stayed in Asia for a **s**. *5550*
24:25 when I have a **convenient s**, I will call for *2540*
2Co 7: 8 made you sorry, though *it were* but for a **s**. *5610*
Gal 6: 9 for in due **s** we shall reap, if we faint not. *2540*
2Ti 4: 2 be instant **in s**, out of season; reprove, *2122*
4: 2 be instant in season, **out of s**; reprove, *171*
Phm 1:15 For perhaps he therefore departed for a **s**, *5610*
Heb 11:25 than to enjoy the pleasures of sin for a **s**; *4340*
1Pe 1: 6 though now for a **s**, if need be, *3641*
Rev 6:11 that they should rest yet for a little **s**, *5550*
20: 3 and after that he must be loosed a little **s**. *5550*

SEASONED (2) [SEASON]

Lk 14:34 have lost his savour, wherewith shall it be **s**? *741*
Col 4: 6 your speech *be* alway with grace, **s** with salt, *741*

SEASONS (12) [SEASON]

Ge 1:14 for signs, and for **s**, and for days, and years: 4150
Ex 18:22 let them judge the people at all **s**: and 6256
18:26 they judged the people at all **s**: the hard 6256
Lev 23: 4 which ye shall proclaim in their **s**. 4150
Ps 16: 7 my reins also instruct me *in* the **night s**. 3915
104:19 He appointed the moon for **s**: the sun 4150
Da 2:21 he changeth the times and the **s**: 2166
Mt 21:41 which shall render him the fruits in their **s**. *2540*
Ac 1: 7 It is not for you to know *the* times or *the* **s**, *2540*
14:17 gave us rain from heaven, and fruitful **s**, *2540*
20:18 what manner I have been with you at all **s**, *5550*
1Th 5: 1 But of the times and the **s**, brethren, *2540*

SEAT (59) [SIT]

Ex 25:17 thou shalt make a **mercy s** *of* pure gold: 3727
25:18 make them, in the two ends of the **mercy s**. 3727
25:19 *even* of the **mercy s** shall ye make 3727
25:20 covering the **mercy s** with their wings, 3727
25:20 toward the **mercy s** shall the faces of 3727
25:21 thou shalt put the **mercy s** above upon 3727
25:22 with thee from above the **mercy s**, 3727
26:34 thou shalt put the **mercy s** upon the ark of 3727
30: 6 before the **mercy s** that *is* over 3727
31: 7 the **mercy s** that *is* thereupon, and all 3727
35:12 *with* the **mercy s**, and the vail of 3727
37: 6 he made the **mercy s** *of* pure gold: 3727
37: 7 he them, on the two ends of the **mercy s**; 3727
37: 8 out of the **mercy s** made he the cherubims 3727
37: 9 covered with their wings over the **mercy s**, 3727
39:35 and the staves thereof, and the **mercy s**, 3727
40:20 and put the **mercy s** above upon the ark: 3727
Lev 16: 2 *place* within the vail before the **mercy s**, 3727
16: 2 I will appear in the cloud upon the **mercy s**. 3727
16:13 the **mercy s** that *is* upon the Testimony, 3727
16:14 sprinkle *it* with his finger upon the **mercy s** 3727
16:14 before the **mercy s** shall he sprinkle of 3727
16:15 sprinkle it upon the **mercy s**, and before 3727
16:15 the mercy seat, and before the **mercy s**: 3727
Nu 7:89 **mercy s** that *was* upon the ark of 3727
Jdg 3:20 God unto thee. And he arose out of *his* **s**. 3678
1Sa 1: 9 Now Eli the priest sat upon a **s** by a post of 3678
4:13 Eli sat upon a **s** *by* the wayside watching: 3678
4:18 that he fell from off the **s** backward by 3678
20:18 be missed, because thy **s** will be empty. 4186
20:25 the king sat upon his **s**, as at other times, 4186
20:25 as at other times, *even* upon a **s** by the wall: 4186
2Sa 23: 8 The Tachmonite that sat in the **s**, 7675
1Ki 2:19 caused a **s** to be set for the king's mother; 3678
10:19 stays on either side on the place of the **s**, 7675
1Ch 28:11 and of the place of the **mercy s**, 3727
Est 3: 1 set his **s** above all the princes that *were* 3678
Job 23: 3 find him! *that* I might come *even* to his **s**! 8499
29: 7 the city, *when* I prepared my **s** in the street; 4186
Ps 1: 1 nor sitteth in the **s** of the scornful. 4186
Pr 9:14 on a **s** in the high places of the city, 3678
Eze 8: 3 where *was* the **s** of the image of jealousy, 4186
28: 2 hast said, I *am* a God, I sit *in* the **s** of God, 4186
Am 6: 3 and cause the **s** of violence to come near; 7675
Mt 23: 2 and the Pharisees sit in Moses' **s**: *2515*
27:19 When he was set down on the **judgment s**, *968*
Jn 19:13 sat down in the **judgment s** in a place *that is* *968*
Ac 18:12 and brought him to the **judgment s**, *968*
18:16 And he drave them from the **judgment s**. *968*
18:17 and beat *him* before the **judgment s**. *968*
25: 6 and the next day sitting in the **judgment s**, *968*
25:10 said Paul, I stand at Cesar's **judgment s**, *968*
25:17 on the morrow I sat on the **judgment s**, and *968*
Ro 14:10 for we shall all stand before the **judgment s** *968*
2Co 5:10 all appear before the **judgment s** of Christ; *968*
Heb 9: 5 cherubims of glory shadowing the **mercy s**; *2435*
Rev 2:13 *even* where Satan's **s** *is*: and thou holdest *2362*
13: 2 his power, and his **s**, and great authority. *2362*
16:10 poured out his vial upon the **s** of the beast; *2362*

SEATED (1) [SIT]

Dt 33:21 there, *in* a portion of the lawgiver, *was he* **s**; 5603

SEATS (11) [SIT]

Mt 21:12 and the **s** of them that sold doves, *2515*
23: 6 at feasts, and the **chief s** in the synagogues, *4410*
Mk 11:15 and the **s** of them that sold doves; *2515*
12:39 And the **chief s** in the synagogues, and *4410*
Lk 1:52 He hath put down the mighty from *their* **s**, *2362*
11:43 for ye love the **uppermost s** in *4410*
20:46 and the **highest s** in the synagogues, and *4410*
Jas 2: 6 and draw you before the **judgment s**? *2922*
Rev 4: 4 about the throne *were* four and twenty **s**: *2362*
4: 4 and upon the **s** I saw four and twenty elders *2362*
11:16 which sat before God on their **s**, *2362*

SEATWARD (1) [SIT]

Ex 37: 9 *even* to the **mercy s** were the faces of 3727

SEBA (4)

Ge 10: 7 **S**, and Havilah, and Sabtah, and Raamah, 5434
1Ch 1: 9 **S**, and Havilah, and Sabta, and Raamah, 5434
Ps 72:10 the kings of Sheba and **S** shall offer gifts. 5434
Isa 43: 3 *for* thy ransom, Ethiopia and **S** for thee. 5434

SEBAM See SHEBAM

SEBAT (1)

Zec 1: 7 which *is* the month **S**, in the second year of 7627

SECACAH (1)

Jos 15:61 the wilderness, Beth-arabah, Middin, and **S**, 5527

SECHU (1)

1Sa 19:22 and came to a great well that *is* in **S**: 7906

SECOND (173) [SECONDARILY, TWO]

Ge 1: 8 and the morning were the **s** day. 8145
2:13 the name of the **s** river *is* Gihon: the same 8145
6:16 **s**, and third *stories* shalt thou make it. 8145
7:11 in the **s** month, the seventeenth day of 8145
8:14 in the **s** month, on the seven and 8145
22:15 unto Abraham out of heaven the **s time**, 8145
30: 7 conceived again, and bare Jacob a **s** son. 8145
30:12 And Zilpah Leah's maid bare Jacob a **s** son. 8145
32:19 so commanded he the **s**, and the third, and 8145
41: 5 he slept and dreamed the **s time**: and 8145
41:43 he made him to ride in the **s** chariot which 4932
41:52 the name of the **s** called he Ephraim: 8145
43:10 surely now we had returned this **s time**. 6471
47:18 they came unto him the **s** year, and 8145
Ex 2:13 when he went out the **s** day, behold, 8145
16: 1 on the fifteenth day of the **s** month after 8145
26: 4 of *another* curtain, in the coupling of the **s**. 8145
26: 5 the curtain that *is* in the coupling of the **s**; 8145
26:10 edge of the curtain which coupleth the **s**. 8145
26:20 for the **s** side of the tabernacle on the north 8145
28:18 the **s** row *shall be* an emerald, a sapphire, 8145
36:11 of *another* curtain, in the coupling of the **s**. 8145
36:12 curtain which *was* in the coupling of the **s**: 8145
36:17 edge of the curtain which coupleth the **s**. 8145
39:11 the **s** row, an emerald, a sapphire, and 8145
40:17 it came to pass in the first month in the **s** 8145
Lev 5:10 And he shall offer the **s** *for* a burnt offering, 8145
13:58 it shall be washed the **s time**, and shall be 8145
Nu 1: 1 on the first *day* of the **s** month, 8145
1: 1 in the **s** year after they were come out of 8145
1:18 together on the first *day* of the **s** month, 8145
2:16 And they shall set forth in the **s rank**. 8145
7:18 On the **s** day Nethaneel the son of Zuar, 8145
9: 1 in the first month of the **s** year after they 8145
9:11 The fourteenth day of the **s** month at even 8145
10: 6 When you blow an alarm the **s time**, then 8145
10:11 it came to pass on the twentieth *day* of the **s** 8145
10:11 *day* of the second month, in the **s** year, 8145
29:17 on the **s** day *ye shall offer* twelve young 8145
Jos 5: 2 again the children of Israel the **s time**. 8145
6:14 the **s** day they compassed the city once, 8145
10:32 which took it on the **s** day, and smote it 8145
19: 1 the **s** lot came forth to Simeon, *even* for 8145
Jdg 6:25 even the **s** bullock of seven years old, and 8145
6:26 take the **s** bullock, and offer a burnt 8145
6:28 the **s** bullock was offered upon the altar that 8145
20:24 against the children of Benjamin the **s** day. 8145
20:25 forth against them out of Gibeah the **s** day, 8145
1Sa 8: 2 was Joel; and the name of his **s**, Abiah: 4932
20:27 *which was* the **s** *day* of the month, 8145
1Sa 20:34 and did eat no meat the **s** day of the month: 8145
26: 8 at once, and I will not *smite* him the **s time**. 8138
2Sa 3: 3 his **s**, Chileab, of Abigail the wife of Nabal 4932
14:29 when he sent again the **s time**, he would 8145
1Ki 6: 1 in the month Zif, which *is* the **s** month, 8145
9: 2 LORD appeared to Solomon the **s time**, 8145
15:25 Israel in the **s** year of Asa king of Judah, 8147
18:34 he said, **Do** *it* **the s time**. And they did *it* 8138
18:34 they **did** *it* **the s time**. And he said, Do *it* 8138
19: 7 angel of the LORD came again the **s time**, 8145
2Ki 1:17 Jehoram reigned in his stead in the **s** year of 8147
9:19 he sent *out* a **s** on horseback, which came to 8145
10: 6 he wrote a letter the **s time** to them, saying, 8145
14: 1 In the **s** year of Joash son of Jehoahaz king 8147
15:32 In the **s** year of Pekah the son of Remaliah 8147
19:29 in the **s** year that which springeth of 8145
23: 4 high priest, and the priests of the **s order**; 4932
25:17 like unto these had the **s** pillar with 8145
25:18 Zephaniah the **s** priest, and the three 4932
1Ch 2:13 and Abinadab the **s**, and Shimma the third, 8145
3: 1 the **s** Daniel, of Abigail the Carmelitess: 8145
3:15 the **s** Jehoiakim, the third Zedekiah, 8145
7:15 and the name of the **s** *was* Zelophehad: 8145
8: 1 Ashbel the **s**, and Aharah the third, 8145
8:39 Jehush the **s**, and Eliphelet the third. 8145
12: 9 Ezer the first, Obadiah the **s**, Eliab 8145
15:18 with them their brethren of the **s degree**, 4932
23:11 Jahath was the chief, and Zizah the **s**: but 8145
23:19 Jeriah the first, Amariah the **s**, Jahaziel 8145
23:20 Michah the first, and Jesiah the **s**. 8145
24: 7 lot came forth to Jehoiarib, the **s** to Jedaiah, 8145
24:23 *of Hebron;* Jeriah *the first,* Amariah the **s**, 8145
25: 9 the **s** *to* Gedaliah, who with his brethren 8145
26: 2 Jediael the **s**, Zebadiah the third, 8145
26: 4 Jehozabad the **s**, Joah the third, and 8145
26:11 Hilkiah the **s**, Tebaliah the third, 8145
27: 4 over the course of the **s** month *was* Dodai 8145
29:22 Solomon the son of David king the **s time**, 8145
2Ch 3: 2 he began to build in the **s** *day* of the second 8145
3: 2 he began to build in the second *day* of the **s** 8145
27: 5 pay unto him, both the **s** year, and the third. 8145
30: 2 to keep the passover in the **s** month. 8145
30:13 feast of unleavened bread in the **s** month, 8145
30:15 on the fourteenth *day* of the **s** month: 8145
35:24 and put him in the **s** chariot that he had; 4932
Ezr 1:10 silver basons of a **s sort** four hundred and 4932
3: 8 Now in the **s** year of their coming unto 8145
3: 8 in the **s** month, began Zerubbabel the son of 8145
4:24 So it ceased unto the **s** year of the reign of 8648
Ne 8:13 on the **s** day were gathered together 8145
11: 9 Judah the son of Senuah *was* **s** over 4932
11:17 Bakbukiah the **s** among his brethren, and 4932
Est 2:14 on the morrow she returned into the **s** house 8145
2:19 virgins were gathered together the **s time**, 8145
7: 2 the king said again unto Esther on the **s** day 8145
9:29 to confirm this **s** letter of Purim. 8145
Job 42:14 the name of the **s**, Kezia; and the name of 8145
Ecc 4: 8 There is one *alone,* and *there is* not a **s**; yea, 8145
4:15 with the **s** child that shall stand *up* in his 8145
Isa 11:11 **s time** to recover the remnant of his people, 8145
37:30 the **s** year that which springeth of the same: 8145
Jer 1:13 of the LORD came unto me the **s time**, 8145
13: 3 of the LORD came unto me the **s time**, 8145
33: 1 the LORD came unto Jeremiah the **s time**, 8145
41: 4 it came to pass the **s** day after *he* had slain 8145
52:22 The **s** pillar also and the pomegranates *were* 8145
52:24 Zephaniah the **s** priest, and the three 4932
Eze 10:14 the **s** face *was* the face of a man, and 8145
43:22 on the **s** day thou shalt offer a kid of 8145
Da 2: 1 in the **s** year of the reign of 8147
7: 5 a **s**, like to a bear, and it raised up itself on 8578
Jnh 3: 1 of the LORD came unto Jonah the **s time**, 8145
Na 1: 9 affliction shall not rise up the **s time**. 6471
Zep 1:10 a howling from the **s**, and a great crashing 4932
Hag 1: 1 In the **s** year of Darius the king, in the sixth 8147
1:15 in the **s** year of Darius the king. 8147
2:10 twentieth *day* of the ninth *month,* in the **s** 8147
Zec 1: 1 In the eighth month, in the **s** year of Darius, 8147
1: 7 *is* the month Sebat, in the **s** year of Darius, 8147
6: 2 and in the **s** chariot black horses; 8145
Mt 21:30 And he came to the **s**, *1208*
22:26 Likewise the **s** also, and the third, unto *1208*
22:39 And the **s** *is* like unto it, Thou shalt love thy *1208*
26:42 He went away again the **s time**, and *1208+1537*
Mk 12:21 And the **s** took her, and died, neither left he *1208*
12:31 And the **s** *is* like, *namely* this, Thou shalt *1208*
14:72 And the **s time** the cock crew. *1208+1537*
Lk 6: 1 to pass on the **s** sabbath **after the first**, *1207*
12:38 And if he shall come in the **s** watch, or *1208*
19:18 And the **s** came, saying, Lord, thy pound *1208*
20:30 And the **s** took her to wife, and he died *1208*
Jn 3: 4 can he enter the **s time** into his mother's *1208*
4:54 This *is* again the **s** miracle *that* Jesus did, *1208*
21:16 He saith to him again the **s time**, Simon, *1208*
Ac 7:13 And at the **s** time Joseph was made known *1208*
10:15 *spake* unto him again the **s time**, *1208+1537*
12:10 they were past the first and the **s** ward, *1208*
13:33 as it is also written in the **s** psalm, Thou art *1208*
1Co 15:47 earthy: the **s** man *is* the Lord from heaven. *1208*
2Co 1:15 you before, that you might have a **s** benefit; *1208*
13: 2 foretell *you,* as if I were present the **s** *time;* *1208*
13: S The **s** *epistle* to the Corinthians was written *1208*
2Th 3: S The **s** *epistle* to the Thessalonians was *1208*
2Ti 4: S The **s** *epistle* unto Timotheus, ordained *1208*
4: S when Paul was brought before Nero the **s** *1208*
Tit 3:10 a heretick after the first and **s** admonition, *1208*
Heb 8: 7 should no place have been sought for the **s**. *1208*
9: 3 And after the **s** vail, the tabernacle which is *1208*
9: 7 But into the **s** *went* the high priest alone *1208*
9:28 the **s time** without sin unto salvation. *1208+1537*
10: 9 away the first, that he may establish the **s**. *1208*
2Pe 3: 1 This **s** epistle, beloved, I now write unto *1208*
Rev 2:11 that overcometh shall not be hurt of the **s** *1208*
4: 7 and the **s** beast like a calf, and the third *1208*
6: 3 And when he had opened the **s** seal, I heard *1208*

Rev 6: 3 I heard the **s** beast say, Come and see. 1208
8: 8 And the **s** angel sounded, and as *it were* a 1208
11:14 The **s** woe is past; *and* behold, the third 1208
16: 3 And the **s** angel poured out his vial upon 1208
20: 6 on such the **s** death hath no power, but 1208
20:14 cast into the lake of fire. This is the **s** death. 1208
21: 8 and brimstone: which is the **s** death. 1208
21:19 the **s**, sapphire; the third, a chalcedony; 1208

SECONDARILY (1) [SECOND]
1Co 12:28 first apostles, **s** prophets, thirdly teachers, 1208

SECRET (68) [SECRETLY, SECRETS]
Ge 49: 6 O my soul, come not thou into their **s**; 5475
Dt 27:15 putteth *it* in *a* **s** *place*. And all the people 5643
29:29 The **s** *things belong* unto the LORD our 5641
Jdg 3:19 said, I have a **s** errand unto thee, O king: 5643
13:18 thou thus after my name, seeing it *is* **s**? 6383
1Sa 5: 9 and they had emerods in their **s parts**. 8368
19: 2 and abide in a **s place**, and hide thyself: 5643
Job 14:13 that thou wouldest **keep** me **s**, until thy 5641
15: 8 Hast thou heard the **s** of God? and dost thou 5475
15:11 with thee? is there *any* **s** thing with thee? 328
20:26 All darkness *shall be* hid in his **s places**: 6845
29: 4 when the **s** of God *was* upon my tabernacle; 5475
40:13 the dust together; *and* bind their faces in **s**. 2934
Ps 10: 8 in the **s places** doth he murder the innocent: 4565
17:12 as it were a young lion lurking in **s places**. 4565
18:11 He made darkness his **s place**; his pavilion 5643
19:12 *his* errors? cleanse thou me from **s** *faults*. 5641
25:14 The **s** of the LORD *is* with them that fear 5475
27: 5 in the **s** of his tabernacle shall he hide me; 5643
31:20 Thou shalt hide them in the **s** of thy 5643
64: 2 Hide me from the **s counsel** of the wicked; 5475
64: 4 That *they* may shoot in **s** at the perfect: 4565
81: 7 I answered thee in the **s place** of thunder: 5643
90: 8 our **s** *sins* in the light of thy countenance. 5956
91: 1 He that dwelleth in the **s place** of the most 5643
139:15 when I was made in **s**, *and* 5643
Pr 3:32 the LORD: but his **s** *is* with the righteous. 5475
9:17 are sweet, and bread *eaten* in **s** is pleasant. 5643
21:14 A gift in **s** pacifieth anger: and a reward in 5643
25: 9 and discover not a **s** *to* another: 5475
27: 5 Open rebuke *is* better than **s** love. 5641
Ecc 12:14 with every **s** *thing*, whether *it be* good, or 5956
SS 2:14 in the **s places** of the stairs, let me see thy 5643
Isa 3:17 and the LORD will discover their **s parts**. 6596
45: 3 hidden riches of **s places**, that thou mayest 4565
45:19 I have not spoken in **s**, in a dark place of 5643
48:16 I have not spoken in **s** from the beginning; 5643
Jer 2:34 I have not found it by **s search**, but upon all 4290
13:17 my soul shall weep in **s places** for *your* 4565
23:24 Can any hide himself in **s places** that I shall 4565
49:10 I have uncovered his **s places**, and he shall 4565
La 3:10 bear lying in wait, *and as* a lion in **s places**. 4565
Eze 7:22 they shall pollute my **s** *place*: for 6845
28: 3 *there is* no **s** *that* they can hide *from* thee: 5640
Da 2:18 of the God of heaven concerning this **s**; 7328
2:19 *was* the **s** revealed unto Daniel in a night 7328
2:22 **s** *things*: he knoweth what *is* in 5642
2:27 The **s** which the king hath demanded 7328
2:30 this **s** *is* not revealed to me for *any* wisdom 7328
2:47 seeing thou couldest reveal this **s**. 7328
4: 9 gods *is* in thee, and no **s** troubleth thee, 7328
Am 3: 7 he revealeth his **s** unto his servants 5475
Mt 6: 4 That thine alms may be in **s**: and thy Father 2927
6: 4 thy Father which seeth in **s** himself shall 2927
6: 6 thy door, pray to thy Father which is in **s**; 2927
6: 6 thy Father which seeth in **s** shall reward 2927
6:18 to fast, but unto thy Father which is in **s**: 2927
6:18 and thy Father, which seeth in **s**, 2927
13:35 I will utter *things which have been* **kept s** 2928
24:26 behold, *he is* in the **s chambers**; believe *it* 5009
Mk 4:22 neither was *any thing* **kept s**, but that it 614
Lk 8:17 For nothing is **s**, that shall not be made 2927
11:33 putteth *it* in a **s place**, neither under a 2927
Jn 7: 4 *there is* no *man that* doeth any *thing* in **s**, 2927
7:10 the feast, not openly, but as it were in **s**. 2927
18:20 always resort; and in **s** have I said nothing. 2927
Ro 16:25 which was **kept s** since the world began, 4601
Eph 5:12 of those *things* which are done of them in **s**. 2931

SECRETLY (20) [SECRET]
Ge 31:27 Wherefore didst thou flee away **s**, and 2244
Dt 13: 6 entice thee **s**, saying, Let us 5643+871.1+1886.1
27:24 that smiteth his neighbour **s**. 5643+871.1+1886.1
28:57 of all *things* **s** in the siege 5643+871.1+1886.1
Jos 2: 1 Nun sent out of Shittim two men to spy **s**, 2791
1Sa 18:22 Commune with David **s**, 3909+871.1+1886.1
23: 9 David knew that Saul **s practised** mischief 2790
2Sa 12:12 For thou didst *it* **s**: but I will 5643+871.1+1886.1
2Ki 17: 9 the children of Israel did **s** *those* things that 2644
Job 4:12 Now a thing was **s brought** to me, and 1589
13:10 if ye do **s** accept persons. 5643+871.1+1886.1
31:27 my heart hath been **s** 5643+871.1+1886.1
Ps 10: 9 He lieth in wait **s** as a lion in 4565+871.1+1886.1
31:20 thou shalt **keep** them **s** in a pavilion from 6845
Jer 37:17 asked him **s** in his house, 5643+871.1+1886.1
38:16 king sware **s** unto Jeremiah, 5643+871.1+1886.1
40:15 to Gedaliah in Mizpah **s**, 5643+871.1+1886.1
Hab 3:14 *was* as to devour the poor **s**. 4565+871.1+1886.1
Jn 11:28 and called Mary her sister **s**, saying, 2977
19:38 disciple of Jesus, but **s** for fear of the Jews, 2928

SECRETS (10) [SECRET]
Dt 25:11 forth her hand, and taketh him by the **s**: 4016
Job 11: 6 that he would shew thee the **s** of wisdom, 8587
Ps 44:21 this out? for he knoweth the **s** of the heart. 8587
Pr 11:13 A talebearer revealeth **s**: but he that is of a 5475
20:19 that goeth about *as* a talebearer revealeth **s**: 5475
Da 2:28 there is a God in heaven that revealeth **s**, 7328
2:29 he that revealeth **s** maketh known to thee 7328
2:47 a Lord of kings, and a revealer of **s**, 7328
Ro 2:16 In the day when God shall judge the **s** of 2927

1Co 14:25 And thus are the **s** of his heart made 2927

SECT (5)
Ac 5:17 with him, (which is the **s** of the Sadducees,) 139
15: 5 But there rose up certain of the **s** of 139
24: 5 and a ringleader of the **s** of the Nazarenes: 139
26: 5 that after the most straitest **s** of our religion I 139
28:22 for as concerning this **s**, we know that every 139

SECU See SECHU

SECUNDUS (1)
Ac 20: 4 of the Thessalonians, Aristarchus and **S**; 4580

SECURE (7) [SECURELY, SECURITY]
Jdg 8:11 and smote the host: for the host was **s**. 983
18: 7 the manner of the Zidonians, quiet and **s**; 982
18:10 ye shall come unto a people **s**, and to a large 982
18:27 unto a people *that were* at quiet and **s**: 982
Job 11:18 thou shalt be **s**, because there is hope; yea, 982
12: 6 and they that provoke God are **s**; 987
Mt 28:14 we will persuade him, and **s** you. 275+4160

SECURELY (2) [SECURE]
Pr 3:29 seeing he dwelleth **s** by thee. 983+3807.1
Mic 2: 8 them that pass by **s** *as men* averse from war. 983

SECURITY (1) [SECURE]
Ac 17: 9 And when they had taken **s** of Jason, and 2425

SEDITION (5) [SEDITIONS]
Ezr 4:15 that they have moved **s** within the same of 849
4:19 *that* rebellion and **s** *have been* made therein. 849
Lk 23:19 (Who for a certain **s** made in the city, and 4714
23:25 And he released unto them him that for **s** 4714
Ac 24: 5 a mover of **s** among all the Jews throughout 4714

SEDITIONS (1) [SEDITION]
Gal 5:20 emulations, wrath, strife, **s**, heresies, 1370

SEDUCE (3) [SEDUCED, SEDUCERS, SEDUCETH, SEDUCING]
Mk 13:22 and shall shew signs and wonders, to **s**, if *it* 635
1Jn 2:26 unto you concerning them that **s** you. 4105
Rev 2:20 and to **s** my servants to commit fornication, 4105

SEDUCED (3) [SEDUCE]
2Ki 21: 9 Manasseh **s** them to do more evil than did 8582
Isa 19:13 they have also **s** Egypt, *even they that are* 8582
Eze 13:10 even because they have **s** my people, 2937

SEDUCERS (1) [SEDUCE]
2Ti 3:13 evil men and **s** shall wax worse and worse, 1114

SEDUCETH (1) [SEDUCE]
Pr 12:26 but the way of the wicked **s** them. 8582

SEDUCING (1) [SEDUCE]
1Ti 4: 1 giving heed to **s** spirits, and doctrines of 4108

SEE (597) [EYESIGHT, FORESAW, FORESEEING, FORESEETH, OVERSEE, SAW, SAWEST, SEEING, SEEN, SEER, SEER'S, SEERS, SEEST, SEETH, SIGHT, SIGHTS]
Ge 2:19 brought *them* unto Adam to **s** what he 7200
8: 8 to **s** if the waters were abated from off 7200
11: 5 the LORD came down to **s** the city and 7200
12:12 when the Egyptians shall **s** thee, that they 7200
18:21 **s** whether they have done altogether 7200
19:21 he said unto him, **S**, I have accepted thee 2009
21:16 Let me not **s** the death of the child. 7200
27: 1 his eyes were dim, so that he could not **s**, 7200
27:27 his raiment, and blessed him, and said, **S**, 7200
31: 5 unto them, I **s** your father's countenance, 7200
31:12 he said, Lift up now thine eyes, and **s**, 7200
31:50 **s**, God *is* witness betwixt me and thee. 7200
32:20 before me, and afterward I will **s** his face; 7200
34: 1 went out to **s** the daughters of the land. 7200
37:14 **s** whether it be well with thy brethren, and 7200
37:20 we shall **s** what will become of his dreams. 7200
39:14 her house, and spake unto them, saying, **S**, 7200
41:41 Pharaoh said unto Joseph, **S**, I have set thee 7200
42: 9 to **s** the nakedness of the land you are 7200
42:12 to **s** the nakedness of the land you are 7200
43: 3 saying, Ye shall not **s** my face, except your 7200
43: 5 man said unto us, Ye shall not **s** my face, 7200
44:23 down with you, ye shall **s** my face no more. 7200
44:26 for we may not **s** the man's face, except our 7200
44:34 lest peradventure I **s** the evil that shall 7200
45:12 your eyes **s**, and the eyes of my brother 7200
45:24 unto them, **S** that ye fall not out by the way. NIH
45:28 *is* yet alive: I will go and **s** him before I die. 7200
48:10 were dim for age, *so that* he could not **s**. 7200
48:11 unto Joseph, I had not thought to **s** thy face: 7200
Ex 1:16 and **s** *them* upon the stools; 7200
3: 3 I will now turn aside, and **s** this great sight, 7200
3: 4 the LORD saw that he turned aside to **s**, 7200
4:18 in Egypt, and **s** whether they be yet alive. 7200
4:21 **s** that thou do all *those* wonders before 7200
5:19 the officers of the children of Israel did **s** 7200
6: 1 Now shalt thou **s** what I will do to Pharaoh: 7200
7: 1 the LORD said unto Moses, **S**, I have 7200
10: 5 that *one* cannot be able to **s** the earth: 7200
10:28 take heed to thyself, **s** my face no more; 7200
10:29 I will **s** thy face again no more. 7200
12:13 where you *are*: and when I **s** the blood, 7200
13:17 the people repent when they **s** war, 7200
14:13 and **s** the salvation of the LORD, 7200
14:13 ye shall **s** them again no more for ever. 7200
16: 7 then ye shall **s** the glory of the LORD; 7200
16:29 **S**, for that the LORD hath given you 7200
16:32 that they may **s** the bread wherewith I have 7200
22: 8 *to* **s** whether he have put his hand unto his NIH

Ex 23: 5 If thou **s** the ass of him that hateth thee 7200
31: 2 **S**, I have called by name Bezaleel the son 7200
33:12 **S**, thou sayest unto me, Bring up this 7200
33:20 he said, Thou canst not **s** my face: for there 7200
33:20 for there shall no man **s** me, and live. 7200
33:23 mine hand, and thou shalt **s** my back parts: 7200
34:10 all the people among which thou *art* shall **s** 7200
35:30 Moses said unto the children of Israel, **S**, 7200
Lev 13: 8 *if* the priest **s** that behold, the scab 7200
13:10 the priest shall **s** *him*: and behold, *if* 7200
13:15 the priest shall **s** the raw flesh, 7200
13:17 the priest shall **s** him: and behold, *if* 7200
13:30 the priest shall **s** the plague: and behold, 7200
14:36 before the priest go *into it* to **s** the plague, 7200
14:36 afterward the priest shall go in to **s** 7200
20:17 **s** her nakedness, and she see his nakedness; 7200
20:17 see her nakedness, and she **s** his nakedness; 7200
Nu 4:20 they shall not go in to **s** when the holy 7200
11:15 and let me not **s** my wretchedness. 7200
11:23 thou shalt **s** now whether my word shall 7200
13:18 **s** the land, what it *is*; and the people that 7200
14:23 Surely they shall not **s** the land which I 7200
14:23 shall any of them that provoked me **s** it: 7200
22:41 that thence he might **s** the utmost part of 7200
23: 9 For from the top of the rocks I **s** him, and 7200
23:13 from whence thou mayest **s** them: 7200
23:13 thou shalt **s** but the utmost part of them, 7200
23:13 part of them, and shalt not **s** them all: 7200
24:17 I shall **s** him, but not now: I shall behold 7200
27:12 **s** the land which I have given unto 7200
32: 8 when I sent them from Kadesh-barnea to **s** 7200
32:11 shall **s** the land which I sware unto 7200
Dt 1:35 men of this evil generation **s** that good land, 7200
1:36 he shall **s** it, and to him will I give the land 7200
3:25 and **s** the good land that *is* beyond Jordan, 7200
3:28 them to inherit the land which thou shalt **s**. 7200
4:28 wood and stone, which neither **s**, nor hear, 7200
18:16 neither let me **s** this great fire any more, 7200
22: 1 Thou shalt not **s** thy brother's ox or his 7200
22: 4 Thou shalt not **s** thy brother's ass or his ox 7200
23:14 that he **s** no unclean thing in thee, and 7200
28:10 all people of the earth shall **s** that thou art 7200
28:34 the sight of thine eyes which thou shalt **s**. 7200
28:67 the sight of thine eyes which thou shalt **s**. 7200
28:68 unto thee, Thou shalt **s** it no more again: 7200
29: 4 eyes to **s**, and ears to hear, unto this day. 7200
29:22 when they **s** the plagues of that land, 7200
30:15 **S**, I have set before thee *this* day life and 7200
32:20 I will **s** what their end *shall be*: for they *are* 7200
32:39 **S** now that I, *even* I, *am* he, and *there is* no 7200
32:52 Yet thou shalt **s** the land before *thee*; but 7200
34: 4 I have **caused** thee **to s** *it* with thine eyes, 7200
Jos 3: 3 When ye **s** the ark of the covenant of 7200
6: 2 the LORD said unto Joshua, **S**, I have 7200
8: 1 **s**, I have given into thy hand the king of Ai, 7200
8: 8 shall ye do. **S**, I have commanded you. 7200
22:10 there an altar by Jordan, a great altar to **s** to. 4758
Jdg 9:37 **S** there come people down by the middle of 2009
14: 8 he turned aside to **s** the carcase of the lion: 7200
16: 5 **s** wherein his great strength *lieth*, and 7200
21:21 **s**, and behold, if the daughters of Shiloh 7200
1Sa 2:32 thou shalt **s** an enemy in *my* habitation, 5027
3: 2 eyes began *to wax* dim, *that* he could not **s**; 7200
4:15 and his eyes were dim, that he could not **s**. 7200
6: 9 **s**, if it goeth up *by* the way of his own coast 7200
6:13 and saw the ark, and rejoiced to **s** *it*. 7200
10:24 **S** ye him whom the LORD hath chosen, 7200
12:16 Now therefore stand and **s** this great thing, 7200
12:17 and **s** that your wickedness *is* great, 7200
14:17 Number now, and **s** who is gone from us. 7200
14:29 **s**, I pray you, how mine eyes have been 7200
14:38 and **s** wherein this sin hath been *this* day. 7200
15:35 Samuel came no more to **s** Saul until 7200
17:28 for thou art come down that *thou* mightest **s** 7200
19: 3 of thee; and what I **s**, that I will tell thee. 7200
19:15 Saul sent the messengers *again* to **s** David, 7200
20:29 get away, I pray thee, and **s** my brethren. 7200
21:14 unto his servants, Lo, you **s** the man *is* mad: 7200
23:22 know and **s** his place where his haunt *is*, 7200
23:23 **S** therefore, and take knowledge of all 7200
24:11 Moreover, my father, **s**, yea see the skirt of 7200
24:11 see, yea **s** the skirt of thy robe in my hand: 7200
24:11 **s** that *there is* neither evil nor transgression 7200
24:15 **s**, and plead my cause, and deliver me out 7200
25:35 **s**, I have hearkened to thy voice, and 7200
26:16 now **s** where the king's spear *is*, and 7200
2Sa 3:13 of thee, that is, Thou shalt not **s** my face, 7200
3:13 when thou comest to **s** my face. 7200
7: 2 **S** now, I dwell in a house of cedar, but 7200
13: 5 when thy father cometh to **s** thee, say unto 7200
13: 5 that I may **s** *it*, and eat *it* at her hand. 7200
13: 6 when the king was come to **s** him, Amnon 7200
14:24 his own house, and let him not **s** my face. 7200
14:30 **S**, Joab's field is near mine, and he hath 7200
14:32 now therefore let me **s** the king's face; and 7200
15: 3 unto him, **S**, thy matters *are* good and right; 7200
15:28 **S**, I will tarry in the plain of the wilderness, 7200
24: 3 *that* the eyes of my lord the king may **s** *it*: 7200
24:13 **s** what answer I shall return *to* him that sent 7200
1Ki 9:12 Hiram came out from Tyre to **s** the cities 7200
12:16 now **s** to thine own house, David. So Israel 7200
14: 4 Ahijah could not **s**; for his eyes were set by 7200
17:23 and Elijah said, **S**, thy son liveth. 7200
20: 7 and **s** how this *man* seeketh mischief: 7200
20:22 and mark, and **s** what thou doest: 7200
22:25 Behold, thou shalt **s** in that day, 7200
2Ki 2:10 *nevertheless*, if thou **s** me *when I am* taken 7200
3:14 I would not look toward thee, nor **s** thee. 7200
3:17 Ye shall not **s** wind, neither shall ye see 7200
3:17 shall not see wind, neither shall ye **s** rain; 7200
5: 7 and **s** how he seeketh a quarrel against me. 7200
6:17 I pray thee, open his eyes, that he may **s**. 7200
6:20 the eyes of these *men*, that they may **s**. 7200
6:32 **S** ye how this son of a murderer hath sent 7200
7: 2 thou shalt **s** *it* with thine eyes, but shall not 7200

2Ki 7:13 that are consumed:) and let us send and **s**. 7200
7:14 the host of the Syrians, saying, Go and **s**. 7200
7:19 thou shalt **s** *it* with thine eyes, but shalt not 7200
8:29 down to **s** Joram the son of Ahab in Jezreel, 7200
9:16 Ahaziah king of Judah was come down to **s** 7200
9:17 Jehu as he came, and said, I **s** a company. 7200
9:34 **Go**, **s** now this cursed *woman*, and 6485
10:16 with me, and **s** my zeal for the LORD. 7200
19:16 open, LORD, thine eyes, and **s**: and 7200
22:20 thine eyes shall not **s** all the evil which I 7200
23:17 he said, What title *is* that that I **s**? And 7200
2Ch 10:16 *and* now, David, **s** to thine own house. 7200
18:16 I did **s** all Israel scattered upon 7200
18:24 thou shalt **s** on that day when thou shalt go 7200
20:17 and **s** the salvation of the LORD with you, 7200
22: 6 to **s** Jehoram the son of Ahab at Jezreel, 7200
24: 5 year to year, and *s that* ye haste the matter. NIH
25:17 Come, let us **s** one another *in* the face. 7200
29: 8 and to hissing, as ye **s** with your eyes. 7200
30: 7 gave them up to desolation, as ye **s**. 7200
34:28 neither shall thine eyes **s** all the evil that I 7200
Ezr 4:14 *it was* not meet for us to **s** the king's 2370
Ne 2:17 I unto them, Ye **s** the distress that we *are* in, 7200
4:11 They shall not know, neither **s**, 7200
9: 9 didst **s** the affliction of our fathers in Egypt, 7200
Est 3: 4 to **s** whether Mordecai's matters would 7200
5:13 long as I **s** Mordecai the Jew sitting at 7200
8: 6 For how can I endure to **s** the evil that shall 7200
8: 6 how can I endure to **s** the destruction of my 7200
Job 3: 9 neither let it **s** the dawning of the day: 7200
6:21 ye **s** *my* casting down, and are afraid. 7200
7: 7 life *is* wind: mine eye shall no more **s** good. 7200
7: 8 The eye of him that hath seen me shall **s** me 7789
9:11 Lo, he goeth by me, and I **s** *him* not: 7200
9:25 than a post: they flee away, they **s** no good. 7200
10:15 therefore **s** thou mine affliction; 7200
17:15 my hope? as for my hope, who shall **s** it? 7789
19:26 this *body*, yet in my flesh shall I **s** God: 2372
19:27 Whom I shall **s** for myself, and mine eyes 2372
20: 9 The eye also *which* saw him shall **s** *him* no NIH
20:17 He shall not **s** the rivers, the floods, 7200
21:20 His eyes shall **s** his destruction, and he shall 7200
22:11 Or darkness, *that* thou canst not **s**; and 7200
22:19 The righteous **s** *it*, and are glad: and 7200
23: 9 *on* the right hand, that I cannot **s** *him:* 7200
24: 1 do they that know him not **s** his days? 2372
24:15 for the twilight, saying, No eye shall **s** me: 7789
28:27 did he **s** it, and declare it; he prepared it, 7200
31: 4 Doth not he **s** my ways, and count all my 7200
33:26 he shall **s** his face with joy: for he will 7200
33:28 into the pit, and his life shall **s** the light. 7200
34:32 *That which* I **s** not teach thou me: if I have 2372
35: 5 Look unto the heavens, and **s**; and 7200
35:14 Although thou sayest thou shalt not **s** him, 7789
36:25 Every man may **s** it; man may behold *it* afar 2372
37:21 now *men* **s** not the bright light which *is* in 7200
Ps 10:11 he hideth his face; he will never **s** *it*. 7200
14: 2 to **s** if there were *any* that did understand, 7200
16:10 neither wilt thou suffer thine Holy One to **s** 7200
22: 7 All they that **s** me laugh me to scorn: 7200
27:13 *I had fainted*, unless I had believed to **s** 7200
31:11 they that did **s** me without fled from me. 7200
34: 8 O taste and **s** that the LORD *is* good: 7200
34:12 *and* loveth *many* days, that *he* may **s** good? 7200
36: 9 fountain of life: in thy light shall we **s** light. 7200
37:34 when the wicked are cut off, thou shalt **s** *it*. 7200
40: 3 many shall **s** *it*, and fear, and shall trust in 7200
41: 6 And if he come to **s** *me*, he speaketh vanity: 7200
49: 9 still live for ever, *and* not **s** corruption. 7200
49:19 of his fathers; they shall never **s** light. 7200
52: 6 The righteous also shall **s**, and fear, and 7200
53: 2 to **s** if there were *any* that did understand, 7200
58: 8 of a woman, *that* they may not **s** the sun. 2372
59:10 God shall let me **s** *my desire* upon mine 7200
63: 2 To **s** thy power and thy glory, so *as* I have 2372
64: 5 snares privily; they say, Who shall **s** them? 7200
64: 8 all that **s** them shall flee away. 7200
66: 5 Come and **s** the works of God: *he is* terrible 7200
69:23 Let their eyes be darkened, that *they* **s** not; 7200
69:32 The humble shall **s** *this, and* be glad: and 7200
74: 9 We **s** not our signs: *there is* no more any 7200
86:17 that they which hate me may **s** *it*, and 7200
89:48 man *is he that* liveth, and shall not **s** death? 7200
91: 8 thou behold and **s** the reward of the wicked. 7200
92:11 Mine eye also shall **s** *my desire* on mine 5027
94: 7 Yet they say, The LORD shall not **s**, 7200
94: 9 he that formed the eye, shall he not **s**? 5027
97: 6 and all the people **s** his glory. 7200
106: 5 That *I* may **s** the good of thy chosen, that *I* 7200
107:24 These **s** the works of the LORD, and 7200
107:42 The righteous shall **s** *it*, and rejoice: and 7200
112: 8 until he **s** *his desire* upon his enemies. 7200
112:10 The wicked shall **s** *it*, and be grieved; 7200
115: 5 speak not: eyes have they, but they **s** not: 7200
118: 7 shall I **s** *my desire* upon them that hate me. 7200
119:74 They that fear thee will be glad when they **s** 7200
128: 5 thou shalt **s** the good of Jerusalem all 7200
128: 6 thou shalt **s** thy children's children, *and* 7200
135:16 speak not; eyes have they, but they **s** not; 7200
139:16 Thine eyes did **s** my substance, yet being 7200
139:24 **s** if *there be any* wicked way in me, and 7200
Pr 24:18 Lest the LORD **s** *it*, and it displease him, 7200
29:16 but the righteous shall **s** their fall. 7200
Ecc 1:10 whereof it may be said, **S**, this *is* new? 7200
2: 3 till I might **s** what *was* that good for 7200
3:18 that *they* might **s** that they themselves are 7200
3:22 for who shall bring him to **s** what shall be 7200
7:11 *by it there is* profit to them that **s** the sun. 7200
8:16 to **s** the business that is done upon 7200
SS 2:14 let me **s** thy countenance, let me hear thy 7200
6:11 I went down into the garden of nuts to **s** 7200
6:11 *and* to **s** whether the vine flourished, *and* 7200
6:13 What will ye **s** in the Shulamite? As it were 2372
7:12 let us **s** if the vine flourish, *whether* 7200
Isa 5:19 that we may **s** *it:* and let the counsel of 7200
Isa 6: 9 and **s** ye **indeed**, but perceive not. 7200+7200
6:10 lest they **s** with their eyes, and hear with 7200
13: 1 which Isaiah the son of Amoz did **s**. 2372
14:16 They that **s** thee shall narrowly look upon 7200
18: 3 the world, and dwellers on the earth, **s** ye, 7200
26:11 *when* thy hand is lifted up, they will not **s**: 2372
26:11 *but* they shall **s**, and be ashamed for *their* 2372
29:18 the eyes of the blind shall **s** out of 7200
30:10 Which say to the seers, **S** not; and to 7200
30:20 but thine eyes shall **s** thy teachers: 7200
32: 3 the eyes of them that **s** shall not be dim, 7200
33:17 Thine eyes shall **s** the king in his beauty: 2372
33:19 Thou shalt not **s** a fierce people, a people of 7200
33:20 thine eyes shall **s** Jerusalem a quiet 7200
35: 2 they shall **s** the glory of the LORD, *and* 7200
37:17 hear; open thine eyes, O LORD, and **s**: 7200
38:11 I said, I shall not **s** the LORD, *even* 7200
40: 5 be revealed, and all flesh shall **s** *it* together: 7200
41:20 That they may **s**, and know, and consider, 7200
42:18 ye deaf; and look, ye blind, that *ye* may **s**. 7200
44: 9 they **s** not, nor know; that they may be 7200
44:18 he hath shut their eyes, that *they* cannot **s**; 7200
48: 6 Thou hast heard, **s** all this; and will not ye 2372
49: 7 a servant of rulers, Kings shall **s** and arise, 7200
52: 8 for they shall **s** eye to eye, when 7200
52:10 all the ends of the earth shall **s** the salvation 7200
52:15 which had not been told them shall they **s**; 7200
53: 2 when we shall **s** him, *there is* no beauty that 7200
53:10 he shall **s** *his* seed, he shall prolong *his* 7200
53:11 He shall **s** of the travail of his soul, *and* 7200
60: 4 Lift up thine eyes round about, and **s**: 7200
60: 5 thou shalt **s**, and flow *together*, and 7200
61: 9 all that **s** them shall acknowledge them, 7200
62: 2 the Gentiles shall **s** thy righteousness, and 7200
64: 9 behold, **s**, we beseech thee, we *are* all thy 5027
66:14 when ye **s** *this*, your heart shall rejoice, 7200
66:18 and they shall come, and **s** my glory. 7200
Jer 1:10 **S**, I have this day set thee over the nations 7200
1:11 And I said, I **s** a rod of an almond tree. 7200
1:13 I said, I **s** a seething pot; and the face 7200
2:10 For pass over the isles of Chittim, and **s**; 7200
2:10 and **s** if there be such a *thing*. 7200
2:19 and **s** that *it is* an evil *thing* and bitter, 7200
2:23 **s** thy way in the valley, know what thou 7200
2:31 O generation, **s** ye the word of the LORD. 7200
3: 2 and **s** where thou hast not been lien with. 7200
4:21 How long shall I **s** the standard, *and* 7200
5: 1 **s** now, and know, and seek in the broad 7200
5:12 neither shall we **s** sword nor famine: 7200
5:21 which have eyes, and **s** not; which have 7200
6:16 the ways, and **s**, and ask for the old paths, 7200
7:12 **s** what I did to it for the wickedness of my 7200
11:20 the heart, let me **s** thy vengeance on them: 7200
12: 4 they said, He shall not **s** our last end. 7200
14:13 say unto them, Ye shall not **s** the sword, 7200
17: 6 and shall not **s** when good cometh; 7200
17: 8 shall not **s** when heat cometh, but her leaf 7200
20:12 the heart, let me **s** thy vengeance on them: 7200
20:18 came I forth out of the womb to **s** labour 7200
22:10 return no more, nor **s** his native country. 7200
22:12 him captive, and shall **s** this land no more. 7200
23:24 in secret places that I shall not **s** him? 7200
30: 6 **s** whether a man doth travail with child? 7200
30: 6 wherefore do I **s** every man *with* his hands 7200
42:14 the land of Egypt, where we shall **s** no war, 7200
42:18 and ye shall **s** this place no more. 7200
51:61 and shalt **s**, and shalt read all these words; 7200
La 1:11 **s**, O LORD, and consider; for I am 7200
1:12 **s** if there be any sorrow like unto my 7200
Eze 8: 6 *and* thou shalt **s** great*er* abominations. 7200
8:13 thou shalt **s** great*er* abominations that they 7200
8:15 thou shalt **s** greater abominations than 7200
12: 2 which have eyes to **s**, and see not; 7200
12: 2 which have eyes to see, and **s** not; 7200
12: 6 cover thy face, that thou **s** not the ground: 7200
12:12 that he **s** not the ground with *his* eyes. 7200
12:13 yet shall he not **s** it, though he shall die 7200
13: 9 mine hand shall be upon the prophets that **s** 2374
13:16 which **s** visions of peace for her, and 2374
13:23 Therefore ye shall **s** no more vanity, 2372
14:22 and ye shall **s** their way and their doings: 7200
14:23 when ye **s** their ways and their doings: 7200
16:37 that they may **s** all thy nakedness. 7200
20:48 all flesh shall **s** that I the LORD have 7200
21:29 Whiles *they* **s** vanity unto thee, whiles *they* 2372
32:31 Pharaoh shall **s** them, and shall be 7200
33: 6 if the watchman **s** the sword come, and 7200
39:21 all the heathen shall **s** my judgment that I 7200
Da 1:10 for why should he **s** your faces worse liking 7200
2: 8 because ye **s** the thing is gone from me. 2370
3:25 and said, Lo, I **s** four men loose, 2370
5:23 iron, wood, and stone, which **s** not, 2370
Joel 2:28 your young men shall **s** visions: 7200
Am 6: 2 Pass ye *unto* Calneh, and **s**; and 7200
Jnh 4: 5 till he might **s** what would become of 7200
Mic 6: 9 and *the man of* wisdom shall **s** thy name: 7200
7:10 she *that is* mine enemy shall **s** *it*, and 7200
7:16 The nations shall **s** and be confounded at all 7200
Hab 1: 1 burden which Habakkuk the prophet did **s**. 2372
2: 1 will watch to **s** what he will say unto me, 7200
Zep 3:15 of thee: thou shalt not **s** evil any more. 7200
Hag 2: 3 how do ye **s** it now? *is it* not in your eyes in 7200
Zec 2: 2 to **s** what *is* the breadth thereof, and what *is* 7200
4:10 shall **s** the plummet in the hand of 7200
5: 2 I answered, I **s** a flying roll; the length 7200
5: 5 and **s** what *is* this that goeth forth. 7200
9: 5 Ashkelon shall **s** *it*, and fear; Gaza also 7200
9: 5 Gaza also *shall* **s** *it*, and be very sorrowful, NIH
10: 7 yea, their children shall **s** *it*, and be glad; 7200
Mal 1: 5 your eyes shall **s**, and ye shall say, 7200
Mt 5: 8 *are* the pure in heart: for they shall **s** God. *3700*
5:16 that they may **s** your good works, and *1492*
7: 5 shalt thou **s clearly** to cast out the mote out *1227*
8: 4 **S** thou tell no *man*; but go thy way, *3708*
9:30 saying, **S** *that* no *man* know *it*. *3708*
Mt 11: 4 again *those things* which ye do hear and **s**: *991*
11: 7 What went ye out into the wilderness to **s**? *2300*
11: 8 But what went ye out for to **s**? A man *1492*
11: 9 But what went ye out for to **s**? A prophet? *1492*
12:38 we would **s** a sign from thee. *1492*
13:13 because they seeing **s** not; and hearing they *991*
13:14 and seeing ye shall **s**, and shall not perceive: *991*
13:15 lest at any time they should **s** with *their* *1492*
13:16 But blessed *are* your eyes, for they **s**: and *991*
13:17 righteous *men* have desired to **s** *those* *1492*
13:17 have desired to see *those things* which ye **s**, *991*
15:31 the lame to walk, and the blind to **s**: *991*
16:28 till they **s** the Son of man coming in his *1492*
22:11 And when the king came in to **s** the guests, *2300*
23:39 Ye shall not **s** me henceforth, till ye shall *1492*
24: 2 **S** ye not all these *things*? verily I say unto *991*
24: 6 **s** that ye be not troubled: for all *these things* *3708*
24:15 shall **s** the abomination of desolation, *1492*
24:30 they shall **s** the Son of man coming in *3700*
24:33 when ye shall **s** all these *things*, know that *1492*
26:58 and sat with the servants, to **s** the end. *1492*
26:64 Hereafter shall ye **s** the Son of man sitting *3700*
27: 4 they said, What *is that* to us? **s** thou *to that*. *3700*
27:24 of the blood of this just *person*: **s** ye *to it*. *3700*
27:49 let us **s** whether Elias will come to save *1492*
28: 1 and the other Mary to **s** the sepulchre. *2334*
28: 6 Come, **s** the place where the Lord lay. *1492*
28: 7 you into Galilee; there shall ye **s** him: *3700*
28:10 go into Galilee, and there shall they **s** me. *3700*
Mk 1:44 **S** thou say nothing to any *man*: but go thy *3708*
4:12 That seeing they may **s**, and not perceive; *991*
5:14 And they went out to **s** what it was that was *1492*
5:15 **s** him that was possessed with the devil, *2334*
5:32 And he looked round about to **s** her that *1492*
6:38 go and **s**. And when they knew, they say, *1492*
8:18 Having eyes, **s** ye not? and having ears, *991*
8:24 and said, I **s** men as trees, walking. *991*
12:15 ye me? bring me a penny, that I may **s** *it*. *1492*
13: 1 **s** what manner of stones and *2396*
13:14 But when ye shall **s** the abomination of *1492*
13:26 shall they **s** the Son of man coming in *3700*
13:29 when ye shall **s** these *things* come to pass, *1492*
14:62 ye shall **s** the Son of man sitting on *3700*
15:32 from the cross, that we may **s** and believe. *1492*
15:36 let us **s** whether Elias will come to take him *1492*
16: 7 there shall ye **s** him, as he said unto you. *3700*
Lk 2:15 and **s** this thing which is come to pass, *1492*
2:26 that *he* should not **s** death, before he had *1492*
3: 6 And all flesh shall **s** the salvation of God. *3700*
6:42 shalt thou **s clearly** to pull out the mote that *1227*
7:22 how that the blind **s**, the lame walk, *308*
7:24 went ye out into the wilderness for to **s**? *2300*
7:25 But what went ye out for to **s**? A man *1492*
7:26 But what went ye out for to **s**? A prophet? *1492*
8:10 that seeing they might not **s**, and *991*
8:16 that they which enter in may **s** the light. *991*
8:20 brethren stand without, desiring to **s** thee. *1492*
8:35 Then they went out to **s** what was done; and *1492*
9: 9 I hear such *things*? And he desired to **s** him. *1492*
9:27 of death, till they **s** the kingdom of God. *1492*
10:23 Blessed *are* the eyes which **s** *the things* that *991*
10:23 *are* the eyes which see *the things* that ye **s**: *991*
10:24 kings have desired to **s** *those things* which *1492*
10:24 have desired to see *those things* which ye **s**, *991*
11:33 that they which come in may **s** the light. *991*
12:54 When ye **s** a cloud rise out of the west, *1492*
12:55 And *when ye* **s** the south wind blow, ye say, NIG
13:28 when ye shall **s** Abraham, and Isaac, and *3700*
13:35 verily I say unto you, Ye shall not **s** me, *1492*
14:18 of ground, and I must needs go and **s** it: *1492*
17:22 when ye shall desire to **s** one of the days of *1492*
17:22 of the Son of man, and ye shall not **s** *it*. *3700*
17:23 And they shall say to you, **S** here; or, *2400*
17:23 they shall say to you, See here; or, **s** there: *2400*
19: 3 And he sought to **s** Jesus who he was; and *1492*
19: 4 climbed up into a sycomore tree to **s** him: *1492*
20:13 they will reverence *him* when they **s** him. *1492*
21:20 And when ye shall **s** Jerusalem compassed *1492*
21:27 shall they **s** the Son of man coming in a *3700*
21:30 ye **s** and know of your own selves that *991*
21:31 when ye **s** these *things* come to pass, *1492*
23: 8 for he was desirous to **s** him of a long *1492*
24:39 handle me, and **s**; for a spirit hath not flesh *1492*
24:39 hath not flesh and bones, as ye **s** me have. *2334*
Jn 1:33 Upon whom thou shalt **s** the Spirit *1492*
1:39 He saith unto them, Come and **s**. They *1492*
1:46 Philip saith unto him, Come and **s**. *1492*
1:50 thou shalt **s** greater *things* than these. *3700*
1:51 Hereafter ye shall **s** heaven open, and *3700*
3: 3 he cannot **s** the kingdom of God. *1492*
3:36 he that believeth not the Son shall not **s** life; *3700*
4:29 Come, **s** a man, which told me all *things* *1492*
4:48 Except ye **s** signs and wonders, ye will not *1492*
6:19 they **s** Jesus walking on the sea, and *2334*
6:30 thou then, that we may **s**, and believe thee? *1492*
6:62 If ye shall **s** the Son of man ascend up *2334*
7: 3 that thy disciples also may **s** the works that *2334*
8:51 keep my saying, he shall never **s** death. *2334*
8:56 Your father Abraham rejoiced to **s** my day: *1492*
9:15 upon mine eyes, and I washed, and do **s**. *991*
9:19 was born blind? how then doth he now **s**? *991*
9:25 I know, that, whereas I was blind, now I **s**. *991*
9:39 this world, that they which **s** not might see; *991*
9:39 this world, that they which see not might **s**; *991*
9:39 and that they which **s** might be made blind. *991*
9:41 but now ye say, We **s**; therefore your sin *991*
11:34 They say unto him, Lord, come and **s**. *1492*
11:40 thou shouldest **s** the glory of God? *3700*
12: 9 but that they might **s** Lazarus also, *1492*
12:21 desired him, saying, Sir, we would **s** Jesus. *1492*
12:40 that they should not **s** with *their* eyes, *1492*
14:19 the world seeth me no more; but ye **s** me: *2334*
16:10 I go to my Father, and ye **s** me no more; *2334*
16:16 A little while, and ye shall not **s** me: and *2334*
16:16 and ye shall **s** me, because I go to *3700*

Jn 16:17 A little while, and ye shall not s me: 2334
16:17 and again, a little while, and ye shall s me: 3700
16:19 I said, A little while, and ye shall not s me: 2334
16:19 and again, a little while, and ye shall s me? 3700
16:22 but I will s you again, and your heart shall 3700
18:26 Did not I s thee in the garden with him? 1492
20:25 Except I shall s in his hands the print of 1492
Ac 2:17 and your young men shall s visions, and 3700
2:27 neither wilt thou suffer thine Holy One to s 1492
2:31 in hell, neither his flesh did s corruption. 1492
2:33 shed forth this, which ye now s and hear. 991
3:16 this *man* strong, whom ye s and know: 2334
7:56 And said, Behold, I s the heavens opened, 2334
8:36 and the eunuch said, S, *here is* water; 2400
13:35 not suffer thine Holy One to s corruption. 1492
15:36 the word of the Lord, *and s* how they do. NIG
19:21 I have been there, I must also s Rome. 1492
19:26 Moreover ye s and hear, that not alone at 2334
20:25 kingdom of God, shall s my face no more. 3700
20:38 that they should s his face no more. 2334
22:11 And when I could not s for the glory of that 1689
22:14 and s *that* Just One, and shouldest hear 1492
23:22 charged *him, S thou* tell no *man* that thou NIG
25:24 ye s this *man*, about whom all the multitude 2334
28:20 to s *you*, and to speak with *you:* because 1492
28:26 and seeing ye shall s, and not perceive: 991
28:27 lest they should s with *their* eyes, and 1492
Ro 1:11 For I long to s you, that I may impart unto 1492
7:23 But I s another law in my members, 991
8:25 But if we hope for that we s not, *then* do we 991
11:8 eyes that *they* should not s, and ears that 991
11:10 that *they* may not s, and bow down their 991
15:21 whom he was not spoken of, they shall s: 3700
15:24 for I trust to s you in my journey, and to be 2300
1Co 1:26 For ye s your calling, brethren, how that not 991
8:10 For if any *man* s thee which hast 1492
13:12 For now we s through a glass, darkly; 991
16:7 For I will not s you now by the way; but I 1492
16:10 s that he may be with you without fear: 991
2Co 8:7 to us, *s* that ye abound in this grace also. NIG
Gal 1:18 years I went up to Jerusalem to s Peter, 2477
6:11 Ye s how large a letter I have written unto 1492
Eph 3:9 And to **make** all *men* s what *is* 5461
5:15 S then that ye walk circumspectly, not as 991
5:33 the wife *s* that she reverence *her* husband. NIG
Php 1:27 that whether I come and s you, or *else* be 1492
2:23 so soon as I shall s how it will go with me. 542
2:28 that, when ye s him again, ye may rejoice, 1492
1Th 2:17 endeavoured the more abundantly to s your 1492
3:6 desiring greatly to s us, as we also *to see* 1492
3:6 greatly to see us, as we also *to s* you: NIG
3:10 day praying exceedingly that *we* might s 1492
5:15 S that none render evil for evil unto any 3708
1Ti 6:16 whom no man hath seen, nor can s: 1492
2Ti 1:4 Greatly desiring to s thee, being mindful of 1492
Heb 2:8 But now we s not yet all *things* put under 3708
2:9 But we s Jesus, who was made a little lower 991
3:19 So we s that they could not enter in because 991
8:5 for, S, saith *he, that* thou make all *things* 3708
10:25 much the more, as ye s the day approaching. 991
11:5 was translated that *he* should not s death; 1492
12:14 without which no *man* shall s the Lord: 3700
12:25 S *that* ye refuse not him that speaketh: for if 991
13:23 with whom, if he come shortly, I will s you. 3700
Jas 2:24 Ye s then how that by works a man is 3708
1Pe 1:8 in whom, though now ye s *him* not, 3708
1:22 *s that ye* love one another with a pure heart NIG
3:10 For he that will love life, and s good days, 1492
2Pe 1:9 and **cannot s far off**, and hath forgotten 3467
1Jn 3:2 be like him; for we shall s him as he is. 3708
5:16 If any *man* s his brother sin a sin *which is* 1492
3Jn 1:14 But I trust *I* shall shortly s thee, and 1492
Rev 1:7 and every eye shall s him, and they *also* 3700
1:12 And I turned to s the voice that spake with 991
3:18 thine eyes *with* eyesalve, that thou mayest s. 991
6:1 one of the four beasts saying, Come and s. 991
6:3 I heard the second beast say, Come and s. 991
6:5 I heard the third beast say, Come and s. 991
6:6 and *s* thou hurt not the oil and the wine. NIG
6:7 voice of the fourth beast say, Come and s. 991
9:20 which neither can s, nor hear, nor walk: 991
11:9 nations shall s their dead bodies three days 991
16:15 lest he walk naked, and they s his shame. 991
18:7 and am no widow, and shall s no sorrow. 1492
18:9 when they shall s the smoke of her burning, 991
19:10 And I said unto me, S *thou do it* not: I am 3708
22:4 And they shall s his face; and his name 3700
22:9 Then saith he unto me, S *thou do it* not: 3708

SEED (279) [SEED'S, SEEDS, SEEDTIME]

Ge 1:11 the herb yielding s, *and* the fruit tree 2233
1:11 his kind, whose s *is* in itself, upon the earth: 2233
1:12 *and* herb yielding s after his kind, and 2233
1:12 whose s *was* in itself, after his kind: 2233
1:29 I have given you every herb bearing s, 2233
1:29 in the which *is* the fruit of a tree yielding s; 2233
3:15 and between thy s and her seed; 2233
3:15 and between thy seed and her s; 2233
4:25 *said she*, hath appointed me another s 2233
7:3 to keep s alive upon the face of all 2233
9:9 with you and with your s after you; 2233
12:7 and said, Unto thy s will I give this land: 2233
13:15 to thee will I give it, and to thy s for ever. 2233
13:16 I will make thy s as the dust of the earth: 2233
13:16 the earth, *then* shall thy s also be numbered. 2233
15:3 Behold, to me thou hast given no s: 2233
15:5 and he said unto him, So shall thy s be. 2233
15:13 Know of a surety that thy s shall be a 2233
15:18 saying, Unto thy s have I given this land, 2233
16:10 I will multiply thy s exceedingly, that it 2233
17:7 thy s after thee in their generations for an 2233
17:7 be a God unto thee, and to thy s after thee. 2233
17:8 I will give unto thee, and to thy s after thee, 2233
17:9 and thy s after thee in their generations. 2233
17:10 between me and you and thy s after thee; 2233
17:12 of any stranger, which *is* not of thy s. 2233
17:19 *and* with his s after him. 2233
19:32 that we may preserve s of our father. 2233
19:34 that we may preserve s of our father. 2233
21:12 her voice; for in Isaac shall thy s be called. 2233
21:13 will I make a nation, because he *is* thy s. 2233
22:17 in multiplying I will multiply thy s as 2233
22:17 thy s shall possess the gate of his enemies; 2233
22:18 in thy s shall all the nations of the earth be 2233
24:7 saying, Unto thy s will I give this land; 2233
24:60 let thy s possess the gate of those which 2233
26:3 for unto thee, and unto thy s, I will give all 2233
26:4 I will make thy s to multiply as the stars of 2233
26:4 and will give unto thy s all these countries; 2233
26:4 in thy s shall all the nations of the earth be 2233
26:24 multiply thy s for my servant Abraham's 2233
28:4 of Abraham, to thee, and to thy s with thee; 2233
28:13 thou liest, to thee will I give it, and to thy s; 2233
28:14 thy s shall be as the dust of the earth, and 2233
28:14 in thy s shall all the families of the earth be 2233
32:12 and make thy s as the sand of the sea, 2233
35:12 and to thy s after thee will I give the land. 2233
38:8 and marry her, and raise up s to thy brother. 2233
38:9 Onan knew that the s should not be his; 2233
38:9 lest that he should give s to his brother. 2233
46:6 into Egypt, Jacob, and all his s with him: 2233
46:7 all his s brought he with him into Egypt. 2233
47:19 and give *us* s, that we may live, and not die, 2233
47:23 lo, *here is* s for you, and ye shall sow 2233
47:24 for s of the field, and for your food, and 2233
48:4 will give this land to thy s after thee *for* an 2233
48:11 and lo, God hath shewed me also thy s. 2233
48:19 his s shall become a multitude of nations. 2233
Ex 16:31 it *was* like coriander s, white; and the taste 2233
28:43 for ever unto him and his s after him. 2233
30:21 and to his s throughout their generations. 2233
32:13 I will multiply your s as the stars of heaven, 2233
32:13 I have spoken of will I give unto your s, 2233
33:1 to Jacob, saying, Unto thy s will I give it: 2233
Lev 11:37 fall upon any sowing s which is to be sown, 2233
11:38 if *any* water be put upon the s, and *any part* 2233
12:2 If a woman have **conceived** s, and born a 2232
15:16 if any man's s of copulation go out from 2233
15:17 every skin, whereon is the s of copulation, 2233
15:18 whom man shall lie *with* s of copulation, 2233
15:32 *of him* whose s goeth from him, and is 2233
18:21 thou shalt not let *any* of thy s pass through 2233
19:19 thou shalt not **sow** thy field **with** mingled s: 2232
20:2 that giveth *any* of his s unto Molech; 2233
20:3 because he hath given of his s unto Molech, 2233
20:4 when he giveth of his s unto Molech, and 2233
21:15 Neither shall he profane his s among his 2233
21:17 Whosoever *he be* of thy s in their 2233
21:21 hath a blemish, of the s of Aaron the priest, 2233
22:3 Whosoever *he be* of all your s among your 2233
22:4 What man soever of the s of Aaron *is* a 2233
22:4 or a man whose s goeth from him; 2233+7902
26:16 ye shall sow your s in vain, for your 2233
27:16 thy estimation shall be according to the s 2233
27:16 a homer of barley s *shall be valued* at fifty 2233
27:30 *whether* of the s of the land, *or* of the fruit 2233
Nu 5:28 shall be free, and shall **conceive** s. 2232+2233
11:7 the manna *was* as coriander s, and 2233
14:24 he went; and his s shall possess it. 2233
16:40 no stranger, which *is* not of the s of Aaron, 2233
18:19 LORD unto thee and to thy s with thee. 2233
20:5 it *is* no place of s, or of figs, or vines, or 2233
24:7 his s *shall be* in many waters, and his king 2233
25:13 he shall have it, and his s after him, 2233
Dt 1:8 to give unto them and to their s after them. 2233
4:37 therefore he chose their s after them, and 2233
10:15 he chose their s after them, *even* you above 2233
11:9 fathers to give unto them and to their s, 2233
11:10 where thou sowedst thy s, and wateredst *it* 2233
14:22 shalt truly tithe all the increase of thy s, 2233
22:9 lest the fruit of *thy* s which thou hast sown, 2233
28:38 Thou shalt carry much s out *into* the field, 2233
28:46 and for a wonder, and upon thy s for ever. 2233
28:59 the plagues of thy s, *even* great plagues, 2233
30:6 the heart of thy s, to love the LORD thy 2233
30:19 that *both* thou and thy s may live: 2233
31:21 be forgotten out of the mouths of their s: 2233
34:4 unto Jacob, saying, I will give it unto thy s: 2233
Jos 24:3 and multiplied his s, and gave him Isaac. 2233
Ru 4:12 of the s which the LORD shall give thee 2233
1Sa 2:20 The LORD give thee s of this woman for 2233
8:15 he will take the tenth of your s, and of your 2233
20:42 and between my s and thy seed for ever. 2233
20:42 and between my seed and thy s for ever. 2233
24:21 that thou wilt not cut off my s after me, and 2233
2Sa 4:8 lord the king this day of Saul, and of his s. 2233
7:12 thy fathers, I will set up thy s after thee, 2233
22:51 unto David, and to his s for evermore. 2233
1Ki 2:33 of Joab, and upon the head of his s for ever: 2233
2:33 upon his s, and upon his house, and 2233
11:14 he *was* of the king's s in Edom. 2233
11:39 And I will for this afflict the s of David, but 2233
18:32 great as would contain two measures of s. 2233
2Ki 5:27 cleave unto thee, and unto thy s for ever. 2233
11:1 she arose and destroyed all the s royal. 2233
17:20 the LORD rejected all the s of Israel, and 2233
25:25 of the s royal, came, and ten men with him, 2233
1Ch 16:13 O ye s of Israel his servant, ye children of 2233
17:11 that I will raise up thy s after thee, 2233
2Ch 20:7 gavest it to the s of Abraham thy friend for 2233
22:10 destroyed all the s royal of the house of 2233
Ezr 2:59 and their s, whether they *were* of Israel: 2233
9:2 that the holy s have mingled themselves 2233
Ne 7:61 nor their s, whether they *were* of Israel. 2233
9:2 the s of Israel separated themselves from all 2233
9:8 to give *it, I say,* to his s, and hast performed 2233
Est 6:13 If Mordecai *be* of the s of the Jews, 2233
9:27 upon their s, and upon all such as joined 2233
9:28 the memorial of them perish from their s. 2233
9:31 had decreed for themselves and for their s, 2233
Est 10:3 his people, and speaking peace to all his s. 2233
Job 5:25 Thou shalt know also that thy s *shall be* 2233
21:8 Their s is established in their sight with 2233
39:12 that he will bring home thy s, and gather *it* 2233
Ps 18:50 to David, and to his s for evermore. 2233
21:10 their s from among the children of men. 2233
22:23 all ye the s of Jacob, glorify him; and 2233
22:23 and fear him, all ye the s of Israel. 2233
22:30 A s shall serve him; it shall be accounted to 2233
25:13 at ease; and his s shall inherit the earth. 2233
37:25 righteous forsaken, nor his s begging bread. 2233
37:26 and lendeth; and his s *is* blessed. 2233
37:28 but the s of the wicked shall be cut off. 2233
69:36 The s also of his servants shall inherit it: 2233
89:4 Thy s will I stablish for ever, and build up 2233
89:29 His s also will I make *to endure* for ever, 2233
89:36 His s shall endure for ever, and his throne 2233
102:28 and their s shall be established before thee. 2233
105:6 O ye s of Abraham his servant, ye children 2233
106:27 To overthrow their s also among 2233
112:2 His s shall be mighty upon earth: 2233
126:6 and weepeth, bearing precious s, 2233
Pr 11:21 but the s of the righteous shall be delivered. 2233
Ecc 11:6 In the morning sow thy s, and in 2233
Isa 1:4 a s of evildoers, children that are 2233
5:10 and the s of a homer shall yield an ephah. 2233
6:13 *so* the holy s *shall be* the substance thereof. 2233
14:20 the s of evildoers shall never be renowned. 2233
17:11 in the morning shalt thou make thy s to 2233
23:3 by great waters the s of Sihor, the harvest 2233
30:23 shall he give the rain of thy s, that thou 2233
41:8 I have chosen, the s of Abraham my friend. 2233
43:5 I will bring thy s from the east, and 2233
44:3 *ground:* I will pour my spirit upon thy s, 2233
45:19 I said not unto the s of Jacob, Seek ye me 2233
45:25 In the LORD shall all the s of Israel be 2233
48:19 Thy s also had been as the sand, and 2233
53:10 he shall see *his* s, he shall prolong *his* days, 2233
54:3 thy s shall inherit the Gentiles, and 2233
55:10 that it may give s to the sower, and bread to 2233
57:3 the s of the adulterer and the whore. 2233
57:4 children of transgression, a s of falsehood, 2233
59:21 of thy mouth, nor out of the mouth of thy s, 2233
59:21 nor out of the mouth of thy seed's s, 2233
61:9 their s shall be known among the Gentiles, 2233
61:9 that they *are* the s *which* the LORD hath 2233
65:9 I will bring forth a s out of Jacob, and 2233
65:23 for they *are* the s of the blessed of 2233
66:22 so shall your s and your name remain. 2233
Jer 2:21 planted thee a noble vine, wholly a right s: 2233
7:15 *even* the whole s of Ephraim. 2233
22:28 he and his s, and are cast into a land which 2233
22:30 for no man of his s shall prosper, 2233
23:8 which led the s of the house of Israel out of 2233
29:32 punish Shemaiah the Nehelamite, and his s: 2233
30:10 and thy s from the land of their captivity; 2233
31:27 and the house of Judah *with* the s of man, 2233
31:27 the seed of man, and *with* the s of beast. 2233
31:36 the s of Israel also shall cease from being a 2233
31:37 I will also cast off all the s of Israel for all 2233
33:22 will I multiply the s of David my servant, 2233
33:26 will I cast away the s of Jacob, and 2233
33:26 that *I* will not take *any* of his s *to be* rulers 2233
33:26 his seed *to be* rulers over the s of Abraham, 2233
35:7 nor sow s, nor plant vineyard, nor have 2233
35:9 neither have we vineyard, nor field, nor s: 2233
36:31 I will punish him and his s and his servants 2233
41:1 of the s royal, and the princes of the king, 2233
46:27 and thy s from the land of their captivity; 2233
49:10 his s is spoiled, and his brethren, and 2233
Eze 17:5 He took also of the s of the land, and 2233
17:13 hath taken of the king's s, and made a 2233
20:5 lifted up mine hand unto the s of the house 2233
43:19 priests the Levites that *be* of the s of Zadok, 2233
44:22 they shall take maidens of the s of 2233
Da 1:3 and of the king's s, and of the princes; 2233
2:43 they shall mingle themselves with the s of 2234
9:1 the son of Ahasuerus, of the s of the Medes, 2233
Joel 1:17 The s is rotten under their clods, the garners 6507
Am 9:13 and the treader of grapes him that soweth s; 2233
Hag 2:19 *Is* the s yet in the barn? yea, as yet the vine, 2233
Zec 8:12 For the s *shall be* prosperous; the vine shall 2233
Mal 2:3 I *will* corrupt your s, and spread dung upon 2233
2:15 That he might seek a godly s. 2233
Mt 13:19 This is he which **received** s by the way 4687
13:20 But he that **received** the s into stony *places,* 4687
13:22 He also that **received** s among the thorns is 4687
13:23 But he that **received** s into the good ground 4687
13:24 a man which sowed good s in his field: 4690
13:27 Sir, didst not thou sow good s in thy field? 4690
13:31 of heaven is like unto a **grain** of mustard s, 2848
13:37 He that soweth the good s is the Son of 4690
13:38 the good s are the children of the kingdom; 4690
17:20 If ye have faith as a **grain** of mustard s, 2848
22:24 his wife, and raise up s unto his brother. 4690
Mk 4:26 as if a man should cast s into the ground, 4703
4:27 day, and the s should spring and grow up, 4703
4:31 *It is* like a **grain** of mustard s, which, 2848
12:19 his wife, and raise up s unto his brother. 4690
12:20 the first took a wife, and dying left no s. 4690
12:21 took her, and died, neither left he *any* s: 4690
12:22 And the seven had her, and left no s: last of 4690
Lk 1:55 to Abraham, and to his s for ever. 4690
8:5 A sower went out to sow his s: and as he 4703
8:11 parable is this: The s is the word of God. 4703
13:19 It is like a **grain** of mustard s, which a man 2848
17:6 If ye had faith as a **grain** of mustard s, 2848
20:28 *his* wife, and raise up s unto his brother. 4690
Jn 7:42 That Christ cometh of the s of David, and 4690
8:33 We be Abraham's s, and were never in 4690
8:37 I know that ye are Abraham's s; but ye seek 4690
Ac 3:25 And in thy s shall all the kindreds of 4690
7:5 and to his s after him, when *as yet* he had 4690
7:6 That his s should sojourn in a strange land; 4690
13:23 Of this *man's* s hath God according to *his* 4690

Ro 1: 3 which was made of the s of David 4690
4:13 or to his s, through the law, but through 4690
4:16 end the promise might be sure to all the s; 4690
4:18 to that which was spoken, So shall thy s be. 4690
9: 7 Neither, because they are the s of Abraham, 4690
9: 7 but, In Isaac shall thy s be called. 4690
9: 8 of the promise are counted for the s. 4690
9:29 Except the Lord of sabaoth had left us a s, 4690
11: 1 of the s of Abraham, of the tribe of 4690
1Co 15:38 pleased him, and to every s his own body. 4690
2Co 9:10 Now he that ministereth s to the sower both 4690
9:10 and multiply your s sown, and increase 4703
11:22 am I. Are they the s of Abraham? so am I. 4690
Gal 3:16 and his s were the promises made. 4690
3:16 but as of one, And to thy s, which is Christ. 4690
3:19 till the s should come to whom the promise 4690
3:29 then are ye Abraham's s, and 4690
2Ti 2: 8 Remember that Jesus Christ of the s of 4690
Heb 2:16 but he took on him the s of Abraham. 4690
11:11 Sara herself received strength to conceive s, 4690
11:18 was said, That in Isaac shall thy s be called: 4690
1Pe 1:23 not of corruptible s, but of incorruptible, 4701
1Jn 3: 9 not commit sin; for his s remaineth in him: 4690
Rev 12:17 to make war with the remnant of her s, 4690

SEED'S (1) [SEED]

Isa 59:21 nor out of the mouth of thy s seed, saith 2233

SEEDS (5) [SEED]

Dt 22: 9 shalt not sow thy vineyard with divers s: 2232
Mt 13: 4 some s fell by the way side, and the fowls NIG
13:32 Which indeed is the least of all s: but 4690
Mk 4:31 is less than all the s that be in the earth: 4690
Gal 3:16 He saith not, And to s, as of many; but as of 4690

SEEDTIME (1) [SEED, TIME]

Ge 8:22 s and harvest, and cold and heat, and 2233

SEEING (116) [SEE]

Ge 15: 2 s I go childless, and the steward of my 2050.1
18:18 S Abraham shall surely become a great 2050.1
19: 1 Lot s them rose up to meet them; and 7200
22:12 s thou hast not withheld thy son, thine 2050.1
24:56 s the LORD hath prospered my way; 2050.1
26:27 s ye hate me, and have sent me away 2050.1
28: 8 Esau s that the daughters of Canaan pleased 7200
44:30 s that his life is bound up in the lad's life; 2050.1
Ex 4:11 the dumb, or deaf, or the s, or the blind? 6493
21: 8 s he hath dealt deceitfully with her. NIH
22:10 or be hurt, or driven away, no man s it: 7200
23: 9 s ye were strangers in the land of Egypt. 3588
Lev 10:17 s it is most holy, and God hath given it you 3588
Nu 15:26 s all the people were in ignorance. 3588
16: 3 s all the congregation are holy, every one of 3588
35:23 s him not, and cast it upon him, that he die, 7200
Jos 17:14 portion to inherit, s I am a great people, 2050.1
22:18 s ye rebel to day against the LORD, NIH
Jdg 13:18 thou thus after my name, s it is secret? 2050.1
17:13 do me good, s I have a Levite to my priest. 3588
19:23 s that this man is come into mine 310+834
21: 7 s we have sworn by the LORD that we 2050.1
21:16 s the women are destroyed out of 3588
Ru 1:21 s the LORD hath testified against me, 2050.1
2:10 take knowledge of me, s I am a stranger? 2050.1
1Sa 16: 1 s I have rejected him from reigning over 2050.1
17:36 s he hath defied the armies of the living 3588
18:23 s that I am a poor man, and 2050.1
24: 6 s he is the anointed of the LORD. 3588
25:26 s the LORD hath withholden thee from 834
28:16 s the LORD is departed from thee, and 2050.1
2Sa 13:39 concerning Amnon, s he was dead. 3588
15:20 s I go whither I may, return thou, and 2050.1
18:22 my son, s that thou hast no tidings ready? 2050.1
19:11 s the speech of all Israel is come to 2050.1
1Ki 1:48 on my throne this day, mine eyes even s it. 7200
11:28 Solomon s the young man that he was 7200
2Ki 10: 2 s your master's sons are with you, and 2050.1
1Ch 12:17 s there is no wrong in mine hands, the God 2050.1
2Ch 2: 6 s the heaven and heaven of heavens cannot 3588
Ezr 9:13 s that thou our God hast punished us less 3588
Ne 2: 2 thy countenance sad, s thou art not sick? 2050.1
Job 14: 5 S his days are determined, the number of his 518
19:28 s the root of the matter is found in me; 2050.1
21:22 s he judgeth those that are high. 2050.1
21:34 s in your answers there remaineth 2050.1
24: 1 s times are not hidden from the Almighty, NIH
28:21 S it is hid from the eyes of all living, and 2050.1
Ps 22: 8 let him deliver him, s he delighted in him. 3588
50:17 S thou hatest instruction, and castest my 2050.1
Pr 3:29 s he dwelleth securely by thee. 2050.1
17:16 to get wisdom, s he hath no heart to it? 2050.1
20:12 The hearing ear, and the s eye, the LORD 7200
Ecc 1: 8 utter it: the eye is not satisfied with s, 7200
2:16 s that which now is, in the days to come 871.1
6:11 S there be many things that increase vanity, 3588
Isa 21: 3 hearing of it; I was dismayed at the s of it. 7200
33:15 of blood, and shutteth his eyes from s evil; 7200
42:20 S many things, but thou observest not; 7200
49:21 s I have lost my children, and 2050.1
Jer 11:15 s she hath wrought lewdness with many, NIH
47: 7 s the LORD hath given it a charge 2050.1
Eze 16:30 s thou doest all these things, the work of an 871.1
17:18 S he despised the oath by breaking 2050.1
21: 4 S then that I will cut off from thee 3282
22:28 them with untempered morter, s vanity, 2374
Da 2:47 of secrets, s thou couldest reveal this secret. 1768
Hos 4: 6 s thou hast forgotten the law of thy God, 2050.1
Mt 5: 1 And s the multitudes, he went up into a 1492
9: 2 Jesus s their faith said unto the sick of 1492
13:13 because they s see not; and hearing they hear 991
13:14 and s ye shall see, and shall not perceive: 991
Mk 4:12 That s they may see, and not perceive; and 991
11:13 And s a fig tree afar off having leaves, 1492
Lk 1:34 How shall this be, s I know not a man? 1893
5:12 who s Jesus fell on his face, and 1492
8:10 that s they might not see, and hearing they 991
23:40 s thou art in the same condemnation? 3754
Jn 2:18 unto us, s that thou doest these things? 3754
9: 7 his way therefore, and washed, and came s. 991
21:21 Peter s him saith to Jesus, Lord, and 1492
Ac 2:15 s it is but the third hour of the day. 1063
2:31 He s this before, spake of the resurrection 4275
3: 3 Who s Peter and John about to go into 1492
7:24 And s one of them suffer wrong, 1492
8: 6 hearing and s the miracles which he did. 991
9: 7 hearing a voice, but s no man. 2334
13:11 shalt be blind, not s the sun for a season. 991
13:46 but s ye put it from you, and 1894
16:27 and s the prison doors open, he drew out 1492
17:24 s that he is Lord of heaven and earth, NIG
17:25 as though he needed any thing, s he giveth NIG
19:36 S then that these things cannot be spoken 3767
24: 2 S that by thee we enjoy great quietness, and NIG
28:26 and s ye shall see, and not perceive: 991
Ro 3:30 S it is one God, which shall justify 1897
1Co 14:16 s he understandeth not what thou sayest? 1894
2Co 3:12 S then that we have such hope, we use 3767
4: 1 Therefore s we have this ministry, as we 2531
11:18 S that many glory after the flesh, I will 1893
11:19 suffer fools gladly, s ye yourselves are wise. NIG
Col 3: 9 s that ye have put off the old man with his NIG
2Th 1: 6 S it is a righteous thing with God to 1512
Heb 4: 6 S therefore it remaineth that some must 1893
4:14 S then that we have a great high priest, 3767
5:11 hard to be uttered, s ye are dull of hearing. 1893
6: 6 s they crucify to themselves the Son of God NIG
7:25 s he ever liveth to make intercession for NIG
8: 4 s that there are priests that offer gifts NIG
11:27 for he endured, as s him who is invisible. 3708
12: 1 Wherefore s we also are compassed about 5105
1Pe 1:22 S ye have purified your souls in obeying NIG
2Pe 2: 8 man dwelling among them, in s and hearing, 990
3:11 S then that all these things shall be NIG
3:14 Wherefore, beloved, s that ye look for 1352
3:17 Ye therefore, beloved, s ye know these 3767

SEEK (244) [SEEKEST, SEEKETH, SEEKING, SOUGHT]

Ge 37:16 he said, I s my brethren: tell me, I pray 1245
43:18 that he may s occasion against us, and fall 1556
Lev 13:36 the priest shall not s for yellow hair: 1239
19:31 neither s after wizards, to be defiled by 1245
Nu 15:39 that ye s not after your own heart and 8446
16:10 with thee: and s ye the priesthood also? 1245
24: 1 to s for enchantments, but he set his face 7125
Dt 4:29 if from thence thou shalt s the LORD thy 1245
4:29 thou shalt find him, if thou s him with all 1875
12: 5 even unto his habitation shall ye s, and 1875
22: 2 it shall be with thee until thy brother s after 1875
23: 6 Thou shalt not s their peace nor their 1875
Ru 3: 1 My daughter, shall I not s rest for thee, 1245
1Sa 9: 3 servants with thee, and arise, go s the asses. 1245
10: 2 The asses which thou wentest to s are 1245
10:14 he said, To s the asses: and when we saw 1245
16:16 to s out a man, who is a cunning player on 1245
23:15 David saw that Saul was come out to s his 1245
23:25 his men went to s him. And they told 1245
24: 2 went to s David and his men upon the rocks 1245
25:26 and they that s evil to my lord, be as Nabal. 1245
25:29 is risen to pursue thee, and to s thy soul: 1245
26: 2 to s David in the wilderness of Ziph. 1245
26:20 for the king of Israel is come out to s a flea, 1245
27: 1 to s me any more in any coast of Israel: 1245
28: 7 S me a woman that hath a familiar spirit, 1245
2Sa 5:17 all the Philistines came up to s David; 1245
1Ki 2:40 went to Gath to Achish to s his servants: 1245
18:10 whither my lord hath not sent to s thee: 1245
19:10 am left; and they s my life, to take it away. 1245
19:14 am left; and they s my life, to take it away. 1245
2Ki 2:16 let them go, we pray thee, and s thy master: 1245
6:19 and I will bring you to the man whom ye s. 1245
1Ch 4:39 of the valley, to s pasture for their flocks. 1245
14: 8 all the Philistines went up to s David. 1245
16:10 let the heart of them rejoice that s 1245
16:11 S the LORD and his strength, seek his 1875
16:11 and his strength, s his face continually. 1245
22:19 and your soul to s the LORD your God; 1875
28: 8 s for all the commandments of the LORD 1875
28: 9 if thou s him, he will be found of thee; but 1875
2Ch 7:14 s my face, and turn from their wicked 1245
11:16 s the LORD God of Israel came to 1245
12:14 he prepared not his heart to s the LORD. 1875
14: 4 commanded Judah to s the LORD God of 1875
15: 2 if ye s him, he will be found of you; but 1875
15:12 they entered into a covenant to s 1875
15:13 That whosoever would not s the LORD 1875
19: 3 and hast prepared thine heart to s God. 1875
20: 3 set himself to s the LORD, and 1875
20: 4 cities of Judah they came to s the LORD. 1245
30:19 That prepareth his heart to s God, 1875
31:21 and in the commandments, to s his God, 1875
34: 3 he began to s after the God of David his 1875
Ezr 4: 2 for we s your God, as ye do; and we do 1875
6:21 to s the LORD God of Israel, did eat, 1875
7:10 For Ezra had prepared his heart to s the law 1875
8:21 to s of him a right way for us, and for our 1245
8:22 God is upon all them for good that s him; 1245
9:12 nor s their peace or their wealth for ever: 1875
Ne 2:10 to s the welfare of the children of Israel. 1245
Job 5: 8 I would s unto God, and unto God would I 1875
7:21 thou shalt s me in the morning, but I shall 7836
8: 5 If thou wouldest s unto God betimes, and 7836
20:10 His children shall s to please the poor, and NIH
Ps 4: 2 will ye love vanity, and s after leasing? 1245
9:10 LORD, hast not forsaken them that s thee. 1875
10: 4 will not s after God: God is not in all his 1875
10:15 the evil man: s out his wickedness till thou 1875
14: 2 were any that did understand, and s God. 1875
22:26 they shall praise the LORD that s him: 1875
24: 6 This is the generation of them that s him, 1875
24: 6 that seek him, that s thy face, O Jacob. 1245
27: 4 I desired of the LORD, that will I s after; 1245
27: 8 When thou saidst, S ye my face; my heart 1245
27: 8 said unto thee, Thy face, LORD, will I s. 1245
34:10 they that s the LORD shall not want any 1875
34:14 and do good; s peace, and pursue it. 1245
35: 4 and put to shame that s after my soul: 1245
38:12 They also that s after my life lay snares for 1245
38:12 they that s my hurt speak mischievous 1875
40:14 confounded together that s after my soul to 1245
40:16 Let all those that s thee rejoice and be glad 1245
53: 2 any that did understand, that did s God. 1875
54: 3 against me, and oppressors s after my soul: 1245
63: 1 thou art my God; early will I s thee: 7836
63: 9 those that s my soul, to destroy it, shall go 1245
69: 6 let not those that s thee be confounded for 1245
69:32 and your heart shall live that s God. 1875
70: 2 and confounded that s after my soul: 1245
70: 4 Let all those that s thee rejoice and be glad 1245
71:13 with reproach and dishonour that s my hurt. 1245
71:24 are brought unto shame, that s my hurt. 1245
83:16 that they may s thy name, O LORD. 1245
104:21 after their prey, and s their meat from God. 1245
105: 3 let the heart of them rejoice that s 1245
105: 4 S the LORD, and his strength: seek his 1875
105: 4 and his strength: s his face evermore. 1245
109:10 let them s their bread also out of their 1875
119: 2 and that s him with the whole heart. 1875
119:45 I will walk at liberty: for I s thy precepts. 1875
119:155 from the wicked: for they s not thy statutes. 1875
119:176 gone astray like a lost sheep; s thy servant; 1245
122: 9 of the LORD our God I will s thy good. 1245
Pr 1:28 they shall s me early, but they shall not 7836
7:15 diligently to s thy face, and I have found 7836
8:17 and those that s me early shall find me. 7836
21: 6 tossed to and fro of them that s death. 1245
23:30 at the wine; they that go to s mixt wine. 2713
23:35 when shall I awake? I will s it yet again. 1245
28: 5 they that s the LORD understand all 1245
29:10 hate the upright: but the just s his soul. 1245
29:26 Many s the ruler's favour; but every man's 1245
Ecc 1:13 I gave my heart to s and search out by 1875
7:25 to s out wisdom, and the reason of things, 1245
8:17 because though a man labour to s it out, 1245
SS 3: 2 I will s him whom my soul loveth: 1245
6: 1 turned aside? that we may s him with thee. 1245
Isa 1:17 s judgment, relieve the oppressed, judge 1875
8:19 S unto them that have familiar spirits, and 1875
8:19 should not a people s unto their God? 1875
9:13 neither do they s the LORD of hosts. 1875
11:10 of the people; to it shall the Gentiles s: 1875
19: 3 they shall s to the idols, and to 1875
26: 9 with my spirit within me will I s thee early: 7836
29:15 Woe unto them that s deep to hide their 6009
31: 1 Holy One of Israel, neither s the LORD. 1875
34:16 S ye out of the book of the LORD, and 1875
41:12 Thou shalt s them, and shalt not find them, 1245
41:17 When the poor and needy s water, and 1245
45:19 not unto the seed of Jacob, S ye me in vain: 1245
51: 1 after righteousness, ye that s the LORD: 1245
55: 6 S ye the LORD while he may be found, 1875
58: 2 Yet they s me daily, and delight to know 1875
Jer 2:24 all they that s her will not weary 1245
2:33 Why trimmest thou thy way to s love? 1245
4:30 lovers will despise thee, they will s thy life. 1245
5: 1 know, and s in the broad places thereof, 1245
11:21 that s thy life, saying, Prophesy not in 1245
19: 7 and by the hands of them that s their lives: 1245
19: 9 they that s their lives, shall straiten them. 1245
21: 7 and into the hand of those that s their life: 1245
22:25 I will give thee into the hand of them that s 1245
29: 7 s the peace of the city whither I have 1875
29:13 ye shall s me, and find me, when ye shall 1245
30:14 lovers have forgotten thee; they s thee not; 1875
34:20 and into the hand of them that s their life: 1245
34:21 into the hand of them that s their life, and 1245
38:16 into the hand of these men that s thy life. 1245
44:30 and into the hand of them that s his life; 1245
45: 5 s them not: for behold, I will bring evil 1245
46:26 into the hand of those that s their lives, 1245
49:37 and before them that s their life: 1245
50: 4 they shall go, and s the LORD their God. 1245
La 1:11 All her people sigh, they s bread; they have 1245
Eze 7:25 they shall s peace, and there shall be none. 1245
7:26 then shall they s a vision of the prophet; but 1245
34: 6 and none did search or s after them. 1245
34:11 will both search my sheep, and s them out. 1239
34:12 so will I s out my sheep, and will deliver 1239
34:16 I will s that which was lost, and bring again 1245
Da 9: 3 to s by prayer and supplications, 1245
Hos 2: 7 she shall s them, but shall not find them: 1245
3: 5 s the LORD their God, and David their 1245
5: 6 and with their herds to s the LORD; 1245
5:15 acknowledge their offence, and s my face: 1245
5:15 in their affliction they will s me early. 7836
7:10 LORD their God, nor s him for all this. 1245
10:12 for it is time to s the LORD, till he come 1875
Am 5: 4 house of Israel, S ye me, and ye shall live: 1875
5: 5 s not Beth-el, nor enter into Gilgal, and 1875
5: 6 S the LORD, and ye shall live; lest he 1875
5: 8 S him that maketh the seven stars and NIH
5:14 S good, and not evil, that ye may live: and 1875
8:12 run to and fro to s the word of the LORD, 1245
Na 3: 7 whence shall I s comforters for thee? 1245
3:11 thou also shalt s strength because of 1245
Zep 2: 3 S ye the LORD, all ye meek of the earth, 1245
2: 3 s righteousness, seek meekness: 1245
2: 3 seek righteousness, s meekness: 1245
Zec 8:21 the LORD, and to s the LORD of hosts: 1245
8:22 strong nations shall come to s the LORD 1245
11:16 neither shall s the young one, nor heal that 1245
12: 9 that I will s to destroy all the nations that 1245
Mal 2: 7 and they should s the law at his mouth: 1245
2:15 That he might s a godly seed. 1245
3: 1 the LORD, whom ye s, shall suddenly 1245

S

Mt 2:13 for Herod will s the young child to destroy 2212
6:32 after all these things do the Gentiles s): 1934
6:33 But s ye first the kingdom of God, and 2212
7: 7 s, and ye shall find; knock, and it shall be 2212
28: 5 for I know that ye s Jesus, which was 2212
Mk 1:37 they said unto him, All men s for thee. 2212
3:32 and thy brethren without s for thee. 2212
8:12 Why doth this generation s after a sign? 1934
16: 6 Ye s Jesus of Nazareth, which was 2212
Lk 11: 9 s, and ye shall find; knock, and it shall be 2212
11:29 they s a sign; and there shall no sign be 1934
12:29 And s not ye what ye shall eat, or what ye 2212
12:30 things do the nations of the world s after: 1934
12:31 But rather s ye the kingdom of God; 2212
13:24 will s to enter in, and shall not be able. 2212
15: 8 the house, and s diligently till she find it? 2212
17:33 Whosoever shall s to save his life shall lose 2212
19:10 For the Son of man is come to s and to save 2212
24: 5 Why s ye the living among the dead? 2212
Jn 1:38 and saith unto them, What s ye? 2212
5:30 is just; because I s not mine own will, 2212
5:44 s not the honour that cometh from God 2212
6:26 Ye s me, not because ye saw the miracles, 2212
7:25 Is not this he, whom they s to kill? 2212
7:34 Ye shall s me, and shall not find me: and 2212
7:36 Ye shall s me, and shall not find me: and 2212
8:21 and ye shall s me, and shall die in your 2212
8:37 but ye s to kill me, because my word hath 2212
8:40 But now ye s to kill me, a man that hath 2212
8:50 And I s not mine own glory: there is one 2212
13:33 Ye shall s me: and as I said unto the Jews, 2212
18: 4 and said unto them, Whom s ye? 2212
18: 7 Then asked he them again, Whom s ye? 2212
18: 8 told you that I am he: if therefore ye s me, 2212
Ac 10:19 said unto him, Behold, three men s thee: 2212
10:21 and said, Behold, I am he whom ye s: 2212
11:25 departed Barnabas to Tarsus, for to s Saul: 327
15:17 That the residue of men might s after 1567
17:27 That they should s the Lord, if haply they 2212
Ro 2: 7 continuance in well doing s for glory 2212
11: 3 and I am left alone, and they s my life. 2212
1Co 1:22 a sign, and the Greeks s after wisdom: 2212
7:27 s not to be loosed. Art thou loosed from a 2212
7:27 Art thou loosed from a wife? s not a wife. 2212
10:24 Let no man s his own, but every man 2212
14:12 s that ye may excel to the edifying of 2212
2Co 12:14 not be burdensome to you: for I s not yours, 2212
13: 3 Since ye s a proof of Christ speaking in me, 2212
Gal 1:10 or do I s to please men? for if I yet pleased 2212
2:17 But if, while we s to be justified by Christ, 2212
Php 2:21 For all s their own, not the things which are 2212
Col 3: 1 with Christ, s those things which are above, 2212
Heb 11: 6 is a rewarder of them that diligently s him. 1567
11:14 things declare plainly that they s a country. 1934
13:14 no continuing city, but we s one to come. 1934
1Pe 3:11 and do good; let him s peace, and ensue it. 2212
Rev 9: 6 And in those days shall men s death, and 2212

SEEKEST (9) [SEEK]

Ge 37:15 the man asked him, saying, What s thou? 1245
Jdg 4:22 and I will shew thee the man whom thou s. 1245
2Sa 17: 3 the man whom thou s is as if all returned: 1245
20:19 thou s to destroy a city and a mother in 1245
1Ki 11:22 thou s to go to thine own country? 1245
Pr 2: 4 If thou s her as silver, and searchest for her 1245
Jer 45: 5 s thou great things for thyself? seek them 1245
Jn 4:27 yet no man said, What s thou? or, 2212
20:15 whom s thou? She, supposing him to be 2212

SEEKETH (42) [SEEK]

1Sa 19: 2 saying, Saul my father s to kill thee: 1245
20: 1 my sin before thy father, that he s my life? 1245
22:23 for he that s my life seeketh thy life: but 1245
22:23 for he that seeketh my life s thy life: but 1245
23:10 thy servant hath certainly heard that Saul s 1245
24: 9 saying, Behold, David s thy hurt? 1245
2Sa 16:11 which came forth of my bowels, s my life: 1245
1Ki 20: 7 pray you, and see how this man s mischief: 1245
2Ki 5: 7 and see how he s a quarrel against me. 579
Job 39:29 From thence she s the prey, and her eyes 2658
Ps 37:32 watcheth the righteous, and s to slay him. 1245
Pr 11:27 He that diligently s good procureth favour: 7836
11:27 he that s mischief, it shall come unto him. 1875
14: 6 A scorner s wisdom, and findeth it not: but 1245
15:14 The heart of him that hath understanding s 1245
17: 9 He that covereth a transgression s love; but 1245
17:11 An evil man s only rebellion: therefore 1245
17:19 and he that exalteth his gate s destruction. 1245
18: 1 s and intermeddleth with all wisdom. 1245
18:15 and the ear of the wise s knowledge. 1245
31:13 She s wool, and flax, and worketh willingly 1875
Ecc 7:28 Which yet my soul s, but I find not: 1245
Isa 40:20 he s unto him a cunning workman to 1245
Jer 5: 1 that executeth judgment, that s the truth; 1245
30:17 saying, This is Zion, whom no man s after. 1875
38: 4 for this man s not the welfare of this 1875
La 3:25 that wait for him, to the soul that s him. 1875
Eze 14:10 as the punishment of him that s unto him; 1875
34:12 As a shepherd s out his flock in the day 1243
Mt 7: 8 that asketh receiveth; and he that s findeth: 2212
12:39 and adulterous generation s after a sign; 1934
16: 4 and adulterous generation s after a sign; 1934
18:12 and s that which is gone astray? 2212
Lk 11:10 and he that s findeth; and to him that 2212
Jn 4:23 for the Father s such to worship him. 2212
7: 4 and he himself s to be known openly. 2212
7:18 He that speaketh of himself s his own 2212
7:18 but he that s his glory that sent him, 2212
8:50 own glory: there is one that s and judgeth. 2212
Ro 3:11 there is none that s after God. NIG
11: 7 Israel hath not obtained that which he s for; 1934
1Co 13: 5 s not her own, is not easily provoked, 2212

SEEKING (14) [SEEK]

Est 10: 3 s the wealth of his people, and 1875
Isa 16: 5 and s judgment, and hasting righteousness. 1875
Mt 12:43 through dry places, s rest, and findeth none. 2212
13:45 like unto a merchant man, s goodly pearls: 2212
Mk 8:11 s of him a sign from heaven, tempting him. 2212
Lk 2:45 they turned back again to Jerusalem, s him. 2212
11:24 he walketh through dry places, s rest; 2212
11:54 and s to catch something out of his mouth, 2212
13: 7 these three years I come s fruit on this fig 2212
Jn 6:24 and came to Capernaum, s for Jesus. 2212
Ac 13: 8 s to turn away the deputy from the faith. 2212
13:11 he went about s some to lead him by 2212
1Co 10:33 Even as I please all men in all things, not s 2212
1Pe 5: 8 walketh about, s whom he may devour: 2212

SEEM (22) [SEEMED, SEEMETH, SEEMLY, UNSEEMLY]

Ge 27:12 I shall s to him as a deceiver; 1961+5869+871.1
Dt 15:18 It shall not s hard unto thee, 5869+871.1
25: 3 thy brother should s vile unto thee. 5869+3807.1
Jos 24:15 if it s evil unto you to serve 5869+871.1
1Sa 24: 4 to him as it shall s good unto thee. 5869+871.1
2Sa 19:37 to him what shall s good unto thee. 5869+871.1
19:38 that which shall s good unto thee: 5869+871.1
1Ki 21: 2 or, if it s good to thee, I will give 5869+871.1
1Ch 13: 2 If it s good unto you, and that it be of NIH
Ezr 5:17 Now therefore, if it s good to the king, NIH
7:18 whatsoever shall s good to thee, and to thy 3191
Ne 9:32 let not all the trouble s little before thee, NIH
Est 5: 4 If it s good unto the king, let the king and NIH
8: 5 the thing s right before the king, and I be 3787
Jer 40: 4 If it s good unto thee to come with 5869+871.1
40: 4 if it s ill unto thee to come with me 5869+871.1
Na 2: 4 they shall s like torches, they shall run like 4758
1Co 11:16 But if any man s to be contentious, we have 1380
12:22 which s to be more feeble, are necessary: 1380
2Co 10: 9 That I may not s as if I would terrify you by 1380
Heb 4: 1 any of you should s to come short of it. 1380
Jas 1:26 If any man among you s to be religious, 1380

SEEMED (16) [SEEM]

Ge 19:14 he s as one that mocked unto 1961+5869+871.1
29:20 they s unto him but a few 1961+5869+871.1
2Sa 3:19 in Hebron all that s good to Israel, 5869+871.1
3:19 that s good to the whole house of 5869+871.1
Ecc 9:13 also under the sun, and it s great unto me: NIH
Jer 18: 4 as s good to the potter to make it. 5869+871.1
27: 5 it unto whom it s meet unto me. 5869+871.1
Mt 11:26 Father: for so it s good in thy sight. 1096
Lk 1: 3 It s good to me also, having had perfect 1380
10:21 Father; for so it s good in thy sight. 1096
24:11 And their words s to them as idle tales, and 5316
Ac 15:25 It s good unto us, being assembled with one 1380
15:28 For it s good to the Holy Ghost, and to us, 1380
Gal 2: 6 But of these who s to be somewhat, 1380
2: 6 for they who s to be somewhat in 1380
2: 9 Cephas, and John, who s to be pillars, 1380

SEEMETH (28) [SEEM]

Lev 14:35 It s to me there is as it were a plague in 7200
Nu 16: 9 S it but a small thing unto you, that the God NIH
Jos 9:25 as it s good and right unto thee to do 5869+871.1
Jdg 10:15 us whatsoever s good unto thee; 5869+871.1
19:24 do with them what s good unto you: 5869+871.1
1Sa 1:23 said unto her, Do what s thee good; 5869+871.1
3:18 let him do what s him good. 5869+871.1
11:10 do with us all that s good unto you. 5869+871.1
14:36 Do whatsoever s good unto thee. 5869+871.1
14:40 Do what s good unto thee. 5869+871.1
18:23 David said, S it to you a light thing 5869+871.1
2Sa 10:12 LORD do that which s him good. 5869+871.1
15:26 him do to me as s good unto him. 5869+871.1
18: 4 What s you best I will do. 5869+871.1
24:22 and offer up what s good unto him: 5869+871.1
Est 3:11 to do with them as it s good to thee. 5869+871.1
Pr 14:12 There is a way which s right unto a 6440+3807.1
16:25 There is a way that s right unto a 6440+3807.1
18:17 He that is first in his own cause s just; but NIH
Jer 26:14 me as s good and meet unto you. 5869+871.1
40: 4 whither it s good and convenient for 5869+871.1
40: 5 go wheresoever it s convenient unto 5869+871.1
Eze 34:18 S it a small thing unto you to have eaten up NIH
Lk 8:18 shall be taken even that which he s to have. 1380
Ac 17:18 other some, He s to be a setter forth of 1380
25:27 For it s to me unreasonable to send a 1380
1Co 3:18 If any man among you s to be wise in this 1380
Heb 12:11 Now no chastening for the present s to be 1380

SEEMLY (2) [SEEM]

Pr 19:10 Delight is not s for a fool; much less for a 5000
26: 1 rain in harvest, so honour is not s for a fool. 5000

SEEN (277) [SEE]

Ge 7: 1 for thee have I s righteous before me in this 7200
8: 5 were the tops of the mountains s. 7200
9:14 that the bow shall be s in the cloud: 7200
22:14 In the mount of the LORD it shall be s. 7200
31:12 for I have s all that Laban doeth unto thee. 7200
31:42 God hath s mine affliction and the labour of 7200
32:30 for I have s God face to face, and my life is 7200
33:10 for therefore I have s thy face, as though I 7200
33:10 as though I had s the face of God, and 7200
45:13 glory in Egypt, and of all that ye have s; 7200
46:30 since I have s thy face, because thou art yet 7200
Ex 3: 7 I have surely s the affliction of my 7200+7200
3: 9 I have also s the oppression wherewith 7200
3:16 and s that which is done to you in Egypt: NIH
10: 6 thy fathers, nor thy fathers' fathers have s, 7200
13: 7 there shall no leavened bread be s with 7200
13: 7 neither shall there be leaven s with thee in 7200
14:13 for the Egyptians whom ye have s to day, 7200
19: 4 Ye have s what I did unto the Egyptians, 7200
20:22 Ye have s that I have talked with you from 7200
32: 9 I have s this people, and behold, it is a 7200
33:23 my back parts: but my face shall not be s. 7200
34: 3 neither let any man be s throughout all 7200
Lev 5: 1 whether he hath s or known of it; if he do 7200
13: 7 after that he hath been s of the priest for his 7200
13: 7 he shall be s of the priest again: 7200
Nu 14:14 that thou LORD art s face to face, and 7200
14:22 Because all those men which have s my 7200
23:21 neither hath he s perverseness in Israel: 7200
27:13 when thou hast s it, thou also shalt be 7200
Dt 1:28 moreover we have s the sons of 7200
1:31 where thou hast s how that the LORD thy 7200
3:21 Thine eyes have s all that the LORD your 7200
4: 3 Your eyes have s what the LORD did 7200
4: 9 forget the things which thine eyes have s, 7200
5:24 we have s this day that God doth talk with 7200
9:13 saying, I have s this people, and behold, 7200
10:21 and terrible things, which thine eyes have s. 7200
11: 2 which have not s the chastisement of 7200
11: 7 your eyes have s all the great acts of 7200
16: 4 there shall be no leavened bread s with thee 7200
21: 7 shed this blood, neither have our eyes s it. 7200
29: 2 Ye have s all that the LORD did before 7200
29: 3 great temptations which thine eyes have s, 7200
29:17 ye have s their abominations, and their 7200
33: 9 and to his mother, I have not s him; 7200
Jos 23: 3 ye have s all that the LORD your God 7200
24: 7 your eyes have s what I have done in 7200
Jdg 2: 7 who had s all the great works of 7200
5: 8 or spear s among forty thousand in Israel? 7200
6:22 I have s an angel of the LORD face to 7200
9:48 What ye have s me do, make haste, and 7200
13:22 shall surely die, because we have s God. 7200
14: 2 I have s a woman in Timnath of 7200
18: 9 for we have s the land, and behold, it is 7200
19:30 There was no such deed done nor s from 7200
1Sa 6:16 when the five lords of the Philistines had s 7200
16:18 I have s a son of Jesse the Beth-lehemite, 7200
17:25 Have ye s this man that is come up? 7200
23:22 his haunt is, and who hath s him there: 7200
24:10 this day thine eyes have s how that 7200
2Sa 17:17 for they might not be s to come into 7200
18:21 to Cushi, Go tell the king what thou hast s. 7200
22:11 and he was s upon the wings of the wind. 7200
1Ki 6:18 all was cedar; there was no stone s. 7200
8: 8 that the ends of the staves were s out in 7200
8: 8 the oracle, and they were not s without: 7200
10: 4 when the queen of Sheba had s all 7200
10: 7 I came, and mine eyes had s it: and behold, 7200
10:12 such almug trees, nor were s unto this day. 7200
13:12 For his sons had s what way the man of 7200
20:13 Hast thou s all this great multitude? 7200
2Ki 9:26 Surely I have s yesterday the blood of 7200
20: 5 I have heard thy prayer, I have s thy tears: 7200
20:15 he said, What have they s in thine house? 7200
20:15 things that are in mine house have they s: 7200
23:29 slew him at Megiddo, when he had s him. 7200
1Ch 29:17 and now have I s with joy thy people, 7200
2Ch 5: 9 were s from the ark before the oracle; 7200
5: 9 the oracle; but they were not s without. 7200
9: 3 when the queen of Sheba had s the wisdom 7200
9: 6 I came, and mine eyes had s it: and behold, 7200
9:11 there were none such s before in the land of 7200
Ezr 3:12 who were ancient men that had s the first 7200
Est 9:26 of that which they had s concerning this 7200
Job 4: 8 Even as I have s, they that plow iniquity, 7200
5: 3 I have s the foolish taking root: but 7200
7: 8 The eye of him that hath s me shall see me 7210
8:18 it shall deny him, saying, I have not s thee. 7200
10:18 given up the ghost, and no eye had s me! 7200
13: 1 mine eye hath s all this, mine ear hath 7200
15:17 and that which I have s I will declare; 2372
20: 7 they which have s him shall say, Where is 7200
27:12 all ye yourselves have s it; why then are ye 2372
28: 7 and which the vulture's eye hath not s: 7805
31:19 If I have s any perish for want of clothing, 7200
33:21 flesh is consumed away, that it cannot be s; 7210
33:21 and his bones that were not s stick out. 7200
38:17 hast thou s the doors of the shadow of 7200
38:22 or hast thou s the treasures of the hail, 7200
Ps 10:14 Thou hast s it; for thou beholdest mischief 7200
18:15 the channels of waters were s, and 7200
35:21 and said, Aha, aha, our eye hath s it. 7200
35:22 This thou hast s, O LORD: keep not 7200
37:25 yet have I not s the righteous forsaken, 7200
37:35 I have s the wicked in great power, and 7200
48: 8 have we s in the city of the LORD of 7200
54: 7 mine eye hath s his desire upon mine 7200
55: 9 for I have s violence and strife in the city. 7200
63: 2 so as I have s thee in the sanctuary. 2372
68:24 They have s thy goings, O God; even 7200
90:15 and the years wherein we have s evil. 7200
98: 3 all the ends of the earth have s the salvation 7200
119:96 I have s an end of all perfection: but 7200
Pr 25: 7 of the prince whom thine eyes have s. 7200
Ecc 1:14 I have s all the works that are done under 7200
3:10 I have s the travail, which God hath given 7200
4: 3 who hath not s the evil work that is done 7200
5:13 There is a sore evil which I have s under 7200
5:18 Behold that which I have s: it is good and 7200
6: 1 There is an evil which I have s under 7200
6: 5 Moreover he hath not s the sun, nor known 7200
6: 6 years twice told, yet hath he s no good: 7200
7:15 All things have I s in the days of my vanity: 7200
8: 9 All this have I s, and applied my heart unto 7200
9:13 This wisdom have I s also under the sun, 7200
10: 5 There is an evil which I have s under 7200
10: 7 I have s servants upon horses, and 7200
Isa 6: 5 for mine eyes have s the King, the LORD 7200
9: 2 The people that walked in darkness have s 7200
16:12 when it is s that Moab is weary on the high 7200
22: 9 Ye have s also the breaches of the city of 7200
38: 5 I have heard thy prayer, I have s thy tears: 7200
39: 4 said he, What have they s in thine house? 7200
39: 4 All that is in mine house have they s: 7200

Isa 44:16 and saith, Aha, I am warm, I have s the fire: 7200
47: 3 be uncovered, yea, thy shame shall be s: 7200
57:18 I have s his ways, and will heal him: I will 7200
60: 2 and his glory shall be s upon thee. 7200
64: 4 neither hath the eye s, O God, besides thee, 7200
66: 8 Who hath heard such *a thing?* who hath s 7200
66:19 heard my fame, neither have s my glory; 7200
Jer 1:12 said the LORD unto me, Thou hast well s: 7200
3: 6 Hast thou s *that* which backsliding Israel 7200
7:11 Behold, even I have s *it,* saith the LORD. 7200
12: 3 thou hast s me, and tried mine heart 7200
13:27 I have s thine adulteries, and thy neighings, 7200
23:13 I have s folly in the prophets of Samaria; 7200
23:14 I have s also in the prophets of Jerusalem a 7200
44: 2 Ye have s all the evil that I have brought 7200
46: 5 Wherefore have I s them dismayed *and* 7200
La 1: 8 because they have s her nakedness: 7200
1:10 for she hath s *that* the heathen entered into 7200
2:14 Thy prophets have s vain and foolish things 2372
2:14 have s for thee false burdens and causes of 2372
2:16 we looked for; we have found, we have s it. 7200
3: 1 I *am* the man *that* hath s affliction by 7200
3:59 O LORD, thou hast s my wrong: 7200
3:60 Thou hast s all their vengeance *and* all their 7200
Eze 8:12 hast thou s what the ancients of the house 7200
8:15 he unto me, Hast thou s *this,* O son of man? 7200
8:17 unto me, Hast thou s *this,* O son of man? 7200
11:24 So the vision that I had s went up from me. 7200
13: 3 follow their own spirit, and have s nothing! 7200
13: 6 They have s vanity and lying divination, 2372
13: 7 Have ye not s a vain vision, and have ye 2372
13: 8 s lies, therefore behold, I *am* against you, 2372
47: 6 hast thou s *this?* Then he brought me, and 7200
Da 2:26 known unto me the dream which I have s, 2370
4: 9 *me* the visions of my dream that I have s, 2370
4:18 This dream I king Nebuchadnezzar have s. 2370
8: 6 which I had s standing before the river, and 7200
8:15 had s the vision, and sought for 7200
9:21 whom I had s in the vision at the beginning, 7200
Hos 6:10 I have s a horrible thing in the house of 7200
Zec 9: 8 any more: for now have I s with mine eyes. 7200
9:14 the LORD shall be s over them, and 7200
10: 2 the diviners have s a lie, and have told false 2372
Mt 2: 2 for we have s his star in the east, and *1492*
6: 1 not your alms before men, to be s of them: *2300*
6: 5 of the streets, that they may be s of men. *5316*
9:33 saying, It was never so s in Israel. *5316*
13:17 and have not s *them;* and to hear *those* *1492*
21:32 when ye had s *it,* repented not afterward, *1492*
23: 5 But all their works they do for to be s of *2300*
Mk 9: 1 till they have s the kingdom of God come *1492*
9: 9 should tell no *man* what *things* they had s, *1492*
16:11 and had been s of her, believed not. *2300*
16:14 they believed not them which had s him *2300*
Lk 1:22 they perceived that he had s a vision in *3708*
2:17 And when they had s *it,* they made known *1492*
2:20 for all *the things* that they had heard and s, *1492*
2:26 before he had s the Lord's Christ. *1492*
2:30 For mine eyes have s thy salvation, *1492*
5:26 saying, We have s strange *things* to day. *1492*
7:22 and tell John what *things* ye have s and *1492*
9:36 days any of *those things* which they had s. *3708*
10:24 and have not s *them;* and to hear *those* *1492*
19:37 for all the mighty works that they had s; *1492*
23: 8 he hoped to have s some miracle done by *1492*
24:23 that *they* had also s a vision of angels, *3708*
24:37 and supposed that *they* had s a spirit. *2334*
Jn 1:18 No *man* hath s God at any time; the only *3708*
3:11 that we do know, and testify that we have s; *3708*
3:32 And what he hath s and heard, that he *3708*
4:45 having s all *the things* that he did at *3708*
5:37 heard his voice at any time, nor s his shape. *3708*
6:14 when they had s the miracle that Jesus did, *1492*
6:36 That ye also have s me, and believe not. *3708*
6:46 Not that any *man* hath s the Father, save he *3708*
6:46 he which is of God, he hath s the Father. *3708*
8:38 I speak *that* which I have s with my Father: *3708*
8:38 ye do *that* which ye have s with your father. *3004*
8:57 fifty years old, and hast thou s Abraham? *3708*
9: 8 they which before had s him that he was *2334*
9:37 Thou hast both s him, and it is he that *3708*
11:45 and had s *the things* which Jesus did, *2300*
14: 7 henceforth ye know him, and have s him. *3708*
14: 9 he that hath s me hath seen the Father; and *3708*
14: 9 he that hath seen me hath s the Father; and *3708*
15:24 but now have they both s and hated both *3708*
20:18 told the disciples that she had s the Lord, *3708*
20:25 said unto him, We have s the Lord. *3708*
20:29 Thomas, because thou hast s me, thou hast *3708*
20:29 blessed *are* they that have not s, and *1492*
Ac 1: 3 being s of them forty days, and speaking of *3700*
1:11 come *in* like manner as ye have s him go *2300*
4:20 but speak *the things* which we have s and *1492*
7:34 I have s, I have seen the affliction of my *1492*
7:34 I have s the affliction of my people which *1492*
7:44 it according to the fashion that he had s. *3708*
9:12 And hath s in a vision a man named *1492*
9:27 declared unto them how he had s the Lord *1492*
10:17 *this* vision which he had s should mean, *1492*
11:13 And he shewed us how he had s an angel in *1492*
11:23 and had s the grace of God, was glad, and *1492*
13:31 And he was s many days of them which *3700*
16:10 And after he had s the vision, *1492*
16:40 and when they had s the brethren, *1492*
21:29 (For they had s **before** with him in the city *4308*
22:15 his witness unto all men of what thou hast s *3708*
26:16 both of *these things* which thou hast s, *1492*
Ro 1:20 from the creation of the world are **clearly** s, *2529*
8:24 but hope that is s is not hope: for what a man *991*
1Co 2: 9 it is written, Eye hath not s, nor ear heard, *1492*
9: 1 have I not s Jesus Christ our Lord? are not *3708*
15: 5 And that he was s of Cephas, then of *3700*
15: 6 he was s of above five hundred brethren at *3700*
15: 7 After that, he was s of James; then of all *3700*
15: 8 And last of all he was s of me also, as of *3700*

2Co 4:18 While we look not at the *things* which are s, *991*
4:18 are seen, but at the *things* which are not s: *991*
4:18 for the *things* which are s *are* temporal; but *991*
4:18 but the *things* which are not s *are* eternal. *991*
Php 4: 9 and received, and heard, and s in me, do: *1492*
Col 2: 1 *for* as many as have not s my face in *3708*
2:18 into *those things* which he hath not s, *3708*
1Ti 3:16 justified in the Spirit, s of angels, *3700*
6:16 whom no man hath s, nor can see: *1492*
Heb 11: 1 hoped for, the evidence of things not s. *991*
11: 3 that *things* which are s were not made of *991*
11: 7 being warned of God of *things* not s as yet, *991*
11:13 but having s them afar off, and *1492*
Jas 5:11 of Job, and have s the end of the Lord; *1492*
1Pe 1: 8 Whom having not s, ye love; in whom, *1492*
1Jn 1: 1 have heard, which we have s with our eyes, *3708*
1: 2 and we have s *it,* and bear witness, and *3708*
1: 3 *That* which we have s and heard declare we *3708*
3: 6 whosoever sinneth hath not s him, *3708*
4:12 No *man* hath s God at any time. If we love *2300*
4:14 And we have s and do testify that *2300*
4:20 that loveth not his brother whom he hath s, *3708*
4:20 how can he love God whom he hath not s? *3708*
3Jn 1:11 but he that doeth evil hath not s God. *3708*
Rev 1:19 Write *the things* which thou hast s, and *1492*
11:19 there was s in his temple the ark of his *3700*
22: 8 heard *them.* And when I had heard and s, *991*

SEER (21) [SEE]

1Sa 9: 9 thus he spake, Come, and let us go to the s: 7200
9: 9 *called* a Prophet was beforetime called a S.) 7200
9:11 and said unto them, Is the s here? 7200
9:19 Samuel answered Saul, and said, I *am* the s: 7200
2Sa 15:27 also unto Zadok the priest, *Art not* thou a s? 7200
24:11 unto the prophet Gad, David's s, saying, 2374
1Ch 9:22 Samuel the s did ordain in their set office. 7200
21: 9 LORD spake unto Gad, David's s, saying, 2374
25: 5 of Heman the king's s in the words of God, 2374
26:28 all that Samuel the s, and Saul the son of 7200
29:29 *are* written in the book of Samuel the s, 7200
29:29 the prophet, and in the book of Gad the s, 2374
2Ch 9:29 in the visions of Iddo the s against 2374
12:15 and of Iddo the s concerning genealogies? 2374
16: 7 at that time Hanani the s came to Asa king 7200
16:10 Asa was wroth with the s, and put him *in* a 7200
19: 2 Jehu the son of Hanani the s went out to 2374
29:25 of Gad the king's s, and Nathan 2374
29:30 the words of David, and of Asaph the s. 2374
35:15 and Heman, and Jeduthun the king's s; 2374
Am 7:12 Amaziah said unto Amos, O thou s, go, 2374

SEER'S (1) [SEE]

1Sa 9:18 Tell me, I pray thee, where the s house *is.* 7200

SEERS (6) [SEE]

2Ki 17:13 by all the prophets, *and by* all the s, saying, 2374
2Ch 33:18 the words of the s that spake to him in 2374
33:19 they *are* written among the sayings of the s. 2374
Isa 29:10 and your rulers, the s hath he covered. 2374
30:10 Which say to the s, See not; and to 7203
Mic 3: 7 Shall the s be ashamed, and the diviners 2374

SEEST (36) [SEE]

Ge 13:15 For all the land which thou s, to thee will I 7200
16:13 that spake unto her, Thou God s me: 7210
31:43 *are* my cattle, and all that thou s *is* mine: 7200
Ex 10:28 for in *that* day thou s my face thou shalt 7200
Dt 4:19 and when thou s the sun, and the moon, and 7200
12:13 burnt offerings in every place that thou s: 7200
20: 1 s horses, and chariots, *and* a people more 7200
21:11 s among the captives a beautiful woman, 7200
Jdg 9:36 Thou s the shadow of the mountains as *if* 7200
1Ki 21:29 S thou how Ahab humbleth himself before 7200
Job 10: 4 thou eyes of flesh? or s thou as man seeth? 7200
Pr 22:29 S thou a man diligent in his business? 2372
26:12 S thou a man wise in his own conceit? 7200
29:20 S thou a man that is hasty in his words? 2372
Ecc 5: 8 If thou s the oppression of the poor, and 7200
Isa 58: 3 have we fasted, *say they,* and thou s not? 7200
58: 7 when thou s the naked, that thou cover him; 7200
Jer 1:11 unto me, saying, Jeremiah, what s thou? 7200
1:13 me the second time, saying, What s thou? 7200
7:17 S thou not what they do in the cities of 7200
20:12 the righteous, *and* s the reins and the heart, 7200
24: 3 LORD unto me, What s thou, Jeremiah? 7200
32:24 is come to pass; and behold, thou s *it.* 7200
Eze 8: 6 unto me, Son of man, s thou what they do? 7200
40: 4 declare all that thou s to the house of Israel. 7200
Da 1:13 and as thou s, deal with thy servants. 7200
Am 7: 8 LORD said unto me, Amos, what s thou? 7200
8: 2 he said, Amos, what s thou? And I said, 7200
Zec 4: 2 And said unto me, What s thou? And I said, 7200
5: 2 he said unto me, What s thou? And I 7200
Mk 5:31 Thou s the multitude thronging thee, and *991*
13: 2 said unto him, S thou these great buildings? *991*
Lk 7:44 and said unto Simon, S thou this woman? *991*
Ac 21:20 and said unto him, Thou s, brother, *2334*
Jas 2:22 S thou how faith wrought with his works, *991*
Rev 1:11 and, What thou s, write in a book, and *991*

SEETH (54) [SEE]

Ge 16:13 Have I also here looked after him that s 7210
44:31 when he s that the lad *is* not *with us,* that he 7200
Ex 4:14 when he s thee, he will be glad in his heart. 7200
12:23 when he s the blood upon the lintel, and 7200
Lev 13:20 if, when the priest s it, behold, it *be* in sight 7200
Dt 32:36 when he s that *their* power is gone, and 7200
1Sa 16: 7 for *the LORD s* not as man seeth; for man NIH
16: 7 for *the LORD seeth* not as man s; for man 7200
2Ki 2:19 of *this* city *is* pleasant, as my lord s: 7200
Job 8:17 about the heap, *and* s the place of stones. 2372
10: 4 thou eyes of flesh? or seest thou as man s? 7200
11:11 he s wickedness also; will he not then 7200
22:14 clouds *are* a covering to him, that he s not; 7200

Job 28:10 and his eye s every precious thing. 7200
28:24 of the earth, *and* s under the whole heaven; 7200
34:21 the ways of man, and he s all his goings. 7200
42: 5 hearing of the ear: but now mine eye s thee. 7200
Ps 37:13 at him: for he s that his day is coming. 7200
49:10 For he s *that* wise *men* die, likewise 7200
58:10 The righteous shall rejoice when he s 2372
Ecc 8:16 (for also *there is that* neither day nor night s 7200
Isa 21: 6 set a watchman, let him declare what he s. 7200
28: 4 which *when* he that looketh upon it s, 7200
29:15 are in the dark, and they say, Who s us? 7200
29:23 when he s his children, the work of mine 7200
47:10 thou hast said, None s me. Thy wisdom and 7200
Eze 8:12 for they say, The LORD s us not; 7200
9: 9 forsaken the earth, and the LORD s not. 7200
12:27 The vision that he s *is* for many days *to* 2372
18:14 that s all his father's sins which he hath 7200
33: 3 *If* when he s the sword come upon the land, 7200
39:15 when *any* s a man's bone, then shall he set 7200
Mt 6: 4 thy Father which s in secret himself shall *991*
6: 6 thy Father which s in secret shall reward *991*
6:18 and thy Father, which s in secret, *991*
Mk 5:38 and s *the* tumult, and them that wept and *2334*
Lk 16:23 and s Abraham afar off, and Lazarus in his *3708*
Jn 1:29 The next day John s Jesus coming unto him, *991*
5:19 of himself, but what he s the Father do: *991*
6:40 that every one which s the Son, and *2334*
9:21 But by what means he now s, we know not; *991*
10:12 s the wolf coming, and leaveth the sheep, *2334*
11: 9 because he s the light of this world. *991*
12:45 And he that s me seeth him that sent me. *2334*
12:45 And he that seeth me s him that sent me. *2334*
14:17 because it s him not, neither knoweth him: *2334*
14:19 a little while, and the world s me no more; *2334*
20: 1 s the stone taken away from the sepulchre. *991*
20: 6 the sepulchre, and s the linen clothes lie, *2334*
20:12 And s two angels in white sitting, the one at *2334*
21:20 s the disciple whom Jesus loved following; *991*
Ro 8:24 for what a man s, why doth he yet hope for? *991*
2Co 12: 6 think of me above *that* which he s me *to be,* *991*
1Jn 3:17 and s his brother hath need, and shutteth up *2334*

SEETHE (9) [SEETHING]

Ex 16:23 will bake *to day,* and s that ye will seethe; 1310
16:23 will bake *to day,* and seethe that ye will s; 1310
23:19 Thou shalt not s a kid in his mother's milk. 1310
29:31 and s his flesh in the holy place. 1310
34:26 Thou shalt not s a kid in his mother's milk. 1310
Dt 14:21 Thou shalt not s a kid in his mother's milk. 1310
2Ki 4:38 and s pottage for the sons of the prophets. 1310
Eze 24: 5 and let them s the bones of it therein. 1310
Zec 14:21 shall come and take of them, and s therein: 1310

SEETHING (3) [SEETHE]

1Sa 2:13 servant came, while the flesh was in s, 1310
Job 41:20 goeth smoke, as *out of* a s pot or caldron. 5301
Jer 1:13 I said, I see a s pot; and the face thereof *is* 5301

SEGUB (3)

1Ki 16:34 up the gates thereof in his youngest *son* S, 7687
1Ch 2:21 threescore years old; and she bare him S. 7687
2:22 S begat Jair, who had three and 7687

SEIR (39)

Ge 14: 6 the Horites in their mount S, unto El-paran, 8165
32: 3 him to Esau his brother unto the land of S, 8165
33:14 to endure, until I come unto my lord unto S. 8165
33:16 Esau returned that day on his way unto S. 8165
36: 8 Thus dwelt Esau in mount S: Esau *is* Edom. 8165
36: 9 Esau the father of the Edomites in mount S: 8165
36:20 These *are* the sons of S the Horite, 8165
36:21 the children of S in the land of Edom. 8165
36:30 of Hori, among their dukes in the land of S. 8165
Nu 24:18 S also shall be a possession for his 8165
Dt 1: 2 the way of mount S unto Kadesh-barnea.) 8165
1:44 as bees do, and destroyed you in S, 8165
2: 1 and we compassed mount S many days. 8165
2: 4 the children of Esau, which dwell in S; 8165
2: 5 I have given mount S unto Esau *for* a 8165
2: 8 which dwelt in S, through the way of 8165
2:12 The Horims also dwelt in S beforetime; but 8165
2:22 to the children of Esau, which dwelt in S, 8165
2:29 (As the children of Esau which dwell in S, 8165
33: 2 from Sinai, and rose up from S unto them; 8165
Jos 11:17 from the mount Halak, that goeth up to S, 8165
12: 7 unto the mount Halak, that goeth up to S; 8165
15:10 from Baalah westward unto mount S, 8165
24: 4 I gave unto Esau mount S, to possess it; 8165
Jdg 5: 4 LORD, when thou wentest out of S, 8165
1Ch 1:38 the sons of S; Lotan, and Shobal, and 8165
4:42 five hundred men, went to mount S, 8165
2Ch 20:10 of Ammon and Moab and mount S, 8165
20:22 Moab, and mount S, which were come 8165
20:23 stood up against the inhabitants of mount S, 8165
20:23 had made an end of the inhabitants of S, 8165
25:11 smote *of* the children of S ten thousand. 8165
25:14 he brought the gods of the children of S, 8165
Isa 21:11 He calleth to me out of S, Watchman, 8165
Eze 25: 8 Because that Moab and S do say, Behold, 8165
35: 2 set thy face against mount S, and 8165
35: 3 Behold, O mount S, I *am* against thee, and 8165
35: 7 Thus will I make mount S most desolate, 8165
35:15 O mount S, and all Idumea, *even* all of it: 8165

SEIRAH See SEIRATH

SEIRATH (1)

Jdg 3:26 beyond the quarries, and escaped unto S. 8167

SEIZE (4) [SEIZED]

Jos 8: 7 up from the ambush, and s **upon** the city: 3423
Job 3: 6 *As for* that night, let darkness s upon it; 3947
Ps 55:15 Let death s upon them, *and* let them go 5377
Mt 21:38 us kill him, and let us s on his inheritance. *2722*

SEIZED (1) [SEIZE]
Jer 49:24 fear hath **s** on *her:* anguish and 2388

SELA (1) [SELA-HAMMAHLEKOTH]
Isa 16: 1 ruler of the land from **S** to the wilderness, 5554

SELAH (75)
2Ki 14: 7 took **S** by war, and called the name of it 5554
Ps 3: 2 *There is* no help for him in God. **S.** 5542
3: 4 and he heard me out of his holy hill. **S.** 5542
3: 8 thy blessing *is* upon thy people. **S.** 5542
4: 2 ye love vanity, *and* seek after leasing? **S.** 5542
4: 4 own heart upon your bed, and be still. **S.** 5542
7: 5 and lay mine honour in the dust. **S.** 5542
9:16 in the work of his own hands. Higgaion. **S.** 5542
9:20 may know themselves *to be but* men. **S.** 5542
20: 3 and accept thy burnt sacrifice. **S.** 5542
21: 2 not withholden the request of his lips. **S.** 5542
24: 6 seek him, that seek thy face, O Jacob. **S.** 5542
24:10 LORD of hosts, he *is* the King of glory. **S.** 5542
32: 4 is turned into the drought of summer. **S.** 5542
32: 5 thou forgavest the iniquity of my sin. **S.** 5542
32: 7 me about *with* songs of deliverance. **S.** 5542
39: 5 man at his best state *is* altogether vanity. **S.** 5542
39:11 like a moth: surely every man *is* vanity. **S.** 5542
44: 8 day long, and praise thy name for ever. **S.** 5542
46: 3 shake with the swelling thereof. **S.** 5542
46: 7 with us; the God of Jacob *is* our refuge. **S.** 5542
46:11 with us; the God of Jacob *is* our refuge. **S.** 5542
47: 4 the excellency of Jacob whom he loved. **S.** 5542
48: 8 our God: God will establish it for ever. **S.** 5542
49:13 yet their posterity approve their sayings. **S.** 5542
49:15 of the grave: for he shall receive me. **S.** 5542
50: 6 for God *is* judge himself. **S.** 5542
52: 3 lying rather than to speak righteousness. **S.** 5542
52: 5 root thee out of the land of the living. **S.** 5542
54: 3 they have not set God before them. **S.** 5542
55: 7 far off, *and* remain in the wilderness. **S.** 5542
55:19 **S.** Because they have no changes, therefore 5542
57: 3 **S.** God shall send forth his mercy and 5542
57: 6 whereof they are fallen *themselves.* **S.** 5542
59: 5 not merciful to any wicked transgressors. **S.** 5542
59:13 ruleth in Jacob unto the ends of the earth. **S.** 5542
60: 4 *it* may be displayed because of the truth. **S.** 5542
61: 4 I will trust in the covert of thy wings. **S.** 5542
62: 4 their mouth, but they curse inwardly. **S.** 5542
62: 8 heart before him: God *is* a refuge for us. **S.** 5542
66: 4 unto thee; they shall sing *to* thy name. **S.** 5542
66: 7 let not the rebellious exalt themselves. **S.** 5542
66:15 of rams; I will offer bullocks with goats. **S.** 5542
67: 1 *and* cause his face to shine upon us; **S.** 5542
67: 4 and govern the nations upon earth. **S.** 5542
68: 7 thou didst march through the wilderness; **S.** 5542
68:19 *benefits, even* the God of our salvation. **S.** 5542
68:32 the earth; O sing *praises unto* the Lord; **S.** 5542
75: 3 *are* dissolved: I bear up the pillars of it. **S.** 5542
76: 3 the shield, and the sword, and the battle. **S.** 5542
76: 9 to save all the meek of the earth. **S.** 5542
77: 3 and my spirit was overwhelmed. **S.** 5542
77: 9 he in anger shut up his tender mercies? **S.** 5542
77:15 thy people, the sons of Jacob and Joseph. **S.** 5542
81: 7 I proved thee at the waters of Meribah. **S.** 5542
82: 2 and accept the persons of the wicked? **S.** 5542
83: 8 they have holpen the children of Lot. **S.** 5542
84: 4 thy house: they will be still praising thee. **S.** 5542
84: 8 my prayer: give ear, O God of Jacob. **S.** 5542
85: 2 thou hast covered all their sin. **S.** 5542
87: 3 *things* are spoken of thee, O city of God. **S.** 5542
87: 6 the people, *that* this *man* was born there. **S.** 5542
88: 7 thou hast afflicted *me with* all thy waves. **S.** 5542
88:10 shall the dead arise *and* praise thee? **S.** 5542
89: 4 build up thy throne to all generations. **S.** 5542
89:37 and *as* a faithful witness in heaven. **S.** 5542
89:45 thou hast covered him with shame. **S.** 5542
89:48 his soul from the hand of the grave? **S.** 5542
140: 3 adder's poison *is* under their lips. **S.** 5542
140: 5 the way side; they have set grins for me. **S.** 5542
140: 8 *lest* they exalt themselves. **S.** 5542
143: 6 soul *thirsteth* after thee, as a thirsty land. **S.** 5542
Hab 3: 3 **S.** His glory covered the heavens, and 5542
3: 9 **S.** Thou didst cleave the earth *with* rivers. 5542
3:13 the foundation unto the neck. **S.** 5542

SELA-HAMMAHLEKOTH (1) [SELA]
1Sa 23:28 they called that place **S.** 5555

SELED (2)
1Ch 2:30 the sons of Nadab; **S**, and Appaim: but 5540
2:30 and Appaim: but **S** died without children. 5540

SELEUCIA (1)
Ac 13: 4 forth by the Holy Ghost, departed unto **S**; *4581*

SELF (6) [HERSELF, HIMSELF, ITSELF, SELFSAME, SELFWILL, SELFWILLED, SELVES, THEMSELVES, THYSELF, YOURSELVES]
Ex 32:13 to whom thou swarest by **thine own s**, 3509.2
Jn 5:30 I can of **mine own s** do nothing: as I hear, *1683*
17: 5 glorify thou me with **thine own s** with *4572*
1Co 4: 3 yea, I judge not **mine own s.** *1683*
Phm 1:19 owest unto me even **thine own s** besides. *4572*
1Pe 2:24 Who **his own s** bare our sins in his own *846*

SELF-CONTROL See TEMPERANCE

SELFSAME (15) [SAME, SELF]
Ge 7:13 In the **s** day entered Noah, and Shem, and 6106
17:23 the flesh of their foreskin in the **s** day, 6106
17:26 In the **s** day was Abraham circumcised, and 6106
Ex 12:17 for in this **s** day have I brought your armies 6106
12:41 thirty years, even the **s** day it came to pass, 6106
12:51 it came to pass the **s** day, *that* the LORD 6106
Lev 23:14 until the **s** day that ye have brought an 6106
23:21 ye shall proclaim on the **s** day, *that* it may 6106
Dt 32:48 the LORD spake unto Moses that **s** day, 6106
Jos 5:11 and parched *corn* in the **s** day. 6106
Eze 40: 1 in the **s** day the hand of the LORD was 6106
Mt 8:13 And his servant was healed in the **s** hour. *1565*
1Co 12:11 all these worketh *that* one and the **s** Spirit, *846*
2Co 5: 5 Now he that hath wrought us for the **s** *thing* *846*
7:11 For behold this **s** *thing,* that ye sorrowed *846*

SELFWILL (1) [SELF, WILL]
Ge 49: 6 and in their **s** they digged down a wall. 7522

SELFWILLED (2) [SELF, WILL]
Tit 1: 7 not **s**, not soon angry, not given to wine, *829*
2Pe 2:10 Presumptuous *are they,* **s**, they are not afraid *829*

SELL (35) [SALE, SELLER, SELLERS, SELLEST, SELLETH, SOLD]
Ge 25:31 Jacob said, **S** me *this* day thy birthright. 4376
37:27 let us **s** him to the Ishmeelites, and let not 4376
Ex 21: 7 if a man **s** his daughter to be a maidservant, 4376
21: 8 to **s** her unto a strange nation he shall have 4376
21:35 they shall **s** the live ox, and divide 4376
22: 1 steal an ox, or a sheep, and kill it, or **s** it; 4376
Lev 25:14 if thou **s ought** unto thy neighbour, 4376+4465
25:15 of years of the fruits he shall **s** unto thee: 4376
25:16 *the years* of the fruits doth he **s** unto thee. 4376
25:29 if a man **s** a dwelling house in a walled city, 4376
25:47 **s** himself unto the stranger *or* sojourner by 4376
Dt 2:28 Thou shalt **s** me meat for money, that I may 7666
14:21 may eat it; or thou mayest **s** *it* unto an alien: 4376
21:14 thou shalt not **s** her **at all** for money, 4376+4376
Jdg 4: 9 for the LORD shall **s** Sisera into the hand 4376
1Ki 21:25 which did **s** himself to work wickedness in 4376
2Ki 4: 7 **s** the oil, and pay thy debt, and live thou 4376
Ne 5: 8 and will you even **s** your brethren? 4376
10:31 or any victuals on the sabbath day to **s**, 4376
Pr 23:23 Buy the truth, and **s** *it* not; *also* wisdom, 4376
Eze 30:12 and **s** the land into the hand of the wicked: 4376
48:14 they shall not **s** of it, neither exchange, 4376
Joel 3: 8 I will **s** your sons and your daughters into 4376
3: 8 they shall **s** them to the Sabeans, to a 4376
Am 8: 5 the new moon be gone, that we may **s** corn? 7666
8: 6 *yea,* and **s** the refuse of the wheat? 7666
Zec 11: 5 they that **s** them say, Blessed *be* 4376
Mt 19:21 go *and* **s** that thou hast, and give to *4453*
25: 9 but go ye rather to them that **s**, and buy for *4453*
Mk 10:21 **s** whatsoever thou hast, and give to *4453*
Lk 12:33 **S** that ye have, and give alms; *4453*
18:22 Yet lackest thou one *thing:* **s** all that thou *4453*
22:36 let him **s** his garment, and buy one. *4453*
Jas 4:13 there a year, and **buy and s**, and get gain: *1710*
Rev 13:17 And that no *man* might buy or **s**, save he *4453*

SELLER (4) [SELL]
Isa 24: 2 as *with* the buyer, so *with* the **s**; 4376
Eze 7:12 let not the buyer rejoice, nor the **s** mourn: 4376
7:13 For the **s** shall not return to that which is 4376
Ac 16:14 a **s of purple**, of the city of Thyatira, *4211*

SELLERS (1) [SELL]
Ne 13:20 **s** of all *kind of* ware lodged without 4376

SELLEST (1) [SELL]
Ps 44:12 Thou **s** thy people for nought, and dost not 4376

SELLETH (7) [SELL]
Ex 21:16 and **s** him, or if he be found in his hand, 4376
Dt 24: 7 and maketh merchandise of him, or **s** him; 4376
Ru 4: 3 **s** a parcel of land, which *was* our brother 4376
Pr 11:26 *shall be* upon the head of him that **s** *it.* 7666
31:24 **s** *it;* and delivereth girdles unto 4376
Na 3: 4 that **s** nations through her whoredoms, and 4376
Mt 13:44 for joy thereof goeth and **s** all that he hath, *4453*

SELVEDGE (2)
Ex 26: 4 the one curtain from the **s** in the coupling; 7098
36:11 of one curtain from the **s** in the coupling: 7098

SELVES (7) [SELF]
Lk 21:30 know of **your own s** that summer is now *1438*
Ac 20:30 Also of your **own s** shall men arise, *846*
2Co 8: 5 but first gave **their own s** to the Lord, and *1438*
13: 5 ye be in the faith; prove **your own s.** *1438*
13: 5 Know ye not **your own s**, how that Jesus *1438*
2Ti 3: 2 For men shall be **lovers of** their **own s**, *5367*
Jas 1:22 not hearers only, deceiving **your own s.** *1438*

SEM (1) [SHEM]
Lk 3:36 which was *the son* of **S**, which was *the son* *4590*

SEMACHIAH (1)
1Ch 26: 7 brethren *were* strong men, Elihu, and **S.** 5565

SEMAKIAH See SEMACHIAH

SEMEI (1)
Lk 3:26 which was *the son* of **S**, which was *the son* *4584*

SEMEIN See SEMEI

SENAAH (2)
Ezr 2:35 The children of **S**, three thousand and 5570
Ne 7:38 The children of **S**, three thousand nine 5570

SENATE (1) [SENATORS]
Ac 5:21 and all the **s** of the children of Israel, and *1087*

SENATORS (1) [SENATE]
Ps 105:22 at his pleasure; and teach his **s** wisdom. 2205

SEND (234) [SENDEST, SENDETH, SENDING, SENT, SENTEST]
Ge 24: 7 he shall **s** his angel before thee, and 7971
24:12 **s** me **good speed** *this* day, 6440+7136+3807.1
24:40 will **s** his angel with thee, and prosper thy 7971
24:54 and he said, **S** me **away** unto my master. 7971
24:56 **s me** away that I may go to my master. 5204.1
27:45 I will **s**, and fetch thee from thence: why 7971
30:25 that Jacob said unto Laban, **S** me **away**, 7971
37:13 come, and I will **s** thee unto them. And he 7971
38:17 he said, I will **s** *thee* a kid from the flock. 7971
38:17 Wilt thou give *me* a pledge, till thou **s** *it?* 7971
42:16 **S** one of you, and let him fetch your 7971
43: 4 If thou wilt **s** our brother with us, we will 7971
43: 5 if thou wilt not **s** *him,* we will not go down: 7971
43: 8 **S** the lad with me, and we will arise and go; 7971
43:14 that he may **s away** your other brother, and 7971
45: 5 for God did **s** me before you to preserve 7971
Ex 3:10 and I will **s** thee unto Pharaoh, 7971
4:13 he said, O my Lord, **s**, I pray thee, by 7971
4:13 by the hand *of him whom* thou wilt **s.** 7971
7: 2 that he **s** the children of Israel out of his 7971
8:21 I will **s** swarms *of flies* upon thee, and 7971
9:14 For I will at this time **s** all my plagues upon 7971
9:19 **S** therefore now, *and* gather thy cattle, and 7971
12:33 that they might **s** them out of the land in 7971
23:20 Behold, I **s** an Angel before thee, to keep 7971
23:27 I will **s** my fear before thee, and 7971
23:28 I will **s** hornets before thee, which shall 7971
33: 2 I will **s** an angel before thee; and I will 7971
33:12 thou hast not let me know whom thou wilt **s** 7971
Lev 16:21 shall **s** *him* **away** by the hand of a fit man 7971
26:22 I will also **s** wild beasts among you, which 7971
26:25 I will **s** the pestilence among you; 7971
26:36 *upon* them that are left *alive* of you I will **s** a 935
Nu 13: 2 **S** thou men, that they may search the land 7971
13: 2 of every tribe of their fathers shall ye **s** a 7971
22:37 **earnestly s** unto thee to call thee? 7971+7971
31: 4 all the tribes of Israel, shall ye **s** to the war. 7971
Dt 1:22 We will **s** men before us, and they shall 7971
7:20 Moreover the LORD thy God will **s** 7971
11:15 I will **s** grass in thy fields for thy cattle, 5414
19:12 the elders of his city shall **s** and fetch him 7971
24: 1 *it* in her hand, and **s** her out of his house. 7971
28:20 The LORD shall **s** upon thee cursing, 7971
28:48 which the LORD shall **s** against thee, 7971
32:24 I will also **s** the teeth of beasts upon them, 7971
Jos 18: 4 I will **s** them, and they shall rise, and 7971
Jdg 13: 8 let the man of God which thou didst **s** come 7971
1Sa 5:11 **S away** the ark of the God of Israel, and 7971
6: 2 tell us wherewith we shall **s** it to his place. 7971
6: 3 If ye **s away** the ark of the God of Israel, 7971
6: 3 the ark of the God of Israel, **s** it not empty; 7971
6: 8 side thereof; and **s** it **away**, that it may go. 7971
9:16 To morrow about *this* time I will **s** thee a 7971
9:26 saying, Up, that I may **s** thee **away.** 7971
11: 3 that we may **s** messengers unto all 7971
12:17 and he shall **s** thunder and rain; 5414
16: 1 go, I will **s** thee to Jesse the Beth-lehemite: 7971
16:11 Samuel said unto Jesse, **S** and fetch him: 7971
16:19 said, **S** me David thy son, which *is* with 7971
20:12 and I then **s** not unto thee, and shew it thee; 7971
20:13 I will shew it thee, and **s** thee **away**, 7971
20:21 behold, I will **s** a lad, *saying,* Go, find out 7971
20:31 Wherefore now **s** and fetch him unto me, 7971
21: 2 thing of the business whereabout I **s** thee, 7971
25:25 young men of my lord, whom thou didst **s.** 7971
2Sa 11: 6 sent to Joab, *saying,* **S** me Uriah the Hittite. 7971
14:32 that I may **s** thee to the king, to say, 7971
15:36 by them ye shall **s** unto me every thing that 7971
17:16 Now therefore **s** quickly, and tell David, 7971
1Ki 8:44 whithersoever thou shalt **s** them, and 7971
18: 1 unto Ahab; and I will **s** rain upon the earth. 5414
18:19 Now therefore **s**, *and* gather to me all Israel 7971
20: 6 Yet I will **s** my servants unto thee to 7971
20: 9 All that thou didst **s** for to thy servant at 7971
20:34 *said Ahab,* I will **s** thee **away** with *this* 7971
2Ki 2:16 some valley. And he said, Ye shall not **s.** 7971
2:17 urged him till *he* was ashamed, he said, **S.** 7971
4:22 said, **S** me, I pray thee, one of the young 7971
5: 5 and I will **s** a letter unto the king of Israel. 7971
5: 7 that this *man* doth **s** unto me to recover a 7971
6:13 Go and spy where he *is,* that I may **s** and 7971
7:13 that are consumed:) and let us **s** and see. 7971
9:17 **s** to meet them, and let him say, *Is it* peace? 7971
15:37 In those days the LORD began to **s** 7971
19: 7 I will **s** a blast upon him, and he shall hear 5414
1Ch 13: 2 let us **s** abroad unto our brethren every 7971
2Ch 2: 3 didst **s** him cedars to build him a house to 7971
2: 7 **S** me now therefore a man cunning to work 7971
2: 8 **S** me also cedar trees, fir trees, and 7971
2:15 hath spoken of, let him **s** unto his servants: 7971
6:27 **s** rain upon thy land, which thou hast given 5414
6:34 enemies by the way that thou shalt **s** them, 7971
7:13 or if I **s** pestilence among my people; 7971
28:16 At that time did king Ahaz **s** unto the kings 7971
32: 9 After this did Sennacherib king of Assyria **s** 7971
Ezr 5:17 let the king **s** his pleasure to us concerning 7972
Ne 2: 5 that thou wouldest **s** me unto Judah, 7971
2: 6 So it pleased the king to **s** me; and I set him 7971
8:10 **s** portions unto *them* for whom nothing is 7971
8:12 to **s** portions, and to make great mirth, 7971
Job 21:11 They **s forth** their little ones like a flock, 7971
38:35 Canst thou **s** lightnings, that they may go, 7971
Ps 20: 2 **S** thee help from the sanctuary, and 7971
43: 3 O **s out** thy light and thy truth: let them 7971
57: 3 He shall **s** from heaven, and save me *from* 7971
57: 3 God shall **s forth** his mercy and his truth. 7971
68: 9 Thou, O God, didst **s** a plentiful rain, 5130
68:33 lo, he doth **s out** his voice, *and that* a 5414
110: 2 The LORD shall **s** the rod of thy strength 7971
118:25 I beseech thee, **s** now **prosperity.** 6743
144: 7 **S** thine hand from above; rid me, and 7971
Pr 10:26 so *is* the sluggard to them that **s** him. 7971

Pr 22:21 the words of truth to them that s unto thee? 7971
25:13 is a faithful messenger to them that s him: 7971
Ecc 10: 1 cause the ointment of the apothecary
to s forth 5042
Isa 6: 8 Whom shall I s, and who will go for us? 7971
6: 8 go for us? Then I said, Here am I; s me. 7971
10: 6 I will s him against a hypocritical nation, 7971
10:16 of hosts, s among his fat ones leanness; 7971
16: 1 S ye the lamb to the ruler of the land from 7971
19:20 he shall s them a saviour, and a great one, 7971
32:20 that s forth thither the feet of the ox and 7971
37: 7 I will s a blast upon him, and he shall hear 5414
57: 9 didst s thy messengers far off, and 7971
66:19 I will s those that escape of them unto 7971
Jer 1: 7 for thou shalt go to all that I shall s thee, 7971
2:10 s unto Kedar, and consider diligently, and 7971
8:17 For behold, I will s serpents, cockatrices, 7971
9:16 I will s a sword after them, till I have 7971
9:17 s for cunning women, that they may come: 7971
16:16 Behold, I will s for many fishers, saith 7971
16:16 after will I s for many hunters, and 7971
24:10 I will s the sword, the famine, and 7971
25: 9 I will s and take all the families of 7971
25:15 all the nations, to whom I s thee, to drink it. 7971
25:16 of the sword that I will s among them. 7971
25:27 of the sword which I will s among you. 7971
27: 3 s them to the king of Edom, and to the king 7971
29:17 Behold, I will s upon them the sword, 7971
29:31 S to all them of the captivity, saying, 7971
42: 5 the LORD thy God shall s thee to us. 7971
42: 6 the LORD our God, to whom we s thee; 7971
43:10 I will s and take Nebuchadrezzar the king 7971
48:12 that I will s unto him wanderers, 7971
49:37 I will s the sword after them, till I have 7971
51: 2 will s unto Babylon fanners, that shall fan 7971
Eze 2: 3 of man, I s thee to the children of Israel, 7971
2: 4 I do s thee unto them; and thou shalt say 7971
5:16 When I shall s upon them the evil arrows of 7971
5:16 and which I will s to destroy you: 7971
5:17 So will I s upon you famine and evil beasts, 7971
7: 3 I will s mine anger upon thee, and 7971
14:13 will s famine upon it, and will cut off man 7971
14:19 Or if I s a pestilence into that land, 7971
14:21 How much more when I s my four sore 7971
28:23 For I will s into her pestilence, and 7971
39: 6 I will s a fire on Magog, and among them 7971
Hos 8:14 I will s a fire upon his cities, and it shall 7971
Joel 2:19 I will s you corn, and wine, and oil, and 7971
Am 1: 4 I will s a fire into the house of Hazael, 7971
1: 7 I will s a fire on the wall of Gaza, 7971
1:10 I will s a fire on the wall of Tyrus, 7971
1:12 I will s a fire upon the Teman, which shall 7971
2: 2 I will s a fire upon Moab, and it shall 7971
2: 5 I will s a fire upon Judah, and it shall 7971
8:11 that I will s a famine in the land, 7971
Mal 2: 2 I will even s a curse upon you, and 7971
3: 1 I will s my messenger, and he shall prepare 7971
4: 5 I will s you Elijah the prophet before 7971
Mt 9:38 that he will s forth labourers into his 1544
10:16 I s you forth as sheep in the midst of 649
10:34 Think not that I am come to s peace on 906
10:34 on earth: I came not to s peace, but a sword. 906
11:10 Behold, I s my messenger before thy face, 649
12:20 till he s forth judgment unto victory. 1544
13:41 The Son of man shall s forth his angels, and 649
14:15 s the multitude away, that they may go into 630
15:23 and besought him, saying, S her away; 630
15:32 and I will not s them away fasting, lest they 630
21: 3 of them; and straightway he will s them. 649
23:34 I s unto you prophets, and wise men, and 649
24:31 And he shall s his angels with a great sound 649
Mk 1: 2 Behold, I s my messenger before thy face, 649
3:14 and that he might s them forth to preach, 649
5:10 would not s them away out of the country. 649
5:12 saying, S us into the swine, that we may 3992
6: 7 and began to s them forth by two and two; 649
6:36 S them away, that they may go into 630
8: 3 And if I s them away fasting to their own 630
11: 3 of him; and straightway he will s him hither. 649
12:13 And they s unto him certain of the Pharisees 649
13:27 And then shall he s his angels, and 649
Lk 7:27 Behold, I s my messenger before thy face, 649
9:12 and said unto him, S the multitude away, 630
10: 2 that he would s forth labourers into his 1544
10: 3 I s you forth as lambs among wolves. 649
11:49 I will s them prophets and apostles, and 649
12:49 I am come to s fire on the earth; and 906
16:24 have mercy on me, and s Lazarus, 3992
16:27 that thou wouldest s him to my father's 3992
20:13 I will s my beloved son: it may be they will 3992
24:49 I s the promise of my Father upon you: 649
Jn 13:20 He that receiveth whomsoever I s receiveth 3992
14:26 whom the Father will s in my name, 3992
15:26 whom I will s unto you from the Father, 3992
16: 7 but if I depart, I will s him unto you. 3992
17: 8 and they have believed that thou didst s me. 649
20:21 as my Father hath sent me, even so s I you. 3992
Ac 3:20 And he shall s Jesus Christ, which before 649
7:34 And now come, I will s thee into Egypt. 649
7:35 the same did God s to be a ruler and 649
10: 5 And now s men to Joppa, and call for one 3992
10:22 by a holy angel to s for thee into his house, 3343
10:32 S therefore to Joppa, and call hither Simon, 3992
11:13 S men to Joppa, and call for Simon, 649
11:29 determined to s relief unto the brethren 3992
15:22 to s chosen men of their own company to 3992
15:23 brethren s greeting unto the brethren which NIG
15:25 to s chosen men unto you with our beloved 3992
22:21 for I will s thee far hence unto the Gentiles. 1821
25: 3 that he would s for him to Jerusalem, 3343
25:21 I commanded him to be kept till I might s 3992
25:25 to Augustus, I have determined to s him. 3992
25:27 For it seemeth to me unreasonable to s a 3992
26:17 from the Gentiles, unto whom now I s thee, 649
1Co 16: 3 them will I s to bring your liberality unto 3992
Php 2:19 But I trust in the Lord Jesus to s Timotheus 3992
2:23 Him therefore I hope to s presently, so 3992
2:25 Yet I supposed it necessary to s to you 3992
2Th 2:11 And for this cause God shall s them strong 3992
Tit 3:12 When I shall s Artemas unto thee, or 3992
Jas 3:11 Doth a fountain s forth at the same place 1032
Rev 1:11 s it unto the seven churches which are in 3992
11:10 and shall s gifts one to another; 3992

SENDEST (6) [SEND]

Dt 15:13 when thou s him out free from thee, 7971
15:18 when thou s him away free from thee; 7971
Jos 1:16 and whithersoever thou s us, we will go. 7971
2Ki 1: 6 that thou s to inquire of Baal-zebub the god 7971
Job 14:20 changest his countenance, and s him away. 7971
Ps 104:30 Thou s forth thy spirit, they are created: 7971

SENDETH (15) [SEND]

Dt 24: 3 it in her hand, and s her out of his house; 7971
1Ki 17:14 until the day that the LORD s rain upon 5414
Job 5:10 the earth, and s waters upon the fields: 7971
12:15 also he s them out, and they overturn 7971
Ps 104:10 He s the springs into the valleys, which run 7971
147:15 He s forth his commandment upon earth: 7971
147:18 He s out his word, and melteth them: 7971
Pr 26: 6 He that s a message by the hand of a fool 7971
SS 1:12 my spikenard s forth the smell thereof. 5414
Isa 18: 2 That s ambassadors by the sea, even in 7971
Mt 5:45 and s rain on the just and on the unjust. 1026
Mk 11: 1 of Olives, he s forth two of his disciples, 649
14:13 And he s forth two of his disciples, and 649
Lk 14:32 he s an ambassage, and desireth conditions 649
Ac 23:26 most excellent governor Felix s greeting. NIG

SENDING (14) [SEND]

2Sa 13:16 this evil in s me away is greater than 7971
2Ch 36:15 by his messengers, rising up betimes, and s; 7971
Est 9:19 good day, and of s portions one to another. 4916
9:22 of s portions one to another, and gifts to 4916
Ps 78:49 and trouble, by s evil angels among them. 4917
Isa 7:25 it shall be for the s forth of oxen, and 4916
Jer 7:25 daily rising up early and s them: 7971
25: 4 rising early and s them; but ye have not 7971
26: 5 and s them, but ye have not hearkened; 7971
29:19 rising up early and s them; but ye would 7971
35:15 rising up early and s them, saying, 7971
44: 4 rising early and s them, saying, Oh, do not 7971
Eze 17:15 he rebelled against him in s his 7971
Ro 8: 3 God s his own Son in the likeness of sinful 3992

SENEH (1)

1Sa 14: 4 was Bozez, and the name of the other S. 5573

SENIR (2)

1Ch 5:23 from Bashan unto Baal-hermon and S, 8149
Eze 27: 5 made all thy ship boards of fir trees of S: 8149

SENNACHERIB (13)

2Ki 18:13 S king of Assyria come up against all 5576
19:16 hear the words of S, which hath sent him to 5576
19:20 me against S king of Assyria I have heard. 5576
19:36 So S king of Assyria departed, and went 5576
2Ch 32: 1 the establishment thereof, S king of Assyria 5576
32: 2 when Hezekiah saw that S was come, and 5576
32: 9 After this did S king of Assyria send his 5576
32:10 Thus saith S king of Assyria, Whereon do 5576
32:22 from the hand of S the king of Assyria, 5576
Isa 36: 1 that S king of Assyria came up against all 5576
37:17 hear all the words of S, which hath sent to 5576
37:21 Whereas thou hast prayed to me against S 5576
37:37 So S king of Assyria departed, and went 5576

SENSE (1) [SENSES, SENSUAL]

Ne 8: 8 gave the s, and caused them to understand 7922

SENSELESS See SILLY; SOTTISH

SENSES (1) [SENSE]

Heb 5:14 even those who by reason of use have their s 145

SENSUAL (2) [SENSE]

Jas 3:15 not from above, but is earthly, s, devilish. 5591
Jude 1:19 s, having not the Spirit. 5591

SENSUALITY See LASCIVIOUSNESS

SENT (690) [SEND]

Ge 3:23 Therefore the LORD God s him forth 7971
8: 7 And he s forth a raven, which went forth to 7971
8: 8 Also he s forth a dove from him, to see if 7971
8:10 again he s forth the dove out of the ark; 7971
8:12 yet other seven days; and s forth the dove; 7971
12:20 they s him away, and his wife, and all that 7971
19:13 and the LORD hath s us to destroy it. 7971
19:29 and s Lot out of the midst of the overthrow, 7971
20: 2 Abimelech king of Gerar s, and took Sarah. 7971
21:14 her shoulder, and the child, and s her away: 7971
24:59 they s away Rebekah their sister, and her 7971
25: 6 s them away from Isaac his son, while he 7971
26:27 ye hate me, and have s me away from you? 7971
26:29 but good, and have s thee away in peace: 7971
26:31 Isaac s them away, and they departed from 7971
27:42 she s and called Jacob her younger son, and 7971
28: 5 Isaac s away Jacob: and he went to 7971
28: 6 s him away to Padan-aram, to take him a 7971
31: 4 Jacob s and called Rachel and Leah to 7971
31:27 that I might have s thee away with mirth, 7971
31:42 surely thou hadst s me away now empty. 7971
32: 3 Jacob s messengers before him to Esau his 7971
32: 5 I have s to tell my lord, that I may find 7971
32:18 it is a present s unto my lord Esau: 7971
32:23 s them over the brook, and sent over that 5674
32:23 over the brook, and s over that he had. 5674
37:14 So he s him out of the vale of Hebron, and 7971
Ge 37:32 they s the coat of many colours, and 7971
38:20 Judah s the kid by the hand of his friend 7971
38:23 I s this kid, and thou hast not found her. 7971
38:25 she s to her father in law, saying, By 7971
41: 8 he s and called for all the magicians of 7971
41:14 Pharaoh s and called Joseph, and 7971
42: 4 Jacob s not with his brethren; 7971
43:34 and s messes unto them from before him: NIH
44: 3 the men were s away, they and their asses. 7971
45: 7 God s me before you to preserve you a 7971
45: 8 So now it was not you that s me hither, but 7971
45:23 to his father he s after this manner; 7971
45:24 So he s his brethren away, and 7971
45:27 wagons which Joseph had s to carry him, 7971
46: 5 in the wagons which Pharaoh had s to carry 7971
46:28 he s Judah before him unto Joseph, to direct 7971
50:16 they s a messenger unto Joseph, saying, 6680
Ex 2: 5 among the flags, she s her maid to fetch it. 7971
3:12 be a token unto thee, that I have s thee: 7971
3:13 The God of your fathers hath s me unto 7971
3:14 of Israel, I AM hath s me unto you. 7971
3:15 and the God of Jacob, hath s me unto you: 7971
4:28 all the words of the LORD who had s him, 7971
5:22 this people? why is it that thou hast s me? 7971
7:16 The LORD God of the Hebrews hath s me 7971
9: 7 Pharaoh s, and behold, there was not one of 7971
9:23 the LORD s thunder and hail, and the fire 5414
9:27 Pharaoh s, and called for Moses and Aaron, 7971
18: 2 Moses' wife, after he had s her back, 7964
24: 5 he s young men of the children of Israel, 7971
Nu 13: 3 s them from the wilderness of Paran: 7971
13:16 the men which Moses s to spy out the land. 7971
13:17 Moses s them to spy out the land of 7971
14:36 the men, which Moses s to search the land, 7971
16:12 Moses s to call Dathan and Abiram, 7971
16:28 ye shall know that the LORD hath s 7971
16:29 of all men; then the LORD hath not s me. 7971
20:14 Moses s messengers from Kadesh unto 7971
20:16 s an angel, and hath brought us forth out of 7971
21: 6 the LORD s fiery serpents among 7971
21:21 Israel s messengers unto Sihon king of 7971
21:32 Moses s to spy out Jaazer, and they took 7971
22: 5 He s messengers therefore unto Balaam 7971
22:10 king of Moab, hath s unto me, saying, 7971
22:15 Balak s yet again princes, more, and 7971
22:40 s to Balaam, and to the princes that were 7971
31: 6 Moses s them to the war, a thousand of 7971
32: 8 when I s them from Kadesh-barnea to see 7971
Dt 2:26 I s messengers out of the wilderness of 7971
9:23 Likewise when the LORD s you from 7971
24: 4 Her former husband, which s her away, 7971
34:11 which the LORD s him to do in the land 7971
Jos 2: 1 Joshua the son of Nun s out of Shittim two 7971
2: 3 the king of Jericho s unto Rahab, saying, 7971
2:21 she s them away, and they departed: and 7971
6:17 because she hid the messengers that we s. 7971
6:25 which Joshua s to spy out Jericho. 7971
7: 2 Joshua s men from Jericho to Ai, which is 7971
7:22 So Joshua s messengers, and they ran unto 7971
8: 3 men of valour, and s them away by night. 7971
8: 9 Joshua therefore s them forth: and 7971
10: 3 of Jerusalem s unto Hoham king of Hebron, 7971
10: 6 the men of Gibeon s unto Joshua to 7971
11: 1 things, that he s to Jobab king of Madon, 7971
14: 7 s me from Kadesh-barnea to espy out 7971
14:11 day as I was in the day that Moses s me: 7971
22: 6 So Joshua blessed them, and s them away: 7971
22: 7 when Joshua s them away also unto their 7971
22:13 the children of Israel s unto the children of 7971
24: 5 I s Moses also and Aaron, and I plagued 7971
24: 9 s and called Balaam the son of Beor to 7971
24:12 I s the hornet before you, which drave them 7971
Jdg 1:23 the house of Joseph s to descry Beth-el. 8446
3:15 by him the children of Israel s a present 7971
3:18 he s away the people that bare the present. 7971
4: 6 she s and called Barak the son of Abinoam 7971
5:15 he was s on foot into the valley. For 7971
6: 8 That the LORD s a prophet unto 7971
6:14 hand of the Midianites: have not I s thee? 7971
6:35 he s messengers throughout all Manasseh; 7971
6:35 he s messengers unto Asher, and 7971
7: 8 he s all the rest of Israel every man unto his 7971
7:24 Gideon s messengers throughout all mount 7971
9:23 God s an evil spirit between Abimelech 7971
9:31 he s messengers unto Abimelech privily, 7971
11:12 Jephthah s messengers unto the king of 7971
11:14 Jephthah s messengers again unto the king 7971
11:17 Israel s messengers unto the king of Edom, 7971
11:17 like manner they s unto the king of Moab: 7971
11:19 Israel s messengers unto Sihon king of 7971
11:28 unto the words of Jephthah which he s him. 7971
11:38 he s her away for two months: and 7971
12: 9 whom he s abroad, and took in thirty 7971
16:18 she s and called for the lords of 7971
18: 2 the children of Dan s of their family five 7971
19:29 and s her into all the coasts of Israel. 7971
20: 6 s her throughout all the country of 7971
20:12 the tribes of Israel s men through all 7971
21:10 the congregation s thither twelve thousand 7971
21:13 the whole congregation s some to speak to 7971
1Sa 4: 4 So the people s to Shiloh, that they might 7971
5: 8 They s therefore and gathered all the lords 7971
5:10 Therefore they s the ark of God to Ekron. 7971
5:11 So they s and gathered together all the lords 7971
6:21 they s messengers to the inhabitants of 7971
10:25 Samuel s all the people away, every man to 7971
11: 7 s them throughout all the coasts of Israel by 7971
12: 8 then the LORD s Moses and Aaron, 7971
12:11 the LORD s Jerubbaal, and Bedan, and 7971
12:18 and the LORD s thunder and rain that day: 5414
13: 2 the rest of the people he s every man to his 7971
15: 1 The LORD s me to anoint thee to be king 7971
15:18 the LORD s thee on a journey, and said, 7971
15:20 have gone the way which the LORD s me, 7971
16:12 he s, and brought him in. Now he was 7971

1Sa 16:19 Wherefore Saul **s** messengers unto Jesse, 7971
16:20 and **s** *them* by David his son unto Saul. 7971
16:22 Saul **s** to Jesse, saying, Let David, I pray 7971
17:31 *them* before Saul: and he **s for** him. 3947
18: 5 David went out whithersoever Saul **s** him, 7971
19:11 Saul also **s** messengers unto David's house, 7971
19:14 And when Saul **s** messengers to take David, 7971
19:15 Saul **s** the messengers *again* to see David, 7971
19:17 **s away** mine enemy, that he is escaped? 7971
19:20 Saul **s** messengers to take David: and 7971
19:21 he **s** other messengers, and they prophesied 7971
19:21 And Saul **s** messengers again the third time, 7971
20:22 *thy way:* for the LORD hath **s** thee **away**. 7971
22:11 the king **s** to call Ahimelech the priest, 7971
25: 5 David **s out** ten young men, and David said 7971
25:14 David **s** messengers out of the wilderness to 7971
25:32 of Israel, which **s** thee this day to meet me: 7971
25:39 David **s** and communed with Abigail, 7971
25:40 unto her, saying, David **s** us unto thee, 7971
26: 4 David therefore **s out** spies, and 7971
30:26 he **s** of the spoil unto the elders of Judah, 7971
31: 9 **s** into the land of the Philistines round 7971
2Sa 2: 5 David **s** messengers unto the men of 7971
3:12 Abner **s** messengers to David on his behalf, 7971
3:14 David **s** messengers to Ish-bosheth Saul's 7971
3:15 Ish-bosheth **s**, and took her from *her* 7971
3:21 David **s** Abner **away**; and he went in peace. 7971
3:22 for he had **s** him **away**, and he was gone in 7971
3:23 he hath **s** him **away**, and he is gone in 7971
3:24 why *is* it *that* thou hast **s** him **away**, and 7971
3:26 from David, he **s** messengers after Abner, 7971
5:11 Hiram king of Tyre **s** messengers to David, 7971
8:10 Toi **s** Joram his son unto king David, 7971
9: 5 king David **s**, and fet him out of the house 7971
10: 2 David **s** to comfort him by the hand of his 7971
10: 3 that he hath **s** comforters unto thee? 7971
10: 3 hath not David *rather* **s** his servants unto 7971
10: 4 *even* to their buttocks, and **s** them **away**. 7971
10: 5 he **s** to meet them, because the men were 7971
10: 6 the children of Ammon **s** and hired 7971
10: 7 when David heard *of it*, he **s** Joab, and all 7971
10:16 Hadarezer **s**, and brought out the Syrians 7971
11: 1 kings go forth *to battle,* that David **s** Joab, 7971
11: 3 David **s** and inquired after the woman. 7971
11: 4 David **s** messengers, and took her; and 7971
11: 5 **s** and told David, and said, I *am* with child. 7971
11: 6 David **s** to Joab, *saying,* Send me Uriah 7971
11: 6 the Hittite. And Joab **s** Uriah to David. 7971
11:14 letter to Joab, and **s** *it* by the hand of Uriah. 7971
11:18 Joab **s** and told David all the things 7971
11:22 shewed David all that Joab had **s** him **for**. 7971
11:27 David **s** and fet her to his house, and 7971
12: 1 the LORD **s** Nathan unto David. And he 7971
12:25 he **s** by the hand of Nathan the prophet; 7971
12:27 Joab **s** messengers to David, and said, 7971
13: 7 David **s** home to Tamar, saying, Go now *to* 7971
14: 2 Joab **s** to Tekoah, and fetcht thence a wise 7971
14:29 Therefore Absalom **s** for Joab, to have sent 7971
14:29 sent for Joab, to have **s** him to the king; 7971
14:29 when he **s** again the second time, he would 7971
14:32 Behold, I **s** unto thee, saying, Come hither, 7971
15:10 Absalom **s** spies throughout all the tribes of 7971
15:12 Absalom **s** *for* Ahithophel the Gilonite, 7971
18: 2 David **s forth** a third part of the people 7971
18:29 When Joab **s** the king's servant, and *me* thy 7971
19:11 king David **s** to Zadok and to Abiathar 7971
19:14 so that they **s** *this word* unto the king, 7971
22:15 he **s out** arrows, and scattered them; 7971
22:17 He **s** from above, he took me; he drew me 7971
24:13 see what answer I shall return *to* him that **s** 7971
24:15 So the LORD **s** a pestilence upon Israel 5414
1Ki 1:44 the king hath **s** with him Zadok the priest, 7971
1:53 So king Solomon **s**, and they brought him 7971
2:25 king Solomon **s** by the hand of Benaiah 7971
2:29 Solomon **s** Benaiah the son of Jehoiada, 7971
2:36 the king **s** and called for Shimei, and 7971
2:42 the king **s** and called for Shimei, and 7971
5: 1 Hiram king of Tyre **s** his servants unto 7971
5: 2 And Solomon **s** to Hiram, saying, 7971
5: 8 Hiram **s** to Solomon, saying, I have 7971
5:14 he **s** them to Lebanon, ten thousand a 7971
7:13 king Solomon **s** and fet Hiram out of Tyre. 7971
8:66 On the eighth day he **s** the people **away**: 7971
9:14 Hiram **s** to the king sixscore talents of gold. 7971
9:27 Hiram **s** in the navy his servants, 7971
12: 3 That they **s** and called him. And Jeroboam 7971
12:18 king Rehoboam **s** Adoram, who *was* over 7971
12:20 that they **s** and called him unto 7971
14: 6 for I *am* **s** to thee *with* heavy *tidings.* 7971
15:18 king Asa **s** them to Ben-hadad, the son of 7971
15:19 I have **s** unto thee a present of silver and 7971
15:20 **s** the captains of the hosts which he had 7971
18:10 whither my lord hath not **s** to seek thee: 7971
18:20 So Ahab **s** unto all the children of Israel, 7971
19: 2 Jezebel **s** a messenger unto Elijah, saying, 7971
20: 2 he **s** messengers to Ahab king of Israel into 7971
20: 5 saying, Although I have **s** unto thee, saying, 7971
20: 7 for he **s** unto me for my wives, and for my 7971
20:10 Ben-hadad **s** unto him, and said, The gods 7971
20:17 Ben-hadad **s out**, and they told him, saying, 7971
20:34 a covenant with him, and **s** him **away**. 7971
21: 8 **s** the letters unto the elders and to 7971
21:11 did as Jezebel had **s** unto them, *and* as *it* 7971
21:11 in the letters which she had **s** unto them. 7971
21:14 they **s** to Jezebel, saying, Naboth is stoned, 7971
2Ki 1: 2 he **s** messengers, and said unto them, Go, 7971
1: 6 turn again unto the king that **s** you, and 7971
1: 9 the king **s** unto him a captain of fifty with 7971
1:11 Again also he **s** unto him another captain of 7971
1:13 he **s** again a captain of the third fifty with 7971
1:16 Forasmuch as thou hast **s** messengers to 7971
2: 2 for the LORD hath **s** me to Beth-el. 7971
2: 4 for the LORD hath **s** me *to* Jericho. 7971
2: 6 here; for the LORD hath **s** me to Jordan. 7971
2:17 They **s** therefore fifty men; and they sought 7971
2Ki 3: 7 and **s** to Jehoshaphat the king of Judah, 7971
5: 6 I have *therewith* **s** Naaman my servant to 7971
5: 8 that he **s** to the king, saying, Wherefore 7971
5:10 Elisha **s** a messenger unto him, saying, Go 7971
5:22 My master hath **s** me, saying, Behold, 7971
6: 9 the man of God **s** unto the king of Israel, 7971
6:10 the king of Israel **s** to the place which 7971
6:14 Therefore **s** he thither horses, and chariots, 7971
6:23 he **s** them **away**, and they went to their 7971
6:32 and *the king* **s** a man from before him: 7971
6:32 See ye how this son of a murderer hath **s** to 7971
7:14 the king **s** after the host of the Syrians, 7971
8: 9 Thy son Ben-hadad king of Syria hath **s** me 7971
9:19 he **s** *out* a second on horseback, which 7971
10: 1 Jehu wrote letters, and **s** *to* Samaria, 7971
10: 5 the bringers up *of the children,* **s** to Jehu, 7971
10: 7 heads in baskets, and **s** him *them* to Jezreel. 7971
10:21 Jehu **s** through all Israel: and all 7971
11: 4 the seventh year Jehoiada **s** and fet 7971
12:18 and **s** *it* to Hazael king of Syria: 7971
14: 8 Amaziah **s** messengers to Jehoash, the son 7971
14: 9 Jehoash the king of Israel **s** to Amaziah 7971
14: 9 The thistle that *was* in Lebanon **s** to 7971
14:19 they **s** after him to Lachish, and slew him 7971
16: 7 So Ahaz **s** messengers to Tiglath-pileser 7971
16: 8 and **s** *it for* a present to the king of Assyria. 7971
16:10 king Ahaz **s** to Urijah the priest the fashion 7971
16:11 to all that king Ahaz had **s** from Damascus: 7971
17: 4 for he had **s** messengers to So king of 7971
17:13 which I **s** to you by my servants 7971
17:25 therefore the LORD **s** lions among them, 7971
17:26 therefore he hath **s** lions among them, 7971
18:14 Hezekiah king of Judah **s** to the king of 7971
18:17 the king of Assyria **s** Tartan and Rabsaris 7971
18:27 Hath my master **s** me to thy master, and 7971
18:27 *hath he* not **s** *me* to the men which sit on NIH
19: 2 he **s** Eliakim, which *was* over 7971
19: 4 whom the king of Assyria his master hath **s** 7971
19: 9 he **s** messengers again unto Hezekiah, 7971
19:16 which hath **s** him to reproach the living 7971
19:20 Then Isaiah the son of Amoz **s** to Hezekiah, 7971
20:12 **s** letters and a present unto Hezekiah: 7971
22: 3 *that* the king **s** Shaphan the son of Azaliah, 7971
22:15 of Israel, Tell the man that **s** you to me, 7971
22:18 to the king of Judah which **s** you to inquire 7971
23: 1 the king **s**, and they gathered unto him all 7971
23:16 **s**, and took the bones out of the sepulchres, 7971
24: 2 the LORD **s** against him bands of 7971
24: 2 and **s** them against Judah to destroy it, 7971
1Ch 8: 8 country of Moab, after he had **s** them **away**; 7971
10: 9 **s** into the land of the Philistines round 7971
12:19 Philistines upon advisement **s** him **away**, 7971
14: 1 Now Hiram king of Tyre **s** messengers to 7971
18:10 He **s** Hadoram his son to king David, 7971
19: 2 David **s** messengers to comfort him 7971
19: 3 that he hath **s** comforters unto thee? 7971
19: 4 hard by *their* buttocks, and **s** them **away**. 7971
19: 5 he **s** to meet them: for the men were greatly 7971
19: 6 the children of Ammon **s** a thousand talents 7971
19: 8 when David heard *of it*, he **s** Joab, and all 7971
19:16 they **s** messengers, and drew forth 7971
21:12 word I shall bring again to him that **s** me. 7971
21:14 So the LORD **s** pestilence upon Israel: and 5414
21:15 God **s** an angel unto Jerusalem to destroy it: 7971
2Ch 2: 3 Solomon **s** to Huram the king of Tyre, 7971
2:11 which he **s** to Solomon, Because 7971
2:13 now I have **s** a cunning man, endued with 7971
7:10 month he **s** the people **away** into their tents, 7971
8:18 Huram **s** him by the hands of his servants 7971
10: 3 they **s** and called him. So Jeroboam and 7971
10:18 king Rehoboam **s** Hadoram that *was* over 7971
16: 2 and **s** to Ben-hadad king of Syria, 7971
16: 3 behold, I have **s** thee silver and gold; go, 7971
16: 4 **s** the captains of his armies against 7971
17: 7 Also in the third year of his reign he **s** to his 7971
17: 8 with them *he* **s** Levites, *even* Shemaiah, NIH
24:19 Yet he **s** prophets to them, to bring them 7971
24:23 **s** all the spoil of them unto the king of 7971
25:13 of the army which Amaziah **s back**, 7725
25:15 he **s** unto him a prophet, which said unto 7971
25:17 **s** to Joash, the son of Jehoahaz, the son of 7971
25:18 Joash king of Israel **s** to Amaziah king of 7971
25:18 **s** to the cedar that *was* in Lebanon, 7971
25:27 they **s** to Lachish after him, and slew him 7971
30: 1 Hezekiah **s** to all Israel and Judah, and 7971
32:21 the LORD **s** an angel, which cut off all 7971
32:31 who **s** unto him to inquire of the wonder 7971
34: 8 he **s** Shaphan the son of Azaliah, and 7971
34:23 of Israel, Tell ye the man that **s** you to me, 7971
34:26 who **s** you to inquire of the LORD, so 7971
34:29 the king **s** and gathered together all 7971
35:21 he **s** ambassadors to him, saying, 7971
36:10 king Nebuchadnezzar **s**, and brought him to 7971
36:15 the LORD God of their fathers **s** to them 7971
Ezr 4:11 This *is* the copy of the letter that they **s** 7972
4:14 therefore have we **s** and certified the king; 7972
4:17 *Then* **s** the king an answer unto Rehum 7972
4:18 The letter which ye **s** unto us *hath been* 7972
5: 6 *this* side the river, **s** unto Darius the king: 7972
5: 7 They **s** a letter unto him, wherein *was* 7972
6:13 to that which Darius the king had **s**, 7972
7:14 Forasmuch as *thou art* **s** of the king, and 7972
8:16 **s** I for Eliezer, for Ariel, for Shemaiah, 7971
8:17 I **s** them **with commandment** unto Iddo 6680
Ne 2: 9 Now the king had **s** captains of the army 7971
6: 2 That Sanballat and Geshem **s** unto me, 7971
6: 3 I **s** messengers unto them, saying, I *am* 7971
6: 4 Yet they **s** unto me four times after this 7971
6: 5 **s** Sanballat his servant unto me in like 7971
6: 8 I **s** unto him, saying, There are no such 7971
6:12 lo, I perceived that God had not **s** him; but 7971
6:17 nobles of Judah **s** many letters unto Tobiah, 1980
6:19 *And* Tobiah **s** letters to put me in fear. 7971
Est 1:22 For he **s** letters into all the king's provinces, 7971
3:13 the letters were **s** by posts into all the king's 7971
Est 4: 4 she **s** raiment to clothe Mordecai, and 7971
5:10 he **s** and called for his friends, and Zeresh 7971
8:10 **s** letters by posts on horseback, *and* 7971
9:20 **s** letters unto all the Jews that *were* in all 7971
9:30 he **s** the letters unto all the Jews, to 7971
Job 1: 4 **s** and called for their three sisters to eat and 7971
1: 5 that Job **s** and sanctified them, and rose up 7971
14: 9 *Yet* through the **s** of water it will bud, and 7381
22: 9 Thou hast **s** widows **away** empty, and 7971
39: 5 Who hath **s out** the wild ass free? or 7971
Ps 18:14 he **s out** his arrows, and scattered them; 7971
18:16 He **s** from above, he took me, he drew me 7971
59: T when Saul **s**, and they watcht the house to 7971
77:17 the skies **s out** a sound: thine arrows also 5414
78:25 eat angels' food: he **s** them meat to the full. 7971
78:45 He **s** divers sorts *of flies* among them, 7971
80:11 She **s out** her boughs unto the sea, and 7971
105:17 He **s** a man before them, *even* Joseph, 7971
105:20 The king **s** and loosed him; *even* the ruler 7971
105:26 He **s** Moses his servant; *and* Aaron whom 7971
105:28 He **s** darkness, and made it dark; and 7971
106:15 their request; but **s** leanness into their soul. 7971
107:20 He **s** his word, and healed them, and 7971
111: 9 He **s** redemption unto his people: he hath 7971
135: 9 *Who* **s** tokens and wonders into the midst 7971
Pr 9: 3 She hath **s forth** her maidens: she crieth 7971
17:11 a cruel messenger shall be **s** against him. 7971
Isa 9: 8 The Lord **s** a word into Jacob, and it hath 7971
20: 1 (when Sargon the king of Assyria **s** him,) 7971
36: 2 the king of Assyria **s** Rabshakeh from 7971
36:12 Hath my master **s** me to thy master and 7971
36:12 *hath he* not **s** *me* to the men that sit upon NIH
37: 2 he **s** Eliakim, who *was* over the household, 7971
37: 4 whom the king of Assyria his master hath **s** 7971
37: 9 when he heard *it*, he **s** messengers to 7971
37:17 which hath **s** to reproach the living God. 7971
37:21 Isaiah the son of Amoz **s** unto Hezekiah, 7971
39: 1 **s** letters and a present to Hezekiah: 7971
42:19 or deaf, as my messenger *that* I **s**? who *is* 7971
43:14 For your sake I have **s** to Babylon, and 7971
48:16 the Lord GOD, and his Spirit, hath **s** me. 7971
55:11 it shall prosper *in the thing* whereto I **s** it. 7971
61: 1 he hath **s** me to bind up the broken-hearted, 7971
Jer 7:25 I have even **s** unto you all my servants 7971
14: 3 their nobles have **s** their little ones to 7971
14:14 I **s** them not, neither have I commanded 7971
14:15 I **s** them not, yet they say, Sword and 7971
19:14 whither the LORD had **s** him to prophesy; 7971
21: 1 when king Zedekiah **s** unto him Pashur 7971
23:21 I have not **s** *these* prophets, yet they ran: 7971
23:32 yet I **s** them not, nor commanded them: 7971
23:38 I have **s** unto you, saying, Ye shall not say, 7971
24: 5 whom I have **s** out of this place *into* 7971
25: 4 the LORD hath **s** unto you all his servants 7971
25:17 to drink, unto whom the LORD had **s** me: 7971
26: 5 whom I **s** unto you, both rising up early, 7971
26:12 The LORD **s** me to prophesy against this 7971
26:15 for of a truth the LORD hath **s** me unto 7971
26:22 Jehoiakim the king **s** men *into* Egypt, 7971
27:15 For I have not **s** them, saith the LORD, 7971
28: 9 that the LORD hath truly **s** him. 7971
28:15 The LORD hath not **s** thee; but 7971
29: 1 **s** from Jerusalem unto the residue of 7971
29: 3 whom Zedekiah king of Judah **s** unto 7971
29: 9 I have not **s** them, saith the LORD. 7971
29:19 which I **s** unto them by my servants 7971
29:20 whom I have **s** from Jerusalem to Babylon: 7971
29:25 Because thou hast **s** letters in thy name unto 7971
29:28 For therefore he **s** unto us *in* Babylon, 7971
29:31 I **s** him not, and he caused you to trust in a 7971
35:15 I have **s** also unto you all my servants 7971
36:14 Therefore all the princes **s** Jehudi the son of 7971
36:21 So the king **s** Jehudi to fet the roll: and 7971
37: 3 Zedekiah the king **s** Jehucal the son of 7971
37: 7 that **s** you unto me to inquire of me; 7971
37:17 Zedekiah the king **s**, and took him *out:* 7971
38:14 Zedekiah the king **s**, and took Jeremiah 7971
39:13 So Nebuzar-adan the captain of the guard **s**, 7971
39:14 Even they **s**, and took Jeremiah out of 7971
40:14 **s** Ishmael the son of Nethaniah to slay 7971
42: 9 unto whom ye **s** me to present your 7971
42:20 when ye **s** me unto the LORD your God, 7971
42:21 nor any *thing* for the which he hath **s** me 7971
43: 1 *for* which the LORD their God had **s** him 7971
43: 2 the LORD our God hath not **s** thee to say, 7971
44: 4 Howbeit I **s** unto you all my servants 7971
48:11 remained in him, and his **s** is not changed. 7381
49:14 an ambassador *is* **s** unto the heathen, 7971
La 1:13 From above hath he **s** fire into my bones, 7971
Eze 2: 9 I looked, behold, a hand *was* **s** unto me; 7971
3: 5 For thou *art* not **s** to a people of a strange 7971
3: 6 Surely, had I **s** thee to them, they would 7971
13: 6 the LORD hath not **s** them: and they have 7971
23:16 and **s** messengers unto them into Chaldea. 7971
23:40 that ye have **s** for men to come from far, 7971
23:40 from far, unto whom a messenger *was* **s**; 7971
31: 4 **s out** her little rivers unto all the trees of 7971
Da 3: 2 Nebuchadnezzar the king **s** to gather 7972
3:28 who hath **s** his angel, and delivered his 7972
5:24 *was* the part of the hand **s** from him; and 7972
6:22 My God hath **s** his angel, and hath shut 7972
10:11 for unto thee am I now **s**. And when he had 7971
Hos 5:13 to the Assyrian, and **s** to king Jareb: 7971
14: 7 the **s** thereof *shall be* as the wine of 2143
Joel 2:25 my great army which I **s** among you. 7971
Am 4:10 I have **s** among you the pestilence after 7971
7:10 Amaziah *the* priest of Beth-el **s** to 7971
Ob 1: 1 an ambassador is **s** among the heathen, 7971
Jnh 1: 4 the LORD **s out** a great wind into the sea, 2904
Mic 6: 4 I **s** before thee Moses, Aaron, and Miriam. 7971
Hag 1:12 as the LORD their God had **s** him, and 7971
Zec 1:10 These *are they* whom the LORD hath **s** to 7971
2: 8 After the glory hath he **s** me unto 7971
2: 9 know that the LORD of hosts hath **s** me. 7971
2:11 the LORD of hosts hath **s** me unto thee. 7971

S

Zec 4: 9 the LORD of hosts hath **s** me unto you. 7971
6:15 the LORD of hosts hath **s** me unto you. 7971
7: 2 When they had **s** *unto* the house of God 7971
7:12 the words which the LORD of hosts hath **s** 7971
9:11 by the blood of thy covenant I have **s forth** 7971
Mal 2: 4 ye shall know that I have **s** this 7971
Mt 2: 8 And he **s** them to Bethlehem, and said, Go *3992*
2:16 and **s forth**, and slew all the children that *649*
10: 5 These twelve Jesus **s forth**, and *649*
10:40 he that receiveth me receiveth him that **s** me. *649*
11: 2 works of Christ, he **s** two of his disciples, *3992*
13:36 Then Jesus **s** the multitude **away**, and *863*
14:10 And he **s**, and beheaded John in the prison. *3992*
14:22 other side, while he **s** the multitudes **away**. *630*
14:23 And when he had **s** the multitudes **away**, *630*
14:35 they **s out** into all that country round about, *649*
15:24 I am not **s** but unto the lost sheep of *649*
15:39 And he **s away** the multitude, and took ship, *630*
20: 2 a penny a day, he **s** them into his vineyard. *649*
21: 1 mount of Olives, then **s** Jesus two disciples, *649*
21:34 he **s** his servants to the husbandmen, *649*
21:36 Again, he **s** other servants moe than the first: *649*
21:37 But last *of all* he **s** unto them his son, saying, *649*
22: 3 And **s forth** his servants to call them that *649*
22: 4 Again, he **s forth** other servants, saying, *649*
22: 7 and he **s forth** his armies, and *3992*
22:16 And they **s out** unto him their disciples with *649*
23:37 and stonest them which are **s** unto thee, *649*
27:19 judgment seat, his wife **s** unto him, saying, *649*
Mk 1:43 charged him, and forthwith **s** him **away**; *1544*
3:31 standing without, **s** unto him, calling him. *649*
4:36 And when they had **s away** the multitude, *863*
6:17 For Herod himself had **s forth** and laid hold *649*
6:27 And immediately the king **s** an executioner, *649*
6:45 unto Bethsaida, while he **s away** the people. *630*
6:46 And when he had **s** them **away**, he departed *657*
8: 9 about four thousand: and he **s** them **away**. *630*
8:26 And he **s** him **away** to his house, saying, *649*
9:37 receiveth not me, but him that **s** me. *649*
12: 2 And at the season he **s** to the husbandmen a *649*
12: 3 and beat *him*, and **s** *him* **away** empty. *649*
12: 4 And again he **s** unto them another servant; *649*
12: 4 and **s** *him* **away** shamefully handled. *649*
12: 5 And again he **s** another; and him they killed, *649*
12: 6 he **s** him also last unto them, saying, *649*
Lk 1:19 and am **s** to speak unto thee, and to shew *649*
1:26 in the sixth month the angel Gabriel was **s** *649*
1:53 and the rich he hath **s** empty **away**. *1821*
4:18 he hath **s** me to heal the broken-hearted, *649*
4:26 But unto none of them was Elias **s**, *3992*
4:43 God to other cities also: for therefore am I **s**. *649*
7: 3 he **s** unto him *the* elders of the Jews, *649*
7: 6 the centurion **s** friends to him, saying unto *3992*
7:10 And they that were **s**, returning to *3992*
7:19 *him* two of his disciples **s** *them* to Jesus, *3992*
7:20 John Baptist hath **s** us unto thee, saying, *649*
8:38 be with him: but Jesus **s** him **away**, saying, *630*
9: 2 And he **s** them to preach the kingdom of *649*
9:48 shall receive me receiveth him that **s** me: *649*
9:52 And **s** messengers before his face: and *649*
10: 1 and **s** them two and two before his face into *649*
10:16 he that despiseth me despiseth him that **s** me. *649*
13:34 and stonest them that are **s** unto thee; *649*
14:17 And **s** his servant at supper time to say to *649*
15:15 and he **s** him into his fields to feed swine. *3992*
19:14 and **s** a message after him, saying, *649*
19:29 *mount* of Olives, he **s** two of his disciples, *649*
19:32 And they that were **s** went their way, and *649*
20:10 And at the season he **s** a servant to *649*
20:10 beat him, and **s** *him* **away** empty. *1821*
20:11 And again he **s** another servant: and *3992*
20:11 *him* shamefully, and **s** *him* **away** empty. *1821*
20:12 And again he **s** a third: and they wounded *3992*
20:20 And they watched *him*, and **s forth** spies, *649*
22: 8 And he **s** Peter and John, saying, Go and *649*
22:35 When I **s** you without purse, and scrip, and *649*
23: 7 he **s** him to Herod, who himself also was at *375*
23:11 a gorgeous robe, and **s** him **again** to Pilate. *375*
23:15 No, nor yet Herod: for I **s** you to him; *375*
Jn 1: 6 There was a man **s** from God, whose name *649*
1: 8 but *was* **s** to bear witness of *that* Light. NIG
1:19 when the Jews **s** priests and Levites from *649*
1:22 that we may give an answer to them that **s** *3992*
1:24 And they which were **s** were of *649*
1:33 but he that **s** me to baptize with water, *3992*
3:17 For God **s** not his Son into the world to *649*
3:28 am not the Christ, but that I am **s** before him. *649*
3:34 For he whom God hath **s** speaketh the words *649*
4:34 My meat is to do the will of him that **s** me, *3992*
4:38 I **s** you to reap *that* whereon ye bestowed no *649*
5:23 honoureth not the Father which hath **s** him. *3992*
5:24 and believeth on him that **s** me, *3992*
5:30 but the will of the Father which hath **s** me. *3992*
5:33 Ye **s** unto John, and he bare witness unto *649*
5:36 witness of me, that the Father hath **s** me. *649*
5:37 And the Father himself, which hath **s** me, *3992*
5:38 for whom he hath **s**, him ye believe not. *649*
6:29 that ye believe on *him* whom he hath **s**. *649*
6:38 own will, but the will of him that **s** me. *3992*
6:39 And this is the Father's will which hath **s** *3992*
6:40 And this is the will of him that **s** me, *3992*
6:44 except the Father which hath **s** me draw *3992*
6:57 As the living Father hath **s** me, and I live by *649*
7:16 My doctrine is not mine, but his that **s** me. *3992*
7:18 but he that seeketh his glory that **s** him, *3992*
7:28 but he that **s** me is true, whom ye know not. *3992*
7:29 for I am from him, and he hath **s** me. *649*
7:32 and the chief priests **s** officers to take him. *649*
7:33 with you, and *then* I go unto him that **s** me. *3992*
8:16 not alone, but I and the Father that **s** me. *3992*
8:18 the Father that **s** me beareth witness of me. *3992*
8:26 but he that **s** me is true; and I speak to *3992*
8:29 And he that **s** me is with me: the Father *3992*
8:42 neither came I of myself, but he **s** me. *649*
9: 4 I must work the works of him that **s** me, *3992*
Jn 9: 7 of Siloam, (which is by interpretation, **S**.) *649*
10:36 and **s** into the world, Thou blasphemest; *649*
11: 3 Therefore *his* sisters **s** unto him, saying, *649*
11:42 *it*, that they may believe that thou hast **s** me. *649*
12:44 believeth not on me, but on him that **s** me. *3992*
12:45 And he that seeth me seeth him that **s** me. *3992*
12:49 but the Father which **s** me, he gave me a *3992*
13:16 neither **he that is s** greater than he that sent *652*
13:16 neither he that is sent greater than he that **s** *3992*
13:20 he that receiveth me receiveth him that **s** *3992*
14:24 is not mine, but the Father's which **s** me. *3992*
15:21 because they know not him that **s** me. *3992*
16: 5 But now I go my way to him that **s** me; and *3992*
17: 3 and Jesus Christ, whom thou hast **s**. *649*
17:18 As thou hast **s** me into the world, even *so* *649*
17:18 even *so* have I also **s** them into the world. *649*
17:21 that the world may believe that thou hast **s** *649*
17:23 that the world may know that thou hast **s** me, *649*
17:25 and these have known that thou hast **s** me. *649*
18:24 Now Annas had **s** him bound unto Caiaphas *649*
20:21 as *my* Father hath **s** me, even *so* send I you. *649*
Ac 3:26 raised up his Son Jesus, **s** him to bless you, *649*
5:21 and **s** to the prison to have them brought. *649*
7:12 corn in Egypt, he **s out** our fathers first. *1821*
7:14 Then **s** Joseph, and called his father Jacob to *649*
8:14 of God, they **s** unto them Peter and John: *649*
9:17 hath **s** me, that thou mightest receive thy *649*
9:30 to Cesarea, and **s** him **forth** to Tarsus. *1821*
9:38 Peter was there, they **s** unto him two men, *649*
10: 8 *these things* unto them, he **s** them to Joppa. *649*
10:17 the men which were **s** from Cornelius had *649*
10:20 doubting nothing: for I have **s** them. *649*
10:21 men which were **s** unto him from Cornelius; *649*
10:29 without gainsaying, as soon as I was **s for**: *3343*
10:29 therefore for what intent ye have **s for** me? *3343*
10:33 Immediately therefore I **s** to thee; and *3992*
10:36 The word which *God* **s** unto the children of *649*
11:11 house where I was, **s** from Cesarea unto me. *649*
11:22 and they **s forth** Barnabas, that *he* should *1821*
11:30 **s** it to the elders by the hands of Barnabas *649*
12:11 that the Lord hath **s** his angel, and *1821*
13: 3 laid *their* hands on them, they **s** *them* **away**. *630*
13: 4 So they, being **s forth** by the Holy Ghost, *1599*
13:15 the prophets the rulers of the synagogue **s** *649*
13:26 to you is the word of this salvation **s**. *649*
15:27 We have **s** therefore Judas and Silas, *649*
16:35 the magistrates **s** the sergeants, saying, *649*
16:36 to Paul, The magistrates have **s** to let you go: *649*
17:10 And the brethren immediately **s away** Paul *1599*
17:14 immediately the brethren **s away** Paul to go *1821*
19:22 So he **s** into Macedonia two of them that *649*
19:31 of Asia, which were his friends, **s** unto him, *3992*
20:17 And from Miletus he **s** to Ephesus, and *3992*
23:30 I **s** straightway to thee, and *3992*
24:24 he **s for** Paul, and heard him concerning *3343*
24:26 wherefore he **s for** him the oftener, and *3343*
28:28 that the salvation of God is **s** unto *649*
Ro 10:15 And how shall they preach, except they be **s**? *649*
16: S *s* by Phebe servant of the church at NIG
1Co 1:17 For Christ **s** me not to baptize, but to preach *649*
4:17 For this cause have I **s** unto you Timotheus, *3992*
2Co 8:18 And we have **s with** him the brother, *4842*
8:22 And we have **s with** them our brother, *4842*
9: 3 Yet have I **s** the brethren, lest our boasting *3992*
12:17 of you by any of them whom I **s** unto you? *649*
12:18 I desired Titus, and with *him* I **s** a brother. *4882*
Gal 4: 4 God **s forth** his Son, made of a woman, *1821*
4: 6 God hath **s forth** the Spirit of his Son into *1821*
Eph 6:22 Whom I have **s** unto you for the same *3992*
Php 2:28 I **s** him therefore the more carefully, that, *3992*
4:16 For even in Thessalonica ye **s** once and *3992*
4:18 the *things which were* **s** from you, NIG
Col 4: 8 Whom I have **s** unto you for the same *3992*
1Th 3: 2 And **s** Timotheus, our brother, and *3992*
3: 5 no longer forbear, I **s** to know your faith, *3992*
2Ti 4:12 And Tychicus have I **s** to Ephesus. *649*
Phm 1:12 Whom I have **s again**: thou therefore *375*
Heb 1:14 **s forth** to minister for them who shall be *649*
Jas 2:25 and had **s** *them* **out** another way? *1544*
1Pe 1:12 with the Holy Ghost **s** *down* from heaven; *649*
2:14 as unto them that are **s** by him for *3992*
1Jn 4: 9 that God **s** his only begotten Son into *649*
4:10 **s** his Son *to be* the propitiation for our sins. *649*
4:14 do testify that the Father **s** the Son *to be* *649*
Rev 1: 1 and he **s** and signified *it* by his angel unto his *649*
5: 6 which are the seven spirits of God **s forth** *649*
22: 6 the Lord God of the holy prophets **s** his *649*
22:16 I Jesus have **s** mine angel to testify unto *3992*

SENTENCE (11) [SENTENCES]
Dt 17: 9 and they shall shew thee the **s** of judgment: 1697
17:10 thou shalt do according to the **s**, which *they* 1697
17:11 According to the **s** of the law which they NIH
17:11 thou shalt not decline from the **s** which they 1697
Ps 17: 2 Let my **s** come forth from thy presence; 4941
Pr 16:10 A **divine s** *is* in the lips of the king: 7081
Ecc 8:11 Because **s** *against* an evil work is not 6599
Jer 4:12 now also will I give **s** against them. 4941
Lk 23:24 And Pilate **gave s** that it should be as they *1948*
Ac 15:19 Wherefore my **s** is, that *we* trouble not *2919*
2Co 1: 9 But we had the **s** of death in ourselves, *610*

SENTENCES (2) [SENTENCE]
Da 5:12 shewing of **hard s**, and dissolving of doubts, 280
8:23 and understanding **dark s**, shall stand up. 2420

SENTEST (4) [SEND]
Ex 15: 7 thou **s forth** thy wrath, *which* consumed 7971
Nu 13:27 We came unto the land whither thou **s** us, 7971
24:12 to thy messengers which thou **s** unto me, 7971
1Ki 5: 8 I have considered *the things* which thou **s** 7971

SENUAH (1)
Ne 11: 9 Judah the son of **S** *was* second over 5574

SEORIM (1)
1Ch 24: 8 The third to Harim, the fourth to **S**, 8188

SEPARATE (32) [SEPARATED, SEPARATETH, SEPARATING, SEPARATION]
Ge 13: 9 **s** thyself, I pray thee, from me: if *thou wilt* 6504
30:40 Jacob did **s** the lambs, and set the faces of 6504
49:26 head of him *that was* **s from** his brethren. 5139
Lev 15:31 Thus shall ye **s** the children of Israel from 5144
22: 2 that they **s** themselves from the holy *things* 5144
Nu 6: 2 woman shall **s** *themselves* to vow a vow of 6381
6: 2 to **s** *themselves* unto the LORD: 5144
6: 3 He shall **s** *himself* from wine and 5144
8:14 Thus shalt thou **s** the Levites from among 914
16:21 **S** yourselves from among this congregation, 914
Dt 19: 2 Thou shalt **s** three cities for thee in the midst 914
19: 7 Thou shalt **s** three cities for thee. 914
29:21 the LORD shall **s** him unto evil out of all 914
Jos 16: 9 the **s** cities for the children of Ephraim 3995
1Ki 8:53 For thou didst **s** them from among all 914
Ezr 10:11 and **s** yourselves from the people of the land, 914
Jer 37:12 to **s** himself thence in the midst of 2505
Eze 41:12 **s place** *at* the end toward the west *was* 1508
41:13 the **s place**, and the building, with the walls 1508
41:14 of the **s place** toward the east, an hundred 1508
41:15 against the **s place** which *was* behind it, 1508
42: 1 chamber that *was* over against the **s place**, 1508
42:10 over against the **s place**, and over against 1508
42:13 which *are* before the **s place**, 1508
Mt 25:32 and he shall **s** them one from another, as a *873*
Lk 6:22 when they shall **s** you *from their company*, *873*
Ac 13: 2 **S** me Barnabas and Saul for the work *873*
Ro 8:35 Who shall **s** us from the love of Christ? *5563*
8:39 shall be able to **s** us from the love of God, *5563*
2Co 6:17 and be ye **s**, saith the Lord, and touch not *873*
Heb 7:26 **s** from sinners, and made higher than *5563*
Jude 1:19 These be they who **s** themselves, sensual, *592*

SEPARATED (33) [SEPARATE]
Ge 13:11 they **s** themselves the one from the other. 6504
13:14 after that Lot was **s** from him, Lift up now 6504
25:23 two manner of people shall be **s** from thy 6504
Ex 33:16 so shall we be **s**, I and thy people, from all 6395
Lev 20:24 which have **s** you from *other* people. 914
20:25 which I have **s** from you as unclean. 914
Nu 16: 9 that the God of Israel hath **s** you from 914
Dt 10: 8 At that time the LORD **s** the tribe of Levi, 914
32: 8 when he **s** the sons of Adam, 6504
33:16 head of him *that was* **s from** his brethren. 5139
1Ch 12: 8 of the Gadites there **s** themselves unto David 914
23:13 Aaron was **s**, that he should sanctify 914
25: 1 the captains of the host **s** to the service of 914
2Ch 25:10 Amaziah **s** them, to wit, the army that was 914
Ezr 6:21 all such as had **s** themselves unto them from 914
8:24 I **s** twelve of the chief of the priests, 914
9: 1 have not **s** themselves from the people of 914
10: 8 himself **s** from the congregation of those that 914
10:16 were **s**, and sat down in the first day of 914
Ne 4:19 and large, and we *are* **s** upon the wall, 6504
9: 2 the seed of Israel **s** themselves from all 914
10:28 all they that had **s** themselves from 914
13: 3 that they **s** from Israel all the mixed 914
Pr 18: 1 having **s** himself, seeketh *and* 6504
19: 4 but the poor is **s** from his neighbour. 6504
Isa 56: 3 The LORD hath **utterly s** me from his 914+914
59: 2 your iniquities have **s** between you and your 914
Hos 4:14 for themselves are **s** with whores, and 6504
9:10 and **s** themselves unto *that* shame; 5144
Ac 19: 9 he departed from them, and **s** the disciples, *873*
Ro 1: 1 *to be* an apostle, **s** unto the gospel of God, *873*
Gal 1:15 who **s** me from my mother's womb, and *873*
2:12 they were come, he withdrew and **s** himself, *873*

SEPARATETH (5) [SEPARATE]
Nu 6: 5 *in* the which he **s** *himself* unto the LORD, 5144
6: 6 All the days that he **s** *himself* unto 5144
Pr 16:28 and a whisperer **s** chief friends. 6504
17: 9 but he that repeateth a matter **s** very friends. 6504
Eze 14: 7 which **s** himself from me, and setteth up his 5144

SEPARATING (1) [SEPARATE]
Zec 7: 3 **s** myself, as I have done these so 5144

SEPARATION (26) [SEPARATE]
Lev 12: 2 according to the days of the **s** for her 5079
12: 5 she shall be unclean two weeks, as *in* her **s**: 5079
15:20 every *thing* that she lieth upon in her **s** shall 5079
15:25 blood many days out of the time of her **s**, 5079
15:25 or if it run beyond the time of her **s**; 5079
15:25 uncleanness shall be as the days of her **s**: 5079
15:26 issue shall be unto her as the bed of her **s**: 5079
15:26 be unclean, as the uncleanness of her **s**. 5079
Nu 6: 4 All the days of his **s** shall he eat nothing 5145
6: 5 All the days of the vow of his **s** there shall 5145
6: 8 All the days of his **s** he *is* holy unto 5145
6:12 unto the LORD the days of his **s**, 5145
6:12 shall be lost, because his **s** was defiled. 5145
6:13 when the days of his **s** are fulfilled: 5145
6:18 the Nazarite shall shave the head of his **s** *at* 5145
6:18 shall take the hair of the head of his **s**, and 5145
6:19 after *the hair of* his **s** is shaven: 5145
6:21 *of* his offering unto the LORD for his **s**, 5145
6:21 so he must do after the law of his **s**. 5145
19: 9 of the children of Israel for a water of **s**: 5079
19:13 the water of **s** was not sprinkled upon him, 5079
19:20 the water of **s** hath not been sprinkled upon 5079
19:21 that he that sprinkleth the water of **s** shall 5079
19:21 he that toucheth the water of **s** shall be 5079
31:23 it shall be purified with the water of **s**: 5079
Eze 42:20 to **make a s** between the sanctuary and 914

SEPHAR (1)
Ge 10:30 as thou goest unto **S**, a mount of the east. 5611

SEPHARAD (1)
Ob 1:20 the captivity of Jerusalem, which *is* in **S**, 5614

SEPHARVAIM (6) [SEPHARVITES]
2Ki 17:24 from **S**, and placed *them* in the cities of 5617
17:31 and Anammelech, the gods of **S**. 5617
18:34 where *are* the gods of **S**, Hena, and Ivah? 5617
19:13 the king of the city of **S**, *of* Hena, and Ivah? 5617
Isa 36:19 where *are* the gods of **S**? and have they 5617
37:13 the king of the city of **S**, Hena, and Ivah? 5617

SEPHARVITES (1) [SEPHARVAIM]
2Ki 17:31 the **S** burnt their children in fire to 5616

SEPULCHRE (54) [SEPULCHRES]
Ge 23: 6 none of us shall withhold from thee his **s**, 6913
Dt 34: 6 but no man knoweth of his **s** unto this day. 6900
Jdg 8:32 was buried in the **s** of Joash his father, in 6913
1Sa 10: 2 thou shalt find two men by Rachel's **s** in 6900
2Sa 2:32 and buried him in the **s** of his father, 6913
4:12 and buried *it* in the **s** of Abner in Hebron. 6913
17:23 died, and was buried in the **s** of his father. 6913
21:14 in Zelah, in the **s** of Kish his father: 6913
1Ki 13:22 thy carcase shall not come unto the **s** of thy 6913
13:31 bury me in the **s** wherein the man of God *is* 6913
2Ki 9:28 buried him in his **s** with his fathers in 6900
13:21 and they cast the man into the **s** of Elisha: 6913
21:26 he was buried in his **s** in the garden of 6900
23:17 *It is* the **s** of the man of God, which came 6913
23:30 *to* Jerusalem, and buried him in his own **s**. 6900
Ps 5: 9 their throat *is* an open **s**; they flatter with 6913
Isa 22:16 that thou hast hewed thee out a **s** here, 6913
22:16 *as he* that heweth him out a **s** on high, *and* 6913
Jer 5:16 Their quiver *is* as an open **s**, they *are* all 6913
Mt 27:60 he rolled a great stone to the door of the **s**, *3419*
27:61 the other Mary, sitting over against the **s**. *5028*
27:64 that the **s** be made sure until the third day, *5028*
27:66 So they went, and made the **s** sure, *5028*
28: 1 and the other Mary to see the **s**. *5028*
28: 8 And they departed quickly from the **s** with *3419*
Mk 15:46 laid him in a **s** which was hewn out of a *3419*
15:46 and rolled a stone unto the door of the **s**. *3419*
16: 2 they came unto the **s** at the rising of *3419*
16: 3 us away the stone from the door of the **s**? *3419*
16: 5 And entering into the **s**, they saw a young *3419*
16: 8 they went out quickly, and fled from the **s**; *3419*
Lk 23:53 and laid it in a **s** *that was* hewn in stone, *3418*
23:55 and beheld the **s**, and how his body was *3419*
24: 1 early in the morning, they came unto the **s**, *3418*
24: 2 found the stone rolled away from the **s**. *3419*
24: 9 And returned from the **s**, and told all these *3419*
24:12 Then arose Peter, and ran unto the **s**; and *3419*
24:22 us astonished, which were early at the **s**; *3419*
24:24 of them which were with us went to the **s**, *3419*
Jn 19:41 and in the garden a new **s**, wherein was *3419*
19:42 of the Jews' preparation *day;* for the **s** was *3419*
20: 1 unto the **s**, and seeth the stone taken away *3419*
20: 1 and seeth the stone taken away from the **s**. *3419*
20: 2 have taken away the Lord out of the **s**, *3419*
20: 3 and *that* other disciple, and came to the **s**. *3419*
20: 4 did outrun Peter, and came first to the **s**. *3419*
20: 6 and went into the **s**, and seeth the linen *3419*
20: 8 which came first to the **s**, and he saw, and *3419*
20:11 But Mary stood without at the **s** weeping: *3419*
20:11 she stooped down, and looked into the **s**, *3419*
Ac 2:29 buried, and his **s** is with us unto this day. *3418*
7:16 laid in the **s** that Abraham bought for a sum *3418*
13:29 *him* down from the tree, and laid *him* in a **s**. *3419*
Ro 3:13 Their throat *is* an open **s**; with their tongues *5028*

SEPULCHRES (16) [SEPULCHRE]
Ge 23: 6 in the choice of our **s** bury thy dead; 6913
2Ki 23:16 he spied the **s** that *were* there in the mount, 6913
23:16 took the bones out of the **s**, and burnt *them* 6913
2Ch 16:14 they buried him in his own **s**, which he had 6913
21:20 city of David, but not in the **s** of the kings. 6913
24:25 they buried him not in the **s** of the kings. 6913
28:27 they brought him not into the **s** of the kings 6913
32:33 they buried him in the chiefest of the **s** of 6913
35:24 was buried in *one of the* **s** of his fathers. 6913
Ne 2: 3 the place of my fathers' **s**, *lieth* waste, and 6913
2: 5 unto the city of my fathers' **s**, that I may 6913
3:16 unto *the place* over against the **s** of David, 6913
Mt 23:27 for ye are like unto whited **s**, which indeed *5028*
23:29 and garnish the **s** of the righteous, *3419*
Lk 11:47 for ye build the **s** of the prophets, and *3419*
11:48 indeed killed them, and ye build their **s**. *3419*

SERAH (2)
Ge 46:17 and Ishui, and Beriah, and **S** their sister: 8294
1Ch 7:30 and Ishuai, and Beriah, and **S** their sister. 8294

SERAIAH (20)
2Sa 8:17 *were* the priests; and **S** *was* the scribe; 8304
2Ki 25:18 the captain of the guard took **S** the chief 8304
25:23 **S** the son of Tanhumeth the Netophathite, 8304
1Ch 4:13 the sons of Kenaz; Othniel, and **S**: and 8304
4:14 **S** begat Joab, the father of the valley of 8304
4:35 of Josibiah, the son of **S**, the son of Asiel, 8304
6:14 Azariah begat **S**, and Seraiah begat 8304
6:14 begat Seraiah, and **S** begat Jehozadak, 8304
Ezr 2: 2 **S**, Reelaiah, Mordecai, Bilshan, Mizpar, 8304
7: 1 Ezra the son of **S**, the son of Azariah, 8304
Ne 10: 2 **S**, Azariah, Jeremiah, 8304
11:11 **S** the son of Hilkiah, the son of Meshullam, 8304
12: 1 of Shealtiel, and Jeshua: **S**, Jeremiah, Ezra, 8304
12:12 of **S**, Meraiah; of Jeremiah, Hananiah; 8304
Jer 36:26 **S** the son of Azriel, and Shelemiah the son 8304
40: 8 **S** the son of Tanhumeth, and the sons of 8304
51:59 prophet commanded **S** the son of Neriah, 8304
51:59 of his reign. And *this* **S** *was* a quiet prince. 8304
51:61 Jeremiah said to **S**, When thou comest *to* 8304
52:24 the captain of the guard took **S** the chief 8304

SERAPHIMS (2)
Isa 6: 2 Above it stood the **s**: each one had six 8314
6: 6 flew one of the **s** unto me, having a live 8314

SERAPHS See SERAPHIMS

SERED (2)
Ge 46:14 sons of Zebulun; **S**, and Elon, and Jahleel. 5624
Nu 26:26 of **S**, the family of the Sardites: of Elon, 5624

SEREDITE See SARDITES

SERGEANTS (2)
Ac 16:35 the magistrates sent the **s**, saying, Let those *4465*
16:38 And the **s** told these words unto *4465*

SERGIUS (1)
Ac 13: 7 with the deputy *of the country,* **S** Paulus, *4588*

SERIOUSNESS See GRAVITY

SERPENT (38) [SERPENT'S, SERPENTS]
Ge 3: 1 Now the **s** was more subtil than any beast 5175
3: 2 the woman said unto the **s**, We may eat of 5175
3: 4 the **s** said unto the woman, Ye shall not 5175
3:13 The **s** beguiled me, and I did eat. 5175
3:14 the LORD God said unto the **s**, 5175
49:17 Dan shall be a **s** by the way, an adder in 5175
Ex 4: 3 he cast it on the ground, and it became a **s**; 5175
7: 9 *it* before Pharaoh, *and* it shall become a **s**. 8577
7:10 and before his servants, and it became a **s**. 8577
7:15 the rod which was turned to a **s** shalt thou 5175
Nu 21: 8 Make thee a fiery **s**, and set it upon a pole: NIH
21: 9 Moses made a **s** of brass, and put it upon a 5175
21: 9 came to pass, that if a **s** had bitten *any* man, 5175
21: 9 when he beheld the **s** of brass, he lived. 5175
2Ki 18: 4 brake in pieces the brasen **s** that Moses had 5175
Job 26:13 his hand hath formed the crooked **s**. 5175
Ps 58: 4 Their poison *is* like the poison of a **s**: 5175
140: 3 They have sharpened their tongues like a **s**; 5175
Pr 23:32 At the last it biteth like a **s**, and 5175
30:19 eagle in the air; the way of a **s** upon a rock; 5175
Ecc 10: 8 whoso breaketh a hedge, a **s** shall bite him. 5175
10:11 Surely the **s** will bite without enchantment; 5175
Isa 14:29 and his fruit *shall be* a **fiery** flying **s**. 8314
27: 1 sword shall punish leviathan the piercing **s**, 5175
27: 1 even leviathan *that* crooked **s**; 5175
30: 6 and old lion, the viper and **fiery** flying **s**, 8314
Jer 46:22 The voice thereof shall go like a **s**; for they 5175
Am 5:19 leaned his hand on the wall, and a **s** bit him. 5175
9: 3 thence will I command the **s**, and he shall 5175
Mic 7:17 They shall lick the dust like a **s**, they shall 5175
Mt 7:10 Or if he ask a fish, will he give him a **s**? *3789*
Lk 11:11 *ask* a fish, will he for a fish give him a **s**? *3789*
Jn 3:14 And as Moses lifted up the **s** in *3789*
2Co 11: 3 as the **s** beguiled Eve through his subtilty, *3789*
Rev 12: 9 the great dragon was cast *out, that* old **s**, *3789*
12:14 and half a time, from the face of the **s**. *3789*
12:15 And the **s** cast out of his mouth water as a *3789*
20: 2 *that* old **s**, which is the devil, and Satan, *3789*

SERPENT'S (2) [SERPENT]
Isa 14:29 for out of the **s** root shall come forth a 5175
65:25 dust *shall be* the **s** meat. They shall not hurt 5175

SERPENTS (13) [SERPENT]
Ex 7:12 every man his rod, and they became **s**: 8577
Nu 21: 6 the LORD sent fiery **s** among the people, 5175
21: 7 that he take away the **s** from us. 5175
Dt 8:15 *wherein were* fiery **s**, and scorpions, and 5175
32:24 upon them, with the poison of **s** of the dust. 2119
Jer 8:17 For behold, I will send **s**, cockatrices, 5175
Mt 10:16 be ye therefore wise as **s**, and harmless as *3789*
23:33 *Ye* **s**, *ye* generation of vipers, how can ye *3789*
Mk 16:18 They shall take up **s**; and if they drink any *3789*
Lk 10:19 I give unto you power to tread on **s** and *3789*
1Co 10: 9 them also tempted, and were destroyed of **s**. *3789*
Jas 3: 7 of birds, and of **s**, and of *things* in the sea, *2062*
Rev 9:19 for their tails *were* like unto **s**, and *3789*

SERUG (5)
Ge 11:20 Reu lived two and thirty years, and begat **S**: 8286
11:21 Reu lived after he begat **S** two hundred 8286
11:22 And **S** lived thirty years, and begat Nahor: 8286
11:23 **S** lived after he begat Nahor two hundred 8286
1Ch 1:26 **S**, Nahor, Terah, 8286

SERVANT (493) [SERVE]
Ge 9:25 a **s** of servants shall he be unto his brethren. 5650
9:26 God of Shem; and Canaan shall be his **s**. 5650
9:27 tents of Shem; and Canaan shall be his **s**. 5650
18: 3 pass not away, I pray thee, from thy **s**: 5650
18: 5 for therefore are you come to your **s**. 5650
19:19 thy **s** hath found grace in thy sight, and 5650
24: 2 Abraham said unto his eldest **s** of his house 5650
24: 5 the **s** said unto him, Peradventure 5650
24: 9 the **s** put his hand under the thigh of 5650
24:10 the **s** took ten camels of the camels of his 5650
24:14 she *that* thou hast appointed for thy **s** Isaac; 5650
24:17 the **s** ran to meet her, and said, Let me, 5650
24:34 And he said, I *am* Abraham's **s**. 5650
24:52 that, when Abraham's **s** heard their words, 5650
24:53 the **s** brought forth jewels of silver, and 5650
24:59 her nurse, and Abraham's **s**, and his men. 5650
24:61 and the **s** took Rebekah, and went his way. 5650
24:65 For she had said unto the **s**, What man *is* 5650
24:65 the **s** had said, It *is* my master: therefore 5650
24:66 the **s** told Isaac all things that he had done. 5650
26:24 multiply thy seed for my **s** Abraham's sake. 5650
32: 4 Thy **s** Jacob saith thus, I have sojourned 5650
32:10 which thou hast shewed unto thy **s**; 5650
32:18 thou shalt say, *They be* thy **s** Jacob's; it *is* a 5650
32:20 Behold, thy **s** Jacob *is* behind us. 5650
33: 5 which God hath graciously given thy **s**. 5650
Ge 33:14 my lord, I pray thee, pass over before his **s**: 5650
39:17 saying, The Hebrew **s**, which thou hast 5650
39:19 After this manner did thy **s** to me; 5650
41:12 a Hebrew, **s** to the captain of the guard; 5650
43:28 Thy **s** our father *is* in good health, he *is* yet 5650
44:10 he with whom it is found shall be my **s**; and 5650
44:17 hand the cup is found, he shall be my **s**; 5650
44:18 said, O my lord, let thy **s**, I pray thee, 5650
44:18 and let not thine anger burn against thy **s**: 5650
44:24 it came to pass when we came up unto thy **s** 5650
44:27 thy **s** my father said unto us, Ye know that 5650
44:30 therefore when I come to thy **s** my father, 5650
44:31 of thy **s** our father with sorrow to the grave. 5650
44:32 For thy **s** became surety for the lad unto my 5650
44:33 let thy **s** abide instead of the lad a bondman 5650
49:15 to bear, and became a **s** unto tribute. 5647
Ex 4:10 nor since thou hast spoken unto thy **s**: 5650
12:44 But every man's **s** that is bought for money, 5650
12:45 and a **hired s** shall not eat thereof. 7916
14:31 and believed the LORD, and his **s** Moses. 5650
21: 2 If thou buy a Hebrew **s**, six years he shall 5650
21: 5 if the **s** shall plainly say, I love my master, 5650
21:20 if a man smite his **s**, or his maid, with a rod, 5650
21:26 if a man smite the eye of his **s**, or the eye of 5650
33:11 his **s** Joshua, the son of Nun, a young man, 8334
Lev 22:10 or a **hired s**, shall not eat *of* the holy *thing.* 7916
25: 6 for thy **s**, and for thy maid, and for thy 5650
25: 6 for thy **hired s**, and for thy stranger that 7916
25:40 *But* as a **hired s**, *and* as a sojourner, 7916
25:50 according to the time of a **hired s** shall it be 7916
25:53 *And* as a yearly **hired s** shall he be with 7916
Nu 11:11 Wherefore hast thou afflicted thy **s**? 5650
11:28 the **s** of Moses, *one* of his young men, 8334
12: 7 My **s** Moses *is* not so, who *is* faithful in all 5650
12: 8 were ye not afraid to speak against my **s** 5650
14:24 my **s** Caleb, because he had another spirit 5650
Dt 3:24 thou hast begun to shew thy **s** thy greatness, 5650
5:15 remember that thou wast a **s** in the land of 5650
15:17 the door, and he shall be thy **s** for ever. 5650
15:18 for he hath been worth a double **hired s** *to* 7916
23:15 Thou shalt not deliver unto his master the **s** 5650
24:14 Thou shalt not oppress a **hired s** *that is* 7916
34: 5 So Moses the **s** of the LORD died there in 5650
Jos 1: 1 Now after the death of Moses the **s** of 5650
1: 2 Moses my **s** is dead; now therefore arise, 5650
1: 7 which Moses my **s** commanded thee: 5650
1:13 Remember the word which Moses the **s** of 5650
1:15 which Moses the LORD'S **s** gave you on 5650
5:14 unto him, What saith my lord unto his **s**? 5650
8:31 As Moses the **s** of the LORD commanded 5650
8:33 as Moses the **s** of the LORD had 5650
9:24 his **s** Moses to give you all the land, 5650
11:12 as Moses the **s** of the LORD commanded. 5650
11:15 As the LORD commanded Moses his **s**, so 5650
12: 6 Them did Moses the **s** of the LORD and 5650
12: 6 Moses the **s** of the LORD gave it *for* a 5650
13: 8 *even* as Moses the **s** of the LORD gave 5650
14: 7 Forty years old *was* I when Moses the **s** of 5650
18: 7 which Moses the **s** of the LORD gave 5650
22: 2 Ye have kept all that Moses the **s** of 5650
22: 4 which Moses the **s** of the LORD gave you 5650
22: 5 which Moses the **s** of the LORD charged 5650
24:29 the **s** of the LORD, died, *being* an hundred 5650
Jdg 2: 8 the **s** of the LORD, died, *being* an hundred 5650
7:10 go thou with Phurah thy **s** down to the host: 5288
7:11 went he down with Phurah his **s** unto 5288
15:18 this great deliverance into the hand of thy **s**: 5650
19: 3 having his **s** with him, and a couple of 5288
19: 9 he, and his concubine, and his **s**, his father 5288
19:11 the **s** said unto his master, Come, I pray 5288
19:13 he said unto his **s**, Come, and let us draw 5288
Ru 2: 5 said Boaz unto his **s** that was set over 5288
2: 6 the **s** that was set over the reapers answered 5288
1Sa 2:13 the priest's **s** came, while the flesh was in 5288
2:15 the priest's **s** came, and said to the man that 5288
3: 9 shalt say, Speak, LORD; for thy **s** heareth. 5650
3:10 Samuel answered, Speak; for thy **s** heareth. 5650
9: 5 Saul said to his **s** that *was* with him, Come, 5288
9: 7 said Saul to his **s**, But behold, *if* we go, 5288
9: 8 the **s** answered Saul again, and said, 5288
9:10 said Saul to his **s**, Well said; come, let us 5288
9:22 Samuel took Saul and his **s**, and 5288
9:27 Bid the **s** pass on before us, (and he passed 5288
10:14 Saul's uncle said unto him and to his **s**, 5288
17:32 thy **s** will go and fight with this Philistine. 5650
17:34 Thy **s** kept his father's sheep, and 5650
17:36 Thy **s** slew both the lion and the bear: and 5650
17:58 *I am* the son of thy **s** Jesse 5650
19: 4 unto him, Let not the king sin against his **s**, 5650
20: 7 say thus, *It is* well; thy **s** shall have peace: 5650
20: 8 Therefore thou shalt deal kindly with thy **s**; 5650
20: 8 for thou hast brought thy **s** into a covenant 5650
22: 8 my son hath stirred up my **s** against me, 5650
22:15 let not the king impute *any* thing unto his **s**, 5650
22:15 for thy **s** knew nothing of all this, less or 5650
23:10 thy **s** hath certainly heard that Saul seeketh 5650
23:11 Will Saul come down, as thy **s** hath heard? 5650
23:11 God of Israel, I beseech thee, tell thy **s**. 5650
25:39 of Nabal, and hath kept his **s** from evil: 5650
25:41 *let* thine handmaid *be* a **s** to wash the feet 8198
26:18 doth my lord thus pursue after his **s**? 5650
26:19 let my lord the king hear the words of his **s**. 5650
27: 5 for why should thy **s** dwell in the royal city 5650
27:12 therefore he shall be my **s** for ever. 5650
28: 2 Surely thou shalt know what thy **s** can do. 5650
29: 3 this David, the **s** of Saul the king of Israel, 5650
29: 8 what hast thou found in thy **s** so long as I 5650
30:13 a young man of Egypt, **s** to an Amalekite; 5650
2Sa 3:18 By the hand of my **s** David I will save my 5650
7: 5 Go and tell my **s** David, Thus saith 5650
7: 8 so shalt thou say unto my **s** David, 5650
7:20 for thou, Lord GOD, knowest thy **s**. 5650
7:21 great things, to make thy **s** know *them.* 5650
7:25 that thou hast spoken concerning thy **s**, 5650
7:26 let the house of thy **s** David be established 5650

S

2Sa 7:27 God of Israel, hast revealed to thy **s**, saying, 5650
7:27 hath thy **s** found in his heart to pray this 5650
7:28 hast promised this goodness unto thy **s**: 5650
7:29 let it please thee to bless the house of thy **s**, 5650
7:29 with thy blessing let the house of thy **s** be 5650
9: 2 *there was* of the house of Saul a **s** whose 5650
9: 2 *Art* thou Ziba? And he said, Thy **s** *is he.* 5650
9: 6 And he answered, Behold thy **s**. 5650
9: 8 he bowed himself, and said, What *is* thy **s**, 5650
9: 9 called to Ziba, Saul's **s**, and said unto him, 5288
9:11 my lord the king hath commanded his **s**, 5650
9:11 commanded his servant, so shall thy **s** do. 5650
11:21 Thy **s** Uriah the Hittite is dead also. 5650
11:24 and thy **s** Uriah the Hittite is dead also. 5650
13:17 he called his **s** that ministered unto him, 5288
13:18 his **s** brought her out, and bolted the door 8334
13:24 said, Behold now, thy **s** hath sheepshearers; 5650
13:24 and his servants go with thy **s**. 5650
13:35 the king's sons come: as thy **s** said, so it is. 5650
14:19 for thy **s** Joab, he bade me, and he put all 5650
14:20 fetch about *this* form of speech hath thy **s** 5650
14:22 To day thy **s** knoweth that I have found 5650
14:22 the king hath fulfilled the request of his **s**. 5650
15: 2 Thy **s** *is* of one of the tribes of Israel. 5650
15: 8 For thy **s** vowed a vow while I abode at 5650
15:21 or life, even there *also* will thy **s** be. 5650
15:34 say unto Absalom, I will be thy **s**, O king; 5650
15:34 as I *have been* thy father's **s** hitherto, so 5650
15:34 servant hitherto, so *will* I now also *be* thy **s**: 5650
16: 1 Ziba the **s** of Mephibosheth met him, with a 5288
18:29 When Joab sent the king's **s**, and *me* thy 5650
18:29 *me* thy **s**, I saw a great tumult, but I knew 5650
19:17 Ziba the **s** of the house of Saul, and 5288
19:19 neither do thou remember *that* which thy **s** 5650
19:20 For thy **s** doth know that I have sinned: 5650
19:26 My lord, O king, my **s** deceived me: 5650
19:26 for thy **s** said, I will saddle me an ass, that I 5650
19:26 go to the king; because thy **s** *is* lame. 5650
19:27 he hath slandered thy **s** unto my lord 5650
19:28 yet didst thou set thy **s** among them that did 5650
19:35 can thy **s** taste what I eat or what I drink? 5650
19:35 should thy **s** be yet a burden unto my lord 5650
19:36 Thy **s** will go a little *way* over Jordan with 5650
19:37 Let thy **s**, I pray thee, turn back again, that I 5650
19:37 behold thy **s** Chimham; let him go over 5650
24:10 O LORD, take away the iniquity of thy **s**; 5650
24:21 is my lord the king come to his **s**? 5650
1Ki 1:19 but Solomon thy **s** hath he not called. 5650
1:26 *even* me thy **s**, and Zadok the priest, and 5650
1:26 and thy **s** Solomon, hath he not called. 5650
1:27 and thou hast not shewed *it* unto thy **s**, 5650
1:51 that he will not slay his **s** with the sword. 5650
2:38 my lord the king hath said, so will thy **s** do. 5650
3: 6 Thou hast shewed unto thy **s** David my 5650
3: 7 thou hast made thy **s** king instead of David 5650
3: 8 thy **s** *is* in the midst of thy people which 5650
3: 9 thy **s** an understanding heart to judge thy 5650
8:24 Who hast kept with thy **s** David my father 5650
8:25 keep with thy **s** David my father that thou 5650
8:26 which thou spakest unto thy **s** David my 5650
8:28 have thou respect unto the prayer of thy **s**, 5650
8:28 which thy **s** prayeth before thee to day: 5650
8:29 which thy **s** shall make towards this place. 5650
8:30 hearken thou to the supplication of thy **s**, 5650
8:52 may be open unto the supplication of thy **s**, 5650
8:53 as thou spakest by the hand of Moses thy **s**, 5650
8:56 he promised by the hand of Moses his **s**. 5650
8:59 that *he* maintain the cause of his **s**, and 5650
8:66 that the LORD had done for David his **s**, 5650
11:11 from thee, and will give it to thy **s**. 5650
11:26 an Ephrathite of Zereda, Solomon's **s**, 5650
11:32 (But he shall have one tribe for my **s** 5650
11:36 that David my **s** may have a light alway 5650
11:38 and my commandments, as David my **s** did; 5650
12: 7 If thou wilt be a **s** unto this people *this* day, 5650
14: 8 *yet* thou hast not been as my **s** David, 5650
14:18 which he spake by the hand of his **s** Ahijah 5650
15:29 which he spake by his **s** Ahijah 5650
16: 9 his **s** Zimri, captain of half *his* chariots, 5650
18: 9 that thou wouldest deliver thy **s** into 5650
18:12 but *I* thy **s** fear the LORD from my youth. 5650
18:36 *that* I *am* thy **s**, and *that* I have done all 5650
18:43 said to his **s**, Go up now, look toward 5288
19: 3 *belongeth* to Judah, and left his **s** there. 5288
20: 9 All that thou didst send for to thy **s** at 5650
20:32 said, Thy **s** Ben-hadad saith, I pray thee, 5650
20:39 Thy **s** went out into the midst of the battle; 5650
20:40 as thy **s** was busy here and there, he was 5650
2Ki 4: 1 saying, Thy **s** my husband is dead; 5650
4: 1 thou knowest that thy **s** did fear 5650
4:12 he said to Gehazi his **s**, Call this 5288
4:24 said to her **s**, Drive, and go *forward;* slack 5288
4:25 that he said to Gehazi his **s**, Behold, 5288
4:38 he said unto his **s**, Set on the great pot, and 5288
5: 6 I have *therewith* sent Naaman my **s** to thee, 5650
5:15 I pray thee, take a blessing of thy **s**. 5650
5:17 be given to thy **s** two mules' burden of 5650
5:17 for thy **s** will henceforth offer neither burnt 5650
5:18 In this thing the LORD pardon thy **s**, 5650
5:18 the LORD pardon thy **s** in this thing. 5650
5:20 the **s** of Elisha the man of God, said, 5288
5:25 And he said, Thy **s** went no whither. 5650
6:15 when the **s** of the man of God was risen 8334
6:15 his **s** said unto him, Alas, my master, 5288
8: 4 the king talked with Gehazi the **s** of 5288
8:13 Hazael said, But what, *is* thy **s** a dog, 5650
9:36 which he spake by his **s** Elijah the Tishbite, 5650
10:10 done *that* which he spake by his **s** Elijah. 5650
14:25 which he spake by the hand of his **s** Jonah, 5650
16: 7 of Assyria, saying, I *am* thy **s** and thy son: 5650
17: 3 Hoshea became his **s**, and gave him 5650
18:12 all that Moses the **s** of the LORD 5650
19:34 mine own sake, and for my **s** David's sake. 5650
20: 6 mine own sake, and for my **s** David's sake. 5650
21: 8 according to all the law that my **s** Moses 5650
2Ki 22:12 and Asahiah a **s** of the king's, saying, 5650
24: 1 and Jehoiakim became his **s** three years: 5650
25: 8 a **s** of the king of Babylon, *unto* Jerusalem: 5650
1Ch 2:34 Sheshan had a **s**, an Egyptian, whose name 5650
2:35 Sheshan gave his daughter to Jarha his **s** to 5650
6:49 according to all that Moses the **s** of God 5650
16:13 O ye seed of Israel his **s**, ye children of 5650
17: 4 Go and tell David my **s**, Thus saith 5650
17: 7 thus shalt thou say unto my **s** David, 5650
17:18 *speak* more to thee for the honour of thy **s**? 5650
17:18 of thy servant? for thou knowest thy **s**. 5650
17:23 that thou hast spoken concerning thy **s** 5650
17:24 *let* the house of David thy **s** *be* established 5650
17:25 hast told thy **s** that *thou* wilt build him a 5650
17:25 thy **s** hath found *in his heart* to pray before 5650
17:26 and hast promised this goodness unto thy **s**: 5650
17:27 let it please thee to bless the house of thy **s**, 5650
21: 8 beseech thee, do away the iniquity of thy **s**; 5650
2Ch 1: 3 which Moses the **s** of the LORD had made 5650
6:15 Thou which hast kept with thy **s** David my 5650
6:16 keep with thy **s** David my father *that* which 5650
6:17 which thou hast spoken unto thy **s** David. 5650
6:19 therefore to the prayer of thy **s**, 5650
6:19 the prayer which thy **s** prayeth before thee: 5650
6:20 to hearken unto the prayer which thy **s** 5650
6:21 therefore unto the supplications of thy **s**, 5650
6:42 remember the mercies of David thy **s**. 5650
13: 6 the **s** of Solomon the son of David, is risen 5650
24: 6 of Moses the **s** of the LORD, 5650
24: 9 **s** of God laid upon Israel in the wilderness. 5650
32:16 LORD God, and against his **s** Hezekiah. 5650
34:20 and Asaiah a **s** of the king's, saying, 5650
Ne 1: 6 that *thou* mayest hear the prayer of thy **s**, 5650
1: 7 which thou commandedst thy **s** Moses. 5650
1: 8 the word that thou commandedst thy **s** 5650
1:11 thine ear be attentive to the prayer of thy **s**, 5650
1:11 thy **s** *this* day, and grant him mercy in 5650
2: 5 and if thy **s** have found favour in thy sight, 5650
2:10 and Tobiah the **s**, the Ammonite, 5650
2:19 Tobiah the **s**, the Ammonite, and 5650
4:22 Let every one with his **s** lodge within 5288
6: 5 sent Sanballat his **s** unto me in like manner 5288
9:14 and laws, by the hand of Moses thy **s**: 5650
10:29 which was given by Moses the **s** of God, 5650
Job 1: 8 unto Satan, Hast thou considered my **s** Job, 5650
2: 3 unto Satan, Hast thou considered my **s** Job, 5650
3:19 *are* there; and the **s** *is* free from his master. 5650
7: 2 As a **s** earnestly desireth the shadow, and 5650
19:16 I called my **s**, and he gave *me* no answer; 5650
41: 4 wilt thou take him for a **s** for ever? 5650
42: 7 me *the thing that is* right, as my **s** Job *hath.* 5650
42: 8 go to my **s** Job, and offer up for yourselves 5650
42: 8 and my **s** Job shall pray for you: 5650
42: 8 me *the thing which is* right, like my **s** Job. 5650
Ps 18: T *A Psalm* of David, the **s** of the LORD, 5650
19:11 Moreover by them *is* thy **s** warned: *and* 5650
19:13 Keep back thy **s** also from presumptuous 5650
27: 9 *far* from me; put not thy **s** away in anger: 5650
31:16 Make thy face to shine upon thy **s**: save me 5650
35:27 hath pleasure in the prosperity of his **s**. 5650
36: T *A Psalm* of David the **s** of the LORD. 5650
69:17 hide not thy face from thy **s**; for I am in 5650
78:70 He chose David also his **s**, and took him 5650
86: 2 my God, save thy **s** that trusteth in thee. 5650
86: 4 Rejoice the soul of thy **s**: for unto thee, 5650
86:16 give thy strength unto thy **s**, and save 5650
89: 3 my chosen, I have sworn unto David my **s**, 5650
89:20 I have found David my **s**; with my holy oil 5650
89:39 Thou hast made void the covenant of thy **s**: 5650
105: 6 O ye seed of Abraham his **s**, ye children of 5650
105:17 *even* Joseph, *who* was sold for a **s**: 5650
105:26 He sent Moses his **s**; *and* Aaron whom he 5650
105:42 his holy promise, *and* Abraham his **s**. 5650
109:28 let them be ashamed; but let thy **s** rejoice. 5650
116:16 Oh LORD, truly I *am* thy **s**; I *am* thy 5650
116:16 I *am* thy **s**, *and* the son of thy handmaid: 5650
119:17 Deal bountifully with thy **s**, *that* I may live, 5650
119:23 *but* thy **s** did meditate in thy statutes. 5650
119:38 Stablish thy word unto thy **s**, who *is* 5650
119:49 Remember the word unto thy **s**, upon which 5650
119:65 Thou hast dealt well with thy **s**, O LORD, 5650
119:76 according to thy word unto thy **s**. 5650
119:84 How many *are* the days of thy **s**? when wilt 5650
119:122 Be surety for thy **s** for good: let not 5650
119:124 Deal with thy **s** according unto thy mercy, 5650
119:125 I *am* thy **s**; give me understanding, that I 5650
119:135 Make thy face to shine upon thy **s**; and 5650
119:140 word *is* very pure: therefore thy **s** loveth it. 5650
119:176 gone astray like a lost sheep; seek thy **s**; 5650
132:10 For thy **s** David's sake turn not away 5650
136:22 *Even* an heritage unto Israel his **s**: for his 5650
143: 2 enter not into judgment with thy **s**: for in 5650
143:12 all them that afflict my soul: for I *am* thy **s**. 5650
144:10 who delivereth David his **s** from the hurtful 5650
Pr 11:29 and the fool *shall be* **s** to the wise of heart. 5650
12: 9 *He that is* despised, and hath a **s**, *is* better 5650
14:35 The king's favour *is* toward a wise **s**: but 5650
17: 2 A wise **s** shall have rule over a son that 5650
19:10 much less for a **s** to have rule over princes. 5650
22: 7 and the borrower *is* **s** to the lender. 5650
29:19 A **s** will not be corrected by words: 5650
29:21 He that delicately bringeth up his **s** from a 5650
30:10 Accuse not a **s** unto his master, lest he 5650
30:22 For a **s** when he reigneth; and a fool when 5650
Ecc 7:21 are spoken; lest thou hear thy **s** curse thee: 5650
Isa 20: 3 Like as my **s** Isaiah hath walked naked and 5650
22:20 that I will call my **s** Eliakim the son of 5650
24: 2 the priest; as *with* the **s**, so *with* his master; 5650
37:35 mine own sake, and for my **s** David's sake. 5650
41: 8 thou, Israel, *art* my **s**, Jacob whom I have 5650
41: 9 and said unto thee, Thou *art* my **s**; 5650
42: 1 Behold my **s**, whom I uphold; mine elect, 5650
42:19 Who *is* blind, but my **s**? or deaf, as my 5650
42:19 is perfect, and blind as the LORD'S **s**? 5650
43:10 the LORD, and my **s** whom I have chosen: 5650
Isa 44: 1 Yet now hear, O Jacob my **s**; and Israel, 5650
44: 2 Fear not, O Jacob, my **s**; and 5650
44:21 O Jacob and Israel; for thou *art* my **s**: 5650
44:21 I have formed thee; thou *art* my **s**: O Israel, 5650
44:26 That confirmeth the word of his **s**, and 5650
48:20 The LORD hath redeemed his **s** Jacob. 5650
49: 3 said unto me, Thou *art* my **s**, O Israel, 5650
49: 5 that formed me from the womb *to be* his **s**, 5650
49: 6 is a light thing that thou shouldest be my **s** 5650
49: 7 to a **s** of rulers, Kings shall see and arise, 5650
50:10 that obeyeth the voice of his **s**, that walketh 5650
52:13 Behold, my **s** shall deal prudently, he shall 5650
53:11 by his knowledge shall my righteous **s** 5650
Jer 2:14 *Is* Israel a **s**? *is* he a homeborn *slave?* why 5650
25: 9 my **s**, and will bring them against this land, 5650
27: 6 Nebuchadnezzar the king of Babylon, my **s**; 5650
30:10 thou not, O my **s** Jacob, saith the LORD; 5650
33:21 my covenant be broken with David my **s**, 5650
33:22 so will I multiply the seed of David my **s**, 5650
33:26 David my **s**, *so* that *I* will not take *any* of 5650
34:16 caused every man his **s**, and every man his 5650
43:10 my **s**, and will set his throne upon these 5650
46:27 O my **s** Jacob, and be not dismayed, 5650
46:28 Fear thou not, O Jacob my **s**, saith 5650
Eze 28:25 their land that I have given to my **s** Jacob. 5650
34:23 and he shall feed them, *even* my **s** David; 5650
34:24 and my **s** David a prince among them; 5650
37:24 David my **s** *shall be* king over them; and 5650
37:25 the land that I have given unto Jacob my **s**, 5650
37:25 my **s** David *shall be* their prince for ever. 5650
Da 6:20 O Daniel, **s** of the living God, is thy God, 5649
9:11 *is* written in the law of Moses the **s** of God, 5650
9:17 hear the prayer of thy **s**, and 5650
10:17 For how can the **s** of this my lord talk with 5650
Hag 2:23 will I take thee, O Zerubbabel, my **s**, 5650
Zec 3: 8 I *will* bring forth my **s** the BRANCH. 5650
Mal 1: 6 son honoureth *his* father, and a **s** his master: 5650
4: 4 Remember ye the law of Moses my **s**, 5650
Mt 8: 6 Lord, my **s** lieth at home sick of the palsy, *3816*
8: 8 the word only, and my **s** shall be healed. *3816*
8: 9 and to my **s**, Do this, and he doeth *it.* *1401*
8:13 And his **s** was healed in the selfsame hour. *3816*
10:24 above *his* master, nor the **s** above his lord. *1401*
10:25 he be as his master, and the **s** as his lord. *1401*
12:18 Behold my **s**, whom I have chosen; my *3816*
18:26 The **s** therefore fell down, and *1401*
18:27 Then the lord of that **s** was moved with *1401*
18:28 But the same **s** went out, and found one of *1401*
18:32 said unto him, O *thou* wicked **s**, I forgave *1401*
20:27 will be chief among you, let him be your **s**: *1401*
23:11 that is greatest among you shall be your **s**. *1249*
24:45 Who then is a faithful and wise **s**, whom his *1401*
24:46 Blessed *is* that **s**, whom his lord when he *1401*
24:48 But *and* if that evil **s** shall say in his heart, *1401*
24:50 The lord of that **s** shall come in a day when *1401*
25:21 Well *done, thou* good and faithful **s**: *1401*
25:23 unto him, Well *done,* good and faithful **s**; *1401*
25:26 said unto him, *Thou* wicked and slothful **s**, *1401*
25:30 And cast ye the unprofitable **s** into outer *1401*
26:51 and stroke a **s** of the high priest's, and *1401*
Mk 9:35 *the same* shall be last of all, and **s** of all. *1249*
10:44 of you will be the chiefest, shall be **s** of all. *1401*
12: 2 at the season he sent to the husbandmen a **s**, *1401*
12: 4 And again he sent unto them another **s**; and *1401*
14:47 and smote a **s** of the high priest, and cut off *1401*
Lk 1:54 He hath holpen his **s** Israel, *3816*
1:69 salvation for us in the house of his **s** David; *3816*
2:29 Lord, now lettest thou thy **s** depart in peace, *1401*
7: 2 And a certain centurion's **s**, who was dear *1401*
7: 3 him that he would come and heal his **s**. *1401*
7: 7 but say in a word, and my **s** shall be healed. *3816*
7: 8 and to my **s**, Do this, and he doeth *it.* *1401*
7:10 found the **s** whole that had been sick. *1401*
12:43 Blessed *is* that **s**, whom his lord when he *1401*
12:45 But and if that **s** say in his heart, My lord *1401*
12:46 The lord of that **s** will come in a day when *1401*
12:47 And that **s**, which knew his lord's will, and *1401*
14:17 And sent his **s** at supper time to say to them *1401*
14:21 So that **s** came, and shewed his lord these *1401*
14:21 master of the house being angry said to his **s**, *1401*
14:22 And the **s** said, Lord, it is done as thou hast *1401*
14:23 And the lord said unto the **s**, Go out into *1401*
16:13 No **s** can serve two masters: for either he *3610*
17: 7 having a **s** plowing or feeding cattle, *1401*
17: 9 Doth he thank that **s** because he did *1401*
19:17 And he said unto him, Well, *thou* good **s**: *1401*
19:22 mouth will I judge thee, *thou* wicked **s**. *1401*
20:10 And at the season he sent a **s** to *1401*
20:11 And again he sent another **s**: and they beat *1401*
22:50 And one of them smote the **s** of the high *1401*
Jn 8:34 Whosoever committeth sin is the **s** of sin. *1401*
8:35 And the **s** abideth not in the house for ever: *1401*
12:26 and where I am, there shall also my **s** be: *1249*
13:16 unto you, The **s** is not greater than his lord; *1401*
15:15 for the **s** knoweth not what his lord doeth: *1401*
15:20 unto you, The **s** is not greater than his lord. *1401*
18:10 and smote the high priest's **s**, and cut off *1401*
Ac 4:25 Who by the mouth of thy **s** David hast said, *3816*
Ro 1: 1 Paul, a **s** of Jesus Christ, called *to be* an *1401*
14: 4 Who art thou that judgest another *man's* **s**? *3610*
16: 1 which is a **s** of the church which is at *1249*
16: S *sent* by Phebe **s** of the church at Cenchrea. *1249*
1Co 7:21 Art thou called *being* a **s**? care not for it: *1401*
7:22 the Lord, *being* a **s**, is the Lord's freeman: *1401*
7:22 he that is called, *being* free, is Christ's **s**. *1401*
9:19 all *men,* yet have I **made** myself **s** unto all, *1402*
Gal 1:10 pleased men, I should not be the **s** of Christ. *1401*
4: 1 as he is a child, differeth nothing from a **s**, *1401*
4: 7 Wherefore thou art no more a **s**, but a son; *1401*
Php 2: 7 and took *upon him* the form of a **s**, and *1401*
Col 4:12 is *one* of you, a **s** of Christ, saluteth you, *1401*
2Ti 2:24 And the **s** of the Lord must not strive; but *1401*
Tit 1: 1 a **s** of God, and an apostle of Jesus Christ, *1401*
Phm 1:16 Not now as a **s**, but above a servant, *1401*
1:16 but above a **s**, a brother beloved, *1401*

Phm 1: S from Rome to Philemon, by Onesimus a **s**. *3610*
Heb 3: 5 verily *was* faithful in all his house, as a **s**, *2324*
Jas 1: 1 a **s** of God and of the Lord Jesus Christ, *1401*
2Pe 1: 1 a **s** and an apostle of Jesus Christ, *1401*
Jude 1: 1 the **s** of Jesus Christ, and brother of James, *1401*
Rev 1: 1 and signified *it* by his angel unto his **s** John: *1401*
15: 3 And they sing the song of Moses the **s** of *1401*

SERVANT'S (9) [SERVE]

Ge 19: 2 into your **s** house, and tarry all night, and 5650
2Sa 7:19 thou hast spoken also of thy **s** house for a 5650
1Ki 11:13 one tribe to thy son for David my **s** sake, 5650
11:34 all the days of his life for David my **s** sake, 5650
2Ki 8:19 not destroy Judah for David his **s** sake, 5650
1Ch 17:17 for thou hast *also* spoken of thy **s** house for 5650
17:19 for thy **s** sake, and according to thine own 5650
Isa 45: 4 For Jacob my **s** sake, and Israel mine elect, 5650
Jn 18:10 off his right ear. The **s** name was Malchus. *1401*

SERVANTS (476) [SERVE]

Ge 9:25 a servant of **s** shall he be unto his brethren. 5650
14:14 he armed his trained ***s***, born in his own NIH
14:15 he and his **s**, by night, and smote them, and 5650
20: 8 called all his **s**, and told all these things in 5650
21:25 which Abimelech's **s** had violently taken 5650
26:14 possession of herds, and great store of **s**: 5657
26:15 For all the wells which his father's **s** had 5650
26:19 Isaac's **s** digged in the valley, and 5650
26:25 tent there: and there Isaac's **s** digged a well. 5650
26:32 that Isaac's **s** came, and told him 5650
27:37 all his brethren have I given to him for **s**; 5650
32:16 he delivered *them* into the hand of his **s**, 5650
32:16 said unto his **s**, Pass over before me, and 5650
40:20 that he made a feast unto all his **s**: 5650
40:20 and of the chief baker among his **s**. 5650
41:10 Pharaoh was wroth with his **s**, and put me 5650
41:37 eyes of Pharaoh, and in the eyes of all his **s**. 5650
41:38 Pharaoh said unto his **s**, Can we find *such* 5650
42:10 my lord, but to buy food are thy **s** come. 5650
42:11 we *are* true *men*, thy **s** are no spies. 5650
42:13 they said, Thy **s** *are* twelve brethren, 5650
44: 7 God forbid that thy **s** should do according 5650
44: 9 With whom*soever* of thy **s** it be found, 5650
44:16 God hath found out the iniquity of thy **s**: 5650
44:16 behold, we *are* my lord's **s**, both we, and 5650
44:19 My lord asked his **s**, saying, Have ye a 5650
44:21 thou saidst unto thy **s**, Bring him down 5650
44:23 thou saidst unto thy **s**, Except your 5650
44:31 thy **s** shall bring down the gray hairs of thy 5650
45:16 and it pleased Pharaoh well, and his **s**. 5650
47: 3 Thy **s** *are* shepherds, both we, *and* also our 5650
47: 4 for thy **s** have no pasture for their flocks; 5650
47: 4 let thy **s** dwell in the land of Goshen. 5650
47:19 and we and our land will be **s** unto Pharaoh: 5650
47:25 of my lord, and we will be Pharaoh's **s**. 5650
50: 2 Joseph commanded his **s** the physicians to 5650
50: 7 with him went up all the **s** of Pharaoh, 5650
50:17 forgive the trespass of the **s** of the God of 5650
50:18 his face; and they said, Behold, we *be* thy **s**. 5650
Ex 5:15 Wherefore dealest thou thus with thy **s**? 5650
5:16 *There is* no straw given unto thy **s**, and 5650
5:16 behold, thy **s** *are* beaten; but the fault *is* in 5650
5:21 in the eyes of his **s**, to put a sword in their 5650
7:10 and before his **s**, and it became a serpent. 5650
7:20 sight of Pharaoh, and in the sight of his **s**; 5650
8: 3 into the house of thy **s**, and upon thy 5650
8: 4 and upon thy people, and upon all thy **s**. 5650
8: 9 for thee, and for thy **s**, and for thy people, 5650
8:11 and from thy **s**, and from thy people; 5650
8:21 upon thy **s**, and upon thy people, and 5650
8:29 from his **s**, and from his people, to morrow: 5650
8:31 from his **s**, and from his people; 5650
9:14 and upon thy **s**, and upon thy people; 5650
9:20 amongst the **s** of Pharaoh made his servants 5650
9:20 amongst the servants of Pharaoh made his **s** 5650
9:21 not the word of the LORD left his **s** 5650
9:30 as for thee and thy **s**, I know that ye will 5650
9:34 and hardened his heart, he and his **s**. 5650
10: 1 hardened his heart, and the heart of his **s**, 5650
10: 6 the houses of all thy **s**, and the houses of all 5650
10: 7 Pharaoh's **s** said unto him, How long shall 5650
11: 3 in the sight of Pharaoh's **s**, and in the sight 5650
11: 8 all these thy **s** shall come down unto me, 5650
12:30 he, and all his **s**, and all the Egyptians; 5650
14: 5 and of his **s** was turned against the people, 5650
32:13 Isaac, and Israel, thy **s**, 5650
Lev 25:42 For they *are* my **s**, which I brought forth 5650
25:55 For unto me the children of Israel *are* **s**; 5650
25:55 they *are* my **s** whom I brought forth out of 5650
Nu 22:18 and said unto the **s** of Balak, 5650
22:22 upon his ass, and his two **s** *were* with him. 5288
31:49 Thy **s** have taken the sum of the men of war 5650
32: 4 *is* a land for cattle, and thy **s** have cattle: 5650
32: 5 let this land be given unto thy **s** for a 5650
32:25 Thy **s** will do as my lord commandeth. 5650
32:27 thy **s** will pass over, every man armed for 5650
32:31 As the LORD hath said unto thy **s**, so 5650
Dt 9:27 Remember thy **s**, Abraham, Isaac, and 5650
29: 2 and unto all his **s**, and unto all his land; 5650
32:36 his people, and repent himself for his **s**, 5650
32:43 for he will avenge the blood of his **s**, and 5650
34:11 and to all his **s**, and to all his land, 5650
Jos 9: 8 they said unto Joshua, We *are* thy **s**. 5650
9: 9 From a very far country thy **s** are come 5650
9:11 and say unto them, We *are* your **s**: 5650
9:24 said, Because it was certainly told thy **s**, 5650
10: 6 Slack not thy hand from thy **s**; 5650
Jdg 3:24 When he was gone out, his **s** came; and 5650
6:27 Gideon took ten men of his **s**, and did as 5650
19:19 and for the young man *which is* with thy **s**: 5650
1Sa 4: 9 that ye be not **s** unto the Hebrews, 5647
8:14 the best *of them*, and give *them* to his **s**. 5650
8:15 and give to his officers, and to his **s**. 5650
8:17 tenth of your sheep: and ye shall be his **s**. 5650
9: 3 Take now one of the **s** with thee, and arise, 5288
1Sa 12:19 Pray for thy **s** unto the LORD thy God, 5650
16:15 Saul's **s** said unto him, Behold now, an evil 5650
16:16 Let our lord now command thy **s** *which are* 5650
16:17 Saul said unto his **s**, Provide me now a man 5650
16:18 answered one of the **s**, and said, Behold, 5288
17: 8 *am* not I a Philistine, and you **s** to Saul? 5650
17: 9 and *to* kill me, then will we be your **s**: 5650
17: 9 then shall ye be our **s**, and serve us. 5650
18: 5 the people, and also in the sight of Saul's **s**. 5650
18:22 Saul commanded his **s**, *saying*, Commune 5650
18:22 hath delight in thee, and all his **s** love thee: 5650
18:23 Saul's **s** spake those words in the ears of 5650
18:24 the **s** of Saul told him, saying, On this 5650
18:26 when his **s** told David these words, 5650
18:30 himself more wisely than all the **s** of Saul; 5650
19: 1 and to all his **s**, that they should kill David. 5650
21: 2 I have appointed *my* **s** to such and such a 5288
21: 7 Now a *certain* man of the **s** of Saul *was* 5650
21:11 the **s** of Achish said unto him, *Is* not this 5650
21:14 said Achish unto his **s**, Lo, you see the man 5650
22: 6 and all his **s** *were* standing about him;) 5650
22: 7 Saul said unto his **s** that stood about him, 5650
22: 9 which *was* set over the **s** of Saul, and said, 5650
22:14 who *is so* faithful among all thy **s** as David, 5650
22:17 the **s** of the king would not put forth their 5650
24: 7 So David stayed his **s** with *these* words, and 376
25: 8 cometh to thine hand unto thy **s**, 5650
25:10 Nabal answered David's **s**, and said, 5650
25:10 there be many **s** now a days that break 5650
25:19 she said unto her **s**, Go on before me; 5288
25:40 when the **s** of David were come to Abigail 5650
25:41 servant to wash the feet of the **s** of my lord. 5650
28: 7 said Saul unto his **s**, Seek me a woman that 5650
28: 7 his **s** said to him, Behold, *there is* a woman 5650
28:23 his **s**, together with the woman, 5650
28:25 she brought *it* before Saul, and before his **s**; 5650
29:10 with thy master's **s** that are come with thee: 5650
2Sa 2:12 and the **s** of Ish-bosheth the son of Saul, 5650
2:13 the **s** of David, went out, and met together 5650
2:15 son of Saul, and twelve of the **s** of David. 5650
2:17 the men of Israel, before the **s** of David. 5650
2:30 there lacked of David's **s** nineteen men and 5650
2:31 the **s** of David had smitten of Benjamin, 5650
3:22 the **s** of David and Joab came from 5650
3:38 the king said unto his **s**, Know ye not that 5650
6:20 to day in the eyes of the handmaids of his **s**, 5650
8: 2 *so* the Moabites became David's **s**, and 5650
8: 6 the Syrians became **s** to David, and 5650
8: 7 of gold that were on the **s** of Hadadezer, 5650
8:14 and all they of Edom became David's **s**. 5650
9:10 Thou therefore, and thy sons, and thy **s**, 5650
9:10 Now Ziba had fifteen sons and twenty **s**. 5650
9:12 all that dwelt in the house of Ziba *were* **s** 5650
10: 2 him by the hand of his **s** for his father. 5650
10: 2 David's **s** came *into* the land of the children 5650
10: 3 hath not David *rather* sent his **s** unto thee, 5650
10: 4 Wherefore Hanun took David's **s**, and 5650
10:19 when all the kings *that were* **s** to Hadarezer 5650
11: 1 sent Joab, and his **s** with him, and all Israel; 5650
11: 9 the king's house with all the **s** of his lord, 5650
11:11 my lord Joab, and the **s** of my lord, 5650
11:13 out to lie on his bed with the **s** of his lord, 5650
11:17 there fell *some* of the people of the **s** of 5650
11:24 shooters shot from off the wall upon thy **s**; 5650
11:24 *some* of the king's **s** be dead, and 5650
12:18 the **s** of David feared to tell him that 5650
12:19 when David saw that his **s** whispered, 5650
12:19 therefore David said unto his **s**, Is the child 5650
12:21 said his **s** unto him, What thing *is* this that 5650
13:24 beseech thee, and his **s** go with thy servant. 5650
13:28 Now Absalom had commanded his **s**, 5288
13:29 the **s** of Absalom did unto Amnon as 5288
13:31 all his **s** stood *by* with their clothes rent. 5650
13:36 the king also and all his **s** wept very sore. 5650
14:30 Therefore he said unto his **s**, See, 5650
14:30 And Absalom's **s** set the field on fire. 5650
14:31 Wherefore have thy **s** set my field on fire? 5650
15:14 David said unto all his **s** that *were* with him 5650
15:15 the king's **s** said unto the king, Behold, 5650
15:15 thy **s** *are ready to do* whatsoever my lord 5650
15:18 all his **s** passed on beside him; and all 5650
16: 6 at David, and at all the **s** of king David: 5650
16:11 to Abishai, and to all his **s**, Behold, my son, 5650
17:20 when Absalom's **s** came to the woman to 5650
18: 7 of Israel were slain before the **s** of David, 5650
18: 9 Absalom met the **s** of David. And Absalom 5650
19: 5 hast shamed *this* day the faces of all thy **s**, 5650
19: 6 that thou regardest neither princes nor **s**: 5650
19: 7 go forth, and speak comfortably unto thy **s**: 5650
19:14 unto the king, Return thou, and all thy **s**. 5650
19:17 his fifteen sons and his twenty **s** with him; 5650
20: 6 take thou thy lord's **s**, and pursue after him, 5650
21:15 his **s** with him, and fought against 5650
21:22 the hand of David, and by the hand of his **s**. 5650
24:20 the king and his **s** coming on toward him: 5650
1Ki 1: 2 Wherefore his **s** said unto him, Let there be 5650
1: 9 and all the men of Judah the king's **s**: 5650
1:33 Take with you the **s** of your lord, and 5650
1:47 moreover the king's **s** came to bless our 5650
2:39 that two of the **s** of Shimei ran away unto 5650
2:39 saying, Behold, thy **s** *be* in Gath. 5650
2:40 and went to Gath to Achish to seek his **s**: 5650
2:40 Shimei went, and brought his **s** from Gath. 5650
3:15 and made a feast to all his **s**. 5650
5: 1 Hiram king of Tyre sent his **s** unto 5650
5: 6 and my **s** shall be with thy servants: 5650
5: 6 and my servants shall be with thy **s**: 5650
5: 6 unto thee will I give hire for thy **s** 5650
5: 9 My **s** shall bring *them* down from Lebanon 5650
8:23 mercy with thy **s** that walk before thee with 5650
8:32 do, and judge thy **s**, condemning 5650
8:36 forgive the sin of thy **s**, and of thy people 5650
9:22 his **s**, and his princes, and his captains, and 5650
9:27 Hiram sent in the navy his **s**, shipmen that 5650
9:27 of the sea, with the **s** of Solomon. 5650
1Ki 10: 5 the sitting of his **s**, and the attendance of his 5650
10: 8 Happy *are* thy men, happy *are* these thy **s**, 5650
10:13 and went to her own country, she and her **s**. 5650
11:17 certain Edomites of his father's **s** with him, 5650
12: 7 to them, then they will be thy **s** for ever. 5650
15:18 and delivered them into the hand of his **s**: 5650
20: 6 Yet I will send my **s** unto thee to morrow 5650
20: 6 search thine house, and the houses of thy **s**; 5650
20:12 in the pavilions, that he said unto his **s**, 5650
20:23 the **s** of the king of Syria said unto him, 5650
20:31 his **s** said unto him, Behold now, we have 5650
22: 3 the king of Israel said unto his **s**, Know ye 5650
22:49 Let my **s** go with thy servants in the ships. 5650
22:49 Let my servants go with thy **s** in the ships. 5650
2Ki 1:13 let my life, and the life of these fifty thy **s**, 5650
2:16 there be with thy **s** fifty strong men; 5650
3:11 one of the king of Israel's **s** answered and 5650
5:13 his **s** came near, and spake unto him, and 5650
5:23 and laid *them* upon two of his **s**; 5288
6: 3 Be content, I pray thee, and go with thy **s**. 5650
6: 8 took counsel with his **s**, saying, In such and 5650
6:11 he called his **s**, and said unto them, Will ye 5650
6:12 one of his **s** said, None, my lord, O king: 5650
7:12 king arose in the night, and said unto his **s**, 5650
7:13 one of his **s** answered and said, Let *some* 5650
9: 7 that I may avenge the blood of my **s** 5650
9: 7 the blood of all the **s** of the LORD, at 5650
9:11 Jehu came forth to the **s** of his lord: and 5650
9:28 his **s** carried him *in a chariot* to Jerusalem, 5650
10: 5 We *are* thy **s**, and will do all that thou shalt 5650
10:19 of Baal, all his **s**, and all his priests; 5647
10:23 here with you none of the **s** of the LORD, 5650
12:20 his **s** arose, and made a conspiracy, 5650
12:21 of Shomer, his **s**, smote him, and he died; 5650
14: 5 that he slew his **s** which had slain the king 5650
17:13 which I sent to you by my **s** the prophets. 5650
17:23 as he had said by all his **s** the prophets. 5650
18:24 of one captain of the least of my master's **s**, 5650
18:26 I pray thee, to thy **s** in the Syrian language; 5650
19: 5 So the **s** of king Hezekiah came to Isaiah. 5650
19: 6 *with* which the **s** of the king of Assyria 5288
21:10 the LORD spake by his **s** the prophets, 5650
21:23 the **s** of Amon conspired against him, and 5650
22: 9 Thy **s** have gathered the money that was 5650
23:30 his **s** carried him *in a chariot* dead from 5650
24: 2 which he spake by his **s** the prophets. 5650
24:10 At that time the **s** of Nebuchadnezzar king 5650
24:11 against the city, and his **s** *did* besiege it. 5650
24:12 and his **s**, and his princes, and his officers: 5650
25:24 Fear not to be the **s** of the Chaldees: 5650
1Ch 18: 2 the Moabites became David's **s**, and 5650
18: 6 the Syrians became David's **s**, and 5650
18: 7 of gold that were on the **s** of Hadarezer, 5650
18:13 and all the Edomites became David's **s**. 5650
19: 2 So the **s** of David came into the land of 5650
19: 3 are not his **s** come unto thee for to search, 5650
19: 4 Wherefore Hanun took David's **s**, and 5650
19:19 when the **s** of Hadarezer saw that they were 5650
19:19 made peace with David, and became his **s**: 5647
20: 8 the hand of David, and by the hand of his **s**. 5650
21: 3 lord the king, *are* they not all my lord's **s**? 5650
2Ch 2: 8 for I know that thy **s** can skill to cut timber 5650
2: 8 and behold, my **s** *shall be* with thy servants, 5650
2: 8 and behold, my servants *shall be* with thy **s**, 5650
2:10 behold, I will give to thy **s**, the hewers that 5650
2:15 lord hath spoken of, let him send unto his **s**: 5650
6:14 and *shewest* mercy unto thy **s**, 5650
6:23 do, and judge thy **s**, by requiting 5650
6:27 forgive the sin of thy **s**, and of thy people 5650
8: 9 Israel did Solomon make no **s** for his work; 5650
8:18 Huram sent him by the hands of his **s** ships, 5650
8:18 and **s** that had knowledge of the sea; 5650
8:18 they went with the **s** of Solomon to Ophir, 5650
9: 4 the sitting of his **s**, and the attendance of his 5650
9: 7 *are* thy men, and happy *are* these thy **s**, 5650
9:10 the **s** also of Huram, and the servants of 5650
9:10 the **s** of Solomon, which brought gold from 5650
9:12 went away to her own land, she and her **s**. 5650
9:21 ships went *to* Tarshish with the **s** of Huram: 5650
10: 7 words to them, they will be thy **s** for ever. 5650
12: 8 Nevertheless they shall be his **s**; that they 5650
24:25 his own **s** conspired against him for 5650
25: 3 that he slew his **s** that had killed the king 5650
32: 9 king of Assyria send his **s** to Jerusalem, 5650
32:16 his **s** spake yet *more* against the LORD 5650
33:24 his **s** conspired against him, and slew him 5650
34:16 saying, All that was committed to thy **s**, 5650
35:23 the king said to his **s**, Have me away; for I 5650
35:24 His **s** therefore took him out of *that* chariot, 5650
36:20 where they were **s** to him and his sons until 5650
Ezr 2:55 The children of Solomon's **s**: the children 5650
2:58 and the children of Solomon's **s**, 5650
2:65 Beside their **s** and their maids, of whom 5650
4:11 Thy **s** the men *on this* side the river, and 5649
5:11 We are the **s** of the God of heaven and 5649
9:11 Which thou hast commanded by thy **s** 5650
Ne 1: 6 for the children of Israel thy **s**, and 5650
1:10 Now these *are* thy **s** and thy people, 5650
1:11 to the prayer of thy **s**, who desire to fear thy 5650
2:20 therefore we his **s** will arise and build: 5650
4:16 *that* the half of my **s** wrought in the work, 5288
4:23 So neither I, nor my brethren, nor my **s**, 5288
5: 5 bondage our sons and our daughters to be **s**, 5650
5:10 I likewise, *and* my brethren, and my **s**, 5288
5:15 *yea*, even their **s** bare rule over the people: 5288
5:16 all my **s** *were* gathered thither unto 5288
7:57 The children of Solomon's **s**: the children 5650
7:60 and the children of Solomon's **s**, 5650
9:10 on all his **s**, and on all the people of his 5650
9:36 we *are* **s** *this* day, and *for* the land that thou 5650
9:36 and the good thereof, behold, we *are* **s** in it: 5650
11: 3 and the children of Solomon's **s**. 5650
13:19 *some* of my **s** set I at the gates, *that* there 5288
Est 1: 3 made a feast unto all his princes and his **s**; 5650
2: 2 said the king's **s** that ministered unto him, 5288

Est 2:18 a great feast unto all his princes and his s, 5650
3: 2 all the king's s, that *were* in the king's gate, 5650
3: 3 the king's s, which *were* in the king's gate, 5650
4:11 All the king's s, and the people of 5650
5:11 him above the princes and s of the king. 5650
6: 3 said the king's s that ministered unto him, 5288
6: 5 the king's s said unto him, Behold, 5288
Job 1:15 they have slain the s with the edge of 5288
1:16 the sheep, and the s, and consumed them; 5288
1:17 slain the s with the edge of the sword; 5288
4:18 Behold, he put no trust in his s; and his 5650
Ps 34:22 The LORD redeemeth the soul of his s: 5650
69:36 The seed also of his s shall inherit it: and 5650
79: 2 The dead bodies of thy s have they given *to* 5650
79:10 of the blood of thy s which is shed. 5650
89:50 Remember, Lord, the reproach of thy s; 5650
90:13 and let it repent thee concerning thy s. 5650
90:16 Let thy work appear unto thy s, and 5650
102:14 For thy s take pleasure in her stones, and 5650
102:28 The children of thy s shall continue, and 5650
105:25 hate his people, to deal subtilly with his s. 5650
113: 1 Praise, O ye s of the LORD, praise 5650
119:91 to thine ordinances: for all *are* thy s. 5650
123: 2 as the eyes of s *look* unto the hand of their 5650
134: 1 ye the LORD, all ye s of the LORD, 5650
135: 1 praise *him*, O ye s of the LORD. 5650
135: 9 O Egypt, upon Pharaoh, and upon all his s. 5650
135:14 and he will repent himself concerning his s. 5650
Pr 29:12 a ruler hearken to lies, all his s *are* wicked. 8334
Ecc 2: 7 I got *me* s and maidens, and had servants 5650
2: 7 and maidens, and had s born in *my* house; NIH
10: 7 I have seen s upon horses, and 5650
10: 7 and princes walking as s upon the earth. 5650
Isa 14: 2 them in the land of the LORD for s 5650
36: 9 of one captain of the least of my master's s, 5650
36:11 unto thy s in the Syrian language; 5650
37: 5 So the s of king Hezekiah came to Isaiah. 5650
37: 6 where*with* the s of the king of Assyria have 5288
37:24 By thy s hast thou reproached the Lord, and 5650
54:17 This *is* the heritage of the s of the LORD, 5650
56: 6 to love the name of the LORD, to be his s, 5650
63:17 Return for thy s sake, the tribes of thine 5650
65: 8 so will I do for my s sakes, that *I* may not 5650
65: 9 shall inherit it, and my s shall dwell there. 5650
65:13 my s shall eat, but ye shall be hungry: 5650
65:13 my s shall drink, but ye shall be thirsty: 5650
65:13 my s shall rejoice, but ye shall be ashamed: 5650
65:14 my s shall sing for joy of heart, but ye shall 5650
65:15 slay thee, and call his s by another name: 5650
66:14 the LORD shall be known towards his s, 5650
Jer 7:25 I have even sent unto you all my s 5650
21: 7 his s, and the people, and such as are left in 5650
22: 2 thy s, and thy people that enter in by these 5650
22: 4 and on horses, he, and his s, and his people. 5650
25: 4 the LORD hath sent unto you all his s 5650
25:19 his s, and his princes, and all his people; 5650
26: 5 To hearken to the words of my s 5650
29:19 which I sent unto them by my s 5650
34:11 caused the s and the handmaids, whom they 5650
34:11 brought them into subjection for s and 5650
34:16 to be unto you for s and for handmaids. 5650
35:15 I have sent also unto you all my s 5650
36:24 nor any of his s that heard all these words. 5650
36:31 and his seed and his s for their iniquity; 5650
37: 2 neither he, nor his s, nor the people of 5650
37:18 or against thy s, or against this people, 5650
44: 4 Howbeit I sent unto you all my s 5650
46:26 king of Babylon, and into the hand of his s: 5650
La 5: 8 S have ruled over us: *there is* none that doth 5650
Eze 38:17 in old time by my s the prophets of Israel, 5650
46:17 give a gift of his inheritance to one of his s, 5650
Da 1:12 Prove thy s, I beseech thee, ten days; and 5650
1:13 and as thou seest, deal with thy s. 5650
2: 4 tell thy s the dream, and we will shew 5649
2: 7 Let the king tell his s the dream, and 5649
3:26 ye s of the most high God, come forth, and 5649
3:28 delivered his s that trusted in him, and 5649
9: 6 Neither have we hearkened unto thy s 5650
9:10 which he set before us by his s 5650
Joel 2:29 also upon the s and upon the handmaids in 5650
Am 3: 7 he revealeth his secret unto his s 5650
Mic 6: 4 and redeemed thee out of the house of s; 5650
Zec 1: 6 which I commanded my s the prophets, 5650
2: 9 and they shall be a spoil to their s: 5647
Mt 13:27 So the s of the householder came and *1401*
13:28 The s said unto him, Wilt thou then *that* we *1401*
14: 2 And said unto his s, This is John *3816*
18:23 which would take account of his s. *1401*
21:34 he sent his s to the husbandmen, that *they* *1401*
21:35 And the husbandmen took his s, and *1401*
21:36 Again, he sent other s moe than the first: *1401*
22: 3 And sent forth his s to call them that were *1401*
22: 4 Again, he sent forth other s, saying, *1401*
22: 6 And the remnant took his s, and *1401*
22: 8 Then saith he to his s, The wedding is *1401*
22:10 So those s went out into the *high*ways, and *1401*
22:13 Then said the king to the s, Bind him hand *1249*
25:14 *who* called his own s, and delivered unto *1401*
25:19 After a long time the lord of those s *1401*
26:58 and went in, and sat with the s, to see *5257*
Mk 1:20 father Zebedee in the ship with the **hired** s, *3411*
13:34 and gave authority to his s, and to every *1401*
14:54 and he sat with the s, and warmed himself *5257*
14:65 the s did strike him with the palms of their *5257*
Lk 12:37 Blessed *are* those s, whom the lord when he *1401*
12:38 and find *them* so, blessed are those s. *1401*
15:17 How many hired s of my father's have NIG
15:19 thy son: make me as one of thy hired *s*. NIG
15:22 But the father said to his s, Bring forth *1401*
15:26 And he called one of the s, and asked what *3816*
17:10 say, We are unprofitable s: *1401*
19:13 And he called his ten s, and delivered them *1401*
19:15 he commanded these s to be called unto *1401*
Jn 2: 5 His mother saith unto the s, Whatsoever he *1249*
2: 9 (but the s which drew the water knew;) *1249*
4:51 his s met him, and told *him*, saying, *1401*
15:15 Henceforth I call you not s; for the servant *1401*
Jn 18:18 And the s and officers stood *there*, who had *1401*
18:26 One of the s of the high priest, being *his* *1401*
18:36 were of this world, then would my s fight, *5257*
Ac 2:18 And on my s and on my handmaidens I *1401*
4:29 and grant unto thy s, that with all boldness *1401*
10: 7 he called two of his **household** s, and *3610*
16:17 These men are the s of the most high God, *1401*
Ro 6:16 that to whom ye yield yourselves s to obey, *1401*
6:16 to obey, *his* s ye are to whom ye obey; *1401*
6:17 that ye were the s of sin, but ye have *1401*
6:18 from sin, ye became the s of righteousness. *1402*
6:19 for as ye have yielded your members s to *1401*
6:19 now yield your members s to righteousness *1401*
6:20 For when ye were the s of sin, ye were free *1401*
6:22 and become s to God, ye have your fruit *1402*
1Co 7:23 bought with a price; be not ye the s of men. *1401*
2Co 4: 5 and ourselves your s for Jesus' sake. *1401*
Eph 6: 5 S, be obedient to *them that are your* masters *1401*
6: 6 but as the s of Christ, doing the will of God *1401*
Php 1: 1 Paul and Timotheus, the s of Jesus Christ, *1401*
Col 3:22 S, obey in all *things your* masters according *1401*
4: 1 give unto *your* s that which is just and *1401*
1Ti 6: 1 Let as many s as are under the yoke count *1401*
Tit 2: 9 *Exhort* s to be obedient unto their own *1401*
1Pe 2:16 cloke of maliciousness, but as the s of God. *1401*
2:18 S, *be* subject to *your* masters with all fear; *3610*
2Pe 2:19 they themselves are the s of corruption: *1401*
Rev 1: 1 to shew unto his s *things* which must *1401*
2:20 and to seduce my s to commit fornication, *1401*
7: 3 till we have sealed the s of our God in their *1401*
10: 7 as he hath declared to his s the prophets. *1401*
11:18 that *thou* shouldest give reward unto thy s *1401*
19: 2 hath avenged the blood of his s at her hand. *1401*
19: 5 all ye his s, and ye that fear him, both *1401*
22: 3 shall be in it; and his s shall serve him: *1401*
22: 6 his s *the things* which must shortly be done. *1401*

SERVANTS' (4) [SERVE]

Ge 46:34 Thy s trade hath been about cattle from our 5650
Ex 8:24 *into* his s houses, and into all the land of 5650
Isa 63:17 Return for thy s sake, the tribes of thine 5650
65: 8 so will I do for my s sakes, that *I* may not 5650

SERVE (209) [BONDSERVANT, BONDSERVICE, EYESERVICE, FELLOWSERVANT, FELLOWSERVANTS, MAIDSERVANT, MAIDSERVANT'S, MAIDSERVANTS, MAIDSERVANTS', MANSERVANT, MANSERVANT'S, MANSERVANTS, MENSERVANTS, SERVANT, SERVANT'S, SERVANTS, SERVANTS', SERVED, SERVEDST, SERVEST, SERVETH, SERVICE, SERVILE, SERVING, SERVITOR, SERVITUDE, WOMENSERVANTS]

Ge 15:13 in a land *that is* not theirs, and shall s them; 5647
15:14 that nation, whom they shall s, will I judge: 5647
25:23 and the elder shall s the younger. 5647
27:29 Let people s thee, and nations bow down to 5647
27:40 shalt thou live, and shalt s thy brother; 5647
29:15 shouldest thou therefore s me for nought? 5647
29:18 I will s thee seven years for Rachel thy 5647
29:25 did not I s with thee for Rachel? wherefore 5647
29:27 thou shalt s with me yet seven other years. 5647
Ex 1:13 **made** the children of Israel to s with 5647
1:14 all their service, wherein they **made** them s, 5647
3:12 ye shall s God upon this mountain. 5647
4:23 unto thee, Let my son go, that he may s me: 5647
7:16 that they may s me in the wilderness: 5647
8: 1 Let my people go, that they may s me. 5647
8:20 Let my people go, that they may s me. 5647
9: 1 Let my people go, that they may s me. 5647
9:13 Let my people go, that they may s me. 5647
10: 3 let my people go, that they may s me. 5647
10: 7 that they may s the LORD their God: 5647
10: 8 unto them, Go, s the LORD your God: 5647
10:11 go now ye *that are* men, and s the LORD; 5647
10:24 unto Moses, and said, Go ye, s the LORD; 5647
10:26 for thereof must we take to s the LORD 5647
10:26 we know not with what we must s 5647
12:31 and go, s the LORD, as ye have said. 5647
14:12 Let us alone, that we may s the Egyptians? 5647
14:12 For *it had been* better for us to s 5647
20: 5 not bow down thyself to them, nor s them: 5647
21: 2 buy a Hebrew servant, six years he shall s: 5647
21: 6 with an aul; and he shall s him for ever. 5647
23:24 nor s them, nor do after their works: 5647
23:25 ye shall s the LORD your God, and 5647
23:33 for if thou s their gods, it will surely be a 5647
Lev 25:39 thou shalt not **compel** him **to** s as a 5647+5656
25:40 *and* shall s thee unto the year of jubile: 5647
Nu 4:24 of the Gershonites, to s, and for burdens: 5647
4:26 all that is made for them: so shall they s. 5647
8:25 the service *thereof*, and shall s no more: 5647
18: 7 the altar, and within the vail; and ye shall s: 5647
18:21 for their service which they s, *even* 5647
Dt 4:19 be driven to worship them, and s them, 5647
4:28 there ye shall s gods, the work of men's 5647
5: 9 bow down thyself unto them, nor s them: 5647
6:13 and s him, and shalt swear by his name. 5647
7: 4 following me, that they may s other gods: 5647
7:16 neither shalt thou s their gods; for that *will* 5647
8:19 other gods, and s them, and worship them, 5647
10:12 to s the LORD thy God with all thy heart 5647
10:20 him shalt thou s, and to him shalt thou 5647
11:13 to s him with all your heart and with all 5647
11:16 and s other gods, and worship them; 5647
12:30 How did these nations s their gods? 5647
13: 2 thou hast not known, and let us s them; 5647
13: 4 and you shall s him, and cleave unto him. 5647
13: 6 saying, Let us go and s other gods, 5647
13:13 saying, Let us go and s other gods, 5647
15:12 be sold unto thee, and s thee six years; 5647
20:11 tributaries unto thee, and they shall s thee. 5647
28:14 *to* the left, to go after other gods to s them. 5647
Dt 28:36 there shalt thou s other gods, wood and 5647
28:48 Therefore shalt thou s thine enemies which 5647
28:64 there thou shalt s other gods, which neither 5647
29:18 to go *and* s the gods of these nations; 5647
30:17 and worship other gods, and s them; 5647
31:20 s them, and provoke me, and break my 5647
Jos 16:10 unto this day, and s under tribute. 5647
22: 5 to s him with all your heart and with all 5647
23: 7 nor cause to swear *by them*, neither s them, 5647
24:14 and s him in sincerity and in truth: 5647
24:14 and in Egypt; and s ye the LORD. 5647
24:15 if it seem evil unto you to s the LORD, 5647
24:15 choose you *this* day whom you will s; 5647
24:15 and my house, we will s the LORD. 5647
24:16 should forsake the LORD, to s other gods; 5647
24:18 *therefore* will we also s the LORD; for he 5647
24:19 unto the people, Ye cannot s the LORD: 5647
24:20 s strange gods, then he will turn and do you 5647
24:21 Nay; but we will s the LORD. 5647
24:22 ye have chosen you the LORD, to s him. 5647
24:24 The LORD our God will we s, and his 5647
Jdg 2:19 in following other gods to s them, and 5647
9:28 and who *is* Shechem, that we should s him? 5647
9:28 s the men of Hamor the father of Shechem: 5647
9:28 of Shechem: for why should we s him? 5647
9:38 Who *is* Abimelech, that we should s him? 5647
1Sa 7: 3 hearts unto the LORD, and s him only: 5647
10: 7 *that* thou do as **occasion** s thee; 3027+4672
11: 1 a covenant with us, and we will s thee. 5647
12:10 the hand of our enemies, and we will s thee. 5647
12:14 s him, and obey his voice, and not rebel 5647
12:20 but s the LORD with all your heart; 5647
12:24 and s him in truth with all your heart: 5647
17: 9 then shall ye be our servants, and s us. 5647
26:19 of the LORD, saying, Go, s other gods. 5647
2Sa 15: 8 *to* Jerusalem, then I will s the LORD. 5647
16:19 again, whom should I s? *should I* not *serve* 5647
16:19 *should I* not s in the presence of his son? NIH
22:44 a people *which* I knew not shall s me. 5647
1Ki 9: 6 but go and s other gods, and worship them: 5647
12: 4 he put upon us, lighter, and we will s thee. 5647
12: 7 wilt s them, and answer them, and 5647
2Ki 10:18 Baal a little; *but* Jehu shall s him much. 5647
17:35 to them, nor s them, nor sacrifice to them: 5647
25:24 in the land, and s the king of Babylon; 5647
1Ch 28: 9 s him with a perfect heart and with a 5647
2Ch 7:19 shall go and s other gods, and 5647
10: 4 that he put upon us, and we will s thee. 5647
29:11 to s him, and that *you* should minister unto 8334
30: 8 s the LORD your God, that the fierceness 5647
33:16 commanded Judah to s the LORD God of 5647
34:33 **made** all that were present in Israel **to** s, 5975
34:33 to serve, *even* to s the LORD their God. 5647
35: 3 s now the LORD your God, and his 5647
Job 21:15 *is* the Almighty, that we should s him? 5647
36:11 s *him*, they shall spend their days in 5647
39: 9 Will the unicorn be willing to s thee, or 5647
Ps 2:11 S the LORD with fear, and rejoice with 5647
18:43 a people *whom* I have not known shall s 5647
22:30 A seed shall s him; it shall be accounted to 5647
72:11 down before him: all nations shall s him. 5647
97: 7 Confounded be all they that s graven 5647
100: 2 S the LORD with gladness: come before 5647
101: 6 that walketh in a perfect way, he shall s me. 8334
102:22 and the kingdoms, to s the LORD. 5647
Isa 14: 3 hard bondage wherein thou wast **made to** s, 5647
19:23 the Egyptians shall s *with* the Assyrians. 5647
43:23 I have not **caused** thee **to** s with an 5647
43:24 thou hast **made** me **to** s with thy sins, 5647
56: 6 to s him, and to love the name of 8334
60:12 kingdom that will not s thee shall perish; 5647
Jer 5:19 shall ye s strangers in a land *that is* not 5647
11:10 and they went after other gods to s them: 5647
13:10 other gods, to s them, and to worship them, 5647
16:13 there shall ye s other gods day and night; 5647
17: 4 I will **cause** thee **to** s thine enemies in 5647
25: 6 go not after other gods to s them, and 5647
25:11 these nations shall s the king of Babylon 5647
25:14 great kings shall s themselves of them also: 5647
27: 6 of the field have I given him also to s him. 5647
27: 7 all nations shall s him, and his son, and 5647
27: 7 and great kings shall s themselves of him. 5647
27: 8 kingdom which will not s the same 5647
27: 9 Ye shall not s the king of Babylon: 5647
27:11 s him, those will I let remain still in their 5647
27:12 and s him and his people, and live. 5647
27:13 nation that will not s the king of Babylon? 5647
27:14 Ye shall not s the king of Babylon: 5647
27:17 unto them; s the king of Babylon, and live: 5647
28:14 that *they* may s Nebuchadnezzar king of 5647
28:14 king of Babylon; and they shall s him: 5647
30: 8 strangers shall no more s themselves of 5647
30: 9 they shall s the LORD their God, and 5647
34: 9 that none should s himself of them, *to wit*, 5647
34:10 that none should s themselves of them any 5647
35:15 go not after other gods to s them, and 5647
40: 9 saying, Fear not to s the Chaldeans: 5647
40: 9 dwell in the land and s the king of Babylon, 5647
40:10 I *will* dwell at Mizpah to s the Chaldeans, 5975
44: 3 *and* to s other gods, whom they knew not, 5647
Eze 20:32 of the countries, to s wood and stone. 8334
20:39 s ye every one his idols, and hereafter *also*, 5647
20:40 of Israel, all of them in the land, s me: 5647
29:18 **caused** his army **to** s a great service against 5647
48:18 shall be for food unto them that s the city. 5647
48:19 they that s the city shall serve it out of all 5647
48:19 they that serve the city shall s it out of all 5647
Da 3:12 they s not thy gods, nor worship the golden 6399
3:14 and Abed-nego, do not ye s my gods, 6399
3:17 our God whom we s *is* able to deliver us 6399
3:18 O king, that we will not s thy gods, 6399
3:28 that they might not s nor worship any god, 6399
7:14 and languages, should s him: 6399
7:27 and all dominions shall s and obey him. 6399
Zep 3: 9 of the LORD, to s him *with* one consent. 5647

Mal 3:14 Ye have said, It is vain to s God: and 5647
Mt 4:10 Lord thy God, and him only shalt thou s. 3000
6:24 No man can s two masters: for either he 1398
6:24 the other. Ye cannot s God and mammon. 1398
Lk 1:74 of our enemies might s him without fear, 3000
4: 8 Lord thy God, and him only shalt thou s. 3000
10:40 care that my sister hath left me to s alone? 1247
12:37 to meat, and will come forth and s them. 1247
15:29 his father, Lo, these many years do I s thee, 1398
16:13 No servant can s two masters: for either he 1398
16:13 the other. Ye cannot s God and mammon. 1398
17: 8 and gird thyself, and s me, till I have eaten 1247
22:26 and he that is chief, as he that doth s. 1247
Jn 12:26 If any man s me, let him follow me; and 1247
12:26 if any man s me, him will my Father 1247
Ac 6: 2 should leave the word of God, and s tables. 1247
7: 7 they come forth, and s me in this place. 3000
27:23 angel of God, whose I am, and whom I s, 3000
Ro 1: 9 whom I s with my spirit in the gospel of his 3000
6: 6 that henceforth we should not s sin. 1398
7: 6 that we should s in newness of spirit, and 1398
7:25 with the mind I myself s the law of God; 1398
9:12 said unto her, The elder shall s the younger. 1398
16:18 For they that are such s not our Lord Jesus 1398
Gal 5:13 to the flesh, but by love s one another. 1398
Col 3:24 of the inheritance: for ye s the Lord Christ. 1398
1Th 1: 9 how ye turned to God from idols to s 1398
2Ti 1: 3 whom I s from my forefathers with pure 3000
Heb 8: 5 Who s unto the example and shadow of 3000
9:14 from dead works to s the living God? 3000
12:28 whereby we may s God acceptably with 3000
13:10 whereof they have no right to eat which s 3000
Rev 7:15 and s him day and night in his temple: 3000
22: 3 shall be in it; and his servants shall s him: 3000

SERVED (74) [SERVE]

Ge 14: 4 Twelve years they s Chedorlaomer, and 5647
29:20 Jacob s seven years for Rachel; and 5647
29:30 and s with him yet seven other years. 5647
30:26 for whom I have s thee, and let me go: 5647
30:29 Thou knowest how I have s thee, and how 5647
31: 6 ye know that with all my power I have s 5647
31:41 I s thee fourteen years for thy two 5647
39: 4 found grace in his sight, and he s him: 8334
40: 4 charged Joseph with them, and he s them: 8334
Dt 12: 2 nations which ye shall possess s their gods, 5647
17: 3 hath gone and s other gods, and 5647
29:26 For they went and s other gods, and 5647
Jos 23:16 have gone and s other gods, and 5647
24: 2 the father of Nachor: and they s other gods. 5647
24:14 put away the gods which your fathers s on 5647
24:15 whether the gods which your fathers s that 5647
24:31 Israel s the LORD all the days of Joshua, 5647
Jdg 2: 7 the people s the LORD all the days of 5647
2:11 in the sight of the LORD, and s Baalim: 5647
2:13 the LORD, and s Baal and Ashtaroth. 5647
3: 6 daughters to their sons, and s their gods. 5647
3: 7 their God, and s Baalim and the groves. 5647
3: 8 the children of Israel s Chushan-rishathaim 5647
3:14 So the children of Israel s Eglon the king of 5647
8: 1 Why hast thou s us thus, that thou calledst 6213
10: 6 s Baalim, and Ashtaroth, and the gods of 5647
10: 6 and forsook the LORD, and s not him. 5647
10:10 have forsaken our God, and also s Baalim. 5647
10:13 Yet ye have forsaken me, and s other gods: 5647
10:16 gods from among them, and s the LORD: 5647
1Sa 7: 4 and Ashtaroth, and s the LORD only. 5647
8: 8 and s other gods, so do they also unto thee. 5647
12:10 and have s Baalim and Ashtaroth: 5647
2Sa 10:19 they made peace with Israel, and s them. 5647
16:19 as I have s in thy father's presence, so will I 5647
1Ki 4:21 and s Solomon all the days of his life. 5647
9: 9 and have worshipped them, and s them: 5647
16:31 and went and s Baal, and worshipped him. 5647
22:53 For he s Baal, and worshipped him, and 5647
2Ki 10:18 and said unto them, Ahab s Baal a little; 5647
17:12 For they s idols, whereof the LORD had 5647
17:16 all the host of heaven, and s Baal. 5647
17:33 feared the LORD, and s their own gods, 5647
17:41 s their graven images, both their children, 5647
18: 7 against the king of Assyria, and s him not. 5647
21: 3 all the host of heaven, and s them. 5647
21:21 and s the idols that his father served, 5647
21:21 and served the idols that his father s, 5647
1Ch 19: 5 and told David how the men were s. NIH
27: 1 their officers that s the king in any matter 8334
2Ch 7:22 and worshipped them, and s them: 5647
24:18 God of their fathers, and s groves and idols: 5647
33: 3 all the host of heaven, and s them. 5647
33:22 Manasseh his father had made, and s them; 5647
Ne 9:35 For they have not s thee in their kingdom, 5647
Est 1:10 the seven chamberlains that s in 8334
Ps 106:36 they s their idols: which were a snare unto 5647
137: 8 he be, that rewardeth thee as thou hast s us. 1580
Ecc 5: 9 is for all: the king himself is s by the field. 5647
Jer 5:19 s strange gods in your land, so shall ye 5647
8: 2 whom they have s, and after whom they 5647
16:11 have s them, and have worshipped them, 5647
22: 9 and worshipped other gods, and s them. 5647
34:14 when he hath s thee six years, thou shalt let 5647
52:12 which s the king of Babylon, 5975+6440+3807.1
Eze 29:18 for the service that he had s against it: 5647
29:20 for his labour wherewith he s against it, 5647
34:27 the hand of those that s themselves of them. 5647
Hos 12:12 Israel s for a wife, and for a wife he kept 5647
Lk 2:37 but s God with fastings and prayers night 3000
Jn 12: 2 they made him a supper; and Martha s: 1247
Ac 13:36 after he had s his own generation by 5256
Ro 1:25 and s the creature more than the Creator, 3000
Php 2:22 the father, he hath s with me in the gospel. 1398

SERVEDST (1) [SERVE]

Dt 28:47 Because thou s not the LORD thy God 5647

SERVEST (2) [SERVE]

Da 6:16 Thy God whom thou s continually, 6399
6:20 is thy God, whom thou s continually, 6399

SERVETH (9) [SERVE]

Nu 3:36 all the vessels thereof, and all that s thereto, 5656
Mal 3:17 as a man spareth his own son that s him. 5647
3:18 between him that s God and him that 5647
3:18 that serveth God and him that s him not. 5647
Lk 22:27 he that sitteth at meat, or he that s? 1247
22:27 at meat? but I am among you as he that s. 1247
Ro 14:18 For he that in these things s Christ is 1398
1Co 14:22 prophesying s not for them that believe not, NIG
Gal 3:19 Wherefore then s the law? It was added NIG

SERVICE (132) [SERVE]

Ge 29:27 we will give thee this also for the s which 5656
30:26 for thou knowest my s which I have done 5656
Ex 1:14 in brick, and in all manner of s in the field: 5656
1:14 all their s, wherein they made them serve, 5656
12:25 he hath promised, that ye shall keep this s. 5656
12:26 say unto you, What mean you by this s? 5656
13: 5 that thou shalt keep this s in this month. 5656
27:19 All the vessels of the tabernacle in all the s 5656
30:16 shalt appoint it for the s of the tabernacle of 5656
31:10 the clothes of s, and the holy garments for 8278
35:19 The clothes of s, to do service in the holy 8278
35:19 to do s in the holy place, the holy garments 8334
35:21 and for all his s, and for the holy garments. 5656
35:24 found shittim wood for any work of the s, 5656
36: 1 manner of work for the s of the sanctuary, 5656
36: 3 for the work of the s of the sanctuary, 5656
36: 5 more than enough for the s of the work, 5656
38:21 for the s of the Levites, by the hand of 5656
39: 1 and scarlet, they made clothes of s, 8278
39: 1 to do s in the holy place, and made the holy 8334
39:40 all the vessels of the s of the tabernacle, 5656
39:41 The clothes of s to do service in the holy 8278
39:41 The clothes of service to do s in the holy 8334
Nu 3: 7 to do the s of the tabernacle. 5656
3: 8 of Israel, to do the s of the tabernacle. 5656
3:26 and the cords of it for all the s thereof. 5656
3:31 and the hanging, and all the s thereof. 5656
4: 4 This shall be the s of the sons of Kohath in 5656
4:19 appoint them every one to his s and to his 5656
4:23 all that enter in to perform the s, to 6633+6635
4:24 This is the s of the families of 5656
4:26 all the instruments of their s, and all that is 5656
4:27 his sons shall be all the s of the sons of 5656
4:27 in all their burdens, and in all their s: 5656
4:28 This is the s of the families of the sons of 5656
4:30 every one that entereth into the s, to do 6635
4:31 according to all their s in the tabernacle of 5656
4:32 all their instruments, and with all their s: 5656
4:33 This is the s of the families of the sons of 5656
4:33 according to all their s, in the tabernacle of 5656
4:35 years old, every one that entereth into the s, 6635
4:37 all that might do s in the tabernacle of 5647
4:39 years old, every one that entereth into the s, 6635
4:41 of all that might do s in the tabernacle of 5647
4:43 years old, every one that entereth into the s, 6635
4:47 every one that came to do the s of 5656
4:47 the s of the burden in the tabernacle of 5656
4:49 every one according to his s, and 5656
7: 5 that they may be to do the s of 5656
7: 5 to every man according to his s. 5656
7: 7 the sons of Gershon, according to their s: 5656
7: 8 the sons of Merari, according unto their s, 5656
7: 9 the s of the sanctuary belonging unto them 5656
8:11 that they may execute the s of the LORD. 5656
8:15 after that shall the Levites go in to do the s 5656
8:19 to do the s of the children of Israel in 5656
8:22 after that went the Levites in to do their s in 5656
8:24 upward they shall go in to wait upon the s 5656
8:25 they shall cease waiting upon the s thereof, 5656
8:26 to keep the charge, and shall do no s. 5656
16: 9 to bring you near to himself to do the s of 5656
18: 4 for all the s of the tabernacle: 5656
18: 6 to do the s of the tabernacle of 5656
18: 7 your priest's office unto you as a s of gift: 5656
18:21 for their s which they serve, even 5656
18:21 even the s of the tabernacle of 5656
18:23 the Levites shall do the s of the tabernacle 5656
18:31 for it is your reward for your s in 5656
Jos 22:27 that we might do the s of the LORD 5656
1Ki 12: 4 make thou the grievous s of thy father, 5656
1Ch 6:31 these are they whom David set over the s of 3027
6:48 of s of the tabernacle of the house of God. 5656
9:13 very able men for the work of the s of 5656
9:19 the Korahites, were over the work of the s, 5656
23:24 that did the work for the s of the house of 5656
23:26 nor any vessels of it for the s thereof. 5656
23:28 Aaron for the s of the house of the LORD, 5656
23:28 and the work of the s of the house of God; 5656
23:32 in the s of the house of the LORD. 5656
24: 3 according to their offices in their s. 5656
24:19 These were the orderings of them in their s 5656
25: 1 the captains of the host separated to the s of 5656
25: 1 of the workmen according to their s was: 5656
25: 6 and harps, for the s of the house of God, 5656
26: 8 able men for strength for the s, 5656
26:30 of the LORD, and in the s of the king. 5656
28:13 for all the work of the s of the house of 5656
28:13 for all the vessels of s in the house of 5656
28:14 of all manner of s; 5656+5656+2050.1
28:14 of every kind of s: 5656+5656+2050.1
28:20 work for the s of the house of the LORD. 5656
28:21 even they shall be with thee for all the s of 5656
28:21 willing skilful man, for any manner of s: 5656
29: 5 is willing to consecrate his s this day unto 3027
29: 7 gave for the s of the house of God of gold 5656
2Ch 8:14 the courses of the priests to their s, and 5656
12: 8 that they may know my s, and the service 5656
12: 8 and the s of the kingdoms of the countries. 5656
24:12 work of the s of the house of the LORD, 5656
29:35 So the s of the house of the LORD was set 5656
31: 2 every man according to his s, the priests 5656
31:16 his daily portion for their s in their charges 5656
31:21 in every work that he began in the s of 5656
34:13 work in any manner of s: 5656+5656+2050.1
35: 2 encouraged them to the s of the house of 5656
35:10 So the s was prepared, and the priests stood 5656
35:15 they might not depart from their s; 5656
35:16 So all the s of the LORD was prepared 5656
Ezr 6:18 for the s of God, which is at Jerusalem; 5673
7:19 thee for the s of the house of thy God, 6402
8:20 the princes had appointed for the s of 5656
Ne 10:32 a shekel for the s of the house of our God; 5656
Ps 104:14 for the cattle, and herb for the s of man: 5656
Jer 22:13 that useth his neighbour's s without wages, 5647
Eze 29:18 his army to serve a great s against Tyrus: 5656
29:18 for the s that he had served against it: 5656
44:14 for all the s thereof, and for all that shall be 5656
Jn 16: 2 killeth you will think that he doeth God s. 2999
Ro 9: 4 the law, and the s of God, and the promises; 2999
12: 1 unto God, which is your reasonable s. 2999
15:31 that my s which I have for Jerusalem may 1248
2Co 9:12 For the administration of this s not only 3009
11: 8 taking wages of them, to do you s. 1248
Gal 4: 8 ye did s unto them which by nature are no 1398
Eph 6: 7 With good will doing s, as to the Lord, and 1398
Php 2:17 upon the sacrifice and s of your faith, 3009
2:30 his life, to supply your lack of s toward me. 3009
1Ti 6: 2 but rather do them s, because they are 1398
Heb 9: 1 covenant had also ordinances of divine s, 2999
9: 6 accomplishing the s of God. 2999
9: 9 that could not make him that did the s 3000
Rev 2:19 I know thy works, and charity, and s, 1248

SERVILE (12) [SERVE]

Lev 23: 7 ye shall do no s work therein. 5656
23: 8 ye shall do no s work therein. 5656
23:21 ye shall do no s work therein: it shall be a 5656
23:25 Ye shall do no s work therein: but ye shall 5656
23:35 ye shall do no s work therein. 5656
23:36 and ye shall do no s work therein. 5656
Nu 28:18 ye shall do no manner of s work therein: 5656
28:25 a holy convocation; ye shall do no s work. 5656
28:26 a holy convocation; ye shall do no s work: 5656
29: 1 a holy convocation; ye shall do no s work: 5656
29:12 ye shall do no s work, and ye shall keep a 5656
29:35 ye shall do no s work therein: 5656

SERVING (7) [SERVE]

Ex 14: 5 that we have let Israel go from s us? 5647
Dt 15:18 hired servant to thee, in s thee six years: 5647
Lk 10:40 But Martha was cumbered about much s, 1248
Ac 20:19 S the Lord with all humility of mind, and 1398
26: 7 instantly s God day and night, hope to 3000
Ro 12:11 in business; fervent in spirit; s the Lord; 1398
Tit 3: 3 deceived, s divers lusts and pleasures, 1398

SERVITOR (1) [SERVE]

2Ki 4:43 his s said, What, should I set this before an 8334

SERVITUDE (2) [SERVE]

2Ch 10: 4 ease thou somewhat the grievous s of thy 5656
La 1: 3 of affliction, and because of great s: 5656

SET (695) [SETTER, SETTEST, SETTETH, SETTING, SETTINGS]

Ge 1:17 God s them in the firmament of the heaven 5414
4:15 the LORD s a mark upon Cain, lest any 7760
6:16 the door of the ark shalt thou s in the side 7760
9:13 I do s my bow in the cloud, and it shall be 5414
17:21 unto thee at this s time in the next year. 4150
18: 8 which he had dressed, and s it before them; 5414
19:16 him forth, and s him without the city. 3240
21: 2 at the s time of which God had spoken to 4150
21:28 Abraham s seven ewe lambs of the flock by 5324
21:29 lambs which thou hast s by themselves? 5324
24:33 there was s meat before him to eat: but 7760
28:11 tarried there all night, because the sun was s; 935
28:12 behold a ladder s up on the earth, and 5324
28:18 s it up for a pillar, and poured oil upon 7760
28:22 this stone, which I have s for a pillar, 7760
30:36 he s three days' journey betwixt himself 7760
30:38 he s the rods which he had pilled before 3322
30:40 s the faces of the flocks toward 5414
31:17 and s his sons and his wives upon camels; 5375
31:21 and s his face toward the mount Gilead. 7760
31:37 s it here before my brethren and 7760
31:45 Jacob took a stone, and s it up for a pillar. 7311
35:14 Jacob s up a pillar in the place where he 5324
35:20 Jacob s a pillar upon her grave: that is 5324
41:33 and wise, and s him over the land of Egypt. 7896
41:41 I have s thee over all the land of Egypt. 5414
43: 9 s him before thee, then let me bear 3322
43:31 and refrained himself, and said, S on bread. 7760
43:32 they s on for him by himself, and for them 7760
44:21 unto me, that I may s mine eyes upon him. 7760
47: 7 Jacob his father, and s him before Pharaoh: 5975
48:20 and he s Ephraim before Manasseh. 7760
Ex 1:11 Therefore they did s over them taskmasters 7760
4:20 s them upon an ass, and he returned to 7392
5:14 which Pharaoh's taskmasters had s over 7760
7:23 neither did he s his heart to this also. 7896
9: 5 the LORD appointed a s time, saying, 4150
13:12 That thou shalt s apart unto the LORD all 5674
19:12 thou shalt s bounds unto the people round 1379
19:23 S bounds about the mount, and sanctify it. 1379
21: 1 judgments which thou shalt s before them. 7760
23:31 I will s thy bounds from the Red sea even 7896
25: 7 stones to be s in the ephod, and in 4394
25:30 thou shalt s upon the table shewbread 5414
26:17 one board, s in order one against another: 7947
26:35 thou shalt s the table without the vail, and 7760
28:11 thou shalt make them to be s in ouches of 5437

Ex 28:17 thou shalt **s** in it settings of stones, 4390
28:20 they shall be **s** in gold in their inclosings. 7660
31: 5 to **s** *them,* and in carving of timber, 4390
32:22 the people, that they *are* **s** on mischief. NIH
35: 9 stones to be **s** for the ephod, and for 4394
35:27 stones to be **s**, for the ephod, and for 4394
35:33 to **s** *them,* and in carving of wood, 4390
37: 3 of gold, *to be* **s** by the four corners of it; NIH
39:10 they **s** in it four rows of stones: *the first* row 4390
39:37 *even with* the lamps to be **s in order**, and 4634
40: 2 **s up** the tabernacle of the tent of 6965
40: 4 **s in order** the things that are to be set in 6186
40: 4 the things that are to be **s in order** upon it; 6187
40: 5 thou shalt **s** the altar of gold for the incense 5414
40: 6 thou shalt **s** the altar of the burnt offering 5414
40: 7 thou shalt **s** the laver between the tent of 5414
40: 8 thou shalt **s up** the court round about, and 7760
40:18 **s up** the boards thereof, and put in the bars 7760
40:20 **s** the staves on the ark, and put the mercy 7760
40:21 **s up** the vail of the covering, and 7760
40:23 he **s** the bread **in order** upon it 6186+6187
40:28 he **s up** the hanging at the door of 7760
40:30 he **s** the laver between the tent of 7760
40:33 and **s up** the hanging of the court gate. 5414
Lev 17:10 I will even **s** my face against *that* soul that 5414
20: 3 I will **s** my face against that man, and 5414
20: 5 I will **s** my face against that man, 7760
20: 6 I will even **s** my face against that soul, and 5414
24: 6 thou shalt **s** them *in* two rows, six on a row, 7760
24: 8 Every sabbath he shall **s** it **in order** before 6186
26: 1 neither shall ye **s up** *any* image of stone in 5414
26:11 I will **s** my tabernacle amongst you: and 5414
26:17 I will **s** my face against you, and ye shall be 5414
Nu 1:51 is to be pitched, the Levites shall **s** it **up**: 6965
2: 9 their armies. *These* shall first **s forth**. 5265
2:16 And they shall **s forth** in the second rank. 5265
2:17 **s forward** *with* the camp of the Levites in 5265
2:17 as they encamp, so shall they **s forward**, 5265
2:34 so they **s forward**, every one after their 5265
4:15 the sanctuary, as the camp is to **s forward**; 5265
5:16 her near, and **s** her before the LORD: 5975
5:18 the priest shall **s** the woman before 5975
5:30 shall **s** the woman before the LORD, and 5975
7: 1 that Moses had fully **s up** the tabernacle, 6965
8:13 thou shalt **s** the Levites before Aaron, and 5975
10:17 and the sons of Merari **s forward**, 5265
10:18 **s forward** according to their armies: 5265
10:21 the Kohathites **s forward**, bearing 5265
10:21 *the other* did **s up** the tabernacle against 6965
10:22 **s forward** according to their armies: 5265
10:25 the camp of the children of Dan **s forward**, 5265
10:28 to their armies, when they **s forward**. 5265
10:35 when the ark **s forward**, that Moses said, 5265
11:24 and **s** them round about the tabernacle. 5975
21: 8 thee a fiery *serpent,* and **s** it upon a pole: 7760
21:10 the children of Israel **s forward**, and 5265
22: 1 the children of Israel **s forward**, and 5265
24: 1 but he **s** his face toward the wilderness. 7896
27:16 of all flesh, **s** a man over the congregation, 6485
27:19 **s** him before Eleazar the priest, and before 5975
27:22 **s** him before Eleazar the priest, and before 5975
29:39 shall do unto the LORD in your **s feasts**, 4150
Dt 1: 8 Behold, I have **s** the land before you: go in 5414
1:21 the LORD thy God hath **s** the land before 5414
4: 8 all this law, which I **s** before you *this* day? 5414
4:44 this *is* the law which Moses **s** before 7760
7: 7 The LORD did not **s** his **love** upon you, 2836
11:26 I **s** before you *this* day a blessing and 5414
11:32 judgments which I **s** before you *this* day. 5414
14:24 thy God shall choose to **s** his name there, 7760
16:22 Neither shalt thou **s** thee **up** *any* image; 6965
17:14 shalt say, I will **s** a king over me, 7760
17:15 Thou shalt **in any wise s** *him* king 7760+7760
17:15 *one* from among thy brethren shalt thou **s** 7760
17:15 thou mayest not **s** a stranger over thee, 5414
19:14 which they of old time have **s** in thine 1379
26: 4 **s** it **down** before the altar of the LORD 3240
26:10 thou shalt **s** it before the LORD thy God, 3240
27: 2 that thou shalt **s** thee **up** great stones, and 6965
27: 4 *that* ye shall **s up** these stones, which I 6965
28: 1 that the LORD thy God will **s** thee on high 5414
28:36 and thy king which thou shalt **s** over thee, 6965
28:56 which would not adventure to **s** the sole of 3322
30: 1 which I have **s** before thee, and thou shalt 5414
30:15 I have **s** before thee *this* day life and good, 5414
30:19 *that* I have **s** before you life and death, 5414
32: 8 he **s** the bounds of the people according to 5324
32:22 **s on fire** the foundations of the mountains. 3857
32:46 **S** your hearts unto all the words which I 7760
Jos 4: 9 Joshua **s up** twelve stones in the midst of 6965
6:26 in his youngest *son* shall he **s up** the gates 5324
8: 8 the city, *that* ye shall **s** the city on fire: 3341
8:12 **s** them to lie in ambush between Beth-el 7760
8:13 when they had **s** the people, *even* all 7760
8:19 took it, and hasted and **s** the city on fire. 3341
10:18 the cave, and **s** men by it for to keep them: 6485
18: 1 **s up** the tabernacle of the congregation 7931
24:25 **s** them a statute and an ordinance in 7760
24:26 great stone, and **s** it **up** there under an oak, 6965
Jdg 1: 8 the edge of the sword, and **s** the city on fire. 7971
6:18 bring forth my present, and **s** *it* before thee. 3240
7: 5 a dog lappeth, him shalt thou **s** by himself; 3322
7:19 *and* they had but **newly s** the watch: 6965+6965
7:22 the LORD **s** every man's sword against 7760
9:25 the men of Shechem **s** liers in wait for him 7760
9:33 thou shalt rise early, and **s** upon the city: 6584
9:49 the hold, and **s** the hold on fire upon them; 3341
15: 5 when he had **s** the brands on fire, he let 1197
16:25 and they **s** him between the pillars. 5975
18:30 the children of Dan **s up** the graven image: 6965
18:31 they **s** them **up** Micah's graven image, 7760
20:22 **s** *their* battle again **in array** in the place 6186
20:29 Israel **s** liers in wait round about Gibeah. 7760
20:36 in wait which they had **s** beside Gibeah. 7760
20:48 also they **s** on fire all the cities that they 7971
Ru 2: 5 said Boaz unto his servant that was **s** over 5324
2: 6 the servant that was **s** over the reapers 5324
1Sa 2: 8 to **s** *them* among princes, and to make them 3427
2: 8 and he hath **s** the world upon them. 7896
5: 2 *into* the house of Dagon, and **s** it by Dagon. 3322
5: 3 took Dagon, and **s** him in his place **again**. 7725
6:18 whereon they **s down** the ark of 3240
7:12 **s** *it* between Mizpeh and Shen, and 7760
8:12 *will* **s** *them* to ear his ground, and to reap his NIH
9:20 lost three days ago, **s** not thy mind on them; 7760
9:23 of which I said unto thee, **S** it by thee. 7760
9:24 *that* which *was* upon it, and **s** *it* before Saul. 7760
9:24 that which is left; **s** *it* before thee, *and* eat: 7760
10:19 said unto him, *Nay,* but **s** a king over us. 7760
12:13 behold, the LORD hath **s** a king over you. 5414
13: 8 according to the **s time** that Samuel *had* 4150
15:11 me that I have **s up** Saul **to be king**: 4427+4428
15:12 he **s** him **up** a place, and is gone about, and 5324
17: 2 **s** the battle **in array** against the Philistines. 6186
17: 8 are ye come out to **s** *your* battle **in array**? 6186
18: 5 Saul **s** him over the men of war, and he was 7760
18:30 of Saul; so that his name was much **s by**. 3365
22: 9 which *was* **s** over the servants of Saul, and 5324
26:24 as thy life was **much s by** this day in mine 1431
26:24 let my life be **much s by** in the eyes of 1431
28:22 and let me **s** a morsel of bread before thee; 7760
2Sa 3:10 to **s up** the throne of David over Israel and 6965
6: 3 they **s** the ark of God upon a new cart, and 7392
6:17 the ark of the LORD, and **s** it in his place, 3322
7:12 thy fathers, I will **s up** thy seed after thee, 6965
10:17 the Syrians **s** *themselves* **in array** against 6186
11:15 **S** ye Uriah in the forefront of the hottest 3051
12:20 they **s** bread before him, and he did eat. 7760
12:30 it was **s** on David's head. And he brought NIH
14:30 and he hath barley there; go and **s** it on fire. 3341
14:30 And Absalom's servants **s** the field on fire. 3341
14:31 Wherefore have thy servants **s** my field on 3341
15:24 they **s down** the ark of God; and 3332
18: 1 **s** captains of thousands and captains of 7760
18:13 thou thyself wouldest have **s** thyself 3320
19:28 yet didst thou **s** thy servant among them 7896
20: 5 he tarried longer than the **s time** which he 4150
23:23 *first* three. And David **s** him over his guard. 7760
1Ki 2:15 *that* all Israel **s** their faces on me, that *I* 7760
2:19 **caused** a seat to **be s** for the king's mother; 7760
2:24 **s** me on the throne of David my father, and 3427
5: 5 whom I will **s** upon thy throne in thy room, 5414
6:19 to **s** there the ark of the covenant of 5414
6:27 he **s** the cherubims within the inner house: 5414
7:16 to **s** upon the tops of the pillars: 5414
7:21 he **s up** the pillars in the porch of 6965
7:21 he **s up** the right pillar, and called the name 6965
7:21 he **s up** the left pillar, and called the name 6965
7:25 the sea *was* **s** above upon them, and all their NIH
7:39 he **s** the sea on the right side of the house 5414
8:21 I have **s** there a place for the ark, wherein *is* 7760
9: 6 *and* my statutes which I have **s** before you, 5414
10: 9 in thee, to **s** thee on the throne of Israel: 5414
12:29 he **s** the one in Beth-el, and the other put he 7760
14: 4 for his eyes were **s** by reason of his age. 6965
15: 4 to **s up** his son after him, and to establish 6965
16:34 **s up** the gates thereof in his youngest *son* 5324
20:12 **S** *yourselves in array.* And they set 7760
20:12 Set *yourselves in array.* And they **s** 7760
21: 9 and **s** Naboth on high among the people: 3427
21:10 **s** two men, sons of Belial, before him, to 3427
21:12 and **s** Naboth on high among the people. 3427
2Ki 4: 4 and thou shalt **s aside** *that* which *is* full. 5265
4:10 let us **s** for him there a bed, and a table, and 7760
4:38 **S on** the great pot, and seethe pottage for 8239
4:43 should I **s** this before an hundred men? 5414
4:44 So he **s** *it* before them, and they did eat, and 5414
6:22 **s** bread and water before them, that they 7760
8:12 their strong holds wilt thou **s** on fire, and 7971
10: 3 **s** *him* on his father's throne, and fight for 7760
12: 4 *account,* the money that every man is **s at**, 6187
12: 9 hole in the lid of it, and **s** it beside the altar, 5414
12:17 and Hazael **s** his face to go up to Jerusalem. 7760
17:10 they **s** them **up** images and groves in every 5324
18:23 if thou be able on thy part to **s** riders upon 5414
20: 1 saith the LORD, **S** thine house **in order**; 6680
21: 7 he **s** a graven image of the grove that he 7760
25:19 out of the city he took an officer that was **s** 6496
25:28 **s** his throne above the throne of the kings 5414
1Ch 6:31 these *are they* whom David **s** over 5975
9:22 Samuel the seer did ordain in their **s office**. 530
9:26 *were* in *their* **s office**, and were over 530
9:31 had the **s office** over the things that were 530
11:14 they **s** themselves in the midst of *that* 3320
11:25 *first* three: and David **s** him over his guard. 7760
16: 1 **s** it in the midst of the tent that David had 3322
19:10 Now when Joab saw that the battle was **s** 6440
19:11 they **s** *themselves* **in array** against 6186
19:17 and **s** *the battle* **in array** against them. 6186
20: 2 stones in it; and it was **s** upon David's head: NIH
21:18 **s up** an altar unto the LORD in 6965
22: 2 he **s** masons to hew wrought stones to build 5975
22:19 Now **s** your heart and your soul to seek 5414
23: 4 four thousand *were* to **s forward** the work 5329
23:31 new moons, and on the **s feasts**, by number, 4150
29: 2 onyx stones, and *stones* to be **s**, 4394
29: 3 I have **s** my **affection** to the house of my 7521
2Ch 2:18 he **s** threescore and ten thousand of them *to* 6213
2:18 hundred overseers to **s** the people **a work**. 5647
3: 5 and **s** thereon palm trees and chains. 5927
4: 4 the sea *was* **s** above upon them, and all their NIH
4: 7 **s** *them* in the temple, five on the right hand, 5414
4:10 he **s** the sea on the right side of the east 5414
4:19 the tables whereon the shewbread *was* **s**; NIH
6:10 am **s** on the throne of Israel, as the LORD 3427
6:13 and had **s** it in the midst of the court: 5414
7:19 which I have **s** before you, and shall go and 5414
9: 8 which delighted in thee to **s** thee on his 5414
11:16 **s** their hearts to seek the LORD God of 5414
13: 3 Abijah **s** the battle **in array** with an army of 631
2Ch 13: 3 Jeroboam also **s** the battle **in array** against 6186
13:11 the *shew*bread also **s** *they* in order upon NIH
14:10 they **s** the battle **in array** in the valley of 6186
17: 2 **s** garrisons in the land of Judah, and in 5414
19: 5 he **s** judges in the land throughout all 5975
19: 8 Moreover in Jerusalem did Jehoshaphat **s** 5975
20: 3 **s** himself to seek the LORD, and 5414
20:17 Ye shall not need to fight in this *battle:* **s** 3320
20:22 the LORD **s** ambushments against 5414
23:10 he **s** all the people, every man having his 5975
23:14 of hundreds that were **s over** the host, 6485
23:19 he **s** the porters at the gates of the house of 5975
23:20 **s** the king upon the throne of the kingdom. 3427
24: 8 **s** it without at the gate of the house of 5414
24:13 they **s** the house of God in his state, and 5975
25:14 **s** them **up** to be his gods, and bowed down 5975
29:25 he **s** the Levites *in* the house of the LORD 5975
29:35 of the house of the LORD was **s in order**. 3559
31: 3 and for the new moons, and for the **s feasts**, 4150
31:15 in the cities of the priests, in *their* **s office**, 530
31:18 for in their **s office** they sanctified 530
32: 6 he **s** captains of war over the people, and 5414
33: 7 he **s** a carved image, the idol which he had 7760
33:19 **s up** groves and graven images, before he 5975
34:12 the sons of the Kohathites, to **s** *it* **forward**; 5329
35: 2 he **s** the priests in their charges, and 5975
Ezr 2:68 for the house of God to **s** it **up** in his place: 5975
3: 3 they **s** the altar upon his bases; for fear *was* 3559
3: 5 of all the **s feasts** of the LORD that were 4150
3: 8 to **s forward** the work of the house of 5329
3: 9 to **s forward** the workmen in the house of 5329
3:10 they **s** the priests in their apparel with 5975
4:10 **s** in the cities of Samaria, and the rest *that* 3488
4:12 have **s up** the walls *thereof,* and joined 3635
4:13 the walls **s up** *again, then* will they not pay 3635
4:16 builded *again,* and the walls thereof **s up**, 3635
5:11 a great king of Israel builded and **s up**. 3635
6:11 and being **s up**, let him be hanged thereon; 2211
6:18 And they **s** the priests in their divisions, and 6966
7:25 *is* in thine hand, **s** magistrates and judges, 4483
9: 9 to **s up** the house of our God, and to repair 7311
Ne 1: 9 that I have chosen to **s** my name there. 7931
2: 6 the king to send me; and I **s** him a time. 5414
3: 1 they sanctified it, and **s up** the doors of it; 5975
3: 3 **s up** the doors thereof, the locks thereof, 5975
3: 6 **s up** the doors thereof, and the locks 5975
3:13 they built it, and **s up** the doors thereof, 5975
3:14 he built it, and **s up** the doors thereof, 5975
3:15 and covered it, and **s up** the doors thereof, 5975
4: 9 **s** a watch against them day and night, 5975
4:13 Therefore **s** I in the lower places behind 5975
4:13 I even **s** the people after *their* families with 5975
5: 7 And I **s** a great assembly against them. 5414
6: 1 (though at that time I had not **s up** 5975
7: 1 I had **s up** the doors, and the porters and 5975
9:37 unto the kings whom thou hast **s** over us 5414
10:33 for the **s feasts**, and for the holy *things,* and 4150
13:11 them together, and **s** them in their place. 5975
13:19 *some* of my servants **s** I at the gates, 5975
Est 2:17 so that he **s** the royal crown upon her head, 7760
3: 1 **s** his seat above all the princes that *were* 7760
6: 8 the crown royal which is **s** upon his head: 5414
8: 2 Esther **s** Mordecai over the house of 7760
Job 5:11 To **s up** on high those that be low; 7760
6: 4 the terrors of God do **s** *themselves* **in array** 6186
7:17 that thou shouldest **s** thine heart upon him? 7896
7:20 why hast thou **s** me as a mark against thee, 7760
9:19 who shall **s** me **a time** *to plead?* 3259
14:13 that thou wouldest appoint me a **s time**, and 2706
16:12 me to pieces, and **s** me **up** for his mark. 6965
19: 8 and he hath **s** darkness in my paths. 7760
30: 1 to have **s** with the dogs of my flock. 7896
30:13 mar my path, they **s forward** my calamity, 3276
33: 5 **s** *thy words* **in order** before me, stand up. 6186
34:14 If he **s** his heart upon *man, if* he gather unto 7760
34:24 without number, and **s** others in their stead. 5975
36:16 **that which** should **be s on** thy table *should* 5183
38:10 it my decreed *place,* and **s** bars and doors, 7760
38:33 canst thou **s** the dominion thereof in 7760
Ps 2: 2 The kings of the earth **s** themselves, and 3320
2: 6 Yet have I **s** my king upon my holy hill of 5250
3: 6 that have **s** *themselves* against me round 7896
4: 3 know that the LORD hath **s apart** *him* 6395
8: 1 who hast **s** thy glory above the heavens. 5414
10: 8 his eyes are **privily s** against the poor. 6845
12: 5 I will **s** *him* in safety *from him that* puffeth 7896
16: 8 I have **s** the LORD always before me: 7737
17:11 they have **s** their eyes bowing down to 7896
19: 4 In them hath he **s** a tabernacle for the sun, 7760
20: 5 name of our God we will **s up** *our* **banners**: 1713
27: 5 he hide me; he shall **s** me **up** upon a rock. 7311
31: 8 thou hast **s** my feet in a large room. 5975
40: 2 **s** my feet upon a rock, *and* established my 6965
50:21 and **s** *them* **in order** before thine eyes. 6186
54: 3 they have not **s** God before them. Selah. 7760
57: 4 I lie *even among* them that are **s on fire**, 3857
62:10 **s** not *your* heart *upon them.* 7896
69:29 let thy salvation, O God, **s** me **up on high**. 7682
73: 9 They **s** their mouth against the heavens, and 8371
73:18 Surely thou didst **s** them in slippery *places:* 7896
74: 4 they **s up** their ensigns *for* signs. 7760
74:17 Thou hast **s** all the borders of the earth: 5324
78: 7 That they might **s** their hope in God, and 7760
78: 8 a generation *that* **s** not their heart **aright**, 3559
85:13 and shall **s** *us* in the way of his steps. 7760
86:14 my soul; and have not **s** thee before them. 7760
89:25 I will **s** his hand also in the sea, and 7760
89:42 Thou hast **s up** the right hand of his 7311
90: 8 Thou hast **s** our iniquities before thee, 7896
91:14 Because he hath **s** his **love** upon me, 2836
91:14 I will **s** him **on high**, because he hath 7682
101: 3 I will **s** no wicked thing before mine eyes: 7896
102:13 time to favour her, yea, the **s time**, is come. 4150
104: 9 Thou hast **s** a bound *that* they may not pass 7760
109: 6 **S** thou a wicked *man* over him: and 6485

Ps 113: 8 That *he* may **s** *him* with princes, *even* with 3427
118: 5 answered me, *and* **s** *me* in a large place. NIH
122: 5 For there are **s** thrones of judgment, 3427
132:11 Of the fruit of thy body will I **s** upon thy 7896
140: 5 by the way side; they have **s** grins for me. 7896
141: 2 Let my prayer be **s forth** before thee *as* 3559
141: 3 **S** a watch, O LORD, before my mouth; 7896
Pr 1:25 ye have **s at nought** all my counsel, and 6544
8:23 I was **s up** from everlasting, from 5258
8:27 when he **s** a compass upon the face of 2710
22:28 ancient landmark, which thy fathers have **s**. 6213
23: 5 Wilt thou **s** thine eyes upon that which is 5774
Ecc 3:11 also he hath **s** the world in their heart, so 5414
7:14 God also hath **s** the one over against 6213
8:11 the heart of the sons of men is **fully s** in 4390
10: 6 Folly is **s** in great dignity, and the rich sit in 5414
12: 9 sought out, *and* **s in order** many proverbs. 8626
SS 5:12 of waters, washed with milk, *and* fitly **s**. 3427
5:14 His hands *are as* gold rings **s** with the beryl: 4390
5:15 of marble, **s** upon sockets of fine gold: 3245
7: 2 thy belly *is like* a heap of wheat **s about** 5473
8: 6 **S** me as a seal upon thine heart, as a seal 7760
Isa 3:24 instead of **well s hair** baldness; and 4639+4748
7: 6 **s a king** in the midst of it, *even* 4427+4428
9:11 Therefore the LORD shall **s up** 7682
11:11 *that* the Lord shall **s** his hand **again** 3254
11:12 he shall **s up** an ensign for the nations, and 5375
14: 1 choose Israel, and **s** them in their own land: 3240
17:10 and shalt **s** it *with* strange slips: 2232
19: 2 I will **s** the Egyptians against the Egyptians: 5526
21: 6 Go, **s** a watchman, let him declare what he 5975
21: 8 and I *am* **s** in my ward whole nights: 5324
22: 7 the horsemen shall **s** themselves **in array** at 7896
23:13 they **s up** the towers thereof, they raised up 6965
27: 4 who would **s** the briers *and* thorns against 5414
27:11 the women come, *and* **s** them **on fire**: for it 215
36: 8 if thou be able on thy part to **s** riders upon 5414
38: 1 saith the LORD, **S** thine house **in order**: 6680
41:19 I will **s** in the desert the fir tree, *and* 7760
42: 4 till he have **s** judgment in the earth: 7760
42:25 it hath **s** him **on fire** round about, yet he 3857
44: 7 shall declare it, and **s** it **in order** for me, 6186
45:20 they have no knowledge that **s up** the wood 5375
46: 7 and **s** him in his place, and he standeth; 3240
49:22 and **s up** my standard to the people: 7311
50: 7 therefore have I **s** my face like a flint, and 7760
57: 7 and high mountain hast thou **s** thy bed: 7760
57: 8 the posts hast thou **s up** thy remembrance: 7760
62: 6 I have **s** watchmen upon thy walls, 6485
66:19 I will **s** a sign among them, and I will send 7760
Jer 1:10 I have this day **s** thee over the nations and 6485
1:15 they shall **s** every one his throne *at* 5414
4: 6 **S up** the standard toward Zion: retire, 5375
5:26 setteth snares; they **s** a trap, they catch men. 5324
6: 1 and **s up** a sign of fire in Beth-haccerem: 5375
6:17 Also I **s** watchmen over you, 6965
6:23 **s in array** as men for war against thee, 6186
6:27 I have **s** thee *for* a tower *and* a fortress 5414
7:12 where I **s** my name at the first, and see what 7931
7:30 they have **s** their abominations in the house 7760
9:13 forsaken my law which I **s** before them, 5414
10:20 my tent any more, and to **s up** my curtains. 6965
11:13 have ye **s up** altars to *that* shameful thing, 7760
21: 8 I **s** before you the way of life, and the way 5414
21:10 For I have **s** my face against this city for 7760
23: 4 I will **s up** shepherds over them which shall 6965
24: 1 two baskets of figs *were* **s** before 3259
24: 6 For I will **s** mine eyes upon them for good, 7760
26: 4 walk in my law, which I have **s** before you, 5414
31:21 **S** thee **up** waymarks, make thee high 5324
31:21 **s** thine heart toward the highway, *even* 7896
31:29 and the children's teeth are **s on edge**. 6949
31:30 the sour grape, his teeth shall be **s on edge**. 6949
32:20 Which hast **s** signs and wonders in the land 7760
32:29 shall come and **s** fire **on** this city, and 3341
32:34 they **s** their abominations in the house, 7760
34:16 whom ye had **s** at liberty at their pleasure, 7971
35: 5 I **s** before the sons of the house of 5414
38:22 Thy friends have **s** thee **on**, and 5496
40:11 that he had **s** over them Gedaliah the son of 6485
42:15 If ye **wholly s** your faces to enter 7760+7760
42:17 So shall it be with all the men that **s** their 7760
43:10 will **s** his throne upon these stones that I 7760
44:10 that I **s** before you and before your fathers. 5414
44:11 I will **s** my face against you for evil, and 7760
44:12 that have **s** their faces to go *into* the land of 7760
49:38 I will **s** my throne in Elam, and will destroy 7760
50: 2 and publish, and **s** up a standard; 5375
50: 9 they shall **s** *themselves* **in array** against 6186
51:12 **S up** the standard upon the walls of 5375
51:12 **s up** the watchmen, prepare the ambushes: 6965
51:27 **S** ye **up** a standard in the land, blow 5375
52:32 **s** his throne above the throne of the kings 5414
La 2:17 he hath **s up** the horn of thine adversaries. 7311
3: 6 He hath **s** me in dark places, as they that be 3427
3:12 his bow, and **s** me as a mark for the arrow. 5324
Eze 2: 2 **s** me upon my feet, that I heard him that 5975
3:24 **s** me upon my feet, and spake with me, and 5975
4: 2 **s** the camp also against it, and set *battering* 5414
4: 2 and **s** *battering* rams against it round about. 7760
4: 3 **s** it *for* a wall of iron between thee and 5414
4: 3 **s** thy face against it, and it shall be 3559
4: 7 Therefore thou shalt **s** thy face toward 3559
5: 5 I have **s** it in the midst of the nations and 7760
6: 2 **s** thy face towards the mountains of Israel, 7760
7:20 beauty of his ornament, he **s** it in majesty: 7760
7:20 therefore have I **s** it far from them. 5414
9: 4 **s a mark** upon the foreheads of 8420+8427
12: 6 for I have **s** thee *for* a sign unto the house 5414
13:17 **s** thy face against the daughters of thy 7760
14: 3 these men have **s up** their idols in their 5927
14: 8 I will **s** my face against that man, and 5414
15: 7 I will **s** my face against them; they shall go 5414
15: 7 when I **s** my face against them. 7760
16:18 thou hast **s** mine oil and mine incense 5414
Eze 16:19 thou hast even **s** it before them for a sweet 5414
17: 4 of traffick; he **s** it in a city of merchants. 7760
17: 5 *it* by great waters, *and* **s** it *as* a willow tree. 7760
17:22 will **s** *it;* I will crop off from the top of his 5414
18: 2 and the children's teeth are **s on edge**? 6949
19: 8 the nations **s** against him on every side 5414
20:46 **s** thy face toward the south, and drop *thy* 7760
21: 2 **s** thy face toward Jerusalem, and drop *thy* 7760
21:15 I have **s** the point of the sword against all 5414
21:16 on the left, whithersoever thy face *is* **s**. 3259
22: 7 In thee have they **s light** by father and 7043
22:10 her **that was s apart** for pollution. 5079
23:24 *which* shall **s** against thee buckler and 7760
23:24 I will **s** judgment before them, and 5414
23:25 I will **s** my jealousy against thee, and 5414
23:41 whereupon thou hast **s** mine incense and 7760
24: 2 the king of Babylon **s** himself against 5564
24: 3 **S on** a pot, set *it* **on**, and also pour water 8239
24: 3 on a pot, **s** *it* **on**, and also pour water into it: 8239
24: 7 she **s** it upon the top of a rock; she poured it 7760
24: 8 I have **s** her blood upon the top of a rock, 5414
24:11 **s** it empty upon the coals thereof, that 5975
24:25 that whereupon they **s** their minds, 4853
25: 2 **s** thy face against the Ammonites, 7760
25: 4 they shall **s** their palaces in thee, and 3427
26: 9 he shall **s** engines of war against thy walls, 5414
26:20 shall **s** thee in the low parts of the earth, 3427
26:20 and I shall **s** glory in the land of the living; 5414
27:10 helmet in thee; they **s forth** thy comeliness. 5414
28: 2 though thou **s** thine heart as the heart of 5414
28: 6 Because thou hast **s** thine heart as the heart 5414
28:14 I have **s** thee *so:* thou wast upon the holy 5414
28:21 **s** thy face against Zidon, and 7760
29: 2 **s** thy face against Pharaoh king of Egypt, 7760
30: 8 when I have **s** a fire in Egypt, and *when* all 5414
30:14 will **s** fire in Zoan, and will execute 5414
30:16 I will **s** fire in Egypt: Sin shall have great 5414
31: 4 the deep **s** him **up on high** with her rivers 7311
32: 8 **s** darkness upon thy land, saith the Lord 5414
32:23 Whose graves are **s** in the sides of the pit, 5414
32:25 They have **s** her a bed in the midst of 5414
33: 2 their coasts, and **s** him for their watchman: 5414
33: 7 I have **s** thee a watchman unto the house of 5414
34:23 I will **s up** one shepherd over them, and 6965
35: 2 **s** thy face against mount Seir, and 7760
37: 1 **s** me **down** in the midst of the valley which 5117
37:26 will **s** my sanctuary in the midst of them for 5414
38: 2 Son of man, **s** thy face against Gog, 7760
39: 9 shall **s on fire** and burn the weapons, 1197
39:15 man's bone, then shall he **s up** a sign by it, 1129
39:21 I will **s** my glory among the heathen, and 5414
40: 2 **s** me upon a very high mountain, by which 5117
40: 4 **s** thine heart upon all that I shall shew thee; 7760
44: 8 ye have **s** keepers of my charge in my 7760
Da 1:11 whom the prince of the eunuchs had **s** over 4487
2:44 shall the God of heaven **s up** a kingdom, 6966
2:49 he **s** Shadrach, Meshach, and Abed-nego, 4483
3: 1 he **s** it **up** in the plain of Dura, in 6966
3: 2 which Nebuchadnezzar the king had **s up**. 6966
3: 3 that Nebuchadnezzar the king had **s up**; 6966
3: 3 the image that Nebuchadnezzar had **s up**. 6966
3: 5 that Nebuchadnezzar the king hath **s up**: 6966
3: 7 that Nebuchadnezzar the king had **s up**. 6966
3:12 There are certain Jews whom thou hast **s** 4483
3:12 the golden image which thou hast **s up**. 6966
3:14 the golden image which I have **s up**? 6966
3:18 the golden image which thou hast **s up**. 6966
5:19 whom he would he **s up**; and whom he 7313
6: 1 It pleased Darius to **s** over the kingdom an 6966
6: 3 the king thought to **s** him over the whole 6966
6:14 and **s** *his* heart on Daniel to deliver him: 7761
7:10 the judgment was **s**, and the books were 3488
8:18 but he touched me, and **s** me upright. 5975
9: 3 I **s** my face unto the Lord God, to seek *by* 5414
9:10 which he **s** before us by his servants 5414
10:10 which **s** me upon my knees and *upon* 5128
10:12 for from the first day that thou didst **s** thine 5414
10:15 I **s** my face toward the ground, and 5414
11:11 he shall **s forth** a great multitude; but 5975
11:13 shall **s forth** a multitude greater than 5975
11:17 He shall also **s** his face to enter with 7760
12:11 the abomination that maketh desolate **s up**, 5414
Hos 2: 3 **s** her as *in* the day that she was born, and 3322
2: 3 **s** her like a dry land, and slay her with 7896
4: 8 and they **s** their heart on their iniquity. 5375
6:11 Also, O Judah, he hath **s** a harvest for thee, 7896
8: 1 *S* the trumpet to thy mouth. *He shall come* NIH
8: 4 They have **s up kings**, but not by me: 4427
11: 8 *how* shall I **s** thee as Zeboim? mine heart is 7760
Joel 2: 5 as a strong people **s in** battle **array**. 6186
Am 7: 8 I *will* **s** a plumbline in the midst of my 7760
8: 5 and the sabbath, that we may **s forth** wheat, 6605
9: 4 I will **s** mine eyes upon them for evil, and 7760
Ob 1: 4 though *thou* **s** thy nest among the stars, 7760
Na 3: 6 thee vile, and will **s** thee as a gazing-stock. 7760
3:13 the gates of thy land shall be **s wide** open 6605
Hab 2: 1 **s** me upon the tower, and will watch to see 3320
2: 9 that *he* may **s** his nest on high, that *he* may 7760
Zec 3: 5 Let them **s** a fair mitre upon his head. 7760
3: 5 So they **s** a fair mitre upon his head, and 7760
5:11 and **s** there upon her own base. 3240
6:11 **s** *them* upon the head of Joshua the son of 7760
8:10 for I **s** all men every one against his 7971
Mal 3:15 yea, they that work wickedness are **s up**; 1129
Mt 5: 1 and when he was **s**, his disciples came unto *2523*
5:14 A city that is **s on** a hill cannot be hid. *2749*
10:35 For I am come to **s** a man **at variance** *1369*
18: 2 unto *him,* and **s** him in the midst of them. *2476*
21: 7 them their clothes, and they **s** *him* thereon. *1940*
25:33 And he shall **s** the sheep on his right hand, *2476*
27:19 When he was **s down** on the judgment seat, *2521*
27:37 And **s up** over his head his accusation *2007*
Mk 1:32 And at even, when the sun did **s**, *1416*
4:21 a bed? *and* not to be **s** on a candlestick? *2007*
6:41 gave *them* to his disciples to **s before** them; *3908*
Mk 8: 6 gave to his disciples to **s before** *them;* and *3908*
8: 6 and they did **s** *them* **before** the people. *3908*
8: 7 commanded to **s** them also **before** *them.* *3908*
9:12 suffer many *things,* and be **s at nought**. *1847*
9:36 a child, and **s** him in the midst of them: *2476*
12: 1 and **s** a hedge **about** *it,* and digged *a place* *4060*
Lk 1: 1 **s forth in order** a declaration of those things *392*
2:34 this *child* is **s** for the fall and rising again of *2749*
4: 9 and **s** him on a pinnacle of the temple, and *2476*
4:18 to **s** at liberty *them that are* bruised, *649*
7: 8 For I also am a man **s** under authority, *5021*
9:16 gave to the disciples to **s before** *3908*
9:47 their heart, took a child, and **s** him by him, *2476*
9:51 he **stedfastly s** his face to go to Jerusalem, *4741*
10: 8 eat such *things* as are **s before** you: *3908*
10:34 and **s** him **on** his own beast, and *1913*
11: 6 to me, and I have nothing to **s before** him: *3908*
19:35 the colt, and they **s** Jesus **thereon**. *1913*
22:55 and were **s down together**, Peter sat down *4776*
23:11 with his men of war **s** him **at nought**, *1848*
Jn 2: 6 And there were **s** there six waterpots of *2749*
2:10 Every man at the beginning doth **s forth** *5087*
3:33 hath **s to** *his* **seal** that God is true. *4972*
6:11 and the disciples to them that were **s down**; *345*
8: 3 and when they had **s** her in the midst, *2476*
13:12 and was **s down** again, he said unto them, *377*
19:29 Now there was **s** a vessel full of vinegar: *2749*
Ac 4: 7 And when they had **s** them in the midst, *2476*
4:11 This is the stone which was **s at nought** of *1848*
5:27 they **s** *them* before the council: *2476*
6: 6 Whom they **s** before the apostles: and *2476*
6:13 And **s up** false witnesses, which said, *2476*
7: 5 in it, no, not so much as to **s** his foot **on**: *968*
7:26 **s** them **at one** *again,* saying, *1515+1519+4900*
12:21 And upon a **s** day Herod, arrayed in royal *5002*
13: 9 with the Holy Ghost, **s** his **eyes** on him, *816*
13:47 *saying,* I have **s** thee to be a light of *5087*
15:16 again the ruins thereof, and I will **s** it **up**: *461*
16:34 he **s meat before** *them,* and rejoiced, *3908+5132*
17: 5 and **s** all the city **on an uproar**, and *2350*
18:10 and no *man* shall **s on** thee to hurt thee: *2007*
19:27 this our craft is in danger to be **s at nought**; *2064*
21: 2 unto Phenicia, we went aboard, and **s forth**. *321*
22:30 brought Paul down, and **s** *him* before them. *2476*
23:24 that they may **s** Paul **on**, and bring *him* safe *1913*
26:32 This man might have been **s at liberty**, *630*
Ro 3:25 Whom God hath **s forth** *to be* a propitiation *4388*
14:10 or why dost thou **s at nought** thy brother? *1848*
1Co 4: 9 For I think that God hath **s forth** us *584*
6: 4 **s** them **to judge** who are least esteemed in *2523*
10:27 whatsoever is **s before** you, eat, asking no *3908*
11:34 And the rest will I **s in order** when I come. *1299*
12:18 But now hath God **s** the members every one *5087*
12:28 And God hath **s** some in the church, *5087*
Gal 3: 1 Jesus Christ hath been **evidently s forth**, *4270*
Eph 1:20 **s** *him* at his own right hand in the heavenly *2523*
Php 1:17 knowing that I am **s** for the defence of *2749*
Col 3: 2 **S** your **affection on** *things* above, not on *5426*
Tit 1: 5 that thou shouldest **s in order** the *things* *1930*
Heb 2: 7 didst **s** him over the works of thy hands: *2525*
6:18 to lay hold upon the hope **s before** *us:* *4295*
8: 1 who is **s** on the right hand of the throne of *2523*
12: 1 with patience the race that is **s before** us, *4295*
12: 2 who for the joy that was **s before** him *4295*
12: 2 is **s down** at the right hand of the throne of *2523*
13:23 ye that *our* brother Timothy is **s at liberty**; *630*
Jas 3: 6 course of nature; and it is **s on fire** of hell. *5394*
Jude 1: 7 strange flesh, are **s forth for** an example, *4295*
Rev 3: 8 I have **s** before thee an open door, and no *1325*
3:21 am **s down** with my Father in his throne. *2523*
4: 2 a throne was **s** in heaven, and one sat on *2749*
10: 2 and he **s** his right foot upon the sea, and *5087*
20: 3 and shut him up, and **s a seal** upon him, *4972*

SETH (8) [SHETH]

Ge 4:25 she bare a son, and called his name **S**: 8352
4:26 to **S**, *to* him also there was born a son; and 8352
5: 3 after his image; and called his name **S**: 8352
5: 4 the days of Adam after he had begotten **S** 8352
5: 6 **S** lived an hundred and five years, and 8352
5: 7 **S** lived after he begat Enos eight hundred 8352
5: 8 all the days of **S** were nine hundred 8352
Lk 3:38 *the son* of Enos, which was *the son* of **S**, *4589*

SETHUR (1)

Nu 13:13 Of the tribe of Asher, **S** the son of Michael. 5639

SETTER (1) [SET]

Ac 17:18 other *some,* He seemeth to be a **s forth** of *2604*

SETTEST (7) [SET]

Dt 23:20 **s** thine hand to in the land whither thou 4916
28: 8 and in all that thou **s** thine hand **unto**; 4916
28:20 in all that thou **s** thine hand **unto** for to do, 4916
Job 7:12 or a whale, that thou **s** a watch over me? 7760
13:27 thou **s a print** upon the heels of my feet. 2707
Ps 21: 3 thou **s** a crown of pure gold on his head. 7896
41:12 and **s** me before thy face for ever. 5324

SETTETH (22) [SET]

Nu 1:51 when the tabernacle **s forward**, the Levites 5265
4: 5 when the camp **s forward**, Aaron shall 5265
Dt 24:15 for he *is* poor, and **s** his heart upon it: 5375
27:16 Cursed *be* he that **s light** by his father or 7034
2Sa 22:34 hinds' *feet:* and **s** me upon my high places. 5975
Job 28: 3 He **s** an end to darkness, and searcheth out 7760
Ps 18:33 hinds' *feet,* and **s** me upon my high places. 5975
36: 4 he **s** himself in a way *that is* not good; 3320
65: 6 Which by his strength **s fast** the mountains; 3559
68: 6 God **s** the solitary in families: he bringeth 3427
75: 7 he putteth down one, and **s up** another. 7311
83:14 and as the flame **s** the mountains **on fire**; 3857
107:41 Yet **s** he the poor **on high** from affliction, 7682
Jer 5:26 *men:* they lay wait, as he that **s** snares; 7918

Jer 43: 3 Baruch the son of Neriah s thee on against 5496
Eze 14: 4 Every man of the house of Israel that s up 5927
14: 7 s up his idols in his heart, and putteth 5927
Da 2:21 he removeth kings, and s up kings: 6966
4:17 he will, and s up over it the basest of men. 6966
Mt 4: 5 and s him on a pinnacle of the temple, *2476*
Lk 8:16 but s *it* on a candlestick, that they *2007*
Jas 3: 6 and s on fire the course of nature; *5394*

SETTING (3) [SET]
Eze 43: 8 In their s of their threshold by my 5414
Mt 27:66 sealing the stone, and s a watch. *3326*
Lk 4:40 Now when the sun was s, all they that had *1416*

SETTINGS (1) [SET]
Ex 28:17 thou shalt set in it s of stones, *even* four 4396

SETTLE (10) [SETTLED, SETTLEST]
1Ch 17:14 I will s him in mine house and in my 5975
Eze 36:11 I will s you after your old estates, and 3427
43:14 *even* to the lower s *shall be* two cubits, 5835
43:14 from the lesser s *even* to the greater settle 5835
43:14 from the lesser settle *even* to the greater s 5835
43:17 the s *shall be* fourteen *cubits* long and 5835
43:20 on the four corners of the s, and upon 5835
45:19 upon the four corners of the s of the altar, 5835
Lk 21:14 S *it* therefore in your hearts, not to meditate *5087*
1Pe 5:10 you perfect, stablish, strengthen, s *you*. *2311*

SETTLED (7) [SETTLE]
1Ki 8:13 a s place for thee to abide in for ever. 4349
2Ki 8:11 he s his countenance stedfastly, until *he* 5975
Ps 119:89 O LORD, thy word *is* s in heaven. 5324
Pr 8:25 Before the mountains were s, before 2883
Jer 48:11 he *hath* s on his lees, and hath not been 8252
Zep 1:12 and punish the men that are s on their lees: 7087
Col 1:23 If ye continue in the faith grounded and s, *1476*

SETTLEMENT See HABITATION

SETTLEST (1) [SETTLE]
Ps 65:10 *thou* s the furrows thereof: thou makest it 5181

SEVEN (463) [SEVENFOLD, SEVENS, SEVENTH]
Ge 5: 7 he begat Enos eight hundred and s years, 7651
5:25 lived an hundred eighty and s years, 7651
5:26 Methuselah lived after he begat Lamech s 7651
5:31 all the days of Lamech were s hundred 7651
5:31 were seven hundred seventy and s years: 7651
7: 4 For yet s days, *and* I will cause it to rain 7651
7:10 it came to pass after s days, that the waters 7651
8:10 he stayed yet other s days; and again he 7651
8:12 he stayed yet other s days; and sent forth 7651
8:14 on the s and twentieth day of the month, 7651
11:21 he begat Serug two hundred and s years, 7651
21:28 Abraham set s ewe lambs of the flock by 7651
21:29 What *mean* these s ewe lambs which thou 7651
21:30 For *these* s ewe lambs shalt thou take of my 7651
23: 1 was an hundred and s and twenty years old: 7651
25:17 an hundred and thirty and s years: 7651
29:18 I will serve thee s years for Rachel thy 7651
29:20 Jacob served s years for Rachel; and 7651
29:27 thou shalt serve with me yet s other years. 7651
29:30 and served with him yet s other years. 7651
31:23 and pursued after him s days' journey; 7651
33: 3 and bowed himself to the ground s times, 7651
41: 2 there came up out of the river s well 7651
41: 3 s other kine came up after them out of 7651
41: 4 leanfleshed kine did eat up the s well 7651
41: 5 s ears of corn came up upon one stalk, rank 7651
41: 6 s thin ears and blasted with the east wind 7651
41: 7 And the s thin ears devoured the seven rank NIH
41: 7 And the seven thin ears devoured the s rank 7651
41:18 there came up out of the river s kine, 7651
41:19 s other kine came up after them, poor and 7651
41:20 the ill favoured kine did eat up the first s fat 7651
41:22 s ears came up in one stalk, full and good: 7651
41:23 s ears, withered, thin, *and* blasted with 7651
41:24 the thin ears devoured the s good ears: 7651
41:26 The s good kine *are* seven years; and 7651
41:26 The seven good kine *are* s years; and 7651
41:26 and the s good ears *are* seven years: 7651
41:26 and the seven good ears *are* s years: 7651
41:27 the s thin and ill favoured kine that came up 7651
41:27 kine that came up after them *are* s years; 7651
41:27 the s empty ears blasted with the east wind 7651
41:27 the east wind shall be s years of famine. 7651
41:29 there come s years of great plenty 7651
41:30 there shall arise after them s years of 7651
41:34 the land of Egypt in the s plenteous years. 7651
41:36 to the land against the s years of famine, 7651
41:47 in the s plenteous years the earth brought 7651
41:48 he gathered up all the food of the s years, 7651
41:53 the s years of plenteousness, that was in 7651
41:54 the s years of dearth began to come, 7651
46:25 bare these unto Jacob: all the souls *were* s. 7651
47:28 of Jacob was an hundred forty and s years. 7651
50:10 he made a mourning for his father s days. 7651
Ex 2:16 Now the priest of Midian had s daughters: 7651
6:16 of Levi *were* an hundred thirty and s years. 7651
6:20 *were* an hundred and thirty and s years. 7651
7:25 s days were fulfilled, after *that* the LORD 7651
12:15 S days shall ye eat unleavened bread; 7651
12:19 S days shall there be no leaven found in 7651
13: 6 S days thou shalt eat unleavened bread, and 7651
13: 7 Unleavened bread shall be eaten s days; 7651
22:30 s days it shall be with his dam; on 7651
23:15 thou shalt eat unleavened bread s days, as I 7651
25:37 thou shalt make the s lamps thereof: and 7651
29:30 priest in his stead shall put them on s days, 7651
29:35 s days shalt thou consecrate them. 7651
29:37 S days thou shalt make an atonement for 7651
34:18 s days thou shalt eat unleavened bread, as I 7651
37:23 he made his s lamps, and his snuffers, and 7651
Ex 38:24 and s hundred and thirty shekels, 7651
38:25 a thousand s hundred and threescore and 7651
38:28 of the thousand s hundred seventy and 7651
Lev 4: 6 sprinkle of the blood s times before 7651
4:17 sprinkle *it* s times before the LORD, 7651
8:11 he sprinkled thereof upon the altar s times, 7651
8:33 tabernacle of the congregation *in* s days, 7651
8:33 an end: for s days shall he consecrate you. 7651
8:35 of the congregation day and night s days, 7651
12: 2 she shall be unclean s days; according to 7651
13: 4 shut up *him that hath* the plague s days: 7651
13: 5 the priest shall shut him up s days more: 7651
13:21 then the priest shall shut him up s days: 7651
13:26 then the priest shall shut him up s days: 7651
13:31 *him that hath* the plague of the scall s days: 7651
13:33 shut up *him that hath* the scall s days more: 7651
13:50 and shut up *it that hath* the plague s days: 7651
13:54 and he shall shut it up s days more: 7651
14: 7 is to be cleansed from the leprosy s times, 7651
14: 8 and shall tarry abroad out of his tent s days. 7651
14:16 shall sprinkle of the oil with his finger s 7651
14:27 in his left hand s times before the LORD: 7651
14:38 of the house, and shut up the house s days: 7651
14:51 and sprinkle the house s times: 7651
15:13 he shall number to himself s days for his 7651
15:19 be blood, she shall be put apart s days: 7651
15:24 be upon him, he shall be unclean s days; 7651
15:28 she shall number to herself s days, and 7651
16:14 of the blood with his finger s times. 7651
16:19 of the blood upon it with his finger s times, 7651
22:27 then it shall be s days under the dam; 7651
23: 6 s days ye must eat unleavened bread. 7651
23: 8 made by fire unto the LORD s days: 7651
23:15 s sabbaths shall be complete: 7651
23:18 ye shall offer with the bread s lambs 7651
23:34 of tabernacles *for* s days unto the LORD. 7651
23:36 S days ye shall offer an offering made by 7651
23:39 ye shall keep a feast unto the LORD s 7651
23:40 rejoice before the LORD your God s days. 7651
23:41 ye shall keep it a feast unto the LORD s 7651
23:42 Ye shall dwell in booths s days; all that are 7651
25: 8 thou shalt number s sabbaths of years unto 7651
25: 8 of years unto thee, s times seven years; 7651
25: 8 of years unto thee, seven times s years; 7651
25: 8 the space of the s sabbaths of years shall be 7651
26:18 I will punish you s *times* more for your 7651
26:21 I will bring s *times* moe plagues upon you 7651
26:24 will punish you yet s *times* for your sins. 7651
26:28 will chastise you s *times* for your sins. 7651
Nu 1:31 *were* fifty and s thousand and four hundred. 7651
1:39 and two thousand and s hundred. 7651
2: 8 *were* fifty and s thousand and four hundred. 7651
2:26 and two thousand and s hundred. 7651
2:31 and fifty and s thousand and six hundred. 7651
3:22 were numbered of them *were* s thousand 7651
4:36 their families were two thousand s hundred 7651
8: 2 the s lamps shall give light over against 7651
12:14 her face, should she not be ashamed s days? 7651
12:14 let her be shut out from the camp s days, 7651
12:15 Miriam was shut out from the camp s days: 7651
13:22 *were.* (Now Hebron was built s years 7651
16:49 were fourteen thousand and s hundred, 7651
19: 4 the tabernacle of the congregation s times: 7651
19:11 *body* of any man shall be unclean s days. 7651
19:14 that *is* in the tent, shall be unclean s days. 7651
19:16 a man, or a grave, shall be unclean s days. 7651
23: 1 Build me here s altars, and prepare me here 7651
23: 1 prepare me here s oxen and seven rams. 7651
23: 1 prepare me here seven oxen and s rams. 7651
23: 4 I have prepared s altars, and I have offered 7651
23:14 built s altars, and offered a bullock and 7651
23:29 Build me here s altars, and prepare me here 7651
23:29 prepare me here s bullocks and seven rams. 7651
23:29 prepare me here seven bullocks and s rams. 7651
26: 7 three thousand and s hundred and thirty. 7651
26:34 fifty and two thousand and s hundred. 7651
26:51 and a thousand s hundred and thirty. 7651
28:11 s lambs of the first year without spot; 7651
28:17 s days shall unleavened bread be eaten. 7651
28:19 and one ram, and s lambs of the first year; 7651
28:21 for every lamb, throughout the s lambs; 7651
28:24 ye shall offer daily, *throughout* the s days, 7651
28:27 one ram, s lambs of the first year; 7651
28:29 deal unto one lamb, throughout the s lambs; 7651
29: 2 s lambs of the first year without blemish: 7651
29: 4 deal for one lamb, throughout the s lambs: 7651
29: 8 one ram, *and* s lambs of the first year; 7651
29:10 deal for one lamb, throughout the s lambs: 7651
29:12 ye shall keep a feast unto the LORD s 7651
29:32 on the seventh day s bullocks, two rams, 7651
29:36 s lambs of the first year without blemish: 7651
31:19 do ye abide without the camp s days: 7651
31:36 s and thirty thousand and five hundred 7651
31:43 thirty thousand *and* s thousand and 7651
31:52 was sixteen thousand s hundred and 7651
Dt 7: 1 s nations greater and mightier than thou; 7651
15: 1 At the end of *every* s years thou shalt make 7651
16: 3 s days shalt thou eat unleavened bread 7651
16: 4 bread seen with thee in all thy coast s days; 7651
16: 9 S weeks shalt thou number unto thee: 7651
16: 9 begin to number the s weeks from *such* 7651
16:13 observe the feast of tabernacles s days, 7651
16:15 S days shalt thou keep a solemn feast unto 7651
28: 7 thee one way, and flee before thee s ways. 7651
28:25 against them, and flee s ways before them: 7651
31:10 saying, At the end of *every* s years, 7651
Jos 6: 4 s priests shall bear before the ark seven 7651
6: 4 seven priests shall bear before the ark s 7651
6: 4 the seventh day ye shall compass the city s 7651
6: 6 let s priests bear seven trumpets of rams' 7651
6: 6 let seven priests bear s trumpets of rams' 7651
6: 8 that the s priests bearing the seven trumpets 7651
6: 8 that the seven priests bearing the s trumpets 7651
6:13 s priests bearing seven trumpets of rams' 7651
6:13 seven priests bearing s trumpets of rams' 7651
Jos 6:15 compassed the city after the same manner s 7651
6:15 only on that day they compassed the city s 7651
18: 2 among the children of Israel s tribes, 7651
18: 5 they shall divide it into s parts: Judah shall 7651
18: 6 therefore describe the land *into* s parts, 7651
18: 9 described it by cities into s parts in a book, 7651
Jdg 6: 1 them into the hand of Midian s years. 7651
6:25 even the second bullock of s years old, and 7651
8:26 a thousand and s hundred *shekels* of gold; 7651
12: 9 for his sons. And he judged Israel s years. 7651
14:12 declare it me *within* the s days of the feast, 7651
14:17 she wept before him the s days, while their 7651
16: 7 If they bind me with s green withs that 7651
16: 8 her s green withs which had not been dried, 7651
16:13 If thou weavest the s locks of my head with 7651
16:19 she caused *him* to shave off the s locks of 7651
20:15 *which* were numbered s hundred chosen 7651
20:16 Among all this people *there were* s hundred 7651
Ru 4:15 which *is* better to thee than s sons, 7651
1Sa 2: 5 so that the barren hath born s; and she that 7651
6: 1 in the country of the Philistines s months. 7651
10: 8 s days shalt thou tarry, till I come to thee, 7651
11: 3 said unto him, Give us s days' respite, 7651
13: 8 he tarried s days, according to the set time 7651
16:10 Jesse made s of his sons to pass before 7651
31:13 under a tree at Jabesh, and fasted s days. 7651
2Sa 2:11 Hebron over the house of Judah was s years 7651
5: 5 In Hebron he reigned over Judah s years 7651
8: 4 thousand *chariots*, and s hundred horsemen, 7651
10:18 David slew *the men of* s hundred chariots 7651
21: 6 Let s men of his sons be delivered unto us, 7651
21: 9 they fell *all* s together, and were put to 7651
23:39 Uriah the Hittite: thirty and s *in* all. 7651
24:13 Shall s years of famine come unto thee in 7651
1Ki 2:11 s years reigned he in Hebron, and thirty and 7651
6: 6 and the third *was* s cubits broad: 7651
6:38 of it. So was he s years in building it. 7651
7:17 s for the one chapiter, and seven for 7651
7:17 one chapiter, and s for the other chapiter. 7651
8:65 s days and seven days, *even* fourteen days. 7651
8:65 seven days and s days, *even* fourteen days. 7651
11: 3 he had s hundred wives, princesses, and 7651
16:15 of Judah did Zimri reign s days in Tirzah. 7651
18:43 *is* nothing. And he said, Go again s times. 7651
19:18 Yet I have left *me* s thousand in Israel, 7651
20:15 all the children of Israel, *being* s thousand. 7651
20:29 they pitched one over against the other s 7651
20:30 and s thousand of the men that were left. 7651
2Ki 3: 9 they fetcht a compass of s days' journey: 7651
3:26 he took with him s hundred men that drew 7651
4:35 the child neesed s times, and the child 7651
5:10 Go and wash in Jordan s times, and 7651
5:14 and dipped *himself* s times in Jordan, 7651
8: 1 it shall also come upon the land s years. 7651
8: 2 sojourned in the land of the Philistines s 7651
8: 3 it came to pass at the s years' end, that 7651
11:21 S years old *was* Jehoash when he *began* to 7651
24:16 *even* s thousand, and craftsmen and smiths 7651
25:27 it came to pass in the s and thirtieth year of 7651
25:27 on the s and twentieth *day* of the month, 7651
1Ch 3: 4 there he reigned s years and six months: 7651
3:24 and Johanan, and Dalaiah, and Anani, s. 7651
5:13 Jorai, and Jachan, and Zia, and Heber, s. 7651
5:18 *were* four and forty thousand s hundred and 7651
7: 5 their genealogies fourscore and s thousand. 7651
9:13 a thousand and s hundred and threescore; 7651
9:25 *were* to come after s days from time to time 7651
10:12 under the oak in Jabesh, and fasted s days. 7651
12:25 for the war, s thousand and one hundred. 7651
12:27 him *were* three thousand and s hundred; 7651
12:34 with shield and spear thirty and s thousand. 7651
15:26 that they offered s bullocks and seven rams. 7651
15:26 that they offered seven bullocks and s rams. 7651
18: 4 s thousand horsemen, and twenty thousand 7651
19:18 David slew of the Syrians s thousand *men* 7651
26:30 men of valour, a thousand and s hundred, 7651
26:32 two thousand and s hundred chief fathers, 7651
29: 4 and s thousand talents of refined silver, 7651
29:27 s years reigned he in Hebron, and thirty and 7651
2Ch 7: 8 same time Solomon kept the feast s days, 7651
7: 9 for they kept the dedication of the altar s 7651
7: 9 of the altar seven days, and the feast s days. 7651
13: 9 himself with a young bullock and s rams, 7651
15:11 s hundred oxen and seven thousand sheep. 7651
15:11 seven hundred oxen and s thousand sheep. 7651
17:11 s thousand and seven hundred rams, and 7651
17:11 seven thousand and s hundred rams, and 7651
17:11 and s thousand and seven hundred he goats. 7651
17:11 and seven thousand and s hundred he goats. 7651
24: 1 Joash *was* s years old when he *began* to 7651
26:13 and s thousand and five hundred, 7651
29:21 they brought s bullocks, and seven rams, 7651
29:21 s rams, and seven lambs, and seven he 7651
29:21 and s lambs, and seven he goats, 7651
29:21 and seven lambs, and s he goats, 7651
30:21 bread s days with great gladness: 7651
30:22 and they did eat throughout the feast s days, 7651
30:23 assembly took counsel to keep other s days: 7651
30:23 and they kept *other* s days *with* gladness. 7651
30:24 a thousand bullocks and s thousand sheep; 7651
35:17 the feast of unleavened bread s days. 7651
Ezr 2: 5 of Arah, s hundred seventy and five. 7651
2: 9 of Zaccai, s hundred and threescore. 7651
2:25 and Beeroth, s hundred and forty and three. 7651
2:33 Hadid, and Ono, s hundred twenty and five. 7651
2:38 a thousand two hundred forty and s. 7651
2:65 of whom *there were* s thousand three 7651
2:65 seven thousand three hundred thirty and s: 7651
2:66 Their horses *were* s hundred thirty and six; 7651
2:67 six thousand s hundred and twenty. 7651
6:22 kept the feast of unleavened bread s days 7651
7:14 of his s counsellers, to inquire concerning 7655
8:35 ninety and six rams, seventy and s lambs, 7657
Ne 7:14 of Zaccai, s hundred and threescore. 7651
7:18 of Adonikam, six hundred threescore and s. 7651

S

Ne 7:19 of Bigvai, two thousand threescore and s. 7651
7:29 and Beeroth, s hundred forty and three. 7651
7:37 Hadid, and Ono, s hundred twenty and one. 7651
7:41 a thousand two hundred forty and s. 7651
7:67 of whom *there were* s thousand three 7651
7:67 seven thousand three hundred thirty and s: 7651
7:68 Their horses, s hundred thirty and six: 7651
7:69 six thousand s hundred and twenty asses. 7651
7:72 and threescore and s priests' garments. 7651
8:18 they kept the feast s days; and on the eighth 7651
Est 1: 1 *over* an hundred and s and 7651
1: 5 both unto great and small, s days, in 7651
1:10 the s chamberlains that served in 7651
1:14 the s princes of Persia and Media, 7651
2: 9 s maidens, *which were* meet to be given 7651
8: 9 an hundred twenty and s provinces, 7651
9:30 s provinces of the kingdom of Ahasuerus, 7651
Job 1: 2 there were born unto him s sons and 7651
1: 3 His substance also was s thousand sheep, 7651
2:13 sat down with him upon the ground s days 7651
2:13 upon the ground seven days and s nights, 7651
5:19 yea, in s there shall no evil touch thee. 7651
42: 8 Therefore take unto you now s bullocks and 7651
42: 8 unto you now seven bullocks and s rams, 7651
42:13 He had also s sons and three daughters. 7658
Ps 12: 6 tried in a furnace of earth, purified s **times**. 7659
119:164 S *times* a day do I praise thee because 7651
Pr 6:16 yea, s *are* an abomination unto him: 7651
9: 1 her house, she hath hewn out her s pillars: 7651
24:16 For a just *man* falleth s *times*, and riseth up 7651
26:16 conceit than s *men* that can render a reason. 7651
26:25 for *there are* s abominations in his heart. 7651
Ecc 11: 2 Give a portion to s, and also to eight; 7651
Isa 4: 1 in that day s women shall take hold of one 7651
11:15 shall smite it in *the* s streams, and 7651
30:26 shall be sevenfold, as the light of s days, 7651
Jer 15: 9 She that hath borne s languisheth: she hath 7651
34:14 At the end of s years let ye go every man 7651
52:25 s men of them that were near the king's 7651
52:30 away captive *of* the Jews s hundred forty 7651
52:31 it came to pass in the s and thirtieth year of 7651
Eze 3:15 remained there astonished among them s 7651
3:16 it came to pass at the end of s days, that 7651
29:17 it came to pass in the s and twentieth year, 7651
39: 9 and they shall burn them with fire s years: 7651
39:12 s months shall the house of Israel be 7651
39:14 after the end of s months shall they search. 7651
40:22 they went up unto it by s steps; and 7651
40:26 *there were* s steps to go up to it, and 7651
41: 3 and the breadth of the door, s cubits. 7651
43:25 S days shalt thou prepare every day a goat 7651
43:26 S days shall they purge the altar and 7651
44:26 they shall reckon unto him s days. 7651
45:21 shall have the passover, a feast of s days; 7620
45:23 s days of the feast he shall prepare a burnt 7651
45:23 s bullocks and seven rams without blemish 7651
45:23 s rams without blemish daily the seven 7651
45:23 seven rams without blemish daily the s 7651
45:25 shall he do the like in the feast *of* the s 7651
Da 3:19 s *times* more than *it was* wont to be heat. 7655
4:16 unto him; and let s times pass over him. 7655
4:23 of the field, till s times pass over him; 7655
4:25 of heaven, and s times shall pass over thee, 7655
4:32 as oxen, and s times shall pass over thee, 7655
9:25 the Messiah the Prince *shall be* s weeks, 7651
Am 5: 8 *Seek him* that maketh the s **stars** and 3598
Mic 5: 5 shall we raise against him s shepherds, and 7651
Zec 3: 9 upon one stone *shall be* s eyes: 7651
4: 2 his s lamps thereon, and seven pipes to 7651
4: 2 and s pipes to the seven lamps, 7651
4: 2 and seven pipes to the s lamps, 7651
4:10 in the hand of Zerubbabel *with* those s; 7651
Mt 12:45 taketh with himself s other spirits more *2033*
15:34 And they said, S, and a few little fishes. *2033*
15:36 And he took the s loaves and the fishes, and *2033*
15:37 the broken *meat* that was left s baskets full. *2033*
16:10 Neither the s loaves of the four thousand, *2033*
18:21 against me, and I forgive him? till s **times**? *2034*
18:22 unto him, I say not unto thee, Until s **times**: *2034*
18:22 seven times: but, Until seventy times s. *2033*
22:25 Now there were with us s brethren: and *2033*
22:28 whose wife shall she be of the s? *2033*
Mk 8: 5 many loaves have ye? And they said, S. *2033*
8: 6 and he took the s loaves, and gave thanks, *2033*
8: 8 of the broken *meat* that was left s baskets. *2033*
8:20 And when the s among four thousand, *2033*
8:20 of fragments took ye up? And they said, S. *2033*
12:20 Now there were s brethren: and the first *2033*
12:22 And the s had her, and left no seed: last of *2033*
12:23 she be of them? for the s had her to wife. *2033*
16: 9 out of whom he had cast s devils. *2033*
Lk 2:36 had lived with a husband s years from her *2033*
8: 2 out of whom went s devils, *2033*
11:26 taketh to *him* s other spirits more wicked *2033*
17: 4 And if he trespass against thee s **times** in a *2034*
17: 4 and s **times** in a day turn again to thee, *2034*
20:29 There were therefore s brethren: and the *2033*
20:31 took her; and in like manner the s also: *2033*
20:33 wife of them is she? for s had her to wife. *2033*
Ac 6: 3 look ye out among you s men of honest *2033*
13:19 And when he had destroyed s nations in *2033*
19:14 And there were s sons of *one* Sceva, a Jew, *2033*
20: 6 Troas in five days; where we abode s days. *2033*
21: 4 finding disciples, we tarried there s days: *2033*
21: 8 the evangelist, which was *one* of the s; *2033*
21:27 And when the s days were almost ended, *2033*
28:14 and were desired to tarry with them s days: *2033*
Ro 11: 4 I have reserved to myself s **thousand** men, *2035*
Heb 11:30 after they were compassed about s days. *2033*
Rev 1: 4 John to the s churches which are in Asia: *2033*
1: 4 from the s spirits which are before his *2033*
1:11 send *it* unto the s churches which are in *2033*
1:12 being turned, I saw s golden candlesticks; *2033*
1:13 And in the midst of the s candlesticks one *2033*
1:16 And he had in his right hand s stars: and *2033*

Rev 1:20 The mystery of the s stars which thou *2033*
1:20 right hand, and the s golden candlesticks. *2033*
1:20 The s stars are the angels of the seven *2033*
1:20 The seven stars are the angels of the s *2033*
1:20 the s candlesticks which thou sawest are *2033*
1:20 which thou sawest are the s churches. *2033*
2: 1 These *things* saith he that holdeth the s *2033*
2: 1 who walketh in the midst of the s golden *2033*
3: 1 These *things* saith he that hath the s spirits *2033*
3: 1 the seven spirits of God, and the s stars; *2033*
4: 5 *there were* s lamps of fire burning before *2033*
4: 5 the throne, which are the s spirits of God. *2033*
5: 1 and on the backside, sealed with s seals. *2033*
5: 5 the book, and to loose the s seals thereof. *2033*
5: 6 *been* slain, having s horns and seven eyes, *2033*
5: 6 *been* slain, having seven horns and s eyes, *2033*
5: 6 which are the s spirits of God sent forth *2033*
8: 2 And I saw the s angels which stood before *2033*
8: 2 and to them were given s trumpets. *2033*
8: 6 And the s angels which had the seven *2033*
8: 6 And the seven angels which had the s *2033*
10: 3 had cried, s thunders uttered their voices. *2033*
10: 4 And when the s thunders had uttered their *2033*
10: 4 Seal *up those things* which the s thunders *2033*
11:13 in the earthquake were slain of men s *2033*
12: 3 having s heads and ten horns, and *2033*
12: 3 and ten horns, and s crowns upon his heads. *2033*
13: 1 having s heads and ten horns, and upon his *2033*
15: 1 s angels having the seven last plagues; *2033*
15: 1 seven angels having the s last plagues; *2033*
15: 6 And the s angels came out of the temple, *2033*
15: 6 having the s plagues, clothed in pure and *2033*
15: 7 And one of the four beasts gave unto the s *2033*
15: 7 s golden vials full of the wrath of God, *2033*
15: 8 till the s plagues of the seven angels were *2033*
15: 8 till the seven plagues of the s angels were *2033*
16: 1 out of the temple saying to the s angels, *2033*
17: 1 And there came one of the s angels which *2033*
17: 1 of the seven angels which had the s vials, *2033*
17: 3 having s heads and ten horns. *2033*
17: 7 which hath the s heads and ten horns. *2033*
17: 9 The s heads are seven mountains, on which *2033*
17: 9 The seven heads are s mountains, on which *2033*
17:10 And there are s kings: five are fallen, and *2033*
17:11 and is of the s, and goeth into perdition. *2033*
21: 9 And there came unto me one of the s angels *2033*
21: 9 the s vials full of the seven last plagues, *2033*
21: 9 the seven vials full of the s last plagues, *2033*

SEVENFOLD (6) [SEVEN]

Ge 4:15 vengeance shall be taken on him s. 7659
4:24 If Cain shall be avenged s, truly Lamech 7659
4:24 truly Lamech seventy and s. 7651
Ps 79:12 render unto our neighbours s into their 7659
Pr 6:31 *if* he be found, he shall restore s; he shall 7659
Isa 30:26 the light of the sun shall be s, as the light of 7659

SEVENS (2) [SEVEN]

Ge 7: 2 beast thou shalt take to thee **by** s, 7651+7651
7: 3 Of fowls also of the air **by** s, 7651+7651

SEVENTEEN (10) [SEVENTEENTH]

Ge 37: 2 Joseph, *being* s years old, 6240+7651
47:28 Jacob lived in the land of Egypt s 6240+7651
Jdg 8:14 *even* **threescore and** s men. 7651+7657+2050.1
1Ki 14:21 and he reigned s years in Jerusalem, 6240+7651
2Ki 13: 1 in Samaria, *and reigned* s years. 6240+7651
1Ch 7:11 *were* s thousand and two hundred 6240+7651
2Ch 12:13 and he reigned s years in Jerusalem, 6240+7651
Ezr 2:39 children of Harim, a thousand and s. 6240+7651
Ne 7:42 children of Harim, a thousand *and* s. 6240+7651
Jer 32: 9 *even* s shekels of silver. 6235+7651+2050.1

SEVENTEENTH (6) [SEVENTEEN]

Ge 7:11 the s day of the month, 6240+7651
8: 4 on the s day of the month, upon 6240+7651
1Ki 22:51 s year of Jehoshaphat king of Judah, 6240+7651
2Ki 16: 1 In the s year of Pekah the son of 6240+7651
1Ch 24:15 The s to Hezir, the eighteenth to 6240+7651
25:24 The s to Joshbekashah, *he,* his sons, 6240+7651

SEVENTH (120) [SEVEN]

Ge 2: 2 on the s day God ended his work which he 7637
2: 2 he rested on the s day from all his work 7637
2: 3 God blessed the s day, and sanctified it: 7637
8: 4 the ark rested in the s month, on 7637
Ex 12:15 bread from the first day until the s day, 7637
12:16 in the s day there shall be a holy 7637
13: 6 in the s day *shall be* a feast to the LORD. 7637
16:26 on the s day, *which is* the sabbath, in it 7637
16:27 of the people on the s day for to gather, 7637
16:29 let no man go out of his place on the s day. 7637
16:30 So the people rested on the s day. 7637
20:10 the s day *is* the sabbath of the LORD thy 7637
20:11 and all that in them *is,* and rested the s day: 7637
21: 2 and in the s he shall go out free for nothing. 7637
23:11 the s *year* thou shalt let it rest and lie still; 7637
23:12 thy work, and on the s day thou shalt rest: 7637
24:16 the s day he called unto Moses out of 7637
31:15 in the s *is* the sabbath of rest, holy to 7637
31:17 on the s day he rested, and was refreshed. 7637
34:21 shalt work, but on the s day thou shalt rest: 7637
35: 2 on the s day there shall be to you a holy 7637
Lev 13: 5 the priest shall look on him the s day: 7637
13: 6 the priest shall look on him again the s day: 7637
13:27 the priest shall look upon him the s day: 7637
13:32 in the s day the priest shall look on 7637
13:34 in the s day the priest shall look on 7637
13:51 he shall look on the plague on the s day: 7637
14: 9 it shall be on the s day, *that* he shall shave 7637
14:39 the priest shall come again the s day, 7637
16:29 *that* in the s month, on the tenth *day* of 7637
23: 3 the s day *is* the sabbath of rest, a holy 7637
23: 8 in the s day *is* a holy convocation: ye shall 7637

Lev 23:16 Even unto the morrow after the s sabbath 7637
23:24 saying, In the s month, in the first *day* of 7637
23:27 Also on the tenth *day* of this s month *there* 7637
23:34 The fifteenth day of this s month *shall be* 7637
23:39 Also in the fifteenth day of the s month, 7637
23:41 ye shall celebrate it in the s month. 7637
25: 4 in the s year shall be a sabbath of rest unto 7637
25: 9 to sound on the tenth *day* of the s month, 7637
25:20 ye shall say, What shall we eat the s year? 7637
Nu 6: 9 his cleansing, on the s day shall he shave it. 7637
7:48 On the s day Elishama the son of 7637
19:12 and on the s day he shall be clean: 7637
19:12 then the s day he shall not be clean. 7637
19:19 unclean on the third day, and on the s day: 7637
19:19 on the s day he shall purify him*self,* and 7637
28:25 on the s day ye shall have a holy 7637
29: 1 in the s month, on the first *day* of 7637
29: 7 ye shall have on the tenth *day* of this s 7637
29:12 on the fifteenth day of the s month ye shall 7637
29:32 on the s day seven bullocks, two rams, *and* 7637
31:19 captives on the third day, and on the s day. 7637
31:24 ye shall wash your clothes on the s day, 7637
Dt 5:14 the s day *is* the sabbath of the LORD thy 7637
15: 9 saying, The s year, the year of release, is at 7651
15:12 in the s year thou shalt let him go free from 7637
16: 8 on the s day *shall be* a solemn assembly to 7637
Jos 6: 4 the s day ye shall compass the city seven 7637
6:15 it came to pass on the s day, that they rose 7637
6:16 it came to pass at the s time, when 7637
19:40 *And* the s lot came out for the tribe of 7637
Jdg 14:15 it came to pass on the s day, that they said 7637
14:17 it came to pass on the s day, that he told 7637
14:18 the men of the city said unto him on the s 7637
2Sa 12:18 it came to pass on the s day, that the child 7637
1Ki 8: 2 the month Ethanim, which *is* the s month. 7637
16:10 the twenty and s year of Asa king of Judah, 7651
16:15 s year of Asa king of Judah did Zimri reign 7651
18:44 it came to pass at the s *time,* that he said, 7637
20:29 that in the s day the battle was joined: 7637
2Ki 11: 4 the s year Jehoiada sent and fet the rulers 7637
12: 1 In the s year of Jehu Jehoash *began* to 7651
13:10 s year of Joash king of Judah *began* 7651
15: 1 s year of Jeroboam king of Israel *began* 7651
18: 9 which *was* the s year of Hoshea son of Elah 7637
25: 8 the fifth month, on the s *day* of the month, 7651
25:25 it came to pass in the s month, *that* Ishmael 7637
1Ch 2:15 Ozem the sixth, David the s: 7637
12:11 Attai the sixth, Eliel the s, 7637
24:10 The s to Hakkoz, the eighth to Abijah, 7637
25:14 The s *to* Jesharelah, *he,* his sons, and 7637
26: 3 Jehohanan the sixth, Elioenai the s. 7637
26: 5 Ammiel the sixth, Issachar the s, 7637
27:10 The s *captain* for the seventh month *was* 7637
27:10 The seventh *captain* for the s month *was* 7637
2Ch 5: 3 king in the feast which *was in* the s month. 7637
7:10 twentieth day of the s month he sent 7637
23: 1 in the s year Jehoiada strengthened himself, 7637
31: 7 and finished *them* in the s month. 7637
Ezr 3: 1 when the s month was come, and 7637
3: 6 From the first day of the s month began 7637
7: 7 in the s year of Artaxerxes the king. 7651
7: 8 which *was in* the s year of the king. 7637
Ne 7:73 when the s month came, the children of 7637
8: 2 upon the first day of the s month. 7637
8:14 dwell in booths in the feast of the s month: 7637
10:31 *that* we would leave the s year, and 7637
Est 1:10 On the s day, when the heart of the king 7637
2:16 the month Tebeth, in the s year of his reign. 7651
Jer 28:17 prophet died the same year in the s month. 7637
41: 1 Now it came to pass in the s month, 7637
52:28 in the s year three thousand Jews and three 7651
Eze 20: 1 it came to pass in the s year, in the fifth 7637
30:20 in the first *month,* in the s *day* of 7651
45:20 thou shalt do the s *day* of the month for 7651
45:25 In the s *month,* in the fifteenth day of 7637
Hag 2: 1 In the s *month,* in the one and twentieth *day* 7637
Zec 7: 5 and s *month,* even those seventy years, 7637
8:19 the fast of the s, and the fast of the tenth, 7637
Mt 22:26 the second also, and the third, unto the s. *2033*
Jn 4:52 Yesterday at the s hour the fever left him. *1442*
Heb 4: 4 For *he* spake in a certain place of the s *day* *1442*
4: 4 And God did rest the s day from all his *1442*
Jude 1:14 And Enoch also, the s from Adam, *1442*
Rev 8: 1 And when he had opened the s seal, *1442*
10: 7 But in the days of the voice of the s angel, *1442*
11:15 And the s angel sounded; and there were *1442*
16:17 And the s angel poured out his vial into *1442*
21:20 the sixth, sardius; the s, chrysolite; *1442*

SEVENTY (61)

Ge 4:24 truly Lamech s and sevenfold. 7657
5:12 Cainan lived s years, and begat Mahalaleel: 7657
5:31 the days of Lamech were seven hundred s 7657
11:26 Terah lived s years, and begat Abram, 7657
12: 4 Abram *was* s and five years old when he 7657
Ex 1: 5 came *out of* the loins of Jacob were s souls: 7657
24: 1 and Abihu, and s of the elders of Israel; 7657
24: 9 and Abihu, and s of the elders of Israel: 7657
38:28 of the thousand seven hundred s and 7657
38:29 the brass of the offering *was* s talents, and 7657
Nu 7:13 thirty *shekels,* one silver bowl of s shekels, 7657
7:19 thirty *shekels,* one silver bowl of s shekels, 7657
7:25 thirty *shekels,* one silver bowl of s shekels, 7657
7:31 thirty *shekels,* one silver bowl of s shekels, 7657
7:37 thirty *shekels,* one silver bowl of s shekels, 7657
7:43 thirty *shekels,* a silver bowl of s shekels, 7657
7:49 thirty *shekels,* one silver bowl of s shekels, 7657
7:55 thirty *shekels,* one silver bowl of s shekels, 7657
7:61 thirty *shekels,* one silver bowl of s shekels, 7657
7:67 thirty *shekels,* one silver bowl of s shekels, 7657
7:73 thirty *shekels,* one silver bowl of s shekels, 7657
7:79 thirty *shekels,* one silver bowl of s shekels, 7657
7:85 an hundred and thirty *shekels,* each bowl s: 7657
11:16 Gather unto me s men of the elders of 7657
11:24 gathered the s men of the elders of 7657

S

Nu 11:25 was upon him, and gave it unto the s elders: 7657
31:32 and s thousand and five thousand sheep, 7657
Jdg 9:56 unto his father, in slaying his s brethren: 7657
2Sa 24:15 Dan even to Beer-sheba s thousand men. 7657
2Ki 10: 1 Ahab had s sons in Samaria. And Jehu 7657
10: 6 Now the king's sons, being s persons, 7657
10: 7 slew s persons, and put their heads in 7657
1Ch 21:14 and there fell of Israel s thousand men. 7657
Ezr 2: 3 two thousand an hundred s and two. 7657
2: 4 of Shephatiah, three hundred s and two. 7657
2: 5 children of Arah, seven hundred s and five. 7657
2:36 house of Jeshua, nine hundred s and three. 7657
2:40 of the children of Hodaviah, s and four. 7657
8: 7 the son of Athaliah, and with him s males. 7657
8:14 Uthai, and Zabbud, and with them s males. 7657
8:35 ninety and six rams, s and seven lambs, 7651
Ne 7: 8 two thousand an hundred s and two. 7657
7: 9 of Shephatiah, three hundred s and two. 7657
7:39 house of Jeshua, nine hundred s and three. 7657
7:43 and of the children of Hodevah, s and four. 7657
11:19 kept the gates, were an hundred s and two. 7657
Est 9:16 slew of their foes s and five thousand, but 7657
Isa 23:15 that Tyre shall be forgotten s years, 7657
23:15 after the end of s years shall Tyre sing as a 7657
23:17 it shall come to pass after the end of s 7657
Jer 25:11 shall serve the king of Babylon s years. 7657
25:12 to pass, when s years are accomplished, 7657
29:10 That after s years be accomplished at 7657
Eze 8:11 there stood before them s men of 7657
41:12 the end toward the west was s cubits broad; 7657
Da 9: 2 that he would accomplish s years in 7657
9:24 S weeks are determined upon thy people 7657
Zec 7: 5 and seventh month, even those s years, 7657
Mt 18:22 Until seven times: but, Until s times seven. 1441
Lk 10: 1 things the Lord appointed other s also, 1440
10:17 And the s returned again with joy, saying, 1440

SEVER (4) [SEVERED]
Ex 8:22 I will s in that day the land of Goshen, 6395
9: 4 the LORD shall s between the cattle of 6395
Eze 39:14 they shall s out men of continual 914
Mt 13:49 and s the wicked from among the just, 873

SEVERAL (12) [SEVERALLY]
Nu 28:13 a s tenth deal of flour mingled with 6241+6241
28:21 A s tenth deal shalt thou offer for 6241+6241
28:29 A s tenth deal unto one lamb, 6241+6241
29:10 A s tenth deal for one lamb, 6241+6241
29:15 a s tenth deal to each lamb of 6241+6241
2Ki 15: 5 the day of his death, and dwelt in a s house. 2669
2Ch 11:12 in every s city he put shields 5892+5892+2050.1
26:21 and dwelt in a s house, being a leper; 2669
28:25 in every s city of Judah he 5892+5892+2050.1
31:19 in every s city, the men that 5892+5892+2050.1
Mt 25:15 to every man according to his s ability; and 2398
Rev 21:21 every s gate was of one pearl: 303+1520

SEVERALLY (1) [SEVERAL]
1Co 12:11 dividing to every man s as he will. 2398

SEVERED (3) [SEVER]
Lev 20:26 have s you from other people, that ye should 914
Dt 4:41 Moses s three cities on this side Jordan 914
Jdg 4:11 had s himself from the Kenites, and 6504

SEVERITY (2)
Ro 11:22 Behold therefore the goodness and s of God: 663
11:22 on them which fell, s; but toward thee, 663

SEW (2) [SEWED, SEWEST, SEWETH, SOW]
Ecc 3: 7 A time to rent, and a time to s; a time to 8609
Eze 13:18 Woe to the women that s pillows to all 8609

SEWED (2) [SEW]
Ge 3: 7 they s fig leaves together, and 8609
Job 16:15 I have s sackcloth upon my skin, and 8609

SEWEST (1) [SEW]
Job 14:17 up in a bag, and thou s up mine iniquity. 2950

SEWETH (1) [SEW]
Mk 2:21 No man also s a piece of new cloth on an 1976

SEXUAL IMMORALITY See FORNICATION

SEXUALLY IMMORAL See WHOREMONGER; WHOREMONGERS

SHAALABBIN (1)
Jos 19:42 And S, and Aijalon, and Jethlah, 8169

SHAALBIM (2)
Jdg 1:35 dwell in mount Heres in Aijalon, and in S: 8169
1Ki 4: 9 in S, and Beth-shemesh, and 8169

SHAALBONITE (2)
2Sa 23:32 Eliahba the S, of the sons of Jashen, 8170
1Ch 11:33 Azmaveth the Baharumite, Eliahba the S, 8170

SHAALIM See SHALIM

SHAAPH (2)
1Ch 2:47 and Geshan, and Pelet, and Ephah, and S. 8174
2:49 She bare also S the father of Madmannah, 8174

SHAARAIM (2)
1Sa 17:52 of the Philistines fell down by the way to S, 8189
1Ch 4:31 and at Beth-birei, and at S. 8189

SHAASHGAZ (1)
Est 2:14 to the custody of S, the king's chamberlain, 8190

SHABBETHAI (3)
Ezr 10:15 Meshullam and S the Levite helped them. 7678
Ne 8: 7 Jamin, Akkub, S, Hodijah, Maaseiah, 7678
11:16 S and Jozabad, of the chief of the Levites, 7678

SHACHIA (1)
1Ch 8:10 Jeuz, and S, and Mirma. These were his 7634

SHADE (1) [SHADY]
Ps 121: 5 the LORD is thy s upon thy right hand. 6738

SHADOW (73) [OVERSHADOW, SHADOWING, SHADOWS]
Ge 19: 8 therefore came they under the s of my roof. 6738
Jdg 9:15 then come and put your trust in my s: 6738
9:36 Thou seest the s of the mountains as if they 6738
2Ki 20: 9 shall the s go forward ten degrees, or 6738
20:10 It is a light thing for the s to go down ten 6738
20:10 but let the s return backward ten degrees. 6738
20:11 he brought the s ten degrees backward, 6738
1Ch 29:15 our days on the earth are as a s, and there is 6738
Job 3: 5 Let darkness and the s of death stain it; 6757
7: 2 As a servant earnestly desireth the s, and 6738
8: 9 because our days upon earth are a s:) 6738
10:21 to the land of darkness and the s of death; 6757
10:22 and of the s of death, without any order, 6757
12:22 and bringeth out to light the s of death. 6757
14: 2 he fleeth also as a s, and continueth not. 6738
16:16 and on mine eyelids is the s of death; 6757
17: 7 of sorrow, and all my members are as a s. 6738
24:17 morning is to them even as the s of death: 6757
24:17 they are in the terrors of the s of death. 6757
28: 3 the stones of darkness, and the s of death. 6757
34:22 There is no darkness, nor s of death, 6757
38:17 hast thou seen the doors of the s of death? 6757
40:22 The shady trees cover him with their s; 6752
Ps 17: 8 the eye, hide me under the s of thy wings, 6738
23: 4 I walk through the valley of the s of death, 6757
36: 7 men put their trust under the s of thy wings. 6738
44:19 and covered us with the s of death. 6757
57: 1 in the s of thy wings will I make my refuge, 6738
63: 7 in the s of thy wings will I rejoice. 6738
80:10 The hills were covered with the s of it, and 6738
91: 1 shall abide under the s of the Almighty. 6738
102:11 My days are like a s that declineth; and 6738
107:10 as sit in darkness and in the s of death, 6757
107:14 them out of darkness and the s of death, 6757
109:23 I am gone like the s when it declineth: I am 6738
144: 4 his days are as a s that passeth away. 6738
Ecc 6:12 of his vain life which he spendeth as a s? 6738
8:13 shall he prolong his days, which are as a s; 6738
SS 2: 3 I sat down under his s with great delight, 6738
Isa 4: 6 there shall be a tabernacle for a s in 6738
9: 2 they that dwell in the land of the s of death, 6757
16: 3 make thy s as the night in the midst of 6738
25: 4 a refuge from the storm, a s from the heat, 6738
25: 5 even the heat with the s of a cloud: 6738
30: 2 of Pharaoh, and to trust in the s of Egypt. 6738
30: 3 the trust in the s of Egypt your confusion. 6738
32: 2 as the s of a great rock in a weary land. 6738
34:15 and lay, and hatch, and gather under her s: 6738
38: 8 I will bring again the s of the degrees, 6738
49: 2 in the s of his hand hath he hid me, and 6738
51:16 have covered thee in the s of mine hand, 6738
Jer 2: 6 a land of drought, and of the s of death, 6757
13:16 he turn it into the s of death, and make it 6757
48:45 They that fled stood under the s of Heshbon 6738
La 4:20 Under his s we shall live among 6738
Eze 17:23 in the s of the branches thereof shall they 6738
31: 6 and under his s dwelt all great nations. 6738
31:12 of the earth are gone down from his s, 6738
31:17 that dwelt under his s in the midst of 6738
Da 4:12 the beasts of the field had s under it, and 2927
Hos 4:13 and elms, because the s thereof is good: 6738
14: 7 They that dwell under his s shall return; 6738
Am 5: 8 and turneth the s of death into the morning, 6757
Jnh 4: 5 made him a booth, and sat under it in the s, 6738
4: 6 that it might be a s over his head, to deliver 6738
Mt 4:16 the region and s of death light is sprung up. 4639
Mk 4:32 fowls of the air may lodge under the s of it. 4639
Lk 1:79 that sit in darkness and in the s of death, 4639
Ac 5:15 that at the least the s of Peter passing by 4639
Col 2:17 Which are a s of things to come; but 4639
Heb 8: 5 s of heavenly things, as Moses was 4639
10: 1 For the law having a s of good things to 4639
Jas 1:17 is no variableness, neither s of turning. 644

SHADOWING (3) [SHADOW]
Isa 18: 1 Woe to the land s with wings, which is 6767
Eze 31: 3 and with a s shrowd, and of a high stature; 6751
Heb 9: 5 And over it the cherubims of glory s 2683

SHADOWS (3) [SHADOW]
SS 2:17 the s flee away, turn, my beloved, and be 6752
4: 6 Until the day break, and the s flee away, 6752
Jer 6: 4 for the s of the evening are stretched out. 6752

SHADRACH (15)
Da 1: 7 to Hananiah, of S; and to Mishael, 7714
2:49 and he set S, Meshach, and Abed-nego, 7715
3:12 of Babylon, S, Meshach, and Abed-nego; 7715
3:13 in his rage and fury commanded to bring S, 7715
3:14 Is it true, O S, Meshach, and Abed-nego, 7715
3:16 S, Meshach, and Abed-nego, answered and 7715
3:19 form of his visage was changed against S, 7715
3:20 men that were in his army to bind S, 7715
3:22 of the fire slew those men that took up S, 7715
3:23 three men, S, Meshach, and Abed-nego, 7715
3:26 and spake, and said, S, Meshach, and 7715
3:26 come hither. Then S, Meshach, and 7715
3:28 said, Blessed be the God of S, Meshach, 7715
3:29 speak any thing amiss against the God of S, 7715
3:30 the king promoted S, Meshach, and 7715

SHADY (2) [SHADE]
Job 40:21 He lieth under the s trees, in the covert of 6628
40:22 The s trees cover him with their shadow; 6628

SHAFT (4)
Ex 25:31 his s, and his branches, his bowls, 3409
37:17 his s, and his branch, his bowls, his knops, 3409
Nu 8: 4 unto the s thereof, unto the flowers thereof, 3409
Isa 49: 2 hath he hid me, and made me a polished s; 2671

SHAGE (1)
1Ch 11:34 Jonathan the son of S the Hararite, 7681

SHAGEE See SHAGE

SHAHAR (1)
Ps 22: T To the chief Musician upon Aijeleth S, 7837

SHAHARAIM (1)
1Ch 8: 8 S begat children in the country of Moab, 7842

SHAHAZIMAH (1)
Jos 19:22 to Tabor, and S, and Beth-shemesh; 7831

SHAHAZUMAH See SHAHAZIMAH

SHAKE (39) [SHAKED, SHAKEN, SHAKETH, SHAKING, SHOOK]
Jdg 16:20 out as at other times before, and s myself. 5287
Ne 5:13 So God s out every man from his house, 5287
Job 4:14 trembling, which made all my bones to s. 6342
15:33 He shall s off his unripe grape as the vine, 2554
16: 4 words against you, and s mine head at you. 5128
Ps 22: 7 shoot out the lip, they s the head, saying, 5128
46: 3 though the mountains s with the swelling 7493
69:23 and make their loins continually to s. 4571
72:16 the fruit thereof shall s like Lebanon: 7493
Isa 2:19 when he ariseth to s terribly the earth. 6206
2:21 when he ariseth to s terribly the earth. 6206
10:15 as if the rod should s itself against them 5130
10:32 he shall s his hand against the mount of 5130
11:15 with his mighty wind shall he s his hand 5130
13: 2 exalt the voice unto them, s the hand, 5130
13:13 Therefore I will s the heavens, and the earth 7264
14:16 the earth to tremble, that did s kingdoms; 7493
24:18 and the foundations of the earth do s. 7493
33: 9 and Bashan and Carmel s off their fruits. 5287
52: 2 S thyself from the dust; arise, and sit down, 5287
Jer 23: 9 because of the prophets; all my bones s; 7363
Eze 26:10 thy walls shall s at the noise of 7493
26:15 Shall not the isles s at the sound of thy fall, 7493
27:28 The suburbs shall s at the sound of the cry 7493
31:16 I made the nations to s at the sound of his 7493
38:20 shall s at my presence, and the mountains 7493
Da 4:14 s off his leaves, and scatter his fruit: 5426
Joel 3:16 and the heavens and the earth shall s: 7493
Am 9: 1 the lintel of the door, that the posts may s: 7493
Hag 2: 6 I will s the heavens, and the earth, and 7493
2: 7 I will s all nations, and the desire of all 7493
2:21 I will s the heavens and the earth; 7493
Zec 2: 9 I will s mine hand upon them, and 5130
Mt 10:14 or city, s off the dust of your feet. 1621
28: 4 And for fear of him the keepers did s, and 4579
Mk 6:11 s off the dust under your feet for a 1621
Lk 6:48 upon that house, and could not s it: 4531
9: 5 s off the very dust from your feet for a 660
Heb 12:26 Yet once more I s not the earth only, but 4579

SHAKED (1) [SHAKE]
Ps 109:25 when they looked upon me they s their 5128

SHAKEN (22) [SHAKE]
Lev 26:36 the sound of a s leaf shall chase them; and 5086
1Ki 14:15 as a reed is s in the water, and he shall root 5110
2Ki 19:21 the daughter of Jerusalem hath s her head at 5128
Ne 5:13 even thus be he s out, and emptied. 5287
Job 16:12 s me to pieces, and set me up for his mark. 6327
38:13 that the wicked might be s out of it? 5287
Ps 18: 7 also of the hills moved and were s, 1607
Isa 37:22 the daughter of Jerusalem hath s her head at 5128
Na 2: 3 and the fir trees shall be terribly s. 7477
3:12 if they be s, they shall even fall into 5128
Mt 11: 7 wilderness to see? A reed s with the wind? 4531
24:29 and the powers of the heavens shall be s: 4531
Mk 13:25 the powers that are in heaven shall be s. 4531
Lk 6:38 and s together, and running over, 4531
7:24 for to see? A reed s with the wind? 4531
21:26 for the powers of heaven shall be s. 4531
Ac 4:31 the place was s where they were assembled 4531
16:26 so that the foundations of the prison were s: 4531
2Th 2: 2 That ye be not soon s in mind, or 4531
Heb 12:27 the removing of those things that are s, 4531
12:27 that those things which cannot be s may 4531
Rev 6:13 when she is s of a mighty wind. 4579

SHAKETH (7) [SHAKE]
Job 9: 6 Which s the earth out of her place, and 7264
Ps 29: 8 The voice of the LORD s the wilderness; 2342
29: 8 the LORD s the wilderness of Kadesh. 2342
60: 2 broken it: heal the breaches thereof; for it s. 4131
Isa 10:15 the saw magnify itself against him that s it? 5130
19:16 of the LORD of hosts, which he s over it. 5130
33:15 that s his hands from holding of bribes, 5287

SHAKING (8) [SHAKE]
Job 41:29 as stubble: he laugheth at the s of a spear. 7494
Ps 44:14 a s of the head among the people. 4493
Isa 17: 6 as the s of an olive tree, two or three berries 5363
19:16 of the s of the hand of the LORD of hosts, 8573
24:13 there shall be as the s of an olive tree, and 5363
30:32 and in battles of s will he fight with it. 8573
Eze 37: 7 behold a s, and the bones came together, 7494
38:19 Surely in that day there shall be a great s in 7494

SHALEM (1)
Ge 33:18 Jacob came to S, a city of Shechem, 8004

SHALIM (1)
1Sa 9: 4 they passed through the land of S, and 8171

SHALISHA (1) [BAAL-SHALISHA]
1Sa 9: 4 passed through the land of S, but 8031

SHALL (9838) [SHALT] See Index of Articles, Etc.

SHALLECHETH (1)
1Ch 26:16 with the gate S, by the causeway of 7996

SHALLEKETH See SHALLECHETH

SHALLUM (27)
2Ki 15:10 S the son of Jabesh conspired against him, 7967
15:13 S the son of Jabesh *began* to reign in 7967
15:14 smote S the son of Jabesh in Samaria, and 7967
15:15 the rest of the acts of S, and his conspiracy 7967
22:14 the wife of S the son of Tikvah, the son of 7967
1Ch 2:40 begat Sisamai, and Sisamai begat S, 7967
2:41 S begat Jekamiah, and Jekamiah begat 7967
3:15 the third Zedekiah, the fourth S. 7967
4:25 S his son, Mibsam his son, Mishma his son. 7967
6:12 Ahitub begat Zadok, and Zadok begat S, 7967
6:13 S begat Hilkiah, and Hilkiah begat Azariah, 7967
7:13 Jahziel, and Guni, and Jezer, and S, 7967
9:17 the porters *were*, S, and Akkub, and 7967
9:17 and their brethren: S *was* the chief; 7967
9:19 And S the son of Kore, the son of Ebiasaph, 7967
9:31 who *was* the firstborn of S the Korahite, 7967
2Ch 28:12 Jehizkiah the son of S, and Amasa the son 7967
34:22 the wife of S the son of Tikvath, the son of 7967
Ezr 2:42 the children of S, the children of Ater, 7967
7: 2 The son of S, the son of Zadok, the son of 7967
10:24 and of the porters; S, and Telem, and Uri. 7967
10:42 S, Amariah, *and* Joseph. 7967
Ne 3:12 next unto him repaired S the son of 7967
7:45 the children of S, the children of Ater, 7967
Jer 22:11 For thus saith the LORD touching S 7967
32: 7 Hanameel the son of S thine uncle *shall* 7967
35: 4 the chamber of Maaseiah the son of S, 7967

SHALLUN (1)
Ne 3:15 the gate of the fountain repaired S the son 7968

SHALMAI (2)
Ezr 2:46 the children of S, the children of Hanan, 8073
Ne 7:48 the children of Hagaba, the children of S, 8014

SHALMAN (1) [SHALMANESER]
Hos 10:14 as S spoiled Beth-arbel in the day of battle: 8020

SHALMANESER (2) [SHALMAN]
2Ki 17: 3 Against him came up S king of Assyria; 8022
18: 9 *that* S king of Assyria came up against 8022

SHALT (1616) [SHALL] See Index of Articles, Etc.

SHAMA (1)
1Ch 11:44 S and Jehiel the sons of Hothan 8091

SHAMARIAH (1)
2Ch 11:19 him children; Jeush, and S, and Zaham. 8114

SHAMBLES (1)
1Co 10:25 Whatsoever is sold in the s, *that* eat, *3111*

SHAME (100) [ASHAMED, SHAMED, SHAMEFASTNESS, SHAMEFUL, SHAMEFULLY, SHAMELESSLY, SHAMETH]
Ex 32:25 naked unto *their* s amongst their enemies:) 8103
Jdg 18: 7 that might put *them* to s in *any* thing; 3637
1Sa 20:34 because his father had done him s. 3637
2Sa 13:13 I, whither shall I cause my s to go? 2781
2Ch 32:21 So he returned with s of face to his own 1322
Job 8:22 They that hate thee shall be clothed with s; 1322
Ps 4: 2 how long *will ye turn* my glory into s? 3639
35: 4 and put to s that seek after my soul: 3637
35:26 let them be clothed with s and 1322
40:14 and put to s that wish me evil. 3637
40:15 Let them be desolate for a reward of their s 1322
44: 7 and hast put them to s that hated us. 954
44: 9 thou hast cast off, and put us to s; and 3637
44:15 and the s of my face hath covered me, 1322
53: 5 thou hast put *them* to s, because God hath 954
69: 7 borne reproach; s hath covered my face. 3639
69:19 my reproach, and my s, and my dishonour: 1322
70: 3 turned back for a reward of their s that say, 1322
71:24 for they are brought unto s, that seek my 2659
83:16 Fill their faces *with* s; that they may seek 7036
83:17 yea, let them be put to s, and perish: 2659
89:45 thou hast covered him with s. Selah. 955
109:29 Let mine adversaries be clothed with s, and 3639
119:31 thy testimonies: O LORD, put me not to s. 954
132:18 His enemies will I clothe with s: but 1322
Pr 3:35 but s shall be the promotion of fools. 7036
9: 7 reproveth a scorner getteth to himself s: 7036
10: 5 sleepeth in harvest *is* a son that causeth s. 954
11: 2 *When* pride cometh, then cometh s: but 7036
12:16 but a prudent *man* covereth s. 7036
13: 5 wicked *man* is loathsome, and cometh to s. 2659
13:18 s *shall be* to him that refuseth instruction: 7036
14:35 but his wrath is *against* him that causeth s. 954
17: 2 shall have rule over a son that causeth s, 954
18:13 he heareth *it*, it *is* folly and s unto him. 3639
19:26 *is* a son that causeth s, and 954
25: 8 when thy neighbour hath put thee to s. 3637
Pr 25:10 Lest he that heareth *it* put thee to s, and 2616
29:15 left *to himself* bringeth his mother to s. 954
Isa 20: 4 *their* buttocks uncovered, *to* the s of Egypt. 6172
22:18 there the chariots of thy glory *shall be* the s 7036
30: 3 shall the strength of Pharaoh be your s, 1322
30: 5 help nor profit, but a s, and also a reproach. 1322
47: 3 shall be uncovered, yea, thy s shall be seen: 2781
50: 6 I hid not my face from s and spitting. 3639
54: 4 for thou shalt not be put to s: 2659
54: 4 for thou shalt forget the s of thy youth, and 1322
61: 7 For your s *you shall have* double; and 1322
Jer 3:24 For s hath devoured the labour of our 1322
3:25 We lie down in our s, and our confusion 1322
13:26 skirts upon thy face, that thy s may appear. 7036
20:18 that my days should be consumed with s? 1322
23:40 a perpetual s, which shall not be forgotten. 3640
46:12 The nations have heard *of* thy s, and thy cry 7036
48:39 how hath Moab turned the back with s! so 954
51:51 s hath covered our faces: for strangers are 3639
Eze 7:18 s *shall be* upon all faces, and baldness upon 955
16:52 bear thine own s for thy sins that thou hast 3639
16:52 be thou confounded also, and bear thy s, 3639
16:54 That thou mayest bear thine own s, and 3639
16:63 open thy mouth any more, because of thy s, 3639
32:24 yet have they borne their s with them that 3639
32:25 yet have they borne their s with them that 3639
32:30 bear their s with them that go down to 3639
34:29 neither bear the s of the heathen any more. 3639
36: 6 because ye have borne the s of the heathen: 3639
36: 7 that *are* about you, they shall bear their s. 3639
36:15 hear in thee the s of the heathen any more, 3639
39:26 After that they have borne their s, and all 3639
44:13 most holy *place*: but they shall bear their s, 3639
Da 12: 2 and some to s *and* everlasting contempt. 2781
Hos 4: 7 *therefore* will I change their glory into s. 7036
4:18 her rulers *with* s do love, Give ye. 7036
9:10 and separated themselves unto *that* s; 1322
10: 6 Ephraim shall receive s, and Israel shall be 1317
Ob 1:10 For *thy* violence against thy brother Jacob s 955
Mic 1:11 inhabitant of Saphir, having *thy* s naked: 1322
2: 6 prophesy to them, *that* they shall not take s. 3639
7:10 and s shall cover her which said unto me, 955
Na 3: 5 thy nakedness, and the kingdoms thy s. 7036
Hab 2:10 Thou hast consulted s to thy house by 1322
2:16 Thou art filled *with* s for glory: drink thou 7036
Zep 3: 5 he faileth not; but the unjust knoweth no s. 1322
3:19 every land where they have been put to s. 1322
Lk 14: 9 thou begin with s to take the lowest room. *152*
Ac 5:41 counted worthy to suffer s for his name. *818*
1Co 4:14 I write not these *things* to s you, but as my *1788*
6: 5 I speak to your s. Is it so, that there is not a *1791*
11: 6 but *if it* be a s for a woman to be shorn or *149*
11:14 if a man have long hair, it is a s unto him? *819*
11:22 church of God, and s them that have not? *2617*
14:35 for it is a s for women to speak in *149*
15:34 knowledge of God: I speak *this* to your s. *1791*
Eph 5:12 For it is a s even to speak of those *things* *149*
Php 3:19 *is their* belly, and *whose* glory *is* in their s, *152*
Heb 6: 6 of God afresh, and put *him* to an open s. *3856*
12: 2 despising the s, and is set down at the right *152*
Jude 1:13 waves of the sea, foaming out their own s; *152*
Rev 3:18 *that* the s of thy nakedness do not appear; *152*
16:15 lest he walk naked, and they see his s. *808*

SHAMED (4) [SHAME]
Ge 38:23 Let her take *it* to her, lest we be s: 937
2Sa 19: 5 Thou hast s *this* day the faces of all thy 954
1Ch 8:12 Eber, and Misham, and S, who built Ono, 8106
Ps 14: 6 You have s the counsel of the poor, because 954

SHAMEFASTNESS (1) [SHAME]
1Ti 2: 9 in modest apparel, with s and sobriety; *127*

SHAMEFUL (2) [SHAME]
Jer 11:13 have ye set up altars to *that* s thing, 1322
Hab 2:16 and s spuing *shall be* on thy glory. 7022

SHAMEFULLY (4) [SHAME]
Hos 2: 5 she that conceived them hath done s: for she 954
Mk 12: 4 in the head, and sent *him* away s handled. *821*
Lk 20:11 and entreated *him* s, and sent *him* away *818*
1Th 2: 2 and were s entreated, as ye know, *5195*

SHAMELESSLY (1) [SHAME]
2Sa 6:20 as one of the vain *fellows* s uncovereth 1540

SHAMER (2)
1Ch 6:46 son of Amzi, the son of Bani, the son of S, 8106
7:34 the sons of S; Ahi, and Rohgah, Jehubbah, 8106

SHAMETH (1) [SHAME]
Pr 28: 7 he that is a companion of riotous *men* s his 3637

SHAMGAR (2)
Jdg 3:31 after him was S the son of Anath, 8044
5: 6 In the days of S the son of Anath, in 8044

SHAMHUTH (1)
1Ch 27: 8 The fifth captain for the fifth month *was* S 8049

SHAMIR (4)
Jos 15:48 in the mountains, S, and Jattir, and Socoh, 8069
Jdg 10: 1 and he dwelt in S in mount Ephraim. 8069
10: 2 three years, and died, and was buried in S. 8069
1Ch 24:24 Michah: of the sons of Michah; S. 8069

SHAMMA (1)
1Ch 7:37 and S, and Shilshah, and Ithran, and Beera. 8037

SHAMMAH (8)
Ge 36:13 Nahath, and Zerah, S, and Mizzah: 8048
36:17 duke Nahath, duke Zerah, duke S, 8048
1Sa 16: 9 Jesse made S to pass by. And he said, 8048
1Sa 17:13 next unto him Abinadab, and the third S. 8048
2Sa 23:11 after him *was* S the son of Agee 8048
23:25 S the Harodite, Elika the Harodite, 8048
23:33 S the Hararite, Ahiam the son of Sharar 8048
1Ch 1:37 of Reuel; Nahath, Zerah, S, and Mizzah. 8048

SHAMMAI (6)
1Ch 2:28 the sons of Onam were, S, and Jada. 8060
2:28 And the sons of S; Nadab, and Abishur. 8060
2:32 the sons of Jada the brother of S; Jether, 8060
2:44 the father of Jorkoam: and Rekem begat S. 8060
2:45 the son of S *was* Maon: and Maon *was* 8060
4:17 and S, and Ishbah the father of Eshtemoa. 8060

SHAMMOTH (1)
1Ch 11:27 S the Harorite, Helez the Pelonite, 8054

SHAMMUA (5)
Nu 13: 4 of the tribe of Reuben, S the son of Zaccur. 8051
2Sa 5:14 S, and Shobab, and Nathan, and Solomon, 8051
1Ch 14: 4 S, and Shobab, Nathan, and Solomon, 8051
Ne 11:17 Abda the son of S, the son of Galal, the son 8051
12:18 Of Bilgah, S; of Shemaiah, Jehonathan; 8051

SHAMSHERAI (1)
1Ch 8:26 And S, and Shehariah, and Athaliah, 8125

SHAPE (2) [SHAPEN, SHAPES]
Lk 3:22 the Holy Ghost descended in a bodily s *1491*
Jn 5:37 heard his voice at any time, nor seen his s. *1491*

SHAPEN (1) [SHAPE]
Ps 51: 5 Behold, I was s in iniquity; and in sin did 2342

SHAPES (1) [SHAPE]
Rev 9: 7 And the s of the locusts *were* like unto *3667*

SHAPHAM (1)
1Ch 5:12 S the next, and Jaanai, and Shaphat in 8223

SHAPHAN (30)
2Ki 22: 3 *that* the king sent S the son of Azaliah, 8227
22: 8 Hilkiah the high priest said unto S 8227
22: 8 Hilkiah gave the book to S, and he read it. 8227
22: 9 S the scribe came to the king, and 8227
22:10 S the scribe shewed the king, saying, 8227
22:10 me a book. And S read it before the king. 8227
22:12 Ahikam the son of S, and Achbor the son 8227
22:12 S the scribe, and Asahiah a servant of 8227
22:14 Ahikam, and Achbor, and S, and Asahiah, 8227
25:22 the son of Ahikam, the son of S, ruler. 8227
2Ch 34: 8 he sent S the son of Azaliah, and Maaseiah 8227
34:15 Hilkiah answered and said to S the scribe, 8227
34:15 And Hilkiah delivered the book to S. 8227
34:16 S carried the book to the king, and 8227
34:18 S the scribe told the king, saying, 8227
34:18 me a book. And S read it before the king. 8227
34:20 Ahikam the son of S, and Abdon the son of 8227
34:20 S the scribe, and Asaiah a servant of 8227
Jer 26:24 of Ahikam the son of S was with Jeremiah, 8227
29: 3 By the hand of Elasah the son of S, and 8227
36:10 in the chamber of Gemariah the son of S 8227
36:11 the son of Gemariah, the son of S, 8227
36:12 Gemariah the son of S, and Zedekiah 8227
39:14 Gedaliah the son of Ahikam the son of S, 8227
40: 5 to Gedaliah the son of Ahikam the son of S, 8227
40: 9 Gedaliah the son of Ahikam the son of S 8227
40:11 Gedaliah the son of Ahikam the son of S; 8227
41: 2 son of Ahikam the son of S with the sword, 8227
43: 6 Gedaliah the son of Ahikam the son of S, 8227
Eze 8:11 midst of them stood Jaazaniah the son of S, 8227

SHAPHAT (8)
Nu 13: 5 Of the tribe of Simeon, S the son of Hori. 8202
1Ki 19:16 Elisha the son of S of Abel-meholah shalt 8202
19:19 and found Elisha the son of S, 8202
2Ki 3:11 and said, Here *is* Elisha the son of S, 8202
6:31 if the head of Elisha the son of S shall stand 8202
1Ch 3:22 Igeal, and Bariah, and Neariah, and S, six. 8202
5:12 the next, and Jaanai, and S in Bashan. 8202
27:29 *were* in the valleys *was* S the son of Adlai: 8202

SHAPHER (2)
Nu 33:23 from Kehelathah, and pitched in mount S. 8234
33:24 they removed from mount S, and 8234

SHAPHIR See SAPHIR

SHARAI (1)
Ezr 10:40 Machnadebai, Shashai, S, 8298

SHARAIM (1)
Jos 15:36 S, and Adithaim, and Gederah, and 8189

SHARAR (1)
2Sa 23:33 Ahiam the son of S the Hararite, 8325

SHARE (1)
1Sa 13:20 to sharpen every man his s, and his coulter, 4282

SHAREZER (2)
2Ki 19:37 and S *his sons* smote him with the sword: 8272
Isa 37:38 and S his sons smote him with the sword; 8272

SHARON (6) [SHARONITE]
1Ch 5:16 in her towns, and in all the suburbs of S, 8289
27:29 over the herds that fed in S *was* Shitrai 8289
SS 2: 1 I am the rose of S, *and* the lily of 8289
Isa 33: 9 S is like a wilderness; and Bashan and 8289
35: 2 the excellency of Carmel and S, they shall 8289
65:10 S shall be a fold of flocks, and the valley of 8289

S

SHARONITE (1) [SHARON]
1Ch 27:29 herds that fed in Sharon *was* Shitrai the **S**: 8290

SHARP (25) [SHARPEN, SHARPENED, SHARPENETH, SHARPER, SHARPLY, SHARPNESS]
Ex 4:25 Zipporah took a **s stone**, and cut off 6864
Jos 5: 2 Make thee **s** knives, and circumcise again 6697
5: 3 Joshua made him **s** knives, and 6697
1Sa 14: 4 *there was* a **s** rock on the one side, and 8127
14: 4 the one side, and a **s** rock on the other side: 8127
Job 41:30 **S** stones *are* under him: he spreadeth sharp 2303
41:30 he spreadeth **s pointed** *things* upon 2742
Ps 45: 5 Thine arrows *are* **s** in the heart of the king's 8150
52: 2 like a **s** rasor, working deceitfully. 3913
57: 4 and arrows, and their tongue a **s** sword. 2299
120: 4 **S** arrows of the mighty, with coals of 8150
Pr 5: 4 as wormwood, **s** as a twoedged sword. 2299
25:18 *is* a maul, and a sword, and a **s** arrow. 8150
Isa 5:28 Whose arrows *are* **s**, and all their bows 8150
41:15 I will make thee a new **s** threshing 2742
49: 2 he hath made my mouth like a **s** sword; 2299
Eze 5: 1 thou, son of man, take thee a **s** knife, 2299
Ac 15:39 And the **contention** was so **s** *between* *3948*
Rev 1:16 out of his mouth went a **s** twoedged sword: *3691*
2:12 These *things* saith he which hath the **s** *3691*
14:14 a golden crown, and in his hand a **s** sickle. *3691*
14:17 is in heaven, he also having a **s** sickle. *3691*
14:18 cried with a loud cry to him that had the **s** *3691*
14:18 Thrust in thy **s** sickle, and gather *3691*
19:15 And out of his mouth goeth a **s** sword, *3691*

SHARPEN (2) [SHARP]
1Sa 13:20 to **s** every man his share, and his coulter, 3913
13:21 and for the axes, and to **s** the goads. 5324

SHARPENED (4) [SHARP]
Ps 140: 3 They have **s** their tongues like a serpent; 8150
Eze 21: 9 A sword, a sword is **s**, and also furbished: 2300
21:10 It is **s** to make a sore slaughter; *it is* 2300
21:11 this sword is **s**, and it *is* furbished, to give it 2300

SHARPENETH (3) [SHARP]
Job 16: 9 his teeth; mine enemy **s** his eyes upon me. 3913
Pr 27:17 Iron **s** iron; so a man sharpeneth 2300
27:17 so a man **s** the countenance of his friend. 2300

SHARPER (2) [SHARP]
Mic 7: 4 the *most* upright *is* **s** than a thorn hedge: NIH
Heb 4:12 powerful, and **s** than any twoedged sword, *5114*

SHARPLY (2) [SHARP]
Jdg 8: 1 And they did chide with him **s**. 2394+871.1
Tit 1:13 Wherefore rebuke them **s**, that they may be *664*

SHARPNESS (1) [SHARP]
2Co 13:10 lest being present I should use **s**, *664*

SHARUHEN (1)
Jos 19: 6 And Beth-lebaoth, and **S**; thirteen cities and 8287

SHASHAI (1)
Ezr 10:40 Machnadebai, **S**, Sharai, 8343

SHASHAK (2)
1Ch 8:14 And Ahio, **S**, and Jeremoth, 8349
8:25 And Iphedeiah, and Penuel, the sons of **S**; 8349

SHATTERED See VEX; VEXATION; VEXED

SHATTERS See SUNDER

SHAUL (7) [SHAULITES]
Ge 46:10 and **S** the son of a Canaanitish woman. 7586
Ex 6:15 and **S** the son of a Canaanitish woman: 7586
Nu 26:13 of **S**, the family of the Shaulites. 7586
1Ch 1:48 **S** of Rehoboth *by* the river reigned in his 7586
1:49 when **S** was dead, Baal-hanan the son of 7586
4:24 and Jamin, Jarib, Zerah, *and* **S**: 7586
6:24 Uriel his son, Uzziah his son, and **S** his son. 7586

SHAULITES (1) [SHAUL]
Nu 26:13 the Zarhites: of Shaul, the family of the **S**. 7587

SHAVE (14) [SHAVED, SHAVEN]
Lev 13:33 shall be shaven, but the scall shall he not **s**; 1548
14: 8 **s off** all his hair, and wash *himself* in water, 1548
14: 9 *that* he shall **s** all his hair **off** his head and 1548
14: 9 even all his hair he shall **s off**: 1548
21: 5 neither shall they **s off** the corner of their 1548
Nu 6: 9 he shall **s** his head in the day of his 1548
6: 9 on the seventh day shall he **s** it. 1548
6:18 the Nazarite shall **s** the head of his 1548
8: 7 let them **s** all their flesh, and let them 5674+8593
Dt 21:12 and she shall **s** her head, and pare her nails; 1548
Jdg 16:19 she **caused** *him* **to s off** the seven locks of 1548
Isa 7:20 In the same day shall the Lord **s** with a 1548
Eze 44:20 Neither shall they **s** their heads, nor suffer 1548
Ac 21:24 with them, that they may **s** *their* heads: *3587*

SHAVED (4) [SHAVE]
Ge 41:14 he **s** *himself*, and changed his raiment, and 1548
2Sa 10: 4 **s off** the *one* half of their beards, and 1548
1Ch 19: 4 **s** them, and cut off their garments in 1548
Job 1:20 **s** his head, and fell down upon the ground, 1494

SHAVEH (1) [SHAVEH KIRIATHAIM]
Ge 14:17 at the valley of **S**, which *is* the king's dale. 7740

SHAVEH KIRIATHAIM (1)
Ge 14: 5 in Ham, and the Emims in **S**, 7741

SHAVEN (7) [SHAVE]
Lev 13:33 He shall be **s**, but the scall shall he not 1548
Nu 6:19 after *the hair of* his separation is **s**: 1548
Jdg 16:17 if I be **s**, then my strength will go from me, 1548
16:22 head began to grow *again* after he was **s**. 1548
Jer 41: 5 having their beards **s**, and their clothes rent, 1548
1Co 11: 5 for *that* is even all one as if she were **s**. *3587*
11: 6 *it* be a shame for a woman to be shorn or **s**, *3587*

SHAVSHA (1)
1Ch 18:16 *were* the priests; and **S** *was* scribe; 7798

SHE (981) [HER, HERS, HERSELF] See Index of Articles, Etc.

SHEAF (9) [SHEAVES]
Ge 37: 7 and lo, my **s** arose, and also stood upright; 485
37: 7 round about, and made obeisance to my **s**. 485
Lev 23:10 ye shall bring a **s** of the firstfruits of your 6016
23:11 And he shall wave the **s** before the LORD, 6016
23:12 ye shall offer that day when ye wave the **s** a 6016
23:15 from the day that ye brought the **s** of 6016
Dt 24:19 hast forgot a **s** in the field, thou shalt not go 6016
Job 24:10 and they take away the **s** *from* the hungry; 6016
Zec 12: 6 the wood, and like a torch of fire in a **s**; 5995

SHEAL (1)
Ezr 10:29 and Adaiah, Jashub, and **S**, and Ramoth. 7594

SHEALTIEL (9)
Ezr 3: 2 Zerubbabel the son of **S**, and his brethren, 7597
3: 8 began Zerubbabel the son of **S**, and 7597
5: 2 rose up Zerubbabel the son of **S**, and 7598
Ne 12: 1 that went up with Zerubbabel the son of **S**, 7597
Hag 1: 1 the prophet unto Zerubbabel the son of **S**, 7597
1:12 Zerubbabel the son of **S**, and Joshua the son 7597
1:14 up the spirit of Zerubbabel the son of **S**, 7597
2: 2 Speak now to Zerubbabel the son of **S**, 7597
2:23 O Zerubbabel, my servant, the son of **S**, 7597

SHEAR (4) [SHEARER, SHEARERS, SHEARING, SHEEPSHEARERS, SHORN]
Ge 31:19 Laban went to **s** his sheep: and Rachel had 1494
38:13 in law goeth up to Timnath to **s** his sheep. 1494
Dt 15:19 thy bullock, nor **s** the firstling of thy sheep. 1494
1Sa 25: 4 in the wilderness that Nabal did **s** his sheep. 1494

SHEARD (1) [SHEARDS]
Isa 30:14 of it a **s** to take fire from the hearth, 2789

SHEARDS (1) [SHEARD]
Eze 23:34 thou shalt break the **s** thereof, and pluck off 2789

SHEARER (1) [SHEAR]
Ac 8:32 and like a lamb dumb before his **s**, so *2751*

SHEARERS (3) [SHEAR]
1Sa 25: 7 now I have heard that thou hast **s**: now thy 1494
25:11 my flesh that I have killed for my **s**, and 1494
Isa 53: 7 as a sheep before her **s** is dumb, so 1494

SHEARIAH (2)
1Ch 8:38 Ishmael, and **S**, and Obadiah, and Hanan. 8187
9:44 Ishmael, and **S**, and Obadiah, and Hanan: 8187

SHEARING (3) [SHEAR]
1Sa 25: 2 and he was **s** his sheep in Carmel. 1494
2Ki 10:12 *And* as he *was at* the **s** house in the way, 1044
10:14 slew them at the pit of the **s** house, 1044

SHEAR-JASHUB (1)
Isa 7: 3 now to meet Ahaz, thou, and **S** thy son, 7610

SHEATH (8)
1Sa 17:51 drew it out of the **s** thereof, and slew him, 8593
2Sa 20: 8 fastened upon his loins in the **s** thereof; 8593
1Ch 21:27 he put up his sword again into the **s** thereof. 5084
Eze 21: 3 will draw forth my sword out of his **s**, and 8593
21: 4 shall my sword go forth out of his **s** against 8593
21: 5 have drawn forth my sword out of his **s**: 8593
21:30 Shall I cause *it* to return into his **s**? I will 8593
Jn 18:11 unto Peter, Put up thy sword into the **s**: *2336*

SHEAVES (9) [SHEAF]
Ge 37: 7 we *were* binding **s** in the field, and lo, 485
37: 7 your **s** stood round about, and 485
Ru 2: 7 and gather after the reapers amongst the **s**: 6016
2:15 Let her glean even among the **s**, and 6016
Ne 13:15 and bringing in **s**, and lading asses; 6194
Ps 126: 6 with rejoicing, bringing his **s** *with him.* 485
129: 7 his hand; nor he that **bindeth s** his bosom. 6014
Am 2:13 as a cart is pressed *that is* full of **s**. 5995
Mic 4:12 for he shall gather them as the **s** into 5995

SHEBA (32) [BEER-SHEBA]
Ge 10: 7 and the sons of Raamah; **S**, and Dedan. 7614
10:28 And Obal, and Abimael, and **S**, 7614
25: 3 Jokshan begat **S**, and Dedan. And the sons 7614
Jos 19: 2 inheritance Beer-sheba, or **S**, and Moladah, 7652
2Sa 20: 1 whose name *was* **S**, the son of Bichri, 7652
20: 2 *and* followed **S** the son of Bichri: 7652
20: 6 Now shall **S** the son of Bichri do us more 7652
20: 7 to pursue after **S** the son of Bichri. 7652
20:10 Abishai his brother pursued after **S** the son 7652
20:13 to pursue after **S** the son of Bichri. 7652
20:21 **S** the son of Bichri by name, 7652
20:22 they cut off the head of **S** the son of Bichri, 7652
1Ki 10: 1 when the queen of **S** heard of the fame of 7614
10: 4 when the queen of **S** had seen all 7614
10:10 the queen of **S** gave to king Solomon. 7614
10:13 king Solomon gave unto the queen of **S** all 7614
1Ch 1: 9 And the sons of Raamah; **S**, and Dedan. 7614
1:22 And Ebal, and Abimael, and **S**, 7614
1:32 And the sons of Jokshan; **S**, and Dedan. 7614
5:13 **S**, and Jorai, and Jachan, and Zia, and 7652
2Ch 9: 1 when the queen of **S** heard of the fame of 7614
9: 3 when the queen of **S** had seen the wisdom 7614
9: 9 spice as the queen of **S** gave king Solomon. 7614
9:12 king Solomon gave to the queen of **S** all her 7614
Job 6:19 the companies of **S** waited for them. 7614
Ps 72:10 the kings of **S** and Seba shall offer gifts. 7614
72:15 and to him shall be given of the gold of **S**: 7614
Isa 60: 6 and Ephah; all they from **S** shall come: 7614
Jer 6:20 cometh there to me incense from **S**, 7614
Eze 27:22 The merchants of **S** and Raamah, they *were* 7614
27:23 Eden, the merchants of **S**, Asshur, *and* 7614
38:13 **S**, and Dedan, and the merchants of 7614

SHEBAH (1) [BEER-SHEBA]
Ge 26:33 he called it **S**: therefore the name of the city 7656

SHEBAM (1)
Nu 32: 3 and Elealeh, and **S**, and Nebo, and Beon, 7643

SHEBANIAH (7)
1Ch 15:24 **S**, and Jehoshaphat, and Nethaneel, and 7645
Ne 9: 4 Jeshua, and Bani, Kadmiel, **S**, Bunni, 7645
9: 5 Hodijah, **S**, *and* Pethahiah, said, Stand up 7645
10: 4 Hattush, **S**, Malluch, 7645
10:10 **S**, Hodijah, Kelita, Pelaiah, Hanan, 7645
10:12 Zaccur, Sherebiah, **S**, 7645
12:14 Of Melicu, Jonathan; of **S**, Joseph; 7645

SHEBARIM (1)
Jos 7: 5 them *from* before the gate *even* unto **S**, 7671

SHEBAT See SEBAT

SHEBER (1)
1Ch 2:48 Caleb's concubine, bare **S**, and Tirhanah. 7669

SHEBNA (9)
2Ki 18:18 **S** the scribe, and Joah the son of Asaph 7644
18:26 **S**, and Joah, unto Rab-shakeh, Speak, 7644
18:37 **S** the scribe, and Joah the son of Asaph 7644
19: 2 **S** the scribe, and the elders of the priests, 7644
Isa 22:15 *even* unto **S**, which *is* over the house, *and* 7644
36: 3 **S** the scribe, and Joah, Asaph's son, 7644
36:11 said Eliakim and **S** and Joah unto 7644
36:22 **S** the scribe, and Joah, the son of Asaph, 7644
37: 2 **S** the scribe, and the elders of the priests 7644

SHEBUEL (3)
1Ch 23:16 *Of* the sons of Gershom, **S** *was* the chief. 7619
25: 4 Uzziel, **S**, and Jerimoth, Hananiah, Hanani, 7619
26:24 **S** the son of Gershom, the son of Moses, 7619

SHECANIAH (2)
1Ch 24:11 The ninth to Jeshua, the tenth to **S**, 7935
2Ch 31:15 and Jeshua, and Shemaiah, Amariah, and **S**, 7935

SHECHANIAH (8)
1Ch 3:21 the sons of Obadiah, the sons of **S**. 7935
3:22 the sons of **S**; Shemaiah: and the sons of 7935
Ezr 8: 3 Of the sons of **S**, of the sons of Pharosh; 7935
8: 5 Of the sons of **S**; the son of Jahaziel, and 7935
10: 2 **S** the son of Jehiel, *one* of the sons of Elam, 7935
Ne 3:29 him repaired also Shemaiah the son of **S**, 7935
6:18 he *was* the son in law of **S** the son of Arah; 7935
12: 3 **S**, Rehum, Meremoth, 7935

SHECHEM (62) [SHECHEM'S, SHECHEMITES, SYCHEM]
Ge 33:18 Jacob came to Shalem, a city of **S**, which *is* 7927
34: 2 when **S** the son of Hamor the Hivite, 7928
34: 4 **S** spake unto his father Hamor, saying, 7928
34: 6 Hamor the father of **S** went out unto Jacob 7928
34: 8 The soul of my son **S** longeth for your 7928
34:11 **S** said unto her father and unto her 7928
34:13 the sons of Jacob answered **S** and Hamor 7928
34:18 words pleased Hamor, and **S** Hamor's son. 7928
34:20 **S** his son came unto the gate of their city, 7928
34:24 unto **S** his son hearkened all that went out 7928
34:26 and **S** his son with the edge of the sword, 7928
35: 4 hid them under the oak which *was* by **S**. 7927
37:12 went to feed their father's flock in **S**. 7927
37:13 Do not thy brethren feed *the flock* in **S**? 7927
37:14 of the vale of Hebron, and he came to **S**. 7927
Nu 26:31 and *of* **S**, the family of the Shechemites: 7928
Jos 17: 2 for the children of **S**, and for the children of 7928
17: 7 Asher *to* Michmethah, that *lieth* before **S**; 7927
20: 7 **S** in mount Ephraim, and Kirjath-arba, 7927
21:21 For they gave them **S** with her suburbs in 7927
24: 1 Joshua gathered all the tribes of Israel to **S**, 7927
24:25 set them a statute and an ordinance in **S**. 7927
24:32 brought up out of Egypt, buried they in **S**, 7927
24:32 father of **S** for an hundred pieces of silver: 7927
Jdg 8:31 his concubine that *was* in **S**, she also bare 7927
9: 1 Abimelech the son of Jerubbaal went to **S** 7927
9: 2 I pray you, in the ears of all the men of **S**, 7927
9: 3 the ears of all the men of **S** all these words: 7927
9: 6 all the men of **S** gathered together, and 7927
9: 6 by the plain of the pillar that *was* in **S**. 7927
9: 7 unto them, Hearken unto me, you men of **S**, 7927
9:18 king over the men of **S**, because he *is* your 7927
9:20 devour the men of **S**, and the house of 7927
9:20 let fire come out from the men of **S**, and 7927
9:23 spirit between Abimelech and the men of **S**; 7927
9:23 the men of **S** dealt treacherously with 7927
9:24 upon the men of **S**, which aided him in 7927
9:25 the men of **S** set liers in wait for him in 7927
9:26 came with his brethren, and went over to **S**: 7927
9:26 the men of **S** put their confidence in him. 7927
9:28 Who *is* Abimelech, and who *is* **S**, that we 7927
9:28 serve the men of Hamor the father of **S**: 7927
9:31 son of Ebed and his brethren be come to **S**; 7927

Jdg 9:34 they laid wait against **S** *in* four companies. 7927
9:39 Gaal went out before the men of **S**, and 7927
9:41 that *they* should not dwell in **S**. 7927
9:46 when all the men of the tower of **S** heard 7927
9:47 that all the men of the tower of **S** were 7927
9:49 that all the men of the tower of **S** died also, 7927
9:57 all the evil of the men of **S** did God render 7927
21:19 highway that goeth up from Beth-el to **S**, 7927
1Ki 12: 1 Rehoboam went *to* **S**: for all Israel were 7927
12: 1 for all Israel were come *to* **S** to make him 7927
12:25 Jeroboam built **S** in mount Ephraim, and 7927
1Ch 6:67 **S** in mount Ephraim with her suburbs; 7927
7:19 Ahian, and **S**, and Likhi, and Aniam. 7928
7:28 **S** also and the towns thereof, unto Gaza and 7927
2Ch 10: 1 Rehoboam went to **S**: for *to* Shechem were 7927
10: 1 for *to* **S** were all Israel come to make him 7927
Ps 60: 6 I will divide **S**, and mete out the valley of 7927
108: 7 I will divide **S**, and mete out the valley of 7927
Jer 41: 5 That there came certain from **S**, 7927

SHECHEM'S (2) [SHECHEM]
Ge 33:19 **S** father, for an hundred pieces of money. 7928
34:26 took Dinah out of **S** house, and went out. 7928

SHECHEMITES (1) [SHECHEM]
Nu 26:31 and *of* Shechem, the family of the **S**: 7930

SHED (52) [SHEDDER, SHEDDETH, SHEDDING]
Ge 9: 6 man's blood, by man shall his blood be **s**: 8210
37:22 **S** no blood, *but* cast him into this pit that *is* 8210
Ex 22: 2 he die, *there shall* no blood *be* **s** for him. NIH
22: 3 upon him, *there shall be* blood **s** for him; NIH
Lev 17: 4 he hath **s** blood; and that man shall be cut 8210
Nu 35:33 be cleansed of the blood that is **s** therein, 8210
35:33 but by the blood of him that **s** it. 8210
Dt 19:10 That innocent blood be not **s** in thy land, 8210
21: 7 and say, Our hands have not **s** this blood, 8210
1Sa 25:26 withholden thee from coming to **s** blood, NIH
25:31 either that thou hast **s** blood causeless, or 8210
25:33 kept me this day from coming to **s** blood, NIH
2Sa 20:10 and **s out** his bowels to the ground, 8210
1Ki 2: 5 **s** the blood of war in peace, and put 7760
2:31 which Joab **s**, from me, and from the house 8210
2Ki 21:16 Moreover Manasseh **s** innocent blood very 8210
24: 4 also *for* the innocent blood that he **s**: for he 8210
1Ch 22: 8 Thou hast **s** blood abundantly, and 8210
22: 8 thou hast **s** much blood upon the earth in 8210
28: 3 *hast been* a man of war, and hast **s** blood. 8210
Ps 79: 3 Their blood have they **s** like water round 8210
79:10 of the blood of thy servants which is **s**. 8210
106:38 **s** innocent blood, *even* the blood of their 8210
Pr 1:16 feet run to evil, and make haste to **s** blood. 8210
6:17 and hands that **s** innocent blood, 8210
Isa 59: 7 and they make haste to **s** innocent blood: 8210
Jer 7: 6 and **s** not innocent blood in this place, 8210
22: 3 neither **s** innocent blood in this place. 8210
22:17 for to **s** innocent blood, and for oppression, 8210
La 4:13 that *have* **s** the blood of the just in the midst 8210
Eze 16:38 that break wedlock and **s** blood are judged; 8210
22: 4 become guilty in thy blood that thou hast **s**; 8210
22: 6 every one were in thee to their power to **s** 8210
22: 9 In thee are men that carry tales to **s** blood: 8210
22:12 In thee have they taken gifts to **s** blood; 8210
22:27 to **s** blood, *and* to destroy souls, to get 8210
23:45 after the manner of *women* that **s** blood; 8210
33:25 your eyes toward your idols, and **s** blood: 8210
35: 5 hast **s** *the blood of* the children of Israel by 5064
36:18 for the blood that they had **s** upon the land, 8210
Joel 3:19 they have **s** innocent blood in their land. 8210
Mt 23:35 all the righteous blood **s** upon the earth, *1632*
26:28 which is **s** for many for the remission of *1632*
Mk 14:24 of the new testament, which is **s** for many. *1632*
Lk 11:50 which was **s** from the foundation of *1632*
22:20 testament in my blood, which is **s** for you. *1632*
Ac 2:33 he hath **s forth** this, which ye now see and *1632*
22:20 the blood of thy martyr Stephen was **s**, *1632*
Ro 3:15 Their feet *are* swift to **s** blood: *1632*
5: 5 the love of God is **s abroad** in our hearts *1632*
Tit 3: 6 Which he **s** on us abundantly through Jesus *1632*
Rev 16: 6 For they have **s** the blood of saints and *1632*

SHEDDER (1) [SHED]
Eze 18:10 a **s** of blood, and *that* doeth the like to *any* 8210

SHEDDETH (2) [SHED]
Ge 9: 6 Whoso **s** man's blood, by man shall his 8210
Eze 22: 3 The city **s** blood in the midst of it, that her 8210

SHEDDING (1) [SHED]
Heb 9:22 and without **s of blood** is no remission. *130*

SHEDEUR (5)
Nu 1: 5 of *the tribe of* Reuben; Elizur the son of **S**. 7707
2:10 of Reuben *shall be* Elizur the son of **S**. 7707
7:30 On the fourth day Elizur the son of **S**, 7707
7:35 this *was* the offering of Elizur the son of **S**. 7707
10:18 and over his host *was* Elizur the son of **S**. 7707

SHEEP (187) [SHEEP'S, SHEEPCOTE, SHEEPCOTES, SHEEPFOLD, SHEEPFOLDS, SHEEPMASTER, SHEEPSHEARERS, SHEEPSKINS, SHEPHERD, SHEPHERD'S, SHEPHERDS, SHEPHERDS']
Ge 4: 2 Abel was a keeper of **s**, but Cain was a 6629
12:16 he had **s**, and oxen, and he asses, and 6629
20:14 Abimelech took **s**, and oxen, and 6629
21:27 Abraham took **s** and oxen, and gave *them* 6629
29: 2 lo, there *were* three flocks of **s** lying by it; 6629
29: 3 watered the **s**, and put the stone again upon 6629
29: 6 Rachel his daughter cometh with the **s**. 6629
29: 7 water ye the **s**, and go *and* feed *them*. 6629
29: 8 from the well's mouth; then we water the **s**. 6629
29: 9 with them, Rachel came with her father's **s**: 6629
29:10 the **s** of Laban his mother's brother, 6629
Ge 30:32 all the brown cattle among the **s**, and 3775
30:33 the goats, and brown amongst the **s**, 3775
30:35 all the brown amongst the **s**, and gave *them* 3775
31:19 Laban went to shear his **s**: and Rachel had 6629
34:28 They took their **s**, and their oxen, and their 6629
38:13 in law goeth up to Timnath to shear his **s**. 6629
Ex 9: 3 the camels, upon the oxen, and upon the **s**: 6629
12: 5 ye shall take *it* out from the **s**, or from 3532
20:24 thy peace offerings, thy **s**, and thine oxen: 6629
22: 1 shall steal an ox, or a **s**, and kill it, or sell it; 7716
22: 1 five oxen for an ox, and four **s** for a sheep. 6629
22: 1 five oxen for an ox, and four sheep for a **s**. 7716
22: 4 his hand alive, whether it be ox, or ass, or **s**; 7716
22: 9 for ass, for **s**, for raiment, *or* for any 7716
22:10 or an ox, or a **s**, or any beast, to keep; 7716
22:30 thou do with thine oxen, *and* with thy **s**: 6629
34:19 thy cattle, *whether* ox or **s**, *that* is male. 7716
Lev 1:10 *namely*, of the **s**, or of the goats, for a burnt 3775
7:23 eat no *manner* fat, of ox, or of **s**, or of goat. 3775
22:19 of the beeves, of the **s**, or of the goats. 3775
22:21 or a freewill offering in beeves or **s**, it shall 6629
22:27 or a **s**, or a goat, is brought forth, then 3775
27:26 man shall sanctify it; whether *it be* ox, or **s**: 7716
Nu 18:17 or the firstling of a **s**, or the firstling of a 3775
22:40 Balak offered oxen and **s**, and sent to 6629
27:17 be not as **s** which have no shepherd. 6629
31:28 of the beeves, and of the asses, and of the **s**: 6629
31:32 and seventy thousand and five thousand **s**, 6629
31:36 and thirty thousand and five hundred **s**: 6629
31:37 the LORD'S tribute of the **s** was six 6629
31:43 *and* seven thousand and five hundred **s**, 6629
32:24 for your little ones, and folds for your **s**; 6792
32:36 fenced cities: and folds for **s**. 6629
Dt 7:13 increase of thy kine, and the flocks of thy **s**, 6629
14: 4 shall eat: the ox, the **s**, and the goat, 3775+7716
14:26 or for **s**, or for wine, or for strong drink, or 6629
15:19 thy bullock, nor shear the firstling of thy **s**. 6629
17: 1 or **s**, wherein is blemish, *or* any evil 7716
18: 3 that offer a sacrifice, whether *it be* ox or **s**; 7716
18: 4 thy oil, and the first of the fleece of thy **s**, 6629
22: 1 not see thy brother's ox or his **s** go astray, 7716
28: 4 increase of thy kine, and the flocks of thy **s**. 6629
28:18 increase of thy kine, and the flocks of thy **s**. 6629
28:31 thy **s** *shall be* given unto thine enemies, 6629
28:51 the increase of thy kine, or flocks of thy **s**, 6629
32:14 Butter of kine, and milk of **s**, with fat of 6629
Jos 6:21 and old, and ox, and **s**, and ass, 7716
7:24 and his **s**, and his tent, and all that he had: 6629
Jdg 6: 4 for Israel, neither **s**, nor ox, nor ass. 7716
1Sa 8:17 He will take the tenth of your **s**: and 6629
14:32 took **s**, and oxen, and calves, and slew *them* 6629
14:34 every man his **s**, and slay *them* here, and 7716
15: 3 and suckling, ox and **s**, camel and ass. 7716
15: 9 the best of the **s**, and of the oxen, and of 6629
15:14 then this bleating of the **s** in mine ears, 6629
15:15 for the people spared the best of the **s** and 6629
15:21 the people took of the spoil, **s** and oxen, 6629
16:11 the youngest, and behold, he keepeth the **s**. 6629
16:19 Send me David thy son, which *is* with the **s**. 6629
17:15 returned from Saul to feed his father's **s** *at* 6629
17:20 left the **s** with a keeper, and took, and went, 6629
17:28 with whom hast thou left those few **s** in 6629
17:34 Thy servant kept his father's **s**, and 6629
22:19 and sucklings, and oxen, and asses, and **s**, 7716
25: 2 he had three thousand **s**, and a thousand 6629
25: 2 and he was shearing his **s** in Carmel. 6629
25: 4 in the wilderness that Nabal did shear his **s**. 6629
25:16 the while we were with them keeping the **s**. 6629
25:18 five **s** ready dressed, and five measures of 6629
27: 9 took away the **s**, and the oxen, and 6629
2Sa 7: 8 from following the **s**, to be ruler over my 6629
17:29 butter, and **s**, and cheese of kine, for David, 6629
24:17 these **s**, what have they done? let thine 6629
1Ki 1: 9 Adonijah slew **s** and oxen and fat cattle by 6629
1:19 and fat cattle and **s** in abundance, 6629
1:25 and fat cattle and **s** in abundance, 6629
4:23 an hundred **s**, beside harts, and roebucks, 6629
8: 5 him before the ark, sacrificing **s** and oxen, 6629
8:63 and an hundred and twenty thousand **s**. 6629
22:17 the hills, as **s** that have not a shepherd: 6629
2Ki 5:26 **s**, and oxen, and menservants, and 6629
1Ch 5:21 *of* **s** two hundred and fifty thousand, and 6629
12:40 wine, and oil, and oxen, and **s** abundantly: 6629
17: 7 the sheepcote, *even* from following the **s**, 6629
21:17 *as for* these **s**, what have they done? 6629
2Ch 5: 6 sacrificed **s** and oxen, which could not be 6629
7: 5 and an hundred and twenty thousand **s**: 6629
14:15 carried away **s** and camels in abundance, 6629
15:11 seven hundred oxen and seven thousand **s**. 6629
18: 2 Ahab killed **s** and oxen for him in 6629
18:16 the mountains, as **s** that have no shepherd: 6629
29:33 six hundred oxen and three thousand **s**. 6629
30:24 a thousand bullocks and seven thousand **s**; 6629
30:24 a thousand bullocks and ten thousand **s**: 6629
31: 6 they also brought in the tithe of oxen and **s**, 6629
Ne 3: 1 the priests, and they built the **s** gate; 6629
3:32 unto the **s** gate repaired the goldsmiths 6629
5:18 *for me* daily *was* one ox *and* six choice **s**; 6629
12:39 the tower of Meah, even unto the **s** gate: 6629
Job 1: 3 His substance also was seven thousand **s**, 6629
1:16 hath burnt up the **s**, and the servants, and 6629
31:20 were *not* warmed with the fleece of my **s**; 3532
42:12 for he had fourteen thousand **s**, and 6629
Ps 8: 7 All **s** and oxen, yea, and the beasts of 6792
44:11 Thou hast given us like **s** appointed for 6629
44:22 we are counted as **s** for the slaughter. 6629
49:14 Like **s** they are laid in the grave; death shall 6629
74: 1 *why* doth thine anger smoke against the **s** 6629
78:52 made his own people to go forth like **s**, and 6629
79:13 **s** of thy pasture will give thee thanks for 6629
95: 7 people of his pasture, and the **s** of his hand. 6629
100: 3 *we are* his people, and the **s** of his pasture. 6629
119:176 I have gone astray like a lost **s**; seek thy 7716
144:13 *that* our **s** may bring forth thousands and 6629
SS 4: 2 Thy teeth *are* like a flock of **s** *that are* even NIH
SS 6: 6 Thy teeth *are* as a flock of **s** which go up 7353
Isa 7:21 man shall nourish a young cow, and two **s**; 6629
13:14 and as a **s** that no *man* taketh up: 6629
22:13 killing **s**, eating flesh, and drinking wine: 6629
53: 6 All we like **s** have gone astray; we have 6629
53: 7 as a **s** before her shearers is dumb, so 7353
Jer 12: 3 pull them out like **s** for the slaughter, and 6629
23: 1 that destroy and scatter the **s** of my pasture! 6629
50: 6 My people hath been lost **s**: their shepherds 6629
50:17 Israel *is* a scattered **s**; the lions have driven 7716
Eze 34: 6 My **s** wandered through all the mountains, 6629
34:11 will both search my **s**, and seek them out. 6629
34:12 that he is among his **s** *that are* scattered; 6629
34:12 so will I seek out my **s**, and will deliver 6629
Hos 12:12 served for a wife, and for a wife he kept **s**. NIH
Joel 1:18 yea, the flocks of **s** are made desolate. 6629
Mic 2:12 I will put them together as the **s** of Bozrah, 6629
5: 8 as a young lion among the flocks of **s**: 6629
Zec 13: 7 the shepherd, and the **s** shall be scattered: 6629
Mt 9:36 scattered abroad, as **s** having no shepherd. *4263*
10: 6 But go rather to the lost **s** of the house of *4263*
10:16 I send you forth as **s** in the midst of wolves: *4263*
12:11 that shall have one **s**, and if it fall into a pit *4263*
12:12 How much then is a man better than a **s**? *4263*
15:24 but unto the lost **s** of the house of Israel. *4263*
18:12 if a man have an hundred **s**, and one of *4263*
18:13 he rejoiceth more of that **s**, than of NIG
25:32 as a shepherd divideth *his* **s** from the goats: *4263*
25:33 And he shall set the **s** on his right hand, but *4263*
26:31 the **s** of the flock shall be scattered abroad. *4263*
Mk 6:34 they were as **s** not having a shepherd: *4263*
14:27 the shepherd, and the **s** shall be scattered. *4263*
Lk 15: 4 What man of you, having an hundred **s**, *4263*
15: 6 for I have found my **s** which was lost. *4263*
Jn 2:14 those that sold oxen and **s** and doves, *4263*
2:15 out of the temple, and the **s** and the oxen; *4263*
5: 2 Now there is at Jerusalem by the **s** *market* a *4262*
10: 2 in by the door is the shepherd of the **s**. *4263*
10: 3 the porter openeth; and the **s** hear his voice: *4263*
10: 3 and he calleth his own **s** by name, and *4263*
10: 4 And when he putteth forth his own **s**, he *4263*
10: 4 he goeth before them, and the **s** follow him: *4263*
10: 7 I say unto you, I am the door of the **s**. *4263*
10: 8 and robbers: but the **s** did not hear them. *4263*
10:11 the good shepherd giveth his life for the **s**. *4263*
10:12 not the shepherd, whose own the **s** are not, *4263*
10:12 wolf coming, and leaveth the **s**, and fleeth: *4263*
10:12 the wolf catcheth them, and scattereth the **s**. *4263*
10:13 he is a hireling, and careth not for the **s**. *4263*
10:14 and know my **s**, and am known of mine. NIG
10:15 the Father: and I lay down my life for the **s**. *4263*
10:16 And other **s** I have, which are not of this *4263*
10:26 because ye are not of my **s**, as I said unto *4263*
10:27 My **s** hear my voice, and I know them, and *4263*
21:16 I love thee. He saith unto him, Feed my **s**. *4263*
21:17 love thee. Jesus saith unto him, Feed my **s**. *4263*
Ac 8:32 was this, He was led as a **s** to the slaughter; *4263*
Ro 8:36 we are accounted as **s** for the slaughter. *4263*
Heb 13:20 *that* great shepherd of the **s**, through *4263*
1Pe 2:25 For ye were as **s** going astray; but are now *4263*
Rev 18:13 and **s**, and horses, and chariots, and slaves, *4263*

SHEEP'S (1) [SHEEP]
Mt 7:15 which come to you in **s** clothing, but *4263*

SHEEPCOTE (2) [SHEEP]
2Sa 7: 8 I took thee from the **s**, from following 5116
1Ch 17: 7 I took thee from the **s**, *even* from following 5116

SHEEPCOTES (1) [SHEEP]
1Sa 24: 3 he came to the **s** by the way, where 1448+6629

SHEEPFOLD (1) [FOLD, SHEEP]
Jn 10: 1 not by the door into the **s**, *833+3588+4263*

SHEEPFOLDS (3) [FOLD, SHEEP]
Nu 32:16 We will build **s** here for our cattle, 1448+6629
Jdg 5:16 Why abodest thou among the **s**, to hear 4942
Ps 78:70 his servant, and took him from the **s**: 4356+6629

SHEEPMASTER (1) [MASTER, SHEEP]
2Ki 3: 4 Mesha king of Moab was a **s**, and 5349

SHEEPSHEARERS (3) [SHEAR, SHEEP]
Ge 38:12 went up unto his **s** to Timnath, he 1494+6629
2Sa 13:23 that Absalom had **s** in Baal-hazor, which *is* 1494
13:24 and said, Behold now, thy servant hath **s**; 1494

SHEEPSKINS (1) [SHEEP, SKIN]
Heb 11:37 they wandered about in **s** and goatskins; *3374*

SHEERAH See SHERAH

SHEET (2) [SHEETS]
Ac 10:11 as *it had been* a great **s** knit at the four *3607*
11: 5 vessel descend, as *it had been* a great **s**, *3607*

SHEETS (2) [SHEET]
Jdg 14:12 I will give you thirty **s** and thirty change of 5466
14:13 shall ye give me thirty **s** and thirty change 5466

SHEHARIAH (1)
1Ch 8:26 And Shamsherai, and **S**, and Athaliah, 7841

SHEKEL (43) [SHEKELS]
Ge 24:22 took a golden earring of **half a s** weight, 1235
Ex 30:13 half a **s** after the shekel of the sanctuary: 8255
30:13 half a shekel after the **s** of the sanctuary: 8255
30:13 (a **s** *is* twenty gerahs:) a half shekel *shall be* 8255
30:13 a half **s** *shall be* the offering of the LORD. 8255
30:15 the poor shall not give less than half a **s**, 8255
30:24 of cassia five hundred *shekels*, after the **s** of 8255
38:24 thirty shekels, after the **s** of the sanctuary. 8255

Ex 38:25 fifteen shekels, after the s of the sanctuary: 8255
38:26 A bekah for every man, that is, half a s, 8255
38:26 is, half a shekel, after the s of the sanctuary, 8255
Lev 5:15 after the s of the sanctuary, for a trespass 8255
27: 3 of silver, after the s of the sanctuary. 8255
27:25 shall be according to the s of the sanctuary: 8255
27:25 the sanctuary: twenty gerahs shall be the s. 8255
Nu 3:47 after the s of the sanctuary shalt thou take 8255
3:47 thou take them: (the s is twenty gerahs:) 8255
3:50 five shekels, after the s of the sanctuary: 8255
7:13 after the s of the sanctuary; 8255
7:19 after the s of the sanctuary; 8255
7:25 after the s of the sanctuary; 8255
7:31 after the s of the sanctuary; 8255
7:37 after the s of the sanctuary; 8255
7:43 after the s of the sanctuary; 8255
7:49 after the s of the sanctuary; 8255
7:55 after the s of the sanctuary; 8255
7:61 after the s of the sanctuary; 8255
7:67 after the s of the sanctuary; 8255
7:73 after the s of the sanctuary; 8255
7:79 after the s of the sanctuary; 8255
7:85 four hundred shekels, after the s of 8255
7:86 shekels apiece, after the s of the sanctuary: 8255
18:16 after the s of the sanctuary, which is twenty 8255
1Sa 9: 8 I have here at hand the fourth part of a s of 8255
2Ki 7: 1 shall a measure of fine flour be sold for a s, 8255
7: 1 two measures of barley for a s, in the gate 8255
7:16 So a measure of fine flour was sold for a s, 8255
7:16 two measures of barley for a s, according to 8255
7:18 Two measures of barley for a s, and 8255
7:18 a shekel, and a measure of fine flour for a s, 8255
Ne 10:32 a s for the service of the house of our God; 8255
Eze 45:12 the s shall be twenty gerahs: 8255
Am 8: 5 the s great, and falsifying the balances by 8255

SHEKELS (96) [SHEKEL]
Ge 23:15 the land is worth four hundred s of silver; 8255
23:16 four hundred s of silver, current money 8255
24:22 two bracelets for her hands of ten s weight NIH
Ex 21:32 he shall give unto their master thirty s of 8255
30:23 of pure myrrh five hundred s, and of sweet NIH
30:23 even two hundred and fifty s, and of sweet NIH
30:23 of sweet calamus two hundred and fifty s, NIH
30:24 of cassia five hundred s, after the shekel of NIH
38:24 nine talents, and seven hundred and thirty s, 8255
38:25 seven hundred and threescore and fifteen s, 8255
38:28 and five s he made hooks for the pillars, NIH
38:29 and two thousand and four hundred s. 8255
Lev 5:15 with thy estimation by s of silver, after 8255
27: 3 even thy estimation shall be fifty s of silver, 8255
27: 4 then thy estimation shall be thirty s. 8255
27: 5 estimation shall be of the male twenty s, 8255
27: 5 twenty shekels, and for the female ten s. 8255
27: 6 thy estimation shall be of the male five s of 8255
27: 6 thy estimation shall be three s of silver. 8255
27: 7 thy estimation shall be fifteen s, and for 8255
27: 7 be fifteen shekels, and for the female ten s. 8255
27:16 seed shall be valued at fifty s of silver. 8255
Nu 3:47 Thou shalt even take five s apiece by 8255
3:50 and five, after the shekel of the sanctuary: NIH
7:13 thirty s, one silver bowl of seventy shekels, NIH
7:13 thirty shekels, one silver bowl of seventy s, 8255
7:14 One spoon of ten s of gold, full of incense: NIH
7:19 thirty s, one silver bowl of seventy shekels, NIH
7:19 thirty shekels, one silver bowl of seventy s, 8255
7:20 One spoon of gold of ten s, full of incense: NIH
7:25 thirty s, one silver bowl of seventy shekels, NIH
7:25 thirty shekels, one silver bowl of seventy s, 8255
7:26 One golden spoon of ten s, full of incense: NIH
7:31 thirty s, one silver bowl of seventy shekels, NIH
7:31 thirty shekels, one silver bowl of seventy s, 8255
7:32 One golden spoon of ten s, full of incense: NIH
7:37 thirty s, one silver bowl of seventy shekels, NIH
7:37 thirty shekels, one silver bowl of seventy s, 8255
7:38 One golden spoon of ten s, full of incense: NIH
7:43 thirty s, a silver bowl of seventy shekels, NIH
7:43 thirty shekels, a silver bowl of seventy s, 8255
7:44 One golden spoon of ten s, full of incense: NIH
7:49 thirty s, one silver bowl of seventy shekels, NIH
7:49 thirty shekels, one silver bowl of seventy s, 8255
7:50 One golden spoon of ten s, full of incense: NIH
7:55 thirty s, one silver bowl of seventy shekels, NIH
7:55 thirty shekels, one silver bowl of seventy s, 8255
7:56 One golden spoon of ten s, full of incense: NIH
7:61 thirty s, one silver bowl of seventy shekels, NIH
7:61 thirty shekels, one silver bowl of seventy s, 8255
7:62 One golden spoon of ten s, full of incense: NIH
7:67 thirty s, one silver bowl of seventy shekels, NIH
7:67 thirty shekels, one silver bowl of seventy s, 8255
7:68 One golden spoon of ten s, full of incense: NIH
7:73 thirty s, one silver bowl of seventy shekels, NIH
7:73 thirty shekels, one silver bowl of seventy s, 8255
7:74 One golden spoon of ten s, full of incense: NIH
7:79 thirty s, one silver bowl of seventy shekels, NIH
7:79 thirty shekels, one silver bowl of seventy s, 8255
7:80 One golden spoon of ten s, full of incense: NIH
7:85 an hundred and thirty s, each bowl seventy: NIH
7:85 four hundred s, after the shekel of NIH
7:86 full of incense, weighing ten s apiece, NIH
7:86 of the spoons was an hundred and twenty s. NIH
18:16 to thine estimation, for the money of five s, 8255
31:52 sixteen thousand seven hundred and fifty s. 8255
Dt 22:19 they shall amerce him in an hundred s of NIH
22:29 unto the damsel's father fifty s of silver, NIH
Jos 7:21 two hundred s of silver, and a wedge of 8255
7:21 a wedge of gold of fifty s weight, then 8255
Jdg 8:26 a thousand and seven hundred s of gold; NIH
17: 2 The eleven hundred s of silver that were NIH
17: 3 when he had restored the eleven hundred s NIH
17: 4 and his mother took two hundred s of silver, NIH
17:10 I will give thee ten s of silver by the year, NIH
1Sa 17: 5 the weight of the coat was five thousand s 8255
17: 7 his spear's head weighed six hundred s of 8255
2Sa 14:26 at two hundred s after the king's weight. 8255
2Sa 18:11 I would have given thee ten s of silver, and NIH
18:12 Though I should receive a thousand s of NIH
21:16 weighed three hundred s of brass in weight, NIH
24:24 and the oxen for fifty s of silver. 8255
1Ki 10:16 six hundred s of gold went to one target. NIH
10:29 went out of Egypt for six hundred s of NIH
2Ki 15:20 of each man fifty s of silver, to give to 8255
1Ch 21:25 the place six hundred s of gold by weight. 8255
2Ch 1:17 Egypt a chariot for six hundred s of silver, NIH
3: 9 the weight of the nails was fifty s of gold. 8255
9:15 six hundred s of beaten gold went to one NIH
9:16 three hundred s of gold went to one shield. NIH
Ne 5:15 and wine, beside forty s of silver; 8255
Jer 32: 9 him the money, even seventeen s of silver. 8255
Eze 4:10 shalt eat shall be by weight, twenty s a day: 8255
45:12 twenty s, five and twenty shekels, 8255
45:12 five and twenty s, fifteen shekels, 8255
45:12 five and twenty shekels, fifteen s, 8255

SHELAH (11) [SHELANITES]
Ge 38: 5 and bare a son; and called his name S: 7956
38:11 thy father's house, till S my son be grown: 7956
38:14 for she saw that S was grown, and she was 7956
38:26 because that I gave her not to S my son. 7956
46:12 and Onan, and S, and Pharez, and Zerah: 7956
Nu 26:20 of S, the family of the Shelanites: 7956
1Ch 1:18 Arphaxad begat S, and Shelah begat Eber. 7974
1:18 Arphaxad begat Shelah, and S begat Eber. 7974
1:24 Shem, Arphaxad, S, 7974
2: 3 The sons of Judah; Er, and Onan, and S: 7956
4:21 The sons of S the son of Judah were, Er 7956

SHELANITES (1) [SHELAH]
Nu 26:20 of Shelah, the family of the S: 8024

SHELEMIAH (10)
1Ch 26:14 the lot eastward fell to S. Then for 8018
Ezr 10:39 And S, and Nathan, and Adaiah, 8018
10:41 Azareel, and S, Shemariah, 8018
Ne 3:30 After him repaired Hananiah the son of S, 8018
13:13 S the priest, and Zadok the scribe, and 8018
Jer 36:14 the son of S, the son of Cushi, unto Baruch, 8018
36:26 S the son of Abdeel, to take Baruch 8018
37: 3 Zedekiah the king sent Jehucal the son of S 8018
37:13 the son of S, the son of Hananiah; 8018
38: 1 Jucal the son of S, and Pashur the son of 8018

SHELEPH (2)
Ge 10:26 and S, and Hazarmaveth, and Jerah, 8026
1Ch 1:20 and S, and Hazarmaveth, and Jerah, 8026

SHELESH (1)
1Ch 7:35 Zophah, and Imna, and S, and Amal. 8028

SHELOMI (1)
Nu 34:27 the children of Asher, Ahihud the son of S. 8015

SHELOMITH (9) [SHELOMOTH]
Lev 24:11 (and his mother's name was S, the daughter 8019
1Ch 3:19 and Hananiah, and S their sister: 8019
23: 9 of Shimei; S, and Haziel, and Haran, three. 8019
23:18 Of the sons of Izhar; S the chief. 8019
26:25 his son, and Zichri his son, and S his son. 8019
26:26 Which S and his brethren were over all 8019
26:28 anything, it was under the hand of S, 8019
2Ch 11:20 him Abijah, and Attai, and Ziza, and S. 8019
Ezr 8:10 of the sons of S; the son of Josiphiah, and 8019

SHELOMOTH (2) [SHELOMITH]
1Ch 24:22 Of the Izharites; S: of the sons of 8013
24:22 Shelomoth: of the sons of S; Jahath. 8013

SHELTER (2)
Job 24: 8 and embrace the rock for want of a s. 4268
Ps 61: 3 For thou hast been a s for me, and a strong 4268

SHELUMIEL (5)
Nu 1: 6 Of Simeon; S the son of Zurishaddai. 8017
2:12 Simeon shall be S the son of Zurishaddai. 8017
7:36 On the fifth day S the son of Zurishaddai, 8017
7:41 this was the offering of S the son of 8017
10:19 of Simeon was S the son of Zurishaddai. 8017

SHEM (17) [SEM]
Ge 5:32 and Noah begat S, Ham, and Japheth. 8035
6:10 begat three sons, S, Ham, and Japheth. 8035
7:13 S, and Ham, and Japheth, the sons of Noah, 8035
9:18 of the ark, were S, and Ham, and Japheth: 8035
9:23 S and Japheth took a garment, and laid it 8035
9:26 he said, Blessed be the LORD God of S; 8035
9:27 and he shall dwell in the tents of S; 8035
10: 1 of the sons of Noah, S, Ham, and Japheth: 8035
10:21 Unto S also, the father of all the children of 8035
10:22 The children of S; Elam, and Asshur, and 8035
10:31 These are the sons of S, after their families, 8035
11:10 These are the generations of S: Shem was 8035
11:10 S was an hundred years old, and 8035
11:11 S lived after he begat Arphaxad five 8035
1Ch 1: 4 Noah, S, Ham, and Japheth. 8035
1:17 The sons of S; Elam, and Asshur, and 8035
1:24 S, Arphaxad, Shelah, 8035

SHEMA (6)
Jos 15:26 Amam, and S, and Moladah, 8090
1Ch 2:43 Korah, and Tappuah, and Rekem, and S. 8087
2:44 S begat Raham, the father of Jorkoam: and 8087
5: 8 the son of S, the son of Joel, who dwelt in 8087
8:13 Beriah also, and S, who were heads of 8087
Ne 8: 4 and S, and Anaiah, and Urijah, and Hilkiah, 8087

SHEMAAH (1)
1Ch 12: 3 then Joash, the sons of S the Gibeathite; 8094

SHEMAIAH (41)
1Ki 12:22 the word of God came unto S the man of 8098
1Ch 3:22 the sons of Shechaniah; S: and the sons of 8098
3:22 the sons of S; Hattush, and Igeal, and 8098
4:37 of Jedaiah, the son of Shimri, the son of S; 8098
5: 4 S his son, Gog his son, Shimei his son, 8098
9:14 S the son of Hasshub, the son of Azrikam, 8098
9:16 Obadiah the son of S, the son of Galal, 8098
15: 8 S the chief, and his brethren two hundred: 8098
15:11 and Joel, S, and Eliel, and Amminadab, 8098
24: 6 S the son of Nethaneel the scribe, one of 8098
26: 4 Moreover the sons of Obed-edom were, S 8098
26: 6 Also unto S his son were sons born, 8098
26: 7 The sons of S; Othni, and Rephael, and 8098
2Ch 11: 2 the word of the LORD came to S the man 8098
12: 5 Then came S the prophet to Rehoboam, and 8098
12: 7 the word of the LORD came to S, saying, 8098
12:15 are they not written in the book of S 8098
17: 8 even S, and Nethaniah, and Zebadiah, and 8098
29:14 and of the sons of Jeduthun; S, and Uzziel. 8098
31:15 Jeshua, and S, Amariah, and Shecaniah, 8098
35: 9 S and Nethaneel, his brethren, and 8098
Ezr 8:13 and S, and with them threescore males. 8098
8:16 for S, and for Elnathan, and for Jarib, and 8098
10:21 and Elijah, and S, and Jehiel, and Uzziah. 8098
10:31 Eliezer, Ishijah, Malchiah, S, Shimeon, 8098
Ne 3:29 After him repaired also S the son of 8098
6:10 Afterward I came unto the house of S 8098
10: 8 Maaziah, Bilgai, S: these were the priests. 8098
11:15 S the son of Hashub, the son of Azrikam, 8098
12: 6 S, and Joiarib, Jedaiah, 8098
12:18 Of Bilgah, Shammua; of S, Jehonathan; 8098
12:34 Judah, and Benjamin, and S, and Jeremiah, 8098
12:35 the son of S, the son of Mattaniah, the son 8098
12:36 S, and Azarael, Milalai, Gilalai, Maai, 8098
12:42 S, and Eleazar, and Uzzi, and Jehohanan, 8098
Jer 26:20 Urijah the son of S of Kirjath-jearim, 8098
29:24 Thus shalt thou also speak to S 8098
29:31 Thus saith the LORD concerning S 8098
29:31 Because that S hath prophesied unto you, 8098
29:32 I will punish S the Nehelamite, and his 8098
36:12 Delaiah the son of S, and Elnathan the son 8098

SHEMARIAH (3)
1Ch 12: 5 and S, and Shephatiah the Haruphite, 8114
Ezr 10:32 Benjamin, Malluch, and S. 8114
10:41 Azareel, and Shelemiah, S, 8114

SHEMEBER (1)
Ge 14: 2 S king of Zeboiim, and the king of Bela, 8038

SHEMER (2)
1Ki 16:24 he bought the hill Samaria of S for two 8106
16:24 after the name of S, owner of the hill, 8106

SHEMIDA (3) [SHEMIDAITES]
Nu 26:32 of S, the family of the Shemidaites: and 8061
Jos 17: 2 of Hepher, and for the children of S: 8061
1Ch 7:19 the sons of S were, Ahian, and Shechem, 8061

SHEMIDAITES (1) [SHEMIDA]
Nu 26:32 of Shemida, the family of the S: and 8062

SHEMINITH (3)
1Ch 15:21 and Azaziah, with harps on the S to excel. 8067
Ps 6: T To the chief Musician on Neginoth upon S, 8067
12: T To the chief Musician upon S, A Psalm of 8067

SHEMIRAMOTH (4)
1Ch 15:18 S, and Jehiel, and Unni, Eliab, and 8070
15:20 S, and Jehiel, and Unni, and Eliab, and 8070
16: 5 S, and Jehiel, and Mattithiah, and Eliab, 8070
2Ch 17: 8 S, and Jehonathan, and Adonijah, and 8070

SHEMUEL (3)
Nu 34:20 children of Simeon, S the son of Ammihud. 8050
1Ch 6:33 a singer, the son of Joel, the son of S, 8050
7: 2 and Jeriel, and Jahmai, and Jibsam, and S, 8050

SHEN (1)
1Sa 7:12 set it between Mizpeh and S, and called 8129

SHENAZAR (1)
1Ch 3:18 Pedaiah, and S, Jecamiah, Hoshama, and 8137

SHENAZZAR See SHENAZAR

SHENIR (2)
Dt 3: 9 call Sirion; and the Amorites call it S;) 8149
SS 4: 8 from the top of S and Hermon, from 8149

SHEPHAM (2)
Nu 34:10 out your east border from Hazar-enan to S: 8221
34:11 the coast shall go down from S to Riblah, 8221

SHEPHATHIAH (1)
1Ch 9: 8 Meshullam the son of S, the son of Reuel, 8203

SHEPHATIAH (12)
2Sa 3: 4 and the fifth, S the son of Abital; 8203
1Ch 3: 3 The fifth, S of Abital: the sixth, Ithream by 8203
12: 5 and Shemariah, and S the Haruphite, 8203
27:16 of the Simeonites, S the son of Maachah: 8203
2Ch 21: 2 and Azariah, and Michael, and S: 8203
Ezr 2: 4 The children of S, three hundred seventy 8203
2:57 The children of S, the children of Hattil, 8203
8: 8 of the sons of S; Zebadiah the son of 8203
Ne 7: 9 The children of S, three hundred seventy 8203
7:59 The children of S, the children of Hattil, 8203
11: 4 the son of Amariah, the son of S, 8203
Jer 38: 1 S the son of Mattan, and Gedaliah the son 8203

SHEPHER See SHAPHER

S

SHEPHERD (43) [HERD, SHEEP]

Ge 46:34 for every s *is* an abomination unto 6629+7462
49:24 (from thence *is* the s, the stone of Israel:) 7462
Nu 27:17 LORD be not as sheep which have no **s**. 7462
1Ki 22:17 upon the hills, as sheep that have no **s**: 7462
2Ch 18:16 the mountains, as sheep that have no **s**: 7462
Ps 23: 1 The LORD *is* my **s**; I shall not want. 7462
80: 1 Give ear, O **S** of Israel, thou that leadest 7462
Ecc 12:11 of assemblies, *which* are given from one **s**. 7462
Isa 40:11 He shall feed his flock like a **s**: he shall 7462
44:28 *He is* my **s**, and shall perform all my 7462
63:11 up out of the sea with the **s** of his flock? 7462
Jer 31:10 and keep him as a **s** *doth* his flock. 7462
43:12 of Egypt, as a **s** putteth on his garment; 7462
49:19 and who *is* that **s** that will stand before me? 7462
50:44 and who *is* that **s** that will stand before me? 7462
51:23 I will also break in pieces with thee the **s** 7462
Eze 34: 5 they were scattered, because *there is* no **s**: 7462
34: 8 because *there was* no **s**, neither did my 7462
34:12 As a **s** seeketh out his flock in the day that 7462
34:23 I will set up one **s** over them, and he shall 7462
34:23 he shall feed them, and he shall be their **s**. 7462
37:24 over them; and they all shall have one **s**: 7462
Am 3:12 As the **s** taketh out of the mouth of the lion 7462
Zec 10: 2 they were troubled, because *there was* no **s**. 7462
11:15 unto thee yet the instruments of a foolish **s**. 7462
11:16 For lo, I *will* raise up a **s** in the land, 7462
11:17 Woe to the idol **s** that leaveth the flock! 7473
13: 7 against my **s**, and against the man *that is* 7462
13: 7 smite the **s**, and the sheep shall be 7462
Mt 9:36 scattered abroad, as sheep having no **s**. *4166*
25:32 as a **s** divideth *his* sheep from the goats: *4166*
26:31 I will smite the **s**, and the sheep of the flock *4166*
Mk 6:34 because they were as sheep not having a **s**: *4166*
14:27 I will smite the **s**, and the sheep shall be *4166*
Jn 10: 2 But he that entereth in by the door is the **s** *4166*
10:11 I am the good **s**: the good shepherd giveth *4166*
10:11 the good **s** giveth his life for the sheep. *4166*
10:12 But *he that is* a hireling, and not the **s**, *4166*
10:14 I am the good **s**, and know my *sheep*, and *4166*
10:16 and there shall be one fold, *and* one **s**. *4166*
Heb 13:20 *that* great **s** of the sheep, through the blood *4166*
1Pe 2:25 but are now returned unto the **S** and *4166*
5: 4 And when the **chief S** shall appear, ye shall *750*

SHEPHERD'S (2) [HERD, SHEEP]

1Sa 17:40 put them in a **s** bag which he had, even in a 7462
Isa 38:12 and is removed from me as a **s** tent: 7473

SHEPHERDS (37) [HERD, SHEEP]

Ge 46:32 the men *are* **s**, for their trade hath 6629+7462
47: 3 Thy servants *are* **s**, both we, *and* 6629+7462
Ex 2:17 the **s** came and drove them away: but 7462
2:19 delivered us out of the hand of the **s**, 7462
1Sa 25: 7 now thy **s** which were with us, we hurt 7462
Isa 13:20 neither shall the **s** make their fold there. 7462
31: 4 when a multitude of **s** is called forth against 7462
56:11 and they *are* **s** *that* cannot understand: 7462
Jer 6: 3 The **s** with their flocks shall come unto her; 7462
23: 4 I will set up **s** over them which shall feed 7462
25:34 Howl, ye **s**, and cry; and wallow yourselves 7462
25:35 the **s** shall have no way to flee, nor 7462
25:36 A voice of the cry of the **s**, and a howling 7462
33:12 shall be a habitation of **s** causing *their* 7462
50: 6 their **s** have caused them to go astray, 7462
Eze 34: 2 prophesy against the **s** of Israel, prophesy, 7462
34: 2 Thus saith the Lord GOD unto the **s**; 7462
34: 2 Woe *be* to the **s** of Israel that do feed 7462
34: 2 should not the **s** feed the flocks? 7462
34: 7 Therefore, ye **s**, hear the word of 7462
34: 8 neither did my **s** search for my flock, but 7462
34: 8 the **s** fed themselves, and fed not my flock; 7462
34: 9 Therefore, O ye **s**, hear the word of 7462
34:10 Behold, I *am* against the **s**; and I will 7462
34:10 neither shall the **s** feed themselves any 7462
Am 1: 2 the habitations of the **s** shall mourn, and 7462
Mic 5: 5 shall we raise against him seven **s**, and 7462
Na 3:18 Thy **s** slumber, O king of Assyria: 7462
Zep 2: 6 coast shall be dwellings *and* cottages for **s**, 7462
Zec 10: 3 Mine anger was kindled against the **s**, and I 7462
11: 3 *There is* a voice of the howling of the **s**; 7462
11: 5 for I am rich: and their own **s** pity them not. 7462
11: 8 Three **s** also I cut off in one month; and 7462
Lk 2: 8 And there were in the same country **s** *4166*
2:15 the **s** said one to another, Let us now go *4166*
2:18 those *things* which were told them by the **s**. *4166*
2:20 And the **s** returned, glorifying and *4166*

SHEPHERDS' (1) [HERD, SHEEP]

SS 1: 8 and feed thy kids beside the **s** tents. 7462

SHEPHI (1) [SHEPHO]

1Ch 1:40 and Manahath, and Ebal, **S**, and Onam. 8195

SHEPHO (1) [SHEPHI]

Ge 36:23 and Manahath, and Ebal, **S**, and Onam. 8195

SHEPHUPHAN (1)

1Ch 8: 5 And Gera, and **S**, and Huram. 8197

SHERAH (1)

1Ch 7:24 (And his daughter *was* **S**, who built 7609

SHEREBIAH (8)

Ezr 8:18 **S**, with his sons and his brethren, eighteen; 8274
8:24 **S**, Hashabiah, and ten of their brethren with 8274
Ne 8: 7 Bani, and **S**, Jamin, Akkub, Shabbethai, 8274
9: 4 **S**, Bani, *and* Chenani, and cried with a loud 8274
9: 5 **S**, Hodijah, Shebaniah, *and* Pethahiah, said, 8274
10:12 Zaccur, **S**, Shebaniah, 8274
12: 8 Binnui, Kadmiel, **S**, Judah, *and* Mattaniah, 8274
12:24 **S**, and Jeshua the son of Kadmiel, 8274

SHERESH (1)

1Ch 7:16 the name of his brother *was* **S**; and his sons 8329

SHEREZER (1)

Zec 7: 2 they had sent *unto* the house of God **S** 8272

SHERIFFS (2)

Da 3: 2 the **s**, and all the rulers of the provinces, 8614
3: 3 the **s**, and all the rulers of the provinces, 8614

SHESHACH (2)

Jer 25:26 and the king of **S** shall drink after them. 8347
51:41 How is **S** taken! and *how* is the praise of 8347

SHESHAI (3)

Nu 13:22 where Ahiman, **S**, and Talmai, the children 8344
Jos 15:14 **S**, and Ahiman, and Talmai, the children of 8344
Jdg 1:10 and they slew **S**, and Ahiman, and Talmai. 8344

SHESHAN (5)

1Ch 2:31 the sons of Ishi; **S**. And the children of 8348
2:31 Sheshan. And the children of **S**; Ahlai. 8348
2:34 Now **S** had no sons, but daughters. 8348
2:34 **S** had a servant, an Egyptian, whose name 8348
2:35 **S** gave his daughter to Jarha his servant to 8348

SHESHBAZZAR (4)

Ezr 1: 8 numbered them unto **S**, the prince of Judah. 8339
1:11 All *these* did **S** bring up with *them of* 8339
5:14 delivered unto *one*, whose name *was* **S**, 8340
5:16 came the same **S**, *and* laid the foundation of 8340

SHETH (2) [SETH]

Nu 24:17 of Moab, and destroy all the children of **S**. 8352
1Ch 1: 1 Adam, **S**, Enosh, 8352

SHETHAR (1)

Est 1:14 **S**, Admatha, Tarshish, Meres, Marsena, *and* 8369

SHETHAR-BOZENAI See SHETHAR-BOZNAI

SHETHAR-BOZNAI (4)

Ezr 5: 3 **S**, and their companions, and said thus unto 8370
5: 6 **S**, and his companions the Apharsachites, 8370
6: 6 **S**, and your companions the Apharsachites, 8370
6:13 *this* side the river, **S**, and their companions, 8370

SHEVA (2)

2Sa 20:25 **S** *was* scribe: and Zadok and Abiathar *were* 7724
1Ch 2:49 **S** the father of Machbenah, and the father 7724

SHEW (228) [SHEWBREAD, SHEWED, SHEWEDST, SHEWEST, SHEWETH, SHEWING]

Ge 12: 1 father's house, unto a land that I will **s** thee: 7200
20:13 This *is* thy kindness which thou shalt **s** unto 6213
24:12 and **s** kindness unto my master Abraham. 6213
40:14 **s** kindness, I pray thee, unto me, and 6213
46:31 go up, and **s** Pharaoh, and say unto him, 5046
Ex 7: 9 unto you, saying, **S** a miracle for you: 5414
9:16 I raised thee up, for to **s** *in* thee my power; 7200
10: 1 that I might **s** these my signs before him: 7896
13: 8 And thou shalt **s** thy son in that day, saying, 5046
14:13 the LORD, which he will **s** to you to day: 6213
18:20 shalt **s** them the way *wherein* they must 3045
25: 9 According to all that I **s** thee, *after* 7200
33:13 **s** me now thy way, that I may know thee, 3045
33:18 And he said, I beseech thee, **s** me thy glory. 7200
33:19 will **s mercy** on whom I will shew mercy. 7355
33:19 will shew mercy on whom I will **s mercy**. 7355
Nu 16: 5 Even to morrow the LORD will **s** who *are* 3045
Dt 1:33 to **s** you by what way ye should go, and in a 7200
3:24 thou hast begun to **s** thy servant thy 7200
5: 5 that time, to **s** you the word of the LORD: 5046
7: 2 with them, nor **s mercy** unto them: 2603
13:17 **s** thee mercy, and have compassion upon 5414
17: 9 they shall **s** thee the sentence of judgment: 5046
17:10 which the LORD shall choose shall **s** thee; 5046
17:11 from the sentence which they shall **s** thee, 5046
28:50 of the old, nor **s favour** to the young: 2603
32: 7 ask thy father, and he will **s** thee; 5046
Jos 2:12 that ye will also **s** kindness unto my 6213
5: 6 sware that *he* would not **s** them the land, 7200
Jdg 1:24 they said unto him, **S** us, we pray thee, 7200
1:24 the city, and we will **s** thee mercy. 5973+6213
4:22 I will **s** thee the man whom thou seekest. 7200
6:17 then **s** me a sign that thou talkest with me. 6213
1Sa 3:15 And Samuel feared to **s** Eli the vision. 5046
8: 9 **s** them the manner of the king that shall 5046
9: 6 peradventure he can **s** us our way that we 5046
9:27 a while, that I may **s** thee the word of God. 8085
10: 8 come to thee, and **s** thee what thou shalt do. 3045
14:12 Come up to us, and we will **s** you a thing. 3045
16: 3 and I will **s** thee what thou shalt do: 3045
20: 2 or small, but that he will **s** it me: 241+1540
20:12 I then send not unto thee, and **s** it thee; 241+1540
20:13 I will **s** it thee, and send thee away, 241+1540
20:14 thou shalt not only while yet I live **s** me 6213
22:17 when he fled, and did not **s** it to me. 241+1540
25: 8 Ask thy young men, and they will **s** thee. 5046
2Sa 2: 6 now the LORD **s** kindness and truth unto 6213
3: 8 which against Judah do **s** kindness *this* day 6213
9: 1 that I may **s** him kindness for Jonathan's 6213
9: 3 that I may **s** the kindness of God unto him? 6213
9: 7 for I will **surely s** thee kindness for 6213+6213
10: 2 I will **s** kindness unto Hanun the son of 6213
15:25 and **s** me *both* it, and his habitation: 7200
22:26 the merciful thou wilt **s** thyself **merciful**, 2616
22:26 the upright man thou wilt **s** thyself **upright**. 8552
22:27 With the pure thou wilt **s** thyself **pure**; and 1305
22:27 the froward thou wilt **s** thyself **unsavoury**. 6617
1Ki 1:52 If he will **s** himself a worthy man, 1961+3807.1
2: 2 and **s** thyself a man; 1961+3807.1
2: 7 **s** kindness unto the sons of Barzillai 6213
18: 1 third year, saying, Go, **s** thyself unto Ahab; 7200
18: 2 Elijah went to **s** himself unto Ahab. 7200
18:15 I will surely **s** myself unto him to day. 7200
2Ki 6:11 Will ye not **s** me which of us *is* for the king 5046
7:12 I will now **s** you what the Syrians have 5046
1Ch 16:23 **s forth** from day to day his salvation. 1319
19: 2 I will **s** kindness unto Hanun the son of 6213
2Ch 16: 9 to **s** himself **strong** in the behalf of *them* 2388
Ezr 2:59 they could not **s** their fathers' house, and 5046
Ne 7:61 they could not **s** their fathers' house, 5046
9:19 to **s** them **light**, and the way wherein they 215
Est 1:11 to **s** the people and the princes her beauty: 7200
2:10 had charged her that she should not **s** *it*. 5046
4: 8 to **s** *it* unto Esther, and to declare *it* unto 7200
Job 10: 2 **s** me wherefore thou contendest with me. 3045
11: 6 that he would **s** thee the secrets of wisdom, 5046
15:17 I will **s** thee, hear me; and that which I have 2331
32: 6 and durst not **s** you mine opinion. 2331
32:10 Hearken to me; I also will **s** mine opinion. 2331
32:17 also my part, I also will **s** mine opinion. 2331
33:23 a thousand, to **s** unto man his uprightness: 5046
36: 2 I will **s** thee that *I have* yet to speak on 2331
Ps 4: 6 *be* many that say, Who will **s** us *any* good? 7200
9: 1 I will **s forth** all thy marvellous works. 5608
9:14 That I may **s forth** all thy praise in 5608
16:11 Thou wilt **s** me the path of life: in thy 3045
17: 7 **S** thy **marvellous** lovingkindness, O thou 6395
18:25 the merciful thou wilt **s** thyself **merciful**; 2616
18:25 an upright man thou wilt **s** thyself **upright**; 8552
18:26 With the pure thou wilt **s** thyself **pure**; and 1305
18:26 the froward thou wilt **s** thyself **froward**. 6617
25: 4 **S** me thy ways, O LORD; teach me thy 3045
25:14 fear him; and he will **s** them his covenant. 3045
39: 6 Surely every man walketh **in a vain s**: 6754
50:23 *aright* will I **s** the salvation of God. 7200
51:15 and my mouth shall **s forth** thy praise. 5046
71:15 My mouth shall **s forth** thy righteousness 5608
79:13 we will **s forth** thy praise to all generations. 5608
85: 7 **S** us thy mercy, O LORD, and grant us thy 7200
86:17 **S** me a token for good; that they which hate 6213
88:10 Wilt thou **s** wonders to the dead? shall 6213
91:16 will I satisfy him, and **s** him my salvation. 7200
92: 2 To **s forth** thy lovingkindness in 5046
92:15 To **s** that the LORD *is* upright: *he is* my 5046
94: 1 to whom vengeance belongeth, **s** thyself. 3313
96: 2 **s forth** his salvation from day to day. 1319
106: 2 the LORD? *who* can **s forth** all his praise? 8085
109:16 Because that he remembered not to **s** 6213
Pr 18:24 that hath friends must **s** himself **friendly**: 7462
Isa 3: 9 The **s** of their countenance doth witness 1971
27:11 he that formed them will **s** them no **favour**. 2603
30:30 shall **s** the lighting down of his arm, 7200
41:22 *them* forth, and **s** us what shall happen: 5046
41:22 let them **s** the former *things*, what they *be*, 5046
41:23 **S** the *things* that are to come hereafter, 5046
43: 9 **s** us former *things?* let them bring forth 8085
43:21 for myself; they shall **s forth** my praise. 5608
44: 7 and shall come, let them **s** unto them. 5046
46: 8 Remember this, and **s yourselves men**: 377
47: 6 thou didst **s** them no mercy; upon 7760
49: 9 to *them* that *are* in darkness, **S** yourselves. 1540
58: 1 **s** my people their transgression, and 5046
60: 6 they shall **s forth** the praises of 1319
Jer 16:10 when thou shalt **s** this people all these 5046
16:13 and night; where I will not **s** you favour. 5414
18:17 I will **s** them the back, and not the face, 7200
33: 3 **s** thee great and mighty *things*, which thou 5046
42: 3 That the LORD thy God may **s** us the way 5046
42:12 I will **s** mercies unto you, that he may have 5414
50:42 they *are* cruel, and will not **s mercy**: 7355
51:31 to **s** the king of Babylon that his city is 5046
Eze 22: 2 yea, thou shalt **s** her all her abominations. 3045
33:31 for with their mouth they **s** much love, *but* 6213
37:18 Wilt thou not **s** us what thou meanest by 5046
40: 4 set thine heart upon all that I shall **s** thee; 7200
40: 4 for to the intent that *I* might **s** *them* unto 7200
43:10 of man, **s** the house to the house of Israel, 5046
43:11 **s** them the form of the house, and 3045
Da 2: 2 the Chaldeans, for to **s** the king his dreams. 5046
2: 4 the dream, and we will **s** the interpretation. 2324
2: 6 if ye **s** the dream, and the interpretation 2324
2: 6 therefore **s** me the dream, and 2324
2: 7 and we will **s** the interpretation of it. 2324
2: 9 I shall know that ye can **s** me 2324
2:10 There is not a man upon the earth that can **s** 2324
2:11 there is none other that can **s** it before 2324
2:16 that *he* would **s** the king the interpretation. 2324
2:24 and I will **s** unto the king the interpretation. 2324
2:27 the soothsayers, **s** unto the king; 2324
4: 2 I thought it good to **s** the signs and 2324
5: 7 **s** me the interpretation thereof, shall be 2324
5:12 be called, and he will **s** the interpretation. 2324
5:15 they could not **s** the interpretation of 2324
9:23 I am come to **s** *thee; for* thou *art* greatly 5046
10:21 I will **s** thee that which is noted in 5046
11: 2 now will I **s** thee the truth. Behold, 5046
Joel 2:30 I will **s** wonders in the heavens and in 5414
Mic 7:15 Egypt will I **s** unto him marvellous *things*. 7200
Na 3: 5 I will **s** the nations thy nakedness, and 7200
Hab 1: 3 Why dost thou **s** me iniquity, and cause *me* 7200
Zec 1: 9 said unto me, I will **s** thee what these *be*. 7200
7: 9 **s** mercy and compassions every man to his 6213
Mt 8: 4 **s** thyself to the priest, and offer the gift that *1166*
11: 4 **s** John **again** *those things* which ye do hear *518*
12:18 and he shall **s** judgment to the Gentiles. *518*
14: 2 works do **s forth** themselves **in** him. *1754*
16: 1 tempting desired him that *he* would **s** them *1925*
16:21 From that time forth began Jesus to **s** unto *1166*
22:19 **S** me the tribute money. And they brought *1925*
24: 1 his disciples came to *him* for to **s** him *1925*
24:24 and shall **s** great signs and wonders; *1325*
Mk 1:44 **s** thyself to the priest, and offer for thy *1166*
6:14 mighty works do **s forth** themselves in *1754*
13:22 and shall **s** signs and wonders, to seduce, *1325*
14:15 And he will **s** you a large upper room *1166*

S

Lk 1:19 unto thee, and to s thee these **glad tidings**. 2097
5:14 no *man:* but go, and s thyself to the priest, 1166
6:47 doeth them, I will s you to whom he is like: 5263
8:39 s how great *things* God hath done unto 1334
17:14 unto them, Go s yourselves unto the priests. 1925
20:24 S me a penny. Whose image and 1925
20:47 and for a s make long prayers: 4392
22:12 And he shall s you a large upper room 1166
Jn 5:20 and he will s him greater works than these, 1166
7:4 If thou do these *things,* s thyself to 5319
11:57 he should s *it,* that they might take him. 3377
14:8 Lord, s us the Father, and it sufficeth us. 1166
14:9 and how sayest thou *then,* S us the Father? 1166
16:13 he speak: and he will s you *things* to come. 312
16:14 shall receive of mine, and shall s *it* unto you. 312
16:15 he shall take of mine, and shall s *it* unto you. 312
16:25 but I shall s you plainly of the Father. 312
Ac 1:24 which knowest the hearts of all *men,* s 322
2:19 And I will s wonders in heaven above, and 1325
7:3 and come into the land which I shall s thee. 1166
9:16 For I will s him how great *things* he must 5263
12:17 *Go* s these *things* unto James, and to 518
16:17 which s unto us the way of salvation. 2605
24:27 and Felix, willing to s the Jews a pleasure, 2698
26:23 and should s light unto the people, and 2605
Ro 2:15 Which s the work of the law written in their 1731
9:17 that I might s my power in thee, and 1731
9:22 willing to s *his* wrath, and to make his 1731
1Co 11:26 ye do s the Lord's death till he come. 2605
12:31 and yet s I unto you a more excellent way. 1166
15:51 Behold, I s you a mystery; We shall not all 3004
2Co 8:24 Wherefore s ye to them, and before 1731
Gal 6:12 As many as desire to **make a fair s** in 2146
Eph 2:7 That in the ages to come he might s 1731
Col 2:15 and powers, he **made a s** of *them* openly, 1165
2:23 Which *things* have indeed a s of wisdom in 3056
1Th 1:9 For they themselves s of us what manner of 518
1Ti 1:16 that in me first Jesus Christ might s **forth** 1731
5:4 let them learn first to s **piety** at home, and 2151
6:15 Which in his times he shall s, *who is* 1166
2Ti 2:15 Study to s thyself approved unto God, 3936
Heb 6:11 And we desire that every one of you do s 1731
6:17 willing more abundantly to s unto the heirs 1925
Jas 2:18 s me thy faith without thy works, and I will 1166
2:18 and I will s thee my faith by my works. 1166
3:13 let him s out of a good conversation his 1166
1Pe 2:9 that ye should s **forth** the praises of him 1804
1Jn 1:2 bear witness, and s unto you *that* eternal life, 518
Rev 1:1 to s unto his servants *things* which must 1166
4:1 I will s thee *things* which must be hereafter. 1166
17:1 I will s unto thee the judgment of the great 1166
21:9 saying, *Come* hither, I will s thee the bride, 1166
22:6 s unto his servants *the things* which must 1166

SHEWBREAD (18) [BREAD, SHEW]

Ex 25:30 thou shalt set upon the table s before 3899+6440
35:13 and all his vessels, and the s, 3899+6440
39:36 all the vessels thereof, and the s, 3899+6440
Nu 4:7 upon the table of s they shall spread a cloth 6440
1Sa 21:6 was no bread there but the s, 3899+6440+1886.1
1Ki 7:48 whereupon the s *was,* 3899+6440+1886.1
1Ch 9:32 s, to prepare *it* every 3899+4635+1886.1
23:29 Both for the s, and for 3899+4635+1886.1
28:16 *by* weight *he gave* gold for the tables of s, 4635
2Ch 2:4 *for* the continual s, and *for* the burnt 4635
4:19 whereon the s *was set;* 3899+6440+1886.1
13:11 the sbread also *set they* in order upon 3899
29:18 and the s table, with all the vessels thereof. 4635
Ne 10:33 For the s, and *for* the continual meat 3899+4635
Mt 12:4 and did eat the s, which was not 740+3588+4286
Mk 2:26 and did eat the s, which is not 740+3588+4286
Lk 6:4 and did take and eat the s, 740+3588+4286
Heb 9:2 and the table, and the s; 740+4286

SHEWED (135) [SHEW]

Ge 19:19 which thou hast s unto me in saving my 6213
24:14 thereby shall I know that thou hast s 6213
32:10 which thou hast s unto thy servant; 6213
39:21 s him mercy, and gave him favour in 5186
41:25 God hath s Pharaoh what he *is* about to do. 5046
41:39 Forasmuch as God hath s thee all this, 3045
48:11 and lo, God hath s me also thy seed. 7200
Ex 15:25 the LORD s him a tree, *which* when he 3384
25:40 which was s thee in the mount. 7200
26:30 thereof which was s thee in the mount. 7200
27:8 as it was s thee in the mount, so shall they 7200
Lev 13:19 somewhat reddish, and it be s to the priest; 7200
13:49 of leprosy, and shall be s unto the priest: 7200
24:12 that the mind of the LORD might be s 6567
Nu 8:4 the pattern which the LORD had s Moses, 7200
13:26 and s them the fruit of the land. 7200
14:11 for all the signs which I have s among 6213
Dt 4:35 Unto thee it was s, that thou mightest know 7200
4:36 upon earth he s thee his great fire; and 7200
5:24 the LORD our God hath s us his glory and 7200
6:22 the LORD s signs and wonders, great and 5414
34:1 the LORD s him all the land of Gilead, 7200
34:12 in all the great terror which Moses s in 6213
Jos 2:12 the LORD, since I have s you kindness, 6213
Jdg 1:25 when he s them the entrance into the city, 7200
4:12 they s Sisera that Barak the son of 5046
8:35 Neither s they kindness to the house of 6213
8:35 all the goodness which he had s unto Israel. 6213
13:10 ran, and s her husband, and said unto him, 5046
13:23 neither would he have s us all these *things,* 7200
16:18 up *this* once, for he hath s me all his heart. 5046
Ru 2:11 unto her, It hath **fully been** s me, 5046+5046
2:19 she s her mother in law with whom she had 5046
3:10 *for* thou hast s **more** kindness in the latter 3190
1Sa 11:9 and s *it* to the men of Jabesh; 5046
15:6 for ye s kindness to all the children of 6213
19:7 and Jonathan s him all those things. 5046
22:21 Abiathar s David that Saul had slain 5046
24:18 thou hast s *this* day how that thou hast dealt 5046
2Sa 2:5 that ye have s this kindness unto your lord, 6213
2Sa 10:2 of Nahash, as his father s kindness unto me. 6213
11:22 and s David all that Joab had sent him for. 5046
1Ki 1:27 and thou hast not s *it* unto thy servant, 3045
3:6 Thou hast s unto thy servant David my 6213
16:27 Omri which he did, and his might that he s, 6213
22:45 and his might that he s, and how he warred, 6213
2Ki 6:6 he s him the place. And he cut down a 7200
8:10 howbeit the LORD hath s me that he shall 7200
8:13 The LORD hath s me *that* thou *shalt be* 7200
11:4 of the LORD, and s them the king's son. 7200
20:13 s them all the house of his precious things, 7200
20:13 all his dominion, that Hezekiah s them not. 7200
20:15 among my treasures that I have not s them. 7200
22:10 Shaphan the scribe s the king, saying, 5046
1Ch 19:2 because his father s kindness to me. 6213
2Ch 1:8 Thou hast s great mercy unto David my 6213
7:10 that the LORD had s unto David, 6213
Ezr 9:8 now for a little space grace hath been *s* from NIH
Est 1:4 When he s the riches of his glorious 7200
2:10 Esther had not s her people nor her kindred: 5046
2:20 Esther had not *yet* s her kindred nor her 5046
3:6 for they had s him the people of Mordecai: 5046
Job 6:14 To him that is afflicted pity *should be* s NIH
Ps 31:21 for he hath s me his **marvellous** kindness 6381
60:3 Thou hast s thy people hard *things:* thou 7200
71:18 until I have s thy strength unto *this* 5046
71:20 *Thou,* which hast s me great and 7200
78:11 and his wonders that he had s them. 7200
98:2 his righteousness hath he **openly** s in 1540
105:27 They s his signs among them, and 7760
111:6 He hath s his people the power of his 5046
118:27 God *is* the LORD, which hath s us **light**: 215
142:2 before him; I s before him my trouble. 5046
Pr 26:26 his wickedness shall be s before the *whole* 1540
Ecc 2:19 where*in* I have s myself **wise** under the sun. 2449
Isa 26:10 Let **favour** be s to the wicked, *yet* will he 2603
39:2 s them the house of his precious things, 7200
39:2 all his dominion, that Hezekiah s them not. 7200
39:4 among my treasures that I have not s them. 7200
40:14 and s to him the way of understanding? 3045
43:12 and have saved, and I have s, 8085
48:3 went forth out of my mouth, and I s them; 8085
48:5 *it* to thee; before it came to pass I s *it* thee: 8085
48:6 will not ye declare *it?* I have s thee new 8085
Jer 24:1 The LORD s me, and, behold, two baskets 7200
38:21 this *is* the word that the LORD hath s me: 7200
Eze 11:25 all the things that the LORD had s me. 7200
20:11 s them my judgments, which *if* a man do, 3045
22:26 neither have they s *difference* between 3045
Am 7:1 Thus hath the Lord GOD s unto me; and 7200
7:4 Thus hath the Lord GOD s unto me: and 7200
7:7 Thus he s me: and behold, the Lord stood 7200
8:1 Thus hath the Lord GOD s unto me: and 7200
Mic 6:8 He hath s thee, O man, what *is* good; and 5046
Zec 1:20 And the LORD s me four carpenters. 7200
3:1 he s me Joshua the high priest standing 7200
Mt 28:11 s unto the chief priests all the *things* that 518
Lk 1:51 He hath s strength with his arm; he hath 4160
1:58 her cousins heard how the Lord had s **great** 3170
4:5 s unto him all the kingdoms of the world in 1166
7:18 And the disciples of John s him of all these 518
10:37 And he said, He that s mercy on him. Then 4160
14:21 s his lord these *things.* Then the master of 518
20:37 dead are raised, even Moses s at the bush, 3377
24:40 he s them *his* hands and *his* feet. 1925
Jn 10:32 Many good works have I s you from my 1166
20:20 said, he s unto them *his* hands and his side. 1166
21:1 After these *things* Jesus s himself again to 5319
21:1 of Tiberias; and on this wise s he *himself.* 5319
21:14 This *is* now the third time *that* Jesus s 5319
Ac 1:3 To whom also he s himself alive after his 3936
3:18 But *those things,* which God **before** had s 4293
4:22 on whom this miracle of healing was s. 1096
7:26 And the next day he s himself unto them as 3700
7:36 after that he had s wonders and signs in 4160
7:52 they have slain them which s **before** of 4293
10:28 God hath s me that *I* should not call any 1166
10:40 raised up the third day, and s him openly; 1325
11:13 And he s us how he had seen an angel in his 518
19:18 and confessed, and s their deeds. 312
20:20 that was profitable *unto you,* but have s you, 312
20:35 I have s you all *things,* how that so 5263
23:22 no *man* that thou hast s these *things* to me. 1718
26:20 But s first unto them of Damascus, 518
28:2 And the barbarous people s us no little 3930
28:21 neither any of the brethren that came s or 518
Ro 1:19 in them; for God hath s *it* unto them. 5319
1Co 10:28 eat not for his sake that s *it,* and 3377
Heb 6:10 of love, which ye have s toward his name, 1731
8:5 to the pattern s to thee in the mount. 1166
Jas 2:13 without mercy, that hath s no mercy; 4160
2Pe 1:14 even as our Lord Jesus Christ hath s me. 1213
Rev 21:10 and high mountain, and s me *that* great city, 1166
22:1 And he s me a pure river of water of life, 1166
22:8 feet of the angel which s me these *things.* 1166

SHEWEDST (2) [SHEW]

Ne 9:10 s signs and wonders upon Pharaoh, and 5414
Jer 11:18 and I know *it:* then thou s me their doings. 7200

SHEWEST (5) [SHEW]

2Ch 6:14 and *s* mercy unto thy servants, NIH
Job 10:16 again thou s thyself **marvellous** upon me. 6381
Jer 32:18 Thou s lovingkindness unto thousands, and 6213
Jn 2:18 said unto him, What sign s thou unto us, 1166
6:30 therefore unto him, What sign s thou then, 4160

SHEWETH (20) [SHEW]

Ge 41:28 What God *is* about to do he s unto Pharaoh. 7200
Nu 23:3 whatsoever he s me I will tell thee. And he 7200
1Sa 22:8 *there is* none that s me that my son 241+1540
22:8 s **unto** me that my son hath stirred up 241+1540
2Sa 22:51 s mercy to his anointed, unto David, and 6213
Job 36:9 he s them their work, and 5046
Job 36:33 The noise thereof s concerning it, the cattle 5046
Ps 18:50 s mercy to his anointed, to David, and 6213
19:1 and the firmament s his handywork. 5046
19:2 and night unto night s knowledge. 2331
37:21 but the righteous s **mercy**, and giveth. 2603
112:5 A good man s **favour**, and lendeth: he will 2603
147:19 He s his word unto Jacob, his statutes and 5046
Pr 12:17 *He that* speaketh truth s **forth** 5046
27:25 the tender grass s itself, and herbs of 7200
Isa 41:26 yea, *there is* none that s, yea, *there is* none 5046
Mt 4:8 and s him all the kingdoms of the world, 1166
Jn 5:20 and s him all *things* that himself doeth: 1166
Ro 9:16 him that runneth, but of God that s **mercy**. 1653
12:8 he that s **mercy**, with cheerfulness. 1653

SHEWING (15) [SHEW]

Ex 20:6 s mercy unto thousands of them that love 6213
Dt 5:10 s mercy unto thousands of them that love 6213
Ps 78:4 s to the generation to come the praises of 5608
SS 2:9 the windows, s himself through the lattice. 6692
Da 4:27 and thine iniquities by s **mercy** to the poor; 2604
5:12 s of hard sentences, and dissolving of 263
Lk 1:80 was in the deserts till the day of his s unto 323
8:1 s **the glad tidings** of the kingdom of God: 2097
Ac 9:39 and s the coats and garments which Dorcas 1925
18:28 s by the scriptures that Jesus was Christ. 1925
2Th 2:4 the temple of God, s himself that he is God. 584
Tit 2:7 In all *things* s thyself a pattern of good 3930
2:7 in doctrine *s* uncorruptness, gravity, NIG
2:10 Not purloining, but s all good fidelity; 1731
3:2 *but* gentle, s all meekness unto all men. 1731

SHIBAH See SHEBAH

SHIBBOLETH (1) [SIBBOLETH]

Jdg 12:6 said they unto him, Say now S: and he said 7641

SHIBMAH (1)

Nu 32:38 (*their* names being changed,) and S: 7643

SHICRON (1)

Jos 15:11 the border was drawn to S, and 7942

SHIELD (45) [SHIELDS]

Ge 15:1 I *am* thy s, *and* thy exceeding great reward. 4043
Dt 33:29 the s of thy help, and who *is* the sword of 4043
Jdg 5:8 was there a s or spear seen among forty 4043
1Sa 17:7 and one bearing a s went before him. 6793
17:41 the man that bare the s *went* before him. 6793
17:45 a sword, and with a spear, and with a s: 3591
2Sa 1:21 for there the s of the mighty is vilely cast 4043
1:21 the s of Saul, *as though he had* not *been* 4043
22:3 *he is* my s, and the horn of my salvation, 4043
22:36 Thou hast also given me the s of thy 4043
1Ki 10:17 three pound *of* gold went to one s: 4043
2Ki 19:32 an arrow there, nor come before it *with* s, 4043
1Ch 12:8 the battle, that could handle s and buckler, 6793
12:24 The children of Judah that bare s and 6793
12:34 with them with s and spear thirty and 6793
2Ch 9:16 hundred *shekels* of gold went to one s. 4043
17:17 *men* with bow and s two hundred thousand. 4043
25:5 forth *to* war, that could handle spear and s. 6793
Job 39:23 against him, the glittering spear and the s. 3591
Ps 3:3 thou, O LORD, *art* a s for me; my glory, 4043
5:12 favour wilt thou compass him as *with* a s. 6793
18:35 Thou hast also given me the s of thy 4043
28:7 The LORD *is* my strength and my s; 4043
33:20 for the LORD: he *is* our help and our s. 4043
35:2 Take hold of s and buckler, and stand up 4043
59:11 and bring them down, O Lord our s. 4043
76:3 the s, and the sword, and the battle. 4043
84:9 O God our s, and look upon the face of 4043
84:11 For the LORD God *is* a sun and s: 4043
91:4 his truth *shall be* thy s and buckler. 6793
115:9 in the LORD: he *is* their help and their s. 4043
115:10 in the LORD: he *is* their help and their s. 4043
115:11 in the LORD: he *is* their help and their s. 4043
119:114 Thou *art* my hiding place and my s: I hope 4043
144:2 my deliverer; my s, and *he* in whom I trust; 4043
Pr 30:5 he *is* a s unto them that put their trust in 4043
Isa 21:5 drink: arise, ye princes, *and* anoint the s. 4043
22:6 *and* horsemen, and Kir uncovered the s. 4043
Jer 46:3 Order ye the buckler and s, and draw near 6793
46:9 and the Libyans, that handle the s; 4043
Eze 23:24 thee buckler and s and helmet round about: 4043
27:10 they hanged the s and helmet in thee; 4043
38:5 with them; all of them *with* s and helmet: 4043
Na 2:3 The s of his mighty *men is* made red, 4043
Eph 6:16 Above all, taking the s of faith, 2375

SHIELDS (23) [SHIELD]

2Sa 8:7 David took the s of gold that were on 7982
1Ki 10:17 *he made* three hundred s *of* beaten gold; 4043
14:26 he took away all the s of gold which 4043
14:27 Rehoboam made in their stead brasen s, 4043
2Ki 11:10 the priest give king David's spears and s, 7982
1Ch 18:7 David took the s of gold that were on 7982
2Ch 9:16 three hundred s *made he of* beaten gold: 4043
11:12 in every several city *he put* s and spears, 6793
12:9 he carried away also the s of gold which 4043
12:10 Instead of which king Rehoboam made s of 4043
14:8 that bare s and drew bows, two hundred 4043
23:9 bucklers, and s, that *had been* king David's, 7982
26:14 prepared for them throughout all the host s, 4043
32:5 and made darts and s in abundance. 4043
32:27 for s, and for all *manner of* pleasant jewels; 4043
Ne 4:16 the s, and the bows, and the habergeons; 4043
Ps 47:9 for the s of the earth *belong* unto God: he is 4043
SS 4:4 a thousand bucklers, all s of mighty *men.* 7982
Isa 37:33 an arrow there, nor come before it *with* s, 4043
Jer 51:11 gather the s: the LORD hath raised up 7982
Eze 27:11 they hanged their s upon thy walls round 7982
38:4 *even* a great company *with* bucklers and s, 4043
39:9 both the s and the bucklers, the bows and 4043

SHIGGAION (1)
Ps 7: T S of David, which he sang unto 7692

SHIGIONOTH (1)
Hab 3: 1 A prayer of Habakkuk the prophet upon S. 7692

SHIHOR (1)
1Ch 13: 5 from S of Egypt even unto the entering of 7883

SHIHOR-LIBNATH (1)
Jos 19:26 and reacheth to Carmel westward, and to S; 7884

SHIKKERON See SHICRON

SHILHI (2)
1Ki 22:42 name *was* Azubah the daughter of S. 7977
2Ch 20:31 name *was* Azubah the daughter of S. 7977

SHILHIM (1)
Jos 15:32 and S, and Ain, and Rimmon: 7978

SHILLEM (2) [SHILLEMITES]
Ge 46:24 Jahzeel, and Guni, and Jezer, and S. 8006
Nu 26:49 of S, the family of the Shillemites. 8006

SHILLEMITES (1) [SHILLEM]
Nu 26:49 of Shillem, the family of the S. 8016

SHILOAH (1)
Isa 8: 6 refuseth the waters of S that go softly, 7975

SHILOH (33) [SHILONITE, SHILONITES, TAANATH-SHILOH]
Ge 49:10 from between his feet, until S come; 7886
Jos 18: 1 children of Israel assembled together *at* S, 7887
18: 8 cast lots for you before the LORD in S. 7887
18: 9 and came *again* to Joshua to the host *at* S. 7887
18:10 Joshua cast lots for them in S before 7887
19:51 divided for an inheritance by lot in S before 7887
21: 2 they spake unto them at S in the land of 7887
22: 9 from the children of Israel out of S, 7887
22:12 of Israel gathered themselves together *at* S, 7887
Jdg 18:31 all the time that the house of God was in S. 7887
21:12 they brought them unto the camp *to* S, 7887
21:19 *there is* a feast of the LORD in S yearly *in* 7887
21:21 if the daughters of S come out to dance in 7887
21:21 every man his wife of the daughters of S, 7887
1Sa 1: 3 to sacrifice unto the LORD of hosts in S. 7887
1: 9 Hannah rose up after *they* had eaten in S, 7887
1:24 him *unto* the house of the LORD *in* S: 7887
2:14 So they did in S unto all the Israelites that 7887
3:21 the LORD appeared again in S: for 7887
3:21 to Samuel in S by the word of the LORD. 7887
4: 3 covenant of the LORD out of S unto us, 7887
4: 4 So the people sent *to* S, that they might 7887
4:12 came *to* S the same day with his clothes 7887
14: 3 the son of Eli, the LORD'S priest in S, 7887
1Ki 2:27 he spake concerning the house of Eli in S. 7887
14: 2 be the wife of Jeroboam; and get thee *to* S: 7887
14: 4 went *to* S, and came *to* the house of Ahijah. 7887
Ps 78:60 So that he forsook the tabernacle of S, 7887
Jer 7:12 go ye now unto my place which *was* in S, 7887
7:14 and to your fathers, as I have done to S. 7887
26: 6 will I make this house like S, and will make 7887
26: 9 This house shall be like S, and this city 7887
41: 5 from S, and from Samaria, *even* fourscore 7887

SHILONI (1)
Ne 11: 5 the son of Zechariah, the son of S. 8023

SHILONITE (5) [SHILOH]
1Ki 11:29 that the prophet Ahijah the S found him in 7888
12:15 which the LORD spake by Ahijah the S 7888
15:29 which he spake by his servant Ahijah the S: 7888
2Ch 9:29 in the prophecy of Ahijah the S, and in 7888
10:15 which he spake by the hand of Ahijah the S 7888

SHILONITES (1) [SHILOH]
1Ch 9: 5 of the S; Asaiah the firstborn, and his sons. 7888

SHILSHAH (1)
1Ch 7:37 and Shamma, and S, and Ithran, and Beera. 8030

SHIMEA (5) [SHIMEAH]
2Sa 21:21 Jonathan the son of S the brother of David 8092
1Ch 3: 5 S, and Shobab, and Nathan, and Solomon, 8092
6:30 S his son, Haggiah his son, Asaiah his son. 8092
6:39 Asaph the son of Berachiah, the son of S, 8092
20: 7 Jonathan the son of S David's brother slew 8092

SHIMEAH (3) [SHIMEA]
2Sa 13: 3 *was* Jonadab, the son of S David's brother: 8093
13:32 the son of S David's brother, answered and 8093
1Ch 8:32 Mikloth begat S. And these also dwelt with 8039

SHIMEAM (1)
1Ch 9:38 Mikloth begat S. And they also dwelt with 8043

SHIMEATH (2) [SHIMEATHITES]
2Ki 12:21 For Jozachar the son of S, and 8100
2Ch 24:26 Zabad the son of S an Ammonitess, and 8100

SHIMEATHITES (1) [SHIMEATH]
1Ch 2:55 the Tirathites, the S, *and* Suchathites. 8101

SHIMEI (42)
Nu 3:18 of Gershon by their families; Libni, and S. 8096
2Sa 16: 5 whose name *was* S, the son of Gera: 8096
16: 7 thus said S when he cursed, Come out, 8096
16:13 S went along on the hill's side over against 8096
19:16 S the son of Gera, a Benjamite, which *was* 8096
19:18 S the son of Gera fell down before the king, 8096
2Sa 19:21 said, Shall not S be put to death for this, 8096
19:23 Therefore the king said unto S, Thou shalt 8096
1Ki 1: 8 S, and Rei, and the mighty *men* which 8096
2: 8 *thou hast* with thee S the son of Gera, 8096
2:36 the king sent and called for S, and said unto 8096
2:38 S said unto the king, The saying *is* good: 8096
2:38 And S dwelt in Jerusalem many days. 8096
2:39 that two of the servants of S ran away unto 8096
2:39 they told S, saying, Behold, thy servants *be* 8096
2:40 S arose, and saddled his ass, and went to 8096
2:40 S went, and brought his servants from 8096
2:41 it was told Solomon that S had gone from 8096
2:42 the king sent and called for S, and said unto 8096
2:44 The king said moreover to S, Thou knowest 8096
4:18 S the son of Elah, in Benjamin: 8096
1Ch 3:19 sons of Pedaiah *were*, Zerubbabel, and S: 8096
4:26 Hamuel his son, Zacchur his son, S his son. 8096
4:27 S had sixteen sons and six daughters; but 8096
5: 4 Shemaiah his son, Gog his son, S his son, 8096
6:17 of the sons of Gershom; Libni, and S. 8096
6:29 Libni his son, S his son, Uzza his son, 8096
6:42 of Ethan, the son of Zimmah, the son of S, 8096
23: 7 Of the Gershonites *were*, Laadan, and S. 8096
23: 9 The sons of S; Shelomith, and Haziel, and 8096
23:10 the sons of S *were*, Jahath, Zina, and Jeush, 8096
23:10 and Beriah. These four *were* the sons of S. 8096
25:17 The tenth *to* S, *he*, his sons, and 8096
27:27 over the vineyards *was* S the Ramathite: 8096
2Ch 29:14 of the sons of Heman; Jehiel, and S: and 8096
31:12 *was* ruler, and S his brother *was* the next. 8096
31:13 the hand of Cononiah and S his brother, 8096
Ezr 10:23 Jozabad, and S, and Kelaiah, (the same *is* 8096
10:33 Eliphelet, Jeremai, Manasseh, *and* S. 8096
10:38 And Bani, and Binnui, S, 8096
Est 2: 5 the son of Jair, the son of S, the son of 8096
Zec 12:13 the family of S apart, and their wives apart; 8097

SHIMEITES See SHIMITES

SHIMEON (1)
Ezr 10:31 Eliezer, Ishijah, Malchiah, Shemaiah, S, 8095

SHIMHI (1)
1Ch 8:21 and Beraiah, and Shimrath, the sons of S; 8096

SHIMI (1) [SHIMITES]
Ex 6:17 Libni, and S, according to their families. 8096

SHIMITES (1) [SHIMI]
Nu 3:21 of the Libnites, and the family of the S: 8097

SHIMMA (1)
1Ch 2:13 and Abinadab the second, and S the third, 8092

SHIMON (1)
1Ch 4:20 the sons of S *were*, Amnon, and Rinnah, 7889

SHIMRATH (1)
1Ch 8:21 Adaiah, and Beraiah, and S, the sons of 8119

SHIMRI (3)
1Ch 4:37 of Allon, the son of Jedaiah, the son of S, 8113
11:45 Jediael the son of S, and Joha his brother, 8113
2Ch 29:13 of the sons of Elizaphan; S, and Jeiel: and 8113

SHIMRITH (1)
2Ch 24:26 and Jehozabad the son of S a Moabitess. 8116

SHIMRON (5) [SHIMRONITES]
Ge 46:13 Tola, and Phuvah, and Job, and S. 8110
Nu 26:24 of S, the family of the Shimronites. 8110
Jos 11: 1 to the king of S, and to the king of 8110
19:15 and S, and Idalah, and Beth-lehem: 8110
1Ch 7: 1 *were*, Tola, and Puah, Jashub, and S, four. 8110

SHIMRONITES (1) [SHIMRON]
Nu 26:24 of Shimron, the family of the S. 8117

SHIMRON-MERON (1)
Jos 12:20 The king of S, one; the king of Achshaph, 8112

SHIMSHAI (4)
Ezr 4: 8 S the scribe wrote a letter against Jerusalem 8124
4: 9 S the scribe, and the rest of their 8124
4:17 *to* S the scribe, and *to* the rest of their 8124
4:23 S the scribe, and their companions, 8124

SHINAB (1)
Ge 14: 2 S king of Admah, and Shemeber king of 8134

SHINAR (7)
Ge 10:10 and Accad, and Calneh, in the land of S. 8152
11: 2 that they found a plain in the land of S; 8152
14: 1 to pass in the days of Amraphel king of S, 8152
14: 9 Amraphel king of S, and Arioch king of 8152
Isa 11:11 from S, and from Hamath, and from 8152
Da 1: 2 which he carried *into* the land of S *to* 8152
Zec 5:11 To build it a house in the land of S: 8152

SHINE (32) [SHINED, SHINETH, SHINING, SHONE]
Nu 6:25 The LORD **make** his face s upon thee, and 215
Job 3: 4 it from above, neither let the light s upon it. 3313
10: 3 and s upon the counsel of the wicked? 3313
11:17 thou shalt s **forth**, thou shalt be as 5774
18: 5 put out, and the spark of his fire shall not s. 5050
22:28 and the light shall s upon thy ways. 5050
36:32 commandeth it *not to* s by *the cloud* that NIH
37:15 and **caused** the light of his cloud **to** s? 3313
41:18 *By* his neesings a light doth s, and his eyes 1984
41:32 He **maketh** a path **to** s after him; *one* would 215
Ps 31:16 **Make** thy face **to** s upon thy servant: 215
67: 1 *and* **cause** his face **to** s upon us; Selah. 215
80: 1 dwellest *between* the cherubims, s **forth**. 3313
Ps 80: 3 us again, O God, and **cause** thy face **to** s; 215
80: 7 O God *of* hosts, and **cause** thy face **to** s; 215
80:19 O LORD God *of* hosts, **cause** thy face **to** s; 215
104:15 *and* oil to **make** *his* face **to** s, and 6670
119:135 **Make** thy face **to** s upon thy servant; and 215
Ecc 8: 1 a man's wisdom **maketh** his face **to** s, and 215
Isa 13:10 and the moon shall not **cause** her light **to** s. 5050
60: 1 Arise, s; for thy light is come, and the glory 215
Jer 5:28 They are waxen fat, they s: yea, 6245
Da 9:17 **cause** thy face **to** s upon thy sanctuary that is 215
12: 3 they that be wise shall s as the brightness of 2094
Mt 5:16 Let your light so s before men, that they *2989*
13:43 Then shall the righteous s **forth** as the sun *1584*
17: 2 and his face did s as the sun, and *2989*
2Co 4: 4 is the image of God, should s unto them. *826*
4: 6 who commanded the light to s out of *2989*
Php 2:15 among whom ye s as lights in the world; *5316*
Rev 18:23 And the light of a candle shall s no more at *5316*
21:23 of the sun, neither of the moon, to s in it: *5316*

SHINED (9) [SHINE]
Dt 33: 2 he s **forth** from mount Paran, and he came 3313
Job 29: 3 When his candle s upon my head, *and* 1984
31:26 If I beheld the sun when it s, or the moon 1984
Ps 50: 2 the perfection of beauty, God hath s. 3313
Isa 9: 2 of death, upon them hath the light s. 5050
Eze 43: 2 many waters: and the earth s with his glory. 215
Ac 9: 3 suddenly there s **round about** him a light *4015*
12: 7 came upon *him*, and a light s in the prison: *2989*
2Co 4: 6 shine out of darkness, hath s in our hearts, *2989*

SHINETH (9) [SHINE]
Job 25: 5 Behold *even* to the moon, and it s not; yea, 166
Ps 139:12 not from thee; but the night s as the day: 215
Pr 4:18 that s **more and more** unto the perfect day. 1980
Mt 24:27 out of the east, and s *even* unto the west; *5316*
Lk 17:24 s unto the other *part* under heaven; *2989*
Jn 1: 5 And the light s in darkness; and *5316*
2Pe 1:19 as unto a light that s in a dark place, *5316*
1Jn 2: 8 darkness is past, and the true light now s. *5316*
Rev 1:16 his countenance *was* as the sun s in his *5316*

SHINING (11) [SHINE]
2Sa 23: 4 out of the earth by **clear** s after rain. 5051
Pr 4:18 the path of the just *is* as the s light, 5051
Isa 4: 5 by day, and the s of a flaming fire by night: 5051
Joel 2:10 and the stars shall withdraw their s: 5051
3:15 and the stars shall withdraw their s. 5051
Hab 3:11 *and* at the s of thy glittering spear. 5051
Mk 9: 3 And his raiment became s, exceeding white *4744*
Lk 11:36 as when the **bright** s of a candle doth give *796*
24: 4 two men stood by them in s garments: *797*
Jn 5:35 He was a burning and a s light: and ye were *5316*
Ac 26:13 s **round about** me and them which *4034*

SHION (1)
Jos 19:19 And Hapharaim, and S, and Anaharath, 7866

SHIP (71) [FORESHIP, SHIPMASTER, SHIPMEN, SHIPPING, SHIPS, SHIPWRACK]
Pr 30:19 the way of a s in the midst of the sea; and 591
Isa 33:21 neither shall gallant s pass thereby. 6716
Eze 27: 5 They have made all thy *s* boards of fir trees NIH
Jnh 1: 3 *to* Joppa; and he found a s going *to* Tarshish: 591
1: 4 in the sea, so that the s was like to be broken. 591
1: 5 cast forth the wares that *were* in the s into 591
1: 5 was gone down into the sides of the s; 5600
Mt 4:21 his brother, in a s with Zebedee their father, *4143*
4:22 And they immediately left the s and *4143*
8:23 And when he was entered into a s, *4143*
8:24 insomuch that the s was covered with *4143*
9: 1 And he entered into a s, and passed over, *4143*
13: 2 unto him, so that he went into a s, and sat; *4143*
14:13 thence by s into a desert place apart: *4143*
14:22 constrained his disciples to get into a s, *4143*
14:24 But the s was now in the midst of the sea, *4143*
14:29 when Peter was come down out of the s, *4143*
14:32 And when they were come into the s, *4143*
14:33 Then they that were in the s came and *4143*
15:39 and took s, and came into the coasts of *4143*
Mk 1:19 who also *were* in the s mending *their* nets. *4143*
1:20 they left their father Zebedee in the s with *4143*
3: 9 that a **small** s should wait on him because *4142*
4: 1 so that he entered into a s, and sat in *4143*
4:36 they took him *even* as he was in the s. *4143*
4:37 and the waves beat into the s, so that it was *4143*
4:38 And he was in the **hinder part of** the s, *4403*
5: 2 And when he was come out of the s, *4143*
5:18 And when he was come into the s, he that *4143*
5:21 And when Jesus was passed over again by s *4143*
6:32 And they departed into a desert place by s *4143*
6:45 constrained his disciples to get into the s, *4143*
6:47 the s was in the midst of the sea, and *4143*
6:51 And he went up unto them into the s; and *4143*
6:54 And when they were come out of the s, *4143*
8:10 And straightway he entered into a s with *4143*
8:13 entering into the s again departed to *4143*
8:14 neither had they in the s with them more *4143*
Lk 5: 3 and taught the people out of the s. *4143*
5: 7 which were in the other s, that *they* should *4143*
8:22 that he went into a s with his disciples: *4143*
8:37 and he went *up* into the s, and *4143*
Jn 6:17 And entered into a s, and went over the sea *4143*
6:19 on the sea, and drawing nigh unto the s: *4143*
6:21 Then they willingly received him into the s: *4143*
6:21 immediately the s was at the land whither *4143*
21: 3 and entered into a s immediately; *4143*
21: 6 Cast the net on the right side of the s, and *4143*
21: 8 And the other disciples came in a **little** s; *4142*
Ac 20:13 And we went before to s, and sailed unto *4143*
20:38 And they accompanied him unto the s. *4143*
21: 2 And finding a s sailing over unto Phenicia, *4143*
21: 3 for there the s was to unlade *her* burden. *4143*
21: 6 taken our leave one of another, we took s; *4143*

Ac 27: 2 And entering into a **s** of Adramyttium, *4143*
27: 6 And there the centurion found a **s** of *4143*
27:10 not only of the lading and **s**, but also of our *4143*
27:11 believed the master and the **owner of the s**, *3490*
27:15 And when the **s** was caught, and could not *4143*
27:17 they used helps, undergirding the **s**; *4143*
27:18 the next *day* they **lightened the s**; *1546+4160*
27:19 with our own hands the tackling of the **s**. *4143*
27:22 of *any man's* life among you, but of the **s**. *4143*
27:30 the shipmen were about to flee out of the **s**, *4143*
27:31 to the soldiers, Except these abide in the **s**, *4143*
27:37 And we were in all in the **s** two hundred *4143*
27:38 they lightened the **s**, and cast out the wheat *4143*
27:39 if it were possible, to thrust in the **s**. *4143*
27:41 where two seas met, they ran the **s** aground; *3491*
27:44 and some on broken pieces of the **s**. *4143*
28:11 And after three months we departed in a **s** *4143*

SHIPHI (1)
1Ch 4:37 Ziza the son of **S**, the son of Allon, the son 8230

SHIPHMITE (1)
1Ch 27:27 for the wine cellars *was* Zabdi the **S**: 8225

SHIPHRAH (1)
Ex 1:15 of which the name of the one *was* **S**, and 8236

SHIPHTAN (1)
Nu 34:24 children of Ephraim, Kemuel the son of **S**. 8204

SHIPMASTER (2) [MASTER, SHIP]
Jnh 1: 6 So the **s** came to him, and 2259+7227+1886.1
Rev 18:17 And every **s**, and all the company in ships, *2942*

SHIPMEN (3) [MAN, SHIP]
1Ki 9:27 **s** that had knowledge of the sea, 376+591
Ac 27:27 about midnight the **s** deemed that they drew *3492*
27:30 And as the **s** were about to flee out of *3492*

SHIPPING (1) [SHIP]
Jn 6:24 they also **took s**, *1519+1684+3588+4143*

SHIPS (39) [SHIP]
Ge 49:13 he *shall be* for a haven of **s**; and his border 591
Nu 24:24 And **s** *shall come* from the coast of Chittim, 6716
Dt 28:68 shall bring thee *into* Egypt again with **s**, 591
Jdg 5:17 why did Dan remain *in* **s**? Asher continued 591
1Ki 9:26 king Solomon made a navy *of* **s** in NIH
22:48 Jehoshaphat made **s** of Tharshish to go to 591
22:48 for the **s** were broken at Ezion-geber. 591
22:49 my servants go with thy servants in the **s**. 591
2Ch 8:18 sent him by the hands of his servants **s**, 591
9:21 For the king's **s** went *to* Tarshish with 591
9:21 every three years once came the **s** of 591
20:36 he joined himself with him to make **s** to go 591
20:36 and they made the **s** in Ezion-geber. 591
20:37 the **s** were broken, that they were not able to 591
Job 9:26 They are passed away as the swift **s**: as 591
Ps 48: 7 Thou breakest the **s** of Tarshish with an east 591
104:26 There go the **s**: *there is* that leviathan, 591
107:23 They that go down to the sea in **s**, that do 591
Pr 31:14 She is like the merchant's **s**; she bringeth her 591
Isa 2:16 upon all the **s** of Tarshish, and upon all 591
23: 1 Howl, ye **s** of Tarshish; for it is laid waste, 591
23:14 Howl, ye **s** of Tarshish: for your strength is 591
43:14 and the Chaldeans, whose cry *is* in the **s**. 591
60: 9 the **s** of Tarshish first, to bring thy sons from 591
Eze 27: 9 all the **s** of the sea with their mariners were 591
27:25 The **s** of Tarshish did sing of thee *in* thy 591
27:29 of the sea, shall come down from their **s**, 591
30: 9 in **s** to make the careless Ethiopians afraid, 6716
Da 11:30 For *the* **s** of Chittim shall come against 6716
11:40 and with horsemen, and with many **s**; 591
Mk 4:36 And there were also with him other **little s**. *4142*
Lk 5: 2 And saw two **s** standing by the lake: but *4143*
5: 3 And he entered into one of the **s**, which was *4143*
5: 7 and filled both the **s**, so that they began to *4143*
5:11 And when they had brought *their* **s** to land, *4143*
Jas 3: 4 Behold also the **s**, which though they be so *4143*
Rev 8: 9 and the third *part* of the **s** were destroyed. *4143*
18:17 every shipmaster, and all the company in **s**, *4143*
18:19 wherein were made rich all that had **s** in *4143*

SHIPWRACK (2) [SHIP]
2Co 11:25 thrice I **suffered s**, a night and a day I have *3489*
1Ti 1:19 put away, concerning faith have **made s**: *3489*

SHISHA (1)
1Ki 4: 3 Elihoreph and Ahiah, the sons of **S**, scribes; 7894

SHISHAK (7)
1Ki 11:40 unto **S** king of Egypt, and was in Egypt 7895
14:25 *that* **S** king of Egypt came up against 7895
2Ch 12: 2 *that* in the fifth year of king Rehoboam **S** 7895
12: 5 together to Jerusalem because of **S**, 7895
12: 5 have I also left you in the hand of **S**. 7895
12: 7 out upon Jerusalem by the hand of **S**. 7895
12: 9 So **S** king of Egypt came up against 7895

SHITRAI (1)
1Ch 27:29 over the herds that fed in Sharon *was* **S** 7061

SHITTAH (1)
Isa 41:19 the **s tree**, and the myrtle, and the oil tree; 7848

SHITTIM (32) [ABEL-SHITTIM]
Ex 25: 5 dyed red, and badgers' skins, and **s** wood, 7848
25:10 they shall make an ark of **s** wood: 7848
25:13 thou shalt make staves of **s** wood, and 7848
25:23 Thou shalt also make a table *of* **s** wood: 7848
25:28 thou shalt make the staves *of* **s** wood, and 7848
26:15 for the tabernacle *of* **s** wood standing up. 7848
26:26 thou shalt make bars *of* **s** wood; five for 7848
Ex 26:32 thou shalt hang it upon four pillars of **s** 7848
26:37 make for the hanging five pillars of **s** *wood*, 7848
27: 1 thou shalt make an altar *of* **s** wood, 7848
27: 6 staves of **s** wood, and overlay them with 7848
30: 1 incense upon: *of* **s** wood shalt thou make it. 7848
30: 5 thou shalt make the staves *of* **s** wood, and 7848
35: 7 dyed red, and badgers' skins, and **s** wood, 7848
35:24 with whom was found **s** wood for any work 7848
36:20 he made boards for the tabernacle *of* **s** 7848
36:31 he made bars of **s** wood; five for the boards 7848
36:36 he made thereunto four pillars of **s** *wood*, 7848
37: 1 Bezaleel made the ark *of* **s** wood: 7848
37: 4 he made staves of **s** wood, and 7848
37:10 he made the table *of* **s** wood: two cubits 7848
37:15 he made the staves *of* **s** wood, and 7848
37:25 he made the incense altar *of* **s** wood: 7848
37:28 he made the staves *of* **s** wood, and 7848
38: 1 he made the altar of burnt offering *of* **s** 7848
38: 6 he made the staves *of* **s** wood, and 7848
Nu 25: 1 Israel abode in **S**, and the people began to 7851
Dt 10: 3 I made an ark of **s** wood, and hewed two 7848
Jos 2: 1 Joshua the son of Nun sent out of **S** two 7851
3: 1 they removed from **S**, and came to Jordan, 7851
Joel 3:18 the LORD, and shall water the valley of **S**. 7851
Mic 6: 5 of Beor answered him; from **S** unto Gilgal; 7851

SHIVERS (1)
Rev 2:27 of a potter *shall* they be **broken to s**: *4937*

SHIZA (1)
1Ch 11:42 Adina the son of **S** the Reubenite, a captain 7877

SHOA (1)
Eze 23:23 all the Chaldeans, Pekod, and **S**, and Koa, 7772

SHOBAB (4)
2Sa 5:14 and **S**, and Nathan, and Solomon, 7727
1Ch 2:18 sons *are* these; Jesher, and **S**, and Ardon. 7727
3: 5 and **S**, and Nathan, and Solomon, four, 7727
14: 4 Shammua, and **S**, Nathan, and Solomon, 7727

SHOBACH (2)
2Sa 10:16 **S** the captain of the host of Hadarezer *went* 7731
10:18 smote **S** the captain of their host, who died 7731

SHOBAI (2)
Ezr 2:42 the children of Hatita, the children of **S**, 7630
Ne 7:45 the children of **S**, an hundred thirty and 7630

SHOBAL (9)
Ge 36:20 Lotan, and **S**, and Zibeon, and Anah, 7732
36:23 the children of **S** *were* these; Alvan, and 7732
36:29 duke Lotan, duke **S**, duke Zibeon, 7732
1Ch 1:38 **S**, and Zibeon, and Anah, and Dishon, and 7732
1:40 The sons of **S**; Alian, and Manahath, and 7732
2:50 of Ephratah; **S** the father of Kirjath-jearim, 7732
2:52 **S** the father of Kirjath-jearim had sons; 7732
4: 1 Hezron, and Carmi, and Hur, and **S**. 7732
4: 2 Reaiah the son of **S** begat Jahath; and 7732

SHOBEK (1)
Ne 10:24 Hallohesh, Pileha, **S**, 7733

SHOBI (1)
2Sa 17:27 that **S** the son of Nahash of Rabbah of 7629

SHOCHO (1)
2Ch 28:18 **S** with the villages thereof, and Timnah 7755

SHOCHOH (2)
1Sa 17: 1 were gathered together *at* **S**, 7755
17: 1 pitched between **S** and Azekah, 7755

SHOCK (1)
Job 5:26 like as a **s of corn** cometh in in his season. 1430

SHOCKS (1)
Jdg 15: 5 burnt up both the **s**, and also the standing 1430

SHOCO (1)
2Ch 11: 7 And Beth-zur, and **S**, and Adullam, 7755

SHOD (4) [UNSHOD]
2Ch 28:15 **s** them, and gave them to eat and to drink, 5274
Eze 16:10 **s** thee *with* badgers' *skin*, and I girded thee 5274
Mk 6: 9 But *be* **s** with sandals; and not put on two *5265*
Eph 6:15 And *your* feet **s** with the preparation of *5265*

SHOE (9) [SHOE'S, SHOELATCHET, SHOES]
Dt 25: 9 loose his **s** from off his foot, and spit in his 5275
25:10 The house of him that hath his **s** loosed. 5275
29: 5 and thy **s** is not waxen old upon thy foot. 5275
Jos 5:15 unto Joshua, Loose thy **s** from off thy foot; 5275
Ru 4: 7 a man plucked off his **s**, and gave *it* to his 5275
4: 8 Buy *it* for thee. So he drew off his **s**. 5275
Ps 60: 8 over Edom will I cast out my **s**: 5275
108: 9 over Edom will I cast out my **s**; 5275
Isa 20: 2 thy loins, and put off thy **s** from thy foot. 5275

SHOE'S (1) [SHOE]
Jn 1:27 whose **s** latchet I am not worthy to unloose. *5266*

SHOELATCHET (1) [LATCHET, SHOE]
Ge 14:23 not *take* from a thread even to a **s**, 5275+8288

SHOES (21) [SHOE]
Ex 3: 5 put off thy **s** from off thy feet, for the place 5275
12:11 your **s** on your feet, and your staff in your 5275
Dt 33:25 Thy **s** *shall be* iron and brass; and as thy 4515
Jos 9: 5 old **s** and clouted upon their feet, and 5275
9:13 our **s** are become old by reason of the very 5275
1Ki 2: 5 his loins, and in his **s** that *were* on his feet. 5275
SS 7: 1 How beautiful are thy feet with **s**, 5275
Isa 5:27 nor the latchet of their **s** be broken: 5275
Eze 24:17 put on thy **s** upon thy feet, and cover not 5275
24:23 your heads, and your **s** upon your feet: 5275
Am 2: 6 for silver, and the poor for a pair of **s**; 5275
8: 6 for silver, and the needy for a pair of **s**; 5275
Mt 3:11 than I, whose **s** I am not worthy to bear: *5266*
10:10 neither two coats, neither **s**, nor yet staves: *5266*
Mk 1: 7 the latchet of whose **s** I am not worthy to *5266*
Lk 3:16 the latchet of whose **s** I am not worthy to *5266*
10: 4 Carry neither purse, nor scrip, nor **s**: and *5266*
15:22 put a ring on his hand, and **s** on *his* feet: *5266*
22:35 I sent you without purse, and scrip, and **s**, *5266*
Ac 7:33 the Lord to him, Put off *thy* **s** from thy feet: *5266*
13:25 whose **s** of *his* feet I am not worthy to *5266*

SHOHAM (1)
1Ch 24:27 Beno, and **S**, and Zaccur, and Ibri. 7719

SHOMER (2)
2Ki 12:21 Jehozabad the son of **S**, his servants, 7763
1Ch 7:32 and **S**, and Hotham, and Shua their sister. 7763

SHONE (7) [SHINE]
Ex 34:29 skin of his face **s** while he talked with him. 7160
34:30 saw Moses, behold, the skin of his face **s**; 7160
34:35 of Moses, that the skin of Moses' face **s**: 7160
2Ki 3:22 the sun **s** upon the water, and the Moabites 2224
Lk 2: 9 the glory of the Lord **s round about** them: *4034*
Ac 22: 6 suddenly there **s** from heaven a great light *4015*
Rev 8:12 and the day **s** not for a third *part* of it, *5316*

SHOOK (12) [SHAKE]
2Sa 6: 6 and took hold of it; for the oxen **s** *it*. 8058
22: 8 the earth **s** and trembled; the foundations of 1607
22: 8 the foundations of heaven moved and **s**, 1607
Ne 5:13 Also I **s** my lap, and said, So God shake out 5287
Ps 18: 7 the earth **s** and trembled; the foundations 1607
68: 8 The earth **s**, the heavens also dropped at 7493
77:18 the world: the earth trembled and **s**. 7493
Isa 23:11 his hand over the sea, he **s** the kingdoms: 7264
Ac 13:51 But they **s off** the dust of their feet against *1621*
18: 6 he **s** *his* raiment, and said unto them, *1621*
28: 5 And he **s off** the beast into the fire, and *660*
Heb 12:26 Whose voice then **s** the earth: but now he *4531*

SHOOT (21) [BOWSHOT, SHOOTERS, SHOOTETH, SHOOTING, SHOT]
Ex 36:33 he made the middle bar to **s** through 1272
1Sa 20:20 I will **s** three arrows on the side *thereof*, as 3384
20:36 Run, find out now the arrows which I **s**. 3384
2Sa 11:20 knew ye not that they would **s** from 3384
2Ki 13:17 he opened *it*. Then Elisha said, **S**. And he 3384
19:32 nor **s** an arrow there, nor come before it 3384
1Ch 5:18 and to **s** with bow, and skilful in war, 1869
2Ch 26:15 to **s** arrows and great stones withal. 3384
Ps 11: 2 that *they* may privily **s** at the upright in 3384
22: 7 they **s out** the lip, they shake the head, 6362
58: 7 *when* he bendeth *his bow to* **s** his arrows, NIH
64: 3 *and* bend *their bows to* **s** their arrows, NIH
64: 4 That *they* may **s** in secret at the perfect: 3384
64: 4 suddenly do they **s** at him, and fear not. 3384
64: 7 God shall **s** at them *with* an arrow; 3384
144: 6 **s out** thine arrows, and destroy them. 7971
Isa 37:33 nor **s** an arrow there, nor come before it 3384
Jer 50:14 bend the bow, **s** at her, spare no arrows: 3034
Eze 31:14 neither **s up** their top among the thick 5414
36: 8 ye shall **s forth** your branches, and 5414
Lk 21:30 When they now **s forth**, ye see and *4261*

SHOOTERS (1) [SHOOT]
2Sa 11:24 the **s** shot from off the wall upon thy 4175

SHOOTETH (3) [SHOOT]
Job 8:16 and his branch **s forth** in his garden, 3318
Isa 27: 8 In measure, when it **s forth**, thou wilt 7971
Mk 4:32 than all herbs, and **s out** great branches; *4160*

SHOOTING (2) [SHOOT]
1Ch 12: 2 in *hurling* stones and **s** arrows out of a bow, NIH
Am 7: 1 beginning of the **s up** of the latter growth; 5927

SHOPHACH (2)
1Ch 19:16 **S** the captain of the host of Hadarezer *went* 7780
19:18 killed **S** the captain of the host. 7780

SHOPHAN See ATROTH SHOPHAN

SHORE (17)
Ge 22:17 and as the sand which *is* upon the sea **s**; 8193
Ex 14:30 saw the Egyptians dead upon the sea **s**. 8193
Jos 11: 4 *even* as the sand that *is* upon the sea **s** in 8193
15: 2 their south border was from the **s** of the salt 7097
Jdg 5:17 Asher continued on the sea **s**, and abode in 2348
1Sa 13: 5 people as the sand which *is* on the sea **s** in 8193
1Ki 4:29 *even* as the sand that *is* on the sea **s**. 8193
9:26 on the **s** of the Red sea, in the land of 8193
Jer 47: 7 against Ashkelon, and against the sea **s**? 2348
Mt 13: 2 sat; and the whole multitude stood on the **s**. *123*
13:48 they drew to **s**, and sat down, and *123*
Mk 6:53 the land of Genesaret, and **drew to** the **s**. *4358*
Jn 21: 4 was now come, Jesus stood on the **s**: *123*
Ac 21: 5 and we kneeled down on the **s**, and prayed. *123*
27:39 but they discovered a certain creek with a **s**, *123*
27:40 the mainsail to the wind, and made toward **s**. *123*
Heb 11:12 as the sand which is by the sea **s** *5491*

SHORELANDS See SUBURBS

SHORN (4) [SHEAR]
SS 4: 2 *are* like a flock of *sheep that are* **even s**, 7094
Ac 18:18 having **s** *his* head in Cenchrea: for he had a *2751*
1Co 11: 6 the woman be not covered, let her also be **s**: *2751*
11: 6 but *if it* be a shame for a woman to be **s** or *2751*

SHORT (13) [SHORTENED, SHORTER, SHORTLY]
Nu 11:23 Is the LORD'S hand **waxed s**? 7114
2Ki 10:32 days the LORD began to **cut** Israel **s**: 7096
Job 17:12 into day: the light *is* s, because of darkness. 7138
20: 5 the triumphing of the wicked *is* s, 4480+7138
Ps 89:47 Remember how s my **time** is: 2465
Ro 3:23 and **come** s of the glory of God; 5302
9:28 the work, and **cut** *it* s in righteousness: 4932
9:28 a s work will the Lord make upon the earth. 4932
1Co 7:29 But this I say, brethren, the time *is* s: 4958
1Th 2:17 being taken from you for a s time in 5610
Heb 4: 1 any of you should seem to **come** s *of it*. 5302
Rev 12:12 he knoweth that he hath *but* a s time. 3641
17:10 he cometh, he must continue a s *space*. 3641

SHORTENED (9) [SHORT]
Ps 89:45 The days of his youth hast thou s: thou hast 7114
102:23 my strength in the way; he s my days. 7114
Pr 10:27 but the years of the wicked shall be s. 7114
Isa 50: 2 Is my hand **s at all**, that *it* cannot 7114+7114
59: 1 Behold, the LORD'S hand is not s, that *it* 7114
Mt 24:22 And except those days should be s, 2856
24:22 for the elect's sake those days shall be s. 2856
Mk 13:20 And except that the Lord had s *those* days, 2856
13:20 whom he hath chosen, he hath s the days. 2856

SHORTER (2) [SHORT]
Isa 28:20 For the bed is s than that *a man* can stretch 7114
Eze 42: 5 Now the upper chambers *were* s: for 7114

SHORTLY (15) [SHORT]
Ge 41:32 by God, and God will s bring it to pass. 4116
Jer 27:16 *shall* now s be brought again from Babylon: 4120
Eze 7: 8 Now will I s pour out my fury upon 4480+7138
Ac 25: 4 he himself would depart s *thither*. 1722+5034
Ro 16:20 shall bruise Satan under your feet s. 1722+5034
1Co 4:19 But I will come to you s, if the Lord will, 5030
Php 2:19 Lord Jesus to send Timotheus s unto you, 5030
2:24 in the Lord that I also myself shall come s. 5030
1Ti 3:14 I unto thee, hoping to come unto thee s: 5030
2Ti 4: 9 Do thy diligence to come s unto me: 5030
Heb 13:23 with whom, if he come s, I will see you. 5030
2Pe 1:14 Knowing that s *I* must put off *this* my 5031
3Jn 1:14 But I trust *I* shall s see thee, and we shall 2112
Rev 1: 1 *things* which must s come to pass; 1722+5034
22: 6 *the things* which must s be done. 1722+5034

SHOSHANNIM (2)
Ps 45: T To the chief Musician upon S, for the sons 7799
69: T To the chief Musician upon S, *A Psalm* of 7799

SHOSHANNIM-EDUTH (1)
Ps 80: T To the chief Musician upon S, A 5715+7799

SHOT (16) [SHOOT]
Ge 40:10 though it budded, *and* her blossoms **s forth**; 5927
49:23 grieved him, and s *at him*, and hated him: 7232
Ex 19:13 shall surely be stoned, or **s through**; 3384+3384
Nu 21:30 We have s at them; Heshbon is perished 3384
1Sa 20:20 on the side *thereof*, as *though* I s at a mark. 7971
20:36 as the lad ran, he s an arrow beyond him. 3384
20:37 place of the arrow which Jonathan had s, 3384
2Sa 11:24 the shooters s from off the wall upon thy 3384
2Ki 13:17 he s. And he said, The arrow of 3384
2Ch 35:23 the archers s at king Josiah; and the king 3384
Ps 18:14 he **s out** lightnings, and discomfited them. 7232
Jer 9: 8 Their tongue *is as* an arrow **s out**; 7819
Eze 17: 6 brought forth branches, and **s forth** sprigs. 7971
17: 7 and **s forth** her branches toward him, 7971
31: 5 of the multitude of waters, when he **s forth**. 7971
31:10 he hath **s up** his top among the thick 5414

SHOULD (783) [SHOULDEST]
Ge 2:18 *It is* not good that the man s be alone; NIH
4:15 upon Cain, lest any finding him s kill him. NIH
18:25 that the righteous s be as the wicked, that be NIH
21: 7 that Sarah s have given children suck? NIH
23: 8 If it be your mind that I s bury my dead out NIH
26: 7 *said he*, the men of the place s kill me for NIH
27:45 why s I be deprived also of you both *in* one NIH
29: 7 neither *is it* time that the cattle s be gathered NIH
29:19 than that I s give her to another man: NIH
30:38 that they s conceive when they came to NIH
33:13 if *men* s overdrive them one day, all NIH
34:31 S he deal with our sister as with a harlot? NIH
38: 9 Onan knew that the seed s not be his; and NIH
38: 9 lest that he s give seed to his brother. NIH
40:15 here also have I done nothing that they s put NIH
43:25 for they heard that they s eat bread there. NIH
44: 7 God forbid that thy servants s do according NIH
44: 8 s we steal out of thy lord's house silver or NIH
44:17 he said, God forbid that I s do so: *but* NIH
44:22 for *if* he s leave his father, *his father* would NIH
47:15 for why s we die in thy presence? for NIH
47:26 *that* Pharaoh s have the fifth *part*; except NIH
Ex 3:11 that I s go unto Pharaoh, and that I should NIH
3:11 that I s bring forth the children of Israel out NIH
5: 2 that I s obey his voice to let Israel go? NIH
14:12 than that we s die in the wilderness. NIH
22: 3 *for* he s make full restitution; if he have NIH
32:12 Wherefore s the Egyptians speak, and say, NIH
35: 1 hath commanded, that *ye* s do them. NIH
39: 7 *that they* s *be* stones for a memorial to NIH
39:23 band round about the hole, *that* it s not rend. NIH
Lev 4:13 *concerning things* which s not be done, NIH
4:22 God *concerning things* which s not be done, NIH
9: 6 which the LORD commanded *that* ye s do: NIH
10:18 s indeed have eaten it in the holy *place*, as I NIH
10:19 s it have been accepted in the sight of NIH
11:43 with them, that ye s be defiled thereby. NIH
20:26 you from *other* people, that *ye* s be mine. NIH
24:23 that they s bring forth him that had cursed NIH
26:13 of Egypt, that *ye* s not be their bondmen; NIH
27:26 which s be the LORD'S firstling, no man NIH
Nu 7: 9 *was that* they s bear upon *their* shoulders. NIH
9: 4 of Israel, that they s keep the passover. NIH
11:13 Whence s I have flesh to give unto all this NIH
12:14 her face, s she not be ashamed seven days? NIH
14: 3 *that* our wives and our children s be a prey? NIH
14:31 your little ones, which ye said s be a prey, NIH
15:34 it was not declared what s be done to him. NIH
20: 4 that we and our cattle s die there? NIH
23:19 God *is* not a man, that he s lie; neither NIH
23:19 neither the son of man, that he s repent: NIH
27: 4 Why s the name of our father be done away NIH
32: 9 that *they* s not go into the land which NIH
35:28 Because he s have remained in the city of NIH
35:32 that he s come again to dwell in the land, NIH
Dt 1:18 you at that time all the things which ye s do. NIH
1:33 to shew you by what way ye s go, and in a NIH
1:39 which ye said s be a prey, and NIH
4: 5 that *ye* s do so in the land whither ye go to NIH
4:21 sware that I s not go over Jordan, and that *I* NIH
4:21 and that *I* s not go in unto *that* good land, NIH
4:42 which s kill his neighbour unawares, NIH
5:25 Now therefore why s we die? for this great NIH
17:16 to the end that he s multiply horses: NIH
20:18 so s ye sin against the LORD your God. NIH
25: 3 *if* he s exceed, and beat him above these NIH
25: 3 then thy brother s seem vile unto thee. NIH
29:18 Lest there s be among you man, or woman, NIH
29:18 lest there s be among you a root that beareth NIH
32:27 lest their adversaries s behave themselves NIH
32:27 *and* lest they s say, Our hand is high, and NIH
32:30 How s one chase a thousand, and two put NIH
Jos 8:29 Joshua commanded that they s take his NIH
8:33 that they s bless the people of Israel. NIH
9:27 this day, in the place which he s choose. NIH
11:20 that *they* s come against Israel *in* battle, that NIH
22:28 when they s *so* say to us or to our NIH
22:29 God forbid that we s rebel against NIH
24:16 God forbid that we s forsake the LORD, NIH
Jdg 8: 6 that we s give bread unto thine army? NIH
8:15 that we s give bread unto thy men *that are* NIH
9: 9 tree said unto them, S I leave my fatness, NIH
9:11 S I forsake my sweetness, and my good NIH
9:13 S I leave my wine, which cheereth God and NIH
9:28 and who *is* Shechem, that we s serve him? NIH
9:28 father of Shechem: for why s we serve him? NIH
9:38 Who *is* Abimelech, that we s serve him? NIH
9:41 that *they* s not dwell in Shechem. NIH
20:38 that they s make a great flame with smoke NIH
21: 3 that there s be to day one tribe lacking in NIH
21:22 unto them at *this* time, *that* you s be guilty. NIH
Ru 1:12 If I s say, I have hope, *if* I should have a NIH
1:12 *if* I s have a husband also to night, and NIH
1:12 husband also to night, and s also bear sons; NIH
1Sa 2:30 of thy father, s walk before me for ever: NIH
8: 7 rejected me, that *I* s not reign over them. NIH
9: 6 he can shew us our way that we s go. NIH
10:22 if the man s yet come thither. NIH
12:21 *s ye go* after vain *things*, which cannot NIH
12:23 God forbid that I s sin against the LORD NIH
15:21 the chief of the things which s have been NIH
15:29 for he *is* not a man, that *he* s repent. NIH
17:26 that he s defy the armies of the living God? NIH
18:18 in Israel, that I s be son in law to the king? NIH
18:19 Saul's daughter s have been given to David, NIH
19: 1 and to all his servants, that they s kill David. NIH
19:17 said unto me, Let me go; why s I kill thee? NIH
20: 2 why s my father hide this thing from me? NIH
20: 5 and I s not fail to sit with the king at meat: NIH
22:13 that *he* s rise against me, to lie in wait, as at NIH
24: 6 The LORD forbid that I s do this thing NIH
26:11 The LORD forbid that *I* s stretch forth NIH
27: 1 *there is* nothing better for me than that I s NIH
27: 5 for why s thy servant dwell in the royal city NIH
27:11 saying, Lest they s tell on us, saying, So did NIH
29: 4 for wherewith s he reconcile himself unto NIH
29: 4 *s it* not *be* with the heads of these men? NIH
2Sa 2:22 wherefore s I smite thee to the ground? how NIH
2:22 s I hold up my face to Joab thy brother? NIH
12:23 now he is dead, wherefore s I fast? can I NIH
13:26 king said unto him, Why s he go with thee? NIH
15:20 s I *this* day make thee go up and down with NIH
16: 9 Why s this dead dog curse my lord NIH
16:19 again, whom s I serve? *should I* not *serve* in NIH
16:19 *s I* not *serve* in the presence of his son? as I NIH
18:12 Though I s receive a thousand *shekels of* NIH
18:13 Otherwise I s have wrought falsehood NIH
19:19 that the king s take *it* to his heart. NIH
19:22 that ye s *this* day be adversaries unto me? NIH
19:34 that I s go up with the king *unto* Jerusalem? NIH
19:35 s thy servant be yet a burden unto my lord NIH
19:36 why s the king recompense *it* me *with* such NIH
19:43 that our advice s not be first had in bringing NIH
20:20 it from me, that I s swallow up or destroy. NIH
21: 5 that devised against us *that* we s be NIH
23:17 it far from me, O LORD, that I s do this: NIH
1Ki 1:27 who s sit on the throne of my lord the king NIH
2: 1 Now the days of David drew nigh that *he* s NIH
2:15 all Israel set their faces on me, that *I* s reign: NIH
6: 6 that *the beams* s not be fastened in the walls NIH
8:36 them the good way wherein they s walk, NIH
11:10 this thing, that *he* s not go after other gods: NIH
14: 2 which told me that I s be king over this NIH
21: 3 that I s give the inheritance of my fathers NIH
2Ki 3:27 he took his eldest son that s have reigned in NIH
4:43 What, s I set this before an hundred men? NIH
6:33 what s I wait for the LORD any longer? NIH
7:19 *if* the LORD s make windows in heaven, NIH
8:13 servant a dog, that he s do this great thing? NIH
11: 9 with them that s go out on the sabbath, and NIH
11:17 that *they* s be the LORD'S people; NIH
17:15 charged them, that *they* s not do like them. NIH
17:28 taught them how they s fear the LORD. NIH
18:35 that the LORD s deliver Jerusalem out of NIH
22:19 that *they* s become a desolation and a curse, NIH
1Ch 9:28 that they s bring them in and out by tale. NIH
1Ch 11:19 that *I* s do this *thing*: shall I drink the blood NIH
16:42 and cymbals for those that s make a sound, NIH
21:17 not on thy people, that *they* s be plagued. NIH
21:18 that David s go up, and set up an altar unto NIH
23:13 that he s sanctify the most holy *things*, he NIH
23:32 that they s keep the charge of the tabernacle NIH
25: 1 of Jeduthun, who s prophesy with harps, NIH
29:14 that we s be able to offer *so* willingly after NIH
2Ch 2: 6 who *am* I then, that I s build him a house, NIH
4:20 that they s burn after the manner before NIH
6:27 them the good way, wherein they s walk; NIH
15:13 the LORD God of Israel s be put to death, NIH
20:21 that s praise the beauty of holiness, as *they* NIH
23:16 that *they* s be the LORD'S people. NIH
23:19 that none *which was* unclean in any thing s NIH
25:13 that *they* s not go with him to battle, fell NIH
29:11 that *you* s minister unto him, and 1961
29:24 and the sin offering *s be made* for all Israel. NIH
30: 1 that *they* s come to the house of the LORD NIH
30: 5 that *they* s come to keep the passover unto NIH
32: 4 Why s the kings of Assyria come, and NIH
32:14 that your God s be able to deliver you out of NIH
Ezr 2:63 that they s not eat of the most holy *things* NIH
4:22 why s damage grow to the hurt of the kings? NIH
7:23 for why s there be wrath against the realm NIH
8:17 I told them what they s say unto Iddo, *and* NIH
8:17 that *they* s bring unto us ministers for NIH
9:14 S we again break thy commandments, and NIH
9:14 so that *there s be* no remnant nor escaping? NIH
10: 5 to swear that *they* s do according to this NIH
10: 7 that *they* s gather themselves together *unto* NIH
10: 8 all his substance s be forfeited, and NIH
Ne 2: 3 why s not my countenance be sad, when NIH
5:12 that *they* s do according to this promise. NIH
6: 3 why s the work cease, whilst I leave it, and NIH
6:11 I said, S such a man as I flee? and who *is* NIH
6:13 that I s be afraid, and do so, and sin, and NIH
7:65 that they s not eat of the most holy *things*, NIH
8:14 that the children of Israel s dwell in booths NIH
8:15 that they s publish and proclaim in all their NIH
9:12 to give them light in the way wherein they s NIH
9:15 promisedst them that *they* s go in to possess NIH
9:19 them light, and the way wherein they s go. NIH
9:23 their fathers, that *they* s go in to possess *it*. NIH
10:37 *that* we s bring the firstfruits of our dough, NIH
11:23 that a certain portion *s be* for the singers, NIH
13: 1 the Moabite s not come into NIH
13: 2 Balaam against them, that *he* s curse them: NIH
13:19 I commanded that the gates s be shut, and NIH
13:19 charged that they s not be opened till after NIH
13:19 *that* there s no burden be brought in on NIH
13:22 I commanded the Levites that they s 1961
13:22 *that* they s come *and* keep the gates, NIH
Est 1: 8 that *they* s do according to every man's NIH
1:22 that every man s bear rule in his own house, NIH
1:22 that it s be published according to NIH
2:10 for Mordecai had charged her that she s not NIH
2:11 how Esther did, and what s become of her. NIH
3:14 that *they* s be ready against that day. NIH
4: 8 to charge her that *she* s go in unto the king, NIH
8:13 that the Jews s be ready against that day to NIH
9:21 that they s keep the fourteenth day of 1961
9:22 that *they* s make them days of feasting and NIH
9:25 s return upon his own head, and that he and NIH
9:25 and his sons s be hanged on the gallows. NIH
9:27 themselves unto them, so as it s not fail, NIH
9:28 *that* these days *s be* remembered and NIH
9:28 *that* these days of Purim s not fail from NIH
Job 3:12 or why the breasts that I s suck? NIH
3:13 For now s I have lien *still* and been quiet, NIH
3:13 have lien *still* and been quiet, I s have slept: NIH
6:10 s I yet have comfort; yea, I would harden NIH
6:11 What *is* my strength, that I s hope? and NIH
6:11 what *is* mine end, that I s prolong my life? NIH
6:14 To him that is afflicted pity *s be shewed* NIH
8: 7 yet thy latter end s greatly increase. NIH
9: 2 of a truth: but how s man be just with God? NIH
9:32 as I *am*, *that* I s answer him, *and* we should NIH
9:32 *and* we s come together in judgment. NIH
10:19 I s have been as though I had not been; I NIH
10:19 I s have been carried from the womb to NIH
11: 2 S not the multitude of words be answered? NIH
11: 2 and s a man full of talk be justified? NIH
11: 3 S thy lies make men hold their peace? and NIH
13: 5 hold your peace, and it s be your wisdom. NIH
13: 9 *Is it* good that he s search you out? or as *one* NIH
15: 2 S a wise *man* utter vain knowledge, and NIH
15: 3 S he reason *with* unprofitable talk? or NIH
15:14 What *is* man, that he s be clean? and NIH
15:14 *is* born of a woman, that he s be righteous? NIH
16: 5 the moving of my lips s asswage *your grief*. NIH
19:28 ye s say, Why persecute we him? seeing NIH
21: 4 *it were so*, why s not my spirit be troubled? NIH
21:15 What *is* the Almighty, that we s serve him? NIH
21:15 what profit s we have, if we pray unto him? NIH
23: 7 so s I be delivered for ever from my judge. NIH
27: 5 God forbid that I s justify you: till I die I NIH
31: 1 mine eyes; why then s I think upon a maid? NIH
31:28 for I s have denied the God *that is* above. NIH
32: 7 Days s speak, and multitude of years should NIH
32: 7 and multitude of years s teach wisdom. NIH
32:13 Lest ye s say, We have found out wisdom: NIH
34: 6 S I lie against my right? my wound *is* NIH
34: 9 It profiteth a man nothing that he s delight NIH
34:10 far be it from God, *that he s do* wickedness; NIH
34:10 the Almighty, *that he s commit* iniquity. NIH
34:23 that *he* s enter into judgment with God. NIH
34:33 *S it be* according to thy mind? he will NIH
36:16 that which s be set on thy table *should be* NIH
36:16 that which should be set on thy table *s be* NIH
41:11 that I s repay *him? whatsoever is* under NIH
Ps 27: 3 Though a host s encamp against me, NIH
27: 3 though war s rise against me, in this *will* I NIH
30: 3 me alive, that I s not go down *to* the pit. NIH
38:16 *Hear me*, lest *otherwise* they s rejoice over NIH

Ps 49: 5 Wherefore s I fear in the days of evil, NIH
49: 9 That he s still live for ever, and not see NIH
69:22 and that which s have been for their welfare, NIH
73:15 I s offend against the generation of thy NIH
78: 5 that they s make them known to their NIH
78: 6 them, even the children which s be born; NIH
78: 6 who s arise and declare them to their NIH
79:10 Wherefore s the heathen say, Where is their NIH
81:14 I s soon have subdued their enemies, and NIH
81:15 The haters of the LORD s have submitted NIH
81:15 but their time s have endured for ever. NIH
81:16 He s have fed them also with the finest of NIH
81:16 with honey out of the rock s I have satisfied NIH
95:11 Unto whom I sware in my wrath that they s NIH
104: 5 the earth, that it s not be removed for ever. NIH
106:23 turn away his wrath, lest he s destroy them. NIH
115: 2 Wherefore s the heathen say, Where is now NIH
119:92 I s then have perished in mine affliction. NIH
139:18 If I s count them, they are moe in number NIH
143: 8 cause me to know the way wherein I s walk; NIH
Pr 8:29 that the waters s not pass his NIH
22: 6 Train up a child in the way he s go: and NIH
22:27 why s he take away thy bed from under NIH
Ecc 2: 3 which they s do under the heaven all NIH
2:18 I s leave it unto the man that shall be after NIH
2:24 than that he s eat and drink, and that he NIH
2:24 that he s make his soul enjoy good in his NIH
3:13 also that every man s eat and drink, and NIH
3:14 God doeth it, that men s fear before him. NIH
3:22 than that a man s rejoice in his own works; NIH
5: 6 wherefore s God be angry at thy voice, and NIH
7:14 to the end that man s find nothing after him. NIH
SS 1: 7 for why s I be as one that turneth aside by NIH
8: 1 when I s find thee without, I would kiss NIH
8: 1 I would kiss thee; yea, I s not be despised. NIH
8: 3 His left hand s be under my head, and NIH
8: 3 my head, and his right hand s embrace me. NIH
Isa 1: 5 Why s ye be stricken any more? ye will NIH
1: 9 we s have been as Sodom, and we should NIH
1: 9 and we s have been like unto Gomorrah. NIH
5: 2 he looked that it s bring forth grapes, and NIH
5: 4 when I looked that it s bring forth grapes, NIH
8:11 instructed me that I s not walk in the way of NIH
8:19 s not a people seek unto their God? for NIH
10:15 as if the rod s shake itself against them that NIH
10:15 as if the staff s lift up itself, as if it were no NIH
36:20 that the LORD s deliver Jerusalem out of NIH
41: 7 fastened it with nails, that it s not be moved. NIH
48:11 will I do it: for how s my name be polluted? NIH
48:19 his name s not have been cut off nor NIH
49:15 that she s not have compassion on the son of NIH
50: 4 that I s know how to speak a word in season NIH
51:14 that he s not die in the pit, nor that his bread NIH
51:14 not die in the pit, nor that his bread s fail. NIH
53: 2 there is no beauty that we s desire him. NIH
54: 9 waters of Noah s no more go over the earth; NIH
57: 6 meat offering. S I receive comfort in these? NIH
57:16 for the spirit s fail before me, and the souls NIH
63:13 in the wilderness, that they s not stumble? NIH
Jer 5:17 which thy sons and thy daughters s eat: NIH
20:18 that my days s be consumed with shame? NIH
23:22 they s have turned them from their evil way, NIH
25:29 my name, and s ye be utterly unpunished? NIH
26:24 that they s not give him into the hand of NIH
27:10 that I s drive you out, and ye should perish. NIH
27:10 that I should drive you out, and ye s perish. NIH
27:17 and live: wherefore s this city be laid waste? NIH
29:26 that ye s be officers in the house of NIH
32:31 that I s remove it from before my face, NIH
32:35 that they s do this abomination, to cause NIH
33:20 that there s not be day and night in their NIH
33:21 that he s not have a son to reign upon his NIH
33:24 that they s be no more a nation before them. NIH
34: 9 That every man s let his manservant, and NIH
34: 9 that none s serve himself of them, to wit, of NIH
34:10 heard that every one s let his manservant, NIH
34:10 that none s serve themselves of them any NIH
37:10 yet s they rise up every man in his tent, and NIH
37:21 Zedekiah the king commanded that they s NIH
37:21 that they s give him daily a piece of bread NIH
39:14 son of Shaphan, that he s carry him home: NIH
40:15 no man shall know it: wherefore s he slay NIH
40:15 which are gathered unto thee s be scattered, NIH
44:14 that they s return into the land of Judah, NIH
46:13 how Nebuchadrezzar king of Babylon s NIH
51:53 Though Babylon s mount up to heaven, and NIH
51:53 though she s fortify the height of her NIH
51:60 book all the evil that s come upon Babylon, NIH
La 1:10 whom thou didst command that they s not NIH
1:16 the comforter that s relieve my soul is far NIH
1:17 that his adversaries s be round about him: NIH
3:26 It is good that a man s both hope and NIH
3:44 a cloud, that our prayer s not pass through. NIH
4:12 the enemy s have entered into the gates of NIH
Eze 8: 6 that I s go far off from my sanctuary? NIH
13:19 to slay the souls that s not die, and to save NIH
13:19 and to save the souls alive that s not live, NIH
13:22 that he s not return from his wicked way, NIH
14: 3 their face: s I be inquired of at all by them? NIH
14:14 they s deliver but their own souls by their NIH
18:23 Have I any pleasure at all that the wicked s NIH
18:23 and not that he s return from his ways, and NIH
19: 9 that his voice s no more be heard upon NIH
20: 9 that it s not be polluted before the heathen, NIH
20:14 that it s not be polluted before the heathen, NIH
20:22 that it s not be polluted in the sight of NIH
20:25 and judgments whereby they s not live; NIH
21:10 s we then make mirth? it contemneth NIH
22:30 that s make up the hedge, and stand in NIH
22:30 me for the land, that I s not destroy it: NIH
24: 8 the top of a rock, that it s not be covered. NIH
33:10 we pine away in them, how s we then live? NIH
34: 2 s not the shepherds feed the flocks? NIH
Da 1: 3 that he s bring certain of the children of NIH
1:10 for why s he see your faces worse liking NIH
Da 1:16 of their meat, and the wine that they s drink; NIH
1:18 that the king had said he s bring them in, NIH
2:13 the decree went forth that the wise men s be NIH
2:18 his fellows s not perish with the rest of NIH
2:29 upon thy bed, what s come to pass hereafter: NIH
2:46 commanded that they s offer an oblation NIH
3:11 that he s be cast into the midst of a burning NIH
3:19 commanded that they s heat the furnace one NIH
5:15 that they s read this writing, and NIH
5:29 that he s be the third ruler in the kingdom. NIH
6: 1 which s be over the whole kingdom; NIH
6: 2 unto them, and the king s have no damage. NIH
6:23 commanded that they s take Daniel up out NIH
7:14 nations, and languages, s serve him: NIH
Hos 10: 3 the LORD; what then s a king do to us? NIH
10:10 It is in my desire that I s chastise them; and NIH
13:13 for he s not stay long in the place of NIH
Joel 2:17 that the heathen s rule over them: NIH
2:17 wherefore s they say among the people, NIH
Jnh 4:11 s not I spare Nineveh, that great city, NIH
Mic 6:16 that I s make thee a desolation, and NIH
Zep 3: 7 so their dwelling s not be cut off, NIH
Hag 1: 2 the time that the LORD'S house s be built. NIH
Zec 7: 3 S I weep in the fifth month, NIH
7: 7 S ye not hear the words which the LORD NIH
7:11 and stopped their ears, that they s not hear. NIH
7:12 lest they s hear the law, and the words NIH
8: 6 s it also be marvellous in my eyes? NIH
Mal 1:13 s I accept this of your hand? saith NIH
2: 7 For the priest's lips s keep knowledge, and NIH
2: 7 and they s seek the law at his mouth: NIH
Mt 2: 4 he demanded of them where Christ s be NIG
2:12 in a dream that they s not return to Herod, NIG
5:29 for thee that one of thy members s perish, NIG
5:29 not that thy whole body s be cast into hell. NIG
5:30 for thee that one of thy members s perish, NIG
5:30 not that thy whole body s be cast into hell. NIG
7:12 whatsoever ye would that men s do to you, NIG
11: 3 Art thou he that s come, or do we look for NIG
12:16 And charged them that they s not make him NIG
13:15 lest at any time they s see with their eyes, NIG
13:15 and s understand with their heart, and NIG
13:15 and s be converted, and I should heal them. NIG
13:15 and should be converted, and I s heal them. NIG
15:33 Whence s we have so much bread in NIG
16:11 that ye s beware of the leaven of NIG
16:20 Then charged he his disciples that they s tell NIG
17:27 Notwithstanding, lest we s offend them, NIG
18:14 that one of these little ones s perish. NIG
18:30 cast him into prison, till he s pay the debt. NIG
18:34 till he s pay all that was due unto him. NIG
19:13 that he s put his hands on them, and pray: NIG
20:10 they supposed that they s have received NIG
20:31 because they s hold their peace: NIG
24:22 And except those days s be shortened, NIG
24:22 be shortened, there s no flesh be saved: 302
25:27 at my coming I s have received mine own 302
26:35 said unto him, Though I s die with thee, 1163
27:20 elders persuaded the multitude that they s NIG
Mk 3: 9 that a small ship s wait on him because NIG
3: 9 of the multitude, lest they s throng him. NIG
3:12 And he straitly charged them that they s not NIG
3:14 that they s be with him, and that he might NIG
4:12 lest at any time they s be converted, and NIG
4:12 and their sins s be forgiven them. NIG
4:22 thing kept secret, but that it s come abroad. NIG
4:26 as if a man s cast seed into the ground, NIG
4:27 And s sleep, and rise night and day, and NIG
4:27 and day, and the seed s spring and grow up, NIG
5:43 And he charged them straitly that no man s NIG
5:43 commanded that something s be given her NIG
6: 8 And commanded them that they s take NIG
6:12 went out, and preached that men s repent. NIG
7:36 And he charged them that they s tell no NIG
8:30 And he charged them that they s tell no man NIG
9: 9 he charged them that they s tell no man NIG
9:10 what the rising from the dead s mean. NIG
9:18 I spake to thy disciples that they s cast him NIG
9:30 and he would not that any man s know it. NIG
9:34 among themselves, who s be the greatest. NIG
10:13 young children to him, that he s touch them: NIG
10:32 began to tell them what things s happen 3195
10:36 What would ye that I s do for you? NIG
10:48 And many charged him that he s hold his NIG
10:51 What wilt thou that I s do unto thee? NIG
11:16 And would not suffer that any man s carry NIG
12:19 that his brother s take his wife, and raise up NIG
13:20 shortened those days, no flesh s be saved: 302
14:31 If I s die with thee, I will not deny thee in 1163
15:11 that he s rather release Barabbas unto them. NIG
15:24 lots upon them, what every man s take. NIG
Lk 1:29 mind what manner of salutation this s be. NIG
1:43 that the mother of my Lord s come to me? NIG
1:57 Now Elisabeth's full time came that she s NIG
1:71 That we s be saved from our enemies, and NIG
2: 1 that all the world s be taxed. NIG
2: 6 the days were accomplished that she s be NIG
2:26 that he s not see death, before he had seen NIG
4:42 stayed him, that he s not depart from them. NIG
5: 7 other ship, that they s come and help them. NIG
6:31 And as ye would that men s do to you, NIG
7: 4 That he was worthy for whom he s do this: NIG
7:19 to Jesus, saying, Art thou he that s come? NIG
7:20 unto thee, saying, Art thou he that s come? NIG
8:12 their hearts, lest they s believe and be saved. NIG
8:56 he charged them that they s tell no man NIG
9:13 except we s go and buy meat for all this NIG
9:31 spake of his decease which he s accomplish 3195
9:46 among them, which of them s be greatest. NIG
9:51 when the time was come that he s be NIG
15:32 It was meet that we s make merry, and NIG
17: 2 than that he s offend one of these little ones. NIG
17: 6 be thou planted in the sea; and it s obey you. 302
17:20 when the kingdom of God s come, NIG
18:39 rebuked him, that he s hold his peace: NIG
Lk 19:11 they thought that the kingdom of God s 3195
19:27 which would not that I s reign over them, NIG
19:40 I tell you that, if these s hold their peace, NIG
20:10 that they s give him of the fruit of NIG
20:20 which s feign themselves just men, that they NIG
20:28 that his brother s take his wife, and raise up NIG
22:23 which of them it was that s do this thing. 3195
22:24 which of them s be accounted the greatest. NIG
23:24 And Pilate gave sentence that it s be as they NIG
24:16 But their eyes were holden that they s not NIG
24:21 But we trusted that it had been he which s 3195
24:47 remission of sins s be preached in his name NIG
Jn 1:31 but that he s be made manifest to Israel, NIG
2:25 And needed not that any s testify of man: NIG
3:15 That whosoever believeth in him s not NIG
3:16 that whosoever believeth in him s not NIG
3:20 to the light, lest his deeds s be reproved. NIG
5:23 That all men s honour the Son, even as they NIG
6:14 This is of a truth that prophet that s come NIG
6:39 that of all which he hath given me I s lose NIG
6:39 but s raise it up again at the last day. NIG
6:64 that believed not, and who s betray him. NIG
6:71 for he it was that s betray him, being one of 3195
7:23 that the law of Moses s not be broken; NIG
7:39 which they that believe on him s receive: 3195
8: 5 law commanded us, that such s be stoned: NIG
8:19 known me, ye s have known my Father also. 302
8:55 and if I s say, I know him not, I shall be a NIG
9: 3 that the works of God s be made manifest in NIG
9:22 he s be put out of the synagogue. NIG
9:41 unto them, If ye were blind, ye s have no sin: 302
11:27 Son of God, which s come into the world. NIG
11:37 have caused that even this man s not have NIG
11:50 that one man s die for the people, and NIG
11:51 he prophesied that Jesus s die for that 3195
11:52 that also he s gather together in one NIG
11:57 he s shew it, that they might take him. NIG
12: 4 Simon's son, which s betray him, 3195
12:23 is come, that the Son of man s be glorified. NIG
12:33 This he said, signifying what death he s die. 3195
12:40 that they s not see with their eyes, NIG
12:40 and be converted, and I s heal them. NIG
12:42 him, lest they s be put out of the synagogue: NIG
12:46 that whosoever believeth on me s not abide NIG
12:49 what I s say, and what I should speak. NIG
12:49 what I should say, and what I s speak. NIG
13: 1 he s depart out of this world unto the Father, NIG
13:11 For he knew who s betray him; therefore NIG
13:15 that ye s do as I have done to you. NIG
13:24 that he s ask who it should be of whom he NIG
13:24 that he should ask who it s be of whom he NIG
13:29 or that he s give something to the poor. NIG
14: 7 known me, ye s have known my Father also: 302
15:16 that you s go and bring forth fruit, and NIG
15:16 forth fruit, and that your fruit s remain: NIG
16: 1 I spoken unto you, that ye s not be offended. NIG
16:30 and needest not that any man s ask thee: NIG
17: 2 that he s give eternal life to as many as thou NIG
18: 4 knowing all things that s come upon him, NIG
18:14 that it was expedient that one man s die for NIG
18:28 into the judgment hall, lest they s be defiled; NIG
18:32 he spake, signifying what death he s die. 3195
18:36 that I s not be delivered to the Jews: NIG
18:37 that I s bear witness unto the truth. NIG
18:39 that I s release unto you one at the passover: NIG
19:31 that the bodies s not remain upon the cross NIG
19:36 were done, that the scripture s be fulfilled, NIG
21:19 signifying by what death he s glorify God. NIG
21:23 the brethren, that that disciple s not die: NIG
21:25 the which, if they s be written every one, NIG
21:25 not contain the books that s be written. NIG
Ac 1: 4 commanded them that they s not depart NIG
2:24 it was not possible that he s be holden of it. NIG
2:25 is on my right hand, that I s not be moved: NIG
2:47 to the church daily such as s be saved. NIG
3:18 that Christ s suffer, he hath so fulfilled. NIG
5:26 the people, lest they s have been stoned. NIG
5:28 Did not we straitly command you that you s NIG
5:40 beaten them, they commanded that they s NIG
6: 2 It is not reason that we s leave the word of NIG
7: 6 That his seed s sojourn in a strange land; NIG
7: 6 and that they s bring them into bondage, and NIG
7:44 that he s make it according to the fashion NIG
8:31 How can I, except some man s guide me? NIG
10:17 what this vision which he had seen s mean, NIG
10:28 God hath shewed me that I s not call any NIG
10:47 forbid water, that these s not be baptized, NIG
11:22 that he s go as far as Antioch. NIG
11:28 signified by the Spirit that there s be great 3195
12:19 and commanded that they s be put to death. NIG
13:28 yet desired they Pilate that he s be slain. NIG
13:46 It was necessary that the word of God s first NIG
14:15 preach unto you that ye s turn from these NIG
15: 2 s go up to Jerusalem unto the apostles and NIG
15: 7 that the Gentiles by my mouth s hear NIG
17:27 That they s seek the Lord, if haply they NIG
18:14 reason would that I s bear with you: NIG
19: 4 that they s believe on him which should NIG
19: 4 that they should believe on him which s NIG
19:27 of the great goddess Diana s be despised, NIG
19:27 and her magnificence s be destroyed, 3195
20:38 he spake, that they s see his face no more. 3195
21: 4 the Spirit, that he s not go up to Jerusalem. NIG
21:16 an old disciple, with whom we s lodge. NIG
21:26 until that an offering s be offered for every NIG
22:22 from the earth: for it is not fit that he s live. NIG
22:24 bade that he s be examined by scourging; NIG
22:29 from him which s have examined him: 3195
23:10 fearing lest Paul s have been pulled in NIG
23:27 of the Jews, and s have been killed of them: 3195
24:23 that he s forbid none of his acquaintance to NIG
24:26 He hoped also that money s have been NIG
25: 4 that Paul s be kept at Cesarea, and that he NIG
26: 8 Why s it be thought a thing incredible with NIG
26: 8 with you, that God s raise the dead? NIG

S

Ac 26:20 that they s repent and turn to God, and NIG
26:22 the prophets and Moses did say s come: 3195
26:23 That Christ s suffer, and that he should be NIG
26:23 that he s be the first that should rise from NIG
26:23 that he should be the first that s rise from NIG
26:23 and s shew light unto the people, and to 3195
27: 1 And when it was determined that we s sail NIG
27:17 fearing lest they s fall into the quicksands, NIG
27:20 lay on us, all hope that we s be saved was NIG
27:21 ye s have hearkened unto me, and not have 1163
27:29 Then fearing lest we s have fallen upon NIG
27:42 lest any of them s swim out, and escape. NIG
27:43 commanded that they which could swim s NIG
28: 6 Howbeit they looked when he s have 3195
28:27 lest they s see with their eyes, and hear with NIG
28:27 and s be converted, and I should heal them. NIG
28:27 and should be converted, and I s heal them. NIG
Ro 2:21 thou that preachest a man s not steal, NIG
2:22 Thou that sayest a man s not commit NIG
4:13 that he s be the heir of the world, NIG
6: 4 even so we also s walk in newness of life. NIG
6: 6 that henceforth we s not serve sin. NIG
6:12 that ye s obey it in the lusts thereof. NIG
7: 4 that ye s be married to another, even to him NIG
7: 4 that we s bring forth fruit unto God. NIG
7: 6 that we s serve in newness of spirit, and NIG
8:26 for we know not what we s pray for as we NIG
11: 8 eyes that they s not see, and ears that they NIG
11: 8 not see, and ears that they s not hear;) NIG
11:11 Have they stumbled that they s fall? NIG
11:25 that ye s be ignorant of this mystery, NIG
11:25 lest ye s be wise in your own conceits; NIG
15:16 That I s be the minister of Jesus Christ to NIG
15:20 lest I s build upon another man's NIG
1Co 1:15 Lest any s say that I had baptized in mine NIG
1:17 lest the cross of Christ s be made of none NIG
1:29 That no flesh s glory in his presence. NIG
2: 5 That your faith s not stand in the wisdom of NIG
4: 3 But with me it is a very small thing that I s NIG
5: 1 that one s have his father's wife. NIG
9:10 that he that ploweth s plow in hope; and 3784
9:10 that he that thresheth in hope s be partaker NIG
9:12 suffer all things, lest we s hinder the gospel NIG
9:14 which preach the gospel s live of the gospel. NIG
9:15 have I written these things, that it s be NIG
9:15 than that any man s make my glorying void. NIG
9:27 to others, I myself s be a castaway. NIG
10: 1 I would not that ye s be ignorant, NIG
10: 6 to the intent we s not lust after evil things, 1510
10:20 I would not that ye s have fellowship with NIG
11:31 would judge ourselves, we s not be judged. 302
11:32 that we s not be condemned with the world. NIG
12:25 That there s be no schism in the body; but NIG
12:25 that the members s have the same care one NIG
2Co 1: 9 that we s not trust in ourselves, but in God NIG
1:17 that with me there s be yea yea, and nay NIG
2: 3 I s have sorrow from them of whom I ought NIG
2: 4 not that you s be grieved, but that ye might NIG
2: 7 comfort him, lest perhaps such a one s be NIG
2:11 Lest Satan s get an advantage of us: for we NIG
4: 4 who is the image of God, s shine unto them. NIG
5:15 that they which live s not henceforth live NIG
8:20 that no man s blame us in this abundance NIG
9: 3 lest our boasting of you s be in vain in this NIG
9: 4 s be ashamed in this same confident NIG
10: 8 For though I s boast somewhat more of our NIG
10: 8 not for your destruction, I s not be ashamed: NIG
11: 3 your minds s be corrupted from NIG
12: 6 lest any man s think of me above that which NIG
12: 7 And lest I s be exalted above measure NIG
12: 7 buffet me, lest I s be exalted above measure. NIG
13: 7 not that we s appear approved, but that ye NIG
13: 7 but that ye s do that which is honest, NIG
13:10 lest being present I s use sharpness, NIG
Gal 1:10 pleased men, I s not be the servant of Christ. NIG
2: 2 lest by any means I s run, or had run, NIG
2: 9 that we s go unto the heathen, and they unto NIG
2:10 Only they would that we s remember NIG
3: 1 that you s not obey the truth, NIG
3:17 that it s make the promise of none effect. NIG
3:19 till the seed s come to whom the promise NIG
3:21 verily righteousness s have been by the law. 302
3:23 shut up unto the faith which s afterwards be NIG
5: 7 who did hinder you that ye s not obey NIG
6:12 only lest they s suffer persecution for NIG
6:14 But God forbid that I s glory, save in NIG
Eph 1: 4 that we s be holy and without blame before NIG
1:12 That we s be to the praise of his glory, NIG
2: 9 Not of works, lest any man s boast. NIG
2:10 which God hath before ordained that we s NIG
3: 6 That the Gentiles s be fellowheirs, and NIG
3: 8 that I s preach among the Gentiles NIG
5:27 or any such thing; but that it s be holy and NIG
Php 1:12 But I would ye s understand, brethren, NIG
2:10 That at the name of Jesus every knee s bow, NIG
2:11 And that every tongue s confess that Jesus NIG
2:27 me also, lest I s have sorrow upon sorrow. NIG
Col 1:19 For it pleased the Father that in him s all NIG
2: 4 lest any man s beguile you with enticing NIG
1Th 3: 3 That no man s be moved by these NIG
3: 4 we told you before that we s suffer 3195
4: 3 that ye s abstain from fornication: NIG
4: 4 That every one of you s know how to NIG
5: 4 that that day s overtake you as a thief. NIG
5:10 or sleep, we s live together with him. NIG
2Th 2:11 strong delusion, that they s believe a lie: NIG
3:10 that if any would not work, neither s he eat. NIG
1Ti 1:16 for a pattern to them which s hereafter NIG
Tit 2:12 and worldly lusts we s live soberly, NIG
3: 7 we s be made heirs according to the hope of NIG
Phm 1:14 that thy benefit s not be as it were of NIG
Heb 2: 1 lest at any time we s let them slip. NIG
2: 9 that he by the grace of God s taste death for NIG
3:18 And to whom sware he that they s not enter NIG
4: 1 any of you s seem to come short of it. NIG
Heb 7:11 priest s rise after the order of Melchisedec, NIG
8: 4 For if he were on earth, he s not be a priest, 302
8: 7 s no place have been sought for the second. 302
9:23 in the heavens s be purified with these; NIG
9:25 Nor yet that he s offer himself often, as NIG
10: 2 that the worshippers once purged s have had NIG
10: 4 blood of bulls and of goats s take away sins. NIG
11: 5 By faith Enoch was translated that he s not NIG
11: 8 which he s after receive for an inheritance, NIG
11:28 lest he that destroyed the firstborn s touch NIG
11:40 that they without us s not be made perfect. NIG
12:19 the word s not be spoken to them any more: NIG
Jas 1:18 that we s be a kind of firstfruits of his NIG
1Pe 1:10 who prophesied of the grace that s come NIG
1:11 and the glory that s follow. 3326+3778
2: 9 that ye s shew forth the praises of him who NIG
2:21 us an example, that ye s follow his steps: NIG
2:24 dead to sins, s live unto righteousness: NIG
3: 9 thereunto called, that ye s inherit a blessing. NIG
4: 2 That he no longer s live the rest of his time NIG
2Pe 2: 6 unto those that after s live ungodly; NIG
3: 9 not willing that any s perish, but that all NIG
3: 9 but that all s come to repentance. NIG
1Jn 3: 1 that we s be called the sons of God: NIG
3:11 the beginning, that we s love one another. NIG
3:23 That we s believe on the name of his Son NIG
4: 3 whereof you have heard that it s come; NIG
2Jn 1: 6 heard from the beginning, ye s walk in it. NIG
Jude 1: 3 exhort you that ye s earnestly contend for NIG
1:18 How that they told you there s be mockers NIG
1:18 who s walk after their own ungodly lusts. NIG
Rev 6: 4 the earth, and that they s kill one another: NIG
6:11 that they s rest yet for a little season, NIG
6:11 that s be killed as they were, should be 3195
6:11 that should be killed as they were, s be NIG
7: 1 that the wind s not blow on the earth, nor on NIG
8: 3 that he s offer it with the prayers of all NIG
9: 4 And it was commanded them that they s not NIG
9: 5 And to them it was given that they s not kill NIG
9: 5 but that they s be tormented five months: NIG
9:20 that they s not worship devils, and idols of NIG
10: 6 are therein, that there s be time no longer: NIG
10: 7 to sound, the mystery of God s be finished, NIG
11:18 that they s be judged, and that thou NIG
12: 6 that they s feed her there a thousand two NIG
13:14 that they s make an image to the beast, NIG
13:15 that the image of the beast s both speak, and NIG
13:15 worship the image of the beast s be killed. NIG
19: 8 And to her was granted that she s be arrayed NIG
19:15 that with it he s smite the nations: NIG
20: 3 that he s deceive the nations no more, NIG
20: 3 till the thousand years s be fulfilled: NIG

SHOULDER (38) [SHOULDERPIECES, SHOULDERS]

Ge 21:14 putting it on her s, and the child, and 7926
24:15 with her pitcher upon her s. 7926
24:45 came forth with her pitcher on her s; 7926
24:46 let down her pitcher from her s, and said, NIH
49:15 bowed his s to bear, and became a servant 7926
Ex 29:22 the fat that is upon them, and the right s; 7785
29:27 the s of the heave offering, which is waved, 7785
Lev 7:32 the right s shall ye give unto the priest for a 7785
7:33 the fat, shall have the right s for his part. 7785
7:34 the heave s have I taken of the children of 7785
8:25 two kidneys, and their fat, and the right s: 7785
8:26 put them on the fat, and upon the right s: 7785
9:21 the right s Aaron waved for a wave offering 7785
10:14 and heave s shall ye eat in a clean place; 7785
10:15 The heave s and the wave breast shall they 7785
Nu 6:19 the priest shall take the sodden s of the ram, 2220
6:20 with the wave breast and heave s: 7785
18:18 the wave breast and as the right s are thine. 7785
Dt 18: 3 and they shall give unto the priest the s, and 2220
Jos 4: 5 ye up every man of you a stone upon his s, 7926
Jdg 9:48 laid it on his s, and said unto the people that 7926
1Sa 9:24 the cook took up the s, and that which was 7785
Ne 9:29 withdrew the s, and hardened their neck, 3802
Job 31:22 Then let mine arm fall from my s blade, 7929
31:36 Surely I would take it upon my s, and 7926
Ps 81: 6 I removed his s from the burden: his hands 7926
Isa 9: 4 the staff of his s, the rod of his oppressor, 7926
9: 6 and the government shall be upon his s: and 7926
10:27 burden shall be taken away from off thy s, 7926
22:22 of the house of David will I lay upon his s; 7926
46: 7 They bear him upon the s, they carry him, 3802
Eze 12: 7 and I bare it upon my s in their sight. 3802
12:12 them shall bear upon his s in the twilight, 3802
24: 4 even every good piece, the thigh, and the s; 3802
29: 7 thou didst break, and rent all their s: 3802
29:18 was made bald, and every s was peeled: 3802
34:21 ye have thrust with side and with s, 3802
Zec 7:11 pulled away the s, and stopped their ears, 3802

SHOULDERPIECES (4) [PIECE, SHOULDER]

Ex 28: 7 It shall have the two s thereof joined at 3802
28:25 put them on the s of the ephod before it. 3802
39: 4 They made s for it, to couple it together: 3802
39:18 put them on the s of the ephod, before it. 3802

SHOULDERS (20) [SHOULDER]

Ge 9:23 laid it upon both their s, and 7926
Ex 12:34 bound up in their clothes upon their s. 7926
28:12 thou shalt put the two stones upon the s of 3802
28:12 the LORD upon his two s for a memorial. 3802
39: 7 he put them on the s of the ephod, that they 3802
Nu 7: 9 was that they should bear upon their s. 3802
Dt 33:12 day long, and he shall dwell between his s. 3802
Jdg 16: 3 bar and all, and put them upon his s, and 3802
1Sa 9: 2 from his s and upward he was higher than 7926
10:23 higher than any of the people from his s 7926
17: 6 his legs, and a target of brass between his s. 3802
1Ch 15:15 of God upon their s with the staves thereon, 3802
2Ch 35: 3 it shall not be a burden upon your s: 3802
Isa 11:14 they shall fly upon the s of the Philistines 3802
14:25 and his burden depart from off their s. 7926
30: 6 they will carry their riches upon the s of 3802
49:22 thy daughters shall be carried upon their s. 3802
Eze 12: 6 In their sight shalt thou bear it upon thy s, 3802
Mt 23: 4 to be borne, and lay them on men's s; 5606
Lk 15: 5 when he hath found it, he layeth it on his s, 5606

SHOULDEST (73) [SHOULD]

Ge 3:11 whereof I commanded thee that thou s not NIH
14:23 lest thou s say, I have made Abram rich: NIH
26:10 and thou s have brought guiltiness upon us. NIH
29:15 s thou therefore serve me for nought? NIH
Nu 11:12 I begotten them, that thou s say unto me, NIH
Dt 4:19 s be driven to worship them, and NIH
26:18 and that thou s keep all his commandments; NIH
29:12 That thou s enter into covenant with NIH
30:12 It is not in heaven, that thou s say, NIH
30:13 Neither is it beyond the sea, that thou s say, NIH
Jdg 11:23 his people Israel, and s thou possess it? NIH
Ru 2:10 that thou s take knowledge of me, seeing I NIH
1Sa 20: 8 for why s thou bring me to thy father? NIH
2Sa 9: 8 that thou s look upon such a dead dog as I NIH
1Ki 1:20 that thou s tell them who shall sit on NIH
2Ki 8:14 He told me that thou s surely recover. NIH
13:19 said, Thou s have smitten five or six times; NIH
14:10 for why s thou meddle to thy hurt, that thou NIH
14:10 that thou s fall, even thou, and Judah with NIH
19:25 that thou s be to lay waste fenced cities into NIH
1Ch 17: 7 that thou s be ruler over my people Israel: NIH
2Ch 19: 2 S thou help the ungodly, and love them that NIH
25:16 forbear; why s thou be smitten? Then NIH
25:19 why s thou meddle to thine hurt, that thou NIH
25:19 that thou s fall, even thou, and Judah with NIH
Job 7:17 What is man, that thou s magnify him? and NIH
7:17 and that thou s set thine heart upon him? NIH
7:18 that thou s visit him every morning, and NIH
10: 3 Is it good unto thee that thou s oppress, NIH
10: 3 that thou s despise the work of thine hands, NIH
38:20 That thou s take it to the bound thereof, and NIH
38:20 that thou s know the paths to the house NIH
Ps 50:16 that thou s take my covenant in thy mouth? NIH
130: 3 If thou, LORD, s mark iniquities, O Lord, NIH
Pr 5: 6 Lest thou s ponder the path of life, her ways NIH
25: 7 than that thou s be put lower in the presence NIH
27:22 Though thou s bray a fool in a mortar NIH
Ecc 5: 5 Better is it that thou s not vow, than that NIH
5: 5 not vow, than that thou s vow and not pay. NIH
7:16 over wise: why s thou destroy thyself? NIH
7:17 why s thou die before thy time? NIH
7:18 It is good that thou s take hold of this; yea, NIH
Isa 37:26 that thou s be to lay waste defenced cities NIH
48: 5 lest thou s say, Mine idol hath done them, NIH
48: 7 lest thou s say, Behold, I knew them. NIH
48:17 which leadeth thee by the way that thou s NIH
49: 6 It is a light thing that thou s be my servant NIH
51:12 that thou s be afraid of a man that shall die, NIH
Jer 14: 8 why s thou be as a stranger in the land, and NIH
14: 9 Why s thou be as a man astonied, as a NIH
29:26 that thou s put him in prison, and in NIH
49:16 though thou s make thy nest as high as NIH
Ob 1:12 thou s not have looked on the day of thy NIH
1:12 neither s thou have rejoiced over NIH
1:12 neither s thou have spoken proudly in NIH
1:13 Thou s not have entered into the gate of my NIH
1:13 thou s not have looked on their affliction in NIH
1:14 Neither s thou have stood in the crossway, NIH
1:14 neither s thou have delivered up those of his NIH
Mt 8: 8 I am not worthy that thou s come under my NIG
18:33 S not thou also have had compassion on 1163
Mk 10:35 we would that thou s do for us whatsoever NIG
Lk 7: 6 for I am not worthy that thou s enter under NIG
Jn 11:40 thou s see the glory of God? NIG
17:15 I pray not that thou s take them out of NIG
17:15 but that thou s keep them from the evil. NIG
Ac 13:47 that thou s be for salvation unto the ends of NIG
22:14 that thou s know his will, and see that Just NIG
22:14 Just One, and s hear the voice of his mouth. NIG
Tit 1: 5 that thou s set in order the things that are NIG
Phm 1:15 a season, that thou s receive him for ever; NIG
Rev 11:18 that thou s give reward unto thy servants NIG
11:18 and s destroy them which destroy the earth. NIG

SHOUT (36) [SHOUTED, SHOUTETH, SHOUTING, SHOUTINGS]

Ex 32:18 It is not the voice of them that s for 6030
Nu 23:21 and the s of a king is among them. 8643
Jos 6: 5 all the people shall s with a great shout; 7321
6: 5 all the people shall shout with a great s; 8643
6:10 saying, Ye shall not s, nor make any noise 7321
6:10 out of your mouth, until the day I bid you s; 7321
6:10 the day I bid you shout; then shall ye s. 7321
6:16 Joshua said unto the people, S; 7321
6:20 the people shouted with a great s, that 8643
1Sa 4: 5 all Israel shouted with a great s, so that 8643
4: 6 the Philistines heard the noise of the s, 8643
4: 6 What meaneth the noise of this great s in 8643
2Ch 13:15 the men of Judah gave a s: and as the men 7321
Ezr 3:11 all the people shouted with a great s, 8643
3:13 s of joy from the noise of the weeping of 8643
3:13 for the people shouted with a loud s, and 8643
Ps 5:11 let them ever s for joy, because 7442
32:11 s for joy, all ye that are upright in heart. 7442
35:27 Let them s for joy, and be glad, that favour 7442
47: 1 s unto God with the voice of triumph. 7321
47: 5 God is gone up with a s, the LORD with 8643
65:13 with corn; they s for joy, they also sing. 7321
132: 9 and let thy saints s for joy. 7442
132:16 and her saints shall s aloud for joy. 7442+7444
Isa 12: 6 Cry out and s, thou inhabitant of Zion: 7442
42:11 let them s from the top of the mountains. 6681
44:23 for the LORD hath done it: s, ye lower 7321
Jer 25:30 he shall give a s, as they that tread 1959+6030
31: 7 and s among the chief of the nations: 6670

S

Jer 50:15 **S** against her round about: she hath given 7321
51:14 and they shall lift up a **s** against thee. 1959
La 3: 8 Also when I cry and **s**, he shutteth out my 7768
Zep 3:14 **s**, O Israel; be glad and rejoice with all 7321
Zec 9: 9 of Zion; **s**, O daughter of Jerusalem: 7321
Ac 12:22 And the people **gave a s**, *saying, It is* *2019*
1Th 4:16 himself shall descend from heaven with a **s**, *2752*

SHOUTED (14) [SHOUT]
Ex 32:17 heard the noise of the people as they **s**, 7452
Lev 9:24 people saw, they **s**, and fell on their faces. 7442
Jos 6:20 So the people **s** when *the priests* blew with 7321
6:20 the people **s** *with* a great shout, that 7321
Jdg 15:14 unto Lehi, the Philistines **s** against him: 7321
1Sa 4: 5 all Israel **s** *with* a great shout, so that 7321
10:24 all the people **s**, and said, God save 7321
17:20 going forth to the fight, and **s** for the battle. 7321
17:52 and **s**, and pursued the Philistines, 7321
2Ch 13:15 as the men of Judah **s**, it came to pass, 7321
Ezr 3:11 all the people **s** *with* a great shout, 7321
3:12 **s aloud** for joy: 6963+7311+8643+871.1+3807.1
3:13 for the people **s** *with* a loud shout, and 7321
Job 38: 7 and all the sons of God **s for joy**? 7321

SHOUTETH (1) [SHOUT]
Ps 78:65 like a mighty *man* that **s** by reason of wine. 7442

SHOUTING (15) [SHOUT]
2Sa 6:15 brought up the ark of the LORD with **s**, 8643
1Ch 15:28 ark of the covenant of the LORD with **s**, 8643
2Ch 15:14 with **s**, and with trumpets, and with cornets. 8643
Job 39:25 the thunder of the captains, and the **s**. 8643
Pr 11:10 and when the wicked perish, *there is* **s**. 7440
Isa 16: 9 for the **s** for thy summer fruits and for thy 1959
16:10 shall be no singing, neither shall there be **s**: 7321
16:10 I have made *their vintage* **s** to cease. 1959
Jer 20:16 cry in the morning, and the **s** at noontide; 8643
48:33 none shall tread *with* **s**; *their* shouting *shall* 1959
48:33 *with* shouting; *their* **s** *shall be* no shouting. 1959
48:33 *with* shouting; *their* shouting *shall be* no **s**. 1959
Eze 21:22 in the slaughter, to lift up the voice with **s**, 8643
Am 1:14 palaces thereof, with **s** in the day of battle, 8643
2: 2 with **s**, *and* with the sound of the trumpet: 8643

SHOUTINGS (1) [SHOUT]
Zec 4: 7 bring forth the headstone *thereof with* **s**, 8663

SHOVEL (1) [SHOVELS]
Isa 30:24 which hath been winnowed with the **s** and 7371

SHOVELS (9) [SHOVEL]
Ex 27: 3 his **s**, and his basons, and his fleshhooks, 3257
38: 3 the **s**, and the basons, *and* the fleshhooks, 3257
Nu 4:14 the fleshhooks, and the **s**, and the basons, 3257
1Ki 7:40 made the lavers, and the **s**, and the basons. 3257
7:45 And the pots, and the **s**, and the basons: and 3257
2Ki 25:14 the **s**, and the snuffers, and the spoons, and 3257
2Ch 4:11 made the pots, and the **s**, and the basons. 3257
4:16 the **s**, and the fleshhooks, and all their 3257
Jer 52:18 the **s**, and the snuffers, and the bowls, and 3257

SHOW See FOREWARN; SHEW

SHOW SYMPATHY See BEMOAN; BEMOANED; BEMOANING

SHOW THE SAME FAVOR See REQUITE; REQUITED; REQUITING

SHOWER (4) [SHOWERS]
Eze 13:11 there shall be an overflowing **s**; and ye, 1653
13:13 there shall be an overflowing **s** in mine 1653
34:26 I will cause the **s** to come down in his 1653
Lk 12:54 straightway ye say, There cometh a **s**; *3655*

SHOWERS (9) [SHOWER]
Dt 32: 2 the tender herb, and as the **s** upon the grass: 7241
Job 24: 8 They are wet with the **s** of the mountains, 2230
Ps 65:10 thou makest it soft with **s**: thou blessest 7241
72: 6 the mown grass: as **s** that water the earth. 7241
Jer 3: 3 Therefore the **s** have been withholden, and 7241
14:22 or can the heavens give **s**? *art* not thou he, 7241
Eze 34:26 in his season; there shall be **s** of blessing. 1653
Mic 5: 7 as the **s** upon the grass, that tarrieth not for 7241
Zec 10: 1 give them **s** of rain, to every one grass in 4306

SHRANK (2)
Ge 32:32 of Israel eat not *of* the sinew which **s**, 5384
32:32 hollow of Jacob's thigh in the sinew that **s**. 5384

SHRED (1)
2Ki 4:39 came and **s** *them* into the pot of pottage: 6398

SHREWD See UNSAVOURY

SHRICH (1)
Isa 34:14 the **s owl** also shall rest there, and find for 3917

SHRINE PROSTITUTE See SODOMITE; SODOMITES

SHRINES (1)
Ac 19:24 which made silver **s** for Diana, *3485*

SHROWD (1)
Eze 31: 3 with a shadowing **s**, and of a high stature; 2793

SHRUBS (1)
Ge 21:15 and she cast the child under one of the **s**. 7880

SHUA (2) [SHUAH]
1Ch 2: 3 him of the daughter of **S** the Canaanitess. 7770
7:32 and Hotham, and **S** their sister. 7774

SHUAH (5) [SHUA]
Ge 25: 2 and Medan, and Midian, and Ishbak, and **S**. 7744
38: 2 of a certain Canaanite, whose name *was* **S**; 7770
38:12 in process of time the daughter of **S** Judah's 7770
1Ch 1:32 and Medan, and Midian, and Ishbak, and **S**. 7744
4:11 Chelub the brother of **S** begat Mehir, 7746

SHUAL (2) [HAZAR-SHUAL]
1Sa 13:17 that leadeth to Ophrah, unto the land of **S**: 7777
1Ch 7:36 and Harnepher, and **S**, and Beri, and Imrah, 7777

SHUBAEL (3)
1Ch 24:20 Levi *were these:* Of the sons of Amram; **S**: 7619
24:20 Shubael: of the sons of **S**; Jehdeiah. 7619
25:20 The thirteenth *to* **S**, *he*, his sons, and 7619

SHUHAM (1) [SHUHAMITES]
Nu 26:42 of **S**, the family of the Shuhamites. 7748

SHUHAMITES (2) [SHUHAM]
Nu 26:42 of Shuham, the family of the **S**. These *are* 7749
26:43 All the families of the **S**, according to those 7749

SHUHITE (5)
Job 2:11 Bildad the **S**, and Zophar the Naamathite: 7747
8: 1 Then answered Bildad the **S**, and said, 7747
18: 1 Then answered Bildad the **S**, and said, 7747
25: 1 Then answered Bildad the **S**, and said, 7747
42: 9 Eliphaz the Temanite and Bildad the **S** *and* 7747

SHULAMITE (2)
SS 6:13 Return, return, O **S**; return, return, that we 7759
6:13 What will ye see in the **S**? As it were 7759

SHULAMMITE See SHULAMITE

SHUMATHITES (1)
1Ch 2:53 the Puhites, and the **S**, and the Mishraites; 8126

SHUN (1) [SHUNNED]
2Ti 2:16 But **s** profane *and* vain babblings: for they *4026*

SHUNAMMITE (8)
1Ki 1: 3 found Abishag a **S**, and brought her to 7767
1:15 and Abishag the **S** ministered unto the king. 7767
2:17 that he give me Abishag the **S** to wife 7767
2:21 Let Abishag the **S** be given to Adonijah thy 7767
2:22 why dost thou ask Abishag the **S** for 7767
2Ki 4:12 he said to Gehazi his servant, Call this **S**. 7767
4:25 his servant, Behold, *yonder is* that **S**: 7767
4:36 he called Gehazi, and said, Call this **S**. 7767

SHUNEM (3)
Jos 19:18 was toward Jezreel, and Chesulloth, and **S**, 7766
1Sa 28: 4 and came and pitched in **S**: 7766
2Ki 4: 8 And it fell on a day, that Elisha passed to **S**, 7766

SHUNI (2) [SHUNITES]
Ge 46:16 **S**, and Ezbon, Eri, and Arodi, and Areli. 7764
Nu 26:15 of **S**, the family of the Shunites: 7764

SHUNITES (1) [SHUNI]
Nu 26:15 the Haggites: of Shuni, the family of the **S**: 7765

SHUNNED (1) [SHUN]
Ac 20:27 For I have not **s** to declare unto you all *5288*

SHUPHAM (1) [SHUPHAMITES]
Nu 26:39 Of **S**, the family of the Shuphamites: 8197

SHUPHAMITES (1) [SHUPHAM]
Nu 26:39 Of Shupham, the family of the **S**: 7781

SHUPPIM (3)
1Ch 7:12 **S** also, and Huppim, the children of Ir, *and* 8206
7:15 took to wife *the sister* of Huppim and **S**, 8206
26:16 To **S** and Hosah *the lot came forth* 8206

SHUR (6)
Ge 16: 7 by the fountain in the way to **S**. 7793
20: 1 dwelled between Kadesh and **S**, and 7793
25:18 they dwelt from Havilah unto **S**, that *is* 7793
Ex 15:22 and they went out into the wilderness of **S**; 7793
1Sa 15: 7 from Havilah *until* thou comest *to* **S**, 7793
27: 8 inhabitants of the land as thou goest to **S**, 7793

SHUSHAN (21)
Ne 1: 1 the twentieth year, as I was in **S** the palace, 7800
Est 1: 2 of his kingdom, which *was* in **S** the palace, 7800
1: 5 the people that were present in **S** the palace, 7800
2: 3 all the fair young virgins unto **S** the palace, 7800
2: 5 *Now* in **S** the palace there was a certain 7800
2: 8 were gathered together unto **S** the palace, 7800
3:15 and the decree was given in **S** the palace. 7800
3:15 to drink; but the city **S** was perplexed. 7800
4: 8 decree that was given at **S** to destroy them, 7800
4:16 together all the Jews that are present in **S**, 7800
8:14 and the decree was given at **S** the palace. 7800
8:15 and the city of **S** rejoiced and was glad. 7800
9: 6 In **S** the palace the Jews slew and 7800
9:11 in **S** the palace was brought before the king. 7800
9:12 destroyed five hundred men in **S** the palace, 7800
9:13 let it be granted to the Jews which *are* in **S** 7800
9:14 the decree was given at **S**; and they hanged 7800
9:15 For the Jews that *were* in **S** gathered 7800
9:15 and slew three hundred men at **S**; 7800
9:18 the Jews that *were* at **S** assembled together 7800
Da 8: 2 when I saw, that I *was* at **S** *in* the palace, 7800

SHUSHAN-EDUTH (1)
Ps 60: T To the chief Musician upon **S**, Michtam of 7802

SHUT (105) [SHUTTETH, SHUTTING]
Ge 7:16 commanded him: and the LORD **s** him in. 5462
19: 6 door unto them, and **s** the door after him, 5462
19:10 into the house to them, and **s** to the door. 5462
Ex 14: 3 in the land, the wilderness hath **s** them in. 5462
Lev 13: 4 the priest shall **s up** *him that hath* 5462
13: 5 the priest shall **s** him **up** seven days more: 5462
13:11 him unclean, *and* shall not **s** him **up**: 5462
13:21 then the priest shall **s** him **up** seven days: 5462
13:26 then the priest shall **s** him **up** seven days: 5462
13:31 the priest shall **s up** *him that hath* 5462
13:33 the priest shall **s up** *him that hath* the scall 5462
13:50 and **s up** *it that hath* the plague seven days: 5462
13:54 and he shall **s** it **up** seven days more: 5462
14:38 the house, and **s up** the house seven days: 5462
14:46 it is **s up** shall be unclean until the even. 5462
Nu 12:14 let her be **s** out from the camp seven days, 5462
12:15 Miriam was **s** out from the camp seven 5462
Dt 11:17 he **s up** the heaven, that there be no rain, 6113
15: 7 nor **s** thine hand from thy poor brother: 7092
32:30 sold them, and the LORD had **s** them **up**? 5462
32:36 is gone, and *there is* none **s up**, or left. 6113
Jos 2: 7 after them were gone out, they **s** the gate. 5462
6: 1 Jericho was **straitly s up** 5462+5462+2050.1
Jdg 3:23 **s** the doors of the parlour upon him, and 5462
9:51 **s** *it* to them, and gat them up to the top of 5462
1Sa 1: 5 but the LORD had **s up** her womb. 5462
1: 6 because the LORD had **s up** her womb. 5462
6:10 to the cart, and **s up** their calves at home: 3607
23: 7 for he is **s in**, by entering into a town that 5462
2Sa 20: 3 So they were **s up** unto the day of their 6887
1Ki 8:35 When heaven is **s up**, and there is no rain, 6113
14:10 *and him that is* **s up** and left in Israel, and 6113
21:21 and *him that is* **s up** and left in Israel, 6113
2Ki 4: 4 thou shalt **s** the door upon thee and 5462
4: 5 and **s** the door upon her and upon her sons, 5462
4:21 and **s** *the door* upon him, and went out. 5462
4:33 **s** the door upon them twain, and 5462
6:32 **s** the door, and hold him fast at the door: 5462
9: 8 and *him that is* **s up** and left in Israel: 6113
14:26 for *there was* not any **s up**, nor any left, 6113
17: 4 therefore the king of Assyria **s** him **up**, and 6113
2Ch 6:26 When the heaven is **s up**, and there is no 6113
7:13 If I **s up** heaven that there be no rain, or if I 6113
28:24 **s up** the doors of the house of the LORD, 5462
29: 7 Also they have **s up** the doors of the porch, 5462
Ne 6:10 the son of Mehetabeel, who *was* **s up**; 6113
6:10 and let us **s** the doors of the temple: 5462
7: 3 let them **s** the doors, and bar *them:* and 1479
13:19 I commanded that the gates should be **s**, 5462
Job 3:10 Because it **s** not **up** the doors of my 5462
11:10 **s up**, or gather together, then who can 5462
38: 8 Or *who* **s up** the sea with doors, when it 5526
41:15 *his* pride, **s up** *together as with* a close seal. 5462
Ps 31: 8 hast not **s** me **up** into the hand of 5462
69:15 and let not the pit **s** her mouth upon me. 332
77: 9 hath he in anger **s up** his tender mercies? 7092
88: 8 *I am* **s up**, and I cannot come forth. 3607
Ecc 12: 4 the doors shall be **s** in the streets, when 5462
SS 4:12 *my* spouse; a spring **s up**, a fountain sealed. 5274
Isa 6:10 and make their ears heavy, and **s** their eyes; 8173
22:22 so he shall open, and none shall **s**; and 5462
22:22 and he shall **s**, and none shall open. 5462
24:10 every house is **s up**, that no *man may* come 5462
24:22 shall be **s up** in the prison, and after many 5462
26:20 thy chambers, and **s** thy doors about thee: 5462
44:18 for he hath **s** their eyes, that *they* cannot 2902
45: 1 leaved gates; and the gates shall not be **s**; 5462
52:15 the kings shall **s** their mouths at him: 7092
60:11 they shall not be **s** day nor night; 5462
66: 9 bring forth, and **s** *the womb?* saith thy God. 6113
Jer 13:19 The cities of the south shall be **s up**, and 5462
20: 9 heart as a burning fire **s up** in my bones, 6113
32: 2 Jeremiah the prophet was **s up** in the court 3607
32: 3 For Zedekiah king of Judah had **s** him **up**, 3607
33: 1 while he was yet **s up** in the court of 6113
36: 5 commanded Baruch, saying, I *am* **s up**; 6113
39:15 while he was **s up** in the court of the prison, 6113
Eze 3:24 unto me, Go, **s** thyself within thine house. 5462
44: 1 which looketh *toward* the east; and it *was* **s**. 5462
44: 2 This gate shall be **s**, it shall not be opened, 5462
44: 2 hath entered in by it, therefore it shall be **s**. 5462
46: 1 the east shall be **s** the six working days; 5462
46: 2 but the gate shall not be **s** until the evening. 5462
46:12 after his going forth *one* shall **s** the gate. 5462
Da 6:22 hath **s** the lions' mouths, that they have not 5463
8:26 wherefore **s** thou **up** the vision; for *it shall* 5640
12: 4 **s up** the words, and seal the book, 5640
Mal 1:10 Who *is there* even among you that would **s** 5462
Mt 6: 6 thy closet, and when thou hast **s** thy door, *2808*
23:13 for ye **s up** the kingdom of heaven against *2808*
25:10 him to the marriage: and the door was **s**. *2808*
Lk 3:20 this above all, that he **s up** John in prison. *2623*
4:25 when the heaven was **s up** three years and *2808*
11: 7 the door is now **s**, and my children are with *2808*
13:25 and hath **s to** the door, and ye begin to stand *608*
Jn 20:19 when the doors were **s** where the disciples *2808*
20:26 *then* came Jesus, the doors being **s**, *2808*
Ac 5:23 The prison truly found we **s** with all safety, *2808*
21:30 the temple: and forthwith the doors were **s**. *2808*
26:10 and many of the saints did I **s up** in prison, *2623*
Gal 3:23 **s up** unto the faith which should afterwards *4788*
Rev 3: 8 thee an open door, and no *man* can **s** it: *2808*
11: 6 These have power to **s** heaven, that it rain *2808*
20: 3 him into the bottomless *pit*, and **s** him **up**, *2808*
21:25 And the gates of it shall not be **s** at all by *2808*

SHUTHALHITES (1) [SHUTHELAH]
Nu 26:35 of Shuthelah, the family of the **S**: 8364

SHUTHELAH (4) [SHUTHALHITES]
Nu 26:35 of **S**, the family of the Shuthalhites: 7803
26:36 these *are* the sons of **S**: of Eran, the family 7803
1Ch 7:20 **S**, and Bered his son, and Tahath his son, 7803

S

1Ch 7:21 his son, and S his son, and Ezer, and Elead, 7803

SHUTHELAHITE See SHUTHALHITES

SHUTTETH (8) [SHUT]
Job 12:14 it cannot be built *again:* he **s up** a man, and 5462
Pr 16:30 He **s** his eyes to devise froward things: 6095
17:28 he that **s** his lips *is esteemed a man* of 331
Isa 33:15 of blood, and **s** his eyes from seeing evil; 6105
La 3:8 when I cry and shout, he **s out** my prayer. 5640
1Jn 3:17 **s up** his bowels *of compassion* from him, *2808*
Rev 3:7 of David, he that openeth, and no *man* **s**; *2808*
3:7 *man* shutteth; and **s**, and no *man* openeth; *2808*

SHUTTING (1) [SHUT]
Jos 2:5 it came to pass *about the time* of **s** of 5462

SHUTTLE (1)
Job 7:6 My days are swifter than a **weaver's s**, and 708

SIA (1) [SIAHA]
Ne 7:47 the children of **S**, the children of Padon, 5517

SIAHA (1) [SIA]
Ezr 2:44 the children of **S**, the children of Padon, 5517

SIBBECAI (2) [SIBBECHAI]
1Ch 11:29 **S** the Hushathite, Ilai the Ahohite, 5444
27:11 for the eighth month *was* **S** the Hushathite, 5444

SIBBECHAI (2) [SIBBECAI]
2Sa 21:18 **S** the Hushathite slew Saph, which *was* of 5444
1Ch 20:4 at which time **S** the Hushathite slew Sippai, 5444

SIBBOLETH (1) [SHIBBOLETH]
Jdg 12:6 he said **S**: for he could not frame to 5451

SIBMAH (4)
Jos 13:19 **S**, and Zareth-shahar in the mount of 7643
Isa 16:8 of Heshbon languish, *and* the vine of **S**: 7643
16:9 with the weeping of Jazer the vine of **S**: 7643
Jer 48:32 O vine of **S**, I will weep for thee with 7643

SIBRAIM (1)
Eze 47:16 Hamath, Berothah, **S**, which *is* between 5453

SICHEM (1)
Ge 12:6 passed through the land unto the place of **S**, 7927

SICK (88) [SICKLY, SICKNESS, SICKNESSES]
Ge 48:1 that *one* told Joseph, Behold, thy father *is* **s**: 2470
Lev 15:33 of her that is **s** of her flowers, and of him 1739
1Sa 19:14 messengers to take David, she said, He *is* **s**. 2470
30:13 left me, because three days agone I **fell s**. 2470
2Sa 12:15 wife bare unto David, and it was **very s**. 605
13:2 *so* vexed, that he **fell s** for his sister Tamar; 2470
13:5 down on thy bed, and **make** thyself **s**: 2470
13:6 So Amnon lay down, and **made** himself **s**: 2470
1Ki 14:1 that time Abijah the son of Jeroboam **fell s**. 2470
14:5 ask a thing of thee for her son; for he *is* **s**: 2470
17:17 the woman, the mistress of the house, **fell s**; 2470
2Ki 1:2 chamber that *was* in Samaria, and was **s**: 2470
8:7 Ben-hadad the king of Syria was **s**; and 2470
8:29 son of Ahab in Jezreel, because he was **s**. 2470
13:14 Now Elisha was **fallen s** of his sickness 2470
20:1 In those days was Hezekiah **s** unto death. 2470
20:12 for he had heard that Hezekiah had been **s**. 2470
2Ch 22:6 son of Ahab at Jezreel, because he was **s**. 2470
32:24 In those days Hezekiah was **s** to the death, 2470
Ne 2:2 thy countenance sad, seeing thou *art* not **s**? 2470
Ps 35:13 *as for* me, when they were **s**, my clothing 2470
Pr 13:12 Hope deferred **maketh** the heart **s**: but 2470
23:35 stricken me, *shalt thou say, and* I was not **s**; 2470
SS 2:5 comfort me with apples: for I *am* **s** of love. 2470
5:8 that ye tell him, that I *am* **s** of love. 2470
Isa 1:5 the whole head *is* **s**, and the whole heart 2483
33:24 the inhabitant shall not say, I am **s**: 2470
38:1 In those days was Hezekiah **s** unto death. 2470
38:9 when he had been **s**, and was recovered of 2470
39:1 for he had heard that he had been **s**, and 2470
Jer 14:18 then behold **them that are s** with famine: 8463
Eze 34:4 neither have ye healed that which was **s**, 2470
34:16 and will strengthen that which was **s**: 2470
Da 8:27 I Daniel fainted, and was **s** *certain* days; 2470
Hos 7:5 have **made** *him* **s** *with* bottles of wine; 2470
Mic 6:13 Therefore also will I **make** *thee* **s** in 2470
Mal 1:8 if ye offer the lame and **s**, *is it* not evil? 2470
1:13 *which was* torn, and the lame, and the **s**; 2470
Mt 4:24 they brought unto him all **s people** *2192+2560*
8:6 my servant lieth at home **s of the palsy**, *3885*
8:14 his wife's mother laid, and **s of a fever**. *4445*
8:16 with *his* word, and healed all that were **s**: *2560*
9:2 they brought to him a **man s of the palsy**, *3885*
9:2 their faith said unto the **s of the palsy**; *3885*
9:6 (then saith he to the **s of the palsy**,) *3885*
9:12 not a physician, but they that are **s**. *2192+2560*
10:8 Heal the **s**, cleanse the lepers, raise the dead, *770*
14:14 toward them, and he healed their **s**. *732*
25:36 I was **s**, and ye visited me: I was in prison, *770*
25:39 Or when saw we thee **s**, *772*
25:43 **s**, and in prison, and ye visited me not. *772*
25:44 or **s**, or in prison, and did not minister unto *772*
Mk 1:30 But Simon's wife's mother lay **s of a fever**, *4445*
1:34 And he healed many *that were* **s** of *2192+2560*
2:3 bringing **one s of the palsy**, *which was* *3885*
2:4 the bed wherein the **s of the palsy** lay. *3885*
2:5 he said unto the **s of the palsy**, Son, *3885*
2:9 is it easier to say to the **s of the palsy**, *3885*
2:10 forgive sins, (he saith to the **s of the palsy**,) *3885*
2:17 need of *the* physician, but they that are **s**: *2560*
6:5 save that he laid *his* hands upon a few **s** *folk*, *732*
6:13 and anointed with oil many *that were* **s**, and *732*
6:55 to carry about in beds those that were **s**, *2560*
Mk 6:56 they laid the **s** in the streets, and *770*
16:18 they shall lay hands on the **s**, and they shall *732*
Lk 4:40 all they that had *any* **s** with divers diseases *770*
5:24 (he said unto the **s of the palsy**,) *3886*
5:31 not a physician; but they that are **s**. *2192+2560*
7:2 unto him, was **s**, and ready to die. *2192+2560*
7:10 found the servant whole that had been **s**. *770*
9:2 the kingdom of God, and to heal the **s**. *770*
10:9 And heal the **s** that are therein, *772*
Jn 4:46 whose son was **s** at Capernaum. *770*
11:1 Now a certain *man* was **s**, *named* Lazarus, *770*
11:2 with her hair, whose brother Lazarus was **s**.) *770*
11:3 Lord, behold, he whom thou lovest is **s**. *770*
11:6 When he had heard therefore that he was **s**, *770*
Ac 5:15 Insomuch that *they* brought forth the **s** into *772*
5:16 bringing **s** *folks*, and *them which were* vexed *772*
9:33 his bed eight years, and was **s of the palsy**. *3886*
9:37 pass in those days, that she was **s**, and died: *770*
19:12 body were brought unto the **s** handkerchiefs *770*
28:8 that the father of Publius lay **s of** a fever *4912*
Php 2:26 because that ye had heard that he had been **s**. *770*
2:27 For indeed he was **s** nigh unto death: but *770*
2Ti 4:20 but Trophimus have I left at Miletum **s**. *770*
Jas 5:14 Is any **s** among you? let him call for *770*
5:15 And the prayer of faith shall save the **s**, and *2577*

SICKLE (12)
Dt 16:9 *as thou* beginnest *to put* the **s** to the corn. 2770
23:25 thou shalt not move a **s** unto thy 2770
Jer 50:16 him that handleth the **s** in the time of 4038
Joel 3:13 Put ye in the **s**, for the harvest is ripe: 4038
Mk 4:29 immediately he putteth in the **s**, because *1407*
Rev 14:14 a golden crown, and in his hand a sharp **s**. *1407*
14:15 sat on the cloud, Thrust in thy **s**, and reap: *1407*
14:16 And he that sat on the cloud thrust in his **s** *1407*
14:17 is in heaven, he also having a sharp **s**. *1407*
14:18 with a loud cry to him that had the sharp **s**, *1407*
14:18 Thrust in thy sharp **s**, and gather *1407*
14:19 And the angel thrust in his **s** into the earth, *1407*

SICKLY (1) [SICK]
1Co 11:30 this cause many *are* weak and **s** among you, *732*

SICKNESS (20) [SICK]
Ex 23:25 I will take **s** away from the midst of thee. 4245
Lev 20:18 a man shall lie with a woman **having** her **s**, 1739
Dt 7:15 the LORD will take away from thee all **s**, 2483
28:61 Also every **s**, and every plague, which *is* 2483
1Ki 8:37 whatsoever plague, whatsoever **s** *there be;* 4245
17:17 his **s** was so sore, that there was no breath 2483
2Ki 13:14 Now Elisha was fallen sick of his **s** whereof 2483
2Ch 6:28 whatsoever sore or whatsoever **s** *there be:* 4245
21:15 thou *shalt* have great **s** by disease of thy 2483
21:15 until thy bowels fall out by reason of the **s** 2483
21:19 his bowels fell out by reason of his **s**: 2483
Ps 41:3 thou wilt make all his bed in his **s**. 2483
Ecc 5:17 *he hath* much sorrow and wrath with his **s**. 2483
Isa 38:9 had been sick, and was recovered of his **s**: 2483
38:12 he will cut me off with **pining s**: from day 1803
Hos 5:13 When Ephraim saw his **s**, and Judah *saw* 2483
Mt 4:23 and healing all *manner of* **s** and all *manner* *3554*
9:35 and healing every **s** and every disease *3554*
10:1 and to heal all *manner of* **s** and all *manner* *3554*
Jn 11:4 This **s** is not unto death, but for the glory of *769*

SICKNESSES (4) [SICK]
Dt 28:59 and sore **s**, and of long continuance. 2483
29:22 the **s** which the LORD hath laid upon it; 8463
Mt 8:17 took our infirmities, and bare our **s**. *3554*
Mk 3:15 And to have power to heal **s**, and to cast out *3554*

SIDDIM (3)
Ge 14:3 these were joined together in the vale of **S**, 7708
14:8 joined battle with them in the vale of **S**; 7708
14:10 the vale of **S** *was* full of slimepits; and 7708

SIDE (444) [ASIDE, BACKSIDE, SIDES, WAYSIDE]
Ge 6:16 the door of the ark shalt thou set in the **s** 6654
38:21 *is* the harlot, that *was* openly by the **way s**? 1870
Ex 2:5 her maidens walked along **by** the river's **s**; 3027
12:7 strike *it* on the two **s posts** and on the upper 4201
12:22 the two **s posts** with the blood that *is* in 4201
12:23 on the two **s posts**, the LORD will pass 4201
17:12 the one on the **one s**, and the other on 2088
17:12 the one side, and the other on the **other s**; 2088
25:12 two rings *shall be* in the one **s** of it, and 6763
25:12 side of it, and two rings in the other **s** of it. 6763
25:32 branches of the candlestick out of the one **s**, 6654
25:32 of the candlestick out of the other **s**: 6654
26:13 a cubit on the one **s**, and a cubit on 2088
26:13 a cubit on the **other s** of that which 2088
26:13 over the sides of the tabernacle on **this s** 2088
26:13 of the tabernacle on this side and on **that s**, 2088
26:18 twenty boards on the south **s** southward. 6285
26:20 for the second **s** of the tabernacle on 6763
26:20 on the north **s** *there shall be* twenty boards: 6285
26:26 five for the boards of the one **s** of 6763
26:27 five bars for the boards of the other **s** of 6763
26:27 five bars for the boards of the **s** of 6763
26:35 on the **s** of the tabernacle toward the south: 6763
26:35 and thou shalt put the table on the north **s**. 6763
27:9 for the south **s** southward *there shall be* 6285
27:9 linen of an hundred cubits long for one **s**: 6285
27:11 likewise for the north **s** in length *there shall* 6285
27:12 *for* the breadth of the court on the west **s** 6285
27:13 the breadth of the court on the east **s** 6285
27:14 The hangings of *one* **s** *of the gate shall be* 3802
27:15 on the other **s** *shall be* hangings, 3802
28:26 which *is* in the **s** of the ephod inward. 5676
32:15 **on the one s** and on the other *were* they 2088
32:26 and said, Who *is* **on** the LORD'S **s**? 3807.1
32:27 Put every man his sword by his **s**, *and* go in 3409
36:11 likewise he made in the uttermost **s** of 8193
36:23 twenty boards for the south **s** southward: 6285
Ex 36:25 for the other **s** of the tabernacle, *which is* 6763
36:31 five for the boards of the one **s** of 6763
36:32 five bars for the boards of the other **s** of 6763
37:3 even two rings upon the one **s** of it, and 6763
37:3 of it, and two rings upon the other **s** of it. 6763
37:8 One cherub on the end on **this s**, and 2088
37:8 another cherub on the *other* end on **that s**: 2088
37:18 of the candlestick out of the one **s** thereof, 6654
37:18 of the candlestick out of the other **s** thereof: 6654
38:9 on the south **s** southward the hangings of 6285
38:11 for the north **s** *the hangings were* an 6285
38:12 for the west **s** *were* hangings of fifty cubits, 6285
38:13 And for the east **s** eastward fifty cubits. 6285
38:14 The hangings of the *one* **s** *of the gate were* 3802
38:15 for the other **s** of the court gate, on this 3802
39:19 which *was* on the **s** of the ephod inward. 5676
40:22 upon the **s** of the tabernacle northward, 3409
40:24 on the **s** of the tabernacle southward. 3409
Lev 1:11 he shall kill it on the **s** of the altar 3409
1:15 the blood thereof shall be wrung out at the **s** 7023
5:9 of the sin offering upon the **s** of the altar; 7023
Nu 2:3 on the **east s** toward the rising of the sun 6924
2:10 On the **south s** *shall be* the standard of 8486
2:18 On the **west s** *shall be* the standard of 3220
2:25 Dan *shall be* on the **north s** by their armies: 6828
3:29 pitch on the **s** of the tabernacle southward. 3409
3:35 *these* shall pitch on the **s** of the tabernacle 3409
10:6 the camps that lie on the **south s** shall take 8486
11:31 as it were a day's journey **on this s**, and 3541
11:31 as it were a day's journey **on the other s**, 3541
16:27 of Korah, Dathan, and Abiram, on **every s**: 5439
21:13 and pitched on the *other* **s** of Arnon, 5676
22:1 pitched in the plains of Moab on *this* **s** 5676
22:24 a wall *being* on **this s**, and a wall on that 2088
22:24 *being* on this side, and a wall on **that s**. 2088
24:6 they spread forth, as gardens by the **river s**, 5104
32:19 not inherit with them on *yonder* **s** Jordan, 5676
32:19 our inheritance is fallen to us on *this* **s** 5676
32:32 inheritance on *this* **s** Jordan *may be* ours. 5676
34:11 Shepham *to* Riblah, on the **east s** of Ain; 6924
34:11 shall reach unto the **s** of the sea of 3802
34:15 on *this* **s** Jordan *near* Jericho eastward, 5676
35:5 the city *on* the east **s** two thousand cubits, 6285
35:5 *on* the south **s** two thousand cubits, and 6285
35:5 *on* the west **s** two thousand cubits, and 6285
35:5 and *on* the north **s** two thousand cubits; 6285
35:14 Ye shall give three cities on *this* **s** Jordan, 5676
Dt 1:1 all Israel on *this* **s** Jordan in the wilderness, 5676
1:5 On *this* **s** Jordan, in the land of Moab, 5676
1:7 the vale, and in the south, and by the sea **s**, 2348
3:8 Amorites the land that *was* on *this* **s** Jordan, 5676
4:32 *ask* from the one **s** of heaven unto the other, 7097
4:41 Moses severed three cities on *this* **s** Jordan 5676
4:46 On *this* **s** Jordan, in the valley over against 5676
4:47 which *were* on *this* **s** Jordan *toward* 5676
4:49 all the plain on *this* **s** Jordan eastward, even 5676
11:30 *Are* they not on the *other* **s** Jordan, by 5676
31:26 put it in the **s** of the ark of the covenant of 6654
Jos 1:14 which Moses gave you on *this* **s** Jordan; 5676
1:15 you on *this* **s** Jordan *toward* the sunrising. 5676
2:10 that *were* on the *other* **s** Jordan, Sihon and 5676
5:1 which *were* on the **s** of Jordan westward, 5676
7:2 on the **east s** of Beth-el, and spake unto 6924
7:7 and dwelt on the *other* **s** Jordan! 5676
8:9 and Ai, on the **west s** of Ai: 3220
8:11 the city, and pitched on the **north s** of Ai: 6828
8:12 and Ai, on the **west s** of the city. 3220
8:22 some **on** this **s**, and some on that side: 4480
8:22 some on this side, and some **on** that **s**: 4480
8:33 stood **on** this **s** the ark and on that side 4480
8:33 and on **that s** before the priests the Levites, 2088
9:1 when all the kings which *were* on *this* **s** 5676
12:1 possessed their land on the *other* **s** Jordan 5676
12:7 the children of Israel smote on *this* **s** Jordan 5676
13:27 Cinnereth on the *other* **s** Jordan eastward. 5676
13:32 on the *other* **s** Jordan, *by* Jericho, eastward. 5676
14:3 and a half tribe on the *other* **s** Jordan: 5676
15:3 it went out to the **south s** to 5045
15:3 ascended up on the **south s** unto 5045
15:7 which *is* on the **south s** of the river: 5045
15:8 of Hinnom unto the south **s** of the Jebusite; 3802
15:10 passed along unto the **s** of mount Jearim, 3802
15:10 on the **north s**, and went down *to* 6828+1886.5
15:11 the border went out unto the **s** of Ekron 3802
16:5 on the **east s** was Ataroth-addar, 4217
16:6 the sea *to* Michmethah on the **north s**; 6828
17:5 which *were* on the *other* **s** Jordan; 5676
17:9 also *was* on the **north s** of the river, 6828
18:12 their border on the north **s** was from 6285
18:12 the border went up to the **s** of Jericho on 3802
18:12 up to the side of Jericho on the **north s**, 6828
18:13 to the **s** of Luz, which *is* Beth-el, 3802
18:13 near the hill that *lieth* on the **south s** of 5045
18:16 to the **s** of Jebusi on the south, and 3802
18:18 passed along toward the **s** over against 3802
18:19 the border passed along to the **s** of 3802
18:20 Jordan was the border of it on the east **s**. 6285
19:14 the border compasseth it on the **north s** *to* 6828
19:27 toward the **north s** *of* Beth-emek, 6828
19:34 and reacheth to Zebulun on the **south s**, and 5045
19:34 reacheth to Asher on the west **s**, and NIH
20:8 on the *other* **s** Jordan *by* Jericho eastward, 5676
22:4 the LORD gave you on the *other* **s** Jordan. 5676
22:7 their brethren on *this* **s** Jordan westward. 5676
24:2 Your fathers dwelt on the *other* **s** of 5676
24:3 Abraham from the *other* **s** of the flood, 5676
24:8 which dwelt on the *other* **s** Jordan; 5676
24:14 fathers served on the *other* **s** of the flood, 5676
24:15 served that *were* on the *other* **s** of the flood, 5676
24:30 on the **north s** of the hill of Gaash. 6828
Jdg 2:9 on the **north s** of the hill Gaash. 6828
7:1 the Midianites were on the **north s** of them, 6828
7:12 as the sand by the sea **s** for multitude. 8193
7:18 blow ye the trumpets also **on every s** of all 5439
7:25 and Zeeb to Gideon on the *other* **s** Jordan. 5676

Jdg 8:34 of all their enemies **on every s**: 4480+5439
10: 8 *other* s Jordan in the land of the Amorites, 5676
11:18 by the **east s** of the land of Moab, 4217+8121
11:18 pitched on the *other* s of Arnon, but 5676
19: 1 sojourning on the s of mount Ephraim, 3411
19:18 toward the s of mount Ephraim; 3411
21:19 which *is* on the **north s** of Beth-el, 4480+6828
21:19 on **the east s** of the highway 4217+8121+1886.1
1Sa 4:18 off the seat backward by the s of the gate, 3027
6: 8 in a coffer by the s thereof; 6654
12:11 out of the hand of your enemies on **every s**, 5439
14: 1 Philistines' garrison, that *is* on the other s. 5676
14: 4 *there was* a sharp rock on the one s, and 5676
14: 4 one side, and a sharp rock on the other s: 5676
14:40 Be ye on one s, and I and Jonathan my son 5676
14:40 and Jonathan my son will be on the other s. 5676
14:47 fought against all his enemies **on every s**, 5439
17: 3 stood on a mountain on the **one s**, 2088
17: 3 Israel stood on a mountain on the **other s**: 2088
20:20 I will shoot three arrows on the s *thereof,* as 6654
20:21 Behold, the arrows *are* **on this s** of thee, 2008
20:25 Abner sat by Saul's s, and David's place 6654
23:26 Saul went on this s of the mountain, and 6654
23:26 and his men on that s of the mountain: 6654
26:13 David went over *to* the *other* s, and 5676
31: 7 Israel that *were* on the *other* s of the valley, 5676
31: 7 *they* that *were* on the *other* s Jordan, 5676
2Sa 2:13 the one on the **one s** of the pool, and 2088+4480
2:13 the other on the **other s** of the pool. 2088+4480
2:16 and *thrust* his sword in his fellow's s; 6654
13:34 people by the way of the hill s behind him. 6654
16:13 Shimei went along on the hill's s over 6763
18: 4 the king stood by the gate s, and all 3027
24: 5 *on* the **right s** of the city that *lieth* in 3225
1Ki 4:24 over all *the region* on *this* s the river, 5676
4:24 over all the kings on *this* s the river: 5676
5: 3 the wars which were **about him on every s**, 5437
5: 4 my God hath given me rest on **every s**, 5439
6: 8 chamber *was* in the right s of the house: 3802
6:31 *and* **s posts** *were* a fifth *part of the wall.* 4201
7: 7 *it was* covered with cedar **from one s of** 4480
7:30 at the s of every addition. 5676
7:39 he put five bases on the right s of the house, 3802
7:39 and five on the left s of the house: 3802
7:39 he set the sea on the right s of the house 3802
7:49 five on the **right s**, and five on the left, 3225
10:19 **on either s** on 2088+2088+4480+4480+2050.1
10:20 twelve lions stood there on **the one s** and 2088
2Ki 3:22 water **on the other s** *as* red as blood: 4480+5048
9:32 to the window, and said, Who *is* **on** my s? 854
12: 9 on the **right s** as one cometh *into* the house 3225
16:14 and put it on the north s of the altar. 3409
1Ch 4:39 *even* unto the east *s* of the valley, to seek NIH
6:78 on the *other* s Jordan *by* Jericho, on the east 5676
6:78 Jordan *by* Jericho, on the east *s* of Jordan, NIH
12:18 *we,* David, and on thy s, thou son of Jesse: 5973
12:37 on the *other* s of Jordan, of the Reubenites, 5676
22:18 he *not* given you rest **on every s**? 4480+5439
26:30 officers among them of Israel on *this* s 5676
2Ch 4: 8 five on the **right s**, and five on the left. 3225
4:10 he set the sea on the right s of the east end, 3802
8:17 to Eloth, at the sea s in the land of Edom. 8193
9:18 stays **on each s** 2088+2088+4480+4480+2050.1
9:19 twelve lions stood there on the **one s** 2088+4480
11:12 having Judah and Benjamin **on** his s. 3807.1
14: 7 and he hath given us rest **on every s**. 4480+5439
20: 2 thee from beyond the sea on this s Syria; NIH
23:10 from the right s of the temple to the left 3802
23:10 of the temple to the left s of the temple, 3802
32:22 and guided them **on every s**. 4480+5439
32:30 brought it straight down to the west *s* of NIH
33:14 on the west *s* of Gihon, in the valley, NIH
Ezr 4:10 the rest *that are on this* s the river, and 5675
4:11 Thy servants the men *on this* s the river, 5675
4:16 shalt have no portion on *this* s the river. 5675
5: 3 governor on *this* s the river, and 5675
5: 6 governor on *this* s the river, and 5675
5: 6 which *were* on *this* s the river, sent unto 5675
6:13 Tatnai, governor on *this* s the river, 5675
8:36 and *to* the governors on *this* s the river: 5676
Ne 3: 7 unto the throne of the governor on *this* s 5676
4:18 every one had his sword girded by his s, 4975
Job 1:10 about all that he hath **on every s**? 4480+5439
18:11 Terrors shall make him afraid **on every s**, 5439
18:12 and destruction *shall be* ready at his s. 6763
19:10 He hath destroyed me **on every s**, and I am 5439
Ps 12: 8 The wicked walk **on every s**, when 5439
31:13 fear *was* **on every s**: while they took 4480+5439
65:12 and the little hills rejoice **on every s**. 2296
71:21 my greatness, and comfort me **on every s**. 5437
91: 7 A thousand shall fall at thy s, and 6654
118: 6 The LORD *is* **on** my s; I will not fear: 3807.1
124: 1 not *been* the LORD who was **on** our s, 3807.1
124: 2 not *been* the LORD who was **on** our s, 3807.1
140: 5 they have spread a net by the **way s**; 3027+4570
Ecc 4: 1 on the s of their oppressors *there was* 3027
Isa 60: 4 and thy daughters shall be nursed at *thy* s. 6654
Jer 6:25 of the enemy *and* fear *is* **on every s**. 4480+5439
20:10 defaming of many, fear **on every s**. 4480+5439
49:29 cry unto them, Fear *is* **on every s**. 4480+5439
52:23 were ninety and six pomegranates on a s; 7307
Eze 1:10 a man, and the face of a lion, on the **right s**: 3225
1:10 they four had the face of an ox on the **left s**, 8040
1:23 which covered on this *s*, and every one had NIH
1:23 which covered on that *s*, their bodies. NIH
4: 4 Lie thou also upon thy left s, and lay 6654
4: 6 lie again on thy right s, and thou shalt bear 6654
4: 8 thou shalt not turn thee from one s to 6654
4: 9 of the days that thou shalt lie upon thy s, 6654
9: 2 *with* linen, with a writer's inkhorn by his s: 4975
9: 3 which *had* the writer's inkhorn by his s; 4975
9:11 which *had* the inkhorn by his s, reported 4975
10: 3 Now the cherubims stood on the **right** s of 3225
11:23 mountain which *is* on the **east s** of the city. 6924
16:33 thee **on every s** for thy whoredom. 4480+5439
Eze 19: 8 the nations set against him **on every s** from 5439
23:22 bring them against thee **on every s**; 4480+5439
25: 9 I *will* open the s of Moab from the cities, 3802
28:23 by the sword upon her **on every s**; 4480+5439
34:21 Because ye have thrust with s and 6654
36: 3 and swallowed you up **on every s**, 4480+5439
37:21 will gather them **on every s**, and 4480+5439
39:17 gather yourselves **on every s** to my 4480+5439
40:10 of the gate eastward *were* three on **this s**, 6311
40:10 *were* three on this side, and three on **that s**; 6311
40:10 and the posts had one measure on **this s** and 6311
40:10 had one measure on this side and on **that s**. 6311
40:12 the little chambers *was* one cubit *on this s*, NIH
40:12 and the space *was* one cubit on **that s**: 6311
40:12 the little chambers *were* six cubits on **this s**, 6311
40:12 cubits on this side, and six cubits on **that s**. 6311
40:18 the pavement by the s of the gates over 3802
40:21 little chambers thereof *were* three on **this s** 6311
40:21 *were* three on this side and three on **that s**; 6311
40:26 one on **this s**, and another on that side, 6311
40:26 one on this side, and another on **that s**, 6311
40:34 posts thereof, on **this s**, and on that side: 6311
40:34 posts thereof, on this side, and on **that s**: 6311
40:37 posts thereof, on **this s**, and on that side: 6311
40:37 posts thereof, on this side, and on **that s**: 6311
40:39 porch of the gate *were* two tables on **this s**, 6311
40:39 two tables on **that s**, to slay thereon 6311
40:40 at the s without, as one goeth up to 3802
40:40 on the other s, which *was* at the porch of 3802
40:41 Four tables *were* on **this s**, and four tables 6311
40:41 four tables on **that** side, by the side of 6311
40:41 four tables on that side, by the s of the gate; 3802
40:44 which *was* at the s of the north gate; 3802
40:44 one at the s of the east gate *having* 3802
40:48 five cubits on **this s**, and five cubits on that 6311
40:48 on this side, and five cubits on **that s**: 6311
40:48 of the gate *was* three cubits on **this s**, 6311
40:48 on this side, and three cubits on **that s**. 6311
40:49 one on **this s**, and another on that side. 6311
40:49 one on this side, and another on **that s**. 6311
41: 1 six cubits broad on the **one s**, and six cubits 6311
41: 1 and six cubits broad on the **other s**, 6311
41: 2 of the door *were* five cubits on the **one s**, 6311
41: 2 the one side, and five cubits on the **other s**: 6311
41: 5 the breadth of *every* **s chamber**, 6763
41: 5 round about the house **on every s**. 5439
41: 6 the **s chambers** *were* three, one over 6763
41: 6 the house for the **s chambers** round about, 6763
41: 7 about still upward to the **s chambers**: 6763
41: 8 the foundations of the **s chambers** *were* a 6763
41: 9 which *was* for the **s chamber** without, *was* 6763
41: 9 place of the **s chambers** that *were* within. 6763
41:10 round about the house **on every s**. 5439+5439
41:11 the doors of the **s chambers** *were* toward 6763
41:15 the galleries thereof on the **one s** and on 6311
41:15 thereof on the one side and on the **other s**, 6311
41:19 man *was* toward the palm tree on the **one s**, 6311
41:19 lion toward the palm tree on the **other s**: 6311
41:26 palm trees on the **one s** and on the other 6311
41:26 trees on the one side and on the **other s**, 6311
41:26 *upon* the **s chambers** of the house, and 6763
42: 9 these chambers *was* the entry on the **east s**, 6921
42:16 He measured the east s with the measuring 7307
42:17 He measured the north s, five hundred 7307
42:18 He measured the south s, five hundred 7307
42:19 He turned about to the west s, *and* 7307
45: 7 for the prince on the **one s** 2088
45: 7 on the **other s** of the oblation of the holy 2088
45: 7 from the west s westward, and from 6285
45: 7 and from the east s eastward: 6285
46:19 the entry, which *was* at the s of the gate, 3802
47: 1 from under from the right s of the house, 3802
47: 1 side of the house, at the south *s* of the altar. NIH
47: 2 behold, there ran out waters on the right s. 3802
47: 7 the river *were* very many trees on the **one s** 2088
47:12 on **this s** and on that side, shall grow all 2088
47:12 on this side and on **that s**, shall grow all 2088
47:15 *be* the border of the land toward the north s, 6285
47:17 border of Hamath. And *this is* the north s. 6285
47:18 the east s ye shall measure from Hauran, 6285
47:18 unto the east sea. And *this is* the east s. 6285
47:19 the south s southward, from Tamar *even* to 6285
47:19 great sea. And *this is* the south s southward. 6285
47:20 The west s also *shall be* the great sea from 6285
47:20 over against Hamath. This *is* the west s. 6285
48: 2 from the east s unto the west side, a *portion* 6285
48: 2 from the east side unto the west s, a *portion* 6285
48: 3 from the east s even unto the west side, 6285
48: 3 from the east side even unto the west s, 6285
48: 4 from the east s unto the west side, a *portion* 6285
48: 4 from the east side unto the west s, a *portion* 6285
48: 5 from the east s unto the west side, a *portion* 6285
48: 5 from the east side unto the west s, a *portion* 6285
48: 6 from the east s even unto the west side, 6285
48: 6 from the east side even unto the west s, 6285
48: 7 from the east s unto the west side, a *portion* 6285
48: 7 from the east side unto the west s, a *portion* 6285
48: 8 of Judah, from the east s unto the west side, 6285
48: 8 of Judah, from the east side unto the west s, 6285
48: 8 from the east s unto the west side: 6285
48: 8 from the east side unto the west s: 6285
48:16 the north s four thousand and five hundred, 6285
48:16 the south s four thousand and five hundred, 6285
48:16 on the east s four thousand and 6285
48:16 the west s four thousand and five hundred. 6285
48:21 on the **one s** and on the other of the holy 2088
48:23 from the east s unto the west side, 6285
48:23 from the east side unto the west s, 6285
48:24 from the east s unto the west side, 6285
48:24 from the east side unto the west s, 6285
48:25 from the east s unto the west side, 6285
48:25 from the east side unto the west s, 6285
48:26 from the east s unto the west side, 6285
48:26 from the east side unto the west s, 6285
48:27 from the east s unto the west side, Gad a 6285
Eze 48:27 from the east side unto the west s, Gad a 6285
48:28 the border of Gad, at the south s southward, 6285
48:30 on the north s, four thousand and 6285
48:32 at the east s four thousand and 6285
48:33 *at* the south s four thousand and 6285
48:34 *At* the west s four thousand and 6285
Da 7: 5 it raised up itself on one s, and *it had* three 7859
10: 4 as I was by the s of the great river, which *is* 3027
11:17 she shall not stand *on his s*, neither be for NIH
12: 5 the one on **this** s of the bank of the river, 2008
12: 5 the other on that s of the bank of the river. 2008
Ob 1:11 In the day that thou stoodest on the **other s**, 5048
Jnh 4: 5 sat on the **east s** of the city, and there made 6924
Zec 4: 3 one upon the right *s* of the bowl, and NIH
4: 3 and the other upon the left *s* thereof. NIH
4:11 trees upon the right *s* of the candlestick NIH
4:11 the candlestick and upon the left *s* thereof? NIH
5: 3 shall be cut off *as* on this *s* according to it; NIH
5: 3 shall be cut off *as* on that *s* according to it. NIH
Mt 8:18 commandment to depart unto the **other s**. *4008*
8:28 And when he was come to the **other s** into *4008*
13: 1 Jesus out of the house, and sat **by** the sea s. *3844*
13: 4 some *seeds* fell **by** the way s, and the fowls *3844*
13:19 is he which received seed **by** the way s. *3844*
14:22 and to go before him unto the **other s**, *4008*
16: 5 his disciples were come to the **other s**, *4008*
20:30 two blind men sitting **by** the way s, *3844*
Mk 2:13 And he went forth again **by** the sea s; and *3844*
4: 1 And he began again to teach **by** the sea s: *3844*
4: 4 some fell by the **way s**, and the fowls of *3598*
4:15 And these are they by the **way s**, where *3598*
4:35 Let us pass over unto the **other s**. *4008*
5: 1 And they came over unto the **other s** of *4008*
5:21 passed over again by ship unto the **other s**, *4008*
6:45 to go to the **other s** before unto Bethsaida, *4008*
8:13 into the ship again departed to the **other s**. *4008*
10: 1 coasts of Judea by the **farther s** of Jordan: *4008*
10:46 of Timeus, sat by the ***high*way s** begging. *3598*
16: 5 saw a young man sitting on the **right s**, *1188*
Lk 1:11 on the **right s** of the altar of incense. *1188*
8: 5 and as he sowed, some fell by the **way s**; *3598*
8:12 Those by the **way s** are they that hear; then *3598*
8:22 Let us go over unto the **other s** of the lake. *4008*
10:31 he saw him, he **passed by on the other s**. *492*
10:32 *on him*, and **passed by on the other s**. *492*
18:35 a certain blind man sat by the **way s** *3598*
19:43 thee round, and keep thee in **on every s**, *3840*
Jn 6:22 **on the other s** of the sea saw that there was *4008*
6:25 had found him **on the other s** of the sea, *4008*
19:18 with him, **on either s one**, *1782+1782+2532*
19:34 of the soldiers with a spear pierced his s, *4125*
20:20 he shewed unto them *his* hands and his s. *4125*
20:25 and thrust my hand into his s, I will not *4125*
20:27 *hither* thy hand, and thrust *it* into my s: *4125*
21: 6 Cast the net on the right s of the ship, and *3313*
Ac 10: 6 a tanner, whose house is **by** the sea s: *3844*
10:32 house of *one* Simon a tanner **by** the sea s: *3844*
12: 7 and he smote Peter on the s, and raised him *4125*
16:13 sabbath we went out of the city **by** a river s, *3844*
2Co 4: 8 *We are* troubled on every *s*, yet not NIG
7: 5 *we were* troubled on every *s*; without *were* NIG
Rev 22: 2 and **of either s** of the river, *1782+1782+2532*

SIDES (48) [SIDE]

Ex 25:14 the staves into the rings by the s of the ark, 6763
25:32 six branches shall come out of the s of it; 6654
26:13 it shall hang over the s of the tabernacle on 6654
26:22 for the s of the tabernacle westward thou 3411
26:23 the corners of the tabernacle in the **two s**. 3411
26:27 of the tabernacle, for the **two s** westward. 3411
27: 7 the staves shall be upon the two s of 6763
28:27 shalt put them on the two s of the ephod 3802
30: 3 the s thereof round about, and the horns 7023
30: 4 upon the two s of it shalt thou make *it;* and 6654
32:15 the tables *were* written on both their s; 5676
36:27 for the s of the tabernacle westward he 3411
36:28 the corners of the tabernacle in the **two s**. 3411
36:32 boards of the tabernacle for the s westward. 3411
37: 5 he put the staves into the rings by the s of 6763
37:18 And six branches going out of the s thereof; 6654
37:26 the s thereof round about, and the horns of 7023
37:27 two corners of it, upon the two s thereof, 6654
38: 7 he put the staves into the rings on the s of 6763
39:20 put them on the two s of the ephod 3802
Nu 33:55 thorns in your s, and shall vex you in 6654
Jos 23:13 scourges in your s, and thorns in your eyes, 6654
Jdg 2: 3 they shall be *as thorns* in your s, and 6654
5:30 of divers colours of needlework on both s, NIH
1Sa 24: 3 and his men remained in the s of the cave. 3411
1Ki 4:24 and he had peace on all s round about him. 5676
6:16 he built twenty cubits on the s of the house, 3411
2Ki 19:23 *to* the s of Lebanon, and will cut down 3411
Ps 48: 2 *is* mount Zion, *on* the s of the north, 3411
128: 3 Thy wife *shall be* as a fruitful vine by the s 3411
Isa 14:13 of the congregation, in the s of the north: 3411
14:15 be brought down to hell, to the s of the pit. 3411
37:24 of the mountains, *to* the s of Lebanon; 3411
66:12 ye shall be borne upon *her* s, and 6654
Jer 6:22 a great nation shall be raised from the s of 3411
48:28 her nest in the s of the hole's mouth. 5676
49:32 I will bring their calamity from all s 5676
Eze 1: 8 of a man under their wings on their four s; 7253
1:17 they went, they went upon their four s; 7253
10:11 they went, they went upon their four s; 7253
32:23 Whose graves are set in the s of the pit, and 3411
41: 2 the s of the door *were* five cubits on the one 3802
41:26 on the s of the porch, and *upon* the side 3802
42:20 He measured it by the four s: it had a wall 7307
46:19 there *was* a place on the **two s** westward. 3411
48: 1 for these are his s east *and* west; a *portion* 6285
Am 6:10 shall say unto *him* that *is* by the s of 3411
Jnh 1: 5 But Jonah was gone down into the s of 3411

SIDON (14) [SIDONIANS, ZIDON]

Ge 10:15 Canaan begat **S** his firstborn, and Heth, 6721

Ge 10:19 the border of the Canaanites was from **S**, 6721
Mt 11:21 **S** they would have repented long ago in *4605*
11:22 for Tyre and **S** at the day of judgment, *4605*
15:21 and departed into the coasts of Tyre and **S**. *4605*
Mk 3: 8 and they about Tyre and **S**, a great *4605*
7:24 and went into the borders of Tyre and **S**, *4605*
7:31 departing from the coasts of Tyre and **S**, *4605*
Lk 4:26 save unto Sarepta, *a city* of **S**, unto a *4605*
6:17 and *from* the sea coast of Tyre and **S**, *4605*
10:13 mighty works had been done in Tyre and **S**, *4605*
10:14 tolerable for Tyre and **S** at the judgment, *4605*
Ac 12:20 highly displeased with them of Tyre and **S**: *4606*
27: 3 And the next *day* we touched at **S**. *4605*

SIDONIANS (5) [SIDON]
Dt 3: 9 (*Which* Hermon the **S** call Sirion; and 6722
Jos 13: 4 Mearah that *is* beside the **S**, unto Aphek, 6722
13: 6 *and* all the **S**, them will I drive out from 6722
Jdg 3: 3 the **S**, and the Hivites that dwelt in mount 6722
1Ki 5: 6 *that* can skill to hew timber like unto the **S**. 6722

SIEGE (17) [BESIEGE]
Dt 20:19 field *is* man's *life*) to employ *them* in the **s**: 4692
28:53 given thee, in the **s**, and in the straitness, 4692
28:55 because he hath nothing left him in the **s**, 4692
28:57 them for want of all *things* secretly in the **s** 4692
1Ki 15:27 and all Israel **laid s** to Gibbethon. 6696
2Ch 32: 9 (but he *himself laid* **s** against Lachish, and NIH
32:10 ye trust, that ye abide in the **s** in Jerusalem? 4692
Isa 29: 3 will **lay s** against thee *with* a mount, and 6696
Jer 19: 9 eat every one the flesh of his friend in the **s** 4692
Eze 4: 2 lay **s** against it, and build a fort against it, 4692
4: 3 be besieged, and thou shalt **lay s** against it. 6696
4: 7 shalt set thy face toward the **s** of Jerusalem, 4692
4: 8 till thou hast ended the days of thy **s**. 4692
5: 2 when the days of the **s** are fulfilled: 4692
Mic 5: 1 he hath laid **s** against us: they shall smite 4692
Na 3:14 Draw thee waters for the **s**, fortify thy 4692
Zec 12: 2 when they shall be in the **s** both against 4692

SIEGEWORKS See BULWARKS

SIEVE (2)
Isa 30:28 to sift the nations with the **s** of vanity: 5299
Am 9: 9 like as *corn* is sifted in a **s**, yet shall not 3531

SIFT (3) [SIFTED]
Isa 30:28 to **s** the nations with the sieve of vanity: 5130
Am 9: 9 I will **s** the house of Israel among all 5128
Lk 22:31 *to have* you, that *he* may **s** *you* as wheat: *4617*

SIFTED (1) [SIFT]
Am 9: 9 like as *corn* is **s** in a sieve, yet shall not 5128

SIGH (7) [SIGHED, SIGHEST, SIGHETH, SIGHING, SIGHS]
Isa 24: 7 vine languisheth, all the merryhearted do **s**. 584
La 1: 4 her priests **s**: her virgins *are* afflicted, and 584
1:11 All her people **s**, they seek bread; they have 584
1:21 They have heard that I **s**; *there is* none to 584
Eze 9: 4 a mark upon the foreheads of the men that **s** 584
21: 6 **S** therefore, thou son of man, with 584
21: 6 and with bitterness **s** before their eyes. 584

SIGHED (3) [SIGH]
Ex 2:23 the children of Israel **s** by reason of 584
Mk 7:34 he **s**, and saith unto him, EPHPHATHA, *4727*
8:12 And he **s deeply** in his spirit, and saith, *389*

SIGHEST (1) [SIGH]
Eze 21: 7 when they say unto thee, Wherefore **s** thou? 584

SIGHETH (1) [SIGH]
La 1: 8 yea, she **s**, and turneth backward. 584

SIGHING (7) [SIGH]
Job 3:24 For my **s** cometh before I eat, and 585
Ps 12: 5 for the **s** of the needy, now will I arise, 603
31:10 life is spent with grief, and my years with **s**: 585
79:11 Let the **s** of the prisoner come before thee, 603
Isa 21: 2 all the **s** thereof have I made to cease. 585
35:10 gladness, and sorrow and **s** shall flee away. 585
Jer 45: 3 I fainted in my **s**, and I find no rest. 585

SIGHS (1) [SIGH]
La 1:22 for my **s** *are* many, and my heart *is* faint. 585

SIGHT (333) [SEE]
Ge 2: 9 to grow every tree that is pleasant to the **s**, 4758
18: 3 if now I have found favour in thy **s**, 5869
19:19 thy servant hath found grace in thy **s**, and 5869
21:11 the thing was very grievous in Abraham's **s** 5869
21:12 Let it not be grievous in thy **s** because 5869
23: 4 I may bury my dead out of my **s**. 6440+3807.1
23: 8 I should bury my dead out of my **s**; 6440+3807.1
32: 5 tell my lord, that I may find grace in thy **s**. 5869
33: 8 *These are* to find grace in the **s** of my lord. 5869
33:10 if now I have found grace in thy **s**, then 5869
33:15 let me find grace in the **s** of my lord. 5869
38: 7 was wicked in the **s** of the LORD; 5869
39: 4 Joseph found grace in his **s**, and he served 5869
39:21 gave him favour in the **s** of the keeper of 5869
47:18 there is not ought left in the **s** of my lord, 6440
47:25 let us find grace in the **s** of my lord, and 5869
47:29 If now I have found grace in thy **s**, put, 5869
Ex 3: 3 I will now turn aside, and see this great **s**, 4758
3:21 I will give this people favour in the **s** of 5869
4:30 and did the signs in the **s** of the people. 5869
7:20 in the **s** of Pharaoh, and in the sight of his 5869
7:20 of Pharaoh, and in the **s** of his servants; 5869
9: 8 it towards the heaven in the **s** of Pharaoh. 5869
11: 3 the LORD gave the people favour in the **s** 5869
11: 3 in the **s** of Pharaoh's servants, and in 5869
Ex 11: 3 and in the **s** of the people.) 5869
12:36 the LORD gave the people favour in the **s** 5869
15:26 wilt do that which is right in his **s**, and 5869
17: 6 Moses did so in the **s** of the elders of Israel. 5869
19:11 in the **s** of all the people upon mount Sinai. 5869
24:17 the **s** of the glory of the LORD *was* like 4758
33:12 and thou hast also found grace in my **s**. 5869
33:13 I pray thee, if I have found grace in thy **s**, 5869
33:13 know thee, that I may find grace in thy **s**: 5869
33:16 and thy people have found grace in thy **s**? 5869
33:17 for thou hast found grace in my **s**, and 5869
34: 9 If now I have found grace in thy **s**, O Lord, 5869
40:38 by night, in the **s** of all the house of Israel, 5869
Lev 10:19 should it have been accepted in the **s** of 5869
13: 3 the plague **in s** *be* deeper than the skin of 4758
13: 4 **in s** *be* not deeper than the skin, and 4758
13: 5 *if* the plague in his **s** be at a stay, *and* 5869
13:20 it *be* **in s** lower than the skin, and the hair 4758
13:25 and it *be* **in s** deeper than the skin; 4758
13:30 behold, *if* it *be* **in s** deeper than the skin; 4758
13:31 it *be* not **in s** deeper than the skin, and 4758
13:32 the scall *be* not **in s** deeper than the skin; 4758
13:34 in the skin, nor *be* **in s** deeper than the skin; 4758
13:37 if the scall be in his **s** at a stay, and 5869
14:37 reddish, which **in s** *are* lower than the wall; 4758
20:17 they shall be cut off in the **s** of their people: 5869
25:53 shall not rule with rigour over him in thy **s**. 5869
26:45 of the land of Egypt in the **s** of the heathen, 5869
Nu 3: 4 priest's office in the **s** of Aaron their father. 6440
11:11 wherefore have I not found favour in thy **s**, 5869
11:15 out of hand, if I have found favour in thy **s**; 5869
13:33 we were in our own **s** as grasshoppers, and 5869
13:33 as grasshoppers, and so we were in their **s**. 5869
19: 5 *one* shall burn the heifer in his **s**; her skin, 5869
20:27 they went up into mount Hor in the **s** of all 5869
25: 6 a Midianitish *woman* in the **s** of Moses, 5869
25: 6 in the **s** of all the congregation of 5869
27:19 and give him a charge in their **s**. 5869
32: 5 said they, if we have found grace in thy **s**, 5869
32:13 that had done evil in the **s** of the LORD, 5869
33: 3 a high hand in the **s** of all the Egyptians. 5869
Dt 4: 6 your understanding in the **s** of the nations, 5869
4:25 shall do evil in the **s** of the LORD thy 5869
4:37 brought thee out in his **s** with his mighty 6440
6:18 *is* right and good in the **s** of the LORD: 5869
9:18 in doing wickedly in the **s** of the LORD, 5869
12:25 *that which is* right in the **s** of the LORD. 5869
12:28 and right in the **s** of the LORD thy God. 5869
17: 2 that hath wrought wickedness in the **s** of 5869
21: 9 *that which is* right in the **s** of the LORD. 5869
28:34 So that thou shalt be mad for the **s** of thine 4758
28:67 for the **s** of thine eyes which thou shalt see. 4758
31: 7 said unto him in the **s** of all Israel, 5869
31:29 ye will do evil in the **s** of the LORD, 5869
34:12 which Moses shewed in the **s** of all Israel. 5869
Jos 3: 7 I begin to magnify thee in the **s** of all Israel, 5869
4:14 magnified Joshua in the **s** of all Israel; 5869
10:12 he said in the **s** of Israel, Sun, stand thou 5869
23: 5 and drive them from out of your **s**; 6440+3807.1
24:17 which did those great signs in our **s**, and 5869
Jdg 2:11 the children of Israel did evil in the **s** of 5869
3: 7 the children of Israel did evil in the **s** of 5869
3:12 the children of Israel did evil again in the **s** 5869
3:12 they had done evil in the **s** of the LORD. 5869
4: 1 the children of Israel again did evil in the **s** 5869
6: 1 the children of Israel did evil in the **s** of 5869
6:17 If now I have found grace in thy **s**, then 5869
6:21 angel of the LORD departed out of his **s**. 5869
10: 6 the children of Israel did evil again in the **s** 5869
13: 1 the children of Israel did evil again in the **s** 5869
Ru 2: 2 glean ears of corn after *him* in whose **s** I 5869
2:13 Let me find favour in thy **s**, my lord; 5869
1Sa 1:18 Let thine handmaid find grace in thy **s**. 5869
12:17 which ye have done in the **s** of the LORD, 5869
15:17 When thou *wast* little in thine own **s**, 5869
15:19 and didst evil in the **s** of the LORD? 5869
16:22 for he hath found favour in my **s**. 5869
18: 5 he was accepted in the **s** of all the people, 5869
18: 5 and also in the **s** of Saul's servants. 5869
29: 6 in with me in the host *is* good in my **s**: 5869
29: 9 to David, I know that thou *art* good in my **s**, 5869
2Sa 6:22 than thus, and will be base in mine own **s**: 5869
7: 9 have cut off all thine enemies out of thy **s**, 6440
7:19 this was yet a small thing in thy **s**, O Lord 5869
12: 9 of the LORD, to do evil in his **s**? 5869
12:11 he shall lie with thy wives in the **s** of this 5869
13: 5 give me meat, and dress the meat in my **s**, 5869
13: 6 make *me* a couple of cakes in my **s**, that I 5869
13: 8 kneaded *it*, and made cakes in his **s**, and 5869
14:22 knoweth that I have found grace in thy **s**, 5869
16: 4 beseech thee *that* I may find grace in thy **s**, 5869
16:22 his father's concubines in the **s** of all Israel. 5869
22:25 according to my cleanness in his **eye s**. 5869
1Ki 8:25 There shall not fail thee a man in my **s** to sit 6440
9: 7 for my name, will I cast out of my **s**; 6440
11: 6 Solomon did evil in the **s** of the LORD, 5869
11:19 Hadad found great favour in the **s** of 5869
11:38 do that *is* right in my **s**, to keep my statutes 5869
14:22 Judah did evil in the **s** of the LORD, and 5869
15:26 he did evil in the **s** of the LORD, and 5869
15:34 he did evil in the **s** of the LORD, and 5869
16: 7 even for all the evil that he did in the **s** of 5869
16:19 sinned in doing evil in the **s** of the LORD, 5869
16:30 Ahab the son of Omri did evil in the **s** of 5869
21:20 thou hast sold thyself to work evil in the **s** 5869
21:25 to work wickedness in the **s** of the LORD, 5869
22:52 he did evil in the **s** of the LORD, and 5869
2Ki 1:13 fifty thy servants, be precious in thy **s**. 5869
1:14 let my life now be precious in thy **s**. 5869
3: 2 he wrought evil in the **s** of the LORD; 5869
3:18 *but* a light thing in the **s** of the LORD: 5869
8:18 and he did evil in the **s** of the LORD. 5869
8:27 did evil in the **s** of the LORD, as *did* 5869
12: 2 Jehoash did *that* which *was* right in the **s** of 5869
13: 2 he did *that* which *was* evil in the **s** of 5869
2Ki 13:11 he did *that* which *was* evil in the **s** of 5869
14: 3 he did *that* which *was* right in the **s** of 5869
14:24 he did *that* which *was* evil in the **s** of 5869
15: 3 he did *that* which *was* right in the **s** of 5869
15: 9 he did *that* which *was* evil in the **s** of 5869
15:18 he did *that* which *was* evil in the **s** of 5869
15:24 he did *that* which *was* evil in the **s** of 5869
15:28 he did *that* which *was* evil in the **s** of 5869
15:34 he did *that* which *was* right in the **s** of 5869
16: 2 did not *that* which *was* right in the **s** of 5869
17: 2 he did *that* which *was* evil in the **s** of 5869
17:17 sold themselves to do evil in the **s** of 5869
17:18 with Israel, and removed them out of his **s**: 6440
17:20 until *he* had cast them out of his **s**. 6440
17:23 the LORD removed Israel out of his **s**, 6440
18: 3 he did *that* which *was* right in the **s** of 5869
20: 3 and have done *that* which *is* good in thy **s**. 5869
21: 2 he did *that* which *was* evil in the **s** of 5869
21: 6 he wrought much wickedness in the **s** of 5869
21:15 they have done *that* which *was* evil in my **s**, 5869
21:16 in doing *that* which *was* evil in the **s** of 5869
21:20 he did *that* which *was* evil in the **s** of 5869
22: 2 he did *that* which *was* right in the **s** of 5869
23:27 I will remove Judah also out of my **s**, 6440
23:32 he did *that* which *was* evil in the **s** of 5869
23:37 he did *that* which *was* evil in the **s** of 5869
24: 3 to remove *them* out of his **s**, for the sins of 6440
24: 9 he did *that* which *was* evil in the **s** of 5869
24:19 he did *that* which *was* evil in the **s** of 5869
1Ch 2: 3 of Judah, was evil in the **s** of the LORD; 5869
19:13 the LORD do *that* which *is* good in his **s**. 5869
22: 8 shed much blood upon the earth in my **s**. 6440
28: 8 in the **s** of all Israel the congregation of 5869
29:25 Solomon exceedingly in the **s** of all Israel, 5869
2Ch 6:16 **s** to sit upon the throne of Israel; 6440+3807.1
7:20 will I cast out of my **s**, and will make it to 6440
20:32 doing *that* which *was* right in the **s** of 5869
22: 4 Wherefore he did evil in the **s** of 5869
24: 2 Joash did *that* which *was* right in the **s** of 5869
25: 2 he did *that* which *was* right in the **s** of 5869
26: 4 he did *that* which *was* right in the **s** of 5869
27: 2 he did *that* which *was* right in the **s** of 5869
28: 1 he did not *that* which *was* right in the **s** of 5869
29: 2 he did *that* which *was* right in the **s** of 5869
32:23 that he was magnified in the **s** of all nations 5869
33: 2 did *that* which *was* evil in the **s** of 5869
33: 6 he wrought much evil in the **s** of 5869
33:22 he did *that* which *was* evil in the **s** of 5869
34: 2 he did *that* which *was* right in the **s** of 5869
36: 5 he did *that* which *was* evil in the **s** of 5869
36: 9 he did *that* which *was* evil in the **s** of 5869
36:12 he did *that* which *was* evil in the **s** of 5869
Ezr 9: 9 hath extended mercy unto us in the **s** of 6440
Ne 1:11 him mercy **in the s** of this man. 6440+3807.1
2: 5 if thy servant have found favour in thy **s**, 6440
8: 5 Ezra opened the book in the **s** of all 5869
Est 2:15 Esther obtained favour in the **s** of all them 5869
2:17 favour in his **s** more than all the virgins; 6440
5: 2 the court, *that* she obtained favour in his **s**: 5869
5: 8 If I have found favour in the **s** of the king, 5869
7: 3 and said, If I have found favour in thy **s**, 5869
8: 5 if I have found favour in his **s**, and the thing 6440
Job 15:15 yea, the heavens are not clean in his **s**. 5869
18: 3 as beasts, *and* reputed vile in your **s**? 5869
19:15 me for a stranger: I am an alien in their **s**. 5869
21: 8 Their seed is established **in** their **s** 6440+3807.1
25: 5 yea, the stars are not pure in his **s**. 5869
34:26 them as wicked *men* in the open **s** of others; 7200
41: 9 shall *not one* be cast down even at the **s** of 4758
Ps 5: 5 The foolish shall not stand in thy **s**: 5869
9:19 let the heathen be judged in thy **s**. 6440
10: 5 thy judgments *are* far above out of his **s**: 5048
19:14 be acceptable in thy **s**, O LORD, 6440
51: 4 have I sinned, and done *this* evil in thy **s**: 5869
72:14 and precious shall their blood be in his **s**. 5869
76: 7 who may stand in thy **s** when once thou art 6440
78:12 Marvellous things did he **in the s** of their 5048
79:10 **s** *by* the revenging of the blood of thy 5869
90: 4 For a thousand years in thy **s** *are but* 5869
98: 2 he openly shewed in the **s** of the heathen. 5869
101: 7 he that telleth lies shall not tarry in my **s**. 5869
116:15 Precious in the **s** of the LORD *is* the death 5869
143: 2 for in thy **s** shall no *man* living be justified. 6440
Pr 1:17 Surely in vain the net *is* spread in the **s** of 5869
3: 4 and good understanding in the **s** of God and 5869
4: 3 and only *beloved* in the **s** of my mother. 6440
Ecc 2:26 to a man that *is* good in his **s** wisdom, 6440
6: 9 Better *is* the **s** of the eyes than 4758
8: 3 Be not hasty to go out of his **s**: stand not in 6440
11: 9 of thine heart, and in the **s** of thine eyes: 4758
Isa 5:21 their own eyes, and prudent in their own **s**! 6440
11: 3 he shall not judge after the **s** of his eyes, 4758
26:17 so have we been in thy **s**, O LORD. 6440
38: 3 and have done *that* which *is* good in thy **s**. 5869
43: 4 Since thou wast precious in my **s**, thou hast 5869
Jer 4: 1 put away thine abominations out of my **s**, 6440
7:15 I will cast you out of my **s**, as I have cast 6440
7:30 children of Judah have done evil in my **s**, 5869
15: 1 cast *them* out of my **s**, and let them go 6440
18:10 If it do evil in my **s**, that *it* obey not my 5869
18:23 neither blot out their sin from thy **s**, 6440+3807.1
19:10 shalt thou break the bottle in the **s** of 5869
32:12 in the **s** of Hanameel mine uncle's *son*, and 5869
34:15 now turned, and had done right in my **s**, 5869
43: 9 in Tahpanhes, in the **s** of the men of Judah; 5869
51:24 evil that they have done in Zion in your **s**, 5869
Eze 4:12 dung that cometh out of man, in their **s**. 5869
5: 8 in the midst of thee in the **s** of the nations. 5869
5:14 about thee, in the **s** of all that pass by. 5869
10: 2 *them* over the city. And he went in in my **s**. 5869
10:19 and mounted up from the earth in my **s**: 5869
12: 3 for removing, and remove by day in their **s**; 5869
12: 3 from thy place to another place in their **s**: 5869
12: 4 thou bring forth thy stuff by day in their **s**, 5869
12: 4 thou shalt go forth at even in their **s**, as they 5869

Eze 12: 5 Dig thou through the wall in their s, and 5869
12: 6 In their s shalt thou bear *it* upon *thy* 5869
12: 7 *and* I bare *it* upon *my* shoulder in their s. 5869
16:41 execute judgments upon thee in the s of 5869
20: 9 among whom they *were,* in whose s I made 5869
20:14 the heathen, in whose s I brought them out. 5869
20:22 that *it* should not be polluted in the s of 5869
20:22 in whose s I brought them forth. 5869
20:43 ye shall lothe yourselves in your own s for 6440
21:23 be unto them as a false divination in their s, 5869
22:16 in thyself in the s of the heathen, 5869
28:18 earth in the s of all them that behold thee. 5869
28:25 shall be sanctified in them in the s of 5869
36:31 shall lothe yourselves in your own s for 6440
36:34 whereas it lay desolate in the s of all that 5869
39:27 am sanctified in them in the s of many 5869
43:11 write *it* in their s, that they may keep 5869
Da 4:11 the s thereof to the end of all the earth: 2379
4:20 and the s thereof to all the earth; 2379
Hos 2: 2 put away her whoredoms out of her s, 6440
2:10 now will I discover her lewdness in the s of 5869
6: 2 will raise us up, and we shall live in his s. 6440
Am 9: 3 though they be hid from my s in the bottom 5869
Jnh 2: 4 I said, I am cast out of thy s; yet I will look 5869
Mal 2:17 Every one that doeth evil *is* good in the s of 5869
Mt 11: 5 The blind **receive** their s, and the lame walk, *308*
11:26 Father: for so it seemed good **in** thy s. *1715*
20:34 and immediately their eyes **received** s, and *308*
Mk 10:51 unto him, Lord, that I might **receive** my s. *308*
10:52 And immediately he **received** his s, and *308*
Lk 1:15 For he shall be great **in the** s of the Lord, *1799*
4:18 and **recovering of** s to the blind, *309*
7:21 and unto many *that were* blind he gave s. *991*
10:21 Father; for so it seemed good **in** thy s. *1715*
15:21 and **in** thy s, and am no more worthy to be *1799*
16:15 men is abomination **in the** s of God. *1799*
18:41 And he said, Lord, that I may **receive** my s. *308*
18:42 And Jesus said unto him, **Receive** thy s: *308*
18:43 And immediately he **received** his s, and *308*
23:48 all the people that came together to that s, *2335*
24:31 and he **vanished out of** their s. *855+1096*
Jn 9:11 and I went and washed, and I **received** s. *308*
9:15 also asked him how he had **received** his s. *308*
9:18 that he had been blind, and **received** his s, *308*
9:18 the parents of him that had **received** his s. *308*
Ac 1: 9 and a cloud received him out of their s. *3788*
4:19 Whether it be right **in the** s of God to *1799*
7:10 wisdom **in the** s of Pharaoh king of Egypt; *1726*
7:31 When Moses saw *it,* he wondered at the s: *3705*
8:21 for thy heart is not right **in the** s of God. *1799*
9: 9 And he was three days without s, and *991*
9:12 *his* hand on him, that he might **receive** his s. *308*
9:17 that thou mightest **receive** thy s, and *308*
9:18 and he **received** s forthwith, and arose, and *308*
10:31 thine alms are had in remembrance **in the** s *1799*
22:13 said unto me, Brother Saul, **receive** thy s. *308*
Ro 3:20 law there shall no flesh be justified **in** his s: *1799*
12:17 Provide *things* honest **in the** s of all men. *1799*
2Co 2:17 of God, **in the** s of God speak we in Christ. *2714*
4: 2 to every man's conscience **in the** s of God. *1799*
5: 7 (For we walk by faith, not by s:) *1491*
7:12 that our care for you **in the** s of God might *1799*
8:21 honest *things,* not only **in the** s of the Lord, *1799*
8:21 sight of the Lord, but also **in the** s of men. *1799*
Gal 3:11 *man* is justified by the law **in the** s of God, *3844*
Col 1:22 unblameable and unreproveable in his s: *2714*
1Th 1: 3 **in the** s of God and our Father; *1715*
1Ti 2: 3 and acceptable **in the** s of God our Saviour; *1799*
6:13 I give thee charge **in the** s of God, *1799*
Heb 4:13 any creature *that is* not manifest **in** his s: *1799*
12:21 And so terrible was the s, *that* Moses said, *5324*
13:21 in you *that which is* well pleasing **in** his s, *1799*
Jas 4:10 Humble yourselves **in the** s of the Lord, *1799*
1Pe 3: 4 which is **in the** s of God of great price. *1799*
1Jn 3:22 do those *things* that are pleasing **in** his s. *1799*
Rev 4: 3 about the throne, **in** s like unto an emerald. *3706*
13:13 from heaven on the earth **in the** s of men, *1799*
13:14 he had power to do **in the** s of the beast; *1799*

SIGHTS (1) [SEE]

Lk 21:11 and **fearful** s and great signs shall there be *5400*

SIGN (76) [SIGNED, SIGNS]

Ex 4: 8 neither hearken to the voice of the first s, 226
4: 8 that they will believe the voice of the latter s. 226
8:23 and thy people: to morrow shall this s be. 226
13: 9 it shall be for a s unto thee upon thine hand, 226
31:13 for it *is* a s between me and you throughout 226
31:17 It *is* a s between me and the children of 226
Nu 16:38 they shall be a s unto the children of Israel. 226
26:10 and fifty men: and they became a s. 5251
Dt 6: 8 thou shalt bind them for a s upon thine hand, 226
11:18 and bind them for a s upon your hand, 226
13: 1 of dreams, and giveth thee a s or a wonder, 226
13: 2 the s or the wonder come to pass, whereof he 226
28:46 they shall be upon thee for a s and for a 226
Jos 4: 6 That this may be a s among you, *that* when 226
Jdg 6:17 then shew me a s that thou talkest with me. 226
20:38 Now there was an **appointed** s between 4150
1Sa 2:34 this *shall be* a s unto thee, that shall come 226
14:10 into our hand: and this *shall be* a s unto us. 226
1Ki 13: 3 he gave a s the same day, saying, This *is* 4159
13: 3 This *is* the s which the LORD hath 4159
13: 5 according to the s which the man of God 4159
2Ki 19:29 this *shall be* a s unto thee, Ye shall eat *this* 226
20: 8 What *shall be* the s that the LORD will heal 226
20: 9 This s shalt thou have of the LORD, 226
2Ch 32:24 he spake unto him, and he gave him a s. 4159
Isa 7:11 Ask thee a s of the LORD thy God; ask it 226
7:14 the Lord himself shall give you a s; 226
19:20 it shall be for a s and for a witness unto 226
20: 3 barefoot three years *for* a s and wonder upon 226
37:30 this *shall be* a s unto thee, Ye shall eat *this* 226
38: 7 this *shall be* a s unto thee from the LORD, 226
38:22 What *is* the s that I shall go up *to* the house 226
55:13 for an everlasting s *that* shall not be cut off. 226
66:19 I will set a s among them, and I will send 226
Jer 6: 1 and set up a **s of fire** in Beth-haccerem: 4864
44:29 this *shall be* a s unto you, saith the LORD, 226
Eze 4: 3 This *shall be* a s to the house of Israel. 226
12: 6 for I have set thee *for* a s unto the house of 4159
12:11 Say, I *am* your s: like as I have done, so 4159
14: 8 will make him a s and a proverb, and I will 226
20:12 my sabbaths, to be a s between me and them, 226
20:20 they shall be a s between me and you, that *ye* 226
24:24 Thus Ezekiel is unto you a s: according to 4159
24:27 thou shalt be a s unto them; and they shall 4159
39:15 a man's bone, then shall he set up a s by it, 6725
Da 6: 8 establish the decree, and s the writing, 7560
Mt 12:38 saying, Master, we would see a s from thee. *4592*
12:39 and adulterous generation seeketh after a s; *4592*
12:39 and there shall no s be given to it, but *4592*
12:39 given to it, but the s of the prophet Jonas: *4592*
16: 1 that *he* would shew them a s from heaven. *4592*
16: 4 and adulterous generation seeketh after a s; *4592*
16: 4 and there shall no s be given unto it, but *4592*
16: 4 given unto it, but the s of the prophet Jonas. *4592*
24: 3 and what *shall be* the s of thy coming, and *4592*
24:30 shall appear the s of the Son of man in *4592*
26:48 Now he that betrayed him gave them a s, *4592*
Mk 8:11 seeking of him a s from heaven, *4592*
8:12 Why doth this generation seek after a s? *4592*
8:12 There shall no s be given unto this *4592*
13: 4 what *shall be* the s when all these *things* *4592*
Lk 2:12 And this *shall be* a s unto you; Ye shall find *4592*
2:34 and for a s which shall be spoken against; *4592*
11:16 tempting *him,* sought of him a s from *4592*
11:29 they seek a s; and there shall no sign be *4592*
11:29 and there shall no s be given it, but the sign *4592*
11:29 be given it, but the s of Jonas the prophet. *4592*
11:30 For as Jonas was a s unto the Ninevites, so *4592*
21: 7 what s *will there be* when these *things* shall *4592*
Jn 2:18 unto him, What s shewest thou unto us, *4592*
6:30 unto him, What s shewest thou then, *4592*
Ac 28:11 in the isle, *whose* s *was* Castor and Pollux. *3902*
Ro 4:11 And he received the s of circumcision, *4592*
1Co 1:22 For the Jews require a s, and the Greeks *4592*
14:22 Wherefore tongues are for a s, not to them *4592*
Rev 15: 1 And I saw another s in heaven, great and *4592*

SIGNED (4) [SIGN]

Da 6: 9 Wherefore king Darius s the writing and 7560
6:10 when Daniel knew that the writing *was* s, 7560
6:12 Hast thou not s a decree, that every man 7560
6:13 nor the decree that thou hast s, but 7560

SIGNET (11) [SIGNETS]

Ge 38:18 Thy s, and thy bracelets, and thy staff that 2368
38:25 *are* these, the s, and bracelets, and staff. 2858
Ex 28:11 in stone, *like* the engravings of a s, 2368
28:21 to their names, *like* the engravings of a s; 2368
28:36 grave upon it, *like* the engravings of a s, 2368
39:14 *like* the engravings of a s, every one with 2368
39:30 it a writing, *like to* the engravings of a s, 2368
Jer 22:24 of Judah were the s upon my right hand, 2368
Da 6:17 the king sealed it with his own s, and 5824
6:17 his own signet, and with the s of his lords; 5824
Hag 2:23 the LORD, and will make thee as a s: 2368

SIGNETS (1) [SIGNET]

Ex 39: 6 graven *as* s are graven, with the names of 2368

SIGNIFICATION (1) [SIGNIFY]

1Co 14:10 in the world, and none of them *is* **without** s. *880*

SIGNIFIED (2) [SIGNIFY]

Ac 11:28 s by the Spirit that there should be great *4591*
Rev 1: 1 and s *it* by his angel unto his servant John: *4591*

SIGNIFIETH (1) [SIGNIFY]

Heb 12:27 And this *word,* Yet once *more,* s *1213*

SIGNIFY (4) [SIGNIFICATION, SIGNIFIED, SIGNIFIETH, SIGNIFYING]

Ac 21:26 to s the accomplishment of the days of *1229*
23:15 ye with the council s to the chief captain *1718*
25:27 not withal to s the crimes *laid* against him. *4591*
1Pe 1:11 Spirit of Christ which was in them did s, *1213*

SIGNIFYING (4) [SIGNIFY]

Jn 12:33 This he said, s what death he should die. *4591*
18:32 which he spake, s what death he should die. *4591*
21:19 s by what death he should glorify God. *4591*
Heb 9: 8 The Holy Ghost this s, that the way into *1213*

SIGNS (53) [SIGN]

Ge 1:14 let them be for s, and for seasons, and 226
Ex 4: 9 if they will not believe also these two s, 226
4:17 rod in thine hand, wherewith thou shalt do s. 226
4:28 and all the s which he had commanded him. 226
4:30 and did the s in the sight of the people. 226
7: 3 multiply my s and my wonders in the land of 226
10: 1 that I might shew these my s before him: 226
10: 2 and my s which I have done amongst them; 226
Nu 14:11 for all the s which I have shewed among 226
Dt 4:34 by s, and by wonders, and by war, and by a 226
6:22 the LORD shewed s and wonders, great 226
7:19 the s, and the wonders, and the mighty hand, 226
26: 8 and with s, and with wonders: 226
29: 3 have seen, the s, and those great miracles: 226
34:11 In all the s and the wonders, which 226
Jos 24:17 and which did those great s in our sight, and 226
1Sa 10: 7 let it be, when these s are come unto thee, 226
10: 9 and all those s came to pass that day. 226
Ne 9:10 And shewedst s and wonders upon Pharaoh, 226
Ps 74: 4 they set up their ensigns *for* s. 226
74: 9 We see not our s: *there is* no more any 226
78:43 How he had wrought his s in Egypt, and 226
105:27 They shewed his s among them, 226
Isa 8:18 whom the LORD hath given me *are* for s 226
Jer 10: 2 and be not dismayed at the s of heaven; 226
32:20 Which hast set s and wonders in the land of 226
32:21 people Israel out of the land of Egypt with s, 226
Da 4: 2 I thought it good to shew the s and 852
4: 3 How great *are* his s! and how mighty *are* his 852
6:27 and he worketh s and wonders in heaven and 852
Mt 16: 3 but can ye not *discern* the s of the times? *4592*
24:24 and shall shew great s and wonders; *4592*
Mk 13:22 and shall shew s and wonders, to seduce, *4592*
16:17 And these s shall follow them that believe; *4592*
16:20 and confirming the word with s following. *4592*
Lk 1:62 And they **made** s to his father, how he *1770*
21:11 and great s shall there be from heaven. *4592*
21:25 And there shall be s in the sun, and in *4592*
Jn 4:48 Except ye see s and wonders, ye will not *4592*
20:30 And many other s truly did Jesus in *4592*
Ac 2:19 in heaven above, and s in the earth beneath; *4592*
2:22 among you by miracles and wonders and s, *4592*
2:43 and s were done by the apostles. *4592*
4:30 and that s and wonders may be done by *4592*
5:12 by the hands of the apostles were many s *4592*
7:36 shewed wonders and s in the land of Egypt, *4592*
8:13 *the* miracles and s *which were* done. *4592*
14: 3 and granted s and wonders to be done by *4592*
Ro 15:19 Through mighty s and wonders, by *4592*
2Co 12:12 Truly the s of an apostle were wrought *4592*
12:12 in s, and wonders, and mighty deeds. *4592*
2Th 2: 9 with all power and s and lying wonders, *4592*
Heb 2: 4 both with s and wonders, and with divers *4592*

SIHON (37)

Nu 21:21 Israel sent messengers unto S king of 5511
21:23 S would not suffer Israel to pass through 5511
21:23 S gathered all his people together, and 5511
21:26 For Heshbon *was* the city of S the king of 5511
21:27 let the city of S be built and prepared: 5511
21:28 out of Heshbon, a flame from the city of S: 5511
21:29 his daughters into captivity unto S king of 5511
21:34 thou shalt do to him as thou didst unto S 5511
32:33 the kingdom of S king of the Amorites, and 5511
Dt 1: 4 After he had slain S the king of 5511
2:24 I have given into thy hand S the Amorite, 5511
2:26 S king of Heshbon *with* words of peace, 5511
2:30 S king of Heshbon would not let us pass by 5511
2:31 I have begun to give S and his land before 5511
2:32 S came out against us, he and all his 5511
3: 2 thou shalt do unto him as thou didst unto S 5511
3: 6 as we did unto S king of Heshbon, 5511
4:46 in the land of S king of the Amorites, 5511
29: 7 S the king of Heshbon, and Og the king of 5511
31: 4 LORD shall do unto them as he did to S 5511
Jos 2:10 S and Og, whom ye utterly destroyed. 5511
9:10 to S king of Heshbon, and to Og king of 5511
12: 2 S king of the Amorites, who dwelt in 5511
12: 5 the border of S king of Heshbon. 5511
13:10 And all the cities of S king of the Amorites, 5511
13:21 all the kingdom of S king of the Amorites, 5511
13:21 Hur, and Reba, *which were* dukes of S, 5511
13:27 the rest of the kingdom of S king of 5511
Jdg 11:19 Israel sent messengers unto S king of 5511
11:20 S trusted not Israel to pass through his 5511
11:20 S gathered all his people together, and 5511
11:21 the LORD God of Israel delivered S and 5511
1Ki 4:19 *in* the country of S king of the Amorites, 5511
Ne 9:22 so they possessed the land of S, and 5511
Ps 135:11 S king of the Amorites, and Og king of 5511
136:19 S king of the Amorites: for his mercy 5511
Jer 48:45 a flame from the midst of S, and 5511

SIHOR (3)

Jos 13: 3 From S, which *is* before Egypt, even unto 7883
Isa 23: 3 by great waters the seed of S, the harvest of 7883
Jer 2:18 the way of Egypt, to drink the waters of S? 7883

SILAS (13) [SILVANUS]

Ac 15:22 and S, chief *men* among the brethren: *4609*
15:27 We have sent therefore Judas and S, *4609*
15:32 And Judas and S, being prophets also *4609*
15:34 Notwithstanding it pleased S to abide there *4609*
15:40 And Paul chose S, and departed, *4609*
16:19 they caught Paul and S, and drew *them* into *4609*
16:25 And at midnight Paul and S prayed, and *4609*
16:29 and fell down before Paul and S, *4609*
17: 4 and consorted with Paul and S; *4609*
17:10 sent away Paul and S by night unto Berea: *4609*
17:14 but S and Timotheus abode there still. *4609*
17:15 and receiving a commandment unto S and *4609*
18: 5 And when S and Timotheus were come *4609*

SILENCE (35) [SILENT]

Jdg 3:19 who said, **Keep** s. And all that stood by 2013
Job 4:16 *there was* s, and I heard a voice, *saying,* 1827
29:21 and waited, and **kept** s at my counsel. 1826
31:34 that I **kept** s, *and* went not out *of* the door? 1826
Ps 31:18 Let the lying lips be **put to** s; which speak 481
32: 3 When I **kept** s, my bones waxed old 2790
35:22 **keep** not s: O Lord, be not far from me. 2790
39: 2 I was dumb *with* s, I held my peace, 1747
50: 3 Our God shall come, and shall not **keep** s: 2790
50:21 These *things* hast thou done, and I **kept** s; 2790
83: 1 **Keep** not thou s, O God: hold not thy 1824
94:17 my help, my soul had almost dwelt *in* s. 1745
115:17 neither any that go down into s. 1745
Ecc 3: 7 a time to **keep** s, and a time to speak; 2814
Isa 15: 1 Ar of Moab is laid waste, *and* **brought to** s; 1820
15: 1 of Moab is laid waste, *and* **brought to** s; 1820
41: 1 **Keep** s before me, O islands; and let 2790
62: 6 make mention of the LORD, keep not s, 1824
65: 6 I will not keep s, but will recompense, 2814
Jer 8:14 for the LORD our God hath **put** us **to** s, 1826
La 2:10 of Zion sit upon the ground, *and* **keep** s: 1826
3:28 He sitteth alone and **keepeth** s, because 1826
Am 5:13 Therefore the prudent shall **keep** s in that 1826

S

Am 8: 3 they shall cast *them* forth with **s**. 2013
Hab 2:20 let all the earth **keep s** before him. 2013
Mt 22:34 heard that he had **put** the Sadducees **to s**, *5392*
Ac 15:12 Then all the multitude **kept s**, and *4601*
21:40 And when there was made a great **s**, *4602*
22: 2 tongue to them, they kept the more **s**: *2271*
1Co 14:28 no interpreter, let him **keep s** in the church; *4601*
14:34 Let your women **keep s** in the churches: *4601*
1Ti 2:11 Let the woman learn in **s** with all *2271*
2:12 usurp authority over the man, but to be in **s**. *2271*
1Pe 2:15 that with well doing *ye* may **put to s** *5392*
Rev 8: 1 there was **s** in heaven about the space of *4602*

SILENT (9) [SILENCE]
1Sa 2: 9 and the wicked shall be **s** in darkness; 1826
Ps 22: 2 and in the night season, and am not **s**. 1747
28: 1 I cry, O LORD, my rock; be not **s** to me: 2790
28: 1 lest, *if* thou be **s** to me, I become like them 2814
30:12 glory may sing *praise* to thee, and not be **s**. 1826
31:17 be ashamed, *and* let them be **s** in the grave. 1826
Isa 47: 5 Sit thou **s**, and get thee into darkness, 1748
Jer 8:14 the defenced cities, and let us be **s** there: 1826
Zec 2:13 **Be s**, O all flesh, before the LORD: for he 2013

SILK (4)
Pr 31:22 of tapestry; her clothing *is* **s** and purple. 8336
Eze 16:10 with fine linen, and I covered thee *with* **s**. 4897
16:13 *of* fine linen, and **s**, and broidered work; 4897
Rev 18:12 and **s**, and scarlet, and all thyine wood, and *4596*

SILLA (1)
2Ki 12:20 the house of Millo, which goeth down *to* **S**. 5538

SILLY (3)
Job 5: 2 the foolish man, and envy slayeth the **s one**. 6601
Hos 7:11 Ephraim also is like a **s** dove, without heart: 6601
2Ti 3: 6 and lead captive **s women** laden with sins, *1133*

SILOAH (1) [SILOAM]
Ne 3:15 the wall of the pool of **S** by the king's 7975

SILOAM (3) [SILOAH]
Lk 13: 4 upon whom the tower in **S** fell, and *4611*
Jn 9: 7 said unto him, Go, wash in the pool of **S**, *4611*
9:11 unto me, Go to the pool of **S**, and wash: *4611*

SILVANUS (4) [SILAS]
2Co 1:19 *even* by me and **S** and Timotheus, was not *4610*
1Th 1: 1 Paul, and **S**, and Timotheus, unto *4610*
2Th 1: 1 Paul, and **S**, and Timotheus, unto *4610*
1Pe 5:12 By **S**, a faithful brother unto you, as I *4610*

SILVER (320) [SILVERLINGS, SILVERSMITH]
Ge 13: 2 *was* very rich in cattle, in **s**, and in gold. 3701
20:16 given thy brother a thousand *pieces* of **s**: 3701
23:15 the land *is worth* four hundred shekels of **s**; 3701
23:16 Abraham weighed to Ephron the **s**, 3701
23:16 four hundred shekels of **s**, current *money* 3701
24:35 **s**, and gold, and menservants, and 3701
24:53 the servant brought forth jewels of **s**, and 3701
37:28 to the Ishmeelites for twenty *pieces* of **s**: 3701
44: 2 put my cup, the **s** cup, in the sack's mouth 3701
44: 8 should we steal out of thy lord's house **s** or 3701
45:22 he gave three hundred *pieces* of **s**, 3701
Ex 3:22 jewels of **s**, and jewels of gold, and 3701
11: 2 jewels of **s**, and jewels of gold. 3701
12:35 they borrowed of the Egyptians jewels of **s**, 3701
20:23 Ye shall not make with me gods of **s**, 3701
21:32 give unto their master thirty shekels *of* **s**, 3701
25: 3 shall take of them; gold, and **s**, and brass, 3701
26:19 thou shalt make forty sockets of **s** under 3701
26:21 their forty sockets *of* **s**; two sockets under 3701
26:25 and their sockets *of* **s**, sixteen sockets; 3701
26:32 *shall be of* gold, upon the four sockets of **s**. 3701
27:10 of the pillars and their fillets *shall be of* **s**. 3701
27:11 the hooks of the pillars and their fillets *of* **s**. 3701
27:17 about the court *shall be* filleted *with* **s**; 3701
27:17 their hooks *shall be of* **s**, and their sockets 3701
31: 4 to work in gold, and in **s**, and in brass, 3701
35: 5 of the LORD; gold, and **s**, and brass, 3701
35:24 Every one that did offer an offering of **s** 3701
35:32 to work in gold, and in **s**, and in brass, 3701
36:24 forty sockets of **s** he made under the twenty 3701
36:26 their forty sockets *of* **s**; two sockets under 3701
36:30 their sockets *were* sixteen sockets *of* **s**, 3701
36:36 and he cast for them four sockets of **s**. 3701
38:10 of the pillars and their fillets *were of* **s**. 3701
38:11 the hooks of the pillars and their fillets *of* **s**. 3701
38:12 the hooks of the pillars and their fillets *of* **s**. 3701
38:17 the hooks of the pillars and their fillets *of* **s**; 3701
38:17 the overlaying of their chapiters *of* **s**; and 3701
38:17 the pillars of the court *were* filleted *with* **s**. 3701
38:19 their hooks *of* **s**, and the overlaying of their 3701
38:19 of their chapiters and their fillets *of* **s**. 3701
38:25 the **s** of them that were numbered of 3701
38:27 of the hundred talents of **s** were cast 3701
Lev 5:15 with thy estimation *by* shekels of **s**, 3701
27: 3 thy estimation shall be fifty shekels of **s**, 3701
27: 6 shall be of the male five shekels of **s**, 3701
27: 6 thy estimation *shall be* three shekels of **s**. 3701
27:16 seed *shall be valued* at fifty shekels of **s**. 3701
Nu 7:13 his offering *was* one **s** charger, the weight 3701
7:13 thirty *shekels*, one **s** bowl of seventy 3701
7:19 He offered *for* his offering one **s** charger, 3701
7:19 thirty *shekels*, one **s** bowl of seventy 3701
7:25 His offering *was* one **s** charger, the weight 3701
7:25 thirty *shekels*, one **s** bowl of seventy 3701
7:31 His offering *was* one **s** charger of 3701
7:31 thirty *shekels*, one **s** bowl of seventy 3701
7:37 His offering *was* one **s** charger, the weight 3701
7:37 thirty *shekels*, one **s** bowl of seventy 3701
7:43 His offering *was* one **s** charger of 3701
7:43 thirty *shekels*, a **s** bowl of seventy shekels, 3701
7:49 His offering *was* one **s** charger, the weight 3701
Nu 7:49 thirty *shekels*, one **s** bowl of seventy 3701
7:55 His offering *was* one **s** charger of 3701
7:55 thirty *shekels*, one **s** bowl of seventy 3701
7:61 His offering *was* one **s** charger, the weight 3701
7:61 thirty *shekels*, one **s** bowl of seventy 3701
7:67 His offering *was* one **s** charger, the weight 3701
7:67 thirty *shekels*, one **s** bowl of seventy 3701
7:73 His offering *was* one **s** charger, the weight 3701
7:73 thirty *shekels*, one **s** bowl of seventy 3701
7:79 His offering *was* one **s** charger, the weight 3701
7:79 thirty *shekels*, one **s** bowl of seventy 3701
7:84 twelve chargers of **s**, twelve silver bowls, 3701
7:84 twelve **s** bowls, twelve spoons of gold: 3701
7:85 Each charger of **s** *weighing* an hundred and 3701
7:85 all the **s** vessels *weighed* two thousand and 3701
10: 2 Make thee two trumpets of **s**; of a whole 3701
22:18 If Balak would give me his house full *of* **s** 3701
24:13 If Balak would give me his house full *of* **s** 3701
31:22 the **s**, the brass, the iron, the tin, and 3701
Dt 7:25 thou shalt not desire the **s** or gold *that is* on 3701
8:13 thy **s** and thy gold is multiplied, and all that 3701
17:17 shall he greatly multiply to himself **s** 3701
22:19 amerce him in an hundred *shekels* of **s**, 3701
22:29 unto the damsel's father fifty *shekels* of **s**, 3701
29:17 their idols, wood and stone, **s** and gold, 3701
Jos 6:19 all the **s**, and gold, and vessels of brass and 3701
6:24 only the **s**, and the gold, and the vessels of 3701
7:21 two hundred shekels *of* **s**, and a wedge of 3701
7:21 in the midst of my tent, and the **s** under it. 3701
7:22 *it was* hid in his tent, and the **s** under it. 3701
7:24 the **s**, and the garment, and the wedge of 3701
22: 8 with **s**, and with gold, and with brass, and 3701
24:32 of Shechem for an hundred **pieces of s**: 7192
Jdg 9: 4 ten *pieces* of **s** out of the house of 3701
16: 5 every one *of us* eleven hundred *pieces* of **s**. 3701
17: 2 The eleven hundred *shekels* of **s** that were 3701
17: 2 also in mine ears, behold, the **s** *is* with me; 3701
17: 3 eleven hundred *shekels* of **s** to his mother, 3701
17: 3 I had wholly dedicated the **s** unto 3701
17: 4 his mother took two hundred *shekels* of **s**, 3701
17:10 I will give thee ten *shekels* of **s** by the year, 3701
1Sa 2:36 crouch to him for a piece of **s** and a morsel 3701
9: 8 here at hand the fourth part of a shekel of **s**: 3701
2Sa 8:10 *Joram* brought with him vessels of **s**, and 3701
8:11 with the **s** and gold that he had dedicated of 3701
18:11 I would have given thee ten *shekels of* **s**, 3701
18:12 a thousand *shekels of* **s** in mine hand, 3701
21: 4 We will have no **s** nor gold of Saul, nor of 3701
24:24 and the oxen for fifty shekels of **s**. 3701
1Ki 7:51 *even* the **s**, and the gold, and the vessels, 3701
10:21 none *were of* **s**: it was nothing accounted of 3701
10:22 and **s**, ivory, and apes, and peacocks. 3701
10:25 vessels of **s**, and vessels of gold, and 3701
10:27 the king made **s** *to be* in Jerusalem as 3701
10:29 out of Egypt for six hundred *shekels* of **s**, 3701
15:15 of the LORD, **s**, and gold, and vessels. 3701
15:18 Asa took all the **s** and the gold that were 3701
15:19 I have sent unto thee a present of **s** and 3701
16:24 hill Samaria of Shemer for two talents of **s**, 3701
20: 3 Thy **s** and thy gold *is* mine; thy wives also 3701
20: 5 Thou shalt deliver me thy **s**, and thy gold, 3701
20: 7 my children, and for my **s**, and for my gold; 3701
20:39 his life, or else thou shalt pay a talent of **s**. 3701
2Ki 5: 5 took with him ten talents of **s**, and 3701
5:22 a talent of **s**, and two changes of garments. 3701
5:23 and bound two talents of **s** in two bags, 3701
6:25 head was *sold* for fourscore *pieces* of **s**, 3701
6:25 of a kab of dove's dung for five *pieces* of **s**. 3701
7: 8 carried thence **s**, and gold, and raiment, and 3701
12:13 *for* the house of the LORD bowls of **s**, 3701
12:13 any vessels of gold, or vessels of **s**, 3701
14:14 he took all the gold and **s**, and all 3701
15:19 Menahem gave Pul a thousand talents of **s**, 3701
15:20 of each man fifty shekels *of* **s**, to give to 3701
16: 8 Ahaz took the **s** and gold that was found *in* 3701
18:14 king of Judah three hundred talents of **s** 3701
18:15 Hezekiah gave *him* all the **s** that was found 3701
20:13 the **s**, and the gold, and the spices, and 3701
22: 4 that he may sum the **s** which is brought *into* 3701
23:33 land to a tribute of an hundred talents of **s**, 3701
23:35 Jehoiakim gave the **s** and the gold to 3701
23:35 he exacted the **s** and the gold of the people 3701
25:15 as *were of* gold, *in* gold, and *of* **s**, *in* silver, 3701
25:15 as *were of* gold, *in* gold, and *of* silver, *in* **s**, 3701
1Ch 18:10 *manner of* vessels of gold and **s** and brass. 3701
18:11 with the **s** and the gold that he brought from 3701
19: 6 a thousand talents of **s** to hire them chariots 3701
22:14 and a thousand thousand talents *of* **s**; 3701
22:16 the gold, the **s**, and the brass, and the iron, 3701
28:14 ***s** also* for all instruments of silver by NIH
28:14 *silver also* for all instruments of **s** by 3701
28:15 for the candlesticks of **s** by weight, *both* for 3701
28:16 and *likewise* **s** for the tables of silver: 3701
28:16 and *likewise* silver for the tables of **s**: 3701
28:17 *likewise* **s** by weight for every bason of NIH
28:17 *silver* by weight for every bason of **s**: 3701
29: 2 the **s** for *things of* silver, and the brass for 3701
29: 2 the silver for *things of* **s**, and the brass for 3701
29: 3 of mine own proper good, *of* gold and **s**, 3701
29: 4 and seven thousand talents of refined **s**, 3701
29: 5 the **s** for *things of* silver, and for all *manner* 3701
29: 5 the silver for *things of* **s**, and for all *manner* 3701
29: 7 *of* **s** ten thousand talents, and *of* brass 3701
2Ch 1:15 the king made **s** and gold at Jerusalem *as* 3701
1:17 a chariot for six hundred *shekels* of **s**, 3701
2: 7 in **s**, and in brass, and in iron, and in purple, 3701
2:14 in **s**, in brass, in iron, in stone, and 3701
5: 1 the **s**, and the gold, and all the instruments, 3701
9:14 the country brought gold and **s** to Solomon. 3701
9:20 none *were of* **s**; it was *not* any thing 3701
9:21 and **s**, ivory, and apes, and peacocks. 3701
9:24 vessels of **s**, and vessels of gold, and 3701
9:27 the king made **s** in Jerusalem as stones, 3701
15:18 had dedicated, **s**, and gold, and vessels. 3701
16: 2 Asa brought out **s** and gold out of 3701
2Ch 16: 3 behold, I have sent thee **s** and gold; go, 3701
17:11 brought Jehoshaphat presents, and tribute **s**; 3701
21: 3 their father gave them great gifts of **s**, and 3701
24:14 and spoons, and vessels of gold and **s**. 3701
25: 6 out of Israel for an hundred talents of **s**. 3701
25:24 *he took* all the gold and the **s**, and all 3701
27: 5 him the same year an hundred talents of **s**, 3701
32:27 he made himself treasuries for **s**, and 3701
36: 3 the land in an hundred talents of **s** 3701
Ezr 1: 4 let the men of his place help him with **s**, 3701
1: 6 strengthened their hands with vessels of **s**, 3701
1: 9 a thousand chargers of **s**, nine and 3701
1:10 **s** basons of a second sort four hundred and 3701
1:11 of **s** *were* five thousand and four hundred. 3701
2:69 five thousand pound *of* **s**, and one hundred 3701
5:14 also of gold and **s** of the house of God, 3702
6: 5 and **s** vessels of the house of God, 3702
7:15 to carry the **s** and gold, which the king and 3702
7:16 all the **s** and gold that thou canst find in all 3702
7:18 to do with the rest of the **s** and gold, 3702
7:22 Unto an hundred talents *of* **s**, and to an 3702
8:25 weighed unto them the **s**, and the gold, and 3701
8:26 their hand six hundred and fifty talents *of* **s**, 3701
8:26 **s** vessels an hundred talents, *and of* gold an 3701
8:28 the **s** and the gold *are* a freewill offering 3701
8:30 and the Levites the weight of the **s**, 3701
8:33 Now on the fourth day was the **s** and 3701
Ne 5:15 and wine, beside forty shekels of **s**; 3701
7:71 two thousand and two hundred pound *of* **s**. 3701
7:72 two thousand pound *of* **s**, and threescore 3701
Est 1: 6 and purple to **s** rings and pillars of marble: 3701
1: 6 the beds *were of* gold and **s**, upon a 3701
3: 9 I will pay ten thousand talents of **s** to 3701
3:11 The **s** *is* given to thee, the people also, 3701
Job 3:15 had gold, who filled their houses *with* **s**: 3701
22:25 and thou shalt have plenty of **s**. 3701
27:16 Though he heap up **s** as the dust, and 3701
27:17 *it* on, and the innocent shall divide the **s**. 3701
28: 1 Surely there is a vein for the **s**, and a place 3701
28:15 neither shall **s** be weighed *for* the price 3701
Ps 12: 6 *as* **s** tried in a furnace of earth, 3701
66:10 proved us: thou hast tried us, as **s** is tried. 3701
68:13 *be as* the wings of a dove covered with **s**, 3701
68:30 *every one* submit himself with pieces of **s**: 3701
105:37 He brought them forth also with **s** and gold: 3701
115: 4 Their idols *are* **s** and gold, the work of 3701
119:72 unto me than thousands of gold and **s**. 3701
135:15 The idols of the heathen *are* **s** and gold, 3701
Pr 2: 4 If thou seekest her as **s**, and searchest for 3701
3:14 of it *is* better than the merchandise of **s**, 3701
8:10 Receive my instruction, and not **s**; and 3701
8:19 fine gold; and my revenue than choice **s**. 3701
10:20 The tongue of the just *is as* choice **s**: 3701
16:16 understanding rather to be chosen than **s**! 3701
17: 3 The fining pot *is* for **s**, and the furnace for 3701
22: 1 *and* loving favour rather than **s** and gold. 3701
25: 4 Take away the dross from the **s**, and 3701
25:11 *is like* apples of gold in pictures of **s**. 3701
26:23 *are like* a potsherd covered with **s** dross. 3701
27:21 *As* the fining pot for **s**, and the furnace for 3701
Ecc 2: 8 I gathered me also **s** and gold, and 3701
5:10 He that loveth **s** shall not be satisfied *with* 3701
5:10 loveth silver shall not be satisfied *with* **s**; 3701
12: 6 Or ever the **s** cord be loosed, or the golden 3701
SS 1:11 make thee borders of gold with studs of **s**. 3701
3:10 He made the pillars thereof *of* **s**, the bottom 3701
8: 9 a wall, we will build upon her a palace of **s**: 3701
8:11 thereof was to bring a thousand *pieces* of **s**. 3701
Isa 1:22 Thy **s** is become dross, thy wine mixt with 3701
2: 7 Their land also is full *of* **s** and gold, 3701
2:20 In that day a man shall cast his idols of **s**, 3701
13:17 against them, which shall not regard **s**; 3701
30:22 also the covering of thy graven images of **s**, 3701
31: 7 every man shall cast away his idols of **s**, 3701
39: 2 the **s**, and the gold, and the spices, and 3701
40:19 it over with gold, and casteth **s** chains. 3701
46: 6 weigh **s** in the balance, *and* hire a 3701
48:10 Behold, I have refined thee, but not with **s**; 3701
60: 9 from far, their **s** and their gold with them, 3701
60:17 for iron I will bring **s**, and for wood brass, 3701
Jer 6:30 Reprobate **s** shall *men* call them, because 3701
10: 4 They deck it with **s** and with gold; 3701
10: 9 **S** spread into plates is brought from 3701
32: 9 the money, *even* seventeen shekels of **s**. 3701
52:19 *in* gold, and *that* which *was of* **s** *in* silver, 3701
52:19 *in* gold, and *that* which *was of* silver *in* **s**, 3701
Eze 7:19 They shall cast their **s** in the streets, and 3701
7:19 their **s** and their gold shall not be able to 3701
16:13 Thus wast thou decked *with* gold and **s**; and 3701
16:17 thy fair jewels of my gold and of my **s**, 3701
22:18 of the furnace; they are *even the* dross *of* **s**. 3701
22:20 *As they* gather **s**, and brass, and iron, and 3701
22:22 As **s** is melted in the midst of the furnace, 3701
27:12 with **s**, iron, tin, and lead, they traded in thy 3701
28: 4 hast gotten gold and **s** into thy treasures: 3701
38:13 to carry away **s** and gold, to take *away* 3701
Da 2:32 his breast and his arms of **s**, his belly and 3702
2:35 the clay, the brass, the **s**, and the gold, 3702
2:45 the brass, the clay, the **s**, and the gold; 3702
5: 2 **s** vessels which his father Nebuchadnezzar 3702
5: 4 of **s**, of brass, of iron, of wood, and 3702
5:23 thou hast praised the gods of **s**, and gold, 3702
11: 8 *and* with their precious vessels *of* **s** and 3701
11:38 **s**, and with precious stones, and pleasant 3701
11:43 power over the treasures of gold and of **s**, 3701
Hos 2: 8 and oil, and multiplied her **s** and gold, 3701
3: 2 I bought her to me for fifteen *pieces* of **s**, 3701
8: 4 *of* their **s** and their gold have they made 3701
9: 6 the pleasant *places* for their **s**, nettles shall 3701
13: 2 have made them molten images of their **s**, 3701
Joel 3: 5 Because ye have taken my **s** and my gold, 3701
Am 2: 6 because they sold the righteous for **s**, and 3701
8: 6 That we may buy the poor for **s**, and 3701
Na 2: 9 Take ye the spoil of **s**, take the spoil of 3701
Hab 2:19 it *is* laid over *with* gold and **s**, and *there is* 3701

S

Zep 1:11 cut down; all they that bear s are cut off. 3701
1:18 Neither their s nor their gold shall be able 3701
Hag 2: 8 The s *is* mine, and the gold *is* mine, 3701
Zec 6:11 take s and gold, and make crowns, and 3701
9: 3 heaped up s as the dust, and fine gold as 3701
11:12 weighed *for* my price thirty *pieces* of s. 3701
11:13 I took the thirty *pieces* of s, and cast them 3701
13: 9 will refine them as s is refined, and will try 3701
14:14 gold, and s, and apparel, in great 3701
Mal 3: 3 he shall sit *as* a refiner and purifier of s: 3701
3: 3 sons of Levi, and purge them as gold and s, 3701
Mt 10: 9 Provide neither gold, nor s, nor brass in your *696*
26:15 covenanted with him for thirty pieces of s. *694*
27: 3 brought again the thirty pieces of s to *694*
27: 5 And he cast down the pieces of s in *694*
27: 6 And the chief priests took the s pieces, and *694*
27: 9 saying, And they took the thirty pieces of s, *694*
Lk 15: 8 Either what woman having ten pieces of s, *1406*
Ac 3: 6 Then Peter said, S and gold have I none; but *694*
17:29 or s, or stone, graven by art and *696*
19:19 and found *it* fifty thousand *pieces* of s. *694*
19:24 which made s shrines for Diana, *693*
20:33 I have coveted no *man's* s, or gold, or *694*
1Co 3:12 s, precious stones, wood, hay, stubble; *696*
2Ti 2:20 there are not only vessels of gold and of s, *693*
Jas 5: 3 Your gold and s is cankered; and the rust of *696*
1Pe 1:18 not redeemed with corruptible *things*, as s *694*
Rev 9:20 idols of gold, and s, and brass, and stone, *693*
18:12 and s, and precious stones, and of pearls, and *696*

SILVERLINGS (1) [SILVER]

Isa 7:23 there were a thousand vines at a thousand s, 3701

SILVERSMITH (1) [SILVER, SMITH]

Ac 19:24 For a certain *man* named Demetrius, a s, *695*

SIMEON (50) [SIMEONITES]

Ge 29:33 me this *son* also: and she called his name S. 8095
34:25 S and Levi, Dinah's brethren, took each 8095
34:30 Jacob said to S and Levi, Ye have troubled 8095
35:23 S, and Levi, and Judah, and Issachar, and 8095
42:24 took from them S, and bound him before 8095
42:36 S *is* not, and ye will take Benjamin *away*: 8095
43:23 And he brought S out unto them. 8095
46:10 the sons of S; Jemuel, and Jamin, and 8095
48: 5 as Reuben and S, they shall be mine. 8095
49: 5 S and Levi *are* brethren; instruments of 8095
Ex 1: 2 Reuben, S, Levi, and Judah, 8095
6:15 the sons of S; Jemuel, and Jamin, and 8095
6:15 these *are* the families of S. 8095
Nu 1: 6 Of S; Shelumiel the son of Zurishaddai. 8095
1:22 Of the children of S, *by* their generations, 8095
1:23 *even* of the tribe of S, *were* fifty and 8095
2:12 which pitch by him *shall be* the tribe of S: 8095
2:12 the captain of the children of S *shall be* 8095
7:36 prince of the children of S, *did offer*: 8095
10:19 of S *was* Shelumiel the son of Zurishaddai. 8095
13: 5 Of the tribe of S, Shaphat the son of Hori. 8095
26:12 The sons of S after their families: 8095
34:20 of the tribe of the children of S, 8095
Dt 27:12 S, and Levi, and Judah, and Issachar, and 8095
Jos 19: 1 the second lot came forth to S, *even* for 8095
19: 1 *even* for the tribe of the children of S 8095
19: 8 children of S according to their families. 8095
19: 9 *was* the inheritance of the children of S: 8095
19: 9 the children of S had their inheritance 8095
21: 4 out of the tribe of S, and out of the tribe of 8099
21: 9 out of the tribe of the children of S, these 8095
Jdg 1: 3 Judah said unto S his brother, Come up 8095
1: 3 with thee into thy lot. So S went with him. 8095
1:17 Judah went with S his brother, and 8095
1Ch 2: 1 Reuben, S, Levi, and Judah, Issachar, and 8095
4:24 The sons of S *were*, Nemuel, and Jamin, 8095
4:42 *even* of the sons of S, five hundred men, 8095
6:65 and out of the tribe of the children of S, and 8095
12:25 Of the children of S, mighty *men* of valour 8095
2Ch 15: 9 of Ephraim and Manasseh, and out of S: 8095
34: 6 and Ephraim, and S, even unto Naphtali, 8095
Eze 48:24 unto the west side, S *shall have* a *portion*. 8095
48:25 by the border of S, from the east side unto 8095
48:33 one gate of S, one gate of Issachar, one gate 8095
Lk 2:25 a man in Jerusalem, whose name *was* S; *4826*
2:34 And S blessed them, and said unto Mary *4826*
3:30 Which was *the son* of S, which was *the son* *4826*
Ac 13: 1 and S that was called Niger, and Lucius of *4826*
15:14 S hath declared how God at the first did *4826*
Rev 7: 7 Of the tribe of S *were* sealed twelve *4826*

SIMEONITES (3) [SIMEON]

Nu 25:14 a prince of a chief house among the S. 8099
26:14 These *are* the families of the S, twenty and 8099
1Ch 27:16 of the S, Shephatiah the son of Maachah: 8099

SIMILITUDE (11) [SIMILITUDES]

Nu 12: 8 and the s of the LORD shall he behold: 8544
Dt 4:12 heard the voice of the words, but saw no s; 8544
4:15 for ye saw no *manner of* s on the day *that* 8544
4:16 the s of any figure, the likeness of male or 8544
2Ch 4: 3 under it *was* the s of oxen, which did 1823
Ps 106:20 Thus they changed their glory into the s of 8403
144:12 polished *after* the s of a palace: 8403
Da 10:16 *one* like the s of the sons of men touched 1823
Ro 5:14 sinned after the s of Adam's transgression, *3667*
Heb 7:15 for that after the s of Melchisedec there *3665*
Jas 3: 9 we men, which are made after the s of God. *3669*

SIMILITUDES (1) [SIMILITUDE]

Hos 12:10 and used s by the ministry of the prophets. 1819

SIMON (69) [PETER, SIMON'S]

Mt 4:18 S called Peter, and Andrew his brother, *4613*
10: 2 The first, S, who is called Peter, and *4613*
10: 4 S the Canaanite, and Judas Iscariot, *4613*
13:55 James, and Joses, and S, and Judas? *4613*
16:16 And S Peter answered and said, Thou art *4613*
16:17 said unto him, Blessed art thou, S Bar-jona: *4613*
17:25 saying, What thinkest thou, S? *4613*
26: 6 was in Bethany, in the house of S the leper, *4613*
27:32 they found a man of Cyrene, S by name: *4613*
Mk 1:16 he saw S and Andrew his brother casting a *4613*
1:29 they entered into the house of S and *4613*
1:36 And S and they that were with him *4613*
3:16 And S he surnamed Peter; *4613*
3:18 and Thaddeus, and S the Canaanite, *4613*
6: 3 of James, and Joses, and of Juda, and S? *4613*
14: 3 And being in Bethany in the house of S *4613*
14:37 and saith unto Peter, S, sleepest thou? *4613*
15:21 And they compel one S a Cyrenian, *4613*
Lk 5: 4 he said unto S, Launch out into the deep, *4613*
5: 5 And S answering said unto him, Master, *4613*
5: 8 When S Peter saw *it*, he fell down at Jesus' *4613*
5:10 of Zebedee, which were partners with S. *4613*
5:10 And Jesus said unto S, Fear not; *4613*
6:14 S, (whom he also named Peter,) and *4613*
6:15 the *son* of Alpheus, and S called Zelotes, *4613*
7:40 S, I have somewhat to say unto thee. *4613*
7:43 S answered and said, I suppose that *he*, to *4613*
7:44 and said unto S, Seest thou this woman? *4613*
22:31 And the Lord said, S, Simon, behold, Satan *4613*
22:31 And the Lord said, Simon, S, behold, Satan *4613*
23:26 they laid hold upon one S, a Cyrenian, *4613*
24:34 is risen indeed, and hath appeared to S. *4613*
Jn 1:40 was Andrew, S Peter's brother. *4613*
1:41 He first findeth his own brother S, and *4613*
1:42 he said, Thou art S the son of Jona: *4613*
6: 8 Andrew, S Peter's brother, saith unto him, *4613*
6:68 Then S Peter answered him, Lord, to whom *4613*
6:71 He spake of Judas Iscariot *the son* of S: *4613*
13: 6 Then cometh he to S Peter: and *Peter* saith *4613*
13: 9 S Peter saith unto him, Lord, not my feet *4613*
13:24 S Peter therefore beckoned to him, that *he* *4613*
13:26 he gave *it* to Judas Iscariot, *the son* of S. *4613*
13:36 S Peter said unto him, Lord, whither goest *4613*
18:10 Then S Peter having a sword drew it, and *4613*
18:15 And S Peter followed Jesus, and *so* *4613*
18:25 And S Peter stood and warmed himself. *4613*
20: 2 and cometh to S Peter, and to the other *4613*
20: 6 Then cometh S Peter following him, and *4613*
21: 2 There were together S Peter, and *4613*
21: 3 S Peter saith unto them, I go a fishing. *4613*
21: 7 Now when S Peter heard that it was *4613*
21:11 S Peter went up, and drew the net to land *4613*
21:15 Jesus saith to S Peter, Simon, *son* of Jonas, *4613*
21:15 Jesus saith to Simon Peter, S, *son* of Jonas, *4613*
21:16 S, *son* of Jonas, lovest thou me? *4613*
21:17 third time, S, *son* of Jonas, lovest thou me? *4613*
Ac 1:13 and S Zelotes, and Judas *the brother* of *4613*
8: 9 But there was a certain man, called S, *4613*
8:13 Then S himself believed also: and when he *4613*
8:18 And when S saw that through laying on of *4613*
8:24 Then answered S, and said, Pray ye to *4613*
9:43 many days in Joppa with one S a tanner. *4613*
10: 5 and call for *one* S, whose surname is Peter: *4613*
10: 6 He lodgeth with one S a tanner, *4613*
10:18 And called, and asked whether S, *4613*
10:32 Send therefore to Joppa, and call hither S, *4613*
10:32 he is lodged in the house of *one* S a tanner *4613*
11:13 Send men to Joppa, and call for S, *4613*
2Pe 1: 1 S Peter, a servant and an apostle of Jesus *4826*

SIMON'S (7) [SIMON]

Mk 1:30 But S wife's mother lay sick of a fever, and *4613*
Lk 4:38 of the synagogue, and entered into S house. *4613*
4:38 And S wife's mother was taken with a great *4613*
5: 3 which was S, and prayed him that *he* would *4613*
Jn 12: 4 S *son*, which should betray him, *4613*
13: 2 of Judas Iscariot, S *son*, to betray him; *4613*
Ac 10:17 Cornelius had made inquiry for S house, *4613*

SIMPLE (20) [SIMPLICITY]

Ps 19: 7 of the LORD *is* sure, making wise the s. 6612
116: 6 The LORD preserveth the s: I was brought 6612
119:130 it giveth understanding unto the s. 6612
Pr 1: 4 To give subtilty to the s, to the young man 6612
1:22 How long, ye s ones, will ye love 6612
1:32 For the turning away of the s shall slay 6612
7: 7 beheld among the s ones, I discerned 6612
8: 5 O ye s, understand wisdom: and, ye fools, 6612
9: 4 Whoso *is* s, let him turn in hither: *as for* 6612
9:13 *she is* s, and knoweth nothing. 6615
9:16 Whoso *is* s, let him turn in hither: and 6612
14:15 The s believeth every word: but the prudent 6612
14:18 The s inherit folly: but the prudent are 6612
19:25 Smite a scorner, and the s will beware: and 6612
21:11 the scorner is punished, the s is made wise: 6612
22: 3 but the s pass on, and are punished. 6612
27:12 *but* the s pass on, *and* are punished. 6612
Eze 45:20 every one that erreth, and for *him that is* s: 6612
Ro 16:18 and fair speeches deceive the hearts of the s. *172*
16:19 *that which is* good, and s concerning evil. *185*

SIMPLICITY (5) [SIMPLE]

2Sa 15:11 they went in their s, and they knew not any 8537
Pr 1:22 How long, ye simple ones, will ye love s? 6612
Ro 12: 8 he that giveth, *let him do it* with s; he that *572*
2Co 1:12 that in s and godly sincerity, not with fleshly *572*
11: 3 your minds should be corrupted from the s *572*

SIMRI (1)

1Ch 26:10 S the chief, (for *though* he was not 8113

SIN (448) [SINFUL, SINNED, SINNER, SINNERS, SINNEST, SINNETH, SINNING, SINS]

Ge 4: 7 if thou doest not well, s lieth at the door. 2403
18:20 and because their s is very grievous; 2403
20: 9 on me and on my kingdom a great s? 2401
31:36 what *is* my s, that thou hast *so* 2403
39: 9 this great wickedness, and s against God? 2398
42:22 saying, Do not s against the child; 2398
50:17 the trespass of thy brethren, and their s; 2403
Ex 10:17 my s only *this* once, and intreat the LORD 2403
16: 1 of Israel came unto the wilderness of S, 5512
17: 1 Israel journeyed from the wilderness of S, 5512
20:20 fear may be before your faces, that ye s not. 2398
23:33 thy land, lest they make thee s against me: 2398
29:14 fire without the camp: it *is* a s offering. 2403
29:36 a bullock *for* a s offering for atonement: 2403
30:10 the blood of the s offering of atonements: 2403
32:21 thou hast brought *so* great a s upon them? 2401
32:30 unto the people, Ye have sinned a great s: 2401
32:30 I shall make an atonement for your s. 2403
32:31 this people have sinned a great s, and 2401
32:32 Yet now, if thou wilt forgive their s; and 2403
32:34 when I visit, I will visit their s upon them. 2403
34: 7 forgiving iniquity and transgression and s, 2403
34: 9 pardon our iniquity and our s, and take us 2403
Lev 4: 2 If a soul shall s through ignorance against 2398
4: 3 If the priest that is anointed do s according 2398
4: 3 do sin according to the s of the people; 819
4: 3 let him bring for his s, which he hath 2403
4: 3 blemish unto the LORD for a s offering. 2403
4: 8 all the fat of the bullock *for* the s offering; 2403
4:13 of Israel s through ignorance, 7686
4:14 When the s, which they have sinned against 2403
4:14 shall offer a young bullock for the s, 2403
4:20 as he did with the bullock for a s offering, 2403
4:21 it *is* a s offering for the congregation. 2403
4:23 Or if his s, wherein he hath sinned, come to 2403
4:24 before the LORD: it *is* a s offering. 2403
4:25 the blood of the s offering with his finger, 2403
4:26 an atonement for him as concerning his s, 2403
4:27 if any one of the common people s through 2398
4:28 Or if his s, which he hath sinned, come to 2403
4:28 for his s which he hath sinned. 2403
4:29 his hand upon the head of the s offering, 2403
4:29 slay the s offering in the place of the burnt 2403
4:32 if he bring a lamb for a s offering, he shall 2403
4:33 his hand upon the head of the s offering, 2403
4:33 slay it for a s offering in the place where 2403
4:34 the blood of the s offering with his finger, 2403
4:35 the priest shall make an atonement for his s 2403
5: 1 if a soul s, and hear the voice of swearing, 2398
5: 6 the LORD for his s which he hath sinned, 2403
5: 6 or a kid of the goats, for a s offering; 2403
5: 6 an atonement for him concerning his s. 2403
5: 7 one for a s offering, and the other for a 2403
5: 8 offer *that* which *is* for the s offering first, 2403
5: 9 of the s offering upon the side of the altar; 2403
5: 9 at the bottom of the altar: it *is* a s offering. 2403
5:10 for him for his s which he had sinned, 2403
5:11 of an ephah of fine flour for a s offering; 2403
5:11 frankincense thereon: for it *is* a s offering. 2403
5:12 by fire unto the LORD: it *is* a s offering. 2403
5:13 his s that he hath sinned in one of these, 2403
5:15 commit a trespass, and s through ignorance, 2398
5:17 if a soul s, and commit any *of these things* 2398
6: 2 If a soul s, and commit a trespass against 2398
6:17 as *is* the s offering, and as the trespass 2403
6:25 This *is* the law of the s offering: 2403
6:25 the s offering be killed before the LORD: 2403
6:26 The priest that offereth it for s shall eat it: 2398
6:30 no s offering, whereof *any* of the blood is 2403
7: 7 As the s offering *is*, so *is* the trespass 2403
7:37 of the s offering, and of the trespass 2403
8: 2 a bullock *for* the s offering, and two rams, 2403
8:14 he brought the bullock *for* the s offering: 2403
8:14 the head of the bullock *for* the s offering. 2403
9: 2 Take thee a young calf for a s offering, and 2403
9: 3 Take ye a kid of the goats for a s offering; 2403
9: 7 offer thy s offering, and thy burnt offering, 2403
9: 8 the altar, and slew the calf of the s offering, 2403
9:10 the caul above the liver of the s offering, 2403
9:15 which *was* the s offering for the people, 2403
9:15 and slew it, and offered it for s, as the first. 2398
9:22 came down from offering of the s offering, 2403
10:16 diligently sought the goat of the s offering, 2403
10:17 Wherefore have ye not eaten the s offering 2403
10:19 *this* day have they offered their s offering 2403
10:19 *if* I had eaten the s offering to day, should 2403
12: 6 or a turtledove, for a s offering, 2403
12: 8 and the other for a s offering: 2403
14:13 the place where he shall kill the s offering 2403
14:13 for as the s offering *is* the priest's, *so is* 2403
14:19 the priest shall offer the s offering, and 2403
14:22 the one shall be a s offering, and the other 2403
14:31 the one *for* a s offering, and the other *for* a 2403
15:15 the one *for* a s offering, and the other *for* a 2403
15:30 priest shall offer the one *for* a s offering, 2403
16: 3 with a young bullock for a s offering, 2403
16: 5 Israel two kids of the goats for a s offering, 2403
16: 6 shall offer *his* bullock of the s offering, 2403
16: 9 lot fell, and offer him *for* a s offering. 2403
16:11 shall bring the bullock of the s offering, 2403
16:11 shall kill the bullock of the s offering 2403
16:15 Then shall he kill the goat of the s offering, 2403
16:25 the fat of the s offering shall he burn upon 2403
16:27 the bullock for the s offering, and the goat 2403
16:27 sin offering, and the goat for the s offering, 2403
19:17 thy neighbour, and not suffer s upon him. 2399
19:22 the LORD for his s which he hath done: 2403
19:22 the s which he hath done shall be forgiven 2403
20:20 they shall bear their s; they shall die 2399
22: 9 lest they bear s for it, and die therefore, if 2399
23:19 one kid of the goats for a s offering, 2403
24:15 Whosoever curseth his God shall bear his s. 2399
Nu 5: 6 woman shall commit any s that men 2403
5: 7 they shall confess their s which they have 2403
6:11 priest shall offer the one for a s offering, 2403
6:14 first year without blemish for a s offering, 2403
6:16 shall offer his s offering, and his burnt 2403
7:16 One kid of the goats for a s offering: 2403
7:22 One kid of the goats for a s offering: 2403
7:28 One kid of the goats for a s offering: 2403

S

Nu 7:34 One kid of the goats for a **s offering**: 2403
7:40 One kid of the goats for a **s offering**: 2403
7:46 One kid of the goats for a **s offering**: 2403
7:52 One kid of the goats for a **s offering**: 2403
7:58 One kid of the goats for a **s offering**: 2403
7:64 One kid of the goats for a **s offering**: 2403
7:70 One kid of the goats for a **s offering**: 2403
7:76 One kid of the goats for a **s offering**: 2403
7:82 One kid of the goats for a **s offering**: 2403
7:87 the kids of the goats for **s offering** twelve. 2403
8: 8 bullock shalt thou take for a **s offering**. 2403
8:12 thou shalt offer the one *for* a **s offering**, 2403
9:13 appointed season, that man shall bear his **s**. 2399
12:11 I beseech thee, lay not the **s** upon us, 2403
15:24 and one kid of the goats for a **s offering**. 2403
15:25 their **s offering** before the LORD, 2403
15:27 if any soul **s** through ignorance, then 2398
15:27 a she goat of the first year for a **s offering**. 2403
16:22 shall one man **s**, and wilt thou be wroth 2398
18: 9 every **s offering** of theirs, and every 2403
18:22 the congregation, lest they bear **s**, and die. 2399
18:32 ye shall bear no **s** by reason of it, when ye 2399
19: 9 of separation: it *is* a **purification for s**. 2403
19:17 of the burnt *heifer* of **purification for s**, 2403
27: 3 but died in his own **s**, and had no sons. 2399
28:15 one kid of the goats for a **s offering** unto 2403
28:22 one goat for a **s offering**, to make an 2403
29: 5 one kid of the goats for a **s offering**, 2403
29:11 One kid of the goats *for* a **s offering**; beside 2403
29:11 beside the **s offering** of atonement, and 2403
29:16 one kid of the goats *for* a **s offering**; beside 2403
29:19 one kid of the goats *for* a **s offering**; beside 2403
29:22 one goat for a **s offering**; beside 2403
29:25 one kid of the goats *for* a **s offering**; beside 2403
29:28 one goat for a **s offering**; beside 2403
29:31 one goat for a **s offering**; beside 2403
29:34 one goat for a **s offering**; beside 2403
29:38 one goat for a **s offering**; beside 2403
32:23 and be sure your **s** will find you out. 2403
33:11 and encamped in the wilderness of **S**. 5512
33:12 their journey out of the wilderness of **S**, 5512
Dt 9:21 I took your **s**, the calf which ye had made, 2403
9:27 nor to their wickedness, nor to their **s**: 2403
15: 9 LORD against thee, and it be **s** unto thee. 2399
19:15 or for any **s**, in any sin that he sinneth: 2403
19:15 or for any sin, in any **s** that he sinneth: 2399
20:18 should ye **s** against the LORD your God. 2398
21:22 if a man have **committed a s** worthy of 2399
22:26 *there is* in the damsel no **s** *worthy* of death: 2399
23:21 require it of thee; and it would be **s** in thee. 2399
23:22 shalt forbear to vow, it shall be no **s** in thee. 2399
24: 4 thou shalt not **cause** the land **to s**, 2398
24:15 cry against thee unto the LORD, and it be **s** unto thee. 2399
24:16 man shall be put to death for his own **s**. 2399
1Sa 2:17 Wherefore the **s** of the young men was very 2403
2:25 If one man **s** against another, the judge 2398
2:25 if a man **s** against the LORD, who shall 2398
12:23 God forbid that I should **s** against 2398
14:33 Behold, the people **s** against the LORD, 2398
14:34 **s** not against the LORD in eating with 2398
14:38 and see wherein this **s** hath been *this* day. 2403
15:23 For rebellion *is as* the **s** of witchcraft, and 2403
15:25 pardon my **s**, and turn again with me, 2403
19: 4 Let not the king **s** against his servant, 2398
19: 5 then wilt thou **s** against innocent blood, 2398
20: 1 what *is* my **s** before thy father, that he 2403
2Sa 12:13 The LORD also hath put away thy **s**; 2403
1Ki 8:34 forgive the **s** of thy people Israel, and 2403
8:35 confess thy name, and turn from their **s**, 2403
8:36 forgive the **s** of thy servants, and of thy 2403
8:46 If they **s** against thee, (for *there is* no man 2398
12:30 this thing became a **s**: for the people went 2403
13:34 this thing became **s** unto the house of 2403
14:16 who did **s**, and who made Israel to sin. 2398
14:16 who did sin, and who made Israel **to s**. 2398
15:26 in his **s** wherewith he made Israel to sin. 2403
15:26 in his sin wherewith he **made** Israel **to s**. 2398
15:30 he sinned, and which he **made** Israel **s**, 2398
15:34 in his **s** wherewith he made Israel to sin. 2403
15:34 in his sin wherewith he **made** Israel **to s**. 2398
16: 2 hast **made** my people Israel **to s**, 2398
16:13 and *by* which they **made** Israel **to s**, 2398
16:19 in his **s** which he did, to make Israel sin. 2403
16:19 in his sin which he did, to **make** Israel **s**. 2398
16:26 in his **s** wherewith he made Israel to sin, 2403
16:26 in his sin wherewith he **made** Israel **to s**, 2398
17:18 art thou come unto me to call my **s** to 5771
21:22 *me* to anger, and **made** Israel **to s**. 2398
22:52 the son of Nebat, who **made** Israel **to s**: 2398
2Ki 3: 3 the son of Nebat, which **made** Israel **to s**; 2398
10:29 who **made** Israel **to s**, Jehu departed not 2398
10:31 sins of Jeroboam, which **made** Israel **to s**. 2398
12:16 **s** money was not brought *into* the house of 2403
13: 2 the son of Nebat, which **made** Israel **to s**; 2398
13: 6 who **made** Israel **s**, *but* walked therein: 2398
13:11 the son of Nebat, who **made** Israel **s**: 2398
14: 6 man shall be put to death for his own **s**. 2399
14:24 the son of Nebat, who **made** Israel **to s**. 2398
15: 9 the son of Nebat, who **made** Israel **to s**. 2398
15:18 the son of Nebat, who **made** Israel **to s**. 2398
15:24 the son of Nebat, who **made** Israel **to s**. 2398
15:28 the son of Nebat, who **made** Israel **to s**. 2398
17:21 the LORD, and **made** them **s** a great sin. 2398
17:21 the LORD, and made them sin a great **s**. 2401
21:11 hath **made** Judah also **to s** with his idols: 2398
21:16 beside his **s** where*with* he made Judah to 2403
21:16 his sin where*with* he **made** Judah **to s**, 2398
21:17 and all that he did, and his **s** that he sinned, 2403
23:15 who **made** Israel **to s**, had made, both that 2398
2Ch 6:22 If a man **s** against his neighbour, and 2398
6:25 forgive the **s** of thy people Israel, and 2403
6:26 confess thy name, *and* turn from their **s**, 2403
6:27 forgive the **s** of thy servants, and of thy 2403
6:36 If they **s** against thee, (for *there is* no man 2398
7:14 will forgive their **s**, and will heal their land. 2403

2Ch 25: 4 but every man shall die for his own **s**. 2399
29:21 for a **s offering** for the kingdom, and 2403
29:23 he goats for the **s offering** before the king 2403
29:24 the **s offering** *should be made* for all Israel. 2403
33:19 all his **s**, and his trespass, and the places 2403
Ezr 6:17 for a **s offering** for all Israel, twelve he 2409
8:35 twelve he goats *for* a **s offering**: 2403
Ne 4: 5 let not their **s** be blotted out from before 2403
6:13 **s**, and *that* they might have *matter* for an 2398
10:33 for the **s offerings** to make an atonement 2403
13:26 Did not Solomon king of Israel **s** by these 2398
13:26 even him did outlandish women **cause to s**. 2398
Job 2:10 In all this did not Job **s** with his lips. 2398
5:24 shalt visit thy habitation, and shalt not **s**. 2398
10: 6 mine iniquity, and searchest after my **s**? 2403
10:14 If I **s**, then thou markest me, and thou wilt 2398
13:23 me to know my transgression and my **s**. 2403
14:16 my steps: dost thou not watch over my **s**? 2403
20:11 His bones are full *of the s of* his youth, NIH
31:30 (Neither have I suffered my mouth to **s** by 2398
34:37 For he addeth rebellion unto his **s**, 2403
35: 3 shall I have, *if I be cleansed* from my **s**? 2403
Ps 4: 4 Stand in awe, and **s** not: commune with 2398
32: 1 *is* forgiven, whose **s** *is* covered. 2401
32: 5 I acknowledged my **s** unto thee, and 2403
32: 5 and thou forgavest the iniquity of my **s**. 2403
38: 3 *there any* rest in my bones because of my **s**. 2403
38:18 mine iniquity; I will be sorry for my **s**. 2403
39: 1 to my ways, that *I* **s** not with my tongue: 2398
40: 6 and **s offering** hast thou not required. 2401
51: 2 mine iniquity, and cleanse me from my **s**. 2403
51: 3 and my **s** *is* ever before me. 2403
51: 5 and in **s** did my mother conceive me. 2399
59: 3 my transgression, nor *for* my **s**, O LORD. 2403
59:12 *For* the **s** of their mouth *and* the words of 2403
85: 2 of thy people, thou hast covered all their **s**. 2403
109: 7 be condemned: and let his prayer become **s**. 2401
109:14 let not the **s** of his mother be blotted out. 2403
119:11 mine heart, that I might not **s** against thee. 2398
Pr 10:16 *tendeth* to life: the fruit of the wicked to **s**. 2403
10:19 the multitude of words there wanteth not **s**: 6588
14: 9 Fools make a mock at **s**: but among 817
14:34 a nation: but **s** *is* a reproach to any people. 2403
20: 9 made my heart clean, I am pure from my **s**? 2403
21: 4 *and* the plowing of the wicked, *is* **s**. 2403
24: 9 The thought of foolishness *is* **s**: and 2403
Ecc 5: 6 not thy mouth to **cause** thy flesh **to s**; 2398
Isa 3: 9 they declare their **s** as Sodom, they hide *it* 2403
5:18 of vanity, and **s** as it were with a cart rope: 2403
6: 7 iniquity is taken away, and thy **s** purged. 2403
27: 9 and this *is* all the fruit to take away his **s**; 2403
30: 1 not of my Spirit, that *they* may add **s** to sin: 2403
30: 1 not of my Spirit, that *they* may add sin to **s**: 2403
31: 7 own hands have made unto you *for* a **s**. 2399
53:10 thou shalt make his soul an **offering for s**, 817
53:12 he bare the **s** of many, and 2399
Jer 16:10 **s** that we have **committed** against 2398+2403
16:18 their iniquity and their **s** double; 2403
17: 1 The **s** of Judah *is* written with a pen of iron, 2403
17: 3 *and* thy high places for **s**, throughout all thy 2403
18:23 neither blot out their **s** from thy sight, but 2403
31:34 and I will remember their **s** no more. 2403
32:35 do this abomination, to **cause** Judah **to s**. 2398
36: 3 that I may forgive their iniquity and their **s**. 2403
51: 5 though their land was filled *with* **s** against 817
La 4: 6 than the **punishment of** the **s** of Sodom, 2403
Eze 3:20 he shall die in his **s**, and his righteousness 2403
3:21 the righteous *man*, that the righteous **s** not, 2398
3:21 he doth not **s**, he shall surely live, because 2398
18:24 in his **s** that he hath sinned, in them shall he 2403
30:15 I will pour my fury upon **S**, the strength of 5512
30:16 **S** shall have great pain, and No shall be 5512
33:14 if he turn from his **s**, and do that which is 2403
40:39 and the **s offering** and the trespass offering. 2403
42:13 the **s offering**, and the trespass offering; 2403
43:19 a young bullock for a **s offering**. 2403
43:21 shalt take the bullock also of the **s offering**, 2403
43:22 the goats without blemish for a **s offering**; 2403
43:25 prepare every day a goat *for* a **s offering**: 2403
44:27 he shall offer his **s offering**, saith the Lord 2403
44:29 the **s offering**, and the trespass offering; 2403
45:17 he shall prepare the **s offering**, and 2403
45:19 shall take of the blood of the **s offering**, 2403
45:22 of the land a bullock *for* a **s offering**. 2403
45:23 and a kid of the goats daily *for* a **s offering**. 2403
45:25 according to the **s offering**, according to 2403
46:20 the trespass offering and the **s offering**, 2403
Da 9:20 confessing my **s** and the sin of my people 2403
9:20 my sin and the **s** of my people Israel, 2403
Hos 4: 8 They eat *up* the **s** of my people, and 2403
8:11 Ephraim hath made many altars to **s**, 2398
8:11 altars to sin, altars shall be unto him to **s**. 2398
10: 8 of Aven, the **s** of Israel, shall be destroyed: 2403
12: 8 shall find none iniquity in me that *were* **s**. 2399
13: 2 now they **s** more and more, and have made 2398
13:12 of Ephraim *is* bound up; his **s** *is* hid. 2403
Am 8:14 They that swear by the **s** of Samaria, and 819
Mic 1:13 she *is* the beginning of the **s** to the daughter 2403
3: 8 Jacob his transgression, and to Israel his **s**. 2403
6: 7 the fruit of my body *for* the **s** of my soul? 2403
Zec 13: 1 to the inhabitants of Jerusalem for **s** and 2403
Mt 12:31 All *manner of* **s** and blasphemy shall be *266*
18:21 how oft shall my brother **s** against me, and I *264*
Jn 1:29 which taketh away the **s** of the world. *266*
5:14 **s** no more, lest a worse *thing* come unto thee. *264*
8: 7 unto them, He that is **without s** among you, *361*
8:11 do I condemn thee: go, and **s** no more. *264*
8:34 Whosoever committeth **s** is the servant of *266*
8:34 committeth sin is the servant of **s**. *266*
8:46 Which of you convinceth me of **s**? And if I *266*
9: 2 saying, Master, who did **s**, this *man*, or *264*
9:41 If ye were blind, ye should have no **s**: *266*
9:41 ye say, We see; therefore your **s** remaineth. *266*
15:22 and spoken unto them, they had not had **s**: *266*
15:22 but now they have no cloke for their **s**. *266*

Jn 15:24 none other *man* did, they had not had **s**: *266*
16: 8 he will reprove the world of **s**, and *266*
16: 9 Of **s**, because they believe not on me; *266*
19:11 delivered me unto thee hath the greater **s**. *266*
Ac 7:60 Lord, lay not this **s** to their charge. *266*
Ro 3: 9 and Gentiles, that *they* are all under **s**; *266*
3:20 for by the law *is* the knowledge of **s**. *266*
4: 8 the man to whom the Lord will not impute **s**. *266*
5:12 as by one man **s** entered into the world, and *266*
5:12 sin entered into the world, and death by **s**; *266*
5:13 For until the law **s** was in the world: but *266*
5:13 but **s** is not imputed when there is no law. *266*
5:20 But where **s** abounded, grace did much more *266*
5:21 That as **s** hath reigned unto death, even so *266*
6: 1 Shall we continue in **s**, that grace may *266*
6: 2 How shall we, that are dead to **s**, live any *266*
6: 6 *him*, that the body of **s** might be destroyed, *266*
6: 6 that henceforth we should not serve **s**. *266*
6: 7 For he that is dead is freed from **s**. *266*
6:10 For in that he died, he died unto **s** once: but *266*
6:11 ye also yourselves to be dead indeed unto **s**, *266*
6:12 Let not **s** therefore reign in your mortal *266*
6:13 *as* instruments of unrighteousness unto **s**: *266*
6:14 For **s** shall not have dominion over you: *266*
6:15 shall we **s**, because we are not under the law, *264*
6:16 whether of **s** unto death, or of obedience *266*
6:17 that ye were the servants of **s**, but ye have *266*
6:18 Being then made free from **s**, ye became *266*
6:20 For when ye were the servants of **s**, ye were *266*
6:22 But now being made free from **s**, and *266*
6:23 For the wages of **s** *is* death; but the gift of *266*
7: 7 *Is* the law **s**? God forbid. Nay, I had not *266*
7: 7 Nay, I had not known **s**, but by the law: for I *266*
7: 8 But **s**, taking occasion by the commandment, *266*
7: 8 For without the law **s** *was* dead. *266*
7: 9 commandment came, **s** revived, and I died. *266*
7:11 For **s**, taking occasion by the commandment, *266*
7:13 But **s**, that it might appear sin, working death *266*
7:13 But sin, that it might appear **s**, working death *266*
7:13 that **s** by the commandment might become *266*
7:14 law is spiritual: but I am carnal, sold under **s**. *266*
7:17 more I that do it, but **s** that dwelleth in me. *266*
7:20 more I that do it, but **s** that dwelleth in me. *266*
7:23 bringing me into captivity to the law of **s** *266*
7:25 law of God; but with the flesh the law of **s**. *266*
8: 2 Jesus hath made me free from the law of **s** *266*
8: 3 and for **s**, condemned sin in the flesh: *266*
8: 3 and for sin, condemned **s** in the flesh: *266*
8:10 *be* in you, the body *is* dead because of **s**; *266*
14:23 of faith: for whatsoever *is* not of faith is **s**. *266*
1Co 6:18 Every **s** that a man doeth is without *265*
8:12 But when ye **s** so against the brethren, and *264*
8:12 their weak conscience, ye **s** against Christ. *264*
15:34 Awake to righteousness, and **s** not: for some *264*
15:56 The sting of death *is* **s**; *266*
15:56 death *is* sin; and the strength of **s** *is* the law. *266*
2Co 5:21 For he hath made him *to be* **s** for us, *266*
5:21 made him *to be* sin for us, who knew no **s**; *266*
Gal 2:17 *is* therefore Christ the minister of **s**? *266*
3:22 But the scripture hath concluded all under **s**, *266*
Eph 4:26 Be ye angry, and **s** not: let not the sun go *264*
2Th 2: 3 and *that* man of **s** be revealed, the son of *266*
1Ti 5:20 Them that **s** rebuke before all, that others *264*
Heb 3:13 be hardened through the deceitfulness of **s**. *266*
4:15 *points* tempted like as *we are*, *yet* without **s**. *266*
9:26 to put away **s** by the sacrifice of himself. *266*
9:28 the second time without **s** unto salvation. *266*
10: 6 *sacrifices* for **s** thou hast had no pleasure. *266*
10: 8 and *offering* for **s** thou wouldest not, *266*
10:18 of these *is*, *there is* no more offering for **s**. *266*
10:26 For if we **s** wilfully after that *we* have *264*
11:25 than to enjoy the pleasures of **s** for a season; *266*
12: 1 and the **s** which doth so easily beset *us*, and *266*
12: 4 yet resisted unto blood, striving against **s**. *266*
13:11 into the sanctuary by the high priest for **s**, *266*
Jas 1:15 when lust hath conceived, it bringeth forth **s**: *266*
1:15 and **s**, when it is finished, bringeth forth *266*
2: 9 ye commit **s**, and are convinced of the law as *266*
4:17 to do good, and doeth *it* not, to him it is **s**. *266*
1Pe 2:22 Who did no **s**, neither was guile found in his *266*
4: 1 hath suffered in the flesh hath ceased from **s**; *266*
2Pe 2:14 full of adultery and that cannot cease from **s**; *266*
1Jn 1: 7 Jesus Christ his Son cleanseth us from all **s**. *266*
1: 8 If we say that we have no **s**, we deceive *266*
2: 1 these *things* write I unto you, that ye **s** not. *264*
2: 1 And if any *man* **s**, we have an advocate with *264*
3: 4 Whosoever committeth **s** transgresseth also *266*
3: 4 the law: for **s** is the transgression of the law. *266*
3: 5 to take away our sins; and in him is no **s**. *266*
3: 8 He that committeth **s** is of the devil; for *266*
3: 9 is born of God doth not commit **s**; *266*
3: 9 and he cannot **s**, because he is born of God. *264*
5:16 If any *man* see his brother **s** a sin *which is* *264*
5:16 If any *man* see his brother sin a **s** *which is* *266*
5:16 he shall give him life for them that **s** not unto *264*
5:16 There is a **s** unto death: I do not say that he *266*
5:17 All unrighteousness is **s**: and there is a sin *266*
5:17 is sin: and there is a **s** not unto death. *266*

SINA (2) [SINAI]

Ac 7:30 **S** an angel of the Lord in a flame of fire in *4614*
7:38 angel which spake to him in the mount **S**, *4614*

SINAI (37) [HOREB, SINA]

Ex 16: 1 of Sin, which *is* between Elim and **S**, 5514
19: 1 day came they *into* the wilderness of **S**. 5514
19: 2 were come *to* the desert of **S**, and 5514
19:11 in the sight of all the people upon mount **S**. 5514
19:18 mount **S** was altogether on a smoke, 5514
19:20 the LORD came down upon mount **S**, 5514
19:23 The people cannot come up to mount **S**: 5514
24:16 glory of the LORD abode upon mount **S**, 5514
31:18 end of communing with him upon mount **S**, 5514
34: 2 come up in the morning unto mount **S**, and 5514
34: 4 in the morning, and went up unto mount **S**, 5514

Ex 34:29 when Moses came down from mount S 5514
34:32 LORD had spoken with him in mount S. 5514
Lev 7:38 the LORD commanded Moses in mount S, 5514
7:38 unto the LORD, in the wilderness of S. 5514
25: 1 the LORD spake unto Moses in mount S, 5514
26:46 the children of Israel in mount S by 5514
27:34 Moses for the children of Israel in mount S. 5514
Nu 1: 1 spake unto Moses in the wilderness of S, 5514
1:19 he numbered them in the wilderness of S. 5514
3: 1 the LORD spake with Moses in mount S. 5514
3: 4 in the wilderness of S, and they had no 5514
3:14 spake unto Moses in the wilderness of S, 5514
9: 1 spake unto Moses in the wilderness of S, 5514
9: 5 first month at even in the wilderness of S: 5514
10:12 their journeys out of the wilderness of S; 5514
26:64 the children of Israel in the wilderness of S. 5514
28: 6 which was ordained in mount S for a sweet 5514
33:15 and pitched in the wilderness of S. 5514
33:16 And they removed from the desert of S, and 5514
Dt 33: 2 The LORD came from S, and rose up 5514
Jdg 5: 5 *even* that S from before the LORD God of 5514
Ne 9:13 Thou camest down also upon mount S, and 5514
Ps 68: 8 *even* S itself *was moved* at the presence of 5514
68:17 *is* among them, *as in* S, in the holy *place*. 5514
Gal 4:24 the one from the mount S, which gendereth *4614*
4:25 For *this* Agar is mount S in Arabia, and *4614*

SINCE (68) [SITH]

Ge 30:30 LORD hath blessed thee s my coming: 3807.1
44:28 is torn in pieces; and I saw him not s: 2008+5704
46:30 s I have seen thy face, because thou *art* yet 310
Ex 4:10 s thou hast spoken unto thy servant: 227+4480
5:23 For s I came to Pharaoh to speak in 227+4480
9:18 s the foundation 3117+4480+1886.1+3807.1
9:24 the land of Egypt s it became a nation. 227+4480
10: 6 s the day that they were upon the earth unto 4480
Nu 22:30 upon which thou hast ridden **ever** s *I* 4480+5750
Dt 4:32 s the day that God created man upon 4480
34:10 there arose not a prophet s in Israel like 5750
Jos 2:12 the LORD, s I have shewed you kindness, 3588
14:10 *even* s the LORD spake this word 227+4480
Ru 2:11 mother in law s the death of thine husband: 310
1Sa 8: 8 s the day that I brought them up out of 4480
9:24 time *hath it* been kept for thee s *I* said, 3807.1
21: 5 s I came out, and the vessels of the young 871.1
29: 3 I have found no *fault* in him s he fell 3117+4480
29: 6 for I have not found evil in thee s the day of 4480
2Sa 7: 6 s the time that I brought up 4480+3807.1
7:11 *as* s the time that I commanded judges *to be* 4480
1Ki 8:16 S the day that I brought forth my people 4480
2Ki 8: 6 all the fruits of the field s the day that she 4480
21:15 s the day their fathers came forth out of 4480
1Ch 17: 5 For I have not dwelt in a house s the day 4480
17:10 s the time that I commanded judges *to be* 4480
2Ch 6: 5 S the day that I brought forth my people out 4480
30:26 for s the time of Solomon the son of David 4480
31:10 S *the people* began to bring the offerings 4480
Ezr 4: 2 we do sacrifice unto him s the days of 4480
5:16 s that time even until now *hath it been* in 4481
9: 7 S the days of our fathers *have* we *been* in a 4480
Ne 8:17 for s the days of Jeshua the son of Nun unto 4480
9:32 s the time of the kings of Assyria unto this 4480
Job 20: 4 this of old, s man was placed upon earth, 4480
38:12 Hast thou commanded the morning s thy 4480
Isa 14: 8 the cedars of Lebanon, *saying,* S thou 227+4480
16:13 hath spoken concerning Moab s that time. 4480
43: 4 S thou wast precious in my sight, 834+4480
44: 7 for me, s I appointed the ancient people? 4480
64: 4 For s **the beginning of the world** 4480+5769
Jer 7:25 S the day that your fathers came forth out 4480
20: 8 For s I spake, I cried out, I cried 1767+4480
31:20 for s I spake against him, I do 1767+4480
44:18 s we left off to burn incense to 227+4480
48:27 for s thou spakest of him, 1767+4480
Da 12: 1 such as never was s there was a nation *even* 4480
Hag 2:16 S those *days* were, when *one* came to 1961+4480
Mt 24:21 such as was not s the beginning of the world *575*
Mk 9:21 How long is it ago s this came unto him? *5613*
Lk 1:70 which have been s the world **began:**) *575*
7:45 this *woman* s **the time** I came in hath *575+3739*
16:16 s that time the kingdom of God is preached, *575*
24:21 to day is the third day s these *things* *575+3739*
Jn 9:32 S the world **began** was it not heard that any *1537*
Ac 3:21 of all his holy prophets s the world **began.** *575*
19: 2 Have ye received the Holy Ghost s ye *1487*
24:11 twelve days s I went up to Jerusalem *575+3739*
Ro 16:25 was kept secret s the **world began,** *166+5550*
1Co 15:21 For s by man *came* death, by man *came* *1894*
2Co 13: 3 S ye seek a proof of Christ speaking in me, *1893*
Col 1: 4 S we heard of your faith in Christ Jesus, and NIG
1: 6 s the day ye heard of *it,* and knew the grace *575*
1: 9 s the day we heard *it,* do not cease to pray *575*
Heb 7:28 which was s the law, *maketh* the Son, *3326*
9:26 must he often have suffered s the foundation *575*
2Pe 3: 4 for s the fathers fell asleep, all *things* *575+3739*
Rev 16:18 such as was not s men were upon *575+3739*

SINCERE (2) [SINCERELY, SINCERITY]

Php 1:10 that ye may be s and without offence till *1506*
1Pe 2: 2 newborn babes, desire the s milk of the word, *97*

SINCERELY (3) [SINCERE]

Jdg 9:16 if ye have done truly and s, 8549+871.1
9:19 dealt truly and s with Jerubbaal and 8549+871.1
Php 1:16 The one preach Christ of contention, not s, *55*

SINCERITY (7) [SINCERE]

Jos 24:14 and serve him in s and in truth: 8549
1Co 5: 8 but with the unleavened bread of s and *1505*
2Co 1:12 that in simplicity and godly s, not with *1505*
2:17 but as of s, but as of God, in the sight of *1505*
8: 8 of others, and to prove the s of your love. *1103*
Eph 6:24 all them that love our Lord Jesus Christ in s. *861*
Tit 2: 7 doctrine *shewing* uncorruptness, gravity, s, *861*

SINEW (3) [SINEWS]

Ge 32:32 of Israel eat not *of* the s which shrank, 1517
32:32 hollow of Jacob's thigh in the s that shrank. 1517
Isa 48: 4 thy neck *is* an iron s, and thy brow brass: 1517

SINEWS (5) [SINEW]

Job 10:11 flesh, and hast fenced me with bones and s. 1517
30:17 in the night season: and my s take no rest. 6207
40:17 the s of his stones are wrapt together. 1517
Eze 37: 6 I will lay s upon you, and will bring up 1517
37: 8 lo, the s and the flesh came up upon them, 1517

SINFUL (8) [SIN]

Nu 32:14 in your fathers' stead, an increase of s men, 2400
Isa 1: 4 Ah s nation, a people laden with iniquity, 2398
Am 9: 8 the eyes of the Lord GOD *are* upon the s 2403
Mk 8:38 words in this adulterous and s generation; *268*
Lk 5: 8 Depart from me; for I am a s man, O Lord. *268*
24: 7 must be delivered into the hands of s men, *268*
Ro 7:13 commandment might become exceeding s. *268*
8: 3 God sending his own Son in the likeness of s *266*

SINFUL NATURE See CARNAL; FLESH

SING (119) [SANG, SINGER, SINGERS, SINGETH, SINGING, SONG, SONGS, SUNG]

Ex 15: 1 and spake, saying, I will s unto the LORD, 7891
15:21 answered them, S ye to the LORD, 7891
32:18 *but* the noise of *them that* s do I hear. 6031
Nu 21:17 this song, Spring up, O well; s ye unto it: 6030
Jdg 5: 3 I, *even* I, will s unto the LORD; 7891
5: 3 I will s *praise* to the LORD God of Israel. 2167
1Sa 21:11 did they not s one to another of him in 6030
2Sa 22:50 and I will s **praises** unto thy name. 2167
1Ch 16: 9 S unto him, sing psalms unto him, talk you 7891
16: 9 Sing unto him, s **psalms** unto him, talk you 2167
16:23 S unto the LORD, all the earth; shew forth 7891
16:33 shall the trees of the wood s **out** at 7442
2Ch 20:22 when they began to s and to praise, 7440
23:13 of musick, and such as taught to s *praise.* NIH
29:30 the princes commanded the Levites to *s* NIH
Job 29:13 I **caused** the widow's heart to s **for joy.** 7442
Ps 7:17 will s *praise* to the name of the LORD 2167
9: 2 I will s *praise* to thy name, O thou most 2167
9:11 S *praises* to the LORD, which dwelleth in 2167
13: 6 I will s unto the LORD, because he hath 7891
18:49 the heathen, and s *praises* unto thy name. 2167
21:13 *so* will we s and praise thy power. 7891
27: 6 I will s, yea, I will sing *praises* unto 7891
27: 6 yea, I will s *praises* unto the LORD. 2167
30: 4 S unto the LORD, O ye saints of his, and 2167
30:12 To the end that *my* glory may s *praise* to 2167
33: 2 s unto him with the psaltery *and* 2167
33: 3 S unto him a new song; play skilfully with 7891
47: 6 S *praises* to God, sing *praises:* sing *praises* 2167
47: 6 s *praises:* sing *praises* unto our King, 2167
47: 6 sing *praises:* s *praises* unto our King, 2167
47: 6 sing *praises* unto our King, s *praises.* 2167
47: 7 the earth: s ye *praises* with understanding. 2167
51:14 my tongue shall s **aloud** of thy 7442
57: 7 my heart is fixed: I will s and give praise. 7891
57: 9 I will s unto thee among the nations. 2167
59:16 I will s of thy power; yea, I will sing aloud 7891
59:16 I will s **aloud** of thy mercy in the morning: 7442
59:17 Unto thee, O my strength, will I s: for God 2167
61: 8 So will I s *praise* unto thy name for ever, 2167
65:13 with corn; they shout for joy, they also s. 7891
66: 2 S **forth** the honour of his name: make his 2167
66: 4 shall worship thee, and shall s unto thee; 2167
66: 4 sing unto thee; they shall s *to* thy name. 2167
67: 4 O let the nations be glad and s **for joy:** 7442
68: 4 S unto God, sing *praises to* his name: 7891
68: 4 Sing unto God, s *praises to* his name: 2167
68:32 S unto God, ye kingdoms of the earth; 7891
68:32 the earth; O s *praises unto* the Lord; Selah. 2167
71:22 unto thee will I s with the harp, O thou 2167
71:23 My lips shall greatly rejoice when I s unto 2167
75: 9 I will s *praises* to the God of Jacob. 2167
81: 1 S **aloud** unto God our strength: make a 7442
89: 1 I will s of the mercies of the LORD for 7891
92: 1 to s *praises* unto thy name, O most High: 2167
95: 1 O come, let us s unto the LORD: let us 7442
96: 1 O s unto the LORD a new song: sing unto 7891
96: 1 new song: s unto the LORD, all the earth. 7891
96: 2 S unto the LORD, bless his name; 7891
98: 1 O s unto the LORD a new song; for he 7891
98: 4 a loud noise, and rejoice, and s *praise.* 2167
98: 5 S unto the LORD with the harp; with 2167
101: 1 I will s of mercy and judgment: unto thee, 7891
101: 1 judgment: unto thee, O LORD, will I s. 2167
104:12 *which* s among the branches. 5414+6963
104:33 I will s unto the LORD as long as I live: 7891
104:33 I will s *praise* to my God while I have my 2167
105: 2 S unto him, sing psalms unto him: talk ye 7891
105: 2 Sing unto him, s **psalms** unto him: talk ye 2167
108: 1 I will s and give praise, even *with* my 7891
108: 3 I will s *praises* unto thee among the nations. 2167
135: 3 s *praises* unto his name; for *it is* pleasant. 2167
137: 3 *saying,* S us *one* of the songs of Zion. 7891
137: 4 How shall we s the LORD'S song in a 7891
138: 1 before the gods will I s *praise* unto thee. 2167
138: 5 they shall s in the ways of the LORD: 7891
144: 9 I will s a new song unto thee, O God: 7891
144: 9 an instrument of ten strings will I s *praises* 2167
145: 7 and shall s of thy righteousness. 7442
146: 2 I will s *praises* unto my God while I have 2167
147: 1 for *it is* good to s *praises* unto our God; 2167
147: 7 S unto the LORD with thanksgiving; 6030
147: 7 s *praise* upon the harp unto our God: 2167
149: 1 S unto the LORD a new song, *and* 7891
149: 3 let them s *praises* unto him with the timbrel 2167
149: 5 in glory: let them s **aloud** upon their beds. 7442
Pr 29: 6 but the righteous doth s and rejoice. 7442
Isa 5: 1 Now will I s to my wellbeloved a song of 7891
12: 5 S unto the LORD; for he hath done 2167
23:15 after the end of seventy years shall Tyre s 7892
23:16 make sweet melody, s many songs, that NIH
24:14 They shall lift up their voice, they shall s, 7442
26:19 Awake and s, ye that dwell in dust: for thy 7442
27: 2 In that day s ye unto her, A vineyard of red 6030
35: 6 as a hart, and the tongue of the dumb s: 7442
38:20 s my songs *to* **the stringed instruments** all 5059
42:10 S unto the LORD a new song, *and* 7891
42:11 let the inhabitants of the rock s, let them 7442
44:23 S, O ye heavens; for the LORD hath done 7442
49:13 S, O heavens; and be joyful, O earth; and 7442
52: 8 *with* the voice together shall they s: 7442
52: 9 Break forth **into joy,** s together, ye waste 7442
54: 1 S, O barren, thou *that* didst not bear; 7442
65:14 my servants shall s for joy of heart, but 7442
Jer 20:13 S unto the LORD, praise ye the LORD: 7891
31: 7 S with gladness for Jacob, and shout among 7442
31:12 they shall come and s in the height of Zion, 7442
51:48 and all that *is* therein, shall s for Babylon: 7442
Eze 27:25 The ships of Tarshish did s of thee *in* thy 7788
Hos 2:15 she shall s there, as *in* the days of her 6030
Zep 2:14 *their* voice shall s in the windows; 7891
3:14 S, O daughter of Zion; shout, O Israel; 7442
Zec 2:10 S and rejoice, O daughter of Zion: for lo, 7442
Ro 15: 9 among the Gentiles, and s unto thy name. *5567*
1Co 14:15 I will s with the spirit, and I will sing with *5567*
14:15 and I will s with the understanding also. *5567*
Heb 2:12 in the midst of the church will I s **praise** *5214*
Jas 5:13 him pray. Is any merry? let him s **psalms.** *5567*
Rev 15: 3 And they s the song of Moses the servant of *103*

SINGED (1)

Da 3:27 nor was a hair of their head s, neither were 2761

SINGER (2) [SING]

1Ch 6:33 Heman a s, the son of Joel, the son of 7891
Hab 3:19 To the **chief** s on my stringed instruments. 5329

SINGERS (38) [SING]

1Ki 10:12 harps also and psalteries for s: 7891
1Ch 9:33 these *are* the s, chief of the fathers of 7891
15:16 *to be* the s with instruments of musick, 7891
15:19 So the s, Heman, Asaph, and Ethan, 7891
15:27 the s, and Chenaniah the master of the song 7891
15:27 the master of the song *with* the s: 7891
2Ch 5:12 Also the Levites *which were* the s, all of 7891
5:13 as the trumpeters and s *were* as one, 7891
9:11 and harps and psalteries for s: 7891
20:21 he appointed s unto the LORD, and 7891
23:13 also the s with instruments of musick, and 7891
29:28 and the s sang, and the trumpeters sounded: 7892
35:15 the s the sons of Asaph *were* in their place, 7891
Ezr 2:41 The s: the children of Asaph, an hundred 7891
2:70 the s, and the porters, and the Nethinims, 7891
7: 7 the s, and the porters, and the Nethinims, 7891
7:24 any of the priests and Levites, s, porters, 2171
10:24 Of the s also; Eliashib: and of the porters; 7891
Ne 7: 1 the porters and the s and the Levites were 7891
7:44 The s: the children of Asaph, an hundred 7891
7:73 the s, and *some* of the people, and 7891
10:28 the priests, the Levites, the porters, the s, 7891
10:39 that minister, and the porters, and the s: 7891
11:22 the s *were* over the business of the house of 7891
11:23 that a certain portion *should be* for the s, 7891
12:28 the sons of the s gathered themselves 7891
12:29 for the s had builded them villages round 7891
12:42 the s sang loud, with Jezrahiah *their* 7891
12:45 both the s and the porters kept the ward of 7891
12:46 and Asaph of old *there were* chief of the s, 7891
12:47 gave the portions of the s and the porters, 7891
13: 5 to the Levites, and the s, and the porters; 7891
13:10 been given *them:* for the Levites and the s, 7891
Ps 68:25 The s went before, the players on 7891
87: 7 As well the s as the players on instruments 7891
Ecc 2: 8 I gat me *men* s and *women* singers, and 7891
2: 8 I gat me *men* singers and *women* s, and 7891
Eze 40:44 the chambers of the s in the inner court, 7891

SINGETH (1) [SING]

Pr 25:20 so *is* he that s songs to a heavy heart. 7891

SINGING (29) [SING]

1Sa 18: 6 s and dancing, to meet king Saul, 7891
2Sa 19:35 can I hear any more the voice of s *men* and 7891
19:35 singing *men* and s *women?* wherefore then 7891
1Ch 6:32 the tabernacle of the congregation with s, 7892
13: 8 with s, and with harps, and with psalteries, 7892
2Ch 23:18 with rejoicing and with s, as it was 7892
30:21 *s* with loud instruments unto the LORD. NIH
35:25 all the s *men* and the singing *women* spake 7891
35:25 the s *women* spake of Josiah in their 7891
Ezr 2:65 *there were* among them two hundred s *men* 7891
2:65 two hundred singing *men* and s *women.* 7891
Ne 7:67 and five s *men* and singing *women.* 7891
7:67 and five singing *men* and s *women.* 7891
12:27 with s, *with* cymbals, psalteries, and 7892
Ps 100: 2 come before his presence with s. 7445
126: 2 filled *with* laughter, and our tongue *with* s: 7440
SS 2:12 the time of the s *of birds* is come, and 2158
Isa 14: 7 at rest, *and* is quiet: they break forth *into* s. 7440
16:10 in the vineyards there shall be no s, 7442
35: 2 and rejoice even *with* joy and s: 7444
44:23 break forth *into* s, ye mountains, O forest, 7440
48:20 with a voice of s declare ye, tell this, 7440
49:13 and break forth *into* s, O mountains: 7440
51:11 shall return, and come with s *unto* Zion; 7440
54: 1 break forth *into* s, and cry aloud, thou *that* 7440
55:12 the hills shall break forth before you *into* s, 7440
Zep 3:17 rest in his love, he will joy over thee with s. 7440
Eph 5:19 s and making melody in your heart to *103*
Col 3:16 s with grace in your hearts to the Lord. *103*

S

SINGLE (2) [SINGLENESS, SINGULAR]

Mt 6:22 if therefore thine eye be **s**, thy whole body *573*
Lk 11:34 therefore when thine eye is **s**, thy whole *573*

SINGLENESS (3) [SINGLE]

Ac 2:46 eat *their* meat with gladness and **s** of heart, *858*
Eph 6: 5 with fear and trembling, in **s** of your heart, *572*
Col 3:22 but in **s** of heart, fearing God: *572*

SINGULAR (1) [SINGLE]

Lev 27: 2 When a man shall **make a s vow**, 5088+6381

SINIM (1)

Isa 49:12 from the west; and these from the land of **S**. 5515

SINITE (2)

Ge 10:17 And the Hivite, and the Arkite, and the **S**, 5513
1Ch 1:15 And the Hivite, and the Arkite, and the **S**, 5513

SINK (6) [SANK, SUNK]

Ps 69: 2 I **s** in deep mire, where *there is* no standing: 2883
69:14 me out of the mire, and let me not **s**: 2883
Jer 51:64 Thus shall Babylon **s**, and shall not rise 8257
Mt 14:30 and beginning to **s**, he cried, saying, Lord, *2670*
Lk 5: 7 filled both the ships, so that they began to **s**. *1036*
9:44 Let these sayings **s down** into your ears: *5087*

SINNED (119) [SIN]

Ex 9:27 and said unto them, I have **s** *this* time: 2398
9:34 he **s** yet more, and hardened his heart, he 2398
10:16 I have **s** against the LORD your God, and 2398
32:30 said unto the people, Ye have **s** a great sin: 2398
32:31 this people have **s** a great sin, and 2398
32:33 Whosoever hath **s** against me, him will I 2398
Lev 4: 3 let him bring for his sin, which he hath **s**, 2398
4:14 which they have **s** against it, is known, then 2398
4:22 When a ruler hath **s**, and done somewhat 2398
4:23 Or if his sin, wherein he hath **s**, come to his 2398
4:28 Or if his sin, which he hath **s**, come to his 2398
4:28 for his sin which he hath **s**. 2398
5: 5 he shall confess that he hath **s** in that *thing:* 2398
5: 6 the LORD for his sin which he hath **s**, 2398
5:10 for him for his sin which he had **s**, 2398
5:11 he that **s** shall bring for his offering 2398
5:13 his sin that he hath **s** in one of these, 2398
6: 4 it shall be, because he hath **s**, and is guilty, 2398
Nu 6:11 for that he **s** by the dead, and shall hallow 2398
12:11 done foolishly, and wherein we have **s**. 2398
14:40 the LORD hath promised: for we have **s**. 2398
21: 7 came to Moses, and said, We have **s**, 2398
22:34 said unto the angel of the LORD, I have **s**; 2398
32:23 behold, ye have **s** against the LORD: 2398
Dt 1:41 unto me, We have **s** against the LORD, 2398
9:16 ye had **s** against the LORD your God, *and* 2398
9:18 because of all your sins which ye **s**, 2398
Jos 7:11 Israel hath **s**, and they have also 2398
7:20 Indeed I have **s** against the LORD God of 2398
Jdg 10:10 We have **s** against thee, both because 2398
10:15 of Israel said unto the LORD, We have **s**: 2398
11:27 Wherefore I have not **s** against thee, but 2398
1Sa 7: 6 said there, We have **s** against the LORD. 2398
12:10 said, We have **s**, because we have forsaken 2398
15:24 Saul said unto Samuel, I have **s**: for I have 2398
15:30 he said, I have **s**: *yet* honour me now, I pray 2398
19: 4 because he hath not **s** against thee, and 2398
24:11 in mine hand, and I have not **s** against thee; 2398
26:21 said Saul, I have **s**: return, my son David: 2398
2Sa 12:13 unto Nathan, I have **s** against the LORD. 2398
19:20 For thy servant doth know that I have **s**: 2398
24:10 I have **s** greatly *in* that I have done: 2398
24:17 Lo, I have **s**, and I have done wickedly: 2398
1Ki 8:33 because they have **s** against thee, and 2398
8:35 is no rain, because they have **s** against thee; 2398
8:47 We have **s**, and have done perversely, 2398
8:50 forgive thy people that have **s** against thee, 2398
15:30 of the sins of Jeroboam which he **s**, 2398
16:13 *by* which they **s**, and *by* which they made 2398
16:19 For his sins which he **s** in doing evil in 2398
18: 9 he said, What have I **s**, that thou wouldest 2398
2Ki 17: 7 that the children of Israel had **s** against 2398
21:17 and all that he did, and his sin that he **s**, 2398
1Ch 21: 8 I have **s** greatly, because I have done this 2398
21:17 even I *it is* that have **s** and done evil indeed; 2398
2Ch 6:24 because they have **s** against thee; 2398
6:26 is no rain, because they have **s** against thee; 2398
6:37 saying, We have **s**, we have done amiss, 2398
6:39 forgive thy people which have **s** against 2398
Ne 1: 6 of Israel, which we have **s** against thee: 2398
1: 6 both I and my father's house have **s**. 2398
9:29 **s** against thy judgments, (which if a man 2398
Job 1: 5 It may be that my sons have **s**, and 2398
1:22 In all this Job **s** not, nor charged God 2398
7:20 I have **s**; what shall I do unto thee, O thou 2398
8: 4 If thy children have **s** against him, and 2398
24:19 *so doth* the grave *those which* have **s**. 2398
33:27 I have **s**, and perverted *that which was* 2398
Ps 41: 4 heal my soul; for I have **s** against thee. 2398
51: 4 have I **s**, and done *this* evil in thy sight: 2398
78:17 they **s** yet more against him by provoking 2398
78:32 For all this they **s** still, and believed not for 2398
106: 6 We have **s** with our fathers, we have 2398
Isa 42:24 the LORD, he against whom we have **s**? 2398
43:27 Thy first father hath **s**, and thy teachers 2398
64: 5 behold, thou art wroth; for we have **s**: 2398
Jer 2:35 with thee, because thou sayest, I have not **s**. 2398
3:25 for we have **s** against the LORD our God, 2398
8:14 because we have **s** against the LORD. 2398
14: 7 are many; we have **s** against thee. 2398
14:20 of our fathers: for we have **s** against thee. 2398
33: 8 whereby they have **s** against me, and I will 2398
33: 8 whereby they have **s**, and whereby they 2398
40: 3 because ye have **s** against the LORD, and 2398
44:23 because ye have **s** against the LORD, and 2398
50: 7 because they have **s** against the LORD, 2398
Jer 50:14 for she hath **s** against the LORD. 2398
La 1: 8 Jerusalem hath **grievously s**; 2398+2399
5: 7 Our fathers have **s**, *and are* not; *and* 2398
5:16 *from* our head: woe unto us, that we have **s**! 2398
Eze 18:24 in his sin that he hath **s**, in them shall he 2398
28:16 of thee *with* violence, and thou hast **s**: 2398
37:23 wherein they have **s**, and will cleanse them: 2398
Da 9: 5 We have **s**, and have committed iniquity, 2398
9: 8 our fathers, because we have **s** against thee. 2398
9:11 of God, because we have **s** against him. 2398
9:15 we have **s**, we have done wickedly. 2398
Hos 4: 7 they were increased, so they **s** against me: 2398
10: 9 thou hast **s** from the days of Gibeah: 2398
Mic 7: 9 because I have **s** against him, until he plead 2398
Hab 2:10 many people, and *hast* **s** *against* thy soul. 2398
Zep 1:17 because they have **s** against the LORD: 2398
Mt 27: 4 I have **s** in that I have betrayed *the* innocent *264*
Lk 15:18 I have **s** against heaven, and before thee, *264*
15:21 I have **s** against heaven, and in thy sight, and *264*
Jn 9: 3 Neither hath this *man* **s**, nor his parents: *264*
Ro 2:12 For as many as have **s** without law shall also *264*
2:12 as many as have **s** in the law shall be judged *264*
3:23 For all have **s**, and come short of the glory of *264*
5:12 passed upon all men, for that all have **s**: *264*
5:14 even over them that had not **s** after *264*
5:16 And not as *it was* by one that **s**, *so is* the gift: *264*
1Co 7:28 But and if thou marry, thou hast not **s**; and *264*
7:28 and if a virgin marry, she hath not **s**. *264*
2Co 12:21 I shall bewail many which have **s already**, *4258*
13: 2 I write to them which **heretofore** have **s**, *4258*
Heb 3:17 *was it* not with them that had **s**, *264*
2Pe 2: 4 For if God spared not the angels that **s**, but *264*
1Jn 1:10 If we say that we have not **s**, we make him a *264*

SINNER (21) [SIN]

Pr 11:31 the earth: much more the wicked and the **s**. 2398
13: 6 but wickedness overthroweth the **s**. 2403
13:22 the wealth of the **s** *is* laid up for the just. 2398
Ecc 2:26 to the **s** he giveth travail, to gather and 2398
7:26 from her; but the **s** shall be taken by her. 2398
8:12 Though a **s** do evil an hundred *times*, and 2398
9: 2 as *is* the good, so *is* the **s**; *and* he that 2398
9:18 of war: but one **s** destroyeth much good. 2398
Isa 65:20 the **s** *being* an hundred years old shall be 2398
Lk 7:37 a woman in the city, which was a **s**, *268*
7:39 *this is* that toucheth him: for she is a **s**. *268*
15: 7 shall be in heaven over one **s** that repenteth, *268*
15:10 the angels of God over one **s** that repenteth. *268*
18:13 his breast, saying, God be merciful to me a **s**. *268*
19: 7 was gone to be guest with a man *that is* a **s**. *268*
Jn 9:16 How can a man *that is* a **s** do such miracles? *268*
9:24 God the praise: we know that this man is a **s**. *268*
9:25 said, Whether he be a **s** *or no*, I know not: *268*
Ro 3: 7 his glory; why yet am I also judged as a **s**? *268*
Jas 5:20 that he which converteth the **s** from the error *268*
1Pe 4:18 where shall the ungodly and the **s** appear? *268*

SINNERS (48) [SIN]

Ge 13:13 and **s** before the LORD exceedingly. 2400
Nu 16:38 The censers of these **s** against their own 2400
1Sa 15:18 and utterly destroy the **s** the Amalekites, 2400
Ps 1: 1 nor standeth in the way of **s**, nor sitteth in 2400
1: 5 nor **s** in the congregation of the righteous. 2400
25: 8 will he teach **s** in the way. 2400
26: 9 Gather not my soul with **s**, nor my life with 2400
51:13 and **s** shall be converted unto thee. 2400
104:35 Let the **s** be consumed out of the earth, and 2400
Pr 1:10 My son, if **s** entice thee, consent thou not. 2400
13:21 Evil pursueth **s**: but to the righteous good 2400
23:17 Let not thine heart envy **s**: but *be thou* in 2400
Isa 1:28 and of the **s** *shall be* together, 2400
13: 9 and he shall destroy the **s** thereof out of it. 2400
33:14 The **s** in Zion are afraid; fearfulness hath 2400
Am 9:10 All the **s** of my people shall die by 2400
Mt 9:10 many publicans and **s** came and sat down *268*
9:11 eateth your Master with publicans and **s**? *268*
9:13 to call *the* righteous, but **s** to repentance. *268*
11:19 a winebibber, a friend of publicans and **s**. *268*
26:45 Son of man is betrayed into the hands of **s**. *268*
Mk 2:15 and **s** sat also together with Jesus and *268*
2:16 Pharisees saw him eat with publicans and **s**, *268*
2:16 he eateth and drinketh with publicans and **s**? *268*
2:17 not to call *the* righteous, but **s** to repentance. *268*
14:41 Son of man is betrayed into the hands of **s**. *268*
Lk 5:30 do ye eat and drink with publicans and **s**? *268*
5:32 not to call *the* righteous, but **s** to repentance. *268*
6:32 have ye? for **s** also love those that love them. *268*
6:33 thank have ye? for **s** also do *even* the same. *268*
6:34 for **s** also lend to sinners, to receive as much *268*
6:34 for sinners also lend to **s**, to receive as much *268*
7:34 a winebibber, a friend of publicans and **s**. *268*
13: 2 Suppose ye that these Galileans were **s** *268*
13: 4 think ye that they were **s** above all men that *3781*
15: 1 him all the publicans and **s** for to hear him. *268*
15: 2 This *man* receiveth **s**, and eateth with them. *268*
Jn 9:31 Now we know that God heareth not **s**: but *268*
Ro 5: 8 in that, while we were yet **s**, Christ died for *268*
5:19 one man's disobedience many were made **s**, *268*
Gal 2:15 *are* Jews by nature, and not **s** of the Gentiles, *268*
2:17 we ourselves also are found **s**, *is* therefore *268*
1Ti 1: 9 for the ungodly and for **s**, for unholy and *268*
1:15 Christ Jesus came into the world to save **s**; *268*
Heb 7:26 separate from **s**, and made higher than *268*
12: 3 such contradiction of **s** against himself, *268*
Jas 4: 8 Cleanse *your* hands, *ye* **s**; and purify *your* *268*
Jude 1:15 of all *their* hard *speeches* which ungodly **s** *268*

SINNEST (1) [SIN]

Job 35: 6 If thou **s**, what doest thou against him? or 2398

SINNETH (22) [SIN]

Nu 15:28 an atonement for the soul that **s ignorantly**, 7683
15:28 when he **s** by ignorance before the LORD, 2398
15:29 that **s through ignorance**, 6213+7684+871.1
Dt 19:15 or for any sin, in any sin that he **s**: 2398
1Ki 8:46 (for *there is* no man that **s** not,) 2398
2Ch 6:36 (for *there is* no man which **s** not,) 2398
Pr 8:36 he that **s** *against* me wrongeth his own soul: 2398
14:21 He that despiseth his neighbour **s**: but 2398
19: 2 and he that hasteth with *his* feet, **s**. 2398
20: 2 *whoso* provoketh him to anger **s** *against* his 2398
Ecc 7:20 man upon earth, that doeth good, and **s** not. 2398
Eze 14:13 when the land **s** against me by trespassing 2398
18: 4 the son *is* mine: the soul that **s**, it shall die. 2398
18:20 The soul that **s**, it shall die. The son shall 2398
33:12 for his *righteousness* in the day that he **s**. 2398
1Co 6:18 he that committeth fornication **s** against his *264*
7:36 so require, let him do what he will, he **s** not: *264*
Tit 3:11 and **s**, being condemned of himself. *264*
1Jn 3: 6 Whosoever abideth in him **s** not: *264*
3: 6 whosoever **s** hath not seen him, *264*
3: 8 the devil; for the devil **s** from the beginning. *264*
5:18 We know that whosoever is born of God **s** *264*

SINNING (2) [SIN]

Ge 20: 6 for I also withheld thee from **s** against me: 2398
Lev 6: 3 any of all *these* that a man doeth, **s** therein: 2398

SINS (172) [SIN]

Lev 16:16 because of their transgressions in all their **s**: 2403
16:21 all their transgressions in all their **s**, putting 2403
16:30 *that* ye may be clean from all your **s** before 2403
16:34 children of Israel for all their **s** once a year. 2403
26:18 punish you seven *times* more for your **s**. 2403
26:21 moe plagues upon you according to your **s**. 2403
26:24 will punish you yet seven *times* for your **s**. 2403
26:28 will chastise you seven *times* for your **s**. 2403
Nu 16:26 of theirs, lest ye be consumed in all their **s**. 2403
Dt 9:18 because of all your **s** which ye sinned, 2403
Jos 24:19 not forgive your transgressions nor your **s**. 2403
1Sa 12:19 for we have added unto all our **s** *this* evil, 2403
1Ki 14:16 give Israel up because of the **s** of Jeroboam, 2403
14:22 they provoked him to jealousy with their **s** 2403
15: 3 he walked in all the **s** of his father, 2403
15:30 Because of the **s** of Jeroboam which he 2403
16: 2 to sin, to provoke me to anger with their **s**; 2403
16:13 For all the **s** of Baasha, and the sins of Elah 2403
16:13 the **s** of Elah his son, *by* which they sinned, 2403
16:19 For his **s** which he sinned in doing evil in 2403
16:31 walk in the **s** of Jeroboam the son of Nebat, 2403
2Ki 3: 3 Nevertheless he cleaved unto the **s** of 2403
10:29 Howbeit *from* the **s** of Jeroboam the son of 2399
10:31 *for* he departed not from the **s** of Jeroboam, 2403
13: 2 followed the **s** of Jeroboam the son of 2403
13: 6 Nevertheless they departed not from the **s** 2403
13:11 he departed not from all the **s** of Jeroboam 2403
14:24 he departed not from all the **s** of Jeroboam 2403
15: 9 he departed not from the **s** of Jeroboam 2403
15:18 he departed not all his days from the **s** of 2403
15:24 he departed not from the **s** of Jeroboam 2403
15:28 he departed not from the **s** of Jeroboam 2403
17:22 For the children of Israel walked in all the **s** 2403
24: 3 for the **s** of Manasseh, according to all that 2403
2Ch 28:10 with you, **s** against the LORD your God? 819
28:13 *already*, ye intend to add *more* to our **s** 2403
Ne 1: 6 confess the **s** of the children of Israel, 2403
9: 2 stood and confessed their **s**, and 2403
9:37 thou hast set over us because of our **s**: 2403
Job 13:23 How many *are* mine iniquities and **s**? 2403
Ps 19:13 **s**; let them not have dominion over me: NIH
25: 7 Remember not the **s** of my youth, nor my 2403
25:18 and my pain; and forgive all my **s**. 2403
51: 9 Hide thy face from my **s**, and blot out all 2399
69: 5 and my **s** are not hid from thee. 819
79: 9 deliver us, and purge away our **s**, for thy 2403
90: 8 our secret **s** in the light of thy countenance. NIH
103:10 He hath not dealt with us after our **s**; 2399
Pr 5:22 he shall be holden with the cords of his **s**. 2403
10:12 stirreth up strifes: but love covereth all **s**. 6588
28:13 He that covereth his **s** shall not prosper: but 6588
Isa 1:18 though your **s** be as scarlet, they shall be as 2399
38:17 for thou hast cast all my **s** behind thy back. 2399
40: 2 of the LORD'S hand double for all her **s**. 2403
43:24 thou hast made me to serve with thy **s**, 2403
43:25 own sake, and will not remember thy **s**. 2403
44:22 thy transgressions, and, as a cloud, thy **s**: 2403
58: 1 and the house of Jacob their **s**. 2403
59: 2 and your **s** have hid *his* face from you, 2403
59:12 before thee, and our **s** testify against us: 2403
Jer 5:25 your **s** have withholden good *things* from 2403
14:10 remember their iniquity, and visit their **s**. 2403
15:13 *that* for all thy **s**, even in all thy borders. 2403
30:14 *because* thy **s** were increased. 2403
30:15 *because* thy **s** were increased, I have done 2403
50:20 the **s** of Judah, and they shall not be found: 2403
La 3:39 a man for the **punishment** of his **s**? 2399
4:13 For the **s** of her prophets, *and* the iniquities 2403
4:22 O daughter of Edom; he will discover thy **s**. 2403
Eze 16:51 hath Samaria committed half of thy **s**; 2403
16:52 **s** that thou hast **committed** more 2403
18:14 that seeth all his father's **s** which he hath 2403
18:21 if the wicked will turn from all his **s** that he 2403
21:24 so that in all your doings your **s** do appear; 2403
23:49 and ye shall bear the **s** of your idols: 2399
33:10 If our transgressions and our **s** *be* upon us, 2403
33:16 None of his **s** that he hath committed shall 2403
Da 4:27 break off thy **s** by righteousness, and 2408
9:16 because for our **s**, and for the iniquities of 2399
9:24 to make an end of **s**, and to make 2403
Hos 8:13 remember their iniquity, and visit their **s**: 2403
9: 9 their iniquity, he will visit their **s**. 2403
Am 5:12 manifold transgressions and your mighty **s**: 2403
Mic 1: 5 all this, and for the **s** of the house of Israel. 2403
6:13 in making *thee* desolate because of thy **s**. 2403
7:19 thou wilt cast all their **s** into the depths of 2403
Mt 1:21 for he shall save his people from their **s**. *266*
3: 6 baptized of him in Jordan, confessing their **s**. *266*
9: 2 be of good cheer; thy **s** be forgiven thee. *266*
9: 5 is easier, to say, *Thy* **s** be forgiven thee; *266*

Mt 9: 6 Son of man hath power on earth to forgive **s**, 266
26:28 is shed for many for the remission of **s**. 266
Mk 1: 4 baptism of repentance for the remission of **s**. 266
1: 5 him in the river *of* Jordan, confessing their **s**. 266
2: 5 sick of the palsy, Son, thy **s** be forgiven thee. 266
2: 7 who can forgive **s** but God only? 266
2: 9 the sick of the palsy, *Thy* **s** be forgiven thee; 266
2:10 Son of man hath power on earth to forgive **s**, 266
3:28 All **s** shall be forgiven unto the sons of men, 265
4:12 and *their* **s** should be forgiven them. 265
Lk 1:77 unto his people by the remission of their **s**, 266
3: 3 baptism of repentance for the remission of **s**; 266
5:20 said unto him, Man, thy **s** are forgiven thee. 266
5:21 Who can forgive **s**, but God alone? 266
5:23 is easier, to say, Thy **s** be forgiven thee; 266
5:24 of man hath power upon earth to forgive **s**, 266
7:47 Her **s**, which are many, are forgiven; 266
7:48 And he said unto her, Thy **s** are forgiven. 266
7:49 Who is this that forgiveth **s** also? 266
11: 4 And forgive us our **s**; for we also forgive 266
24:47 remission of **s** should be preached in his 266
Jn 8:21 and ye shall seek me, and shall die in your **s**: 266
8:24 unto you, that ye shall die in your **s**: 266
8:24 not that I am *he*, ye shall die in your **s**. 266
9:34 Thou wast altogether born in **s**, and dost thou 266
20:23 Whose soever **s** ye remit, they are remitted 266
20:23 *and* whose soever **s** ye retain, they are NIG
Ac 2:38 name of Jesus Christ for the remission of **s**, 266
3:19 be converted, that your **s** may be blotted out, 266
5:31 repentance to Israel, and forgiveness of **s**. 266
10:43 believeth in him shall receive remission of **s**. 266
13:38 is preached unto you the forgiveness of **s**: 266
22:16 arise, and be baptized, and wash away thy **s**, 266
26:18 that they may receive forgiveness of **s**, and 266
Ro 3:25 for the remission of **s** that are past, 265
4: 7 are forgiven, and whose **s** are covered. 266
7: 5 the motions of **s**, which were by the law, 266
11:27 unto them, when I shall take away their **s**. 266
1Co 15: 3 how that Christ died for our **s** according to 266
15:17 your faith *is* vain; ye are yet in your **s**. 266
Gal 1: 4 Who gave himself for our **s**, that he might 266
Eph 1: 7 the forgiveness of **s**, according to the riches 3900
2: 1 who were dead in trespasses and **s**; 266
2: 5 Even when we were dead in **s**, 3900
Col 1:14 through his blood, *even* the forgiveness of **s**: 266
2:11 in putting off the body of the **s** of the flesh, 266
2:13 being dead in *your* **s** and 3900
1Th 2:16 they might be saved, to fill up their **s** alway: 266
1Ti 5:22 no *man*, neither be partaker of other *men's* **s**: 266
5:24 Some men's **s** are open beforehand, 266
2Ti 3: 6 and lead captive silly women laden with **s**, 266
Heb 1: 3 when he had by himself purged our **s**, 266
2:17 to make reconciliation for the **s** of 266
5: 1 he may offer both gifts and sacrifices for **s**: 266
5: 3 the people, so also for himself, to offer for **s**. 266
7:27 first for his own **s**, *and* then for the people's: 266
8:12 and their **s** and their iniquities will I 266
9:28 So Christ was once offered to bear the **s** of 266
10: 2 should have had no more conscience of **s**. 266
10: 3 a remembrance *again made* of **s** every year. 266
10: 4 of bulls and of goats should take away **s**. 266
10:11 which can never take away **s**: 266
10:12 he had offered one sacrifice for **s** for ever, 266
10:17 And their **s** and iniquities will I remember no 266
10:26 there remaineth no more sacrifice for **s**, 266
Jas 5:15 and if he have committed **s**, they shall be 266
5:20 from death, and shall hide a multitude of **s**. 266
1Pe 2:24 Who his own self bare our **s** in his own body 266
2:24 that we, being dead to **s**, should live unto 266
3:18 For Christ also hath once suffered for **s**, 266
4: 8 for charity shall cover the multitude of **s**. 266
2Pe 1: 9 forgotten that *he* was purged from his old **s**. 266
1Jn 1: 9 If we confess our **s**, he is faithful and just to 266
1: 9 he is faithful and just to forgive us *our* **s**, and 266
2: 2 And he is the propitiation for our **s**: and 266
2: 2 but also for *the* **s** *of* the whole world. NIG
2:12 *your* **s** are forgiven you for his name's sake. 266
3: 5 that he was manifested to take away our **s**; 266
4:10 sent his Son *to be* the propitiation for our **s**. 266
Rev 1: 5 and washed us from our **s** in his own blood, 266
18: 4 that ye be not partakers of her **s**, and that ye 266
18: 5 For her **s** have reached unto heaven, and God 266

SION (8) [ZION]

Dt 4:48 even unto mount **S**, which *is* Hermon, 7865
Mt 21: 5 Tell ye the daughter of **S**, Behold, thy King 4622
Jn 12:15 Fear not, daughter of **S**: behold, thy King 4622
Ro 9:33 I lay in **S** a stumblingstone and rock of 4622
11:26 There shall come out of **S** the Deliverer, 4622
Heb 12:22 But ye are come unto mount **S**, and 4622
1Pe 2: 6 I lay in **S** a chief corner stone, elect, 4622
Rev 14: 1 and lo, a Lamb stood on the mount **S**, and 4622

SIPHMOTH (1)

1Sa 30:28 to *them* which *were* in **S**, and to *them* 8224

SIPPAI (1)

1Ch 20: 4 time Sibbechai the Hushathite slew **S**, 5598

SIR (12) [SIRS]

Ge 43:20 said, O **s**, we came indeed down at the first 113
Mt 13:27 the householder came and said unto him, **S**, 2962
21:30 And he answered and said, I *go*, **s**: and 2962
27:63 Saying, **S**, we remember that that deceiver 2962
Jn 4:11 The woman saith unto him, **S**, thou hast 2962
4:15 **S**, give me this water, that I thirst not, 2962
4:19 The woman saith unto him, **S**, I perceive 2962
4:49 unto him, **S**, come down ere my child die. 2962
5: 7 **S**, I have no man, when the water is 2962
12:21 and desired him, saying, **S**, we would see 2962
20:15 him to be the gardener, saith unto him, **S**, 2962
Rev 7:14 And I said unto him, **S**, thou knowest. 2962

SIRAH (1)

2Sa 3:26 brought him again from the well of **S**: 5626

SIRION (2)

Dt 3: 9 (*Which* Hermon the Sidonians call **S**; and 8303
Ps 29: 6 a calf; Lebanon and **S** like a young unicorn. 8303

SIRS (7) [SIR]

Ac 7:26 them at one *again*, saying, **S**, ye are brethren; 435
14:15 And saying, **S**, why do ye these *things*? We 435
16:30 And brought them out, and said, **S**, 2962
19:25 and said, **S**, ye know that by this craft we 435
27:10 And said unto them, **S**, I perceive that *this* 435
27:21 and said, **S**, *ye* should have hearkened unto 435
27:25 Wherefore, **s**, be of good cheer: for I believe 435

SISAMAI (2)

1Ch 2:40 Eleasah begat **S**, and Sisamai begat 5581
2:40 begat Sisamai, and **S** begat Shallum, 5581

SISERA (21)

Jdg 4: 2 the captain of whose host *was* **S**, which 5516
4: 7 I will draw unto thee to the river Kishon **S**, 5516
4: 9 for the LORD shall sell **S** into the hand of 5516
4:12 they shewed **S** that Barak the son of 5516
4:13 **S** gathered together all his chariots, 5516
4:14 LORD hath delivered **S** into thine hand: 5516
4:15 the LORD discomfited **S**, and all *his* 5516
4:15 so that **S** lighted down off *his* chariot, and 5516
4:16 all the host of **S** fell upon the edge of 5516
4:17 Howbeit **S** fled away on his feet to the tent 5516
4:18 Jael went out to meet **S**, and said unto him, 5516
4:22 behold, as Barak pursued **S**, Jael came out 5516
4:22 **S** lay dead, and the nail *was* in his temples. 5516
5:20 the stars in their courses fought against **S**. 5516
5:26 with the hammer she smote **S**, she smote 5516
5:28 The mother of **S** looked out at a window, 5516
5:30 to **S** a prey of divers colours, a prey of 5516
1Sa 12: 9 he sold them into the hand of **S**, captain of 5516
Ezr 2:53 The children of Barkos, the children of **S**, 5516
Ne 7:55 the children of **S**, the children of Tamah, 5516
Ps 83: 9 as *to* **S**, as *to* Jabin, at the brook of Kison: 5516

SISMAI See SISAMAI

SISTER (109) [SISTER'S, SISTERS]

Ge 4:22 iron: and the **s** of Tubal-cain *was* Naamah. 269
12:13 Say, I pray thee, thou *art* my **s**: that it may be 269
12:19 Why saidst thou, She *is* my **s**? so I might 269
20: 2 Abraham said of Sarah his wife, She *is* my **s**: 269
20: 5 Said he not unto me, She *is* my **s**? and she, 269
20:12 yet indeed *she is* my **s**; she *is* the daughter of 269
24:30 when he heard the words of Rebekah his **s**, 269
24:59 they sent away Rebekah their **s**, and her 269
24:60 and said unto her, Thou *art* our **s**, 269
25:20 of Padan-aram, the **s** to Laban the Syrian. 269
26: 7 *him* of his wife; and he said, She *is* my **s**: 269
26: 9 how saidst thou, She *is* my **s**? And Isaac said 269
28: 9 the **s** of Nebajoth, to be his wife. 269
30: 1 bare Jacob no *children*, Rachel envied her **s**; 269
30: 8 great wrestlings have I wrestled with my **s**, 269
34:13 said, because he had defiled Dinah their **s**: 269
34:14 to give our **s** to one that is uncircumcised; 269
34:27 the city, because they had defiled their **s**. 269
34:31 Should he deal with our **s** as with a harlot? 269
36: 3 Ishmael's daughter, **s** of Nebajoth. 269
36:22 and Hemam; and Lotan's **s** *was* Timna. 269
46:17 and Ishui, and Beriah, and Serah their **s**: 269
Ex 2: 4 his **s** stood afar off, to wit what would be 269
2: 7 said his **s** to Pharaoh's daughter, Shall I go 269
6:20 Amram took him Jochebed his **father's s** to 1733
6:23 of Amminadab, **s** of Naashon, to wife; 269
15:20 the **s** of Aaron, took a timbrel in her hand; 269
Lev 18: 9 The nakedness of thy **s**, the daughter of thy 269
18:11 begotten of thy father, she *is* thy **s**, thou shalt 269
18:12 not uncover the nakedness of thy father's **s**: 269
18:13 not uncover the nakedness of thy mother's **s**: 269
18:18 Neither shalt thou take a wife to her **s**, to vex 269
20:17 if a man shall take his **s**, his father's 269
20:19 not uncover the nakedness of thy mother's **s**, 269
20:19 of thy mother's sister, nor of thy father's **s**: 269
21: 3 And for his **s** a virgin, that is nigh unto him, 269
Nu 6: 7 for his brother, or for his **s**, when they die: 269
25:18 the daughter of a prince of Midian, their **s**, 269
26:59 and Moses, and Miriam their **s**. 269
Dt 27:22 Cursed *be* he that lieth with his **s**, 269
Jdg 15: 2 *is* not her younger **s** fairer than she? take her, 269
Ru 1:15 thy **s in law** is gone back unto her people, 2994
1:15 her gods: return thou after thy **s in law**. 2994
2Sa 13: 1 that Absalom the son of David had a fair **s**, 269
13: 2 *so* vexed, that he fell sick for his **s** Tamar; 269
13: 4 I love Tamar, my brother Absalom's **s**. 269
13: 5 let my **s** Tamar come, and give me meat, and 269
13: 6 let Tamar my **s** come, and make *me* a couple 269
13:11 and said unto her, Come lie with me, my **s**. 269
13:20 hold now thy peace, my **s**: he *is* thy brother; 269
13:22 because he had forced his **s** Tamar. 269
13:32 from the day that he forced his **s** Tamar. 269
17:25 of Nahash, **s** to Zeruiah Joab's mother. 269
1Ki 11:19 that he gave him *to* wife the **s** of his own 269
11:19 his own wife, the **s** of Tahpenes the queen. 269
11:20 the **s** of Tahpenes bare him Genubath his 269
2Ki 11: 2 the daughter of king Joram, **s** of Ahaziah, 269
1Ch 1:39 Hori, and Homam: and Timna *was* Lotan's **s**. 269
3: 9 sons of the concubines, and Tamar their **s**. 269
3:19 and Hananiah, and Shelomith their **s**: 269
4: 3 and the name of their **s** *was* Hazelelponi: 269
4:19 the sons of *his* wife Hodiah the **s** of Naham, 269
7:15 Machir took to wife *the* **s** of Huppim and NIH
7:18 his **s** Hammoleketh bare Ishod, and Abiezer, 269
7:30 and Ishuai, and Beriah, and Serah their **s**. 269
7:32 and Shomer, and Hotham, and Shua their **s**. 269
2Ch 22:11 the priest, (for she was the **s** of Ahaziah,) 269
Job 17:14 to the worm, *Thou art* my mother, and my **s**. 269
Pr 7: 4 Say unto wisdom, Thou *art* my **s**; and 269
SS 4: 9 hast ravished my heart, my **s**, *my* spouse; 269
4:10 How fair is thy love, my **s**, *my* spouse! 269
4:12 A garden inclosed *is* my **s**, *my* spouse; 269
5: 1 I am come into my garden, my **s**, *my* spouse: 269
5: 2 my **s**, my love, my dove, my undefiled: 269
8: 8 We have a little **s**, and she hath no breasts: 269
8: 8 what shall we do for our **s** in the day when 269
Jer 3: 7 And her treacherous **s** Judah saw *it*. 269
3: 8 yet her treacherous **s** Judah feared not, but 269
3:10 yet for all this her treacherous **s** Judah hath 269
22:18 or, Ah **s**! they shall not lament for him, 269
Eze 16:45 thou *art* the **s** of thy sisters, which lothed 269
16:46 thine elder **s** *is* Samaria, she and 269
16:46 thy younger **s**, that dwelleth at thy right 269
16:48 the Lord GOD, Sodom thy **s** hath not done, 269
16:49 this was the iniquity of thy **s** Sodom, pride, 269
16:56 For thy **s** Sodom was not mentioned by thy 269
22:11 another in thee hath humbled his **s**, 269
23: 4 *were* Aholah the elder, and Aholibah her **s**: 269
23:11 when her **s** Aholibah saw *this*, she was more 269
23:11 in her whoredoms more than her **s** in *her* 269
23:18 like as my mind was alienated from her **s**. 269
23:31 Thou hast walked in the way of thy **s**; 269
23:33 desolation, *with* the cup of thy **s** Samaria. 269
44:25 or for **s** that hath had no husband, 269
Mt 12:50 the same is my brother, and **s**, and mother. 79
Mk 3:35 the same is my brother, and my **s**, and mother. 79
Lk 10:39 And she had a **s** called Mary, which also sat at 79
10:40 dost thou not care that my **s** hath left me to 79
Jn 11: 1 the town of Mary and her **s** Martha. 79
11: 5 Jesus loved Martha, and her **s**, and Lazarus. 79
11:28 and called Mary her **s** secretly, saying, 79
11:39 Martha, the **s** of him that was dead, saith unto 79
19:25 and his mother's **s**, Mary the *wife* of 79
Ro 16: 1 I commend unto you Phebe our **s**, which is a 79
16:15 and his **s**, and Olympas, and all the saints 79
1Co 7:15 or a **s** is not under bondage in such *cases*: but 79
9: 5 Have we not power to lead about a **s**, a wife, 79
Jas 2:15 If a brother or **s** be naked, and destitute of 79
2Jn 1:13 The children of thy elect **s** greet thee. Amen. 79

SISTER'S (7) [SISTER]

Ge 24:30 the earring and bracelets upon his **s** hands, 269
29:13 when Laban heard the tidings of Jacob his **s** 269
Lev 20:17 he hath uncovered his **s** nakedness; he shall 269
1Ch 7:15 and Shuppim, whose **s** name *was* Maachah;) 269
Eze 23:32 Thou shalt drink *of* thy **s** cup deep and large: 269
Ac 23:16 And when Paul's **s** son heard of *their* lying in 79
Col 4:10 saluteth you, and Marcus, **s son** to Barnabas, 431

SISTERS (19) [SISTER]

Jos 2:13 my **s**, and all that they have, and deliver our 269
1Ch 2:16 Whose **s** *were* Zeruiah, and Abigail. And 269
Job 1: 4 sent and called for their three **s** to eat and 269
42:11 all his **s**, and all *they that had been of* his 269
Eze 16:45 thou *art* the sister of thy **s**, which lothed their 269
16:51 hast justified thy **s** in all thine abominations 269
16:52 Thou also, which hast judged thy **s**, 269
16:52 thy shame, in that thou hast justified thy **s**. 269
16:55 When thy **s**, Sodom and her daughters, 269
16:61 when thou shalt receive thy **s**, thine elder and 269
Hos 2: 1 Ammi; and to your **s**, Ruhamah. 269
Mt 13:56 And his **s**, are they not all with us? Whence 79
19:29 or **s**, or father, or mother, or wife, or children, 79
Mk 6: 3 and are not his **s** here with us? And they were 79
10:29 or **s**, or father, or mother, or wife, or children, 79
10:30 and **s**, and mothers, and children, and lands, 79
Lk 14:26 and children, and brethren, and **s**, yea, 79
Jn 11: 3 Therefore *his* **s** sent unto him, saying, Lord, 79
1Ti 5: 2 as mothers; the younger as **s**, with all purity. 79

SIT (113) [DOWNSITTING, SAT, SATEST, SEAT, SEATED, SEATS, SEATWARD, SITTEST, SITTETH, SITTING]

Ge 27:19 arise, I pray thee, **s** and eat of my venison, 3427
Nu 32: 6 brethren go to war, and shall ye **s** here? 3427
Jdg 5:10 ye that **s** in judgment, and walk by the way. 3427
Ru 3:18 said she, **S still**, my daughter, until thou 3427
4: 1 *Ho*, such a one, turn aside, **s down** here. 3427
4: 2 elders of the city, and said, **S** ye **down** here. 3427
1Sa 9:22 **made** them **s** in the chiefest place among 5414
16:11 for we will not **s down** till he come hither. 5437
20: 5 I should **not fail to s** with the king at meat: 3427
2Sa 19: 8 Behold, the king doth **s** in the gate. 3427
1Ki 1:13 after me, and he shall **s** upon my throne? 3427
1:17 after me, and he shall **s** upon my throne. 3427
1:20 that *thou* shouldest tell them who shall **s** on 3427
1:24 after me, and he shall **s** upon my throne? 3427
1:27 who should **s** on the throne of my lord 3427
1:30 and he shall **s** upon my throne in my stead; 3427
1:35 that he may come and **s** upon my throne; 3427
1:48 which hath given *one* to **s** on my throne *this* 3427
3: 6 that thou hast given him a son to **s** on his 3427
8:20 **s** on the throne of Israel, as the LORD 3427
8:25 man in my sight to **s** on the throne of Israel; 3427
2Ki 7: 3 to another, Why **s** we here until we die? 3427
7: 4 if we **s** still here, we die also. Now therefore NIH
10:30 thy children of the fourth *generation* shall **s** 3427
15:12 Thy sons shall **s** on the throne of Israel unto 3427
18:27 *hath he* not *sent me* to the men which **s** on 3427
1Ch 28: 5 he hath chosen Solomon my son to **s** upon 3427
2Ch 6:16 in my sight to **s** upon the throne of Israel; 3427
Ps 26: 5 of evildoers; and will not **s** with the wicked. 3427
69:12 They that **s** in the gate speak against me; 3427
107:10 Such as **s** in darkness and in the shadow of 3427
110: 1 said unto my Lord, **S** thou at my right hand, 3427
119:23 Princes also did **s** *and* speak against me: *but* 3427
127: 2 to **s up** late, to eat the bread of sorrows: 3427
132:12 their children also shall **s** upon thy throne 3427
Ecc 10: 6 in great dignity, and the rich **s** in low place. 3427
Isa 3:26 she *being* desolate shall **s** upon the ground. 3427
14:13 I will **s** also upon the mount of 3427
16: 5 he shall **s** upon it in truth in the tabernacle 3427

S

Isa 30: 7 concerning this, Their strength *is* to **s still.** 7674
36:12 *hath he* not *sent me* to the men that **s** upon 3427
42: 7 them that **s in** darkness out of the prison 3427
47: 1 Come down, and **s** in the dust, O virgin 3427
47: 1 daughter of Babylon, **s** on the ground: 3427
47: 5 **S** thou silent, and get thee into darkness, 3427
47: 8 I shall not **s** *as* a widow, neither shall I 3427
47:14 *be* a coal to warm at, *nor* fire to **s** before it. 3427
52: 2 the dust; arise, *and* **s down,** O Jerusalem: 3427
Jer 8:14 Why do we **s still?** assemble yourselves, 3427
13:13 even the kings that **s** upon David's throne, 3427
13:18 to the queen, Humble yourselves, **s down:** 3427
16: 8 to **s** with them to eat and to drink. 3427
33:17 David shall never want a man to **s** upon 3427
36:15 **S down** now, and read it in our ears. 3427
36:30 He shall have none to **s** upon the throne of 3427
48:18 come down from *thy* glory, and **s** in thirst; 3427
La 1: 1 How doth the city **s** solitary, *that was* full 3427
2:10 The elders of the daughter of Zion **s** upon 3427
Eze 26:16 they shall **s** upon the ground, and 3427
28: 2 hast said, I *am* a God, I **s** *in* the seat of God, 3427
33:31 they **s** before thee *as* my people, and 3427
44: 3 he shall **s** in it to eat bread before 3427
Da 7: 9 cast *down,* and the Ancient of days did **s,** 3488
7:26 the judgment shall **s,** and they shall take 3488
Joel 3:12 for there will I **s** to judge all the heathen 3427
Mic 4: 4 they shall **s** every man under his vine and 3427
7: 8 when I **s** in darkness, the LORD *shall be* a 3427
Zec 3: 8 thou, and thy fellows that **s** before thee: 3427
6:13 and shall **s** and rule upon his throne: 3427
Mal 3: 3 he shall **s** *as* a refiner and purifier of silver: 3427
Mt 8:11 and shall **s down** with Abraham, and Isaac, *347*
14:19 And he commanded the multitude to **s down** *347*
15:35 And he commanded the multitude to **s down** *377*
19:28 when the Son of man shall **s** in the throne *2523*
19:28 ye also shall **s** upon twelve thrones, *2523*
20:21 Grant that these my two sons may **s,** *2523*
20:23 baptized *with:* but to **s** on my right hand, *2523*
22:44 unto my Lord, **S** thou on my right hand, *2521*
23: 2 and the Pharisees **s** in Moses' seat: *2523*
25:31 then shall he **s** upon the throne of his glory: *2523*
26:36 **S** ye here, while I go and pray yonder. *2523*
Mk 6:39 **make** all **s down** by companies upon *347*
8: 6 And he commanded the people to **s down** on *377*
10:37 said unto him, Grant unto us that we may **s,** *2523*
10:40 But to **s** on my right hand and on my left *2523*
12:36 said to my Lord, **S** thou on my right hand, *2521*
14:32 his disciples, **S** ye here, while I shall pray. *2523*
Lk 1:79 To give light to them that **s** in darkness and *2521*
9:14 **Make** them **s down** by fifties in a *2625*
9:15 And they did so, and **made** *them* all **s down.** *347*
12:37 and **make** them to **s down to meat,** and *347*
13:29 and shall **s down** in the kingdom of God. *347*
14: 8 a wedding, **s** not **down** in the highest room; *2625*
14:10 go and **s down** in the lowest room; *377*
14:10 presence of them that **s at meat with** thee. *4873*
16: 6 and **s down** quickly, and write fifty. *2523*
17: 7 from the field, Go and **s down to meat?** *377*
20:42 said to my Lord, **S** thou on my right hand, *2521*
22:30 **s** on thrones judging the twelve tribes of *2523*
22:69 Hereafter shall the Son of man **s** on *2521*
Jn 6:10 And Jesus said, Make the men **s down.** *377*
Ac 2:30 *he* would raise up Christ to **s** on his throne; *2523*
2:34 unto my Lord, **S** thou on my right hand, *2521*
8:31 that *he* would come up and **s** with him. *2523*
1Co 8:10 knowledge **s at meat** in the idol's temple, *2621*
Eph 2: 6 **made** *us* **s together** in heavenly *places* in *4776*
Heb 1:13 **S** on my right hand, until I make thine *2521*
Jas 2: 3 say unto him, **S** thou here in a good place; *2521*
2: 3 thou there, or **s** here under my footstool: *2521*
Rev 3:21 To him that overcometh will I grant to **s** *2523*
17: 3 I saw a woman **s** upon a scarlet coloured *2521*
18: 7 I **s** a queen, and am no widow, and shall see *2521*
19:18 and of them that **s** on them, and the flesh of *2521*

SITH (3) [SINCE]

Jer 15: 7 *s* they return not from their ways. NIH
23:38 **s** ye say, The burden of the LORD; 518
Eze 35: 6 **s** thou hast not hated blood, even blood shall 518

SITHRI See ZITHRI

SITNAH (1)

Ge 26:21 for that also: and he called the name of it **S.** 7856

SITTEST (7) [SITH]

Ex 18:14 why **s** thou thyself alone, and all the people 3427
Dt 6: 7 shalt talk of them when thou **s** in thine 3427
11:19 speaking of them when thou **s** in thine 3427
Ps 50:20 Thou **s** *and* speakest against thy brother; 3427
Pr 23: 1 When thou **s** to eat with a ruler, 3427
Jer 22: 2 that **s** upon the throne of David, thou, and 3427
Ac 23: 3 for **s** thou to judge me after the law, and *2521*

SITTETH (42) [SITH]

Ex 11: 5 from the firstborn of Pharaoh that **s** upon 3427
Lev 15: 4 every thing, whereon he **s,** shall be unclean. 3427
15: 6 he that **s** on *any* thing whereon he sat that 3427
15:20 every *thing* also that she **s** upon shall be 3427
15:23 or on *any* thing whereon she **s,** when he 3427
15:26 whatsoever she **s** upon shall be unclean, 3427
Dt 17:18 when he **s** upon the throne of his kingdom, 3427
1Ki 1:46 also Solomon **s** on the throne of 3427
Est 6:10 Mordecai the Jew, that **s** at the king's gate: 3427
Ps 1: 1 of sinners, nor **s** in the seat of the scornful. 3427
2: 4 He that **s** in the heavens shall laugh: 3427
10: 8 He **s** in the lurking places of the villages: 3427
29:10 The LORD **s** upon the flood; yea, 3427
29:10 the flood; yea, the LORD **s** King for ever. 3427
47: 8 God **s** upon the throne of his holiness. 3427
99: 1 he **s** *between* the cherubims; let the earth be 3427
Pr 9:14 For she **s** at the door of her house, on a seat 3427
20: 8 A king that **s** in the throne of judgment 3427
31:23 when he **s** among the elders of the land. 3427

SS 1:12 While the king *s* at his table, my spikenard NIH
Isa 28: 6 for a spirit of judgment to him that **s** in 3427
40:22 *It is* he that **s** upon the circle of the earth, 3427
Jer 17:11 *As* the partridge **s** *on eggs,* and 1716
29:16 of the king that **s** upon the throne of David, 3427
La 3:28 He **s** alone and keepeth silence, because 3427
Zec 1:11 behold, all the earth **s still,** and is at rest. 3427
5: 7 this *is* a woman that **s** in the midst of 3427
Mt 23:22 throne of God, and by him that **s** thereon. *2521*
Lk 14:28 **s** not **down** first, and counteth the cost, *2523*
14:31 **s** not **down** first, and consulteth whether he *2523*
22:27 he that **s at meat,** or he that serveth? *345*
22:27 *is* not he that **s at meat**? but I am among you *345*
1Co 14:30 If *any thing* be revealed to another that **s** *2521*
Col 3: 1 where Christ **s** on the right hand of God. *2521*
2Th 2: 4 so that he as God **s** in the temple of God, *2523*
Rev 5:13 *be* unto him that **s** upon the throne, and *2521*
6:16 hide us from the face of him that **s** on *2521*
7:10 Salvation to our God which **s** upon *2521*
7:15 he that **s** on the throne shall dwell among *2521*
17: 1 of the great whore that **s** upon many waters: *2521*
17: 9 seven mountains, on which the woman **s.** *2521*
17:15 where the whore **s,** are peoples, and *2521*

SITTING (43) [SITH]

Dt 22: 6 the dam **s** upon the young, or upon 7257
Jdg 3:20 he was **s** in a summer parlour, which he had 3427
1Ki 10: 5 the **s** of his servants, and the attendance of 4186
13:14 man of God, and found him **s** under an oak: 3427
22:19 I saw the LORD **s** on his throne, and 3427
2Ki 4:38 the sons of the prophets *were* **s** before him: 3427
9: 5 the captains of the host *were* **s;** 3427
2Ch 9: 4 the **s** of his servants, and the attendance of 4186
9:18 stays on each side of the **s** place, and 3427
18:18 I saw the LORD **s** upon his throne, and 3427
Ne 2: 6 said unto me, (the queen also **s** by him,) 3427
Est 5:13 long as I see Mordecai the Jew **s** at 3427
Isa 6: 1 died I saw also the Lord **s** upon a throne, 3427
Jer 17:25 and princes **s** upon the throne of David, 3427
22: 4 house kings **s** upon the throne of David, 3427
22:30 **s** upon the throne of David, and ruling any 3427
38: 7 the king then **s** in the gate of Benjamin; 3427
La 3:63 Behold their **s down,** and their rising up; 3427
Mt 9: 9 named Matthew, **s** at the receipt of custom: *2521*
11:16 It is like unto children **s** in the markets, and *2521*
20:30 two blind men **s** by the way side, *2521*
21: 5 and **s** upon an ass, and a colt the foal of an *1910*
26:64 Hereafter shall ye see the Son of man **s** on *2521*
27:36 And **s down** they watched him there; *2521*
27:61 other Mary, **s** over against the sepulchre. *2521*
Mk 2: 6 But there were certain of the scribes **s** there, *2521*
2:14 he saw Levi the *son* of Alpheus **s** at *2521*
5:15 **s,** and clothed, and in his right mind: *2521*
14:62 ye shall see the Son of man **s** on the right *2521*
16: 5 they saw a young man **s** on the right side, *2521*
Lk 2:46 **s** in the midst of the doctors, both hearing *2516*
5:17 doctors of the law **s** *by,* which were come *2521*
5:27 named Levi, **s** at the receipt of custom: *2521*
7:32 They are like unto children **s** in *2521*
8:35 **s** at the feet of Jesus, clothed, and in his *2521*
10:13 ago repented, **s** in sackcloth and ashes. *2521*
Jn 2:14 and doves, and the changers of money **s:** *2521*
12:15 behold, thy King cometh, **s** on an ass's colt. *2521*
20:12 And seeth two angels in white **s,** the one at *2516*
Ac 2: 2 it filled all the house where they were **s.** *2521*
8:28 and **s** in his chariot read Esaias the prophet. *2521*
25: 6 and the next day **s** in the judgment seat, *2523*
Rev 4: 4 the seats I saw four and twenty elders **s,** *2521*

SITUATE (3) [SITUATION]

1Sa 14: 5 The forefront of the one *was* **s** northward 4690
Eze 27: 3 O thou that art **s** at the entry of the sea, 3427
Na 3: 8 populous No, that was **s** among the rivers, 3427

SITUATION (2) [SITUATE]

2Ki 2:19 I pray thee, the **s** of *this* city *is* pleasant, 4186
Ps 48: 2 Beautiful for **s,** the joy of the whole earth, 5131

SIVAN (1)

Est 8: 9 that *is,* the month **S,** on the three and 5510

SIX (202) [SIXSCORE, SIXTH]

Ge 7: 6 Noah *was* **s** hundred years old when 8337
7:11 In the **s** hundredth year of Noah's life, 8337
8:13 it came to pass in the **s** hundredth and 8337
16:16 Abram *was* fourscore and **s** years old, 8337
30:20 with me, because I have born him **s** sons: 8337
31:41 two daughters, and **s** years for thy cattle: 8337
46:26 all the souls *were* threescore and **s;** 8337
Ex 12:37 about **s** hundred thousand on foot *that were* 8337
14: 7 And he took **s** hundred chosen chariots, and 8337
16:26 **S** days ye shall gather it; but on the seventh 8337
20: 9 **S** days shalt thou labour, and do all thy 8337
20:11 For *in* **s** days the LORD made heaven and 8337
21: 2 a Hebrew servant, **s** years he shall serve: 8337
23:10 **s** years thou shalt sow thy land, and 8337
23:12 **S** days thou shalt do thy work, and on 8337
24:16 and the cloud covered it **s** days: 8337
25:32 **s** branches shall come out of the sides of it; 8337
25:33 in the **s** branches that come out of 8337
25:35 according to the **s** branches that proceed out 8337
26: 9 **s** curtains by themselves, and shalt double 8337
26:22 westward thou shalt make **s** boards. 8337
28:10 **S** of their names on one stone, and the *other* 8337
28:10 the *other* **s** names of the rest on the other 8337
31:15 **S** days may work be done; but in 8337
31:17 for *in* **s** days the LORD made heaven and 8337
34:21 **S** days thou shalt work, but on the seventh 8337
35: 2 **S** days shall work be done, but on 8337
36:16 and **s** curtains by themselves. 8337
36:27 the tabernacle westward he made **s** boards. 8337
37:18 **s** branches going out of the sides thereof; 8337
37:19 throughout the **s** branches going out of 8337
37:21 according to the **s** branches going out of it. 8337

Ex 38:26 for **s** hundred thousand and three thousand 8337
Lev 12: 5 of her purifying threescore and **s** days. 8337
23: 3 **S** days shall work be done: but the seventh 8337
24: 6 thou shalt set them *in* two rows, **s** on a row, 8337
25: 3 **S** years thou shalt sow thy field, and 8337
25: 3 **s** years thou shalt prune thy vineyard, and 8337
Nu 1:21 *were* forty and **s** thousand and 8337
1:25 and five thousand **s** hundred and fifty. 8337
1:27 and fourteen thousand and **s** hundred. 8337
1:46 Even all they that were numbered were **s** 8337
2: 4 and fourteen thousand and **s** hundred. 8337
2: 9 and **s** thousand and four hundred, 8337
2:11 *were* forty and **s** thousand and 8337
2:15 and five thousand and **s** hundred and fifty. 8337
2:31 fifty and seven thousand and **s** hundred. 8337
2:32 their hosts *were* **s** hundred thousand 8337
3:28 *were* eight thousand and **s** hundred, 8337
3:34 upward, *were* **s** thousand and two hundred. 8337
4:40 two thousand and **s** hundred and thirty. 8337
7: 3 **s** covered wagons, and twelve oxen; 8337
11:21 amongst whom I *am, are* **s** hundred 8337
26:41 and five thousand and **s** hundred. 8337
26:51 **s** hundred thousand and a thousand seven 8337
31:32 was **s** hundred thousand and 8337
31:37 the LORD'S tribute of the sheep was **s** 8337
31:38 the beeves *were* thirty and **s** thousand; of 8337
31:44 And thirty and **s** thousand beeves, 8337
35: 6 the Levites *there shall be* **s** cities for refuge, 8337
35:13 *of these* cities which ye shall give **s** cities 8337
35:15 These **s** cities shall be a refuge, *both* for 8337
Dt 5:13 **S** days thou shalt labour, and do all thy 8337
15:12 be sold unto thee, and serve thee **s** years; 8337
15:18 servant *to thee,* in serving thee **s** years: 8337
16: 8 **S** days thou shalt eat unleavened bread: and 8337
Jos 6: 3 the city once. Thus shalt thou do **s** days. 8337
6:14 returned *into* the camp: so they did **s** days. 8337
7: 5 of Ai smote of them about thirty and **s** men: 8337
15:59 and Eltekon; **s** cities with their villages. 8337
15:62 and En-gedi; **s** cities with their villages. 8337
Jdg 3:31 which slew *of* the Philistines **s** hundred 8337
12: 7 Jephthah judged Israel **s** years. Then died 8337
18:11 **s** hundred men appointed *with* weapons of 8337
18:16 the **s** hundred men appointed *with* their 8337
18:17 **s** hundred men that were appointed *with* 8337
20:15 and **s** thousand men that drew sword, 8337
20:47 **s** hundred men turned and fled to 8337
Ru 3:15 he measured **s** *measures* of barley, and 8337
3:17 These **s** *measures* of barley gave he me; 8337
1Sa 13: 5 **s** thousand horsemen, and people as 8337
13:15 present with him, about **s** hundred men. 8337
14: 2 the people that *were* with him *were* about **s** 8337
17: 4 whose height *was* **s** cubits and a span. 8337
17: 7 his spear's head *weighed* **s** hundred shekels 8337
23:13 *which were* about **s** hundred, arose and 8337
27: 2 he passed over with the **s** hundred men that 8337
30: 9 and the **s** hundred men that *were* with him, 8337
2Sa 2:11 of Judah was seven years and **s** months. 8337
5: 5 over Judah seven years and **s** months: 8337
6:13 the ark of the LORD had gone **s** paces, 8337
15:18 **s** hundred men which came after him from 8337
21:20 that had on every hand **s** fingers, and 8337
21:20 on every foot **s** toes, four and twenty *in* 8337
1Ki 6: 6 the middle *was* **s** cubits broad, and the third 8337
10:14 in one year was **s** hundred threescore 8337
10:14 hundred threescore and **s** talents of gold, 8337
10:16 **s** hundred *shekels* of gold went to one 8337
10:19 The throne had **s** steps, and the top of 8337
10:20 one side and on the other upon the **s** steps: 8337
10:29 went out of Egypt for **s** hundred *shekels* of 8337
11:16 (For **s** months did Joab remain there with 8337
16:23 twelve years: **s** years reigned he in Tirzah. 8337
2Ki 5: 5 **s** thousand *pieces* of gold, and ten changes 8337
11: 3 her hid *in* the house of the LORD **s** years. 8337
13:19 shouldest have smitten five or **s** times; 8337
15: 8 reign over Israel in Samaria **s** months. 8337
1Ch 3: 4 *These* **s** were born unto him in Hebron; and 8337
3: 4 there he reigned seven years and **s** months: 8337
3:22 and Bariah, and Neariah, and Shaphat, **s.** 8337
4:27 Shimei had sixteen sons and **s** daughters; 8337
7: 2 and twenty thousand and **s** hundred. 8337
7: 4 **s** and thirty thousand *men:* for they had 8337
7:40 to battle *was* twenty and **s** thousand men. 8337
8:38 Azel had **s** sons, whose names *are* these, 8337
9: 6 and their brethren, **s** hundred and ninety. 8337
9: 9 nine hundred and fifty and **s.** 8337
9:44 Azel had **s** sons, whose names *are* these, 8337
12:24 spear *were* **s** thousand and eight hundred, 8337
12:26 of Levi four thousand and **s** hundred. 8337
12:35 and eight thousand and **s** hundred. 8337
20: 6 **s** *on each hand,* and six *on each foot:* and 8337
20: 6 six *on each hand,* and **s** *on each foot:* and 8337
21:25 So David gave to Ornan for the place **s** 8337
23: 4 and **s** thousand *were* officers and judges: 8337
25: 3 and Jeshaiah, Hashabiah, and Mattithiah, **s,** 8337
26:17 Eastward *were* **s** Levites, northward four a 8337
2Ch 1:17 brought forth out of Egypt a chariot for **s** 8337
2: 2 and **s** hundred to oversee them. 8337
2:17 and three thousand and **s** hundred. 8337
2:18 **s** hundred overseers to set the people a 8337
3: 8 fine gold, *amounting* to **s** hundred talents. 8337
9:13 to Solomon in one year was **s** hundred 8337
9:13 and threescore and **s** talents of gold; 8337
9:15 **s** hundred *shekels* of beaten gold went to 8337
9:18 *there were* **s** steps to the throne, with a 8337
9:19 one side and on the other upon the **s** steps. 8337
16: 1 In the **s** and thirtieth year of the reign of 8337
22:12 he was with them hid in the house of God **s** 8337
26:12 of valour *were* two thousand and **s** hundred. 8337
29:33 the consecrated *things were* **s** hundred oxen 8337
35: 8 **s** hundred *small cattle,* and three hundred 8337
Ezr 2:10 children of Bani, **s** hundred forty and two. 8337
2:11 of Bebai, **s** hundred twenty and three. 8337
2:13 of Adonikam, **s** hundred sixty and six. 8337
2:13 of Adonikam, six hundred sixty and **s.** 8337
2:14 of Bigvai, two thousand fifty and **s.** 8337

S

Ezr 2:22 The men of Netophah, fifty and **s**. 8337
2:26 and Gaba, **s** hundred twenty and one. 8337
2:30 of Magbish, an hundred fifty and **s**. 8337
2:35 three thousand and **s** hundred and thirty. 8337
2:60 of Nekoda, **s** hundred fifty and two. 8337
2:66 horses *were* seven hundred thirty and **s**; 8337
2:67 **s** thousand seven hundred and twenty. 8337
8:26 I even weighed unto their hand **s** hundred 8337
8:35 ninety and **s** rams, seventy and 8337
Ne 5:18 *me* daily *was* one ox *and* **s** choice sheep; 8337
7:10 children of Arah, **s** hundred fifty and two. 8337
7:15 of Binnui, **s** hundred forty and eight. 8337
7:16 of Bebai, **s** hundred twenty and eight. 8337
7:18 **s** hundred threescore and seven. 8337
7:20 children of Adin, **s** hundred fifty and five. 8337
7:30 and Geba, **s** hundred twenty and one. 8337
7:62 of Nekoda, **s** hundred forty and two. 8337
7:68 Their horses, seven hundred thirty and **s**: 8337
7:69 **s** thousand seven hundred and twenty asses. 8337
Est 2:12 *to wit,* **s** months with oil of myrrh, and 8337
2:12 **s** months with sweet odours, and with *other* 8337
Job 5:19 He shall deliver thee in **s** troubles: yea, 8337
42:12 **s** thousand camels, and a thousand yoke of 8337
Pr 6:16 These **s** *things* doth the LORD hate: yea, 8337
Isa 6: 2 each one had **s** wings; with twain he 8337
Jer 34:14 when he hath served thee **s** years, thou shalt 8337
52:23 were ninety and **s** pomegranates on a side; 8337
52:30 persons *were* four thousand and **s** hundred. 8337
Eze 9: 2 **s** men came from the way of the higher 8337
40: 5 in the man's hand a measuring reed of **s** 8337
40:12 the little chambers *were* **s** cubits on this 8337
40:12 cubits on this side, and **s** cubits on that side. 8337
41: 1 **s** cubits broad on the one side, and 8337
41: 1 and **s** cubits broad on the other side, 8337
41: 3 the door, **s** cubits; and the breadth of 8337
41: 5 he measured the wall of the house, **s** cubits; 8337
41: 8 chambers *were* a full reed of **s** great cubits. 8337
46: 1 the east shall be shut the **s** working days; 8337
46: 4 day *shall be* **s** lambs without blemish, 8337
46: 6 without blemish, and **s** lambs, and a ram: 8337
Da 3: 1 *and* the breadth thereof **s** cubits: 8353
Mt 17: 1 And after **s** days Jesus taketh Peter, James, *1803*
Mk 9: 2 And after **s** days Jesus taketh with *him* *1803*
Lk 4:25 was shut up three years and **s** months, *1803*
13:14 There are **s** days in which *men* ought to *1803*
Jn 2: 6 And there were set there **s** waterpots of *1803*
2:20 and **s** years was this temple in building, *1803*
12: 1 Then Jesus **s** days before the passover came *1803*
Ac 11:12 Moreover these **s** brethren accompanied *1803*
18:11 he continued *there* a year and **s** months, *1803*
Jas 5:17 *by the space of* three years and **s** months. *1803*
Rev 4: 8 And the four beasts had each of them **s** *1803*
13:18 number *is* **S hundred threescore** *and* **six**. *5516*
13:18 number *is* **Six hundred threescore** *and* **s**. *5516*
14:20 of a thousand *and* **s hundred** furlongs. *1812*

SIXSCORE (2) [SIX]

1Ki 9:14 Hiram sent to the king **s** 3967+6242+2050.1
Jnh 4:11 wherein are more than **s** thousand 6240+8147

SIXTEEN (23) [SIXTEENTH]

Ge 46:18 she bare unto Jacob, *even* **s** souls. 6240+8337
Ex 26:25 and their sockets *of* silver, **s** sockets; 6240+8337
36:30 their sockets *were* **s** sockets *of* silver, 6240+8337
Nu 26:22 **threescore and s** thousand 7657+8337+2050.1
31:40 the persons *were* **s** thousand; of 6240+8337
31:46 And **s** thousand persons;) 6240+8337
31:52 was **s** thousand seven hundred and 6240+8337
Jos 15:41 **s** cities with their villages. 6240+8337
19:22 *at* Jordan: **s** cities with their villages. 6240+8337
2Ki 13:10 in Samaria, *and reigned* **s** years. 6240+8337
14:21 which *was* **s** years old, and made him 6240+8337
15: 2 **S** years old was he when he *began* to 6240+8337
15:33 and he reigned **s** years in Jerusalem. 6240+8337
16: 2 reigned **s** years in Jerusalem, and 6240+8337
1Ch 4:27 Shimei had **s** sons and six daughters; 6240+8337
24: 4 **s** chief *men* of the house of *their* 6240+8337
2Ch 13:21 and two sons, and **s** daughters. 6240+8337
26: 1 who *was* **s** years old, and made him 6240+8337
26: 3 **S** years old *was* Uzziah when he 6240+8337
27: 1 and he reigned **s** years in Jerusalem. 6240+8337
27: 8 and reigned **s** years in Jerusalem. 6240+8337
28: 1 and he reigned **s** years in Jerusalem: 6240+8337
Ac 27:37 ship two hundred **threescore** *and* **s** *1440+1803*

SIXTEENTH (3) [SIXTEEN]

1Ch 24:14 fifteenth to Bilgah, the **s** to Immer, 6240+8337
25:23 The **s** to Hananiah, *he,* his sons, and 6240+8337
2Ch 29:17 in the **s** day of the first month they 6240+8337

SIXTH (47) [SIX]

Ge 1:31 and the morning were the **s** day. 8345
30:19 conceived again, and bare Jacob the **s** son. 8345
Ex 16: 5 that on the **s** day they shall prepare *that* 8345
16:22 *that* on the **s** day they gathered twice as 8345
16:29 he giveth you on the **s** day the bread of two 8345
26: 9 shalt double the **s** curtain in the forefront of 8345
Lev 25:21 my blessing upon you in the **s** year, 8345
Nu 7:42 On the **s** day Eliasaph the son of Deuel, 8345
29:29 on the **s** day eight bullocks, two rams, *and* 8345
Jos 19:32 The **s** lot came out to the children of 8345
2Sa 3: 5 the **s**, Ithream, by Eglah David's wife. 8345
1Ki 16: 8 **s** year of Asa king of Judah *began* Elah 8337
2Ki 18:10 *even* in the **s** year of Hezekiah, that *is* 8337
1Ch 2:15 Ozem the **s**, David the seventh: 8345
3: 3 of Abital: the **s**, Ithream by Eglah his wife. 8345
12:11 Attai the **s**, Eliel the seventh, 8345
24: 9 The fifth to Malchijah, the **s** to Mijamin, 8345
25:13 The **s** *to* Bukkiah, *he,* his sons, and 8345
26: 3 Elam the fifth, Jehohanan the **s**, 8345
26: 5 Ammiel the **s**, Issachar the seventh, 8345
27: 9 The **s** *captain* for the sixth month *was* Ira 8345
27: 9 The sixth *captain* for the **s** month *was* Ira 8345
Ezr 6:15 which *was in* the **s** year of the reign of 8353

Ne 3:30 Hanun the **s** son of Zalaph, another piece. 8345
Eze 4:11 also water by measure, the **s** *part* of a hin: 8345
8: 1 it came to pass in the **s** year, in the sixth 8345
8: 1 in the **s** *month,* in the fifth *day* of 8345
39: 2 **leave** but **the s part** of thee, and will cause 8338
45:13 the **s** *part* of an ephah of a homer of wheat, 8345
45:13 ye shall **give the s part** of an ephah of a 8341
46:14 the **s** *part* of an ephah, and the third *part* of 8345
Hag 1: 1 in the **s** month, in the first day of 8345
1:15 the four and twentieth day of the **s** month, 8345
Mt 20: 5 Again he went out about the **s** and *1623*
27:45 Now from the **s** hour there was darkness *1623*
Mk 15:33 And when the **s** hour was come, there was *1623*
Lk 1:26 And in the **s** month the angel Gabriel was *1623*
1:36 and this is the **s** month with her, who was *1623*
23:44 And it was about the **s** hour, and there was *1623*
Jn 4: 6 on the well: *and* it was about the **s** hour. *1623*
19:14 of the passover, and about the **s** hour: *1623*
Ac 10: 9 up upon the house to pray about the **s** hour: *1623*
Rev 6:12 And I beheld when he had opened the **s** *1623*
9:13 And the **s** angel sounded, and I heard a *1623*
9:14 Saying to the **s** angel which had *1623*
16:12 And the **s** angel poured out his vial upon *1623*
21:20 The fifth, sardonyx; the **s**, sardius; *1623*

SIXTY (15) [SIXTYFOLD, THREESCORE]

Ge 5:15 Mahalaleel lived **s** and five years, and 8346
5:18 Jared lived an hundred **s** and two years, 8346
5:20 all the days of Jared were nine hundred **s** 8346
5:21 Enoch lived **s** and five years, and 8346
5:23 all the days of Enoch were three hundred **s** 8346
5:27 days of Methuselah were nine hundred **s** 8346
Lev 27: 3 twenty years old even unto **s** years old, 8346
27: 7 if *it be* from **s** years old and above; if *it be* a 8346
Nu 7:88 *were* twenty and four bullocks, the rams **s**, 8346
7:88 four bullocks, the rams sixty, the he goats **s**, 8346
7:88 he goats sixty, the lambs of the first year **s**. 8346
Ezr 2:13 of Adonikam, six hundred **s** and six. 8346
Mt 13:23 some an hundred*fold,* some **s**, some thirty. *1835*
Mk 4: 8 and some **s**, and some an hundred. *1835*
4:20 some thirty*fold,* some **s**, and some an *1835*

SIXTYFOLD (1) [SIXTY]

Mt 13: 8 some an hundred*fold,* some **s**, some *1835*

SIZE (5)

Ex 36: 9 four cubits: the curtains *were* all of one **s**. 4060
36:15 the eleven curtains *were* of one **s**. 4060
1Ki 6:25 cherubims *were* of one measure and one **s**. 7095
7:37 had one casting, one measure, *and* one **s**. 7095
1Ch 23:29 and for all *manner of* measure and **s**; 4060

SKIES (5) [SKY]

2Sa 22:12 dark waters, *and* thick clouds of the **s**. 7834
Ps 18:11 *were* dark waters *and* thick clouds of the **s**. 7834
77:17 the **s** sent out a sound: thine arrows also 7834
Isa 45: 8 and let the **s** pour down righteousness: 7834
Jer 51: 9 unto heaven, and is lifted up *even* to the **s**. 7834

SKILFUL (7) [SKILL]

1Ch 5:18 **s** in war, *were* four and forty thousand 3925
15:22 instructed about the song, because he *was* **s**. 995
28:21 willing **s** *man,* for any *manner of* service: 2451
2Ch 2:14 **s** to work in gold, and in silver, in brass, 3045
Eze 21:31 the hand of brutish men, *and* **s** to destroy. 2796
Da 1: 4 **s** in all wisdom, and cunning in knowledge, 7919
Am 5:16 and such as are **s** of lamentation to wailing. 3045

SKILFULLY (1) [SKILL]

Ps 33: 3 him a new song; play **s** with a loud noise. 3190

SKILFULNESS (1) [SKILL]

Ps 78:72 and guided them by the **s** of his hands. 8394

SKILL (7) [SKILFUL, SKILFULLY, SKILFULNESS, UNSKILFUL]

1Ki 5: 6 **can s** to hew timber like unto 3045
2Ch 2: 7 that can **s** to grave with the cunning *men* 3045
2: 8 for I know that thy servants can **s** to cut 3045
34:12 all that could **s** of instruments of musick. 995
Ecc 9:11 nor yet favour to men of **s**; 3045
Da 1:17 and **s** in all learning and wisdom: 7919
9:22 I am now come forth to **give** thee **s** and 7919

SKIN (77) [FORESKIN, FORESKINS, GOATSKINS, SHEEPSKINS, SKINS]

Ex 22:27 his covering only, it *is* his raiment for his **s**: 5785
29:14 of the bullock, and his **s**, and his dung, 5785
34:29 that Moses wist not that the **s** of his face 5785
34:30 saw Moses, behold, the **s** of his face shone; 5785
34:35 of Moses, that the **s** of Moses' face shone: 5785
Lev 4:11 the **s** of the bullock, and all his flesh, 5785
7: 8 *even* the priest shall have to himself the **s** of 5785
11:32 vessel of wood, or raiment, or **s**, or sack, 5785
13: 2 When a man shall have in the **s** of his flesh 5785
13: 2 it be in the **s** of his flesh like the plague of 5785
13: 3 the priest shall look on the plague in the **s** 5785
13: 3 the plague in sight *be* deeper than the **s** of 5785
13: 4 If the bright spot *be* white in the **s** of his 5785
13: 4 in sight *be* not deeper than the **s**, and 5785
13: 5 at a stay, *and* the plague spread not in the **s**; 5785
13: 6 and the plague spread not in the **s**, 5785
13: 7 But if the scab spread much abroad in the **s**, 5785
13: 8 the scab spreadeth in the **s**, then the priest 5785
13:10 *if* the rising *be* white in the **s**, and it have 5785
13:11 It *is* an old leprosy in the **s** of his flesh, and 5785
13:12 if a leprosy break out abroad in the **s**, and 5785
13:12 the leprosy cover all the **s** of *him that hath* 5785
13:18 in which, *even* in the **s** thereof, was a boil, 5785
13:20 it *be* in sight lower than the **s**, and the hair 5785
13:21 *if* it *be* not lower than the **s**, but *be* 5785
13:22 if it spread much abroad in the **s**, then 5785
13:24 in the **s** whereof *there is* a hot burning, and 5785

Lev 13:25 and it *be* in sight deeper than the **s**; 5785
13:26 it *be* no lower than the *other* **s**, but *be* 5785
13:27 *and* if it be spread much abroad in the **s**, 5785
13:28 *and* spread not in the **s**, but it *be* somewhat 5785
13:30 behold, *if* it *be* in sight deeper than the **s**; 5785
13:31 it *be* not in sight deeper than the **s**, and 5785
13:32 the scall *be* not in sight deeper than the **s**; 5785
13:34 behold, *if* the scall be not spread in the **s**, 5785
13:34 the skin, nor *be* in sight deeper than the **s**; 5785
13:35 if the scall spread much in the **s** after his 5785
13:36 behold, *if* the scall be spread in the **s**, 5785
13:38 a woman have in the **s** of their flesh bright 5785
13:39 *if* the bright spots in the **s** of their flesh *be* 5785
13:39 it *is* a freckled spot *that* groweth in the **s**: 5785
13:43 as the leprosy appeareth in the **s** of 5785
13:48 whether in a **s**, or in any thing made of 5785
13:48 in a skin, or in any thing made of **s**; 5785
13:49 or in the **s**, either in the warp, or in 5785
13:49 or in the woof, or in any thing of **s**; 5785
13:51 or in a **s**, *or* in any work that is made of 5785
13:51 in a skin, *or* in any work that is made of **s**; 5785
13:52 in woollen or in linen, or any thing of **s**, 5785
13:53 or in the woof, or in any thing of **s**; 5785
13:56 or out of the **s**, or out of the warp, or out of 5785
13:57 or in the woof, or in any thing of **s**; 5785
13:58 whatsoever thing of **s** *it be,* which thou 5785
15:17 every garment, and every **s**, whereon is 5785
Nu 19: 5 her **s**, and her flesh, and her blood, with her 5785
Job 2: 4 the LORD, and said, **S** for skin, yea, 5785
2: 4 the LORD, and said, Skin for **s**, yea, 5785
7: 5 my **s** is broken, and become loathsome. 5785
10:11 Thou hast clothed me with **s** and flesh, and 5785
16:15 I have sewed sackcloth upon my **s**, and 1539
18:13 It shall devour the strength of his **s**: 5785
19:20 My bone cleaveth to my **s** and to my flesh, 5785
19:20 and I am escaped with the **s** of my teeth. 5785
19:26 *though* after my **s** *worms* destroy this *body,* 5785
30:30 My **s** is black upon me, and my bones are 5785
41: 7 Canst thou fill his **s** with barbed irons? or 5785
Ps 102: 5 of my groaning my bones cleave to my **s**. 1320
Jer 13:23 Can the Ethiopian change his **s**, or 5785
La 3: 4 My flesh and my **s** hath he made old; 5785
4: 8 their **s** cleaveth to their bones; it is 5785
5:10 Our **s** was black like an oven because of 5785
Eze 16:10 shod thee *with* badgers' **s**, and I girded thee NIH
37: 6 and cover you with **s**, and put breath in you, 5785
37: 8 upon them, and the **s** covered them above: 5785
Mic 3: 2 who pluck off their **s** from off them, and 5785
3: 3 my people, and flay their **s** from off them; 5785
Mk 1: 6 and with a girdle of a **s** about his loins; *1193*

SKINK See SNAIL

SKINS (24) [SKIN]

Ge 3:21 wife did the LORD God make coats of **s**, 5785
27:16 she put the **s** of the kids of the goats upon 5785
Ex 25: 5 rams' **s** dyed red, and badgers' skins, and 5785
25: 5 dyed red, and badgers' **s**, and shittim wood, 5785
26:14 a covering for the tent *of* rams' **s** dyed red, 5785
26:14 and a covering above of badgers' **s**. 5785
35: 7 rams' **s** dyed red, and badgers' skins, and 5785
35: 7 dyed red, and badgers' **s**, and shittim wood, 5785
35:23 goats' *hair,* and red **s** of rams, and 5785
35:23 of rams, and badgers' **s**, brought *them.* 5785
36:19 he made a covering for the tent *of* rams' **s** 5785
36:19 and a covering of badgers' **s** above *that.* 5785
39:34 the covering of rams' **s** dyed red, and 5785
39:34 the covering of badgers' **s**, and the vail of 5785
Lev 13:59 *in* the warp, or woof, or any thing of **s**, 5785
16:27 they shall burn in the fire their **s**, and their 5785
Nu 4: 6 shall put thereon the covering of badgers' **s**, 5785
4: 8 the same with a covering of badgers' **s**, 5785
4:10 thereof within a covering of badgers' **s**, 5785
4:11 cover it with a covering of badgers' **s**, and 5785
4:12 cover them with a covering of badgers' **s**, 5785
4:14 spread upon it a covering of badgers' **s**, 5785
4:25 the covering of the **badgers' s** that *is* above 8476
31:20 all that is made of **s**, and all work of goats' 5785

SKIP (1) [SKIPPED, SKIPPEDST, SKIPPING]

Ps 29: 6 He **maketh** them also **to s** like a calf; 7540

SKIPPED (2) [SKIP]

Ps 114: 4 The mountains **s** like rams, *and* the little 7540
114: 6 Ye mountains, *that* ye **s** like rams; *and* 7540

SKIPPEDST (1) [SKIP]

Jer 48:27 since thou spakest of him, thou **s for joy**. 5110

SKIPPING (1) [SKIP]

SS 2: 8 upon the mountains, **s** upon the hills. 7092

SKIRT (12) [SKIRTS]

Dt 22:30 his father's wife, nor discover his father's **s**. 3671
27:20 because he uncovereth his father's **s**. 3671
Ru 3: 9 spread therefore thy **s** over thine handmaid; 3671
1Sa 15:27 he laid hold upon the **s** of his mantle, and 3671
24: 4 and cut off the **s** of Saul's robe privily. 3671
24: 5 smote him, because he had cut off Saul's **s**. 3671
24:11 see, yea see the **s** of thy robe in my hand: 3671
24:11 for in that I cut off the **s** of thy robe, and 3671
Eze 16: 8 I spread my **s** over thee, and covered thy 3671
Hag 2:12 If one bear holy flesh in the **s** of his 3671
2:12 and with his **s** do touch bread, or pottage, or 3671
Zec 8:23 even shall take hold of the **s** of him that is a 3671

SKIRTS (7) [SKIRT]

Ps 133: 2 that went down to the **s** of his garments; 6310
Jer 2:34 Also in thy **s** is found the blood of the souls 3671
13:22 For the greatness of thine iniquity are thy **s** 7757
13:26 Therefore will I discover thy **s** upon thy 7757
La 1: 9 Her filthiness *is* in her **s**; she remembereth 7757
Eze 5: 3 a few in number, and bind them in thy **s**. 3671
Na 3: 5 I will discover thy **s** upon thy face, and 7757

SKULL (5)
Jdg 9:53 Abimelech's head, and all to brake his s. 1538
2Ki 9:35 they found no more of her than the s, and 1538
Mt 27:33 that is to say, a place of a s, *2898*
Mk 15:22 being interpreted, The place of a s. *2898*
Jn 19:17 forth into a place called *the place* of a s, *2898*

SKY (7) [SKIES]
Dt 33:26 in thy help, and in his excellency *on* the s. 7834
Job 37:18 Hast thou with him spread out the s, 7834
Mt 16: 2 *It will be* fair weather: for the s is red. *3772*
16: 3 for the s is red and lowring. O *ye* *3772*
16: 3 ye can discern the face of the s; *3772*
Lk 12:56 ye can discern the face of the s and of *3772*
Heb 11:12 *so many* as the stars of the s in multitude, *3772*

SLACK (8) [SLACKED, SLACKNESS]
Dt 7:10 he will not be s to him that hateth him, 309
23:21 LORD thy God, thou shalt not s to pay it: 309
Jos 10: 6 S not thy hand from thy servants; 7503
18: 3 How long *are* you s to go to possess 7503
2Ki 4:24 and go *forward;* s not *thy* riding for me, 6113
Pr 10: 4 *He becometh* poor that dealeth *with* a s 7423
Zep 3:16 *and to* Zion, Let not thine hands be s. 7503
2Pe 3: 9 The Lord is not s concerning *his* promise, *1019*

SLACKED (1) [SLACK]
Hab 1: 4 Therefore the law is s, and judgment doth 6313

SLACKNESS (1) [SLACK]
2Pe 3: 9 *his* promise, as some *men* count s; *1022*

SLAIN (183) [SLAY]
Ge 4:23 for I have s a man to my wounding, and 2026
34:27 The sons of Jacob came upon the s, and 2491
Lev 14:51 dip them in the blood of the s bird, and 7819
26:17 and ye shall be s before your enemies; 5062
Nu 11:22 Shall the flocks and the herds be s for them, 7819
14:16 therefore he hath s them in the wilderness. 7819
19:16 whosoever toucheth one **that is** s with a 2491
19:18 a bone, or one s, or one dead, or a grave: 2491
22:33 surely now also I had s thee, and saved her 2026
23:24 eat *of* the prey, and drink the blood of the s. 2491
25:14 Now the name of the Israelite that was s, 5221
25:14 *even* that was s with the Midianitish 5221
25:15 Midianitish woman that was s *was* Cozbi, 5221
25:18 which was s in the day of the plague for 5221
31: 8 beside *the rest of* them **that were** s; 2491
31:19 whosoever hath touched *any* s, purify *both* 2491
Dt 1: 4 After he had s Sihon the king of 5221
21: 1 If *one* be found s in the land which 2491
21: 1 *and* it be not known who hath s him: 5221
21: 2 cities which *are* round about him that is s: 2491
21: 3 *that* the city *which is* next unto the s *man,* 2491
21: 6 *that are* next unto the s *man,* shall wash 2491
28:31 Thine ox *shall be* s before thine eyes, and 2873
32:42 *and that* with the blood of the s and of 2491
Jos 11: 6 will I deliver them up all s before Israel: 2491
13:22 the sword among them that were s by them. 2491
Jdg 9:18 have s his sons, threescore and ten persons, 2026
15:16 with the jaw of an ass have I s a thousand 5221
20: 4 the husband of the woman that was s, 7523
20: 5 me by night, *and* thought to have s me: 2026
1Sa 4:11 sons of Eli, Hophni and Phinehas, were s. 4191
18: 7 Saul hath s his thousands, and David his ten 5221
19: 6 *As* the LORD liveth, he shall not be s. 4191
19:11 thy life to night, to morrow thou *shalt be* s. 4191
20:32 and said unto him, Wherefore shall he be s? 4191
21:11 Saul hath s his thousands, and David his ten 5221
22:21 Abiathar shewed David that Saul had s 2026
31: 1 and fell down s in mount Gilboa. 2491
31: 8 when the Philistines came to strip the s, 2491
2Sa 1:16 I have s the LORD'S anointed. 4191
1:19 The beauty of Israel *is* s upon thy high 2491
1:22 From the blood of the s, from the fat of 2491
1:25 *thou wast* s in thine high places. 2491
3:30 he had s their brother Asahel at Gibeon in 4191
4:11 when wicked men have s a righteous 2026
12: 9 hast s him with the sword of the children of 2026
13:30 Absalom hath s all the king's sons, and 5221
13:32 Let not my lord suppose *that* they have s all 4191
18: 7 Where the people of Israel were s before 5062
21:12 when the Philistines had s Saul in Gilboa: 5221
21:16 *with* a new *sword,* thought to have s David. 5221
1Ki 1:19 he hath s oxen and fat cattle and sheep in 2076
1:25 hath s oxen and fat cattle and sheep in 2076
9:16 s the Canaanites that dwelt in the city, and 2026
11:15 of the host was gone up to bury the s, 2491
13:26 which hath torn him, and s him, 4191
16:16 hath conspired, and hath also s the king: 5221
19: 1 withal how he had s all the prophets with 2026
19:10 and s thy prophets with the sword; 2026
19:14 and s thy prophets with the sword; 2026
2Ki 3:23 the kings are **surely** s, and they have 2717+2717
11: 2 from among the king's sons which were s; 4191
11: 2 from Athaliah, so that he was not s. 4191
11: 8 that cometh within the ranges, let him be s: 4191
11:15 Let her not be s *in* the house of the LORD. 4191
11:16 *into* the king's house: and there was she s. 4191
14: 5 that he slew his servants which had s 5221
1Ch 5:22 For there fell down many s, because 2491
10: 1 and fell down s in mount Gilboa. 2491
10: 8 when the Philistines came to strip the s, 2491
11:11 he lift up his spear against three hundred s 2491
2Ch 13:17 there fell down s of Israel five hundred 2491
21:13 also hast s thy brethren of thy father's 2026
22: 1 Arabians to the camp had s all the eldest. 2026
22: 9 when they had s him, they buried him: 4191
22:11 from among the king's sons that were s, 4191
23:14 followeth her, let him be s with the sword. 4191
23:21 after that they had s Athaliah with 4191
28: 9 ye have s them in a rage *that* reacheth up 2026
Est 7: 4 to be destroyed, to be s, and to perish. 2026
9:11 On that day the number of those that were s 2026
Est 9:12 The Jews have s and destroyed five 2026
Job 1:15 they have s the servants with the edge of 5221
1:17 s the servants with the edge of the sword; 5221
39:30 up blood: and where the s *are,* there *is* she. 2491
Ps 62: 3 ye shall be s all of you: as a bowing wall 7523
88: 5 the dead, like the s that lie in the grave, 2491
89:10 broken Rahab in pieces, as one that is s; 2491
Pr 7:26 yea, many strong *men have been* s by her. 2026
22:13 *is* a lion without, I shall be s in the streets. 7523
24:11 unto death, and *those that are* ready to be s; 2027
Isa 10: 4 and they shall fall under the s. 2026
14:19 *and as* the raiment of those that are s, 2026
14:20 hast destroyed thy land, *and* s thy people: 2026
22: 2 thy s *men are* not slain with the sword, nor 2491
22: 2 thy slain *men are* not s with the sword, nor 2491
26:21 her blood, and shall no more cover her s. 2026
27: 7 is he s according to the slaughter of them 2026
27: 7 to the slaughter of them that are s by him? 2026
34: 3 Their s also shall be cast out, and their stink 2491
66:16 and the s of the LORD shall be many. 2491
Jer 9: 1 night for the s of the daughter of my 2491
14:18 the field, then behold the s with the sword: 2491
18:21 *let* their young men *be* s by the sword in 5221
25:33 the s of the LORD shall be at that day 2491
33: 5 whom I have s in mine anger and in my 5221
41: 4 came to pass the second day after *he* had s 4191
41: 9 whom he had s because of Gedaliah, 5221
41: 9 of Nethaniah filled it *with them that were* s. 2491
41:16 after *that* he had s Gedaliah the son of 5221
41:18 Ishmael the son of Nethaniah had s 5221
51: 4 Thus the s shall fall in the land of 2491
51:47 and all her s shall fall in the midst of her. 2491
51:49 As Babylon *hath caused* the s of Israel to 2491
51:49 at Babylon shall fall the s of all the earth. 2491
La 2:20 the prophet be s in the sanctuary of 2026
2:21 thou hast s *them* in the day of thine anger; 2026
3:43 thou hast s, thou hast not pitied. 2026
4: 9 *They that be* s with the sword are better 2491
4: 9 are better than *they that be* s with hunger: 2491
Eze 6: 4 I will cast down your s *men* before your 2491
6: 7 the s shall fall in the midst of you, and 2491
6:13 when their s *men* shall be among their idols 2491
9: 7 the house, and fill the courts *with* the s: 2491
11: 6 Ye have multiplied your s in this city, 2491
11: 6 ye have filled the streets thereof *with* the s. 2491
11: 7 Your s whom ye have laid in the midst of 2491
16:21 That thou hast s my children, and 7819
21:14 doubled the third time, the sword of the s: 2491
21:14 it *is* the sword of the great *men that are* s, 2491
21:29 the necks of *them that are* s of the wicked, 2491
23:39 For when they had s their children to their 7819
26: 6 *are* in the field shall be s by the sword; 2026
28: 8 thou shalt die the deaths of *them that are* s 2491
30: 4 when the s shall fall in Egypt, and 2491
30:11 against Egypt, and fill the land *with* the s. 2491
31:17 him unto *them that be* s with the sword; 2491
31:18 with *them that be* s with the sword. 2491
32:20 the midst of *them that are* s by the sword: 2491
32:21 they lie uncircumcised, s by the sword. 2491
32:22 all of them s, fallen by the sword: 2491
32:23 all of them s, fallen by the sword, 2491
32:24 all of them s, fallen by the sword, 2491
32:25 in the midst of the s with all her multitude: 2491
32:25 all of them uncircumcised, s by the sword: 2491
32:25 he is put in the midst of *them that be* s. 2491
32:26 all of them uncircumcised, s by the sword, 2490
32:28 shalt lie with *them that are* s with 2491
32:29 are laid by *them that were* s by the sword: 2491
32:30 which are gone down with the s; 2491
32:30 they lie uncircumcised with *them that be* s 2491
32:31 and all his army s by the sword, 2491
32:32 with *them that are* s with the sword, 2491
35: 8 I will fill his mountains *with* his s *men:* in 2491
35: 8 shall they fall *that are* s with the sword. 2491
37: 9 O breath, and breathe upon these s, that 2026
Da 2:13 went forth that the wise *men* should be s; 6992
2:13 they sought Daniel and his fellows to be s. 6992
5:30 *was* Belshazzar the king of the Chaldeans s. 6992
7:11 I beheld *even* till the beast *was* s, and 6992
11:26 shall overflow: and many shall fall down s. 2491
Hos 6: 5 I have s them by the words of my mouth: 2026
Am 4:10 your young men have I s with the sword, 2026
Na 3: 3 *there is* a multitude of s, and a great 2491
Zep 2:12 Ethiopians also, ye *shall be* s by my sword. 2491
Lk 9:22 scribes, and be s, and be raised the third day. *615*
Ac 2:23 and by wicked hands have crucified and s: *337*
5:36 who was s; and all, as many as obeyed him, *337*
7:42 have ye offered to me s **beasts** and *4968*
7:52 they have s them which shewed before of *615*
13:28 *yet* desired they Pilate that he should be s. *337*
23:14 that *we* will eat nothing until we have s Paul. *615*
Eph 2:16 by the cross, having s the enmity thereby: *615*
Heb 11:37 were tempted, were s with the sword: *599+5408*
Rev 2:13 who was s among you, where Satan *615*
5: 6 stood a Lamb as *it had been* s, having seven *4969*
5: 9 for thou wast s, and hast redeemed us to *4969*
5:12 Worthy is the Lamb that was s to receive *4969*
6: 9 of them that were s for the word of God, *4969*
11:13 in the earthquake were s of men seven *615*
13: 8 Lamb s from the foundation of the world. *4969*
18:24 and of all that were s upon the earth. *4969*
19:21 And the remnant were s with the sword of *615*

SLANDER (3) [SLANDERED, SLANDERERS, SLANDEREST, SLANDERETH, SLANDEROUSLY, SLANDERS]
Nu 14:36 by bringing up a s upon the land, 1681
Ps 31:13 For I have heard the s of many: fear *was* on 1681
Pr 10:18 lying lips, and he that uttereth a s, *is* a fool. 1681

SLANDERED (1) [SLANDER]
2Sa 19:27 he hath s thy servant unto my lord the king; 7270

SLANDERERS (1) [SLANDER]
1Ti 3:11 *be* grave, not s, sober, faithful in all *things.* *1228*

SLANDEREST (1) [SLANDER]
Ps 50:20 thou s thine own mother's son. 1848+5414

SLANDERETH (1) [SLANDER]
Ps 101: 5 Whoso privily s his neighbour, him will I 3960

SLANDEROUSLY (1) [SLANDER]
Ro 3: 8 And not *rather,* (as we be s **reported,** and *987*

SLANDERS (2) [SLANDER]
Jer 6:28 *are* all grievous revolters, walking with s: 7400
9: 4 every neighbour will walk *with* s. 7400

SLANG (1)
1Sa 17:49 s *it,* and smote the Philistine in his 7049

SLAUGHTER (56)
Ge 14:17 after his return from the s of Chedorlaomer, 5221
Jos 10:10 and slew them *with* a great s at Gibeon, and 4347
10:20 an end of slaying them *with* a very great s, 4347
Jdg 11:33 plain of the vineyards, *with* a very great s. 4347
15: 8 he smote them hip and thigh *with* a great s: 4347
1Sa 4:10 there was a very great s; for there fell of 4347
4:17 there hath been also a great s among 4046
6:19 smitten *many* of the people *with* a great s. 4347
14:14 s, which Jonathan and his armourbearer **made,** 4347+5221
14:30 for had there not been now a much greater s 4347
17:57 as David returned from the s of 5221
18: 6 when David was returned from the s of 5221
19: 8 and slew them *with* a great s; 4347
23: 5 their cattle, and smote them *with* a great s. 4347
2Sa 1: 1 when David was returned from the s of 5221
17: 9 There is a s among the people that follow 4046
18: 7 there was there a great s that day *of* twenty 4046
1Ki 20:21 and slew the Syrians with a great s. 4347
2Ch 13:17 and his people slew them *with* a great s: 4347
25:14 after that Amaziah was come from the s of 5221
28: 5 of Israel, who smote him *with* a great s. 4347
Est 9: 5 s, and destruction, and did what they would 2027
Ps 44:22 day long; we are counted as sheep for the s. 2878
Pr 7:22 as an ox goeth to the s, or as a fool to 2874
Isa 10:26 to the s of Midian at the rock Oreb: 4347
14:21 Prepare s for his children for the iniquity of 4293
27: 7 is he slain according to the s of them that 2027
30:25 streams of waters in the day of the great s, 2027
34: 2 he hath delivered them to the s. 2874
34: 6 and a great s in the land of Idumea. 2874
53: 7 he is brought as a lamb to the s, and as a 2874
65:12 and ye shall all bow down to the s: 2874
Jer 7:32 of the son of Hinnom, but the valley of s: 2028
11:19 like a lamb *or* an ox *that* is brought to the s; 2873
12: 3 pull them out like sheep for the s, and 2878
12: 3 and prepare them for the day of s. 2028
19: 6 of the son of Hinnom, but The valley of s. 2028
25:34 for the days of your s and of your 2873
48:15 chosen young men are gone down to the s, 2874
50:27 all her bullocks; let them go down to the s: 2874
51:40 I will bring them down like lambs to the s, 2873
Eze 9: 2 and every man a s weapon in his hand; 4660
21:10 It is sharpened to make a **sore** s; *it is* 2873+2874
21:15 ah, *it is* made bright, *it is* wrapt up for the s. 2874
21:22 to open the mouth in the s, 7524
21:28 for the s *it is* furbished, to consume because 2874
26:15 the s is **made** in the midst of thee? 2026+2027
Hos 5: 2 the revolters are profound to make s, 7819
Ob 1: 9 of the mount of Esau may be cut off by s. 6993
Zec 11: 4 LORD my God; Feed the flock of the s; 2028
11: 7 I will feed the flock of s, *even* you, O poor 2028
Ac 8:32 was this, He was led as a sheep to the s; *4967*
9: 1 and s against the disciples of the Lord, *5408*
Ro 8:36 we are accounted as sheep for the s. *4967*
Heb 7: 1 who met Abraham returning from the s of *2871*
Jas 5: 5 have nourished your hearts, as in a day of s. *4967*

SLAVE (1) [SLAVES]
Jer 2:14 *is* he a homeborn s? why is he spoiled? NIH

SLAVE DRIVERS See TASKMASTERS

SLAVE MASTERS See TASKMASTERS

SLAVE TRADERS See MENSTEALERS

SLAVES (1) [SLAVE]
Rev 18:13 and chariots, and s, and souls of men. *4983*

SLAY (117) [MANSLAYER, MANSLAYERS, SLAIN, SLAYER, SLAYETH, SLAYING, SLEW, SLEWEST]
Ge 4:14 *that* every one that findeth me shall s me. 2026
18:25 to s the righteous with the wicked: 4191
20: 4 Lord, wilt thou s also a righteous nation? 2026
20:11 and they will s me for my wife's sake. 2026
22:10 his hand, and took the knife to s his son. 7819
27:41 are at hand; then will I s my brother Jacob. 2026
34:30 themselves together against me, and s me; 5221
37:18 they conspired against him to s him. 4191
37:20 and let us s him, and cast him into some pit, 2026
37:26 What profit *is it* if we s our brother, and 2026
42:37 saying, S my two sons, if I bring him not to 4191
43:16 *these* men home, and s, and make ready; 2873
Ex 2:15 heard this thing, he sought to s Moses. 2026
4:23 behold, I will s thy son, *even* thy firstborn. 2026
5:21 to put a sword in their hand to s us. 2026
21:14 upon his neighbour, to s him with guile; 2026
23: 7 and the innocent and righteous s thou not: 2026
29:16 thou shalt s the ram, and thou shalt take his 7819
32:12 to s them in the mountains, and to consume 2026
32:27 s every man his brother, and every man his 2026
Lev 4:29 s the sin offering in the place of the burnt 7819

S

Lev 4:33 **s** it for a sin offering in the place where 7819
14:13 he shall **s** the lamb in the place where he 7819
20:15 be put to death: and ye shall **s** the beast. 2026
Nu 19: 3 and *one* shall **s** her before his face: 7819
25: 5 **S** ye every one his men that were joined 2026
35:19 The revenger of blood himself shall **s** 4191
35:19 when he meeteth him, he shall **s** him. 4191
35:21 the revenger of blood shall **s** the murderer, 4191
Dt 9:28 he hath brought them out to **s** them in 4191
19: 6 because the way is long, and **s** him; 5221+5315
27:25 Cursed *be* he that taketh reward to **s** 5221+5315
Jos 13:22 did the children of Israel **s** with the sword 2026
Jdg 8:19 ye had saved them alive, I would not **s** you. 2026
8:20 unto Jether his firstborn, Up, *and* **s** them. 2026
9:54 said unto him, Draw thy sword, and **s** me, 4191
1Sa 2:25 because the LORD would **s** them. 4191
5:10 God of Israel to us, to **s** us and our people. 4191
5:11 own place, that it **s** us not, and our people: 4191
14:34 man his sheep, and **s** *them* here, and eat; 7819
15: 3 **s** both man and woman, infant and 4191
19: 5 innocent blood, to **s** David without a cause? 4191
19:11 to watch him, and to **s** him in the morning: 4191
19:15 him up to me in the bed, that I may **s** him. 4191
20: 8 if there be in me iniquity, **s** me thyself; 4191
20:33 it was determined of his father to **s** David. 4191
22:17 Turn, and **s** the priests of the LORD; 4191
2Sa 1: 9 Stand, I pray thee, upon me, and **s** me: 4191
3:37 not of the king to **s** Abner the son of Ner. 4191
21: 2 Saul sought to **s** them in his zeal to 5221
1Ki 1:51 he will not **s** his servant with the sword. 4191
3:26 the living child, and **in no wise s** it. 4191+4191
3:27 the living child, and **in no wise s** it: 4191+4191
15:28 of Asa king of Judah did Baasha **s** him, 4191
17:18 my sin to remembrance, and to **s** my son? 4191
18: 9 thy servant into the hand of Ahab, to **s** me? 4191
18:12 and he cannot find thee, he shall **s** me: 2026
18:14 Behold, Elijah *is here:* and he shall **s** me. 2026
19:17 escapeth the sword of Hazael shall Jehu **s**: 4191
19:17 from the sword of Jehu shall Elisha **s**. 4191
20:36 art departed from me, a lion shall **s** thee. 5221
2Ki 8:12 their young *men* wilt thou **s** with the sword, 2026
10:25 and to the captains, Go in, *and* **s** them; 5221
17:26 behold, they **s** them, because they know not 4191
2Ch 20:23 **utterly to s** and destroy *them:* and 2763
23:14 **S** her not *in* the house of the LORD. 4191
Ne 4:11 and **s** them, and cause the work to cease. 2026
6:10 for they will come to **s** thee; yea, in 2026
6:10 yea, in the night will they come to **s** thee. 2026
Est 8:11 to destroy, to **s**, and to cause to perish, 2026
Job 9:23 If the scourge **s** suddenly, he will laugh at 4191
13:15 Though he **s** me, *yet* will I trust in him: but 6991
20:16 of asps: the viper's tongue shall **s** him. 2026
Ps 34:21 Evil shall **s** the wicked: and they that hate 4191
37:14 *and* to **s** such as be of upright conversation. 2873
37:32 the righteous, and seeketh to **s** him. 4191
59:11 **S** them not, lest my people forget: 2026
94: 6 They **s** the widow and the stranger, and 2026
109:16 that *he* might even **s** the broken in heart. 4191
139:19 Surely thou wilt **s** the wicked, O God: 6991
Pr 1:32 For the turning away of the simple shall **s** 2026
Isa 11: 4 with the breath of his lips shall he **s** 4191
14:30 with famine, and he shall **s** thy remnant. 2026
27: 1 and he shall **s** the dragon that *is* in the sea. 2026
65:15 for the Lord GOD shall **s** thee, and call his 4191
Jer 5: 6 Wherefore a lion out of the forest shall **s** 5221
15: 3 the sword to **s**, and the dogs to tear, and 2026
18:23 me to **s** *me:* forgive not their iniquity, 4194
20: 4 and shall **s** them with the sword. 5221
29:21 and he shall **s** them before your eyes; 5221
40:14 the son of Nethaniah to **s** thee? 5221+5315
40:15 I will **s** Ishmael the son of Nethaniah, and 5221
40:15 know *it:* wherefore should he **s** thee, 5221+5315
41: 8 them that said unto Ishmael, **S** us not: 4191
50:27 **S** all her bullocks; let them go down to 2717
Eze 9: 6 **S** utterly old *and* young, both maids, and 2026
13:19 to **s** the souls that should not die, and 4191
23:47 they shall **s** their sons and their daughters, 2026
26: 8 He shall **s** with the sword thy daughters in 2026
26:11 he shall **s** thy people by the sword, and 2026
40:39 to **s** thereon the burnt offering and the sin 7819
44:11 they shall **s** the burnt offering and 7819
Da 2:14 which was gone forth to **s** the wise *men* of 6992
Hos 2: 3 set her like a dry land, and **s** her with thirst. 4191
9:16 yet will I **s** *even* the beloved *fruit* of their 4191
Am 2: 3 will **s** all the princes thereof with him, 2026
9: 1 and I will **s** the last of them with the sword: 2026
9: 4 I command the sword, and it shall **s** them: 2026
Hab 1:17 and not spare continually to **s** the nations? 2026
Zec 11: 5 Whose possessors **s** them, and 2026
Lk 11:49 and *some* of them they shall **s** and persecute: *615*
19:27 bring hither, and **s** *them* before me. *2695*
Jn 5:16 and sought to **s** him, because he had done *615*
Ac 5:33 cut *to the heart,* and took counsel to **s** them. *337*
9:29 the Grecians: but they went about to **s** him. *337*
11: 7 saying unto me, Arise, Peter; **s** and eat. *2380*
Rev 9:15 and a year, for to **s** the third *part* of men. *615*

SLAYER (19) [SLAY]

Nu 35:11 that the **s** may flee thither, which killeth 7523
35:24 the congregation shall judge between the **s** 5221
35:25 the congregation shall deliver the **s** out of 7523
35:26 if the **s** shall at any time come *without* 7523
35:27 and the revenger of blood kill the **s**; 7523
35:28 after the death of the high priest the **s** shall 7523
Dt 4:42 That the **s** might flee thither, which should 7523
19: 3 three parts, that every **s** may flee thither. 7523
19: 4 this *is* the case of the **s**, which shall flee 7523
19: 6 Lest the avenger of the blood pursue the **s**, 7523
Jos 20: 3 That the **s** that killeth *any* person unawares 7523
20: 5 they shall not deliver the **s** up into his hand; 7523
20: 6 shall the **s** return, and come unto his own 7523
21:13 her suburbs, *to be* a city of refuge for the **s**; 7523
21:21 *to be* a city of refuge for the **s**; 7523
21:27 her suburbs, *to be* a city of refuge for the **s**; 7523
21:32 her suburbs, *to be* a city of refuge for the **s**; 7523
Jos 21:38 her suburbs, *to be* a city of refuge for the **s**; 7523
Eze 21:11 to give it into the hand of the **s**. 2026

SLAYETH (5) [SLAY]

Ge 4:15 said unto him, Therefore whosoever **s** Cain, 2026
Dt 22:26 and **s** him, even so *is* this matter: 7523
Job 5: 2 the foolish man, and envy **s** the silly one. 4191
Eze 28: 9 Wilt thou yet say before him that **s** thee, 2026
28: 9 and no God, in the hand of him that **s** thee. 2490

SLAYING (7) [SLAY]

Jos 8:24 when Israel had made an end of **s** all 2026
10:20 the children of Israel had made an end of **s** 5221
Jdg 9:56 unto his father, in **s** his seventy brethren: 2026
1Ki 17:20 widow with whom I sojourn, by **s** her son? 4191
Isa 22:13 and gladness, **s** oxen, and killing sheep, 2026
57: 5 **s** the children in the valleys under the clifts 7819
Eze 9: 8 while they were **s** them, and I *was* left, 5221

SLEEP (82) [ASLEEP, SLEEPER, SLEEPEST, SLEEPETH, SLEEPING, SLEPT]

Ge 2:21 the LORD God caused a **deep s** to fall 8639
15:12 was going down, a **deep s** fell upon Abram; 8639
28:11 his pillows, and **lay down** in that place **to s**. 7901
28:16 Jacob awaked out of his **s**, and he said, 8142
31:40 and my **s** departed from mine eyes. 8142
Ex 22:27 wherein shall he **s**? and it shall come to 7901
Dt 24:12 *be* poor, thou shalt not **s** with his pledge: 7901
24:13 that he may **s** in his own raiment, and 7901
31:16 Behold, thou shalt **s** with thy fathers; 7901
Jdg 16:14 he awaked out of his **s**, and went away with 8142
16:19 she **made** him **s** upon her knees; and 3462
16:20 he awoke out of his **s**, and said, I will go 8142
1Sa 3: 3 God *was,* and Samuel was laid down *to s;* NIH
26:12 a **deep s** from the LORD was fallen upon 8639
2Sa 7:12 thou shalt **s** with thy fathers, I will set up 7901
1Ki 1:21 when my lord the king shall **s** with his 7901
Est 6: 1 On that night could not the king **s**, and 8142
Job 4:13 of the night, when **deep s** falleth on men. 8639
7:21 for now shall I **s** in the dust; and thou shalt 7901
14:12 shall not awake, nor be raised out of their **s**. 8142
33:15 of the night, when **deep s** falleth upon men, 8639
Ps 4: 8 I will both lay me down in peace, and **s**: 3462
13: 3 mine eyes, lest I **s** the *sleep of* death; 3462
13: 3 lighten mine eyes, lest I sleep the *s of* death; NIH
76: 5 are spoiled, they have slept their **s**: 8142
76: 6 and horse *are* **cast into a dead s**. 7290
78:65 the Lord awaked as one out of **s**, *and* like a 3463
90: 5 them away as with a flood; they are *as* a **s**: 8142
121: 4 keepeth Israel shall neither slumber nor **s**. 3462
127: 2 of sorrows: *for* so he giveth his beloved **s**. 8142
132: 4 I will not give **s** to mine eyes, *or* slumber to 8153
Pr 3:24 shalt lie down, and thy **s** shall be sweet. 8142
4:16 For they **s** not, except they have done 3462
4:16 their **s** is taken away, unless they cause 8142
6: 4 Give not **s** to thine eyes, nor slumber to 8142
6: 9 How long wilt thou **s**, O sluggard? 7901
6: 9 when wilt thou arise out of thy **s**? 8142
6:10 *Yet* a little **s**, a little slumber, a little folding 8142
6:10 a little folding of the hands to **s**: 7901
19:15 Slothfulness casteth into a **deep s**; and 8639
20:13 Love not **s**, lest thou come to poverty; 8142
24:33 *Yet* a little **s**, a little slumber, a little folding 8142
24:33 a little folding of the hands to **s**: 7901
Ecc 5:12 The **s** of a labouring *man is* sweet, 8142
5:12 of the rich will not suffer him to **s**. 3462
8:16 neither day nor night seeth **s** with his eyes:) 8142
SS 5: 2 I **s**, but my heart waketh: *it is* the voice of 3463
Isa 5:27 none shall slumber nor **s**; neither shall 3462
29:10 poured out upon you the spirit of **deep s**, 8639
Jer 31:26 and beheld; and my **s** was sweet unto me. 8142
51:39 **s** a perpetual sleep, and not wake, saith 3462
51:39 sleep a perpetual **s**, and not wake, saith 8142
51:57 and they shall **s** a perpetual sleep, 3462
51:57 and they shall sleep a perpetual **s**, 8142
Eze 34:25 in the wilderness, and **s** in the woods. 3462
Da 2: 1 was troubled, and his **s** brake from him. 8142
6:18 before him; and his **s** went from him. 8139
8:18 I was **in a deep s** on my face toward 7290
10: 9 was I **in a deep s** on my face, and my face 7290
12: 2 many of them that **s** in the dust of the earth 3463
Zec 4: 1 as a man that is wakened out of his **s**, 8142
Mt 1:24 Then Joseph being raised from **s** did as *5258*
26:45 unto them, **S** on now, and take your rest: *2518*
Mk 4:27 And should **s**, and rise night and day, and *2518*
14:41 unto them, **S** on now, and take your rest: *2518*
Lk 9:32 they that were with him were heavy with **s**: *5258*
22:46 And said unto them, Why **s** ye? rise and *2518*
Jn 11:11 but I go, that I may **awake** him **out of s**. *1852*
11:12 his disciples, Lord, if he **s**, he shall do well. *2837*
11:13 that he had spoken of taking of rest in **s**. *5258*
Ac 13:36 **fell on s**, and was laid unto his fathers, and *2837*
16:27 of the prison **awaking out of** his **s**, *1096+1853*
20: 9 named Eutychus, being fallen into a deep **s**: *5258*
20: 9 he sunk down with **s**, and fell down from *5258*
Ro 13:11 that now *it is* high time to awake out of **s**: *5258*
1Co 11:30 and sickly among you, and many **s**. *2837*
15:51 We shall not all **s**, but we shall all be *2837*
1Th 4:14 them also which **s** in Jesus will God bring *2837*
5: 6 Therefore let us not **s**, as *do* others; but *2518*
5: 7 For they that **s** sleep in the night; and *2518*
5: 7 For they that sleep **s** in the night; and *2518*
5:10 died for us, that, whether we wake or **s**, *2518*

SLEEPER (1) [SLEEP]

Jnh 1: 6 said unto him, What meanest thou, O **s**? 7290

SLEEPEST (4) [SLEEP]

Ps 44:23 Awake, why **s** thou, O Lord? arise, cast *us* 3462
Pr 6:22 when thou **s**, it shall keep thee; and 7901
Mk 14:37 and saith unto Peter, Simon, **s** thou? *2518*
Eph 5:14 Awake thou that **s**, and arise from the dead, *2518*

SLEEPETH (7) [SLEEP]

1Ki 18:27 *or* peradventure he **s**, and must be awaked. 3463
Pr 10: 5 he that **s** in harvest *is* a son that causeth 7290
Hos 7: 6 their baker **s** all the night; *in* the morning it 3463
Mt 9:24 for the maid is not dead, but **s**. And they *2518*
Mk 5:39 and weep? the damsel is not dead, but **s**. *2518*
Lk 8:52 he said, Weep not; she is not dead, but **s**. *2518*
Jn 11:11 he saith unto them, Our friend Lazarus **s**; *2837*

SLEEPING (6) [SLEEP]

1Sa 26: 7 Saul lay **s** within the trench, and his spear 3463
Isa 56:10 **s**, lying down, loving to slumber. 1957
Mk 13:36 Lest coming suddenly he find you **s**. *2518*
14:37 and findeth them **s**, and saith unto Peter, *2518*
Lk 22:45 to his disciples, he found them **s** for sorrow, *2837*
Ac 12: 6 the same night Peter was **s** between two *2837*

SLEIGHT (1)

Eph 4:14 every wind of doctrine, by the **s** of men, *2940*

SLEPT (49) [SLEEP]

Ge 2:21 a deep sleep to fall upon Adam, and he **s**: 3462
41: 5 he **s** and dreamed the second time: and 3462
2Sa 11: 9 Uriah **s** *at* the door of the king's house with 7901
1Ki 2:10 So David **s** with his fathers, and was buried 7901
3:20 while thine handmaid **s**, and laid it in her 3463
11:21 when Hadad heard in Egypt that David **s** 7901
11:43 Solomon **s** with his fathers, and was buried 7901
14:20 he **s** with his fathers, and Nadab his son 7901
14:31 Rehoboam **s** with his fathers, and 7901
15: 8 Abijam **s** with his fathers; and they buried 7901
15:24 Asa **s** with his fathers, and was buried with 7901
16: 6 So Baasha **s** with his fathers, and 7901
16:28 So Omri **s** with his fathers, and was buried 7901
19: 5 as he lay and **s** under a juniper tree, 3462
22:40 So Ahab **s** with his fathers; and Ahaziah his 7901
22:50 Jehoshaphat **s** with his fathers, and 7901
2Ki 8:24 Joram **s** with his fathers, and was buried 7901
10:35 Jehu **s** with his fathers: and they buried him 7901
13: 9 Jehoahaz **s** with his fathers; and they buried 7901
13:13 Joash **s** with his fathers; and Jeroboam sat 7901
14:16 Jehoash **s** with his fathers, and was buried 7901
14:22 after that the king **s** with his fathers. 7901
14:29 Jeroboam **s** with his fathers, *even* with 7901
15: 7 So Azariah **s** with his fathers; and 7901
15:22 Menahem **s** with his fathers; and 7901
15:38 Jotham **s** with his fathers, and was buried 7901
16:20 Ahaz **s** with his fathers, and was buried 7901
20:21 Hezekiah **s** with his fathers: and 7901
21:18 Manasseh **s** with his fathers, and 7901
24: 6 So Jehoiakim **s** with his fathers: and 7901
2Ch 9:31 Solomon **s** with his fathers, and he was 7901
12:16 Rehoboam **s** with his fathers, and 7901
14: 1 So Abijah **s** with his fathers, and 7901
16:13 Asa **s** with his fathers, and died in the one 7901
21: 1 Now Jehoshaphat **s** with his fathers, and 7901
26: 2 after that the king **s** with his fathers. 7901
26:23 So Uzziah **s** with his fathers, and 7901
27: 9 Jotham **s** with his fathers, and they buried 7901
28:27 Ahaz **s** with his fathers, and they buried 7901
32:33 Hezekiah **s** with his fathers, and they buried 7901
33:20 So Manasseh **s** with his fathers, and 7901
Job 3:13 lien *still* and been quiet, I should have **s**: 3462
Ps 3: 5 I laid me down and **s**; I awaked; for 3462
76: 5 are spoiled, they have **s** their sleep: 5123
Mt 13:25 But while men **s**, his enemy came and *2518*
25: 5 they all slumbered and **s**. *2518*
27:52 and many bodies of saints which **s** arose, *2837*
28:13 by night, and stole him *away* while we **s**. *2837*
1Co 15:20 *and* become the firstfruits of them that **s**. *2837*

SLEW (196) [SLAY]

Ge 4: 8 rose up against Abel his brother, and **s** him. 2026
4:25 another seed instead of Abel, whom Cain **s**. 2026
34:25 upon the city boldly, and **s** all the males. 2026
34:26 they **s** Hamor and Shechem his son with 2026
38: 7 sight of the LORD; and the LORD **s** him. 4191
38:10 the LORD: wherefore he **s** him also. 4191
49: 6 for in their anger they **s** a man, and in their 2026
Ex 2:12 he **s** the Egyptian, and hid him in the sand. 5221
13:15 that the LORD **s** all the firstborn in 2026
Lev 8:15 he **s** *it;* and Moses took the blood, and put *it* 7819
8:23 he **s** *it;* and Moses took of the blood of it, 7819
9: 8 the altar, and **s** the calf of the sin offering, 7819
9:12 he **s** the burnt offering; and Aaron's sons 7819
9:15 and **s** it, and offered it for sin, as the first. 7819
9:18 He **s** also the bullock and the ram *for* a 7819
Nu 31: 7 and they **s** all the males. 2026
31: 8 they **s** the kings of Midian, beside *the rest* 2026
31: 8 Balaam also the son of Beor they **s** with 2026
Jos 8:21 then they turned again, and **s** the men of Ai. 5221
9:26 the children of Israel, that they **s** them not. 2026
10:10 **s** them *with* a great slaughter at Gibeon, 5221
10:11 the children of Israel **s** with the sword. 2026
10:26 and **s** them, and hanged them on five trees: 4191
11:17 kings he took, and smote them, and **s** them. 4191
Jdg 1: 4 they **s** *of* them in Bezek ten thousand men. 5221
1: 5 they **s** the Canaanites and the Perizzites. 5221
1:10 they **s** Sheshai, and Ahiman, and Talmai. 5221
1:17 they **s** the Canaanites that inhabited 5221
3:29 they **s** *of* Moab at that time about ten 5221
3:31 which **s** *of* the Philistines six hundred men 5221
7:25 they **s** Oreb upon the rock Oreb, and Zeeb 2026
7:25 Zeeb they **s** at the winepress of Zeeb, and 2026
8:17 tower of Penuel, and **s** the men of the city. 2026
8:18 What manner of men *were they* whom ye **s** 2026
8:21 **s** Zebah and Zalmunna, and took away 2026
9: 5 **s** his brethren the sons of Jerubbaal, 2026
9:24 Abimelech their brother, which **s** them; 2026
9:44 *people* that *were* in the fields, and **s** them. 5221
9:45 **s** the people that *was* therein, and 2026
9:54 that *men* say not of me, A woman **s** him. 2026
12: 6 and **s** him at the passages of Jordan: 7819
14:19 **s** thirty men of them, and took their spoil, 5221

S

Jdg 15:15 took it, and s a thousand men therewith. 5221
16:24 of our country, which s many of us. 2491
16:30 So the dead which he s at his death were 4191
16:30 were moe than *they* which he s in his life. 4191
20:45 and s two thousand men of them. 5221
1Sa 1:25 they s a bullock, and brought the child to 7819
4: 2 they s of the army in the field about four 5221
11:11 s the Ammonites until the heat of the day: 5221
14:13 and his armourbearer s after him. 4191
14:32 oxen, and calves, and s *them* on the ground: 7819
14:34 ox with him *that* night, and s *them* there. 7819
17:35 by his beard, and smote him, and s him. 4191
17:36 Thy servant s both the lion and the bear: 5221
17:50 a stone, and smote the Philistine, and s him; 4191
17:51 and s him, and cut off his head therewith. 4191
18:27 and s of the Philistines two hundred men; 5221
19: 5 s the Philistine, and the LORD wrought a 5221
19: 8 and s them *with* a great slaughter; 5221
22:18 s on that day fourscore and five persons 4191
29: 5 Saul s his thousands, and David his ten 5221
30: 2 they s not any, either great or small, but 4191
31: 2 the Philistines s Jonathan, and Abinadab, 5221
2Sa 1:10 s him, because I was sure that he could not 4191
3:30 So Joab and Abishai his brother s Abner, 2026
4: 7 s him, and beheaded him, and took his 4191
4:10 I took hold of him, and s him in Ziklag, 2026
4:12 and they s them, and cut off their hands and 2026
8: 5 David s of the Syrians two and 5221
10:18 David s *the men of* seven hundred chariots 2026
14: 6 but the one smote the other, and s him. 4191
14: 7 for the life of his brother whom he s; 2026
18:15 and smote Absalom, and s him. 4191
21: 1 bloody house, because he s the Gibeonites. 4191
21:18 Sibbechai the Hushathite s Saph, 5221
21:19 s *the brother of* Goliath the Gittite, 5221
21:21 son of Shimea the brother of David s him. 5221
23: 8 eight hundred, whom he s at one time. 2491
23:12 and defended it, and s the Philistines: 5221
23:18 and s them, and had the name among three. 2491
23:20 many acts, he s two lionlike men of Moab: 5221
23:20 s a lion in the midst of a pit in time of 5221
23:21 he s an Egyptian, a goodly man: and 5221
23:21 and s him with his own spear. 2026
1Ki 1: 9 Adonijah s sheep and oxen and fat cattle by 2076
2: 5 whom he s, and shed the blood of war in 2026
2:32 better than he, and s them with the sword, 2026
2:34 went up, and fell upon him, and s him: 4191
11:24 when David s them *of Zobah: and* 2026
13:24 a lion met him by the way, and s him: 4191
16:11 *that* he s all the house of Baasha: 5221
18:13 when Jezebel s the prophets of the LORD, 2026
18:40 to the brook Kishon, and s them there. 7819
19:21 s them, and boiled their flesh with 2076
20:20 they s every one his man: and the Syrians 5221
20:21 and s the Syrians with a great slaughter. 5221
20:29 the children of Israel s *of* the Syrians an 5221
20:36 from him, a lion found him, and s him. 5221
2Ki 9:31 *Had* Zimri peace, who s his master? 2026
10: 7 s seventy persons, and put their heads in 7819
10: 9 I conspired against my master, and s him: 2026
10: 9 and slew him: but who s all these? 5221
10:11 So Jehu s all that remained of the house of 5221
10:14 s them at the pit of the shearing house, 7819
10:17 he s all that remained unto Ahab in 5221
11:18 s Mattan the priest of Baal before the altars. 2026
11:20 they s Athaliah with the sword *beside* 4191
12:20 s Joash *in* the house of Millo, 5221
14: 5 that he s his servants which had slain 5221
14: 6 the children of the murderers he s not: 4191
14: 7 He s *of* Edom in the valley of salt ten 5221
14:19 sent after him to Lachish, and s him there. 4191
15:10 and s him, and reigned in his stead. 4191
15:14 and s him, and reigned in his stead. 4191
15:30 and s him, and reigned in his stead, 4191
16: 9 *the people of* it captive to Kir, and s Rezin. 4191
17:25 lions among them, which s *some* of them. 2026
21:23 and s the king in his own house. 4191
21:24 the people of the land s all them that had 5221
23:20 he s all the priests of the high places that 2076
23:29 he s him at Megiddo, when he had seen 4191
25: 7 they s the sons of Zedekiah before his eyes, 7819
25:21 and s them at Riblah in the land of Hamath. 4191
1Ch 2: 3 in the sight of the LORD; and he s him. 4191
7:21 men of Gath that were born in *that* land s, 2026
10: 2 the Philistines s Jonathan, and Abinadab, 5221
10:14 therefore he s him, and turned the kingdom 4191
11:14 and delivered it, and s the Philistines; 5221
11:20 he s *them,* and had a name among the three. 2491
11:22 many acts; he s two lionlike men of Moab: 5221
11:22 and s a lion in a pit in a snowy day. 5221
11:23 he s an Egyptian, a man of *great* stature, 5221
11:23 and s him with his own spear. 2026
18: 5 David s of the Syrians two and 5221
18:12 Moreover Abishai the son of Zeruiah s of 5221
19:18 David s of the Syrians seven thousand *men* 2026
20: 4 at which time Sibbechai the Hushathite s 5221
20: 5 Elhanan the son of Jair s Lahmi the brother 5221
20: 7 the son of Shimea David's brother s him. 5221
2Ch 13:17 his people s them *with* a great slaughter: 5221
21: 4 s all his brethren with the sword, and 2026
22: 8 that ministered to Ahaziah, he s them. 2026
22:11 him from Athaliah, so that she s him not. 4191
23:15 gate *by* the king's house, they s her there. 4191
23:17 s Mattan the priest of Baal before the altars. 2026
24:22 his father had done to him, but s his son. 2026
24:25 and s him on his bed, and he died: 2026
25: 3 that he s his servants that had killed 2026
25: 4 he s not their children, but *did* as it is 4191
25:27 sent to Lachish after him, and s him there. 4191
28: 6 For Pekah the son of Remaliah s in Judah 2026
28: 7 s Maaseiah the king's son, and Azrikam 2026
32:21 they that came forth of his own bowels s 5307
33:24 against him, and s him in his own house. 4191
33:25 the people of the land s all them that had 5221
36:17 who s their young men with the sword in 2026

Ne 9:26 s thy prophets which testified against them 2026
Est 9: 6 in Shushan the palace the Jews s and 2026
9:10 the enemy of the Jews, s they; 2026
9:15 and s three hundred men at Shushan; 2026
9:16 s of their foes seventy and five thousand, 2026
Ps 78:31 s the fattest of them, and smote down 2026
78:34 When he s them, then they sought him: and 2026
105:29 their waters into blood, and s their fish. 4191
135:10 smote great nations, and s mighty kings; 2026
136:18 s famous kings: for his mercy *endureth* for 2026
Isa 66: 3 He that killeth an ox *is as if* he s a man; 5221
Jer 20:17 Because he s me not from the womb; or 4191
26:23 who s him with the sword, and cast his 5221
39: 6 the king of Babylon s the sons of Zedekiah 7819
39: 6 also the king of Babylon s all the nobles of 7819
41: 2 s him, whom the king of Babylon had made 4191
41: 3 Ishmael also s all the Jews that were with 5221
41: 7 that Ishmael the son of Nethaniah s them, 7819
41: 8 and s them not among their brethren. 4191
52:10 the king of Babylon s the sons of Zedekiah 7819
52:10 he s also all the princes of Judah in Riblah. 7819
La 2: 4 s all *that were* pleasant to the eye, in 2026
Eze 9: 7 And they went forth, and s in the city. 5221
23:10 her daughters, and s her with the sword: 2026
40:41 whereupon they s *their sacrifices.* 7819
40:42 wherewith they s the burnt offering 7819
Da 3:22 the flame of the fire s those men that took 6992
5:19 whom he would he s; and whom he would 6992
Mt 2:16 s all the children that were in Bethlehem, *337*
21:39 and cast *him* out of the vineyard, and s *him.* *615*
22: 6 and entreated *them* spitefully, and s *them.* *615*
23:35 whom ye s between the temple and *5407*
Lk 13: 4 whom the tower in Siloam fell, and s them, *615*
Ac 5:30 up Jesus, whom ye s and hanged on a tree. *1315*
10:39 whom they s and hanged on a tree: *337*
22:20 and kept the raiment of them that s him. *337*
Ro 7:11 deceived me, and by it s *me.* *615*
1Jn 3:12 was of *that* wicked one, and s his brother. *4969*
3:12 And wherefore s he him? Because his own *4969*

SLEWEST (1) [SLAY]
1Sa 21: 9 whom thou s in the valley of Elah, behold, 5221

SLIDDEN (1) [SLIDE]
Jer 8: 5 is this people of Jerusalem s **back** *by* a 7725

SLIDE (3) [BACKSLIDER, BACKSLIDING, BACKSLIDINGS, SLIDDEN, SLIDETH]
Dt 32:35 recompence; their foot shall s in *due* time: 4131
Ps 26: 1 also in the LORD; *therefore* I shall not s. 4571
37:31 God *is* in his heart; none of his steps shall s. 4571

SLIDETH (1) [SLIDE]
Hos 4:16 For Israel s **back** as a backsliding heifer: 5637

SLIGHTLY (2)
Jer 6:14 hurt of *the daughter of* my people s, 5921+7043
8:11 hurt of the daughter of my people s, 5921+7043

SLIME (2) [SLIMEPITS]
Ge 11: 3 brick for stone, and s had they for morter. 2564
Ex 2: 3 daubed it with s and with pitch, and put 2564

SLIMEPITS (1) [PIT, SLIME]
Ge 14:10 the vale of Siddim *was* **full of** s; 875+875+2564

SLING (8) [SLINGERS, SLINGS, SLINGSTONES]
Jdg 20:16 every one could s stones at a hair *breadth,* 7049
1Sa 17:40 even in a scrip; and his s *was* in his hand: 7050
17:50 David prevailed over the Philistine with a s 7050
25:29 them shall he s **out** *as out* of the middle of a 7049
25:29 he sling out *as out* of the middle of a s. 7050
Pr 26: 8 As he *that* bindeth a stone in a s, so *is* he 4773
Jer 10:18 I will s **out** the inhabitants of the land at 7049
Zec 9:15 shall devour, and subdue *with* s stones; 7050

SLINGERS (1) [SLING]
2Ki 3:25 howbeit the s went about *it,* and smote it. 7051

SLINGS (1) [SLING]
2Ch 26:14 habergeons, and bows, and s to cast stones. 7050

SLINGSTONES (1) [SLING, STONE]
Job 41:28 s are turned with him into stubble. 68+7050

SLIP (5) [SLIPPERY, SLIPPETH, SLIPS, SLIPT]
2Sa 22:37 steps under me; so that my feet did not s. 4571
Job 12: 5 He that is ready to s with *his* feet *is as* a 4571
Ps 17: 5 goings in thy paths, *that* my footsteps s not. 4131
18:36 my steps under me, that my feet did not s. 4571
Heb 2: 1 lest at any time we should let *them* s. *3901*

SLIPPERY (3) [SLIP]
Ps 35: 6 Let their way be dark and s: and let 2519
73:18 Surely thou didst set them in s *places:* thou 2513
Jer 23:12 be unto them as s *ways* in the darkness: 2519

SLIPPETH (3) [SLIP]
Dt 19: 5 the head s from the helve, and lighteth upon 5394
Ps 38:16 when my foot s, they magnify *themselves* 4131
94:18 When I said, My foot s; thy mercy, 4131

SLIPS (1) [SLIP]
Isa 17:10 and shalt set it *with* strange s: 2156

SLIPT (2) [SLIP]
1Sa 19:10 he s **away** out of Saul's presence, and 6362
Ps 73: 2 almost gone; my steps had well nigh s. 8210

SLOTHFUL (15) [SLOTHFULNESS]
Jdg 18: 9 be not s to go, *and* to enter to possess 6101
Pr 12:24 bear rule: but the s shall be under tribute. 7423
12:27 The s *man* roasteth not that which he took 7423
15:19 The way of the s *man is* as a hedge of 6102
18: 9 He also that is s in his work *is* brother to 7503
19:24 A s *man* hideth his hand in *his* bosom, and 6102
21:25 The desire of the s killeth him; for his 6102
22:13 The s *man* saith, *There is* a lion without, 6102
24:30 I went by the field of the s, and by 376+6102
26:13 The s *man* saith, *There is* a lion in the way; 6102
26:14 upon his hinges, so *doth* the s upon his bed. 6102
26:15 The s hideth his hand in *his* bosom; 6102
Mt 25:26 said unto him, *Thou* wicked and s servant, *3636*
Ro 12:11 Not s in business; fervent in spirit; *3636*
Heb 6:12 That ye be not s, but followers of them who *3576*

SLOTHFULNESS (2) [SLOTHFUL]
Pr 19:15 S casteth into a deep sleep; and an idle soul 6103
Ecc 10:18 By **much** s the building decayeth; and 6103

SLOW (15) [SLOWLY]
Ex 4:10 but I *am* s of speech, and of a slow tongue. 3515
4:10 but I *am* slow of speech, and of a s tongue. 3515
Ne 9:17 s to anger, and of great kindness, and 750
Ps 103: 8 gracious, s to anger, and plenteous in mercy. 750
145: 8 s to anger, and of great mercy. 750
Pr 14:29 *He that is* s to wrath *is* of great 750
15:18 but *he that is* s to anger appeaseth strife. 750
16:32 *He that is* s to anger *is* better than 750
Joel 2:13 s to anger, and of great kindness, and 750
Jnh 4: 2 s to anger, and of great kindness, and 750
Na 1: 3 The LORD *is* s to anger, and great in 750
Lk 24:25 s of heart to believe all that the prophets *1021*
Tit 1:12 *are* alway liars, evil beasts, s bellies. *692*
Jas 1:19 be swift to hear, s to speak, slow to wrath: *1021*
1:19 be swift to hear, slow to speak, s to wrath: *1021*

SLOWLY (1) [SLOW]
Ac 27: 7 And when we had **sailed** s many days, and *1020*

SLUCES (1)
Isa 19:10 all that make s *and* ponds for fish. 7938

SLUG See SNAIL

SLUGGARD (6)
Pr 6: 6 Go to the ant, thou s; consider her ways, 6102
6: 9 How long wilt thou sleep, O s? when wilt 6102
10:26 the eyes, so *is* the s to them that send him. 6102
13: 4 The soul of the s desireth, and *hath* nothing: 6102
20: 4 The s will not plow by reason of the cold; 6102
26:16 The s *is* wiser in his own conceit than seven 6102

SLUMBER (10) [SLUMBERED, SLUMBERETH, SLUMBERINGS]
Ps 121: 3 be moved: he that keepeth thee will not s. 5123
121: 4 he that keepeth Israel shall neither s nor 5123
132: 4 sleep to mine eyes, *or* s to mine eyelids, 8572
Pr 6: 4 sleep to thine eyes, nor s to thine eyelids. 8572
6:10 *Yet* a little sleep, a little s, a little folding of 8572
24:33 *Yet* a little sleep, a little s, a little folding of 8572
Isa 5:27 none shall s nor sleep; neither shall 5123
56:10 sleeping, lying down, loving to s. 5123
Na 3:18 Thy shepherds s, O king of Assyria: 5123
Ro 11: 8 God hath given them the spirit of s, *2659*

SLUMBERED (1) [SLUMBER]
Mt 25: 5 the bridegroom tarried, they all s and slept. *3573*

SLUMBERETH (1) [SLUMBER]
2Pe 2: 3 lingereth not, and their damnation s not. *3573*

SLUMBERINGS (1) [SLUMBER]
Job 33:15 sleep falleth upon men, in s upon the bed; 8572

SLY See BACKBITING; BACKBITINGS

SMALL (97) [SMALLEST]
Ge 19:11 the house with blindness, both s and great; 6996
30:15 *Is it* a s **matter** that thou hast taken my 4592
Ex 9: 9 it shall become s **dust** in all the land of Egypt, 80
16:14 upon the face of the wilderness *there lay* a s 1851
16:14 *as* s as the hoar frost on the ground. 1851
18:22 but every s matter they shall judge: 6996
18:26 but every s matter they judged themselves. 6996
30:36 thou shalt beat *some* of it **very** s, and put of 1854
Lev 16:12 his hands full of sweet incense **beaten** s, 1851
Nu 16: 9 *Seemeth it but* a s **thing** unto you, that 4592
16:13 *Is it* a s **thing** that thou hast brought us up 4592
32:41 and took the s **towns** thereof, 2333
Dt 1:17 you shall hear the s as well as the great; 6996
9:21 and stamped it, *and* **ground** *it* **very** s, 2912
9:21 *it* very small, *even* until *it was as* s as dust: 1854
25:13 in thy bag divers weights, a great and a s. 6996
25:14 house divers measures, a great and a s. 6996
32: 2 as the s **rain** upon the tender herb, and 8164
1Sa 5: 9 both s and great, and they had emerods in 6996
20: 2 my father will do nothing *either* great or s, 6996
30: 2 either great or s, but carried *them* away, 6996
30:19 neither s nor great, neither sons nor 6996
2Sa 7:19 this was yet a s **thing** in thy sight, O Lord 6994
17:13 until there be not one s **stone** found there. 6872
22:43 did I **beat** them *as* s as the dust of the earth, 7833
1Ki 2:20 she said, I desire one s petition of thee; 6996
19:12 in the fire: and after the fire a still s voice. 1851
22:31 saying, Fight neither with s nor great, 6996
2Ki 19:26 Therefore their inhabitants *were* of s power, 7116
23: 2 and all the people, both s and great: 6996
23: 6 **stampt** *it* s to powder, and cast the powder 1854
23:15 *and* **stampt** *it* s to powder, and burnt 1854
25:26 both s and great, and the captains of 6996
1Ch 17:17 *yet* this was a s **thing** in thine eyes, O God; 6994
25: 8 ward against *ward,* as well the s as 6996
26:13 they cast lots, as well the s as the great, 6996
2Ch 15:13 whether s or great, whether man or woman. 6996
18:30 saying, Fight ye not with s or great, 6996
24:24 For the army of the Syrians came with a s 4705

S

2Ch 31:15 by courses, as well *to* the great as *to* the **s**: 6996
34:30 the Levites, and all the people, great and **s**: 6996
35: 8 six hundred *s cattle,* and three hundred NIH
35: 9 for passover *offerings* five thousand *s cattle,* NIH
36:18 great and **s**, and the treasures of the house 6996
Est 1: 5 both unto great and **s**, seven days, in 6996
1:20 their husbands honour, both to great and **s**. 6996
Job 3:19 The **s** and great *are* there; and the servant *is* 6996
8: 7 Though thy beginning was **s**, yet thy latter 4705
15:11 *Are* the consolations of God **s** with thee? 4592
36:27 For he **maketh s** the drops of water: 1639
37: 6 likewise *to* the **s** rain, and *to* the great rain 4306
Ps 18:42 did I **beat** them **s** as the dust before 7833
104:25 both **s** and great beasts. 6996
115:13 that fear the LORD, *both* **s** and great. 6996
119:141 I *am* **s** and despised: *yet* do not I forget thy 6810
Pr 24:10 in the day of adversity, thy strength *is* **s**. 6862
Ecc 2: 7 s[S] cattle above all that were in Jerusalem 6629
Isa 1: 9 had left unto us a **very s** remnant, 4592+3509.1
7:13 *Is it* a **s thing** for you to weary men, but 4592
16:14 the remnant *shall be* very **s** *and* feeble. 4213
22:24 and the issue, all vessels of **s quantity**, 6996
29: 5 of thy strangers shall be like **s** dust, 1851
37:27 Therefore their inhabitants *were* of **s** power, 7116
40:15 are counted as the **s dust** of the balance: 7834
41:15 **beat** *them* **s**, and shalt make the hills as 1854
43:23 Thou hast not brought me the **s cattle** of 7716
54: 7 For a **s** moment have I forsaken thee; but 6996
60:22 a thousand, and a **s one** a strong nation: 6810
Jer 16: 6 the great and the **s** shall die in this land: 6996
30:19 also glorify them, and they shall not be **s**. 6819
44:28 Yet a **s** number that escape the sword shall 4962
49:15 I will make thee **s** among the heathen, *and* 6996
Eze 16:20 *Is this* of thy whoredoms a **s matter**, 4592
34:18 *Seemeth it* a **s thing** unto you to have eaten 4592
Da 11:23 and shall become strong with a **s** people. 4592
Am 7: 2 *by* whom shall Jacob arise? for he *is* **s**. 6996
7: 5 *by* whom shall Jacob arise? for he *is* **s**. 6996
8: 5 **making** the ephah **s**, and the shekel great, 6994
Ob 1: 2 I have made thee **s** among the heathen: 6996
Zec 4:10 For who hath despised the day of **s** *things?* 6996
Mk 3: 9 that a **s ship** should wait on him because *4142*
8: 7 And they had a few **s fishes**: and *2485*
Jn 2:15 when he had made a scourge of **s cords**, *4979*
6: 9 hath five barley loaves, and two **s fishes**: *3795*
Ac 12:18 there was no **s** stir among the soldiers, *3641*
15: 2 and Barnabas had no **s** dissension and *3641*
19:23 And the same time there arose no **s** stir *3641*
19:24 brought no **s** gain unto the craftsmen; *3641*
26:22 this day, witnessing both to **s** and great, *3398*
27:20 no **s** tempest lay on *us,* all hope that we *3641*
1Co 4: 3 But with me it is a **very s** *thing* that I *1646*
Jas 3: 4 *yet* are they turned about with a **very s** *1646*
Rev 11:18 and them that fear thy name, **s** and great; *3398*
13:16 *both* **s** and great, rich and poor, free and *3398*
19: 5 and ye that fear him, both **s** and great. *3398*
19:18 *men,* both free and bond, both **s** and great. *3398*
20:12 the dead, **s** and great, stand before God; *3398*

SMALL COPPER COINS See MITES

SMALLEST (2) [SMALL]
1Sa 9:21 a Benjamite, of the **s** of the tribes of Israel? 6996
1Co 6: 2 are ye unworthy to judge the **s matters**? *1646*

SMALLEST LETTER See JOT

SMALLEST STROKE See TITTLE

SMART (1)
Pr 11:15 He that is surety for a stranger shall **s** 7321+7451

SMELL (20) [SMELLED, SMELLETH, SMELLING, SWEETSMELLING]
Ge 27:27 he smelled the **s** of his raiment, and 7381
27:27 the **s** of my son *is* as the smell of a field 7381
27:27 the smell of my son *is* as the **s** of a field 7381
Ex 30:38 to **s** thereto, shall even be cut off from his 7306
Lev 26:31 I will not **s** the savour of your sweet 7306
Dt 4:28 which neither see, nor hear, nor eat, nor **s**. 7306
Ps 45: 8 All thy garments **s** *of* myrrh, and aloes, *and* NIH
115: 6 hear not: noses have they, but they **s** not: 7306
SS 1:12 my spikenard sendeth forth the **s** thereof. 7381
2:13 vines *with* the tender grape give a *good* **s**. 7381
4:10 and the **s** of thine ointments than all spices! 7381
4:11 the **s** of thy garments *is* like the smell of 7381
4:11 the smell of thy garments *is* like the **s** of 7381
7: 8 the vine, and the **s** of thy nose like apples; 7381
7:13 The mandrakes give a **s**, and at our gates 7381
Isa 3:24 *that* instead of **sweet s** there shall be stink; 1314
Da 3:27 nor the **s** of fire had passed on them. 7382
Hos 14: 6 be as the olive tree, and his **s** as Lebanon. 7381
Am 5:21 and I will not **s** in your solemn assemblies. 7306
Php 4:18 an odour of a **sweet s**, a sacrifice *2175*

SMELLED (2) [SMELL]
Ge 8:21 the LORD **s** a sweet savour; and 7306
27:27 he **s** the smell of his raiment, and 7306

SMELLETH (1) [SMELL]
Job 39:25 he **s** the battle afar off, the thunder of 7306

SMELLING (3) [SMELL]
SS 5: 5 my fingers *with* **sweet s** myrrh, upon 5674
5:13 his lips *like* lilies, dropping **sweet s** myrrh. 5674
1Co 12:17 the whole *were* hearing, where *were* the **s**? *3750*

SMITE (125) [SMITERS, SMITEST, SMITETH, SMITING, SMITTEN, SMOTE, SMOTEST]
Ge 8:21 neither will I again **s** any more every *thing* 5221
32: 8 **s** it, then the *other* company which is left 5221
32:11 lest he will come and **s** me, *and* the mother 5221
Ex 3:20 **s** Egypt with all my wonders which I will 5221
7:17 I will **s** with the rod that *is* in mine hand 5221
8: 2 behold, I will **s** all thy borders with frogs: 5062
8:16 out thy rod, and **s** the dust of the land, 5221
9:15 that I may **s** thee and thy people with 5221
12:12 will **s** all the firstborn in the land of Egypt, 5221
12:13 to destroy *you,* when I **s** the land of Egypt. 5221
12:23 For the LORD will pass through to **s** 5062
12:23 to come in unto your houses to **s** *you.* 5062
17: 6 thou shalt **s** the rock, and there shall come 5221
21:18 one **s** another with a stone, or with *his* fist, 5221
21:20 if a man **s** his servant, or his maid, with a 5221
21:26 if a man **s** the eye of his servant, or the eye 5221
21:27 if he **s out** his manservant's tooth, or 5307
Nu 14:12 I will **s** them with the pestilence, and 5221
22: 6 *that* we may **s** them, and *that* I may drive 5221
24:17 shall **s** the corners of Moab, and destroy all 4272
25:17 Vex the Midianites, and **s** them: 5221
35:16 if he **s** him with an instrument of iron, so 5221
35:17 if he **s** him with throwing a stone, 5221
35:18 Or *if* he **s** him with a hand weapon of 5221
35:21 Or in enmity **s** him with his hand, that he 5221
Dt 7: 2 thou shalt **s** them, *and* utterly destroy them; 5221
13:15 Thou shalt **surely s** the inhabitants of 5221+5221
19:11 **s** him mortally that he die, and fleeth into 5221
20:13 thou shalt **s** every male thereof with 5221
28:22 The LORD shall **s** thee with a 5221
28:27 The LORD will **s** thee with the botch of 5221
28:28 The LORD shall **s** thee with madness, and 5221
28:35 The LORD shall **s** thee in the knees, and 5221
33:11 **s** through the loins of them that rise against 4272
Jos 7: 3 or three thousand men go up and **s** Ai; 5221
10: 4 and help me, that we may **s** Gibeon: 5221
10:19 your enemies, and **s the hindmost** of them; 2179
12: 6 of the LORD and the children of Israel **s**: 5221
13:12 for these did Moses **s**, and cast them out. 5221
Jdg 6:16 and thou shalt **s** the Midianites as one man. 5221
20:31 they began to **s** of the people, *and* kill, as at 5221
20:39 Benjamin began to **s** *and* kill of the men of 5221
21:10 **s** the inhabitants of Jabesh-gilead with 5221
1Sa 15: 3 Now go and **s** Amalek, and utterly destroy 5221
17:46 I will **s** thee, and take thine head from thee; 5221
18:11 I will **s** David even to the wall *with it.* And 5221
19:10 Saul sought to **s** David even to the wall 5221
20:33 Saul cast a javelin at him to **s** him: 5221
23: 2 Shall I go and **s** these Philistines? 5221
23: 2 Go, and **s** the Philistines, and save Keilah. 5221
26: 8 now therefore let me **s** him, I pray thee, 5221
26: 8 and I will not **s** him the second time. NIH
26:10 the LORD liveth, the LORD shall **s** him; 5062
2Sa 2:22 wherefore should I **s** thee to the ground? 5221
5:24 before thee, to **s** the host of the Philistines. 5221
13:28 and when I say unto you, **S** Amnon; 5221
15:14 and **s** the city with the edge of the sword. 5221
17: 2 him shall flee; and I will **s** the king only: 5221
18:11 why didst thou not **s** him there to 5221
1Ki 14:15 For the LORD shall **s** Israel, as a reed is 5221
20:35 the word of the LORD, **S** me, I pray thee. 5221
20:35 I pray thee. And the man refused to **s** him. 5221
20:37 another man, and said, **S** me, I pray thee. 5221
2Ki 3:19 ye shall **s** every fenced city, and 5221
6:18 said, **S** this people, I pray thee, 5221
6:21 shall I **s** *them?* shall I smite *them?* 5221
6:21 shall I smite *them?* shall I **s** *them?* 5221
6:22 Thou shalt not **s** *them:* wouldest thou smite 5221
6:22 Thou shalt not smite *them:* wouldest thou **s** 5221
9: 7 thou shalt **s** the house of Ahab thy master, 5221
9:27 and said, **S** him also in the chariot. 5221
13:17 for thou shalt **s** the Syrians in Aphek, 5221
13:18 unto the king of Israel, **S** upon the ground. 5221
13:19 *it:* whereas now thou shalt **s** Syria 5221
1Ch 14:15 for God is gone forth before thee to **s** 5221
2Ch 21:14 *with* a great plague will the LORD **s** thy 5062
Ps 121: 6 The sun shall not **s** thee by day, nor 5221
141: 5 Let the righteous **s** me; *it shall be* a 1986
Pr 19:25 **S** a scorner, and the simple will beware: 5221
Isa 3:17 Therefore the Lord will **s with a scab** 5596
10:24 he shall **s** thee with a rod, and shall lift up 5221
11: 4 he shall **s** the earth with the rod of his 5221
11:15 shall **s** it in *the* seven streams, and 5221
19:22 the LORD shall **s** Egypt: *he* shall smite 5062
19:22 *he* shall **s** and heal *it:* and they shall return 5062
49:10 neither shall the heat nor sun **s** them: 5221
58: 4 debate, and to **s** with the fist of wickedness: 5221
Jer 18:18 let us **s** him with the tongue, and let us not 5221
21: 6 I will **s** the inhabitants of this city, both 5221
21: 7 he shall **s** them with the edge of the sword; 5221
43:11 he shall **s** the land of Egypt, *and* 5221
46:13 should come and **s** the land of Egypt. 5221
49:28 Nebuchadrezzar king of Babylon shall **s**, 5221
Eze 5: 2 take a third *part, and* **s** about it with a knife: 5221
6:11 **S** with thine hand, and stamp with thy foot, 5221
9: 5 Go ye after him through the city, and **s**: 5221
21:12 upon my people: **s** therefore upon *thy* thigh. 5606
21:14 **s** *thine* hands together, and let the sword be 5221
21:17 I will also **s** mine hands together, and I will 5221
32:15 when I shall **s** all them that dwell therein, 5221
39: 3 I will **s** thy bow out of thy left hand, and 5221
Am 3:15 I will **s** the winter house with the summer 5221
6:11 he will **s** the great house *with* breaches, and 5221
9: 1 he said, **S** the lintel of the door, that 5221
Mic 5: 1 they shall **s** the judge of Israel with a rod 5221
Na 2:10 the knees **s together**, and much pain *is* in 6375
Zec 9: 4 her out, and he will **s** her power in the sea; 5221
10:11 shall **s** the waves in the sea, and all 5221
11: 6 they shall **s** the land, and out of their hand 3807
12: 4 I will **s** every horse with astonishment, and 5221
12: 4 will **s** every horse of the people with 5221
13: 7 **s** the shepherd, and the sheep shall be 5221
14:12 **s** all the people that have fought against 5062
14:18 where*with* the LORD will **s** the heathen 5062
Mal 4: 6 lest I come and **s** the earth *with* a curse. 5221
Mt 5:39 whosoever shall **s** thee on thy right cheek, *4474*
24:49 And shall begin to **s** *his* fellowservants, and *5180*
26:31 I will **s** the shepherd, and the sheep of *3960*
Mk 14:27 I will **s** the shepherd, and the sheep shall be *3960*
Lk 22:49 unto him, Lord, shall we **s** with the sword? *3960*
Ac 23: 2 that stood by him to **s** him on the mouth. *5180*
23: 3 God shall **s** thee, *thou* whited wall: *5180*
2Co 11:20 exalt himself, if a man **s** you on the face. *1194*
Rev 11: 6 and to **s** the earth with all plagues, as often *3960*
19:15 that with it he should **s** the nations: *3960*

SMITERS (1) [SMITE]
Isa 50: 6 I gave my back to the **s**, and my cheeks to 5221

SMITEST (2) [SMITE]
Ex 2:13 the wrong, Wherefore **s** thou thy fellow? 5221
Jn 18:23 of the evil: but if well, why **s** thou me? *1194*

SMITETH (13) [SMITE]
Ex 21:12 He that **s** a man, so that he die, shall be 5221
21:15 he that **s** his father, or his mother, shall be 5221
Dt 25:11 husband out of the hand of him that **s** him, 5221
27:24 Cursed *be* he that **s** his neighbour secretly. 5221
Jos 15:16 He that **s** Kirjath-sepher, and taketh it, 5221
Jdg 1:12 He that **s** Kirjath-sepher, and taketh it, 5221
2Sa 5: 8 **s** the Jebusites, and the lame and the blind, 5221
1Ch 11: 6 Whosoever **s** the Jebusites first shall be 5221
Job 26:12 by his understanding he **s through** 4272
Isa 9:13 For the people turneth not unto him that **s** 5221
La 3:30 He giveth *his* cheek to him that **s** him: he is 5221
Eze 7: 9 ye shall know that I *am* the LORD that **s**. 5221
Lk 6:29 *And* unto him that **s** thee on the *one* cheek *5180*

SMITH (3) [COPPERSMITH, GOLDSMITH, GOLDSMITH'S, GOLDSMITHS, SILVERSMITH, SMITHS]
1Sa 13:19 Now there was no **s** found throughout all 2796
Isa 44:12 The **s** *with* the tongs both worketh in 1270+2796
54:16 I have created the **s** that bloweth the coals 2796

SMITHS (4) [SMITH]
2Ki 24:14 and all the craftsmen and **s**: 4525
24:16 craftsmen and **s** a thousand, all *that were* 4525
Jer 24: 1 with the carpenters and **s**, from Jerusalem, 4525
29: 2 Jerusalem, and the carpenters, and the **s**, 4525

SMITING (5) [SMITE]
Ex 2:11 he spied an Egyptian **s** a Hebrew, *one* of his 5221
2Sa 8:13 from **s** of the Syrians in the valley of salt, 5221
1Ki 20:37 smote him, so that in **s** he wounded *him.* 5221
2Ki 3:24 they went forward **s** the Moabites, even in 5221
Mic 6:13 Therefore also will I make *thee* sick in **s** 5221

SMITTEN (63) [SMITE]
Ex 7:25 after *that* the LORD had **s** the river. 5221
9:31 the flax and the barley was **s**: for the barley 5221
9:32 the wheat and the rye were not **s**: for they 5221
22: 2 be found breaking up, and be **s** that he die, 5221
Nu 14:42 that ye be not **s** before your enemies. 5062
22:28 that thou hast **s** me these three times? 5221
22:32 Wherefore hast thou **s** thine ass these three 5221
33: 4 which the LORD had **s** among them: 5221
Dt 1:42 lest ye be **s** before your enemies. 5062
28: 7 rise up against thee *to be* **s** before thy face: 5062
28:25 The LORD shall cause thee *to be* **s** before 5062
Jdg 1: 8 **s** it with the edge of the sword, and set 5221
20:32 They *are* **s down** before us, as at the first. 5062
20:36 children of Benjamin saw that they were **s**: 5062
20:39 Surely they are **s down** before us, 5062+5062
1Sa 4: 2 Israel was **s** before the Philistines: 5062
4: 3 Wherefore hath the LORD **s** us to day 5062
4:10 Israel was **s**, and they fled every man into 5062
5:12 the men that died not were **s** with 5221
6:19 the LORD had **s** *many* of the people *with* 5221
7:10 and they were **s** before Israel. 5062
13: 4 all Israel heard say *that* Saul had **s** a 5221
30: 1 and **s** Ziklag, and burnt it with fire; 5221
2Sa 2:31 the servants of David had **s** of Benjamin, 5221
8: 9 that David had **s** all the host of Hadadezer, 5221
8:10 had fought against Hadadezer, and **s** him: 5221
10:15 when the Syrians saw that they were **s** 5062
10:19 saw that they were **s** before Israel, 5062
11:15 ye from him, that he may be **s**, and die. 5221
1Ki 8:33 When thy people Israel be **s down** before 5062
11:15 after he had **s** every male in Edom; 5221
2Ki 2:14 when he also had **s** the waters, they parted 5221
3:23 surely slain, and they have **s** one another: 5221
13:19 *Thou* shouldest have **s** five or six times; 5221
13:19 hadst thou **s** Syria till *thou* hadst consumed 5221
14:10 Thou hast **indeed s** Edom, and 5221+5221
1Ch 18: 9 **s** all the host of Hadarezer king of Zobah; 5221
18:10 had fought against Hadarezer, and **s** him; 5221
2Ch 20:22 were come against Judah; and they were **s**. 5062
25:16 forbear; why shouldest thou be **s**? Then 5221
25:19 Thou sayest, Lo, thou hast **s** the Edomites; 5221
26:20 to go out, because the LORD had **s** him. 5060
28:17 again the Edomites had come and **s** Judah, 5221
Job 16:10 they have **s** me upon the cheek 5221
Ps 3: 7 for thou hast **s** all mine enemies *upon* 5221
69:26 For they persecute *him* whom thou hast **s**; 5221
102: 4 My heart is **s**, and withered like grass; so 5221
143: 3 he hath **s** my life **down** to the ground; 1792
Isa 5:25 his hand against them, and hath **s** them: 5221
24:12 and the gate is **s** *with* destruction. 3807
27: 7 Hath he **s** him, as he smote those that smote 5221
53: 4 him stricken, **s** of God, and afflicted. 5221
Jer 2:30 In vain have I **s** your children; 5221
14:19 why hast thou **s** us, and *there is* no healing 5221
37:10 For though ye had **s** the whole army of 5221
Eze 22:13 I have **s** mine hand at thy dishonest gain 5221
33:21 came unto me, saying, The city is **s**. 5221
40: 1 the fourteenth year after that the city was **s**, 5221
Hos 6: 1 heal us; he hath **s**, and he will bind us up. 5221
9:16 Ephraim is **s**, their root is dried up, 5221
Am 4: 9 I have **s** you with blasting and mildew: 5221
Ac 23: 3 commandest me to be **s** contrary to *5180*
Rev 8:12 and the third *part* of the sun was **s**, and *4141*

SMOKE (45) [SMOKING]

Ge 19:28 the **s** of the country went up as the smoke 7008
19:28 the smoke of the country went up as the **s** 7008
Ex 19:18 mount Sinai was altogether on a **s**, because 6225
19:18 the **s** thereof ascended as the smoke of a 6227
19:18 the smoke thereof ascended as the **s** of a 6227
Dt 29:20 and his jealousy shall **s** against that man, 6225
Jos 8:20 the **s** of the city ascended up to heaven, and 6227
8:21 that the **s** of the city ascended, then 6227
Jdg 20:38 that they should make a great flame with **s** 6227
20:40 to arise up out of the city *with* a pillar of **s**, 6227
2Sa 22: 9 There went up a **s** out of his nostrils, and 6227
Job 41:20 Out of his nostrils goeth **s**, as *out of* a 6227
Ps 18: 8 There went up a **s** out of his nostrils, and 6227
37:20 into **s** shall they consume *away*. 6227
68: 2 As **s** is driven away, *so* drive *them* away: 6227
74: 1 *why* doth thine anger **s** against the sheep of 6225
102: 3 For my days are consumed like **s**, and 6227
104:32 he toucheth the hills, and they **s**. 6225
119:83 For I am become like a bottle in the **s**; 7008
144: 5 touch the mountains, and they shall **s**. 6225
Pr 10:26 as **s** to the eyes, so *is* the sluggard to them 6227
SS 3: 6 out of the wilderness like pillars of **s**, 6227
Isa 4: 5 a cloud and **s** by day, and the shining of a 6227
6: 4 that cried, and the house was filled *with* **s**. 6227
9:18 they shall mount up *like* the lifting up of **s**. 6227
14:31 for there shall come from the north a **s**, and 6227
34:10 nor day; the **s** thereof shall go up for ever: 6227
51: 6 for the heavens shall vanish away like **s**, 6227
65: 5 These *are* a **s** in my nose, a fire that burneth 6227
Hos 13: 3 the floor, and as the **s** out of the chimney. 6227
Joel 2:30 in the earth, blood, and fire, and pillars of **s**. 6227
Na 2:13 I will burn her chariots in the **s**, and 6227
Ac 2:19 blood, and fire, and vapour of **s**: *2586*
Rev 8: 4 And the **s** of the incense, *which came* with *2586*
9: 2 and there arose a **s** out of the pit, as *2586*
9: 2 out of the pit, as the **s** of a great furnace; *2586*
9: 2 the air were darkened by reason of the **s** of *2586*
9: 3 And there came out of the **s** locusts upon *2586*
9:17 mouths issued fire and **s** and brimstone. *2586*
9:18 the fire, and by the **s**, and by the brimstone, *2586*
14:11 And the **s** of their torment ascendeth up for *2586*
15: 8 And the temple was filled with **s** from *2586*
18: 9 when they shall see the **s** of her burning, *2586*
18:18 And cried when they saw the **s** of her *2586*
19: 3 And her **s** rose up for ever and ever. *2586*

SMOKING (5) [SMOKE]

Ge 15:17 behold a **s** furnace, and a burning lamp that 6227
Ex 20:18 noise of the trumpet, and the mountain **s**: 6226
Isa 7: 4 for the two tails of these **s** firebrands, 6226
42: 3 and the **s** flax shall he not quench: 3544
Mt 12:20 he not break, and **s** flax shall he not quench, *5188*

SMOOTH (6) [SMOOTHER, SMOOTHETH]

Ge 27:11 brother *is* a hairy man, and I *am* a **s** man: 2509
27:16 upon his hands, and upon the **s** of his neck: 2513
1Sa 17:40 chose him five **s** stones out of the brook, 2512
Isa 30:10 speak unto us **s** *things*, prophesy deceits: 2513
57: 6 Among the **s** *stones* of the stream *is* thy 2511
Lk 3: 5 and the rough ways *shall be* made **s**; *3006*

SMOOTHER (2) [SMOOTH]

Ps 55:21 *The words of* his mouth were **s** than butter, 2505
Pr 5: 3 a honeycomb, and her mouth *is* **s** than oil: 2509

SMOOTHETH (1) [SMOOTH]

Isa 41: 7 he that **s** *with* the hammer him that smote 2505

SMOTE (230) [SMITE]

Ge 14: 5 **s** the Rephaims in Ashteroth Karnaim, and 5221
14: 7 **s** all the country of the Amalekites, and 5221
14:15 and **s** them, and pursued them unto Hobah, 5221
19:11 they **s** the men that *were at* the door of 5221
36:35 who **s** Midian in the field of Moab, 5221
Ex 7:20 and **s** the waters that *were* in the river, 5221
8:17 **s** the dust of the earth, and it became lice in 5221
9:25 the hail **s** throughout all the land of Egypt 5221
9:25 the hail **s** every herb of the field, and brake 5221
12:27 when he **s** the Egyptians, and delivered our 5062
12:29 that at midnight the LORD **s** all 5221
21:19 his staff, then shall he that **s** *him* be quit: 5221
Nu 3:13 *for* on the day that I **s** all the firstborn in 5221
8:17 on the day that I **s** every firstborn in 5221
11:33 the LORD **s** the people *with* a very great 5221
14:45 **s** them, and discomfited them, *even* unto 5221
20:11 and with his rod he **s** the rock twice: 5221
21:24 Israel **s** him with the edge of the sword, 5221
21:35 So they **s** him, and his sons, and all his 5221
22:23 Balaam **s** the ass, to turn her *into* the way. 5221
22:25 foot against the wall: and he **s** her again. 5221
22:27 was kindled, and he **s** the ass with a staff. 5221
24:10 and he **s** his hands **together**: 5606
32: 4 *Even* the country which the LORD **s** 5221
35:21 he that **s** *him* shall surely be put to death; 5221
Dt 2:33 we **s** him, and his sons, and all his people. 5221
3: 3 we **s** him until none was left to him 5221
4:46 whom Moses and the children of Israel **s**, 5221
25:18 by the way, and **s the hindmost** of thee, 2179
29: 7 out against us unto battle, and we **s** them: 5221
Jos 7: 5 the men of Ai **s** of them about thirty and 5221
7: 5 and **s** them in the going down: 5221
8:22 they **s** them, so that *they* let none of them 5221
8:24 *unto* Ai, and **s** it with the edge of the sword. 5221
9:18 the children of Israel **s** them not, because 5221
10:10 and **s** them to Azekah, and unto Makkedah. 5221
10:26 afterward Joshua **s** them, and slew them, 5221
10:28 **s** it with the edge of the sword, and the king 5221
10:30 he **s** it with the edge of the sword, and all 5221
10:32 **s** it with the edge of the sword, and all 5221
10:33 Joshua **s** him and his people, until *he* had 5221
10:35 **s** it with the edge of the sword, and all 5221
10:37 **s** it with the edge of the sword, and the king 5221
10:39 they **s** them with the edge of the sword, and 5221
Jos 10:40 So Joshua **s** all the country of the hills, and 5221
10:41 Joshua **s** them from Kadesh-barnea even 5221
11: 8 who **s** them, and chased them unto great 5221
11: 8 they **s** them, until *they* left them none 5221
11:10 and **s** the king thereof with the sword: 5221
11:11 they **s** all the souls that *were* therein with 5221
11:12 **s** them with the edge of the sword, *and* 5221
11:14 every man they **s** with the edge of 5221
11:17 kings he took, and **s** them, and slew them. 5221
12: 1 which the children of Israel **s**, and 5221
12: 7 the children of Israel **s** on *this* side Jordan 5221
13:21 whom Moses **s** with the princes of Midian, 5221
19:47 **s** it with the edge of the sword, and 5221
20: 5 because he **s** his neighbour unwittingly, and 5221
Jdg 1:25 they **s** the city with the edge of the sword; 5221
3:13 went and **s** Israel, and possessed the city of 5221
4:21 **s** the nail into his temples, and fastened *it* 8628
5:26 with the hammer she **s** Sisera, she smote off 1986
5:26 she **s off** his head, when she had pierced 4277
7:13 a tent, and **s** it that it fell, and overturned it, 5221
8:11 east of Nobah and Jogbehah, and **s** the host: 5221
9:43 and he rose up against them, and **s** them. 5221
11:21 into the hand of Israel, and they **s** them: 5221
11:33 he **s** them from Aroer, even till thou come 5221
12: 4 the men of Gilead **s** Ephraim, because 5221
15: 8 he **s** them hip and thigh *with* a great 5221
18:27 they **s** them with the edge of the sword, and 5221
20:35 the LORD **s** Benjamin before Israel: and 5062
20:37 **s** all the city with the edge of the sword. 5221
20:48 **s** them with the edge of the sword, as well 5221
1Sa 4: 8 these *are* the Gods that **s** the Egyptians with 5221
5: 6 **s** them with emerods, *even* Ashdod and 5221
5: 9 he **s** the men of the city, both small and 5221
6: 9 we shall know that *it is* not his hand *that* **s** 5060
6:19 he **s** the men of Beth-shemesh, because 5221
6:19 even he **s** of the people fifty thousand 5221
7:11 pursued the Philistines, and **s** them, 5221
13: 3 Jonathan **s** the garrison of the Philistines 5221
14:31 they **s** the Philistines that day from 5221
14:48 **s** the Amalekites, and delivered Israel out 5221
15: 7 Saul **s** the Amalekites from Havilah *until* 5221
17:35 **s** him, and delivered *it* out of his mouth: 5221
17:35 *him* by his beard, and **s** him, and slew him. 5221
17:49 slang *it*, and **s** the Philistine in his forehead, 5221
17:50 a stone, and **s** the Philistine, and slew him; 5221
19:10 and he **s** the javelin into the wall: 5221
22:19 **s** he with the edge of the sword, both men 5221
23: 5 and **s** them *with* a great slaughter. 5221
24: 5 that David's heart **s** him, because he had 5221
25:38 ten days *after*, that the LORD **s** Nabal, 5062
27: 9 David **s** the land, and left neither man nor 5221
30:17 David **s** them from the twilight even unto 5221
2Sa 1:15 fall upon him. And he **s** him that he died. 5221
2:23 **s** him under the fifth *rib*, that the spear 5221
3:27 **s** him there *under* the fifth *rib*, that he died, 5221
4: 6 they **s** him under the fifth *rib*: and Rechab 5221
4: 7 they **s** him, and slew him, and 5221
5:20 and David **s** them there, and said, 5221
5:25 **s** the Philistines from Geba until thou come 5221
6: 7 God **s** him there for *his* error; and there he 5221
8: 1 that David **s** the Philistines, and 5221
8: 2 he **s** Moab, and measured them with a line, 5221
8: 3 David **s** also Hadadezer, the son of Rehob, 5221
10:18 **s** Shobach the captain of their host, 5221
11:21 Who **s** Abimelech the son of Jerubbesheth? 5221
14: 6 but the one **s** the other, and slew him. 5221
14: 7 they said, Deliver him that **s** his brother, 5221
18:15 armour compassed about and **s** Absalom, 5221
20:10 so he **s** him therewith in the fifth *rib*, and 5221
21:17 and **s** the Philistine, and killed him. 5221
23:10 **s** the Philistines until his hand was weary, 5221
24:10 David's heart **s** him after that he had 5221
24:17 when he saw the angel that **s** the people, 5221
1Ki 15:20 **s** Ijon, and Dan, and Abel-beth-maachah, 5221
15:27 Baasha **s** him at Gibbethon, 5221
15:29 *that* he **s** all the house of Jeroboam; 5221
16:10 Zimri went in and **s** him, and killed him, 5221
20:21 **s** the horses and chariots, and slew 5221
20:37 the man **s** him, so that in smiting he 5221
22:24 and **s** Micaiah on the cheek, and said, 5221
22:34 **s** the king of Israel between the joints of 5221
2Ki 2: 8 **s** the waters, and they were divided hither 5221
2:14 **s** the waters, and said, Where *is* the LORD 5221
3:24 the Israelites rose up and **s** the Moabites, so 5221
3:25 howbeit the slingers went about *it*, and **s** it. 5221
6:18 he **s** them with blindness according to 5221
8:21 **s** the Edomites which compassed him 5221
9:24 **s** Jehoram between his arms, and the arrow 5221
10:25 they **s** them with the edge of the sword; 5221
10:32 Hazael **s** them in all the coasts of Israel; 5221
12:21 of Shomer, his servants, **s** him, and he died; 5221
13:18 the ground. And he **s** thrice, and stayed. 5221
15: 5 the LORD **s** the king, so that he was a 5060
15:10 **s** him before the people, and slew him, and 5221
15:14 and **s** Shallum the son of Jabesh in Samaria, 5221
15:16 Menahem **s** Tiphsah, and all that *were* 5221
15:16 opened not *to him*, therefore he **s** *it; and* 5221
15:25 against him, and **s** him in Samaria, 5221
15:30 **s** him, and slew him, and reigned in his 5221
18: 8 He **s** the Philistines, *even* unto Gaza, and 5221
19:35 **s** in the camp of the Assyrians an hundred 5221
19:37 and Sharezer *his sons* **s** him with the sword: 5221
25:21 the king of Babylon **s** them, and slew them 5221
25:25 **s** Gedaliah, that he died, and the Jews and 5221
1Ch 1:46 which **s** Midian in the field of Moab, 5221
4:41 **s** their tents, and the habitations that were 5221
4:43 they **s** the rest of the Amalekites that were 5221
13:10 he **s** him, because he put his hand to 5221
14:11 to Baal-perazim; and David **s** them there. 5221
14:16 they **s** the host of the Philistines from 5221
18: 1 that David **s** the Philistines, and 5221
18: 2 he **s** Moab; and the Moabites became 5221
18: 3 David **s** Hadarezer king of Zobah unto 5221
20: 1 And Joab **s** Rabbah, and destroyed it. 5221
21: 7 with this thing; therefore he **s** Israel. 5221
2Ch 13:15 that God **s** Jeroboam and all Israel before 5062
14:12 So the LORD **s** the Ethiopians before Asa, 5062
14:14 they **s** all the cities round about Gerar; 5221
14:15 They **s** also the tents of cattle, and 5221
16: 4 they **s** Ijon, and Dan, and Abel-maim, and 5221
18:23 and **s** Micaiah upon the cheek, and said, 5221
18:33 **s** the king of Israel between the joints of 5221
21: 9 **s** the Edomites which compassed him in, 5221
21:18 after all this the LORD **s** him in his 5062
22: 5 at Ramoth-gilead: and the Syrians **s** Joram. 5221
25:11 and **s** *of* the children of Seir ten thousand. 5221
25:13 **s** three thousand of them, and took much 5221
28: 5 they **s** him, and carried away a great 5221
28: 5 of Israel, who **s** him *with* a great slaughter. 5221
28:23 unto the gods of Damascus, which **s** him: 5221
Ne 13:25 **s** certain of them, and pluckt off their hair, 5221
Est 9: 5 Thus the Jews **s** all their enemies *with* 5221
Job 1:19 **s** the four corners of the house, and it fell 5060
2: 7 **s** Job with sore boils from the sole of his 5221
Ps 60: T **s** of Edom in the valley of salt twelve 5221
78:20 Behold, he **s** the rock, that the waters 5221
78:31 and **s down** the chosen *men* of Israel. 3766
78:51 **s** all the firstborn in Egypt; the chief of 5221
78:66 he **s** his enemies in the hinder parts: he put 5221
105:33 He **s** their vines also and their fig trees; and 5221
105:36 He **s** also all the firstborn in their land, 5221
135: 8 Who **s** the firstborn of Egypt, both of man 5221
135:10 Who **s** great nations, and slew mighty 5221
136:10 To him that **s** Egypt in their firstborn: 5221
136:17 To him which **s** great kings: for his mercy 5221
SS 5: 7 found me, they **s** me, they wounded me; 5221
Isa 10:20 shall no more again stay upon him that **s** 5221
14: 6 He who **s** the people in wrath *with* a 5221
14:29 the rod of him that **s** thee is broken: 5221
27: 7 smitten him, as he **s** those that smote him? 4347
27: 7 smitten him, as he smote those that **s** him? 5221
30:31 be beaten down, *which* **s** with a rod. 5221
37:36 **s** in the camp of the Assyrians an hundred 5221
37:38 and Sharezer his sons **s** him with the sword; 5221
41: 7 *with* the hammer him that **s** the anvil, 1986
57:17 of his covetousness was I wroth, and **s** him: 5221
60:10 for in my wrath I **s** thee, but in my favour 5221
Jer 20: 2 Pashur **s** Jeremiah the prophet, and put him 5221
31:19 that I was instructed, I **s** upon *my* thigh: 5606
37:15 **s** him, and put him *in* prison *in* the house of 5221
41: 2 **s** Gedaliah the son of Ahikam the son of 5221
46: 2 which Nebuchadrezzar king of Babylon **s** 5221
47: 1 the Philistines, before that Pharaoh **s** Gaza. 5221
52:27 the king of Babylon **s** them, and put them 5221
Da 2:34 which **s** the image upon his feet *that were* 4223
2:35 the stone that **s** the image became a great 4223
5: 6 and his knees **s** one against another. 5368
8: 7 and **s** the ram, and brake his two horns: 5221
Jnh 4: 7 and it **s** the gourd, that it withered. 5221
Hag 2:17 I **s** you with blasting and with mildew and 5221
Mt 26:51 servant of the high priest's, and **s off** his ear. *851*
26:67 **s** *him* **with the palms of** their **hands**, *4474*
26:68 unto us, *thou* Christ, Who is he that **s** thee? *3817*
27:30 and took the reed, and **s** him on the head. *5180*
Mk 14:47 and **s** a servant of the high priest, and *3817*
15:19 And they **s** him on the head with a reed, *5180*
Lk 18:13 unto heaven, but **s** upon his breast, saying, *5180*
22:50 And one of them **s** the servant of the high *3960*
22:63 that held Jesus mocked him, and **s** *him*. *1194*
22:64 saying, Prophesy, who is it that **s** thee? *3817*
23:48 were done, **s** their breasts, and returned. *5180*
Jn 18:10 and **s** the high priest's servant, and cut off *3817*
19: 3 and they **s** him **with** their **hands**. *1325+4475*
Ac 7:24 him that was oppressed, and **s** the Egyptian: *3960*
12: 7 and he **s** Peter on the side, and raised him *3960*
12:23 And immediately *the* angel of the Lord **s** *3960*

SMOTEST (1) [SMITE]

Ex 17: 5 thy rod, wherewith thou **s** the river, take in 5221

SMYRNA (2)

Rev 1:11 and unto **S**, and unto Pergamos, and *4667*
2: 8 And unto the angel of the church in **S** write; *4668*

SNAIL (2)

Lev 11:30 and the lizard, and the **s**, and the mole. 2546
Ps 58: 8 As a **s** *which* melteth, let *every one of them* 7642

SNARE (47) [ENSNARED, SNARED, SNARES]

Ex 10: 7 How long shall this *man* be a **s** unto us? 4170
23:33 their gods, it will surely be a **s** unto thee. 4170
34:12 lest it be for a **s** in the midst of thee: 4170
Dt 7:16 their gods; for that *will be* a **s** unto thee. 4170
Jdg 2: 3 and their gods shall be a **s** unto you. 4170
8:27 which *thing* became a **s** unto Gideon, and 4170
1Sa 18:21 that she may be a **s** to him, and that 4170
28: 9 wherefore then **layest** thou a **s** for my life, 5367
Job 18: 8 by his own feet, and he walketh upon a **s**. 7639
18:10 The **s** *is* laid for him in the ground, and 2256
Ps 69:22 Let their table become a **s** before them: and 6341
91: 3 Surely he shall deliver thee from the **s** of 6341
106:36 their idols: which were a **s** unto them. 4170
119:110 The wicked have laid a **s** for me: yet I erred 6341
124: 7 Our soul is escaped as a bird out of the **s** of 6341
124: 7 the **s** is broken, and we are escaped. 6341
140: 5 The proud have hid a **s** for me, and cords; 6341
141: 9 Keep me from the **s** *which* they have laid 6341
142: 3 I walked have they privily laid a **s** for me. 6341
Pr 7:23 as a bird hasteth to the **s**, and knoweth not 6341
18: 7 and his lips *are* the **s** of his soul. 4170
20:25 *It is* a **s** to the man *who* devoureth *that* 4170
22:25 thou learn his ways, and get a **s** to thy soul. 4170
29: 6 the transgression of an evil man *there is* a **s**: 4170
29: 8 Scornful men **bring** a city **into a s**: but 6315
29:25 The fear of man bringeth a **s**: but 4170
Ecc 9:12 and as the birds that are caught in the **s**; 6341
Isa 8:14 and for a **s** to the inhabitants of Jerusalem. 4170
24:17 Fear, and the pit, and the **s**, *are* upon thee, 6341
24:18 the midst of the pit shall be taken in the **s**: 6341

S

Isa 29:21 **lay a s** for him that reproveth in the gate, 6983
Jer 48:43 Fear, and the pit, and the **s**, *shall be* upon 6341
48:44 up out of the pit shall be taken in the **s**: 6341
50:24 I have **laid a s** for thee, and thou art also 3369
La 3:47 Fear and a **s** is come upon us, desolation 6354
Eze 12:13 upon him, and he shall be taken in my **s**: 4686
17:20 he shall be taken in my **s**, and I will bring 4686
Hos 5: 1 because ye have been a **s** on Mizpah, and 6341
9: 8 the prophet *is* a **s** of a fowler in all his 6341
Am 3: 5 Can a bird fall in a **s** upon the earth, 6341
3: 5 shall *one* take up a **s** from the earth, and 6341
Lk 21:35 For as a **s** shall it come on all them that *3803*
Ro 11: 9 Let their table be made a **s**, and a trap, and *3803*
1Co 7:35 not that I may cast a **s** upon you, but *1029*
1Ti 3: 7 he fall into reproach and the **s** of the devil. *3803*
6: 9 that will be rich fall into temptation and a **s**, *3803*
2Ti 2:26 recover themselves out of the **s** of the devil, *3803*

SNARED (9) [SNARE]
Dt 7:25 nor take *it* unto thee, lest thou be **s** therein: 3369
12:30 Take heed to thyself that thou be not **s** by 5367
Ps 9:16 the wicked is **s** in the work of his own 5367
Pr 6: 2 Thou art **s** with the words of thy mouth, 3369
12:13 The wicked is **s** by the transgression of *his* 4170
Ecc 9:12 so *are* the sons of men **s** in an evil time, 3369
Isa 8:15 fall, and be broken, and be **s**, and be taken. 3369
28:13 and be broken, and **s**, and taken. 3369
42:22 *they are* all of them **s** in holes, and they are 6351

SNARES (14) [SNARE]
Jos 23:13 they shall be **s** and traps unto you, and 6341
2Sa 22: 6 me about; the **s** of death prevented me: 4170
Job 22:10 Therefore **s** *are* round about thee, and 6341
40:24 it with his eyes: *his* nose pierceth through **s**. 4170
Ps 11: 6 Upon the wicked he shall rain **s**, fire and 6341
18: 5 me about: the **s** of death prevented me. 4170
38:12 They also that seek after my life **lay s** *for* 5367
64: 5 they commune of laying **s** privily; they say, 4170
Pr 13:14 of life, to depart from the **s** of death. 4170
14:27 of life, to depart from the **s** of death. 4170
22: 5 Thorns *and* **s** *are* in the way of the froward: 6341
Ecc 7:26 whose heart *is* **s** and nets, *and* her hands *as* 4685
Jer 5:26 *men:* they lay wait, as he that setteth **s**; 3353
18:22 a pit to take me, and hid **s** for my feet. 6341

SNATCH (1)
Isa 9:20 he shall **s** on the right hand, and be hungry; 1504

SNEERED See DERIDED

SNORTING (1)
Jer 8:16 The **s** of his horses was heard from Dan: 5170

SNOUT (1)
Pr 11:22 *As* a jewel of gold in a swine's **s**, *so is* a fair 639

SNOW (24) [SNOWY]
Ex 4: 6 it out, behold, his hand *was* leprous as **s**. 7950
Nu 12:10 behold, Miriam *became* leprous, *white* as **s**: 7950
2Sa 23:20 slew a lion in the midst of a pit in time of **s**: 7950
2Ki 5:27 out from his presence a leper *as white* as **s**. 7950
Job 6:16 reason of the ice, *and* wherein the **s** is hid: 7950
9:30 If I wash myself with **s** water, and make my 7950
24:19 Drought and heat consume the **s** waters: *so* 7950
37: 6 For he saith to the **s**, Be thou *on* the earth; 7950
38:22 thou entered into the treasures of the **s**? 7950
Ps 51: 7 wash me, and I shall be whiter than **s**. 7950
68:14 kings in it, it was *white* as **s** in Salmon. 7949
147:16 He giveth **s** like wool: he scattereth 7950
148: 8 Fire, and hail; **s**, and vapour; stormy wind 7950
Pr 25:13 As the cold of **s** in the time of harvest, *so* 7950
26: 1 As **s** in summer, and as rain in harvest, so 7950
31:21 She is not afraid of the **s** for her household: 7950
Isa 1:18 be as scarlet, they shall be as white as **s**; 7950
55:10 the **s** from heaven, and returneth not thither, 7950
Jer 18:14 Will *a man* leave the **s** of Lebanon *which* 7950
La 4: 7 Her Nazarites were purer than **s**, they were 7950
Da 7: 9 whose garment *was* white as **s**, and the hair 8517
Mt 28: 3 like lightning, and his raiment white as **s**: *5510*
Mk 9: 3 became shining, exceeding white as **s**; *5510*
Rev 1:14 hairs *were* white like wool, *as* white as **s**; *5510*

SNOWY (1) [SNOW]
1Ch 11:22 and slew a lion in a pit in a **s** day. 7950

SNUFFDISHES (3) [DISH, SNUFFETH]
Ex 25:38 and the **s** thereof, *shall be of* pure gold. 4289
37:23 and his snuffers, and his **s**, *of* pure gold. 4289
Nu 4: 9 and his **s**, and all the oil vessels thereof, 4289

SNUFFED (2) [SNUFFETH]
Jer 14: 6 they **s up** the wind like dragons; 7602
Mal 1:13 what a weariness *is it!* and ye have **s** at it, 5301

SNUFFERS (6) [SNUFFETH]
Ex 37:23 and his **s**, and his snuffdishes, *of* pure gold. 4457
1Ki 7:50 the **s**, and the basons, and the spoons, and 4212
2Ki 12:13 **s**, basons, trumpets, any vessels of gold, or 4212
25:14 the **s**, and the spoons, and all the vessels of 4212
2Ch 4:22 the **s**, and the basons, and the spoons, and 4212
Jer 52:18 the **s**, and the bowls, and the spoons, and 4212

SNUFFETH (1) [SNUFFDISHES, SNUFFED, SNUFFERS]
Jer 2:24 *that* **s up** the wind at her pleasure; 7602

SO (1689) [FORSOMUCH, HOWSOEVER, INSOMUCH, SOEVER, WHATSOEVER, WHENSOEVER, WHEREINSOEVER, WHERESOEVER, WHITHERSOEVER, WHOMSOEVER, WHOSO, WHOSOEVER]
Ge 1: 7 *were* above the firmament: and it was **s**. 3651
1: 9 and let the dry *land* appear: and it was **s**. 3651
Ge 1:11 *is* in itself, upon the earth: and it was **s**. 3651
1:15 to give light upon the earth: and it was **s**. 3651
1:24 of the earth after his kind: and it was **s**. 3651
1:27 **S** God created man in his own image, 2050.1
1:30 every green herb for meat: and it was **s**. 3651
3:24 **S** he drove out the man; and he placed at 2050.1
6:22 to all that God commanded him, **s** did he. 3651
8:11 **s** Noah knew that the waters were abated 2050.1
11: 8 **S** the LORD scattered them abroad from 2050.1
12: 4 **S** Abram departed, as the LORD had 2050.1
12:19 **s** I might have taken her to me to wife: 2050.1
13: 6 **s that** they could not dwell together. 2050.1
13:16 **s that** if a man can number the dust of 834
15: 5 and he said unto him, **S** shall thy seed be. 3541
18: 5 And they said, **S** do, as thou hast said. 3651
19: 7 I pray you, brethren, do not **s** wickedly. NIH
19:11 **s that** they wearied themselves to find 2050.1
19:18 Lot said unto them, Oh, not **s**, my Lord: NIH
20:17 **S** Abraham prayed unto God: and 2050.1
21: 6 *s that* all that hear will laugh with me. NIH
22: 8 **s** they went both of them together. 2050.1
22:19 **S** Abraham returned unto his young men, 2050.1
24:46 **s** I drank, and she made the camels drink 2050.1
25:22 and she said, **If** *it be* **s**, why *am* I thus? 518+3651
27: 1 his eyes were dim, **s that** he could **not** see, 4480
27:20 How *is* it *that* thou hast found *it* **s** quickly, NIH
27:23 brother Esau's hands: **s** he blessed him. 2050.1
28:21 **S that** I come again to my father's house 2050.1
29:26 It must not be **s** done in our country, 3651
29:28 Jacob did **s**, and fulfilled her week: and 3651
30:33 **S** shall my righteousness answer for me 2050.1
30:42 **S** the feebler were Laban's, and 2050.1
31:21 **S** he fled with all that he had; and he rose 2050.1
31:28 thou hast now done foolishly in **s** doing. NIH
31:36 that thou hast **s** hotly pursued after me? NIH
32:19 **s** commanded he the second, and the third, 1571
32:21 **S** went the present over before him: and 2050.1
33:16 **S** Esau returned that day on his way unto 2050.1
34:12 **Ask** me **never s much** dowry and 3966+7235
35: 6 **S** Jacob came to Luz, which *is* in the land 2050.1
37:14 **S** he sent him out of the vale of Hebron, 2050.1
40: 7 Wherefore look ye **s** sadly to day? NIH
41: 4 and fat kine. **S** Pharaoh awoke. 2050.1
41:13 to pass, as he interpreted to us, **s** it was; 3651
41:21 as at the beginning. **S** I awoke. 2050.1
41:39 *there is* none **s** discreet and wise as thou NIH
41:57 that the famine was **s** sore in all lands. NIH
42:20 **s** shall your words be verified, and 2050.1
42:20 and ye shall not die. And they did **s**. 3651
42:34 *that* ye *are* true *men:* **s** will I deliver you NIH
43: 6 Israel said, Wherefore dealt ye **s** ill with me, NIH
43:11 said unto them, If *it must be* **s** now, do this; 3651
43:34 five times **s much as** any of theirs. 4480+7235
44: 5 he divineth? ye have done evil in **s** doing. NIH
44:17 he said, God forbid that I should do **s**: *but* 2063
45: 8 **S** now *it was* not you *that* sent me hither, 2050.1
45:21 the children of Israel did **s**: and Joseph gave 3651
45:24 **S** he sent his brethren away, and 2050.1
47:13 **s that** the land of Egypt and *all* the land 2050.1
47:20 over them: **s** the land became Pharaoh's. 2050.1
47:28 **s** the whole age of Jacob was an hundred 2050.1
48:10 were dim for age, **s** *that* he could not see. NIH
48:18 said unto his father, Not **s**, my father: 3651
49:17 **s that** his rider shall fall backward. 2050.1
50: 3 for **s** are fulfilled the days of those which 3651
50:17 **S** shall ye say unto Joseph, Forgive, I pray 3541
50:26 **S** Joseph died, *being* an hundred and 2050.1
Ex 1:10 and **s** get them up out of the land. NIH
2:18 How *is it that* you are come **s** soon to day? NIH
4:26 **S** he let him go: then she said, A bloody 2050.1
5:12 **S** the people were scattered abroad 2050.1
5:22 wherefore hast thou **s** evil entreated this NIH
6: 9 Moses spake **s** unto the children of Israel: 3651
7: 6 the LORD commanded them, **s** did they. 3651
7:10 they did **s** as the LORD had commanded: 3651
7:20 Moses and Aaron did **s**, as the LORD 3651
7:22 of Egypt did **s** with their enchantments: 3651
8: 7 the magicians did **s** with their 3651
8:17 they did **s**; for Aaron stretched out his hand 3651
8:18 the magicians did **s** with their enchantments 3651
8:18 **s** there were lice upon man, and 2050.1
8:24 the LORD did **s**; and there came a 3651
8:26 Moses said, It is not meet **s** to do; for we 3651
9:24 **S** there was hail, and fire mingled with 2050.1
10:10 Let the LORD be **s** with you, as I will let 3651
10:11 Not **s**: go now ye *that are* men, and 3651
10:15 **s that** the land was darkened; 2050.1
10:20 **s that** he would not let the children of 2050.1
11:10 **s that** he would not let the children of 2050.1
12:28 commanded Moses and Aaron, **s** did they. 3651
12:36 **s that** they lent unto them *such things as* 2050.1
12:50 commanded Moses and Aaron, **s** did they. 3651
14: 4 know that I *am* the LORD. And they did **s**. 3651
14:20 **s that** the one came not near the other all 2050.1
14:25 **s that** the Egyptians said, Let us flee 2050.1
16:18 there remained not **s much as** one of them. 5704
15:22 **S** Moses brought Israel from the Red sea, 2050.1
16:17 the children of Israel did **s**, and gathered, 3651
16:30 **S** the people rested on the seventh day. 2050.1
16:34 **s** Aaron laid it up before the Testimony, 2050.1
17: 6 Moses did **s** in the sight of the elders of 3651
17:10 **S** Joshua did as Moses had said to him, 2050.1
18:22 **s** shall it be easier for thyself, and 2050.1
18:23 God command thee *s*, then thou shalt be NIH
18:24 **S** Moses hearkened to the voice of his 2050.1
19:16 **s that** all the people that *was* in the camp 2050.1
19:25 **S** Moses went down unto the people, and 2050.1
21:12 He that smiteth a man, **s that** he die, 2050.1
21:22 **s that** her fruit depart *from her*, and 2050.1
22: 6 **s that** the stacks of corn, or the standing 2050.1
25: 9 even **s** shall ye make *it*. 3651
25:33 **s** in the six branches that come out of 3651
27: 8 thee in the mount, **s** shall they make *it*. 3651
28: 7 and **s** it shall be joined together. NIH
30:21 **S** they shall wash their hands and 2050.1
Ex 30:23 and of sweet cinnamon **half s much**, 4276
32:21 that thou hast brought **s** great a sin upon NIH
32:24 **S** they gave *it* me: then I cast it into 2050.1
33:16 **s** shall we be separated, I and thy people, 2050.1
36: 6 **S** the people were restrained from 2050.1
36:13 the taches: **s** it became one tabernacle. 2050.1
37:19 **s** throughout the six branches going out of 3651
39:32 the LORD commanded Moses, **s** did they. 3651
39:42 **s** the children of Israel made all the work. 3651
39:43 had commanded, *even* **s** had they done it: 3651
40:16 that the LORD commanded him, **s** did he. 3651
40:33 court gate. **S** Moses finished the work. 2050.1
Lev 4:20 for a sin offering, **s** shall he do with this: 3651
7: 7 As the sin offering *is*, **s** *is* the trespass 3509.1
8:34 **s** the LORD hath commanded to do, NIH
8:35 that ye die not: for **s** I am commanded. 3651
8:36 **S** Aaron and his sons did all things which 2050.1
10: 5 **S** they went near, and carried them in 2050.1
10:13 made by fire: for **s** I am commanded. 3651
11:32 until the even; **s** it shall be cleansed. 2050.1
14:13 *is* the priest's, **s** *is* the trespass offering: NIH
14:21 cannot get **s** *much;* then he shall take one NIH
16: 4 wash his flesh in water, and **s** put them on. NIH
16:16 **s** shall he do for the tabernacle of 3651
24:19 as he hath done, **s** shall it be done to him; 3651
24:20 in a man, **s** shall it be done to him *again*. 3651
26:15 **s that** *ye* will not do all my 3807.1
27:12 valuest it, *who art* the priest, **s** shall it be. 3651
27:14 the priest shall estimate it, **s** shall it stand. 3651
Nu 1:19 **s** he numbered them in the wilderness of 2050.1
1:45 **S** were all those that were numbered of 2050.1
1:54 the LORD commanded Moses, **s** did they. 3651
2:17 as they encamp, **s** shall they set forward, 3651
2:34 **s** they pitched by their standards, and so 3651
2:34 **s** they set forward, every one after their 3651
4:26 that is made for them: **s** shall they serve. 2050.1
5: 4 the children of Israel did **s**, and put them 3651
5: 4 unto Moses, **s** did the children of Israel. 3651
6:21 **s** he must do after the law of his separation. 3651
8: 3 Aaron did **s**; he lighted the lamps thereof 3651
8: 4 shewed Moses, **s** he made the candlestick. 3651
8: 7 their clothes, and **s** make themselves clean. NIH
8:20 **s** did the children of Israel unto them. 3651
8:22 the Levites, **s** did they unto them. 3651
9: 5 **s** did the children of Israel. 3651
9:14 to the manner thereof, **s** shall he do: 3651
9:16 **S** it was alway: the cloud covered it *by day*, 3651
9:20 **s** it was, when the cloud was a few days NIH
9:21 **s** it was, when the cloud abode from even NIH
12: 7 My servant Moses *is* not **s**, who *is* faithful 3651
13:21 **S** they went up, and searched the land 2050.1
13:33 and **s** we were in their sight. 3651
14:28 spoken in mine ears, **s** will I do to you: 3651
15:12 **s** shall ye do to *every* one according to their 3602
15:14 unto the LORD; as ye do, **s** he shall do. 3651
15:15 as ye *are*, **s** shall the stranger be before 3509.1
15:20 of the threshingfloor, **s** shall ye heave it. 3651
16:27 **S** they gat up from the tabernacle of 2050.1
17:11 Moses did **s**: as the LORD commanded NIH
17:11 as the LORD commanded him, **s** did he. 3651
20: 8 **s** thou shalt give the congregation and 2050.1
21:35 **S** they smote him, and his sons, and 2050.1
22:30 was I ever wont to do **s** unto thee? And he 3541
22:35 **S** Balaam went with the princes of Balak. 2050.1
25: 8 **S** the plague was stayed from the children 2050.1
31: 5 **S** there were delivered out of 2050.1
32:23 if ye will not do **s**, behold, ye have sinned 3651
32:28 **S** concerning them Moses commanded 2050.1
32:31 hath said unto thy servants, **s** will we do. 3651
35: 7 **S** all the cities which ye shall give to NIH
35:16 of iron, **s that** he die, he *is* a murderer: 2050.1
35:29 **S** these *things* shall be for a statute of 2050.1
35:33 **S** ye shall not pollute the land wherein ye 2050.1
36: 3 **s** shall it be taken from the lot of our 2050.1
36: 4 **s** shall their inheritance be taken away 2050.1
36: 7 **S** shall not the inheritance of the children 2050.1
36:10 **s** did the daughters of Zelophehad: 3651
Dt 1:11 **make** you a thousand times **s many moe** 3254
1:15 **S** I took the chief of your tribes, 2050.1
1:43 **S** I spake unto you; and you would not 2050.1
1:46 **S** ye abode in Kadesh many days, 2050.1
2: 5 their land, no, not **s much as** a foot breadth; 5704
2:16 **S** it came to pass, when all the men of 2050.1
3: 3 **S** the LORD our God delivered into our 2050.1
3:21 **s** shall the LORD do unto all 3651
3:29 **S** we abode in the valley over against 2050.1
4: 5 that *ye* should do **s** in the land whither ye 3651
4: 7 For what nation *is there* **s** great, who hath NIH
4: 7 *so* great, who hath God **s** nigh unto them, NIH
4: 8 what nation *is there* **s** great, that hath NIH
4: 8 that hath statutes and judgments **s** NIH
7: 4 **s** will the anger of the LORD be kindled 2050.1
7:19 **s** shall the LORD thy God do unto all 3651
8: 5 **s** the LORD thy God chasteneth thee. NIH
8:20 before your face, **s** shall ye perish; 3651
9: 3 **s** shalt thou drive them out, and 2050.1
9: 8 **s that** the LORD was angry with you to 2050.1
9:15 **S** I turned and came down from 2050.1
12: 4 Ye shall not do **s** unto the LORD your 3651
12:10 round about, **s that** ye dwell in safety; 2050.1
12:22 and the hart is eaten, **s** thou shalt eat them: 3651
12:30 serve their gods? even **s** will I do likewise. 3651
12:31 Thou shalt not do **s** unto the LORD thy 3651
13: 5 **S** shalt thou put the evil away from 2050.1
14:24 for thee, **s that** thou art not able to carry it; 3588
17: 7 **S** thou shalt put the evil away from 2050.1
18:14 thy God hath not suffered thee **s** *to do*. 3651
19:10 *for* an inheritance, and **s** blood be upon thee. NIH
19:19 **s** shalt thou put the evil away from among 2050.1
20:18 **s** should ye sin against the LORD your 2050.1
21: 9 **S** shalt thou put away the *guilt of* 2050.1
21:21 **s** shalt thou put evil away from among 2050.1
22: 3 **s** shalt thou do with his raiment; and with 3651
22: 5 for all that do **s** *are* abomination unto 428
22:21 **s** shalt thou put evil away from among 2050.1

S

Dt 22:22 s shalt thou put away evil from Israel. 2050.1
22:24 s thou shalt put away evil from among 2050.1
22:26 and slayeth him, even s is this matter: 3651
24: 8 commanded them, s ye shall observe to do. NIH
25: 9 S shall it be done unto that man that will 3602
28:34 S that thou shalt be mad for the sight of 2050.1
28:54 S that the man that is tender among you, NIH
28:55 S that he will not give to any of them of NIH
28:63 s the LORD will rejoice over you to 3651
29:22 S that the generation to come of your 2050.1
30:17 s that thou wilt not hear, but shalt be 2050.1
31:17 s that they will say in that day, Are not 2050.1
32:12 S the LORD alone did lead him, and NIH
33:25 and as thy days, s shall thy strength be. NIH
34: 5 S Moses the servant of the LORD died 2050.1
34: 8 s the days of weeping and mourning for 2050.1
Jos 1: 5 as I was with Moses, s I will be with thee: NIH
1:17 in all things, s will we hearken unto thee: 3651
2:21 According unto your words, s be it. 3651
2:23 S the two men returned, and 2050.1
3: 7 as I was with Moses, s I will be with thee. NIH
4: 8 of Israel did s as Joshua commanded, NIH
5:15 thou standest is holy. And Joshua did s. 3651
6:11 S the ark of the LORD compassed 2050.1
6:14 returned into the camp: s they did six days. 3541
6:20 S the people shouted when the priests 2050.1
6:20 s that the people went up into the city, 2050.1
6:27 S the LORD was with Joshua; and 2050.1
7: 4 S there went up thither of the people 2050.1
7:16 S Joshua rose up early in the morning, 2050.1
7:22 S Joshua sent messengers, and they ran 2050.1
7:26 S the LORD turned from the fierceness 2050.1
8: 3 S Joshua arose, and all the people of war, 2050.1
8:22 s they were in the midst of Israel, 2050.1
8:22 s that they let none of them remain or 5704
8:25 s it was, that all that fell that day, both of NIH
9:26 s did he unto them, and delivered them out 3651
10: 1 her king, s he had done to Ai and her king; 3651
10: 7 S Joshua ascended from Gilgal, he, and 2050.1
10:13 S the sun stood still in the midst of 2050.1
10:23 they did s, and brought forth those five 3651
10:39 s he did to Debir, and to the king thereof; 3651
10:40 S Joshua smote all the country of 2050.1
11: 7 S Joshua came, and all the people of war 2050.1
11:15 s did Moses command Joshua, and so 3651
11:15 Moses command Joshua, and s did Joshua; 3651
11:16 S Joshua took all that land, the hills, and 2050.1
11:23 S Joshua took the whole land, 2050.1
14: 5 s the children of Israel did, and 3651
14:11 even s is my strength now, for war, 3509.1
14:12 if s be the LORD will be with me, then 194
15: 7 s northward, looking toward Gilgal, that is NIH
16: 4 S the children of Joseph, Manasseh and 2050.1
19:51 S they made an end of dividing 2050.1
21:40 S all the cities for the children of Merari by NIH
22: 6 S Joshua blessed them, and sent them 2050.1
22:25 s shall your children make our children 2050.1
22:28 when they should s say to us or to our NIH
23:15 s shall the LORD bring upon you all evil 3651
24:10 s I delivered you out of his hand. 2050.1
24:25 S Joshua made a covenant with 2050.1
24:28 S Joshua let the people depart, every man 2050.1
Jdg 1: 3 into thy lot. S Simeon went with him. 2050.1
1: 7 as I have done, s God hath requited me. 3651
1:35 s that they became tributaries. 2050.1
2:14 s that they could not any longer stand 2050.1
2:17 of the LORD; but they did not s. 3651
3:14 S the children of Israel served Eglon 2050.1
3:22 s that he could not draw the dagger out of 3588
3:30 S Moab was subdued that day under 2050.1
4:14 S Barak went down from mount Tabor, 2050.1
4:15 s that Sisera lighted down off his chariot, 2050.1
4:21 he was fast asleep and weary. S he died. 2050.1
4:23 S God subdued on that day Jabin the king 2050.1
5:28 Why is his chariot s long in coming? NIH
5:31 S let all thine enemies perish, O LORD: 3651
6: 3 s it was, when Israel had sown, that NIH
6:20 and pour out the broth. And he did s. 3651
6:27 s it was, because he feared his father's NIH
6:38 it was s: for he rose up early on 3651
6:40 God did s that night: for it was dry upon 3651
7: 1 s that the host of the Midianites were on 2050.1
7: 5 S he brought down the people unto 2050.1
7: 8 S the people took victuals in their hand, 2050.1
7:15 it was s, when Gideon heard the telling of NIH
7:17 it shall be that, as I do, s shall ye do. 3651
7:19 S Gideon, and the hundred men that were 2050.1
8:18 they answered, As thou art, s were they; 3644
8:21 for as the man is, s is his strength. NIH
8:28 s that they lifted up their heads no more. 2050.1
9:49 s that all the men of the tower of 2050.1
10: 9 s that Israel was sore distressed. 2050.1
11: 5 it was s, that when the children of Ammon NIH
11:10 if we do not s according to thy words. 3651
11:21 s Israel possessed all the land of 2050.1
11:23 S now the LORD God of Israel hath 2050.1
11:24 S whomsoever the LORD our God shall 2050.1
11:32 S Jephthah passed over unto the children 2050.1
12: 5 it was s, that when those Ephraimites which NIH
13:19 S Manoah took a kid with a meat 2050.1
14:10 S his father went down unto the woman: 2050.1
14:10 a feast; for s used the young men to do. 3651
14:15 ye called us to take that we have? is it not s? NIH
15:11 they did unto me, s have I done unto them. 3651
16: 9 the fire. S his strength was not known. 2050.1
16:16 s that his soul was vexed unto death; NIH
16:30 S the dead which he slew at his death 2050.1
17:10 and thy victuals. S the Levite went in. 2050.1
18:21 S they turned and departed, and put 2050.1
19: 4 s they did eat and drink, and lodged there. 2050.1
19:21 S he brought him into his house, and 2050.1
19:23 nay, I pray you, do not s wickedly; NIH
19:24 but unto this man do not s vile a thing. 2063
19:25 s the man took his concubine, and 2050.1
19:30 it was s, that all that saw it said, There was NIH

Jdg 20:11 S all the men of Israel were gathered 2050.1
20:36 S the children of Benjamin saw that they 2050.1
20:46 S that all which fell that day of Benjamin 2050.1
21:14 and yet s they sufficed them not. 3651
21:23 the children of Benjamin did s, and 3651
Ru 1:17 the LORD do s to me, and more also, 3541
1:19 S they two went until they came to 2050.1
1:22 S Naomi returned, and Ruth 2050.1
2: 7 s she came, and hath continued even from 2050.1
2:17 S she gleaned in the field until even, and 2050.1
2:23 S she kept fast by the maidens of Boaz to 2050.1
4: 8 Buy it for thee. S he drew off his shoe. 2050.1
4:13 S Boaz took Ruth, and she was his wife: 2050.1
1Sa 1: 7 as he did s year by year, when she went up 3651
1: 7 house of the LORD, s she provoked her; 3651
1: 9 S Hannah rose up after they had eaten in 2050.1
1:18 S the woman went her way, and did eat, 2050.1
1:23 S the woman abode, and gave her son 2050.1
2: 3 Talk no more s exceeding proudly; let not NIH
2: 5 s that the barren hath born seven; and 5704
2:14 S they did in Shiloh unto all the Israelites 3602
2:21 s that she conceived, and bare three sons 2050.1
3: 9 S Samuel went and lay down in his place. 2050.1
3:17 God do s to thee, and more also, if thou 3541
4: 4 S the people sent to Shiloh, that they 2050.1
4: 5 a great shout, s that the earth rang again. 2050.1
5: 7 when the men of Ashdod saw that it was s, 3651
5: 9 it was s, that after they had carried it about, NIH
5:11 S they sent and gathered together all 2050.1
6:10 the men did s; and took two milch kine, 3651
7:13 S the Philistines were subdued, and 2050.1
8: 8 served other gods, s do they also unto thee. 3651
9:10 S they went unto the city where the man 2050.1
9:21 s to me? 1697+2088+1886.1+1886.1+3509.1
9:24 S Saul did eat with Samuel that day. 2050.1
10: 9 it was s, that when he had turned his back to NIH
11: 7 s shall it be done unto his oxen. 3541
11:11 it was s on the morrow, that Saul put NIH
11:11 s that two of them were not left together. 2050.1
12:18 S Samuel called unto the LORD; and 2050.1
13:22 S it came to pass in the day of battle, 2050.1
14:15 s it was a very great trembling. 2050.1
14:23 S the LORD saved Israel that day: 2050.1
14:24 S none of the people tasted any food. 2050.1
14:44 Saul answered, God do s and more also: 3541
14:45 S the people rescued Jonathan, that he 2050.1
14:47 S Saul took the kingdom over Israel, and 2050.1
15: 6 S the Kenites departed from among 2050.1
15:31 S Samuel turned again after Saul; and 2050.1
15:33 s shall thy mother be childless among 3651
16:13 S Samuel rose up, and went to Ramah. 2050.1
16:23 s Saul was refreshed, and was well, and 2050.1
17:27 S shall it be done to the man that killeth 3541
17:50 S David prevailed over the Philistine with 2050.1
18:30 of Saul; s that his name was much set by. 2050.1
19:12 S Michal let David down through a 2050.1
19:17 Why hast thou deceived me s, and 3602
19:18 S David fled, and escaped, and came to 2050.1
20: 2 father hide this thing from me? it is not s. NIH
20:13 The LORD do s and much more to 3541
20:16 S Jonathan made a covenant with 2050.1
20:24 S David hid himself in the field: and 2050.1
20:34 S Jonathan arose from the table in fierce 2050.1
21: 6 S the priest gave him hallowed bread: for 2050.1
22:14 who is s faithful among all thy servants as NIH
23: 5 S David and his men went to Keilah, and 2050.1
23: 5 S David saved the inhabitants of Keilah. 2050.1
24: 7 S David stayed his servants with these 2050.1
25:12 S David's young men turned their way, 2050.1
25:20 it was s, as she rode on the ass, that she NIH
25:21 s that nothing was missed of all that 2050.1
25:22 S and more also do God unto the enemies 3541
25:25 for as his name is, s is he; Nabal is his 3651
25:35 S David received of her hand that which 2050.1
26: 7 S David and Abishai came to the people 2050.1
26:12 S David took the spear and the cruse of 2050.1
26:24 s let my life be much set by in the eyes of 3651
26:25 S David went on his way, and 2050.1
27: 1 of Israel: s shall I escape out of his hand. 2050.1
27:11 S did David, and so will be his manner all 3541
27:11 s will be his manner all the while he 3541
28:23 S he arose from the earth, and sat upon 2050.1
29: 8 s long as I have been with thee unto 3117+4480
29:11 S David and his men rose up early to 2050.1
30: 3 S David and his men came to the city, 2050.1
30: 9 S David went, he and the six hundred 2050.1
30:10 s faint that they could not go over 4480
30:21 s faint that they could not follow David, 4480
30:23 said David, Ye shall not do s, my brethren, 3651
30:24 s shall his part be that tarrieth by 2050.1
30:25 it was s from that day forward, that he made NIH
31: 6 S Saul died, and his three sons, and 2050.1
2Sa 1: 2 s it was, when he came to David, that he fell NIH
1:10 S I stood upon him, and slew him, 2050.1
2: 2 S David went up thither, and his two 2050.1
2:16 fellow's side; s they fell down together: 2050.1
2:28 S Joab blew a trumpet, and all the people 2050.1
2:31 s that three hundred and threescore men NIH
3: 9 S do God to Abner, and more also, except, 3541
3: 9 hath sworn to David, even s I do to him; 3651
3:20 S Abner came to David to Hebron, and 2050.1
3:30 S Joab and Abishai his brother slew 2050.1
3:34 falleth before wicked men, s fellest thou. NIH
3:35 S do God to me, and more also, 3541
5: 3 S all the elders of Israel came to the king 2050.1
5: 9 S David dwelt in the fort, and called it 2050.1
5:25 David did s, as the LORD had 3651
6:10 S David would not remove the ark of 2050.1
6:12 S David went and brought up the ark of 2050.1
6:13 it was s, that when they that bare the ark of NIH
6:15 S David and all the house of Israel 2050.1
6:19 a flagon of wine. S all the people 2050.1
7: 8 Now therefore s shalt thou say unto my 3541
7:17 this vision, s did Nathan speak unto David. 3651
8: 2 s the Moabites became David's servants, NIH

2Sa 9:11 his servant, s shall thy servant do. 3651
9:13 S Mephibosheth dwelt in Jerusalem: 2050.1
10:14 S Joab returned from the children of 2050.1
10:19 S the Syrians feared to help the children 2050.1
11:12 S Uriah abode in Jerusalem that day, 2050.1
11:20 if s be that the king's wrath arise, and he say 518
11:20 Wherefore approached ye s nigh unto NIH
11:22 S the messenger went, and came and 2050.1
12:31 S David and all the people returned unto 2050.1
13: 2 Amnon was s vexed, that he fell sick for his NIH
13: 6 S Amnon lay down, and made himself 2050.1
13: 8 S Tamar went to her brother Amnon's 2050.1
13:15 s that the hatred wherewith he hated her 3588
13:20 S Tamar remained desolate in her brother 2050.1
13:35 sons come: as thy servant said, s it is. 3651
13:38 S Absalom fled, and went to Geshur, and 2050.1
14: 3 S Joab put the words in her mouth. 2050.1
14: 7 s they shall quench my coal which is left, NIH
14:17 s is my lord the king to discern good and 3651
14:23 S Joab arose and went to Geshur, and 2050.1
14:24 S Absalom returned to his own house, 2050.1
14:25 s much praised as Absalom for his beauty: 3966
14:28 S Absalom dwelt two full years in 2050.1
14:33 S Joab came to the king, and told him: 2050.1
15: 2 it was s, that when any man that had a NIH
15: 5 it was s, that when any man came nigh to NIH
15: 6 s Absalom stole the hearts of the men of 2050.1
15: 9 in peace. S he arose, and went to Hebron. 2050.1
15:34 s will I now also be thy servant: 2050.1
15:37 S Hushai David's friend came into 2050.1
16:10 s let him curse, because the LORD hath 3588
16:10 then say, Wherefore hast thou done s? 3651
16:19 s will I be in thy presence. 3651
16:22 S they spread Absalom a tent upon 2050.1
16:23 s was all the counsel of Ahithophel both 3651
17: 3 s all the people shall be in peace. NIH
17:12 S shall we come upon him in some place 2050.1
17:12 him there shall not be left s much as one. 1571
17:26 S Israel and Absalom pitched in the land 2050.1
18: 6 S the people went out into the field 2050.1
19:13 God do s to me, and more also, if thou be 3541
19:14 s that they sent this word unto the king, 2050.1
19:15 S the king returned, and came to Jordan. 2050.1
20: 2 S every man of Israel went up from after 2050.1
20: 3 S they were shut up unto the day of their 2050.1
20: 5 S Amasa went to assemble the men of 2050.1
20:10 s he smote him therewith in the fifth rib, 2050.1
20:10 S Joab and Abishai his brother pursued 2050.1
20:18 at Abel: and s they ended the matter. 3651
20:21 The matter is not s: but a man of mount 3651
22: 4 s shall I be saved from mine enemies. 2050.1
22:35 s that a bow of steel is broken by mine 2050.1
22:37 under me; s that my feet did not slip. 2050.1
23: 5 Although my house be not s with God; 3651
24: 8 S when they had gone through all 2050.1
24:13 S Gad came to David, and told him, and 2050.1
24:15 S the LORD sent a pestilence upon 2050.1
24:24 S David bought the threshingfloor and 2050.1
24:25 S the LORD was intreated for the land, 2050.1
1Ki 1: 3 S they sought for a fair damsel 2050.1
1: 6 any time in saying, Why hast thou done s? 3602
1:30 even s will I certainly do this day. 3588
1:36 LORD God of my lord the king say s too. 3651
1:37 even s be he with Solomon, and make his 3651
1:38 S Zadok the priest, and Nathan 2050.1
1:40 s that the earth rent with the sound of 2050.1
1:45 s that the city rang again. 2050.1
1:53 S king Solomon sent, and they brought 2050.1
2: 7 for s they came to me when I fled because 3651
2:10 S David slept with his fathers, and 2050.1
2:23 God do s to me, and more also, 3541
2:27 S Solomon thrust out Abiathar from 2050.1
2:34 S Benaiah the son of Jehoiada went up, 2050.1
2:38 the king hath said, s will thy servant do. 3651
2:46 S the king commanded Benaiah the son 2050.1
3: 9 is able to judge this thy s great a people? NIH
3:12 s that there was none like thee before thee, 834
3:13 s that there shall not be any among the kings 834
4: 1 S king Solomon was king over all Israel. 2050.1
5: 4 s that there is neither adversary nor evil NIH
5:10 S Hiram gave Solomon cedar trees and 2050.1
5:18 s they prepared timber and stones to build 2050.1
6: 7 s that there was neither hammer nor axe 2050.1
6: 9 S he built the house, and finished it; and 2050.1
6:14 S Solomon built the house, and 2050.1
6:20 and s covered the altar which was of cedar. NIH
6:21 S Solomon overlaid the house within with 2050.1
6:26 ten cubits, and s was it of the other cherub. 3651
6:27 s that the wing of the one touched 2050.1
6:33 S also made he for the door of the temple 3651
6:38 of it. S was he seven years in building it. 2050.1
7: 9 and s on the outside toward the great court. NIH
7:18 and s did he for the other chapiter. 3651
7:22 s was the work of the pillars finished. 2050.1
7:40 S Hiram made an end of doing all 2050.1
7:51 S was ended all the work that king 2050.1
8:11 S that the priests could not stand to 2050.1
8:25 s that thy children take heed to their way, 7535
8:46 s that they carry them away captives unto 2050.1
8:48 s return unto thee with all their heart, and NIH
8:54 it was s, that when Solomon had made an NIH
8:63 S the king and all the children of Israel 2050.1
9:25 the LORD. S he finished the house. 2050.1
10:13 S she turned and went to her own 2050.1
10:23 S king Solomon exceeded all the kings of 2050.1
10:29 s for all the kings of the Hittites, and for 3651
11:19 s that he gave him to wife the sister of 2050.1
12:12 S Jeroboam and all the people came to 2050.1
12:16 S when all Israel saw that the king 2050.1
12:16 David. S Israel departed unto their tents. 2050.1
12:19 S Israel rebelled against the house of 2050.1
12:32 offered upon the altar (s did he in Beth-el,) 3651
12:33 S he offered upon the altar which he had 2050.1
13: 4 s that he could not pull it in again to him. 2050.1
13: 9 For s was it charged me by the word of 3651

1Ki 13:10 **S** he went another way, and returned not 2050.1
13:13 **S** they saddled him the ass: and he rode 2050.1
13:19 **S** he went back with him, and did eat 2050.1
14: 4 Jeroboam's wife did **s**, and arose, and 3651
14: 6 it was ***s***, when Ahijah heard the sound of NIH
14:28 it was ***s***, when the king went *into* the house NIH
15:20 **S** Ben-hadad hearkened unto king Asa, 2050.1
16: 6 **S** Baasha slept with his fathers, and 2050.1
16:22 **s** Tibni died, and Omri reigned. 2050.1
16:28 **S** Omri slept with his fathers, and 2050.1
17: 5 **S** he went and did according unto 2050.1
17:10 **S** he arose and went to Zarephath. 2050.1
17:17 his sickness was **s** sore, that there was no 3966
18: 4 For it was ***s***, when Jezebel cut off NIH
18: 6 **S** they divided the land between them to 2050.1
18:12 ***s*** when I come and tell Ahab, and he cannot NIH
18:16 **S** Obadiah went to meet Ahab, and 2050.1
18:20 **S** Ahab sent unto all the children of 2050.1
18:42 **S** Ahab went up to eat and to drink. 2050.1
19: 2 **S** let the gods do *to me,* and more also, 3541
19:13 it was ***s***, when Elijah heard *it,* that he NIH
19:19 **S** he departed thence, and found Elisha 2050.1
20:10 said, The gods do **s** unto me, and more also, 3541
20:19 **S** these young men of the princes of 2050.1
20:25 he hearkened unto their voice, and did **s**. 3651
20:29 ***s*** it was, that in the seventh day the battle NIH
20:32 **S** they girded sackcloth on their loins, and 2050.1
20:34 **S** he made a covenant with him, and 2050.1
20:37 **s that** in smiting he wounded *him.* 2050.1
20:38 **S** the prophet departed, and waited for 2050.1
20:40 **S** *shall* thy judgment *be;* thyself hast 3651
21: 5 said unto him, Why is thy spirit **s sad**, 5620
21: 8 **S** she wrote letters in Ahab's name, and 2050.1
22: 8 Jehoshaphat said, Let not the king say **s**. 3651
22:12 all the prophets prophesied **s**, saying, Go up 3651
22:15 **S** he came to the king. And the king said 2050.1
22:22 and prevail also: go forth, and do **s**. 3651
22:29 **S** the king of Israel and Jehoshaphat 2050.1
22:37 **S** the king died, and was brought *to* 2050.1
22:40 **S** Ahab slept with his fathers; and 2050.1
2Ki 1:17 **S** he died according to the word of 2050.1
2: 2 leave thee. **S** they went down *to* Beth-el. 2050.1
2: 4 not leave thee. **S** they came *to* Jericho. 2050.1
2: 8 **s that** they two went over on dry *ground.* 2050.1
2:10 *I am* taken from thee, it shall be **s** unto thee; 3651
2:10 so unto thee; but if not, it shall not be ***s***. NIH
2:22 **S** the waters were healed unto this day, 2050.1
3: 9 **S** the king of Israel went, and the king of 2050.1
3:12 **S** the king of Israel and Jehoshaphat and 2050.1
3:24 **s that** they fled before them: 2050.1
4: 5 **S** she went from him, and shut the door 2050.1
4: 8 ***s*** it was, *that* as oft as he passed by, NIH
4:25 **S** she went and came unto the man of 2050.1
4:36 **S** he called her. And when she was come 2050.1
4:40 **S** they poured out for the men to eat. 2050.1
4:44 **S** he set *it* before them, and they did eat, 2050.1
5: 8 it was ***s***, when Elisha the man of God had NIH
5: 9 **S** Naaman came with his horses and 2050.1
5:12 **S** he turned and went away in a rage. 2050.1
5:19 **S** he departed from him a little way. 2050.1
5:21 **S** Gehazi followed after Naaman. 2050.1
6: 4 **S** he went with them. And when they 2050.1
6:23 **S** the bands of Syria came no more into 2050.1
6:29 **S** we boiled my son, and did eat him: and 2050.1
6:31 he said, God do **s** and more also to me, 3541
7:10 **S** they came and called unto the porter of 2050.1
7:16 **S** a measure of fine flour was *sold* for a 2050.1
7:20 **s** it fell out unto him: for the people trode 3651
8: 6 **S** the king appointed unto her a certain 2050.1
8: 9 **S** Hazael went to meet him, and took a 2050.1
8:14 **S** he departed from Elisha, and came to 2050.1
8:15 and spread *it* on his face, **s that** he died: 2050.1
8:21 **S** Joram went over to Zair, and all 2050.1
9: 4 **S** the young man, *even* the young man 2050.1
9:14 **S** Jehu the son of Jehoshaphat the son of 2050.1
9:16 **S** Jehu rode *in a chariot,* and went to 2050.1
9:18 **S** there went one on horseback to meet 2050.1
9:22 **s long as** the whoredoms of thy mother 5704
9:22 and her witchcrafts *are* ***s*** many? NIH
9:27 *And they did* ***s*** at the going up to Gur, NIH
9:33 **S** they threw her down: and *some* of her 2050.1
9:37 ***s*** that they shall not say, This *is* Jezebel. NIH
10:11 **S** Jehu slew all that remained of the house 2050.1
10:16 **S** they made him ride in his chariot. 2050.1
10:21 **s that** there was not a man left that came 2050.1
11: 2 from Athaliah, **s that** he was not slain. 2050.1
11: 6 **s** shall ye keep the watch of the house, 2050.1
12: 6 **s**, *that* in the three and twentieth year NIH
12:10 it was ***s***, when they saw that *there was* much NIH
13: 5 **s that** they went out from under the hand 2050.1
13:24 **S** Hazael king of Syria died; and 2050.1
15: 5 **s that** he was a leper unto the day of his 2050.1
15: 7 **S** Azariah slept with his fathers; and 2050.1
15:12 fourth *generation.* And **s** it came to pass. 3651
15:20 **S** the king of Assyria turned back, and 2050.1
16: 7 **S** Ahaz sent messengers to Tiglath-pileser 2050.1
16:11 **s** Urijah the priest made *it* against king 3651
17: 4 for he had sent messengers to **S** king of 5471
17: 7 For ***s*** it was, that the children of Israel had NIH
17:23 **S** was Israel carried away out of their 2050.1
17:25 ***s*** it was at the beginning of their dwelling NIH
17:32 **S** they feared the LORD, and made unto 2050.1
17:41 **S** these nations feared the LORD, and 2050.1
17:41 as did their fathers, ***s*** do they unto this day. NIH
18: 5 **s that** after him was none like him among 2050.1
18:21 **s** *is* Pharaoh king of Egypt unto all that 3651
19: 5 **S** the servants of king Hezekiah came to 2050.1
19: 8 **S** Rab-shakeh returned, and found 2050.1
19:36 **S** Sennacherib king of Assyria departed, 2050.1
22:14 **S** Hilkiah the priest, and Ahikam, and 2050.1
23:18 **S** they let his bones alone, with the bones 2050.1
24: 6 **S** Jehoiakim slept with his fathers: and 2050.1
25: 6 **S** they took the king, and brought him up 2050.1
25:21 **S** Judah was carried away out of their 2050.1
1Ch 9: 1 **S** all Israel were reckoned by 2050.1
9:23 **S** they and their children had 2050.1
10: 4 **S** Saul took a sword, and fell upon it. 2050.1
10: 6 **S** Saul died, and his three sons, and all his 2050.1
10:13 **S** Saul died for his transgression which he 2050.1
11: 6 **S** Joab the son of Zeruiah went first up, 2050.1
11: 9 **S** David waxed greater and greater: 2050.1
13: 4 the congregation said that *they* would do **s**: 3651
13: 5 **S** David gathered all Israel together, 2050.1
13:13 **S** David brought not the ark *home* to 2050.1
14:11 **S** they came up to Baal-perazim; and 2050.1
15:14 **S** the priests and the Levites sanctified 2050.1
15:17 **S** the Levites appointed Heman the son of 2050.1
15:19 **S** the singers, Heman, Asaph, and Ethan, 2050.1
15:25 **S** David, and the elders of Israel, and 2050.1
16: 1 **S** they brought the ark of God, and set it 2050.1
16:37 **S** he left there before the ark of 2050.1
17:15 this vision, **s** did Nathan speak unto David. 3651
18:14 **S** David reigned over all Israel, and 2050.1
19: 2 **S** the servants of David came into 2050.1
19: 7 **S** they hired thirty and two thousand 2050.1
19:14 **S** Joab and the people that *were* with him 2050.1
19:17 **S when** David had put the battle in array 2050.1
20: 3 Even **s** dealt David with all the cities of 3651
21: 3 **make** his people an hundred times
s many moe 3254
21:11 **S** Gad came to David, and said unto him, 2050.1
21:14 **S** the LORD sent pestilence upon Israel: 2050.1
21:25 **S** David gave to Ornan for the place six 2050.1
22: 5 **S** David prepared abundantly before his 2050.1
23: 1 **S when** David was old and full of days, 2050.1
25: 7 **S** the number of them, with their brethren 2050.1
29:14 that we should be able to offer ***s*** NIH
2Ch 1: 3 **S** Solomon, and all the congregation with 2050.1
1:10 can judge this thy people, *that is* ***s*** great? NIH
1:17 **s** brought they out *horses* for all the kings 3651
2: 3 house to dwell therein, *even* ***s*** *deal with me.* NIH
5:14 **S that** the priests could not stand to 2050.1
6:16 **s that** thy children take heed to their way to 518
6:31 **s long as** they live in 3117+3605+1886.1
7: 5 **s** the king and all the people dedicated 2050.1
7:21 **s that** he shall say, Why hath the LORD 2050.1
8:14 for **s** had David the man of God 3651
8:16 ***S*** the house of the LORD was perfected. NIH
9:12 **S** she turned, and went away to her own 2050.1
10: 3 **S** Jeroboam and all Israel came and 2050.1
10:12 **S** Jeroboam and all the people came to 2050.1
10:15 **S** the king hearkened not unto the people: 2050.1
10:16 own house. **S** all Israel went to their tents. 2050.1
11:17 **S** they strengthened the kingdom of 2050.1
12: 9 **S** Shishak king of Egypt came up against 2050.1
12:13 **S** king Rehoboam strengthened himself in 2050.1
13: 9 **s** that whosoever cometh to consecrate NIH
13:13 **s** they were before Judah, and 2050.1
13:17 **s** there fell down slain of Israel five 2050.1
14: 1 **S** Abijah slept with his fathers, and 2050.1
14: 7 on every side. **S** they built and prospered. 2050.1
14:12 **S** the LORD smote the Ethiopians 2050.1
15:10 **S** they gathered themselves together *at* 2050.1
17:10 **s that** they made no war against 2050.1
18: 7 Jehoshaphat said, Let not the king say **s**. 3651
18:11 all the prophets prophesied **s**, saying, Go up 3651
18:21 shalt also prevail: go out, and do *even* **s**. 3651
18:28 **S** the king of Israel and Jehoshaphat 2050.1
18:29 **S** the king of Israel disguised himself; 2050.1
19:10 ***s*** wrath come upon you, and upon your NIH
20: 6 **s that** none is able to withstand thee? 2050.1
20:20 your God, **s** shall you be established; 2050.1
20:20 believe his prophets, **s** shall ye prosper. 2050.1
20:25 in gathering of the spoil, it was **s** much. 3588
20:30 **S** the realm of Jehoshaphat was quiet: 2050.1
21:10 **S** the Edomites revolted from under 2050.1
21:17 **s that** there was never a son left him, 2050.1
21:19 **s** he died of sore diseases. And his people 2050.1
22: 1 **S** Ahaziah the son of Jehoram king of 2050.1
22: 9 **S** the house of Ahaziah had no power to 2050.1
22:11 **S** Jehoshabeath, the daughter of king 2050.1
22:11 from Athaliah, **s that** she slew him not. 2050.1
23: 8 **S** the Levites and all Judah did according 2050.1
23:15 **S** they laid hands on her; and when she 2050.1
24:13 **S** the workmen wrought, and the work 2050.1
24:24 **S** they executed judgment against Joash. 2050.1
25:21 **S** Joash the king of Israel went up; and 2050.1
26:23 **S** Uzziah slept with his fathers, and 2050.1
27: 5 **S much** did the children of Ammon pay 2063
27: 6 **S** Jotham became mighty, because 2050.1
28:14 **S** the armed men left the captives and 2050.1
29:17 **s** they sanctified the house of the LORD 2050.1
29:22 **S** they killed the bullocks, and the priests 2050.1
29:25 for ***s*** *was* the commandment of the LORD NIH
29:34 **s that** they could not flay all the burnt 2050.1
29:35 **S** the service of the house of the LORD 2050.1
30: 5 **S** they established a decree to make 2050.1
30: 6 **S** the posts went with the letters from 2050.1
30: 9 **s** that *they shall* come again into this land: 2050.1
30:10 **S** the posts passed from city to city 2050.1
30:26 **S** there was great joy in Jerusalem: 2050.1
32: 4 **S** there was gathered much people 2050.1
32:17 **s** shall not the God of Hezekiah deliver his 3651
32:21 **S** he returned with shame of face to his 2050.1
32:23 **s that** he was magnified in the sight of all 2050.1
32:26 **s that** the wrath of the LORD came not 2050.1
33: 8 **s that** they will take heed to do all that 518+7535
33: 9 **S** Manasseh made Judah and 2050.1
33:20 **S** Manasseh slept with his fathers, and 2050.1
34: 6 ***s did he*** in the cities of Manasseh, and NIH
34:26 of the LORD, **s** shall ye say unto him, 3541
34:28 **S** they brought the king word again. 2050.1
35: 6 **S** kill the passover, and 2050.1
35:10 **S** the service was prepared, and 2050.1
35:12 of Moses. And **s** *did they* with the oxen. 3651
35:16 **S** all the service of the LORD was 2050.1
Ezr 2:70 **S** the priests, and the Levites, and 2050.1
3:13 **S that** the people could not discern 2050.1
4:13 ***s*** thou shalt endamage the revenue of NIH
4:15 **s** shalt thou find in the book of 2050.3
Ezr 4:24 **S** it ceased unto the second year of 1934+2050.3
5:17 whether it be **s**, that a decree *was* made of NIH
6:13 the king had sent, **s** they did speedily. 3660
8:23 **S** we fasted and besought our God for 2050.1
8:30 **S** took the priests and the Levites 2050.1
9: 2 **s that** the holy seed have mingled 2050.1
9:14 **s** that *there should be* no remnant nor NIH
10:12 loud voice, As thou hast said, **s** must we do. 3651
10:16 the children of the captivity did **s**. And Ezra 3651
Ne 2: 4 **S** I prayed to the God of heaven. 2050.1
2: 6 **S** it pleased the king to send me; and I set 2050.1
2:11 **S** I came to Jerusalem, and was there 2050.1
2:15 by the gate of the valley, and ***s*** returned. NIH
2:18 **S** they strengthened their hands for *this* 2050.1
4: 6 **S** built we the wall; and all the wall was 2050.1
4:10 **s that** we are not able to build the wall. 2050.1
4:18 his sword girded by his side, and ***s*** builded. NIH
4:21 **S** we laboured in the work: and half of 2050.1
4:23 **S** neither I, nor my brethren, nor my 2050.1
5:12 of them; **s** will we do as thou sayest. 3651
5:13 **S** God shake out every man from his house, 3602
5:15 but **s** did not I, because of the fear of God. 3651
6: 3 a great work, **s that** I cannot come down: 2050.1
6:13 do **s**, and sin, and *that* they might have 3651
6:15 **S** the wall was finished in the twenty and 2050.1
7:73 **S** the priests, and the Levites, and 2050.1
8: 8 **S** they read in the book in the law of God 2050.1
8:11 **S** the Levites stilled all the people, 2050.1
8:16 **S** the people went forth, and 2050.1
8:17 day had not the children of Israel done **s**. 3651
9:10 **S** didst thou get thee a name, as *it is* this 2050.1
9:11 **s that** they went through the midst of 2050.1
9:21 the wilderness, ***s that*** they lacked nothing; NIH
9:22 **s** they possessed the land of Sihon, and 2050.1
9:24 **S** the children went in and possessed 2050.1
9:25 **s** they did eat, and were filled, and 2050.1
9:28 **s that** they had the dominion over them: 2050.1
12:40 **S** stood the two *companies of them that* 2050.1
12:43 **s that** the joy of Jerusalem was heard 2050.1
13:20 **S** the merchants and sellers of all *kind of* 2050.1
13:21 if ye do ***s*** again, I will lay hands on you. NIH
Est 1: 8 for **s** the king had appointed to all 3651
1:13 (for **s** *was* the king's manner towards all 3651
1:17 **s that** *they* shall despise their husbands in 3807.1
2: 4 the thing pleased the king; and he did **s**. 3651
2: 8 **S** it came to pass, when the king's 2050.1
2:12 (for **s** were the days of their purifications 3651
2:16 **S** Esther was taken unto king Ahasuerus 2050.1
2:17 **s that** he set the royal crown upon her 2050.1
3: 2 for the king had **s** commanded concerning 3651
4: 4 **S** Esther's maids and her chamberlains 2050.1
4: 6 **S** Hatach went forth to Mordecai unto 2050.1
4:16 **s** will I go in unto the king, which *is* not 3651
4:17 **S** Mordecai went his way, and 2050.1
5: 2 it was ***s***, when the king saw Esther NIH
5: 2 **S** Esther drew near, and touched the top 2050.1
5: 5 **S** the king and Haman came to 2050.1
5:13 **s long as** I see Mordecai the Jew 3605+871.1
6: 6 **S** Haman came in. And the king said unto 2050.1
6:10 and do *even* **s** to Mordecai the Jew, 3651
7: 1 **S** the king and Haman came to banquet 2050.1
7: 5 that durst presume in his heart to do **s**? 3651
7:10 **S** they hanged Haman on the gallows that 2050.1
8: 4 **S** Esther arose, and stood before the king, 2050.1
8:14 ***S*** the posts that rode upon mules *and* NIH
9:14 the king commanded it **s** to be done: and 3651
9:27 unto them, **s** as it should not fail, 2050.1
Job 1: 3 **s that** this man was the greatest of all 2050.1
1: 5 it was **s**, when the days of *their* feasting 3588
1:12 **S** Satan went forth from the presence of 2050.1
2: 7 **S** went Satan forth from the presence of 2050.1
2:13 **S** they sat down with him upon 2050.1
5:12 **s that** their hands cannot perform *their* 2050.1
5:16 **S** the poor hath hope, and 2050.1
5:27 **s** it *is;* hear it, and know thou *it* for thy 3651
7: 3 **S** am I made to possess months of vanity, 3651
7: 9 **s** he that goeth down *to* the grave shall 3651
7:15 **S that** my soul chooseth strangling, *and* 2050.1
7:20 **s that** I am a burden to myself? 2050.1
8:13 **S** *are* the paths of all that forget God; and 3651
9: 2 I know *it is* **s** of a truth: but how should 3651
9:30 **make** my hands **never s clean**; 1253+2141+871.1
9:35 and not fear him; but *it is* not **s** with me. 3651
13: 9 man mocketh another, do ye ***s*** mock him? NIH
14:12 **S** man lieth down, and riseth not: till 2050.1
21: 4 if *it were* ***s***, why should not my spirit be NIH
23: 7 **s** should I be delivered for ever from my 2050.1
24:19 ***s doth*** the grave *those which* have sinned. NIH
24:25 if *it be* not ***s*** now, who will make me a liar, NIH
27: 6 heart shall not reproach *me* **s long as** I live. 4480
32: 1 **S** these three men ceased to answer Job, 2050.1
32:22 *in* ***s*** *doing* my Maker would soon take me NIH
33:20 **S that** his life abhorreth bread, and 2050.1
34:25 in the night, **s that** they are destroyed. 2050.1
34:28 **S that** *they* cause the cry of the poor to 3807.1
35:15 because *it is* not ***s***, he hath visited *in* his NIH
36:16 Even **s** would he have removed thee out of 637
41:10 None *is* ***s*** fierce that dare stir him up: who NIH
41:16 One is **s** near to another, that no air can NIH
42: 7 it was ***s***, that after the LORD had spoken NIH
42: 9 **S** Eliphaz the Temanite and Bildad 2050.1
42:12 **S** the LORD blessed the latter end of 2050.1
42:15 women found ***s*** fair as the daughters of Job: NIH
42:17 **S** Job died, *being* old and full of days. 2050.1
Ps 1: 4 The ungodly *are* not **s**: but *are* like the chaff 3651
7: 7 **S** shall the congregation of the people 2050.1
18: 3 **s** shall I be saved from mine enemies. 2050.1
18:34 **s that** a bow of steel is broken *by* mine 2050.1
21:13 ***s*** will we sing and praise thy power. NIH
22: 1 *why art thou* ***s*** far from helping me, *and* NIH
26: 6 **s** will I compass thine altar, O LORD: 2050.1
35:25 say in their hearts, Ah, **s** would we have it: NIH
37: 3 ***s*** shalt thou dwell in the land, and NIH
40:12 **s that** I am not able to look *up;* they are 2050.1
42: 1 **s** panteth my soul after thee, O God. 3651

S

Ps 45:11 S shall the king greatly desire thy beauty: 2050.1
48: 5 They saw it, and s they marvelled; 3651
48: 8 s have we seen in the city of the LORD of 3651
48:10 s is thy praise unto the ends of the earth: 3651
58: 5 voice of charmers, charming never s wisely. NIH
58:11 S that a man shall say, Verily there is a 2050.1
61: 8 S will I sing praise unto thy name for ever, 3651
63: 2 s as I have seen thee in the sanctuary. 3651
64: 8 S they shall make their own tongue to fall 2050.1
65: 9 them corn, when thou hast s provided for it. 3651
68: 2 smoke is driven away, s drive them away: NIH
68: 2 s let the wicked perish at the presence of NIH
72: 7 s long as the moon endureth. 1097+5704
73:20 s, O Lord, when thou awakest, thou shalt NIH
73:22 S foolish was I, and ignorant: I was as a 2050.1
77: 4 I am s troubled that I cannot speak. NIH
77:13 who is s great a God as our God? NIH
78:21 s a fire was kindled against Jacob, and 2050.1
78:29 S they did eat, and were well filled: for he 2050.1
78:53 led them on safely, s that they feared not: 2050.1
78:60 S that he forsook the tabernacle of 2050.1
78:72 S he fed them according to the integrity 2050.1
79:13 S we thy people and sheep of thy pasture 2050.1
80:12 s that all they which pass by the way do 2050.1
80:18 S will not we go back from thee: 2050.1
81:12 S I gave them up unto their own heart's 2050.1
83:15 S persecute them with thy tempest, and 3651
90:11 even according to thy fear, s is thy wrath. NIH
90:12 S teach us to number our days, that we may 3651
102: 4 like grass; s that I forget to eat my bread. 3588
102:15 S the heathen shall fear the name of 2050.1
103: 5 s that thy youth is renewed like the eagle's. NIH
103:11 s great is his mercy toward them that fear NIH
103:12 s far hath he removed our transgressions NIH
103:13 s the LORD pitieth them that fear him. NIH
103:15 as a flower of the field, s he flourisheth. 3651
104:25 S is this great and wide sea, wherein are NIH
106: 9 s he led them through the depths, 2050.1
106:30 and s the plague was stayed. NIH
106:32 s that it went ill with Moses for their 2050.1
106:33 s that he spake unadvisedly with his lips. 2050.1
107: 2 Let the redeemed of the LORD say s, NIH
107:29 a calm, s that the waves thereof are still. 2050.1
107:30 s he bringeth them unto their desired 2050.1
107:38 s that they are multiplied greatly; 2050.1
109:17 As he loved cursing, s let it come unto 2050.1
109:17 not in blessing, s let it be far from him. 2050.1
109:18 s let it come into his bowels like water, 2050.1
115: 8 s is every one that trusteth in them. NIH
119:27 s shall I talk of thy wondrous works. 2050.1
119:42 S shall I have wherewith to answer him 2050.1
119:44 S shall I keep thy law continually for ever 2050.1
119:88 s shall I keep the testimony of thy mouth. 2050.1
119:134 of man: s will I keep thy precepts. 2050.1
123: 2 s our eyes wait upon the LORD our God, 3651
125: 2 s the LORD is round about his people 2050.1
127: 2 for s he giveth his beloved sleep. 3651
127: 4 a mighty man; s are children of the youth. 3651
135:18 s is every one that trusteth in them. NIH
147:20 He hath not dealt s with any nation: and 3651
Pr 1:19 S are the ways of every one that is greedy 3651
2: 2 S that thou incline thine ear unto 3807.1
3: 4 S shalt thou find favour and 2050.1
3:10 S shall thy barns be filled with plenty, 2050.1
3:22 S shall they be life unto thy soul, and 2050.1
6:11 S shall thy poverty come as one that 2050.1
6:29 S he that goeth in to his neighbour's wife; 3651
7:13 S she caught him, and kissed him, and 2050.1
10:25 s is the wicked no more: but the righteous 2050.1
10:26 s is the sluggard to them that send him. 3651
11:19 s he that pursueth evil pursueth it to his 2050.1
11:22 s is a fair woman which is without NIH
15: 7 but the heart of the foolish doeth not s. 3651
19:24 and will not s much as bring it to his 1571
20:30 s do stripes the inward parts of the belly. 2050.1
23: 7 For as he thinketh in his heart, s is he: Eat 3651
24:14 S shall the knowledge of wisdom be unto 3651
24:29 s to him as he hath done to me: 834+3509.1
24:34 S shall thy poverty come as one that 2050.1
25:12 s is a wise reprover upon an obedient ear. NIH
25:13 s is a faithful messenger to them that send NIH
25:16 eat s much as is sufficient for thee, 1767
25:17 lest he be weary of thee, and s hate thee. NIH
25:20 s is he that singeth songs to a heavy heart. 2050.1
25:23 s doth an angry countenance a backbiting 2050.1
25:25 s is good news from a far country. 2050.1
25:27 s for men to search their own glory is not 2050.1
26: 1 s honour is not seemly for a fool. 3651
26: 2 s the curse causeless shall not come. 3651
26: 7 s is a parable in the mouth of fools. 2050.1
26: 8 a sling, s is he that giveth honour to a fool. 3651
26: 9 s is a parable in the mouth of fools. 2050.1
26:11 to his vomit, s a fool returneth to his folly. NIH
26:14 s doth the slothful upon his bed. 2050.1
26:19 S is the man that deceiveth his neighbour, 3651
26:20 s where there is no talebearer, the strife 2050.1
26:21 s is a contentious man to kindle strife. 2050.1
27: 8 s is a man that wandereth from his place. 3651
27: 9 s doth the sweetness of a man's friend by 2050.1
27:17 s a man sharpeneth the countenance of 2050.1
27:18 s he that waiteth on his master shall be 2050.1
27:19 to face, s the heart of man to man. 3651
27:20 s the eyes of man are never satisfied. 2050.1
27:21 furnace for gold; s is a man to his praise. 2050.1
28:15 s is a wicked ruler over the poor people. NIH
30:33 s the forcing of wrath bringeth forth 2050.1
31:11 s that he shall have no need of spoil. 2050.1
Ecc 2: 9 S I was great, and increased more than all 2050.1
2:15 to the fool, s it happeneth even to me; 1571
3:11 s that no man can find out 834+1097+4480
3:19 as the one dieth, s dieth the other; yea, 3651
3:19 s that a man hath no preeminence above 2050.1
4: 1 S I returned, and considered all 2050.1
5:16 that in all points as he came, s shall he go: 3651
6: 2 s that he wanteth nothing for his soul of 2050.1
Ecc 6: 3 s that the days of his years be many, and 2050.1
7: 6 under a pot, s is the laughter of the fool: 3651
8:10 s I saw the wicked buried, who had come 3651
8:10 forgotten in the city where they had s done: 3651
9: 2 as is the good, s is the sinner; and he that 3509.1
9:12 s are the sons of men snared in an evil 3509.1
10: 1 s doth a little folly him that is in reputation NIH
11: 5 even s thou knowest not the works of God 3602
SS 2: 2 s is my love among the daughters. 3651
2: 3 the wood, s is my beloved among the sons. 3651
5: 9 another beloved, that thou dost s charge us? 3602
Isa 5:24 s their root shall be as rottenness, and NIH
6:13 when they cast their leaves: s the holy seed NIH
10: 7 Howbeit he meaneth not s, neither doth his 3651
10: 7 not so, neither doth his heart think s; 3651
10:11 her idols, s do to Jerusalem and her idols? 3651
10:26 s shall he lift it up after the manner of 2050.1
14:24 as I have thought, s shall it come to pass; 3651
14:24 and as I have purposed, s shall it stand: NIH
16: 2 s the daughters of Moab shall be at the fords NIH
16: 6 and his wrath: but his lies shall not be s. 3651
18: 4 For s the LORD said unto me, I will take 3541
20: 2 And he did s, walking naked and barefoot. 3651
20: 4 S shall the king of Assyria lead away 3651
21: 1 s it cometh from the desert, from a terrible NIH
22:22 s he shall open, and none shall shut; and 2050.1
23: 1 s that there is no house, no entering in: NIH
23: 5 s shall they be sorely pained at the report 3509.1
24: 2 as with the people, s with the priest; 3509.1
24: 2 as with the servant, s with his master; 3509.1
24: 2 as with the maid, s with her mistress; 3509.1
24: 2 as with the buyer, s with the seller; 3509.1
24: 2 as with the lender, s with the borrower; 3509.1
24: 2 of usury, s with the giver of usury to him. 3509.1
26:17 s have we been in thy sight, O LORD. 3651
28: 8 and filthiness, s that there is no place clean. NIH
29: 8 s shall the multitude of all the nations be, 3651
30:14 s that there shall not be found in 2050.1
31: 4 s shall the LORD of hosts come down to 3651
31: 5 s will the LORD of hosts defend 3651
36: 6 s is Pharaoh king of Egypt to all that trust 3651
37: 5 S the servants of king Hezekiah came to 2050.1
37: 8 S Rabshakeh returned, and found the king 2050.1
37:37 S Sennacherib king of Assyria departed, 2050.1
38: 8 S the sun returned ten degrees, by which 2050.1
38:13 that, as a lion, s will he break all my bones: 3651
38:14 Like a crane or a swallow, s did I chatter: 3651
38:16 s wilt thou recover me, and make me to 2050.1
40:20 s impoverished that he hath no oblation 5533
41: 7 S the carpenter encouraged the goldsmith, 2050.1
47: 7 s that thou didst not lay these things to thy NIH
47:12 if s be thou shalt be able to profit, if so 194
47:12 be able to profit, if s be thou mayest prevail. 194
52:14 his visage was s marred more than any 3651
52:15 S shall he sprinkle many nations; the kings 3651
53: 7 is dumb, s he openeth not his mouth. 2050.1
54: 9 s have I sworn that I would not be wroth 3651
55: 9 s are my ways higher than your ways, and 3651
55:11 S shall my word be that goeth forth out of 3651
59:19 S shall they fear the name of the LORD 2050.1
60:15 s that no man went through thee, I will 2050.1
61:11 s the Lord GOD will cause righteousness 3651
62: 5 a virgin, s shall thy sons marry thee: NIH
62: 5 the bride, s shall thy God rejoice over thee. NIH
63: 8 that will not lie: s he was their Saviour. 2050.1
63:14 s didst thou lead thy people, to make 3651
65: 8 s will I do for my servants' sakes, that I 3651
66:13 mother comforteth, s will I comfort you; 3651
66:22 s shall your seed and your name remain. 3651
Jer 2:26 is found, s is the house of Israel ashamed; 3651
2:36 Why gaddest thou about s much to change NIH
3:20 s have you dealt treacherously with me, 3651
5:19 s shall ye serve strangers in a land that is 3651
5:27 of birds, s are their houses full of deceit: 3651
5:31 and my people love to have it s: 3651
6: 7 s she casteth out her wickedness: 3651
9:10 s that none can pass through them; neither 4480
10:18 will distress them, that they may find it s. NIH
11: 4 s shall ye be my people, and I will be 2050.1
11: 5 answered I, and said, S be it, O LORD. 543
13: 2 S I got a girdle, according to the word of 2050.1
13: 5 S I went, and hid it by Euphrates, as 2050.1
13:11 s have I caused to cleave unto me the whole 3651
17:11 s he that getteth riches, and not by right, NIH
18: 4 s he made it again another vessel, 2050.1
18: 6 s are ye in mine hand, O house of Israel. 3651
19:11 Even s will I break this people and this 3602
21: 2 if s be that the LORD will deal with us 194
24: 2 which could not be eaten, they were s bad. 4480
24: 3 that cannot be eaten, they are s evil. 4480
24: 5 s will I acknowledge them that are carried 3651
24: 8 which cannot be eaten, they are s evil; 4480
24: 8 S will I give Zedekiah the king of Judah, 3651
26: 3 If s be they will hearken, and turn every man 194
26: 7 S the priests and the prophets and all 2050.1
28: 6 the LORD do s: the LORD perform thy 3651
28:11 Even s will I break the yoke of 3602
28:17 S Hananiah the prophet died the same 2050.1
29:17 that cannot be eaten, they are s evil. 4480
30: 7 for that day is great, s that none is like it: 4480
31:28 s will I watch over them, to build, and 3651
32: 8 S Hanameel mine uncle's son came to me 2050.1
32:11 S I took the evidence of the purchase, 2050.1
32:42 s will I bring upon them all the good that I 3651
33:22 s will I multiply the seed of David my 3651
33:26 s that I will not take any of his seed to be NIH
34: 5 s shall they burn odours for thee; 3651
35:11 of the Syrians: s we dwell at Jerusalem. 2050.1
36:14 S Baruch the son of Neriah took the roll 2050.1
36:15 in our ears. S Baruch read it in their ears. 2050.1
36:21 S the king sent Jehudi to fet the roll: and 2050.1
37:14 s Irijah took Jeremiah, and brought him to 2050.1
38: 6 but mire: s Jeremiah sunk in the mire. 2050.1
38:11 S Ebed-melech took the men with him, 2050.1
38:12 under the cords. And Jeremiah did s. 3651
Jer 38:13 S they drew up Jeremiah with cords, and 2050.1
38:16 S Zedekiah the king sware secretly unto 2050.1
38:20 s it shall be well unto thee, and thy soul 2050.1
38:23 S they shall bring out all thy wives and 2050.1
38:27 S they left off speaking with him; for 2050.1
38:28 S Jeremiah abode in the court of 2050.1
39:13 S Nebuzar-adan the captain of the guard 2050.1
39:14 him home: s he dwelt among the people. 2050.1
40: 5 S the captain of the guard gave him 2050.1
41: 7 it was s, when they came into the midst of NIH
41: 8 S he forbare, and slew them not among 2050.1
41:14 S all the people that Ishmael had carried 2050.1
42:17 S shall it be with all the men that set their 2050.1
42:18 s shall my fury be poured forth upon you, 3651
42:20 s declare unto us, and we will do it. 3651
43: 4 S Johanan the son of Kareah, and all 2050.1
43: 7 S they came into the land of Egypt: 2050.1
44:14 S that none of the remnant of Judah, 2050.1
44:22 S that the LORD could no longer bear, 2050.1
46:18 and as Carmel by the sea, s shall he come. NIH
48:30 it shall not be s; his lies shall not so 3651
48:30 shall not be so; his lies shall not s effect it. 3651
48:39 s shall Moab be a derision and a 2050.1
50:40 s shall no man abide there, neither shall any NIH
51: 8 balm for her pain, if s be she may be healed. 194
51:49 s at Babylon shall fall the slain of all 1571
51:60 S Jeremiah wrote in a book all the evil 2050.1
52: 5 S the city was besieged unto the eleventh 2050.1
52: 6 s that there was no bread for the people 2050.1
52:26 S Nebuzar-adan the captain of the guard 2050.1
La 2:22 s that in the day of the LORD'S anger 2050.1
3:29 mouth in the dust; if s be there may be hope. 194
4:14 s that men could not touch their garments. 871.1
5:20 us for ever, and forsake us s long time? 753
Eze 1:18 they were s high that they were dreadful; NIH
1:28 s was the appearance of the brightness 3651
3: 2 S I opened my mouth, and he caused me 2050.1
3:14 S the spirit lifted me up, and took me 2050.1
4: 5 s shalt thou bear the iniquity of the house 2050.1
5:15 S it shall be a reproach and a taunt, 2050.1
5:17 S will I send upon you famine and 2050.1
6:14 S will I stretch out mine hand upon them, 2050.1
8: 5 S I lift up mine eyes the way toward 2050.1
8:10 S I went in and saw; and behold every 2050.1
11:24 S the vision that I had seen went up from 2050.1
12: 7 I did s as I was commanded: I brought forth 3651
12:11 as I have done, s shall it be done unto them: 3651
13:14 S will I break down the wall that ye have 2050.1
13:14 s that the foundation thereof shall be 2050.1
14:15 they spoil it, s that it be desolate, that no 2050.1
14:17 s that I cut off man and beast from it: 2050.1
15: 6 s will I give the inhabitants of Jerusalem. 3651
16:16 things shall not come, neither shall it be s. NIH
16:42 S will I make my fury towards thee to 2050.1
16:44 As is the mother, s is her daughter. NIH
17: 6 s it became a vine, and brought forth 2050.1
18: 4 s also the soul of the son is mine: 3509.1
18:30 s iniquity shall not be your ruin. 2050.1
19:14 s that she hath no strong rod to be a 2050.1
20:36 s will I plead with you, saith the Lord 3651
21:24 s that in all your doings your sins do 3807.1
22:20 to melt it; s will I gather you in mine anger 3651
22:22 s shall ye be melted in the midst thereof; 3651
23:18 S she discovered her whoredoms, and 2050.1
23:27 s that thou shalt not lift up thine eyes 2050.1
23:44 s went they in unto Aholah and 3651
24:18 S I spake unto the people in the morning: 2050.1
24:19 these things are to us, that thou doest s? NIH
28:14 I have set thee s: thou wast upon the holy NIH
31: 9 s that all the trees of Eden, that were in 2050.1
33: 7 S thou, O son of man, I have set thee a 2050.1
34:12 s will I seek out my sheep, and will deliver 3651
35:15 it was desolate, s will I do unto thee: 3651
36:38 s shall the waste cities be filled with flocks 3651
37: 7 S I prophesied as I was commanded: and 2050.1
37:10 S I prophesied as he commanded me, and 2050.1
37:23 s shall they be my people, and I will be 2050.1
38:20 S that the fishes of the sea, and the fowls 2050.1
39: 7 S will I make my holy name known in 2050.1
39:10 S that they shall take no wood out of 2050.1
39:22 S the house of Israel shall know that I am 2050.1
39:23 their enemies: s fell they all by the sword. 2050.1
40: 5 s he measured the breadth of the building, 2050.1
40:47 S he measured the court, an hundred 2050.1
41: 4 S he measured the length thereof, 2050.1
41: 7 s increased from the lowest chamber to 3651
41:13 S he measured the house, an hundred 2050.1
41:18 s that a palm tree was between a cherub 2050.1
41:19 S that the face of a man was toward 2050.1
43: 5 S the spirit took me up, and brought me 2050.1
43:15 S the altar shall be four cubits; and 2050.1
43:27 that upon the eight day, and s forward, NIH
45:20 s thou shalt do the seventh day of 3651
45:20 is simple: s shall ye reconcile the house. 2050.1
47:21 S shall ye divide this land unto you 2050.1
Da 1: 5 s nourishing them three years, that at 2050.1
1:14 S he consented to them in this matter, and 2050.1
2: 2 S they came and stood before the king. 2050.1
2:15 Why is the decree s hasty from the king? NIH
2:42 s the kingdom shall be partly strong, and NIH
3:17 If it be s, our God whom we serve is able to NIH
5: 6 s that the joints of his loins were loosed, 2050.3
6:23 S Daniel was taken up out of the den, and 2050.3
6:28 S this Daniel prospered in the reign of 2050.3
7:16 S he told me, and made me know 2050.3
8: 4 s that no beasts might stand before him, 2050.1
8:17 S he came near where I stood: and 2050.1
10: 7 s that they fled to hide themselves. 2050.1
11: 9 S the king of the south shall come into his 2050.1
11:15 S the king of the north shall come, and 2050.1
11:30 s shall he do; he shall even return, and 2050.1
Hos 1: 3 S he went and took Gomer the daughter 2050.1
3: 2 S I bought her to me for fifteen pieces of 2050.1
3: 3 for another man: s will I also be for thee. 2050.1
4: 7 were increased, s they sinned against me: 3651

Hos 6: 9 s the company of priests murder in the way NIH
8: 7 if s be it yield, the strangers shall swallow it 194
10:15 S shall Beth-el do unto you because of your 3602
11: 2 they called them, s they went from them: 3651
13: 6 to their pasture, s were they filled; 2050.1
14: 2 s will we render the calves of our lips. 2050.1
Joel 2: 4 and as horsemen, s shall they run. 3651
3:17 S shall ye know that I am the LORD 2050.1
Am 3:12 s shall the children of Israel be taken out 3651
4: 8 S two or three cities wandered unto one 2050.1
5: 9 s that the spoiled shall come against 2050.1
5:14 s the LORD, the God of hosts, shall be 3651
Ob 1:16 s shall all the heathen drink continually, NIH
Jnh 1: 3 s he paid the fare thereof, and went down 2050.1
1: 4 s that the ship was like to be broken. 2050.1
1: 6 S the shipmaster came to him, and 2050.1
1: 6 if s be that God will think upon us, that we 194
1: 7 S they cast lots, and the lot fell upon 2050.1
1:12 the sea; s shall the sea be calm unto you: 2050.1
1:15 S they took up Jonah, and cast him forth 2050.1
3: 3 S Jonah arose, and went unto Nineveh, 2050.1
3: 5 S the people of Nineveh believed God, 2050.1
4: 5 S Jonah went out of the city, and sat on 2050.1
4: 6 S Jonah was exceeding glad of the gourd. 2050.1
Mic 2: 2 s they oppress a man and his house, 2050.1
5:14 midst of thee: s will I destroy thy cities. 2050.1
7: 3 his mischievous desire: s they wrap it up. 2050.1
Zep 3: 6 cities are destroyed, s that there is no man, NIH
3: 7 s their dwelling should not be cut off, 2050.1
Hag 2: 5 s my spirit remaineth among you: 2050.1
2:14 S is this people, and so is this nation before 3651
2:14 this people, and s is this nation before me, 3651
2:14 s is every work of their hands; and 3651
Zec 1: 6 to our doings, s hath he dealt with us. 3651
1:14 S the angel that communed with me said 2050.1
1:21 s that no man did lift up his head: 6310+3509.1
3: 5 S they set a fair mitre upon his head, and 2050.1
4: 4 S I answered and spake to the angel that 2050.1
6: 7 S they walked to and fro through 2050.1
7: 3 as I have done these s many years? 4100+3509.1
7:13 s they cried, and I would not hear, saith 3651
8:13 s will I save you, and ye shall be a blessing: 3651
8:15 S again have I thought in these days to do 3651
10: 1 s the LORD shall make bright clouds, and NIH
11:11 s the poor of the flock that waited upon me 3651
11:12 S they weighed for my price thirty pieces 2050.1
14:15 s shall be the plague of the horse, of 3651
Mal 3:13 What have we spoken s much against thee? NIH
Mt 1:17 S all the generations from Abraham to 3767
3:15 said unto him, Suffer it to be s now: NIG
5:12 for s persecuted they the prophets which 3779
5:16 Let your light s shine before men, that they 3779
5:19 and shall teach men s, 3779
5:47 than others? do not even the publicans s? 3779
6:30 if God s clothe the grass of the field, 3779
7:12 should do to you, do ye even s to them: 3779
7:17 Even s every good tree bringeth forth good 3779
8:10 I have not found s great faith, no not in 5118
8:13 as thou hast believed, s be it done unto thee. NIG
8:28 s that no man might pass by that way. 5620
8:31 S the devils besought him, saying, If thou 1161
9:19 and followed him, and s did his disciples. NIG
9:33 saying, It was never s seen in Israel. 3779
11:26 Even s, Father: for so it seemed good in thy 3483
11:26 Father: for s it seemed good in thy sight. 3779
12:40 s shall the Son of man be three days and 3779
12:45 Even s shall it be also unto this wicked 3779
13: 2 s that he went into a ship, and sat; 5620
13:27 S the servants of the householder came and 1161
13:32 s that the birds of the air come and lodge in 5620
13:40 s shall it be in the end of this world. 3779
13:49 S shall it be at the end of the world: 3779
15:33 we have s much bread in the wilderness, 5118
15:33 as to fill s great a multitude? 5118
18:13 And if s be that he find it, verily I say unto NIG
18:14 Even s it is not the will of your Father 3779
18:31 S when his fellowservants saw what was 1161
18:35 S likewise shall my heavenly Father do also 2532
19: 8 but from the beginning it was not s. 3779
19:10 If the case of the man be s with his wife, 3779
19:12 which were s born from their mother's 3779
20: 8 S when even was come, the lord of 1161
20:16 S the last shall be first, and the first last: 3779
20:26 But it shall not be s among you: but 3779
20:34 S Jesus had compassion on them, and 1161
22:10 S those servants went out into 2532
23:28 Even s ye also outwardly appear righteous 3779
24:27 s shall also the coming of the Son of man 3779
24:33 S likewise ye, when ye shall see all these 3779
24:37 But as the days of Noe were, s shall also 3779
24:39 s shall also the coming of the Son of man 3779
24:46 his lord when he cometh shall find s doing. 3779
25: 9 Not s; lest there be not enough for us and NIG
25:20 And s he that had received five talents came NIG
27:64 s the last error shall be worse than the first. 2532
27:66 S they went, and made the sepulchre sure, 1161
28:15 S they took the money, and did as they 1161
Mk 2: 2 them, no, not s much as about the door: 3366
2: 8 that they s reasoned within themselves, 3779
3:20 s that they could not so much as eat bread 5620
3:20 so that they could not s much as eat bread. 3383
4: 1 s that he entered into a ship, and sat in 5620
4:17 in themselves, and s endure but for a time; NIG
4:26 And he said, S is the kingdom of God, as if 3779
4:32 s that the fowls of the air may lodge under 5620
4:37 beat into the ship, s that it was now full. 5620
4:40 he said unto them, Why are ye s fearful? 3779
6:31 and they had no leisure s much as to 2532+3761
7:18 Are ye s without understanding also? 3779
7:36 s much the more a great deal they NIG
8: 8 S they did eat, and were filled: and 1161
9: 3 s as no fuller on earth can white them. 3634
10: 8 s then they are no more twain, but 5620
10:43 But s shall it not be among you: but 3779
13:29 S ye in like manner, when ye shall 2532+3779
Mk 14:59 But neither s did their witness agree 3779
15: 5 answered nothing; s that Pilate marvelled. 5620
15:15 And s Pilate, willing to content the people, NIG
15:39 saw that he s cried out, and gave up 3779
16:19 S then after the Lord had spoken unto them, 3767
Lk 1:21 that he tarried s long in the temple. NIG
1:60 and said, Not s; but he shall be called John. NIG
2: 6 And s it was that, while they were there, NIG
2:21 which was s named of the angel before he NIG
5: 7 both the ships, s that they began to sink. 5620
5:10 And s was also James, and John, the sons 3668
5:15 But s much the more went there a fame NIG
6: 3 Have ye not read s much as this, NIG
6:10 And he did s: and his hand was restored 3779
6:26 s did their fathers to the false 846+2596+3588
7: 9 I have not found s great faith, no, not in 5118
9:15 And they did s, and made them all sit 3779
10:21 even s, Father; for so it seemed good in thy 3483
10:21 Father; for s it seemed good in thy sight. 3779
11: 2 Thy will be done, as in heaven, s in earth. 2532
11:30 s shall also the Son of man be to this 3779
12:21 S is he that layeth up treasure for himself, 3779
12:28 If then God s clothe the grass, which is to 3779
12:38 or come in the third watch, and find them s, 3779
12:43 his lord when he cometh shall find s doing. 3779
12:54 ye say, There cometh a shower; and s it is. 3779
14:21 S that servant came, and shewed his lord 2532
14:33 S likewise, whosoever he be of you that 3767
16: 5 S he called every one of his lord's debtors 2532
16:26 s that they which would pass from hence to 3704
17:10 S likewise ye, when ye shall have done all 3779
17:24 s shall also the Son of man be in his day. 3779
17:26 s shall it be also in the days of the Son of 3779
18:13 would not lift up s much as his eyes unto 3761
18:39 but he cried s much the more, Thou Son of NIG
20:15 S they cast him out of the vineyard, and 2532
20:20 that s they might deliver him unto NIG
21:31 S likewise ye, when ye see these things 3779
21:34 and s that day come upon you unawares. NIG
22:26 But ye shall not be s: but he that is greatest 3779
24:24 and found it even s as the women had said: 3779
Jn 3: 8 s is every one that is born of the Spirit. 3779
3:14 even s must the Son of man be lifted up: 3779
3:16 For God s loved the world, that he gave his 3779
4:40 S when the Samaritans were come unto 3767
4:46 S Jesus came again into Cana of Galilee, 3767
4:53 S the father knew that it was at the same 3767
5:21 and quickeneth them; even s the Son 3779
5:26 s hath he given to the Son to have life in 3779
6: 9 but what are they among s many? 5118
6:10 S the men sat down, in number about five 3767
6:19 S when they had rowed about five and 3767
6:57 s he that eateth me, even he shall live by 2532
7:43 S there was a division among the people 3767
8: 7 S when they continued asking him, he lift 1161
8:59 through the midst of them, and s passed by. 3779
10:15 knoweth me, even s know I the Father: 2504
11:28 And when she had s said, she went her 3778
12:37 he had done s many miracles before them, 5118
12:50 even as the Father said unto me, s I speak. 3779
13:12 S after he had washed their feet, and 3767
13:13 and Lord: and ye say well; for s I am. NIG
13:33 I go, ye cannot come; s now I say to you. 2532
14: 2 if it were not s, I would have told you. I go NIG
14: 9 Have I been s long time with you, and 5118
14:31 Father gave me commandment, even s I do. 3779
15: 8 bear much fruit; s shall ye be my disciples. 2532
15: 9 Father hath loved me, s have I loved you: 2504
17:18 even s have I also sent them into the world. NIG
18:15 followed Jesus, and s did another disciple: NIG
18:22 saying, Answerest thou the high priest s? 3779
20: 4 S they ran both together: and the other 1161
20:20 And when he had s said, he shewed unto 3778
20:21 my Father hath sent me, even s send I you. NIG
21:11 and for all there were s many, yet was not 5118
21:15 S when they had dined, Jesus saith to 3767
Ac 1:11 shall s come in like manner as ye have seen 3779
3:12 or why look ye s earnestly on us, as though NIG
3:18 that Christ should suffer, he hath s fulfilled. 3779
4:21 S when they had further threatened them, 1161
5: 8 me whether ye sold the land for s much? 5118
5: 8 so much? And she said, Yea, for s much. 5118
5:32 and s is also the Holy Ghost, whom God NIG
7: 1 said the high priest, Are these things s? 3779
7: 5 in it, no, not s much as to set his foot on: 3761
7: 8 and s Abraham begat Isaac, and 3779
7:15 S Jacob went down into Egypt, and died, 1161
7:19 s that they cast out their young children, 3588
7:51 Holy Ghost: as your fathers did, s do ye. 2532
8:32 his shearer, s opened he not his mouth: 3779
10:14 But Peter said, Not s, Lord; for I have 3365
11: 8 But I said, Not s, Lord: for nothing 3365
12: 8 And s he did. And he saith unto him, 3779
12:15 she constantly affirmed that it was even s. 3779
13: 4 S they, being sent forth by the Holy Ghost, 3767
13: 8 But Elymas the sorcerer (for s is his name 3779
13:47 For s hath the Lord commanded us, 3779
14: 1 and s spake, that a great multitude both of 3779
15:30 S when they were dismissed, they came to 3767
15:39 And the contention was s sharp between NIG
15:39 and s Barnabas took Mark, and sailed unto NIG
16: 5 And s were the churches established in 3767
16:26 s that the foundations of the prison were 5620
17:11 whether those things were s. 3779
17:33 S Paul departed from among them. 3779
19: 2 We have not s much as heard 235+3761
19:10 s that all they which dwelt in Asia heard 5620
19:12 S that from his body were brought 2532+5620
19:14 a Jew, and chief of the priests, which did s. 3778
19:16 s that they fled out of that house naked and 5620
19:20 S mightily grew the word of God and 3779
19:22 S he sent into Macedonia two of them that 1161
19:27 S that not only this our craft is in danger to 1161
20:11 even till break of day, s he departed. 3779
20:13 for s had he appointed, minding himself to 3779
Ac 20:24 s that I might finish my course with joy, 5613
20:35 I have shewed you all things, how that s 3779
21:11 S shall the Jews at Jerusalem bind the man 3779
21:35 And when he came upon the stairs, s it was, 4819
22:24 know wherefore they cried s against him. 3779
23: 7 And when he had s said, there arose a 3778
23:11 s must thou bear witness also at Rome. 3779
23:18 S he took him, and brought him to the chief 3767
23:22 S the chief captain then let the young man 3767
24: 9 saying that these things were s. 3779
24:14 s worship I the God of my fathers, 3779
27:17 strake sail, and s were driven. 3779
27:44 And s it came to pass, that they escaped all 3779
28: 9 S when this was done, others also, 3767
28:14 seven days: and s we went toward Rome. 3779
Ro 1:15 S, as much as in me is, I am ready to preach 3779
1:20 s that they are without excuse: 1519+3588
4:18 that which was spoken, S shall thy seed be. 3779
5: 3 And not only s, but we glory in tribulations NIG
5:11 And not only s, but we also joy in God NIG
5:12 and s death passed upon all men, for that all 3779
5:15 not as the offence, s also is the free gift. 3779
5:16 not as it was by one that sinned, s is the gift: NIG
5:18 even s by the righteousness of one the free 3779
5:19 s by the obedience of one shall many be 3779
5:21 even s might grace reign through 3779
6: 3 s many of us as were baptized into Jesus 3745
6: 4 even s we also should walk in newness of 3779
6:19 even s now yield your members servants to 3779
7: 2 the law to her husband s long as he liveth; NIG
7: 3 S then if, while her husband liveth, she be 686
7: 3 s that she is no adulteress, though she be 3588
7:25 S then with the mind I myself serve the law 686
8: 8 S then they that are in the flesh cannot 1161
8: 9 if s be that the Spirit of God dwell in you. 1512
8:17 if s be that we suffer with him, that we 1512
9:16 S then it is not of him that willeth, nor of 686
10:17 S then faith cometh by hearing, 686
11: 5 Even s then at this present time also there is 3779
11:16 and if the root be holy, s are the branches. 2532
11:26 And s all Israel shall be saved: as it is 3779
11:31 Even s have these also now not believed, 3779
12: 5 S we, being many, are one body in Christ, 3779
12:20 for in s doing thou shalt heap coals of fire 3778
14:12 S then every one of us shall give account of 686
15:19 s that from Jerusalem, and round about 5620
15:20 Yea, s have I strived to preach the gospel, 3779
1Co 1: 7 S that ye come behind in no gift; 5620
2:11 even s the things of God knoweth no man, 3779
3: 7 S then neither is he that planteth any thing, 5620
3:15 he himself shall be saved; yet s as by fire. 3779
4: 1 Let a man s account of us, as of 3779
5: 1 such fornication as is not s much as named 3761
5: 3 concerning him that hath s done this deed, 3779
6: 5 Is it s, that there is not a wise man amongst 3779
7:17 Lord hath called every one, s let him walk. 3779
7:17 let him walk. And s ordain I in all churches. 3779
7:26 I say, that it is good for a man s to be. 3779
7:36 and need s require, let him do what he will, 3779
7:37 and hath s decreed in his heart that he will 3778
7:38 S then he that giveth her in marriage doeth 5620
7:40 But she is happier if she s abide, after my 3779
8:12 But when ye sin s against the brethren, and 3779
9:14 Even s hath the Lord ordained that they 3779
9:15 things, that it should be s done unto me: 3779
9:24 the prize? S run, that ye may obtain. 3779
9:26 I therefore s run, not as uncertainly; so 3779
9:26 s fight I, not as one that beateth the air: 3779
11:12 even s is the man also by the woman; 3779
11:28 and s let him eat of that bread, and drink of 3779
12:12 being many, are one body: s also is Christ. 3779
13: 2 s that I could remove mountains, and 5620
14: 9 S likewise you, except ye utter by 3779
14:10 s many kinds of voices in the world, and 5118
14:12 Even s ye, forasmuch as ye are zealous of 3779
14:25 and s falling down on his face he will 3779
15:11 or they, s we preach, and so ye believed. 3779
15:11 or they, so we preach, and s ye believed. 3779
15:15 not up, if s be that the dead rise not. 686+1512
15:22 even s in Christ shall all be made alive. 3779
15:42 S also is the resurrection of the dead. It is 3779
15:45 And s it is written, The first man Adam was 3779
15:54 S when this corruptible shall have put on 1161
16: 1 to the churches of Galatia, even s do ye. 3779
2Co 1: 5 s our consolation also aboundeth by Christ. 3779
1: 7 s shall ye be also of the consolation. 3779
1:10 Who delivered us from s great a death, and 5082
2: 7 S that contrariwise ye ought rather to 5620
3: 7 s that the children of Israel could not 5620
4:12 S then death worketh in us, but life in you. 5620
5: 3 s be that being clothed we shall not be 2532
7: 7 mind toward me; s that I rejoiced the more. 5620
7:14 even s our boasting, which I made before 3779
8: 6 s he would also finish in you the same 3779
8:11 s there may be a performance also out of 3779
9: 7 in his heart, s let him give; not grudgingly, NIG
10: 7 as he is Christ's, even s are we Christ's. 3779
11: 3 s your minds should be corrupted from 3779
11: 9 to you, and s will I keep myself. NIG
11:22 s am I. Are they Israelites? so am I. Are NIG
11:22 s am I. Are they the seed of Abraham? so NIG
11:22 Are they the seed of Abraham? s am I. 2504
12:16 But be it s, I did not burden you: 1510
Gal 1: 6 I marvel that you are s soon removed from 3779
1: 9 As we said before, s say I now again, If any 2532
3: 3 Are ye s foolish? having begun in 3779
3: 4 Have ye suffered s many things in vain? 5118
3: 9 S then they which be of faith are blessed 5620
4: 3 Even s we, when we were children, were in 3779
4:29 was born after the Spirit, even s it is now. 3779
4:31 S then, brethren, we are not children of 686
5:17 s that ye cannot do the things that ye 2443
6: 2 and s fulfil the law of Christ. 3779
Eph 2:15 of twain one new man, s making peace; NIG
4:20 But ye have not s learned Christ; 3779

Eph 4:21 If s be that ye have heard him, and 1489
5:24 s *let* the wives *be* to their own husbands in 3779
5:28 S ought men to love their wives as their 3779
5:33 s love his wife even as himself; 3779
Php 1:13 S that my bonds in Christ are manifest in 5620
1:20 *s* now also Christ shall be magnified in my NIG
2:23 s soon as I shall see how it will go 302+5613
3:17 and mark them which walk s as ye have us 3779
4: 1 my joy and crown, s stand fast in the Lord, 3779
Col 2: 6 Christ Jesus the Lord, *s* walk ye in him: NIG
3:13 even as Christ forgave you, s also *do* ye. 3779
1Th 1: 7 S that ye were ensamples to all that believe 5620
1: 8 s that we need not to speak any *thing.* 5620
2: 4 in trust with the gospel, *even* s we speak; 3779
2: 8 S being affectionately desirous of you, 3779
4: 1 *s* ye would abound more *and more.* NIG
4:14 *even* s them also which sleep in Jesus will 3779
4:17 and s shall we ever be with the Lord. 3779
5: 2 of the Lord s cometh as a thief in the night. 3779
2Th 1: 4 S that we ourselves glory in you in 5620
2: 4 s that he as God sitteth in the temple of 5620
3:17 is the token in every epistle: s I write. 3779
1Ti 1: 4 than godly edifying which is in faith: *s do.* NIG
3:11 Even s *must their* wives *be* grave, 5615
6:20 and oppositions of science falsely s called: NIG
2Ti 3: 8 s do these also resist the truth: 3779
Heb 1: 4 Being made s much better than the angels, 5118
2: 3 we escape, if we neglect s great salvation; NIG
3:11 S I sware in my wrath, They shall not enter 5613
3:19 S we see that they could not enter in 2532
4: 7 in David, To day, after s long a time; 5118
5: 3 s also for himself, to offer for sins. 3779
5: 5 S also Christ glorified not himself to be 3779
6:15 And s, after he had patiently endured, 3779
7: 9 And as *I* may s[s] say, Levi also, 2031
7:22 s much was Jesus made a surety of a better 5118
9:28 S Christ was once offered to bear the sins 3779
10:25 *one another:* and s much the more, 5118
10:33 companions of them that were s used. 3779
11: 3 s that *things* which are seen were not 1519+3588
11:12 *s many* as the stars of the sky in multitude, NIG
12: 1 about with s great a cloud of witnesses, 5118
12: 1 and the sin which doth s easily beset *us,* and NIG
12:20 And if *s much as* a beast touch NIG
12:21 And s terrible was the sight, *that* Moses 3779
13: 6 S that we may boldly say, The Lord *is* my 5620
Jas 1:11 s also shall the rich *man* fade away in his 3779
2:12 S speak ye, and so do, as they that shall be 3779
2:12 So speak ye, and s do, as they that shall be 3779
2:17 Even s faith, if it hath not works, is dead, 3779
2:26 is dead, s faith without works is dead also. 3779
3: 4 which though they be s great, and 5082
3: 5 Even s the tongue is a little member, and 3779
3: 6 s is the tongue amongst our members, 3779
3:10 My brethren, these *things* ought not s to be. 3779
3:12 s *can* no fountain *both* yield salt water and 3779
1Pe 1:15 s be ye holy in all *manner of* conversation; 2532
2: 3 If s be ye have tasted that the Lord *is* 1512
2:15 For s is the will of God, that with well 3779
3:17 For *it is* better, if the will of God be s[s], 2309
4:10 *even* s minister the same one to another, NIG
5:13 saluteth you; and *s doth* Marcus my son. NIG
2Pe 1:11 For s an entrance shall be ministered unto 3779
1Jn 2: 6 abideth in him ought himself also s to walk, 3779
4:11 Beloved, if God s loved us, we ought also 3779
4:17 because as he is, s are we in this world. 2532
Rev 1: 7 shall wail because of him. Even s, Amen. 3483
2:15 S hast thou also them that hold the doctrine 3779
3:16 S *then* because thou art lukewarm, and 3779
8:12 s as the third *part* of them was darkened 2443
13:13 s that he maketh fire come down from 2532
16: 7 Even s, Lord God Almighty, true and 3483
16:18 s mighty an earthquake, *and* so great. 3779
16:18 so mighty an earthquake, *and* s great. 3779
17: 3 S he carried me away in the spirit into 2532
18: 7 s much torment and sorrow give her: 5118
18:17 one hour s great riches is come to nought. 5118
22:20 Amen. Even s, come, Lord Jesus. 3483

SOAKED (1)
Isa 34: 7 their land shall be s with blood, and 7301

SOAP See FULLER; SOPE

SOBER (12) [SOBRIETY]
2Co 5:13 or whether we be s, *it is* for your cause. 4993
1Th 5: 6 as *do* others; but let us watch and be s. 3525
5: 8 But let us, who are of the day, be s, 3525
1Ti 3: 2 vigilant, s, of good behaviour, given to 4998
3:11 not slanderers, s, faithful in all *things.* 3524
Tit 1: 8 a lover of good *men,* s, just, holy, 4998
2: 2 That the aged men be s, grave, temperate, 3524
2: 4 they may teach the young *women* to be s, 4994
2: 6 *men* likewise exhort to be s minded. 4993
1Pe 1:13 be s, and hope to the end for the grace that 3525
4: 7 be ye therefore s, and watch unto prayer. 4993
5: 8 Be s, be vigilant; because your adversary 3525

SOBERLY (2) [SOBRIETY]
Ro 12: 3 but to think s, according as God hath dealt 4993
Tit 2:12 and worldly lusts we should live s, 4996

SOBERNESS (1) [SOBRIETY]
Ac 26:25 but speak forth *the* words of truth and s. 4997

SOBRIETY (2) [SOBER, SOBERLY, SOBERNESS]
1Ti 2: 9 modest apparel, with shamefastness and s; 4997
2:15 in faith and charity and holiness with s. 4997

SOCHO (1)
1Ch 4:18 Heber the father of S, and Jekuthiel 7755

SOCHOH (1)
1Ki 4:10 to him *pertained* S, and all the land of 7755

SOCKET (1) [SOCKETS]
Ex 38:27 of the hundred talents, a talent for a s. 134

SOCKETS (54) [SOCKET]
Ex 26:19 thou shalt make forty s of silver under 134
26:19 two s under one board for his two tenons, 134
26:19 two s under another board for his two 134
26:21 their forty s *of* silver; two sockets under one 134
26:21 two s under one board, and two sockets 134
26:21 one board, and two s under another board. 134
26:25 and their s *of* silver, sixteen sockets; 134
26:25 and their sockets *of* silver, sixteen s; 134
26:25 two s under one board, and two sockets 134
26:25 one board, and two s under another board. 134
26:32 *shall be of* gold, upon the four s of silver. 134
26:37 and thou shalt cast five s of brass for them. 134
27:10 and their twenty s *shall be of* brass; 134
27:11 his twenty pillars and their twenty s *of* brass; 134
27:12 fifty cubits: their pillars ten, and their s ten. 134
27:14 their pillars three, and their s three. 134
27:15 *cubits:* their pillars three, and their s three. 134
27:16 their pillars *shall be* four, and their s four. 134
27:17 hooks *shall be of* silver, and their s *of* brass. 134
27:18 *of* fine twined linen, and their s *of* brass. 134
35:11 and his boards, his bars, his pillars, and his s, 134
35:17 their s, and the hanging for the door of 134
36:24 forty s of silver he made under the twenty 134
36:24 two s under one board for his two tenons, 134
36:24 two s under another board for his two 134
36:26 their forty s *of* silver; two sockets under one 134
36:26 two s under one board, and two sockets 134
36:26 one board, and two s under another board. 134
36:30 their s *were* sixteen sockets *of* silver, 134
36:30 their sockets *were* sixteen s *of* silver, 134
36:30 sockets *of* silver, under every board two s. 134
36:36 *of* gold; and he cast for them four s of silver. 134
36:38 with gold: but their five s *were of* brass. 134
38:10 *were* twenty, and their brasen s twenty; 134
38:11 *were* twenty, and their s *of* brass twenty; 134
38:12 fifty cubits, their pillars ten, and their s ten; 134
38:14 their pillars three, and their s three. 134
38:15 their pillars three, and their s three. 134
38:17 the s for the pillars *were of* brass; the hooks 134
38:19 pillars *were* four, and their s *of* brass four; 134
38:27 of silver were cast the s of the sanctuary, 134
38:27 of the sanctuary, and the s of the vail; 134
38:27 an hundred s of the hundred talents, a talent 134
38:30 therewith he made the s to the door of 134
38:31 the s of the court round about, and 134
38:31 the s of the court gate, and all the pins of 134
39:33 his boards, his bars, and his pillars, and his s, 134
39:40 and his s, and the hanging for the court gate, 134
40:18 fastened his s, and set up the boards thereof, 134
Nu 3:36 and the s thereof, and all the vessels thereof, 134
3:37 and their s, and their pins, and their cords. 134
4:31 and the pillars thereof, and s thereof, 134
4:32 their s, and their pins, and their cords, 134
SS 5:15 *as* pillars of marble, set upon s of fine gold: 134

SOCO See SHOCHO; SHOCO; SOCHO

SOCOH (2)
Jos 15:35 Jarmuth, and Adullam, S, and Azekah, 7755
15:48 in the mountains, Shamir, and Jattir, and S, 7755

SOD (2) [SODDEN]
Ge 25:29 Jacob s pottage: and Esau came from 2102
2Ch 35:13 the *other* holy *offerings* s they in pots, and 1310

SODA See NITRE

SODDEN (6) [SOD]
Ex 12: 9 s at all with water, but roast with 1310+1311
Lev 6:28 the earthen vessel wherein it is s shall be 1310
6:28 if it be s in a brasen pot, it shall be both 1310
Nu 6:19 the priest shall take the s shoulder of 1311
1Sa 2:15 for he will not have s flesh of thee, but raw. 1310
La 4:10 The hands of the pitiful women have s their 1310

SODERING (1)
Isa 41: 7 smote the anvil, saying, It *is* ready for the s: 1694

SODI (1)
Nu 13:10 the tribe of Zebulun, Gaddiel the son of S. 5476

SODOM (48) [SODOMA, SODOMITE, SODOMITES]
Ge 10:19 as thou goest unto S, and Gomorrah, and 5467
13:10 before the LORD destroyed S and 5467
13:12 of the plain, and pitched his tent toward S. 5467
13:13 the men of S *were* wicked and 5467
14: 2 *That these* made war with Bera king of S, 5467
14: 8 there went out the king of S, and the king 5467
14:10 the kings of S and Gomorrah fled, and 5467
14:11 they took all the goods of S and Gomorrah, 5467
14:12 who dwelt in S, and his goods, and 5467
14:17 the king of S went out to meet him after his 5467
14:21 the king of S said unto Abram, Give me 5467
14:22 Abram said to the king of S, I have lift up 5467
18:16 rose up from thence, and looked toward S: 5467
18:20 Because the cry of S and Gomorrah is 5467
18:22 their faces from thence, and went toward S: 5467
18:26 If I find in S fifty righteous within the city, 5467
19: 1 there came two angels to S at even; and 5467
19: 1 Sodom at even; and Lot sat in the gate of S: 5467
19: 4 the men of the city, *even* the men of S, 5467
19:24 the LORD rained upon S and 5467
19:28 he looked toward S and Gomorrah, and 5467
Dt 29:23 like the overthrow of S, and Gomorrah, 5467
32:32 For their vine *is* of the vine of S, and of 5467
Isa 1: 9 we should have been as S, *and* we should 5467
1:10 the word of the LORD, ye rulers of S; 5467
3: 9 they declare their sin as S, they hide *it* not. 5467
13:19 shall be as when God overthrew S and 5467
Jer 23:14 they are all of them unto me as S, and 5467
49:18 As *in* the overthrow of S and Gomorrah 5467
50:40 As God overthrew S and Gomorrah and 5467
La 4: 6 greater than the punishment of the sin of S, 5467
Eze 16:46 at thy right hand, *is* S and her daughters. 5467
16:48 the Lord GOD, S thy sister hath not done, 5467
16:49 this was the iniquity of thy sister S, pride, 5467
16:53 the captivity of S and her daughters, and 5467
16:55 When thy sisters, S and her daughters, 5467
16:56 For thy sister S was not mentioned by thy 5467
Am 4:11 as God overthrew S and Gomorrah, and 5467
Zep 2: 9 Surely Moab shall be as S, and the children 5467
Mt 10:15 It shall be more tolerable for the land of S 4670
11:23 have been done in thee, had been done in S, 4670
11:24 for the land of S in the day of judgment, 4670
Mk 6:11 It shall be more tolerable for S and 4670
Lk 10:12 it shall be more tolerable in that day for S, 4670
17:29 But the *same* day that Lot went out of S it 4670
2Pe 2: 6 And turning the cities of S and 4670
Jude 1: 7 *Even* as S and Gomorrha, and the cities 4670
Rev 11: 8 which spiritually is called S and Egypt, 4670

SODOMA (1) [SODOM]
Ro 9:29 we had been as S, and been made like unto 4670

SODOMITE (1) [SODOM]
Dt 23:17 of Israel, nor a s of the sons of Israel. 6948

SODOMITES (4) [SODOM]
1Ki 14:24 there were also s in the land: *and* they did 6945
15:12 he took away the s out of the land, and 6945
22:46 the remnant of the s, which remained in 6945
2Ki 23: 7 he brake down the houses of the s, 6945

SOEVER (16) [EVER, SO]
Lev 15: 9 what saddle s he rideth upon that hath 834+3605
17: 3 What man s *there be* of the house of 376+376
22: 4 What man s of the seed of Aaron *is* a 376+376
Dt 12:32 What thing s I command you, 834+3605
2Sa 15:35 *that* what thing s thou shalt hear out 834+3605
24: 3 how many s they be, an hundredfold, 3509.1
1Ki 8:38 and supplication s be *made* by any man, 3605
2Ch 6:29 what supplication s shall be *made* of any 834
19:10 what cause s shall come to you of 834+3605
Mk 3:28 blasphemies wherewith s they shall 302+3745
6:10 In what place s ye enter into a 1437+3699
11:24 What *things* s ye desire, when ye pray, 302
Jn 5:19 for what *things* s he doeth, these also 302+3739
20:23 Whose s sins ye remit, they are remitted unto 302
20:23 *and* whose s *sins* ye retain, they are retained. 302
Ro 3:19 Now we know that what *things* s the law 3745

SOFT (8) [SOFTER, SOFTLY]
Job 23:16 For God maketh my heart s, and 7401
41: 3 unto thee? will he speak s *words* unto thee? 7390
Ps 65:10 thou makest it s with showers: 4127
Pr 15: 1 A s answer turneth away wrath: but 7390
25:15 and a s tongue breaketh the bone. 7390
Mt 11: 8 A man clothed in s raiment? behold, 3120
11: 8 they that wear s *clothing* are in kings' 3120
Lk 7:25 A man clothed in s raiment? Behold, 3120

SOFTER (1) [SOFT]
Ps 55:21 his words were s than oil, yet *were* they 7401

SOFTLY (7) [SOFT]
Ge 33:14 I will lead on s, according as 328+3807.1
Jdg 4:21 went s unto him, and 3814+871.1+1886.1
Ru 3: 7 *of corn:* and she came s, 3909+871.1+1886.1
1Ki 21:27 and fasted, and lay in sackcloth, and went s. 328
Isa 8: 6 the waters of Shiloah that go s, 328+3807.1
38:15 himself hath done *it:* I shall go s all my 1718
Ac 27:13 And when the south wind blew s, 5285

SOIL (1)
Eze 17: 8 It *was* planted in a good s by great waters, 7704

SOJOURN (33) [SOJOURNED, SOJOURNER, SOJOURNERS, SOJOURNETH, SOJOURNING]
Ge 12:10 Abram went down into Egypt to s there; 1481
19: 9 said *again,* This one *fellow* came in to s, 1481
26: 3 S in this land, and I will be with thee, and 1481
47: 4 For to s in the land are we come; 1481
Ex 12:48 when a stranger shall s with thee, and 1481
Lev 17: 8 or of the strangers which s among you, 1481
17:10 or of the strangers that s among you, 1481
17:13 or of the strangers that s among you, 1481
19:33 if a stranger s with thee in your land, 1481
20: 2 or of the strangers that s in Israel, 1481
25:45 of the strangers that do s among you, 1481
Nu 9:14 if a stranger shall s among you, and 1481
15:14 if a stranger s with you, or whosoever *be* 1481
Jdg 17: 8 to s where he could find *a place:* 1481
17: 9 I go to s where I may find *a place.* 1481
Ru 1: 1 went to s in the country of Moab, 1481
1Ki 17:20 evil upon the widow with whom I s, 1481
2Ki 8: 1 and s wheresoever thou canst sojourn: 1481
8: 1 and sojourn wheresoever thou canst s: 1481
Ps 120: 5 Woe is me, that I s *in* Mesech, *that* I dwell 1481
Isa 23: 7 her own feet shall carry her afar off to s. 1481
52: 4 went down aforetime *into* Egypt to s there; 1481
Jer 42:15 faces to enter *into* Egypt, and go to s there; 1481
42:17 set their faces to go *into* Egypt to s there; 1481
42:22 the place whither ye desire to go *and* to s. 1481
43: 2 thee to say, Go not *into* Egypt to s there: 1481
44:12 faces to go *into* the land of Egypt to s there, 1481
44:14 which are gone into the land of Egypt to s 1481
44:28 that are gone into the land of Egypt to s 1481
La 4:15 the heathen, They shall no more s *there.* 1481
Eze 20:38 them forth out of the country where they s, 4033
47:22 to the strangers that s among you, 1481
Ac 7: 6 his seed should s in a strange land; 1510+3941

SOJOURNED (12) [SOJOURN]
Ge 20: 1 between Kadesh and Shur, and s in Gerar. 1481
21:23 and to the land wherein thou hast s. 1481
21:34 Abraham s in the Philistines' land many 1481
32: 4 I have s with Laban, and stayed *there* until 1481
35:27 *is* Hebron, where Abraham and Isaac s. 1481
Dt 18: 6 where he s, and come with all the desire of 1481
26: 5 s there with a few, and became there a 1481
Jdg 17: 7 of Judah, who *was* a Levite, and he s there. 1481
19:16 also of mount Ephraim; and he s in Gibeah: 1481
2Ki 8: 2 s in the land of the Philistines seven years. 1481
Ps 105:23 *into* Egypt; and Jacob s in the land of Ham. 1481
Heb 11: 9 By faith he s in the land of promise, as *in* a *3939*

SOJOURNER (8) [SOJOURN]
Ge 23: 4 I *am* a stranger and a s with you: give me a 8453
Lev 22:10 eat *of* the holy *thing:* a s of the priest's, 8453
25:35 *yea, though he be* a stranger, or a s; that he 8453
25:40 *and* as a s, he shall be with thee, *and* 8453
25:47 if a s or stranger wax rich by thee, and 1616
25:47 sell himself unto the stranger *or* s by thee, 8453
Nu 35:15 for the stranger, and for the s among them: 8453
Ps 39:12 with thee, *and* a s, as all my fathers *were.* 8453

SOJOURNERS (3) [SOJOURN]
Lev 25:23 for ye *were* strangers and s with me. 8453
2Sa 4: 3 to Gittaim, and were s there until this day.) 1481
1Ch 29:15 before thee, and s, as *were* all our fathers: 8453

SOJOURNETH (15) [SOJOURN]
Ex 3:22 of her that s in her house, jewels of silver, 1481
12:49 and unto the stranger that s among you. 1481
Lev 16:29 or a stranger that s among you: 1481
17:12 neither shall any stranger that s among you 1481
18:26 nor any stranger that s among you: 1481
25: 6 and for thy stranger that s with thee, 1481
Nu 15:15 also for the stranger that s *with you,* an 1481
15:16 and for the stranger that s with you. 1481
15:26 and the stranger that s among them; 1481
15:29 and for the stranger that s among them. 1481
19:10 unto the stranger that s among them, for a 1481
Jos 20: 9 and for the stranger that s among them, 1481
Ezr 1: 4 remaineth in any place where he s, 1481
Eze 14: 7 or of the stranger that s in Israel, 1481
47:23 to pass, *that* in what tribe the stranger s, 1481

SOJOURNING (3) [SOJOURN]
Ex 12:40 Now the s of the children of Israel, 4186
Jdg 19: 1 that there was a certain Levite s on the side 1481
1Pe 1:17 pass the time of your s *here* in fear: *3940*

SOLACE (1)
Pr 7:18 the morning: let us s ourselves with loves. 5965

SOLD (82) [SELL]
Ge 25:33 to him: and he s his birthright unto Jacob. 4376
31:15 for he hath s us, and hath quite devoured 4376
37:28 s Joseph to the Ishmeelites for twenty 4376
37:36 the Medanites s him into Egypt unto 4376
41:56 the storehouses, and s unto the Egyptians; 7666
42: 6 he *it was* that s to all the people of the land: 7666
45: 4 Joseph your brother, whom ye s into Egypt. 4376
45: 5 angry with yourselves, that ye s me hither: 4376
47:20 for the Egyptians s every man his field, 4376
47:22 gave them: wherefore they s not their lands. 4376
Ex 22: 3 then he shall be s for his theft. 4376
Lev 25:23 The land shall not be s for ever: for the land 4376
25:25 hath s away *some* of his possession, and 4376
25:25 shall he redeem **that which** his brother s. 4465
25:27 the overplus unto the man to whom he s it; 4376
25:28 **that which is** s shall remain in the hand of 4465
25:29 redeem it within a whole year after it is s; 4465
25:33 the house **that was** s, and the city of his 4465
25:34 of the suburbs of their cities may not be s; 4376
25:39 by thee be waxen poor, and be s unto thee; 4376
25:42 they shall not be s as bondmen. 4376+4466
25:48 After *that* he is s he may be redeemed 4376
25:50 that he was s to him unto the year of jubile: 4376
27:20 or if he have s the field to another man, 4376
27:27 it shall be s according to thy estimation. 4376
27:28 of his possession, shall be s or redeemed: 4376
Dt 15:12 be s unto thee, and serve thee six years; 4376
28:68 there ye shall be s unto your enemies for 4376
32:30 except their Rock had s them, and 4376
Jdg 2:14 he s them into the hands of their enemies 4376
3: 8 he s them into the hand of 4376
4: 2 the LORD s them into the hand of Jabin 4376
10: 7 he s them into the hands of the Philistines, 4376
1Sa 12: 9 he s them into the hand of Sisera, captain of 4376
1Ki 21:20 thou hast s thyself to work evil in the sight 4376
2Ki 6:25 until an ass's head was s for fourscore NIH
7: 1 a measure of fine flour *be* s for a shekel, NIH
7:16 So a measure of fine flour was s for a NIH
17:17 s themselves to do evil in the sight of 4376
Ne 5: 8 the Jews, which were s unto the heathen; 4376
5: 8 or shall they be s unto us? Then held they 4376
13:15 *them* in the day wherein they s victuals. 4376
13:16 s on the sabbath unto the children of Judah, 4376
Est 7: 4 For we are s, I and my people, to be 4376
7: 4 if we had been s for bondmen and 4376
Ps 105:17 *even* Joseph, *who* was s for a servant: 4376
Isa 50: 1 of my creditors *is it* to whom I have s 4376
50: 1 for your iniquities have you s yourselves, 4376
52: 3 Ye have s yourselves for nought; 4376
Jer 34:14 a Hebrew, which hath been s unto thee; 4376
La 5: 4 for money; our wood is s *unto us.* 4242+871.1
Eze 7:13 the seller shall not return to that which is s, 4465
Joel 3: 3 and s a girl for wine, that they might drink. 4376
3: 6 the children of Jerusalem have ye s unto 4376
3: 7 out of the place whither ye have s them, 4376
Am 2: 6 because they s the righteous for silver, and 4376
Mt 10:29 Are not two sparrows s for a farthing? and *4453*
13:46 went and s all that he had, and bought it. *4097*
18:25 his lord commanded him to be s, and *4097*
21:12 and cast out all them that s and bought in *4453*
21:12 and the seats of them that s doves, *4453*
26: 9 For this ointment might have been s for *4097*
Mk 11:15 and began to cast out them that s and *4453*
11:15 and the seats of them that s doves; *4453*
14: 5 For it might have been s for more than *4097*
Lk 12: 6 Are not five sparrows s for two farthings, *4453*
17:28 did eat, they drank, they bought, they s, *4453*
19:45 and began to cast out them that s therein, *4453*
Jn 2:14 And found in the temple those that s oxen *4453*
2:16 And said unto them that s doves, *4453*
12: 5 Why was not this ointment s for three *4097*
Ac 2:45 And s their possessions and goods, and *4097*
4:34 were possessors of lands or houses s them, *4453*
4:34 brought the prices of the *things* that were s, *4097*
4:37 s *it,* and brought the money, and laid *it* at *4453*
5: 1 with Sapphira his wife, s a possession, *4453*
5: 4 and after it was s, was it not in thine own *4097*
5: 8 Tell me whether ye s the land for so much? *591*
7: 9 moved with envy, s Joseph into Egypt: *591*
Ro 7:14 law is spiritual: but I am carnal, s under sin. *4097*
1Co 10:25 Whatsoever is s in the shambles, *that* eat, *4453*
Heb 12:16 who for one morsel of meat s his birthright. *591*

SOLDIER (5) [FELLOWSOLDIER, SOLDIERS, SOLDIERS']
Jn 19:23 and made four parts, to every s a part; *4757*
Ac 10: 7 a devout s of them that waited on him *4757*
28:16 to dwell by himself with a s that kept him. *4757*
2Ti 2: 3 as a good s of Jesus Christ. *4757*
2: 4 please him who hath **chosen** *him* **to be a** s. *4758*

SOLDIERS (29) [SOLDIER]
1Ch 7: 4 *were* bands of s for war, six and 6635
7:11 two hundred s, *fit to* go out *for* war NIH
2Ch 25:13 the s of the army which Amaziah sent back, 1121
Ezr 8:22 ashamed to require of the king a band *of* s NIH
Isa 15: 4 the **armed** s of Moab shall cry out; 2502
Mt 8: 9 a man under authority, having s under me: *4757*
27:27 Then the s of the governor took Jesus into *4757*
27:27 and gathered unto him the whole band *of* s. NIG
28:12 they gave large money unto the s, *4757*
Mk 15:16 And the s led him away into the hall, *4757*
Lk 3:14 And *the* s likewise demanded of him, *4754*
7: 8 having under me s, and I say unto one, Go, *4757*
23:36 And the s also mocked him, coming to *him,* *4757*
Jn 19: 2 And the s platted a crown of thorns, and *4757*
19:23 Then the s, when they had crucified Jesus, *4757*
19:24 cast lots. These *things* therefore the s did. *4757*
19:32 Then came the s, and brake the legs of *4757*
19:34 But one of the s with a spear pierced his *4757*
Ac 12: 4 delivered *him* to four quaternions of s to *4757*
12: 6 night Peter was sleeping between two s, *4757*
12:18 there was no small stir among the s, *4757*
21:32 Who immediately took s and centurions, *4757*
21:32 when they saw the chief captain and the s, *4757*
21:35 that he was borne of the s for the violence *4757*
23:10 commanded the s to go down, and to take *4753*
23:23 Make ready two hundred s to go to *4757*
27:31 Then the s, as it was commanded them, *4757*
27:31 Paul said to the centurion and to the s, *4757*
27:32 Then the s cut off the ropes of the boat, and *4757*

SOLDIERS' (1) [SOLDIER]
Ac 27:42 And the s counsel was to kill the prisoners, *4757*

SOLE (12) [SOLES]
Ge 8: 9 the dove found no rest for the s of her foot, 3709
Dt 28:35 from the s of thy foot unto the top of thy 3709
28:56 which would not adventure to set the s of 3709
28:65 neither shall the s of thy foot have rest: 3709
Jos 1: 3 Every place that the s of your foot shall 3709
2Sa 14:25 from the s of his foot even to the crown of 3709
2Ki 19:24 with the s of my feet have I dried up all 3709
Job 2: 7 smote Job with sore boils from the s of his 3709
Isa 1: 6 From the s of the foot even unto the head 3709
37:25 with the s of my feet have I dried up all 3709
Eze 1: 7 the s of their feet *was* like the sole of a 3709
1: 7 the sole of their feet *was* like the s of a 3709

SOLEMN (29) [SOLEMNITIES, SOLEMNITY, SOLEMNLY]
Lev 23:36 it *is* a s **assembly**; *and* ye shall do no 6116
Nu 10:10 in your s **days**, and in the beginnings of 4150
15: 3 or in a freewill offering, or in your s **feasts**, 4150
29:35 the eighth day ye shall have a s **assembly**; 6116
Dt 16: 8 on the seventh day *shall be* a s **assembly** to 6116
16:15 Seven days shalt thou **keep a** s **feast** unto 2287
2Ki 10:20 Jehu said, Proclaim a s **assembly** for Baal. 6116
2Ch 2: 4 and on the s **feasts** of the LORD our God. 4150
7: 9 in the eighth day they made a s **assembly**: 6116
8:13 and on the new moons, and on the s **feasts**, 4150
Ne 8:18 on the eighth day *was* a s **assembly**, 6116
Ps 81: 3 in the time appointed, on our s **feast** day. 2282
92: 3 the psaltery; upon the harp with a s **sound**. 1902
Isa 1:13 *it is* iniquity, even the s **meeting**. 6116
La 1: 4 because none come to the s **feasts**. 4150
2: 6 the LORD hath caused the s **feasts** and 4150
2: 7 of the LORD, as *in* the day of a s **feast**. 4150
2:22 Thou hast called as *in* a s day my terrors 4150
Eze 36:38 as the flock of Jerusalem in her s **feasts**; 4150
46: 9 come before the LORD in the s **feasts**, 4150
Hos 2:11 and her sabbaths, and all her s **feasts**. 4150
9: 5 What will ye do in the s day, and in the day 4150
12: 9 in tabernacles, as *in* the days of the s **feast**. 4150
Joel 1:14 call a s **assembly**, gather the elders *and* 6116
2:15 in Zion, sanctify a fast, call a s **assembly**: 6116
Am 5:21 and I will not smell in your s **assemblies**. 6116
Na 1:15 O Judah, keep thy s **feasts**, perform thy 2282
Zep 3:18 *them that are* sorrowful for the s **assembly**, 4150
Mal 2: 3 your faces, *even* the dung of your s **feasts**; 2282

SOLEMNITIES (3) [SOLEMN]
Isa 33:20 Look upon Zion, the city of our s: 4150
Eze 45:17 in the sabbaths in all s of the house of 4150
46:11 in the s the meat offering shall be an ephah 4150

SOLEMNITY (2) [SOLEMN]
Dt 31:10 in the s of the year of release, in the feast of 4150
Isa 30:29 as *in* the night when a holy s is kept; 2282

SOLEMNLY (2) [SOLEMN]
Ge 43: 3 man did s **protest** unto us, saying, 5749+5749
1Sa 8: 9 howbeit yet **protest** s unto them, and 5749+5749

SOLES (7) [SOLE]
Dt 11:24 Every place whereon the s of your feet 3709
Jos 3:13 as soon as the s of the feet of the priests 3709
4:18 the s of the priests' feet were lift up unto 3709
1Ki 5: 3 until the LORD put them under the s of 3709
Isa 60:14 bow themselves down at the s of thy feet; 3709
Eze 43: 7 and the place of the s of my feet, 3709
Mal 4: 3 for they shall be ashes under the s of your 3709

SOLITARILY (1) [SOLITARY]
Mic 7:14 which dwell s *in* the wood, in 910+3807.1

SOLITARY (7) [SOLITARILY]
Job 3: 7 Lo, let that night be s, let no joyful voice 1565
30: 3 For want and famine *they were* s; flying 1565
Ps 68: 6 God setteth the s in families: he bringeth 3173
107: 4 They wandered in the wilderness in a s 3452
Isa 35: 1 and the s **place** shall be glad *for* them; 6723
La 1: 1 How doth the city sit s, *that was* full of 910
Mk 1:35 and departed into a s place, and *2048*

SOLOMON (281) [JEDIDIAH, SOLOMON'S]
2Sa 5:14 Shammua, and Shobab, and Nathan, and S, 8010
12:24 she bare a son, and he called his name S: 8010
1Ki 1:10 and the mighty *men,* and S his brother, 8010
1:11 spake unto Bath-sheba the mother of S, 8010
1:12 thine own life, and the life of thy son S. 8010
1:13 Assuredly S thy son shall reign after me, 8010
1:17 *saying,* Assuredly S thy son shall reign 8010
1:19 but S thy servant hath he not called. 8010
1:21 and my son S shall be *counted* offenders. 8010
1:26 and thy servant S, hath he not called. 8010
1:30 Assuredly S thy son shall reign after me, 8010
1:33 cause S my son to ride upon mine own 8010
1:34 with the trumpet, and say, God save king S. 8010
1:37 even so be he with S, and make his throne 8010
1:38 caused S to ride upon king David's mule, 8010
1:39 of oil out of the tabernacle, and anointed S. 8010
1:39 and all the people said, God save king S. 8010
1:43 Verily our lord king David hath made S 8010
1:46 also S sitteth on the throne of the kingdom. 8010
1:47 God make the name of S better than thy 8010
1:50 Adonijah feared because of S, and arose, 8010
1:51 it was told S, saying, Behold, 8010
1:51 Behold, Adonijah feareth king S: 8010
1:51 Let king S swear unto me to day that he 8010
1:52 S said, If he will shew himself a worthy 8010
1:53 So king S sent, and they brought him down 8010
1:53 he came and bowed himself to king S: and 8010
1:53 and S said unto him, Go to thine house. 8010
2: 1 and he charged S his son, saying, 8010
2:12 sat S upon the throne of David his father; 8010
2:13 came to Bath-sheba the mother of S. 8010
2:17 he said, Speak, I pray thee, unto S the king, 8010
2:19 Bath-sheba therefore went unto king S, 8010
2:22 king S answered and said unto his mother, 8010
2:23 king S sware by the LORD, saying, God 8010
2:25 king S sent by the hand of Benaiah the son 8010
2:27 So S thrust out Abiathar from being priest 8010
2:29 it was told king S that Joab was fled unto 8010
2:29 S sent Benaiah the son of Jehoiada, saying, 8010
2:41 it was told S that Shimei had gone from 8010
2:45 king S *shall be* blessed, and the throne of 8010
2:46 kingdom was established in the hand of S. 8010
3: 1 S made affinity with Pharaoh king of 8010
3: 3 S loved the LORD, walking in the statutes 8010
3: 4 a thousand burnt offerings did S offer up on 8010
3: 5 In Gibeon the LORD appeared to S in a 8010
3: 6 S said, Thou hast shewed unto thy servant 8010
3:10 the Lord, that S had asked this thing. 8010
3:15 S awoke; and behold, *it was* a dream. 8010
4: 1 So king S was king over all Israel. 8010
4: 7 S had twelve officers over all Israel, which 8010
4:11 which had Taphath the daughter of S to 8010
4:15 he also took Basmath the daughter of S to 8010
4:21 S reigned over all kingdoms from the river 8010
4:21 and served S all the days of his life. 8010
4:25 Dan even to Beer-sheba, all the days of S. 8010
4:26 S had forty thousand stalls of horses for his 8010
4:27 those officers provided victual for king S, 8010
4:29 God gave S wisdom and 8010
4:34 came of all people to hear the wisdom of S, 8010
5: 1 king of Tyre sent his servants unto S; 8010
5: 2 And S sent to Hiram, saying, 8010
5: 7 to pass, when Hiram heard the words of S, 8010
5: 8 Hiram sent to S, saying, I have considered 8010
5:10 So Hiram gave S cedar trees and fir trees 8010
5:11 S gave Hiram twenty thousand measures of 8010
5:11 pure oil: thus gave S to Hiram year by year. 8010
5:12 the LORD gave S wisdom, as he promised 8010
5:12 there was peace between Hiram and S; and 8010
5:13 king S raised a levy out of all Israel; and 8010
5:15 S had threescore and ten thousand that bare 8010
6: 2 the house which king S built for 8010
6:11 the word of the LORD came to S, saying, 8010
6:14 So S built the house, and finished it. 8010
6:21 So S overlaid the house within with pure 8010
7: 1 S was building his own house thirteen 8010
7: 8 S made also a house for Pharaoh's 8010
7:13 And king S sent and fet Hiram out of Tyre. 8010
7:14 he came to king S, and wrought all his 8010
7:40 made king S *for* the house of the LORD: 8010
7:45 which Hiram made to king S *for* the house 8010

S

1Ki 7:47 S left all the vessels *unweighed,* because 8010
7:48 S made all the vessels that *pertained unto* 8010
7:51 So was ended all the work that king S made 8010
7:51 S brought in the *things* which David his 8010
8: 1 S assembled the elders of Israel, and all 8010
8: 1 children of Israel, unto king S *in* Jerusalem, 8010
8: 2 king S at the feast in the month Ethanim, 8010
8: 5 king S, and all the congregation of Israel, 8010
8:12 spake S, The LORD said that *he* would 8010
8:22 S stood before the altar of the LORD in 8010
8:54 *that* when S had made an end of praying all 8010
8:63 S offered a sacrifice of peace offerings, 8010
8:65 at that time S held a feast, and all Israel 8010
9: 1 when S had finished the building of 8010
9: 2 That the LORD appeared to S the second 8010
9:10 when S had built the two houses, the house 8010
9:11 of Tyre had furnished S with cedar trees 8010
9:11 king S gave Hiram twenty cities in the land 8010
9:12 to see the cities which S had given him; 8010
9:15 this *is* the reason of the levy which king S 8010
9:17 S built Gezer, and Beth-horon the nether, 8010
9:19 all the cities of store that S had, and cities 8010
9:19 that which S desired to build in Jerusalem, 8010
9:21 upon those did S levy a tribute of 8010
9:22 of the children of Israel did S make no 8010
9:24 unto her house which *S* had built for her: NIH
9:25 three times in a year did S offer burnt 8010
9:26 king S made a navy *of ships* in 8010
9:27 of the sea, with the servants of S. 8010
9:28 and twenty talents, and brought *it* to king S. 8010
10: 1 of S concerning the name of the LORD, 8010
10: 2 when she was come to S, she communed 8010
10: 3 S told her all her questions: there was not 8010
10:10 which the queen of Sheba gave to king S. 8010
10:13 king S gave unto the queen of Sheba all her 8010
10:13 besides *that* which S gave her of his royal 8010
10:14 Now the weight of gold that came to S in 8010
10:16 king S made two hundred targets *of* beaten 8010
10:21 was nothing accounted of in the days of S. 8010
10:23 So king S exceeded all the kings of 8010
10:24 all the earth sought to S, to hear his 8010
10:26 S gathered together chariots and horsemen: 8010
10:28 And S had horses brought out of Egypt, and 8010
11: 1 king S loved many strange women, 8010
11: 2 after their gods: S clave unto these in love. 8010
11: 4 For it came to pass, when S was old, 8010
11: 5 For S went after Ashtoreth the goddess of 8010
11: 6 S did evil in the sight of the LORD, and 8010
11: 7 did S build a high place for Chemosh, 8010
11: 9 And the LORD was angry with S, because 8010
11:11 Wherefore the LORD said unto S, 8010
11:14 the LORD stirred up an adversary unto S, 8010
11:25 was an adversary to Israel all the days of S, 8010
11:27 S built Millo, *and* repaired the breaches of 8010
11:28 S seeing the young man that he was 8010
11:31 will rent the kingdom out of the hand of S, 8010
11:40 S sought therefore to kill Jeroboam. 8010
11:40 and was in Egypt until the death of S. 8010
11:41 the rest of the acts of S, and all that he did, 8010
11:41 not written in the book of the acts of S? 8010
11:42 the time that S reigned in Jerusalem over 8010
11:43 S slept with his fathers, and was buried in 8010
12: 2 he was fled from the presence of king S, 8010
12: 6 that stood before S his father while he *yet* 8010
12:21 kingdom again to Rehoboam the son of S. 8010
12:23 the son of S, king of Judah, and unto all 8010
14:21 Rehoboam the son of S reigned in Judah. 8010
14:26 all the shields of gold which S had made. 8010
2Ki 21: 7 to S his son, In this house, and 8010
23:13 which S the king of Israel had builded for 8010
24:13 cut in pieces all the vessels of gold which S 8010
25:16 the bases which S had made for the house 8010
1Ch 3: 5 and Shobab, and Nathan, and S, four, 8010
6:10 in the temple that S built in Jerusalem:) 8010
6:32 until S had built the house of the LORD in 8010
14: 4 Shammua, and Shobab, Nathan, and S, 8010
18: 8 wherewith S made the brasen sea, and 8010
22: 5 my son *is* young and tender, and 8010
22: 6 he called for S his son, and charged him to 8010
22: 7 David said to S, My son, *as for* me, it was 8010
22: 9 for his name shall be S, and I will give 8010
22:17 all the princes of Israel to help S his son, 8010
23: 1 *of* days, he made S his son king over Israel. 8010
28: 5 he hath chosen S my son to sit upon 8010
28: 6 he said unto me, S thy son, he shall build 8010
28: 9 thou, S my son, know thou the God of thy 8010
28:11 David gave to S his son the pattern of 8010
28:20 David said to S his son, Be strong and 8010
29: 1 S my son, whom alone God hath chosen, *is* 8010
29:19 give unto S my son a perfect heart, to keep 8010
29:22 they made S the son of David king 8010
29:23 S sat on the throne of the LORD as king 8010
29:24 submitted themselves unto S the king. 8010
29:25 the LORD magnified S exceedingly in 8010
29:28 honour: and S his son reigned in his stead. 8010
2Ch 1: 1 S the son of David was strengthened in his 8010
1: 2 S spake unto all Israel, to the captains of 8010
1: 3 So S, and all the congregation with him, 8010
1: 5 and S and the congregation sought *unto* it. 8010
1: 6 S went up thither to the brasen altar before 8010
1: 7 In that night did God appear unto S, and 8010
1: 8 S said unto God, Thou hast shewed great 8010
1:11 God said to S, Because this was in thine 8010
1:13 S came *from his journey* to the high place 8010
1:14 S gathered chariots and horsemen: and 8010
1:16 And S had horses brought out of Egypt, and 8010
2: 1 S determined to build a house for the name 8010
2: 2 S told out threescore and ten thousand men 8010
2: 3 S sent to Huram the king of Tyre, saying, 8010
2:11 which he sent to S, Because the LORD 8010
2:17 S numbered all the strangers that *were* in 8010
3: 1 S began to build the house of the LORD at 8010
3: 3 Now these *are the things wherein* S was 8010
4:11 to make for king S for the house of God; 8010
4:16 did Huram his father make to king S for 8010
2Ch 4:18 Thus S made all these vessels in great 8010
4:19 S made all the vessels that *were for* 8010
5: 1 Thus all the work that S made for the house 8010
5: 1 S brought in *all the things* that David his 8010
5: 2 S assembled the elders of Israel, and all 8010
5: 6 Also king S, and all the congregation of 8010
6: 1 said S, The LORD hath said that *he* would 8010
6:13 For S had made a brasen scaffold, of five 8010
7: 1 Now when S had made an end of praying, 8010
7: 5 king S offered a sacrifice of twenty and 8010
7: 7 Moreover S hallowed the middle of 8010
7: 7 the brasen altar which S had made was not 8010
7: 8 Also at the same time S kept the feast seven 8010
7:10 and to S, and to Israel his people. 8010
7:11 Thus S finished the house of the LORD, 8010
7:12 the LORD appeared to S by night, and 8010
8: 1 wherein S had built the house of 8010
8: 2 the cities which Huram had restored to S, 8010
8: 2 S built them, and caused the children of 8010
8: 3 S went *to* Hamath-zobah, and 8010
8: 6 all the store cities that S had, and all 8010
8: 6 all that S desired to build in Jerusalem, and 8010
8: 8 them did S make to pay tribute until this 8010
8: 9 of the children of Israel did S make no 8010
8:11 S brought up the daughter of Pharaoh out 8010
8:12 S offered burnt offerings unto the LORD 8010
8:16 Now all the work of S was prepared unto 8010
8:17 went S to Ezion-geber, and to Eloth, at 8010
8:18 they went with the servants of S to Ophir, 8010
8:18 talents of gold, and brought *them* to king S. 8010
9: 1 the queen of Sheba heard of the fame of S, 8010
9: 1 she came to prove S with hard questions at 8010
9: 1 when she was come to S, she communed 8010
9: 2 S told her all her questions: and there was 8010
9: 2 there was nothing hid from S which he told 8010
9: 3 queen of Sheba had seen the wisdom of S, 8010
9: 9 spice as the queen of Sheba gave king S. 8010
9:10 the servants of S, which brought gold from 8010
9:12 king S gave to the queen of Sheba all her 8010
9:13 Now the weight of gold that came to S in 8010
9:14 of the country brought gold and silver to S. 8010
9:15 king S made two hundred targets *of* beaten 8010
9:20 all the drinking vessels of king S *were of* 8010
9:20 *not* any thing accounted of in the days of S. 8010
9:22 king S passed all the kings of the earth in 8010
9:23 kings of the earth sought the presence of S, 8010
9:25 S had four thousand stalls for horses and 8010
9:28 they brought unto S horses out of Egypt, 8010
9:29 Now the rest of the acts of S, first and last, 8010
9:30 S reigned in Jerusalem over all Israel forty 8010
9:31 S slept with his fathers, and he was buried 8010
10: 2 whither he had fled from the presence of S 8010
10: 6 stood before S his father while he *yet* lived, 8010
11: 3 Speak unto Rehoboam the son of S, king of 8010
11:17 made Rehoboam the son of S strong, 8010
11:17 they walked in the way of David and S. 8010
12: 9 also the shields of gold which S had made. 8010
13: 6 the servant of S the son of David, is risen 8010
13: 7 themselves against Rehoboam the son of S, 8010
30:26 for since the time of S the son of David 8010
33: 7 God had said to David and to S his son, 8010
35: 3 Put the holy ark in the house which S 8010
35: 4 and according to the writing of S his son. 8010
Ne 12:45 commandment of David, *and* of S his son. 8010
13:26 Did not S king of Israel sin by these *things?* 8010
Ps 72: T *A Psalm* for S. 8010
127: T A Song of degrees for S. 8010
Pr 1: 1 The proverbs of S the son of David, king of 8010
10: 1 The proverbs of S. A wise son maketh a 8010
25: 1 These *are* also proverbs of S, which 8010
SS 1: 5 as the tents of Kedar, as the curtains of S. 8010
3: 9 King S made himself a chariot of the wood 8010
3:11 behold king S with the crown where*with* 8010
8:11 S had a vineyard at Baal-hamon; he let out 8010
8:12 thou, O S, *must have* a thousand, and 8010
Jer 52:20 which king S had made in the house of 8010
Mt 1: 6 David the king begat S of *her that had been* *4672*
1: 7 And S begat Roboam; and Roboam begat *4672*
6:29 That even S in all his glory was not arrayed *4672*
12:42 parts of the earth to hear the wisdom of S; *4672*
12:42 and behold, a greater than S *is* here. *4672*
Lk 11:31 parts of the earth to hear the wisdom of S; *4672*
11:31 and behold, a greater than S *is* here. *4672*
12:27 *that* S in all his glory was not arrayed like *4672*
Ac 7:47 But S built him a house. *4672*

SOLOMON'S (25) [SOLOMON]

1Ki 4:22 S provision for one day was thirty measures 8010
4:27 for all that came unto king S table, 8010
4:30 S wisdom excelled the wisdom of all 8010
5:16 Besides the chief of S officers which *were* 8010
5:18 S builders and Hiram's builders did hew 8010
6: 1 in the fourth year of S reign over Israel, 8010
9: 1 all S desire which he was pleased to do, 8010
9:16 it *for* a present unto his daughter, S wife. 8010
9:23 chief of the officers that *were* over S work, 8010
10: 4 when the queen of Sheba had seen all S 8010
10:21 all king S drinking vessels *were of* gold, 8010
11:26 an Ephrathite of Zereda, S servant, 8010+3807.1
1Ch 3:10 S son *was* Rehoboam, Abia his son, Asa his 8010
2Ch 7:11 all that came into S heart to make in 8010
8:10 these *were* the chief of king S 8010+3807.1
Ezr 2:55 The children of S servants: the children of 8010
2:58 and the children of S servants, 8010
Ne 7:57 The children of S servants: the children of 8010
7:60 and the children of S servants, 8010
11: 3 and the children of S servants. 8010
SS 1: 1 The song of songs, which *is* S. 8010+3807.1
3: 7 Behold his bed, which *is* S; 8010+3807.1
Jn 10:23 And Jesus walked in the temple in S porch. *4672*
Ac 3:11 unto them in the porch that is called S, *4672*
5:12 they were all with one accord in S porch. *4672*

SOME (231) [SOMEBODY, SOMETHING, SOMETIME, SOMETIMES, SOMEWHAT]

Ge 19:19 the mountain, lest *s* evil take me, and I die: NIH
27: 3 go out to the field, and take me *s* venison; NIH
30:35 *and* every one that had *s* white in it, and NIH
33:15 Let me now leave with thee *s* of the folk NIH
37:20 and cast him into s pit, and we will say, 259
37:20 we will say, *S* evil beast hath devoured him: NIH
47: 2 he took s of his brethren, *even* five 4480+7097
Ex 16:17 did so, and gathered, s[S] more, some less. 1886.1
16:17 did so, and gathered, some more, s[S] less. 1886.1
16:20 s of them left of it until the morning, and 376
16:27 *that* there went out *s* of the people on NIH
30:36 thou shalt beat *s* of it very small, and put of NIH
Lev 4: 7 the priest shall put *s* of the blood upon NIH
4:17 the priest shall dip his finger *in s* of NIH
4:18 he shall put *s* of the blood upon the horns of NIH
14:14 the priest shall take *s* of the blood of NIH
14:15 the priest shall take *s* of the log of oil, and NIH
14:25 the priest shall take *s* of the blood of NIH
14:27 priest shall sprinkle with his right finger *s* NIH
25:25 hath sold away *s* of his possession, and NIH
27:16 if a man shall sanctify unto the LORD *s* NIH
Nu 5:20 *s* man hath lain with thee beside thine NIH
21: 1 against Israel, and took *s* of them prisoners. NIH
27:20 thou shalt put *s* of thine honour upon him, NIH
31: 3 Arm s of yourselves unto the war, and 376
Dt 24: 1 because he hath found s uncleanness in her: 1697
Jos 8:22 s on this side, and some on that side: 428
8:22 some on this side, and s on that side: 428
Jdg 21:13 the whole congregation sent *s* to speak to NIH
Ru 2:16 let fall also *s* of the handfuls of purpose for NIH
1Sa 8:11 and *s* shall run before his chariots. NIH
13: 7 *s of the* Hebrews went over Jordan *to* NIH
24:10 *s* bade *me* kill thee: but *mine eye* spared NIH
27: 5 let them give me a place in s town in 259
2Sa 11:17 there fell *s* of the people of the servants of NIH
11:24 *s* of the king's servants be dead, and NIH
17: 9 he is hid now in s pit, or in some *other* 259
17: 9 is hid now in some pit, or in s *other* place: 259
17: 9 when *s* of them be overthrown at the first, NIH
17:12 So shall we come upon him in s place 259
1Ki 14:13 in him there is found *s* good thing toward NIH
2Ki 2:16 cast him upon s mountain, or into some 259
2:16 him upon some mountain, or into s valley. 259
5:13 *if* the prophet had bid thee *do s* great thing, NIH
7: 9 *s* mischief will come upon us: NIH
7:13 his servants answered and said, Let *s* take, NIH
9:33 *s* of her blood was sprinkled on the wall, NIH
17:25 lions among them, which slew *s* of them. NIH
1Ch 4:42 *s* of them, *even* of the sons of Simeon, NIH
9:29 *S* of them also *were* appointed to oversee NIH
9:30 *s* of the sons of the priests made NIH
12:19 there fell *s* of Manasseh to David, when he NIH
2Ch 12: 7 but I will grant them s deliverance; 4592+3509.1
16:10 of this *thing.* And Asa oppressed *s* of NIH
17:11 Also *s* of the Philistines brought NIH
20: 2 there came *s* that told Jehoshaphat, saying, NIH
Ezr 2:68 *s* of the chief of the fathers, when they came NIH
2:70 *s* of the people, and the singers, and NIH
7: 7 there went up *s* of the children of Israel, NIH
10:44 *s* of them had wives by *whom* they had NIH
Ne 2:12 arose in the night, I and *s* few men with me; NIH
5: 3 *S* also there were that said, We *have* NIH
5: 5 *s* of our daughters are brought unto bondage NIH
6: 2 let us meet together in *s one of* the villages NIH
7:70 s of the chief of the fathers gave unto 4480+7117
7:71 *s* of the chief of the fathers gave to NIH
7:73 *s* of the people, and the Nethinims, and NIH
11:25 *s* of the children of Judah dwelt at NIH
12:44 at that time were s appointed over 376
13:15 In those days saw I in Judah *s* treading wine NIH
13:19 *s* of my servants set I at the gates, *that* there NIH
Job 24: 2 *S* remove the landmarks; they violently take NIH
Ps 20: 7 S *trust* in chariots, and some in horses: but 428
20: 7 Some *trust* in chariots, and s in horses: but 428
69:20 I looked *for s* to take pity, but *there was* NIH
Pr 4:16 is taken away, unless they cause *s* to fall. NIH
Jer 49: 9 would they not leave *s* gleaning grapes? NIH
Eze 6: 8 that ye may have *s* that shall escape NIH
Da 8:10 it cast down *s* of the host and of the stars to NIH
11:35 *s* of them of understanding shall fall, to try NIH
12: 2 s to everlasting life, and some to shame *and* 428
12: 2 and s to shame *and* everlasting contempt. 428
Am 4:11 I have overthrown *s* of you, as God NIH
Ob 1: 5 to thee, would they not leave *s* grapes? NIH
Mt 13: 4 s *seeds* fell by the way side, and the fowls *3739*
13: 5 S fell upon stony *places,* where they had not *243*
13: 7 And s fell among thorns; and the thorns *243*
13: 8 s an hundred*fold,* some sixty*fold,* some *3739*
13: 8 some an hundred*fold,* s sixty*fold,* some *3739*
13: 8 some an hundred*fold,* some sixty*fold,* s *3739*
13:23 s an hundred*fold,* some sixty, some thirty. *3739*
13:23 some an hundred*fold,* s sixty, some thirty. *3739*
13:23 some an hundred*fold,* some sixty, s thirty. *3739*
16:14 S *say that thou art* John the Baptist: *3588*
16:14 s, Elias; and others, Jeremias, or one of *243*
16:28 I say unto you, There be s standing here, *5100*
19:12 For there are *s* eunuchs, which were so NIG
19:12 and there are *s* eunuchs, which were made NIG
23:34 and *s* of them ye shall kill and crucify; and NIG
23:34 *s* of them shall ye scourge in your NIG
27:47 S of them that stood there, when they heard *5100*
28:11 s of the watch came into the city, and *5100*
28:17 they worshipped him: but s doubted. *3588*
Mk 2: 1 he entered into Capernaum after *s* days; NIG
4: 4 s fell by the way side, and the fowls of *3739*
4: 5 And s fell on stony ground, where it had not *243*
4: 7 And s fell among thorns, and the thorns grew *243*
4: 8 s thirty, and some sixty, and some an *1520*
4: 8 and s sixty, and some an hundred. *1520*
4: 8 and some sixty, and s an hundred. *1520*
4:20 s thirty*fold,* some sixty, and some an *1520*
4:20 some thirty*fold,* s sixty, and some an *1520*

Mk 4:20 thirtyfold, some sixty, and s an hundred. 1520
7: 2 And when they saw s of his disciples eat 5100
8:28 but s say, Elias; and others, One of 243
9: 1 That there be s of them that stand here, 5100
12: 5 him they killed, and many others; beating s, 3588
12: 5 many others; beating some, and killing s. 3588
14: 4 And there were s that had indignation 5100
14:65 And s began to spit on him, and to cover 5100
15:35 And s of them that stood by, when they 5100
Lk 8: 5 and as he sowed, s fell by the way side; and 3739
8: 6 And s fell upon a rock; and as soon as it 2087
8: 7 And s fell among thorns; and the thorns 2087
9: 7 because that it was said of s, 5100
9: 8 And of s, that Elias had appeared; and 5100
9:19 but s say, Elias; and others say, that one of 243
9:27 tell you of a truth, there be s standing here, 5100
11:15 But s of them said, He casteth out devils 5100
11:49 and s of them they shall slay and persecute: NIG
13: 1 There were present at that season s that told 5100
19:39 And s of the Pharisees from among 5100
21: 5 And as s spake of the temple, how it was 5100
21:16 s of you shall they cause to be put to death. NIG
23: 8 he hoped to have seen s miracle done by 5100
Jn 3:25 Then there arose a question between s of NIG
6:64 But there are s of you that believe not. 5100
7:12 for s said, He is a good man: others said, 3588
7:25 Then said s of them of Jerusalem, Is not 5100
7:41 But s said, Shall Christ come out of Galilee? 243
7:44 And s of them would have taken him; but 5100
9: 9 S said, This is he: others said, He is like him: 243
9:16 Therefore said s of the Pharisees, This man 5100
9:40 And s of the Pharisees which were with him NIG
10: 1 but climbeth up s other way, the same is a 237
11:37 And s of them said, Could not this man, 5100
11:46 But s of them went their ways to 5100
13:29 For s of them thought, because Judas had 5100
16:17 Then said s of his disciples among NIG
Ac 5:15 passing by might overshadow s of them. 5100
8: 9 giving out that himself was s great one: 5100
8:31 How can I, except s man should guide me? 5100
8:34 prophet this? of himself, or of s other man? 5100
11:20 And s of them were men of Cyprus and 5100
13:11 he went about seeking s to lead him by NIG
15:36 And s days after Paul said unto Barnabas, 5100
17: 4 And s of them believed, and consorted with 5100
17:18 And s said, What will this babbler say? 5100
17:18 other s, He seemeth to be a setter forth of NIG
17:21 but either to tell, or to hear s new thing.) 5100
17:32 resurrection of the dead, s mocked: 3303+3588
18:23 And after he had spent s time there, he 5100
19:32 S therefore cried one thing, and 243+3303
19:32 therefore cried one thing, and s another: NIG
21:34 And s cried one thing, some another, 243
21:34 And some cried one thing, s another, NIG
27:27 deemed that they drew near to s country; 5100
27:34 Wherefore I pray you to take s meat: for this NIG
27:36 all of good cheer, and they also took s meat. NIG
27:44 s on boards, and some on broken pieces of 3739
27:44 and s on broken pieces of the ship. 3739
28:24 And s believed the things which were 3588
28:24 which were spoken, and s believed not. 3588
Ro 1:11 that I may impart unto you s spiritual gift, 5100
1:13 that I might have s fruit among you also, 5100
3: 3 For what if s did not believe? shall their 5100
3: 8 and as s affirm that we say,) 5100
5: 7 yet peradventure for a good man s would 5100
11:14 are my flesh, and might save s of them. 5100
11:17 And if s of the branches be broken off, and 5100
15:15 I have written the more boldly unto you in s 575
1Co 4:18 Now s are puffed up, as though I would not 5100
6:11 And such were s of you: but ye are washed, 5100
8: 7 for s with conscience of the idol unto this 5100
9:22 to all men, that I might by all means save s. 5100
10: 7 Neither be ye idolaters, as were s of them; 5100
10: 8 as s of them committed, and fell in one day 5100
10: 9 as s of them also tempted, and 5100
10:10 as s of them also murmured, and 5100
12:28 And God hath set s in the church, 3739
15: 6 unto this present, but s are fallen asleep. 5100
15:12 how say s among you that there is no 5100
15:34 for s have not the knowledge of God: 5100
15:35 But s man will say, How are the dead 5100
15:37 it may chance of wheat, or of s other grain: 5100
2Co 3: 1 as s others, epistles of commendation to 5100
10: 2 wherewith I think to be bold against s, 5100
10:12 compare ourselves with s that commend 5100
Gal 1: 7 but there be s that trouble you, and 5100
Eph 4:11 And he gave s, apostles; and some, 3303+3588
4:11 and s, prophets; and some, evangelists; and 3588
4:11 and s, evangelists; and some, pastors and 3588
4:11 evangelists; and s, pastors and teachers; 3588
Php 1:15 S indeed preach Christ even of envy and 5100
1:15 of envy and strife; and s also of good will: 5100
1Th 3: 5 lest by s means the tempter have tempted 3381
2Th 3:11 For we hear that there are s which walk 5100
1Ti 1: 3 that thou mightest charge s that they teach 5100
1: 6 From which s having swerved have turned 5100
1:19 which s having put away, concerning faith 5100
4: 1 that in the latter times s shall depart from 5100
5:15 For s are already turned aside after Satan. 5100
5:24 S men's sins are open beforehand, 5100
5:24 to judgment; and s men they follow after. 5100
5:25 Likewise also the good works of s are NIG
6:10 which while s coveted after, they have 5100
6:21 Which s professing have erred concerning 5100
2Ti 2:18 is past already; and overthrow the faith of s. 5100
2:20 and s to honour, and some to dishonour. 3739
2:20 and some to honour, and s to dishonour. 3739
Heb 3: 4 For every house is builded by s man; but 5100
3:16 For s, when they had heard, did provoke: 5100
4: 6 it remaineth that s must enter therein, 5100
10:25 as the manner of s is; but exhorting one 5100
11:40 God having provided s better thing for us, 5100
13: 2 for thereby s have entertained angels 5100
1Pe 4:12 as though s strange thing happened unto NIG
2Pe 3: 9 his promise, as s men count slackness; 5100
3:16 in which are s things hard to be understood, 5100
Jude 1:22 And of s have compassion, making a 3303+3739
Rev 2:10 the devil shall cast s of you into prison, NIG

SOMEBODY (2) [SOME]

Lk 8:46 And Jesus said, S hath touched me: for I 5100
Ac 5:36 rose up Theudas, boasting himself to be s; 5100

SOMETHING (8) [SOME, THING]

1Sa 20:26 for he thought, S hath befallen him, he is 4745
Mk 5:43 commanded that s should be given her to NIG
Lk 11:54 and seeking to catch s out of his mouth, 5100
Jn 13:29 or that he should give s to the poor. 5100
Ac 3: 5 unto them, expecting to receive s of them. 5100
23:15 as though ye would inquire s more 3588
23:18 man unto thee, who hath s to say unto thee. 5100
Gal 6: 3 For if a man think himself to be s, when he 5100

SOMETIME (3) [SOME, TIME]

Col 1:21 that were s alienated and enemies in your 4218
3: 7 In the which ye also walked s, when ye 4218
1Pe 3:20 Which s were disobedient, when once 4218

SOMETIMES (3) [SOME, TIME]

Eph 2:13 But now in Christ Jesus ye who s were far 4218
5: 8 For ye were s darkness, but now are ye 4218
Tit 3: 3 For we ourselves also were s foolish, 4218

SOMEWHAT (25) [SOME, WHAT]

Lev 4:13 they have done s against any of 259
4:22 done s through ignorance against any of 259
4:27 while he doeth s against any of 259
13: 6 if the plague be s dark, and the plague 3544
13:19 and s reddish, and it be shewed to the priest; 125
13:21 it be not lower than the skin, but be s dark; 3544
13:24 have a white bright spot, s reddish, or white; 125
13:26 no lower than the other skin, but be s dark; 3544
13:28 and spread not in the skin, but it be s dark; 3544
13:56 the plague be s dark after the washing of it; 3544
1Ki 2:14 said moreover, I have s to say unto thee. 1697
2Ki 5:20 I will run after him, and take s of him. 3972
2Ch 10: 4 ease thou s the grievous servitude of thy 7043
10: 9 Ease s the yoke that thy father did put upon 7043
10:10 but make thou it s lighter for us; 7043
Lk 7:40 unto him, Simon, I have s to say unto thee. 5100
Ac 23:20 as though they would inquire s of him more 5100
25:26 examination had, I might have s to write. 5100
Ro 15:24 first I be s filled with your company. 575+3313
2Co 5:12 that you may have s to answer them which NIG
10: 8 For though I should boast s more of our 5100
Gal 2: 6 But of these who seemed to be s, 5100
2: 6 for they who seemed to be s in conference NIG
Heb 8: 3 necessity that this man have s also to offer. 5100
Rev 2: 4 Nevertheless I have s against thee, because NIG

SON (2374) [SON'S, SONS, SONS']

Ge 4:17 of the city, after the name of his s, Enoch. 1121
4:25 she bare a s, and called his name Seth: 1121
4:26 to Seth, to him also there was born a s; and 1121
5: 3 and begat a s in his own likeness, NIH
5:28 and two years, and begat a s: 1121
9:24 knew what his younger s had done unto 1121
11:31 Terah took Abram his s, and Lot the son of 1121
11:31 Lot the s of Haran his son's son, and Sarai 1121
11:31 Lot the son of Haran his son's s, and Sarai 1121
11:31 his daughter in law, his s Abram's wife; 1121
12: 5 Lot his brother's s, and all their substance 1121
14:12 they took Lot, Abram's brother's s, 1121
16:11 shalt bear a s, and shalt call his name 1121
16:15 Hagar bare Abram a s: and Abram called 1121
17:16 will bless her, and give thee a s also of her: 1121
17:19 Sarah thy wife shall bear thee a s indeed; 1121
17:23 Abraham took Ishmael his s, and all that 1121
17:25 Ishmael his s was thirteen years old, 1121
17:26 Abraham circumcised, and Ishmael his s. 1121
18:10 and lo, Sarah thy wife shall have a s. 1121
18:14 to the time of life, and Sarah shall have a s. 1121
19:12 s in law, and thy sons, and thy daughters, 2860
19:37 the firstborn bare a s, and called his name 1121
19:38 she also bare a s, and called his name 1121
21: 2 and bare Abraham a s in his old age, 1121
21: 3 Abraham called the name of his s that was 1121
21: 4 Abraham circumcised his s Isaac being 1121
21: 5 when his s Isaac was born unto him. 1121
21: 7 for I have born him a s in his old age. 1121
21: 9 And Sarah saw the s of Hagar the Egyptian, 1121
21:10 Cast out this bondwoman and her s: 1121
21:10 for the s of this bondwoman shall not be 1121
21:10 bondwoman shall not be heir with my s, 1121
21:11 in Abraham's sight because of his s. 1121
21:13 also of the s of the bondwoman will I make 1121
21:23 nor with my s, nor with my son's son: 5209
21:23 nor with my son, nor with my son's s: 5220
22: 2 he said, Take now thy s, thine only son 1121
22: 2 Take now thy son, thine only s Isaac, NIH
22: 3 Isaac his s, and clave the wood for 1121
22: 6 burnt offering, and laid it upon Isaac his s; 1121
22: 7 he said, Here am I, my s. And he said, 1121
22: 8 Abraham said, My s, God will provide 1121
22: 9 bound Isaac his s, and laid him on the altar 1121
22:10 his hand, and took the knife to slay his s. 1121
22:12 seeing thou hast not withheld thy s, thine 1121
22:12 not withheld thy son, thine only s from me. NIH
22:13 up for a burnt offering in the stead of his s. 1121
22:16 hast not withheld thy s, thine only son: 1121
22:16 hast not withheld thy son, thine only s: NIH
23: 8 and intreat for me to Ephron the s of Zohar, 1121
24: 3 that thou shalt not take a wife unto my s of 1121
24: 4 and take a wife unto my s Isaac. 1121
24: 5 must I needs bring thy s again unto the land 1121
24: 6 Beware thou that thou bring not my s 1121
24: 7 thou shalt take a wife unto my s from 1121
24: 8 my oath: only bring not my s thither again. 1121
Ge 24:15 s of Milcah, the wife of Nahor, 1121
24:24 I am the daughter of Bethuel the s of 1121
24:36 Sarah my master's wife bare a s to my 1121
24:37 Thou shalt not take a wife to my s of 1121
24:38 to my kindred, and take a wife unto my s. 1121
24:40 thou shalt take a wife for my s of my 1121
24:44 hath appointed out for my master's s. 1121
24:47 The daughter of Bethuel, Nahor's s, 1121
24:48 my master's brother's daughter unto his s. 1121
25: 6 sent them away from Isaac his s, while he 1121
25: 9 in the field of Ephron the s of Zohar 1121
25:11 of Abraham, that God blessed his s Isaac; 1121
25:12 Abraham's s, whom Hagar the Egyptian, 1121
25:19 are the generations of Isaac, Abraham's s: 1121
27: 1 he called Esau his eldest s, and said unto 1121
27: 1 his eldest son, and said unto him, My s: 1121
27: 5 heard when Isaac spake to Esau his s. 1121
27: 6 Rebekah spake unto Jacob her s, saying, 1121
27: 8 Now therefore, my s, obey my voice 1121
27:13 said unto him, Upon me be thy curse, my s: 1121
27:15 took goodly raiment of her eldest s Esau, 1121
27:15 and put them upon Jacob her younger s: 1121
27:17 had prepared, into the hand of her s Jacob. 1121
27:18 and he said, Here am I; who art thou, my s? 1121
27:20 Isaac said unto his s, How is it that thou 1121
27:20 it that thou hast found it so quickly, my s? 1121
27:21 I pray thee, that I may feel thee, my s, 1121
27:21 whether thou be my very s Esau or not. 1121
27:24 he said, Art thou my very s Esau? And he 1121
27:26 Come near now, and kiss me, my s. 1121
27:27 the smell of my s is as the smell of a field 1121
27:32 And he said, I am thy s, thy firstborn Esau. 1121
27:37 and what shall I do now unto thee, my s? 1121
27:42 these words of Esau her elder s were told to 1121
27:42 she sent and called Jacob her younger s, 1121
27:43 Now therefore, my s, obey my voice; and 1121
28: 5 s of Bethuel the Syrian, the brother of 1121
28: 9 the daughter of Ishmael Abraham's s, 1121
29: 5 unto them, Know ye Laban the s of Nahor? 1121
29:12 and that he was Rebekah's s: 1121
29:13 heard the tidings of Jacob his sister's s, 1121
29:32 bare a s, and she called his name Reuben: 1121
29:33 she conceived again, and bare a s; and said, 1121
29:33 he hath therefore given me this s also: NIH
29:34 she conceived again, and bare a s; and said, 1121
29:35 she conceived again, and bare a s: and 1121
30: 5 And Bilhah conceived, and bare Jacob a s. 1121
30: 6 also heard my voice, and hath given me a s: 1121
30: 7 conceived again, and bare Jacob a second s. 1121
30:10 And Zilpah Leah's maid bare Jacob a s. 1121
30:12 Zilpah Leah's maid bare Jacob a second s. 1121
30:17 she conceived, and bare Jacob the fifth s. 1121
30:19 conceived again, and bare Jacob the sixth s. 1121
30:23 she conceived, and bare a s; and said, 1121
30:24 The LORD shall add to me another s. 1121
34: 2 when Shechem the s of Hamor the Hivite, 1121
34: 8 The soul of my s Shechem longeth for your 1121
34:18 pleased Hamor, and Shechem Hamor's s. 1121
34:20 Shechem his s came unto the gate of their 1121
34:24 unto Shechem his s hearkened all that went 1121
34:26 Shechem his s with the edge of the sword, 1121
35:17 Fear not; thou shalt have this s also. 1121
36:10 Eliphaz the s of Adah the wife of Esau, 1121
36:10 Reuel the s of Bashemath the wife of Esau. 1121
36:12 Timna was concubine to Eliphaz Esau's s; 1121
36:15 the sons of Eliphaz the firstborn s of Esau; NIH
36:17 these are the sons of Reuel Esau's s; 1121
36:32 Bela the s of Beor reigned in Edom: and 1121
36:33 Jobab the s of Zerah of Bozrah reigned in 1121
36:35 Husham died, and Hadad the s of Bedad, 1121
36:38 Baal-hanan the s of Achbor reigned in his 1121
36:39 Baal-hanan the s of Achbor died, and 1121
37: 3 because he was the s of his old age: 1121
37:34 his loins, and mourned for his s many days. 1121
37:35 For I will go down into the grave unto my s 1121
38: 3 she conceived, and bare a s; and he called 1121
38: 4 she conceived again, and bare a s; and 1121
38: 5 she yet again conceived, and bare a s; and 1121
38:11 father's house, till Shelah my s be grown: 1121
38:26 because that I gave her not to Shelah my s. 1121
42:38 he said, My s shall not go down with you; 1121
43:29 brother Benjamin, his mother's s, and said, 1121
43:29 he said, God be gracious unto thee, my s. 1121
45: 9 and say unto him, Thus saith thy s Joseph, 1121
45:28 It is enough; Joseph my s is yet alive: 1121
46:10 and Shaul the s of a Canaanitish woman. 1121
47:29 he called his s Joseph, and said unto him, 1121
48: 2 Behold, thy s Joseph cometh unto thee: 1121
48:19 his father refused, and said, I know it, my s, 1121
49: 9 from the prey, my s, thou art gone up: 1121
50:23 s of Manasseh were brought up upon 1121
Ex 1:16 the stools; if it be a s, then ye shall kill him: 1121
1:22 Every s that is born ye shall cast into 1121
2: 2 the woman conceived, and bare a s: and 1121
2:10 Pharaoh's daughter, and he became her s. 1121
2:22 she bare him a s, and he called his name 1121
4:22 Israel is my s, even my firstborn: 1121
4:23 I say unto thee, Let my s go, that he may 1121
4:23 behold, I will slay thy s, even thy firstborn. 1121
4:25 cut off the foreskin of her s, and cast it at 1121
6:15 and Shaul the s of a Canaanitish woman: 1121
6:25 Eleazar Aaron's s took him one of 1121
10: 2 that thou mayest tell in the ears of thy s, 1121
10: 2 of thy son's s, what things I have wrought 1121
13: 8 thou shalt shew thy s in that day, saying, 1121
13:14 it shall be when thy s asketh thee in time to 1121
20:10 thou, nor thy s, nor thy daughter, 1121
21: 9 if he have betrothed her unto his s, he shall 1121
21:31 Whether he have gored a s, or have gored a 1121
23:12 and the s of thy handmaid, and the stranger, 1121
29:30 And that s that is priest in his stead shall 1121
31: 2 I have called by name Bezaleel the s of Uri, 1121
31: 2 of Uri, the s of Hur, of the tribe of Judah: 1121
31: 6 the s of Ahisamach, of the tribe of Dan: 1121
32:29 even every man upon his s, and upon his 1121

Ex	33:11	servant Joshua, the **s** of Nun, a young man,	1121
	35:30	hath called by name Bezaleel the **s** of Uri,	1121
	35:30	of Uri, the **s** of Hur, of the tribe of Judah;	1121
	35:34	*both* he, and Aholiab, the **s** of Ahisamach,	1121
	38:21	the hand of Ithamar, **s** to Aaron the priest.	1121
	38:22	Bezaleel the **s** of Uri, the son of Hur, of	1121
	38:22	of Uri, the **s** of Hur, of the tribe of Judah,	1121
	38:23	**s** of Ahisamach, of the tribe of Dan,	1121
Lev	12: 6	are fulfilled, for a **s**, or for a daughter,	1121
	21: 2	for his **s**, and for his daughter, and for his	1121
	24:10	the **s** of an Israelitish woman, whose father	1121
	24:10	*this* **s** of the Israelitish *woman* and a man of	1121
	24:11	the Israelitish woman's **s** blasphemed	1121
	25:49	Either his uncle, or his uncle's **s**,	1121
Nu	1: 5	*tribe of* Reuben; Elizur the **s** of Shedeur.	1121
	1: 6	Of Simeon; Shelumiel the **s** of Zurishaddai.	1121
	1: 7	Of Judah; Nahshon the **s** of Amminadab.	1121
	1: 8	Of Issachar; Nethaneel the **s** of Zuar.	1121
	1: 9	Of Zebulun; Eliab the **s** of Helon.	1121
	1:10	of Ephraim; Elishama the **s** of Ammihud:	1121
	1:10	of Manasseh; Gamaliel the **s** of Pedahzur.	1121
	1:11	Of Benjamin; Abidan the **s** of Gideoni.	1121
	1:12	Of Dan; Ahiezer the **s** of Ammishaddai.	1121
	1:13	Of Asher; Pagiel the **s** of Ocran.	1121
	1:14	Of Gad; Eliasaph the **s** of Deuel.	1121
	1:15	Of Naphtali; Ahira the **s** of Enan.	1121
	1:20	Israel's **eldest s**, *by* their generations,	1060
	2: 3	Nahshon the **s** of Amminadab *shall be*	1121
	2: 5	Nethaneel the **s** of Zuar *shall be* captain of	1121
	2: 7	Eliab the **s** of Helon *shall be* captain of	1121
	2:10	of Reuben *shall be* Elizur the **s** of Shedeur.	1121
	2:12	*shall be* Shelumiel the **s** of Zurishaddai.	1121
	2:14	of Gad *shall be* Eliasaph the **s** of Reuel.	1121
	2:18	*shall be* Elishama the **s** of Ammihud.	1121
	2:20	*shall be* Gamaliel the **s** of Pedahzur.	1121
	2:22	Benjamin *shall be* Abidan the **s** of Gideoni.	1121
	2:25	*shall be* Ahiezer the **s** of Ammishaddai.	1121
	2:27	of Asher *shall be* Pagiel the **s** of Ocran.	1121
	2:29	of Naphtali *shall be* Ahira the **s** of Enan.	1121
	3:24	Gershonites *shall be* Eliasaph the **s** of Lael.	1121
	3:30	*shall be* Elizaphan the **s** of Uzziel.	1121
	3:32	Eleazar the **s** of Aaron the priest *shall be*	1121
	3:35	of Merari *was* Zuriel the **s** of Abihail:	1121
	4:16	*to* the office of Eleazar the **s** of Aaron	1121
	4:28	hand of Ithamar the **s** of Aaron the priest.	1121
	4:33	under the hand of Ithamar the **s** of Aaron	1121
	7: 8	under the hand of Ithamar the **s** of Aaron	1121
	7:12	first day was Nahshon the **s** of Amminadab,	1121
	7:17	this *was* the offering of Nahshon the **s** of	1121
	7:18	On the second day Nethaneel the **s** of Zuar,	1121
	7:23	this *was* the offering of Nethaneel the **s** of	1121
	7:24	On the third day Eliab the **s** of Helon,	1121
	7:29	this *was* the offering of Eliab the **s** of	1121
	7:30	On the fourth day Elizur the **s** of Shedeur,	1121
	7:35	this *was* the offering of Elizur the **s** of	1121
	7:36	On the fifth day Shelumiel the **s** of	1121
	7:41	this *was* the offering of Shelumiel the **s** of	1121
	7:42	On the sixth day Eliasaph the **s** of Deuel,	1121
	7:47	this *was* the offering of Eliasaph the **s** of	1121
	7:48	On the seventh day Elishama the **s** of	1121
	7:53	this *was* the offering of Elishama the **s** of	1121
	7:54	On the eighth day *offered* Gamaliel the **s** of	1121
	7:59	this *was* the offering of Gamaliel the **s** of	1121
	7:60	On the ninth day Abidan the **s** of Gideoni,	1121
	7:65	this *was* the offering of Abidan the **s** of	1121
	7:66	On the tenth day Ahiezer the **s** of	1121
	7:71	this *was* the offering of Ahiezer the **s** of	1121
	7:72	On the eleventh day Pagiel the **s** of Ocran,	1121
	7:77	this *was* the offering of Pagiel the **s** of	1121
	7:78	On the twelfth day Ahira the **s** of Enan,	1121
	7:83	this *was* the offering of Ahira the **s** of Enan.	1121
	10:14	over his host *was* Nahshon the **s** of	1121
	10:15	of Issachar *was* Nethaneel the **s** of Zuar.	1121
	10:16	of Zebulun *was* Eliab the **s** of Helon.	1121
	10:18	over his host *was* Elizur the **s** of Shedeur.	1121
	10:19	*was* Shelumiel the **s** of Zurishaddai.	1121
	10:20	of Gad *was* Eliasaph the **s** of Deuel.	1121
	10:22	over his host *was* Elishama the **s** of	1121
	10:23	Manasseh *was* Gamaliel the **s** of Pedahzur.	1121
	10:24	of Benjamin *was* Abidan the **s** of Gideoni.	1121
	10:25	over his host *was* Ahiezer the **s** of	1121
	10:26	of Asher *was* Pagiel the **s** of Ocran.	1121
	10:27	of Naphtali *was* Ahira the **s** of Enan.	1121
	10:29	the **s** of Raguel the Midianite,	1121
	11:28	Joshua the **s** of Nun, the servant of Moses,	1121
	13: 4	tribe of Reuben, Shammua the **s** of Zaccur.	1121
	13: 5	the tribe of Simeon, Shaphat the **s** of Hori.	1121
	13: 6	tribe of Judah, Caleb the **s** of Jephunneh.	1121
	13: 7	the tribe of Issachar, Igal the **s** of Joseph.	1121
	13: 8	the tribe of Ephraim, Oshea the **s** of Nun.	1121
	13: 9	the tribe of Benjamin, Palti the **s** of Raphu.	1121
	13:10	the tribe of Zebulun, Gaddiel the **s** of Sodi.	1121
	13:11	the tribe of Manasseh, Gaddi the **s** of Susi.	1121
	13:12	the tribe of Dan, Ammiel the **s** of Gemalli.	1121
	13:13	the tribe of Asher, Sethur the **s** of Michael.	1121
	13:14	tribe of Naphtali, Nahbi the **s** of Vophsi.	1121
	13:15	Of the tribe of Gad, Geuel the **s** of Machi.	1121
	13:16	Moses called Oshea the **s** of Nun, Jehoshua.	1121
	14: 6	Joshua the **s** of Nun, and Caleb the son of	1121
	14: 6	son of Nun, and Caleb the **s** of Jephunneh,	1121
	14:30	save Caleb the **s** of Jephunneh, and	1121
	14:30	son of Jephunneh, and Joshua the **s** of Nun.	1121
	14:38	Joshua the **s** of Nun, and Caleb the son of	1121
	14:38	son of Nun, and Caleb the **s** of Jephunneh,	1121
	16: 1	Now Korah, the **s** of Izhar, the son of	1121
	16: 1	the **s** of Kohath, the son of Levi, and	1121
	16: 1	the **s** of Levi, and Dathan and Abiram,	1121
	16: 1	On, the **s** of Peleth, sons of Reuben,	1121
	16:37	Speak unto Eleazar the **s** of Aaron	1121
	20:25	Take Aaron and Eleazar his **s**, and	1121
	20:26	and put them upon Eleazar his **s**:	1121
	20:28	and put them upon Eleazar his **s**;	1121
	22: 2	Balak the **s** of Zippor saw all that Israel had	1121
	22: 4	Balak the **s** of Zippor *was* king of	1121
	22: 5	unto Balaam the **s** of Beor to Pethor,	1121
Nu	22:10	Balak the **s** of Zippor, king of Moab,	1121
	22:16	to him, Thus saith Balak the **s** of Zippor,	1121
	23:18	hear; hearken unto me, thou **s** of Zippor:	1121
	23:19	neither the **s** of man, that he should repent:	1121
	24: 3	Balaam the **s** of Beor hath said, and	1121
	24:15	Balaam the **s** of Beor hath said, and	1121
	25: 7	when Phinehas, the **s** of Eleazar, the son of	1121
	25: 7	the son of Eleazar, the **s** of Aaron the priest,	1121
	25:11	Phinehas, the **s** of Eleazar, the son of Aaron	1121
	25:11	the son of Eleazar, the **s** of Aaron the priest,	1121
	25:14	*was* Zimri, the **s** of Salu, a prince of a chief	1121
	26: 1	and unto Eleazar the **s** of Aaron the priest,	1121
	26: 5	Reuben, the **eldest s** of Israel: the children	1060
	26:33	Zelophehad the **s** of Hepher had no sons,	1121
	26:65	save Caleb the **s** of Jephunneh, and	1121
	26:65	son of Jephunneh, and Joshua the **s** of Nun.	1121
	27: 1	the **s** of Hepher, the son of Gilead, the son	1121
	27: 1	the **s** of Gilead, the son of Machir,	1121
	27: 1	the son of Gilead, the **s** of Machir,	1121
	27: 1	the son of Machir, the **s** of Manasseh,	1121
	27: 1	of the families of Manasseh the **s** of Joseph:	1121
	27: 4	among his family, because he hath no **s**?	1121
	27: 8	have no **s**, then ye shall cause his	1121
	27:18	Take thee Joshua the **s** of Nun, a man in	1121
	31: 6	and Phinehas the **s** of Eleazar the priest,	1121
	31: 8	Balaam also the **s** of Beor they slew with	1121
	32:12	Save Caleb the **s** of Jephunneh	1121
	32:12	the Kenezite, and Joshua the **s** of Nun:	1121
	32:28	Joshua the **s** of Nun, and the chief fathers	1121
	32:33	unto half the tribe of Manasseh the **s** of	1121
	32:39	the children of Machir the **s** of Manasseh	1121
	32:40	Moses gave Gilead unto Machir the **s** of	1121
	32:41	Jair the **s** of Manasseh went and took	1121
	34:17	Eleazar the priest, and Joshua the **s** of Nun.	1121
	34:19	tribe of Judah, Caleb the **s** of Jephunneh.	1121
	34:20	of Simeon, Shemuel the **s** of Ammihud.	1121
	34:21	tribe of Benjamin, Elidad the **s** of Chislon.	1121
	34:22	of the children of Dan, Bukki the **s** of Jogli.	1121
	34:23	of Manasseh, Hanniel the **s** of Ephod.	1121
	34:24	of Ephraim, Kemuel the **s** of Shiphtan.	1121
	34:25	of Zebulun, Elizaphan the **s** of Parnach.	1121
	34:26	children of Issachar, Paltiel the **s** of Azzan.	1121
	34:27	children of Asher, Ahihud the **s** of Shelomi.	1121
	34:28	of Naphtali, Pedahel the **s** of Ammihud.	1121
	36: 1	the **s** of Machir, the son of Manasseh, of	1121
	36: 1	the son of Machir, the **s** of Manasseh, of	1121
	36:12	of the sons of Manasseh the **s** of Joseph,	1121
Dt	1:31	as a man doth bear his **s**, in all the way that	1121
	1:36	Save Caleb the **s** of Jephunneh, he shall see	1121
	1:38	*But* Joshua the **s** of Nun, which standeth	1121
	3:14	Jair the **s** of Manasseh took all the country	1121
	5:14	thou, nor thy **s**, nor thy daughter, nor thy	1121
	6: 2	thou, and thy **s**, and thy son's son, all	1121
	6: 2	thou, and thy son, and thy son's **s**, all	1121
	6:20	*And* when thy **s** asketh thee in time to	1121
	6:21	thou shalt say unto thy **s**, We were	1121
	7: 3	thy daughter thou shalt not give unto his **s**,	1121
	7: 3	nor his daughter shalt thou take unto thy **s**.	1121
	7: 4	For they will turn away thy **s** from	1121
	8: 5	as a man chasteneth his **s**, *so* the LORD	1121
	10: 6	Eleazar his **s** ministered in the priest's	1121
	11: 6	the sons of Eliab, the **s** of Reuben:	1121
	12:18	thy **s**, and thy daughter, and	1121
	13: 6	the **s** of thy mother, or thy son, or	1121
	13: 6	or thy **s**, or thy daughter, or the wife of thy	1121
	16:11	thy **s**, and thy daughter, and	1121
	16:14	thy **s**, and thy daughter, and	1121
	18:10	found among you *any one* that maketh his **s**	1121
	21:15	and *if* the firstborn **s** be hers that was hated:	1121
	21:16	*that* he may not make the **s** of the beloved	1121
	21:16	beloved firstborn before the **s** of the hated,	1121
	21:17	he shall acknowledge the **s** of the hated *for*	1121
	21:18	If a man have a stubborn and rebellious **s**,	1121
	21:20	This our **s** *is* stubborn and rebellious,	1121
	23: 4	they hired against thee Balaam the **s** of	1121
	28:56	towards her **s**, and towards her daughter,	1121
	31:23	he gave Joshua the **s** of Nun a charge,	1121
	32:44	of the people, he and Hoshea the **s** of Nun.	1121
	34: 9	Joshua the **s** of Nun was full *of* the spirit of	1121
Jos	1: 1	that the LORD spake unto Joshua the **s** of	1121
	2: 1	Joshua the **s** of Nun sent out of Shittim two	1121
	2:23	came to Joshua the **s** of Nun, and told him	1121
	6: 6	Joshua the **s** of Nun called the priests, and	1121
	6:26	in his youngest ***s*** shall he set up the gates of	NIH
	7: 1	for Achan, the **s** of Carmi, the son of Zabdi,	1121
	7: 1	of Carmi, the **s** of Zabdi, the son of Zerah,	1121
	7: 1	of Carmi, the son of Zabdi, the **s** of Zerah,	1121
	7:18	Achan, the **s** of Carmi, the son of Zabdi,	1121
	7:18	of Carmi, the **s** of Zabdi, the son of Zerah,	1121
	7:18	of Carmi, the son of Zabdi, the **s** of Zerah,	1121
	7:19	said unto Achan, My **s**, give, I pray thee,	1121
	7:24	took Achan the **s** of Zerah, and the silver,	1121
	13:22	Balaam also the **s** of Beor, the soothsayer,	1121
	13:31	the children of Machir the **s** of Manasseh,	1121
	14: 1	Joshua the **s** of Nun, and the heads of	1121
	14: 6	Caleb the **s** of Jephunneh the Kenezite said	1121
	14:13	gave unto Caleb the **s** of Jephunneh Hebron	1121
	14:14	became the inheritance of Caleb the **s** of	1121
	15: 6	up *to* the stone of Bohan the **s** of Reuben:	1121
	15: 8	the border went up *by* the valley of the **s** of	1121
	15:13	unto Caleb the **s** of Jephunneh he gave a	1121
	15:17	Othniel the **s** of Kenaz, the brother of	1121
	17: 2	Manasseh the **s** of Joseph by their families.	1121
	17: 3	Zelophehad, the **s** of Hepher, the son of	1121
	17: 3	the **s** of Gilead, the son of Machir,	1121
	17: 3	the son of Gilead, the **s** of Machir,	1121
	17: 3	the **s** of Manasseh, had no sons, but	1121
	17: 4	before Joshua the **s** of Nun, and before	1121
	18:16	*lieth* before the valley of the **s** of Hinnom,	1121
	18:17	descended *to* the stone of Bohan the **s** of	1121
	19:49	to Joshua the **s** of Nun among them:	1121
	19:51	Joshua the **s** of Nun, and the heads of	1121
	21: 1	unto Joshua the **s** of Nun, and unto	1121
	21:12	gave they to Caleb the **s** of Jephunneh for	1121
	22:13	Phinehas the **s** of Eleazar the priest,	1121
Jos	22:20	Did not Achan the **s** of Zerah commit a	1121
	22:31	Phinehas the **s** of Eleazar the priest said	1121
	22:32	Phinehas the **s** of Eleazar the priest, and	1121
	24: 9	Balak the **s** of Zippor, king of Moab, arose	1121
	24: 9	called Balaam the **s** of Beor to curse you:	1121
	24:29	that Joshua the **s** of Nun, the servant of	1121
	24:33	Eleazar the **s** of Aaron died; and	1121
	24:33	in a hill that pertained to Phinehas his **s**,	1121
Jdg	1:13	Othniel the **s** of Kenaz, Caleb's younger	1121
	2: 8	Joshua the **s** of Nun, the servant of	1121
	3: 9	*even* Othniel the **s** of Kenaz,	1121
	3:11	And Othniel the **s** of Kenaz died.	1121
	3:15	Ehud the **s** of Gera, a Benjamite, a man	1121
	3:31	after him was Shamgar the **s** of Anath,	1121
	4: 6	called Barak the **s** of Abinoam out of	1121
	4:12	they shewed Sisera that Barak the **s** of	1121
	5: 1	and Barak the **s** of Abinoam on that day,	1121
	5: 6	In the days of Shamgar the **s** of Anath,	1121
	5:12	thy captivity captive, thou **s** of Abinoam.	1121
	6:11	his **s** Gideon threshed wheat by	1121
	6:29	Gideon the **s** of Joash hath done this thing.	1121
	6:30	Bring out thy **s**, that he may die:	1121
	7:14	save the sword of Gideon the **s** of Joash,	1121
	8:13	Gideon the **s** of Joash returned from battle	1121
	8:22	both thou, and thy **s**, and thy son's son also:	1121
	8:22	both thou, and thy son, and thy son's **s** also:	1121
	8:23	over you, neither shall my **s** rule over you:	1121
	8:29	Jerubbaal the **s** of Joash went and dwelt in	1121
	8:31	she also bare him a **s**, whose name he	1121
	8:32	Gideon the **s** of Joash died in a good old	1121
	9: 1	Abimelech the **s** of Jerubbaal went to	1121
	9: 5	notwithstanding yet Jotham the youngest **s**	1121
	9:18	made Abimelech, the **s** of his maidservant,	1121
	9:26	Gaal the **s** of Ebed came with his brethren,	1121
	9:28	Gaal the **s** of Ebed said, Who *is* Abimelech,	1121
	9:28	*is* not *he* the **s** of Jerubbaal? and Zebul his	1121
	9:30	city heard the words of Gaal the **s** of Ebed,	1121
	9:31	Gaal the **s** of Ebed and his brethren be	1121
	9:35	Gaal the **s** of Ebed went out, and stood *in*	1121
	9:57	upon them came the curse of Jotham the **s**	1121
	10: 1	arose to defend Israel Tola the **s** of Puah,	1121
	10: 1	of Puah, the **s** of Dodo, a man of Issachar;	1121
	11: 1	*man* of valour, and he *was* the **s** of a harlot:	1121
	11: 2	for thou *art* the **s** of a strange woman.	1121
	11:25	any thing better than Balak the **s** of Zippor,	1121
	11:34	beside her he had neither **s** nor daughter.	1121
	12:13	after him Abdon the **s** of Hillel,	1121
	12:15	Abdon the **s** of Hillel the Pirathonite died,	1121
	13: 3	but thou shalt conceive, and bear a **s**.	1121
	13: 5	For lo, thou *shalt* conceive, and bear a **s**;	1121
	13: 7	Behold, thou *shalt* conceive, and bear a **s**;	1121
	13:24	the woman bare a **s**, and called his name	1121
	15: 6	the **s in law** of the Timnite, because he had	2860
	17: 2	Blessed *be thou* of the LORD, my **s**.	1121
	17: 3	unto the LORD from my hand for my **s**,	1121
	18:30	Jonathan, the **s** of Gershom, the son of	1121
	18:30	the **s** of Manasseh, he and his sons were	1121
	19: 5	the damsel's father said unto his **s in law**,	2860
	20:28	Phinehas, the **s** of Eleazar, the son of	1121
	20:28	the son of Eleazar, the **s** of Aaron,	1121
Ru	4:13	gave her conception, and she bare a **s**.	1121
	4:17	a name, saying, There is a **s** born to Naomi;	1121
1Sa	1: 1	the **s** of Jeroham, the son of Elihu, the son	1121
	1: 1	the **s** of Elihu, the son of Tohu, the son of	1121
	1: 1	the **s** of Tohu, the son of Zuph,	1121
	1: 1	son of Tohu, the **s** of Zuph, an Ephrathite:	1121
	1:20	that she bare a **s**, and called his name	1121
	1:23	and gave her **s** suck until she weaned him.	1121
	3: 6	he answered, I called not, my **s**; lie down	1121
	3:16	Eli called Samuel, and said, Samuel, my **s**.	1121
	4:16	And he said, What is there done, my **s**?	1121
	4:20	*unto her,* Fear not; for thou hast born a **s**.	1121
	7: 1	sanctified Eleazar his **s** to keep the ark of	1121
	9: 1	the **s** of Abiel, the son of Zeror, the son of	1121
	9: 1	the son of Abiel, the **s** of Zeror, the son of	1121
	9: 1	the son of Zeror, the **s** of Bechorath,	1121
	9: 1	of Bechorath, the **s** of Aphiah, a Benjamite,	1121
	9: 2	he had a **s**, whose name *was* Saul, a choice	1121
	9: 3	Kish said to Saul his **s**, Take now one of	1121
	10: 2	for you, saying, What shall I do for my **s**?	1121
	10:11	What *is* this *that* is come unto the **s** of	1121
	10:21	and Saul the **s** of Kish was taken:	1121
	13:16	Jonathan his **s**, and the people that were	1121
	13:22	and with Jonathan his **s** was there found.	1121
	14: 1	that Jonathan the **s** of Saul said unto	1121
	14: 3	Ahiah, the **s** of Ahitub, Ichabod's brother,	1121
	14: 3	the **s** of Phinehas, the son of Eli,	1121
	14: 3	the son of Phinehas, the **s** of Eli,	1121
	14:39	though it be in Jonathan my **s**, he shall	1121
	14:40	and Jonathan my **s** will be on the other side.	1121
	14:42	Cast *lots* between me and Jonathan my **s**.	1121
	14:50	host *was* Abner, the **s** of Ner, Saul's uncle.	1121
	14:51	Ner the father of Abner *was* the **s** of Abiel.	1121
	16:18	I have seen a **s** of Jesse the Beth-lehemite,	1121
	16:19	said, Send me David thy **s**, which *is* with	1121
	16:20	sent *them* by David his **s** unto Saul.	1121
	17:12	Now David *was* the **s** of that Ephrathite of	1121
	17:17	Jesse said unto David his **s**, Take now for	1121
	17:55	of the host, Abner, whose **s** *is* this youth?	1121
	17:56	Inquire thou whose **s** the stripling *is*.	1121
	17:58	to him, Whose **s** *art* thou, *thou* young man?	1121
	17:58	*I am* the **s** of thy servant Jesse	1121
	18:18	that I should be **s in law** to the king?	2860
	18:21	Thou shalt *this* day be my **s in law** in	2859
	18:22	now therefore be the king's **s in law**.	2859
	18:23	to you a light *thing* to be a king's **s in law**,	2859
	18:26	David well to be the king's **s in law**:	2859
	18:27	that he might be the king's **s in law**.	2859
	19: 1	Saul spake to Jonathan his **s**, and to all his	1121
	19: 2	Jonathan Saul's **s** delighted much in David:	1121
	20:27	Saul said unto Jonathan his **s**,	1121
	20:27	Wherefore cometh not the **s** of Jesse to	1121
	20:30	Thou **s** of the perverse rebellious *woman*,	1121
	20:30	the **s** of Jesse to thine own confusion,	1121
	20:31	For as long as the **s** of Jesse liveth upon	1121

1Sa 22: 7 will the **s** of Jesse give every one of you 1121
22: 8 *there is* none that sheweth me that my **s** 1121
22: 8 son hath made *a league* with the **s** of Jesse, 1121
22: 8 sheweth unto me that my **s** hath stirred up 1121
22: 9 said, I saw the **s** of Jesse coming to Nob, 1121
22: 9 to Nob, to Ahimelech the **s** of Ahitub: 1121
22:11 the **s** of Ahitub, and all his father's house, 1121
22:12 Saul said, Hear now, thou **s** of Ahitub. 1121
22:13 thou and the **s** of Jesse, in that thou hast 1121
22:14 which *is* the king's **s in law**, and goeth at 2860
22:20 one of the sons of Ahimelech the **s** of 1121
23: 6 when Abiathar the **s** of Ahimelech fled to 1121
23:16 Jonathan Saul's **s** arose, and went to David 1121
24:16 Saul said, *Is* this thy voice, my **s** David? 1121
25: 8 hand unto thy servants, and to thy **s** David. 1121
25:10 who *is* the **s** of Jesse? there be many 1121
25:17 for he *is such* a **s** of Belial, that *a man* 1121
25:44 David's wife, to Phalti the **s** of Laish, 1121
26: 5 Abner the **s** of Ner, the captain of his host: 1121
26: 6 to Abishai the **s** of Zeruiah, brother to Joab, 1121
26:14 to Abner the **s** of Ner, saying, Answerest 1121
26:17 and said, *Is* this thy voice, my **s** David? 1121
26:21 return, my **s** David: for I will no more do 1121
26:25 said to David, Blessed *be* thou, my **s** David: 1121
27: 2 unto Achish, the **s** of Maoch, king of Gath. 1121
30: 7 Ahimelech's **s**, I pray thee, bring me hither 1121
2Sa 1: 4 and Saul and Jonathan his **s** are dead also. 1121
1: 5 thou that Saul and Jonathan his **s** be dead? 1121
1:12 for Jonathan his **s**, and for the people of 1121
1:13 I *am* the **s** of a stranger, an Amalekite. 1121
1:17 over Saul and over Jonathan his **s**: 1121
2: 8 Abner the **s** of Ner, captain of Saul's host, 1121
2: 8 took Ish-bosheth the **s** of Saul, and 1121
2:10 Ish-bosheth Saul's **s** *was* forty years old 1121
2:12 Abner the **s** of Ner, and the servants of 1121
2:12 the servants of Ish-bosheth the **s** of Saul, 1121
2:13 Joab the **s** of Zeruiah, and the servants of 1121
2:15 which *pertained* to Ish-bosheth the **s** of 1121
3: 3 Absalom the **s** of Maacah the daughter of 1121
3: 4 the fourth, Adonijah the **s** of Haggith; and 1121
3: 4 and the fifth, Shephatiah the **s** of Abital; 1121
3:14 sent messengers to Ish-bosheth Saul's **s**, 1121
3:15 *even* from Phaltiel the **s** of Laish. 1121
3:23 Abner the **s** of Ner came to the king, and 1121
3:25 Thou knowest Abner the **s** of Ner, that he 1121
3:28 ever from the blood of Abner the **s** of Ner: 1121
3:37 not of the king to slay Abner the **s** of Ner. 1121
4: 1 when Saul's **s** heard that Abner was dead in 1121
4: 2 Saul's **s** had two men *that were* captains of 1121
4: 4 Jonathan, Saul's **s**, had a son *that was* lame 1121
4: 4 had a **s** *that was* lame of *his* feet, *and* 1121
4: 8 Behold the head of Ish-bosheth the **s** of 1121
7:14 I will be his father, and he shall be my **s**. If 1121
8: 3 the **s** of Rehob, king of Zobah, 1121
8:10 Toi sent Joram his **s** unto king David, 1121
8:12 of Hadadezer, **s** of Rehob, king of Zobah. 1121
8:16 Joab the **s** of Zeruiah *was* over the host; 1121
8:16 Jehoshaphat the **s** of Ahilud *was* recorder; 1121
8:17 Zadok the **s** of Ahitub, and Ahimelech 1121
8:17 Ahimelech the **s** of Abiathar, *were* 1121
8:18 Benaiah the **s** of Jehoiada *was over* both 1121
9: 3 Jonathan hath yet a **s**, *which is* lame on *his* 1121
9: 4 of Machir, the **s** of Ammiel, in Lo-debar. 1121
9: 5 of Machir, the **s** of Ammiel, from Lo-debar. 1121
9: 6 the **s** of Jonathan, the son of Saul, 1121
9: 6 the son of Jonathan, the **s** of Saul, 1121
9: 9 I have given unto thy master's **s** all that 1121
9:10 that thy master's **s** may have food to eat: 1121
9:10 Mephibosheth thy master's **s** shall eat bread 1121
9:12 Mephibosheth had a young **s**, whose name 1121
10: 1 and Hanun his **s** reigned in his stead. 1121
10: 2 I will shew kindness unto Hanun the **s** of 1121
11:21 Who smote Abimelech the **s** of 1121
11:27 and she became his wife, and bare him a **s**. 1121
12:24 she bare a **s**, and he called his name 1121
13: 1 that Absalom the **s** of David had a fair 1121
13: 1 and Amnon the **s** of David loved her. 1121
13: 3 the **s** of Shimeah David's brother: 1121
13: 4 Why *art* thou, *being* the king's **s**, lean from 1121
13:25 Nay, my **s**, let us not all now go, 1121
13:32 the **s** of Shimeah David's brother, answered 1121
13:37 the **s** of Ammihud, king of Geshur. 1121
13:37 And *David* mourned for his **s** every day. 1121
14: 1 Now Joab the **s** of Zeruiah perceived that 1121
14:11 to destroy any more, lest they destroy my **s**. 1121
14:11 there shall not one hair of thy **s** fall to 1121
14:16 my **s** together out of the inheritance of God. 1121
15:27 Ahimaaz thy **s**, and Jonathan the son of 1121
15:27 thy son, and Jonathan the **s** of Abiathar. 1121
15:36 Ahimaaz Zadok's *s*, and NIH
15:36 Zadok's *son*, and Jonathan Abiathar's *s*; and NIH
16: 3 the king said, And where *is* thy master's **s**? 1121
16: 5 whose name *was* Shimei, the **s** of Gera: 1121
16: 8 kingdom into the hand of Absalom thy **s**: 1121
16: 9 said Abishai the **s** of Zeruiah unto the king, 1121
16:11 and to all his servants, Behold, my **s**, 1121
16:19 *should I* not *serve* in the presence of his **s**? 1121
17:25 which Amasa *was* a man's **s**, whose name 1121
17:27 that Shobi the **s** of Nahash of Rabbah of 1121
17:27 Machir the **s** of Ammiel of Lo-debar, and 1121
18: 2 a third part under the hand of Abishai the **s** 1121
18:12 put forth mine hand against the king's **s**: 1121
18:18 I have no **s** to keep my name in 1121
18:19 said Ahimaaz the **s** of Zadok, Let me now 1121
18:20 no tidings, because the king's **s** is dead. 1121
18:22 said Ahimaaz the **s** of Zadok yet again to 1121
18:22 Joab said, Wherefore wilt thou run, my **s**, 1121
18:27 like the running of Ahimaaz the **s** of Zadok. 1121
18:33 thus he said, O my **s** Absalom, my son, 1121
18:33 my son Absalom, my **s**, my son Absalom: 1121
18:33 my son Absalom, my son, my **s** Absalom: 1121
18:33 died for thee, O Absalom, my **s**, my son. 1121
18:33 died for thee, O Absalom, my son, my **s**. 1121
19: 2 that day *how* the king was grieved for his **s**. 1121
19: 4 O my **s** Absalom, O Absalom, my son, 1121

2Sa 19: 4 son Absalom, O Absalom, my **s**, my son. 1121
19: 4 son Absalom, O Absalom, my son, my **s**. 1121
19:16 Shimei the **s** of Gera, a Benjamite, 1121
19:18 Shimei the **s** of Gera fell down before 1121
19:21 Abishai the **s** of Zeruiah answered and said, 1121
19:24 Mephibosheth the **s** of Saul came down to 1121
20: 1 *was* Sheba, the **s** of Bichri, a Benjamite: 1121
20: 1 neither have we inheritance in the **s** of 1121
20: 2 *and* followed Sheba the **s** of Bichri: 1121
20: 6 Now shall Sheba the **s** of Bichri do us more 1121
20: 7 to pursue after Sheba the **s** of Bichri. 1121
20:10 brother pursued after Sheba the **s** of Bichri. 1121
20:13 to pursue after Sheba the **s** of Bichri. 1121
20:21 Sheba the **s** of Bichri by name, 1121
20:22 they cut off the head of Sheba the **s** of 1121
20:23 Benaiah the **s** of Jehoiada *was* over 1121
20:24 Jehoshaphat the **s** of Ahilud *was* recorder: 1121
21: 7 the **s** of Jonathan the son of Saul, because 1121
21: 7 the son of Jonathan the **s** of Saul, because 1121
21: 7 between David and Jonathan the **s** of Saul. 1121
21: 8 whom she brought up for Adriel the **s** of 1121
21:12 the bones of Jonathan his **s** from the men of 1121
21:13 of Saul and the bones of Jonathan his **s**; 1121
21:14 Jonathan his **s** buried they in the country of 1121
21:17 Abishai the **s** of Zeruiah succoured him, 1121
21:19 where Elhanan the **s** of Jaare-oregim, 1121
21:21 Jonathan the **s** of Shimea the brother of 1121
23: 1 David the **s** of Jesse said, and the man *who* 1121
23: 9 after him *was* Eleazar the **s** of Dodo 1121
23:11 after him *was* Shammah the **s** of Agee 1121
23:18 the brother of Joab, the **s** of Zeruiah, 1121
23:20 Benaiah the **s** of Jehoiada, the son of a 1121
23:20 the **s** of a valiant man, of Kabzeel, who had 1121
23:22 These *things* did Benaiah the **s** of Jehoiada, 1121
23:24 Elhanan the **s** of Dodo *of* Beth-lehem, 1121
23:26 the Paltite, Ira the **s** of Ikkesh the Tekoite, 1121
23:29 Heleb the **s** of Baanah, a Netophathite, 1121
23:29 Ittai the **s** of Ribai out of Gibeah of 1121
23:33 Ahiam the **s** of Sharar the Hararite, 1121
23:34 Eliphelet the **s** of Ahasbai, the son of 1121
23:34 son of Ahasbai, the **s** of the Maachathite, 1121
23:34 Eliam the **s** of Ahithophel the Gilonite, 1121
23:36 Igal the **s** of Nathan of Zobah, Bani 1121
23:37 armourbearer to Joab the **s** of Zeruiah, 1121
1Ki 1: 5 Adonijah the **s** of Haggith exalted himself, 1121
1: 7 he conferred with Joab the **s** of Zeruiah, 1121
1: 8 Benaiah the **s** of Jehoiada, and Nathan 1121
1:11 Hast thou not heard that Adonijah the **s** of 1121
1:12 own life, and the life of thy **s** Solomon. 1121
1:13 Assuredly Solomon thy **s** shall reign after 1121
1:17 *saying,* Assuredly Solomon thy **s** shall 1121
1:21 my **s** Solomon shall be *counted* offenders. 1121
1:26 Benaiah the **s** of Jehoiada, and thy servant 1121
1:30 Assuredly Solomon thy **s** shall reign after 1121
1:32 the prophet, and Benaiah the **s** of Jehoiada. 1121
1:33 cause Solomon my **s** to ride upon mine own 1121
1:36 Benaiah the **s** of Jehoiada answered 1121
1:38 Benaiah the **s** of Jehoiada, and 1121
1:42 Jonathan the **s** of Abiathar the priest came: 1121
1:44 Benaiah the **s** of Jehoiada, and 1121
2: 1 and he charged Solomon his **s**, saying, 1121
2: 5 also what Joab the **s** of Zeruiah did to me, 1121
2: 5 unto Abner the **s** of Ner, and unto Amasa 1121
2: 5 unto Amasa the **s** of Jether, whom he slew, 1121
2: 8 *thou hast* with thee Shimei the **s** of Gera, 1121
2:13 Adonijah the **s** of Haggith came to 1121
2:22 the priest, and for Joab the **s** of Zeruiah. 1121
2:25 by the hand of Benaiah the **s** of Jehoiada; 1121
2:29 Solomon sent Benaiah the **s** of Jehoiada, 1121
2:32 knowing *thereof, to wit,* Abner the **s** of Ner, 1121
2:32 host of Israel, and Amasa the **s** of Jether, 1121
2:34 So Benaiah the **s** of Jehoiada went up, and 1121
2:35 the king put Benaiah the **s** of Jehoiada in 1121
2:39 unto Achish **s** of Maachah king of Gath. 1121
2:46 So the king commanded Benaiah the **s** of 1121
3: 6 that thou hast given him a **s** to sit on his 1121
3:20 at midnight, and took my **s** from beside me, 1121
3:21 it was not my **s**, which I did bear. 1121
3:22 the living *is* my **s**, and the dead *is* thy son. 1121
3:22 the living *is* my son, and the dead *is* thy **s**. 1121
3:22 the dead *is* thy **s**, and the living *is* my son. 1121
3:22 the dead *is* thy son, and the living *is* my **s**. 1121
3:23 This *is* my **s** that liveth, and thy son *is* 1121
3:23 *is* my son that liveth, and thy **s** *is* the dead: 1121
3:23 thy **s** *is* the dead, and my son *is* the living. 1121
3:23 thy son *is* the dead, and my **s** *is* the living. 1121
3:26 for her bowels yerned upon her **s**, and 1121
4: 2 he had; Azariah the **s** of Zadok the priest, 1121
4: 3 Jehoshaphat the **s** of Ahilud, the recorder. 1121
4: 4 Benaiah the **s** of Jehoiada *was* over 1121
4: 5 Azariah the **s** of Nathan *was* over 1121
4: 5 Zabud the **s** of Nathan *was* principal 1121
4: 6 Adoniram the **s** of Abda *was* over 1121
4: 8 The **s** of Hur, in mount Ephraim: 1121
4: 9 The **s** of Dekar, in Makaz, and in Shaalbim, 1121
4:10 The **s** of Hesed, in Aruboth; to him 1121
4:11 The **s** of Abinadab, *in* all the region of Dor; 1121
4:12 Baana the **s** of Ahilud; *to him pertained* 1121
4:13 The **s** of Geber, in Ramoth-gilead; to him 1121
4:13 to him *pertained* the towns of Jair the **s** of 1121
4:14 Ahinadab the **s** of Iddo *had* Mahanaim: 1121
4:16 Baanah the **s** of Hushai *was* in Asher and 1121
4:17 Jehoshaphat the **s** of Paruah, in Issachar: 1121
4:18 Shimei the **s** of Elah, in Benjamin: 1121
4:19 Geber the **s** of Uri *was* in the country of 1121
5: 5 spake unto David my father, saying, Thy **s**, 1121
5: 7 which hath given unto David a wise **s** over 1121
7:14 He *was* a widow's **s** of the tribe of 1121
8:19 thy **s** that shall come forth out of thy loins, 1121
11:12 *but* I will rend it out of the hand of thy **s**. 1121
11:13 will give one tribe to thy **s** for David my 1121
11:20 sister of Tahpenes bare him Genubath his **s**, 1121
11:23 *another* adversary, Rezon the **s** of Eliadah, 1121
11:26 Jeroboam the **s** of Nebat, an Ephrathite of 1121
11:36 unto his **s** will I give one tribe, that David 1121

1Ki 11:43 and Rehoboam his **s** reigned in his stead. 1121
12: 2 to pass, when Jeroboam the **s** of Nebat, 1121
12:15 the Shilonite unto Jeroboam the **s** of Nebat. 1121
12:16 neither *have we* inheritance in the **s** of 1121
12:21 again to Rehoboam the **s** of Solomon. 1121
12:23 the **s** of Solomon, king of Judah, and 1121
13:11 his **s** came and told him all the works that 1121
14: 1 At that time Abijah the **s** of Jeroboam fell 1121
14: 5 cometh to ask a thing of thee for her **s**; 1121
14:20 and Nadab his **s** reigned in his stead. 1121
14:21 Rehoboam the **s** of Solomon reigned in 1121
14:31 And Abijam his **s** reigned in his stead. 1121
15: 1 the **s** of Nebat reigned Abijam over Judah. 1121
15: 4 to set up his **s** after him, and to establish 1121
15: 8 and Asa his **s** reigned in his stead. 1121
15:18 the **s** of Tabrimon, the son of Hezion, 1121
15:18 of Tabrimon, the **s** of Hezion, king of Syria, 1121
15:24 and Jehoshaphat his **s** reigned in his stead. 1121
15:25 Nadab the **s** of Jeroboam *began* to reign 1121
15:27 Baasha the **s** of Ahijah, of the house of 1121
15:33 **s** of Ahijah to reign over all Israel in 1121
16: 1 the word of the LORD came to Jehu the **s** 1121
16: 3 like the house of Jeroboam the **s** of Nebat. 1121
16: 6 and Elah his **s** reigned in his stead. 1121
16: 7 also by the hand of the prophet Jehu the **s** 1121
16: 8 **s** of Baasha to reign over Israel in Tirzah, 1121
16:13 the sins of Elah his **s**, *by* which they sinned, 1121
16:21 half of the people followed Tibni the **s** of 1121
16:22 people that followed Tibni the **s** of Ginath: 1121
16:26 in all the way of Jeroboam the **s** of Nebat, 1121
16:28 and Ahab his **s** reigned in his stead. 1121
16:29 Ahab the **s** of Omri to reign over Israel: 1121
16:29 Ahab the **s** of Omri reigned over Israel in 1121
16:30 Ahab the **s** of Omri did evil in the sight of 1121
16:31 walk in the sins of Jeroboam the **s** of Nebat, 1121
16:34 set up the gates thereof in his youngest *s* NIH
16:34 which he spake by Joshua the **s** of Nun. 1121
17:12 I may go in and dress it for me and my **s**, 1121
17:13 and after make for thee and for thy **s**. 1121
17:17 *that* the **s** of the woman, the mistress of 1121
17:18 my sin to remembrance, and to slay my **s**? 1121
17:19 he said unto her, Give me thy **s**. And he 1121
17:20 with whom I sojourn, by slaying her **s**? 1121
17:23 and Elijah said, See, thy **s** liveth. 1121
19:16 Jehu the **s** of Nimshi shalt thou anoint to be 1121
19:16 Elisha the **s** of Shaphat of Abel-meholah 1121
19:19 and found Elisha the **s** of Shaphat, 1121
21:22 like the house of Jeroboam the **s** of Nebat, 1121
21:22 like the house of Baasha the **s** of Ahijah, 1121
22: 8 *is* yet one man, Micaiah the **s** of Imlah, 1121
22: 9 said, Hasten *hither* Micaiah the **s** of Imlah. 1121
22:11 Zedekiah the **s** of Chenaanah made him 1121
22:24 Zedekiah the **s** of Chenaanah went near, 1121
22:26 of the city, and to Joash the king's **s**; 1121
22:40 and Ahaziah his **s** reigned in his stead. 1121
22:41 Jehoshaphat the **s** of Asa *began* to reign 1121
22:49 said Ahaziah the **s** of Ahab unto 1121
22:50 and Jehoram his **s** reigned in his stead. 1121
22:51 Ahaziah the **s** of Ahab *began* to reign over 1121
22:52 in the way of Jeroboam the **s** of Nebat, 1121
2Ki 1:17 the **s** of Jehoshaphat king of Judah; 1121
1:17 king of Judah; because he had no **s**. 1121
3: 1 Now Jehoram the **s** of Ahab *began* to reign 1121
3: 3 unto the sins of Jeroboam the **s** of Nebat, 1121
3:11 and said, Here *is* Elisha the **s** of Shaphat, 1121
3:27 he took his eldest **s** that should have 1121
4: 6 that she said unto her **s**, Bring me yet a 1121
4:16 to the time of life, thou shalt embrace a **s**. 1121
4:17 bare a **s** at that season that Elisha had said 1121
4:28 she said, Did I desire a **s** of my lord? did I 1121
4:36 come in unto him, he said, Take up thy **s**. 1121
4:37 and took up her **s**, and went out. 1121
6:28 This woman said unto me, Give thy **s**, 1121
6:28 to day, and we will eat my **s** to morrow. 1121
6:29 So we boiled my **s**, and did eat him: and 1121
6:29 next day, Give thy **s**, that we may eat him: 1121
6:29 that we may eat him: and she hath hid her **s**. 1121
6:31 if the head of Elisha the **s** of Shaphat shall 1121
6:32 See ye how this **s** of a murderer hath sent to 1121
8: 1 whose **s** he had restored to life, saying, 1121
8: 5 the woman, whose **s** he had restored to life, 1121
8: 5 O king, this *is* the woman, and this *is* her **s**, 1121
8: 9 Thy **s** Ben-hadad king of Syria hath sent 1121
8:16 in the fifth year of Joram the **s** of Ahab 1121
8:16 Jehoram the **s** of Jehoshaphat king of Judah 1121
8:24 and Ahaziah his **s** reigned in his stead. 1121
8:25 In the twelfth year of Joram the **s** of Ahab 1121
8:25 of Jehoram king of Judah *begin* to reign. 1121
8:27 for he *was* the **s in law** of the house of 2860
8:28 he went with Joram the **s** of Ahab to 1121
8:29 Ahaziah the **s** of Jehoram king of Judah 1121
8:29 down to see Joram the **s** of Ahab in Jezreel, 1121
9: 2 look out there Jehu the **s** of Jehoshaphat 1121
9: 2 the son of Jehoshaphat the **s** of Nimshi, 1121
9: 9 like the house of Jeroboam the **s** of Nebat, 1121
9: 9 like the house of Baasha the **s** of Ahijah: 1121
9:14 So Jehu the **s** of Jehoshaphat the son of 1121
9:14 So Jehu the son of Jehoshaphat the **s** of 1121
9:20 the driving *is* like the driving of Jehu the **s** 1121
9:29 in the eleventh year of Joram the **s** of Ahab 1121
10:15 he lighted on Jehonadab the **s** of Rechab 1121
10:23 Jehu went, and Jehonadab the **s** of Rechab, 1121
10:29 Howbeit *from* the sins of Jeroboam the **s** of 1121
10:35 And Jehoahaz his **s** reigned in his stead 1121
11: 1 mother of Ahaziah saw that her **s** was dead, 1121
11: 2 took Joash the **s** of Ahaziah, and stale him 1121
11: 4 the LORD, and shewed them the king's **s**. 1121
11:12 he brought forth the king's **s**, and put 1121
12:21 For Jozachar the **s** of Shimeath, and 1121
12:21 Jehozabad the **s** of Shomer, his servants, 1121
12:21 and Amaziah his **s** reigned in his stead. 1121
13: 1 twentieth year of Joash the **s** of Ahaziah 1121
13: 1 **s** of Jehu *began* to reign over Israel in 1121
13: 2 followed the sins of Jeroboam the **s** of 1121
13: 3 into the hand of Ben-hadad the **s** of Hazael, 1121

S

2Ki 13: 9 and Joash his **s** reigned in his stead. 1121
13:10 **s** of Jehoahaz to reign over Israel in 1121
13:11 all the sins of Jeroboam the **s** of Nebat, 1121
13:24 and Ben-hadad his **s** reigned in his stead. 1121
13:25 Jehoash the **s** of Jehoahaz took again out of 1121
13:25 of Ben-hadad the **s** of Hazael the cities, 1121
14: 1 In the second year of Joash **s** of Jehoahaz 1121
14: 1 Amaziah the **s** of Joash king of Judah. 1121
14: 8 the **s** of Jehoahaz son of Jehu, king of 1121
14: 8 the son of Jehoahaz **s** of Jehu, king of 1121
14: 9 Give thy daughter to my **s** to wife: 1121
14:13 the **s** of Jehoash the son of Ahaziah, 1121
14:13 the son of Jehoash the **s** of Ahaziah, 1121
14:16 and Jeroboam his **s** reigned in his stead. 1121
14:17 Amaziah the **s** of Joash king of Judah lived 1121
14:17 **s** of Jehoahaz king of Israel fifteen years. 1121
14:23 In the fifteenth year of Amaziah the **s** of 1121
14:23 **s** of Joash king of Israel *began* to reign in 1121
14:24 all the sins of Jeroboam the **s** of Nebat, 1121
14:25 the **s** of Amittai, the prophet, which *was* of 1121
14:27 by the hand of Jeroboam the **s** of Joash. 1121
14:29 and Zachariah his **s** reigned in his stead. 1121
15: 1 **s** of Amaziah king of Judah to reign. 1121
15: 5 Jotham the king's **s** *was* over the house, 1121
15: 7 and Jotham his **s** reigned in his stead. 1121
15: 8 **s** of Jeroboam reign over Israel in Samaria 1121
15: 9 from the sins of Jeroboam the **s** of Nebat, 1121
15:10 Shallum the **s** of Jabesh conspired against 1121
15:13 Shallum the **s** of Jabesh *began* to reign in 1121
15:14 For Menahem the **s** of Gadi went up from 1121
15:14 smote Shallum the **s** of Jabesh in Samaria, 1121
15:17 Menahem the **s** of Gadi to reign over Israel, 1121
15:18 from the sins of Jeroboam the **s** of Nebat, 1121
15:22 and Pekahiah his **s** reigned in his stead. 1121
15:23 **s** of Menahem *began* to reign over Israel in 1121
15:24 from the sins of Jeroboam the **s** of Nebat, 1121
15:25 Pekah the **s** of Remaliah, a captain of his, 1121
15:27 **s** of Remaliah *began* to reign over Israel in 1121
15:28 from the sins of Jeroboam the **s** of Nebat, 1121
15:30 Hoshea the **s** of Elah made a conspiracy 1121
15:30 against Pekah the **s** of Remaliah, 1121
15:30 in the twentieth year of Jotham the **s** of 1121
15:32 In the second year of Pekah the **s** of 1121
15:32 the **s** of Uzziah king of Judah to reign. 1121
15:37 king of Syria, and Pekah the **s** of Remaliah. 1121
15:38 and Ahaz his **s** reigned in his stead. 1121
16: 1 In the seventeenth year of Pekah the **s** of 1121
16: 1 **s** of Jotham king of Judah *began* to reign. 1121
16: 3 yea, and made his **s** to pass through the fire, 1121
16: 5 Pekah **s** of Remaliah king of Israel came up 1121
16: 7 saying, I *am* thy servant and thy **s**: 1121
16:20 and Hezekiah his **s** reigned in his stead. 1121
17: 1 **s** of Elah to reign in Samaria over Israel 1121
17:21 they made Jeroboam the **s** of Nebat king: 1121
18: 1 year of Hoshea **s** of Elah king of Israel, 1121
18: 1 *that* Hezekiah the **s** of Ahaz king of Judah 1121
18: 9 which *was* the seventh year of Hoshea **s** of 1121
18:18 there came out to them Eliakim the **s** of 1121
18:18 and Joah the **s** of Asaph the recorder. 1121
18:26 said Eliakim the **s** of Hilkiah, and Shebna, 1121
18:37 came Eliakim the **s** of Hilkiah, which *was* 1121
18:37 and Joah the **s** of Asaph the recorder, 1121
19: 2 to Esai the prophet the **s** of Amoz. 1121
19:20 Isaiah the **s** of Amoz sent to Hezekiah, 1121
19:37 And Esarhaddon his **s** reigned in his stead. 1121
20: 1 the prophet Isaiah the **s** of Amoz came to 1121
20:12 the **s** of Baladan, king of Babylon, 1121
20:21 and Manasseh his **s** reigned in his stead. 1121
21: 6 he made his **s** pass through the fire, and 1121
21: 7 to Solomon his **s**, In this house, and 1121
21:18 and Amon his **s** reigned in his stead. 1121
21:24 the people of the land made Josiah his **s** 1121
21:26 and Josiah his **s** reigned in his stead. 1121
22: 3 *that* the king sent Shaphan the **s** of Azaliah, 1121
22: 3 the **s** of Meshullam, the scribe, *to* the house 1121
22:12 Ahikam the **s** of Shaphan, and Achbor 1121
22:12 Achbor the **s** of Michaiah, and Shaphan 1121
22:14 the wife of Shallum the **s** of Tikvah, the son 1121
22:14 the **s** of Harhas, keeper of the wardrobe; 1121
23:10 that no man might make his **s** or his 1121
23:15 the high place which Jeroboam the **s** of 1121
23:30 the people of the land took Jehoahaz the **s** 1121
23:34 Pharaoh-nechoh made Eliakim the **s** of 1121
24: 6 and Jehoiachin his **s** reigned in his stead. 1121
25:22 even over them he made Gedaliah the **s** of 1121
25:22 the son of Ahikam, the **s** of Shaphan, ruler. 1121
25:23 even Ishmael the **s** of Nethaniah, and 1121
25:23 Johanan the **s** of Careah, and Seraiah 1121
25:23 Seraiah the **s** of Tanhumeth 1121
25:23 Jaazaniah the **s** of a Maachathite, they and 1121
25:25 *that* Ishmael the **s** of Nethaniah, the son of 1121
25:25 the **s** of Elishama, of the seed royal, came, 1121
1Ch 1:43 the children of Israel; Bela the **s** of Beor: 1121
1:44 Jobab the **s** of Zerah of Bozrah reigned in 1121
1:46 Husham was dead, Hadad the **s** of Bedad, 1121
1:49 Baal-hanan the **s** of Achbor reigned in his 1121
2:18 Caleb the **s** of Hezron begat *children* of 1121
2:45 the **s** of Shammai *was* Maon: and 1121
2:50 These were the sons of Caleb the **s** of Hur, 1121
3: 2 Absalom the **s** of Maachah the daughter of 1121
3: 2 the fourth, Adonijah the **s** of Haggith: 1121
3:10 Solomon's **s** *was* Rehoboam, Abia his son, 1121
3:10 Abia his **s**, Asa his son, Jehoshaphat his 1121
3:10 Abia his son, Asa his **s**, Jehoshaphat his 1121
3:10 his son, Asa his son, Jehoshaphat his **s**, 1121
3:11 Joram his **s**, Ahaziah his son, Joash his son, 1121
3:11 Joram his son, Ahaziah his **s**, Joash his son, 1121
3:11 Joram his son, Ahaziah his son, Joash his **s**, 1121
3:12 Amaziah his **s**, Azariah his son, Jotham his 1121
3:12 his son, Azariah his **s**, Jotham his son, 1121
3:12 his son, Azariah his son, Jotham his **s**, 1121
3:13 Ahaz his **s**, Hezekiah his son, Manasseh his 1121
3:13 Ahaz his son, Hezekiah his **s**, Manasseh his 1121
3:13 his son, Hezekiah his son, Manasseh his **s**, 1121
3:14 Amon his **s**, Josiah his son. 1121

1Ch 3:14 Amon his son, Josiah his **s**. 1121
3:16 Jeconiah his **s**, Zedekiah his son. 1121
3:16 Jeconiah his son, Zedekiah his **s**. 1121
3:17 the sons of Jeconiah; Assir, Salathiel his **s**, 1121
3:19 the **s** of Zerubbabel; Meshullam, and 1121
4: 2 Reaiah the **s** of Shobal begat Jahath; and 1121
4: 8 and the families of Aharhel the **s** of Harum. 1121
4:15 the sons of Caleb the **s** of Jephunneh; Iru, 1121
4:21 The sons of Shelah the **s** of Judah *were*, Er 1121
4:25 Shallum his **s**, Mibsam his son, Mishma his 1121
4:25 his son, Mibsam his **s**, Mishma his son. 1121
4:25 his son, Mibsam his son, Mishma his **s**. 1121
4:26 Hamuel his **s**, Zacchur his son, Shimei his 1121
4:26 his son, Zacchur his **s**, Shimei his son. 1121
4:26 his son, Zacchur his son, Shimei his **s**. 1121
4:34 and Jamlech, and Joshah the **s** of Amaziah, 1121
4:35 Joel, and Jehu the **s** of Josibiah, the son of 1121
4:35 the **s** of Seraiah, the son of Asiel, 1121
4:35 the son of Seraiah, the **s** of Asiel, 1121
4:37 Ziza the **s** of Shiphi, the son of Allon, 1121
4:37 the **s** of Allon, the son of Jedaiah, the son 1121
4:37 the son of Allon, the **s** of Jedaiah, the son 1121
4:37 the son of Jedaiah, the **s** of Shimri, 1121
4:37 the son of Shimri, the **s** of Shemaiah; 1121
5: 1 unto the sons of Joseph the **s** of Israel: 1121
5: 4 Shemaiah his **s**, Gog his son, Shimei his 1121
5: 4 his son, Gog his **s**, Shimei his son, 1121
5: 4 his son, Gog his son, Shimei his **s**, 1121
5: 5 Micah his **s**, Reaia his son, Baal his son, 1121
5: 5 Micah his son, Reaia his **s**, Baal his son, 1121
5: 5 Micah his son, Reaia his son, Baal his **s**, 1121
5: 6 Beerah his **s**, whom Tilgath-pilneser king 1121
5: 8 Bela the **s** of Azaz, the son of Shema, 1121
5: 8 the **s** of Shema, the son of Joel, who dwelt 1121
5: 8 the son of Shema, the **s** of Joel, who dwelt 1121
5:14 These *are* the children of Abihail the **s** of 1121
5:14 the **s** of Jaroah, the son of Gilead, the son 1121
5:14 the son of Jaroah, the **s** of Gilead, the son 1121
5:14 the son of Gilead, the **s** of Michael, 1121
5:14 the **s** of Jeshishai, the son of Jahdo, the son 1121
5:14 of Jeshishai, the **s** of Jahdo, the son of Buz; 1121
5:14 of Jeshishai, the son of Jahdo, the **s** of Buz; 1121
5:15 Ahi the **s** of Abdiel, the son of Guni, 1121
5:15 Ahi the son of Abdiel, the **s** of Guni, 1121
6:20 Libni his **s**, Jahath his son, Zimmah his son, 1121
6:20 Libni his son, Jahath his **s**, Zimmah his son, 1121
6:20 Libni his son, Jahath his son, Zimmah his **s**, 1121
6:21 Joah his **s**, Iddo his son, Zerah his son, 1121
6:21 Joah his son, Iddo his **s**, Zerah his son, 1121
6:21 Joah his son, Iddo his son, Zerah his **s**, 1121
6:21 Iddo his son, Zerah his son, Jeaterai his **s**. 1121
6:22 Amminadab his **s**, Korah his son, Assir his 1121
6:22 his son, Korah his **s**, Assir his son, 1121
6:22 his son, Korah his son, Assir his **s**, 1121
6:23 Elkanah his **s**, and Ebiasaph his son, and 1121
6:23 and Ebiasaph his **s**, and Assir his son, 1121
6:23 and Ebiasaph his son, and Assir his **s**, 1121
6:24 Tahath his **s**, Uriel his son, Uzziah his son, 1121
6:24 Tahath his son, Uriel his **s**, Uzziah his son, 1121
6:24 his son, Uzziah his **s**, and Shaul his son. 1121
6:24 his son, Uzziah his son, and Shaul his **s**. 1121
6:26 Zophai his **s**, and Nahath his son, 1121
6:26 Zophai his son, and Nahath his **s**, 1121
6:27 Eliab his **s**, Jeroham his son, Elkanah his 1121
6:27 Eliab his son, Jeroham his **s**, Elkanah his 1121
6:27 his son, Jeroham his son, Elkanah his **s**. 1121
6:29 Mahli, Libni his **s**, Shimei his son, Uzza his 1121
6:29 Libni his son, Shimei his **s**, Uzza his son, 1121
6:29 Libni his son, Shimei his son, Uzza his **s**, 1121
6:30 Shimea his **s**, Haggiah his son, Asaiah his 1121
6:30 his son, Haggiah his **s**, Asaiah his son. 1121
6:30 his son, Haggiah his son, Asaiah his **s**. 1121
6:33 Heman a singer, the **s** of Joel, the son of 1121
6:33 a singer, the son of Joel, the **s** of Shemuel, 1121
6:34 The **s** of Elkanah, the son of Jeroham, 1121
6:34 the **s** of Jeroham, the son of Eliel, the son 1121
6:34 of Jeroham, the **s** of Eliel, the son of Toah, 1121
6:34 of Jeroham, the son of Eliel, the **s** of Toah, 1121
6:35 The **s** of Zuph, the son of Elkanah, the son 1121
6:35 The son of Zuph, the **s** of Elkanah, the son 1121
6:35 the **s** of Mahath, the son of Amasai, 1121
6:35 the son of Mahath, the **s** of Amasai, 1121
6:36 The **s** of Elkanah, the son of Joel, the son of 1121
6:36 the **s** of Joel, the son of Azariah, 1121
6:36 the son of Joel, the **s** of Azariah, 1121
6:36 the son of Azariah, the **s** of Zephaniah, 1121
6:37 The **s** of Tahath, the son of Assir, the son of 1121
6:37 The son of Tahath, the **s** of Assir, the son of 1121
6:37 the son of Assir, the **s** of Ebiasaph, the son 1121
6:37 the son of Ebiasaph, the **s** of Korah, 1121
6:38 The **s** of Izhar, the son of Kohath, the son 1121
6:38 the **s** of Kohath, the son of Levi, the son of 1121
6:38 of Kohath, the **s** of Levi, the son of Israel. 1121
6:38 of Kohath, the son of Levi, the **s** of Israel. 1121
6:39 *even* Asaph the **s** of Berachiah, the son of 1121
6:39 the son of Berachiah, the **s** of Shimea, 1121
6:40 The **s** of Michael, the son of Baaseiah, 1121
6:40 The son of Michael, the **s** of Baaseiah, 1121
6:40 the son of Baaseiah, the **s** of Malchiah, 1121
6:41 The **s** of Ethni, the son of Zerah, the son of 1121
6:41 The son of Ethni, the **s** of Zerah, the son of 1121
6:41 of Ethni, the son of Zerah, the **s** of Adaiah, 1121
6:42 The **s** of Ethan, the son of Zimmah, the son 1121
6:42 The son of Ethan, the **s** of Zimmah, the son 1121
6:42 the son of Zimmah, the **s** of Shimei, 1121
6:43 The **s** of Jahath, the son of Gershom, 1121
6:43 the **s** of Gershom, the son of Levi. 1121
6:43 the son of Gershom, the **s** of Levi. 1121
6:44 Ethan the **s** of Kishi, the son of Abdi, 1121
6:44 of Kishi, the **s** of Abdi, the son of Malluch, 1121
6:44 of Kishi, the son of Abdi, the **s** of Malluch, 1121
6:45 The **s** of Hashabiah, the son of Amaziah, 1121
6:45 the **s** of Amaziah, the son of Hilkiah, 1121
6:45 the son of Amaziah, the **s** of Hilkiah, 1121
6:46 The **s** of Amzi, the son of Bani, the son of 1121

1Ch 6:46 The son of Amzi, the **s** of Bani, the son of 1121
6:46 of Amzi, the son of Bani, the **s** of Shamer, 1121
6:47 The **s** of Mahli, the son of Mushi, the son 1121
6:47 the **s** of Mushi, the son of Merari, the son 1121
6:47 of Mushi, the **s** of Merari, the son of Levi. 1121
6:47 of Mushi, the son of Merari, the **s** of Levi. 1121
6:50 Eleazar his **s**, Phinehas his son, Abishua his 1121
6:50 Eleazar his son, Phinehas his **s**, Abishua his 1121
6:50 his son, Phinehas his son, Abishua his **s**, 1121
6:51 Bukki his **s**, Uzzi his son, Zerahiah his son, 1121
6:51 Bukki his son, Uzzi his **s**, Zerahiah his son, 1121
6:51 Bukki his son, Uzzi his son, Zerahiah his **s**, 1121
6:52 Meraioth his **s**, Amariah his son, Ahitub his 1121
6:52 his son, Amariah his **s**, Ahitub his son, 1121
6:52 his son, Amariah his son, Ahitub his **s**, 1121
6:53 Zadok his **s**, Ahimaaz his son. 1121
6:53 Zadok his son, Ahimaaz his **s**. 1121
6:56 they gave to Caleb the **s** of Jephunneh. 1121
7:16 Maachah the wife of Machir bare a **s**, and 1121
7:17 the **s** of Machir, the son of Manasseh. 1121
7:17 the son of Machir, the **s** of Manasseh. 1121
7:20 Bered his **s**, and Tahath his son, and 1121
7:20 Tahath his **s**, and Eladah his son, and 1121
7:20 and Eladah his **s**, and Tahath his son, 1121
7:20 and Eladah his son, and Tahath his **s**, 1121
7:21 Zabad his **s**, and Shuthelah his son, and 1121
7:21 and Shuthelah his **s**, and Ezer, and Elead, 1121
7:23 and bare a **s**, and he called his name Beriah, 1121
7:25 Rephah *was* his **s**, also Resheph, and 1121
7:25 and Telah his **s**, and Tahan his son, 1121
7:25 and Telah his son, and Tahan his **s**, 1121
7:26 Laadan his **s**, Ammihud his son, 1121
7:26 Laadan his son, Ammihud his **s**, 1121
7:26 his son, Ammihud his son, Elishama his **s**, 1121
7:27 Non his **s**, Jehoshua his son. 1121
7:27 Non his son, Jehoshua his **s**. 1121
7:29 In these dwelt the children of Joseph the **s** 1121
7:35 the **s** of his brother Helem; Zophah, and 1121
8:30 his firstborn **s** Abdon, and Zur, and Kish, 1121
8:34 the **s** of Jonathan *was* Merib-baal; and 1121
8:37 Rapha *was* his **s**, Eleasah his son, Azel his 1121
8:37 *was* his son, Eleasah his **s**, Azel his son: 1121
8:37 *was* his son, Eleasah his son, Azel his **s**: 1121
9: 4 Uthai the **s** of Ammihud, the son of Omri, 1121
9: 4 the **s** of Omri, the son of Imri, the son of 1121
9: 4 son of Omri, the **s** of Imri, the son of Bani, 1121
9: 4 son of Omri, the son of Imri, the **s** of Bani, 1121
9: 4 of the children of Pharez the **s** of Judah. 1121
9: 7 Sallu the **s** of Meshullam, the son of 1121
9: 7 the **s** of Hodaviah, the son of Hasenuah, 1121
9: 7 the son of Hodaviah, the **s** of Hasenuah, 1121
9: 8 Ibneiah the **s** of Jeroham, and Elah the son 1121
9: 8 Elah the **s** of Uzzi, the son of Michri, and 1121
9: 8 the **s** of Michri, and Meshullam the son of 1121
9: 8 Meshullam the **s** of Shephathiah, the son of 1121
9: 8 the **s** of Reuel, the son of Ibnijah; 1121
9: 8 the son of Reuel, the **s** of Ibnijah; 1121
9:11 Azariah the **s** of Hilkiah, the son of 1121
9:11 the **s** of Meshullam, the son of Zadok, 1121
9:11 the **s** of Zadok, the son of Meraioth, the son 1121
9:11 the son of Zadok, the **s** of Meraioth, the son 1121
9:11 the son of Meraioth, the **s** of Ahitub, 1121
9:12 Adaiah the **s** of Jeroham, the son of Pashur, 1121
9:12 the **s** of Pashur, the son of Malchijah, and 1121
9:12 the **s** of Malchijah, and Maasiai the son of 1121
9:12 Maasiai the **s** of Adiel, the son of Jahzerah, 1121
9:12 the **s** of Jahzerah, the son of Meshullam, 1121
9:12 the son of Jahzerah, the **s** of Meshullam, 1121
9:12 the **s** of Meshillemith, the son of Immer; 1121
9:12 the son of Meshillemith, the **s** of Immer; 1121
9:14 Shemaiah the **s** of Hasshub, the son of 1121
9:14 the **s** of Azrikam, the son of Hashabiah, 1121
9:14 the son of Azrikam, the **s** of Hashabiah, 1121
9:15 and Galal, and Mattaniah the **s** of Micah, 1121
9:15 of Micah, the **s** of Zichri, the son of Asaph; 1121
9:15 of Micah, the son of Zichri, the **s** of Asaph; 1121
9:16 Obadiah the **s** of Shemaiah, the son of 1121
9:16 the **s** of Galal, the son of Jeduthun, and 1121
9:16 the **s** of Jeduthun, and Berechiah the son of 1121
9:16 Berechiah the **s** of Asa, the son of Elkanah, 1121
9:16 Berechiah the son of Asa, the **s** of Elkanah, 1121
9:19 Shallum the **s** of Kore, the son of Ebiasaph, 1121
9:19 the **s** of Ebiasaph, the son of Korah, and 1121
9:19 the **s** of Korah, and his brethren, 1121
9:20 Phinehas the **s** of Eleazar was the ruler over 1121
9:21 *And* Zechariah the **s** of Meshelemiah *was* 1121
9:36 his firstborn **s** Abdon, then Zur, and Kish, 1121
9:40 the **s** of Jonathan *was* Merib-baal: and 1121
9:43 Rephaiah his **s**, Eleasah his son, Azel his 1121
9:43 his son, Eleasah his **s**, Azel his son. 1121
9:43 his son, Eleasah his son, Azel his **s**. 1121
10:14 turned the kingdom unto David the **s** of 1121
11: 6 So Joab the **s** of Zeruiah went first up, and 1121
11:12 after him *was* Eleazar the **s** of Dodo, 1121
11:22 Benaiah the **s** of Jehoiada, the son of a 1121
11:22 the **s** of a valiant man of Kabzeel, who had 1121
11:24 These *things* did Benaiah the **s** of Jehoiada, 1121
11:26 Elhanan the **s** of Dodo of Beth-lehem, 1121
11:28 Ira the **s** of Ikkesh the Tekoite, Abi-ezer 1121
11:30 Heled the **s** of Baanah the Netophathite, 1121
11:31 Ithai the **s** of Ribai of Gibeah, 1121
11:34 Jonathan the **s** of Shage the Hararite, 1121
11:35 Ahiam the **s** of Sacar the Hararite, 1121
11:35 of Sacar the Hararite, Eliphal the **s** of Ur, 1121
11:37 Hezro the Carmelite, Naarai the **s** of Ezbai, 1121
11:38 brother of Nathan, Mibhar the **s** of Haggeri, 1121
11:39 the armourbearer of Joab the **s** of Zeruiah, 1121
11:41 Uriah the Hittite, Zabad the **s** of Ahlai, 1121
11:42 Adina the **s** of Shiza the Reubenite, 1121
11:43 Hanan the **s** of Maachah, and Joshaphat 1121
11:45 Jediael the **s** of Shimri, and Joha his 1121
12: 1 himself close because of Saul the **s** of Kish: 1121
12:18 *we*, David, and on thy side, thou **s** of Jesse: 1121
15:17 So the Levites appointed Heman the **s** of 1121
15:17 of his brethren, Asaph the **s** of Berechiah; 1121

1Ch 15:17 their brethren, Ethan the **s** of Kushaiah; 1121
16:38 Obed-edom also the **s** of Jeduthun and 1121
17:13 I will be his father, and he shall be my **s**: 1121
18:10 He sent Hadoram his **s** to king David, 1121
18:12 Moreover Abishai the **s** of Zeruiah slew of 1121
18:15 Joab the **s** of Zeruiah *was* over the host; 1121
18:15 and Jehoshaphat the **s** of Ahilud, recorder. 1121
18:16 Zadok the **s** of Ahitub, and Abimelech 1121
18:16 Abimelech the **s** of Abiathar, *were* 1121
18:17 Benaiah the **s** of Jehoiada *was* over 1121
19: 1 Ammon died, and his **s** reigned in his stead. 1121
19: 2 I will shew kindness unto Hanun the **s** of 1121
20: 5 Elhanan the **s** of Jair slew Lahmi 1121
20: 6 and he also was the **s** of the giant. 3205
20: 7 Jonathan the **s** of Shimea David's brother 1121
22: 5 Solomon my **s** *is* young and tender, and 1121
22: 6 he called for Solomon his **s**, and 1121
22: 7 David said to Solomon, My **s**, *as for* me, 1121
22: 9 Behold, a **s** *shall be* born to thee, who shall 1121
22:10 he shall be my **s**, and I *will be* his father; 1121
22:11 Now, my **s**, the LORD be with thee; and 1121
22:17 the princes of Israel to help Solomon his **s**, 1121
23: 1 he made Solomon his **s** king over Israel. 1121
24: 6 Shemaiah the **s** of Nethaneel the scribe, 1121
24: 6 Ahimelech the **s** of Abiathar, and *before* 1121
24:29 the **s** of Kish *was* Jerahmeel. 1121
26: 1 Of the Korhites *was* Meshelemiah the **s** of 1121
26: 6 Also unto Shemaiah his **s** were sons born, 1121
26:14 *for* Zechariah his **s**, a wise counseller, 1121
26:24 Shebuel the **s** of Gershom, the son of 1121
26:24 the **s** of Moses, *was* ruler of the treasures. 1121
26:25 Rehabiah his **s**, and Jeshaiah his son, and 1121
26:25 Jeshaiah his **s**, and Joram his son, and 1121
26:25 Joram his **s**, and Zichri his son, and 1121
26:25 and Zichri his **s**, and Shelomith his son. 1121
26:25 and Zichri his son, and Shelomith his **s**. 1121
26:28 Saul the **s** of Kish, and Abner the son of 1121
26:28 Abner the **s** of Ner, and Joab the son of 1121
26:28 and Joab the **s** of Zeruiah, had dedicated; 1121
27: 2 month *was* Jashobeam the **s** of Zabdiel: 1121
27: 5 third month *was* Benaiah the **s** of Jehoiada, 1121
27: 6 and *in* his course *was* Ammizabad his **s**. 1121
27: 7 of Joab, and Zebadiah his **s** after him: 1121
27: 9 month *was* Ira the **s** of Ikkesh the Tekoite: 1121
27:16 the Reubenites *was* Eliezer the **s** of Zichri: 1121
27:16 Shephatiah the **s** of Maachah: 1121
27:17 Of the Levites, Hashabiah the **s** of Kemuel: 1121
27:18 of Issachar, Omri the **s** of Michael: 1121
27:19 Of Zebulun, Ishmaiah the **s** of Obadiah: 1121
27:19 of Naphtali, Jerimoth the **s** of Azriel: 1121
27:20 of Ephraim, Hoshea the **s** of Azaziah: 1121
27:20 tribe of Manasseh, Joel the **s** of Pedaiah: 1121
27:21 in Gilead, Iddo the **s** of Zechariah: 1121
27:21 of Benjamin, Jaasiel the **s** of Abner: 1121
27:22 Of Dan, Azareel the **s** of Jeroham. 1121
27:24 Joab the **s** of Zeruiah began to number, but 1121
27:25 treasures *was* Azmaveth the **s** of Adiel: 1121
27:25 the castles, *was* Jehonathan the **s** of Uzziah: 1121
27:26 of the ground *was* Ezri the **s** of Chelub: 1121
27:29 in the valleys *was* Shaphat the **s** of Adlai: 1121
27:32 Jehiel the **s** of Hachmoni *was* with 1121
27:34 after Ahithophel *was* Jehoiada the **s** of 1121
28: 5 he hath chosen Solomon my **s** to sit upon 1121
28: 6 he said unto me, Solomon thy **s**, he shall 1121
28: 6 for I have chosen him to be my **s**, and I will 1121
28: 9 thou, Solomon my **s**, know thou the God of 1121
28:11 David gave to Solomon his **s** the pattern of 1121
28:20 And David said to Solomon his **s**, Be strong 1121
29: 1 Solomon my **s**, whom alone God hath 1121
29:19 give unto Solomon my **s** a perfect heart, 1121
29:22 they made Solomon the **s** of David king 1121
29:26 Thus David the **s** of Jesse reigned over all 1121
29:28 and Solomon his **s** reigned in his stead. 1121
2Ch 1: 1 Solomon the **s** of David was strengthened 1121
1: 5 that Bezaleel the **s** of Uri, the son of Hur, 1121
1: 5 the son of Uri, the **s** of Hur, had made, 1121
2:12 who hath given to David the king a wise **s**, 1121
2:14 The **s** of a woman of the daughters of Dan, 1121
6: 9 thy **s** which shall come forth out of thy 1121
9:29 the seer against Jeroboam the **s** of Nebat? 1121
9:31 and Rehoboam his **s** reigned in his stead. 1121
10: 2 when Jeroboam the **s** of Nebat, who *was* in 1121
10:15 the Shilonite to Jeroboam the **s** of Nebat. 1121
10:16 *we have* none inheritance in the **s** of Jesse: 1121
11: 3 Speak unto Rehoboam the **s** of Solomon, 1121
11:17 made Rehoboam the **s** of Solomon strong, 1121
11:18 daughter of Jerimoth the **s** of David *to* wife, 1121
11:18 Abihail the daughter of Eliab the **s** of Jesse; 1121
11:22 Rehoboam made Abijah the **s** of Maachah 1121
12:16 and Abijah his **s** reigned in his stead. 1121
13: 6 Yet Jeroboam the **s** of Nebat, the servant of 1121
13: 6 the servant of Solomon the **s** of David, 1121
13: 7 against Rehoboam the **s** of Solomon, 1121
14: 1 Asa his **s** reigned in his stead. In his days 1121
15: 1 the spirit of God came upon Azariah the **s** 1121
17: 1 Jehoshaphat his **s** reigned in his stead, and 1121
17:16 next him *was* Amasiah the **s** of Zichri, 1121
18: 7 the same *is* Micaiah the **s** of Imla. 1121
18: 8 said, Fetch quickly Micaiah the **s** of Imla. 1121
18:10 Zedekiah the **s** of Chenaanah had made him 1121
18:23 Zedekiah the **s** of Chenaanah came near, 1121
18:25 of the city, and to Joash the king's **s**; 1121
19: 2 Jehu the **s** of Hanani the seer went out to 1121
19:11 Zebadiah the **s** of Ishmael, the ruler of 1121
20:14 upon Jahaziel the **s** of Zechariah, the son of 1121
20:14 the **s** of Benaiah, the son of Jeiel, the son of 1121
20:14 the son of Benaiah, the **s** of Jeiel, the son of 1121
20:14 the son of Jeiel, the **s** of Mattaniah, 1121
20:34 written in the book of Jehu the **s** of Hanani, 1121
20:37 Eliezer the **s** of Dodavah of Mareshah 1121
21: 1 And Jehoram his **s** reigned in his stead. 1121
21:17 so that there was never a **s** left him, 1121
22: 1 Ahaziah his youngest **s** king in his stead: 1121
22: 1 So Ahaziah the **s** of Jehoram king of Judah 1121
22: 5 went with Jehoram the **s** of Ahab king of 1121

2Ch 22: 6 Azariah the **s** of Jehoram king of Judah 1121
22: 6 to see Jehoram the **s** of Ahab at Jezreel, 1121
22: 7 with Jehoram against Jehu the **s** of Nimshi, 1121
22: 9 said they, he *is* the **s** of Jehoshaphat, 1121
22:10 mother of Ahaziah saw that her **s** was dead, 1121
22:11 took Joash the **s** of Ahaziah, and stole him 1121
23: 1 Azariah the **s** of Jeroham, and Ishmael 1121
23: 1 Ishmael the **s** of Jehohanan, and Azariah 1121
23: 1 Azariah the **s** of Obed, and Maaseiah 1121
23: 1 Maaseiah the **s** of Adaiah, and Elishaphat 1121
23: 1 Elishaphat the **s** of Zichri, into covenant 1121
23: 3 unto them, Behold, the king's **s** shall reign, 1121
23:11 they brought out the king's **s**, and put upon 1121
24:20 the spirit of God came upon Zechariah the **s** 1121
24:22 his father had done to him, but slew his **s**. 1121
24:26 Zabad the **s** of Shimeath an Ammonitess, 1121
24:26 Jehozabad the **s** of Shimrith a Moabitess. 1121
24:27 And Amaziah his **s** reigned in his stead. 1121
25:17 sent to Joash, the **s** of Jehoahaz, the son of 1121
25:17 the **s** of Jehu, king of Israel, saying, Come, 1121
25:18 Give thy daughter to my **s** to wife: 1121
25:23 the **s** of Joash, the son of Jehoahaz, 1121
25:23 the son of Joash, the **s** of Jehoahaz, 1121
25:25 Amaziah the **s** of Joash king of Judah lived 1121
25:25 **s** of Jehoahaz king of Israel fifteen years. 1121
26:21 and Jotham his **s** *was* over the king's house, 1121
26:22 Isaiah the prophet, the **s** of Amoz, write. 1121
26:23 and Jotham his **s** reigned in his stead. 1121
27: 9 and Ahaz his **s** reigned in his stead. 1121
28: 3 incense in the valley of the **s** of Hinnom, 1121
28: 6 For Pekah the **s** of Remaliah slew in Judah 1121
28: 7 slew Maaseiah the king's **s**, and Azrikam 1121
28:12 Azariah the **s** of Johanan, Berechiah the son 1121
28:12 Berechiah the **s** of Meshillemoth, and 1121
28:12 Jehizkiah the **s** of Shallum, and Amasa 1121
28:12 son of Shallum, and Amasa the **s** of Hadlai, 1121
28:27 and Hezekiah his **s** reigned in his stead. 1121
29:12 Mahath the **s** of Amasai, and Joel the son of 1121
29:12 son of Amasai, and Joel the **s** of Azariah, 1121
29:12 Kish the **s** of Abdi, and Azariah the son of 1121
29:12 son of Abdi, and Azariah the **s** of Jehalelel: 1121
29:12 Joah the **s** of Zimmah, and Eden the son of 1121
29:12 the son of Zimmah, and Eden the **s** of Joah: 1121
30:26 for since the time of Solomon the **s** of 1121
31:14 Kore the **s** of Imnah the Levite, the porter 1121
32:20 the prophet Isaiah the **s** of Amoz, prayed 1121
32:32 the **s** of Amoz, *and* in the book of the kings 1121
32:33 And Manasseh his **s** reigned in his stead. 1121
33: 6 the fire in the valley of the **s** of Hinnom: 1121
33: 7 had said to David and to Solomon his **s**, 1121
33:20 and Amon his **s** reigned in his stead. 1121
33:25 the people of the land made Josiah his **s** 1121
34: 8 he sent Shaphan the **s** of Azaliah, and 1121
34: 8 and Joah the **s** of Joahaz the recorder, 1121
34:20 Ahikam the **s** of Shaphan, and Abdon 1121
34:20 Abdon the **s** of Micah, and Shaphan 1121
34:22 the wife of Shallum the **s** of Tikvath, 1121
34:22 the **s** of Hasrah, keeper of the wardrobe; 1121
35: 3 the **s** of David king of Israel did build; 1121
35: 4 according to the writing of Solomon his **s**. 1121
36: 1 the people of the land took Jehoahaz the **s** 1121
36: 8 and Jehoiachin his **s** reigned in his stead. 1121
Ezr 3: 2 stood up Jeshua the **s** of Jozadak, and 1121
3: 2 Zerubbabel the **s** of Shealtiel, and 1121
3: 8 began Zerubbabel the **s** of Shealtiel, and 1121
3: 8 Jeshua the **s** of Jozadak, and the remnant of 1121
5: 1 the prophet, and Zechariah the **s** of Iddo, 1247
5: 2 rose up Zerubbabel the **s** of Shealtiel, and 1247
5: 2 Jeshua the **s** of Jozadak, and began to build 1247
6:14 the prophet and Zechariah the **s** of Iddo. 1247
7: 1 Ezra the **s** of Seraiah, the son of Azariah, 1121
7: 1 the **s** of Azariah, the son of Hilkiah, 1121
7: 1 the son of Azariah, the **s** of Hilkiah, 1121
7: 2 The **s** of Shallum, the son of Zadok, the son 1121
7: 2 the **s** of Zadok, the son of Ahitub, 1121
7: 2 the son of Zadok, the **s** of Ahitub, 1121
7: 3 The **s** of Amariah, the son of Azariah, 1121
7: 3 the **s** of Azariah, the son of Meraioth, 1121
7: 3 the son of Azariah, the **s** of Meraioth, 1121
7: 4 The **s** of Zerahiah, the son of Uzzi, the son 1121
7: 4 the **s** of Uzzi, the son of Bukki, 1121
7: 4 the son of Uzzi, the **s** of Bukki, 1121
7: 5 The **s** of Abishua, the son of Phinehas, 1121
7: 5 the **s** of Phinehas, the son of Eleazar, 1121
7: 5 the son of Phinehas, the **s** of Eleazar, 1121
7: 5 of Eleazar, the **s** of Aaron the chief priest: 1121
8: 4 Elihoenai the **s** of Zerahiah, and with him 1121
8: 5 the **s** of Jahaziel, and with him three 1121
8: 6 Ebed the **s** of Jonathan, and with him fifty 1121
8: 7 Jeshaiah the **s** of Athaliah, and with him 1121
8: 8 Zebadiah the **s** of Michael, and with him 1121
8: 9 Obadiah the **s** of Jehiel, and with him two 1121
8:10 the **s** of Josiphiah, and with him an hundred 1121
8:11 Zechariah the **s** of Bebai, and with him 1121
8:12 Johanan the **s** of Hakkatan, and with him an 1121
8:18 of Mahli, the **s** of Levi, the son of Israel; 1121
8:18 of Mahli, the son of Levi, the **s** of Israel; 1121
8:33 hand of Meremoth the **s** of Uriah the priest; 1121
8:33 with him *was* Eleazar the **s** of Phinehas; 1121
8:33 with them *was* Jozabad the **s** of Jeshua, and 1121
8:33 and Noadiah the **s** of Binnui, Levites; 1121
10: 2 Shechaniah the **s** of Jehiel, *one* of the sons 1121
10: 6 went into the chamber of Johanan the **s** of 1121
10:15 Only Jonathan the **s** of Asahel and 1121
10:15 Jahaziah the **s** of Tikvah were employed 1121
10:18 *namely,* of the sons of Jeshua the **s** of 1121
Ne 1: 1 The words of Nehemiah the **s** of Hachaliah. 1121
3: 2 next to them builded Zaccur the **s** of Imri. 1121
3: 4 next unto them repaired Meremoth the **s** of 1121
3: 4 Meremoth the son of Urijah, the **s** of Koz. 1121
3: 4 next unto them repaired Meshullam the **s** of 1121
3: 4 the son of Berechiah, the **s** of Meshezabeel. 1121
3: 4 next unto them repaired Zadok the **s** of 1121
3: 6 old gate repaired Jehoiada the **s** of Paseah, 1121
3: 6 and Meshullam the **s** of Besodeiah; 1121

Ne 3: 8 Next unto him repaired Uzziel the **s** of 1121
3: 8 Next unto him also repaired Hananiah the **s** 1121
3: 9 next unto them repaired Rephaiah the **s** of 1121
3:10 next unto them repaired Jedaiah the **s** of 1121
3:10 next unto him repaired Hattush the **s** of 1121
3:11 Malchijah the **s** of Harim, and Hashub 1121
3:11 Hashub the **s** of Pahath-moab, repaired 1121
3:12 next unto him repaired Shallum the **s** of 1121
3:14 the dung gate repaired Malchiah the **s** of 1121
3:15 repaired Shallun the **s** of Col-hozeh, 1121
3:16 After him repaired Nehemiah the **s** of 1121
3:17 repaired the Levites, Rehum the **s** of Bani. 1121
3:18 their brethren, Bavai the **s** of Henadad, 1121
3:19 next to him repaired Ezer the **s** of Jeshua, 1121
3:20 After him Baruch the **s** of Zabbai earnestly 1121
3:21 After him repaired Meremoth the **s** of 1121
3:21 son of Urijah the **s** of Koz another piece, 1121
3:23 After him repaired Azariah the **s** of 1121
3:23 of Maaseiah the **s** of Ananiah by his house. 1121
3:24 After him repaired Binnui the **s** of Henadad 1121
3:25 Palal the **s** of Uzai, over against the turning 1121
3:25 After him Pedaiah the **s** of Parosh. 1121
3:29 After them repaired Zadok the **s** of Immer 1121
3:29 After him repaired also Shemaiah the **s** of 1121
3:30 After him repaired Hananiah the **s** of 1121
3:30 Hanun the sixth **s** of Zalaph, another piece. 1121
3:30 After him repaired Meshullam the **s** of 1121
3:31 **s** unto the place of the Nethinims, 1121
6:10 the **s** of Delaiah the son of Mehetabeel, 1121
6:10 the son of Delaiah the **s** of Mehetabeel, 1121
6:18 he *was* the **s in law** of Shechaniah the son 2860
6:18 he *was* the son in law of Shechaniah the **s** 1121
6:18 his **s** Johanan had taken the daughter of 1121
6:18 daughter of Meshullam the **s** of Berechiah. 1121
8:17 for since the days of Jeshua the **s** of Nun 1121
10: 1 the **s** of Hachaliah, and Zidkijah, 1121
10: 9 both Jeshua the **s** of Azaniah, Binnui of 1121
10:38 the priest the **s** of Aaron shall be with 1121
11: 4 Athaiah the **s** of Uzziah, the son of 1121
11: 4 the **s** of Zechariah, the son of Amariah, 1121
11: 4 the son of Zechariah, the **s** of Amariah, 1121
11: 4 the son of Amariah, the **s** of Shephatiah, 1121
11: 4 the son of Shephatiah, the **s** of Mahalaleel, 1121
11: 5 Maaseiah the **s** of Baruch, the son of 1121
11: 5 the **s** of Col-hozeh, the son of Hazaiah, 1121
11: 5 the **s** of Hazaiah, the son of Adaiah, the son 1121
11: 5 the **s** of Adaiah, the son of Joiarib, 1121
11: 5 the son of Adaiah, the **s** of Joiarib, 1121
11: 5 the son of Joiarib, the **s** of Zechariah, 1121
11: 5 the son of Zechariah, the **s** of Shiloni. 1121
11: 7 Sallu the **s** of Meshullam, the son of Joed, 1121
11: 7 the **s** of Joed, the son of Pedaiah, the son of 1121
11: 7 the son of Joed, the **s** of Pedaiah, the son of 1121
11: 7 the son of Pedaiah, the **s** of Kolaiah, 1121
11: 7 the **s** of Maaseiah, the son of Ithiel, the son 1121
11: 7 the **s** of Ithiel, the son of Jesaiah. 1121
11: 7 the son of Ithiel, the **s** of Jesaiah. 1121
11: 9 Joel the **s** of Zichri *was* their overseer: 1121
11: 9 Judah the **s** of Senuah *was* second over 1121
11:10 the priests: Jedaiah the **s** of Joiarib, Jachin, 1121
11:11 Seraiah the **s** of Hilkiah, the son of 1121
11:11 the **s** of Meshullam, the son of Zadok, 1121
11:11 the **s** of Zadok, the son of Meraioth, the son 1121
11:11 the son of Zadok, the **s** of Meraioth, the son 1121
11:11 the son of Meraioth, the **s** of Ahitub, 1121
11:12 Adaiah the **s** of Jeroham, the son of 1121
11:12 the **s** of Pelaliah, the son of Amzi, the son 1121
11:12 the son of Pelaliah, the **s** of Amzi, the son 1121
11:12 the son of Amzi, the **s** of Zechariah, the son 1121
11:12 the **s** of Pashur, the son of Malchiah, 1121
11:12 the son of Pashur, the **s** of Malchiah, 1121
11:13 Amashai the **s** of Azareel, the son of 1121
11:13 the **s** of Ahasai, the son of Meshillemoth, 1121
11:13 the **s** of Meshillemoth, the son of Immer, 1121
11:13 the son of Meshillemoth, the **s** of Immer, 1121
11:14 *was* Zabdiel, the **s** of *one of* the great *men*. 1121
11:15 Shemaiah the **s** of Hashub, the son of 1121
11:15 the **s** of Azrikam, the son of Hashabiah, 1121
11:15 the **s** of Hashabiah, the son of Bunni; 1121
11:15 the son of Hashabiah, the **s** of Bunni; 1121
11:17 Mattaniah the **s** of Micha, the son of Zabdi, 1121
11:17 of Micha, the **s** of Zabdi, the son of Asaph, 1121
11:17 of Micha, the son of Zabdi, the **s** of Asaph, 1121
11:17 Abda the **s** of Shammua, the son of Galal, 1121
11:17 the **s** of Galal, the son of Jeduthun. 1121
11:17 the son of Galal, the **s** of Jeduthun. 1121
11:22 at Jerusalem *was* Uzzi the **s** of Bani, 1121
11:22 the **s** of Hashabiah, the son of Mattaniah, 1121
11:22 the **s** of Mattaniah, the son of Micha. 1121
11:22 the son of Mattaniah, the **s** of Micha. 1121
11:24 Pethahiah the **s** of Meshezabeel, of 1121
11:24 of the children of Zerah the **s** of Judah, 1121
12: 1 went up with Zerubbabel the **s** of Shealtiel, 1121
12:23 even until the days of Johanan the **s** of 1121
12:24 Sherebiah, and Jeshua the **s** of Kadmiel, 1121
12:26 These *were* in the days of Joiakim the **s** of 1121
12:26 the **s** of Jozadak, and in the days of 1121
12:35 *namely,* Zechariah the **s** of Jonathan, 1121
12:35 the **s** of Shemaiah, the son of Mattaniah, 1121
12:35 the **s** of Mattaniah, the son of Michaiah, 1121
12:35 the **s** of Michaiah, the son of Zaccur, 1121
12:35 the **s** of Zaccur, the son of Asaph: 1121
12:35 the son of Zaccur, the **s** of Asaph: 1121
12:45 of David, *and* of Solomon his **s**. 1121
13:13 next to them *was* Hanan the **s** of Zaccur, 1121
13:13 the son of Zaccur, the **s** of Mattaniah: 1121
13:28 of Joiada, the **s** of Eliashib the high priest, 1121
13:28 *was* **s in law** to Sanballat the Horonite: 2860
Est 2: 5 the **s** of Jair, the son of Shimei, the son of 1121
2: 5 the son of Jair, the **s** of Shimei, the son of 1121
2: 5 son of Shimei, the **s** of Kish, a Benjamite; 1121
3: 1 Haman the **s** of Hammedatha the Agagite, 1121
3:10 gave it unto Haman the **s** of Hammedatha 1121
8: 5 Haman the **s** of Hammedatha the Agagite, 1121
9:10 The ten sons of Haman the **s** of 1121

S

Est 9:24 Because Haman the s of Hammedatha, 1121
Job 18:19 He shall neither have s nor nephew among 5209
25: 6 and the s of man, which is a worm? 1121
32: 2 was kindled the wrath of Elihu the s of 1121
32: 6 Elihu the s of Barachel the Buzite answered 1121
35: 8 thy righteousness may profit the s of man. 1121
Ps 2: 7 LORD hath said unto me, Thou art my S; 1121
2:12 Kiss the S, lest he be angry, and ye perish 1248
3: T of David, when he fled from Absalom his s. 1121
8: 4 and the s of man, that thou visitest him? 1121
50:20 thou slanderest thine own mother's s. 1121
72: 1 and thy righteousness unto the king's s. 1121
72:20 The prayers of David the s of Jesse are 1121
80:17 upon the s of man whom thou madest 1121
86:16 and save the s of thine handmaid. 1121
89:22 nor the s of wickedness afflict him. 1121
116:16 am thy servant, and the s of thy handmaid: 1121
144: 3 or the s of man, that thou makest account of 1121
146: 3 nor in the s of man, in whom there is no 1121
Pr 1: 1 The proverbs of Solomon the s of David, 1121
1: 8 My s, hear the instruction of thy father, and 1121
1:10 My s, if sinners entice thee, consent thou 1121
1:15 My s, walk not thou in the way with them; 1121
2: 1 My s, if thou wilt receive my words, and 1121
3: 1 My s, forget not my law; but let thine heart 1121
3:11 My s, despise not the chastening of 1121
3:12 even as a father the s in whom he 1121
3:21 My s, let not them depart from thine eyes: 1121
4: 3 For I was my father's s, tender and 1121
4:10 Hear, O my s, and receive my sayings; and 1121
4:20 My s, attend to my words; incline thine ear 1121
5: 1 My s, attend unto my wisdom, and 1121
5:20 why wilt thou, my s, be ravisht with a 1121
6: 1 My s, if thou be surety for thy friend, 1121
6: 3 Do this now, my s, and deliver thyself, 1121
6:20 My s, keep thy father's commandment, and 1121
7: 1 My s, keep my words, and lay up my 1121
10: 1 A wise s maketh a glad father: but a foolish 1121
10: 1 a foolish s is the heaviness of his mother. 1121
10: 5 He that gathereth in summer is a wise s: but 1121
10: 5 he that sleepeth in harvest is a s that 1121
13: 1 A wise s heareth his father's instruction: 1121
13:24 He that spareth his rod hateth his s: but 1121
15:20 A wise s maketh a glad father: but a foolish 1121
17: 2 A wise servant shall have rule over a s that 1121
17:25 A foolish s is a grief to his father, and 1121
19:13 A foolish s is the calamity of his father: and 1121
19:18 Chasten thy s while there is hope, and 1121
19:26 is a s that causeth shame, and 1121
19:27 Cease, my s, to hear the instruction that 1121
23:15 My s, if thine heart be wise, my heart shall 1121
23:19 my s, and be wise, and guide thine heart in 1121
23:26 My s, give me thine heart, and let thine 1121
24:13 My s, eat thou honey, because it is good; 1121
24:21 My s, fear thou the LORD and the king: 1121
27:11 My s, be wise, and make my heart glad, 1121
28: 7 Whoso keepeth the law is a wise s: but 1121
29:17 Correct thy s, and he shall give thee rest; 1121
29:21 shall have him become his s at the length. 4497
30: 1 The words of Agur the s of Jakeh, even 1121
31: 2 What, my s? and what, the son of my 1248
31: 2 what, the s of my womb? and what, the son 1248
31: 2 of my womb? and what, the s of my vows? 1248
Ecc 1: 1 the s of David, king in Jerusalem. 1121
5:14 he begetteth a s, and there is nothing in his 1121
10:17 when thy king is the s of nobles, and 1121
12:12 further, by these, my s, be admonished: 1121
Isa 1: 1 The vision of Isaiah the s of Amoz, 1121
2: 1 The word that Isaiah the s of Amoz saw 1121
7: 1 it came to pass in the days of Ahaz the s of 1121
7: 1 the s of Uzziah king of Judah, that Rezin 1121
7: 1 and Pekah the s of Remaliah, king of Israel, 1121
7: 3 to meet Ahaz, thou, and Shear-jashub thy s, 1121
7: 4 Rezin with Syria, and of the s of Remaliah. 1121
7: 5 Ephraim, and the s of Remaliah, 1121
7: 6 king in the midst of it, even the s of Tabeal: 1121
7: 9 and the head of Samaria is Remaliah's s. 1121
7:14 bear a S, and shall call his name Immanuel. 1121
8: 2 and Zechariah the s of Jeberechiah. 1121
8: 3 and she conceived, and bare a s. 1121
8: 6 and rejoice in Rezin and Remaliah's s; 1121
9: 6 unto us a child is born, unto us a S is given: 1121
13: 1 which Isaiah the s of Amoz did see. 1121
14:12 from heaven, O Lucifer, s of the morning! 1121
14:22 remnant, and s, and nephew, saith 5209
19:11 I am the s of the wise, the son of ancient 1121
19:11 the son of the wise, the s of ancient kings? 1121
20: 2 spake the LORD by Isaiah the s of Amoz, 1121
22:20 that I will call my servant Eliakim the s of 1121
36: 3 Hilkiah's s, which was over the house, and 1121
36: 3 and Joah, Asaph's s, the recorder. 1121
36:22 came Eliakim, the s of Hilkiah, that was 1121
36:22 and Joah, the s of Asaph, the recorder, 1121
37: 2 unto Isaiah the prophet the s of Amoz. 1121
37:21 Isaiah the s of Amoz sent unto Hezekiah, 1121
37:38 and Esar-haddon his s reigned in his stead. 1121
38: 1 Isaiah the prophet the s of Amoz came unto 1121
39: 1 the s of Baladan, king of Babylon, 1121
49:15 not have compassion on the s of her womb? 1121
51:12 of the s of man which shall be made as 1121
56: 2 and the s of man that layeth hold on it; 1121
56: 3 Neither let the s of the stranger, that hath 1121
Jer 1: 1 The words of Jeremiah the s of Hilkiah, 1121
1: 2 days of Josiah the s of Amon king of Judah, 1121
1: 3 It came also in the days of Jehoiakim the s 1121
1: 3 of Zedekiah the s of Josiah king of Judah, 1121
6:26 as for an only s, most bitter lamentation: NIH
7:31 which is in the valley of the s of Hinnom, 1121
7:32 nor the valley of the s of Hinnom, but 1121
15: 4 of Manasseh the s of Hezekiah king of 1121
19: 2 go forth unto the valley of the s of Hinnom, 1121
19: 6 nor The valley of the s of Hinnom, but The 1121
20: 1 Now Pashur the s of Immer the priest, 1121
21: 1 sent unto him Pashur the s of Melchiah, 1121
21: 1 Zephaniah the s of Maaseiah the priest, 1121

Jer 22:11 Shallum the s of Josiah king of Judah, 1121
22:18 Jehoiakim the s of Josiah king of Judah; 1121
22:24 though Coniah the s of Jehoiakim king of 1121
24: 1 Jeconiah the s of Jehoiakim king of Judah, 1121
25: 1 of Jehoiakim the s of Josiah king of Judah, 1121
25: 3 From the thirteenth year of Josiah the s of 1121
26: 1 s of Josiah king of Judah came this word 1121
26:20 Urijah the s of Shemaiah of Kirjath-jearim, 1121
26:22 namely, Elnathan the s of Achbor, and 1121
26:24 Nevertheless the hand of Ahikam the s of 1121
27: 1 s of Josiah king of Judah came this word 1121
27: 7 serve him, and his s, and his son's son, 1121
27: 7 serve him, and his son, and his son's s, 1121
27:20 s of Jehoiakim king of Judah from 1121
28: 1 that Hananiah the s of Azur the prophet, 1121
28: 4 Jeconiah the s of Jehoiakim king of Judah, 1121
29: 3 By the hand of Elasah the s of Shaphan, 1121
29: 3 of Shaphan, and Gemariah the s of Hilkiah, 1121
29:21 of Ahab the s of Kolaiah, and of Zedekiah, 1121
29:21 and of Zedekiah, the s of Maaseiah, 1121
29:25 to Zephaniah the s of Maaseiah the priest, 1121
31:20 Is Ephraim my dear s? is he a pleasant 1121
32: 7 Hanameel the s of Shallum thine uncle 1121
32: 8 So Hanameel mine uncle's s came to me in 1121
32: 9 bought the field of Hanameel my uncle's s, 1121
32:12 the purchase unto Baruch the s of Neriah, 1121
32:12 the s of Maaseiah, in the sight of Hanameel 1121
32:12 in the sight of Hanameel mine uncle's s, and NIH
32:16 the purchase unto Baruch the s of Neriah, 1121
32:35 which are in the valley of the s of Hinnom, 1121
33:21 that he should not have a s to reign upon 1121
35: 1 of Jehoiakim the s of Josiah king of Judah, 1121
35: 3 I took Jaazaniah the s of Jeremiah, the son 1121
35: 3 the s of Habaziniah, and his brethren, and 1121
35: 4 of Hanan, the s of Igdaliah, a man of God, 1121
35: 4 the chamber of Maaseiah the s of Shallum, 1121
35: 6 for Jonadab the s of Rechab our father 1121
35: 8 s of Rechab our father in all that he hath 1121
35:14 The words of Jonadab the s of Rechab, 1121
35:16 Because the sons of Jonadab the s of 1121
35:19 Jonadab the s of Rechab shall not want a 1121
36: 1 of Jehoiakim the s of Josiah king of Judah, 1121
36: 4 Jeremiah called Baruch the s of Neriah: 1121
36: 8 Baruch the s of Neriah did according to all 1121
36: 9 of Jehoiakim the s of Josiah king of Judah, 1121
36:10 in the chamber of Gemariah the s of 1121
36:11 When Michaiah the s of Gemariah, the son 1121
36:11 the son of Gemariah, the s of Shaphan, 1121
36:12 Delaiah the s of Shemaiah, and 1121
36:12 Elnathan the s of Achbor, and 1121
36:12 Gemariah the s of Shaphan, and 1121
36:12 Zedekiah the s of Hananiah, and all 1121
36:14 Therefore all the princes sent Jehudi the s 1121
36:14 the s of Shelemiah, the son of Cushi, 1121
36:14 the s of Cushi, unto Baruch, saying, 1121
36:14 So Baruch the s of Neriah took the roll in 1121
36:26 the king commanded Jerahmeel the s of 1121
36:26 Seraiah the s of Azriel, and Shelemiah 1121
36:26 Shelemiah the s of Abdeel, to take Baruch 1121
36:32 it to Baruch the scribe, the s of Neriah; 1121
37: 1 king Zedekiah the s of Josiah reigned 1121
37: 1 instead of Coniah the s of Jehoiakim, 1121
37: 3 Zedekiah the king sent Jehucal the s of 1121
37: 3 Zephaniah the s of Maaseiah the priest to 1121
37:13 the s of Shelemiah, the son of Hananiah; 1121
37:13 the son of Shelemiah, the s of Hananiah; 1121
38: 1 Shephatiah the s of Mattan, and 1121
38: 1 Gedaliah the s of Pashur, and Jucal the son 1121
38: 1 Jucal the s of Shelemiah, and Pashur 1121
38: 1 and Pashur the s of Malchiah, 1121
38: 6 cast him into the dungeon of Malchiah the s 1121
39:14 committed him unto Gedaliah the s of 1121
39:14 the son of Ahikam the s of Shaphan, 1121
40: 5 he said, Go back also to Gedaliah the s of 1121
40: 5 the son of Ahikam the s of Shaphan, 1121
40: 6 went Jeremiah unto Gedaliah the s of 1121
40: 7 the s of Ahikam governor in the land, 1121
40: 8 even Ishmael the s of Nethaniah, and 1121
40: 8 Seraiah the s of Tanhumeth, and the sons of 1121
40: 8 Jezaniah the s of a Maachathite, they and 1121
40: 9 Gedaliah the s of Ahikam the son of 1121
40: 9 Gedaliah the son of Ahikam the s of 1121
40:11 that he had set over them Gedaliah the s of 1121
40:11 the son of Ahikam the s of Shaphan; 1121
40:13 Moreover Johanan the s of Kareah, and 1121
40:14 Ishmael the s of Nethaniah to slay thee? 1121
40:14 Gedaliah the s of Ahikam believed them 1121
40:15 Johanan the s of Kareah spake to Gedaliah 1121
40:15 I will slay Ishmael the s of Nethaniah, and 1121
40:16 Gedaliah the s of Ahikam said unto 1121
40:16 Ahikam said unto Johanan the s of Kareah, 1121
41: 1 that Ishmael the s of Nethaniah the son of 1121
41: 1 that Ishmael the son of Nethaniah the s of 1121
41: 1 came unto Gedaliah the s of Ahikam to 1121
41: 2 arose Ishmael the s of Nethaniah, and 1121
41: 2 smote Gedaliah the s of Ahikam the son of 1121
41: 2 smote Gedaliah the son of Ahikam the s of 1121
41: 6 Ishmael the s of Nethaniah went forth from 1121
41: 6 Come to Gedaliah the s of Ahikam. 1121
41: 7 that Ishmael the s of Nethaniah slew them, 1121
41: 9 Ishmael the s of Nethaniah filled it with 1121
41:10 committed to Gedaliah the s of Ahikam: 1121
41:10 Ishmael the s of Nethaniah carried them 1121
41:11 when Johanan the s of Kareah, and all 1121
41:11 heard of all the evil that Ishmael the s of 1121
41:12 went to fight with Ishmael the s of 1121
41:13 with Ishmael saw Johanan the s of Kareah, 1121
41:14 and went unto Johanan the s of Kareah. 1121
41:15 Ishmael the s of Nethaniah escaped from 1121
41:16 took Johanan the s of Kareah, and all 1121
41:16 recovered from Ishmael the s of Nethaniah, 1121
41:16 after that he had slain Gedaliah the s of 1121
41:18 Ishmael the s of Nethaniah had slain 1121
41:18 had slain Gedaliah the s of Ahikam, 1121
42: 1 Johanan the s of Kareah, and Jezaniah 1121

Jer 42: 1 Jezaniah the s of Hoshaiah, and all 1121
42: 8 called he Johanan the s of Kareah, and 1121
43: 2 spake Azariah the s of Hoshaiah, and 1121
43: 2 Johanan the s of Kareah, and all the proud 1121
43: 3 Baruch the s of Neriah setteth thee on 1121
43: 4 So Johanan the s of Kareah, and all 1121
43: 5 Johanan the s of Kareah, and all 1121
43: 6 the s of Ahikam the son of Shaphan, 1121
43: 6 the son of Ahikam the s of Shaphan, 1121
43: 6 the prophet, and Baruch the s of Neriah. 1121
45: 1 prophet spake unto Baruch the s of Neriah, 1121
45: 1 in the fourth year of Jehoiakim the s of 1121
46: 2 of Jehoiakim the s of Josiah king of Judah. 1121
49:18 neither shall a s of man dwell in it. 1121
49:33 abide there, nor any s of man dwell in it. 1121
50:40 neither shall any s of man dwell therein. 1121
51:43 neither doth any s of man pass thereby. 1121
51:59 commanded Seraiah the s of Neriah, 1121
51:59 the son of Neriah, the s of Maaseiah, 1121
Eze 1: 3 the s of Buzi, in the land of the Chaldeans 1121
2: 1 S of man, stand upon thy feet, and I will 1121
2: 3 he said unto me, S of man, I send thee to 1121
2: 6 thou, s of man, be not afraid of them, 1121
2: 8 thou, s of man, hear what I say unto thee; 1121
3: 1 unto me, S of man, eat that thou findest; 1121
3: 3 he said unto me, S of man, cause thy belly 1121
3: 4 he said unto me, S of man, go, get thee unto 1121
3:10 Moreover he said unto me, S of man, all 1121
3:17 S of man, I have made thee a watchman 1121
3:25 thou, O s of man, behold, they shall put 1121
4: 1 Thou also, s of man, take thee a tile, and 1121
4:16 he said unto me, S of man, behold, 1121
5: 1 thou, s of man, take thee a sharp knife, 1121
6: 2 S of man, set thy face towards 1121
7: 2 Also, thou s of man, thus saith the Lord 1121
8: 5 said he unto me, S of man, lift up thine 1121
8: 6 S of man, seest thou what they do? 1121
8: 8 he unto me, S of man, dig now in the wall: 1121
8:11 in the midst of them stood Jaazaniah the s 1121
8:12 said he unto me, S of man, hast thou seen 1121
8:15 unto me, Hast thou seen this, O s of man? 1121
8:17 unto me, Hast thou seen this, O s of man? 1121
11: 1 among whom I saw Jaazaniah the s of 1121
11: 1 Pelatiah the s of Benaiah, princes of 1121
11: 2 said he unto me, S of man, these are 1121
11: 4 against them, prophesy, O s of man. 1121
11:13 that Pelatiah the s of Benaiah died. 1121
11:15 S of man, thy brethren, even thy brethren, 1121
12: 2 S of man, thou dwellest in the midst of a 1121
12: 3 Therefore thou s of man, prepare thee stuff 1121
12: 9 S of man, hath not the house of Israel, 1121
12:18 S of man, eat thy bread with quaking, and 1121
12:22 S of man, what is that proverb that ye have 1121
12:27 S of man, behold, they of the house of 1121
13: 2 S of man, prophesy against the prophets of 1121
13:17 Likewise thou s of man, set thy face against 1121
14: 3 S of man, these men have set up their idols 1121
14:13 S of man, when the land sinneth against me 1121
14:20 they shall deliver neither s nor daughter; 1121
15: 2 S of man, What is the vine tree more than 1121
16: 2 S of man, cause Jerusalem to know her 1121
17: 2 S of man, put forth a riddle, and speak a 1121
18: 4 the father, so also the soul of the s is mine: 1121
18:10 If he beget a s that is a robber, a shedder of 1121
18:14 Now lo, if he beget a s, that seeth all his 1121
18:19 doth not the s bear the iniquity of 1121
18:19 When the s hath done that which is lawful 1121
18:20 The s shall not bear the iniquity of 1121
18:20 shall the father bear the iniquity of the s: 1121
20: 3 S of man, speak unto the elders of Israel, 1121
20: 4 Wilt thou judge them, s of man, wilt thou 1121
20:27 Therefore, s of man, speak unto the house 1121
20:46 S of man, set thy face toward the south, and 1121
21: 2 S of man, set thy face toward Jerusalem, 1121
21: 6 Sigh therefore, thou s of man, with 1121
21: 9 S of man, prophesy, and say, Thus saith 1121
21:10 it contemneth the rod of my s, as every tree. 1121
21:12 Cry and howl, s of man: for it shall be upon 1121
21:14 s of man, prophesy, and smite thine hands 1121
21:19 Also, thou s of man, appoint thee two ways, 1121
21:28 thou, s of man, prophesy and say, 1121
22: 2 Now, thou s of man, wilt thou judge, wilt 1121
22:18 S of man, the house of Israel is to me 1121
22:24 S of man, say unto her, Thou art the land 1121
23: 2 S of man, there were two women, 1121
23:36 S of man, wilt thou judge Aholah and 1121
24: 2 S of man, write thee the name of the day, 1121
24:16 S of man, behold, I take away from thee 1121
24:25 Also, thou s of man, shall it not be in 1121
25: 2 S of man, set thy face against 1121
26: 2 S of man, because that Tyrus hath said 1121
27: 2 Now, thou s of man, take up a lamentation 1121
28: 2 S of man, say unto the prince of Tyrus, 1121
28:12 S of man, take up a lamentation upon 1121
28:21 S of man, set thy face against Zidon, and 1121
29: 2 S of man, set thy face against Pharaoh king 1121
29:18 S of man, Nebuchadrezzar king of Babylon 1121
30: 2 S of man, prophesy and say, Thus saith 1121
30:21 S of man, I have broken the arm of Pharaoh 1121
31: 2 S of man, speak unto Pharaoh king of 1121
32: 2 S of man, take up a lamentation for 1121
32:18 S of man, wail for the multitude of Egypt, 1121
33: 2 S of man, speak to the children of thy 1121
33: 7 So thou, O s of man, I have set thee a 1121
33:10 Therefore, O thou s of man, speak unto 1121
33:12 Therefore, thou s of man, say unto 1121
33:24 S of man, they that inhabit those wastes of 1121
33:30 Also, thou s of man, the children of thy 1121
34: 2 S of man, prophesy against the shepherds 1121
35: 2 S of man, set thy face against mount Seir, 1121
36: 1 Also, thou s of man, prophesy unto 1121
36:17 S of man, when the house of Israel dwelt in 1121
37: 3 unto me, S of man, can these bones live? 1121
37: 9 prophesy, s of man, and say to the wind, 1121
37:11 he said unto me, S of man, these bones are 1121

Eze 37:16 Moreover, thou **s** of man, take thee one 1121
38: 2 **S** of man, set thy face against Gog, the land 1121
38:14 **s** of man, prophesy and say unto Gog, 1121
39: 1 Therefore thou **s** of man, prophesy against 1121
39:17 thou **s** of man, thus saith the Lord GOD; 1121
40: 4 **S** of man, behold with thine eyes, and 1121
43: 7 he said unto me, **S** of man, the place of my 1121
43:10 Thou **s** of man, shew the house to the house 1121
43:18 he said unto me, **S** of man, thus saith 1121
44: 5 **S** of man, mark well, and behold with thine 1121
44:25 or for mother, or for **s**, or for daughter, 1121
47: 6 he said unto me, **S** of man, hast thou seen 1121
Da 3:25 the form of the fourth *is* like the **S** of God. 1247
5:22 thou his **s**, O Belshazzar, hast not humbled 1247
7:13 *one* like the **S** of man came with the clouds 1247
8:17 he said unto me, Understand, O **s** of man: 1121
9: 1 In the first year of Darius the **s** of 1121
Hos 1: 1 the **s** of Beeri, in the days of Uzziah, 1121
1: 1 in the days of Jeroboam the **s** of Joash, 1121
1: 3 which conceived, and bare him a **s**. 1121
1: 8 she conceived, and bare a **s**. 1121
11: 1 I loved him, and called my **s** out of Egypt. 1121
13:13 he *is* an unwise **s**; for he should not stay 1121
Joel 1: 1 LORD that came to Joel the **s** of Pethuel. 1121
Am 1: 1 in the days of Jeroboam the **s** of Joash king 1121
7:14 *was* no prophet, neither *was* I a prophet's **s**; 1121
8:10 I will make it as the mourning of an only **s**, NIH
Jnh 1: 1 LORD came unto Jonah the **s** of Amittai, 1121
Mic 6: 5 what Balaam the **s** of Beor answered him; 1121
7: 6 For the **s** dishonoureth the father, 1121
Zep 1: 1 which came unto Zephaniah the **s** of Cushi, 1121
1: 1 the **s** of Gedaliah, the son of Amariah, 1121
1: 1 the **s** of Amariah, the son of Hizkiah, 1121
1: 1 the son of Amariah, the **s** of Hizkiah, 1121
1: 1 in the days of Josiah the **s** of Amon, king of 1121
Hag 1: 1 prophet unto Zerubbabel the **s** of Shealtiel, 1121
1: 1 to Joshua the **s** of Josedech the high priest, 1121
1:12 Zerubbabel the **s** of Shealtiel, and 1121
1:12 Joshua the **s** of Josedech the high priest, 1121
1:14 the spirit of Zerubbabel the **s** of Shealtiel, 1121
1:14 the spirit of Joshua the **s** of Josedech 1121
2: 2 Speak now to Zerubbabel the **s** of Shealtiel, 1121
2: 2 to Joshua the **s** of Josedech the high priest 1121
2: 4 be strong, O Joshua, **s** of Josedech, the high 1121
2:23 my servant, the **s** of Shealtiel, 1121
Zec 1: 1 the **s** of Berechiah, the son of Iddo 1121
1: 1 the **s** of Iddo the prophet, saying, 1121
1: 7 the **s** of Berechiah, the son of Iddo 1121
1: 7 the **s** of Iddo the prophet, saying, 1121
6:10 go *into* the house of Josiah the **s** of 1121
6:11 set *them* upon the head of Joshua the **s** of 1121
6:14 to Jedaiah, and to Hen the **s** of Zephaniah, 1121
12:10 as one mourneth for *his* only **s**, and shall be NIH
Mal 1: 6 A **s** honoureth *his* father, and a servant his 1121
3:17 as a man spareth his own **s** that serveth 1121
Mt 1: 1 the **s** of David, the son of Abraham. 5207
1: 1 the son of David, the **s** of Abraham. 5207
1:20 saying, Joseph, *thou* **s** of David, fear not to 5207
1:21 And she shall bring forth a **s**, and thou shalt 5207
1:23 and shall bring forth a **s**, and they shall call 5207
1:25 till she had brought forth her firstborn **s**: 5207
2:15 saying, Out of Egypt have I called my **s**. 5207
3:17 saying, This is my beloved **S**, in whom I 5207
4: 3 to him, he said, If thou be the **S** of God, 5207
4: 6 If thou be the **S** of God, cast thyself down: 5207
4:21 James the *s* of Zebedee, and John his NIG
7: 9 whom if his **s** ask bread, will he give him a 5207
8:20 the **S** of man hath not where to lay *his* head. 5207
8:29 we to do with thee, Jesus, *thou* **S** of God? 5207
9: 2 **S**, be of good cheer; thy sins be forgiven 5043
9: 6 But that ye may know that the **S** of man 5207
9:27 crying, and saying, *Thou* **S** of David, 5207
10: 2 the *s* of Zebedee, and John his brother; NIG
10: 3 James the *s* of Alpheus, and Lebbeus, NIG
10:23 cities of Israel, till the **S** of man be come. 5207
10:37 and he that loveth **s** or daughter more than 5207
11:19 The **S** of man came eating and drinking, 5207
11:27 and no *man* knoweth the **S**, but the Father; 5207
11:27 save the **S**, and *he* to whomsoever the Son 5207
11:27 *he* to whomsoever the **S** will reveal *him.* 5207
12: 8 For the **S** of man is Lord even of 5207
12:23 and said, Is this the **s** of David? 5207
12:32 speaketh a word against the **S** of man, 5207
12:40 so shall the **S** of man be three days and 5207
13:37 He that soweth the good seed is the **S** of 5207
13:41 The **S** of man shall send forth his angels, 5207
13:55 Is not this the carpenter's **s**? is not his 5207
14:33 saying, Of a truth thou art the **S** of God. 5207
15:22 mercy on me, O Lord, *thou* **S** of David; 5207
16:13 Whom do men say that I the **S** of man am? 5207
16:16 Thou art the Christ, the **S** of the living God. 5207
16:27 For the **S** of man shall come in the glory of 5207
16:28 till they see the **S** of man coming in his 5207
17: 5 which said, This is my beloved **S**, in whom 5207
17: 9 Tell the vision to no *man,* until the **S** of 5207
17:12 Likewise shall also the **S** of man suffer of 5207
17:15 Lord, have mercy on my **s**: for he is 5207
17:22 The **S** of man shall be betrayed into 5207
18:11 For the **S** of man is come to save that which 5207
19:28 when the **S** of man shall sit in the throne of 5207
20:18 the **S** of man shall be betrayed unto 5207
20:28 Even as the **S** of man came not to be 5207
20:30 mercy on us, O Lord, *thou* **S** of David. 5207
20:31 mercy on us, O Lord, *thou* **S** of David. 5207
21: 9 cried, saying, Hosanna to the **S** of David: 5207
21:15 and saying, Hosanna to the **S** of David; 5207
21:28 and he came to the first, and said, **S**, 5043
21:37 But last of *all* he sent unto them his **s**, 5207
21:37 his son, saying, They will reverence my **s**. 5207
21:38 But when the husbandmen saw the **s**, 5207
22: 2 which made a marriage for his **s**, 5207
22:42 whose **s** is he? They say unto him, *The Son* 5207
22:42 is he? They say unto him, *The* **S** of David. NIG
22:45 then call him Lord, how is he his **s**? 5207
23:35 unto the blood of Zacharias **s** of Barachias, 5207
Mt 24:27 so shall also the coming of the **S** of man be. 5207
24:30 shall appear the sign of the **S** of man in 5207
24:30 they shall see the **S** of man coming in 5207
24:37 so shall also the coming of the **S** of man be. 5207
24:39 so shall also the coming of the **S** of man be. 5207
24:44 for in such an hour as you think not the **S** of 5207
25:13 nor the hour wherein the **S** of man cometh. 5207
25:31 When the **S** of man shall come in his glory, 5207
26: 2 the **S** of man is betrayed to be crucified. 5207
26:24 The **S** of man goeth as it is written of him: 5207
26:24 woe unto that man by whom the **S** of man 5207
26:45 the **S** of man is betrayed into the hands of 5207
26:63 us whether thou be the Christ, the **S** of God. 5207
26:64 Hereafter shall ye see the **S** of man sitting 5207
27:40 If thou be the **S** of God, come down from 5207
27:43 have him: for he said, I am the **S** of God. 5207
27:54 saying, Truly this was the **S** of God. 5207
28:19 and of the **S**, and of the Holy Ghost: 5207
Mk 1: 1 of the gospel of Jesus Christ, the **S** of God; 5207
1:11 *saying,* Thou art my beloved **S**, in whom I 5207
1:19 he saw James the *s* of Zebedee, and John his NIG
2: 5 of the palsy, **S**, thy sins be forgiven thee. 5043
2:10 But that ye may know that the **S** of man 5207
2:14 he saw Levi the *s* of Alpheus sitting at NIG
2:28 Therefore the **S** of man is Lord also of 5207
3:11 and cried, saying, Thou art the **S** of God. 5207
3:17 And James the *s* of Zebedee, and John NIG
3:18 and James the *s* of Alpheus, and Thaddeus, NIG
5: 7 Jesus, *thou* **S** of the most high God? 5207
6: 3 the **s** of Mary, the brother of James, and 5207
8:31 that the **S** of man must suffer many *things,* 5207
8:38 of him also shall the **S** of man be ashamed, 5207
9: 7 of the cloud, saying, This is my beloved **S**: 5207
9: 9 till the **S** of man were risen from the dead. 5207
9:12 and how it is written of the **S** of man, 5207
9:17 said, Master, I have brought unto thee my **s**, 5207
9:31 The **S** of man is delivered into the hands of 5207
10:33 the **S** of man shall be delivered unto 5207
10:45 For even the **S** of man came not to be 5207
10:46 blind Bartimeus, the **s** of Timeus, 5207
10:47 and say, Jesus, *thou* **S** of David, 5207
10:48 *Thou* **S** of David, have mercy on me. 5207
12: 6 Having yet therefore one **s**, 5207
12: 6 saying, They will reverence my **s**. 5207
12:35 How say the scribes that Christ is the **S** of 5207
12:37 him Lord; and whence is he *then* his **s**? 5207
13:12 the brother to death, and the father the **s**; 5043
13:26 shall they see the **S** of man coming in 5207
13:32 are in heaven, neither the **S**, but the Father. 5207
13:34 *For the* **S** *of man is* as a man taking a far NIG
14:21 The **S** of man indeed goeth, as it is written 5207
14:21 woe to that man by whom the **S** of man is 5207
14:41 the **S** of man is betrayed into the hands of 5207
14:61 Art thou the Christ, the **S** of the Blessed? 5207
14:62 ye shall see the **S** of man sitting on the right 5207
15:39 he said, Truly this man was the **S** of God. 5207
Lk 1:13 and thy wife Elisabeth shall bear thee a **s**, 5207
1:31 and bring forth a **s**, and shalt call his name 5207
1:32 and shall be called the **S** of the Highest: 5207
1:35 be born of thee shall be called the **S** of God. 5207
1:36 she hath also conceived a **s** in her old age: 5207
1:57 be delivered; and she brought forth a **s**. 5207
2: 7 And she brought forth her firstborn **s**, and 5207
2:48 and his mother said unto him, **S**, why hast 5043
3: 2 the word of God came unto John the **s** of 5207
3:22 which said, Thou art my beloved **S**; 5207
3:23 the **s** of Joseph, which was *the son* of Heli, 5207
3:23 the son of Joseph, which was *the* **s** of Heli, NIG
3:24 Which was *the* **s** of Matthat, which was NIG
3:24 which was *the* **s** of Levi, which was *the son* NIG
3:24 *the son* of Levi, which was *the* **s** of Melchi, NIG
3:24 which was *the* **s** of Janna, which was NIG
3:24 *the son* of Janna, which was *the* **s** of Joseph, NIG
3:25 Which was *the* **s** of Mattathias, which was NIG
3:25 which was *the* **s** of Amos, which was NIG
3:25 which was *the* **s** of Naum, which was NIG
3:25 *the son* of Naum, which was *the* **s** of Esli, NIG
3:25 *the son* of Esli, which was *the* **s** of Nagge, NIG
3:26 Which was *the* **s** of Maath, which was NIG
3:26 which was *the* **s** of Mattathias, which was NIG
3:26 which was *the* **s** of Semei, which was NIG
3:26 which was *the* **s** of Joseph, which was NIG
3:26 *the son* of Joseph, which was *the* **s** of Juda, NIG
3:27 Which was *the* **s** of Joanna, which was NIG
3:27 *son* of Joanna, which was *the* **s** of Rhesa, NIG
3:27 *son* of Rhesa, which was *the* **s** of Zorobabel, NIG
3:27 which was *the* **s** of Salathiel, which was NIG
3:27 *son* of Salathiel, which was *the* **s** of Neri, NIG
3:28 Which was *the* **s** of Melchi, which was NIG
3:28 which was *the* **s** of Addi, which was *the son* NIG
3:28 *the son* of Addi, which was *the* **s** of Cosam, NIG
3:28 which was *the* **s** of Elmodam, which was NIG
3:28 *the son* of Elmodam, which was *the* **s** of Er, NIG
3:29 Which was *the* **s** of Jose, which was *the son* NIG
3:29 *the son* of Jose, which was *the* **s** of Eliezer, NIG
3:29 *the son* of Eliezer, which was *the* **s** of Jorim, NIG
3:29 which was *the* **s** of Matthat, which was NIG
3:29 *the son* of Matthat, which was *the* **s** of Levi, NIG
3:30 Which was *the* **s** of Simeon, which was NIG
3:30 which was *the* **s** of Juda, which was *the son* NIG
3:30 *the son* of Juda, which was *the* **s** of Joseph, NIG
3:30 *the son* of Joseph, which was *the* **s** of Jonan, NIG
3:30 *son* of Jonan, which was *the* **s** of Eliakim, NIG
3:31 Which was *the* **s** of Melea, which was NIG
3:31 *son* of Melea, which was *the* **s** of Menan, NIG
3:31 *son* of Menan, which was *the* **s** of Mattatha, NIG
3:31 which was *the* **s** of Nathan, which was NIG
3:31 *son* of Nathan, which was *the* **s** of David, NIG
3:32 Which was *the* **s** of Jesse, which was NIG
3:32 which was *the* **s** of Obed, which was *the son* NIG
3:32 *the son* of Obed, which was *the* **s** of Booz, NIG
3:32 *the son* of Booz, which was *the* **s** of Salmon, NIG
3:32 *son* of Salmon, which was *the* **s** of Naasson, NIG
3:33 Which was *the* **s** of Aminadab, which was NIG
3:33 which was *the* **s** of Aram, which was NIG
Lk 3:33 *the son* of Aram, which was *the* **s** of Esrom, NIG
3:33 which was *the* **s** of Phares, which was NIG
3:33 *the son* of Phares, which was *the* **s** of Juda, NIG
3:34 Which was *the* **s** of Jacob, which was NIG
3:34 *the son* of Jacob, which was *the* **s** of Isaac, NIG
3:34 *son* of Isaac, which was *the* **s** of Abraham, NIG
3:34 which was *the* **s** of Thara, which was NIG
3:34 *son* of Thara, which was *the* **s** of Nachor, NIG
3:35 Which was *the* **s** of Saruch, which was NIG
3:35 which was *the* **s** of Ragau, which was NIG
3:35 which was *the* **s** of Phalec, which was NIG
3:35 which was *the* **s** of Heber, which was NIG
3:35 *the son* of Heber, which was *the* **s** of Sala, NIG
3:36 Which was *the* **s** of Cainan, which was NIG
3:36 which was *the* **s** of Arphaxad, which was NIG
3:36 which was *the* **s** of Sem, which was *the son* NIG
3:36 *the son* of Sem, which was *the* **s** of Noe, NIG
3:36 *the son* of Noe, which was *the* **s** of Lamech, NIG
3:37 Which was *the* **s** of Mathusala, which was NIG
3:37 which was *the* **s** of Enoch, which was NIG
3:37 *the son* of Enoch, which was *the* **s** of Jared, NIG
3:37 *son* of Jared, which was *the* **s** of Maleleel, NIG
3:37 *son* of Maleleel, which was *the* **s** of Cainan, NIG
3:38 Which was *the* **s** of Enos, which was *the son* NIG
3:38 *the son* of Enos, which was *the* **s** of Seth, NIG
3:38 which was *the* **s** of Adam, which was NIG
3:38 *the son* of Adam, which was *the* **s** of God. NIG
4: 3 said unto him, If thou be the **S** of God, 5207
4: 9 and said unto him, If thou be the **S** of God, 5207
4:22 And they said, Is not this Joseph's **s**? 5207
4:41 and saying, Thou art Christ the **S** of God. 5207
5:24 But that ye may know that the **S** of man 5207
6: 5 That the **S** of man is Lord also of 5207
6:15 James the *s* of Alpheus, and Simon called NIG
6:22 your name as evil, for the **S** of man's sake. 5207
7:12 the only **s** of his mother, and she was a 5207
7:34 The **S** of man is come eating and drinking; 5207
8:28 with thee, Jesus, *thou* **S** of God most high? 5207
9:22 The **S** of man must suffer many *things,* and 5207
9:26 of him shall the **S** of man be ashamed, 5207
9:35 of the cloud, saying, This is my beloved **S**: 5207
9:38 Master, I beseech thee, look upon my **s**: 5207
9:41 and suffer you? Bring thy **s** hither. 5207
9:44 for the **S** of man shall be delivered into 5207
9:56 For the **S** of man is not come to destroy 5207
9:58 the **S** of man hath not where to lay *his* head. 5207
10: 6 And if the **s** of peace be there, your peace 5207
10:22 and no *man* knoweth who the **S** is, but 5207
10:22 but the **S**, and *he* to whom the Son will 5207
10:22 and *he* to whom the **S** will reveal *him.* 5207
11:11 *If* a **s** shall ask bread of any of you that is a 5207
11:30 shall also the **S** of man be to this 5207
12: 8 him shall the **S** of man also confess before 5207
12:10 shall speak a word against the **S** of man, 5207
12:40 for the **S** of man cometh at an hour when ye 5207
12:53 The father shall be divided against the **s**, 5207
12:53 against the son, and the **s** against the father; 5207
15:13 And not many days after the younger **s** 5207
15:19 And am no more worthy to be called thy **s**: 5207
15:21 And the **s** said unto him, Father, I have 5207
15:21 and am no more worthy to be called thy **s**. 5207
15:24 For this my **s** was dead, and is alive again; 5207
15:25 Now his elder **s** was in the field: and as he 5207
15:30 But as soon as this thy **s** was come, 5207
15:31 **S**, thou art ever with me, and all that I have 5043
16:25 But Abraham said, **S**, remember that thou 5043
17:22 to see one of the days of the **S** of man, 5207
17:24 so shall also the **S** of man be in his day. 5207
17:26 shall it be also in the days of the **S** of man. 5207
17:30 Even thus shall it be in the day when the **S** 5207
18: 8 Nevertheless when the **S** of man cometh, 5207
18:31 the **S** of man shall be accomplished. 5207
18:38 he cried, saying, Jesus, *thou* **S** of David, 5207
18:39 *so* much the more, *Thou* **S** of David, 5207
19: 9 forsomuch as he also is a **s** of Abraham. 5207
19:10 For the **S** of man is come to seek and 5207
20:13 I will send my beloved **s**: it may be they 5207
20:41 How say they that Christ is David's **s**? 5207
20:44 calleth him Lord, how is he then his **s**? 5207
21:27 shall they see the **S** of man coming in a 5207
21:36 to pass, and to stand before the **S** of man. 5207
22:22 And truly the **S** of man goeth, as it was 5207
22:48 betrayest thou the **S** of man with a kiss? 5207
22:69 Hereafter shall the **S** of man sit on the right 5207
22:70 said they all, Art thou then the **S** of God? 5207
24: 7 The **S** of man must be delivered into 5207
Jn 1:18 the only begotten **S**, which is in the bosom 5207
1:34 and bare record that this is the **S** of God. 5207
1:42 he said, Thou art Simon the **s** of Jona: 5207
1:45 Jesus of Nazareth, the **s** of Joseph. 5207
1:49 unto him, Rabbi, thou art the **S** of God; 5207
1:51 and descending upon the **S** of man. 5207
3:13 *even* the **S** of man which is in heaven. 5207
3:14 *even* so must the **S** of man be lifted up: 5207
3:16 the world, that he gave his only begotten **S**, 5207
3:17 For God sent not his **S** into the world to 5207
3:18 in the name of the only begotten **S** of God. 5207
3:35 The Father loveth the **S**, and hath given all 5207
3:36 He that believeth on the **S** hath everlasting 5207
3:36 he that believeth not the **S** shall not see life; 5207
4: 5 of ground that Jacob gave to his **s** Joseph. 5207
4:46 whose **s** was sick at Capernaum. 5207
4:47 that he would come down, and heal his **s**: 5207
4:50 saith unto him, Go *thy way;* thy **s** liveth. 5207
4:51 met him, and told *him,* saying, Thy **s** liveth. 3816
4:53 the which Jesus said unto him, Thy **s** liveth: 5207
5:19 The **S** can do nothing of himself, but 5207
5:19 he doeth, these also doeth the **S** likewise. 5207
5:20 For the Father loveth the **S**, and 5207
5:21 so the **S** quickeneth whom he will. 5207
5:22 hath committed all judgment unto the **S**: 5207
5:23 That all *men* should honour the **S**, even as 5207
5:23 He that honoureth not the **S** honoureth not 5207
5:25 when the dead shall hear the voice of the **S** 5207
5:26 hath he given to the **S** to have life in 5207

Jn 5:27 judgment also, because he is the S of man. 5207
6:27 which the S of man shall give unto you: 5207
6:40 that every one which seeth the S, and 5207
6:42 the s of Joseph, whose father and mother 5207
6:53 Except ye eat the flesh of the S of man, and 5207
6:62 if ye shall see the S of man ascend up 5207
6:69 thou art that Christ, the S of the living God. 5207
6:71 He spake of Judas Iscariot the s of Simon: NIG
8:28 When ye have lift up the S of man, then 5207
8:35 in the house for ever: but the s abideth ever. 5207
8:36 If the S therefore shall make you free, 5207
9:19 And they asked them, saying, Is this your s, 5207
9:20 We know that this is our s, and that he was 5207
9:35 Dost thou believe on the S of God? 5207
10:36 because I said, I am the S of God? 5207
11: 4 that the S of God might be glorified 5207
11:27 that thou art the Christ, the S of God, 5207
12: 4 Simon's s, which should betray him, NIG
12:23 that the S of man should be glorified. 5207
12:34 sayest thou, The S of man must be lift up? 5207
12:34 man must be lift up? who is this S of man? 5207
13: 2 of Judas Iscariot, Simon's s, to betray him; NIG
13:26 he gave it to Judas Iscariot, the s of Simon. NIG
13:31 Now is the S of man glorified, and God is 5207
14:13 that the Father may be glorified in the S. 5207
17: 1 glorify thy S, that thy Son also may glorify 5207
17: 1 thy Son, that thy S also may glorify thee: 5207
17:12 none of them is lost, but the s of perdition; 5207
19: 7 because he made himself the S of God. 5207
19:26 unto his mother, Woman, behold thy s. 5207
20:31 that Jesus is the Christ, the S of God; 5207
21:15 saith to Simon Peter, Simon, s of Jonas, NIG
21:16 Simon, s of Jonas, lovest thou me? NIG
21:17 Simon, s of Jonas, lovest thou me? NIG
Ac 1:13 James the s of Alpheus, and Simon Zelotes, NIG
3:13 of our fathers, hath glorified his S Jesus; 3816
3:26 you first God, having raised up his S Jesus, 3816
4:36 being interpreted, The s of consolation,) 5207
7:21 him up, and nourished him for her own s. 5207
7:56 the S of man standing on the right hand of 5207
8:37 I believe that Jesus Christ is the S of God. 5207
9:20 in the synagogues, that he is the S of God. 5207
13:21 and God gave unto them Saul the s of Cis, 5207
13:22 and said, I have found David the s of Jesse, NIG
13:33 Thou art my S, this day have I begotten 5207
16: 1 the s of a certain woman, 5207
23: 6 I am a Pharisee, the s of a Pharisee: 5207
23:16 And when Paul's sister's s heard of their 5207
Ro 1: 3 Concerning his S Jesus Christ our Lord, 5207
1: 4 And declared to be the S of God with 5207
1: 9 I serve with my spirit in the gospel of his S, 5207
5:10 reconciled to God by the death of his S, 5207
8: 3 God sending his own S in the likeness of 5207
8:29 to be conformed to the image of his S, 5207
8:32 He that spared not his own S, but 5207
9: 9 time will I come, and Sara shall have a s. 5207
1Co 1: 9 fellowship of his S Jesus Christ our Lord. 5207
4:17 who is my beloved s, and faithful in 5043
15:28 shall the S also himself be subject unto him 5207
2Co 1:19 For the S of God, Jesus Christ, who was 5207
Gal 1:16 To reveal his S in me, that I might preach 5207
2:20 the flesh I live by the faith of the S of God, 5207
4: 4 God sent forth his S, made of a woman, 5207
4: 6 God hath sent forth the Spirit of his S into 5207
4: 7 thou art no more a servant, but a s; 5207
4: 7 and if a s, then an heir of God through 5207
4:30 Cast out the bondwoman and her s: for 5207
4:30 for the s of the bondwoman shall not be 5207
4:30 not be heir with the s of the freewoman. 5207
Eph 4:13 and of the knowledge of the S of God, 5207
Php 2:22 the proof of him, that, as a s with the father, 5043
Col 1:13 us into the kingdom of his dear S: 5207
4:10 and Marcus, sister's s to Barnabas, 431
1Th 1:10 And to wait for his S from heaven, 5207
2Th 2: 3 man of sin be revealed, the s of perdition; 5207
1Ti 1: 2 Unto Timothy, my own s in the faith: 5043
1:18 This charge I commit unto thee, s Timothy, 5043
2Ti 1: 2 To Timothy, my dearly beloved s: Grace, 5043
2: 1 Thou therefore, my s, be strong in the grace 5043
Tit 1: 4 mine own s after the common faith: 5043
Phm 1:10 I beseech thee for my s Onesimus, whom I 5043
Heb 1: 2 in these last days spoken unto us by his S, 5207
1: 5 Thou art my S, this day have I begotten 5207
1: 5 to him a Father, and he shall be to me a S? 5207
1: 8 But unto the S he saith, Thy throne, O God, 5207
2: 6 or the s of man, that thou visitest him? 5207
3: 6 But Christ as a S over his own house; 5207
4:14 Jesus the S of God, let us hold fast our 5207
5: 5 but he that said unto him, Thou art my S, 5207
5: 8 Though he were a S, yet learned he 5207
6: 6 seeing they crucify to themselves the S of 5207
7: 3 of life; but made like unto the S of God; 5207
7:28 which was since the law, maketh the S, 5207
10:29 who hath trodden under foot the S of God, 5207
11:17 the promises offered up his only begotten s, NIG
11:24 refused to be called the s of Pharaoh's 5207
12: 5 My s, despise not thou the chastening of 5207
12: 6 and scourgeth every s whom he receiveth. 5207
12: 7 for what s is he whom the father chasteneth 5207
Jas 2:21 when he had offered Isaac his s upon 5207
1Pe 5:13 saluteth you; and so doth Marcus my s. 5207
2Pe 1:17 This is my beloved S, in whom I am well 5207
2:15 following the way of Balaam the s of Bosor, NIG
1Jn 1: 3 with the Father, and with his S Jesus Christ. 5207
1: 7 the blood of Jesus Christ his S cleanseth us 5207
2:22 that denieth the Father and the S. 5207
2:23 Whosoever denieth the S, the same hath not 5207
2:23 he that acknowledgeth the S hath the Father NIG
2:24 ye also shall continue in the S, and in 5207
3: 8 For this purpose the S of God was 5207
3:23 believe on the name of his S Jesus Christ, 5207
4: 9 that God sent his only begotten S into 5207
4:10 sent his S to be the propitiation for our sins. 5207
4:14 do testify that the Father sent the S to be 5207
4:15 Whosoever shall confess that Jesus is the S 5207
1Jn 5: 5 he that believeth that Jesus is the S of God? 5207
5: 9 of God which he hath testified of his S. 5207
5:10 He that believeth on the S of God hath 5207
5:10 not the record that God gave of his S. 5207
5:11 to us eternal life, and this life is in his S. 5207
5:12 He that hath the S hath life; and he that 5207
5:12 he that hath not the S of God hath not life. 5207
5:13 that believe on the name of the S of God; 5207
5:13 that ye may believe on the name of the S of 5207
5:20 And we know that the S of God is come, 5207
5:20 him that is true, even in his S Jesus Christ. 5207
2Jn 1: 3 the S of the Father, in truth and love. 5207
1: 9 of Christ, he hath both the Father and the S. 5207
Rev 1:13 candlesticks one like unto the S of man, 5207
2:18 These things saith the S of God, who hath 5207
14:14 upon the cloud one sat like unto the S of 5207
21: 7 and I will be his God, and he shall be my s. 5207

SON'S (22) [SON]

Ge 11:31 Lot the son of Haran his s son, and Sarai 1121
16:15 Abram called his s name, which Hagar 1121
21:23 nor with my son, nor with my s son: 5220
24:51 and go, and let her be thy master's s wife, 1121
27:25 near to me, and I will eat of my s venison, 1121
27:31 my father arise, and eat of his s venison, 1121
30:14 Give me, I pray thee, of thy s mandrakes. 1121
30:15 wouldest thou take away my s mandrakes 1121
30:15 lie with thee to night for thy s mandrakes. 1121
30:16 for surely I have hired thee with my s 1121
37:32 know now whether it be thy s coat or no. 1121
37:33 he knew it, and said, It is my s coat; an evil 1121
Ex 10: 2 of thy s son, what things I have wrought in 1121
Lev 18:10 The nakedness of thy s daughter, or of thy 1121
18:15 she is thy s wife; thou shalt not uncover her 1121
18:17 neither shalt thou take her s daughter, or 1121
Dt 6: 2 thou, and thy son, and thy s son, all 1121
Jdg 8:22 both thou, and thy son, and thy s son also: 1121
1Ki 11:35 I will take the kingdom out of his s hand, 1121
21:29 in his s days will I bring the evil upon his 1121
Pr 30: 4 and what is his s name, if thou canst tell? 1121
Jer 27: 7 shall serve him, and his son, and his s son, 1121

SONG (78) [SING]

Ex 15: 1 the children of Israel this s unto 7892
15: 2 The LORD is my strength and s, and he is 2176
Nu 21:17 Israel sang this s, Spring up, O well; 7892
Dt 31:19 Now therefore write ye this s for you, 7892
31:19 that this s may be a witness for me against 7892
31:21 that this s shall testify against them as a 7892
31:22 Moses therefore wrote this s the same day, 7892
31:30 congregation of Israel the words of this s, 7892
32:44 spake all the words of this s in the ears of 7892
Jdg 5:12 awake, awake, utter a s: arise, Barak, and 7892
2Sa 22: 1 s in the day that the LORD had delivered 7892
1Ch 6:31 the service of s in the house of the LORD, 7892
15:22 chief of the Levites, was for s: 4853
15:22 he instructed about the s, because he was 4853
15:27 Chenaniah the master of the s with 4853
25: 6 father for s in the house of the LORD, 7892
2Ch 29:27 the s of the LORD began also with 7892
Job 30: 9 now am I their s, yea, I am their byword. 5058
Ps 18: T s in the day that the LORD delivered him 7892
28: 7 and with my s will I praise him. 7892
30: T S at the dedication of the house of David. 7892
33: 3 Sing unto him a new s; play skilfully with a 7892
40: 3 he hath put a new s in my mouth, 7892
42: 8 in the night his s shall be with me, and 7892
45: T the sons of Korah, Maschil, A S of loves. 7892
46: T for the sons of Korah, A S upon Alamoth. 7892
48: T A S and Psalm for the sons of Korah. 7892
65: T chief Musician, A Psalm and S of David. 7892
66: T To the chief Musician, A S or Psalm. 7892
67: T chief Musician on Neginoth, A Psalm or S. 7892
68: T the chief Musician, A Psalm or S of David. 7892
69:12 and I was the s of the drunkards. 5058
69:30 I will praise the name of God with a s; and 7892
75: T Al-taschith, A Psalm or S of Asaph. 7892
76: T on Neginoth, A Psalm or S of Asaph. 7892
77: 6 I call to remembrance my s in the night: 5058
83: T A S or Psalm of Asaph. 7892
87: T A Psalm or S for the sons of Korah. 7892
88: T A S or Psalm for the sons of Korah. To 7892
92: T A Psalm or S for the sabbath day. 7892
96: 1 O sing unto the LORD a new s: sing unto 7892
98: 1 O sing unto the LORD a new s; for he 7892
108: T A S or Psalm of David. 7892
118:14 The LORD is my strength and s, and 2176
120: T A S of degrees. 7892
121: T A S of degrees. 7892
122: T A S of degrees of David. 7892
123: T A S of degrees. 7892
124: T A S of degrees of David. 7892
125: T A S of degrees. 7892
126: T A S of degrees. 7892
127: T A S of degrees for Solomon. 7892
128: T A S of degrees. 7892
129: T A S of degrees. 7892
130: T A S of degrees. 7892
131: T A S of degrees of David. 7892
132: T A S of degrees. 7892
133: T A S of degrees of David. 7892
134: T A S of degrees. 7892
137: 3 us away captive required of us a s; 1697+7892
137: 4 How shall we sing the LORD'S s in a 7892
144: 9 I will sing a new s unto thee, O God: 7892
149: 1 Sing unto the LORD a new s, and 7892
Ecc 7: 5 than for a man to hear the s of fools. 7892
SS 1: 1 The s of songs, which is Solomon's. 7892
Isa 5: 1 Now will I sing to my wellbeloved a s of 7892
12: 2 JEHOVAH is my strength and my s; 2176
24: 9 They shall not drink wine with a s; 7892
26: 1 In that day shall this s be sung in the land 7892
30:29 Ye shall have a s, as in the night when a 7892
42:10 Sing unto the LORD a new s, and 7892
La 3:14 to all my people; and their s all the day. 5058
Eze 33:32 thou art unto them as a very lovely s of one 7892
Rev 5: 9 And they sung a new s, saying, Thou art 5603
14: 3 And they sung as it were a new s before 5603
14: 3 and no man could learn that s but 5603
15: 3 And they sing the s of Moses the servant of 5603
15: 3 and the s of the Lamb, saying, Great and 5603

SONGS (20) [SING]

Ge 31:27 and with s, with tabret, and with harp? 7892
1Ki 4:32 and his s were a thousand and five. 7892
1Ch 25: 7 that were instructed in the s of the LORD, 7892
Ne 12:46 and s of praise and thanksgiving unto God. 7892
Job 35:10 God my Maker, who giveth s in the night; 2158
Ps 32: 7 thou shalt compass me about with s of 7438
119:54 Thy statutes have been my s in the house of 2158
137: 3 saying, Sing us one of the s of Zion. 7892
Pr 25:20 so is he that singeth s to a heavy heart. 7892
SS 1: 1 The song of s, which is Solomon's. 7892
Isa 23:16 make sweet melody, sing many s, that thou 7892
24:16 uttermost part of the earth have we heard s, 2158
35:10 come to Zion with s and everlasting joy 7440
38:20 we will sing my s to the stringed 5058
Eze 26:13 I will cause the noise of thy s to cease; and 7892
Am 5:23 Take thou away from me the noise of thy s; 7892
8: 3 the s of the temple shall be howlings in that 7892
8:10 and all your s into lamentation; 7892
Eph 5:19 in psalms and hymns and spiritual s, 5603
Col 3:16 in psalms and hymns and spiritual s, 5603

SONS (1076) [SON]

Ge 5: 4 and he begat s and daughters: 1121
5: 7 seven years, and begat s and daughters: 1121
5:10 fifteen years, and begat s and daughters: 1121
5:13 forty years, and begat s and daughters: 1121
5:16 thirty years, and begat s and daughters: 1121
5:19 hundred years, and begat s and daughters: 1121
5:22 hundred years, and begat s and daughters: 1121
5:26 and two years, and begat s and daughters: 1121
5:30 and five years, and begat s and daughters: 1121
6: 2 That the s of God saw the daughters of men 1121
6: 4 when the s of God came in unto 1121
6:10 Noah begat three s, Shem, Ham, and 1121
6:18 thy s, and thy wife, and thy sons' wives 1121
7: 7 his s, and his wife, and his sons' wives with 1121
7:13 the s of Noah, and Noah's wife, and 1121
7:13 the three wives of his s with them, into 1121
8:16 and thy s, and thy sons' wives with thee. 1121
8:18 his s, and his wife, and his sons' wives with 1121
9: 1 God blessed Noah and his s, and said unto 1121
9: 8 unto Noah, and to his s with him, saying, 1121
9:18 the s of Noah, that went forth of the ark, 1121
9:19 These are the three s of Noah: and of them 1121
10: 1 Now these are the generations of the s of 1121
10: 1 and unto them were s born after the flood. 1121
10: 2 The s of Japheth; Gomer, and Magog, and 1121
10: 3 the s of Gomer; Ashkenaz, and Riphath, 1121
10: 4 the s of Javan; Elishah, and Tarshish, 1121
10: 6 the s of Ham; Cush, and Mizraim, and 1121
10: 7 the s of Cush; Seba, and Havilah, and 1121
10: 7 and the s of Raamah; Sheba, and Dedan. 1121
10:20 These are the s of Ham, after their families, 1121
10:25 unto Eber were born two s: the name of one 1121
10:29 and Jobab: all these were the s of Joktan. 1121
10:31 These are the s of Shem, after their 1121
10:32 These are the families of the s of Noah, 1121
11:11 hundred years, and begat s and daughters. 1121
11:13 three years, and begat s and daughters. 1121
11:15 three years, and begat s and daughters. 1121
11:17 thirty years, and begat s and daughters. 1121
11:19 nine years, and begat s and daughters. 1121
11:21 seven years, and begat s and daughters. 1121
11:23 hundred years, and begat s and daughters. 1121
11:25 nineteen years, and begat s and daughters. 1121
19:12 thy s, and thy daughters, and 1121
19:14 Lot went out, and spake unto his s in law, 2860
19:14 one that mocked unto his s in law. 2860
23: 3 and spake unto the s of Heth, saying, 1121
23:11 in the presence of the s of my people give I 1121
23:16 had named in the audience of the s of Heth, 1121
23:20 of a buryingplace by the s of Heth. 1121
25: 3 the s of Dedan were Asshurim, and 1121
25: 4 the s of Midian; Ephah, and Epher, and 1121
25: 6 unto the s of the concubines, 1121
25: 9 his s Isaac and Ishmael buried him in 1121
25:10 which Abraham purchased of the s of Heth: 1121
25:13 these are the names of the s of Ishmael, 1121
25:16 These are the s of Ishmael, and these are 1121
27:29 and let thy mother's s bow down to thee: 1121
29:34 unto me, because I have born him three s: 1121
30:20 with me, because I have born him six s: 1121
30:35 and gave them into the hand of his s. 1121
31: 1 he heard the words of Laban's s, saying, 1121
31:17 and set his s and his wives upon camels; 1121
31:28 hast not suffered me to kiss my s and my 1121
31:55 kissed his s and his daughters, and 1121
32:22 his eleven s, and passed over the ford 3206
34: 5 now his s were with his cattle in the field: 1121
34: 7 the s of Jacob came out of the field when 1121
34:13 the s of Jacob answered Shechem and 1121
34:25 that two of the s of Jacob, Simeon and 1121
34:27 The s of Jacob came upon the slain, and 1121
35: 5 and they did not pursue after the s of Jacob. 1121
35:22 Israel heard it. Now the s of Jacob were 1121
35:23 The s of Leah; Reuben, Jacob's firstborn, 1121
35:24 The s of Rachel; Joseph, and Benjamin: 1121
35:25 the s of Bilhah, Rachel's handmaid; Dan, 1121
35:26 the s of Zilpah, Leah's handmaid; Gad, 1121
35:26 these are the s of Jacob, which were born to 1121
35:29 and his s Esau and Jacob buried him. 1121
36: 5 these are the s of Esau, which were born 1121
36: 6 his s, and his daughters, and all the persons 1121
36:10 These are the names of Esau's s; 1121
36:11 the s of Eliphaz were Teman, Omar, Zepho, 1121
36:12 these were the s of Adah Esau's wife. 1121
36:13 these are the s of Reuel; Nahath, and Zerah, 1121

Ge 36:13 these were the **s** of Bashemath Esau's wife. 1121
36:14 these were the **s** of Aholibamah, 1121
36:15 These *were* dukes of the **s** of Esau: the sons 1121
36:15 the **s** of Eliphaz the firstborn *son* of Esau; 1121
36:16 the land of Edom; these *were* the **s** of Adah. 1121
36:17 these *are* the **s** of Reuel Esau's son; 1121
36:17 these *are* the **s** of Bashemath Esau's wife. 1121
36:18 these *are* the **s** of Aholibamah Esau's wife; 1121
36:19 These *are* the **s** of Esau, who *is* Edom, and 1121
36:20 These *are* the **s** of Seir the Horite, 1121
37: 2 the lad *was* with the **s** of Bilhah, and 1121
37: 2 and with the **s** of Zilpah, his father's wives: 1121
37:35 all his **s** and all his daughters rose up to 1121
41:50 unto Joseph were born two **s** before 1121
42: 1 Jacob said unto his **s**, Why do ye look one 1121
42: 5 the **s** of Israel came to buy *corn* among 1121
42:11 We *are* all one man's **s**; we *are* true *men*, 1121
42:13 the **s** of one man in the land of Canaan; 1121
42:32 We *be* twelve brethren, **s** of our father; one 1121
42:37 saying, Slay my two **s**, if I bring him not to 1121
44:27 Ye know that my wife bare me two *s*: NIH
46: 5 and the **s** of Israel carried Jacob their father, 1121
46: 7 His **s**, and his sons' sons with him, 1121
46: 7 His sons, and his sons' **s** with him, 1121
46: 8 which came into Egypt, Jacob and his **s**: 1121
46: 9 the **s** of Reuben; Hanoch, and Phallu, and 1121
46:10 the **s** of Simeon; Jemuel, and Jamin, and 1121
46:11 the **s** of Levi; Gershon, Kohath, and Merari. 1121
46:12 the **s** of Judah; Er, and Onan, and Shelah, 1121
46:12 the **s** of Pharez were Hezron and Hamul. 1121
46:13 the **s** of Issachar; Tola, and Phuvah, and 1121
46:14 the **s** of Zebulun; Sered, and Elon, and 1121
46:15 These *be* the **s** of Leah, which she bare unto 1121
46:15 all the souls of his **s** and his daughters *were* 1121
46:16 the **s** of Gad; Ziphion, and Haggi, Shuni, 1121
46:17 the **s** of Asher; Jimnah, and Ishuah, and 1121
46:17 and the **s** of Beriah; Heber, and Malchiel. 1121
46:18 These *are* the **s** of Zilpah, whom Laban 1121
46:19 The **s** of Rachel Jacob's wife; Joseph, and 1121
46:21 the **s** of Benjamin *were* Belah, and Becher, 1121
46:22 These *are* the **s** of Rachel, which were born 1121
46:23 And the **s** of Dan; Hushim. 1121
46:24 the **s** of Naphtali; Jahzeel, and Guni, and 1121
46:25 These *are* the **s** of Bilhah, which Laban 1121
46:27 the **s** of Joseph, which were born him in 1121
48: 1 he took with him his two **s**, Manasseh and 1121
48: 5 now thy two **s**, Ephraim and Manasseh, 1121
48: 8 Israel beheld Joseph's **s**, and said, Who *are* 1121
48: 9 Joseph said unto his father, They *are* my **s**, 1121
49: 1 Jacob called unto his **s**, and said, 1121
49: 2 and hear, ye **s** of Jacob; 1121
49:33 had made an end of commanding his **s**, 1121
50:12 his **s** did unto him according as he 1121
50:13 For his **s** carried him into the land of 1121
Ex 3:22 ye shall put *them* upon your **s**, and 1121
4:20 Moses took his wife and his **s**, and set them 1121
6:14 The **s** of Reuben the firstborn of Israel; 1121
6:15 the **s** of Simeon; Jemuel, and Jamin, and 1121
6:16 these *are* the names of the **s** of Levi 1121
6:17 The **s** of Gershon; Libni, and Shimi, 1121
6:18 the **s** of Kohath; Amram, and Izhar, and 1121
6:19 the **s** of Merari; Mahali and Mushi: 1121
6:21 the **s** of Izhar; Korah, and Nepheg, and 1121
6:22 the **s** of Uzziel; Mishael, and Elzaphan, 1121
6:24 the **s** of Korah; Assir, and Elkanah, and 1121
10: 9 our old, with our **s** and with our daughters, 1121
12:24 an ordinance to thee and to thy **s** for ever. 1121
18: 3 her two **s**; of which the name of the one 1121
18: 5 came with his **s** and his wife unto Moses 1121
18: 6 and thy wife, and her two **s** with her. 1121
21: 4 and she have born him **s** or daughters; 1121
22:29 the firstborn of thy **s** shalt thou give unto 1121
27:21 his **s** shall order it from evening to morning 1121
28: 1 his **s** with him, from among the children of 1121
28: 1 and Abihu, Eleazar and Ithamar, Aaron's **s**. 1121
28: 4 his **s**, that he may minister unto me in 1121
28:40 for Aaron's **s** thou shalt make coats, and 1121
28:41 upon Aaron thy brother, and his **s** with him; 1121
28:43 they shall be upon Aaron, and upon his **s**, 1121
29: 4 his **s** thou shalt bring unto the door of 1121
29: 8 thou shalt bring his **s**, and put coats upon 1121
29: 9 Aaron and his **s**, and put the bonnets on 1121
29: 9 and thou shalt consecrate Aaron and his **s**. 1121
29:10 his **s** shall put their hands upon the head of 1121
29:15 his **s** shall put their hands upon the head of 1121
29:19 his **s** shall put their hands upon the head of 1121
29:20 upon the tip of the right ear of his **s**, and 1121
29:21 upon his **s**, and upon the garments of his 1121
29:21 and upon the garments of his **s** with him: 1121
29:21 and his **s**, and his sons' garments with him. 1121
29:24 hands of Aaron, and in the hands of his **s**; 1121
29:27 *is* for Aaron, and of *that* which *is* for his **s**: 1121
29:32 and his **s** shall eat the flesh of the ram, 1121
29:35 thus shalt thou do unto Aaron, and to his **s**, 1121
29:44 I will sanctify also both Aaron and his **s**, 1121
30:19 and his **s** shall wash their hands and 1121
30:30 thou shalt anoint Aaron and his **s**, and 1121
31:10 the garments of his **s**, to minister in 1121
32: 2 of your **s**, and of your daughters, and 1121
32:26 all the **s** of Levi gathered themselves 1121
34:16 thou take of their daughters unto thy **s**, and 1121
34:16 make thy **s** go a whoring after their gods. 1121
34:20 All the firstborn of thy **s** thou shalt redeem: 1121
35:19 the garments of his **s**, to minister in 1121
39:27 *of* woven work for Aaron, and for his **s**, 1121
40:12 his **s** unto the door of the tabernacle of 1121
40:14 thou shalt bring his **s**, and clothe them with 1121
40:31 and Aaron and his **s** washed their hands and 1121
Lev 1: 5 the priests, Aaron's **s**, shall bring the blood, 1121
1: 7 the **s** of Aaron the priest shall put fire upon 1121
1: 8 the priests, Aaron's **s**, shall lay the parts, 1121
1:11 the priests, Aaron's **s**, shall sprinkle his 1121
2: 2 he shall bring it to Aaron's **s** the priests: 1121
3: 2 Aaron's **s** the priests shall sprinkle 1121
3: 5 Aaron's **s** shall burn it on the altar upon 1121
Lev 3: 8 Aaron's **s** shall sprinkle the blood thereof 1121
3:13 the **s** of Aaron shall sprinkle the blood 1121
6: 9 Command Aaron and his **s**, saying, This *is* 1121
6:14 the **s** of Aaron shall offer it before 1121
6:16 remainder thereof shall Aaron and his **s** eat: 1121
6:20 This *is* the offering of Aaron and of his **s**, 1121
6:22 the priest of his **s** that is anointed in his 1121
6:25 Speak unto Aaron and to his **s**, saying, 1121
7:10 and dry, shall all the **s** of Aaron have, 1121
7:33 He among the **s** of Aaron, that offereth 1121
7:34 unto his **s** by a statute for ever from among 1121
7:35 of Aaron, and of the anointing of his **s**, 1121
8: 2 Take Aaron and his **s** with him, and 1121
8: 6 Moses brought Aaron and his **s**, and 1121
8:13 Moses brought Aaron's **s**, and put coats 1121
8:14 his **s** laid their hands upon the head of 1121
8:18 his **s** laid their hands upon the head of 1121
8:22 his **s** laid their hands upon the head of 1121
8:24 he brought Aaron's **s**, and Moses put of 1121
8:30 upon his **s**, and upon his sons' garments 1121
8:30 and his **s**, and his sons' garments with him. 1121
8:31 Moses said unto Aaron and to his **s**, 1121
8:31 Aaron and his **s** shall eat it. 1121
8:36 his **s** did all things which the LORD 1121
9: 1 *that* Moses called Aaron and his **s**, and 1121
9: 9 the **s** of Aaron brought the blood unto him: 1121
9:12 Aaron's **s** presented unto him the blood, 1121
9:18 Aaron's **s** presented unto him the blood, 1121
10: 1 Nadab and Abihu, the **s** of Aaron, 1121
10: 4 the **s** of Uzziel the uncle of Aaron, and 1121
10: 6 unto Eleazar and unto Ithamar his **s**, 1121
10: 9 nor strong drink, thou, nor thy **s** with thee, 1121
10:12 and unto Ithamar his **s** that were left; 1121
10:14 and thy **s**, and thy daughters with thee: 1121
10:16 Ithamar the **s** of Aaron which were left 1121
13: 2 the priest, or unto one of his **s** the priests: 1121
16: 1 after the death of the two **s** of Aaron, 1121
17: 2 unto his **s**, and unto all the children of 1121
21: 1 Speak unto the priests the **s** of Aaron, and 1121
21:24 to his **s**, and unto all the children of Israel. 1121
22: 2 Speak unto Aaron and to his **s**, that they 1121
22:18 to his **s**, and unto all the children of Israel, 1121
26:29 ye shall eat the flesh of your **s**, and the flesh 1121
Nu 2:14 the captain of the **s** of Gad *shall be* Eliasaph 1121
2:18 the captain of the **s** of Ephraim *shall be* 1121
2:22 the captain of the **s** of Benjamin *shall be* 1121
3: 2 these *are* the names of the **s** of Aaron; 1121
3: 3 These *are* the names of the **s** of Aaron, 1121
3: 9 give the Levites unto Aaron and to his **s**: 1121
3:10 And thou shalt appoint Aaron and his **s**, and 1121
3:17 these were the **s** of Levi by their names; 1121
3:18 these *are* the names of the **s** of Gershon by 1121
3:19 the **s** of Kohath by their families; Amram, 1121
3:20 the **s** of Merari by their families; Mahli, 1121
3:25 the charge of the **s** of Gershon in 1121
3:29 The families of the **s** of Kohath shall pitch 1121
3:36 charge of the **s** of Merari *shall be* 1121
3:38 *shall be* Moses, and Aaron and his **s**, 1121
3:48 is *to be* redeemed, unto Aaron and to his **s**. 1121
3:51 were redeemed unto Aaron and to his **s**, 1121
4: 2 Take the sum of the **s** of Kohath from 1121
4: 2 sons of Kohath from among the **s** of Levi, 1121
4: 4 This *shall be* the service of the **s** of Kohath 1121
4: 5 his **s**, and they shall take down the covering 1121
4:15 his **s** have made an end of covering 1121
4:15 the **s** of Kohath shall come to bear *it:* but 1121
4:15 These *things are* the burden of the **s** of 1121
4:19 holy *things:* Aaron and his **s** shall go in, 1121
4:22 Take also the sum of the **s** of Gershon, 1121
4:27 his **s** shall be all the service of the sons of 1121
4:27 his sons shall be all the service of the **s** of 1121
4:28 This *is* the service of the families of the **s** of 1121
4:29 *As for* the **s** of Merari, thou shalt number 1121
4:33 This *is* the service of the families of the **s** of 1121
4:34 the **s** of the Kohathites after their families, 1121
4:38 those that were numbered of the **s** of 1121
4:41 of the families of the **s** of Gershon, 1121
4:42 numbered of the families of the **s** of Merari, 1121
4:43 numbered of the families of the **s** of Merari, 1121
6:23 Speak unto Aaron and unto his **s**, saying, 1121
7: 7 four oxen he gave unto the **s** of Gershon, 1121
7: 8 eight oxen he gave unto the **s** of Merari, 1121
7: 9 unto the **s** of Kohath he gave none: because 1121
8:13 before his **s**, and offer them *for* an offering 1121
8:19 to his **s** from among the children of Israel, 1121
8:22 before Aaron, and before his **s**: 1121
10: 8 the **s** of Aaron, the priests, shall blow with 1121
10:17 the **s** of Gershon and the sons of Merari set 1121
10:17 of Gershon and the **s** of Merari set forward, 1121
13:33 the **s** of Anak, *which come* of the giants: 1121
16: 1 Dathan and Abiram, the **s** of Eliab, and On, 1121
16: 1 the son of Peleth, **s** of Reuben, took *men:* 1121
16: 7 *ye take* too much upon you, ye **s** of Levi. 1121
16: 8 unto Korah, Hear, I pray you, ye **s** of Levi: 1121
16:10 and all thy brethren the **s** of Levi with thee: 1121
16:12 to call Dathan and Abiram, the **s** of Eliab: 1121
16:27 and their **s**, and their little children. 1121
18: 1 Thou and thy **s** and thy father's house with 1121
18: 1 thy **s** with thee shall bear the iniquity of 1121
18: 2 thy **s** with thee *shall minister* before 1121
18: 7 thy **s** with thee shall keep your priest's 1121
18: 8 and to thy **s**, by an ordinance for ever. 1121
18: 9 *shall be* most holy for thee and for thy **s**. 1121
18:11 to thy **s** and to thy daughters with thee, by a 1121
18:19 and thy **s** and thy daughters with thee, 1121
21:29 he hath given his **s** that escaped, and 1121
21:35 smote him, and his **s**, and all his people, 1121
26: 8 And the **s** of Pallu; Eliab. 1121
26: 9 the **s** of Eliab; Nemuel, and Dathan, and 1121
26:12 The **s** of Simeon after their families: 1121
26:19 The **s** of Judah *were* Er and Onan: and Er 1121
26:20 And the **s** of Judah after their families were, 1121
26:21 the **s** of Pharez were; of Hezron, the family 1121
26:23 *Of* the **s** of Issachar after their families: 1121
26:26 *Of* the **s** of Zebulun after their families: 1121
Nu 26:28 The **s** of Joseph after their families *were* 1121
26:29 *Of* the **s** of Manasseh: of Machir, the family 1121
26:30 These *are* the **s** of Gilead: *of* Jeezer, 1121
26:33 Zelophehad the son of Hepher had no **s**, 1121
26:35 These *are* the **s** of Ephraim after their 1121
26:36 these *are* the **s** of Shuthelah: of Eran, 1121
26:37 These *are* the families of the **s** of Ephraim 1121
26:37 These *are* the **s** of Joseph after their 1121
26:38 The **s** of Benjamin after their families: 1121
26:40 the **s** of Bela were Ard and Naaman: 1121
26:41 These *are* the **s** of Benjamin after their 1121
26:42 These *are* the **s** of Dan after their families: 1121
26:45 Of the **s** of Beriah: of Heber, the family of 1121
26:47 These *are* the families of the **s** of Asher 1121
26:48 *Of* the **s** of Naphtali after their families: 1121
27: 3 but died in his own sin, and had no **s**. 1121
36: 1 of the families of the **s** of Joseph, 1121
36: 3 *if* they be married to any of the **s** of 1121
36: 5 The tribe of the **s** of Joseph hath said well. 1121
36:11 were married unto their father's brothers' **s**: 1121
36:12 of the **s** of Manasseh the son of Joseph, 1121
Dt 1:28 moreover we have seen the **s** of 1121
2:33 we smote him, and his **s**, and all his people. 1121
4: 9 but teach them thy **s**, and thy sons' sons; 1121
4: 9 but teach them thy sons, and thy sons' **s**; 1121
11: 6 did unto Dathan and Abiram, the **s** of Eliab, 1121
12:12 ye, and your **s**, and your daughters, and 1121
12:31 for even their **s** and their daughters they 1121
18: 5 of the LORD, him and his **s** for ever. 1121
21: 5 the priests the **s** of Levi shall come near; 1121
21:16 when he maketh his **s** to inherit *that* which 1121
23:17 of Israel, nor a sodomite of the **s** of Israel. 1121
28:32 Thy **s** and thy daughters *shall be* given unto 1121
28:41 Thou shalt beget **s** and daughters, but 1121
28:53 the flesh of thy **s** and of thy daughters, 1121
31: 9 delivered it unto the priests the **s** of Levi, 1121
32: 8 when he separated the **s** of Adam, 1121
32:19 because of the provoking of his **s**, 1121
Jos 7:24 his **s**, and his daughters, and his oxen, and 1121
15:14 Caleb drove thence the three **s** of Anak, 1121
17: 3 son of Manasseh, had no **s**, but daughters: 1121
17: 6 Manasseh had an inheritance among his **s**: 1121
17: 6 the rest of Manasseh's **s** had the land of 1121
24:32 **s** of Hamor the father of Shechem for an 1121
Jdg 1:20 and he expelled thence the three **s** of Anak. 1121
3: 6 gave their daughters to their **s**, and 1121
8:19 *were* my brethren, *even* the **s** of my mother: 1121
8:30 and ten **s** of his body begotten: 1121
9: 2 either that all the **s** of Jerubbaal, *which are* 1121
9: 5 slew his brethren the **s** of Jerubbaal, 1121
9:18 have slain his **s**, threescore and ten persons, 1121
9:24 and ten **s** of Jerubbaal might come, 1121
10: 4 he had thirty **s** that rode on thirty ass colts, 1121
11: 2 Gilead's wife bare him **s**; and *his* wife's 1121
11: 2 *his* wife's **s** grew up, and they thrust out 1121
12: 9 he had thirty **s**, and thirty daughters, 1121
12: 9 in thirty daughters from abroad for his **s**. 1121
12:14 he had forty **s** and thirty nephews, that rode 1121
17: 5 and teraphim, and consecrated one of his **s**, 1121
17:11 young man was unto him as one of his **s**. 1121
18:30 his **s** were priests to the tribe of Dan until 1121
19:22 the men of the city, certain **s** of Belial, 1121
Ru 1: 1 of Moab, he, and his wife, and his two **s**. 1121
1: 2 the name of his two **s** Mahlon and Chilion, 1121
1: 3 and she was left, and her two **s**. 1121
1: 5 the woman was left of her two **s** and 3206
1:11 *are there* yet *any mo*e **s** in my womb, 1121
1:12 also to night, and should also bear **s**; 1121
4:15 which *is* better to thee than seven **s**, 1121
1Sa 1: 3 the two **s** of Eli, Hophni and Phinehas, 1121
1: 4 and to all her **s** and her daughters, portions: 1121
1: 8 *am* not I better to thee than ten **s**? 1121
2:12 Now the **s** of Eli *were* sons of Belial; 1121
2:12 Now the sons of Eli *were* **s** of Belial; 1121
2:21 and bare three **s** and two daughters. 1121
2:22 and heard all that his **s** did unto all Israel; 1121
2:24 Nay, my **s**; for *it is* no good report that I 1121
2:29 honourest thy **s** above me, to make 1121
2:34 that shall come upon thy two **s**, on Hophni 1121
3:13 because his **s** made themselves vile, and 1121
4: 4 the two **s** of Eli, Hophni and Phinehas, 1121
4:11 the two **s** of Eli, Hophni and Phinehas, 1121
4:17 thy two **s** also, Hophni and Phinehas, 1121
8: 1 that he made his **s** judges over Israel. 1121
8: 3 his **s** walked not in his ways, but 1121
8: 5 thou art old, and thy **s** walk not in thy ways: 1121
8:11 He will take your **s**, and appoint *them* for 1121
12: 2 grayheaded; and behold, my **s** *are* with you: 1121
14:49 Now the **s** of Saul were Jonathan, and 1121
16: 1 for I have provided me a king among his **s**. 1121
16: 5 he sanctified Jesse and his **s**, and 1121
16:10 Jesse made seven of his **s** to pass before 1121
17:12 whose name *was* Jesse; and he had eight **s**: 1121
17:13 the three eldest **s** of Jesse went *and* 1121
17:13 the names of his three **s** that went to 1121
22:20 one of the **s** of Ahimelech the son of 1121
28:19 to morrow *shalt* thou and thy **s** *be* with me: 1121
30: 3 their wives, and their **s**, and their daughters, 1121
30: 6 every man for his **s** and for his daughters: 1121
30:19 neither **s** nor daughters, neither spoil, 1121
31: 2 followed hard upon Saul and upon his **s**; 1121
31: 2 and Abinadab, and Malchishua, Saul's **s**. 1121
31: 6 his three **s**, and his armourbearer, and 1121
31: 7 that Saul and his **s** were dead, they forsook 1121
31: 8 and his three **s** fallen in mount Gilboa. 1121
31:12 the bodies of his **s** from the wall of 1121
2Sa 2:18 there were three **s** of Zeruiah there, Joab, 1121
3: 2 unto David were **s** born in Hebron: and 1121
3:39 these men the **s** of Zeruiah *be* too hard for 1121
4: 2 the **s** of Rimmon a Beerothite, of 1121
4: 5 the **s** of Rimmon the Beerothite, Rechab 1121
4: 9 the **s** of Rimmon the Beerothite, and 1121
5:13 there were yet **s** and daughters born to 1121
6: 3 Uzzah and Ahio, the **s** of Abinadab, 1121
8:18 and David's **s** were chief rulers. 1121

2Sa 9:10 Thou therefore, and thy **s**, and thy servants, 1121
9:10 Now Ziba had fifteen **s** and 1121
9:11 shall eat at my table, as one of the king's **s**. 1121
13:23 and Absalom invited all the king's **s**. 1121
13:27 let Amnon and all the king's **s** go with him. 1121
13:29 all the king's **s** arose, and every man gat 1121
13:30 Absalom hath slain all the king's **s**, and 1121
13:32 have slain all the young men the king's **s**; 1121
13:33 to think *that* all the king's **s** are dead: 1121
13:35 unto the king, Behold, the king's **s** come: 1121
13:36 the king's **s** came, and lift up their voice 1121
14: 6 thy handmaid had two **s**, and they two 1121
14:27 unto Absalom there were born three **s**, and 1121
15:27 your two **s** with you, Ahimaaz thy son, and 1121
15:36 *they have* there with them their two **s**, 1121
16:10 have I to do with you, ye **s** of Zeruiah? 1121
19: 5 the lives of thy **s** and of thy daughters, and 1121
19:17 his fifteen **s** and his twenty servants with 1121
19:22 have I to do with you, ye **s** of Zeruiah, 1121
21: 6 Let seven men of his **s** be delivered unto us, 1121
21: 8 the king took the two **s** of Rizpah 1121
21: 8 the five **s** of Michal the daughter of Saul, 1121
21:16 which *was* of the **s** of the giant, 3211
21:18 slew Saph, which *was* of the **s** of the giant. 3211
23: 6 *the* **s** *of* Belial *shall be* all of them as thorns NIH
23:32 *of* the **s** of Jashen, Jonathan, 1121
1Ki 1: 9 called all his brethren the king's **s**, and all 1121
1:19 hath called all the **s** of the king, and 1121
1:25 hath called all the king's **s**, and the captains 1121
2: 7 shew kindness unto the **s** of Barzillai 1121
4: 3 Elihoreph and Ahiah, the **s** of Shisha, 1121
4:31 and Chalcol, and Darda, the **s** of Mahol: 1121
11:20 household among the **s** of Pharaoh. 1121
12:31 the people, which were not of the **s** of Levi. 1121
13:12 For his **s** had seen what way the man of 1121
13:13 he said unto his **s**, Saddle me the ass. 1121
13:27 he spake to his **s**, saying, Saddle me the ass. 1121
13:31 that he spake to his **s**, saying, When I am 1121
18:31 the number of the tribes of the **s** of Jacob, 1121
20:35 a certain man of the **s** of the prophets said 1121
21:10 set two men, **s** of Belial, before him, to bear 1121
2Ki 2: 3 the **s** of the prophets that *were at* Beth-el 1121
2: 5 the **s** of the prophets that *were* at Jericho 1121
2: 7 And fifty men of the **s** of the prophets went, 1121
2:15 when the **s** of the prophets which *were* to 1121
4: 1 wives of the **s** of the prophets unto Elisha, 1121
4: 1 to take unto him my two **s** to be bondmen. 3206
4: 4 shut the door upon thee and upon thy **s**, 1121
4: 5 and shut the door upon her and upon her **s**, 1121
4:38 the **s** of the prophets *were* sitting before 1121
4:38 and seethe pottage for the **s** of the prophets. 1121
5:22 two young men of the **s** of the prophets: 1121
6: 1 the **s** of the prophets said unto Elisha, 1121
9:26 and the blood of his **s**, saith the LORD; 1121
10: 1 Ahab had seventy **s** in Samaria. And Jehu 1121
10: 2 seeing your master's **s** *are* with you, and 1121
10: 3 out the best and meetest of your master's **s**, 1121
10: 6 ye the heads of the men your master's **s**, 1121
10: 6 Now the king's **s**, *being* seventy persons, 1121
10: 7 that they took the king's **s**, and 1121
10: 8 have brought the heads of the king's **s**. 1121
11: 2 stale him from among the king's **s** which 1121
15:12 Thy **s** shall sit on the throne of Israel unto 1121
17:17 they caused their **s** and their daughters to 1121
19:37 Sharezer *his* **s** smote him with the sword: NIH
20:18 of thy **s** that shall issue from thee, 1121
25: 7 they slew the **s** of Zedekiah before his eyes, 1121
1Ch 1: 5 The **s** of Japheth; Gomer, and Magog, and 1121
1: 6 the **s** of Gomer; Ashchenaz, and Riphath, 1121
1: 7 the **s** of Javan; Elishah, and Tarshish, 1121
1: 8 The **s** of Ham; Cush, and Mizraim, Put, and 1121
1: 9 the **s** of Cush; Seba, and Havilah, and 1121
1: 9 And the **s** of Raamah; Sheba, and Dedan. 1121
1:17 The **s** of Shem; Elam, and Asshur, and 1121
1:19 unto Eber were born two **s**: the name of 1121
1:23 and Jobab. All these *were* the **s** of Joktan. 1121
1:28 The **s** of Abraham; Isaac, and Ishmael. 1121
1:31 and Kedemah. These *are* the **s** of Ishmael. 1121
1:32 Now the **s** of Keturah, 1121
1:32 And the **s** of Jokshan; Sheba, and Dedan. 1121
1:33 the **s** of Midian; Ephah, and Epher, and 1121
1:33 and Eldaah. All these *are* the **s** of Keturah. 1121
1:34 begat Isaac. The **s** of Isaac; Esau and Israel. 1121
1:35 The **s** of Esau; Eliphaz, Reuel, and Jeush, 1121
1:36 The **s** of Eliphaz; Teman, and Omar, Zephi, 1121
1:37 The **s** of Reuel; Nahath, Zerah, Shammah, 1121
1:38 the **s** of Seir; Lotan, and Shobal, and 1121
1:39 the **s** of Lotan; Hori, and Homam: and 1121
1:40 The **s** of Shobal; Alian, and Manahath, and 1121
1:40 And the **s** of Zibeon; Aiah, and Anah. 1121
1:41 The **s** of Anah; Dishon. And the sons of 1121
1:41 the **s** of Dishon; Amram, and Eshban, and 1121
1:42 The **s** of Ezer; Bilhan, and Zavan, *and* 1121
1:42 *and* Jakan. The **s** of Dishan; Uz, and Aran. 1121
2: 1 These *are* the **s** of Israel; Reuben, Simeon, 1121
2: 3 The **s** of Judah; Er, and Onan, and Shelah: 1121
2: 4 and Zerah. All the **s** of Judah *were* five. 1121
2: 5 The **s** of Pharez; Hezron, and Hamul. 1121
2: 6 the **s** of Zerah; Zimri, and Ethan, and 1121
2: 7 the **s** of Carmi; Achar, the troubler of 1121
2: 8 And the **s** of Ethan; Azariah. 1121
2: 9 The **s** also of Hezron, that were born unto 1121
2:16 the **s** of Zeruiah; Abishai, and Joab, and 1121
2:18 her **s** *are* these; Jesher, and Shobab, and 1121
2:23 All these *belonged to* the **s** of Machir 1121
2:25 the **s** of Jerahmeel the firstborn of Hezron 1121
2:27 the **s** of Ram the firstborn of Jerahmeel 1121
2:28 the **s** of Onam were, Shammai, and Jada. 1121
2:28 the **s** of Shammai; Nadab, and Abishur. 1121
2:30 the **s** of Nadab; Seled, and Appaim: but 1121
2:31 the **s** of Appaim; Ishi. And the sons of Ishi; 1121
2:31 the **s** of Ishi; Sheshan. And the children of 1121
2:32 the **s** of Jada the brother of Shammai; 1121
2:33 the **s** of Jonathan; Peleth, and Zaza. 1121
2:33 and Zaza. These were the **s** of Jerahmeel. 1121

1Ch 2:34 Now Sheshan had no **s**, but daughters. 1121
2:42 Now the **s** of Caleb the brother of 1121
2:42 and the **s** of Mareshah the father of Hebron. 1121
2:43 the **s** of Hebron; Korah, and Tappuah, and 1121
2:47 the **s** of Jahdai; Regem, and Jotham, and 1121
2:50 These were the **s** of Caleb the son of Hur, 1121
2:52 Shobal the father of Kirjath-jearim had **s**; 1121
2:54 The **s** of Salma; Beth-lehem, and 1121
3: 1 Now these were the **s** of David, which were 1121
3: 9 *These were* all the **s** of David, beside 1121
3: 9 beside the **s** of the concubines, and 1121
3:15 the **s** of Josiah *were*, the firstborn Johanan, 1121
3:16 the **s** of Jehoiakim: Jeconiah his son, 1121
3:17 the **s** of Jeconiah; Assir, Salathiel his son, 1121
3:19 And the **s** of Pedaiah *were*, Zerubbabel, and 1121
3:21 the **s** of Hananiah; Pelatiah, and Jesaiah: 1121
3:21 the **s** of Rephaiah, the sons of Arnan, 1121
3:21 the **s** of Arnan, the sons of Obadiah, 1121
3:21 the sons of Arnan, the **s** of Obadiah, 1121
3:21 the sons of Obadiah, the **s** of Shechaniah. 1121
3:22 the **s** of Shechaniah; Shemaiah: and 1121
3:22 the **s** of Shemaiah; Hattush, and Igeal, and 1121
3:23 The **s** of Neariah; Elioenai, and Hezekiah, 1121
3:24 the **s** of Elioenai *were*, Hodaiah, and 1121
4: 1 The **s** of Judah; Pharez, Hezron, and Carmi, 1121
4: 4 These *are* the **s** of Hur, the firstborn of 1121
4: 6 These *were* the **s** of Naarah. 1121
4: 7 the **s** of Helah *were*, Zereth, and Jezoar, 1121
4:13 the **s** of Kenaz; Othniel, and Seraiah: and 1121
4:13 and Seraiah: and the **s** of Othniel; Hathath. 1121
4:15 the **s** of Caleb the son of Jephunneh; Iru, 1121
4:15 and Naam: and the **s** of Elah, even Kenaz. 1121
4:16 the **s** of Jehaleleel; Ziph, and Ziphah, Tiria, 1121
4:17 the **s** of Ezra *were*, Jether, and Mered, and 1121
4:18 these *are* the **s** of Bithiah the daughter of 1121
4:19 the **s** of *his* wife Hodiah the sister of 1121
4:20 the **s** of Shimon *were*, Amnon, and Rinnah, 1121
4:20 the **s** of Ishi *were*, Zoheth, and Ben-zoheth. 1121
4:21 The **s** of Shelah the son of Judah *were*, Er 1121
4:24 The **s** of Simeon *were*, Nemuel, and Jamin, 1121
4:26 the **s** of Mishma; Hamuel his son, 1121
4:27 Shimei had sixteen **s** and six daughters; 1121
4:42 *even* of the **s** of Simeon, five hundred men, 1121
4:42 and Rephaiah, and Uzziel, the **s** of Ishi. 1121
5: 1 Now the **s** of Reuben the firstborn of Israel, 1121
5: 1 his birthright was given unto the **s** of 1121
5: 3 The **s**, *I say*, of Reuben the firstborn of 1121
5: 4 The **s** of Joel; Shemaiah his son, Gog his 1121
5:18 The **s** of Reuben, and the Gadites, and 1121
6: 1 The **s** of Levi; Gershon, Kohath, and 1121
6: 2 the **s** of Kohath; Amram, Izhar, and 1121
6: 3 The **s** also of Aaron; Nadab, and Abihu, 1121
6:16 The **s** of Levi; Gershom, Kohath, and 1121
6:17 these *be* the names of the **s** of Gershom; 1121
6:18 the **s** of Kohath *were*, Amram, and Izhar, 1121
6:19 The **s** of Merari; Mahli, and Mushi. 1121
6:22 The **s** of Kohath; Amminadab his son, 1121
6:25 the **s** of Elkanah; Amasai, and Ahimoth. 1121
6:26 the **s** of Elkanah; Zophai his son, and 1121
6:28 the **s** of Samuel; the firstborn Vashni, and 1121
6:29 The **s** of Merari; Mahli, Libni his son, 1121
6:33 Of the **s** of the Kohathites: Heman a singer, 1121
6:44 their brethren the **s** of Merari *stood* on 1121
6:49 his **s** offered upon the altar of the burnt 1121
6:50 these *are* the **s** of Aaron; Eleazar his son, 1121
6:54 of the **s** of Aaron, of the families of 1121
6:57 to the **s** of Aaron they gave the cities of 1121
6:61 unto the **s** of Kohath, which were left of 1121
6:62 to the **s** of Gershom throughout their 1121
6:63 Unto the **s** of Merari *were given* by lot, 1121
6:66 *the residue* of the families of the **s** of 1121
6:70 for the family of the remnant of the **s** of 1121
6:71 Unto the **s** of Gershom *were given* out of 1121
7: 1 Now the **s** of Issachar *were*, Tola, and 1121
7: 2 the **s** of Tola; Uzzi, and Rephaiah, and 1121
7: 3 the **s** of Uzzi; Izrahiah: and the sons of 1121
7: 3 the **s** of Izrahiah; Michael, and Obadiah, 1121
7: 4 *men:* for they had many wives and **s**. 1121
7: 6 *The* **s** *of* Benjamin; Bela, and Becher, and NIH
7: 7 the **s** of Bela; Ezbon, and Uzzi, and Uzziel, 1121
7: 8 the **s** of Becher; Zemira, and Joash, and 1121
7: 8 and Alameth. All these *are* the **s** of Becher. 1121
7:10 The **s** also of Jediael; Bilhan: and the sons 1121
7:10 the **s** of Bilhan; Jeush, and Benjamin, and 1121
7:11 All these the **s** of Jediael, by the heads of 1121
7:12 children of Ir, *and* Hushim, the **s** of Aher. 1121
7:13 The **s** of Naphtali; Jahziel, and Guni, and 1121
7:13 and Jezer, and Shallum, the **s** of Bilhah. 1121
7:14 The **s** of Manasseh; Ashriel, whom she 1121
7:16 and his **s** *were* Ulam and Rakem. 1121
7:17 the **s** of Ulam; Bedan. These *were* the sons 1121
7:17 These *were* the **s** of Gilead, the son of 1121
7:19 the **s** of Shemida were, Ahian, and 1121
7:20 the **s** of Ephraim; Shuthelah, and Bered his 1121
7:30 The **s** of Asher; Imnah, and Isuah, and 1121
7:31 the **s** of Beriah; Heber, and Malchiel, 1121
7:33 the **s** of Japhlet; Pasach, and Bimhal, and 1121
7:34 the **s** of Shamer; Ahi, and Rohgah, 1121
7:36 The **s** of Zophah; Suah, and Harnepher, and 1121
7:38 the **s** of Jether; Jephunneh, and Pispah, and 1121
7:39 the **s** of Ulla; Arah, and Haniel, and Rezia. 1121
8: 3 the **s** of Bela were, Addar, and Gera, and 1121
8: 6 these *are* the **s** of Ehud: these *are* the heads 1121
8:10 These *were* his **s**, heads of the fathers. 1121
8:12 The **s** of Elpaal; Eber, and Misham, and 1121
8:16 and Ispah, and Joha, the **s** of Beriah; 1121
8:18 and Jezliah, and Jobab, the **s** of Elpaal; 1121
8:21 and Beraiah, and Shimrath, the **s** of Shimhi; 1121
8:25 and Penuel, the **s** of Shashak; 1121
8:27 and Eliah, and Zichri, the **s** of Jeroham. 1121
8:35 the **s** of Micah *were*, Pithon, and Melech, 1121
8:38 And Azel had six **s**, whose names *are* these, 1121
8:38 and Hanan. All these *were* the **s** of Azel. 1121
8:39 the **s** of Eshek his brother *were*, Ulam his 1121
8:40 the **s** of Ulam were mighty men of valour, 1121

1Ch 8:40 archers, and had many **s**, and sons' sons, 1121
8:40 and sons' **s**, an hundred and fifty. 1121
8:40 fifty. All these *are* of the **s** of Benjamin. 1121
9: 5 Asaiah the firstborn, and his **s**. 1121
9: 6 of the **s** of Zerah; Jeuel, and their brethren, 1121
9: 7 of the **s** of Benjamin; Sallu the son of 1121
9:14 the son of Hashabiah, of the **s** of Merari; 1121
9:30 *some* of the **s** of the priests made 1121
9:32 of the **s** of the Kohathites, *were* over 1121
9:41 the **s** of Micah *were*, Pithon, and Melech, 1121
9:44 And Azel had six **s**, whose names *are* these, 1121
9:44 and Hanan: these *were* the **s** of Azel. 1121
10: 2 followed hard after Saul, and after his **s**; 1121
10: 2 and Malchishua, the **s** of Saul. 1121
10: 6 his three **s**, and all his house died together. 1121
10: 7 that Saul and his **s** were dead, then 1121
10: 8 and his **s** fallen in mount Gilboa. 1121
10:12 the bodies of his **s**, and brought them to 1121
11:34 The **s** of Hashem the Gizonite, Jonathan 1121
11:44 and Jehiel the **s** of Hothan the Aroerite, 1121
11:46 the **s** of Elnaam, and Ithmah the Moabite, 1121
12: 3 Joash, the **s** of Shemaah the Gibeathite; 1121
12: 3 Jeziel, and Pelet, the **s** of Azmaveth; and 1121
12: 7 and Zebadiah, the **s** of Jeroham of Gedor. 1121
12:14 These *were* of the **s** of Gad, captains of 1121
14: 3 and David begat moe **s** and daughters. 1121
15: 5 Of the **s** of Kohath; Uriel the chief, and 1121
15: 6 Of the **s** of Merari; Asaiah the chief, and 1121
15: 7 Of the **s** of Gershom; Joel the chief, and 1121
15: 8 Of the **s** of Elizaphan; Shemaiah the chief, 1121
15: 9 Of the **s** of Hebron; Eliel the chief, and 1121
15:10 Of the **s** of Uzziel; Amminadab the chief, 1121
15:17 of the **s** of Merari their brethren, Ethan 1121
16:42 of God. And the **s** of Jeduthun *were* porters. 1121
17:11 thy seed after thee, which shall be of thy **s**; 1121
18:17 the **s** of David *were* chief about the king. 1121
21:20 and his four **s** with him hid themselves. 1121
23: 6 them *into* courses among the **s** of Levi, 1121
23: 8 The **s** of Laadan; the chief *was* Jehiel, and 1121
23: 9 The **s** of Shimei; Shelomith, and Haziel, 1121
23:10 And the **s** of Shimei *were*, Jahath, Zina, and 1121
23:10 Beriah. These four *were* the **s** of Shimei. 1121
23:11 Jeush and Beriah had not many **s**; therefore 1121
23:12 The **s** of Kohath; Amram, Izhar, Hebron, 1121
23:13 The **s** of Amram; Aaron and Moses: and 1121
23:13 the most holy *things*, he and his **s** for ever, 1121
23:14 his **s** were named of the tribe of Levi. 1121
23:15 The **s** of Moses *were*, Gershom, and 1121
23:16 *Of* the **s** of Gershom, Shebuel *was* 1121
23:17 the **s** of Eliezer *were*, Rehabiah the chief. 1121
23:17 Eliezer had none other **s**; but the sons of 1121
23:17 but the **s** of Rehabiah were very many. 1121
23:18 *Of* the **s** of Izhar; Shelomith the chief. 1121
23:19 *Of* the **s** of Hebron; Jeriah the first, 1121
23:20 *Of* the **s** of Uzziel; Michah the first, and 1121
23:21 The **s** of Merari; Mahli, and Mushi. 1121
23:21 Mushi. The **s** of Mahli; Eleazar, and Kish. 1121
23:22 Eleazar died, and had no **s**, but daughters: 1121
23:22 and their brethren the **s** of Kish took them. 1121
23:23 The **s** of Mushi; Mahli, and Eder, and 1121
23:24 These *were* the **s** of Levi after the house of 1121
23:28 Because their office *was* to wait on the **s** of 1121
23:32 the charge of the **s** of Aaron their brethren, 1121
24: 1 Now *these are* the divisions of the **s** of 1121
24: 1 The **s** of Aaron; Nadab, and Abihu, 1121
24: 3 both Zadok of the **s** of Eleazar, and 1121
24: 3 and Ahimelech of the **s** of Ithamar, 1121
24: 4 there were moe chief men found of the **s** of 1121
24: 4 the sons of Eleazar than of the **s** of Ithamar; 1121
24: 4 Among the **s** of Eleazar *there were* sixteen 1121
24: 4 eight among the **s** of Ithamar according to 1121
24: 5 were of the **s** of Eleazar, and of the sons of 1121
24: 5 the sons of Eleazar, and of the **s** of Ithamar. 1121
24:20 the rest of the **s** of Levi *were these:* Of 1121
24:20 of Levi *were these:* Of the **s** of Amram; 1121
24:20 Shubael: of the **s** of Shubael; Jehdeiah. 1121
24:21 of the **s** of Rehabiah, the first *was* Isshiah. 1121
24:22 Shelomoth: of the **s** of Shelomoth; Jahath. 1121
24:23 the **s** *of Hebron;* Jeriah *the first,* Amariah 1121
24:24 *Of* the **s** of Uzziel; Michah: of the sons of 1121
24:24 Michah: of the **s** of Michah; Shamir. 1121
24:25 *was* Isshiah: of the **s** of Isshiah; Zechariah. 1121
24:26 The **s** of Merari *were* Mahli and Mushi: 1121
24:26 and Mushi: the **s** of Jaaziah; Beno. 1121
24:27 The **s** of Merari by Jaaziah; Beno, and 1121
24:28 Of Mahli *came* Eleazar, who had no **s**. 1121
24:30 The **s** also of Mushi; Mahli, and Eder, and 1121
24:30 These *were* the **s** of the Levites after 1121
24:31 **s** of Aaron in the presence of David 1121
25: 1 separated to the service of the **s** of Asaph, 1121
25: 2 Of the **s** of Asaph; Zaccur, and Joseph, and 1121
25: 2 the **s** of Asaph under the hands of Asaph, 1121
25: 3 the **s** of Jeduthun; Gedaliah, and Zeri, and 1121
25: 4 the **s** of Heman; Bukkiah, Mattaniah, 1121
25: 5 All these *were* the **s** of Heman the king's 1121
25: 5 God gave to Heman fourteen **s** and 1121
25: 9 who with his brethren and **s** *were* twelve: 1121
25:10 *he*, his **s**, and his brethren, *were* twelve: 1121
25:11 *he*, his **s**, and his brethren, *were* twelve: 1121
25:12 *he*, his **s**, and his brethren, *were* twelve: 1121
25:13 *he*, his **s**, and his brethren, *were* twelve: 1121
25:14 *he*, his **s**, and his brethren, *were* twelve: 1121
25:15 *he*, his **s**, and his brethren, *were* twelve: 1121
25:16 *he*, his **s**, and his brethren, *were* twelve: 1121
25:17 *he*, his **s**, and his brethren, *were* twelve: 1121
25:18 *he*, his **s**, and his brethren, *were* twelve: 1121
25:19 *he*, his **s**, and his brethren, *were* twelve: 1121
25:20 *he*, his **s**, and his brethren, *were* twelve: 1121
25:21 *he*, his **s**, and his brethren, *were* twelve: 1121
25:22 *he*, his **s**, and his brethren, *were* twelve: 1121
25:23 *he*, his **s**, and his brethren, *were* twelve: 1121
25:24 *he*, his **s**, and his brethren, *were* twelve: 1121
25:25 *he*, his **s**, and his brethren, *were* twelve: 1121
25:26 *he*, his **s**, and his brethren, *were* twelve: 1121
25:27 *he*, his **s**, and his brethren, *were* twelve: 1121

1Ch 25:28 *he,* his s, and his brethren, *were* twelve: 1121
25:29 *he,* his s, and his brethren, *were* twelve: 1121
25:30 *he,* his s, and his brethren, *were* twelve: 1121
25:31 *he,* his s, and his brethren, *were* twelve. 1121
26: 1 the son of Kore, of the s of Asaph. 1121
26: 2 the s of Meshelemiah *were,* Zechariah 1121
26: 4 Moreover the s of Obed-edom *were,* 1121
26: 6 Also unto Shemaiah his son were s born, 1121
26: 7 The s of Shemaiah; Othni, and Rephael, 1121
26: 8 All these of the s of Obed-edom: they and 1121
26: 8 they and their s and their brethren, 1121
26: 9 Meshelemiah had s and brethren, 1121
26:10 of the children of Merari, had s; 1121
26:11 all the s and brethren of Hosah *were* 1121
26:15 to his s the house of Asuppim. 1121
26:19 of the porters among the s of Kore, 1121
26:19 sons of Kore, and among the s of Merari. 1121
26:21 *As concerning* the s of Laadan; the sons of 1121
26:21 the s of the Gershonite Laadan, 1121
26:22 The s of Jehieli; Zetham, and Joel his 1121
26:29 his s *were* for the outward business over 1121
27:32 the son of Hachmoni *was* with the king's s: 1121
28: 1 of his s, with the officers, and *with* 1121
28: 4 among the s of my father he liked me to 1121
28: 5 of all my s, (for the LORD hath given me 1121
28: 5 (for the LORD hath given me many s,) 1121
29:24 and all the s likewise of king David, 1121
2Ch 5:12 of Jeduthun, with their s and their brethren, 1121
11:14 his s had cast them off from executing 1121
11:21 begat twenty and eight s, and 1121
13: 5 to him and to his s *by* a covenant of salt? 1121
13: 8 the LORD in the hand of the s of David; 1121
13: 9 the s of Aaron, and the Levites, and 1121
13:10 *are* the s of Aaron, and the Levites *wait* 1121
13:21 begat twenty and two s, and 1121
20:14 of Mattaniah, a Levite of the s of Asaph, 1121
21: 2 he had brethren the s of Jehoshaphat, 1121
21: 2 all these *were* the s of Jehoshaphat king of 1121
21: 7 to give a light to him and to his s for ever. 1121
21:17 king's house, and his s also, and his wives; 1121
21:17 save Jehoahaz, the youngest of his s. 1121
22: 8 the s of the brethren of Ahaziah, 1121
22:11 stole him from among the king's s that 1121
23: 3 as the LORD hath said of the s of David. 1121
23:11 Jehoiada and his s anointed him, and said, 1121
24: 3 two wives; and he begat s and daughters. 1121
24: 7 For the s of Athaliah, *that* wicked woman, 1121
24:25 for the blood of the s of Jehoiada the priest, 1121
24:27 Now *concerning* his s, and the greatness of 1121
26:18 but to the priests the s of Aaron, 1121
28: 8 s, and daughters, and took also away much 1121
29: 9 our s and our daughters and our wives *are* 1121
29:11 My s, be not now negligent: for the LORD 1121
29:12 son of Azariah, of the s of the Kohathites: 1121
29:12 of the s of Merari, Kish the son of Abdi, 1121
29:13 of the s of Elizaphan; Shimri, and Jeiel: 1121
29:13 of the s of Asaph; Zechariah, and 1121
29:14 of the s of Heman; Jehiel, and Shimei: and 1121
29:14 of the s of Jeduthun; Shemaiah, and Uzziel. 1121
29:21 he commanded the priests the s of Aaron to 1121
31:18 their wives, and their s, and their daughters, 1121
31:19 Also of the s of Aaron the priests, 1121
32:33 chiefest of the sepulchres of the s of David: 1121
34:12 Obadiah, the Levites, of the s of Merari; 1121
34:12 and Meshullam, of the s of the Kohathites, 1121
35:14 the priests the s of Aaron *were busied* in 1121
35:14 and for the priests the s of Aaron. 1121
35:15 the singers the s of Asaph *were* in their 1121
36:20 his s until the reign of the kingdom of 1121
Ezr 3: 9 stood Jeshua *with* his s and his brethren, 1121
3: 9 and his brethren, Kadmiel and his s, 1121
3: 9 Kadmiel and his sons, the s of Judah, 1121
3: 9 the s of Henadad, *with* their sons and 1121
3: 9 *with* their s and their brethren the Levites. 1121
3:10 the Levites the s of Asaph with cymbals, 1121
6:10 pray for the life of the king, and of his s. 1123
7:23 against the realm of the king and his s? 1123
8: 2 Of the s of Phinehas; Gershom: of the sons 1121
8: 2 of the s of Ithamar; Daniel: of the sons of 1121
8: 2 Daniel: of the s of David; Hattush. 1121
8: 3 Of the s of Shechaniah, of the sons of 1121
8: 3 the sons of Shechaniah, of the s of Pharosh; 1121
8: 4 Of the s of Pahath-moab; Elihoenai the son 1121
8: 5 Of the s of Shechaniah; the son of Jahaziel, 1121
8: 6 Of the s also of Adin; Ebed the son of 1121
8: 7 of the s of Elam; Jeshaiah the son of 1121
8: 8 of the s of Shephatiah; Zebadiah the son of 1121
8: 9 Of the s of Joab; Obadiah the son of Jehiel, 1121
8:10 of the s of Shelomith; the son of Josiphiah, 1121
8:11 of the s of Bebai; Zechariah the son of 1121
8:12 of the s of Azgad; Johanan the son of 1121
8:13 of the last s of Adonikam, whose names *are* 1121
8:14 Of the s also of Bigvai; Uthai, and Zabbud, 1121
8:15 and found there none of the s of Levi. 1121
8:18 of the s of Mahli, the son of Levi, the son 1121
8:18 with his s and his brethren, eighteen; 1121
8:19 with him Jeshaiah of the s of Merari, 1121
8:19 of Merari, his brethren and their s, twenty; 1121
9: 2 daughters for themselves, and for their s: 1121
9:12 give not your daughters unto their s, 1121
9:12 neither take their daughters unto your s, 1121
10: 2 *one* of the s of Elam, answered and 1121
10:18 among the s of the priests there were found 1121
10:18 *namely,* of the s of Jeshua the son of 1121
10:20 of the s of Immer; Hanani, and Zebadiah. 1121
10:21 of the s of Harim; Maaseiah, and Elijah, 1121
10:22 of the s of Pashur; Elioenai, Maaseiah, 1121
10:25 of the s of Parosh; Ramiah, and Jeziah, and 1121
10:26 of the s of Elam; Mattaniah, Zechariah, 1121
10:27 of the s of Zattu; Elioenai, Eliashib, 1121
10:28 Of the s also of Bebai; Jehohanan, 1121
10:29 of the s of Bani; Meshullam, Malluch, and 1121
10:30 of the s of Pahath-moab; Adna, and Chelal, 1121
10:31 *of* the s of Harim; Eliezer, Ishijah, 1121
10:33 Of the s of Hashum; Mattenai, Mattathah, 1121
Ezr 10:34 Of the s of Bani; Maadai, Amram, and Uel, 1121
10:43 Of the s of Nebo; Jeiel, Mattithiah, Zabad, 1121
Ne 3: 3 the fish gate did the s of Hassenaah build, 1121
4:14 your s, and your daughters, your wives, and 1121
5: 2 We, our s, and our daughters, *are* many: 1121
5: 5 we bring into bondage our s and our 1121
10: 9 Binnui of the s of Henadad, Kadmiel; 1121
10:28 their wives, their s, and their daughters, 1121
10:30 the land, nor take their daughters for our s: 1121
10:36 Also the firstborn of our s, and of our 1121
11: 6 All the s of Perez that dwelt at Jerusalem 1121
11: 7 these *are* the s of Benjamin; Sallu the son 1121
11:22 Of the s of Asaph, the singers *were* over 1121
12:23 The s of Levi, the chief of the fathers, 1121
12:28 the s of the singers gathered themselves 1121
12:35 *certain* of the priests' s with trumpets; 1121
13:25 shall not give your daughters unto their s, 1121
13:25 nor take their daughters unto your s, or 1121
13:28 *one* of the s of Joiada, the son of Eliashib 1121
Est 9:10 The ten s of Haman the son of 1121
9:12 the palace, and the ten s of Haman; 1121
9:13 let Haman's ten s be hanged upon 1121
9:14 and they hanged Haman's ten s. 1121
9:25 and his s should be hanged on the gallows. 1121
Job 1: 2 there were born unto him seven s and 1121
1: 4 his s went and feasted *in their* houses, 1121
1: 5 It may be that my s have sinned, and 1121
1: 6 Now there was a day when the s of God 1121
1:13 there was a day when his s and 1121
1:18 Thy s and thy daughters *were* eating and 1121
2: 1 Again there was a day when the s of God 1121
14:21 His s come to honour, and he knoweth *it* 1121
38: 7 and all the s of God shouted for joy? 1121
38:32 or canst thou guide Arcturus with his s? 1121
42:13 He had also seven s and three daughters. 1121
42:16 and saw his s, and his sons' sons, 1121
42:16 and saw his sons, and his sons' s, 1121
Ps 4: 2 O ye s of men, how long *will ye turn* my 1121
31:19 them that trust in thee before the s of men! 1121
33:13 from heaven; he beholdeth all the s of men. 1121
42: T chief Musician, Maschil, for the s of Korah. 1121
44: T To the chief Musician for the s of Korah, 1121
45: T for the s of Korah, Maschil, A Song of 1121
46: T To the chief Musician for the s of Korah, 1121
47: T chief Musician, A Psalm for the s of Korah. 1121
48: T A Song *and* Psalm for the s of Korah. 1121
49: T chief Musician, A Psalm for the s of Korah. 1121
57: 4 *even* the s of men, whose teeth *are* spears 1121
58: 1 do ye judge uprightly, O ye s of men? 1121
77:15 thy people, the s of Jacob and Joseph. 1121
84: T upon Gittith, A Psalm for the s of Korah. 1121
85: T chief Musician, A Psalm for the s of Korah. 1121
87: T A Psalm *or* Song for the s of Korah. 1121
88: T A Song *or* Psalm for the s of Korah. To 1121
89: 6 *who* among the s of the mighty can be 1121
106:37 they sacrificed their s and their daughters 1121
106:38 *even* the blood of their s and of their 1121
144:12 That our s *may be* as plants grown up in 1121
145:12 To make known to the s of men his mighty 1121
Pr 8: 4 I call; and my voice *is* to the s of man. 1121
8:31 and my delights *were* with the s of men. 1121
Ecc 1:13 this sore travail hath God given to the s of 1121
2: 3 till I might see what *was* that good for the s 1121
2: 8 and the delights of the s of men, 1121
3:10 which God hath given to the s of men to be 1121
3:18 heart concerning the estate of the s of men, 1121
3:19 For that which befalleth the s of men 1121
8:11 the heart of the s of men is fully set in them 1121
9: 3 also the heart of the s of men is full *of* evil, 1121
9:12 so *are* the s of men snared in an evil time, 1121
SS 2: 3 of the wood, so *is* my beloved among the s. 1121
Isa 37:38 Sharezer his s smote him with the sword; 1121
39: 7 of thy s that shall issue from thee, 1121
43: 6 bring my s from far, and my daughters 1121
45:11 Ask me of *things* to come concerning my s, 1121
49:22 they shall bring thy s in *their* arms, and 1121
51:18 *There is* none to guide her among all the s 1121
51:18 hand of all the s *that* she hath brought up. 1121
51:20 Thy s have fainted, they lie at the head of 1121
52:14 and his form more than the s of men: 1121
56: 5 a name better than *of* s and *of* daughters: 1121
56: 6 Also the s of the stranger, that join 1121
57: 3 draw near hither, ye s of the sorceress, 1121
60: 4 thy s shall come from far, and 1121
60: 9 to bring thy s from far, their silver and 1121
60:10 the s of strangers shall build up thy walls, 1121
60:14 The s also of them that afflicted thee shall 1121
61: 5 the s of the alien *shall be* your plowmen 1121
62: 5 marrieth a virgin, *so* shall thy s marry thee: 1121
62: 8 the s of the stranger shall not drink thy 1121
Jer 3:24 and their herds, their s and their daughters. 1121
5:17 *which* thy s and thy daughters should eat: 1121
6:21 and the s together shall fall upon them; 1121
7:31 to burn their s and their daughters in 1121
11:22 their s and their daughters shall die by 1121
13:14 even the fathers and the s together, saith 1121
14:16 them, their wives, nor their s, nor their 1121
16: 2 neither shalt thou have s nor daughters in 1121
16: 3 For thus saith the LORD concerning the s 1121
19: 5 to burn their s with fire *for* burnt offerings 1121
19: 9 I will cause them to eat the flesh of their s 1121
29: 6 Take ye wives, and beget s and daughters; 1121
29: 6 take wives for your s, and give your 1121
29: 6 that they may bear s and daughters; 1121
32:19 *are* open upon all the ways of the s of men: 1121
32:35 to cause their s and their daughters to pass 1121
35: 3 all his s, and the whole house of 1121
35: 4 into the chamber of the s of Hanan, the son 1121
35: 5 I set before the s of the house of 1121
35: 6 no wine, *neither* ye, nor your s for ever: 1121
35: 8 we, our wives, our s, nor our daughters; 1121
35:14 that he commanded his s not to drink wine, 1121
35:16 Because the s of Jonadab the son of Rechab 1121
39: 6 the king of Babylon slew the s of Zedekiah 1121
40: 8 Johanan and Jonathan the s of Kareah, and 1121
Jer 40: 8 the s of Ephai the Netophathite, and 1121
48:46 for thy s are taken captives, and 1121
49: 1 thus saith the LORD; Hath Israel no s? 1121
52:10 the king of Babylon slew the s of Zedekiah 1121
La 4: 2 The precious s of Zion, comparable to fine 1121
Eze 5:10 Therefore the fathers shall eat the s in 1121
5:10 of thee, and the s shall eat their fathers; 1121
14:16 they shall deliver neither s nor daughters; 1121
14:18 they shall deliver neither s nor daughters, 1121
14:22 be brought forth, *both* s and daughters: 1121
16:20 Moreover thou hast taken thy s and thy 1121
20:31 when *ye* make your s to pass through 1121
23: 4 were mine, and they bare s and daughters. 1121
23:10 they took her s and her daughters, and slew 1121
23:25 they shall take thy s and thy daughters; and 1121
23:37 have also caused their s, whom they bare 1121
23:47 they shall slay their s and their daughters, 1121
24:21 your s and your daughters whom ye have 1121
24:25 set their minds, their s and their daughters, 1121
40:46 these *are* the s of Zadok among the sons of 1121
40:46 these *are* the sons of Zadok among the s of 1121
44:15 the priests the Levites, the s of Zadok, 1121
46:16 If the prince give a gift unto any of his s, 1121
46:18 he shall give his s inheritance out of his 1121
48:11 priests that are sanctified of the s of Zadok; 1121
Da 5:21 he *was* driven from the s of men; and 1123
10:16 *one* like the similitude of the s of men 1121
11:10 his s shall be stirred up, and shall assemble 1121
Hos 1:10 unto them, *Ye are* the s of the living God. 1121
Joel 1:12 joy is withered away from the s of men. 1121
2:28 your s and your daughters shall prophesy, 1121
3: 8 I will sell your s and your daughters into 1121
Am 2:11 I raised up of your s for prophets, and 1121
7:17 thy s and thy daughters shall fall by 1121
Mic 5: 7 not for man, nor waiteth for the s of men. 1121
Zec 9:13 raised up thy s, O Zion, against thy sons, 1121
9:13 O Zion, against thy s, O Greece, and 1121
Mal 3: 3 he shall purify the s of Levi, and 1121
3: 6 therefore ye s of Jacob are not consumed. 1121
Mt 20:20 mother of Zebedee's children with her s, *5207*
20:21 Grant that these my two s may sit, *5207*
21:28 A *certain* man had two s; and he came to *5043*
26:37 with *him* Peter and the two s of Zebedee, *5207*
Mk 3:17 which is, The s of thunder:) *5207*
3:28 All sins shall be forgiven unto the s of men, *5207*
10:35 And James and John, the s of Zebedee, *5207*
Lk 5:10 *was* also James, and John, *the* s of Zebedee, *5207*
11:19 by whom do your s cast *them* out? *5207*
15:11 And he said, A certain man had two s: *5207*
Jn 1:12 to them gave he power to become the s of *5043*
21: 2 and the s of Zebedee, and two other of his NIG
Ac 2:17 and your s and your daughters shall *5207*
7:16 of the s of Emmor the *father* of Sychem. *5207*
7:29 the land of Madian, where he begat two s. *5207*
19:14 And there were seven s of *one* Sceva, *5207*
Ro 8:14 by the Spirit of God, they are the s of God. *5207*
8:19 for the manifestation of the s of God. *5207*
1Co 4:14 but as my beloved s I warn *you.* *5043*
2Co 6:18 and ye shall be my s and daughters, *5207*
Gal 4: 5 that we might receive the **adoption of s**. *5206*
4: 6 And because ye are s, God hath sent forth *5207*
4:22 For it is written, that Abraham had two s, *5207*
Eph 3: 5 was not made known unto the s of men, *5207*
Php 2:15 and harmless, the s of God without rebuke, *5043*
Heb 2:10 by whom *are* all *things,* in bringing many s *5207*
7: 5 And verily they that are of the s of Levi *5207*
11:21 was a dying, blessed both the s of Joseph; *5207*
12: 7 God dealeth with you as with s; *5207*
12: 8 then are ye bastards, and not s. *5207*
1Jn 3: 1 that we should be called the s of God: *5043*
3: 2 now are we the s of God, and it doth not yet *5043*

SONS' (26) [SON]

Ge 6:18 and thy wife, and thy s wives with thee. 1121
7: 7 and his wife, and his s wives with him, 1121
8:16 and thy sons, and thy s wives with thee. 1121
8:18 and his wife, and his s wives with him: 1121
46: 7 His sons, and his s sons with him, 1121
46: 7 his s daughters, and all his seed brought he 1121
46:26 out of his loins, besides Jacob's s wives, 1121
Ex 29:21 and his sons, and his s garments with him: 1121
29:28 his s by a statute for ever from 1121+3807.1
29:29 the holy garments of Aaron shall be his s 1121
39:41 his s garments, to minister in the priest's 1121
Lev 2: 3 offering *shall be* Aaron's and his s: 1121+3807.1
2:10 offering *shall be* Aaron's and his s: 1121+3807.1
7:31 but the breast shall be Aaron's and his s. 1121
8:27 upon his s hands, and waved them *for* a 1121
8:30 his sons, and upon his s garments with him; 1121
8:30 and his sons, and his s garments with him. 1121
10:13 because it *is* thy due, and thy s due, 1121
10:14 for *they be* thy due, and thy s due, 1121
10:15 it shall be thine, and thy s with thee, by a 1121
24: 9 it shall be Aaron's and his s; and 1121+3807.1
Dt 4: 9 but teach them thy sons, and thy s sons; 1121
1Ch 8:40 and s sons, an hundred and fifty. 1121
Job 42:16 and saw his sons, and his s sons, 1121
Eze 46:16 inheritance thereof shall be his s; 1121+3807.1
46:17 but his inheritance shall be his s for them. 1121

SOON (65) [SOONER]

Ge 18:33 as s as he had left communing with 834+3509.1
27:30 as s as Isaac had made an end of 834+3509.1
44: 3 As s as the morning was light, the men 2050.1
Ex 2:18 How *is it that* you are come so s to day? 4116
9:29 As s as I am gone out of the city, 3509.1
32:19 as s as he came nigh unto the camp, 834+3509.1
Dt 4:26 that ye shall s utterly perish from off 4116
Jos 2: 7 as s as they which pursued after 834+3509.1
2:11 And as s as we had heard *these things,* 2050.1
3:13 as s as the soles of the feet of the priests 3509.1
8:19 they ran as s as *he* had stretched out his 3509.1
8:29 as s as the sun was down, 3509.1
Jdg 8:33 to pass, as s as Gideon was dead, 834+3509.1
9:33 *that* in the morning, as s as the sun is up, 3509.1

S

1Sa 9:13 **As s as** ye be come *into* the city, ye shall 3509.1
13:10 that **as s as** he had made an end of 3509.1
20:41 *And* **as s as** the lad was gone, 2050.1
29:10 **and as s as** ye be up early in the morning, 2050.1
2Sa 6:18 **And as s as** David had made an end of 2050.1
13:36 **as s as** he had made an end of speaking, 3509.1
15:10 **As s as** ye hear the sound of the trumpet, 3509.1
22:45 **as s as** they hear, they shall be obedient 3807.1
1Ki 16:11 to reign, **as s as** he sat on his throne, 3509.1
18:12 come to pass, *as s as* I am gone from thee, NIH
20:36 **behold, as s as** thou art departed from me, 2009
20:36 **And as s as** he was departed from him, a 2050.1
2Ki 10:2 Now **as s as** this letter cometh to you, 3509.1
10:25 **as s as** he had made an end of offering 3509.1
14:5 **as s as** the kingdom was confirmed 834+3509.1
2Ch 31:5 **as s as** the commandment came abroad, 3509.1
Job 32:22 my Maker would **s** take me away. 4592+3509.1
Ps 18:44 **As s as** they hear *of me*, they shall obey 3807.1
37:2 For they shall **s** be cut down like the grass, 4120
58:3 they go astray **as s as** they be **born**, 990+4480
68:31 Ethiopia shall **s** stretch out her hands unto NIH
81:14 I should **s** have subdued their 4592+3509.1
90:10 sorrow; for it is **s** cut off, and we fly away. 2440
106:13 They **s** forgat his works; they waited not for 4116
Pr 14:17 *He that is* **s** angry dealeth foolishly: and 7116
Isa 66:8 for **as s as** Zion travailed, she brought forth 1571
Eze 23:16 **as s as** she saw them with her eyes, 3807.1
Mt 21:20 How **s** is the fig tree withered away! 3916
Mk 1:42 And as **s** as he had spoken, immediately NIG
5:36 **As s as** Jesus heard the word *that was* 2112
11:2 and **as s as** ye be entered into it, ye shall 2112
14:45 And as **s** as he was come, he goeth NIG
Lk 1:23 And it came to pass *that*, **as s as** the days of 5613
1:44 **as s as** the voice of thy salutation sounded 5613
8:6 and as **s** as it was sprung up, it withered NIG
15:30 But **as s as** this thy son was come, 3753
22:66 And **as s as** it was day, the elders of 5613
23:7 And as **s** as he knew that he belonged unto NIG
Jn 11:20 **as s as** she heard that Jesus was coming, 5613
11:29 **As s as** she heard *that*, she arose quickly, 5613
16:21 but **as s as** she is delivered of the child, 3752
18:6 **As s** then **as** he had said unto them, I am 5613
21:9 **As s** then **as** they were come to land, 5613
Ac 10:29 without gainsaying, as **s** as I was sent for: NIG
12:18 Now as **s** as it was day, there was no small NIG
Gal 1:6 **s** removed from him that called you into 5030
Php 2:23 **so s as** I shall see how it will go with 302+5613
2Th 2:2 That ye be not **s** shaken in mind, or 5030
Tit 1:7 not selfwilled, not **s angry**, not given to 3711
Rev 10:10 and **as s as** I had eaten it, my belly was 3753
12:4 for to devour her child **as s as** it was born. 3752

SOONER (2) [SOON]

Heb 13:19 do this, that I may be restored to you the **s**. 5030
Jas 1:11 For the sun is no **s** risen with a burning heat, NIG

SOOTHED See MOLLIFIED

SOOTHSAYER (1) [SOOTHSAYERS, SOOTHSAYING]

Jos 13:22 Balaam also the son of Beor, the **s**, did 7080

SOOTHSAYER'S See MEONENIM

SOOTHSAYERS (6) [SOOTHSAYER]

Isa 2:6 *are* **s** like the Philistines, and they please 6049
Da 2:27 the magicians, the **s**, shew unto the king; 1505
4:7 the astrologers, the Chaldeans, and the **s**: 1505
5:7 in the astrologers, the Chaldeans, and the **s**. 1505
5:11 astrologers, Chaldeans, *and* **s**; 1505
Mic 5:12 thine hand; and thou shalt have no *more* **s**: 6049

SOOTHSAYING (1) [SOOTHSAYER]

Ac 16:16 which brought her masters much gain by **s**: 3132

SOP (4)

Jn 13:26 He it is, to whom I shall give a **s**, 5596
13:26 dipped *it*. And when he had dipped the **s**, 5596
13:27 And after the **s** Satan entered into him. 5596
13:30 having received the **s** went immediately 5596

SOPATER (1)

Ac 20:4 And there accompanied him into Asia **S** of 4986

SOPE (2)

Jer 2:22 wash thee with nitre, and take thee much **s**, 1287
Mal 3:2 he *is* like a refiner's fire, and like fullers' **s**: 1287

SOPHERETH (2)

Ezr 2:55 the children of Sotai, the children of **S**, 5618
Ne 7:57 the children of Sotai, the children of **S**, 5618

SORCERER (2) [SORCERY]

Ac 13:6 they found a certain **s**, a false prophet, 3097
13:8 But Elymas the **s** (for so is his name by 3097

SORCERERS (6) [SORCERY]

Ex 7:11 Pharaoh also called the wise men and the **s**: 3784
Jer 27:9 nor to your **s**, which speak unto you, 3786
Da 2:2 and the **s**, and the Chaldeans, 3784
Mal 3:5 I will be a swift witness against the **s**, and 3784
Rev 21:8 and whoremongers, and **s**, and idolaters, 5332
22:15 and **s**, and whoremongers, and murderers, 5333

SORCERESS (1) [SORCERY]

Isa 57:3 draw near hither, ye sons of the **s**, the seed 6049

SORCERIES (5) [SORCERY]

Isa 47:9 their perfection for the multitude of thy **s**, 3785
47:12 and with the multitude of thy **s**, 3785
Ac 8:11 of long time *he* had bewitched them with **s**. 3095
Rev 9:21 nor of their **s**, nor of their fornication, 5331
18:23 for by thy **s** were all nations deceived. 5331

SORCERY (1) [SORCERER, SORCERERS, SORCERESS, SORCERIES]

Ac 8:9 which beforetime in the *same* city **used s**, 3096

SORE (98) [SORELY, SORER, SORES]

Ge 19:9 And they pressed **s** upon the man, *even* Lot, 3966
20:8 in their ears: and the men were **s** afraid. 3966
31:30 **s longedst** after thy father's house, 3700+3700
34:25 when they were **s**, that two of the sons of 3510
41:56 the famine **waxed s** in the land of Egypt. 2388
41:57 that the famine was *so* **s** in all lands. 2388
43:1 And the famine *was* **s** in the land. 3515
47:4 for the famine *is* **s** in the land of Canaan: 3515
47:13 for the famine *was* very **s**, so that the land 3515
50:10 with a great and very **s** lamentation: 3515
Ex 14:10 marched after them; and they were **s** afraid: 3966
Lev 13:42 or bald forehead, a white reddish **s**; 5061
13:43 *if* the rising of the **s** *be* white reddish in his 5061
Nu 22:3 Moab was **s** afraid of the people, because 3966
Dt 6:22 shewed signs and wonders, great and **s**, 7451
28:35 with a **s** botch that cannot be healed, 7451
28:59 and **s** sicknesses, and of long continuance. 7451
Jos 9:24 we were **s** afraid of our lives because of 3966
Jdg 10:9 of Ephraim; so that Israel was **s** distressed. 3966
14:17 he told her, because she **lay s upon** him: 6693
15:18 he was **s** athirst, and called on the LORD, 3966
20:34 men out of all Israel, and the battle was **s**: 3513
21:2 up their voices, and **wept s**; 1058+1065+1419
1Sa 1:6 her adversary also **provoked** her **s**, 3707+3708
1:10 prayed unto the LORD, and **wept s**. 1058+1058
5:7 for his hand is **s** upon us, and upon Dagon 7185
14:52 there was **s** war against the Philistines all 2389
17:24 the man, fled from him, and were **s** afraid. 3966
21:12 was **s** afraid of Achish the king of Gath. 3966
28:15 Saul answered, I am **s** distressed; for 3966
28:20 was **s** afraid, because of the words of 3966
28:21 saw that he was **s** troubled, and said unto 3966
31:3 the battle **went s** against Saul, and 3513
31:3 and he was **s** wounded of the archers. 3966
31:4 would not; for he was **s** afraid: 3966
2Sa 2:17 there was a very **s** battle that day; 7186
13:36 and all his servants **wept** very **s**. 1058+1065
1Ki 17:17 his sickness was so **s**, that there was no 2389
18:2 And *there was* a **s** famine in Samaria. 2389
2Ki 3:26 Moab saw that the battle was too **s** for him, 2388
6:11 king of Syria was **s troubled** for this thing; 5590
20:3 And Hezekiah **wept s**. 1058+1065+1419
1Ch 10:3 the battle **went s** against Saul, and 3513
10:4 would not; for he was **s** afraid. 3966
2Ch 6:28 whatsoever **s** or whatsoever sickness *there* 5061
6:29 when every one shall know his own **s** and 5061
21:19 so he died of **s** diseases. And his people 7451
28:19 **transgressed s** against the LORD. 4603+4604
35:23 Have me away; for I am **s** wounded. 3966
Ezr 10:1 children: for the people **wept** very **s**. 1058+1059
Ne 2:2 sorrow of heart. Then I was very **s** afraid, 7235
13:8 it grieved me **s**: therefore I cast forth all 3966
Job 2:7 smote Job with **s** boils from the sole of his 7451
5:18 For he **maketh s**, and bindeth up: 3510
Ps 2:5 and vex them in his **s displeasure**. 2740
6:3 My soul is also **s** vexed: but thou, 3966
6:10 all mine enemies be ashamed and **s** vexed: 3966
38:2 in me, and thy hand **presseth** me **s**. 5181+5921
38:8 I am feeble and **s** broken: I have 3966+5704
38:11 and my friends stand aloof from my **s**; 5061
44:19 Though thou hast **s broken** us in the place 1794
55:4 My heart is **s pained** within me: and 2342
71:20 which hast shewed me great and **s** troubles, 7451
77:2 my **s** ran in the night, and ceased not: 3027
118:13 Thou hast **thrust s** at me that *I* might 1760+1760
118:18 The LORD hath **chastened** me **s**: 3256+3256
Ecc 1:13 this **s** travail hath God given to the sons of 7451
4:8 This *is* also vanity, yea, it *is* a **s** travail. 7451
5:13 There is a **s** evil *which* I have seen under 2470
5:16 this also *is* a **s** evil, *that* in all points as he 2470
Isa 27:1 In that day the LORD with his **s** and great 7186
38:3 And Hezekiah **wept s**. 1058+1065+1419
59:11 like bears, and **mourn s** like doves: 1897+1897
64:9 Be not wroth **very s**, O LORD, 3966+5704
64:12 hold thy peace, and afflict us **very s**? 3966+5704
Jer 13:17 mine eye shall **weep s**, and run down 1830+1830
22:10 *but* **weep s** for him that goeth away: 1058+1058
50:12 Your mother shall be **s** confounded; 3966
52:6 the famine was **s** in the city, so that there 2388
La 1:2 She **weepeth s** in the night, and 1058+1058
3:52 Mine enemies **chased** me **s**, like a 6679+6679
Eze 14:21 How much more when I send my four **s** 7451
21:10 is sharpened to make a **s slaughter**; 2873+2874
27:35 their kings shall be **s afraid**, they 8175+8178
Da 6:14 was **s** displeased with himself, and set *his* 7690
Mic 2:10 it shall destroy *you*, even *with* a **s** 4834
Zec 1:2 The LORD hath been **s displeased** 7107+7110
1:15 I am very **s displeased** with 7107+7110
Mt 17:6 *it*, they fell on their face, and were **s** afraid. 4970
17:15 for he is lunatick, and **s** vexed: for ofttimes 2560
21:15 to the Son of David; they were **s displeased**, 23
Mk 6:51 they were **s** amazed in themselves beyond 3029
9:6 not what to say; for they were **s afraid**. 1630
9:26 and rent him **s**, and came out of *him*: and 4183
14:33 and began to be **s amazed**, and to be very 1568
Lk 2:9 round about them: and they were **s** afraid. 3173
Ac 20:37 And *they* all wept **s**, and fell on Paul's 2425
Rev 16:2 grievous **s** upon the men which had 1668

SOREK (1)

Jdg 16:4 that he loved a woman in the valley of **S**, 7796

SORELY (2) [SORE]

Ge 49:23 The archers have **s grieved** him, and shot *at* 4843
Isa 23:5 shall they be **s pained** *at* the report of Tyre. 2342

SORER (1) [SORE]

Heb 10:29 Of how much **s** punishment, suppose ye, 5501

SORES (4) [SORE]

Isa 1:6 *but* wounds, and bruises, and putrifying **s**: 4347
Lk 16:20 which was laid at his gate, **full of s**, 1669
16:21 moreover the dogs came and licked his **s**. 1668
Rev 16:11 of heaven because of their pains and their **s**, 1668

SORROW (70) [SORROWED, SORROWETH, SORROWFUL, SORROWING, SORROWS, SORRY]

Ge 3:16 I will greatly multiply thy **s** and 6093
3:16 in **s** thou shalt bring forth children; and 6089
3:17 in **s** shalt thou eat *of* it all the days of thy 6093
42:38 shall ye bring down my gray hairs with **s** to 3015
44:29 ye shall bring down my gray hairs with **s** to 7451
44:31 of thy servant our father with **s** to the grave. 3015
Ex 15:14 **s** shall take hold on the inhabitants of 2427
Lev 26:16 consume the eyes, and **cause s** of heart: 1727
Dt 28:65 and failing of eyes, and **s** of mind: 1671
1Ch 4:9 saying, Because I bare *him* with **s**. 6090
Ne 2:2 this *is* nothing *else* but **s** of heart. Then I 7455
Est 9:22 which was turned unto them from **s** to joy, 3015
Job 3:10 *mother's* womb, nor hid **s** from mine eyes. 5999
6:10 yea, I would harden myself in **s**; let him not 2427
17:7 Mine eye also is dim by reason of **s**, and 3708
41:22 and **s** is turned into joy before him. 1670
Ps 13:2 in my soul, *having* **s** in my heart daily? 3015
38:17 to halt, and my **s** *is* continually before me. 4341
39:2 *even* from good; and my **s** was stirred. 3511
55:10 mischief also and **s** *are* in the midst of it. 5999
90:10 yet *is* their strength labour and **s**; 205
107:39 low through oppression, affliction, and **s**. 3015
116:3 gat hold upon me: I found trouble and **s**. 3015
Pr 10:10 He that winketh *with* the eye causeth **s**: but 6094
10:22 it maketh rich, and he addeth no **s** with it. 6089
15:13 but by **s** of the heart the spirit *is* broken. 6094
17:21 He that begetteth a fool *doeth it* to his **s**: 8424
23:29 who hath **s**? who hath contentions? who hath 17
Ecc 1:18 he that increaseth knowledge increaseth **s**. 4341
5:17 *he hath* much **s** and wrath with his sickness. 3707
7:3 **S** *is* better than laughter: for by the sadness 3708
11:10 Therefore remove **s** from thy heart, and 3708
Isa 5:30 behold darkness *and* **s**, and the light is 6862
14:3 the LORD shall give thee rest from thy **s**, 6090
17:11 heap in the day of grief and of desperate **s**. 3511
29:2 and there shall be heaviness and **s**: 592
35:10 gladness, and **s** and sighing shall flee away. 3015
50:11 have of mine hand; ye shall lie down in **s**. 4620
51:11 joy; *and* **s** and mourning shall flee away. 3015
65:14 ye shall cry for **s** of heart, and shall howl 3511
Jer 8:18 *When* I would comfort myself against **s**, 3015
20:18 I forth out of the womb to see labour and **s**, 3015
30:15 thy **s** *is* incurable for the multitude of thine 4341
31:12 and they shall not **s** any more at all. 1669
31:13 and make them rejoice from their **s**. 3015
45:3 for the LORD hath added grief to my **s**; 4341
49:23 *there is* **s** on the sea; it cannot be quiet. 1674
51:29 the land shall tremble and **s**: for every 2342
La 1:12 see if there be any **s** like unto my sorrow, 4341
1:12 see if there be any sorrow like unto my **s**, 4341
1:18 I pray you, all people, and behold my **s**: 4341
3:65 Give them **s** of heart, thy curse unto them. 4044
Eze 23:33 shalt be filled *with* drunkenness and **s**, 3015
Hos 8:10 they shall **s** a little for the burden of 2490
Lk 22:45 his disciples, he found them sleeping for **s**, 3077
Jn 16:6 *things* unto you, **s** hath filled your heart. 3077
16:20 but your **s** shall be turned into joy. 3077
16:21 A woman when she is in travail hath **s**, 3077
16:22 And ye now therefore have **s**: but I will see 3077
Ro 9:2 great heaviness and continual **s** in my heart. 3601
2Co 2:3 I should have **s** from *them of* whom I ought 3077
2:7 should be swallowed up with overmuch **s**. 3077
7:10 For godly **s** worketh repentance to salvation 3077
7:10 but the **s** of the world worketh death. 3077
Php 2:27 me also, lest I should have **s** upon sorrow. 3077
2:27 me also, lest I should have sorrow upon **s**. 3077
1Th 4:13 them which are asleep, that ye **s** not, 3076
Rev 18:7 so much torment and **s** give her: 3997
18:7 and am no widow, and shall see no **s**. 3997
21:4 be no more death, neither **s**, nor crying, 3997

SORROWED (2) [SORROW]

2Co 7:9 made sorry, but that ye **s** to repentance: 3076
7:11 For behold this selfsame *thing*, that ye **s** 3076

SORROWETH (1) [SORROW]

1Sa 10:2 **s** for you, saying, What shall I do for my 1672

SORROWFUL (18) [SORROW]

1Sa 1:15 No, my lord, I *am* a woman of a **s** spirit: 7186
Job 6:7 my soul refused to touch *are* as my **s** meat. 1741
Ps 69:29 I *am* poor and **s**: let thy salvation, O God, 3510
Pr 14:13 Even in laughter the heart is **s**; and the end 3510
Jer 31:25 and I have replenished every **s** soul. 1669
Zep 3:18 I will gather *them that are* **s** for the solemn 3013
Zec 9:5 Gaza also *shall see it*, and be very **s**, and 2342
Mt 19:22 man heard *that* saying, he went away **s**: 3076
26:22 And they were exceeding **s**, and 3076
26:37 and began to be **s** and very heavy. 3076
26:38 My soul is **exceeding s**, *even* unto death: 4036
Mk 14:19 And they began to be **s**, and to say unto him 3076
14:34 My soul is **exceeding s** unto death: 4036
Lk 18:23 And when he heard this, he was **very s**: 4036
18:24 And when Jesus saw that he was **very s**, 4036
Jn 16:20 and ye shall be **s**, but your sorrow shall be 3076
2Co 6:10 As **s**, yet alway rejoicing; as poor, 3076
Php 2:28 ye may rejoice, and *that* I may be the **less s**. 253

SORROWING (2) [SORROW]

Lk 2:48 behold, thy father and I have sought thee **s**. 3600
Ac 20:38 **S** most *of all* for the words which he spake, 3600

SORROWS (22) [SORROW]

Ex 3:7 of their taskmasters; for I know their **s**; 4341

2Sa 22: 6 The s of hell compassed me about; 2256
Job 9:28 I am afraid of all my s, I know that thou 6094
21:17 upon them! God distributeth s in his anger. 2256
39: 3 forth their young ones, they cast out their s. 2256
Ps 16: 4 Their s shall be multiplied that hasten after 6094
18: 4 The s of death compassed me, and 2256
18: 5 The s of hell compassed me about: 2256
32:10 Many shall be to the wicked: but he that 4341
116: 3 The s of death compassed me, and the pains 2256
127: 2 up early, to sit up late, to eat the bread of s: 6089
Ecc 2:23 For all his days are s, and his travail grief; 4341
Isa 13: 8 s shall take hold of them; they shall be in 2256
53: 3 a man of s, and acquainted with grief: 4341
53: 4 he hath borne our griefs, and carried our s: 4341
Jer 13:21 shall not s take thee, as a woman in travail? 2256
49:24 and s have taken her as a woman in travail. 2256
Da 10:16 by the vision my s are turned upon me, and 6735
Hos 13:13 The s of a travailing woman shall come 2256
Mt 24: 8 All these are the beginning of s. 5604
Mk 13: 8 and troubles: these are the beginnings of s. 5604
1Ti 6:10 pierced themselves through with many s. 3601

SORRY (14) [SORROW]
1Sa 22: 8 there is none of you that is s for me, or 2470
Ne 8:10 neither be ye s; for the joy of the LORD is 6087
Ps 38:18 mine iniquity; I will be s for my sin. 1672
Isa 51:19 are come unto thee; who shall be s for thee? 5110
Mt 14: 9 And the king was s: nevertheless for 3076
17:23 be raised again. And they were exceeding s. 3076
18:31 they were very s, and came and told unto 3076
Mk 6:26 And the king was exceeding s; yet for his 4036
2Co 2: 2 For if I make you s, who is he then 3076
2: 2 but the same which is made s by me? 3076
7: 8 For though I made you s with a letter, I do 3076
7: 8 that the same epistle hath made you s, 3076
7: 9 not that ye were made s, but that ye 3076
7: 9 for ye were made s after a godly manner, 3076

SORT (21) [SORTS]
Ge 6:19 two of every s shalt thou bring into the ark, NIH
6:20 two of every s shall come unto thee, to keep NIH
7:14 fowl after his kind, every bird of every s. 3671
2Ki 24:14 save the poorest s of the people of the land. 1803
1Ch 24: 5 they divided by lot, one s with another; NIH
29:14 willingly after this s? for all things come of NIH
2Ch 30: 5 it of a long time in such s as it was written. NIH
Ezr 1:10 silver basons of a second s four hundred 4932
4: 8 Jerusalem to Artaxerxes the king in this s: 3660
Ne 6: 4 they sent unto me four times after this s; 1697
Eze 23:42 with the men of the common s were brought 120
39: 4 thee unto the ravenous birds of every s, 3671
44:30 of every s of your oblations, shall be NIH
Da 1:10 than the children which are of your s? 1524
3:29 no other God that can deliver after this s. 3509.4
Ac 17: 5 unto them certain lewd fellows of the baser s, 60
Ro 15:15 written the more boldly unto you in some s, 3313
1Co 3:13 shall try every man's work of what s it is. 3697
2Co 7:11 thing, that ye sorrowed after a godly s, 2596
2Ti 3: 6 For of this s are they which creep into NIG
3Jn 1: 6 forward on their journey after a godly s, 516

SORTS (7) [SORT]
Dt 22:11 Thou shalt not wear a garment of divers s, 8162
Ne 5:18 and once in ten days store of all s of wine: NIH
Ps 78:45 He sent divers s of flies among them, 6157
105:31 there came divers s of flies, and lice in all 6157
Ecc 2: 8 musical instruments, and that
of all s. 7705+7705
Eze 27:24 were thy merchants in all s of things, 4360
38: 4 all of them clothed with all s of armour, 4358

SOSIPATER (1)
Ro 16:21 and Lucius, and Jason, and S, my kinsmen, 4989

SOSTHENES (2)
Ac 18:17 Then all the Greeks took S, the chief ruler 4988
1Co 1: 1 through the will of God, and S our brother, 4988

SOTAI (2)
Ezr 2:55 the children of S, the children of Sophereth, 5479
Ne 7:57 the children of S, the children of Sophereth, 5479

SOTTISH (1)
Jer 4:22 they are s children, and they have none 5530

SOUGHT (126) [SEEK]
Ge 43:30 he s where to weep; and he entered into his 1245
Ex 2:15 heard this thing, he s to slay Moses. 1245
4:19 for all the men are dead which s thy life. 1245
4:24 that the LORD met him, and s to kill him. 1245
33: 7 that every one which s the LORD went 1245
Lev 10:16 Moses diligently s the goat of the sin 1875+1875
Nu 35:23 and was not his enemy, neither s his harm: 1245
Dt 13:10 he hath s to thrust thee away from 1245
Jos 2:22 the pursuers s them throughout all the way, 1245
Jdg 14: 4 that he s an occasion against the Philistines: 1245
18: 1 in those days the tribe of the Danites s them 1245
1Sa 10:21 when they s him, he could not be found. 1245
13:14 the LORD hath s him a man after his own 1245
14: 4 by which Jonathan s to go over unto 1245
19:10 Saul s to smite David even to the wall with 1245
23:14 Saul s him every day, but God delivered 1245
27: 4 to Gath: and he s no more again for him. 1245
2Sa 3:17 Ye s for David in times past to be king 1245
4: 8 son of Saul thine enemy, which s thy life; 1245
17:20 when they had s and could not find them, 1245
21: 2 Saul s to slay them in his zeal to 1245
1Ki 1: 2 Let there be s for my lord the king a young 1245
1: 3 So they s for a fair damsel throughout all 1245
10:24 all the earth s to Solomon, to hear his 1245
11:40 Solomon s therefore to kill Jeroboam. 1245
2Ki 2:17 and they s three days, but found him not. 1245
1Ch 15:13 for that we s him not after the due order. 1875
26:31 year of the reign of David they were s for, 1875
2Ch 1: 5 Solomon and the congregation s unto it. 1875
9:23 all the kings of the earth s the presence of 1245
14: 7 because we have s the LORD our God, 1875
14: 7 we have s him, and he hath given us rest on 1875
15: 4 of Israel, and s him, he was found of them. 1245
15:15 and s him with their whole desire; 1245
16:12 yet in his disease he s not to the LORD, 1875
17: 3 of his father David, and s not unto Baalim; 1875
17: 4 s to the LORD God of his father, and 1875
22: 9 he s Ahaziah: and they caught him, (for he 1245
22: 9 who s the LORD with all his heart. 1875
25:15 Why hast thou s after the gods of 1875
25:20 because they s after the gods of Edom. 1875
26: 5 he s God in the days of Zechariah, who had 1875
26: 5 as long as he s the LORD, God made him 1875
Ezr 2:62 These s their register among those that 1245
Ne 7:64 These s their register among those that 1245
12:27 they s the Levites out of all their places, 1245
Est 2: 2 Let there be fair young virgins s for 1245
2:21 and s to lay hand on the king Ahasuerus. 1245
3: 6 wherefore Haman s to destroy all the Jews 1245
6: 2 who s to lay hand on the king Ahasuerus. 1245
9: 2 to lay hand on such as s their hurt: 1245
Ps 34: 4 I s the LORD, and he heard me, and 1875
37:36 yea, I s him, but he could not be found. 1245
77: 2 In the day of my trouble I s the Lord: 1875
78:34 When he slew them, then they s him: and 1875
86:14 the assemblies of violent men have s after 1245
111: 2 s out of all them that have pleasure therein. 1875
119:10 With my whole heart have I s thee: O let 1875
119:94 save me; for I have s thy precepts. 1875
Ecc 2: 3 I s in mine heart to give myself unto wine, 8446
7:29 but they have s out many inventions. 1245
12: 9 and s out, and set in order many proverbs. 2713
12:10 The Preacher s to find out acceptable 1245
SS 3: 1 By night on my bed I s him whom my soul 1245
3: 1 soul loveth: I s him, but I found him not. 1245
3: 2 soul loveth: I s him, but I found him not. 1245
5: 6 I s him, but I could not find him; I called 1245
Isa 62:12 shalt be called, S out, A city not forsaken. 1875
65: 1 I am s of them that asked not for me: I am 1875
65: 1 for me: I am found of them that s me not: 1245
65:10 lie down in, for my people that have s me. 1875
Jer 8: 2 whom they have s, and whom they have 1875
10:21 and have not s the LORD: 1875
26:21 his words, the king s to put him to death: 1245
44:30 of Babylon, his enemy, and that s his life. 1245
50:20 the iniquity of Israel shall be s for, and 1245
La 1:19 while they s their meat, to relieve their 1245
Eze 22:30 I s for a man among them, that should 1245
26:21 shalt be no more: though thou be s for, 1245
34: 4 neither have ye s that which was lost; 1245
Da 2:13 they s Daniel and his fellows to be slain. 1156
4:36 my counsellers and my lords s unto me; 1156
6: 4 princes s to find occasion against Daniel 1156
8:15 and s for the meaning, then, behold, 1245
Ob 1: 6 searched out! how are his hid things s up! 1158
Zep 1: 6 those that have not s the LORD, nor 1245
Zec 6: 7 s to go that they might walk to and 1245
Mt 2:20 for they are dead which s the young child's 2212
21:46 But when they s to lay hands on him, 2212
26:16 And from that time he s opportunity to 2212
26:59 the council, s false witness against Jesus, 2212
Mk 11:18 heard it, and s how they might destroy him: 2212
12:12 And they s to lay hold on him, but 2212
14: 1 the scribes s how they might take him by 2212
14:11 And he s how he might conveniently betray 2212
14:55 all the council s for witness against Jesus to 2212
Lk 2:44 and they s him among their kinsfolk and 327
2:48 thy father and I have s thee sorrowing. 2212
2:49 he said unto them, How is it that ye s me? 2212
4:42 and the people s him, and came unto him, 2212
5:18 and they s means to bring him in, and to lay 2212
6:19 And the whole multitude s to touch him: 2212
11:16 tempting him, s of him a sign from heaven. 2212
13: 6 and he came and s fruit thereon, 2212
19: 3 And he s to see Jesus who he was; and 2212
19:47 and the chief of the people s to destroy him, 2212
20:19 the scribes the same hour s to lay hands on 2212
22: 2 and scribes s how they might kill him; 2212
22: 6 s opportunity to betray him unto them in 2212
Jn 5:16 and s to slay him, because he had done 2212
5:18 Therefore the Jews s the more to kill him, 2212
7: 1 in Jewry, because the Jews s to kill him. 2212
7:11 Then the Jews s him at the feast, and said, 2212
7:30 Then they s to take him: but no man laid 2212
10:39 Therefore they s again to take him: but 2212
11: 8 Master, the Jews of late s to stone thee; 2212
11:56 Then s they for Jesus, and spake among 2212
19:12 And from thenceforth Pilate s to release 2212
Ac 12:19 And when Herod had s for him, and 1934
17: 5 and s to bring them out to the people. 2212
Ro 9:32 Because they s it not by faith, but as it were NIG
10:20 saith, I was found of them that s me not; 2212
1Th 2: 6 Nor of men s we glory, neither of you, 2212
2Ti 1:17 was in Rome, he s me out very diligently, 2212
Heb 8: 7 should no place have been s for the second. 2212
12:17 though he s it carefully with tears. 1567

SOUL (458) [SOUL'S, SOULS]
Ge 2: 7 breath of life; and man became a living s. 5315
12:13 and my s shall live because of thee. 5315
17:14 that s shall be cut off from his people; 5315
19:20 (is it not a little one?) and my s shall live. 5315
27: 4 that my s may bless thee before I die. 5315
27:19 eat of my venison, that thy s may bless me. 5315
27:25 my son's venison, that my s may bless thee. 5315
27:31 his son's venison, that thy s may bless me. 5315
34: 3 his s clave unto Dinah the daughter of 5315
34: 8 The s of my son Shechem longeth for your 5315
35:18 as her s was in departing (for she died) 5315
42:21 in that we saw the anguish of his s, when he 5315
49: 6 O my s, come not thou into their secret; 5315
Ex 12:15 that s shall be cut off from Israel. 5315
12:19 even that s shall be cut off from 5315
Ex 30:12 man a ransom for his s unto the LORD, 5315
31:14 that s shall be cut off from amongst his 5315
Lev 4: 2 If a s shall sin through ignorance against 5315
5: 1 if a s sin, and hear the voice of swearing, 5315
5: 2 Or if a s touch any unclean thing, 5315
5: 4 Or if a s swear, pronouncing with his lips to 5315
5:15 If a s commit a trespass, and sin through 5315
5:17 if a s sin, and commit any of these things 5315
6: 2 If a s sin, and commit a trespass against 5315
7:18 the s that eateth of it shall bear his iniquity. 5315
7:20 the s that eateth of the flesh of the sacrifice 5315
7:20 even that s shall be cut off from his people. 5315
7:21 Moreover the s that shall touch any unclean 5315
7:21 even that s shall be cut off from his people. 5315
7:25 even the s that eateth it shall be cut off 5315
7:27 Whatsoever s it be that eateth any manner 5315
7:27 even that s shall be cut off from his people. 5315
17:10 I will even set my face against that s that 5315
17:11 blood that maketh an atonement for the s. 5315
17:12 of Israel, No s of you shall eat blood, 5315
17:15 every s that eateth that which died of itself, 5315
19: 8 that s shall be cut off from among his 5315
20: 6 the s that turneth after such as have familiar 5315
20: 6 I will even set my face against that s, and 5315
22: 3 that s shall be cut off from my presence: 5315
22: 6 The s which hath touched any such shall be 5315
22:11 if the priest buy any s with his money, 5315
23:29 For whatsoever s it be that shall not be 5315
23:30 whatsoever s it be that doeth any work in 5315
23:30 the same s will I destroy from among his 5315
26:11 amongst you: and my s shall not abhor you. 5315
26:15 or if your s abhor my judgments, so that ye 5315
26:30 of your idols, and my s shall abhor you. 5315
26:43 and because their s abhorred my statutes. 5315
Nu 9:13 even the same s shall be cut off from 5315
11: 6 now our s is dried away: there is nothing at 5315
15:27 if any s sin through ignorance, then he shall 5315
15:28 the priest shall make an atonement for the s 5315
15:30 the s that doeth ought presumptuously, 5315
15:30 that s shall be cut off from among his 5315
15:31 that s shall utterly be cut off; 5315
19:13 and that s shall be cut off from Israel: 5315
19:20 that s shall be cut off from among 5315
19:22 the s that toucheth it shall be unclean until 5315
21: 4 the s of the people was much discouraged 5315
21: 5 and our s loatheth this light bread. 5315
30: 2 or swear an oath to bind his s with a bond; 5315
30: 4 her bond wherewith she hath bound her s, 5315
30: 4 every bond wherewith she hath bound her s 5315
30: 5 her bonds wherewith she hath bound her s, 5315
30: 6 out of her lips, wherewith she bound her s; 5315
30: 7 her bonds wherewith she bound her s shall 5315
30: 8 wherewith she bound her s, of none effect: 5315
30:10 or bound her s by a bond with an oath; 5315
30:11 every bond wherewith she bound her s shall 5315
30:12 or concerning the bond of her s, shall not 5315
30:13 and every binding oath to afflict the s, 5315
31:28 one s of five hundred, both of the persons, 5315
Dt 4: 9 heed to thyself, and keep thy s diligently, 5315
4:29 him with all thy heart and with all thy s. 5315
6: 5 and with all thy s, and with all thy might. 5315
10:12 God with all thy heart and with all thy s, 5315
11:13 him with all your heart and with all your s, 5315
11:18 these my words in your heart and in your s, 5315
12:15 all thy gates, whatsoever thy s lusteth after, 5315
12:20 eat flesh, because thy s longeth to eat flesh; 5315
12:20 eat flesh, whatsoever thy s lusteth after. 5315
12:21 thou shalt eat in thy gates whatsoever thy s 5315
13: 3 God with all your heart and with all your s. 5315
13: 6 or thy friend, which is as thine own s, 5315
14:26 money for whatsoever thy s lusteth after, 5315
14:26 or for whatsoever thy s desireth: 5315
26:16 them with all thine heart, and with all thy s. 5315
30: 2 with all thine heart, and with all thy s; 5315
30: 6 and with all thy s, that thou mayest live. 5315
30:10 God with all thine heart, and with all thy s. 5315
Jos 22: 5 him with all your heart and with all your s. 5315
Jdg 5:21 O my s, thou hast trodden down strength. 5315
10:16 his s was grieved for the misery of Israel. 5315
16:16 so that his s was vexed unto death; 5315
1Sa 1:10 she was in bitterness of s, and prayed unto 5315
1:15 have poured out my s before the LORD. 5315
1:26 O my lord, as thy s liveth, my lord, 5315
2:16 then take as much as thy s desireth; 5315
17:55 As thy s liveth, O king, I cannot tell. 5315
18: 1 that the s of Jonathan was knit with the soul 5315
18: 1 that the soul of Jonathan was knit with the s 5315
18: 1 and Jonathan loved him as his own s. 5315
18: 3 because he loved him as his own s. 5315
20: 3 as thy s liveth, there is but a step between 5315
20: 4 Whatsoever thy s desireth, I will even do it 5315
20:17 for he loved him as he loved his own s. 5315
23:20 to all the desire of thy s to come down; 5315
24:11 yet thou huntest my s to take it. 5315
25:26 as the LORD liveth, and as thy s liveth, 5315
25:29 is risen to pursue thee, and to seek thy s: 5315
25:29 the s of my lord shall be bound in 5315
26:21 my s was precious in thine eyes this day: 5315
30: 6 because the s of all the people was grieved, 5315
2Sa 4: 9 who hath redeemed my s out of all 5315
5: 8 and the blind, that are hated of David's s, 5315
11:11 as thou livest, and as thy s liveth, I will not 5315
13:39 the s of king David longed to go forth unto NIH
14:19 woman answered and said, As thy s liveth, 5315
1Ki 1:29 that hath redeemed my s out of all distress, 5315
2: 4 truth with all their heart and with all their s, 5315
8:48 with all their s, in the land of their enemies, 5315
11:37 thou shalt reign according to all that thy s 5315
17:21 let this child's s come into him again. 5315
17:22 the s of the child came into him again, and 5315
2Ki 2: 2 and as thy s liveth, I will not leave thee. 5315
2: 4 and as thy s liveth, I will not leave thee. 5315
2: 6 and as thy s liveth, I will not leave thee. 5315
4:27 Let her alone; for her s is vexed within her: 5315
4:30 and as thy s liveth, I will not leave thee. 5315

2Ki 23: 3 statutes with all their heart and all their s, 5315
23:25 with all his s, and with all his might, 5315
1Ch 22:19 and your s to seek the LORD your God; 5315
2Ch 6:38 with all their s in the land of their captivity, 5315
15:12 with all their heart and with all their s; 5315
34:31 with all his heart, and with all his s, 5315
Job 3:20 is in misery, and life unto the bitter in s; 5315
6: 7 The things that my s refused to touch are as 5315
7:11 I will complain in the bitterness of my s. 5315
7:15 So that my s chooseth strangling, and 5315
9:21 I were perfect, yet would I not know my s: 5315
10: 1 My s is weary of my life; I will leave my 5315
10: 1 I will speak in the bitterness of my s. 5315
12:10 In whose hand is the s of every living thing, 5315
14:22 and his s within him shall mourn. 5315
16: 4 I also could speak as ye do: if your s were 5315
19: 2 How long will ye vex my s, and break me 5315
21:25 another dieth in the bitterness of his s, and 5315
23:13 and what his s desireth, even that he doeth. 5315
24:12 and the s of the wounded crieth out: 5315
27: 2 and the Almighty, who hath vexed my s; 5315
27: 8 hath gained, when God taketh away his s? 5315
30:15 they pursue my s as the wind: and 5082
30:16 now my s is poured out upon me; the days 5315
30:25 was not my s grieved for the poor? 5315
31:30 mouth to sin by wishing a curse to his s.) 5315
33:18 He keepeth back his s from the pit, and 5315
33:20 life abhorreth bread, and his s dainty meat. 5315
33:22 his s draweth near unto the grave, and 5315
33:28 He will deliver his s from going into 5315
33:30 To bring back his s from the pit, to be 5315
Ps 3: 2 Many there be which say of my s, There is 5315
6: 3 My s is also sore vexed: but thou, 5315
6: 4 Return, O LORD, deliver my s: O save 5315
7: 2 Lest he tear my s like a lion, rending it in 5315
7: 5 Let the enemy persecute my s, and take it; 5315
11: 1 how say ye to my s, Flee as a bird to your 5315
11: 5 him that loveth violence his s hateth. 5315
13: 2 How long shall I take counsel in my s, 5315
16: 2 O my s, thou hast said unto the LORD, NIH
16:10 For thou wilt not leave my s in hell; 5315
17:13 deliver my s from the wicked, which is thy 5315
19: 7 of the LORD is perfect, converting the s: 5315
22:20 Deliver my s from the sword; my darling 5315
22:29 and none can keep alive his own s. 5315
23: 3 He restoreth my s: he leadeth me in 5315
24: 4 who hath not lift up his s unto vanity, 5315
25: 1 Unto thee, O LORD, do I lift up my s. 5315
25:13 His s shall dwell at ease; and his seed shall 5315
25:20 O keep my s, and deliver me: let me not be 5315
26: 9 Gather not my s with sinners, nor my life 5315
30: 3 thou hast brought up my s from the grave: 5315
31: 7 thou hast known my s in adversities; 5315
31: 9 with grief, yea, my s and my belly. 5315
33:19 To deliver their s from death, and to keep 5315
33:20 Our s waiteth for the LORD: he is our 5315
34: 2 My s shall make her boast in the LORD: 5315
34:22 The LORD redeemeth the s of his 5315
35: 3 say unto my s, I am thy salvation. 5315
35: 4 and put to shame that seek after my s: 5315
35: 7 without cause they have digged for my s. 5315
35: 9 my s shall be joyful in the LORD: it shall 5315
35:12 me evil for good to the spoiling of my s. 5315
35:13 I humbled my s with fasting; and my prayer 5315
35:17 rescue my s from their destructions, 5315
40:14 confounded together that seek after my s to 5315
41: 4 heal my s; for I have sinned against thee. 5315
42: 1 so panteth my s after thee, O God. 5315
42: 2 My s thirsteth for God, for the living God: 5315
42: 4 these things, I pour out my s in me: 5315
42: 5 Why art thou cast down, O my s? and 5315
42: 6 O my God, my s is cast down within me: 5315
42:11 Why art thou cast down, O my s? and 5315
43: 5 Why art thou cast down, O my s? and 5315
44:25 For our s is bowed down to the dust: 5315
49: 8 (For the redemption of their s is precious, 5315
49:15 God will redeem my s from the power of 5315
49:18 Though whiles he lived he blessed his s: 5315
54: 3 against me, and oppressors seek after my s: 5315
54: 4 the Lord is with them that uphold my s. 5315
55:18 He hath delivered my s in peace from 5315
56: 6 mark my steps, when they wait for my s. 5315
56:13 For thou hast delivered my s from death: 5315
57: 1 for my s trusteth in thee: yea, in the shadow 5315
57: 4 My s is among lions: and I lie even among 5315
57: 6 a net for my steps; my s is bowed down: 5315
59: 3 For lo, they lie in wait for my s: the mighty 5315
62: 1 Truly my s waiteth upon God: from him 5315
62: 5 My s, wait thou only upon God; for my 5315
63: 1 my s thirsteth for thee, my flesh longeth for 5315
63: 5 My s shall be satisfied as with marrow and 5315
63: 8 My s followeth hard after thee: thy right 5315
63: 9 those that seek my s, to destroy it, shall go 5315
66: 9 Which holdeth our s in life, and 5315
66:16 I will declare what he hath done for my s. 5315
69: 1 for the waters are come in unto my s. 5315
69:10 I wept, and chastened my s with fasting, 5315
69:18 Draw nigh unto my s, and redeem it: 5315
70: 2 and confounded that seek after my s: 5315
71:10 they that lay wait for my s take counsel 5315
71:13 and consumed that are adversaries to my s; 5315
71:23 and my s, which thou hast redeemed. 5315
72:14 He shall redeem their s from deceit and 5315
74:19 O deliver not the s of thy turtledove unto 5315
77: 2 ceased not: my s refused to be comforted. 5315
78:50 he spared not their s from death, but 5315
84: 2 My s longeth, yea, even fainteth for 5315
86: 2 Preserve my s; for I am holy: O thou my 5315
86: 4 Rejoice the s of thy servant: for unto thee, 5315
86: 4 for unto thee, O Lord, do I lift up my s. 5315
86:13 thou hast delivered my s from the lowest 5315
86:14 of violent men have sought after my s; 5315
88: 3 For my s is full of troubles: and my life 5315
88:14 LORD, why castest thou off my s? 5315
89:48 shall he deliver his s from the hand of 5315
Ps 94:17 my help, my s had almost dwelt in silence. 5315
94:19 within me thy comforts delight my s. 5315
94:21 together against the s of the righteous, 5315
103: 1 Bless the LORD, O my s: and all that is 5315
103: 2 O my s, and forget not all his benefits: 5315
103:22 of his dominion: bless the LORD, O my s. 5315
104: 1 Bless the LORD, O my s. O LORD my 5315
104:35 Bless thou the LORD, O my s. Praise ye 5315
106:15 their request; but sent leanness into their s. 5315
107: 5 Hungry and thirsty, their s fainted in them. 5315
107: 9 For he satisfieth the longing s, and 5315
107: 9 and filleth the hungry s with goodness. 5315
107:18 Their s abhorreth all manner of meat; and 5315
107:26 their s is melted because of trouble. 5315
109:20 and of them that speak evil against my s. 5315
109:31 to save him from those that condemn his s. 5315
116: 4 O LORD, I beseech thee, deliver my s. 5315
116: 7 Return unto thy rest, O my s; for 5315
116: 8 For thou hast delivered my s from death, 5315
119:20 My s breaketh for the longing that it hath 5315
119:25 My s cleaveth unto the dust: quicken thou 5315
119:28 My s melteth for heaviness: strengthen thou 5315
119:81 My s fainteth for thy salvation: but I hope 5315
119:109 My s is continually in my hand: yet do I not 5315
119:129 therefore doth my s keep them. 5315
119:167 My s hath kept thy testimonies; and I love 5315
119:175 Let my s live, and it shall praise thee; and 5315
120: 2 Deliver my s, O LORD, from lying lips, 5315
120: 6 My s hath long dwelt with him that hateth 5315
121: 7 thee from all evil: he shall preserve thy s. 5315
123: 4 Our s is exceedingly filled with 5315
124: 4 the stream had gone over our s: 5315
124: 5 Then the proud waters had gone over our s. 5315
124: 7 Our s is escaped as a bird out of the snare 5315
130: 5 my s doth wait, and in his word do I hope. 5315
130: 6 My s waiteth for the Lord more than they 5315
131: 2 his mother: my s is even as a weaned child. 5315
138: 3 strengthenedst me with strength in my s. 5315
139:14 and that my s knoweth right well. 5315
141: 8 in thee is my trust; leave not my s destitute. 5315
142: 4 refuge failed me; no man cared for my s. 5315
142: 7 Bring my s out of prison, that I may praise 5315
143: 3 For the enemy hath persecuted my s; 5315
143: 6 my s thirsteth after thee, as a thirsty land. 5315
143: 8 I should walk; for I lift up my s unto thee. 5315
143:11 for thy righteousness' sake bring my s out 5315
143:12 and destroy all them that afflict my s: 5315
146: 1 ye the LORD. Praise the LORD, O my s. 5315
Pr 2:10 and knowledge is pleasant unto thy s; 5315
3:22 So shall they be life unto thy s, and grace to 5315
6:30 if he steal to satisfy his s when he is 5315
6:32 he that doeth it destroyeth his own s. 5315
8:36 that sinneth against me wrongeth his own s: 5315
10: 3 The LORD will not suffer the s of 5315
11:17 The merciful man doeth good to his own s: 5315
11:25 The liberal s shall be made fat: and he that 5315
13: 2 the s of the transgressors shall eat violence. 5315
13: 4 The s of the sluggard desireth, and 5315
13: 4 but the s of the diligent shall be made fat. 5315
13:19 The desire accomplished is sweet to the s: 5315
13:25 righteous eateth to the satisfying of his s: 5315
15:32 refuseth instruction despiseth his own s: 5315
16:17 he that keepeth his way preserveth his s. 5315
16:24 sweet to the s, and health to the bones. 5315
18: 7 and his lips are the snare of his s. 5315
19: 2 Also, that the s be without knowledge, it is 5315
19: 8 He that getteth wisdom loveth his own s: 5315
19:15 and an idle s shall suffer hunger. 5315
19:16 the commandment keepeth his own s; 5315
19:18 and let not thy s spare for his crying. 5315
20: 2 him to anger sinneth against his own s. 5315
21:10 The s of the wicked desireth evil: 5315
21:23 and his tongue keepeth his s from troubles. 5315
22: 5 he that doth keep his s shall be far from 5315
22:23 and spoil the s of those that spoiled them. 5315
22:25 learn his ways, and get a snare to thy s. 5315
23:14 the rod, and shalt deliver his s from hell. 5315
24:12 heart consider it? and he that keepeth thy s, 5315
24:14 the knowledge of wisdom be unto thy s: 5315
25:13 for he refresheth the s of his masters. 5315
25:25 As cold waters to a thirsty s, so is good 5315
27: 7 The full s loatheth a honeycomb; but to 5315
27: 7 to the hungry s every bitter thing is sweet. 5315
29:10 hate the upright: but the just seek his s. 5315
29:17 yea, he shall give delight unto thy s. 5315
29:24 is partner with a thief hateth his own s: 5315
Ecc 2:24 that he should make his s enjoy good in his 5315
4: 8 do I labour, and bereave my s of good? 5315
6: 2 that he wanteth nothing for his s of all that 5315
6: 3 his s be not filled with good, and also that 5315
7:28 Which yet my s seeketh, but I find not: 5315
SS 1: 7 Tell me, O thou whom my s loveth, 5315
3: 1 on my bed I sought him whom my s loveth: 5315
3: 2 I will seek him whom my s loveth: 5315
3: 3 to whom I said, Saw ye him whom my s 5315
3: 4 but I found him whom my s loveth: 5315
5: 6 my s failed when he spake: I sought him, 5315
6:12 my s made me like the chariots of 5315
Isa 1:14 and your appointed feasts my s hateth: 5315
3: 9 Woe unto their s! for they have rewarded 5315
10:18 and of his fruitful field, both s and body: 5315
26: 8 the desire of our s is to thy name, and to 5315
26: 9 With my s have I desired thee in the night; 5315
29: 8 but he awaketh, and his s is empty: 5315
29: 8 behold, he is faint, and his s hath appetite: 5315
32: 6 to make empty the s of the hungry, and 5315
38:15 softly all my years in the bitterness of my s. 5315
38:17 thou hast in love to my s delivered it from 5315
42: 1 mine elect, in whom my s delighteth; 5315
44:20 that he cannot deliver his s, nor say, Is there 5315
51:23 which have said to thy s, Bow down, 5315
53:10 when thou shalt make his s an offering for 5315
53:11 He shall see of the travail of his s, and 5315
53:12 he hath poured out his s unto death: 5315
55: 2 and let your s delight itself in fatness. 5315
Isa 55: 3 hear, and your s shall live; and I will make 5315
58: 3 wherefore have we afflicted our s, and 5315
58: 5 a day for a man to afflict his s? is it to bow 5315
58:10 if thou draw out thy s to the hungry, and 5315
58:10 to the hungry, and satisfy the afflicted s; 5315
58:11 satisfy thy s in drought, and make fat thy 5315
61:10 my s shall be joyful in my God; 5315
66: 3 and their s delighteth in their abominations. 5315
Jer 4:10 whereas the sword reacheth unto the s). 5315
4:19 my peace, because thou hast heard, O my s, 5315
4:31 for my s is wearied because of murderers. 5315
5: 9 shall not my s be avenged on such a nation 5315
5:29 shall not my s be avenged on such a nation 5315
6: 8 O Jerusalem, lest my s depart from thee; 5315
9: 9 shall not my s be avenged on such a nation 5315
12: 7 I have given the dearly beloved of my s 5315
13:17 my s shall weep in secret places for your 5315
14:19 hath thy s lothed Zion? why hast thou 5315
18:20 for they have digged a pit for my s. 5315
20:13 for he hath delivered the s of the poor from 5315
31:12 their s shall be as a watered garden; and 5315
31:14 I will satiate the s of the priests with 5315
31:25 For I have satiated the weary s, and I have 5315
31:25 and I have replenished every sorrowful s. 5315
32:41 with my whole heart and with my whole s. 5315
38:16 As the LORD liveth, that made us this s, 5315
38:17 thy s shall live, and this city shall not be 5315
38:20 shall be well unto thee, and thy s shall live. 5315
50:19 his s shall be satisfied upon mount Ephraim 5315
51: 6 of Babylon, and deliver every man his s: 5315
51:45 deliver ye every man his s from the fierce 5315
La 1:11 pleasant things for meat to relieve the s: 5315
1:16 the comforter that should relieve my s is far 5315
2:12 when their s was poured out into their 5315
3:17 thou hast removed my s far off from peace: 5315
3:20 My s hath them still in remembrance, and 5315
3:24 The LORD is my portion, saith my s; 5315
3:25 that wait for him, to the s that seeketh him. 5315
3:58 thou hast pleaded the causes of my s; 5315
Eze 3:19 his iniquity; but thou hast delivered thy s. 5315
3:21 he is warned; also thou hast delivered thy s. 5315
4:14 behold, my s hath not been polluted: 5315
18: 4 as the s of the father, so also the soul of 5315
18: 4 the father, so also the s of the son is mine: 5315
18: 4 son is mine: the s that sinneth, it shall die. 5315
18:20 The s that sinneth, it shall die. The son shall 5315
18:27 is lawful and right, he shall save his s alive. 5315
24:21 of your eyes, and that which your s pitieth; 5315
33: 5 he that taketh warning shall deliver his s. 5315
33: 9 his iniquity; but thou hast delivered thy s. 5315
Hos 9: 4 for their bread for their s shall not come 5315
Jnh 2: 5 waters compassed me about, even to the s: 5315
2: 7 When my s fainted within me I 5315
Mic 6: 7 the fruit of my body for the sin of my s? 5315
7: 1 to eat: my s desired the firstripe fruit. 5315
Hab 2: 4 his s which is lifted up is not upright in 5315
2:10 many people, and hast sinned against thy s. 5315
Zec 11: 8 my s lothed them, and their soul also 5315
11: 8 lothed them, and their s also abhorred me. 5315
Mt 10:28 kill the body, but are not able to kill the s: 5590
10:28 fear him which is able to destroy both s 5590
12:18 my beloved, in whom my s is well pleased: 5590
16:26 gain the whole world, and lose his own s? 5590
16:26 shall a man give in exchange for his s? 5590
22:37 and with all thy s, and with all thy mind. 5590
26:38 My s is exceeding sorrowful, even unto 5590
Mk 8:36 gain the whole world, and lose his own s? 5590
8:37 shall a man give in exchange for his s? 5590
12:30 and with all thy s, and with all thy mind, 5590
12:33 and with all the s, and with all the strength, 5590
14:34 My s is exceeding sorrowful unto death: 5590
Lk 1:46 Mary said, My s doth magnify the Lord, 5590
2:35 a sword shall pierce through thy own s 5590
10:27 and with all thy s, and with all thy strength, 5590
12:19 And I will say to my s, Soul, thou hast 5590
12:19 And I will say to my soul, S, thou hast 5590
12:20 this night thy s shall be required of thee: 5590
Jn 12:27 Now is my s troubled; and what shall I say? 5590
Ac 2:27 Because thou wilt not leave my s in hell, 5590
2:31 of Christ, that his s was not left in hell, 5590
2:43 And fear came upon every s: and 5590
3:23 And it shall come to pass, that every s, 5590
4:32 believed were of one heart and of one s: 5590
Ro 2: 9 upon every s of man that doeth evil, 5590
13: 1 Let every s be subject unto the higher 5590
1Co 15:45 The first man Adam was made a living s; 5590
2Co 1:23 I call God for a record upon my s, 5590
1Th 5:23 and I pray God your whole spirit and s and 5590
Heb 4:12 piercing even to the dividing asunder of s 5590
6:19 Which hope we have as an anchor of the s, 5590
10:38 my s shall have no pleasure in him. 5590
10:39 of them that believe to the saving of the s. 5590
Jas 5:20 error of his way shall save a s from death, 5590
1Pe 2:11 from fleshly lusts, which war against the s; 5590
2Pe 2: 8 vexed his righteous s from day to day with 5590
3Jn 1: 2 and be in health, even as thy s prospereth. 5590
Rev 16: 3 and every living s died in the sea. 5590
18:14 And the fruits that thy s lusted after are 5590

SOUL'S (1) [SOUL]

Job 16: 4 as ye do: if your soul were in my s stead, 5315

SOULS (78) [SOUL]

Ge 12: 5 and the s that they had gotten in Haran; 5315
46:15 all the s of his sons and his daughters were 5315
46:18 these she bare unto Jacob, even sixteen s. 5315
46:22 were born to Jacob: all the s were fourteen. 5315
46:25 bare these unto Jacob: all the s were seven. 5315
46:26 All the s that came with Jacob into Egypt, 5315
46:26 all the s were threescore and six; 5315
46:27 which were born him in Egypt, were two s: 5315
46:27 all the s of the house of Jacob, which came 5315
Ex 1: 5 all the s that came out of the loins of Jacob 5315
1: 5 out of the loins of Jacob were seventy s: 5315
12: 4 take it according to the number of the s; 5315

Ex 30:15 to make an atonement for your **s**. 5315
30:16 to make an atonement for your **s**. 5315
Lev 16:29 ye shall afflict your **s**, and do no work *at* 5315
16:31 ye shall afflict your **s**, *by* a statute for ever. 5315
17:11 the altar to make an atonement for your **s**: 5315
18:29 even the **s** that commit *them* shall be cut off 5315
20:25 ye shall not make your **s** abominable by 5315
23:27 ye shall afflict your **s**, and offer an offering 5315
23:32 a sabbath of rest, and ye shall afflict your **s**: 5315
Nu 16:38 censers of these sinners against their own **s**, 5315
29: 7 and ye shall afflict your **s**: 5315
30: 9 wherewith they have bound their **s**, 5315
31:50 to make an atonement for our **s** before 5315
Jos 10:28 them, and all the **s** that *were* therein; 5315
10:30 of the sword, and all the **s** that *were* therein; 5315
10:32 of the sword, and all the **s** that *were* therein, 5315
10:35 all the **s** that *were* therein he utterly 5315
10:37 and all the **s** that *were* therein; 5315
10:37 it utterly, and all the **s** that *were* therein. 5315
10:39 utterly destroyed all the **s** that *were* therein; 5315
11:11 they smote all the **s** that *were* therein with 5315
23:14 ye know in all your hearts and in all your **s**, 5315
1Sa 25:29 the **s** of thine enemies, them shall he sling 5315
Ps 72:13 needy, and shall save the **s** of the needy. 5315
97:10 he preserveth the **s** of his saints; 5315
Pr 11:30 a tree of life; and he that winneth **s** *is* wise. 5315
14:25 A true witness delivereth **s**: but a deceitful 5315
Isa 57:16 before me, and the **s** *which* I have made. 5397
Jer 2:34 Also in thy skirts is found the blood of the **s** 5315
6:16 and ye shall find rest for your **s**. 5315
26:19 *might* we procure great evil against our **s**. 5315
44: 7 commit ye *this* great evil against your **s**, 5315
La 1:19 they sought their meat, to relieve their **s**. 5315
Eze 7:19 they shall not satisfy their **s**, neither fill 5315
13:18 upon the head of every stature to hunt **s**! 5315
13:18 Will ye hunt the **s** of my people, and will ye 5315
13:18 will ye save the **s** alive *that come* unto you? 5315
13:19 to slay the **s** that should not die, and to save 5315
13:19 and to save the **s** alive that should not live, 5315
13:20 where*with* ye there hunt the **s** to make *them* 5315
13:20 them from your arms, and will let the **s** go, 5315
13:20 *even* the **s** that ye hunt to make *them* fly. 5315
14:14 *but* their own **s** by their righteousness, 5315
14:20 deliver their own **s** by their righteousness. 5315
18: 4 Behold, all **s** *are* mine; as the soul of 5315
22:25 they have devoured **s**; they have taken 5315
22:27 to shed blood, *and* to destroy **s**, to get 5315
Mt 11:29 in heart: and ye shall find rest unto your **s**. *5590*
Lk 21:19 In your patience possess ye your **s**. *5590*
Ac 2:41 added *unto them* about three thousand **s**. *5590*
7:14 and all his kindred, threescore and fifteen **s**. *5590*
14:22 Confirming the **s** of the disciples, *and* *5590*
15:24 subverting your **s**, saying, *Ye must* be *5590*
27:37 ship two hundred threescore *and* sixteen **s**. *5590*
1Th 2: 8 but also our own **s**, because ye were dear *5590*
Heb 13:17 for they watch for your **s**, as they that must *5590*
Jas 1:21 which is able to save your **s**. *5590*
1Pe 1: 9 of your faith, *even* the salvation of *your* **s**. *5590*
1:22 Seeing ye have purified your **s** in obeying *5590*
2:25 unto the Shepherd and Bishop of your **s**. *5590*
3:20 that is, eight **s** were saved by water. *5590*
4:19 the keeping of their **s** *to him* in well doing, *5590*
2Pe 2:14 cannot cease from sin; beguiling unstable **s**: *5590*
Rev 6: 9 I saw under the altar the **s** of them that were *5590*
18:13 and chariots, and slaves, and **s** of men. *5590*
20: 4 *I saw* the **s** of them that were beheaded for *5590*

SOUND (89) [SOUNDED, SOUNDETH, SOUNDING, SOUNDNESS, SOUNDS]

Ex 28:35 his **s** shall be heard when he goeth in unto 6963
Lev 25: 9 thou **cause** the trumpet of the jubile **to s** 5674
25: 9 **make** the trumpet **s** throughout all your 5674
26:36 the **s** of a shaken leaf shall chase them; and 6963
Nu 10: 7 shall blow, but you shall not **s an alarm**. 7321
Jos 6: 5 *and* when ye hear the **s** of the trumpet, 6963
6:20 when the people heard the **s** of the trumpet, 6963
2Sa 5:24 when thou hearest the **s** of a going in 6963
6:15 and with the **s** of the trumpet. 6963
15:10 As soon as ye hear the **s** of the trumpet, 6963
1Ki 1:40 so that the earth rent with the **s** of them. 6963
1:41 when Joab heard the **s** of the trumpet, he 6963
14: 6 *so,* when Ahijah heard the **s** of her feet, 6963
18:41 drink; for *there is* a **s** of abundance of rain. 6963
2Ki 6:32 *is* not the **s** of his master's feet behind him? 6963
1Ch 14:15 when thou shalt hear a **s** of going in 6963
15:19 *were appointed* to **s** with cymbals of brass; 8085
15:28 with **s** of the cornet, and with trumpets, and 6963
16: 5 but Asaph **made a s** with cymbals; 8085
16:42 cymbals for those that should **make a s**, 8085
2Ch 5:13 to make one **s** to be heard in praising and 6963
Ne 4:20 *therefore* ye hear the **s** of the trumpet, 6963
Job 15:21 A dreadful **s** *is* in his ears: in prosperity 6963
21:12 and harp, and rejoice at the **s** of the organ. 6963
37: 2 and the **s** *that* goeth out of his mouth. 1899
39:24 neither believeth he that *it is* the **s** of 6963
Ps 47: 5 a shout, the LORD with the **s** of a trumpet. 6963
77:17 the skies sent out a **s**: thine arrows also 6963
89:15 *is* the people that know the **joyful s**: 8643
92: 3 the psaltery; upon the harp with a **solemn s**. 1902
98: 6 **s** of cornet make a joyful noise before 6963
119:80 Let my heart be **s** in thy statutes; that I be 8549
150: 3 Praise him with the **s** of the trumpet: 8629
Pr 2: 7 He layeth up **s wisdom** for the righteous: 8454
3:21 thine eyes: keep **s wisdom** and discretion: 8454
8:14 Counsel *is* mine, and **s wisdom**: I *am* 8454
14:30 A **s** heart *is* the life of the flesh: but 4832
Ecc 12: 4 when the **s** of the grinding is low, and 6963
Isa 16:11 Wherefore my bowels shall **s** like a harp for 1993
Jer 4:19 hast heard, O my soul, the **s** of the trumpet, 6963
4:21 the standard, *and* hear the **s** of the trumpet? 6963
6:17 *saying,* Hearken to the **s** of the trumpet. 6963
8:16 the whole land trembled at the **s** of 6963
25:10 the **s** of the millstones, and the light of 6963
42:14 nor hear the **s** of the trumpet, nor have 6963
48:36 Therefore mine heart shall **s** for Moab like 1993
Jer 48:36 mine heart shall **s** like pipes for the men of 1993
50:22 A **s** of battle *is* in the land, and of great 6963
51:54 A **s** of a cry *cometh* from Babylon, and 6963
Eze 10: 5 the **s** of the cherubims' wings was heard 6963
26:13 the **s** of thy harps shall be no more heard. 6963
26:15 Shall not the isles shake at the **s** of thy fall, 6963
27:28 The suburbs shall shake at the **s** of the cry 6963
31:16 I made the nations to shake at the **s** of his 6963
33: 4 whosoever heareth the **s** of the trumpet, 6963
33: 5 He heard the **s** of the trumpet, and took not 6963
Da 3: 5 *That* at what time ye hear the **s** of 7032
3: 7 when all the people heard the **s** of 7032
3:10 that every man that shall hear the **s** of 7032
3:15 that at what time ye hear the **s** of the cornet, 7032
Joel 2: 1 and **s an alarm** in my holy mountain: 7321
Am 2: 2 *and* with the **s** of the trumpet: 6963
6: 5 That chant to the **s** of the viol, *and* invent to 6310
Mt 6: 2 *thine* alms, do not **s a trumpet** before thee, *4537*
24:31 And he shall send his angels with a great **s** *5456*
Lk 15:27 because he hath received him *safe and* **s**. *5198*
Jn 3: 8 and thou hearest the **s** thereof, but canst not *5456*
Ac 2: 2 And suddenly there came a **s** from heaven *2279*
Ro 10:18 their **s** went into all the earth, and *5353*
1Co 14: 7 *And* even *things* without life giving **s**, *5456*
14: 8 For if the trumpet give an uncertain **s**, *5456*
15:52 for the **trumpet** shall **s**, and the dead shall *4537*
1Ti 1:10 other *thing that* is contrary to **s** doctrine; *5198*
2Ti 1: 7 but of power, and of love, and of a **s mind**. *4995*
1:13 Hold fast the form of **s** words, which thou *5198*
4: 3 come when they will not endure **s** doctrine; *5198*
Tit 1: 9 that he may be able by **s** doctrine both to *5198*
1:13 that they may be **s** in the faith; *5198*
2: 1 But speak thou *the things* which become **s** *5198*
2: 2 grave, temperate, **s** in faith, in charity, *5198*
2: 8 **S** speech that cannot be condemned; that he *5199*
Heb 12:19 And the **s** of a trumpet, and the voice of *2279*
Rev 1:15 and his voice as the **s** of many waters. *5456*
8: 6 seven trumpets prepared themselves to **s**. *4537*
8:13 of the three angels, which are yet to **s**. *4537*
9: 9 the **s** of their wings *was* as the sound of *5456*
9: 9 the sound of their wings *was* as the **s** of *5456*
10: 7 when he shall begin to **s**, the mystery of *4537*
18:22 the **s** of a millstone shall be heard no more *5456*

SOUNDED (18) [SOUND]

Ex 19:19 when the voice of the trumpet **s long**, and 1980
1Sa 20:12 when I have **s** my father about to morrow 2713
2Ch 7: 6 and the priests **s trumpets** before them, and 2690
13:14 and the priests **s** with the trumpets. 2690
23:13 of the land rejoiced, and **s** with trumpets, 8628
29:28 and the singers sang, and the trumpeters **s**: 2690
Ne 4:18 And he that **s** the trumpet *was* by me. 8628
Lk 1:44 as soon as the voice of thy salutation **s** in *1096*
Ac 27:28 And **s**, and found *it* twenty fathoms: and *1001*
27:28 they **s** again, and found *it* fifteen fathoms. *1001*
1Th 1: 8 For from you **s out** the word of the Lord *1837*
Rev 8: 7 The first angel **s**, and there followed hail *4537*
8: 8 And the second angel **s**, and as *it were* a *4537*
8:10 And the third angel **s**, and there fell a great *4537*
8:12 And the fourth angel **s**, and the third *part* of *4537*
9: 1 And the fifth angel **s**, and I saw a star fall *4537*
9:13 And the sixth angel **s**, and I heard a voice *4537*
11:15 And the seventh angel **s**; and there were *4537*

SOUNDETH (1) [SOUND]

Ex 19:13 when the trumpet **s long**, they shall come 4900

SOUNDING (7) [SOUND]

1Ch 15:16 psalteries and harps and cymbals, **s**, 8085
2Ch 5:12 and twenty priests **s** with trumpets:) 2690
13:12 his priests with **s** trumpets to cry alarm 8643
Ps 150: 5 praise him upon the **high s** cymbals. 8643
Isa 63:15 the **s** of thy bowels and of thy mercies 1995
Eze 7: 7 and not the **s again** of the mountains. 1906
1Co 13: 1 I am become *as* **s** brass, or a tinkling *2278*

SOUNDNESS (4) [SOUND]

Ps 38: 3 *There is* no **s** in my flesh because of thine 4974
38: 7 and *there is* no **s** in my flesh. 4974
Isa 1: 6 foot even unto the head *there is* no **s** in it; 4974
Ac 3:16 this **perfect s** in the presence of you all. *3647*

SOUNDS (1) [SOUND]

1Co 14: 7 harp, except they give a distinction in the **s**, *5353*

SOUR (5)

Isa 18: 5 and the **s grape** is ripening in the flower, 1155
Jer 31:29 The fathers have eaten a **s grape**, and 1155
31:30 every man that eateth the **s grape**, his teeth 1155
Eze 18: 2 The fathers have eaten **s grapes**, and 1155
Hos 4:18 Their drink is **s**; they have committed 5493

SOUTH (143) [SOUTHWARD]

Ge 12: 9 going on still toward the **s**. 5045
13: 1 all that he had, and Lot with him, into the **s**. 5045
13: 3 he went on his journeys from the **s** even to 5045
20: 1 from thence toward the **s** country, 5045
24:62 for he dwelt in the **s** country. 5045
28:14 to the east, and to the north, and to the **s**: 5045
Ex 26:18 boards on the **s** side southward. 5045+1886.5
26:35 on the side of the tabernacle toward the **s**: 8486
27: 9 for the **s** side southward *there shall be* 5045
36:23 twenty boards for the **s** side southward: 5045
38: 9 on the **s** side southward the hangings of 5045
Nu 2:10 On the **s side** *shall be* the standard of 8486
10: 6 the camps that lie on the **s side** shall take 8486
13:22 they ascended by the **s**, and came unto 5045
13:29 The Amalekites dwell in the land of the **s**: 5045
21: 1 Arad the Canaanite, which dwelt *in* the **s**, 5045
33:40 which dwelt in the **s** in the land of Canaan, 5045
34: 3 your **s** quarter shall be from the wilderness 5045
34: 3 your **s** border shall be the outmost coast of 5045
34: 4 your border shall turn from the **s** to 5045
34: 4 the going forth thereof shall be from the **s** 5045
Nu 35: 5 *on* the **s** side two thousand cubits, and 5045
Dt 1: 7 in the vale, and in the **s**, and by the sea side, 5045
33:23 possess thou the west and the **s**. 1864
34: 3 the **s**, and the plain of the valley of Jericho, 5045
Jos 10:40 of the **s**, and of the vale, and of the springs, 5045
11: 2 of the plains **s** of Cinneroth, and in 5045
11:16 all the **s** *country,* and all the land of 5045
12: 3 and from the **s**, under Ashdoth-pisgah: 8486
12: 8 in the **s** *country;* the Hittites, the Amorites, 5045
13: 4 From the **s**, all the land of the Canaanites, 8486
15: 1 *was* the uttermost part of the **s** *coast.* 8486
15: 2 their **s** border was from the shore of the salt 5045
15: 3 it went out to the **s side** to 5045
15: 3 ascended up on the **s side** unto 5045
15: 4 were at the sea: this shall be your **s** coast. 5045
15: 7 which *is* on the **s side** of the river: 5045
15: 8 unto the **s** side of the Jebusite; 4480+5045
15:19 a blessing; for thou hast given me a **s** land; 5045
18: 5 Judah shall abide in their coast on the **s**, 5045
18:13 near the hill that *lieth* on the **s side** of 5045
18:15 the **s** quarter *was* from the end of 5045+1886.5
18:16 to the side of Jebusi on the **s**, and 5045
18:19 bay of the salt sea at the **s** end of Jordan: 5045
18:19 south end of Jordan: this *was* the **s** coast. 5045
19: 8 cities to Baalath-beer, Ramath of the **s**. 5045
19:34 reacheth to Zebulun on the **s side**, and 5045
Jdg 1: 9 and in the **s**, and in the valley. 5045
1:15 for thou hast given me a **s** land; give me 5045
1:16 of Judah, which *lieth* in the **s** of Arad; 5045
21:19 to Shechem, and on the **s** of Lebonah. 5045
1Sa 20:41 David arose out of *a place* toward the **s**, and 5045
23:19 of Hachilah, which *is* on the **s** of Jeshimon? 3225
23:24 of Maon, in the plain on the **s** of Jeshimon. 3225
27:10 Against the **s** of Judah, and against 5045
27:10 against the **s** of the Jerahmeelites, and 5045
27:10 and against the **s** of the Kenites. 5045
30: 1 that the Amalekites had invaded the **s**, and 5045
30:14 We made an invasion *upon* the **s** of 5045
30:14 to Judah, and upon the **s** of Caleb; 5045
30:27 to *them* which *were* in **s** Ramoth, and 5045
2Sa 24: 7 they went out to the **s** of Judah, *even to* 5045
1Ki 7:25 three looking toward the **s**, and 5045
7:39 of the house eastward over against the **s**. 5045
1Ch 9:24 toward the east, west, north, and **s**. 5045
2Ch 4: 4 three looking toward the **s**, and 5045
4:10 of the east end, over against the **s**. 5045+1886.5
28:18 of the **s** of Judah, and had taken 5045
Job 9: 9 and Pleiades, and the chambers of the **s**. 8486
37: 9 Out of the **s** cometh the whirlwind: and 2315
37:17 when he quieteth the earth by the **s** *wind?* 1864
39:26 *and* stretch her wings toward the **s**? 8486
Ps 75: 6 the east, nor from the west, nor from the **s**. 4057
78:26 and by his power he brought in the **s wind**. 8486
89:12 The north and the **s** thou hast created them: 3225
107: 3 the west, from the north, and from the **s**. 3220
126: 4 O LORD, as the streams in the **s**. 5045
Ecc 1: 6 The wind goeth toward the **s**, and 1864
11: 3 if the tree fall toward the **s**, or toward 1864
SS 4:16 Awake, O north wind; and come thou **s**; 8486
Isa 21: 1 As whirlwinds in the **s** pass through; *so* 5045
30: 6 The burden of the beasts of the **s**: into 5045
43: 6 Give *up;* and to the **s**, Keep not back: 8486
Jer 13:19 The cities of the **s** shall be shut up, and 5045
17:26 and from the mountains, and from the **s**, 5045
32:44 of the valley, and in the cities of the **s**: 5045
33:13 in the cities of the **s**, and in the land of 5045
Eze 20:46 set thy face toward the **s**, and 8486+1886.5
20:46 drop *thy word* toward the **s**, and 1864
20:46 prophesy against the forest of the **s** field; 5045
20:47 say to the forest of the **s**, Hear the word of 5045
20:47 all faces from the **s** to the north shall be 5045
21: 4 against all flesh from the **s** *to* the north: 5045
40: 2 which *was* as the frame of a city on the **s**. 5045
40:24 After that he brought me toward the **s**, and 1864
40:24 the south, and behold a gate toward the **s**: 1864
40:27 *was* a gate in the inner court toward the **s**: 1864
40:27 he measured from gate to gate toward the **s** 1864
40:28 he brought me to the inner court by the **s** 1864
40:28 he measured the **s** gate according to these 1864
40:44 and their prospect *was* toward the **s**: 1864
40:45 whose prospect *is* toward the **s**, 1864
41:11 the north, and another door toward the **s**: 1864
42:12 the **s** *was* a door in the head of the way, 1864
42:13 The north chambers *and* the **s** chambers, 1864
42:18 He measured the **s** side, five hundred reeds, 1864
46: 9 shall go out *by* the way of the **s** gate; 5045
46: 9 he that entereth *by* the way of the **s** gate 5045
47: 1 side of the house, at the **s** *side* of the altar. 5045
47:19 the **s** side southward, from Tamar *even* to 5045
47:19 *is* the **s** side southward. 8486+1886.5+1886.5
48:10 toward the **s** five and twenty thousand *in* 5045
48:16 the **s** side four thousand and five hundred, 5045
48:17 toward the **s** two hundred and fifty, and 5045
48:28 the border of Gad, at the **s** side southward, 5045
48:33 *at* the **s** side four thousand and five hundred 5045
Da 8: 9 toward the **s**, and toward the east, and 5045
11: 5 the king of the **s** shall be strong, and *one* of 5045
11: 6 for the king's daughter of the **s** shall come 5045
11: 9 So the king of the **s** shall come into *his* 5045
11:11 the king of the **s** shall be moved with 5045
11:14 many stand up against the king of the **s**: 5045
11:15 the arms of the **s** shall not withstand, 5045
11:25 his courage against the king of the **s** with a 5045
11:25 the king of the **s** shall be stirred up to battle 5045
11:29 he shall return, and come toward the **s**; 5045
11:40 at the time of the end shall the king of the **s** 5045
Ob 1:19 *they of* the **s** shall possess the mount of 5045
1:20 shall possess the cities of the **s**. 5045
Zec 6: 6 the grisled go forth toward the **s** country. 8486
7: 7 when *men* inhabited the **s** and the plain? 5045
9:14 and shall go with whirlwinds of the **s**. 8486
14: 4 the north, and half of it toward the **s**. 5045
14:10 plain from Geba to Rimmon **s** of Jerusalem: 5045
Mt 12:42 *The* queen of the **s** shall rise up in *3558*
Lk 11:31 *The* queen of the **s** shall rise up in *3558*

Lk 12:55 And when *ye see* the **s wind** blow, ye say, *3558*
13:29 and *from* the **s**, and shall sit down in *3558*
Ac 8:26 go toward the **s** unto the way that goeth *3314*
27:12 and lieth toward the **s west** and north west. *3047*
27:13 And when the **s wind** blew softly, *3558*
28:13 and after one day the **s wind** blew, and *3558*
Rev 21:13 on the **s** three gates; and on the west three *3558*

SOUTHWARD (24) [SOUTH]
Ge 13:14 **s**, and eastward, and westward: 5045+1886.5
Ex 26:18 twenty boards on the south side **s**. 8486+1886.5
27: 9 for the south side **s** *there shall be* 8486+1886.5
36:23 twenty boards for the south side **s**: 8486+1886.5
38: 9 on the south side **s** the hangings of 8486+1886.5
40:24 on the side of the tabernacle **s**. 5045+1886.5
Nu 3:29 on the side of the tabernacle **s**. 8486+1886.5
13:17 Get you up this *way* **s**, and 5045+871.1+1886.1
Dt 3:27 **s**, and eastward, and behold *it* with 8486+1886.5
Jos 15: 1 the wilderness of Zin **s** *was* 5045+1886.5
15: 2 from the bay that looketh **s**: 5045+1886.5
15:21 the coast of Edom **s** were Kabzeel, 5045+1886.5
17: 9 *unto* the river Kanah, **s** of the river: 5045+1886.5
17:10 **S** *it was* Ephraim's, and 5045+1886.5
18:13 the side of Luz, which *is* Beth-el, **s**; 5045+1886.5
18:14 compassed the corner of the sea **s**, 5045+1886.5
18:14 hill that *lieth* before Beth-horon **s**; 5045+1886.5
1Sa 14: 5 and the other **s** over against Gibeah. 4480+5045
1Ch 26:15 To Obed-edom **s**; and to his sons 5045+1886.5
26:17 **s** four a day, and toward Asuppim 5045+1886.5
Eze 47:19 the south side **s**, from Tamar *even* 8486+1886.5
47:19 to the great sea. And *this is* the south side **s**. 5045
48:28 border of Gad, at the south side **s**, 8486+1886.5
Da 8: 4 and northward, and **s**; 5045+1886.5

SOW (37) [SEW, SOWED, SOWEDST, SOWER, SOWEST, SOWETH, SOWING, SOWN]
Ge 47:23 *here is* seed for you, and ye shall **s** the land. 2232
Ex 23:10 six years thou shalt **s** thy land, and 2232
Lev 19:19 shalt not **s** thy field **with** mingled **seed**: 2232
25: 3 Six years thou shalt **s** thy field, and 2232
25: 4 thou shalt neither **s** thy field, nor prune thy 2232
25:11 ye shall not **s**, neither reap that which 2232
25:20 behold, we shall not **s**, nor gather in our 2232
25:22 ye shall **s** the eighth year, and eat *yet* of old 2232
26:16 ye shall **s** your seed in vain, for your 2232
Dt 22: 9 shalt not **s** thy vineyard with divers **seeds**: 2232
2Ki 19:29 in the third year **s** ye, and reap, and 2232
Job 4: 8 and **s** wickedness, reap the same. 2232
31: 8 *Then* let me **s**, and let another eat; yea, 2232
Ps 107:37 **s** the fields, and plant vineyards, which may 2232
126: 5 They that **s** in tears shall reap in joy. 2232
Ecc 11: 4 He that observeth the wind shall not **s**; and 2232
11: 6 In the morning **s** thy seed, and in 2232
Isa 28:24 Doth the plowman plow all day to **s**? 2232
30:23 that thou shalt **s** the ground withal; 2232
32:20 Blessed *are* ye that **s** beside all waters, 2232
37:30 in the third year **s** ye, and reap, and 2232
Jer 4: 3 fallow ground, and **s** not among thorns. 2232
31:27 that I will **s** the house of Israel and 2232
35: 7 nor **s** seed, nor plant vineyard, nor have 2232
Hos 2:23 I will **s** her unto me in the earth; and I will 2232
10:12 **S** to yourselves in righteousness, reap in 2232
Mic 6:15 Thou shalt **s**, but thou shalt not reap; 2232
Zec 10: 9 I will **s** them among the people: and they 2232
Mt 6:26 for they **s** not, neither do they reap, *4687*
13: 3 saying, Behold, a sower went forth to **s**; *4687*
13:27 Sir, didst not thou **s** good seed in thy field? *4687*
Mk 4: 3 Behold, there went out a sower to **s**: *4687*
Lk 8: 5 A sower went out to **s** his seed: and as he *4687*
12:24 for they neither **s** nor reap; which neither *4687*
19:21 not down, and reapest that thou didst not **s**. *4687*
19:22 I laid not down, and reaping that I did not **s**: *4687*
2Pe 2:22 The **s** that was washed to *her* wallowing in 5300

SOWED (10) [SOW]
Ge 26:12 Isaac **s** in that land, and received in 2232
Jdg 9:45 beat down the city, and **s** it *with* salt. 2232
Mt 13: 4 And when he **s**, some *seeds* fell by the way *4687*
13:24 unto a man which **s** good seed in his field: *4687*
13:25 enemy came and **s** tares among the wheat, *4687*
13:31 which a man took, and **s** in his field: *4687*
13:39 The enemy that **s** them is the devil; *4687*
25:26 thou knewest that I reap where I **s** not, and *4687*
Mk 4: 4 And it came to pass, as *he* **s**, some fell by *4687*
Lk 8: 5 and as he **s**, some fell by the way side; and *4687*

S

SOWEDST (1) [SOW]
Dt 11:10 where thou **s** thy seed, and wateredst *it* with 2232

SOWER (8) [SOW]
Isa 55:10 that it may give seed to the **s**, and bread to 2232
Jer 50:16 Cut off the **s** from Babylon, and him that 2232
Mt 13: 3 saying, Behold, a **s** went forth to sow; *4687*
13:18 Hear ye therefore the parable of the **s**. *4687*
Mk 4: 3 Hearken; Behold, there went out a **s** to sow: *4687*
4:14 The **s** soweth the word. *4687*
Lk 8: 5 A **s** went out to sow his seed: and as he *4687*
2Co 9:10 Now he that ministereth seed to the **s** both *4687*

SOWEST (3) [SOW]
1Co 15:36 *that* which thou **s** is not quickened, *4687*
15:37 And *that* which thou **s**, thou sowest not that *4687*
15:37 thou **s** not that body that shall be, but *4687*

SOWETH (15) [SOW]
Pr 6:14 deviseth mischief continually; he **s** discord. 7971
6:19 and he that **s** discord among brethren. 7971
11:18 *to* him that **s** righteousness *shall be* a sure 2232
16:28 A froward man **s** strife: and a whisperer 7971
22: 8 He that **s** iniquity shall reap vanity: and 2232
Am 9:13 and the treader of grapes him that **s** seed; 4900
Mt 13:37 He that **s** the good seed is the Son of man; *4687*
Mk 4:14 The sower **s** the word. *4687*
Jn 4:36 that both he that **s** and he that reapeth may *4687*
4:37 And herein is *that* saying true, One **s**, *4687*
2Co 9: 6 But this *I say*, He which **s** sparingly shall *4687*
9: 6 he which **s** bountifully shall reap also *4687*
Gal 6: 7 for whatsoever a man **s**, that shall he also *4687*
6: 8 For he that **s** to his flesh shall of the flesh *4687*
6: 8 he that **s** to the Spirit shall of the Spirit reap *4687*

SOWING (2) [SOW]
Lev 11:37 if *any part* of their carcase fall upon any **s** 2221
26: 5 and the vintage shall reach unto the **s time**: 2233

SOWN (32) [SOW]
Ex 23:16 thy labours, which thou hast **s** in the field: 2232
Lev 11:37 fall upon any sowing seed which is to be **s**, 2232
Dt 21: 4 which is neither eared nor **s**, and shall strike 2232
22: 9 lest the fruit of *thy* seed which thou hast **s**, 2232
29:23 salt, *and* burning, *that* it is not **s**, 2232
Jdg 6: 3 *so* it was, when Israel had **s**, that 2232
Ps 97:11 Light is **s** for the righteous, and 2232
Isa 19: 7 every thing **s** by the brooks, shall wither, 4218
40:24 not be planted; yea, they shall not be **s**: 2232
61:11 as the garden causeth the **things that are s** 2221
Jer 2: 2 in the wilderness, in a land *that was* not **s**. 2232
12:13 They have **s** wheat, but shall reap thorns: 2232
Eze 36: 9 turn unto you, and ye shall be tilled and **s**: 2232
Hos 8: 7 For they have **s** the wind, and they shall 2232
Na 1:14 *that* no more of thy name be **s**: 2232
Hag 1: 6 Ye have **s** much, and bring in little; *ye* eat, 2232
Mt 13:19 catcheth away that which was **s** in his heart. *4687*
25:24 reaping where thou hast not **s**, and *4687*
Mk 4:15 they by the way side, where the word is **s**; *4687*
4:15 taketh away the word that was **s** in their *4687*
4:16 And these are they likewise which are **s** on *4687*
4:18 And these are they which are **s** among *4687*
4:20 And these are they which are **s** on good *4687*
4:31 which, when it is **s** in the earth, *4687*
4:32 But when it is **s**, it groweth up, and *4687*
1Co 9:11 If we have **s** unto you spiritual *things, is it* *4687*
15:42 It is **s** in corruption; it is raised in *4687*
15:43 It is **s** in dishonour; it is raised in glory: it is *4687*
15:43 it is **s** in weakness; it is raised in power: *4687*
15:44 It is **s** a natural body; it is raised a spiritual *4687*
2Co 9:10 and multiply your **seed s**, and increase *4703*
Jas 3:18 And the fruit of righteousness is **s** in peace *4687*

SPACE (27)
Ge 29:14 And he abode with him the **s** of a month. 3117
32:16 and put a **s** betwixt drove and drove. 7305
Lev 25: 8 the **s** of the seven sabbaths of years shall be 3117
25:30 if it be not redeemed within the **s** of a full 4390
Dt 2:14 the **s** in which we came from 3117
Jos 3: 4 Yet there shall be a **s** between you and it, 7350
1Sa 26:13 hill afar off; a great **s** *being* between them: 4725
Ezr 9: 8 now for a little **s** grace hath been *shewed* 7281
Jer 28:11 **within the s** of two full years. 5750+871.1
Eze 40:12 The **s** also before the little chambers *was* 1366
40:12 and the **s** *was* one cubit on that side: 1366
Lk 22:59 And about the **s** of one hour **after** another *1339*
Ac 5: 7 And it was about the **s** of three hours **after**, *1292*
5:34 to put the apostles forth a **little s**; *1024*
7:42 sacrifices *by the s of* forty years in NIG
13:20 *them* judges about *the s of* four hundred NIG
13:21 tribe of Benjamin, *by the s of* forty years. NIG
15:33 And after they had **tarried** *there* a **s**, *4160+5550*
19: 8 and spake boldly **for the s** of three months, *1909*
19:10 And this continued **by the s** of two years; *1909*
19:34 all with one voice about **the s** of two hours *1909*
20:31 that *by the s of* three years I ceased not to NIG
Jas 5:17 it rained not on the earth *by the s of* three NIG
Rev 2:21 And I gave her **s** to repent of her *5550*
8: 1 there was silence in heaven about the **s** of NIG
14:20 by the **s of** a thousand *and* six hundred *575*
17:10 he cometh, he must continue a short *s*. NIG

SPAIN (2)
Ro 15:24 Whensoever I take my journey into **S**, I will *4681*
15:28 them this fruit, I will come by you into **S**. *4681*

SPAKE (588) [SPEAK]
Ge 8:15 And God **s** unto Noah, saying, 1696
9: 8 God **s** unto Noah, and to his sons with him, 559
16:13 she called the name of the LORD that **s** 1696
18:29 he **s** unto him yet again, and said, 1696
19:14 Lot went out, and **s** unto his sons in law, 1696
21:22 Phichol the chief captain of his host **s** unto 559
22: 7 Isaac **s** unto Abraham his father, and said, 559
23: 3 and **s** unto the sons of Heth, saying, 1696
23:13 he **s** unto Ephron in the audience of 1696
24: 7 which **s** unto me, and that sware unto me, 1696
24:30 his sister, saying, Thus **s** the man unto me; 1696
27: 5 Rebekah heard when Isaac **s** to Esau his 1696
27: 6 Rebekah **s** unto Jacob her son, saying, 559
29: 9 while he yet **s** with them, Rachel came with 1696
31:11 And the angel of God **s** unto me in a dream, 559
31:29 the God of your father **s** unto me yesternight, 559
34: 3 the damsel, and **s** kindly unto the damsel. 1696
34: 4 Shechem **s** unto his father Hamor, saying, 559
35:15 name of the place where God **s** with him, 1696
39:10 came to pass, as she **s** to Joseph day by day, 1696
39:14 of her house, and **s** unto them, saying, See, 559
39:17 she **s** unto him according to these words, 1696
39:19 which she **s** unto him, saying, After this 1696
41: 9 **s** the chief butler unto Pharaoh, saying, 1696
42: 7 unto them, and **s** roughly unto them; 1696
42:14 That *is it* that I **s** unto you, saying, Ye *are* 1696
42:22 saying, **S** I not unto you, saying, Do not sin 559
42:23 *them;* for he **s unto** them by an interpreter. 996
42:30 **s** roughly to us, and took us for spies of 1696
42:37 Reuben **s** unto his father, saying, Slay my 559
43: 3 Judah **s** unto him, saying, The man did 559
43:27 your father well, the old man of whom ye **s**? 559
43:29 younger brother, of whom ye **s** unto me? 559
44: 6 and he **s** unto them these *same* words. 1696
46: 2 God **s** unto Israel in the visions of the night, 559
Ge 47: 5 Pharaoh **s** unto Joseph, saying, Thy father 559
49:28 this *is it* that their father **s** unto them, and 1696
50: 4 Joseph **s** unto the house of Pharaoh, saying, 1696
50:17 And Joseph wept when they **s** unto him. 1696
50:21 he comforted them, and **s** kindly unto them. 1696
Ex 1:15 the king of Egypt **s** to the Hebrew midwives, 559
4:30 Aaron **s** all the words which the LORD 1696
5:10 and they **s** to the people, saying, 559
6: 2 God **s** unto Moses, and said unto him, I *am* 1696
6: 9 Moses **s** so unto the children of Israel: but 1696
6:10 And the LORD **s** unto Moses, saying, 1696
6:12 Moses **s** before the LORD, saying, 1696
6:13 the LORD **s** unto Moses and unto Aaron, 1696
6:27 *These are* they which **s** to Pharaoh king of 1696
6:28 LORD **s** unto Moses in the land of Egypt, 1696
6:29 That the LORD **s** unto Moses, saying, 1696
7: 7 three years old, when they **s** unto Pharaoh. 1696
7: 8 the LORD **s** unto Moses and unto Aaron, 559
7:19 the LORD **s** unto Moses, Say unto Aaron, 559
8: 1 the LORD **s** unto Moses, Go unto Pharaoh, 559
8: 5 the LORD **s** unto Moses, Say unto Aaron, 559
12: 1 the LORD **s** unto Moses and Aaron in 559
13: 1 And the LORD **s** unto Moses, saying, 1696
14: 1 And the LORD **s** unto Moses, saying, 1696
15: 1 **s**, saying, I will sing unto the LORD, for he 559
16: 9 Moses **s** unto Aaron, Say unto all 559
16:10 as Aaron **s** unto the whole congregation of 1696
16:11 And the LORD **s** unto Moses, saying, 1696
19:19 Moses **s**, and God answered him by a 1696
19:25 went down unto the people, and **s** unto them. 559
20: 1 And God **s** all these words, saying, 1696
25: 1 And the LORD **s** unto Moses, saying, 1696
30:11 And the LORD **s** unto Moses, saying, 1696
30:17 And the LORD **s** unto Moses, saying, 1696
30:22 Moreover the LORD **s** unto Moses, 1696
31: 1 And the LORD **s** unto Moses, saying, 1696
31:12 And the LORD **s** unto Moses, saying, 559
33:11 the LORD **s** unto Moses face to face, as a 1696
34:34 **s** unto the children of Israel *that* which he 1696
35: 4 Moses **s** unto all the congregation of 559
36: 5 they **s** unto Moses, saying, The people bring 559
40: 1 And the LORD **s** unto Moses, saying, 1696
Lev 1: 1 **s** unto him out of the tabernacle of 1696
4: 1 And the LORD **s** unto Moses, saying, 1696
5:14 And the LORD **s** unto Moses, saying, 1696
6: 1 And the LORD **s** unto Moses, saying, 1696
6: 8 And the LORD **s** unto Moses, saying, 1696
6:19 And the LORD **s** unto Moses, saying, 1696
6:24 And the LORD **s** unto Moses, saying, 1696
7:22 And the LORD **s** unto Moses, saying, 1696
7:28 And the LORD **s** unto Moses, saying, 1696
8: 1 And the LORD **s** unto Moses, saying, 1696
10: 3 This *is it* that the LORD **s**, saying, 1696
10: 8 And the LORD **s** unto Aaron, saying, 1696
10:12 Moses **s** unto Aaron, and unto Eleazar and 1696
11: 1 the LORD **s** unto Moses and to Aaron, 1696
12: 1 And the LORD **s** unto Moses, saying, 1696
13: 1 the LORD **s** unto Moses and Aaron, 1696
14: 1 And the LORD **s** unto Moses, saying, 1696
14:33 the LORD **s** unto Moses and unto Aaron, 1696
15: 1 the LORD **s** unto Moses and to Aaron, 1696
16: 1 the LORD **s** unto Moses after the death of 1696
17: 1 And the LORD **s** unto Moses, saying, 1696
18: 1 And the LORD **s** unto Moses, saying, 1696
19: 1 And the LORD **s** unto Moses, saying, 1696
20: 1 And the LORD **s** unto Moses, saying, 1696
21:16 And the LORD **s** unto Moses, saying, 1696
22: 1 And the LORD **s** unto Moses, saying, 1696
22:17 And the LORD **s** unto Moses, saying, 1696
22:26 And the LORD **s** unto Moses, saying, 1696
23: 1 And the LORD **s** unto Moses, saying, 1696
23: 9 And the LORD **s** unto Moses, saying, 1696
23:23 And the LORD **s** unto Moses, saying, 1696
23:26 And the LORD **s** unto Moses, saying, 1696
23:33 And the LORD **s** unto Moses, saying, 1696
24: 1 And the LORD **s** unto Moses, saying, 1696
24:13 And the LORD **s** unto Moses, saying, 1696
24:23 Moses **s** to the children of Israel, that they 1696
25: 1 the LORD **s** unto Moses in mount Sinai, 1696
27: 1 And the LORD **s** unto Moses, saying, 1696
Nu 1: 1 the LORD **s** unto Moses in the wilderness 1696
2: 1 the LORD **s** unto Moses and unto Aaron, 1696
3: 1 Moses in the day that the LORD **s** with 1696
3: 5 And the LORD **s** unto Moses, saying, 1696
3:11 And the LORD **s** unto Moses, saying, 1696
3:14 the LORD **s** unto Moses in the wilderness 1696
3:44 And the LORD **s** unto Moses, saying, 1696
4: 1 the LORD **s** unto Moses and unto Aaron, 1696
4:17 the LORD **s** unto Moses and unto Aaron, 1696
4:21 And the LORD **s** unto Moses, saying, 1696
5: 1 And the LORD **s** unto Moses, saying, 1696
5: 4 as the LORD **s** unto Moses, so did 1696
5: 5 And the LORD **s** unto Moses, saying, 1696
5:11 And the LORD **s** unto Moses, saying, 1696
6: 1 And the LORD **s** unto Moses, saying, 1696
6:22 And the LORD **s** unto Moses, saying, 1696
7: 4 And the LORD **s** unto Moses, saying, 559
7:89 the two cherubims: and he **s** unto him. 1696
8: 1 And the LORD **s** unto Moses, saying, 1696
8: 5 And the LORD **s** unto Moses, saying, 1696
8:23 And the LORD **s** unto Moses, saying, 1696
9: 1 the LORD **s** unto Moses in the wilderness 1696
9: 4 Moses **s** unto the children of Israel, 1696
9: 9 And the LORD **s** unto Moses, saying, 1696
10: 1 And the LORD **s** unto Moses, saying, 1696
11:25 **s** unto him, and took of the spirit that *was* 1696
12: 1 and Aaron **s** against Moses because 1696
12: 4 And the LORD **s** suddenly unto Moses, and 559
13: 1 And the LORD **s** unto Moses, saying, 1696
14: 7 they **s** unto all the company of the children 559
14:26 the LORD **s** unto Moses and unto Aaron, 1696
15: 1 And the LORD **s** unto Moses, saying, 1696
15:17 And the LORD **s** unto Moses, saying, 1696
15:37 And the LORD **s** unto Moses, saying, 559
16: 5 he **s** unto Korah and unto all his company, 1696

Nu 16:20 the LORD **s** unto Moses and unto Aaron, 1696
16:23 And the LORD **s** unto Moses, saying, 1696
16:26 he **s** unto the congregation, saying, Depart, 1696
16:36 And the LORD **s** unto Moses, saying, 1696
16:44 And the LORD **s** unto Moses, saying, 1696
17: 1 And the LORD **s** unto Moses, saying, 1696
17: 6 Moses **s** unto the children of Israel, and 1696
17:12 the children of Israel **s** unto Moses, saying, 559
18: 8 the LORD **s** unto Aaron, Behold, I also 1696
18:20 the LORD **s** unto Aaron, Thou shalt have 559
18:25 And the LORD **s** unto Moses, saying, 1696
19: 1 the LORD **s** unto Moses and unto Aaron, 1696
20: 3 the people chode with Moses, and **s**, saying, 559
20: 7 And the LORD **s** unto Moses, saying, 1696
20:12 the LORD **s** unto Moses and Aaron, 559
20:23 the LORD **s** unto Moses and Aaron in 559
21: 5 the people **s** against God, and 1696
21:16 that *is* the well whereof the LORD **s** unto 559
22: 7 and **s** unto him the words of Balak. 1696
24:12 **S** I not also to thy messengers which thou 1696
25:10 And the LORD **s** unto Moses, saying, 1696
25:16 And the LORD **s** unto Moses, saying, 1696
26: 1 that the LORD **s** unto Moses and 559
26: 3 Eleazar the priest **s** with them in the plains 1696
26:52 And the LORD **s** unto Moses, saying, 1696
27: 6 And the LORD **s** unto Moses, saying, 559
27:15 And Moses **s** unto the LORD, saying, 1696
28: 1 And the LORD **s** unto Moses, saying, 1696
30: 1 Moses **s** unto the heads of the tribes 1696
31: 1 And the LORD **s** unto Moses, saying, 1696
31: 3 Moses **s** unto the people, saying, Arm some 1696
31:25 And the LORD **s** unto Moses, saying, 559
32: 2 children of Reuben came and **s** unto Moses, 559
32:25 and the children of Reuben **s** unto Moses, 559
33:50 the LORD **s** unto Moses in the plains of 1696
34: 1 And the LORD **s** unto Moses, saying, 1696
34:16 And the LORD **s** unto Moses, saying, 1696
35: 1 the LORD **s** unto Moses in the plains of 1696
35: 9 And the LORD **s** unto Moses, saying, 1696
36: 1 and **s** before Moses, and before the princes, 1696
Dt 1: 1 These *be* the words which Moses **s** unto all 1696
1: 3 *that* Moses **s** unto the children of Israel, 1696
1: 6 The LORD our God **s** unto us in Horeb, 1696
1: 9 I **s** unto you at that time, saying, I am not 559
1:43 So I **s** unto you; and you would not hear, 1696
2: 1 of the Red sea, as the LORD **s** unto me: 1696
2: 2 And the LORD **s** unto me, saying, 559
2:17 That the LORD **s** unto me, saying, 1696
4:12 the LORD **s** unto you out of the midst of 1696
4:15 **s** unto you in Horeb out of the midst of 1696
4:45 which Moses **s** unto the children of Israel, 1696
5:22 These words the LORD **s** unto all your 1696
5:28 voice of your words, when ye **s** unto me; 1696
9:10 which the LORD **s** with you in the mount 1696
9:13 Furthermore the LORD **s** unto me, saying, 559
10: 4 which the LORD **s** unto you in the mount 1696
13: 2 to pass, whereof he **s** unto thee, saying, 1696
27: 9 and the priests the Levites **s** unto all Israel, 1696
28:68 by the way where*of* I **s** unto thee, Thou shalt 559
31: 1 and **s** these words unto all Israel. 1696
31:30 Moses **s** in the ears of all the congregation 1696
32:44 **s** all the words of this song in the ears of 1696
32:48 the LORD **s** unto Moses that selfsame 1696
Jos 1: 1 that the LORD **s** unto Joshua the son of 559
1:12 half the tribe of Manasseh, **s** Joshua, saying, 559
3: 6 Joshua **s** unto the priests, saying, Take up 559
4: 1 that the LORD **s** unto Joshua, saying, 559
4: 8 of Jordan, as the LORD **s** unto Joshua, 1696
4:12 children of Israel, as Moses **s** unto them: 1696
4:15 And the LORD **s** unto Joshua, saying, 559
4:21 And he **s** unto the children of Israel, saying, 559
7: 2 **s** unto them, saying, Go up and view 559
9:11 and all the inhabitants of our country **s** to us, 559
9:22 called for them, and he **s** unto them, saying, 1696
10:12 **s** Joshua to the LORD in the day when 1696
14:10 *even* since the LORD **s** this word unto 1696
14:12 whereof the LORD **s** in that day; 1696
17:14 the children of Joseph **s** unto Joshua, 1696
17:17 Joshua **s** unto the house of Joseph, *even* to 559
20: 1 The LORD also **s** unto Joshua, saying, 1696
20: 2 whereof I **s** unto you by the hand of Moses: 1696
21: 2 they **s** unto them at Shiloh in the land of 1696
22: 8 he **s** unto them, saying, Return with much 559
22:15 of Gilead, and they **s** with them, saying, 1696
22:30 of Gad and the children of Manasseh **s**, 1696
23:14 the LORD your God **s** concerning you; 1696
24:27 words of the LORD which he **s** unto us: 1696
Jdg 2: 4 when the angel of the LORD **s** these 1696
8: 8 thence *to* Penuel, and **s** unto them likewise: 1696
8: 9 he **s** also unto the men of Penuel, saying, 559
9: 3 his mother's brethren **s** of him in the ears of 1696
9:37 Gaal **s** again and said, See there come 1696
15:13 they **s** unto him, saying, No; but we will bind 559
19:22 **s** to the master of the house, the old man, 559
Ru 4: 1 the kinsman of whom Boaz **s** came by; 1696
1Sa 1:13 Now Hannah, she **s** in her heart; only her 1696
7: 3 Samuel **s** unto all the house of Israel, saying, 559
9: 9 thus he **s**, Come, and let us go to the seer: 559
9:17 Behold the man whom I **s** to thee of: 559
10:16 whereof Samuel **s**, he told him not. 559
16: 4 Samuel did *that* which the LORD **s**, and 1696
17:23 and **s** according to the same words: 1696
17:26 David **s** to the men that stood by him, 559
17:28 Eliab his eldest brother heard when he **s** 1696
17:30 and **s** after the same manner: 559
17:31 when the words were heard which David **s**, 1696
18:23 Saul's servants **s** those words in the ears of 1696
18:24 told him, saying, On this manner **s** David. 1696
19: 1 Saul **s** to Jonathan his son, and to all his 1696
19: 4 Jonathan **s** good of David unto Saul his 1696
20:26 Nevertheless Saul **s** not any thing that day: 1696
25: 9 they **s** to Nabal according to all those words 1696
25:40 they **s** unto her, saying, David sent us unto 1696
28:12 the woman **s** to Saul, saying, Why hast thou 559
28:17 LORD hath done to him, as he **s** by me: 1696

1Sa 30: 6 for the people **s** of stoning him, because 559
2Sa 3:19 Abner also **s** in the ears of Benjamin: and 1696
5: 1 **s**, saying, Behold, we *are* thy bone and 559
5: 6 which **s** unto David, saying, Except thou 559
7: 7 **s** I a word with any of the tribes of Israel, 1696
12:18 we **s** unto him, and he would not hearken 1696
13:22 Absalom **s** unto his brother Amnon neither 1696
14: 4 when the woman of Tekoah **s** to the king, 559
17: 6 to Absalom, Absalom **s** unto him, saying, 559
20:18 she **s**, saying, They were wont to speak in 559
22: 1 David **s** unto the LORD the words of this 1696
23: 2 The Spirit of the LORD **s** by me, and 1696
23: 3 of Israel said, the Rock of Israel **s** to me, 1696
24:17 David **s** unto the LORD when he saw 559
1Ki 1:11 Wherefore Nathan **s** unto Bath-sheba 559
1:42 while he yet **s**, behold, Jonathan the son of 1696
2: 4 his word which he **s** concerning me, 1696
2:27 which he **s** concerning the house of Eli in 1696
3:22 *is* my son. Thus they **s** before the king. 1696
3:26 **s** the woman whose the living child *was* unto 559
4:32 he **s** three thousand proverbs: and his songs 1696
4:33 he **s** of trees, from the cedar tree that *is* in 1696
4:33 he **s** also of beasts, and of fowl, and 1696
5: 5 as the LORD **s** unto David my father, 1696
6:12 with thee, which I **s** unto David thy father: 1696
8:12 **s** Solomon, The LORD said that *he* would 559
8:15 which **s** with his mouth unto David my 1696
8:20 LORD hath performed his word that he **s**, 1696
12: 3 Israel came, and **s** unto Rehoboam, saying, 1696
12: 7 they **s** unto him, saying, If thou wilt be a 1696
12:10 that were grown up with him **s** unto him, 1696
12:10 thou speak unto this people that **s** unto thee, 1696
12:14 **s** to them after the counsel of the young 1696
12:15 which the LORD **s** by Ahijah the Shilonite 1696
13:18 an angel **s** unto me by the word of 1696
13:26 word of the LORD, which he **s** unto him. 1696
13:27 he **s** to his sons, saying, Saddle me the ass. 1696
13:31 that he **s** to his sons, saying, When I am 559
14:18 which he **s** by the hand of his servant 1696
15:29 which he **s** by his servant Ahijah 1696
16:12 which he **s** against Baasha by Jehu 1696
16:34 which he **s** by Joshua the son of Nun. 1696
17:16 word of the LORD, which he **s** by Elijah. 1696
20:28 **s** unto the king of Israel, and said, Thus saith 559
21: 2 Ahab **s** unto Naboth, saying, Give me thy 1696
21: 6 Because I **s** unto Naboth the Jezreelite, and 1696
21:23 of Jezebel also **s** the LORD, saying, 1696
22:13 that was gone to call Micaiah **s** unto him, 1696
22:38 unto the word of the LORD which he **s**. 1696
2Ki 1: 9 he **s** unto him, Thou man of God, the king 1696
2:22 to the saying of Elisha which he **s**. 1696
5:13 and **s** unto him, and said, My father, 1696
7:17 who **s** when the king came down to him. 1696
8: 1 **s** Elisha unto the woman, whose son he had 1696
9:12 he said, Thus and thus **s** he to me, saying, 559
9:36 which he **s** by his servant Elijah 1696
10:10 which the LORD **s** concerning the house 1696
10:10 for the LORD hath done *that* which he **s** 1696
10:17 saying of the LORD, which he **s** to Elijah. 1696
14:25 which he **s** by the hand of his servant 1696
15:12 word of the LORD which he **s** unto Jehu, 1696
17:26 Wherefore they **s** to the king of Assyria, 559
18:28 **s**, saying, Hear the word of the great king, 1696
21:10 the LORD **s** by his servants the prophets, 1696
22:19 when thou heardest what I **s** against this 1696
24: 2 which he **s** by his servants the prophets. 1696
25:28 he **s** kindly to him, and set his throne above 1696
1Ch 15:16 David **s** to the chief of the Levites to appoint 559
17: 6 **s** I a word to any of the judges of Israel, 1696
21: 9 the LORD **s** unto Gad, David's seer, 1696
21:19 which he **s** in the name of the LORD. 1696
2Ch 1: 2 Solomon **s** unto all Israel, to the captains of 559
6: 4 he **s** with his mouth to my father David, 1696
10: 3 and all Israel came and **s** to Rehoboam, 1696
10: 7 they **s** unto him, saying, If thou be kind to 1696
10:10 that were brought up with him **s** unto him, 1696
10:10 Thus shalt thou answer the people that **s** 1696
10:15 which he **s** by the hand of Ahijah 1696
18:12 the messenger that went to call Micaiah **s** to 1696
18:19 one **s** saying after this manner, and 559
30:22 Hezekiah **s** comfortably unto all the Levites 1696
32: 6 the city, and **s** comfortably to them, saying, 1696
32:16 his servants **s** yet *more* against the LORD 1696
32:19 they **s** against the God of Jerusalem, 1696
32:24 and he **s** unto him, and he gave him a sign. 559
33:10 the LORD **s** to Manasseh, and to his 1696
33:18 the words of the seers that **s** to him in 1696
34:22 and they **s** to her to that *effect*. 1696
35:25 the singing *women* **s** of Josiah in their 559
Ne 4: 2 he **s** before his brethren and the army of 559
8: 1 they **s** unto Ezra the scribe to bring the book 559
13:24 their children **s** half in the speech of 1696
Est 3: 4 when they **s** daily unto him, and 559
4:10 Again Esther **s** unto Hatach, and gave him 559
8: 3 Esther **s** yet again before the king, and 1696
Job 2:13 seven nights, and none **s** a word unto him: 1696
3: 2 And Job **s**, and said, 6030
19:18 despised me; I arose, and they **s** against me. 1696
29:22 After my words they **s** not again; and NIH
32:16 (for they **s** not, but stood still, *and* 1696
35: 1 Elihu **s** moreover, and said, 6030
Ps 18: T who **s** unto the LORD the words of this 1696
33: 9 For he **s**, and it was *done*; he commanded, 559
39: 3 the fire burned: *then* **s** I with my tongue, 1696
78:19 Yea, they **s** against God; they said, Can 1696
99: 7 He **s** unto them in the cloudy pillar: 1696
105:31 He **s**, and there came divers sorts *of flies*, 559
105:34 He **s**, and the locusts came, and caterpillars, 559
106:33 so that he **s** **unadvisedly** with his lips. 981
Pr 30: 1 the man **s** unto Ithiel, even unto Ithiel and 5002
SS 2:10 My beloved **s**, and said unto me, Rise up, 6030
5: 6 my soul failed when he **s**: I sought him, but 1696
Isa 7:10 Moreover the LORD **s** again unto Ahaz, 1696
8: 5 The LORD **s** also unto me again, saying, 1696
8:11 For the LORD **s** thus to me with a strong 559

Isa 20: 2 At the same time **s** the LORD by Isaiah 1696
65:12 when I **s**, ye did not hear; but did evil 1696
66: 4 did answer; when I **s**, they did not hear: 1696
Jer 7:13 I **s** unto you, rising up early and speaking, 1696
7:22 For I **s** not unto your fathers, 1696
8: 6 and heard, *but* they **s** not aright: 1696
14:14 I commanded them, neither **s** unto them: 1696
19: 5 nor **s** *it*, neither came *it* into my mind: 1696
20: 8 For since I **s**, I cried out, I cried violence 1696
22:21 I **s** unto thee in thy prosperity; *but* 1696
25: 2 The which Jeremiah the prophet **s** unto all 1696
26:11 **s** the priests and the prophets unto 559
26:12 **s** Jeremiah unto all the princes and to all 559
26:17 **s** to all the assembly of the people, saying, 559
26:18 **s** to all the people of Judah, saying, 559
27:12 I **s** also to Zedekiah king of Judah 1696
27:16 Also I **s** to the priests and to all this people, 1696
28: 1 **s** unto me in the house of the LORD, 559
28:11 Hananiah **s** in the presence of all the people, 559
30: 4 these *are* the words that the LORD **s** 1696
31:20 for since I **s** against him, I do earnestly 1696
34: 6 Jeremiah the prophet **s** all these words unto 1696
36: 2 all the nations, from the day I **s** unto thee, 1696
37: 2 which he **s** by the prophet Jeremiah. 1696
38: 8 the king's house, and **s** to the king, saying, 1696
40:15 Johanan the son of Kareah **s** to Gedaliah in 559
43: 2 **s** Azariah the son of Hoshaiah, and 559
45: 1 The word that Jeremiah the prophet **s** unto 1696
46:13 The word that the LORD **s** to Jeremiah 1696
50: 1 The word that the LORD **s** against 1696
51:12 done that which he **s** against the inhabitants 1696
52:32 **s** kindly unto him, and set his throne above 1696
Eze 1:28 my face, and I heard a voice of one that **s**. 1696
2: 2 the spirit entered into me when he **s** unto 1696
2: 2 my feet, that I heard him that **s** unto me. 1696
3:24 and **s** with me, and said unto me, Go, 1696
10: 2 he **s** unto the man clothed with linen, and 559
11:25 I **s** unto them of the captivity all the things 1696
24:18 So I **s** unto the people in the morning: and 1696
Da 1: 3 the king **s** unto Ashpenaz the master of his 559
2: 4 **s** the Chaldeans to the king in Syriack, 1696
3: 9 They **s** and said to the king 6032
3:14 Nebuchadnezzar **s** and said unto them, *Is it* 6032
3:19 *therefore* he **s**, and commanded that *they* 6032
3:24 *and* **s**, and said unto his counsellers, 6032
3:26 *and* **s**, and said, Shadrach, Meshach, and 6032
3:28 *Then* Nebuchadnezzar **s**, and said, 6032
4:19 The king **s**, and said, Belteshazzar, let not 6032
4:30 The king **s**, and said, *Is* not this great 6032
5: 7 *And* the king **s**, and said to the wise *men* of 6032
5:10 *and* the queen **s** and said, O king, live for 6032
5:13 *And* the king **s** and said unto Daniel, 6032
6:12 **s** before the king concerning the king's 560
6:16 *Now* the king **s** and said unto Daniel, 6032
6:20 *and* the king **s** and said to Daniel, O Daniel, 6032
7: 2 Daniel **s** and said, I saw in my vision by 6032
7:11 voice of the great words which the horn **s**: 4449
7:20 a mouth that **s** very great *things*, whose 4449
8:13 saint said unto that certain *saint* which **s**, 1696
9: 6 which **s** in thy name to our kings, 1696
9:12 which he **s** against us, and against our 1696
10:16 **s**, and said unto him that stood before me, 1696
Hos 12: 4 him *in* Beth-el, and there he **s** with us; 1696
13: 1 When Ephraim **s** trembling, he exalted 1696
Jnh 2:10 the LORD **s** unto the fish, and it vomited 559
Hag 1:13 **s** Haggai the LORD'S messenger in 559
Zec 1:21 he **s**, saying, These *are* the horns which have 559
3: 4 and **s** unto those that stood before him, 559
4: 4 and **s** to the angel that talked with me, 559
4: 6 he answered and **s** unto me, saying, This *is* 559
6: 8 he upon me, and **s** unto me, saying, Behold, 1696
Mal 3:16 they that feared the LORD **s** often one to 1696
Mt 9:18 While he **s** these *things* unto them, behold, *2980*
9:33 when the devil was cast out, the dumb **s**: *2980*
12:22 that the blind and dumb both **s** and saw. *2980*
13: 3 And he **s** many *things* unto them in *2980*
13:33 Another parable **s** he unto them; *2980*
13:34 All these *things* **s** Jesus unto the multitude *2980*
13:34 and without a parable **s** he not unto them: *2980*
14:27 But straightway Jesus **s** unto them, saying, *2980*
16:11 How *is it that* ye do not understand that I **s** *3004*
17: 5 While he yet **s**, behold, a bright cloud *2980*
17:13 Then the disciples understood that he **s** unto *3004*
21:45 they perceived that he **s** of them. *3004*
22: 1 and **s** unto them again by parables, *3004*
23: 1 Then **s** Jesus to the multitude, and to his *2980*
26:47 And while he yet **s**, lo, Judas, one of *2980*
28:18 And Jesus came and **s** unto them, saying, *2980*
Mk 3: 9 And he **s** to his disciples, that a small ship *3004*
4:33 And with many such parables **s** he the word *2980*
4:34 But without a parable **s** he not unto them: *2980*
5:35 While he yet **s**, there came from the ruler of *2980*
7:35 of his tongue was loosed, and he **s** plain. *2980*
8:32 And he **s** *that* saying openly. And Peter *2980*
9:18 I **s** to thy disciples that they should cast him *3004*
12:26 how in the bush God **s** unto him, saying, *3004*
14:31 But he **s** the more vehemently, If I should *3004*
14:39 and prayed, and **s** the same words. *3004*
14:43 while he yet **s**, cometh Judas, one of *2980*
Lk 1:42 And she **s** **out** with a loud voice, *400*
1:55 (As he **s** to our fathers), to Abraham, and *2980*
1:64 and his tongue *loosed*, and he **s**, and *2980*
1:70 (As he **s** by the mouth of his holy prophets, *2980*
2:38 **s** of him to all them that looked for *2980*
2:50 not the saying which he **s** unto them. *2980*
4:36 and **s** among themselves, saying, What a *4814*
5:36 And he **s** also a parable unto them; No *man* *3004*
6:39 And he **s** a parable unto them, Can *3004*
7:39 had bidden him saw *it*, he **s** within himself, *3004*
8: 4 to him out of every city, he **s** by a parable: *3004*
8:49 While he yet **s**, there cometh one from *2980*
9:11 and **s** unto them of the kingdom of God, *2980*
9:31 **s** of his decease which he should *3004*
9:34 While he thus **s**, there came a cloud, and *3004*
11:14 when the devil was gone out, the dumb **s**; *2980*

S

Lk 11:27 as he s these *things,* a certain woman of *3004*
11:37 And as *he* s, a certain Pharisee besought *2980*
12:16 And he s a parable unto them, saying, *3004*
13: 6 He s also this parable; A certain *man* had a *3004*
14: 3 And Jesus answering s unto the lawyers *3004*
15: 3 And he s this parable unto them, saying, *3004*
18: 1 And he s a parable unto them *to this end,* *3004*
18: 9 And he s this parable unto certain which *3004*
19:11 these *things,* he added and s a parable, *3004*
20: 2 And s unto him, saying, Tell us, by what *3004*
21: 5 And as some s of the temple, how it was *3004*
21:29 And he s to them a parable; Behold the fig *3004*
22:47 And while he yet s, behold a multitude, and *2980*
22:60 while he yet s, the cock crew. *2980*
22:65 And many other *things* blasphemously s *3004*
23:20 willing to release Jesus, s again to *them.* *4377*
24: 6 remember how he s unto you when he was *2980*
24:36 And as they thus s, Jesus himself stood in *2980*
24:44 These *are* the words which I s unto you, *2980*
Jn 1:15 and cried, saying, This was he of whom I s, *3004*
2:21 But he s of the temple of his body. *3004*
6:71 He s of Judas Iscariot *the son* of Simon: *3004*
7:13 Howbeit no *man* s openly of him for fear of *2980*
7:39 (But this s he of the Spirit, which they that *3004*
7:46 Never man s like this man. *2980*
8:12 Then s Jesus again unto them, saying, I am *2980*
8:20 These words s Jesus in the treasury, as he *2980*
8:27 They understood not that he s to them of *3004*
8:30 As he s these *words,* many believed on *2980*
9:22 These *words* s his parents, because *3004*
9:29 We know that God s unto Moses: *as for* this *2980*
10: 6 This parable s Jesus unto them: but *3004*
10: 6 *things* they were which he s unto them. *2980*
10:41 all *things* that John s of this *man* were true. *3004*
11:13 Howbeit Jesus s of his death: but *3004*
11:51 And this s he not of himself: but being high *3004*
11:56 and s among themselves, as they stood in *3004*
12:29 it thundered: others said, An angel s to him. *2980*
12:36 These *things* s Jesus, and departed, and *2980*
12:38 which he s, Lord, who hath believed our *3004*
12:41 when he saw his glory, and s of him. *2980*
13:22 one on another, doubting of whom he s. *3004*
13:24 should ask who it should be of whom he s. *3004*
13:28 knew for what intent he s this unto him. *3004*
17: 1 These *words* s Jesus, and lift up his eyes to *2980*
18: 9 the saying might be fulfilled, which he s, *3004*
18:16 and s unto her that kept the door, and *3004*
18:20 answered him, I s openly to the world; *2980*
18:32 which he s, signifying what death he should *3004*
21:19 This s he, signifying by what death he *3004*
Ac 1:16 mouth of David s **before** concerning Judas, *4302*
2:31 *this* before, s of the resurrection of Christ, *2980*
4: 1 And as they s unto the people, the priests, *2980*
4:31 and they s the word of God with boldness. *2980*
6:10 the wisdom and the spirit by which he s. *2980*
7: 6 And God s on this wise, That his seed *2980*
7:38 the angel which s to him in the mount Sina, *2980*
8: 6 gave heed unto those *things* which Philip s, *3004*
8:26 And *the* angel of the Lord s unto Philip, *2980*
9:29 And he s boldly in the name of the Lord *2980*
10: 7 And when the angel which s unto Cornelius *2980*
10:15 And *the* voice *s* unto him again the second NIG
10:44 While Peter yet s these words, the Holy *2980*
11:20 s unto the Grecians, preaching the Lord *2980*
13:45 s **against** those *things* which were spoken by *483*
14: 1 and so s, that a great multitude both of *2980*
16:13 s unto the women which resorted *thither.* *2980*
16:32 And they s unto him the word of the Lord, *2980*
18: 9 Then s the Lord to Paul in the night by a *3004*
18:25 he s and taught diligently the *things* of *2980*
19: 6 and they s with tongues, and prophesied. *2980*
19: 8 and s **boldly** for the space of three months, *3955*
19: 9 but s **evil** of *that* way before the multitude, *2551*
20:38 most *of all* for the words which he s, *3004*
21:40 he s **unto** *them* in the Hebrew tongue, *4377*
22: 2 (And when they heard that he s in *4377*
22: 9 they heard not the voice of him that s to *2980*
26:24 And as he thus s **for** himself, Festus said *626*
28:19 But when the Jews s **against** *it,* I was *483*
28:21 that came shewed or s any harm of thee. *2980*
28:25 Well s the Holy Ghost by Esaias *2980*
1Co 13:11 When I was a child, I s as a child, *2980*
14: 5 I would that ye all s with tongues, but *2980*
2Co 7:14 but as we s all *things* to you in truth, even *2980*
Gal 4:15 Where is then the blessedness you s of? for NIG
Heb 1: 1 in divers manners s in time past unto *2980*
4: 4 For *he* s in a certain place of the seventh *3004*
7:14 of which tribe Moses s nothing concerning *2980*
12:25 not who refused him that s on earth, *5537*
2Pe 1:21 holy men of God s *as they were* moved by *2980*
Rev 1:12 And I turned to see the voice that s with *2980*
10: 8 And the voice which I heard from heaven s *2980*
13:11 two horns like a lamb, and he s as a dragon. *2980*

SPAKEST (10) [SPEAK]
Jdg 13:11 *Art* thou the man that s unto the woman? 1696
17: 2 s of also in mine ears, behold, the silver *is* 559
1Sa 28:21 unto thy words which thou s unto me. 1696
1Ki 8:24 thou s also with thy mouth, and 1696
8:26 which thou s unto thy servant David my 1696
8:53 as thou s by the hand of Moses thy servant, 1696
2Ch 6:15 s with thy mouth, and hast fulfilled *it* with 1696
Ne 9:13 s with them from heaven, and gavest them 1696
Ps 89:19 thou s in vision to thy holy one, and saidst, 1696
Jer 48:27 for since thou s of him, thou skippedst for 1697

SPAN (8) [SPANNED]
Ex 28:16 a s *shall be* the length thereof, and a span 2239
28:16 and a s *shall be* the breadth thereof. 2239
39: 9 a s *was* the length thereof, and a span 2239
39: 9 and a s the breadth thereof, *being* doubled. 2239
1Sa 17: 4 whose height *was* six cubits and a s. 2239
Isa 40:12 meted out heaven with the s, and 2239
La 2:20 eat their fruit, *and* children of a s **long**? 2949
Eze 43:13 the edge thereof round about *shall be* a s: 2239

SPANNED (1) [SPAN]
Isa 48:13 and my right hand hath s the heavens: 2946

SPARE (40) [SPARED, SPARETH, SPARING, SPARINGLY]
Ge 18:24 not s the place for the fifty righteous that 5375
18:26 then I will s all the place for their sakes. 5375
Dt 13: 8 neither shalt thou s, neither shalt thou 2550
29:20 The LORD will not s him, but then 5545
1Sa 15: 3 destroy all that they have, and s them not; 2550
Ne 13:22 s me according to the greatness of 2347+5921
Job 6:10 harden myself in sorrow; let him not s: 2550
16:13 cleaveth my reins asunder, and doth not s; 2550
20:13 *Though* he s it, and forsake it not; but 2550
27:22 For *God* shall cast upon him, and not s: 2550
30:10 far from me, and s not to spit in my face. 2820
Ps 39:13 O s me, that I may recover strength, before 8159
72:13 He shall s the poor and needy, and 2347+5921
Pr 6:34 he will not s in the day of vengeance. 2550
19:18 is hope, and let not thy soul s for his crying. 5375
Isa 9:19 fuel of the fire: no man shall s his brother. 2550
13:18 of the womb; their eye shall not s children. 2347
30:14 that is broken in pieces; he shall not s: 2550
54: 2 s not, lengthen thy cords, and 2820
58: 1 Cry aloud, s not, lift up thy voice like a 2820
Jer 13:14 I will not pity, nor s, nor have mercy, but 2347
21: 7 he shall not s them, neither have pity, 2347
50:14 bend the bow, shoot at her, s no arrows: 2550
51: 3 s ye not her young men; destroy ye utterly 2550
Eze 5:11 also diminish *thee;* neither shall mine eye s, 2347
7: 4 mine eye shall not s thee, neither will I 2347
7: 9 mine eye shall not s, neither will I have 2347
8:18 mine eye shall not s, neither will I have 2347
9: 5 let not your eye s, neither have ye pity: 2347
9:10 *as for* me also, mine eye shall not s, 2347
24:14 neither will I s, neither will I repent; 2347
Joel 2:17 S thy people, O LORD, and give not thine 2347
Jnh 4:11 should not I s Nineveh, *that* great city, 2347
Hab 1:17 and not s continually to slay the nations? 2550
Mal 3:17 I will s them, as a man spareth his own son 2550
Lk 15:17 of my father's **have** bread **enough and to** s, *4052*
Ro 11:21 *take heed* lest he also s not thee. *5339*
1Co 7:28 shall have trouble in the flesh: but I s you. *5339*
2Co 1:23 that to s you I came not as yet unto Corinth. *5339*
13: 2 all other, that, if I come again, I will not s: *5339*

SPARED (12) [SPARE]
1Sa 15: 9 Saul and the people s Agag, and the best of 2550
15:15 for the people s the best of the sheep and 2550
24:10 *mine eye* s thee; and I said, I will not put 2347
2Sa 12: 4 he s to take of his own flock and of his own 2550
21: 7 the king s Mephibosheth, the son of 2550
2Ki 5:20 my master hath s Naaman this Syrian, 2820
Ps 78:50 he s not their soul from death, but 2820
Eze 20:17 Nevertheless mine eye s them from 2347
Ro 8:32 He that s not his own Son, but *5339*
11:21 For if God s not the natural branches, *5339*
2Pe 2: 4 For if God s not the angels that sinned, but *5339*
2: 5 And s not the old world, but saved Noah *5339*

SPARETH (4) [SPARE]
Pr 13:24 He that s his rod hateth his son: but he that 2820
17:27 He that hath knowledge s his words: *and* 2820
21:26 day long: but the righteous giveth and s not. 2820
Mal 3:17 as a man s his own son that serveth him. 2550

SPARING (1) [SPARE]
Ac 20:29 wolves enter in among you, not s the flock. *5339*

SPARINGLY (2) [SPARE]
2Co 9: 6 But this *I say,* He which soweth s shall reap *5340*
9: 6 which soweth sparingly shall reap also s; *5340*

SPARK (2) [SPARKS]
Job 18: 5 put out, and the s of his fire shall not shine. 7632
Isa 1:31 the maker of it as a s, and they shall both 5213

SPARKLED (1)
Eze 1: 7 they s like the colour of burnished brass. 5340

SPARKS (4) [SPARK]
Job 5: 7 unto trouble, as the s fly upward. 1121+7565
41:19 go burning lamps, *and* s of fire leap out. 3590
Isa 50:11 that compass *yourselves* about with s: 2131
50:11 your fire, and in the s *that* ye have kindled. 2131

SPARROW (2) [SPARROWS]
Ps 84: 3 the s hath found a house, and the swallow a 6833
102: 7 and am as a s alone upon the housetop. 6833

SPARROWS (4) [SPARROW]
Mt 10:29 Are not two s sold for a farthing? and *4765*
10:31 ye are of more value than many s. *4765*
Lk 12: 6 Are not five s sold for two farthings, and *4765*
12: 7 ye are of more value than many s. *4765*

SPAT (1) [SPIT]
Jn 9: 6 he s on the ground, and made clay of *4429*

SPEAK (513) [SPAKE, SPAKEST, SPEAKER, SPEAKEST, SPEAKETH, SPEAKING, SPEAKINGS, SPEECH, SPEECHES, SPEECHLESS, SPOKEN, SPOKESMAN, UNSPEAKABLE]
Ge 18:27 I have taken upon me to s unto the Lord, 1696
18:30 Oh let not the Lord be angry, and I will s: 1696
18:31 I have taken upon me to s unto the Lord: 1696
18:32 be angry, and I will s yet but *this* once: 1696
24:33 I have told mine errand. And he said, **S on.** 1696
24:50 we cannot s unto thee bad or good. 1696
27: 6 I heard thy father s unto Esau thy brother, 1696
31:24 Take heed that thou s not to Jacob either 1696
31:29 Take thou heed that thou s not to Jacob 1696
32: 4 Thus shall ye s unto my lord Esau; 559
32:19 On this manner shall you s unto Esau, 1696
37: 4 and could not s peaceably unto him. 1696
44:16 what shall we s? or how shall we clear 1696
44:18 s a word in my lord's ears, and let not thine 1696
50: 4 s, I pray you, in the ears of Pharaoh, saying, 1696
Ex 4:14 I know that he can s **well**. And also, 1696+1696
4:15 thou shalt s unto him, and put words in his 1696
5:23 For since I came to Pharaoh to s in thy 1696
6:11 Go in, s unto Pharaoh king of Egypt, 1696
6:29 s thou unto Pharaoh king of Egypt all that I 1696
7: 2 Thou shalt s all that I command thee: and 1696
7: 2 Aaron thy brother shall s unto Pharaoh, 1696
7: 9 When Pharaoh shall s unto you, saying, 1696
11: 2 S now in the ears of the people, and 1696
12: 3 S ye unto all the congregation of Israel, 1696
14: 2 S unto the children of Israel, that they turn 1696
14:15 s unto the children of Israel, that they go 1696
16:12 s unto them, saying, At even ye shall eat 1696
19: 6 These *are* the words which thou shalt s unto 1696
19: 9 that the people may hear when I s with 1696
20:19 S thou with us, and we will hear: 1696
20:19 but let not God s with us, lest we die. 1696
23: 2 neither shalt thou s in a cause to decline 6030
23:22 indeed obey his voice, and do all that I s; 1696
25: 2 S unto the children of Israel, that they bring 1696
28: 3 thou shalt s unto all *that are* wise hearted, 1696
29:42 where I will meet you, to s there unto thee. 1696
30:31 thou shalt s unto the children of Israel, 1696
31:13 S thou also unto the children of Israel, 1696
32:12 Wherefore should the Egyptians s, and say, 559
34:34 went in before the LORD to s with him, 1696
34:35 face again, until he went in to s with him. 1696
Lev 1: 2 S unto the children of Israel, and say unto 1696
4: 2 S unto the children of Israel, saying, If a 1696
6:25 S unto Aaron and to his sons, saying, 1696
7:23 S unto the children of Israel, saying, 1696
7:29 S unto the children of Israel, saying, 1696
9: 3 unto the children of Israel thou shalt s, 1696
11: 2 S unto the children of Israel, saying, 1696
12: 2 S unto the children of Israel, saying, If a 1696
15: 2 S unto the children of Israel, and say unto 1696
16: 2 said unto Moses, S unto Aaron thy brother, 1696
17: 2 S unto Aaron, and unto his sons, and 1696
18: 2 S unto the children of Israel, and say unto 1696
19: 2 S unto all the congregation of the children 1696
21: 1 S unto the priests the sons of Aaron, and 559
21:17 S unto Aaron, saying, Whosoever *he be* of 1696
22: 2 S unto Aaron and to his sons, that they 1696
22:18 S unto Aaron, and to his sons, and unto all 1696
23: 2 S unto the children of Israel, and say unto 1696
23:10 S unto the children of Israel, and say unto 1696
23:24 S unto the children of Israel, saying, In 1696
23:34 S unto the children of Israel, saying, The 1696
24:15 thou shalt s unto the children of Israel, 1696
25: 2 S unto the children of Israel, and say unto 1696
27: 2 S unto the children of Israel, and say unto 1696
Nu 5: 6 S unto the children of Israel, When a man 1696
5:12 S unto the children of Israel, and say unto 1696
6: 2 S unto the children of Israel, and say unto 1696
6:23 S unto Aaron and unto his sons, saying, 1696
7:89 of the congregation to s with him, 1696
8: 2 S unto Aaron, and say unto him, 1696
9:10 S unto the children of Israel, saying, If any 1696
12: 6 in a vision, *and* will s unto him in a dream. 1696
12: 8 With him will I s mouth to mouth, 1696
12: 8 were ye not afraid to s against my servant 1696
14:15 which have heard the fame of thee will s, 559
15: 2 S unto the children of Israel, and say unto 1696
15:18 S unto the children of Israel, and say unto 1696
15:38 S unto the children of Israel, and bid them 1696
16:24 S unto the congregation, saying, Get you up 1696
16:37 S unto Eleazar the son of Aaron the priest, 559
17: 2 S unto the children of Israel, and take of 1696
18:26 Thus s unto the Levites, and say unto them, 1696
19: 2 saying, S unto the children of Israel, 1696
20: 8 and s ye unto the rock before their eyes; 1696
21:27 Wherefore they that s **in proverbs** say, 4911
22: 8 word again, as the LORD shall s unto me: 1696
22:35 only the word that I shall s unto thee, 1696
22:35 I shall speak unto thee, that thou shalt s. 1696
22:38 that God putteth in my mouth, that shall I s. 1696
23: 5 Return unto Balak, and thus thou shalt s. 1696
23:12 Must I not take heed to s that which 1696
24:13 *but* what the LORD saith, that will I s? 1696
27: 7 The daughters of Zelophehad s right: 1696
27: 8 thou shalt s unto the children of Israel, 1696
33:51 S unto the children of Israel, and say unto 1696
35:10 S unto the children of Israel, and say unto 1696
Dt 3:26 s no more unto me of this matter. 1696
5: 1 judgments which I s in your ears *this* day, 1696
5:27 s thou unto us all that the LORD our God 1696
5:27 that the LORD our God shall s unto thee; 1696
5:31 I will s unto thee all the commandments, 1696
9: 4 S not thou in thine heart, after that 559
11: 2 for *I s* not with your children which have NIH
18:18 he shall s unto them all that I shall 1696
18:19 my words which he shall s in my name, 1696
18:20 which shall presume to s a word in my 1696
18:20 which I have not commanded him to s, or 1696
18:20 or that shall s in the name of other gods, 1696
20: 2 priest shall approach and s unto the people, 1696
20: 5 the officers shall s unto the people, saying, 1696
20: 8 the officers shall s further unto the people, 1696
25: 8 of his city shall call him, and s unto him: 1696
26: 5 thou shalt s and say before the LORD thy 6030
27:14 the Levites shall s, and say unto all the men 6030
31:28 that I may s these words in their ears, 1696
32: 1 Give ear, O ye heavens, and I will s; and 1696
Jos 4:10 commanded Joshua to s unto the people, 1696
20: 2 S to the children of Israel, saying, 1696
22:24 In time to come your children might s unto 559
Jdg 5:10 S, ye that ride on white asses, ye that sit in 7878
6:39 hot against me, and I will s but *this* once: 1696
9: 2 S, I pray you, in the ears of all the men of 1696

Jdg 19: 3 to s friendly unto her, *and* to bring her 1696
19:30 of it, take advice, and s *your minds.* 1696
21:13 the whole congregation sent *some* to s to 1696
1Sa 3: 9 he call thee, that thou shalt say, S, LORD; 1696
3:10 Samuel answered, S; for thy servant 1696
25:17 a son of Belial, that *a man* cannot s to him. 1696
25:24 s in thine audience, and hear the words of 1696
2Sa 3:19 Abner went also to s in the ears of David in 1696
3:27 Joab took him aside in the gate to s with 1696
7:17 all this vision, so did Nathan s unto David. 1696
13:13 Now therefore, I pray thee, s unto the king; 1696
14: 3 to the king, and s on this manner unto him. 1696
14:12 s *one* word unto my lord the king. 1696
14:13 for the king doth s this thing as one which 1696
14:15 that I am come to s of this thing unto my 1696
14:15 handmaid said, I will now s unto the king; 1696
14:18 woman said, Let my lord the king now s. 1696
17: 6 shall we do *after* his saying? if not; s thou. 1696
19: 7 and s comfortably unto thy servants: 1696
19:10 why s ye **not a word** of bringing the king 2790
19:11 S unto the elders of Judah, saying, 1696
20:16 Come near hither, that I may s with thee. 1696
20:18 were **wont to** s in old time, saying, 1696+1696
1Ki 2:17 he said, S, I pray thee, unto Solomon 559
2:18 Well; I will s for thee unto the king. 1696
2:19 king Solomon, to s unto him for Adonijah. 1696
12: 7 s good words to them, then they will be thy 1696
12:10 Thus shalt thou s unto this people that spake 559
12:23 S unto Rehoboam, the son of Solomon, 559
21:19 thou shalt s unto him, saying, Thus saith 1696
21:19 thou shalt s unto him, saying, Thus saith 1696
22:13 of one of them, and s *that which is* good. 1696
22:14 the LORD saith unto me, that will I s. 1696
22:24 of the LORD from me to s unto thee? 1696
2Ki 18:19 S ye now to Hezekiah, Thus saith the great 559
18:26 and Joah, unto Rab-shakeh, S, I pray thee, 1696
18:27 to thy master, and to thee, to s these words? 1696
19:10 Thus shall ye s to Hezekiah king of Judah, 559
1Ch 17:15 all this vision, so did Nathan s unto David. 1696
17:18 What can David *s* more to thee for NIH
2Ch 10: 7 and please them, and s good words to them, 1696
11: 3 S unto Rehoboam the son of Solomon, 559
18:12 be like one of theirs, and s thou good. 1696
18:13 even what my God saith, that will I s. 1696
18:23 of the LORD from me to s unto thee? 1696
32:17 God of Israel, and to s against him, saying, 559
Ne 13:24 could not s in the Jews' language, but 1696
Est 5:14 to morrow s thou unto the king that 559
6: 4 to s unto the king to hang Mordecai on 559
Job 7:11 I will s in the anguish of my spirit; 1696
8: 2 How long wilt thou s these *things?* and 4448
9:19 If *I s* of strength, lo, *he is* strong: and if of NIH
9:35 *Then* would I s, and not fear him; but *it is* 1696
10: 1 I will s in the bitterness of my soul. 1696
11: 5 O that God would s, and open his lips 1696
12: 8 Or s to the earth, and it shall teach thee: and 7878
13: 3 Surely I would s to the Almighty, and 1696
13: 7 Will you s wickedly for God? and 1696
13:13 that I may s, and let come on me what *will.* 1696
13:22 or let me s, and answer thou me. 1696
16: 4 I also could s as ye *do:* if your soul were in 1696
16: 6 Though I s, my grief is not asswaged: and 1696
18: 2 of words? mark, and afterwards we will s. 1696
21: 3 Suffer me that I may s; and after that I have 1696
27: 4 My lips shall not s wickedness, nor my 1696
32: 7 Days should s, and multitude of years 1696
32:20 I will s, that I may be refreshed: I will open 1696
33:31 unto me: hold thy peace, and I will s. 1696
33:32 answer me: s, for I desire to justify thee. 1696
34:33 and not I: therefore s what thou knowest. 1696
36: 2 I will shew thee that *I have* yet to s on 4405
37:20 Shall it be told him that I s? if a man speak, 1696
37:20 if a man s, surely he shall be swallowed up. 559
41: 3 unto thee? will he s soft *words* unto thee? 1696
42: 4 Hear, I beseech thee, and I will s: I will 1696
Ps 2: 5 shall he s unto them in his wrath, and 1696
5: 6 Thou shalt destroy them that s leasing: 1696
12: 2 They s vanity every one with his 1696
12: 2 *and* with a double heart do they s. 1696
17:10 own fat: *with* their mouth they s proudly. 1696
28: 3 which s peace to their neighbours, but 1696
29: 9 in his temple doth every one s of *his* glory. 559
31:18 which s grievous things proudly and 1696
35:20 For they s not peace: but they devise 1696
35:28 my tongue shall s of thy righteousness *and* 1897
38:12 they that seek my hurt s mischievous 1696
40: 5 s *of them,* they are moe than can be 1696
41: 5 Mine enemies s evil of me, When shall he 559
45: 1 I s of the things which I have made touching 559
49: 3 My mouth shall s of wisdom; and 1696
50: 7 Hear, O my people, and I will s; O Israel, 1696
52: 3 *and* lying rather than to s righteousness. 1696
58: 1 Do ye indeed s righteousness, 1696
59:12 and for cursing and lying *which* they s. 5608
63:11 the mouth of them that s lies shall be 1696
69:12 They that sit in the gate s against me; and 7878
71:10 For mine enemies s against me; and they that 559
73: 8 and s wickedly *concerning* oppression: 1696
73: 8 *concerning* oppression: they s loftily. 1696
73:15 If I say, I will s thus; behold, I should 5608
75: 5 your horn on high: s *not* with a stiff neck. 1696
77: 4 I am *so* troubled that I cannot s. 1696
85: 8 I will hear what God the LORD will s: 1696
85: 8 for he will s peace unto his people, and 1696
94: 4 *long* shall they utter *and* s hard *things? and* 1696
109:20 and of them that s evil against my soul. 1696
115: 5 They have mouths, but they s not: 1696
115: 7 neither s they through their throat. 1897
119:23 Princes also did sit *and* s against me: *but* 1696
119:46 I will s of thy testimonies also before kings, 1696
119:172 My tongue shall s of thy word: for all thy 6030
120: 7 *for* peace: but when I s, they *are* for war. 1696
127: 5 they shall s with the enemies in the gate. 1696
135:16 They have mouths, but they s not; 1696
139:20 For they s against thee wickedly, *and* 559

Ps 145: 5 I will s of the glorious honour of thy 7878
145: 6 *men* shall s of the might of thy terrible acts: 559
145:11 They shall s of the glory of thy kingdom, 559
145:21 My mouth shall s the praise of the LORD: 1696
Pr 8: 6 Hear, for I will s of excellent things; and 1696
8: 7 For my mouth shall s truth; and 1897
23: 9 S not in the ears of a fool: for he will 1696
23:16 shall rejoice, when thy lips s right things. 1696
Ecc 3: 7 a time to keep silence, and a time to s; 1696
SS 7: 9 **causing** the lips of *those that are* asleep **to** s. 1680
Isa 8:10 to nought; s the word, and it shall not stand: 1696
8:20 if they s not according to this word, *it is* 559
14:10 All they shall s and say unto thee, Art thou 6030
19:18 the land of Egypt s the language of Canaan, 1696
28:11 and another tongue will he s to this people. 1696
29: 4 *and* shalt s out of the ground, and 1696
30:10 Prophesy not unto us right *things,* s unto us 1696
32: 4 the stammerers shall be ready to s plainly. 1696
32: 6 For the vile person will s villany, and 1696
36:11 and Joah unto Rabshakeh, S, I pray thee, 1696
36:11 and s not to us in the Jews' language, 1696
36:12 to thy master and to thee to s these words? 1696
37:10 Thus shall ye s to Hezekiah king of Judah, 559
40: 2 S ye comfortably to Jerusalem, and 1696
41: 1 let them come near; then let them s: let us 1696
45:19 I the LORD s righteousness, I declare 1696
50: 4 to s a word **in season** to *him that is* weary: 5790
52: 6 *know* in that day that I *am* he that doth s: 1696
56: 3 hath joined himself to the LORD, s, saying, 559
59: 4 *they* trust in vanity, and s lies; 1696
63: 1 I that s in righteousness, mighty to save. 1696
Jer 1: 6 said I, Ah, Lord GOD, behold, I cannot s: 1696
1: 7 whatsoever I command thee thou shalt s. 1696
1:17 and s unto them all that I command thee: 1696
5: 5 unto the great men, and will s unto them; 1696
5:14 Because ye s this word, behold, I will make 1696
6:10 To whom shall I s, and give warning, 1696
7:27 Therefore thou shalt s all these words unto 1696
9: 5 one his neighbour, and will not s the truth: 1696
9: 5 they have taught their tongue to s lies, *and* 1696
9:22 S, Thus saith the LORD, Even 1696
10: 5 They *are* upright as the palm tree, but s not: 1696
11: 2 s unto the men of Judah, and to 1696
12: 6 though they s fair *words* unto thee. 1696
13:12 Therefore thou shalt s unto them this word; 559
18: 7 *At what* instant I shall s concerning a 1696
18: 9 *at what* instant I shall s concerning a nation, 1696
18:11 s to the men of Judah, and to the inhabitants 559
18:20 Remember that I stood before thee to s 1696
20: 9 of him, nor s any more in his name. 1696
22: 1 of the king of Judah, and s there this word, 1696
23:16 they s a vision of their own heart, *and* 1696
23:28 hath my word, let him s my word faithfully. 1696
26: 2 and s unto all the cities of Judah, 1696
26: 2 all the words that I command thee to s unto 1696
26: 8 commanded *him* to s unto all the people, 1696
26:15 unto you to s all these words in your ears. 1696
27: 9 to your sorcerers, which s unto you, saying, 559
27:14 the words of the prophets that s unto you, 559
28: 7 thou now this word that I s in thine ears, 1696
29:24 *Thus* shalt thou also s to Shemaiah 559
32: 4 shall s with him mouth to mouth, and 1696
34: 2 Go and s to Zedekiah king of Judah, and 559
34: 3 he shall s with thee mouth to mouth, and 1696
35: 2 s unto them, and bring them *into* the house 1696
38:20 voice of the LORD, which I s unto thee: 1696
39:16 Go and s to Ebed-melech the Ethiopian, 559
Eze 2: 1 stand upon thy feet, and I will s unto thee. 1696
2: 7 thou shalt s my words unto them, 1696
3: 1 this roll, and go s unto the house of Israel. 1696
3: 4 of Israel, and s with my words unto them. 1696
3:10 all my words that I shall s unto thee receive 1696
3:11 s unto them, and tell them, Thus saith 1696
3:27 when I s with thee, I will open thy mouth, 1696
11: 5 LORD fell upon me, and said unto me, S; 559
12:25 I will s, and the word that I shall speak 1696
12:25 the word that I shall s shall come to pass; 1696
14: 4 Therefore s unto them, and say unto them, 1696
17: 2 **s a parable** unto the house of Israel; 4911+4912
20: 3 s unto the elders of Israel, and say unto 1696
20:27 s unto the house of Israel, and say unto 1696
20:49 they say of me, Doth he not s parables? 4911
24:21 S unto the house of Israel, Thus saith 559
24:27 and thou shalt s, and be no more dumb: 1696
29: 3 S, and say, Thus saith the Lord GOD; 1696
31: 2 s unto Pharaoh king of Egypt, and to his 559
32:21 The strong among the mighty shall s to him 1696
33: 2 s to the children of thy people, and say unto 1696
33: 8 if thou dost not s to warn the wicked from 1696
33:10 thou son of man, s unto the house of Israel; 559
33:10 Thus ye s, saying, If our transgressions and 559
33:24 inhabit those wastes of the land of Israel s, 559
33:30 s one to another, every one to his brother, 1696
37:18 when the children of thy people shall s unto 559
39:17 S unto every feathered fowl, and to every 559
Da 2: 9 and corrupt words to s before me, 560
3:29 which s any thing amiss against the God of 560
7:25 he shall s *great* words against the most 4449
10:11 understand the words that I s unto thee, and 1696
10:19 I was strengthened, and said, Let my lord s; 1696
11:27 and they shall s lies at one table; 1696
11:36 shall s marvellous *things* against the God of 1696
Hos 2:14 the wilderness, and s comfortably unto her 1696
Hab 2: 3 but at the end it shall s, and not lie: 6315
Zep 3:13 of Israel shall not do iniquity, nor s lies; 1696
Hag 2: 2 S now to Zerubbabel the son of Shealtiel, 559
2:21 S to Zerubbabel, governor of Judah, saying, 559
Zec 2: 4 unto him, Run, s to this young man, saying, 1696
6:12 s unto him, saying, Thus speaketh 559
7: 3 *And* to s unto the priests which *were* in 559
7: 5 S unto all the people of the land, and to 559
8:16 S ye every man the truth to his neighbour; 1696
9:10 he shall s peace unto the heathen: and 1696
Mt 8: 8 but s the word only, and my servant shall *3004*
10:19 take no thought how or what ye shall s: *2980*

Mt 10:19 given you in that *same* hour what ye shall s. *2980*
10:20 For it is not ye that s, but the Spirit of your *2980*
10:27 I tell you in darkness, *that* s ye in light: *3004*
12:34 s good *things?* for out of the abundance of *2980*
12:36 That every idle word that men shall s, *2980*
12:46 stood without, desiring to s with him. *2980*
12:47 stand without, desiring to s with thee. *2980*
13:13 Therefore s I to them in parables: because *2980*
15:31 when they saw the dumb to s, the maimed *2980*
Mk 1:34 and suffered not the devils to s, because *2980*
2: 7 Why doth this *man* thus s blasphemies? *2980*
7:37 both the deaf to hear, and the dumb to s. *2980*
9:39 in my name, that can lightly s **evil** of me. *2551*
12: 1 And he began to s unto them by parables. *3004*
13:11 take no thought beforehand what ye shall s, *2980*
13:11 shall be given you in that hour, that s ye: *2980*
13:11 for it is not ye that s, but the Holy Ghost. *2980*
14:71 *saying,* I know not this man of whom ye s. *3004*
16:17 out devils; they shall s with new tongues; *2980*
Lk 1:19 and am sent to s unto thee, and to shew thee *2980*
1:20 thou shalt be dumb, and not able to s, *2980*
1:22 he came out, he could not s unto them: *2980*
4:41 he rebuking *them* suffered them not to s: *2980*
6:26 unto you, when all men shall s well of you: *3004*
7:15 he that was dead sat up, and began to s. *2980*
7:24 he began to s unto the people concerning *3004*
11:53 and to **provoke** him **to** s of many *things:* *653*
12:10 And whosoever shall s a word against *3004*
12:13 Master, s to my brother, that *he* divide *3004*
20: 9 Then began he to s to the people this *3004*
Jn 1:37 And the two disciples heard him s, and *2980*
1:40 One of the two which heard John s, and NIG
3:11 We s that we do know, and testify that we *2980*
4:26 saith unto her, I that s unto thee am *he.* *2980*
6:63 the words that I s unto you, *they* are spirit, *2980*
7:17 it be of God, or *whether* I s of myself. *2980*
8:26 I s to the world those *things* which I have *3004*
8:28 my Father hath taught me, I s these *things.* *2980*
8:38 I s *that* which I have seen with my Father: *2980*
9:21 he is of age; ask him: he shall s for himself. *2980*
12:49 what I should say, and what I should s. *2980*
12:50 whatsoever I s therefore, even as the Father *2980*
12:50 even as the Father said unto me, so I s. *2980*
13:18 I s not of you all: I know whom I have *3004*
14:10 the words that I s unto you, I speak not of *2980*
14:10 that I speak unto you, I s not of myself: *2980*
16:13 for he shall not s of himself; but *2980*
16:13 whatsoever he shall hear, *that* shall he s: *2980*
16:25 when I shall no more s unto you in *2980*
17:13 and these *things* I s in the world, that they *2980*
Ac 2: 4 and began to s with other tongues, as *2980*
2: 6 that every man heard them s in his own *2980*
2: 7 Behold, are not all these which s Galileans? *2980*
2:11 we do hear them s in our tongues *2980*
2:29 let *me* freely s unto you of the patriarch *3004*
4:17 that *they* s henceforth to no man in this *2980*
4:18 commanded them not to s at all nor teach in *5350*
4:20 but s *the things* which we have seen and *2980*
4:29 that with all boldness *they* may s thy word, *2980*
5:20 s in the temple to the people all the words *2980*
5:40 that *they* should not s in the name of Jesus, *2980*
6:11 We have heard him s blasphemous words *2980*
6:13 This man ceaseth not to s blasphemous *2980*
10:32 who, when he cometh, shall s unto thee. *2980*
10:46 For they heard them s with tongues, and *2980*
11:15 And as I began to s, the Holy Ghost fell on *2980*
14: 9 The same heard Paul s: who stedfastly *2980*
18: 9 Be not afraid, but s, and hold not thy peace: *2980*
18:26 And he began to s **boldly** in the synagogue: *3955*
21:37 unto the chief captain, May I s unto thee? *3004*
21:37 unto thee? Who said, **Canst** thou s Greek? *1097*
21:39 suffer me to s unto the people. *2980*
23: 5 Thou shalt not s evil of the ruler of thy *3004*
24:10 the governor had beckoned unto him to s, *3004*
26: 1 Thou art permitted to s for thyself. *3004*
26:25 but s **forth** *the* words of truth and soberness. *669*
26:26 of these *things,* before whom also I s freely: *2980*
28:20 to see *you,* and to s **with** *you:* because *4354*
Ro 3: 5 who taketh vengeance? (I s as a man) *3004*
6:19 I s after the manner of men because of *3004*
7: 1 (for I s to them that know the law,) *2980*
11:13 For I s to you Gentiles, inasmuch as I am *3004*
15:18 For I will not dare to s of any of *those* *2980*
1Co 1:10 that ye all s the same *thing,* and *that* there *3004*
2: 6 Howbeit we s wisdom among *them that are* *2980*
2: 7 But we s the wisdom of God in a mystery, *2980*
2:13 Which *things* also we s, not in the words *2980*
3: 1 could not s unto you as unto spiritual, but *2980*
6: 5 I s to your shame. Is it so, that there is not a *3004*
7: 6 But I s this by permission, *and* not of *3004*
7:12 But to the rest s I, not the Lord: If any *3004*
7:35 And this I s for your own profit; not that I *3004*
10:15 I s as to wise *men;* judge ye what I say. *3004*
12:30 do all s with tongues? do all interpret? *2980*
13: 1 Though I s with the tongues of men and *2980*
14: 6 except I shall s to you either by revelation, *2980*
14: 9 what is spoken? for ye shall s into the air. *2980*
14:18 I s with tongues more than you all: *2980*
14:19 Yet in the church I had rather s five words *2980*
14:21 and other lips will I s unto this people; *2980*
14:23 and all s with tongues, and there come in *2980*
14:27 If any *man* s in an *unknown* tongue, *let it* *2980*
14:28 and let him s to himself, and to God. *2980*
14:29 Let the prophets s two or three, and let *2980*
14:34 for it is not permitted unto them to s; but *2980*
14:35 for it is a shame for women to s in *2980*
14:39 and forbid not to s with tongues. *2980*
15:34 knowledge of God: I s *this* to your shame. *3004*
2Co 2:17 of God, in the sight of God s we in Christ. *2980*
4:13 I spoken; we also believe, and therefore s; *2980*
6:13 in the same, (I s as unto *my* children,) *3004*
7: 3 I s not *this* to condemn *you:* for I have said *3004*
8: 8 I s not by commandment, but by occasion *3004*
11:17 *That* which I s, I speak *it* not after the Lord, *2980*
11:17 I s *it* not after the Lord, but as *it were* *2980*

2Co 11:21 I s as concerning reproach, as though we 3004
11:21 whereinsoever any is bold, (I s foolishly,) 3004
11:23 (I s as a fool) I am more; in labours more 2980
12:19 we s before God in Christ: but we do all 2980
Gal 3:15 Brethren, I s after the manner of men; 3004
Eph 4:25 s every man truth with his neighbour: 2980
5:12 For it is a shame even to s of those things 3004
5:32 but I s concerning Christ and the church. 3004
6:20 that therein I may s boldly, as I ought to 3955
6:20 therein I may speak boldly, as I ought to s. 2980
Php 1:14 are much more bold to s the word without 2980
4:11 Not that I s in respect of want: for I have 3004
Col 4: 3 to s the mystery of Christ, for which I am 2980
4: 4 I may make it manifest, as I ought to s. 2980
1Th 1: 8 so that we need not to s any thing. 2980
2: 2 we were bold in our God to s unto you 2980
2: 4 put in trust with the gospel, even so we s; 2980
2:16 Forbidding us to s to the Gentiles that they 2980
1Ti 2: 7 (I s the truth in Christ, and lie not;) 3004
5:14 to the adversary to s reproachfully. 3059
Tit 2: 1 But s thou the things which become sound 2980
2:15 These things s, and exhort, and rebuke with 2980
3: 2 To s evil of no man, to be no brawlers, but 987
Heb 2: 5 the world to come, whereof we s: 2980
6: 9 accompany salvation, though we thus s. 2980
9: 5 of which we cannot now s particularly. 3004
Jas 1:19 be swift to hear, slow to s, slow to wrath: 2980
2:12 So s ye, and so do, as they that shall be 2980
4:11 S not evil one of another, brethren. He that 2635
1Pe 2:12 whereas they s against you as evildoers, 2635
3:10 from evil, and his lips that they s no guile: 2980
3:16 that, whereas they s evil of you, as of 2635
4:11 If any man s, let him speak as the oracles of 2980
4:11 man speak, let him s as the oracles of God; NIG
2Pe 2:10 they are not afraid to s evil of dignities. 987
2:12 s evil of the things that they understand not; 987
2:18 For when they s great swelling words of 5350
1Jn 4: 5 therefore s they of the world, and the world 2980
2Jn 1:12 and s face to face, that our joy may be full. 2980
3Jn 1:14 shortly see thee, and we shall s face to face. 2980
Jude 1: 8 despise dominion, and s evil of dignities. 987
1:10 But these s evil of those things which they 987
Rev 2:24 not known the depths of Satan, as they s; 3004
13:15 that the image of the beast should both s, 2980

SPEAKER (2) [SPEAK]

Ps 140:11 Let not an evil s be established in 376+3956
Ac 14:12 Mercurius, because he was the chief s. 3056

SPEAKEST (17) [SPEAK]

1Sa 9:21 wherefore then s thou so to me? 1696
2Sa 19:29 Why s thou any more of thy matters? 1696
2Ki 6:12 the words that thou s in thy bedchamber. 1696
Job 2:10 Thou s as one of the foolish women 1696
Ps 50:20 Thou sittest and s against thy brother; 1696
51: 4 that thou mightest be justified when thou s, 1696
Isa 40:27 Why sayest thou, O Jacob, and s, O Israel, 1696
Jer 40:16 do this thing: for thou s falsely of Ishmael. 1696
43: 2 saying unto Jeremiah, Thou s falsely: 1696
Eze 3:18 nor s to warn the wicked from his wicked 1696
Zec 13: 3 for thou s lies in the name of the LORD: 1696
Mt 13:10 Why s thou unto them in parables? 2980
Lk 12:41 s thou this parable unto us, or even to all? 3004
Jn 16:29 Lo, now s thou plainly, and speakest no 2980
16:29 speakest thou plainly, and s no proverb. 3004
19:10 saith Pilate unto him, S thou not unto me? 2980
Ac 17:19 what this new doctrine, whereof thou s, is? 2980

SPEAKETH (74) [SPEAK]

Ge 45:12 that it is my mouth that s unto you. 1696
Ex 33:11 face to face, as a man s unto his friend. 1696
Nu 23:26 saying, All that the LORD s, that I must 1696
Dt 18:22 When a prophet s in the name of 1696
1Ki 20: 5 said, Thus s Ben-hadad, saying, Although I 559
Job 2:10 speakest as one of the foolish women s. 1696
17: 5 He that s flattery to his friends, even 5046
33:14 For God s once, yea twice, yet man 1696
Ps 12: 3 and the tongue that s proud things: 1696
15: 2 and s the truth in his heart. 1696
37:30 The mouth of the righteous s wisdom, and 1897
41: 6 if he come to see me, he s vanity: his heart 1696
144: 8 Whose mouth s vanity, and their right hand 1696
144:11 whose mouth s vanity, and their right hand 1696
Pr 2:12 man, from the man that s froward things; 1696
6:13 winketh with his eyes, he s with his feet, 4448
6:19 A false witness that s lies, and he that 6315
10:32 but the mouth of the wicked s frowardness. NIH
12:17 He that s truth sheweth forth righteousness: 6315
12:18 There is that s like the piercings of a sword: 981
14:25 but a deceitful witness s lies. 6315
16:13 of kings; and they love him that s right. 1696
19: 5 and he that s lies shall not escape. 6315
19: 9 and he that s lies shall perish. 6315
21:28 but the man that heareth, s constantly. 1696
26:25 When he s fair, believe him not: for there 6963
Isa 9:17 and an evildoer, and every mouth s folly. 1696
32: 7 lying words, even when the needy s right. 1696
33:15 that walketh righteously, and s uprightly; 1696
Jer 9: 8 tongue is as an arrow shot out; it s deceit: 1696
9: 8 one s peaceably to his neighbour with his 1696
10: 1 Hear ye the word which the LORD s unto 1696
28: 2 Thus s the LORD of hosts, the God of 559
29:25 Thus s the LORD of hosts, the God of 559
30: 2 Thus s the LORD God of Israel, saying, 559
Eze 10: 5 the voice of the Almighty God when he s. 1696
Am 5:10 and they abhor him that s uprightly. 1696
Hag 1: 2 Thus s the LORD of hosts, saying, This 559
Zec 6:12 Thus s the LORD of hosts, saying, 559
7: 9 Thus s the LORD of hosts, saying, Execute 559
Mt 10:20 but the Spirit of your Father which s in you. 2980
12:32 And whosoever s a word against the Son of 3004
12:32 but whosoever s against the Holy Ghost, 3004
12:34 of the abundance of the heart the mouth s. 2980
Lk 5:21 saying, Who is this which s blasphemies? 2980
6:45 of the abundance of the heart his mouth s. 2980
Jn 3:31 is of the earth is earthly, and s of the earth: 2980
3:34 For he whom God hath sent s the words of 2980
7:18 He that s of himself seeketh his own glory: 2980
7:26 he s boldly, and they say nothing unto him. 2980
8:44 When he s a lie, he speaketh of his own: 2980
8:44 When he speaketh a lie, he s of his own: 2980
19:12 whosoever maketh himself a king s against 483
Ac 2:25 For David s concerning him, I foresaw 3004
8:34 I pray thee, of whom s the prophet this? 3004
Ro 10: 6 But the righteousness which is of faith s on 3004
1Co 14: 2 For he that s in an unknown tongue 2980
14: 2 in an unknown tongue s not unto men, 2980
14: 2 him; howbeit in the spirit he s mysteries. 2980
14: 3 But he that prophesieth s unto men to 2980
14: 4 He that s in an unknown tongue edifieth 2980
14: 5 prophesieth than he that s with tongues, 2980
14:11 I shall be unto him that s a barbarian, and 2980
14:11 and he that s shall be a barbarian unto me. 2980
14:13 Wherefore let him that s in an unknown 2980
1Ti 4: 1 Now the Spirit s expressly, that in the latter 3004
Heb 11: 4 of his gifts: and by it he being dead yet s. 2980
12: 5 which s unto you as unto children, 1256
12:24 that s better things than that of Abel. 2980
12:25 See that ye refuse not him that s: for if they 2980
12:25 we turn away from him that s from heaven: NIG
Jas 4:11 He that s evil of his brother, and judgeth his 2635
4:11 s evil of the law, and judgeth the law: 2635
Jude 1:16 their mouth s great swelling words, having 2980

SPEAKING (62) [SPEAK]

Ge 24:15 before he had done s, that behold, 1696
24:45 before I had done s in mine heart, behold, 1696
Ex 34:33 till Moses had done s with them, he put a 1696
Nu 7:89 he heard the voice of one s unto him from 1696
16:31 as he had made an end of s all these words, 1696
Dt 4:33 Did ever people hear the voice of God s out 1696
5:26 that hath heard the voice of the living God s 1696
11:19 s of them when thou sittest in thine house, 1696
20: 9 when the officers have made an end of s 1696
32:45 Moses made an end of s all these words to 1696
Jdg 15:17 to pass, when he had made an end of s, 1696
Ru 1:18 to go with her, then she left s unto her. 1696
1Sa 18: 1 when he made an end of s unto Saul, 1696
24:16 when David had made an end of s these 1696
2Sa 13:36 as soon as he had made an end of s, 1696
2Ch 36:12 prophet s from the mouth of the LORD. NIH
Est 10: 3 of his people, and s peace to all his seed. 1696
Job 1:16 While he was yet s, there came also 1696
1:17 While he was yet s, there came also 1696
1:18 While he was yet s, there came also 1696
4: 2 but who can withhold himself from s? 4405
32:15 they answered no more: they left off s. 4405
Ps 34:13 tongue from evil, and thy lips from s guile. 1696
58: 3 go astray as soon as they be born, s lies. 1696
Isa 58: 9 the putting forth of the finger, and s vanity; 1696
58:13 thine own pleasure, nor s thine own words: 1696
59:13 s oppression and revolt, conceiving and 1696
65:24 and whiles they are yet s, I will hear. 1696
Jer 7:13 rising up early and s, but ye heard not; 1696
25: 3 I have spoken unto you, rising early and s; 1696
26: 7 all the people heard Jeremiah s these words 1696
26: 8 when Jeremiah had made an end of s all 1696
35:14 I have spoken unto you, rising early and s; 1696
38: 4 all the people, in s such words unto them: 1696
38:27 So they left off s with him; for the matter 2790
43: 1 that when Jeremiah had made an end of s 1696
Eze 43: 6 I heard him s unto me out of the house; 1696
Da 7: 8 eyes of man, and a mouth s great things. 4449
8:13 I heard one saint s, and another saint said 1696
8:18 Now as he was s with me, I was in a deep 1696
9:20 whiles I was s, and praying, and 1696
9:21 Yea, whiles I was s in prayer, even the man 1696
Mt 6: 7 that they shall be heard for their much s. 4180
Lk 5: 4 Now when he had left s, he said unto 2980
Ac 1: 3 s of the things pertaining to the kingdom of 3004
7:44 as he had appointed, s unto Moses, 2980
13:43 who, s to them, persuaded them to continue 4354
14: 3 therefore abode they s boldly in the Lord, 3955
20:30 s perverse things, to draw away disciples 2980
26:14 I heard a voice s unto me, and saying in 2980
1Co 12: 3 that no man s by the Spirit of God calleth 2980
14: 6 brethren, if I come unto you s with tongues, 2980
2Co 13: 3 Since ye seek a proof of Christ s in me, 2980
Eph 4:15 But s the truth in love, may grow up into 226
4:31 wrath, and anger, and clamour, and evil s, 988
5:19 S to yourselves in psalms and hymns and 2980
1Ti 4: 2 S lies in hypocrisy, having their conscience 5573
5:13 busybodies, s things which they ought not. 2980
1Pe 4: 4 to the same excess of riot, s evil of you: 987
2Pe 2:16 the dumb ass s with man's voice forbad 5350
3:16 s in them of these things; in which are some 2980
Rev 13: 5 And there was given unto him a mouth s 2980

SPEAKINGS (1) [SPEAK]

1Pe 2: 1 and hypocrisies, and envies, and all evil s, 2636

SPEAR (45) [SPEAR'S, SPEARMEN, SPEARS]

Jos 8:18 Stretch out the s that is in thy hand toward 3591
8:18 Joshua stretched out the s that he had in his 3591
8:26 wherewith he stretched out the s, 3591
Jdg 5: 8 or s seen among forty thousand in Israel? 7420
1Sa 13:22 that there was neither sword nor s found in 2595
17: 7 the staff of his s was like a weaver's beam; 2595
17:45 a sword, and with a s, and with a shield: 2595
17:47 the LORD saveth not with sword and s: 2595
21: 8 is there not here under thine hand s or 2595
22: 6 having his s in his hand, and all his servants 2595
26: 7 and his s stuck in the ground at his bolster: 2595
26: 8 with the s even to the earth at once, and 2595
26:11 take thou now the s that is at his bolster, 2595
26:12 So David took the s and the cruse of water 2595
26:16 now see where the king's s is, and the cruse 2595
26:22 and said, Behold, the king's s; 2595
2Sa 1: 6 behold, Saul leaned upon his s; 2595
2:23 s smote him under the fifth rib, that 2595
2:23 fifth rib, that the s came out behind him; 2595
21:16 the weight of whose s weighed three 7013
21:19 the staff of whose s was like a weaver's 2595
23: 7 be fenced with iron and the staff of a s; 2595
23: 8 he lift up his s against eight hundred, NIH
23:18 he lift up his s against three hundred, and 2595
23:21 the Egyptian had a s in his hand; but 2595
23:21 plucked the s out of the Egyptian's hand, 2595
23:21 and slew him with his own s. 2595
1Ch 11:11 he lift up his s against three hundred slain 2595
11:20 for lifting up his s against three hundred, 2595
11:23 in the Egyptian's hand was a s like a 2595
11:23 pluckt the s out of the Egyptian's hand, and 2595
11:23 and slew him with his own s. 2595
12:24 and s were six thousand and eight hundred, 7420
12:34 with shield and s thirty and seven thousand. 2595
20: 5 whose s staff was like a weaver's beam. 2595
2Ch 25: 5 forth to war, that could handle s and shield. 7420
Job 39:23 against him, the glittering s and the shield. 2595
41:26 the s, the dart, nor the habergeon. 2595
41:29 he laugheth at the shaking of a s. 3591
Ps 35: 3 Draw out also the s, and stop the way 2595
46: 9 the bow, and cutteth the s in sunder; 2595
Jer 6:23 They shall lay hold on bow and s; they are 3591
Na 3: 3 both the bright sword and the glittering s: 2595
Hab 3:11 and at the shining of thy glittering s. 2595
Jn 19:34 But one of the soldiers with a s pierced his 3057

SPEAR'S (1) [SPEAR]

1Sa 17: 7 his s head weighed six hundred shekels of 2595

SPEARMEN (2) [MAN, SPEAR]

Ps 68:30 Rebuke the company of s, the multitude of 7070
Ac 23:23 and ten, and s two hundred, 1187

SPEARS (16) [SPEAR]

1Sa 13:19 Lest the Hebrews make them swords or s: 2595
2Ki 11:10 hundreds did the priest give king David's s 2595
2Ch 11:12 in every several city he put shields and s, 7420
14: 8 had an army of men that bare targets and s, 7420
23: 9 delivered to the captains of hundreds s, 2595
26:14 s, and helmets, and habergeons, and bows, 7420
Ne 4:13 with their swords, their s, and their bows. 7420
4:16 the other half of them held both the s, 7420
4:21 half of them held the s from the rising of 7420
Job 41: 7 with barbed irons? or his head with fish s? 6767
Ps 57: 4 whose teeth are s and arrows, and 2595
Isa 2: 4 and their s into pruninghooks: 2595
Jer 46: 4 furbish the s, and put on the brigandines. 7420
Eze 39: 9 the s, and they shall burn them with fire 7420
Joel 3:10 into swords, and your pruninghooks into s: 7420
Mic 4: 3 and their s into pruninghooks: 2595

SPECIAL (2) [ESPECIALLY, SPECIALLY]

Dt 7: 6 chosen thee to be a s people unto himself, 5459
Ac 19:11 And God wrought s miracles 3588+3750+5177

SPECIALLY (6) [SPECIAL]

Dt 4:10 S the day that thou stoodest before NIH
Ac 25:26 and s before thee, O king Agrippa, that, 3122
1Ti 4:10 Saviour of all men, s of those that believe. 3122
5: 8 and s for those of his own house, he hath 3122
Tit 1:10 and deceivers, s they of the circumcision: 3122
Phm 1:16 s to me, but how much more unto thee, 3122

SPECK OF SAWDUST See MOTE

SPECKLED (11)

Ge 30:32 removing from thence all the s and 5348
30:32 and the spotted and s among the goats: 5348
30:33 every one that is not s and spotted amongst 5348
30:35 all the she goats that were s and spotted, 5348
30:39 forth cattle ringstraked, s, and spotted. 5348
31: 8 If he said thus, The s shall be thy wages; 5348
31: 8 be thy wages; then all the cattle bare s: 5348
31:10 the cattle were ringstraked, s, and grisled. 5348
31:12 the cattle are ringstraked, s, and grisled: 5348
Jer 12: 9 Mine heritage is unto me as a s bird, 6641
Zec 1: 8 him were there red horses, s, and white. 8320

SPECTACLE (1)

1Co 4: 9 for we are made a s unto the world, and 2302

SPED (1) [SPEED]

Jdg 5:30 Have they not s? have they not divided 4672

SPEECH (49) [SPEAK]

Ge 4:23 ye wives of Lamech, hearken unto my s: 565
11: 1 earth was of one language, and of one s. 1697
11: 7 they may not understand one another's s. 8193
Ex 4:10 but I am slow of s, and of a slow tongue. 6310
Dt 22:14 give occasions of s against her, and 1697
22:17 he hath given occasions of s against her, 1697
32: 2 drop as the rain, my s shall distil as the dew, 565
2Sa 14:20 To fetch about this form of s hath thy 1697
19:11 seeing the s of all Israel is come to the king, 1697
1Ki 3:10 the s pleased the Lord, that Solomon had 1697
2Ch 32:18 they cried with a loud voice in the Jews' s 3066
Ne 13:24 their children spake half in the s of Ashdod, 797
Job 12:20 He removeth away the s of the trusty, and 8193
13:17 Hear diligently my s, and my declaration 4405
21: 2 Hear diligently my s, and let this be your 4405
24:25 me a liar, and make my s nothing worth? 4405
29:22 not again; and my s dropped upon them. 4405
37:19 for we cannot order our s by reason of NIH
Ps 17: 6 incline thine ear unto me, and hear my s. 565
19: 2 Day unto day uttereth s, and night unto night 562
19: 3 There is no s nor language, where their voice 562
Pr 7:21 With her much fair s she caused him to 3948
17: 7 Excellent s becometh not a fool: much less 8193
SS 4: 3 like a thread of scarlet, and thy s is comely: 4057
Isa 28:23 and hear my voice; hearken, and hear my s. 565

Isa 29: 4 thy **s** shall be low out of the dust, and 565
29: 4 and thy **s** shall whisper out of the dust. 565
32: 9 ye careless daughters, give ear unto my **s**. 565
33:19 a people of a deeper **s** than *thou* canst 8193
Jer 31:23 As yet they shall use this **s** in the land of 1697
Eze 1:24 the voice of **s**, as the noise of a host: 1999
3: 5 thou *art* not sent to a people of a strange **s** 8193
3: 6 Not to many people of a strange **s** and of a 8193
Hab 3: 2 I have heard thy **s**, *and* was afraid: 8088
Mt 26:73 art *one* of them; for thy **s** bewrayeth thee. *2981*
Mk 7:32 *was* deaf, and had an **impediment in** his **s**; *3424*
14:70 art a Galilean, and thy **s** agreeth *thereto*. *2981*
Jn 8:43 Why do ye not understand my **s**? *even* *2981*
Ac 14:11 their voices, saying **in the s of Lycaonia**, *3072*
20: 7 and continued *his* **s** until midnight. *3056*
1Co 2: 1 came not with excellency of **s** or *3056*
2: 4 And my **s** and my preaching *was* not with *3056*
4:19 not the **s** of them which are puffed up, but *3056*
2Co 3:12 such hope, we use great **plainness of s**: *3954*
7: 4 Great *is* my **boldness of s** toward you, *3954*
10:10 presence *is* weak, and *his* **s** contemptible. *3056*
11: 6 But though *I be* rude in **s**, yet not in *3056*
Col 4: 6 Let your **s** *be* alway with grace, *3056*
Tit 2: 8 Sound **s** that cannot be condemned; that he *3056*

SPEECHES (7) [SPEAK]

Nu 12: 8 even apparently, and not in **dark s**; 2420
Job 6:26 the **s** of one that is desperate, *which are* as 561
15: 3 or *with* **s** wherewith he can do no good? 4405
32:14 neither will I answer him with your **s**. 561
33: 1 hear my **s**, and hearken to all my words. 4405
Ro 16:18 and **fair s** deceive the hearts of the simple. *2129*
Jude 1:15 of all *their* hard **s** which ungodly sinners NIG

SPEECHLESS (3) [SPEAK]

Mt 22:12 having a wedding garment? And he was **s**. *5392*
Lk 1:22 for he beckoned unto them, and remained **s**. *2974*
Ac 9: 7 the men which journeyed with him stood **s**, *1769*

SPEED (11) [SPED, SPEEDILY, SPEEDY]

Ge 24:12 **send** me **good s** *this* day, and 6440+7136+3807.1
1Sa 20:38 cried after the lad, **Make s**, haste, stay not. 4120
2Sa 15:14 **make s** to depart, lest he overtake us 4116
1Ki 12:18 Therefore king Rehoboam **made s** to get *him* 553
2Ch 10:18 king Rehoboam **made s** to get *him* up to *his* 553
Ezr 6:12 have made a decree; let it be done **with s**. 629
Isa 5:19 Let him **make s**, *and* hasten his work, 4116
5:26 and behold, they shall come with **s** swiftly: 4120
Ac 17:15 for to come to him **with all s**, *5030+5613*
2Jn 1:10 not into *your* house, neither bid him **God s**: *5463*
1:11 For he that biddeth him **God s** is partaker *5463*

SPEEDILY (19) [SPEED]

Ge 44:11 they **s** took down every man his sack to 4116
1Sa 27: 1 **s escape** into the land of 4422+4422
2Sa 17:16 of the wilderness, but **s pass over**; 5674+5674
2Ch 35:13 and **divided** *them* **s** among all the people. 7323
Ezr 6:13 Darius the king had sent, so they did **s**. 629
7:17 That thou mayest buy **s** with this money 629
7:21 of heaven, shall require of you, *it* be done **s**, 629
7:26 let judgment be executed **s** upon him, 629
Est 2: 9 and he **s** gave her her things for purification, 926
Ps 31: 2 Bow down thine ear to me; deliver me **s**: 4120
69:17 thy servant; for I am in trouble: hear me **s**. 4118
79: 8 let thy tender mercies **s** prevent us: for we 4118
102: 2 in the day *when* I call answer me **s**. 4118
143: 7 Hear me **s**, O LORD: my spirit faileth: 4118
Ecc 8:11 *against* an evil work is not executed **s**, 4120
Isa 58: 8 and thine health shall spring forth **s**: 4120
Joel 3: 4 **s** will I return your recompence upon your 4120
Zec 8:21 Let us **go s** to pray before 1980+1980
Lk 18: 8 I tell you that he will avenge them **s**. *1722+5034*

SPEEDY (1) [SPEED]

Zep 1:18 for he shall make even a **s** riddance of all 926

SPELT See RIE

SPEND (7) [SPENDEST, SPENDETH, SPENT]

Dt 32:23 upon them; I will **s** mine arrows upon them. 3615
Job 21:13 They **s** their days in wealth, and in a 3615
36:11 serve *him*, they shall **s** their days in 3615
Ps 90: 9 we **s** our years as a tale *that is told*. 3615
Isa 55: 2 Wherefore do ye **s** money for *that which is* 8254
Ac 20:16 because he would not **s** the **time** in Asia: *5551*
2Co 12:15 And I will very gladly **s** and be spent for *1159*

SPENDEST (1) [SPEND]

Lk 10:35 and whatsoever thou **s more**, when I come *4325*

SPENDETH (3) [SPEND]

Pr 21:20 of the wise; but a foolish man **s** it **up**. 1104
29: 3 he that keepeth company with harlots **s** *his* 6
Ecc 6:12 all the days of his vain life which he **s** as a 6213

SPENT (19) [SPEND]

Ge 21:15 the water was **s** in the bottle, and she cast 3615
47:18 *it* from my lord, how that our money is **s**; 8552
Lev 26:20 your strength shall be **s** in vain: for your 8552
Jdg 19:11 when they *were* by Jebus, the day was far **s**; 7286
1Sa 9: 7 for the bread is **s** in our vessels, and *there is* 235
Job 7: 6 a weaver's shuttle, and are **s** without hope. 3615
Ps 31:10 For my life is **s** with grief, and my years 3615
Isa 49: 4 I have **s** my strength for nought, and 3615
Jer 37:21 until all the bread in the city were **s**. 8552
Mk 5:26 many physicians, and had **s** all that she had, *1159*
6:35 And when the day was now far **s**, *1096*
Lk 8:43 which had **s** all *her* living upon physicians, *4321*
15:14 And when he had **s** all, there arose a mighty *1159*
24:29 and the day is **far s**. *2235+2827*
Ac 17:21 strangers which were there **s** their **time** in *2119*
18:23 And after he had **s** some time *there*, he *4160*
27: 9 Now when much time was **s**, and *1230*
Ro 13:12 The night is **far s**, the day is at hand: let us *4298*

2Co 12:15 I will very gladly spend and be **s** for you; *1550*

SPEW See BELCH; SPUE

SPICE (5) [SPICED, SPICERY, SPICES]

Ex 35:28 **s**, and oil for the light, and for the anointing 1314
1Ki 10:15 *of* the traffick of the **s** merchants, and *of* all NIH
2Ch 9: 9 neither was there any such **s** as the queen of 1314
SS 5: 1 I have gathered my myrrh with my **s**; I have 1313
Eze 24:10 and **s** it well, and let the bones be burnt. 7543

SPICED (1) [SPICE]

SS 8: 2 I would cause thee to drink of **s** wine, of 7544

SPICERY (1) [SPICE]

Ge 37:25 from Gilead with their camels bearing **s** 5219

SPICES (31) [SPICE]

Ge 43:11 **s**, and myrrh, nuts, and almonds: 5219
Ex 25: 6 **s** for anointing oil, and for sweet incense, 1314
30:23 Take thou also unto thee principal **s**, 1314
30:34 Take unto thee **sweet s**, stacte, and onycha, 5561
30:34 *these* **sweet s** with pure frankincense: 5561
35: 8 **s** for anointing oil, and for the sweet 1314
37:29 and the pure incense of **sweet s**, 5561
1Ki 10: 2 *with* camels that bare **s**, and very much 1314
10:10 of **s** very great store, and precious stones: 1314
10:10 there came no more such abundance of **s** as 1314
10:25 and armour, and **s**, horses, and mules, 1314
2Ki 20:13 the **s**, and the precious ointment, and all 1314
1Ch 9:29 and the oil, and the frankincense, and the **s**. 1314
9:30 of the priests made the ointment of the **s**. 1314
2Ch 9: 1 camels that bare **s**, and gold in abundance, 1314
9: 9 of **s** great abundance, and precious stones: 1314
9:24 raiment, harness, and **s**, horses, and mules, 1314
16:14 divers kinds *of* **s** prepared by NIH
32:27 for **s**, and for shields, and for all *manner of* 1314
SS 4:10 and the smell of thine ointments than all **s**! 1314
4:14 myrrh and aloes, with all the chief **s**: 1314
4:16 my garden, *that* the **s** thereof may flow out. 1314
5:13 His cheeks *are* as a bed of **s**, *as* sweet 1314
6: 2 to the beds of **s**, to feed in the gardens, and 1314
8:14 or to a young hart upon the mountains of **s**. 1314
Isa 39: 2 the **s**, and the precious ointment, and all 1314
Eze 27:22 occupied in thy fairs with chief of all **s**, 1314
Mk 16: 1 and Salome, had bought *sweet* **s**, that they *759*
Lk 23:56 they returned, and prepared **s** and ointments; *759*
24: 1 bringing the **s** which they had prepared, and *759*
Jn 19:40 and wound it in linen clothes with the **s**, *759*

SPIDER (1) [SPIDER'S]

Pr 30:28 The **s** taketh hold with her hands, and *is* in 8079

SPIDER'S (2) [SPIDER]

Job 8:14 be cut off, and whose trust *shall be* a **s** web. 5908
Isa 59: 5 cockatrice' eggs, and weave the **s** web: 5908

SPIED (6) [SPY]

Ex 2:11 he **s** an Egyptian smiting a Hebrew, *one* of 7200
Jos 6:22 the two men that had **s out** the country, 7270
2Ki 9:17 he **s** the company of Jehu as he came, and 7200
13:21 they **s** a band *of men*; and they cast the man 7200
23:16 he **s** the sepulchres that *were* there in 7200
23:24 all the abominations that were **s** in the land 7200

SPIES (14) [SPY]

Ge 42: 9 of them, and said unto them, Ye *are* **s**; 7270
42:11 we *are* true *men*, thy servants are no **s**. 7270
42:14 *is it* that I spake unto you, saying, Ye *are* **s**: 7270
42:16 else by the life of Pharaoh surely ye *are* **s**. 7270
42:30 to us, and took us for **s** of the country. 7270
42:31 unto him, We *are* true *men*; we are no **s**: 7270
42:34 shall I know that ye *are* no **s**, but *that* ye *are* 7270
Nu 21: 1 *tell* that Israel came *by* the way of the **s**; 871
Jos 6:23 the young men that were **s** went in, and 7270
Jdg 1:24 the **s** saw a man come forth out of the city, 8104
1Sa 26: 4 David therefore sent out **s**, and 7270
2Sa 15:10 Absalom sent **s** throughout all the tribes of 7270
Lk 20:20 And they watched *him*, and sent forth **s**, *1455*
Heb 11:31 when she had received the **s** with peace. *2605*

SPIKENARD (5)

SS 1:12 my **s** sendeth forth the smell thereof. 5373
4:13 with pleasant fruits; camphire, with **s**, 5373
4:14 **S** and saffron; calamus and cinnamon, 5373
Mk 14: 3 box of ointment of **s** very precious; *3487+4101*
Jn 12: 3 took Mary a pound of ointment of **s**, *3487+4101*

SPILLED (3) [SPILT]

Ge 38: 9 brother's wife, that he **s** *it* on the ground, 7843
Mk 2:22 and the wine is **s**, and the bottles will be *1632*
Lk 5:37 and be **s**, and the bottles shall perish. *1632*

SPILT (1) [SPILLED]

2Sa 14:14 needs die, and *are* as water **s** on the ground, 5064

SPIN (3) [SPUN]

Ex 35:25 all the women that were wise hearted did **s** 2901
Mt 6:28 they grow; they toil not, neither do they **s**: *3514*
Lk 12:27 they toil not, they **s** not; and yet I say unto *3514*

SPINDLE (1)

Pr 31:19 She layeth her hands to the **s**, and her hands 3601

SPIRIT (505) [SPIRITS, SPIRITUAL, SPIRITUALLY]

Ge 1: 2 the **S** of God moved upon the face of 7307
6: 3 My **s** shall not always strive with man, 7307
41: 8 it came to pass in the morning that his **s** 7307
41:38 as this *is*, a man in whom the **s** of God *is*? 7307
45:27 the **s** of Jacob their father revived: 7307
Ex 6: 9 hearkened not unto Moses for anguish of **s**, 7307
28: 3 whom I have filled with the **s** of wisdom, 7307
31: 3 I have filled him *with* the **s** of God, 7307

Ex 35:21 every one whom his **s** made willing, *and* 7307
35:31 he hath filled him *with* the **s** of God, 7307
Lev 20:27 A man also or woman that hath a **familiar s**, 178
Nu 5:14 the **s** of jealousy come upon him, and he be 7307
5:14 or if the **s** of jealousy come upon him, and 7307
5:30 Or when the **s** of jealousy cometh upon 7307
11:17 I will take of the **s** which *is* upon thee, and 7307
11:25 took of the **s** that *was* upon him, and gave *it* 7307
11:25 to pass, that when the **s** rested upon them, 7307
11:26 the **s** rested upon them; and they *were* of 7307
11:29 that the LORD would put his **s** upon 7307
14:24 because he had another **s** with him, and 7307
24: 2 and the **s** of God came upon him. 7307
27:18 a man in whom *is* the **s**, and lay thine hand 7307
Dt 2:30 for the LORD thy God hardened his **s**, and 7307
34: 9 Joshua the son of Nun was full *of* the **s** of 7307
Jos 5: 1 neither was there **s** in them any more, 7307
Jdg 3:10 the **s** of the LORD came upon him, and 7307
6:34 the **s** of the LORD came upon Gideon, 7307
9:23 God sent an evil **s** between Abimelech 7307
11:29 the **s** of the LORD came upon Jephthah, 7307
13:25 the **s** of the LORD began to move him at 7307
14: 6 the **s** of the LORD came mightily upon 7307
14:19 the **s** of the LORD came upon him, and 7307
15:14 the **s** of the LORD came mightily upon 7307
15:19 his **s** came again, and he revived: 7307
1Sa 1:15 my lord, I *am* a woman of a sorrowful **s**: 7307
10: 6 the **s** of the LORD will come upon thee, 7307
10:10 the **s** of God came upon him, and 7307
11: 6 the **s** of God came upon Saul when he 7307
16:13 the **s** of the LORD came upon David from 7307
16:14 the **s** of the LORD departed from Saul, 7307
16:14 an evil **s** from the LORD troubled him. 7307
16:15 an evil **s** from God troubleth thee. 7307
16:16 when the evil **s** from God is upon thee, 7307
16:23 when the *evil* **s** from God was upon Saul, 7307
16:23 was well, and the evil **s** departed from him. 7307
18:10 that the evil **s** from God came upon Saul, 7307
19: 9 the evil **s** from the LORD was upon Saul, 7307
19:20 the **s** of God was upon the messengers of 7307
19:23 the **s** of God was upon him also, and 7307
28: 7 Seek me a woman that hath a **familiar s**, 178
28: 7 *there is* a woman that hath a **familiar s** at 178
28: 8 divine unto me by the **familiar s**, and 178
30:12 he had eaten, his **s** came again to him: 7307
2Sa 23: 2 The **S** of the LORD spake by me, and 7307
1Ki 10: 5 of the LORD; there was no more **s** in her. 7307
18:12 that the **s** of the LORD shall carry thee 7307
21: 5 said unto him, Why is thy **s** so sad, 7307
22:21 there came forth a **s**, and stood before 7307
22:22 I will be a lying **s** in the mouth of all his 7307
22:23 the LORD hath put a lying **s** in the mouth 7307
22:24 Which way went the **s** of the LORD from 7307
2Ki 2: 9 let a double portion of thy **s** be upon me. 7307
2:15 The **s** of Elijah doth rest on Elisha. 7307
2:16 lest peradventure the **s** of the LORD hath 7307
1Ch 5:26 the God of Israel stirred up the **s** of Pul 7307
5:26 the **s** of Tilgath-pilneser king of Assyria, 7307
10:13 asking *counsel* of *one that had* a **familiar s**, 178
12:18 the **s** came upon Amasai, *who was* chief of 7307
28:12 the pattern of all that he had by the **s**, of 7307
2Ch 9: 4 of the LORD; there was no more **s** in her. 7307
15: 1 the **s** of God came upon Azariah the son of 7307
18:20 there came out a **s**, and stood before 7307
18:21 be a lying **s** in the mouth of all his prophets. 7307
18:22 the LORD hath put a lying **s** in the mouth 7307
18:23 Which way went the **s** of the LORD from 7307
20:14 came the **s** of the LORD in the midst of 7307
21:16 up against Jehoram the **s** of the Philistines, 7307
24:20 the **s** of God came upon Zechariah the son 7307
33: 6 dealt with a **familiar s**, and with wizards: 178
36:22 the LORD stirred up the **s** of Cyrus king 7307
Ezr 1: 1 the LORD stirred up the **s** of Cyrus king 7307
1: 5 with all *them* whose **s** God had raised, 7307
Ne 9:20 Thou gavest also thy good **s** to instruct 7307
9:30 testifiedst against them by thy **s** in thy 7307
Job 4:15 a **s** passed before my face; the hair of my 7307
6: 4 the poison whereof drinketh up my **s**: 7307
7:11 I will speak in the anguish of my **s**; 7307
10:12 and thy visitation hath preserved my **s**. 7307
15:13 That thou turnest thy **s** against God, and 7307
20: 3 the **s** of my understanding causeth me to 7307
21: 4 *so*, why should not my **s** be troubled? 7307
26: 4 and whose **s** came from thee? 5397
26:13 By his **s** he hath garnished the heavens; 7307
27: 3 **s** in me, and the **s** of God *is* in my nostrils; 7307
32: 8 *there is* a **s** in man: and the inspiration of 7307
32:18 *of* matter, the **s** within me constraineth me. 7307
33: 4 The **S** of God hath made me, and the breath 7307
34:14 upon *man*, *if* he gather unto himself his **s** 7307
Ps 31: 5 Into thine hand I commit my **s**: thou hast 7307
32: 2 and in whose **s** *there is* no guile. 7307
34:18 and saveth such as be of a contrite **s**. 7307
51:10 O God; and renew a right **s** within me. 7307
51:11 and take not thy holy **S** from me. 7307
51:12 and uphold me *with thy* free **s**. 7307
51:17 The sacrifices of God *are* a broken **s**: 7307
76:12 He shall cut off the **s** of princes: *he is* 7307
77: 3 I complained, and my **s** was overwhelmed. 7307
77: 6 own heart: and my **s** made diligent search. 7307
78: 8 and whose **s** was not stedfast with God. 7307
104:30 Thou sendest forth thy **s**, they are created: 7307
106:33 Because they provoked his **s**, so that he 7307
139: 7 Whither shall I go from thy **s**? or 7307
142: 3 When my **s** was overwhelmed within me, 7307
143: 4 Therefore is my **s** overwhelmed within me; 7307
143: 7 my **s** faileth: hide not thy face from me, 7307
143:10 thy **s** *is* good; lead me into the land of 7307
Pr 1:23 behold, I will pour out my **s** unto you, I will 7307
11:13 he that is of a faithful **s** concealeth 7307
14:29 but *he that is* hasty of **s** exalteth folly. 7307
15: 4 but perverseness therein *is* a breach in the **s**. 7307
15:13 but by sorrow of the heart the **s** *is* broken. 7307
16:18 and a haughty **s** before a fall. 7307
16:19 Better *it is to be* of an humble **s** with 7307

S

Pr 16:32 he that ruleth his s than he that taketh a 7307
17:22 a medicine: but a broken s drieth the bones. 7307
17:27 a man of understanding is of an excellent s. 7307
18:14 The s of a man will sustain his infirmity; 7307
18:14 but a wounded s who can bear? 7307
20:27 The s of man is the candle of the LORD, 5397
25:28 He that hath no rule over his own s is like a 7307
29:23 but honour shall uphold the humble in s. 7307
Ecc 1:14 and behold, all is vanity and vexation of s. 7307
1:17 I perceived that this also is vexation of s. 7307
2:11 all was vanity and vexation of s, and 7307
2:17 unto me: for all is vanity and vexation of s. 7307
2:26 This also is vanity and vexation of s. 7307
3:21 Who knoweth the s of man that goeth 7307
3:21 the s of the beast that goeth downward to 7307
4: 4 This is also vanity and vexation of s. 7307
4: 6 hands full with travail and vexation of s. 7307
4:16 Surely this also is vanity and vexation of s. 7307
6: 9 this is also vanity and vexation of s. 7307
7: 8 the patient in s is better than the proud in 7307
7: 8 patient in spirit is better than the proud in s. 7307
7: 9 Be not hasty in thy s to be angry: for anger 7307
8: 8 There is no man that hath power over the s 7307
8: 8 hath power over the spirit to retain the s; 7307
10: 4 If the s of the ruler rise up against thee, 7307
11: 5 thou knowest not what is the way of the s, 7307
12: 7 and the s shall return unto God who gave it. 7307
Isa 4: 4 the midst thereof by the s of judgment, 7307
4: 4 spirit of judgment, and by the s of burning. 7307
11: 2 the S of the LORD shall rest upon him, 7307
11: 2 the s of wisdom and understanding, 7307
11: 2 understanding, the s of counsel and might, 7307
11: 2 the s of knowledge and of the fear of 7307
19: 3 the s of Egypt shall fail in the midst 7307
19:14 The LORD hath mingled a perverse s in 7307
26: 9 with my s within me will I seek thee early: 7307
28: 6 for a s of judgment to him that sitteth in 7307
29: 4 as of one that hath a familiar s, out of 178
29:10 poured out upon you the s of deep sleep, 7307
29:24 They also that erred in s shall come to 7307
30: 1 that cover with a covering, but not of my S, 7307
31: 3 not God; and their horses flesh, and not s. 7307
32:15 Until the s be poured upon us from on high, 7307
34:16 and his s it hath gathered them. 7307
38:16 and in all these things is the life of my s: 7307
40: 7 the s of the LORD bloweth upon it: 7307
40:13 Who hath directed the s of the LORD, or 7307
42: 1 soul delighteth; I have put my s upon him: 7307
42: 5 upon it, and s to them that walk therein: 7307
44: 3 dry ground: I will pour my s upon thy seed, 7307
48:16 the Lord GOD, and his S, hath sent me. 7307
54: 6 thee as a woman forsaken and grieved in s, 7307
57:15 him also that is of a contrite and humble s, 7307
57:15 to revive the s of the humble, and to revive 7307
57:16 for the s should fail before me, and 7307
59:19 the s of the LORD shall lift up a standard 7307
59:21 My s that is upon thee, and my words 7307
61: 1 The S of the Lord GOD is upon me; 7307
61: 3 the garment of praise for the s of heaviness; 7307
63:10 they rebelled, and vexed his holy S: 7307
63:11 where is he that put his holy S within him? 7307
63:14 the S of the LORD caused him to rest: 7307
65:14 of heart, and shall howl for vexation of s. 7307
66: 2 even to him that is poor and of a contrite s, 7307
Jer 51:11 the LORD hath raised up the s of 7307
Eze 1:12 whither the s was to go, they went; and 7307
1:20 Whithersoever the s was to go, they went, 7307
1:20 to go, they went, thither was their s to go; 7307
1:20 for the s of the living creature was in 7307
1:21 for the s of the living creature was in 7307
2: 2 the s entered into me when he spake unto 7307
3:12 the s took me up, and I heard behind me a 7307
3:14 So the s lifted me up, and took me away, 7307
3:14 and I went in bitterness, in the heat of my s; 7307
3:24 the s entered into me, and set me upon my 7307
8: 3 the s lift me up between the earth and 7307
10:17 these lift up themselves also: for the s of 7307
11: 1 Moreover the s lift me up, and brought me 7307
11: 5 the S of the LORD fell upon me, and 7307
11:19 and I will put a new s within you; 7307
11:24 Afterwards the s took me up, and 7307
11:24 brought me in vision by the S of God into 7307
13: 3 that follow their own s, and have seen 7307
18:31 and make you a new heart and a new s: 7307
21: 7 every s shall faint, and all knees shall be 7307
36:26 give you, and a new s will I put within you: 7307
36:27 I will put my s within you, and cause you to 7307
37: 1 carried me out in the s of the LORD, and 7307
37:14 shall put my s in you, and ye shall live, 7307
39:29 for I have poured out my s upon the house 7307
43: 5 So the s took me up, and brought me into 7307
Da 2: 1 wherewith his s was troubled, and his sleep 7307
2: 3 and my s was troubled to know the dream. 7307
4: 8 and in whom is the s of the holy gods: 7308
4: 9 I know that the s of the holy gods is in thee, 7308
4:18 for the s of the holy gods is in thee. 7308
5:11 in whom is the s of the holy gods; 7308
5:12 Forasmuch as an excellent s, and 7308
5:14 that the s of the gods is in thee, and 7308
6: 3 princes, because an excellent s was in him; 7308
7:15 I Daniel was grieved in my s in the midst of 7308
Hos 4:12 for the s of whoredoms hath caused them to 7307
5: 4 for the s of whoredoms is in the midst of 7307
Joel 2:28 that I will pour out my s upon all flesh; 7307
2:29 in those days will I pour out my s. 7307
Mic 2: 7 of Jacob, is the s of the LORD straitened? 7307
2:11 If a man walking in the s and falsehood do 7307
3: 8 truly I am full of power by the s of 7307
Hag 1:14 the LORD stirred up the s of Zerubbabel 7307
1:14 the s of Joshua the son of Josedech the high 7307
1:14 and the s of all the remnant of the people; 7307
2: 5 of Egypt, so my s remaineth among you: 7307
Zec 4: 6 Not by might, nor by power, but by my s, 7307
6: 8 have quieted my s in the north country. 7307
7:12 hath sent in his s by the former prophets: 7307

Zec 12: 1 and formeth the s of man within him. 7307
12:10 the s of grace and of supplications: 7307
13: 2 and the unclean s to pass out of the land. 7307
Mal 2:15 Yet had he the residue of the s. And 7307
2:15 Therefore take heed to your s, and let none 7307
2:16 therefore take heed to your s, that ye deal 7307
Mt 3:16 he saw the S of God descending like a 4151
4: 1 Then was Jesus led up of the S into 4151
5: 3 Blessed are the poor in s: for theirs is 4151
10:20 the S of your Father which speaketh in you. 4151
12:18 I will put my s upon him, and he shall shew 4151
12:28 But if I cast out devils by the S of God, 4151
12:43 When the unclean s is gone out of a man, 4151
14:26 the sea, they were troubled, saying, It is a s; 5326
22:43 How then doth David in s call him Lord, 4151
26:41 the s indeed is willing, but the flesh is 4151
Mk 1:10 and the S like a dove descending upon him: 4151
1:12 And immediately the S driveth him into 4151
1:23 in their synagogue a man with an unclean s; 4151
1:26 And when the unclean s had torn him, and 4151
2: 8 when Jesus perceived in his s that they so 4151
3:30 Because they said, He hath an unclean s. 4151
5: 2 out of the tombs a man with an unclean s, 4151
5: 8 Come out of the man, thou unclean s. 4151
6:49 they supposed it had been a s, and 5326
7:25 whose young daughter had an unclean s, 4151
8:12 And he sighed deeply in his s, and saith, 4151
9:17 unto thee my son, which hath a dumb s: 4151
9:20 he saw him, straightway the s tare him; 4151
9:25 he rebuked the foul s, saying unto him, 4151
9:25 Thou dumb and deaf s, I charge thee, 4151
9:26 And the s cried, and rent him sore, and NIG
14:38 The s truly is ready, but the flesh is weak. 4151
Lk 1:17 And he shall go before him in the s and 4151
1:47 And my s hath rejoiced in God my Saviour. 4151
1:80 and waxed strong in s, and was in 4151
2:27 And he came by the S into the temple: and 4151
2:40 and waxed strong in s, filled with wisdom: 4151
4: 1 and was led by the S into the wilderness, 4151
4:14 And Jesus returned in the power of the S 4151
4:18 The S of the Lord is upon me, 4151
4:33 which had a s of an unclean devil, and 4151
8:29 (For he had commanded the unclean s to 4151
8:55 And her s came again, and she arose 4151
9:39 a s taketh him, and he suddenly crieth out; 4151
9:42 tare him. And Jesus rebuked the unclean s, 4151
9:55 Ye know not what manner of s ye are of. 4151
10:21 In that hour Jesus rejoiced in s, and said, 4151
11:13 give the Holy S to them that ask him? 4151
11:24 When the unclean s is gone out of a man, 4151
13:11 there was a woman which had a s of 4151
23:46 Father, into thy hands I commend my s: 4151
24:37 and supposed that they had seen a s. 4151
24:39 for a s hath not flesh and bones, as ye see 4151
Jn 1:32 I saw the S descending from heaven like a 4151
1:33 Upon whom thou shalt see the S 4151
3: 5 Except a man be born of water and of the S, 4151
3: 6 and that which is born of the S is spirit. 4151
3: 6 and that which is born of the Spirit is s. 4151
3: 8 so is every one that is born of the S. 4151
3:34 for God giveth not the S by measure unto 4151
4:23 worshippers shall worship the Father in s 4151
4:24 God is a S: and they that worship him must 4151
4:24 that worship him must worship him in s 4151
6:63 It is the s that quickeneth; the flesh 4151
6:63 unto you, they are s, and they are life. 4151
7:39 (But this spake he of the S, which they that 4151
11:33 he groaned in the s, and was troubled, 4151
13:21 he was troubled in s, and testified, and said, 4151
14:17 Even the S of truth; whom the world cannot 4151
15:26 even the S of truth, which proceedeth from 4151
16:13 Howbeit when he, the S of truth, is come, 4151
Ac 2: 4 other tongues, as the S gave them utterance. 4151
2:17 I will pour out of my S upon all flesh: 4151
2:18 I will pour out in those days of my S; 4151
5: 9 agreed together to tempt the S of the Lord? 4151
6:10 the wisdom and the s by which he spake. 4151
7:59 and saying, Lord Jesus, receive my s. 4151
8:29 Then the S said unto Philip, Go near, and 4151
8:39 the S of the Lord caught away Philip, 4151
10:19 the S said unto him, Behold, three men 4151
11:12 And the S bade me go with them, 4151
11:28 signified by the S that there should be great 4151
16: 7 into Bithynia: but the S suffered them not. 4151
16:16 a certain damsel possessed with a s of 4151
16:18 being grieved, turned and said to the s, 4151
17:16 for them at Athens, his s was stirred in him, 4151
18: 5 Paul was pressed in s, and testified to 4151
18:25 and being fervent in the s, he spake and 4151
19:15 And the evil s answered and said, Jesus I 4151
19:16 And the man in whom the evil s was leapt 4151
19:21 things were ended, Paul purposed in the s, 4151
20:22 I go bound in the s unto Jerusalem, 4151
21: 4 who said to Paul through the S, that he 4151
23: 8 there is no resurrection, neither angel nor s: 4151
23: 9 but if a s or an angel hath spoken to him, 4151
Ro 1: 4 according to the S of holiness, by 4151
1: 9 whom I serve with my s in the gospel of his 4151
2:29 of the heart, in the s, and not in the letter; 4151
7: 6 that we should serve in newness of s, and 4151
8: 1 who walk not after the flesh, but after the S. 4151
8: 2 For the law of the S of life in Christ Jesus 4151
8: 4 who walk not after the flesh, but after the S. 4151
8: 5 they that are after the S the things of 4151
8: 5 that are after the Spirit the things of the S. 4151
8: 9 but in the S, if so be that the Spirit of God 4151
8: 9 if so be that the S of God dwell in you. 4151
8: 9 Now if any man have not the S of Christ, 4151
8:10 but the S is life because of righteousness. 4151
8:11 But if the S of him that raised up Jesus 4151
8:11 mortal bodies by his S that dwelleth in you. 4151
8:13 if ye through the S do mortify the deeds of 4151
8:14 For as many as are led by the S of God, 4151
8:15 For ye have not received the s of bondage 4151
8:15 but ye have received the S of adoption, 4151

Ro 8:16 The S itself beareth witness with our spirit, 4151
8:16 The Spirit itself beareth witness with our s, 4151
8:23 which have the firstfruits of the S, 4151
8:26 Likewise the S also helpeth our infirmities: 4151
8:26 the S itself maketh intercession for us with 4151
8:27 hearts knoweth what is the mind of the S, 4151
11: 8 God hath given them the s of slumber, 4151
12:11 in business; fervent in s; serving the Lord; 4151
15:19 and wonders, by the power of the S of God; 4151
15:30 Christ's sake, and for the love of the S, 4151
1Co 2: 4 but in demonstration of the S and of power: 4151
2:10 God hath revealed them unto us by his S: 4151
2:10 for the S searcheth all things, yea, the deep 4151
2:11 a man, save the s of man which is in him? 4151
2:11 of God knoweth no man, but the S of God. 4151
2:12 not the s of the world, but the Spirit which 4151
2:12 of the world, but the S which is of God; 4151
2:14 receiveth not the things of the S of God: 4151
3:16 and that the S of God dwelleth in you? 4151
4:21 a rod, or in love, and in the s of meekness? 4151
5: 3 I verily, as absent in body, but present in s, 4151
5: 4 when ye are gathered together, and my s, 4151
5: 5 that the s may be saved in the day of 4151
6:11 of the Lord Jesus, and by the S of our God. 4151
6:17 But he that is joined unto the Lord is one s. 4151
6:20 your body, and in your s, which are God's. 4151
7:34 that she may be holy both in body and in s: 4151
7:40 and I think also that I have the S of God. 4151
12: 3 that no man speaking by the S of God 4151
12: 4 there are diversities of gifts, but the same S. 4151
12: 7 But the manifestation of the S is given to 4151
12: 8 For to one is given by the S the word of 4151
12: 8 the word of knowledge by the same S; 4151
12: 9 To another faith by the same S; to another 4151
12: 9 another the gifts of healing by the same S; 4151
12:11 these worketh that one and the selfsame S, 4151
12:13 For by one S are we all baptized into one 4151
12:13 and have been all made to drink into one S. 4151
14: 2 howbeit in the s he speaketh mysteries. 4151
14:14 my s prayeth, but my understanding is 4151
14:15 I will pray with the s, and will pray with 4151
14:15 I will sing with the s, and I will sing with 4151
14:16 Else when thou shalt bless with the s, 4151
15:45 the last Adam was made a quickening s. 4151
16:18 For they have refreshed my s and yours: 4151
2Co 1:22 and given the earnest of the S in our hearts. 4151
2:13 I had no rest in my s, because I found not 4151
3: 3 with ink, but with the S of the living God; 4151
3: 6 not of the letter, but of the s: 4151
3: 6 for the letter killeth, but the s giveth life. 4151
3: 8 How shall not the ministration of the s be 4151
3:17 Now the Lord is that S: and where 4151
3:17 where the S of the Lord is, there is liberty. 4151
3:18 glory to glory, even as by the S of the Lord. 4151
4:13 We having the same s of faith, according as 4151
5: 5 also hath given unto us the earnest of the S. 4151
7: 1 from all filthiness of the flesh and s, 4151
7:13 because his s was refreshed by you all. 4151
11: 4 or if ye receive another s, which ye have 4151
12:18 walked we not in the same s? walked we 4151
Gal 3: 2 Received ye the S by the works of the law, 4151
3: 3 having begun in the S, are ye now made 4151
3: 5 He therefore that ministereth to you the S, 4151
3:14 that we might receive the promise of the S 4151
4: 6 God hath sent forth the S of his Son into 4151
4:29 persecuted him that was born after the S, 4151
5: 5 For we through the S wait for the hope of 4151
5:16 Walk in the S, and ye shall not fulfil 4151
5:17 For the flesh lusteth against the S, and 4151
5:17 the Spirit, and the S against the flesh: 4151
5:18 But if ye be led of the S, ye are not under 4151
5:22 But the fruit of the S is love, joy, peace, 4151
5:25 If we live in the S, let us also walk in 4151
5:25 live in the Spirit, let us also walk in the S. 4151
6: 1 restore such a one in the s of meekness; 4151
6: 8 he that soweth to the S shall of the Spirit 4151
6: 8 he that soweth to the Spirit shall of the S 4151
6:18 of our Lord Jesus Christ be with your s. 4151
Eph 1:13 ye were sealed with that holy S of promise, 4151
1:17 may give unto you the s of wisdom and 4151
2: 2 the s that now worketh in the children of 4151
2:18 both have access by one S unto the Father. 4151
2:22 for a habitation of God through the S. 4151
3: 5 his holy apostles and prophets by the S; 4151
3:16 to be strengthened with might by his S in 4151
4: 3 Endeavouring to keep the unity of the S in 4151
4: 4 There is one body, and one S, even as ye 4151
4:23 And be renewed in the s of your mind; 4151
4:30 And grieve not the holy S of God, 4151
5: 9 (For the fruit of the S is in all goodness and 4151
5:18 wherein is excess; but be filled with the S; 4151
6:17 and the sword of the S, which is the word 4151
6:18 with all prayer and supplication in the S, 4151
Php 1:19 and the supply of the S of Jesus Christ, 4151
1:27 of your affairs, that ye stand fast in one s, 4151
2: 1 if any fellowship of the S, if any bowels 4151
3: 3 which worship God in the s, and rejoice in 4151
Col 1: 8 also declared unto us your love in the S. 4151
2: 5 yet am I with you in the s, joying and 4151
1Th 4: 8 who hath also given unto us his holy S. 4151
5:19 Quench not the S. 4151
5:23 and I pray God your whole s and soul and 4151
2Th 2: 2 or be troubled, neither by s, nor by word, 4151
2: 8 whom the Lord shall consume with the s of 4151
2:13 to salvation through sanctification of the S 4151
1Ti 3:16 justified in the S, seen of angels, 4151
4: 1 Now the S speaketh expressly, that in 4151
4:12 in charity, in s, in faith, in purity. 4151
2Ti 1: 7 For God hath not given us the s of fear; but 4151
4:22 The Lord Jesus Christ be with thy s. Grace 4151
Phm 1:25 of our Lord Jesus Christ be with your s. 4151
Heb 4:12 even to the dividing asunder of soul and s, 4151
9:14 who through the eternal S offered himself 4151
10:29 and hath done despite unto the S of grace? 4151
Jas 2:26 For as the body without the s is dead, so 4151

S

Jas 4: 5 the **s** that dwelleth in us lusteth to envy? *4151*
1Pe 1: 2 through sanctification of the **S**, *4151*
1:11 what manner of time the **S** of Christ which *4151*
1:22 the **S** unto unfeigned love of the brethren, *4151*
3: 4 *even the ornament* of a meek and quiet **s**, *4151*
3:18 death in the flesh, but quickened by the **S**: *4151*
4: 6 the flesh, but live according to God in the **s**. *4151*
4:14 happy *are ye;* for the **s** of glory and of God *4151*
1Jn 3:24 in us, by the **S** which he hath given us. *4151*
4: 1 believe not every **s**, but try the spirits *4151*
4: 2 Hereby know ye the **S** of God: Every spirit *4151*
4: 2 Every **s** that confesseth that Jesus Christ is *4151*
4: 3 And every **s** that confesseth not that Jesus *4151*
4: 3 and this is *that* **s** of antichrist, whereof you NIG
4: 6 Hereby know we the **s** of truth, and *4151*
4: 6 we the spirit of truth, and the **s** of error. *4151*
4:13 he in us, because he hath given us of his **S**. *4151*
5: 6 And it is the **S** that beareth witness, because *4151*
5: 6 that beareth witness, because the **S** is truth. *4151*
5: 8 the **S**, and the water, and the blood: *4151*
Jude 1:19 sensual, having not the **S**. *4151*
Rev 1:10 I was in the **s** on the Lord's day, and *4151*
2: 7 let him hear what the **S** saith unto *4151*
2:11 let him hear what the **S** saith unto *4151*
2:17 let him hear what the **S** saith unto *4151*
2:29 let him hear what the **S** saith unto *4151*
3: 6 let him hear what the **S** saith unto *4151*
3:13 let him hear what the **S** saith unto *4151*
3:22 let him hear what the **S** saith unto *4151*
4: 2 And immediately I was in the **s**: and *4151*
11:11 a half the **s** of life from God entered into *4151*
14:13 Yea, saith the **S**, that they may rest from *4151*
17: 3 So he carried me away in the **s** into *4151*
18: 2 and the hold of every foul **s**, and a cage of *4151*
19:10 for the testimony of Jesus is the **s** of *4151*
21:10 And he carried me away in the **s** to a great *4151*
22:17 And the **S** and the bride say, Come. And let *4151*

[HOLY] SPIRIT See [HOLY] GHOST

SPIRITIST See WIZARD

SPIRITS (46) [SPIRIT]

Lev 19:31 Regard not them that have **familiar s**, 178
20: 6 that turneth after such as have **familiar s**, 178
Nu 16:22 said, O God, the God of the **s** of all flesh, 7307
27:16 the LORD, the God of the **s** of all flesh, 7307
Dt 18:11 or a consulter with **familiar s**, or a wizard, 178
1Sa 28: 3 Saul had put away those that had **familiar s**, 178
28: 9 he hath cut off those that have **familiar s**, 178
2Ki 21: 6 and dealt with **familiar s** and wizards: 178
23:24 Moreover the *workers with* **familiar s**, and 178
Ps 104: 4 Who maketh his angels **s**; his ministers a 7307
Pr 16: 2 own eyes; but the LORD weigheth the **s**. 7307
Isa 8:19 Seek unto them that have **familiar s**, and 178
19: 3 to them that have **familiar s**, and to 178
Zec 6: 5 These *are* the four **s** of the heavens, 7307
Mt 8:16 and he cast out the **s** with *his* word, and *4151*
10: 1 he gave them power against unclean **s**, *4151*
12:45 taketh with himself seven other **s** more *4151*
Mk 1:27 commandeth he even the unclean **s**, *4151*
3:11 And unclean **s**, when they saw him, *4151*
5:13 And the unclean **s** went out, and *4151*
6: 7 two; and gave them power over unclean **s**; *4151*
Lk 4:36 and power he commandeth the unclean **s**, *4151*
6:18 And they that were vexed with unclean **s**: *4151*
7:21 *their* infirmities and plagues, and of evil **s**; *4151*
8: 2 which had been healed of evil **s** and *4151*
10:20 rejoice not, that the **s** are subject unto you; *4151*
11:26 taketh to *him* seven other **s** more wicked *4151*
Ac 5:16 and *them which were* vexed with unclean **s**: *4151*
8: 7 For unclean **s**, crying with loud voice, *4151*
19:12 from them, and the evil **s** went out of them. *4151*
19:13 had evil **s** the name of the Lord Jesus, *4151*
1Co 12:10 to another discerning of **s**; *4151*
14:32 And the **s** of the prophets are subject to *4151*
1Ti 4: 1 giving heed to seducing **s**, and doctrines of *4151*
Heb 1: 7 Who maketh his angels **s**, and his ministers *4151*
1:14 Are they not all ministering **s**, sent forth to *4151*
12: 9 rather be in subjection unto the Father of **s**, *4151*
12:23 and to the **s** of just *men* made perfect, *4151*
1Pe 3:19 he went and preached unto the **s** in prison; *4151*
1Jn 4: 1 but try the **s** whether they are of God: *4151*
Rev 1: 4 from the seven **s** which are before his *4151*
3: 1 These *things* saith he that hath the seven **s** *4151*
4: 5 the throne, which are the seven **s** of God. *4151*
5: 6 which are the seven **s** of God sent forth into *4151*
16:13 And I saw three unclean **s** like frogs *come* *4151*
16:14 For they are the **s** of devils, working *4151*

SPIRITUAL (28) [SPIRIT]

Hos 9: 7 the **s** man *is* mad, for the multitude of thine 7307
Ro 1:11 that I may impart unto you some **s** gift, *4152*
7:14 For we know that the law is **s**: but I am *4152*
15:27 **s** *things,* their duty is also to minister unto *4152*
1Co 2:13 comparing **s** *things* with spiritual. *4152*
2:13 comparing spiritual *things* with **s**. *4152*
2:15 But he that is **s** judgeth all *things,* yet he *4152*
3: 1 could not speak unto you as unto **s**, but *4152*
9:11 If we have sown unto you **s** *things, is it* a *4152*
10: 3 And did all eat the same **s** meat; *4152*
10: 4 And did all drink the same **s** drink: for they *4152*
10: 4 for they drank of *that* **s** Rock that followed *4152*
12: 1 Now concerning **s** *gifts,* brethren, I would *4152*
14: 1 and desire **s** *gifts,* but rather that ye may *4152*
14:12 forasmuch as ye are zealous of **s** *gifts,* seek *4151*
14:37 any *man* think himself to be a prophet, or **s**, *4152*
15:44 is sown a natural body; it is raised a **s** body. *4152*
15:44 is a natural body, and there is a **s** body. *4152*
15:46 Howbeit *that was* not first *which is* **s**, but *4152*
15:46 *is* natural; *and* afterward *that which is* **s**. *4152*
Gal 6: 1 man be overtaken in a fault, ye which are **s**, *4152*
Eph 1: 3 who hath blessed us with all **s** blessings in *4152*
5:19 in psalms and hymns and **s** songs, *4152*
6:12 against **s** wickedness in high *places.* *4152*
Col 1: 9 his will in all wisdom and **s** understanding; *4152*
3:16 another in psalms and hymns and **s** songs, *4152*
1Pe 2: 5 as lively stones, are built *up* a **s** house, *4152*
2: 5 a holy priesthood, to offer up **s** sacrifices, *4152*

SPIRITUALLY (3) [SPIRIT]

Ro 8: 6 but to be **s** minded *is* life and peace. *4151*
1Co 2:14 know *them,* because they are **s** discerned. *4153*
Rev 11: 8 which **s** is called Sodom and Egypt, *4153*

SPIT (11) [SPAT, SPITTED, SPITTING, SPITTLE]

Lev 15: 8 if he that hath the issue **s** upon him that is 7556
Nu 12:14 If her father had **but s** in her face, 3417+3417
Dt 25: 9 and **s** in his face, and shall answer and say, 3417
Job 30:10 far from me, and spare not to **s** in my face. 7536
Mt 26:67 Then did they **s** in his face, and *1716*
27:30 And they **s** upon him, and took the reed, *1716*
Mk 7:33 his ears, and he **s**, and touched his tongue; *4429*
8:23 and when he had **s** on his eyes, and put *his* *4429*
10:34 and shall **s upon** him, and shall kill him: *1716*
14:65 And some began to **s on** him, and to cover *1716*
15:19 and did **s upon** him, and bowing *their* *1716*

SPITE (1) [SPITEFULLY]

Ps 10:14 seen *it;* for thou beholdest mischief and **s**, 3708

SPITEFULLY (2) [SPITE]

Mt 22: 6 and **entreated** *them* **s**, and slew *them.* *5195*
Lk 18:32 and **s entreated**, and spitted on: *5195*

SPITTED (1) [SPIT]

Lk 18:32 and spitefully entreated, and **s on**: *1716*

SPITTING (1) [SPIT]

Isa 50: 6 I hid not my face from shame and **s**. 7536

SPITTLE (3) [SPIT]

1Sa 21:13 and let his **s** fall down upon his beard. 7388
Job 7:19 nor let me alone till I swallow down my **s**? 7536
Jn 9: 6 and made clay of the **s**, and he anointed *4427*

SPLENDID See GOODLIER; GOODLIEST; GOODLY

SPLINT See ROLLER

SPLIT See CLAVE

SPOIL (118) [SPOILED, SPOILER, SPOILERS, SPOILEST, SPOILETH, SPOILING, SPOILS]

Ge 49:27 the prey, and at night he shall divide the **s**. 7998
Ex 3:22 and ye shall **s** the Egyptians. 5337
15: 9 I will overtake, I will divide the **s**; 7998
Nu 31: 9 **took** the **s** of all their cattle, and all their 962
31:11 they took all the **s**, and all the prey, *both* of 7998
31:12 the prey, and the **s**, unto Moses, and 7998
31:53 (*For* the men of war had **taken s**, every man 962
Dt 2:35 and the **s** of the cities which we took. 7998
3: 7 all the cattle, and the **s** of the cities, we took 7998
13:16 thou shalt gather all the **s** of it into 7998
13:16 all the **s** thereof every whit, for the LORD 7998
20:14 all that is in the city, *even* all the **s** thereof, 7998
20:14 thou shalt eat the **s** of thine enemies, 7998
Jos 8: 2 only the **s** thereof, and the cattle thereof, 7998
8:27 the **s** of that city Israel took for a prey unto 7998
11:14 all the **s** of these cities, and the cattle, 7998
22: 8 divide the **s** of your enemies with your 7998
Jdg 5:30 *meet* for the necks of *them that take* the **s**? 7998
14:19 took their **s**, and gave change *of garments* 2488
1Sa 14:30 of the **s** of their enemies which they found? 7998
14:32 the people flew upon the **s**, and took sheep, 7998
14:36 **s** them until the morning light, and let us not 962
15:19 didst fly upon the **s**, and didst evil in 7998
15:21 the people took of the **s**, sheep and oxen, 7998
30:16 of all the great **s** that they had taken out of 7998
30:19 neither sons nor daughters, neither **s**, 7998
30:20 *other* cattle, and said, This *is* David's **s**. 7998
30:22 we will not give them *ought* of the **s** that 7998
30:26 he sent of the **s** unto the elders of Judah, 7998
30:26 Behold a present for you of the **s** of 7998
2Sa 3:22 a troop, and brought in a great **s** with them: 7998
8:12 of Amalek, and of the **s** of Hadadezer, 7998
12:30 he brought forth the **s** of the city in great 7998
23:10 the people returned after him only to **s**. 6584
2Ki 3:23 one another: now therefore, Moab, to the **s**. 7998
21:14 become a prey and a **s** to all their enemies; 4933
1Ch 20: 2 he brought also exceeding much **s** *out* of 7998
2Ch 14:13 and they carried away very much **s**. 7998
14:14 for there was *exceeding* much **s** in them. 961
15:11 of the **s** *which* they had brought, 7998
20:25 his people came to take away the **s** of them, 7998
20:25 they were three days in gathering of the **s**, 7998
24:23 sent all the **s** of them unto the king of 7998
25:13 three thousand of them, and took much **s**. 961
28: 8 took also away much **s** from them, and 7998
28: 8 from them, and brought the **s** to Samaria. 7998
28:14 the **s** before the princes and all 961
28:15 with the **s** clothed all *that were* naked 7998
Ezr 9: 7 and to a **s**, and to confusion of face, 961
Est 3:13 and *to take* the **s** of them for a prey. 7998
8:11 and *to take* the **s** of them for a prey, 7998
9:10 but on the **s** laid they not their hand. 961
Job 29:17 and pluckt the **s** out of his teeth. 2964
Ps 44:10 and they which hate us **s** for themselves. 8154
68:12 she that tarried at home divided the **s**. 7998
89:41 All that pass by the way **s** him: he is a 8155
109:11 he hath; and let the strangers **s** his labour. 962
119:162 at thy word, as one that findeth great **s**. 7998
Pr 1:13 we shall fill our houses *with* **s**: 7998
16:19 than to divide the **s** with the proud. 7998
22:23 and **s** the soul of those that spoiled them. 6906
24:15 of the righteous; **s** not his resting place: 7703
31:11 in her, so that he shall have no need of **s**. 7998
SS 2:15 the foxes, the little foxes, that **s** the vines: 2254
Isa 3:14 the **s** of the poor *is* in your houses. 1500
8: 4 the **s** of Samaria shall be taken away before 7998
9: 3 *and* as *men* rejoice when they divide the **s**. 7998
10: 6 to take the **s**, and to take the prey, and 7998
11:14 they shall **s** them of the east together: 962
17:14 This *is* the portion of them that **s** us, and 8154
33: 1 when thou shalt cease to **s**, thou shalt be 7703
33: 4 your **s** shall be gathered *like* the gathering 7998
33:23 is the prey of a great **s** divided; the lame 7998
42:22 *for* a **s**, and none saith, Restore. 4933
42:24 Who gave Jacob for a **s**, and Israel to 4933
53:12 and he shall divide the **s** with the strong; 7998
Jer 5: 6 *and* a wolf of the evenings shall **s** them, 7703
6: 7 violence and **s** is heard in her; before me 7701
15:13 thy treasures will I give to the **s** without 957
17: 3 thy substance *and* all thy treasures to the **s**, 957
20: 5 which shall **s** them, and take them, and 962
20: 8 I spake, I cried out, I cried violence and **s**; 7701
30:16 they that **s** thee shall be a spoil, and all that 7601
30:16 they that spoil thee shall be a **s**, and all that 4933
47: 4 Because of the day that cometh to **s** all 7703
47: 4 for the LORD *will* **s** the Philistines, 7703
49:28 go up to Kedar, and **s** the men of the east. 7703
49:32 and the multitude of their cattle a **s**: 7998
50:10 Chaldea shall be a **s**: all that spoil her shall 7998
50:10 all that **s** her shall be satisfied, saith 7997
Eze 7:21 and to the wicked of the earth for a **s**; 7998
14:15 they **s** it, so that it be desolate, that no man 7921
25: 7 and will deliver thee for a **s** to the heathen; 957
26: 5 and it shall become a **s** to the nations. 957
26:12 they shall **make a s** of thy riches, and 7997
29:19 and **take** her **s**, and take her prey; 7997+7998
32:12 they shall **s** the pomp of Egypt, and all 7703
38:12 To **take a s**, and to take a prey; to 7997+7998
38:13 unto thee, Art thou come to **take a s**? 7997+7998
38:13 *away* cattle and goods, to take a great **s**? 7998
39:10 they shall **s** those that spoiled them, and 7997
45: 9 remove violence and **s**, and 7701
Da 11:24 among them the prey, and **s**, and riches: 7998
11:33 by flame, by captivity, and by **s**, *many* days. 961
Hos 10: 2 down their altars, he shall **s** their images. 7703
13:15 he shall **s** the treasure of all pleasant 8154
Na 2: 9 **Take** ye **the s** of silver, take the spoil of 962
2: 9 ye the spoil of silver, **take the s** of gold: 962
Hab 2: 8 all the remnant of the people shall **s** thee; 7997
2:17 the **s** of beasts, *which* made them afraid, 7701
Zep 2: 9 the residue of my people shall **s** them, and 962
Zec 2: 9 and they shall be a **s** to their servants: 7998
14: 1 thy **s** shall be divided in the midst of thee. 7998
Mt 12:29 and **s** his goods, except he first bind *1283*
12:29 strong *man?* and then he will **s** his house. *1283*
Mk 3:27 and **s** his goods, except he will first bind *1283*
3:27 strong *man;* and then he will **s** his house. *1283*
Col 2: 8 Beware lest any *man* **s** you through *4812*

SPOILED (55) [SPOIL]

Ge 34:27 **s** the city, because they had defiled their 962
34:29 and **s** even all that *was* in the house. 962
Ex 12:36 *as they required.* And they **s** the Egyptians. 5337
Dt 28:29 shalt be only oppressed and **s** evermore, 1497
Jdg 2:14 them into the hands of spoilers that **s** them. 8155
2:16 them out of the hand of those that **s** them. 8154
1Sa 14:48 Israel out of the hands of them that **s** them. 8154
17:53 after the Philistines, and they **s** their tents. 8155
2Ki 7:16 went out, and **s** the tents of the Syrians. 962
2Ch 14:14 they **s** all the cities; for there was *exceeding* 962
Job 12:17 He leadeth counsellers away **s**, and 7758
12:19 He leadeth princes away **s**, and 7758
Ps 76: 5 The stouthearted are **s**, they have slept their 7997
Pr 22:23 and spoil the soul of those that **s** them. 6906
Isa 13:16 their houses shall be **s**, and their wives 8155
18: 2 trodden down, whose land the rivers have **s**. 958
18: 7 under foot, whose land the rivers have **s**, 958
24: 3 shall be utterly emptied, and **utterly s**: 962+962
33: 1 to thee that spoilest, and thou *wast* not **s**; 7703
33: 1 thou shalt cease to spoil, thou shalt be **s**; 7703
42:22 this *is* a people robbed and **s**; *they are* all of 8154
Jer 2:14 *is* he a homeborn *slave? why* is he **s**? 957
4:13 than eagles. Woe unto us! for we are **s**. 7703
4:20 destruction is cried; for the whole land is **s**: 7703
4:20 suddenly are my tents **s**, *and* my curtains in 7703
4:30 when thou art **s**, what wilt thou do? 7703
9:19 wailing is heard out of Zion, How are we **s**! 7703
10:20 My tabernacle is **s**, and all my cords are 7703
21:12 deliver *him that is* **s** out of the hand of 1497
22: 3 deliver the **s** out of the hand of 1497
25:36 *shall be heard:* for the LORD *hath* **s** their 7703
48: 1 for it is **s**: Kiriathaim is confounded *and* 7703
48:15 Moab is **s**, and gone up *out of* her cities, 7703
48:20 and cry; tell ye *it* in Arnon, that Moab is **s**, 7703
49: 3 Howl, O Heshbon, for Ai is **s**: cry, 7703
49:10 his seed is **s**, and his brethren, and 7703
51:55 Because the LORD *hath* **s** Babylon, and 7703
Eze 18: 7 hath **s** none by violence, hath given his 1497
18:12 the poor and needy, hath **s** by violence, 1497
18:16 neither hath **s** by violence, *but* hath given 1497
18:18 **s** *his* brother by violence, and did *that* 1497
23:46 and *will* give them to be removed and **s**. 957
39:10 they shall spoil those that **s** them, and 7997
Hos 10:14 thy people, and all thy fortresses shall be **s**, 7703
10:14 as Shalman **s** Beth-arbel in the day of 7701
Am 3:11 from thee, and thy palaces shall be **s**. 962
5: 9 That strengtheneth the **s** against the strong, 7701
5: 9 so that the **s** shall come against the fortress. 7701
Mic 2: 4 *and* say, We be **utterly s**: 7703+7703
Hab 2: 8 Because thou hast **s** many nations, all 7997
Zec 2: 8 he sent me unto the nations which **s** you: 7997
11: 2 cedar is fallen; because the mighty are **s**: 7703
11: 3 of the shepherds; for their glory is **s**: 7703
11: 3 of young lions; for the pride of Jordan is **s**. 7703
Col 2:15 *And* having **s** principalities and powers, *554*

SPOILER (9) [SPOIL]

Isa 16: 4 thou a covert to them from the face of the **s**: 7703

S

Isa 16: 4 the extortioner is at an end, the **s** ceaseth, 7701
21: 2 dealeth treacherously, and the **s** spoileth. 7703
Jer 6:26 for the **s** shall suddenly come upon us. 7703
15: 8 mother of the young men a **s** at noonday: 7703
48: 8 the **s** shall come upon every city, and 7703
48:18 for the **s** of Moab shall come upon thee, 7703
48:32 the **s** is fallen upon thy summer fruits and 7703
51:56 Because the **s** is come upon her, *even* upon 7703

SPOILERS (7) [SPOIL]
Jdg 2:14 he delivered them into the hands of **s** that 8154
1Sa 13:17 the **s** came out of the camp of 7843
14:15 the garrison, and the **s**, they also trembled, 7843
2Ki 17:20 and delivered them into the hand of **s**, 8154
Jer 12:12 The **s** are come upon all high places 7703
51:48 for the **s** shall come unto her from 7703
51:53 *yet* from me shall **s** come unto her, saith 7703

SPOILEST (1) [SPOIL]
Isa 33: 1 Woe to thee that **s**, and thou *wast* not 7703

SPOILETH (4) [SPOIL]
Ps 35:10 and the needy from him that **s** him? 1497
Isa 21: 2 dealeth treacherously, and the spoiler **s**. 7703
Hos 7: 1 *and* the troop *of robbers* **s** without. 6584
Na 3:16 the cankerworm **s**, and flieth away. 6584

SPOILING (5) [SPOIL]
Ps 35:12 They rewarded me evil for good *to* the **s** of 7908
Isa 22: 4 of the **s** of the daughter of my people. 7701
Jer 48: 3 *be* from Horonaim, **s** and great destruction. 7701
Hab 1: 3 for **s** and violence *are* before me: and 7701
Heb 10:34 and took joyfully the **s** of your goods, *724*

SPOILS (5) [SPOIL]
Jos 7:21 When I saw among the **s** a goodly 7998
1Ch 26:27 Out of the **s** **won** in battles did they 7998
Isa 25:11 their pride together with the **s** of their hands. 698
Lk 11:22 wherein he trusted, and divideth his **s**. *4661*
Heb 7: 4 patriarch Abraham gave the tenth of the **s**. *205*

SPOKEN (287) [SPEAK]
Ge 12: 4 as the LORD had **s** unto him; 1696
18:19 upon Abraham that which he hath **s** of him. 1696
19:21 *this* city, for the which thou hast **s**. 1696
21: 1 and the LORD did unto Sarah as he had **s**. 1696
21: 2 at the set time of which God had **s** to him. 1696
24:51 master's son's wife, as the LORD hath **s**. 1696
28:15 until I have done *that* which I have **s** to thee 1696
41:28 This *is* the thing which I have **s** unto 1696
44: 2 did according to the word that Joseph had **s**. 1696
Ex 4:10 nor since thou hast **s** unto thy servant: 1696
4:30 words which the LORD had **s** unto Moses, 1696
9:12 as the LORD had **s** unto Moses. 1696
9:35 of Israel go; as the LORD had **s** by Moses. 1696
10:29 Moses said, Thou hast **s** well, I will see thy 1696
19: 8 said, All that the LORD hath **s** we will do. 1696
32:13 all this land that I have **s** of will I give unto 559
32:34 unto *the place* of which I have **s** unto thee: 1696
33:17 I will do this thing also that thou hast **s**: 1696
34:32 the LORD had **s** with him in mount Sinai. 1696
Lev 10:11 hath **s** unto them by the hand of Moses. 1696
Nu 1:48 For the LORD had **s** unto Moses, saying, 1696
10:29 for the LORD hath **s** good concerning 1696
12: 2 Hath the LORD indeed **s** only by Moses? 1696
12: 2 hath he not **s** also by us? And the LORD 1696
14:17 be great, according as thou hast **s**, saying, 1696
14:28 as ye have **s** in mine ears, so will I do to 1696
15:22 which the LORD hath **s** unto Moses, 1696
21: 7 for we have **s** against the LORD, and 1696
23: 2 Balak did as Balaam had **s**; and Balak and 1696
23:17 said unto him, What hath the LORD **s**? 1696
23:19 shall he not do *it*? or hath he **s**, and shall he 1696
Dt 1:14 The thing which thou hast **s** is good *for us* 1696
5:28 of this people, which they have **s** unto thee: 1696
5:28 they have well *said* all that they have **s**. 1696
6:19 from before thee, as the LORD hath **s**. 1696
13: 5 he hath **s** to turn *you* away from 1696
18:17 They have well **s** *that* which they have NIH
18:17 have well *spoken that* which they have **s**. 1696
18:21 the word which the LORD hath not **s**? 1696
18:22 *is* the thing which the LORD hath not **s**, 1696
18:22 the prophet hath **s** it presumptuously: 1696
26:19 unto the LORD thy God, as he hath **s**. 1696
Jos 6: 8 to pass, when Joshua had **s** unto the people, 559
21:45 the LORD had **s** unto the house of Israel; 1696
Ru 2:13 for that thou hast **s** friendly unto thine 1696
1Sa 1:16 of my complaint and grief have I **s** hitherto. 1696
3:12 *things* which I have **s** concerning his house: 1696
20:23 the matter which thou and I have **s** of, 1696
25:30 all the good that he hath **s** concerning thee, 1696
2Sa 2:27 unless thou hadst **s**, surely then in 1696
3:18 then do *it*: for the LORD hath **s** of David, 559
6:22 and of the maidservants which thou hast **s** of, 559
7:19 thou hast **s** also of thy servant's house for a 1696
7:25 the word that thou hast **s** concerning thy 1696
7:29 hast **s** *it*: and with thy blessing let the house 1696
14:19 left from ought that my lord the king hath **s**: 1696
17: 6 saying, Ahithophel hath **s** after this manner: 1696
1Ki 2:23 if Adonijah have not **s** this word against his 1696
12: 9 this people, who have **s** to me, saying, 1696
13: 3 This *is* the sign which the LORD hath **s**; 1696
13:11 the words which he had **s** unto the king, 1696
14:11 of the air eat: for the LORD hath **s** *it*. 1696
18:24 the people answered and said, It is well **s**. 1697
21: 4 which Naboth the Jezreelite had **s** to him: 1696
22:23 the LORD hath **s** evil concerning thee. 1696
22:28 all in peace, the LORD hath not **s** by me. 1696
2Ki 1:17 the word of the LORD which Elijah had **s**. 1696
4:13 wouldest thou be **s** for to the king, or to 1696
7:18 it came to pass as the man of God had **s** to 1696
19:21 This *is* the word that the LORD hath **s** 1696
20: 9 the LORD will do the thing that he hath **s**: 1696
20:19 the word of the LORD which thou hast **s**. 1696
1Ch 17:17 for thou hast *also* **s** of thy servant's house 1696
17:23 let the thing that thou hast **s** concerning thy 1696
2Ch 2:15 and the wine, which my lord hath **s** of, 559
6:10 hath performed his word that he hath **s**: 1696
6:17 which thou hast **s** unto thy servant David. 1696
10: 9 which have **s** to me, saying, Ease somewhat 1696
18:22 and the LORD hath **s** evil against thee. 1696
18:27 in peace, *then* hath not the LORD **s** by me. 1696
36:22 that the word of the LORD **s** by the mouth NIH
Ezr 8:22 because we had **s** unto the king, saying, 559
Ne 2:18 as also the king's words that he had **s** unto 559
Est 6:10 let nothing fail of all that thou hast **s**. 1696
7: 9 who had **s** good for the king, standeth in 1696
Job 21: 3 and after that I have **s**, mock on. 1696
32: 4 Now Elihu had waited till Job had **s**, 1697
33: 2 my mouth, my tongue hath **s** in my mouth. 1696
33: 8 Surely thou hast **s** in mine hearing, and 559
34:35 Job hath **s** without knowledge, and 1696
40: 5 Once have I **s**; but I will not answer: yea, 1696
42: 7 that after the LORD had **s** these words 1696
42: 7 for ye have not **s** of me *the thing that is* 1696
42: 8 in that ye have not **s** of me *the thing which* 1696
Ps 50: 1 hath **s**, and called the earth from the rising 1696
60: 6 God hath **s** in his holiness; I will rejoice, 1696
62:11 God hath **s** once; twice have I heard this; 1696
66:14 my mouth hath **s**, when I was in trouble. 1696
87: 3 Glorious *things* are **s** of thee, O city of God. 1696
108: 7 God hath **s** in his holiness; I will rejoice, 1696
109: 2 they have **s** against me *with* a lying tongue. 1696
116:10 I believed, therefore have I **s**: I was greatly 1696
Pr 15:23 and a word **s** in due season, how good *is it*! NIH
25:11 A word fitly **s** *is like* apples of gold in 1696
Ecc 7:21 Also take no heed unto all words that are **s**; 1696
SS 8: 8 sister in the day when she shall be **s** for? 1696
Isa 1: 2 for the LORD hath **s**, I have nourished and 1696
1:20 for the mouth of the LORD hath **s** *it*. 1696
16:13 This *is* the word that the LORD hath **s** 1696
16:14 now the LORD hath **s**, saying, 1696
21:17 for the LORD God of Israel hath **s** *it*. 1696
22:25 it shall be cut off: for the LORD hath **s** *it*. 1696
23: 4 for the sea hath **s**, *even* the strength of 559
24: 3 for the LORD hath **s** this word. 1696
25: 8 off all the earth: for the LORD hath **s** *it*. 1696
31: 4 For thus hath the LORD **s** unto me, Like as 559
37:22 This *is* the word which the LORD hath **s** 1696
38: 7 the LORD will do this thing that he hath **s**; 1696
38:15 he hath both **s** unto me, and himself hath 559
39: 8 the word of the LORD which thou hast **s**. 1696
40: 5 for the mouth of the LORD hath **s** *it*. 1696
45:19 I have not **s** in secret, in a dark place of 1696
46:11 yea, I have **s** *it*, I will also bring it to pass; 1696
48:15 I, *even* I, have **s**; yea, I have called him: 1696
48:16 I have not **s** in secret from the beginning; 1696
58:14 for the mouth of the LORD hath **s** *it*. 1696
59: 3 your lips have **s** lies, your tongue hath 1696
Jer 3: 5 thou hast **s** and done evil *things* as thou 1696
4:28 because I have **s** *it*, I have purposed *it*, and 1696
9:12 to whom the mouth of the LORD hath **s**, 1696
13:15 be not proud: for the LORD hath **s**. 1696
23:21 I have not **s** to them, yet they prophesied. 1696
23:35 and, What hath the LORD **s**? 1696
23:37 and, What hath the LORD **s**? 1696
25: 3 I have **s** unto you, rising early and 1696
26:16 for he hath **s** to us in the name of 1696
27:13 as the LORD hath **s** against the nation that 1696
29:23 have **s** lying words in my name, which I 1696
30: 2 Write thee all the words that I have **s** unto 1696
32:24 what thou hast **s** is come to pass; and 1696
33:24 thou not what this people have **s**, 1696
35:14 notwithstanding I have **s** unto you, 1696
35:17 because I have **s** unto them, but they have 1696
36: 2 write therein all the words that I have **s** 1696
36: 4 which he had **s** unto him, upon a roll of a 1696
38: 1 heard the words that Jeremiah had **s** unto 1696
44:16 *As for* the word that thou hast **s** unto us in 1696
44:25 your wives have both **s** with your mouths, 1696
48: 8 shall be destroyed, as the LORD hath **s**. 559
51:62 O LORD, thou hast **s** against this place, 1696
Eze 5:13 they shall know that I the LORD have **s** *it* 1696
5:15 in furious rebukes. I the LORD have **s** *it*. 1696
5:17 sword upon thee. I the LORD have **s** *it*. 1696
12:28 the word which I have **s** shall be done, 1696
13: 7 have ye not **s** a lying divination, whereas ye 559
13: 7 The LORD saith *it*; albeit I have not **s**? 1696
13: 8 Because ye have **s** vanity, and seen lies, 1696
14: 9 if the prophet be deceived when he hath **s** a 1696
17:21 ye shall know that I the LORD have **s** *it*. 1696
17:24 I the LORD have **s** and have done *it*. 1696
21:32 for I the LORD have **s** *it*. 1696
22:14 I the LORD have **s** *it*, and will do *it*. 1696
22:28 Lord GOD, when the LORD hath not **s**. 1696
23:34 for I have **s** *it*, saith the Lord GOD. 1696
24:14 I the LORD have **s** *it*: it shall come to 1696
26: 5 for I have **s** *it*, saith the Lord GOD: and 1696
26:14 for I the LORD have **s** *it*, saith the Lord 1696
28:10 for I have **s** *it*, saith the Lord GOD. 1696
30:12 hand of strangers: I the LORD have **s** *it*. 1696
34:24 among them; I the LORD have **s** *it*. 1696
35:12 thou hast **s** against the mountains of Israel, 559
36: 5 Surely in the fire of my jealousy have I **s** 1696
36: 6 I have **s** in my jealousy and in my fury, 1696
36:36 I the LORD have **s** *it*, and I will do *it*. 1696
37:14 shall ye know that I the LORD have **s** *it*, 1696
38:17 *Art* thou he of whom I have **s** in old time by 1696
38:19 *and* in the fire of my wrath have I **s**, 1696
39: 5 for I have **s** *it*, saith the Lord GOD. 1696
39: 8 this *is* the day whereof I have **s**. 1696
Da 4:31 O king Nebuchadnezzar, to thee it is **s**; 560
10:11 when he had **s** this word unto me, I stood 1696
10:15 when he had **s** such words unto me, I set 1696
10:19 when he had **s** unto me, I was strengthened, 1696
Hos 7:13 yet they have **s** lies against me. 1696
10: 4 They have **s** words, swearing falsely in 1696
12:10 I have also **s** by the prophets, and I have 1696
Joel 3: 8 a people far off: for the LORD hath **s** *it*. 1696
Am 3: 1 Hear this word that the LORD hath **s** 1696
3: 8 the Lord GOD hath **s**, who can but 1696
5:14 God of hosts, shall be with you, as ye have **s**. 559
Ob 1:12 neither shouldest thou have **s** proudly in 6310
1:18 house of Esau; for the LORD hath **s** *it*. 1696
Mic 4: 4 the mouth of the LORD of hosts hath **s** *it*. 1696
6:12 the inhabitants thereof have **s** lies, and 1696
Zec 10: 2 For the idols have **s** vanity, and the diviners 1696
Mal 3:13 What have we **s** so much against thee? 1696
Mt 1:22 that it might be fulfilled which was **s** of *3004*
2:15 that it might be fulfilled which was **s** of *3004*
2:17 Then was fulfilled that which was **s** by *3004*
2:23 that it might be fulfilled which was **s** by *3004*
3: 3 For this is he that was **s** of by the prophet *3004*
4:14 That it might be fulfilled which was **s** by *3004*
8:17 That it might be fulfilled which was **s** by *3004*
12:17 That it might be fulfilled which was **s** by *3004*
13:35 That it might be fulfilled which was **s** by *3004*
21: 4 that it might be fulfilled which was **s** by *3004*
22:31 have ye not read that which was **s** unto you *3004*
24:15 **s** of by Daniel the prophet, stand in the holy *3004*
26:65 his clothes, saying, He hath **s** **blasphemy**; *987*
27: 9 Then was fulfilled that which was **s** by *3004*
27:35 that it might be fulfilled which was **s** by *3004*
Mk 1:42 And as soon as he had **s**, immediately *3004*
5:36 As soon as Jesus heard the word *that was* **s**, *2980*
12:12 for they knew that he had **s** the parable *3004*
13:14 **s** of by Daniel the prophet, standing where *3004*
14: 9 *this* also that she hath done shall be **s** of for *2980*
16:19 So then after the Lord had **s** unto them, *2980*
Lk 2:33 at those *things* which were **s** of him. *2980*
2:34 and for a sign which shall be **s** **against**; *483*
12: 3 Therefore whatsoever ye have **s** in darkness *3004*
12: 3 *that* which ye have **s** in the ear in closets *2980*
18:34 neither knew they the *things* which were **s**. *3004*
19:28 And when he had thus **s**, he went before, *3004*
20:19 for they perceived that he had **s** this parable *3004*
24:25 heart to believe all that the prophets have **s**: *2980*
24:40 And when he had thus **s**, he shewed them *3004*
Jn 4:50 the word that Jesus had **s** unto him, *3004*
9: 6 When he had thus **s**, he spat on the ground, *3004*
11:13 they thought that he had **s** of taking of rest *3004*
11:43 And when he thus had **s**, he cried with a *3004*
12:48 the word that I have **s**, the same shall judge *2980*
12:49 For I have not **s** of myself; but the Father *2980*
14:25 These *things* have I **s** unto you, being *yet* *2980*
15: 3 through the word which I have **s** unto you. *2980*
15:11 These *things* have I **s** unto you, that my joy *2980*
15:22 If I had not come and **s** unto them, they had *2980*
16: 1 These *things* have I **s** unto you, that ye *2980*
16:25 These *things* have I **s** unto you in proverbs: *2980*
16:33 These *things* I have **s** unto you, that in me *2980*
18: 1 When Jesus had **s** these *words*, he went *3004*
18:22 And when he had thus **s**, one of the officers *3004*
18:23 Jesus answered him, If I have **s** evil, *2980*
20:18 and *that* he had **s** these *things* unto her. *3004*
21:19 And when he had **s** this, he saith unto him, *3004*
Ac 1: 9 And when he had **s** these *things*, while they *3004*
2:16 But this is that which was **s** by the prophet *3004*
3:21 **s** by the mouth of all his holy prophets *2980*
3:24 those that follow after, as many as have **s**, *2980*
8:24 that none of *these things* which ye have **s** *3004*
9:27 and that he had **s** to him, and how he had *2980*
13:40 upon you, which is **s** of in the prophets; *3004*
13:45 spake against those *things* which were **s** by *3004*
13:46 of God should first have been **s** to you: *2980*
16:14 unto the *things* which were **s** of Paul. *2980*
19:36 then that these *things* **cannot be s against**, *368*
19:41 And when he had thus **s**, he dismissed *3004*
20:36 And when he had thus **s**, he kneeled down, *3004*
23: 9 but if a spirit or an angel hath **s** to him, *2980*
26:30 And when he had thus **s**, the king rose up, *3004*
27:11 more than those *things* which were **s** by *3004*
27:35 And when he had thus **s**, he took bread, and *3004*
28:22 we know that every where it is **s** **against**. *483*
28:24 some believed the *things* which were **s**, *3004*
28:25 after that Paul had **s** one word, *3004*
Ro 1: 8 that your faith is **s of** throughout the whole *2605*
4:18 according to that which was **s**, So shall thy *3004*
14:16 Let not then your good be **evil s of**: *987*
15:21 To whom he was not **s** of, they shall see: *312*
1Co 10:30 why am I **evil s of** for *that for* which I give *987*
14: 9 how shall it be known what is **s**? *2980*
2Co 4:13 I believed, *and* therefore have I **s**; *2980*
Heb 1: 2 Hath in these last days **s** unto us by *his* Son, *2980*
2: 2 For if the word **s** by angels was stedfast, *2980*
2: 3 which at the first began to be **s** by the Lord, *2980*
3: 5 of those *things* which were to be **s** after; *2980*
4: 8 would he not afterward have **s** of another *2980*
7:13 For he of whom these *things* are **s** *3004*
8: 1 Now of the *things* which we have **s** *this is* *3004*
9:19 For when Moses had **s** every precept to all *2980*
12:19 the **word** should not be **s** to them any more: *3056*
13: 7 who have **s** unto you the word of God: *2980*
Jas 5:10 who have **s** in the name of the Lord, *2980*
1Pe 4:14 on their part he is **evil s of**, but on your part *987*
2Pe 2: 2 of whom the way of truth shall be **evil s of**. *987*
3: 2 which were **s before** by the holy prophets, *4302*
Jude 1:15 which ungodly sinners have **s** against him. *2980*
1:17 **s before** of the apostles of our Lord Jesus *4302*

SPOKES (1)
1Ki 7:33 their naves, and their felloes, and their **s**, 2840

SPOKESMAN (1) [MAN, SPEAK]
Ex 4:16 he shall be thy **s** unto the people: and 1696

SPONGE See SPUNGE

SPOON (12) [SPOONS]
Nu 7:14 One **s** of ten *shekels* of gold, full *of* 3709
7:20 One **s** of gold of ten *shekels*, full *of* 3709
7:26 One golden **s** of ten *shekels*, full *of* incense: 3709
7:32 One golden **s** *of* ten *shekels*, full *of* incense: 3709

S

Nu 7:38 One golden **s** of ten *shekels,* full *of* incense: 3709
7:44 One golden **s** of ten *shekels,* full *of* incense: 3709
7:50 One golden **s** of ten *shekels,* full *of* incense: 3709
7:56 One golden **s** of ten *shekels,* full *of* incense: 3709
7:62 One golden **s** of ten *shekels,* full *of* incense: 3709
7:68 One golden **s** of ten *shekels,* full *of* incense: 3709
7:74 One golden **s** of ten *shekels,* full *of* incense: 3709
7:80 One golden **s** of ten *shekels,* full *of* incense: 3709

SPOONS (12) [SPOON]
Ex 25:29 **s** thereof, and covers thereof, and 3709
37:16 his **s**, and his bowls, and *his* covers to cover 3709
Nu 4: 7 the **s**, and the bowls, and covers to cover 3709
7:84 twelve silver bowls, twelve **s** of gold: 3709
7:86 The golden **s** *were* twelve, full *of* incense, 3709
7:86 all the gold of the **s** *was* an hundred and 3709
1Ki 7:50 and the **s**, and the censers *of* pure gold; 3709
2Ki 25:14 the **s**, and all the vessels of brass wherewith 3709
2Ch 4:22 the basons, and the **s**, and the censers, 3709
24:14 to offer *withal,* and **s**, and vessels of gold 3709
Jer 52:18 the **s**, and all the vessels of brass wherewith 3709
52:19 the candlesticks, and the **s**, and the cups; 3709

SPORT (6) [SPORTING]
Jdg 16:25 Call for Samson, that he may **make** us **s**. 7832
16:25 of the prison house; and he **made** them **s**: 6711
16:27 women, that beheld while Samson **made s**. 7832
Pr 10:23 *It is* as **s** to a fool to do mischief: but a man 7814
26:19 his neighbour, and saith, Am not I **in s**? 7832
Isa 57: 4 Against whom do ye **s** yourselves? 6026

SPORTING (2) [SPORT]
Ge 26: 8 behold, Isaac *was* **s with** Rebekah his wife. 6711
2Pe 2:13 **s** themselves with their own deceivings *1792*

SPOT (25) [SPOTS, SPOTTED, UNSPOTTED]
Lev 13: 2 or **bright s**, and it be in the skin of his flesh 934
13: 4 If the **bright s** *be* white in the skin of his 934
13:19 or a **bright s**, white, *and* somewhat reddish, 934
13:23 if the **bright s** stay in his place, *and* 934
13:24 *flesh* that burneth have a white **bright s**, 934
13:25 *if* the hair in the **bright s** be turned white, 934
13:26 *there be* no white hair in the **bright s**, and 934
13:28 if the **bright s** stay in his place, *and* 934
13:39 it *is* a **freckled s** *that* groweth in the skin: 933
14:56 a rising, and for a scab, and for a **bright s**: 934
Nu 19: 2 that they bring thee a red heifer **without s**, 8549
28: 3 two lambs of the first year **without s** day 8549
28: 9 day two lambs of the first year **without s**, 8549
28:11 seven lambs of the first year **without s**; 8549
29:17 fourteen lambs of the first year **without s**; 8549
29:26 fourteen lambs of the first year **without s**: 8549
Dt 32: 5 their **s** *is* not *the spot* of his children: 3971
32: 5 their spot *is* not *the* **s** of his children: NIH
Job 11:15 then shalt thou lift up thy face without **s**; 3971
SS 4: 7 *art* all fair, my love; *there is* no **s** in thee. 3971
Eph 5:27 not having **s**, or wrinkle, or any such *thing;* *4696*
1Ti 6:14 thou keep *this* commandment **without s**, *784*
Heb 9:14 Spirit offered himself **without s** to God, *299*
1Pe 1:19 as of a lamb without blemish and **without s**: *784*
2Pe 3:14 of him in peace, **without s**, and blameless. *784*

SPOTS (6) [SPOT]
Lev 13:38 have in the skin of their flesh **bright s**, 934
13:38 their flesh bright spots, *even* white **bright s**; 934
13:39 *if* the **bright s** in the skin of their flesh *be* 934
Jer 13:23 change his skin, or the leopard his **s**? 2272
2Pe 2:13 **S** *they are* and blemishes, *4696*
Jude 1:12 These are **s** in your feasts of charity when *4694*

SPOTTED (7) [SPOT]
Ge 30:32 from thence all the speckled and **s** cattle, 2921
30:32 and the **s** and speckled among the goats: 2921
30:33 *is* not speckled and **s** amongst the goats, 2921
30:35 the he goats that were ringstraked and **s**, 2921
30:35 all the she goats that were speckled and **s**, 2921
30:39 forth cattle ringstraked, speckled, and **s**. 2921
Jude 1:23 hating even the garment **s** by the flesh. *4695*

SPOUSE (6) [SPOUSES]
SS 4: 8 *my* **s**, with me from Lebanon: 3618
4: 9 hast ravished my heart, my sister, *my* **s**; 3618
4:10 How fair is thy love, my sister, *my* **s**! 3618
4:11 Thy lips, O *my* **s**, drop *as* the honeycomb: 3618
4:12 A garden inclosed *is* my sister, *my* **s**; 3618
5: 1 I am come into my garden, my sister, *my* **s**: 3618

SPOUSES (2) [SPOUSE]
Hos 4:13 and your **s** shall commit adultery. 3618
4:14 nor your **s** when they commit adultery: 3618

SPRANG (8) [SPRING]
Ge 41: 6 blasted with the east wind **s up** after them. 6779
Mk 4: 5 and immediately it **s up**, because *it* had no *1816*
4: 8 and did yield fruit that **s up** and increased; *305*
Lk 8: 7 and the thorns **s up with** *it,* and choked it. *4855*
8: 8 and **s up**, and bare fruit an hundredfold. *5453*
Ac 16:29 and **s in**, and came trembling, and *1530*
Heb 7:14 For *it is* evident that our Lord **s** out of Juda; *393*
11:12 Therefore **s** there even of one, and him as *1080*

SPREAD (109) [OVERSPREAD, SPREADEST, SPREADETH, SPREADING, SPREADINGS]
Ge 10:18 the families of the Canaanites **s abroad**. 6327
28:14 thou shalt **s abroad** to the west, and to 6555
33:19 a parcel of a field, where he had **s** his tent, 5186
35:21 and **s** his tent beyond the tower of Edar. 5186
Ex 9:29 I will **s abroad** my hands unto the LORD; 6566
9:33 **s abroad** his hands unto the LORD: 6566
37: 9 the cherubims **s out** *their* wings on high, 6566
40:19 he **s abroad** the tent over the tabernacle, 6566
Lev 13: 5 at a stay, *and* the plague **s** not in the skin; 6581
13: 6 and the plague **s** not in the skin, 6581
13: 7 if the scab **s much abroad** in 6581+6581
13:22 if it **s much abroad** in the skin, then 6581+6581
13:23 in his place, *and* **s** not, it *is* a burning boil; 6581
13:27 *and* if it be **s much abroad** in 6581+6581
13:28 *and* **s** not in the skin, but it *be* somewhat 6581
13:32 *if* the scall **s** not, and there be in it no 6581
13:34 behold, *if* the scall be not **s** in the skin, 6581
13:35 if the scall **s much** in the skin after 6581+6581
13:36 behold, *if* the scall be **s** in the skin, 6581
13:51 if the plague be **s** in the garment, either in 6581
13:53 behold, the plague be not **s** in the garment, 6581
13:55 changed his colour, and the plague be not **s**; 6581
14:39 *if* the plague be **s** in the walls of the house; 6581
14:44 and behold, *if* the plague be **s** in the house, 6581
14:48 behold, the plague hath not **s** in the house, 6581
Nu 4: 6 shall **s** over *it* a cloth wholly of blue, and 6566
4: 7 upon the table of shewbread they shall **s** a 6566
4: 8 they shall **s** upon them a cloth of scarlet, 6566
4:11 upon the golden altar they shall **s** a cloth of 6566
4:13 from the altar, and **s** a purple cloth thereon: 6566
4:14 they shall **s** upon it a covering of badgers' 6566
11:32 they **s** *them* **all abroad** for 7849+7849
24: 6 As the valleys are they **s forth**, as gardens 5186
Dt 22:17 they shall **s** the cloth before the elders of 6566
Jdg 8:25 We will willingly give *them.* And they **s** a 6566
15: 9 pitched in Judah, and **s** themselves in Lehi. 5203
Ru 3: 9 **s** therefore thy skirt over thine handmaid; 6566
1Sa 30:16 behold *they were* **s abroad** upon all 5203
2Sa 5:18 and **s** themselves in the valley of Rephaim 5203
5:22 and **s** themselves in the valley of Rephaim. 5203
16:22 So they **s** Absalom a tent upon the top of 5186
17:19 and **s** a covering over the well's mouth, 6566
17:19 well's mouth, and **s** ground corn thereon; 7849
21:10 and **s** it for her upon the rock, 5186
22:43 mire of the street, *and* did **s** them **abroad**. 7554
1Ki 6:32 **s** gold upon the cherubims, and upon 7286
8: 7 For the cherubims **s forth** *their* two wings 6566
8:22 and **s forth** his hands *toward* heaven: 6566
8:38 and **s forth** his hands towards this house: 6566
8:54 from kneeling on his knees with his hands **s** 6566
2Ki 8:15 and **s** *it* on his face, so that he died: 6566
19:14 of the LORD, and **s** it before the LORD. 6566
1Ch 14: 9 and **s** themselves in the valley of Rephaim. 6584
14:13 again **s** themselves **abroad** in the valley. 6584
28:18 that **s out** *their wings,* and covered the ark 6566
2Ch 3:13 **s** themselves **forth** twenty cubits: 6566
5: 8 For the cherubims **s forth** *their* wings over 6566
6:12 of Israel, and **s forth** his hands: 6566
6:13 and **s forth** his hands towards heaven, 6566
6:29 and shall **s forth** his hands in this house: 6566
26: 8 his name **s abroad** even to the entering in 1980
26:15 his name **s** far abroad; for he was 3318
Ezr 9: 5 **s out** my hands unto the LORD my God, 6566
Job 29:19 My root *was* **s out** by the waters, and 6605
37:18 Hast thou with him **s out** the sky, *which is* 7554
Ps 105:39 He **s** a cloud for a covering; and fire to give 6566
140: 5 cords; they have **s** a net by the way side; 6566
Pr 1:17 Surely in vain the net *is* **s** in the sight of any 2219
Isa 1:15 when ye **s forth** your hands, I will hide 6566
14:11 the worm is **s** under thee, and the worms 3331
19: 8 they that **s** nets upon the waters shall 6566
25: 7 and the vail that is **s** over all nations. 5259
25:11 he shall **s forth** his hands in the midst of 6566
33:23 their mast, they could not **s** the sail: 6566
37:14 of the LORD, and **s** it before the LORD. 6566
42: 5 he that **s forth** the earth, and that which 7554
58: 5 to **s** sackcloth and ashes *under him?* wilt 3331
65: 2 I have **s out** mine hands all the day unto a 6566
Jer 8: 2 they shall **s** them before the sun, and 7849
10: 9 Silver **s into plates** is brought from 7554
43:10 and he shall **s** his royal pavilion over them. 5186
48:40 an eagle, and shall **s** his wings over Moab. 6566
49:22 as the eagle, and **s** his wings over Bozrah: 6566
La 1:10 The adversary hath **s** out his hand upon all 6566
1:13 he hath **s** a net for my feet, he hath turned 6566
Eze 2:10 he **s** it before me; and it *was* written within 6566
12:13 My net also will I **s** upon him, and he shall 6566
16: 8 I **s** my skirt over thee, and covered thy 6566
17:20 I will **s** my net upon him, and he shall be 6566
19: 8 the provinces, and **s** their net over him: 6566
26:14 thou shalt be *a place* to **s** nets upon; 4894
32: 3 **s out** my net over thee with a company of 6566
47:10 they shall be a **place to s forth** nets; 4894
Hos 5: 1 a snare on Mizpah, and a net **s** upon Tabor. 6566
7:12 they shall go, I will **s** my net upon them; 6566
14: 6 His branches shall **s**, and his beauty shall be 1980
Joel 2: 2 as the morning **s** upon the mountains: 6566
Hab 1: 8 their horsemen shall **s** themselves, and 6335
Zec 1:17 through prosperity shall yet be **s abroad**; 6327
2: 6 for I have **s** you **abroad** as the four winds 6566
Mal 2: 3 your seed, and **s** dung upon your faces, 2219
Mt 9:31 **s abroad** his **fame** in all that country. *1310*
21: 8 And a very great multitude **s** their garments *4766*
Mk 1:28 And immediately his fame **s abroad** *1831*
6:14 heard *of him;* (for his name was **s abroad**:) *5318*
11: 8 And many **s** their garments in the way: and *4766*
Lk 19:36 as he went, they **s** their clothes in the way. *5291*
Ac 4:17 But that it **s** no further among the people, *1268*
1Th 1: 8 place your faith to God-ward is **s abroad**; *1831*

SPREADEST (1) [SPREAD]
Eze 27: 7 was that **which** thou **s forth** to be thy sail; 4666

SPREADETH (14) [SPREAD]
Lev 13: 8 the scab **s** in the skin, then the priest shall 6581
Dt 32:11 **s abroad** her wings, taketh them, 6566
Job 9: 8 Which alone **s out** the heavens, and 5186
26: 9 face of *his* throne, *and* **s** his cloud upon it. 6576
36:30 he **s** his light upon it, and covereth 6566
41:30 he **s** sharp pointed *things* upon the mire. 7502
Pr 29: 5 A man that flattereth his neighbour **s** a net 6566
Isa 25:11 as he that swimmeth **s forth** *his hands* to 6566
40:19 the goldsmith **s** it **over** with gold, and 7554
40:22 and **s** them **out** as a tent to dwell in: 4969
44:24 that **s abroad** the earth by myself; 7554
Jer 4:31 *that* bewaileth herself, *that* **s** her hands, 6566
17: 8 *that* **s out** her roots by the river, and 7971
La 1:17 Zion **s forth** her hands, *and there is* none to 6566

SPREADING (4) [SPREAD]
Lev 13:57 it *is* a **s** *plague:* thou shalt burn that wherein 6524
Ps 37:35 and **s** himself like a green bay tree. 6168
Eze 17: 6 it grew, and became a **s** vine of low stature, 5628
26: 5 It shall be *a place for* the **s** of nets in 4894

SPREADINGS (1) [SPREAD]
Job 36:29 Also can *any* understand the **s** of 4666

SPRIGS (2)
Isa 18: 5 he shall both cut off the **s** with pruning 2150
Eze 17: 6 brought forth branches, and shot forth **s**. 6288

SPRING (23) [DAYSPRING, SPRANG, SPRINGETH, SPRINGING, SPRINGS, SPRUNG, WATERSPRINGS, WELLSPRING]
Nu 21:17 Israel sang this song, **S up**, O well; sing ye 5927
Dt 8: 7 depths that **s out** of the valleys and hills; 3318
Jdg 19:25 when the day began to **s**, they let her go. 5927
1Sa 9:26 it came to pass about the **s** of the day, 5927
2Ki 2:21 he went forth unto the **s** of the waters, and 4161
Job 5: 6 neither doth trouble **s** out of the ground; 6779
38:27 **cause** the bud of the tender herb **to s forth**? 6779
Ps 85:11 Truth shall **s out** of the earth; and 6779
92: 7 When the wicked **s** as the grass, and 6524
Pr 25:26 *is as* a troubled fountain, and a corrupt **s**. 4726
SS 4:12 *my* spouse; a **s** shut up, a fountain sealed. 1530
Isa 42: 9 before they **s forth** I tell you of them. 6779
43:19 I will do a new *thing;* now it shall **s forth**; 6779
44: 4 they shall **s up** *as* among the grass, 6779
45: 8 and let righteousness **s up** together; 6779
58: 8 and thine health shall **s forth** speedily: 6779
58:11 and like a **s** of water, whose waters fail not. 4161
61:11 **causeth** the things that are sown in it **to s forth**; 6779
61:11 **cause** righteousness and praise **to s forth** 6779
Eze 17: 9 it shall wither *in* all the leaves of her **s**, 6780
Hos 13:15 his **s** shall become dry, and his fountain 4726
Joel 2:22 for the pastures of the wilderness do **s**, 1876
Mk 4:27 and day, and the seed should **s** and grow up, *985*

SPRINGETH (4) [SPRING]
1Ki 4:33 even unto the hyssop that **s out** of the wall: 3318
2Ki 19:29 the second year **that which s of the same**; 7823
Isa 37:30 the second year **that which s of the same**: 7823
Hos 10: 4 thus judgment **s up** as hemlock in 6524

SPRINGING (5) [SPRING]
Ge 26:19 and found there a well of **s** water. 2416
2Sa 23: 4 *as* the tender grass *s* out of the earth by clear NIH
Ps 65:10 with showers: thou blessest the **s** thereof. 6780
Jn 4:14 him a well of water **s up** into everlasting life. *242*
Heb 12:15 lest any root of bitterness **s** up trouble *you,* *5453*

SPRINGS (16) [SPRING]
Dt 4:49 the sea of the plain, under the **s** of Pisgah. 794
Jos 10:40 of the vale, and of the **s**, and all their kings: 794
12: 8 in the **s**, and in the wilderness, and in 794
15:19 me a south land; give me also **s** of water. 1543
15:19 he gave her the upper **s**, and the nether 1543
15:19 her the upper springs, and the nether **s**. 1543
Jdg 1:15 me a south land; give me also **s** of water. 1543
1:15 Caleb gave her the upper **s** and the nether 1543
1:15 gave her the upper springs and the nether **s**. 1543
Job 38:16 Hast thou entered into the **s** of the sea? or 5033
Ps 87: 7 *shall be there:* all my **s** *are* in thee. 4599
104:10 He sendeth the **s** into the valleys, *which* run 4599
Isa 35: 7 a pool, and the thirsty land **s** of water: 4002
41:18 a pool of water, and the dry land **s** of water. 4161
49:10 even by the **s** of water shall he guide them. 4002
Jer 51:36 I will dry up her sea, and make her **s** dry. 4726

SPRINKLE (31) [SPRINKLED, SPRINKLETH, SPRINKLING]
Ex 9: 8 let Moses **s** it towards the heaven in 2236
29:16 and **s** *it* round about upon the altar. 2236
29:20 and **s** the blood upon the altar round about. 2236
29:21 **s** *it* upon Aaron, and upon his garments, 5137
Lev 1: 5 **s** the blood round about upon the altar that 2236
1:11 shall **s** his blood round about upon the altar. 2236
3: 2 Aaron's sons the priests shall **s** the blood 2236
3: 8 Aaron's sons shall **s** the blood thereof 2236
3:13 the sons of Aaron shall **s** the blood thereof 2236
4: 6 **s** of the blood seven times before 5137
4:17 **s** *it* seven times before the LORD, 5137
5: 9 he shall **s** of the blood of the sin offering 5137
7: 2 the blood thereof shall he **s** round about 2236
14: 7 he shall **s** upon him that is to be cleansed 5137
14:16 shall **s** of the oil with his finger seven times 5137
14:27 the priest shall **s** with his right finger *some* 5137
14:51 running water, and **s** the house seven times: 5137
16:14 **s** *it* with his finger upon the mercy seat 5137
16:14 before the mercy seat shall he **s** of 5137
16:15 **s** it upon the mercy seat, and before 5137
16:19 he shall **s** of the blood upon it with his 5137
17: 6 the priest shall **s** the blood upon the altar of 2236
Nu 8: 7 **S** water of purifying upon them, and 5137
18:17 thou shalt **s** their blood upon the altar, and 2236
19: 4 **s** of her blood directly before the tabernacle 5137
19:18 **s** *it* upon the tent, and upon all the vessels, 5137
19:19 the clean *person* shall **s** upon the unclean 5137
2Ki 16:15 **s** upon it all the blood of the burnt offering, 2236
Isa 52:15 So shall he **s** many nations; the kings shall 5137
Eze 36:25 will I **s** clean water upon you, and ye shall 2236
43:18 offerings thereon, and to **s** blood thereon. 2236

SPRINKLED (25) [SPRINKLE]
Ex 9:10 Moses **s** it *up* toward heaven; and it became 2236
24: 6 and half of the blood he **s** on the altar. 2236
24: 8 the blood, and **s** *it* on the people, and said, 2236

S

Lev 6:27 when there is **s** of the blood thereof upon 5137
6:27 thou shalt wash that whereon it was **s** in 5137
8:11 And he **s** thereof upon the altar seven times, 5137
8:19 Moses **s** the blood upon the altar round 2236
8:24 Moses **s** the blood upon the altar round 2236
8:30 **s** *it* upon Aaron, *and* upon his garments, 5137
9:12 which he **s** round about upon the altar. 2236
9:18 which he **s** upon the altar round about, 2236
Nu 19:13 the water of separation was not **s** upon him, 2236
19:20 the water of separation hath not been **s** 2236
2Ki 9:33 *some* of her blood was **s** on the wall, and 5137
16:13 **s** the blood of his peace offerings, upon 2236
2Ch 29:22 received the blood, and **s** *it* on the altar: 2236
29:22 the rams, they **s** the blood upon the altar: 2236
29:22 and they **s** the blood upon the altar. 2236
30:16 the priests **s** the blood, *which they received* 2236
35:11 and the priests **s** *the blood* from their hands, 2236
Job 2:12 and **s** dust upon their heads toward heaven. 2236
Isa 63: 3 their blood shall be **s** upon my garments, 5137
Heb 9:19 and **s** both the book, and all the people, *4472*
9:21 Moreover he **s** with blood both *4472*
10:22 having *our* hearts **s** from an evil *4472*

SPRINKLETH (2) [SPRINKLE]
Lev 7:14 it shall be the priest's that **s** the blood of 2236
Nu 19:21 that he that **s** the water of separation shall 5137

SPRINKLING (4) [SPRINKLE]
Heb 9:13 and the ashes of a heifer **s** the unclean, *4472*
11:28 he kept the passover, and the **s** of blood, *4378*
12:24 and to the blood of **s**, that speaketh better *4473*
1Pe 1: 2 and **s** of the blood of Jesus Christ: *4473*

SPROUT (1)
Job 14: 7 that it will **s** again, and that the tender 2498

SPRUNG (7) [SPRING]
Ge 41:23 blasted with the east wind, **s up** after them: 6779
Lev 13:42 it *is* a leprosy **s up** in his bald head, or his 6524
Mt 4:16 the region and shadow of death light is **s up**. *393*
13: 5 and forthwith they **s up**, because *they* had *1816*
13: 7 and the thorns **s up**, and choked them: *305*
13:26 But when the blade was **s up**, and *985*
Lk 8: 6 and as soon as it was **s up**, it withered *5453*

SPUE (4) [SPUED, SPUING]
Lev 18:28 That the land **s** not you **out** also, when ye 6958
20:22 I bring you to dwell therein, **s** you not **out**. 6958
Jer 25:27 **s**, and fall, and rise no more, because of 7006
Rev 3:16 cold nor hot, I will **s** thee out of my mouth. *1692*

SPUED (1) [SPUE]
Lev 18:28 as it **s out** the nations that *were* before you. 6958

SPUING (1) [SPUE]
Hab 2:16 and **shameful s** *shall be* on thy glory. 7022

SPUN (2) [SPIN]
Ex 35:25 brought that which they had **s**, *both* of blue, 4299
35:26 stirred them up in wisdom **s** goats' *hair*. 2901

SPUNGE (3)
Mt 27:48 and took a **s**, and filled *it* with vinegar, and *4699*
Mk 15:36 And one ran and filled a **s** *full* of vinegar, *4699*
Jn 19:29 and they filled a **s** with vinegar, and put *it* *4699*

SPY (12) [ESPIED, ESPY, SPIED, SPIES]
Nu 13:16 men which Moses sent to **s out** the land. 8446
13:17 Moses sent them to **s out** the land of 8446
21:32 Moses sent to **s out** Jaazer, and they took 7270
Jos 2: 1 sent out of Shittim two men to **s** secretly, 7270
6:25 which Joshua sent to **s out** Jericho. 7270
Jdg 18: 2 to **s out** the land, and to search it; 7270
18:14 answered the five men that went to **s out** 7270
18:17 the five men that went to **s out** the land 7270
2Sa 10: 3 and to **s** it **out**, and to overthrow it? 7270
2Ki 6:13 Go and **s** where he *is*, that I may send and 7200
1Ch 19: 3 and to overthrow, and to **s out** the land? 7270
Gal 2: 4 who came in privily to **s out** our liberty *2684*

SQUADS OF FOUR SOLDIERS See QUATERNIONS

SQUARE (3) [FOURSQUARE, SQUARED, SQUARES, STONESQUARERS]
1Ki 7: 5 all the doors and posts *were* **s**, *with* 7251
Eze 43:16 twelve broad, **s** in the four squares thereof. 7251
45: 2 five hundred *in breadth*, **s** round about; 7251

SQUARED (1) [SQUARE]
Eze 41:21 The posts of the temple *were* **s**, *and* the face 7251

SQUARES (2) [SQUARE]
Eze 43:16 twelve broad, square in the four **s** thereof. 7253
43:17 and fourteen broad in the four **s** thereof; 7253

STABILITY (1) [STABLE]
Isa 33: 6 and knowledge shall be the **s** of thy times, 530

STABLE (2) [STABILITY, UNSTABLE]
1Ch 16:30 the world also shall be **s**, that it be not 3559
Eze 25: 5 And I will make Rabbah a **s** for camels, and 5116

STABLISH (15) [STABLISHED, STABLISHETH]
2Sa 7:13 I will **s** the throne of his kingdom for ever. 3559
1Ch 17:11 be of thy sons; and I will **s** his kingdom. 3559
17:12 me a house, and I will **s** his throne for ever. 3559
18: 3 as he went to **s** his dominion by the river 5324
2Ch 7:18 will I **s** the throne of thy kingdom, 6965
Est 9:21 To **s** *this* among them, that they should 6965
Ps 89: 4 Thy seed will I **s** for ever, and build up thy 3559
119:38 **S** thy word unto thy servant, who *is* 6965
Isa 9: 7 to **s** it with judgment and with justice from 5582
Ro 16:25 Now to him that is of power to **s** you *4741*
1Th 3:13 To the end *he* may **s** your hearts *4741*
2Th 2:17 and **s** you in every good word and work. *4741*
3: 3 who shall **s** you, and keep *you* from evil. *4741*
Jas 5: 8 Be ye also patient; **s** your hearts: for *4741*
1Pe 5:10 make you perfect, **s**, strengthen, settle *you*. *4741*

STABLISHED (10) [STABLISH]
Lev 25:30 house that *is* in the walled city shall be **s** 6965
Dt 19:15 of three witnesses, shall the matter be **s**. 6965
1Sa 20:31 thou shalt not be **s**, nor thy kingdom. 3559
2Sa 7:16 thy kingdom shall be **s** for ever before thee: 539
7:16 before thee: thy throne shall be **s** for ever. 3559
2Ch 17: 5 Therefore the LORD **s** the kingdom in his 3559
Ps 93: 1 the world also is **s**, *that* it cannot be moved. 3559
148: 6 He hath also **s** them for ever and ever: 5975
Col 2: 7 and built up in him, and **s** in the faith, *950*
2Pe 1:12 ye know *them*, and be **s** in the present truth. *4741*

STABLISHETH (3) [STABLISH]
Pr 29: 4 The king by judgment **s** the land: but 5975
Hab 2:12 a town with blood, and **s** a city by iniquity! 3559
2Co 1:21 Now he which **s** us with you in Christ, and *950*

STACHYS (1)
Ro 16: 9 our helper in Christ, and **S** my beloved. *4720*

STACKS (1)
Ex 22: 6 so that the **s of corn**, or the standing corn, 1430

STACTE (1)
Ex 30:34 sweet spices, **s**, and onycha, and galbanum; 5198

STADIA See FURLONGS

STAFF (43) [HANDSTAVES, STAVES]
Ge 32:10 for with my **s** I passed over this Jordan; 4731
38:18 thy bracelets, and thy **s** that *is* in thine hand. 4294
38:25 *are* these, the signet, and bracelets, and **s**. 4294
Ex 12:11 shoes on your feet, and your **s** in your hand; 4731
21:19 walk abroad upon his **s**, then shall he that 4938
Lev 26:26 *And* when I have broken the **s** of your 4294
Nu 13:23 and they bare it between two upon a **s**; 4132
22:27 was kindled, and he smote the ass with a **s**. 4731
Jdg 6:21 forth the end of the **s** that *was* in his hand, 4938
1Sa 17: 7 the **s** of his spear *was* like a weaver's beam; 6086
17:40 he took his **s** in his hand, and chose him 4731
2Sa 3:29 or that leaneth on a **s**, or that falleth on 6418
21:19 the **s** of whose spear *was* like a weaver's 6086
23: 7 be fenced *with* iron and the **s** of a spear; 6086
23:21 he went down to him with a **s**, and 7626
2Ki 4:29 take my **s** in thine hand, and go *thy way:* if 4938
4:29 and lay my **s** upon the face of the child. 4938
4:31 and laid the **s** upon the face of the child; 4938
18:21 thou trustest upon the **s** of this bruised reed, 4938
1Ch 11:23 he went down to him with a **s**, and 7626
20: 5 whose spear **s** *was* like a weaver's beam. 6086
Ps 23: 4 thy rod and thy **s** they comfort me. 4938
105:16 the land: he brake the whole **s** of bread. 4294
Isa 3: 1 and from Judah the stay and the **s**, 4938
9: 4 the **s** of his shoulder, the rod of his 4294
10: 5 and the **s** in their hand *is* mine indignation. 4294
10:15 as if the **s** should lift up *itself, as if it were* 4294
10:24 shall lift up his **s** against thee, after 4294
14: 5 The LORD hath broken the **s** of 4294
28:27 the fitches are beaten out with a **s**, and 4294
30:32 *in* every *place* where the grounded **s** shall 4294
36: 6 thou trustest in the **s** of this broken reed, 4938
Jer 48:17 How is the strong **s** broken, *and* 4294
Eze 4:16 I will break the **s** of bread in Jerusalem: 4294
5:16 upon you, and will break your **s** of bread: 4294
14:13 will break the **s** of the bread thereof, and 4294
29: 6 they have been a **s** of reed to the house of 4938
Hos 4:12 and their **s** declareth unto them: 4731
Zec 8: 4 every man with his **s** in his hand for very 4938
11:10 I took my **s**, *even* Beauty, and cut it 4731
11:14 I cut asunder mine other **s**, *even* Bands, 4731
Mk 6: 8 nothing for *their* journey, save a **s** only; *4464*
Heb 11:21 worshipped, *leaning* upon the top of his **s**. *4464*

STAFFS See STAVES

STAG See HART

STAGGER (3) [STAGGERED, STAGGERETH]
Job 12:25 he **maketh** them to **s** like a drunken *man*. 8582
Ps 107:27 **s** like a drunken *man*, and are at their wit's 5128
Isa 29: 9 *with* wine; they **s**, but not *with* strong drink. 5128

STAGGERED (1) [STAGGER]
Ro 4:20 He **s** not at the promise of God through *1252*

STAGGERETH (1) [STAGGER]
Isa 19:14 as a drunken *man* **s** in his vomit. 8582

STAIN (3)
Job 3: 5 Let darkness and the shadow of death **s** it; 1350
Isa 23: 9 to **s** the pride of all glory, *and* to bring into 2490
63: 3 my garments, and I will **s** all my raiment. 1351

STAIRS (10)
1Ki 6: 8 they went up with **winding s** into 3883
2Ki 9:13 and put *it* under him on the top of the **s**, and 4609
Ne 3:15 unto the **s** that go down from the city of 4609
9: 4 stood up upon the **s** of the Levites, Jeshua, 4608
12:37 they went up by the **s** of the city of David, 4609
SS 2:14 in the secret places of the **s**, let me see thy 4095
Eze 40: 6 went up the **s** thereof, and measured 4609
43:17 and his **s** *shall* look toward the east. 4609
Ac 21:35 And when he came upon the **s**, so it was, *304*
21:40 Paul stood on the **s**, and beckoned with *304*

STAKES (2)
Isa 33:20 not one of the **s** thereof shall ever be 3489
54: 2 lengthen thy cords, and strengthen thy **s**; 3489

STALE (2) [STEAL]
Ge 31:20 Jacob **s away unawares** to Laban 1589+3820
2Ki 11: 2 **s** him from among the king's sons which 1589

STALK (3) [STALKS]
Ge 41: 5 seven ears of corn came up upon one **s**, 7070
41:22 seven ears came up in one **s**, full and good: 7070
Hos 8: 7 it hath no **s**: the bud shall yield no meal: if 7054

STALKS (1) [STALK]
Jos 2: 6 hid them with the **s** of flax, which she had 6086

STALL (3) [STALLED, STALLS]
Am 6: 4 and the calves out of the midst of the **s**; 4770
Mal 4: 2 go forth, and grow up as calves of the **s**. 4770
Lk 13:15 sabbath loose his ox or *his* ass from the **s**, *5336*

STALLED (1) [STALL]
Pr 15:17 love is, than a **s** ox and hatred therewith. 75

STALLS (4) [STALL]
1Ki 4:26 Solomon had forty thousand **s** of horses for 723
2Ch 9:25 And Solomon had four thousand **s** for horses 723
32:28 **s** for all *manner of* beasts, and cotes for 723
Hab 3:17 the fold, and *there shall be* no herd in the **s**: 7517

STAMMERERS (1) [STAMMERING]
Isa 32: 4 the tongue of the **s** shall be ready to speak 5926

STAMMERING (2) [STAMMERERS]
Isa 28:11 For with **s** lips and another tongue will he 3934
33:19 of a **s** tongue, *that thou canst* not 3932

STAMP (2) [STAMPED, STAMPING, STAMPT]
2Sa 22:43 I did **s** them as the mire of the street, *and* 1854
Eze 6:11 thine hand, and **s** with thy foot, and say, 7554

STAMPED (7) [STAMP]
Dt 9:21 with fire, and **s** it, *and* ground *it* very small, 3807
2Ch 15:16 and **s** *it*, and burnt *it* at the brook Kidron. 1854
Eze 25: 6 **s** with the feet, and rejoiced in heart with 7554
Da 7: 7 and **s** the residue with the feet of it: 7512
7:19 in pieces, and **s** the residue with his feet; 7512
8: 7 him down to the ground, and **s upon** him: 7429
8:10 of the stars to the ground, and **s** upon them. 7429

STAMPING (1) [STAMP]
Jer 47: 3 At the noise of the **s** of the hoofs of his 8161

STAMPT (2) [STAMP]
2Ki 23: 6 **s** *it* **small** to powder, and cast the powder 1854
23:15 *and* **s** *it* **small** to powder, and burnt 1854

STANCHED (1)
Lk 8:44 and immediately her issue of blood **s**. *2476*

STAND (274) [STANDEST, STANDETH, STANDING, STOOD, STOODEST]
Ge 19: 9 they said, **S** back. And they said *again, This* 5066
24:13 Behold, I **s** *here* by the well of water; and 5324
24:43 Behold, I **s** by the well of water; and it shall 5324
Ex 7:15 thou shalt **s** by the river's brink against he 5324
8:20 early in the morning, and **s** before Pharaoh; 3320
9:11 the magicians could not **s** before Moses 5975
9:13 and **s** before Pharaoh, and say unto him, 3320
14:13 **s still**, and see the salvation of the LORD, 3320
17: 6 I will **s** before thee there upon the rock in 5975
17: 9 to morrow I will **s** on the top of the hill 5324
18:14 all the people **s** by thee from morning unto 5324
33:10 all the people saw the cloudy pillar **s** *at* 5975
33:21 a place by me, and thou shalt **s** upon a rock: 5324
Lev 18:23 neither shall any woman **s** before a beast to 5975
19:16 neither shalt thou **s** against the blood of thy 5975
26:37 ye shall have no **power to s** before your 8617
27:14 as the priest shall estimate it, so shall it **s**. 6965
27:17 according to thy estimation it shall **s**. 6965
Nu 1: 5 these *are* the names of the men that shall **s** 5975
9: 8 **S still**, and I will hear what the LORD 5975
11:16 that they may **s** there with thee. 3320
16: 9 to **s** before the congregation to minister 5975
23: 3 **S** by thy burnt offering, and I will go: 3320
23:15 unto Balak, **S** here by thy burnt offering, 3320
27:21 he shall **s** before Eleazar the priest, 5975
30: 4 all her vows shall **s**, and every bond 6965
30: 4 wherewith she hath bound her soul shall **s**. 6965
30: 5 wherewith she hath bound her soul, shall **s**: 6965
30: 7 day that he heard *it*: then her vows shall **s**, 6965
30: 7 wherewith she bound her soul shall **s**. 6965
30: 9 have bound their souls, shall **s** against her. 6965
30:11 all her vows shall **s**, and every bond 6965
30:11 bond wherewith she bound her soul shall **s**. 6965
30:12 concerning the bond of her soul, shall not **s**: 6965
35:12 until he **s** before the congregation in 5975
Dt 5:31 **s** thou here by me, and I will speak unto 5975
7:24 there shall no man *be able to* **s** before thee, 3320
9: 2 *of whom* thou hast heard *say*, Who can **s** 3320
10: 8 to **s** before the LORD to minister unto 5975
11:25 There shall no man *be able to* **s** before you: 3320
18: 5 to **s** to minister in the name of the LORD, 5975
18: 7 as all his brethren the Levites *do*, which **s** 5975
19:17 between whom the controversy *is*, shall **s** 5975
24:11 Thou shalt **s** abroad, and the man to whom 5975
25: 8 *if* he **s** *to it*, and say, I like not to take her; 5975
27:12 These shall **s** upon mount Gerizzim to bless 5975
27:13 these shall **s** upon mount Ebal to curse; 5975
29:10 Ye **s** *this* day all of you before the LORD 5324
Jos 1: 5 There shall not any man *be able to* **s** before 3320
3: 8 water of Jordan, ye shall **s still** in Jordan. 5975
3:13 from above; and they shall **s** *upon* a heap. 5975

Jos 7:12 Therefore the children of Israel could not s 6965
7:13 thou canst not s before thine enemies, 6965
10: 8 there shall not a man of them s before thee. 5975
10:12 of Israel, Sun, s thou still upon Gibeon; 1826
20: 4 shall s at the entering of the gate of the city, 5975
20: 6 until he s before the congregation for 5975
23: 9 no man hath been able to s before you unto 5975
Jdg 2:14 that they could not any longer s before their 5975
4:20 S in the door of the tent, and it shall be, 5975
1Sa 6:20 Who is able to s before this holy LORD 5975
9:27 s thou still a while, that I may shew thee 5975
12: 7 Now therefore s still, that I may reason 3320
12:16 Now therefore s and see this great thing, 3320
14: 9 we will s still in our place, and will not go 5975
16:22 Let David, I pray thee, s before me; 5975
19: 3 s beside my father in the field where thou 5975
2Sa 1: 9 S, I pray thee, upon me, and slay me: 5975
18:30 king said unto him, Turn aside, and s here. 3320
1Ki 1: 2 let her s before the king, and let her cherish 5975
8:11 So that the priests could not s to minister 5975
10: 8 which s continually before thee, and 5975
17: 1 God of Israel liveth, before whom I s, 5975
18:15 LORD of hosts liveth, before whom I s, 5975
19:11 and s upon the mount before the LORD. 5975
2Ki 3:14 of hosts liveth, before whom I s, surely, 5975
5:11 s, and call on the name of the LORD his 5975
5:16 before whom I s, I will receive none. 5975
6:31 the son of Shaphat shall s on him this day. 5975
10: 4 stood not before him: how then shall we s? 5975
1Ch 21:16 saw the angel of the LORD s between 5975
23:30 to s every morning to thank and praise 5975
2Ch 5:14 So that the priests could not s to minister by 5975
9: 7 which s continually before thee, and 5975
20: 9 we s before this house, and in thy presence, 5975
20:17 s ye still, and see the salvation of 5975
29:11 for the LORD hath chosen you to s before 5975
34:32 caused all that were present in Jerusalem and Benjamin to s 5975
35: 5 s in the holy place according to 5975
Ezr 9:15 for we cannot s before thee because of this. 5975
10:13 much rain, and we are not able to s without, 5975
10:14 Let now our rulers of all the congregation s, 5975
Ne 7: 3 while they s by, let them shut the doors, 5975
9: 5 S up and bless the LORD your God for 6965
Est 3: 4 to see whether Mordecai's matters would s: 5975
8:11 to s for their life, to destroy, to slay, and 5975
Job 8:15 shall lean upon his house, but it shall not s: 5975
19:25 that he shall s at the latter day upon 6965
30:20 hear me: I s up, and thou regardest me not. 5975
33: 5 set thy words in order before me, s up. 3320
37:14 s still, and consider the wondrous works of 5975
38:14 as clay to the seal; and they s as a garment. 3320
41:10 him up: who then is able to s before me? 3320
Ps 1: 5 Therefore the ungodly shall not s in 6965
4: 4 S in awe, and sin not: commune with your 7264
5: 5 The foolish shall not s in thy sight: 3320
20: 8 and fallen: but we are risen, and s upright. 5749
24: 3 and who shall s in his holy place? 6965
30: 7 thou hast made my mountain to s strong: 5975
33: 8 let all the inhabitants of the world s in awe 1481
35: 2 and buckler, and s up for mine help. 6965
38:11 and my friends s aloof from my sore; 5975
38:11 from my sore; and my kinsmen s afar off. 5975
45: 9 right hand did s the queen in gold of Ophir. 5324
73: 7 Their eyes s out with fatness: they have 3318
76: 7 who may s in thy sight when once thou art 5975
78:13 and he made the waters to s as a heap. 5324
89:28 and my covenant shall s fast with him. 539
89:43 and hast not made him to s in the battle. 6965
94:16 who will s up for me against the workers of 3320
109: 6 over him: and let Satan s at his right hand. 5975
109:31 For he shall s at the right hand of the poor, 5975
111: 8 They s fast for ever and ever, and are done 5564
122: 2 Our feet shall s within thy gates, 5975
130: 3 mark iniquities, O Lord, who shall s? 5975
134: 1 which by night s in the house of 5975
135: 2 Ye that s in the house of the LORD, in 5975
147:17 ice like morsels: who can s before his cold? 5975
Pr 12: 7 but the house of the righteous shall s. 5975
19:21 the counsel of the LORD, that shall s. 6965
22:29 he shall s before kings; he shall not stand 3320
22:29 he shall not s before mean men. 3320
25: 6 and s not in the place of great men: 5975
27: 4 but who is able to s before envy? 5975
Ecc 4:15 with the second child that shall s up in his 5975
8: 3 s not in an evil thing; for he doeth 5975
Isa 7: 7 Thus saith the Lord GOD, It shall not s, 6965
8:10 speak the word, and it shall not s: 6965
11:10 which shall s for an ensign of the people; 5975
14:24 and as I have purposed, so shall it s: 6965
21: 8 I s continually upon the watchtower in 5975
27: 9 the groves and images shall not s up. 6965
28:18 and your agreement with hell shall not s; 6965
32: 8 and by liberal things shall he s. 6965
40: 8 but the word of our God shall s for ever. 6965
44:11 let them s up; yet they shall fear, and 5975
46:10 My counsel shall s, and I will do all my 6965
47:12 S now with thine enchantments, and 5975
47:13 s up, and save thee from these things that 5975
48:13 when I call unto them, they s up together. 5975
50: 8 let us s together: who is mine adversary? let 5975
51:17 Awake, awake, s up, O Jerusalem, 6965
61: 5 strangers shall s and feed your flocks, and 5975
65: 5 Which say, S by thyself, come not near to 7126
Jer 6:16 S ye in the ways, and see, and ask for 5975
7: 2 S in the gate of the LORD'S house, and 5975
7:10 come and s before me in this house, which 5975
14: 6 the wild asses did s in the high places, 5975
15:19 thee again, and thou shalt s before me: 5975
17:19 s in the gate of the children of the people, 5975
26: 2 S in the court of the LORD'S house, and 5975
35:19 not want a man to s before me for ever. 5975
44:28 shall know whose words shall s, mine, or 6965
44:29 shall surely s against you for evil: 6965+6965
46: 4 and s forth with your helmets; 3320
Jer 46:14 say ye, S fast, and prepare thee; for 3320
46:21 they did not s, because the day of their 5975
48:19 inhabitant of Aroer, s by the way and espy; 5975
49:19 who is that shepherd that will s before me? 5975
50:44 who is that shepherd that will s before me? 5975
51:50 escaped the sword, go away, s not still: 5975
Eze 2: 1 s upon thy feet, and I will speak unto thee. 5975
13: 5 to s in the battle in the day of the LORD. 5975
17:14 that by keeping of his covenant it might s. 5975
22:30 s in the gap before me for the land, that I 5975
27:29 from their ships, they shall s upon the land; 5975
29: 7 and madest all their loins to be at a s. 5976
31:14 neither their trees s up in their height, 5975
33:26 Ye s upon your sword, ye work 5975
44:11 they shall s before them to minister unto 5975
44:15 they shall s before me to offer unto me 5975
44:24 in controversy they shall s in judgment; 5975
46: 2 shall s by the post of the gate, and 5975
47:10 that the fishers shall s upon it from En-gedi 5975
Da 1: 4 such as had ability in them to s in 5975
1: 5 that at the end thereof they might s before 5975
2:44 all these kingdoms, and it shall s for ever. 6966
7: 4 made s upon the feet as a man, and a man's 6966
8: 4 so that no beasts might s before him, 5975
8: 7 there was no power in the ram to s before 5975
8:22 four kingdoms shall s up out of the nation, 5975
8:23 understanding dark sentences, shall s up. 5975
8:25 he shall also s up against the Prince of 5975
10:11 words that I speak unto thee, and s upright: 5975
11: 2 there shall s up yet three kings in Persia; 5975
11: 3 a mighty king shall s up, that shall rule 5975
11: 4 when he shall s up, his kingdom shall be 5975
11: 6 of the arm; neither shall he s, nor his arm: 5975
11: 7 out of a branch of her roots shall one s up 5975
11:14 in those times there shall many s up against 5975
11:16 his own will, and none shall s before him: 5975
11:16 he shall s in the glorious land, which by his 5975
11:17 she shall not s on his side, neither be for 5975
11:20 shall s up in his estate a raiser of taxes in 5975
11:21 in his estate shall s up a vile person, to 5975
11:25 and mighty army; but he shall not s: 5975
11:31 arms shall s on his part, and they shall 5975
12: 1 at that time shall Michael s up, the great 5975
12:13 and s in thy lot at the end of the days. 5975
Am 2:15 Neither shall he s that handleth the bow; 5975
Mic 5: 4 he shall s and feed in the strength of 5975
Na 1: 6 Who can s before his indignation? and 5975
2: 8 S, stand, shall they cry; but none shall look 5975
2: 8 Stand, s, shall they cry; but none shall look 5975
Hab 2: 1 I will s upon my watch, and set me upon 5975
Zec 3: 7 thee places to walk among these that s by. 5975
4:14 that s by the Lord of the whole earth. 5975
14: 4 his feet shall s in that day upon the mount 5975
14:12 consume away while they s upon their feet, 5975
Mal 3: 2 who shall s when he appeareth? for he is 5975
Mt 12:25 or house divided against itself shall not s: 2476
12:26 how shall then his kingdom s? 2476
12:47 thy mother and thy brethren s without, 2476
20: 6 unto them, Why s ye here all the day idle? 2476
24:15 s in the holy place, (whoso readeth, let him 2476
Mk 3: 3 man which had the withered hand, S forth. 1453
3:24 against itself, that kingdom cannot s. 2476
3:25 divided against itself, that house cannot s. 2476
3:26 be divided, he cannot s, but hath an end. 2476
9: 1 That there be some of them that s here, 2476
11:25 And when ye s praying, forgive, if ye have 4739
Lk 1:19 I am Gabriel, that s in the presence of God; 3936
6: 8 Rise up, and s forth in the midst. 2476
8:20 Thy mother and thy brethren s without, 2476
11:18 against himself, how shall his kingdom s? 2476
13:25 and ye begin to s without, and to knock at 2476
21:36 to pass, and to s before the Son of man. 2476
Jn 11:42 of the people which s by I said it, that they 4026
Ac 1:11 of Galilee, why s ye gazing up into heaven? 2476
4:10 even by him doth this man s here before 3936
5:20 s and speak in the temple to the people all 2476
8:38 And he commanded the chariot to s still: 2476
10:26 But Peter took him up, saying, S up; 450
14:10 Said with a loud voice, S upright on thy feet. 450
25:10 said Paul, I s at Cæsar's judgment seat, 2476
26: 6 And now I s and am judged for the hope of 2476
26:16 But rise, and s upon thy feet: for I have 2476
Ro 5: 2 access by faith into this grace wherein we s, 2476
9:11 of God according to election might s, 3306
14: 4 holden up: for God is able to make him s. 2476
14:10 for we shall all s before the judgment seat 3936
1Co 2: 5 That your faith should not s in the wisdom 1510
15: 1 also you have received, and wherein ye s; 2476
15:30 And why s we in jeopardy every hour? 2793
16:13 Watch ye, s fast in the faith, quit you like 4739
2Co 1:24 are helpers of your joy: for by faith ye s. 2476
Gal 4:20 to change my voice; for I s in doubt of you. 639
5: 1 S fast therefore in the liberty wherewith 4739
Eph 6:11 that ye may be able to s against the wiles of 2476
6:13 in the evil day, and having done all, to s. 2476
6:14 S therefore, having your loins girt about 2476
Php 1:27 of your affairs, that ye s fast in one spirit, 4739
4: 1 my joy and crown, so s fast in the Lord, 4739
Col 4:12 that ye may s perfect and complete in all 2476
1Th 3: 8 For now we live, if ye s fast in the Lord. 4739
2Th 2:15 s fast, and hold the traditions which ye 4739
Jas 2: 3 S thou there, or sit here under my footstool: 2476
1Pe 5:12 this is the true grace of God wherein ye s. 2476
Rev 3:20 Behold, I s at the door, and knock: if any 2476
6:17 wrath is come; and who shall be able to s? 2476
10: 5 And the angel which I saw s upon the sea 2476
15: 2 s on the sea of glass, having the harps of 2476
18:15 shall s afar off for the fear of her torment, 2476
20:12 the dead, small and great, s before God; 2476

STANDARD (18) [STANDARD-BEARER, STANDARDS]

Nu 1:52 every man by his own s, throughout their 1714
2: 2 children of Israel shall pitch by his own s, 1714
2: 3 s of the camp of Judah pitch throughout 1714
Nu 2:10 On the south side shall be the s of the camp 1714
2:18 On the west side shall be the s of the camp 1714
2:25 The s of the camp of Dan shall be on 1714
10:14 In the first place went the s of the camp of 1714
10:18 the s of the camp of Reuben set forward 1714
10:22 the s of the camp of the children of 1714
10:25 the s of the camp of the children of Dan set 1714
Isa 49:22 the Gentiles, and set up my s to the people: 5251
59:19 the spirit of the LORD shall lift up a s 5127
62:10 out the stones; lift up a s for the people. 5251
Jer 4: 6 Set up the s toward Zion: retire, stay not: 5251
4:21 How long shall I see the s, and hear 5251
50: 2 the nations, and publish, and set up a s; 5251
51:12 Set up the s upon the walls of Babylon, 5251
51:27 Set ye up a s in the land, blow the trumpet 5251

STANDARD-BEARER (1) [BEAR, STANDARD]

Isa 10:18 and they shall be as when a s fainteth. 5263

STANDARDS (3) [STANDARD]

Nu 2:17 every man in his place by their s. 1714
2:31 They shall go hindmost with their s. 1714
2:34 so they pitched by their s, and so they set 1714

STANDEST (6) [STAND]

Ge 24:31 of the LORD; wherefore s thou without? 5975
Ex 3: 5 for the place whereon thou s is holy 5975
Jos 5:15 for the place whereon thou s is holy. 5975
Ps 10: 1 Why s thou afar off, O LORD? why hidest 5975
Ac 7:33 for the place where thou s is holy ground. 2476
Ro 11:20 they were broken off, and thou s by faith. 2476

STANDETH (30) [STAND]

Nu 14:14 that thy cloud s over them, and that thou 5975
Dt 1:38 s before thee, he shall go in thither: 5975+3807.1
17:12 will not hearken unto the priest that s to 5975
29:15 with him that s here with us this day before 5975
Jdg 16:26 may feel the pillars whereupon the house s, 3559
Est 6: 5 unto him, Behold, Haman s in the court. 5975
7: 9 good for the king, s in the house of Haman. 5975
Ps 1: 1 nor s in the way of sinners, nor sitteth in 5975
26:12 My foot s in an even place: in 5975
33:11 The counsel of the LORD s for ever, 5975
82: 1 God s in the congregation of the mighty; 5324
119:161 a cause: but my heart s in awe of thy word. 6342
Pr 8: 2 She s in the top of high places by the way, 5324
SS 2: 9 behold, he s behind our wall, he looketh 5975
Isa 3:13 The LORD s up to plead, and standeth to 5324
3:13 up to plead, and s to judge the people. 5975
46: 7 and set him in his place, and he s; 5975
59:14 away backward, and justice s afar off: 5975
Da 12: 1 the great prince which s for the children of 5975
Zec 11:16 that that is broken, nor feed that that s still: 5324
Jn 1:26 but there s one among you, whom ye know 2476
3:29 which s and heareth him, rejoiceth greatly 2476
Ro 14: 4 to his own master he s or falleth. Yea, 4739
1Co 7:37 Nevertheless he that s stedfast in his heart, 2476
8:13 I will eat no flesh while the world s, lest I 1519
10:12 Wherefore let him that thinketh he s take 2476
2Ti 2:19 Nevertheless the foundation of God s sure, 2476
Heb 10:11 And every priest s daily ministering and 2476
Jas 5: 9 the judge s before the door. 2476
Rev 10: 8 the hand of the angel which s upon the sea 2476

STANDING (55) [STAND]

Ex 22: 6 stacks of corn, or the s corn, or the field, 7054
26:15 for the tabernacle of shittim wood s up. 5975
36:20 for the tabernacle of shittim wood, s up. 5975
Lev 26: 1 neither rear you up a s image, 4676
Nu 22:23 the ass saw the angel of the LORD s in 5324
22:31 he saw the angel of the LORD s in 5324
Dt 23:25 When thou comest into the s corn of thy 7054
23:25 move a sickle unto thy neighbour's s corn. 7054
Jdg 15: 5 he let them go into the s corn of 7054
15: 5 also the s corn, with the vineyards and 7054
1Sa 19:20 Samuel s as appointed over them, the spirit 5975
22: 6 and all his servants were s about him;) 5324
1Ki 13:25 in the way, and the lion s by the carcase: 5975
13:28 and the ass and the lion s by the carcase: 5975
22:19 all the host of heaven s by him on his right 5975
2Ch 9:18 sitting place, and two lions s by the stays: 5975
18:18 all the host of heaven s on his right hand 5975
Est 5: 2 when the king saw Esther the queen s in 5975
Ps 69: 2 I sink in deep mire, where there is no s: 4613
107:35 He turneth the wilderness into a s water, and 98
114: 8 Which turned the rock into a s water, the flint 98
Da 8: 6 which I had seen s before the river, and 5975
Am 9: 1 I saw the Lord s upon the altar: and he said, 5324
Mic 1:11 of Beth-ezel; he shall receive of you his s. 5979
5:13 and thy s images out of the midst of thee; 4676
Zec 3: 1 he shewed me Joshua the high priest s 5975
3: 1 and Satan s at his right hand to resist him. 5975
6: 5 which go forth from s before the Lord of all 3320
Mt 6: 5 for they love to pray s in the synagogues 2476
16:28 I say unto you, There be some s here, 2476
20: 3 and saw others s idle in the marketplace, 2476
20: 6 and found others s idle, and saith unto 2476
Mk 3:31 his brethren and his mother, and, s without, 2476
13:14 by Daniel the prophet, s where it ought not, 2476
Lk 1:11 s on the right side of the altar of incense. 2476
5: 2 And saw two ships s by the lake: but 2476
9:27 I tell you of a truth, there be some s here, 2476
18:13 s afar off, would not lift up so much as his 2476
Jn 8: 9 left alone, and the woman s in the midst. 2476
19:26 saw his mother, and the disciple s by, 3936
20:14 and saw Jesus s, and knew not that it was 2476
Ac 2:14 But Peter, s up with the eleven, lift up his 2476
4:14 And beholding the man which was healed s 2476
5:23 and the keepers s without before the doors: 2476
5:25 the men whom ye put in prison are s in 2476
7:55 and Jesus s on the right hand of God, 2476
7:56 the Son of man s on the right hand of God. 2476
22:20 I also was s by, and consenting unto his 2186
24:21 this one voice, that I cried s among them, 2476

S

Heb 9: 8 while as the first tabernacle was yet s: 4714
2Pe 3: 5 and the earth s out of the water and in 4921
Rev 7: 1 And after these *things* I saw four angels s 2476
11: 4 the two candlesticks s before the God of 2476
18:10 S afar off for the fear of her torment, 2476
19:17 And I saw an angel s in the sun; and 2476

STANK (3) [STINK]

Ex 8:14 them together upon heaps: and the land s. 887
16:20 until the morning, and it bred worms, and s: 887
2Sa 10: 6 when the children of Ammon saw that they s 887

STAR (15) [STARE, STARS]

Nu 24:17 there shall come a S out of Jacob, and 3556
Am 5:26 and Chiun your images, the s of your god, 3556
Mt 2: 2 for we have seen his s in the east, and 792
2: 7 inquired of them diligently what time the s 792
2: 9 and lo, the s, which they saw in the east, 792
2:10 When they saw the s, they rejoiced *with* 792
Ac 7:43 of Moloch, and the s of your god Remphan, 798
1Co 15:41 for *one* s differeth from *another* star in glory. 792
15:41 for *one* star differeth from *another* s in glory. 792
2Pe 1:19 and the **day** s arise in your hearts: 5459
Rev 2:28 And I will give him the morning s. 792
8:10 and there fell a great s from heaven, 792
8:11 And the name of the s is called Wormwood: 792
9: 1 and I saw a s fall from heaven unto the earth: 792
22:16 of David, *and* the bright and morning s. 792

STARE (1)

Ps 22:17 tell all my bones: they look *and* s upon me. 7200

STARGAZERS (1) [GAZE, STAR]

Isa 47:13 the astrologers, the s, 2374+3556+871.1+1886.1

STARS (51) [STAR]

Ge 1:16 light to rule the night: *he made* the s also. 3556
15: 5 Look now towards heaven, and tell the s, 3556
22:17 multiply thy seed as the s of the heaven, 3556
26: 4 I will make thy seed to multiply as the s of 3556
37: 9 and the eleven s made obeisance to me. 3556
Ex 32:13 I will multiply your seed as the s of heaven, 3556
Dt 1:10 you *are this* day as the s of heaven for 3556
4:19 thou seest the sun, and the moon, and the s, 3556
10:22 made thee as the s of heaven for multitude. 3556
28:62 whereas ye were as the s of heaven for 3556
Jdg 5:20 the s in their courses fought against Sisera. 3556
1Ch 27:23 increase Israel like to the s of the heavens. 3556
Ne 4:21 the rising of the morning till the s appeared. 3556
9:23 children also multipliedst thou as the s 3556
Job 3: 9 Let the s of the twilight thereof be dark; 3556
9: 7 and it riseth not; and sealeth up the s. 3556
22:12 behold the height of the s, how high they 3556
25: 5 yea, the s are not pure in his sight. 3556
38: 7 When the morning s sang together, and 3556
Ps 8: 3 the work of thy fingers, the moon and the s, 3556
136: 9 The moon and s to rule by night: for his 3556
147: 4 He telleth the number of the s; he calleth 3556
148: 3 sun and moon: praise him, all ye s of light. 3556
Ecc 12: 2 the sun, or the light, or the moon, or the s, 3556
Isa 13:10 For the s of heaven and the constellations 3556
14:13 I will exalt my throne above the s of God: 3556
Jer 31:35 the moon and of the s for a light by night, 3556
Eze 32: 7 the heaven, and make the s thereof dark; 3556
Da 8:10 *some* of the host and of the s to the ground, 3556
12: 3 turn many to righteousness as the s for ever 3556
Joel 2:10 and the s shall withdraw their shining: 3556
3:15 and the s shall withdraw their shining. 3556
Am 5: 8 *Seek him* that maketh the **seven** s and 3598
Ob 1: 4 though *thou* set thy nest among the s, 3556
Na 3:16 thy merchants above the s of heaven: 3556
Mt 24:29 and the s shall fall from heaven, and 792
Mk 13:25 And the s of heaven shall fall, 792
Lk 21:25 in the sun, and in the moon, and in the s; 798
Ac 27:20 And when neither sun nor s in many days 798
1Co 15:41 of the moon, and another glory of the s: 792
Heb 11:12 *so many* as the s of the sky in multitude, and 798
Jude 1:13 wandering s, to whom is reserved 792
Rev 1:16 And he had in his right hand seven s: and 792
1:20 The mystery of the seven s which thou 792
1:20 The seven s are the angels of the seven 792
2: 1 These *things* saith he that holdeth the seven s 792
3: 1 the seven spirits of God, and the seven s; 792
6:13 And the s of heaven fell unto the earth, 792
8:12 *part* of the moon, and the third *part* of the s; 792
12: 1 and upon her head a crown of twelve s: 792
12: 4 And his tail drew the third *part* of the s of 792

STATE (14)

Ge 43: 7 The man asked us straitly of our s, and NIH
2Ch 24:13 they set the house of God in his s, and 4971
Est 1: 7 according to the s of the king. 3027
2:18 gave gifts, according to the s of the king. 3027
Ps 39: 5 verily every man **at** his **best** s *is* altogether 5324
Pr 27:23 Be thou diligent to know the s of thy 6440
28: 2 knowledge the s *thereof* shall be prolonged. 3651
Isa 22:19 and from thy s shall he pull thee down. 4612
Mt 12:45 the last s of that man is worse than the first. NIG
Lk 11:26 the last s of that man is worse than the first. NIG
Php 2:19 of good comfort, when I know your s. 3588+4012
2:20 who will naturally care for your s. 3588+4012
4:11 for I have learned, in whatsoever s I am, NIG
Col 4: 7 All my s shall Tychicus declare unto you, 2596

STATELY (1)

Eze 23:41 satest upon a s bed, and a table prepared 3520

STATION (1)

Isa 22:19 I will drive thee from thy s, and from thy 4673

STATURE (17)

Nu 13:32 that we saw in it *are* men of a **great** s. 4060
1Sa 16: 7 his countenance, or on the height of his s; 6967
2Sa 21:20 where was a man of *great* s, that had on 4067
1Ch 11:23 a man of *great* s, five cubits *high;* and in 4060
20: 6 where was a man of *great* s, whose fingers 4060
SS 7: 7 This thy s is like to a palm tree, and 6967
Isa 10:33 the high ones of s *shall be* hewn down, and 6967
45:14 of Ethiopia and of the Sabeans, men of s, 4060
Eze 13:18 make kerchiefs upon the head of every s to 6967
17: 6 and became a spreading vine of low s, 6967
19:11 her s was exalted among the thick 6967
31: 3 with a shadowing shrowd, and of a high s; 6967
Mt 6:27 thought can add one cubit unto his s? 2244
Lk 2:52 And Jesus increased in wisdom and s, and 2244
12:25 taking thought can add to his s one cubit? 2244
19: 3 not for the press, because he was little of s. 2244
Eph 4:13 unto the measure of the s of the fulness of 2244

STATUTE (35) [STATUTES]

Ex 15:25 there he made for them a s and 2706
27:21 *it shall be* a s for ever unto their generations 2708
28:43 *it shall be* a s for ever unto him and his seed 2708
29: 9 office shall be theirs for a perpetual s: 2708
29:28 his sons' by a s for ever from the children 2706
30:21 it shall be a s for ever to them, *even* to him 2706
Lev 3:17 *It shall be* a perpetual s for your 2708
6:18 *It shall be* a s for ever in your generations 2706
6:22 *it is* a s for ever unto the LORD; it shall be 2706
7:34 unto his sons by a s for ever from among 2706
7:36 *by* a s for ever throughout their generations. 2708
10: 9 *it shall be* a s for ever throughout your 2708
10:15 and thy sons' with thee, by a s for ever; 2706
16:29 *this* shall be a s for ever unto you: *that* in 2708
16:31 ye shall afflict your souls, *by* a s for ever. 2708
16:34 this shall be an everlasting s unto you, 2708
17: 7 This shall be a s for ever unto them 2708
23:14 *it shall be* a s for ever throughout your 2708
23:21 s for ever in all your dwellings throughout 2708
23:31 *it shall be* a s for ever throughout your 2708
23:41 *It shall be* a s for ever in your generations: 2708
24: 3 *it shall be* a s for ever in your generations. 2708
24: 9 the LORD made by fire, *by* a perpetual s. 2706
Nu 18:11 to thy daughters with thee, by a s for ever: 2706
18:19 and thy daughters with thee, by a s for ever: 2706
18:23 *it shall be* a s for ever throughout your 2708
19:10 sojourneth among them, for a s for ever. 2708
19:21 it shall be a perpetual s unto them, that he 2708
27:11 it shall be unto the children of Israel a s of 2708
35:29 So these *things* shall be for a s of judgment 2708
Jos 24:25 set them a s and an ordinance in Shechem. 2706
1Sa 30:25 that he made it a s and an ordinance for 2706
Ps 81: 4 For this *was* a s for Israel, *and* a law of 2706
Da 6: 7 consulted together to establish a royal s, 7010
6:15 Persians *is,* That no decree nor s which 7010

STATUTES (132) [STATUTE]

Ge 26: 5 my commandments, my s, and my laws. 2708
Ex 15:26 to his commandments, and keep all his s, 2706
18:16 and I do make *them* know the s of God, and 2706
Lev 10:11 s which the LORD hath spoken unto them 2706
18: 5 Ye shall therefore keep my s, and my 2708
18:26 Ye shall therefore keep my s and my 2708
19:19 Ye shall keep my s. Thou shalt not let thy 2708
19:37 Therefore shall ye observe all my s, and all 2708
20: 8 ye shall keep my s, and do them: I *am* 2708
20:22 Ye shall therefore keep all my s, and all my 2708
25:18 Wherefore ye shall do my s, and keep my 2708
26: 3 If ye walk in my s, and keep my 2708
26:15 if ye shall despise my s, or if your soul 2708
26:43 and because their soul abhorred my s. 2708
26:46 These *are* the s and judgments and laws, 2706
Nu 30:16 These *are* the s, which the LORD 2706
Dt 4: 1 O Israel, unto the s and unto the judgments, 2706
4: 5 Behold, I have taught you s and judgments, 2706
4: 6 which shall hear all these s, and say, 2706
4: 8 that hath s and judgments *so* righteous as 2706
4:14 commanded me at that time to teach you s 2706
4:40 Thou shalt keep therefore his s, and his 2706
4:45 and the s, and the judgments, 2706
5: 1 the s and judgments which I speak in your 2706
5:31 the s, and the judgments, which thou shalt 2706
6: 1 the s, and the judgments, 2706
6: 2 to keep all his s and his commandments, 2708
6:17 his testimonies, and his s, which he hath 2706
6:20 and the s, and the judgments, 2706
6:24 LORD commanded us to do all these s, 2706
7:11 and the s, and the judgments, 2706
8:11 his judgments, and his s, which I command 2708
10:13 commandments of the LORD, and his s, 2708
11: 1 his s, and his judgments, and 2708
11:32 ye shall observe to do all the s and 2706
12: 1 These *are* the s and judgments, which ye 2706
16:12 and thou shalt observe and do these s. 2706
17:19 keep all the words of this law and these s, 2706
26:16 thy God hath commanded thee to do these s 2706
26:17 to keep his s, and his commandments, and 2706
27:10 do his commandments and his s, which I 2706
28:15 and his s which I command thee *this* day; 2708
28:45 and his s which he commanded thee: 2708
30:10 his s which are written in this book of 2708
30:16 and his s and his judgments, 2708
2Sa 22:23 and *as for* his s, I did not depart from them. 2708
1Ki 2: 3 to keep his s, *and* his commandments, and 2708
3: 3 walking in the s of David his father: 2708
3:14 to keep my s and my commandments, 2706
6:12 if thou wilt walk in my s, and execute my 2708
8:58 and his s, and his judgments, 2706
8:61 to walk in his s, and to keep his 2706
9: 4 *and* wilt keep my s and my judgments: 2706
9: 6 *and* my s which I have set before you, 2708
11:11 thou hast not kept my covenant and my s, 2708
11:33 *to keep* my s and my judgments, as *did* 2708
11:34 he kept my commandments and my s: 2708
11:38 to keep my s and my commandments, 2708
2Ki 17: 8 walked in the s of the heathen, whom 2708
17:13 and keep my commandments *and* my s, 2708
17:15 they rejected his s, and his covenant that he 2706
17:19 walked in the s of Israel which they made. 2708
2Ki 17:34 neither do they after their s, or after their 2708
17:37 the s, and the ordinances, and the law, and 2706
23: 3 his s with all *their* heart and all *their* soul, 2708
1Ch 22:13 if thou takest heed to fulfil the s and 2706
29:19 thy s, and to do all *these things,* and 2706
2Ch 7:17 and shalt observe my s and my judgments; 2706
7:19 and forsake my s and my commandments, 2708
19:10 and commandment, s and judgments, 2706
33: 8 according to the whole law and the s and 2706
34:31 his testimonies, and his s, with all his heart, 2706
Ezr 7:10 to do *it,* and to teach in Israel s and 2706
7:11 of the LORD, and of his s to Israel. 2706
Ne 1: 7 nor the s, nor the judgments, 2706
9:13 and true laws, good s and commandments: 2706
9:14 commandedst them precepts, s, and laws, 2706
10:29 our Lord, and his judgments and his s; 2706
Ps 18:22 and I did not put away his s from me. 2708
19: 8 The s of the LORD *are* right, rejoicing 6490
50:16 What hast thou to do to declare my s, or 2706
89:31 If they break my s, and keep not my 2708
105:45 That they might observe his s, and keep his 2706
119: 5 that my ways were directed to keep thy s! 2706
119: 8 I will keep thy s: O forsake me not utterly. 2706
119:12 *art* thou, O LORD: teach me thy s. 2706
119:16 I will delight myself in thy s: I will not 2708
119:23 *but* thy servant did meditate in thy s. 2706
119:26 and thou heardest me: teach me thy s. 2706
119:33 Teach me, O LORD, the way of thy s; and 2706
119:48 I have loved; and I will meditate in thy s. 2706
119:54 Thy s have been my songs in the house of 2706
119:64 is full *of* thy mercy: teach me thy s. 2706
119:68 *art* good, and doest good; teach me thy s. 2706
119:71 have been afflicted; that I might learn thy s. 2706
119:80 Let my heart be sound in thy s; that I be not 2706
119:83 in the smoke; *yet* do I not forget thy s. 2706
119:112 I have inclined mine heart to perform thy s 2706
119:117 I will have respect unto thy s continually. 2706
119:118 trodden down all them that err from thy s: 2706
119:124 unto thy mercy, and teach me thy s. 2706
119:135 shine upon thy servant; and teach me thy s. 2706
119:145 hear me, O LORD: I will keep thy s. 2706
119:155 far from the wicked: for they seek not thy s. 2706
119:171 when thou hast taught me thy s. 2706
147:19 his s and his judgments unto Israel. 2706
Jer 44:10 nor in my s, that I set before you and before 2708
44:23 nor walked in his law, nor in his s, nor in 2708
Eze 5: 6 my s more than the countries that *are* round 2708
5: 6 and my s, they have not walked in them. 2708
5: 7 *and* have not walked in my s, neither have 2708
11:12 for ye have not walked in my s, 2706
11:20 That they may walk in my s, and keep mine 2708
18: 9 Hath walked in my s, and hath kept my 2708
18:17 my judgments, hath walked in my s; 2708
18:19 *and* hath kept all my s, and hath done them, 2708
18:21 keep all my s, and do that which is lawful 2708
20:11 I gave them my s, and shewed them my 2708
20:13 they walked not in my s, and they despised 2708
20:16 walked not in my s, but polluted my 2708
20:18 Walk ye not in the s of your fathers, 2706
20:19 walk in my s, and keep my judgments, and 2708
20:21 they walked not in my s, neither kept my 2708
20:24 had despised my s, and had polluted my 2708
20:25 Wherefore I gave them also s *that were* not 2706
33:15 walk in the s of life, without committing 2708
36:27 cause you to walk in my s, and ye shall 2706
37:24 and observe my s, and do them. 2708
44:24 my laws and my s in all mine assemblies; 2708
Mic 6:16 For the s of Omri are kept, and all 2708
Zec 1: 6 my words and my s, which I commanded 2706
Mal 4: 4 for all Israel, *with* the s and judgments. 2706

STAVES (49) [STAFF]

Ex 25:13 thou shalt make s of shittim wood, and 905
25:14 thou shalt put the s into the rings by the sides 905
25:15 The s shall be in the rings of the ark: 905
25:27 rings be for places of the s to bear the table. 905
25:28 thou shalt make the s *of* shittim wood, and 905
27: 6 thou shalt make s for the altar, staves of 905
27: 6 s of shittim wood, and overlay them with 905
27: 7 the s shall be put into the rings, and 905
27: 7 the s shall be upon the two sides of the altar, 905
30: 4 they shall be for places for the s to bear it 905
30: 5 thou shalt make the s *of* shittim wood, and 905
35:12 The ark, and the s thereof, *with* the mercy 905
35:13 his s, and all his vessels, and the shewbread, 905
35:15 the incense altar and his s, and the anointing 905
35:16 his s, and all his vessels, the laver and his 905
37: 4 he made s of shittim wood, and 905
37: 5 he put the s into the rings by the sides of 905
37:14 the places for the s to bear the table. 905
37:15 he made the s *of* shittim wood, and 905
37:27 to be places for the s to bear it withal. 905
37:28 he made the s *of* shittim wood, and 905
38: 5 of the grate of brass, *to be* places for the s. 905
38: 6 he made the s *of* shittim wood, and 905
38: 7 he put the s into the rings on the sides of 905
39:35 and the s thereof, and the mercy seat, 905
39:39 his s, and all his vessels, the laver and his 905
40:20 set the s on the ark, and put the mercy seat 905
Nu 4: 6 wholly of blue, and shall put in the s thereof. 905
4: 8 badgers' skins, and shall put in the s thereof. 905
4:11 badgers' skins, and shall put to the s thereof: 905
4:14 of badgers' skins, and put to the s of it. 905
21:18 the direction of the lawgiver, with their s. 4938
1Sa 17:43 *Am* I a dog, that thou comest to me with s? 4731
1Ki 8: 7 covered the ark and the s thereof above. 905
8: 8 they drew out the s, that the ends of 905
8: 8 that the ends of the s were seen out in 905
1Ch 15:15 upon their shoulders with the s thereon, 4133
2Ch 5: 8 covered the ark and the s thereof above. 905
5: 9 they drew out the s *of the ark,* that the ends 905
5: 9 s were seen from the ark before the oracle; 905
Hab 3:14 Thou didst strike through with his s 4294
Zec 11: 7 I took unto me two s; the one I called 4731
Mt 10:10 neither two coats, neither shoes, nor yet s: 4464

S

Mt 26:47 him a great multitude with swords and **s**, *3586*
26:55 a thief with swords and **s** for to take me? *3586*
Mk 14:43 him a great multitude with swords and **s**, *3586*
14:48 a thief, with swords and *with* **s** to take me? *3586*
Lk 9:3 neither **s**, nor scrip, neither bread, *4464*
22:52 as against a thief, with swords and **s**? *3586*

STAY (33) [STAYED, STAYETH, STAYS]
Ge 19:17 behind thee, neither **s** thou in all the plain; 5975
Ex 9:28 I will let you go, and ye shall **s** no longer. 5975
Lev 13:5 *if* the plague in his sight be **at a s**, *and* 5975
13:23 if the bright spot **s** in his place, *and* 5975
13:28 if the bright spot **s** in his place, *and* 5975
13:37 if the scall be in his sight **at a s**, and 5975
Jos 10:19 **s** you not, *but* pursue after your enemies, 5975
Ru 1:13 would ye **s** for them from having husbands? 5702
1Sa 15:16 **S**, and I will tell thee what the LORD hath 7503
20:38 cried after the lad, Make speed, haste, **s** not. 5975
2Sa 22:19 of my calamity: but the LORD was my **s**. 4937
24:16 **s** now thine hand. And the angel of 7503
1Ch 21:15 *It is* enough, **s** now thine hand. 7503
Job 37:4 he will not **s** them when his voice is heard. 6117
38:37 or who can **s** the bottles of heaven, 7901
Ps 18:18 of my calamity: but the LORD was my **s**. 4937
Pr 28:17 shall flee to the pit; let no man **s** him. 8551
SS 2:5 **S** me with flagons, comfort me with apples: 5564
Isa 3:1 and from Judah the **s** and the staff, 4937
3:1 the whole **s** of bread, and the whole stay of 4937
3:1 stay of bread, and the whole **s** of water, 4937
10:20 shall no more again **s** upon him that smote 8172
10:20 shall **s** upon the LORD, the Holy One of 8172
19:13 *even they that are* the **s** of the tribes thereof. 6438
29:9 **S** yourselves, and wonder; cry ye out, and 4102
30:12 and perverseness, and **s** thereon: 8172
31:1 **s** on horses, and trust in chariots, because 8172
48:2 and **s** themselves upon the God of Israel; 5564
50:10 name of the LORD, and **s** upon his God. 8172
Jer 4:6 retire, **s** not: for I will bring evil from 5975
20:9 weary with forbearing, and I could not **s**. NIH
Da 4:35 none can **s** his hand, or say unto him, 4223
Hos 13:13 for he should not **s** long in *the place of* 5975

STAYED (31) [STAY]
Ge 8:10 he **s** yet other seven days; and again he sent 2342
8:12 he **s** yet other seven days; and sent forth 3176
32:4 sojourned with Laban, and **s** *there* until now: 309
Ex 10:24 only let your flocks and your herds be **s**: 3322
17:12 Aaron and Hur **s up** his hands, the one on 8551
Nu 16:48 and the living; and the plague was **s**. 6113
16:50 of the congregation: and the plague was **s**. 6113
25:8 So the plague was **s** from the children of 6113
Dt 10:10 I **s** in the mount, according to the first time, 5975
Jos 10:13 the sun stood still, and the moon **s**, until 5975
1Sa 20:19 *when* thou hast **s three days**, *then* 8027
24:7 So David **s** his servants with *these* words, 8156
30:9 where those that were left behind **s**. 5975
2Sa 17:17 Now Jonathan and Ahimaaz **s** by En-rogel; 5975
24:21 that the plague may be **s** from the people. 6113
24:25 the land, and the plague was **s** from Israel. 6113
1Ki 22:35 the king was **s up** in *his* chariot against 5975
2Ki 4:6 *There is* not a vessel more. And the oil **s**. 5975
13:18 the ground. And he smote thrice, and **s**. 5975
15:20 turned back, and **s** not there in the land. 5975
1Ch 21:22 that the plague may be **s** from the people. 6113
2Ch 18:34 howbeit the king of Israel **s** *himself* **up** in 5975
Job 38:11 and here shall thy proud waves be **s**? 7896
Ps 106:30 and *so* the plague was **s**. 6113
Isa 26:3 *whose* mind *is* **s** *on thee:* because 5564
La 4:6 as in a moment, and no hands **s** on her. 2342
Eze 31:15 floods thereof, and the great waters were **s**: 3607
Hag 1:10 Therefore the heaven over you is **s** from 3607
1:10 from dew, and the earth is **s** *from* her fruit. 3607
Lk 4:42 sought him, and came unto him, and **s** him, *2722*
Ac 19:22 but he himself **s** in Asia for a season. *1907*

STAYETH (1) [STAY]
Isa 27:8 he **s** his rough wind in the day of the east 1898

STAYS (4) [STAY]
1Ki 10:19 *there were* **s** on either side on the place of 3027
10:19 of the seat, and two lions stood beside the **s**. 3027
2Ch 9:18 **s** on each side of the sitting place, and 3027
9:18 and two lions standing by the **s**: 3027

STEAD (94) [STEADS]
Ge 22:13 up for a burnt offering **in the s** of his son. 8478
30:2 he said, *Am* I **in** God's **s**, who hath 8478
36:33 the son of Zerah of Bozrah reigned **in** his **s**. 8478
36:34 of the land of Temani reigned **in** his **s**. 8478
36:35 in the field of Moab, reigned **in** his **s**: 8478
36:36 and Samlah of Masrekah reigned **in** his **s**. 8478
36:37 of Rehoboth *by* the river reigned **in** his **s**. 8478
36:38 the son of Achbor reigned **in** his **s**. 8478
36:39 of Achbor died, and Hadar reigned **in** his **s**: 8478
Ex 29:30 *And* that son that is priest **in** his **s** shall put 8478
Lev 6:22 priest of his sons that is anointed **in** his **s** 8478
16:32 in the priest's office **in** his father's **s**, 8478
Nu 32:14 ye are risen up **in** your fathers' **s**, 8478
Dt 2:12 from before them, and dwelt **in** their **s**; 8478
2:21 they succeeded them, and dwelt **in** their **s**: 8478
2:22 and dwelt **in** their **s** *even* unto this day: 8478
2:23 destroyed them, and dwelt **in** their **s**.) 8478
10:6 son ministered in the priest's office **in** his **s**. 8478
Jos 5:7 their children, *whom* he raised up **in** their **s**, 8478
2Sa 10:1 and Hanun his son reigned **in** his **s**. 8478
16:8 of Saul, **in** whose **s** thou hast reigned; 8478
1Ki 1:30 and he shall sit upon my throne **in** my **s**; 8478
1:35 my throne; for he shall be king **in** my **s**: 8478
11:43 and Rehoboam his son reigned **in** his **s**. 8478
14:20 and Nadab his son reigned **in** his **s**. 8478
14:27 king Rehoboam made **in** their **s** brasen 8478
14:31 And Abijam his son reigned **in** his **s**. 8478
15:8 of David: and Asa his son reigned **in** his **s**. 8478
15:24 and Jehoshaphat his son reigned **in** his **s**. 8478
1Ki 15:28 did Baasha slay him, and reigned **in** his **s**. 8478
16:6 in Tirzah: and Elah his son reigned **in** his **s**. 8478
16:10 of Asa king of Judah, and reigned **in** his **s**. 8478
16:28 and Ahab his son reigned **in** his **s**. 8478
22:40 and Ahaziah his son reigned **in** his **s**. 8478
22:50 and Jehoram his son reigned **in** his **s**. 8478
2Ki 1:17 Jehoram reigned **in** his **s** in the second year 8478
3:27 eldest son that should have reigned **in** his **s**, 8478
8:15 so that he died: and Hazael reigned **in** his **s**. 8478
8:24 and Ahaziah his son reigned **in** his **s**. 8478
10:35 And Jehoahaz his son reigned **in** his **s**. 8478
12:21 and Amaziah his son reigned **in** his **s**. 8478
13:9 and Joash his son reigned **in** his **s**. 8478
13:24 and Ben-hadad his son reigned **in** his **s**. 8478
14:16 and Jeroboam his son reigned **in** his **s**. 8478
14:29 and Zachariah his son reigned **in** his **s**. 8478
15:7 and Jotham his son reigned **in** his **s**. 8478
15:10 and slew him, and reigned **in** his **s**. 8478
15:14 and slew him, and reigned **in** his **s**. 8478
15:22 and Pekahiah his son reigned **in** his **s**. 8478
15:30 and slew him, and reigned **in** his **s**, 8478
15:38 and Ahaz his son reigned **in** his **s**. 8478
16:20 and Hezekiah his son reigned **in** his **s**. 8478
19:37 And Esarhaddon his son reigned **in** his **s**. 8478
20:21 and Manasseh his son reigned **in** his **s**. 8478
21:18 of Uzza: and Amon his son reigned **in** his **s**. 8478
21:24 the land made Josiah his son king **in** his **s**. 8478
21:26 of Uzza: and Josiah his son reigned **in** his **s**. 8478
23:30 and made him king **in** his father's **s**. 8478
24:6 and Jehoiachin his son reigned **in** his **s**. 8478
24:17 Mattaniah his father's brother king **in** his **s**, 8478
1Ch 1:44 the son of Zerah of Bozrah reigned **in** his **s**. 8478
1:45 the land of the Temanites reigned **in** his **s**. 8478
1:46 in the field of Moab, reigned **in** his **s**: 8478
1:47 Samlah of Masrekah reigned **in** his **s**. 8478
1:48 of Rehoboth *by* the river reigned **in** his **s**. 8478
1:49 the son of Achbor reigned **in** his **s**. 8478
1:50 was dead, Hadad reigned **in** his **s**: 8478
19:1 Ammon died, and his son reigned **in** his **s**. 8478
29:28 and Solomon his son reigned **in** his **s**. 8478
2Ch 1:8 and hast made me to reign **in** his **s**. 8478
9:31 and Rehoboam his son reigned **in** his **s**. 8478
12:16 and Abijah his son reigned **in** his **s**. 8478
14:1 Asa his son reigned **in** his **s**. In his days 8478
17:1 Jehoshaphat his son reigned **in** his **s**, and 8478
21:1 And Jehoram his son reigned **in** his **s**. 8478
22:1 Ahaziah his youngest son king **in** his **s**: 8478
24:27 And Amaziah his son reigned **in** his **s**. 8478
26:23 a leper: and Jotham his son reigned **in** his **s**. 8478
27:9 of David: and Ahaz his son reigned **in** his **s**. 8478
28:27 and Hezekiah his son reigned **in** his **s**. 8478
32:33 And Manasseh his son reigned **in** his **s**. 8478
33:20 and Amon his son reigned **in** his **s**. 8478
33:25 the land made Josiah his son king **in** his **s**. 8478
36:1 made him king **in** his father's **s** in 8478
36:8 and Jehoiachin his son reigned **in** his **s**. 8478
Job 16:4 as ye *do:* if your soul were **in** my soul's **s**, 8478
33:6 I *am* according to thy wish **in** God's **s**: 3807.1
34:24 without number, and set others **in** their **s**. 8478
Pr 11:8 of trouble, and the wicked cometh **in** his **s**. 8478
Ecc 4:15 the second child that shall stand *up* **in** his **s**. 8478
Isa 37:38 and Esar-haddon his son reigned **in** his **s**. 8478
Jer 29:26 thee priest **in the s of** Jehoiada the priest, 8478
2Co 5:20 we pray *you* **in** Christ's **s**, be ye reconciled *5228*
Phm 1:13 that in thy **s** he might have ministered unto *5228*

STEADFAST (1) [STEDFAST]
Job 11:15 yea, thou shalt be **s**, and shalt not fear. 3332

STEADS (1) [STEAD]
1Ch 5:22 And they dwelt **in** their **s** until the captivity. 8478

STEADY (1)
Ex 17:12 his hands were **s** until the going down of 530

STEAL (22) [MENSTEALERS, STALE, STEALETH, STEALING, STEALTH, STOLE, STOLEN]
Ge 31:27 flee away secretly, and **s away from** me; 1589
44:8 should we **s** out of thy lord's house silver or 1589
Ex 20:15 Thou shalt not **s**. 1589
22:1 If a man shall **s** an ox, or a sheep, and 1589
Lev 19:11 Ye shall not **s**, neither deal falsely, 1589
Dt 5:19 Neither shalt thou **s**. 1589
2Sa 19:3 as people being ashamed **s away** when they 1589
Pr 6:30 if he **s** to satisfy his soul when he is hungry; 1589
30:9 **s**, and take the name of my God *in vain*. 1589
Jer 7:9 *Will ye* **s**, murder, and commit adultery, 1589
23:30 that **s** my words every one from his 1589
Mt 6:19 and where thieves break through and **s**: *2813*
6:20 where thieves do not break through nor **s**: *2813*
19:18 shalt not commit adultery, Thou shalt not **s**, *2813*
27:64 and **s** him *away*, and say unto the people, *2813*
Mk 10:19 not commit adultery, Do not kill, Do not **s**, *2813*
Lk 18:20 not commit adultery, Do not kill, Do not **s**, *2813*
Jn 10:10 but for to **s**, and to kill, and to destroy: *2813*
Ro 2:21 thou that preachest *a man* should not **s**, *2813*
2:21 *a man* should not steal, dost thou **s**? *2813*
13:9 Thou shalt not kill, Thou shalt not **s**, *2813*
Eph 4:28 Let him that stole **s** no more: but rather let *2813*

STEALETH (3) [STEAL]
Ex 21:16 he that **s** a man, and selleth him, or if he be 1589
Job 27:20 a tempest **s** him **away** in the night. 1589
Zec 5:3 for every one that **s** shall be cut off *as* on 1589

STEALING (2) [STEAL]
Dt 24:7 If a man be found **s** any of his brethren of 1589
Hos 4:2 and killing, and **s**, and committing adultery, 1589

STEALTH (1) [STEAL]
2Sa 19:3 the people gat them by **s** that day *into* 1589

STEDFAST (10) [STEADFAST, STEDFASTLY, STEDFASTNESS]
Ps 78:8 and whose spirit was not **s** with God. 539
78:37 neither were they **s** in his covenant. 539
Da 6:26 **s** for ever, and his kingdom *that* which shall 7011
1Co 7:37 Nevertheless he that standeth **s** in *his* heart, *1476*
15:58 my beloved brethren, be ye **s**, unmoveable, *1476*
2Co 1:7 And our hope of you *is* **s**, knowing, that as *949*
Heb 2:2 For if the word spoken by angels was **s**, and *949*
3:14 if we hold the beginning of *our* confidence **s** *949*
6:19 both sure and **s**, and which entereth into that *949*
1Pe 5:9 Whom resist **s** in the faith, knowing that *4731*

STEDFASTLY (10) [STEDFAST]
Ru 1:18 When she saw that she *was* **s minded** to go 553
2Ki 8:11 he settled his countenance **s**, until *he* was 7760
Lk 9:51 he **s set** his face to go to Jerusalem, *4741*
Ac 1:10 And while they **looked s** toward heaven as *816*
2:42 And they **continued s** in the apostles' *4342*
6:15 all that sat in the council, **looking s** on him, *816*
7:55 **looked** up **s** into heaven, and saw the glory *816*
14:9 who **s beholding** him, and perceiving that he *816*
2Co 3:7 that the children of Israel could not **s behold** *816*
3:13 that the children of Israel could not **s look** to *816*

STEDFASTNESS (2) [STEDFAST]
Col 2:5 your order, and the **s** of your faith in Christ. *4733*
2Pe 3:17 error of the wicked, fall from your own **s**. *4740*

STEEL (4)
2Sa 22:35 so that a bow of **s** is broken *by* mine arms. 5154
Job 20:24 *and* the bow of **s** shall strike him through. 5154
Ps 18:34 so that a bow of **s** is broken *by* mine arms. 5154
Jer 15:12 iron break the northern iron and the **s**? 5178

STEEP (5)
Eze 38:20 the **s places** shall fall, and every wall shall 4095
Mic 1:4 the waters *that are* poured down a **s place**. 4174
Mt 8:32 ran violently down a **s place** into the sea, *2911*
Mk 5:13 the herd ran violently down a **s place** into *2911*
Lk 8:33 the herd ran violently down a **s place** into *2911*

STEM (1)
Isa 11:1 there shall come forth a rod out of the **s** of 1503

STEP (2) [FOOTSTEPS, STEPPED, STEPPETH, STEPS]
1Sa 20:3 *there is* but a **s** between me and death. 6587
Job 31:7 If my **s** hath turned out of the way, and 838

STEPHANAS (4)
1Co 1:16 And I baptized also the household of **S**: *4734*
16:15 brethren, (ye know the house of **S**, *4734*
16:17 I am glad of the coming of **S** and *4734*
16: S Corinthians was written from Philippi by **S**, *4734*

STEPHEN (7)
Ac 6:5 and they chose **S**, a man full of faith and *4736*
6:8 And **S**, full of faith and power, did great *4736*
6:9 of Cilicia and of Asia, disputing with **S**. *4736*
7:59 And they stoned **S**, calling upon *God*, and *4736*
8:2 And devout men carried **S** *to his burial*, and *4736*
11:19 arose about **S** travelled as far as Phenice, *4736*
22:20 And when the blood of thy martyr **S** was *4736*

STEPPED (1) [STEP]
Jn 5:4 first after the troubling of the water **s in**, *1684*

STEPPETH (1) [STEP]
Jn 5:7 I am coming, another **s down** before me. *2597*

STEPS (38) [STEP]
Ex 20:26 Neither shalt thou go up by **s** unto mine 4609
2Sa 22:37 Thou hast enlarged my **s** under me; so 6806
1Ki 10:19 The throne had six **s**, and the top of 4609
10:20 the one side and on the other upon the six **s**: 4609
2Ch 9:18 *there were* six **s** to the throne, with a 4609
9:19 the one side and on the other upon the six **s**. 4609
Job 14:16 For now thou numberest my **s**: dost thou 6806
18:7 The **s** of his strength shall be straitened, and 6806
23:11 My foot hath held his **s**, his way have I kept, 838
29:6 When *I* washed my **s** with butter, and 1978
31:4 not he see my ways, and count all my **s**? 6806
31:37 declare unto him the number of my **s**; 6806
Ps 17:11 They have now compassed us *in* our **s**: 838
18:36 Thou hast enlarged my **s** under me, that my 6806
37:23 The **s** of a *good* man are ordered by 4703
37:31 God *is* in his heart; none of his **s** shall slide. 838
44:18 neither have our **s** declined from thy way; 838
56:6 they hide themselves, they mark my **s**, 6119
57:6 They have prepared a net for my **s**; my soul 6471
73:2 were almost gone; my **s** had well nigh slipt. 838
85:13 and shall set *us* in the way of his **s**. 6471
119:133 Order my **s** in thy word: and let not any 6471
Pr 4:12 When thou goest thy **s** shall not be 6806
5:5 go down *to* death; her **s** take hold on hell. 6806
16:9 his way: but the LORD directeth his **s**. 6806
Isa 26:6 the feet of the poor, *and* the **s** of the needy. 6471
Jer 10:23 *it is* not in man that walketh to direct his **s**. 6806
La 4:18 They hunt our **s**, that *we* cannot go in our 6806
Eze 40:22 they went up unto it by seven **s**; and 4609
40:26 *there were* seven **s** to go up to it, and 4609
40:31 and the going up to it *had* eight **s**. 4609
40:34 that side: and the going up to it *had* eight **s**. 4609
40:37 that side: and the going up to it *had* eight **s**. 4609
40:49 *he brought me* by the **s** whereby they went 4609
Da 11:43 and the Ethiopians *shall be* at his **s**. 4703
Ro 4:12 who also walk in the **s** of *that* faith of our *2487*
2Co 12:18 same spirit? *walked we* not in the same **s**? *2487*
1Pe 2:21 us an example, that ye should follow his **s**: *2487*

STERN (1)
Ac 27:29 they cast four anchors out of the **s**, and *4403*

S

STEW See POTTAGE

STEWARD (13) [STEWARDS, STEWARDSHIP]
Ge 15: 2 the s of my house is this Eliezer of 1121+4943
43:19 they came near to the s of 376+834+5921
44: 1 he commanded the s of his house, 834+5921
44: 4 Joseph said unto his s, Up, 834+1004+5921
1Ki 16: 9 of Arza s of his house in Tirzah. 834+5921
Mt 20: 8 the lord of the vineyard saith unto his s, 2012
Lk 8: 3 And Joanna the wife of Chuza Herod's s, 2012
12:42 Who then is that faithful and wise s, 3623
16: 1 was a certain rich man, which had a s; 3623
16: 2 for thou mayest be no longer s. 3621
16: 3 Then the s said within himself, What shall I 3623
16: 8 And the lord commended the unjust s, 3623
Tit 1: 7 bishop must be blameless, as the s of God; 3623

STEWARDS (4) [STEWARD]
1Ch 28: 1 the s over all the substance and 8269
1Co 4: 1 of Christ, and s of the mysteries of God. 3623
4: 2 Moreover it is required in s, that a man be 3623
1Pe 4:10 as good s of the manifold grace of God. 3623

STEWARDSHIP (3) [STEWARD]
Lk 16: 2 give an account of thy s; for thou mayest be 3622
16: 3 for my lord taketh away from me the s: 3622
16: 4 what to do, that, when I am put out of the s, 3622

STICK (14) [CANDLESTICK, CANDLESTICKS, STICKETH, STICKS, STUCK]
2Ki 6: 6 he cut down a s, and cast it in thither; 6086
Job 33:21 and his bones that were not seen s out. 8192
41:17 they s together, that they cannot be 3920
Ps 38: 2 For thine arrows s fast in me, and thy hand 5181
La 4: 8 it is withered, it is become like a s. 6086
Eze 29: 4 I will cause the fish of thy rivers to s unto 1692
29: 4 all the fish of thy rivers shall s unto thy 1692
37:16 take thee one s, and write upon it, 6086
37:16 take another s, and write upon it, 6086
37:16 the s of Ephraim, and for all the house of 6086
37:17 join them one to another into one s; and 6086
37:19 Behold, I will take the s of Joseph, which is 6086
37:19 even with the s of Judah, and make them 6086
37:19 make them one s, and they shall be one in 6086

STICKETH (1) [STICK]
Pr 18:24 there is a friend that s closer than a brother. 1695

STICKS (6) [STICK]
Nu 15:32 they found a man that gathered s upon 6086
15:33 they that found him gathering s brought 6086
1Ki 17:10 the widow woman was there gathering of s: 6086
17:12 behold, I am gathering two s, that I may go 6086
Eze 37:20 the s whereon thou writest shall be in thine 6086
Ac 28: 3 And when Paul had gathered a bundle of s, 5434

STIFF (4) [STIFFENED, STIFFNECKED]
Dt 31:27 For I know thy rebellion, and thy s neck: 7186
Ps 75: 5 your horn on high: speak not with a s neck. 6277
Jer 17:23 made their neck s, that they might not hear, 7185
Eze 2: 4 they are impudent children and s hearted. 2389

STIFFENED (1) [STIFF]
2Ch 36:13 he s his neck, and hardened his heart from 7185

STIFFNECKED (9) [NECK, STIFF]
Ex 32: 9 and behold, it is a s people: 6203+7186
33: 3 midst of thee; for thou art a s people: 6203+7186
33: 5 children of Israel, Ye are a s people: 6203+7186
34: 9 for it is a s people; and pardon our 6203+7186
Dt 9: 6 for thou art a s people. 6203+7186
9:13 and behold, it is a s people: 6203+7186
10:16 foreskin of your heart, and be no more s. 6203
2Ch 30: 8 Now be ye not s, as your fathers 6203+7185
Ac 7:51 Ye s and uncircumcised in heart and ears, 4644

STILL (101) [STILLED, STILLEST, STILLETH]
Ge 12: 9 going on s toward the south. 5265+2050.1
41:21 they were s ill favoured, as at the beginning. NIH
Ex 9: 2 refuse to let them go, and wilt hold them s, 5750
14:13 stand s, and see the salvation of 3320
15:16 of thine arm they shall be as s as a stone; 1826
23:11 seventh year thou shalt let it rest and lie s; 5203
Lev 13:57 if it appear s in the garment, either in 5750
Nu 9: 8 Stand s, and I will hear what the LORD 5975
14:38 men that went to search the land, lived s. NIH
Jos 3: 8 water of Jordan, ye shall stand s in Jordan. 5975
10:12 of Israel, Sun, stand thou s upon Gibeon; 1826
10:13 the sun stood s, and the moon stayed, 1826
10:13 So the sun stood s in the midst of heaven, 5975
11:13 as for the cities that stood s in their 5975
24:10 therefore he blessed you s: 1288+1288
Jdg 18: 9 are ye s? be not slothful to go, and to enter 2814
Ru 3:18 said she, Sit s, my daughter, until thou 3427
1Sa 9:27 stand thou s a while, that I may shew thee 5975
12: 7 Now therefore stand s, that I may reason 3320
12:25 if ye shall s do wickedly, ye shall be 7489+7489
14: 9 we will stand s in our place, and will not 5975
26:25 great things, and also shalt s prevail. 3201+3201
2Sa 2:23 where Asahel fell down and died stood s. 5975
2:28 all the people stood s, and pursued after 5975
11: 1 But David tarried s at Jerusalem. NIH
14:32 had been good for me to have been there s: 5750
16: 5 he came forth, and cursed s as he came. NIH
18:30 And he turned aside, and stood s. 5975
20:12 the man saw that all the people stood s, 5975
20:12 that every one that came by him stood s. 5975
1Ki 19:12 in the fire: and after the fire a s small voice. 1827
22: 3 we be s, and take it not out of the hand of 2814
2Ki 2:11 s went on, and talked, that behold, 1980+1980
7: 4 if we sit s here, we die also. Now therefore 3427
12: 3 the people s sacrificed and burnt incense in 5750
15: 4 and burnt incense s on the high places. 5750
15:35 and burnt incense s in the high places. 5750
2Ch 20:17 stand ye s, and see the salvation of NIH
22: 9 had no power to keep s the kingdom. 6113
33:17 Nevertheless the people did sacrifice s in 5750
Ne 12:39 and they stood s in the prison gate. 5975
Job 2: 3 s he holdeth fast his integrity, 5750
2: 9 unto him, Dost thou s retain thine integrity? 5750
3:13 For now should I have lien s and been quiet, NIH
4:16 It stood s, but I could not discern the form 5975
20:13 it not; but keep it s within his mouth: 4513
32:16 but stood s, and answered no more:) 5975
37:14 stand s, and consider the wondrous works 5975
Ps 4: 4 your own heart upon your bed, and be s. 1826
8: 2 that thou mightest s the enemy and 7673
23: 2 he leadeth me beside the s waters. 4496
46:10 Be s, and know that I am God: I will be 7503
49: 9 That he should s live for ever, and not see 5750
68:21 the hairy scalp of such a one as goeth on s 1980
76: 8 from heaven; the earth feared, and was s, 8252
78:32 For all this they sinned s, and believed not 5750
83: 1 hold not thy peace, and be not s, O God. 8252
84: 4 they will be s praising thee. Selah. 5750
92:14 They shall s bring forth fruit in old age; 5750
107:29 a calm, so that the waves thereof are s. 2814
139:18 the sand: when I awake, I am s with thee. 5750
Ecc 12: 9 he s taught the people knowledge; 5750
Isa 5:25 turned away, but his hand is stretched out s. 5750
9:12 turned away, but his hand is stretched out s. 5750
9:17 turned away, but his hand is stretched out s. 5750
9:21 turned away, but his hand is stretched out s. 5750
10: 4 turned away, but his hand is stretched out s. 5750
23: 2 Be s, ye inhabitants of the isle; thou whom 1826
30: 7 concerning this, Their strength is to sit s. 7674
42:14 I have been s, and refrained myself: 2790
Jer 8:14 Why do we sit s? assemble yourselves, and 3427
23:17 They say s unto them that despise me, 559+559
27:11 those will I let remain s in their own land, 3240
31:20 I do earnestly remember him s: 5750
42:10 If ye will s abide in this land, then will I 7725
47: 6 up thyself into thy scabbard, rest, and be s. 1826
51:50 escaped the sword, go away, stand not s: 5975
La 3:20 soul hath them s in remembrance, 2142+2142
Eze 33:30 the children of thy people s are talking NIH
41: 7 a winding about s upward 4605+1886.5+3807.1
41: 7 s upward round about 4605+1886.5+3807.1
41: 7 the breadth of the house was s upward, NIH
Hab 3:11 and moon stood s in their habitation: 5975
Zec 1:11 behold, all the earth sitteth s, and is at rest. 3427
11:16 that is broken, nor feed that that standeth s: 5324
Mt 20:32 And Jesus stood s, and called them, and 2476
Mk 4:39 the wind, and said unto the sea, Peace, be s. 5392
10:49 And Jesus stood s, and commanded him to 2476
Lk 7:14 and they that bare him stood s. And he 2476
Jn 7: 9 words unto them, he abode s in Galilee. NIG
11: 6 he abode two days s in the same place NIG
11:20 and met him: but Mary sat s in the house. NIG
Ac 8:38 And he commanded the chariot to stand s: 2476
15:34 it pleased Silas to abide there s. NIG
17:14 but Silas and Timotheus abode there s. 5278
Ro 11:23 they also, if they bide not s in unbelief, 1961
1Ti 1: 3 As I besought thee to abide s at Ephesus, NIG
Rev 22:11 He that is unjust, let him be unjust s: and 2089
22:11 and he which is filthy, let him be filthy s: 2089
22:11 he that is righteous, let him be righteous s: 2089
22:11 and he that is holy, let him be holy s. 2089

STILLBORN See UNTIMELY

STILLED (2) [STILL]
Nu 13:30 Caleb s the people before Moses, and said, 2013
Ne 8:11 So the Levites s all the people, saying, 2814

STILLEST (1) [STILL]
Ps 89: 9 when the waves thereof arise, thou s them. 7623

STILLETH (1) [STILL]
Ps 65: 7 Which s the noise of the seas, the noise of 7623

STING (2) [STINGETH, STINGS]
1Co 15:55 O death, where is thy s? O grave, where is 2759
15:56 The s of death is sin; 2759

STINGETH (1) [STING]
Pr 23:32 it biteth like a serpent, and s like an adder. 6567

STINGS (1) [STING]
Rev 9:10 and there were s in their tails: 2759

STINK (8) [STANK, STINKETH, STINKING, STUNK]
Ge 34:30 Ye have troubled me to make me to s 887
Ex 7:18 is in the river shall die, and the river shall s; 887
16:24 it did not s, neither was there any worm 887
Ps 38: 5 My wounds s and are corrupt because of my 887
Isa 3:24 that instead of sweet smell there shall be s; 4716
34: 3 their s shall come up out of their carcases, 889
Joel 2:20 his s shall come up, and his ill savour shall 889
Am 4:10 I have made the s of your camps to come up 889

STINKETH (2) [STINK]
Isa 50: 2 their fish s, because there is no water, and 887
Jn 11:39 saith unto him, Lord, by this time he s: 3605

STINKING (1) [STINK]
Ecc 10: 1 of the apothecary to send forth a s savour: 887

STIR (20) [STIRRED, STIRRETH, STIRS]
Nu 24: 9 who shall s him up? Blessed is he that 6965
Job 17: 8 the innocent shall s up himself against 5782
41:10 None is so fierce that dare s him up: who 5782
Ps 35:23 S up thyself, and awake to my judgment, 5782
78:38 anger away, and did not s up all his wrath. 5782
80: 2 Benjamin and Manasseh s up thy strength, 5782
Pr 15: 1 away wrath: but grievous words s up anger. 5927
SS 2: 7 that ye s not up, nor awake my love, till he 5782
3: 5 that ye s not up, nor awake my love, till he 5782
8: 4 that ye s not up, nor awake my love, 5782
Isa 10:26 the LORD of hosts shall s up a scourge 5782
13:17 Behold, I will s up the Medes against them, 5782
42:13 he shall s up jealousy like a man of war: 5782
Da 11: 2 shall s up all against the realm of Grecia. 5782
11:25 he shall s up his power and his courage 5782
Ac 12:18 there was no small s among the soldiers, 5017
19:23 And the same time there arose no small s 5017
2Ti 1: 6 remembrance that thou s up the gift of God, 329
2Pe 1:13 to s you up by putting you in 1326
3: 1 in both which I s up your pure minds by 1326

STIRRED (23) [STIR]
Ex 35:21 every one whose heart s him up, and 5375
35:26 all the women whose heart s them up in 5375
36: 2 even every one whose heart s him up to 5375
1Sa 22: 8 sheweth unto me that my son hath s up my 6965
26:19 If the LORD have s thee up against me, 5496
1Ki 11:14 the LORD s up an adversary unto 6965
11:23 God s him up another adversary, Rezon 6965
21:25 the LORD, whom Jezebel his wife s up. 5496
1Ch 5:26 the God of Israel s up the spirit of Pul king 5782
2Ch 21:16 Moreover the LORD s up against 5782
36:22 the LORD s up the spirit of Cyrus king of 5782
Ezr 1: 1 the LORD s up the spirit of Cyrus king of 5782
Ps 39: 2 even from good; and my sorrow was s. 5916
Da 11:10 his sons shall be s up, and shall assemble a 1624
11:10 shall he return, and be s up, even to his 1624
11:25 the king of the south shall be s up to battle 1624
Hag 1:14 the LORD s up the spirit of Zerubbabel 5782
Ac 6:12 And they s up the people, and the elders, 4787
13:50 But the Jews s up the devout and 3951
14: 2 But the unbelieving Jews s up the Gentiles, 1892
17:13 they came thither also, and s up the people. 4531
17:16 for them at Athens, his spirit was s in him, 3947
21:27 s up all the people, and laid hands on him, 4797

STIRRETH (8) [STIR]
Dt 32:11 As an eagle s up her nest, fluttereth over 5782
Pr 10:12 Hatred s up strifes: but love covereth all 5782
15:18 A wrathful man s up strife: but he that is 1624
28:25 He that is of a proud heart s up strife: but 1624
29:22 An angry man s up strife, and a furious 1624
Isa 14: 9 it s up the dead for thee, even all the chief 5782
64: 7 that s up himself to take hold of thee: 5782
Lk 23: 5 saying, He s up the people, 383

STIRS (1) [STIR]
Isa 22: 2 Thou that art full of s, a tumultuous city, 8663

STOCK (8) [STOCKS]
Lev 25:47 by thee, or to the s of the stranger's family: 6133
Job 14: 8 and the s thereof die in the ground; 1503
Isa 40:24 yea, their s shall not take root in the earth: 1503
44:19 shall I fall down to the s of a tree? 944
Jer 2:27 Saying to a s, Thou art my father; and to a 6086
10: 8 and foolish: the s is a doctrine of vanities. 6086
Ac 13:26 children of the s of Abraham, and 1085
Php 3: 5 of the s of Israel, of the tribe of Benjamin, 1085

STOCKS (9) [STOCK]
Job 13:27 Thou puttest my feet also in the s, and 5465
33:11 He putteth my feet in the s, he marketh all 5465
Pr 7:22 or as a fool to the correction of the s; 5914
Jer 3: 9 committed adultery with stones and with s. 6086
20: 2 put him in the s that were in the high gate 4115
20: 3 Pashur brought forth Jeremiah out of the s. 4115
29:26 shouldest put him in prison, and in the s. 6729
Hos 4:12 My people ask counsel at their s, and 6086
Ac 16:24 and made their feet fast in the s. 3586

STOICKS (1)
Ac 17:18 and of the S, encountered him. 4770

STOLE (4) [STEAL]
2Sa 15: 6 Absalom s the hearts of the men of Israel. 1589
2Ch 22:11 s him from among the king's sons that were 1589
Mt 28:13 by night, and s him away while we slept. 2813
Eph 4:28 Let him that s steal no more: but rather let 2813

STOLEN (15) [STEAL]
Ge 30:33 the sheep, that shall be counted s with me. 1589
31:19 Rachel had s the images that were her 1589
31:26 that thou hast s away unawares to 1589+3824
31:30 yet wherefore hast thou s my gods? 1589
31:32 For Jacob knew not that Rachel had s them. 1589
31:39 whether s by day, or stolen by night. 1589
31:39 whether stolen by day, or s by night. 1589
40:15 For indeed I was s away out of 1589+1589
Ex 22: 7 to keep, and it be s out of the man's house; 1589
22:12 if it be s from him, he shall make 1589+1589
Jos 7:11 have also s, and dissembled also, and 1589
2Sa 19:41 our brethren the men of Judah s thee away, 1589
21:12 which had s them from the street of 1589
Pr 9:17 S waters are sweet, and bread eaten in 1589
Ob 1: 5 would they not have s till they had enough? 1589

STOMACH'S (1) [STOMACHER]
1Ti 5:23 but use a little wine for thy s sake and 4751

STOMACHER (1) [STOMACH'S]
Isa 3:24 instead of a s a girding of sackcloth; and 6614

STONE (192) [BRIMSTONE, CHALKSTONES, HAILSTONES, HAIL-STONES, HEADSTONE, SLINGSTONES, STONE'S, STONED, STONES, STONESQUARERS, STONEST, STONING, STONY, STUMBLINGSTONE]
Ge 2:12 land is good: there is bdellium and the onyx s. 68
11: 3 they had brick for s, and slime had they for 68
28:18 and took the s that he had put for his pillows, 68
28:22 this s, which I have set for a pillar, shall be 68

Ge 29: 2 and a great **s** *was* upon the well's mouth. 68
29: 3 and they rolled the **s** from the well's mouth, 68
29: 3 put the **s** again upon the well's mouth in his 68
29: 8 and *till* they roll the **s** from the well's mouth; 68
29:10 rolled the **s** from the well's mouth, and 68
31:45 And Jacob took a **s**, and set it up *for* a pillar. 68
35:14 where he talked with him, *even* a pillar of **s**: 68
49:24 (from thence *is* the shepherd, the **s** of Israel:) 68
Ex 4:25 Zipporah took a **sharp s**, and cut off 6864
7:19 both in *vessels of* wood, and in *vessels of* **s**. 68
8:26 before their eyes, and will they not **s** us? 5619
15: 5 they sank into the bottom as a **s**. 68
15:16 of thine arm they shall be *as* still as a **s**; 68
17: 4 this people? they be almost ready to **s** me. 5619
17:12 they took a **s**, and put *it* under him, and he sat 68
20:25 if thou wilt make me an altar of **s**, thou shalt 68
20:25 of stone, thou shalt not build it *of* **hewn s**: 1496
21:18 one smite another with a **s**, or with *his* fist, 68
24:10 as it were a paved work of a **sapphire s**, 5601
24:12 and I will give thee tables of **s**, and a law, and 68
28:10 Six of their names on one **s**, and the *other* six 68
28:10 the *other* six names of the rest on the other **s**, 68
28:11 *With* the work of an engraver in **s**, *like* 68
31:18 two tables of Testimony, tables of **s**, 68
34: 1 Hew thee two tables of **s** like unto the first: 68
34: 4 he hewed two tables of **s** like unto the first; 68
34: 4 and took in his hand the two tables of **s**. 68
Lev 20: 2 the people of the land shall **s** him with 7275
20:27 they shall **s** them with stones: their blood 7275
24:14 his head, and let all the congregation **s** him. 7275
24:16 congregation shall **certainly s** him: 7275+7275
24:23 out of the camp, and **s** him with stones. 7275
26: 1 neither shall ye set up *any* image of **s** in your 68
Nu 14:10 all the congregation bade **s** them with 7275
15:35 all the congregation shall **s** him with stones 7275
35:17 if he smite him with throwing a **s**, 68
35:23 Or with any **s**, wherewith *a man* may die, 68
Dt 4:13 and he wrote them upon two tables of **s**. 68
4:28 wood and **s**, which neither see, nor hear, 68
5:22 he wrote them in two tables of **s**, and 68
9: 9 up into the mount to receive the tables of **s**, 68
9:10 the LORD delivered unto me two tables of **s** 68
9:11 *that* the LORD gave me the two tables of **s**, 68
10: 1 Hew thee two tables of **s** like unto the first, 68
10: 3 and hewed two tables of **s** like unto the first, 68
13:10 thou shalt **s** him with stones, that he die; 5619
17: 5 and shalt **s** them with stones, till they die. 5619
21:21 all the men of his city shall **s** him with 7275
22:21 the men of her city shall **s** her with stones 5619
22:24 ye shall **s** them with stones that they die; 5619
28:36 there shalt thou serve other gods, wood and **s**. 68
28:64 nor thy fathers have known, *even* wood and **s**. 68
29:17 their idols, wood and **s**, silver and gold, 68
Jos 4: 5 take ye up every man of you a **s** upon his 68
15: 6 the border went up *to* the **s** of Bohan the son 68
18:17 descended *to* the **s** of Bohan the son of 68
24:26 took a great **s**, and set it up there under an 68
24:27 Behold, this **s** shall be a witness unto us; 68
Jdg 9: 5 *being* threescore and ten persons, upon one **s**: 68
9:18 upon one **s**, and have made Abimelech, 68
1Sa 6:14 stood there, where *there was* a great **s**: 68
6:15 of gold *were*, and put *them* on the great **s**: 68
6:18 even unto the great **s** *of* Abel, NIH
6:18 *which* **s** *remaineth* unto this day in the field NIH
7:12 Samuel took a **s**, and set *it* between Mizpeh 68
14:33 roll a great **s** unto me *this* day. 68
17:49 took thence a **s**, and slang *it*, and smote 68
17:49 his forehead, that the **s** sunk into his forehead; 68
17:50 over the Philistine with a sling and with a **s**, 68
20:19 was *in hand*, and shalt remain by the **s** Ezel. 68
25:37 heart died within him, and he became *as* a **s**. 68
2Sa 17:13 until there be not one **small s** found there. 6872
20: 8 When they *were* at the great **s** which *is* in 68
1Ki 1: 9 and oxen and fat cattle by the **s** of Zoheleth, 68
6: 7 was built *of* **s** made ready *before it was* 68
6:18 all *was* cedar; there was no **s** seen. 68
6:36 the inner court *with* three rows of **hewed s**, 1496
8: 9 nothing in the ark save the two tables of **s**, 68
21:10 *then* carry him out, and **s** him, that he may 5619
2Ki 3:25 every good piece of land cast every man his **s**, 68
12:12 hewers of **s**, and to buy timber and 68
12:12 hewed **s** to repair the breaches of the house of 68
19:18 but the work of men's hands, wood and **s**: 68
22: 6 to buy timber and hewn **s** to repair the house. 68
1Ch 22:14 timber also and **s** have I prepared; and 68
22:15 hewers and workers of **s** and timber, and 68
2Ch 2:14 in silver, in brass, in iron, in **s**, and in timber, 68
34:11 and builders gave they *it*, to buy hewn **s**, 68
Ne 4: 3 go up, he shall even break down their **s** wall. 68
9:11 into the deeps, as a **s** into the mighty waters. 68
Job 28: 2 of the earth, and brass *is* molten *out of* the **s**. 68
38: 6 or who laid the corner **s** thereof; 68
38:30 The waters are hid as *with* a **s**, and the face of 68
41:24 His heart is as firm as a **s**; yea, as hard as a 68
Ps 91:12 *their* hands, lest thou dash thy foot against a **s**. 68
118:22 The **s** *which* the builders refused is become 68
118:22 refused is become the head ***s*** of the corner. NIH
Pr 17: 8 A gift *is as* a precious **s** in the eyes of him that 68
24:31 and the **s** wall thereof was broken down. 68
26: 8 As *he that* bindeth a **s** in a sling, so *is* he that 68
26:27 and he that rolleth a **s**, it will return upon him. 68
27: 3 A **s** *is* heavy, and the sand weighty; but 68
Isa 8:14 for a **s** of stumbling and for a rock of offence 68
28:16 Behold, I lay in Zion for a foundation a **s**, 68
28:16 lay in Zion for a foundation a stone, a tried **s**, 68
28:16 a precious corner ***s***, a sure foundation: NIH
37:19 but the work of men's hands, wood and **s**: 68
Jer 2:27 and to a **s**, Thou hast brought me forth: 68
51:26 they shall not take of thee a **s** for a corner, 68
51:26 a stone for a corner, nor a **s** for foundations; 68
51:63 *that* thou shalt bind a **s** to it, and cast it into 68
La 3: 9 He hath inclosed my ways with **hewn s**, 1496
3:53 my life in the dungeon, and cast a **s** upon me. 68
Eze 1:26 of a throne, as the appearance of a sapphire **s**: 68
10: 1 appeared over them as it were a sapphire **s**, 68
Eze 10: 9 of the wheels *was* as the colour of a beryl **s**. 68
16:40 they shall **s** thee with stones, and thrust thee 7275
20:32 families of the countries, to serve wood and **s**. 68
23:47 the company shall **s** them with stones, and 7275
28:13 every precious **s** *was* thy covering, 68
40:42 the four tables *were* of hewn **s** for the burnt 68
Da 2:34 Thou sawest till that a **s** was cut out without 69
2:35 the **s** that smote the image became a great 69
2:45 Forasmuch as thou sawest that the **s** was cut 69
5: 4 of silver, of brass, of iron, of wood, and of **s**. 69
5:23 gold, of brass, iron, wood, and **s**, which see 69
6:17 a **s** was brought, and laid upon the mouth of 69
Am 5:11 ye have built houses of **hewn s**, but ye shall 1496
Hab 2:11 For the **s** shall cry out of the wall, and 68
2:19 Awake; to the dumb **s**, Arise, it shall teach! 68
Hag 2:15 from before a **s** was laid upon a stone in 68
2:15 from before a stone was laid upon a **s** in 68
Zec 3: 9 For behold the **s** that I have laid before 68
3: 9 before Joshua; upon one **s** *shall be* seven eyes: 68
7:12 they made their hearts *as* an **adamant s**, 8068
12: 3 Jerusalem a burdensome **s** for all people: 68
Mt 4: 6 at any time thou dash thy foot against a **s**. *3037*
7: 9 if his son ask bread, will he give him a **s**? *3037*
21:42 The **s** which the builders rejected, *3037*
21:44 And whosoever shall fall on this **s** shall be *3037*
24: 2 There shall not be left here one **s** upon *3037*
27:60 he rolled a great **s** to the door of *3037*
27:66 sealing the **s**, and setting a watch. *3037*
28: 2 came and rolled back the **s** from the door, *3037*
Mk 12:10 The **s** which the builders rejected is become *3037*
13: 2 there shall not be left one **s** upon another, *3037*
15:46 rolled a **s** unto the door of the sepulchre. *3037*
16: 3 Who shall roll us away the **s** from the door *3037*
16: 4 they saw that the **s** was rolled away: *3037*
Lk 4: 3 command this **s** that it be made bread. *3037*
4:11 at any time thou dash thy foot against a **s**. *3037*
11:11 of you that is a father, will he give him a **s**? *3037*
19:44 they shall not leave in thee one **s** upon *3037*
20: 6 if we say, Of men; all the people will **s** us: *2642*
20:17 The **s** which the builders rejected, *3037*
20:18 Whosoever shall fall upon that **s** shall be *3037*
21: 6 in the which there shall not be left one **s** *3037*
23:53 laid it in a sepulchre *that was* **hewn in s**, *2991*
24: 2 And they found the **s** rolled away from *3037*
Jn 1:42 which is by interpretation, A **s**. *4074*
2: 6 And there were set there six waterpots of **s**, *3035*
8: 7 sin among you, let him first cast a **s** at her. *3037*
10:31 Then the Jews took up stones again to **s** *3034*
10:32 for which of those works do ye **s** me? *3034*
10:33 saying, For a good work we **s** thee not; *3034*
11: 8 Master, the Jews of late sought to **s** thee; *3034*
11:38 the grave. It was a cave, and a **s** lay upon it. *3037*
11:39 Jesus said, Take ye away the **s**. Martha, *3037*
11:41 Then they took away the **s** *from the place* *3037*
20: 1 seeth the **s** taken away from the sepulchre. *3037*
Ac 4:11 This is the **s** which was set at nought of you *3037*
14: 5 to use *them* despitefully, and to **s** them, *3036*
17:29 or silver, or **s**, graven by art and *3037*
2Co 3: 3 not in tables **of s**, but in fleshy tables of *3035*
Eph 2:20 Christ himself being the chief corner ***s***; NIG
1Pe 2: 4 To whom coming, *as unto* a living **s**, *3037*
2: 6 Behold, I lay in Sion a chief corner **s**, elect, *3037*
2: 7 the **s** which the builders disallowed, *3037*
2: 8 And a **s** of stumbling, and a rock of *3037*
Rev 2:17 and will give him a white **s**, and in *5586*
2:17 and in the **s** a new name written, *5586*
4: 3 to look upon like a jasper and a sardine **s**: *3037*
9:20 idols of gold, and silver, and brass, and **s**, *3035*
16:21 *every* ***s*** about the weight of a talent: NIG
17: 4 with gold and precious **s** and pearls, *3037*
18:21 And a mighty angel took up a **s** like a great *3037*
21:11 her light *was* like unto a **s** most precious, *3037*
21:11 *even* like a jasper **s**, clear as crystal; *3037*

STONE'S (1) [STONE]

Lk 22:41 And he was withdrawn from them about a **s** *3037*

STONED (22) [STONE]

Ex 19:13 he shall **surely** be **s**, or shot through; 5619+5619
21:28 the ox shall be **surely s**, and his flesh 5619+5619
21:29 the ox shall be **s**, and his owner also shall 5619
21:32 shekels *of* silver, and the ox shall be **s**. 5619
Nu 15:36 and **s** him with stones, and he died; 7275
Jos 7:25 all Israel **s** him *with* stones, and 7275
7:25 with fire, after they had **s** them with stones. 5619
1Ki 12:18 all Israel **s** him with stones, that he died. 7275
21:13 the city, and **s** him with stones, that he died. 5619
21:14 to Jezebel, saying, Naboth is **s**, and is dead. 5619
21:15 when Jezebel heard that Naboth was **s**, and 5619
2Ch 10:18 the children of Israel **s** him with stones, 7275
24:21 **s** him *with* stones at the commandment of 7275
Mt 21:35 beat one, and killed another, and **s** another. *3036*
Jn 8: 5 law commanded us, that such should be **s**: *3036*
Ac 5:26 the people, lest they should have been **s**. *3034*
7:58 and **s** *him:* and the witnesses laid down *3036*
7:59 And they **s** Stephen, calling upon *God*, and *3036*
14:19 and, having **s** Paul, drew *him* out of *3034*
2Co 11:25 once was I **s**, thrice I suffered shipwrack, *3034*
Heb 11:37 They were **s**, they were sawn asunder, *3034*
12:20 it shall be **s**, or thrust through with a dart: *3036*

STONES (175) [STONE]

Ge 28:11 he took of the **s** of *that* place, and put *them for* 68
31:46 Jacob said unto his brethren, Gather **s**; and 68
31:46 and they took **s**, and made a heap: 68
Ex 25: 7 Onyx **s**, and stones to be set in the ephod, and 68
25: 7 **s** to be set in the ephod, and in the breastplate. 68
28: 9 thou shalt take two onyx **s**, and grave on them 68
28:11 shalt thou engrave the two **s** with the names of 68
28:12 thou shalt put the two **s** upon the shoulders of 68
28:12 *for* **s** of memorial unto the children of Israel: 68
28:17 thou shalt set in it settings of **s**, *even* four 68
28:17 set in it settings of stones, *even* four rows of **s**: 68
28:21 the **s** shall be with the names of the children 68
Ex 31: 5 in cutting of **s**, to set *them*, and in carving of 68
35: 9 onyx **s**, and stones to be set for the ephod, 68
35: 9 **s** to be set for the ephod, and for 68
35:27 the rulers brought onyx **s**, and stones to be set, 68
35:27 **s** to be set, for the ephod, and for 68
35:33 in the cutting of **s**, to set *them*, and in carving 68
39: 6 they wrought onyx **s** inclosed *in* ouches *of* 68
39: 7 *that they should be* **s** for a memorial to 68
39:10 they set in it four rows of **s**: *the first* row *was* 68
39:14 the **s** *were* according to the names of 68
Lev 14:40 they take away the **s** in which the plague *is*, 68
14:42 they shall take other **s**, and put *them* in 68
14:42 and put *them* in the place of *those* **s**; 68
14:43 after *that* he hath taken away the **s**, and 68
14:45 the **s** of it, and the timber thereof, and all 68
20: 2 the people of the land shall stone him with **s**. 68
20:27 they shall stone them with **s**: their blood *shall* 68
21:20 be scurvy, or scabbed, or hath his **s** broken; 810
24:23 cursed out of the camp, and stone him with **s**. 68
Nu 14:10 all the congregation bade stone them with **s**. 68
15:35 all the congregation shall stone him with **s** 68
15:36 the camp, and stoned him with **s**, and he died; 68
Dt 8: 9 a land whose **s** *are* iron, and out of whose hills 68
13:10 And thou shalt stone him with **s**, that he die; 68
17: 5 and shalt stone them with **s**, till they die. 68
21:21 all the men of his city shall stone him with **s**, 68
22:21 the men of her city shall stone her with **s** that 68
22:24 and ye shall stone them with **s** that they die; 68
23: 1 He that is wounded in the **s**, or hath *his* 1795
27: 2 that thou shalt set thee up great **s**, and 68
27: 4 *that* ye shall set up these **s**, which I command 68
27: 5 altar unto the LORD thy God, an altar of **s**: 68
27: 6 the altar of the LORD thy God *of* whole **s**: 68
27: 8 thou shalt write upon the **s** all the words of 68
Jos 4: 3 twelve **s**, and ye shall carry them over with 68
4: 6 to come, saying, What mean ye by these **s**? 68
4: 7 these **s** shall be for a memorial unto 68
4: 8 took up twelve **s** out of the midst of Jordan, 68
4: 9 Joshua set up twelve **s** in the midst of Jordan, 68
4:20 those twelve **s**, which they took out of Jordan, 68
4:21 in time to come, saying, What *mean* these **s**? 68
7:25 all Israel stoned him *with* **s**, and burned them 68
7:25 with fire, after they had stoned them with **s**. 68
7:26 they raised over him a great heap of **s** unto 68
8:29 raise thereon a great heap of **s**, *that remaineth* 68
8:31 an altar of whole **s**, over which no *man* hath 68
8:32 he wrote there upon the **s** a copy of the law of 68
10:11 that the LORD cast down great **s** from 68
10:18 Roll great **s** upon the mouth of the cave, and 68
10:27 laid great **s** in the cave's mouth, *which remain* 68
Jdg 20:16 every one could sling **s** at a hair *breadth*, and 68
1Sa 17:40 and chose him five smooth **s** out of the brook, 68
2Sa 12:30 *was* a talent of gold with the precious **s**: 68
16: 6 he cast **s** at David, and at all the servants of 68
16:13 as he went, and threw **s** at him, and cast dust. 68
18:17 and laid a very great heap of **s** upon him: 68
1Ki 5:17 they brought great **s**, costly stones, *and* 68
5:17 great stones, costly **s**, *and* hewed stones, 68
5:17 great stones, costly stones, *and* hewed **s**, 68
5:18 they prepared timber and **s** to build the house. 68
7: 9 All these *were of* costly **s**, according to 68
7: 9 according to the measures of **hewed s**, 1496
7:10 the foundation *was of* costly **s**, *even* great 68
7:10 *even* great **s**, stones of ten cubits, and 68
7:10 **s** of ten cubits, and stones of eight cubits. 68
7:10 stones of ten cubits, and **s** of eight cubits. 68
7:11 above *were* costly **s**, after the measures of 68
7:11 after the measures of **hewed s**, and cedars. 1496
7:12 about *was with* three rows *of* **hewed s**, 1496
10: 2 and very much gold, and precious **s**: 68
10:10 and of spices very great store, and precious **s**: 68
10:11 great plenty of almug trees, and precious **s**. 68
10:27 the king made silver *to be* in Jerusalem as **s**, 68
12:18 and all Israel stoned him with **s**, that he died. 68
15:22 they took away the **s** of Ramah, and 68
18:31 Elijah took twelve **s**, according to the number 68
18:32 *with* the **s** he built an altar in the name of 68
18:38 the **s**, and the dust, and licked up the water 68
21:13 the city, and stoned him with **s**, that he died. 68
2Ki 3:19 and mar every good piece of land with **s**. 68
3:25 only in Kir haraseth left *they* the **s** thereof; 68
16:17 under it, and put it upon a pavement of **s**. 68
1Ch 12: 2 the right hand and the left in *hurling* **s** and 68
20: 2 talent of gold, and *there were* precious **s** in it; 68
22: 2 he set masons to hew wrought **s** to build 68
29: 2 onyx **s**, and *stones* to be set, glistering stones, 68
29: 2 onyx stones, and ***s*** to be set, NIH
29: 2 glistering **s**, and of divers colours, and 68
29: 2 all *manner of* precious **s**, and marble stones in 68
29: 2 precious stones, and marble **s** in abundance. 68
29: 8 they with whom *precious* **s** were found gave 68
2Ch 1:15 and gold at Jerusalem *as plenteous* as **s**, 68
3: 6 he garnished the house with precious **s** for 68
9: 1 and gold in abundance, and precious **s**: 68
9: 9 and of spices great abundance, and precious **s**: 68
9:10 brought algum trees and precious **s**. 68
9:27 the king made silver in Jerusalem as **s**, and 68
10:18 and the children of Israel stoned him with **s**, 68
16: 6 they carried away the **s** of Ramah, and 68
24:21 stoned him *with* **s** at the commandment of 68
26:14 habergeons, and bows, and slings to cast **s**. 68
26:15 to shoot arrows and great **s** withal. 68
32:27 for precious **s**, and for spices, and for shields, 68
Ezr 5: 8 which *is* builded *with* great **s**, and timber *is* 69
6: 4 *With* three rows of great **s**, and a row of new 69
Ne 4: 2 will they revive the **s** out of the heaps of 68
Job 5:23 For thou shalt be in league with the **s** of 68
6:12 *Is* my strength the strength of **s**? or *is* my flesh 68
8:17 about the heap, *and* seeth the place of **s**. 68
14:19 The waters wear the **s**: thou washest away 68
22:24 and *the gold of* Ophir as the **s** of the brooks. 6697
28: 3 the **s** of darkness, and the shadow of death. 68
28: 6 The **s** of it *are* the place of sapphires: and 68
40:17 the sinews of his **s** are wrapt together. 6344
41:30 Sharp **s** *are* under him: he spreadeth sharp 2789

S

Ps 102:14 For thy servants take pleasure in her s, and 68
137: 9 and dasheth thy little ones against the s. 5553
144:12 that our daughters may be as corner s, 2106
Ecc 3: 5 A time to cast away s, and a time to gather 68
3: 5 away stones, and a time to gather s together; 68
10: 9 Whoso removeth s shall be hurt therewith; 68
Isa 5: 2 gathered out the s thereof, and planted it 5619
9:10 fallen down, but we will build with hewn s: 1496
14:19 with a sword, that go down to the s of the pit; 68
27: 9 when he maketh all the s of the altar as 68
34:11 the line of confusion, and the s of emptiness. 68
54:11 I will lay thy s with fair colours, and lay thy 68
54:12 and all thy borders of pleasant s. 68
57: 6 Among the smooth s of the stream is thy NIH
60:17 and for wood brass, and for s iron: 68
62:10 cast up, cast up the highway; gather out the s; 68
Jer 3: 9 committed adultery with s and with stocks. 68
43: 9 Take great s in thine hand, and hide them in 68
43:10 will set his throne upon these s that I have 68
La 3:16 He hath also broken my teeth with gravel s, 2687
4: 1 the s of the sanctuary are poured out in the top 68
Eze 16:40 they shall stone thee with s, and thrust thee 68
23:47 And the company shall stone them with s, and 68
26:12 they shall lay thy s and thy timber and 68
27:22 of all spices, and with all precious s, and gold. 68
28:14 and down in the midst of the s of fire. 68
28:16 from the midst of the s of fire. 68
Da 11:38 and with precious s, and pleasant things. 68
Mic 1: 6 I will pour down the s thereof into the valley, 68
Zec 5: 4 it with the timber thereof and the s thereof. 68
9:15 they shall devour, and subdue with sling s; 68
9:16 for they shall be as the s of a crown, lifted up 68
Mt 3: 9 that God is able of these s to raise up 3037
4: 3 command that these s be made bread. 3037
Mk 5: 5 crying, and cutting himself with s. 3037
12: 4 and at him they cast s, and wounded him in 3036
13: 1 see what manner of s and what buildings 3037
Lk 3: 8 That God is able of these s to raise up 3037
19:40 the s would immediately cry out. 3037
21: 5 how it was adorned with goodly s and gifts, 3037
Jn 8:59 Then took they up s to cast at him: but 3037
10:31 Then the Jews took up s again to stone him. 3037
1Co 3:12 silver, precious s, wood, hay, stubble; 3037
2Co 3: 7 written and engraven in s, was glorious, 3037
1Pe 2: 5 Ye also, as lively s, are built up a spiritual 3037
Rev 18:12 and precious s, and of pearls, and 3037
18:16 with gold, and precious s, and pearls: 3037
21:19 garnished with all manner of precious s. 3037

STONESQUARERS (1) [SQUARE, STONE]

1Ki 5:18 Hiram's builders did hew them, and the s: 1382

STONEST (2) [STONE]

Mt 23:37 and s them which are sent unto thee, 3036
Lk 13:34 and s them that are sent unto thee; 3036

STONING (1) [STONE]

1Sa 30: 6 for the people spake of s him, because 5619

STONY (7) [STONE]

Ps 141: 6 When their judges are overthrown in s 5553
Eze 11:19 I will take the s heart out of their flesh, and 68
36:26 I will take away the s heart out of your flesh, 68
Mt 13: 5 Some fell upon s places, where they had 4075
13:20 But he that received the seed into s places, 4075
Mk 4: 5 And some fell on s ground, where it had 4075
4:16 they likewise which are sown on s ground; 4075

STOOD (339) [STAND]

Ge 18: 2 and looked, and lo, three men s by him: 5324
18: 8 he s by them under the tree, and they did 5975
18:22 but Abraham s yet before the LORD. 5975
19:27 to the place where he s before the LORD: 5975
23: 3 Abraham s up from before his dead, and 6965
23: 7 Abraham s up, and bowed himself to 6965
24:30 and behold, he s by the camels at the well. 5975
28:13 the LORD s above it, and said, 5324
37: 7 and lo, my sheaf arose, and also s upright; 5324
37: 7 your sheaves s round about, and 5437
41: 1 and behold, he s by the river. 5975
41: 3 s by the other kine upon the brink of 5975
41:17 behold, I s upon the bank of the river: 5975
41:46 Joseph was thirty years old when he s 5975
43:15 went down to Egypt, and s before Joseph. 5975
45: 1 himself before all them that s by him; 5324
45: 1 there s no man with him, while Joseph 5975
Ex 2: 4 his sister s afar off, to wit what would be 3320
2:17 Moses s up and helped them, and 6965
5:20 met Moses and Aaron, who s in the way, 5324
9:10 ashes of the furnace, and s before Pharaoh; 5975
14:19 from before their face, and s behind them: 5975
15: 8 the floods s upright as a heap, and 5324
18:13 the people s by Moses from the morning 5975
19:17 and they s at the nether part of the mount. 3320
20:18 people saw it, they removed, and s afar off. 5975
20:21 the people s afar off, and Moses drew near 5975
32:26 Moses s in the gate of the camp, and said, 5975
33: 8 s every man at his tent door, and 5324
33: 9 s at the door of the tabernacle, and 5975
34: 5 s with him there, and proclaimed the name 3320
Lev 9: 5 drew near and s before the LORD. 5975
Nu 11:32 the people s up all that day, and all that 6965
12: 5 s in the door of the tabernacle, and 5975
16:18 s in the door of the tabernacle of 5975
16:27 s in the door of their tents, and their wives, 5324
16:48 he s between the dead and the living; and 5975
22:22 the angel of the LORD s in the way for an 3320
22:24 the angel of the LORD s in a path of 5975
22:26 went further, and s in a narrow place, 5975
23: 6 lo, he s by his burnt sacrifice, he, and 5324
23:17 he s by his burnt offering, and the princes 5324
27: 2 they s before Moses, and before Eleazar 5975
Dt 4:11 ye came near and s under the mountain; 5975
5: 5 (I s between the LORD and you at that 5975
Dt 31:15 the pillar of the cloud s over the door of 5975
Jos 3:16 the waters which came down from above s 5975
3:17 s firm on dry ground in the midst of Jordan, 5975
4: 3 out of the place where the priests' feet s 4673
4: 9 which bare the ark of the covenant s: 4673
4:10 For the priests which bare the ark s in 5975
5:13 there s a man over against him with his 5975
8:33 s on this side the ark and on that side before 5975
10:13 the sun s still, and the moon stayed, 1826
10:13 So the sun s still in the midst of heaven, 5975
11:13 as for the cities that s still in their strength, 5975
20: 9 of blood, until he s before the congregation. 5975
21:44 there s not a man of all their enemies before 5975
Jdg 3:19 And all that s by him went out from him. 5975
6:31 Joash said unto all that s against him, Will 5975
7:21 they s every man in his place round about 5975
9: 7 he went and s in the top of mount Gerizim, 5975
9:35 and s in the entering of the gate of the city: 5975
9:44 and s in the entering of the gate of the city: 5975
16:29 two middle pillars upon which the house s, 3559
18:16 of Dan, s by the entering of the gate. 5324
18:17 the priest s in the entering of the gate with 5324
20:28 the son of Aaron, s before it in those days,) 5975
1Sa 1:26 I am the woman that s by thee here, 5324
3:10 s, and called as at other times, Samuel, 3320
4:20 the time of her death the women that s 5324
6:14 a Beth-shemite, and s there, where there 5975
10:23 when he s among the people, he was higher 3320
16:21 David came to Saul, and s before him: and 5975
17: 3 the Philistines s on a mountain on the one 5975
17: 3 Israel s on a mountain on the other side: 5975
17: 8 he s and cried unto the armies of Israel, 5975
17:26 David spake to the men that s by him, 5975
17:51 s upon the Philistine, and took his sword, 5975
22: 7 Saul said unto his servants that s about him, 5324
22:17 the king said unto the footmen that s about 5324
26:13 and s on the top of a hill afar off; 5975
2Sa 1:10 So I s upon him, and slew him, because 5975
2:23 where Asahel fell down and died s still. 5975
2:25 became one troop, and s on the top of a hill. 5975
2:28 all the people s still, and pursued after 5975
13:31 all his servants s by with their clothes rent. 5324
15: 2 up early, and s beside the way of the gate: 5975
18: 4 the king s by the gate side, and all 5975
18:30 stand here. And he turned aside, and s still. 5975
20:11 one of Joab's men s by him, and said, 5975
20:12 when the man saw that all the people s still, 5975
20:12 saw that every one that came by him s still. 5975
20:15 bank against the city, and it s in the trench: 5975
23:12 he s in the midst of the ground, and 3320
1Ki 1:28 the king's presence, and s before the king. 5975
3:15 s before the ark of the covenant of 5975
3:16 unto the king, and s before him. 5975
7:25 It s upon twelve oxen, three looking toward 5975
8:14 (and all the congregation of Israel s;) 5975
8:22 Solomon s before the altar of the LORD 5975
8:55 he s, and blessed all the congregation of 5975
10:19 of the seat, and two lions s beside the stays. 5975
10:20 twelve lions s there on the one side and 5975
12: 6 that s before Solomon his father while he 5975
12: 8 up with him, and which s before him: 5975
13: 1 and Jeroboam s by the altar to burn incense. 5975
13:24 was cast in the way, and the ass s by it, 5975
13:24 stood by it, the lion also s by the carcase. 5975
19:13 and s in the entering in of the cave. 5975
22:21 s before the LORD, and said, I will 5975
2Ki 2: 7 of the prophets went, and s to view afar off: 5975
2: 7 to view afar off: and they two s by Jordan. 5975
2:13 and went back, and s by the bank of Jordan; 5975
3:21 on armour, and upward, and s in the border. 5975
4:12 when he had called her, she s before him. 5975
4:15 when he had called her, she s in the door. 5975
5: 9 and s at the door of the house of Elisha. 5975
5:15 his company, and came, and s before him: 5975
5:25 he went in, and s before his master. 5975
8: 9 and came and s before him, and said, 5975
9:17 there s a watchman on the tower in Jezreel, 5975
10: 4 said, Behold, two kings s not before him: 5975
10: 9 s, and said to all the people, Ye be 5975
11:11 the guard s, every man with his weapons in 5975
11:14 behold, the king s by a pillar, as the manner 5975
13:21 of Elisha, he revived, and s up on his feet. 6965
18:17 and s by the conduit of the upper pool, 5975
18:28 Rab-shakeh s and cried with a loud voice in 5975
23: 3 the king s by a pillar, and made a covenant 5975
23: 3 And all the people s to the covenant. 5975
1Ch 6:39 his brother Asaph, who s on his right hand, 5975
6:44 their brethren the sons of Merari s on NIH
21: 1 Satan s up against Israel, and 5975
21:15 the angel of the LORD s by 5975
28: 2 David the king s up upon his feet, and 6965
2Ch 3:13 they s on their feet, and their faces were 5975
4: 4 It s upon twelve oxen, three looking toward 5975
5:12 s at the east end of the altar, and with them 5975
6: 3 and all the congregation of Israel s. 5975
6:12 he s before the altar of the LORD in 5975
6:13 upon it he s, and kneeled down upon his 5975
7: 6 trumpets before them, and all Israel s. 5975
9:19 twelve lions s there on the one side and 5975
10: 6 s before Solomon his father while he yet 5975
10: 8 brought up with him, that s before him. 5975
13: 4 Abijah s up upon mount Zemaraim, 6965
18:20 s before the LORD, and said, I will entice 5975
20: 5 Jehoshaphat s in the congregation of Judah 5975
20:13 all Judah s before the LORD, with their 5975
20:19 s up to praise the LORD God of Israel 6965
20:20 Jehoshaphat s and said, Hear me, O Judah, 5975
20:23 Moab s up against the inhabitants of mount 5975
23:13 the king s at his pillar at the entering in, and 5975
24:20 which s above the people, and said unto 5975
28:12 s up against them that came from the war, 6965
29:26 the Levites s with the instruments of David, 5975
30:16 they s in their place after their manner, 5975
34:31 the king s in his place, and made a 5975
35:10 the priests s in their place, and the Levites 5975
Ezr 2:63 holy things till there s up a priest with Urim 5975
3: 2 s up Jeshua the son of Jozadak, and 6965
3: 9 s Jeshua with his sons and his brethren, 5975
10:10 Ezra the priest s up, and said unto them, 6965
Ne 7:65 things, till there s up a priest with Urim 5975
8: 4 Ezra the scribe s upon a pulpit of wood, 5975
8: 4 beside him s Mattithiah, and Shema, and 5975
8: 5 and when he opened it, all the people s up: 5975
8: 7 the law: and the people s in their place. NIH
9: 2 s and confessed their sins, and the iniquities 5975
9: 3 they s up in their place, and read in 6965
9: 4 s up upon the stairs of the Levites, Jeshua, 6965
12:39 and they s still in the prison gate. 5975
12:40 So s the two companies of them that gave 5975
Est 5: 1 and s in the inner court of the king's house, 5975
5: 9 that he s not up, nor moved for him, he was 6965
7: 7 Haman s up to make request for his life to 5975
8: 4 So Esther arose, and s before the king, 5975
9:16 s for their lives, and had rest from their 5975
Job 4:15 before my face; the hair of my flesh s up: 5568
4:16 It s still, but I could not discern the form 5975
29: 8 and the aged arose, and s up. 5975
30:28 I s up, and I cried in the congregation. 6965
32:16 but s still, and answered no more:) 5975
Ps 33: 9 it was done; he commanded, and it s fast. 5975
104: 6 the waters s above the mountains. 5975
106:23 had not Moses his chosen s before him in 5975
106:30 s up Phinehas, and executed judgment: 5975
Isa 6: 2 Above it s the seraphims: each one had six 5975
36: 2 he s by the conduit of the upper pool in 5975
36:13 Rabshakeh s, and cried with a loud voice in 5975
Jer 15: 1 Though Moses and Samuel s before me, 5975
18:20 Remember that I s before thee to speak 5975
19:14 he s in the court of the LORD'S house; 5975
23:18 For who hath s in the counsel of 5975
23:22 if they had s in my counsel, and had caused 5975
28: 5 in the presence of all the people that s in 5975
36:21 in the ears of all the princes which s beside 5975
44:15 all the women that s by, a great multitude, 5975
46:15 they s not, because the LORD did drive 5975
48:45 They that fled s under the shadow of 5975
La 2: 4 he s with his right hand as an adversary, 5324
Eze 1:21 when those s, these stood; and when those 5975
1:21 when those stood, these s; and when those 5975
1:24 when they s, they let down their wings. 5975
1:25 when they s, and had let down their wings. 5975
3:23 behold, the glory of the LORD s there, 5975
8:11 there s before them seventy men of 5975
8:11 in the midst of them s Jaazaniah the son of 5975
9: 2 they went in, and s beside the brasen altar. 5975
10: 3 Now the cherubims s on the right side of 5975
10: 4 and s over the threshold of the house; NIH
10: 6 then he went in, and s beside the wheels. 5975
10:17 When they s, these stood; and when they 5975
10:17 When they stood, these s; and when they 5975
10:18 of the house, and s over the cherubims. 5975
10:19 every one s at the door of the east gate of 5975
11:23 s upon the mountain which is on the east 5975
21:21 For the king of Babylon s at the parting of 5975
37:10 they lived, and s up upon their feet, 5975
40: 3 and a measuring reed; and he s in the gate. 5975
43: 6 me out of the house; and the man s by me. 5975
47: 1 for the forefront of the house s toward NIH
Da 1:19 Azariah: therefore s they before the king. 5975
2: 2 So they came and s before the king. 5975
2:31 brightness was excellent, s before thee; 6966
3: 3 they s before the image that 6966
7:10 ten thousand times ten thousand s before 6966
7:16 I came near unto one of them that s by, 6966
8: 3 there s before the river a ram which had 5975
8:15 there s before me as the appearance of a 5975
8:17 So he came near where I s: and when he 5977
8:22 that being broken, whereas four s up for it, 5975
10:11 spoken this word unto me, I s trembling. 5975
10:16 spake, and said unto him that s before me, 5975
11: 1 even I, s to confirm and to strengthen him. 5977
12: 5 and behold, there s other two, 5975
Hos 10: 9 there they s: the battle in Gibeah against 5975
Am 7: 7 the Lord s upon a wall made by a 5324
Ob 1:14 Neither shouldest thou have s in 5975
Hab 3: 6 He s, and measured the earth: he beheld, 5975
3:11 The sun and moon s still in their habitation: 5975
Zec 1: 8 he s among the myrtle trees that were in 5975
1:10 the man that s among the myrtle trees 5975
1:11 the LORD that s among the myrtle trees, 5975
3: 3 filthy garments, and s before the angel. 5975
3: 4 and spake unto those that s before him, 5975
3: 5 And the angel of the LORD s by. 5975
Mt 2: 9 and s over where the young child was. 2476
12:46 his mother and his brethren s without, 2476
13: 2 sat; and the whole multitude s on the shore. 2476
20:32 And Jesus s still, and called them, and said, 2476
26:73 And after a while came unto him they that s 2476
27:11 And Jesus s before the governor: and 2476
27:47 Some of them that s there, when they heard 2476
Mk 10:49 And Jesus s still, and commanded him to 2476
11: 5 And certain of them that s there said unto 2476
14:47 And one of them that s by drew a sword, 3936
14:60 And the high priest s up in the midst, and 450
14:69 and began to say to them that s by, This is 3936
14:70 they that s by said again to Peter, 3936
15:35 And some of them that s by, when they 3936
15:39 which s over against him, saw that he so 3936
Lk 4:16 on the sabbath day, and s up for to read. 450
4:39 And he s over her, and rebuked the fever; 2186
5: 1 of God, he s by the lake of Gennesaret, 2476
6: 8 in the midst. And he arose and s forth. 2476
6:17 and s in the plain, and the company of his 2476
7:14 and they that bare him s still. And he said, 2476
7:38 And s at his feet behind him weeping, and 2476
9:32 his glory, and the two men that s with him. 4921
10:25 a certain lawyer s up, and tempted him, 450
17:12 ten men that were lepers, which s afar off: 2476
18:11 The Pharisee s and prayed thus with 2476
18:40 And Jesus s, and commanded him to be 2476

S

Lk 19: 8 And Zacchaeus **s**, and said unto the Lord; 2476
19:24 And he said unto them that **s by**, Take from *3936*
23:10 And the chief priests and scribes **s** and *2476*
23:35 And the people **s** beholding. And the rulers *2476*
23:49 **s** afar off, beholding these *things.* *2476*
24: 4 two men **s by** them in shining garments: *2186*
24:36 Jesus himself **s** in the midst of them, and *2476*
Jn 1:35 Again the next day *after* John **s**, and two of *2476*
6:22 when the people which **s** on the other side *2476*
7:37 Jesus **s** and cried, saying, If any *man* thirst, *2476*
11:56 as they **s** in the temple, What think ye, *2476*
12:29 that **s** *by,* and heard *it,* said that it *2476*
18: 5 which betrayed him, **s** with them. *2476*
18:16 But Peter **s** at the door without. Then went *2476*
18:18 officers **s** *there,* who had made a fire of *2476*
18:18 and Peter **s** with them, and warmed himself. *2476*
18:22 one of the officers which **s by** stroke Jesus *3936*
18:25 And Simon Peter **s** and warmed himself. *2476*
19:25 Now there **s** by the cross of Jesus his *2476*
20:11 But Mary **s** without at the sepulchre *2476*
20:19 came Jesus and **s** in the midst, and *2476*
20:26 and **s** in the midst, and said, Peace *be* unto *2476*
21: 4 was now come, Jesus **s** on the shore: *2476*
Ac 1:10 two men **s by** them in white apparel; *3936*
1:15 And in those days Peter **s up** in the midst of *450*
3: 8 And he leaping up **s**, and walked, and *2476*
4:26 The kings of the earth **s up**, and the rulers *3936*
5:34 Then **s** there **up** one in the council, *450*
9: 7 And the men which journeyed with him **s** *2476*
9:39 and all the widows **s by** him weeping, and *3936*
10:17 and **s before** the gate, *2186*
10:30 a man **s** before me in bright clothing, *2476*
11:13 which **s** and said unto him, Send men to *2476*
11:28 And there **s up** one of them named Agabus, *450*
12:14 ran in, and told how Peter **s** before the gate. *2476*
13:16 Then Paul **s up**, and beckoning with *his* hand *450*
14:20 as the disciples **s round about** him, *2944*
16: 9 There **s** a man of Macedonia, and *2476*
17:22 Then Paul **s** in the midst of Mars' hill, and *2476*
21:40 Paul **s** on the stairs, and beckoned with *2476*
22:13 and **s**, and said unto me, Brother Saul, *2186*
22:25 Paul said unto the centurion that **s** by, Is it *2476*
23: 2 that **s by** him to smite him on the mouth. *3936*
23: 4 And they that **s by** said, Revilest thou *3936*
23:11 And the night following the Lord **s by** him, *2186*
24:20 doing in me, while I **s** before the council, *2476*
25: 7 came down from Jerusalem **s round about**, *4026*
25:18 Against whom when the accusers **s** *up,* they *2476*
27:21 But after long abstinence Paul **s** *forth* in *2476*
27:23 For there **s by** me this night *the* angel of *3936*
2Ti 4:16 At my first answer no *man* **s with** me, but *4836*
4:17 Notwithstanding the Lord **s with** me, and *3936*
Heb 9:10 *Which* **s** only in meats and drinks, and NIG
Rev 5: 6 **s** a Lamb as *it had been* slain, having seven *2476*
7: 9 **s** before the throne, and before the Lamb, *2476*
7:11 And all the angels **s** round about the throne, *2476*
8: 2 And I saw the seven angels which **s** before *2476*
8: 3 And another angel came and **s** at the altar, *2476*
11: 1 and the angel **s**, saying, Rise, and *2476*
11:11 into them, and they **s** upon their feet; *2476*
12: 4 the dragon **s** before the woman which was *2476*
13: 1 And I **s** upon the sand of the sea, and saw a *2476*
14: 1 and lo, a Lamb **s** on the mount Sion, and *2476*
18:17 and as many as trade by sea, **s** afar off, *2476*

STOODEST (3) [STAND]
Nu 22:34 for I knew not that thou **s** in the way 5324
Dt 4:10 *Specially* the day that thou **s** before 5975
Ob 1:11 In the day that thou **s** on the other side, 5975

STOOL (1) [FOOTSTOOL, STOOLS]
2Ki 4:10 and a table, and a **s**, and a candlestick: 3678

STOOLS (1) [STOOL]
Ex 1:16 the Hebrew women, and see *them* upon the **s**; 70

STOOP (4) [STOOPED, STOOPETH, STOOPING]
Job 9:13 his anger, the proud helpers do **s** under him. 7817
Pr 12:25 Heaviness in the heart of man **maketh** it **s**; 7812
Isa 46: 2 They **s**, they bow down together; 7164
Mk 1: 7 of whose shoes I am not worthy to **s down** *2955*

STOOPED (7) [STOOP]
Ge 49: 9 he **s down**, he couched as a lion, and as an 3766
1Sa 24: 8 David **s** *with his* face to the earth, and 6915
28:14 he **s** *with his* face to the ground, and 6915
2Ch 36:17 or maiden, old man, or **him that s for age**: 3486
Jn 8: 6 But Jesus **s** down, and with *his* finger wrote *2955*
8: 8 And again he **s** down, and wrote on *2955*
20:11 she **s down, and looked** into the sepulchre, *3879*

STOOPETH (1) [STOOP]
Isa 46: 1 Bel boweth down, Nebo **s**, their idols were 7164

STOOPING (2) [STOOP]
Lk 24:12 and **s down**, he beheld the linen clothes laid *3879*
Jn 20: 5 And he **s down, and looking** in, saw *3879*

STOP (7) [STOPPED, STOPPETH, STOPT, UNSTOPPED]
1Ki 18:44 and get thee down, that the rain **s** thee not. 6113
2Ki 3:19 **s** all wells of water, and mar every good 5640
2Ch 32: 3 his mighty **men** to **s** the waters of 5640
Ps 35: 3 **s** *the way* against them that persecute me: 5462
107:42 rejoice: and all iniquity shall **s** her mouth. 7092
Eze 39:11 it *shall* **s** the *noses of the* passengers: and 2629
2Co 11:10 no *man* shall **s** me of this boasting in *5420*

STOPPED (14) [STOP]
Ge 8: 2 and the windows of heaven were **s**, 5534
26:15 the Philistims had **s** them, and filled them 5640
26:18 for the Philistims had **s** them after the death 5640
Lev 15: 3 or his flesh be **s** from his issue, it *is* his 2856
2Ki 3:25 they **s** all the wells of water, and felled all 5640
2Ch 32:30 This same Hezekiah also **s** the upper 5640
Ne 4: 7 *and* that the breaches began to be **s**, then 5640
Ps 63:11 the mouth of them that speak lies shall be **s**. 5534
Jer 51:32 *that* the passages are **s**, and the reeds they 8610
Zec 7:11 and **s** their ears, that *they* should not hear. 3513
Ac 7:57 and **s** their ears, and ran upon him with one *4912*
Ro 3:19 that every mouth may be **s**, and all *5420*
Tit 1:11 Whose **mouths** must be **s**, who subvert *1993*
Heb 11:33 obtained promises, **s** the mouths of lions, *5420*

STOPPETH (4) [STOP]
Job 5:16 poor hath hope, and iniquity **s** her mouth. 7092
Ps 58: 4 *they are* like the deaf adder *that* **s** her ear; 331
Pr 21:13 Whoso **s** his ears at the cry of the poor, 331
Isa 33:15 that **s** his ears from hearing of blood, and 331

STOPT (1) [STOP]
2Ch 32: 4 who **s** all the fountains, and the brook that 5640

STORE (25) [STOREHOUSE, STOREHOUSES]
Ge 26:14 of herds, and **great s** of servants: 7227
41:36 *that* food shall be for **s** to the land against 6487
Lev 25:22 her fruits come in ye shall eat *of* the old **s**. NIH
26:10 ye shall eat **old s**, and bring forth 3462+3465
Dt 28: 5 Blessed *shall be* thy basket and thy **s**. 4863
28:17 Cursed *shall be* thy basket and thy **s**. 4863
32:34 *Is* not this **laid up in s** with me, *and* 3647
1Ki 9:19 all the cities of **s** that Solomon had, 4543
10:10 of spices very **great s**, and precious stones: 7235
2Ki 20:17 *that* which thy fathers have **laid up in s** unto 686
1Ch 29:16 all this **s** that we have prepared to build 1995
2Ch 8: 4 all the **s** cities, which he built in Hamath. 4543
8: 6 all the **s** cities that Solomon had, and all 4543
11:11 and **s** of victual, and *of* oil and wine. 214
16: 4 and all the **s** cities of Naphtali. 4543
17:12 and he built in Judah castles, and cities of **s**. 4543
31:10 and that which is left *is* this **great s**. 1995
Ne 5:18 and once in ten days **s** of all *sorts of* wine: 7235
Ps 144:13 **all manner of s**: 413+2177+2177+4480
Isa 39: 6 *that* which thy fathers have **laid up in s** until 686
Am 3:10 who **s up** violence and robbery in their 686
Na 2: 9 for *there is* none end of the **s** *and* glory out 8498
1Co 16: 2 week let every one of you lay by him **in s**, *2343*
1Ti 6:19 **Laying up in s** for themselves a good *597*
2Pe 3: 7 are now, by the same word are **kept in s**, *2343*

STOREHOUSE (2) [HOUSE, STORE]
Mal 3:10 Bring ye all the tithes into the **s**, that 214+1004
Lk 12:24 which neither have **s** nor barn; and God *5009*

STOREHOUSES (6) [HOUSE, STORE]
Ge 41:56 Joseph opened all **the s**, 834+871.1+1992.1
Dt 28: 8 command the blessing upon thee in thy **s**, 618
1Ch 27:25 and over the **s** in the fields, in the cities, and 214
2Ch 32:28 **S** also for the increase of corn, and wine, 4543
Ps 33: 7 as a heap: he layeth up the depth in **s**. 214
Jer 50:26 her from the utmost border, open her **s**: 3965

STORIES (5) [STORY]
Ge 6:16 second, and third **s** shalt thou make it. NIH
Eze 41:16 the galleries round about on their three **s**, NIH
42: 3 *was* gallery against gallery in three **s**. NIH
42: 6 For they *were* in three **s**, but had not pillars NIH
Am 9: 6 *It is* he that buildeth his **s** in the heaven, and 4609

STORK (5)
Lev 11:19 the **s**, the heron after her kind, and 2624
Dt 14:18 the **s**, and the heron after her kind, and 2624
Ps 104:17 *as for* the **s**, the fir trees *are* her house. 2624
Jer 8: 7 the **s** in the heaven knoweth her appointed 2624
Zec 5: 9 for they had wings like the wings of a **s**: 2624

STORM (14) [STORMY]
Job 21:18 and as chaff that the **s** carrieth away. 5492
27:21 and **as a s hurleth** him out of his place. 8175
Ps 55: 8 I would hasten my escape from the windy **s** 5584
83:15 and make them afraid with thy **s**. 5492
107:29 He maketh the **s** a calm, so that the waves 5591
Isa 4: 6 and for a covert from **s** and from rain 2230
25: 4 a refuge from the **s**, a shadow from 2230
25: 4 when the blast of the terrible ones *is* as a **s** 2230
28: 2 as a tempest of hail *and* a destroying **s**, 8178
29: 6 *with* **s** and tempest, and the flame of 5492
Eze 38: 9 Thou shalt ascend and come like a **s**, 7722
Na 1: 3 *hath* his way in the whirlwind and in the **s**, 8183
Mk 4:37 And there arose a great **s** of wind, and *2978*
Lk 8:23 there came down a **s** of wind on the lake; *2978*

STORMY (4) [STORM]
Ps 107:25 For he commandeth, and raiseth the **s** wind, 5591
148: 8 and vapour; **s** wind fulfilling his word: 5591
Eze 13:11 shall fall; and a **s** wind shall rent *it.* 5591
13:13 I will even rent *it with* a **s** wind in my fury; 5591

STORY (2) [STORIES]
2Ch 13:22 *are* written in the **s** of the prophet Iddo. 4097
24:27 behold they *are* written in the **s** of the book 4097

STOUT (4) [STOUTHEARTED, STOUTNESS]
Job 4:11 the **s lion's** whelps are scattered abroad. 3833
Isa 10:12 I will punish the fruit of the **s** heart of 1433
Da 7:20 whose look *was* more **s** than his fellows. 7260
Mal 3:13 Your words have been **s** against me, 2388

STOUTHEARTED (2) [HEART, STOUT]
Ps 76: 5 The **s** are spoiled, they have slept their 47+3820
Isa 46:12 Hearken unto me, ye **s**, that *are* far from 47+3820

STOUTNESS (1) [STOUT]
Isa 9: 9 that say in the pride and **s** of heart, 1433

STRAIGHT (28) [STRAIGHTWAY]
Jos 6: 5 shall ascend up every man **s before** him. 5048
6:20 every man **s before** him, and they took 5048
1Sa 6:12 the kine **took** the **s** way to the way of 3474
2Ch 32:30 **brought** it **s** down to the west *side* of 3474
Ps 5: 8 **make** thy way **s** before my face. 3474
Pr 4:25 and let thine eyelids **look s** before thee. 3474
Ecc 1:15 *That which is* crooked cannot be **made s**: 8626
7:13 for who can **make** *that* **s**, which he hath 8626
Isa 40: 3 **make s** in the desert a highway for our 3474
40: 4 the crooked shall be **made s**, and the rough 4334
42:16 light before them, and crooked things **s**. 4334
45: 2 and **make** the crooked places **s**: 3474
Jer 31: 9 to walk by the rivers of waters in a **s** way, 3477
Eze 1: 7 their feet *were* **s** feet; and the sole of their 3477
1: 9 they went every one **s forward.** 413+5676+6440
1:12 they went every one **s forward**: 413+5676+6440
1:23 under the firmament *were* their wings **s**, 3477
10:22 they went every one **s forward.** 413+5676+6440
Mt 3: 3 ye the way of the Lord, make his paths **s**. *2117*
Mk 1: 3 ye the way of the Lord, make his paths **s**. *2117*
Lk 3: 4 ye the way of the Lord, make his paths **s**. *2117*
3: 5 and the crooked shall be **made s**, and *2117*
13:13 and immediately she was **made s**, and *461*
Jn 1:23 **Make s** the way of the Lord, as said *2116*
Ac 9:11 and go into the street which is called **S**, and *2117*
16:11 we **came with a s course** to Samothracia, *2113*
21: 1 we came with a **s course** unto Cos, and *2113*
Heb 12:13 And make **s** paths for your feet, lest *that* *3717*

STRAIGHTWAY (42) [STRAIGHT]
1Sa 9:13 be come *into* the city, ye shall **s** find him, 3651
28:20 Saul fell **s** all along on the earth, and 4116
Pr 7:22 He goeth after her **s**, as an ox goeth to 6597
Da 10:17 for me, **s** there remained no strength in me, 6258
Mt 3:16 he was baptized, went up **s** out of the water: *2112*
4:20 And they **s** left *their* nets, and *2112*
14:22 And **s** Jesus constrained his disciples to get *2112*
14:27 But **s** Jesus spake unto them, saying, Be of *2112*
21: 2 and **s** ye shall find an ass tied, and a colt *2112*
21: 3 hath need of them; and **s** he will send them. *2112*
25:15 his several ability; and **s** took his journey. *2112*
27:48 And **s** one of them ran, and took a spunge, *2112*
Mk 1:10 And **s** coming up out of the water, he saw *2112*
1:18 And **s** they forsook their nets, and *2112*
1:20 And **s** he called them: and they left their *2112*
1:21 **s** on the sabbath day he entered into *2112*
2: 2 And **s** many were gathered together, *2112*
3: 6 **s** took counsel with the Herodians against *2112*
5:29 And **s** the fountain of her blood was dried *2112*
5:42 And **s** the damsel arose, and walked; *2112*
6:25 And she came in **s** with haste unto the king, *2112*
6:45 And **s** he constrained his disciples to get *2112*
6:54 come out of the ship, **s** they knew him, *2112*
7:35 And **s** his ears were opened, *2112*
8:10 And **s** he entered into a ship with his *2112*
9:15 And **s** all the people, when they beheld *2112*
9:20 and when he saw him, **s** the spirit tare him; *2112*
9:24 And **s** the father of the child cried out, and *2112*
11: 3 need of him; and **s** he will send him hither. *2112*
14:45 he goeth **s** to him, and saith, Master, *2112*
15: 1 And **s** in the morning the chief priests held *2112*
Lk 5:39 No *man* also having drunk old *wine* **s** *2112*
8:55 And her spirit came again, and she arose **s**: *3916*
12:54 the west, **s** ye say, There cometh a shower; *2112*
14: 5 will not **s** pull him out on the sabbath day? *2112*
Jn 13:32 him in himself, and shall **s** glorify him. *2112*
Ac 5:10 Then fell she down **s** at his feet, and *3916*
9:20 And **s** he preached Christ in *2112*
16:33 and was baptized, he and all his, **s**. *3916*
22:29 Then **s** they departed from him which *2112*
23:30 I sent **s** to thee, and gave commandment to *1824*
Jas 1:24 **s** forgetteth what manner of *man* he was. *2112*

STRAIN (1)
Mt 23:24 which **s out** a gnat, and swallow a camel. *1368*

STRAIT (10) [STRAITEN, STRAITENED, STRAITENETH, STRAITEST, STRAITLY, STRAITNESS, STRAITS]
1Sa 13: 6 the men of Israel saw that they were **in a s**, 6887
2Sa 24:14 David said unto Gad, I am in a great **s**: 6887
2Ki 6: 1 the place where we dwell with thee is too **s** 6862
1Ch 21:13 And David said unto Gad, I am **in a** great **s**: 6887
Job 36:16 would he have removed thee out of the **s** 6862
Isa 49:20 in thine ears, The place *is* too **s** for me: 6862
Mt 7:13 Enter ye in at the **s** gate: for wide *is* *4728*
7:14 Because **s** *is* the gate, and narrow *is* *4728*
Lk 13:24 Strive to enter in at the **s** gate: for many, *4728*
Php 1:23 For I am **in a s** betwixt two, having a desire *4912*

STRAITEN (1) [STRAIT]
Jer 19: 9 and they that seek their lives, shall **s** them. 6693

STRAITENED (8) [STRAIT]
Job 18: 7 The steps of his strength shall be **s**, and 3334
37:10 is given: and the breadth of the waters is **s**. 4164
Pr 4:12 When thou goest thy steps shall not be **s**; 3334
Eze 42: 6 *the building* was **s** more than the lowest and 680
Mic 2: 7 of Jacob, is the spirit of the LORD **s**? 7114
Lk 12:50 and how am I **s** till it be accomplished! *4912*
2Co 6:12 Ye are not **s** in us, *4729*
6:12 in us, but ye are **s** in your own bowels. *4729*

STRAITENETH (1) [STRAIT]
Job 12:23 he enlargeth the nations, and **s** them *again.* 5148

STRAITEST (1) [STRAIT]
Ac 26: 5 that after the **most s** sect of our religion I *196*

STRAITLY (11) [STRAIT]
Ge 43: 7 The man **asked** us **s** of our state, and 7592+7592
Ex 13:19 for he had **s sworn** the children of 7650+7650
Jos 6: 1 Now Jericho was **s shut up** 5462+5462+2050.1
1Sa 14:28 **s charged** the people **with an oath**, 7650+7650
Mt 9:30 and Jesus **s charged** them, saying, See *that* *1690*

S

Mk 1:43 And he **s charged** him, and forthwith sent *1690*
3:12 And he **s** charged them that they should not *4183*
5:43 And he charged them **s** that no *man* should *4183*
Lk 9:21 And he **s charged** them, and *2008*
Ac 4:17 among the people, let us **s threaten** them, *546*
5:28 Did not we **s command** you that *you* *3852+3853*

STRAITNESS (5) [STRAIT]
Dt 28:53 hath given thee, in the siege, and in the **s**, 4689
28:55 nothing left him in the siege, and in the **s**, 4689
28:57 of all *things* secretly in the siege and **s**, 4689
Job 36:16 *into* a broad place, where *there is* no **s**; 4164
Jer 19: 9 the flesh of his friend in the siege and **s**, 4689

STRAITS (2) [STRAIT]
Job 20:22 fulness of his sufficiency he shall be **in s**: 3334
La 1: 3 her persecutors overtook her between the **s**. 4712

STRAKE (3) [STRIKE]
2Sa 12:15 the LORD **s** the child that Uriah's wife 5062
20:10 bowels to the ground, and **s** him not again; NIH
Ac 27:17 the quicksands, **s** sail, and so were driven. *5465*

STRAKES (2)
Ge 30:37 pilled white **s** in them, and made the white 6479
Lev 14:37 *be* in the walls of the house with **hollow s**, 8258

STRANDS See WIRES

STRANGE (76) [STRANGELY, STRANGER, STRANGER'S, STRANGERS, STRANGERS']
Ge 35: 2 Put away the **s** gods that *are* among you, 5236
35: 4 they gave unto Jacob all the **s** gods which 5236
42: 7 **made** himself **s** unto them, and 5234
Ex 2:22 he said, I have been a stranger in a **s** land. 5237
18: 3 for he said, I have been an alien in a **s** land: 5237
21: 8 to sell her unto a **s** nation he shall have no 5237
30: 9 Ye shall offer no **s** incense thereon, nor 2114
Lev 10: 1 offered **s** fire before the LORD, 2114
Nu 3: 4 when they offered **s** fire before the LORD, 2114
26:61 when they offered **s** fire before the LORD. 2114
Dt 32:12 lead him, and *there was* no **s** god with him. 5236
32:16 They provoked him to jealousy with **s** *gods*, 2114
Jos 24:20 serve **s** gods, then he will turn and do you 5236
24:23 *said he*, the **s** gods which *are* among you, 5236
Jdg 10:16 they put away the **s** gods from among them, 5236
11: 2 for thou *art* the son of a **s** woman. 312
1Sa 7: 3 *then* put away the **s** gods and Ashtaroth 5236
1Ki 11: 1 king Solomon loved many **s** women, 5237
11: 8 likewise did he for all his **s** wives, 5237
2Ki 19:24 I have digged and drunk **s** waters, and 2114
2Ch 14: 3 For he took away the altars of the **s** *gods*, 5236
33:15 he took away the **s** gods, and the idol out of 5236
Ezr 10: 2 have taken **s** wives of the people of 5237
10:10 have transgressed, and have taken **s** wives, 5237
10:11 people of the land, and from the **s** wives. 5237
10:14 let all *them* which have taken **s** wives in our 5237
10:17 **s** wives by the first day of the first month. 5237
10:18 there were found that had taken **s** wives: 5237
10:44 All these had taken **s** wives: and *some* of 5237
Ne 13:27 to transgress against our God in marrying **s** 5237
Job 19: 3 ashamed *that* you **make** yourselves **s** to me. 1970
19:17 My breath is **s** to my wife, though I 2114
31: 3 a **s punishment** to the workers of iniquity? 5235
Ps 44:20 or stretched out our hands to a **s** god; 2114
81: 9 There shall no **s** god be in thee; 2114
81: 9 neither shall thou worship *any* **s** god. 5236
114: 1 of Jacob from a people of **s language**; 3937
137: 4 we sing the LORD'S song in a **s** land? 5236
144: 7 of great waters, from the hand of **s** children; 5236
144:11 and deliver me from the hand of **s** children, 5236
Pr 2:16 To deliver thee from the **s** woman, 2114
5: 3 For the lips of a **s** *woman* drop *as* a 2114
5:20 be ravisht with a **s** *woman*, and embrace 2114
6:24 from the flattery of the tongue of a **s** 5237
7: 5 That *they* may keep thee from the **s** woman, 2114
20:16 and take a pledge of him for a **s** *woman*. 5237
21: 8 The way of man *is* froward and **s**: but *as for* 2054
22:14 The mouth of **s** *women is* a deep pit: he that 2114
23:27 a deep ditch; and a **s** *woman is* a narrow pit. 5237
23:33 Thine eyes shall behold **s** *women*, and 2114
27:13 and take a pledge of him for a **s** *woman*. 5237
Isa 17:10 pleasant plants, and shalt set it *with* **s** slips: 2114
28:21 that he may do his work, his **s** work; 2114
28:21 and bring to pass his act, his **s** act. 5237
43:12 when *there was* no **s** *god* among you: 2114
Jer 2:21 the degenerate plant of a **s** vine unto me? 5237
5:19 served **s** gods in your land, so shall ye serve 5236
8:19 their graven images, *and* with **s** vanities? 5236
Eze 3: 5 For thou *art* not sent to a people of a **s** 6012
3: 6 Not to many people of a **s** speech and of a 6012
Da 11:39 he do in the most strong holds with a **s** god, 5236
Hos 5: 7 for they have begotten **s** children: now shall 2114
8:12 my law, *but* they were counted as a **s** *thing*. 2114
Zep 1: 8 and all such as are clothed with **s** apparel. 5237
Mal 2:11 and hath married the daughter of a **s** god. 5236
Lk 5:26 saying, We have seen **s** *things* to day. *3861*
Ac 7: 6 That his seed should sojourn in a **s** land; *245*
17:18 He seemeth to be a setter forth of **s** gods: *3581*
17:20 For thou bringest certain **s** *things* to our *3579*
26:11 I persecuted *them* even unto **s** cities. *1854*
Heb 11: 9 as *in* a **s** *country*, dwelling in tabernacles *245*
13: 9 carried about with divers and **s** doctrines. *3581*
1Pe 4: 4 Wherein they **think it s** that you run not *3579*
4:12 **think it** not **s** concerning the fiery trial *3579*
4:12 as though *some* **s** *thing* happened unto you: *3581*
Jude 1: 7 and going after **s** flesh, are set forth for an *2087*

STRANGELY (1) [STRANGE]
Dt 32:27 adversaries should **behave** themselves **s**, 5234

STRANGER (129) [STRANGE]
Ge 15:13 Know of a surety that thy seed shall be a **s** 1616
17: 8 after thee, the land wherein thou art a **s**, 4033
17:12 or bought with money of any **s**, 1121+5236
17:27 and bought with money of the **s**, 1121+5236
23: 4 I *am* a **s** and a sojourner with you: give me 1616
28: 4 mayest inherit the land wherein thou art a **s**, 4033
37: 1 dwelt in the land wherein his father was a **s**, 4033
Ex 2:22 he said, I have been a **s** in a strange land. 1616
12:19 whether he be a **s**, or born in the land. 1616
12:43 There shall no **s** eat thereof: 1121+5236
12:48 when a **s** shall sojourn with thee, and 1616
12:49 and unto the **s** that sojourneth among you. 1616
20:10 thy cattle, nor thy **s** that *is* within thy gates: 1616
22:21 Thou shalt neither vex a **s**, nor oppress him: 1616
23: 9 Also thou shalt not oppress a **s**: for ye know 1616
23: 9 for ye know the heart of a **s**, seeing ye were 1616
23:12 thy handmaid, and the **s**, may be refreshed. 1616
29:33 a **s** shall not eat *thereof*, because they *are* 2114
30:33 or whosoever putteth *any* of it upon a **s**, 2114
Lev 16:29 or a **s** that sojourneth among you: 1616
17:12 neither shall any **s** that sojourneth among 1616
17:15 or a **s**, he shall both wash his clothes, and 1616
18:26 nor any **s** that sojourneth among you: 1616
19:10 thou shalt leave them for the poor and **s**: 1616
19:33 if a **s** sojourn with thee in your land, 1616
19:34 *But* the **s** that dwelleth with you shall be 1616
22:10 There shall no **s** eat *of* the holy *thing*: a 2114
22:12 daughter also be *married* unto a **s**, 376+2114
22:13 but there shall no **s** eat thereof. 2114
23:22 shalt leave them unto the poor, and to the **s**: 1616
24:16 as well the **s**, as he that is born in the land, 1616
24:22 as well for the **s**, as for one of your own 1616
25: 6 and for thy **s** that sojourneth with thee, 8453
25:35 *yea, though he be* a **s**, or a sojourner; 1616
25:47 if a sojourner or **s** wax rich by thee, and 8453
25:47 sell himself unto the **s** *or* sojourner by thee, 1616
Nu 1:51 the **s** that cometh nigh shall be put to death. 2114
3:10 the **s** that cometh nigh shall be put to death. 2114
3:38 the **s** that cometh nigh shall be put to death. 2114
9:14 if a **s** shall sojourn among you, and 1616
9:14 both for the **s**, and for him that was born in 1616
15:14 if a **s** sojourn with you, or whosoever *be* 1616
15:15 also for the **s** that sojourneth *with you*, an 1616
15:15 ye *are*, so shall the **s** be before the LORD. 1616
15:16 and for the **s** that sojourneth with you. 1616
15:26 and the **s** that sojourneth among them; 1616
15:29 and for the **s** that sojourneth among them. 1616
15:30 *whether he be* born in the land, or a **s**, 1616
16:40 **s**, which *is* not of the seed of Aaron, 376+2214
18: 4 and a **s** shall not come nigh unto you. 2114
18: 7 the **s** that cometh nigh shall be put to death. 2114
19:10 unto the **s** that sojourneth among them, 1616
35:15 for the **s**, and for the sojourner among 1616
Dt 1:16 and his brother, and the **s** *that is* with him. 1616
5:14 thy cattle, nor thy **s** that *is* within thy gates; 1616
10:18 the fatherless and widow, and loveth the **s**, 1616
10:19 Love ye therefore the **s**: for ye were 1616
14:21 thou shalt give it unto the **s** that *is* in thy 1616
14:29 the **s**, and the fatherless, and the widow, 1616
16:11 the **s**, and the fatherless, and the widow, 1616
16:14 the **s**, and the fatherless, and the widow, 1616
17:15 thou mayest not set a **s** over thee, 376+5237
23: 7 because thou wast a **s** in his land. 1616
23:20 Unto a **s** thou mayest lend upon usury; but 5237
24:17 shalt not pervert the judgment of the **s**, 1616
24:19 it shall be for the **s**, for the fatherless, and 1616
24:20 it shall be for the **s**, for the fatherless, and 1616
24:21 it shall be for the **s**, for the fatherless, and 1616
25: 5 dead shall not marry without unto a **s**: 376+2214
26:11 and the Levite, and the **s** that *is* among you. 1616
26:12 the **s**, the fatherless, and the widow, 1616
26:13 unto the **s**, to the fatherless, and to 1616
27:19 *be* he that perverteth the judgment of the **s**, 1616
28:43 The **s** that *is* within thee shall get up above 1616
29:11 your wives, and thy **s** that *is* in thy camp, 1616
29:22 the **s** that shall come from a far land, 5237
31:12 and thy **s** that *is* within thy gates, 1616
Jos 8:33 as well the **s**, as he that was born among 1616
20: 9 and for the **s** that sojourneth among them, 1616
Jdg 19:12 will not turn aside hither into the city of a **s**, 5237
Ru 2:10 take knowledge of me, seeing I *am* a **s**? 5237
2Sa 1:13 I *am* the son of a **s**, an Amalekite. 376+1616
15:19 the king: for thou *art* a **s**, and also an exile. 5237
1Ki 3:18 *there was* no **s** with us in the house, 2114
8:41 Moreover concerning a **s**, that *is* not of thy 5237
8:43 do according to all that the **s** calleth to thee 5237
2Ch 6:32 Moreover concerning the **s**, which *is* not of 5237
6:33 do according to all that the **s** calleth to thee 5237
Job 15:19 was given, and no **s** passed among them. 2114
19:15 and my maidens, count me for a **s**: 2114
31:32 The **s** did not lodge in the street: *but* 1616
Ps 39:12 for I *am* a **s** with thee, *and* a sojourner, 1616
69: 8 I am become a **s** unto my brethren, and 2114
94: 6 They slay the widow and the **s**, and 1616
119:19 I *am* a **s** in the earth: hide not thy 1616
Pr 2:16 *even* from the **s** *which* flattereth with her 5237
5:10 and thy labours *be* in the house of a **s**; 5237
5:20 and embrace the bosom of a **s**? 5237
6: 1 *if* thou hast stricken thy hand with a **s**, 2114
7: 5 from the **s** *which* flattereth with her words. 5237
11:15 He that is surety for a **s** shall smart *for it*: 2114
14:10 and a **s** doth not intermeddle with his joy. 2114
20:16 Take his garment that is surety *for* a **s**: and 2114
27: 2 own mouth; a **s**, and not thine own lips. 5237
27:13 Take his garment that is surety *for* a **s**, and 2114
Ecc 6: 2 power to eat thereof, but a **s** eateth it: 376+5237
Isa 56: 3 Neither let the son of the **s**, that hath joined 5236
56: 6 Also the sons of the **s**, that join themselves 5236
62: 8 the sons of the **s** shall not drink thy wine, 5236
Jer 7: 6 *If* ye oppress not the **s**, the fatherless, and 1616
14: 8 why shouldest thou be as a **s** in the land, 1616
22: 3 to the **s**, the fatherless, nor the widow, 1616
Eze 14: 7 or of the **s** that sojourneth in Israel, 1616
22: 7 have they dealt by oppression with the **s**: 1616
22:29 they have oppressed the **s** wrongfully. 1616
44: 9 No **s**, uncircumcised in heart, 1121+5236
44: 9 of any **s** that *is* among the children of 1121+5236
Eze 47:23 to pass, *that* in what tribe the **s** sojourneth, 1616
Ob 1:12 of thy brother in the day that he became a **s**; 5235
Zec 7:10 nor the fatherless, the **s**, nor the poor; 1616
Mal 3: 5 that turn aside the **s** *from his right*, and 1616
Mt 25:35 me drink: I was a **s**, and ye took me in: *3581*
25:38 When saw we thee a **s**, and took *thee* in? or *3581*
25:43 I was a **s**, and ye took me not in: naked, and *3581*
25:44 or a **s**, or naked, or sick, or in prison, and *3581*
Lk 17:18 returned to give glory to God, save this **s**. *241*
24:18 Art thou only a **s** in Jerusalem, and hast not *3939*
Jn 10: 5 And a **s** will they not follow, but will flee *245*
Ac 7:29 and was a **s** in the land of Madian, where he *3941*

STRANGER'S (2) [STRANGE]
Lev 22:25 Neither from a **s** hand shall ye offer 1121+5236
25:47 by thee, or to the stock of the **s** family: 1616

STRANGERS (79) [STRANGE]
Ge 31:15 Are we not counted of him **s**? for he hath 5237
36: 7 the land wherein they were **s** could not bear 4033
Ex 6: 4 of their pilgrimage, wherein they were **s**. 1481
22:21 for ye were **s** in the land of Egypt. 1616
23: 9 seeing ye were **s** in the land of Egypt. 1616
Lev 17: 8 or of the **s** which sojourn among you, 1616
17:10 or of the **s** that sojourn among you, 1616
17:13 or of the **s** that sojourn among you, 1616
19:34 for ye were **s** in the land of Egypt: 1616
20: 2 or of the **s** that sojourn in Israel, that giveth 1616
22:18 of the house of Israel, or of the **s** in Israel, 1616
25:23 for ye *were* **s** and sojourners with me. 1616
25:45 Moreover of the children of the **s** that do 8453
Dt 10:19 for ye were **s** in the land of Egypt. 1616
24:14 of thy **s** that *are* in thy land within thy 1616
31:16 go a whoring after the gods of the **s** of 5236
Jos 8:35 and the **s** that were conversant among them. 1616
2Sa 22:45 **S** shall submit themselves unto me: 1121+5236
22:46 **S** shall fade away, and they shall be 1121+5236
1Ch 16:19 ye were *but* few, even a few, and **s** in it. 1481
22: 2 David commanded to gather together the **s** 1616
29:15 For we *are* **s** before thee, and sojourners, 1616
2Ch 2:17 Solomon numbered all the **s** that *were* 376+1616
15: 9 the **s** with them out of Ephraim and 1481
30:25 and the **s** that came out of the land of Israel, 1616
Ne 9: 2 separated themselves from all **s**, 1121+5236
13:30 Thus cleansed I them from all **s**, and 5236
Ps 18:44 **s** shall submit themselves unto me. 1121+5236
18:45 The **s** shall fade away, and be afraid 1121+5236
54: 3 For **s** are risen up against me, and 2114
105:12 men in number; yea, *very* few, and **s** in it. 1481
109:11 that he hath; and let the **s** spoil his labour. 2114
146: 9 The LORD preserveth the **s**; he relieveth 1616
Pr 5:10 Lest **s** be filled *with* thy wealth; and 2114
Isa 1: 7 **s** devour it in your presence, and *it is* 2114
1: 7 and *it is* desolate, as overthrown by **s**. 2114
2: 6 they please themselves in the children of **s**. 5237
5:17 the waste places of the fat ones shall **s** eat. 1481
14: 1 the **s** shall be joined with them, and 1616
25: 2 a palace of **s** to be no city; it shall never be 2114
25: 5 Thou shalt bring down the noise of **s**, as 2114
29: 5 Moreover the multitude of thy **s** shall be 2114
60:10 the sons of **s** shall build up thy walls, and 5236
61: 5 **s** shall stand and feed your flocks, and 2114
Jer 2:25 for I have loved **s**, and after them will I go. 2114
3:13 hast scattered thy ways to the **s** under every 2114
5:19 shall ye serve **s** in a land *that is* not yours. 2114
30: 8 **s** shall no more serve themselves of him: 2114
35: 7 live many days in the land where ye *be* **s**. 1481
51:51 for **s** are come into the sanctuaries of 2114
La 5: 2 Our inheritance is turned to **s**, our houses to 2114
Eze 7:21 I will give it into the hands of the **s** for a 2114
11: 9 deliver you into the hands of **s**, and 2114
16:32 *which* taketh **s** instead of her husband. 2114
28: 7 Behold therefore, I *will* bring **s** upon thee, 2114
28:10 of the uncircumcised by the hand of **s**: 2114
30:12 and all that is therein, by the hand of **s**: 2114
31:12 **s**, the terrible of the nations, have cut him 2114
44: 7 ye have brought *into my sanctuary* **s**, 1121+5236
47:22 to the **s** that sojourn among you, 1616
Hos 7: 9 **S** have devoured his strength, and 2114
8: 7 if so be it yield, *the* **s** shall swallow it up. 2114
Joel 3:17 there shall no **s** pass through her any more. 2214
Ob 1:11 in the day that the **s** carried away captive 2114
Mt 17:25 or tribute? of their own children, or of **s**? *245*
17:26 Peter saith unto him, Of **s**. Jesus saith unto *245*
27: 7 with them the potter's field, to bury **s** in. *3581*
Jn 10: 5 from him: for they know not the voice of **s**. *245*
Ac 2:10 and **s** of Rome, Jews and proselytes, *1927*
13:17 exalted the people when *they* **dwelt as s** in *3940*
17:21 **s** which were there spent their time in *3581*
Eph 2:12 and **s** from the covenants of promise, *3581*
2:19 Now therefore ye are no more **s** and *3581*
1Ti 5:10 brought up children, if she have **lodged s**, *3580*
Heb 11:13 and confessed that they were **s** and *3581*
13: 2 Be not forgetful to **entertain s**: for thereby *5381*
1Pe 1: 1 to the **s** scattered throughout Pontus, *3927*
2:11 I beseech *you* as **s** and pilgrims, *3941*
3Jn 1: 5 thou doest to the brethren, and to **s**; *3581*

STRANGERS' (1) [STRANGE]
Pr 5:17 be only thine own, and not **s** with thee. 2114

STRANGLED (4) [STRANGLING]
Na 2:12 **s** for his lionesses, and filled his holes *with* 2614
Ac 15:20 and *from* things **s**, and *from* blood. *4156*
15:29 and from **things s**, and from fornication: *4156*
21:25 and from **s**, and from fornication. *4156*

STRANGLING (1) [STRANGLED]
Job 7:15 So that my soul chooseth **s**, *and* 4267

STRAW (16)
Ge 24:25 We have both **s** and provender enough, and 8401
24:32 gave **s** and provender for the camels, and 8401
Ex 5: 7 Ye shall no more give the people **s** to make 8401

Ex 5: 7 let them go and gather **s** for themselves. 8401
5:10 Thus saith Pharaoh, I will not give you **s**. 8401
5:11 get you **s** where you can find *it:* yet not 8401
5:12 land of Egypt to gather stubble instead of **s**. 8401
5:13 *your* daily tasks, as when there was **s**. 8401
5:16 *There is* no **s** given unto thy servants, and 8401
5:18 for there shall no **s** be given you, yet shall 8401
Jdg 19:19 Yet there is both **s** and provender for our 8401
1Ki 4:28 Barley also and **s** for the horses and 8401
Job 41:27 He esteemeth iron as **s**, *and* brass as rotten 8401
Isa 11: 7 and the lion shall eat **s** like the ox. 8401
25:10 *even* as **s** is trodden down for the dunghill. 4963
65:25 and the lion shall eat **s** like the bullock: 8401

STRAWED (5) [STROWED]

Ex 32:20 **s** *it* upon the water, and made the children 2219
Mt 21: 8 from the trees, and **s** *them* in the way. *4766*
25:24 and gathering where thou hast not **s**: *1287*
25:26 I sowed not, and gather where I have not **s**: *1287*
Mk 11: 8 off the trees, and **s** *them* in the way. *4766*

STREAKED See RINGSTRAKED

STREAM (12) [STREAMS]

Nu 21:15 *at* the **s** of the brooks that goeth down to 793
Job 6:15 *and* as the **s** of brooks they pass away; 650
Ps 124: 4 the **s** had gone over our soul: 5158
Isa 27:12 the channel of the river unto the **s** of Egypt, 5158
30:28 his breath, as an overflowing **s**, shall reach 5158
30:33 like a **s** of brimstone, doth kindle it. 5158
57: 6 Among the smooth *stones* of the **s** *is* thy 5158
66:12 the glory of the Gentiles like a flowing **s**: 5158
Da 7:10 A fiery **s** issued and came forth from before 5103
Am 5:24 as waters, and righteousness as a mighty **s**. 5158
Lk 6:48 the **s** beat vehemently upon that house, and *4215*
6:49 against which the **s** did beat vehemently, *4215*

STREAMS (12) [STREAM]

Ex 7:19 upon their **s**, upon their rivers, and 5104
8: 5 forth thine hand with thy rod over the **s**, 5104
Ps 46: 4 the **s** whereof shall make glad the city of 6388
78:16 He brought **s** also out of the rock, and 5140
78:20 waters gushed out, and the **s** overflowed; 5158
126: 4 O LORD, as the **s** in the south. 650
SS 4:15 well of living waters, and **s** from Lebanon. 5140
Isa 11:15 shall smite it in *the* seven **s**, and make *men* 5158
30:25 **s** of waters in the day of the great slaughter, 2988
33:21 *be* unto us a place of broad rivers *and* **s**; 2975
34: 9 the **s** thereof shall be turned into pitch, and 5158
35: 6 shall waters break out, and **s** in the desert. 5158

STREET (36) [STREETS]

Ge 19: 2 Nay; but we will abide in the **s** all night. 7339
Dt 13:16 the spoil of it into the midst of the **s** thereof, 7339
Jos 2:19 go out of the doors of thy house into the **s**, 2351
Jdg 19:15 went in, he sat him down in a **s** of the city: 7339
19:17 he saw a wayfaring man in the **s** of the city: 7339
19:20 wants *lie* upon me; only lodge not in the **s**. 7339
2Sa 21:12 which had stolen them from the **s** of 7339
22:43 I did stamp them as the mire of the **s**, *and* 2351
2Ch 29: 4 and gathered them together into the east **s**, 7339
32: 6 gathered them together to him in the **s** of 7339
Ezr 10: 9 all the people sat in the **s** of the house of 7339
Ne 8: 1 into the **s** that *was* before the water gate; 7339
8: 3 he read therein before the **s** that *was* before 7339
8:16 in the **s** of the water gate, and in the street 7339
8:16 and in the **s** of the gate of Ephraim. 7339
Est 4: 6 forth to Mordecai unto the **s** of the city, 7339
6: 9 bring him on horseback through the **s** of 7339
6:11 brought him on horseback through the **s** of 7339
Job 18:17 and he shall have no name in the **s**. 2351
29: 7 the city, *when* I prepared my seat in the **s**; 7339
31:32 The stranger did not lodge in the **s**: *but* 2351
Pr 7: 8 Passing through the **s** near her corner; and 7784
Isa 42: 2 nor cause his voice to be heard in the **s**. 2351
51:23 and as the **s**, to them that went over. 2351
59:14 for truth is fallen in the **s**, and equity cannot 7339
Jer 37:21 daily a piece of bread out of the bakers' **s**, 2351
La 2:19 that faint for hunger in the top of every **s**. 2351
4: 1 are poured out in the top of every **s**. 2351
Eze 16:24 and hast made thee a high place in every **s**. 7339
16:31 and makest thine high place in every **s**; 7339
Da 9:25 the **s** shall be built again, and the wall, 7339
Ac 9:11 and go into the **s** which is called Straight, *4505*
12:10 they went out, and passed on through one **s**; *4505*
Rev 11: 8 And their dead bodies *shall lie* in the **s** of *4113*
21:21 and the **s** of the city *was* pure gold, as *it* *4113*
22: 2 In the midst of the **s** of it, and of either side *4113*

STREETS (65) [STREET]

2Sa 1:20 in Gath, publish *it* not in the **s** of Askelon; 2351
1Ki 20:34 thou shalt make **s** for thee in Damascus, 2351
Ps 18:42 I did cast them out as the dirt in the **s**. 2351
55:11 and guile depart not from her **s**. 7339
144:13 forth thousands and ten thousands in our **s**: 2351
144:14 that *there be* no complaining in our **s**. 7339
Pr 1:20 she uttereth her voice in the **s**: 7339
5:16 *and* rivers of waters in the **s**. 7339
7:12 now in the **s**, and lieth in wait at every 7339
22:13 *is* a lion without, I shall be slain in the **s**. 7339
26:13 *There is* a lion in the way; a lion *is* in the **s**. 7339
Ecc 12: 4 the doors shall be shut in the **s**, when 7784
12: 5 and the mourners go about the **s**: 7784
SS 3: 2 go about the city in the **s** and in the broad 7784
Isa 5:25 carcases were torn in the midst of the **s**. 2351
10: 6 to tread them down like the mire of the **s**. 2351
15: 3 In their **s** they shall gird themselves with 2351
15: 3 in their **s**, every one shall howl, weeping 7339
24:11 *There is* a crying for wine in the **s**; all joy is 2351
51:20 they lie at the head of all the **s**, as a wild 2351
Jer 5: 1 ye to and fro through the **s** of Jerusalem, 2351
7:17 cities of Judah and in the **s** of Jerusalem? 2351
7:34 from the **s** of Jerusalem, the voice of mirth, 2351
9:21 *and* the young men from the **s**. 7339
Jer 11: 6 in the **s** of Jerusalem, saying, Hear ye 2351
11:13 *according to* the number of the **s** of 2351
14:16 shall be cast out in the **s** of Jerusalem 2351
33:10 in the **s** of Jerusalem, that are desolate, 2351
44: 6 cities of Judah and in the **s** of Jerusalem; 2351
44: 9 land of Judah, and in the **s** of Jerusalem? 2351
44:17 cities of Judah, and in the **s** of Jerusalem: 2351
44:21 in the **s** of Jerusalem, ye, and your fathers, 2351
48:38 the housetops of Moab, and in the **s** thereof: 7339
49:26 Therefore her young men shall fall in her **s**, 7339
50:30 Therefore shall her young men fall in the **s**, 7339
51: 4 and *they that are* thrust through in her **s**. 2351
La 2:11 and the sucklings swoon in the **s** of the city. 7339
2:12 when they swooned as the wounded in the **s** 7339
2:21 and the old lie on the ground in the **s**: 2351
4: 5 that did feed delicately are desolate in the **s**: 2351
4: 8 than a coal; they are not known in the **s**: 2351
4:14 They have wandered *as* blind *men* in the **s**, 2351
4:18 hunt our steps, that *we* cannot go in our **s**: 7339
Eze 7:19 They shall cast their silver in the **s**, and 2351
11: 6 ye have filled the **s** thereof *with* the slain. 2351
26:11 of his horses shall he tread down all thy **s**: 2351
28:23 into her pestilence, and blood into her **s**; 2351
Am 5:16 Wailing *shall be* in all **s**; and they shall say 7339
Mic 7:10 she be trodden down as the mire of the **s**. 2351
Na 2: 4 The chariots shall rage in the **s**, they shall 2351
3:10 were dashed in pieces at the top of all the **s**: 2351
Zep 3: 6 I made their **s** waste, that none passeth by: 2351
Zec 8: 4 and old women dwell in the **s** of Jerusalem, 7339
8: 5 the **s** of the city shall be full *of* boys and 7339
8: 5 *of* boys and girls playing in the **s** thereof. 7339
9: 3 the dust, and fine gold as the mire of the **s**. 2351
10: 5 *enemies* in the mire of the **s** in the battle: 2351
Mt 6: 2 do in the synagogues and in the **s**, *4505*
6: 5 the synagogues and in the corners of the **s**, *4113*
12:19 shall any *man* hear his voice in the **s**. *4113*
Mk 6:56 they laid the sick in the **s**, and besought him *58*
Lk 10:10 go *your ways* out into the **s** of the same, *4113*
13:26 thy presence, and thou hast taught in our **s**. *4113*
14:21 Go out quickly into the **s** and lanes of *4113*
Ac 5:15 that *they* brought forth the sick into the **s**, *4113*

STRENGTH (242) [STRENGTHEN, STRENGTHENED, STRENGTHENEDST, STRENGTHENETH, STRENGTHENING, STRONG, STRONGER, STRONGEST, STRONGLY]

Ge 4:12 it shall not henceforth yield unto thee her **s**; 3581
49: 3 my might, and the beginning of my **s**, 202
49:24 his bow abode in **s**, and the arms of his 386
Ex 13: 3 for by **s** of hand the LORD brought you 2392
13:14 By **s** of hand the LORD brought us out 2392
13:16 for by **s** of hand the LORD brought us 2392
14:27 the sea returned to his **s** when the morning 386
15: 2 The LORD *is* my **s** and song, and he is 5797
15:13 thou hast guided *them* in thy **s** unto thy 5797
Lev 26:20 your **s** shall be spent in vain: for your land 3581
Nu 23:22 he hath as it were the **s** of an unicorn. 8443
24: 8 he hath as it were the **s** of an unicorn: 8443
Dt 21:17 for he *is* the beginning of his **s**; the right of 202
33:25 brass; and as thy days, *so shall* thy **s** *be*. 1679
Jos 11:13 *as for* the cities that stood still in their **s**, 8510
14:11 as my **s** *was* then, even so *is* my strength 3581
14:11 even so *is* my **s** now, for war, both to go 3581
Jdg 5:21 O my soul, thou hast trodden down **s**. 5797
8:21 for as the man *is, so is* his **s**. And Gideon 1369
16: 5 see wherein his great **s** *lieth,* and by what 3581
16: 6 wherein thy great **s** *lieth,* and 3581
16: 9 it toucheth the fire. So his **s** was not known. 3581
16:15 hast not told me wherein thy great **s** *lieth.* 3581
16:17 my **s** will go from me, and I shall become 3581
16:19 to afflict him, and his **s** went from him. 3581
1Sa 2: 4 and they that stumbled are girt with **s**. 2428
2: 9 in darkness; for by **s** shall no man prevail. 3581
2:10 he shall give **s** unto his king, and exalt 5797
15:29 also the **S** of Israel will not lie nor repent: 5331
28:20 there was no **s** in him; for he had eaten no 3581
28:22 eat, that thou mayest have **s**, when thou 3581
2Sa 22:33 God *is* my **s** *and* power: and he maketh my 4581
22:40 For thou hast girded me with **s** to battle. 2428
1Ki 19: 8 went in the **s** of that meat forty days and 3581
2Ki 9:24 **drew** a bow **with** his **full s**, 3027+4390+871.1
18:20 *I have* counsel and **s** for the war. 1369
19: 3 to the birth, and *there is* not **s** to bring forth. 3581
1Ch 16:11 Seek the LORD and his **s**, seek his face 5797
16:27 **s** and gladness *are* in his place. 5797
16:28 give unto the LORD glory and **s**. 5797
26: 8 able men for **s** for the service, 3581
29:12 *it is* to make great, and to **give s** unto all. 2388
2Ch 6:41 thy resting place, thou, and the ark of thy **s**: 5797
13:20 Neither did Jeroboam recover **s** again in 3581
Ne 4:10 The **s** of the bearers of burdens is decayed, 3581
8:10 for the joy of the LORD *is* your **s**. 4581
Job 6:11 What *is* my **s**, that I should hope? and 3581
6:12 *Is* my **s** the strength of stones? or *is* my 3581
6:12 *Is* my strength the **s** of stones? or *is* my 3581
9: 4 *He is* wise in heart, and mighty in **s**: 3581
9:19 If *I speak* of **s**, lo, *he is* strong: and if of 3581
12:13 With him *is* wisdom and **s**, he hath counsel 1369
12:16 With him *is* **s** and wisdom: the deceived 5797
12:21 and weakeneth the **s** of the mighty. 4206
18: 7 The steps of his **s** shall be straitened, and 202
18:12 His **s** shall be hunger-bitten, and 202
18:13 It shall devour the **s** of his skin: *even* 905
18:13 *even* the firstborn of death shall devour his **s**. 905
21:23 One dieth in his full **s**, *being* wholly at ease 6106
23: 6 great power? No; but he would put *s* in me. NIH
26: 2 *how* savest thou the arm *that hath* no **s**? 5797
30: 2 whereto *might* the **s** of their hands profit 3581
36: 5 and despiseth not *any: he is* mighty **in s** *and* 3581
36:19 *no,* not gold, nor all the forces of **s**. 3581
37: 6 the small rain, and *to* the great rain of his **s**. 5797
39:11 Wilt thou trust him, because his **s** *is* great? 3581
39:19 Hast thou given the horse **s**? hast thou 1369
39:21 paweth in the valley, and rejoiceth in *his* **s**. 3581
Job 40:16 his **s** *is* in his loins, and his force *is* in 3581
41:22 In his neck remaineth **s**, and sorrow is 5797
Ps 8: 2 sucklings hast thou ordained **s** because 5797
18: 1 I will love thee, O LORD, my **s**. 2391
18: 2 my God, my **s**, in whom I will trust; 6697
18:32 *It is* God that girdeth me *with* **s**, and 2428
18:39 For thou hast girded me *with* **s** unto 2428
19:14 O LORD, my **s**, and my redeemer. 6697
20: 6 heaven with the saving **s** of his right hand. 1369
21: 1 The king shall joy in thy **s**, O LORD; and 5797
21:13 Be thou exalted, LORD, in thine own **s**: *so* 5797
22:15 My **s** is dried up like a potsherd; and 3581
22:19 O LORD: O my **s**, haste thee to help me. 360
27: 1 the LORD *is* the **s** of my life; of whom 4581
28: 7 The LORD *is* my **s** and my shield; 5797
28: 8 The LORD *is* their **s**, and he *is* the saving 5797
28: 8 and he *is* the saving **s** of his anointed. 4581
29: 1 give unto the LORD glory and **s**. 5797
29:11 The LORD will give **s** unto his people; 5797
31: 4 have laid privily for me: for thou *art* my **s**. 4581
31:10 my **s** faileth because of mine iniquity, and 3581
33:16 a mighty *man* is not delivered by much **s**. 3581
33:17 neither shall he deliver *any* by his great **s**. 2428
37:39 *he is* their **s** in the time of trouble. 4581
38:10 My heart panteth, my **s** faileth me: as for 3581
39:13 O spare me, that I may **recover s**, before I 1082
43: 2 For thou *art* the God of my **s**: why dost 4581
46: 1 God *is* our refuge and **s**, a very present help 5797
52: 7 Lo, *this is* the man *that* made not God his **s**; 4581
54: 1 by thy name, and judge me by thy **s**. 1369
59: 9 *Because of* his **s** will I wait upon thee: 5797
59:17 Unto thee, O my **s**, will I sing: for God *is* 5797
60: 7 *is* mine; Ephraim also *is* the **s** of mine head; 4581
62: 7 the rock of my **s**, *and* my refuge, *is* in God. 5797
65: 6 Which by his **s** setteth fast the mountains; 3581
68:28 Thy God hath commanded thy **s**: 5797
68:34 Ascribe ye **s** unto God: his excellency *is* 5797
68:34 *is* over Israel, and his **s** *is* in the clouds. 5797
68:35 the God of Israel *is* he that giveth **s** and 5797
71: 9 old age; forsake me not when my **s** faileth. 3581
71:16 I will go in the **s** of the Lord GOD: I will 1369
71:18 until I have shewed thy **s** unto *this* 2220
73: 4 no bands in their death: but their **s** *is* firm. 193
73:26 *but* God *is* the **s** of my heart, and 6697
74:13 Thou didst divide the sea by thy **s**: 5797
77:14 thou hast declared thy **s** among the people. 5797
78: 4 his **s**, and his wonderful works that he hath 5807
78:51 the chief of *their* **s** in the tabernacles of Ham: 202
78:61 delivered his **s** into captivity, and his glory 5797
80: 2 and Benjamin and Manasseh stir up thy **s**, 1369
81: 1 Sing aloud unto God our **s**: make a joyful 5797
84: 5 Blessed *is* the man whose **s** *is* in thee; 5797
84: 7 They go from **s** to strength, *every one of* 2428
84: 7 They go from strength to **s**, *every one of* 2428
86:16 give thy **s** unto thy servant, and save 5797
88: 4 into the pit: I am as a man *that hath* no **s**: 353
89:17 For thou *art* the glory of their **s**: and in thy 5797
90:10 if by reason of **s** *they be* fourscore years, 1369
90:10 yet *is* their **s** labour and sorrow; 7296
93: 1 the LORD is clothed with **s**, *wherewith* he 5797
95: 4 of the earth: the **s** of the hills *is* his also. 8443
96: 6 **s** and beauty *are* in his sanctuary. 5797
96: 7 give unto the LORD glory and **s**. 5797
99: 4 The king's **s** also loveth judgment; 5797
102:23 He weakened my **s** in the way; 3581
103:20 the LORD, ye his angels, that excel in **s**, 3581
105: 4 Seek the LORD, and his **s**: seek his face 5797
105:36 firstborn in their land, the chief of all their **s**. 202
108: 8 *is* mine; Ephraim also *is* the **s** of mine head; 4581
110: 2 The LORD shall send the rod of thy **s** out 5797
118:14 The LORD *is* my **s** and song, and 5797
132: 8 into thy rest; thou, and the ark of thy **s**. 5797
138: 3 *and* strengthenedst me *with* **s** in my soul. 5797
140: 7 O GOD the Lord, the **s** of my salvation, 5797
144: 1 Blessed *be* the LORD my **s**, 6697
147:10 He delighteth not in the **s** of the horse: 1369
Pr 8:14 I *am* understanding; I have **s**. 1369
10:29 The way of the LORD *is* **s** to the upright: 4581
14: 4 but much increase *is* by the **s** of the ox. 3581
20:29 The glory of young men *is* their **s**: and 3581
21:22 casteth down the **s** of the confidence 5797
24: 5 yea, a man of knowledge increaseth **s**. 3581
24:10 faint in the day of adversity, thy **s** *is* small. 3581
31: 3 Give not thy **s** unto women, nor thy ways to 2428
31:17 She girdeth her loins with **s**, and 5797
31:25 **S** and honour *are* her clothing; and she shall 5797
Ecc 9:16 said I, Wisdom *is* better than **s**: 1369
10:10 whet the edge, then must he put to more **s**: 2428
10:17 due season, for **s**, and not for drunkenness. 1369
Isa 5:22 and men of **s** to mingle strong drink: 2428
10:13 By the **s** of my hand I have done *it,* and 3581
12: 2 for the LORD JEHOVAH *is* my **s** and 5797
17:10 hast not been mindful of the rock of thy **s**, 4581
23: 4 *even* the **s** of the sea, saying, I travail not, 4581
23:10 O daughter of Tarshish: *there is* no more **s**. 4206
23:14 ships of Tarshish: for your **s** is laid waste. 4581
25: 4 For thou hast been a **s** to the poor, 4581
25: 4 a **s** to the needy in his distress, a refuge 4581
26: 4 in the LORD JEHOVAH *is* everlasting **s**: 6697
27: 5 Or let him take hold of my **s**, *that* he may 4581
28: 6 for **s** to them that turn the battle to the gate. 1369
30: 2 to strengthen themselves in the **s** of 4581
30: 3 Therefore shall the **s** of Pharaoh be your 4581
30: 7 I cried concerning this, Their **s** *is* to sit still. 7293
30:15 and in confidence shall be your **s**: 1369
33: 6 the stability of thy times, *and* **s** of salvation: 2633
36: 5 vain words) *I have* counsel and **s** for war: 1369
37: 3 to the birth, and *there is* not **s** to bring forth. 3581
40: 9 good tidings, lift up thy voice with **s**; 3581
40:29 to *them that have* no might he increaseth **s**. 6109
40:31 wait upon the LORD shall renew *their* **s**; 3581
41: 1 O islands; and let the people renew *their* **s**: 3581
42:25 the fury of his anger, and the **s** of battle: 5807
44:12 and worketh it with the **s** of his arms: 3581
44:12 yea, he is hungry, and his **s** faileth: 3581

Isa 45:24 in the LORD have I righteousness and **s**: 5797
49: 4 I have spent my **s** for nought, and in vain: 3581
49: 5 of the LORD, and my God shall be my **s**. 5797
51: 9 Awake, awake, put on **s**, O arm of 5797
52: 1 Awake, awake; put on thy **s**, O Zion; put on 5797
62: 8 by his right hand, and by the arm of his **s**, 5797
63: 1 travelling in the greatness of his **s**? 3581
63: 6 and I will bring down their **s** to the earth. 5332
63:15 where *is* thy zeal and thy **s**, the sounding of 1369
Jer 16:19 my **s**, and my fortress, and my refuge in 5797
20: 5 Moreover I will deliver all the **s** of this city, 2633
51:53 she should fortify the height of her **s**, 5797
La 1: 6 they are gone without **s** before the pursuer. 3581
1:14 he hath made my **s** to fall, the Lord hath 3581
3:18 My **s** and my hope is perished from 5331
Eze 24:21 the excellency of your **s**, the desire of your 5797
24:25 *be* in the day when I take from them their **s**, 4581
30:15 will pour my fury upon Sin, the **s** of Egypt; 4581
30:18 the pomp of her **s** shall cease in her: *as for* 5797
33:28 and the pomp of her **s** shall cease; 5797
Da 2:37 thee a kingdom, power, and **s**, and glory. 8632
2:41 there shall be in it of the **s** of the iron, 5326
10: 8 great vision, and there remained no **s** in me: 3581
10: 8 in me into corruption, and I retained no **s**. 3581
10:16 turned upon me, and I have retained no **s**. 3581
10:17 straightway there remained no **s** in me, 3581
11: 2 by his **s** through his riches he shall stir up 2393
11:15 neither *shall there be any* **s** to withstand. 3581
11:17 He shall also set his face to enter with the **s** 8633
11:31 they shall pollute the sanctuary *of* **s**, and 4581
Hos 7: 9 Strangers have devoured his **s**, and 3581
12: 3 and by his **s** he had power with God: 202
Joel 2:22 the fig tree and the vine do yield their **s**. 2428
3:16 and the **s** of the children of Israel. 4581
Am 3:11 he shall bring down thy **s** from thee, and 5797
6:13 we not taken to us horns by our own **s**? 2392
Mic 5: 4 shall stand and feed in the **s** of the LORD, 5797
Na 3: 9 Ethiopia and Egypt *were* her **s**, and *it was* 6109
3:11 thou also shalt seek **s** because of the enemy. 4581
Hab 3:19 The Lord GOD *is* my **s**, and he will make 2428
Hag 2:22 I will destroy the **s** of the kingdoms of 2392
Zec 12: 5 The inhabitants of Jerusalem *shall be* my **s** in 556
Mk 12:30 and with all thy mind, and with all thy **s**: *2479*
12:33 and with all the **s**, and to love *his* neighbour *2479*
Lk 1:51 He hath shewed **s** with his arm; he hath *2904*
10:27 and with all thy **s**, and with all thy mind; *2479*
Ac 3: 7 his feet and ankle bones **received s**, *4732*
9:22 But Saul **increased** the more **in s**, and *1743*
Ro 5: 6 For when we were yet **without s**, in due time *772*
1Co 15:56 of death *is* sin; and the **s** of sin *is* the law. *1411*
2Co 1: 8 we were pressed out of measure, above **s**, *1411*
12: 9 for my **s** is made perfect in weakness. *1411*
Heb 9:17 otherwise it is of no **s** at all whilst *2480*
11:11 Through faith also Sara herself received **s** *1411*
Rev 1:16 countenance *was* as the sun shineth in his **s**. *1411*
3: 8 for thou hast a little **s**, and hast kept my *1411*
5:12 and **s**, and honour, and glory, and blessing. *2479*
12:10 and **s**, and the kingdom of our God, and *1411*
17:13 shall give their power and **s** unto the beast. *1849*

STRENGTHEN (32) [STRENGTH]
Dt 3:28 and encourage him, and **s** him: 553
Jdg 16:28 I pray thee, and **s** me, I pray thee, 2388
1Ki 20:22 **s** thyself, and mark, and see what thou 2388
Ezr 6:22 to **s** their hands in the work of the house of 2388
Ne 6: 9 Now therefore, *O God,* **s** my hands. 2388
Job 16: 5 *But* I would **s** you with my mouth, and 553
Ps 20: 2 from the sanctuary, and **s** thee out of Zion; 5582
27:14 of good courage, and he shall **s** thine heart: 553
31:24 of good courage, and he shall **s** your heart, 553
41: 3 The LORD will **s** him upon the bed of 5582
68:28 **s**, O God, that which thou hast wrought for 5810
89:21 be established: mine arm also shall **s** him. 553
119:28 **s** thou me according unto thy word. 6965
Isa 22:21 **s** him *with* thy girdle, and I will commit thy 2388
30: 2 to **s** themselves in the strength of Pharaoh, 5810
33:23 they could not well **s** their mast, they could 2388
35: 3 **S** ye the weak hands, and confirm 2388
41:10 I will **s** thee; yea, I will help thee; yea, I will 553
54: 2 lengthen thy cords, and **s** thy stakes; 2388
Jer 23:14 they **s** also the hands of evildoers, that none 2388
Eze 7:13 neither shall any **s** himself in the iniquity of 2388
16:49 neither did she **s** the hand of the poor and 2388
30:24 I will **s** the arms of the king of Babylon, 2388
30:25 I will **s** the arms of the king of Babylon, 2388
34:16 was broken, and will **s** that which was sick: 2388
Da 11: 1 *even* I, stood to confirm and to **s** him. 4581
Am 2:14 the strong shall not **s** his force, neither shall 553
Zec 10: 6 I will **s** the house of Judah, and I will save 1396
10:12 I will **s** them in the LORD; and they shall 1396
Lk 22:32 when thou art converted, **s** thy brethren. *4741*
1Pe 5:10 make you perfect, stablish, **s**, settle *you.* *4599*
Rev 3: 2 Be watchful, and **s** the *things* which remain, *4741*

STRENGTHENED (39) [STRENGTH]
Ge 48: 2 and Israel **s** himself, and sat upon the bed. 2388
Jdg 3:12 the LORD **s** Eglon the king of Moab 2388
7:11 afterward shall thine hands be **s** to go down 2388
1Sa 23:16 *into* the wood, and **s** his hand in God. 2388
2Sa 2: 7 Therefore now let your hands be **s**, and 2388
1Ch 11:10 who **s** themselves with him in his kingdom, 2388
2Ch 1: 1 Solomon the son of David was **s** in his 2388
11:17 So they **s** the kingdom of Judah, and 2388
12: 1 had **s** himself, he forsook the law of 2393
12:13 So king Rehoboam **s** himself in Jerusalem, 2388
13: 7 have **s** themselves against Rehoboam the son 553
17: 1 in his stead, and **s** himself against Israel. 2388
21: 4 he **s** himself, and slew all his brethren with 2388
23: 1 in the seventh year Jehoiada **s** himself, and 2388
24:13 set the house of God in his state, and **s** it. 553
25:11 Amaziah **s** himself, and led forth his 2388
26: 8 in of Egypt: for he **s** *himself* exceedingly. 2388
28:20 unto him, and distressed him, but **s** him not. 2388
32: 5 Also he **s** himself, and built up all the wall 2388
Ezr 1: 6 all *they that were* about them **s** their hands 2388
7:28 I was **s** as the hand of the LORD my God 2388
Ne 2:18 So they **s** their hands for *this* good *work.* 2388
Job 4: 3 and thou hast **s** the weak hands. 2388
4: 4 was falling, and thou hast **s** the feeble knees. 553
Ps 52: 7 his riches, *and* **s** himself in his wickedness. 5810
147:13 For he hath **s** the bars of thy gates; he hath 2388
Pr 8:28 when *he* **s** the fountains of the deep: 5810
Eze 13:22 **s** the hands of the wicked, that *he* should 2388
34: 4 The diseased have ye not **s**, neither have ye 2388
Da 10:18 like the appearance of a man, and he **s** me, 2388
10:19 I was **s**, and said, Let my lord speak; 2388
10:19 said, Let my lord speak; for thou hast **s** me. 2388
11: 6 begat her, and he that **s** her in *these* times. 2388
11:12 ten thousands: but he shall not be **s** *by it.* 5810
Hos 7:15 Though I have bound *and* **s** their arms, 2388
Ac 9:19 And when he had received meat, he was **s**. *1765*
Eph 3:16 to be **s** with might by his Spirit in the inner *2901*
Col 1:11 **S** with all might, according to his glorious *1412*
2Ti 4:17 the Lord stood with me, and **s** me; *1743*

STRENGTHENEDST (1) [STRENGTH]
Ps 138: 3 *and* **s** me *with* strength in my soul. 7292

STRENGTHENETH (7) [STRENGTH]
Job 15:25 and **s** himself against the Almighty. 1396
Ps 104:15 to shine, and bread *which* **s** man's heart. 5582
Pr 31:17 her loins with strength, and **s** her arms. 553
Ecc 7:19 Wisdom **s** the wise more than ten mighty 5810
Isa 44:14 which he **s** for himself among the trees of 553
Am 5: 9 That **s** the spoiled against the strong, so 1082
Php 4:13 I can do all *things* through Christ which **s** *1743*

STRENGTHENING (2) [STRENGTH]
Lk 22:43 an angel unto him from heaven, **s** him. *1765*
Ac 18:23 and Phrygia in order, **s** all the disciples. *1991*

STRETCH (50) [OUTSTRETCHED, STRETCHED, STRETCHEDST, STRETCHEST, STRETCHETH, STRETCHING]
Ex 3:20 I will **s out** my hand, and smite Egypt with 7971
7: 5 when I **s forth** mine hand upon Egypt, and 5186
7:19 **s out** thine hand upon the waters of Egypt, 5186
8: 5 **S forth** thine hand with thy rod over 5186
8:16 **S out** thy rod, and smite the dust of 5186
9:15 For now I will **s out** my hand, that I may 7971
9:22 **S forth** thine hand toward heaven, 5186
10:12 **S out** thine hand over the land of Egypt for 5186
10:21 **S out** thine hand toward heaven, 5186
14:16 **s out** thine hand over the sea, and divide it: 5186
14:26 unto Moses, **S out** thine hand over the sea, 5186
25:20 the cherubims shall **s forth** *their* wings on 6566
Jos 8:18 **S out** the spear that *is* in thy hand toward 5186
1Sa 24: 6 to **s forth** mine hand against him, 7971
26: 9 for who can **s forth** his hand against 7971
26:11 The LORD forbid that *I* should **s forth** 7971
26:23 I would not **s forth** mine hand against 7971
2Sa 1:14 How wast thou not afraid to **s forth** thine 7971
2Ki 21:13 I will **s** over Jerusalem the line of Samaria, 5186
Job 11:13 and **s out** thine hands toward him; 6566
30:24 Howbeit *he* will not **s out** *his* hand to 7971
39:26 *and* **s** her wings toward the south? 6566
Ps 68:31 Ethiopia shall soon **s out** her hands unto 7323
138: 7 thou shalt **s forth** thine hand against 7971
143: 6 I **s forth** my hands unto thee: my soul 6566
Isa 28:20 For the bed is shorter than that *a man* can **s** 8311
31: 3 When the LORD shall **s out** his hand, 5186
34:11 he shall **s out** upon it the line of confusion, 5186
54: 2 let them **s forth** the curtains of thine 5186
Jer 6:12 for I will **s out** my hand upon 5186
10:20 *there is* none to **s forth** my tent any more, 5186
15: 6 therefore will I **s out** my hand against thee, 5186
51:25 I will **s out** mine hand upon thee, and 5186
Eze 6:14 So will I **s out** mine hand upon them, and 5186
14: 9 I will **s out** my hand upon him, and 5186
14:13 will I **s out** mine hand upon it, and 5186
25: 7 I will **s out** mine hand upon thee, and 5186
25:13 I will also **s out** mine hand upon Edom, and 5186
25:16 I *will* **s out** mine hand upon the Philistines, 5186
30:25 and he shall **s** it **out** upon the land of Egypt. 5186
35: 3 and I will **s out** mine hand against thee, and 5186
Da 11:42 He shall **s forth** his hand also upon 7971
Am 6: 4 **s** themselves upon their couches, and 5628
Zep 1: 4 I will also **s out** mine hand upon Judah, and 5186
2:13 he will **s out** his hand against the north, 5186
Mt 12:13 saith he to the man, **S forth** thine hand. *1614*
Mk 3: 5 he saith unto the man, **S forth** thine hand. *1614*
Lk 6:10 he said unto the man, **S forth** thy hand. *1614*
Jn 21:18 thou shalt **s forth** thy hands, and *1614*
2Co 10:14 For we **s** not ourselves **beyond** *our* *5239*

STRETCHED (71) [STRETCH]
Ge 22:10 Abraham **s forth** his hand, and took 7971
48:14 Israel **s out** his right hand, and laid *it* upon 7971
Ex 6: 6 and I will redeem you with a **s out** arm, and 5186
8: 6 Aaron **s out** his hand over the waters of 5186
8:17 for Aaron **s out** his hand with his rod, and 5186
9:23 Moses **s forth** his rod toward heaven: and 5186
10:13 Moses **s forth** his rod over the land of 5186
10:22 Moses **s forth** his hand toward heaven; 5186
14:21 Moses **s out** his hand over the sea; and 5186
14:27 Moses **s forth** his hand over the sea, and 5186
Dt 4:34 and by a **s out** arm, and by great terrors, 5186
5:15 through a mighty hand and by a **s out** arm: 5186
7:19 and the mighty hand, and the **s out** arm, 5186
9:29 by thy mighty power and by thy **s out** arm. 5186
11: 2 his mighty hand, and his **s out** arm, 5186
Jos 8:18 Joshua **s out** the spear that *he had* in his 5186
8:19 they ran as soon as *he* had **s out** his hand: 5186
8:26 hand back, wherewith he **s out** the spear, 5186
2Sa 24:16 when the angel **s out** his hand *upon* 7971
1Ki 6:27 they **s forth** the wings of the cherubims, 6566
8:42 of thy strong hand, and of thy **s out** arm;) 5186
17:21 he **s** himself upon the child three times, 4058
2Ki 4:34 he **s** himself upon the child; and the flesh of 1457
4:35 fro; and went up, and **s** himself upon him: 1457
17:36 of Egypt with great power and a **s out** arm, 5186
1Ch 21:16 having a drawn sword in his hand **s out** 5186
2Ch 6:32 and thy mighty hand, and thy **s out** arm; 5186
Job 38: 5 or who hath **s** the line upon it? 5186
Ps 44:20 or **s out** our hands to a strange god; 6566
88: 9 upon thee, I have **s out** my hands unto thee. 7849
136: 6 To him that **s out** the earth above 7554
136:12 With a strong hand, and with a **s out** arm: 5186
Pr 1:24 I have **s out** my hand, and no man 5186
Isa 3:16 walk with **s forth** necks and wanton eyes, 5186
5:25 he hath **s forth** his hand against them, and 5186
5:25 not turned away, but his hand *is* **s out** still. 5186
9:12 not turned away, but his hand *is* **s out** still. 5186
9:17 not turned away, but his hand *is* **s out** still. 5186
9:21 not turned away, but his hand *is* **s out** still. 5186
10: 4 not turned away, but his hand *is* **s out** still. 5186
14:26 this *is* the hand that is **s out** upon all 5186
14:27 who shall disannul *it?* and his hand *is* **s out**, 5186
16: 8 her branches are **s out**, they are gone over 5203
23:11 He **s out** his hand over the sea, he shook 5186
42: 5 he that created the heavens, and **s** them **out**; 5186
45:12 have **s out** the heavens, and all their host 5186
51:13 that hath **s forth** the heavens, and laid 5186
Jer 6: 4 for the shadows of the evening are **s out**. 5186
10:12 hath **s out** the heavens by his discretion. 5186
32:17 the earth by thy great power and **s out** arm, 5186
32:21 and with a **s out** arm, and with great terror; 5186
51:15 hath **s out** the heaven by his understanding. 5186
La 2: 8 he hath **s out** a line, he hath not withdrawn 5186
Eze 1:11 their wings *were* **s** upward; two *wings* of 6504
1:22 **s forth** over their heads above. 5186
10: 7 *one* cherub **s forth** his hand from between 7971
16:27 I have **s out** my hand over thee, and 5186
20:33 with a **s out** arm, and with fury poured out, 5186
20:34 with a **s out** arm, and with fury poured out. 5186
Hos 7: 5 of wine; he **s out** his hand with scorners. 4900
Am 6: 7 the banquet of them that **s** themselves shall 5628
Zec 1:16 and a line shall be **s forth** upon Jerusalem. 5186
Mt 12:13 And he **s** *it* **forth**; and it was restored *1614*
12:49 And he **s forth** his hand toward his *1614*
14:31 And immediately Jesus **s forth** *his* hand, *1614*
26:51 one of them which were with Jesus **s out** *1614*
Mk 3: 5 And he **s** *it* **out**: and his hand was restored *1614*
Lk 22:53 the temple, ye **s forth** no hands against me: *1614*
Ac 12: 1 Now about that time Herod the king **s forth** *1911*
26: 1 Then Paul **s forth** the hand, and *1614*
Ro 10:21 All day long have I **s forth** my hands unto *1600*

STRETCHEDST (1) [STRETCH]
Ex 15:12 Thou **s out** thy right hand, the earth 5186

STRETCHEST (1) [STRETCH]
Ps 104: 2 who **s out** the heavens like a curtain: 5186

STRETCHETH (7) [STRETCH]
Job 15:25 For he **s out** his hand against God, and 5186
26: 7 He **s out** the north over the empty place, 5186
Pr 31:20 She **s out** her hand to the poor; yea, 6566
Isa 40:22 that **s out** the heavens as a curtain, and 5186
44:13 The carpenter **s out** *his* rule; he marketh it 5186
44:24 all *things;* that **s forth** the heavens alone; 5186
Zec 12: 1 which **s forth** the heavens, and layeth 5186

STRETCHING (2) [STRETCH]
Isa 8: 8 the **s out** of his wings shall fill the breadth 4298
Ac 4:30 By **s forth** thine hand to heal; and *1614*

STRICKEN (18) [STRIKE]
Ge 18:11 and Sarah *were* old *and* **well s** in age; 935
24: 1 Abraham was old, *and* **well s** in age: and 935
Jos 13: 1 Now Joshua was old *and* **s** in years; and 935
13: 1 Thou art old *and* **s** in years, and 935
23: 1 that Joshua waxed old *and* **s** in age. 935
23: 2 and said unto them, I am old *and* **s** in age: 935
Jdg 5:26 she had pierced and **s through** his temples. 2498
1Ki 1: 1 Now king David was old *and* **s** in years; and 935
Pr 6: 1 *if* thou hast **s** thy hand with a stranger, 8628
23:35 They have **s** me, *shalt thou say, and* I was 5221
Isa 1: 5 Why should ye be **s** any more? ye will 5221
16: 7 shall ye mourn; surely *they are* **s**. 5218
53: 4 yet we did esteem him **s**, smitten of God, 5060
53: 8 for the transgression of my people was he **s**. 5061
Jer 5: 3 thou hast **s** them, but they have not grieved; 5221
La 4: 9 **s through** for *want of* the fruits of the field. 1856
Lk 1: 7 and they both were *now* **well s** in years. *4260*
1:18 an old man, and my wife **well s** in years. *4260*

STRIFE (39) [STRIVE]
Ge 13: 7 there was a **s** between the herdmen of 7379
13: 8 Let there be no **s**, I pray thee, between me 4808
Nu 27:14 in the **s** of the congregation, to sanctify me 4808
Dt 1:12 and your burden, and your **s**? 7379
Jdg 12: 2 my people were at great **s** with the children 7379
2Sa 19: 9 all the people were **at s** throughout all 1777
Ps 31:20 secretly in a pavilion from the **s** of tongues. 7379
55: 9 for I have seen violence and **s** in the city. 7379
80: 6 Thou makest us a **s** unto our neighbours: 4066
106:32 They angered *him* also at the waters of **s**, so 4808
Pr 15:18 A wrathful man stirreth up **s**: but *he that is* 4066
15:18 but *he that is* slow to anger appeaseth **s**. 7379
16:28 A froward man soweth **s**: and a whisperer 4066
17: 1 than a house full *of* sacrifices with **s**. 7379
17:14 The beginning of **s** *is as* when one letteth 4066
17:19 He loveth transgression that loveth **s**: *and* 4683
20: 3 *It is* an honour for a man to cease from **s**: 7379
22:10 go out; yea, **s** and reproach shall cease. 1779
26:17 *and* meddleth with **s** *belonging* not to him, 7379
26:20 where *there is* no talebearer, the **s** ceaseth. 4066
26:21 to fire; so *is* a contentious man to kindle **s**. 7379
28:25 He that is of a proud heart stirreth up **s**: but 4066
29:22 An angry man stirreth up **s**, and a furious 4066
30:33 so the forcing of wrath bringeth forth **s**. 7379
Isa 58: 4 ye fast for **s** and debate, and to smite with 7379

Jer 15:10 that thou hast borne me a man of s and 7379
Eze 47:19 from Tamar *even* to the waters of s *in* 4808
48:28 from Tamar *unto* the waters of s *in* Kadesh, 4808
Hab 1: 3 and there are *that* raise up s and contention. 7379
Lk 22:24 And there was also a s among them, which *5379*
Ro 13:13 and wantonness, not in s and envying. *2054*
1Co 3: 3 and s, and divisions, are ye not carnal, and *2054*
Gal 5:20 emulations, wrath, s, seditions, heresies, *2052*
Php 1:15 indeed preach Christ even of envy and s; *2054*
2: 3 *Let* nothing *be done* through s or vainglory; *2052*
1Ti 6: 4 cometh envy, s, railings, evil surmisings, *2054*
Heb 6:16 for confirmation *is* to them an end of all s. *485*
Jas 3:14 ye have bitter envying and s in your hearts, *2052*
3:16 and s *is,* there *is* confusion and every evil *2052*

STRIFES (4) [STRIVE]
Pr 10:12 Hatred stirreth up s: but love covereth all 4066
2Co 12:20 envyings, wraths, s, backbitings, *2052*
1Ti 6: 4 but doting about questions and s **of words**, *3055*
2Ti 2:23 knowing that they do gender s. *3163*

STRIKE (12) [STRAKE, STRICKEN, STRIKER, STRIKETH, STROKE, STROKES, STROOKE, STRUCK]
Ex 12: 7 s *it* on the two side posts and on the upper 5414
12:22 s the lintel and the two side posts with 5060
Dt 21: 4 shall s **off** the heifer's **neck** there in 6202
2Ki 5:11 s his hand over the place, and recover 5130
Job 17: 3 who *is* he *that* will s hands with me? 8628
20:24 *and* the bow of steel shall s him **through**. 2498
Ps 110: 5 The Lord at thy right hand shall s **through** 4272
Pr 7:23 Till a dart s **through** his liver; as a bird 6398
17:26 just *is* not good, *nor* to s princes for equity. 5221
22:26 Be not thou *one* of them that s hands, *or* 8628
Hab 3:14 Thou didst s **through** with his staves 5344
Mk 14:65 s him **with the palms of** their **hands**. *906+4475*

STRIKER (2) [STRIKE]
1Ti 3: 3 Not given to wine, no s, not greedy of filthy *4131*
Tit 1: 7 not soon angry, not given to wine, no s, *4131*

STRIKETH (3) [STRIKE]
Job 34:26 He s them as wicked *men* in the open sight 5606
Pr 17:18 A man void of understanding s hands, *and* 8628
Rev 9: 5 the torment of a scorpion, when he s a man. *3817*

STRING (2) [STRINGED, STRINGS]
Ps 11: 2 they make ready their arrow upon the s, 3499
Mk 7:35 and the s of his tongue was loosed, and *1199*

STRINGED (3) [STRING]
Ps 150: 4 praise him with s **instruments** and organs. 4482
Isa 38:20 **sing** my songs *to* **the s instruments** all 5059
Hab 3:19 To the chief singer on my s **instruments**. 5058

STRINGS (4) [STRING]
Ps 21:12 *arrows* upon thy s against the face of them. 4340
33: 2 the psaltery *and* an **instrument of ten s**. 6218
92: 3 Upon an **instrument of ten s**, and upon 6218
144: 9 an **instrument of ten s** will I sing *praises* 6218

STRIP (7) [STRIPPED, STRIPT]
Nu 20:26 s Aaron of his garments, and put them upon 6584
1Sa 31: 8 when the Philistines came to s the slain, 6584
1Ch 10: 8 when the Philistines came to s the slain, 6584
Isa 32:11 s ye, and make ye bare, and gird *sackcloth* 6584
Eze 16:39 they shall s thee also of thy clothes, and 6584
23:26 They shall also s thee **out of** thy clothes, 6584
Hos 2: 3 Lest I s her naked, and set her as *in* the day 6584

STRIPE (2) [STRIPES]
Ex 21:25 for burning, wound for wound, s for stripe. 2250
21:25 for burning, wound for wound, stripe for s. 2250

STRIPES (17) [STRIPE]
Dt 25: 3 Forty s he may **give** him, *and* not exceed: 5221
25: 3 beat him above these *with* many s, then 4347
2Sa 7:14 and with the s of the children of men: 5061
Ps 89:32 with the rod, and their iniquity with s. 5061
Pr 17:10 a wise *man* than an hundred s into a fool. 5221
19:29 for scorners, and s for the back of fools. 4112
20:30 so *do* s the inward parts of the belly. 4347
Isa 53: 5 upon him; and with his s we are healed. 2250
Lk 12:47 to his will, shall be beaten with many *s*. NIG
12:48 and did commit *things* worthy of s, *4127*
12:48 shall be beaten with few *s*. For unto NIG
Ac 16:23 And when they had laid many s upon them, *4127*
16:33 same hour of the night, and washed *their* s; *4127*
2Co 6: 5 In s, in imprisonments, in tumults, *4127*
11:23 In s above measure, in prisons more *4127*
11:24 Of the Jews five times received I forty *s* NIG
1Pe 2:24 by whose s ye were healed. *3468*

STRIPLING (1)
1Sa 17:56 king said, Inquire thou whose son the s *is*. 5958

STRIPPED (6) [STRIP]
Nu 20:28 Moses s Aaron of his garments, and 6584
1Sa 31: 9 s **off** his armour, and sent into the land of 6584
1Ch 10: 9 when they had s him, they took his head, 6584
Job 22: 6 and s the naked of their clothing. 6584
Mt 27:28 And they s him, and put on him a scarlet *1562*
Lk 10:30 which s him **of** his **raiment**, and *1562*

STRIPT (7) [STRIP]
Ge 37:23 that they s Joseph **out of** his coat, 6584
Ex 33: 6 the children of Israel s themselves of their 5337
1Sa 18: 4 Jonathan s himself of the robe that *was* 6584
19:24 he s **off** his clothes also, and 6584
2Ch 20:25 which they s **off** for themselves, 5337
Job 19: 9 He hath s me of my glory, and taken 6584
Mic 1: 8 I will wail and howl, I will go s and naked: 7758

STRIVE (22) [STRIFE, STRIFES, STRIVED, STRIVEN, STRIVETH, STRIVING, STRIVINGS, STROVE]
Ge 6: 3 My spirit shall not always s with man, 1777
26:20 the herdmen of Gerar did s with Isaac's 7378
Ex 21:18 if men s **together**, and one smite another 7378
21:22 If men s, and hurt a woman with child, so 5327
Dt 25:11 When men s together one with another, 5327
33: 8 *with* whom thou didst s at the waters of 7378
Jdg 11:25 did he **ever** s against Israel, or did he 7378+7378
Job 33:13 Why dost thou s against him? for he giveth 7378
Ps 35: 1 O LORD, with them that s **with** me: 3401
Pr 3:30 S not with a man without cause, if he have 7378
25: 8 Go not forth hastily to s, lest *thou know not* 7378
Isa 41:11 and they that s **with** thee shall perish. 7379
45: 9 *Let* the potsherd *s* with the potsherds of NIH
Hos 4: 4 Yet let no man s, nor reprove another: 7378
4: 4 for thy people *are* as they that s with 7378
Mt 12:19 He shall not s, nor cry; neither shall any *2051*
Lk 13:24 S to enter in at the strait gate: for many, I say *75*
Ro 15:30 that *ye* s **together with** me in *your* prayers *4865*
2Ti 2: 5 And if a man also s **for masteries**, *yet* is he *118*
2: 5 *yet* is he not crowned, except he s lawfully. *118*
2:14 that *they* s not **about words** to no profit, *3054*
2:24 And the servant of the Lord must not s; but *3164*

STRIVED (1) [STRIVE]
Ro 15:20 Yea, so have I s to preach the gospel, *5389*

STRIVEN (1) [STRIVE]
Jer 50:24 because thou hast s against the LORD. 1624

STRIVETH (2) [STRIVE]
Isa 45: 9 Woe unto him that s with his maker! 7378
1Co 9:25 And every *man* that s **for the mastery** is *75*

STRIVING (3) [STRIVE]
Php 1:27 with one mind s **together** for the faith of *4866*
Col 1:29 I also labour, s according to his working, *75*
Heb 12: 4 not yet resisted unto blood, s against sin. *464*

STRIVINGS (3) [STRIVE]
2Sa 22:44 Thou also hast delivered me from the s of 7379
Ps 18:43 Thou hast delivered me from the s of 7379
Tit 3: 9 and contentions, and s about the law; *3163*

STROKE (14) [STRIKE]
Dt 17: 8 and plea, and between s and stroke, 5061
17: 8 and plea, and between stroke and s, 5061
19: 5 his hand **fetcheth a s** with the axe to cut 5080
21: 5 every controversy and every s be *tried:* 5061
Est 9: 5 all their enemies *with* the s of the sword, 4347
Job 23: 2 my s is heavier than my groaning. 3027
36:18 *beware* lest he take thee away with *his* s: 5607
Ps 39:10 Remove thy s away from me: I am 5061
Isa 14: 6 the people in wrath *with* a continual s, 4347
30:26 and healeth the s of their wound. 4273
Eze 24:16 from thee the desire of thine eyes with a s: 4046
Mt 26:51 and s a servant of the high priest's, and *3960*
Lk 22:64 they s him on the face, and asked him, *5180*
Jn 18:22 s Jesus **with the palm of** his **hand**, *1325+4475*

STROKES (1) [STRIKE]
Pr 18: 6 into contention, and his mouth calleth for s. 4112

STRONG (255) [STRENGTH]
Ge 49:14 Issachar *is* a s ass couching down between 1634
49:24 the arms of his hands were **made** s by 6339
Ex 6: 1 for with a s hand shall he let them go, and 2389
6: 1 with a s hand shall he drive them out of his 2389
10:19 the LORD turned a mighty s west wind, 2389
13: 9 for with a s hand hath the LORD brought 2389
14:21 LORD caused the sea to go *back* by a s 5794
Lev 10: 9 Do not drink wine nor s **drink**, thou, 7941
Nu 6: 3 separate *himself* from wine and s **drink**, 7941
6: 3 no vinegar of wine, or vinegar of s **drink**, 7941
13:18 whether they *be* s or weak, few or many; 2389
13:19 dwell in, whether in tents, or in s **holds**; 4013
13:28 Nevertheless the people *be* s that dwell in 5794
20:20 him with much people, and with a s hand. 2389
21:24 the border of the children of Ammon *was* s. 5794
24:21 S *is* thy dwelling place, and thou puttest thy 386
28: 7 s **wine** to be poured unto the LORD *for* a 7941
Dt 2:36 there was not one city too s for us: 7682
11: 8 that ye may be s, and go in and possess 2388
14:26 or for s **drink**, or for whatsoever thy soul 7941
29: 6 neither have you drunk wine or s **drink**: 7941
31: 6 Be s and of a good courage, fear not, nor be 2388
31: 7 of all Israel, Be s and of a good courage: 2388
31:23 said, Be s and of a good courage: 2388
Jos 1: 6 Be s and of a good courage: for unto this 2388
1: 7 Only be thou s and very courageous, 2388
1: 9 Be s and of a good courage; be not afraid, 2388
1:18 to death: only be s and of a good courage. 2388
10:25 nor be dismayed, be s and of good courage: 2388
14:11 As yet I *am as* s *this* day as *I was* in the day 2389
17:13 when the children of Israel were **waxen** s, 2388
17:18 have iron chariots, *and* though they *be* s. 2389
19:29 turneth *to* Ramah, and to the s city Tyre; 4013
23: 9 out from before you great nations and s: 6099
Jdg 1:28 it came to pass, when Israel was s, that they 2388
6: 2 in the mountains, and caves, and s **holds**. 4679
9:51 there was a s tower within the city, and 5797
13: 4 drink not wine nor s **drink**, and eat not any 7941
13: 7 now drink no wine nor s **drink**, neither eat 7941
13:14 neither let her drink wine or s **drink**, 7941
14:14 and out of the s came forth sweetness. 5794
18:26 when Micah saw that they *were* too s for 2389
1Sa 1:15 I have drunk neither wine nor s **drink**, but 7941
4: 9 Be s, and quit yourselves like men, O ye 2388
14:52 when Saul saw any s man, or any valiant 1368
23:14 David abode in the wilderness in s **holds**, 4679
23:19 hide himself with us in s **holds** in the wood, 4679
23:29 and dwelt in s **holds** at En-gedi. 4679

2Sa 3: 6 that Abner **made** himself s for the house of 2388
5: 7 Nevertheless David took the s **hold** of 4686
10:11 If the Syrians be too s for me, then 2388
10:11 if the children of Ammon be too s for thee, 2388
11:25 **make** thy battle *more* s against the city, and 2388
15:12 the conspiracy was s; for the people 533
16:21 shall the hands of all that *are* with thee be s. 2388
22:18 He delivered me from my s enemy, *and* 5794
22:18 that hated me: for they were too s for me. 553
24: 7 came *to* the s **hold** of Tyre, and *to* all 4013
1Ki 2: 2 be thou s therefore, and shew thyself a 2388
8:42 of thy s hand, and of thy stretched out arm;) 2389
19:11 a great and s wind rent the mountains, and 2389
2Ki 2:16 be with thy servants fifty s men; 1121+2428
8:12 their s **holds** wilt thou set on fire, and 4013
24:16 a thousand, all *that were* s *and* apt for war, 1368
1Ch 19:12 If the Syrians be too s for me, then thou 2388
19:12 if the children of Ammon be too s for thee, 2388
22:13 be s, and of good courage; dread not, nor be 2388
26: 7 whose brethren *were* s men, Elihu, and 2428
26: 9 Meshelemiah had sons and brethren, s men, 2428
28:10 a house for the sanctuary: be s, and do *it*. 2388
28:20 Be s and of good courage, and do *it:* fear 2388
2Ch 11:11 he fortified the s **holds**, and put captains in 4694
11:12 and spears, and **made** them exceeding s, 2388
11:17 and **made** Rehoboam the son of Solomon s, 553
15: 7 Be ye s therefore, and let not your hands be 2388
16: 9 to **shew** himself s in the behalf of *them* 2388
25: 8 if thou *wilt* go, do *it*, be s for the battle: 2388
26:15 he was marvellously helped, till he was s. 2388
26:16 when he was s, his heart was lifted up to *his* 2393
32: 7 Be s and courageous, be not afraid nor 2388
Ezr 9:12 that ye may be s, and eat the good of 2388
Ne 1:10 by thy great power, and by thy s hand. 2389
9:25 they took s cities, and a fat land, and 1219
Job 8: 2 the words of thy mouth *be like* a s wind? 3524
9:19 If *I speak* of strength, lo, *he is* s: and if of 533
30:21 with thy s hand thou opposest thyself 6108
33:19 and the multitude of his bones *with* s *pain:* 386
37:18 *which is* s, *and* as a molten looking glass? 2389
39:28 upon the crag of the rock, and the s **place**. 4686
40:18 His bones *are as* s **pieces** of brass; his bones 650
Ps 10:10 that the poor may fall by his s *ones*. 6099
18:17 He delivered me from my s enemy, and 5794
18:17 which hated me: for they were too s for me. 553
19: 5 *and* rejoiceth as a s *man* to run a race. 1368
22:12 s *bulls* of Bashan have beset me round. 47
24: 8 the LORD s and mighty, the LORD 5808
30: 7 thou hast made my mountain to stand s: 5797
31: 2 be thou my s rock, for a house of defence to 4581
31:21 me his marvellous kindness in a s city. 4692
35:10 the poor from him that is too s for him, 2389
38:19 But mine enemies *are* lively, *and* they are s: 6105
60: 9 Who will bring me *into* the s city? who will 4692
61: 3 for me, *and* a s tower from the enemy. 5797
71: 3 Be thou my s habitation, whereunto *I* may 6697
71: 7 unto many; but thou *art* my s refuge. 5797
80:15 the branch *that* thou **madest** s for thyself. 553
80:17 upon the son of man *whom* thou **madest** s 553
89: 8 of hosts, who *is* a s LORD like unto thee? 2626
89:10 thou hast scattered thine enemies with thy s 5797
89:13 s is thy hand, *and* high is thy right hand. 5810
89:40 thou hast brought his s **holds** to ruin. 4013
108:10 Who will bring me *into* the s city? who will 4013
136:12 With a s hand, and with a stretched out 2389
144:14 *That* our oxen *may be* s **to labour**; 5445
Pr 7:26 yea, many s *men have been* slain by her. 6099
10:15 The rich *man's* wealth *is* his s city: 5797
11:16 retaineth honour: and s *men* retain riches. 6184
14:26 In the fear of the LORD *is* s confidence: 5797
18:10 The name of the LORD *is* a s tower: 5797
18:11 The rich *man's* wealth *is* his s city, and as a 5797
18:19 offended *is harder to be won* than a s city: 5797
20: 1 Wine *is* a mocker, s **drink** *is* raging: and 7941
21:14 and a reward in the bosom s wrath. 5794
24: 5 A wise man *is* s; yea, a man of knowledge 5797
30:25 The ants *are* a people not s, yet they 5794
31: 4 to drink wine; nor for princes s **drink**: 7941
31: 6 Give s **drink** unto him that is ready to 7941
Ecc 9:11 nor the battle to the s, neither yet bread to 1368
12: 3 the s men shall bow themselves, and 2428
SS 8: 6 for love *is* s as death; jealousy *is* cruel as 5794
Isa 1:31 the s shall be as tow, and the maker of it as 2634
5:11 the morning, *that* they may follow s **drink**; 7941
5:22 and men of strength to mingle s **drink**: 7941
8: 7 s and many, *even* the king of Assyria, and 6099
8:11 For the LORD spake thus to me with a s 2393
17: 9 In that day shall his s cities be as a forsaken 4581
23:11 *city*, to destroy the s **holds** thereof. 4581
24: 9 s **drink** shall be bitter to them that drink it. 7941
25: 3 Therefore shall the s people glorify thee, 5794
26: 1 We have a s city; salvation will *God* 5797
27: 1 s sword shall punish leviathan the piercing 2389
28: 2 the LORD hath a mighty and s one, 533
28: 7 and through s **drink** are out of the way; 7941
28: 7 and the prophet have erred through s **drink**, 7941
28: 7 they are out of the way through s **drink**; 7941
28:22 ye not mockers, lest your bands be **made** s: 2388
29: 9 they stagger, but not *with* s **drink**. 7941
31: 1 in horsemen, because they are very s; but 6105
31: 9 he shall pass over *to* his s **hold** for fear, 5553
35: 4 that are of a fearful heart, Be s, fear not: 2388
40:10 the Lord GOD will come with s *hand*, and 2389
40:26 of *his* might, for that *he is* s in power; 533
41:21 bring forth your s *reasons*, saith the King of 6110
53:12 and he shall divide the spoil with the s; 6099
56:12 and we will fill ourselves with s **drink**; 7941
60:22 a thousand, and a small one a s nation: 6099
Jer 8:16 at the sound of the neighing of his s **ones**; 47
21: 5 with an outstretched hand and with a s arm, 2389
32:21 with a s hand, and with a stretched out arm, 2389
47: 3 of his s *horses*, at the rushing of his chariots, 47
48:14 We *are* mighty and s men for the war? 2428
48:17 How is the s staff broken, *and* the beautiful 5797
48:18 upon thee, *and* he shall destroy thy s **holds**. 4013

S

Jer 48:41 the s **holds** are surprised, and the mighty 4679
49:19 of Jordan against the habitation of the s: 386
50:34 Their redeemer *is* s; the LORD of hosts *is* 2389
50:44 of Jordan unto the habitation of the s: 386
51:12 **make** the watch s, set up the watchmen, 2388
La 2: 2 wrath the s **holds** of the daughter of Judah; 4013
2: 5 he hath destroyed his s **holds**, and 4013
Eze 3: 8 I have made thy face s against their faces, 2389
3: 8 and thy forehead s against their foreheads. 2389
3:14 but the hand of the LORD was s upon me. 2388
7:24 I will also make the pomp of the s to cease; 5794
19:11 she had s rods for the sceptres of them that 5797
19:12 her s rods were broken and withered; 5797
19:14 that she hath no s rod *to be* a sceptre to 5797
22:14 thine heart endure, or can thine hands be s, 2388
26:11 thy s garrisons shall go down to the ground. 5797
26:17 which wast s in the sea, she and 2389
30:21 to bind it, to **make** it s to hold the sword. 2388
30:22 his arms, the s, and that which was broken; 2389
32:21 The s among the mighty shall speak to him 410
34:16 I will destroy the fat and the s; I will feed 2389
Da 2:40 the fourth kingdom shall be s as iron: 8624
2:42 *so* the kingdom shall be partly s, and 8624
4:11 was s, and the height thereof reached unto 8631
4:20 that thou sawest, which grew, and was s, 8631
4:22 O king, that art grown and become s: 8631
7: 7 dreadful and terrible, and s exceedingly; 8624
8: 8 when he was s, the great horn was broken; 6105
10:19 peace *be* unto thee, be s, yea, be strong. 2388
10:19 peace *be* unto thee, be strong, yea, be s. 2388
11: 5 the king of the south shall be s, and *one* of 2388
11: 5 he shall be s above him, and 2388
11:23 and shall become s with a small people. 6105
11:24 forecast his devices against the s **holds**, 4013
11:32 people that do know their God shall be s, 2388
11:39 Thus shall he do in the **most** s holds with a 4581
Joel 1: 6 s, and without number, whose teeth *are* 6099
2: 2 a great people and a s; there hath not been 6099
2: 5 the stubble, as a s people set in battle array. 6099
2:11 for *he is* s that executeth his word: for 6099
3:10 into spears: let the weak say, I *am* s. 1368
Am 2: 9 of the cedars, and he *was* s as the oaks; 2634
2:14 the s shall not strengthen his force, 2389
5: 9 That strengtheneth the spoiled against the s, 5794
Mic 2:11 prophesy unto thee of wine and of s **drink**; 7941
4: 3 many people, and rebuke s nations afar off; 6099
4: 7 and her that was cast far off a s nation: 6099
4: 8 the s **hold** of the daughter of Zion, 6077
5:11 of thy land, and throw down all thy s **holds**: 4013
6: 2 and ye s foundations of the earth: 386
Na 1: 7 *is* good, a s **hold** in the day of trouble; 4581
2: 1 watch the way, **make** *thy* loins s, 2388
3:12 All thy s **holds** *shall be like* fig trees with 4013
3:14 waters for the siege, fortify thy s **holds**: 4013
3:14 and tread the morter, **make** s the brickkiln. 2388
Hab 1:10 they shall deride every s **hold**; for they 4013
Hag 2: 4 Yet now be s, O Zerubbabel, saith 2388
2: 4 be s, O Joshua, son of Josedech, the high 2388
2: 4 be s, all ye people of the land, saith 2388
Zec 8: 9 Let your hands be s, ye that hear in these 2388
8:13 a blessing: fear not, *but* let your hands be s. 2388
8:22 s nations shall come to seek the LORD of 6099
9: 3 Tyrus did build herself a s **hold**, and 4692
9:12 Turn ye to the s **hold**, ye prisoners of hope: 1225
Mt 12:29 Or else how can one enter into a s *man's* *2478*
12:29 except he first bind the s *man?* and then *2478*
Mk 3:27 No *man* can enter into a s *man's* house, and *2478*
3:27 except he will first bind the s *man;* and then *2478*
Lk 1:15 and shall drink neither wine nor s **drink**; *4608*
1:80 and **waxed** s in spirit, and was in *2901*
2:40 and **waxed** s in spirit, filled with wisdom: *2901*
11:21 When a s *man* armed keepeth his palace, *2478*
Ac 3:16 faith in his name hath **made** this *man* s, *4732*
Ro 4:20 but was s in faith, giving glory to God; *1743*
15: 1 that are s ought to bear the infirmities of *1415*
1Co 4:10 we *are* weak, but ye *are* s; ye *are* *2478*
16:13 fast in the faith, quit you like men, be s. *2901*
2Co 10: 4 God to the pulling down of s **holds**;) *3794*
12:10 for when I am weak, then am I s. *1415*
13: 9 are glad, when we are weak, and ye are s: *1415*
Eph 6:10 be s in the Lord, and in the power of his *1743*
2Th 2:11 And for this cause God shall send them s *1753*
2Ti 2: 1 be s in the grace that is in Christ Jesus. *1743*
Heb 5: 7 and supplications with s crying and *2478*
5:12 as have need of milk, and not of s meat. *4731*
5:14 But s meat belongeth to *them that are* of *4731*
6:18 God to lie, we might have a s consolation, *2478*
11:34 out of weakness were **made** s, waxed *1743*
1Jn 2:14 because ye are s, and the word of God *2478*
Rev 5: 2 And I saw a s angel proclaiming with a *2478*
18: 2 And he cried mightily with a s voice, *3173*
18: 8 for s *is* the Lord God who judgeth her. *2478*

STRONGER (21) [STRENGTH]
Ge 25:23 *the one* people shall be s than *the other* 553
30:41 whensoever the s cattle did conceive, 7194
30:42 the feebler were Laban's, and the s Jacob's. 7194
Nu 13:31 against the people; for they *are* s than we. 2389
Jdg 14:18 what *is* s than a lion? And he said unto 5794
2Sa 1:23 swifter than eagles, they were s than lions. 1396
3: 1 David **waxed** s and stronger, and the house 1980
3: 1 David waxed stronger and s, and the house 2390
13:14 but, being s than she, forced her, and 2388
1Ki 20:23 therefore they were s than we; but let us 2388
20:23 and surely we shall be s than they. 2388
20:25 *and* surely we shall be s than they. 2388
Job 17: 9 clean hands shall be s **and stronger**. 555+3254
17: 9 clean hands shall be **stronger and** s. 555+3254
Ps 105:24 and **made** them s than their enemies. 6105
142: 6 from my persecutors; for they are s than I. 553
Jer 20: 7 thou art s **than** I, and hast prevailed: I am 2388
31:11 from the hand of *him that was* s than he. 2389
Lk 11:22 But when a s **than** he shall come upon *him,* *2478*
1Co 1:25 and the weakness of God is s **than** men. *2478*
10:22 the Lord to jealousy? are we s **than** he? *2478*

STRONGEST (1) [STRENGTH]
Pr 30:30 A lion *which is* s among beasts, and 1368

STRONGLY (1) [STRENGTH]
Ezr 6: 3 and *let* the foundations thereof *be* s **laid**; 5446

STROOKE (1) [STRIKE]
1Sa 2:14 he s *it* into the pan, or kettle, or caldron, 5221

STROVE (14) [STRIVE]
Ge 26:20 of the well Esek; because they s with him. 6229
26:21 digged another well, and s for that also: 7378
26:22 digged another well; and for that they s not: 7378
Ex 2:13 two men of the Hebrews s **together**: 5327
Lev 24:10 and a man of Israel s **together** in the camp; 5327
Nu 20:13 the children of Israel s with the LORD, 7378
26: 9 who s against Moses and against Aaron in 5327
26: 9 of Korah, when they s against the LORD: 5327
2Sa 14: 6 they two s **together** in the field, and 5327
Ps 60: T when he s with Aram-naharaim and 5327
Da 7: 2 the four winds of the heaven s upon 1519
Jn 6:52 The Jews therefore s amongst themselves, *3164*
Ac 7:26 day he shewed himself unto them as they s, *3164*
23: 9 and s, saying, We find no evil in this man: *1264*

STROWED (1) [STRAWED]
2Ch 34: 4 s *it* upon the graves of them that had 2236

STRUCK (1) [STRIKE]
2Ch 13:20 and the LORD s him, and he died. 5062

STRUGGLED (1)
Ge 25:22 the children s **together** within her; and 7533

STUBBLE (18)
Ex 5:12 of Egypt to **gather** s instead of straw. 7179+7197
15: 7 forth thy wrath, *which* consumed them as s. 7179
Job 13:25 and fro? and wilt thou pursue the dry s? 7179
21:18 They are as s before the wind, and as chaff 8401
41:28 slingstones are turned with him into s. 7179
41:29 Darts are counted as s: he laugheth at 7179
Ps 83:13 them like a wheel; as the s before the wind. 7179
Isa 5:24 Therefore as the fire devoureth the s, and 7179
33:11 shall conceive chaff, ye shall bring forth s: 7179
40:24 the whirlwind shall take them away as s. 7179
41: 2 *to* his sword, *and* as driven s *to* his bow. 7179
47:14 Behold, they shall be as s; the fire shall 7179
Jer 13:24 Therefore will I scatter them as the s that 7179
Joel 2: 5 noise of a flame of fire that devoureth the s, 7179
Ob 1:18 the house of Esau for s, and they shall 7179
Na 1:10 they shall be devoured as s fully dry. 7179
Mal 4: 1 yea, and all that do wickedly, shall be s: 7179
1Co 3:12 silver, precious stones, wood, hay, s; *2562*

STUBBORN (5) [STUBBORNNESS]
Dt 21:18 If a man have a s and rebellious son, 5637
21:20 This our son *is* s and rebellious, he will not 5637
Jdg 2:19 their own doings, nor from their s way. 7186
Ps 78: 8 their fathers, a s and rebellious generation; 5637
Pr 7:11 (She *is* loud and s; her feet abide not in her 5637

STUBBORNNESS (2) [STUBBORN]
Dt 9:27 look not unto the s of this people, nor to 7190
1Sa 15:23 and s *is as* iniquity and idolatry. 6484

STUCK (3) [STICK]
1Sa 26: 7 and his spear s in the ground *at* his bolster: 4600
Ps 119:31 I have s unto thy testimonies: O LORD, 1692
Ac 27:41 and the forepart s **fast**, and *2043*

STUDIETH (2) [STUDY]
Pr 15:28 The heart of the righteous s to answer: but 1897
24: 2 For their heart s destruction, and their lips 1897

STUDS (1)
SS 1:11 We will make thee borders of gold with s 5351

STUDY (3) [STUDIETH]
Ecc 12:12 and much s *is* a weariness of the flesh. 3854
1Th 4:11 And that *ye* s to be quiet, and to do your *5389*
2Ti 2:15 S to shew thyself approved unto God, *4704*

STUFF (16)
Ge 31:37 Whereas thou hast searched all my s, 3627
31:37 hast thou found of all thy household s? 3627
45:20 Also regard not your s; for the good of all 3627
Ex 22: 7 unto his neighbour money or s to keep, 3627
36: 7 For the s *they had* was sufficient for all 4399
Jos 7:11 they have put *it* even amongst their own s. 3627
1Sa 10:22 Behold, he hath hid himself among the s. 3627
25:13 and two hundred abode by the s. 3627
30:24 so *shall* his part *be* that tarrieth by the s: 3627
Ne 13: 8 I cast forth all the household s of Tobiah 3627
Eze 12: 3 prepare thee s for removing, and remove by 3627
12: 4 shalt thou bring forth thy s by day in their 3627
12: 4 by day in their sight, as s for removing: 3627
12: 7 I brought forth my s by day, as stuff for 3627
12: 7 as s for captivity, and in the even I digged 3627
Lk 17:31 upon the housetop, and his s in the house, *4632*

STUMBLE (19) [STUMBLED, STUMBLETH, STUMBLING, STUMBLINGBLOCK, STUMBLINGBLOCKS, STUMBLINGSTONE]
Pr 3:23 *in* thy way safely, and thy foot shall not s. 5062
4:12 and when thou runnest, thou shalt not s. 3782
4:19 as darkness: they know not at what they s. 3782
Isa 5:27 None *shall be* weary nor s amongst them; 3782
8:15 among them shall s, and fall, and 3782
28: 7 they err in vision, they s *in* judgment. 6328
59:10 we s at noonday as *in* the night; *we are* in 3782
63:13 in the wilderness, *that* they should not s? 3782
Jer 13:16 before your feet s upon the dark mountains, 5062
18:15 they have **caused** them **to** s in their ways 3782
20:11 therefore my persecutors shall s, and 3782
31: 9 in a straight way, wherein they shall not s: 3782
46: 6 they shall s, and fall toward the north by 3782
50:32 the most proud shall s and fall, and 3782
Da 11:19 but he shall s and fall, and not be found. 3782
Na 2: 5 they shall s in their walk; they shall make 3782
3: 3 of *their* corpses; they s upon their corpses: 3782
Mal 2: 8 ye have **caused** many **to** s at the law; 3782
1Pe 2: 8 *even to them* which s at the word, *4350*

STUMBLED (6) [STUMBLE]
1Sa 2: 4 and they that s are girt with strength. 3782
1Ch 13: 9 his hand to hold the ark; for the oxen s. 8058
Ps 27: 2 upon me to eat up my flesh, they s and fell. 3782
Jer 46:12 for the mighty *man* hath s against 3782
Ro 9:32 the law. For they s at *that* stumblingstone; *4350*
11:11 say then, Have they s that they should fall? *4417*

STUMBLETH (4) [STUMBLE]
Pr 24:17 and let not thine heart be glad when he s: 3782
Jn 11: 9 he s not, because he seeth the light of this *4350*
11:10 he s, because there is no light in him. *4350*
Ro 14:21 nor *any thing* whereby thy brother s, or *4350*

STUMBLING (3) [STUMBLE]
Isa 8:14 for a stone of s and for a rock of offence to 5063
1Pe 2: 8 And a stone of s, and a rock of offence, *4348*
1Jn 2:10 and there is none **occasion of** s in him. *4625*

STUMBLINGBLOCK (12) [STUMBLE]
Lev 19:14 nor put a s before the blind, but shalt fear 4383
Isa 57:14 take up the s out of the way of my people. 4383
Eze 3:20 and I lay a s before him, he shall die: 4383
7:19 because it is the s of their iniquity. 4383
14: 3 put the s of their iniquity before their face: 4383
14: 4 putteth the s of his iniquity before his face, 4383
14: 7 putteth the s of his iniquity before his face, 4383
Ro 11: 9 and a s, and a recompence unto them: *4625*
14:13 that no *man* put a s or an occasion to fall in *4348*
1Co 1:23 unto the Jews a s, and unto the Greeks *4625*
8: 9 of yours become a s to them that are weak. *4348*
Rev 2:14 who taught Balac to cast a s before *4625*

STUMBLINGBLOCKS (2) [STUMBLE]
Jer 6:21 I will lay s before this people, and 4383
Zep 1: 3 fishes of the sea, and the s with the wicked; 4384

STUMBLINGSTONE (2) [STONE, STUMBLE]
Ro 9:32 the law. For they stumbled at *that* s; *3037+4348*
9:33 I lay in Sion a s and rock of offence: *3037+4348*

STUMP (4)
1Sa 5: 4 only *the* s *of* Dagon was left to him. NIH
Da 4:15 Nevertheless leave the s of his roots in 6136
4:23 yet leave the s of the roots thereof in 6136
4:26 whereas they commanded to leave the s of 6136

STUNK (1) [STINK]
Ex 7:21 the river s, and the Egyptians could not drink 887

STUPID See UNLEARNED

SUAH (1)
1Ch 7:36 S, and Harnepher, and Shual, and Beri, and 5477

SUBDUE (8) [SUBDUED, SUBDUEDST, SUBDUETH]
Ge 1:28 multiply, and replenish the earth, and s it: 3533
1Ch 17:10 Moreover I will s all thine enemies. 3665
Ps 47: 3 He shall s the people under us, and 1696
Isa 45: 1 hand I have holden, to s nations before him; 7286
Da 7:24 from the first, and he shall s three kings. 8214
Mic 7:19 he will s our iniquities; and thou wilt cast 3533
Zec 9:15 they shall devour, and s *with* sling stones; 3533
Php 3:21 he is able even to s all *things* unto himself. *5293*

SUBDUED (19) [SUBDUE]
Nu 32:22 the land be s before the LORD: then 3533
32:29 and the land shall be s before you; 3533
Dt 20:20 city that maketh war with thee, until it be s. 3381
Jos 18: 1 And the land was s before them. 3533
Jdg 3:30 So Moab was s that day under the hand of 3665
4:23 So God s on that day Jabin the king of 3665
8:28 Thus was Midian s before the children of 3665
11:33 Thus the children of Ammon were s before 3665
1Sa 7:13 So the Philistines were s, and they came no 3665
2Sa 8: 1 David smote the Philistines, and s them: 3665
8:11 he had dedicated of all nations which he s; 3533
22:40 them that rose up against me hast thou s 3766
1Ch 18: 1 s them, and took Gath and her towns out of 3665
20: 4 the children of the giant: and they were s. 3665
22:18 the land is s before the LORD, and before 3533
Ps 18:39 thou hast s under me those that rose up 3766
81:14 I should soon have s their enemies, and 3665
1Co 15:28 And when all *things* shall be s unto him, *5293*
Heb 11:33 Who through faith s kingdoms, *2610*

SUBDUEDST (1) [SUBDUE]
Ne 9:24 thou s before them the inhabitants of 3665

SUBDUETH (3) [SUBDUE]
Ps 18:47 avengeth me, and s the people under me. 1696
144: 2 whom I trust; who s my people under me. 7286
Da 2:40 s all *things:* and as iron that breaketh all 2827

SUBJECT (17) [SUBJECTED, SUBJECTION]
Lk 2:51 came to Nazareth, and was s unto them: *5293*
10:17 even the devils are s unto us through thy *5293*
10:20 rejoice not, that the spirits are s unto you; *5293*
Ro 8: 7 for it is not s to the law of God, *5293*
8:20 For the creature was **made** s to vanity, *5293*
13: 1 Let every soul be s unto the higher powers. *5293*

Ro 13: 5 Wherefore *ye* must needs be **s**, not only for *5293*
1Co 14:32 And the spirits of the prophets are **s to** *5293*
15:28 shall the Son also himself be **s** unto him *5293*
Eph 5:24 Therefore as the church is **s** unto Christ, so *5293*
Col 2:20 living in the world, are ye **s to ordinances**, *1379*
Tit 3: 1 Put them in mind to be **s** to principalities *5293*
Heb 2:15 death were all their lifetime **s** to bondage. *1777*
Jas 5:17 Elias was a man **s to like passions** as we *3663*
1Pe 2:18 Servants, *be* **s to** *your* masters with all fear; *5293*
3:22 and powers being **made s** unto him. *5293*
5: 5 all *of you* be **s** one to another, and *5293*

SUBJECTED (1) [SUBJECT]
Ro 8:20 by reason of him who hath **s** *the same,* in *5293*

SUBJECTION (14) [SUBJECT]
Ps 106:42 they were **brought into s** under their hand. 3665
Jer 34:11 **brought** them **into s** for servants and 3533
34:16 to return, and **brought** them **into s**, to be 3533
1Co 9:27 I keep under my body, and **bring** *it* **into s**: *1396*
2Co 9:13 your professed **s** unto the gospel of Christ, *5292*
Gal 2: 5 To whom we gave place by **s**, no, not for an *5292*
1Ti 2:11 Let the woman learn in silence with all **s**. *5292*
3: 4 having *his* children in **s** with all gravity; *5292*
Heb 2: 5 For unto *the* angels hath he not **put in s** *5293*
2: 8 Thou hast **put** all *things* **in s** under his feet. *5293*
2: 8 For in that *he* **put** all **in s under** him, *5293*
12: 9 shall we not much rather be **in s** unto *5293*
1Pe 3: 1 ye wives, *be* **in s** to your own husbands; *5293*
3: 5 being **in s** unto their own husbands: *5293*

SUBMISSIVE See SUBJECTION

SUBMIT (12) [SUBMITTED, SUBMITTING]
Ge 16: 9 thy mistress, and **s** thyself under her hands. 6031
2Sa 22:45 Strangers shall **s** themselves unto me: 3584
Ps 18:44 the strangers shall **s** themselves unto me. 3584
66: 3 shall thine enemies **s** themselves unto thee. 3584
68:30 *till every one* **s** himself with pieces of 7511
1Co 16:16 That ye **s** yourselves unto such, and *5293*
Eph 5:22 **s** yourselves unto your own husbands, *5293*
Col 3:18 **s** yourselves unto your own husbands, *5293*
Heb 13:17 have the rule over you, and **s** yourselves: *5226*
Jas 4: 7 **S** yourselves therefore to God. Resist *5293*
1Pe 2:13 **S** yourselves to every ordinance of man for *5293*
5: 5 *ye* younger, **s** yourselves unto the elder. *5293*

SUBMITTED (3) [SUBMIT]
1Ch 29:24 **s** themselves unto Solomon the king. 5414
Ps 81:15 The haters of the LORD should have **s** 3584
Ro 10: 3 have not **s** themselves unto *5293*

SUBMITTING (1) [SUBMIT]
Eph 5:21 **S** yourselves one to another in the fear of *5293*

SUBORNED (1)
Ac 6:11 Then they **s** men, which said, We have *5260*

SUBSCRIBE (2) [SUBSCRIBED]
Isa 44: 5 another shall **s** *with* his hand unto 3789
Jer 32:44 **s** evidences, and seal *them,* and 3789

SUBSCRIBED (2) [SUBSCRIBE]
Jer 32:10 I **s** the evidence, and sealed *it,* and 3789
32:12 in the presence of the witnesses that **s** 3789

SUBSTANCE (50)
Ge 7: 4 every **living s** that I have made will I 3351
7:23 every **living s** was destroyed which *was* 3351
12: 5 all their **s** that they had gathered, and 7399
13: 6 for their **s** was great, so that they could not 7399
15:14 afterward shall they come out with great **s**. 7399
34:23 *Shall* not their cattle and their **s** and 7075
36: 6 his cattle, and all his beasts, and all his **s**, 7075
Dt 11: 6 and all the **s** that *was* in their possession, 3351
33:11 his **s**, and accept the work of his hands: 2428
Jos 14: 4 their suburbs for their cattle and for their **s**. 7075
1Ch 27:31 All these *were* the rulers of the **s** which *was* 7399
28: 1 the stewards over all the **s** and 7399
2Ch 21:17 carried away all the **s** that was found in 7399
31: 3 portion of his **s** for the burnt offerings, 7399
32:29 for God had given him **s** very much. 7399
35: 7 these *were* of the king's **s**. 7399
Ezr 8:21 and for our little ones, and for all our **s**. 7399
10: 8 all his **s** should be forfeited, and 7399
Job 1: 3 His **s** also was seven thousand sheep, and 4735
1:10 his hands, and his **s** is increased in the land. 4735
5: 5 and the robber swalloweth up their **s**. 2428
6:22 or, Give a reward for me of your **s**? 3581
15:29 not be rich, neither shall his **s** continue, 2428
20:18 according to *his* **s** *shall* the restitution *be,* 2428
22:20 Whereas our **s** is not cut down, but 7009
30:22 me to ride *upon it,* and dissolvest my **s**. 8454
Ps 17:14 and leave the rest of their *s* to their babes. NIH
105:21 him lord of his house, and ruler of all his **s**: 7075
139:15 My **s** was not hid from thee, when I was 6108
139:16 eyes did see my **s**, **yet being unperfect**; 1564
Pr 1:13 We shall find all precious **s**, we shall fill 1952
3: 9 Honour the LORD with thy **s**, and 1952
6:31 he shall give all the **s** of his house. 1952
8:21 *I* may cause those that love me to inherit **s**; 3426
10: 3 but he casteth away the **s** of the wicked. 1942
12:27 but the **s** of a diligent man *is* precious. 1952
28: 8 by usury and unjust gain increaseth his **s**, 1952
29: 3 company with harlots spendeth *his* **s**. 1952
SS 8: 7 if a man would give all the **s** of his house 1952
Isa 6:13 teil tree, and as an oak, whose **s** *is* in them, 4678
6:13 *so* the holy seed *shall be* the **s** thereof. 4678
Jer 15:13 Thy **s** and thy treasures will I give to 2428
17: 3 I will give thy **s** *and* all thy treasures to 2428
Hos 12: 8 I am become rich, I have found me out **s**: 202
Ob 1:13 nor have laid *hands* on their **s** in the day of 2428
Mic 4:13 their **s** unto the Lord of the whole earth. 2428
Lk 8: 3 which ministered unto him of their **s**. *5225*
15:13 and there wasted his **s** with riotous living. *3776*
Heb 10:34 have in heaven a better and an enduring **s**. *5223*
11: 1 Now faith is the **s** of *things* hoped for, *5287*

SUBTIL (3) [SUBTILTY]
Ge 3: 1 Now the serpent was more **s** than any beast 6175
2Sa 13: 3 and Jonadab *was* a very **s** man. 2450
Pr 7:10 *with* the attire of a harlot, and **s** of heart. 5341

SUBTILLY (3) [SUBTILTY]
1Sa 23:22 it is told me *that* he **dealeth very s**. 6191+6191
Ps 105:25 hate his people, to **deal s** with his servants. 5230
Ac 7:19 The same **dealt s with** our kindred, and *2686*

SUBTILTY (6) [SUBTIL, SUBTILLY]
Ge 27:35 Thy brother came with **s**, and hath taken 4820
2Ki 10:19 Jehu did *it* in **s**, to the intent that *he* might 6122
Pr 1: 4 To give **s** to the simple, to the young man 6195
Mt 26: 4 consulted that they might take Jesus by **s**, *1388*
Ac 13:10 And said, O full of all **s** and all mischief, *1388*
2Co 11: 3 as the serpent beguiled Eve through his **s**, *3834*

SUBURBS (115)
Lev 25:34 the field of the **s** of their cities may not be 4054
Nu 35: 2 ye shall give *also* unto the Levites **s** for 4054
35: 3 the **s** of them shall be for their cattle, and 4054
35: 4 the **s** of the cities, which ye shall give unto 4054
35: 5 this shall be to them the **s** of the cities. 4054
35: 7 eight cities: them *shall ye give* with their **s**. 4054
Jos 14: 4 save cities to dwell *in,* with their **s** for their 4054
21: 2 to dwell in, with the **s** thereof for our cattle. 4054
21: 3 of the LORD, these cities and their **s**. 4054
21: 8 lot unto the Levites these cities with their **s**, 4054
21:11 of Judah, with the **s** thereof round about it. 4054
21:13 of Aaron the priest Hebron with her **s**, 4054
21:13 refuge for the slayer; and Libnah with her **s**, 4054
21:14 Jattir with her **s**, and Eshtemoa with her 4054
21:14 with her suburbs, and Eshtemoa with her **s**, 4054
21:15 Holon with her **s**, and Debir with her 4054
21:15 with her suburbs, and Debir with her **s**, 4054
21:16 Ain with her **s**, and Juttah with her suburbs, 4054
21:16 Juttah with her **s**, *and* Beth-shemesh with 4054
21:16 her suburbs, *and* Beth-shemesh with her **s**; 4054
21:17 Gibeon with her **s**, Geba with her suburbs, 4054
21:17 Gibeon with her suburbs, Geba with her **s**, 4054
21:18 Anathoth with her **s**, and Almon with her 4054
21:18 with her suburbs, and Almon with her **s**; 4054
21:19 the priests, *were* thirteen cities with their **s**. 4054
21:21 For they gave them Shechem with her **s** in 4054
21:21 refuge for the slayer; and Gezer with her **s**, 4054
21:22 Kibzaim with her **s**, and Beth-horon with 4054
21:22 her suburbs, and Beth-horon with her **s**; 4054
21:23 out of the tribe of Dan, Eltekeh with her **s**, 4054
21:23 with her suburbs, Gibbethon with her **s**, 4054
21:24 Aijalon with her **s**, Gath-rimmon with her 4054
21:24 with her suburbs, Gath-rimmon with her **s**; 4054
21:25 Tanach with her **s**, and Gath-rimmon with 4054
21:25 her suburbs, and Gath-rimmon with her **s**; 4054
21:26 All the cities *were* ten with their **s** for 4054
21:27 *they gave* Golan in Bashan with her **s**, 4054
21:27 and Beeshterah with her **s**; two cities. 4054
21:28 Kishon with her **s**, Dabareh with her 4054
21:28 with her suburbs, Dabareh with her **s**, 4054
21:29 Jarmuth with her **s**, En-gannim with her 4054
21:29 with her suburbs, En-gannim with her **s**; 4054
21:30 Mishal with her **s**, Abdon with her suburbs, 4054
21:30 Mishal with her suburbs, Abdon with her **s**, 4054
21:31 Helkath with her **s**, and Rehob with her 4054
21:31 with her suburbs, and Rehob with her **s**; 4054
21:32 of Naphtali, Kedesh in Galilee with her **s**, 4054
21:32 Hammoth-dor with her **s**, and Kartan with 4054
21:32 with her suburbs, and Kartan with her **s**; 4054
21:33 families *were* thirteen cities with their **s**. 4054
21:34 Jokneam with her **s**, and Kartah with her 4054
21:34 with her suburbs, and Kartah with her **s**, 4054
21:35 Dimnah with her **s**, Nahalal with her 4054
21:35 with her suburbs, Nahalal with her **s**; 4054
21:36 Bezer with her **s**, and Jahazah with her 4054
21:36 with her suburbs, and Jahazah with her **s**, 4054
21:37 Kedemoth with her **s**, and Mephaath with 4054
21:37 with her suburbs, and Mephaath with her **s**; 4054
21:38 tribe of Gad, Ramoth in Gilead with her **s**, 4054
21:38 for the slayer; and Mahanaim with her **s**, 4054
21:39 Heshbon with her **s**, Jazer with her suburbs; 4054
21:39 Heshbon with her suburbs, Jazer with her **s**; 4054
21:41 *were* forty and eight cities with their **s**. 4054
21:42 These cities were every one with their **s** 4054
2Ki 23:11 which *was* in the **s**, and burnt the chariots 6503
1Ch 5:16 in her towns, and in all the **s** of Sharon, 4054
6:55 of Judah, and the **s** thereof round about it. 4054
6:57 Libnah with her **s**, and Jattir, and 4054
6:57 and Jattir, and Eshtemoa, with their **s**, 4054
6:58 Hilen with her **s**, Debir with her suburbs, 4054
6:58 Hilen with her suburbs, Debir with her **s**, 4054
6:59 Ashan with her **s**, and Beth-shemesh with 4054
6:59 her suburbs, and Beth-shemesh with her **s**: 4054
6:60 Geba with her **s**, and Alemeth with her 4054
6:60 Alemeth with her **s**, and Anathoth with her 4054
6:60 with her suburbs, and Anathoth with her **s**. 4054
6:64 gave to the Levites *these* cities with their **s**. 4054
6:67 Shechem in mount Ephraim with her **s**; 4054
6:67 *they gave* also Gezer with her **s**, 4054
6:68 Jokmeam with her **s**, and Beth-horon with 4054
6:68 her suburbs, and Beth-horon with her **s**, 4054
6:69 Aijalon with her **s**, and Gath-rimmon with 4054
6:69 her suburbs, and Gath-rimmon with her **s**: 4054
6:70 Aner with her **s**, and Bileam with her 4054
6:70 with her suburbs, and Bileam with her **s**, 4054
6:71 Golan in Bashan with her **s**, and Ashtaroth 4054
6:71 with her suburbs, and Ashtaroth with her **s**: 4054
6:72 Kedesh with her **s**, Daberath with her 4054
6:72 with her suburbs, Daberath with her **s**, 4054
6:73 Ramoth with her **s**, and Anem with her 4054
6:73 with her suburbs, and Anem with her **s**: 4054
1Ch 6:74 Mashal with her **s**, and Abdon with her 4054
6:74 with her suburbs, and Abdon with her **s**, 4054
6:75 Hukok with her **s**, and Rehob with her 4054
6:75 with her suburbs, and Rehob with her **s**: 4054
6:76 Kedesh in Galilee with her **s**, and Hammon 4054
6:76 Hammon with her **s**, and Kirjathaim with 4054
6:76 her suburbs, and Kirjathaim with her **s**. 4054
6:77 Rimmon with her **s**, Tabor with her 4054
6:77 with her suburbs, Tabor with her **s**: 4054
6:78 Bezer in the wilderness with her **s**, and 4054
6:78 with her suburbs, and Jahzah with her **s**, 4054
6:79 Kedemoth also with her **s**, and Mephaath 4054
6:79 with her suburbs, and Mephaath with her **s**: 4054
6:80 Ramoth in Gilead with her **s**, and 4054
6:80 with her suburbs, and Mahanaim with her **s**, 4054
6:81 Heshbon with her **s**, and Jazer with her 4054
6:81 with her suburbs, and Jazer with her **s**. 4054
13: 2 and Levites *which are* in their cities *and* **s**, 4054
2Ch 11:14 For the Levites left their **s** and 4054
31:19 *which were* in the fields of the **s** of their 4054
Eze 27:28 The **s** shall shake at the sound of the cry of 4054
45: 2 fifty cubits round about *for* the **s** thereof. 4054
48:15 *place* for the city, for dwelling, and for **s**: 4054
48:17 the **s** of the city shall be toward the north 4054

SUBVERT (2) [SUBVERTED, SUBVERTING]
La 3:36 To **s** a man in his cause, the Lord approveth 5791
Tit 1:11 must be stopped, who **s** whole houses, *396*

SUBVERTED (1) [SUBVERT]
Tit 3:11 Knowing that *he that is* such is **s**, and *1612*

SUBVERTING (2) [SUBVERT]
Ac 15:24 **s** your souls, saying, *Ye must* be *384*
2Ti 2:14 to no profit, *but* to the **s** of the hearers. *2692*

SUCATHITES See SUCHATHITES

SUCCEED (1) [SUCCEEDED, SUCCEEDEST, SUCCESS]
Dt 25: 6 *that* the firstborn which she beareth shall **s** 6965

SUCCEEDED (3) [SUCCEED]
Dt 2:12 the children of Esau **s** them, when they had 3423
2:21 and they **s** them, and dwelt in their stead: 3423
2:22 they **s** them, and dwelt in their stead *even* 3423

SUCCEEDEST (2) [SUCCEED]
Dt 12:29 and thou **s** them, and dwellest in their land; 3423
19: 1 thou **s** them, and dwellest in their cities, 3423

SUCCESS (1) [SUCCEED]
Jos 1: 8 and then thou shalt **have good s**. 7919

SUCCOTH (18)
Ge 33:17 Jacob journeyed to **S**, and built him a 5523
33:17 the name of the place is called **S**. 5523
Ex 12:37 of Israel journeyed from Rameses to **S**, 5523
13:20 they took their journey from **S**, and 5523
Nu 33: 5 removed from Rameses, and pitched in **S**. 5523
33: 6 they departed from **S**, and pitched in 5523
Jos 13:27 and Beth-nimrah, and **S**, and Zaphon, 5523
Jdg 8: 5 he said unto the men of **S**, Give, I pray you, 5523
8: 6 the princes of **S** said, *Are* the hands of 5523
8: 8 him as the men of **S** had answered *him.* 5523
8:14 caught a young man of the men of **S**, and 5523
8:14 he described unto him the princes of **S**, and 5523
8:15 he came unto the men of **S**, and said, 5523
8:16 and with them he taught the men of **S**. 5523
1Ki 7:46 in the clay ground between **S** and Zarthan. 5523
2Ch 4:17 in the clay ground between **S** and 5523
Ps 60: 6 and mete out the valley of **S**. 5523
108: 7 and mete out the valley of **S**. 5523

SUCCOTH-BENOTH (1)
2Ki 17:30 the men of Babylon made **S**, and the men 5524

SUCCOUR (3) [SUCCOURED, SUCCOURER]
2Sa 8: 5 when the Syrians of Damascus came to **s** 5826
18: 3 now *it is* better that thou **s** us out of 5826
Heb 2:18 he is able to **s** them that are tempted. *997*

SUCCOURED (2) [SUCCOUR]
2Sa 21:17 Abishai the son of Zeruiah **s** him, and 5826
2Co 6: 2 and in the day of salvation have I **s** thee: *997*

SUCCOURER (1) [SUCCOUR]
Ro 16: 2 for she hath been a **s** of many, and *4368*

SUCH (249)
Ge 4:20 he was the father of **s** as dwell in tents, and NIH
4:20 as dwell in tents, and *of* **s** *as have* cattle. NIH
4:21 he was the father of all **s** as handle the harp NIH
27: 4 **s as** I love, and bring *it* to me, that I 834+3509.1
27: 9 meat for thy father, **s as** he loveth: 834+3509.1
27:14 savoury meat, **s as** his father loved. 834+3509.1
27:46 **s as** these *which are* of the daughters of 3509.1
30:32 among the goats: and *of* **s** shall be my hire. NIH
41:19 **s** as I never saw in all the land of Egypt for 2007
41:38 Can we find *s a one* as this *is,* a man in NIH
44:15 wot ye not that **s** a man as I can certainly 834
Ex 9:18 **s** as hath not been in Egypt since 834
9:24 **s as** there was none like it in all the land of 834
10:14 before them there were no **s** locusts as they, 3651
10:14 as they, neither after them shall be **s**. 3651
11: 6 **s** as there was none like it, nor shall be like it 834
12:36 that they lent unto them *s things as they* NIH
18:21 **s** as fear God, men of truth, NIH
18:21 place **s** over them, *to be* rulers of thousands, NIH
34:10 **s** as have not been done in all the earth, 834
Lev 10:19 and **s** things have befallen me: 3509.1
11:34 *that* on which *s* water cometh shall be NIH
11:34 all drink that may be drunk in every *s* vessel NIH

S

Lev 14:22 or two young pigeons, **s as** he is able to get; 834
14:30 or of the young pigeons, **s** as he can get; 4480
14:31 *Even* **s as** he is able to get, the one *for* a sin 834
20: 6 the soul that turneth after **s** as have familiar NIH
22: 6 The soul which hath touched *any* **s** shall 2050.2
27: 9 all that *any man* giveth of **s** unto NIH
Nu 8:16 instead of **s** as open every womb, NIH
Dt 4:32 whether there hath been *any* **s** *thing* as this NIH
5:29 O that there were **s** a heart in them, 2088
13:11 shall do no more any **s** wickedness as this is 1697
13:14 *that* **s** abomination is wrought among you; 2063
16: 9 begin to number the seven weeks from **s** NIH
17: 4 *that* **s** abomination is wrought in Israel: 2088
19:20 shall henceforth commit no more any **s** evil 2088
25:16 For all that do **s** *things, and* all that do 428
Jdg 3: 2 at the least **s as** before knew nothing thereof: 834
13:23 as *at this* time have told us **s** *things* as these. NIH
18:23 that thou comest with **s** a company? NIH
19:30 There was no **s** *deed* done 2063+1886.1+3509.1
Ru 4: 1 *Ho,* **s a one**, turn aside, sit down here. 492+6423
1Sa 2:23 And he said unto them, Why do ye **s** things? 428
4: 7 hath not been **s** *a thing* heretofore. 2088+3509.1
21: 2 appointed *my* servants to **s and such** 492+6423
21: 2 appointed *my* servants to **such and s** 492+6423
25:17 for he *is* **s** a son of Belial, that *a man* cannot NIH
2Sa 9: 8 that thou shouldest look upon **s** a dead dog NIH
12: 8 moreover have given unto thee **s** 2007+3509.1
12: 8 given unto thee such and **s things**. 2007+3509.1
13:12 for no **s** thing ought to be done in Israel: 3651
13:18 for with **s** robes were the king's daughters 3651
14:13 hast thou thought **s** a thing against 3509.1
16: 2 that **s** as be faint in the wilderness may 1886.1
19:36 the king recompense *it* me *with* **s** a reward? 2088
1Ki 10:10 there came no more **s** abundance of spices 1931
10:12 there came no **s** almug trees, nor were seen 3651
2Ki 6: 8 In **s** and such a place *shall be* my camp. 6423
6: 8 In such and **s** a place *shall be* my camp. 492
6: 9 Beware that *thou* pass not **s** a place; 2088
7:19 windows in heaven, might **s** a thing be? 3509.1
19:29 *this* year **s things as grow of themselves,** 5599
21:12 I *am* bringing **s** evil upon Jerusalem and NIH
23:22 Surely there was not holden **s** a passover 3509.1
25:15 *and* **s** *things as were of* gold, *in* gold, and *of* 834
1Ch 12:33 Of Zebulun, **s** as went forth to battle, NIH
12:36 **s** as went forth to battle, expert in war, NIH
29:25 bestowed upon him **s** royal majesty as had NIH
2Ch 1:12 **s** as none of the kings have had that *have* 3651
4: 6 **s** things as they offered for the burnt NIH
9: 9 neither was there any **s** spice as the queen 1931
9:11 there were none **s** seen before in the land 3509.1
11:16 after them out of all the tribes of Israel **s** 1886.1
23:13 of musick, and **s** as taught to *sing* praise. NIH
24:12 Jehoiada gave it to **s** as did the work of NIH
24:12 also **s** as wrought iron and brass to mend NIH
30: 5 for they had not done *it* of a long *time in* **s** NIH
35:18 neither did all the kings of Israel keep **s** a 3509.1
Ezr 4:10 *are on this* side the river, and **at s a time.** 3706
4:11 men *on this* side the river, and **at s a time.** 3706
4:17 beyond the river: Peace, and **at s a time.** 3706
6:21 all **s as** had separated themselves unto 1886.1
7:12 of heaven, perfect *peace,* and **at s a time.** 3706
7:25 the river, all **s** as know the laws of thy God; NIH
7:27 which hath put **s** *a thing* as this in the king's NIH
8:31 and of **s** as lay in wait by the way. NIH
9:13 and hast given us **s** deliverance as this; NIH
10: 3 **s as** are born of them, according to 1886.1
Ne 6: 8 There are no **s** things *done* as thou 428+3509.1
6:11 I said, Should **s** a man as I flee? and who *is* 3644
Est 2: 9 with **s things as belonged** to her, and seven 4490
4:11 except **s** to whom the king shall hold 834+4480
4:14 art come to the kingdom for **s** a time as this? NIH
9: 2 to lay hand on **s** as sought their hurt: NIH
9:27 all **s** as joined themselves unto them, 1886.1
Job 12: 3 yea, who knoweth not **s** *things* **as** these? 3644
14: 3 dost thou open thine eyes upon **s a one,** 2088
15:13 and lettest **s** words go out of thy mouth? NIH
16: 2 I have heard many **s** *things:* miserable 3509.1
18:21 Surely **s** *are* the dwellings of the wicked, and 428
23:14 and many **s** *things are* with him. 2007+3509.1
Ps 25:10 truth unto **s** as keep his covenant and NIH
27:12 up against me, and **s** as breathe out cruelty. NIH
34:18 and saveth **s** as be of a contrite spirit. NIH
37:14 *and* to slay **s** as be of upright conversation. NIH
37:22 For **s** as be blessed of him shall inherit NIH
40: 4 not the proud, nor **s** as turn aside to lies. NIH
40:16 let **s** as love thy salvation say continually, NIH
50:21 thou thoughtest that I was altogether **s** *a one* NIH
55:20 He hath put forth his hands against **s** as be NIH
68:21 the hairy scalp of **s** a one as goeth on still in NIH
70: 4 let **s** as love thy salvation say continually, NIH
73: 1 to Israel, *even* to **s** as are of a clean heart. NIH
103:18 To **s** as keep his covenant, and to those that NIH
107:10 **S** as sit in darkness and in the shadow of NIH
125: 5 As for **s** as turn aside *unto* their crooked 1886.1
139: 6 **S** knowledge *is* too wonderful for me; it is NIH
144:15 Happy *is that* people, that is **in s a case:** 3602
Pr 11:20 **s** *as are* upright in *their* way *are* his delight. NIH
28: 4 but **s** as keep the law contend with them. NIH
30:20 **S** *is* the way of an adulterous woman; 3651
31: 8 of all **s** as are appointed to destruction. NIH
Ecc 4: 1 the tears of **s** as were oppressed, and 1886.1
Isa 9: 1 Nevertheless the dimness *shall* not *be* **s as** 834
10:20 and **s as are escaped** of the house of Jacob, 6413
20: 6 in that day, Behold, **s** *is* our expectation, 3541
37:30 Ye shall eat *this* year **s as growth of itself**; 5599
58: 5 Is it **s** a fast that I have chosen? 2088+3509.1
66: 8 Who hath heard **s** *a thing?* who 2088+3509.1
66: 8 **s** *things?* Shall the earth be made to 428+3509.1
Jer 2:10 and see if there be **s** *a thing.* 2088+3509.1
5: 9 my soul be avenged on **s** a nation as this? 3509.1
5:29 shall not my soul be avenged on **s a** nation as 834
9: 9 my soul be avenged on **s** a nation **as** this? 3509.1
15: 2 **S as** *are* for death, to death; and such as *are* 834
15: 2 and **s as** *are* for the sword, to the sword; and 834
15: 2 **s as** *are* for the famine, to the famine; and 834
Jer 15: 2 and **s as** *are* for the captivity, to the captivity. 834
18:13 who hath heard **s** *things:* the virgin 428+3509.1
21: 7 **s** as are left in this city from 1886.1
38: 4 in speaking **s** words unto them: 3509.1
43:11 *and deliver* **s** *as are* for death to death; 834
43:11 **s** *as are* for captivity to captivity; and such *as* 834
43:11 and **s** *as are* for the sword to the sword. 834
44:14 for none shall return but **s** as shall escape. 518
Eze 17:15 shall he escape that doeth **s** *things?* or 428
18:14 and considereth, and doeth not **s like,** 3509.1
Da 1: 4 **s as** *had* ability in them to stand in the king's 834
2:10 *that* asked **s** things at any magician, 1836+3509.4
10:15 when he had spoken **s** words unto me, 3509.1
11:32 **s** as do wickedly against the covenant shall NIH
12: 1 **s as** never was since there was a nation *even* 834
Am 5:16 **s** as are skilful of lamentation to wailing. NIH
Mic 5:15 upon the heathen, **s as** they have not heard. 834
Zep 1: 8 all **s as** are clothed with strange apparel. 1886.1
Mt 9: 8 which had given **s** power unto men. *5108*
18: 5 And whoso shall receive one **s** little child in *5108*
19:14 unto me: for of **s** is the kingdom of heaven. *5108*
24:21 **s as** was not since the beginning of *3634*
24:44 for in **s** an hour as you think not the Son of *3739*
26:18 Go into the city to **s a man,** and say unto *1170*
Mk 4:18 are sown among thorns; **s** as hear the word, *3588*
4:20 **s as** hear the word, and receive *it,* and *3748*
4:33 And with many **s** parables spake he *5108*
6: 2 that even **s** mighty works are wrought by *5108*
7: 8 cups: and many other **s** like *things* ye do. *5108*
7:13 and many **s** like *things* do ye. *5108*
9:37 Whosoever shall receive one of **s** children *5108*
10:14 them not: for of **s** is the kingdom of God. *5108*
13: 7 for **s** *things* must needs be; but the end *shall* NIG
13:19 **s** as was not from the beginning of *5108*
Lk 9: 9 of whom I hear **s** *things?* And he desired to *5108*
10: 7 and drinking **s** *things* **as** they **give:** *3588+3844*
10: 8 eat **s** *things* as are set before you: *3588*
11:41 But rather give alms *of* **s** *things* as *you* *3588*
13: 2 because they suffered **s** *things?* *5108*
18:16 them not: for of **s** is the kingdom of God. *5108*
Jn 4:23 for the Father seeketh **s** to worship him. *5108*
7:32 people murmured **s** *things* concerning him; *3778*
8: 5 commanded us, that **s** should be stoned: *5108*
9:16 How can a man *that is* a sinner do **s** *5108*
Ac 2:47 And the Lord added to the church daily **s** as *3588*
3: 6 have I none; but **s** as I have give I thee: *3739*
15:24 to whom we gave no **s** commandment: NIG
16:24 Who, having received **s** a charge, *5108*
18:15 look ye *to it;* for I will be no judge of **s** *3778*
21:25 concluded that they observe no **s** *thing,* *5108*
22:22 said, Away with **s** *a fellow* from the earth: *5108*
25:18 none accusation of **s** *things* as I supposed: NIG
25:20 because I doubted of **s** *manner of* questions, *3778*
26:29 both almost, and altogether **s as** *3697+5108*
28:10 they laded *us* with **s** *things* as were *3588*
Ro 1:32 that they which commit **s** *things* are worthy *5108*
2: 2 truth against them which commit **s** *things.* *5108*
2: 3 that judgest them which do **s** *things,* and *5108*
16:18 For *they that are* **s** serve not our Lord Jesus *5108*
1Co 5: 1 and **s** fornication as is not so much as *5108*
5: 5 To deliver **s a one** unto Satan for *5108*
5:11 or an extortioner; with **s a one** no not to eat. *5108*
6:11 And **s** were some of you: but ye are *3778*
7:15 or a sister is not under bondage in **s** *cases:* *5108*
7:28 Nevertheless **s** shall have trouble in *5108*
10:13 taken you but **s** as is common to man: NIG
11:16 we have no **s** custom, neither the churches *5108*
15:48 *is* the earthy, **s** *are they* also *that are* earthy: *5108*
15:48 **s** *are they* also *that are* heavenly. *5108*
16:16 That ye submit yourselves unto **s,** and *5108*
16:18 therefore acknowledge ye *them that are* **s.** *5108*
2Co 2: 6 Sufficient to **s** *a man is* this punishment, *5108*
2: 7 comfort *him,* lest perhaps **s a one** should be *5108*
3: 4 And **s** trust have we through Christ to *5108*
3:12 Seeing then that we have **s** hope, we use *5108*
10:11 Let **s a one** think this, that, such as we are *5108*
10:11 **s as** we are in word by letters when we are *3634*
10:11 **s** *will we be* also in deed when we are *5108*
11:13 For **s** *are* false apostles, deceitful workers, *5108*
12: 2 **s a one** caught up to the third heaven. *5108*
12: 3 And I knew **s** a man, (whether in the body, *5108*
12: 5 Of **s a one** will I glory: yet of myself I will *5108*
12:20 I shall not find you **s as** I would, and *that* I *3634*
12:20 *that* I shall be found unto you **s as** ye would *3634*
Gal 5:21 drunkenness, revellings, and **s** like: *3778*
5:21 that they which do **s** *things* shall not inherit *5108*
5:23 against **s** there is no law. *5108*
6: 1 restore **s a one** in the spirit of meekness; *5108*
Eph 5:27 or any **s** *thing;* but that it should be holy *5108*
Php 2:29 with all gladness; and hold **s** in reputation: *5108*
1Th 4: 6 that the Lord *is* the avenger of all **s,** *3778*
2Th 3:12 Now *them that are* **s** we command and *5108*
1Ti 6: 5 gain is godliness: from **s** withdraw thyself. *5108*
2Ti 3: 5 the power thereof: from **s** turn away. *3778*
Tit 3:11 Knowing that *he that is* **s** is subverted, and *5108*
Phm 1: 9 *thee,* being **s a one** as Paul the aged, *5108*
Heb 5:12 and are become **s** as have need of milk, and NIG
7:26 For **s** a high priest became us, *who is* holy, *5108*
8: 1 We have **s** a high priest, who is set on *5108*
11:14 For they that say **s** *things* declare plainly *5108*
12: 3 For consider him that endured **s** *5108*
13: 5 *and be* content with **s** *things* as ye have: *3588*
13:16 for with **s** sacrifices God is well pleased. *5108*
Jas 4:13 or to morrow we will go into **s** a city, *3592*
4:16 in your boastings: all **s** rejoicing is evil. *5108*
2Pe 1:17 when there came **s** a voice to him from *5107*
3:14 seeing that ye look for **s** *things,* be diligent *3778*
3Jn 1: 8 We therefore ought to receive **s,** that we *5108*
Rev 5:13 and **s** as are in the sea, and all that are in *3739*
16:18 **s** as was not since men were upon the earth, *3634*
20: 6 on **s** the second death hath no power, but *3778*

SUCHATHITES (1)

1Ch 2:55 the Tirathites, the Shimeathites, *and* **S.** 7756

SUCK (19) [SUCKED, SUCKING, SUCKLING, SUCKLINGS]

Ge 21: 7 that Sarah should have **given** children **s**? 3243
Dt 32:13 he **made** him **to s** honey out of the rock, 3243
33:19 for they shall **s** *of* the abundance of 3243
1Sa 1:23 and **gave** her son **s** until she weaned him. 3243
1Ki 3:21 I rose in the morning to **give** my child **s,** 3243
Job 3:12 or why the breasts that I should **s**? 3243
20:16 He shall **s** the poison of asps: the viper's 3243
39:30 Her young ones also **s up** blood: and where 5966
Isa 60:16 Thou shalt also **s** the milk of the Gentiles, 3243
60:16 the Gentiles, and shalt **s** the breast of kings: 3243
66:11 That ye may **s,** and be satisfied with 3243
66:12 shall ye **s,** ye shall be borne upon *her* sides, 3243
La 4: 3 the breast, they **give s** to their young ones: 3243
Eze 23:34 Thou shalt even drink it and **s** *it* **out,** and 4680
Joel 2:16 the children, and **those that s** the breasts: 3243
Mt 24:19 and to them that **give s** in those days. *2337*
Mk 13:17 and to them that **give s** in those days. *2337*
Lk 21:23 and to them that **give s,** in those days, *2337*
23:29 and the paps which never **gave s.** *2337*

SUCKED (2) [SUCK]

SS 8: 1 my brother, that **s** the breasts of my mother! 3243
Lk 11:27 bare thee, and the paps which thou hast **s.** *2337*

SUCKING (5) [SUCK]

Nu 11:12 as a nursing father beareth the **s child,** 3243
1Sa 7: 9 Samuel took a **s** lamb, and offered it *for* a 2461
Isa 11: 8 the **s child** shall play on the hole of the asp, 3243
49:15 Can a woman forget her **s child,** that *she* 5764
La 4: 4 The tongue of the **s child** cleaveth to 3243

SUCKLING (3) [SUCK]

Dt 32:25 the **s** *also* with the man of gray hairs. 3243
1Sa 15: 3 infant and **s,** ox and sheep, camel and ass. 3243
Jer 44: 7 off from you man and woman, child and **s,** 3243

SUCKLINGS (4) [SUCK]

1Sa 22:19 children and **s,** and oxen, and asses, and 3243
Ps 8: 2 **s** hast thou ordained strength because 3243
La 2:11 and the **s** swoon in the streets of the city. 3243
Mt 21:16 of babes and **s** thou hast perfected praise? *2337*

SUDDEN (3) [SUDDENLY]

Job 22:10 round about thee, and **s** fear troubleth thee; 6597
Pr 3:25 Be not afraid of **s** fear, neither of 6597
1Th 5: 3 then **s** destruction cometh upon them, *160*

SUDDENLY (41) [SUDDEN]

Nu 6: 9 if any man die **very s** by him, 6597+6621+871.1
12: 4 the LORD spake **s** unto Moses, and 6597
35:22 if he thrust him **s** without enmity, or 6621+871.1
Dt 7: 4 be kindled against you, and destroy thee **s.** 4118
Jos 10: 9 Joshua therefore came unto them **s,** *and* 6597
11: 7 against them by the waters of Merom **s;** 6597
2Sa 15:14 lest he overtake us **s,** and bring evil upon 4116
2Ch 29:36 the people: for the thing was *done* **s.** 6597+871.1
Job 5: 3 taking root: but **s** I cursed his habitation. 6597
9:23 If the scourge slay **s,** he will laugh at 6597
Ps 6:10 let them return *and* be ashamed **s.** 7281
64: 4 **s** do they shoot at him, and fear not. 6597
64: 7 *with* an arrow; **s** shall they be wounded. 6597
Pr 6:15 Therefore shall his calamity come **s;** 6597
6:15 **s** shall he be broken without remedy. 6621
24:22 For their calamity shall rise **s;** and 6597
29: 1 shall **s** be destroyed, and that without 6621
Ecc 9:12 in an evil time, when it falleth **s** upon them. 6597
Isa 29: 5 passeth away: yea, it shall be at an instant **s.** 6597
30:13 whose breaking cometh **s** at an instant. 6597
47:11 desolation shall come upon thee **s,** 6597
48: 3 I did *them* **s,** and they came to pass. 6597
Jer 4:20 **s** are my tents spoiled, *and* my curtains in a 6597
6:26 for the spoiler shall **s** come upon us. 6597
15: 8 I have caused *him* to fall upon it **s,** and 6597
18:22 when thou shalt bring a troop **s** upon them: 6597
49:19 I will **s** make him run away from her: and 7280
50:44 I will make them **s** run away from her: and 7280
51: 8 Babylon is **s** fallen and destroyed: howl for 6597
Hab 2: 7 Shall they not rise up **s** that *shall* bite thee, 6621
Mal 3: 1 whom ye seek, shall **s** come to his temple, 6597
Mk 9: 8 And **s,** when they had looked round about, *1819*
13:36 Lest coming **s** he find you sleeping. *1810*
Lk 2:13 And **s** there was with the angel a multitude *1810*
9:39 a spirit taketh him, and he **s** crieth out; *1810*
Ac 2: 2 And **s** there came a sound from heaven as of *869*
9: 3 **s** there shined round about him a light from *1810*
16:26 And **s** there was a great earthquake, so *869*
22: 6 **s** there shone from heaven a great light *1810*
28: 6 should have swollen, or fallen down dead **s:** *869*
1Ti 5:22 Lay hands **s** on no *man,* neither be partaker *5030*

SUE (1)

Mt 5:40 And if any man will **s** thee **at the law,** and *2919*

SUFFER (96) [LONGSUFFERING, SUFFERED, SUFFEREST, SUFFERETH, SUFFERING, SUFFERINGS]

Ex 12:23 will not **s** the destroyer to come in unto 5414
22:18 Thou shalt not **s** a witch **to live.** 2421
Lev 2:13 **s** the salt of the covenant of thy God
to be lacking 7673
19:17 thy neighbour, and not **s** sin upon him. 5375
22:16 Or **s** them **to bear** the iniquity of trespass, 5375
Nu 21:23 Sihon would not **s** Israel to pass through his 5414
Jos 10:19 of them; **s** them not to enter into their cities: 5414
Jdg 1:34 for they would not **s** them to come down to 5414
15: 1 But her father would not **s** him to go in. 5414
16:26 **S** me that I may feel the pillars whereupon 3240
2Sa 14:11 that thou wouldest **not s** the revengers of 4480
1Ki 15:17 that *he* might not **s** *any* to go out or come in 5414
Est 3: 8 it *is* not for the king's profit to **s** them. 3240
Job 9:18 He will not **s** me to take my breath, but 5414

S

Job 21: 3 **S** me that I may speak; and after that I have 5375
24:11 *and* tread *their* winepresses, and **s thirst.** 6770
36: 2 **S** me a little, and I will shew thee that *I* 3803
Ps 9:13 consider my trouble *which I* **s** of them that NIH
16:10 neither wilt thou **s** thine Holy One to see 5414
34:10 The young lions do lack, and **s hunger**: 7456
55:22 he shall never **s** the righteous to be moved. 5414
88:15 ready to die from *my* youth *up: while* I **s** 5375
89:33 take from him, nor **s** my faithfulness **to fail.** 8266
101: 5 a high look and a proud heart will not I **s.** 3201
121: 3 He will not **s** thy foot to be moved: he that 5414
Pr 10: 3 not **s** the soul of the righteous **to famish**: 7456
19:15 deep sleep; and an idle soul shall **s hunger.** 7456
19:19 *A man* of great wrath *shall* **s** punishment: 5375
Ecc 5: 6 **S** not thy mouth to cause thy flesh to sin; 5414
5:12 the abundance of the rich will not **s** him to 3240
Eze 44:20 their heads, nor **s** *their* locks **to grow long**; 7971
Mt 3:15 answering said unto him, **S** *it to be so* now: *863*
8:21 Lord, **s** me first to go and bury my father. *2010*
8:31 **s** us to go away into the herd of swine. *2010*
16:21 and **s** many *things* of the elders and *3958*
17:12 Likewise shall also the Son of man **s** of *3958*
17:17 how long shall I **s** you? bring him hither to *430*
19:14 **S** little children, and forbid them not, *863*
23:13 neither **s** ye them that are entering to go in. *863*
Mk 7:12 And ye **s** him no more to do ought for his *863*
8:31 that the Son of man must **s** many *things,* *3958*
9:12 that he must **s** many *things,* and be set at *3958*
9:19 how long shall I **s** you? bring him unto me. *430*
10:14 **S** the little children to come unto me, and *863*
11:16 And would not **s** that any *man* should carry *863*
Lk 8:32 they besought him that he would **s** them to *2010*
9:22 The Son of man must **s** many *things,* and *3958*
9:41 how long shall I be with you, and **s** you? *430*
9:59 Lord, **s** me first to go and bury my father. *2010*
17:25 But first must he **s** many *things,* and *3958*
18:16 **S** little children to come unto me, and *863*
22:15 to eat this passover with you before I **s**: *3958*
22:51 And Jesus answered and said, **S** ye thus far. *1439*
24:46 and thus it behoved Christ to **s,** and to rise *3958*
Ac 2:27 neither wilt thou **s** thine Holy One to see *1325*
3:18 that Christ should **s,** he hath so fulfilled. *3958*
5:41 counted worthy to **s shame** for his name. *818*
7:24 And seeing one *of them* **s wrong,** he defended *91*
9:16 great *things* he must **s** for my name's sake. *3958*
13:35 not **s** thine Holy One to see corruption. *1325*
21:39 **s** me to speak unto the people. *2010*
26:23 That Christ should **s,** *and* that he *should be* 3805
Ro 8:17 be that we **s with** *him,* that we may be also *4841*
1Co 3:15 *man's* work shall be burnt, he shall **s loss**: *2210*
4:12 we bless; being persecuted, we **s** *it:* *430*
6: 7 why do ye not rather **s** *yourselves to* be NIG
9:12 **s** all *things,* lest we should hinder *4722*
10:13 who will not **s** you to be tempted above that *1439*
12:26 And whether one member **s,** all *3958*
12:26 all the members **s with** *it;* or one member *4841*
2Co 1: 6 of the same sufferings which we also **s**: *3958*
11:19 For ye **s** fools gladly, seeing ye *yourselves* *430*
11:20 For ye **s,** if a man bring you into bondage, *430*
Gal 5:11 why do I yet **s persecution**? *1377*
6:12 only lest they should **s persecution** for *1377*
Php 1:29 to believe on him, but also to **s** for his sake; *3958*
4:12 to be hungry, both to abound and to **s need.** *5302*
1Th 3: 4 you before that we should **s tribulation**; *2346*
2Th 1: 5 of the kingdom of God, for which ye also **s**: *3958*
1Ti 2:12 But I **s** not a woman to teach, nor to usurp *2010*
4:10 therefore we both labour and **s reproach,** *3679*
2Ti 1:12 For the which cause I also **s** these *things:* *3958*
2: 9 Wherein I **s trouble,** as an evil doer, *2553*
2:12 If we **s,** we shall also reign with *him:* if we *5278*
3:12 godly in Christ Jesus shall **s persecution.** *1377*
Heb 11:25 Choosing rather to **s affliction with** *4778*
13: 3 with *them; and* them which **s adversity,** *2558*
13:22 brethren, **s** the word of exhortation: *430*
1Pe 2:20 ye do well, and **s** *for it,* ye take it patiently, *3958*
3:14 But and if ye **s** for righteousness' sake, *3958*
3:17 that *ye* **s** for well doing, than for evil doing. *3958*
4:15 But let none of you **s** as a murderer, or *as* a *3958*
4:16 Yet if *any man* **s** as a Christian, let him not NIG
4:19 Wherefore let them that **s** according to *3958*
Rev 2:10 none *of those things* which thou shalt **s.** *3958*
11: 9 shall not **s** their dead bodies to be put in *863*

SUFFERED (50) [SUFFER]

Ge 20: 6 therefore **s** I thee not to touch her. 5414
31: 7 ten times; but God **s** him not to hurt me. 5414
31:28 hast not **s** me to kiss my sons and my 5203
Dt 8: 3 **s** thee **to hunger,** and fed thee with manna, 7456
18:14 the LORD thy God hath not **s** thee so 5414
Jdg 3:28 toward Moab, and **s** not a man to pass over. 5414
1Sa 24: 7 and **s** them not to rise against Saul. 5414
2Sa 21:10 **s** neither the birds of the air to rest on them 5414
1Ch 16:21 He **s** no man to do them wrong: yea, 3240
Job 31:30 (Neither have I **s** my mouth to sin by 5414
Ps 105:14 He **s** no man to do them wrong: yea, 3240
Jer 15:15 know that for thy sake I have **s** rebuke. 5375
Mt 3:15 us to fulfil all righteousness. Then he **s** him. *863*
19: 8 of the hardness of your hearts **s** you to put *2010*
24:43 would not have **s** his house to be broken up. *1439*
27:19 for I have **s** many *things* this day in a dream *3958*
Mk 1:34 and **s** not the devils to speak, because *863*
5:19 Howbeit Jesus **s** him not, but saith unto him, *863*
5:26 And had **s** many *things* of many physicians, *3958*
5:37 And he **s** no *man* to follow him, save Peter, *863*
10: 4 Moses **s** to write a bill of divorcement, and *2010*
Lk 4:41 And he rebuking *them* **s** them not to speak: *1439*
8:32 them to enter into them. And he **s** them. *2010*
8:51 the house, he **s** no *man* to go in, save Peter, *863*
12:39 not have **s** his house to be broken through. *863*
13: 2 the Galileans, because they **s** such *things?* *3958*
24:26 Ought not Christ to have **s** these *things,* and *3958*
Ac 13:18 years **s** he their **manners** in the wilderness. *5159*
14:16 Who in times past **s** all nations to walk in *1439*
16: 7 go into Bithynia: but the Spirit **s** them not. *1439*
17: 3 that Christ must needs have **s,** and *3958*
19:30 in unto the people, the disciples **s** him not. *1439*
28:16 Paul was **s** to dwell by himself with a *2010*
2Co 7:12 nor for his cause that **s wrong,** but that our *91*
11:25 thrice I **s shipwrack,** a night and a day I *3489*
Gal 3: 4 Have ye **s** so many *things* in vain? if *it be* *3958*
Php 3: 8 for whom I have **s** the **loss** of all *things,* and *2210*
1Th 2: 2 But even after that we had **s before,** and *4310*
2:14 for ye also have **s** like *things* of your own *3958*
Heb 2:18 For in that he himself hath **s** being tempted, *3958*
5: 8 he obedience by *the things* which he **s**; *3958*
7:23 *they* were **not s** to continue by reason of *2967*
9:26 must he often have **s** since the foundation *3958*
13:12 with his own blood, **s** without the gate. *3958*
1Pe 2:21 because Christ also **s** for us, leaving us an *3958*
2:23 when he **s,** he threatened not; but *3958*
3:18 For Christ also hath once **s** for sins, the just *3958*
4: 1 then as Christ hath **s** for us in the flesh, *3958*
4: 1 for he that hath **s** in the flesh hath ceased *3958*
5:10 after that ye have **s** a while, make you *3958*

SUFFEREST (1) [SUFFER]

Rev 2:20 because thou **s** *that* woman Jezebel, *1439*

SUFFERETH (5) [SUFFER]

Ps 66: 9 soul in life, and **s** not our feet to be moved. 5414
107:38 and **s** not their cattle **to decrease.** 4591
Mt 11:12 until now the kingdom of heaven **s violence,** *971*
Ac 28: 4 the sea, yet Vengeance **s** not to live. *1439*
1Co 13: 4 Charity **s long,** *and* is kind; charity envieth *3114*

SUFFERING (5) [SUFFER]

Ac 27: 7 the wind not **s** us, we sailed under Crete, *4330*
Heb 2: 9 for the **s** of death, crowned with glory and *3804*
Jas 5:10 for an example of **s affliction,** and *2552*
1Pe 2:19 toward God endure grief, **s** wrongfully. *3958*
Jude 1: 7 an example, **s** the vengeance of eternal fire. *5254*

SUFFERINGS (10) [SUFFER]

Ro 8:18 For I reckon that the **s** of *this* present time *3804*
2Co 1: 5 For as the **s** of Christ abound in us, so *3804*
1: 6 of the same **s** which we also suffer: *3804*
1: 7 that as you are partakers of the **s,** so *3804*
Php 3:10 his resurrection, and the fellowship of his **s,** *3804*
Col 1:24 Who now rejoice in my **s** for you, and *3804*
Heb 2:10 captain of their salvation perfect through **s.** *3804*
1Pe 1:11 when it testified beforehand the **s** of Christ, *3804*
4:13 inasmuch as ye are partakers of Christ's **s**; *3804*
5: 1 and a witness of the **s** of Christ, and also a *3804*

SUFFICE (7) [SUFFICED, SUFFICETH, SUFFICIENCY, SUFFICIENT, SUFFICIENTLY]

Nu 11:22 and the herds be slain for them, to **s** them? 4672
11:22 be gathered together for them, to **s** them? 4672
Dt 3:26 the LORD said unto me, Let it **s** thee; 7227
1Ki 20:10 if the dust of Samaria shall **s** for handfuls 5606
Eze 44: 6 let it **s** you of all your abominations, 7227
45: 9 Let it **s** you, O princes of Israel: 7227
1Pe 4: 3 For the time past of *our* life may **s** us to have *713*

SUFFICED (3) [SUFFICE]

Jdg 21:14 and yet so they **s** them not. 4672
Ru 2:14 and she did eat, and was **s,** and left. 7646
2:18 to her that she had reserved after she was **s.** 7648

SUFFICETH (1) [SUFFICE]

Jn 14: 8 Lord, shew us the Father, and it **s** us. *714*

SUFFICIENCY (3) [SUFFICE]

Job 20:22 In the fulness of his **s** he shall be in straits: 5607
2Co 3: 5 *thing* as of ourselves; but our **s** *is* of God; *2426*
9: 8 always having all **s** in all *things,* may abound *841*

SUFFICIENT (13) [SUFFICE]

Ex 36: 7 For the stuff *they had* was **s** for all the work 1767
Dt 15: 8 shalt surely lend him **s for** his need, *in that* 1767
33: 7 let his hands *be* **s** for him; and be thou a 7227
Pr 25:16 eat **so much as is s** for thee, lest thou be 1767
Isa 40:16 Lebanon *is* not **s** to burn, nor the beasts 1767
40:16 nor the beasts thereof **s** *for* a burnt offering. 1767
Mt 6:34 of itself. **S** unto the day *is* the evil thereof. *713*
Lk 14:28 the cost, whether he have **s** to finish it? *3588*
Jn 6: 7 Two hundred pennyworth of bread is not **s** *714*
2Co 2: 6 **S** to such *a man is* this punishment, *2425*
2:16 unto life. And who *is* **s** for these *things?* *2425*
3: 5 Not that we are **s** of ourselves to think any *2425*
12: 9 And he said unto me, My grace is **s** for thee: *714*

SUFFICIENTLY (2) [SUFFICE]

2Ch 30: 3 had not sanctified themselves **s,** 4078+3807.1
Isa 23:18 to eat **s,** and for durable clothing. 7654+3807.1

SUIT (3) [SUITS]

Jdg 17:10 and a **s** of apparel, and thy victuals. 6187
2Sa 15: 4 that every man which hath *any* **s** or 7379
Job 11:19 yea, many shall **make s** unto thee. 2470

SUITS (1) [SUIT]

Isa 3:22 The **changeable s of apparel,** and 4254

SUKKIIMS (1)

2Ch 12: 3 the Lubims, the **S,** and the Ethiopians. 5525

SUKKITES See SUKKIIMS

SULPHUR See BRIMSTONE

SUM (21)

Ex 21:30 If there be laid on him a **s of money,** then 3724
30:12 When thou takest the **s** of the children of 7218
38:21 This is the **s** of the tabernacle, *even* of 6485
Nu 1: 2 Take ye the **s** of all the congregation of 7218
1:49 neither take the **s** of them among 7218
4: 2 Take the **s** of the sons of Kohath from 7218
4:22 Take also the **s** of the sons of Gershon, 7218
26: 2 Take the **s** of all the congregation of 7218
26: 4 *Take the* **s** *of the people,* from twenty years NIH
31:26 Take the **s** of the prey that was taken, *both* 7218
31:49 Thy servants have taken the **s** of the men of 7218
2Sa 24: 9 Joab gave *up* the **s** of the number of 4557
2Ki 22: 4 that he may **s** the silver which is brought 8552
1Ch 21: 5 Joab gave the **s** of the number of the people 4557
Est 4: 7 of the **s** of the money that Haman had 6575
Ps 139:17 O God: how great is the **s** of them! 7218
Eze 28:12 Thou sealest up the **s,** full *of* wisdom, and 8508
Da 7: 1 the dream, *and* told the **s** of the matters. 7217
Ac 7:16 **s** of money of the sons of Emmor the *father* *5092*
22:28 With a great **s** obtained I this freedom. *2774*
Heb 8: 1 *things* which we have spoken *this is* the **s**: *2774*

SUMMER (27)

Ge 8:22 **s** and winter, and day and night shall not 7019
Jdg 3:20 he was sitting in a **s** parlour, which he had 4747
3:24 Surely he covereth his feet in *his* **s** 4747
2Sa 16: 1 an hundred of **s fruits,** and a bottle of wine. 7019
16: 2 and **s fruit** for the young men to eat; 7019
Ps 32: 4 my moisture is turned into the drought of **s.** 7019
74:17 of the earth: thou hast made **s** and winter. 7019
Pr 6: 8 Provideth her meat in the **s,** *and* 7019
10: 5 He that gathereth in **s** *is* a wise son: *but* 7019
26: 1 As snow in **s,** and as rain in harvest, so 7019
30:25 yet they prepare their meat in the **s**; 7019
Isa 16: 9 for the shouting for thy **s fruits** and for thy 7019
18: 6 the fowls shall **s** upon them, and all 6972
28: 4 *and* as the hasty fruit before the **s**; 7019
Jer 8:20 is past, the **s** is ended, and we are not saved. 7019
40:10 **s fruits,** and oil, and put *them* in your 7019
40:12 and gathered wine and **s fruits** very much. 7019
48:32 the spoiler is fallen upon thy **s fruits** and 7019
Da 2:35 became like the chaff of the **s** 7007
Am 3:15 I will smite the winter house with the **s** 7019
8: 1 unto me: and behold, a basket of **s fruit.** 7019
8: 2 I said, A basket of **s fruit.** Then said 7019
Mic 7: 1 am as when they have gathered the **s fruits,** 7019
Zec 14: 8 the hinder sea: in **s** and in winter shall it be. 7019
Mt 24:32 putteth forth leaves, ye know that **s** *is* nigh: *2330*
Mk 13:28 putteth forth leaves, ye know that **s** is near: *2330*
Lk 21:30 know of your own selves that **s** is now nigh *2330*

SUMPTUOUSLY (1)

Lk 16:19 and fine linen, and fared **s** every day: *2988*

SUN (160) [SUNRISING]

Ge 15:12 when the **s** was going down, a deep sleep 8121
15:17 when the **s** went down, and it was dark, 8121
19:23 The **s** was risen upon the earth when Lot 8121
28:11 there all night, because the **s** was set; 8121
32:31 as he passed over Penuel the **s** rose upon 8121
37: 9 the **s** and the moon and the eleven stars 8121
Ex 16:21 and when the **s** waxed hot, it melted. 8121
17:12 were steady until the going down of the **s.** 8121
22: 3 If the **s** be risen upon him, *there shall be* 8121
22:26 thou shalt deliver it unto him by that the **s** 8121
Lev 22: 7 when the **s** is down, he shall be clean, and 8121
Nu 2: 3 on the east side toward the **rising of the s** 4217
25: 4 them up before the LORD against the **s,** 8121
Dt 4:19 when thou seest the **s,** and the moon, and 8121
11:30 by the way where the **s** goeth down, in 8121
16: 6 at the going down of the **s,** at the season 8121
17: 3 either the **s,** or moon, or any of the host of 8121
23:11 when the **s** is down, he shall come into 8121
24:13 the pledge again when the **s** goeth down, 8121
24:15 his hire, neither shall the **s** go down upon it; 8121
33:14 the precious fruits brought forth by the **s,** 8121
Jos 1: 4 great sea *toward* the going down of the **s,** 8121
8:29 as soon as the **s** was down, 8121
10:12 he said in the sight of Israel, **S,** stand thou 8121
10:13 the **s** stood still, and the moon stayed, 8121
10:13 So the **s** stood still in the midst of heaven, 8121
10:27 pass at the time of the going down of the **s,** 8121
12: 1 *other* side Jordan toward the rising of the **s,** 8121
Jdg 5:31 *let* them that love him *be* as the **s** when he 8121
8:13 returned from battle before the **s** was up, 2775
9:33 *that* in the morning, as soon as the **s** is up, 8121
14:18 on the seventh day before the **s** went down, 2775
19:14 the **s** went down upon them *when they* 8121
1Sa 11: 9 To morrow, by *that time* the **s** be hot, 8121
2Sa 2:24 the **s** went down when they were come to 8121
3:35 or ought else, till the **s** be down. 8121
12:11 he with thy wives in the sight of this **s.** 8121
12:12 this thing before all Israel, and before the **s.** 8121
23: 4 *when* the **s** riseth, *even* a morning without 8121
1Ki 22:36 the host about the going down of the **s,** 8121
2Ki 3:22 the **s** shone upon the water, and 8121
23: 5 to the **s,** and to the moon, and to 8121
23:11 that the kings of Judah had given to the **s,** 8121
23:11 and burnt the chariots of the **s** with fire. 8121
2Ch 18:34 about the time of the **s** going down he died. 8121
Ne 7: 3 of Jerusalem be opened until the **s** be hot; 8121
Job 8:16 He *is* green before the **s,** and his branch 8121
9: 7 Which commandeth the **s,** and it riseth not; 2775
30:28 I went mourning without the **s**: I stood up, 2535
31:26 If I beheld the **s** when it shined, or the moon 216
Ps 19: 4 In them hath he set a tabernacle for the **s,** 8121
50: 1 called the earth from the rising of the **s** unto 8121
58: 8 of a woman, *that* they may not see the **s.** 8121
72: 5 They shall fear thee as long as the **s** and 8121
72:17 name shall be continued as long as the **s**: 8121
74:16 thou hast prepared the light and the **s.** 8121
84:11 For the LORD God *is* a **s** and shield: 8121
89:36 for ever, and his throne as the **s** before me. 8121
104:19 for seasons: the **s** knoweth his going down. 8121
104:22 The **s** ariseth, they gather themselves 8121
113: 3 From the rising of the **s** unto the going 8121
121: 6 The **s** shall not smite thee by day, nor 8121
136: 8 The **s** to rule by day: for his mercy *endureth* 8121
148: 3 Praise ye him, **s** and moon: praise him, 8121
Ecc 1: 3 all his labour which he taketh under the **s**? 8121

S

Ecc 1: 5 The **s** also ariseth, and the sun goeth down, 8121
1: 5 the **s** goeth down, and hasteth to his place 8121
1: 9 and *there is* no new *thing* under the **s**. 8121
1:14 seen all the works that are done under the **s**; 8121
2:11 and *there was* no profit under the **s**. 8121
2:17 the work that is wrought under the **s** *is* 8121
2:18 my labour which I *had* taken under the **s**: 8121
2:19 I have shewed myself wise under the **s**. 8121
2:20 of all the labour which I took under the **s**. 8121
2:22 wherein he *hath* laboured under the **s**? 8121
3:16 moreover I saw under the **s** the place of 8121
4: 1 the oppressions that *are* done under the **s**: 8121
4: 3 seen the evil work that is done under the **s**. 8121
4: 7 I returned, and I saw vanity under the **s**. 8121
4:15 all the living which walk under the **s**, 8121
5:13 is a sore evil *which* I have seen under the **s**, 8121
5:18 he taketh under the **s** all the days of his life, 8121
6: 1 is an evil which I have seen under the **s**, 8121
6: 5 Moreover he hath not seen the **s**, nor known 8121
6:12 a man what shall be after him under the **s**? 8121
7:11 *by it there is* profit to them that see the **s**. 8121
8: 9 unto every work that is done under the **s**: 8121
8:15 a man hath no better *thing* under the **s**, 8121
8:15 his life, which God giveth him under the **s**. 8121
8:17 find out the work that is done under the **s**: 8121
9: 3 among all *things* that are done under the **s**, 8121
9: 6 ever in any *thing* that is done under the **s**. 8121
9: 9 which he hath given thee under the **s**, 8121
9: 9 in thy labour which thou takest under the **s**. 8121
9:11 I returned, and saw under the **s**, that 8121
9:13 This wisdom have I seen also under the **s**, 8121
10: 5 is an evil *which* I have seen under the **s**, 8121
11: 7 *thing it is* for the eyes to behold the **s**: 8121
12: 2 While the **s**, or the light, or the moon, or 8121
SS 1: 6 because the **s** hath looked upon me: 8121
6:10 clear as the **s**, *and* terrible as *an army* with 2535
Isa 13:10 the **s** shall be darkened in his going forth, 8121
24:23 shall be confounded, and the **s** ashamed, 2535
30:26 of the moon shall be as the light of the **s**, 2535
30:26 the light of the **s** shall be sevenfold, as 2535
38: 8 which is gone down in the **s** dial of Ahaz, 8121
38: 8 So the **s** returned ten degrees, by which 8121
41:25 from the rising of the **s** shall he call upon 8121
45: 6 they may know from the rising of the **s**, 8121
49:10 neither shall the heat nor **s** smite them: 8121
59:19 and his glory from the rising of the **s**. 8121
60:19 The **s** shall be no more thy light by day; 8121
60:20 Thy **s** shall no more go down; neither shall 8121
Jer 8: 2 they shall spread them before the **s**, and 8121
15: 9 her **s** is gone down while *it was* yet day: 8121
31:35 which giveth the **s** for a light by day, *and* 8121
Eze 8:16 and they worshipped the **s** towards the east. 8121
32: 7 I will cover the **s** with a cloud, and 8121
Da 6:14 he laboured till the going down of the **s** to 8122
Joel 2:10 the **s** and the moon shall be dark, and 8121
2:31 The **s** shall be turned into darkness, and 8121
3:15 The **s** and the moon shall be darkened, and 8121
Am 8: 9 that I will cause the **s** to go down at noon, 8121
Jnh 4: 8 it came to pass, when the **s** did arise, 8121
4: 8 the **s** beat upon the head of Jonah, that he 8121
Mic 3: 6 the **s** shall go down over the prophets, and 8121
Na 3:17 *but* when the **s** ariseth they flee away, and 8121
Hab 3:11 The **s** *and* moon stood still in *their* 8121
Mal 1:11 For from the rising of the **s** even unto 8121
4: 2 unto you that fear my name shall the **S** of 8121
Mt 5:45 for he maketh his **s** to rise on the evil and *2246*
13: 6 And when the **s** was up, they were *2246*
13:43 Then shall the righteous shine forth as the **s** *2246*
17: 2 and his face did shine as the **s**, and *2246*
24:29 of those days shall the **s** be darkened, *2246*
Mk 1:32 And at even, when the **s** did set, *2246*
4: 6 But when the **s** was up, it was scorched; *2246*
13:24 the **s** shall be darkened, and the moon shall *2246*
16: 2 unto the sepulchre at the rising of the **s**. *2246*
Lk 4:40 Now when the **s** was setting, all they that *2246*
21:25 And there shall be signs in the **s**, and in *2246*
23:45 And the **s** was darkened, and the vail of *2246*
Ac 2:20 The **s** shall be turned into darkness, and *2246*
13:11 shalt be blind, not seeing the **s** for a season. *2246*
26:13 above the brightness of the **s**, shining round *2246*
27:20 And when neither **s** nor stars in many days *2246*
1Co 15:41 *There is* one glory of the **s**, and *2246*
Eph 4:26 let not the **s** go down upon your wrath: *2246*
Jas 1:11 For the **s** is no sooner risen with a burning *2246*
Rev 1:16 his countenance *was* as the **s** shineth in his *2246*
6:12 and the **s** became black as sackcloth of hair, *2246*
7:16 neither shall the **s** light on them, nor any *2246*
8:12 and the third *part* of the **s** was smitten, and *2246*
9: 2 and the **s** and the air were darkened by *2246*
10: 1 and his face *was* as *it were* the **s**, and *2246*
12: 1 a woman clothed with the **s**, and the moon *2246*
16: 8 fourth angel poured out his vial upon the **s**; *2246*
19:17 And I saw an angel standing in the **s**; and *2246*
21:23 And the city had no need of the **s**, neither of *2246*
22: 5 they need no candle, neither light of the **s**; *2246*

SUNDER (7) [SUNDERED]

Ps 46: 9 the bow, and **cutteth** the spear **in s**; 7112
107:14 of death, and **brake** their bands **in s**. 5423
107:16 gates of brass, and **cut** the bars of iron **in s**. 1438
Isa 27: 9 the altar as chalkstones that are **beaten in s**, 5310
45: 2 gates of brass, and **cut in s** the bars of iron: 1438
Na 1:13 off thee, and will **burst** thy bonds **in s**. 5423
Lk 12:46 and will **cut** him **in s**, and will appoint *him* *1371*

SUNDERED (1) [SUNDER]

Job 41:17 they stick together, that they cannot be **s**. 6504

SUNDRY (1)

Heb 1: 1 God, who **at s** times and in divers manners *3588*

SUNG (6) [SING]

Ezr 3:11 they **s** together by course in praising and 6030
Isa 26: 1 In that day shall this song be **s** in the land 7891
Mt 26:30 And when they had **s a hymn**, they went *5214*
Mk 14:26 And when they had **s a hymn**, they went *5214*
Rev 5: 9 And they **s** a new song, saying, Thou art *103*
14: 3 And they **s** as *it were* a new song before *103*

SUNK (7) [SINK]

1Sa 17:49 that the stone **s** into his forehead; 2883
2Ki 9:24 at his heart, and he **s down** in his chariot. 3766
Ps 9:15 The heathen are **s down** in the pit *that* they 2883
Jer 38: 6 but mire: so Jeremiah **s** in the mire. 2883
38:22 thy feet are **s** in the mire, *and* they are 2883
La 2: 9 Her gates are **s** into the ground; he hath 2883
Ac 20: 9 he **s down** with sleep, and fell down from *2702*

SUNRISING (10) [RISE, SUN]

Nu 21:11 which *is* before Moab, toward the **s**. 4217+8121
34:15 Jordan *near* Jericho eastward, toward the **s**. 4217
Dt 4:41 on *this* side Jordan toward the **s**; 4217+8121
4:47 on *this* side Jordan *toward* the **s**; 4217+8121
Jos 1:15 you on *this* side Jordan *toward* the **s**. 4217+8121
13: 5 all Lebanon, *toward* the **s**, 4217+8121+1886.1
19:12 **s** unto the border of Chisloth-tabor, 4217+8121
19:27 turneth *toward* **the s** *to* 4217+8121+1886.1
19:34 upon Jordan *toward* **the s**. 4217+8121+1886.1
Jdg 20:43 over against Gibeah toward the **s**. 4217+8121

SUP (3) [SUPPED, SUPPER]

Hab 1: 9 their faces shall **s up** *as* the east wind, and 4041
Lk 17: 8 Make ready wherewith I may **s**, and *1172*
Rev 3:20 and will **s** with him, and he with me. *1172*

SUPERFLUITY (1) [SUPERFLUOUS]

Jas 1:21 lay apart all filthiness and **s** of naughtiness, *4050*

SUPERFLUOUS (3) [SUPERFLUITY]

Lev 21:18 or he that hath a flat nose, or any thing **s**, 8311
22:23 or a lamb that **hath any thing s** or 8311
2Co 9: 1 to the saints, it is **s** for me to write to you: *4053*

SUPERSCRIPTION (5)

Mt 22:20 saith unto them, Whose *is* this image and **s**? *1923*
Mk 12:16 saith unto them, Whose *is* this image and **s**? *1923*
15:26 And the **s** of his accusation was written *1923*
Lk 20:24 Whose image and **s** hath it? They answered *1923*
23:38 And a **s** also was written over him in letters *1923*

SUPERSTITION (1) [SUPERSTITIOUS]

Ac 25:19 questions against him of their own **s**, *1175*

SUPERSTITIOUS (1) [SUPERSTITION]

Ac 17:22 I perceive that in all *things* ye are **too s**. *1174*

SUPERVISION See SCHOOLMASTER

SUPPED (1) [SUP]

1Co 11:25 when *he* had **s**, saying, This cup is the new *1172*

SUPPER (14) [SUP]

Mk 6:21 that Herod on his birthday made a **s** to his *1173*
Lk 14:12 When thou makest a dinner or a **s**, call not *1173*
14:16 A certain man made a great **s**, and *1173*
14:17 And sent his servant at **s** time to say to *1173*
14:24 men which were bidden shall taste of my **s**. *1173*
22:20 Likewise also the cup after **s**, saying, *1172*
Jn 12: 2 There they made him a **s**; and Martha *1173*
13: 2 And **s** being ended, the devil having now *1173*
13: 4 He riseth from **s**, and laid aside *his* *1173*
21:20 which also leaned on his breast at **s**, and *1173*
1Co 11:20 one place, *this* is not to eat the Lord's **s**. *1173*
11:21 every one taketh before *other* his own **s**: *1173*
Rev 19: 9 are called unto the marriage **s** of the Lamb. *1173*
19:17 gather yourselves together unto the **s** of *1173*

SUPPLANT (1) [SUPPLANTED]

Jer 9: 4 for every brother will **utterly s**, 6117+6117

SUPPLANTED (1) [SUPPLANT]

Ge 27:36 for he hath **s** me these two times: he took 6117

SUPPLE (1)

Eze 16: 4 neither wast thou washed in water to **s** *thee;* 4935

SUPPLIANTS (1)

Zep 3:10 From beyond the rivers of Ethiopia my **s**, 6282

SUPPLICATION (39) [SUPPLICATIONS]

1Sa 13:12 and I have not **made s** unto the LORD: 2470
1Ki 8:28 to his **s**, O LORD my God, to hearken 8467
8:30 hearken thou to the **s** of thy servant, and 8467
8:33 pray, and **make s** unto thee in this house: 2603
8:38 and **s** soever be *made* by any man, 8467
8:45 hear thou *in* heaven their prayer and their **s**, 8467
8:47 **make s** unto thee in the land of them *that* 2603
8:49 and their **s** *in* heaven thy dwelling place, 8467
8:52 That thine eyes may be open unto the **s** of 8467
8:52 unto the **s** of thy people Israel, to hearken 8467
8:54 all this prayer and **s** unto the LORD, 8467
8:59 wherewith I have **made s** before 2603
9: 3 and thy **s**, that thou hast **made** before me: 8467
2Ch 6:19 to his **s**, O LORD my God, to hearken 8467
6:24 pray and **make s** before thee in this house; 2603
6:29 *or* what **s** soever shall be *made* of any man, 8467
6:35 from the heavens their prayer and their **s**, 8467
33:13 heard his **s**, and brought him again *to* 8467
Est 4: 8 to **make s** unto him, and to make request 2603
Job 8: 5 and **make** thy **s** to the Almighty; 2603
9:15 *but* I would **make s** to my judge. 2603
Ps 6: 9 The LORD hath heard my **s**; the LORD 8467
30: 8 O LORD; and unto the LORD I **made s**. 2603
55: 1 O God; and hide not thyself from my **s**. 8467
119:170 Let my **s** come before thee: deliver me 8467
142: 1 voice unto the LORD did I **make** my **s**. 2603
Isa 45:14 they shall **make s** unto thee, *saying,* Surely 6419
Jer 36: 7 It may be they will present their **s** before 8467
37:20 let my **s**, I pray thee, be accepted before 8467
38:26 I presented my **s** before the king, 8467
42: 2 our **s** be accepted before thee, and pray for 8467
42: 9 unto whom ye sent me to present your **s** 8467
Da 6:11 and **making s** before his God. 2604
9:20 presenting my **s** before the LORD my God 8467
Hos 12: 4 he wept, and **made s** unto him: he found 2603
Ac 1:14 continued with one accord in prayer and **s**, *1162*
Eph 6:18 always with all prayer and **s** in the Spirit, *1162*
6:18 with all perseverance and **s** for all saints; *1162*
Php 4: 6 **s** with thanksgiving let your requests be *1162*

SUPPLICATIONS (21) [SUPPLICATION]

2Ch 6:21 Hearken therefore unto the **s** of thy servant, 8469
6:39 their prayer and their **s**, and maintain their 8467
Job 41: 3 Will he make many **s** unto thee? will he 8469
Ps 28: 2 Hear the voice of my **s**, when I cry unto 8469
28: 6 because he hath heard the voice of my **s**. 8469
31:22 the voice of my **s** when I cried unto thee. 8469
86: 6 my prayer; and attend to the voice of my **s**. 8469
116: 1 he hath heard my voice *and* my **s**. 8469
130: 2 thine ears be attentive to the voice of my **s**. 8469
140: 6 my God: hear the voice of my **s**, O LORD. 8469
143: 1 my prayer, O LORD, give ear to my **s**: 8469
Jer 3:21 weeping *and* **s** of the children of Israel: 8469
31: 9 with weeping, and with **s** will I lead them: 8469
Da 9: 3 to seek *by* prayer and **s**, with fasting, and 8469
9:17 his **s**, and cause thy face to shine upon thy 8469
9:18 for we do not present our **s** before thee for 8469
9:23 At the beginning of thy **s** 8469
Zec 12:10 of Jerusalem, the spirit of grace and of **s**: 8469
1Ti 2: 1 therefore that, first of all, **s**, prayers, *1162*
5: 5 and continueth in **s** and prayers night and *1162*
Heb 5: 7 up prayers and **s** with strong crying and *2428*

SUPPLIED (2) [SUPPLY]

1Co 16:17 which was lacking on your part they have **s**. *378*
2Co 11: 9 brethren which came from Macedonia **s**: *4322*

SUPPLIES See CELLARS; STUFF

SUPPLIETH (2) [SUPPLY]

2Co 9:12 service not only **s** the want of the saints, *4322*
Eph 4:16 and compacted by that which every joint **s**, *2024*

SUPPLY (5) [SUPPLIED, SUPPLIETH]

2Co 8:14 your abundance *may be a* **s** for their want, NIG
8:14 that their abundance also may be *a* **s** for NIG
Php 1:19 and the **s** of the Spirit of Jesus Christ, *2024*
2:30 *his* life, to **s** your lack of service toward me. *378*
4:19 But my God shall **s** all your need according *4137*

SUPPORT (2)

Ac 20:35 so labouring *ye* ought to **s** the weak, *482*
1Th 5:14 comfort the feebleminded, **s** the weak, *472*

SUPPORTS See UNDERSETTERS

SUPPOSE (10) [SUPPOSED, SUPPOSING]

2Sa 13:32 Let not my lord **s** *that* they have slain all 559
Lk 7:43 said, I **s** that *he,* to whom he forgave most. *5274*
12:51 **S** ye that I am come to give peace on earth? *1380*
13: 2 **S** ye that these Galileans were sinners *1380*
Jn 21:25 I **s** that even the world itself could not *3633*
Ac 2:15 as ye **s**, seeing it is *but* the third hour of *5274*
1Co 7:26 I **s** therefore that this is good for the present *3543*
2Co 11: 5 For I **s** I was not a whit behind the very *3049*
Heb 10:29 **s** ye, shall he be thought worthy, *1380*
1Pe 5:12 as I **s**, I have written briefly, exhorting, and *3049*

SUPPOSED (8) [SUPPOSE]

Mt 20:10 they **s** that they should have received more; *3543*
Mk 6:49 they **s** *it* had been a spirit, and cried out: *1380*
Lk 3:23 about thirty years of age, being (as was **s**) *3543*
24:37 affrighted, and **s** that *they* had seen a spirit. *1380*
Ac 7:25 For he **s** his brethren would have *3543*
21:29 whom they **s** that Paul had brought into *3543*
25:18 none accusation of *such things* as I **s**: *5282*
Php 2:25 Yet I **s** it necessary to send to you *2233*

SUPPOSING (7) [SUPPOSE]

Lk 2:44 **s** him to have been in the company, *3543*
Jn 20:15 She, **s** him to be the gardener, saith unto *1380*
Ac 14:19 *him* out of the city, **s** he had been dead. *3543*
16:27 **s** that the prisoners had been fled. *3543*
27:13 **s** that *they* had obtained *their* purpose, *1380*
Php 1:16 **s** to add affliction to my bonds: *3633*
1Ti 6: 5 of the truth, **s** that gain is godliness: *3543*

SUPREME (1)

1Pe 2:13 Lord's sake: whether *it be* to the king, as **s**; *5242*

SUPREME COMMANDER See TARTAN

SUR (1)

2Ki 11: 6 a third *part shall be* at the gate of **S**; and 5495

SURE (41) [SURELY, SURETIES, SURETISHIP, SURETY]

Ge 23:17 all the borders round about, were **made s** 6965
23:20 were **made s** unto Abraham for a 6965
Ex 3:19 I am **s** that the king of Egypt will not let 3045
Nu 32:23 and be **s** your sin will find you out. 3045
Dt 12:23 Only be **s** that thou eat not the blood: 2388
1Sa 2:35 I will build him a **s** house; and he shall walk 539
20: 7 be **s** that evil is determined by him. 3045
25:28 will certainly make my lord a **s** house; 539
2Sa 1:10 I was **s** that he could not live after *that* he 3045
23: 5 ordered in all *things,* and **s**: 8104
1Ki 11:38 and build thee a **s** house, as I built for David, 539
Ne 9:38 because of all this we make a **s** covenant, 548
Job 24:22 he riseth up, and no *man* is **s** of life. 539
Ps 19: 7 the testimony of the LORD *is* **s**, 539

S

Ps 93: 5 Thy testimonies are very **s**: 539
111: 7 and judgment; all his commandments *are* **s**. 539
Pr 6: 3 go, humble thyself, and **make s** thy friend. 7292
11:15 smart *for it:* and he that hateth suretiship *is* **s**. 982
11:18 *to* him that soweth righteousness *shall be* a **s** 571
Isa 22:23 I will fasten him *as* a nail in a **s** place; and 539
22:25 shall the nail that is fastened in the **s** place be 539
28:16 corner *stone,* a **s foundation**: 3245+4143
32:18 in **s** dwellings, and in quiet resting places; 4009
33:16 *shall be* given him; his waters *shall be* **s**. 539
55: 3 with you, *even* the **s** mercies of David. 539
Da 2:45 *is* certain, and the interpretation thereof **s**. 540
4:26 thy kingdom *shall be* **s** unto thee, after that 7011
Mt 27:64 that the sepulchre be **made s** until the third *805*
27:65 go your way, **make** *it* as **s** as you can. *805*
27:66 So they went, and **made** the sepulchre **s**, *805*
Lk 10:11 notwithstanding be ye **s** of this, that *1097*
Jn 6:69 and are **s** that thou art *that* Christ, *1097*
16:30 Now are we **s** that thou knowest all *things,* *1492*
Ac 13:34 I will give you the **s** mercies of David. *4103*
Ro 2: 2 But we are **s** that the judgment of God is *1492*
4:16 to the end the promise might be **s** to all *949*
15:29 And I am **s** that, when I come unto you, *1492*
2Ti 2:19 the foundation of God standeth **s**, *4731*
Heb 6:19 both **s** and stedfast, and which entereth into *804*
2Pe 1:10 to make your calling and election **s**: *949*
1:19 We have also a **more s** word of prophecy; *949*

SURELY (284) [SURE]

Ge 2:17 thou eatest thereof thou shalt **s die**. 4191+4191
3: 4 unto the woman, Ye shall not **s die**: 4191+4191
9: 5 And **s** your blood of your lives will I require; 389
18:18 Seeing that Abraham shall **s become** 1961+1961
20: 7 know thou that thou shalt **s die**, thou, 4191+4191
20:11 **S** the fear of God *is* not in this place; 7535
26:11 his wife shall **s be put to death**. 4191+4191
28:16 and he said, **S** the LORD is in this place; 403
28:22 me I will **s give the tenth** unto thee. 6237+6237
29:14 to him, **S** thou *art* my bone and my flesh. 389
29:32 **S** the LORD hath looked upon my 3588
30:16 for **s** I have **hired** thee with my son's 7936+7936
31:42 **s** thou hadst sent me away now empty. 3588
32:12 I will **s do** thee **good**, and make thy 3190+3190
42:16 or else by the life of Pharaoh **s** ye *are* spies. 3588
43:10 **s** now we had returned this second time. 3588
44:28 from me, and I said, **S** he is torn in pieces; 389
46: 4 I will also **s bring** thee **up** *again:* and 5927+5927
50:24 God will **s visit** you, and bring you 6485+6485
50:25 God will **s visit** you, and ye shall 6485+6485
Ex 2:14 and said, **S** *this* thing is known. 403
3: 7 I have **s seen** the affliction of my 7200+7200
3:16 I have **s visited** you, and *seen* that 6485+6485
4:25 said, **S** a bloody husband *art* thou to me. 3588
11: 1 **s thrust** you **out** hence altogether. 1644+1644
13:19 saying, God will **s visit** you; 6485+6485
18:18 Thou wilt **s wear away**, both thou, 5034+5034
19:12 the mount shall be **s put to death**: 4191+4191
19:13 he shall **s be stoned**, or shot through; 5619+5619
21:12 that he die, shall be **s put to death**. 4191+4191
21:15 his mother, shall be **s put to death**. 4191+4191
21:16 his hand, he shall **s be put to death**. 4191+4191
21:17 his mother, shall **s** be **put to death**. 4191+4191
21:20 his hand; he shall be **s punished**. 5358+5358
21:22 he shall be **s punished**, according as 6064+6064
21:28 the ox shall be **s stoned**, and 5619+5619
21:36 he shall **s pay** ox for ox; and 7999+7999
22: 6 the fire shall **s make restitution**. 7999+7999
22:14 not with it, he shall **s make** *it* **good**. 7999+7999
22:16 he shall **s endow** her to be his wife. 4117+4117
22:19 with a beast shall **s** be **put to death**. 4191+4191
22:23 at all unto me, I will **s hear** their cry; 8085+8085
23: 4 shalt **s bring** it **back** to him **again**. 7725+7725
23: 5 help him, thou shalt **s help** with him. 5800+5800
23:33 their gods, it will **s** be a snare unto thee. 3588
31:14 defileth it shall **s** be **put to death**: 4191+4191
31:15 he shall **s** be **put to death**. 4191+4191
40:15 for their anointing shall **s be** an everlasting 1961
Lev 20: 2 he shall **s** be **put to death**: 4191+4191
20: 9 or his mother shall be **s put to death**: 4191+4191
20:10 adulteress shall **s** be **put to death**. 4191+4191
20:11 both of them shall **s** be **put to death**; 4191+4191
20:12 both of them shall **s** be **put to death**: 4191+4191
20:13 they shall **s** be **put to death**; their 4191+4191
20:15 a beast, he shall **s** be **put to death**: 4191+4191
20:16 they shall **s** be **put to death**; their 4191+4191
20:27 is a wizard, shall **s** be **put to death**: 4191+4191
24:16 he shall **s** be **put to death**, *and* all 4191+4191
24:17 any man shall **s** be **put to death**. 4191+4191
27:29 *but* shall **s** be **put to death**. 4191+4191
Nu 13:27 and **s** it floweth with milk and honey; 1571
14:23 **S** they shall **not** see the land which I sware 518
14:35 **s** do it unto all this evil congregation, 518+3808
15:35 The man shall be **s put to death**: 4191+4191
18:15 firstborn of man shalt thou **s redeem**, 6299+6299
22:33 **s** now also I had slain thee, and saved her 3588
23:23 **S** *there is* no enchantment against Jacob, 3588
26:65 They shall **s die** in the wilderness. 4191+4191
27: 7 thou shalt **s give** them a possession 5414+5414
32:11 **S none** of the men that came up out of 518
35:16 the murderer shall **s** be **put to death**. 4191+4191
35:17 the murderer shall **s** be **put to death**. 4191+4191
35:18 the murderer shall **s** be **put to death**. 4191+4191
35:21 smote *him* shall **s** be **put to death**; 4191+4191
35:31 but he shall be **s put to death**. 4191+4191
Dt 1:35 **S** there shall **not** one of these men of this 518
4: 6 **S** this great nation *is* a wise and 7535
8:19 against you *this* day that ye shall **s perish**. 6+6
13: 9 thou shalt **s kill** him; thine hand shall 2026+2026
13:15 Thou shalt **s smite** the inhabitants of 5221+5221
15: 8 shalt **s lend** him sufficient for his 5670+5670
15:10 Thou shalt **s give** him, and 5414+5414
16:15 of thine hands, therefore thou shalt **s** rejoice. 389
22: 4 **s** help him to **lift** *them* **up again**. 6965+6965
23:21 thy God will **s require** it of thee; 1875+1875
30:18 that ye shall **s perish**, *and that* ye shall not 6+6
Dt 31:18 I will **s hide** my face in that day for 5641+5641
Jos 14: 9 **S** the land whereon thy feet have 518+3808
Jdg 3:24 **S** he covereth his feet in *his* summer 389
4: 9 she said, I will **s go** with thee: 1980+1980
6:16 **S** I will be with thee, and thou shalt smite 3588
11:31 shall **s** be the LORD'S, and I will offer it NIH
13:22 **s die**, because we have seen God. 4191+4191
15:13 **s** we will not **kill** thee. And they 4191+4191
20:39 they said, **S** they are smitten down before us, 389
21: 5 He shall **s** be **put to death**. 4191+4191
Ru 1:10 **S** we will return with thee unto thy people. 3588
1Sa 9: 6 all that he saith **cometh s to pass**: 935+935
14:39 be in Jonathan my son, he shall **s die**. 4191+4191
14:44 for thou shalt **s die**, Jonathan. 4191+4191
15:32 Agag said, **S** the bitterness of death is past. 403
16: 6 said, **S** the LORD'S anointed *is* before him. 389
17:25 **s** to defy Israel is he come up: and it shall 3588
20:26 he *is* not clean; **s** *he is* not clean. 3588
20:31 fetch him unto me, for he shall **s die**. 1121+4194
22:16 Thou shalt **s die**, Ahimelech, thou, 4191+4191
22:22 *was* there, that he would **s tell** Saul: 5046+5046
24:20 I know well that thou shalt **s be king**, 4427+4427
25:21 **S** in vain have I kept all that this *fellow* hath 389
25:34 **s** there had not been left unto Nabal by 3588
28: 2 David said to Achish, **S** thou shalt 3651+3807.1
29: 6 said unto him, **S**, *as* the LORD liveth, 3588
30: 8 for thou shalt **s overtake** *them,* and 5381+5381
2Sa 2:27 **s** then in the morning the people had gone 3588
9: 7 for I will **s shew** thee kindness for 6213+6213
11:23 **S** the men prevailed against us, and 3588
12: 5 that hath done this *thing* shall **s die**: 1121+4194
12:14 also that is born unto thee shall **s die**. 4191+4191
15:21 **s** in what place my lord the king shall 518+3588
18: 2 will **s go forth** with you myself also. 3318+3318
20:18 They shall **s ask** *counsel* at Abel: 7592+7592
24:24 but I will **s buy** *it* of thee at a price: 7069+7069
1Ki 2:37 know for certain that thou shalt **s die**: 4191+4191
2:42 any whither, that thou shalt **s die**? 4191+4191
8:13 I have **s built** thee a house to dwell 1129+1129
11: 2 *for* **s** they will turn away your heart after 403
11:11 I will **s rend** the kingdom from thee, 7167+7167
13:32 of Samaria, shall **s come to pass**. 1961+1961
18:15 I will **s** shew myself unto him to day. 3588
20:23 and **s** we shall be stronger than they. 518+3808
20:25 *and* **s** we shall be stronger than they. 518+3808
22:32 that they said, **S** it *is* the king of Israel. 389
2Ki 1: 4 thou art gone up, but shalt **s die**. 4191+4191
1: 6 thou art gone up, but shalt **s die**. 4191+4191
1:16 thou art gone up, but shalt **s die**. 4191+4191
3:14 of hosts liveth, before whom I stand, **s**, 3588
3:23 the kings are **s slain**, and they have 2717+2717
5:11 He will **s come out** to me, and stand, 3318+3318
8:10 hath shewed me that he shall **s die**. 4191+4191
8:14 me *that* thou shouldest **s recover**. 2421+2421
9:26 **S** I have seen yesterday the blood of 518+3808
18:30 The LORD will **s deliver** us, and 5337+5337
23:22 **S** there was not holden such a passover 3588
24: 3 **S** at the commandment of the LORD came 389
Est 6:13 but shalt **s fall** before him. 5307+5307
Job 8: 6 **s** now he would awake for thee, and 3588
13: 3 **S** I would speak to the Almighty, and 199
13:10 He will **s reprove** you, if ye do 3198+3198
14:18 **s** the mountain falling cometh to nought, 199
18:21 **S** such *are* the dwellings of the wicked, and 389
20:20 **S** he shall not feel quietness in his belly, 3588
28: 1 **S** there is a vein for the silver, and a place 3588
31:36 **S** I would take it upon my shoulder, 518+3808
33: 8 **S** thou hast spoken in mine hearing, and 389
34:12 Yea, **s** God will not do wickedly, neither will 551
34:31 **S** it *is meet to be* said unto God, I have 3588
35:13 **S** God will not hear vanity, neither will 389
37:20 if a man speak, **s** he shall be swallowed up. 3588
40:20 **S** the mountains bring him forth food, 3588
Ps 23: 6 **S** goodness and mercy shall follow me all 389
32: 6 **s** in the floods of great waters they shall not 7535
39: 6 **S** every man walketh in a vain shew: 389
39: 6 **s** they are disquieted in vain: he heapeth up 389
39:11 like a moth: **s** every man *is* vanity. Selah. 389
62: 9 **S** men of low degree *are* vanity, *and* men of 389
73:18 **S** thou didst set them in slippery *places:* thou 389
76:10 **S** the wrath of man shall praise thee: 3588
77:11 **s** I will remember thy wonders of old. 3588
85: 9 **S** his salvation *is* nigh them that fear him; 389
91: 3 **S** he shall deliver thee from the snare of 3588
112: 6 **S** he shall not be moved for ever: 3588
131: 2 **S** I have behaved and quieted myself, 518+3808
132: 3 **S** I will **not** come into the tabernacle of my 518
139:11 If I say, **S** the darkness shall cover me; 389
139:19 **S** thou wilt slay the wicked, O God: 518
140:13 **S** the righteous shall give thanks unto thy 389
Pr 1:17 **S** in vain the net *is* spread in the sight of 3588
3:34 **S** he scorneth the scorners: but he giveth 518
10: 9 He that walketh uprightly walketh **s**: but 983
22:16 that giveth to the rich, *shall* **s** *come* to want. 389
23:18 **For s** there is an end; and 518+3588
30: 2 **S** I *am* more brutish than *any* man, and 3588
30:33 **S** the churning of milk bringeth forth 3588
Ecc 4:16 **S** this also *is* vanity and vexation of spirit. 3588
7: 7 **S** oppression maketh a wise *man* mad; and 3588
8:12 yet **s** I know that it shall be well with them 3588
10:11 **S** the serpent will bite without enchantment; 518
Isa 7: 9 not believe, **s** ye shall not be established. 3588
14:24 **S** as I have thought, so shall it come to 518+3808
16: 7 shall ye mourn; **s** *they are* stricken. 389
19:11 **S** the princes of Zoan *are* fools, the counsel 389
22:14 **S** this iniquity shall **not** be purged from you 518
22:17 and will **s cover** thee. 5844+5844
22:18 will **s violently turn and toss** 6801+6801+6802
29:16 **S** your turning of *things* upside down shall 518
36:15 The LORD will **s deliver** us: 5337+5337
40: 7 bloweth upon it: **s** the people *is* grass. 403
45:14 unto thee, *saying,* **S** God *is* in thee; 389
45:24 **S**, shall *one* say, in the LORD have I 389
49: 4 *yet* **s** my judgment *is* with the LORD, and 403
49:18 thou shalt **s** clothe thee with them all, NIH
Isa 53: 4 **S** he hath borne our griefs, and carried our 403
54:15 they shall **s gather together**, *but* 1481+1481
60: 9 **S** the isles shall wait for me, and the ships 3588
62: 8 **S** I will **no** more give thy corn *to be* meat for 518
63: 8 For he said, **S** they *are* my people, 389
Jer 2:35 am innocent, **s** his anger shall turn from me. 389
3:20 **S** *as* a wife treacherously departeth from her 403
4:10 **s** thou hast greatly deceived this people 403
5: 2 **s** they swear falsely. 3651+3807.1
5: 4 Therefore I said, **S** these *are* poor; they are 389
8:13 I will **s consume** them, saith 622+5486
16:19 **S** our fathers have inherited lies, vanity, and 389
22: 6 *yet* **s** I will make thee a wilderness *and* 518+3808
22:22 **s** then shalt thou be ashamed and 3588
24: 8 **s** thus saith the LORD, So will I give 3588
26: 8 took him, saying, Thou shalt **s die**. 4191+4191
26:15 ye shall **s** bring innocent blood upon 3588
31:18 I have **s heard** Ephraim bemoaning 8085+8085
31:19 **S** after that I was turned, I repented; and 3588
31:20 I will **s have mercy** upon him, 7355+7355
32: 4 shall **s** be **delivered** into the hand of 5414
34: 3 shalt **s** be **taken**, and delivered into 8610+8610
36:16 will **s tell** the king of all these words. 5046+5046
37: 9 Chaldeans shall **s depart** from us: 1980+1980
38: 3 This city shall **s** be **given** into 5414+5414
38:15 wilt thou not **s put** me **to death**? 4191+4191
39:18 For I will **s deliver** thee, and 4422+4422
44:25 We will **s** perform our vows that we have 6213
44:25 ye will **s accomplish** your vows, and 6965+6965
44:25 and **s perform** your vows. 6213+6213
44:29 shall **s stand** against you for evil: 6965+6965
46:18 **S** as Tabor *is* among the mountains, and 3588
49:12 but thou shalt **s drink** *of it.* 8354+8354
49:20 **S** the least of the flock shall draw 518+3808
49:20 **s** he shall make their habitations 518+3808
50:45 **S** the least of the flock shall draw 518+3808
50:45 **s** he shall make *their* habitation 518+3808
51:14 *saying,* **S** I will fill thee *with* men, 518+3588
51:56 God of recompences shall **s requite**. 7999+7999
La 3: 3 **S** against me is he turned; he turneth his 389
Eze 3: 6 **S**, had I sent thee to them, they would 518+3808
3:18 unto the wicked, Thou shalt **s die**; 4191+4191
3:21 he shall **s live**, because he is warned; 2421+2421
5:11 **S**, because thou hast defiled my 518+3808
17:16 **s** in the place *where* the king *dwelleth* 518+3808
17:19 **s** mine oath that he hath despised, and 518+3808
18: 9 he *is* just, he shall **s live**, saith 2421+2421
18:13 **s die**; his blood shall be upon him. 4191+4191
18:17 iniquity of his father, he shall **s live**. 2421+2421
18:19 and hath done them, he shall **s live**. 2421+2421
18:21 is lawful and right, he shall **s live**, 2421+2421
18:28 he shall **s live**, he shall not die. 2421+2421
20:33 **s** with a mighty hand, and with a 518+3808
31:11 the heathen; he shall **s deal** with him: 6213+6213
33: 8 O wicked *man,* thou shalt **s die**; 4191+4191
33:13 to the righteous, *that* he shall **s live**; 2421+2421
33:14 unto the wicked, Thou shalt **s die**; 4191+4191
33:15 he shall **s live**, he shall not die. 2421+2421
33:16 is lawful and right; he shall **s live**. 2421+2421
33:27 **s** *they* that *are* in the wastes shall fall 518+3808
34: 8 **s** because my flock became a prey, 518+3808
36: 5 **S** in the fire of my jealousy have I 518+3808
36: 7 **S** the heathen that *are* about you, 518+3808
38:19 **S** in that day there shall be a great 518+3808
Hos 5: 9 have I made known that which shall **s** be. 539
12:11 **s** they are vanity: they sacrifice bullocks in 389
Am 3: 7 **S** the Lord GOD will do nothing, but he 3588
5: 5 for Gilgal shall **s go into captivity**, 1540+1540
7:11 Israel shall **s** be **led away captive** 1540+1540
7:17 Israel shall **s go into captivity** forth 1540+1540
8: 7 **S** I will **never** forget any of 518+5331+3807.1
Mic 2:12 I will **s assemble**, O Jacob, all of thee; 622+622
2:12 I will **s gather** the remnant of Israel; 6908+6908
Hab 2: 3 because it will **s come**, it will not tarry. 935+935
Zep 2: 9 **S** Moab shall be as Sodom, and the children 3588
3: 7 I said, **S** thou wilt fear me, thou wilt receive 389
Mt 26:73 said to Peter, **S** thou also art *one* of them; *230*
Mk 14:70 said again to Peter, **S** thou art *one* of them: *230*
Lk 1: 1 which are **most s believed** among us, *4135*
4:23 Ye will **s** say unto me this proverb, *3843*
Jn 17: 8 and have known **s** that I came out from thee, *230*
Heb 6:14 **S** blessing I will bless thee, and *2229+3375*
Rev 22:20 these *things* saith, **S** I come quickly. *3483*

SURETIES (1) [SURE]

Pr 22:26 strike hands, *or* of them that are **s** for debts. 6148

SURETISHIP (1) [SURE]

Pr 11:15 smart *for it:* and he that hateth **s** *is* sure. 8628

SURETY (14) [SURE]

Ge 15:13 **Know of a s** that thy seed shall be a 3045+3045
18:13 **I of a s** bear *a child,* which am old? 552+637
26: 9 and said, Behold, **of a s** she *is* thy wife: 389
43: 9 I will be **s for** him; of my hand shalt thou 6148
44:32 For thy servant **became s** for the lad unto 6148
Job 17: 3 Lay down now, **put** me **in a s** with thee; 6148
Ps 119:122 Be **s for** thy servant for good: let not 6148
Pr 6: 1 My son, if thou be **s for** thy friend, *if* thou 6148
11:15 He that is **s** for a stranger shall smart *for it:* 6148
17:18 **becometh s** in the presence of his 6148+6161
20:16 Take his garment that is **s** *for* a stranger, 6148
27:13 Take his garment that is **s** *for* a stranger, 6148
Ac 12:11 he said, Now I know **of a s**, that the Lord *230*
Heb 7:22 much was Jesus made a **s** of a better *1450*

SURFEITING (1)

Lk 21:34 any time your hearts be overcharged with **s**, *2897*

SURMISINGS (1)

1Ti 6: 4 cometh envy, strife, railings, evil **s**, *5283*

SURNAME (8) [SURNAMED]

Isa 44: 5 and **s** *himself* by the name of Israel. 3655

S

Mt 10: 3 and Lebbeus, whose **s** was Thaddeus; *1941*
Ac 10: 5 and call for *one* Simon, whose **s** is Peter: *1941*
10:32 and call hither Simon, whose **s** is Peter; *1941*
11:13 and call for Simon, whose **s** is Peter; *1941*
12:12 the mother of John, whose **s** was Mark; *1941*
12:25 took with *them* John, whose **s** was Mark. *1941*
15:37 to take with *them* John, whose **s** was Mark. *2564*

SURNAMED (8) [SURNAME]
Isa 45: 4 I have **s** thee, though thou hast not known 3655
Mk 3:16 And Simon he **s** Peter; *2007*
3:17 (and he **s** them Boanerges, which is, *2007+3686*
Lk 22: 3 Then entered Satan into Judas **s** Iscariot, *1941*
Ac 1:23 who was **s** Justus, and Matthias. *1941*
4:36 who by the apostles was **s** Barnabas, *1941*
10:18 which was **s** Peter, were lodged there. *1941*
15:22 *namely,* Judas **s** Barsabas, and Silas, *1941*

SURPRISED (3)
Isa 33:14 are afraid; fearfulness hath **s** the hypocrites. 270
Jer 48:41 the strong holds are **s**, and the mighty 8610
51:41 *how* is the praise of the whole earth **s**! 8610

SURVIVE See ABIDE; ABIDETH; ABIDING

SURVIVORS See RESIDUE

SUSA See SHUSHAN; SUSANCHITES

SUSANCHITES (1)
Ezr 4: 9 the **S**, the Dehavites, *and* the Elamites, 7801

SUSANNA (1)
Lk 8: 3 and **S**, and many others, which ministered *4677*

SUSI (1)
Nu 13:11 the tribe of Manasseh, Gaddi the son of **S**. 5485

SUSPENSE See TARRIED; TARRIEST; TARRIETH; TARRY; TARRYING

SUSPICIONS See SURMISINGS

SUSTAIN (4) [SUSTAINED, SUSTENANCE]
1Ki 17: 9 a widow woman there to **s** thee. 3557
Ne 9:21 forty years didst thou **s** them in 3557
Ps 55:22 upon the LORD, and he shall **s** thee: 3557
Pr 18:14 The spirit of a man will **s** his infirmity; but 3557

SUSTAINED (3) [SUSTAIN]
Ge 27:37 and with corn and wine have I **s** him: 5564
Ps 3: 5 and slept; I awaked; for the LORD **s** me. 5564
Isa 59:16 unto him; and his righteousness, it **s** him. 5564

SUSTENANCE (3) [SUSTAIN]
Jdg 6: 4 left no **s** for Israel, neither sheep, nor ox, 4241
2Sa 19:32 he had **provided** the king of **s** while he lay 3557
Ac 7:11 great affliction: and our fathers found no **s**. *5527*

SWADDLED (2) [SWADDLING]
La 2:22 those that I have **s** and brought up hath 2946
Eze 16: 4 wast not salted at all, nor **s at all**. 2853+2853

SWADDLING (3) [SWADDLED]
Job 38: 9 and thick darkness a **s band** for it, 2854
Lk 2: 7 and **wrapped** him **in s clothes**, and *4683*
2:12 shall find *the* babe **wrapped in s clothes**, *4683*

SWALLOW (23) [SWALLOWED, SWALLOWETH]
Nu 16:30 the earth open her mouth, and **s** them **up**, 1104
16:34 for they said, Lest the earth **s** us **up** *also*. 1104
2Sa 20:19 why wilt thou **s up** the inheritance of 1104
20:20 be it from me, that I should **s up** or destroy. 1104
Job 7:19 nor let me alone till I **s down** my spittle? 1104
20:18 for shall he restore, and shall not **s** *it* **down**: 1104
Ps 21: 9 the LORD shall **s** them **up** in his wrath, 1104
56: 1 for man would **s** me **up**; he fighting daily 7602
56: 2 Mine enemies would daily **s** *me* **up**: 7602
57: 3 the reproach of him that would **s** me **up**. 7602
69:15 neither let the deep **s** me **up**, and let not 1104
84: 3 the **s** a nest for herself, where she may lay 1866
Pr 1:12 Let us **s** them **up** alive as the grave; and 1104
26: 2 as the **s** by flying, so the curse causeless 1866
Ecc 10:12 but the lips of a fool will **s up** himself. 1104
Isa 25: 8 He will **s up** death in victory; and the Lord 1104
38:14 Like a crane *or* a **s**, so did I chatter: I did 5693
Jer 8: 7 and the **s** observe the time of their coming; 5693
Hos 8: 7 if so be it yield, *the* strangers shall **s** it **up**. 1104
Am 8: 4 Hear this, O ye that **s up** the needy, even to 7602
Ob 1:16 they shall **s down**, and they shall be as 3886
Jnh 1:17 had prepared a great fish to **s up** Jonah. 1104
Mt 23:24 which strain out a gnat, and **s** a camel. *2666*

SWALLOWED (26) [SWALLOW]
Ex 7:12 but Aaron's rod **s up** their rods. 1104
15:12 out thy right hand, the earth **s** them. 1104
Nu 16:32 **s** them **up**, and their houses, and all 1104
26:10 **s** them **up** together with Korah, when that 1104
Dt 11: 6 **s** them **up**, and their households, and 1104
2Sa 17:16 lest the king be **s up**, and all the people that 1104
Job 6: 3 of the sea: therefore my words are **s up**. 3886
20:15 He hath **s down** riches, and he shall vomit 1104
37:20 if a man speak, surely he shall be **s up**. 1104
Ps 35:25 let them not say, We have **s** him **up**. 1104
106:17 The earth opened and **s up** Dathan, and 1104
124: 3 they had **s** us **up** quick, when their wrath 1104
Isa 28: 7 through strong drink, they are **s up** of wine, 1104
49:19 and they that **s** thee **up** shall be far away. 1104
Jer 51:34 he hath **s** me **up** like a dragon, 1104
51:44 out of his mouth that which he hath **s up**: 1105
La 2: 2 The Lord hath **s up** all the habitations of 1104
2: 5 he hath **s up** Israel, he hath swallowed up 1104
2: 5 up Israel, he hath **s up** all her palaces: 1104
La 2:16 they say, We have **s** *her* **up**: certainly this *is* 1104
Eze 36: 3 *you* desolate, and **s** you **up** on every side, 7602
Hos 8: 8 Israel is **s up**: now shall they be among 1104
1Co 15:54 that is written, Death is **s up** in victory. *2666*
2Co 2: 7 one should be **s up** with overmuch sorrow. *2666*
5: 4 that mortality might be **s up** of life. *2666*
Rev 12:16 **s up** the flood which the dragon cast out of *2666*

SWALLOWETH (2) [SWALLOW]
Job 5: 5 and the robber **s up** their substance. 7602
39:24 He **s** the ground with fierceness and rage: 1572

SWAN (2)
Lev 11:18 the **s**, and the pelican, and the gier eagle, 8580
Dt 14:16 The little owl, and the great owl, and the **s**, 8580

SWARE (78) [SWEAR]
Ge 21:31 because there they **s** both of them. 7650
24: 7 spake unto me, and that **s** unto me, saying, 7650
24: 9 and **s** to him concerning that matter. 7650
25:33 Swear to me *this* day; and he **s** to him: 7650
26: 3 I will perform the oath which I **s** unto 7650
26:31 in the morning, and **s** one to another: 7650
31:53 And Jacob **s** by the fear of his father Isaac. 7650
47:31 he **s** unto him. And Israel bowed himself 7650
50:24 land unto the land which he **s** to Abraham, 7650
Ex 13: 5 which he **s** unto thy fathers to give thee, 7650
13:11 as he **s** unto thee and to thy fathers, and 7650
33: 1 unto the land which I **s** unto Abraham, 7650
Nu 14:16 people into the land which he **s** unto them, 7650
14:23 Surely they shall not see the land which I **s** 7650
14:30 *concerning* which I **s** to make you 3027+5375
32:10 kindled the same time, and he **s**, saying, 7650
32:11 shall see the land which I **s** unto Abraham, 7650
Dt 1: 8 possess the land which the LORD **s** unto 7650
1:34 your words, and was wroth, and **s**, saying, 7650
1:35 which I **s** to give unto your fathers, 7650
2:14 among the host, as the LORD **s** unto them. 7650
4:21 **s** that I should not go over Jordan, and 7650
4:31 of thy fathers which he **s** unto them. 7650
6:10 into the land which he **s** unto thy fathers, 7650
6:18 possess the good land which the LORD **s** 7650
6:23 to give us the land which he **s** unto our 7650
7:12 and the mercy which he **s** unto thy fathers: 7650
7:13 in the land which he **s** unto thy fathers to 7650
8: 1 possess the land which the LORD **s** unto 7650
8:18 his covenant which he **s** unto thy fathers, 7650
9: 5 word which the LORD **s** unto thy fathers, 7650
10:11 which I **s** unto their fathers to give unto 7650
11: 9 which the LORD **s** unto your fathers to 7650
11:21 in the land which the LORD **s** unto your 7650
26: 3 LORD **s** unto our fathers for to give us. 7650
28:11 in the land which the LORD **s** unto thy 7650
30:20 land which the LORD **s** unto thy fathers, 7650
31:20 into the land which I **s** unto their fathers, 7650
31:21 I have brought them into the land which I **s**. 7650
31:23 of Israel into the land which I **s** unto them: 7650
34: 4 This *is* the land which I **s** unto Abraham, 7650
Jos 1: 6 which I **s** unto their fathers to give them. 7650
5: 6 unto whom the LORD **s** that *he* would not 7650
5: 6 which the LORD **s** unto their fathers that 7650
6:22 and all that she hath, as ye **s** unto her. 7650
9:15 the princes of the congregation **s** unto them. 7650
9:20 because of the oath which we **s** unto them. 7650
14: 9 Moses **s** on that day, saying, Surely 7650
21:43 land which he **s** to give unto their fathers; 7650
21:44 according to all that he **s** unto their fathers: 7650
Jdg 2: 1 have brought you unto the land which I **s** 7650
1Sa 19: 6 Saul **s**, *As* the LORD liveth, he shall not 7650
20: 3 David **s** moreover, and said, Thy father 7650
24:22 David **s** unto Saul. And Saul went home; 7650
28:10 Saul **s** to her by the LORD, saying, *As* 7650
2Sa 3:35 David **s**, saying, So do God to me, and 7650
19:23 shalt not die. And the king **s** unto him. 7650
21:17 the men of David **s** unto him, saying, 7650
1Ki 1:29 the king **s**, and said, *As* the LORD liveth, 7650
1:30 Even as I **s** unto thee by the LORD God of 7650
2: 8 and I **s** to him by the LORD, saying, 7650
2:23 king Solomon **s** by the LORD, saying, 7650
2Ki 25:24 Gedaliah **s** to them, and to their men, and 7650
2Ch 15:14 they **s** unto the LORD with a loud voice, 7650
Ezr 10: 5 do according to this word. And they **s**. 7650
Ps 95:11 *Unto* whom I **s** in my wrath that they 7650
132: 2 How he **s** unto the LORD, *and* 7650
Jer 38:16 So Zedekiah the king **s** secretly unto 7650
40: 9 of Ahikam the son of Shaphan **s** unto them 7650
Eze 16: 8 I **s** unto thee, and entered into a covenant 7650
Da 12: 7 **s** by him that liveth for ever that *it shall be* 7650
Mk 6:23 And he **s** unto her, Whatsoever thou shalt *3660*
Lk 1:73 The oath which he **s** to our father Abraham, *3660*
Heb 3:11 So I **s** in my wrath, They shall not enter *3660*
3:18 And to whom **s** he that *they* should not *3660*
6:13 could swear by no greater, he **s** by himself, *3660*
7:21 unto him, The Lord **s** and will not repent, *3660*
Rev 10: 6 And **s** by him that liveth for ever and ever, *3660*

SWAREST (5) [SWEAR]
Ex 32:13 to whom thou **s** by thine own self, and 7650
Nu 11:12 unto the land which thou **s** unto their 7650
Dt 26:15 as thou **s** unto our fathers, a land that 7650
1Ki 1:17 thou **s** by the LORD thy God unto thine 7650
Ps 89:49 *which* thou **s** unto David in thy truth? 7650

SWARM (3) [SWARMS]
Ex 8:24 there came a grievous **s** *of flies* into 6157
8:24 the land was corrupted by reason of the **s** 6157
Jdg 14: 8 *there was* a **s** of bees and honey in 5712

SWARMS (5) [SWARM]
Ex 8:21 I will send **s** *of flies* upon thee, and 6157
8:21 of the Egyptians shall be full of **s** *of flies,* 6157
8:22 that no **s** *of flies* shall be there; 6157
8:29 I will intreat the LORD that the **s** *of flies* 6157
8:31 and he removed the **s** *of flies* from Pharaoh, 6157

SWEAR (60) [FORSWEAR, SWARE, SWAREST, SWEARERS, SWEARETH, SWEARING, SWORN]
Ge 21:23 **s** unto me here by God that thou wilt not 7650
21:24 And Abraham said, I will **s**. 7650
24: 3 I will **make** thee **s** by the LORD, the God 7650
24:37 my master **made** me **s**, saying, Thou shalt 7650
25:33 Jacob said, **S** to me *this* day; and he sware 7650
47:31 he said, **S** unto me. And he sware unto him. 7650
50: 5 My father **made** me **s**, saying, Lo, I die: 7650
50: 6 thy father, according as he **made** thee **s**. 7650
Ex 6: 8 *concerning* the which I did **s** to give 3027+5375
Lev 5: 4 Or if a soul **s**, pronouncing with *his* lips to 7650
19:12 ye shall not **s** by my name falsely, 7650
Nu 30: 2 or **s** an oath to bind his soul with a bond; 7650
Dt 6:13 and serve him, and shalt **s** by his name. 7650
10:20 to him shalt thou cleave, and **s** by his name. 7650
Jos 2:12 I pray you, **s** unto me by the LORD, 7650
2:17 this thine oath which thou hast **made** us **s**. 7650
2:20 of thine oath which thou hast **made** us **to s**. 7650
23: 7 nor **cause to s** *by them,* neither serve them, 7650
Jdg 15:12 Samson said unto them, **S** unto me, that ye 7650
1Sa 20:17 Jonathan caused David to **s** again, because 7650
24:21 **S** now therefore unto me by the LORD, 7650
30:15 he said, **S** unto me by God, that thou wilt 7650
2Sa 19: 7 for I **s** by the LORD, if thou go not forth, 7650
1Ki 1:13 lord O king, **s** unto thine handmaid, saying, 7650
1:51 Let king Solomon **s** unto me to day that he 7650
2:42 Did I not **make** thee to **s** by the LORD, 7650
8:31 an oath be laid upon him to **cause** him **to s**, 422
2Ch 6:22 and an oath be laid upon him to **make** him **s**, 422
36:13 who had **made** him **s** by God: 7650
Ezr 10: 5 **made** the chief priests, the Levites, and all Israel, **to s** 7650
Ne 13:25 off their hair, and **made** them **s** by God, 7650
Isa 3: 7 In that day shall he **s**, saying, I will not be a 5375
19:18 of Canaan, and **s** to the LORD of hosts: 7650
45:23 every knee shall bow, every tongue shall **s**. 7650
48: 1 which **s** by the name of the LORD, and 7650
65:16 he that sweareth in the earth shall **s** by 7650
Jer 4: 2 thou shalt **s**, The LORD liveth, in truth, 7650
5: 2 The LORD liveth; surely they **s** falsely. 7650
7: 9 **s** falsely, and burn incense unto Baal, and 7650
12:16 to **s** by my name, The LORD liveth; 7650
12:16 as they taught my people to **s** by Baal; then 7650
22: 5 I **s** by myself, saith the LORD, 7650
32:22 which thou didst **s** to their fathers to give 7650
Hos 4:15 up *to* Beth-aven, nor **s**, The LORD liveth. 7650
Am 8:14 They that **s** by the sin of Samaria, and say, 7650
Zep 1: 5 that worship *and* that **s** by the LORD, 7650
1: 5 by the LORD, and that **s** by Malcham; 7650
Mt 5:34 But I say unto you, **S** not at all; neither by *3660*
5:36 Neither shalt thou **s** by thy head, because *3660*
23:16 Whosoever shall **s** by the temple, *3660*
23:16 whosoever shall **s** by the gold of *3660*
23:18 And, Whosoever shall **s** by the altar, it is *3660*
23:20 Whoso therefore shall **s** by the altar, *3660*
23:21 And whoso shall **s** by the temple, *3660*
23:22 And he that shall **s** by heaven, sweareth by *3660*
26:74 Then began he to curse and to **s**, *saying,* I *3660*
Mk 14:71 But he began to curse and to **s**, *saying,* I *3660*
Heb 6:13 because he could **s** by no greater, he sware *3660*
6:16 For men verily **s** by the greater: and an oath *3660*
Jas 5:12 **s** not, neither by heaven, neither by *3660*

SWEARERS (1) [SWEAR]
Mal 3: 5 against false **s**, and against those that 7650

SWEARETH (11) [SWEAR]
Lev 6: 3 and lieth concerning it, and **s** falsely; 7650
Ps 15: 4 *He that* **s** to *his own* hurt, and changeth not. 7650
63:11 in God; every one that **s** by him shall glory: 7650
Ecc 9: 2 *and* he that **s**, as he that feareth an oath. 7650
Isa 65:16 he that **s** in the earth shall swear by the God 7650
Zec 5: 3 every one that **s** shall be cut off *as* on that 7650
5: 4 into the house of him that **s** falsely by my 7650
Mt 23:18 but whosoever **s** by the gift that is upon it, *3660*
23:20 the altar, **s** by it, and by all *things* thereon. *3660*
23:21 **s** by it, and by him that dwelleth therein. *3660*
23:22 **s** by the throne of God, and by him that *3660*

SWEARING (4) [SWEAR]
Lev 5: 1 and hear the voice of **s**, and *is* a witness, 423
Jer 23:10 for because of **s** the land mourneth; 423
Hos 4: 2 By **s**, and lying, and killing, and stealing, 422
10: 4 **s** falsely in making a covenant: 422

SWEAT (3)
Ge 3:19 In the **s** of thy face shalt thou eat bread, 2188
Eze 44:18 *themselves* with any thing that causeth **s**. 3154
Lk 22:44 his **s** was as it were great drops of blood *2402*

SWEEP (3) [SWEEPING, SWEPT]
Isa 14:23 I will **s** it with the besom of destruction, 2894
28:17 the hail shall **s away** the refuge of lies, and 3261
Lk 15: 8 and **s** the house, and seek diligently till she *4563*

SWEEPING (1) [SWEEP]
Pr 28: 3 poor *is like* a **s** rain which leaveth no food. 5502

SWEET (108) [SWEETER, SWEETLY, SWEETNESS, SWEETSMELLING]
Ge 8:21 the LORD smelled a **s** savour; and 5207
Ex 15:25 into the waters, the waters were **made s**: 4985
25: 6 spices for anointing oil, and for **s** incense, 5561
29:18 it *is* a **s** savour, an offering made by fire 5207
29:25 for a **s** savour before the LORD: 5207
29:41 to the drink offering thereof, for a **s** savour, 5207
30: 7 Aaron shall burn thereon **s** incense every 5561
30:23 and of **s** cinnamon half so much, 1314
30:23 and of **s** calamus two hundred and 1314
30:34 Take unto thee **s spices**, stacte, and onycha, 5561
30:34 *these* **s spices** with pure frankincense: 5561
31:11 **s** incense for the holy *place:* according to 5561

Ex 35: 8 for anointing oil, and for the **s** incense, 5561
35:15 the **s** incense, and the hanging for the door 5561
35:28 for the anointing oil, and for the **s** incense. 5561
37:29 and the pure incense of **s spices**, 5561
39:38 the **s** incense, and the hanging for 5561
40:27 he burnt **s** incense thereon; as the LORD 5561
Lev 1: 9 by fire, of a **s** savour unto the LORD. 5207
1:13 by fire, of a **s** savour unto the LORD. 5207
1:17 by fire, of a **s** savour unto the LORD. 5207
2: 2 by fire, of a **s** savour unto the LORD: 5207
2: 9 by fire, of a **s** savour unto the LORD. 5207
2:12 they shall not be burnt on the altar for a **s** 5207
3: 5 by fire, of a **s** savour unto the LORD. 5207
3:16 of the offering made by fire for a **s** savour: 5207
4: 7 of the altar of **s** incense before the LORD, 5561
4:31 the priest shall burn *it* upon the altar for a **s** 5207
6:15 shall burn *it upon* the altar *for* a **s** savour, 5207
6:21 thou offer *for* a **s** savour unto the LORD. 5207
8:21 it *was* a burnt sacrifice for a **s** savour, *and* 5207
8:28 they *were* consecrations for a **s** savour: it *is* 5207
16:12 and his hands full of **s** incense beaten small, 5561
17: 6 burn the fat for a **s** savour unto the LORD. 5207
23:13 by fire unto the LORD *for* a **s** savour: 5207
23:18 made by fire, of **s** savour unto the LORD. 5207
26:31 will not smell the savour of your **s odours**. 5207
Nu 4:16 the **s** incense, and the daily meat offering, 5561
15: 3 to make a **s** savour unto the LORD, of 5207
15: 7 *of* wine, *for* a **s** savour unto the LORD. 5207
15:10 by fire, of a **s** savour unto the LORD. 5207
15:13 by fire, of a **s** savour unto the LORD. 5207
15:14 by fire, of a **s** savour unto the LORD; 5207
15:24 for a **s** savour unto the LORD, with his 5207
18:17 by fire, for a **s** savour unto the LORD. 5207
28: 2 made by fire, *for* a **s** savour unto me, 5207
28: 6 which was ordained in mount Sinai for a **s** 5207
28: 8 by fire, *of* a **s** savour unto the LORD. 5207
28:13 *for* a burnt offering *of* a **s** savour, 5207
28:24 by fire, *of* a **s** savour unto the LORD: 5207
28:27 ye shall offer the burnt offering for a **s** 5207
29: 2 ye shall offer a burnt offering for a **s** savour 5207
29: 6 according unto their manner, for a **s** savour, 5207
29: 8 offering unto the LORD *for* a **s** savour; 5207
29:13 by fire, *of* a **s** savour unto the LORD; 5207
29:36 by fire, *of* a **s** savour unto the LORD: 5207
2Sa 23: 1 of Jacob, and the **s** psalmist of Israel, said, 5273
2Ch 2: 4 *and* to burn before him **s** incense, and 5561
13:11 evening burnt sacrifices and **s** incense: 5561
16:14 in the bed which was filled *with* **s odours** 1314
Ezr 6:10 That they may offer sacrifices of **s savours** 5208
Ne 8:10 drink the **s**, and send portions unto *them* for 4477
Est 2:12 six months with **s odours**, and with *other* 1314
Job 20:12 Though wickedness be **s** in his mouth, 4985
21:33 The clods of the valley shall be **s** unto him, 4985
38:31 Canst thou bind the **s influences** of 4575
Ps 55:14 We **took s** counsel together, *and* 4985
104:34 My meditation of him shall be **s**: I will be 6149
119:103 How **s** are thy words unto my taste! 4452
141: 6 they shall hear my words; for they are **s**. 5276
Pr 3:24 shalt lie down, and thy sleep shall be **s**. 6149
9:17 Stolen waters are **s**, and bread *eaten* in 4985
13:19 The desire accomplished is **s** to the soul: 6149
16:24 **s** to the soul, and health to the bones. 4966
20:17 Bread of deceit *is* **s** to a man; but 6156
23: 8 shalt thou vomit up, and lose thy **s** words. 5273
24:13 and the honeycomb, *which is* **s** to thy taste: 4966
27: 7 *to* the hungry soul every bitter *thing is* **s**. 4966
Ecc 5:12 The sleep of a labouring *man is* **s**, 4966
11: 7 Truly the light *is* **s**, and a pleasant *thing it is* 4966
SS 2: 3 and his fruit *was* **s** to my taste. 4966
2:14 for **s** *is* thy voice, and thy countenance *is* 6156
5: 5 my fingers *with* **s smelling** myrrh, upon 5674
5:13 cheeks *are* as a bed of spices, *as* **s** flowers: 4840
5:13 lips *like* lilies, dropping **s smelling** myrrh. 5674
5:16 His mouth *is* **most s**: yea, he *is* altogether 4477
Isa 3:24 *that* instead of **s smell** there shall be stink; 1314
5:20 that put bitter for **s**, and sweet for bitter! 4966
5:20 that put bitter for sweet, and **s** for bitter! 4966
23:16 **make s** melody, sing many songs, that thou 3190
43:24 Thou hast bought me no **s cane** with 7070
49:26 with their own blood, as with **s wine**: 6071
Jer 6:20 and the **s** cane from a far country? 2896
6:20 nor your sacrifices **s** unto me. 6149
31:26 and beheld; and my sleep was **s** unto me. 6149
Eze 6:13 the place where they did offer **s** savour to 5207
16:19 thou hast even set it before them for a **s** 5207
20:28 there also they made their **s** savour, and 5207
20:41 I will accept you with *your* **s** savour, 5207
Da 2:46 offer an oblation and **s odours** unto him. 5208
Am 9:13 the mountains shall drop **s wine**, and all 6071
Mic 6:15 and **s wine**, but shalt not drink wine. 8492
Mk 16: 1 and Salome, had bought *s* spices, that they NIG
2Co 2:15 For we are unto God a **s savour** of Christ, *2175*
Php 4:18 an odour of a **s smell**, a sacrifice *2175*
Jas 3:11 send forth at the same place **s** *water* *1099*
Rev 10: 9 but it shall be in thy mouth **s** as honey. *1099*
10:10 it up; and it was in my mouth **s** as honey: *1099*

SWEETER (3) [SWEET]
Jdg 14:18 the sun went down, What *is* **s** than honey? 4966
Ps 19:10 **s** also than honey and the honeycomb. 4966
119:103 my taste! *yea, s* than honey to my mouth! NIH

SWEETLY (2) [SWEET]
Job 24:20 forget him; the worm shall **feed s on** him; 4988
SS 7: 9 for my beloved, that goeth *down* **s**, 4339+3807.1

SWEETNESS (5) [SWEET]
Jdg 9:11 Should I forsake my **s**, and my good fruit, 4987
14:14 and out of the strong came forth **s**. 4966
Pr 16:21 and the **s** of the lips increaseth learning. 4986
27: 9 *doth* the **s** of a man's friend by hearty 4986
Eze 3: 3 and it was in my mouth as honey for **s**. 4966

SWEETSMELLING (1) [SMELL, SWEET]
Eph 5: 2 and a sacrifice to God for a **s** savour. *2175*

SWELL (4) [SWELLED, SWELLING, SWELLINGS, SWOLLEN]
Nu 5:21 make thy thigh to rot, and thy belly to **s**; 6639
5:22 to **make** *thy* belly **to s**, and *thy* thigh to rot: 6638
5:27 and her belly shall **s**, and her thigh shall rot: 6638
Dt 8: 4 neither did thy foot **s**, these forty years. 1216

SWELLED (1) [SWELL]
Ne 9:21 clothes waxed not old, and their feet **s** not. 1216

SWELLING (7) [SWELL]
Ps 46: 3 *though* the mountains shake with the **s** 1346
Isa 30:13 **s out** in a high wall, whose breaking 1158
Jer 12: 5 then how wilt thou do in the **s** of Jordan? 1347
49:19 he shall come up like a lion from the **s** of 1347
50:44 he shall come up like a lion from the **s** of 1347
2Pe 2:18 For when they speak **great s** *words* of *5246*
Jude 1:16 their mouth speaketh **great s** *words*, *5246*

SWELLINGS (1) [SWELL]
2Co 12:20 strifes, backbitings, whisperings, **s**, tumults: *5450*

SWEPT (4) [SWEEP]
Jdg 5:21 The river of Kishon **s** them **away**, 1640
Jer 46:15 Why are thy valiant *men* **s away**? 5502
Mt 12:44 he findeth *it* empty, **s**, and garnished. *4563*
Lk 11:25 he cometh, he findeth *it* **s** and garnished. *4563*

SWERVED (1)
1Ti 1: 6 From which some having **s** have turned aside *795*

SWIFT (20) [SWIFTER, SWIFTLY]
Dt 28:49 the end of the earth, *as* **s** as the eagle flieth; NIH
1Ch 12: 8 *were* as **s** as the roes upon the mountains: 4116
Job 9:26 They are passed away as the **s** ships: as 16
24:18 He *is* **s** as the waters; their portion is cursed 7031
Pr 6:18 feet that be **s** in running to mischief, 4116
Ecc 9:11 under the sun, that the race *is* not to the **s**, 7031
Isa 18: 2 *saying,* Go, ye **s** messengers, to a nation 7031
19: 1 the LORD rideth upon a **s** cloud, and 7031
30:16 and, We will ride upon the **s**; therefore shall 7031
30:16 therefore shall they that pursue you be **s**. 7043
66:20 and upon mules, and upon **s beasts**, 3753
Jer 2:23 *thou art* a **s** dromedary traversing her ways; 7031
46: 6 Let not the **s** flee away, nor the mighty *man* 7031
Am 2:14 Therefore the flight shall perish from the **s**, 7031
2:15 *he that is* **s** of foot shall not deliver *himself*: 7031
Mic 1:13 of Lachish, bind the chariot to the **s beast**: 7409
Mal 3: 5 I will be a **s** witness against the sorcerers, 4116
Ro 3:15 Their feet *are* **s** to shed blood: *3691*
Jas 1:19 let every man be **s** to hear, slow to speak, *5036*
2Pe 2: 1 and bring upon themselves **s** destruction. *5031*

SWIFTER (6) [SWIFT]
2Sa 1:23 they were **s** than eagles, they were stronger 7043
Job 7: 6 My days are **s** than a weaver's shuttle, and 7043
9:25 Now my days are **s** than a post: they flee 7043
Jer 4:13 his horses are **s** than eagles. Woe unto us! 7043
La 4:19 Our persecutors are **s** than the eagles of 7031
Hab 1: 8 Their horses also are **s** than the leopards, 7043

SWIFTLY (4) [SWIFT]
Ps 147:15 *upon* earth: his word runneth **very s**. 4120+5704
Isa 5:26 and behold, they shall come with speed **s**: 7031
Da 9:21 the beginning, being caused to fly **s**, 3288+871.1
Joel 3: 4 **s** *and* speedily will I return your 7031

SWIM (6) [SWIMMEST, SWIMMETH]
2Ki 6: 6 and cast *it* in thither; and the iron did **s**. 6687
Ps 6: 6 all the night **make** I my bed to **s**; 7811
Isa 25:11 swimmeth spreadeth forth *his hands* to **s**: 7811
Eze 47: 5 for the waters were risen, waters to **s** in, 7813
Ac 27:42 lest any *of them* should **s out**, and escape. *1579*
27:43 commanded that they which could **s** should *2860*

SWIMMEST (1) [SWIM]
Eze 32: 6 with thy blood the land wherein thou **s**, 6824

SWIMMETH (1) [SWIM]
Isa 25:11 as he that **s** spreadeth forth *his hands* to 7811

SWINE (16) [SWINE'S]
Lev 11: 7 the **s**, though he divide the hoof, and 2386
Dt 14: 8 the **s**, because it divideth the hoof, 2386
Mt 7: 6 neither cast ye your pearls before **s**, *5519*
8:30 off from them a herd of many **s** feeding. *5519*
8:31 suffer us to go away into the herd of **s**. *5519*
8:32 come out, they went into the herd of **s**: *5519*
8:32 the whole herd of **s** ran violently down a *5519*
Mk 5:11 the mountains a great herd of **s** feeding. *5519*
5:12 saying, Send us into the **s**, that we may *5519*
5:13 spirits went out, and entered into the **s**: *5519*
5:14 And they that fed the **s** fled, and told *it* in *5519*
5:16 with the devil, and *also* concerning the **s**. *5519*
Lk 8:32 And there was there a herd of many **s** *5519*
8:33 out of the man, and entered into the **s**: *5519*
15:15 and he sent him into his fields to feed **s**. *5519*
15:16 his belly with the husks that the **s** did eat: *5519*

SWINE'S (4) [SWINE]
Pr 11:22 *As* a jewel of gold in a **s** snout, *so is* a fair 2386
Isa 65: 4 which eat **s** flesh, and broth of abominable 2386
66: 3 an oblation, *as if he offered* **s** blood; 2386
66:17 eating **s** flesh, and the abomination, and 2386

SWOLLEN (1) [SWELL]
Ac 28: 6 they looked when he should have **s**, *4092*

SWOON (1) [SWOONED]
La 2:11 and the sucklings **s** in the streets of the city. 5848

SWOONED (1) [SWOON]
La 2:12 when they **s** as the wounded in the streets 5848

SWORD (424) [SWORDS]
Ge 3:24 a flaming **s** which turned every way, 2719
27:40 by thy **s** shalt thou live, and shalt serve thy 2719
31:26 my daughters, as captives taken with the **s**? 2719
34:25 took each man his **s**, and came upon 2719
34:26 and Shechem his son with the edge of the **s**, 2719
48:22 out of the hand of the Amorite with my **s** 2719
Ex 5: 3 fall upon us with pestilence, or with the **s**. 2719
5:21 to put a **s** in their hand to slay us. 2719
15: 9 I will draw my **s**, my hand shall destroy 2719
17:13 and his people with the edge of the **s**. 2719
18: 4 and delivered me from the **s** of Pharaoh: 2719
22:24 shall wax hot, and I will kill you with the **s**; 2719
32:27 Put every man his **s** by his side, *and* go in 2719
Lev 26: 6 neither shall the **s** go through your land. 2719
26: 7 and they shall fall before you by the **s**. 2719
26: 8 your enemies shall fall before you by the **s**. 2719
26:25 I will bring a **s** upon you, that shall avenge 2719
26:33 the heathen, and will draw out a **s** after you: 2719
26:36 they shall flee, as fleeing from a **s**; and 2719
26:37 as it were before a **s**, when none pursueth: 2719
Nu 14: 3 to fall by the **s**, *that* our wives and 2719
14:43 there before you, and ye shall fall by the **s**: 2719
19:16 one that is slain with a **s** in the open fields, 2719
20:18 lest I come out against thee with the **s**. 2719
21:24 Israel smote him with the edge of the **s**, 2719
22:23 in the way, and his **s** drawn in his hand: 2719
22:29 I would there were a **s** in mine hand, 2719
22:31 in the way, and his **s** drawn in his hand: 2719
31: 8 also the son of Beor they slew with the **s**. 2719
Dt 13:15 of that city with the edge of the **s**, 2719
13:15 the cattle thereof, with the edge of the **s**. 2719
20:13 every male thereof with the edge of the **s**: 2719
28:22 with the **s**, and with blasting, and 2719
32:25 The **s** without, and terror within, 2719
32:41 If I whet my glittering **s**, and mine hand 2719
32:42 with blood, and my **s** shall devour flesh; 2719
33:29 and who *is* the **s** of thy excellency! 2719
Jos 5:13 against him with his **s** drawn in his hand: 2719
6:21 and sheep, and ass, with the edge of the **s**. 2719
8:24 they were all fallen on the edge of the **s**, 2719
8:24 *unto* Ai, and smote it with the edge of the **s**. 2719
10:11 whom the children of Israel slew with the **s**. 2719
10:28 smote it with the edge of the **s**, and the king 2719
10:30 he smote it with the edge of the **s**, and all 2719
10:32 smote it with the edge of the **s**, and all 2719
10:35 smote it with the edge of the **s**, and all 2719
10:37 smote it with the edge of the **s**, and the king 2719
10:39 they smote them with the edge of the **s**, and 2719
11:10 and smote the king thereof with the **s**: 2719
11:11 that *were* therein with the edge of the **s**, 2719
11:12 smote them with the edge of the **s**, *and* 2719
11:14 man they smote with the edge of the **s**, 2719
13:22 did the children of Israel slay with the **s** 2719
19:47 smote it with the edge of the **s**, and 2719
24:12 *but* not with thy **s**, nor with thy bow. 2719
Jdg 1: 8 smitten it with the edge of the **s**, and set 2719
1:25 they smote the city with the edge of the **s**; 2719
4:15 with the edge of the **s** before Barak; 2719
4:16 host of Sisera fell upon the edge of the **s**; 2719
7:14 This *is* nothing else save the **s** of Gideon 2719
7:18 say, *The s* of the LORD, and of Gideon. NIH
7:20 The **s** of the LORD, and of Gideon. 2719
7:22 the LORD set every man's **s** against his 2719
8:10 and twenty thousand men that drew **s**. 2719
8:20 the youth drew not his **s**: for he feared, 2719
9:54 and said unto him, Draw thy **s**, and slay me, 2719
18:27 they smote them with the edge of the **s**, and 2719
20: 2 four hundred thousand footmen that drew **s**. 2719
20:15 and six thousand men that drew **s**, 2719
20:17 four hundred thousand men that drew **s**: 2719
20:25 thousand men; all these drew the **s**. 2719
20:35 and an hundred men: all these drew the **s**. 2719
20:37 smote all the city with the edge of the **s**. 2719
20:46 and five thousand men that drew the **s**; 2719
20:48 smote them with the edge of the **s**, as well 2719
21:10 of Jabesh-gilead with the edge of the **s**, 2719
1Sa 13:22 that there was neither **s** nor spear found in 2719
14:20 every man's **s** was against his fellow, *and* 2719
15: 8 all the people with the edge of the **s**. 2719
15:33 As thy **s** hath made women childless, so 2719
17:39 David girded his **s** upon his armour, and 2719
17:45 Thou comest to me with a **s**, and with a 2719
17:47 know that the LORD saveth not with **s** 2719
17:50 but *there was* no **s** in the hand of David. 2719
17:51 took his **s**, and drew it out of the sheath 2719
18: 4 even to his **s**, and to his bow, and to his 2719
21: 8 there not here under thine hand spear or **s**? 2719
21: 8 for I have neither brought my **s** nor my 2719
21: 9 priest said, The **s** of Goliath the Philistine, 2719
22:10 and gave him the **s** of Goliath the Philistine. 2719
22:13 in that thou hast given him bread and a **s**, 2719
22:19 smote he with the edge of the **s**, both men 2719
22:19 and asses, and sheep, with the edge of the **s**. 2719
25:13 unto his men, Gird you on every man his **s**. 2719
25:13 they girded on every man his **s**; and 2719
25:13 his sword; and David also girded on his **s**: 2719
31: 4 Draw thy **s**, and thrust me through 2719
31: 4 therefore Saul took a **s**, and fell upon it. 2719
31: 5 he fell likewise upon his **s**, and died with 2719
2Sa 1:12 of Israel; because they were fallen by the **s**. 2719
1:22 and the **s** of Saul returned not empty. 2719
2:16 and *thrust* his **s** in his fellow's side; 2719
2:26 and said, Shall the **s** devour for ever? 2719
3:29 or that falleth on the **s**, or that lacketh 2719
11:25 for the **s** devoureth one as well as another: 2719
12: 9 thou hast killed Uriah the Hittite with the **s**, 2719
12: 9 hast slain him with the **s** of the children of 2719

2Sa 12:10 the s shall never depart from thine house, 2719
15:14 and smite the city with the edge of the s. 2719
18: 8 more people that day than the s devoured. 2719
20: 8 upon it a girdle with a s fastened upon his 2719
20:10 Amasa took no heed to the s that *was* in 2719
21:16 he being girded *with* a new *s*, thought to NIH
23:10 was weary, and his hand clave unto the s: 2719
24: 9 thousand valiant men that drew the s; 2719
1Ki 1:51 that he will not slay his servant with the s. 2719
2: 8 I will not put thee to death with the s. 2719
2:32 better than he, and slew them with the s, 2719
3:24 the king said, Bring me a s. And they 2719
3:24 And they brought a s before the king. 2719
19: 1 how he had slain all the prophets with the s. 2719
19:10 and slain thy prophets with the s; 2719
19:14 and slain thy prophets with the s; 2719
19:17 *that* him that escapeth the s of Hazael shall 2719
19:17 him that escapeth from the s of Jehu shall 2719
2Ki 6:22 whom thou hast taken captive with thy s 2719
8:12 their young *men* wilt thou slay with the s, 2719
10:25 they smote them with the edge of the s; 2719
11:15 him that followeth her kill with the s. 2719
11:20 they slew Athaliah with the s *beside* 2719
19: 7 I will cause him to fall by the s in his own 2719
19:37 and Sharezer *his sons* smote him with the s: 2719
1Ch 5:18 men *able to* bear buckler and s, and 2719
10: 4 Draw thy s, and thrust me through 2719
10: 4 So Saul took a s, and fell upon it. 2719
10: 5 he fell likewise on the s, and died. 2719
21: 5 and an hundred thousand men that drew s: 2719
21: 5 and ten thousand men that drew s. 2719
21:12 while that the s of thine enemies overtaketh 2719
21:12 or else three days the s of the LORD, 2719
21:16 having a drawn s in his hand stretched out 2719
21:27 he put up his s again into the sheath 2719
21:30 of the s of the angel of the LORD. 2719
2Ch 20: 9 *as* the s, judgment, or pestilence, or famine, 2719
21: 4 slew all his brethren with the s, and 2719
23:14 followeth her, let him be slain with the s. 2719
23:21 after that they had slain Athaliah with the s. 2719
29: 9 our fathers have fallen by the s, and 2719
32:21 his own bowels slew him there with the s. 2719
36:17 who slew their young men with the s in 2719
36:20 them that had escaped from the s carried he 2719
Ezr 9: 7 to the s, to captivity, and to a spoil, and 2719
Ne 4:18 every one had his s girded by his side, and 2719
Est 9: 5 all their enemies *with* the stroke of the s, 2719
Job 1:15 slain the servants with the edge of the s; 2719
1:17 slain the servants with the edge of the s; 2719
5:15 he saveth the poor from the s, from their 2719
5:20 and in war from the power of the s. 2719
15:22 of darkness, and he *is* waited for of the s. 2719
19:29 Be ye afraid of the s: for wrath *bringeth* 2719
19:29 for wrath *bringeth* the punishments of the s, 2719
20:25 yea, the **glistering** s cometh out of his gall: 1300
27:14 If his children be multiplied, *it is* for the s: 2719
33:18 the pit, and his life from perishing by the s. 7973
36:12 they shall perish by the s, and they shall die 7973
39:22 neither turneth he back from the s. 2719
40:19 he that made him can make his s to 2719
41:26 The s of him that layeth at him cannot hold: 2719
Ps 7:12 If he turn not, he will whet his s; he hath 2719
17:13 my soul from the wicked, *which is* thy s: 2719
22:20 Deliver my soul from the s; my darling 2719
37:14 The wicked have drawn out the s, and 2719
37:15 Their s shall enter into their own heart, and 2719
42:10 *As* with a s in my bones, mine enemies 7524
44: 3 not the land in possession by their own s, 2719
44: 6 in my bow, neither shall my s save me. 2719
45: 3 Gird thy s upon *thy* thigh, O *most* mighty, 2719
57: 4 and arrows, and their tongue a sharp s. 2719
63:10 They shall fall by the s: they shall be a 2719
64: 3 Who whet their tongue like a s, *and* 2719
76: 3 the shield, and the s, and the battle. 2719
78:62 He gave his people over also unto the s; 2719
78:64 Their priests fell by the s; and their widows 2719
89:43 Thou hast also turned the edge of his s, and 2719
144:10 David his servant from the hurtful s. 2719
149: 6 and a twoedged s in their hand; 2719
Pr 5: 4 bitter as wormwood, sharp as a twoedged s. 2719
12:18 is that speaketh like the piercings of a s: 2719
25:18 *is* a maul, and a s, and a sharp arrow. 2719
SS 3: 8 every man *hath* his s upon his thigh 2719
Isa 1:20 and rebel, ye shall be devoured *with* the s: 2719
2: 4 nation shall not lift up s against nation, 2719
3:25 Thy men shall fall by the s, and thy mighty 2719
13:15 that is joined *unto them* shall fall by the s. 2719
14:19 thrust through with a s, that go down to 2719
21:15 from the drawn s, and from the bent bow, 2719
22: 2 thy slain *men are* not slain with the s, nor 2719
27: 1 strong s shall punish leviathan the piercing 2719
31: 8 shall the Assyrian fall with the s, not of a 2719
31: 8 the s, not of a mean man, shall devour him: 2719
31: 8 he shall flee from the s, and his young men 2719
34: 5 For my s shall be bathed in heaven: behold, 2719
34: 6 The s of the LORD is filled *with* blood, 2719
37: 7 I will cause him to fall by the s in his own 2719
37:38 and Sharezer his sons smote him with the s; 2719
41: 2 he gave *them* as the dust *to* his s, *and* 2719
49: 2 he hath made my mouth like a sharp s; 2719
51:19 and destruction, and the famine, and the s: 2719
65:12 Therefore will I number you to the s, and 2719
66:16 by his s will the LORD plead with all 2719
Jer 2:30 your own s hath devoured your prophets, 2719
4:10 whereas the s reacheth unto the soul). 2719
5:12 upon us; neither shall we see s nor famine: 2719
5:17 wherein thou trustedst, with the s. 2719
6:25 for the s of the enemy *and* fear *is* on every 2719
9:16 I will send a s after them, till I have 2719
11:22 the young men shall die by the s; their sons 2719
12:12 for the s of the LORD *shall* devour from 2719
14:12 I will consume them by the s, and by 2719
14:13 say unto them, Ye shall not see the s, 2719
14:15 S and famine shall not be in this land; 2719
14:15 By s and famine shall those prophets be 2719

Jer 14:16 because of the famine and the s; 2719
14:18 the field, then behold the slain with the s: 2719
15: 2 such as *are* for the s, to the sword; and 2719
15: 2 such as *are* for the sword, to the s; and 2719
15: 3 the s to slay, and the dogs to tear, and 2719
15: 9 the residue of them will I deliver to the s 2719
16: 4 they shall be consumed by the s, and 2719
18:21 pour out their *blood* by the force of the s; 2719
18:21 *let* their young men *be* slain by the s in 2719
19: 7 I will cause them to fall by the s before 2719
20: 4 they shall fall by the s of their enemies, and 2719
20: 4 and shall slay them with the s. 2719
21: 7 from the s, and from the famine, 2719
21: 7 he shall smite them with the edge of the s; 2719
21: 9 that abideth in this city shall die by the s, 2719
24:10 I will send the s, the famine, and 2719
25:16 of the s that I will send among them. 2719
25:27 of the s which I will send among you. 2719
25:29 for I *will* call for a s upon all 2719
25:31 he will give them *that are* wicked to the s, 2719
26:23 who slew him with the s, and cast his dead 2719
27: 8 with the s, and with the famine, and 2719
27:13 thou and thy people, by the s, by 2719
29:17 Behold, I will send upon them the s, 2719
29:18 I will persecute them with the s, with 2719
31: 2 The people which were left of the s found 2719
32:24 because of the s, and *of* the famine, and 2719
32:36 the hand of the king of Babylon by the s, 2719
33: 4 thrown down by the mounts, and by the s; 2719
34: 4 of thee, Thou shalt not die by the s: 2719
34:17 to the s, to the pestilence, and to 2719
38: 2 that remaineth in this city shall die by the s, 2719
39:18 thou shalt not fall by the s, but thy life shall 2719
41: 2 of Ahikam the son of Shaphan with the s, 2719
42:16 come to pass, *that* the s, which ye feared, 2719
42:17 they shall die by the s, by the famine, and 2719
42:22 know certainly that ye shall die by the s, 2719
43:11 and such *as are* for the s to the sword. 2719
43:11 and such *as are* for the sword to the s. 2719
44:12 they shall *even* be consumed by the s, *and* 2719
44:12 the greatest, by the s and by the famine: 2719
44:13 by the s, by the famine, and by 2719
44:18 have been consumed by the s and by 2719
44:27 land of Egypt shall be consumed by the s 2719
44:28 Yet a small number that escape the s shall 2719
46:10 the s shall devour, and it shall be satiate 2719
46:14 for the s shall devour round about thee. 2719
46:16 land of our nativity, from the oppressing s. 2719
47: 6 O thou s of the LORD, how long *will it be* 2719
48: 2 O Madmen; the s shall pursue thee. 2719
48:10 cursed *be* he that keepeth back his s from 2719
49:37 I will send the s after them, till I have 2719
50:16 for fear of the oppressing s they shall turn 2719
50:35 A s *is* upon the Chaldeans, saith 2719
50:36 A s *is* upon the liars; and they shall dote: 2719
50:36 a s *is* upon her mighty *men;* and they shall 2719
50:37 A s *is* upon their horses, and upon their 2719
50:37 a s *is* upon her treasures; and they shall be 2719
51:50 Ye that have escaped the s, go *away,* stand 2719
La 1:20 abroad the s bereaveth, at home *there is* as 2719
2:21 and my young men are fallen by the s; 2719
4: 9 *They that be* slain with the s are better than 2719
5: 9 our lives because of the s of the wilderness. 2719
Eze 5: 2 the wind; and I will draw out a s after them. 2719
5:12 a third *part* shall fall by the s round about 2719
5:12 and I will draw out a s after them. 2719
5:17 and I will bring the s upon thee. 2719
6: 3 *will* bring a s upon you, and I will destroy 2719
6: 8 that shall escape the s among the nations, 2719
6:11 for they shall fall by the s, by the famine, 2719
6:12 *he* that *is* near shall fall by the s; and he that 2719
7:15 The s *is* without, and the pestilence and 2719
7:15 he that *is* in the field shall die with the s; 2719
11: 8 Ye have feared the s; and I will bring a 2719
11: 8 I will bring a s upon you, saith the Lord 2719
11:10 Ye shall fall by the s; I will judge you in 2719
12:14 and I will draw out the s after them. 2719
12:16 I will leave a few men of them from the s, 2719
14:17 Or *if* I bring a s upon that land, and say, 2719
14:17 that land, and say, S, go through the land; 2719
14:21 the s, and the famine, and the noisome 2719
17:21 with all his bands shall fall by the s, 2719
21: 3 will draw forth my s out of his sheath, and 2719
21: 4 shall my s go forth out of his sheath against 2719
21: 5 have drawn forth my s out of his sheath: 2719
21: 9 Say, A s, a sword is sharpened, and 2719
21: 9 a s is sharpened, and also furbished: 2719
21:11 this s is sharpened, and it *is* furbished, 2719
21:12 terrors by reason of the s shall be upon my 2719
21:13 and what if *the s* contemn even the rod? NIH
21:14 let the s be doubled the third time, 2719
21:14 be doubled the third time, the s of the slain: 2719
21:14 it *is* the s of the great *men that are* slain, 2719
21:15 I have set the point of the s against all their 2719
21:19 that the s of the king of Babylon may come: 2719
21:20 that the s may come to Rabbath of 2719
21:28 even say thou, The s, the sword *is* drawn: 2719
21:28 even say thou, The sword, the s *is* drawn: 2719
23:10 and her daughters, and slew her with the s: 2719
23:25 and thy remnant shall fall by the s: 2719
24:21 whom ye have left shall fall by the s. 2719
25:13 and they of Dedan shall fall by the s. 2719
26: 6 *are* in the field shall be slain by the s; 2719
26: 8 He shall slay with the s thy daughters in 2719
26:11 he shall slay thy people by the s, and 2719
28:23 of her by the s upon her on every side; 2719
29: 8 I *will* bring a s upon thee, and cut off man 2719
30: 4 the s shall come upon Egypt, and great pain 2719
30: 5 is in league, shall fall with them by the s. 2719
30: 6 tower of Syene shall they fall in it by the s, 2719
30:17 and of Phi-beseth shall fall by the s: 2719
30:21 to bind it, to make it strong to hold the s. 2719
30:22 and I will cause the s to fall out of his hand. 2719
30:24 king of Babylon, and put my s in his hand: 2719
30:25 when I shall put my s into the hand of 2719

Eze 31:17 with him unto *them that be* slain with the s; 2719
31:18 with *them that be* slain with the s. 2719
32:10 when I shall brandish my s before them; 2719
32:11 The s of the king of Babylon shall come 2719
32:20 in the midst of *them that are* slain by the s: 2719
32:20 she is delivered *to* the s: draw her and 2719
32:21 they lie uncircumcised, slain by the s. 2719
32:22 about him: all of them slain, fallen by the s: 2719
32:23 all of them slain, fallen by the s, 2719
32:24 her grave, all of them slain, fallen by the s, 2719
32:25 all of them uncircumcised, slain by the s: 2719
32:26 all of them uncircumcised, slain by the s, 2719
32:28 shalt lie with *them that are* slain with the s. 2719
32:29 are laid by *them that were* slain by the s: 2719
32:30 with *them that be* slain by the s, 2719
32:31 and all his army slain by the s, 2719
32:32 with *them that are* slain with the s, 2719
33: 2 unto them, When I bring the s upon a land, 2719
33: 3 *If* when he seeth the s come upon the land, 2719
33: 4 if the s come, and take him away, his blood 2719
33: 6 if the watchman see the s come, and 2719
33: 6 if the s come, and take *any* person from 2719
33:26 Ye stand upon your s, ye work 2719
33:27 that *are* in the wastes shall fall by the s, 2719
35: 5 force of the s in the time of their calamity, 2719
35: 8 shall they fall *that are* slain with the s. 2719
38: 8 the land *that is* brought back from the s, 2719
38:21 I will call *for* a s against him throughout all 2719
38:21 every man's s shall be against his brother. 2719
39:23 of their enemies: so fell they all by the s. 2719
Da 11:33 yet they shall fall by the s, and by flame, 2719
Hos 1: 7 nor by s, nor by battle, by horses, nor by 2719
2:18 I will break the bow and the s and the battle 2719
7:16 their princes shall fall by the s for the rage 2719
11: 6 the s shall abide on his cities, and 2719
13:16 they shall fall by the s: their infants shall be 2719
Joel 2: 8 *when* they fall upon the s, they shall not be 7973
Am 1:11 he did pursue his brother with the s, 2719
4:10 your young men have I slain with the s, and 2719
7: 9 against the house of Jeroboam with the s. 2719
7:11 Jeroboam shall die by the s, and Israel shall 2719
7:17 and thy daughters shall fall by the s, 2719
9: 1 and I will slay the last of them with the s: 2719
9: 4 thence will I command the s, and it shall 2719
9:10 the sinners of my people shall die by the s, 2719
Mic 4: 3 nation shall not lift up a s against nation, 2719
5: 6 shall waste the land of Assyria with the s, 2719
6:14 thou deliverest will I give up to the s. 2719
Na 2:13 and the s shall devour thy young lions: 2719
3: 3 The horseman lifteth up both the bright s 2719
3:15 the s shall cut thee off, it shall eat thee up 2719
Zep 2:12 Ethiopians also, ye *shall be* slain by my s. 2719
Hag 2:22 every one by the s of his brother. 2719
Zec 9:13 and made thee as the s of a mighty *man.* 2719
11:17 the s *shall be* upon his arm, and upon his 2719
13: 7 Awake, O s, against my shepherd, and 2719
Mt 10:34 on earth: I came not to send peace, but a s. 3162
26:51 and drew his s, and stroke a servant of 3162
26:52 unto him, Put up again thy s into his place: 3162
26:52 for all they that take the s shall perish with 3162
26:52 that take the sword shall perish with the s. 3162
Mk 14:47 And one of them that stood by drew a s, 3162
Lk 2:35 a s shall pierce through thy own soul also,) 4501
21:24 And they shall fall by the edge of the s, and 3162
22:36 and he that hath no s, let him sell his 3162
22:49 unto him, Lord, shall we smite with the s? 3162
Jn 18:10 Then Simon Peter having a s drew it, and 3162
18:11 unto Peter, Put up thy s into the sheath: 3162
Ac 12: 2 killed James the brother of John with the s. 3162
16:27 he drew out his s, and would have killed 3162
Ro 8:35 or famine, or nakedness, or peril, or s? 3162
13: 4 be afraid; for he beareth not the s in vain: 3162
Eph 6:17 and the s of the Spirit, which is the word of 3162
Heb 4:12 powerful, and sharper than any twoedged s, 3162
11:34 violence of fire, escaped the edge of the s, 3162
11:37 were tempted, were slain with the s: 3162
Rev 1:16 out of his mouth went a sharp twoedged s: 4501
2:12 *things* saith he which hath the sharp s 4501
2:16 will fight against them with the s of my 4501
6: 4 and there was given unto him a great s. 3162
6: 8 to kill with s, and with hunger, and 4501
13:10 he that killeth with the s must be killed with 3162
13:10 with the sword must be killed with the s. 3162
13:14 which had the wound by a s, and did live. 3162
19:15 And out of his mouth goeth a sharp s, 4501
19:21 And the remnant were slain with the s of 4501
19:21 which *s* proceeded out of his mouth: NIG

SWORDS (24) [SWORD]

1Sa 13:19 Lest the Hebrews make *them* s or spears: 2719
2Ki 3:26 with him seven hundred men that drew s, 2719
Ne 4:13 the people after *their* families with their s, 2719
Ps 55:21 were softer than oil, yet *were they* **drawn** s. 6609
59: 7 s *are* in their lips: for who, *say they,* doth 2719
Pr 30:14 whose teeth *are as* s, and their jaw teeth *as* 2719
SS 3: 8 They all hold s, *being* expert in war: 2719
Isa 2: 4 they shall beat their s into plowshares, and 2719
21:15 For they fled from the s, from the drawn 2719
Eze 16:40 and thrust thee through with their s. 2719
23:47 with stones, and dispatch them with their s; 2719
28: 7 they shall draw their s against the beauty of 2719
30:11 they shall draw their s against Egypt, and 2719
32:12 By the s of the mighty will I cause thy 2719
32:27 they have laid their s under their heads, but 2719
38: 4 and shields, all of them handling s: 2719
Joel 3:10 Beat your plowshares into s, and 2719
Mic 4: 3 they shall beat their s into plowshares, and 2719
Mt 26:47 and with him a great multitude with s and 3162
26:55 Are ye come out as against a thief with s 3162
Mk 14:43 and with him a great multitude with s and 3162
14:48 a thief, with s and *with* staves to take me? 3162
Lk 22:38 And they said, Lord, behold, here *are* two s. 3162
22:52 as against a thief, with s and staves? 3162

SWORN (48) [SWEAR]
Ge 22:16 said, By myself have I **s**, saith the LORD, 7650
Ex 13:19 for he had **straitly s** the children of 7650+7650
17:16 Because the LORD hath **s** 3027+3678+5921
Lev 6: 5 Or all *that* about which he hath **s** falsely; 7650
Dt 7: 8 he would keep the oath which he had **s** unto 7650
13:17 multiply thee, as he hath **s** unto thy fathers; 7650
19: 8 as he hath **s** unto thy fathers, and give thee 7650
28: 9 people unto himself, as he hath **s** unto thee, 7650
29:13 as he hath **s** unto thy fathers, to Abraham, 7650
31: 7 hath **s** unto their fathers to give them; 7650
Jos 9:18 the princes of the congregation had **s** unto 7650
9:19 We have **s** unto them by the LORD God 7650
Jdg 2:15 and as the LORD had **s** unto them: 7650
21: 1 Now the men of Israel had **s** in Mizpeh, 7650
21: 7 seeing we have **s** by the LORD that *we* 7650
21:18 for the children of Israel have **s**, saying, 7650
1Sa 3:14 I have **s** unto the house of Eli, 7650
20:42 forasmuch as we have **s** both of us in 7650
2Sa 3: 9 as the LORD hath **s** to David, even so I do 7650
21: 2 and the children of Israel had **s** unto them: 7650
2Ch 15:15 for they had **s** with all their heart, and 7650
Ne 6:18 For *there were* many in Judah **s** unto 1167+7621
9:15 the land which thou hadst **s** to give them. 3027
Ps 24: 4 up his soul unto vanity, nor **s** deceitfully. 7650
89: 3 my chosen, I have **s** unto David my servant, 7650
89:35 Once have I **s** by my holiness that I will not 7650
102: 8 they that are mad against me are **s** against 7650
110: 4 The LORD hath **s**, and will not repent, 7650
119:106 I have **s**, and I will perform *it*, that *I* will 7650
132:11 The LORD hath **s** *in* truth unto David; 7650
Isa 14:24 The LORD of hosts hath **s**, saying, 7650
45:23 I have **s** by myself, the word is gone out of 7650
54: 9 for *as* I have **s** that the waters of Noah 7650
54: 9 have I **s** that *I* would not be wroth with 7650
62: 8 The LORD hath **s** by his right hand, and 7650
Jer 5: 7 and **s** by *them that are* no gods: 7650
11: 5 That *I* may perform the oath which I have **s** 7650
44:26 Behold, I have **s** by my great name, 7650
49:13 For I have **s** by myself, saith the LORD, 7650
51:14 The LORD of hosts hath **s** by himself, 7650
Eze 21:23 in their sight, to them that have **s** oaths: 7650
Am 4: 2 The Lord GOD hath **s** by his holiness, 7650
6: 8 The Lord GOD hath **s** by himself, saith 7650
8: 7 The LORD hath **s** by the excellency of 7650
Mic 7:20 which thou hast **s** unto our fathers from 7650
Ac 2:30 knowing that God had **s** with an oath to *3660*
7:17 which God had **s** to Abraham, the people *3660*
Heb 4: 3 as *he* said, As I have **s** in my wrath, if they *3660*

SYCAMINE (1)
Lk 17: 6 ye might say unto this **s tree**, Be thou *4807*

SYCAMORE-FIG See SYCOMORE

SYCHAR (1)
Jn 4: 5 he to a city of Samaria, which is called **S**, *4965*

SYCHEM (2) [SHECHEM]
Ac 7:16 And were carried over into **S**, and laid in *4966*
7:16 of the sons of Emmor the *father* of **S**. *4966*

SYCOMORE (7) [SYCOMORES]
1Ki 10:27 cedars made he *to be* as the **s trees** that *are* 8256
1Ch 27:28 the **s trees** that *were* in the low plains *was* 8256
2Ch 1:15 cedar trees made he as the **s trees** that *are* 8256
9:27 cedar trees made he as the **s trees** that *are* 8256
Ps 78:47 vines with hail, and their **s trees** with frost. 8256
Am 7:14 I *was* a herdman, and a gatherer of **s fruit**: 8256
Lk 19: 4 and climbed up into a **s tree** to see him: *4809*

SYCOMORES (1) [SYCOMORE]
Isa 9:10 the **s** are cut down, but we will change 8256

SYENE (2)
Eze 29:10 from the tower of **S** even unto the border of 5482
30: 6 from the tower of **S** shall they fall in it by 5482

SYNAGOGUE (43) [SYNAGOGUE'S, SYNAGOGUES]
Mt 12: 9 was departed thence, he went into their **s**: *4864*
13:54 he taught them in their **s**, insomuch that *4864*
Mk 1:21 on the sabbath day he entered into the **s**, *4864*
1:23 And there was in their **s** a man with an *4864*
1:29 when they were come out of the **s**, *4864*
3: 1 And he entered again into the **s**; and *4864*
5:22 there cometh one of the **rulers of the s**, *752*
5:36 he saith unto the **ruler of the s**, Be not *752*
5:38 he cometh to the house of the **ruler of the s**, *752*
6: 2 day was come, he began to teach in the **s**: *4864*
Lk 4:16 he went into the **s** on the sabbath day, *4864*
4:20 And the eyes of all *them that were* in the **s** *4864*
4:28 And all *they* in the **s**, when they heard these *4864*
4:33 And in the **s** there was a man, which had a *4864*
4:38 And he arose out of the **s**, and entered into *4864*
6: 6 that he entered into the **s** and taught: *4864*
7: 5 loveth our nation, and he hath built us a **s**. *4864*
8:41 named Jairus, and he was a ruler of the **s**: *4864*
13:14 And the **ruler of the s** answered with *752*
Jn 6:59 These *things* said he in the **s**, as he taught in *4864*
9:22 he *was* Christ, he should be **put out of the s**. *656*
12:42 *him*, lest they should be **put out of the s**: *656*
18:20 I ever taught in the **s**, and in the temple, *4864*
Ac 6: 9 Then there arose certain of the **s**, which is *4864*
6: 9 which is called *the* **s** of the Libertines, and NIG
13:14 and went into the **s** on the sabbath day, and *4864*
13:15 the prophets the **rulers of the s** sent unto *752*
13:42 And when the Jews were gone out of the **s**, *4864*
14: 1 that they went *both* together into the **s** of *4864*
17: 1 to Thessalonica, where was a **s** of the Jews: *4864*
17:10 who coming *thither* went into the **s** of *4864*
17:17 Therefore disputed he in the **s** with *4864*
18: 4 And he reasoned in the **s** every sabbath, and *4864*
18: 7 whose house joined hard to the **s**. *4864*
18: 8 And Crispus, the *chief* **ruler of the s**, *752*
18:17 the *chief* **ruler of the s**, and beat *him* before *752*
18:19 but he himself entered into the **s**, and *4864*
18:26 And he began to speak boldly in the **s**: *4864*
19: 8 And he went into the **s**, and spake boldly *4864*
22:19 beat in every **s** them that believed on thee: *4864*
26:11 And I punished them oft in every **s**, and *4864*
Rev 2: 9 are Jews, and are not, but *are* the **s** of Satan. *4864*
3: 9 Behold, I *will* make *them* of the **s** of Satan, *4864*

SYNAGOGUE'S (2) [SYNAGOGUE]
Mk 5:35 there came from the **ruler of the s** *house* *752*
Lk 8:49 there cometh one from the **ruler of the s** *752*

SYNAGOGUES (24) [SYNAGOGUE]
Ps 74: 8 they have burnt up all the **s** of God in 4150
Mt 4:23 teaching in their **s** and preaching the gospel *4864*
6: 2 as the hypocrites do in the **s** and in *4864*
6: 5 *are*: for they love to pray standing in the **s** *4864*
9:35 teaching in their **s**, and preaching *4864*
10:17 and they will scourge you in their **s**; *4864*
23: 6 rooms at feasts, and the chief seats in the **s**, *4864*
23:34 *some* of them shall ye scourge in your **s**, *4864*
Mk 1:39 And he preached in their **s** throughout all *4864*
12:39 And the chief seats in the **s**, and *4864*
13: 9 to councils; and in the **s** ye shall be beaten: *4864*
Lk 4:15 And he taught in their **s**, being glorified of *4864*
4:44 And he preached in the **s** of Galilee. *4864*
11:43 for ye love the uppermost seats in the **s**, and *4864*
12:11 And when they bring you unto the **s**, and *4864*
13:10 And he was teaching in one of the **s** on *4864*
20:46 and the highest seats in the **s**, and the chief *4864*
21:12 persecute *you*, delivering *you* up to *the* **s**, *4864*
Jn 16: 2 They shall put you **out of the s**: yea, the time *656*
Ac 9: 2 desired of him letters to Damascus to the **s**, *4864*
9:20 straightway he preached Christ in the **s**, *4864*
13: 5 they preached the word of God in the **s** of *4864*
15:21 being read in the **s** every sabbath day. *4864*
24:12 the people, neither in the **s**, nor in the city: *4864*

SYNTYCHE (1)
Php 4: 2 I beseech Euodias, and beseech **S**, that *they* *4941*

SYRACUSE (1)
Ac 28:12 And landing at **S**, we tarried *there* three *4946*

SYRIA (75) [SYRIA-DAMASCUS, SYRIA-MAACHAH, SYRIACK, SYRIAN, SYRIANS, SYROPHENICIAN]
Jdg 10: 6 the gods of **S**, and the gods of Zidon, and 758
2Sa 8: 6 Then David put garrisons in **S** of Damascus: 758
8:12 Of **S**, and of Moab, and of the children of 758
15: 8 vowed a vow while I abode at Geshur in **S**, 758
1Ki 10:29 kings of the Hittites, and for the kings of **S**, 758
11:25 and he abhorred Israel, and reigned over **S**. 758
15:18 of Tabrimon, the son of Hezion, king of **S**, 758
19:15 anoint Hazael to be king over **S**: 758
20: 1 Ben-hadad the king of **S** gathered all his host 758
20:20 Ben-hadad the king of **S** escaped on a horse 758
20:22 for at the return of the year the king of **S** will 758
20:23 the servants of the king of **S** said unto him, 758
22: 1 continued three years without war between **S** 758
22: 3 take it not out of the hand of the king of **S**? 758
22:31 But the king of **S** commanded his thirty and 758
2Ki 5: 1 captain of the host of the king of **S**, 758
5: 1 the LORD had given deliverance unto **S**: 758
5: 5 the king of **S** said, Go to, go, and I will send 758
6: 8 Then the king of **S** warred against Israel, and 758
6:11 Therefore the heart of the king of **S** was sore 758
6:23 So the bands of **S** came no more into 758
6:24 that Ben-hadad king of **S** gathered all his 758
7: 5 come to the uttermost part of the camp of **S**, 758
8: 7 Ben-hadad the king of **S** was sick; and it was 758
8: 9 Thy son Ben-hadad king of **S** hath sent me to 758
8:13 shewed me *that* thou *shalt be* king over **S**. 758
8:28 against Hazael king of **S** in Ramoth-gilead; 758
8:29 when he fought against Hazael king of **S**. 758
9:14 and all Israel, because of Hazael king of **S**. 758
9:15 when he fought with Hazael king of **S**.) 758
12:17 Hazael king of **S** went up, and fought against 758
12:18 king's house, and sent *it* to Hazael king of **S**: 758
13: 3 them into the hand of Hazael king of **S**, 758
13: 4 because the king of **S** oppressed them. 758
13: 7 for the king of **S** had destroyed them, and 758
13:17 and the arrow of deliverance from **S**: 758
13:19 hadst thou smitten **S** till *thou* hadst 758
13:19 consumed *it*: whereas now thou shalt smite **S** 758
13:22 Hazael king of **S** oppressed Israel all 758
13:24 So Hazael king of **S** died; and Ben-hadad his 758
15:37 to send against Judah Rezin the king of **S**, 758
16: 5 Rezin king of **S** and Pekah son of Remaliah 758
16: 6 At that time Rezin king of **S** recovered Elath 758
16: 6 Rezin king of Syria recovered Elath to **S**, 758
16: 7 and save me out of the hand of the king of **S**, 758
2Ch 1:17 and *for* the kings of **S**, by their means. 758
16: 2 and sent to Ben-hadad king of **S**, 758
16: 7 Because thou hast relied on the king of **S**, 758
16: 7 is the host of the king of **S** escaped out of 758
18:10 With these thou shalt push **S** until they be 758
18:30 Now the king of **S** had commanded 758
20: 2 thee from beyond the sea on this side **S**; 758
22: 5 against Hazael king of **S** at Ramoth-gilead: 758
22: 6 when he fought with Hazael king of **S**. 758
24:23 *that* the host of **S** came up against him: 758
28: 5 delivered him into the hand of the king of **S**; 758
28:23 Because the gods of the kings of **S** help 758
Isa 7: 1 *that* Rezin the king of **S**, and Pekah the son 758
7: 2 **S** is confederate with Ephraim. 758
7: 4 for the fierce anger of Rezin with **S**, and 758
7: 5 Because **S**, Ephraim, and the son of 758
7: 8 For the head of **S** *is* Damascus, and the head 758
17: 3 from Damascus, and the remnant of **S**: 758
Eze 16:57 time of *thy* reproach of the daughters of **S**, 758
27:16 **S** *was* thy merchant by reason of 758
Hos 12:12 Jacob fled *into* the country of **S**, and 758
Am 1: 5 the people of **S** shall go into captivity unto 758
Mt 4:24 And his fame went throughout all **S**: and *4947*
Lk 2: 2 made when Cyrenius was governor of **S**.) *4947*
Ac 15:23 the Gentiles in Antioch and **S** and Cilicia: *4947*
15:41 And he went through **S** and Cilicia, *4947*
18:18 and sailed thence into **S**, and with him *4947*
20: 3 wait for him, as he was about to sail into **S**, *4947*
21: 3 and sailed into **S**, and landed at Tyre: *4947*
Gal 1:21 Afterwards I came into the regions of **S** and *4947*

SYRIACK (1) [SYRIA]
Da 2: 4 spake the Chaldeans to the king **in S**, O king, 762

SYRIA-DAMASCUS (1) [DAMASCUS, SYRIA]
1Ch 18: 6 David put *garrisons* in **S**; and 758+1834

SYRIA-MAACHAH (1) [SYRIA]
1Ch 19: 6 and out of **S**, and out of Zobah. 758

SYRIAN (12) [SYRIA]
Ge 25:20 the daughter of Bethuel the **S** of Padan-aram, 761
25:20 of Padan-aram, the sister to Laban the **S**. 761
28: 5 son of Bethuel the **S**, the brother of Rebekah, 761
31:20 Jacob stale away unawares to Laban the **S**, 761
31:24 God came to Laban the **S** in a dream by 761
Dt 26: 5 A **S** ready to perish *was* my father, and 761
2Ki 5:20 my master hath spared Naaman this **S**, 761
18:26 pray thee, to thy servants **in the S language**; 762
Ezr 4: 7 of the letter *was* written **in the S tongue**, 762
4: 7 and interpreted **in the S tongue**. 762
Isa 36:11 unto thy servants **in the S language**; 762
Lk 4:27 them was cleansed, saving Naaman the **S**. *4948*

SYRIAN PHOENICIA See SYROPHENICIAN

SYRIANS (61) [SYRIA]
2Sa 8: 5 when the **S** of Damascus came to succour 758
8: 5 David slew of the **S** two and 758
8: 6 the **S** became servants to David, and 758
8:13 from smiting of the **S** in the valley of salt, 758
10: 6 Ammon sent and hired the **S** of Beth-rehob, 758
10: 6 and the **S** of Zoba, twenty thousand footmen, 758
10: 8 the **S** of Zoba, and of Rehob, and Ish-tob, 758
10: 9 of Israel, and put *them* in array against the **S**: 758
10:11 If the **S** be too strong for me, then thou shalt 758
10:13 *were* with him, unto the battle against the **S**: 758
10:14 when the children of Ammon saw that the **S** 758
10:15 when the **S** saw that they were smitten 758
10:16 brought out the **S** that *were* beyond the river: 758
10:17 the **S** set *themselves* in array against David, 758
10:18 the **S** fled before Israel; and David slew 758
10:18 *the men of* seven hundred chariots of the **S**, 758
10:19 So the **S** feared to help the children of 758
1Ki 20:20 and the **S** fled; and Israel pursued them: and 758
20:21 and slew the **S** with a great slaughter. 758
20:26 that Ben-hadad numbered the **S**, and went up 758
20:27 flocks of kids; but the **S** filled the country. 758
20:28 saith the LORD, Because the **S** have said, 758
20:29 the children of Israel slew *of* the **S** an 758
22:11 With these shalt thou push the **S**, 758
22:35 was stayed up in *his* chariot against the **S**, 758
2Ki 5: 2 the **S** had gone out *by* companies, and 758
6: 9 a place; for thither the **S** are come down. 758
7: 4 come, and let us fall unto the host of the **S**: 758
7: 5 in the twilight, to go unto the camp of the **S**: 758
7: 6 For the Lord had made the host of the **S** to 758
7:10 We came to the camp of the **S**, and behold, 758
7:12 I will now shew you what the **S** have done to 758
7:14 the king sent after the host of the **S**, saying, 758
7:15 which the **S** had cast away in their haste. 758
7:16 went out, and spoiled the tents of the **S**. 758
8:28 in Ramoth-gilead; and the **S** wounded Joram. 761
8:29 which the **S** had given him at Ramah, 761
9:15 of the wounds which the **S** had given him, 761
13: 5 they went out from under the hand of the **S**: 758
13:17 for thou shalt smite the **S** in Aphek, till *thou* 758
16: 6 the **S** came *to* Elath, and dwelt there unto 726
24: 2 bands of the **S**, and bands of the Moabites, 758
1Ch 18: 5 when the **S** of Damascus came to help 758
18: 5 David slew of the **S** two and 758
18: 6 the **S** became David's servants, and 758
19:10 of Israel, and put *them* in array against the **S**. 758
19:12 If the **S** be too strong for me, then thou shalt 758
19:14 him drew nigh before the **S** unto the battle; 758
19:15 when the children of Ammon saw that the **S** 758
19:16 when the **S** saw that they were put to 758
19:16 drew forth the **S** that *were* beyond the river: 758
19:17 had put the battle in array against the **S**, 758
19:18 the **S** fled before Israel; and David slew of 758
19:18 David slew of the **S** seven thousand *men* 758
19:19 neither would the **S** help the children of 758
2Ch 18:34 up in *his* chariot against the **S** until the even: 758
22: 5 at Ramoth-gilead: and the **S** smote Joram. 7421
24:24 For the army of the **S** came with a small 758
Isa 9:12 The **S** before, and the Philistines behind; and 758
Jer 35:11 and for fear of the army of the **S**: 758
Am 9: 7 from Caphtor, and the **S** from Kir? 758

SYROPHENICIAN (1) [PHENICIA, SYRIA]
Mk 7:26 The woman was a Greek, a **S** by nation; *4949*

T

TAANACH (6)
Jos 12:21 The king of T, one; the king of Megiddo, 8590
17:11 the inhabitants of T and her towns, and 8590
Jdg 1:27 and her towns, nor T and her towns, 8590
5:19 fought the kings of Canaan in T by 8590
1Ki 4:12 *to him pertained* T and Megiddo, and 8590
1Ch 7:29 T and her towns, Megiddo and her towns, 8590

TAANATH-SHILOH (1) [SHILOH]
Jos 16: 6 the border went about eastward *unto* T, and 8387

TABALIAH See TEBALIAH

TABBAOTH (2)
Ezr 2:43 the children of Hasupha, the children of T, 2884
Ne 7:46 the children of Hashupha, the children of T, 2884

TABBATH (1)
Jdg 7:22 *and* to the border of Abel-meholah, unto T. 2888

TABEAL (1)
Isa 7: 6 a king in the midst of it, *even* the son of T: 2870

TABEEL (1)
Ezr 4: 7 T, and the rest of their companions, 2870

TABERAH (2)
Nu 11: 3 he called the name of the place T: because 8404
Dt 9:22 at T, and at Massah, and 8404

TABERNACLE (328) [TABERNACLES]
Ex 25: 9 *after* the pattern of the t, and the pattern of 4908
26: 1 Moreover thou shalt make the t *with* ten 4908
26: 6 with the taches: and it shall be one t. 4908
26: 7 *of* goats' *hair* to be a covering upon the t: 4908
26: 9 the sixth curtain in the forefront of the t. 168
26:12 shall hang over the backside of the t. 4908
26:13 it shall hang over the sides of the t on this 4908
26:15 thou shalt make boards for the t *of* shittim 4908
26:17 shalt thou make for all the boards of the t. 4908
26:18 thou shalt make the boards for the t, 4908
26:20 for the second side of the t on the north 4908
26:22 for the sides of the t westward thou shalt 4908
26:23 for the corners of the t in the two sides. 4908
26:26 five for the boards of the one side of the t, 4908
26:27 bars for the boards of the other side of the t, 4908
26:27 five bars for the boards of the side of the t, 4908
26:30 thou shalt rear up the t according to 4908
26:35 table on the side of the t toward the south: 4908
27: 9 thou shalt make the court of the t: for 4908
27:19 All the vessels of the t in all the service 4908
27:21 In the t of the congregation without the vail, 168
28:43 when they come in unto the t of 168
29: 4 unto the door of the t of the congregation, 168
29:10 be brought before the t of the congregation: 168
29:11 *by* the door of the t of the congregation. 168
29:30 when he cometh into the t of 168
29:32 *by* the door of the t of the congregation. 168
29:42 the t of the congregation before the LORD: 168
29:43 and *the t* shall be sanctified by my glory. NIH
29:44 And I will sanctify the t of the congregation, 168
30:16 shalt appoint it for the service of the t of 168
30:18 thou shalt put it between the t of 168
30:20 When they go into the t of the congregation, 168
30:26 thou shalt anoint the t of the congregation 168
30:36 put of it before the Testimony in the t of 168
31: 7 The t of the congregation, and the ark of 168
31: 7 *is* thereupon, and all the furniture of the t, 168
33: 7 Moses took the t, and pitched it without 168
33: 7 and called it the T of the Congregation. 168
33: 7 went out unto the T of the Congregation, 168
33: 8 to pass, when Moses went out unto the t, 168
33: 8 after Moses, until he was gone into the t. 168
33: 9 it came to pass, as Moses entered into the t, 168
33: 9 stood *at* the door of the t, and *the LORD* 168
33:10 saw the cloudy pillar stand *at* the t door: 168
33:11 a young man, departed not out of the t. 168
35:11 The t, his tent, and his covering, his taches, 4908
35:15 for the door at the entering in of the t, 4908
35:18 The pins of the t, and the pins of the court, 4908
35:21 to the work of the t of the congregation, 168
36: 8 the t made ten curtains *of* fine twined linen, 4908
36:13 another with the taches: so it became one t. 4908
36:14 *of* goats' *hair* for the tent over the t: 4908
36:20 he made boards for the t *of* shittim wood, 4908
36:22 thus did he make for all the boards of the t. 4908
36:23 he made boards for the t; twenty boards for 4908
36:25 for the other side of the t, *which is* toward 4908
36:27 for the sides of the t westward he made six 4908
36:28 two boards made he for the corners of the t 4908
36:31 five for the boards of the one side of the t, 4908
36:32 bars for the boards of the other side of the t, 4908
36:32 five bars for the boards of the t for the sides 4908
36:37 he made a hanging for the t door *of* blue, 168
38: 8 which assembled *at* the door of the t of 168
38:20 all the pins of the t, and of the court round 4908
38:21 This is the sum of the t, *even* of 4908
38:21 *even* of the t of Testimony, as it was 4908
38:30 to the door of the t of the congregation, 168
38:31 all the pins of the t, and all the pins of 4908
39:32 Thus was all the work of the t of the tent of 4908
39:33 they brought the t unto Moses, the tent, 4908
39:38 and the hanging for the t door, 168
Ex 39:40 and all the vessels of the service of the t, 4908
40: 2 set up the t of the tent of the congregation. 4908
40: 5 and put the hanging of the door to the t. 4908
40: 6 door of the t of the tent of the congregation. 4908
40: 9 anoint the t, and all that *is* therein, and 4908
40:12 his sons unto the door of the t of 168
40:17 *day* of the month, *that* the t was reared up. 4908
40:18 Moses reared up the t, and fastened his 4908
40:19 he spread abroad the tent over the t, and 4908
40:21 he brought the ark into the t, and set up 4908
40:22 upon the side of the t northward, without 4908
40:24 the table, on the side of the t southward. 4908
40:28 he set up the hanging at the door of the t. 4908
40:29 door of the t of the tent of the congregation, 4908
40:33 he reared up the court round about the t 4908
40:34 and the glory of the LORD filled the t. 4908
40:35 the glory of the LORD filled the t. 4908
40:36 the cloud was taken up from over the t, 4908
40:38 For the cloud of the LORD *was* upon the t 4908
Lev 1: 1 spake unto him out of the t of 168
1: 3 the t of the congregation before the LORD. 168
1: 5 *is by* the door of the t of the congregation. 168
3: 2 kill it *at* the door of the t of 168
3: 8 and kill it before the t of the congregation: 168
3:13 and kill it before the t of the congregation: 168
4: 4 the t of the congregation before the LORD; 168
4: 5 and bring it to the t of the congregation: 168
4: 7 which *is* in the t of the congregation; 168
4: 7 which *is at* the door of the t of 168
4:14 bring him before the t of the congregation. 168
4:16 bullock's blood to the t of the congregation: 168
4:18 that *is* in the t of the congregation, and shall 168
4:18 which *is at* the door of the t of 168
6:16 in the court of the t of the congregation they 168
6:26 in the court of the t of the congregation. 168
6:30 t of the congregation to reconcile *withal* in 168
8: 3 unto the door of the t of the congregation. 168
8: 4 unto the door of the t of the congregation. 168
8:10 anointed the t and all that *was* therein, 4908
8:31 Boil the flesh *at* the door of the t of 168
8:33 ye shall not go out of the door of the t of 168
8:35 Therefore shall ye abide *at* the door of the t 168
9: 5 commanded before the t of the congregation: 168
9:23 Aaron went into the t of the congregation, 168
10: 7 ye shall not go out from the door of the t of 168
10: 9 when ye go into the t of the congregation, 168
12: 6 unto the door of the t of the congregation, 168
14:11 *at* the door of the t of the congregation: 168
14:23 unto the door of the t of the congregation, 168
15:14 unto the door of the t of the congregation, 168
15:29 to the door of the t of the congregation. 168
15:31 when they defile my t that *is* among them. 4908
16: 7 *at* the door of the t of the congregation. 168
16:16 so shall he do for the t of the congregation, 168
16:17 there shall be no man in the t of 168
16:20 the holy *place*, and the t of the congregation, 168
16:23 Aaron shall come into the t of 168
16:33 he shall make an atonement for the t of 168
17: 4 bringeth it not unto the door of the t of 168
17: 4 the LORD before the t of the LORD; 4908
17: 5 unto the door of the t of the congregation, 168
17: 6 *at* the door of the t of the congregation, 168
17: 9 bringeth it not unto the door of the t of 168
19:21 unto the door of the t of the congregation, 168
24: 3 the Testimony, in the t of the congregation, 168
26:11 I will set my t amongst you: and my soul 4908
Nu 1: 1 in the t of the congregation, on the first *day* 168
1:50 thou shalt appoint the Levites over the t of 4908
1:50 they shall bear the t, and all the vessels 4908
1:50 unto it, and shall encamp round about the t. 4908
1:51 when the t setteth forward, the Levites shall 4908
1:51 when the t is to be pitched, the Levites 4908
1:53 the Levites shall pitch round about the t of 4908
1:53 the Levites shall keep the charge of the t of 4908
2: 2 far off about the t of the congregation shall 168
2:17 the t of the congregation shall set forward 168
3: 7 before the t of the congregation, 168
3: 7 the congregation, to do the service of the t. 4908
3: 8 they shall keep all the instruments of the t of 168
3: 8 children of Israel, to do the service of the t. 4908
3:23 shall pitch behind the t westward. 4908
3:25 the charge of the sons of Gershon in the t of 168
3:25 of the congregation *shall be* the t, 4908
3:25 the hanging for the door of the t of 168
3:26 which *is* by the t, and by the altar round 4908
3:29 shall pitch on the side of the t southward. 4908
3:35 *these* shall pitch on the side of the t 4908
3:36 sons of Merari *shall be* the boards of the t, 4908
3:38 those that encamp before the t toward 4908
3:38 *even* before the t of the congregation 168
4: 3 to do the work in the t of the congregation. 168
4: 4 sons of Kohath in the t of the congregation, 168
4:15 sons of Kohath in the t of the congregation. 168
4:16 *and* the oversight of all the t, and of all that 4908
4:23 to do the work in the t of the congregation. 168
4:25 they shall bear the curtains of the t, and 4908
4:25 the t of the congregation, his covering, and 168
4:25 the hanging for the door of the t of 168
4:26 which *is* by the t and by the altar round 4908
4:28 sons of Gershon in the t of the congregation: 168
4:30 to do the work of the t of the congregation. 168
4:31 according to all their service in the t of 168
4:31 the boards of the t, and the bars thereof, 4908
4:33 all their service, in the t of the congregation, 168
4:35 for the work in the t of the congregation: 168
4:37 all that *might* do service in the t of 168
4:39 for the work in the t of the congregation, 168
4:41 of all that *might* do service in the t of 168
4:43 for the work in the t of the congregation, 168
4:47 the service of the burden in the t of 168
5:17 of the dust that is in the floor of the t 4908
6:10 to the door of the t of the congregation: 168
6:13 he shall be brought unto the door of the t of 168
6:18 *at* the door of the t of the congregation, 168
7: 1 on the day that Moses had fully set up the t, 4908
Nu 7: 3 an ox: and they brought them before the t. 4908
7: 5 that they may be to do the service of the t of 168
7:89 when Moses was gone into the t of 168
8: 9 thou shalt bring the Levites before the t of 168
8:15 to do the service of the t of the congregation: 168
8:19 of Israel in the t of the congregation, 168
8:22 in the t of the congregation before Aaron, 168
8:24 upon the service of the t of the congregation: 168
8:26 shall minister with their brethren in the t of 168
9:15 on the day that the t was reared up, 4908
9:15 the cloud covered the t, *namely*, the tent of 4908
9:15 at even there was upon the t as it were 4908
9:17 And when the cloud was taken up from the t, 168
9:18 as long as the cloud abode upon the t they 4908
9:19 when the cloud tarried long upon the t 4908
9:20 when the cloud was a few days upon the t; 4908
9:22 or a year, that the cloud tarried upon the t, 4908
10: 3 thee at the door of the t of the congregation. 168
10:11 *that* the cloud was taken up from off the t 4908
10:17 the t was taken down; and the sons of 4908
10:17 sons of Merari set forward, bearing the t. 4908
10:21 *the other* did set up the t against they came. 4908
11:16 bring them unto the t of the congregation, 168
11:24 the people, and set them round about the t. 168
11:26 were written, but went not out unto the t: 168
12: 4 Come out ye three unto the t of 168
12: 5 stood *in* the door of the t, and called Aaron 168
12:10 the cloud departed from off the t; and 168
14:10 the glory of the LORD appeared in the t of 168
16: 9 to do the service of the t of the LORD, 4908
16:18 stood *in* the door of the t of the congregation 168
16:19 unto the door of the t of the congregation: 168
16:24 Get you up from about the t of Korah, 4908
16:27 So they gat up from the t of Korah, Dathan, 4908
16:42 that they looked toward the t of 168
16:43 Aaron came before the t of the congregation. 168
16:50 unto the door of the t of the congregation: 168
17: 4 thou shalt lay them up in the t of 168
17: 7 rods before the LORD in the t of Witness. 168
17: 8 that on the morrow Moses went into the t of 168
17:13 near unto the t of the LORD shall die: 4908
18: 2 thy sons with thee *shall minister* before the t 168
18: 3 keep thy charge, and the charge of all the t: 168
18: 4 keep the charge of the t of the congregation, 168
18: 4 the congregation, for all the service of the t: 168
18: 6 to do the service of the t of the congregation. 168
18:21 *even* the service of the t of the congregation. 168
18:22 come nigh the t of the congregation, 168
18:23 the Levites shall do the service of the t of 168
18:31 for it *is* your reward for your service in the t 168
19: 4 sprinkle of her blood directly before the t of 168
19:13 not himself, defileth the t of the LORD; 4908
20: 6 unto the door of the t of the congregation, 168
25: 6 who *were* weeping *before* the door of the t 168
27: 2 *by* the door of the t of the congregation, 168
31:30 which keep the charge of the t of 4908
31:47 which kept the charge of the t of 4908
31:54 and brought it into the t of the congregation, 168
Dt 31:14 present yourselves in the t of 168
31:14 presented themselves in the t of 168
31:15 the LORD appeared in the t in a pillar of a 168
31:15 of the cloud stood over the door of the t. 168
Jos 18: 1 and set up the t of the congregation there. 168
19:51 *at* the door of the t of the congregation. 168
22:19 wherein the LORD'S t dwelleth, and 4908
22:29 of the LORD our God that *is* before his t. 4908
1Sa 2:22 *at* the door of the t of the congregation. 168
2Sa 6:17 in the midst of the t that David had pitched 168
7: 6 but have walked in a tent and in a t. 4908
1Ki 1:39 the priest took a horn of oil out of the t, 168
2:28 And Joab fled unto the t of the LORD, and 168
2:29 that Joab was fled unto the t of the LORD; 168
2:30 Benaiah came to the t of the LORD, and 168
8: 4 the t of the congregation, and all the holy 168
8: 4 all the holy vessels that *were* in the t, 168
1Ch 6:32 of the t of the congregation with singing, 168
6:48 *of* service of the t of the house of God. 4908
9:19 of the service, keepers of the gates of the t: 168
9:21 of the door of the t of the congregation. 168
9:23 *namely*, the house of the t, by wards. 168
16:39 before the t of the LORD in the high place 4908
17: 5 tent to tent, and from *one* t *to another*. 4908
21:29 For the t of the LORD, which Moses 4908
23:26 *they* shall no *more* carry the t, nor any 4908
23:32 that they should keep the charge of the t of 168
2Ch 1: 3 for there was the t of the congregation of 168
1: 5 he put before the t of the LORD: 4908
1: 6 which *was* at the t of the congregation, and 168
1:13 from before the t of the congregation, and 168
5: 5 the t of the congregation, and all the holy 168
5: 5 all the holy vessels that *were* in the t, these 168
24: 6 congregation of Israel, for the t of Witness? 168
Job 5:24 thou shalt know that thy t *shall be in* peace; 168
18: 6 The light shall be dark in his t, and 168
18:14 His confidence shall be rooted out of his t, 168
18:15 It shall dwell in his t, because *it is* none of 168
19:12 against me, and encamp round about my t. 168
20:26 it shall go ill with him that is left in his t. 168
29: 4 when the secret of God *was* upon my t; 168
31:31 If the men of my t said not, O that we had of 168
36:29 of the clouds, *or* the noise of his t? 5521
Ps 15: 1 LORD, who shall abide in thy t? who shall 168
19: 4 the world. In them hath he set a t for the sun, 168
27: 5 in the secret of his t shall he hide me; 168
27: 6 will I offer in his t sacrifices of joy; 168
61: 4 I will abide in thy t for ever: I will trust in 168
76: 2 In Salem also is his t, and his dwelling 5520
78:60 So that he forsook the t of Shiloh, the tent 4908
78:67 Moreover he refused the t of Joseph, and 168
132: 3 Surely I will not come into the t of my 168
Pr 14:11 but the t of the upright shall flourish. 168
Isa 4: 6 there shall be a t for a shadow in 5521
16: 5 he shall sit upon it in truth in the t of David, 168
33:20 a t *that* shall not be taken down; 168
Jer 10:20 My t is spoiled, and all my cords are broken: 168

T

La 2: 4 to the eye, in the t of the daughter of Zion: 168
2: 6 he hath violently taken away his t, as if it 7900
Eze 37:27 My t also shall be with them: yea, I will be 4908
41: 1 other side, which was the breadth of the t. 168
Am 5:26 But ye have borne the t of your Moloch and 5522
9:11 In that day will I raise up the t of David 5521
Ac 7:43 ye took up the t of Moloch, and the star of 4633
7:44 Our fathers had the t of Witness in 4633
7:46 and desired to find a t for the God of Jacob. 4638
15:16 and will build again the t of David, 4633
2Co 5: 1 our earthly house of this t were dissolved, 4636
5: 4 For we that are in this t do groan, 4636
Heb 8: 2 and of the true t, which the Lord pitched, 4633
8: 5 of God when he was about to make the t: 4633
9: 2 For there was a t made; the first, wherein 4633
9: 3 the t which is called the holiest of all; 4633
9: 6 the priests went always into the first t, 4633
9: 8 while as the first t was yet standing: 4633
9:11 by a greater and more perfect t, not made 4633
9:21 he sprinkled with blood both the t, 4633
13:10 they have no right to eat which serve the t. 4633
2Pe 1:13 I think it meet, as long as I am in this t, 4638
1:14 that shortly I must put off this my t, 4638
Rev 13: 6 and his t, and them that dwell in heaven. 4633
15: 5 the temple of the t of the testimony in 4633
21: 3 the t of God is with men, and he will dwell 4633

TABERNACLES (30) [TABERNACLE]
Lev 23:34 feast of t for seven days unto the LORD. 5521
Nu 24: 5 are thy tents, O Jacob, and thy t, O Israel! 4908
Dt 16:13 Thou shalt observe the feast of t seven 5521
16:16 in the feast of weeks, and in the feast of t: 5521
31:10 of the year of release, in the feast of t, 5521
2Ch 8:13 in the feast of weeks, and in the feast of t. 5521
Ezr 3: 4 They kept also the feast of t, as it is written, 5521
Job 11:14 and let not wickedness dwell in thy t. 168
12: 6 The t of robbers prosper, and they that 168
15:34 and fire shall consume the t of bribery. 168
22:23 thou shalt put away iniquity far from thy t. 168
Ps 43: 3 bring me unto thy holy hill, and to thy t. 4908
46: 4 the holy place of the t of the most High. 4908
78:51 the chief of their strength in the t of Ham: 168
83: 6 The t of Edom, and the Ishmaelites; 168
84: 1 How amiable are thy t, O LORD of hosts! 4908
118:15 and salvation is in the t of the righteous: 168
132: 7 We will go into his t: we will worship at 4908
Da 11:45 he shall plant the t of his palace between 168
Hos 9: 6 shall possess them: thorns shall be in their t. 168
12: 9 of Egypt will yet make thee to dwell in t, 168
Zec 14:16 LORD of hosts, and to keep the feast of t. 5521
14:18 that come not up to keep the feast of t. 5521
14:19 that come not up to keep the feast of t. 5521
Mal 2:12 out of the t of Jacob, and him that offereth 168
Mt 17: 4 if thou wilt, let us make here three t: 4633
Mk 9: 5 and let us make three t; one for thee, and 4633
Lk 9:33 and let us make three t; one for thee, and 4633
Jn 7: 2 Now the Jews' feast of t was at hand. 4634
Heb 11: 9 as in a strange country, dwelling in t with 4633

TABITHA (2)
Ac 9:36 was at Joppa a certain disciple named T, 5000
9:40 and turning him to the body said, T, arise. 5000

TABLE (73) [TABLES]
Ex 25:23 Thou shalt also make a t of shittim wood: 7979
25:27 be for places of the staves to bear the t. 7979
25:28 that the t may be borne with them. 7979
25:30 thou shalt set upon the t shewbread before 7979
26:35 thou shalt set the t without the vail, and 7979
26:35 the candlestick over against the t on 7979
26:35 and thou shalt put the t on the north side. 7979
30:27 the t and all his vessels, and the candlestick 7979
31: 8 the t and his furniture, and the pure 7979
35:13 The t, and his staves, and all his vessels, 7979
37:10 he made the t of shittim wood: two cubits 7979
37:14 the places for the staves to bear the t. 7979
37:15 and overlaid them with gold, to bear the t. 7979
37:16 he made the vessels which were upon the t, 7979
39:36 The t, and all the vessels thereof, and 7979
40: 4 thou shalt bring in the t, and set in order 7979
40:22 he put the t in the tent of the congregation, 7979
40:24 over against the t, on the side of 7979
Lev 24: 6 a row, upon the pure t before the LORD. 7979
Nu 3:31 the t, and the candlestick, and the altars, 7979
4: 7 upon the t of shewbread they shall spread a 7979
Jdg 1: 7 cut off, gathered their meat under my t: 7979
1Sa 20:29 Therefore he cometh not unto the king's t. 7979
20:34 So Jonathan arose from the t in fierce 7979
2Sa 9: 7 and thou shalt eat bread at my t continually. 7979
9:10 master's son shall eat bread alway at my t. 7979
9:11 said the king, he shall eat at my t, 7979
9:13 for he did eat continually at the king's t; 7979
19:28 among them that did eat at thine own t. 7979
1Ki 2: 7 and let them be of those that eat at thy t: 7979
4:27 for all that came unto king Solomon's t, 7979
7:48 the altar of gold, and the t of gold, 7979
10: 5 the meat of his t, and the sitting of his 7979
13:20 it came to pass, as they sat at the t, that 7979
18:19 four hundred, which eat at Jezebel's t. 7979
2Ki 4:10 and a t, and a stool, and a candlestick: 7979
1Ch 28:16 of shewbread, for every t, 7979+7979+2050.1
2Ch 9: 4 the meat of his t, and the sitting of his 7979
13:11 also set they in order upon the pure t; 7979
29:18 the shewbread t, with all the vessels 7979
Ne 5:17 Moreover there were at my t an hundred 7979
Job 36:16 that which should be set on thy t should be 7979
Ps 23: 5 Thou preparest a t before me in 7979
69:22 Let their t become a snare before them: and 7979
78:19 Can God furnish a t in the wilderness? 7979
128: 3 children like olive plants round about thy t. 7979
Pr 3: 3 write them upon the t of thine heart: 3871
7: 3 write them upon the t of thine heart. 3871
9: 2 her wine; she hath also furnished her t. 7979
SS 1:12 While the king sitteth at his t, my spikenard 4524
Isa 21: 5 Prepare the t, watch in the watchtower, eat, 7979
30: 8 write it before them in a t, and note it in a 3871
65:11 that prepare a t for that troop, and 7979
Jer 17: 1 it is graven upon the t of their heart, and 3871
Eze 23:41 a stately bed, and a t prepared before it, 7979
39:20 Thus ye shall be filled at my t with horses 7979
41:22 This is the t that is before the LORD. 7979
44:16 they shall come near to my t, to minister 7979
Da 11:27 and they shall speak lies at one t; 7979
Mal 1: 7 The t of the LORD is contemptible. 7979
1:12 ye say, The t of the LORD is polluted; 7979
Mt 15:27 the crumbs which fall from their masters' t. 5132
Mk 7:28 yet the dogs under the t eat of 5132
Lk 1:63 And he asked for a writing t, and wrote, 4093
16:21 crumbs which fell from the rich man's t: 5132
22:21 him that betrayeth me is with me on the t. 5132
22:30 may eat and drink at my t in my kingdom, 5132
Jn 12: 2 of them that sat at the t with him. 4873
13:28 Now no man at the t knew for what intent he 345
Ro 11: 9 Let their t be made a snare, and a trap, and 5132
1Co 10:21 ye cannot be partakers of the Lord's t, and 5132
10:21 of the Lord's table, and of the t of devils. 5132
Heb 9: 2 and the t, and the shewbread; 5132

TABLES (56) [TABLE, TABLETS]
Ex 24:12 I will give thee t of stone, and a law, and 3871
31:18 two t of Testimony, tables of stone, 3871
31:18 two tables of Testimony, t of stone, 3871
32:15 the two t of the Testimony were in his 3871
32:15 the t were written on both their sides; 3871
32:16 the t were the work of God, and the writing 3871
32:16 was the writing of God, graven upon the t. 3871
32:19 he cast the t out of his hands, and 3871
34: 1 Hew thee two t of stone like unto the first: 3871
34: 1 I will write upon these t the words that 3871
34: 1 tables the words that were in the first t, 3871
34: 4 he hewed two t of stone like unto the first; 3871
34: 4 and took in his hand the two t of stone. 3871
34:28 he wrote upon the t the words of 3871
34:29 the two t of Testimony in Moses' hand, 3871
Dt 4:13 and he wrote them upon two t of stone. 3871
5:22 he wrote them in two t of stone, and 3871
9: 9 up into the mount to receive the t of stone, 3871
9: 9 even the t of the covenant which 3871
9:10 the LORD delivered unto me two t of 3871
9:11 that the LORD gave me the two t of stone, 3871
9:11 tables of stone, even the t of the covenant. 3871
9:15 the two t of the covenant were in my two 3871
9:17 I took the two t, and cast them out of my 3871
10: 1 Hew thee two t of stone like unto the first, 3871
10: 2 I will write on the t the words that were in 3871
10: 2 that were in the first t which thou brakest, 3871
10: 3 hewed two t of stone like unto the first, and 3871
10: 3 the mount, having the two t in mine hand. 3871
10: 4 he wrote on the t, according to the first 3871
10: 5 and put the t in the ark which I had made; 3871
1Ki 8: 9 There was nothing in the ark save the two t 3871
1Ch 28:16 by weight he gave gold for the t of 7979
28:16 and likewise silver for the t of silver: 7979
2Ch 4: 8 He made also ten t, and placed them in 7979
4:19 the t whereon the shewbread was set; 7979
5:10 There was nothing in the ark save the two t 3871
Isa 28: 8 For all t are full of vomit and filthiness, so 7979
Eze 40:39 in the porch of the gate were two t on this 7979
40:39 two t on that side, to slay thereon the burnt 7979
40:40 to the entry of the north gate, were two t; 7979
40:40 was at the porch of the gate, were two t. 7979
40:41 Four t were on this side, and four tables on 7979
40:41 four t on that side, by the side of the gate; 7979
40:41 eight t, whereupon they slew their 7979
40:42 the four t were of hewn stone for the burnt 7979
40:43 and upon the t was the flesh of the offering. 7979
Hab 2: 2 Write the vision, and make it plain upon t, 3871
Mt 21:12 and overthrew the t of the moneychangers, 5132
Mk 7: 4 of cups, and pots, brasen vessels, and of t. 2825
11:15 and overthrew the t of the money-changers, 5132
Jn 2:15 the changers' money, and overthrew the t; 5132
Ac 6: 2 should leave the word of God, and serve t. 5132
2Co 3: 3 not in t of stone, but in fleshy tables of 4109
3: 3 tables of stone, but in fleshy t of the heart. 4109
Heb 9: 4 rod that budded, and the t of the covenant; 4109

TABLETS (3) [TABLES]
Ex 35:22 and earrings, and rings, and t, 3558
Nu 31:50 chains, and bracelets, rings, earrings, and t, 3558
Isa 3:20 and the t, and the earrings, 1004+5315

TABOR (10) [AZNOTH-TABOR, CHISLOTH-TABOR]
Jos 19:22 the coast reacheth to T, and Shahazimah, 8396
Jdg 4: 6 saying, Go and draw toward mount T, and 8396
4:12 son of Abinoam was gone up to mount T. 8396
4:14 So Barak went down from mount T, and 8396
8:18 of men were they whom ye slew at T? 8396
1Sa 10: 3 thou shalt come to the plain of T, and 8396
1Ch 6:77 with her suburbs, T with her suburbs: 8396
Ps 89:12 T and Hermon shall rejoice in thy name. 8396
Jer 46:18 Surely as T is among the mountains, and 8396
Hos 5: 1 snare on Mizpah, and a net spread upon T. 8396

TABRET (4) [TABRETS]
Ge 31:27 and with songs, with t, and with harp? 8596
1Sa 10: 5 and a t, and a pipe, and a harp, before them; 8596
Job 17: 6 of the people; and aforetime I was as a t. 8611
Isa 5:12 and the viol, the t, and pipe, and wine, 8596

TABRETS (5) [TABRET]
1Sa 18: 6 with t, with joy, and with instruments of 8596
Isa 24: 8 The mirth of t ceaseth, the noise of them 8596
30:32 lay upon him, it shall be with t and harps: 8596
Jer 31: 4 thou shalt again be adorned with thy t, and 8596
Eze 28:13 the workmanship of thy t and of thy pipes 8596

TABRIMMON See TABRIMON

TABRIMON (1)
1Ki 15:18 the son of T, the son of Hezion, king of 2886

TABRING (1)
Na 2: 7 the voice of doves, t upon their breasts. 8608

TACHES (10)
Ex 26: 6 thou shalt make fifty t of gold, and 7165
26: 6 and couple the curtains together with the t: 7165
26:11 thou shalt make fifty t of brass, and put 7165
26:11 put the t into the loops, and couple the tent 7165
26:33 thou shalt hang up the vail under the t, 7165
35:11 his t, and his boards, his bars, his pillars, 7165
36:13 he made fifty t of gold, and coupled 7165
36:13 the curtains one unto another with the t: 7165
36:18 he made fifty t of brass to couple the tent 7165
39:33 his t, his boards, his bars, and his pillars, 7165

TACHMONITE (1)
2Sa 23: 8 The T that sat in the seat, chief among 8461

TACKLING (1) [TACKLINGS]
Ac 27:19 out with our own hands the t of the ship. 4631

TACKLINGS (1) [TACKLING]
Isa 33:23 Thy t are loosed; they could not well 2256

TADMOR (2)
1Ki 9:18 and T in the wilderness, in the land, 8412
2Ch 8: 4 he built T in the wilderness, and all 8412

TAHAN (2) [TAHANITES]
Nu 26:35 of T, the family of the Tahanites. 8465
1Ch 7:25 and Telah his son, and T his son, 8465

TAHANITES (1) [TAHAN]
Nu 26:35 of Tahan, the family of the T. 8470

TAHAPANES (1) [TAHPANHES]
Jer 2:16 and T have broken the crown of thy head. 8471

TAHASH See THAHASH

TAHATH (6)
Nu 33:26 from Makheloth, and encamped at T. 8480
33:27 they departed from T, and pitched at Tarah. 8480
1Ch 6:24 T his son, Uriel his son, Uzziah his son, 8480
6:37 The son of T, the son of Assir, the son of 8480
7:20 T his son, and Eladah his son, and 8480
7:20 his son, and Eladah his son, and T his son, 8480

TAHKEMONITE See TACHMONITE

TAHPANHES (5) [TAHAPANES, TEHAPHNEHES]
Jer 43: 7 of the LORD: thus came they even to T. 8471
43: 8 word of the LORD unto Jeremiah in T, 8471
43: 9 is at the entry of Pharaoh's house in T, 8471
44: 1 at T, and at Noph, and in the country of 8471
46:14 in Migdol, and publish in Noph and in T: 8471

TAHPENES (3)
1Ki 11:19 of his own wife, the sister of T the queen. 8472
11:20 the sister of T bare him Genubath his son, 8472
11:20 whom T weaned in Pharaoh's house: 8472

TAHREA (1)
1Ch 9:41 and Melech, and T, and Ahaz. 8475

TAHTIM-HODSHI (1)
2Sa 24: 6 they came to Gilead, and to the land of T; 8483

TAIL (10) [TAILS]
Ex 4: 4 Put forth thine hand, and take it by the t. 2180
Dt 28:13 shall make thee the head, and not the t; 2180
28:44 he shall be the head, and thou shalt be the t. 2180
Jdg 15: 4 turned t to tail, and put a firebrand in 2180
15: 4 turned tail to t, and put a firebrand in 2180
Job 40:17 He moveth his t like a cedar: the sinews of 2180
Isa 9:14 LORD will cut off from Israel head and t, 2180
9:15 the prophet that teacheth lies, he is the t. 2180
19:15 which the head or t, branch or rush, 2180
Rev 12: 4 And his t drew the third part of the stars of 3769

TAILS (6) [TAIL]
Jdg 15: 4 put a firebrand in the midst between two t. 2180
Isa 7: 4 neither be fainthearted for the two t of 2180
Rev 9:10 And they had t like unto scorpions, and 3769
9:10 and there were stings in their t: 3769
9:19 their power is in their mouth, and in their t: 3769
9:19 for their t were like unto serpents, and 3769

TAKE (874) [OVERTAKE, TAKEN, TAKER, TAKEST, TAKETH, TAKING, TOOK, TOOKEST, UNTAKEN]
Ge 3:22 t also of the tree of life, and eat, and 3947
6:21 t thou unto thee of all food that is eaten, 3947
7: 2 Of every clean beast thou shalt t to thee by 3947
12:19 behold thy wife, t her, and go thy way. 3947
13: 9 if thou wilt t the left hand, then I will go to NIH
14:21 me the persons, and t the goods to thyself. 3947
14:23 That I will not t from a thread even to a NIH
14:23 that I will not t any thing that is thine, 3947
14:24 and Mamre; let them t their portion. 3947
15: 9 T me a heifer of three years old, and a she 3947
19:15 Arise, t thy wife, and thy two daughters, 3947
19:19 the mountain, lest some evil t me, and I die: 1692
21:30 For these seven ewe lambs shalt thou t of 3947
22: 2 he said, T now thy son, thine only son 3947
23:13 t it of me, and I will bury my dead there. 3947
24: 3 that thou shalt not t a wife unto my son of 3947
24: 4 my kindred, and t a wife unto my son Isaac. 3947
24: 7 thou shalt t a wife unto my son from 3947
24:37 Thou shalt not t a wife to my son of 3947

T

Ge 24:38 to my kindred, and **t** a wife unto my son. 3947
24:40 thou shalt **t** a wife for my son of my 3947
24:48 which had led me in the right way to **t** my 3947
24:51 **t** *her,* and go, and let her be thy master's 3947
27: 3 Now therefore **t**, I pray thee, thy weapons, 5375
27: 3 go out to the field, and **t** me *some* venison; 6679
27:46 if Jacob **t** a wife of the daughters of Heth, 3947
28: 1 Thou shalt not **t** a wife of the daughters of 3947
28: 2 **t** thee a wife from thence of the daughters 3947
28: 6 to Padan-aram, to **t** him a wife from thence; 3947
28: 6 Thou shalt not **t** a wife of the daughters of 3947
30:15 wouldest thou **t away** my son's mandrakes 3947
31:24 **T heed** that thou speak not to Jacob either 8104
31:29 **T** thou **heed** that thou speak not to Jacob 8104
31:31 Peradventure thou wouldest **t by force** thy 1497
31:32 thou what *is* thine with me, and **t** *it* to thee. 3947
31:50 if thou shalt **t** *other* wives beside my 3947
33:11 **T**, I pray thee, my blessing that is brought 3947
33:12 Let us **t** our **journey**, and let us go, and 5265
34: 9 unto us, and **t** our daughters unto you. 3947
34:16 we will **t** your daughters to us, and we will 3947
34:17 will we **t** our daughter, and we will be 3947
34:21 let us **t** their daughters to us for wives, and 3947
38:23 Judah said, Let her **t** *it* to her, lest we be 3947
41:34 **t up the fifth** *part* of the land of Egypt in 2567
42:33 **t** *food for* the famine of your households, 3947
42:36 ye will **t** Benjamin *away:* all these things 3947
43:11 **t** of the best fruits in the land in your 3947
43:12 **t** double money in your hand; and 3947
43:13 **T** also your brother, and arise, go again 3947
43:18 and **t** us for bondmen, and our asses. 3947
44:29 if ye **t** this also from me, and 3947
45:18 **t** your father and your households, and 3947
45:19 **t** you wagons out of the land of Egypt for 3947
Ex 2: 9 **T** this child **away**, and nurse it for me, and 1980
4: 4 Put forth thine hand, and **t** it by the tail. 270
4: 9 that thou shalt **t** of the water of the river, 3947
4:17 thou shalt **t** this rod in thine hand, 3947
6: 7 I will **t** you to me for a people, and I will be 3947
7: 9 **T** thy rod, and cast *it* before Pharaoh, *and* 3947
7:15 to a serpent shalt thou **t** in thine hand. 3947
7:19 **T** thy rod, and stretch out thine hand upon 3947
8: 8 that he may **t away** the frogs from me, and 5493
9: 8 **T** to you handfuls of ashes of the furnace, 3947
10:17 that he may **t away** from me this death 5493
10:26 for thereof must we **t** to serve the LORD 3947
10:28 Get thee from me, **t heed** to thyself, see my 8104
12: 3 In the tenth *day* of this month they shall **t** to 3947
12: 4 his neighbour next unto his house **t** *it* 3947
12: 5 ye shall **t** *it* **out** from the sheep, or from 3947
12: 7 they shall **t** of the blood, and strike *it* on 3947
12:21 **t** you a lamb according to your families, 3947
12:22 ye shall **t** a bunch of hyssop, and dip *it* in 3947
12:32 Also **t** your flocks and your herds, as ye 3947
15:14 sorrow shall **t hold** on the inhabitants of 270
15:15 of Moab, trembling shall **t hold** upon them; 270
16:16 **t** ye every man for *them* which *are* in his 3947
16:33 **T** a pot, and put an omer full of manna 3947
17: 5 and **t** with thee of the elders of Israel; 3947
17: 5 smotest the river, **t** in thine hand, and go. 3947
19:12 saying, **T heed** to yourselves, *that ye* go *not* 8104
20: 7 Thou shalt not **t** the name of the LORD 5375
21:10 If he **t** him another *wife;* her food, 3947
21:14 thou shalt **t** him from mine altar, that he 3947
22:26 **at all t** thy neighbour's raiment
to pledge, 2254+2254
23: 8 thou shalt **t** no gift: for the gift blindeth 3947
23:25 I will **t** sickness **away** from the midst of 5493
25: 2 with his heart ye shall **t** my offering. 3947
25: 3 this *is* the offering which ye shall **t** of them; 3947
26: 5 that the loops may **t hold** one of another. 6901
28: 1 **t** thou unto thee Aaron thy brother, and 7126
28: 5 they shall **t** gold, and blue, and purple, and 3947
28: 9 thou shalt **t** two onyx stones, and grave on 3947
29: 1 **T** one young bullock, and two rams without 3947
29: 5 thou shalt **t** the garments, and put upon 3947
29: 7 shalt thou **t** the anointing oil, and pour *it* 3947
29:12 thou shalt **t** of the blood of the bullock, 3947
29:13 thou shalt **t** all the fat that covereth 3947
29:15 Thou shalt also **t** one ram; and Aaron and 3947
29:16 thou shalt **t** his blood, and sprinkle *it* round 3947
29:19 thou shalt **t** the other ram; and Aaron and 3947
29:20 **t** of his blood, and put *it* upon the tip of 3947
29:21 thou shalt **t** of the blood that *is* upon 3947
29:22 Also thou shalt **t** of the ram the fat and 3947
29:26 thou shalt **t** the breast of the ram of Aaron's 3947
29:31 thou shalt **t** the ram of the consecration, 3947
30:16 thou shalt **t** the atonement money of 3947
30:23 **T** thou also unto thee principal spices, 3947
30:34 **T** unto thee sweet spices, stacte, and 3947
33:23 I will **t away** mine hand, and thou shalt see 5493
34: 9 and our sin, and **t** us **for** thine **inheritance**. 5157
34:12 **T heed** to thyself, lest thou make a 8104
34:16 thou **t** of their daughters unto thy sons, and 3947
35: 5 **T** ye from amongst you an offering unto 3947
40: 9 thou shalt **t** the anointing oil, and anoint 3947
Lev 2: 2 he shall **t** thereout his **handful** 4393+7061+7062
2: 9 the priest shall **t** from the meat offering a 7311
3: 4 with the kidneys, it shall he **t away**. 5493
3: 9 it shall he **t off** hard by the back bone; 5493
3:10 with the kidneys, it shall he **t away**. 5493
3:15 with the kidneys, it shall he **t away**. 5493
4: 5 the priest that is anointed shall **t** of 3947
4: 8 he shall **t off** from it all the fat of 7311
4: 9 with the kidneys, it shall he **t away**, 5493
4:19 he shall **t** all his fat from him, and burn *it* 7311
4:25 the priest shall **t** of the blood of the sin 3947
4:30 the priest shall **t** of the blood thereof with 3947
4:31 he shall **t away** all the fat thereof, as the fat 5493
4:34 the priest shall **t** of the blood of the sin 3947
4:35 he shall **t away** all the fat thereof, as the fat 5493
5:12 the priest shall **t** his **handful** 4393+7061+7062
6:10 **t up** the ashes which the fire hath 7311
6:15 he shall **t** of it his handful, of the flour of 7311
7: 4 with the kidneys, it shall he **t away**: 5493

Lev 8: 2 **T** Aaron and his sons with him, and 3947
9: 2 **T** thee a young calf for a sin offering, and 3947
9: 3 **T** ye a kid of the goats for a sin offering; 3947
10:12 **T** the meat offering that remaineth of 3947
14: 4 shall the priest command to **t** for him that is 3947
14: 6 he shall **t** it, and the cedar wood, and 3947
14:10 on the eighth day he shall **t** two he lambs 3947
14:12 the priest shall **t** one he lamb, and offer him 3947
14:14 the priest shall **t** *some* of the blood of 3947
14:15 the priest shall **t** *some* of the log of oil, and 3947
14:21 he shall **t** one lamb *for* a trespass offering 3947
14:24 the priest shall **t** the lamb of the trespass 3947
14:25 the priest shall **t** *some* of the blood of 3947
14:40 the priest shall command that they **t away** 2502
14:42 they shall **t** other stones, and put *them* in 3947
14:42 he shall **t** other morter, and shall plaister 3947
14:49 he shall **t** to cleanse the house two birds, 3947
14:51 he shall **t** the cedar wood, and the hyssop, 3947
15:14 on the eighth day he shall **t** to him two 3947
15:29 on the eighth day she shall **t** unto her two 3947
16: 5 he shall **t** of the congregation of 3947
16: 7 he shall **t** the two goats, and present them 3947
16:12 he shall **t** a censer full of burning coals of 3947
16:14 he shall **t** of the blood of the bullock, and 3947
16:18 shall **t** of the blood of the bullock, and 3947
18:17 neither shalt thou **t** her son's daughter, or 3947
18:18 Neither shalt thou **t** a wife to her sister, 3947
20:14 if a man **t** a wife and her mother, it *is* 3947
20:17 if a man shall **t** his sister, his father's 3947
20:21 if a man shall **t** his brother's wife, it *is* an 3947
21: 7 They shall not **t** a wife *that is* a whore, or 3947
21: 7 neither shall they **t** a woman put away from 3947
21:13 And he shall **t** a wife in her virginity. 3947
21:14 or profane, *or* a harlot, these shall he not **t**: 3947
21:14 he shall **t** a virgin of his own people to 3947
22: 5 or a man of whom he may **t uncleanness**, 2930
23:40 ye shall **t** you on the first day the boughs of 3947
24: 5 thou shalt **t** fine flour, and bake twelve 3947
25:36 **T** thou no usury of him, or increase: but 3947
25:46 ye shall **t** them **as an inheritance** for your 5157
Nu 1: 2 **T** ye the sum of all the congregation of 5375
1:49 neither **t** the sum of them among 5375
1:51 setteth forward, the Levites shall **t** it **down**: 3381
3:40 upward, and **t** the number of their names. 5375
3:41 thou shalt **t** the Levites for me (I *am* 3947
3:45 **T** the Levites instead of all the firstborn 3947
3:47 Thou shalt even **t** five shekels apiece by 3947
3:47 after the shekel of the sanctuary shalt thou **t** 3947
4: 2 **T** the sum of the sons of Kohath from 5375
4: 5 they shall **t down** the covering vail, and 3381
4: 9 they shall **t** a cloth of blue, and cover 3947
4:12 they shall **t** all the instruments of ministry, 3947
4:13 they shall **t away** the **ashes** from the altar, 1878
4:22 **T** also the sum of the sons of Gershon, 5375
5:17 the priest shall **t** holy water in an earthen 3947
5:17 the floor of the tabernacle the priest shall **t**, 3947
5:25 the priest shall **t** the jealousy offering out of 3947
5:26 the priest shall **t** a **handful** of the offering, 7061
6:18 shall **t** the hair of the head of his separation, 3947
6:19 the priest shall **t** the sodden shoulder of 3947
7: 5 **T** *it* of them, that they may be to do 3947
8: 6 **T** the Levites from among the children of 3947
8: 8 let them **t** a young bullock with his meat 3947
8: 8 another young bullock shalt thou **t** for a sin 3947
10: 6 lie on the south side shall **t** their **journey**: 5265
11:17 I will **t** of the spirit which *is* upon thee, and 680
16: 3 said unto them, *Ye* **t** too much upon you, NIH
16: 6 **T** you censers, Korah, and all his company; 3947
16: 7 *ye* **t** too much upon you, ye sons of Levi. NIH
16:17 **t** every man his censer, and put incense in 3947
16:37 that he **t up** the censers out of the burning, 7311
16:46 **T** a censer, and put fire therein from off 3947
17: 2 **t** of every one of them a rod according to 3947
17:10 thou shalt **quite t away** their murmurings 3615
18:26 When ye **t** of the children of Israel 3947
19: 4 Eleazar the priest shall **t** of her blood with 3947
19: 6 the priest shall **t** cedar wood, and hyssop, 3947
19:17 for an unclean *person* they shall **t** of 3947
19:18 a clean person shall **t** hyssop, and dip *it* in 3947
20: 8 **T** the rod, and gather thou the assembly 3947
20:25 **T** Aaron and Eleazar his son, and 3947
21: 7 that he **t away** the serpents from us. 5493
23:12 Must I not **t heed** to speak that which 8104
25: 4 **T** all the heads of the people, and 3947
26: 2 **T** the sum of all the congregation of 5375
26: 4 *T the sum of the people,* from twenty years NIH
27:18 **T** thee Joshua the son of Nun, a man in 3947
31:26 **T** the sum of the prey that was taken, *both* 5375
31:29 **T** *it* of their half, and give *it* unto Eleazar 3947
31:30 thou shalt **t** one portion of fifty, of 3947
34:18 ye shall **t** one prince of every tribe, 3947
35:31 Moreover ye shall **t** no satisfaction for 3947
35:32 ye shall **t** no satisfaction for him that is fled 3947
Dt 1: 7 **t** your **journey**, and go *to* the mount of 5265
1:13 **T** ye wise men, and understanding, and 3051
1:40 **t** your **journey** into the wilderness *by* 5265
2: 4 **t** ye good **heed** unto yourselves therefore: 8104
2:24 **t** your **journey**, and pass over the river 5265
4: 9 Only **t heed** to thyself, and keep thy soul 8104
4:15 **T** ye therefore good **heed** unto yourselves; 8104
4:23 **T heed** unto yourselves, lest ye forget 8104
4:34 **t** him a nation from the midst of *another* 3947
5:11 Thou shalt not **t** the name of the LORD 5375
7: 3 nor his daughter shalt thou **t** unto thy son. 3947
7:15 the LORD will **t away** from thee all 5493
7:25 or gold *that is* on them, nor **t** *it* unto thee, 3947
10:11 Arise, **t** thy journey before the people, 1980
11:16 **T heed** to yourselves, that your heart be not 8104
12:13 **T heed** to thyself that thou offer not thy 8104
12:19 **T heed** to thyself that thou forsake not 8104
12:26 thou shalt **t**, and go unto the place which 5375
12:30 **T heed** to thyself that thou be not snared by 8104
15:17 thou shalt **t** an aul, and thrust *it* through his 3947
16:19 shalt not respect persons, neither **t** a gift: 3947
20: 7 he die in the battle, and another man **t** her. 3947

Dt 20:14 all the spoil thereof, shalt thou **t** unto thyself; 962
20:19 a long time, in making war against it to **t** it, 8610
21: 3 even the elders of that city shall **t** a heifer, 3947
22: 6 thou shalt not **t** the dam with the young: 3947
22: 7 let the dam go, and **t** the young to thee; 3947
22:13 If any man **t** a wife, and go in unto her, and 3947
22:15 **t** and bring forth *the tokens of* the damsel's 3947
22:18 the elders of that city shall **t** *that* man and 3947
22:30 A man shall not **t** his father's wife, 3947
24: 4 may not **t** her again to be his wife, 3947
24: 6 **t** the nether or the upper millstone to **pledge**: 2254
24: 8 **T heed** in the plague of leprosy, that *thou* 8104
24:17 nor **t** a widow's raiment **to pledge**: 2254
25: 5 **t** her to him to wife, and perform the duty 3947
25: 7 if the man like not to **t** his brother's wife, 3947
25: 8 *if* he stand *to it,* and say, I like not to **t** her; 3947
26: 2 That thou shalt **t** of the first of all the fruit 3947
26: 4 the priest shall **t** the basket out of thine 3947
27: 9 **T heed**, and hearken, O Israel; 5535
31:26 **T** this book of the law, and put it in the side 3947
32:41 and mine hand **t hold** on judgment; 270
Jos 3: 6 **T up** the ark of the covenant, and pass over 5375
3:12 **t** ye twelve men out of the tribes of Israel, 3947
4: 2 **T** you twelve men out of the people, out of 3947
4: 3 **T** you hence out of the midst of Jordan, 5375
4: 5 **t** ye **up** every man of you a stone upon his 7311
6: 6 **T up** the ark of the covenant, and let seven 5375
6:18 when ye **t** of the accursed thing, and 3947
7:13 until ye **t away** the accursed thing from 5493
7:14 the family which the LORD shall **t** shall 3920
7:14 the household which the LORD shall **t** 3920
8: 1 **t** all the people of war with thee, and arise, 3947
8: 2 shall ye **t for a prey** unto yourselves: 962
8:29 should **t** his carcase **down** from the tree, 3381
9:11 **T** victuals with you for the journey, and 3947
10:42 and their land did Joshua **t** *at* one time, 3920
11:12 did Joshua **t**, and smote them with the edge 3920
20: 4 they shall **t** him into the city unto them, and 622
22: 5 But **t** diligent **heed** to do the commandment 8104
22:19 and **t possession** among us: 270
23:11 **T** good **heed** therefore unto yourselves, that 8104
Jdg 4: 6 **t** with thee ten thousand men of 3947
5:30 *meet* for the necks of *them that* **t** the spoil? NIH
6:20 **T** the flesh and the unleavened *cakes,* and 3947
6:25 unto him, **T** thy father's young bullock, 3947
6:26 **t** the second bullock, and offer a burnt 3947
7:24 **t** before them the waters unto Beth-barah 3920
14: 3 that thou goest to **t** a wife of 3947
14: 8 after a time he returned to **t** her, and 3947
14:15 have ye called us to **t that** we **have**? *is it* 3423
15: 2 **t** her, I pray thee, instead of her. 1961+3807.1
19:30 of it, **t advice**, and speak *your minds.* 5779
20:10 we will **t** ten men of an hundred throughout 3947
Ru 2:10 that *thou* shouldest **t knowledge** of me, 5234
2:19 blessed be he that did **t knowledge** of thee. 5234
1Sa 2:16 *then* **t** *as much* as thy soul desireth; 3947
2:16 *it me* now: and if not, I will **t** *it* by force. 3947
6: 7 make a new cart, and **t** two milch kine, 3947
6: 8 **t** the ark of the LORD, and lay it upon 3947
8:11 He will **t** your sons, and appoint *them* for 3947
8:13 he will **t** your daughters to be 3947
8:14 he will **t** your fields, and your vineyards, 3947
8:15 he will **t the tenth** of your seed, and 6237
8:16 he will **t** your menservants, and your 3947
8:17 He will **t the tenth** of your sheep: and 6237
9: 3 **T** now one of the servants with thee, 3947
9: 5 *caring* for the asses, and **t thought** for us. 1672
16: 2 LORD said, **T** a heifer with thee, and say, 3947
17:17 **T** now for thy brethren an ephah of this 3947
17:18 how thy brethren fare, and **t** their pledge. 3947
17:46 will smite thee, and **t** thine head from thee; 5493
19: 2 **t heed** to thyself until the morning, and 8104
19:14 when Saul sent messengers to **t** David, she 3947
19:20 Saul sent messengers to **t** David: and 3947
20:21 the arrows *are* on this side of thee, **t** them; 3947
21: 9 if thou wilt **t** that, take *it:* for *there is* no 3947
21: 9 **t** *it:* for *there is* no other save that here. 3947
23:23 **t knowledge** of all the lurking places where 3045
23:26 and his men round about to **t** them. 8610
24:11 yet thou huntest my soul to **t** it. 3947
25:11 Shall I then **t** my bread, and my water, and 3947
25:39 with Abigail, to **t** her to him to wife. 3947
25:40 sent us unto thee, to **t** thee to him to wife. 3947
26:11 **t** thou now the spear that *is at* his bolster, 3947
2Sa 2:21 of the young men, and **t** thee his armour. 3947
4:11 your hand, and **t** you **away** from the earth? 1197
5: 6 Except thou **t away** the blind and the lame, 5493
12: 4 he spared to **t** of his own flock and of his 3947
12:11 and I will **t** thy wives before thine eyes, and 3947
12:28 and encamp against the city, and **t** it: 3920
12:28 lest I **t** the city, and it be called after my 3920
13:33 let not my lord the king **t** the thing to his 7760
15:20 I may, return thou, and **t back** thy brethren: 7725
16: 9 me go over, I pray thee, and **t off** his head. 5493
19:19 that the king should **t** *it* to his heart. 7760
19:30 said unto the king, Yea, let him **t** all, 3947
20: 6 **t** thou thy lord's servants, and pursue after 3947
24:10 **t away** the iniquity of thy servant; 5674
24:22 Let my lord the king **t** and offer up what 3947
1Ki 1:33 **T** with you the servants of your lord, and 3947
2: 4 saying, If thy children **t heed** to their way, 8104
2:31 that thou mayest **t away** the innocent 5493
8:25 so that thy children **t heed** to their way, 8104
11:31 And he said to Jeroboam, **T** thee ten pieces: 3947
11:34 Howbeit I will not **t** the whole kingdom out 3947
11:35 I will **t** the kingdom out of his son's hand, 3947
11:37 I will **t** thee, and thou shalt reign according 3947
14: 3 **t** with thee ten loaves, and cracknels, and 3947
14:10 will **t away** the remnant of the house of 1197
16: 3 I will **t away** the posterity of Baasha, and 1197
18:40 said unto them, **T** the prophets of Baal; 8610
19: 4 *is* enough; now, O LORD, **t away** my life; 3947
19:10 am left; and they seek my life, to **t** it **away**. 3947
19:14 am left; and they seek my life, to **t** it **away**. 3947
20: 6 they shall put *it* in their hand, and **t** *it* **away**. 3947

T

1Ki 20:18 they be come out for peace, **t** them alive; 8610
20:18 they be come out for war, **t** them alive. 8610
20:24 do this thing, **T** the kings **away**, every man 5493
21:15 **t possession** of the vineyard of Naboth 3423
21:16 Naboth the Jezreelite, to **t possession** of it. 3423
21:21 will **t away** thy posterity, and will cut off 1197
22: 3 **t** it not out of the hand of the king of Syria? 3947
22:26 **T** Micaiah, and carry him back unto Amon 3947
2Ki 2: 1 when the LORD would **t up** Elijah *into* 5927
2: 3 Knowest thou that the LORD will **t away** 3947
2: 5 Knowest thou that the LORD will **t away** 3947
4: 1 the creditor is come to **t** unto him my two 3947
4:29 **t** my staff in thine hand, and go *thy way:* if 3947
4:36 come in unto him, he said, **T up** thy son. 5375
5:15 I pray thee, **t** a blessing of thy servant. 3947
5:16 And he urged him to **t** *it;* but he refused. 3947
5:20 I will run after him, and **t** somewhat of him. 3947
5:23 Naaman said, Be content, **t** two talents. 3947
6: 2 **t** thence every man a beam, and let us make 3947
6: 7 Therefore said he, **T** *it* **up** to thee. And he 7311
6:32 a murderer hath sent to **t away** mine head? 5493
7:13 his servants answered and said, Let *some* **t**, 3947
8: 8 **T** a present in thine hand, and go, meet 3947
9: 1 **t** this box of oil in thine hand, and go *to* 3947
9: 3 **t** the box of oil, and pour *it* on his head, 3947
9:17 **T** a horseman, and send to meet them, and 3947
9:25 **T up**, *and* cast him in the portion of 5375
9:26 Now therefore **t** *and* cast him into the plat 5375
10: 6 **t** ye the heads of the men your master's 3947
10:14 he said, **T** them alive. And they took them 8610
12: 5 Let the priests **t** *it* to them, every man of his 3947
13:15 Elisha said unto him, **T** bow and arrows. 3947
13:18 he said, **T** the arrows. And he took *them.* 3947
18:32 **t** you **away** to a land like your own land, 3947
19:30 of Judah shall *yet* again **t root** downward, 8328
20: 7 Isaiah said, **T** a lump of figs. And they took 3947
20:18 shall they **t** *away;* and they shall be 3947
1Ch 7:21 they came down to **t** *away* their cattle. 3947
17:13 I will not **t** my mercy **away** from him, as I 5493
21:23 **T** *it* to thee, and let my lord the king do *that* 3947
21:24 for I will not **t** *that* which *is* thine for 5375
28:10 **T heed** now; for the LORD hath chosen 7200
2Ch 6:16 that thy children **t heed** to their way to 8104
18:25 **T** ye Micaiah, and carry him back to Amon 3947
19: 6 said to the judges, **T heed** what ye do: 7200
19: 7 **t heed** and do *it:* for *there is* no iniquity 8104
20:25 his people came to **t away** the spoil of them, 962
32:18 to trouble them; that they might **t** the city. 3920
33: 8 that they will **t heed** to do all that I have 8104
Ezr 4:22 **T heed** now that ye fail not to do this: why 2095
5:14 those did Cyrus the king **t** out of the temple 5312
5:15 said unto him, **T** these vessels, go, 5376
9:12 neither **t** their daughters unto your sons, 5375
Ne 5: 2 we **t up** corn *for them,* that we may eat, 3947
6: 7 and let us **t counsel** together. 3289
10:30 the land, nor **t** their daughters for our sons: 3947
10:38 with the Levites, when the Levites **t tithes**: 6237
13:25 nor **t** their daughters unto your sons, or 5375
Est 3:13 and *to* **t** the spoil of them for a prey. NIH
4: 4 and to **t away** his sackcloth from him: 5493
6:10 *and* **t** the apparel and the horse, 3947
8:11 and *to* **t** the spoil of them for a prey, NIH
Job 7:21 and **t away** mine iniquity? 5674
9:18 He will not suffer me to **t** my breath, but 7725
9:34 Let him **t** his rod **away** from me, and let not 5493
10:20 let me alone, that I may **t comfort** a little, 1082
11:18 *and* thou shalt **t** thy **rest** in safety. 7901
13:14 Wherefore do I **t** my flesh in my teeth, and 5375
18: 9 The grin shall **t** *him* by the heel, *and* 270
21:12 They **t** the timbrel and harp, and rejoice at 5375
23:10 he knoweth the way that I **t**: *when* he hath 5978
24: 2 they **violently t away** flocks, and 1497
24: 3 they **t** the widow's ox **for a pledge**. 2254
24: 9 from the breast, and **t a pledge** of the poor. 2254
24:10 and they **t away** the sheaf *from* the hungry; 5375
27:20 Terrors **t hold on** him as waters, a tempest 5381
30:17 the night season: and my sinews **t** no **rest**. 7901
31:36 Surely I would **t** it upon my shoulder, *and* 5375
32:22 *so doing* my Maker would soon **t** me **away**. 5375
36:17 judgment and justice **t hold on** *thee.* 8551
36:18 *beware* lest he **t** thee **away** with *his* stroke: 5496
36:21 **T heed**, regard not iniquity: for this hast 8104
38:13 That *it* might **t hold** of the ends of the earth, 270
38:20 That thou shouldest **t** it to the bound 3947
41: 4 wilt thou **t** him for a servant for ever? 3947
42: 8 Therefore **t** unto you now seven bullocks 3947
Ps 2: 2 the rulers **t counsel** together, against 3245
7: 5 the enemy persecute my soul, and **t** *it;* yea, 5381
13: 2 How long shall I **t** counsel in my soul, 7896
16: 4 not offer, nor **t up** their names into my lips. 5375
27:10 forsake me, then the LORD will **t** me **up**. 622
31:13 against me, they devised to **t away** my life. 3947
35: 2 **T hold** of shield and buckler, and stand up 2388
39: 1 I said, I will **t heed** to my ways, that *I* sin 8104
50: 9 I will **t** no bullock out of thy house, *nor* he 3947
50:16 *that* thou shouldest **t** my covenant in thy 5375
51:11 and **t** not thy holy Spirit from me. 3947
52: 5 he shall **t** thee **away**, and pluck thee out of 2846
58: 9 he shall **t** them **away as with a whirlwind**, 8175
69:20 I looked *for some* to **t pity**, but *there was* 5110
69:24 and let thy wrathful anger **t hold** of them. 5381
71:10 they that lay wait for my soul **t counsel** 3289
71:11 persecute and **t** him; for *there is* none to 8610
80: 9 didst **cause** it **to t deep root**, and 8327+8328
81: 2 **T** a psalm, and bring hither the timbrel, 5375
83:12 **t** to ourselves the houses of God
in possession. 3423
89:33 will I not **utterly t** from him, 6331
102:14 For thy servants **t pleasure** in her stones, 7521
102:24 **t** me not **away** in the midst of my days: 5927
109: 8 his days be few; *and* let another **t** his office. 3947
116:13 I will **t** the cup of salvation, and call upon 5375
119:43 **t** not the word of truth utterly out of my 5337
139: 9 *If* I **t** the wings of the morning, *and* dwell in 5375
139:20 *and* thine enemies **t** *thy name* in vain. 5375

Pr 2:19 neither **t** they **hold** of the paths of life. 5381
4:13 **T fast hold** of instruction; let *her* not go: 2388
5: 5 go down *to* death; her steps **t hold** on hell. 8551
5:22 His own iniquities shall **t** the wicked 3920
6:25 neither let her **t** thee with her eyelids. 3947
6:27 Can a man **t** fire in his bosom, and 2846
7:18 let us **t** our **fill** of love until the morning: 7301
20:16 **T** his garment that is surety *for* a stranger: 3947
20:16 **t a pledge** of him for a strange *woman.* 2254
22:27 why should he **t away** thy bed from under 3947
25: 4 **T away** the dross from the silver, and 1898
25: 5 **T away** the wicked *from* before the king, 1898
27:13 **T** his garment that is surety *for* a stranger, 3947
27:13 **t a pledge** of him for a strange *woman.* 2254
30: 9 steal, and **t** the name of my God *in vain.* 8610
Ecc 5:15 shall **t** nothing of his labour, which he may 5375
5:19 to **t** his portion, and to rejoice in his labour; 5375
7:18 *It is* good that thou shouldest **t hold** of this; 270
7:21 Also **t** no **heed** unto all words that 3820+5414
SS 2:15 **T** us the foxes, the little foxes, that spoil 270
7: 8 I will **t hold** of the boughs thereof: 270
Isa 1:25 away thy dross, and **t away** all thy tin: 5493
3: 1 doth **t away** from Jerusalem and 5493
3: 6 When a man shall **t hold** of his brother *of* 8610
3:18 In that day the Lord will **t away** the bravery 5493
4: 1 in that day seven women shall **t hold** of one 2388
4: 1 called by thy name, to **t away** our reproach. 622
5: 5 I *will* **t away** the hedge thereof, and it shall 5493
5:23 **t away** the righteousness of the righteous 5493
7: 4 say unto him, **T heed**, and be quiet; 8104
8: 1 **T** thee a great roll, and write in it with a 3947
8:10 **T counsel together**, and it shall 5779+6098
10: 2 to **t away** the right **from** the poor of my 1497
10: 6 to **t** the spoil, and to take the prey, and 7997
10: 6 to **t** the prey, and to tread them down like 962
13: 8 sorrows shall **t hold** of *them;* they shall be in 270
14: 2 the people shall **t** them, and bring them to 3947
14: 2 they shall **t** them **captives**, whose captives 7617
14: 4 That thou shalt **t up** this proverb against 5375
16: 3 **T** counsel, execute judgment; make thy 935
18: 4 I will **t** my **rest**, and I will consider in my 8252
18: 5 and **t away** *and* cut down the branches. 5493
23:16 **T** a harp, go about the city, thou harlot that 3947
25: 8 the rebuke of his people shall he **t away** 5493
27: 5 Or let him **t hold** of my strength, *that* he 2388
27: 6 **cause** them that come of Jacob **to t root**: 8327
27: 9 and this *is* all the fruit to **t away** his sin; 5493
28:19 From the time that it goeth forth it shall **t** 3947
30: 1 the LORD, that **t** counsel, but not of me; 6213
30:14 of it a sheard to **t** fire from the hearth, 2846
30:14 or to **t** water *withal* out of the pit. 2834
33:23 of a great spoil divided; the lame **t** the prey. 962
36:17 **t** you **away** to a land like your own land, 3947
37:31 house of Judah shall again **t** root downward, NIH
38:21 Let them **t** a lump of figs, and lay *it* for a 5375
39: 7 which thou shalt beget, shall they **t away**; 3947
40:24 yea, their stock shall not **t root** in the earth: 8327
40:24 the whirlwind shall **t** them **away** as stubble. 5375
44:15 for he will **t** thereof, and warm himself; 3947
45:21 *them* near; yea, let them **t counsel** together: 3289
47: 2 **T** the millstones, and grind meal: 3947
47: 3 I will **t** vengeance, and I will not meet *thee* 3947
56: 4 that please me, and **t hold** of my covenant; 2388
57:13 vanity shall **t** *them:* but he that putteth his 3947
57:14 **t up** the stumblingblock out of the way of 7311
58: 2 they **t delight in** approaching to God. 2654
58: 9 Here I *am.* If thou **t away** from the midst of 5493
64: 7 that stirreth up himself to **t hold** of thee: 2388
66:21 I will also **t** of them for priests *and* 3947
Jer 2:22 wash thee with nitre, and **t** thee **much** sope, 7235
3:14 I will **t** you one of a city, and two of a 3947
4: 4 **t away** the foreskins of your heart, ye men 5493
5:10 **t away** her battlements; for they *are* not 5493
7:29 and **t up** a lamentation on high places; 5375
9: 4 **T** ye **heed** every one of his neighbour, and 8104
9:10 For the mountains will I **t up** a weeping 5375
9:18 them make haste, and **t up** a wailing for us, 5375
13: 4 **T** the girdle that thou hast got, which *is* 3947
13: 6 to Euphrates, and **t** the girdle from thence, 3947
13:21 shall not sorrows **t** thee, as a woman in 270
15:15 **t** me not **away** in thy longsuffering: 3947
15:19 if thou **t forth** the precious from the vile, 3318
16: 2 Thou shalt not **t** thee a wife, neither shalt 3947
17:21 **T heed** to yourselves, and bear no burden 8104
18:22 for they have digged a pit to **t** me, and 3920
19: 1 **t** of the ancients of the people, and of NIH
20: 5 and **t** them, and carry them to Babylon. 3947
20:10 and we shall **t** our revenge on him. 3947
25: 9 will send and **t** all the families of the north, 3947
25:10 Moreover I will **t** from them the voice of mirth, 6
25:15 **T** the wine cup of this fury at mine hand, 3947
25:28 if they refuse to **t** the cup at thine hand to 3947
29: 6 **T** ye wives, and beget sons and daughters; 3947
29: 6 **t** wives for your sons, and give your 3947
32: 3 of the king of Babylon, and he shall **t** it; 3920
32:14 **T** these evidences, this evidence of 3947
32:24 they are come *unto* the city to **t** it; 3920
32:25 the field for money, and **t witnesses**; 5707+5749
32:28 king of Babylon, and he shall **t** it: 3920
32:44 **t witnesses** in the land of Benjamin, 5707+5749
33:26 that *I* will not **t** *any* of his seed *to be* rulers 3947
34:22 against it, and **t** it, and burn it with fire: 3920
36: 2 **T** thee a roll of a book, and write therein all 3947
36:14 **T** in thine hand the roll wherein thou hast 3947
36:26 to **t** Baruch the scribe and Jeremiah 3947
36:28 **T** thee again another roll, and write in it all 3947
37: 8 this city, and **t** it, and burn it with fire. 3920
38: 3 king of Babylon's army, which shall **t** it. 3920
38:10 **T** from hence thirty men with thee, and 3947
38:10 **t up** Jeremiah the prophet out of 5927
39:12 **T** him, and look well to him, and do him no 3947
43: 9 **T** great stones in thine hand, and hide them 3947
43:10 and **t** Nebuchadrezzar the king of Babylon, 3947
44:12 I will **t** the remnant of Judah, that have set 3947
46:11 Go up *into* Gilead, and **t** balm, O virgin, 3947

Jer 49:29 their flocks shall they **t** *away:* they shall 3947
49:29 they shall **t** to themselves their curtains, 5375
50:15 **t vengeance** upon her; as she hath done, 5358
51: 8 **t** balm for her pain, if so be she may be 3947
51:26 they shall not **t** of thee a stone for a corner, 3947
51:36 thy cause, and **t vengeance** for thee; 5358+5360
La 2:13 What *thing* shall I **t to witness** for thee? 5749
Eze 4: 1 **t** thee a tile, and lay it before thee, and 3947
4: 3 Moreover **t** thou unto thee an iron pan, and 3947
4: 9 **T** thou also unto thee wheat, and barley, 3947
5: 1 thou, son of man, **t** thee a sharp knife, 3947
5: 1 **t** thee a barber's rasor, and cause *it* to pass 3947
5: 1 **t** thee balances to weigh, and divide 3947
5: 2 thou shalt **t** a third *part, and* smite about it 3947
5: 3 Thou shalt also **t** thereof a few in number, 3947
5: 4 **t** of them again, and cast them into 3947
10: 6 saying, **T** fire from between the wheels, 3947
11:18 they shall **t away** all the detestable things 5493
11:19 I will **t** the stony heart out of their flesh, 5493
14: 5 That *I* may **t** the house of Israel in their 8610
15: 3 will *men* **t** a pin of it to hang any vessel 3947
16:16 of thy garments thou didst **t**, and 3947
16:39 shall **t** thy fair jewels, and leave thee naked 3947
17:22 I will also **t** of the highest branch of 3947
19: 1 Moreover **t** thou **up** a lamentation for 5375
21:26 Remove the diadem, and **t off** the crown: 7311
22:16 thou shalt **t** thine **inheritance** in thyself in 2490
23:25 they shall **t away** thy nose and thine ears; 5493
23:25 they shall **t** thy sons and thy daughters; and 3947
23:26 of thy clothes, and **t away** thy fair jewels. 3947
23:29 shall **t** *away* all thy labour, and shall leave 3947
24: 5 **T** the choice of the flock, and burn also 3947
24: 8 fury to come up to **t vengeance**; 5358+5359
24:16 I **t away** from thee the desire of thine eyes 3947
24:25 *shall it* not *be* in the day when I **t** from 3947
26:17 they shall **t up** a lamentation for thee, and 5375
27: 2 son of man, **t up** a lamentation for Tyrus; 5375
27:32 in their wailing they shall **t up** a 5375
28:12 **t up** a lamentation upon the king of Tyrus, 5375
29:19 he shall **t** her multitude, and take her spoil, 5375
29:19 and **t** her **spoil**, and take her prey; 7997+7998
29:19 and take her spoil, and **t** her **prey**; 957+962
30: 4 they shall **t** *away* her multitude, and 3947
32: 2 **t up** a lamentation for Pharaoh king of 5375
33: 2 if the people of the land **t** a man of their 3947
33: 4 if the sword come, and **t** him **away**, 3947
33: 6 and **t** *any* person from among them, 3947
36:24 For I will **t** you from among the heathen, 3947
36:26 I will **t away** the stony heart out of your 5493
37:16 **t** thee one stick, and write upon it, 3947
37:16 **t** another stick, and write upon it, 3947
37:19 Behold, I *will* **t** the stick of Joseph, 3947
37:21 I *will* **t** the children of Israel from among 3947
38:12 To **t a spoil**, and to take a prey; to 7997+7998
38:12 To take a spoil, and to **t a prey**; to turn 957+962
38:13 Art thou come to **t a spoil**? 7997+7998
38:13 thou gathered thy company to **t a prey**? 957+962
38:13 and gold, to **t** *away* cattle and goods, 3947
38:13 *away* cattle and goods, to **t** a great spoil? 7997
39:10 So that they shall **t** no wood out of 5375
43:20 thou shalt **t** of the blood thereof, and put *it* 3947
43:21 Thou shalt **t** the bullock also of the sin 3947
44:22 Neither shall they **t** for their wives a 3947
44:22 they shall **t** maidens of the seed of 3947
45: 9 **t away** your exactions from my people, 7311
45:18 thou shalt **t** a young bullock without 3947
45:19 the priest shall **t** of the blood of the sin 3947
46:18 Moreover the prince shall not **t** of 3947
Da 6:23 commanded that *they* should **t** Daniel **up** 5267
7:18 the saints of the most High shall **t** 6902
7:26 they shall **t away** his dominion, to consume 5709
11:15 up a mount, and **t** the most fenced cities: 3920
11:18 his face unto the isles, and shall **t** many: 3920
11:31 shall **t away** the daily *sacrifice,* and 5493
Hos 1: 2 **t** unto thee a wife of whoredoms and 3947
1: 6 but I will **utterly t** them **away**. 5375+5375
2: 9 and **t** *away* my corn in the time thereof, and 3947
2:17 For I will **t away** the names of Baalim out 5493
4:10 they have left off to **t heed** to the LORD. 8104
4:11 and wine and new wine **t** *away* the heart. 3947
5:14 I will **t away**, and none shall rescue *him.* 5375
11: 4 I was to them as they that **t off** the yoke on 7311
14: 2 **T** with you words, and turn to the LORD: 3947
14: 2 **T away** all iniquity, and receive *us* 5375
Am 3: 5 shall *one* **t up** a snare from the earth, and 5927
4: 2 that he will **t** you **away** with hooks, and 5375
5: 1 Hear ye this word which I **t up** against you, 5375
5:11 and ye **t** from him burdens of wheat: 3947
5:12 they **t** a bribe, and they turn aside the poor 3947
5:23 **T** thou **away** from me the noise of thy 5493
6:10 a man's uncle shall **t** him **up**, and he that 5375
9: 2 into hell, thence shall mine hand **t** them; 3947
9: 3 I will search and **t** them out thence; 3947
Jnh 1:12 **T** me **up**, and cast me forth into the sea; 5375
4: 3 O LORD, **t**, I beseech thee, 3947
Mic 2: 2 they covet fields, and **t** *them* **by violence**; 1497
2: 2 by violence; and houses, and **t** *them* **away**: 5375
2: 4 In that day shall *one* **t up** a parable against 5375
2: 6 to them, *that* they shall not **t** shame. 5253
6:14 thou shalt **t hold**, but shalt not deliver; and 5253
Na 1: 2 the LORD will **t vengeance** on his 5358
2: 9 **T** ye **the spoil** of silver, take the spoil of 962
2: 9 ye the spoil of silver, **t the spoil** of gold: 962
Hab 1:10 for they shall heap dust, and **t** it. 3920
1:15 They **t up** all of them with the angle, 5927
2: 6 Shall not all these **t up** a parable against 5375
Zep 3:11 I will **t away** out of the midst of thee them 5493
Hag 1: 8 I will **t pleasure** in it, and I will be 7521
2:23 will I **t** thee, O Zerubbabel, my servant, 3947
Zec 1: 6 did they not **t hold** of your fathers? 5381
3: 4 **T away** the filthy garments from him. 5493
6:10 **T** of *them of* the captivity, *even* of Heldai, 3947
6:11 **t** silver and gold, and make crowns, and 3947
8:23 **t hold** out of all languages of the nations, 2388
8:23 even shall **t hold** of the skirt of him that is a 2388

T

Zec 9: 7 I will t away his blood out of his mouth, 5493
11:15 T unto thee yet the instruments of a foolish 3947
14:21 they that sacrifice shall come and t of them, 3947
Mal 2: 3 and one shall t you away with it. 5375
2:15 Therefore t heed to your spirit, and let none 8104
2:16 therefore t heed to your spirit, that ye deal 8104
Mt 1:20 fear not to t unto thee Mary thy wife: 3880
2:13 and t the young child and his mother, and 3880
2:20 and t the young child and his mother, and 3880
5:40 and t away thy coat, let him have thy cloke 2983
6: 1 T heed that ye do not your alms before 4337
6:25 T no thought for your life, what ye shall 3309
6:28 And why t ye thought for raiment? 3309
6:31 Therefore t no thought, saying, What shall 3309
6:34 T therefore no thought for the morrow: 3309
6:34 for the morrow shall t thought for 3309
9: 6 Arise, t up thy bed, and go unto thine house. 142
10:19 t no thought how or what ye shall speak: 3309
11:12 and the violent t it by force. 726
11:29 T my yoke upon you, and learn of me; for I 142
15:26 It is not meet to t the children's bread, and 2983
16: 5 the other side, they had forgotten to t bread. 2983
16: 6 T heed and beware of the leaven of 3708
16:24 and t up his cross, and follow me. 142
17:25 of whom do the kings of the earth t custom 2983
17:27 and t up the fish that first cometh up; 142
17:27 that t, and give unto them for me and thee. 2983
18:10 T heed that ye despise not one of these 3708
18:16 hear thee, then t with thee one or two more, 3880
18:23 which would t account of his servants. 4868
20:14 T that thine is, and go thy way: I will give 142
22:13 Bind him hand and foot, and t him away, 142
24: 4 unto them, T heed that no man deceive you. 991
24:17 come down to t any thing out of his house: 142
24:18 is in the field return back to t his clothes. 142
25:28 T therefore the talent from him, and give it 142
26: 4 And consulted that they might t Jesus by 2902
26:26 and gave it to the disciples, and said, T, eat; 2983
26:45 unto them, Sleep on now, and t your rest: 373
26:52 for all they that t the sword shall perish 2983
26:55 a thief with swords and staves for to t me? 4815
Mk 2: 9 or to say, Arise, and t up thy bed, and walk? 142
2:11 and t up thy bed, and go thy way into thine 142
4:24 he said unto them, T heed what you hear: 991
6: 8 And commanded them that they should t 142
7:27 for it is not meet to t the children's bread, 2983
8:14 Now the disciples had forgotten to t bread, 2983
8:15 And he charged them, saying, T heed, 3708
8:34 and t up his cross, and follow me. 142
10:21 and come, t up the cross, and follow me. 142
12:19 that his brother should t his wife, and 2983
13: 5 to say, T heed lest any man deceive you: 991
13: 9 But t heed to yourselves: for they shall 991
13:11 t no thought beforehand what ye shall 4305
13:15 neither enter therein, to t any thing out of his 142
13:16 not turn back again for to t up his garment. 142
13:23 But t ye heed: behold, I have foretold you 991
13:33 T ye heed, watch and pray: for ye know not 991
14: 1 the scribes sought how they might t him by 2902
14:22 brake it, and gave to them, and said, T, eat: 2983
14:36 unto thee; t away this cup from me: 3911
14:41 unto them, Sleep on now, and t your rest: 373
14:44 is he; t him, and lead him away safely. 2902
14:48 with swords and with staves to t me? 4815
15:24 lots upon them, what every man should t. 142
15:36 see whether Elias will come to t him down. 2507
16:18 They shall t up serpents; and if they drink 142
Lk 1:25 on me, to t away my reproach among men. 851
5:24 and t up thy couch, and go into thine house. 142
6: 4 of God, and did t and eat the shewbread, 2983
6:29 away thy cloke forbid not to t thy coat also. NIG
8:18 T heed therefore how ye hear: 991
9: 3 T nothing for your journey, neither staves, 142
9:23 him deny himself, and t up his cross daily, 142
10:35 the host, and said unto him, T care of him; 1959
11:35 T heed therefore that the light which is in 4648
12:11 t ye no thought how or what thing ye shall 3309
12:15 T heed, and beware of covetousness: 3708
12:19 t thine ease, eat, drink, and be merry. 373
12:22 T no thought for your life, what ye shall 3309
12:26 is least, why t ye thought for the rest? 3309
14: 9 thou begin with shame to t the lowest 2722
16: 6 T thy bill, and sit down quickly, and 1209
16: 7 unto him, T thy bill, and write fourscore. 1209
17: 3 T heed to yourselves: If thy brother 4337
17:31 let him not come down to t it away: 142
19:24 T from him the pound, and give it to him 142
20:20 men, that they might t hold of his words, 1949
20:26 And they could not t hold of his words 1949
20:28 that his brother should t his wife, and 2983
21: 8 And he said, T heed that ye be not deceived: 991
21:34 And t heed to yourselves, lest at any time 4337
22:17 T this, and divide it among yourselves: 2983
22:36 a purse, let him t it, and likewise his scrip: 142
Jn 2:16 them that sold doves, T these things hence; 142
5: 8 saith unto him, Rise, t up thy bed, and walk. 142
5:11 same said unto me, T up thy bed, and walk. 142
5:12 said unto thee, T up thy bed, and walk? 142
6: 7 that every one of them may t a little. 2983
6:15 that they would come and t him by force, 726
7:30 Then they sought to t him: but no man laid 4084
7:32 and the chief priests sent officers to t him. 4084
10:17 I lay down my life, that I might t it again. 2983
10:18 lay it down, and I have power to t it again. 2983
10:39 Therefore they sought again to t him: but 4084
11:39 Jesus said, T ye away the stone. Martha, 142
11:48 and t away both our place and nation. 142
11:57 he should shew it, that they might t him. 4084
16:15 that he shall t of mine, and shall shew it 2983
17:15 I pray not that thou shouldest t them out of 142
18:31 T ye him, and judge him according to your 2983
19: 6 T ye him, and crucify him: for I find no 2983
19:38 besought Pilate that he might t away 142
20:15 thou hast laid him, and I will t him away. 142
Ac 1:20 and his bishoprick let another t. 2983
Ac 1:25 That he may t part of this ministry and 2983
5:35 t heed to yourselves what ye intend to do 4337
12: 3 he proceeded further to t Peter also. 4815
15:14 to t out of them a people for his name. 2983
15:37 And Barnabas determined to t with them 4838
15:38 But Paul thought not good to t him with 4838
20:13 unto Assos, there intending to t in Paul: 353
20:26 Wherefore I t you to record this day, that I 3143
20:28 T heed therefore unto yourselves, and to all 4337
21:24 Them t, and purify thyself with them, and 3880
22:26 saying, T heed what thou doest: 3708
23:10 and to t him by force from among them, and 726
24: 8 by examining of whom thyself mayest t NIG
27:33 Paul besought them all to t meat, saying, 3335
27:34 Wherefore I pray you to t some meat: 4355
Ro 11:21 t heed lest he also spare not thee. NIG
11:27 unto them, when I shall t away their sins. 851
15:24 Whensoever I t my journey into Spain, 4198
1Co 3:10 But let every man t heed how he buildeth 991
6: 7 Why do ye not rather t wrong? why do ye not 91
6:15 shall I then t the members of Christ, and 142
8: 9 But t heed lest by any means this liberty of 991
9: 9 out the corn. Doth God t care for oxen? 3199
10:12 that thinketh he standeth t heed lest he fall. 991
11:24 given thanks, he brake it, and said, T, eat: 2983
2Co 8: 4 t upon us the fellowship of the ministering NIG
11:20 if a man devour you, if a man t of you, if a 2983
12:10 Therefore I t pleasure in infirmities, 2106
Gal 5:15 t heed ye be not consumed one of another. 991
Eph 6:13 Wherefore t unto you the whole armour of 353
6:17 And t the helmet of salvation, and 1209
Col 4:17 T heed to the ministry which thou hast 991
1Ti 3: 5 how shall he t care of the church of God?) 1959
4:16 T heed unto thyself, and unto the doctrine; 1907
2Ti 4:11 T Mark, and bring him with thee: for he is 353
Heb 3:12 T heed, brethren, lest there be in any of you 991
7: 5 to t tithes of the people according to the law, 586
10: 4 of bulls and of goats should t away sins. 851
10:11 which can never t away sins: 4014
Jas 5:10 T, my brethren, the prophets, who have 2983
1Pe 2:20 for your faults, ye shall t it patiently? 5278
2:20 do well, and suffer for it, ye t it patiently, 5278
2Pe 1:19 whereunto ye do well that ye t heed, 4337
1Jn 3: 5 that he was manifested to t away our sins; 142
Rev 3:11 which thou hast, that no man t thy crown. 2983
5: 9 Thou art worthy to t the book, and to open 2983
6: 4 power was given to him that sat thereon to t 2983
10: 8 t the little book which is open in the hand 2983
10: 9 And he said unto me, T it, and eat it up; 2983
22:17 let him t the water of life freely. 2983
22:19 And if any man shall t away from the words 851
22:19 God shall t away his part out of the book of 851

TAKEN (338) [TAKE]

Ge 2:22 which the LORD God had t from man, 3947
2:23 because she was t out of Man. 3947
3:19 unto the ground; for out of it wast thou t: 3947
3:23 to till the ground from whence he was t. 3947
4:15 vengeance shall be t on him sevenfold. 5358
12:15 and the woman was t into Pharaoh's house. 3947
12:19 so I might have t her to me to wife: now 3947
14:14 Abram heard that his brother was t captive, 7617
18:27 I have t upon me to speak unto the Lord, 2974
18:31 I have t upon me to speak unto the Lord: 2974
20: 3 for the woman which thou hast t; 3947
21:25 Abimelech's servants had violently t away. 1497
27:33 where is he that hath t venison, and 6679
27:35 with subtilty, and hath t away thy blessing. 3947
27:36 behold, now he hath t away my blessing. 3947
30:15 Is it a small matter that thou hast t my 3947
30:23 and said, God hath t away my reproach: 622
31: 1 Jacob hath t away all that was our father's; 3947
31: 9 Thus God hath t away the cattle of your 5337
31:16 For all the riches which God hath t from 5337
31:26 my daughters, as captives t with the sword? NIH
31:34 Now Rachel had t the images, and put them 3947
Ex 14:11 hast thou t us away to die in 3947
25:15 rings of the ark: they shall not be t from it. 5493
40:36 when the cloud was t up from over 5927
40:37 if the cloud were not t up, then 5927
40:37 journeyed not till the day that it was t up. 5927
Lev 4:10 As it was t off from the bullock of 7311
4:31 as the fat is t away from off the sacrifice of 5493
4:35 as the fat of the lamb is t away from 5493
6: 2 or in a thing t away by violence, or 1498
7:34 the heave shoulder have I t of the children 3947
14:43 after that he hath t away the stones, and 2502
24: 8 being t from the children of Israel by an NIH
Nu 3:12 I have t the Levites from among 3947
5:13 neither she be t with the manner; 8610
8:16 children of Israel, have I t them unto me. 3947
8:18 I have t the Levites for all the firstborn of 3947
9:17 when the cloud was t up from 5927
9:21 that the cloud was t up in the morning, then 5927
9:21 by day or by night that the cloud was t up, 5927
9:22 but when it was t up, they journeyed. 5927
10:11 that the cloud was t up from off 5927
10:17 the tabernacle was t down; and the sons of 3381
16:15 I have not t one ass from them, 5375
18: 6 I have t your brethren the Levites from 3947
21:26 t all his land out of his hand, even unto 3947
31:26 Take the sum of the prey that was t, both of 7628
31:49 Thy servants have t the sum of the men of 5375
31:53 (For the men of war had t spoil, every man 962
36: 3 shall their inheritance be t from 1639
36: 3 shall it be t from the lot of our inheritance. 1639
36: 4 shall their inheritance be t away from 1639
Dt 4:20 the LORD hath t you, and brought you 3947
20: 7 hath betrothed a wife, and hath not t her? 3947
21:10 and thou hast t them captive, 7617+7628
24: 1 When a man hath t a wife, and married her, 3947
24: 5 When a man hath t a new wife, he shall not 3947
24: 5 and shall cheer up his wife which he hath t. 3947
26:14 neither have I t away ought thereof for any 1197
28:31 thine ass shall be violently t away from 1497
Jos 7:11 for they have even t of the accursed thing, 3947
7:15 that he that is t with the accursed thing 3920
7:16 by their tribes; and the tribe of Judah was t: 3920
7:17 the Zarhites man by man; and Zabdi was t: 3920
7:18 son of Zerah, of the tribe of Judah, was t. 3920
8: 8 it shall be, when ye have t the city, that ye 8610
8:21 all Israel saw that the ambush had t 3920
10: 1 Jerusalem had heard how Joshua had t Ai, 3920
Jdg 1: 8 had t it, and smitten it with the edge of 3920
11:36 forasmuch as the LORD hath t vengeance 6213
14: 9 he told not them that he had t the honey out 7287
15: 6 because he had t his wife, and given her to 3947
17: 2 shekels of silver that were t from thee, 3947
18:24 Ye have t away my gods which I made, 3947
1Sa 4:11 the ark of God was t; and the two sons of 3947
4:17 Phinehas, are dead, and the ark of God is t. 3947
4:19 heard the tidings that the ark of God was t, 3947
4:21 because the ark of God was t, and because 3947
4:22 from Israel: for the ark of God is t. 3947
7:14 the cities which the Philistines had t from 3947
10:20 to come near, the tribe of Benjamin was t. 3920
10:21 the family of Matri was t, and Saul the son 3920
10:21 was taken, and Saul the son of Kish was t: 3920
12: 3 whose ox have I t? or whose ass have I 3947
12: 3 or whose ass have I t? or whom have I 3947
12: 4 neither hast thou t ought of any man's 3947
14:41 a perfect lot. And Saul and Jonathan were t: 3920
14:42 and Jonathan my son. And Jonathan was t. 3920
21: 6 that was t from before the LORD, 5493
21: 6 hot bread in the day when it was t away. 3947
30: 2 had t the women captives, that were 7617
30: 3 and their daughters, were t captives. 7617
30: 5 David's two wives were t captives, 7617
30:16 of all the great spoil that they had t out of 3947
30:19 nor any thing that they had t to them: 3947
2Sa 12: 9 hast t his wife to be thy wife, and hast slain 3947
12:10 hast t the wife of Uriah the Hittite to be thy 3947
12:27 and have t the city of waters. 3920
16: 8 and, behold, thou art t to thy mischief, NIH
18: 9 he was t up between the heaven and 5414
18:18 Now Absalom in his lifetime had t and 3947
23: 6 because they cannot be t with hands: 3947
1Ki 7: 8 whom he had t to wife, like unto this porch. 3947
9: 9 have t hold upon other gods, and 2388
9:16 t Gezer, and burnt it with fire, and slain 3920
16:18 to pass, when Zimri saw that the city was t, 3920
21:19 Hast thou killed, and also t possession? 3423
22:43 the high places were not t away 5493
2Ki 2: 9 do for thee, before I be t away from thee. 3947
2:10 nevertheless, if thou see me when I am t 3947
2:16 the spirit of the LORD hath t him up, 5375
4:20 when he had t him, and brought him to his 5375
6:22 whom thou hast t captive with thy sword 7617
12: 3 the high places were not t away: the people 5493
13:25 which he had t out of the hand of Jehoahaz 3947
14: 4 Howbeit the high places were not t away: 5493
18:10 of Hoshea king of Israel, Samaria was t. 3920
18:22 and whose altars Hezekiah hath t away, 5493
24: 7 for the king of Babylon had t from the river 3947
1Ch 24: 6 one principal household being t for Eleazar, 270
24: 6 taken for Eleazar, and one t for Ithamar. 270
2Ch 15: 8 out of the cities which he had t from mount 3920
15:17 the high places were not t away out of 5493
17: 2 of Ephraim, which Asa his father had t. 3920
19: 3 in that thou hast t away the groves out of 1197
20:33 Howbeit the high places were not t away: 5493
28:11 which ye have t captive of your brethren: 7617
28:18 had t Beth-shemesh, and Ajalon, and 3920
30: 2 For the king had t counsel, and his princes, 3289
32:12 Hath not the same Hezekiah t away his 5493
Ezr 9: 2 For they have t of their daughters for 5375
10: 2 have t strange wives of the people of 3427
10:10 and have t strange wives, 3427
10:14 let all them which have t strange wives in 3427
10:17 made an end with all the men that had t 3427
10:18 there were found that had t strange wives: 3427
10:44 All these had t strange wives: and some of 5375
Ne 5:15 had t of them bread and wine, beside forty 3947
6:18 his son Johanan had t the daughter of 3947
Est 2:15 who had t her for his daughter, was come 3947
2:16 So Esther was t unto king Ahasuerus into 3947
8: 2 which he had t from Haman, and gave it 5674
Job 1:21 the LORD hath t away; blessed be 3947
16:12 he hath also t me by my neck, and 270
19: 9 of my glory, and t the crown from my head. 5493
20:19 he hath violently t away a house which he 1497
22: 6 For thou hast t a pledge from thy brother 2254
24:24 they are t out of the way as all other, and 7092
27: 2 God liveth, who hath t away my judgment; 5493
28: 2 Iron is t out of the earth, and brass is 3947
30:16 the days of affliction have t hold upon me. 270
34: 5 and God hath t away my judgment. 5493
34:20 the mighty shall be t away without hand. 5493
Ps 9:15 in the net which they hid is their own foot t. 3920
10: 2 let them be t in the devices that they have 8610
40:12 mine iniquities have t hold upon me, so 5381
59:12 the words of their lips let them even be t in 3920
83: 3 They have t crafty counsel against thy 6191
85: 3 Thou hast t away all thy wrath: thou hast 622
119:53 Horror hath t hold upon me because of 270
119:111 Thy testimonies have I t as an heritage for 5157
119:143 Trouble and anguish have t hold on me: 4672
Pr 3:26 and shall keep thy foot from being t. 3921
4:16 their sleep is t away, unless they cause 1497
6: 2 thou art t with the words of thy mouth, 3920
7:20 He hath t a bag of money with him, 3947
11: 6 transgressors shall be t in their own 3920
Ecc 2:18 I hated all my labour which I had t under 6001
3:14 can be put to it, nor any thing t from it: 1639
7:26 from her; but the sinner shall be t by her. 3920
9:12 as the fishes that are t in an evil net, and 270
Isa 6: 6 which he had t with the tongs from off 3947
6: 7 thine iniquity is t away, and thy sin purged. 5493
7: 5 have t evil counsel against thee, saying, 3289
8: 4 the spoil of Samaria shall be t away before 5375

Isa 8:15 fall, and be broken, and be snared, and be t. 3920
10:27 that his burden shall be t away from off thy 5493
10:29 they have t up their lodging at Geba; 4411
16:10 gladness is t away, and joy out of 622
17: 1 Damascus is t away from being a city, and 5493
21: 3 pangs have t hold upon me, as the pangs of 270
23: 8 Who hath t this counsel against Tyre, 3289
24:18 the midst of the pit shall be t in the snare: 3920
28:13 and be broken, and snared, and t. 3920
33:20 a tabernacle that shall not be t down; 6813
36: 7 and whose altars Hezekiah hath t away, 5493
41: 9 Thou whom I have t from the ends of 2388
49:24 Shall the prey be t from the mighty, or 3947
49:25 the captives of the mighty shall be t away, 3947
51:22 I have t out of thine hand the cup of 3947
52: 5 that my people is t away for nought? 3947
53: 8 He was t from prison and from judgment: 3947
57: 1 merciful men are t away, none considering 622
57: 1 considering that the righteous is t away 622
64: 6 like the wind, have t us away. 5375
Jer 6:11 even the husband with the wife shall be t, 3920
6:24 anguish hath t hold of us, and pain, as of a 2388
8: 9 men are ashamed, they are dismayed and t: 3920
8:21 am black; astonishment hath t hold on me. 2388
12: 2 hast planted them, yea, they have t root: 8327
16: 5 for I have t away my peace from this people, 622
29:22 of them shall be t up a curse by all 3947
34: 3 shalt surely be t, and delivered into 8610+8610
38:23 shalt be t by the hand of the king of 8610
38:28 prison until the day that Jerusalem was t: 3920
38:28 and he was there when Jerusalem was t. 3920
39: 5 when they had t him, they brought him up 3947
40: 1 when he had t him being bound in chains 3947
40:10 and dwell in your cities that ye have t. 8610
48: 1 Kiriathaim is confounded and t: Misgab is 3920
48: 7 and in thy treasures, thou shalt also be t: 3920
48:33 and gladness is t from the plentiful field, 622
48:41 Kerioth is t, and the strong holds are 3920
48:44 he that getteth up out of the pit shall be t in 3920
48:46 for thy sons are t captives, and 3947
49:20 of the LORD, that he hath t against Edom; 3289
49:24 sorrows have t her as a woman in travail. 270
49:30 Babylon hath t counsel against you, 3289+6098
50: 2 say, Babylon is t, Bel is confounded, 3920
50: 9 against her; from thence she shall be t: 3920
50:24 thou art also t, O Babylon, and thou wast 3920
50:45 the LORD, that he hath t against Babylon; 3289
51:31 king of Babylon that his city is t at one end, 3920
51:41 How is Sheshach t! and how is t the praise of 3920
51:56 upon Babylon, and her mighty men are t, 3920
La 2: 6 he hath violently t away his tabernacle, 2554
4:20 was t in their pits, of whom we said, 3920
Eze 12:13 upon him, and he shall be t in my snare: 8610
15: 3 Shall wood be t thereof to do any work? or 3947
16:17 Thou hast also t thy fair jewels of my gold 3947
16:20 Moreover thou hast t thy sons and thy 3947
16:37 with whom thou hast t pleasure, and all 6149
17:12 hath t the king thereof, and the princes 3947
17:13 hath t of the king's seed, and made a 3947
17:13 with him, and hath t an oath of him: 935
17:13 he hath also t the mighty of the land: 3947
17:20 he shall be t in my snare, and I will bring 8610
18: 8 upon usury, neither hath t any increase, 3947
18:13 given forth upon usury, and hath t increase: 3947
18:17 That hath t off his hand from the poor, 7725
19: 4 he was t in their pit, and they brought him 8610
19: 8 their net over him: he was t in their pit. 8610
21:23 the iniquity, that they may be t. 8610
21:24 ye shall be t with the hand. 8610
22:12 In thee have they t gifts to shed blood; 3947
22:12 thou hast t usury and increase, and 3947
22:25 they have t the treasure and 3947
25:15 t vengeance with a despiteful heart, 5358+5359
27: 5 they have t cedars from Lebanon to make 3947
33: 6 among them, he is t away in his iniquity; 3947
36: 3 ye are t up in the lips of talkers, and are an 5927
Da 5: 2 t out of the temple which was in Jerusalem; 5312
5: 3 t out of the temple of the house of God 5312
6:23 So Daniel was t up out of the den, and 5267
7:12 the beasts, they had their dominion t away: 5709
8:11 by him the daily sacrifice was t away, and 7311
11:12 And when he hath t away the multitude, his 5375
12:11 time that the daily sacrifice shall be t away, 5493
Hos 4: 3 the fishes of the sea also shall be t away. 622
Joel 3: 5 Because ye have t my silver and my gold, 3947
Am 3: 4 lion cry out of his den, if he have t nothing? 3920
3: 5 the earth, and have t nothing at all? 3920+3920
3:12 shall the children of Israel be t out that 5337
4:10 the sword, and have t away your horses; 7628
6:13 Have we not t to us horns by our own 3947
Mic 2: 9 from their children have ye t away my 3947
4: 9 for pangs have t thee as a woman in travail. 2388
Zep 3:15 The LORD hath t away thy judgments, 5493
Zec 14: 2 the city shall be t, and the houses rifled, 3920
Mt 4:24 sick people that were t with divers diseases 4912
9:15 when the bridegroom shall be t from 522
13:12 from him shall be t away even that he hath. 142
16: 7 saying, It is because we have t no bread. 2983
21:43 The kingdom of God shall be t from you, 142
24:40 the one shall be t, and the other left. 3880
24:41 the one shall be t, and the other left. 3880
25:29 from him that hath not shall be t away even 142
27:59 And when Joseph had t the body, 2983
28:12 and had t counsel, they gave large money 2983
Mk 2:20 when the bridegroom shall be t away from 522
4:25 from him shall be t even that which he hath. 142
6:41 And when he had t the five loaves and 2983
9:36 and when he had t him in his arms, he said 1723
Lk 1: 1 Forasmuch as many have t in hand to set 2021
4:38 And Simon's wife's mother was t with a 4912
5: 5 toiled all the night, and have t nothing: 2983
5: 9 the draught of the fishes which they had t: 4815
5:18 in a bed a man which was t with a palsy: 3886
5:35 when the bridegroom shall be t away from 522
5:36 the piece that was t out of the new agreeth NIG

Lk 8:18 from him shall be t even that which he 142
8:37 from them; for they were t with great fear: 4912
9:17 there was t up of fragments that remained to 142
10:42 which shall not be t away from her. 851
11:52 for ye have t away the key of knowledge: 142
17:34 the one shall be t, and the other shall be 3880
17:35 the one shall be t, and the other left. 3880
17:36 the one shall be t, and the other left. 3880
19: 8 t any thing from any man
by false accusation, 4811
19:26 even that he hath shall be t away from him. 142
Jn 7:44 And some of them would have t him; but 4084
8: 3 Pharisees brought unto him a woman t in 2638
8: 4 Master, this woman was t in adultery, in 2638
13:12 and had t his garments, and was set down 2983
19:31 be broken, and that they might be t away. 142
20: 1 seeth the stone t away from the sepulchre. 142
20: 2 They have t away the Lord out of 142
20:13 Because they have t away my Lord, and 142
Ac 1: 2 Until the day in which he was t up, after that 353
1: 9 things, while they beheld, he was t up; 1869
1:11 which is t up from you into heaven, shall so 353
1:22 unto that same day that he was t up from us, 353
2:23 ye have t, and by wicked hands have 2983
8: 7 with them: and many t with palsies, 3886
8:33 In his humiliation his judgment was t away: 142
8:33 for his life is t from the earth. 142
17: 9 And when they had t security of Jason, and 2983
20: 9 down from the third loft, and was t up dead. 142
21: 6 And when we had t our leave one of 782
23:27 This man was t of the Jews, and 4815
27:17 Which when they had t up, they used helps, 142
27:20 that we should be saved was then t away. 4014
27:33 and continued fasting, having t nothing. 4355
27:40 And when they had t up the anchors, 4014
Ro 9: 6 though the word of God hath t none effect. 1601
1Co 5: 2 this deed might be t away from among you. 1808
10:13 There hath no temptation t you but such as 2983
2Co 3:16 turn to the Lord, the vail shall be t away. 4014
1Th 2:17 being t from you for a short time in 642
2Th 2: 7 letteth will let, until he be t out of the way. 1096
1Ti 5: 9 Let not a widow be t into the number 2639
2Ti 2:26 who are t captive by him at his will. 2221
Heb 5: 1 For every high priest t from among men is 2983
2Pe 2:12 brute beasts, made to be t and destroyed, 259
Rev 5: 8 And when he had t the book, the four 2983
11:17 because thou hast t to thee thy great power, 2983
19:20 And the beast was t, and with him the false 4084

TAKER (1) [TAKE]

Isa 24: 2 as with the t of usury, so with the giver of 5378

TAKEST (9) [TAKE]

Ex 4: 9 the water which thou t out of the river 3947
30:12 When thou t the sum of the children of 5375
Jdg 4: 9 notwithstanding the journey that thou t 1980
1Ch 22:13 if thou t heed to fulfil the statutes and 8104
Ps 104:29 thou t away their breath, they die, and 622
144: 3 what is man, that thou t knowledge of him? 3045
Ecc 9: 9 in thy labour which thou t under the sun. 6001
Isa 58: 3 our soul, and thou t no knowledge? 3045
Lk 19:21 thou t up that thou layedst not down, and 142

TAKETH (74) [TAKE]

Ex 20: 7 hold him guiltless that t his name in vain. 5375
Dt 5:11 hold him guiltless that t his name in vain. 5375
10:17 which regardeth not persons, nor t reward: 3947
24: 6 to pledge: for he t a man's life to pledge. 2254
25:11 forth her hand, and t him by the secrets: 2388
27:25 Cursed be he that t reward to slay an 3947
32:11 t them, beareth them on her wings: 3947
Jos 7:14 that the tribe which the LORD t shall 3920
15:16 He that smiteth Kirjath-sepher, and t it, 3920
Jdg 1:12 He that smiteth Kirjath-sepher, and t it, 3920
1Sa 17:26 and t away the reproach from Israel? 5493
1Ki 14:10 as a man t away dung, till it be all gone. 1197
Job 5: 5 t it even out of the thorns, and the robber 3947
5:13 He t the wise in their own craftiness: and 3920
9:12 Behold, he t away, who can hinder him? 2862
12:20 and t away the understanding of the aged. 3947
12:24 He t away the heart of the chief of 5493
21: 6 am afraid, and trembling t hold on my flesh. 270
27: 8 he hath gained, when God t away his soul? 7953
40:24 He t it with his eyes: his nose pierceth 3947
Ps 15: 3 nor t up a reproach against his neighbour. 5375
15: 5 to usury, nor t reward against the innocent. 3947
118: 7 The LORD t my part with them that 3807.1
137: 9 Happy shall he be that t and dasheth thy 270
147:10 he t not pleasure in the legs of a man. 7521
147:11 The LORD t pleasure in them that fear 7521
149: 4 For the LORD t pleasure in his people: 7521
Pr 1:19 which t away the life of the owners thereof. 3947
16:32 he that ruleth his spirit than he that t a city. 3920
17:23 A wicked man t a gift out of the bosom to 3947
25:20 As he that t away a garment in cold 5710
26:17 to him, is like one that t a dog by the ears. 2388
30:28 The spider t hold with her hands, and is in 8610
Ecc 1: 3 of all his labour which he t under the sun? 5998
2:23 yea, his heart t not rest in the night. 7901
5:18 to enjoy the good of all his labour that he t 5998
Isa 13:14 and as a sheep that no man t up: 6908
40:15 he t up the isles as a very little thing 5190
44:14 down cedars, and t the cypress and the oak, 3947
51:18 neither is there any that t her by the hand of 2388
56: 6 polluting it, and t hold of my covenant; 2388
Eze 16:32 which t strangers instead of her husband. 3947
33: 4 sound of the trumpet, and t not warning; 2094
33: 5 But he that t warning shall deliver his soul. 2094
Am 3:12 As the shepherd t out of the mouth of 5337
Mt 4: 5 Then the devil t him up into the holy city, 3880
4: 8 the devil t him up into an exceeding high 3880
9:16 for that which is put in to fill it up t from 142
10:38 And he that t not his cross, and 2983
12:45 t with himself seven other spirits more 3880

Mt 17: 1 And after six days Jesus t Peter, James, and 3880
Mk 2:21 else the new piece that filled it up t away 142
4:15 t away the word that was sown in their 142
5:40 he t the father and the mother of 3880
9: 2 And after six days Jesus t with him Peter, 3880
9:18 And wheresoever he t him, he teareth him: 2638
14:33 And he t with him Peter and James and 3880
Lk 6:29 him that t away thy cloke forbid not to take 142
6:30 of him that t away thy goods ask them not 142
8:12 and t away the word out of their hearts, 142
9:39 a spirit t him, and he suddenly crieth out; 2983
11:22 he t from him all his armour wherein he 142
11:26 t to him seven other spirits more wicked 3880
16: 3 for my lord t away from me the stewardship: 851
Jn 1:29 of God, which t away the sin of the world. 142
10:18 No man t it from me, but I lay it down of 142
15: 2 in me that beareth not fruit he t away: 142
16:22 and your joy no man t from you. 142
21:13 and t bread, and giveth them, and 2983
Ro 3: 5 Is God unrighteous who t vengeance? 2018
1Co 3:19 He t the wise in their own craftiness. 1405
11:21 For in eating every one t before other his 4301
Heb 5: 4 And no man t this honour unto himself, but 2983
10: 9 He t away the first, that he may establish 337

TAKING (20) [TAKE]

2Ch 19: 7 nor respect of persons, nor t of gifts. 4727
Job 5: 3 I have seen the foolish t root: but 8327
Ps 119: 9 by t heed thereto according to thy word. 8104
Jer 50:46 At the noise of the t of Babylon the earth is 8610
Eze 25:12 the house of Judah by t vengeance, 5358+5359
Hos 11: 3 Ephraim also to go, t them by their arms; 3947
Mt 6:27 Which of you by t thought can add one 3309
Mk 13:34 the Son of man is as a man t a far journey, 590
Lk 4: 5 the devil, t him up into a high mountain, 321
12:25 And which of you with t thought can add 3309
19:22 t up that I laid not down, and reaping that I 142
Jn 11:13 they thought that he had spoken of t of rest 2838
Ro 7: 8 But sin, t occasion by the commandment, 2983
7:11 For sin, t occasion by the commandment, 2983
2Co 2:13 but t my leave of them, I went from thence 657
11: 8 t wages of them, to do you service. 2983
Eph 6:16 Above all, t the shield of faith, wherewith ye 353
2Th 1: 8 t vengeance on them that know not God, 1325
1Pe 5: 2 t the oversight thereof, not by constraint, 1983
3Jn 1: 7 they went forth, t nothing of the Gentiles. 2983

TALE (5) [TALEBEARER, TALES]

Ex 5: 8 the t of the bricks, which they did make 4971
5:18 yet shall ye deliver the t of bricks. 8506
1Sa 18:27 and they gave them in full t to the king, 4390
1Ch 9:28 that they should bring them in and out by t. 4557
Ps 90: 9 we spend our years as a t that is told. 1899

TALEBEARER (6) [BEAR, TALE]

Lev 19:16 go up and down as a t among thy people: 7400
Pr 11:13 A t revealeth secrets: but he that is of 1980+7400
18: 8 The words of a t are as wounds, and 5372
20:19 He that goeth about as a t revealeth secrets: 7400
26:20 so where there is no t, the strife ceaseth. 5372
26:22 The words of a t are as wounds, and 5372

TALENT (14) [TALENTS]

Ex 25:39 Of a t of pure gold shall he make it, with all 3603
37:24 Of a t of pure gold made he it, and all 3603
38:27 of the hundred talents, a t for a socket. 3603
2Sa 12:30 the weight whereof was a t of gold with 3603
1Ki 20:39 his life, or else thou shalt pay a t of silver. 3603
2Ki 5:22 a t of silver, and two changes of garments. 3603
23:33 an hundred talents of silver, and a t of gold. 3603
1Ch 20: 2 found it to weigh a t of gold, and 3603
2Ch 36: 3 an hundred talents of silver and a t of gold. 3603
Zec 5: 7 behold, there was lift up a t of lead: and 3603
Mt 25:24 Then he which had received the one t came 5007
25:25 and went and hid thy t in the earth: 5007
25:28 Take therefore the t from him, and give it 5007
Rev 16:21 every stone about the weight of a t: 5006

TALENTS (51) [TALENT]

Ex 38:24 was twenty and nine t, and seven hundred 3603
38:25 of the congregation was an hundred t, 3603
38:27 of the hundred t of silver were cast 3603
38:27 an hundred sockets of the hundred t, 3603
38:29 the brass of the offering was seventy t, and 3603
1Ki 9:14 Hiram sent to the king sixscore t of gold. 3603
9:28 four hundred and twenty t, and brought it to 3603
10:10 the king an hundred and twenty t of gold, 3603
10:14 six hundred threescore and six t of gold, 3603
16:24 hill Samaria of Shemer for two t of silver, 3603
2Ki 5: 5 took with him ten t of silver, and 3603
5:23 Naaman said, Be content, take two t. 3603
5:23 and bound two t of silver in two bags, 3603
15:19 Menahem gave Pul a thousand t of silver, 3603
18:14 king of Judah three hundred t of silver 3603
18:14 talents of silver and thirty t of gold. 3603
23:33 put the land to a tribute of an hundred t of 3603
1Ch 19: 6 the children of Ammon sent a thousand t of 3603
22:14 the LORD an hundred thousand t of gold, 3603
22:14 and a thousand thousand t of silver; 3603
29: 4 Even three thousand t of gold, of the gold 3603
29: 4 and seven thousand t of refined silver, 3603
29: 7 of the house of God of gold five thousand t 3603
29: 7 of silver ten thousand t, and of brass 3603
29: 7 of brass eighteen thousand t, and 3603
29: 7 and one hundred thousand t of iron. 3603
2Ch 3: 8 with fine gold, amounting to six hundred t. 3603
8:18 thence four hundred and fifty t of gold, 3603
9: 9 the king an hundred and twenty t of gold, 3603
9:13 and threescore and six t of gold; 3603
25: 6 out of Israel for an hundred t of silver. 3603
25: 9 what shall we do for the hundred t which I 3603
27: 5 him the same year an hundred t of silver, 3603
36: 3 condemned the land in an hundred t of 3603
Ezr 7:22 Unto an hundred t of silver, and to an 3604

Ezr 8:26 their hand six hundred and fifty t of silver, 3603
8:26 silver vessels an hundred t, and of gold an 3603
8:26 hundred talents, and of gold an hundred t; 3603
Est 3: 9 I will pay ten thousand t of silver to 3603
Mt 18:24 unto him, which ought him ten thousand t. 5007
25:15 And unto one he gave five t, to another 5007
25:16 Then he that had received the five t went 5007
25:16 with the same, and made them other five t. 5007
25:20 And so he that had received five t came and 5007
25:20 five talents came and brought other five t, 5007
25:20 Lord, thou deliveredst unto me five t: 5007
25:20 I have gained besides them five t moe. 5007
25:22 He also that had received two t came and 5007
25:22 said, Lord, thou deliveredst unto me two t: 5007
25:22 I have gained two other t besides them. 5007
25:28 and give it unto him which hath ten t. 5007

TALES (2) [TALE]
Eze 22: 9 In thee are men that **carry** t to shed blood: 7400
Lk 24:11 And their words seemed to them as **idle** t, 3026

TALITHA (1)
Mk 5:41 by the hand, and said unto her, T CUMI; 5008

TALK (24) [TALKED, TALKERS, TALKEST, TALKETH, TALKING]
Nu 11:17 I will come down and t with thee there: 1696
Dt 5:24 we have seen this day that God doth t with 1696
6: 7 shalt t of them when thou sittest in thine 1696
1Sa 2: 3 T no more so exceeding proudly; let not 1696
2Ki 18:26 t not with us in the Jews' language in 1696
1Ch 16: 9 unto him, t you of all his wondrous works. 7878
Job 11: 2 and should a man **full of** t be justified? 8193
13: 7 for God? and t deceitfully for him? 1696
15: 3 Should he reason with unprofitable t? or 1697
Ps 69:26 they t to the grief of those whom thou hast 5608
71:24 My tongue also shall t of thy righteousness 1897
77:12 also of all thy work, and t of thy doings. 7878
105: 2 unto him: t ye of all his wondrous works. 7878
119:27 so shall I t of thy wondrous works. 7878
145:11 glory of thy kingdom, and t of thy power; 1696
Pr 6:22 and when thou awakest, it shall t with thee. 7878
14:23 but the t of the lips tendeth only to penury. 1697
24: 2 and their lips t of mischief. 1696
Ecc 10:13 the end of his t is mischievous madness. 6310
Jer 12: 1 yet let me t with thee of thy judgments. 1696
Eze 3:22 into the plain, and I will there t with thee. 1696
Da 10:17 For how can the servant of this my lord t 1696
Mt 22:15 how they might entangle him in his t. 3056
Jn 14:30 Hereafter I will not t much with you: 2980

TALKED (42) [TALK]
Ge 4: 8 Cain t with Abel his brother: and it came to 559
17: 3 on his face: and God t with him, saying, 1696
35:13 from him in the place where he t with him. 1696
35:14 Jacob set up a pillar in the place where he t 1696
45:15 and after that his brethren t with him. 1696
Ex 20:22 Ye have seen that I have t with you from 1696
33: 9 and the LORD t with Moses. 1696
34:29 skin of his face shone while he t with him. 1696
34:31 returned unto him: and Moses t with them. 1696
Dt 5: 4 The LORD t with you face to face in 1696
Jdg 14: 7 he went down, and t with the woman; and 1696
1Sa 14:19 it came to pass, while Saul t unto the priest, 1696
17:23 as he t with them, behold, there came up 1696
1Ki 1:22 lo, while she yet t with the king, Nathan 1696
2Ki 2:11 as they still went on, and t, that behold, 1696
6:33 while he yet t with them, behold, 1696
8: 4 the king t with Gehazi the servant of 1696
2Ch 25:16 it came to pass, as he t with him, that 1696
Jer 38:25 if the princes hear that I have t with thee, 1696
Da 9:22 he informed me, and t with me, and said, 1696
Zec 1: 9 the angel that t with me said unto me, 1696
1:13 the LORD answered the angel that t with 1696
1:19 I said unto the angel that t with me, 1696
2: 3 the angel that t with me went forth, and 1696
4: 1 the angel that t with me came again, and 1696
4: 4 and spake to the angel that t with me, 1696
4: 5 Then the angel that t with me answered and 1696
5: 5 the angel that t with me went forth, and 1696
5:10 said I to the angel that t with me, 1696
6: 4 and said unto the angel that t with me, 1696
Mt 12:46 While he yet t to the people, behold, 2980
Mk 6:50 And immediately he t with them, and 2980
Lk 9:30 And behold, there t **with** him two men, 4814
24:14 And they t together of all these things 3656
24:32 while he t with us by the way, and while he 2980
Jn 4:27 and marvelled that he t with the woman: 2980
Ac 10:27 And as he t **with** him, he went in, and 4926
20:11 broken bread, and eaten, and t a long while, 3656
26:31 they t between themselves, saying, 2980
Rev 17: 1 and t with me, saying unto me, 2980
21: 9 and t with me, saying, Come hither, I will 2980
21:15 And he that t with me had a golden reed to 2980

TALKERS (2) [TALK]
Eze 36: 3 ye are taken up in the lips of t, and are an 3956
Tit 1:10 are many unruly and **vain** t and deceivers, 3151

TALKEST (3) [TALK]
Jdg 6:17 then shew me a sign that thou t with me. 1696
1Ki 1:14 while thou yet t there with the king, 1696
Jn 4:27 seekest thou? or, Why t thou with her? 2980

TALKETH (2) [TALK]
Ps 37:30 and his tongue t of judgment. 1696
Jn 9:37 both seen him, and it is he that t with thee. 2980

TALKING (9) [TALK]
Ge 17:22 he left off t with him, and God went up 1696
1Ki 18:27 either he is t, or he is pursuing, or he is in a 7879
Est 6:14 while they were yet t with him, came 1696
Job 29: 9 The princes refrained t, and laid their hand 4405
Eze 33:30 the children of thy people still are t against 1696

Mt 17: 3 unto them Moses and Elias t with him. 4814
Mk 9: 4 with Moses: and they were t **with** Jesus. 4814
Eph 5: 4 Neither filthiness, nor **foolish** t, nor jesting, 3473
Rev 4: 1 was as it were of a trumpet t with me; 2980

TALL (5) [TALLER]
Dt 2:10 a people great, and many, and t, as 7311
2:21 A people great, and many, and t, as 7311
9: 2 A people great and t, the children of 7311
2Ki 19:23 will cut down the t cedar trees thereof, and 6967
Isa 37:24 I will cut down the t cedars thereof, and 6967

TALLER (1) [TALL]
Dt 1:28 The people is greater and t than we; 7311

TALMAI (6)
Nu 13:22 where Ahiman, Sheshai, and T, 8526
Jos 15:14 Sheshai, and Ahiman, and T, the children 8526
Jdg 1:10 and they slew Sheshai, and Ahiman, and T. 8526
2Sa 3: 3 Maacah the daughter of T king of Geshur; 8526
13:37 Absalom fled, and went to T, the son of 8526
1Ch 3: 2 Maachah the daughter of T king of Geshur: 8526

TALMON (5)
1Ch 9:17 and T, and Ahiman, and their brethren: 2929
Ezr 2:42 the children of Ater, the children of T, 2929
Ne 7:45 the children of Ater, the children of T, 2929
11:19 T, and their brethren that kept the gates, 2929
12:25 Obadiah, Meshullam, T, Akkub, 2929

TAMAH (1)
Ne 7:55 the children of Sisera, the children of T, 8547

TAMAR (24) [BAAL-TAMAR, HAZAZON-TAMAR, HAZEZON-TAMAR]
Ge 38: 6 for Er his firstborn, whose name was T. 8559
38:11 said Judah to T his daughter in law, 8559
38:11 as his brethren did. And T went and 8559
38:13 it was told T, saying, Behold thy father in 8559
38:24 T thy daughter in law hath played 8559
Ru 4:12 house of Pharez, whom T bare unto Judah, 8559
2Sa 13: 1 David had a fair sister, whose name was T; 8559
13: 2 so vexed, that he fell sick for his sister T; 8559
13: 4 Amnon said unto him, I love T, my brother 8559
13: 5 let my sister T come, and give me meat, 8559
13: 6 let T my sister come, and make me a 8559
13: 7 David sent home to T, saying, Go now to 8559
13: 8 So T went to her brother Amnon's house; 8559
13:10 Amnon said unto T, Bring the meat into 8559
13:10 T took the cakes which she had made, and 8559
13:19 T put ashes on her head, and rent her 8559
13:20 So T remained desolate in her brother 8559
13:22 because he had forced his sister T. 8559
13:32 from the day that he forced his sister T. 8559
14:27 and one daughter, whose name was T: 8559
1Ch 2: 4 T his daughter in law bare him Pharez and 8559
3: 9 sons of the concubines, and T their sister. 8559
Eze 47:19 from T even to the waters of strife in 8559
48:28 the border shall be even from T unto 8559

TAMBOURINE; TAMBOURINES See TABRET; TABRETS; TIMBREL

TAME (2) [TAMED]
Mk 5: 4 in pieces: neither could any man t him. 1150
Jas 3: 8 But the tongue can no man t; it is an unruly 1150

TAMED (2) [TAME]
Jas 3: 7 is t, and hath been tamed of mankind: 1150
3: 7 is tamed, and hath been t of mankind: 1150

TAMMUZ (1)
Eze 8:14 behold, there sat women weeping for T. 8542

TANACH (1)
Jos 21:25 T with her suburbs, and Gath-rimmon with 8590

TANHUMETH (2)
2Ki 25:23 Seraiah the son of T the Netophathite, and 8576
Jer 40: 8 Seraiah the son of T, and the sons of Ephai 8576

TANNER (3)
Ac 9:43 many days in Joppa with one Simon a t. 1038
10: 6 He lodgeth with one Simon a t, 1038
10:32 he is lodged in the house of one Simon a t 1038

TAPESTRY (2)
Pr 7:16 I have deckt my bed with **coverings of** t, 4765
31:22 She maketh herself **coverings of** t; 4765

TAPHATH (1)
1Ki 4:11 which had T the daughter of Solomon to 2955

TAPPUAH (6) [BETH-TAPPUAH]
Jos 12:17 The king of T, one; the king of Hepher, 8599
15:34 And Zanoah, and En-gannim, T, and Enam, 8599
16: 8 The border went out from T westward unto 8599
17: 8 Now Manasseh had the land of T: but 8599
17: 8 T on the border of Manasseh belonged to 8599
1Ch 2:43 Korah, and T, and Rekem, and Shema. 8599

TAR PITS See SLIMEPITS

TARAH (2)
Nu 33:27 departed from Tahath, and pitched at T. 8646
33:28 they removed from T, and pitched in 8646

TARALAH (1)
Jos 18:27 And Rekem, and Irpeel, and T, 8634

TARE (4) [TEAR]
2Sa 13:31 and t his garments, and lay on the earth; 7167

2Ki 2:24 and t forty and two children of them. 1234
Mk 9:20 he saw him, straightway the spirit t him; 4682
Lk 9:42 t him. And Jesus rebuked the unclean spirit, 4952

TAREA (1)
1Ch 8:35 and Melech, and T, and Ahaz. 8390

TARES (8)
Mt 13:25 enemy came and sowed t among the wheat, 2215
13:26 brought forth fruit, then appeared the t also. 2215
13:27 in thy field? from whence then hath it t? 2215
13:29 lest while ye gather up the t, ye root up also 2215
13:30 Gather ye together first the t, and bind them 2215
13:36 Declare unto us the parable of the t of 2215
13:38 but the t are the children of the wicked one; 2215
13:40 As therefore the t are gathered and burnt in 2215

TARGET (3) [TARGETS]
1Sa 17: 6 and a t of brass between his shoulders. 3591
1Ki 10:16 six hundred shekels of gold went to one t. 6793
2Ch 9:15 shekels of beaten gold went to one t. 6793

TARGETS (3) [TARGET]
1Ki 10:16 king Solomon made two hundred t of 6793
2Ch 9:15 king Solomon made two hundred t of 6793
14: 8 Asa had an army of men that bare t and 6793

TARPELITES (1)
Ezr 4: 9 the T, the Apharsites, the Archevites, 2967

TARRIED (32) [TARRY]
Ge 24:54 the men that were with him, and t **all night**; 3885
28:11 t there **all night**, because the sun was set; 3885
31:54 did eat bread, and t **all night** in the mount. 3885
Nu 9:19 when the cloud t **long** upon the tabernacle 748
9:22 a year, that the cloud t upon the tabernacle, 748
Jdg 3:25 they t till they were ashamed: and behold, 2342
3:26 Ehud escaped while they t, and passed 4102
19: 8 they t until afternoon, and they did eat both 4102
Ru 2: 7 until now, that she t a little in the house. 3427
1Sa 13: 8 he t seven days, according to the set time 3176
14: 2 Saul t in the uttermost part of Gibeah under 3427
2Sa 11: 1 But David t still at Jerusalem. 3427
15:17 after him, and t in a place that was far off. 5975
15:29 of God again to Jerusalem: and they t there. 3427
20: 5 he t **longer** than the set time which he had 309
2Ki 2:18 came again to him, (for he t at Jericho,) 3427
1Ch 20: 1 David t at Jerusalem. And Joab smote 3427
Ps 68:12 she that t at home divided the spoil. 5116
Mt 25: 5 While the bridegroom t, they all slumbered 5549
Lk 1:21 marvelled that he t so **long** in the temple. 5549
2:43 the child Jesus t **behind** in Jerusalem; 5278
Jn 3:22 and there he t with them, and baptized. 1304
Ac 9:43 that he t many days in Joppa with one 3306
15:33 And after they had t there **a space**, 4160+5550
18:18 And Paul after this t there yet a good while, 4357
20: 5 These going before t **for** us at Troas. 3306
20:15 we arrived at Samos, and t at Trogyllium; 3306
21: 4 finding disciples, we t there seven days: 1961
21:10 And as we t there many days, there came 1961
25: 6 And when he had t among them more than 1304
27:33 This day is the fourteenth day that ye have t 4328
28:12 landing at Syracuse, we t there three days. 1961

TARRIEST (1) [TARRY]
Ac 22:16 And now why t thou? arise, and 3195

TARRIETH (2) [TARRY]
1Sa 30:24 so shall his part be that t by the stuff: 3427
Mic 5: 7 showers upon the grass, that t not for man, 6960

TARRY (51) [TARRIED, TARRIEST, TARRIETH, TARRYING]
Ge 19: 2 t **all night**, and wash your feet, and ye shall 3885
27:44 t with him a few days, until thy brother's 3427
30:27 t: for I have learned by experience that NIH
45: 9 of all Egypt: come down unto me, t not: 5975
Ex 12:39 were thrust out of Egypt, and could not t, 4102
24:14 he said unto the elders, T ye here for us, 3427
Lev 14: 8 shall t **abroad** out of his tent seven days. 3427
Nu 22:19 I pray you, t ye also here this night, 3427
Jdg 5:28 in coming? why t the wheels of his chariots? 309
6:18 And he said, I will t until thou come again. 3427
19: 6 and t **all night**, and let thine heart be merry. 3885
19: 9 towards evening, I pray you t **all night**: 3885
19:10 the man would not t that **night**, but he rose 3885
Ru 1:13 Would ye t for them till they were grown? 7663
3:13 T this night, and it shall be in the morning, 3885
1Sa 1:23 thee good; t until thou have weaned him; 3427
10: 8 seven days shalt thou t, till I come to thee, 3176
14: 9 say thus unto us, T until we come to you; 1826
2Sa 10: 5 T at Jericho until your beards be grown, 3427
11:12 T here to day also, and to morrow I will let 3427
15:28 See, I will t in the plain of the wilderness, 4102
18:14 said Joab, I may not t thus with thee. 3176
19: 7 there will not t one with thee this night: 3885
2Ki 2: 2 Elijah said unto Elisha, T here, I pray thee; 3427
2: 4 said unto him, Elisha, t here, I pray thee; 3427
2: 6 Elijah said unto him, T, I pray thee, here; 3427
7: 9 if we t till the morning light, some mischief 2442
9: 3 Then open the door, and flee, and t not. 2442
14:10 glory of this, and t at home: for why 3427
1Ch 19: 5 T at Jericho until your beards be grown, 3427
Ps 101: 7 he that telleth lies shall not t in my sight. 3559
Pr 23:30 They that t **long** at the wine; they that go to 309
Isa 46:13 not be far off, and my salvation shall not t: 309
Jer 14: 8 man that turneth aside to t **for a night**? 3885
Hab 2: 3 though it t, wait for it; because it will 4102
2: 3 because it will surely come, it will not t. 309
Mt 26:38 unto death: t ye here, and watch with me. 3306
Mk 14:34 sorrowful unto death: t ye here, and watch. 3306
Lk 24:29 is far spent. And he went in to t with them. 3306
24:49 but t ye in the city of Jerusalem, until ye be 2523
Jn 4:40 they besought him that he would t with 3306

T

Jn 21:22 If I will that he **t** till I come, what *is that* to 3306
21:23 but, If I will that he **t** till I come, what *is* 3306
Ac 10:48 Then prayed they him to **t** certain days. 1961
18:20 When they desired *him* to **t** longer time 3306
28:14 and were desired to **t** with them seven days: 1961
1Co 11:33 ye come together to eat, **t** one **for** another. 1551
16: 7 but I trust to **t** a while with you, if the Lord 1961
16: 8 But I will **t** at Ephesus until Pentecost. 1961
1Ti 3:15 But if I **t long**, that thou mayest know how 1019
Heb 10:37 he that shall come will come, and will not **t**. 5549

TARRYING (2) [TARRY]
Ps 40:17 and my deliverer; **make** no **t**, O my God. 309
70: 5 and my deliverer; O LORD, **make** no **t**. 309

TARSHISH (24) [THARSHISH]
Ge 10: 4 Elishah, and **T**, Kittim, and Dodanim. 8659
1Ch 1: 7 Elishah, and **T**, Kittim, and Dodanim. 8659
2Ch 9:21 For the king's ships went *to* **T** with 8659
9:21 every three years once came the ships of **T** 8659
20:36 himself with him to make ships to go *to* **T**: 8659
20:37 that they were not able to go to **T**. 8659
Est 1:14 **T**, Meres, Marsena, *and* Memucan, 8659
Ps 48: 7 Thou breakest the ships of **T** with an east 8659
72:10 The kings of **T** and *of* the isles shall bring 8659
Isa 2:16 upon all the ships of **T**, and upon all 8659
23: 1 Howl, ye ships of **T**; for it is laid waste, so 8659
23: 6 Pass ye over to **T**; howl, ye inhabitants of 8659
23:10 thy land as a river, O daughter of **T**: 8659
23:14 Howl, ye ships of **T**: for your strength is 8659
60: 9 the ships of **T** first, to bring thy sons from 8659
66:19 *to* **T**, Pul, and Lud, that draw the bow, 8659
Jer 10: 9 Silver spread into plates is brought from **T**, 8659
Eze 27:12 **T** *was* thy merchant by reason of 8659
27:25 The ships of **T** did sing of thee *in* thy 8659
38:13 Sheba, and Dedan, and the merchants of **T**, 8659
Jnh 1: 3 Jonah rose up to flee unto **T** from 8659
1: 3 *to* Joppa; and he found a ship going *to* **T**: 8659
1: 3 to go with them unto **T** from the presence 8659
4: 2 Therefore I fled before unto **T**: for I knew 8659

TARSUS (5)
Ac 9:11 house of Judas for *one* called Saul, of **T**: 5018
9:30 down to Cesarea, and sent him forth to **T**. 5019
11:25 Then departed Barnabas to **T**, for to seek 5019
21:39 Paul said, I am a man *which am* a Jew of **T**, 5018
22: 3 *which am* a Jew, born in **T**, *a city* in Cilicia, 5019

TARTAK (1)
2Ki 17:31 the Avites made Nibhaz and **T**, and 8662

TARTAN (2)
2Ki 18:17 the king of Assyria sent **T** and Rabsaris 8661
Isa 20: 1 In the year that **T** came unto Ashdod, 8661

TASK (2) [TASKMASTERS, TASKS]
Ex 5:14 Wherefore have ye not fulfilled your **t** in 2706
5:19 *ought* from your bricks of *your* daily **t**. 1697

TASKMASTERS (6) [MASTER, TASK]
Ex 1:11 Therefore they did set over them **t** to 4522+8269
3: 7 have heard their cry by reason of their **t**; 5065
5: 6 Pharaoh commanded the same day the **t** of 5065
5:10 the **t** of the people went out, and 5065
5:13 the **t** hasted *them*, saying, Fulfil your 5065
5:14 which Pharaoh's **t** had set over them, 5065

TASKS (1) [TASK]
Ex 5:13 Fulfil your works, *your* daily **t**, as when 1697

TASTE (22) [TASTED, TASTETH]
Ex 16:31 the **t** of it *was* like wafers *made* with honey. 2940
Nu 11: 8 and the **t** of it was as the taste of fresh oil. 2940
11: 8 and the taste of it was as the **t** of fresh oil. 2940
1Sa 14:43 I **did but t** a little honey with the end 2938+2938
2Sa 3:35 and more also, if I **t** bread, or ought else, 2938
19:35 can thy servant **t** what I eat or what I drink? 2938
Job 6: 6 or is there *any* **t** in the white of an egg? 2940
6:30 cannot my **t** discern perverse things? 2441
12:11 ear try words? and the mouth **t** his meat? 2938
Ps 34: 8 O **t** and see that the LORD *is* good: 2938
119:103 How sweet are thy words unto my **t**! 2441
Pr 24:13 the honeycomb, *which is* sweet to thy **t**: 2441
SS 2: 3 and his fruit *was* sweet to my **t**. 2441
Jer 48:11 therefore his **t** remained in him, and 2940
Jnh 3: 7 man nor beast, herd nor flock, **t** any thing: 2938
Mt 16:28 standing here, which shall not **t** of death, 1089
Mk 9: 1 that stand here, which shall not **t** of death, 1089
Lk 9:27 standing here, which shall not **t** of death, 1089
14:24 which were bidden shall **t** of my supper. 1089
Jn 8:52 keep my saying, he shall never **t** of death. 1089
Col 2:21 (Touch not; **t** not; handle not; 1089
Heb 2: 9 that he by the grace of God should **t** death 1089

TASTED (8) [TASTE]
1Sa 14:24 So none of the people **t** *any* food. 2938
14:29 because I **t** a little of this honey. 2938
Da 5: 2 Belshazzar, whiles *he* **t** the wine, 2942
Mt 27:34 when he had **t** *thereof*, he would not drink. 1089
Jn 2: 9 When the ruler of the feast had **t** the water 1089
Heb 6: 4 and have **t** of the heavenly gift, and 1089
6: 5 And have **t** the good word of God, and 1089
1Pe 2: 3 If so be ye have **t** that the Lord *is* gracious. 1089

TASTELESS See UNSAVOURY

TASTETH (1) [TASTE]
Job 34: 3 the ear trieth words, as the mouth **t** meat. 2938

TASTY See SAVOURY

TATNAI (4)
Ezr 5: 3 At the same time came to them **T**, 8674
5: 6 The copy of the letter that **T**, governor on 8674
6: 6 Now *therefore*, **T**, governor beyond 8674
6:13 **T**, governor on *this* side the river, 8674

TATTENAI See TATNAI

TATTLERS (1)
1Ti 5:13 not only idle, but **t** also and busybodies, 5397

TAUGHT (81) [TEACH]
Dt 4: 5 I have **t** you statutes and judgments, 3925
31:22 the same day, and **t** it the children of Israel. 3925
Jdg 8:16 and with them he **t** the men of Succoth. 3045
2Ki 17:28 **t** them how they should fear the LORD. 3384
2Ch 6:27 when thou hast **t** them the good way, 3384
17: 9 they **t** in Judah, and *had* the book of the law 3925
17: 9 all the cities of Judah, and **t** the people. 3925
23:13 of musick, and such as **t** to *sing* praise. 3045
30:22 **t** the good **knowledge** of 7919+7922
35: 3 said unto the Levites that **t** all Israel, 995
Ne 8: 9 the Levites that **t** the people, said unto all 995
Ps 71:17 O God, thou hast **t** me from my youth: and 3925
119:102 from thy judgments: for thou hast **t** me. 3384
119:171 when thou hast **t** me thy statutes. 3925
Pr 4: 4 He **t** me also, and said unto me, Let thine 3384
4:11 I have **t** thee in the way of wisdom; I have 3384
31: 1 the prophecy that his mother **t** him. 3256
Ecc 12: 9 was wise, he still **t** the people knowledge; 3925
Isa 29:13 their fear towards me is **t** *by* the precept of 3925
40:13 or *being* his counseller hath **t** him? 3045
40:14 **t** him in the path of judgment, and 3925
40:14 **t** him knowledge, and shewed to him 3925
54:13 all thy children *shall be* **t** of the LORD; 3928
Jer 2:33 hast thou also **t** the wicked ones thy ways. 3925
9: 5 they have **t** their tongue to speak lies, *and* 3925
9:14 after Baalim, which their fathers **t** them: 3925
12:16 as they **t** my people to swear by Baal; then 3925
13:21 for thou hast **t** them *to be* captains, *and* 3925
28:16 thou hast **t** rebellion against the LORD. 1696
29:32 he hath **t** rebellion against the LORD. 1696
32:33 though *I* **t** them, rising up early and 3925
Eze 23:48 that all women may be **t** not to do after 3256
Hos 10:11 Ephraim *is as* a heifer *that is* **t**, *and* 3925
11: 3 I **t** Ephraim also **to go**, taking them by their 7270
Zec 13: 5 for man **t** me *to keep cattle* from my youth. 7069
Mt 5: 2 he opened his mouth, and **t** them, saying, 1321
7:29 For he **t** them as *one* having authority, and 1321
13:54 he **t** them in their synagogue, insomuch that 1321
28:15 took the money, and did as they were **t**: 1321
Mk 1:21 day he entered into the synagogue, and **t**. 1321
1:22 for he **t** them as *one* that had authority, and 1321
2:13 multitude resorted unto him, and he **t** them. 1321
4: 2 And he **t** them many *things* by parables, 1321
6:30 what they had done, and what they had **t**. 1321
9:31 For he **t** his disciples, and said unto them, 1321
10: 1 and, as he was wont, he **t** them again. 1321
11:17 And he **t**, saying unto them, Is it not 1321
12:35 and said, while he **t** in the temple, 1321
Lk 4:15 And he **t** in their synagogues, 1321
4:31 of Galilee, and **t** them on the sabbath days. 1321
5: 3 sat down, and **t** the people out of the ship. 1321
6: 6 that he entered into the synagogue and **t**: 1321
11: 1 us to pray, as John also **t** his disciples. 1321
13:26 thy presence, and thou hast **t** in our streets. 1321
19:47 And he **t** daily in the temple. But the chief 1321
20: 1 as he **t** the people in the temple, and 1321
Jn 6:45 the prophets, And they shall be all **t** of God. 1318
6:59 he in the synagogue, as he **t** in Capernaum. 1321
7:14 feast Jesus went up into the temple, and **t**. 1321
7:28 Then cried Jesus in the temple as he **t**, 1321
8: 2 unto him; and he sat down, and **t** them. 1321
8:20 Jesus in the treasury, as he **t** in the temple: 1321
8:28 but as my Father hath **t** me, I speak these 1321
18:20 I ever **t** in the synagogue, and in the temple, 1321
Ac 4: 2 Being grieved that they **t** the people, and 1321
5:21 into the temple early in the morning, and **t**. 1321
11:26 and **t** much people, and the disciples were 1321
14:21 and had **t** many, they returned *again* to 3100
15: 1 came down from Judea **t** the brethren, 1321
18:25 and **t** diligently the *things* of the Lord, 1321
20:20 and have **t** you publickly, and from house 1321
22: 3 **t** according to the perfect manner of the law 3811
Gal 1:12 neither was I **t** *it*, but by the revelation of 1321
6: 6 Let him that is **t** in the word communicate 2727
Eph 4:21 and have been **t** by him, as the truth is in 1321
Col 2: 7 stablished in the faith, as ye have been **t**, 1321
1Th 4: 9 for ye yourselves are **t of God** to love one 2312
2Th 2:15 hold the traditions which ye have been **t**, 1321
Tit 1: 9 fast the faithful word as *he* hath been **t**, 1322
1Jn 2:27 and is no lie, and even as it hath **t** you, 1321
Rev 2:14 who **t** Balac to cast a stumblingblock 1321

TAUNT (2) [TAUNTING]
Jer 24: 9 a reproach and a proverb, a **t** and a curse, 8148
Eze 5:15 So it shall be a reproach and a **t**, 1422

TAUNTING (1) [TAUNT]
Hab 2: 6 and a **t** proverb against him, and say, 4426

TAVERNS (1)
Ac 28:15 us as far as Appii forum, and The three **t**: 4999

TAX BOOTH See RECEIPT OF CUSTOM

TAX COLLECTOR See PUBLICAN

TAXATION (1) [TAXED, TAXES, TAXING]
2Ki 23:35 of every one according to his **t**, to give *it* 6187

TAXED (4) [TAXATION]
2Ki 23:35 he **t** the land to give the money according 6186
Lk 2: 1 that all the world should be **t**. 583
2: 3 And all went to be **t**, every one into his own 583
2: 5 To be **t** with Mary his espoused wife, 583

TAXES (1) [TAXATION]
Da 11:20 shall stand up in his estate a raiser of **t** *in* 5065

TAXING (2) [TAXATION]
Lk 2: 2 (*And* this **t** was first made when Cyrenius 582
Ac 5:37 rose up Judas of Galilee in the days of the **t**, 582

TEACH (109) [TAUGHT, TEACHER, TEACHERS, TEACHEST, TEACHETH, TEACHING]
Ex 4:12 thy mouth, and **t** thee what thou shalt say. 3384
4:15 his mouth, and will **t** you what ye shall do. 3384
18:20 thou shalt **t** them ordinances and laws, and 2094
24:12 I have written; that thou mayest **t** them. 3384
35:34 he hath put in his heart that *he* may **t**, 3384
Lev 10:11 that *ye* may **t** the children of Israel all 3384
14:57 To **t** when *it is* unclean, and when *it is* 3384
Dt 4: 1 and unto the judgments, which I **t** you, 3925
4: 9 but **t** them thy sons, and thy sons' sons; 3045
4:10 the earth, and *that* they may **t** their children. 3925
4:14 LORD commanded me at that time to **t** 3925
5:31 and the judgments, which thou shalt **t** them, 3925
6: 1 the LORD your God commanded to **t** you, 3925
6: 7 thou shalt **t** them **diligently** unto thy 8150
11:19 ye shall **t** them your children, speaking of 3925
17:11 sentence of the law which they shall **t** thee, 3384
20:18 That they **t** you not to do after all their 3925
24: 8 to all that the priests the Levites shall **t** you: 3384
31:19 song for you, and **t** it the children of Israel: 3925
33:10 They shall **t** Jacob thy judgments, and 3384
Jdg 3: 2 to **t** them war, at the least such as before 3925
13: 8 **t** us what we shall do unto the child that 3384
1Sa 12:23 but I will **t** you the good and the right way: 3384
2Sa 1:18 (Also he bade *them* **t** the children of Judah 3925
1Ki 8:36 that thou **t** them the good way wherein they 3384
2Ki 17:27 let him **t** them the manner of the God of 3384
2Ch 17: 7 and to Michaiah, to **t** in the cities of Judah. 3925
Ezr 7:10 to do *it*, and to **t** in Israel statutes and 3925
7:25 thy God; and **t** ye them that know *them* not. 3046
Job 6:24 **T** me, and I will hold my tongue: and 3384
8:10 Shall not they **t** thee, *and* tell thee, and 3384
12: 7 ask now the beasts, and they shall **t** thee; 3384
12: 8 Or speak to the earth, and it shall **t** thee: 3384
21:22 Shall *any* **t** God knowledge? seeing he 3925
27:11 I will **t** you by the hand of God: *that* which 3384
32: 7 and multitude of years should **t** wisdom. 3045
33:33 hold thy peace, and I shall **t** thee wisdom. 502
34:32 *That which* I see not **t** thou me: if I have 3384
37:19 **T** us what we shall say unto him; *for* we 3045
Ps 25: 4 me thy ways, O LORD; **t** me thy paths. 3925
25: 5 Lead me in thy truth, and **t** me: for thou *art* 3925
25: 8 will he **t** sinners in the way. 3384
25: 9 and the meek will he **t** his way. 3925
25:12 him shall he **t** in the way *that* he shall 3384
27:11 **T** me thy way, O LORD, and lead me in a 3384
32: 8 and **t** thee in the way which thou shalt go: 3384
34:11 I will **t** you the fear of the LORD. 3925
45: 4 thy right hand shall **t** thee terrible *things*. 3384
51:13 *Then* will I **t** transgressors thy ways; and 3925
60: T Michtam of David, to **t**; 3925
86:11 **T** me thy way, O LORD; I will walk in 3384
90:12 So **t** *us* to number our days, that we may 3045
105:22 at his pleasure; and **t** his senators **wisdom**. 2449
119:12 *art* thou, O LORD: **t** me thy statutes. 3925
119:26 and thou heardest me: **t** me thy statutes. 3925
119:33 **T** me, O LORD, the way of thy statutes; 3384
119:64 is full *of* thy mercy: **t** me thy statutes. 3925
119:66 **T** me good judgment and knowledge: for I 3925
119:68 *art* good, and doest good; **t** me thy statutes. 3925
119:108 O LORD, and **t** me thy judgments. 3925
119:124 unto thy mercy, and **t** me thy statutes. 3925
119:135 upon thy servant; and **t** me thy statutes. 3925
132:12 and my testimony that I shall **t** them, 3925
143:10 **T** me to do thy will; for thou *art* my God: 3925
Pr 9: 9 **t** a just *man*, and he will increase in 3045
Isa 2: 3 he will **t** us of his ways, and we will walk 3384
28: 9 Whom shall he **t** knowledge? and whom 3384
28:26 instruct him to discretion, *and* doth **t** him. 3384
Jer 9:20 **t** your daughters wailing, and every one her 3925
31:34 they shall **t** no more every man his 3925
Eze 44:23 they shall **t** my people *the difference* 3384
Da 1: 4 whom *they* might **t** the learning and 3925
Mic 3:11 the priests thereof **t** for hire, and 3384
4: 2 he will **t** us of his ways, and we will walk 3384
Hab 2:19 Awake; to the dumb stone, Arise, it shall **t**! 3384
Mt 5:19 least commandments, and shall **t** men so, 1321
5:19 **t** *them*, the same shall be called great in 1321
11: 1 he departed thence to **t** and to preach in 1321
28:19 Go ye therefore, and **t** all nations, 3100
Mk 4: 1 And he began again to **t** by the sea side: 1321
6: 2 was come, he began to **t** in the synagogue: 1321
6:34 and he began to **t** them many *things*. 1321
8:31 And he began to **t** them, that the Son of 1321
Lk 11: 1 Lord, **t** us to pray, as John also taught his 1321
12:12 For the Holy Ghost shall **t** you in the same 1321
Jn 7:35 among the Gentiles, and **t** the Gentiles? 1321
9:34 altogether born in sins, and dost thou **t** us? 1321
14:26 he shall **t** you all *things*, and bring all 1321
Ac 1: 1 of all that Jesus began both to do and **t**, 1321
4:18 commanded them not to speak at all nor **t** 1321
5:28 you that *you* should not **t** in this name? 1321
5:42 they ceased not to **t** and preach Jesus 1321
16:21 And **t** customs, which are not lawful for us 2605
1Co 4:17 as I **t** every where in every church. 1321
11:14 Doth not even nature itself **t** you, that, if a 1321
14:19 that *by my voice* I might **t** others also, 2727
1Ti 1: 3 charge some that *they* **t** no **other doctrine**, 2085
2:12 But I suffer not a woman to **t**, nor to usurp 1321
3: 2 given to hospitality, **apt to t**; 1317
4:11 These *things* command and **t**. 1321
6: 2 of the benefit. These *things* **t** and exhort. 1321
6: 3 If any *man* **t otherwise**, and consent not to 2085
2Ti 2: 2 who shall be able to **t** others also. 1321
2:24 but be gentle unto all *men*, **apt to t**, patient, 1317
Tit 2: 4 they may **t** the young *women* **to be sober**, 4994

T

Heb 5:12 ye have need that *one* t you again which *be* 1321
8:11 And they shall not t every man his 1321
1Jn 2:27 in you, and ye need not that any *man* t you: 1321
Rev 2:20 to t and to seduce my servants to commit 1321

TEACHER (6) [TEACH]
1Ch 25: 8 the small as the great, the t as the scholar. 995
Hab 2:18 the molten image, and a t of lies, that 3384
Jn 3: 2 we know that thou art a t come from God: 1320
Ro 2:20 An instructor of the foolish, a t of babes, 1320
1Ti 2: 7 a t of the Gentiles in faith and verity. 1320
2Ti 1:11 and an apostle, and a t of the Gentiles. 1320

TEACHERS (14) [TEACH]
Ps 119:99 I have more understanding than all my t: 3925
Pr 5:13 have not obeyed the voice of my t, 3384
Isa 30:20 yet shall not thy t be removed into a corner 3384
30:20 any more, but thine eyes shall see thy t: 3384
43:27 and thy t have transgressed against me. 3887
Ac 13: 1 that was at Antioch certain prophets and t; 1320
1Co 12:28 thirdly t, after that miracles, then gifts of 1320
12:29 *are* all t? *are* all workers of miracles? 1320
Eph 4:11 some, evangelists; and some, pastors and t; 1320
1Ti 1: 7 Desiring to be **t of the law**; 3547
2Ti 4: 3 own lusts shall they heap to themselves t, 1320
Tit 2: 3 not given to much wine, **t of good things**; 2567
Heb 5:12 For when for the time ye ought to be t, 1320
2Pe 2: 1 even as there shall be **false** t among you, 5572

TEACHEST (8) [TEACH]
Ps 94:12 O LORD, and t him out of thy law; 3925
Mt 22:16 thou art true, and t the way of God in truth, 1321
Mk 12:14 of men, but t the way of God in truth: 1321
Lk 20:21 we know that thou sayest and t rightly, 1321
20:21 person *of any*, but t the way of God truly: 1321
Ac 21:21 that thou t all the Jews which are among 1321
Ro 2:21 Thou therefore which t another, 1321
2:21 which teachest another, t thou not thyself? 1321

TEACHETH (16) [TEACH]
2Sa 22:35 He t my hands to war; so that a bow of 3925
Job 35:11 Who t us more than the beasts of the earth, 502
36:22 God exalteth by his power: who t like him? 3384
Ps 18:34 He t my hands to war, so that a bow of 3925
94:10 he that t man knowledge, *shall not he* 3925
144: 1 which t my hands to war, *and* my fingers to 3925
Pr 6:13 speaketh with his feet, he t with his fingers; 3384
16:23 The heart of the wise t his mouth, and 7919
Isa 9:15 and the prophet that t lies, he *is* the tail. 3384
48:17 I *am* the LORD thy God which t thee to 3925
Ac 21:28 that t all *men* every where against 1321
Ro 12: 7 *our* ministering: or he that t, on teaching; 1321
1Co 2:13 not in the words which man's wisdom t, 1318
2:13 but which the Holy Ghost t; 1318
Gal 6: 6 unto him that t in all good *things*. 2727
1Jn 2:27 as the same anointing t you of all *things*, 1321

TEACHING (25) [TEACH]
2Ch 15: 3 and without a t priest, and without law. 3384
Jer 32:33 t *them*, yet they have not hearkened to 3925
Mt 4:23 t in their synagogues and preaching 1321
9:35 t in their synagogues, and preaching 1321
15: 9 t for doctrines the commandments of men. 1321
21:23 of the people came unto him as he was t, 1321
26:55 I sat daily with you t in the temple, and 1321
28:20 T them to observe all *things* whatsoever I 1321
Mk 6: 6 And he went round about the villages, t. 1321
7: 7 t for doctrines the commandments of men. 1321
14:49 I was daily with you in the temple t, and 1321
Lk 5:17 as he was t, that there were Pharisees and 1321
13:10 And he was t in one of the synagogues on 1321
13:22 t, and journeying towards Jerusalem. 1321
21:37 And in the day time he was t in the temple; 1321
23: 5 up the people, t throughout all Jewry, 1321
Ac 5:25 are standing in the temple, and t the people. 1321
15:35 t and preaching the word of the Lord, 1321
18:11 six months, t the word of God among them. 1321
28:31 t those *things* which concern the Lord Jesus 1321
Ro 12: 7 *our* ministering: or he that teacheth, on t; 1319
Col 1:28 every man, and t every man in all wisdom; 1321
3:16 t and admonishing one another in psalms 1321
Tit 1:11 t *things* which *they* ought not, for filthy 1321
2:12 T us that denying ungodliness and worldly 3811

TEAR (13) [TARE, TEARETH, TEARS, TORN]
Jdg 8: 7 I will t your flesh with the thorns of 1758
Ps 7: 2 Lest he t my soul like a lion, rending *it* in 2963
35:15 I knew *it* not; they did t *me*, and ceased not: 7167
50:22 lest I t *you* **in pieces**, and *there be* none to 2963
Jer 15: 3 the dogs to t, and the fowls of the heaven, 5498
16: 7 Neither shall *men* t *themselves* for them in 6536
Eze 13:20 I will t them from your arms, and will let 7167
13:21 Your kerchiefs also will I t, and deliver my 7167
Hos 5:14 I, *even* I, will t and go away; I will take 2963
13: 8 them like a lion: the wild beast shall t them. 1234
Am 1:11 his anger did t perpetually, and he kept his 2963
Na 2:12 The lion did t **in pieces** enough for his 2963
Zec 11:16 flesh of the fat, and t their claws **in pieces**. 6561

TEARETH (6) [TEAR]
Dt 33:20 and t the arm with the crown of the head. 2963
Job 16: 9 He t *me in* his wrath, who hateth me: 2963
18: 4 He t himself in his anger: shall the earth be 2963
Mic 5: 8 and t **in pieces**, and none can deliver. 2963
Mk 9:18 And wheresoever he taketh him, he t him: 4486
Lk 9:39 and it t him that he foameth again, and 4682

TEARS (36) [TEAR]
2Ki 20: 5 I have heard thy prayer, I have seen thy t: 1832
Est 8: 3 besought him with t to put away 1058
Job 16:20 *but* mine eye poureth out *t* unto God. NIH
Ps 6: 6 bed to swim; I water my couch with my t. 1832
39:12 ear unto my cry; hold not thy peace at my t: 1832
42: 3 My t have been my meat day and night, 1832
56: 8 put thou my t into thy bottle: *are they* not in 1832
80: 5 Thou feedest them with the bread of t; and 1832
80: 5 and givest them t to drink *in great* measure. 1832
116: 8 mine eyes from t, *and* my feet from falling. 1832
126: 5 They that sow in t shall reap in joy. 1832
Ecc 4: 1 the t of such as were oppressed, and 1832
Isa 16: 9 I will water thee *with* my t, O Heshbon, 1832
25: 8 the Lord GOD will wipe away t from off 1832
38: 5 I have heard thy prayer, I have seen thy t: 1832
Jer 9: 1 mine eyes a fountain of t, that I might weep 1832
9:18 that our eyes may run down *with* t, and 1832
13:17 run down *with* t, because the LORD'S 1832
14:17 Let mine eyes run down *with* t night and 1832
31:16 voice from weeping, and thine eyes from t: 1832
La 1: 2 in the night, and her t *are* on her cheeks: 1832
2:11 Mine eyes do fail with t, my bowels are 1832
2:18 let t run down like a river day and night: 1832
Eze 24:16 nor weep, neither shall thy t run down. 1832
Mal 2:13 covering the altar of the LORD *with* t, 1832
Mk 9:24 cried out, and said with t, Lord, I believe; 1144
Lk 7:38 and began to wash his feet with t, and 1144
7:44 but she hath washed my feet with t, and 1144
Ac 20:19 of mind, and *with* many t, and temptations, 1144
20:31 not to warn every one night and day with t. 1144
2Co 2: 4 of heart I wrote unto you with many t; 1144
2Ti 1: 4 desiring to see thee, being mindful of thy t, 1144
Heb 5: 7 t unto him that was able to save him from 1144
12:17 though he sought it carefully with t. 1144
Rev 7:17 God shall wipe away all t from their eyes. 1144
21: 4 And God shall wipe away all t from their 1144

TEATS (3)
Isa 32:12 They *shall* lament for the t, for the pleasant 7699
Eze 23: 3 there they bruised the t of their virginity. 1717
23:21 in bruising thy t by the Egyptians for 1717

TEBAH (1)
Ge 22:24 she bare also T, and Gaham, and Thahash, 2875

TEBALIAH (1)
1Ch 26:11 Hilkiah the second, T the third, 2882

TEBETH (1)
Est 2:16 which *is* the month T, in the seventh year 2887

TEDIOUS (1)
Ac 24: 4 that I be not further t unto thee, 1465

TEETH (49) [TOOTH]
Ge 49:12 *be* red with wine, and *his* t white with milk. 8127
Nu 11:33 while the flesh *was* yet between their t, 8127
Dt 32:24 I will also send the t of beasts upon them, 8127
1Sa 2:13 with a fleshhook of three t in his hand; 8127
Job 4:10 and the t of the young lions, are broken. 8127
13:14 Wherefore do I take my flesh in my t, and 8127
16: 9 he gnasheth upon me with his t; 8127
19:20 and I am escaped with the skin of my t. 8127
29:17 the wicked, and pluckt the spoil out of his t. 8127
41:14 of his face? his t *are* terrible round about. 8127
Ps 3: 7 thou hast broken the t of the ungodly. 8127
35:16 *they* gnashed upon me *with* their t. 8127
37:12 the just, and gnasheth upon him *with* his t. 8127
57: 4 whose t *are* spears and arrows, and 8127
58: 6 Break their t, O God, in their mouth: 8127
58: 6 break out the **great** t of the young lions, 4459
112:10 he shall gnash *with* his t, and melt away: 8127
124: 6 who hath not given us *as* a prey to their t. 8127
Pr 10:26 As vinegar to the t, and as smoke to 8127
30:14 whose t *are as* swords, and their jaw teeth 8127
30:14 *are as* swords, and their **jaw** t *as* knives, 4973
SS 4: 2 Thy t *are* like a flock of *sheep that are* even 8127
6: 6 Thy t *are* as a flock of sheep which go up 8127
Isa 41:15 a new sharp threshing instrument having t: 6374
Jer 31:29 and the children's t are set on edge. 8127
31:30 the sour grape, his t shall be set on edge. 8127
La 2:16 they hiss and gnash the t: they say, 8127
3:16 He hath also broken my t with gravel 8127
Eze 18: 2 and the children's t are set on edge? 8127
Da 7: 5 ribs in the mouth of it between the t of it: 8128
7: 7 strong exceedingly; and it had great iron t: 8128
7:19 whose t *were of* iron, and his nails *of* brass; 8128
Joel 1: 6 whose t *are* the teeth of a lion, and he hath 8127
1: 6 whose teeth *are* the t of a lion, and he hath 8127
Am 4: 6 I also have given you cleanness of t in all 8127
Mic 3: 5 that bite with their t, and cry, Peace; 8127
Zec 9: 7 and his abominations from between his t: 8127
Mt 8:12 there shall be weeping and gnashing of t. 3599
13:42 there shall be wailing and gnashing of t. 3599
13:50 there shall be wailing and gnashing of t. 3599
22:13 there shall be weeping and gnashing of t. 3599
24:51 there shall be weeping and gnashing of t. 3599
25:30 there shall be weeping and gnashing of t. 3599
27:44 crucified with him, **cast** the same **in** his t. 3679
Mk 9:18 and gnasheth with his t, and pineth away: 3599
Lk 13:28 There shall be weeping and gnashing of t, 3599
Ac 7:54 and they gnashed on him *with their* t. 3599
Rev 9: 8 and their t were as *the teeth* of lions. 3599
9: 8 and their teeth were as *the* t of lions. NIG

TEHAPHNEHES (1) [TAHPANHES]
Eze 30:18 At T also the day shall be darkened, when I 8471

TEHINNAH (1)
1Ch 4:12 and Paseah, and T the father of Irnahash. 8468

TEIL (1)
Isa 6:13 as a **t tree**, and as an oak, whose substance *is* 424

TEKEL (2)
Da 5:25 MENE, MENE, T, UPHARSIN. 8625
5:27 T; Thou art weighed in the balances, and 8625

TEKOA (6) [TEKOAH, TEKOITE, TEKOITES]
1Ch 2:24 wife bare him Ashur the father of T. 8620
4: 5 Ashur the father of T had two wives, Helah 8620
2Ch 11: 6 built even Beth-lehem, and Etam, and T, 8620
20:20 and went forth into the wilderness of T: 8620
Jer 6: 1 blow the trumpet in T, and set up a sign of 8620
Am 1: 1 who was among the herdmen of T, 8620

TEKOAH (3) [TEKOA]
2Sa 14: 2 Joab sent to T, and fetcht thence a wise 8620
14: 4 when the woman of T spake to the king, 8621
14: 9 the woman of T said unto the king, 8621

TEKOITE (3) [TEKOA]
2Sa 23:26 the Paltite, Ira the son of Ikkesh the T, 8621
1Ch 11:28 Ira the son of Ikkesh the T, Abi-ezer 8621
27: 9 month *was* Ira the son of Ikkesh the T: 8621

TEKOITES (2) [TEKOA]
Ne 3: 5 next unto them the T repaired; but 8621
3:27 After them the T repaired another piece, 8621

TEL-ABIB (1)
Eze 3:15 I came to them of the captivity *at* T, 8512

TELAH (1)
1Ch 7:25 and T his son, and Tahan his son, 8520

TELAIM (1)
1Sa 15: 4 numbered them in T, two hundred thousand 2923

TELASSAR (1) [THELASAR]
Isa 37:12 and the children of Eden which *were* in T? 8515

TELEM (2)
Jos 15:24 Ziph, and T, and Bealoth, 2928
Ezr 10:24 and of the porters; Shallum, and T, and Uri. 2928

TEL-HARESHA (1) [TEL-HARSA]
Ne 7:61 T, Cherub, Addon, and Immer: 8521

TEL-HARSA (1) [TEL-HARESHA]
Ezr 2:59 T, Cherub, Addan, *and* Immer: 8521

TELL (217) [FORETELL, FORETOLD, TELLEST, TELLETH, TELLING, TOLD]
Ge 12:18 why didst thou not t me that she *was* thy 5046
15: 5 Look now towards heaven, and t the stars, 5608
21:26 neither didst thou t me, neither yet heard I 5046
22: 2 one of the mountains which I will t thee of. 559
24:23 t me, I pray thee: is there room *in* thy 5046
24:49 deal kindly and truly with my master, t me: 5046
24:49 if not, t me; that I may turn to the right 5046
26: 2 dwell in the land which I shall t thee of: 559
29:15 for nought? t me, what *shall* thy wages *be?* 5046
31:27 didst not t me, that I might have sent thee 5046
32: 5 I have sent to t my lord, that I may find 5046
32:29 asked *him*, and said, T *me*, I pray thee, 5046
37:16 t me, I pray thee, where they feed *their* 5046
40: 8 *belong* to God? t me *them*, I pray you. 5608
43: 6 *as* to t the man whether ye had yet a 5046
43:22 we cannot t who put our money in our 3045
45:13 you shall t my father of all my glory in 5046
49: 1 that I may t you *that* which shall befall you 5046
Ex 9: 1 unto Moses, Go in unto Pharaoh, and t him, 1696
10: 2 that thou mayest t in the ears of thy son, 5608
14:12 *Is* not this the word that we did t thee in 1696
19: 3 house of Jacob, and t the children of Israel; 5046
Lev 14:35 the house shall come and t the priest, 5046
Nu 14:14 they will t *it* to the inhabitants of this land: 559
21: 1 heard *t* that Israel came *by* the way of NIH
23: 3 and whatsoever he sheweth me I will t thee. 5046
Dt 17:11 according to the judgment which they shall t 559
32: 7 shew thee; thy elders, and they will t thee. 559
Jos 7:19 t me now what thou hast done; hide *it* not 5046
Jdg 14:16 father nor my mother, and shall I t *it* thee? 5046
16: 6 Delilah said to Samson, T me, I pray thee, 5046
16:10 now t me, I pray thee, wherewith thou 5046
16:13 t me wherewith thou mightest be bound. 5046
20: 3 of Israel, T *us*, how was this wickedness? 1696
Ru 3: 4 and he will t thee what thou shalt do. 5046
4: 4 but if thou wilt not redeem *it*, *then* t me, 5046
1Sa 6: 2 t us wherewith we shall send it to his place. 3045
9: 8 I give to the man of God, to t us our way. 5046
9:18 said, T me, I pray thee, where the seer's 5046
9:19 and will t thee all that *is* in thine heart. 5046
10:15 Saul's uncle said, T me, I pray thee, 5046
14:43 to Jonathan, T me what thou hast done. 5046
15:16 I will t thee what the LORD hath said to 5046
17:55 *As* thy soul liveth, O king, I cannot t. 3045
19: 3 of thee; and what I see, that I will t thee. 5046
20: 9 come upon thee, then would not I t it thee? 5046
20:10 said David to Jonathan, Who shall t me? 5046
22:22 that he would **surely** t Saul: 5046+5046
23:11 God of Israel, I beseech thee, t thy servant. 5046
27:11 saying, Lest they should t on us, saying, 5046
2Sa 1: 4 I pray thee, t me. And he answered, 5046
1:20 T *it* not in Gath, publish *it* not in the streets 5046
7: 5 Go and t my servant David, Thus saith 559
12:18 the servants of David feared to t him that 5046
12:18 if we t him *that* the child is dead? 559
12:22 Who can t *whether* GOD will be gracious 3045
13: 4 wilt thou not t me? And Amnon said unto 5046
15:35 thou shalt t *it* to Zadok and Abiathar 5046
17:16 therefore send quickly, and t David, saying, 5046
18:21 to Cushi, Go t the king what thou hast seen. 5046
1Ki 1:20 that *thou* shouldest t them who shall sit on 5046
14: 3 he shall t thee what shall become of 5046
14: 7 Go, t Jeroboam, Thus saith the LORD God 559
18: 8 I *am*: go, t thy lord, Behold, Elijah *is here*. 559
18:11 Go, t thy lord, Behold, Elijah *is here*. 559
18:12 *so* when I come and t Ahab, and he cannot 5046
18:14 Go, t thy lord, Behold, Elijah *is here:* and 559
20: 9 of Ben-hadad, T my lord the king, 559
20:11 T *him*, Let not him that girdeth on *his* 1696

1Ki 22:16 shall I adjure thee that thou t me nothing 1696
22:18 Did I not t thee that he would prophesy no 559
2Ki 4: 2 t me, what hast thou in the house? And she 5046
7: 9 that we may go and t the king's household. 5046
8: 4 saying, T me, I pray thee, all the great 5608
9:12 they said, *It is* false; t us now. And he said, 5046
9:15 escape out of the city to go to t *it* in Jezreel. 5046
20: 5 and t Hezekiah the captain of my people, 559
22:15 God of Israel, T the man that sent you to me, 559
1Ch 17: 4 Go and t David my servant, Thus saith 559
17:10 Furthermore I t thee that the LORD will 5046
21:10 Go and t David, saying, Thus saith 1696
2Ch 18:17 Did I not t thee *that* he would not prophesy 559
34:23 of Israel, T ye the man that sent you to me, 559
Job 1:15 and I only am escaped alone to t thee. 5046
1:16 and I only am escaped alone to t thee. 5046
1:17 and I only am escaped alone to t thee. 5046
1:19 and I only am escaped alone to t thee. 5046
8:10 *and* t thee, and utter words out of their heart? 559
12: 7 the fowls of the air, and they shall t thee: 5046
34:34 Let men of understanding t me, and let a 559
Ps 22:17 I may t all my bones: they look *and* 5608
26: 7 and t of all thy wondrous works. 5608
48:12 go round about her: t the towers thereof. 5608
48:13 that ye may t *it* to the generation following. 5608
50:12 If I were hungry, I would not t thee: for 559
Pr 30: 4 and what *is* his son's name, if thou canst t? 3045
Ecc 6:12 for who can t a man what shall be after him 5046
8: 7 for who can t him when it shall be? 5046
10:14 a man cannot t what shall be; and 3045
10:14 and what shall be after him, who can t him? 5046
10:20 that which hath wings shall t the matter. 5046
SS 1: 7 T me, O thou whom my soul loveth, 5046
5: 8 that ye t him, that I *am* sick of love. 5046
Isa 5: 5 I will t you what I *will* do to my vineyard: 3045
6: 9 he said, Go, and t this people, Hear ye 559
19:12 *are* thy wise *men?* and let them t thee now, 5046
42: 9 before they spring forth I t you of them. 8085
45:21 T ye, and bring *them* near; yea, let them 5046
48:20 with a voice of singing declare ye, t this, 8085
Jer 15: 2 thou shalt t them, Thus saith the LORD; 559
19: 2 proclaim there the words that I shall t thee, 1696
23:27 which they t every man to his neighbour, 5608
23:28 that hath a dream, let him t a dream; 5608
23:32 do t them, and cause my people to err by 5608
28:13 Go and t Hananiah, saying, Thus saith 559
34: 2 of Judah, and t him, Thus saith the LORD; 559
35:13 Go and t the men of Judah and 559
36:16 We will **surely** t the king of all these 5046+5046
36:17 they asked Baruch, saying, T us now, 5046
48:20 cry; t ye *it* in Arnon, that Moab is spoiled, 5046
Eze 3:11 speak unto them, and t them, Thus saith 559
12:23 T them therefore, Thus saith the Lord 559
17:12 Know ye not what these *things mean?* t 559
24:19 Wilt thou not t us what these *things are* to 5046
Da 2: 4 t thy servants the dream, and we will shew 560
2: 7 Let the king t his servants the dream, and 560
2: 9 therefore t me the dream, and I shall know 560
2:36 we will t the interpretation thereof before 560
4: 9 t *me* the visions of my dream that I have 560
Joel 1: 3 T ye your children of it, and *let* your 5608
1: 3 *let* your children *t* their children, and NIH
Jnh 1: 8 said they unto him, T us, we pray thee, 5046
3: 9 Who can t *if* God will turn and repent, and 3045
Mt 8: 4 See thou t no *man;* but go thy way, *3004*
10:27 What I t you in darkness, *that* speak ye in *3004*
16:20 t no *man* that he was Jesus the Christ. *3004*
17: 9 T the vision to no *man,* until the Son of *3004*
18:15 go and t him his **fault** between thee and *1651*
18:17 neglect to hear them, t *it* unto the church: *3004*
21: 5 T ye the daughter of Sion, Behold, *3004*
21:24 will ask you one thing, which if ye t me, *3004*
21:24 I in like wise will t you by what authority I *3004*
21:27 they answered Jesus, and said, We cannot t. *1492*
21:27 Neither t I you by what authority I do *3004*
22: 4 saying, T them which are bidden, Behold, *3004*
22:17 T us therefore, What thinkest thou? Is it *3004*
24: 3 T us, when shall these *things* be? *3004*
26:63 that thou t us whether thou be the Christ, *3004*
28: 7 t his disciples that he is risen from *3004*
28: 9 And as they went to t his disciples, behold, *518*
28:10 go t my brethren that they go into Galilee, *518*
Mk 1:30 sick of a fever, and anon they t him of her. *3004*
5:19 t them how great *things* the Lord hath done *312*
7:36 And he charged them that they should t no *3004*
8:26 go into the town, nor t *it* to any in the town. *3004*
8:30 And he charged them that they should t no *3004*
9: 9 he charged them that they should t no *man* *1334*
10:32 began to t them what *things* should happen *3004*
11:29 I will t you by what authority I do these *3004*
11:33 and said unto Jesus, We cannot t. *1492*
11:33 Neither do I t you by what authority I do *3004*
13: 4 T us, when shall these *things* be? and *3004*
16: 7 t his disciples and Peter that he goeth *3004*
Lk 4:25 But I t you of a truth, many widows were in *3004*
5:14 And he charged him to t no *man:* but go, *3004*
7:22 and t John what *things* ye have seen and *518*
7:42 T me therefore, which of them will love *3004*
8:56 he charged them that they should t no *man* *3004*
9:21 commanded *them* to t no *man* that *thing;* *3004*
9:27 But I t you of a truth, there be some *3004*
10:24 For I t you, that many prophets and *3004*
12:51 on earth? I t you, Nay; but rather division: *3004*
12:59 I t thee, thou shalt not depart thence, *3004*
13: 3 I t you, Nay: but, except ye repent, ye shall *3004*
13: 5 I t you, Nay: but, except ye repent, ye shall *3004*
13:27 But he shall say, I t you, I know you not *3004*
13:32 Go ye, and t that fox, Behold, I cast out *3004*
17:34 I t you, in that night there shall be two *men* *3004*
18: 8 I t you that he will avenge them speedily. *3004*
18:14 I t you, this man went down to his house *3004*
19:40 and said unto them, I t you that, *3004*
20: 2 And spake unto him, saying, T us, by what *3004*
20: 7 that *they* could not t whence *it was.* *1492*
20: 8 Neither t I you by what authority I do *3004*
Lk 22:34 And he said, I t thee, Peter, *the* cock shall *3004*
22:67 t us. And he said unto them, If I tell you, *3004*
22:67 unto them, If I t you, you will not believe: *3004*
Jn 3: 8 but canst not t whence it cometh, and *1492*
3:12 ye believe, if I t you *of* heavenly *things?* *3004*
4:25 when he is come, he will t us all *things.* *312*
8:14 but ye cannot t whence I come, and *1492*
8:45 And because I t *you* the truth, ye believe *3004*
10:24 to doubt? If thou be the Christ, t us plainly. *3004*
12:22 and again Andrew and Philip t Jesus. *3004*
13:19 Now I t you before it come, that, when it is *3004*
16: 7 Nevertheless I t you the truth; It is *3004*
16:18 A little while? we cannot t what he saith. *1492*
18:34 of thyself, or did others t *it* thee of me? *3004*
20:15 if thou have borne him *hence,* t me where *3004*
Ac 5: 8 T me whether ye sold the land for so *3004*
10: 6 he shall t thee what thou oughtest to do. *2980*
11:14 Who shall t thee words, whereby thou and *2980*
15:27 who shall also t *you* the same *things* by *518*
17:21 but *either* to t, or to hear some new *thing.)* *3004*
22:27 and said unto him, T me, art thou a *3004*
23:17 for he hath a certain *thing* to t him. *518*
23:19 asked *him,* What is that thou hast to t me? *518*
23:22 charged *him, See thou* t no *man* that thou *1583*
2Co 12: 2 years ago, (whether in the body, I cannot t; *1492*
12: 2 or whether out of the body, I cannot t: *1492*
12: 3 in the body, or out of the body, I cannot t: *1492*
Gal 4:16 your enemy, because I t you **the truth**? *226*
4:21 T me, ye that desire to be under the law, *3004*
5:21 of the which I t you **before**, as I have also *4302*
Php 3:18 you often, and now t *you* even weeping, *3004*
Heb 11:32 for the time would fail me to t of Gedeon, *1334*
Rev 17: 7 I will t thee the mystery of the woman, and *3004*

TELLEST (1) [TELL]

Ps 56: 8 Thou t my wanderings: put thou my tears 5608

TELLETH (7) [TELL]

2Sa 7:11 Also the LORD t thee that he will make 5046
2Ki 6:12 t the king of Israel the words that thou 5046
Ps 41: 6 to itself; *when* he goeth abroad, he t *it.* 1696
101: 7 he that t lies shall not tarry in my sight. 1696
147: 4 He t the number of the stars; he calleth 4487
Jer 33:13 hands of him that t *them,* saith the LORD. 4487
Jn 12:22 Philip cometh and t Andrew: and *3004*

TELLING (3) [TELL]

Jdg 7:15 so, when Gideon heard the t of the dream, 4557
2Sa 11:19 When thou hast made an end of t 1696
2Ki 8: 5 *as* he was t the king how he had restored a 5608

TEL-MELAH (2)

Ezr 2:59 these *were* they which went up from T, 8528
Ne 7:61 these *were* they which went up *also* from T, 8528

TEMA (5)

Ge 25:15 Hadar, and T, Jetur, Naphish, and 8485
1Ch 1:30 and Dumah, Massa, Hadad, and T, 8485
Job 6:19 The troops of T looked, the companies of 8485
Isa 21:14 The inhabitants of the land of T brought 8485
Jer 25:23 T, and Buz, and all *that are* in the utmost 8485

TEMAH See TAMAH; THAMAH

TEMAN (11) [TEMANI, TEMANITE, TEMANITES]

Ge 36:11 the sons of Eliphaz were T, Omar, Zepho, 8487
36:15 duke T, duke Omar, duke Zepho, 8487
36:42 Duke Kenaz, duke T, duke Mibzar, 8487
1Ch 1:36 T, and Omar, Zephi, and Gatam, Kenaz, 8487
1:53 Duke Kenaz, duke T, duke Mibzar, 8487
Jer 49: 7 LORD of hosts; *Is* wisdom no more in T? 8487
49:20 hath purposed against the inhabitants of T: 8487
Eze 25:13 I will make it desolate from T; and they of 8487
Am 1:12 I will send a fire upon the T, which shall 8487
Ob 1: 9 thy mighty *men,* O T, shall be dismayed, 8487
Hab 3: 3 God came from T, and the Holy One from 8487

TEMANI (1) [TEMAN]

Ge 36:34 Husham of the land of T reigned in his 8489

TEMANITE (6) [TEMAN]

Job 2:11 Eliphaz the T, and Bildad the Shuhite, and 8489
4: 1 Then Eliphaz the T answered and said, 8489
15: 1 Then answered Eliphaz the T, and said, 8489
22: 1 Then Eliphaz the T answered and said, 8489
42: 7 the LORD said to Eliphaz the T, 8489
42: 9 So Eliphaz the T and Bildad the Shuhite 8489

TEMANITES (1) [TEMAN]

1Ch 1:45 Husham of the land of the T reigned in his 8489

TEMENI (1)

1Ch 4: 6 and Hepher, and T, and Haahashtari. 8488

TEMPER (1) [TEMPERANCE, TEMPERATE, TEMPERED, UNTEMPERED]

Eze 46:14 *part* of a hin of oil, to t with the fine flour; 7450

TEMPERANCE (4) [TEMPER]

Ac 24:25 t, and judgment to come, Felix trembled, *1466*
Gal 5:23 Meekness, t: against such there is no law. *1466*
2Pe 1: 6 And to knowledge t; and to temperance *1466*
1: 6 and to t patience; and to patience godliness; *1466*

TEMPERATE (3) [TEMPER]

1Co 9:25 t in all *things.* Now they *do it* to obtain a *1467*
Tit 1: 8 a lover of good *men,* sober, just, holy, t; *1468*
2: 2 grave, t, sound in faith, in charity, *4998*

TEMPERED (3) [TEMPER]

Ex 29: 2 cakes unleavened t with oil, and 1101
30:35 the apothecary, t **together**, pure *and* holy: 4414
1Co 12:24 but God hath t the body **together**, *4786*

TEMPEST (18) [TEMPESTUOUS]

Job 9:17 For he breaketh me with a t, and 8183
27:20 a t stealeth him away in the night. 5492
Ps 11: 6 fire and brimstone, and a horrible t: 7307
55: 8 my escape from the windy storm *and* t. 5591
83:15 So persecute them with thy t, and 5591
Isa 28: 2 *which* as a t of hail *and* a destroying storm, 2230
29: 6 *with* storm and t, and the flame of 5591
30:30 *with* scattering, and t, and hailstones. 2230
32: 2 from the wind, and a covert from the t; 2230
54:11 **tossed with** t, *and* not comforted, behold, 5590
Am 1:14 with a t in the day of the whirlwind: 5591
Jnh 1: 4 there was a mighty t in the sea, so that 5591
1:12 for I know that for my sake this great t *is* 5591
Mt 8:24 And behold, there arose a great t in the sea, *4578*
Ac 27:18 And we being exceedingly **tossed with a** t, *5492*
27:20 no small t lay on *us,* all hope that we *5494*
Heb 12:18 nor unto blackness, and darkness, and t, *2366*
2Pe 2:17 clouds that are carried with a t; *2978*

TEMPESTUOUS (4) [TEMPEST]

Ps 50: 3 and it shall be very t round about him. 8175
Jnh 1:11 unto us? for the sea wrought, and was t. 5590
1:13 the sea wrought, and was t against them. 5590
Ac 27:14 But not long after there arose against it a t *5189*

TEMPLE (204) [TEMPLES]

1Sa 1: 9 a seat by a post of the t of the LORD. 1964
3: 3 ere the lamp of God went out in the t of 1964
2Sa 22: 7 he did hear my voice out of his t, and 1964
1Ki 6: 3 the porch before the t of the house, 1964
6: 5 round about, *both* of the t and of the oracle: 1964
6:17 the house, that *is,* the t before it, was forty 1964
6:33 So also made he for the door of the t posts 1964
7:21 he set up the pillars in the porch of the t: 1964
7:50 for the doors of the house, *to wit,* of the t. 1964
2Ki 11:10 that *were* in the t of the LORD. 1004
11:11 from the right corner of the t to the left 1004
11:11 of the temple to the left corner of the t, 1004
11:11 of the temple, *along* by the altar and the t. 1004
11:13 she came to the people *into* the t of 1004
18:16 *gold from* the doors of the t of the LORD, 1964
23: 4 to bring forth out of the t of the LORD all 1964
24:13 of Israel had made in the t of the LORD, 1964
1Ch 6:10 in the t that Solomon built in Jerusalem:) 1004
10:10 and fastened his head *in* the t of Dagon. 1004
2Ch 3:17 he reared up the pillars before the t, one on 1964
4: 7 and set *them* in the t, five on the right hand, 1964
4: 8 placed *them* in the t, five on the right side, 1964
4:22 and the doors of the house of the t, 1964
23:10 from the right side of the t to the left side of 1004
23:10 side of the temple to the left side of the t, 1004
23:10 *along* by the altar and the t, by the king 1004
26:16 went into the t of the LORD to burn 1964
27: 2 howbeit he entered not into the t of 1964
29:16 t of the LORD into the court of the house 1964
35:20 all this, when Josiah had prepared the t, 1004
36: 7 and put them in his t at Babylon. 1964
Ezr 3: 6 the foundation of the t of the LORD was 1964
3:10 laid the foundation of the t of the LORD, 1964
4: 1 the t unto the LORD God of Israel; 1964
5:14 which Nebuchadnezzar took out of the t 1965
5:14 brought them into the t of Babylon, 1965
5:14 those did Cyrus the king take out of the t of 1965
5:15 carry them into the t that *is* in Jerusalem, 1965
6: 5 forth out of the t which *is* at Jerusalem, 1965
6: 5 brought *again* unto the t which *is* at 1965
Ne 6:10 within the t, and let us shut the doors of 1964
6:10 and let us shut the doors of the t: 1964
6:11 *being* as I *am,* would go into the t to save 1964
Ps 5: 7 in thy fear will I worship toward thy holy t. 1964
11: 4 The LORD *is* in his holy t, the LORD'S 1964
18: 6 he heard my voice out of his t, and my cry 1964
27: 4 of the LORD, and to inquire in his t. 1964
29: 9 in his t doth every one speak of *his* glory. 1964
48: 9 O God, in the midst of thy t. 1964
65: 4 goodness of thy house, *even* of thy holy t. 1964
68:29 Because of thy t at Jerusalem shall kings 1964
79: 1 thy holy t have they defiled; they have laid 1964
138: 2 I will worship toward thy holy t, and 1964
Isa 6: 1 high and lifted up, and his train filled the t. 1964
44:28 and *to* the t, Thy foundation shall be laid. 1964
66: 6 of noise from the city, a voice from the t, 1964
Jer 7: 4 saying, The t of the LORD, The temple of 1964
7: 4 The t of the LORD, The temple of 1964
7: 4 The t of the LORD, *are* these. 1964
24: 1 two baskets of figs *were* set before the t of 1964
50:28 LORD our God, the vengeance of his t. 1964
51:11 of the LORD, the vengeance of his t. 1964
Eze 8:16 behold, *at* the door of the t of the LORD, 1964
8:16 *with* their backs toward the t of 1964
41: 1 Afterward he brought me to the t, and 1964
41: 4 and the breadth, twenty cubits, before the t: 1964
41:15 with the inner t, and the porches of 1964
41:20 palm trees made, and *on* the wall of the t. 1964
41:21 The posts of the t *were* squared, *and* 1964
41:23 And the t and the sanctuary had two doors. 1964
41:25 on the doors of the t, cherubims and 1964
42: 8 and lo, before the t *were* an hundred cubits. 1964
Da 5: 2 taken out of the t which *was* in Jerusalem; 1965
5: 3 t of the house of God which *was* at 1965
Am 8: 3 the songs of the t shall be howlings in that 1964
Jnh 2: 4 yet I will look again toward thy holy t. 1964
2: 7 prayer came in unto thee, into thine holy t. 1964
Mic 1: 2 against you, the Lord from his holy t. 1964
Hab 2:20 the LORD *is* in his holy t: let all the earth 1964
Hag 2:15 laid upon a stone in the t of the LORD: 1964
2:18 the foundation of the LORD'S t was laid, 1964
Zec 6:12 and he shall build the t of the LORD: 1964
6:13 Even he shall build the t of the LORD; 1964
6:14 for a memorial in the t of the LORD. 1964
6:15 and build in the t of the LORD, 1964
8: 9 of hosts was laid, that the t might be built. 1964
Mal 3: 1 ye seek, shall suddenly come to his t, 1964

T

Mt 4: 5 and setteth him on a pinnacle of the **t**, *2411*
12: 5 days the priests in the **t** profane the sabbath, *2411*
12: 6 That in this place is *one* greater than the **t**. *2411*
21:12 And Jesus went into the **t** of God, and *2411*
21:12 out all them that sold and bought in the **t**, *2411*
21:14 *the* blind and *the* lame came to him in the **t**; *2411*
21:15 and the children crying in the **t**, and saying, *2411*
21:23 And when he was come into the **t**, the chief *2411*
23:16 which say, Whosoever shall swear by the **t**, *3485*
23:16 whosoever shall swear by the gold of the **t**, *3485*
23:17 the gold, or the **t** that sanctifieth the gold? *3485*
23:21 And whoso shall swear by the **t**, *3485*
23:35 whom ye slew between the **t** and the altar. *3485*
24: 1 Jesus went out, and departed from the **t**: *2411*
24: 1 *him* for to shew him the buildings of the **t**. *2411*
26:55 I sat daily with you teaching in the **t**, and *2411*
26:61 I am able to destroy the **t** of God, and *3485*
27: 5 he cast down the pieces of silver in the **t**, *3485*
27:40 *Thou* that destroyest the **t**, and buildest *it* in *3485*
27:51 the vail of the **t** was rent in twain from *3485*
Mk 11:11 Jesus entered into Jerusalem, and into the **t**: *2411*
11:15 and Jesus went into the **t**, and began to cast *2411*
11:15 cast out them that sold and bought in the **t**, *2411*
11:16 *man* should carry *any* vessel through the **t**. *2411*
11:27 and as he was walking in the **t**, there come *2411*
12:35 and said, while he taught in the **t**, *2411*
13: 1 And as he went out of the **t**, one of his *2411*
13: 3 the mount of Olives over against the **t**, *2411*
14:49 I was daily with you in the **t** teaching, and *2411*
14:58 I will destroy this **t** that is made with hands, *3485*
15:29 *thou* that destroyest the **t**, and buildest *it* in *3485*
15:38 And the vail of the **t** was rent in twain from *3485*
Lk 1: 9 when he went into the **t** of the Lord. *3485*
1:21 marvelled that he tarried *so* long in the **t**. *3485*
1:22 perceived that he had seen a vision in the **t**: *3485*
2:27 And he came by the Spirit into the **t**: and *2411*
2:37 which departed not from the **t**, but *2411*
2:46 after three days they found him in the **t**, *2411*
4: 9 and set him on a pinnacle of the **t**, and *2411*
11:51 which perished between the altar and the **t**: *3624*
18:10 Two men went up into the **t** to pray; *2411*
19:45 And he went into the **t**, and began to cast *2411*
19:47 And he taught daily in the **t**. But the chief *2411*
20: 1 as he taught the people in the **t**, and *2411*
21: 5 And as some spake of the **t**, how it was *2411*
21:37 in the day time he was teaching in the **t**; *2411*
21:38 came early in the morning to him in the **t**, *2411*
22:52 and captains of the **t**, and the elders, *2411*
22:53 When I was daily with you in the **t**, *2411*
23:45 and the vail of the **t** was rent in the midst. *3485*
24:53 And were continually in the **t**, praising and *2411*
Jn 2:14 And found in the **t** those that sold oxen and *2411*
2:15 he drove *them* all out of the **t**, and the sheep *2411*
2:19 Destroy this **t**, and in three days I will raise *3485*
2:20 Forty and six years was this **t** in building, *3485*
2:21 But he spake of the **t** of his body. *3485*
5:14 Afterward Jesus findeth him in the **t**, and *2411*
7:14 midst of the feast Jesus went up into the **t**, *2411*
7:28 Then cried Jesus in the **t** as he taught, *2411*
8: 2 in the morning he came again into the **t**, *2411*
8:20 Jesus in the treasury, as he taught in the **t**: *2411*
8:59 but Jesus hid himself, and went out of the **t**, *2411*
10:23 And Jesus walked in the **t** in Solomon's *2411*
11:56 as they stood in the **t**, What think ye, *2411*
18:20 I ever taught in the synagogue, and in the **t**, *2411*
Ac 2:46 continuing daily with one accord in the **t**, *2411*
3: 1 John went up together into the **t** at the hour *2411*
3: 2 whom they laid daily at the gate of the **t** *2411*
3: 2 to ask alms of them that entered into the **t**; *2411*
3: 3 seeing Peter and John about to go into the **t**, *2411*
3: 8 walked, and entered with them into the **t**, *2411*
3:10 sat for alms at the Beautiful gate of the **t**: *2411*
4: 1 and the captain of the **t**, and the Sadducees, *2411*
5:20 speak in the **t** to the people all the words of *2411*
5:21 they entered into the **t** early in the morning, *2411*
5:24 the *high* priest and the captain of the **t** and *2411*
5:25 whom ye put in prison are standing in the **t**, *2411*
5:42 And daily in the **t**, and in every house, they *2411*
19:27 also that the **t** of the great goddess Diana *2411*
21:26 himself with them entered into the **t**, *2411*
21:27 when they saw him in the **t**, stirred up all *2411*
21:28 and further brought Greeks also into the **t**, *2411*
21:29 supposed that Paul had brought into the **t**.) *2411*
21:30 they took Paul, and drew him out of the **t**: *2411*
22:17 even while I prayed in the **t**, I was in a *2411*
24: 6 Who also hath gone about to profane the **t**: *2411*
24:12 And they neither found me in the **t** *2411*
24:18 Jews from Asia found me purified in the **t**, *2411*
25: 8 neither against the **t**, nor *yet* against Cesar, *2411*
26:21 these causes the Jews caught me in the **t**, *2411*
1Co 3:16 Know ye not that ye are the **t** of God, and *3485*
3:17 If any *man* defile the **t** of God, him shall *3485*
3:17 for the **t** of God is holy, which *temple* ye *3485*
3:17 the temple of God is holy, which ***t*** ye are. NIG
6:19 know ye not that your body is the **t** of *3485*
8:10 hast knowledge sit at meat in the **idol's t**, *1493*
9:13 about holy *things* live of *the things of* the **t**? *2411*
2Co 6:16 And what agreement hath the **t** of God with *3485*
6:16 for ye are the **t** of the living God; as God *3485*
Eph 2:21 together groweth unto a holy **t** in the Lord: *3485*
2Th 2: 4 so that he as God sitteth in the **t** of God, *3485*
Rev 3:12 will I make a pillar in the **t** of my God, *3485*
7:15 and serve him day and night in his **t**: *3485*
11: 1 and measure the **t** of God, and the altar, and *3485*
11: 2 But the court which is without the **t** leave *3485*
11:19 And the **t** of God was opened in heaven, *3485*
11:19 there was seen in his **t** the ark of his *3485*
14:15 And another angel came out of the **t**, *3485*
14:17 And another angel came out of the **t** which *3485*
15: 5 the **t** of the tabernacle of the testimony in *3485*
15: 6 And the seven angels came out of the **t**, *3485*
15: 8 And the **t** was filled with smoke from *3485*
15: 8 and no *man* was able to enter into the **t**, *3485*
16: 1 And I heard a great voice out of the **t** *3485*
16:17 there came a great voice out of the **t** of *3485*
Rev 21:22 And I saw no **t** therein: for the Lord God *3485*
21:22 God Almighty and the Lamb are the **t** of it. *3485*

TEMPLE SERVANTS See NETHINIMS

TEMPLES (9) [TEMPLE]

Jdg 4:21 smote the nail into his **t**, and fastened *it* into 7541
4:22 Sisera lay dead, and the nail *was* in his **t**. 7541
5:26 she had pierced and stricken through his **t**. 7541
SS 4: 3 thy **t** *are* like a piece of a pomegranate 7541
6: 7 As a piece of a pomegranate *are* thy **t** 7541
Hos 8:14 hath forgotten his Maker, and buildeth **t**; 1964
Joel 3: 5 have carried into your **t** my goodly pleasant 1964
Ac 7:48 Howbeit the most High dwelleth not in **t** *3485*
17:24 earth, dwelleth not in **t** made with hands; *3485*

TEMPORAL (1)

2Co 4:18 for the *things* which are seen *are* **t**; but *4340*

TEMPORARY See TEMPORAL

TEMPORARY RESIDENT See SOJOURN; SOJOURNED; SOJOURNER; SOJOURNERS; SOJOURNETH; SOJOURNING

TEMPT (14) [TEMPTATION, TEMPTATIONS, TEMPTED, TEMPTER, TEMPTETH, TEMPTING]

Ge 22: 1 that God did **t** Abraham, and said unto him, 5254
Ex 17: 2 with me? wherefore do ye **t** the LORD? 5254
Dt 6:16 Ye shall not **t** the LORD your God, as ye 5254
Isa 7:12 I will not ask, neither will I **t** the LORD. 5254
Mal 3:15 yea, *they that* **t** God are even delivered. 974
Mt 4: 7 Thou shalt not **t** the LORD thy God. *1598*
22:18 and said, Why **t** ye me, *ye* hypocrites? *3985*
Mk 12:15 said unto them, Why **t** ye me? *3985*
Lk 4:12 is said, Thou shalt not **t** the Lord thy God. *1598*
20:23 and said unto them, Why **t** ye me? *3985*
Ac 5: 9 How *is it* that ye have agreed together to **t** *3985*
15:10 Now therefore why **t** ye God, to put a yoke *3985*
1Co 7: 5 that Satan **t** you not for your incontinency. *3985*
10: 9 Neither let us **t** Christ, as some of them also *1598*

TEMPTATION (16) [TEMPT]

Ps 95: 8 *and* as *in* the day of **t** in the wilderness: 4531
Mt 6:13 And lead us not into **t**, but deliver us from *3986*
26:41 Watch and pray, that ye enter not into **t**: *3986*
Mk 14:38 Watch ye and pray, lest ye enter into **t**. *3986*
Lk 4:13 And when the devil had ended all the **t**, *3986*
8:13 a while believe, and in time of **t** fall away. *3986*
11: 4 And lead us not into **t**; but deliver us from *3986*
22:40 said unto them, Pray that *ye* enter not into **t**. *3986*
22:46 sleep ye? rise and pray, lest ye enter into **t**. *3986*
1Co 10:13 There hath no **t** taken you but such as is *3986*
10:13 will with the **t** also make a way to escape, *3986*
Gal 4:14 And my **t** which was in my flesh ye *3986*
1Ti 6: 9 But they that will be rich fall into **t** and *3986*
Heb 3: 8 in the day of **t** in the wilderness: *3986*
Jas 1:12 Blessed *is* the man that endureth **t**: *3986*
Rev 3:10 I also will keep thee from the hour of **t**, *3986*

TEMPTATIONS (8) [TEMPT]

Dt 4:34 by **t**, by signs, and by wonders, and by war, 4531
7:19 The great **t** which thine eyes saw, and 4531
29: 3 The great **t** which thine eyes have seen, 4531
Lk 22:28 which have continued with me in my **t**. *3986*
Ac 20:19 of mind, and *with* many tears, and **t**, *3986*
Jas 1: 2 count *it* all joy when ye fall into divers **t**; *3986*
1Pe 1: 6 ye are in heaviness through manifold **t**: *3986*
2Pe 2: 9 knoweth *how* to deliver the godly out of **t**, *3986*

TEMPTED (25) [TEMPT]

Ex 17: 7 because they **t** the LORD, saying, Is 5254
Nu 14:22 have **t** me *now* these ten times, and 5254
Dt 6:16 LORD your God, as ye **t** *him* in Massah. 5254
Ps 78:18 they **t** God in their heart by asking meat for 5254
78:41 they turned *back* and **t** God, and limited 5254
78:56 Yet they **t** and provoked the most high 5254
95: 9 When your fathers **t** me, proved me, and 5254
106:14 in the wilderness, and **t** God in the desert. 5254
Mt 4: 1 into the wilderness to be **t** of the devil. *3985*
Mk 1:13 in the wilderness forty days, **t** of Satan; *3985*
Lk 4: 2 Being forty days **t** of the devil. And in *3985*
10:25 lawyer stood up, and **t** him, saying, Master, *1598*
1Co 10: 9 as some of them also **t**, and were destroyed *3985*
10:13 who will not suffer you to be **t** above that *3985*
Gal 6: 1 considering thyself, lest thou also be **t**. *3985*
1Th 3: 5 lest by some means the tempter have **t** you, *3985*
Heb 2:18 For in that he himself hath suffered being **t**, *3985*
2:18 he is able to succour them that are **t**. *3985*
3: 9 When your fathers **t** me, proved me, and *3985*
4:15 was in all *points* **t** like as *we are, yet* *3985*
11:37 they were sawn asunder, were **t**, *3985*
Jas 1:13 Let no *man* say when he is **t**, I am tempted *3985*
1:13 *man* say when he is tempted, I am **t** of God: *3985*
1:13 for God **cannot be t** with evil, *551+1510*
1:14 But every man is **t**, when he is drawn away *3985*

TEMPTER (2) [TEMPT]

Mt 4: 3 And when the **t** came to him, he said, *3985*
1Th 3: 5 lest by some means the **t** have tempted you, *3985*

TEMPTETH (1) [TEMPT]

Jas 1:13 be tempted with evil, neither **t** he any *man*: *3985*

TEMPTING (7) [TEMPT]

Mt 16: 1 **t** desired him that *he* would shew them a *3985*
19: 3 came unto him, **t** him, and saying unto him, *3985*
22:35 asked *him a question*, **t** him, and saying, *3985*
Mk 8:11 seeking of him a sign from heaven, **t** him. *3985*
10: 2 for a man to put away *his* wife? **t** him. *3985*
Lk 11:16 **t** *him*, sought of him a sign from heaven. *3985*
Jn 8: 6 This they said, **t** him, that they might have *3985*

TEN (248) [TEN'S, TENS, TENTH]

Ge 5:14 of Cainan were nine hundred and **t** years: 6235
16: 3 after Abram had dwelt **t** years in the land of 6235
18:32 Peradventure **t** shall be found there. And he 6235
24:10 the servant took **t** camels of the camels of 6235
24:22 two bracelets for her hands of **t** *shekels* 6235
24:55 abide with us *a few* days, at the least **t**; 6218
31: 7 and changed my wages **t** times; 6235
31:41 and thou hast changed my wages **t** times. 6235
32:15 forty kine, and **t** bulls, twenty she asses, 6235
32:15 and ten bulls, twenty she asses, and **t** foals. 6235
42: 3 Joseph's **t** brethren went down to buy corn 6235
45:23 **t** asses laden with the good things of Egypt, 6235
45:23 **t** she asses laden with corn and bread and 6235
46:27 came into Egypt, *were* **threescore and t**. 7657
50: 3 mourned for him **threescore and t** 7657
50:22 and Joseph lived an hundred and **t** years. 6235
50:26 *being* an hundred and **t** years old: 6235
Ex 15:27 of water, and **threescore and t** palm trees: 7657
26: 1 *with* **t** curtains *of* fine twined linen, 6235
26:16 **T** cubits *shall be* the length of a board, and 6235
27:12 their pillars **t**, and their sockets ten. 6235
27:12 their pillars ten, and their sockets **t**. 6235
34:28 of the covenant, the **t** commandments. 6235
36: 8 made **t** curtains *of* fine twined linen, 6235
36:21 The length of a board *was* **t** cubits, and 6235
38:12 their pillars **t**, and their sockets ten; 6235
38:12 their pillars ten, and their sockets **t**; 6235
Lev 26: 8 an hundred of you shall put **t thousand** to 7233
26:26 **t** women shall bake your bread in one oven, 6235
27: 5 and for the female **t** shekels. 6235
27: 7 and for the female **t** shekels. 6235
Nu 7:14 One spoon of **t** *shekels* of gold, full *of* 6235
7:20 One spoon of gold of **t** *shekels*, full *of* 6235
7:26 One golden spoon of **t** *shekels*, full *of* 6235
7:32 One golden spoon *of* **t** *shekels*, full *of* 6235
7:38 One golden spoon of **t** *shekels*, full *of* 6235
7:44 One golden spoon of **t** *shekels*, full *of* 6235
7:50 One golden spoon of **t** *shekels*, full *of* 6235
7:56 One golden spoon of **t** *shekels*, full *of* 6235
7:62 One golden spoon of **t** *shekels*, full *of* 6235
7:68 One golden spoon of **t** *shekels*, full *of* 6235
7:74 One golden spoon of **t** *shekels*, full *of* 6235
7:80 One golden spoon of **t** *shekels*, full *of* 6235
7:86 full *of* incense, *weighing* **t** *shekels* apiece, 6235
11:19 nor two days, nor five days, neither **t** days, 6235
11:32 he that gathered least gathered **t** homers: 6235
14:22 have tempted me *now* these **t** times, and 6235
29:23 And on the fourth day **t** bullocks, two rams, 6235
33: 9 of water, and **threescore and t** palm trees; 7657
Dt 4:13 you to perform, *even* **t** commandments; 6235
10: 4 to the first writing, the **t** commandments, 6235
10:22 down into Egypt with **threescore and t** 7657
32:30 two put **t thousand** to flight, except their 7233
33: 2 and he came with **t thousands** of saints: 7233
33:17 they *are* the **t thousands** of Ephraim, and 7233
Jos 15:57 and Timnah; **t** cities with their villages. 6235
17: 5 there fell **t** portions to Manasseh, beside 6235
21: 5 out of the half tribe of Manasseh, **t** cities. 6235
21:26 All the cities *were* **t** with their suburbs for 6235
22:14 with him **t** princes, of each chief house a 6235
24:29 died, *being* an hundred and **t** years old. 6235
Jdg 1: 4 they slew *of* them in Bezek **t** thousand men. 6235
1: 7 **Threescore and t** kings, having their 7657
2: 8 died, *being* an hundred and **t** years old. 6235
3:29 they slew *of* Moab at that time about **t** 6235
4: 6 take with thee **t** thousand men of 6235
4:10 he went up with **t** thousand men at his feet: 6235
4:14 and **t** thousand men after him. 6235
6:27 Gideon took **t** men of his servants, and 6235
7: 3 and there remained **t** thousand. 6235
8:30 Gideon had **threescore and t** sons of his 7657
9: 2 *which are* **threescore and t** persons, 7657
9: 4 they gave him **threescore and t** *pieces* of 7657
9: 5 *being* **threescore and t** persons, upon one 7657
9:18 **threescore and t** persons, upon one stone, 7657
9:24 the cruelty *done* to the **threescore and t** 7657
12:11 judged Israel; and he judged Israel **t** years. 6235
12:14 that rode on **threescore and t** ass colts: 7651
17:10 I will give thee **t** *shekels* of silver by 6235
20:10 we will take **t** men of an hundred 6235
20:10 and a thousand out of **t thousand**, 7233
20:34 there came against Gibeah **t** thousand 6235
Ru 1: 4 and they dwelled there about **t** years. 6235
4: 2 he took **t** men of the elders of the city, and 6235
1Sa 1: 8 *am* not I better to thee than **t** sons? 6235
6:19 fifty thousand and **threescore and t** men: 7657
15: 4 and **t** thousand men of Judah. 6235
17:17 of this parched *corn*, and these **t** loaves, 6235
17:18 carry these **t** cheeses unto the captain of 6235
18: 7 his thousands, and David his **t thousands**. 7233
18: 8 have ascribed unto David **t thousands**, 7233
21:11 his thousands, and David his **t thousands**? 7233
25: 5 David sent out **t** young men, and 6235
25:38 it came to pass about **t** days *after*, that 6235
29: 5 his thousands, and David his **t thousands**? 7233
2Sa 15:16 the king left **t** women, *which were* 6235
18: 3 now *thou art* worth **t** thousand of us: 6235
18:11 I would have given thee **t** *shekels of* silver, 6235
18:15 **t** young men that bare Joab's armour 6235
19:43 We have **t** parts in the king, and we have 6235
20: 3 the king took the **t** women *his* concubines, 6235
1Ki 4:23 **T** fat oxen, and twenty oxen out of 6235
5:14 to Lebanon, **t** thousand a month *by* courses: 6235
5:15 Solomon had **threescore and t** thousand 7657
6: 3 **t** cubits *was* the breadth thereof before 6235
6:23 cherubims *of* olive tree, each **t** cubits high. 6235
6:24 the uttermost part of the other *were* **t** cubits. 6235
6:25 the other cherub *was* **t** cubits: both 6235
6:26 The height of the one cherub *was* **t** cubits, 6235
7:10 stones of **t** cubits, and stones of eight 6235
7:23 **t** cubits from the one brim to the other: 6235
7:24 **t** in a cubit, compassing the sea round 6235

1Ki 7:27 he made t bases of brass; four cubits *was* 6235
7:37 After this *manner* he made the t bases: 6235
7:38 made he t lavers of brass: one laver 6235
7:38 upon every one of the t bases one laver. 6235
7:43 the t bases, and ten lavers on the bases; 6235
7:43 the ten bases, and t lavers on the bases; 6235
11:31 he said to Jeroboam, Take thee t pieces: 6235
11:31 of Solomon, and will give t tribes to thee: 6235
11:35 and will give it unto thee, *even* t tribes. 6235
14: 3 take with thee t loaves, and cracknels, and 6235
2Ki 5: 5 took with him t talents of silver, and 6235
5: 5 *pieces* of gold, and t changes of raiment. 6235
13: 7 and t chariots, and ten thousand footmen; 6235
13: 7 and ten chariots, and t thousand footmen; 6235
14: 7 He slew *of* Edom in the valley of salt t 6235
15:17 over Israel, *and reigned* t years in Samaria. 6235
20: 9 shall the shadow go forward t degrees, or 6235
20: 9 forward ten degrees, or go back t degrees? 6235
20:10 thing for the shadow to go down t degrees: 6235
20:10 let the shadow return backward t degrees. 6235
20:11 he brought the shadow t degrees backward, 6235
24:14 *even* t thousand captives, and all 6240
25:25 and t men with him, and smote Gedaliah, 6235
1Ch 6:61 the half *tribe* of Manasseh, by lot, t cities. 6235
21: 5 Judah *was* four hundred **threescore and t** 7657
29: 7 thousand talents and t **thousand** drams, 7239
29: 7 *of* silver t thousand talents, and *of* brass 6235
2Ch 2: 2 Solomon told out **threescore and t** 7657
2:18 he set **threescore and t** thousand of them 7657
4: 1 and t cubits the height thereof. 6235
4: 2 Also he made a molten sea of t cubits from 6235
4: 3 t in a cubit, compassing the sea round 6235
4: 6 He made also t lavers, and put five on 6235
4: 7 he made t candlesticks of gold according to 6235
4: 8 He made also t tables, and placed *them* in 6235
14: 1 In his days the land was quiet t years. 6235
25:11 smote *of* the children of Seir t thousand. 6235
25:12 *other* t thousand *left* alive did the children 6235
27: 5 t thousand measures of wheat, and 6235
27: 5 of wheat, and t thousand of barley. 6235
29:32 was **threescore and t** bullocks, an hundred 7657
30:24 a thousand bullocks and t thousand sheep: 6235
36: 9 three months and t days in Jerusalem: 6235
36:21 to fulfil **threescore and t** years. 7657
Ezr 1:10 basons of a second sort four hundred and t, 6235
8:12 and with him an hundred and t males. 6235
8:24 and t of their brethren with them, 6235
Ne 4:12 by them came, they said unto us t times, 6235
5:18 and once in t days store of all *sorts of* wine: 6235
11: 1 to bring one of t to dwell in Jerusalem 6235
Est 3: 9 I will pay t thousand talents of silver to 6235
9:10 The t sons of Haman the son of 6235
9:12 the palace, and the t sons of Haman; 6235
9:13 let Haman's t sons be hanged upon 6235
9:14 and they hanged Haman's t sons. 6235
Job 19: 3 These t times have ye reproached me: 6235
Ps 3: 6 I will not be afraid of t **thousands** of 7233
33: 2 the psaltery *and* an **instrument of t strings.** 6218
90:10 of our years *are* **threescore** years **and t**; 7657
91: 7 thy side, and **t thousand** at thy right hand; 7233
92: 3 Upon an **instrument of t strings,** and 6218
144: 9 an **instrument of t strings** will I sing 6218
144:13 and **t thousands** in our streets: 7231
Ecc 7:19 Wisdom strengtheneth the wise more than t 6235
SS 5:10 and ruddy, the chiefest among t **thousand.** 7233
Isa 5:10 t acres of vineyard shall yield one bath, and 6235
38: 8 the sun dial of Ahaz, t degrees backward. 6235
38: 8 So the sun returned t degrees, by which 6235
Jer 41: 1 princes of the king, even t men with him, 6235
41: 2 the t men that were with him, and 6235
41: 8 t men were found among them that said 6235
42: 7 it came to pass after t days, that the word of 6235
Eze 40:11 the breadth of the entry of the gate, t cubits; 6235
41: 2 the breadth of the door *was* t cubits; and 6235
42: 4 before the chambers *was* a walk of t cubits 6235
45: 1 and the breadth *shall be* t thousand. 6235
45: 3 and the breadth of t thousand: 6235
45: 5 *the* t thousand of breadth, shall also 6235
45:14 out of the cor, *which is* a homer of t baths; 6235
45:14 homer of ten baths; *for* t baths *are* a homer: 6235
48: 9 *in* length, and *of* t thousand *in* breadth. 6235
48:10 and toward the west t thousand *in* breadth, 6235
48:10 toward the east t thousand *in* breadth, and 6235
48:13 *in* length, and t thousand *in* breadth: 6235
48:13 and the breadth t thousand. 6235
48:18 holy *portion shall be* t thousand eastward, 6235
48:18 and t thousand westward: 6235
Da 1:12 Prove thy servants, I beseech thee, t days; 6235
1:14 in this matter, and proved them t days. 6235
1:15 at the end of t days their countenances 6235
1:20 he found them t times better than all 6235
7: 7 that *were* before it; and it had t horns. 6236
7:10 **t thousand** times ten thousand stood before 7240
7:10 ten thousand times t **thousand** stood before 7240
7:20 of the t horns that *were* in his head, and 6236
7:24 the t horns out of this kingdom *are* ten 6236
7:24 the ten horns out of this kingdom *are* t 6236
11:12 and he shall cast down *many* t **thousands**: 7239
Am 5: 3 went forth *by* an hundred shall leave t, 6235
6: 9 if there remain t men in one house, 6235
Mic 6: 7 *or* with t **thousands** of rivers of oil? 7233
Hag 2:16 heap of twenty *measures*, there were *but* t: 6235
Zec 1:12 hast had indignation these **threescore and t** 7657
5: 2 and the breadth thereof t cubits. 6235
8:23 In those days *it shall come to pass,* that t 6235
Mt 18:24 which ought him **t thousand** talents. *3463*
20:24 And when the t heard *it,* they were moved *1176*
25: 1 of heaven be likened unto t virgins, *1176*
25:28 and give *it* unto him which hath t talents. *1176*
Mk 10:41 And when the t heard *it,* they began to be *1176*
Lk 14:31 consulteth whether he be able with t *1176*
15: 8 Either what woman having t pieces of *1176*
17:12 there met him t men *that were* lepers, *1176*
17:17 answering said, Were there not t cleansed? *1176*
19:13 And he called his t servants, and *1176*
Lk 19:13 and delivered them t pounds, and said unto *1176*
19:16 Lord, thy pound hath gained t pounds. *1176*
19:17 very little, have thou authority over t cities. *1176*
19:24 and give *it* to him that hath t pounds. *1176*
19:25 they said unto him, Lord, he hath t pounds.) *1176*
Ac 23:23 and horsemen **threescore** *and* t, and *1440*
25: 6 had tarried among them more than t days, *1176*
1Co 4:15 For though you have **t thousand** instructors *3463*
14:19 than **t thousand** words in an *unknown* *3463*
Jude 1:14 the Lord cometh with **t thousands** of his *3461*
Rev 2:10 and ye shall have tribulation t days: *1176*
5:11 the number of them was t **thousand** times *3461*
5:11 them was ten thousand times **t thousand,** *3461*
12: 3 having seven heads and t horns, and *1176*
13: 1 having seven heads and t horns, and *1176*
13: 1 and upon his horns t crowns, and upon his *1176*
17: 3 having seven heads and t horns. *1176*
17: 7 which hath the seven heads and t horns. *1176*
17:12 And the t horns which thou sawest are ten *1176*
17:12 And the ten horns which thou sawest are t *1176*
17:16 And the t horns which thou sawest upon *1176*

TEN'S (1) [TEN]

Ge 18:32 And he said, I will not destroy *it* for t sake. 6235

TEND (1) [TENDETH]

Pr 21: 5 The thoughts of the diligent *t* only to NIH

TENDER (40) [TENDERHEARTED, TENDERNESS]

Ge 18: 7 fetcht a calf t and good, and gave *it* unto a 7390
29:17 Leah was t eyed; but Rachel was beautiful 7390
33:13 My lord knoweth that the children *are* t, 7390
Dt 28:54 *So that* the man *that is* t among you, and 7390
28:56 The t and delicate *woman* among you, 7390
32: 2 as the small rain upon the t **herb,** and as 1877
2Sa 23: 4 *as* the t **grass** *springing* out of the earth by 1877
2Ki 22:19 Because thine heart was t, and thou hast 7401
1Ch 22: 5 Solomon my son *is* young and t, and 7390
29: 1 *is yet* young and t, and the work *is* great: 7390
2Ch 13: 7 when Rehoboam was young and t hearted, 7390
34:27 Because thine heart was t, and thou didst 7401
Job 14: 7 that the t **branch** thereof will not cease. 3127
38:27 to cause the bud of the t **herb** to spring 1877
Ps 25: 6 thy **t mercies** and thy lovingkindnesses; 7356
40:11 Withhold not thou thy **t mercies** from me, 7356
51: 1 of thy **t mercies** blot out my transgressions. 7356
69:16 according to the multitude of thy **t mercies.** 7356
77: 9 hath he in anger shut up his t **mercies**? 7356
79: 8 let thy **t mercies** speedily prevent us: 7356
103: 4 thee *with* lovingkindness and **t mercies;** 7356
119:77 Let thy **t mercies** come *unto* me, that I may 7356
119:156 Great *are* thy **t mercies,** O LORD: 7356
145: 9 and his **t mercies** *are* over all his works. 7356
Pr 4: 3 t and only *beloved* in the sight of my 7390
12:10 but the **t mercies** of the wicked *are* cruel. 7356
27:25 the **t grass** sheweth itself, and herbs of 1877
SS 2:13 the vines *with* the **t grape** give a *good* 5563
2:15 spoil the vines: for our vines *have* **t grapes.** 5563
7:12 *whether* the **t grape** appear, *and* 5563
Isa 47: 1 for thou shalt no more be called t and 7390
53: 2 he shall grow up before him as a **t plant,** 3126
Eze 17:22 off from the top of his young twigs a **t one,** 7390
Da 1: 9 and **t love** with the prince of the eunuchs. 7356
4:15 of iron and brass, in the **t grass** of the field; 1883
4:23 of iron and brass, in the **t grass** of the field; 1883
Mt 24:32 When his branch is yet t, and putteth forth *527*
Mk 13:28 When her branch is yet t, and putteth forth *527*
Lk 1:78 Through the **t mercy** of our God; *1650+4698*
Jas 5:11 that the Lord is very pitiful, and of **t mercy.** *3629*

TENDERHEARTED (1) [HEART, TENDER]

Eph 4:32 one to another, t, forgiving one another, *2155*

TENDERNESS (1) [TENDER]

Dt 28:56 foot upon the ground for delicateness and t, 7391

TENDETH (5) [TEND]

Pr 10:16 The labour of the righteous *t* to life: the fruit NIH
11:19 As righteousness *t* to life: so he that NIH
11:24 more than is meet, but *it t* to poverty. NIH
14:23 but the talk of the lips *t* only to penury. NIH
19:23 The fear of the LORD *t* to life: and *he that* NIH

TENONS (6)

Ex 26:17 Two t *shall there be* in one board, set in 3027
26:19 two sockets under one board for his two t, 3027
26:19 sockets under another board for his two t. 3027
36:22 One board had two t, equally distant one 3027
36:24 two sockets under one board for his two t, 3027
36:24 sockets under another board for his two t. 3027

TENOR (2)

Ge 43: 7 we told him according to the t of these 6310
Ex 34:27 for after the t of these words I have made a 6310

TENS (3) [TENS]

Ex 18:21 rulers of fifties, and rulers of t: 6235
18:25 of hundreds, rulers of fifties, and rulers of t. 6235
Dt 1:15 captains over t, and officers among your 6235

TENT (98) [TENTMAKERS, TENTS]

Ge 9:21 and he was uncovered within his t. 168
12: 8 pitched his t, *having* Beth-el on the west, 168
13: 3 unto the place where his t had been at 168
13:12 the plain, and **pitched** his t toward Sodom. 167
13:18 Abram **removed** his t, and came and 167
18: 1 he sat *in* the t door in the heat of the day; 168
18: 2 *them,* he ran to meet them from the t door, 168
18: 6 Abraham hastened into the t unto Sarah, 168
18: 9 thy wife? And he said, Behold, in the t. 168
18:10 Sarah heard *it in* the t door, which was 168
24:67 Isaac brought her into his mother Sarah's t, 168
26:17 **pitched** his t in the valley of Gerar, and 2583
26:25 name of the LORD, and pitched his t there: 168
Ge 31:25 Now Jacob had pitched his t in the mount: 168
31:33 Laban went into Jacob's t, and into Leah's 168
31:33 into Leah's t, and into the two maidservants' 168
31:33 went he out of Leah's t, and entered into 168
31:33 of Leah's tent, and entered into Rachel's t. 168
31:34 Laban searched all the t, but found *them* not. 168
33:18 and **pitched** his t before the city. 2583
33:19 a parcel of a field, where he had spread his t, 168
35:21 and spread his t beyond the tower of Edar. 168
Ex 18: 7 of *their* welfare; and they came into the t. 168
26:11 and couple the t together, that it may be one. 168
26:12 that remaineth of the curtains of the t, 168
26:13 in the length of the curtains of the t, 168
26:14 thou shalt make a covering for the t *of* rams' 168
26:36 shalt make a hanging for the door of the t, 168
33: 8 stood every man *at* his t door, and 168
33:10 and worshipped, every man *in* his t door. 168
35:11 his t, and his covering, his taches, and 168
36:14 he made curtains *of* goats' *hair* for the t over 168
36:18 he made fifty taches of brass to couple the t 168
36:19 he made a covering for the t *of* rams' skins 168
39:32 of the t of the congregation finished: 168
39:33 the t, and all his furniture, his taches, 168
39:40 the tabernacle, for the t of the congregation, 168
40: 2 the tabernacle of the t of the congregation. 168
40: 6 of the tabernacle of the t of the congregation. 168
40: 7 thou shalt set the laver between the t of 168
40:19 he spread abroad the t over the tabernacle, 168
40:19 and put the covering of the t above upon it; 168
40:22 he put the table in the t of the congregation, 168
40:24 he put the candlestick in the t of 168
40:26 he put the golden altar in the t of 168
40:29 of the tabernacle of the t of the congregation, 168
40:30 he set the laver between the t of 168
40:32 When they went into the t of 168
40:34 a cloud covered the t of the congregation, 168
40:35 Moses was not able to enter into the t of 168
Lev 14: 8 shall tarry abroad out of his t seven days. 168
Nu 3:25 the t, the covering thereof, and the hanging 168
9:15 *namely,* the t of the Testimony: 168
11:10 their families, every man in the door of his t: 168
19:14 This *is* the law, when a man dieth in a t: 168
19:14 all that come into the t, and all that *is* in 168
19:14 come into the tent, and all that *is* in the t, 168
19:18 sprinkle *it* upon the t, and upon all 168
25: 8 he went after the man of Israel into the t, 6898
Jos 7:21 they *are* hid in the earth in the midst of my t, 168
7:22 sent messengers, and they ran unto the t; 168
7:22 *it was* hid in his t, and the silver under it. 168
7:23 And they took them out of the midst of the t, 168
7:24 and his sheep, and his t, and all that he had: 168
Jdg 4:11 pitched his t unto the plain of Zaanaim, 168
4:17 Howbeit Sisera fled away on his feet to the t 168
4:18 when he had turned in unto her into the t, 168
4:20 Stand *in* the door of the t, and it shall be, 168
4:21 Jael Heber's wife took a nail of the t, and 168
4:22 when he came into her *t,* behold, Sisera lay NIH
5:24 blessed shall she be above women in the t. 168
7: 8 all *the rest of* Israel every man unto his t, 168
7:13 came unto a t, and smote it that it fell, and 168
7:13 it fell, and overturned it, that the t lay along. 168
20: 8 We will not any *of us* go to his t, 168
1Sa 4:10 and they fled every man into his t: 168
13: 2 rest of the people he sent every man to his t. 168
17:54 *to* Jerusalem; but he put his armour in his t. 168
2Sa 7: 6 but have walked in a t and in a tabernacle. 168
16:22 So they spread Absalom a t upon the top of 168
18:17 and all Israel fled every one to his t. 168
19: 8 for Israel had fled every man to his t. 168
20:22 they retired from the city, every man to his t. 168
2Ki 7: 8 they went into one t, and did eat and drink, 168
7: 8 entered into another t, and carried thence 168
1Ch 15: 1 for the ark of God, and pitched for it a t. 168
16: 1 set it in the midst of the t that David had 168
17: 5 have gone from t to tent, and from *one* 168
17: 5 have gone from tent to t, and from *one* 168
2Ch 1: 4 for he had pitched a t for it at Jerusalem. 168
25:22 and they fled every man to his t. 168
Ps 78:60 of Shiloh, the t *which* he placed among men; 168
Isa 13:20 neither shall the Arabian **pitch t** there; 167
38:12 and is removed from me as a shepherd's t: 168
40:22 and spreadeth them out as a t to dwell in: 168
54: 2 Enlarge the place of thy t, and let them 168
Jer 10:20 *there is* none to stretch forth my t any more, 168
37:10 *yet* should they rise up every man in his t, 168

TENTH (81) [TENS]

Ge 8: 5 the waters decreased continually until the t 6224
8: 5 in the t *month,* on the first *day* of 6224
28:22 me I will **surely give the t** unto thee. 6237+6237
Ex 12: 3 In the t *day* of this month they shall take to 6218
16:36 Now an omer *is* the t *part* of an ephah. 6224
29:40 with the one lamb a **t deal** of flour mingled 6241
Lev 5:11 t *part* of an ephah of fine flour for a sin 6224
6:20 the t *part* of an ephah of fine flour *for* a 6224
14:10 **three t deals** of fine flour *for* a meat 6241+7969
14:21 **one t deal** of fine flour mingled with 259+6241
16:29 on the t *day* of the month, ye shall afflict 6218
23:13 two **t deals** *of* fine flour mingled with oil, 6241
23:17 habitations two wave loaves of two **t deals**: 6241
23:27 Also on the t *day* of this seventh month 6218
24: 5 two **t deals** shall be *in* one cake. 6241
25: 9 to sound on the t *day* of the seventh month, 6218
27:32 the t shall be holy unto the LORD. 6224
Nu 5:15 the t *part* of an ephah of barley meal; 6224
7:66 On the t day Ahiezer the son of 6224
15: 4 **t deal** *of* flour mingled with the fourth *part* 6241
15: 6 **t deals** *of* flour mingled with the third *part* 6241
15: 9 **t deals** *of* flour mingled with half a hin of 6241
18:21 I have given the children of Levi all the t in 4643
18:26 it for the LORD, *even* a t *part* of the tithe. 4643
28: 5 a t *part* of an ephah *of* flour for a meat 6224
28: 9 and two **t deals** *of* flour *for* a meat offering, 6241
28:12 three **t deals** *of* flour *for* a meat offering, 6241
28:12 and two **t deals** *of* flour *for* a meat offering, 6241

T

Nu 28:13 a **several t deal** of flour mingled 6241+6241
28:20 three **t deals** shall ye offer for a bullock, 6241
28:20 for a bullock, and two **t deals** for a ram; 6241
28:21 A **several t deal** shalt thou offer for 6241+6241
28:28 three **t deals** unto one bullock, two tenth 6241
28:28 unto one bullock, two **t deals** unto one ram, 6241
28:29 A **several t deal** unto one lamb, 6241+6241
29: 3 three **t deals** for a bullock, *and* two tenth 6241
29: 3 for a bullock, *and* two **t deals** for a ram, 6241
29: 4 one **t deal** for one lamb, throughout 6241
29: 7 ye shall have on the **t** *day* of this seventh 6218
29: 9 three **t deals** to a bullock, *and* two tenth 6241
29: 9 to a bullock, *and* two **t deals** to one ram, 6241
29:10 A **several t deal** for one lamb, 6241+6241
29:14 three **t deals** unto every bullock of 6241
29:14 two **t deals** to each ram of the two rams, 6241
29:15 a **several t deal** to each lamb of 6241+6241
Dt 23: 2 even *to* his **t** generation shall he not enter 6224
23: 3 even *to* their **t** generation shall they not 6224
Jos 4:19 the people came up out of Jordan on the **t** 6218
1Sa 8:15 he will **take the t** of your seed, and of your 6237
8:17 He will **take the t** of your sheep: and 6237
2Ki 25: 1 in the **t** month, in the tenth *day* of 6224
25: 1 the tenth month, in the **t** *day* of the month, 6218
1Ch 12:13 Jeremiah the **t**, Machbanai the eleventh. 6224
24:11 The ninth to Jeshua, the **t** to Shecaniah, 6224
25:17 The **t** *to* Shimei, *he,* his sons, and 6224
27:13 The **t** *captain* for the tenth month *was* 6224
27:13 The tenth *captain* for the **t** month *was* 6224
Ezr 10:16 sat down in the first day of the **t** month to 6224
Est 2:16 into his house royal in the **t** month, 6224
Isa 6:13 yet in it *shall be* a **t**, and *it* shall return, and 6224
Jer 32: 1 in the **t** year of Zedekiah king of Judah, 6224
39: 1 in the **t** month, came Nebuchadrezzar king 6224
52: 4 in the **t** month, in the tenth *day* of 6224
52: 4 the tenth month, in the **t** *day* of the month, 6218
52:12 the fifth month, in the **t** *day* of the month, 6218
Eze 20: 1 in the fifth *month,* the **t** *day* of the month, 6218
24: 1 Again in the ninth year, in the **t** month, 6224
24: 1 the tenth month, in the **t** *day* of the month, 6218
29: 1 In the **t** year, in the tenth *month,* in 6224
29: 1 in the **t** *month,* in the twelfth *day* of 6224
33:21 in the **t** *month,* in the fifth *day* of 6224
40: 1 of the year, in the **t** *day* of the month, 6218
45:11 that the bath may contain the **t part** of a 4643
45:11 and the ephah the **t** *part* of a homer: 6224
45:14 *ye shall offer* the **t part** of a bath out of 4643
Zec 8:19 the fast of the seventh, and the fast of the **t**, 6224
Jn 1:39 him that day: for it was about the **t** hour. *1182*
Heb 7: 2 To whom also Abraham gave a **t** *part* of all; *1181*
7: 4 patriarch Abraham gave the **t** of the spoils. *1181*
Rev 11:13 and the **t** *part* of the city fell, and in *1182*
21:20 the ninth, a topaz; the **t**, a chrysoprasus; *1182*

TENTMAKERS (1) [MAKE, TENT]

Ac 18: 3 for *by* their occupation they were **t**. *4635*

TENTS (66) [TENT]

Ge 4:20 he was the father of such as dwell in **t**, and 168
9:27 and he shall dwell in the **t** of Shem; 168
13: 5 with Abram, had flocks, and herds, and **t**. 168
25:27 and Jacob *was* a plain man, dwelling in **t**. 168
31:33 and into the two maidservants' **t**; 168
Ex 16:16 ye every man for *them* which *are* in his **t**. 168
Nu 1:52 the children of Israel shall **pitch** their **t**, 2583
9:17 there the children of Israel **pitched** their **t**. 2583
9:18 upon the tabernacle they **rested in** the **t**. 2583
9:20 of the LORD they **abode in** their **t**, 2583
9:22 the children of Israel **abode in** their **t**, and 2583
9:23 of the LORD they **rested in** the **t**, 2583
13:19 dwell in, whether in **t**, or in strong holds; 4264
16:26 from the **t** of these wicked men, and 168
16:27 stood *in* the door of their **t**, and their wives, 168
24: 2 he saw Israel abiding *in his* **t** according to NIH
24: 5 How goodly are thy **t**, O Jacob, *and* 168
Dt 1:27 ye murmured in your **t**, and said, 168
1:33 to search you out a place to **pitch** your **t** *in,* 2583
5:30 Go say to them, Get you into your **t** again. 168
11: 6 their **t**, and all the substance that *was* in their 168
16: 7 shalt turn in the morning, and go unto thy **t**. 168
33:18 in thy going out; and, Issachar, in thy **t**. 168
Jos 3:14 when the people removed from their **t**, 168
22: 4 get ye unto your **t**, *and* unto the land of your 168
22: 6 sent them away: and they went unto their **t**. 168
22: 7 Joshua sent them away also unto their **t**, 168
22: 8 Return with much riches unto your **t**, and 168
Jdg 6: 5 they came up with their cattle and their **t**, 168
8:11 of them that dwelt in **t** on the east of Nobah 168
1Sa 17:53 the Philistines, and they spoiled their **t**. 4264
2Sa 11:11 The ark, and Israel, and Judah, abide in **t**; 5521
20: 1 the son of Jesse: every man to his **t**, O Israel. 168
1Ki 8:66 went unto their **t** joyful and glad of heart for 168
12:16 to your **t**, O Israel: now see to thine own 168
12:16 David. So Israel departed unto their **t**. 168
2Ki 7: 7 left their **t**, and their horses, and their asses, 168
7:10 and asses tied, and the **t** as they *were.* 168
7:16 went out, and spoiled the **t** of the Syrians. 4264
8:21 the chariots: and the people fled into their **t**. 168
13: 5 the children of Israel dwelt in their **t**, 168
14:12 and they fled every man to their **t**. 168
1Ch 4:41 smote their **t**, and the habitations that were 168
5:10 they dwelt in their **t** throughout all the east 168
2Ch 7:10 month he sent the people away into their **t**, 168
10:16 every man to your **t**, O Israel: *and* now, 168
10:16 thine own house. So all Israel went to their **t**. 168
14:15 They smote also the **t** of cattle, and 168
31: 2 to praise in the gates of the **t** of 4264
Ezr 8:15 and there **abode** we **in t** three days: 2583
Ps 69:25 be desolate; *and* let none dwell in their **t**. 168
78:55 made the tribes of Israel to dwell in their **t**. 168
84:10 than to dwell in the **t** of wickedness. 168
106:25 murmured in their **t**, *and* hearkened not unto 168
120: 5 *in* Mesech, *that* I dwell in the **t** of Kedar! 168
SS 1: 5 as the **t** of Kedar, as the curtains of Solomon. 168
1: 8 and feed thy kids beside the shepherds' **t**. 4908
Jer 4:20 suddenly are my **t** spoiled, *and* my curtains 168
6: 3 they shall pitch *their* **t** against her round 168
30:18 I *will* bring again the captivity of Jacob's **t**, 168
35: 7 but all your days ye shall dwell in **t**; 168
35:10 we have dwelt in **t**, and have obeyed, and 168
49:29 Their **t** and their flocks shall they take *away:* 168
Hab 3: 7 I saw the **t** of Cushan in affliction: *and* 168
Zec 12: 7 The LORD also shall save the **t** of Judah 168
14:15 and of all the beasts that shall be in these **t**, 4264

TERAH (11) [THARA]

Ge 11:24 lived nine and twenty years, and begat **T**: 8646
11:25 Nahor lived after he begat **T** an hundred 8646
11:26 **T** lived seventy years, and begat Abram, 8646
11:27 Now these *are* the generations of **T**: 8646
11:27 **T** begat Abram, Nahor, and Haran; and 8646
11:28 Haran died before his father **T** in the land 8646
11:31 **T** took Abram his son, and Lot the son of 8646
11:32 the days of **T** were two hundred and 8646
11:32 five years: and **T** died in Haran. 8646
Jos 24: 2 *even* **T**, the father of Abraham, and 8646
1Ch 1:26 Serug, Nahor, **T**, 8646

TERAPHIM (6)

Jdg 17: 5 and **t**, and consecrated one of his sons, 8655
18:14 **t**, and a graven image, and a molten image? 8655
18:17 the ephod, and the **t**, and the molten image: 8655
18:18 the ephod, and the **t**, and the molten image. 8655
18:20 the **t**, and the graven image, and went in 8655
Hos 3: 4 and without an ephod, and *without* **t**: 8655

TEREBINTH See TEIL

TERESH (2)

Est 2:21 Bigthan and **T**, of those which kept 8657
6: 2 that Mordecai had told of Bigthana and **T**, 8657

TERMED (2)

Isa 62: 4 Thou shalt no more be **t** Forsaken; 559
62: 4 neither shall thy land any more be **t** 559

TERRACES (1)

2Ch 9:11 the king made *of* the algum trees **t** to 4546

TERRESTRIAL (2)

1Co 15:40 *are* also celestial bodies, and bodies **t**: *1919*
15:40 *is* one, and the *glory* of the **t** *is* another. *1919*

TERRIBLE (52) [TERRIFY]

Ex 34:10 for it *is* a **t** thing that I will do with thee. 3372
Dt 1:19 *through* all that great and **t** wilderness, 3372
7:21 thy God *is* among you, a mighty God and **t**. 3372
8:15 led thee through *that* great and **t** wilderness, 3372
10:17 of lords, a great God, a mighty, and a **t**, 3372
10:21 and **t** *things,* which thine eyes have seen. 3372
Jdg 13: 6 the countenance of an angel of God, very **t**: 3372
2Sa 7:23 to do for you great things and **t**, for thy 3372
Ne 1: 5 the great and **t** God, that keepeth covenant 3372
4:14 *which is* great and **t**, and fight for your 3372
9:32 the great, the mighty, and the **t** God, 3372
Job 37:22 out of the north: with God *is* **t** majesty. 3372
39:20 a grasshopper? the glory of his nostrils *is* **t**. 367
41:14 doors of his face? his teeth *are* **t** round about. 367
Ps 45: 4 and thy right hand shall teach thee **t** *things.* 3372
47: 2 For the LORD most High *is* **t**; *he is* a 3372
65: 5 *By* **t** *things* in righteousness wilt thou 3372
66: 3 Say unto God, How **t** *art thou in* thy works! 3372
66: 5 *he is* **t** *in his* doing toward the children of 3372
68:35 O God, *thou art* **t** out of thy holy places: 3372
76:12 of princes: *he is* **t** to the kings of the earth. 3372
99: 3 Let them praise thy great and **t** name; *for* it 3372
106:22 land of Ham, *and* **t** *things* by the Red sea. 3372
145: 6 *men* shall speak of the might of thy **t acts**: 3372
SS 6: 4 as Jerusalem, **t** as *an army* with banners. 366
6:10 as the sun, *and* **t** as *an army* with banners? 366
Isa 13:11 and will lay low the haughtiness of the **t**. 6184
18: 2 to a people **t** from their beginning hitherto; 3372
18: 7 from a people **t** from their beginning 3372
21: 1 *so* it cometh from the desert, from a **t** land. 3372
25: 3 the city of the **t** nations shall fear thee. 6184
25: 4 when the blast of the **t ones** *is* as a storm 6184
25: 5 the branch of the **t ones** shall be brought 6184
29: 5 the multitude of the **t ones** *shall be* as chaff 6184
29:20 For the **t one** is brought **to nought**, and 6184
49:25 and the prey of the **t** shall be delivered: 6184
64: 3 When thou didst **t things** *which* we looked 3372
Jer 15:21 I will redeem thee out of the hand of the **t**. 6184
20:11 the LORD *is* with me as a mighty **t one**: 6184
La 5:10 black like an oven because of the **t** famine. 2152
Eze 1:22 creature *was* as the colour of the **t** crystal, 3372
28: 7 strangers upon thee, the **t** of the nations: 6184
30:11 his people with him, the **t** of the nations, 6184
31:12 strangers, the **t** of the nations, have cut him 6184
32:12 to fall, the **t** of the nations, all of them: 6184
Da 2:31 before thee; and the form thereof *was* **t**. 1763
7: 7 dreadful and **t**, and strong exceedingly; 574
Joel 2:11 the day of the LORD *is* great and very **t**; 3372
2:31 and the **t** day of the LORD come. 3372
Hab 1: 7 They *are* **t** and dreadful: their judgment and 366
Zep 2:11 The LORD *will be* **t** unto them: for he will 3372
Heb 12:21 And so **t** was the sight, *that* Moses said, *5398*

TERRIBLENESS (3) [TERRIFY]

Dt 26: 8 with great **t**, and with signs, and 4172
1Ch 17:21 to make thee a name of greatness and **t**, 3372
Jer 49:16 Thy **t** hath deceived thee, *and* the pride of 8606

TERRIBLY (3) [TERRIFY]

Isa 2:19 when he ariseth to **shake t** the earth. 6206
2:21 when he ariseth to **shake t** the earth. 6206
Na 2: 3 and the fir trees shall be **t shaken**. 7477

TERRIFIED (4) [TERRIFY]

Dt 20: 3 neither be ye **t** because of them; 6206
Lk 21: 9 hear of wars and commotions, be not **t**: *4422*
24:37 But they were **t** and affrighted, and *4422*
Php 1:28 And in nothing **t** by *your* adversaries: *4426*

TERRIFIEST (1) [TERRIFY]

Job 7:14 me with dreams, and **t** me through visions: 1204

TERRIFY (4) [TERRIBLE, TERRIBLENESS, TERRIBLY, TERRIFIED, TERRIFIEST, TERROR, TERRORS]

Job 3: 5 upon it; let the blackness of the day **t** it. 1204
9:34 away from me, and let not his fear **t** me: 1204
31:34 or did the contempt of families **t** me, that I 2865
2Co 10: 9 That I may not seem as if *I* would **t** you by *1629*

TERROR (29) [TERRIFY]

Ge 35: 5 the **t** of God was upon the cities that *were* 2847
Lev 26:16 I will even appoint over you **t**, consumption, 928
Dt 32:25 The sword without, and **t** within, 367
34:12 in all the great **t** which Moses shewed in 4172
Jos 2: 9 that your **t** is fallen upon us, and that all 367
Job 31:23 For destruction from God *was* a **t** to me, 6343
33: 7 Behold, my **t** shall not make thee afraid, 367
Ps 91: 5 Thou shalt not be afraid for the **t** by night; 6343
Isa 10:33 of hosts, shall lop the bough with **t**: 4637
19:17 the land of Judah shall be a **t** unto Egypt, 2283
33:18 Thine heart shall meditate **t**. Where *is* 367
54:14 and from **t**; for it shall not come near thee. 4288
Jer 17:17 Be not a **t** unto me: thou *art* my hope in 4288
20: 4 I will make thee a **t** to thyself, and to all thy 4032
32:21 with a stretched out arm, and with great **t**; 4172
Eze 26:17 which cause their **t** *to be* on all that haunt it. 2851
26:21 I will make thee a **t**, and thou *shalt be* no 1091
27:36 thou shalt be a **t**, and never *shalt be* any 1091
28:19 thou shalt be a **t**, and never *shalt* thou *be* 1091
32:23 which caused **t** in the land of the living. 2851
32:24 which caused their **t** in the land of 2851
32:25 though their **t** was caused in the land of 2851
32:26 though they caused their **t** in the land of 2851
32:27 though *they were* the **t** of the mighty in 2851
32:30 with their **t** *they are* ashamed of their 2851
32:32 For I have caused my **t** in the land of 2851
Ro 13: 3 For rulers are not a **t** to good works, but *5401*
2Co 5:11 Knowing therefore the **t** of the Lord, *5401*
1Pe 3:14 happy *are ye:* and be not afraid of their **t**, *5401*

TERRORS (15) [TERRIFY]

Dt 4:34 and by a stretched out arm, and by great **t**, 4172
Job 6: 4 the **t** of God do set *themselves* in array 1161
18:11 **T** shall make him afraid on every side, and 1091
18:14 and it shall bring him to the king of **t**. 1091
20:25 sword cometh out of his gall: **t** *are* upon him. 367
24:17 if *one* know *them, they are in* the **t** of 1091
27:20 **T** take hold on him as waters, a tempest 1091
30:15 **T** are turned upon me: they pursue my soul 1091
Ps 55: 4 and the **t** of death are fallen upon me. 367
73:19 they are utterly consumed with **t**. 1091
88:15 youth *up: while* I suffer thy **t** I am distracted. 367
88:16 wrath goeth over me; thy **t** have cut me off. 1161
Jer 15: 8 to fall upon it suddenly, and **t** *upon* the city. 928
La 2:22 Thou hast called as *in* a solemn day my **t** 4032
Eze 21:12 **t** by reason of the sword shall be upon my 4048

TERTIUS (1)

Ro 16:22 I **T**, who wrote *this* epistle, salute you in *5060*

TERTULLUS (2)

Ac 24: 1 and *with* a certain orator *named* **T**, *5061*
24: 2 And when he was called *forth,* **T** began to *5061*

TESTAMENT (14) [TESTIFY]

Mt 26:28 For this is my blood of the new **t**, which is *1242*
Mk 14:24 unto them, This is my blood of the new **t**, *1242*
Lk 22:20 saying, This cup *is* the new **t** in my blood, *1242*
1Co 11:25 saying, This cup is the new **t** in my blood: *1242*
2Co 3: 6 hath made us able ministers of the new **t**; *1242*
3:14 untaken away in the reading of the old **t**; *1242*
Heb 7:22 much was Jesus made a surety of a better **t**. *1242*
9:15 this cause he is the mediator of the new **t**, *1242*
9:15 transgressions that were under the first **t**, *1242*
9:16 For where a **t** *is,* there must also of *1242*
9:17 For a **t** *is* of force after *men* are dead: *1242*
9:18 Whereupon neither the first *t* was dedicated NIG
9:20 This *is* the blood of the **t** which God hath *1242*
Rev 11:19 was seen in his temple the ark of his **t**: *1242*

TESTATOR (2) [TESTIFY]

Heb 9:16 must also of necessity be the death of the **t**. *1303*
9:17 it is of no strength at all whilst the **t** liveth. *1303*

TESTIFIED (24) [TESTIFY]

Ex 21:29 it hath been **t** to his owner, and he hath not 5749
Dt 19:18 *and* hath **t** falsely against his brother; 6030
Ru 1:21 seeing the LORD hath **t** against me, and 6030
2Sa 1:16 for thy mouth hath **t** against thee, saying, 6030
2Ki 17:13 Yet the LORD **t** against Israel, and 5749
17:15 his testimonies which he **t** against them; 5749
2Ch 24:19 unto the LORD; and they **t** against them: 5749
Ne 9:26 slew thy prophets which **t** against them to 5749
13:15 I **t** *against them* in the day wherein they 5749
13:21 I **t** against them, and said unto them, 5749
Jn 4:39 which **t**, He told me all that ever I did. *3140*
4:44 For Jesus himself **t**, that a prophet hath no *3140*
13:21 and **t**, and said, Verily, verily, I say unto *3140*
Ac 8:25 when they had **t** and preached the word of *1263*
18: 5 and **t** to the Jews *that* Jesus *was* Christ. *1263*
23:11 for as thou hast **t** of me in Jerusalem, so *1263*
28:23 he expounded and **t** the kingdom of God, *1263*
1Co 15:15 we have **t** of God that he raised up Christ: *3140*
1Th 4: 6 as we also have forewarned you and **t**. *1263*
1Ti 2: 6 a ransom for all, to be **t** in due time. *3142*
Heb 2: 6 But one in a certain place **t**, saying, What is *1263*
1Pe 1:11 when it **t beforehand** the sufferings of *4303*
1Jn 5: 9 witness of God which he hath **t** of his Son. *3140*
3Jn 1: 3 and **t** of the truth *that is* in thee, *3140*

TESTIFIEDST (2) [TESTIFY]
Ne 9:29 t against them, that *thou* mightest bring 5749
9:30 t against them by thy spirit in thy prophets: 5749

TESTIFIETH (5) [TESTIFY]
Hos 7:10 the pride of Israel t to his face: and they do 6030
Jn 3:32 And what he hath seen and heard, that he t; 3140
21:24 This is the disciple which t of these *things,* 3140
Heb 7:17 For *he* t, Thou *art* a priest for ever after 3140
Rev 22:20 He which t these *things* saith, Surely I 3140

TESTIFY (29) [TESTAMENT, TESTATOR, TESTIFIED, TESTIFIEDST, TESTIFIETH, TESTIFYING, TESTIMONIES, TESTIMONY]
Nu 35:30 one witness shall not t against *any* person 6030
Dt 8:19 I t against you *this* day that ye shall surely 5749
19:16 man to t against him *that which is* wrong; 6030
31:21 that this song shall t against them as a 6030
32:46 Set your hearts unto all the words which I t 5749
Ne 9:34 where*with* thou didst t against them. 5749
Job 15: 6 and not I; yea, thine own lips t against thee. 6030
Ps 50: 7 O Israel, and I will t against thee: 5749
81: 8 Hear, O my people, and I will t unto thee: 5749
Isa 59:12 before thee, and our sins t against us: 6030
Jer 14: 7 though our iniquities t against us, 6030
Hos 5: 5 the pride of Israel doth t to his face: 6030
Am 3:13 Hear ye, and t in the house of Jacob, 5749
Mic 6: 3 wherein have I wearied thee? t against me. 6030
Lk 16:28 that he may t unto them, lest they also 1263
Jn 2:25 And needed not that any should t of man: 3140
3:11 that we do know, and t that we have seen; 3140
5:39 and they are they which t of me. 3140
7: 7 but me it hateth, because I t of it, that 3140
15:26 from the Father, he shall t of me: 3140
Ac 2:40 And with many other words did he t and 1263
10:42 to t that it is he which was ordained of God 1263
20:24 to t the gospel of the grace of God. 1263
26: 5 me from the beginning, if they would t, 3140
Gal 5: 3 For I t again to every man that is 3143
Eph 4:17 This I say therefore, and t in the Lord, 3143
1Jn 4:14 do t that the Father sent the Son *to be* 3140
Rev 22:16 I Jesus have sent mine angel to t unto you 3140
22:18 For I t unto every *man* that heareth 4828

TESTIFYING (3) [TESTIFY]
Ac 20:21 T both to the Jews, and *also* to the Greeks, 1263
Heb 11: 4 that he was righteous, God t of his gifts: 3140
1Pe 5:12 t that this is the true grace of God wherein 1957

TESTIMONIES (36) [TESTIFY]
Dt 4:45 These *are* the t, and the statutes, and 5713
6:17 his t, and his statutes, which he hath 5713
6:20 What *mean* the t, and the statutes, and 5713
1Ki 2: 3 and his judgments, and his t, 5715
2Ki 17:15 and his t which he testified against them; 5715
23: 3 to keep his commandments and his t and 5715
1Ch 29:19 thy t, and thy statutes, and to do all *these* 5715
2Ch 34:31 and his t, and his statutes, with all his heart, 5715
Ne 9:34 unto thy commandments and thy t, 5715
Ps 25:10 unto such as keep his covenant and his t. 5713
78:56 the most high God, and kept not his t: 5713
93: 5 Thy t are very sure: holiness becometh 5713
99: 7 they kept his t, and the ordinance *that* he 5713
119: 2 Blessed *are* they that keep his t, *and* 5713
119:14 I have rejoiced in the way of thy t, as *much* 5715
119:22 and contempt; for I have kept thy t. 5713
119:24 Thy t also *are* my delight *and* 5713
119:31 I have stuck unto thy t: O LORD, put me 5715
119:36 Incline my heart unto thy t, and not to 5715
119:46 I will speak of thy t also before kings, and 5713
119:59 on my ways, and turned my feet unto thy t. 5713
119:79 unto me, and those that have known thy t. 5713
119:95 me to destroy me: *but* I will consider thy t. 5713
119:99 my teachers: for thy t *are* my meditation. 5715
119:111 Thy t have I taken as an heritage for ever: 5715
119:119 the earth *like* dross: therefore I love thy t. 5713
119:125 me understanding, that I may know thy t. 5713
119:129 Thy t *are* wonderful: therefore doth my 5715
119:138 Thy t *that* thou hast commanded *are* 5713
119:144 The righteousness of thy t *is* everlasting: 5715
119:146 unto thee; save me, and I shall keep thy t. 5713
119:152 Concerning thy t, I have known of old that 5713
119:157 *yet* do I not decline from thy t. 5715
119:167 My soul hath kept thy t; and *I* love them 5713
119:168 I have kept thy precepts and thy t: for all 5713
Jer 44:23 in his law, nor in his statutes, nor in his t; 5715

TESTIMONY (76) [TESTIFY]
Ex 16:34 so Aaron laid it up before the T, to be kept. 5715
25:16 thou shalt put into the ark the T which I 5715
25:21 in the ark thou shalt put the T that I shall 5715
25:22 cherubims which *are* upon the ark of the T, 5715
26:33 in thither within the vail the ark of the T: 5715
26:34 the ark of the T in the most holy *place.* 5715
27:21 which *is* before the T, Aaron and his sons 5715
30: 6 it before the vail that *is* by the ark of the T, 5715
30: 6 before the mercy seat that *is* over the T, 5715
30:26 and the ark of the T, 5715
30:36 put of it before the T in the tabernacle of 5715
31: 7 the ark of the T, and the mercy seat that *is* 5715
31:18 two tables of T, tables of stone, 5715
32:15 the two tables of the T *were* in his hand: 5715
34:29 with the two tables of T in Moses' hand, 5715
38:21 *even* of the tabernacle of T, as it was 5715
39:35 The ark of the T, and the staves thereof, 5715
40: 3 thou shalt put therein the ark of the T, and 5715
40: 5 gold for the incense before the ark of the T, 5715
40:20 he took and put the T into the ark, and 5715
40:21 the covering, and covered the ark of the T; 5715
Lev 16:13 cover the mercy seat that *is* upon the T, 5715
24: 3 Without the vail of the T, in the tabernacle 5715
Nu 1:50 the Levites over the tabernacle of T, 5715
1:53 shall pitch round about the tabernacle of T, 5715
Nu 1:53 shall keep the charge of the tabernacle of T. 5715
4: 5 and cover the ark of T with it: 5715
7:89 the mercy seat that *was* upon the ark of T, 5715
9:15 the tabernacle, *namely,* the tent of the T: 5715
10:11 taken up from off the tabernacle of the T. 5715
17: 4 tabernacle of the congregation before the T, 5715
17:10 Bring Aaron's rod again before the T, 5715
Jos 4:16 the priests that bear the ark of the T, 5715
Ru 4: 7 to his neighbour: and this *was* a t in Israel. 8584
2Ki 11:12 the crown upon him, and *gave him* the T; 5715
2Ch 23:11 and *gave him* the T, and made him king. 5715
Ps 19: 7 the t of the LORD *is* sure, making wise 5715
78: 5 For he established a t in Jacob, and 5715
81: 5 This he ordained in Joseph *for* a t, when he 5715
119:88 so shall I keep the t of thy mouth. 5715
122: 4 tribes of the LORD, *unto* the t of Israel, 5715
132:12 and my t that I shall teach them, 5713
Isa 8:16 Bind up the t, seal the law among my 8584
8:20 To the law and to the t: if they speak not 8584
Mt 8: 4 offer the gift that Moses commanded for a t 3142
10:18 for a t against them and the Gentiles. 3142
Mk 1:44 Moses commanded, for a t unto them. 3142
6:11 shake off the dust under your feet for a t 3142
13: 9 and kings for my sake, for a t against them. 3142
Lk 5:14 as Moses commanded, for a t unto them. 3142
9: 5 dust from your feet for a t against them. 3142
21:13 And it shall turn to you for a t. 3142
Jn 3:32 he testifieth; and no *man* receiveth his t. 3141
3:33 He that hath received his t hath set to *his* 3141
5:34 But I receive not t from man: 3141
8:17 in your law, that the t of two men is true. 3141
21:24 these *things:* and we know that his t is true. 3141
Ac 13:22 to whom also he **gave** t, and said, I have 3140
14: 3 which **gave** t unto the word of his grace, 3140
22:18 for they will not receive thy t concerning 3141
1Co 1: 6 Even as the t of Christ was confirmed in 3142
2: 1 declaring unto you the t of God. 3142
2Co 1:12 the t of our conscience, that in simplicity 3142
2Th 1:10 (because our t among you was believed) 3142
2Ti 1: 8 therefore ashamed of the t of our Lord, 3142
Heb 3: 5 for a t of those *things* which were to be 3142
11: 5 for before his translation he had this t, 3140
Rev 1: 2 and of the t of Jesus Christ, and of all 3141
1: 9 word of God, and for the t of Jesus Christ. 3141
6: 9 word of God, and for the t which they held: 3141
11: 7 And when they shall have finished their t, 3141
12:11 of the Lamb, and by the word of their t; 3141
12:17 of God, and have the t of Jesus Christ. 3141
15: 5 the temple of the tabernacle of the t in 3142
19:10 and of thy brethren that have the t of Jesus: 3141
19:10 for the t of Jesus is the spirit of prophecy. 3141

TETRARCH (7)
Mt 14: 1 At that time Herod the t heard of the fame 5076
Lk 3: 1 and Herod being t of Galilee, and 5075
3: 1 and his brother Philip t of Iturea and of 5075
3: 1 and Lysanias the t of Abilene, 5075
3:19 But Herod the t, being reproved by him for 5076
9: 7 Now Herod the t heard of all that was done 5076
Ac 13: 1 had been brought up with Herod the t, 5076

THADDEUS (2)
Mt 10: 3 and Lebbeus, whose surname was T; 2280
Mk 3:18 and T, and Simon the Canaanite, 2280

THAHASH (1)
Ge 22:24 and Gaham, and T, and Maachah. 8477

THAMAH (1)
Ezr 2:53 the children of Sisera, the children of T, 8547

THAMAR (1)
Mt 1: 3 And Judas begat Phares and Zara of T; and 2283

THAN (483)
Ge 3: 1 Now the serpent was **more** subtil t any 4480
4:13 My punishment *is* greater t *I* can bear. 4480
19: 9 will we deal worse with thee, t with them. 4480
25:23 *the one* people shall be stronger t *the other* 4480
26:16 from us; for thou art much mightier t we. 4480
29:19 t that I should give her to another man: 4480
29:30 he loved also Rachel **more** t Leah, and 4480
34:19 he *was* **more** honourable t all the house of 4480
36: 7 For their riches were more t that they might 4480
37: 3 Now Israel loved Joseph **more** t all his 4480
37: 4 father loved him **more** t all his brethren, 4480
38:26 and said, She hath been **more** righteous t I; 4480
39: 9 *There is* none greater in this house t I; 4480
41:40 only *in* the throne will I be greater t thou. 4480
48:19 truly his younger brother shall be greater t 4480
Ex 1: 9 of Israel *are* moe and mightier t we: 4480
14:12 t that we should die in the wilderness. 4480
18:11 Now I know that the LORD *is* greater t all 4480
30:15 the poor shall not give less t half a shekel, 4480
36: 5 The people bring much more t enough for 4480
Lev 13: 3 the plague in sight *be* deeper t the skin of 4480
13: 4 in sight *be* not deeper t the skin, and 4480
13:20 it *be* in sight lower t the skin, and the hair 4480
13:21 if it *be* not lower t the skin, but *be* 4480
13:25 and it *be* in sight deeper t the skin; 4480
13:26 it *be* no lower t the *other* skin, but *be* 4480
13:30 behold, if it *be* in sight deeper t the skin; 4480
13:31 it *be* not in sight deeper t the skin, and 4480
13:32 the scall *be* not in sight deeper t the skin; 4480
13:34 in the skin, nor *be* in sight deeper t the skin; 4480
14:37 reddish, which in sight *are* lower t the wall; 4480
27: 8 if he be poorer t thy estimation, then 4480
Nu 3:46 of Israel, which are more t the Levites; 5921
13:31 the people; for they *are* stronger t we. 4480
14:12 of thee a greater nation and mightier t they. 4480
22:15 more, and **more** honourable t they. 4480
24: 7 his king shall be higher t Agag, and 4480
Dt 1:28 The people *is* greater and taller t we; 4480
4:38 and mightier t thou *art,* to bring thee in, 4480
Dt 7: 1 seven nations greater and mightier t thou; 4480
7: 7 ye were **moe** in number t any people; 4480
7:17 in thine heart, These nations *are* moe t I; 4480
9: 1 nations greater and mightier t thyself, 4480
9:14 of thee a nation mightier and greater t they. 4480
11:23 greater nations and mightier t yourselves. 4480
20: 1 and chariots, *and* a people more t thou, 4480
Jos 10: 2 because it *was* greater t Ai, and all the men 4480
10:11 *they were* moe which died with hailstones t 4480
Jdg 2:19 corrupted *themselves* **more** t their fathers, 4480
8: 2 of Ephraim better t the vintage of Abi-ezer? 4480
11:25 now *art* thou any thing better t Balak 4480
14:18 sun went down, What *is* sweeter t honey? 4480
14:18 what *is* stronger t a lion? And he said unto 4480
15: 2 *is* not her younger sister fairer t she? 4480
15: 3 Now shall I be **more** blameless t 4480
16:30 were moe t *they* which he slew in his life. 4480
Ru 3:10 kindness in the latter end t at the beginning, 4480
3:12 howbeit there is a kinsman nearer t I. 4480
4:15 which *is* better to thee t seven sons, 4480
1Sa 1: 8 *am* not I better to thee t ten sons? 4480
9: 2 the children of Israel a goodlier person t he: 4480
9: 2 upward *he was* higher t any of the people. 4480
10:23 he was higher t any of the people from his 4480
15:22 to obey *is* better t sacrifice, *and* to hearken 4480
15:22 *and* to hearken t the fat of rams. 4480
15:28 to a neighbour of thine, *that is* better t thou. 4480
18:30 *that* David behaved himself **more** wisely t 4480
24:17 said to David, Thou *art* **more** righteous t I: 4480
27: 1 *there is* nothing better for me t **that** I 3588
2Sa 1:23 they were swifter t eagles, they were 4480
1:23 than eagles, they were stronger t lions. 4480
6:22 I will yet be **more** vile t thus, and will be 4480
13:14 but, being stronger t she, forced her, and 4480
13:15 t the love wherewith he had loved her. 4480
13:16 this evil in sending me away *is* greater t 4480
17:14 *is* better t the counsel of Ahithophel. 4480
18: 8 the wood devoured more people that day t 4480
19: 7 that *will be* worse unto thee t all the evil 4480
19:43 and we have also **more** *right* in David t ye: 4480
19:43 fiercer t the words of the men of Israel. 4480
20: 5 he tarried longer t the set time which he 4480
20: 6 of Bichri do us **more** harm t *did* Absalom: 4480
23:23 He was **more** honourable t the thirty, but 4480
1Ki 1:37 make his throne greater t the throne of my 4480
1:47 God make the name of Solomon better t 4480
1:47 and make his throne greater t thy throne. 4480
2:32 upon two men **more** righteous and better t 4480
4:31 For he was wiser t all men; than Ethan 4480
4:31 t Ethan the Ezrahite, and Heman, and 4480
12:10 My little *finger* shall be thicker t my 4480
16:25 and did worse t all that *were* before him. 4480
16:33 t all the kings of Israel that were before 4480
19: 4 my life; for I *am* not better t my fathers. 4480
20:23 therefore they were stronger t we; but let us 4480
20:23 and surely we shall be stronger t they. 4480
20:25 *and* surely we shall be stronger t they. 4480
21: 2 I will give thee for it a better vineyard t it; 4480
2Ki 5:12 better t all the waters of Israel? 4480
6:16 for *they* that *be* with us *are* moe t *they* that 4480
9:35 they found no more of her t the skull, 518+3588
21: 9 Manasseh seduced them to do **more** evil t 4480
1Ch 4: 9 Jabez was **more** honourable t his brethren: 4480
11:21 he was **more** honourable t the two; 871.1
24: 4 the sons of Eleazar t of the sons of Ithamar; 4480
2Ch 10:10 My little *finger* shall be thicker t my 4480
20:25 **more** t they could carry away: 369+3807.1
21:13 father's house, *which were* better t thyself: 4480
25: 9 is able to give thee much more t this. 4480
29:34 **more** upright in heart to sanctify themselves t 4480
30:18 **otherwise** t it was written. 3808+871.1+3509.1
32: 7 for *there be* moe with us t with him: 4480
33: 9 to err, *and* to do worse t the heathen, 4480
Ezr 9:13 punished us less t our iniquities *deserve,* 4480
Est 1:19 royal estate unto another *that is* better t she. 4480
2:17 favour in his sight **more** t all the virgins; 4480
4:13 *in* the king's house, **more** t all the Jews. 4480
6: 6 delight to do honour **more** t to myself? 3148
Job 3:21 and dig for it **more** t for hid treasures; 4480
4:17 Shall mortal man be **more** just t God? 4480
4:17 shall a man be **more** pure t his Maker? 4480
6: 3 For now it would be heavier t the sand of 4480
7: 6 My days are swifter t a weaver's shuttle, 4480
7:15 *and* death **rather** t my life. 4480
9:25 Now my days are swifter t a post: they flee 4480
11: 6 that God exacteth of thee *less* t thine 4480
11: 8 deeper t hell; what canst thou know? 4480
11: 9 The measure thereof *is* longer t the earth, 4480
11: 9 longer than the earth, and broader t the sea. 4480
11:17 *thine* age shall be clearer t the noonday; 4480
15:10 and very aged men, much elder t thy father. 4480
23: 2 my stroke is heavier t my groaning. 5921
23:12 of his mouth **more** t my necessary *food.* 4480
30: 1 now *they that are* younger t I have me in 4480
30: 8 of base men: they were viler t the earth. 4480
32: 2 because he justified himself **rather** t God. 4480
32: 4 had spoken, because they *were* elder t he. 4480
33:12 will answer thee, that God is greater t man. 4480
33:25 His flesh shall be fresher t a child's: 4480
34:19 regardeth the rich **more** t the poor? 6440+3807.1
34:23 For he will not lay upon man more *t right;* NIH
35: 2 My righteousness *is* **more** t God's? 4480
35: 5 behold the clouds *which* are higher t thou. 4480
35:11 Who teacheth us **more** t the beasts of 4480
35:11 and maketh us wiser t the fowls of heaven? 4480
36:21 for this hast thou chosen **rather** t affliction. 4480
42:12 the latter end of Job **more** t his beginning: 4480
Ps 4: 7 **more** t *in* the time *that* their corn and 4480
8: 5 For thou hast made him a little lower t 4480
19:10 **More** to be desired *are they* t gold, yea, 4480
19:10 *are they* than gold, yea, t much fine gold: 4480
19:10 sweeter also t honey and the honeycomb. 4480
37:16 A little that a righteous *man* hath *is* better t 4480
40: 5 speak *of them,* they are moe t can be 4480
40:12 that I am not able to look *up;* they are moe t 4480

Ps 45: 2 Thou art fairer t the children of men: 4480
51: 7 wash me, and I shall be whiter t snow. 4480
52: 3 Thou lovest evil more t good; and 4480
52: 3 and lying rather t to speak righteousness. 4480
55:21 The words of his mouth were smoother t NIH
55:21 his words were softer t oil, yet were they 4480
61: 2 lead me to the rock that is higher t I. 4480
62: 9 they are altogether lighter t vanity. 4480
63: 3 Because thy lovingkindness is better t life, 4480
69: 4 a cause are moe t the hairs of mine head: 4480
69:31 This also shall please the LORD better t 4480
73: 7 they have more t heart could wish. 5674
76: 4 Thou art more glorious and excellent t 4480
84:10 For a day in thy courts is better t a 4480
84:10 t to dwell in the tents of wickedness. 4480
87: 2 of Zion more t all the dwellings of Jacob. 4480
89:27 higher t the kings of the earth. 3807.1
93: 4 The LORD on high is mightier t the noise 4480
93: 4 yea, t the mighty waves of the sea. NIH
105:24 and made them stronger t their enemies. 4480
118: 8 It is better to trust in the LORD t to put 4480
118: 9 It is better to trust in the LORD t to put 4480
119:72 The law of thy mouth is better unto me t 4480
119:98 hast made me wiser t mine enemies: 4480
119:99 I have more understanding t all my 4480
119:100 I understand more t the ancients, because 4480
119:103 yea, sweeter t honey to my mouth! 4480
130: 6 My soul waiteth for the Lord more t they 4480
130: 6 I say, more t they that watch for NIH
139:18 they are moe in number t the sand: 4480
142: 6 my persecutors; for they are stronger t I. 4480
Pr 3:14 For the merchandise of it is better t 4480
3:14 of silver, and the gain thereof t fine gold. 4480
3:15 She is more precious t rubies: and all 4480
5: 3 and her mouth is smoother t oil: 4480
8:10 and knowledge rather t choice gold. 4480
8:11 For wisdom is better t rubies; and all 4480
8:19 My fruit is better t gold, yea, than fine 4480
8:19 fruit is better than gold, yea, t fine gold; 4480
8:19 fine gold; and my revenue t choice silver. 4480
11:24 there is that withholdeth more t is meet, 4480
12: 9 is better t he that honoureth himself, and 4480
12:26 The righteous is more excellent t his 4480
15:16 Better is little with the fear of the LORD t 4480
15:17 love is, t a stalled ox and hatred therewith. 4480
16: 8 Better is a little with righteousness t great 4480
16:16 How much better is it to get wisdom t gold! 4480
16:16 to get understanding rather to be chosen t 4480
16:19 t to divide the spoil with the proud. 4480
16:32 He that is slow to anger is better t 4480
16:32 he that ruleth his spirit t he that taketh a 4480
17: 1 t a house full of sacrifices with strife. 4480
17:10 A reproof entereth more into a wise man t 4480
17:12 meet a man, rather t a fool in his folly. 408
18:19 A brother offended is harder to be won t a 4480
18:24 there is a friend that sticketh closer t a 4480
19: 1 t he that is perverse in his lips, and is a 4480
19:22 and a poor man is better t a liar. 4480
21: 3 more acceptable to the LORD t sacrifice. 4480
21: 9 t with a brawling woman in a wide house. 4480
21:19 t with a contentious and an angry woman. 4480
22: 1 A good name is rather to be chosen t great 4480
22: 1 and loving favour rather t silver and gold. 4480
25: 7 t that thou shouldest be put lower in 4480
25:24 t with a brawling woman and in a wide 4480
26:12 there is more hope of a fool t of him. 4480
26:16 The sluggard is wiser in his own conceit t 4480
27: 3 but a fool's wrath is heavier t them both. 4480
27: 5 Open rebuke is better t secret love. 4480
27:10 for better is a neighbour that is near t a 4480
28: 6 t he that is perverse in his ways, though he 4480
28:23 afterwards shall find more favour t he that 4480
29:20 there is more hope of a fool t of him. 4480
30: 2 Surely I am more brutish t any man, and 4480
Ecc 1:16 have gotten more wisdom t all they that 5921
2: 9 increased more t all that were before me in 4480
2:16 of the wise more t of the fool for ever; 5973
2:24 t that he should eat and drink, and that he NIH
2:25 or who else can hasten hereunto, more t I? 4480
3:22 t that a man should rejoice in his own 4480
4: 2 dead more t the living which are yet alive. 4480
4: 3 Yea, better is he t both they, which hath not 4480
4: 6 t both the hands full with travail and 4480
4: 9 Two are better t one; because they have a 4480
4:13 and a wise child t an old and foolish king, 4480
5: 1 be more ready to hear, t to give 4480
5: 5 t that thou shouldest vow and not pay. 4480
5: 8 for he that is higher t the highest 4480+5921
5: 8 and there be higher t they. 5921
6: 3 I say, that an untimely birth is better t he. 4480
6: 5 nor known any thing: this hath more rest t 4480
6: 8 For what hath the wise more t the fool? 4480
6: 9 Better is the sight of the eyes t 4480
6:10 he contend with him that is mightier t he. 4480
7: 1 A good name is better t precious ointment; 4480
7: 1 the day of death t the day of one's birth. 4480
7: 2 t to go to the house of feasting: 4480
7: 3 Sorrow is better t laughter: for by 4480
7: 5 t for a man to hear the song of fools. 4480
7: 8 Better is the end of a thing t the beginning 4480
7: 8 the patient in spirit is better t the proud in 4480
7:10 that the former days were better t these? 4480
7:19 Wisdom strengtheneth the wise more t ten 4480
7:26 I find more bitter t death the woman, 4480
8:15 t to eat, and to drink, and to be merry: 518+3588
9: 4 for a living dog is better t a dead lion. 4480
9:16 said I, Wisdom is better t strength: 4480
9:17 more t the cry of him that ruleth among 4480
9:18 Wisdom is better t weapons of war: but 4480
SS 1: 2 of his mouth: for thy love is better t wine. 4480
1: 4 we will remember thy love more t wine: 4480
4:10 how much better is thy love t wine! and 4480
4:10 the smell of thine ointments t all spices! 4480
5: 9 What is thy beloved more t another 4480
5: 9 what is thy beloved more t another 4480
Isa 13:12 I will make a man more precious t fine 4480
13:12 even a man t the golden wedge of Ophir. 4480
28:20 For the bed is shorter t that a man can 4480
28:20 the covering narrower t that he can wrap 3509.1
33:19 a people of a deeper speech t thou canst 4480
40:17 they are counted to him less t nothing, and 4480
52:14 his visage was so marred more t any man, 4480
52:14 and his form more t the sons of men: 4480
54: 1 for more are the children of the desolate t 4480
55: 9 For as the heavens are higher t the earth, so 4480
55: 9 so are my ways higher t your ways, and 4480
55: 9 and my thoughts t your thoughts. 4480
56: 5 a name better t of sons and of daughters: 4480
57: 8 discovered thyself to another t me, 854+4480
65: 5 come not near to me; for I am holier t thou. NIH
Jer 3:11 justified herself more t treacherous Judah. 4480
4:13 his horses are swifter t eagles. Woe unto 4480
5: 3 they have made their faces harder t a rock; 4480
7:26 their neck: they did worse t their fathers. 4480
8: 3 death shall be chosen rather t life by all 4480
16:12 ye have done worse t your fathers; 4480
20: 7 thou art stronger t I, and hast prevailed: 2388
31:11 the hand of him that was stronger t he. 4480
46:23 because they are more t the grasshoppers, 4480
La 4: 6 t the punishment of the sin of Sodom, 4480
4: 7 Her Nazarites were purer t snow, they were 4480
4: 7 purer than snow, they were whiter t milk, 4480
4: 7 they were more ruddy in body t rubies, 4480
4: 8 Their visage is blacker t a coal; they are not 4480
4: 9 are better t they that be slain with hunger: 4480
4:19 Our persecutors are swifter t the eagles of 4480
Eze 3: 9 As an adamant harder t flint have I made 4480
5: 6 into wickedness more t the nations, 4480
5: 6 my statutes more t the countries that are 4480
5: 7 Because ye multiplied more t the nations 4480
6:14 more desolate t the wilderness toward 4480
8:15 thou shalt see greater abominations t these. 4480
15: 2 What is the vine tree more t any tree, or 4480
15: 2 t a branch which is among the trees of NIH
16:47 wast corrupted more t they in all thy ways. 4480
16:51 multiplied thine abominations more t they, 4480
16:52 hast committed more abominable t they: 4480
16:52 they are more righteous t thou: yea, 4480
23:11 more corrupt in her inordinate love t she, 4480
23:11 in her whoredoms more t her sister in her 4480
28: 3 Behold, thou art wiser t Daniel; there is no 4480
36:11 will do better unto you t at your 4480
42: 5 for the galleries were higher t these, 4480
42: 5 t the lower, and than the middlemost of 4480
42: 5 and t the middlemost of the building. 4480
42: 6 the building was straitened more t 4480
Da 1:10 liking t the children which are of your sort? 4480
1:15 fatter in flesh t all the children which did 4480
1:20 he found them ten times better t all 5921
2:30 any wisdom that I have more t any living, 4481
3:19 seven times more t it was wont to be heat. 1768
7:20 whose look was more stout t his fellows. 4481
8: 3 one was higher t the other, and the higher 4480
11: 2 and the fourth shall be far richer t they all: 4480
11: 8 he shall continue more years t the king of 4480
11:13 shall set forth a multitude greater t 4480
Hos 2: 7 for then was it better with me t now. 227+4480
6: 6 the knowledge of God more t burnt 4480
Am 6: 2 be they better t these kingdoms? or 4480
6: 2 or their border greater t your border? 4480
Jnh 4: 3 for it is better for me to die t to live. 4480
4: 8 and said, It is better for me to die t to live. 4480
4:11 wherein are more t sixscore thousand 4480
Mic 7: 4 the most upright is sharper t a thorn hedge: 4480
Na 3: 8 Art thou better t populous No, that was 4480
Hab 1: 8 Their horses also are swifter t the leopards, 4480
1: 8 and are more fierce t the evening wolves: 4480
1:13 Thou art of purer eyes t to behold evil, and 4480
1:13 the man that is more righteous t he? 4480
Hag 2: 9 latter house shall be greater t of the former, 4480
Mt 3:11 but he that cometh after me is mightier t I, 2478
5:37 for whatsoever is more t these cometh of 4053
5:47 what do ye more t others? do not even NIG
6:25 ye shall put on. Is not the life more t meat, 4183
6:25 more than meat, and the body t raiment? NIG
6:26 Are ye not much better t they? 1308
10:15 in the day of judgment, t for that city. 2228
10:31 ye are of more value t many sparrows. 1308
10:37 or mother more t me is not worthy of me: 5228
10:37 or daughter more t me is not worthy of me. 5228
11: 9 yea, I say unto you, and more t a prophet. 4053
11:11 hath not risen a greater t John the Baptist: 3187
11:11 in the kingdom of heaven is greater t he. 3187
11:22 and Sidon at the day of judgment, t for you. 2228
11:24 Sodom in the day of judgment, t for thee. 2228
12: 6 That in this place is one greater t 3187
12:12 How much then is a man better t a sheep? 1308
12:41 and behold, a greater t Jonas is here. 4183
12:42 and behold, a greater t Solomon is here. 4183
12:45 seven other spirits more wicked t himself, 4191
12:45 the last state of that man is worse t the first. 5501
18: 8 rather t having two hands or two feet to be 2228
18: 9 rather t having two eyes to be cast into 2228
18:13 he rejoiceth more of that sheep, t of 2228
19:24 t for a rich man to enter into the kingdom 2228
21:36 he sent other servants moe t the first: 4183
23:15 twofold more the child of hell t 1362
26:53 he shall presently give me more t twelve 2228
27:64 so the last error shall be worse t the first. 5501
Mk 1: 7 There cometh one mightier t I after me, 2478
4:31 is less t all the seeds that be in the earth: 3398
4:32 and becometh greater t all herbs, and 3187
6:11 in the day of judgment, t for that city. 2228
8:14 they in the ship with them more t one loaf. 1508
9:43 t having two hands to go into hell, into 2228
9:45 t having two feet to be cast into hell, 2228
9:47 t having two eyes to be cast into hell fire: 2228
10:25 t for a rich man to enter into the kingdom 2228
12:31 none other commandment greater t these. 3187
12:33 is more t all whole burnt offerings and 4183
Mk 12:43 That this poor widow hath cast more in, t 4183
14: 5 For it might have been sold for more t 1883
Lk 3:13 Exact no more t that which is appointed 3844
3:16 but one mightier t I cometh, the latchet of 2478
7:26 I say unto you, and much more t a prophet. 4054
7:28 is not a greater prophet t John the Baptist: 3187
7:28 least in the kingdom of God is greater t he. 3187
10:12 in that day for Sodom, t for that city. 2228
10:14 and Sidon at the judgment, t for you. 2228
11:22 But when a stronger t he shall come upon 2478
11:26 seven other spirits more wicked t himself; 4191
11:26 the last state of that man is worse t the first. 5501
11:31 and behold, a greater t Solomon is here. 4183
11:32 and behold, a greater t Jonas is here. 4183
12: 7 ye are of more value t many sparrows. 1308
12:23 The life is more t meat, and the body is 4183
12:23 than meat, and the body is more t raiment. NIG
12:24 how much more are ye better t the fowls? 1308
14: 8 lest a more honourable man t thou be 1784
15: 7 more t over ninety and nine just persons 2228
16: 8 generation wiser t the children of light. 5228
16:17 earth to pass, t one tittle of the law to fail. 2228
17: 2 t that he should offend one of these little 2228
18:14 to his house justified rather t the other: 2228
18:25 t for a rich man to enter into the kingdom 2228
21: 3 that this poor widow hath cast in more t 4183
Jn 1:50 thou shalt see greater things t these. 3187
3:19 and men loved darkness rather t light, 2228
4: 1 and baptized moe disciples t John, 2228
4:12 Art thou greater t our father Jacob, 3187
5:20 he will shew him greater works t these, 3187
5:36 But I have greater witness t that of John: 3187
7:31 will he do moe miracles t these which this NIG
8:53 Art thou greater t our father Abraham, 3187
10:29 which gave them me, is greater t all; 3187
12:43 For they loved the praise of men more t 2260
13:16 The servant is not greater t his lord; 3187
13:16 neither he that is sent greater t he that sent 3187
14:12 and greater works t these shall he do; 3187
14:28 the Father: for my Father is greater t I. 3187
15:13 Greater love hath no man t this, that a man 3187
15:20 The servant is not greater t his lord. 3187
21:15 son of Jonas, lovest thou me more t these? 4183
Ac 4:19 God to hearken unto you more t unto God, 2228
5:29 said, We ought to obey God rather t men. 2228
15:28 to lay upon you no greater burden t these 4133
17:11 These were more noble t those in 2104
20:35 It is more blessed to give t to receive. 2228
23:13 And they were more t forty which had made NIG
23:21 for there lie in wait for him of them moe t NIG
25: 6 he had tarried among them more t ten days, 2228
26:22 saying none other things t those which 1622
27:11 more t those things which were spoken by 2228
Ro 1:25 and served the creature more t the Creator, 3844
3: 9 are we better t they? No, in no wise: for we NIG
8:37 more t conquerors through him that loved 5245
12: 3 not to think of himself more highly t he 3844
13:11 for now is our salvation nearer t when we 2228
1Co 1:25 Because the foolishness of God is wiser t 4680
1:25 the weakness of God is stronger t men. 2478
3:11 For other foundation can no man lay t that 3844
7: 9 for it is better to marry t to burn. 2228
9:15 t that any man should make my glorying 2228
10:22 the Lord to jealousy? are we stronger t he? 2478
14: 5 for greater is he that prophesieth t he that 2228
14:18 I speak with tongues more t you all: 3123
14:19 t ten thousand words in an unknown 2228
15:10 but I laboured more abundantly t they all: 4054
2Co 1:13 t what you read or acknowledge; 235+2228
Gal 1: 8 preach any other gospel unto you t that 3844
1: 9 any other gospel unto you t that ye have 3844
4:27 children t she which hath a husband. 2228+3123
Eph 3: 8 who am less t the least of all saints, NIG
Php 2: 3 let each esteem other better t themselves. 5242
1Ti 1: 4 rather t godly edifying which is in faith: 2228
5: 8 denied the faith, and is worse t an infidel. 5501
2Ti 3: 4 lovers of pleasures more t lovers of God; 2228
Phm 1:21 knowing that thou wilt also do more t I 5228
Heb 1: 4 Being made so much better t the angels, 2909
1: 4 obtained a more excellent name t they. 3844
2: 7 Thou madest him a little lower t the angels; 3844
2: 9 who was made a little lower t the angels, 3844
3: 3 was counted worthy of more glory t Moses, 3844
3: 3 the house hath more honour t the house. NIG
4:12 and sharper t any twoedged sword, 5228
7:26 and made higher t the heavens; 5308
9:23 themselves with better sacrifices t these. 3844
11: 4 unto God a more excellent sacrifice t Cain, 3844
11:25 t to enjoy the pleasures of sin for a season; 2228
11:26 greater riches t the treasures in Egypt: 3187
12:24 that speaketh better things t that of Abel. 3844
1Pe 1: 7 being much more precious t of gold that NIG
3:17 ye suffer for well doing, t for evil doing. 2228
2Pe 2:20 the latter end is worse with them t 5501
2:21 to have known the way of righteousness, t, 2228
1Jn 3:20 God is greater t our heart, and knoweth all 3187
4: 4 is he that is in you, t he that is in the world. 2228
3Jn 1: 4 I have no greater joy t to hear that my 3186
Rev 2:19 and the last to be more t the first. 4183

THANK (27) [THANKED, THANKFUL, THANKFULNESS, THANKING, THANKS, THANKSGIVING, THANKSGIVINGS, THANKWORTHY, UNTHANKFUL]

1Ch 16: 4 to t and praise the LORD God of Israel: 3034
16: 7 to t the LORD into the hand of Asaph 3034
23:30 to stand every morning to t and praise 3034
29:13 we t thee, and praise thy glorious name. 3034
2Ch 29:31 t offerings into the house of the LORD. 8426
29:31 brought in sacrifices and t offerings; 8426
33:16 thereon peace offerings and t offerings, 8426
Da 2:23 I t thee, and praise thee, O thou God of my 3029
Mt 11:25 that time Jesus answered and said, I t thee, 1843
Lk 6:32 love them which love you, what t have ye? 5485

Lk 6:33 which do good to you, what t have ye? *5485*
6:34 whom ye hope to receive, what t have ye? *5485*
10:21 and said, I t thee, O Father, Lord of heaven *1843*
17: 9 Doth he t that servant because he did *2192+5485*
18:11 and prayed thus with himself, God, I t thee, *2168*
Jn 11:41 Father, I t thee that thou hast heard me. *2168*
Ro 1: 8 I t my God through Jesus Christ for you all, *2168*
7:25 I t God through Jesus Christ our Lord. So *2168*
1Co 1: 4 I t my God always on your behalf, for *2168*
1:14 I t God that I baptized none of you, but *2168*
14:18 I t my God, I speak with tongues more than *2168*
Php 1: 3 I t my God upon every remembrance of *2168*
1Th 2:13 For this cause also t we God without *2168*
2Th 1: 3 We are bound to t God always for you, *2168*
1Ti 1:12 And I t Christ Jesus our Lord, *2192+5485*
2Ti 1: 3 I t God, whom I serve from *my* *2192+5485*
Phm 1: 4 I t my God, making mention of thee always *2168*

THANKED (3) [THANK]
2Sa 14:22 his face, and bowed himself, and t the king: 1288
Ac 28:15 Paul saw, he t God, and took courage. *2168*
Ro 6:17 But God be t, that ye were the servants of *5485*

THANKFUL (3) [THANK]
Ps 100: 4 be t unto him, *and* bless his name. 3034
Ro 1:21 glorified *him* not as God, neither were t; *2168*
Col 3:15 also ye are called in one body; and be ye t. *2170*

THANKFULNESS (1) [THANK]
Ac 24: 3 in all places, most noble Felix, with all t. *2169*

THANKING (1) [THANK]
2Ch 5:13 to be heard in praising and t the LORD; 3034

THANKS (73) [THANK]
2Sa 22:50 Therefore I will **give** t unto thee, 3034
1Ch 16: 8 **Give** t unto the LORD, call upon his 3034
16:34 O **give** t unto the LORD; for *he is* good; 3034
16:35 that *we* may **give** t to thy holy name, 3034
16:41 to **give** t to the LORD, because his mercy 3034
25: 3 a harp, to **give** t and to praise the LORD. 3034
2Ch 31: 2 to **give** t, and to praise in the gates of 3034
Ezr 3:11 in praising and **giving** t unto the LORD; 3034
Ne 12:24 over against them, to praise *and* to **give** t, 3034
12:31 two great *companies of them that gave* t, 8426
12:38 the other *company of them that gave* t went 8426
12:40 *of them that gave* t in the house of God, 8426
Ps 6: 5 of thee: in the grave who shall **give** thee t? 3034
18:49 Therefore will I **give** t unto thee, 3034
30: 4 **give** t at the remembrance of his holiness. 3034
30:12 my God, I will **give** t unto thee for ever. 3034
35:18 I will **give** thee t in the great congregation: 3034
75: 1 Unto thee, O God, do we **give** t, *unto thee* 3034
75: 1 do we give thanks, *unto thee* do we **give** t: 3034
79:13 sheep of thy pasture will **give** thee t for 3034
92: 1 *It is* a good *thing* to **give** t unto the LORD, 3034
97:12 **give** t at the remembrance of his holiness. 3034
105: 1 O **give** t unto the LORD; call upon his 3034
106: 1 O **give** t unto the LORD; for *he is* good: 3034
106:47 to **give** t unto thy holy name, *and* 3034
107: 1 O **give** t unto the LORD, for *he is* good: 3034
118: 1 O **give** t unto the LORD; for *he is* good: 3034
118:29 O **give** t unto the LORD; for *he is* good: 3034
119:62 At midnight I will rise to **give** t unto thee 3034
122: 4 to **give** t unto the name of the LORD. 3034
136: 1 O **give** t unto the LORD; for *he is* good: 3034
136: 2 O **give** t unto the God of gods: for his 3034
136: 3 O **give** t to the Lord of lords: for his mercy 3034
136:26 O **give** t unto the God of heaven: for his 3034
140:13 Surely the righteous shall **give** t unto thy 3034
Da 6:10 prayed, and **gave** t before his God, as he 3029
Mt 15:36 and **gave** t, and brake *them,* and gave to his *2168*
26:27 and **gave** t, and gave *it* to them, saying, *2168*
Mk 8: 6 and **gave** t, and brake, and gave to his *2168*
14:23 and when he had **given** t, he gave *it* to *2168*
Lk 2:38 in that instant **gave** t *likewise* **unto** the Lord, *437*
17:16 down on *his* face at his feet, **giving** him t: *2168*
22:17 and **gave** t, and said, Take this, and *2168*
22:19 and **gave** t, and brake *it,* and gave unto *2168*
Jn 6:11 and when he had **given** t, he distributed to *2168*
6:23 eat bread, after that the Lord had **given** t:) *2168*
Ac 27:35 and **gave** t to God in presence of *them* all: *2168*
Ro 14: 6 eateth to the Lord, for he **giveth** God t; *2168*
14: 6 to the Lord he eateth not, and **giveth** God t. *2168*
16: 4 unto whom not only I **give** t, but also all *2168*
1Co 10:30 I evil spoken of for *that for* which I **give** t? *2168*
11:24 And when he had **given** t, he brake *it,* and *2168*
14:16 the unlearned say Amen at thy **giving** of t, *2169*
14:17 For thou verily **givest** t well, but the other *2168*
15:57 But t *be* to God, which giveth us *5485*
2Co 1:11 t may be **given** by many on our behalf. *2168*
2:14 Now t *be* unto God, which always causeth *5485*
8:16 But t *be* to God, which put the same earnest *5485*
9:15 T *be* unto God for his unspeakable gift. *5485*
Eph 1:16 Cease not to **give** t for you, *2168*
5: 4 are not convenient: but rather **giving** of t. *2169*
5:20 **Giving** t always for all *things* unto God and *2168*
Col 1: 3 We **give** t to God and the Father of our *2168*
1:12 **Giving** t unto the Father, which hath made *2168*
3:17 **giving** t to God and the Father by him. *2168*
1Th 1: 2 We **give** t to God always for you all, *2168*
3: 9 For what t can we render to God again for *2169*
5:18 In every *thing* **give** t: for this *is* the will of *2168*
2Th 2:13 But we are bound to **give** t alway to God *2168*
1Ti 2: 1 prayers, intercessions, *and* **giving** of t, *2169*
Heb 13:15 the fruit of *our* lips **giving** t to his name. *3670*
Rev 4: 9 honour and t to him that sat on the throne, *2169*
11:17 Saying, We **give** thee t, O Lord God *2168*

THANKSGIVING (28) [GIVE, THANK]
Lev 7:12 If he offer it for a t, then he shall offer with 8426
7:12 he shall offer with the sacrifice of t 8426
7:13 the sacrifice of t of his peace offerings. 8426
7:15 t shall be eaten the same day that it is 8426
Lev 22:29 when ye will offer a sacrifice of t unto 8426
Ne 11:17 *was* the principal to begin the t in prayer: 3034
12: 8 *which was* over the t, he and his brethren. 1960
12:46 and songs of praise and t unto God. 3034
Ps 26: 7 That *I* may publish with the voice of t, and 8426
50:14 Offer unto God t; and pay thy vows unto 8426
69:30 with a song; and will magnify him with t. 8426
95: 2 Let us come before his presence with t, *and* 8426
100: 4 Enter *into* his gates with t, *and* into his 8426
107:22 let them sacrifice the sacrifices of t, and 8426
116:17 I will offer to thee the sacrifice of t, and 8426
147: 7 Sing unto the LORD with t; sing *praise* 8426
Isa 51: 3 found therein, t, and the voice of melody. 8426
Jer 30:19 out of them shall proceed t and the voice of 8426
Am 4: 5 offer a **sacrifice of** t with leaven, and 8426
Jnh 2: 9 I will sacrifice unto thee with the voice of t; 8426
2Co 4:15 that the abundant grace might through the t *2169*
9:11 which causeth through us t to God. *2169*
Php 4: 6 supplication with t let your requests be *2169*
Col 2: 7 have been taught, abounding therein with t. *2169*
4: 2 in prayer, and watch in the same with t; *2169*
1Ti 4: 3 to be received with t of them which believe *2169*
4: 4 to be refused, if it be received with t: *2169*
Rev 7:12 and t, and honour, and power, and might, *2169*

THANKSGIVINGS (2) [GIVE, THANK]
Ne 12:27 both with t, and with singing, 8426
2Co 9:12 but is abundant also by many t unto God; *2169*

THANKWORTHY (1) [THANK, WORTH]
1Pe 2:19 For this *is* t, if a man for conscience toward *5485*

THARA (1) [TERAH]
Lk 3:34 which was *the son* of T, which was *the son* *2291*

THARSHISH (4) [TARSHISH]
1Ki 10:22 For the king had at sea a navy of T with 8659
10:22 once in three years came the navy of T, 8659
22:48 Jehoshaphat made ships of T to go to Ophir 8659
1Ch 7:10 and Zethan, and T, and Ahishahar. 8659

THAT (12914) [THOSE] See Index of Articles, Etc.

THE (64039) See Index of Articles, Etc.

THEATRE (2)
Ac 19:29 they rushed with one accord into the t. *2302*
19:31 *he* would not adventure himself into the t. *2302*

THEBEZ (3)
Jdg 9:50 went Abimelech to T, and 8405
9:50 and encamped against T, and took it. 8405
2Sa 11:21 upon him from the wall, that he died in T? 8405

THEE (3826) [THOU] See Index of Articles, Etc.

THEE-WARD (1) [THOU]
1Sa 19: 4 his works *have been* to t very good: 3509.2

THEFT (2) [THEFTS, THIEF, THIEVES]
Ex 22: 3 have nothing, then he shall be sold for his t. 1591
22: 4 If the t be certainly found in his hand alive, 1591

THEFTS (3) [THEFT]
Mt 15:19 murders, adulteries, fornications, t, *2829*
Mk 7:22 T, covetousness, wickedness, deceit, *2829*
Rev 9:21 nor of their fornication, nor of their t. *2809*

THEIR (3931) [THEY] See Index of Articles, Etc.

THEIRS (21) [THEY]
Ge 15:13 a stranger in a land *that is* not t, 1992.1+3807.1
34:23 and every beast of t *be* ours? 3963.1
43:34 mess was five times so much as any of t. 3963.1
Ex 29: 9 the priest's office shall be t for a 1992.1+3807.1
Lev 18:10 not uncover: for t *is* thine own nakedness. 2007
Nu 16:26 these wicked men, and touch nothing of t, 1992.1
18: 9 every oblation of t, every meat offering 3963.1
18: 9 every meat offering of t, and every sin 3963.1
18: 9 every sin offering of t, and every trespass 3963.1
18: 9 of theirs, and every trespass offering of t, 3963.1
Jos 21:10 had: for t was the first lot. 1992.1+3807.1
1Ch 6:54 the Kohathites: for t was the lot. 1992.1+3807.1
2Ch 18:12 be like one of t, and speak thou good. 1992.1
Jer 44:28 words shall stand, mine, or t. 4480+1992.1
Eze 7:11 nor of their multitude, nor of any of t: 1992.1
44:29 dedicate thing in Israel shall be t. 1992.1+3807.1
Hab 1: 6 possess the dwelling places *that are* not t. 2050.2
Mt 5: 3 poor in spirit: for t is the kingdom of heaven. *846*
5:10 for t is the kingdom of heaven. *846*
1Co 1: 2 of Jesus Christ our Lord, both t and ours: *846*
2Ti 3: 9 be manifest unto all *men,* as t also was. *1565*

THELASAR (1) [TELASSAR]
2Ki 19:12 and the children of Eden which *were* in T? 8515

THEM (6429) [THEY] See Index of Articles, Etc.

THEMSELVES (409) [SELF, THEY]
Ge 3: 7 fig leaves together, and made t aprons. 1992.1
3: 8 his wife hid t from the presence of NIH
13:11 and they separated t the one from the other. NIH
19:11 so that they wearied t to find the door. NIH
21:28 ewe lambs of the flock **by** t. 905+2006.1+3807.1
21:29 which thou hast set **by** t? 905+3807.1+5089.1
30:40 he put his own flocks **by** t, and 905+3807.1
32:16 of his servants, every drove **by** t; 905+3807.1
33: 6 they and their children, and they bowed t. NIH
33: 7 with her children came near, and bowed t: NIH
Ge 33: 7 Joseph near and Rachel, and they bowed t. NIH
34:30 they shall gather t together against me, and NIH
42: 6 bowed down t before him *with* their faces to NIH
43:26 the house, and bowed t to him to the earth. NIH
43:32 for them **by** t, and for 905+3807.1+3963.1
43:32 did eat with him, **by** t: 905+3807.1+3963.1
Ex 5: 7 let them go and gather straw for t. 1992.1
11: 8 bow down t unto me, saying, Get thee out, NIH
12:39 had they prepared for t *any* victual. 1992.1
18:26 but every small matter they judged t. 1992
19:22 which come near to the LORD, sanctify t, NIH
26: 9 thou shalt couple five curtains **by** t, 905+3807.1
26: 9 six curtains **by** t, and shalt double 905+3807.1
32: 1 the people gathered t together unto Aaron, NIH
32: 7 out of the land of Egypt, have corrupted t: NIH
32:26 all the sons of Levi gathered t together unto NIH
33: 6 the children of Israel stript t of their NIH
36:16 he coupled five curtains **by** t, and 905+3807.1
36:16 by themselves, and six curtains **by** t. 905+3807.1
Lev 15:18 they shall *both* bathe t in water, and NIH
22: 2 that they separate t from the holy *things* of NIH
Nu 6: 2 woman shall separate t to vow a vow of a NIH
6: 2 of a Nazarite, to separate t unto the LORD: NIH
8: 7 wash their clothes, and *so* make t clean. NIH
10: 3 all the assembly shall assemble t to thee at NIH
10: 4 thousands of Israel, shall gather t unto thee. NIH
11:32 they spread *them* all abroad for t round 1992.1
16: 3 they gathered t together against Moses and NIH
20: 2 they gathered t together against Moses and NIH
27: 3 t together against the LORD in NIH
Dt 7:20 are left, and hide t from thee, be destroyed. NIH
9:12 t; they are quickly turned aside out of NIH
31:14 presented t in the tabernacle of NIH
31:20 shall have eaten and filled t, and waxen fat; NIH
32: 5 They have corrupted t, their spot *is* not NIH
32:27 lest their adversaries should behave t NIH
32:31 our Rock, even our enemies t *being* judges. NIH
Jos 8:27 of that city Israel took for a prey unto t, 1992.1
9: 2 That they gathered t together, to fight with NIH
10: 5 gathered t together, and went up, they and NIH
10:13 until the people had avenged t upon their NIH
10:16 kings fled, and hid t in a cave at Makkedah. NIH
11:14 children of Israel took for a prey unto t; 1992.1
22:12 of Israel gathered t together *at* Shiloh, NIH
24: 1 and they presented t before God. NIH
Jdg 2:12 bowed t unto them, and provoked NIH
2:17 after other gods, and bowed t unto them: NIH
2:19 and corrupted t more than their fathers, NIH
5: 2 when the people willingly offered t. NIH
5: 9 that offered t willingly among the people. NIH
7: 2 lest Israel vaunt t against me, saying, NIH
7:23 the men of Israel gathered t together out of NIH
7:24 all the men of Ephraim gathered t together, NIH
10:17 the children of Israel assembled t together, NIH
12: 1 the men of Ephraim **gathered t together,** 6817
15: 9 and pitched in Judah, and spread t in Lehi. NIH
20: 2 presented t in the assembly of the people of NIH
20:14 the children of Benjamin gathered t together NIH
20:20 the men of Israel put t in array to fight NIH
20:22 the people the men of Israel encouraged t, NIH
20:22 place where they put t in array the first day. NIH
20:30 put t in array against Gibeah, as at other NIH
20:33 their place, and put t in array at Baal-tamar: NIH
20:37 the liers in wait drew t along, and smote all NIH
1Sa 2: 5 *They that were* full have hired out t for NIH
3:13 because his sons made t vile, and 1992.1
4: 2 the Philistines put t in array against Israel: NIH
8: 4 all the elders of Israel gathered t together, NIH
13: 5 the Philistines gathered t together to fight NIH
13: 6 the people did hide t in caves, and NIH
13:11 *that* the Philistines gathered t together *at* NIH
14:11 both of them discovered t unto the garrison NIH
14:11 forth out of the holes where they had hid t. NIH
14:20 the people that *were* with him assembled t, NIH
14:22 of Israel which had hid t in mount Ephraim, NIH
21: 4 if the young men have kept t at least from NIH
22: 2 *that was* discontented, gathered t unto him; NIH
28: 4 the Philistines gathered t together, and came NIH
2Sa 2:25 the children of Benjamin gathered t together NIH
5:18 and spread t in the valley of Rephaim. NIH
5:22 and spread t in the valley of Rephaim. NIH
10: 8 *were* **by** t in the field. 905+3807.1+3963.1
10:15 before Israel, they gathered t together. NIH
10:17 And the Syrians set t in array against David, NIH
16:14 came weary, and refreshed t there. NIH
22:45 Strangers shall submit t unto me: as soon as NIH
1Ki 8: 2 all the men of Israel assembled t unto king NIH
8:47 *Yet* if they shall bethink t in the land 3963.1
18:23 let them choose one bullock for t, and 1992.1
18:28 and cut t after their manner with knives and NIH
20:12 Set *yourselves in array.* And they set t *in* NIH
2Ki 2:15 and bowed t to the ground before him. NIH
7:12 are they gone out of the camp to hide t in NIH
8:20 hand of Judah, and made a king over t. 1992.1
17:17 sold t to do evil in the sight of the LORD, NIH
17:32 made unto t of the lowest of them priests 1992.1
19:29 shall eat *this* year **such things as grow of** t, 5599
1Ch 11: 1 all Israel gathered t to David unto Hebron, NIH
11:10 who strengthened t with him in his NIH
11:14 they set t in the midst of *that* parcel, and NIH
12: 8 of the Gadites there separated t unto David NIH
13: 2 *and* suburbs, that they may gather t unto us: NIH
14: 9 and spread t in the valley of Rephaim. NIH
14:13 the Philistines yet again spread t abroad in NIH
15:14 the Levites sanctified t to bring up the ark NIH
19: 6 saw that they had made t odious to David, NIH
19: 7 the children of Ammon gathered t together NIH
19: 9 come *were* **by** t in the field. 905+3807.1+3963.1
19:11 they set t in array against the children of NIH
21:20 the angel; and his four sons with him hid t. NIH
29:24 submitted t unto Solomon the king. 3027
2Ch 3:13 The wings of these cherubims spread t forth NIH
5: 3 Wherefore all the men of Israel assembled t NIH
6:37 *Yet* if they bethink t in the land whither 3963.1
7: 3 they bowed t *with their* faces to the ground NIH

T

2Ch 7:14 shall humble t, and pray, and seek my face, NIH
12: 6 the princes of Israel and the king humbled t; NIH
12: 7 when the LORD saw that they humbled t, NIH
12: 7 to Shemaiah, saying, They have humbled t; NIH
13: 7 have strengthened t against Rehoboam NIH
14:13 that they could not recover t; 1992.1
15:10 So they gathered t together at Jerusalem in NIH
20: 4 Judah gathered t together, to ask help of NIH
20:25 which they stript off for t, 1992.1
20:26 on the fourth day they assembled t in NIH
21: 8 dominion of Judah, and made t a king. 1992.1
29:15 their brethren, and sanctified t, and came, NIH
29:29 and all that were present with him bowed t, NIH
29:34 and until the other priests had sanctified t: NIH
29:34 upright in heart to sanctify t than the priests. NIH
30: 3 the priests had not sanctified t sufficiently, NIH
30: 3 neither had the people gathered t together to NIH
30:11 and Manasseh and of Zebulun humbled t, NIH
30:15 sanctified t, and brought in the burnt NIH
30:18 Issachar, and Zebulun, had not cleansed t, NIH
30:24 and a great number of priests sanctified t. NIH
31:18 for in their set office they sanctified t in NIH
32: 8 the people rested t upon the words of NIH
35:14 afterward they made ready for t, and 1992.1
35:14 therefore the Levites prepared for t, and 1992.1
Ezr 3: 1 the people gathered t together as one man to NIH
6:20 for their brethren the priests, and for t. 1992.1
6:21 all such as had separated t unto them from NIH
9: 1 have not separated t from the people of NIH
9: 2 they have taken of their daughters for t, 1992.1
9: 2 that the holy seed have mingled t with NIH
10: 7 that they should gather t together unto NIH
10: 9 Benjamin gathered t together unto NIH
Ne 4: 2 will they fortify t? will they sacrifice? 1992.1
8: 1 all the people gathered t together as one NIH
8:16 and brought them, and made t booths, 1992.1
9: 2 the seed of Israel separated t from all NIH
9:25 and delighted t in thy great goodness. NIH
10:28 all they that had separated t from the people NIH
11: 2 that willingly offered t to dwell at NIH
12:28 the sons of the singers gathered t together, NIH
12:30 the priests and the Levites purified t, and NIH
13:22 the Levites that they should cleanse t, NIH
Est 8:11 were in every city to gather t together, NIH
8:13 that day to avenge t on their enemies. NIH
9: 2 The Jews gathered t together in their cities NIH
9:15 the Jews that were in Shushan gathered t NIH
9:16 in the king's provinces gathered t together, NIH
9:27 upon all such as joined t unto them, so as it NIH
9:31 as they had decreed for t and 5315+3963.1
Job 1: 6 God came to present t before the LORD, NIH
2: 1 God came to present t before the LORD, NIH
3:14 which built desolate places for t; 4123.1
6: 4 the terrors of God do set t in array against NIH
16:10 they have gathered t together against me. NIH
24: 4 the poor of the earth hide t together. NIH
24:16 which they had marked for t in 4123.1
29: 8 The young men saw me, and hid t: and NIH
30:14 in the desolation they rolled t upon me. NIH
34:22 where the workers of iniquity may hide t. NIH
39: 3 They bow t, they bring forth their young NIH
41:23 they are firm in t; they cannot be moved. 2050.2
41:25 by reason of breakings they purify t. NIH
Ps 2: 2 The kings of the earth set t, and the rulers NIH
3: 6 that have set t against me round about. NIH
9:20 that the nations may know t to be but men. 1992
18:44 the strangers shall submit t unto me. NIH
35:15 they rejoiced, and gathered t together: NIH
35:15 yea, the abjects gathered t together against NIH
35:26 and dishonour that magnify t against me. NIH
37:11 shall delight t in the abundance of peace. NIH
38:16 my foot slippeth, they magnify t against me. NIH
44:10 and they which hate us spoil for t. 4123.1
49: 6 and boast t in the multitude of their riches; NIH
56: 6 They gather t together, they hide NIH
56: 6 they hide t, they mark my steps, when they NIH
57: 6 into the midst whereof they are fallen t. NIH
59: 4 They run and prepare t without my fault: NIH
64: 5 They encourage t in an evil matter: 4123.1
64: 8 make their own tongue to fall upon t: 4123.1
66: 3 shall thine enemies submit t unto thee. NIH
66: 7 let not the rebellious exalt t. Selah. NIH
80: 6 and our enemies laugh among t. 4123.1
81:15 LORD should have submitted t unto him: NIH
94: 4 and all the workers of iniquity boast t? NIH
94:21 They gather t together against the soul of NIH
97: 7 serve graven images, that boast t of idols: NIH
104:22 they gather t together, and lay them down in NIH
106:28 They joined t also unto Baal-peor, and NIH
109:29 let them cover t with their own confusion, NIH
140: 8 not his wicked device; lest they exalt t. NIH
Pr 23: 5 for riches certainly make t wings; they fly 2050.2
28:28 When the wicked rise, men hide t: but NIH
Ecc 3:18 that they might see that they t are beasts. 1992
11: 3 be full of rain, they empty t upon the earth: NIH
12: 3 the strong men shall bow t, and the grinders NIH
Isa 2: 6 they please t in the children of strangers. NIH
3: 9 for they have rewarded evil unto t. 1992.1
8:21 they shall fret t, and curse their king and NIH
10:31 the inhabitants of Gebim gather t to flee. NIH
15: 3 In their streets they shall gird t with NIH
22: 7 the horsemen shall set t in array at the gate. NIH
30: 2 to strengthen t in the strength of Pharaoh, NIH
46: 2 but t are gone into captivity. 5315+3963.1
47:14 they shall not deliver t from 5315+3963.1
48: 2 For they call t of the holy city, and NIH
48: 2 holy city, and stay t upon the God of Israel; NIH
49:18 all these gather t together, and come to thee. NIH
56: 6 that join t to the LORD, to serve him, and NIH
59: 6 neither shall they cover t with their works: NIH
60: 4 all they gather t together, they come to thee: NIH
60:14 all they that despised thee shall bow t down NIH
66:17 They that sanctify t, and purify themselves NIH
66:17 purify t in the gardens behind one tree in NIH
Jer 2:24 all they that seek her will not weary t; in her NIH
Jer 4: 2 the nations shall bless t in him, and in him NIH
5: 7 assembled t by troops in the harlots' houses. NIH
5:22 though the waves thereof toss t, yet can they NIH
7:19 do they not provoke t to the confusion of 3963.1
9: 5 speak lies, and weary t to commit iniquity. NIH
11:17 which they have done against t to 1992.1
12:13 they have put t to pain, but shall not profit: NIH
16: 6 neither shall men lament for them, nor cut t, NIH
16: 6 cut themselves, nor make t bald for them: NIH
16: 7 Neither shall men tear t for them in NIH
25:14 and great kings shall serve t of them also: 1992
27: 7 and great kings shall serve t of him. NIH
30: 8 and strangers shall no more serve t of him: NIH
30:21 their nobles shall be of t, and 5105.2
34:10 that none should serve t of them any more, NIH
41: 5 having cut t, with offerings and incense in NIH
49:29 away: they shall take to t their curtains, 1992.1
50: 9 they shall set t in array against her; NIH
La 2:10 they have girded t with sackcloth: NIH
4:14 they have polluted t with blood, so that men NIH
Eze 6: 9 they shall lothe t for the evils 6440+1992.1
7:18 They shall also gird t with sackcloth, and NIH
10:17 these lift up t also: for the spirit of 3963.1
10:22 river of Chebar, their appearances and t: 3963.1
14:18 but they only shall be delivered t. 3963.1
26:16 they shall clothe t with trembling; they shall NIH
27:30 their heads, they shall wallow t in the ashes: NIH
27:31 they shall make t utterly bald for thee, and NIH
31:14 trees by the waters exalt t for their height, NIH
34: 2 to the shepherds of Israel that do feed t! 3963.1
34: 8 the shepherds fed t, and fed not my flock; 3963.1
34:10 shall the shepherds feed t any more; 3963.1
34:27 of the hand of those that served t of them. NIH
37:23 Neither shall they defile t any more with NIH
43:26 and purify it; and they shall consecrate t. 2050.2
44:18 they shall not gird t with any thing that NIH
44:25 shall come at no dead person to defile t: NIH
44:25 that hath had no husband, they may defile t. NIH
45: 5 the ministers of the house, have for t, 1992.1
Da 2:43 they shall mingle t with the seed of men: NIH
10: 7 fell upon them, so that they fled to hide t. NIH
11: 6 in the end of years they shall join t together; NIH
11:14 also the robbers of thy people shall exalt t to NIH
Hos 1:11 appoint t one head, and they shall come 1992.1
4:14 for t are separated with whores, and 1992
7:14 they assemble t for corn and wine, and NIH
9: 9 They have deeply corrupted t, as in the days NIH
9:10 and separated t unto that shame; NIH
10:10 they shall bind t in their two furrows. 3963.1
Am 2: 8 they lay t down upon clothes laid to pledge NIH
6: 4 stretch t upon their couches, and eat NIH
6: 5 and invent to t instruments of musick, 1992.1
6: 6 and anoint t with the chief ointments: NIH
6: 7 the banquet of them that stretched t shall be NIH
9: 3 though they hide t in the top of Carmel, NIH
Mic 3: 4 as they have behaved t ill in their doings. NIH
Hab 1: 7 and their dignity shall proceed of t. 5105.2
1: 8 their horsemen shall spread t, and NIH
2:13 the people shall weary t for very vanity? NIH
Zep 2: 8 and magnified t against their border. NIH
2:10 magnified t against the people of NIH
Zec 4:12 pipes empty the golden oil out of t? 1992.1
11: 5 possessors slay them, and hold t not guilty: NIH
12: 3 all that burden t with it shall be cut in NIH
12: 7 Jerusalem do not magnify t against Judah. NIH
Mt 9: 3 certain of the scribes said within t, 1438
14: 2 mighty works do shew forth t in him. NIG
14:15 may go into the villages, and buy t victuals. 1438
16: 7 And they reasoned among t, saying, It is 1438
19:12 which have made t eunuchs for 1438
21:25 And they reasoned with t, saying, If we 1438
21:38 the son, they said among t, This is the heir; 1438
23: 4 they t will not move them with one of their NIG
Mk 1:27 insomuch that they questioned among t, 846
2: 8 in his spirit that they so reasoned within t, 1438
4:17 And have no root in t, and so endure but 1438
6:14 mighty works do shew forth t in him. NIG
6:30 And the apostles gathered t together unto NIG
6:36 and into the villages, and buy t bread: 1438
6:51 they were sore amazed in t beyond 1438
8:16 And they reasoned among t, saying, It is 240
9: 2 them up into a high mountain apart by t: 3441
9: 8 no man any more, save Jesus only with t. 1438
9:10 And they kept that saying with t, 1438
9:34 for by the way they had disputed among t, 240
10:26 saying among t, Who then can be saved? 1438
11:31 And they reasoned with t, saying, If we 1438
12: 7 But those husbandmen said amongst t, This 1438
14: 4 were some that had indignation within t, 1438
15:31 mocking said among t with the scribes, 240
16: 3 And they said among t, Who shall roll us 1438
Lk 4:36 and spake among t, saying, What a word is 240
7:30 rejected the counsel of God against t, 1438
7:49 sat at meat with him began to say within t, 1438
18: 9 which trusted in t that they were righteous, 1438
20: 5 And they reasoned with t, saying, If we 1438
20:14 they reasoned among t, saying, This is 1438
20:20 which should feign t just men, that they 1438
22:23 And they began to inquire among t, which 1438
23:12 for before they were at enmity between t. 1438
24:12 he beheld the linen clothes laid by t, and 3441
Jn 6:52 The Jews therefore strove amongst t, saying, 240
7:35 Then said the Jews among t, Whither will 1438
11:55 Jerusalem before the passover, to purify t. 1438
11:56 and spake among t, as they stood in 240
12:19 The Pharisees therefore said among t, 1438
16:17 Then said some of his disciples among t, 240
17:13 that they might have my joy fulfilled in t. 846
18:18 and they warmed t: and Peter stood with NIG
18:28 and they t went not into the judgment hall, 846
19:24 They said therefore among t, Let us not rent 240
Ac 4:15 out of the council, they conferred among t, 240
5:36 of men, about four hundred, joined t: NIG
11:26 that a whole year they assembled t with NIG
15:32 And Judas and Silas, being prophets also t, 846
Ac 16:37 but let them come t and fetch us out. 846
18: 6 And when they opposed t, and blasphemed, NIG
21:25 that they keep t from things offered to idols, 846
23:12 and bound t under a curse, 1438
23:21 which have bound t with an oath, 1438
24:15 hope towards God, which they t also allow, 846
26:31 gone aside, they talked between t, saying, 240
27:40 they committed t unto the sea, and NIG
27:43 could swim should cast t first into the sea, NIG
28: 4 they said among t, No doubt this man is a 240
28:25 And when they agreed not among t, 240
28:29 and had great reasoning among t. 1438
Ro 1:22 Professing t to be wise, they became fools, NIG
1:24 to dishonour their own bodies between t: 1438
1:27 receiving in t that recompence of their error 1438
2:14 these, having not the law, are a law unto t: 1438
10: 3 have not submitted t unto the righteousness NIG
13: 2 they that resist shall receive to t damnation. 1438
1Co 6: 9 nor abusers of t with mankind, NIG
16:15 that they have addicted t to the ministry of 1438
2Co 5:15 live should not henceforth live unto t, 1438
8: 3 beyond their power they were **willing of t**; 830
10:12 ourselves with some that commend t: 1438
10:12 but they measuring t by themselves, and 1438
10:12 but they measuring themselves by t, and 1438
10:12 and comparing t amongst themselves, 1438
10:12 and comparing themselves amongst t, 1438
11:13 transforming t into the apostles of Christ. NIG
Gal 6:13 For neither they t who are circumcised 3588
Eph 4:19 Who being past feeling have given t over 1438
Php 2: 3 of mind let each esteem other better than t. 1438
1Th 1: 9 For **they t** shew of us what manner of 846
1Ti 1:10 for them that defile t with mankind, NIG
2: 9 that women adorn t in modest apparel, 1438
3:13 a deacon well purchase to t a good degree, 1438
6:10 and pierced t through with many sorrows. 1438
6:19 Laying up in store for t a good foundation 1438
2Ti 2:25 In meekness instructing those that **oppose t**; 475
2:26 And that they may recover t out of the snare NIG
4: 3 after their own lusts shall they heap to t 1438
Tit 1:12 One of t, even a prophet of their own, said, 846
Heb 6: 6 seeing they crucify to t the Son of God 1438
9:23 the heavenly things t with better sacrifices 846
1Pe 1:12 that not unto t, but unto us they did 1438
3: 5 who trusted in God, adorned t, being in 1438
2Pe 2: 1 and bring upon t swift destruction. 1438
2:13 sporting t with their own deceivings while NIG
2:19 they t are the servants of corruption: 846
Jude 1: 7 in like manner giving t over to fornication, 3778
1:10 brute beasts, in those things they corrupt t. NIG
1:12 they feast with you, feeding t without fear: 1438
1:19 These be they who separate t, sensual, 1438
Rev 6:15 and every free man, hid t in the dens and 1438
8: 6 had the seven trumpets prepared t to sound. 1438

THEN (2168)

Ge 3: 5 t your eyes shall be opened, and ye shall 2050.1
4:26 t began men to call upon the name of 227
8: 9 t he put forth his hand, and took her, and 2050.1
12: 6 And the Canaanite was t in the land. 227
13: 7 and the Perizzite dwelled t in the land. 227
13: 9 take the left hand, t I will go to the right; 2050.1
13: 9 to the right hand, t I will go to the left. 2050.1
13:11 T Lot chose him all the plain of Jordan; 2050.1
13:16 the earth, t shall thy seed also be numbered. NIH
13:18 T Abram removed his tent, and came and 2050.1
17:17 T Abraham fell upon his face, and 2050.1
18:15 T Sarah denied, saying, I laughed not; 2050.1
18:26 t I will spare all the place for their sakes. 2050.1
19:15 t the angels hastened Lot, saying, Arise, 2050.1
19:24 T the LORD rained upon Sodom and 2050.1
20: 9 T Abimelech called Abraham, and 2050.1
21:32 t Abimelech rose up, and Phichol 2050.1
22: 4 T on the third day Abraham lift up his 2050.1
24: 8 t thou shalt be clear from this my oath: 2050.1
24:41 T shalt thou be clear from this my oath, 227
24:50 T Laban and Bethuel answered and said, 2050.1
25: 1 T again Abraham took a wife, and 2050.1
25: 8 T Abraham gave up the ghost, and 2050.1
25:34 T Jacob gave Esau bread and pottage of 2050.1
26:12 T Isaac sowed in that land, and 2050.1
26:26 T Abimelech went to him from Gerar, 2050.1
27:41 at hand; t will I slay my brother Jacob. 2050.1
27:45 t I will send, and fetch thee from thence: 2050.1
28: 9 T went Esau unto Ishmael, and took unto 2050.1
28:21 in peace; t shall the LORD be my God: 2050.1
29: 1 T Jacob went on his journey, and 2050.1
29: 8 the well's mouth; t we water the sheep. 2050.1
29:25 t hast thou beguiled me? 2050.1
30:14 T Rachel said to Leah, Give me, I pray 2050.1
31: 8 thy wages; t all the cattle bare speckled: 2050.1
31: 8 thy hire; t bare all the cattle ringstraked. 2050.1
31:16 now t, whatsoever God hath said unto 2050.1
31:17 T Jacob rose up, and set his sons and his 2050.1
31:25 T Laban overtook Jacob. Now Jacob had 2050.1
31:33 T went he out of Leah's tent, and 2050.1
31:54 T Jacob offered sacrifice upon the mount, 2050.1
32: 7 T Jacob was greatly afraid and distressed: 2050.1
32: 8 t the other company which is left shall 2050.1
32:18 T thou shalt say, They be thy servant 2050.1
33: 6 T the handmaidens came near, they and 2050.1
33:10 t receive my present at my hand: 2050.1
34:16 T will we give our daughters unto you, 2050.1
34:17 t will we take our daughter, and we will 2050.1
35: 2 T Jacob said unto his household, and 2050.1
37:28 T there passed by Midianites 2050.1
38:11 T said Judah to Tamar his daughter in 2050.1
38:21 T he asked the men of that place, saying, 2050.1
39: 9 how t can I do this great wickedness, and 2050.1
41: 9 T spake the chief butler unto Pharaoh, 2050.1
41:14 T Pharaoh sent and called Joseph, and 2050.1
42:25 T Joseph commanded to fill their sacks 2050.1
42:34 t shall I know that ye are no spies, but 2050.1
42:38 t shall ye bring down my gray hairs with 2050.1
43: 9 t let me bear the blame for ever: 2050.1

Ge 44: 8 how t should we steal out of thy lord's 2050.1
44:11 T they speedily took down every man his 2050.1
44:13 T they rent their clothes, and laded every 2050.1
44:18 T Judah came near unto him, and said, 2050.1
44:26 brother be with us, t will we go down: 2050.1
44:32 t I shall bear the blame to my father for 2050.1
45: 1 T Joseph could not refrain himself before 2050.1
47: 1 T Joseph came and told Pharaoh, and 2050.1
47: 6 t make them rulers over my cattle. 2050.1
47:23 T Joseph said unto the people, Behold, 2050.1
49: 4 t defiledst thou *it:* he went up to my couch. 227
Ex 1:16 if it *be* a son, t ye shall kill him: 2050.1
1:16 but if it *be* a daughter, t she shall live. 2050.1
2: 7 T said his sister to Pharaoh's daughter, 2050.1
4:25 T Zipporah took a sharp stone, and 2050.1
4:26 t she said, A bloody husband *thou art,* 227
4:31 t they bowed their heads and worshipped. 2050.1
5:15 T the officers of the children of Israel 2050.1
6: 1 T the LORD said unto Moses, 2050.1
6:12 how t shall Pharaoh hear me, who *am* of 2050.1
7: 9 t thou shalt say unto Aaron, Take thy rod, 2050.1
7:11 T Pharaoh also called the wise men and 2050.1
8: 8 T Pharaoh called for Moses and Aaron, 2050.1
8:19 T the magicians said unto Pharaoh, 2050.1
9: 1 T the LORD said unto Moses, Go in 2050.1
10:16 T Pharaoh called for Moses and Aaron in 2050.1
12:21 T Moses called for all the elders of Israel, 2050.1
12:44 hast circumcised him, t shall he eat thereof. 227
12:48 and t let him come near and keep it; 227
13:13 not redeem *it,* t thou shalt break his neck: 2050.1
15: 1 T sang Moses and the children of Israel this 227
15:15 T the dukes of Edom shall be amazed; 227
16: 4 T said the LORD unto Moses, Behold, 2050.1
16: 6 t ye shall know that the LORD hath 2050.1
16: 7 t ye shall see the glory of the LORD; 2050.1
17: 8 T came Amalek, and fought with Israel in 2050.1
18:12 T Jethro, Moses' father in law, 2050.1
18:23 God command thee *so,* t thou shalt be 2050.1
19: 5 t ye shall be a peculiar treasure unto me 2050.1
21: 3 t his wife shall go out with him. 2050.1
21: 6 T his master shall bring him unto 2050.1
21: 8 to himself, t shall he let her be redeemed: 2050.1
21:11 t shall she go out free without money. 2050.1
21:13 t I will appoint thee a place whither he 2050.1
21:19 his staff, t shall he that smote *him* be quit: 2050.1
21:23 t thou shalt give life for life, 2050.1
21:28 t the ox shall be surely stoned, and 2050.1
21:30 t he shall give *for* the ransom of his life 2050.1
21:35 t they shall sell the live ox, and divide 2050.1
22: 3 t he shall be sold for his theft. 2050.1
22: 8 t the master of the house shall be brought 2050.1
22:11 *T* shall an oath of the LORD be between NIH
22:13 *t* let him bring it *for* witness, *and* he shall NIH
23:22 t I will be an enemy unto thine enemies, 2050.1
24: 9 T went up Moses, and Aaron, Nadab, and 2050.1
29: 7 T shalt thou take the anointing oil, and 2050.1
29:20 T shalt thou kill the ram, and take of his 2050.1
29:34 t thou shalt burn the remainder with fire: 2050.1
30:12 t shall they give every man a ransom for 2050.1
32:24 t I cast it into the fire, and there came out 2050.1
32:26 T Moses stood in the gate of the camp, 2050.1
34:20 *him* not, t shalt thou break his neck. 2050.1
36: 1 T wrought Bezaleel and Aholiab, and 2050.1
40:34 T a cloud covered the tent of 2050.1
40:37 t they journeyed not till the day that it 2050.1
Lev 1:14 t he shall bring his offering of 2050.1
3: 7 t shall he offer it before the LORD. 2050.1
3:12 t he shall offer it before the LORD. 2050.1
4: 3 t let him bring for his sin, which he hath 2050.1
4:14 t the congregation shall offer a young 2050.1
4:28 t he shall bring his offering, a kid of 2050.1
5: 1 do not utter *it,* t he shall bear his iniquity. 2050.1
5: 3 he knoweth *of it,* t he shall be guilty. 2050.1
5: 4 when he knoweth *of it,* t he shall be 2050.1
5: 7 t he shall bring for his trespass, which he 2050.1
5:11 t he that sinned shall bring for his 2050.1
5:12 T shall he bring it to the priest, and 2050.1
5:15 t he shall bring for his trespass unto 2050.1
6: 4 T it shall be, because he hath sinned, and 2050.1
7:12 t he shall offer with the sacrifice of 2050.1
10: 3 T Moses said unto Aaron, This *is it* that 2050.1
12: 2 t she shall be unclean seven days; 2050.1
12: 4 she shall *t* continue in the blood of her NIH
12: 5 t she shall be unclean two weeks, as *in* 2050.1
12: 8 t she shall bring two turtles, or two young 2050.1
13: 2 t he shall be brought unto Aaron 2050.1
13: 4 t the priest shall shut up *him that hath* 2050.1
13: 5 t the priest shall shut him up seven days 2050.1
13: 8 t the priest shall pronounce him unclean: 2050.1
13: 9 t he shall be brought unto the priest; 2050.1
13:13 T the priest shall consider: and behold, 2050.1
13:17 t the priest shall pronounce *him* clean *that* 2050.1
13:21 t the priest shall shut him up seven days: 2050.1
13:22 t the priest shall pronounce him unclean: 2050.1
13:25 T the priest shall look upon it: and 2050.1
13:26 t the priest shall shut him up seven days: 2050.1
13:27 t the priest shall pronounce him unclean: 2050.1
13:30 T the priest shall see the plague: and 2050.1
13:30 t the priest shall pronounce him unclean: 2050.1
13:31 t the priest shall shut up *him that hath* 2050.1
13:34 t the priest shall pronounce him clean: 2050.1
13:36 T the priest shall look on him: and 2050.1
13:39 T the priest shall look: and behold, *if* 2050.1
13:43 T the priest shall look upon it: and 2050.1
13:54 T the priest shall command that they 2050.1
13:56 t he shall rend it out of the garment, or 2050.1
13:58 t it shall be washed the second time, and 2050.1
14: 4 T shall the priest command to take for 2050.1
14:21 cannot get *so much;* t he shall take one 2050.1
14:36 T the priest shall command that they 2050.1
14:38 T the priest shall go out of the house to 2050.1
14:40 T the priest shall command that they take 2050.1
14:44 T the priest shall come and look, and 2050.1
14:48 t the priest shall pronounce the house 2050.1
15: 8 t he shall wash his clothes, and 2050.1

Lev 15:13 t he shall number to himself seven days 2050.1
15:16 t he shall wash all his flesh in water, 2050.1
15:28 t she shall number to herself seven days, 2050.1
16:15 T shall he kill the goat of the sin offering, 2050.1
17:15 unclean until the even: t shall he be clean. 2050.1
17:16 his flesh; t he shall bear his iniquity. 2050.1
19:23 t ye shall count the fruit thereof as 2050.1
20: 5 T I will set my face against that man, 2050.1
22:14 t he shall put the fifth *part* thereof unto it, 2050.1
22:27 t it shall be seven days under the dam; 2050.1
23:10 t ye shall bring a sheaf of the firstfruits of 2050.1
23:19 T ye shall sacrifice one kid of the goats 2050.1
25: 2 t shall the land keep a sabbath unto 2050.1
25: 9 T shalt thou cause the trumpet of 2050.1
25:21 T I will command my blessing upon you 2050.1
25:25 t shall he redeem that which his brother 2050.1
25:27 T let him count the years of the sale 2050.1
25:28 t that which is sold shall remain in 2050.1
25:29 t he may redeem it within a whole year 2050.1
25:30 t the house that *is* in the walled city shall 2050.1
25:33 t the house that was sold, and the city of 2050.1
25:35 decay with thee; t thou shalt relieve him: 2050.1
25:41 And *t* shall he depart from thee, *both* he and NIH
25:52 t he shall count with him, *and* 2050.1
25:54 t he shall go out in the year of jubile, 2050.1
26: 4 T I will give you rain in due season, 2050.1
26:18 t I will punish you seven *times* more for 2050.1
26:24 T will I also walk contrary unto you, and 2050.1
26:28 T I will walk contrary unto you **also** in 2050.1
26:34 T shall the land enjoy her sabbaths, as long 227
26:34 *even* t shall the land rest, and enjoy her 227
26:41 **if** t their uncircumcised hearts be 176+227
26:41 they t accept of the punishment of their 227
26:42 T will I remember my covenant with 2050.1
27: 4 t thy estimation shall be thirty shekels. 2050.1
27: 5 t thy estimation shall be of the male 2050.1
27: 6 t thy estimation shall be of the male five 2050.1
27: 7 t thy estimation shall be fifteen shekels, 2050.1
27: 8 t he shall present himself before 2050.1
27:10 t it and the exchange thereof shall be 2050.1
27:11 t he shall present the beast before 2050.1
27:13 t he shall add a fifth *part* thereof unto thy 2050.1
27:14 t the priest shall estimate it, whether it be 2050.1
27:15 t he shall add the fifth *part* of the money 2050.1
27:16 t thy estimation shall be according to 2050.1
27:18 t the priest shall reckon unto him 2050.1
27:19 t he shall add the fifth *part* of the money 2050.1
27:23 T the priest shall reckon unto him 2050.1
27:27 t he shall redeem *it* according to thine 2050.1
27:27 t it shall be sold according to thy 2050.1
27:33 t both it and the change thereof shall be 2050.1
Nu 2: 7 *T* the tribe of Zebulun: and Eliab the son of NIH
2:14 T the tribe of Gad: and the captain of 2050.1
2:17 T the tabernacle of the congregation shall 2050.1
2:22 T the tribe of Benjamin: and the captain 2050.1
2:29 T the tribe of Naphtali: and the captain of 2050.1
5: 7 T they shall confess their sin which they 2050.1
5:15 T shall the man bring his wife unto 2050.1
5:21 T the priest shall charge the woman with 2050.1
5:25 T the priest shall take the jealousy 2050.1
5:27 t it shall come to pass, *that,* if she be 2050.1
5:28 t she shall be free, and shall conceive 2050.1
5:31 T shall the man be guiltless from iniquity, 2050.1
6: 9 t he shall shave his head in the day of his 2050.1
7:89 t he heard the voice of one speaking unto 2050.1
8: 8 T let them take a young bullock with his 2050.1
9:17 t after that the children of Israel 2050.1
9:19 t the children of Israel kept the charge of 2050.1
9:21 up in the morning, t they journeyed: 2050.1
10: 4 *but* with one *trumpet,* t the princes, 2050.1
10: 5 t the camps that lie on the east parts shall 2050.1
10: 6 t the camps that lie on the south side shall 2050.1
10: 9 t ye shall blow an alarm with 2050.1
11:10 T Moses heard the people weep 2050.1
12: 8 wherefore t were ye not afraid to speak 2050.1
14: 5 T Moses and Aaron fell on their faces 2050.1
14: 8 t he will bring us into this land, and 2050.1
14:13 T the Egyptians shall hear *it,* (for thou 2050.1
14:15 t the nations which have heard the fame 2050.1
14:45 T the Amalekites came down, and 2050.1
15: 4 T shall he that offereth his offering unto 2050.1
15: 9 T shall he bring with a bullock a meat 2050.1
15:19 T it shall be, *that* when ye eat of 2050.1
15:24 T it shall be, if *ought* be committed by 2050.1
15:27 t he shall bring a she goat of the first year 2050.1
16: 3 wherefore t lift you up yourselves above 2050.1
16:29 of all men; *t* the LORD hath not sent me. NIH
16:30 t ye shall understand that these men have 2050.1
18:26 t ye shall offer up a heave offering of it 2050.1
18:30 t it shall be counted unto the Levites as 2050.1
19: 7 T the priest shall wash his clothes, and 2050.1
19:12 t the seventh day he shall not be clean. 2050.1
20: 1 T came the children of Israel, *even* 2050.1
20:19 drink *of* thy water, t I will pay for it: 2050.1
21: 1 t he fought against Israel, and took *some* 2050.1
21: 2 t I will utterly destroy their cities. 2050.1
21:17 T Israel sang this song, Spring up, O well; 227
22:31 T the LORD opened the eyes of 2050.1
27: 1 T came the daughters of Zelophehad, 2050.1
27: 8 t ye shall cause his inheritance to pass 2050.1
27: 9 t ye shall give his inheritance unto his 2050.1
27:10 t ye shall give his inheritance unto his 2050.1
27:11 t ye shall give his inheritance unto his 2050.1
30: 4 t all her vows shall stand, and every bond 2050.1
30: 7 that he heard *it:* t her vows shall stand, 2050.1
30: 8 t he shall make her vow which she 2050.1
30:11 t all her vows shall stand, and every bond 2050.1
30:12 *t* whatsoever proceeded out of her lips NIH
30:14 t he establisheth all her vows, or all her 2050.1
30:15 heard *them;* t he shall bear her iniquity. 2050.1
32:22 t afterward ye shall return, and 2050.1
32:29 t ye shall give them the land of Gilead for 2050.1
33:52 T ye shall drive out all the inhabitants of 2050.1
33:55 t it shall come to pass, *that those* which 2050.1
34: 3 T your south quarter shall be from 2050.1

Nu 35:11 T ye shall appoint you cities to be cities 2050.1
35:24 T the congregation shall judge between 2050.1
36: 3 t shall their inheritance be taken from 2050.1
36: 4 t shall their inheritance be put unto 2050.1
Dt 1:29 T I said unto you, Dread not, neither be 2050.1
1:41 T ye answered and said unto me, 2050.1
2: 1 T we turned, and took our journey into 2050.1
2:32 T Sihon came out against us, he and 2050.1
3: 1 T we turned, and went up the way to 2050.1
3:20 *t* shall ye return every man unto his NIH
4:41 T Moses severed three cities on *this* side 227
5:25 our God any more, t we shall die. 2050.1
6:12 *T* beware lest thou forget the LORD, NIH
6:21 T thou shalt say unto thy son, We were 2050.1
8:10 t thou shalt bless the LORD thy God for 2050.1
8:14 T thine heart be lifted up, and thou forget 2050.1
9: 9 t I abode in the mount forty days and 2050.1
9:23 t you rebelled against the commandment 2050.1
11:17 *t* the LORD'S wrath be kindled against NIH
11:23 T will the LORD drive out all these 2050.1
12:11 T there shall be a place which 2050.1
12:21 t thou shalt kill of thy herd and of thy 2050.1
13:14 T shalt thou inquire, and make search, 2050.1
14:25 T shalt thou turn *it* into money, and 2050.1
15:12 t in the seventh year thou shalt let him go 2050.1
15:17 T thou shalt take an aul, and thrust *it* 2050.1
17: 5 T shalt thou bring forth that man or 2050.1
17: 8 t shalt thou arise, and get thee up into 2050.1
18: 7 T he shall minister in the name of 2050.1
19: 9 t shalt thou add three cities moe for thee, 2050.1
19:12 T the elders of his city shall send and 2050.1
19:17 T both the men, between whom 2050.1
19:19 T shall ye do unto him, as he had thought 2050.1
20:10 fight against it, t proclaim peace unto it. 2050.1
20:11 of peace, and open unto thee, t it shall be, 2050.1
20:12 war against thee, t thou shalt besiege it: 2050.1
21: 2 T thy elders and thy judges shall come 2050.1
21:12 T thou shalt bring her home to thine 2050.1
21:14 t thou shalt let her go whither she will; 2050.1
21:16 T it shall be, when he maketh his sons to 2050.1
21:19 T shall his father and his mother lay hold 2050.1
22: 2 t thou shalt bring it unto thine own house, 2050.1
22: 8 t thou shalt make a battlement for thy 2050.1
22:15 T shall the father of the damsel, and 2050.1
22:21 T they shall bring out the damsel to 2050.1
22:22 t they shall both of them die, *both* 2050.1
22:24 T ye shall bring them both out unto 2050.1
22:25 t the man only that lay with her shall die: 2050.1
22:29 T the man that lay with her shall give 2050.1
23: 9 t keep thee from every wicked thing. 2050.1
23:10 t shall he go abroad out of the camp, 2050.1
23:24 t thou mayest eat grapes thy fill at thine 2050.1
23:25 t thou mayest pluck the ears with thine 2050.1
24: 1 t let him write her a bill of divorcement, 2050.1
24: 7 t that thief shall die; and thou shalt put 2050.1
25: 1 t they shall justify the righteous, and 2050.1
25: 3 t thy brother should seem vile unto thee. 2050.1
25: 7 t let his brother's wife go up to the gate 2050.1
25: 8 T the elders of his city shall call him, and 2050.1
25: 9 T shall his brother's wife come unto him 2050.1
25:12 T thou shalt cut off her hand, thine eye 2050.1
26:13 T thou shalt say before the LORD thy 2050.1
28:59 T the LORD will make thy plagues 2050.1
29:20 t the anger of the LORD and his jealousy 227
29:25 T *men* shall say, Because they have 2050.1
30: 3 That t the LORD thy God will turn thy 2050.1
31:17 T my anger shall be kindled against them 2050.1
31:20 t will they turn unto other gods, and 2050.1
32:15 thou art covered *with fatness;* t 2050.1
33:28 Israel t shall dwell *in* safety alone: 2050.1
Jos 1: 8 for t thou shalt make thy way prosperous, 227
1: 8 and t thou shalt have good success. 227
1:10 T Joshua commanded the officers of 2050.1
1:15 t ye shall return unto the land of your 2050.1
2:15 T she let them down by a cord through 2050.1
2:20 t we will be quit of thine oath which thou 2050.1
3: 3 t ye shall remove from your place, and 2050.1
4: 4 T Joshua called the twelve men, whom he 2050.1
4: 7 T ye shall answer them, That the waters 2050.1
4:22 T ye shall let your children know, 2050.1
6:10 the day I bid you shout; t shall ye shout. 2050.1
7:21 t I coveted them, and took them; 2050.1
8: 7 T ye shall rise up from the ambush, and 2050.1
8:21 t they turned again, and slew the men of 2050.1
8:30 T Joshua built an altar unto the LORD God 227
10:12 T spake Joshua to the LORD in the day 227
10:22 T said Joshua, Open the mouth of 2050.1
10:29 T Joshua passed from Makkedah, and 2050.1
10:33 T Horam king of Gezer came up to help 227
14: 6 T the children of Judah came unto Joshua 2050.1
14:11 as my strength *was* t, even so *is* my strength 227
14:12 t I shall *be able to* drive them out, as 2050.1
15: 1 *This* t was the lot of the tribe of 2050.1
17:15 *t* get thee up to the wood *country,* and NIH
19:12 *t* goeth out to Daberath, and goeth up *to* NIH
19:29 *t* the coast turneth *to* Ramah, and to NIH
19:34 *t* the coast turneth westward *to* NIH
20: 5 t they shall not deliver the slayer up into 2050.1
20: 6 t shall the slayer return, and come unto his 227
21: 1 T came near the heads of the fathers of 2050.1
22: 1 T Joshua called the Reubenites, and 227
22: 7 also unto their tents, t he blessed them, 2050.1
22:19 *t* pass ye over unto the land of NIH
22:21 T the children of Reuben and the children 2050.1
23:16 t shall the anger of the LORD be 2050.1
24: 9 T Balak the son of Zippor, king of Moab, 2050.1
24:20 t he will turn and do you hurt, 2050.1
Jdg 2:18 t the LORD was with the judge, and 2050.1
3:23 T Ehud went forth through the porch, and 2050.1
4: 8 If thou wilt go with me, t I will go: 2050.1
4: 8 if thou wilt not go with me, *t* I will not go. NIH
4:21 T Jael Heber's wife took a nail of 2050.1
5: 1 T sang Deborah and Barak the son of 2050.1
5: 8 chose new gods; t *was* war in the gates: 227
5:11 t shall the people of the LORD go down to 227

T

Jdg 5:13 T he made him that remaineth have 227
5:19 t fought the kings of Canaan in Taanach by 227
5:22 T were the horsehoofs broken by the means 227
6:13 be with us, why t is all this befallen us? 2050.1
6:17 t shew me a sign that thou talkest with 2050.1
6:21 T the angel of the LORD put forth 2050.1
6:21 the unleavened *cakes.* T the angel of 2050.1
6:24 T Gideon built an altar there unto 2050.1
6:27 T Gideon took ten men of his servants, 2050.1
6:30 T the men of the city said unto Joash, 2050.1
6:33 T all the Midianites and the Amalekites 2050.1
6:37 *it be* dry upon all the earth *beside,* t 2050.1
7: 1 T Jerubbaal, who *is* Gideon, and all 2050.1
7:11 T went he down with Phurah his servant 2050.1
7:18 t blow ye the trumpets also on every side 2050.1
7:24 T all the men of Ephraim gathered 2050.1
8: 3 T their anger was abated toward him, 227
8: 7 t I will tear your flesh with the thorns of 2050.1
8:18 T said he unto Zebah and Zalmunna, 2050.1
8:21 T Zebah and Zalmunna said, Rise thou, 2050.1
8:22 T the men of Israel said unto Gideon, 2050.1
9:12 T said the trees unto the vine, Come thou, 2050.1
9:14 T said all the trees unto the bramble, 2050.1
9:15 *t* come *and* put your trust in my shadow: NIH
9:19 If ye t have dealt truly and sincerely with 2050.1
9:19 *t* rejoice ye in Abimelech, and let him also NIH
9:23 T God sent an evil spirit between 2050.1
9:29 my hand; t would I remove Abimelech. 2050.1
9:33 t mayest thou do to them as thou shalt 2050.1
9:38 T said Zebul unto him, Where *is* now thy 2050.1
9:50 T went Abimelech to Thebez, and 2050.1
9:54 T he called hastily unto the young man 2050.1
10:17 T the children of Ammon were gathered 2050.1
11: 3 T Jephthah fled from his brethren, and 2050.1
11:11 T Jephthah went with the elders of 2050.1
11:17 T Israel sent messengers unto the king of 2050.1
11:18 T they went along through 2050.1
11:29 T the spirit of the LORD came upon 2050.1
11:31 T it shall be, that whatsoever cometh 2050.1
12: 3 wherefore t are ye come up unto me this 2050.1
12: 4 T Jephthah gathered together all the men 2050.1
12: 6 T said they unto him, Say now 2050.1
12: 6 T they took him, and slew him at 2050.1
12: 7 T died Jephthah the Gileadite, and 2050.1
12:10 T died Ibzan, and was buried at 2050.1
13: 6 T the woman came and told her husband, 2050.1
13: 8 T Manoah intreated the LORD, and 2050.1
13:21 T Manoah knew that he *was* an angel of 227
14: 3 T his father and his mother said unto him, 2050.1
14: 5 T went Samson down, and his father and 2050.1
14:12 t I will give you thirty sheets and 2050.1
14:13 t shall ye give me thirty sheets and 2050.1
15: 6 T the Philistines said, Who hath done 2050.1
15: 9 T the Philistines went up, and pitched in 2050.1
15:11 T three thousand men of Judah went to 2050.1
16: 1 T went Samson to Gaza, and saw there a 2050.1
16: 7 t shall I be weak, and be as another man. 2050.1
16: 8 T the lords of the Philistines brought up 2050.1
16:11 t shall I be weak, and be as another man. 2050.1
16:17 t my strength will go from me, and I shall 2050.1
16:18 T the lords of the Philistines came up 2050.1
16:23 T the lords of the Philistines gathered 2050.1
16:31 T his brethren and all the house of his 2050.1
17:13 T said Micah, Now know I that 2050.1
18: 7 T the five men departed, and came to 2050.1
18:14 T answered the five men that went to spy 2050.1
18:18 T said the priest unto them, What do ye? 2050.1
19:26 T came the woman in the dawning of 2050.1
19:28 T the man took her *up* upon an ass, and 2050.1
20: 1 T all the children of Israel went out, and 2050.1
20: 3 T said the children of Israel, Tell *us,* how 2050.1
20:26 T all the children of Israel, and all 2050.1
21:16 T the elders of the congregation said, 2050.1
21:19 T they said, Behold, *there is* a feast of 2050.1
21:21 t come ye out of the vineyards, and 2050.1
Ru 1: 6 T she arose with her daughters in law, 2050.1
1: 9 T she kissed them; and they lift up their 2050.1
1:18 go with her, t she left speaking unto her. 2050.1
1:21 why *t* call ye me Naomi, seeing the LORD NIH
2: 5 T said Boaz unto his servant that was set 2050.1
2: 8 T said Boaz unto Ruth, Hearest thou not, 2050.1
2:10 T she fell on her face, and bowed herself 2050.1
2:13 T she said, Let me find favour in thy 2050.1
3: 1 T Naomi her mother in law said unto her, 2050.1
3:13 t will I do the part of a kinsman to thee, 2050.1
3:18 T said she, Sit still, my daughter, 2050.1
4: 1 T went Boaz up *to* the gate, and sat him 2050.1
4: 4 but if thou wilt not redeem *it,* *t* tell me, NIH
4: 5 T said Boaz, What day thou buyest 2050.1
1Sa 1: 8 T said Elkanah her husband to her, 2050.1
1:11 t I will give him unto the LORD all 2050.1
1:17 T Eli answered and said, Go in peace: 2050.1
1:22 *t* I will bring him, that he may appear before NIH
2:16 *t* take *as much* as thy soul desireth; NIH
2:16 t he would answer him, *Nay;* but 2050.1
3:10 T Samuel answered, Speak; for thy 2050.1
3:16 T Eli called Samuel, and said, Samuel, 2050.1
6: 3 t ye shall be healed, and it shall be known to 227
6: 4 T said they, What *shall be* the trespass 2050.1
6: 6 Wherefore t do ye harden your hearts, 2050.1
6: 9 *t* he hath done us this great evil: NIH
6: 9 t we shall know that *it is* not his hand *that* 2050.1
7: 3 *t* put away the strange gods and Ashtaroth NIH
7: 4 T the children of Israel did put away 2050.1
7:12 T Samuel took a stone, and set *it* between 2050.1
8: 4 T all the elders of Israel gathered 2050.1
9: 4 t they passed through the land of Shalim, 2050.1
9: 7 T said Saul to his servant, But behold, 2050.1
9:10 T said Saul to his servant, Well said; 2050.1
9:18 T Saul drew near to Samuel in the gate, 2050.1
9:21 t speakest thou so to me? 2050.1
10: 1 T Samuel took a vial of oil, and poured *it* 2050.1
10: 2 t thou shalt find two men by Rachel's 2050.1
10: 3 T shalt thou go on forward from thence, 2050.1
10:11 t the people said one to another, 2050.1

1Sa 10:25 T Samuel told the people the manner of 2050.1
11: 1 T Nahash the Ammonite came up, and 2050.1
11: 3 and t, if *there be* no man to save us, we 2050.1
11: 4 T came the messengers *to* Gibeah of 2050.1
11:14 T said Samuel to the people, Come, and 2050.1
12: 8 t the LORD sent Moses and Aaron, 2050.1
12:14 t shall both ye and also the king that 2050.1
12:15 t shall the hand of the LORD be against 2050.1
12:21 for *t should ye go* after vain *things,* which NIH
13: 6 t the people did hide themselves in caves, 2050.1
14: 8 T said Jonathan, Behold, we will pass 2050.1
14: 9 t we will stand still in our place, and 2050.1
14:10 Come up unto us; t we will go up: 2050.1
14:17 T said Saul unto the people that *were* 2050.1
14:28 T answered one of the people, and said, 2050.1
14:29 T said Jonathan, My father hath troubled 2050.1
14:33 T they told Saul, saying, Behold, 2050.1
14:36 T said the priest, Let us draw near hither 2050.1
14:40 T said he unto all Israel, Be ye on one 2050.1
14:43 T Saul said to Jonathan, Tell me what 2050.1
14:46 T Saul went up from following 2050.1
15:10 T came the word of the LORD unto 2050.1
15:14 What *meaneth* t this bleating of the sheep 2050.1
15:16 T Samuel said unto Saul, Stay, and I will 2050.1
15:19 Wherefore t didst thou not obey the voice 2050.1
15:30 T he said, I have sinned: *yet* honour me 2050.1
15:32 T said Samuel, Bring you hither to me 2050.1
15:34 T Samuel went to Ramah; and Saul went 2050.1
16: 8 T Jesse called Abinadab, and made him 2050.1
16: 9 T Jesse made Shammah to pass by. 2050.1
16:13 T Samuel took the horn of oil, and 2050.1
16:18 T answered one of the servants, and said, 2050.1
17: 9 and *to* kill me, t will we be your servants: 2050.1
17: 9 t shall ye be our servants, and serve us. 2050.1
17:45 T said David to the Philistine, 2050.1
18: 3 T Jonathan and David made a covenant, 2050.1
18:30 T the princes of the Philistines went 2050.1
19: 5 wherefore t wilt thou sin against innocent 2050.1
19:22 T went he also to Ramah, and came to a 2050.1
20: 4 T said Jonathan unto David, 2050.1
20: 6 If thy father at all miss me, t say, 2050.1
20: 7 *t* be sure that evil is determined by him. NIH
20: 9 come upon thee, t would not I tell it thee? 2050.1
20:10 T said David to Jonathan, Who shall tell 2050.1
20:12 and I t send not unto thee, and shew it thee; 227
20:13 t I will shew it thee, and send thee away, 2050.1
20:18 T Jonathan said to *David,* To morrow *is* 2050.1
20:19 *t* thou shalt go down quickly, and come to NIH
20:21 this side of thee, take them; t come thou: 2050.1
20:30 T Saul's anger was kindled against 2050.1
21: 1 T came David to Nob to Ahimelech 2050.1
21:14 T said Achish unto his servants, Lo, 2050.1
21:14 *t* have ye brought him to me? NIH
22: 5 T David departed, and came *into* 2050.1
22: 7 T Saul said unto his servants that stood 2050.1
22: 9 T answered Doeg the Edomite, which 2050.1
22:11 T the king sent to call Ahimelech 2050.1
22:14 T Ahimelech answered the king, and 2050.1
22:15 Did I t begin to inquire of God for 3117+1886.1
23: 1 T they told David, saying, Behold, 2050.1
23: 3 how much more t if we come *to* Keilah 2050.1
23: 4 T David inquired of the LORD yet 2050.1
23:10 T said David, O LORD God of Israel, 2050.1
23:12 T said David, Will the men of Keilah 2050.1
23:13 T David and his men, *which were* about 2050.1
23:19 T came up the Ziphites to Saul to Gibeah, 2050.1
24: 2 T Saul took three thousand chosen men 2050.1
24: 4 T David arose, and cut off the skirt of 2050.1
25:11 Shall I t take my bread, and my water, 2050.1
25:18 T Abigail made haste, and took two 2050.1
25:31 my lord, t remember thine handmaid. 2050.1
26: 2 T Saul arose, and went down to 2050.1
26: 6 T answered David and said to Ahimelech 2050.1
26: 8 T said Abishai to David, God hath 2050.1
26:13 T David went over *to* the *other* side, and 2050.1
26:14 T Abner answered and said, Who *art* thou 2050.1
26:15 wherefore t hast thou not kept thy lord 2050.1
26:21 T said Saul, I have sinned: return, my son 2050.1
26:25 T Saul said to David, Blessed *be* thou, 2050.1
27: 6 T Achish gave him Ziklag that day: 2050.1
28: 7 T said Saul unto his servants, Seek me a 2050.1
28: 9 wherefore t layest thou a snare for my 2050.1
28:11 T said the woman, Whom shall I bring up 2050.1
28:16 T said Samuel, Wherefore then dost thou 2050.1
28:16 Wherefore t dost thou ask of me, 2050.1
28:20 T Saul fell straightway all along on 2050.1
28:25 T they arose up, and went away that 2050.1
29: 3 T said the princes of the Philistines, 2050.1
29: 6 T Achish called David, and said unto 2050.1
30: 4 T David and the people that *were* with 2050.1
30:22 T answered all the wicked men and 2050.1
30:23 T said David, Ye shall not do so, 2050.1
31: 4 T said Saul unto his armourbearer, Draw 2050.1
2Sa 1:11 T David took hold on his clothes, and 2050.1
2:15 T there arose and went over by number 2050.1
2:20 T Abner looked behind him, and said, *Art* 2050.1
2:22 how t should I hold up my face to Joab 2050.1
2:26 T Abner called to Joab, and said, Shall 2050.1
2:26 how long shall it be t, ere thou bid 2050.1
2:27 surely t in the morning the people had gone 227
3: 8 T was Abner very wroth for the words of 2050.1
3:16 T said Abner unto him, Go, return. 2050.1
3:18 Now t do *it:* for the LORD hath spoken 2050.1
3:24 T Joab came to the king, and said, 2050.1
5: 1 T came all the tribes of Israel to David 2050.1
5:24 *that* t thou shalt bestir thyself: 227
5:24 for t shall the LORD go out before thee, 227
6:20 T David returned to bless his household. 2050.1
7:18 T went king David in, and sat before 2050.1
8: 6 T David put garrisons in Syria of 2050.1
8:10 T Toi sent Joram his son unto king 2050.1
9: 5 T king David sent, and fet him out of 2050.1
9: 9 T the king called to Ziba, Saul's servant, 2050.1
9:11 T said Ziba unto the king, According to 2050.1
10: 2 T said David, I will shew kindness unto 2050.1

2Sa 10: 5 until your beards be grown, and *t* return. NIH
10:11 be too strong for me, t thou shalt help me: 2050.1
10:11 for thee, t I will come and help thee. 2050.1
10:14 *t* fled they *also* before Abishai, and NIH
11:10 why *t* didst thou not go down unto thine NIH
11:11 shall I t go into mine house, to eat and 2050.1
11:18 T Joab sent and told David all the things 2050.1
11:21 t say thou, Thy servant Uriah the Hittite 2050.1
11:25 T David said unto the messenger, 2050.1
12:18 how will he t vex himself, if we tell him 2050.1
12:20 T David arose from the earth, and 2050.1
12:20 t he came to his own house; and when he 2050.1
12:21 T said his servants unto him, What thing 2050.1
13: 7 T David sent home to Tamar, saying, 2050.1
13:15 T Amnon hated her exceedingly; so 2050.1
13:17 T he called his servant that ministered 2050.1
13:18 T his servant brought her out, and 2050.1
13:26 T said Absalom, If not, I pray thee, 2050.1
13:28 Smite Amnon; t kill him, fear not: 2050.1
13:29 T all the king's sons arose, and 2050.1
13:31 T the king arose, and tare his garments, 2050.1
14:11 T said she, I pray thee, let the king 2050.1
14:12 T the woman said, Let thine handmaid, 2050.1
14:13 Wherefore t hast thou thought such a 2050.1
14:17 T thine handmaid said, The word of my 2050.1
14:18 T the king answered and said unto 2050.1
14:31 T Joab arose, and came to Absalom unto 2050.1
15: 2 t Absalom called unto him, and said, 2050.1
15: 8 *to* Jerusalem, t I will serve the LORD. 2050.1
15:10 t ye shall say, Absalom reigneth in 2050.1
15:19 T said the king to Ittai the Gittite, 2050.1
15:33 t thou shalt be a burden unto me: 2050.1
15:34 t mayest thou for me defeat the counsel 2050.1
16: 4 T said the king to Ziba, Behold, thine *are* 2050.1
16: 9 T said Abishai the son of Zeruiah unto 2050.1
16:10 Who shall t say, Wherefore hast thou 2050.1
16:20 T said Absalom to Ahithophel, 2050.1
16:21 t shall the hands of all that *are* with thee 2050.1
17: 5 T said Absalom, Call now Hushai 2050.1
17:13 t shall all Israel bring ropes to that city, 2050.1
17:15 T said Hushai unto Zadok and 2050.1
17:22 T David arose, and all the people that 2050.1
17:24 T David came to Mahanaim. 2050.1
18:14 T said Joab, I may not tarry thus with 2050.1
18:19 T said Ahimaaz the son of Zadok, Let me 2050.1
18:21 T said Joab to Cushi, Go tell the king 2050.1
18:22 T said Ahimaaz the son of Zadok yet 2050.1
18:23 T Ahimaaz ran *by* the way of the plain, 2050.1
19: 6 *this* day, t it had pleased thee well. 227+3588
19: 8 T the king rose, and sat in the gate. 2050.1
19:12 wherefore t are ye the last to bring back 2050.1
19:35 and singing *women?* wherefore t 2050.1
19:40 T the king went on to Gilgal, and 2050.1
19:42 wherefore t be ye angry for this matter? 2050.1
19:43 why t did ye despise us, that our advice 2050.1
20: 4 T said the king to Amasa, Assemble me 2050.1
20:16 T cried a wise woman out of the city, 2050.1
20:17 I *am he.* T she said unto him, 2050.1
20:18 T she spake, saying, They were wont to 2050.1
20:22 T the woman went unto all the people in 2050.1
21: 1 T there was a famine in the days of David 2050.1
21:17 T the men of David sware unto him, saying, 227
21:18 t Sibbechai the Hushathite slew Saph, 227
22: 8 T the earth shook and trembled; 2050.1
22:43 T did I beat them *as* small as the dust of 2050.1
23:14 David *was* t in a hold, and the garrison of 227
23:14 of the Philistines *was* t in Beth-lehem. 227
24: 6 T they came to Gilead, and to the land of 2050.1
1Ki 1: 5 T Adonijah the son of Haggith exalted 2050.1
1:13 my throne? why t doth Adonijah reign? 2050.1
1:28 T king David answered and said, Call me 2050.1
1:31 T Bath-sheba bowed *with her* face *to* 2050.1
1:35 T ye shall come up after him, that he may 2050.1
2:12 T sat Solomon upon the throne of David 2050.1
2:20 T she said, I desire one small petition of 2050.1
2:23 T king Solomon sware by the LORD, 2050.1
2:28 T tidings came to Joab: for Joab had 2050.1
2:29 T Solomon sent Benaiah the son of 2050.1
2:43 Why t hast thou not kept the oath of 2050.1
3:14 did walk, t I will lengthen thy days. 2050.1
3:16 T came there two women, *that were* harlots, 227
3:23 T said the king, The one saith, This *is* my 2050.1
3:26 T spake the woman whose the living 2050.1
3:27 T the king answered and said, Give her 2050.1
6:10 *t* he built chambers against all the house, NIH
6:12 t will I perform my word with thee, 2050.1
7: 7 T he made a porch for the throne where 2050.1
7:38 T made he ten lavers of brass: one laver 2050.1
8: 1 T Solomon assembled the elders of Israel, 227
8:12 T spake Solomon, The LORD said that *he* 227
8:32 T hear thou *in* heaven, and do, and 2050.1
8:34 T hear thou *in* heaven, and forgive the sin 2050.1
8:36 T hear thou *in* heaven, and forgive the sin 2050.1
8:39 T hear thou *in* heaven thy dwelling place, 2050.1
8:45 T hear thou *in* heaven their prayer and 2050.1
8:49 T hear thou their prayer and 2050.1
9: 5 T I will establish the throne of thy 2050.1
9: 7 T will I cut off Israel out of the land 2050.1
9:11 *that* t king Solomon gave Hiram twenty 227
9:24 had built for her: t did he build Millo. 227
11: 7 T did Solomon build a high place for 227
11:22 T Pharaoh said unto him, But what *hast* 2050.1
12: 5 yet *for* three days, t come again to me. 2050.1
12: 7 t they will be thy servants for ever. 2050.1
12:18 T king Rehoboam sent Adoram, who *was* 2050.1
12:25 T Jeroboam built Shechem in mount 2050.1
12:27 t shall the heart of this people turn again 2050.1
13:15 T he said unto him, Come home with me, 2050.1
13:31 t bury me in the sepulchre wherein 2050.1
15:18 T Asa took all the silver and the gold that 2050.1
15:22 T king Asa made a proclamation 2050.1
16: 1 T the word of the LORD came to Jehu 2050.1
16:21 T were the people of Israel divided into two 227
18:21 if Baal, *t* follow him. And the people NIH
18:22 T said Elijah unto the people, I, *even* I 2050.1

T

1Ki 18:38 T the fire of the LORD fell, and 2050.1
19: 2 T Jezebel sent a messenger unto Elijah, 2050.1
19: 5 behold t, an angel touched him, and 2050.1
19:20 and my mother, and t I will follow thee. NIH
19:21 T he arose, and went after Elijah, and 2050.1
20: 7 T the king of Israel called all the elders of 2050.1
20:14 T he said, Who shall order the battle? 2050.1
20:15 T he numbered the young men of 2050.1
20:33 T he said, Go ye, bring him. 2050.1
20:33 T Ben-hadad came forth to him; and 2050.1
20:34 T *said Ahab,* I will send thee away with 2050.1
20:36 T said he unto him, Because thou hast not 2050.1
20:37 T he found another man, and said, 2050.1
20:39 t shall thy life be for his life, or else thou 2050.1
21:10 t carry him out, and stone him, that he may NIH
21:13 T they carried him forth out of the city, 2050.1
21:14 T they sent to Jezebel, saying, Naboth is 2050.1
22: 6 T the king of Israel gathered the prophets 2050.1
22: 9 T the king of Israel called an officer, and 2050.1
22:47 *There was* t no king in Edom: a deputy 2050.1
22:49 T said Ahaziah the son of Ahab unto 227
2Ki 1: 1 T Moab rebelled against Israel after 2050.1
1: 9 T the king sent unto him a captain of fifty 2050.1
1:10 t let fire come down from heaven, and 2050.1
3:27 T he took his eldest son that should have 2050.1
4: 3 T he said, Go, borrow thee vessels abroad 2050.1
4: 7 T she came and told the man of God. 2050.1
4:14 he said, What t *is* to be done for her? 2050.1
4:20 he sat on her knees till noon, and t died. NIH
4:24 T she saddled an ass, and said to her 2050.1
4:28 T she said, Did I desire a son of my lord? 2050.1
4:29 T he said to Gehazi, Gird up thy loins, 2050.1
4:35 T he returned, and walked in the house to 2050.1
4:37 T she went in, and fell at his feet, and 2050.1
4:41 he said, T bring meal. And he cast *it* into 2050.1
5:13 thou not have done *it?* how much rather t, 2050.1
5:14 T went he down, and dipped *himself* 2050.1
5:17 Shall there not t, I pray thee, 2050.1
6: 8 T the king of Syria warred against Israel, 2050.1
6:31 T he said, God do so and more also to 2050.1
7: 1 T Elisha said, Hear ye the word of 2050.1
7: 2 T a lord on whose hand the king leaned 2050.1
7: 4 t the famine *is* in the city, and we shall 2050.1
7: 9 T they said one to another, We do not 2050.1
8: 1 T spake Elisha unto the woman, 2050.1
8:16 Jehoshaphat *being* t king of Judah, 2050.1
8:22 this day. T Libnah revolted at the same time. 227
9: 3 T take the box of oil, and pour *it* on his 2050.1
9: 3 T open the door, and flee, and tarry not. 2050.1
9:11 T Jehu came forth to the servants of his 2050.1
9:13 T they hasted, and took every man his 2050.1
9:15 t let none go forth *nor* escape out of the city NIH
9:19 T he sent *out* a second on horseback, 2050.1
9:25 T said *Jehu* to Bidkar his captain, 2050.1
10: 4 not before him: how t shall we stand? 2050.1
10: 6 T he wrote a letter the second time to 2050.1
12: 7 T king Jehoash called for Jehoiada 2050.1
12:17 T Hazael king of Syria went up, and 227
13:17 he opened *it.* T Elisha said, Shoot. 2050.1
13:19 t hadst thou smitten Syria till *thou* hadst 227
14: 8 T Amaziah sent messengers to Jehoash, 227
15:16 T Menahem smote Tiphsah, and all that 227
16: 5 T Rezin king of Syria and Pekah son of 227
17: 5 T the king of Assyria came up throughout 2050.1
17:27 T the king of Assyria commanded, 2050.1
17:28 T one of the priests whom they had 2050.1
18:24 How t wilt thou turn away the face of one 2050.1
18:26 T said Eliakim the son of Hilkiah, and 2050.1
18:28 T Rab-shakeh stood and cried with a loud 2050.1
18:31 t eat ye every man of his own vine, and NIH
18:37 T came Eliakim the son of Hilkiah, 2050.1
19:20 T Isaiah the son of Amoz sent to 2050.1
20: 2 T he turned his face to the wall, and 2050.1
20:14 T came Isaiah the prophet unto king 2050.1
20:19 T said Hezekiah unto Isaiah, Good *is* 2050.1
23:17 T he said, What title *is* that that I see? 2050.1
24: 1 t he turned and rebelled against him. 2050.1
1Ch 1:29 t Kedar, and Adbeel, and Mibsam, 2050.1
2:24 t Abiah Hezron's wife bare him Ashur 2050.1
6:32 t they waited on their office according to NIH
9:36 t Zur, and Kish, and Baal, and Ner, and 2050.1
10: 4 T said Saul to his armourbearer, Draw 2050.1
10: 7 t they forsook their cities, and fled: 2050.1
11: 1 T all Israel gathered themselves to David 2050.1
11:16 David *was* t in the hold, and the Philistines' 227
11:16 the Philistines' garrison *was* t at Beth-lehem. 227
12: 3 The chief *was* Ahiezer, t Joash, the sons 2050.1
12:18 T the spirit came upon Amasai, *who was* 2050.1
12:18 T David received them, and made them 2050.1
14:11 T David said, God hath broken in upon 2050.1
14:15 *that* t thou shalt go out to battle: 227
15: 2 T David said, None ought to carry the ark of 227
16: 7 T on that day David delivered first *this* 227
16:33 T shall the trees of the wood sing out at 227
17: 2 T Nathan said unto David, Do all that *is* 2050.1
18: 6 T David put *garrisons* in Syria-damascus; 2050.1
19: 5 T there went *certain,* and told David how 2050.1
19: 5 until your beards be grown, and t return. NIH
19:12 be too strong for me, t thou shalt help me: 2050.1
19:12 be too strong for thee, t I will help thee. 2050.1
19:15 into the city. T Joab came *to* Jerusalem. 2050.1
21: 3 why t doth my lord require this *thing?* why NIH
21:16 T David and the elders *of Israel, who* 2050.1
21:18 T the angel of the LORD commanded 2050.1
21:22 T David said to Ornan, Grant me 2050.1
21:28 Ornan the Jebusite, t he sacrificed there. 2050.1
22: 1 T David said, This *is* the house of 2050.1
22: 6 T he called for Solomon his son, and 2050.1
22:13 T shalt thou prosper, if thou takest heed to 227
26:14 T *for* Zechariah his son, a wise 2050.1
28: 2 T David the king stood up upon his feet, 2050.1
28:11 T David gave to Solomon his son 2050.1
29: 5 who t *is* willing to consecrate his service NIH
29: 6 T the chief of the fathers and princes of 2050.1
29: 9 T the people rejoiced, for that they 2050.1
1Ch 29:23 T Solomon sat on the throne of 2050.1
2Ch 1: 2 T Solomon spake unto all Israel, to 2050.1
1:13 T Solomon came *from his journey* to 2050.1
2: 6 who *am* I t, that I should build him a 2050.1
2:11 T Huram the king of Tyre answered in 2050.1
3: 1 T Solomon began to build the house of 2050.1
5: 2 T Solomon assembled the elders of Israel, 227
5:11 *and* did not t wait by course: NIH
5:13 that t the house was filled *with* a cloud, NIH
6: 1 T said Solomon, The LORD hath said that 227
6:17 Now t, O LORD God of Israel, let thy 2050.1
6:23 T hear thou from heaven, and do, and 2050.1
6:25 T hear thou from the heavens, and 2050.1
6:27 T hear thou *from* heaven, and forgive 2050.1
6:29 T what prayer *or* what supplication soever NIH
6:30 T hear thou from heaven thy dwelling 2050.1
6:33 T hear thou from the heavens, *even* from 2050.1
6:35 T hear thou from the heavens their prayer 2050.1
6:39 T hear thou from the heavens, *even* from 2050.1
7: 4 T the king and all the people offered 2050.1
7:14 t will I hear from heaven, and 2050.1
7:18 T will I stablish the throne of thy 2050.1
7:20 T will I pluck them up by the roots out of 2050.1
8:12 T Solomon offered burnt offerings unto 227
8:17 T went Solomon to Ezion-geber, and 227
10:18 T king Rehoboam sent Hadoram that *was* 2050.1
12: 5 T came Shemaiah the prophet to 2050.1
13:15 T the men of Judah gave a shout: and 2050.1
14:10 T Asa went out against him, and they set 2050.1
16: 2 T Asa brought out silver and gold out of 2050.1
16: 6 T Asa the king took all Judah; and 2050.1
16:10 T Asa was wroth with the seer, and 2050.1
18:16 T he said, I did see all Israel scattered 2050.1
18:20 T there came out a spirit, and 2050.1
18:23 T Zedekiah the son of Chenaanah came 2050.1
18:25 T the king of Israel said, Take ye 2050.1
18:27 t hath not the LORD spoken by me. NIH
20: 2 T there came *some* that told Jehoshaphat, 2050.1
20: 9 in our affliction, t thou wilt hear and help. 2050.3
20:14 T upon Jahaziel the son of Zechariah, 2050.1
20:27 T they returned, every man of Judah and 2050.1
20:37 T Eliezer the son of Dodavah of 2050.1
21: 9 T Jehoram went forth with his princes, 2050.1
23:11 T they brought out the king's son, and 2050.1
23:13 T Athaliah rent her clothes, and said, 2050.1
23:14 T Jehoiada the priest brought out 2050.1
23:17 T all the people went *to* the house of 2050.1
24:17 to the king. T the king hearkened unto them. 227
25:10 T Amaziah separated them, to wit, 2050.1
25:16 T the prophet forbare, and said, I know 2050.1
25:17 T Amaziah king of Judah took advice, 2050.1
26: 1 T all the people of Judah took Uzziah, 2050.1
26:19 T Uzziah was wroth, and *had* a censer in 2050.1
28:12 T certain of the heads of the children of 2050.1
28:15 their brethren: t they returned *to* Samaria. 2050.1
29:12 T the Levites arose, Mahath the son of 2050.1
29:18 T they went in to Hezekiah the king, and 2050.1
29:20 T Hezekiah the king rose early, and 2050.1
29:31 T Hezekiah answered and said, Now ye 2050.1
30:15 T they killed the passover on 2050.1
30:27 T the priests the Levites arose and 2050.1
31: 1 *all.* T all the children of Israel returned, 2050.1
31: 9 T Hezekiah questioned with the priests 2050.1
31:11 T Hezekiah commanded to prepare 2050.1
32:18 T they cried with a loud voice in 2050.1
33:13 T Manasseh knew that the LORD he 2050.1
34:18 T Shaphan the scribe told the king, 2050.1
34:29 T the king sent and gathered together all 2050.1
36: 1 T the people of the land took Jehoahaz 2050.1
Ezr 1: 5 T rose up the chief of the fathers of Judah 2050.1
3: 2 T stood up Jeshua the son of Jozadak, 2050.1
3: 9 T stood Jeshua *with* his sons and 2050.1
4: 2 T they came to Zerubbabel, and to 2050.1
4: 4 T the people of the land weakened 2050.1
4: 9 T *wrote* Rehum the chancellor, 116
4:13 walls set up *again,* t will they not pay toll, NIH
4:17 T sent the king an answer unto Rehum NIH
4:24 T ceased the work of the house of 116+871.2
5: 1 T the prophets, Haggai the prophet, and 2050.1
5: 2 T rose up Zerubbabel the son of 116+871.2
5: 4 T said we unto them after this manner, 116
5: 5 t they returned answer by letter concerning 116
5: 9 T asked we those elders, *and* said unto them 116
5:16 T came the same Sheshbazzar, *and* laid 116
6: 1 T Darius the king made a decree, and 116+871.2
6:13 T Tatnai, governor on *this* side the river, 116
8:16 T sent I for Eliezer, for Ariel, 2050.1
8:21 T I proclaimed a fast there, at the river 2050.1
8:24 T I separated twelve of the chief of 2050.1
8:31 T we departed from the river of Ahava on 2050.1
9: 4 T were assembled unto me every one that 2050.1
10: 5 T arose Ezra, and made the chief priests, 2050.1
10: 6 T Ezra rose up from before the house of 2050.1
10: 9 T all the men of Judah and 2050.1
10:12 T all the congregation answered and 2050.1
Ne 2: 2 sorrow of heart. T I was very sore afraid, 2050.1
2: 4 T the king said unto me, For what dost 2050.1
2: 9 T I came to the governors beyond 2050.1
2:14 T I went on to the gate of the fountain, 2050.1
2:15 T went I up in the night by the brook, and 2050.1
2:17 T said I unto them, Ye see the distress 2050.1
2:18 T I told them of the hand of my God 2050.1
2:20 T answered I them, and said unto them, 2050.1
3: 1 T Eliashib the high priest rose up with his 2050.1
4: 7 to be stopped, t they were very wroth, 2050.1
5: 7 T I consulted with myself, and I rebuked 2050.1
5: 8 T held they their peace, and 2050.1
5:12 T said they, We will restore *them,* and 2050.1
5:12 T I called the priests, and took an oath of 2050.1
6: 5 T sent Sanballat his servant unto me in 2050.1
6: 8 T I sent unto him, saying, There are no 2050.1
8:10 T he said unto them, Go *your way,* eat 2050.1
9: 4 T stood up upon the stairs of the Levites, 2050.1
9: 5 T the Levites, Jeshua and Kadmiel, Bani, 2050.1
12:31 T I brought up the princes of Judah upon 2050.1
Ne 13: 9 T I commanded, and they cleansed 2050.1
13:11 T contended I with the rulers, and said, 2050.1
13:12 T brought all Judah the tithe of the corn 2050.1
13:17 T I contended with the nobles of Judah, 2050.1
13:21 T I testified against them, and said unto 2050.1
13:27 Shall we t hearken unto you to do all this 2050.1
Est 1:13 T the king said to the wise *men,* which 2050.1
2: 2 T said the king's servants that ministered 2050.1
2:13 T thus came *every* maiden unto the king; 2050.1
2:18 T the king made a great feast unto all his 2050.1
2:19 t Mordecai sat in the king's gate. 2050.1
3: 3 T the king's servants, which *were* in 2050.1
3: 5 him reverence, t was Haman full *of* wrath. NIH
3:12 T were the king's scribes called on 2050.1
4: 4 T was the queen exceedingly grieved; 2050.1
4: 5 T called Esther for Hatach, *one* of 2050.1
4:13 T Mordecai commanded to answer 2050.1
4:14 t shall there enlargement and NIH
4:15 T Esther bade *them* return Mordecai *this* 2050.1
5: 3 T said the king unto her, What wilt thou, 2050.1
5: 5 T the king said, Cause Haman to make 2050.1
5: 7 T answered Esther, and said, My petition 2050.1
5: 9 T went Haman forth that day joyful and 2050.1
5:14 T said Zeresh his wife and all his friends 2050.1
5:14 t go thou in merrily with the king unto 2050.1
6: 3 T said the king's servants that ministered 2050.1
6:10 T the king said to Haman, Make haste, 2050.1
6:11 T took Haman the apparel and the horse, 2050.1
6:13 T said his wise *men* and Zeresh his wife 2050.1
7: 3 T Esther the queen answered and said, 2050.1
7: 5 T the king Ahasuerus answered and 2050.1
7: 6 T Haman was afraid before the king and 2050.1
7: 8 T the king returned out of the palace 2050.1
7: 8 bed whereon Esther *was.* T said the king, 2050.1
7: 9 T the king said, Hang him thereon. 2050.1
7:10 T was the king's wrath pacified. 2050.1
8: 4 T the king held out the golden sceptre 2050.1
8: 7 T the king Ahasuerus said unto Esther 2050.1
8: 9 T were the king's scribes called at that 2050.1
9:13 T said Esther, If it please the king, let it 2050.1
9:29 T Esther the queen, the daughter of 2050.1
Job 1: 7 T Satan answered the LORD, and said, 2050.1
1: 9 T Satan answered the LORD, and said, 2050.1
1:20 T Job arose, and rent his mantle, and 2050.1
2: 9 T said his wife unto him, Dost thou still 2050.1
3:13 I should have slept: t had I been at rest, 227
4: 1 T Eliphaz the Temanite answered and 2050.1
4:15 T a spirit passed before my face; the hair 2050.1
6:10 T should I yet have comfort; yea, I would 2050.1
7:14 T thou scarest me with dreams, and 2050.1
8: 1 T answered Bildad the Shuhite, and said, 2050.1
8:18 t *it* shall deny him, *saying,* I have not 2050.1
9: 1 T Job answered and said, 2050.1
9:29 *If* I be wicked, **why** t labour 2088+4100+3807.1
9:35 T would I speak, and not fear him; but *it is* NIH
10:14 t thou markest me, and thou wilt not 2050.1
10:18 Wherefore t hast thou brought me forth 2050.1
10:20 cease t, and let me alone, that I may take 2050.1
11: 1 T answered Zophar the Naamathite, and 2050.1
11:10 or gather together, t who can hinder him? 2050.1
11:11 will he not t consider *it?* 2050.1
11:15 For t shalt thou lift up thy face without spot; 227
13:20 unto me: t will I not hide myself from thee. 227
13:22 T call thou, and I will answer: or let me 2050.1
15: 1 T answered Eliphaz the Temanite, and 2050.1
16: 1 T Job answered and said, 2050.1
16:22 t I shall go the way *whence* I shall not 2050.1
18: 1 T answered Bildad the Shuhite, and said, 2050.1
19: 1 T Job answered and said, 2050.1
20: 1 T answered Zophar the Naamathite, and 2050.1
21:34 How t comfort ye me in vain, seeing *in* 2050.1
22: 1 T Eliphaz the Temanite answered and 2050.1
22:24 T shalt thou lay up gold as dust, and 2050.1
22:26 For t shalt thou have thy delight in 227
22:29 t thou shalt say, *There is* lifting up; 2050.1
23: 1 T Job answered and said, 2050.1
25: 1 T answered Bildad the Shuhite, and said, 2050.1
25: 4 How t can man be justified with God? or 2050.1
27:12 seen *it;* why t are ye thus altogether vain? 2050.1
28:20 Whence t cometh wisdom? and where *is* 2050.1
28:27 T did he see it, and declare it; he prepared it, 227
29:11 When the ear heard *me,* t it blessed me, 2050.1
29:18 T I said, I shall die in my nest, and I shall 2050.1
30:26 t evil came *unto me:* and when I waited 2050.1
31: 1 why t should I think upon a maid? 2050.1
31: 8 T let me sow, and let another eat; yea, NIH
31:10 T let my wife grind unto another, and NIH
31:14 What t shall I do when God riseth up? 2050.1
31:22 T let mine arm fall from *my* shoulder blade, NIH
32: 2 T was kindled the wrath of Elihu the son 2050.1
32: 5 *these* three men, t his wrath was kindled. 2050.1
33:16 T he openeth the ears of men, and sealeth 227
33:24 T he is gracious unto him, and saith, 2050.1
34:29 giveth quietness, who t can make trouble? NIH
34:29 he hideth *his* face, who t can behold him? 2050.1
36: 9 T he sheweth them their work, and 2050.1
36:18 t a great ransom cannot deliver thee. 2050.1
37: 8 T the beasts go into dens, and remain in 2050.1
38: 1 T the LORD answered Job out of 2050.1
38:21 Knowest thou *it,* because thou wast t born? 227
40: 3 T Job answered the LORD, and said, 2050.1
40: 6 T answered the LORD unto Job out of 2050.1
40:14 T will I also confess unto thee that thine 2050.1
41:10 him up: who t is able to stand before me? 2050.1
42: 1 T Job answered the LORD, and said, 2050.1
42:11 T came there unto him all his brethren, 2050.1
Ps 2: 5 T shall he speak unto them in his wrath, and 227
18: 7 T the earth shook and trembled; 2050.1
18:15 T the channels of waters were seen, and 2050.1
18:42 T did I beat them small as the dust before 2050.1
19:13 t shall I be upright, and I shall be innocent 227
27:10 t the LORD will take me up. 2050.1
39: 3 the fire burned: t spake I with my tongue, NIH
40: 7 T said I, Lo, I come: in the volume of 227
43: 4 T will I go unto the altar of God, 2050.1

T

Ps 50:18 t thou consentedst with him, and 2050.1
51:13 T will I teach transgressors thy ways; and NIH
51:19 T shalt thou be pleased with the sacrifices of 227
51:19 burnt offering and whole *burnt offering:* t 227
55: 6 *for* t would I fly away, and be at rest. NIH
55: 7 Lo, t would I wander far off, *and* remain in NIH
55:12 t I could have borne *it:* neither *was it* he 2050.1
55:12 t I would have hid myself from him: 2050.1
56: 9 When I cry *unto thee,* t shall mine enemies 227
67: 6 T shall the earth yield her increase; *and* NIH
69: 4 t I restored *that* which I took not away. 227
73:17 sanctuary of God; t understood I their end. NIH
78:34 When he slew them, t they sought him: 2050.1
78:65 T the Lord awaked as one out of sleep, 2050.1
80:12 Why hast thou t broken down her hedges, NIH
89:19 T thou spakest in vision to thy holy one, and 227
89:32 T will I visit their transgression with 2050.1
96:12 t shall all the trees of the wood rejoice 227
106:12 T believed they his words; they sang his 2050.1
106:30 T stood up Phinehas, and 2050.1
107: 6 T they cried unto the LORD in their 2050.1
107:13 T they cried unto the LORD in their 2050.1
107:19 T they cry unto the LORD in their 2050.1
107:28 T they cry unto the LORD in their 2050.1
107:30 T are they glad because they be quiet; so 2050.1
116: 4 T called I upon the name of the LORD; 2050.1
119: 6 T shall I not be ashamed, when I have 227
119:92 I should t have perished in mine affliction. 227
124: 3 T they had swallowed us up quick, 233
124: 4 T the waters had overwhelmed us, 233
124: 5 T the proud waters had gone over our soul. 233
126: 2 T was our mouth filled *with* laughter, and 227
126: 2 t said they among the heathen, The LORD 227
142: 3 within me, t thou knewest my path. 2050.1
Pr 1:28 T shall they call upon me, but I will not 227
2: 5 T shalt thou understand the fear of 227
2: 9 T shalt thou understand righteousness, and 227
3:23 T shalt thou walk *in* thy way safely, and 227
8:30 T I was by him, *as* one brought up *with* 2050.1
11: 2 *When* pride cometh, t cometh shame: but 2050.1
15:11 **how much more** t the hearts of 637+3588
18: 3 t cometh also contempt, and with ignominy NIH
20:14 but when he is gone his way, t he boasteth. 227
20:24 can a man t understand his own way? 2050.1
24:14 hast found *it,* t there shall be a reward, 2050.1
24:32 T I saw, *and* considered *it* well: I looked 2050.1
Ecc 2:11 T I looked on all the works that my hands 2050.1
2:13 T I saw that wisdom excelleth folly, 2050.1
2:15 T said I in my heart, As it happeneth to 2050.1
2:15 even to me; and why was I t more wise? 227
2:15 T I said in my heart, that this also *is* 2050.1
4: 7 T I returned, and I saw vanity under 2050.1
4:11 Again, if two lie together, t they have 2050.1
8:15 T I commended mirth, because a man 2050.1
8:17 T I beheld all the work of God, that a 2050.1
9:16 T said I, Wisdom *is* better than strength: 2050.1
10:10 the edge, t must he put to more strength: 2050.1
12: 7 T shall the dust return to the earth as it 2050.1
SS 8:10 t was I in his eyes as one that found favour. 227
Isa 5:17 T shall the lambs feed after their manner, 2050.1
6: 5 T said I, Woe *is* me! for I am undone; 2050.1
6: 6 T flew one of the seraphims unto me, 2050.1
6: 8 go for us? T I said, Here *am* I; send me. 2050.1
6:11 T said I, Lord, how long? And he 2050.1
7: 3 T said the LORD unto Isaiah, Go forth 2050.1
8: 3 T said the LORD to me, Call his name 2050.1
14:25 t shall his yoke depart from off them, and 2050.1
14:32 What shall *one* t answer the messengers 2050.1
24:23 T the moon shall be confounded, and 2050.1
28:18 t ye shall be trodden down by it. 2050.1
30:23 T shall he give the rain of thy seed, 2050.1
31: 8 T shall the Assyrian fall with the sword, 2050.1
32:16 T judgment shall dwell in the wilderness, 2050.1
33:23 T is the prey of a great spoil divided; 227
35: 5 T the eyes of the blind shall be opened, and 227
35: 6 T shall the lame *man* leap as a hart, and 227
36: 3 T came forth unto him Eliakim, 2050.1
36: 9 How t wilt thou turn away the face of one 2050.1
36:11 T said Eliakim and Shebna and Joah unto 2050.1
36:13 T Rabshakeh stood, and cried with a loud 2050.1
36:22 T came Eliakim, the son of Hilkiah, 2050.1
37:21 T Isaiah the son of Amoz sent unto 2050.1
37:36 T the angel of the LORD went forth, 2050.1
38: 2 T Hezekiah turned his face toward 2050.1
38: 4 T came the word of the LORD to Isaiah, 2050.1
39: 3 T came Isaiah the prophet unto king 2050.1
39: 4 T said he, What have they seen in thine 2050.1
39: 5 T said Isaiah to Hezekiah, Hear the word 2050.1
39: 8 T said Hezekiah to Isaiah, Good *is* 2050.1
40:18 To whom t will ye liken God? or 2050.1
40:25 To whom t will ye liken me, or shall I be 2050.1
41: 1 let them come near; t let them speak: let us 227
44:15 T shall it be for a man to burn: for he will 2050.1
48:18 t had thy peace been as a river, and 2050.1
49: 4 T I said, I have laboured in vain, I have 2050.1
49:21 T shalt thou say in thine heart, Who hath 2050.1
58: 8 T shall thy light break forth as the morning, 227
58: 9 T shalt thou call, and the LORD shall 227
58:10 t shall thy light rise in obscurity, and 2050.1
58:14 T shalt thou delight thyself in the LORD; 227
60: 5 T thou shalt see, and flow *together,* and 227
63:11 T he remembered the days of old, Moses, 2050.1
66:12 t shall ye suck, ye shall be borne upon *her* 2050.1
Jer 1: 4 T the word of the LORD came unto me, 2050.1
1: 6 T said I, Ah, Lord GOD, behold, 2050.1
1: 9 T the LORD put forth his hand, and 2050.1
1:12 T said the LORD unto me, Thou hast 2050.1
1:14 T the LORD said unto me, Out of 2050.1
2:21 how t art thou turned *into* the degenerate 2050.1
4: 1 out of my sight, t shalt thou not remove. 2050.1
4:10 (T said I, Ah, Lord GOD! surely thou 2050.1
5: 7 they t committed adultery, and 2050.1
5:19 t shalt thou answer them, Like as ye have 2050.1
7: 7 T will I cause you to dwell in this place, 2050.1
7:34 T will I cause to cease from the cities of 2050.1

Jer 8: 5 Why *t* is this people of Jerusalem slidden NIH
8:22 why t is not the health of the daughter of 3588
11: 5 T answered I, and said, So be it, 2050.1
11: 6 T the LORD said unto me, Proclaim all 2050.1
11:12 T shall the cities of Judah and 2050.1
11:15 when thou doest evil, t thou rejoicest. 227
11:18 I know *it:* t thou shewedst me their doings. 227
12: 5 t how canst thou contend with horses? 2050.1
12: 5 *they wearied thee,* t how wilt thou do in 2050.1
12:16 t shall they be built in the midst of my 2050.1
13: 7 T I went to Euphrates, and digged, and 2050.1
13: 8 T the word of the LORD came unto me, 2050.1
13:13 T shalt thou say unto them, Thus saith 2050.1
13:23 t may ye also do good, that are accustomed NIH
14:11 T said the LORD unto me, Pray not for 2050.1
14:13 T said I, Ah Lord GOD! behold, 2050.1
14:14 T the LORD said unto me, The prophets 2050.1
14:18 t behold the slain with the sword: 2050.1
14:18 t behold them that are sick with famine: 2050.1
15: 1 T said the LORD unto me, 2050.1
15: 2 t thou shalt tell them, Thus saith 2050.1
15:19 t will I bring thee again, *and* thou shalt 2050.1
16:11 T shalt thou say unto them, Because your 2050.1
17:25 T shall there enter into the gates of this 2050.1
17:27 t will I kindle a fire in the gates thereof, 2050.1
18: 3 T I went down *to* the potter's house, and 2050.1
18: 5 T the word of the LORD came to me, 2050.1
18:10 not my voice, t I will repent of the good, 2050.1
18:18 T said they, Come, and let us devise 2050.1
19:10 T shalt thou break the bottle in the sight 2050.1
19:14 T came Jeremiah from Tophet, 2050.1
20: 2 T Pashur smote Jeremiah the prophet, 2050.1
20: 3 T said Jeremiah unto him, The LORD 2050.1
20: 9 T I said, I will not make mention of him, 2050.1
21: 3 T said Jeremiah unto them, Thus shall ye 2050.1
22: 4 t shall there enter in by the gates of this 2050.1
22: 9 T they shall answer, Because they have 2050.1
22:15 and justice, *and* t *it was* well with him? 227
22:16 t *it was* well *with him: was* not this to know 227
22:22 surely t shalt thou be ashamed and 227
23:22 t they should have turned them from their 2050.1
23:33 thou shalt t say unto them, What burden? 2050.1
24: 3 T said the LORD unto me, What seest 2050.1
25:17 T took I the cup at the LORD'S hand, 2050.1
25:28 t shalt thou say unto them, Thus saith 2050.1
26: 6 T will I make this house like Shiloh, and 2050.1
26:10 t they came up from the king's house 2050.1
26:11 T spake the priests and the prophets unto 2050.1
26:12 T spake Jeremiah unto all the princes and 2050.1
26:16 T said the princes and all the people unto 2050.1
26:17 T rose up certain of the elders of the land, 2050.1
27: 7 t many nations and great kings shall serve NIH
27:22 t will I bring them up, and restore them to 2050.1
28: 5 T the prophet Jeremiah said unto 2050.1
28: 9 t shall the prophet be known, that NIH
28:10 T Hananiah the prophet took the yoke 2050.1
28:12 T the word of the LORD came unto 2050.1
28:15 T said the prophet Jeremiah unto 2050.1
29:12 T shall ye call upon me, and ye shall go 2050.1
29:30 T came the word of the LORD unto 2050.1
31:13 T shall the virgin rejoice in the dance, 227
31:36 t the seed of Israel also shall cease from NIH
32: 2 For t the king of Babylon's army besieged 227
32: 8 T I knew that this *was* the word of 2050.1
32:26 T came the word of the LORD unto 2050.1
33:21 T may also my covenant be broken with NIH
33:26 T will I cast away the seed of Jacob, and 1571
34: 6 T Jeremiah the prophet spake all these 2050.1
34:10 any more, t they obeyed, and let *them* go. 2050.1
35: 3 T I took Jaazaniah the son of Jeremiah, 2050.1
35:12 T came the word of the LORD unto 2050.1
36: 4 T Jeremiah called Baruch the son of 2050.1
36:10 T read Baruch in the book the words of 2050.1
36:12 T he went down *into* the king's house, 2050.1
36:13 T Michaiah declared unto them all 2050.1
36:18 T Baruch answered them, He pronounced 2050.1
36:19 T said the princes unto Baruch, Go, 2050.1
36:27 T the word of the LORD came to 2050.1
36:32 T took Jeremiah another roll, and gave it 2050.1
37: 5 T Pharaoh's army was come forth out of 2050.1
37: 6 T came the word of the LORD unto 2050.1
37:12 T Jeremiah went forth out of Jerusalem to 2050.1
37:14 T said Jeremiah, *It is* false; I fall not 2050.1
37:17 T Zedekiah the king sent, and took him 2050.1
37:21 T Zedekiah the king commanded that 2050.1
38: 1 T Shephatiah the son of Mattan, and 2050.1
38: 5 T Zedekiah the king said, Behold, he *is* in 2050.1
38: 6 T took they Jeremiah, and cast him into 2050.1
38: 7 the king t sitting in the gate of Benjamin; 2050.1
38:10 T the king commanded Ebed-melech 2050.1
38:14 T Zedekiah the king sent, and 2050.1
38:15 T Jeremiah said unto Zedekiah, If I 2050.1
38:17 T said Jeremiah unto Zedekiah, 2050.1
38:17 t thy soul shall live, and this city shall not 2050.1
38:18 t shall this city be given into the hand of 2050.1
38:24 T said Zedekiah unto Jeremiah, Let no 2050.1
38:26 T thou shalt say unto them, I presented 2050.1
38:27 T came all the princes unto Jeremiah, and 2050.1
39: 4 t they fled, and went forth out of the city 2050.1
39: 6 T the king of Babylon slew the sons of 2050.1
39: 9 T Nebuzar-adan the captain of the guard 2050.1
40: 6 T went Jeremiah unto Gedaliah the son of 2050.1
40: 8 T they came to Gedaliah to Mizpah, 2050.1
40:15 T Johanan the son of Kareah spake to 2050.1
41: 2 T arose Ishmael the son of Nethaniah, 2050.1
41:10 T Ishmael carried away captive all 2050.1
41:12 T they took all the men, and went to fight 2050.1
41:13 that *were* with him, t they were glad. 2050.1
41:16 T took Johanan the son of Kareah, and 2050.1
42: 1 T all the captains of the forces, and 2050.1
42: 4 T Jeremiah the prophet said unto them, 2050.1
42: 5 T they said to Jeremiah, The LORD be a 2050.1
42: 8 T called he Johanan the son of Kareah, 2050.1
42:10 t will I build you, and not pull *you* down, 2050.1
42:16 T it shall come to pass, *that* the sword, 2050.1

Jer 43: 2 T spake Azariah the son of Hoshaiah, and 2050.1
43: 8 T came the word of the LORD unto 2050.1
44:15 T all the men which knew that their 2050.1
44:17 for t had we plenty of victuals, and NIH
44:20 T Jeremiah said unto all the people, to 2050.1
47: 2 t the men shall cry, and all the inhabitants 2050.1
49: 1 why t doth their king inherit Gad, and NIH
49: 2 t shall Israel be heir unto them that were 2050.1
51:48 T the heaven and the earth, and all that *is* 2050.1
51:62 T shalt thou say, O LORD, thou hast 2050.1
52: 7 T the city was broken up, and all the men 2050.1
52: 9 T they took the king, and carried him up 2050.1
52:11 T he put out the eyes of Zedekiah; and 2050.1
52:15 T Nebuzar-adan the captain of the guard 2050.1
La 3:54 over mine head; t I said, I am cut off. NIH
Eze 3: 3 T did I eat *it;* and it was in my mouth as 2050.1
3:12 T the spirit took me up, and I heard 2050.1
3:15 T I came to them of the captivity *at* 2050.1
3:23 T I arose, and went forth into the plain: 2050.1
3:24 T the spirit entered into me, and set me 2050.1
4:14 T said I, Ah Lord GOD, behold, 2050.1
4:15 T he said unto me, Lo, I have given thee 2050.1
5: 1 t take thee balances to weigh, and 2050.1
5: 4 T take of them again, and cast them into 2050.1
6:13 T shall ye know that I *am* the LORD, 2050.1
7:26 t shall they seek a vision of the prophet; 2050.1
8: 2 T I beheld, and lo, a likeness as 2050.1
8: 5 T said he unto me, Son of man, lift up 2050.1
8: 8 T said he unto me, Son of man, dig now 2050.1
8:12 T said he unto me, Son of man, hast thou 2050.1
8:14 T he brought me to the door of the gate of 2050.1
8:15 T said he unto me, Hast thou seen *this,* O 2050.1
8:17 T he said unto me, Hast thou seen *this,* O 2050.1
9: 6 T they began at the ancient men which 2050.1
9: 9 T said he unto me, The iniquity of 2050.1
10: 1 T I looked, and behold, in the firmament 2050.1
10: 4 T the glory of the LORD went up from 2050.1
10: 6 t he went in, and stood beside the wheels. 2050.1
10:18 T the glory of the LORD departed from 2050.1
11: 2 T said he unto me, Son of man, these *are* 2050.1
11:13 T fell I down upon my face, and 2050.1
11:22 T did the cherubims lift up their wings, 2050.1
11:25 T I spake unto them of the captivity all 2050.1
12: 4 T shalt thou bring forth thy stuff by day 2050.1
14: 1 T came certain of the elders of Israel unto 2050.1
14:13 t will I stretch out mine hand upon it, and 2050.1
16: 9 T washed I thee with water; yea, 2050.1
16:53 t *will I bring again* the captivity of thy 2050.1
16:55 t thou and thy daughters shall return to 2050.1
16:61 T thou shalt remember thy ways, and 2050.1
18:13 shall he t live? he shall not live: he hath 2050.1
19: 5 t she took another of her whelps, *and* 2050.1
19: 8 T the nations set against him on every 2050.1
20: 2 T came the word of the LORD unto me, 2050.1
20: 7 T said I unto them, Cast ye away every 2050.1
20: 8 t I said, *I* will pour out my fury upon 2050.1
20:13 t I said, *I* would pour out my fury upon 2050.1
20:21 t I said, *I* would pour out my fury upon 2050.1
20:28 t they saw every high hill, and all 2050.1
20:29 T I said unto them, What *is* the high place 2050.1
20:49 T said I, Ah Lord GOD, they say of me, 2050.1
21: 4 **Seeing** t that I will cut off from thee 3282
21:10 should we t make mirth? it contemneth 176
22: 3 T say thou, Thus saith the Lord GOD, 2050.1
23:13 T I saw that she was defiled, *that* they 2050.1
23:18 t my mind was alienated from her, like as 2050.1
23:39 t they came the same day into my 2050.1
23:43 T said I unto *her that was* old *in* 2050.1
24:11 T set it empty upon the coals thereof, that 2050.1
24:20 T I answered them, The word of 2050.1
26:16 T all the princes of the sea shall come 2050.1
28:25 t shall they dwell in their land that I have 2050.1
32: 4 T will I leave thee upon the land, I will 2050.1
32:14 T will I make their waters deep, and 227
32:15 t shall they know that I *am* the LORD. 2050.1
33: 4 T whosoever heareth the sound of 2050.1
33:10 pine away in them, how should we t live? 2050.1
33:23 T the word of the LORD came unto me, 2050.1
33:29 T shall they know that I *am* the LORD, 2050.1
33:33 t shall they know that a prophet hath been 2050.1
36:25 T will I sprinkle clean water upon you, 2050.1
36:31 T shall ye remember your own evil ways, 2050.1
36:36 T the heathen that are left round about 2050.1
37: 9 T said he unto me, Prophesy unto 2050.1
37:11 T he said unto me, Son of man, these 2050.1
37:14 t shall ye know that I the LORD have 2050.1
37:16 t take another stick, and write upon it, 2050.1
39:15 man's bone, t shall he set up a sign by it, 2050.1
39:28 T shall they know that I *am* the LORD 2050.1
40: 6 T came he unto the gate which looketh 2050.1
40: 9 T measured he the porch of the gate, 2050.1
40:13 He measured t the gate from the roof of 2050.1
40:17 T brought he me into the outward court, 2050.1
40:19 T he measured the breadth from 2050.1
41: 3 T went he inward, and measured the post 2050.1
42: 1 T he brought me forth into the utter court, 2050.1
42:13 T said he unto me, The north chambers 2050.1
42:14 When the priests enter *therein,* t 2050.1
44: 1 T he brought me back the way of the gate 2050.1
44: 2 T said the LORD unto me; This gate 2050.1
44: 4 T brought he me the way of the north 2050.1
46: 2 t he shall go forth; but the gate shall not 2050.1
46:12 *one* shall t open him the gate that looketh 2050.1
46:12 t he shall go forth; and after his going 2050.1
46:17 t it shall be his to the year of liberty; 2050.1
46:20 T said he unto me, This *is* the place 2050.1
46:21 T he brought me forth into the utter court, 2050.1
46:24 T said he unto me, These *are* the places 2050.1
47: 2 T brought he me out *of* the way of 2050.1
47: 6 hast thou seen *this?* T he brought me, and 2050.1
47: 8 T said he unto me, These waters issue out 2050.1
Da 1:10 t shall ye make *me* endanger my head to 2050.1
1:11 T said Daniel to Melzar, whom the prince 2050.1
1:13 T let our countenances be looked upon 2050.1
1:18 t the prince of the eunuchs brought them 2050.1

Da 2: 2 **T** the king commanded to call 2050.1
2: 4 **T** spake the Chaldeans to the king in 2050.1
2:14 **T** Daniel answered with counsel and 116+871.2
2:15 **T** Arioch made the thing known to Daniel. 116
2:16 **T** Daniel went in, and desired of the king 2050.3
2:17 **T** Daniel went to his house, and made 116
2:19 **T** *was* the secret revealed unto Daniel in a 116
2:19 **T** Daniel blessed the God of heaven. 116
2:25 **T** Arioch brought in Daniel before the king 116
2:35 **T** was the iron, the clay, the brass, 116+871.2
2:46 **T** the king Nebuchadnezzar fell upon 116+871.2
2:48 **T** the king made Daniel a great man, and 116
2:49 **T** Daniel requested of the king, and he set 2050.3
3: 2 **T** Nebuchadnezzar the king sent to gather 2050.3
3: 3 **T** the princes, the governors and 116+871.2
3: 4 **T** a herald cried aloud, To you it is 2050.3
3:13 **T** Nebuchadnezzar in *his* rage and 116+871.2
3:13 Abed-nego. **T** they brought these men 116+871.2
3:19 **T** was Nebuchadnezzar full *of* fury, 116+871.2
3:21 **T** these men were bound in their 116+871.2
3:24 **T** Nebuchadnezzar the king was astonied, 116
3:26 **T** Nebuchadnezzar came near to 116+871.2
3:26 come *hither.* **T** Shadrach, Meshach, 116+871.2
3:28 **T** Nebuchadnezzar spake, and said, NIH
3:30 **T** the king promoted Shadrach, 116+871.2
4: 7 **T** came in the magicians, 116+871.2
4:19 **T** Daniel, whose name *was* Belteshazzar, 116
5: 3 **T** they brought the golden vessels 116+871.2
5: 6 **T** the king's countenance was changed, 116
5: 8 **T** came in all the king's wise *men:* but 116
5: 9 **T** *was* king Belshazzar greatly troubled, and 116
5:13 **T** was Daniel brought in before 116+871.2
5:17 **T** Daniel answered and said before 116+871.2
5:24 **T** *was* the part of 116+4481+6925+871.2
5:29 **T** commanded Belshazzar, and 116+871.2
6: 3 **T** this Daniel was preferred above 116
6: 4 **T** the presidents and princes sought to find 116
6: 5 **T** said these men, We shall not find any 116
6: 6 **T** these presidents and princes assembled 116
6:11 **T** these men assembled, and found Daniel 116
6:12 **T** they came near, and spake before 116+871.2
6:13 **T** answered they and said before 116+871.2
6:14 **T** the king, when he heard *these* words, was 116
6:15 **T** these men assembled unto the king, 116+871.2
6:16 **T** the king commanded, and 116+871.2
6:18 **T** the king went to his palace, and passed 116
6:19 **T** the king arose very early in 116+871.2
6:21 **T** said Daniel unto the king, O king, live for 116
6:23 **T** was the king exceeding glad for 116+871.2
6:25 **T** king Darius wrote unto all people, 116+871.2
7: 1 visions of his head upon his bed: **t** 116+871.2
7:11 I beheld **t** because of the voice of 116+871.2
7:19 **T** I would know the truth of the fourth beast, 116
8: 3 **T** I lifted up mine eyes, and saw, and 2050.1
8:13 **T** I heard one saint speaking, and 2050.1
8:14 **t** shall the sanctuary be cleansed. 2050.1
8:15 and sought for the meaning, **t** behold, 2050.1
10: 5 **T** I lift up mine eyes, and looked, and 2050.1
10: 9 **t** was I in a deep sleep on my face, and 2050.1
10:12 **T** said he unto me, Fear not, Daniel: 2050.1
10:16 **t** I opened my mouth, and spake, and 2050.1
10:18 **T** there came again and touched me *one* 2050.1
10:20 **T** said he, Knowest thou wherefore I 2050.1
11:10 **t** shall he return, and be stirred up, 2050.1
11:19 **T** he shall turn his face towards the fort 2050.1
11:20 **T** shall stand up in his estate a raiser of 2050.1
11:28 **T** shall he return *into* his land with great 2050.1
12: 5 **T** I Daniel looked, and behold, 2050.1
12: 8 **t** said I, O my lord, what *shall be* the end 2050.1
Hos 1: 9 **T** said *God,* Call his name Lo-ammi: 2050.1
1:11 **T** shall the children of Judah and 2050.1
2: 7 shall not find *them:* **t** shall she say, I will 2050.1
2: 7 **for t** *was it* better with me than now. 3588
3: 1 **T** said the LORD unto me, Go yet, 2050.1
5:13 **t** went Ephraim to the Assyrian, and 2050.1
6: 3 **T** shall we know, *if* we follow on to know 2050.1
7: 1 **t** the iniquity of Ephraim was discovered, 2050.1
10: 3 the LORD; what **t** should a king do to us? NIH
11: 1 **t** I loved him, and called my son out of 2050.1
11:10 **t** the children shall tremble from the west. 2050.1
Joel 2:18 **T** will the LORD be jealous for his land, 2050.1
2:23 Be glad **t**, ye children of Zion, and 2050.1
3:17 **t** shall Jerusalem be holy, and there shall 2050.1
Am 6: 2 **t** go down *to* Gath of the Philistines: *be* 2050.1
6:10 **T** shall he say, Hold thy tongue: for *we* 2050.1
7: 2 **t** I said, O Lord GOD, forgive, I beseech 2050.1
7: 5 **T** said I, O Lord GOD, cease, I beseech 2050.1
7: 8 **T** said the Lord, Behold, I *will* set a 2050.1
7:10 **T** Amaziah *the* priest of Beth-el sent to 2050.1
7:14 **T** answered Amos, and said to Amaziah, 2050.1
8: 2 **T** said the LORD unto me, The end is 2050.1
Jnh 1: 5 **T** the mariners were afraid, and 2050.1
1: 8 **T** said they unto him, Tell us, we pray 2050.1
1:10 **T** were the men exceedingly afraid, 2050.1
1:11 **T** said they unto him, What shall we do 2050.1
1:16 **T** the men feared the LORD 2050.1
2: 1 **T** Jonah prayed unto the LORD his God 2050.1
2: 4 **T** I said, I am cast out of thy sight; yet I 2050.1
4: 4 **T** said the LORD, Doest thou well to be 2050.1
4:10 **T** said the LORD, Thou hast had pity on 2050.1
Mic 3: 4 **T** shall they cry unto the LORD, but he will 227
3: 7 **T** shall the seers be ashamed, and 2050.1
5: 3 **t** the remnant of his brethren shall return 2050.1
5: 5 **t** shall we raise against him seven 2050.1
7:10 **T** she *that is* mine enemy shall see *it,* and 2050.1
Hab 1:11 **T** shall *his* mind change, and he shall pass 227
Zep 3: 9 For **t** will I turn to the people a pure 227
3:11 for **t** I will take away out of the midst of thee 227
Hag 1: 3 **T** came the word of the LORD by 2050.1
1:12 **T** Zerubbabel the son of Shealtiel, and 2050.1
1:13 **T** spake Haggai the LORD'S messenger 2050.1
2:13 **T** said Haggai, If *one that is* unclean *by* a 2050.1
2:14 **T** answered Haggai, and said, So *is* this 2050.1
Zec 1: 9 **T** said I, O my lord, what *are* these? 2050.1
1:12 **T** the angel of the LORD answered and 2050.1

Zec 1:18 **T** lift I up mine eyes, and saw, and 2050.1
1:21 **T** said I, What come these to do? And he 2050.1
2: 2 **T** said I, Whither goest thou? And he said 2050.1
3: 7 **t** thou shalt also judge my house, and 2050.1
4: 5 **T** the angel that talked with me answered 2050.1
4: 6 **T** he answered and spake unto me, 2050.1
4:11 **T** answered I, and said unto him, 2050.1
4:14 **T** said he, These *are* the two anointed 2050.1
5: 1 **T** I turned, and lift up mine eyes, and 2050.1
5: 3 **T** said he unto me, This *is* the curse that 2050.1
5: 5 **T** the angel that talked with me went 2050.1
5: 9 **T** lift I up mine eyes, and looked, and 2050.1
5:10 **T** said I to the angel that talked with me, 2050.1
6: 4 **T** I answered and said unto the angel that 2050.1
6: 8 **T** cried he upon me, and spake unto me, 2050.1
6:11 **T** take silver and gold, and make crowns, 2050.1
7: 4 **T** came the word of the LORD of hosts 2050.1
11: 9 **T** said I, I will not feed you: that that 2050.1
11:14 **T** I cut asunder mine other staff, *even* 2050.1
13: 3 **t** his father and his mother that begat him 2050.1
13: 6 **T** he shall answer, *Those with* which I 2050.1
14: 3 **T** shall the LORD go forth, and 2050.1
Mal 1: 6 if **t** I *be* a father, where *is* mine honour? 2050.1
3: 4 **T** shall the offering of Judah and 2050.1
3:16 **T** they that feared the LORD spake often 227
3:18 **T** shall ye return, and discern between 2050.1
Mt 1:19 **T** Joseph her husband, being a just *man,* 1161
1:24 **T** Joseph being raised from sleep did as 1161
2: 7 **T** Herod, when he had privily called 5119
2:16 **T** Herod, when he saw that he was mocked 5119
2:17 **T** was fulfilled that which was spoken by 5119
3: 5 **T** went out to him Jerusalem, and all Judea, 5119
3:13 **T** cometh Jesus from Galilee to Jordan unto 5119
3:15 fulfil all righteousness. **T** he suffered him. 5119
4: 1 **T** was Jesus led up of the Spirit into 5119
4: 5 **T** the devil taketh him *up* into the holy city, 5119
4:10 **T** saith Jesus unto him, Get thee hence, 5119
4:11 **T** the devil leaveth him, and behold, 5119
5:24 thy brother, and **t** come and offer thy gift. 5119
7: 5 and **t** shalt thou see clearly to cast out 5119
7:11 If ye **t**, being evil, know how to give good 3767
7:23 And **t** will I profess unto them, I never 5119
8:26 **T** he arose, and rebuked the winds and 5119
9: 6 (**t** saith he to the sick of the palsy,) 5119
9:14 **T** came to him the disciples of John, 5119
9:15 be taken from them, and **t** shall they fast. 5119
9:29 **T** touched he their eyes, saying, 5119
9:37 **T** saith he unto his disciples, The harvest 5119
11:20 **T** began he to upbraid the cities wherein 5119
12:12 How much **t** is a man better than a sheep? 3767
12:13 **T** saith he to the man, Stretch forth thine 5119
12:14 **T** the Pharisees went out, and held a 1161
12:22 **T** was brought unto him one possessed with 5119
12:26 how shall **t** his kingdom stand? 3767
12:28 **t** the kingdom of God is come unto you. 686
12:29 strong *man?* and **t** he will spoil his house. 5119
12:38 **T** certain of the scribes and of the Pharisees 5119
12:44 **T** he saith, I will return into my house from 5119
12:45 **T** goeth he, and taketh with himself seven 5119
12:47 **T** one said unto him, Behold, thy mother 1161
13:19 **t** cometh the wicked one, and catcheth away NIG
13:26 forth fruit, **t** appeared the tares also. 5119
13:27 in thy field? from whence **t** hath it tares? 3767
13:28 Wilt thou **t** *that* we go and gather them up? 3767
13:36 **T** Jesus sent the multitude away, and 5119
13:43 **T** shall the righteous shine forth as the sun 5119
13:52 **T** said he unto them, Therefore every scribe 1161
13:56 Whence **t** hath this *man* all these *things?* 3767
14:33 **T** they that were in the ship came and 1161
15: 1 **T** came to Jesus scribes and Pharisees, 5119
15:12 **T** came his disciples, and said unto him, 5119
15:15 **T** answered Peter and said unto him, 1161
15:21 **T** Jesus went thence, and departed into 2532
15:25 **T** came she and worshipped him, saying, 1161
15:28 **T** Jesus answered and said unto her, 5119
15:32 **T** Jesus called his disciples unto *him,* and 1161
16: 6 **T** Jesus said unto them, Take heed and 1161
16:12 **T** understood they how that he bade *them* 5119
16:20 **T** charged he his disciples that they should 5119
16:22 **T** Peter took him, and began to rebuke him, 2532
16:24 **T** said Jesus unto his disciples, If any *man* 5119
16:27 and **t** he shall reward every man according 5119
17: 4 **T** answered Peter, and said unto Jesus, 1161
17:10 Why **t** say the scribes that Elias must first 3767
17:13 **T** the disciples understood that he spake 5119
17:17 **T** Jesus answered and said, O faithless and 1161
17:19 **T** came the disciples to Jesus apart, 5119
17:26 saith unto him, **T** are the children free. 686+1065
18:16 hear *thee,* **t** take with thee one or two more, NIG
18:21 **T** came Peter to him, and said, Lord, 5119
18:27 **T** the lord of that servant was moved with 1161
18:32 **T** his lord, after that he had called him, 5119
19: 7 Why did Moses **t** command to give a 3767
19:13 **T** were there brought unto him little 5119
19:23 **T** said Jesus unto his disciples, Verily I say 1161
19:25 saying, Who **t** can be saved? 686
19:27 **T** answered Peter and said unto him, 5119
20:20 **T** came to him the mother of Zebedee's 5119
21: 1 mount of Olives, **t** sent Jesus two disciples, 5119
21:25 say unto us, Why did ye not **t** believe him? 3767
22: 8 **T** saith he to his servants, The wedding is 5119
22:13 **T** said the king to the servants, Bind him 5119
22:15 **T** went the Pharisees, and took counsel 5119
22:21 **T** saith he unto them, Render therefore 5119
22:35 **T** one of them, *which was* a lawyer, 2532
22:43 How **t** doth David in spirit call him Lord, 3767
22:45 If David **t** call him Lord, how is he his son? 3767
23: 1 **T** spake Jesus to the multitude, and to his 5119
23:32 Fill ye up **t** the measure of your fathers. 2532
24: 9 **T** shall they deliver you up to be afflicted, 5119
24:10 And **t** shall many be offended, and 5119
24:14 unto all nations; and **t** shall the end come. 5119
24:16 **T** let them which be in Judea flee into 5119
24:21 For **t** shall be great tribulation, such as was 5119
24:23 **T** if any *man* shall say unto you, Lo, here *is* 5119

Mt 24:30 And **t** shall appear the sign of the Son of 5119
24:30 and **t** shall all the tribes of the earth mourn, 5119
24:40 **T** shall two be in the field; the one shall be 5119
24:45 Who **t** is a faithful and wise servant, 686
25: 1 **T** shall the kingdom of heaven be likened 5119
25: 7 **T** all those virgins arose, and trimmed their 5119
25:16 **T** he that had received the five talents went 1161
25:24 **T** he which had received the one talent 2532
25:27 and **t** at my coming I should have received NIG
25:31 **t** shall he sit upon the throne of his glory: 5119
25:34 **T** shall the King say unto them on his right 5119
25:37 **T** shall the righteous answer him, saying, 5119
25:41 **T** shall he say also unto them on the left 5119
25:44 **T** shall they also answer him, saying, Lord, 5119
25:45 **T** shall he answer them, saying, Verily I 5119
26: 3 **T** assembled together the chief priests, and 5119
26:14 **T** one of the twelve, called Judas Iscariot, 5119
26:25 **T** Judas, which betrayed him, answered and 1161
26:31 **T** saith Jesus unto them, All ye shall be 5119
26:36 **T** cometh Jesus with them unto a place 5119
26:38 **T** saith he unto them, My soul is exceeding 5119
26:45 **T** cometh he to his disciples, and saith unto 5119
26:50 **T** came they, and laid hands on Jesus, and 5119
26:52 **T** said Jesus unto him, Put up again thy 5119
26:54 *But* how **t** shall the scriptures be fulfilled, 3767
26:56 **T** all the disciples forsook him, and fled. 5119
26:65 **T** the high priest rent his clothes, saying, 5119
26:67 **T** did they spit in his face, and 5119
26:74 **T** began he to curse and to swear, *saying,* I 5119
27: 3 **T** Judas, which had betrayed him, when he 5119
27: 9 **T** was fulfilled that which was spoken by 5119
27:13 **T** said Pilate unto him, Hearest thou not 5119
27:16 And they had **t** a notable prisoner, 5119
27:22 What shall I do **t** with Jesus which is called 3767
27:25 **T** answered all the people, and said, 2532
27:26 **T** released he Barabbas unto them: 5119
27:27 **T** the soldiers of the governor took Jesus 5119
27:38 **T** were there two thieves crucified with 5119
27:58 **T** Pilate commanded the body to be 5119
28:10 **T** said Jesus unto them, Be not afraid: 5119
28:16 **T** the eleven disciples went *away* into 1161
Mk 2:20 and **t** shall they fast in those days. 5119
3:27 strong *man;* and **t** he will spoil his house. 5119
3:31 There came **t** *his* brethren and his mother, 3767
4:13 and how **t** will ye know all parables? NIG
4:28 first the blade, **t** the ear, after that the full 1534
7: 1 **T** came together unto him the Pharisees, 2532
7: 5 **T** the Pharisees and scribes asked him, 1899
10: 8 **so t** they are no more twain, but one flesh. 5620
10:21 **T** Jesus beholding him loved him, and 1161
10:26 among themselves, Who **t** can be saved? 2532
10:28 **T** Peter began to say unto him, Lo, we have 2532
11:31 he will say, Why **t** did ye not believe him? 3767
12:18 **T** come unto him *the* Sadducees, which say 2532
12:37 him Lord; and whence is he **t** his son? NIG
13:14 **t** let them that be in Judea flee to 5119
13:21 And **t** if any *man* shall say to you, Lo, here 5119
13:26 And **t** shall they see the Son of man coming 5119
13:27 And **t** shall he send his angels, and 5119
14:63 **T** the high priest rent his clothes, and saith, 1161
15:12 What will ye **t** *that* I shall do *unto him* 3767
15:14 **T** Pilate said unto them, Why, what evil 1161
16:19 So **t** after the Lord had spoken unto them, 3303
Lk 1:34 **T** said Mary unto the angel, How shall this 1161
2:28 **T** took he him *up* in his arms, and 2532
3: 7 **T** said he to the multitude that came forth 3767
3:10 asked him, saying, What shall we do **t**? 3767
3:12 **T** came also publicans to be baptized, and 1161
5:35 and **t** shall they fast in those days. 5119
5:36 **t** both the new maketh a rent, and the piece NIG
6: 9 **T** said Jesus unto them, I will ask you one 3767
6:42 and **t** shalt thou see clearly to pull out 5119
7: 6 **T** Jesus went with them. And when he was 1161
7:22 **T** Jesus answering said unto them, Go *your* 2532
7:31 Whereunto **t** shall I liken the men of this 3767
8:12 **t** cometh the devil, and taketh away 1534
8:19 **T** came to him *his* mother and his brethren, 1161
8:24 Master, master, we perish. **T** he rose, 1161
8:33 **T** went the devils out of the man, and 1161
8:35 **T** they went out to see what was done; and 1161
8:37 **T** the whole multitude of the country of 2532
9: 1 **T** he called his twelve disciples together, 1161
9:12 **t** came the twelve, and said unto him, 1161
9:16 **T** he took the five loaves and the two 1161
9:46 **T** there arose a reasoning among them, 1161
10:37 **T** said Jesus unto him, Go, and do thou 3767
11:13 If ye **t**, being evil, know how to give good 3767
11:26 **T** goeth he, and taketh to *him* seven other 5119
11:45 **T** answered one of the lawyers, and 1161
12:20 **t** whose shall *those things* be, which thou 1161
12:26 If ye **t** be not able *to do that thing which is* 3767
12:28 If **t** God so clothe the grass, which is to day 1161
12:41 **T** Peter said unto him, Lord, speakest thou 1161
12:42 Who **t** is *that* faithful and wise steward, 686
13: 7 **T** said he unto the dresser of his vineyard, 1161
13: 9 and if not, **t** after that thou shalt cut it down. NIG
13:15 The Lord **t** answered him, and said, 3767
13:18 **T** said he, Unto what is the kingdom of 1161
13:23 **T** said one unto him, Lord, are there few 1161
13:26 **T** shall ye begin to say, We have eaten and 5119
14:10 **t** shalt thou have worship in the presence of 5119
14:12 **T** said he also to him that bade him, 1161
14:16 **T** said he unto him, A certain man made a 1161
14:21 shewed his lord these *things.* **T** the master 5119
15: 1 **T** drew near unto him all the publicans and 1161
16: 3 **T** the steward said within himself, 1161
16: 7 **T** said he to another, And how much owest 1899
16:27 **T** he said, I pray thee therefore, father, 1161
17: 1 **T** said he unto the disciples, It is impossible 1161
18:26 they that heard *it* said, Who **t** can be saved? 2532
18:28 **T** Peter said, Lo, we have left all, 1161
18:31 **T** he took unto *him* the twelve, and 1161
19:15 **t** he commanded these servants to be called 2532
19:16 **T** came the first, saying, Lord, thy pound 1161
19:23 Wherefore **t** gavest not thou my money 2532

Lk 20: 5 he will say, Why **t** believed ye him not? 3767
20: 9 **T** began he to speak to the people this 1161
20:13 **T** said the lord of the vineyard, What shall I 1161
20:17 and said, What is this **t** that is written, 3767
20:27 **T** came to *him* certain of the Sadducees, 1161
20:39 **T** certain of the scribes answering said, 1161
20:44 calleth him Lord, how is he **t** his son? 2532
20:45 **T** in the audience of all the people he said 1161
21:10 **T** said he unto them, Nation shall rise 5119
21:20 **t** know that the desolation thereof is nigh. 5119
21:21 **T** let them which are in Judea flee to 5119
21:27 And **t** shall they see the Son of man coming 5119
21:28 to pass, **t** look up, and lift up your heads; NIG
22: 3 **T** entered Satan into Judas surnamed 1161
22: 7 **T** came the day of unleavened bread, 1161
22:36 **T** said he unto them, But now, he that hath 3767
22:52 **T** Jesus said unto the chief priests, and 1161
22:54 **T** took they him, and led *him*, and 1161
22:70 **T** said they all, Art thou then the Son of 1161
22:70 said they all, Art thou **t** the Son of God? 3767
23: 4 **T** said Pilate to the chief priests and *to* 1161
23: 9 **T** he questioned *with* him in many words; 1161
23:30 **T** shall they begin to say to the mountains, 5119
23:34 **T** said Jesus, Father, forgive them; for they 1161
24:12 **T** arose Peter, and ran unto the sepulchre; 1161
24:25 **T** he said unto them, O fools, and slow of 2532
24:45 **T** opened he their understanding, that *they* 5119
Jn 1:21 And they asked him, What **t**? Art thou 3767
1:22 **T** said they unto him, Who art thou? 3767
1:25 and said unto him, Why baptizest thou **t**, 3767
1:38 **T** Jesus turned, 1161
2:10 *men* have well drunk, **t** that which is worse: 5119
2:18 **T** answered the Jews and said unto him, 3767
2:20 **T** said the Jews, Forty and six years was 3767
3:25 **T** there arose a question between *some* of 3767
4: 5 **T** cometh he to a city of Samaria, which is 3767
4: 9 **T** saith the woman of Samaria unto him, 3767
4:11 from whence **t** hast thou *that* living water? 3767
4:28 The woman **t** left her waterpot, and 3767
4:30 **T** they went out of the city, and came unto 3767
4:35 are yet four months, and **t** cometh harvest? NIG
4:45 **T** when he was come into Galilee, 3767
4:48 **T** said Jesus unto him, Except ye see signs 3767
4:52 **T** inquired he of them the hour when he 3767
5: 4 whosoever **t** first after the troubling of 3767
5:12 **T** asked they him, What man is that which 3767
5:19 **T** answered Jesus and said unto them, 3767
6: 5 When Jesus **t** lift up *his* eyes, 3767
6:14 **T** *those* men, when they had seen 3767
6:21 **T** they willingly received him into the ship: 3767
6:28 **T** said they unto him, What shall we do, 3767
6:30 unto him, What sign shewest thou **t**, 3767
6:32 **T** Jesus said unto them, Verily, verily, I say 3767
6:34 **T** said they unto him, Lord, evermore give 3767
6:41 The Jews **t** murmured at him, because 3767
6:42 how *is it* **t** *that* he saith, I came down from 3767
6:53 **T** Jesus said unto them, Verily, verily, I say 3767
6:67 **T** said Jesus unto the twelve, Will ye also 3767
6:68 **T** Simon Peter answered him, Lord, 3767
7: 6 **T** Jesus said unto them, My time is not yet 3767
7:10 **t** went he also up unto the feast, not openly, 5119
7:11 **T** the Jews sought him at the feast, and 3767
7:25 **T** said some of them of Jerusalem, Is not 3767
7:28 **T** cried Jesus in the temple as he taught, 3767
7:30 **T** they sought to take him: but no *man* laid 3767
7:33 **T** said Jesus unto them, Yet a little while 3767
7:33 I with you, and **t** I go unto him that sent me. NIG
7:35 **T** said the Jews among themselves, 3767
7:45 **T** came the officers to the chief priests and 3767
7:47 **T** answered them the Pharisees, Are ye also 3767
8:12 **T** spake Jesus again unto them, saying, 3767
8:19 **T** said they unto him, Where is thy Father? 3767
8:21 **T** said Jesus again unto them, I go my way, 3767
8:22 **T** said the Jews, Will he kill himself? 3767
8:25 **T** said they unto him, Who art thou? 3767
8:28 **T** said Jesus unto them, When ye have lift 3767
8:28 **t** shall ye know that I am *he*, and *that* I do 5119
8:31 **T** said Jesus to those Jews which believed 3767
8:31 in my word, **t** are ye my disciples indeed; NIG
8:41 **T** said they to him, We be not born of 3767
8:48 **T** answered the Jews, and said unto him, 3767
8:52 **T** said the Jews unto him, Now we know 3767
8:57 **T** said the Jews unto him, Thou art not yet 3767
8:59 **T** took they up stones to cast at him: but 3767
9:12 **T** said they unto him, Where is he? He said, 3767
9:15 **T** again the Pharisees also asked him how 3767
9:19 was born blind? how **t** doth he now see? 3767
9:24 **T** again called they the man that was blind, 3767
9:26 **T** said they to him again, What did he to 1161
9:28 **T** they reviled him, and said, Thou art his 3767
10: 7 **T** said Jesus unto them again, Verily, 3767
10:24 **T** came the Jews round about him, and 3767
10:31 **T** the Jews took up stones again to stone 3767
11: 7 **T** after that saith he to *his* disciples, Let us 1899
11:12 **T** said his disciples, Lord, if he sleep, 3767
11:14 **T** said Jesus unto them plainly, 3767+5119
11:16 **T** said Thomas, which is called Didymus, 3767
11:17 **T** when Jesus came, he found that he had 3767
11:20 **T** Martha, as soon as she heard that Jesus 3767
11:21 **T** said Martha unto Jesus, Lord, if thou 3767
11:31 The Jews **t** which were with her in 3767
11:32 **T** when Mary was come where Jesus was, 3767
11:36 **T** said the Jews, Behold, how he loved him. 3767
11:41 **T** they took away the stone *from the place* 3767
11:45 **T** many of the Jews which came to Mary, 3767
11:47 **T** gathered the chief priests and 3767
11:53 **T** from that day forth they took counsel 3767
11:56 **T** sought they for Jesus, and spake among 3767
12: 1 **T** Jesus six days before the passover came 3767
12: 3 **T** took Mary a pound of ointment of 3767
12: 4 **T** saith one of his disciples, Judas Iscariot, 3767
12: 7 **T** said Jesus, Let her alone: against the day 3767
12:16 **t** remembered they that these *things* were 5119
12:28 **T** came there a voice from heaven, 3767
12:35 **T** Jesus said unto them, Yet a little while is 3767
Jn 13: 6 **T** cometh he to Simon Peter: and 3767
13:14 If I **t**, *your* Lord and Master, have washed 3767
13:22 **T** the disciples looked one on another, 3767
13:25 He **t** lying on Jesus' breast saith unto him, 1161
13:27 **T** said Jesus unto him, That thou doest, 3767
13:30 He **t** having received the sop went 3767
14: 9 and how sayest thou **t**, Shew us the Father? NIG
16:17 **T** said *some* of his disciples among 3767
18: 3 Judas **t**, having received a band *of men*, and 3767
18: 6 As soon **t** as he had said unto them, I am 3767
18: 7 **T** asked he them again, Whom seek ye? 3767
18:10 **T** Simon Peter having a sword drew it, and 3767
18:11 **T** said Jesus unto Peter, Put up thy sword 3767
18:12 **T** the band and the captain and officers of 3767
18:16 **T** went out *that* other disciple, which was 3767
18:17 **T** saith the damsel that kept the door unto 3767
18:19 The high priest **t** asked Jesus of his 3767
18:27 Peter **t** denied again: and immediately 3767
18:28 **T** led they Jesus from Caiaphas unto 3767
18:29 Pilate **t** went out unto them, and said, What 3767
18:31 **T** said Pilate unto them, Take ye him, and 3767
18:33 **T** Pilate entered into the judgment hall 3767
18:36 of this world, **t** would my servants fight, NIG
18:37 therefore said unto him, Art thou a king **t**? 3766
18:40 **T** cried they all again, saying, Not this *man*, 3767
19: 1 **T** Pilate therefore took Jesus, and 5119
19: 5 **T** came Jesus forth, wearing the crown of 3767
19:10 **T** saith Pilate unto him, Speakest thou not 3767
19:16 **T** delivered he him therefore unto them to 5119
19:20 This title **t** read many of the Jews: for 3767
19:21 **T** said the chief priests of the Jews to 3767
19:23 **T** the soldiers, when they had crucified 3767
19:27 **T** saith he to the disciple, Behold thy 1534
19:32 **T** came the soldiers, and brake the legs of 3767
19:40 **T** took they the body of Jesus, and wound it 3767
20: 2 **T** she runneth, and cometh to Simon Peter, 3767
20: 6 **T** cometh Simon Peter following him, and 3767
20: 8 **T** went in also *that* other disciple, 3767+5119
20:10 **T** the disciples went away again unto their 3767
20:19 **T** the same day at evening, being the first 3767
20:20 **T** were the disciples glad, when they saw 3767
20:21 **T** said Jesus to them again, Peace *be* unto 3767
20:26 **t** came Jesus, the doors being shut, NIG
20:27 **T** saith he to Thomas, Reach hither thy 1534
21: 5 **T** Jesus saith unto them, Children, have ye 3767
21: 9 As soon **t** as they were come to land, 3767
21:13 Jesus **t** cometh, and taketh bread, and 3767
21:20 **T** Peter, turning about, seeth the disciple 1161
21:23 **T** went this saying abroad among 3767
Ac 1:12 **T** returned they unto Jerusalem from 5119
2:38 **T** Peter said unto them, Repent, and 1161
2:41 **T** they that gladly received his word were 3767
3: 6 **T** Peter said, Silver and gold have I none; 1161
4: 8 **T** Peter, filled with the Holy Ghost, 5119
5: 9 **T** Peter said unto her, How *is it* that ye 1161
5:10 **T** fell she down straightway at his feet, and 1161
5:17 **T** the high priest rose up, and all they that 1161
5:25 **T** came one and told them, saying, Behold, 1161
5:26 **T** went the captain with the officers, and 5119
5:29 **T** Peter and the *other* apostles answered 1161
5:34 **T** stood there up one in the council, 1161
6: 2 **T** the twelve called the multitude of 1161
6: 9 **T** there arose certain of the synagogue, 1161
6:11 **T** they suborned men, which said, We have 5119
7: 1 **T** said the high priest, Are these *things* so? 1161
7: 4 **T** came he out of the land of the Chaldeans, 5119
7:14 **T** sent Joseph, and called his father Jacob 1161
7:29 **T** fled Moses at this saying, and was a 1161
7:32 and the God of Jacob. **T** Moses trembled, 1161
7:33 **T** said the Lord to him, Put off *thy* shoes 1161
7:42 **T** God turned, and gave them up to worship 1161
7:57 **T** they cried out with a loud voice, and 1161
8: 5 **T** Philip went down to the city of Samaria, 1161
8:13 **T** Simon himself believed also: and 1161
8:17 **T** laid they *their* hands on them, and 5119
8:24 **T** answered Simon, and said, Pray ye to 1161
8:29 **T** the Spirit said unto Philip, Go near, and 1161
8:35 **T** Philip opened his mouth, 1161
9:13 **T** Ananias answered, Lord, I have heard by 1161
9:19 **T** was Saul certain days with the disciples 1161
9:25 **T** the disciples took him by night, and 1161
9:31 **T** had the churches rest throughout all 3767
9:39 **T** Peter arose and went with them. When he 1161
10:21 **T** Peter went down to the men which were 1161
10:23 **T** called he them in, and lodged *them*. And 3767
10:34 **T** Peter opened *his* mouth, and said, Of a 1161
10:46 and magnify God. **T** answered Peter, 5119
10:48 **T** prayed they him to tarry certain days. 5119
11:16 **T** remembered I the word of the Lord, 1161
11:17 Forasmuch **t** as God gave them the like gift 3767
11:18 **T** hath God also to the Gentiles granted 686
11:22 **T** tidings of these *things* came unto the ears 1161
11:25 **T** departed Barnabas to Tarsus, for to seek 1161
11:29 **T** the disciples, every man according to his 1161
12: 3 (**T** were the days of unleavened bread.) 1161
12:15 it was *even* so. **T** said they, It is his angel. 1161
13: 9 **T** Saul, (who also *is called* Paul,) 1161
13:12 **T** the deputy, when he saw what was done, 5119
13:16 **T** Paul stood up, and beckoning with *his* 1161
13:46 **T** Paul and Barnabas waxed bold, and said, 1161
14:13 **T** the priest of Jupiter, which was before 1161
15:12 **T** all the multitude kept silence, and 1161
15:22 **T** pleased it the apostles and elders, 5119
16: 1 **T** came he to Derbe and Lystra: and 1161
16:29 **T** he called for a light, and sprang in, and 1161
17:14 And **t** immediately the brethren sent away 5119
17:18 **T** certain philosophers of the Epicureans, 1161
17:22 **T** Paul stood in the midst of Mars' hill, and 1161
17:29 **Forasmuch t** as we are the offspring of 3767
18: 9 **T** spake the Lord to Paul in the night by a 1161
18:17 **T** all the Greeks took Sosthenes, the *chief* 1161
18:18 and **t** took his leave of the brethren, and NIG
19: 3 unto them, Unto what **t** were ye baptized? 3767
19: 4 **T** said Paul, John verily baptized *with* 1161
19:13 **T** certain of the vagabond Jews, exorcists, 1161
Ac 19:36 **Seeing t** that these *things* cannot be spoken 3767
21:13 **T** Paul answered, What mean ye to weep 1161
21:26 **T** Paul took the men, and the next day 5119
21:33 **T** the chief captain came near, and 5119
22:22 and **t** lift up their voices, and said, NIG
22:27 **T** the chief captain came, and said unto 1161
22:29 **T** straightway they departed from him 3767
23: 3 **T** said Paul unto him, God shall smite thee, 5119
23: 5 **T** said Paul, I wist not, brethren, that he 5037
23:17 **T** Paul called one of the centurions unto 1161
23:19 **T** the chief captain took him by the hand, 1161
23:22 So the chief captain **t** let the young man NIG
23:27 **t** came I with an army, and rescued him, NIG
23:31 **T** the soldiers, as it was commanded them, 3767
24:10 **T** Paul, after that the governor had 1161
25: 2 **T** the high priest and the chief of the Jews 1161
25:10 **T** said Paul, I stand at Cesar's judgment 1161
25:12 **T** Festus, when he had conferred with 5119
25:22 **T** Agrippa said unto Festus, I would also 1161
26: 1 **T** Agrippa said unto Paul, Thou art 1161
26: 1 **T** Paul stretched forth the hand, and 5119
26:20 and **t** to the Gentiles, that *they* should repent NIG
26:28 **T** Agrippa said unto Paul, Almost thou 1161
26:32 **T** said Agrippa unto Festus, This man 1161
27:20 that we should be saved was **t** taken away. 3062
27:29 **T** fearing lest we should have fallen upon 5037
27:32 **T** the soldiers cut off the ropes of the boat, 5119
27:36 **T** were they all of good cheer, and 1161
28: 1 **t** they knew that the island was called 5119
Ro 3: 1 What advantage **t** hath the Jew? or 3767
3: 6 **for t** how shall God judge the world? 1893
3: 9 What **t**? are we better *than they?* No, in no 3767
3:27 Where *is* boasting **t**? It is excluded. By 3767
3:31 Do we **t** make void the law through faith? 3767
4: 1 What shall we say **t** that Abraham our 3767
4: 9 *Cometh* this blessedness **t** upon 3767
4:10 How was it **t** reckoned? when he was in 3767
5: 9 Much more **t**, being now justified by his 3767
6: 1 What shall we say **t**? Shall we continue in 3767
6:15 What **t**? shall we sin, because we are not 3767
6:18 Being **t** made free from sin, ye became 1161
6:21 What fruit had ye **t** *in those things* whereof 5119
7: 3 So **t** if, while *her* husband liveth, she be 3767
7: 7 What shall we say **t**? *Is* the law sin? 3767
7:13 Was **t** that which is good made death unto 3767
7:16 If **t** I do that which I would not, I consent 1161
7:17 Now **t** it is no more I that do it, but sin that 1161
7:21 I find **t** a law, that, when I would do good, 686
7:25 So **t** with the mind I myself serve the law 3767
8: 8 **So t** they that are in the flesh cannot please 1161
8:17 And if children, **t** heirs; heirs of God, and 2532
8:25 see not, **t** do we with patience wait for *it*. NIG
8:31 What shall we **t** say to these *things?* If God 3767
9:14 What shall we say **t**? *Is there* 3767
9:16 So **t** *it is* not of him that willeth, nor of him 3767
9:19 Thou wilt say **t** unto me, Why doth he yet 3767
9:30 What shall we say **t**? That the Gentiles, 3767
10:14 How **t** shall they call on *him* in whom they 3767
10:17 **So t** faith *cometh* by hearing, 686
11: 1 I say **t**, Hath God cast away his people? 3767
11: 5 *Even* so **t** at *this* present time also there is a 3767
11: 6 And if by grace, **t** *is it* no more of works: NIG
11: 6 But if *it be* of works, **t** is it no more grace: NIG
11: 7 What **t**? Israel hath not obtained that which 3767
11:11 I say **t**, Have they stumbled that they 3767
11:19 Thou wilt say **t**, The branches were broken 3767
12: 6 Having **t** gifts differing according to 1161
13: 3 Wilt thou **t** not be afraid of the power? 1161
14:12 So **t** every one of us shall give account of 3767
14:16 Let not **t** your good be evil spoken of: 3767
15: 1 We **t** that are strong ought to bear 1161
1Co 3: 5 Who **t** is Paul, and who *is* Apollos, but 3767
3: 7 **So t** neither is he that planteth any *thing*, 5620
4: 5 and **t** shall every man have praise of God. 5119
5:10 for **t** must ye needs go out of the world. 686
6: 4 If **t** ye have judgments *of things* pertaining 3767
6:15 shall I **t** take the members of Christ, and 3767
7:38 **So t** he that giveth *her* in marriage doeth 5620
9:18 What is my reward **t**? *Verily* that, when I 3767
10:19 What say I **t**? that the idol is any *thing*, or 3767
12:28 **t** gifts of healings, helps, governments, 1534
13:10 **t** that which is in part shall be done away. 5119
13:12 through a glass, darkly; but **t** face to face: 5119
13:12 but **t** shall I know even as also I am known. 5119
14:15 What is it **t**? I will pray with the spirit, and 3767
14:26 How is it **t**, brethren? when ye come 3767
15: 5 that he was seen of Cephas, **t** of the twelve: 1534
15: 7 he was seen of James; **t** of all the apostles. 1534
15:13 of the dead, **t** is Christ **not** risen: 3761
15:14 **t** *is* our preaching vain, and your faith *is* also 686
15:16 if the dead rise not, **t** is **not** Christ raised: 3761
15:18 **T** they also which are fallen asleep in Christ 686
15:24 **T** *cometh* the end, when he shall have 1534
15:28 **t** shall the Son also himself be subject unto 5119
15:29 at all? why are they **t** baptized for the dead? 2532
15:54 **t** shall be brought to pass the saying that is 5119
2Co 2: 2 who is he **t** that maketh me glad, but 2532
3:12 **Seeing t** that we have such hope, we use 3767
4:12 **So t** death worketh in us, but life in you. 5620
5:14 that if one died for all, **t** were all dead: 686
5:20 *Now* **t** we are ambassadors for Christ, 3767
6: 1 We **t**, *as* workers together *with him*, 1161
12:10 for when I am weak, **t** am I strong. 5119
Gal 1:18 **T** after three years I went up to Jerusalem 1899
2: 1 **T** fourteen years after I went up again to 1899
2:21 *come* by the law, **t** Christ is dead in vain. 686
3: 9 **So t** they which be of faith are blessed with 5620
3:19 Wherefore **t** *serveth* the law? It was added 3767
3:21 *Is* the law **t** against the promises of God? 3767
3:29 **t** are ye Abraham's seed, and heirs according 686
4: 7 if a son, **t** an heir of God through Christ. 2532
4: 8 Howbeit **t**, when ye knew not God, ye did 5119
4:15 Where is **t** the blessedness ye spake of? 3767
4:29 But as **t** he that was born after the flesh 5119
4:31 **So t**, brethren, we are not children of 686

Gal 5:11 t is the offence of the cross ceased. 686
5:16 *This* I say t, Walk in the Spirit, and ye shall 1161
6: 4 and t shall he have rejoicing in himself 5119
Eph 5:15 See t that ye walk circumspectly, not as 3767
Php 1:18 What t? notwithstanding, every way, 1063
Col 3: 1 If ye t be risen with Christ, seek those 3767
3: 4 t shall ye also appear with him in glory. 5119
1Th 4: 1 Furthermore t we beseech you, brethren, 3767
4:17 T we which are alive *and* remain shall be 1899
5: 3 t sudden destruction cometh upon them, 5119
2Th 2: 8 And t shall *that* Wicked be revealed, 5119
1Ti 2:13 For Adam was first formed, t Eve. 1534
3: 2 A bishop t must be blameless, the husband 3767
3:10 t let them use the office of a deacon, 1534
Heb 2:14 Forasmuch t as the children are partakers of 3767
4: 8 t would he not afterward have spoken of NIG
4:14 **Seeing** t that we have a great high priest, 3767
7:27 first for his own sins, *and* t for the people's: 1899
8: 7 t should no place have been sought for NIG
9: 1 T verily the first *covenant* had also 3767
9: 9 Which *was* a figure for the time t present, NIG
9:26 For t must he often have suffered since 1893
10: 2 For t would they not have ceased to be 1893
10: 7 T said I, Lo, I come (in the volume of 5119
10: 9 T said he, Lo, I come to do thy will, 5119
12: 8 are partakers, t are ye bastards, and not sons. 686
12:26 Whose voice t shook the earth: but now he 5119
Jas 1:15 T when lust hath conceived, it bringeth 1534
2: 4 Are ye not t partial in yourselves, and 2532
2:24 Ye see t how that by works a man is 5106
3:17 t peaceable, gentle, *and* easy to be 1899
4:14 for a little *time,* and t vanisheth away. 1899
1Pe 4: 1 **Forasmuch** t **as** Christ hath suffered for us 3767
2Pe 3: 6 Whereby the world that t was, 5119
3:11 Seeing t that all these *things shall* be 3767
1Jn 1: 5 This t is the message which we have heard 2532
3:21 us not, t have we confidence towards God. NIG
Rev 3:16 So t because thou art lukewarm, and NIG
22: 9 T saith he unto me, See *thou do it* not: for I 2532

THENCE (145) [THENCEFORTH]

Ge 2:10 from t it was parted, and became into four 8033
11: 8 abroad from t upon the face of all the earth: 8033
11: 9 from t did the LORD scatter them abroad 8033
12: 8 he removed from t unto a mountain on 8033
18:16 the men rose up from t, and looked toward 8033
18:22 the men turned their faces from t, and 8033
20: 1 Abraham journeyed from t toward 8033
24: 7 thou shalt take a wife unto my son from t. 8033
26:17 Isaac departed t, and pitched his tent 4480+8033
26:22 he removed from t, and digged another 8033
26:23 And he went up from t to Beer-sheba. 8033
27: 9 fetch me from t two good kids of the goats; 8033
27:45 I will send, and fetch thee from t: why 8033
28: 2 take thee a wife from t of the daughters of 8033
28: 6 to Padan-aram, to take him a wife from t; 8033
30:32 removing from t all the speckled and 8033
42: 2 you down thither, and buy for us from t; 8033
42:26 asses with the corn, and departed t. 4480+8033
49:24 (from t *is* the shepherd, the stone of Israel:) 8033
Nu 13:23 cut down from t a branch with one cluster 8033
13:24 the children of Israel cut down from t. 8033
21:12 From t they removed, and pitched in 8033
21:13 From t they removed, and pitched on 8033
21:16 from t *they went* to Beer: that *is* the well 8033
22:41 that t he might see the utmost part of 4480+8033
23:13 not see them all: and curse me them from t. 8033
23:27 that thou mayest curse me them from t. 8033
Dt 4:29 if from t thou shalt seek the LORD thy 8033
5:15 thee out t through a mighty hand 4480+8033
6:23 he brought us out from t, that he might 8033
10: 7 From t they journeyed *unto* Gudgodah; and 8033
19:12 of his city shall send and fetch him t, 4480+8033
22: 8 upon thine house, if any man fall from t. 5105.2
24:18 LORD thy God redeemed thee t: 4480+8033
30: 4 from t will the LORD thy God gather 8033
30: 4 gather thee, and from t will he fetch thee: 8033
Jos 6:22 bring out t the woman, and all that 4480+8033
13: 4 *From* t it passed toward Ammon, and NIH
15:14 Caleb drove t the three sons of Anak, 4480+8033
15:15 he went up t to the inhabitants of 4480+8033
18:13 the border went over from t toward Luz, 8033
18:14 the border was drawn *t,* and compassed NIH
19:13 from t passeth on along on the east to 8033
19:34 goeth out from t to Hukkok, and 8033
Jdg 1:11 from t he went against the inhabitants of 8033
1:20 he expelled t the three sons of Anak. 4480+8033
8: 8 he went up t *to* Penuel, and 4480+8033
18:11 there went from t of the family of 8033
18:13 they passed t *unto* mount Ephraim, 4480+8033
19:18 the side of mount Ephraim; from t *am* I. 8033
21:24 the children of Israel departed t at that time, 8033
21:24 they went out from t every man to his 8033
1Sa 4: 4 that they might bring from t the ark of 8033
10: 3 shalt thou go on forward from t, and 8033
10:23 they ran and fetched him t: and 4480+8033
17:49 took t a stone, and slang *it,* and 4480+8033
22: 1 David therefore departed t, and escaped to 8033
22: 3 David went t *to* Mizpeh of Moab: 4480+8033
23:29 David went up from t, and dwelt in strong 8033
2Sa 6: 2 of Judah, to bring up from t the ark of God, 8033
14: 2 fetcht t a wise woman, and said unto 4480+8033
16: 5 t came out a man of the family of 4480+8033
21:13 he brought up from t the bones of Saul and 8033
1Ki 1:45 they are come up from t rejoicing, so 8033
2:36 and go not forth t any whither. 4480+8033
9:28 fet from t gold, four hundred and 8033
12:25 went out from t, and built Penuel. 8033
19:19 So he departed t, and found Elisha 4480+8033
2Ki 2:21 there shall not be from t any more death or 8033
2:23 he went up from t *unto* Beth-el: and as he 8033
2:25 he went from t to mount Carmel, and 8033
2:25 and from t he returned *to* Samaria. 8033
6: 2 take t every man a beam, and let us 4480+8033
7: 8 carried t silver, and gold, and 4480+8033
2Ki 7: 8 carried t *also,* and went and hid *it.* 4480+8033
10:15 when he was departed t, he lighted on 8033
17:27 one of the priests whom ye brought from t; 8033
17:33 the nations whom they carried away from t. 8033
23:12 brake *them* down from t, and cast the dust 8033
24:13 he carried out t all the treasures of 4480+8033
1Ch 13: 6 up t the ark of God the LORD, 4480+8033
2Ch 8:18 took t four hundred and fifty talents 4480+8033
26:20 and they thrust him out from t; 8033
Ezr 6: 6 *are* beyond the river, be ye far from t: 8536
Ne 1: 9 *yet* will I gather them from t, and will bring 8033
Job 39:29 From t she seeketh the prey, *and* her eyes 8033
Isa 52:11 Depart ye, depart ye, go ye out from t, 8033
65:20 There shall be no more t an infant of 4480+8033
Jer 5: 6 every one that goeth out t shall be 2007+4480
13: 6 go to Euphrates, and take the girdle from t, 8033
22:24 right hand, yet would I pluck thee t; 4480+8033
36:29 shall cause to cease from t man and 5089.1
37:12 to separate himself t in the midst of 4480+8033
38:11 took t old cast clouts and old rotten 4480+8033
43:12 and he shall go forth from t in peace. 8033
49:16 I will bring thee down from t, saith 8033
49:38 will destroy from t the king and the princes, 8033
50: 9 array against her; from t she shall be taken: 8033
Eze 11:18 and all the abominations thereof from t. 5089.1
Hos 2:15 I will give her her vineyards from t, and 8033
Am 6: 2 see; and from t go ye *to* Hamath the great: 8033
9: 2 t shall mine hand take them; 4480+8033
9: 2 *to* heaven, t will I bring them down: 4480+8033
9: 3 I will search and take them out t; 8033
9: 3 t will I command the serpent, and 4480+8033
9: 4 t will I command the sword, and 4480+8033
Ob 1: 4 t will I bring thee down, saith 4480+8033
Mt 4:21 And going on **from** t, he saw other two 1564
5:26 Thou shalt by no means come out t, 1564
9: 9 And as Jesus passed forth **from** t, he saw a 1564
9:27 And when Jesus departed t, two blind men 1564
10:11 in it is worthy; and there abide till ye **go** t. 1831
11: 1 he departed t to teach and to preach in their 1564
12: 9 And when he was departed t, he went into 1564
12:15 Jesus knew *it,* he withdrew himself **from** t: 1564
13:53 had finished these parables, he departed t. 1564
14:13 When Jesus heard *of it,* he departed t by 1564
15:21 Then Jesus went t, and departed into 1564
15:29 And Jesus departed from t, and came nigh 1564
19:15 he laid *his* hands on them, and departed t. 1564
Mk 1:19 And when he had gone a little further t, 1564
6: 1 And he went out **from** t, and came into his 1564
6:11 nor hear you, when ye depart t, 1564
7:24 And **from** t he arose, and went into 1564
9:30 **And** they departed t, and passed through 2547
10: 1 **And** he rose **from** t, 2547
Lk 9: 4 ye enter into, there abide, and t depart. 1564
12:59 I tell thee, thou shalt not depart t, till thou 1564
16:26 they pass to us, that *would come* **from** t. 1564
Jn 4:43 Now after two days he departed t, and 1564
11:54 went t unto a country near to 1564
Ac 7: 4 **and from** t, when his father was dead, 2547
13: 4 and **from** t they sailed to Cyprus. 1564
14:26 **And** t sailed to Antioch, from whence they 2547
16:12 **And from** t to Philippi, which is the chief 2547
18: 7 And he departed t, and entered into a 1564
18:18 and **sailed** t into Syria, and with him 1602
20:15 **And** we sailed t, and came the next *day* 2547
21: 1 unto Rhodes, **and from** t unto Patara: 2547
27: 4 **And** when we had launched **from** t, 2547
27:12 the more part advised to depart t **also,** 2547
27:13 loosing *t,* they sailed close by Crete. NIG
28:13 **And from** t we fet a compass, 3606
28:15 **And from** t, when the brethren heard of us, 2547
2Co 2:13 of them, I went from t into Macedonia. NIG

THENCEFORTH (4) [THENCE]

Lev 22:27 t it shall be accepted for an offering made 1973
2Ch 32:23 in the sight of all nations from t. 310+3651
Mt 5:13 it is t good for nothing, but to be cast out, 2089
Jn 19:12 *And* **from** t Pilate sought to release 1537+3778

THEOPHILUS (2)

Lk 1: 3 write unto thee in order, most excellent T, 2321
Ac 1: 1 The former treatise have I made, O T, of all 2321

THERE (2299)

Ge 1: 3 God said, Let t be light: and there was light. NIH
1: 3 God said, Let there be light: and t was light. NIH
1: 6 Let t be a firmament in the midst of NIH
1:14 Let t be lights in the firmament of NIH
1:30 wherein *t is* life, *I have given* every green NIH
2: 5 and t *was* not a man to till the ground. NIH
2: 6 t went up a mist from the earth, and NIH
2: 8 and t he put the man whom he had formed. 8033
2:11 the whole land of Havilah, where *t is* gold; NIH
2:12 *is* good: t *is* bdellium and the onyx stone. 8033
2:20 for Adam t was not found a help meet for NIH
4:26 to Seth, *to* him also t was born a son; and NIH
6: 4 T were giants in the earth in those days; and NIH
7: 9 T went in two and two unto Noah into NIH
9:11 neither shall t any more be a flood to NIH
11: 2 in the land of Shinar; and they dwelt t. 8033
11: 7 us go down, and t confound their language, 8033
11: 9 the LORD did t confound the language of NIH
11:31 and they came unto Haran, and dwelt t. 8033
12: 7 t builded he an altar unto the LORD, 8033
12: 8 t he builded an altar unto the LORD, and 8033
12:10 t was a famine in the land: and Abram went NIH
12:10 Abram went down into Egypt to sojourn t; 8033
13: 4 the altar, which he had made t at the first: 8033
13: 4 t Abram called on the name of the LORD. 8033
13: 7 t was a strife between the herdmen of NIH
13: 8 Let t be no strife, I pray thee, between me NIH
13:18 and built t an altar unto the LORD. 8033
14: 8 t went out the king of Sodom, and the king NIH
14:10 of Sodom and Gomorrah fled, and fell t; 8033
14:13 t came one that had escaped, and NIH
Ge 18:24 Peradventure t **be** fifty righteous within 3426
18:28 Peradventure t shall lack five of the fifty NIH
18:28 he said, If I find t forty and five, I will not 8033
18:29 Peradventure t shall be forty found there. NIH
18:29 Peradventure there shall be forty found t. 8033
18:30 Peradventure t shall thirty be found there. NIH
18:30 Peradventure there shall thirty be found t. 8033
18:30 he said, I will not do *it,* if I find thirty t. 8033
18:31 Peradventure t shall be twenty found there. NIH
18:31 Peradventure there shall be twenty found t. 8033
18:32 Peradventure ten shall be found t. And he 8033
19: 1 t came two angels to Sodom at even; and NIH
19:31 *t is* not a man in the earth to come in unto NIH
21:31 because t they sware both of them. 8033
21:33 called t on the name of the LORD, 8033
22: 2 offer him t for a burnt offering upon one of 8033
22: 9 Abraham built an altar t, and laid the wood 8033
23:13 *it* of me, and I will bury my dead t. 8033+1886.5
24:23 **is** t room *in* thy father's house for us to 3426
24:33 t was set *meat* before him to eat: but NIH
25:10 t was Abraham buried, and 8033+1886.5
25:24 behold, *t were* twins in her womb. NIH
26: 1 t was a famine in the land, besides the first NIH
26: 8 to pass, when he had been t a long time, 8033
26:17 his tent in the valley of Gerar, and dwelt t. 8033
26:19 and found t a well of springing water. 8033
26:25 he builded an altar t, and called upon 8033
26:25 name of the LORD, and pitched his tent t: 8033
26:25 and t Isaac's servants digged a well. 8033
26:28 we said, Let t be now an oath betwixt us, NIH
28:11 tarried t all night, because the sun was set; 8033
29: 2 lo, t *were* three flocks of sheep lying by it; 8033
31:14 *Is* t yet any portion or inheritance for us in NIH
31:46 a heap: and they did eat t upon the heap. 8033
32: 4 with Laban, and stayed *t* until now: NIH
32:13 he lodged t that *same* night; and took of 8033
32:24 t wrestled a man with him until the breaking NIH
32:29 ask after my name? And he blessed him t. 8033
33:20 he erected t an altar, and called it 8033
35: 1 Arise, go up to Beth-el, and dwell t: 8033
35: 1 make t an altar unto God, that appeared 8033
35: 3 I will make t an altar unto God, 8033
35: 7 he built t an altar, and called the place 8033
35: 7 because t God appeared unto him, when he 8033
35:16 t was but a little way to come to Ephrath: NIH
36:31 before t reigned *any* king over the children NIH
37:24 and the pit *was* empty, *t was* no water in it. NIH
37:28 t passed by Midianites merchantmen; and NIH
38: 2 Judah saw t a daughter of a certain 8033
38:21 they said, T was no harlot in this *place.* NIH
38:22 place said, *that* t was no harlot in this *place.* NIH
39: 9 *T is* none greater in this house than I; NIH
39:11 *t was* none of the men of the house there NIH
39:11 *there was* none of the men of the house t 8033
39:20 *were* bound: and he was t in the prison. 8033
39:22 whatsoever they did t, he was the doer *of* 8033
40: 8 a dream, and *t is* no interpreter of it. NIH
40:17 in the uppermost basket *t was* of all *manner* NIH
41: 2 t came up out of the river seven well NIH
41: 8 *t was* none that could interpret them unto NIH
41:12 *t was* there with us a young man, a Hebrew, NIH
41:12 *there was* t with us a young man, a Hebrew, 8033
41:15 a dream, and *t is* none that can interpret it: NIH
41:18 t came up out of the river seven kine, NIH
41:24 but *t was* none that could declare *it* to me. NIH
41:29 t come seven years of great plenty NIH
41:30 t shall arise after them seven years of NIH
41:39 *t is* none so discreet and wise as thou *art:* NIH
41:54 but in all the land of Egypt t was bread. NIH
42: 1 Now when Jacob saw that t **was** corn in 3426
42: 2 Behold, I have heard that t **is** corn in Egypt: 3426
42:16 be proved, whether *t be any* truth in you: NIH
43:25 for they heard that they should eat bread t. 8033
43:30 into *his* chamber, and wept t. 8033+1886.5
44:14 came to Joseph's house; for he *was* yet t: 8033
45: 1 t stood no man with him, while Joseph NIH
45: 6 yet *t are* five years, *in* the which *there shall* NIH
45: 6 *in* the which *t shall* neither *be* earing nor NIH
45:11 t will I nourish thee; for yet *there are* five 8033
45:11 for yet *t are* five years of famine; lest thou, NIH
46: 3 for I will t make of thee a great nation. 8033
47:13 *t was* no bread in all the land; for the famine NIH
47:18 t is not ought left in the sight of my lord, NIH
48: 7 when yet *t was* but a little way to come unto NIH
48: 7 I buried her t in the way of Ephrath; 8033
49:31 T they buried Abraham and Sarah 8033+1886.5
49:31 t they buried Isaac and Rebekah 8033+1886.5
49:31 his wife; and t I buried Leah. 8033+1886.5
50: 5 of Canaan, t shalt thou bury me. 8033+1886.5
50: 9 t went up with him both chariots and NIH
50:10 t they mourned with a great and very sore 8033
Ex 1: 8 Now t arose up a new king over Egypt, NIH
1:10 to pass, that, when t falleth out any war, NIH
2: 1 t went a man of the house of Levi, and NIH
2:12 and when he saw that *t was* no man, NIH
5: 9 Let t more work be laid upon the men, NIH
5:13 *your* daily tasks, as when t was straw. NIH
5:16 *T is* no straw given unto thy servants, and NIH
5:18 for t shall no straw be given you, yet shall NIH
7:19 *that* t may be blood throughout all the land NIH
7:21 t was blood throughout all the land of NIH
8:10 that thou mayest know that *t is* none like NIH
8:15 when Pharaoh saw that t was respite, he NIH
8:18 so t were lice upon man, and upon beast. NIH
8:22 that no swarms *of flies* shall be t; 8033
8:24 t came a grievous swarm *of flies* into NIH
8:31 and from his people; t remained not one. NIH
9: 3 *t shall be* a very grievous murrain. NIH
9: 4 t shall nothing die of all *that is* NIH
9: 7 t was not one of the cattle of the Israelites NIH
9:14 that thou mayest know that *t is* none like me NIH
9:22 that t may be hail in all the land of Egypt, NIH
9:24 So t was hail, and fire mingled with the hail, NIH
9:24 such as t was none like it in all the land of NIH
9:26 where the children of Israel *were,* was t no NIH

T

Ex 9:28 that t be no *more* mighty thunderings and NIH
9:29 shall cease, neither shall t be any more hail; NIH
10:14 very grievous *were they;* before them t were NIH
10:15 t remained not any green thing in the trees, NIH
10:19 t remained not one locust in all the coasts of NIH
10:21 that t may be darkness over the land of NIH
10:22 t was a thick darkness in all the land of NIH
10:26 go with us; t shall not a hoof be left behind; NIH
11: 6 t shall be a great cry throughout all the land NIH
11: 6 such as t was none like it, nor shall be like it NIH
12:16 in the first day *t shall be* a holy NIH
12:16 in the seventh day t shall be a holy NIH
12:19 Seven days shall t be no leaven found in NIH
12:30 and t was a great cry in Egypt; NIH
12:30 for *t was* not a house where *there was* not NIH
12:30 for *there was* not a house where *t was* not NIH
12:43 the passover: T shall no stranger eat thereof: NIH
13: 3 *place:* t shall no leavened bread be eaten. NIH
13: 7 t shall no leavened bread be seen with thee, NIH
13: 7 neither shall t be leaven seen with thee in all NIH
14:11 Because *t were* no graves in Egypt, NIH
14:28 t remained not so much as one of them. NIH
15:25 t he made for them a statute and 8033
15:25 and an ordinance, and t he proved them, 8033
15:27 and they encamped t by the waters. 8033
16:14 upon the face of the wilderness *t lay* a small NIH
16:24 not stink, neither was t any worm therein. NIH
16:26 *which is* the sabbath, in it t shall be none. NIH
16:27 *that* t went out *some* of the people on NIH
17: 1 and *t was* no water for the people to drink. NIH
17: 3 the people thirsted t for water; and 8033
17: 6 I will stand before thee t upon the rock in 8033
17: 6 the rock, and t shall come water out of it, NIH
19: 2 and t Israel camped before the mount. 8033
19:13 T shall not a hand touch it, but he shall NIH
19:16 that t were thunders and lightnings, and NIH
21:30 If t be laid on him a sum of money, then NIH
22: 2 that he die, *t shall* no blood *be shed* for him. NIH
22: 3 upon him, *t shall be* blood *shed* for him; NIH
23:26 T shall nothing cast their young, nor be NIH
24:10 *t was* under his feet as it were a paved work NIH
24:12 Come up to me into the mount, and be t: 8033
25:22 t I will meet with thee, and I will commune 8033
25:35 *t shall be* a knop under two branches of NIH
26:17 Two tenons *shall t be* in one board, set in NIH
26:20 on the north side *t shall be* twenty boards: NIH
27: 9 for the south side southward *t shall be* NIH
27:11 likewise for the north side in length *t shall* NIH
28:32 t shall be a hole in the top of it, in the midst NIH
29:42 where I will meet you, to speak t unto thee. 8033
29:43 t I will meet with the children of 8033+1886.5
30:12 that t be no plague amongst them, NIH
30:34 of each shall t be a like *weight:* NIH
32:17 unto Moses, *T is* a noise of war in the camp. NIH
32:24 cast it into the fire, and t came out this calf. NIH
32:28 t fell of the people that day about three NIH
33:20 my face: for t shall no man see me, and live. NIH
33:21 *t is* a place by me, and thou shalt stand upon NIH
34: 2 present thyself t to me in the top of 8033
34: 5 stood with him t, and proclaimed the name 8033
34:28 he was t with the LORD forty days and 8033
35: 2 on the seventh day t shall be to you a holy NIH
36:30 t were eight boards; and their sockets *were* NIH
39:23 *t was* a hole in the midst of the robe, as NIH
40:30 and the altar, and put water t, 8033+1886.5
Lev 6:27 when t is sprinkled of the blood thereof upon 834
7: 7 *t is* one law for them: the priest that maketh NIH
8:31 t eat it with the bread that *is* in the basket of 8033
9:24 t came a fire out from before the LORD, NIH
10: 2 t went out fire from the LORD, and NIH
11:36 or pit, *wherein t is* plenty of water, NIH
13:10 and *t be* quick raw flesh in the rising; NIH
13:19 in the place of the boil t be a white rising, NIH
13:21 *t be* no white hairs therein, and *if it be* not NIH
13:24 Or if t be *any* flesh, in the skin whereof NIH
13:24 in the skin whereof *t is* a hot burning, and NIH
13:26 *t be* no white hair in the bright spot, and NIH
13:30 *t be* in it a yellow thin hair; then the priest NIH
13:31 the skin, and *that t is* no black hair in it; NIH
13:32 t be in it no yellow hair, and the scall *be* not NIH
13:37 and *that* t is black hair grown up therein; NIH
13:42 if t be in the bald head, or bald forehead, NIH
14:35 It seemeth to me *t is* as it were a plague in NIH
16:17 t shall be no man in the tabernacle of NIH
16:23 into the holy *place,* and shall leave them t: 8033
17: 3 What man soever *t be* of the house of Israel, NIH
17: 8 Whatsoever man *t be* of the house of Israel, NIH
17:10 whatsoever man *t be* of the house of Israel, NIH
17:13 whatsoever man *t be* of the children of NIH
20:14 that t be no wickedness among you. NIH
21: 1 T shall none be defiled for the dead among NIH
22:10 T shall no stranger eat *of* the holy *thing:* a NIH
22:13 but t shall no stranger eat thereof. NIH
22:21 be accepted; t shall be no blemish therein. NIH
23:27 month *t shall be* a day of atonement: NIH
25:51 If *t be* yet many years *behind,* according NIH
25:52 if t remain but few years unto the year of NIH
Nu 1: 4 with you t shall be a man of every tribe; NIH
1:53 that t be no wrath upon the congregation of NIH
5:13 be defiled, and *t be* no witness against her, NIH
6: 5 All the days of the vow of his separation t NIH
8:19 that t be no plague among the children of NIH
9: 6 t were *certain* men, who were defiled by NIH
9:15 at even t was upon the tabernacle as it were NIH
9:17 t the children of Israel pitched their tents. 8033
11: 6 *t is* nothing at all, beside *this* manna, NIH
11:16 that they may stand t with thee. 8033
11:17 I will come down and talk with thee t: and 8033
11:26 t remained two *of the* men in the camp, NIH
11:27 And t ran a young man, and told Moses, and NIH
11:31 t went forth a wind from the LORD, and NIH
11:34 because t they buried the people that lusted. 8033
12: 6 If t be a prophet among you, *I* the LORD NIH
13:20 or lean, whether **t be** wood therein, or not. 3426
13:28 moreover we saw the children of Anak t. 8033

Nu 13:33 t we saw the giants, the sons of Anak, 8033
14:35 shall be consumed, and t they shall die. 8033
14:43 and the Canaanites *are* t before you, 8033
16:35 And t came out a fire from the LORD, and NIH
16:46 for t is wrath gone out from the LORD; NIH
18: 5 that t be no wrath any more upon NIH
19:18 upon the persons that were t, and upon him 8033
20: 1 and Miriam died t, and was buried there. 8033
20: 1 and Miriam died there, and was buried t. 8033
20: 2 t was no water for the congregation: and NIH
20: 4 that we and our cattle should die t? 8033
20: 5 neither *is t any* water to drink. NIH
20:26 be gathered *unto his people,* and shall die t. 8033
20:28 and Aaron died t in the top of the mount: 8033
21: 5 for *t is* no bread, neither *is there any* water; NIH
21: 5 for *there is* no bread, neither *is t any* water; NIH
21:28 For t is a fire gone out of Heshbon, a flame NIH
21:32 and drove out the Amorites that *were* t. 8033
21:35 his people, until t was none left him alive: NIH
22: 5 Behold, t is a people come out from Egypt: NIH
22:11 Behold, *t is* a people come out of Egypt, NIH
22:29 I would **t were** a sword in mine hand, 3426
23:23 Surely *t is* no enchantment against Jacob, NIH
23:23 neither *is t* any divination against Israel: NIH
24:17 t shall come a Star out of Jacob, and NIH
26:62 t was no inheritance given them among NIH
26:64 among these t was not a man of them whom NIH
26:65 t was not left a man of them, save Caleb NIH
31: 5 So t were delivered out of the thousands of NIH
31:16 t was a plague among the congregation of NIH
31:49 our charge, and t lacketh not one man of us. NIH
32:26 our cattle, shall be t in the cities of Gilead: 8033
33: 9 and ten palm trees; and they pitched t. 8033
33:38 died t, in the fortieth year after the children 8033
35: 6 the Levites *t shall be* six cities for refuge, NIH
Dt 1: 2 (*T are* eleven days' *journey* from Horeb *by* NIH
1:28 we have seen the sons of the Anakims t. 8033
1:35 Surely t shall not one of these men of this NIH
1:46 according unto the days that ye abode *t.* NIH
2:36 t was not one city too strong for us: NIH
3: 4 t was not a city which we took not from NIH
3:24 for what God *is t* in heaven or in earth, NIH
4: 7 For what nation *is t so* great, who hath God NIH
4: 8 what nation *is t so* great, that hath statutes NIH
4:28 t ye shall serve gods, the work of men's 8033
4:32 whether t hath been *any such thing* as this NIH
4:35 he *is* God; *t is* none else besides him. NIH
4:39 and upon the earth beneath: *t is* none else. NIH
5:26 For who *is t of* all flesh, that hath heard NIH
5:29 O that t were such a heart in them, that they NIH
7:14 t shall not be male or female barren among NIH
7:24 t shall no man *be able to* stand before thee, NIH
8:15 and drought, where *t was* no water; NIH
10: 5 t they be, as the LORD commanded me. 8033
10: 6 t Aaron died, and there he was buried; 8033
10: 6 there Aaron died, and t he was buried; 8033
11:17 that t be no rain, and *that* the land yield not NIH
11:25 T shall no man *be able to* stand before you: NIH
12: 5 out of all your tribes to put his name t, 8033
12: 7 t ye shall eat before the LORD your God, 8033
12:11 t shall be a place which the LORD your NIH
12:11 shall choose to cause his name to dwell t; 8033
12:14 t thou shalt offer thy burnt offerings, and 8033
12:14 and t thou shalt do all that I command thee. 8033
12:21 to put his name t be too far from thee, 8033
13: 1 If t arise among you a prophet, or a dreamer NIH
13:12 LORD thy God hath given thee to dwell t, 8033
13:17 t shall cleave nought of the cursed thing to NIH
14:23 which he shall choose to place his name t, 8033
14:24 thy God shall choose to set his name t, 8033
14:26 thou shalt eat t before the LORD thy God, 8033
15: 4 Save when t shall be no poor among you; NIH
15: 7 If t be among you a poor man of one of thy NIH
15: 9 Beware that t be not a thought in thy wicked NIH
15:21 if t be *any* blemish therein, *as if it be* lame, NIH
16: 2 LORD shall choose to place his name t. 8033
16: 4 t shall be no leavened bread seen with thee NIH
16: 4 neither shall t *any thing* of the flesh, NIH
16: 6 t thou shalt sacrifice the passover at even, 8033
16:11 thy God hath chosen to place his name t. 8033
17: 2 If t be found among you, within any of thy NIH
17: 8 If t arise a matter too hard for thee in NIH
17:12 to minister t before the LORD thy God, 8033
18: 7 *do,* which stand t before the LORD. 8033
18:10 T shall not be found among you *any one* NIH
20: 5 What man *is t* that hath built a new house, NIH
20: 7 what man *is t* that hath betrothed a wife, NIH
20: 8 What man *is t that is* fearful and NIH
21: 4 shall strike off the heifer's neck t in 8033
22:26 *t is* in the damsel no sin *worthy* of death: NIH
22:27 damsel cried, and *t was* none to save her. NIH
23:10 If t be among you any man, that is not clean NIH
23:17 T shall be no whore of the daughters of NIH
25: 1 If t be a controversy between men, and NIH
26: 2 thy God shall choose to place his name t. 8033
26: 5 sojourned t with a few, and became there a 8033
26: 5 became t a nation, great, mighty, and 8033
27: 5 t shalt thou build an altar unto the LORD 8033
27: 7 shalt eat t, and rejoice before the LORD 8033
28:32 and *t shall be* no might in thine hand. NIH
28:36 t shalt thou serve other gods, wood and 8033
28:64 t thou shalt serve other gods, which neither 8033
28:65 the LORD shall give thee t a trembling 8033
28:68 t ye shall be sold unto your enemies for 8033
29:18 Lest t should **be** among you man, or 3426
29:18 lest t should **be** among you a root that 3426
31:26 that it may be t for a witness against thee. 8033
32:12 and *t was* no strange god with him. NIH
32:28 neither *is t any* understanding in them. NIH
32:36 power is gone, and *t is* none shut up, or left. NIH
32:39 *even* I, *am* he, and *t is* no god with me: NIH
32:39 neither *is t any* that can deliver out of my NIH
33:19 t they shall offer sacrifices of 8033
33:21 because t, *in* a portion of the lawgiver, 8033
33:26 *T is* none like unto the God of Jeshurun, NIH

Dt 34: 5 So Moses the servant of the LORD died t 8033
34:10 t arose not a prophet since in Israel like unto NIH
Jos 1: 5 T shall not any man *be able to* stand before NIH
2: 1 named Rahab, and lodged t. 8033+1886.5
2: 2 t came men in hither to night of the children NIH
2: 4 T came men unto me, but I wist not NIH
2:11 neither did t remain any more courage in NIH
2:16 hide yourselves t three days, 8033+1886.5
2:22 unto the mountain, and abode t three days, 8033
3: 1 and lodged t before they passed over. 8033
3: 4 Yet t shall be a space between you and it, NIH
4: 8 where they lodged, and laid them down t. 8033
4: 9 and they are t unto this day. 8033
5: 1 neither was t spirit in them any more, NIH
5:13 t stood a man over against him with his NIH
7: 4 So t went up thither of the people about NIH
7:13 *T is* an accursed thing in the midst of thee, NIH
8:11 now *t was* a valley between them and Ai. NIH
8:14 he wist not that *t were* liers in ambush NIH
8:17 t was not a man left in Ai or Beth-el, NIH
8:32 he wrote t upon the stones a copy of 8033
8:35 T was not a word of all that Moses NIH
9:23 t shall none of you be freed from being NIH
10: 8 t shall not a man of them stand before thee. NIH
10:14 t was no day like that before it or after it, NIH
11:11 utterly destroying *them:* t was not any left NIH
11:19 T was not a city that made peace with NIH
11:22 T was none of the Anakims left in the land NIH
11:22 in Gath, and in Ashdod, t remained. NIH
13: 1 t remaineth *yet* very much land to be NIH
14:12 in that day how the Anakims *were* t, 8033
17: 1 T was also a lot for the tribe of Manasseh; NIH
17: 2 T was also *a lot* for the rest of the children NIH
17: 5 t fell ten portions to Manasseh, beside NIH
17:15 cut down for thyself t in the land of 8033
18: 1 set up the tabernacle of the congregation t. 8033
18: 2 t remained among the children of Israel NIH
18:10 t Joshua divided the land unto the children 8033
21:44 t stood not a man of all their enemies before NIH
21:45 T failed not ought of any good thing which NIH
22:10 the half tribe of Manasseh built t an altar by 8033
22:17 although t was a plague in the congregation NIH
24:26 a great stone, and set it up t under an oak, 8033
Jdg 1: 7 brought him *to* Jerusalem, and t he died. 8033
2: 5 and they sacrificed t unto the LORD. 8033
2:10 t arose another generation after them, NIH
3:29 all men of valour; and t escaped not a man. NIH
4:16 edge of the sword; *and* t was not a man left. NIH
4:17 for *t was* peace between Jabin the king of NIH
4:20 inquire of thee, and say, **Is** t any man here? 3426
5: 8 was t a shield or spear seen among forty NIH
5:11 t shall they rehearse the righteous acts of 8033
5:14 Out of Ephraim *was t* a root of them against NIH
5:15 For the divisions of Reuben *t were* great NIH
5:16 For the divisions of Reuben *t were* great NIH
5:27 where he bowed, t he fell down dead. 8033
6:11 t came an angel of the LORD, and NIH
6:21 and t rose up fire out of the rock, NIH
6:24 Gideon built an altar t unto the LORD, 8033
6:39 and upon all the ground let t be dew. NIH
6:40 and t was dew on all the ground. NIH
7: 3 t returned of the people twenty and NIH
7: 3 two thousand; and t remained ten thousand. NIH
7: 4 the water, and I will try them for thee t: 8033
7:13 *t was* a man that told a dream unto his NIH
8:10 for t fell an hundred and twenty thousand NIH
9:21 and fled, and went to Beer, and dwelt t, 8033
9:36 t come people down from the top of NIH
9:37 See t come people down by the middle of NIH
9:51 But t was a strong tower within the city, and NIH
10: 1 after Abimelech t arose to defend Israel NIH
11: 3 t were gathered vain men to Jephthah, and NIH
12: 6 t fell at that time of the Ephraimites forty NIH
13: 2 t was a certain man of Zorah, of the family NIH
14: 3 *Is* t never a woman among the daughters of NIH
14: 8 *t was* a swarm of bees and honey in NIH
14:10 Samson made t a feast; for so used 8033
15:19 *was* in the jaw, and t came water thereout; NIH
16: 1 and saw t a harlot, and went in unto her. 8033
16: 9 Now *t were* men lying in wait, abiding with NIH
16:12 *t were* liers in wait abiding in the chamber. NIH
16:17 T hath not come a rasor upon mine head; NIH
16:27 the lords of the Philistines *were* t; 8033+1886.5
16:27 *t were* upon the roof about three thousand NIH
17: 1 t was a man of mount Ephraim, whose NIH
17: 6 In those days *t was* no king in Israel, *but* NIH
17: 7 t was a young man out of Beth-lehem-judah NIH
17: 7 who *was* a Levite, and he sojourned t. 8033
18: 1 In those days *t was* no king in Israel: and NIH
18: 2 to the house of Micah, they lodged t. 8033
18: 7 *t was* no magistrate in the land, that might NIH
18:10 a place where *t is* no want of any thing that NIH
18:11 t went from thence of the family of NIH
18:14 Do ye know that **t is** in these houses an 3426
18:28 *t was* no deliverer, because it *was* far from NIH
19: 1 in those days, when *t was* no king in Israel, NIH
19: 1 that t was a certain Levite sojourning on NIH
19: 2 was t four whole months. 8033
19: 4 so they did eat and drink, and lodged t. 8033
19: 7 law urged him: therefore he lodged t again. 8033
19:10 *t were* with him two asses saddled, NIH
19:15 for *t was* no man that took them into *his* NIH
19:16 t came an old man from his work out of NIH
19:18 and *t is* no man that receiveth me to house. NIH
19:19 Yet **t is** both straw and provender for our 3426
19:19 **t is** bread and wine also for me, and for thy 3426
19:19 with thy servants: *t is* no want of any thing. NIH
19:30 T was no such *deed* done nor seen from NIH
20:16 Among all this people *t were* seven hundred NIH
20:26 sat t before the LORD, and fasted that day 8033
20:27 (for the ark of the covenant of God *was* t in 8033
20:34 t came against Gibeah ten thousand chosen NIH
20:38 Now t was an appointed sign between NIH
20:44 t fell of Benjamin eighteen thousand men; NIH
21: 1 T shall not any of us give his daughter unto NIH

T

Jdg 21: 2 abode t till even before God, and lift up 8033
21: 3 that t should be to day one tribe lacking in NIH
21: 4 built t an altar, and offered burnt offerings 8033
21: 5 Who is t among all the tribes of Israel that NIH
21: 6 T is one tribe cut off from Israel this day. NIH
21: 8 What one is t of the tribes of Israel that NIH
21: 8 t came none to the camp from Jabesh-gilead NIH
21: 9 t were none of the inhabitants of NIH
21: 9 none of the inhabitants of Jabesh-gilead t. 8033
21:17 T must be an inheritance for them that be NIH
21:19 t is a feast of the LORD in Shiloh yearly in NIH
21:25 In those days t was no king in Israel: NIH
Ru 1: 1 judges ruled, that t was a famine in the land. NIH
1: 2 into the country of Moab, and continued t. 8033
1: 4 and they dwelled t about ten years. 8033
1:11 are t yet any moe sons in my womb, NIH
1:17 thou diest, will I die, and t will I be buried: 8033
3:12 howbeit t is a kinsman nearer than I. 3426
4: 1 Boaz up to the gate, and sat him down t: 8033
4: 4 for t is none to redeem it besides thee; and NIH
4:17 it a name, saying, T is a son born to Naomi; NIH
1Sa 1: 1 Now t was a certain man of NIH
1: 3 Phinehas, the priests of the LORD, were t. 8033
1:11 and t shall no rasor come upon his head. NIH
1:22 before the LORD, and t abide for ever. 8033
1:28 And he worshipped the LORD t. 8033
2: 2 T is none holy as the LORD: for there is NIH
2: 2 for t is none beside thee: neither is there any NIH
2: 2 neither is t any rock like our God. NIH
2:27 t came a man of God unto Eli, and said unto NIH
2:31 that t shall not be an old man in thine house. NIH
2:32 t shall not be an old man in thine house for NIH
3: 1 in those days; t was no open vision. NIH
4: 4 were t with the ark of the covenant of God. 8033
4: 7 for t hath not been such a thing heretofore. NIH
4:10 t was a very great slaughter; for there fell of NIH
4:10 for t fell of Israel thirty thousand footmen. NIH
4:12 t ran a man of Benjamin out of the army, NIH
4:16 And he said, What is t done, my son? NIH
4:17 t hath been also a great slaughter among NIH
5:11 for t was a deadly destruction throughout all NIH
5:11 the city; the hand of God was very heavy t. 8033
6: 7 on which t hath come no yoke, and tie NIH
6:14 a Beth-shemite, and stood t, where there 8033
6:14 stood there, where t was a great stone: NIH
7: 6 and fasted on that day, and said t, 8033
7:14 t was peace between Israel and NIH
7:17 for t was his house; and there he judged 8033
7:17 t he judged Israel; and there he built an 8033
7:17 and t he built an altar unto the LORD. 8033
9: 1 Now t was a man of Benjamin, whose name NIH
9: 2 t was not among the children of Israel a NIH
9: 4 the land of Shalim, and t they were not: NIH
9: 6 t is in this city a man of God, and he is an NIH
9: 7 t is not a present to bring to the man of God: NIH
9:12 for t is a sacrifice of the people to day in NIH
10: 3 t shall meet thee three men going up to God 8033
10:24 that t is none like him among all the people? NIH
10:26 t went with him a band of men, NIH
11: 3 then, if t be no man to save us, we will NIH
11:13 T shall not a man be put to death this day: NIH
11:14 us go to Gilgal, and renew the kingdom t. 8033
11:15 t they made Saul king before the LORD in 8033
11:15 t they sacrificed sacrifices of peace 8033
11:15 t Saul and all the men of Israel rejoiced 8033
13:19 Now t was no smith found throughout all NIH
13:22 that t was neither sword nor spear found in NIH
13:22 and with Jonathan his son was t found. NIH
14: 4 t was a sharp rock on the one side, and NIH
14: 6 for t is no restraint to the LORD to save by NIH
14:15 And t was trembling in the host, in the field, NIH
14:17 and his armourbearer were not t. NIH
14:20 and t was a very great discomfiture. NIH
14:25 a wood; and t was honey upon the ground. NIH
14:30 for had t not been now a much greater NIH
14:34 his ox with him that night, and slew them t. 8033
14:39 t was not a man among all the people that NIH
14:45 t shall not one hair of his head fall to NIH
14:52 t was sore war against the Philistines all NIH
16:11 T remaineth yet the youngest, and behold, NIH
17: 3 other side: and t was a valley between them. NIH
17: 4 t went out a champion out of the camp of NIH
17:23 behold, t came up the champion, NIH
17:29 What have I now done? Is t not a cause? NIH
17:34 t came a lion and a bear, and took a lamb NIH
17:46 that all the earth may know that t is a God 3426
17:50 but t was no sword in the hand of David. NIH
18:10 and t was a javelin in Saul's hand. NIH
19: 8 t was war again: and David went out, and NIH
19:16 come in, behold t was an image in the bed, NIH
20: 3 t is but a step between me and death. NIH
20: 6 for t is a yearly sacrifice there for all NIH
20: 6 for there is a yearly sacrifice t for all 8033
20: 8 if t be in me iniquity, slay me thyself; 3426
20:12 if t be good toward David, and I then NIH
20:21 for t is peace to thee, and no hurt; as NIH
20:29 he hath commanded me to be t: and now, NIH
21: 3 of bread in mine hand, or what t is present. NIH
21: 4 T is no common bread under mine hand, but NIH
21: 4 under mine hand, but t is hallowed bread; 3426
21: 6 So the priest gave him hallowed bread: for t NIH
21: 6 hallowed bread: for there was no bread t 8033
21: 7 man of the servants of Saul was t that day, 8033
21: 8 is t not here under thine hand spear or 3426
21: 9 take it: for t is no other save that here. NIH
21: 9 David said, T is none like that; give it me. NIH
22: 2 t were with him about four hundred men. NIH
22: 8 t is none that sheweth me that my son hath NIH
22: 8 t is none of you that is sorry for me, or NIH
22:22 it that day, when Doeg the Edomite was t, 8033
23:22 his haunt is, and who hath seen him t: 8033
23:27 t came a messenger unto Saul, saying, NIH
24:11 see that t is neither evil nor transgression in NIH
25: 2 t was a man in Maon, whose possessions NIH
25: 7 neither was t ought missing unto them, NIH

1Sa 25:10 t be many servants now a days that break NIH
25:13 t went up after David about four hundred NIH
25:34 surely t had not been left unto Nabal by NIH
26:15 for t came one of the people in to destroy NIH
27: 1 t is nothing better for me than that I should NIH
27: 5 town in the country, that I may dwell t: 8033
28: 7 t is a woman that hath a familiar spirit at NIH
28:10 t shall no punishment happen to thee for NIH
28:20 t was no strength in him; for he had eaten NIH
30:17 t escaped not a man of them, save four NIH
30:19 t was nothing lacking to them, neither small NIH
31:12 and came to Jabesh, and burnt them t. 8033
2Sa 1:21 Ye mountains of Gilboa, let t be no dew, NIH
1:21 be no dew, neither let t be rain upon you, NIH
1:21 for t the shield of the mighty is vilely cast 8033
2: 4 t they anointed David king over the house 8033
2:15 t arose and went over by number twelve of NIH
2:17 t was a very sore battle that day; and NIH
2:18 t were three sons of Zeruiah there, Joab, NIH
2:18 there were three sons of Zeruiah t, Joab, 8033
2:23 he fell down t, and died in the same place: 8033
2:30 t lacked of David's servants nineteen men NIH
3: 1 Now t was long war between the house of NIH
3: 6 while t was war between the house of Saul NIH
3:27 smote him t under the fifth rib, that he died, 8033
3:29 let t not fail from the house of Joab one that NIH
3:38 Know ye not that t is a prince and a great NIH
4: 3 and were sojourners t until this day.) 8033
5:13 t were yet sons and daughters born to NIH
5:20 and David smote them t, and said, 8033
5:21 t they left their images, and David and 8033
6: 7 God smote him t for his error; and there he 8033
6: 7 his error; and t he died by the ark of God. 8033
7:22 for t is none like thee, neither is there any NIH
7:22 like thee, neither is t any God beside thee, NIH
9: 1 Is t yet any that is left of the house of Saul, 3426
9: 2 t was of the house of Saul a servant whose NIH
9: 3 Is t not yet any of the house of Saul, NIH
10:18 the captain of their host, who died t. 8033
11: 8 t followed him a mess of meat from NIH
11:17 t fell some of the people of the servants of NIH
12: 1 said unto him, T were two men in one city; NIH
12: 4 t came a traveller unto the rich man, and NIH
13:16 she said unto him, T is no cause: this evil in NIH
13:30 king's sons, and t is not one of them left. NIH
13:34 t came much people by the way of the hill NIH
13:38 and went to Geshur, and was t three years. 8033
14: 6 t was none to part them, but the one smote NIH
14:11 t shall not one hair of thy son fall to NIH
14:25 in all Israel t was none to be so NIH
14:25 crown of his head t was no blemish in him. NIH
14:27 unto Absalom t were born three sons, and NIH
14:30 field is near mine, and he hath barley t; 8033
14:32 It had been good for me to have been t still: 8033
14:32 if t be any iniquity in me, let him kill me. NIH
15: 3 t is no man deputed of the king to hear thee. NIH
15:13 t came a messenger to David, saying, NIH
15:21 or life, even t also will thy servant be. 8033
15:28 until t come word from you to certify me. NIH
15:29 God again to Jerusalem: and they tarried t. 8033
15:35 hast thou not t with thee Zadok and 8033
15:36 they have t with them their two sons, 8033
16:14 came weary, and refreshed themselves t. 8033
17: 9 T is a slaughter among the people that NIH
17:12 of all the men that are with him t shall not NIH
17:13 until t be not one small stone found there. NIH
17:13 until there be not one small stone found t. 8033
17:22 by the morning light t lacked not one of NIH
18: 7 t was there a great slaughter that day of NIH
18: 7 there was t a great slaughter that day of 8033
18: 8 For the battle was t scattered over the face 8033
18:11 why didst thou not smite him t to 8033
18:13 for t is no matter hid from the king, and NIH
18:25 If he be alone, t is tidings in his mouth. NIH
19: 7 t will not tarry one with thee this night: NIH
19:17 t were a thousand men of Benjamin with NIH
19:18 t went over a ferry boat to carry over NIH
19:22 shall t any man be put to death this day in NIH
20: 1 And t happened to be there a man of Belial, 8033
20: 1 And there happened to be t a man of Belial, NIH
20: 7 t went out after him Joab's men, and NIH
21: 1 t was a famine in the days of David three NIH
21:18 that t was again a battle with the Philistines NIH
21:19 t was again a battle in Gob with NIH
21:20 t was yet a battle in Gath, where was a man NIH
22: 9 T went up a smoke out of his nostrils, and NIH
22:42 They looked, but t was none to save; NIH
23: 9 when they defied the Philistines that were t 8033
24: 9 t were in Israel eight hundred thousand NIH
24:13 that t be three days' pestilence in thy land? NIH
24:15 t died of the people from Dan even to NIH
24:25 And David built t an altar unto the LORD, 8033
1Ki 1: 2 Let t be sought for my lord the king a young NIH
1:14 while thou yet talkest t with the king, 8033
1:34 Nathan the prophet anoint him t king over 8033
1:52 t shall not a hair of him fall to the earth: NIH
2: 4 all their soul, t shall not fail thee (said he) 3807.1
2:33 shall t be peace for ever from the LORD. NIH
2:36 dwell t, and go not forth thence any 8033
3: 2 t was no house built unto the name of NIH
3: 4 the king went to Gibeon to sacrifice t; 8033
3:12 so that t was none like thee before thee, NIH
3:13 that t shall not be any among the kings like NIH
3:16 came t two women, that were harlots, NIH
3:18 t was no stranger with us in the house, NIH
4:34 t came of all people to hear the wisdom of NIH
5: 4 that t is neither adversary nor evil occurrent. NIH
5: 6 for thou knowest that t is not among us any NIH
5: 9 will cause them to be discharged t, and 8033
5:12 t was peace between Hiram and Solomon; NIH
6: 7 that t was neither hammer nor axe nor any NIH
6:18 all was cedar; t was no stone seen. NIH
6:19 to set t the ark of the covenant of 8033
7: 4 t were windows in three rows, and light was NIH
7:24 under the brim of it round about t were NIH

1Ki 7:29 and upon the ledges t was a base above: and NIH
7:34 t were four undersetters to the four corners NIH
7:35 in the top of the base was t a round compass NIH
8: 8 seen without: and t they are unto this day. 8033
8: 9 T was nothing in the ark save the two tables NIH
8: 9 of stone, which Moses put t at Horeb, 8033
8:21 I have set t a place for the ark, wherein is 8033
8:23 t is no God like thee, in heaven above, or NIH
8:25 T shall not fail thee a man in my sight to sit NIH
8:29 which thou hast said, My name shall be t: 8033
8:35 t is no rain, because they have sinned NIH
8:37 If t be in the land famine, if there be NIH
8:37 if t be pestilence, blasting, mildew, locust, NIH
8:37 mildew, locust, or if t be caterpillar; NIH
8:37 whatsoever sickness t be; NIH
8:46 (for t is no man that sinneth not,) NIH
8:56 t hath not failed one word of all his good NIH
8:60 the LORD is God, and that t is none else. NIH
8:64 for t he offered burnt offerings, and meat 8033
9: 3 thou hast built, to put my name t for ever; 8033
9: 3 and mine heart shall be t perpetually. 8033
9: 5 T shall not fail thee a man upon the throne NIH
10: 3 t was not any thing hid from the king, NIH
10: 5 of the LORD; t was no more spirit in her. NIH
10:10 t came no more such abundance of spices as NIH
10:12 t came no such almug trees, nor were seen NIH
10:19 t were stays on either side on the place of NIH
10:20 twelve lions stood t on the one side and 8033
10:20 t was not the like made in any kingdom. NIH
11:16 (For six months did Joab remain t with all 8033
11:36 which I have chosen me to put my name t. 8033
12:20 t was none that followed the house of NIH
13: 1 t came a man of God out of Judah by NIH
13:11 Now t dwelt an old prophet in Beth-el; and NIH
13:17 Thou shalt eat no bread nor drink water t, 8033
14: 2 behold, t is Ahijah the prophet, which told 8033
14:13 in him t is found some good thing toward NIH
14:21 of all the tribes of Israel, to put his name t. 8033
14:24 t were also sodomites in the land: and NIH
14:30 t was war between Rehoboam and NIH
15: 6 t was war between Rehoboam and NIH
15: 7 t was war between Abijam and Jeroboam. NIH
15:16 t was war between Asa and Baasha king of NIH
15:19 T is a league between me and thee, and NIH
15:32 t was war between Asa and Baasha king of NIH
17: 1 t shall not be dew nor rain these years, but NIH
17: 4 have commanded the ravens to feed thee t. 8033
17: 7 because t had been no rain in the land. NIH
17: 9 which belongeth to Zidon, and dwell t: 8033
17: 9 I have commanded a widow woman t to 8033
17:10 the widow woman was t gathering of 8033
17:17 so sore, that t was no breath left in him. NIH
18: 2 And t was a sore famine in Samaria. NIH
18:10 thy God liveth, t is no nation or kingdom, 3426
18:10 He is not t; he took an oath of the kingdom NIH
18:26 t was no voice, nor any that answered. NIH
18:29 that t was neither voice, nor any to answer, NIH
18:40 down to the brook Kishon, and slew them t. 8033
18:41 drink; for t is a sound of abundance of rain. NIH
18:43 went up, and looked, and said, T is nothing. NIH
18:44 Behold, t ariseth a little cloud out of the sea, NIH
18:45 and wind, and t was a great rain. NIH
19: 3 belongeth to Judah, and left his servant t. 8033
19: 6 t was a cake baken on the coals, and a cruse NIH
19: 9 he came thither unto a cave, and lodged t; 8033
19:13 t came a voice unto him, and said, NIH
20: 1 t were thirty and two kings with him, and NIH
20:13 t came a prophet unto Ahab king of Israel, NIH
20:17 T are men come out of Samaria. NIH
20:28 t came a man of God, and spake unto NIH
20:30 t a wall fell upon twenty and NIH
20:40 as thy servant was busy here and t, he was 2008
21:13 t came in two men, children of Belial, and NIH
21:25 (But t was none like unto Ahab, which did NIH
22: 7 Is t not here a prophet of the LORD NIH
22: 8 T is yet one man, Micaiah the son of Imlah, NIH
22:21 t came forth a spirit, and stood before NIH
22:36 t went a proclamation throughout the host NIH
22:47 T was then no king in Edom: a deputy was NIH
2Ki 1: 3 Is it not because t is not a God in Israel, NIH
1: 6 T came a man up to meet us, and said unto NIH
1: 6 Is it not because t is not a God in Israel, NIH
1:10 t came down fire from heaven, and NIH
1:14 t came fire down from heaven, and burnt up NIH
1:16 t is no God in Israel to inquire of his word? NIH
2:11 t appeared a chariot of fire, and horses of NIH
2:16 t be with thy servants fifty strong men; 3426
2:21 cast the salt in t, and said, Thus saith 8033
2:21 t shall not be from thence any more death or NIH
2:23 t came forth little children out of the city, NIH
2:24 t came forth two she bears out of the wood, NIH
3: 9 t was no water for the host, and for NIH
3:11 Is t not here a prophet of the LORD, NIH
3:20 t came water by the way of Edom, and NIH
3:27 t was great indignation against Israel: and NIH
4: 1 Now t cried a certain woman of the wives NIH
4: 6 he said unto her, T is not a vessel more. NIH
4:10 let us set for him t a bed, and a table, and 8033
4:11 turned into the chamber, and lay t. 8033+1886.5
4:31 but t was neither voice, nor hearing. NIH
4:38 t was a dearth in the land; and the sons of NIH
4:40 O thou man of God, t is death in the pot. NIH
4:41 they may eat. And t was no harm in the pot. NIH
4:42 t came a man from Baal-shalisha, and NIH
5: 8 he shall know that t is a prophet in Israel. 3426
5:15 now I know that t is no God in all the earth, NIH
5:17 Naaman said, Shall t not then, I pray thee, NIH
5:18 into the house of Rimmon to worship t, 8033
5:22 even now t be come to me from mount NIH
6: 2 let us make us a place t, where we may 8033
6:10 and warned him of, and saved himself t, 8033
6:25 t was a great famine in Samaria: and NIH
6:26 t cried a woman unto him, saying, Help, NIH
7: 3 t were four leprous men at the entering in of NIH
7: 4 the famine is in the city, and we shall die t: 8033

T

2Ki 7: 5 camp of Syria, behold, *t was* no man there. NIH
7: 5 camp of Syria, behold, *there was* no man t. 8033
7:10 behold, *t was* no man there, neither voice of NIH
7:10 behold, *there was* no man t, neither voice 8033
9: 2 look out t Jehu the son of Jehoshaphat 8033
9:10 *t shall be* none to bury *her.* And he opened NIH
9:16 and went to Jezreel; for Joram lay t. 8033
9:17 t stood a watchman on the tower in Jezreel, NIH
9:18 So t went one on horseback to meet him, NIH
9:23 said to Ahaziah, *T is* treachery, O Ahaziah. NIH
9:27 And he fled *to* Megiddo, and died t. 8033
9:32 t looked out to him two *or* three eunuchs. NIH
10: 2 *t are* with you chariots and horses, a fenced NIH
10: 8 t came a messenger, and told him, saying, NIH
10:10 Know now that t shall fall unto the earth NIH
10:21 so that t was not a man left that came not. NIH
10:23 look that **t be** here with you none of 3426
11:16 *into* the king's house: and t was she slain. 8033
12:10 when they saw that *t was* much money in NIH
12:13 Howbeit t were not made *for* the house of NIH
13: 6 t remained the grove also in Samaria.) NIH
14: 9 t passed by a wild beast that *was* in NIH
14:19 sent after him to Lachish, and slew him t. 8033
14:26 for *t was* not any shut up, nor any left, NIH
15:20 turned back, and stayed not t in the land. 8033
16: 6 came *to* Elath, and dwelt t unto this day. 8033
17:11 t they burnt incense in all the high places, 8033
17:18 t was none left but the tribe of Judah only. NIH
17:25 it was at the beginning of their dwelling t, 8033
17:27 let them go and dwell t, and let him teach 8033
18:18 t came out to them Eliakim the son of NIH
19: 3 the birth, and *t is* not strength to bring forth. NIH
19:32 nor shoot an arrow t, nor come before it 8033
20:13 t was nothing in his house, nor in all his NIH
20:15 t is nothing among my treasures that I have NIH
22: 7 Howbeit t was no reckoning made with NIH
23:16 he spied the sepulchres that *were* t in 8033
23:20 the high places that *were* t upon the altars, 8033
23:22 Surely t was not holden such a passover NIH
23:25 like unto him was t no king before him, NIH
23:25 neither after him arose t *any* like him. NIH
23:27 house of which I said, My name shall be t. 8033
23:34 and he came *to* Egypt, and died t. 8033
25: 3 t was no bread for the people of the land. NIH
25:23 to Gedaliah *to* Mizpah, even Ishmael NIH
1Ch 3: 4 t he reigned seven years and six months: 8033
4:23 t they dwelt with the king for his work. 8033
4:40 for *they* of Ham had dwelt t of old. 8033
4:41 the habitations that were found t, 8033+1886.5
4:41 because *t was* pasture there for their flocks. NIH
4:41 because *there was* pasture t for their flocks. 8033
4:43 were escaped, and dwelt t unto this day. 8033
5:22 For t fell down many slain, because the war NIH
11:13 t the Philistines were gathered together to NIH
12: 8 of the Gadites t separated themselves unto NIH
12:16 And t came of the children of Benjamin and NIH
12:17 seeing *t is* no wrong in mine hands, the God NIH
12:19 t fell *some* of Manasseh to David, when he NIH
12:20 t fell to him of Manasseh, Adnah, and NIH
12:22 For at *that* time day by day t came to David NIH
12:39 t they were with David three days, eating 8033
12:40 sheep abundantly: for *t was* joy in Israel. NIH
13:10 hand to the ark: and t he died before God. 8033
14:11 to Baal-perazim; and David smote them t. 8033
14:12 when they had left their gods t, David gave 8033
16:37 So he left t before the ark of the covenant 8033
17:20 O LORD, *t is* none like thee, neither *is* NIH
17:20 like thee, neither *is t any* God besides thee, NIH
19: 5 t went *certain,* and told David how the men NIH
20: 2 of gold, and *t were* precious stones in it; NIH
20: 4 that t arose war at Gezer with NIH
20: 5 t was war again with the Philistines; and NIH
20: 6 yet again t was war at Gath, where was a NIH
21:14 and t fell of Israel seventy thousand men. NIH
21:26 And David built t an altar unto the LORD, 8033
21:28 of Ornan the Jebusite, then he sacrificed t. 8033
22:15 Moreover *t are* workmen with thee in NIH
22:16 and the brass, and the iron, *t is* no number. NIH
24: 4 t were moe chief men found of the sons of NIH
24: 4 Among the sons of Eleazar *t were* sixteen NIH
26:31 t were found among them mighty *men* of NIH
27:24 because t fell wrath for it against Israel; NIH
28:21 *t shall be* with thee for all *manner of* NIH
29:15 earth *are* as a shadow, and *t is* none abiding. NIH
2Ch 1: 3 for t was the tabernacle of the congregation 8033
1:12 neither shall t any after thee have the like. NIH
5: 9 not seen without. And it is unto this day. 8033
5:10 *T was* nothing in the ark save the two tables NIH
6: 5 build a house *in,* that my name might be t; 8033
6: 6 that my name might be t; 8033
6:14 *t is* no God like thee in the heaven, nor in NIH
6:16 T shall not fail thee a man in my sight to sit NIH
6:20 hast said that *thou* wouldest put thy name t; 8033
6:26 t is no rain, because they have sinned NIH
6:28 If t be dearth in the land, if there be NIH
6:28 if t be pestilence, if there be blasting, or NIH
6:28 if t be blasting, or mildew, locusts, or NIH
6:28 or whatsoever sickness *t be:* NIH
6:36 (for *t is* no man which sinneth not,) NIH
7: 7 for t he offered burnt offerings, and the fat 8033
7:13 If I shut up heaven that t be no rain, or if I NIH
7:16 this house, that my name may be t for ever: 8033
7:16 and mine heart shall be t perpetually. 8033
7:18 T shall not fail thee a man *to be* ruler in NIH
8: 2 and caused the children of Israel to dwell t. 8033
9: 2 t was nothing hid from Solomon which he NIH
9: 4 of the LORD; t was no more spirit in her. NIH
9: 9 neither was t any such spice as the queen of NIH
9:11 t were none such seen before in the land of NIH
9:18 *t were* six steps to the throne, with a NIH
9:19 twelve lions stood t on the one side and 8033
9:19 T was not the like made in any kingdom. NIH
12:13 of all the tribes of Israel, to put his name t. 8033
12:15 *t were* wars between Rehoboam and NIH
13: 2 t was war between Abijah and Jeroboam. NIH

2Ch 13: 7 t are gathered unto him vain men, NIH
13: 8 and *t are* with you golden calves, NIH
13:17 t fell down slain of Israel five hundred NIH
14: 9 t came out against them Zerah the Ethiopian NIH
14:14 for t was *exceeding* much spoil in them. NIH
15: 5 in those times *t was* no peace to him that NIH
15:19 t was no *more* war unto the five and NIH
16: 3 *T is* a league between me and thee, as *there* NIH
16: 3 as *t was* between my father and thy father: NIH
18: 6 *Is t* not here a prophet of the LORD NIH
18: 7 *T is* yet one man, by whom *we* may inquire NIH
18:20 t came out a spirit, and stood before NIH
19: 3 Nevertheless t are good things found in NIH
19: 7 do *it:* for *t is* no iniquity with the LORD NIH
20: 2 t came *some* that told Jehoshaphat, saying, NIH
20: 2 T cometh a great multitude against thee NIH
20: 6 in thine hand *is t not* power and might, so NIH
20:26 of Berachah; for t they blessed the LORD: 8033
21:12 t came a writing to him from Elijah NIH
21:17 so that t was never a son left him, NIH
23:15 gate *by* the king's house, they slew her t. 8033
24:11 when they saw that *t was* much money, NIH
25: 7 t came a man of God to him, saying, NIH
25:18 t passed by a wild beast that *was* in NIH
25:27 sent to Lachish after him, and slew him t. 8033
28: 9 a prophet of the LORD was t, 8033
28:10 *are* t not *with* you, *even* with you, NIH
28:13 is great, and *t is* fierce wrath against Israel. NIH
28:18 and the villages thereof: and they dwelt t. 8033
30:13 t assembled *at* Jerusalem much people to NIH
30:17 For *t were* many in the congregation that NIH
30:26 So t was great joy in Jerusalem: for since NIH
30:26 of Israel *t was* not the like in Jerusalem. NIH
32: 4 So t was gathered much people together, NIH
32: 7 for *t be* moe with us than with him: NIH
32:14 Who *was t* among all the gods of those NIH
32:21 his own bowels slew him t with the sword. 8033
32:25 therefore t was wrath upon him, and NIH
34:13 of the Levites *t were* scribes, and officers, NIH
35:18 t was no passover like to that, kept in Israel NIH
36:16 against his people, till *t was* no remedy. NIH
36:23 Who *is t* among you of all his people? NIH
Ezr 1: 3 Who *is t* among you of all his people? NIH
2:63 holy *things* till t stood *up* a priest with Urim NIH
2:65 of whom *t were* seven thousand three NIH
2:65 *t were* among them two hundred singing NIH
4:20 T have been mighty kings also over NIH
5:17 let t be search made in the king's treasure NIH
5:17 which *is* t at Babylon, whether it be *so,* 8536
6: 2 t was found at Achmetha, in the palace that NIH
6:12 caused his name to dwell t destroy all kings 8536
7: 7 t went up *some* of the children of Israel, NIH
7:23 for why should t be wrath against the realm NIH
8:15 and t abode we in tents three days: 8033
8:15 and found t none of the sons of Levi. 8033
8:21 I proclaimed a fast t, at the river Ahava, 8033
8:25 his lords, and all Israel *t* present, had NIH
8:32 came *to* Jerusalem, and abode t three days. 8033
9:14 that *t should be* no remnant nor escaping? NIH
10: 1 t assembled unto him out of Israel a very NIH
10: 2 yet now **t is** hope in Israel concerning this 3426
10:18 among the sons of the priests t were found NIH
Ne 1: 3 The remnant that are left of the captivity t 8033
1: 9 though t were of you cast out unto NIH
1: 9 place that I have chosen to set my name t. 8033
2:10 t was come a man to seek the welfare of NIH
2:11 I came to Jerusalem, and was t three days. 8033
2:12 neither *was t any* beast with me, save NIH
2:14 *t was* no place for the beast *that was* under NIH
4:10 burdens is decayed, and *t is* much rubbish; NIH
5: 1 t was a great cry of the people and of their NIH
5: 2 For **t were** that said, We, our sons, and 3426
5: 3 *Some* also **t were** that said, We *have* 3426
5: 4 **T were** also that said, We have borrowed 3426
5:17 Moreover *t were* at my table an hundred NIH
6: 1 and *that* t was no breach left therein; NIH
6: 7 at Jerusalem, saying, *T is* a king in Judah: NIH
6: 8 T are no such things *done* as thou sayest, NIH
6:11 who *is t,* that, *being* as I *am,* would go into NIH
6:18 For *t were* many in Judah sworn unto him, NIH
7:65 *things,* till t stood *up* a priest with Urim NIH
7:67 of whom *t were* seven thousand three NIH
8:17 done so. And t was very great gladness. NIH
12:46 and Asaph of old *t were* chief of the singers, NIH
13:16 T dwelt men of Tyre also therein, which NIH
13:19 *that* t should no burden be brought in on NIH
13:26 among many nations was t no king like him, NIH
Est 1:18 Thus *shall t* arise too much contempt and NIH
1:19 let t go a royal commandment from him, NIH
2: 2 Let t be fair young virgins sought for NIH
2: 5 *Now* in Shushan the palace t was a certain NIH
3: 8 **T is** a certain people scattered abroad and 3426
3:12 t was written according to all that 871.1+2050.2
4: 3 *t was* great mourning among the Jews, and NIH
4:11 *t is* one law of his to put *him* to death, NIH
4:14 *then* shall t enlargement and NIH
6: 3 unto him, T is nothing done for him. NIH
7: 7 for he saw that t was evil determined NIH
Job 1: 1 T was a man in the land of Uz, whose name NIH
1: 2 t were born unto him seven sons and NIH
1: 6 Now t was a day when the sons of God NIH
1: 8 that *t is* none like him in the earth, a perfect NIH
1:13 t was a day when his sons and his daughters NIH
1:14 And t came a messenger unto Job, and said, NIH
1:16 yet speaking, t came also another, and said, NIH
1:17 yet speaking, t came also another, and said, NIH
1:18 t came also another, and said, Thy sons and NIH
1:19 t came a great wind from the wilderness, NIH
2: 1 Again t was a day when the sons of God NIH
2: 3 that *t is* none like him in the earth, a perfect NIH
3: 3 *it was* said, T is a man child conceived. NIH
3:17 T the wicked cease *from* troubling; and 8033
3:17 *from* troubling; and t the weary be at rest. 8033
3:18 *T* the prisoners rest together; they hear not NIH
3:19 The small and great *are* t; and the servant *is* 8033

Job 4:16 *t was* silence, and I heard a voice, *saying,* NIH
5: 1 Call now, if **t be** *any* that will answer thee; 3426
5: 4 in the gate, neither *is* t any to deliver *them.* NIH
5:19 yea, in seven t shall no evil touch thee. NIH
6: 6 or **is t** *any* taste in the white of an egg? 3426
6:30 **Is t** iniquity in my tongue? cannot my taste 3426
7: 1 *Is t* not an appointed time to man upon NIH
9:33 Neither **is t** *any* daysman betwixt us, 3426
10: 7 *t is* none that can deliver out of thine hand. NIH
11:18 And thou shalt be secure, because **t is** hope; 3426
12:14 shutteth up a man, and t can be no opening. NIH
12:24 wander in a wilderness *where t is* no way. NIH
14: 7 For **t is** hope of a tree, if it be cut down, 3426
15:11 with thee? is t *any* secret thing with thee? NIH
17: 2 *Are t* not mockers with me? and *doth not* NIH
19: 7 not heard: I cry aloud, but *t is* no judgment. NIH
19:29 that ye may know *t is* a judgment. NIH
20:21 *T shall* none of his meat *be* left; therefore NIH
21:33 after him, as *t are* innumerable before him. NIH
21:34 seeing *in* your answers t remaineth NIH
22:29 then thou shalt say, *T is* lifting up; NIH
23: 7 T the righteous *might* dispute with him; so 8033
23: 8 he *is* not *t;* and backward, but I cannot NIH
25: 3 **Is t** *any* number of his armies? and 3426
28: 1 Surely **t is** a vein for the silver, and a place 3426
28: 7 *T is* a path which no fowl knoweth, and NIH
30:26 when I waited for light, t came darkness. NIH
31: 2 For what portion of God *is t* from above? NIH
32: 5 When Elihu saw that *t was* no answer in NIH
32: 8 *t is* a spirit in man: and the inspiration of NIH
32:12 *t was* none of you that convinced Job, *or* NIH
33: 9 I *am* innocent; neither *is t* iniquity in me. NIH
33:23 If **t be** a messenger with him, 3426
34:22 *T is* no darkness, nor shadow of death, NIH
35:12 T they cry, but none giveth answer, 8033
36:16 *into* a broad place, where *t is* no straitness; NIH
36:18 Because *t is* wrath, *beware* lest he take thee NIH
38:26 *is;* on the wilderness, wherein *t is* no man; NIH
39:30 up blood: and where the slain *are,* t *is* she. 8033
41:33 Upon earth **t is not** his like, who is made 369
42:11 came t unto him all his brethren, and all his NIH
Ps 3: 2 Many *t be* which say of my soul, *There is* NIH
3: 2 say of my soul, *T is* no help for him in God. NIH
4: 6 *T be* many that say, Who will shew us *any* NIH
5: 9 For *t is* no faithfulness in their mouth; NIH
6: 5 For in death *t is* no remembrance of thee: NIH
7: 2 *it* in pieces, while *t is* none to deliver. NIH
7: 3 have done this; if **t be** iniquity in my hands; 3426
14: 1 The fool hath said in his heart, *T is* no God. NIH
14: 1 *t is* none that doeth good. NIH
14: 2 to see if **t were** *any* that did understand, 3426
14: 3 *t is* none that doeth good, no, not one. NIH
14: 5 T were they in great fear: for God *is* in 8033
16:11 at thy right hand *t are* pleasures for NIH
18: 8 T went up a smoke out of his nostrils, and NIH
18:41 *t was* none to save *them: even* unto NIH
19: 3 *T is* no speech nor language, *where* their NIH
19: 6 and t is nothing hid from the heat thereof. NIH
19:11 *and* in keeping of them *t is* great reward. NIH
22:11 for trouble *is* near; for *t is* none to help. NIH
30: 9 What profit *is t* in my blood, when I go NIH
32: 2 and in whose spirit *t is* no guile. NIH
33:16 T is no king saved by the multitude of a NIH
34: 9 for *t is* no want to them that fear him. NIH
36: 1 *that t is* no fear of God before his eyes. NIH
36:12 T are the workers of iniquity fallen: 8033
38: 3 *T is* no soundness in my flesh because NIH
38: 3 neither *is t any* rest in my bones because NIH
38: 7 and *t is* no soundness in my flesh. NIH
45:12 the daughter of Tyre *shall be t* with a gift; NIH
46: 4 *T is* a river, the streams whereof shall make NIH
48: 6 Fear took hold upon them t, *and* pain, as of 8033
50:22 tear *you* in pieces, and *t be* none to deliver. NIH
53: 1 The fool hath said in his heart, *T is* no God. NIH
53: 1 *t is* none that doeth good. NIH
53: 2 to see if **t were** *any* that did understand, 3426
53: 3 *t is* none that doeth good, no, not one. NIH
53: 5 T were they in great fear, *where* no fear 8033
55:18 *was* against me: for t were many with me. NIH
58:11 Verily *t is* a reward for the righteous: NIH
66: 6 the flood on foot: t did we rejoice in him. 8033
68:27 T *is* little Benjamin *with* their ruler, 8033
69: 2 I sink in deep mire, where *t is* no standing: NIH
69:20 *for some* to take pity, but *t was* none; NIH
69:35 that they may dwell t, and have it in 8033
71:11 and take him; for *t is* none to deliver *him.* NIH
72:16 T shall be a handful of corn in the earth NIH
73: 4 For *t are* no bands in their death: but NIH
73:11 and **is t** knowledge in the most High? 3426
73:25 *t is* none upon earth *that* I desire beside NIH
74: 9 *t is* no more any prophet: neither *is there* NIH
74: 9 neither *is t* among us any that knoweth how NIH
75: 8 For in the hand of the LORD *t is* a cup, NIH
76: 3 T brake he the arrows of the bow, 8033+1886.5
79: 3 and *t was* none to bury *them.* NIH
81: 9 T shall no strange god be in thee; NIH
86: 8 Among the gods *t is* none like unto thee, NIH
86: 8 neither *are t any works* like unto thy works. NIH
87: 4 Tyre, with Ethiopia; this *man* was born t. 8033
87: 6 *up* the people, *that* this *man* was born t. 8033
87: 7 *shall be* t: all my springs *are* in thee. NIH
91:10 T shall no evil befall thee, neither shall *any* NIH
92:15 my rock, and *t is* no unrighteousness in him. NIH
104:26 T go the ships: *there is* that leviathan, 8033
104:26 *t is* that leviathan, *whom* thou hast made to NIH
105:31 t came divers sorts *of flies, and* lice in all NIH
105:37 *t was* not *one* feeble *person* among their NIH
106:11 their enemies: t was not one of them left. NIH
107:12 they fell down, and *t was* none to help. NIH
107:36 t he maketh the hungry to dwell, that they 8033
107:40 in the wilderness, *where t is* no way. NIH
109:12 Let t be none to extend mercy unto him: NIH
109:12 neither let t be any to favour his fatherless NIH
112: 4 Unto the upright t ariseth light in NIH
122: 5 For t are set thrones of judgment, 8033+1886.5

T

Ps 130: 4 t is forgiveness with thee, that thou mayest NIH
130: 7 for with the LORD t is mercy, and NIH
132:17 T will I make the horn of David to bud: 8033
133: 3 for t the LORD commanded the blessing, 8033
135:17 neither is t any breath in their mouths. 3426
137: 1 of Babylon, t we sat down, yea, we wept, 8033
137: 3 For t they that carried us away captive 8033
139: 4 For t is not a word in my tongue, but lo, NIH
139: 8 If I ascend up into heaven, thou art t: if I 8033
139: 8 if I make my bed in hell, behold, thou art t. NIH
139:10 Even t shall thy hand lead me, and thy right 8033
139:16 when as yet t was none of them. NIH
139:24 see if t be any wicked way in me, and NIH
142: 4 but t was no man that would know me: NIH
144:14 that t be no breaking in, nor going out; NIH
144:14 that t be no complaining in our streets. NIH
146: 3 nor in the son of man, in whom t is no help. NIH
Pr 7:10 t met him a woman with the attire of a NIH
8: 8 t is nothing froward or perverse in them. NIH
8:24 When t were no depths, I was brought forth; NIH
8:24 when t were no fountains abounding with NIH
8:27 When he prepared the heavens, I was t: 8033
9:18 he knoweth not that the dead are t; and 8033
10:19 In the multitude of words t wanteth not sin: NIH
11:10 and when the wicked perish, t is shouting. NIH
11:14 in the multitude of counsellers t is safety. NIH
11:24 T is that scattereth, and yet increaseth; and 3426
11:24 t is that withholdeth more than is meet, but NIH
12:18 T is that speaketh like the piercings of a 3426
12:21 T shall no evil happen to the just: but NIH
12:28 and in the pathway thereof t is no death. NIH
13: 7 T is that maketh himself rich, yet hath 3426
13: 7 t is that maketh himself poor, yet hath great NIH
13:23 t is that is destroyed for want of judgment. 3426
14: 9 at sin: but among the righteous t is favour. NIH
14:12 T is a way which seemeth right unto a man, 3426
14:23 In all labour t is profit: but the talk of NIH
16:25 T is a way that seemeth right unto a man, 3426
16:27 up evil: and in his lips t is as a burning fire. NIH
17:16 Wherefore is t a price in the hand of a fool NIH
18:24 t is a friend that sticketh closer than a 3426
19:18 Chasten thy son while t is hope, and let not 3426
19:21 T are many devices in a man's heart; NIH
20:15 T is gold, and a multitude of rubies: but 3426
21:20 T is treasure to be desired and oil in NIH
21:30 T is no wisdom nor understanding nor NIH
22:13 The slothful man saith, T is a lion without, NIH
23:18 For surely t is an end; and thine expectation 3426
24: 6 and in multitude of counsellers t is safety. NIH
24:14 thou hast found it, then t shall be a reward, 3426
24:20 For t shall be no reward to the evil man; NIH
25: 4 and t shall come forth a vessel for the finer. NIH
26:12 t is more hope of a fool than of him. NIH
26:13 slothful man saith, T is a lion in the way; NIH
26:20 Where no wood is, t the fire goeth out: so NIH
26:20 so where t is no talebearer, the strife NIH
26:25 for t are seven abominations in his heart. NIH
28:12 righteous men do rejoice, t is great glory: NIH
29: 6 In the transgression of an evil man t is a NIH
29: 9 whether he rage or laugh, t is no rest. NIH
29:18 Where t is no vision, the people perish: but NIH
29:20 t is more hope of a fool than of him. NIH
30:11 T is a generation that curseth their father, NIH
30:12 T is a generation that are pure in their own NIH
30:13 T is a generation, O how lofty are their NIH
30:14 T is a generation, whose teeth are as NIH
30:15 T are three things that are never satisfied, NIH
30:18 T be three things which are too wonderful NIH
30:24 T be four things which are little upon NIH
30:29 T be three things which go well, yea, NIH
30:31 and a king, against whom t is no rising up. NIH
Ecc 1: 9 and t is no new thing under the sun. NIH
1:10 Is t any thing whereof it may be said, See, 3426
1:11 T is no remembrance of former things; NIH
1:11 t be any remembrance of things that are to NIH
2:11 of spirit, and t was no profit under the sun. NIH
2:16 For t is no remembrance of the wise more NIH
2:21 For t is a man whose labour is in wisdom, 3426
2:24 T is nothing better for a man, than that he NIH
3: 1 To every thing t is a season, and a time to NIH
3:12 I know that t is no good in them, but for a NIH
3:16 that wickedness was t; 8033+1886.5
3:16 that iniquity was t. 8033+1886.5
3:17 for t is a time there for every purpose and NIH
3:17 for there is a time t for every purpose and 8033
3:22 Wherefore I perceive that t is nothing NIH
4: 1 on the side of their oppressors t was power; NIH
4: 8 T is one alone, and there is not a second; 3426
4: 8 There is one alone, and t is not a second; NIH
4: 8 yet is t no end of all his labour; neither is NIH
4:16 T is no end of all the people, even of all that NIH
5: 7 and many words t are also divers vanities: NIH
5: 8 highest regardeth; and t be higher than they. NIH
5:11 what good is t to the owners thereof, NIH
5:13 T is a sore evil which I have seen under 3426
5:14 begetteth a son, and t is nothing in his hand. NIH
6: 1 T is an evil which I have seen under 3426
6:11 Seeing t be many things that increase 3426
7:11 and by it t is profit to them that see the sun. NIH
7:15 t is a just man that perisheth in his 3426
7:15 t is a wicked man that prolongeth his life in 3426
7:20 For t is not a just man upon earth, that doeth NIH
8: 4 Where the word of a king is, t is power: and NIH
8: 6 Because to every purpose t is time and 3426
8: 8 T is no man that hath power over the spirit NIH
8: 8 t is no discharge in that war; neither shall NIH
8: 9 t is a time wherein one man ruleth over NIH
8:14 T is a vanity which is done upon the earth; 3426
8:14 that t be just men, unto whom it happeneth 3426
8:14 t be wicked men, to whom it happeneth 3426
8:16 (for also t is that neither day nor night seeth NIH
9: 2 t is one event to the righteous, and to NIH
9: 3 under the sun, that t is one event unto all: NIH
9: 4 For to him that is joined to all the living t is 3426
9:10 for t is no work, nor device, nor knowledge, NIH

Ecc 9:14 T was a little city, and few men within it; NIH
9:14 t came a great king against it, and NIH
9:15 Now t was found in it a poor wise man, and NIH
10: 5 T is an evil which I have seen under 3426
11: 3 the place where the tree falleth, t it shall be. 8033
12:12 of making many books t is no end; and NIH
SS 4: 4 whereon t hang a thousand bucklers, NIH
4: 7 art all fair, my love; t is no spot in thee. NIH
6: 6 and t is not one barren among them. NIH
6: 8 T are threescore queens, and NIH
7:12 bud forth: t will I give thee my loves. 8033
8: 5 t thy mother brought thee forth: 8033+1886.5
8: 5 t she brought thee forth that bare 8033+1886.5
Isa 1: 6 even unto the head t is no soundness in it; NIH
2: 7 gold, neither is t any end of their treasures; NIH
2: 7 neither is t any end of their chariots: NIH
3:24 that instead of sweet smell t shall be stink; NIH
4: 6 t shall be a tabernacle for a shadow in NIH
5: 6 but t shall come up briers and thorns: NIH
5: 8 that lay field to field, till t be no place, NIH
6:12 t be a great forsaking in the midst of NIH
7:23 where t were a thousand vines at a thousand NIH
7:25 t shall not come thither the fear of briers NIH
8:20 this word, it is because t is no light in them. NIH
9: 7 his government and peace t shall be no end, NIH
10:14 t was none that moved the wing, or NIH
11: 1 t shall come forth a rod out of the stem of NIH
11:10 in that day t shall be a root of Jesse, NIH
11:16 t shall be a highway for the remnant of his NIH
13:20 neither shall the Arabian pitch tent t; 8033
13:20 shall the shepherds make their fold t. 8033
13:21 wild beasts of the desert shall lie t; and 8033
13:21 owls shall dwell t, and satyrs shall dance 8033
13:21 shall dwell there, and satyrs shall dance t. 8033
14:31 for t shall come from the north a smoke, NIH
15: 6 the grass faileth, t is no green thing. NIH
16:10 in the vineyards t shall be no singing, NIH
16:10 be no singing, neither shall t be shouting: NIH
17: 9 children of Israel: and t shall be desolation. NIH
19:15 Neither shall t be any work for Egypt, NIH
19:19 In that day shall t be an altar to the LORD NIH
19:23 In that day shall t be a highway out of NIH
22:18 t shalt thou die, and there 8033+1886.5
22:18 t the chariots of thy glory shall be 8033+1886.5
23: 1 so that t is no house, no entering in: NIH
23:10 daughter of Tarshish: t is no more strength. NIH
23:12 to Chittim; t also shalt thou have no rest. 8033
24:11 T is a crying for wine in the streets; all joy NIH
24:13 t shall be as the shaking of an olive tree, and NIH
27:10 t shall the calf feed, and there shall he lie 8033
27:10 t shall he lie down, and consume 8033
28: 8 and filthiness, so that t is no place clean. NIH
28:10 line upon line; here a little, and t a little: 8033
28:13 line upon line; here a little, and t a little; 8033
29: 2 and t shall be heaviness and sorrow: NIH
30:14 that t shall not be found in the bursting of it NIH
30:25 t shall be upon every high mountain, and NIH
30:28 t shall be a bridle in the jaws of the people, NIH
33:21 t the glorious LORD will be unto us a 8033
34:12 none shall be t, and all her princes shall be 8033
34:14 the shrich owl also shall rest t, and find for 8033
34:15 T shall the great owl make her 8033+1886.5
34:15 t shall the vultures also be gathered, 8033
35: 8 a highway shall be t, and a way, and it shall 8033
35: 9 No lion shall be t, nor any ravenous beast 8033
35: 9 shall go up thereon, it shall not be found t; 8033
35: 9 found there; but the redeemed shall walk t: NIH
37: 3 the birth, and t is not strength to bring forth. NIH
37:33 nor shoot an arrow t, nor come before it 8033
39: 2 t was nothing in his house, nor in all his NIH
39: 4 t is nothing among my treasures that I have NIH
39: 8 For t shall be peace and truth in my days. NIH
40:28 t is no searching of his understanding. NIH
41:17 t is none, and their tongue faileth for thirst, NIH
41:26 yea, t is none that sheweth, yea, there is NIH
41:26 yea, t is none that declareth, yea, NIH
41:26 yea, t is none that heareth your words. NIH
41:28 For I beheld, and t was no man; NIH
41:28 and t was no counseller, that, NIH
43:10 before me t was no God formed, NIH
43:10 no God formed, neither shall t be after me. NIH
43:11 the LORD; and beside me t is no saviour. NIH
43:12 when t was no strange god among you: NIH
43:13 t is none that can deliver out of my hand: NIH
44: 6 I am the last; and besides me t is no God. NIH
44: 8 Is t a God besides me? yea, there is no 3426
44: 8 yea, t is no God; I know not any. NIH
44:19 neither is t knowledge nor understanding to NIH
44:20 nor say, Is t not a lie in my right hand? NIH
45: 5 I am the LORD, and t is none else, there is NIH
45: 5 there is none else, t is no God besides me: NIH
45: 6 and from the west, that t is none besides me. NIH
45: 6 I am the LORD, and t is none else. NIH
45:14 in thee; and t is none else, there is no God. NIH
45:14 in thee; and there is none else, t is no God. NIH
45:18 I am the LORD; and t is none else. NIH
45:21 t is no God else beside me; a just God and NIH
45:21 just God and a saviour; t is none beside me. NIH
45:22 the earth: for I am God, and t is none else. NIH
46: 9 for I am God, and t is none else; I am God, NIH
46: 9 none else; I am God, and t is none like me, NIH
47: 1 t is no throne, O daughter of the Chaldeans; NIH
47:14 t shall not be a coal to warm at, nor fire to NIH
48:16 from the time that it was, t am I: 8033
48:22 T is no peace, saith the LORD, unto NIH
50: 2 Wherefore, when I came, was t no man? NIH
50: 2 when I called, was t none to answer? Is my NIH
50: 2 because t is no water, and dieth for thirst. NIH
51:18 T is none to guide her among all the sons NIH
51:18 neither is t any that taketh her by the hand NIH
52: 1 for henceforth t shall no more come into NIH
52: 4 down aforetime into Egypt to sojourn t; 8033
53: 2 t is no beauty that we should desire him. NIH
57:10 thy way; yet saidst thou not, T is no hope: NIH
57:21 T is no peace, saith my God, to the wicked. NIH

Isa 59: 8 and t is no judgment in their goings: NIH
59:11 we look for judgment, but t is none; NIH
59:15 it displeased him that t was no judgment. NIH
59:16 he saw that t was no man, and NIH
59:16 and wondered that t was no intercessor: NIH
63: 3 of the people t was none with me: NIH
63: 5 I looked, and t was none to help; and NIH
63: 5 and I wondered that t was none to uphold: NIH
64: 7 t is none that calleth upon thy name, NIH
65: 9 and my servants shall dwell t. 8033+1886.5
65:20 T shall be no more thence an infant of days, NIH
Jer 2:10 and see if t be such a thing. NIH
2:25 thou saidst, T is no hope: no; for I have NIH
3: 3 and t hath been no latter rain; NIH
3: 6 green tree, and t hath played the harlot. 8033
4:25 lo, t was no man, and all the birds of NIH
5: 1 a man, if t be any that executeth judgment, 3426
6:14 Peace, peace; when t is no peace. NIH
6:20 To what purpose cometh t to me incense NIH
7: 2 proclaim t this word, and say, Hear 8033
7:32 they shall bury in Tophet, till t be no place. 369
8:11 Peace, peace; when t is no peace. NIH
8:13 t shall be no grapes on the vine, nor figs on NIH
8:14 the defenced cities, and let us be silent t: 8033
8:22 Is t no balm in Gilead; is there no physician NIH
8:22 no balm in Gilead; is t no physician there? NIH
8:22 no balm in Gilead; is there no physician t? 8033
10: 6 Forasmuch as t is none like unto thee, NIH
10: 7 all their kingdoms, t is none like unto thee. NIH
10:13 t is a multitude of waters in the heavens, NIH
10:14 is falsehood, and t is no breath in them. NIH
10:20 t is none to stretch forth my tent any more, NIH
11:23 t shall be no remnant of them: for I will NIH
13: 4 and hide it t in a hole of the rock. 8033
13: 6 which I commanded thee to hide t. 8033
14: 4 for t was no rain in the earth, the plowmen NIH
14: 5 and forsook it, because t was no grass. NIH
14: 6 their eyes did fail, because t was no grass. NIH
14:19 thou smitten us, and t is no healing for us? NIH
14:19 we looked for peace, and t is no good; and NIH
14:22 Are t any among the vanities of 3426
16:13 t shall ye serve other gods day and night; 8033
16:19 vanity, and things wherein t is no profit. NIH
17:25 shall t enter into the gates of this city kings NIH
18: 2 t I will cause thee to hear my 8033+1886.5
18:12 they said, T is no hope: but we will walk NIH
19: 2 proclaim t the words that I shall tell thee, 8033
19:11 them in Tophet, till t be no place to bury. NIH
20: 6 t thou shalt die, and shalt be buried there, 8033
20: 6 shalt be buried t, thou, and all thy friends, 8033
22: 1 of the king of Judah, and speak t this word, 8033
22: 4 shall t enter in by the gates of this house NIH
22:26 where ye were not born; and t shall ye die. 8033
26:20 t was also a man that prophesied in NIH
27:22 t shall they be until the day that I 8033+1886.5
29: 6 that ye may be increased t, and 8033
30:13 T is none to plead thy cause, that thou NIH
31: 6 For t shall be a day, that the watchmen 3426
31:17 t is hope in thine end, saith the LORD, 3426
31:24 t shall dwell in Judah itself, and in all NIH
32: 5 t shall he be until I visit him, saith 8033
32:17 out arm, and t is nothing too hard for thee: NIH
32:27 of all flesh: is t any thing too hard for me? NIH
33:10 Again t shall be heard in this place, which NIH
33:20 that t should not be day and night in their NIH
36:12 lo, all the princes sat t, even Elishama 8033
36:22 t was a fire on the hearth burning before NIH
36:32 t were added besides unto them many like NIH
37:10 t remained but wounded men among them, NIH
37:13 a captain of the ward was t, whose name 8033
37:16 and Jeremiah had remained t many days; 8033
37:17 and said, Is t any word from the LORD? 3426
37:17 Jeremiah said, T is: for, said he, thou shalt 3426
37:20 the house of Jonathan the scribe, lest I die t. 8033
38: 6 in the dungeon t was no water, but mire: NIH
38: 9 he is: for t is no more bread in the city. NIH
38:26 me to return to Jonathan's house, to die t. 8033
38:28 and he was t when Jerusalem was taken. NIH
41: 1 and t they did eat bread together in Mizpah. 8033
41: 3 the Chaldeans that were found t, and 8033
41: 5 That t came certain from Shechem, NIH
42:14 have hunger of bread; and t will we dwell: 8033
42:15 to enter into Egypt, and go to sojourn t; 8033
42:16 shall overtake you t in the land of Egypt, 8033
42:16 shall follow close after you t in Egypt; 8033
42:16 after you there in Egypt; and t ye shall die. 8033
42:17 set their faces to go into Egypt to sojourn t; 8033
43: 2 thee to say, Go not into Egypt to sojourn t: 8033
44:12 to go into the land of Egypt to sojourn t, 8033
44:14 are gone into the land of Egypt to sojourn t, 8033
44:14 they have a desire to return to dwell t: 8033
44:27 and by the famine, until t be an end of them. NIH
44:28 are gone into the land of Egypt to sojourn t, 8033
46:17 They did cry t, Pharaoh king of Egypt is 8033
47: 7 the sea shore? t hath he appointed it. 8033
48: 2 T shall be no more praise of Moab: NIH
48:38 T shall be lamentation generally upon all NIH
49:18 saith the LORD, no man shall abide t, 8033
49:23 t is sorrow on the sea; it cannot be quiet. NIH
49:33 t shall no man abide there, nor any son of NIH
49:33 there shall no man abide t, nor any son of 8033
49:36 t shall be no nation whither the outcasts of NIH
50: 3 For out of the north t cometh up a nation NIH
50:20 shall be sought for, and t shall be none; NIH
50:39 the wild beasts of the islands shall dwell t, 8033
50:40 so shall no man abide t, neither shall any 8033
51:16 t is a multitude of waters in the heavens; NIH
51:17 is falsehood, and t is no breath in them. NIH
52: 6 that t was no bread for the people of NIH
52:23 t were ninety and six pomegranates on a NIH
52:34 t was a continual diet given him of the king NIH
La 1:12 see if t be any sorrow like unto my sorrow, 3426
1:17 her hands, and t is none to comfort her: NIH
1:20 the sword bereaveth, at home t is as death. NIH
1:21 heard that I sigh; t is none to comfort me: NIH

La 3:29 mouth in the dust; if so be **t** may be hope. NIH
4:15 the heathen, They shall no more sojourn ***t***. NIH
5: 8 ***t*** *is* none that doth deliver *us* out of their NIH
Eze 1: 3 the hand of the LORD was **t** upon him. 8033
1:25 **t** was a voice from the firmament that *was* NIH
2: 5 yet shall know that **t** hath been a prophet NIH
2:10 ***t*** *was* written therein lamentations, and NIH
3:15 remained **t** astonished among them seven 8033
3:22 the hand of the LORD was **t** upon me; 8033
3:22 into the plain, and I will **t** talk with thee. 8033
3:23 behold, the glory of the LORD stood **t**, 8033
4:14 neither came **t** abominable flesh into my NIH
7:11 of theirs: neither *shall* ***t*** *be* wailing for them. NIH
7:25 they shall seek peace, and ***t*** *shall be* none. NIH
8: 1 that the hand of the Lord GOD fell **t** upon 8033
8: 4 the glory of the God of Israel *was* **t**, 8033
8:11 **t** stood before them seventy men of NIH
8:14 behold, **t** sat women weeping for Tammuz. 8033
10: 1 **t** appeared over them as it were a sapphire NIH
10: 8 **t** appeared in the cherubims the form of a NIH
12:13 yet shall he not see it, though he shall die **t**. 8033
12:24 For **t** shall be no more any vain vision nor NIH
12:28 **T** shall none of my words be prolonged any NIH
13:10 and ***t*** *was* no peace; and one built up a wall, NIH
13:11 **t** shall be an overflowing shower; and ye, NIH
13:13 **t** shall be an overflowing shower in mine NIH
13:16 and ***t*** *is* no peace, saith the Lord GOD. NIH
13:20 where*with* ye **t** hunt the souls to make *them* 8033
17: 7 **T** was also another great eagle with great NIH
17:20 will plead with him **t** *for* his trespass that he 8033
20:28 they offered **t** their sacrifices, and 8033
20:28 **t** they presented the provocation of their 8033
20:28 **t** also they made their sweet savour, and 8033
20:28 and poured out **t** their drink offerings. 8033
20:35 and **t** will I plead with you face to face. 8033
20:40 Lord GOD, **t** shall all the house of Israel, 8033
20:40 **t** will I accept them, and there will I require 8033
20:40 **t** will I require your offerings, and 8033
20:43 **t** shall ye remember your ways, and all 8033
22:20 and I will leave *you* ***t***, and melt you. NIH
22:25 ***T*** *is* a conspiracy of her prophets in NIH
23: 2 Son of man, **t** were two women, NIH
23: 3 **t** were their breasts pressed, and 8033+1886.5
23: 3 **t** they bruised the teats of their virginity. 8033
28: 3 ***t*** *is* no secret *that* they can hide *from* thee: NIH
28:24 **t** shall be no more a pricking brier unto NIH
29:14 and they shall be **t** a base kingdom. 8033
30:13 **t** shall be no more a prince of the land of NIH
30:18 when I shall break **t** the yokes of Egypt: 8033
32:22 Asshur *is* **t** and all her company: his graves 8033
32:24 **T** *is* Elam and all her multitude round about 8033
32:26 **T** *is* Meshech, Tubal, and all her multitude: 8033
32:29 **T** *is* Edom, her kings, and all her 8033+1886.5
32:30 **T** *be* the princes of the north, all of 8033+1886.5
34: 5 were scattered, because ***t*** *is* no shepherd: NIH
34: 8 because ***t*** *was* no shepherd, neither did my NIH
34:14 **t** shall they lie in a good fold, and *in* a fat 8033
34:26 in his season; **t** shall be showers of blessing. NIH
35:10 will possess it; whereas the LORD was **t**: 8033
37: 2 ***t*** *were* very many in the open valley; NIH
37: 7 **t** was a noise, and behold a shaking, and NIH
37: 8 them above: but ***t*** *was* no breath in them. NIH
38:19 Surely in that day **t** shall be a great shaking NIH
39:11 *that* I will give unto Gog a place **t** of graves 8033
39:11 **t** shall they bury Gog and all his multitude: 8033
39:28 and have left none of them any more **t**. 8033
40: 3 me thither, and behold, ***t*** *was* a man, NIH
40:16 ***t*** *were* narrow windows to the little NIH
40:17 lo, ***t*** *were* chambers, and a pavement made NIH
40:25 ***t*** *were* windows in it and in the arches NIH
40:26 ***t*** *were* seven steps to go up to it, and NIH
40:27 **t** *was* a gate in the inner court toward NIH
40:29 ***t*** *were* windows in it and in the arches NIH
40:33 ***t*** *were* windows therein and in the arches NIH
40:49 ***t*** *were* pillars by the posts, one on this side, NIH
41: 7 ***t*** *was* an enlarging, and a winding about still NIH
41:25 ***t*** *were made* on them, on the doors of NIH
41:25 ***t*** *were* thick planks upon the face of NIH
41:26 ***t*** *were* narrow windows and palm trees on NIH
42:13 *things:* **t** shall they lay the most holy *things,* 8033
42:14 **t** they shall lay their garments wherein they 8033
45: 2 Of this **t** shall be for the sanctuary five NIH
46:19 **t** *was* a place on the two sides westward. 8033
46:21 in every corner of the court ***t*** *was* a court. NIH
46:22 In the four corners of the court ***t*** *were* courts NIH
46:23 ***t*** *was* a row *of building* round about in NIH
47: 2 behold, **t** ran out waters on the right side. NIH
47: 9 and **t** shall be a very great multitude of fish, 8033
47:23 **t** shall ye give *him* his inheritance, saith 8033
48:35 *that* day *shall be,* The LORD *is* **t**. 8033+1886.5
Da 2: 9 me the dream, ***t*** *is but* one decree for you: NIH
2:10 **T is** not a man upon the earth that can shew 383
2:10 therefore ***t*** *is* no king, lord, nor ruler, NIH
2:11 **t is** none other that can shew it before 383
2:28 **t is** a God in heaven that revealeth secrets, 383
2:41 but **t** shall be in it of the strength of the iron, NIH
3:12 **T are** certain Jews whom thou hast set over 383
3:29 **t is** no other God that can deliver after this 383
4:31 **t** fell a voice from heaven, *saying,* O king NIH
5:11 **T is** a man in thy kingdom, in whom *is* 383
6: 4 neither was **t** any error or fault found in NIH
7: 8 **t** came up among them another little horn, NIH
7: 8 before whom **t** were three of the first NIH
7:14 ***t*** *was* given him dominion, and glory, and NIH
8: 3 **t** stood before the river a ram which had two NIH
8: 4 neither *was* ***t*** *any* that could deliver out of NIH
8: 7 **t** was no power in the ram to stand before NIH
8: 7 **t** was none that could deliver the ram out of NIH
8:15 **t** stood before me as the appearance of a NIH
10: 8 and **t** remained no strength in me: NIH
10:13 and I remained **t** with the kings of Persia. 8033
10:17 straightway **t** remained no strength in me, NIH
10:17 strength in me, neither is **t** breath left in me. NIH
10:18 **t** came again and touched me *one* like NIH
10:21 ***t*** *is* none that holdeth with me in these NIH
Da 11: 2 **t** *shall* stand up yet three kings in Persia; NIH
11:14 in those times **t** shall many stand up against NIH
11:15 neither *shall* **t** *be any* strength to withstand. NIH
12: 1 **t** shall be a time of trouble, such as never NIH
12: 1 such as never was since **t** was a nation *even* NIH
12: 5 and behold, **t** stood other two, NIH
12:11 ***t*** *shall be* a thousand two hundred and NIH
Hos 1:10 not my people, **t** it shall be said unto them, NIH
2:15 she shall sing **t**, as *in* the days of 8033+1886.5
4: 1 because ***t*** *is* no truth, nor mercy, NIH
4: 9 **t** shall be, like people, like priest: and I will NIH
6: 7 **t** have they dealt treacherously against me. 8033
6:10 **t** *is* the whoredom of Ephraim, Israel is 8033
7: 7 ***t*** *is* none among them that calleth unto me. NIH
7: 9 yea, gray hairs are **here and t** upon him, 2236
9:12 *that* ***t*** *shall* not *be* a man *left:* yea, NIH
9:15 wickedness *is* in Gilgal, for **t** I hated them: 8033
10: 9 **t** they stood: the battle in Gibeah against 8033
12: 4 him *in* Beth-el, and **t** he spake with us; 8033
12:11 *Is* ***t*** iniquity *in* Gilead? surely they are NIH
13: 4 but me: for ***t*** *is* no saviour beside me. NIH
13: 8 and **t** will I devour them like a lion: 8033
Joel 2: 2 **t** hath not been ever the like, neither shall 1930.2
3: 2 will plead with them **t** for my people and 8033
3:12 for **t** will I sit to judge all the heathen round 8033
3:17 **t** shall no strangers pass through her any NIH
Am 3: 6 shall **t** be evil in a city, and the LORD NIH
3:11 An adversary ***t*** *shall be* even round about NIH
4: 7 when ***t*** *were* yet three months to the harvest: NIH
5: 2 upon her land; ***t*** *is* none to raise her up. NIH
5: 6 and ***t*** *be* none to quench *it* in Beth-el. NIH
6: 9 if **t** remain ten men in one house, that they NIH
6:10 sides of the house, *Is* **t** yet *any* with thee? NIH
6:12 will *one* plow **t** with oxen? for ye have NIH
7:12 and **t** eat bread, and prophesy there: 8033
7:12 and there eat bread, and prophesy **t**: 8033
8: 3 ***t*** *shall be* many dead bodies in every place; NIH
Ob 1: 7 under thee: ***t*** *is* none understanding in him. NIH
1:17 shall be deliverance, and **t** shall be holiness; NIH
1:18 **t** shall not be *any* remaining of the house of NIH
Jnh 1: 4 **t** was a mighty tempest in the sea, so NIH
4: 5 **t** made him a booth, and sat under it in 8033
Mic 3: 7 cover their lips; for ***t*** *is* no answer of God. NIH
4: 9 *is* **t** no king in thee? is thy counseller NIH
4:10 *even* to Babylon; **t** shalt thou be delivered; 8033
4:10 **t** the LORD shall redeem thee from 8033
6:10 **Are t** yet the treasures of wickedness *in* 786
7: 1 ***t*** *is* no cluster to eat: my soul desired NIH
7: 2 ***t*** *is* none upright among men: they all lie in NIH
Na 1:11 **T** is *one* come out of thee, that imagineth NIH
2: 9 for ***t*** *is* none end of the store *and* glory out NIH
3: 3 ***t*** *is* a multitude of slain, and a great number NIH
3: 3 and ***t*** *is* none end of *their* corpses; NIH
3:15 **T** shall the fire devour thee; the sword shall 8033
3:19 ***T*** *is* no healing of thy bruise; thy wound *is* NIH
Hab 1: 3 and **t** are *that* raise up strife and contention. NIH
2:19 and ***t*** *is* no breath at all in the midst of it. NIH
3: 4 his hand: and **t** *was* the hiding of his power. 8033
3:17 the fold, and ***t*** *shall be* no herd in the stalls: NIH
Zep 1:10 *that* ***t*** *shall be* the noise of a cry from NIH
1:14 the mighty *man* shall cry **t** bitterly. 8033
2: 5 destroy thee, that **t** shall be no inhabitant. NIH
2:15 in her heart, I *am,* and ***t*** *is* none beside me: NIH
3: 6 cities are destroyed, so that **t** is no man, NIH
3: 6 there is no man, that **t** is none inhabitant. NIH
Hag 1: 6 *ye* clothe you, but **t is none** warm; and he 369
2:14 and *that* which they offer **t** *is* unclean. 8033
2:16 came to a heap of twenty *measures,* **t** were NIH
2:16 *vessels out of* the press, **t** were *but* twenty. NIH
Zec 1: 8 and behind him *were* **t** red horses, speckled, NIH
5: 7 behold, **t** *was* lift up a talent of lead: and NIH
5: 9 **t** came out two women, and the wind *was* in NIH
5:11 be established, and set **t** upon her own base. 8033
6: 1 **t** came four chariots out from between two NIH
8: 4 **T** shall yet old men and old women dwell in NIH
8:10 For before these days **t** was no hire for man, NIH
8:10 neither *was* ***t*** *any* peace to him that went out NIH
8:20 *It shall* yet *come to pass,* that **t** shall come NIH
10: 2 were troubled, because ***t*** *was* no shepherd. NIH
11: 3 ***T*** *is* a voice of the howling of NIH
12:11 In that day shall **t** be a great mourning in NIH
13: 1 In that day **t** shall be a fountain opened to NIH
14: 4 the west, *and* ***t*** *shall be* a very great valley; NIH
14: 9 in that day shall **t** be one LORD, and NIH
14:11 and **t** shall be no more utter destruction; NIH
14:18 that *have* no *rain;* **t** shall be the plague, NIH
14:20 In that day shall **t** be upon the bells of NIH
14:21 in that day **t** shall be no more the Canaanite NIH
Mal 1:10 Who *is* ***t*** even among you that would shut NIH
3:10 that **t** may be meat in mine house, and NIH
3:10 that ***t*** *shall* not *be room* enough *to receive* NIH
Mt 2: 1 **t** came wise men from the east to Jerusalem, NIG
2:13 and be thou **t** until I bring thee word: *1563*
2:15 And was **t** until the death of Herod: that it *1563*
2:18 In Rama was **t** a voice heard, lamentation, NIG
4:25 And **t** followed him great multitudes *of* NIG
5:23 **and t** rememberest that thy brother hath *2546*
5:24 Leave **t** thy gift before the altar, and go thy *1563*
6:21 your treasure is, **t** will your heart be also. *1563*
7: 9 Or what man is **t** of you, whom if his son NIG
7:13 and many **t** be which go in thereat: NIG
7:14 leadeth unto life, and few **t** be that find it. NIG
8: 2 **t** came a leper and worshipped him, saying, NIG
8: 5 **t** came unto him a centurion, NIG
8:12 **t** shall be weeping and gnashing of teeth. *1563*
8:24 **t** arose a great tempest in the sea, NIG
8:26 and the sea; and **t** was a great calm. NIG
8:28 **t** met him two possessed with devils, NIG
8:30 And **t** was a good way off from them a herd NIG
9:18 **t** came a *certain* ruler, and worshipped him, NIG
10:11 it is worthy; **and t** abide till ye go thence. *2546*
10:26 for **t** is nothing covered, that shall not be NIG
11:11 Among *them that are* born of women **t** hath NIG
12:10 **t** was a man which had *his* hand withered. NIG
12:11 unto them, What man shall **t** be among you, NIG
Mt 12:39 and **t** shall no sign be given to it, but NIG
12:45 than himself, and they enter in and dwell **t**: *1563*
13:42 **t** shall be wailing and gnashing of teeth. *1563*
13:50 **t** shall be wailing and gnashing of teeth. *1563*
13:58 And he did not many mighty works **t**, *1563*
14:23 the evening was come, he was **t** alone. *1563*
15:29 went up into a mountain, and sat down **t**. *1563*
16: 4 and **t** shall no sign be given unto it, but NIG
16:28 I say unto you, **T** be some standing here, NIG
17: 3 **t** appeared unto them Moses and NIG
17:14 **t** came to him a *certain* man, kneeling down NIG
18:20 in my name, **t** am I in the midst of them. *1563*
19: 2 followed him; and he healed them **t**. *1563*
19:12 For **t** are *some* eunuchs, which were so NIG
19:12 and **t** are *some* eunuchs, which were made NIG
19:12 and **t** be eunuchs, which have made NIG
19:13 Then were **t** brought unto him little NIG
19:17 ***t*** *is* none good but one, *that is,* God: but NIG
21:17 of the city into Bethany; and he lodged **t**. *1563*
21:33 **T** was a certain householder, which planted NIG
22:11 he saw **t** a man which had not on a wedding *1563*
22:13 **t** shall be weeping and gnashing of teeth. *1563*
22:23 which say that **t** is no resurrection, and NIG
22:25 Now **t** were with us seven brethren: and NIG
24: 2 **T** shall not be left here one stone upon NIG
24: 7 and **t** shall be famines, and pestilences, and NIG
24:22 be shortened, **t** should no flesh be saved: NIG
24:23 shall say unto you, Lo, here *is* Christ, or **t**; *5602*
24:24 For **t** shall arise false Christs, and NIG
24:28 **t** will the eagles be gathered together. *1563*
24:51 **t** shall be weeping and gnashing of teeth. *1563*
25: 6 And at midnight **t** was a cry made, Behold, NIG
25: 9 *Not so;* lest **t** be not enough for us and you: NIG
25:25 in the earth: lo, **t** thou hast *that is* thine. NIG
25:30 **t** shall be weeping and gnashing of teeth. *1563*
26: 5 Not on the feast *day,* lest **t** be an uproar NIG
26: 7 **T** came unto him a woman having an NIG
26:13 **t** shall also *this,* that this *woman* hath done, NIG
26:71 saw him, and said unto them that were **t**, *1563*
27:36 And sitting down they watched him **t**; *1563*
27:38 Then were **t** two thieves crucified with him, NIG
27:45 Now from the sixth hour **t** was darkness NIG
27:47 Some of them that stood **t**, when they heard *1563*
27:55 And many women were **t** beholding afar *1563*
27:57 **t** came a rich man of Arimathea, NIG
27:61 And **t** was Mary Magdalene, and the other *1563*
28: 2 And behold, **t** was a great earthquake: NIG
28: 7 before you into Galilee; **t** shall ye see him: *1563*
28:10 go into Galilee, **and t** shall they see me. *2546*
Mk 1: 5 And **t** went out unto him all the land of NIG
1: 7 **T** cometh one mightier than I after me, NIG
1:11 And **t** came a voice from heaven, NIG
1:13 And he was **t** in the wilderness forty days, *1563*
1:23 And **t** was in their synagogue a man with an NIG
1:35 departed into a solitary place, **and t** prayed. *2546*
1:38 the next towns, that I may preach **t also**: *2546*
1:40 And **t** came a leper to him, beseeching him, NIG
2: 2 insomuch that **t** was no room to receive NIG
2: 6 But **t** were certain of the scribes sitting NIG
2: 6 there were certain of the scribes sitting **t**, *1563*
2:15 for **t** were many, and they followed him. NIG
3: 1 **t** was a man there which had a withered NIG
3: 1 there was a man **t** which had a withered *1563*
3:31 **T** came then *his* brethren and his mother, NIG
4: 1 **t** was gathered unto him a great multitude, NIG
4: 3 Behold, **t** went out a sower to sow: NIG
4:22 For **t** is nothing hid, which shall not be NIG
4:36 And **t** were also with him other little ships. NIG
4:37 And **t** arose a great storm of wind, and NIG
4:39 the wind ceased, and **t** was a great calm. NIG
5: 2 immediately **t** met him out of the tombs a NIG
5:11 Now **t** was there nigh unto the mountains a NIG
5:11 Now there was **t** nigh unto the mountains a *1563*
5:22 **t** cometh one of the rulers of the synagogue, NIG
5:35 **t** came from the ruler of the synagogue's NIG
6: 5 And he could **t** do no mighty work, *1563*
6:10 **t** abide till ye depart from that place. *1563*
6:31 for **t** were many coming and going, and they NIG
7: 4 And many other *things* **t** be, which they NIG
7:15 **T** is nothing from without a man, NIG
8:12 **T** shall no sign be given unto this NIG
9: 1 That **t** be some of them that stand here, NIG
9: 4 And **t** appeared unto them Elias with NIG
9: 7 And **t** was a cloud that overshadowed them: NIG
9:39 for **t** is no *man* which shall do a miracle in NIG
10:17 **t** came one running, and kneeled to him, NIG
10:18 ***t*** *is* none good but one, *that is,* God. NIG
10:29 **T** is no *man* that hath left house, or NIG
11: 5 And certain of them that stood **t** said unto *1563*
11:27 **t** come to him the chief priests, and NIG
12:18 which say **t** is no resurrection; NIG
12:20 Now **t** were seven brethren: and the first NIG
12:31 **T** is none other commandment greater than NIG
12:32 for **t** is one God; and there is none other but NIG
12:32 there is one God; and **t** is none other but he: NIG
12:42 And **t** came a certain poor widow, and NIG
13: 2 **t** shall not be left one stone upon another, NIG
13: 8 and **t** shall be earthquakes in divers places, NIG
13: 8 and **t** shall be famines and troubles: NIG
13:21 say to you, Lo, here *is* Christ; or lo, *he is* **t**; *1563*
14: 2 Not on the feast *day,* lest **t** be an uproar of NIG
14: 3 **t** came a woman having an alabaster box of NIG
14: 4 And **t** were some that had indignation NIG
14:13 **t** shall meet you a man bearing a pitcher of NIG
14:15 *and* prepared: **t** make ready for us. *1563*
14:51 And **t** followed him a certain young man, NIG
14:57 And **t** arose certain, and bare false witness NIG
14:66 **t** cometh one of the maids of the high priest: NIG
15: 7 And **t** was *one* named Barabbas, *which lay* NIG
15:33 **t** was darkness over the whole land until NIG
15:40 **T** were also women looking on afar off: NIG
16: 7 **t** shall ye see him, as he said unto you. *1563*
Lk 1: 5 **T** was in the days of Herod, the king of NIG
1:11 And **t** appeared unto him an angel of NIG
1:33 and of his kingdom **t** shall be no end. NIG

Lk 1:45 for t shall be a performance of those *things* NIG
1:61 T is none of thy kindred that is called by NIG
2: 1 *that* t went out a decree from Cesar NIG
2: 6 And so it was *that,* while they were t, 1563
2: 7 because t was no room for them in the inn. NIG
2: 8 And t were in the same country shepherds NIG
2:13 And suddenly t was with the angel a NIG
2:25 And behold, t was a man in Jerusalem, NIG
2:36 And t was *one* Anna, a prophetess, NIG
4:14 t went out a fame of him through all NIG
4:17 And t was delivered unto him the book of NIG
4:33 And in the synagogue t was a man, NIG
5:15 *much* the more went t a fame abroad of NIG
5:17 that t were Pharisees and doctors of the law NIG
5:29 and t was a great company of publicans and NIG
6: 6 t was a man whose right hand was 1563
6:19 for t went virtue out of him, and NIG
7:12 behold, t was a dead man carried out, NIG
7:16 And t came a fear on all: NIG
7:28 Among *those that are* born of women t is NIG
7:41 T was a certain creditor which had two NIG
8:23 t came down a storm of wind on the lake; NIG
8:24 and they ceased, and t was a calm. NIG
8:27 t met him out of the city a certain man, NIG
8:32 And t was there a herd of many swine NIG
8:32 And there was t a herd of many swine 1563
8:41 t came a man named Jairus, and he was a NIG
8:49 t cometh one from the ruler of NIG
9: 4 ye enter into, t abide, and thence depart. 1563
9:17 t was taken up of fragments that remained NIG
9:27 I tell you of a truth, t be some standing here, NIG
9:30 And behold, t talked with him two men, NIG
9:34 t came a cloud, and overshadowed them: NIG
9:35 And t came a voice out of the cloud, saying, NIG
9:46 Then t arose a reasoning among them, NIG
10: 6 And if the son of peace be t, your peace 1563
10:31 And by chance t came down a certain priest NIG
11:26 than himself; and they enter in, and dwell t: 1563
11:29 and t shall no sign be given it, but the sign NIG
12: 1 when t were gathered together an NIG
12: 2 For t is nothing covered, that shall not be NIG
12:18 and t will I bestow all my fruits and 1563
12:34 your treasure is, t will your heart be also. 1563
12:52 For from henceforth t shall be five in one NIG
12:54 straightway ye say, T cometh a shower; NIG
12:55 the south wind blow, ye say, T will be heat; NIG
13: 1 T were present at that season some that told NIG
13:11 t was a woman which had a spirit of NIG
13:14 T are six days in which *men* ought to work: NIG
13:23 one unto him, Lord, are t few that be saved? NIG
13:28 T shall be weeping and gnashing of teeth, 1563
13:30 t are last which shall be first, and there are NIG
13:30 be first, and t are first which shall be last. NIG
13:31 The same day t came certain *of* NIG
14: 2 t was a certain man before him, NIG
14:22 as thou hast commanded, and yet t is room. NIG
14:25 And t went great multitudes with him: and NIG
15:10 t is joy in the presence of the angels of God NIG
15:13 t wasted his substance with riotous living. 1563
15:14 t arose a mighty famine in that land; NIG
16: 1 T was a certain rich man, which had a NIG
16:19 T was a certain rich man, which was NIG
16:20 And t was a certain beggar named Lazarus, NIG
16:26 between us and you t is a great gulf fixed: NIG
17:12 t met him ten men *that were* lepers, NIG
17:17 answering said, Were t not ten cleansed? NIG
17:18 T are not found that returned to give glory NIG
17:21 or, lo t: for behold, the kingdom of God is 1563
17:23 they shall say to you, See here; or, see t: 1563
17:34 in that night t shall be two *men* in one bed; NIG
18: 2 Saying, T was in a city a judge, NIG
18: 3 And t was a widow in that city; and NIG
18:29 T is no *man* that hath left house, or parents, NIG
19: 2 And behold, *t was* a man named Zaccheus, NIG
20:27 which deny that t is any resurrection; NIG
20:29 T were therefore seven brethren: and NIG
21: 6 in the which t shall not be left one stone NIG
21: 7 what sign *will t be* when these *things* shall NIG
21:11 and great signs shall t be from heaven. NIG
21:18 But t shall not a hair of your head perish. NIG
21:23 for t shall be great distress in the land, and NIG
21:25 And t shall be signs in the sun, and in NIG
22:10 t shall a man meet you, bearing a pitcher of NIG
22:12 large upper room furnished: t make ready. 1563
22:24 And t was also a strife among them, which NIG
22:43 And t appeared an angel unto him from NIG
23:27 And t followed him a great company of NIG
23:32 And t were also two other, malefactors, NIG
23:33 t they crucified him, and the malefactors, 1563
23:44 t was a darkness over all the earth until NIG
23:50 And behold, *t was* a man named Joseph, NIG
24:18 which are come to pass t in these days? 846
Jn 1: 6 T was a man sent from God, whose name NIG
1:26 but t standeth one among you, whom ye NIG
1:46 Can t any good *thing* come out of Nazareth? NIG
2: 1 And the third day t was a marriage in Cana NIG
2: 1 of Galilee; and the mother of Jesus was t: 1563
2: 6 And t were set there six waterpots of stone, NIG
2: 6 And there were set t six waterpots of stone, 1563
2:12 and they continued t not many days. 1563
3: 1 T was a man of the Pharisees, NIG
3:22 and t he tarried with them, and baptized. 1563
3:23 to Salim, because t was much water there: NIG
3:23 to Salim, because there was much water t: 1563
3:25 Then t arose a question between *some* of NIG
4: 6 Now Jacob's well was t. Jesus therefore, 1563
4: 7 T cometh a woman of Samaria to draw NIG
4:35 T are yet four months, and *then* cometh NIG
4:40 tarry with them: and he abode t two days. 1563
4:46 And t was a certain nobleman, whose son NIG
5: 1 After this t was a feast of the Jews; and NIG
5: 2 Now t is at Jerusalem by the sheep *market* a NIG
5: 5 And a certain man was t, which had an 1563
5:32 T is another that beareth witness of me; and NIG
5:45 t is *one* that accuseth you, *even* Moses, NIG

Jn 6: 3 a mountain, and t he sat with his disciples. 1563
6: 9 T is a lad here, which hath five barley NIG
6:10 Now t was much grass in the place. So NIG
6:22 the sea saw that t was none other boat there, NIG
6:22 sea saw that there was none other boat t, 1563
6:23 (Howbeit t came other boats from Tiberias NIG
6:24 therefore saw that Jesus was not t, 1563
6:64 But t are some of you that believe not. NIG
7: 4 For *t is* no *man that* doeth any *thing* in NIG
7:12 And t was much murmuring among NIG
7:43 So t was a division among the people NIG
8:44 not in the truth, because t is no truth in him. NIG
8:50 own glory: t is *one* that seeketh and judgeth. NIG
9:16 And t was a division among them. NIG
10:16 and t shall be one fold, *and* one shepherd. NIG
10:19 T was a division therefore again among NIG
10:40 John at first baptized; and t he abode. 1563
10:42 And many believed on him t. 1563
11: 9 Are t not twelve hours in the day? NIG
11:10 he stumbleth, because t is no light in him. NIG
11:15 I am glad for your sakes that I was not t, 1563
11:31 saying, She goeth unto the grave to weep t. 1563
11:54 and t continued with his disciples. 2546
12: 2 T they made him a supper; and Martha 1563
12: 9 of the Jews therefore knew that he was t: 1563
12:20 And t were certain Greeks among them that NIG
12:26 and where I am, t shall also my servant be: 1563
12:28 Then came t a voice from heaven, *saying,* I NIG
13:23 Now t was leaning on Jesus' bosom one of NIG
14: 3 that where I am, *t* ye may be also. NIG
18:18 officers stood *t,* who had made a fire of NIG
19:25 Now t stood by the cross of Jesus his NIG
19:29 Now t was set a vessel full of vinegar: and NIG
19:34 and forthwith came t out blood and water. NIG
19:39 And t came also Nicodemus, which at NIG
19:41 Now in the place where he was crucified t NIG
19:42 T laid they Jesus therefore because of 1563
21: 2 T were together Simon Peter, and NIG
21: 9 they saw a fire of coals t, and fish laid 2749
21:11 and for all t were so many, *yet* was not NIG
21:25 And t are also many other *things* which NIG
Ac 2: 2 And suddenly t came a sound from heaven NIG
2: 3 And t appeared unto them cloven tongues NIG
2: 5 And t were dwelling at Jerusalem Jews, NIG
2:41 the same day t were added *unto them* about NIG
4:12 Neither is t salvation in any other: for there NIG
4:12 for t is none other name under heaven given NIG
4:34 Neither was t any among them that lacked: NIG
5:16 T came also a multitude *out* of the cities NIG
5:34 Then stood t up one in the council, NIG
6: 1 t arose a murmuring of the Grecians against NIG
6: 9 Then t arose certain of the synagogue, NIG
7:11 Now t came a dearth over all the land of NIG
7:12 But when Jacob heard that t was corn in NIG
7:30 t appeared to him in the wilderness of NIG
8: 1 And at that time t was a great persecution NIG
8: 8 And t was great joy in that city. NIG
8: 9 But t was a certain man, called Simon, NIG
9: 3 suddenly t shined round about him a light NIG
9:10 And t was a certain disciple at Damascus, NIG
9:18 And immediately t fell from his eyes as it NIG
9:33 And t he found a certain man named 1563
9:36 Now t was at Joppa a certain disciple NIG
9:38 disciples had heard that Peter was t, 846+1722
10: 1 T was a certain man in Cesarea called NIG
10:13 And t came a voice to him, Rise, Peter; kill, NIG
10:18 which was surnamed Peter, were lodged t. 1759
11:11 immediately t were three men already come NIG
11:28 And t stood up one of them named Agabus, NIG
11:28 signified by the Spirit that t should be great NIG
12:18 t was no small stir among the soldiers, NIG
12:19 down from Judea to Cesarea, and *t* abode. NIG
13: 1 Now t were in the church that was at NIG
13:11 And immediately t fell on him a mist and NIG
13:25 not *he.* But behold, t cometh *one* after me, NIG
14: 5 And when t was an assault made both of NIG
14: 7 And t they preached the gospel. 2546
14: 8 And t sat a certain man at Lystra, NIG
14:19 And t came thither *certain* Jews from NIG
14:28 And t they abode long time with 1563
15: 5 But t rose up certain of the sect of NIG
15: 7 And when t had been much disputing, Peter NIG
15:33 And after they had tarried *t* a space, NIG
15:34 Notwithstanding it pleased Silas to abide t 846
16: 1 and behold, a certain disciple was t, 1563
16: 9 T stood a man of Macedonia, and NIG
16:15 and abide t. And she constrained us. NIG
16:26 And suddenly t was a great earthquake, so NIG
17: 7 saying that t is another king, *one* Jesus. NIG
17:14 but Silas and Timotheus abode t still. 1563
17:21 strangers which were t spent their time in 1927
18:11 And he continued *t* a year and six months, NIG
18:18 And Paul *after this* tarried *t* yet a good NIG
18:19 And he came to Ephesus, and left them t: but 846
18:23 And after he had spent some time t, he NIG
19: 2 much as heard whether t be *any* Holy NIG
19:14 And t were seven sons of *one* Sceva, a Jew, NIG
19:21 to Jerusalem, saying, After I have been t, 1563
19:23 And the same time t arose no small stir NIG
19:35 what man is t that knoweth not how that NIG
19:38 any *man,* the law is open, and t are deputies: NIG
19:40 t being no cause whereby we may give an NIG
20: 3 And *t* abode three months: and when NIG
20: 4 And t accompanied him into Asia Sopater NIG
20: 8 And t were many lights in the upper NIG
20: 9 And t sat in a window a certain young man NIG
20:13 unto Assos, t intending to take in Paul: 1564
20:22 the *things* that shall befall me t: 846+1722
21: 3 for t the ship was to unlade *her* burden. 1566
21: 4 finding disciples, we tarried t seven days: 846
21:10 And as we tarried *t* many days, there came NIG
21:10 t came down from Judea a certain prophet, NIG
21:16 T went with us also *certain* of the disciples NIG
21:20 how many thousands of Jews t are which NIG
21:40 And when t was made a great silence, NIG

Ac 22: 5 to Damascus, to bring them which were t, 1566
22: 6 suddenly t shone from heaven a great light NIG
22:10 and t it shall be told thee of all *things* 2546
22:12 a good report of all the Jews which dwelt *t,* NIG
23: 7 t arose a dissension between the Pharisees NIG
23: 8 For the Sadducees say that t is no NIG
23: 9 And t arose a great cry: and the scribes *that* NIG
23:10 And when t arose a great dissension, NIG
23:21 for t lie in wait for him of them moe *than* NIG
24:11 that t are *yet* but twelve days since I went NIG
24:15 that t shall be a resurrection of the dead, NIG
25: 5 this man, if t be any *wickedness* in him. NIG
25: 9 and t be judged of these *things* before me? 1563
25:11 if t be none *of these things* whereof these NIG
25:14 And when they had been t many days, 1563
25:14 T is a certain man left in bonds by Felix: NIG
25:20 and t be judged of these *matters.* 2546
27: 6 And t the centurion found a ship of 2546
27:12 might attain to Phenice, *and t* to winter; NIG
27:14 But not long after t arose against it a NIG
27:22 for t shall be no loss of *any man's* life NIG
27:23 For t stood by me this night *the* angel of NIG
27:34 for t shall not a hair fall from the head of NIG
28: 3 t came a viper out of the heat, and NIG
28:12 landing at Syracuse, we tarried *t* three days. NIG
28:18 because t was no cause of death in me. NIG
28:23 a day, t came many to him into *his* lodging; NIG
Ro 2:11 For t is no respect of persons with God. NIG
3: 1 the Jew? or what profit *is t* of circumcision? NIG
3:10 is written, T is none righteous, no, not one: NIG
3:11 T is none that understandeth, there is none NIG
3:11 t is none that seeketh after God. NIG
3:12 t is none that doeth good, no, not one. NIG
3:18 T is no fear of God before their eyes. NIG
3:20 Therefore by the deeds of the law t shall no NIG
3:22 all them that believe: for t is no difference: NIG
4:15 for where no law is, *t is* no transgression. NIG
5:13 but sin is not imputed when t is no law. NIG
8: 1 *T is* therefore now no condemnation to NIG
9:14 *Is t* unrighteousness with God? God forbid. NIG
9:26 t shall they be called the children of 1563
10:12 For t is no difference between the Jew and NIG
11: 5 at *this* present time also t is a remnant NIG
11:26 T shall come out of Sion the Deliverer, and NIG
13: 1 For t is no power but of God: the powers NIG
13: 9 and if *t be* any other commandment, it is NIG
14:14 that *t is* nothing unclean of itself: NIG
15:12 T shall be a root of Jesse, and he that *shall* NIG
1Co 1:10 and *that* t be no divisions among you; NIG
1:11 of Chloe, that t are contentions among you. NIG
3: 3 for whereas *t is* among you envying, and NIG
5: 1 It is reported commonly *that t is* fornication NIG
6: 5 it so, that t is not a wise *man* amongst you? NIG
6: 7 therefore t is utterly a fault among you, NIG
7:34 T is difference *also* between a wife and a NIG
8: 4 and that *t is* none other God but one. NIG
8: 5 For though t be that are called gods, NIG
8: 5 (as t be gods many, and lords many,) NIG
8: 6 But to us *t is but* one God, the Father, NIG
8: 7 Howbeit *t is* not in every *man that* NIG
10:13 T hath no temptation taken you but such as NIG
11:18 I hear that t be divisions among you; NIG
11:19 For t must be also heresies among you, NIG
12: 4 Now t are diversities of gifts, but the same NIG
12: 5 And t are differences of administrations, but NIG
12: 6 And t are diversities of operations, but it is NIG
12:25 That t should be no schism in the body; but NIG
13: 8 but whether *t be* prophecies, they shall fail; NIG
13: 8 whether *t be* tongues, they shall cease; NIG
13: 8 whether *t be* knowledge, it shall vanish NIG
14:10 T are, it may be, NIG
14:23 and t come in *those that are* unlearned, or NIG
14:24 and t come in one that believeth not, or NIG
14:28 But if t be no interpreter, let him keep NIG
15:12 how say some among you that t is no NIG
15:13 But if t be no resurrection of the dead, then NIG
15:39 but *t is* one *kind of* flesh of men, NIG
15:40 *T are* also celestial bodies, and NIG
15:41 *T is* one glory of the sun, and another glory NIG
15:44 T is a natural body, and there is a spiritual NIG
15:44 is a natural body, and t is a spiritual body. NIG
16: 2 that t be no gatherings when I come. NIG
16: 9 unto me, and *t are* many adversaries. NIG
2Co 1:17 that with me t should be yea yea, and nay NIG
3:17 where the Spirit of the Lord *is,* t *is* liberty. 1563
8:11 perform the doing *of it;* that as *t was* a NIG
8:11 *t may be* a performance also out of that NIG
8:12 For if t be first a willing mind, *it is* accepted NIG
8:14 for your want: that t may be equality: NIG
12: 7 t was given to me a thorn in the flesh, NIG
12:20 lest *t be* debates, envyings, wraths, strifes, NIG
Gal 1: 7 but t be some that trouble you, and NIG
3:21 for if t had been a law given which could NIG
3:28 T is neither Jew nor Greek, there is neither NIG
3:28 Jew nor Greek, t is neither bond nor free, NIG
3:28 bond nor free, t is neither male nor female: NIG
5:23 against such t is no law. NIG
Eph 4: 4 *T is* one body, and one Spirit, even as ye are NIG
6: 9 neither is t respect of persons with him. NIG
Php 2: 1 If *t be* therefore any consolation in Christ, NIG
4: 8 if *t be* any virtue, and if *there be* any praise, NIG
4: 8 if *there be* any virtue, and if *t be* any praise, NIG
Col 3:11 Where t is neither Greek nor Jew, NIG
3:25 he hath done: and t is no respect of persons. NIG
2Th 2: 3 for *that day shall not come,* except t come a NIG
3:11 For we hear that *t are* some which walk NIG
1Ti 1:10 if *t be* any other *thing that* is contrary to NIG
2: 5 For *t is* one God, and one mediator between NIG
2Ti 2:20 But in a great house t are not only vessels of NIG
4: 8 Henceforth t is laid up for me a crown of NIG
Tit 1:10 For t are many unruly and vain talkers and NIG
3:12 for I have determined t to winter. 1563
Phm 1:23 T salute thee Epaphras, my fellowprisoner NIG
Heb 3:12 lest t be in any of you an evil heart of NIG
4: 9 T remaineth therefore a rest to the people of NIG

T

Heb 4:13 Neither is **t** any creature *that is* not manifest NIG
7: 8 **t** he *receiveth them,* of whom it is *1563*
7:11 what further need *was* **t** that another priest NIG
7:12 **t** is made of necessity a change also of NIG
7:15 for that after the similitude of Melchisedec **t** NIG
7:18 For **t** is verily a disannulling of NIG
8: 4 seeing that **t** are priests that offer gifts NIG
9: 2 For **t** was a tabernacle made; the first, NIG
9:16 For where a testament *is,* **t** must also of NIG
10: 3 But in those *sacrifices* **t** *is* a remembrance NIG
10:18 Now where remission of these *is,* **t** *is* no NIG
10:26 **t** remaineth no more sacrifice for sins, NIG
11:12 Therefore sprang **t** even of one, and him as NIG
12:16 Lest **t** *be* any fornicator, or profane *person,* NIG
Jas 2: 2 For if **t** come unto your assembly a man NIG
2: 2 **t** come in also a poor *man* in vile raiment; NIG
2: 3 Stand thou **t**, or sit here under my footstool: *1563*
2:19 Thou believest that **t** is one God; thou doest NIG
3:16 and strife *is,* **t** *is* confusion and every evil *1563*
4:12 **T** is one lawgiver, who is able to save and NIG
4:13 and continue **t** a year, and buy and sell, and *1563*
2Pe 1:17 when **t** came such a voice to him from NIG
2: 1 But **t** were false prophets also among NIG
2: 1 even as **t** shall be false teachers among you, NIG
3: 3 that **t** shall come in the last days scoffers, NIG
1Jn 2:10 and **t** is none occasion of stumbling in him. NIG
2:18 even now are **t** many antichrists; *1096*
4:18 **T** is no fear in love; but perfect love casteth NIG
5: 7 For **t** are three that bear record in heaven, NIG
5: 8 And **t** are three that bear witness in earth, NIG
5:16 **T** is a sin unto death: I do not say that he NIG
5:17 is sin: and **t** is a sin not unto death. NIG
2Jn 1:10 If **t** come any unto you, and bring not this NIG
Jude 1: 4 For **t** are certain men crept in unawares, NIG
1:18 How that they told you **t** should be mockers NIG
Rev 2:14 thou hast **t** them that hold the doctrine of *1563*
4: 3 and *t was* a rainbow round about the throne, NIG
4: 5 *t were* seven lamps of fire burning before NIG
4: 6 And before the throne *t was* a sea of glass NIG
6: 4 And **t** went out another horse *that was* red: NIG
6: 4 and **t** was given unto him a great sword. NIG
6:12 sixth seal, and lo, **t** was a great earthquake; NIG
7: 4 *and t were* sealed an hundred *and* forty *and* NIG
8: 1 **t** was silence in heaven about the space of NIG
8: 3 and **t** was given unto him much incense, NIG
8: 5 and **t** were voices, and thunderings, and NIG
8: 7 and **t** followed hail and fire mingled with NIG
8:10 and **t** fell a great star from heaven, NIG
9: 2 and **t** arose a smoke out of the pit, as NIG
9: 3 And **t** came out of the smoke locusts upon NIG
9:10 and **t** were stings in their tails: NIG
9:12 behold, **t** come two woes more hereafter. NIG
10: 6 are therein, that **t** should be time no longer: NIG
11: 1 And **t** was given me a reed like unto a rod: NIG
11:13 And the same hour was **t** a great earthquake, NIG
11:15 and **t** were great voices in heaven, saying, NIG
11:19 **t** was seen in his temple the ark of his NIG
11:19 and **t** were lightnings, and voices, and NIG
12: 1 And **t** appeared a great wonder in heaven; NIG
12: 3 And **t** appeared another wonder in heaven; NIG
12: 6 that they should feed her **t** a thousand two *1563*
12: 7 And **t** was war in heaven: Michael and NIG
13: 5 And **t** was given unto him a mouth speaking NIG
14: 8 And **t** followed another angel, saying, NIG
16: 2 and **t** fell a noisome and grievous sore upon NIG
16:17 **t** came a great voice out of the temple of NIG
16:18 And **t** were voices, and thunders, and NIG
16:18 and **t** was a great earthquake, such as was NIG
16:21 And **t** fell upon men a great hail out of NIG
17: 1 And **t** came one of the seven angels which NIG
17:10 And **t** are seven kings: five are fallen, and NIG
20:11 and **t** was found no place for them. NIG
21: 1 were passed away; and **t** was no more sea. NIG
21: 4 and **t** shall be no more death, NIG
21: 4 nor crying, neither shall **t** be any more pain: NIG
21: 9 And **t** came unto me one of the seven angels NIG
21:25 at all by day: for **t** shall be no night there. NIG
21:25 at all by day: for there shall be no night **t**. *1563*
21:27 And **t** shall in no wise enter into it any *thing* NIG
22: 2 either side of the river, *was t* the tree of life, NIG
22: 3 And **t** shall be no more curse: but the throne NIG
22: 5 And **t** shall be no night there; and they need NIG
22: 5 And there shall be no night **t**; and they need *1563*

THEREABOUT (1) [ABOUT]

Lk 24: 4 they were *much* perplexed **t**, behold, *3778+4012*

THEREAT (3) [AT]

Ex 30:19 wash their hands and their feet **t**: 4480+5105.2
40:31 washed their hands and their feet **t**: 4480+5105.2
Mt 7:13 and many there be which go in **t**: *846+1223*

THEREBY (21) [BY]

Ge 24:14 **t** shall I know that thou hast 871.1+1886.3
Lev 11:43 that ye should be defiled **t**. 871.1+3963.1
Job 22:21 **t** good shall come *unto* thee. 871.1+1992.1
Pr 20: 1 is deceived **t** is not wise. 871.1+2050.2
Ecc 10: 9 wood shall be endangered **t**. 871.1+3963.1
Isa 33:21 with oars, neither shall gallant ship pass **t**. 5105.2
Jer 18:16 every one that passeth **t** shall be 5921+1886.3
19: 8 every one that passeth **t** shall be astonished 5921
51:43 neither doth *any* son of man pass **t**. 871.1+2006.1
Eze 12: 5 wall in their sight, and carry out **t**. 871.1+2050.2
12:12 dig through the wall to carry out **t**: 871.1+2050.2
33:12 he shall not fall **t** in the day that he 871.1+1886.3
33:18 he shall even die **t**. 871.1+1992.1
33:19 is lawful and right, he shall live **t**. 5921+1992.1
Zec 9: 2 Hamath also shall border **t**; Tyrus, 871.1+1886.3
Jn 11: 4 the Son of God might be glorified **t**. *846+1223*
Eph 2:16 by the cross, having slain the enmity **t**: *846+1722*
Heb 12:11 unto them which are exercised **t**. *846+1223*
12:15 up trouble *you,* and **t** many be defiled; *1223*
13: 2 for **t** some have entertained angels *1223*
1Pe 2: 2 milk of the word, that ye may grow **t**: *1722*

THEREFORE (1237)

Ge 2:24 **T** shall a man leave his father and his 3651+5921
3:23 **T** the LORD God sent him forth from 2050.1
4:15 the LORD said unto him, **T** 3651+3807.1
11: 9 **T** is the name of it called Babel; 3651+5921
12:12 **T** it shall come to pass, when 2050.1
12:19 now **t** behold thy wife, take *her,* and 2050.1
17: 9 Thou shalt keep my covenant **t**, thou, and 2050.1
18: 5 for **t** are you come to your servant. 3651+5921
18:12 **T** Sarah laughed within herself, saying, 2050.1
19: 8 for **t** came they under the shadow of 3651+5921
19:22 **T** the name of the city was called 3651+5921
20: 6 thee from sinning against me: **t** 3651+5921
20: 7 Now **t** restore the man *his* wife; for he *is* 2050.1
20: 8 **T** Abimelech rose early in the morning, 2050.1
21:23 Now **t** swear unto me here by God that 2050.1
23:15 betwixt me and thee? bury **t** thy dead. 2050.1
24:65 **t** she took a vail, and covered herself. 2050.1
25:30 same red *pottage;* for I *am* faint: **t** 3651+5921
26:33 he called it Shebah: **t** the name of 3651+5921
27: 3 Now **t** take, I pray thee, thy weapons, 2050.1
27: 8 Now **t**, my son, obey my voice according 2050.1
27:28 **T** God give thee of the dew of heaven, 2050.1
27:43 Now **t**, my son, obey my voice; and arise, 2050.1
29:15 shouldest thou **t** serve me for nought? 2050.1
29:32 now **t** my husband will love me. 3588
29:33 he hath **t** given me this *son* also: 2050.1
29:34 because I have born him three sons: **t** 3651+5921
29:35 Now will I praise the LORD: **t** 3651+5921
30: 6 me a son: **t** called she his name Dan. 3651+5921
30:15 Rachel said, **T** he shall lie with 3651+3807.1
31:44 Now **t** come thou, let us make a covenant, I 6258
31:48 thee *this* day. **T** was the name of it 3651+5921
32:32 **T** the children of Israel eat not *of* 3651+5921
33:10 for **t** I have seen thy face, as though I 3651+5921
33:17 made booths for his cattle: **t** 3651+5921
34:21 **t** let them dwell in the land, and 2050.1
37:20 Come now **t**, and let us slay him, and 2050.1
38:29 upon thee: **t** his name was called Pharez. 2050.1
41:33 Now **t** let Pharaoh look out a man 2050.1
42:21 we would not hear; **t** is this distress 3651+5921
42:22 **t**, behold, also his blood is required. 2050.1
44:30 Now **t** when I come to thy servant my 3509.1
44:33 Now **t**, I pray thee, let thy servant abide 2050.1
45: 5 Now **t** be not grieved, nor angry with 2050.1
47: 4 now **t**, we pray thee, let thy servants 2050.1
50: 5 Now **t** let me go up, I pray thee, and 2050.1
50:21 Now **t** fear ye not: I will nourish you and 2050.1
Ex 1:11 **T** they did set over them taskmasters to 2050.1
1:20 **T** God dealt well with the midwives: and 2050.1
3: 9 Now **t**, behold, the cry of the children of 2050.1
3:10 Come now **t**, and I will send thee unto 2050.1
4:12 Now **t** go, and I will be with thy mouth, 2050.1
5: 8 for they *be* idle; **t** they cry, saying, 3651+5921
5:17 *ye are* idle: **t** ye say, Let us go *and* 3651+5921
5:18 Go **t** now, *and* work; for there shall no 2050.1
9:19 Send **t** now, *and* gather thy cattle, and all 2050.1
10:17 Now **t** forgive, I pray thee, my sin only 2050.1
12:17 **t** shall ye observe this day in your 2050.1
13:10 Thou shalt **t** keep this ordinance in his 2050.1
13:15 the firstborn of beast: **t** I sacrifice to 3651+5921
15:23 for they *were* bitter: **t** the name of it 3651+5921
16:29 hath given you the sabbath, **t** 3651+5921
19: 5 Now **t**, if ye will obey my voice indeed, 2050.1
31:14 Ye shall keep the sabbath **t**; for it *is* holy 2050.1
32:10 Now **t** let me alone, that my wrath may 2050.1
32:34 **T** now go, lead the people unto *the place* 2050.1
33: 5 **t** now put off thy ornaments from thee, 2050.1
33:13 Now **t**, I pray thee, if I have found grace 2050.1
Lev 8:35 **T** shall ye abide *at* the door of 2050.1
9: 8 Aaron **t** went unto the altar, and slew 2050.1
11:44 ye shall **t** sanctify yourselves, and 2050.1
11:45 ye shall **t** be holy, for I *am* holy. 2050.1
13:52 He shall **t** burn *that* garment, 2050.1
16: 4 **t** shall he wash his flesh in water, and *so* 2050.1
17:12 **T** I said unto the children of Israel, 3651+5921
17:14 **t** I said unto the children of Israel, 2050.1
18: 5 Ye shall **t** keep my statutes, and my 2050.1
18:25 **t** I do visit the iniquity thereof upon it, 2050.1
18:26 Ye shall **t** keep my statutes and my 2050.1
18:30 **T** ye shall keep mine ordinance, that *ye* 2050.1
19: 8 **T** *every one* that eateth it shall bear his 2050.1
19:37 **T** shall ye observe all my statutes, and all 2050.1
20: 7 Sanctify yourselves **t**, and be ye holy: 2050.1
20:22 Ye shall **t** keep all my statutes, and all my 2050.1
20:23 all these *things,* **and t** I abhorred them. 2050.1
20:25 Ye shall **t** put difference between clean 2050.1
21: 6 they do offer: **t** they shall be holy. 2050.1
21: 8 Thou shalt sanctify him **t**; for he offereth 2050.1
22: 9 They shall **t** keep mine ordinance, 2050.1
22: 9 for it, and die **t**, if they profane it: 871.1+2050.2
22:31 **T** shall ye keep my commandments, and 2050.1
25:17 Ye shall not **t** oppress one another; 2050.1
Nu 3:12 of Israel: **t** the Levites shall be mine; 2050.1
11:18 **t** the LORD will give you flesh, and 2050.1
14:16 **t** he hath slain them in the wilderness. 2050.1
14:43 **t** the LORD will not be with you. 2050.1
16:38 before the LORD, **t** they are hallowed: 2050.1
18: 7 **T** thou and thy sons with thee shall keep 2050.1
18:24 have given to the Levites to inherit: **t** 3651+5921
18:30 **T** thou shalt say unto them, When ye 2050.1
20:12 **t** ye shall not bring this congregation into 3651
21: 7 **T** the people came to Moses, and said, 2050.1
22: 5 He sent messengers **t** unto Balaam 2050.1
22: 6 Come now **t**, I pray thee, curse me this 2050.1
22:17 come **t**, I pray thee, curse me this people. 2050.1
22:19 Now **t**, I pray you, tarry ye also here *this* 2050.1
22:34 now **t**, if it displease thee, I will get me 2050.1
24:11 **T** now flee thou to thy place: I thought to 2050.1
24:14 come *t, and* I will advertise thee what this NIH
27: 4 Give unto us *t* a possession among NIH
31:17 Now **t** kill every male among the little 2050.1
31:50 We have **t** brought an oblation for 2050.1
35:34 Defile not **t** the land which ye shall 2050.1
Dt 2: 4 take ye good heed unto yourselves **t**: 2050.1
4: 1 Now **t** hearken, O Israel, unto the statutes 2050.1
4: 6 Keep **t** and do *them;* for this *is* your 2050.1
4:15 Take ye **t** good heed unto yourselves; for 2050.1
4:37 **t** he chose their seed after them, and 2050.1
4:39 Know **t** *this* day, and consider *it* in thine 2050.1
4:40 Thou shalt keep **t** his statutes, and his 2050.1
5:15 by a stretched out arm: **t** the LORD 3651+5921
5:25 Now **t** why should we die? for this great 2050.1
5:32 Ye shall observe to do **t** as the LORD 2050.1
6: 3 Hear **t**, O Israel, and observe to do *it;* that 2050.1
7: 9 Know **t** that the LORD thy God, he *is* 2050.1
7:11 Thou shalt **t** keep the commandments, 2050.1
8: 6 **T** thou shalt keep the commandments of 2050.1
9: 3 Understand **t** *this* day, that the LORD 2050.1
9: 6 Understand **t**, that the LORD thy God 2050.1
9:26 I prayed **t** unto the LORD, and said, 2050.1
10:16 Circumcise **t** the foreskin of your heart, 2050.1
10:19 Love ye **t** the stranger: for ye were 2050.1
11: 1 **T** thou shalt love the LORD thy God, 2050.1
11: 8 **T** shall ye keep all the commandments 2050.1
11:18 **T** shall ye lay up these my words in your 2050.1
14: 7 not the hoof; *t* they *are* unclean unto you. NIH
15:11 shall never cease out of the land: **t** 3651+5921
15:15 LORD thy God redeemed thee: **t** 3651+5921
16: 2 Thou shalt **t** sacrifice the passover unto 2050.1
16:15 of thine hands, **t** thou shalt surely rejoice. 2050.1
18: 2 **T** shall they have no inheritance among 2050.1
23:14 before thee; **t** shall thy camp be holy: 2050.1
24:18 thy God redeemed thee thence: **t** 3651+5921
24:22 a bondman in the land of Egypt: **t** 3651+5921
25:19 **T** it shall be, when the LORD thy God 2050.1
26:16 thou shalt **t** keep and do them with all 2050.1
27: 4 **T** it shall be when ye be gone over 2050.1
27:10 Thou shalt **t** obey the voice of 2050.1
28:48 **T** shalt thou serve thine enemies which 2050.1
29: 9 Keep **t** the words of this covenant, and 2050.1
30:19 **t** choose life, that *both* thou and thy seed 2050.1
31:19 Now **t** write ye this song for you, 2050.1
31:22 Moses **t** wrote this song the same day, 2050.1
Jos 1: 2 now **t** arise, go over this Jordan, thou, and 2050.1
2:12 Now **t**, I pray you, swear unto me by 2050.1
3:12 Now **t** take ye twelve men out of 2050.1
4:17 Joshua **t** commanded the priests, saying, 2050.1
7:12 **T** the children of Israel could not stand 2050.1
7:14 In the morning **t** ye shall be brought 2050.1
8: 6 as at the first: **t** we will flee before them. 2050.1
8: 9 Joshua **t** sent them forth: and they went to 2050.1
9: 6 now **t** make ye a league with us. 6258
9:11 **t** now make ye a league with us. 6258
9:19 of Israel: now **t** we may not touch them. 6258
9:23 Now **t** ye *are* cursed, and there shall none 6258
9:24 **t** we were sore afraid of our lives because 2050.1
10: 5 **T** the five kings of the Amorites, the king 2050.1
10: 9 Joshua **t** came unto them suddenly, *and* 2050.1
13: 7 Now **t** divide this land for an inheritance 6258
14: 4 **t** they gave no part unto the Levites in 2050.1
14:12 Now **t** give me this mountain, 2050.1
14:14 Hebron **t** became the inheritance of 3651+5921
17: 1 man of war, **t** he had Gilead and Bashan. 2050.1
17: 4 **T** according to the commandment of 2050.1
18: 6 Ye shall **t** describe the land *into* seven 2050.1
19: 9 **t** the children of Simeon had their 2050.1
19:47 **t** the children of Dan went up to fight 2050.1
22: 4 **t** now return ye, and get ye unto your 2050.1
22:26 **T** we said, Let us now prepare to build us 2050.1
22:28 **T** said we, that it shall be, when they 2050.1
23: 6 Be ye **t** very courageous to keep and 2050.1
23:11 Take good heed **t** unto yourselves, that ye 2050.1
23:15 **T** it shall come to pass, *that* as all good 2050.1
24:10 unto Balaam; **t** he blessed you still: 2050.1
24:14 Now **t** fear the LORD, and serve him in 2050.1
24:18 *t* will we also serve the LORD; for he *is* NIH
24:23 Now **t** put away, *said he,* the strange gods 2050.1
24:27 it shall be **t** a witness unto you, lest ye 2050.1
Jdg 2:23 **T** the LORD left those nations, without 2050.1
3: 8 **T** the anger of the LORD was hot 2050.1
3:25 **t** they took a key, and opened *them:* and 2050.1
6:32 **T** on that day he called him Jerubbaal, 2050.1
7: 3 Now **t** go to, proclaim in the ears of 2050.1
8: 7 **T** when the LORD hath delivered 3651+3807.1
9:16 Now **t**, if ye have done truly and 2050.1
9:32 Now **t** up by night, thou and the people 2050.1
11: 8 **T** we turn again to thee now, 3651+3807.1
11:13 **t** restore those *lands* again peaceably. 2050.1
11:26 why **t** did ye not recover *them* within that 2050.1
13: 4 Now **t** beware, I pray thee, and drink not 2050.1
14: 2 now **t** get her for me to wife. 2050.1
15: 2 hated her; **t** I gave her to thy companion: 2050.1
16:12 Delilah **t** took new ropes, and bound him 2050.1
17: 3 now **t** I will restore it unto thee. 2050.1
18:14 now **t** consider what ye have to do. 2050.1
19: 7 in law urged him: **t** he lodged there again. 2050.1
20:13 Now **t** deliver *us* the men, the children of 2050.1
20:42 **T** they turned *their backs* before the men 2050.1
21:20 **T** they commanded the children of 2050.1
Ru 3: 3 Wash *thyself* **t**, and anoint thee, and 2050.1
3: 9 spread **t** thy skirt over thine handmaid; 2050.1
4: 8 **T** the kinsman said unto Boaz, Buy *it* for 2050.1
1Sa 1: 7 provoked her; **t** she wept, and did not eat. 2050.1
1:13 **t** Eli thought she had been drunken. 2050.1
1:28 **T** also I have lent him to the LORD; 2050.1
3: 9 **T** Eli said unto Samuel, Go, lie down: 2050.1
3:14 **t** I have sworn unto the house of 3651+3807.1
5: 5 **T** neither the priests of Dagon, 3651+5921
5: 8 They sent **t** and gathered all the lords of 2050.1
5:10 **T** they sent the ark of God *to* Ekron. 2050.1
6: 7 Now **t** make a new cart, and take two 2050.1
8: 9 Now **t** hearken unto their voice: 2050.1
9:13 Now **t** get you up; for about *this* time ye 2050.1
10:12 who *is* their father? **T** it became a 3651+5921
10:19 Now **t** present yourselves before 2050.1
10:22 **T** they inquired of the LORD further, 2050.1
11:10 **T** the men of Jabesh said, To morrow we 2050.1
12: 7 Now **t** stand still, that I may reason with 2050.1

T

1Sa 12:13 Now t behold the king whom ye have 2050.1
12:16 Now t stand and see this great thing, which 1571
13:12 T said I, The Philistines will come down 2050.1
13:12 I forced myself t, and offered a burnt 2050.1
14:41 T Saul said unto the LORD God of 2050.1
15: 1 now t hearken thou unto the voice of 2050.1
15:25 Now t, I pray thee, pardon my sin, and 2050.1
17:51 T David ran, and stood upon 2050.1
18:13 T Saul removed him from him, and 2050.1
18:22 love thee: now t be the king's son in law. 2050.1
19: 2 now t, I pray thee, take heed to thyself 2050.1
20: 8 T thou shalt deal kindly with thy servant; 2050.1
20:29 see my brethren. T he cometh not 3651+5921
21: 3 Now t what is under thine hand? give *me* 2050.1
22: 1 David t departed thence, and escaped to 2050.1
23: 2 T David inquired of the LORD, saying, 2050.1
23:20 Now t, O king, come down according to 2050.1
23:23 See t, and take knowledge of all 2050.1
23:28 went against the Philistines: t 3651+5921
24:15 The LORD t be judge, and 2050.1
24:21 Swear now t unto me by the LORD, 2050.1
25:17 Now t know and consider what thou wilt 2050.1
25:26 Now t, my lord, *as* the LORD liveth, 2050.1
26: 4 David t sent out spies, and 2050.1
26: 8 now t let me smite him, I pray thee, 2050.1
26:19 Now t, I pray thee, let my lord the king 2050.1
26:20 Now t, let not my blood fall to the earth 2050.1
27:12 t he shall be my servant for ever. 2050.1
28: 2 Achish said to David, T will I 3651+3807.1
28:15 t I have called thee, that *thou* mayest 2050.1
28:18 t hath the LORD done this thing 3651+5921
28:22 Now t, I pray thee, hearken thou also 2050.1
31: 4 t Saul took a sword, and fell upon it. 2050.1
2Sa 2: 7 T now let your hands be strengthened, 2050.1
4:11 shall I not t now require his blood of your 2050.1
5:20 as the breach of waters. T he called 3651+5921
6:21 t will I play before the LORD. 2050.1
6:23 T Michal the daughter of Saul had no 2050.1
7: 8 Now t so shalt thou say unto my servant 2050.1
7:27 I will build thee a house: t hath thy 3651+5921
7:29 T now let it please thee to bless the house 2050.1
9:10 Thou t, and thy sons, and thy servants, 2050.1
12:10 Now t the sword shall never depart from 2050.1
12:16 David t besought God for the child; and 2050.1
12:19 t David said unto his servants, Is the child 2050.1
12:28 Now t gather the rest of the people 2050.1
13:13 Now t, I pray thee, speak unto the king; 2050.1
13:33 Now t let not my lord the king take 2050.1
14:15 Now t that I am come to speak of this 2050.1
14:17 t the LORD thy God will be with thee. 2050.1
14:21 t, bring the young man Absalom again. 2050.1
14:26 *the hair* was heavy on him, t he polled it:) 2050.1
14:29 T Absalom sent for Joab, to have sent 2050.1
14:30 T he said unto his servants, See, 2050.1
14:32 now t let me see the king's face; and 2050.1
15:29 Zadok t and Abiathar carried the ark of 2050.1
15:35 t it shall be, *that* what thing soever thou 2050.1
17:11 T I counsel *that* all Israel be generally 3588
17:16 Now t send quickly, and tell David, 2050.1
18: 3 t now *it is* better that thou succour us out 2050.1
19: 7 Now t arise, go forth, and 2050.1
19:10 Now t why speak ye not a word of 2050.1
19:20 t, behold, I am come the first *this* day of 2050.1
19:23 T the king said unto Shimei, Thou shalt 2050.1
19:27 of God: do t what *is* good in thine eyes. 2050.1
19:28 What right t have I yet to cry any more 2050.1
22:25 T the LORD hath recompensed me 2050.1
22:50 T I will give thanks unto thee, 3651+5921
23:17 t he would not drink it. These *things* did 2050.1
23:19 t he was their captain: howbeit he 2050.1
1Ki 1:12 Now t come, let me, I pray thee, give thee 2050.1
2: 2 be thou strong t, and shew thyself a man; 2050.1
2: 6 Do t according to thy wisdom, and let not 2050.1
2: 9 Now t hold him not guiltless: for thou *art* 2050.1
2:19 Bath-sheba t went unto king Solomon, 2050.1
2:24 Now t, *as* the LORD liveth, which hath 2050.1
2:33 Their blood shall t return upon the head 2050.1
2:44 t the LORD shall return thy wickedness 2050.1
3: 9 Give t thy servant an understanding heart 2050.1
5: 6 Now t command thou that they hew me 2050.1
8:25 T now, LORD God of Israel, keep with 2050.1
8:61 Let your heart t be perfect with 2050.1
9: 9 served them: t hath the LORD 3651+5921
10: 9 t made he thee king, to do judgment and 2050.1
11:40 Solomon sought t to kill Jeroboam. 2050.1
12: 4 now t make thou the grievous service of 2050.1
12:18 T king Rehoboam made speed to get *him* 2050.1
12:24 They hearkened t to the word of 2050.1
13:26 t the LORD hath delivered him unto 2050.1
14:10 T, behold, I will bring evil upon 3651+3807.1
14:12 Arise thou t, get thee to thine own house: 2050.1
18:19 Now t send, *and* gather to me all Israel 2050.1
18:23 Let them t give us two bullocks; and 2050.1
20:23 Their gods *are* gods of the hills; t 3651+5921
20:28 t will I deliver all this great multitude into 2050.1
20:42 t thy life shall go for his life, and 2050.1
22:19 t the word of the LORD: 3651+3807.1
22:23 Now t, behold, the LORD hath put a 2050.1
2Ki 1: 4 Now t thus saith the LORD, 3651+3807.1
1: 6 of Baal-zebub the god of Ekron? t 3651+3807.1
1:14 t let my life now be precious in thy sight. 2050.1
1:16 t thou shalt not come down off *that* 3651+3807.1
2:17 They sent t fifty men; and they sought 2050.1
3:23 one another: now t, Moab, to the spoil. 2050.1
4:33 He went in t, and shut the door upon 2050.1
5:15 now t, I pray thee, take a blessing of thy 2050.1
5:27 The leprosy t of Naaman shall cleave 2050.1
6: 7 T said he, Take *it* up to thee. And he put 2050.1
6:11 T the heart of the king of Syria was sore 2050.1
6:14 T sent he thither horses, and chariots, and 2050.1
7: 4 Now t come, and let us fall unto the host 2050.1
7: 9 now t come, that we may go and tell 2050.1
7:12 t are they gone out of the camp to hide 2050.1
7:14 They took t two chariot horses; and 2050.1
9:26 Now t take *and* cast him into the plat *of* 2050.1

2Ki 10:19 Now t call unto me all the prophets of 2050.1
12: 7 now t receive no *more* money of your 2050.1
14:11 T Jehoash king of Israel went up; and he 2050.1
15:16 they opened not *to him,* t he smote *it; and* 2050.1
17: 4 t the king of Assyria shut him up, and 2050.1
17:18 T the LORD was very angry with Israel, 2050.1
17:25 t the LORD sent lions among them, 2050.1
17:26 t he hath sent lions among them, 2050.1
18:23 Now t, I pray thee, give pledges to my 2050.1
19:18 and stone: t they have destroyed them. 2050.1
19:19 Now t, O LORD our God, I beseech 2050.1
19:26 T their inhabitants *were* of small power, 2050.1
19:28 t I will put my hook in thy nose, and 2050.1
19:32 T thus saith the LORD 3651+3807.1
21:12 T thus saith the LORD God of 3651+3807.1
22:17 t my wrath shall be kindled against this 2050.1
22:20 Behold t, I will gather thee unto 3651+3807.1
1Ch 10:14 t he slew him, and turned the kingdom 2050.1
11: 3 T came all the elders of Israel to the king 2050.1
11: 7 David dwelt in the castle; t 3651+5921
11:19 T he would not drink it. These *things* did 2050.1
14:11 like the breaking forth of waters: t 3651+5921
14:14 T David inquired again of God; and God 2050.1
14:16 David t did as God commanded him: 2050.1
17: 7 Now t thus shalt thou say unto my 2050.1
17:23 T now, LORD, let the thing that thou 2050.1
17:25 that *thou* wilt build him a house: t 3651+5921
17:27 Now t let it please thee to bless the house 2050.1
21: 7 with this thing; t he smote Israel. 2050.1
21:12 Now t advise thyself what word I shall 2050.1
22: 5 I will t now make preparation for it. NIH
22:16 Arise t, and be doing, and the LORD be NIH
22:19 arise t, and build ye the sanctuary of 2050.1
23:11 t they were in one reckoning, 2050.1
24: 2 t Eleazar and Ithamar executed 2050.1
28: 8 Now t in the sight of all Israel 2050.1
29:13 Now t, our God, we thank thee, and 2050.1
2Ch 2: 7 Send me now t a man cunning to work in 2050.1
2:15 Now t the wheat, and the barley, the oil, 2050.1
6:10 The LORD t hath performed his word 2050.1
6:16 Now t, O LORD God of Israel, 2050.1
6:19 Have respect t to the prayer of thy 2050.1
6:21 Hearken t unto the supplications of thy 2050.1
6:41 Now t arise, O LORD God, into thy 2050.1
7:22 served them: t hath he brought all 3651+5921
9: 8 t made he thee king over them, to do 2050.1
10: 4 now t ease thou somewhat the grievous 2050.1
12: 5 t have I also left you in the hand of Shishak. NIH
12: 7 t I will not destroy them, but I will grant NIH
14: 7 T he said unto Judah, Let us build these 2050.1
15: 7 Be ye strong t, and let not your hands be 2050.1
16: 7 t is the host of the king of Syria 3651+5921
16: 9 t from henceforth thou shalt have wars. 3588
17: 5 T the LORD stablished the kingdom in 2050.1
18: 5 T the king of Israel gathered together *of* 2050.1
18:12 let thy word t, I pray thee, be like one of 2050.1
18:16 let them return t every man to his house in NIH
18:18 Again he said, T hear the word of 3651+3807.1
18:22 Now t behold, the LORD hath put a 2050.1
18:31 T they compassed about him to fight: but 2050.1
18:33 t he said to *his* chariot man, Turn thine 2050.1
19: 2 t *is* wrath upon thee from 2063+871.1+2050.1
20:26 for there they blessed the LORD: t 3651+5921
28:11 Now hear me t, and deliver the captives 2050.1
28:23 t will I sacrifice to them, that they may help NIH
30: 7 *who* t gave them up to desolation, as ye 2050.1
30:17 t the Levites had the charge of the killing 2050.1
32:15 Now t let not Hezekiah deceive you, 2050.1
32:25 t there was wrath upon him, and 2050.1
34:25 t my wrath shall be poured out upon this 2050.1
35:14 t the Levites prepared for themselves, and 2050.1
35:24 His servants t took him out of *that* 2050.1
36:17 T he brought upon them the king of 2050.1
Ezr 2:62 t were they, as polluted, put from 2050.1
4:14 t have we sent and certified the king; 1836+5922
5:17 Now t, if *it seem* good to the king, 2050.3
6: 6 Now t, Tatnai, governor beyond the river, NIH
9:12 Now t give not your daughters unto their 6258
10: 3 Now t let us make a covenant with our 2050.1
10:11 Now t make confession unto the LORD 2050.1
Ne 2:20 t we his servants will arise and build: 2050.1
4:13 T set I in the lower places behind 2050.1
4:20 In what place t ye hear the sound of NIH
5: 2 t we take up corn *for them,* that we may 2050.1
6: 7 Come now t, and let us take counsel 2050.1
6: 9 Now t, *O God,* strengthen my hands. 2050.1
6:13 T *was* he hired, that I should be 4616+3807.1
7:64 t were they, as polluted, put from 2050.1
9:27 T thou deliveredst them into the hand of 2050.1
9:28 t leftest thou them in the hand of their 2050.1
9:30 t gavest thou them into the hand of 2050.1
9:32 Now t, our God, the great, the mighty, 2050.1
13: 8 t I cast forth all the household stuff of 2050.1
13:28 the Horonite: t I chased him from me. 2050.1
Est 1:12 t was the king very wroth, and his anger 2050.1
2:23 t they were both hanged on a tree: 2050.1
3: 8 t it *is* not for the king's profit to suffer 2050.1
9:19 T the Jews of the villages, that dwelt 3651+5921
9:26 T for all the words of this letter, and 3651+5921
Job 5:17 t despise not thou the chastening of 2050.1
6: 3 t my words are swallowed up. 3651+5921
6:28 Now t be content, look upon me; for *it is* 2050.1
7:11 T I will not refrain my mouth; I will speak 1571
9:22 This *is* one *thing,* t I said *it,* He 3651+5921
10:15 of confusion; t see thou mine affliction; 2050.1
11: 6 Know t that God exacteth of thee *less* than 3588
17: 4 hid their heart from understanding: t 3651+5921
20: 2 T do my thoughts cause me to 3651+3807.1
20:21 t shall no *man* look for his goods. 3651+5921
21:14 T they say unto God, Depart from us; 2050.1
22:10 T snares *are* round about thee, and 3651+5921
23:15 T am I troubled at his presence: 3651+5921
32:10 T I said, Hearken to me; I also will 3651+3807.1
34:10 T hearken unto me, ye men of 3651+3807.1
34:25 T he knoweth their works, and 3651+3807.1

Job 34:33 and not I: t speak what thou knowest. 2050.1
35:14 *is* before him; t trust thou in him. 2050.1
35:16 T doth Job open his mouth in vain; 2050.1
37:24 Men do t fear him: he respecteth 3651+3807.1
42: 3 counsel without knowledge? t 3651+3807.1
42: 8 T take unto you now seven bullocks and 2050.1
Ps 1: 5 T the ungodly shall not stand in 3651+5921
2:10 Be wise now t, O ye kings: be instructed, 2050.1
7: 7 for their sakes t return thou on high. 2050.1
16: 9 T my heart is glad, and my glory 3651+3807.1
18:24 T hath the LORD recompensed me 2050.1
18:49 T will I give thanks unto thee, 3651+5921
21:12 T shalt thou make them turn their back, 3588
25: 8 Good and upright *is* the LORD: t 3651+5921
26: 1 also in the LORD; t I shall not slide. NIH
27: 6 t will I offer in his tabernacle sacrifices of 2050.1
28: 7 t my heart greatly rejoiceth; and with my 2050.1
31: 3 t for thy name's sake lead me, and 2050.1
36: 7 t the children of men put their trust under 2050.1
40:12 hairs of mine head: t my heart faileth me. 2050.1
42: 6 t will I remember thee from the land 3651+5921
45: 2 grace is poured into thy lips: t 3651+5921
45: 7 hatest wickedness: t God, thy God, 3651+5921
45:17 be remembered in all generations: t 3651+5921
46: 2 T will not we fear, though the earth 3651+5921
55:19 have no changes, t they fear not God. 2050.1
59: 5 Thou t, O LORD God *of* hosts, the God 2050.1
63: 7 t in the shadow of thy wings will I 2050.1
73: 6 T pride compasseth them about as 3651+3807.1
73:10 T his people return hither: and 3651+3807.1
78:21 T the LORD heard *this,* and 3651+3807.1
78:33 T their days did he consume in vanity, 2050.1
91:14 set his love upon me, t will I deliver him: 2050.1
106:23 T he said that *he* would destroy them, 2050.1
106:26 T he lifted up his hand against them, 2050.1
106:40 T was the wrath of the LORD kindled 2050.1
107:12 T he brought down their heart with 2050.1
110: 7 shall drink of the brook in the way: t 3651+5921
116: 2 t will I call upon *him* as long as I live. 2050.1
116:10 I believed, t have I spoken: I was greatly 3588
118: 7 t shall I see *my desire* upon them that 2050.1
119:104 thy precepts I get understanding: t 3651+5921
119:119 the wicked of the earth *like* dross: t 3651+3807.1
119:127 T I love thy commandments above 3651+5921
119:128 T I esteem all *thy* precepts 3651+5921
119:129 t doth my soul keep them. 3651+5921
119:140 word *is* very pure: t thy servant loveth it. 2050.1
139:19 O God: depart from me t, ye bloody men. 2050.1
143: 4 T is my spirit overwhelmed within me; 2050.1
Pr 1:31 T shall they eat of the fruit of their own 2050.1
4: 7 *is* the principal thing; t get wisdom: NIH
5: 7 Hear me now t, O ye children, and 2050.1
6:15 T shall his calamity come suddenly; 3651+5921
6:34 t he will not spare in the day of 2050.1
7:15 T came I forth to meet thee, 3651+5921
7:24 Hearken unto me now t, O ye children, 2050.1
8:32 Now t hearken unto me, O ye children: 2050.1
17:11 t a cruel messenger shall be sent against 2050.1
17:14 t leave off contention, before *it* be 2050.1
20: 4 t shall he beg in harvest, and 2050.1
20:19 t meddle not with him that flattereth *with* 2050.1
Ecc 2: 1 prove thee with mirth, t enjoy pleasure: 2050.1
2:17 T I hated life; because the work that is 2050.1
2:20 T I went about to cause my heart to 2050.1
5: 2 upon earth: t let thy words be few. 3651+5921
8: 6 t the misery of man *is* great upon him. 3588
8:11 t the heart of the sons of men is fully 3651+5921
11:10 T remove sorrow from thy heart, and 2050.1
SS 1: 3 t do the virgins love thee. 3651+5921
Isa 1:24 T saith the Lord, the LORD of 3651+3807.1
2: 6 T thou hast forsaken thy people the house 3588
2: 9 humbleth himself; t forgive them not. 2050.1
3:17 T the Lord will smite with a scab 2050.1
5:13 T my people are gone into 3651+3807.1
5:14 T hell hath enlarged herself, 3651+3807.1
5:24 T as the fire devoureth the stubble, 3651+3807.1
5:25 T is the anger of the LORD kindled 3651+5921
7:14 T the Lord himself shall give you a 3651+3807.1
8: 7 Now t behold, the Lord bringeth up 3651+3807.1
9:11 T the LORD shall set up the adversaries 2050.1
9:14 T the LORD will cut off from Israel 2050.1
9:17 T the Lord shall have no joy in their 3651+5921
10:16 T shall the Lord, the Lord of hosts, 3651+3807.1
10:24 T thus saith the Lord GOD of 3651+3807.1
12: 3 T with joy shall ye draw water out of 2050.1
13: 7 T shall all hands be faint, and 3651+5921
13:13 T I will shake the heavens, and 3651+5921
15: 4 t the armed soldiers of Moab shall 3651+5921
15: 7 T the abundance they have gotten, 3651+5921
16: 7 T shall Moab howl for Moab, 3651+3807.1
16: 9 T I will bewail with the weeping of 3651+5921
17:10 t shalt thou plant pleasant plants, and 3651+5921
21: 3 T are my loins filled *with* pain: 3651+5921
22: 4 T said I, Look away from me; I will 3651+5921
24: 6 T hath the curse devoured the earth, 3651+5921
24: 6 t the inhabitants of the earth are 3651+5921
25: 3 T shall the strong people glorify 3651+5921
26:14 t hast thou visited and 3651+3807.1
27: 9 By this t shall the iniquity of Jacob 3651+3807.1
27:11 it *is* a people of no understanding: t 3651+5921
28:16 T thus saith the Lord GOD, 3651+3807.1
28:22 Now t be ye not mockers, lest your bands 2050.1
29:14 T, behold, I will proceed to do a 3651+3807.1
29:22 T thus saith the LORD, 3651+3807.1
30: 3 T shall the strength of Pharaoh be your 2050.1
30: 7 t have I cried concerning this, 3651+3807.1
30:13 T this iniquity shall be to you as a 3651+3807.1
30:16 will flee upon horses; t shall ye flee: 3651+5921
30:16 t shall they that pursue you be swift. 3651+5921
30:18 t will the LORD wait, that *he* may 3651+3807.1
30:18 unto you, and t will he be exalted, 3651+3807.1
36: 8 Now t give pledges, I pray thee, to my 2050.1
37:19 and stone: t they have destroyed them. 2050.1
37:20 Now t, O LORD our God, save us from 2050.1
37:27 T their inhabitants *were* of small power, 2050.1

Isa 37:29 t will I put my hook in thy nose, and 2050.1
37:33 T thus saith the LORD 3651+3807.1
38:20 t we will sing my songs *to* the stringed 2050.1
42:25 T he hath poured upon him the fury of his 2050.1
43: 4 t will I give men for thee, and people for 2050.1
43:12 t ye *are* my witnesses, saith the LORD, 2050.1
43:28 T I have profaned the princes of 2050.1
47: 8 T hear now this, *thou that art* given to 2050.1
47:11 T shall evil come upon thee; thou shalt 2050.1
50: 7 For the Lord GOD will help me; t 3651+5921
50: 7 therefore shall I not be confounded: t 3651+5921
51:11 T the redeemed of the LORD shall 2050.1
51:21 T hear now this, thou afflicted, and 3651+3807.1
52: 5 Now t, what have I here, saith 2050.1
52: 6 T my people shall know my name: 3651+3807.1
52: 6 my people shall know my name: t 3651+3807.1
53:12 T will I divide him *a portion* with 3651+3807.1
57:10 hast found the life of thine hand; t 3651+5921
59: 9 T is judgment far from us, 3651+5921
59:16 t his arm brought salvation unto him; and 2050.1
60:11 T thy gates shall be open continually; 2050.1
61: 7 they shall rejoice in their portion: t 3651+3807.1
63: 5 t mine own arm brought salvation unto 2050.1
63:10 t he was turned to be their enemy, *and* 2050.1
65: 7 t will I measure their former work into 2050.1
65:12 T will I number you to the sword, and 2050.1
65:13 T thus saith the Lord GOD, 3651+3807.1
Jer 1:17 Thou t gird up thy loins, and arise, and 2050.1
2:19 know t and see that *it is* an evil *thing* and 2050.1
2:33 thou thy way to seek love? t 3651+3807.1
3: 3 T the showers have been withholden, and 2050.1
5: 4 T I said, Surely these *are* poor; they are 2050.1
5:27 so *are* their houses full *of* deceit: t 3651+5921
6:11 T I am full *of* the fury of the LORD; 2050.1
6:15 neither could they blush: t 3651+3807.1
6:18 T hear, ye nations, and know, 3651+3807.1
6:21 T thus saith the LORD, Behold, 3651+3807.1
7:14 T will I do unto *this* house, which is 2050.1
7:16 T pray not thou for this people, neither 2050.1
7:20 T thus saith the Lord GOD; 3651+3807.1
7:27 T thou shalt speak all these words unto 2050.1
7:32 T, behold, the days come, saith 3651+3807.1
8:10 T will I give their wives unto 3651+3807.1
8:12 neither could they blush: t 3651+3807.1
9: 7 T thus saith the LORD of hosts, 3651+3807.1
9:15 T thus saith the LORD of hosts, 3651+3807.1
10:21 have not sought the LORD: t 3651+5921
11: 8 t I will bring upon them all the words of 2050.1
11:11 T thus saith the LORD, Behold, 3651+3807.1
11:14 T pray not thou for this people, neither 2050.1
11:21 T thus saith the LORD of the men 3651+3807.1
11:22 T thus saith the LORD of hosts, 3651+3807.1
12: 8 out against me: t have I hated it. 3651+5921
13:12 T thou shalt speak unto them this word; 2050.1
13:24 T will I scatter them as the stubble that 2050.1
13:26 T will I discover thy skirts upon 1571+2050.1
14:10 t the LORD doth not accept them; 2050.1
14:15 T thus saith the LORD 3651+3807.1
14:17 T thou shalt say this word unto them; Let 2050.1
14:22 t we will wait upon thee: for thou hast 2050.1
15: 6 t will I stretch out my hand against thee, 2050.1
15:19 T thus saith the LORD, If thou 3651+3807.1
16:13 T will I cast you out of this land into a 2050.1
16:14 T behold, the days come, saith 3651+3807.1
16:21 T behold, I *will* this once cause 3651+3807.1
18:11 Now t go to, speak to the men of Judah, 2050.1
18:13 T thus saith the LORD; Ask ye 3651+3807.1
18:21 T deliver up their children to 3651+3807.1
19: 6 T behold, the days come, saith 3651+3807.1
20:11 *is* with me as a mighty terrible one: t 3651+5921
22:18 T thus saith the LORD 3651+3807.1
23: 2 T thus saith the LORD God of 3651+3807.1
23: 7 T behold, the days come, saith 3651+3807.1
23:15 T thus saith the LORD of hosts 3651+3807.1
23:30 T behold, I *am* against 3651+3807.1
23:32 t they shall not profit this people at all, 2050.1
23:38 t thus saith the LORD; 3651+3807.1
23:39 T behold, I, even I, will utterly 3651+3807.1
25: 8 T thus saith the LORD of hosts; 3651+3807.1
25:27 T thou shalt say unto them, Thus saith 2050.1
25:30 T prophesy thou against them all these 2050.1
26:13 T now amend your ways and 2050.1
27: 9 T hearken not ye to your prophets, nor to 2050.1
27:14 T hearken not unto the words of 2050.1
28:16 T thus saith the LORD; Behold, 3651+3807.1
29:20 Hear ye t the word of the LORD, all *ye* 2050.1
29:27 Now t why hast thou not reproved Jeremiah 6258
29:28 For t he sent unto us *in* Babylon, 3651+5921
29:32 T thus saith the LORD; Behold, 3651+3807.1
30:10 T fear thou not, O my servant Jacob, 2050.1
30:16 T all they that devour thee shall be 3651+3807.1
31: 3 t *with* lovingkindness have I drawn 3651+5921
31:12 T they shall come and sing in the height 2050.1
31:20 I do earnestly remember him still: t 3651+5921
32:23 t thou hast caused all this evil to come 2050.1
32:28 T thus saith the LORD; Behold, 3651+3807.1
32:36 now t thus saith the LORD, 3651+3807.1
34:12 T the word of the LORD came to 2050.1
34:17 T thus saith the LORD; Ye have 3651+3807.1
35:17 T thus saith the LORD God of 3651+3807.1
35:19 T thus saith the LORD of hosts, 3651+3807.1
36: 6 T go thou, and read in the roll, 2050.1
36:14 T all the princes sent Jehudi the son of 2050.1
36:30 T thus saith the LORD of 3651+3807.1
37:20 T hear now, I pray thee, O my lord 2050.1
38: 4 T the princes said unto the king, 2050.1
40: 3 his voice, t this thing is come upon you. 2050.1
42:15 now t hear the word of 3651+3807.1
42:22 Now t know certainly that ye shall die by 2050.1
44: 7 T now thus saith the LORD, the God of 2050.1
44:11 T thus saith the LORD of hosts, 3651+3807.1
44:22 t is your land a desolation, and an 2050.1
44:23 t this evil is happened unto you, as *at* 3651+5921
44:26 T hear ye the word of the LORD, 3651+3807.1
48:11 t his taste remained in him, and 3651+5921
Jer 48:12 T behold, the days come, saith 3651+3807.1
48:31 T will I howl for Moab, and I will 3651+5921
48:36 T mine heart shall sound for Moab 3651+5921
49: 2 T behold, the days come, saith 3651+3807.1
49:20 T hear the counsel of the LORD, 3651+3807.1
49:26 T her young men shall fall in her 3651+3807.1
50:18 T thus saith the LORD of hosts, 3651+3807.1
50:30 T shall her young men fall in 3651+3807.1
50:39 T the wild beasts of the desert with 3651+3807.1
50:45 T hear ye the counsel of 3651+3807.1
51: 7 of her wine; t the nations are mad. 3651+5921
51:36 T thus saith the LORD; Behold, 3651+3807.1
51:47 T behold, the days come, that I will 3651+3807.1
La 1: 8 grievously sinned; t she is removed: 3651+5921
1: 9 last end; t she came down wonderfully: 2050.1
2: 8 t he made the rampart and the wall to 2050.1
3:21 This I recall to my mind, t have I 3651+5921
3:24 saith my soul; t will I hope in him. 3651+5921
Eze 3:17 t hear the word at my mouth, and 2050.1
4: 7 T thou shalt set thy face toward the siege 2050.1
5: 7 T thus saith the Lord GOD; 3651+3807.1
5: 8 T thus saith the Lord GOD; 3651+3807.1
5:10 T the fathers shall eat the sons in 3651+3807.1
5:11 t will I also diminish *thee;* neither shall 2050.1
7:20 of their detestable things therein: t 3651+5921
8:18 T will I also deal in fury: mine eye shall 1571
11: 4 T prophesy against them, 3651+3807.1
11: 7 T thus saith the Lord GOD; 3651+3807.1
11:16 T say, Thus saith the Lord GOD; 3651+3807.1
11:17 T say, Thus saith the Lord GOD; 3651+3807.1
12: 3 T thou son of man, prepare thee stuff for 2050.1
12:23 Tell them t, Thus saith the Lord 3651+3807.1
12:28 T say unto them, Thus saith 3651+3807.1
13: 8 T thus saith the Lord GOD; 3651+3807.1
13: 8 seen lies, t behold, I *am* against 3651+3807.1
13:13 T thus saith the Lord GOD; I will 3651+3807.1
13:23 T ye shall see no more vanity, 3651+3807.1
14: 4 T speak unto them, and say unto 3651+3807.1
14: 6 T say unto the house of Israel, 3651+3807.1
15: 6 T thus saith the Lord GOD; 3651+3807.1
16:27 Behold t, I have stretched out my hand 2050.1
16:34 is given unto thee, t thou art contrary. 2050.1
16:37 Behold t, I will gather all thy 3651+3807.1
16:43 fretted me in all these *things;* behold t, 2050.1
16:50 t I took them away as I saw *good.* 2050.1
17:19 T thus saith the Lord GOD; *As* I 3651+3807.1
18:30 T I will judge you, O house of 3651+3807.1
20:27 T, son of man, speak unto 3651+3807.1
21: 4 t shall my sword go forth out of his 3651+3807.1
21: 6 Sigh t, thou son of man, with 2050.1
21:12 my people: smite t upon *thy* thigh. 3651+3807.1
21:14 Thou t, son of man, prophesy, and 2050.1
21:24 T thus saith the Lord GOD; 3651+3807.1
22: 4 art come *even* unto thy years: t 3651+5921
22:13 Behold t, I have smitten mine hand at thy 2050.1
22:19 T thus saith the Lord GOD; 3651+3807.1
22:19 ye are all become dross, behold t, 3651+3807.1
22:31 T have I poured out mine indignation 2050.1
23:22 T, O Aholibah, thus saith the Lord 3651+3807.1
23:31 t will I give her cup into thine hand. 2050.1
23:35 T thus saith the Lord GOD; 3651+3807.1
23:35 t bear thou also thy lewdness and thy 2050.1
24: 9 T thus saith the Lord GOD; 3651+3807.1
25: 4 Behold t, I *will* deliver thee to 3651+3807.1
25: 7 Behold t, I will stretch out mine 3651+3807.1
25: 9 T behold, I *will* open the side of 3651+3807.1
25:13 T thus saith the Lord GOD; I will 3651+3807.1
25:16 T thus saith the Lord GOD; 3651+3807.1
26: 3 T thus saith the Lord GOD; 3651+3807.1
28: 6 T thus saith the Lord GOD; 3651+3807.1
28: 7 Behold t, I *will* bring strangers 3651+3807.1
28:16 t I will cast thee as profane out of 2050.1
28:18 t will I bring forth a fire from the midst of 2050.1
29: 8 T thus saith the Lord GOD; 3651+3807.1
29:10 Behold t, I *am* against thee, and 3651+3807.1
29:19 T thus saith the Lord GOD; 3651+3807.1
30:22 T thus saith the Lord GOD; 3651+3807.1
31: 5 T his height was exalted above all 3651+5921
31:10 T thus saith the Lord GOD; 3651+3807.1
31:11 I have t delivered him into the hand of 2050.1
32: 3 I will t spread out my net over thee with a 2050.1
33: 7 t thou shalt hear the word at my mouth, 2050.1
33:10 T, O thou son of man, speak unto 2050.1
33:12 T, thou son of man, say unto the children 2050.1
34: 7 T, ye shepherds, hear the word of 3651+3807.1
34: 9 T, O ye shepherds, hear the word 3651+3807.1
34:20 T thus saith the Lord GOD unto 3651+3807.1
34:22 T will I save my flock, and they shall no 2050.1
35: 6 T, *as* I live, saith the Lord GOD, I 3651+3807.1
35:11 T, *as* I live, saith the Lord GOD, 3651+3807.1
36: 3 T prophesy and say, Thus saith 3651+3807.1
36: 4 T, ye mountains of Israel, hear 3651+3807.1
36: 5 T thus saith the Lord GOD; 3651+3807.1
36: 6 Prophesy t concerning the land of 3651+3807.1
36: 7 T thus saith the Lord GOD; 3651+3807.1
36:14 T thou shalt devour men no more, 3651+3807.1
36:22 T say unto the house of Israel, 3651+3807.1
37:12 T prophesy and say unto them, 3651+3807.1
38:14 T, son of man, prophesy and 3651+3807.1
39: 1 T thou son of man, prophesy against 2050.1
39:23 t hid I my face from them, and gave them 2050.1
39:25 T thus saith the Lord GOD; 3651+3807.1
41: 7 t the breadth of the house *was still* 3651+5921
42: 6 pillars as the pillars of the courts: t 3651+5921
44: 2 hath entered in by it, t it shall be shut. 2050.1
44:12 house of Israel to fall into iniquity; t 3651+5921
Da 1: 8 t he requested of the prince of 2050.1
1:19 and Azariah: t stood they before the king. 2050.1
2: 6 t shew me the dream, and the interpretation 3861
2: 9 t tell me the dream, and I shall know that 3861
2:10 t *there is* no king, lord, 1768+3606+6903
2:24 T Daniel went in unto Arioch, 1836+3606+6903
3: 7 T at that time, when all 1836+3606+6903
3:19 *t* he spake, and commanded that *they* should NIH
3:22 T because the king's 1836+3606+6903
Da 3:29 T I make a decree, That every people, 2050.3
4: 6 T made I a decree to bring in all 4481+2050.3
8: 8 T the he goat waxed very great: and 2050.1
9:11 t the curse is poured upon us, and 2050.1
9:14 T hath the LORD watched upon 2050.1
9:17 Now t, O our God, hear the prayer of thy 2050.1
9:23 t understand the matter, and consider 2050.1
9:25 Know t and understand, *that* from 2050.1
10: 8 T I was left alone, and saw this great 2050.1
11:30 t he shall be grieved, and return, and 2050.1
11:44 t he shall go forth with great fury to 2050.1
Hos 2: 2 let her t put away her whoredoms out of 2050.1
2: 6 T behold, I will hedge up thy way 3651+3807.1
2: 9 T will I return, and take *away* my 3651+3807.1
2:14 T behold, I *will* allure her, and 3651+3807.1
4: 3 T shall the land mourn, and 3651+5921
4: 5 T shalt thou fall *in the* day, and 2050.1
4: 7 *t* will I change their glory into shame. NIH
4:13 the shadow thereof *is* good: t 3651+5921
4:14 t the people *that* doth not understand shall 2050.1
5: 5 t shall Israel and Ephraim fall in their 2050.1
5:10 *t* I will pour out my wrath upon them like NIH
5:12 T *will* I *be* unto Ephraim as a moth, and 2050.1
6: 5 T have I hewed *them* by 3651+5921
8: 6 the workman made it; t it *is* not God: but 2050.1
9: 9 *t* he will remember their iniquity, he will NIH
10:14 T shall a tumult arise among thy people, 2050.1
12: 6 T turn thou to thy God: keep mercy and 2050.1
12:14 t shall he leave his blood upon him, and 2050.1
13: 3 T they shall be as the morning 3651+3807.1
13: 6 their heart was exalted; t have they 3651+5921
13: 7 T I will be unto them as a lion: as a 2050.1
Joel 2:12 T also now, saith the LORD, turn ye 2050.1
Am 2:14 T the flight shall perish from the swift, 2050.1
3: 2 of all the families of the earth: t 3651+5921
3:11 T thus saith the Lord GOD; 3651+3807.1
4:12 T thus will I do unto thee, O Israel: 3651+3807.1
5:11 Forasmuch t as your treading *is* upon 3282
5:13 T the prudent shall keep silence in 3651+3807.1
5:16 T the LORD, the God of hosts, 3651+3807.1
5:27 T will I cause you to go into captivity 2050.1
6: 7 T now shall they go captive with 3651+3807.1
6: 8 t will I deliver up the city with all that is 2050.1
7:16 Now t hear thou the word of the LORD: 2050.1
7:17 T thus saith the LORD; Thy wife 3651+3807.1
Jnh 4: 2 when I was yet in my country? T I 3651+5921
4: 3 T now, O LORD, take, I beseech thee, 2050.1
Mic 1: 6 T I will make Samaria as a heap of 2050.1
1: 8 T I will wail and howl, I will go 2088+5921
1:14 T shalt thou give presents to 3651+3807.1
2: 3 T thus saith the LORD; Behold, 3651+3807.1
2: 5 T thou shalt have none that shall 3651+3807.1
3: 6 T night *shall be* unto you, that *ye* 3651+3807.1
3:12 T shall Zion for your sake be 3651+3807.1
5: 3 T will he give them up, until 3651+3807.1
6:13 T also will I make *thee* sick in smiting 2050.1
6:16 t ye shall bear the reproach of my people. 2050.1
7: 7 T I will look unto the LORD; I will wait 2050.1
Hab 1: 4 T the law is slacked, and 3651+5921
1: 4 t wrong judgment proceedeth. 3651+5921
1:15 t they rejoice and are glad. 3651+5921
1:16 T they sacrifice unto their net, and 3651+5921
1:17 Shall they t empty their net, and 3651+5921
Zep 1:13 T their goods shall become a booty, and 2050.1
2: 9 T *as* I live, saith the LORD of 3651+3807.1
3: 8 T wait ye upon me, saith 3651+3807.1
Hag 1: 5 Now t thus saith the LORD of hosts; 2050.1
1:10 T the heaven over you is stayed from 3651+5921
Zec 1: 3 T say thou unto them, Thus saith 2050.1
1:16 T thus saith the LORD; I am 3651+3807.1
7:12 t came a great wrath from the LORD of 2050.1
7:13 T it is come to pass, *that* as he cried, and 2050.1
8:19 cheerful feasts; t love the truth and peace. 2050.1
10: 2 they comfort in vain: t they went 3651+5921
Mal 2: 9 T have I also made you contemptible and 2050.1
2:15 T take heed to your spirit, and let none 2050.1
2:16 t take heed to your spirit, that ye deal not 2050.1
3: 6 t ye sons of Jacob are not consumed. 2050.1
Mt 3: 8 Bring forth t fruits meet for repentance: *3767*
3:10 t every tree which bringeth not forth good *3767*
5:19 Whosoever t shall break one of these least *3767*
5:23 T if thou bring thy gift to the altar, and *3767*
5:48 Be ye t perfect, even as your Father which *3767*
6: 2 T when thou doest *thine* alms, do not sound *3767*
6: 8 Be not ye t like unto them: for your Father *3767*
6: 9 After this manner t pray ye: Our Father *3767*
6:22 if t thine eye be single, thy whole body *3767*
6:23 If t the light that is in thee be darkness, *3767*
6:25 T I say unto you, Take no thought *1223+3778*
6:31 T take no thought, saying, What shall we *3767*
6:34 Take t no thought for the morrow: for *3767*
7:12 T all *things* whatsoever ye would that men *3767*
7:24 T whosoever heareth these sayings of mine, *3767*
9:38 Pray ye t the Lord of the harvest, that he *3767*
10:16 be ye t wise as serpents, and harmless as *3767*
10:26 Fear them not t: for there is nothing *3767*
10:31 Fear ye not t, ye are of more value than *3767*
10:32 Whosoever t shall confess me before men, *3767*
12:27 t they shall be your judges. *1223+3778*
13:13 T speak I to them in parables: *1223+3778*
13:18 Hear ye t the parable of the sower. *3767*
13:40 As t the tares are gathered and burnt in *3767*
13:52 T every scribe *which is* instructed *1223+3778*
14: 2 and t mighty works do shew forth *1223+3778*
18: 4 Whosoever t shall humble himself as this *3767*
18:23 T is the kingdom of heaven likened *1223+3778*
18:26 The servant t fell down, and *3767*
19: 6 What t God hath joined together, let not *3767*
19:27 and followed thee; what shall we have t? *686*
21:40 When the lord t of the vineyard cometh, *3767*
21:43 T say I unto you, The kingdom of *1223+3778*
22: 9 Go ye t into the highways, *3767*
22:17 Tell us t, What thinkest thou? Is it lawful to *3767*
22:21 Render t unto Cesar the *things* which are *3767*
22:28 T in the resurrection whose wife shall she *3767*

Mt 23: 3 All t whatsoever they bid you observe, 3767
23:14 t ye shall receive the greater damnation. 1223
23:20 Whoso t shall swear by the altar, 3767
24:15 When ye t shall see the abomination of 3767
24:42 Watch t: for ye know not what hour your 3767
24:44 T be ye also ready: for in such an 1223+3778
25:13 Watch t, for ye know neither the day nor 3767
25:27 Thou oughtest t to have put my money to 3767
25:28 Take t the talent from him, and give *it* unto 3767
27:17 T when they were gathered together, Pilate 3767
27:64 Command t that the sepulchre be made sure 3767
28:19 Go ye t, and teach all nations, 3767
Mk 1:38 preach there also: for t came I forth. 1519+3778
2:28 T the Son of man is Lord also of 5620
6:14 and t mighty works do shew forth 1223+3778
6:19 T Herodias had a quarrel against him, and 1161
8:38 Whosoever t shall be ashamed of me and 1063
10: 9 What t God hath joined together, let not 3767
11:24 T I say unto you, What *things* soever 1223+3778
12: 6 Having yet t one son, his wellbeloved, 3767
12: 9 What shall t the lord of the vineyard do? 3767
12:23 In the resurrection t, when they shall rise, 3767
12:24 Do ye not t err, because ye know not 1223+3778
12:27 the God of the living: ye t do greatly err. 3767
12:37 David t himself calleth him Lord; and 3767
13:35 Watch ye t: for ye know not when 3767
Lk 1:35 t also *that* holy thing which shall be born of 1352
3: 8 Bring forth t fruits worthy of repentance, 3767
3: 9 every tree t which bringeth not forth good 3767
4: 7 If thou t wilt worship me, all shall be thine. 3767
4:43 to other cities also: for t am I sent. 1519+3778
6:36 Be ye t merciful, as your Father also is 3767
7:42 Tell me t, which of them will love him 3767
8:18 Take heed t how ye hear: for whosoever 3767
10: 2 T said he unto them, The harvest truly *is* 3767
10: 2 pray ye t the Lord of the harvest, that he 3767
10:40 to serve alone? bid her t that she help me. 3767
11:19 t shall they be your judges. 1223+3778
11:34 t when thine eye is single, thy whole body 3767
11:35 Take heed t that the light which is in thee 3767
11:36 If thy whole body t *be* full of light, 3767
11:49 T also said the wisdom of God, I will 1223+3778
12: 3 T whatsoever ye have spoken in 473+3739
12: 7 Fear not t: ye are of more value than many 3767
12:22 T I say unto you, Take no thought 1223+3778
12:40 Be ye t ready also: for the Son of man 3767
13:14 in them t come and be healed, and not on 3767
14:20 married a wife, and t I cannot come. 1223+3778
15:28 t came his father out and intreated him. 3767
16:11 If t ye have not been faithful in 3767
16:27 Then he said, I pray thee t, father, that thou 3767
19:12 He said t, A certain nobleman went into a 3767
20:15 and killed *him.* What t shall the lord of 3767
20:25 Render t unto Cesar the *things* which be 5106
20:29 There were t seven brethren: and the first 3767
20:33 T in the resurrection whose wife of them is 3767
20:44 David t calleth him Lord, how is he then 3767
21: 8 time draweth near: go ye not t after them. 3767
21:14 Settle *it* t in your hearts, not to meditate 3767
21:36 Watch ye t, and pray always, that ye may 3767
23:16 I will t chastise him, and release *him.* 3767
23:20 Pilate t, willing to release Jesus, spake 3767
23:22 in him: I will t chastise him, and let *him* go. 3767
Jn 1:31 t am I come baptizing with water. 1223+3778
2:22 When t he was risen from the dead, 3767
3:29 this my joy t is fulfilled. 3767
4: 1 When t the Lord knew how the Pharisees 3767
4: 6 Jesus t, being wearied with *his* journey, 3767
4:33 T said the disciples one to another, 3767
5:10 The Jews t said unto him that was cured, 3767
5:16 And t did the Jews persecute Jesus, 1223+3778
5:18 T the Jews sought the more to kill 1223+3778
6:13 T they gathered *them* together, and 3767
6:15 When Jesus t perceived that they would 3767
6:24 When the people t saw that Jesus was not 3767
6:30 They said t unto him, What sign shewest 3767
6:43 Jesus t answered and said unto them, 3767
6:45 Every *man* t that hath heard, and 3767
6:52 The Jews t strove amongst themselves, 3767
6:60 Many t of his disciples, when they had 3767
6:65 And he said, T said I unto you, 1223+3778
7: 3 His brethren t said unto him, Depart hence, 3767
7:22 Moses t gave unto you circumcision, 1223+3778
7:40 Many of the people t, when they heard *this* 3767
8:13 The Pharisees t said unto him, Thou bearest 3767
8:24 I said t unto you, that ye shall die in your 3767
8:36 If the Son t shall make you free, ye shall be 3767
8:47 ye t hear *them* not, because ye are 1223+3778
9: 7 He went his way t, and washed, and 3767
9: 8 The neighbours t, and they which before 3767
9:10 T said they unto him, How were thine eyes 3767
9:16 T said some of the Pharisees, This man is 3767
9:23 T said his parents, He is of age; 1223+3778
9:41 now ye say, We see; t your sin remaineth. 3767
10:17 T doth *my* Father love me, because 1223+3778
10:19 There was a division t again among 3767
10:39 T they sought again to take him: but 3767
11: 3 T *his* sisters sent unto him, saying, Lord, 3767
11: 6 When he had heard t that he was sick, he 3767
11:33 When Jesus t saw her weeping, and 3767
11:38 Jesus t again groaning in himself cometh to 3767
11:54 Jesus t walked no more openly among 3767
12: 9 of the Jews t knew that he was there: 3767
12:17 The people t that was with him when he 3767
12:19 The Pharisees t said among themselves, 3767
12:21 The same came t to Philip, which was of 3767
12:29 The people t, that stood *by,* and heard *it,* 3767
12:39 T they could not believe, because 1223+3778
12:50 whatsoever I speak t, even as the Father 3767
13:11 t said he, Ye are not all clean. 1223+3778
13:24 Simon Peter t beckoned to him, that *he* 3767
13:31 T, when he was gone out, Jesus said, 3767
15:19 of the world, t the world hateth you. 1223+3778
16:15 t said I, that he shall take of mine, 1223+3778
16:18 They said t, What is this that he saith, A 3767
Jn 16:22 And ye now t have sorrow: but I will see 3767
18: 4 Jesus t, knowing all *things* that should 3767
18: 8 have told you that I am *he:* if t ye seek me, 3767
18:25 They said t unto him, Art not thou also *one* 3767
18:31 The Jews t said unto him, It is not lawful 3767
18:37 Pilate t said unto him, Art thou a king 3767
18:39 will ye t *that* I release unto you the King of 3767
19: 1 Then Pilate t took Jesus, and 3767
19: 4 Pilate t went forth again, and saith unto 3767
19: 6 the chief priests t and officers saw him, 3767
19: 8 When Pilate t heard that saying, he was 3767
19:11 t he that delivered me unto thee hath 1223+3778
19:13 When Pilate t heard that saying, he brought 3767
19:16 Then delivered he him t unto them to be 3767
19:24 They said t among themselves, Let us not 3767
19:24 did cast lots. These *things* t the soldiers did. 3767
19:26 When Jesus t saw *his* mother, and 3767
19:30 When Jesus t had received the vinegar, 3767
19:31 The Jews t, because it was the preparation, 3767
19:38 He came t, and took the body of Jesus. 3767
19:42 There laid they Jesus t because of the Jews' 3767
20: 3 Peter t went forth, and *that* other disciple, 3767
20:25 The other disciples t said unto him, 3767
21: 6 They cast t, and now they were not able to 3767
21: 7 T that disciple whom Jesus loved saith unto 3767
Ac 1: 6 When they t were come together, 3767
2:26 T did my heart rejoice, and 1223+3778
2:30 T being a prophet, and knowing that God 3767
2:33 T being by the right hand of God exalted, 3767
2:36 T let all the house of Israel know assuredly, 3767
3:19 Repent ye t, and be converted, that your 3767
8: 4 T they that were scattered abroad went 3767
8:22 Repent t of this thy wickedness, and 3767
10:20 Arise t, and get *thee* down, and go with 235
10:29 T came I *unto you* without 1352+2532
10:29 I ask t for what intent ye have sent for me? 3767
10:32 Send t to Joppa, and call hither Simon, 3767
10:33 Immediately t I sent to thee; and thou hast 3767
10:33 Now t are we all here present before God, 3767
12: 5 Peter t was kept in prison: but prayer was 3767
13:38 Be it known unto you t, men *and* brethren, 3767
13:40 Beware t, lest that come upon you, which is 3767
14: 3 Long time t abode they speaking boldly in 3767
15: 2 When t Paul and Barnabas had no small 3767
15:10 Now t why tempt ye God, to put a yoke 3767
15:27 We have sent t Judas and Silas, who shall 3767
16:11 T loosing from Troas, we came with a 3767
16:36 let you go: now t depart, and go in peace. 3767
17:12 T many of them believed; also of 3767
17:17 T disputed he in the synagogue with 3767
17:20 we would know t what these *things* mean. 3767
17:23 Whom t ye ignorantly worship, him declare 3767
19:32 Some t cried one *thing,* and some another: 3767
20:11 When he t was come up *again,* and 1161
20:28 Take heed t unto yourselves, and to all 3767
20:31 T watch, and remember, that *by the space* 1352
21:22 What is it t? the multitude must needs 3767
21:23 Do t this that we say to thee: We have four 3767
23:15 Now t ye with the council signify to 3767
25: 5 Let them t, said he, which among you are 3767
25:17 T, when they were come hither, 3767
26:22 Having t obtained help of God, I continue 3767
28:20 For this cause t have I called for you, to see 3767
28:28 Be it known t unto you, that the salvation 3767
Ro 2: 1 T thou art inexcusable, O man, 1352
2:21 Thou t which teachest another, 3767
2:26 T if the uncircumcision keep 3767
3:20 T by the deeds of the law there shall no 1360
3:28 T we conclude that a man is justified by 3767
4:16 T *it is* of faith, that *it might be* by 1223+3778
4:22 And t it was imputed to him for 1352
5: 1 T being justified by faith, we have peace 3767
5:18 T as by the offence of one *judgment* 686+3767
6: 4 T we are buried with him by baptism into 3767
6:12 Let not sin t reign in your mortal body, 3767
8: 1 *There is* t now no condemnation to them 686
8:12 T, brethren, we are debtors, not to 686+3767
9:18 T hath he mercy on whom he will 686+3767
11:22 Behold t the goodness and severity of God: 3767
12: 1 I beseech you t, brethren, by the mercies of 3767
12:20 T if thine enemy hunger, feed him; if he 3767
13: 2 Whosoever t resisteth the power, 5620
13: 7 Render t to all *their* dues: tribute to whom 3767
13:10 t love *is* the fulfilling of the law. 3767
13:12 let us t cast off the works of darkness, and 3767
14: 8 whether we live t, or die, we are the Lord's. 3767
14:13 Let us not t judge one another any more: 3767
14:19 Let us t follow *after* the *things* which 686+3767
15:17 I have t whereof *I* may glory through Jesus 3767
15:28 When t I have performed this, and 3767
16:19 unto all *men.* I am glad t on your behalf: 3767
1Co 3:21 T let no *man* glory in men. For all *things* 5620
4: 5 T judge nothing before the time, until 5620
5: 7 Purge out t the old leaven, that ye may be a 3767
5: 8 T let us keep the feast, not with old leaven, 5620
5:13 T put away from among yourselves *that* 2532
6: 7 Now t there is utterly a fault among you, 3767
6:20 t glorify God in your body, and in your 1211
7: 8 I say t to the unmarried and widows, It is 1161
7:26 I suppose t that this is good for the present 3767
8: 4 As concerning t the eating of those things 3767
9:26 I t so run, not as uncertainly; so fight I, 5106
10:31 Whether t ye eat, or drink, or 3767
11:20 When ye come together t into one place, 3767
12:15 of the body; is it t not of the body? 3778+3844
12:16 of the body; is it t not of the body? 3778+3844
14:11 T if I know not the meaning of the voice, 3767
14:23 If t the whole church be come together into 3767
15:11 T whether *it were* I or they, so we preach, 3767
15:58 T, my beloved brethren, be ye stedfast, 5620
16:11 Let no *man* t despise him: but conduct him 3767
16:18 t acknowledge ye *them that are* such. 3767
2Co 1:17 When I t was thus minded, did I use 3767
4: 1 T seeing we have this ministry, 1223+3778
4:13 is written, I believed, *and* t have I spoken; 1352
2Co 4:13 have I spoken; we also believe, and t speak; 1352
5: 6 T *we are* always confident, knowing that, 3767
5:11 Knowing t the terror of the Lord, 3767
5:17 T if any *man be* in Christ, *he is* a new 5620
7: 1 Having t these promises, dearly beloved, 3767
7:13 T we were comforted in your 1223+3778
7:16 I rejoice t that I have confidence in you in 3767
8: 7 T, as ye abound in every *thing, in* faith, and 235
8:11 Now t perform the doing *of it;* that as *there* 2532
9: 5 T I thought it necessary to exhort 3767
11:15 T *it is* no great *thing* if his ministers also be 3767
12: 9 Most gladly t will I rather glory in my 3767
12:10 T I take pleasure in infirmities, 1352
13:10 T I write these *things* being absent, 1223+3778
Gal 2:17 found sinners, *is* t Christ the minister of sin? 687
3: 5 He t that ministereth to you the Spirit, and 3767
3: 7 Know ye t that they which are of faith, 686
4:16 Am I t become your enemy, because I tell 5620
5: 1 Stand fast t in the liberty wherewith Christ 3767
6:10 As we have t opportunity, let us do 686+3767
Eph 2:19 Now t ye are no more strangers and 3767
4: 1 I t, the prisoner of the Lord, beseech you 3767
4:17 This I say t, and testify in the Lord, that ye 3767
5: 1 Be ye t followers of God, as dear children; 3767
5: 7 Be not ye t partakers with them. 3767
5:24 T as the church is subject unto Christ, so 235
6:14 Stand t, having your loins girt about with 3767
Php 2: 1 If *there be* t any consolation in Christ, 3767
2:23 Him t I hope to send presently, so soon as 3767
2:28 I sent him t the more carefully, that, 3767
2:29 Receive him t in the Lord with all gladness; 3767
3:15 Let us t, as many as *be* perfect, be thus 3767
4: 1 T, my brethren dearly beloved and 5620
Col 2: 6 As ye have t received Christ Jesus 3767
2:16 Let no *man* t judge you in meat, 3767
3: 5 Mortify t your members which are upon 3767
3:12 Put on t, as the elect of God, holy and 3767
1Th 3: 7 T, brethren, we were comforted over 1223+3778
4: 8 He t that despiseth, despiseth not man, but 5105
5: 6 T let us not sleep, as *do* others; but 686+3767
2Th 2:15 T, brethren, stand fast, and hold 686+3767
1Ti 2: 1 I exhort t that, first of all, supplications, 3767
2: 8 I will t that men pray every where, 3767
4:10 For t we both labour and 1519+3778
5:14 I will t that the younger *women* marry, 3767
2Ti 1: 8 Be not thou t ashamed of the testimony of 3767
2: 1 Thou t, my son, be strong in the grace that 3767
2: 3 Thou t endure hardness, as a good soldier 3767
2:10 T I endure all *things* for the elects' 1223+3778
2:21 If a man t purge himself from these, 3767
4: 1 I charge *thee* t before God, and the Lord 3767
Phm 1:12 thou t receive him, that is, mine own 1161
1:15 For perhaps he t departed for a 1223+3778
1:17 If thou count me t a partner, receive him as 3767
Heb 1: 9 t God, *even* thy God, hath anointed 1223+3778
2: 1 T we ought to give the more earnest 1223+3778
4: 1 Let us t fear, lest, a promise being left *us* of 3767
4: 6 Seeing t it remaineth that some *must* enter 3767
4: 9 There remaineth t a rest to the people of 686
4:11 Let us labour t to enter into that rest, 3767
4:16 Let us t come boldly unto the throne of 3767
6: 1 T leaving the principles of the doctrine of 1352
7:11 If t perfection were by the Levitical 3767
9:23 *It was* t necessary that the patterns of *things* 3767
10:19 Having t, brethren, boldness to enter into 3767
10:35 Cast not away t your confidence, 3767
11:12 T sprang there even of one, and him as 1352
13:13 Let us go forth t unto him without 5106
13:15 By him t let us offer the sacrifice of praise 3767
Jas 4: 4 whosoever t will be a friend of the world is 3767
4: 7 Submit yourselves t to God. Resist 3767
4:17 T to him that knoweth to do good, and 3767
5: 7 Be patient t, brethren, unto the coming of 3767
1Pe 2: 7 Unto you t which believe *he is* precious: 3767
4: 7 be ye t sober, and watch unto prayer. 3767
5: 6 Humble yourselves t under the mighty 3767
2Pe 3:17 Ye t, beloved, **seeing** ye know *these things* 3767
1Jn 2:24 Let *that* t abide in you, which ye have 3767
3: 1 t the world knoweth us not, because 1223+3778
4: 5 t speak they of the world, and 1223+3778
3Jn 1: 8 We t ought to receive such, that we might 3767
Jude 1: 5 I will t put you in remembrance, though ye NIG
Rev 2: 5 Remember t from whence thou art fallen, 3767
3: 3 Remember t how thou hast received and 3767
3: 3 If t thou shalt not watch, I will come on 3767
3:19 and chasten: be zealous t, and repent. 3767
7:15 T are they before the throne of God, 1223+3778
12:12 T rejoice, ye heavens, and ye that 1223+3778
18: 8 T shall her plagues come in one day, 1223+3778

THEREFROM (3) [FROM]

Jos 23: 6 that *ye* turn not aside t *to* the right 4480+5105.2
2Ki 3: 3 Israel to sin; he departed not t. 4480+5089.1
13: 2 Israel to sin; he departed not t. 4480+5089.1

THEREIN (230) [IN]

Ge 9: 7 in the earth, and multiply t. 871.1+1886.3
18:24 for the fifty righteous that *are* t? 7130+871.1
23:11 the cave that *is* t, I give it thee; 871.1+2050.2
23:17 the cave which *was* t, and all 871.1+2050.2
23:20 the field, and the cave that *is* t, 871.1+2050.2
34:10 dwell and trade you t, and get you 1886.3
34:10 and get you possessions t. 871.1+1886.3
34:21 let them dwell in the land, and trade t; 1886.3
47:27 they had possession t, and grew, 871.1+1886.3
49:32 of the cave that *is* t *was* from 871.1+2050.2
Ex 2: 3 and with pitch, and put the child t; 871.1+1886.3
5: 9 the men, that they may labour t; 871.1+1886.3
16:24 neither was there any worm t. 871.1+2050.2
16:33 put an omer full of manna t, 8033+1886.5
21:33 cover it, and an ox or an ass fall t; 8033+1886.5
29:29 to be anointed t, and to be 871.1+1992.1
30:18 the altar, and thou shalt put water t. 8033+1886.5
31:14 for whosoever doeth *any* work t, 871.1+1886.3
35: 2 whosoever doeth work t shall be 871.1+2050.2

Ex 40: 3 thou shalt put t the ark of the Testimony, 8033
40: 7 and the altar, and shalt put water t. 8033
40: 9 all that *is* t, and shalt hallow it, 871.1+2050.2
Lev 6: 3 that a man doeth, sinning t: 2007+871.1+1886.1
6: 7 that he hath done in trespassing t. 871.1+1886.3
8:10 the tabernacle and all that *was* t, 871.1+2050.2
10: 1 put fire t, and put incense thereon, 871.1+2006.1
13:21 *there be* no white hairs t, and *if* it 871.1+1886.3
13:37 *that* there is black hair grown up t; 871.1+2050.2
18: 4 keep mine ordinances, to walk t: 871.1+1992.1
18:30 and that ye defile not yourselves t: 871.1+1992.1
20:22 whither I bring you to dwell t, 871.1+1886.3
22:21 there shall be no blemish t. 871.1+2050.2
23: 3 ye shall do no work *t*: it *is* the sabbath of NIH
23: 7 ye shall do no servile work *t*. NIH
23: 8 ye shall do no servile work *t*. NIH
23:21 ye shall do no servile work *t*: *it shall be* a NIH
23:25 Ye shall do no servile work *t*: but ye shall NIH
23:35 ye shall do no servile work *t*. NIH
23:36 *and* ye shall do no servile work *t*. NIH
25:19 eat *your* fill, and dwell t in safety. 5921+1886.3
26:32 your enemies which dwell t shall 871.1+1886.3
Nu 4:16 of all that t *is*, in the sanctuary, 871.1+2050.2
13:18 it *is*; and the people that dwelleth t, 5921+1886.3
13:20 whether there be wood t, or not. 871.1+1886.3
14:30 I sware to make you dwell t, 871.1+1886.3
16: 7 put fire t, and put incense in them 871.1+2006.1
16:46 put fire t from off the altar, and 5921+1886.3
28:18 ye shall do no *manner of* servile work *t*: NIH
29: 7 your souls: ye shall not do any work *t*: NIH
29:35 ye shall do no servile work *t*: NIH
32:40 son of Manasseh; and he dwelt t. 871.1+1886.3
33:53 *of* the land, and dwell t: 871.1+1886.3
35:33 of the blood that is shed t, 871.1+1886.3
Dt 2:10 (The Emims dwelt t in times past, 871.1+1886.3
2:20 giants dwelt t in old time; and 871.1+1886.3
7:25 *it* unto thee, lest thou be snared t: 871.1+2050.2
8:12 and hast built goodly houses, and dwelt *t*; NIH
10:14 the earth *also*, with all that t *is*. 871.1+1886.3
11:31 ye shall possess it, and dwell t. 871.1+1886.3
13:15 all that *is* t, and the cattle thereof, 871.1+1886.3
15:21 if there be *any* blemish t, *as if it be* 871.1+2050.2
16: 8 LORD thy God: thou shalt do no work *t*. NIH
17:14 and shalt dwell t, and shalt say, 871.1+1886.3
17:19 shall read t all the days of his life: 871.1+2050.2
20:11 *that* all the people that is found t 871.1+1886.3
26: 1 and possessest it, and dwellest t; 871.1+1886.3
28:30 a house, and thou shalt not dwell t: 871.1+2050.2
29:23 nor any grass groweth t, 871.1+1886.3
Jos 1: 8 thou shalt meditate t day and 871.1+2050.2
1: 8 according to all that is written t: 871.1+2050.2
6:17 all that *are* t, to the LORD: 834+871.1+1886.3
6:24 city with fire, and all that *was* t: 871.1+1886.3
10:28 them, and all the souls that *were* t; 871.1+1886.3
10:30 and all the souls that *were* t; 871.1+1886.3
10:32 and all the souls that *were* t, 871.1+1886.3
10:35 all the souls that *were* t he utterly 871.1+1886.3
10:37 all the souls that *were* t; 871.1+1886.3
10:37 all the souls that *were* t. 871.1+1886.3
10:39 destroyed all the souls that *were* t; 871.1+1886.3
11:11 they smote all the souls that *were* t 871.1+1886.3
19:47 dwelt t, and called Leshem, Dan, 871.1+1886.3
19:50 and he built the city, and dwelt t. 871.1+1886.3
21:43 and they possessed it, and dwelt t. 871.1+1886.3
Jdg 2:22 the way of the LORD to walk t, 871.1+3963.1
8:25 did cast t every man the earrings of 8033+1886.5
9:45 slew the people that *was* t, 871.1+1886.3
16:30 upon all the people that *were* t. 871.1+2050.2
18: 7 saw the people that *were* t, 7130+871.1+1886.3
18:28 And they built a city, and dwelt t. 871.1+1886.3
1Sa 30: 2 the women captives, that *were* t: 871.1+1886.3
2Sa 12:31 forth the people that *were* t, 871.1+1886.3
1Ki 8:16 to build a house, that my name might be t; 8033
11:24 dwelt t, and reigned in Damascus. 871.1+1886.3
12:25 in mount Ephraim, and dwelt t; 871.1+1886.3
2Ki 2:20 Bring me a new cruse, and put salt t. 8033
12: 9 the priests that kept the door put t 8033+1886.5
13: 6 who made Israel sin, *but* walked t: 871.1+1886.3
13:11 made Israel sin: *but* he walked t. 871.1+1886.3
15:16 all that *were* t, and the coasts 871.1+1886.3
15:16 all the women t that were with child he 1886.3
1Ch 16:32 the fields rejoice, and all that *is* t. 871.1+2050.2
21:22 build an altar t unto the LORD: 871.1+2050.2
2Ch 2: 3 to build him a house to dwell t, 871.1+2050.2
5:10 the two tables which Moses put *t* at Horeb, NIH
20: 8 they dwelt t, and have built thee a 871.1+1886.3
20: 8 thee a sanctuary t for thy name, 871.1+1886.3
Ezr 4:19 and sedition *have been* made t. 871.2+1886.9
6: 2 t *was* a record thus written: 1459+871.2+1886.9
Ne 6: 1 and *that* there was no breach left t; 871.1+1886.3
7: 4 the people *were* few t, 8432+871.1+1886.3
7: 5 up at the first, and found written t, 871.1+2050.2
8: 3 he read t before the street that *was* 871.1+2050.2
9: 6 all *things* that *are* t, the seas, and 5921+1886.3
9: 6 all that *is* t, and thou preservest 871.1+1992.1
13: 1 t was found written, that 871.1+2050.2
13:16 There dwelt men of Tyre also t, 871.1+1886.3
Job 3: 7 let no joyful voice come t. 871.1+2050.2
20:18 the restitution *be*, and he shall not rejoice *t*. NIH
Ps 24: 1 the world, and they that dwell t. 871.1+1886.3
37:29 the land, and dwell t for ever. 5921+1886.3
68:10 Thy congregation hath dwelt t: 871.1+1886.3
69:34 and every *thing* that moveth t. 871.1+3963.1
69:36 that love his name shall dwell t. 871.1+1886.3
96:12 field be joyful, and all that *is* t: 871.1+2050.2
98: 7 the world, and they that dwell t. 871.1+1886.3
104:26 *whom* thou hast made to play t. 871.1+2050.2
107:34 wickedness of them that dwell t. 871.1+1886.3
111: 2 out of all them that have pleasure t. 1992.1
119:35 for t do I delight. 871.1+2050.2
146: 6 and earth, the sea, and all that t is: 871.1+3963.1
Pr 15: 4 t *is* a breach in the spirit. 871.1+1886.3
22:14 that is abhorred of the LORD shall fall t. 8033
26:27 Whoso diggeth a pit shall fall t: 871.1+1886.3
Ecc 2:21 t shall he leave it *for* his portion. 871.1+2050.2
Isa 5: 2 of it, and also made a winepress t: 871.1+2050.2
7: 6 let us make a breach t for us, and set a 5089.1
24: 6 and they that dwell t are desolate: 871.1+1886.3
33:24 the people that dwell t *shall be* 871.1+1886.3
34: 1 let the earth hear, and **all that is** t; 4393
34:17 to generation shall they dwell t. 871.1+1886.3
35: 8 though fools, shall not err *t*. NIH
42: 5 and spirit to them that walk t: 871.1+1886.3
42:10 ye that go down to the sea, and **all that is** t; 4393
44:23 O forest, and every tree t: 871.1+2050.2
51: 3 joy and gladness shall be found t, 871.1+1886.3
51: 6 they that dwell t shall die in like manner: 1886.3
59: 8 goeth t shall not know peace. 871.1+1886.3
Jer 4:29 and not a man dwell t. 871.1+2006.1
6:16 walk t, and ye shall find rest for 871.1+1886.3
6:16 But they said, We will not walk *t*. NIH
8:16 the city, and those that dwell t. 871.1+1886.3
9:13 my voice, neither walked t; 871.1+1886.3
12: 4 wickedness of them that dwell t? 871.1+1886.3
17:24 the sabbath day, to do no work t; 871.1+2050.2
23:12 they shall be driven on, and fall t: 871.1+1886.3
27:11 and they shall till it, and dwell t. 871.1+1886.3
36: 2 write t all the words that I have 413+1886.3
36:29 Why hast thou written t, saying, 5921+1886.3
36:32 who wrote t from the mouth of 5921+1886.3
44: 2 and no man dwelleth t, 871.1+1992.1
47: 2 shall overflow the land, and **all that is** t; 4393
47: 2 the city, and them that dwell t: 871.1+1886.3
48: 9 without any to dwell t. 871.1+2006.1
50: 3 and none shall dwell t: 871.1+1886.3
50:39 and the owls shall dwell t: 871.1+1886.3
50:40 shall any son of man dwell t. 871.1+1886.3
51:48 and the earth, and all that *is* t, 871.1+1992.1
Eze 2: 9 and lo, a roll of a book *was* t; 871.1+2050.2
2:10 *there was* written t lamentations, 413+1886.3
7:20 *and* of their detestable things t: 871.1+2050.2
12:19 her land may be desolate from **all that is** t, 4393
12:19 violence of all them that dwell t. 871.1+1886.3
14:22 t shall be left a remnant that shall 871.1+1886.3
20:47 south to the north shall be burnt t. 871.1+1886.3
24: 5 seethe the bones of it t. 8432+871.1+1886.3
24: 6 to the pot whose scum *is* t, 871.1+1886.3
28:26 they shall dwell safely t, and 5921+1886.3
30:12 and **all that is** t, by the hand of strangers: 4393
32:15 I shall smite all them that dwell t, 871.1+1886.3
37:25 they shall dwell t, *even* they, and 5921+1886.3
40:33 *there were* windows t and in 2050.2+3807.1
42:14 When the priests enter *t*, then shall they not NIH
44:14 and for all that shall be done t. 871.1+2050.2
Da 5: 2 and his concubines, might drink t. 871.2+1952.1
Hos 4: 3 one that dwelleth t shall languish, 871.1+1886.3
14: 9 but the transgressors shall fall t. 871.1+3963.1
Am 6: 8 will I deliver up the city with **all that is** t. 4393
8: 8 every one mourn that dwelleth t? 871.1+1886.3
9: 5 and all that dwell t shall mourn: 871.1+1886.3
Mic 1: 2 hearken, O earth, and **all that t is**: 4393
7:13 be desolate because of them that dwell t, 1886.3
Na 1: 5 yea, the world, and all that dwell t. 871.1+1886.3
Hab 2: 8 *of* the city, and *of* all that dwell t. 871.1+1886.3
2:17 *of* the city, and *of* all that dwell t. 871.1+1886.3
2:18 the maker of his work trusteth t, 5921+2050.2
Zec 2: 4 of men and cattle t: 8432+871.1+1886.3
6: 6 The black horses which *are* t go 871.1+1886.3
13: 8 two parts t shall be cut off *and* die; 871.1+1886.3
13: 8 die; but the third shall be left t. 871.1+1886.3
14:21 and take of them, and seethe t: 871.1+1886.3
Mt 23:21 sweareth by it, and by him that dwelleth t. *846*
Mk 10:15 as a little child, he shall not enter t. *846+1519*
13:15 neither enter *t*, to take any *thing* out of his NIG
Lk 10: 9 And heal the sick that are t, *846+1722*
18:17 as a little child shall in no wise enter t. *846+1519*
19:45 and began to cast out them that sold t, *846+1722*
Jn 12: 6 and had the bag, and bare what was put *t*. NIG
Ac 1:20 be desolate, and let no man dwell t: *846+1722*
14:15 and the sea, and all *things* that are t: *846+1722*
17:24 that made the world and all *things* t, *846+1722*
27: 6 sailing into Italy; and he put us t. *846+1519*
Ro 1:17 For t is the righteousness of God *846+1722*
6: 2 that are dead to sin, live any longer t? *846+1722*
1Co 7:24 he is called, t abide with God. *1722+3778*
Eph 6:20 that t I may speak boldly, as I ought to *846+1722*
Php 1:18 I t do rejoice, yea, and will rejoice. *1722+3778*
Col 2: 7 abounding t with thanksgiving. *846+1722*
Heb 4: 6 it remaineth that some *must* enter t, *846+1519*
10: 8 neither hadst pleasure *t*: which are offered NIG
13: 9 profited them that have been **occupied** t. *4043*
Jas 1:25 continueth *t*, he being not a forgetful hearer, NIG
2Pe 2:20 they are again entangled t, and overcome, *3778*
3:10 and the works that are t shall be burnt up. *1722*
Rev 1: 3 keep those *things* which are written t: *846+1722*
10: 6 and the *things* that t are, and the earth, *846+1722*
10: 6 and the *things* that t are, and the sea, *846+1722*
10: 6 the sea, and the *things* which are t, *846+1722*
11: 1 and the altar, and them that worship t. *846+1722*
13:12 them which dwell t to worship *846+1722*
21:22 And I saw no temple t: for the Lord *846+1722*

THEREINTO (1) [INTO]

Lk 21:21 them that are in the countries enter t. *846+1519*

THEREOF (908) [OF]

Ge 2:17 for in the day that thou eatest t thou shalt 4480
2:19 every living creature, that *was* the name t. 2050.2
2:21 his ribs, and closed up the flesh instead t; 5089.1
3: 5 doth know that in the day ye eat t, 4480+5105.2
3: 6 she took of the fruit t, and did eat, and 2050.2
4: 4 the firstlings of his flock and of the fat t. 2006.1
6:16 door of the ark shalt thou set in the side t; 1886.3
9: 4 flesh with the life t, *which is* the blood 2050.2
9: 4 *which is* the blood t, shall you not eat. 2050.2
40:10 the clusters t brought forth ripe grapes: 1886.3
40:18 and said, This *is* the interpretation t: 2050.2
41: 8 of Egypt, and all the wise men t: 1886.3
45:16 the fame *t* was heard *in* Pharaoh's house, NIH
47:21 borders of Egypt even to the *other* end t. 1930.2
Ex 3:20 wonders which I will do in the midst t: 2050.2
5: 8 you shall not diminish *ought* t: 4480+5105.2
9:18 since the foundation t even until now. 1886.3
10:26 for t must we take to serve 4480+5105.2
12: 9 with his legs, and with the purtenance t. 2050.2
12:43 There shall no stranger eat t: 871.1+2050.2
12:44 then shall he eat t. 871.1+2050.2
12:45 and a hired servant shall not eat t. 871.1+2050.2
12:46 neither shall ye break a bone t. 871.1+2050.2
12:48 uncircumcised person shall eat t. 871.1+2050.2
16:31 the house of Israel called the name t 2050.2
19:18 the smoke t ascended as the smoke of a 2050.2
22:11 the owner of it shall accept *t*, and he shall NIH
22:12 shall make restitution unto the owner t. 2050.2
22:14 or die, the owner t *being* not with it, 2050.2
22:15 *But* if the owner t *be* with it, he shall not 2050.2
23:10 thy land, and shalt gather in the fruits t: 1886.3
25: 9 the pattern of all the instruments t, even 2050.2
25:10 two cubits and a half *shall be* the length t, 2050.2
25:10 a cubit and a half the breadth t, and 2050.2
25:10 and a cubit and a half the height t. 2050.2
25:12 for it, and put *them* in the four corners t; 2050.2
25:17 two cubits and a half *shall be* the length t, 1886.3
25:17 and a cubit and a half the breadth t. 1886.3
25:19 ye make the cherubims on the two ends t. 2050.2
25:23 two cubits *shall be* the length t, and 2050.2
25:23 a cubit the breadth t, and a cubit and 2050.2
25:23 and a cubit and a half the height t. 2050.2
25:25 golden crown to the border t round about. 2050.2
25:26 the four corners that *are* on the four feet t. 2050.2
25:29 thou shalt make the dishes t, and 2050.2
25:29 spoons t, and covers thereof, and 2050.2
25:29 and covers t, and bowls thereof, 2050.2
25:29 and covers thereof, and bowls t, 2050.2
25:37 thou shalt make the seven lamps t: and 1886.3
25:37 they shall light the lamps t, that they may 1886.3
25:38 the tongs t, and the snuffdishes thereof, 1886.3
25:38 the snuffdishes t, *shall be of* pure gold. 1886.3
26:30 t which was shewed thee in the mount. 2050.2
27: 1 and the height t *shall be* three cubits. 2050.2
27: 2 horns of it upon the four corners t: 4480+5105.2
27: 3 all the vessels t thou shalt make *of* brass. 2050.2
27: 4 four brasen rings in the four corners t. 2050.2
27:10 the twenty pillars t and their twenty 2050.2
27:19 of the tabernacle in all the service t, 2050.2
27:19 all the pins t, and all the pins of the court, 2050.2
28: 7 It shall have the two shoulderpieces *t* joined NIH
28: 7 *thereof* joined at the two edges t; 2050.2
28: 8 be of the same, according to the work t; 1930.2
28:16 a span *shall be* the length t, and a span 2050.2
28:16 and a span *shall be* the breadth t. 2050.2
28:26 ends of the breastplate in the border t, 2050.2
28:27 towards the forepart t, over against 2050.2
28:27 over against *the other* coupling t, 2050.2
28:28 t unto the rings of the ephod with a lace 2050.2
28:32 be a hole in the top of it, in the midst t: 2050.2
28:33 and of scarlet, round about the hem t; 2050.2
29:33 a stranger shall not eat *t*, because they *are* NIH
29:41 according to the drink offering t, 1886.3+3807.1
30: 2 A cubit *shall be* the length t, and a cubit 2050.2
30: 2 length thereof, and a cubit the breadth t; 2050.2
30: 2 two cubits *shall be* the height t: the horns 2050.2
30: 2 the horns t *shall be* of the same. 2050.2
30: 3 the top t, and the sides thereof round 2050.2
30: 3 the sides t round about, and the horns 2050.2
30: 3 thereof round about, and the horns t; 2050.2
30: 4 by the two corners t, upon the two sides 2050.2
30:37 according to the composition t: 1886.3
35:12 The ark, and the staves t, *with* the mercy 2050.2
36:29 coupled together at the head t, to one 2050.2
37: 6 two cubits and a half *was* the length t, 1886.3
37: 6 and one cubit and a half the breadth t. 1886.3
37: 8 made he the cherubims on the two ends t. 2050.2
37:10 two cubits *was* the length t, and a cubit 2050.2
37:10 a cubit the breadth t, and a cubit and 2050.2
37:10 and a cubit and a half the height t: 2050.2
37:12 made a crown of gold for the border t 2050.2
37:13 four corners that *were* in the four feet t. 2050.2
37:18 six branches going out of the sides t; 1886.3
37:18 of the candlestick out of the one side t, 1886.3
37:18 of the candlestick out of the other side t: 1886.3
37:24 pure gold made he it, and all the vessels t. 1886.3
37:25 height of it; the horns t were of the same. 2050.2
37:26 the sides t round about, and the horns of 2050.2
37:27 two rings of gold for it under the crown t, 2050.2
37:27 two corners of it, upon the two sides t, 2050.2
38: 1 five cubits *was* the length t, and 2050.2
38: 1 and five cubits the breadth t; 2050.2
38: 1 and three cubits the height t. 2050.2
38: 2 he made the horns t on the four corners of 2050.2
38: 2 of it; the horns t were of the same: 2050.2
38: 3 all the vessels t made he *of* brass. 2050.2
38: 4 compass t beneath unto the midst of it. 2050.2
39: 5 *was* of the same, according to the work t; 1930.2
39: 9 a span *was* the length t, and a span 2050.2
39: 9 and a span the breadth t, *being* doubled. 2050.2
39:20 of it, over against the *other* coupling t, 2050.2
39:35 and the staves t, and the mercy seat, 2050.2
39:36 all the vessels t, and the shewbread, 2050.2
39:37 The pure candlestick, *with* the lamps t, 1886.3
39:37 and all the vessels t, and the oil for light, 1886.3
40: 4 in the candlestick, and light the lamps t. 1886.3
40: 9 shalt hallow it, and all the vessels t: 2050.2
40:18 set up the boards t, and put in the bars 2050.2
40:18 put in the bars t, and reared up his pillars. 2050.2
Lev 1:15 the blood t shall be wrung out at the side 2050.2
1:17 he shall cleave it with the wings t, *but* 2050.2
2: 2 take thereout his handful of the flour t, 1886.3
2: 2 of the oil t, with all the frankincense 1886.3
2: 2 of the oil thereof, with all the frankincense t; 1886.3
2: 9 take from the meat offering a memorial t, 1886.3
2:16 *part* of the beaten corn t, and *part* of 1886.3
2:16 beaten corn thereof, and *part* of the oil t, 1886.3
2:16 the oil thereof, with all the frankincense t: 1886.3
3: 8 Aaron's sons shall sprinkle the blood t 2050.2

Lev 3: 9 the fat **t**, *and* the whole rump, it shall he 2050.2
3:13 the blood **t** upon the altar round about. 2050.2
3:14 he shall offer **t** his offering, 4480+5105.2
4:30 the priest shall take of the blood **t** with 1886.3
4:30 shall pour out all the blood **t** at 1886.3
4:31 he shall take away all the fat **t**, as the fat 1886.3
4:34 shall pour out all the blood **t** at 1886.3
4:35 he shall take away all the fat **t**, as the fat 1886.3
5:12 a memorial **t**, and burn *it* on the altar, 1886.3
6:15 of the oil **t**, and all the frankincense 1886.3
6:16 the remainder **t** shall Aaron and 4480+5089.1
6:20 of it in the morning, and half **t** at night. 1886.3
6:27 Whatsoever shall touch the flesh **t** shall 1886.3
6:27 when there is sprinkled of the blood **t** 1886.3
6:29 the males among the priests shall eat **t**: 1886.3
7: 2 the blood **t** shall he sprinkle round about 2050.2
7: 3 he shall offer of it all the fat **t**; the rump, 2050.2
7: 6 Every male among the priests shall eat **t**: 5105.2
7:19 *as for* the flesh, all that be clean shall eat **t**. 1320
8:11 he sprinkled **t** upon the altar seven 4480+5105.2
9:13 unto him, with the pieces **t**, and the head: 1886.3
9:17 took a handful **t**, and burnt *it* upon 4480+5089.1
11:39 he that toucheth the carcase **t** shall be 1886.3
13: 4 and the hair **t** be not turned white; 1886.3
13:18 in which, *even* in the skin **t**, was a boil, and 3588
13:20 the skin, and the hair **t** be turned white; 1886.3
14:45 the timber **t**, and all the morter of 2050.2
17:13 he shall even pour out the blood **t**, and 2050.2
17:14 of all flesh; the blood of it *is* for the life **t**: 2050.2
17:14 for the life of all flesh *is* the blood **t**: 2050.2
18:25 therefore I do visit the iniquity **t** upon it, 1886.3
19:23 shall count the fruit **t** as uncircumcised: 2050.2
19:24 in the fourth year all the fruit **t** shall be 2050.2
19:25 in the fifth year shall ye eat of the fruit **t**, 2050.2
19:25 that *it* may yield unto you the increase **t**: 2050.2
22:13 but there shall no stranger eat **t**. 871.1+2050.2
22:14 he shall put the fifth *part* **t** unto it, and 2050.2
22:24 neither shall you make *any* offering **t** in NIH
23:10 shall reap the harvest **t**, then ye shall 1886.3
23:13 the meat offering **t** *shall be* two tenth 2050.2
23:13 the drink offering **t** *shall be of* wine, 1886.4
24: 5 take fine flour, and bake twelve cakes **t**: 1886.3
25: 3 thy vineyard, and gather in the fruit **t**; 1886.3
25: 7 thy land, shall all the increase **t** be meat. 1886.3
25:10 *all* the land unto all the inhabitants **t**: 1886.3
25:12 ye shall eat the increase **t** out of the field. 1886.3
25:16 of years thou shalt increase the price **t**, 2050.2
25:27 let him count the years of the sale **t**, and 2050.2
27:10 then it and the exchange **t** shall be holy. 2050.2
27:13 he shall add a fifth *part* **t** unto thy 2050.2
27:16 shall be according to the seed **t**: 2050.2
27:21 the possession **t** shall be the priest's. 2050.2
27:31 he shall add thereto the fifth *part* **t**. 2050.2
27:33 both it and the change **t** shall be holy; 2050.2
Nu 1:50 over all the vessels **t**, and over all *things* 2050.2
1:50 bear the tabernacle, and all the vessels **t**; 2050.2
2: 6 those that were numbered **t**, *were* fifty 2050.2
2: 8 those that were numbered **t**, *were* fifty 2050.2
2:11 those that were numbered **t**, *were* forty 2050.2
3:25 the covering **t**, and the hanging for 1930.2
3:26 and the cords of it for all the service **t**. 2050.2
3:31 and the hanging, and all the service **t**. 2050.2
3:36 the bars **t**, and the pillars thereof, and 2050.2
3:36 the pillars **t**, and the sockets thereof, and 2050.2
3:36 the sockets **t**, and all the vessels thereof, 2050.2
3:36 all the vessels **t**, and all that serveth 2050.2
4: 6 of blue, and shall put in the staves **t**. 2050.2
4: 8 and shall put in the staves **t**. 2050.2
4: 9 his snuffdishes, and all the oil vessels **t**, 1886.3
4:10 all the vessels **t** within a covering of 1886.3
4:11 and shall put to the staves **t**: 2050.2
4:14 they shall put upon it all the vessels **t**, 2050.2
4:16 *is*, in the sanctuary, and in the vessels **t**. 2050.2
4:31 the bars **t**, and the pillars thereof, and 2050.2
4:31 and the pillars **t**, and sockets thereof, 2050.2
4:31 and the pillars thereof, and sockets **t**, 2050.2
5: 7 his trespass with the principal **t**, 2050.2
5: 7 add unto it the fifth *part* **t**, and give *it* 2050.2
5:26 *even* the memorial **t**, and burn *it* upon 1886.3
7: 1 sanctified it, and all the instruments **t**, 2050.2
7: 1 both the altar and all the vessels **t**, and 2050.2
7:13 the weight **t** *was* an hundred and 1886.3
8: 3 he lighted the lamps **t** over against 1886.3
8: 4 unto the shaft **t**, unto the flowers thereof, 1886.3
8: 4 unto the flowers **t**, *was* beaten work: 1886.3
8:25 they shall cease waiting upon the service **t**, NIH
9: 3 according to all the ceremonies **t**, shall ye 2050.2
9:14 according to the manner **t**, so shall he do: 2050.2
11: 7 and the colour **t** as the colour of bdellium. 2050.2
13:32 *is* a land that eateth up the inhabitants **t**; 1886.3
18:28 ye shall give **t** the LORD'S heave 4480+5105.2
18:29 of all the best **t**, *even* the hallowed *part* 2050.2
18:29 *even* the hallowed *part* **t** out of it. 2050.2
18:30 When ye have heaved the best **t** from it, 2050.2
21:25 in Heshbon, and in all the villages **t**. 1886.3
21:32 they took the villages **t**, and drove out 1886.3
26:56 According to the lot shall the possession **t** 2050.2
28: 7 the drink offering **t** *shall be* the fourth 2050.2
28: 8 the morning, and as the drink offering **t**, 2050.2
28: 9 mingled with oil, and the drink offering **t**: 2050.2
29:19 the meat offering **t**, and their drink 1886.3
32:33 the land, with the cities **t** in the coasts, 1886.3
32:41 and took the small towns **t**, 1992.1
32:42 and the villages **t**, and called it Nobah, 1886.3
34: 2 the land of Canaan with the coasts **t**:) 1886.3
34: 4 the going forth **t** shall be from the south 2050.2
34:12 this shall be your land with the coasts **t** 1886.3
Dt 3:11 nine cubits *was* the length **t**, and 1886.3
3:12 half mount Gilead, and the cities **t**, gave I 2050.2
3:17 the coast **t**, from Chinnereth even unto NIH
9:21 I cast the dust **t** into the brook that 2050.2
12:15 the unclean and the clean may eat **t**, as of 5105.2
13:15 and all that *is* therein, and the cattle **t**, 1886.3
13:16 spoil of it into the midst of the street **t**, 1886.3
13:16 all the spoil **t** every whit, for the LORD 1886.3

Dt 15:23 Only thou shalt not eat the blood **t**; 2050.2
20:13 thou shalt smite every male **t** with 1886.3
20:14 all that is in the city, *even* all the spoil **t**, 1886.3
20:19 thou shalt not destroy the trees **t** by 1886.3
26:14 I have not eaten **t** in my mourning, 4480+5105.2
26:14 neither have I taken away *ought* **t** 4480+5105.2
26:14 *use*, nor given *ought* **t** for the dead: 4480+5105.1
28:30 and shalt not gather the grapes **t**. 5105.2
28:31 thine eyes, and thou shalt not eat **t**: 4480+5105.2
29:23 *And that* the whole land **t** *is* brimstone, 1886.3
33:16 precious things of the earth and fulness **t**, 1886.3
Jos 6: 2 the king **t**, *and* the mighty *men* of valour. 1886.3
6:26 he shall lay the foundation **t** in his 5089.1
7:14 shall come according to the families **t**; NIH
8: 2 only the spoil **t**, and the cattle thereof, 1886.3
8: 2 only the spoil thereof, and the cattle **t**, 1886.3
9: 1 the Hivite, and the Jebusite, heard **t**; NIH
10: 2 than Ai, and all the men **t** *were* mighty. 1886.3
10:28 the king **t** he utterly destroyed, them, 1886.3
10:30 the king **t**, into the hand of Israel; 1886.3
10:30 did unto the king **t** as he did unto the king 1886.3
10:37 the king **t**, and all the cities thereof, 1886.3
10:37 all the cities **t**, and all the souls that *were* 1886.3
10:39 and the king **t**, and all the cities thereof; 1886.3
10:39 and the king thereof, and all the cities **t**; 1886.3
10:39 so he did to Debir, and to the king **t**; 1886.3
11:10 and smote the king **t** with the sword: 1886.3
13:23 the border **t**. This *was* the inheritance of NIH
13:23 their families, the cities and villages **t**. 2006.1
15: 7 and the goings out **t** were at En-rogel: 2050.2
15:12 the coast **t**. This *is* the coast of the children NIH
15:47 and the great sea, and the border **t**. NIH
16: 3 and the goings out **t** are at the sea. 2050.2
16: 8 and the goings out **t** were at the sea. 2050.2
18:12 the goings out **t** were at the wilderness of NIH
18:14 the goings out **t** were at Kirjath-baal, 2050.2
18:20 by the coasts **t** round about, according to 1886.3
19:14 the outgoings **t** are *in* the valley of 2050.2
19:29 the outgoings **t** are at the sea from 2050.2
19:33 and the outgoings **t** were *at* Jordan: 2050.2
21: 2 dwell in, with the suburbs **t** for our cattle. 2006.1
21:11 with the suburbs **t** round about it. 1886.3
21:12 the fields of the city, and the villages **t**, 1886.3
22: 7 unto the *other* half **t** gave Joshua among 2050.2
23:14 *and* not one thing hath failed **t**. 4480+5105.2
Jdg 1:18 Also Judah took Gaza with the coast **t**, 1886.3
1:18 Askelon with the coast **t**, and Ekron with 1886.3
1:18 coast thereof, and Ekron with the coast **t**. 1886.3
1:26 built a city, and called the name **t** Luz: 1886.3
1:26 which *is* the name **t** unto this day. 1886.3
3: 2 at the least such as before knew nothing **t**: 3963.1
5:23 curse ye bitterly the inhabitants **t**; 1886.3
7:15 the interpretation **t**, that he worshipped, 2050.2
8:14 the elders **t**, *even* threescore 1886.3
8:27 Gideon made an ephod **t**, and put it in his 2050.2
14: 9 he took **t** in his hands, and went on eating, NIH
15:19 wherefore he called the name **t** 1886.3
17: 4 who made **t** a graven image and a molten 1930.2
1Sa 5: 6 *even* Ashdod and the coasts **t**. 1886.3
6: 8 trespass offering, in a coffer by the side **t**; 2050.2
7:14 the coasts **t** did Israel deliver out of 4993.1
17:51 drew it out of the sheath **t**, and slew him, 1886.3
20:20 I will shoot three arrows on the side **t**, as NIH
28:24 and did bake unleavened bread **t**: 1930.2
2Sa 20: 8 fastened upon his loins in the sheath **t**; 1886.3
23:16 nevertheless he would not drink **t**, but 3963.1
1Ki 2:32 my father David not knowing **t**, *to wit*, NIH
3:27 and in no wise slay it: she *is* the mother **t**. 2050.2
6: 2 the length **t** *was* threescore cubits, and 2050.2
6: 2 the breadth **t** twenty *cubits*, and the height 2050.2
6: 2 and the height **t** thirty cubits. 2050.2
6: 3 twenty cubits *was* the length **t**, 2050.2
6: 3 ten cubits *was* the breadth **t** before 2050.2
6:20 and twenty cubits in the height **t**: 2050.2
6:38 house finished throughout all the parts **t**, 2050.2
7: 2 the length **t** *was* an hundred cubits, and 2050.2
7: 2 the breadth **t** fifty cubits, and the height 2050.2
7: 2 fifty cubits, and the height **t** thirty cubits, 2050.2
7: 6 the length **t** *was* fifty cubits, and 2050.2
7: 6 and the breadth **t** thirty cubits: 2050.2
7:21 right pillar, and called the name **t** Jachin: 2050.2
7:21 the left pillar, and called the name **t** Boaz. 2050.2
7:26 the brim **t** was wrought like the brim of a 2050.2
7:27 four cubits the breadth **t**, and three cubits 1886.3
7:30 the four corners **t** had undersetters: under 2050.2
7:31 the mouth **t** *was* round *after* the work of 1886.3
7:35 on the top of the base the ledges **t** and 1886.3
7:35 and the borders **t** *were* of the same. 1886.3
7:36 For on the plates of the ledges **t**, and 1886.3
7:36 on the borders **t**, he graved cherubims, 1886.3
8: 7 covered the ark and the staves **t** above. 2050.2
13:26 him back from the way heard **t**, he said, NIH
15:21 when Baasha heard **t**, that he left off NIH
15:22 the timber **t**, where*with* Baasha had 1886.3
16:34 he laid the foundation **t** in Abiram his 1886.3
16:34 set up the gates **t** in his youngest *son* 1886.3
17:13 make me **t** a little cake first, and 4480+8033
2Ki 2:12 the chariot of Israel, and the horsemen **t**. 2050.2
3:25 only in Kir-haraseth left *they* the stones **t**; 1886.3
4:39 gathered **t** wild gourds his lap full, 4480+5105.2
4:40 *is* death in the pot. And they could not eat **t**. NIH
4:42 and full ears of corn in the husk **t**. 2050.2
4:43 They shall eat, and shall leave **t**. NIH
4:44 left **t**, according to the word of the LORD. NIH
7: 2 *it* with thine eyes, but shalt not eat **t**. 4480+8033
7:19 *it* with thine eyes, but shalt not eat **t**. 4480+8033
13:14 the chariot of Israel, and the horsemen **t**. 2050.2
15:16 and the coasts **t** from Tirzah: 1886.3
16:10 of it, according to all the workmanship **t**. 1930.2
17:24 and dwelt in the cities **t**. 1886.3
18: 8 *even* unto Gaza, and the borders **t**, 1886.3
19:23 will cut down the tall cedar trees **t**, *and* 2050.2
19:23 trees thereof, *and* the choice fir trees **t**: 2050.2
19:29 and plant vineyards, and eat the fruits **t**. 3963.1
22:16 this place, and upon the inhabitants **t**, 2050.2

2Ki 22:19 against the inhabitants **t**, that *they* should 2050.2
23: 6 cast the powder **t** upon the graves of 1886.3
1Ch 2:23 from them, with Kenath, and the towns **t**, 1886.3
6:55 and the suburbs **t** round about it. 1886.3
6:56 the fields of the city, and the villages **t**, 1886.3
7:28 habitations *were*, Beth-el and the towns **t**, 1886.3
7:28 and westward Gezer, with the towns **t**; 1886.3
7:28 Shechem also and the towns **t**, unto Gaza 1886.3
7:28 towns thereof, unto Gaza and the towns **t**: 1886.3
8:12 who built Ono, and Lod, with the towns **t**: 1886.3
9:27 the opening **t** every morning pertained to NIH
16:32 Let the sea roar, and the fulness **t**: let 2050.2
21:27 put up his sword again into the sheath **t**. 1886.3
23:26 nor any vessels of it for the service **t**. 2050.2
28:11 of the houses **t**, and of the treasuries 2050.2
28:11 of the treasuries **t**, and of the upper 2050.2
28:11 of the upper chambers **t**, and of the inner 2050.2
28:11 of the inner parlours **t**, and of the place of 2050.2
28:15 for every candlestick, and *for* the lamps **t**: 1886.3
28:15 the candlestick, and *also for* the lamps **t**, 1886.3
2Ch 3: 7 and the walls **t**, and the doors thereof, 2050.2
3: 7 walls thereof, and the doors **t**, with gold; 2050.2
3: 8 and the breadth **t** twenty cubits: 2050.2
4: 1 twenty cubits the length **t**, and 2050.2
4: 1 twenty cubits the breadth **t**, and ten cubits 2050.2
4: 1 and ten cubits the height **t**. 2050.2
4: 2 in compass, and five cubits the height **t**; 2050.2
4:22 the inner doors **t** for the most holy *place*, 2050.2
5: 8 covered the ark and the staves **t** above. 2050.2
13:11 the candlestick of gold with the lamps **t**, 1886.3
13:19 Beth-el with the towns **t**, and Jeshanah 1886.3
13:19 Jeshanah with the towns **t**, and Ephrain 1886.3
13:19 and Ephrain with the towns **t**. 1886.3
16: 6 the timber **t**, where*with* Baasha was a 1886.3
28:18 Shocho with the villages **t**, and Timnah 1886.3
28:18 Timnah with the villages **t**, Gimzo also 1886.3
28:18 Gimzo also and the villages **t**: 1886.3
29:18 with all the vessels **t**, and the shewbread 2050.2
29:18 shewbread table, with all the vessels **t**. 2050.2
32: 1 the establishment **t**, Sennacherib king of NIH
34:24 this place, and upon the inhabitants **t**, 2050.2
34:27 against the inhabitants **t**, and 2050.2
36:19 burnt all the palaces **t** with fire, and 1886.3
36:19 and destroyed all the goodly vessels **t**. 1886.3
Ezr 4:12 have set up the walls **t**, and joined NIH
4:16 be builded *again*, and the walls **t** set up, 1886.7
6: 3 and *let* the foundations **t** *be* strongly laid; 1958.2
6: 3 the height **t** threescore cubits, *and* 1886.8
6: 3 *and* the breadth **t** threescore cubits; 1886.8
9: 9 to repair the desolations **t**, and to give us 2050.2
10:14 the elders of every city, and the judges **t**, 1886.3
Ne 1: 3 and the gates **t** are burnt with fire. 1886.3
2: 3 and the gates **t** are consumed with fire? 1886.3
2:13 and the gates **t** were consumed with fire. 1886.3
2:17 and the gates **t** are burnt with fire: 1886.3
3: 3 who *also* laid the beams **t**, and set up 1930.2
3: 3 set up the doors **t**, the locks thereof, and 2050.2
3: 3 the locks **t**, and the bars thereof. 2050.2
3: 3 the locks thereof, and the bars **t**. 2050.2
3: 6 they laid the beams **t**, and set up the doors 1930.2
3: 6 set up the doors **t**, and the locks thereof, 2050.2
3: 6 and the locks **t**, and the bars thereof. 2050.2
3: 6 and the locks thereof, and the bars **t**. 2050.2
3:13 they built it, and set up the doors **t**, 2050.2
3:13 the locks **t**, and the bars thereof, and 2050.2
3:13 the bars **t**, and a thousand cubits on 2050.2
3:14 he built it, and set up the doors **t**, 2050.2
3:14 the locks **t**, and the bars thereof. 2050.2
3:14 the locks thereof, and the bars **t**. 2050.2
3:15 and covered it, and set up the doors **t**, 2050.2
3:15 the locks **t**, and the bars thereof, and 2050.2
3:15 the bars **t**, and the wall of the pool of 2050.2
4: 6 wall was joined together unto the half **t**: 1886.3
6:16 that when all our enemies heard **t**, and NIH
9:36 gavest unto our fathers to eat the fruit **t** 1886.3
9:36 to eat the fruit thereof and the good **t**, 1886.3
11:25 *in* the villages **t**, and at Dibon, and *in* 1886.3
11:25 *in* the villages **t**, and at Jekabzeel, and 1886.3
11:25 and at Jekabzeel, and *in* the villages **t**, 1886.3
11:27 and at Beer-sheba, and *in* the villages **t**, 1886.3
11:28 and at Mekonah, and in the villages **t**, 1886.3
11:30 the fields **t**, *at* Azekah, and *in* the villages 1886.3
11:30 *at* Azekah, and *in* the villages **t**. 1886.3
13:14 house of my God, and for the offices **t**. 2050.2
Est 1:22 every province according to the writing **t**, 1886.3
2:22 Esther certified the king **t** in Mordecai's NIH
3:12 every province according to the writing **t**, 1886.3
8: 9 on the three and twentieth *day* **t**; 871.1+2050.2
8: 9 every province according to the writing **t**, 1886.3
9:18 together on the thirteenth *day* **t**, 871.1+2050.2
9:18 and on the fourteenth **t**; 871.1+2050.2
Job 3: 9 Let the stars of the twilight **t** be dark; 2050.2
4:12 and mine ear received a little **t**. 4480+1930.2
4:16 but I could not discern the form **t**: 1930.2
9: 6 out of her place, and the pillars **t** tremble. 1886.3
9:24 he covereth the faces of the judges **t**; 1886.3
11: 9 The measure **t** *is* longer than the earth, 1886.3
14: 7 that the tender branch **t** will not cease. 2050.2
14: 8 Though the root **t** wax old in the earth, 2050.2
14: 8 and the stock **t** die in the ground; 2050.2
15:29 neither shall he prolong the perfection **t** 3963.1
24: 2 they violently take away flocks, and feed **t**. NIH
24:13 they know not the ways **t**, nor abide in 2050.2
24:13 the ways thereof, nor abide in the paths **t**. 2050.2
26: 5 under the waters, and the inhabitants **t**. 1992.1
28:13 Man knoweth not the price **t**; neither is it 1886.3
28:15 shall silver be weighed *for* the price **t**. 1886.3
28:22 We have heard the fame **t** with our ears. 1886.3
28:23 God understandeth the way **t**, and 1886.3
28:23 way thereof, and he knoweth the place **t**. 1886.3
31:17 the fatherless hath not eaten **t**; 4480+5089.1
31:38 or that the furrows likewise **t** complain; 1886.3
31:39 If I have eaten the fruits **t** without money, 1886.3
31:39 caused the owners **t** to lose their life: 1886.3
36:27 pour down rain according to the vapour **t**: 2050.2

Job 36:33 The noise t sheweth concerning it, 2050.2
38: 5 Who hath laid the measures t, if thou 1886.3
38: 6 Whereupon are the foundations t 1886.3
38: 6 or who laid the corner stone t; 1886.3
38: 9 When I made the cloud the garment t, 2050.2
38:19 and *as for* darkness, where *is* the place t, 2050.2
38:20 That thou shouldest take it to the bound t, 2050.2
38:20 shouldest know the paths to the house t? 2050.2
38:33 canst thou set the dominion t in the earth? 2050.2
Ps 19: 6 and there is nothing hid from the heat t. 2050.2
24: 1 earth *is* the LORD'S, and the fulness t; 1886.3
34: 2 the humble shall hear *t*, and be glad. NIH
46: 3 *Though* the waters t roar *and* be troubled, 2050.2
46: 3 the mountains shake with the swelling t. 2050.2
48:12 and go round about her: tell the towers t. 1886.3
50: 1 rising of the sun unto the going down t. 2050.2
50:12 for the world *is* mine, and the fulness t. 1886.3
55:10 night they go about it upon the walls t: 1886.3
55:11 Wickedness *is* in the midst t: deceit and 1886.3
60: 2 heal the breaches t; for it shaketh. 1886.3
65:10 *Thou* waterest the ridges t abundantly: 1886.3
65:10 *thou* settlest the furrows t: thou makest it 1886.3
65:10 thou blessest the springing t. 1886.3
71:15 all the day; for I know not the numbers *t*. NIH
72:16 the fruit t shall shake like Lebanon: 2050.2
74: 6 now they break down the carved work t 1886.3
75: 3 and all the inhabitants t *are* dissolved: 1886.3
75: 8 the dregs t, all the wicked of the earth 1886.3
80:10 the boughs t *were like* the goodly cedars. 1886.3
89: 9 when the waves t arise, thou stillest them. 2050.2
89:11 *as for* the world and the fulness t, 1886.3
96:11 be glad; let the sea roar, and the fulness t. 2050.2
97: 1 let the multitude of isles be glad *t*. NIH
98: 7 Let the sea roar, and the fulness t; 2050.2
102:14 in her stones, and favour the dust t. 1886.3
103:16 and the place t shall know it no more. 2050.2
107:25 which lifteth up the waves t. 2050.2
107:29 storm a calm, so that the waves t are still. 1992.1
137: 2 our harps upon the willows in the midst t. 1886.3
137: 7 *it*, rase *it*, *even* to the foundation t. 871.1+1886.3
Pr 1:19 taketh away the life of the owners t. 2050.2
3:14 of silver, and the gain t than fine gold. 1886.3
12:28 and *in* the pathway *t there is* no death. NIH
14:12 but the end t *are* the ways of death. 1886.3
16:25 but the end t *are* the ways of death. 1886.3
16:33 the whole disposing t *is* of the LORD. 2050.2
18:21 and they that love it shall eat the fruit t. 1886.3
20:21 but the end t shall not be blessed. 1886.3
21:22 down the strength of the confidence t. 1886.3
24:31 *and* nettles had covered the face t, and 2050.2
24:31 and the stone wall t was broken down. 2050.2
25: 8 *thou know not* what to do in the end t, 1886.3
27:18 keepeth the fig tree shall eat the fruit t: 1886.3
28: 2 of a land many *are* the princes t: 1886.3
28: 2 knowledge the state *t* shall be prolonged. NIH
Ecc 5:11 what good *is there* to the owners t, 1886.3
5:13 *namely*, riches kept for the owners t to 2050.2
5:19 hath given him power to eat t, 4480+5105.2
6: 2 God giveth him not power to eat t, 4480+5105.2
7: 8 *is* the end of a thing than the beginning t: 2050.2
SS 1:12 my spikenard sendeth forth the smell t. 2050.2
3:10 He made the pillars t *of* silver, the bottom 2050.2
3:10 the bottom t *of* gold, the covering of it *of* 2050.2
3:10 the midst t being paved *with* love, 2050.2
4:16 my garden, *that* the spices t may flow out. 2050.2
7: 8 I will take hold of the boughs t: 2050.2
8: 6 the coals t *are* coals of fire, *which hath* a 1886.3
8:11 every one for the fruit t was to bring a 2050.2
8:12 those that keep the fruit t two hundred. 2050.2
Isa 3:14 ancients of his people, and the princes t: 2050.2
4: 4 the midst t by the spirit of judgment, 1886.3
5: 2 gathered out the stones t, and planted it 1930.2
5: 5 I *will* take away the hedge t, and it shall 2050.2
5: 5 *and* break down the wall t, and it shall be 2050.2
5:30 and the light is darkened in the heavens t. 1886.3
6:13 *so* the holy seed *shall be* the substance t. 1886.3
13: 9 and he shall destroy the sinners t out of it. 1886.3
13:10 the constellations t shall not give their 1992.1
14:17 as a wilderness, and destroyed the cities t; 2050.2
15: 8 the howling t unto Eglaim, and 1886.3
15: 8 and the howling t *unto* Beer-elim. 1886.3
16: 8 have broken down the principal plants t, 1886.3
17: 6 *or* five in the outmost fruitful branches t, 1886.3
19: 3 the spirit of Egypt shall fail in the midst t; 2050.2
19: 3 and I will destroy the counsel t: 2050.2
19:10 they shall be broken *in* the purposes t, 1886.3
19:13 *even they that are* the stay of the tribes t. 1886.3
19:14 mingled a perverse spirit in the midst t: 1886.3
19:14 have caused Egypt to err in every work t, 1930.2
19:17 every one that maketh mention t shall be 1886.3
19:19 and a pillar at the border t to the LORD. 1886.3
21: 2 all the sighing t have I made to cease. 1886.3
22:11 ye have not looked unto the Maker t, 1886.3
23:11 *city*, to destroy the strong holds t. 1886.3
23:13 they set up the towers t, they raised up 2050.2
23:13 they raised up the palaces t; 1886.3
24: 1 and scattereth abroad the inhabitants t. 1886.3
24: 5 also is defiled under the inhabitants t; 1886.3
24:20 the transgression t shall be heavy upon it; 1886.3
27:10 he lie down, and consume the branches t. 1886.3
27:11 When the boughs t are withered, 1886.3
28:25 When he hath made plain the face t, 1886.3
30:27 *with* his anger, and the burden *t is* heavy: NIH
30:33 the pile t *is* fire and much wood; 1886.3
31: 4 to fight for mount Zion, and for the hill t. 1886.3
33:20 not one of the stakes t shall ever be 2050.2
33:20 neither shall any of the cords t be broken. 2050.2
34: 9 the streams t shall be turned into pitch, 1886.3
34: 9 the dust t into brimstone, and the land 1886.3
34: 9 and the land t shall become burning pitch. 1886.3
34:10 nor day; the smoke t shall go up for ever: 1886.3
34:12 They shall call the nobles t *to* 1886.3
34:13 nettles and brambles in the fortresses t: 1886.3
37:24 I will cut down the tall cedars t, *and* 2050.2
37:24 cedars thereof, *and* the choice fir trees t: 2050.2

Isa 37:30 and plant vineyards, and eat the fruit t. 3963.1
40: 6 all the goodliness t *is* as the flower of 2050.2
40:16 nor the beasts t sufficient *for* a burnt 2050.2
40:22 and the inhabitants t *are* as grasshoppers; 1886.3
41: 9 called thee from the chief men t, and 1886.3
42:10 is therein; the isles, and the inhabitants t. 1992.1
42:11 the cities t lift up *their voice*, the villages 2050.2
44:15 for he will take t, and 4480+1992.1
44:16 He burneth part t in the fire; with part 2050.2
44:16 with part t he eateth flesh; he roasteth 2050.2
44:17 the residue t he maketh a god, *even* his 2050.2
44:19 also I have baked bread upon the coals t; 2050.2
44:19 I make the residue t an abomination? 2050.2
44:26 and I will raise up the decayed places t: 1886.3
48:19 offspring of thy bowels like the gravel t; 2050.2
62: 1 until the righteousness t go forth as 1886.3
62: 1 and the salvation t as a lamp *that* burneth. 1886.3
Jer 1:13 and the face t *is* towards the north. 2050.2
1:15 against all the walls t round about, and 1886.3
1:18 against the princes t, against the priests 1886.3
1:18 against the priests t, and against 1886.3
2: 7 to eat the fruit t and the goodness thereof; 1886.3
2: 7 to eat the fruit thereof and the goodness t; 1886.3
4:26 all the cities t were broken down at 2050.2
5: 1 and know, and seek in the broad places t, 1886.3
5:22 though the waves t toss themselves, 2050.2
5:31 *it* so: and what will ye do in the end t? 1886.3
6:24 We have heard the fame t: our hands wax 2050.2
11:19 Let us destroy the tree with the fruit t, 2050.2
14: 2 Judah mourneth, and the gates t languish; 1886.3
14: 8 of Israel, the saviour t in time of trouble, 2050.2
17:27 will I kindle a fire in the gates t, and 1886.3
19: 8 and hiss because of all the plagues t. 1886.3
19:12 to the inhabitants t, and *even* make this 2050.2
20: 5 all the labours t, and all the precious 1886.3
20: 5 all the precious things t, and all 1886.3
21:14 I will kindle a fire in the forest t, and 1886.3
23:14 and the inhabitants t as Gomorrah. 1886.3
25: 9 against the inhabitants t, and against all 1886.3
25:18 and the kings t, *and* the princes thereof, 1886.3
25:18 and the kings thereof, *and* the princes t, 1886.3
26:15 upon this city, and upon the inhabitants t: 1886.3
29: 7 for in the peace t shall ye have peace. 1886.3
30:18 the palace shall remain after the manner t. 2050.2
31:23 in the land of Judah and in the cities t, 2050.2
31:24 *in* all the cities t together, husbandmen, 2050.2
31:35 which divideth the sea when the waves t 2050.2
33: 2 Thus saith the LORD the maker t, 1886.3
33:12 and without beast, and in all the cities t, 2050.2
34: 1 and against all the cities t, saying, 1886.3
34:18 in twain, and passed between the parts t, 2050.2
46: 8 the city and the inhabitants t. 871.1+1886.3
46:22 The voice t shall go like a serpent; 1886.3
48: 9 for the cities t shall be desolate, without 1886.3
48:38 housetops of Moab, and in the streets t: 1886.3
49:13 all the cities t shall be perpetual wastes. 1886.3
49:17 and shall hiss at all the plagues t. 1886.3
49:18 and Gomorrah and the neighbour *cities* t, 1886.3
49:21 the noise t was heard in the Red sea. 1886.3
49:32 I will bring their calamity from all sides t, 2050.2
50:29 it round about; let none t escape: 1886.3+3807.1
50:40 and Gomorrah and the neighbour *cities* t, 1886.3
51:28 the captains t, and all the rulers thereof, 1886.3
51:28 all the rulers t, and all the land of his 1886.3
51:42 with the multitude of the waves t. 2050.2
52:21 and the thickness t *was* four fingers: 2050.2
La 2: 2 polluted the kingdom and the princes t. 1886.3
4:11 and it hath devoured the foundations t. 1886.3
Eze 1: 4 out of the midst t as the colour of amber, 1886.3
1: 5 Also out of the midst t *came* the likeness 1886.3
4: 9 in one vessel, and make thee bread t, 3963.1
4: 9 and ninety days shalt thou eat t. 5105.2
5: 3 Thou shalt also take t a few in 4480+8033
5: 4 *for* t shall a fire come forth into all 4480+5105.2
7:12 for wrath *is* upon all the multitude t. 1886.3
7:13 vision *is* touching the whole multitude t, 1886.3
7:14 for my wrath *is* upon all the multitude t. 1886.3
9: 4 abominations that be done in the midst t. 1886.3
10: 7 took *t*, and put *it* into the hands of *him that* NIH
11: 6 ye have filled the streets t *with* the slain. 1886.3
11: 9 I will bring you out of the midst t, and 1886.3
11:11 neither shall ye be the flesh in the midst t; 1886.3
11:18 shall take away all the detestable things t 1886.3
11:18 and all the abominations t from thence. 1886.3
13:14 so that the foundation t shall be 2050.2
13:14 and ye shall be consumed in the midst t: 1886.3
14:13 will break the staff of the bread t, 1886.3+3807.1
15: 3 Shall wood be taken t to do *any* 4480+5105.2
17: 6 and the roots t were under him: 2050.2
17: 9 shall he not pull up the roots t, and cut off 1886.3
17: 9 and cut off the fruit t, that it wither? 1886.3
17: 9 many people to pluck it up by the roots t. 1886.3
17:12 hath taken the king t, and the princes 1886.3
17:12 the princes t, and led them with him to 1886.3
17:23 in the shadow of the branches t shall they 2050.2
19: 7 the land was desolate, and the fulness t, 1886.3
20:29 the name t is called Bamah unto this day. 1886.3
22:21 and ye shall be melted in the midst t. 1886.3
22:22 so shall ye be melted in the midst t; 1886.3
22:25 conspiracy of her prophets in the midst t, 1886.3
22:25 made her many widows in the midst t. 1886.3
22:27 Her princes in the midst t *are* like wolves 1886.3
23:34 thou shalt break the sheards t, and 1886.3
24: 4 Gather the pieces t into it, *even* every 1886.3
24:11 set it empty upon the coals t, that 1886.3
27: 9 the wise *men* t were in thee thy calkers: 1886.3
31:15 I restrained the floods t, and the great 1886.3
32: 7 the heaven, and make the stars t dark; 1992.1
32:12 and all the multitude t shall be destroyed. 1886.3
32:13 I will destroy also all the beasts t from 1886.3
38:13 with all the young lions t, shall say unto 1886.3
40: 6 went up the stairs t, and measured 2050.2
40: 9 the posts t, two cubits; and the porch of 2050.2
40:20 he measured the length t, and the breadth 2050.2
40:20 the length thereof, and the breadth t. 2050.2

Eze 40:21 the little chambers t *were* three on this 2050.2
40:21 the posts t and the arches thereof were 2050.2
40:21 the arches t were after the measure of 2050.2
40:21 the length t *was* fifty cubits, and 2050.2
40:22 and the arches t *were* before them. 2050.2
40:24 he measured the posts t and the arches 2050.2
40:24 the arches t according to these measures. 2050.2
40:25 in it and in the arches t round about, 2050.2
40:26 to it, and the arches t *were* before them: 2050.2
40:26 and another on that side, upon the posts t. 2050.2
40:29 the little chambers t, and the posts 2050.2
40:29 the posts t, and the arches thereof, 2050.2
40:29 the posts thereof, and the arches t, 2050.2
40:29 in it and in the arches t round about: 2050.2
40:31 the arches t *were* toward the utter court; 2050.2
40:31 and palm trees *were* upon the posts t: 2050.2
40:33 the little chambers t, and the posts 2050.2
40:33 and the posts t, and the arches thereof, 2050.2
40:33 and the posts thereof, and the arches t, 2050.2
40:33 and in the arches t round about: 2050.2
40:34 the arches t *were* toward the outward 2050.2
40:34 palm trees *were* upon the posts t, on this 2050.2
40:36 The little chambers t, the posts thereof, 2050.2
40:36 the posts t, and the arches thereof, and 2050.2
40:36 the arches t, and the windows to it round 2050.2
40:37 the posts t *were* toward the utter court; 2050.2
40:37 palm trees *were* upon the posts t, on this 2050.2
40:38 entries t *were* by the posts of the gates, 1886.3
41: 2 he measured the length t, forty cubits: 2050.2
41: 4 So he measured the length t, 2050.2
41:12 and the length t ninety cubits. 2050.2
41:13 and the building, with the walls t, 1886.3
41:15 the galleries t on the one side and on 1886.3
41:22 cubits high, and the length t two cubits; 2050.2
41:22 the corners t, and the length thereof, and 2050.2
41:22 the length t, and the walls thereof, 2050.2
41:22 and the walls t, *were of* wood: 2050.2
42: 7 the length t *was* fifty cubits. 2050.2
43:11 the fashion t, and the goings out thereof, 2050.2
43:11 the goings out t, and the comings in 2050.2
43:11 the comings in t, and all the forms 2050.2
43:11 all the forms t, and all the ordinances 2050.2
43:11 all the ordinances t, and all the forms 2050.2
43:11 all the forms t, and all the laws thereof: 2050.2
43:11 all the forms thereof, and all the laws t: 2050.2
43:11 that they may keep the whole form t, and 2050.2
43:11 and all the ordinances t, and do them. 2050.2
43:12 limit t round about *shall be* most holy. 2050.2
43:13 the border t by the edge thereof round 1886.3
43:13 the border thereof by the edge t round 1886.3
43:16 twelve broad, square in the four squares t. 2050.2
43:17 and fourteen broad in the four squares t; 1886.3
43:17 the bottom t *shall be* a cubit about; and 1886.3
43:20 thou shalt take of the blood t, and put *it* 2050.2
44: 5 house of the LORD, and all the laws t; 2050.2
44:14 for all the service t, and for all that shall 2050.2
45: 1 This *shall be* holy in all the borders t 1886.3
45: 2 fifty cubits round about *for* the suburbs t. 2050.2
45:11 the measure t shall be after the homer. 2050.2
46: 8 and he shall go forth by the way t. 2050.2
46:16 the inheritance t shall be his sons'; 2050.2
47:11 the miry places t and the marishes thereof 2050.2
47:11 and the marishes t shall not be healed; 2050.2
47:12 by the river upon the bank t, on this side 2050.2
47:12 neither shall the fruit t be consumed: 2050.2
47:12 the fruit t shall be for meat, and the leaf 2050.2
47:12 be for meat, and the leaf t for medicine. 1930.2
48:10 of the LORD shall be in the midst t. 2050.2
48:15 and the city shall be in the midst t. 2050.2
48:16 these *shall be* the measures t; the north 1886.3
48:18 the increase t shall be for food unto them 2050.2
48:21 of the house *shall be* in the midst t. 2050.2
Da 1: 5 that at the end t they might stand before 3963.1
2: 5 with the interpretation t, ye shall be cut in 1886.8
2: 6 shew the dream, and the interpretation t, 1886.8
2: 6 me the dream, and the interpretation t. 1886.8
2: 9 that ye can shew me the interpretation t. 1886.8
2:26 I have seen, and the interpretation t? 1886.8
2:31 before thee; and the form t *was* terrible. 1886.8
2:36 we will tell the interpretation t before 1886.8
2:45 *is* certain, and the interpretation t sure. 1886.8
3: 1 *and* the breadth t six cubits: 1886.8
4: 7 make known unto me the interpretation t. 1886.8
4: 9 that I have seen, and the interpretation t. 1886.8
4:10 of the earth, and the height t *was* great. 1886.8
4:11 the height t reached unto heaven, and 1886.8
4:11 the sight t to the end of all the earth: 1886.8
4:12 The leaves t *were* fair, and the fruit 1886.8
4:12 the fruit t much, and in it *was* meat for 1886.8
4:12 fowls of the heaven dwelt in the boughs t, 1958.2
4:18 O Belteshazzar, declare the interpretation t, NIH
4:19 or the interpretation t, trouble thee. NIH
4:19 and the interpretation t to thine enemies. 1886.8
4:20 the heaven, and the sight t to all the earth; 1886.8
4:21 the fruit t much, and in it *was* meat for 1886.8
4:23 yet leave the stump of the roots t in 1958.2
5: 7 shew me the interpretation t, shall be 1886.8
5: 8 known to the king the interpretation t. 1886.8
5:15 make known unto me the interpretation t: 1886.8
5:16 make known to me the interpretation t, 1886.8
7: 4 I beheld till the wings t were pluckt, and 1886.9
9:26 the end t *shall be* with a flood, and 2050.2
Hos 2: 9 take *away* my corn in the time t, and 2050.2
2: 9 my wine in the season t, and will recover 2050.2
4:13 and elms, because the shadow t *is* good: 1886.3
8:14 and it shall devour the palaces t. 1886.3
9: 4 all that eat t shall be polluted: 2050.2
10: 5 for the people t shall mourn over it, and 2050.2
10: 5 the priests t *that* rejoiced on it, 5921+2050.2
10: 5 for the glory t, because it is departed from NIH
14: 7 the sent t *shall be* as the wine of Lebanon. 2050.2
Joel 1: 7 *it* away; the branches t are made white. 1886.3
Am 1: 3 I will not turn away *the punishment* t; 5105.2
1: 6 I will not turn away *the punishment* t; 5105.2
1: 7 of Gaza, which shall devour the palaces t: 1886.3

Am 1: 9 I will not turn away *the punishment* t; 5105.2
1:10 which shall devour the palaces t. 1886.3
1:11 I will not turn away *the punishment* t; 5105.2
1:13 I will not turn away *the punishment* t; 5105.2
1:14 it shall devour the palaces t, 1886.3
2: 1 I will not turn away *the punishment* t; 5105.2
2: 3 I will cut off the judge from the midst t, 1886.3
2: 3 will slay all the princes t with him, 1886.3
2: 4 I will not turn away *the punishment* t; 5105.2
2: 6 I will not turn away *the punishment* t; 5105.2
3: 9 behold the great tumults in the midst t, 1886.3
3: 9 and the oppressed in the midst t. 1886.3
8:10 an only *son,* and the end t as a bitter day. 1886.3
9:11 that is fallen, and close up the breaches t; 2006.1
9:14 plant vineyards, and drink the wine t; 3963.1
Jnh 1: 3 so he paid the fare t, and went down into 1886.3
Mic 1: 6 I will pour down the stones t into 1886.3
1: 6 and I will discover the foundations t. 1886.3
1: 7 all the graven images t shall be beaten to 1886.3
1: 7 all the hires t shall be burnt with the fire, 1886.3
1: 7 and all the idols t will I lay desolate: 1886.3
3:11 The heads t judge for reward, and 1886.3
3:11 the priests t teach for hire, and 1886.3
3:11 and the prophets t divine for money: 1886.3
5: 6 and the land of Nimrod in the entrances t: 1886.3
6:12 For the rich *men* t are full *of* violence, 1886.3
6:12 the inhabitants t have spoken lies, and 1886.3
6:16 and the inhabitants t a hissing: 1886.3
Na 1: 8 he will make an utter end of the place t, 1886.3
2: 5 they shall make haste *to* the wall t, and 1886.3
Hab 2:18 image that the maker t hath graven it; 2050.2
Zep 1:13 plant vineyards, but not drink the wine t. 3963.1
3: 5 The just LORD *is* in the midst t; he will 1886.3
Zec 2: 2 to see what *is* the breadth t, and what *is* 1886.3
2: 2 breadth thereof, and what *is* the length t. 1886.3
3: 9 behold, I *will* engrave the graving t, 1886.3
4: 2 seven lamps, which *were* upon the top t: 1886.3
4: 3 and the other upon the left *side* t. 1886.3
4: 7 he shall bring forth the headstone *t with* NIH
4:11 the candlestick and upon the left *side* t? 1886.3
5: 2 the length t *is* twenty cubits, and 1886.3
5: 2 and the breadth t ten cubits. 1886.3
5: 4 shall consume it with the timber t and 2050.2
5: 4 it with the timber thereof and the stones t. 2050.2
5: 8 cast the weight of lead upon the mouth t. 1886.3
7: 7 and the cities t round about her, 1886.3
8: 5 *of* boys and girls playing in the streets t. 1886.3
9: 1 and Damascus *shall be* the rest t: 2050.2
14: 4 shall cleave in the midst t toward the east 2050.2
Mal 1:12 the fruit t, *even* his meat, *is* contemptible. 2050.2
Mt 2:16 and in all the coasts t, from two years old *846*
6:34 of itself. Sufficient unto the day *is* the evil t. *846*
12:36 they shall give account t in the day of *4012*
13:32 of the air come and lodge in the branches t. *846*
13:44 and for joy t goeth and selleth all that he *846*
14:13 when the people had heard *t*, they followed NIG
21:43 given to a nation bringing forth the fruits t. *846*
22: 7 But when the king heard *t*, he was wroth: NIG
27:34 when he had tasted *t*, he would not drink. NIG
Mk 6:16 But when Herod heard *t*, he said, It is John, NIG
Lk 19:33 the owners t said unto them, Why loose ye *846*
21:20 then know that the desolation t is nigh. *846*
22:16 unto you, I will not any more eat t, *846+1537*
Jn 3: 8 and thou hearest the sound t, but canst not *846*
4:12 and drank t himself, and his children, *846+1537*
6:50 from heaven, that a man may eat t, *846+1537*
7: 7 I testify of it, that the works t are evil. *846*
Ac 15:16 and I will build again the ruins t, and I will *846*
Ro 6:12 that *ye* should obey it in the lusts t. *846*
13:14 provision for the flesh, to *fulfil* the lusts *t*. NIG
1Co 9: 7 a vineyard, and eateth not of the fruit t? *846*
9:23 that I might be partaker t with *you.* *846*
10:26 For the earth *is* the Lord's, and the fulness t. *846*
10:28 for the earth *is* the Lord's, and the fulness t: *846*
2Ti 3: 5 a form of godliness, but denying the power t: *846*
Heb 7:18 for the weakness and unprofitableness t. *846*
Jas 1:11 and the flower t falleth, and the grace of *846*
1Pe 1:24 and the flower t falleth away: *846*
5: 2 taking the oversight *t*, not by constraint, but NIG
1Jn 2:17 And the world passeth away, and the lust t: *846*
Rev 5: 2 to open the book, and to loose the seals t? *846*
5: 5 open the book, and to loose the seven seals t. *846*
5: 9 to take the book, and to open the seals t: *846*
16:12 and the water t was dried up, that the way of *846*
16:21 for the plague t was exceeding great. *846*
21:15 the city, and the gates t, and the wall thereof. *846*
21:15 the city, and the gates thereof, and the wall t. *846*
21:17 And he measured the wall t, an hundred *and* *846*
21:23 did lighten it, and the Lamb *is* the light t. *846*

THEREON (66) [ON]

Ge 35:14 he poured a drink offering t, and 5921+1886.3
35:14 and he poured oil t. 5921+1886.3
Ex 17:12 and put *it* under him, and he sat t; 5921+1886.3
20:24 shalt sacrifice t thy burnt offerings, 5921+2050.2
20:26 thy nakedness be not discovered t. 5921+2050.2
30: 7 Aaron shall burn t sweet incense 5921+2050.2
30: 9 Ye shall offer no strange incense t, 5921+2050.2
30: 9 shall ye pour drink offering t. 5921+2050.2
40:27 he burnt sweet incense t; as 5921+2050.2
40:35 because the cloud abode t, and 5921+2050.2
Lev 2: 1 oil upon it, and put frankincense t: 5921+1886.3
2: 6 part it in pieces, and pour oil t: 5921+1886.3
2:15 oil upon it, and lay frankincense t: 5921+1886.3
5:11 shall he put *any* frankincense t: 5921+1886.3
6:12 he shall burn t the fat of the peace 5921+1886.3
10: 1 put incense t, and offered strange 5921+1886.3
11:38 *any part* of their carcase fall t, it *shall be* 5921
Nu 4: 6 shall put t the covering of badgers' 5921+2050.2
4: 7 put t the dishes, and the spoons, 5921+2050.2
4: 7 and the continual bread shall be t: 5921+2050.2
4:13 and spread a purple cloth t: 5921+2050.2
5:15 oil upon it, nor put frankincense t; 5921+2050.2
9:22 remaining t, the children of Israel 5921+2050.2
16:18 laid incense t, and stood *in* 5921+1992.1
Dt 27: 6 thou shalt offer burnt offerings t 5921+2050.2
Jos 8:29 raise t a great heap of stones, 5921
8:31 they offered t burnt offerings unto 5921+2050.2
22:23 or if to offer t burnt offering or 5921+2050.2
22:23 or if to offer peace offerings t, 5921+2050.2
2Sa 17:19 and spread ground corn t; 5921+2050.2
19:26 I may ride t, and go to the king; 5921+1886.3
1Ki 6:35 he carved *t* cherubims and palm trees and NIH
13:13 saddled him the ass: and he rode t, 5921+2050.2
2Ki 16:12 to the altar, and offered t. 5921+2050.2
1Ch 12:17 the God of our fathers look *t*, and rebuke *it.* NIH
15:15 their shoulders with the staves t, 5921+1992.1
2Ch 3: 5 and set t palm trees and chains. 5921+2050.2
3:14 and wrought cherubims t. 5921+2050.2
33:16 sacrificed t peace offerings and 5921+2050.2
Ezr 3: 2 of Israel, to offer burnt offerings t, 5921+2050.2
3: 3 they offered burnt offerings t unto 5921+2050.2
6:11 being set up, let him be hanged t; 5922+1958.2
Est 5:14 that Mordecai may be hanged t: 5921+2050.2
7: 9 Then the king said, Hang him t. 5921+2050.2
Isa 30:12 and perverseness, and stay t: 5921+2050.2
35: 9 nor *any* ravenous beast shall go up t, 5089.1
Eze 15: 3 a pin of it to hang any vessel t? 5921+2050.2
40:39 to slay t the burnt offering and 413+1992.1
43:18 to offer burnt offerings t, and 5921+2050.2
43:18 and to sprinkle blood t. 5921+2050.2
Zec 4: 2 his seven lamps t, and seven pipes to 1886.3
Mt 21: 7 on them their clothes, and they set *him* t. *1883*
21:19 he came to it, and found nothing t, *846+1722*
23:20 sweareth by it, and by all *things* t. *846+1883*
23:22 of God, and by him that sitteth t. *846+1883*
Mk 11:13 if haply he might find any *thing* t: *846+1722*
14:72 And when he **thought** t, he wept. *1911*
Lk 13: 6 and he came and sought fruit t, *846+1722*
19:35 upon the colt, and they **set** Jesus t. *1913*
Jn 12:14 when he had found a young ass, sat t; *846+1909*
21: 9 of coals there, and fish **laid** t, and bread. *1945*
1Co 3:10 laid the foundation, and another **buildeth** t. *2026*
Rev 5: 3 was able to open the book, neither to look t. *846*
5: 4 and to read the book, neither to look t. *846*
6: 4 *power* was given to him that sat t to take *1909*
21:12 twelve angels, and names **written** *t*on, *1924*

THEREOUT (2) [OUT]

Lev 2: 2 he shall take t his handful of 4480+8033
Jdg 15:19 in the jaw, and there came water t; 4480+5105.2

THERETO (20) [TO]

Ex 25:24 and make t a crown *of* gold round about. 2050.2
29:41 shalt do t according to the meat offering of NIH
30:38 to smell t, shall even be cut off 871.1+1886.3
Lev 5:16 and shall add the fifth *part* t, 5921+2050.2
6: 5 shall add the fifth *part* more t, *and* give it 2050.2
18:23 woman stand before a beast to lie down t: 1886.3
20:16 lie down t, thou shalt kill the woman and 1886.3
27:27 and shall add a fifth *part* of it t: 5921
27:31 he shall add t the fifth *part* thereof. 5921+2050.2
Nu 3:36 the vessels thereof, and all that serveth t, 2050.2
19:17 water shall be put t in a vessel: 5921+2050.2
Dt 12:32 not add t, nor diminish from it. 5921+2050.2
Jdg 11:17 the king of Edom would not hearken *t*. And NIH
1Ch 22:14 I prepared; and thou mayest add t. 5921+1992.1
2Ch 10:14 your yoke heavy, but I will add t: 5921+2050.2
21:11 commit fornication, and compelled Judah *t*. NIH
Ps 119: 9 by taking heed *t* according to thy word. NIH
Isa 44:15 graven image, and falleth down t. 3807.1+4123.1
Mk 14:70 art a Galilean, and thy speech agreeth *t*. NIG
Gal 3:15 no *man* disannulleth, or added t. NIG

THEREUNTO (9) [UNTO]

Ex 32: 8 have sacrificed t, and said, 2050.2+3807.1
36:36 he made t four pillars of shittim 1886.3+3807.1
37:11 t a crown *of* gold round about. 2050.2+3807.1
37:12 Also he made t a border of a 2050.2+3807.1
Dt 1: 7 unto all *the places* nigh t, in the plain, 2050.2
Eph 6:18 and watching t with all *846+1519+3778*
1Th 3: 3 know that we are appointed t. *1519+3778*
Heb 10: 1 year continually make the comers *t* perfect. NIG
1Pe 3: 9 knowing that ye are t called, that ye *1519+3778*

THEREUPON (5) [UPON]

Ex 31: 7 the mercy seat that *is* t, and all 5921+2050.2
Eze 16:16 and playedst the harlot t: 5921+1992.1
Zep 2: 7 house of Judah; they shall feed t: 5921+1992.1
1Co 3:10 let every man take heed how he **buildeth** t. *2026*
3:14 *man's* work abide which he hath **built** t, *2026*

THEREWITH (36) [WITH]

Ex 22: 6 be consumed *t*; he that kindled the fire shall NIH
30:26 tabernacle of the congregation t, 871.1+2050.2
38:30 t he made the sockets to the door 871.1+1886.3
Lev 7: 7 the priest that maketh atonement t 871.1+2050.2
8: 7 and bound *it* unto him t. 871.1+2050.2
15:32 goeth from him, and is defiled t; 871.1+1886.3
18:23 with any beast to defile *thyself* t: 871.1+1886.3
22: 8 he shall not eat to defile *himself* t: 871.1+1886.3
Dt 16: 3 shalt thou eat unleavened bread t, 5921+2050.2
23:13 thou shalt dig t, and shalt turn 871.1+1886.3
Jdg 15:15 took it, and slew a thousand men t. 871.1+1886.3
16:12 bound him t, and said unto him, 871.1+1992.1
1Sa 12: 3 *any* bribe to blind mine eyes t? 871.1+2050.2
17:51 slew him, and cut off his head t. 871.1+1886.3
31: 4 and thrust me through t; 871.1+1886.3
2Sa 20:10 so he smote him t in the fifth *rib,* 871.1+1886.3
2Ki 5: 6 I have t sent Naaman my servant to thee, NIH
12:14 t the house of the LORD. 871.1+2050.2
1Ch 10: 4 and thrust me through t; 871.1+1886.3
23: 5 which I made, *said David,* to praise *t*. NIH
2Ch 16: 6 and he built t Geba and Mizpah. 871.1+1992.1
Pr 15:16 than great treasure and trouble t. 871.1+2050.2
15:17 than a stalled ox and hatred t. 871.1+2050.2
17: 1 *is* a dry morsel, and quietness t, 871.1+1886.3
25:16 lest thou be filled t, and vomit it. 5105.2
Ecc 1:13 given to the sons of man to be exercised t. 871.1
2: 6 to water t the wood that bringeth forth 4480
10: 9 removeth stones shall be hurt t; 871.1+1992.1
Isa 10:15 itself against him that heweth t? 871.1+2050.2
Eze 4:15 and thou shalt prepare thy bread t. 5921+1992.1
Joel 2:19 and oil, and ye shall be satisfied t: 854+2050.2
Php 4:11 in whatsoever *state* I am, *t* to be content. NIG
1Ti 6: 8 having food and raiment let us be t content. *3778*
Jas 3: 9 T bless we God, even the Father; and *846+1722*
3: 9 and t curse we men, which are made *846+1722*
3Jn 1:10 and not content t, neither doth he *1909+3778*

THESE (1225) [THIS]

Ge 2: 4 T *are* the generations of the heavens and 428
6: 9 T *are* the generations of Noah: Noah was a 428
9:19 T *are* the three sons of Noah: and of them 428
10: 1 Now t *are* the generations of the sons of 428
10: 5 By t were the isles of the Gentiles divided in 428
10:20 T *are* the sons of Ham, after their families, 428
10:29 and Jobab: all t *were* the sons of Joktan. 428
10:31 T *are* the sons of Shem, after their families, 428
10:32 T *are* the families of the sons of Noah, 428
10:32 by t were the nations divided in the earth 428
11:10 T *are* the generations of Shem: Shem *was* an 428
11:27 Now t *are* the generations of Terah: 428
14: 2 *That* t made war with Bera king of Sodom, NIH
14: 3 All t were joined together in the vale of 428
14:13 and t *were* confederate with Abram. 1992
15: 1 After t things the word of the LORD came 428
15:10 he took unto him all t, and divided them in 428
19: 8 only unto t men do nothing; for therefore 411
20: 8 and told all t things in their ears: 428
21:29 What *mean* t seven ewe lambs which thou 428
21:30 For *t* seven ewe lambs shalt thou take of my NIH
22: 1 it came to pass after t things, that God did 428
22:20 it came to pass after t things, that it was told 428
22:23 t eight Milcah did bear to Nahor, 428
23: 1 *t were* the years of the life of Sarah. NIH
24:28 and told *them of* her mother's house t things. 428
25: 4 Eldaah. All t *were* the children of Keturah. 428
25: 7 t *are* the days of the years of Abraham's life 428
25:12 Now t *are* the generations of Ishmael, 428
25:13 t *are* the names of the sons of Ishmael, 428
25:16 T *are* the sons of Ishmael, and these *are* their 428
25:16 t *are* their names, by their towns, and 428
25:17 t *are* the years of the life of Ishmael, 428
25:19 t *are* the generations of Isaac, 428
26: 3 I will give all t countries, and I will perform 411
26: 4 and will give unto thy seed all t countries; 411
27:36 for he hath supplanted me t two times: he 2088
27:42 t words of Esau her elder son were told to NIH
27:46 such as t *which are* of the daughters of 428
29:13 to his house. And he told Laban all t things. 428
31:43 *T* daughters *are* my daughters, and *these* NIH
31:43 *t* children *are* my children, and *these* cattle NIH
31:43 *t* cattle *are* my cattle, and all that thou seest NIH
31:43 what can I do *this* day unto t my daughters, 428
32:17 goest thou? and whose *are* t before thee? 428
33: 8 *T are* to find grace in the sight of my lord. NIH
34:21 T men *are* peaceable with us; therefore 428
35:26 t *are* the sons of Jacob, which were born to 428
36: 1 Now t *are* the generations of Esau, who *is* 428
36: 5 t *are* the sons of Esau, which were born unto 428
36: 9 t *are* the generations of Esau the father of 428
36:10 T *are* the names of Esau's sons; Eliphaz 428
36:12 t *were* the sons of Adah Esau's wife. 428
36:13 t *are* the sons of Reuel; Nahath, and Zerah, 428
36:13 t were the sons of Bashemath Esau's wife. 428
36:14 t were the sons of Aholibamah, the daughter 428
36:15 T *were* dukes of the sons of Esau: the sons 428
36:16 t *are* the dukes *that came* of Eliphaz in 428
36:16 the land of Edom; t *were* the sons of Adah. 428
36:17 t *are* the sons of Reuel Esau's son; 428
36:17 t *are* the dukes *that came* of Reuel in 428
36:17 t *are* the sons of Bashemath Esau's wife. 428
36:18 t *are* the sons of Aholibamah Esau's wife; 428
36:18 t *were* the dukes *that came* of Aholibamah 428
36:19 T *are* the sons of Esau, who *is* Edom, and 428
36:19 of Esau, who *is* Edom, and t *are* their dukes. 428
36:20 T *are* the sons of Seir the Horite, 428
36:21 t *are* the dukes of the Horites, the children of 428
36:23 the children of Shobal *were* t; Alvan, and 428
36:24 And t *are* the children of Zibeon; both Ajah, 428
36:25 the children of Anah *were* t; Dishon, and 428
36:26 t *are* the children of Dishon; Hemdan, and 428
36:27 The children of Ezer *are* t; Bilhan, and 428
36:28 The children of Dishan *are* t; Uz, and Aran. 428
36:29 T *are* the dukes *that came* of the Horites; 428
36:30 t *are* the dukes *that came* of Hori, 428
36:31 t *are* the kings that reigned in the land of 428
36:40 t *are* the names of the dukes *that came* of 428
36:43 t *be* the dukes of Edom, according to their 428
37: 2 T *are* the generations of Jacob. Joseph, 428
38:25 By the man, whose t *are, am* I with child: 428
38:25 whose *are* t, the signet, and bracelets, and 428
39: 7 it came to pass after t things, that his 428
39:17 she spake unto him according to t words, 428
40: 1 it came to pass after t things, *that* the butler 428
42:36 ye will take Benjamin *away:* all t **things** 5089.1
43: 7 we told him according to the tenor of t 428
43:16 Bring *t* men home, and slay, and NIH
43:16 for *t* men shall dine with me at noon. NIH
44: 6 and he spake unto them t *same* words. 428
44: 7 unto him, Wherefore saith my lord t words? 428
45: 6 For t two years *hath* the famine *been* in 2088
46: 8 And t *are* the names of the children of Israel, 428
46:15 T *be* the sons of Leah, which she bare unto 428
46:18 T *are* the sons of Zilpah, whom Laban gave 428
46:18 t she bare unto Jacob, *even* sixteen souls. 428
46:22 T *are* the sons of Rachel, which were born to 428
46:25 T *are* the sons of Bilhah, which Laban gave 428
46:25 his daughter, and she bare t unto Jacob: 428
48: 1 it came to pass after t things, that *one* told 428
48: 8 beheld Joseph's sons, and said, Who *are* t? 428
49:28 All t *are* the twelve tribes of Israel: and 428
Ex 1: 1 Now t *are* the names of the children of 428

T

Ex 4: 9 if they will not believe also t two signs, 428
6:14 T be the heads of their fathers' houses: 428
6:14 and Carmi: t be the families of Reuben. 428
6:15 t are the families of Simeon. 428
6:16 t are the names of the sons of Levi according 428
6:19 t are the families of Levi according to their 428
6:24 Abiasaph: t are the families of the Korhites. 428
6:25 t are the heads of the fathers of the Levites 428
6:26 T are that Aaron and Moses, to whom NIH
6:27 T are they which spake to Pharaoh king of NIH
6:27 from Egypt: t are that Moses and Aaron. NIH
10: 1 that I might shew t my signs before him: 428
11: 8 all t thy servants shall come down unto me, 428
11:10 and Aaron did all t wonders before Pharaoh: 428
14:20 to them, but it gave light by night to t so NIH
15:26 I will put none of t diseases upon thee, NIH
19: 6 T are the words which thou shalt speak unto 428
19: 7 laid before their faces all t words which 428
20: 1 And God spake all t words, saying, 428
21: 1 Now t are the judgments which thou shalt 428
21:11 if he do not t three unto her, then shall she 428
24: 8 hath made with you concerning all t words. 428
25:39 pure gold shall he make it, with all t vessels. 428
28: 4 t are the garments which they shall make; 428
30:34 t sweet spices with pure frankincense: NIH
32: 4 they said, T be thy gods, O Israel, 428
32: 8 and said, T be thy gods, O Israel, 428
33: 4 when the people heard t evil tidings, they 2088
34: 1 I will write upon t tables the words that NIH
34:27 said unto Moses, Write thou t words: 428
34:27 for after the tenor of t words I have made a 428
35: 1 T are the words which the LORD hath 428
Lev 2: 8 that is made of t things unto the LORD: 428
5: 4 of it, then he shall be guilty in one of t. 428
5: 5 when he shall be guilty in one of t things, 428
5:13 his sin that he hath sinned in one of t, 428
5:17 commit any of t things which are forbidden NIH
6: 3 in any of all t that a man doeth, sinning NIH
11: 2 T are the beasts which ye shall eat among 2063
11: 4 Nevertheless t shall ye not eat of them that 2088
11: 9 T shall ye eat of all that are in the waters: 2088
11:13 t are they which ye shall have in 428
11:21 Yet t may ye eat of every flying creeping 2088
11:22 Even t of them ye may eat; the locust after 428
11:24 for t ye shall be unclean: 428
11:29 T also shall be unclean unto you among 2088
11:31 T are unclean to you among all that creep: 428
16: 4 t are holy garments; therefore shall he wash 1992
18:24 Defile not you yourselves in any of t things: 428
18:24 t the nations are defiled which I cast out 428
18:26 and shall not commit any of t abominations; 428
18:27 (For all t abominations have the men of 411
18:29 For whosoever shall commit any of t 428
18:30 that ye commit not any one of t abominable NIH
20:23 for they committed all t things, and therefore 428
21:14 or profane, or a harlot, t shall he not take: 428
22:22 ye shall not offer t unto the LORD, 428
22:25 ye offer the bread of your God of any of t; 428
23: 2 be holy convocations, even t are my feasts. 428
23: 4 T are the feasts of the LORD, even holy 428
23:37 T are the feasts of the LORD, which ye 428
25:54 if he be not redeemed in t years, then 428
26:14 and will not do all t commandments; 428
26:23 if ye will not be reformed by me by t things, 428
26:46 T are the statutes and judgments and laws, 428
27:34 T are the commandments, which the LORD 428
Nu 1: 5 t are the names of the men that shall stand 428
1:16 T were the renowned of the congregation, 428
1:17 Aaron took t men which are expressed by 428
1:44 T are those that were numbered, 428
2: 9 their armies. T shall first set forth. NIH
2:32 T are those which were numbered of 428
3: 1 T also are the generations of Aaron and 428
3: 2 t are the names of the sons of Aaron; 428
3: 3 T are the names of the sons of Aaron, 428
3:17 And t were the sons of Levi by their names; 428
3:18 t are the names of the sons of Gershon by 428
3:20 T are the families of the Levites according to 428
3:21 t are the families of the Gershonites. 428
3:27 t are the families of the Kohathites. 428
3:33 of the Mushites: t are the families of Merari. 428
3:35 t shall pitch on the side of the tabernacle NIH
4:15 T things are the burden of the sons of 428
4:37 T were they that were numbered of 428
4:41 T are they that were numbered of 428
4:45 T be those that were numbered of 428
5:23 And the priest shall write t curses in a book, 428
13: 4 t were their names: of the tribe of Reuben, 428
13:16 T are the names of the men which Moses 428
14:22 have tempted me now t ten times, and 2088
14:39 Moses told t sayings unto all the children of 428
15:13 All that are born of the country shall do t 428
15:22 and not observed all t commandments, 428
16:14 wilt thou put out the eyes of t men? we will 1992
16:26 from the tents of t wicked men, and 428
16:28 the LORD hath sent me to do all t works; 428
16:29 If t men die the common death of all men, or 428
16:30 ye shall understand that t men have 428
16:31 as he had made an end of speaking all t 428
16:38 The censers of t sinners against their own 428
21:25 Israel took all t cities: and Israel dwelt in all 428
22: 9 and said, What men are t with thee? 428
22:28 that thou hast smitten me t three times? 2088
22:32 Wherefore hast thou smitten thine ass t 2088
22:33 saw me, and turned from me t three times: 2088
24:10 thou hast altogether blessed them t three 2088
26: 7 T are the families of the Reubenites: and 428
26:14 T are the families of the Simeonites, twenty 428
26:18 T are the families of the children of Gad 428
26:22 T are the families of Judah according to 428
26:25 T are the families of Issachar according to 428
26:27 T are the families of the Zebulunites 428
26:30 T are the sons of Gilead: of Jeezer, 428
26:34 T are the families of Manasseh, and 428
26:35 T are the sons of Ephraim after their 428

Nu 26:36 t are the sons of Shuthelah: of Eran, 428
26:37 T are the families of the sons of Ephraim 428
26:37 T are the sons of Joseph after their families. 428
26:41 T are the sons of Benjamin after their 428
26:42 T are the sons of Dan after their families: 428
26:42 T are the families of Dan after their families. 428
26:47 T are the families of the sons of Asher 428
26:50 T are the families of Naphtali according to 428
26:51 T were the numbered of the children of 428
26:53 Unto t the land shall be divided for an 428
26:57 t are they that were numbered of the Levites 428
26:58 T are the families of the Levites: the family 428
26:63 T are they that were numbered by Moses 428
26:64 among t there was not a man of them whom 428
27: 1 t are the names of his daughters; Mahlah, 428
28:23 Ye shall offer t beside the burnt offering in 428
29:39 T things ye shall do unto the LORD in your 428
30:16 T are the statutes, which the LORD 428
31:16 Behold, t caused the children of Israel, 2007
33: 1 T are the journeys of the children of Israel, 428
33: 2 t are their journeys according to their goings 428
34:17 T are the names of the men which shall 428
34:19 the names of the men are t: Of the tribe of 428
34:29 T are they whom the LORD commanded to 428
35:13 of t cities which ye shall give six cities shall NIH
35:15 T six cities shall be a refuge, both for 428
35:24 the revenger of blood according to t 428
35:29 So t things shall be for a statute of judgment 428
36:13 T are the commandments and the judgments, 428
Dt 1: 1 T be the words which Moses spake unto all 428
1:35 Surely there shall not one of t men of this 428
2: 7 t forty years the LORD thy God hath been 2088
3: 5 All t cities were fenced with high walls, 428
3:21 your God hath done unto t two kings: 428
4: 6 which shall hear all t statutes, and say, 428
4:30 all t things are come upon thee, even in 428
4:42 that fleeing unto one of t cities he might live: 411
4:45 T are the testimonies, and the statutes, and 428
5:22 T words the LORD spake unto all your 428
6: 1 Now t are the commandments, the statutes, 2088
6: 6 t words, which I command thee this day, 428
6:24 the LORD commanded us to do all t 428
6:25 if we observe to do all t commandments 2088
7:12 if ye hearken to t judgments, and keep, and 428
7:17 say in thine heart, T nations are moe than I; 428
8: 2 God led thee t forty years in the wilderness, 2088
8: 4 neither did thy foot swell, t forty years. 2088
9: 4 for the wickedness of t nations the LORD 428
9: 5 for the wickedness of t nations the LORD 428
10:21 that hath done for thee t great and terrible 428
11:18 Therefore shall ye lay up t my words in your 428
11:22 For if ye shall diligently keep all t 2088
11:23 will the LORD drive out all t nations from 428
12: 1 T are the statutes and judgments, which ye 428
12:28 and hear all t words which I command thee, 428
12:30 How did t nations serve their gods? 428
14: 4 T are the beasts which ye shall eat: the ox, 2088
14: 7 Nevertheless t ye shall not eat of them that 2088
14: 9 T ye shall eat of all that are in the waters: 2088
14:12 t are they of which ye shall not eat: 2088
15: 5 to observe to do all t commandments which 2088
16:12 and thou shalt observe and do t statutes. 428
17:19 keep all the words of this law and t statutes, 428
18:12 For all that do t things are an abomination 428
18:12 of t abominations the LORD thy God doth 428
18:14 For t nations, which thou shalt possess, 428
19: 9 If thou shalt keep all t commandments to 2088
19: 9 add three cities moe for thee, beside t three: 428
19:11 that he die, and fleeth into one of t cities: 411
20:15 which are not of the cities of t nations. 428
20:16 of the cities of t people, which the LORD 428
22:17 yet t are the tokens of my daughter's 428
23:18 for even both t are abomination unto 1992.1
25: 3 and beat him above t with many stripes, then 428
26:16 God hath commanded thee to do t statutes 428
27: 4 that ye shall set up t stones, which I 428
27:12 T shall stand upon mount Gerizzim to bless 428
27:13 And t shall stand upon mount Ebal to curse; 428
28: 2 all t blessings shall come on thee, and 428
28:15 that all t curses shall come upon thee, and 428
28:45 Moreover all t curses shall come upon thee, 428
28:65 among t nations shalt thou find no ease, 1992
29: 1 T are the words of the covenant, which 428
29:18 to go and serve the gods of t nations; 1992
30: 1 when all t things are come upon thee, 428
30: 7 the LORD thy God will put all t curses 428
31: 1 and spake t words unto all Israel. 428
31: 3 he will destroy t nations from before thee, 428
31:17 Are not t evils come upon us, because our 428
31:28 that I may speak t words in their ears, 428
32:45 Moses made an end of speaking all t words 428
Jos 2:11 as soon as we had heard t things, our hearts NIH
4: 6 saying, What mean you by t stones? 428
4: 7 t stones shall be for a memorial unto 428
4:21 time to come, saying, What mean t stones? 428
9:13 t bottles of wine, which we filled, were new; 428
9:13 t our garments and our shoes are become old 428
10:16 t five kings fled, and hid themselves in a 428
10:24 put your feet upon the necks of t kings. 428
10:42 all t kings and their land did Joshua take at 428
11: 5 when all t kings were met together, 428
11:14 all the spoil of t cities, and the cattle, 428
12: 1 Now t are the kings of the land, which 428
12: 7 t are the kings of the country which Joshua 428
13:12 for t did Moses smite, and cast them out. 3963.1
13:32 T are the countries which Moses did 428
14: 1 t are the countries which the children of 428
14:10 me alive, as he said, t forty and five years, 2088
17: 2 t were the male children of Manasseh 428
17: 3 t are the names of his daughters, Mahlah, 428
17: 9 t cities of Ephraim are among the cities of 428
19: 8 all the villages that were round about t cities 428
19:16 to their families, t cities with their villages. 428
19:31 to their families, t cities with their villages. 428
19:48 to their families, t cities with their villages. 428

Jos 19:51 T are the inheritances, which Eleazar 428
20: 9 T were the cities appointed for all 428
21: 3 of the LORD, t cities and their suburbs. 428
21: 8 unto the Levites t cities with their suburbs, 428
21: 9 t cities which are here mentioned by name, 428
21:42 T cities were every one with their suburbs 428
21:42 round about them: thus were all t cities. 428
22: 3 Ye have not left your brethren t many days 2088
23: 3 your God hath done unto all t nations 428
23: 4 I have divided unto you by lot t nations that 428
23: 7 That ye come not among t nations, these that 428
23: 7 these nations, t that remain amongst you; 428
23:12 cleave unto the remnant of t nations, 428
23:12 even t that remain among you, and 428
23:13 drive out any of t nations from before you; 428
24:26 Joshua wrote t words in the book of the law 428
24:29 it came to pass after t things, that Joshua 428
Jdg 2: 4 when the angel of the LORD spake t words 428
3: 1 Now t are the nations which the LORD left, 428
9: 3 ears of all the men of Shechem all t words: 428
13:23 neither would he have shewed us all t things, 428
13:23 as at this time have told us such things as t. 2063
16:15 thou hast mocked me t three times, and 2088
18:14 Do ye know that there is in t houses an 428
18:18 t went into Micah's house, and fetched 428
19:13 let us draw near to one of t places to lodge NIH
20:17 that drew sword: all t were men of war. 2088
20:25 eighteen thousand men; all t drew the sword. 428
20:35 and an hundred men: all t drew the sword. 428
20:44 thousand men; all t were men of valour. 428
20:46 drew the sword; all t were men of valour. 428
Ru 3:17 T six measures of barley gave he me; 428
4:18 Now t are the generations of Pharez: 428
1Sa 4: 8 who shall deliver us out of the hand of t 428
4: 8 t are the Gods that smote the Egyptians with 428
6:17 t are the golden emerods which 428
10: 7 let it be, when t signs are come unto thee, 428
14: 6 let us go over unto the garrison of t 428
14: 8 we will pass over unto t men, and we will NIH
14:49 the names of his two daughters were t; NIH
16:10 unto Jesse, The LORD hath not chosen t. 428
17:17 of this parched corn, and t ten loaves, 2088
17:18 carry t ten cheeses unto the captain of their 428
17:39 David said unto Saul, I cannot go with t; 428
18:26 when his servants told David t words, 428
21: 5 kept from us about t **three days**, 8032+8543
21:12 David laid up t words in his heart, and 428
23: 2 Shall I go and smite t Philistines? 428
24: 7 So David stayed his servants with t words, NIH
24:16 when David had made an end of speaking t 428
25:37 his wife had told him t things, that his heart 428
29: 3 What do t Hebrews here? And Achish said 428
29: 3 which hath been with me t days, or 2088
29: 3 or t years, and I have found no fault in him 2088
29: 4 should it not be with the heads of t men? 1992
31: 4 lest t uncircumcised come and thrust me 428
2Sa 3: 5 T were born to David in Hebron. 428
3:39 t men the sons of Zeruiah be too hard for 428
5:14 t be the names of those that were born unto 428
7:17 According to all t words, and according to 428
7:21 own heart, hast thou done all t great things, 2088
13:21 when king David heard of all t things, he 428
14:19 he put all t words in the mouth of thine 428
16: 2 said unto Ziba, What meanest thou by t? 428
21:22 T four were born to the giant in Gath, and 428
23: 1 Now t be the last words of David. David 428
23: 8 T be the names of the mighty men whom 428
23:17 T things did these three mighty men. 428
23:17 These things did t three mighty men. NIH
23:22 T things did Benaiah the son of Jehoiada, 428
24:17 t sheep, what have they done? let thine hand, 428
24:23 All t things did Araunah, as a king, NIH
1Ki 4: 2 t were the princes which he had; Azariah 428
4: 8 t are their names: The son of Hur, in mount 428
7: 9 All t were of costly stones, according to 428
7:45 all t vessels, which Hiram made to king 428
8:59 let t my words, wherewith I have made 428
9:13 What cities are t which thou hast given me, 428
9:23 T were the chief of the officers that were 428
10: 8 Happy are thy men, happy are t thy servants, 428
10:10 t which the queen of Sheba gave to king NIH
11: 2 their gods: Solomon clave unto t in love. 1992.1
17: 1 there shall not be dew nor rain t years, but 428
17:17 it came to pass after t things, that the son of 428
18:36 and that I have done all t things at thy word. 428
20:19 So t young men of the princes of 428
21: 1 it came to pass after t things, that Naboth 428
22:11 With t shalt thou push the Syrians, 428
22:17 the LORD said, T have no master: let them 428
22:23 lying spirit in the mouth of all t thy prophets, 428
2Ki 1: 7 came up to meet you, and told you t words? 428
1:13 let my life, and the life of t fifty thy servants, 428
2:21 saith the LORD, I have healed t waters; 428
3:10 that the LORD hath called t three kings 428
3:13 for the LORD hath called t three kings 428
6:20 open the eyes of t men, that they may see. 428
7: 8 when t lepers came to the uttermost part of 428
10: 9 and slew him: but who slew all t? 428
17:41 So t nations feared the LORD, and served 428
18:27 to thy master, and to thee, to speak t words? 428
20:14 and said unto him, What said t men? 428
21:11 Because Manasseh king of Judah hath done t 428
23:16 of God proclaimed, who proclaimed t words. 428
23:17 proclaimed t things that thou hast done 428
25:16 the brass of all t vessels was without weight. 428
25:17 like unto t had the second pillar with 428
25:20 Nebuzar-adan captain of the guard took t, 3963.1
1Ch 1:23 and Jobab. All t were the sons of Joktan. 428
1:29 T are their generations: The firstborn of 428
1:31 and Kedemah. T are the sons of Ishmael. 428
1:33 and Eldaah. All t are the sons of Keturah. 428
1:43 Now t are the kings that reigned in the land 428
1:54 duke Iram. T are the dukes of Edom. 428
2: 1 T are the sons of Israel; Reuben, Simeon, 428
2:18 her sons are t; Jesher, and Shobab, and 428

1Ch 2:23 All t *belonged to* the sons of Machir 428
2:33 and Zaza. T were the sons of Jerahmeel. 428
2:50 T were the sons of Caleb the son of Hur, 428
2:55 T *are* the Kenites that came of Hemath, 1992
3: 1 Now t were the sons of David, which were 428
3: 4 *T* six were born unto him in Hebron; and NIH
3: 5 t were born unto him in Jerusalem; Shimea, 428
3: 9 *T were* all the sons of David, beside NIH
4: 2 T *are* the families of the Zorathites. 428
4: 3 t *were of* the father of Etam; Jezreel, and 428
4: 4 T *are* the sons of Hur, the firstborn of 428
4: 6 and Haahashtari. T *were* the sons of Naarah. 428
4:12 father of Irnahash. T *are* the men of Rechah. 428
4:18 t *are* the sons of Bithiah the daughter of 428
4:22 Jashubi-lehem. And *t are* ancient things. NIH
4:23 T *were* the potters, and those that dwelt 1992
4:31 T *were* their cities unto the reign of David. 428
4:33 T *were* their habitations, and 2088
4:38 T mentioned by *their* names *were* princes in 428
4:41 t written by name came in the days of 428
5:14 T *are* the children of Abihail the son of Huri, 428
5:17 All t were reckoned by genealogies in 3963.1
5:24 t *were* the heads of the house of their fathers, 428
6:17 And t *be* the names of the sons of Gershom; 428
6:19 t *are* the families of the Levites according to 428
6:31 t *are they* whom David set over the service 428
6:33 t *are* they that waited with their children. 428
6:50 And t *are* the sons of Aaron; Eleazar his son, 428
6:54 Now t *are* their dwelling places throughout 428
6:64 the children of Israel gave to the Levites *t* NIH
6:65 t cities, which are called by *their* names. 428
7: 8 and Alameth. All t *are* the sons of Becher. 428
7:11 All t the sons of Jediael, by the heads of 428
7:17 T *were* the sons of Gilead, the son of 428
7:29 In t dwelt the children of Joseph the son of 428
7:33 and Ashvath. T *are* the children of Japhlet. 428
7:40 All t *were* the children of Asher, heads of 428
8: 6 t *are* the sons of Ehud: these *are* the heads of 428
8: 6 t *are* the heads of the fathers of 428
8:10 Mirma. T *were* his sons, heads of the fathers. 428
8:28 T *were* heads of the fathers, by their 428
8:28 chief *men.* T dwelt in Jerusalem. 428
8:32 t also dwelt with their brethren in 1992
8:38 whose names *are* t, Azrikam, Bocheru, and 428
8:38 and Hanan. All t *were* the sons of Azel. 428
8:40 and fifty. All t *are* of the sons of Benjamin. 428
9: 9 All t men *were* chief of the fathers in 428
9:22 All t which were chosen to be porters in 3963.1
9:22 T were reckoned by their genealogy in their 1992
9:26 For t Levites, the four chief porters, *were* in 1992
9:33 t *are* the singers, chief of the fathers of 428
9:34 T chief fathers of the Levites *were* chief 428
9:34 their generations; t dwelt at Jerusalem. 428
9:44 whose names *are* t, Azrikam, Bocheru, and 428
9:44 and Hanan: t *were* the sons of Azel. 428
10: 4 lest t uncircumcised come and abuse me. 428
11:10 T also *are* the chief of the mighty *men* whom 428
11:19 t men that have put their lives in jeopardy? 428
11:19 drink it. T *things* did *these* three mightiest. 428
11:19 drink it. These *things* did *t* three mightiest. NIH
11:24 T *things* did Benaiah the son of Jehoiada, 428
12: 1 Now t *are* they that came to David to Ziklag, 428
12:14 T *were* of the sons of Gad, captains of 428
12:15 T *are* they that went over Jordan in the first 428
12:23 t *are* the numbers of the bands that were 428
12:38 All t men of war, that could keep rank, 428
14: 4 Now t *are* the names of *his* children which 428
17:15 According to all t words, and according to 428
17:19 in making known all *t* great things. NIH
18:11 the gold that he brought from all *t* nations; NIH
20: 8 T were born unto the giant in Gath; and 411
21:17 *as for* t sheep, what have they done? 428
23: 9 T *were* the chief of the fathers of Laadan. 428
23:10 and Beriah. T four *were* the sons of Shimei. 428
23:24 T *were* the sons of Levi after the house of 428
24: 1 Now *t are* the divisions of the sons of NIH
24:19 T *were* the orderings of them in their service 428
24:20 the rest of the sons of Levi *were t*: Of NIH
24:30 T *were* the sons of the Levites after 428
24:31 T likewise cast lots over against their 1992
25: 5 All t *were* the sons of Heman the king's seer 428
25: 6 All t *were* under the hands of their father for 428
26: 8 All t of the sons of Obed-edom: they and 428
26:12 Among t *were* the divisions of the porters, 428
26:19 T *are* the divisions of the porters among 428
27:22 T *were* the princes of the tribes of Israel. 428
27:31 All t *were* the rulers of the substance which 428
29:17 heart I have willingly offered all t *things:* 428
29:19 to do all *t things,* and to build the palace, NIH
2Ch 3: 3 Now t *are the things wherein* Solomon was 428
3:13 The wings of t cherubims spread themselves 428
4:18 Thus Solomon made all t vessels in great 428
5: 5 t did the priests *and* the Levites bring up. 3963.1
8:10 t *were* the chief of king Solomon's officers, 428
9: 7 *are* thy men, and happy *are* t thy servants, 428
14: 7 Let us build t cities, and make about *them* 428
14: 8 all t *were* mighty *men* of valour. 428
15: 8 when Asa heard t words, and the prophecy 428
17:14 t *are* the numbers of them according to 428
17:19 T waited on the king, besides *those* whom 428
18:10 With t thou shalt push Syria until they be 428
18:16 the LORD said, T have no master; let them 428
18:22 a lying spirit in the mouth of t thy prophets, 428
21: 2 all t *were* the sons of Jehoshaphat king of 428
24:26 t *are* they that conspired against him; 428
29:32 all t *were* for a burnt offering to the LORD. 428
32: 1 After t things, and the establishment *thereof,* 428
35: 7 t *were* of the king's substance. 428
36:18 of his princes; all *t* he brought *to* Babylon. NIH
Ezr 1:11 All *t* did Sheshbazzar bring up with *them of* NIH
2: 1 Now t *are* the children of the province that 428
2:59 t *were* they which went up from Tel-melah, 428
2:62 T sought their register *among* those that 428
4:21 Give ye now commandment to cause t men 479
5: 9 to build this house, and to make up t walls? 1836
Ezr 5:11 build the house that was builded t many 1836
5:15 said unto him, Take t vessels, go, carry them 412
6: 8 t Jews for the building of this house of God: 479
6: 8 forthwith expences be given unto t men, 479
7: 1 Now after t things, in the reign of Artaxerxes 428
8: 1 T *are* now the chief of their fathers, and 428
8:13 whose names *are* t, Eliphelet, Jeiel, and 428
9: 1 Now when t *things* were done, the princes 428
9:14 join in affinity with the people of t 428
10:44 All t had taken strange wives: and *some* of 428
Ne 1: 4 when I heard t words, *that* I sat down and 428
1:10 Now t *are* thy servants and thy people, 1992
4: 2 and said, What do *t* feeble Jews? NIH
5: 6 angry when I heard their cry and t words. 428
6: 6 mayest be their king, according to t words. 428
6: 7 be reported to the king according to t words. 428
6:14 and Sanballat according to t their works, 428
6:16 all the heathen that *were* about us saw *t* NIH
7: 6 T *are* the children of the province, that went 428
7:61 t *were* they which went up *also* from 428
7:64 T sought their register *among* those that 428
10: 8 Bilgai, Shemaiah: t *were* the priests. 428
11: 3 Now t *are* the chief of the province that 428
11: 7 t *are* the sons of Benjamin; Sallu the son of 428
12: 1 Now t *are* the priests and the Levites that 428
12: 7 T *were* the chief of the priests and of their 428
12:26 T *were* in the days of Joiakim the son of 428
13:26 Did not Solomon king of Israel sin by t 428
Est 1: 5 when t days were expired, the king made a 428
2: 1 After t things, when the wrath of king 428
3: 1 After t things did king Ahasuerus promote 428
4:11 to come in unto the king t thirty days. 2088
9:20 Mordecai wrote t things, and sent letters 428
9:26 Wherefore they called t days Purim after 428
9:27 that they would keep t two days according to 428
9:28 *that* t days *should be* remembered and 428
9:28 *that* t days of Purim should not fail from 428
9:31 To confirm t days of Purim in their times 428
9:32 the decree of Esther confirmed t matters of 428
Job 8: 2 How long wilt thou speak t *things?* and 428
10:13 t *things* hast thou hid in thine heart: I know 428
12: 3 yea, who knoweth not such *things* as t? 428
12: 9 Who knoweth not in all t that the hand of 428
19: 3 T ten times have ye reproached me: you are 2088
26:14 Lo, t *are* parts of his ways: but how little a 428
32: 1 So t three men ceased to answer Job, 428
32: 5 *was* no answer in the mouth of *t* three men, NIH
33:29 all t *things* worketh God oftentimes with 428
42: 7 that after the LORD had spoken t words 428
Ps 15: 5 He that doeth t *things* shall never be moved. 428
42: 4 When I remember t *things,* I pour out my 428
50:21 T *things* hast thou done, and I kept silence; 428
57: 1 my refuge, until *t* calamities be overpast. NIH
73:12 Behold, t *are* the ungodly, who prosper in 428
104:27 T wait all upon thee; that *thou* mayest 3963.1
107:24 T see the works of the LORD, and 1992
107:43 will observe t *things,* even they shall 428
Pr 6:16 T six *things* doth the LORD hate: yea, 2007
24:23 T *things* also *belong* to the wise. *It is* not 428
25: 1 T *are* also proverbs of Solomon, which 428
Ecc 7:10 that the former days were better than t? 428
11: 9 that for all t *things* God will bring thee into 428
12:12 further, by t, my son, be admonished: 1992
Isa 7: 4 neither be fainthearted for the two tails of t 428
34:16 no one of t shall fail, none shall want her 2007
36:12 to thy master and to thee to speak t words? 428
36:20 Who *are they* amongst all the gods of t 428
38:16 by t *things men* live, and in all these 1992.1
38:16 and in all t *things is* the life of my spirit: 2006.1
39: 3 and said unto him, What said t men? 428
40:26 behold who hath created t *things,* that 428
42:16 T things will I do unto them, and not forsake 428
44:21 Remember t, O Jacob and Israel; for thou *art* 428
45: 7 and create evil: I the LORD do all t *things.* 428
47: 7 that thou didst not lay t *things* to thy heart, 428
47: 9 t two *things* shall come to thee *in* a moment 428
47:13 save thee from *t things* that shall come upon NIH
48:14 which among them hath declared t *things?* 428
49:12 Behold, t shall come from far: and lo, 428
49:12 lo, t from the north and from the west; and 428
49:12 from the west; and t from the land of Sinim. 428
49:18 all t gather themselves together, *and* 3963.1
49:21 Who hath begotten me t, seeing I have lost 428
49:21 who hath brought up t? Behold, I was left 428
49:21 I was left alone; t, where *had* they *been?* 428
51:19 T two *things* are come unto thee; who shall 2007
57: 6 meat offering. Should I receive comfort in t? 428
60: 8 Who *are* t *that* fly as a cloud, and as 428
64:12 Wilt thou refrain thyself for t *things,* O 428
65: 5 T *are* a smoke in my nose, a fire that burneth 428
Jer 2:34 not found it by secret search, but upon all t. 428
3: 7 I said after she had done all t *things,* Turn 428
3:12 Go and proclaim t words toward the north, 428
4:18 thy doings have procured t *things* unto thee; 428
5: 4 Therefore I said, Surely t *are* poor; they are 1992
5: 5 t have altogether broken the yoke, *and* 1992
5: 9 Shall I not visit for t *things?* saith 428
5:19 Wherefore doth the LORD our God all t 428
5:25 Your iniquities have turned away t *things,* 428
5:29 Shall I not visit for t *things?* saith 428
7: 2 that enter in at t gates to worship 428
7: 4 The temple of the LORD, *are* t. 1992
7:10 We are delivered to do all t abominations? 428
7:13 And now, because ye have done all t works, 428
7:27 Therefore thou shalt speak all t words unto 428
9: 9 Shall I not visit them for t *things?* saith 428
9:24 for in t *things* I delight, saith the LORD. 428
9:26 for all *t* nations *are* uncircumcised, and NIH
10:11 from the earth, and from under t heavens. 429
11: 6 Proclaim all t words in the cities of Judah, 428
13:22 Wherefore come t *things* upon me? 428
14:22 upon thee: for thou hast made all t *things.* 428
16:10 when thou shalt shew this people all t words, 428
17:20 of Jerusalem, that enter in by t gates: 428
20: 1 heard *that* Jeremiah prophesied t things. 428
Jer 22: 2 and thy people that enter in by t gates: 428
22: 5 if ye will not hear t words, I swear by 428
23:21 I have not sent *t* prophets, yet they ran: NIH
24: 5 Like t good figs, so will I acknowledge them 428
25: 9 against all t nations round about, and 428
25:11 t nations shall serve the king of Babylon 428
25:30 Therefore prophesy thou against them all t 428
26: 7 all the people heard Jeremiah speaking t 428
26:10 When the princes of Judah heard t things, 428
26:15 unto you to speak all t words in your ears. 428
27: 6 now have I given all t lands into the hand of 428
27:12 king of Judah according to all t words, 428
28:14 a yoke of iron upon the neck of all t nations, 428
29: 1 Now t *are* the words of the letter that 428
30: 4 t *are* the words that the LORD spake 428
30:15 I have done t **things** unto thee. 428
31:21 O virgin of Israel, turn again to t thy cities, 428
32:14 Take t evidences, this evidence of 428
34: 6 Jeremiah the prophet spake all t words unto 428
34: 7 for t defenced cities remained of the cities 2007
36:16 We will surely tell the king of all t words. 428
36:17 How didst thou write all t words at his 428
36:18 He pronounced all t words unto me with his 428
36:24 nor any of his servants that heard all t words. 428
38: 9 t men have done evil in all that they have 428
38:12 Put now *t* old cast clouts and rotten rags NIH
38:16 neither will I give thee into the hand of t 428
38:24 Let no man know of t words, and thou shalt 428
38:27 he told them according to all t words that 428
43: 1 God had sent him to them, *even* all t words; 428
43:10 will set his throne upon t stones that I have 428
45: 1 when he had written t words in a book at 428
51:60 *even* all t words that are written against 428
51:61 and shalt see, and shalt read all t words; 428
52:20 the brass of all t vessels was without weight. 428
52:22 and the pomegranates *were* like unto t. 428
La 1:16 For t *things* I weep; mine eye, mine eye 428
4: 9 for t pine away, stricken through for *want* 1992
5:17 heart is faint; for t *things* our eyes are dim. 428
Eze 1:21 When those went, *t* went; and when those NIH
1:21 when those stood, *t* stood; and when those NIH
8:15 thou shalt see greater abominations than t. 428
10:17 When they stood, *t* stood; and when they NIH
10:17 *t* lift up themselves *also:* for the spirit of NIH
11: 2 t *are* the men that devise mischief, and give 428
14: 3 t men have set up their idols in their heart, 428
14:14 Though t three men, Noah, Daniel, and Job, 428
14:16 *Though* t three men *were* in it, *as* I live, 428
14:18 Though t three men *were* in it, *as* I live, 428
16: 5 eye pitied thee, to do any of t unto thee, 428
16:20 t hast thou sacrificed unto them to be 3963.1
16:30 seeing thou doest all t *things,* the work of an 428
16:43 hast fretted me in all t *things;* behold 428
17:12 Know ye not what t *things mean?* tell *them,* 428
17:18 hath done all t *things,* he shall not escape. 428
18:10 *that* doeth the like to *any* one of t *things,* 428
18:13 he hath done all t abominations; he shall 428
23:10 T discovered her nakedness: they took her 1992
23:30 *I will do* t *things* unto thee, because 428
24:19 Wilt thou not tell us what t *things are* to us, 428
27:21 and goats: in t *were they* thy merchants. 3963.1
27:24 T *were* thy merchants in all sorts of things, 1992
30:17 and t *cities* shall go into captivity. 2007
35:10 T two nations and these two countries 1886.1
35:10 and t two countries shall be mine, NIH
36:20 T *are* the people of the LORD, and 428
37: 3 said unto me, Son of man, can t bones live? 428
37: 4 Prophesy upon t bones, and say unto them, 428
37: 5 Thus saith the Lord GOD unto t bones; 428
37: 9 O breath, and breathe upon t slain, that they 428
37:11 t bones *are* the whole house of Israel: 428
37:18 thou not shew us what thou meanest by t? 428
40:24 the arches thereof according to t measures. 428
40:28 he measured the south gate according to t 428
40:29 the arches thereof, according to t measures: 428
40:32 he measured the gate according to t 428
40:33 *were* according to t measures: 428
40:35 and measured *it* according to t measures; 428
40:46 t *are* the sons of Zadok among the sons of 1992
42: 5 for the galleries were higher than t, than 2007
42: 9 from under t chambers *was* the entry on 428
43:13 t *are* the measures of the altar after 428
43:18 T *are* the ordinances of the altar in the day 428
43:27 when *t* days are expired, it shall be, NIH
46:22 t four corners *were* of one measure. 3963.1
46:24 unto me, T *are* the places of them that boil, 428
47: 8 T waters issue out toward the east country, 428
47: 9 of fish, because t waters shall come thither: 428
48: 1 Now t *are* the names of the tribes. From 428
48: 1 for t are his sides east *and* west; a *portion* NIH
48:16 t *shall be* the measures thereof; the north 428
48:29 t *are* their portions, saith the Lord GOD. 428
48:30 t *are* the goings out of the city: on the north 428
Da 1: 6 Now among t were of the children of 1992.1
1:17 As for t four children, God gave them 428
2:28 the visions of thy head upon thy bed, *are* t; 1836
2:40 all *things:* and as iron that breaketh all t, 459
2:44 in the days of t kings shall the God of 581
2:44 break in pieces and consume all t kingdoms, 459
3:12 t men, O king, have not regarded thee: 479
3:13 Then they brought t men before the king. 479
3:21 t men were bound in their coats, their hosen, 479
3:23 t three men, Shadrach, Meshach, and 479
3:27 being gathered together, saw t men, 479
6: 2 over t three presidents; of whom Daniel 1952.1
6: 5 said t men, We shall not find any occasion 479
6: 6 t presidents and princes assembled *together* 459
6:11 t men assembled, and found Daniel praying 479
6:14 the king, when he heard *t* words, was sore NIH
6:15 t men assembled unto the king, and said unto 479
7:17 T great beasts, which *are* four, *are* four 459
10:21 *there is* none that holdeth with me in t 428
11: 6 and he that strengthened her in *t* times. NIH
11:27 both t kings' hearts *shall be* to do 1992.1
11:41 t shall escape out of his hand, *even* Edom, 428

Da 12: 6 How long *shall it be to* the end of **t** NIH
12: 7 the holy people, all **t** *things* shall be finished. 428
12: 8 my lord, what *shall be* the end of **t** *things?* 428
Hos 2:12 **T** *are* my rewards that my lovers have given NIH
14: 9 he shall understand **t** *things?* prudent, and 428
Am 6: 2 *be they* better than **t** kingdoms? or 428
Mic 2: 7 *are* **t** his doings? do not my words do good 428
Hab 2: 6 Shall not all **t** take up a parable against 3963.1
Hag 2:13 *is* unclean *by* a dead body touch any of **t**, 428
Zec 1: 9 said I, O my lord, what *are* **t**? And the angel 428
1: 9 me said unto me, I will shew thee what **t** *be.* 428
1:10 **T** *are they* whom the LORD hath sent to 428
1:12 *against* which thou hast had indignation **t** 2088
1:19 the angel that talked with me, What *be* **t**? 428
1:19 **T** *are* the horns which have scattered Judah, 428
1:21 said I, What come **t** to do? And he spake, 428
1:21 **T** *are* the horns which have scattered Judah, 428
1:21 **t** are come to fray them, to cast out the horns 428
3: 7 I will give thee places to walk among **t** that 428
4: 4 talked with me, saying, What *are* **t**, my lord? 428
4: 5 Knowest thou not what **t** *be?* And I said, No, 428
4:11 What *are* **t** two olive trees upon the right *side* 428
4:12 What *be* **t** two olive branches which through NIH
4:13 Knowest thou not what **t** *be?* And I said, No, 428
4:14 said he, **T** *are* the two anointed ones, 428
5:10 with me, Whither do **t** bear the ephah? 1992
6: 4 that talked with me, What *are* **t**, my lord? 428
6: 5 **T** *are* the four spirits of the heavens, 428
6: 8 **t** that go toward the north country have NIH
7: 3 as I have done **t** so many years? 2088
8: 6 eyes of the remnant of this people in **t** days, 1992
8: 9 ye that hear in **t** days these words by 428
8: 9 ye that hear in these days **t** words by 428
8:10 For before **t** days there was no hire for 1992
8:12 of this people to possess all **t** *things.* 428
8:15 So again have I thought in **t** days to do well 428
8:16 **T** *are* the things that ye shall do; Speak ye 428
8:17 for all **t** *are things* that I hate, saith 428
13: 6 unto him, What *are* **t** wounds in thine hands? 428
14:15 and of all the beasts that shall be in **t** tents, 1992
Mt 1:20 But while he thought on **t** *things,* behold, *3778*
2: 3 When Herod the king had heard *t things,* he NIG
3: 9 that God is able of **t** stones to raise up *3778*
4: 3 command that **t** stones be made bread. *3778*
4: 9 saith unto him, All **t** *things* will I give thee, *3778*
5:19 shall break one of **t** least commandments, *3778*
5:37 for whatsoever is more than **t** cometh of *3778*
6:29 all his glory was not arrayed like one of **t**. *3778*
6:32 (For after all **t** *things* do the Gentiles seek): *3778*
6:32 knoweth that ye have need of all **t** *things.* *3778*
6:33 and all **t** *things* shall be added unto you. *3778*
7:24 Therefore whosoever heareth **t** sayings of *3778*
7:26 And every one that heareth **t** sayings of *3778*
7:28 to pass, when Jesus had ended **t** sayings, *3778*
9:18 While he spake **t** *things* unto them, behold, *3778*
10: 2 Now the names of the twelve apostles are **t**; *3778*
10: 5 **T** twelve Jesus sent forth, and *3778*
10:42 **t** little ones a cup of cold *water* only in *3778*
11:25 thou hast hid **t** *things* from the wise and *3778*
13:34 All **t** *things* spake Jesus unto the multitude *3778*
13:51 Have ye understood all **t** *things?* They say *3778*
13:53 *that* when Jesus had finished **t** parables, *3778*
13:54 this *man* this wisdom, and *t* mighty works? NIG
13:56 Whence then hath this *man* all **t** *things?* *3778*
15:20 **T** are *the things* which defile a man: but *3778*
18: 6 But whoso shall offend one of **t** little ones *3778*
18:10 Take heed that ye despise not one of **t** little *3778*
18:14 that one of **t** little ones should perish. *3778*
19: 1 *that* when Jesus had finished **t** sayings, *3778*
19:20 All **t** *things* have I kept from my youth up: *3778*
20:12 **T** last have wrought *but* one hour, and *3778*
20:21 unto him, Grant that **t** my two sons may sit, *3778*
21:16 said unto him, Hearest thou what **t** say? *3778*
21:23 By what authority doest thou **t** *things?* and *3778*
21:24 tell you by what authority I do **t** *things.* *3778*
21:27 Neither tell I you by what authority I do **t** *3778*
22:22 When they had heard *t words,* they NIG
22:40 On **t** two commandments hang all the law *3778*
23:23 **t** ought *ye* to have done, and not to leave *3778*
23:36 All **t** *things* shall come upon this *3778*
24: 2 See ye not all **t** *things?* verily I say unto *3778*
24: 3 Tell us, when shall **t** *things* be? *3778*
24: 6 for all *t things* must come to pass, but NIG
24: 8 All **t** *are* the beginning of sorrows. *3778*
24:33 when ye shall see all **t** *things,* know that it *3778*
24:34 shall not pass, till all **t** *things* be fulfilled. *3778*
25:40 *it* unto one of the least of **t** my brethren, *3778*
25:45 as ye did *it* not to one of the least of **t**, *3778*
25:46 And **t** shall go away into everlasting *3778*
26: 1 when Jesus had finished all **t** sayings, *3778*
26:62 what *is it which* **t** witness against thee? *3778*
Mk 2: 8 Why reason ye **t** *things* in your hearts? *3778*
4:11 all *t things* are done in parables: NIG
4:15 And **t** are they by the way side, where *3778*
4:16 And **t** are they likewise which are sown on *3778*
4:18 And **t** are they which are sown among *3778*
4:20 And **t** are they which are sown on good *3778*
6: 2 From whence hath this *man* **t** *things?* and *3778*
7:23 All **t** evil *things* come from within, and *3778*
8: 4 From whence can a man satisfy **t** *men* with *3778*
9:42 And whosoever shall offend one of *t* little NIG
10:20 all **t** have I observed from my youth. *3778*
11:28 By what authority doest thou **t** *things?* and *3778*
11:28 who gave thee this authority to do **t** *things?* *3778*
11:29 I will tell you by what authority I do **t** *3778*
11:33 I tell you by what authority I do **t** *things.* *3778*
12:31 is none other commandment greater than **t**. *3778*
12:40 **t** shall receive greater damnation. *3778*
13: 2 said unto him, Seest thou **t** great buildings? *3778*
13: 4 Tell us, when shall **t** *things* be? and *3778*
13: 4 what *shall be* the sign when all **t** *things* *3778*
13: 8 troubles: **t** *are* the beginnings of sorrows. *3778*
13:29 when ye shall see **t** *things* come to pass, *3778*
13:30 shall not pass, till all **t** *things* be done. *3778*
14:60 what *is it which* **t** witness against thee? *3778*
Mk 16:17 And **t** signs shall follow them that believe; *3778*
Lk 1:19 unto thee, and to shew thee **t** glad tidings. *3778*
1:20 until the day that **t** *things* shall be *3778*
1:65 all **t** sayings were noised abroad throughout *3778*
2:19 But Mary kept all **t** things, and *3778*
2:51 his mother kept all **t** sayings in her heart. *3778*
3: 8 That God is able of **t** stones to raise up *3778*
4:28 when they heard **t** *things,* were filled with *3778*
5:27 And after **t** *things* he went forth, and saw a *3778*
7: 9 When Jesus heard **t** *things,* he marvelled at *3778*
7:18 of John shewed him of all **t** *things.* *3778*
8: 8 And when he said **t** *things,* he cried, He that *3778*
8:13 and **t** have no root, which for a while *3778*
8:21 my brethren are **t** which hear the word of *3778*
9:28 to pass about an eight days after **t** sayings, *3778*
9:44 Let **t** sayings sink down into your ears: *3778*
10: 1 After **t** *things* the Lord appointed other *3778*
10:21 that thou hast hid **t** *things* from the wise *3778*
10:36 Which now of **t** three, thinkest thou, *3778*
11:27 as he spake **t** *things,* a certain woman of *3778*
11:42 **t** ought *ye* to have done, and not to leave *3778*
11:53 And as he said **t** *things* unto them, *3778*
12:27 all his glory was not arrayed like one of **t**. *3778*
12:30 For all **t** *things* do the nations of the world *3778*
12:30 your Father knoweth that ye have need of **t** *3778*
12:31 and all **t** *things* shall be added unto you. *3778*
13: 2 Suppose ye that **t** Galileans were sinners *3778*
13: 7 *t* three years I come seeking fruit on this fig NIG
13:16 whom Satan hath bound, lo *t* eighteen years, NIG
13:17 And when he had said **t** *things,* all his *3778*
14: 6 And they could not answer him again to **t** *3778*
14:15 with *him* heard **t** *things,* he said unto him, *3778*
14:21 shewed his lord **t** *things.* Then the master of *3778*
15:26 and asked what **t** *things* meant. *3778*
15:29 *his* father, Lo, **t many** years do I serve thee, *5118*
16:14 heard all **t** *things:* and they derided him. *3778*
17: 2 than that he should offend one of **t** little *3778*
18:21 All **t** have I kept from my youth up. *3778*
18:22 Now when Jesus heard **t** *things,* he said *3778*
18:34 And they understood none of **t** *things:* and *3778*
19:11 And as they heard **t** *things,* he added and *3778*
19:15 he commanded **t** servants to be called unto *3778*
19:40 I tell you that, if **t** should hold their peace, *3778*
20: 2 by what authority doest thou **t** *things?* or *3778*
20: 8 Neither tell I you by what authority I do **t** *3778*
20:16 He shall come and destroy **t** husbandmen, *3778*
21: 4 For all **t** have of their abundance cast in *3778*
21: 6 *As for* **t** *things* which ye behold, the days *3778*
21: 7 saying, Master, but when shall **t** *things* be? *3778*
21: 7 what sign *will there be* when **t** *things* shall *3778*
21: 9 for **t** *things* must first come to pass; but *3778*
21:12 But before all **t**, they shall lay their hands *3778*
21:22 For **t** be *the* days of vengeance, that all *3778*
21:28 And when **t** *things* begin to come to pass, *3778*
21:31 when ye see **t** *things* come to pass, *3778*
21:36 escape all **t** *things* that shall come to pass, *3778*
23:31 For if they do **t** *things* in a green tree, *3778*
23:49 stood afar off, beholding **t** *things.* *3778*
24: 9 and told all **t** *things* unto the eleven, and *3778*
24:10 which told **t** *things* unto the apostles. *3778*
24:14 And they talked together of all **t** *things* *3778*
24:17 What *manner of* communications *are* **t** that *3778*
24:18 which are come to pass there in **t** days? *3778*
24:21 to day is the third day since **t** *things* were *3778*
24:26 Ought not Christ to have suffered **t** *things,* *3778*
24:44 **T** *are* the words which I spake unto you, *3778*
24:48 And ye are witnesses of **t** *things.* *3778*
Jn 1:28 **T** *things* were done in Bethabara beyond *3778*
1:50 thou shalt see greater *things* than **t**. *3778*
2:16 them that sold doves, Take **t** *things* hence; *3778*
2:18 unto us, seeing that thou doest **t** *things?* *3778*
3: 2 for no *man* can do **t** miracles that thou *3778*
3: 9 and said unto him, How can **t** *things* be? *3778*
3:10 master of Israel, and knowest not **t** *things?* *3778*
3:22 After **t** *things* came Jesus and his disciples *3778*
5: 3 In **t** lay a great multitude of impotent *folk,* *3778*
5:16 he had done **t** *things* on the sabbath day. *3778*
5:19 he doeth, **t** also doeth the Son likewise. *3778*
5:20 and he will shew him greater works than **t**, *3778*
5:34 but **t** *things* I say, that ye might be saved. *3778*
6: 1 After **t** *things* Jesus went over the sea of *3778*
6: 5 Whence shall we buy bread, that **t** may eat? *3778*
6:59 **T** *things* said he in the synagogue, as he *3778*
7: 1 After **t** *things* Jesus walked in Galilee: *3778*
7: 4 If thou do **t** *things,* shew thyself to *3778*
7: 9 When he had said **t** *words* unto them, *3778*
7:31 will he do moe miracles than **t** which this *3778*
8:20 **T** words spake Jesus in the treasury, as he *3778*
8:28 my Father hath taught me, I speak **t** *things.* *3778*
8:30 As he spake **t** *words,* many believed on *3778*
9:22 **T** *words* spake his parents, because *3778*
9:40 which were with him heard **t** *words,* *3778*
10:19 again among the Jews for **t** sayings. *3778*
10:21 **T** are not the words of him that hath a *3778*
11:11 **T** *things* said he: and after that he saith unto *3778*
12:16 **T** *things* understood not his disciples at *3778*
12:16 remembered they that **t** *things* were written *3778*
12:16 and *that* they had done **t** *things* unto him. *3778*
12:36 **T** *things* spake Jesus, and departed, and *3778*
12:41 **T** *things* said Esaias, when he saw his *3778*
13:17 If ye know **t** *things,* happy are ye if ye do *3778*
14:12 and greater *works* than **t** shall he do; *3778*
14:25 **T** *things* have I spoken unto you, being *yet* *3778*
15:11 **T** *things* have I spoken unto you, that my *3778*
15:17 **T** *things* I command you, that ye love one *3778*
15:21 But all **t** *things* will they do unto you for *3778*
16: 1 **T** *things* have I spoken unto you, that ye *3778*
16: 3 And **t** *things* will they do unto you, because *3778*
16: 4 But **t** *things* have I told you, that when *3778*
16: 4 And **t** *things* I said not unto you at *3778*
16: 6 But because I have said **t** *things* unto you, *3778*
16:25 **T** *things* have I spoken unto you in *3778*
16:33 **T** *things* I have spoken unto you, that in me *3778*
17: 1 **T** *words* spake Jesus, and lift up his eyes to *3778*
17:11 but **t** are in the world, and I come to thee. *3778*
Jn 17:13 and **t** *things* I speak in the world, that they *3778*
17:20 Neither pray I for **t** alone, but for them also *3778*
17:25 and **t** have known that thou hast sent me. *3778*
18: 1 When Jesus had spoken **t** *words,* he went *3778*
18: 8 therefore ye seek me, let **t** go their way: *3778*
19:24 cast lots. **T** *things* therefore the soldiers did. *3778*
19:36 For **t** *things* were done, that the scripture *3778*
20:18 and *that* he had spoken **t** *things* unto her. *3778*
20:31 But **t** are written, that ye might believe that *3778*
21: 1 After **t** *things* Jesus shewed himself again *3778*
21:15 *son* of Jonas, lovest thou me more than **t**? *3778*
21:24 This is the disciple which testifieth of **t** *3778*
21:24 and wrote **t** *things:* and we know that his *3778*
Ac 1: 9 And when he had spoken **t** *things,* while *3778*
1:14 **T** all continued with one accord in prayer *3778*
1:21 Wherefore of **t** men which have companied NIG
1:24 shew whether of **t** two thou hast chosen, *3778*
2: 7 are not all **t** which speak Galileans? *3778*
2:13 mocking said, *T men* are full of new wine. NIG
2:15 For **t** are not drunken, as ye suppose, *3778*
2:22 Ye men of Israel, hear **t** words; Jesus of *3778*
3:24 have likewise foretold of **t** days. *3778*
4:16 Saying, What shall we do to **t** men? for that *3778*
5: 5 And Ananias hearing **t** words fell down, *3778*
5: 5 great fear came on all them that heard **t** *3778*
5:11 and upon as many as heard **t** *things.* *3778*
5:24 and the chief priests heard **t** things, *3778*
5:32 And we are his witnesses of **t** things; and *so* *3778*
5:35 what ye intend to do as touching **t** men. *3778*
5:36 For before **t** days rose up Theudas, *3778*
5:38 Refrain from **t** men, and let them alone: *3778*
7: 1 Then said the high priest, Are **t** *things* so? *3778*
7:50 Hath not my hand made all **t** *things?* *3778*
7:54 When they heard **t** *things,* they were cut to *3778*
8:24 that none of *t things* which ye have spoken NIG
10: 8 And when he had declared all *t things* unto NIG
10:44 While Peter yet spake **t** words, the Holy *3778*
10:47 forbid water, that **t** should not be baptized, *3778*
11:12 Moreover **t** six brethren accompanied me, *3778*
11:18 When they heard **t** *things,* they held their *3778*
11:22 Then tidings of **t** *things* came unto the ears *846*
11:27 And in **t** days came prophets from *3778*
12:17 *Go* shew **t** *things* unto James, and to *3778*
13:42 the Gentiles besought that **t** words might be *3778*
14:15 why do ye **t** *things?* We also are men of *3778*
14:15 preach unto you that *ye* should turn from **t** *3778*
14:18 And with **t** sayings scarce restrained they *3778*
15:17 saith the Lord, who doeth all **t** *things.* *3778*
15:28 to lay upon you no greater burden than **t** *3778*
16:17 **T** men are the servants of the most high *3778*
16:20 saying, **T** men, being Jews, do exceedingly *3778*
16:38 And the sergeants told **t** words unto *3778*
17: 6 **T** that have turned the world upside down *3778*
17: 7 **t** all do contrary to the decrees of Cesar, *3778*
17: 8 rulers of the city, when they heard **t** *things.* *3778*
17:11 **T** were more noble than those in *3778*
17:20 would know therefore what **t** *things* mean. *3778*
18: 1 After **t** *things* Paul departed from Athens, *3778*
19:21 After **t** *things* were ended, Paul purposed in *3778*
19:28 And when they heard *t sayings,* they were NIG
19:36 then that **t** *things* cannot be spoken against, *3778*
19:37 For ye have brought *hither* **t** men, *3778*
20: 5 **T** going before tarried for us at Troas. *3778*
20:24 But none of **t** *things* move me, neither count NIG
20:34 that **t** hands have ministered unto my *3778*
21:12 And when we heard **t** *things,* both we, and *3778*
21:38 which before **t** days madest an uproar, and *3778*
23:22 *man* that thou hast shewed **t** *things* to me. *3778*
24: 8 of all **t** *things,* whereof we accuse him. *3778*
24: 9 also assented, saying that **t** *things* were so. *3778*
24:20 Or else let **t** same *here* say, if they have *3778*
24:22 And when Felix heard **t** *things,* having *3778*
25: 9 and there be judged of **t** *things* before me? *3778*
25:11 if there be none *of* **t** *things* whereof these NIG
25:11 if there be none *of these things* whereof **t** *3778*
25:20 and there be judged of **t** *matters.* *3778*
26:16 a witness both of *t things* which thou hast NIG
26:21 For **t** causes the Jews caught me in *3778*
26:26 For the king knoweth of **t** *things,* before *3778*
26:26 for I am persuaded that none of **t** *things* are *3778*
26:29 and altogether such as I am, except **t** bonds. *3778*
27:31 to the soldiers, Except **t** abide in the ship, *3778*
28:29 And when he had said **t** *words,* the Jews *3778*
Ro 2:14 **t**, having not the law, are a law unto *3778*
8:31 then say to **t** *things?* If God *be* for us, *3778*
8:37 in all **t** *things* we are more than conquerors *3778*
9: 8 of the flesh, **t** *are* not the children of God: *3778*
11:24 how much more shall **t**, which be *3778*
11:31 *Even* so have **t** also now not believed, *3778*
14:18 For he that in **t** *things* serveth Christ *is* *3778*
15:23 But now having no more place in **t** parts, *3778*
15:23 having a great desire **t** many years to come NIG
1Co 4: 6 And **t** *things,* brethren, I have in a figure *3778*
4:14 I write not **t** *things* to shame you, but *3778*
9: 8 Say I **t** *things* as a man? or saith not the law *3778*
9:15 But I have used none of **t** *things:* neither *3778*
9:15 have I written **t** *things,* that it should be *3778*
10: 6 Now **t** *things* were our examples, to *3778*
10:11 Now all **t** *things* happened unto them for *3778*
12: 2 carried away unto *t* dumb idols, *even* as ye NIG
12:11 But all **t** worketh *that* one and the selfsame *3778*
12:23 upon **t** we bestow more abundant honour; *3778*
13:13 now abideth faith, hope, charity, **t** three; *3778*
13:13 these three; but the greatest of **t** *is* charity. *3778*
2Co 2:16 And who *is* sufficient for **t** *things?* *3778*
7: 1 Having therefore **t** promises, *3778*
13:10 Therefore I write **t** *things* being absent, *3778*
Gal 2: 6 But of **t** who seemed to be somewhat, *3588*
4:24 for **t** are the two covenants; the one from *3778*
5:17 and **t** are contrary the one to the other: so *3778*
5:19 which are *t;* Adultery, fornication, NIG
Eph 5: 6 of **t** *things* cometh the wrath of God upon *3778*
Php 4: 8 if *there be* any praise, think on **t** *things.* *3778*
Col 3: 8 But now you also put off all *t;* anger, wrath, NIG
3:14 And above all **t** *things put on* charity, *3778*

Col 4:11 **T** only *are my* fellowworkers unto *3778*
1Th 3: 3 That no *man* should be moved by **t** *3778*
4:18 Wherefore comfort one another with **t** *3778*
2Th 2: 5 I was yet with you, I told you **t** *things?* *3778*
1Ti 3:10 And let **t** also first be proved; then let them *3778*
3:14 **T** *things* write I unto thee, hoping to come *3778*
4: 6 **t** *things,* thou shalt be a good minister of *3778*
4:11 **T** *things* command and teach. *3778*
4:15 Meditate upon **t** *things;* give thyself wholly *3778*
5: 7 And **t** *things* give in charge, that they may *3778*
5:21 that thou observe **t** *things* without *3778*
6: 2 of the benefit. **T** *things* teach and exhort. *3778*
6:11 flee **t** *things;* and follow *after* *3778*
2Ti 1:12 For the which cause I also suffer **t** *things:* *3778*
2:14 Of **t** *things* put *them* in remembrance, *3778*
2:21 If a man therefore purge himself from **t**, *3778*
3: 8 so do **t** also resist the truth: *3778*
Tit 2:15 **T** *things* speak, and exhort, and rebuke with *3778*
3: 8 **t** *things* I will that thou affirm constantly, *3778*
3: 8 **T** *things* are good and profitable unto men. *3778*
Heb 1: 2 Hath in **t** last days spoken unto us by *his* *3778*
7:13 For he of whom **t** *things* are spoken *3778*
9: 6 Now when **t** *things* were thus ordained, *3778*
9:23 in the heavens should be purified with **t**; *3778*
9:23 themselves with better sacrifices than **t**. *3778*
10:18 Now where remission of **t** *is, there is* no *3778*
11:13 **T** all died in faith, not having received *3778*
11:39 And **t** all, having obtained a good report *3778*
Jas 3:10 My brethren, **t** *things* ought not so to be. *3778*
1Pe 1:20 but was manifest in *t* last times for you, NIG
2Pe 1: 4 that by **t** you might be partakers of *3778*
1: 8 For if **t** *things* be in you, and abound, *3778*
1: 9 But he that lacketh **t** *things* is blind, and *3778*
1:10 for if ye do **t** *things,* ye shall never fall: *3778*
1:12 of **t** *things,* though ye know *them,* *3778*
1:15 to have **t** *things* always in remembrance. *3778*
2:12 But **t**, as natural brute beasts, made to be *3778*
2:17 **T** are wells without water, clouds that are *3778*
3:11 then that all **t** *things shall* be dissolved, *3778*
3:16 speaking in them of **t** *things;* in which are *3778*
3:17 beloved, seeing ye know **t** *things* before, NIG
1Jn 1: 4 And **t** *things* write we unto you, that your *3778*
2: 1 **t** *things* write I unto you, that ye sin not. *3778*
2:26 **T** *things* have I written unto you *3778*
5: 7 and the Holy Ghost: and **t** three are one. *3778*
5: 8 and the blood: and *t* three agree in one. NIG
5:13 **T** *things* have I written unto you that *3778*
Jude 1: 8 Likewise also **t** *filthy* dreamers defile *3778*
1:10 But **t** speak evil of those *things* which they *3778*
1:12 **T** are spots in your feasts of charity when *3778*
1:14 prophesied of **t**, saying, Behold, *3778*
1:16 **T** are murmurers, complainers, *3778*
1:19 **T** be they who separate themselves, *3778*
Rev 2: 1 **T** *things* saith he that holdeth the seven *3592*
2: 8 **T** *things* saith the first and the last, *3592*
2:12 **T** *things* saith he which hath the sharp *3592*
2:18 **T** *things* saith the Son of God, who hath his *3592*
3: 1 **T** *things* saith he that hath the seven spirits *3592*
3: 7 **T** *things* saith he *that is* holy, he *that is* true, *3592*
3:14 **T** *things* saith the Amen, the faithful and *3592*
7: 1 And after **t** *things* I saw four angels *3778*
7:13 What are **t** which are arrayed in white *3778*
7:14 **T** are they which came out of great *3778*
9:18 By **t** three was the third *part* of men killed, *3778*
9:20 **t** plagues *yet* repented not of the works of *3778*
11: 4 **T** are the two olive trees, and the two *3778*
11: 6 **T** have power to shut heaven, that it rain *3778*
11:10 **t** two prophets tormented them that dwelt *3778*
14: 4 **T** are they which were not defiled with *3778*
14: 4 **T** are they which follow the Lamb *3778*
14: 4 **T** were redeemed from among men, *3778*
16: 9 of God, which hath power over **t** plagues: *3778*
17:13 **T** have one mind, and shall give their *3778*
17:14 **T** shall make war with the Lamb, and *3778*
17:16 **t** shall hate the whore, and shall make her *3778*
18: 1 And after **t** *things* I saw another angel come *3778*
18:15 The merchants of **t** *things,* which were *3778*
19: 1 And after **t** *things* I heard a great voice of *3778*
19: 9 unto me, **T** are the true sayings of God. *3778*
19:20 *T* both were cast alive into a lake of fire NIG
21: 5 Write: for **t** words are true and faithful. *3778*
22: 6 unto me, **T** sayings *are* faithful and true: *3778*
22: 8 And I John saw **t** *things,* and heard *them.* *3778*
22: 8 of the angel which shewed me **t** *things.* *3778*
22:16 to testify unto you **t** *things* in the churches. *3778*
22:18 If any *man* shall add unto **t** *things,* God *3778*
22:20 He which testifieth **t** *things* saith, Surely I *3778*

THESSALONIANS (5) [THESSALONICA]

Ac 20: 4 and of the **T**, Aristarchus and Secundus; *2331*
1Th 1: 1 unto the church of the **T** *which is* in God *2331*
5: S The first *epistle* unto the **T** was written *2331*
2Th 1: 1 unto the church of the **T** in God our Father *2331*
3: S The second *epistle* to the **T** was written *2331*

THESSALONICA (6) [THESSALONIANS]

Ac 17: 1 and Apollonia, they came to **T**, *2332*
17:11 These were more noble than those in **T**, *2332*
17:13 But when the Jews of **T** had knowledge *2332*
27: 2 a Macedonian of **T**, being with us. *2331*
Php 4:16 For even in **T** ye sent once and again unto *2332*
2Ti 4:10 *this* present world, and is departed unto **T**; *2332*

THEUDAS (1)

Ac 5:36 For before these days rose up **T**, *2333*

THEY (7376) [THEIR, THEIRS, THEM, THEMSELVES] See Index of Articles, Etc.

THICK (39) [THICKER, THICKNESS]

Ex 10:22 there was a **t** darkness in all the land of 653
19: 9 Lo, I come unto thee in a **t** cloud, 5645
19:16 a **t** cloud upon the mount, and the voice of 3515
20:21 Moses drew near unto the **t darkness** 6205
Lev 23:40 the boughs of **t** trees, and willows of 5687
Dt 4:11 *with* darkness, clouds, and **t darkness**. 6205
5:22 of the cloud, and of the **t darkness**, *with* a 6205
32:15 thou art waxed fat, thou art **grown t**, 5666
2Sa 18: 9 the mule went under the **t boughs** of a great 7730
22:12 dark waters, *and* **t clouds** of the skies. 5645
1Ki 7: 6 and the **t beam** *were* before them. 5646
7:26 it *was* a handbreadth **t**, and the brim thereof 5672
8:12 said that *he* would dwell in the **t darkness**. 6205
2Ki 8:15 that he took a **t cloth**, and dipt *it* in water, 4346
2Ch 6: 1 said that *he* would dwell in the **t darkness**. 6205
Ne 8:15 palm branches, and branches of **t** trees, 5687
Job 15:26 *his* neck, upon the **t** bosses of his bucklers: 5672
22:14 **T clouds** *are* a covering to him, that he 5645
26: 8 He bindeth up the waters in his **t clouds**; 5645
37:11 Also by watering he wearieth the **t cloud**: 5645
38: 9 and **t darkness** a swaddling band for it, 6205
Ps 18:11 *were* dark waters *and* **t clouds** of the skies. 5645
18:12 *that was* before him his **t clouds** passed, 5645
74: 5 as he had lifted up axes upon the **t** trees. 5442
Isa 44:22 I have blotted out, as a **t cloud**, 5645
Eze 6:13 every green tree, and under every **t** oak, 5687
8:11 his hand; and a **t** cloud of incense went up. 6282
19:11 stature was exalted among the **t branches**, 5688
20:28 all the **t** trees, and they offered there their 5687
31: 3 and his top was among the **t boughs**. 5688
31:10 hath shot up his top among the **t boughs**, 5688
31:14 shoot up their top among the **t boughs**, 5688
41:12 the wall of the building *was* five cubits **t** 7341
41:25 *there were* **t** planks upon the face of 5646
41:26 side chambers of the house, and **t planks**. 5646
Joel 2: 2 a day of clouds and of **t darkness**, 6205
Hab 2: 6 and to him that ladeth himself with **t clay**! 5671
Zep 1:15 a day of clouds and **t darkness**, 6205
Lk 11:29 when the people were **gathered t together**, *1865*

THICKER (2) [THICK]

1Ki 12:10 My little *finger* shall be **t** than my father's 5666
2Ch 10:10 My little *finger* shall be **t** than my father's 5666

THICKET (2) [THICKETS]

Ge 22:13 behold behind *him* a ram caught in a **t** by 5442
Jer 4: 7 The lion is come up from his **t**, and 5441

THICKETS (4) [THICKET]

1Sa 13: 6 in **t**, and in rocks, and in high places, and 2337
Isa 9:18 shall kindle in the **t** of the forest, and 5442
10:34 he shall cut down the **t** of the forest with 5442
Jer 4:29 they shall go into **t**, and climb up upon 5645

THICKNESS (4) [THICK]

2Ch 4: 5 the **t** of it *was* a handbreadth, and the brim 5672
Jer 52:21 and the **t** thereof *was* four fingers: 5672
Eze 41: 9 The **t** of the wall, which *was* for the side 7341
42:10 The chambers *were* in the **t** of the wall of 7341

THIEF (28) [THEFT]

Ex 22: 2 If a **t** be found breaking up, and be smitten 1590
22: 7 if the **t** be found, let him pay double. 1590
22: 8 If the **t** be not found, then the master of 1590
Dt 24: 7 that **t** shall die; and thou shalt put evil away 1590
Job 24:14 and needy, and in the night is as a **t**. 1590
30: 5 (they cried after them as *after* a **t**;) 1590
Ps 50:18 When thou sawest a **t**, then 1590
Pr 6:30 *Men* do not despise a **t**, if he steal to satisfy 1590
29:24 Whoso is partner with a **t** hateth his own 1590
Jer 2:26 As the **t** is ashamed when he is found, so 1590
Hos 7: 1 the **t** cometh in, *and* the troop *of robbers* 1590
Joel 2: 9 they shall enter in at the windows like a **t**. 1590
Zec 5: 4 and it shall enter into the house of the **t**, and 1590
Mt 24:43 known in what watch the **t** would come, *2812*
26:55 Are ye come out as against a **t** with swords *3027*
Mk 14:48 as against a **t**, with swords and *with* staves *3027*
Lk 12:33 where no **t** approacheth, neither moth *2812*
12:39 had known what hour the **t** would come, *2812*
22:52 as against a **t**, with swords and staves? *3027*
Jn 10: 1 other way, the same is a **t** and a robber. *2812*
10:10 The **t** cometh not, but for to steal, and *2812*
12: 6 but because he was a **t**, and had the bag, *2812*
1Th 5: 2 of the Lord so cometh as a **t** in the night. *2812*
5: 4 that *that* day should overtake you as a **t**. *2812*
1Pe 4:15 *or as* a **t**, or *as* an evildoer, or as a busybody *2812*
2Pe 3:10 But the day of the Lord will come as a **t** in *2812*
Rev 3: 3 I will come on thee as a **t**, and thou shalt *2812*
16:15 Behold, I come as a **t**. Blessed *is* he that *2812*

THIEVES (16) [THEFT]

Isa 1:23 princes *are* rebellious, and companions of **t**: 1590
Jer 48:27 was he found among **t**? for since thou 1590
49: 9 if **t** by night, they will destroy till they have 1590
Ob 1: 5 If **t** came to thee, if robbers by night, 1590
Mt 6:19 and where **t** break through and steal: *2812*
6:20 and where **t** do not break through nor steal: *2812*
21:13 of prayer; but ye have made it a den of **t**. *3027*
27:38 Then were there two **t** crucified with him, *3027*
27:44 The **t** also, which were crucified with him, *3027*
Mk 11:17 of prayer? but ye have made it a den of **t**. *3027*
15:27 And with him they crucify two **t**; the one *3027*
Lk 10:30 and fell among **t**, which stripped him of his *3027*
10:36 neighbour unto him that fell among the **t**? *3027*
19:46 of prayer: but ye have made it a den of **t**. *3027*
Jn 10: 8 All that ever came before me are **t** and *2812*
1Co 6:10 Nor **t**, nor covetous, nor drunkards, *2812*

THIGH (21) [THIGHS]

Ge 24: 2 Put, I pray thee, thy hand under my **t**: 3409
24: 9 the servant put his hand under the **t** of 3409
32:25 against him, he touched the hollow of his **t**; 3409
32:25 the hollow of Jacob's **t** was out of joint, 3409
32:31 rose upon him, and he halted upon his **t**. 3409
32:32 which *is* upon the hollow of the **t**, unto this 3409
32:32 he touched the hollow of Jacob's **t** in 3409
47:29 thy hand under my **t**, and deal kindly and 3409
Nu 5:21 when the LORD doth make thy **t** to rot, 3409
Nu 5:22 to make *thy* belly to swell, and *thy* **t** to rot: 3409
5:27 and her belly shall swell, and her **t** shall rot: 3409
Jdg 3:16 gird it under his raiment upon his right **t**. 3409
3:21 took the dagger from his right **t**, and 3409
15: 8 them hip and **t** *with* a great slaughter: 3409
Ps 45: 3 Gird thy sword upon *thy* **t**, O *most* mighty, 3409
SS 3: 8 every man *hath* his sword upon his **t** 3409
Isa 47: 2 thy locks, make bare the leg, uncover the **t**, 7785
Jer 31:19 that I was instructed, I smote upon *my* **t**: 3409
Eze 21:12 my people: smite therefore upon *thy* **t**. 3409
24: 4 every good piece, the **t**, and the shoulder; 3409
Rev 19:16 on *his* vesture and on his **t** a name written, *3382*

THIGHS (3) [THIGH]

Ex 28:42 from the loins even unto the **t** they shall 3409
SS 7: 1 the joints of thy **t** *are* like jewels, the work 3409
Da 2:32 arms of silver, his belly and his **t** of brass, 3410

THIMNATHAH (1)

Jos 19:43 And Elon, and **T**, and Ekron, 8553

THIN (9)

Ge 41: 6 seven **t** ears and blasted with the east wind 1851
41: 7 the seven **t** ears devoured the seven rank 1851
41:23 withered, **t**, *and* blasted with the east wind, 1851
41:24 the **t** ears devoured the seven good ears: 1851
41:27 the seven **t** and ill favoured kine that came 7534
Ex 39: 3 they did beat the gold into **t plates**, and 6341
Lev 13:30 *there be* in it a yellow **t** hair; then the priest 1851
1Ki 7:29 oxen *were certain* additions **made** of **t** 4174
Isa 17: 4 *that* the glory of Jacob shall be **made t**, and 1809

THINE (933) [THOU]

Ge 13:14 Lift up now **t** eyes, and look from 3509.2
14:20 which hath delivered **t** enemies into thy 3509.2
14:23 I will not take any thing that *is* **t**, 3509.2+3807.1
15: 4 unto him, saying, This shall not be **t** heir; 3509.2
15: 4 he that shall come forth out of **t own** 3509.2
15: 4 out of thine own bowels shall be **t** heir. 3509.2
20: 7 surely die, thou, and all that *are* **t**. 3509.2+3807.1
21:18 lift up the lad, and hold him in **t** hand; 3509.3
22: 2 Take now thy son, **t** only *son* Isaac, 3509.2
22:12 he said, Lay not **t** hand upon the lad, 3509.2
22:12 not withheld thy son, **t** only *son* from me. 3509.2
22:16 hast not withheld thy son, **t** only *son:* 3509.2
30:27 if I have found favour in **t** eyes, 3509.2
31:12 he said, Lift up now **t** eyes, and see, 3509.2
31:32 discern thou what *is* **t** with me, 3509.2+3807.1
38:18 and thy staff that *is* in **t** hand. 3509.2
40:13 three days shall Pharaoh lift up **t** head, 3509.2
44:18 let not **t** anger burn against thy servant: 3509.2
46: 4 and Joseph shall put his hand upon **t** eyes. 3509.2
47:19 Wherefore shall we die before **t** eyes, 3509.2
48: 6 shall be **t**, *and* shall be called 3509.2+3807.1
49: 8 thy hand *shall be* in the neck of **t** 3509.2
Ex 4: 2 said unto him, What *is* that in **t** hand? 3509.2
4: 4 Put forth **t** hand, and take it by the tail. 3509.2
4: 6 unto him, Put now **t** hand into thy bosom. 3509.2
4: 7 he said, Put **t** hand into thy bosom again 3509.2
4:17 thou shalt take this rod in **t** hand, 3509.2
4:21 which I have put in **t** hand: 3509.2
5:16 but the fault *is* in **t own** people. 3509.2
7:15 to a serpent shalt thou take in **t** hand. 3509.2
7:19 stretch out **t** hand upon the waters of 3509.2
8: 3 which shall go up and come into **t** house, 3509.2
8: 3 into **t** ovens, and into thy 3509.2
8: 5 Stretch forth **t** hand with thy rod over 3509.2
9:14 time send all my plagues upon **t** heart, 3509.2
9:22 Stretch forth **t** hand toward heaven, 3509.2
10:12 Stretch out **t** hand over the land of Egypt 3509.2
10:21 Stretch out **t** hand toward heaven, 3509.2
13: 9 it shall be for a sign unto thee upon **t** 3509.2
13: 9 for a memorial between **t** eyes, that 3509.2
13:16 it shall be for a token upon **t** hand, and 3509.2
13:16 and for frontlets between **t** eyes: 3509.2
14:16 stretch out **t** hand over the sea, and 3509.2
14:26 Stretch out **t** hand over the sea, 3509.2
15: 7 in the greatness of **t** excellency thou hast 3509.2
15:16 by the greatness of **t** arm they shall be *as* 3509.2
15:17 them in the mountain of **t** inheritance, 3509.2
17: 5 smotest the river, take in **t** hand, and go. 3509.2
20:24 peace offerings, thy sheep, and **t** oxen: 3509.2
22:30 Likewise shalt thou do with **t** oxen, *and* 3509.2
23: 1 put not **t** hand with the wicked to be an 3509.2
23: 4 If thou meet **t** enemy's ox or his ass 3509.2
23:12 that **t** ox and thine ass may rest, and 3509.2
23:12 that thine ox and **t** ass may rest, and 3509.2
23:22 I will be an enemy unto **t** enemies, and 3509.2
23:22 and an adversary unto **t** adversaries. 3509.2
23:27 I will make all **t** enemies turn their backs 3509.2
32:13 to whom thou swarest by **t own self**, and 3509.2
34: 9 and our sin, and take us for **t** inheritance. NIH
Lev 2:13 with all **t** offerings thou shalt offer salt. 3509.2
10:15 it shall be **t**, and thy sons' with 3509.2+3807.1
18:10 for theirs *is* **t own** nakedness. 3509.2
18:14 not approach to his wife: she *is* **t** aunt. 3509.2
19:17 Thou shalt not hate thy brother in **t** heart: 3509.2
27:23 he shall give **t** estimation in that day, *as* a 3509.2
27:27 he shall redeem *it* according to **t** 3509.2
Nu 5:20 *some* man hath lain with thee beside **t** 3509.3
10:35 LORD, and let **t** enemies be scattered; 3509.2
18: 9 This shall be **t** of the most holy 3509.2+3807.1
18:11 this *is* **t**; the heave offering of 3509.2+3807.1
18:13 unto the LORD, shall be **t**; 3509.2+3807.1
18:13 every one *that is* clean in **t** house shall eat 3509.2
18:14 thing devoted in Israel shall be **t**. 3509.2+3807.1
18:15 *it be* of men or beasts, shall be **t**: 3509.2+3807.1
18:16 according to **t** estimation, *for* the money 3509.2
18:18 the flesh of them shall be **t**, as 3509.2+3807.1
18:18 and as the right shoulder are **t**. 3509.2+3807.1
18:20 **t** inheritance among the children of Israel. 3509.2
22:30 the ass said unto Balaam, *Am* not I **t** ass, 3509.2
22:30 ridden ever since *I was* **t** unto this day? 3509.2
22:32 Wherefore hast thou smitten **t** ass these 3509.2

T

Nu 27:18 *is* the spirit, and lay **t** hand upon him; 3509.2
27:20 thou shalt put *some* of **t** honour upon 3509.2
Dt 3:21 **T** eyes have seen all that the LORD 3509.2
3:27 lift up **t** eyes westward, and northward, 3509.2
3:27 eastward, and behold *it* with **t** eyes: 3509.2
4: 9 lest thou forget the things which **t** eyes 3509.2
4:19 lest thou lift up **t** eyes unto heaven, and 3509.2
4:39 *this* day, and consider *it* in **t** heart, 3509.2
5:14 thy maidservant, nor **t** ox, nor thine ass, 3509.2
5:14 thy maidservant, nor thine ox, nor **t** ass, 3509.2
6: 5 love the LORD thy God with all **t** heart, 3509.2
6: 6 thee *this* day, shall be in **t** heart: 3509.2
6: 7 shalt talk of them when thou sittest in **t** 3509.2
6: 8 thou shalt bind them for a sign upon **t** 3509.2
6: 8 they shall be as frontlets between **t** eyes. 3509.2
6:19 To cast out all **t** enemies from before 3509.2
7:13 thy land, thy corn, and thy wine, and **t** oil, 3509.2
7:16 **t** eye shall have no pity upon them: 3509.2
7:17 If thou shalt say in **t** heart, These nations 3509.2
7:19 The great temptations which **t** eyes saw, 3509.2
7:24 he shall deliver their kings into **t** hand, 3509.2
7:26 thou bring an abomination into **t** house, 3509.2
8: 2 prove thee, to know what *was* in **t** heart, 3509.2
8: 5 Thou shalt also consider in **t** heart, that, 3509.2
8:14 **t** heart be lifted up, and thou forget 3509.2
8:17 thou say in **t** heart, My power and 3509.2
9: 4 Speak not thou in **t** heart, after that 3509.2
9: 5 or for the uprightness of **t** heart, 3509.2
9:26 destroy not thy people and **t** inheritance, 3509.2
9:29 Yet they *are* thy people and **t** inheritance, 3509.2
10:21 terrible *things*, which **t** eyes have seen. 3509.2
11:14 gather in thy corn, and thy wine, and **t** oil. 3509.2
11:19 speaking of them when thou sittest in **t** 3509.2
11:20 them upon the door posts of **t** house, 3509.2
12:17 or heave offering of **t** hand: 3509.2
12:18 God in all that thou puttest **t** hands unto. 3509.2
13: 6 or thy friend, which *is* as **t own** soul, 3509.2
13: 8 neither shall **t** eye pity him, neither shalt 3509.2
13: 9 **t** hand shall be first upon him to put him 3509.2
13:17 nought of the cursed thing to **t** hand: 3509.2
14:23 of **t** oil, and the firstlings of thy herds and 3509.2
14:25 bind up the money in **t** hand, and shalt go 3509.2
14:26 thou shalt rejoice, thou and **t** household, 3509.2
14:28 all the tithe of **t** increase the same year, 3509.2
14:29 all the work of **t** hand which thou doest. 3509.2
15: 3 *that* which is **t** with thy brother thine hand 3509.2
15: 3 *that* which is thine with thy brother **t** hand 3509.2
15: 7 nor shut **t** hand from thy poor brother: 3509.2
15: 8 thou shalt open **t** hand wide unto him, 3509.2
15: 9 **t** eye be evil against thy poor brother, and 3509.2
15:10 **t** heart shall not be grieved when thou 3509.2
15:10 and in all that thou puttest **t** hand unto. 3509.2
15:11 Thou shalt open **t** hand wide unto thy 3509.2
15:16 because he loveth thee and **t** house, 3509.2
16:10 a tribute of a freewill offering of **t** hand, 3509.2
16:15 in all the works of **t** hands, therefore 3509.2
18:21 if thou say in **t** heart, How shall we know 3509.2
19:13 **T** eye shall not pity him, but thou shalt 3509.2
19:14 which they of old time have set in **t** 3509.2
19:21 **t** eye shall not pity; *but* life *shall go* for 3509.2
20: 1 When thou goest out to battle against **t** 3509.2
20:13 thy God hath delivered it into **t** hands, 3509.2
20:14 thou shalt eat the spoil of **t** enemies, 3509.2
21:10 When thou goest forth to war against **t** 3509.2
21:10 thy God hath delivered them into **t** hands, 3509.2
21:12 thou shalt bring her home to **t** house; and 3509.2
21:13 shall remain in **t** house, and bewail her 3509.2
22: 2 thou shalt bring it unto **t own** house, and 3509.2
22: 8 that thou bring not blood upon **t** house, 3509.2
23: 9 When the host goeth forth against **t** 3509.2
23:14 and to give up **t** enemies before thee; 3509.2
23:20 **t** hand to in the land whither thou goest to 3509.2
23:24 thou mayest eat grapes thy fill at **t own** 3509.2
23:25 thou mayest pluck the ears with **t** hand; 3509.2
24:19 When thou cuttest down **t** harvest in thy 3509.2
24:19 may bless thee in all the work of **t** hands. 3509.2
24:20 When thou beatest **t** olive tree, thou shalt 3509.2
25:12 cut off her hand, **t** eye shall not pity *her.* 3509.2
25:14 Thou shalt not have in **t** house divers 3509.2
25:19 thee rest from all **t** enemies round about, 3509.2
26: 4 the priest shall take the basket out of **t** 3509.2
26:11 unto **t** house, thou, and the Levite, and 3509.2
26:12 all the tithes of **t** increase the third year, 3509.2
26:16 keep and do them with all **t** heart, 3509.2
28: 7 The LORD shall cause **t** enemies that 3509.2
28: 8 and in all that thou settest **t** hand unto; 3509.2
28:12 and to bless all the work of **t** hand: 3509.2
28:20 all that thou settest **t** hand unto for to do, 3509.2
28:25 cause thee *to be* smitten before **t** enemies: 3509.2
28:31 **T** ox *shall be* slain before thine eyes, and 3509.2
28:31 Thine ox *shall be* slain before **t** eyes, and 3509.2
28:31 **t** ass *shall be* violently taken away from 3509.2
28:31 thy sheep *shall be* given unto **t** enemies, 3509.2
28:32 **t** eyes shall look, and fail *with longing* for 3509.2
28:32 and *there shall be* no might in **t** hand. 3509.2
28:34 the sight of **t** eyes which thou shalt see. 3509.2
28:40 the oil; for **t** olive shall cast *his fruit.* 3509.2
28:48 Therefore shalt thou serve **t** enemies 3509.2
28:53 thou shalt eat the fruit of **t own** body, 3509.2
28:53 wherewith **t** enemies shall distress thee: 3509.2
28:55 wherewith **t** enemies shall distress thee in 3509.2
28:57 wherewith **t** enemy shall distress thee in 3509.2
28:67 for the fear of **t** heart where*with* thou 3509.2
28:67 the sight of **t** eyes which thou shalt see. 3509.2
29: 3 The great temptations which **t** eyes have 3509.2
30: 2 with all **t** heart, and with all thy soul; 3509.2
30: 4 If *any* of **t** be driven out unto the outmost 3509.2
30: 6 the LORD thy God will circumcise **t** 3509.2
30: 6 to love the LORD thy God with all **t** 3509.2
30: 7 will put all these curses upon **t** enemies, 3509.2
30: 9 thee plenteous in every work of **t** hand, 3509.2
30:10 unto the LORD thy God with all **t** heart, 3509.2
30:17 if **t** heart turn away, so that thou wilt not 3509.2
33:10 and whole *burnt sacrifice* upon **t** altar. 3509.2
33:29 **t** enemies shall be found liars unto thee; 3509.2

Dt 34: 4 I have caused thee to see *it* with **t** eyes, 3509.2
Jos 2: 3 to thee, which are entered into **t** house: 3509.3
2:17 We *will be* blameless of this **t** oath which 3509.3
2:20 we will be quit of **t** oath which thou hast 3509.3
6: 2 I have given into **t** hand Jericho, and 3509.2
7:13 thou canst not stand before **t** enemies, 3509.2
8:18 toward Ai; for I will give it into **t** hand. 3509.2
9:25 now, behold, we *are* in **t** hand: as it 3509.2
10: 8 for I have delivered them into **t** hand; 3509.2
14: 9 trodden shall be **t** inheritance, 3509.2+3807.1
17:18 the mountain shall be **t**; for it *is* a wood, 3509.2
17:18 the outgoings of it shall be **t**: for 3509.2+3807.1
Jdg 4: 7 and I will deliver him into **t** hand. 3509.2
4: 9 that thou takest shall not be for **t** honour; 3509.2
4:14 LORD hath delivered Sisera into **t** hand: 3509.2
5:31 So let all **t** enemies perish, O LORD: 3509.2
6:39 Let not **t** anger be hot against me, and 3509.2
7: 7 and deliver the Midianites into **t** hand: 3509.2
7: 9 for I have delivered it into **t** hand. 3509.2
7:11 afterward shall **t** hands be strengthened to 3509.2
8: 6 of Zebah and Zalmunna now in **t** hand, 3509.2
8: 6 that we should give bread unto **t** army? 3509.2
8:15 of Zebah and Zalmunna now in **t** hand, 3509.2
9:29 Increase **t** army, and come out. 3509.2
11:36 taken vengeance for thee of **t** enemies, 3509.2
12: 1 we will burn **t** house upon thee with fire. 3509.2
16:15 I love thee, when **t** heart *is* not with me? 3509.2
18:19 lay **t** hand upon thy mouth, and go with 3509.2
19: 5 Comfort **t** heart *with* a morsel of bread, 3509.2
19: 6 tarry all night, and let **t** heart be merry. 3509.2
19: 8 father said, Comfort **t** heart, I pray thee. 3509.2
19: 9 lodge here, that **t** heart may be merry; 3509.2
19:22 forth the man that came into **t** house, 3509.2
20:28 for to morrow I will deliver them into **t** 3509.2
Ru 2: 9 *Let* **t** eyes *be* on the field that they do 3509.3
2:10 Why have I found grace in **t** eyes, 3509.2
2:11 in law since the death of **t** husband: 3509.3
2:13 for that thou hast spoken friendly unto **t** 3509.2
3: 9 she answered, I *am* Ruth **t** handmaid: 3509.2
3: 9 spread therefore thy skirt over **t** 3509.2
4:11 that is come into **t** house like Rachel 3509.2
4:15 of *thy* life, and a nourisher of **t** old age: 3509.3
1Sa 1:11 look on the affliction of **t** handmaid, 3509.2
1:11 not forget **t** handmaid, but wilt give unto 3509.2
1:11 wilt give unto **t** handmaid a man child, 3509.2
1:16 Count not **t** handmaid for a daughter of 3509.2
1:18 Let **t** handmaid find grace in thy sight. 3509.2
2:31 that I will cut off **t** arm, and the arm of 3509.2
2:31 that there shall not be an old man in **t** 3509.2
2:32 there shall not be an old man in **t** house 3509.2
2:33 the man of **t**, *whom* I shall not cut off 3509.2
2:33 *shall be* to consume **t** eyes, and to grieve 3509.2
2:33 consume thine eyes, and to grieve **t** heart: 3509.2
2:33 all the increase of **t** house shall die in 3509.2
2:36 *that* every one that is left in **t** house shall 3509.2
9:19 and will tell thee all that *is* in **t** heart. 3509.2
9:20 as for **t** asses that were lost three days 3509.2
14: 7 said unto him, Do all that *is* in **t** heart: 3509.2
14:19 said unto the priest, Withdraw **t** hand. 3509.2
15:17 When thou *wast* little in **t own** sight, 3509.2
15:28 hath given it to a neighbour of **t**, *that is* 3509.2
16: 1 fill **t** horn *with* oil, and go, I will send 3509.2
17:28 thy pride, and the naughtiness of **t** heart; 3509.2
17:46 smite thee, and take **t** head from thee; 3509.2
20: 3 knoweth that I have found grace in **t** eyes; 3509.2
20:29 and now, if I have found favour in **t** eyes, 3509.2
20:30 the son of Jesse to **t own** confusion, 3509.2
21: 3 Now therefore what is under **t** hand? 3509.2
21: 8 is there not here under **t** hand spear or 3509.2
22:14 thy bidding, and *is* honourable in **t** house? 3509.2
23: 4 I will deliver the Philistines into **t** hand. 3509.2
24: 4 I will deliver **t** enemy into thine hand, 3509.2
24: 4 I will deliver thine enemy into **t** hand, 3509.2
24:10 this day **t** eyes have seen how that 3509.2
24:15 my cause, and deliver me out of **t** hand. 3509.2
24:18 the LORD had delivered me into **t** hand, 3509.2
24:20 of Israel shall be established in **t** hand. 3509.2
25: 6 peace *be to* **t** house, and peace *be unto* all 3509.2
25: 8 let the young men find favour in **t** eyes: 3509.2
25: 8 whatsoever cometh to **t** hand unto thy 3509.2
25:24 *let this* iniquity *be:* and let **t** handmaid, 3509.2
25:24 speak in **t** audience, and hear the words 3509.2
25:24 and hear the words of **t** handmaid. 3509.2
25:25 I **t** handmaid saw not the young men of 3509.2
25:26 *from* avenging thyself with **t own** hand, 3509.2
25:26 now let **t** enemies, and they that seek evil 3509.2
25:27 now this blessing which **t** handmaid hath 3509.2
25:28 forgive the trespass of **t** handmaid: 3509.2
25:29 the souls of **t** enemies, them shall he sling 3509.2
25:31 with my lord, then remember **t** handmaid. 3509.2
25:35 said unto her, Go up in peace to **t** house; 3509.3
25:41 *let* **t** handmaid *be* a servant to wash 3509.2
26: 8 God hath delivered **t** enemy into thine 3509.2
26: 8 God hath delivered thine enemy into **t** 3509.2
26:21 my soul was precious in **t** eyes this day: 3509.2
27: 5 If I have now found grace in **t** eyes, 3509.2
28:16 from thee, and is become **t** enemy? 3509.2
28:17 hath rent the kingdom out of **t** hand, 3509.2
28:21 **t** handmaid hath obeyed thy voice, and 3509.2
28:22 hearken thou also unto the voice of **t** 3509.2
2Sa 1:14 wast thou not afraid to stretch forth **t** 3509.2
1:25 *thou wast* slain in **t** high places. 3509.2
3:21 that thou mayest reign over all that **t** heart 3509.2
4: 8 of Ish-bosheth the son of Saul **t** enemy, 3509.2
5:19 deliver the Philistines into **t** hand. 3509.2
7: 3 to the king, Go, do all that *is* in **t** heart; 3509.2
7: 9 have cut off all **t** enemies out of thy sight, 3509.2
7:11 caused thee to rest from all **t** enemies. 3509.2
7:16 **t** house and thy kingdom shall be 3509.2
7:21 and according to **t own** heart, 3509.2
11:10 *then* didst thou not go down unto **t** house? 3509.2
12:10 sword shall never depart from **t** house, 3509.2
12:11 up evil against thee out of **t own** house, 3509.2
12:11 I will take thy wives before **t** eyes, and 3509.2
13:10 *into* the chamber, that I may eat of **t** hand. 3509.3

2Sa 14: 7 the whole family is risen against **t** 3509.2
14: 8 Go to **t** house, and I will give charge 3509.3
14:12 woman said, Let **t** handmaid, I pray thee, 3509.2
14:17 **t** handmaid said, The word of my lord 3509.2
14:19 he put all these words in the mouth of **t** 3509.2
16: 4 Behold, **t** *are* all that *pertained* 3509.2+3807.1
17:11 and *that* thou go to battle in **t own** person. 3509.2
19: 6 In that thou lovest **t** enemies, and hatest 3509.2
19:27 do therefore what *is* good in **t** eyes. 3509.2
19:28 among them that did eat at **t own** table. 3509.2
20:17 unto him, Hear the words of **t** handmaid. 3509.2
22:28 **t** eyes *are* upon the haughty, *that* thou 3509.2
24:13 wilt thou flee three months before **t** 3509.2
24:16 stay now **t** hand. And the angel of 3509.2
24:17 let **t** hand, I pray thee, be against me, and 3509.2
1Ki 1:12 that thou mayest save **t own** life, and 3509.3
1:13 O king, swear unto **t** handmaid, saying, 3509.2
1:17 by the LORD thy God unto **t** handmaid, 3509.2
1:53 Solomon said unto him, Go to **t** house. 3509.2
2:26 Get thee *to* Anathoth, unto **t own** fields; 3509.2
2:37 thy blood shall be upon **t own** head. 3509.2
2:44 Thou knowest all the wickedness which **t** 3509.2
2:44 return thy wickedness upon **t own** head; 3509.2
3:11 nor hast asked the life of **t** enemies; 3509.2
3:20 while **t** handmaid slept, and laid it in her 3509.2
3:26 neither mine nor **t**, *but* divide *it.* 3509.3+3807.1
8:18 Whereas it was in **t** heart to build a house 3509.2
8:18 thou didst well that it was in **t** heart. 3509.2
8:24 hast fulfilled *it* with **t** hand, as *it is* this 3509.2
8:29 That **t** eyes may be open toward this 3509.2
8:31 the oath come before **t** altar in this house: 3509.2
8:51 For they *be* thy people, and **t** inheritance, 3509.2
8:52 That **t** eyes may be open unto 3509.2
8:53 to be **t** inheritance, as thou 3509.2+3807.1
11:22 thou seekest to go to **t own** country? 3509.2
12:16 now see to **t own** house, David. So Israel 3509.2
13: 8 If thou wilt give me half **t** house, I will 3509.2
13:18 Bring him back with thee into **t** house, 3509.2
14:12 thou therefore, get thee to **t own** house: 3509.3
17:11 I pray thee, a morsel of bread in **t** hand. 3509.3
19:10 thrown down **t** altars, and slain thy 3509.2
19:14 thrown down **t** altars, and slain thy 3509.2
20: 4 I *am* **t**, and all that I have. 3509.2+3807.1
20: 6 they shall search **t** house, and the houses 3509.2
20: 6 *that* whatsoever *is* pleasant in **t** eyes, 3509.2
20:13 behold, I will deliver it into **t** hand *this* 3509.2
20:28 will I deliver all this great multitude into **t** 3509.2
21: 7 *and* eat bread, and let **t** heart be merry: 3509.2
21:19 of Naboth shall dogs lick thy blood, even **t**. 859
21:22 will make **t** house like the house of 3509.2
22:34 Turn **t** hand, and carry me out of the host; 3509.2
2Ki 4: 2 **T** handmaid hath not any thing in 3509.2
4:16 man of God, do not lie unto **t** handmaid. 3509.2
4:29 take my staff in **t** hand, and go *thy way:* if 3509.2
7: 2 thou shalt see *it* with **t** eyes, but shalt not 3509.2
7:19 thou shalt see *it* with **t** eyes, but shalt not 3509.2
8: 1 go thou and **t** household, and 3509.3
8: 8 Take a present in **t** hand, and go, meet 3509.2
9: 1 take this box of oil in **t** hand, and go *to* 3509.2
10: 5 do thou *that* which *is* good in **t** eyes. 3509.2
10:15 and said to him, Is **t** heart right, 3509.2
10:15 If it be, give *me* **t** hand. And he gave *him* 3509.2
13:16 king of Israel, Put **t** hand upon the bow. 3509.2
14:10 and **t** heart hath lifted thee up: 3509.2
19:16 LORD, bow down **t** ear, and hear: open, 3509.2
19:16 open, LORD, **t** eyes, and see: and 3509.2
19:22 *thy* voice, and lift up **t** eyes on high? 3509.2
20: 1 saith the LORD, Set **t** house in order; 3509.2
20:15 he said, What have they seen in **t** house? 3509.2
20:17 that all that *is* in **t** house, and *that* which 3509.2
22:19 Because **t** heart was tender, and thou hast 3509.2
22:20 **t** eyes shall not see all the evil which I 3509.2
1Ch 4:10 that **t** hand might be with me, and 3509.2
12:18 of the captains, *and he said,* **T** 3509.2+3807.1
12:18 *be* unto thee, and peace *be* to **t** helpers; 3509.2
14:10 Go up; for I will deliver them into **t** hand. 3509.2
17: 2 said unto David, Do all that *is* in **t** heart; 3509.2
17: 8 cut off all **t** enemies from before thee, 3509.2
17:10 Moreover I will subdue all **t** enemies. 3509.2
17:17 *yet* this was a small thing in **t** eyes, 3509.2
17:19 and according to **t own** heart, 3509.2
17:22 thou make **t own** people for ever; 3509.2+3807.1
21:12 while that the sword of **t** enemies 3509.2
21:15 *It is* enough, stay now **t** hand. 3509.2
21:17 let **t** hand, I pray thee, O LORD my 3509.2
21:24 for I will not take *that* which *is* **t** 3509.2+3807.1
29:11 **T**, O LORD, *is* the greatness, 3509.2+3807.1
29:11 and in the earth *is* **t**; thine *is* the kingdom, NIH
29:11 earth *is thine;* **t** *is* the kingdom, 3509.2+3807.1
29:12 in **t** hand *is* power and might; and in thine 3509.2
29:12 in **t** hand *it is* to make great, and to give 3509.2
29:14 of thee, and of **t** own have we given thee. 3509.2
29:16 for **t** holy name *cometh* of thine hand, 3509.2
29:16 for thine holy name *cometh* of **t** hand, 3509.2
29:16 *cometh* of thine hand, and *is* all **t own**. 3509.2
2Ch 1:11 Because this was in **t** heart, and thou hast 3509.2
1:11 or honour, nor the life of **t** enemies, 3509.2
6: 8 Forasmuch as it was in **t** heart to build a 3509.2
6: 8 thou didst well *in* that it was in **t** heart: 3509.2
6:15 hast fulfilled *it* with **t** hand, as *it is* this 3509.2
6:20 That **t** eyes may be open upon this house 3509.2
6:22 the oath come before **t** altar in this house; 3509.2
6:40 **t** eyes be open, and *let* thine ears *be* attent 3509.2
6:40 *let* **t** ears *be* attent unto the prayer *that is* 3509.2
6:42 turn not away the face of **t** anointed: 3509.2
9: 5 which I heard in mine own land of **t** acts, 3509.2
10:16 *and* now, David, see to **t own** house. 3509.2
16: 7 of the king of Syria escaped out of **t** hand. 3509.2
16: 8 he delivered them into **t** hand. 3509.2
18:33 he said to *his* chariot man, Turn **t** hand, 3509.2
19: 3 and hast prepared **t** heart to seek God. 3509.2
20: 6 in **t** hand *is there not* power and might, so 3509.2
25:15 deliver their own people out of **t** hand? 3509.2
25:19 and **t** heart lifteth thee up to boast: 3509.2
25:19 why shouldest thou meddle to *t* hurt, NIH

T

2Ch 26:18 neither *shall it be for* t honour from 3509.2
34:27 Because t heart was tender, and 3509.2
34:28 neither shall t eyes see all the evil that I 3509.2
Ezr 7:14 to the law of thy God which *is* in t hand; 3509.5
7:25 *is* in t hand, set magistrates and judges, 3509.5
Ne 1: 6 Let t ear now be attentive, and thine eyes 3509.2
1: 6 ear now be attentive, and t eyes open, 3509.2
1:11 let now t ear be attentive to the prayer of 3509.2
6: 8 but thou feignest them out of **t own** heart. 3509.2
Job 1:11 put forth t hand now, and touch all that he 3509.2
1:12 only upon himself put not forth t hand. 3509.2
2: 5 put forth t hand now, and touch his bone 3509.2
2: 6 said unto Satan, Behold, he *is* in t hand; 3509.2
2: 9 Dost thou still retain t integrity? 3509.2
5:25 and t offspring as the grass of the earth. 3509.2
7: 8 shall see me no *more:* t eyes *are* upon me, 3509.2
7:17 that thou shouldest set t heart upon him? 3509.2
10: 3 that thou shouldest despise the work of t 3509.2
10: 7 *is* none that can deliver out of t hand. 3509.2
10: 8 T hands have made me and fashioned me 3509.2
10:13 these *things* hast thou hid in t heart: 3509.2
10:17 and increasest t indignation upon me; 3509.2
11: 4 doctrine *is* pure, and I am clean in t eyes. 3509.2
11: 6 that God exacteth of thee *less* than t 3509.2
11:13 If thou prepare t heart, and stretch out 3509.2
11:13 and stretch out t hands toward him; 3509.2
11:14 If iniquity *be* in t hand, put it far away, 3509.2
11:17 And *t* age shall be clearer than the noonday; NIH
13:21 Withdraw t hand far from me: and let not 3509.2
13:24 thy face, and holdest me for t enemy? 3509.2
14: 3 dost thou open t eyes upon such a one, 3509.2
14:15 thou wilt have a desire to the work of t 3509.2
15: 5 For thy mouth uttereth t iniquity, and 3509.2
15: 6 **T own** mouth condemneth thee, and 3509.2
15: 6 not I; yea, **t own** lips testify against thee. 3509.2
15:12 Why doth t heart carry thee away? and 3509.2
15:12 thee away? and what do t eyes wink at, 3509.2
22: 5 and t iniquities infinite? 3509.2
22:22 and lay up his words in t heart. 3509.2
22:30 it is delivered by the pureness of t hands. 3509.2
35: 7 thou him? or what receiveth he of t hand? 3509.2
40:14 will I also confess unto thee that **t own** 3509.2
41: 8 Lay t hand upon him, remember 3509.2
Ps 2: 8 I shall give *thee* the heathen *for* t 3509.2
6: 1 O LORD, rebuke me not in t anger, 3509.2
7: 6 Arise, O LORD, in t anger, lift up 3509.2
8: 2 ordained strength because of t enemies, 3509.2
10:12 Arise, O LORD; O God, lift up t hand: 3509.2
10:17 their heart, thou wilt cause t ear to hear: 3509.2
16:10 neither wilt thou suffer t Holy One to see 3509.2
17: 2 let t eyes behold the things that are equal. 3509.2
17: 6 t ear unto me, *and* hear my speech. 3509.2
20: 4 Grant thee according to **t own** heart, and 3509.2
21: 8 T hand shall find out all thine enemies: 3509.2
21: 8 Thine hand shall find out all t enemies: 3509.2
21: 9 as a fiery oven in the time of t anger: 3509.2
21:12 *when* thou shalt make ready *t arrows* upon NIH
21:13 thou exalted, LORD, in **t own** strength: 3509.2
26: 6 so will I compass t altar, O LORD: 3509.2
26: 8 and the place where t honour dwelleth. 3509.2
27:14 and he shall strengthen t heart: 3509.2
28: 9 Save thy people, and bless t inheritance: 3509.2
31: 2 Bow down t ear to me; deliver me 3509.2
31: 5 Into t hand I commit my spirit: thou hast 3509.2
31:22 my haste, I am cut off from before t eyes: 3509.2
37: 4 he shall give thee the desires of t heart. 3509.2
38: 2 For t arrows stick fast in me, and 3509.2
38: 3 soundness in my flesh because of t anger; 3509.2
39:10 I am consumed by the blow of t hand. 3509.2
44: 3 t arm, and the light of thy countenance, 3509.2
45: 5 T arrows *are* sharp in the heart of 3509.2
45:10 and consider, and incline t ear; 3509.3
45:10 forget also **t own** people, and thy father's 3509.3
50:20 thou slanderest **t own** mother's son. 3509.2
50:21 and set *them* in order before t eyes. 3509.2
51:19 then shall they offer bullocks upon t altar. 3509.2
56: 7 in *t* anger cast down the people, O God. NIH
66: 3 through the greatness of thy power shall t 3509.2
68: 9 whereby thou didst confirm t inheritance, 3509.2
68:23 may be dipped in the blood of *t* enemies, NIH
69: 9 For the zeal of t house hath eaten me up; 3509.2
69:24 Pour out t indignation upon them, and 3509.2
71: 2 incline t ear unto me, and save me. 3509.2
71:16 of thy righteousness, *even* of t only. 3509.2
74: 1 *why* doth t anger smoke against the sheep 3509.2
74: 2 the rod of t inheritance, *which* thou hast 3509.2
74: 4 T enemies roar in the midst of thy 3509.2
74:16 The day *is* t, the night also *is* 3509.2+3807.1
74:16 day *is* thine, the night also *is* t: 3509.2+3807.1
74:22 Arise, O God, plead **t own** cause: 3509.2
74:23 Forget not the voice of t enemies: 3509.2
77:15 Thou hast with *t* arm redeemed thy people, NIH
77:17 out a sound: t arrows also went abroad. 3509.2
79: 1 the heathen are come into t inheritance; 3509.2
83: 2 For lo, t enemies make a tumult: and 3509.2
84: 3 *even* t altars, O LORD of hosts, 3509.2
84: 9 and look upon the face of t anointed. 3509.2
85: 3 *thyself* from the fierceness of t anger. 3509.2
85: 4 and cause t anger towards us to cease. 3509.2
85: 5 wilt thou draw out t anger to all 3509.2
86: 1 Bow down t ear, O LORD, hear me: 3509.2
86:16 and save the son of t handmaid. 3509.2
88: 2 before thee: incline t ear unto my cry; 3509.2
89:10 thou hast scattered t enemies with thy 3509.2
89:11 The heavens *are* t, the earth also 3509.2+3807.1
89:11 *are* thine, the earth also *is* t: 3509.2+3807.1
89:38 thou hast been wroth with t anointed. 3509.2
89:51 Wherewith t enemies have reproached, 3509.2
89:51 reproached the footsteps of t anointed. 3509.2
90: 7 For we are consumed by t anger, and 3509.2
90:11 Who knoweth the power of t anger? 3509.2
91: 8 Only with t eyes shalt thou behold and 3509.2
92: 9 For lo, t enemies, O LORD, for lo, 3509.2
92: 9 O LORD, for lo, t enemies shall perish; 3509.2
93: 5 holiness becometh t house, O LORD, 3509.2
Ps 94: 5 O LORD, and afflict t heritage. 3509.2
102: 2 I am in trouble; incline t ear unto me: 3509.2
102:10 Because of t indignation and thy wrath: 3509.2
103: 3 Who forgiveth all t iniquities; 3509.3
104:28 thou openest t hand, they are filled *with* 3509.2
106: 5 that *I* may glory with t inheritance. 3509.2
110: 1 until I make t enemies thy footstool. 3509.2
110: 2 rule thou in the midst of t enemies. 3509.2
119:91 They continue *this* day according to t 3509.2
119:94 I *am* t, save me; for I have sought 3509.2+3807.1
119:173 Let t hand help me; for I have chosen thy 3509.2
128: 2 For thou shalt eat the labour of t hands: 3509.2
128: 3 as a fruitful vine by the sides of t house: 3509.2
130: 2 let t ears be attentive to the voice of my 3509.2
132:10 sake turn not away the face of t anointed. 3509.2
138: 7 thou shalt stretch forth t hand against 3509.2
138: 8 forsake not the works of **t own** hands. 3509.2
139: 5 and before, and laid t hand upon me. 3509.2
139:16 T eyes did see my substance, yet being 3509.2
139:20 *and* t enemies take *thy name* in vain. 3509.2
144: 6 shoot out t arrows, and destroy them. 3509.2
144: 7 Send t hand from above; rid me, and 3509.2
145:16 Thou openest t hand, and satisfiest 3509.2
Pr 2: 2 So that *thou* incline t ear unto wisdom, 3509.2
2: 2 *and* apply t heart to understanding; 3509.2
2:10 When wisdom entereth into t heart, and 3509.2
3: 1 but let t heart keep my commandments: 3509.2
3: 3 write them upon the table of t heart: 3509.2
3: 5 Trust in the LORD with all t heart; and 3509.2
3: 5 and lean not unto **t own** understanding. 3509.2
3: 7 Be not wise in **t own** eyes: fear 3509.2
3: 9 and with the firstfruits of all t increase: 3509.2
3:21 My son, let not them depart from t eyes: 3509.2
3:27 when it is in the power of t hand to do *it.* 3509.2
4: 4 said unto me, Let t heart retain my words: 3509.2
4: 9 She shall give to t head an ornament of 3509.2
4:20 my words; incline t ear unto my sayings. 3509.2
4:21 Let them not depart from t eyes; 3509.2
4:21 keep them in the midst of t heart. 3509.2
4:25 Let t eyes look right on, and let thine 3509.2
4:25 and let t eyelids look straight before thee. 3509.2
5: 1 *and* bow t ear to my understanding: 3509.2
5: 9 Lest thou give t honour unto others, and 3509.2
5:15 Drink waters out of **t own** cistern, and 3509.2
5:15 and running waters out of **t own** well. 3509.2
5:17 Let them be only **t own**, and 3509.2+3807.1
6: 4 Give not sleep to t eyes, nor slumber to 3509.2
6: 4 to thine eyes, nor slumber to t eyelids. 3509.2
6:21 Bind them continually upon t heart, *and* 3509.2
6:25 Lust not after her beauty in t heart; 3509.2
7: 2 live; and my law as the apple of t eye. 3509.2
7: 3 write them upon the table of t heart. 3509.2
7:25 Let not t heart decline to her ways, go not 3509.2
20:13 open t eyes, *and* thou shalt be satisfied 3509.2
22:17 Bow down t ear, and hear the words of 3509.2
22:17 and apply t heart unto my knowledge. 3509.2
23: 4 not to be rich: cease from **t own** wisdom. 3509.2
23: 5 Wilt thou set t eyes upon that which is 3509.2
23:12 Apply t heart unto instruction, and 3509.2
23:12 and t ears to the words of knowledge. 3509.2
23:15 My son, if t heart be wise, my heart shall 3509.2
23:17 Let not t heart envy sinners: but *be thou* 3509.2
23:18 and t expectation shall not be cut off. 3509.2
23:19 and be wise, and guide t heart in the way. 3509.2
23:26 give me t heart, and let thine eyes 3509.2
23:26 and let t eyes observe my ways. 3509.2
23:33 T eyes shall behold strange *women,* and 3509.2
23:33 and t heart shall utter perverse things. 3509.2
24:17 Rejoice not when t enemy falleth, and 3509.2
24:17 let not t heart be glad when he stumbleth: 3509.2
24:27 in the field; and afterwards build t house. 3509.2
25: 7 of the prince whom t eyes have seen. 3509.2
25:10 to shame, and t infamy turn not away. 3509.2
25:21 If t enemy *be* hungry, give him bread to 3509.2
27: 2 *man* praise thee, and not **t own** mouth; 3509.2
27: 2 a stranger, and not **t own** lips. 3509.2
27:10 **T own** friend, and thy father's friend, 3509.2
30:32 thought evil, *lay* t hand upon thy mouth. NIH
Ecc 5: 2 let not t heart be hasty to utter *any* thing 3509.2
5: 6 and destroy the work of t hands? 3509.2
7:18 yea, also from this withdraw not t hand: 3509.2
7:22 For oftentimes also **t own** heart knoweth 3509.2
11: 6 and in the evening withhold not t hand: 3509.2
11: 9 walk in the ways of t heart, and in 3509.2
11: 9 of thine heart, and in the sight of t eyes: 3509.2
SS 4: 9 thou hast ravished my heart with one of t 3509.3
4:10 the smell of t ointments than all spices! 3509.3
6: 5 Turn away t eyes from me, for they have 3509.3
7: 4 t eyes *like* the *fish*pools in Heshbon, 3509.3
7: 5 T head upon thee *is* like Carmel, and 3509.3
7: 5 and the hair of t head like purple; 3509.3
8: 6 Set me as a seal upon t heart, as a seal 3509.2
8: 6 upon thine heart, as a seal upon t arm: 3509.2
Isa 6: 7 t iniquity is taken away, and thy sin 3509.2
12: 1 t anger is turned away, and 3509.2
14:13 For thou hast said in t heart, I will ascend 3509.2
26:11 the fire of t enemies shall devour them. 3509.2
30:20 but t eyes shall see thy teachers: 3509.2
30:21 t ears shall hear a word behind thee, 3509.2
33:17 T eyes shall see the king in his beauty: 3509.2
33:18 T heart shall meditate terror. Where *is* 3509.2
33:20 t eyes shall see Jerusalem a quiet 3509.2
37:17 Incline t ear, O LORD, and hear; 3509.2
37:17 hear; open t eyes, O LORD, and see: 3509.2
37:23 *thy* voice, and lifted up t eyes on high? 3509.2
38: 1 saith the LORD, Set t house in order: 3509.2
39: 4 said he, What have they seen in t house? 3509.2
39: 6 that all that *is* in t house, and *that* which 3509.2
42: 6 will hold t hand, and will keep thee, and 3509.2
43:24 thou hast wearied me with t iniquities. 3509.2
44: 3 and my blessing upon t offspring: 3509.2
45:14 unto thee, and they shall be t: 3509.3+3807.1
47: 6 and given them into t hand: 3509.3
47: 8 that sayest in t heart, I *am,* and none else 1886.3
47: 9 the great abundance of t enchantments. 3509.3
Isa 47:10 thou hast said in t heart, I *am,* and 3509.3
47:12 Stand now with t enchantments, and 3509.3
48: 8 from that time *that* t ear was not opened: 3509.2
49:18 Lift up t eyes round about, and behold: 3509.3
49:20 lost the other, shall say again in t ears, 3509.3
49:21 shalt thou say in t heart, Who hath 3509.3
51:22 I have taken out of t hand the cup of 3509.3
54: 2 let them stretch forth the curtains of t 3509.3
54: 5 For thy Maker *is* t husband; the LORD 3509.3
57:10 thou hast found the life of t hand; 3509.3
58: 7 thou hide not thyself from **t own** flesh? 3509.2
58: 8 and t health shall spring forth speedily: 3509.2
58:13 shalt honour him, not doing **t own** ways, 3509.2
58:13 own ways, nor finding **t own** pleasure, 3509.2
58:13 own pleasure, nor speaking *t own* words: NIH
60: 4 Lift up t eyes round about, and see: 3509.3
60: 5 flow *together,* and t heart shall fear, and 3509.3
60:17 and t exactors righteousness. 3509.3
60:20 for the LORD shall be t 3509.3+3807.1
62: 8 give thy corn *to be* meat for t enemies; 3509.3
63: 2 Wherefore *art thou* red in t apparel, and 3509.2
63:17 servants' sake, the tribes of t inheritance. 3509.2
63:19 We are *t*: thou never barest rule over them; NIH
64: 2 to make thy name known to t adversaries, 3509.2
64: 8 and we all *are* the work of t hand. 3509.2
Jer 2: 2 of thy youth, the love of t espousals, 3509.3
2:19 **T own** wickedness shall correct thee, and 3509.3
2:22 *yet* t iniquity *is* marked before me, 3509.3
2:37 from him, and t hands upon thine head: 3509.3
2:37 from him, and thine hands upon t head: 3509.3
3: 2 Lift up t eyes unto the high places, and 3509.3
3:13 Only acknowledge t iniquity, that thou 3509.3
4: 1 if thou wilt put away t abominations out 3509.2
4:14 wash t heart from wickedness, 3509.3
4:18 *is* bitter, because it reacheth unto t heart. 3509.3
5: 3 O LORD, *are* not t eyes upon the truth? 3509.2
5:17 they shall eat up t harvest, and thy bread, 3509.2
5:17 they shall eat up thy flocks and t herds: 3509.2
6: 9 turn back t hand as a grapegatherer into 3509.2
7:29 Cut off t hair, *O Jerusalem,* and cast *it* 3509.3
9: 6 T habitation *is* in the midst of deceit; 3509.2
10:24 not in t anger, lest thou bring me to 3509.2
13:22 if thou say in t heart, Wherefore come 3509.3
13:22 For the greatness of t iniquity are thy 3509.3
13:27 I have seen t adulteries, and 3509.3
13:27 t abominations on the hills in the fields. 3509.3
15:14 I will make *thee* to pass with t enemies 3509.2
17: 4 shalt discontinue from t heritage that I 3509.2
17: 4 I will cause thee to serve t enemies in 3509.2
18:23 deal *thus* with them in the time of t anger. 3509.2
20: 4 t eyes *shall* behold *it;* and I will give all 3509.2
20: 6 all that dwell in t house shall go into 3509.2
22:17 t eyes and thine heart *are* not but for thy 3509.2
22:17 thine eyes and t heart *are* not but for thy 3509.2
25:28 if they refuse to take the cup at t hand to 3509.2
28: 7 thou now this word that I speak in t ears, 3509.2
30:14 cruel one, for the multitude of t iniquity; 3509.3
30:15 Why criest thou for t affliction? 3509.3
30:15 incurable for the multitude of t iniquity: 3509.3
30:16 all t adversaries, every one of them, 3509.3
31:16 from weeping, and t eyes from tears: 3509.3
31:17 there is hope in t end, saith the LORD, 3509.3
31:21 set t heart toward the highway, *even* 3509.3
32: 7 Hanameel the son of Shallum t uncle 3509.2
32: 7 right of redemption *is* t to buy *it.* 3509.2+3807.1
32: 8 for the right of inheritance *is* t, 3509.2+3807.1
32: 8 *is* thine, and the redemption *is* t; 3509.2+3807.1
32:19 for t eyes *are* open upon all the ways of 3509.2
34: 3 t eyes shall behold the eyes of the king of 3509.2
36:14 Take in t hand the roll wherein thou hast 3509.2
38:12 rotten rags under t armholes under 3509.2
38:17 with fire; and thou shalt live, and t house: 3509.2
40: 4 from the chains which *were* upon t hand. 3509.2
42: 2 a few of many, as t eyes do behold us:) 3509.2
43: 9 Take great stones in t hand, and 3509.2
49:16 deceived thee, *and* the pride of t heart, 3509.2
51:13 t end is come, *and* the measure of thy 3509.3
La 2:14 they have not discovered t iniquity, 3509.3
2:16 All t enemies have opened their mouth 3509.3
2:17 he hath caused *t* enemy to rejoice over thee, NIH
2:17 he hath set up the horn of t adversaries. 3509.3
2:18 no rest; let not the apple of t eye cease. 3509.3
2:19 pour out t heart like water before the face 3509.3
2:21 thou hast slain *them* in the day of t anger; 3509.2
3:56 hide not t ear at my breathing, at my cry. 3509.2
4:22 The punishment of t iniquity is 3509.3
4:22 he will visit t iniquity, O daughter of 3509.3
Eze 3:10 I shall speak unto thee receive in t heart, 3509.2
3:10 in thine heart, and hear with t ears. 3509.2
3:18 but his blood will I require at t hand. 3509.2
3:20 but his blood will I require at t hand. 3509.2
3:24 unto me, Go, shut thyself within t house. 3509.2
4: 7 t arm *shall be* uncovered, and thou shalt 3509.2
5: 1 cause *it* to pass upon t head and upon thy 3509.2
5: 9 the like, because of all t abominations. 3509.3
5:11 with all t abominations, therefore will I 3509.3
6:11 Smite with t hand, and stamp with thy 3509.2
7: 3 will recompense upon thee all t 3509.3
7: 4 t abominations shall be in the midst of 3509.3
7: 8 will recompense thee for all t 3509.3
7: 9 t abominations *that* are in the midst of 3509.3
8: 5 lift up t eyes now the way towards 3509.2
10: 2 fill t hand *with* coals of fire from between 3509.2
16: 6 and saw thee polluted in **t own** blood, 3509.3
16: 7 t hair is grown, whereas thou *wast* naked 3509.3
16:11 I put bracelets upon t hands, and a chain 3509.3
16:12 earrings in t ears, and a beautiful crown 3509.3
16:12 and a beautiful crown upon t head. 3509.3
16:15 thou didst trust in **t own** beauty, and 3509.3
16:22 in all t abominations and thy whoredoms 3509.3
16:27 have diminished t ordinary *food,* and 3509.3
16:30 How weak is t heart, saith the Lord 3509.3
16:31 In that thou buildest t eminent place in 3509.3
16:31 and makest t high place in every street; 3509.3
16:39 they shall throw down t eminent place, 3509.3

T

Eze 16:41 they shall burn t houses with fire, and 3509.3
16:43 I also will recompense thy way upon t head, NIH
16:43 *this* lewdness above all t abominations. 3509.3
16:46 t elder sister *is* Samaria, she and 3509.3
16:51 thou hast multiplied t abominations more 3509.3
16:51 hast justified thy sisters in all t 3509.3
16:52 bear t own shame for thy sins that thou 3509.3
16:54 That thou mayest bear t own shame, and 3509.3
16:58 borne thy lewdness and t abominations, 3509.3
16:61 thy sisters, t elder and thy younger: 3509.3
21:14 smite t hands together, and let the sword be NIH
22: 4 hast defiled *thyself* in t idols which thou 3509.3
22:14 Can t heart endure, or can thine hands be 3509.3
22:14 heart endure, or can t hands be strong, 3509.3
22:16 thou shalt take t inheritance in thyself in NIH
23:25 they shall take away thy nose and t ears; 3509.3
23:27 thou shalt not lift up t eyes unto them, 3509.3
23:31 therefore will I give her cup into t hand. 3509.3
23:34 and pluck off t own breasts: 3509.3
24:16 I take away from thee the desire of t eyes 3509.2
24:17 bind the tire of t head upon thee, and 3509.2
24:26 to cause *thee* to hear *it* with t ears? NIH
25: 6 Because thou hast clapped t hands, and NIH
27: 6 *Of* the oaks of Bashan have they made t 3509.3
27:10 and of Lud and of Phut were in t army, 3509.3
27:11 The men of Arvad with t army *were* upon NIH
27:15 isles *were* the merchandise of t hand: 3509.3
28: 2 Because t heart *is* lifted up, and thou hast 3509.2
28: 2 thou set t heart as the heart of God: 3509.2
28: 4 with t understanding thou hast gotten thee 3509.2
28: 5 t heart is lifted up because of thy riches: 3509.2
28: 6 Because thou hast set t heart as the heart 3509.2
28:17 T heart was lifted up because of thy 3509.2
28:18 by the multitude of t iniquities, 3509.2
33: 8 but his blood will I require at t hand. 3509.2
35:11 I will even do according to t anger, and 3509.2
35:11 according to t envy which thou hast used 3509.2
37:17 and they shall become one in t hand. 3509.2
37:20 shall be in t hand before their eyes. 3509.2
38: 4 and all t army, horses and horsemen, 3509.2
38:12 to turn t hand upon the desolate places 3509.2
39: 3 will cause t arrows to fall out of thy right 3509.2
40: 4 behold with t eyes, and hear with thine 3509.2
40: 4 hear with t ears, and set thine heart upon 3509.2
40: 4 set t heart upon all that I shall shew thee; 3509.2
44: 5 behold with t eyes, and hear with thine 3509.2
44: 5 hear with t ears all that I say unto thee 3509.2
44:30 that he may cause the blessing to rest in t 3509.2
Da 2:38 of the heaven hath he given into t hand, 3509.5
3:17 he will deliver *us* out of t hand, O king. 3509.5
4:19 the interpretation thereof to t enemies. 3509.5
4:27 t iniquities by shewing mercy to the poor; 3509.5
5:22 O Belshazzar, hast not humbled t heart, 3509.5
9:16 let t anger and thy fury be turned away 3509.2
9:18 O my God, incline t ear, and hear; 3509.2
9:18 open t eyes, and behold our desolations, 3509.2
9:19 do; defer not, for t own sake, O my God: 3509.2
10:12 for from the first day that thou didst set t 3509.2
Hos 9: 7 for the multitude of t iniquity, and 3509.2
13: 9 hast destroyed thyself; but in me *is* t help. 3509.2
14: 1 thy God; for thou hast fallen by t iniquity. 3509.2
Joel 2:17 and give not t heritage to reproach, 3509.2
Ob 1: 3 The pride of t heart hath deceived thee, 3509.2
1:15 thy reward shall return upon t own head. 3509.2
Jnh 1: 8 this evil *is* upon us; What *is* t occupation? 3509.2
2: 7 came in unto thee, into t holy temple. 3509.2
Mic 4:10 redeem thee from the hand of t enemies. 3509.3
4:13 for I will make t horn iron, and I will 3509.3
5: 9 T hand shall be lift up upon thine 3509.2
5: 9 Thine hand shall be lift up upon t 3509.2
5: 9 and all t enemies shall be cut off. 3509.2
5:12 I will cut off witchcrafts out of t hand; 3509.2
5:13 thou shalt no more worship the work of t 3509.2
7:14 with thy rod, the flock of t heritage, 3509.2
Na 3:13 shall be set wide open unto t enemies: 3509.3
Hab 3: 8 *was* t anger against the rivers? *was* thy 3509.2
3: 8 that thou didst ride upon t horses *and* 3509.2
3:11 at the light of t arrows they went, *and* 3509.2
3:13 *even* for salvation with t anointed; 3509.2
3:15 Thou didst walk through the sea *with* t 3509.2
Zep 3:15 thy judgments, he hath cast out t enemy: 3509.3
3:16 *and to* Zion, Let not t hands be slack. 3509.3
Zec 3: 4 I have caused t iniquity to pass from thee, 3509.2
5: 5 Lift up now t eyes, and see what *is* this 3509.2
13: 6 What *are* these wounds in t hands? 3509.2
Mt 5:25 Agree with t adversary quickly, whiles thou 4771
5:33 but shalt perform unto the Lord t oaths: 4771
5:43 shalt love thy neighbour, and hate t enemy. 4771
6: 2 Therefore when thou doest t alms, do not NIG
6: 4 That t alms may be in secret: and 4771
6:13 For t is the kingdom, and the power, and 4771
6:17 anoint t head, and wash thy face; 4771
6:22 if therefore t eye be single, thy whole body 4771
6:23 But if t eye be evil, thy whole body shall be 4771
7: 3 considerest not the beam that is in t own 4774
7: 4 Let me pull out the mote out of t eye; 4771
7: 4 and behold, a beam *is* in t own eye? 4771
7: 5 first cast out the beam out of t own eye; 4771
9: 6 Arise, take up thy bed, and go unto t house. 4771
12:13 saith he to the man, Stretch forth t hand. 4771
18: 9 And if t eye offend thee, pluck it out, and 4771
20:14 Take *that* t *is,* and go thy way: I will give 4674
20:15 do what I will with mine own? Is t eye evil, 4771
22:44 till I make t enemies thy footstool? 4771
25:25 in the earth: lo, *there* thou hast *that is* t. 4674
Mk 2:11 up thy bed, and go thy way into t house. 4771
3: 5 he saith unto the man, Stretch forth t hand. 4771
9:47 And if t eye offend thee, pluck it out: it is 4771
12:36 till I make t enemies thy footstool. 4771
Lk 4: 7 therefore wilt worship me, all shall be t. 4771
5:24 and take up thy couch, and go into t house. 4771
5:33 of the Pharisees; but t eat and drink? 4674
6:41 perceivest not the beam that is in t own 2398
6:42 let me pull out the mote that is in t eye, 4771
6:42 not the beam that is in t own eye? 4771
Lk 6:42 cast out first the beam out of t own eye, 4771
7:44 I entered into t house, thou gavest me no 4771
8:39 Return to t own house, and shew how great 4771
11:34 therefore when t eye is single, thy whole 4771
11:34 but when t eye is evil, thy body also *is* full NIG
12:19 take t ease, eat, drink, *and* be merry. NIG
12:58 When thou goest with t adversary to 4771
15:31 art ever with me, and all that I have is t. 4674
19:22 Out of t own mouth will I judge thee, 4771
19:42 but now they are hid from t eyes. 4771
19:43 that t enemies shall cast a trench about 4771
20:43 Till I make t enemies thy footstool. 4771
22:42 nevertheless not my will, but t, be done. 4674
Jn 2:17 The zeal of t house hath eaten me up. 4771
8:10 Woman, where are those t accusers? 4771
9:10 they unto him, How were t eyes opened? 4771
9:17 thou of him, that he hath opened t eyes? 4771
9:26 did he to thee? how opened he t eyes? 4771
17: 5 glorify thou me with t own self with 4572
17: 6 t they were, and thou gavest them me; and 4674
17: 9 which thou hast given me; for they are t. 4674
17:10 And all mine are t, and thine are mine; and 4674
17:10 And all mine are thine, and t are mine; and 4674
17:11 keep through t own name those whom thou 4771
18:35 T own nation and the chief priests have 4674
Ac 2:27 neither wilt thou suffer t Holy One to see 4771
4:30 By stretching forth t hand to heal; and 4771
5: 3 why hath Satan filled t heart to lie to 4771
5: 4 Whiles it remained, was it not t own? and 4771
5: 4 after it was sold, was it not in t own power? 4674
5: 4 why hast thou conceived this thing in t 4771
8:22 if perhaps the thought of t heart may be 4771
8:37 If thou believest with all t heart, NIG
10: 4 t alms are come up for a memorial before 4771
10:31 t alms are had in remembrance in the sight 4771
13:35 not suffer t Holy One to see corruption. 4771
23:35 said he, when t accusers are also come. 4771
Ro 10: 6 Say not in t heart, Who shall ascend into 4771
10: 9 shalt believe in t heart that God hath raised 4771
11: 3 thy prophets, and digged down t altars; 4771
12:20 Therefore if t enemy hunger, feed him; 4771
1Co 10:29 I say, not t own, but of the other's: 1438
1Ti 5:23 thy stomach's sake and t often infirmities. 4771
Phm 1:19 owest unto me even t own self besides. 4572
Heb 1:10 and the heavens are the works of t hands: 4771
1:13 until I make t enemies thy footstool? 4771
Rev 3:18 and anoint t eyes *with* eyesalve, that thou 4771

THING (548) [ANYTHING, NOTHING, SOMETHING, THINGS, THINGS']

Ge 1:24 creeping t, and beast of the earth after his 7431
1:25 every t that creepeth upon the earth after 7431
1:26 over every creeping t that creepeth upon 7431
1:28 over every living t that moveth upon 2416
1:30 to every t that creepeth upon the earth, NIH
1:31 God saw every t that he had made, and 3605
6: 7 and the creeping t, and the fowls of the air; 7431
6:17 *and* every t that *is* in the earth shall die. NIH
6:19 of every living t of all flesh, two of every NIH
6:20 of every creeping t of the earth after his 7431
7: 8 and of every t that creepeth upon the earth, NIH
7:14 every creeping t that creepeth upon 7431
7:21 of every creeping t that creepeth upon 8318
8: 1 every living t, and all the cattle that *was* 2416
8:17 Bring forth with thee every living t that *is* 2416
8:17 of every creeping t that creepeth upon 7431
8:19 every creeping t, and every fowl, *and* 7431
8:21 neither will I again smite any more every t NIH
9: 3 Every moving t that liveth shall be meat 7431
14:23 that I will not take any t that *is* thine, 3605
18:14 Is any t too hard for the LORD? At 1697
18:17 Shall I hide from Abraham *that* t which I NIH
19:21 See, I have accepted thee concerning this t, 1697
19:22 for I cannot do any t till thou be come 1697
20:10 sawest thou, that thou hast done this t? 1697
21:11 the t was very grievous in Abraham's sight 1697
21:26 I wot not who hath done this t: 1697
22:12 the lad, neither do thou any t unto him: 3972
22:16 for because thou hast done this t, and 1697
24:50 said, The t proceedeth from the LORD: 1697
30:31 Jacob said, Thou shalt not give me any t: 3972
30:31 if thou wilt do this t for me, I will again 1697
34: 7 which t ought not to be done. 3651
34:14 they said unto them, We cannot do this t, 1697
34:19 the young man deferred not to do the t, 1697
38:10 *the* t which he did displeased the LORD: NIH
39: 9 neither hath he kept back any t from me 3972
39:23 not to any t *that was* under his hand; 3605+3972
41:28 This *is* the t which I have spoken unto 1697
41:32 *it is* because the t *is* established by God, 1697
41:37 the t was good in the eyes of Pharaoh, and 1697
44: 7 thy servants should do according to this t: 1697
Ex 1:18 Why have ye done this t, and have saved 1697
2:14 and said, Surely *this* t is known. 1697
2:15 Now when Pharaoh heard this t, he sought 1697
9: 5 To morrow the LORD shall do this t in 1697
9: 6 the LORD did that t on the morrow, and 1697
10:15 there remained not any green t in the trees, 3418
12:24 ye shall observe this t for an ordinance to 1697
16:14 of the wilderness *there lay* a small round t, 2636
16:16 This *is* the t which the LORD hath 1697
16:32 This *is* the t which the LORD 1697
18:11 for in the t wherein they dealt proudly *he* 1697
18:14 What *is* this t that thou doest to the people? 1697
18:17 unto him, The t that thou doest *is* not good. 1697
18:18 for *this* t *is* too heavy for thee; thou art not 1697
18:23 If thou shalt do this t, and God command 1697
20: 4 any likeness *of any* t that *is* in heaven NIH
20:17 his ass, nor any t that *is* thy neighbour's. 3605
22: 9 for any manner of lost t, which *another* NIH
22:15 if it *be* a hired t, it came for his hire. NIH
29: 1 this *is* the t that thou shalt do unto them to 1697
33:17 I will do this t also that thou hast spoken: 1697
34:10 for it *is* a terrible t that I will do with thee. NIH
35: 4 This *is* the t which the LORD 1697
Lev 2: 3 *it is a* t most holy of the offerings of NIH
2:10 *it is a* t most holy of the offerings of 6944+6944
4:13 the t be hid from the eyes of the assembly, 1697
5: 2 Or if a soul touch any unclean t, whether *it* 1697
5: 5 shall confess that he hath sinned in that t: NIH
5:16 for the harm that he hath done in the holy t, NIH
6: 2 or in a t taken away by violence, or 1498
6: 4 or the t which he hath deceitfully gotten, 1886.1
6: 4 him to keep, or the lost t which he found, NIH
6: 7 it shall be forgiven him for any t of all that NIH
7:19 the flesh that toucheth any unclean t shall NIH
7:21 any unclean t, *as* the uncleanness of man, NIH
7:21 or any abominable unclean t, and eat of NIH
8: 5 This *is* the t which the LORD commanded 1697
9: 6 This *is* the t which the LORD commanded 1697
11:10 and of any living t which *is* in the waters, 5315
11:21 flying creeping t that goeth upon *all* four, 8318
11:35 every t whereupon *any part* of their carcase NIH
11:41 every creeping t that creepeth upon 8318
11:43 with any creeping t that creepeth, 8318
11:44 *of* creeping t that creepeth upon the earth. 8318
12: 4 she shall touch no hallowed t, nor come into NIH
13:48 whether in a skin, or in any t made of skin; 3605
13:49 the warp, or in the woof, or in any t of skin; 3627
13:52 in woollen or in linen, or any t of skin, 3627
13:53 the warp, or in the woof, or in any t of skin; 3627
13:54 priest shall command that they wash *the* t NIH
13:57 the warp, or in the woof, or in any t of skin; 3627
13:58 whatsoever t of skin *it be,* which thou shalt 3627
13:59 *in* the warp, or woof, or any t of skins, 3627
15: 4 every t, whereon he sitteth, shall be 3627
15: 6 he that sitteth on *any* t whereon he sat that 3627
15:10 whosoever toucheth any t that was under NIH
15:20 every t that she lieth upon in her separation NIH
15:20 every t also that she sitteth upon shall be NIH
15:22 whosoever toucheth any t that she sat upon 3627
15:23 or on *any* t whereon she sitteth, when he 3627
17: 2 This *is* the t which the LORD hath 1697
19: 8 he hath profaned the hallowed t of NIH
19:26 Ye shall not eat *any* t with the blood: NIH
20:17 it *is* a wicked t; and they shall be cut off in 2617
20:21 take his brother's wife, it *is* an unclean t: 5079
20:25 by any *manner of living* t that creepeth *on* NIH
21:18 he that hath a flat nose, or any t superfluous, NIH
22: 4 whoso toucheth any t *that is* unclean *by* NIH
22: 5 Or whosoever toucheth any creeping t, 8318
22:10 There shall no stranger eat *of* the holy t: a NIH
22:10 a hired servant, shall not eat *of* the holy t. NIH
22:14 if a man eat *of* the holy t unwittingly, then NIH
22:14 shall give *it* unto the priest with the holy t. NIH
22:23 or a lamb that hath any t superfluous or 8311
23:37 and drink offerings, every t upon his day: 1697
27:23 in that day, *as* a holy t unto the LORD. NIH
27:28 Notwithstanding no devoted t, that a man 2764
27:28 every devoted t *is* most holy unto 2764
Nu 4:15 they shall not touch *any* holy t, lest they die. NIH
16: 9 *Seemeth it but* a small t unto you, that 4592
16:13 *Is it* a small t that thou hast brought us up 4592
16:30 if the LORD make a new t, and the earth 1278
17:13 Whosoever cometh any t near unto 3605
18: 7 your priest's office for every t of the altar, 1697
18:14 Every t devoted in Israel shall be thine. 3605
18:15 Every t that openeth the matrix in all flesh, 3605
20:19 without *doing* any t *else,* go through on my 1697
22:38 have I now any power at all to say any t? 3972
30: 1 This *is* the t which the LORD hath 1697
31:23 Every t that may abide the fire, ye shall 1697
32:20 Moses said unto them, If ye will do this t, 1697
35:22 have cast upon him any t without laying of 3627
36: 6 This *is* the t which the LORD doth 1697
Dt 1:14 The t which thou hast spoken *is* good *for us* 1697
1:32 Yet in this t ye did not believe the LORD 1697
4:18 The likeness of any t that creepeth on NIH
4:23 the likeness of any t, which the LORD thy NIH
4:25 *or* the likeness of any t, and shall do evil in NIH
4:32 whether there hath been *any such* t as this NIH
4:32 hath been *any such thing* as this great t *is,* 1697
5: 8 any likeness *of any* t that *is* in heaven NIH
5:21 or his ass, or any t that *is* thy neighbour's. NIH
7:26 thine house, lest thou be a cursed t like it: 2764
7:26 shalt utterly abhor it; for it *is* a cursed t. 2764
8: 9 thou shalt not lack any t in it; NIH
12:32 What t soever I command you, observe to 1697
13:14 behold, *if it be* truth, *and* the t certain, *that* 1697
13:17 there shall cleave nought of the cursed t to 2764
14: 3 Thou shalt not eat any abominable t. NIH
14:19 every creeping t that flieth *is* unclean unto 8318
14:21 Ye shall not eat of any t that dieth of itself: 3605
15:10 that for this t the LORD thy God shall 1697
15:15 I command thee this t to day. 1697
16: 4 neither shall there *any* t of the flesh, NIH
17: 4 and behold, *it is* true, *and* the t certain, 1697
17: 5 which have committed that wicked t, 1697
18:22 if the t follow not, nor come to pass, that *is* 1697
18:22 that *is* the t which the LORD hath not 1697
22: 3 with all lost t of thy brother's, which he NIH
22:20 if this t be true, *and the tokens of* virginity 1697
23: 9 then keep thee from every wicked t. 1697
23:14 that he see no unclean t in thee, and 1697
23:19 usury of any t that is lent upon usury: 1697
24:10 When thou dost lend thy brother any t, 3972
24:18 I command thee to do this t. 1697
24:22 I command thee to do this t. 1697
26:11 thou shalt rejoice in every good t which NIH
31:13 which have not known *any* t, may hear, and NIH
32:47 For it *is* not a vain t for you; because it *is* 1697
32:47 through this t ye shall prolong *your* days in 1697
Jos 4:10 until every t was finished that the LORD 1697
6:18 wise keep *yourselves* from the accursed t, 2764
6:18 when ye take of the accursed t, and 2764
7: 1 committed a trespass in the accursed t: 2764
7: 1 the tribe of Judah, took of the accursed t: 2764
7:11 for they have even taken of the accursed t, 2764
7:13 *There is* an accursed t in the midst of thee, 2764
7:13 until ye take away the accursed t from 2764

Jos 7:15 *that* he that is taken with the **accursed t** 2764
9:24 because of you, and have done this **t**. 1697
14: 6 Thou knowest the **t** that the LORD said 1697
21:45 There failed not ought of any good **t** which 1697
22:20 Zerah commit a trespass in the **accursed t**, 2764
22:24 we have not *rather* done it for fear of *this* **t**, 1697
22:33 And the **t** pleased the children of Israel; and 1697
23:14 that not one **t** hath failed of all the good 1697
23:14 unto you, *and* not one **t** hath failed thereof. 1697
Jdg 6:29 said one to another, Who hath done this **t**? 1697
6:29 Gideon the son of Joash hath done this **t**. 1697
8:27 which *t* became a snare unto Gideon, and NIH
11:25 now *art* thou **any t better** than Balak 2896+2896
11:37 unto her father, Let this **t** be done for me: 1697
13: 4 nor strong drink, and eat not any unclean *t*: NIH
13: 7 neither eat any unclean *t*: for the child shall NIH
13:14 She may not eat of any *t* that cometh of NIH
13:14 nor eat any unclean *t*: all that I commanded NIH
18: 7 that might put *them* to shame in *any* **t**; 1697
18:10 a place where *there is* no want of any **t** that 1697
19:19 with thy servants: *there is* no want of any **t**. 1697
19:24 but unto this man do not so vile a **t**. 1697
20: 9 now this *shall be* the **t** which we will do to 1697
21:11 this *is* the **t** that ye shall do, Ye shall utterly 1697
Ru 3:18 in rest, until he have finished the **t** *this* day. 1697
1Sa 3:11 to Samuel, Behold, I will do a **t** in Israel, 1697
3:17 What *is* the **t** that *the LORD* hath said 1697
3:17 if thou hide *any* **t** from me of all the things 1697
4: 7 for there hath not been such *a t* heretofore. NIH
8: 6 the **t** displeased Samuel, when they said, 1697
12:16 Now therefore stand and see this great **t**, 1697
14:12 Come up to us, and we will shew you a **t**. 1697
15: 9 every **t** *that was* vile and refuse, that they 4399
18:20 and they told Saul, and the **t** pleased him. 1697
18:23 Seemeth it to you a light *t* to be a king's son NIH
20: 2 why should my father hide this **t** from me? 1697
20:26 Nevertheless Saul spake not **any t** that day: 3972
20:39 the lad knew not **any t**: only Jonathan and 3972
21: 2 Let no man know **any t** of the business 3972
22:15 let not the king impute *any* **t** unto his 1697
24: 6 The LORD forbid that I should do this **t** 1697
25:15 we were not hurt, neither missed we **any t**, 3972
26:16 This **t** *is* not good that thou hast done. 1697
28:10 no punishment happen to thee for this **t**. 1697
28:18 hath the LORD done this **t** unto thee this 1697
30:19 nor any *t* that they had taken to them: NIH
2Sa 2: 6 this kindness, because ye have done this **t**. 1697
3:13 one **t** I require of thee, that is, Thou shalt 1697
7:19 this was yet a **small t** in thy sight, O Lord 6994
11:11 and *as* thy soul liveth, I will not do this **t**. 1697
11:25 say unto Joab, Let not this **t** displease thee, 1697
11:27 the **t** that David had done displeased 1697
12: 5 the man that hath done this *t* shall surely NIH
12: 6 because he did this **t**, and because he had 1697
12:12 I will do this **t** before all Israel, and 1697
12:21 What **t** *is* this that thou hast done? 1697
13: 2 Amnon thought it hard for him to do **any t** 3972
13:12 for no such **t** ought to be done in Israel: NIH
13:20 he *is* thy brother; regard not this **t**. So 1697
13:33 let not my lord the king take the **t** to his 1697
14:13 hast thou thought such a **t** against 2088
14:13 for the king doth speak this **t** as one which 1697
14:15 that I am come to speak of this **t** unto my 1697
14:18 I pray thee, the **t** that I shall ask thee. 1697
14:20 of speech hath thy servant Joab done this **t**: 1697
14:21 unto Joab, Behold now, I have done this **t**: 1697
15:11 in their simplicity, and they knew not any **t**. 1697
15:35 *that* what **t** soever thou shalt hear out of 1697
15:36 by them ye shall send unto me every **t** that 1697
17:19 corn thereon; and the **t** was not known. 1697
24: 3 why doth my lord the king delight in this **t**? 1697
1Ki 1:27 Is this **t** done by my lord the king, and 1697
3:10 the Lord, that Solomon had asked this **t**. 1697
3:11 Because thou hast asked this **t**, and hast not 1697
10: 3 there was not *any* **t** hid from the king, 1697
11:10 And had commanded him concerning this **t**, 1697
12:24 man to his house; for this **t** is from me. 1697
12:30 this **t** became a sin: for the people went *to* 1697
13:33 After this **t** Jeroboam returned not from his 1697
13:34 this **t** became sin unto the house of 1697
14: 5 the wife of Jeroboam cometh to ask a **t** of 1697
14:13 in him there is found *some* good **t** toward 1697
15: 5 turned not aside from any *t* that he NIH
16:31 as if it had been a **light t** for him to walk in 7043
20: 9 this **t** I may not do. And the messengers 1697
20:24 do this **t**, Take the kings away, every man 1697
20:33 whether *any t would come* from him, NIH
2Ki 2:10 he said, Thou hast asked a **hard t**: 7185
3:18 *but* a **light t** in the sight of the LORD: 7043
4: 2 Thine handmaid hath not **any t** in 3605
5:13 *if* the prophet had bid thee *do some* great **t**, 1697
5:18 In this **t** the LORD pardon thy servant, 1697
5:18 the LORD pardon thy servant in this **t**. 1697
6:11 king of Syria was sore troubled for this **t**; 1697
7: 2 make windows in heaven, might this **t** be? 1697
7:19 in heaven, might such a **t** be? 1697+1886.1
8: 9 even *of* every **good t** of Damascus, 2898
8:13 a dog, that he should do this great **t**? 1697
11: 5 saying, This *is* the **t** that ye shall do; 1697
17:12 had said unto them, Ye shall not do this **t**. 1697
20: 9 that the LORD will do the **t** that he hath 1697
20:10 It is a **light t** for the shadow to go down ten 7043
1Ch 2: 7 who transgressed in the **t accursed**. 2764
11:19 that *I* should do this *t*: shall I drink NIH
13: 4 for the **t** was right in the eyes of all 1697
17:17 *yet* this was a **small t** in thine eyes, O God; 6994
17:23 let the **t** that thou hast spoken concerning 1697
21: 3 doth my lord require this *t*? why will he be NIH
21: 7 God was displeased with this **t**; therefore 1697
21: 8 sinned greatly, because I have done this **t**: 1697
2Ch 9:20 it was *not* **any t** accounted of in the days of 3972
11: 4 man to his house, for this **t** is done of me. 1697
16:10 of this *t*. And Asa oppressed *some* of NIH
23: 4 This *is* the **t** that ye shall do; A third *part* of 1697
23:19 that none *which was* unclean in any **t** 1697

2Ch 29:36 the people: for the **t** was *done* suddenly. 1697
30: 4 the **t** pleased the king and all 1697
Ezr 7:27 which hath put *such a t* as this in the king's NIH
9: 3 when I heard this **t**, I rent my garment and 1697
10: 2 there is hope in Israel concerning this *t*. NIH
10:13 are many that have transgressed in this **t**. 1697
Ne 2:19 and said, What *is* this **t** that ye do? 1697
13:17 What evil **t** *is* this that ye do, and 1697
Est 2: 4 And the **t** pleased the king; and he did so. 1697
2:22 the **t** was known to Mordecai, who told *it* 1697
5:14 the **t** pleased Haman; and he caused 1697
6:13 all his friends every *t* that had befallen him. NIH
8: 5 the **t** seem right before the king, and I *be* 1697
Job 3:25 For the **t** which I greatly feared is come NIH
4:12 Now a **t** was secretly brought to me, and 1697
6: 8 God would grant *me* the **t** that I **long for**! 8615
9:22 This *is* one *t*, therefore I said *it*, He NIH
12:10 In whose hand *is* the soul of every living *t*, NIH
13:28 he, as a **rotten t**, consumeth, as a garment 7538
14: 4 Who can bring a clean *t* out of an unclean? NIH
15:11 with thee? is there *any* secret **t** with thee? 1697
22:28 Thou shalt also decree a **t**, and it shall be 562
23:14 For he performeth the **t that is appointed** 2706
26: 3 hast thou plentifully declared the **t as it is**? 8454
28:10 and his eye seeth every **precious t**. 3366
28:11 the **t that is hid** bringeth he forth *to* light. 8587
33:32 If *thou* hast **any t to say**, answer me: speak, 4405
39: 8 and he searcheth after every **green t**. 3387
42: 2 I know that thou canst do every *t*, and NIH
42: 7 for ye have not spoken of me *the t that is* NIH
42: 8 in that ye have not spoken of me *the t which* NIH
Ps 2: 1 and the people imagine a vain *t*? NIH
27: 4 One *t* have I desired of the LORD, that NIH
33:17 A horse *is* a **vain t** for safety: neither shall 8267
34:10 seek the LORD shall not want any good *t*. NIH
38:20 because I follow *the t that* good *is*. NIH
69:34 the seas, and every *t* that moveth therein. NIH
84:11 no good *t* will he withhold from them that NIH
89:34 nor alter the **t that is gone out** of my lips. 4161
92: 1 *It is* a good *t* to give thanks unto NIH
101: 3 I will set no wicked **t** before mine eyes: 1697
141: 4 Incline not my heart to *any* evil **t**, 1697
145:16 and satisfiest the desire of every **living t**. 2416
150: 6 Let every *t that hath* breath praise NIH
Pr 4: 7 Wisdom *is* the **principal t**; *therefore* 7225
18:22 *Whoso* findeth a wife findeth a good *t*, and NIH
22:18 For *it is* a pleasant *t* if thou keep them NIH
25: 2 *It is* the glory of God to conceal a **t**: but 1697
27: 7 *to* the hungry soul every bitter *t is* sweet. NIH
Ecc 1: 9 The **t** that hath been, *it is* that which shall 4100
1: 9 and *there is* no new *t* under the sun. NIH
1:10 Is there *any* **t** whereof it may be said, See, 1697
3: 1 To every *t there is* a season, and a time to NIH
3:11 He hath made every *t* beautiful in his time: NIH
3:14 be put to it, **nor any t** taken from it: 369+2050.1
3:19 befalleth beasts; even **one t** befalleth them: 259
5: 2 let not thine heart be hasty to utter *any* **t** 1697
6: 5 nor known *any t*: this hath more rest than NIH
7: 8 Better *is* the end of a **t** than the beginning 1697
8: 1 and who knoweth the interpretation of a **t**? 1697
8: 3 stand not in an evil **t**; for he doeth 1697
8: 5 the commandment shall feel no evil **t**: 1697
8:15 a man hath no better *t* under the sun, NIH
9: 5 the dead know not **any t**, neither have they 3972
9: 6 for ever in any *t* that is done under the sun. NIH
11: 7 a pleasant *t it is* for the eyes to behold NIH
12:14 with every secret *t*, whether *it be* good, or NIH
Isa 7:13 *Is it* a **small t** for you to weary men, but 4592
15: 6 the grass faileth, there is no **green t**. 3418
17:13 and like a **rolling t** before the whirlwind. 1534
19: 7 **every t** sown by the brooks, shall wither, 3605
29:16 shall the **t framed** say of him that framed 3336
29:21 and turn aside the just for a **t of nought**. 8414
38: 7 that the LORD will do this **t** that he hath 1697
40:15 he taketh up the isles as a **very little t**. 1851
41:12 shall be as nothing, and as a **t of nought**. 657
43:19 I will do a new *t*; now it shall spring forth; NIH
49: 6 It is a light **t** that thou shouldest be my NIH
52:11 touch no unclean *t*; go ye out of the midst of NIH
55:11 and it shall prosper *in the t* whereto I sent it. NIH
64: 6 we are all as an unclean *t*, and all our NIH
66: 8 Who hath heard such a *t*? who hath seen NIH
Jer 2:10 and see if there be such a *t*. NIH
2:19 and see that *it is* an evil *t* and bitter, NIH
5:30 and **horrible t** is committed in the land; 8186
7:23 this **t** commanded I them, saying, Obey my 1697
11:13 have ye set up altars to *that* **shameful t**, 1322
14:14 a **t of nought**, and the deceit of their heart. 457
18:13 virgin of Israel hath done a very **horrible t**. 8186
22: 4 For if ye do this **t** indeed, then shall there 1697
23:14 in the prophets of Jerusalem a **horrible t**: 8186
31:22 for the LORD hath created a new *t* in NIH
32:27 of all flesh: is there any **t** too hard for me? 1697
33:14 that I will perform *that* good **t** which I have 1697
38: 5 for the king *is* not *he that* can do *any* **t** 1697
38:14 king said unto Jeremiah, I *will* ask thee a **t**; 1697
40: 3 his voice, therefore this **t** is come upon you. 1697
40:16 the son of Kareah, Thou shalt not do this **t**: 1697
42: 3 we may walk, and the **t** that we may do. 1697
42: 4 *that* whatsoever **t** the LORD shall answer 1697
42:21 nor any *t* for the which he hath sent me unto NIH
44: 4 Oh, do not this abominable **t** that I hate. 1697
44:17 we will certainly do whatsoever **t** goeth 1697
La 2:13 What *t* shall I take to witness for thee? NIH
2:13 what *t* shall I liken to thee, O daughter of NIH
Eze 8:17 Is it a **light t** to the house of Judah that *they* 7043
14: 9 be deceived when he hath spoken a **t**, 1697
16:47 as *if that were* a very little *t*, thou wast NIH
34:18 *Seemeth it* a **small t** unto you to have eaten 4592
44:18 they shall not gird *themselves* with any **t** NIH
44:29 every **dedicate t** in Israel shall be theirs. 2764
44:31 The priests shall not eat *of* **any t** that is 3605
47: 9 *that* every **t** that liveth, which moveth, 5315
47: 9 every *t* shall live whither the river cometh. NIH
48:12 *a t* most holy by the border of the Levites. NIH

Da 2: 5 to the Chaldeans, The **t** is gone from me: 4406
2: 8 because ye see the **t** is gone from me. 4406
2:11 And *it is* a rare **t** that the king requireth, and 4406
2:15 Then Arioch made the **t** known to Daniel. 4406
2:17 made the **t** known to Hananiah, Mishael, 4406
3:29 which speak **any t amiss** against the God 7960
4:33 The same hour was the **t** fulfilled upon 4406
5:15 could not shew the interpretation of the **t**: 4406
5:26 This *is* the interpretation of the **t**: MENE; 4406
6:12 The king answered and said, The **t** *is* true, 4406
10: 1 In the third year of Cyrus king of Persia a **t** 1697
10: 1 the **t** *was* true, but the time appointed *was* 1697
10: 1 he understood the **t**, and had understanding 1697
Hos 6:10 I have seen a **horrible t** in the house of 8186
8: 3 Israel hath cast off *the t that is* good: NIH
8:12 *but* they were counted as a strange *t*. NIH
Am 6:13 *Ye* which rejoice in a **t** of nought, 1697
Jnh 3: 7 man nor beast, herd nor flock, taste **any t**: 3972
Mal 1:14 sacrificeth unto the Lord a corrupt *t*: for I NIH
Mt 8:33 and told every *t*, and what was befallen to NIG
18:19 earth as touching any **t** that they shall ask, *4229*
19:16 Good Master, what good *t* shall I do, NIG
20:20 and desiring a certain *t* of him. NIG
21:24 said unto them, I also will ask you one **t**, *3056*
24:17 come down to take any *t* out of his house: NIG
Mk 1:27 among themselves, saying, What *t* is this? NIG
4:22 neither was *any t* kept secret, but that it NIG
5:32 round about to see her that had done this *t*. NIG
7:18 that whatsoever *t* from without entereth into NIG
9:22 if thou canst do any *t*, have compassion on NIG
10:21 and said unto him, One *t* thou lackest: NIG
11:13 if haply he might find any *t* thereon: NIG
13:15 neither enter *therein*, to take any *t* out of his NIG
16: 8 neither said they any *t* to any *man*; for they NIG
16:18 if they drink any deadly *t*, it shall not hurt NIG
Lk 1:35 also *that* **holy t** which shall be born of thee *40*
2:15 and see this **t** which is come to pass, *4487*
6: 9 I will ask you one *t*; Is it lawful on NIG
8:17 neither *any t* hid, that shall not be known NIG
9:21 And commanded *them* to tell no *man* that *t*; NIG
10:42 But one *t* is needful: and Mary hath chosen NIG
12:11 no thought how or what *t* ye shall answer, NIG
12:26 then be not able *to do that t which is* least, NIG
18:22 Yet lackest thou one *t*: sell all that thou NIG
19: 8 if I have taken any *t* from any *man* by false NIG
20: 3 said unto them, I will also ask you one **t**; *3056*
22:23 which of them it was that should do this *t*. NIG
22:35 and shoes, lacked ye any *t*? And they said, NIG
Jn 1: 3 without him was not any *t* made that was NIG
1:46 Can there any good *t* come out of Nazareth? NIG
5:14 sin no more, lest a worse *t* come unto thee. NIG
7: 4 For *there is* no *man that* doeth any *t* in NIG
9:25 one *t* I know, that, whereas I was blind, NIG
9:30 Why herein is a marvellous *t*, that ye know NIG
14:14 If ye shall ask any *t* in my name, I will do NIG
18:34 answered him, Sayest thou this *t* of thyself, NIG
Ac 5: 4 why hast thou conceived this **t** in thine *4229*
10:14 for I have never eaten any *t that is* common NIG
10:28 Ye know how that it is an unlawful *t* for a NIG
12:12 And when he had considered *the t*, he came NIG
17:21 but *either* to tell, or to hear some new *t*.) NIG
17:25 as though he needed any *t*, seeing he giveth NIG
19:32 Some therefore cried one *t*, and NIG
19:39 But if ye inquire any *t* concerning other NIG
21:25 concluded that they observe no such *t*, save NIG
21:34 And some cried one *t*, some another, NIG
23:17 for he hath a certain *t* to tell him. NIG
25: 8 against Cesar, have I offended any *t at all*. NIG
25:11 or have committed any *t* worthy of death, NIG
25:26 Of whom I have no certain *t* to write unto NIG
26: 8 Why should it be thought *a t* incredible with NIG
26:10 Which *t* I also did in Jerusalem: and NIG
26:26 for this *t* was not done in a corner. NIG
Ro 7:18 dwelleth no good *t*: for to will is present NIG
8:33 Who shall lay any **t** to the charge of God's NIG
9:20 Shall **the t** formed say to him that formed *3588*
13: 6 attending continually upon this very *t*. NIG
13: 8 Owe no *man* any *t*, but to love one another: NIG
14:14 to him that esteemeth any *t* to be unclean, NIG
14:21 nor *any t* whereby thy brother stumbleth, or NIG
14:22 not himself in *that t* which he alloweth. NIG
1Co 1: 5 That in every *t* ye are enriched by him, NIG
1:10 that ye all speak the same *t*, and *that* there NIG
2: 2 For I determined not to know any *t* among NIG
3: 7 neither is he that planteth any *t*, neither he NIG
4: 3 But with me it is a very small *t* that I should NIG
8: 2 And if any *man* think that *he* knoweth any *t*, NIG
8: 7 this hour, eat *it* as a **t offered unto an idol**; *1494*
9:11 great *t* if we shall reap your carnal *things?* NIG
9:17 For if I do this *t* willingly, I have a reward: NIG
10:19 that the idol is any *t*, or that which is NIG
10:19 is offered in sacrifice to idols is any *t*? NIG
14:30 If *any t* be revealed to another that sitteth NIG
14:35 And if they will learn any *t*, let them ask NIG
2Co 2:10 To whom ye forgive any *t*, I *forgive* also: NIG
2:10 for if I forgave any *t*, to whom I forgave *it*, NIG
3: 5 of ourselves to think any *t* as of ourselves; NIG
5: 5 hath wrought us for the selfsame *t is* God, NIG
6: 3 Giving no offence in any *t*, that the ministry NIG
6:17 and touch not the unclean *t*; and I will NIG
7:11 For behold this selfsame *t*, that ye sorrowed NIG
7:14 For if I have boasted any *t* to him of you, NIG
8: 7 as ye abound in every *t*, *in* faith, and NIG
9:11 Being enriched in every *t* to all NIG
10: 5 **every** high **t** that exalteth itself against *3956*
11:15 Therefore *it is* no great *t* if his ministers also NIG
12: 8 For this *t* I besought the Lord thrice, that it NIG
Gal 4:18 to be zealously affected always in a good *t*, NIG
5: 6 availeth any *t*, nor uncircumcision; NIG
6:15 availeth any *t*, nor uncircumcision, NIG
Eph 4:28 working with *his* hands the *t which is* good, NIG
5:24 wives *be* to their own husbands in every *t*. NIG
5:27 or any such *t*; but that it should be holy and NIG
6: 8 Knowing that whatsoever good *t* any man NIG
Php 1: 6 Being confident of this very *t*, that he which NIG

T

Php 3:13 *this* one *t I do,* forgetting those *things which* NIG
3:15 and if in any *t* ye be otherwise minded, NIG
3:16 by the same rule, *let us* mind the same *t.* NIG
4: 6 but in every *t* by prayer and supplication NIG
1Th 1: 8 so that we need not to speak any *t.* NIG
5:18 In every *t* give thanks: for this *is* the will of NIG
2Th 1: 6 Seeing *it is* a righteous *t* with God to NIG
1Ti 1:10 if *there be* any other *t that* is contrary to NIG
2Ti 1:14 *That* **good t** which was committed unto *2570*
Tit 2: 8 be ashamed, having no evil *t* to say of you. NIG
Phm 1: 6 every good *t* which is in you in Christ Jesus. NIG
Heb 10:29 an unholy *t,* and hath done despite unto NIG
10:31 *It is* a fearful *t* to fall into the hands of NIG
11:40 God having provided some better *t* for us, NIG
13: 9 For *it is* a good *t* that the heart be NIG
Jas 1: 7 think that he shall receive any *t* of the Lord. NIG
1Pe 4:12 as though *some* strange *t* happened unto NIG
2Pe 3: 8 be not ignorant of this one *t,* that one day *is* NIG
1Jn 2: 8 unto you, which *t* is true in him and in you: NIG
5:14 that, if we ask any *t* according to his will, NIG
Rev 2:15 doctrine of the Nicolaitans, which *t* I hate. NIG
9: 4 neither any green *t,* neither any tree; NIG
21:27 And there shall in no wise enter into it any *t* NIG

THINGS (1161) [THING]

Ge 7:23 the **creeping t,** and the fowl of the heaven; 7431
9: 3 as the green herb have I given you all *t.* NIH
15: 1 After these t the word of the LORD came 1697
20: 8 and told all these **t** in their ears: 1697
22: 1 it came to pass after these **t,** that God did 1697
22:20 it came to pass after these **t,** that it was told 1697
24: 1 the LORD had blessed Abraham **in all t.** 3605
24:28 told *them of* her mother's house these **t.** 1697
24:53 to her brother and to her mother **precious t.** 4030
24:66 the servant told Isaac all **t** that he had done. 1697
29:13 to his house. And he told Laban all these **t.** 1697
39: 7 it came to pass after these **t,** that his 1697
40: 1 it came to pass after these **t,** *that* the butler 1697
42:36 ye will take Benjamin *away:* all **these t** 5089.1
45:23 ten asses laden with the **good t** of Egypt, 2898
48: 1 it came to pass after these **t,** that *one* told 1697
Ex 10: 2 **what t** I have wrought in Egypt, and my 834
12:36 that they lent unto them *such t as they* NIH
23:13 in all *t* that I have said unto you be NIH
25:22 of all *t* which I will give thee in NIH
28:38 *t,* which the children of Israel shall hallow NIH
29:33 they shall eat those *t* wherewith NIH
29:35 according to all *t* which I have commanded NIH
40: 4 set in order the **t** that are to be set in order NIH
Lev 2: 8 that is made of these *t* unto the LORD: NIH
4: 2 (*concerning t* which ought not to be done), NIH
4:13 *concerning t* which should not be done, NIH
4:22 God *concerning t* which should not be done, NIH
4:27 *concerning t* which ought not to be done, NIH
5: 2 or the carcase of unclean **creeping t,** and 8318
5: 5 when he shall be guilty in one of these *t,* NIH
5:15 in the holy *t* of the LORD; NIH
5:17 commit any *of these t* which are forbidden NIH
8:36 his sons did all **t** which the LORD 1697
10:19 the LORD; and such **t** have befallen me: 428
11:23 all *other* flying **creeping t,** which have four 8318
11:29 the **creeping t** that creep upon the earth; 8318
11:42 all **creeping t** that creep upon the earth, 8318
14:11 those *t,* before the LORD, *at* the door of NIH
15:10 he that beareth *any of* those *t* shall wash his NIH
15:27 whosoever toucheth those *t* shall be NIH
18:24 Defile not you yourselves in any of these *t.* NIH
20:23 for they committed all these *t,* and therefore NIH
22: 2 from the holy *t* of the children of Israel, NIH
22: 2 name *in those t* which they hallow unto me: NIH
22: 3 that goeth unto the holy *t* which the children NIH
22: 4 he shall not eat of the holy *t,* until he be NIH
22: 6 shall not eat of the holy *t,* unless he wash NIH
22: 7 shall afterward eat of the holy *t,* because NIH
22:12 she may not eat of an offering of the holy *t.* NIH
22:15 they shall not profane the holy *t* of NIH
22:16 when they eat their holy *t:* for I the LORD NIH
26:23 if ye will not be reformed by me by these *t,* NIH
Nu 1:50 and over all *t* that *belong* to it: NIH
4: 4 of the congregation, *about* the most holy *t:* NIH
4:15 These *t are* the burden of the sons of Kohath NIH
4:19 when they approach unto the most holy *t:* NIH
4:20 they shall not go in to see when the holy *t* NIH
5: 9 every offering of all the holy *t* of NIH
5:10 every man's hallowed *t* shall be his: NIH
15:13 country shall do these *t* after this manner, NIH
18: 8 all the hallowed *t* of the children of Israel; NIH
18: 9 This shall be thine of the most holy *t,* NIH
18:19 All the heave offerings of the holy *t,* which NIH
18:32 neither shall ye pollute the holy *t* of NIH
29:39 These *t* ye shall do unto the LORD in your NIH
31:20 of goats' *hair,* and all **t made** of wood. 3627
35:29 So these *t* shall be for a statute of judgment NIH
Dt 1:18 I commanded you at that time all the **t** 1697
4: 7 as the LORD our God *is* in all *t that* we NIH
4: 9 lest thou forget the **t** which thine eyes have 1697
4:30 all these **t** are come upon thee, *even* in 1697
6:11 houses full *of* all good *t,* which thou filledst NIH
10:21 and terrible *t,* which thine eyes have seen. NIH
12: 8 Ye shall not do after all *the t* that we do NIH
12:26 Only thy holy *t* which thou hast, and NIH
18:12 For all that do these *t are* an abomination NIH
25:16 For all that do such *t, and* all that do NIH
26:13 I have brought away the hallowed *t* out of NIH
28:47 of heart, for the abundance of all *t;* NIH
28:48 in want of all *t:* and he shall put a yoke of NIH
28:57 for she shall eat them for want of all *t* NIH
29:29 The secret *t belong* unto the LORD our NIH
29:29 *those t* which are revealed *belong* unto us NIH
30: 1 when all these **t** are come upon thee, 1697
32:35 the **t that shall come** upon them make 6264
33:13 for the **precious t** of heaven, for the dew, 4022
33:14 for the **precious t** put forth by the moon, 4022
33:15 for the **chief t** of the ancient mountains, 7218
33:15 and for the **precious t** of the lasting hills, 4022

Dt 33:16 for the **precious t** of the earth and 4022
Jos 1:17 as we hearkened unto Moses in all *t,* NIH
2:11 as soon as we had heard *these t,* our hearts NIH
2:23 of Nun, and told him all *t* that befell them: NIH
11: 1 when Jabin king of Hazor had heard *those t,* NIH
23:14 **t** which the LORD your God spake 1697
23:15 *that* as all good **t** are come upon you, 1697
23:15 shall the LORD bring upon you all evil **t,** 1697
24:29 it came to pass after these **t,** that Joshua 1697
Jdg 13:23 neither would he have shewed us all these *t,* NIH
13:23 as *at this* time have told us *such t* as these. NIH
18:27 And they took *the t* which Micah had made, NIH
Ru 4: 7 concerning changing, for to confirm all **t;** 1697
1Sa 2:23 he said unto them, Why do ye such **t?** for I 1697
3:12 In that day I will perform against Eli all *t* NIH
3:17 if thou hide *any* thing from me of all the **t** 1697
12:21 *should ye go* after vain *t,* which cannot NIH
12:24 for consider how **great t** he hath **done** for 1431
15:21 **t** which should have been **utterly destroyed,** 2764
19: 7 and Jonathan shewed him all those **t.** 1697
25:37 his wife had told him these **t,** that his heart 1697
26:25 thou shalt both **do great t,** and 6213+6213
2Sa 7:21 own heart, hast thou done all these **great t,** 1420
7:23 to do for you **great t** and terrible, for thy 1420
11:18 told David all the **t concerning** the war; 1697
12: 8 given unto thee such and **such t.** 2007+3509.1
13:21 when king David heard of all these **t,** he 1697
14:20 of God, to know all *t* that *are* in the earth. NIH
23: 5 ordered in all *t,* and sure: NIH
23:17 These *t* did *these* three mighty *men.* NIH
23:22 These *t* did Benaiah the son of Jehoiada, NIH
24:12 I offer thee three *t;* choose thee one of them, NIH
24:23 All *these t* did Araunah, *as* a king, give unto NIH
1Ki 4:33 and of fowl, and of **creeping t,** 7431
5: 8 I have considered *the t* which thou sentest NIH
7:51 Solomon brought in the *t* which David his NIH
15:15 he brought in *the t* which his father had NIH
15:15 *the t* which himself had dedicated, *into* NIH
17:17 it came to pass after these **t,** *that* the son of 1697
18:36 and *that* I have done all these **t** at thy word. 1697
21: 1 it came to pass after these **t,** *that* Naboth 1697
21:26 according to all *t* as did the Amorites, NIH
2Ki 8: 4 all the great *t* that Elisha hath done. NIH
11: 9 to all *t* that Jehoiada the priest commanded: NIH
12: 4 All the money of the dedicated *t* that is NIH
12:18 took all the hallowed *t* that Jehoshaphat, NIH
12:18 his own hallowed *t,* and all the gold that NIH
14: 3 he did according to all *t* as Joash his father NIH
17: 9 the children of Israel did secretly *those* **t** 1697
17:11 wrought wicked **t** to provoke the LORD to 1697
19:29 eat *this* year **such t as grow of themselves,** 5599
20:13 them all the house of his **precious t,** 5238
20:15 All *the t* that *are* in mine house have they NIH
23:17 proclaimed these **t** that thou hast done 1697
25:15 *and* such *t* as *were of* gold, *in* gold, and *of* NIH
1Ch 4:22 and Jashubi-lehem. And *these are* ancient **t.** 1697
9:31 over the **t that were made** in the pans. 4639
11:19 drink it. These *t* did *these* three mightiest. NIH
11:24 These *t* did Benaiah the son of Jehoiada, NIH
17:19 in making known all *these* **great t.** 1420
21:10 I offer thee three *t:* choose thee one of them, NIH
23:13 that he should sanctify the most holy *t,* he NIH
23:28 in the purifying of all holy *t,* and the work NIH
26:20 and over the treasures of the dedicate *t.* NIH
26:26 of the dedicate *t,* which David the king, NIH
28:12 and of the treasuries of the dedicate *t:* NIH
28:14 *He gave* of gold by weight for *t of* gold, NIH
29: 2 my God the gold for *t to be made of* gold, NIH
29: 2 the silver for *t of* silver, and the brass for NIH
29: 2 the brass for *t of* brass, the iron for *things of* NIH
29: 2 the iron for *t of* iron, and wood for *things of* NIH
29: 2 for *things of* iron, and wood for *t of* wood; NIH
29: 5 The gold for *t of* gold, and the silver for NIH
29: 5 the silver for *t of* silver, and for all *manner* NIH
29:14 willingly after this *sort?* for all *t come* of NIH
29:17 heart I have willingly offered all these *t:* NIH
29:19 and to do all *these t,* and to build the palace, NIH
2Ch 3: 3 Now these *are the t wherein* Solomon was NIH
4: 6 such **t** as they **offered** for the burnt offering 4639
5: 1 Solomon brought in *all the t* that David his NIH
12:12 and also in Judah **t** went well. 1697
15:18 he brought *into* the house of God *the t* that NIH
19: 3 Nevertheless there are good **t** found in thee, 1697
21: 3 of gold, and of **precious t,** with fenced 4030
23: 8 all Judah did according to all *t* that Jehoiada NIH
24: 7 also all the dedicate *t* of the house of NIH
29:33 the consecrated *t were* six hundred oxen NIH
31: 5 the tithe of all *t* brought they in abundantly. NIH
31: 6 the tithe of holy *t* which were consecrated NIH
31:12 and the tithes and the dedicate *t* faithfully: NIH
31:14 of the LORD, and the most holy *t.* NIH
32: 1 After these **t,** and the establishment *thereof,* 1697
Ezr 1: 6 and with beasts, and with **precious t,** 4030
2:63 that they should not eat of the most holy *t* NIH
7: 1 Now after these **t,** in the reign of 1697
9: 1 Now when these *t* were done, the princes NIH
Ne 6: 8 There are no such **t** *done* as thou sayest, but 1697
6:16 *t,* they were much cast down in their own NIH
7:65 that they should not eat of the most holy *t,* NIH
9: 6 all *t* that *are* therein, the seas, and all that *is* NIH
10:33 for the holy *t,* and for the sin offerings to NIH
12:47 they sanctified *holy t* unto the Levites; and NIH
13:26 *t?* yet among many nations was there no NIH
Est 2: 1 After these **t,** when the wrath of king 1697
2: 3 let their **t for purification** be given *them:* 8562
2: 9 he speedily gave her her **t for purification,** 8562
2: 9 with **such t as belonged** to her, and seven 4490
2:12 with *other* **t for the purifying** of 8562
3: 1 After these **t** did king Ahasuerus promote 1697
5:11 all *the t* where*in* the king had promoted NIH
9:20 Mordecai wrote these **t,** and sent letters 1697
Job 5: 9 Which doeth great *t* and unsearchable; NIH
5: 9 unsearchable; marvellous *t* without number: NIH
6: 7 **The t** *that* my soul refused to touch *are* as 1992
6:30 cannot my taste discern **perverse t?** 1942

Job 8: 2 How long wilt thou speak these *t?* and NIH
9:10 Which doeth great *t* past finding out; yea, NIH
10:13 these *t* hast thou hid in thine heart: I know NIH
12: 3 yea, who knoweth not such *t* as these? NIH
12:22 He discovereth deep *t* out of darkness, and NIH
13:20 Only do not two *t* unto me: then will I not NIH
13:26 For thou writest bitter *t* against me, and NIH
14:19 thou washest away the **t which grow** out of 5599
16: 2 I have heard many such *t:* miserable NIH
22:18 Yet he filled their houses *with* good *t:* but NIH
23:14 for me: and many such *t are* with him. NIH
26: 5 Dead *t* are formed from under the waters, NIH
33:29 all these *t* worketh God oftentimes with NIH
37: 5 great *t* doeth he, which we cannot NIH
41:30 he spreadeth sharp pointed *t* upon the mire. NIH
41:34 He beholdeth all high *t:* he *is* a king over all NIH
42: 3 *t* too wonderful for me, which I knew not. NIH
Ps 8: 6 thy hands; thou hast put all *t* under his feet: NIH
12: 3 *and* the tongue that speaketh proud *t:* NIH
15: 5 He that doeth these *t* shall never be moved. NIH
17: 2 let thine eyes behold the **t that are equal.** 4339
31:18 which speak **grievous t** proudly and 6277
35:11 they laid to my charge *t* that I knew not. NIH
38:12 that seek my hurt speak **mischievous t,** 1942
42: 4 When I remember these *t,* I pour out my NIH
45: 1 I speak of the **t** which I have **made** 4639
45: 4 thy right hand shall teach thee terrible *t.* NIH
50:21 These *t* hast thou done, and I kept silence; NIH
57: 2 unto God that performeth *all t* for me. NIH
60: 3 Thou hast shewed thy people hard *t:* thou NIH
65: 5 *By* terrible *t* in righteousness wilt thou NIH
71:19 *is* very high, who hast done great *t:* O God, NIH
72:18 God of Israel, who only doeth wondrous *t.* NIH
78:12 **Marvellous t** did he in the sight of their 6382
86:10 and doest wondrous *t:* thou *art* God alone. NIH
87: 3 Glorious *t* are spoken of thee, O city of NIH
94: 4 *long* shall they utter *and* speak hard *t? and* NIH
98: 1 for he hath done marvellous *t:* his right NIH
103: 5 Who satisfieth thy mouth with good *t; so* NIH
104:25 wherein *are* **t creeping** innumerable, 7431
106:21 which had done great *t* in Egypt; NIH
106:22 land of Ham, *and* terrible *t* by the Red sea. NIH
107:43 will observe these *t,* even they shall NIH
113: 6 Who humbleth *himself* to behold *the t that* NIH
119:18 that I may behold wondrous *t* out of thy NIH
119:128 all *thy* precepts concerning all *t* to be right; NIH
126: 2 The LORD hath done great **t** for them. NIH
126: 3 The LORD hath done great **t** for us; NIH
131: 1 in great *matters,* or in *t* too high for me. NIH
148:10 all cattle; **creeping t,** and flying fowl: 7431
Pr 2:12 from the man that speaketh **froward t;** 8419
3:15 all the **t** thou canst desire are not to be NIH
6:16 These six *t* doth the LORD hate: yea, NIH
8: 6 Hear, for I will speak of **excellent t;** and 5057
8: 6 and the opening of my lips *shall be* **right t.** 4339
8:11 all the **t** that may be desired are not to be NIH
15:28 the mouth of the wicked poureth out evil *t.* NIH
16: 4 The LORD hath made all *t* for himself: NIH
16:30 He shutteth his eyes to devise **froward t:** 8419
22:20 Have not I written to thee **excellent t** in 7991
23:16 shall rejoice, when thy lips speak **right t.** 4339
23:33 and thine heart shall utter **perverse t.** 8419
24:23 These *t* also *belong* to the wise. *It is* not NIH
26:10 The great *God* that formed all *t* both NIH
28: 5 they that seek the LORD understand all *t.* NIH
28:10 the upright shall have good *t* in possession. NIH
30: 7 Two *t* have I required of thee; deny me NIH
30:15 There are three *t that* are never satisfied, NIH
30:15 *yea,* four *t* say not, *It is* enough: NIH
30:18 There be three *t which* are too wonderful NIH
30:21 For three *t* the earth is disquieted, and NIH
30:24 There be four *t which are* little upon NIH
30:29 There be three *t* which go well, yea, four are NIH
Ecc 1: 8 All **t** *are* full of labour; man cannot utter *it:* 1697
1:11 *There is* no remembrance of former *t;* NIH
1:11 *t* that are to come with *those* that shall come NIH
1:13 search out by wisdom concerning all *t* that NIH
6:11 Seeing there be many **t** that increase vanity, 1697
7:15 All *t* have I seen in the days of my vanity: NIH
7:25 the reason *of t,* and to know the wickedness NIH
9: 2 All *t come* alike to all: *there is* one event to NIH
9: 3 This *is* an evil among all *t* that are done NIH
10:19 maketh merry: but money answereth all *t.* NIH
11: 9 that for all these *t* God will bring thee into NIH
Isa 12: 5 the LORD; for he hath done **excellent t:** 1348
25: 1 thy name; for thou hast done **wonderful t;** 6382
25: 6 hosts make unto all people a feast of **fat t,** 8081
25: 6 wines on the lees, of **fat t** full of marrow, 8081
29:16 Surely your turning *of t* upside down shall NIH
30:10 Prophesy not unto us right *t,* speak unto us NIH
30:10 speak unto us smooth *t,* prophesy deceits: NIH
32: 8 the liberal deviseth liberal *t;* and by liberal NIH
32: 8 liberal *things;* and by liberal *t* shall he stand. NIH
34: 1 the world, and **all t** that come forth of it. 3605
38:16 by these *t* men live, and in all these *things is* NIH
38:16 and in all these *t is* the life of my spirit: NIH
39: 2 shewed them the house of his **precious t,** 5238
40:26 behold who hath created these *t,* that NIH
41:22 let them shew the former *t,* what they *be,* NIH
41:22 end of them; or declare us *t* for to come. NIH
41:23 Shew the *t* that are to come hereafter, NIH
42: 9 the former *t are* come to pass, and NIH
42: 9 are come to pass, and new *t* do I declare: NIH
42:16 light before them, and **crooked t** straight. 4625
42:16 These **t** will I do unto them, and not forsake 1697
42:20 Seeing many *t,* but thou observest not; NIH
43: 9 shew us former *t?* let them bring forth their NIH
43:18 Remember ye not the former *t,* neither NIH
43:18 former *things,* neither consider the *t* of old. NIH
44: 7 the *t* that are coming, and shall come, NIH
44: 9 their delectable *t* shall not profit; and NIH
44:24 I *am* the LORD that maketh all *t;* that NIH
45: 7 and create evil: I the LORD do all these *t.* NIH
45:11 Ask me of *t* to come concerning my sons, NIH
45:19 I declare **t that are right.** 4339

T

Isa 46: 9 Remember the former t of old: for I am NIH
46:10 from ancient times the t that are not yet NIH
47: 7 so that thou didst not lay these t to thy heart, NIH
47: 9 these two t shall come to thee in a moment NIH
47:13 save thee from these t that shall come upon NIH
48: 3 I have declared the former t from NIH
48: 6 it? I have shewed thee new t from this time, NIH
48: 6 even hidden t, and thou didst not know NIH
48:14 which among them hath declared these t? NIH
51:19 These two t are come unto thee; who shall NIH
56: 4 choose the t that please me, and take hold of NIH
61:11 as the garden causeth the **t that are sown** 2221
64: 3 When thou didst **terrible t** which we 3372
64:11 and all our **pleasant t** are laid waste. 4261
64:12 Wilt thou refrain thyself for these t, O NIH
65: 4 and broth of abominable t is in their vessels; NIH
66: 2 For all those t hath mine hand made, and NIH
66: 2 and all those t have been, saith the LORD: NIH
66: 8 t? Shall the earth be made to bring forth in NIH
Jer 2: 8 and walked after t that do not profit. NIH
3: 5 and done evil t as thou couldest. NIH
3: 7 I said after she had done all these t, Turn NIH
4:18 thy doings have procured these t unto thee; NIH
5: 9 Shall I not visit for these t? saith NIH
5:19 the LORD our God all these t unto us? NIH
5:25 Your iniquities have turned away these t, NIH
5:25 your sins have withholden good t from you. NIH
5:29 Shall I not visit for these t? saith NIH
8:13 the t that I have given them shall pass away NIH
9: 9 Shall I not visit them for these t? saith NIH
9:24 for in these t I delight, saith the LORD. NIH
10:16 for he is the former of all t; and Israel is NIH
13:22 Wherefore come these t upon me? NIH
14:22 upon thee: for thou hast made all these t. NIH
16:18 of their detestable and **abominable t.** 8441
16:19 vanity, and t wherein there is no profit. NIH
17: 9 The heart is deceitful above all t, and NIH
18:13 who hath heard such t: the virgin of Israel NIH
20: 1 heard that Jeremiah prophesied these **t.** 1697
20: 5 all the **precious t** thereof, and all 3366
21:14 and it shall devour **all t** round about it. 3605
26:10 When the princes of Judah heard these **t,** 1697
30:15 I have done **these t** unto thee. 428
31: 5 and shall **eat** them **as common t.** 2490
33: 3 and mighty t, which thou knowest not. NIH
42: 5 if we do not even according to all **t** for 1697
44:18 we have wanted all t, and have been NIH
45: 5 seekest thou great t for thyself? seek them NIH
51:19 for he is the former of all t: and Israel is NIH
La 1: 7 of her miseries all her **pleasant t** that she 4262
1:10 spread out his hand upon all her **pleasant t:** 4261
1:11 they have given their **pleasant t** for meat to 4261
1:16 For these t I weep; mine eye, mine eye NIH
2:14 have seen vain and **foolish t** for thee: 8602
5:17 heart is faint; for these t our eyes are dim. NIH
Eze 5:11 my sanctuary with all thy **detestable t,** 8251
7:20 and of their **detestable t** therein: 8251
8:10 behold every form of **creeping t,** and 7431
11: 5 for I know the **t that come into** your mind, 4609
11:18 they shall take away all the **detestable t** 8251
11:21 walketh after the heart of their **detestable t** 8251
11:25 I spake unto them of the captivity all the **t** 1697
16:16 the like t shall not come, neither shall it be NIH
16:30 seeing thou doest all these t, the work of an NIH
16:43 hast fretted me in all these t; behold NIH
17:12 Know ye not what these t mean? tell them, NIH
17:15 shall he escape that doeth such t? or shall he NIH
17:18 hath done all these t, he shall not escape. NIH
18:10 and that doeth the like to any one of these t, NIH
20:40 of your oblations, with all your holy t. NIH
22: 8 Thou hast despised mine holy t, and hast NIH
22:25 they have taken the treasure and **precious t;** 3366
22:26 have profaned mine holy t: they have put no NIH
23:30 I will do these t unto thee, because thou hast NIH
24:19 Wilt thou not tell us what these t are to us, NIH
27:24 These were thy merchants in **all sorts of t,** 4360
37:23 nor with their **detestable t,** nor with any of 8251
38:10 that at the same time shall **t** come into thy 1697
38:20 and all **creeping t** that creep upon the earth, 7431
42:13 t: there shall they lay the most holy things, NIH
42:13 things: there shall they lay the most holy t, NIH
42:14 shall approach to those t which are for NIH
44: 8 ye have not kept the charge of mine holy t: NIH
44:13 nor to come near to any of my holy t, in NIH
44:30 And the first of all the firstfruits of all t, and NIH
Da 2:10 that asked such **t** at any magician, or 4406
2:22 secret t: he knoweth what is in the darkness, NIH
2:40 subdueth all t: and as iron that breaketh all NIH
7: 8 eyes of man, and a mouth speaking great t. NIH
7:16 made me know the interpretation of the **t.** 4406
7:20 a mouth that spake very great t, whose look NIH
10:21 there is none that holdeth with me in these t, NIH
11:36 shall speak marvellous t against the God of NIH
11:38 and with precious stones, and **pleasant t.** 2532
11:43 and over all the precious t of Egypt: NIH
12: 7 the holy people, all these t shall be finished. NIH
12: 8 O my lord, what shall be the end of these t? NIH
Hos 2:18 and with the **creeping t** of the ground: 7431
8:12 I have written to him the **great t** of my law, 7230
9: 3 and they shall eat unclean t in Assyria. NIH
14: 9 he shall understand these t? prudent, and NIH
Joel 2:20 come up, because he hath done **great t.** 1431
2:21 and rejoice: for the LORD will do **great t.** 1431
3: 5 into your temples my goodly **pleasant t:** 4261
Ob 1: 6 How are the t of Esau searched out! how are NIH
1: 6 searched out! how are his **hid t** sought up! 4710
Mic 7:15 of Egypt will I shew unto him marvellous t. NIH
Hab 1:14 as the **creeping t,** that have no ruler over 7431
Zep 1: 2 I will utterly consume all t from off NIH
Zec 4:10 For who hath despised the day of small t? NIH
8:12 of this people to possess all these t. NIH
8:16 These are the **t** that ye shall do; Speak ye 1697
8:17 for all these are t that I hate, saith NIH
Mt 1:20 But while he thought on these t, behold, NIG
2: 3 When Herod the king had heard these t, he NIG

Mt 4: 9 saith unto him, All these t will I give thee, NIG
6: 8 for your Father knoweth what t ye have NIG
6:32 (For after all these t do the Gentiles seek): NIG
6:32 knoweth that ye have need of all these t. NIG
6:33 and all these t shall be added unto you. NIG
6:34 for the morrow shall take thought for the t NIG
7:11 in heaven give good t to them that ask him? NIG
7:12 Therefore all t whatsoever ye would that NIG
9:18 While he spake these t unto them, behold, NIG
11: 4 shew John again those t which ye do hear NIG
11:25 thou hast hid these t from the wise and NIG
11:27 All t are delivered unto me of my Father: NIG
12:34 speak good t? for out of the abundance of NIG
12:35 treasure of the heart bringeth forth good t: NIG
12:35 out of the evil treasure bringeth forth evil t. NIG
13: 3 And he spake many t unto them in parables, NIG
13:17 righteous men have desired to see those t NIG
13:17 and to hear those t which ye hear, NIG
13:34 All these t spake Jesus unto the multitude in NIG
13:35 I will utter t which have been kept secret NIG
13:41 gather out of his kingdom all **t that offend,** 4625
13:51 Have ye understood all these t? They say NIG
13:52 which bringeth forth out of his treasure t NIG
13:56 Whence then hath this man all these t? NIG
15:18 But those t which proceed out of the mouth NIG
15:20 These are the t which defile a man: but NIG
16:21 and suffer many t of the elders and NIG
16:23 for thou savourest not the t that be of God, NIG
17:11 Elias truly shall first come, and restore all t. NIG
19:20 All these t have I kept from my youth up: NIG
19:26 but with God all t are possible. NIG
21:15 and scribes saw the wonderful t that he did, NIG
21:22 And all t, whatsoever ye shall ask in prayer, NIG
21:23 By what authority doest thou these t? and NIG
21:24 will tell you by what authority I do these t. NIG
21:27 tell I you by what authority I do these t. NIG
22: 4 my fatlings are killed, and all t are ready: NIG
22:21 unto Cesar the t which are Cesar's; NIG
22:21 and unto God the t that are God's. NIG
23:20 sweareth by it, and by all t thereon. NIG
23:36 All these t shall come upon this generation. NIG
24: 2 See ye not all these t? verily I say unto you, NIG
24: 3 Tell us, when shall these t be? NIG
24: 6 for all these t must come to pass, but NIG
24:33 when ye shall see all these t, know that it is NIG
24:34 shall not pass, till all these t be fulfilled. NIG
25:21 thou hast been faithful over a few t, I will NIG
25:21 many t: enter thou into the joy of thy lord. NIG
25:23 thou hast been faithful over a few t, I will NIG
25:23 many t: enter thou into the joy of thy lord. NIG
27:13 Hearest thou not how many t they witness NIG
27:19 I have suffered many t this day in a dream NIG
27:54 and those t that were done, they feared NIG
28:11 shewed unto the chief priests all the t that NIG
28:20 Teaching them to observe all t whatsoever I NIG
Mk 1:44 offer for thy cleansing those t which Moses NIG
2: 8 Why reason ye these t in your hearts? NIG
3: 8 when they had heard what great t he did, NIG
4: 2 And he taught them many t by parables, and NIG
4:11 are without, all these t are done in parables: NIG
4:19 and the lusts of other t entering in, NIG
4:34 he expounded all t to his disciples. NIG
5:19 tell them how great t the Lord hath done for NIG
5:20 began to publish in Decapolis how great t NIG
5:26 And had suffered many t of many NIG
6: 2 From whence hath this man these t? and NIG
6:20 he did many t, and heard him gladly. NIG
6:30 and told him all t, both what they had done, NIG
6:34 and he began to teach them many t. NIG
7: 4 And many other t there be, which they have NIG
7: 8 and cups: and many other such like t ye do. NIG
7:13 have delivered: and many such like t do ye. NIG
7:15 but the t which come out of him, those are NIG
7:23 All these evil t come from within, and NIG
7:37 saying, He hath done all t well: NIG
8:31 that the Son of man must suffer many t, and NIG
8:33 for thou savourest not the t that be of God, NIG
8:33 that be of God, but the t that be of men. NIG
9: 9 should tell no man what t they had seen, NIG
9:12 and restoreth all t; and how it is written of NIG
9:12 that he must suffer many t, and be set at NIG
9:23 all t are possible to him that believeth. NIG
10:27 with God: for with God all t are possible. NIG
10:32 began to tell them what t should happen NIG
11:11 when he had looked round about upon all t, NIG
11:23 shall believe that those t which he saith NIG
11:24 What t soever ye desire, when ye pray, NIG
11:28 By what authority doest thou these t? and NIG
11:28 who gave thee this authority to do these t? NIG
11:29 will tell you by what authority I do these t. NIG
11:33 do I tell you by what authority I do these t. NIG
12:17 Render to Cesar the t that are Cesar's, and NIG
12:17 are Cesar's, and to God the t that are God's. NIG
13: 4 Tell us, when shall these t be? and NIG
13: 4 what shall be the sign when all these t shall NIG
13: 7 for such t must needs be; but the end shall NIG
13:23 ye heed: behold, I have foretold you all t. NIG
13:29 when ye shall see these t come to pass, NIG
13:30 shall not pass, till all these t be done. NIG
14:36 Abba, Father, all t are possible unto thee; NIG
15: 3 the chief priests accused him of many t: NIG
15: 4 behold how many t they witness against NIG
Lk 1: 1 **t** which are most surely believed among us, 4229
1: 3 having had perfect understanding of all t NIG
1: 4 thou mightest know the certainty of those **t,** 3056
1:20 until the day that these t shall be performed, NIG
1:45 for there shall be a performance of those t NIG
1:49 he that is mighty hath done to me **great t;** 3167
1:53 He hath filled the hungry with good t; and NIG
2:18 t which were told them by the shepherds. NIG
2:19 But Mary kept all these **t,** and 4487
2:20 praising God for all the t that they had heard NIG
2:33 his mother marvelled at those t which were NIG
2:39 And when they had performed all t NIG
3:18 And many other t in his exhortation NIG

Lk 4:28 when they heard these t, were filled with NIG
5:26 saying, We have seen strange t to day. NIG
5:27 And after these t he went forth, and saw a NIG
6:46 Lord, Lord, and do not the t which I say? NIG
7: 9 When Jesus heard these t, he marvelled at NIG
7:18 disciples of John shewed him of all these t. NIG
7:22 and tell John what t ye have seen and heard; NIG
8: 8 And when he had said these t, he cried, He that NIG
8:39 shew how great t God hath done unto thee. NIG
8:39 city how great t Jesus had done unto him. NIG
9: 9 of whom I hear such t? And he desired to NIG
9:22 The Son of man must suffer many t, and NIG
9:36 told no man in those days any of those t NIG
9:43 But while they wondered every one at all t NIG
10: 1 After these t the Lord appointed other NIG
10: 7 eating and drinking such t as they give: NIG
10: 8 receive you, eat such t as are set before you: NIG
10:21 that thou hast hid these t from the wise and NIG
10:22 All t are delivered to me of my Father: and NIG
10:23 Blessed are the eyes which see the t that ye NIG
10:24 kings have desired to see those t which ye NIG
10:24 and to hear those t which ye hear, NIG
10:41 thou art careful and troubled about many t: NIG
11:27 as he spake these t, a certain woman of NIG
11:41 But rather give alms of such t as you have; NIG
11:41 and, behold, all t are clean unto you. NIG
11:53 And as he said these t unto them, the scribes NIG
11:53 and to provoke him to speak of many t: NIG
12:15 the abundance of the t which he possesseth. NIG
12:20 then whose shall those t be, which thou hast NIG
12:30 For all these t do the nations of the world NIG
12:30 knoweth that ye have need of these t. NIG
12:31 and all these t shall be added unto you. NIG
12:48 and did commit t worthy of stripes, NIG
13: 2 the Galileans, because they suffered such t? NIG
13:17 And when he had said these t, all his NIG
13:17 all the people rejoiced for all the glorious t NIG
14: 6 they could not answer him again to these t. NIG
14:15 with him heard these t, he said unto him, NIG
14:17 were bidden, Come; for all t are now ready. NIG
14:21 shewed his lord these t. Then the master of NIG
15:26 the servants, and asked what these t meant. NIG
16:14 heard all these t: and they derided him. NIG
16:25 thou in thy lifetime receivedst thy good t, NIG
16:25 and likewise Lazarus evil t: but now he is NIG
17: 9 he did the t that were commanded him? NIG
17:10 when ye shall have done all those t which NIG
17:25 But first must he suffer many t, and NIG
18:22 Now when Jesus heard these t, he said unto NIG
18:27 The t which are unpossible with men are NIG
18:31 all t that are written by the prophets NIG
18:34 And they understood none of these t: and NIG
18:34 neither knew they the t which were spoken. NIG
19:11 And as they heard these t, he added and NIG
19:42 thy day, the t which belong unto thy peace! NIG
20: 2 by what authority doest thou these t? or NIG
20: 8 tell I you by what authority I do these t. NIG
20:25 therefore unto Cesar the t which be Cesar's, NIG
20:25 and unto God the t which be God's. NIG
21: 6 As for these t which ye behold, the days NIG
21: 7 saying, Master, but when shall these t be? NIG
21: 7 what sign will there be when these t shall NIG
21: 9 for these t must first come to pass; but NIG
21:22 that all t which are written may be fulfilled. NIG
21:26 for looking after those t which are coming NIG
21:28 And when these t begin to come to pass, NIG
21:31 when ye see these t come to pass, NIG
21:36 to escape all these t that shall come to pass, NIG
22:37 for the t concerning me have an end. NIG
22:65 And many other t blasphemously spake NIG
23: 8 because he had heard many t of him; NIG
23:14 touching those t whereof ye accuse him: NIG
23:31 For if they do these t in a green tree, NIG
23:48 beholding the t which were done, NIG
23:49 stood afar off, beholding these t. NIG
24: 9 and told all these t unto the eleven, and NIG
24:10 which told these t unto the apostles. NIG
24:14 And they talked together of all these t NIG
24:18 hast not known the t which are come to pass NIG
24:19 unto them, What t? And they said unto him, NIG
24:21 to day is the third day since these t were NIG
24:26 Ought not Christ to have suffered these t, NIG
24:27 all the scriptures the t concerning himself. NIG
24:35 And they told what t were done in the way, NIG
24:44 was yet with you, that all t must be fulfilled, NIG
24:48 And ye are witnesses of these t. NIG
Jn 1: 3 All t were made by him; and without him NIG
1:28 These t were done in Bethabara beyond NIG
1:50 thou shalt see greater t than these. NIG
2:16 them that sold doves, Take these t hence; NIG
2:18 thou unto us, seeing that thou doest these t? NIG
3: 9 and said unto him, How can these t be? NIG
3:10 a master of Israel, and knowest not these t? NIG
3:12 If I have told you earthly t, and ye believe NIG
3:12 shall ye believe, if I tell you of heavenly t? NIG
3:22 After these t came Jesus and his disciples NIG
3:35 the Son, and hath given all t into his hand. NIG
4:25 when he is come, he will tell us all t. NIG
4:29 a man, which told me all t that ever I did: NIG
4:45 having seen all the t that he did at Jerusalem NIG
5:16 he had done these t on the sabbath day. NIG
5:19 for what t soever he doeth, these also doeth NIG
5:20 and sheweth him all t that himself doeth: NIG
5:34 but these t I say, that ye might be saved. NIG
6: 1 After these t Jesus went over the sea of NIG
6:59 These t said he in the synagogue, as he NIG
7: 1 After these t Jesus walked in Galilee: for he NIG
7: 4 If thou do these t, shew thyself to the world. NIG
7:32 people murmured such t concerning him; NIG
8:26 I have many t to say and to judge of you: NIG
8:26 I speak to the world those t which I have NIG
8:28 my Father hath taught me, I speak these t. NIG
8:29 for I do always those t that please him. NIG
10: 6 they understood not what t they were which NIG
10:41 all t that John spake of this man were true. NIG

T

Jn 11:11 These t said he: and after that he saith unto NIG
11:45 and had seen the t which Jesus did, NIG
11:46 and told them what t Jesus had done. NIG
12:16 These t understood not his disciples at NIG
12:16 remembered they that these t were written NIG
12:16 and that they had done these t unto him. NIG
12:36 These t spake Jesus, and departed, and NIG
12:41 These t said Esaias, when he saw his glory, NIG
13: 3 knowing that the Father had given all t NIG
13:17 If ye know these t, happy are ye if ye do NIG
13:29 Buy those t that we have need of against NIG
14:25 These t have I spoken unto you, being yet NIG
14:26 he shall teach you all t, and bring all things NIG
14:26 and bring all t to your remembrance, NIG
15:11 These t have I spoken unto you, that my joy NIG
15:15 for all t that I have heard of my Father I NIG
15:17 These t I command you, that ye love one NIG
15:21 But all these t will they do unto you for my NIG
16: 1 These t have I spoken unto you, that ye NIG
16: 3 And these t will they do unto you, because NIG
16: 4 But these t have I told you, that when NIG
16: 4 And these t I said not unto you at NIG
16: 6 But because I have said these t unto you, NIG
16:12 I have yet many t to say unto you, but NIG
16:13 he speak: and he will shew you t to come. NIG
16:15 All t that the Father hath are mine: therefore NIG
16:25 These t have I spoken unto you in proverbs: NIG
16:30 Now are we sure that thou knowest all t, NIG
16:33 These t I have spoken unto you, that in me NIG
17: 7 Now they have known that all t whatsoever NIG
17:13 and these t I speak in the world, that they NIG
18: 4 knowing all t that should come upon him, NIG
19:24 cast lots. These t therefore the soldiers did. NIG
19:28 Jesus knowing that all t were now NIG
19:36 For these t were done, that the scripture NIG
20:18 and that he had spoken these t unto her. NIG
21: 1 After these t Jesus shewed himself again to NIG
21:17 thou knowest all t; thou knowest that I love NIG
21:24 is the disciple which testifieth of these t, NIG
21:24 and wrote these t: and we know that his NIG
21:25 And there are also many other t which Jesus NIG
Ac 1: 3 speaking of the t pertaining to the kingdom NIG
1: 9 And when he had spoken these t, while they NIG
2:44 were together, and had all t common; NIG
3:18 But those t, which God before had shewed NIG
3:21 t, which God hath spoken by the mouth of NIG
3:22 him shall ye hear in all t whatsoever he NIG
4:20 but speak the t which we have seen and NIG
4:25 and the people imagine vain t? NIG
4:32 neither said any of them that ought of the t NIG
4:32 was his own; but they had all t common. NIG
4:34 brought the prices of the t that were sold, NIG
5: 5 fear came on all them that heard these t. NIG
5:11 and upon as many as heard these t. NIG
5:24 and the chief priests heard these t, 3056
5:32 And we are his witnesses of these t; and so 4487
7: 1 Then said the high priest, Are these t so? NIG
7:50 Hath not my hand made all these t? NIG
7:54 When they heard these t, they were cut to NIG
8: 6 gave heed unto those t which Philip spake, NIG
8:12 the t concerning the kingdom of God, NIG
8:24 that none of these t which ye have spoken NIG
9:16 For I will shew him how great t he must NIG
10: 8 And when he had declared all these t unto NIG
10:12 and **creeping t**, and fowls of the air. 2062
10:33 to hear all t that are commanded thee of NIG
10:39 And we are witnesses of all t which he did NIG
11: 6 and **creeping t**, and fowls of the air. 2062
11:18 When they heard these t, they held their NIG
11:22 Then tidings of these t came unto the ears of NIG
12:17 Go shew these t unto James, and to NIG
13:39 t, from which ye could not be justified by NIG
13:45 spake against those t which were spoken by NIG
14:15 why do ye these t? We also are men of like NIG
14:15 and the sea, and all t that are therein: NIG
15: 4 they declared all t that God had done with NIG
15:17 saith the Lord, who doeth all these t. NIG
15:20 and from **t strangled**, and from blood. 3588
15:27 who shall also tell you the same t by mouth. NIG
15:28 no greater burden than these necessary t; NIG
15:29 and from **t strangled**, and from fornication: 4156
16:14 that she attended unto the t which were NIG
17: 8 rulers of the city, when they heard these t. NIG
17:11 scriptures daily, whether those t were so. NIG
17:20 For thou bringest certain strange t to our NIG
17:20 would know therefore what these t mean. NIG
17:22 I perceive that in all t ye are too NIG
17:24 God that made the world and all t therein, NIG
17:25 he giveth to all life, and breath, and all t; NIG
18: 1 After these t Paul departed from Athens, NIG
18:17 And Gallio cared for none of those t. NIG
18:25 and taught diligently the t of the Lord, NIG
19: 8 persuading the t concerning the kingdom of NIG
19:21 After these t were ended, Paul purposed in NIG
19:36 then that these t cannot be spoken against, NIG
20:22 not knowing the t that shall befall me there: NIG
20:24 But none of these t move me, neither count NIG
20:30 speaking perverse t, to draw away disciples NIG
20:35 I have shewed you all t, how that so NIG
21:12 And when we heard these t, both we, and NIG
21:19 he declared particularly what t God had NIG
21:24 all may know that those t, whereof they NIG
21:25 keep themselves from **t offered to idols**, 1494
22:10 there it shall be told thee of all t which are NIG
23:22 no man that thou hast shewed these t to me. NIG
24: 8 of all these t, whereof we accuse him. NIG
24: 9 also assented, saying that these t were so. NIG
24:13 Neither can they prove the t whereof they NIG
24:14 believing all t which are written in the law NIG
24:22 And when Felix heard these t, having more NIG
25: 9 and there be judged of these t before me? NIG
25:11 if there be none of these t whereof these NIG
25:18 none accusation of such t as I supposed: NIG
26: 2 all the t whereof I am accused of the Jews: NIG
26: 9 that I ought to do many t contrary to NIG
Ac 26:16 a witness both of these t which thou hast NIG
26:16 of those t in the which I will appear unto NIG
26:22 saying none other t than those which NIG
26:26 For the king knoweth of these t, before NIG
26:26 for I am persuaded that none of these t are NIG
27:11 more than those t which were spoken by NIG
28:10 they laded us with such t as were necessary. NIG
28:24 And some believed the t which were NIG
28:31 teaching those t which concern the Lord NIG
Ro 1:20 For the invisible t of him from the creation NIG
1:20 being understood by the **t that are made**, 4161
1:23 and fourfooted beasts, and **creeping t**. 2062
1:28 to do those t which are not convenient; NIG
1:30 inventors of evil t, disobedient to parents, NIG
1:32 that they which commit such t are worthy of NIG
2: 1 for thou that judgest doest the same t. NIG
2: 2 to truth against them which commit such t. NIG
2: 3 that judgest them which do such t, and NIG
2:14 do by nature the t contained in the law, NIG
2:18 and approvest the t that are more excellent, NIG
3:19 Now we know that what t soever the law NIG
4:17 calleth those t which be not as though they NIG
6:21 in those t whereof ye are now ashamed? NIG
6:21 for the end of those t is death. NIG
8: 5 are after the flesh do mind the t of the flesh; NIG
8: 5 they that are after the Spirit the t of NIG
8:28 And we know that all t work together for NIG
8:31 then say to these t? If God be for us, NIG
8:32 he not with him also freely give us all t? NIG
8:37 in all these t we are more than conquerors NIG
8:38 nor principalities, nor powers, nor t present, NIG
8:38 nor things present, nor t to come, NIG
10: 5 That the man which doeth those t shall live NIG
10:15 of peace, and bring glad tidings of good t! NIG
11:36 to him, are all t: to whom be glory for ever. NIG
12:16 Mind not high t, but condescend to men of NIG
12:17 Provide t honest in the sight of all men. NIG
14: 2 For one believeth that he may eat all t: NIG
14:18 For he that in these t serveth Christ is NIG
14:19 follow after the t which make for peace, NIG
14:19 and t wherewith one may edify another. NIG
14:20 All t indeed are pure; but it is evil for that NIG
15: 4 For whatsoever t were written aforetime NIG
15:17 Jesus Christ in those t which pertain to God. NIG
15:18 For I will not dare to speak of any of those t NIG
15:27 t, their duty is also to minister unto them in NIG
15:27 is also to minister unto them in carnal t. NIG
1Co 1:27 But God hath chosen the foolish t of NIG
1:27 God hath chosen the weak t of the world to NIG
1:27 world to confound the t which are mighty; NIG
1:28 And base t of the world, and things which NIG
1:28 and t which are despised, hath God chosen, NIG
1:28 hath God chosen, yea, and t which are not, NIG
1:28 which are not, to bring to nought t that are: NIG
2: 9 the t which God hath prepared for them that NIG
2:10 for the Spirit searcheth all t, yea, the deep NIG
2:10 searcheth all things, yea, the **deep t** of God. 899
2:11 For what man knoweth the t of a man, NIG
2:11 even so the t of God knoweth no man, but NIG
2:12 that we might know the t that are freely NIG
2:13 Which t also we speak, not in the words NIG
2:13 comparing spiritual t with spiritual. NIG
2:14 But the natural man receiveth not the t of NIG
2:15 But he that is spiritual judgeth all t, yet he NIG
3:21 let no man glory in men. For all t are yours; NIG
3:22 or death, or t present, or things to come; NIG
3:22 or death, or things present, or t to come; NIG
4: 5 who both will bring to light the hidden t of NIG
4: 6 And these t, brethren, I have in a figure NIG
4:13 are the offscouring of all t unto this day. NIG
4:14 I write not these t to shame you, but as my NIG
6: 3 how much more t that pertain to this life? NIG
6: 4 ye have judgments of t pertaining to this NIG
6:12 All t are lawful unto me, but all things are NIG
6:12 lawful unto me, but all t are not expedient: NIG
6:12 all t are lawful for me, but I will not be NIG
7: 1 Now concerning the t whereof ye wrote NIG
7:32 He that is unmarried careth for the t that NIG
7:33 But he that is married careth for the t that NIG
7:34 The unmarried woman careth for the t of NIG
7:34 she that is married careth for the t of NIG
8: 1 Now as touching **t offered unto idols**, 1494
8: 4 **t that are offered in sacrifice unto idols**, 1494
8: 6 of whom are all t, and we in him; NIG
8: 6 by whom are all t, and we by him. NIG
8:10 to eat those t which are **offered to idols**; 1494
9: 8 Say I these t as a man? or saith not the law NIG
9:11 If we have sown unto you spiritual t, is it a NIG
9:11 a great thing if we shall reap your carnal t? NIG
9:12 suffer all t, lest we should hinder the gospel NIG
9:13 about holy t live of the things of the temple? NIG
9:13 about holy things live of the t of the temple? NIG
9:15 But I have used none of these t: neither NIG
9:15 have I written these t, that it should be NIG
9:22 I am made all t to all men, that I might by NIG
9:25 t. Now they do it to obtain a corruptible NIG
10: 6 Now these t were our examples, to NIG
10: 6 to the intent we should not lust after evil t, NIG
10:11 Now all these t happened unto them for NIG
10:20 But I say, that the t which the Gentiles NIG
10:23 All t are lawful for me, but all things are not NIG
10:23 lawful for me, but all t are not expedient: NIG
10:23 all t are lawful for me, but all things edify NIG
10:23 things are lawful for me, but all t edify not. NIG
10:33 Even as I please all men in all t, not seeking NIG
11: 2 that you remember me in all t, and keep NIG
11:12 man also by the woman; but all t of God. NIG
13: 7 Beareth all t, believeth all things, hopeth all NIG
13: 7 Beareth all things, believeth all t, hopeth all NIG
13: 7 all things, hopeth all t, endureth all things. NIG
13: 7 all things, hopeth all things, endureth all t. NIG
13:11 I became a man, I put away childish t. NIG
14: 7 And even t without life giving sound, NIG
14:26 Let all t be done unto edifying. NIG
14:37 let him acknowledge that the t that I write NIG
1Co 14:40 Let all t be done decently and in order. NIG
15:27 For he hath put all t under his feet. NIG
15:27 all t are put under him, it is manifest that he NIG
15:27 is excepted, which did put all t under him. NIG
15:28 And when all t shall be subdued unto him, NIG
15:28 be subject unto him that put all t under him, NIG
16:14 Let all your t be done with charity. NIG
2Co 1:13 For we write none other t unto you, NIG
1:17 or the t that I purpose, do I purpose NIG
2: 9 of you, whether ye be obedient in all t. NIG
2:16 unto life. And who is sufficient for these t? NIG
4: 2 But have renounced the hidden t of NIG
4:15 For all t are for your sakes, that NIG
4:18 While we look not at the t which are seen, NIG
4:18 are seen, but at the t which are not seen: NIG
4:18 for the t which are seen are temporal; but NIG
4:18 but the t which are not seen are eternal. NIG
5:10 that every one may receive the t done in his NIG
5:17 old t are past away; behold, all things are NIG
5:17 are past away; behold, all t are become new. NIG
5:18 And all t are of God, who hath reconciled NIG
6: 4 But in all t approving ourselves as NIG
6:10 as having nothing, and yet possessing all t. NIG
7:11 In all t ye have approved yourselves to be NIG
7:14 but as we spake all t to you in truth, even so NIG
7:16 that I have confidence in you in all t. NIG
8:21 Providing for honest t, not only in the sight NIG
8:22 have oftentimes proved diligent in many t, NIG
9: 8 always having all sufficiency in all t, may NIG
10: 7 Do ye look on t after the outward NIG
10:13 But we will not boast of t without our NIG
10:15 Not boasting of t without our measure, NIG
10:16 not to boast in another man's line of t made NIG
11: 6 made manifest among you in all t. NIG
11: 9 in all t I have kept myself from being NIG
11:28 Besides those t that are without, that which NIG
11:30 I will glory of the t which concern mine NIG
12:19 but we do all t, dearly beloved, for your NIG
13:10 Therefore I write these t being absent, NIG
Gal 1:20 Now the t which I write unto you, behold, NIG
2:18 For if I build again the t which I destroyed, NIG
3: 4 Have ye suffered so many t in vain? if it be NIG
3:10 t which are written in the book of the law to NIG
4:24 Which t are an allegory: for these are NIG
5:17 so that ye cannot do the t that ye would. NIG
5:21 that they which do such t shall not inherit NIG
6: 6 unto him that teacheth in all good t. NIG
Eph 1:10 might gather together in one all t in Christ, NIG
1:11 all t after the counsel of his own will: NIG
1:22 And hath put all t under his feet, and NIG
1:22 gave him to be the head over all t to NIG
3: 9 in God, who created all t by Jesus Christ: NIG
4:10 above all heavens, that he might fill all t.) NIG
4:15 may grow up into him in all t, which is NIG
5: 6 of these t cometh the wrath of God upon NIG
5:12 For it is a shame even to speak of those t NIG
5:13 But all t that are reproved are made NIG
5:20 Giving thanks always for all t unto God and NIG
6: 9 And, ye masters, do the same t unto them, NIG
6:21 in the Lord, shall make known to you all t: NIG
Php 1:10 That ye may approve t that are excellent; NIG
1:12 that the t which happened unto me have NIG
2: 4 Look not every man on his own t, but NIG
2: 4 but every man also on the t of others. NIG
2:10 of t in heaven, and things in earth, and NIG
2:10 and t in earth, and things under the earth; NIG
2:10 and things in earth, and t under the earth; NIG
2:14 Do all t without murmurings and NIG
2:21 not the t which are Jesus Christ's. NIG
3: 1 To write the same t to you, to me indeed is NIG
3: 7 But what t were gain to me, those I counted NIG
3: 8 and I count all t but loss for the excellency NIG
3: 8 for whom I have suffered the loss of all t, NIG
3:13 this one thing I do, forgetting those t which NIG
3:13 reaching forth unto those t which are NIG
3:19 glory is in their shame, who mind earthly t.) NIG
3:21 he is able even to subdue all t unto himself. NIG
4: 8 Finally, brethren, whatsoever t are true, NIG
4: 8 whatsoever t are honest, whatsoever things NIG
4: 8 whatsoever t are just, whatsoever things are NIG
4: 8 things are just, whatsoever t are pure, NIG
4: 8 things are pure, whatsoever t are lovely, NIG
4: 8 are lovely, whatsoever t are of good report; NIG
4: 8 and if there be any praise, think on these t. NIG
4: 9 Those t, which ye have both learned, and NIG
4:12 in all t I am instructed both to be full and NIG
4:13 I can do all t through Christ which NIG
4:18 having received of Epaphroditus the t which NIG
Col 1:16 For by him were all t created, that are in NIG
1:16 all t were created by him, and for him: NIG
1:17 And he is before all t, and by him all things NIG
1:17 is before all things, and by him all t consist. NIG
1:18 that in all t he might have the preeminence. NIG
1:20 by him to reconcile all t unto himself; NIG
1:20 I say, whether they be t in earth, or things in NIG
1:20 they be things in earth, or t in heaven. NIG
2:17 Which are a shadow of t to come; but NIG
2:18 intruding into those t which he hath not NIG
2:23 Which t have indeed a shew of wisdom in NIG
3: 1 with Christ, seek those t which are above, NIG
3: 2 Set your affection on t above, not on things NIG
3: 2 on things above, not on t on the earth. NIG
3:14 And above all these t put on charity, NIG
3:20 obey your parents in all t: for this is well NIG
3:22 obey in all t your masters according to NIG
4: 9 They shall make known unto you all t NIG
1Th 2:14 for ye also have suffered like t of your own NIG
5:21 Prove all t; hold fast that which is good. NIG
2Th 2: 5 when I was yet with you, I told you these t? NIG
3: 4 and will do the t which we command you. NIG
1Ti 3:11 not slanderers, sober, faithful in all t. NIG
3:14 These t write I unto thee, hoping to come NIG
4: 6 t, thou shalt be a good minister of Jesus NIG
4: 8 godliness is profitable unto all t, having NIG
4:11 These t command and teach. NIG

1Ti 4:15 Meditate upon these *t;* give thyself wholly NIG
5: 7 And these *t* give in charge, that they may be NIG
5:13 speaking *t* which they ought not. NIG
5:21 that thou observe these *t* without preferring NIG
6: 2 of the benefit. These *t* teach and exhort. NIG
6:11 flee these *t;* and follow *after* righteousness, NIG
6:13 who quickeneth all *t,* and *before* Christ NIG
6:17 who giveth us richly all *t* to enjoy; NIG
2Ti 1:12 For the which cause I also suffer these *t:* NIG
1:18 in how many *t* he ministered *unto me* at NIG
2: 2 And *the t* that thou hast heard of me among NIG
2: 7 the Lord give thee understanding in all *t.* NIG
2:10 Therefore I endure all *t* for the elects' sakes, NIG
2:14 Of these *t* put *them* in remembrance, NIG
3:14 But continue thou in *the t* which thou hast NIG
4: 5 But watch thou in all *t,* endure afflictions, NIG
Tit 1: 5 that thou shouldest set in order the *t* that are NIG
1:11 teaching *t* which *they* ought not, for filthy NIG
1:15 Unto the pure all *t are* pure: but unto them NIG
2: 1 But speak thou *the t* which become sound NIG
2: 3 given to much wine, **teachers of good t;** 2567
2: 7 In all *t* shewing thyself a pattern of good NIG
2: 9 to please *them* well in all *t;* not answering NIG
2:10 the doctrine of God our Saviour in all *t.* NIG
2:15 These *t* speak, and exhort, and rebuke with NIG
3: 8 these *t* I will that thou affirm constantly, NIG
3: 8 These *t* are good and profitable unto men. NIG
Heb 1: 2 whom he hath appointed heir of all *t,* by NIG
1: 3 upholding all *t* by the word of his power, NIG
2: 1 earnest heed to the *t* which we have heard, NIG
2: 8 Thou hast put all *t* in subjection under his NIG
2: 8 But now we see not yet all *t* put under him. NIG
2:10 for whom *are* all *t,* and by whom *are* all NIG
2:10 by whom *are* all *t,* in bringing many sons NIG
2:17 Wherefore in all *t* it behoved him to be NIG
2:17 faithful high priest *in t* pertaining to God, NIG
3: 4 by some *man;* but he that built all *t is* God. NIG
3: 5 for a testimony of those *t* which were to be NIG
4:13 but all *t are* naked and opened unto the eyes NIG
5: 1 is ordained for men *in t* pertaining to God, NIG
5: 8 *yet* learned he obedience by *the t* which he NIG
5:11 Of whom we have **many** t to say, and 4183
6: 9 we are persuaded better *t* of you, and NIG
6: 9 and *t* that accompany salvation, though we NIG
6:18 That by two immutable **t,** in which *it was* 4229
7:13 For he of whom these *t* are spoken NIG
8: 1 Now of the *t* which we have spoken *this is* NIG
8: 5 shadow of heavenly *t,* as Moses was NIG
8: 5 saith *he, that* thou make all *t* according to NIG
9: 6 Now when these *t* were thus ordained, NIG
9:11 being come a high priest of good *t* to come, NIG
9:22 And almost all *t* are by the law purged with NIG
9:23 necessary that the patterns of *t* in NIG
9:23 the heavenly *t* themselves with better NIG
10: 1 For the law having a shadow of good *t* to NIG
10: 1 to come, *and* not the very image of the **t,** 4229
11: 1 Now faith is the substance of *t* hoped for, NIG
11: 1 *things* hoped for, the evidence of **t** not seen. 4229
11: 3 that *t* which are seen were not made of NIG
11: 3 seen were not made of *t* which do appear. NIG
11: 7 being warned of God of *t* not seen as yet, NIG
11:14 For they that say such *t* declare plainly that NIG
11:20 and Esau concerning *t* to come. NIG
12:24 that speaketh better *t* than *that of* Abel. NIG
12:27 the removing of those *t* that are shaken, NIG
12:27 as of *t* that are made, that those *things* NIG
12:27 that those *t* which cannot be shaken may NIG
13: 5 *and be* content with such *t* as ye have: NIG
13:18 in all *t* willing to live honestly. NIG
Jas 2:16 notwithstanding ye give them not those *t* NIG
3: 2 For *in* many *t* we offend all. If any *man* NIG
3: 5 is a little member, and boasteth **great t.** 3173
3: 7 and of *t* in the sea, is tamed, and hath been NIG
3:10 My brethren, these *t* ought not so to be. NIG
5:12 But above all *t,* my brethren, swear not, NIG
1Pe 1:12 but unto us they did minister the **t,** 846
1:12 which *t the* angels desire to look into. NIG
1:18 not redeemed with corruptible *t, as* silver NIG
4: 7 But the end of all *t* is at hand: be ye NIG
4: 8 And above all *t* have fervent charity among NIG
4:11 that God in all *t* may be glorified through NIG
2Pe 1: 3 hath given unto us all *t* that *pertain* unto life NIG
1: 8 For if these *t* be in you, and abound, NIG
1: 9 But he that lacketh these *t* is blind, and NIG
1:10 for if ye do these *t,* ye shall never fall: NIG
1:12 of these *t,* though ye know *them,* NIG
1:15 to have these *t* always in remembrance. NIG
2:12 speak evil of *the t* that they understand not; NIG
3: 4 all *t* continue as *they were* from NIG
3:11 then that all these *t shall* be dissolved, NIG
3:14 seeing that ye look for such *t,* be diligent NIG
3:16 speaking in them of these *t;* in which are NIG
3:16 in which are some *t* hard to be understood, NIG
3:17 beloved, seeing ye know *these t* before, NIG
1Jn 1: 4 And these *t* write we unto you, that your joy NIG
2: 1 these *t* write I unto you, that ye sin not. NIG
2:15 the world, neither the *t* that are in the world. NIG
2:20 from the Holy One, and ye know all *t.* NIG
2:26 These *t* have I written unto you concerning NIG
2:27 as the same anointing teacheth you of all *t,* NIG
3:20 is greater than our heart, and knoweth all *t.* NIG
3:22 and do those *t* that are pleasing in his sight. NIG
5:13 These *t* have I written unto you that believe NIG
2Jn 1: 8 that we lose not *those t* which we have NIG
1:12 Having many *t* to write unto you, I would NIG
3Jn 1: 2 I wish above all *t* that thou mayest prosper NIG
1:13 I had many *t* to write, NIG
Jude 1:10 But these speak evil of those *t* which they NIG
1:10 in those *t* they corrupt themselves. NIG
Rev 1: 1 to shew unto his servants *t* which must NIG
1: 2 of Jesus Christ, and of all *t* that he saw. NIG
1: 3 and keep those *t* which are written therein: NIG
1:19 Write *the t* which thou hast seen, and NIG
1:19 and *the t* which are, and *the things* which NIG
1:19 and *the t* which shall be hereafter; NIG

Rev 2: 1 These *t* saith he that holdeth the seven stars NIG
2: 8 These *t* saith the first and the last, NIG
2:10 Fear none *of those t* which thou shalt suffer: NIG
2:12 These *t* saith he which hath the sharp sword NIG
2:14 But I have a few *t* against thee, because NIG
2:14 to eat **t sacrificed unto idols,** and 1494
2:18 These *t* saith the Son of God, who hath his NIG
2:20 Notwithstanding I have a few *t* against thee, NIG
2:20 and to eat **t sacrificed unto idols.** 1494
3: 1 These *t* saith he that hath the seven spirits of NIG
3: 2 and strengthen the *t* which remain, NIG
3: 7 These *t* saith he *that is* holy, he *that is* true, NIG
3:14 These *t* saith the Amen, the faithful and NIG
4: 1 I will shew thee *t* which must be hereafter. NIG
4:11 for thou hast created all *t,* and for thy NIG
7: 1 And after these *t* I saw four angels standing NIG
10: 4 Seal *up those t* which the seven thunders NIG
10: 6 and the *t* that therein are, and the earth, and NIG
10: 6 and the *t* that therein are, and the sea, and NIG
10: 6 and the sea, and the *t* which are therein, NIG
13: 5 given unto him a mouth speaking great *t* NIG
18: 1 And after these *t* I saw another angel come NIG
18:14 and all *t which were* dainty and goodly are NIG
18:15 The merchants of these *t,* which were made NIG
19: 1 And after these *t* I heard a great voice of NIG
20:12 the dead were judged out of those *t* which NIG
21: 4 more pain: for the former *t* are passed away. NIG
21: 5 the throne said, Behold, I make all *t* new. NIG
21: 7 He that overcometh shall inherit all *t;* and NIG
22: 6 servants the *t* which must shortly be done. NIG
22: 8 And I John saw these *t,* and heard *them.* NIG
22: 8 feet of the angel which shewed me these *t.* NIG
22:16 to testify unto you these *t* in the churches. NIG
22:18 If any *man* shall add unto these *t,* God shall NIG
22:19 *from* the *t* which are written in this book. NIG
22:20 He which testifieth these *t* saith, Surely I NIG

THINGS' (1) [THING]

Col 3: 6 For which *t* sake the wrath of God cometh NIG

THINK (65) [BETHINK, THINKEST, THINKETH, THINKING, THOUGHT, THOUGHTEST, THOUGHTS]

Ge 40:14 But **t on** me when it shall be well with thee, 2142
Nu 36: 6 marry to whom they **t best;** 2896+5869+871.1
2Sa 13:33 to **t** *that* all the king's sons are dead: 559
2Ch 13: 8 now ye **t** to withstand the kingdom of 559
Ne 5:19 **T** upon me, my God, for good, *according to* 2142
6: 6 saith *it, that* thou and the Jews **t** to rebel: 2803
6:14 **t** thou upon Tobiah and Sanballat according 2142
Est 4:13 **T** not with thyself that *thou* shalt escape *in* 1819
Job 31: 1 mine eyes; why then should I **t** upon a maid? 995
41:32 after him; *one* would **t** the deep to be hoary. 2803
Ecc 8:17 though a wise *man* **t** to know *it,* yet shall he 559
Isa 10: 7 meaneth not so, neither doth his heart **t** so; 2803
Jer 23:27 Which **t** to cause my people to forget my 2803
29:11 For I know the thoughts that I **t** towards 2803
Eze 38:10 thy mind, and thou shalt **t** an evil thought: 2803
Da 7:25 most High, and **t** to change times and laws: 5452
Jnh 1: 6 if so be that God will **t** upon us, that we 6245
Zec 11:12 If ye **t** good, give *me* my price; 5869+871.1
Mt 3: 9 And **t** not to say within yourselves, *1380*
5:17 **T** not that I am come to destroy the law, or *3543*
6: 7 as the heathen *do:* for they **t** that they shall *1380*
9: 4 Wherefore **t** ye evil in your hearts? *1760*
10:34 **T** not that I am come to send peace on *3543*
18:12 How **t** ye? if a man have an hundred sheep, *1380*
21:28 But what **t** you? A *certain* man had two *1380*
22:42 Saying, What **t** ye of Christ? whose son is *1380*
24:44 for in such an hour as you **t** not the Son of *1380*
26:66 What **t** ye? They answered and said, He is *1380*
Mk 14:64 what **t** ye? And they all condemned him to *5316*
Lk 12:40 of man cometh at an hour when ye **t** not. *1380*
13: 4 **t** ye that they were sinners above all men *1380*
Jn 5:39 for in them ye **t** ye have eternal life: *1380*
5:45 Do not **t** that I will accuse you to *1380*
11:56 as they stood in the temple, What **t** ye, *1380*
16: 2 that whosoever killeth you will **t** that he *1380*
Ac 13:25 *his* course, he said, Whom **t** ye that I am? *5282*
17:29 we ought not to **t** that the Godhead is like *3543*
26: 2 I **t** myself happy, king Agrippa, because *2233*
Ro 12: 3 not to **t** *of himself* more **highly** than he *5252*
12: 3 *of himself* more highly than he ought to **t;** *5426*
12: 3 but to **t** soberly, according as God hath *5426*
1Co 4: 6 that ye might learn in us not to **t** *of men* *5426*
4: 9 For I **t** that God hath set forth us *1380*
7:36 But if any *man* **t** that *he* behaveth himself *3543*
7:40 and I **t** also that *I* have the Spirit of God. *1380*
8: 2 And if any *man* **t** that *he* knoweth any *1380*
12:23 the body, which we **t** to be less honourable, *1380*
14:37 If any *man* **t** himself to be a prophet, or *1380*
2Co 3: 5 Not that we are sufficient of ourselves to **t** *3049*
10: 2 wherewith I **t** to be bold against some, *3049*
10: 2 which **t** of us as if we walked according to *3049*
10: 7 let him of himself **t** this again, that, as he *is* *3049*
10:11 Let such a one **t** this, that, such as we are in *3049*
11:16 I say again, Let no *man* **t** me a fool; *1380*
12: 6 lest any *man* should **t** of me above *that* *3049*
12:19 **t** you that we excuse ourselves unto you? *1380*
Gal 6: 3 For if a man **t** himself to be something, *1380*
Eph 3:20 abundantly above all that we ask or **t,** *3539*
Php 1: 7 Even as it is meet for me to **t** this of you all, *5426*
4: 8 if *there be* any praise, **t** on these *things.* *3049*
Jas 1: 7 For let not that man **t** that he shall receive *3633*
4: 5 Do ye **t** that the scripture saith in vain, *1380*
1Pe 4: 4 Wherein they **t it strange** that you run not *3579*
4:12 **t it** not **strange** concerning the fiery trial *3579*
2Pe 1:13 Yea, I **t** it meet, as long as I am in this *2233*

THINKEST (9) [THINK]

2Sa 10: 3 said unto Hanun their lord, **T** 5869+871.1
1Ch 19: 3 **T** thou that David doth honour thy 5869+871.1
Job 35: 2 **T** thou this to be right, *that* thou saidst, 2803
Mt 17:25 saying, What **t** thou, Simon? *1380*
Mt 22:17 Tell us therefore, What **t** thou? Is it lawful *1380*
26:53 **T** thou that I cannot now pray to my Father, *1380*
Lk 10:36 Which now of these three, **t** thou, *1380*
Ac 28:22 But we desire to hear of thee what thou **t:** *5426*
Ro 2: 3 And **t** thou this, O man, that judgest them *3049*

THINKETH (6) [THINK]

2Sa 18:27 Me **t** the running of the foremost *is* like 7200
Ps 40:17 and needy; *yet* the Lord **t** upon me: 2803
Pr 23: 7 For as he **t** in his heart, so *is* he: Eat and 8176
1Co 10:12 Wherefore let him that **t** he standeth take *1380*
13: 5 her own, is not easily provoked, **t** no evil; *3049*
Php 3: 4 If any other *man* **t** that *he hath whereof he* *1380*

THINKING (2) [THINK]

2Sa 4:10 **t** to have brought good tidings, 5869+871.1
5: 6 in hither: **t,** David cannot come in hither. 559

THIRD (182) [THREE]

Ge 1:13 and the morning were the **t** day. 7992
2:14 the name of the **t** river *is* Hiddekel: that *is it* 7992
6:16 second, and **t** *stories* shalt thou make it. 7992
22: 4 on the **t** day Abraham lift up his eyes, and 7992
31:22 it was told Laban on the **t** day that Jacob 7992
32:19 the **t,** and all that followed the droves, 7992
34:25 it came to pass on the **t** day, when they 7992
40:20 it came to pass the **t** day, *which was* 7992
42:18 Joseph said unto them the **t** day, This do, 7992
50:23 Joseph saw Ephraim's children of the **t** 8029
Ex 19: 1 In the **t** month, when the children of Israel 7992
19:11 be ready against the **t** day: for the third day 7992
19:11 for the **t** day the LORD will come down in 7992
19:15 unto the people, Be ready against the **t** day: 7969
19:16 it came to pass on the **t** day in the morning, 7992
20: 5 of the fathers upon the children unto the **t** 8029
28:19 the **t** row a ligure, an agate, and 7992
34: 7 unto the **t** and to the fourth *generation.* 8029
39:12 the **t** row, a ligure, an agate, and 7992
Lev 7:17 on the **t** day shall be burnt with fire. 7992
7:18 peace offerings be eaten at all on the **t** day, 7992
19: 6 if ought remain until the **t** day, it shall be 7992
19: 7 if it be eaten at all on the **t** day, it *is* 7992
Nu 2:24 And they shall go forward in the **t rank.** 7992
7:24 On the **t** day Eliab the son of Helon, 7992
14:18 of the fathers upon the children unto the **t** 8029
15: 6 flour mingled with the **t** *part* of a hin of oil. 7992
15: 7 for a drink offering thou shalt offer the **t** 7992
19:12 He shall purify himself with it on the **t** day, 7992
19:12 if he purify not himself the **t** day, then 7992
19:19 sprinkle upon the unclean on the **t** day, 7992
28:14 the **t** *part* of a hin unto a ram, and a fourth 7992
29:20 on the **t** day eleven bullocks, two rams, 7992
31:19 and your captives on the **t** day, 7992
Dt 5: 9 of the fathers upon the children unto the **t** 8029
23: 8 of the LORD *in* their **t** generation. 7992
26:12 all the tithes of thine increase the **t** year, 7992
Jos 9:17 and came unto their cities on the **t** day. 7992
19:10 the **t** lot came up for the children of 7992
Jdg 20:30 the children of Benjamin on the **t** day, 7992
1Sa 3: 8 the LORD called Samuel again the **t time.** 7992
17:13 unto him Abinadab, and the **t** Shammah. 7992
19:21 Saul sent messengers again the **t time,** and 7992
20: 5 myself in the fields unto the **t** *day* at even. 7992
20:12 *or* the **t** *day,* and behold, *if there be* good 7992
30: 1 his men were come to Ziklag on the **t** day, 7992
2Sa 1: 2 It came even to pass on the **t** day, that 7992
3: 3 the **t,** Absalom the son of Maacah 7992
18: 2 David sent forth a **t part** of the people 7992
18: 2 a **t part** under the hand of Abishai the son 7992
18: 2 a **t part** under the hand of Ittai the Gittite. 7992
1Ki 3:18 it came to pass the **t** day after that I was 7992
6: 6 and the **t** *was* seven cubits broad: 7992
6: 8 and out of the middle into the **t.** 7992
12:12 all the people came to Rehoboam the **t** day, 7992
12:12 saying, Come to me again the **t** day. 7992
15:28 Even in the **t** year of Asa king of Judah did 7969
15:33 In the **t** year of Asa king of Judah *began* 7969
18: 1 of the LORD came to Elijah in the **t** year, 7992
18:34 he said, **Do** *it* **the t time.** And they did *it* 8027
18:34 *it* the third time. And they **did** *it* **the t time.** 8027
22: 2 It came to pass on the **t** year, that 7992
2Ki 1:13 he sent again a captain of the **t** fifty with 7992
1:13 the **t** captain of fifty went up, and came 7992
11: 5 A **t** *part* of you that enter in on the sabbath 7992
11: 6 a **t** *part shall be* at the gate of Sur; and 7992
11: 6 and a **t** *part* at the gate behind the guard: 7992
18: 1 Now it came to pass in the **t** year of Hoshea 7969
19:29 in the **t** year sow ye, and reap, and 7992
20: 5 on the **t** day thou shalt go up *unto* the house 7992
20: 8 up *into* the house of the LORD the **t** day? 7992
1Ch 2:13 Abinadab the second, and Shimma the **t,** 7992
3: 2 The **t,** Absalom the son of Maachah 7992
3:15 the **t** Zedekiah, the fourth Shallum. 7992
8: 1 Ashbel the second, and Aharah the **t,** 7992
8:39 Jehush the second, and Eliphelet the **t.** 7992
12: 9 the first, Obadiah the second, Eliab the **t,** 7992
23:19 Jahaziel the **t,** and Jekameam the fourth. 7992
24: 8 The **t** to Harim, the fourth to Seorim, 7992
24:23 Jahaziel the **t,** Jekameam the fourth. 7992
25:10 The **t** *to* Zaccur, *he,* his sons, and 7992
26: 2 Jediael the second, Zebadiah the **t,** 7992
26: 4 Joah the **t,** and Sacar the fourth, and 7992
26:11 Hilkiah the second, Tebaliah the **t,** 7992
27: 5 The **t** captain of the host for the third month 7992
27: 5 The third captain of the host for the **t** month 7992
2Ch 10:12 all the people came to Rehoboam on the **t** 7992
10:12 saying, Come again to me on the **t** day. 7992
15:10 together at Jerusalem in the **t** month, 7992
17: 7 Also in the **t** year of his reign he sent to his 7969
23: 4 A **t** *part* of you entering on the sabbath, 7992
23: 5 a **t** *part shall be* at the king's house; and 7992
23: 5 and a **t** *part* at the gate of the foundation: 7992
27: 5 unto him, both the second year, and the **t.** 7992
31: 7 In the **t** month they began to lay 7992

T

Ezr 6:15 this house was finished on the t day of 8532
Ne 10:32 to charge ourselves yearly with the t *part* of 7992
Est 1: 3 In the t year of his reign, he made a feast 7969
5: 1 Now it came to pass on the t day, 7992
8: 9 scribes called at that time in the t month, 7992
Job 42:14 and the name of the t, Keren-happuch. 7992
Isa 19:24 In that day shall Israel be the t with Egypt 7992
37:30 in the t year sow ye, and reap, and 7992
Jer 38:14 t entry that *is* in the house of the LORD: 7992
Eze 5: 2 Thou shalt burn with fire a t *part* in 7992
5: 2 thou shalt take a t *part, and* smite about it 7992
5: 2 a t *part* thou shalt scatter in the wind; and 7992
5:12 A t *part* of thee shall die with 7992
5:12 a t *part* shall fall by the sword round about 7992
5:12 I will scatter a t *part* into all the winds, and 7992
10:14 the t the face of a lion, and the fourth 7992
21:14 let the sword be doubled the t **time**, 7992
31: 1 in the t *month,* in the first *day* of the month, 7992
46:14 of an ephah, and the t *part* of a hin of oil, 7992
Da 1: 1 In the t year of the reign of Jehoiakim king 7969
2:39 another t kingdom of brass, which shall 8523
5: 7 and shall be the t ruler in the kingdom. 8523
5:16 and shalt be the t ruler in the kingdom. 8531
5:29 that *he* should be the t ruler in the kingdom. 8531
8: 1 In the t year of the reign of king Belshazzar 7969
10: 1 In the t year of Cyrus king of Persia a thing 7969
Hos 6: 2 in the t day he will raise us up, and we shall 7992
Zec 6: 3 in the t chariot white horses; and in 7992
13: 8 *and* die; but the t shall be left therein. 7992
13: 9 I will bring the t *part* through the fire, and 7992
Mt 16:21 and be killed, and be raised *again* the t day. *5154*
17:23 the t day he shall be raised *again.* And they *5154*
20: 3 And he went out about the t hour, and *5154*
20:19 and the t day he shall rise again. *5154*
22:26 the second also, and the t, unto the seventh. *5154*
26:44 away again, and prayed the t **time**, *1537+5154*
27:64 that the sepulchre be made sure until the t *5154*
Mk 9:31 after that he is killed, he shall rise the t day. *5154*
10:34 kill him: and the t day he shall rise again. *5154*
12:21 neither left he *any* seed: and the t likewise. *5154*
14:41 And he cometh the t **time**, and saith unto *5154*
15:25 And it was the t hour, and they crucified *5154*
Lk 9:22 and be slain, and be raised the t day. *5154*
12:38 or come in the t watch, and find *them* so, *5154*
13:32 and the t *day* I shall be perfected. *5154*
18:33 to death: and the t day he shall rise again. *5154*
20:12 And again he sent a t: and they wounded *5154*
20:31 And the t took her; and in like manner *5154*
23:22 And he said unto them the t **time**, Why, *5154*
24: 7 and be crucified, and the t day rise again. *5154*
24:21 to day is the t day since these *things* were *5154*
24:46 and to rise from the dead the t day: *5154*
Jn 2: 1 And the t day there was a marriage in Cana *5154*
21:14 This *is* now the t **time** *that* Jesus shewed *5154*
21:17 He saith unto him the t **time**, Simon, *son* of *5154*
21:17 because he said unto him the t **time**, *5154*
Ac 2:15 seeing it is *but* the t hour of the day. *5154*
10:40 Him God raised up the t day, and *5154*
20: 9 and fell down from the t **loft**, and *5152*
23:23 two hundred, at the t hour of the night; *5154*
27:19 And the t *day* we cast *out* with our own *5154*
1Co 15: 4 that he rose *again* the t day according to *5154*
2Co 12: 2 such a one caught up to the t heaven. *5154*
12:14 the t *time* I am ready to come to you; *5154*
13: 1 This *is* the t *time* I am coming to you. *5154*
Rev 4: 7 and the t beast had a face as a man, and *5154*
6: 5 And when he had opened the t seal, I heard *5154*
6: 5 I heard the t beast say, Come and see. *5154*
8: 7 and the t *part* of trees was burnt up, and all *5154*
8: 8 and the t *part* of the sea became blood; *5154*
8: 9 And the t *part* of the creatures which were *5154*
8: 9 and the t *part* of the ships were destroyed. *5154*
8:10 And the t angel sounded, and there fell a *5154*
8:10 and it fell upon the t *part* of the rivers, and *5154*
8:11 the t *part* of the waters became wormwood; *5154*
8:12 and the t *part* of the sun was smitten, and *5154*
8:12 and the t *part* of the moon, and the third *5154*
8:12 *part* of the moon, and the t *part* of the stars; *5154*
8:12 so as the t *part* of them was darkened and *5154*
8:12 and the day shone not for a t *part* of it, *5154*
9:15 and a year, for to slay the t *part* of men. *5154*
9:18 By these three was the t *part* of men killed, *5154*
11:14 *and* behold, the t woe cometh quickly. *5154*
12: 4 And his tail drew the t *part* of the stars of *5154*
14: 9 And *the* t angel followed them, saying with *5154*
16: 4 And the t angel poured out his vial upon *5154*
21:19 the second, sapphire; the t, a chalcedony; *5154*

THIRDLY (1) [THREE]
1Co 12:28 t teachers, after that miracles, then gifts of *5154*

THIRST (31) [ATHIRST, BLOODTHIRSTY, THIRSTED, THIRSTETH, THIRSTY]
Ex 17: 3 and our children and our cattle with t? 6772
Dt 28:48 in t, and in nakedness, and in want of all 6772
29:19 of mine heart, to add drunkenness *to* t: 6771
Jdg 15:18 now shall I die for t, and fall into the hand 6772
2Ch 32:11 over yourselves to die by famine and by t, 6772
Ne 9:15 water for them out of the rock for their t, 6772
9:20 and gavest them water for their t. 6772
Job 24:11 *and* tread *their* winepresses, and **suffer** t. 6770
Ps 69:21 and in my t they gave me vinegar to drink. 6772
104:11 of the field: the wild asses quench their t. 6772
Isa 5:13 and their multitude dried up with t. 6772
41:17 *there is* none, *and* their tongue faileth for t, 6772
49:10 They shall not hunger nor t; neither shall 6770
50: 2 because *there is* no water, and dieth for t. 6772
Jer 2:25 from being unshod, and thy throat from t: 6773
48:18 come down from *thy* glory, and sit in t; 6772
La 4: 4 child cleaveth to the roof of his mouth for t: 6772
Hos 2: 3 set her like a dry land, and slay her with t. 6772
Am 8:11 nor a t for water, but of hearing the words 6772
8:13 the fair virgins and young men faint for t. 6772
Mt 5: 6 which do hunger and t after righteousness: *1372*
Jn 4:13 Whosoever drinketh of this water shall t *1372*
4:14 the water that I shall give him shall never t; *1372*
4:15 Sir, give me this water, that I t not, *1372*
6:35 and he that believeth on me shall never t. *1372*
7:37 Jesus stood and cried, saying, If any *man* t, *1372*
19:28 the scripture might be fulfilled, saith, I t. *1372*
Ro 12:20 feed him; if he t, give him drink: *1372*
1Co 4:11 and t, and are naked, and are buffeted, and *1372*
2Co 11:27 in hunger and t, in fastings often, in cold *1373*
Rev 7:16 shall hunger no more, neither t any more; *1372*

THIRSTED (2) [THIRST]
Ex 17: 3 the people t there for water; and the people 6770
Isa 48:21 they t not *when* he led them through 6770

THIRSTETH (4) [THIRST]
Ps 42: 2 My soul t for God, for the living God: 6770
63: 1 my soul t for thee, my flesh longeth for 6770
143: 6 my soul *t* after thee, as a thirsty land. Selah. NIH
Isa 55: 1 Ho, every one that t, come ye to the waters, 6771

THIRSTY (17) [THIRST]
Jdg 4:19 pray thee, a little water to drink; for I am t. 6770
2Sa 17:29 and weary, and t, in the wilderness. 6771
Ps 63: 1 in a dry and t land, where no water is; 5889
107: 5 Hungry and t, their soul fainted in them. 6771
143: 6 my soul *thirsteth* after thee, as a t land. 5889
Pr 25:21 and if he *be* t, give him water to drink: 6771
25:25 *As* cold waters to a t soul, so *is* good news 5889
Isa 21:14 of Tema brought water to him that was t, 6771
29: 8 or as when a t *man* dreameth, and behold, 6771
32: 6 and he will cause the drink of the t to fail. 6771
35: 7 a pool, and the t **land** springs of water: 6774
44: 3 For I will pour water upon *him that is* t, and 6771
65:13 my servants shall drink, but ye shall be t: 6770
Eze 19:13 in the wilderness, in a dry and t ground. 6772
Mt 25:35 I was t, and ye gave me drink: I was a *1372*
25:37 and fed *thee?* or t, and gave *thee* drink? *1372*
25:42 no meat: I was t, and ye gave me no drink: *1372*

THIRTEEN (15) [THIRTEENTH]
Ge 17:25 Ishmael his son *was* t years old, 6240+7969
Nu 3:43 and **threescore and** t. 7657+7969+2050.1
3:46 **threescore and** t of 7657+7969+1886.1+2050.1
29:13 t young bullocks, two rams, *and* 6240+7969
29:14 unto every bullock of the t bullocks, 6240+7969
Jos 19: 6 Sharuhen; t cities and their villages: 6240+7969
21: 4 out of the tribe of Benjamin, t cities. 6240+7969
21: 6 tribe of Manasseh in Bashan, t cities. 6240+7969
21:19 *were* t cities with their suburbs. 6240+7969
21:33 *were* t cities with their suburbs. 6240+7969
1Ki 7: 1 was building his own house t years, 6240+7969
1Ch 6:60 their families *were* t cities. 6240+7969
6:62 tribe of Manasseh in Bashan, t cities. 6240+7969
26:11 and brethren of Hosah *were* t. 6240+7969
Eze 40:11 *and* the length of the gate, t cubits. 6240+7969

THIRTEENTH (11) [THIRTEEN]
Ge 14: 4 and *in* the t year they rebelled. 6240+7969
1Ch 24:13 The t to Huppah, the fourteenth to 6240+7969
25:20 The t *to* Shubael, *he,* his sons, and 6240+7969
Est 3:12 called on the t day of the first month, 6240+7969
3:13 upon the t *day* of the twelfth month, 6240+7969
8:12 *namely,* upon the t *day* of the twelfth 6240+7969
9: 1 on the t day of the same, 6240+7969
9:17 On the t day of the month Adar; and 6240+7969
9:18 together on the t *day* thereof, 6240+7969
Jer 1: 2 of Judah, in the t year of his reign. 6240+7969
25: 3 From the t year of Josiah the son of 6240+7969

THIRTIETH (9) [THIRTY]
2Ki 15:13 the nine and t year of Uzziah king of Judah; 7970
15:17 t year of Azariah king of Judah *began* 7970
25:27 t year of the captivity of Jehoiachin king of 7970
2Ch 15:19 unto the five and t year of the reign of Asa. 7970
16: 1 t year of the reign of Asa Baasha king of 7970
Ne 5:14 the two and t year of Artaxerxes the king, 7970
13: 6 t year of Artaxerxes king of Babylon came 7970
Jer 52:31 t year of the captivity of Jehoiachin king of 7970
Eze 1: 1 Now it came to pass in the t year, in 7970

THIRTY (174) [THIRTIETH, THIRTYFOLD]
Ge 5: 3 Adam lived an hundred and t years, and 7970
5: 5 Adam lived were nine hundred and t years: 7970
5:16 he begat Jared eight hundred and t years, 7970
6:15 it fifty cubits, and the height of it t cubits. 7970
11:12 Arphaxad lived five and t years, and 7970
11:14 And Salah lived t years, and begat Eber: 7970
11:16 Eber lived four and t years, and 7970
11:17 he begat Peleg four hundred and t years, 7970
11:18 And Peleg lived t years, and begat Reu: 7970
11:20 Reu lived two and t years, and begat Serug: 7970
11:22 And Serug lived t years, and begat Nahor: 7970
18:30 Peradventure there shall t be found there. 7970
18:30 he said, I will not do *it,* if I find t there. 7970
25:17 an hundred and t and seven years: 7970
32:15 T milch camels with their colts, forty kine, 7970
41:46 Joseph *was* t years old when he stood 7970
46:15 his sons and his daughters *were* t and three. 7970
47: 9 my pilgrimage *are* an hundred and t years: 7970
Ex 6:16 years of the life of Levi *were* an hundred t 7970
6:18 of the life of Kohath *were* an hundred t 7970
6:20 *were* an hundred and t and seven years. 7970
12:40 in Egypt, *was* four hundred and t years. 7970
12:41 at the end of the four hundred and t years, 7970
21:32 he shall give unto their master t shekels *of* 7970
26: 8 The length of one curtain *shall be* t cubits, 7970
36:15 The length of one curtain *was* t cubits, and 7970
38:24 and seven hundred and t shekels, 7970
Lev 12: 4 the blood of her purifying three and t days; 7970
27: 4 then thy estimation shall be t shekels. 7970
Nu 1:35 *were* t and two thousand and two hundred. 7970
1:37 *were* t and five thousand and four hundred. 7970
2:21 *were* t and two thousand and two hundred. 7970
2:23 *were* t and five thousand and four hundred. 7970
4: 3 From t years old and upward even until 7970
4:23 From t years old and upward until fifty 7970
4:30 From t years old and upward even unto 7970
4:35 From t years old and upward even unto 7970
4:39 From t years old and upward even unto 7970
4:40 were two thousand and six hundred and t. 7970
4:43 From t years old and upward even unto 7970
4:47 From t years old and upward even unto 7970
7:13 t *shekels,* one silver bowl of seventy 7970
7:19 t *shekels,* one silver bowl of seventy 7970
7:25 t *shekels,* one silver bowl of seventy 7970
7:31 t *shekels,* one silver bowl of seventy 7970
7:37 t *shekels,* one silver bowl of seventy 7970
7:43 t *shekels,* a silver bowl of seventy shekels, 7970
7:49 t *shekels,* one silver bowl of seventy 7970
7:55 t *shekels,* one silver bowl of seventy 7970
7:61 t *shekels,* one silver bowl of seventy 7970
7:67 t *shekels,* one silver bowl of seventy 7970
7:73 t *shekels,* one silver bowl of seventy 7970
7:79 t *shekels,* one silver bowl of seventy 7970
7:85 and t *shekels,* each bowl seventy: 7970
20:29 they mourned for Aaron t days, *even* all 7970
26: 7 three thousand and seven hundred and t. 7970
26:37 t and two thousand and five hundred. 7970
26:51 and a thousand seven hundred and t. 7970
31:35 t and two thousand persons in all, 7970
31:36 seven and t thousand and five hundred 7970
31:38 the beeves *were* t and six thousand; of 7970
31:39 the asses *were* t thousand and five hundred; 7970
31:40 of which the LORD'S tribute *was* t and 7970
31:43 t thousand *and* seven thousand and 7970
31:44 And t and six thousand beeves, 7970
31:45 And t thousand asses and five hundred, 7970
Dt 2:14 the brook Zered, *was* t and eight years; 7970
34: 8 for Moses in the plains of Moab t days: 7970
Jos 7: 5 the men of Ai smote of them about t and 7970
8: 3 Joshua chose out t thousand mighty *men* of 7970
12:24 king of Tirzah, one: all the kings t and one. 7970
Jdg 10: 4 he had t sons that rode on thirty ass colts, 7970
10: 4 he had thirty sons that rode on t ass colts, 7970
10: 4 they had t cities, which are called 7970
12: 9 he had t sons, and thirty daughters, 7970
12: 9 t daughters, *whom* he sent abroad, and 7970
12: 9 took in t daughters from abroad for his 7970
12:14 he had forty sons and t nephews, that rode 7970
14:11 that they brought t companions to be with 7970
14:12 I will give you t sheets and thirty change of 7970
14:12 you thirty sheets and t change of garments: 7970
14:13 shall ye give me t sheets and thirty change 7970
14:13 me thirty sheets and t change of garments. 7970
14:19 slew t men of them, and took their spoil, 7970
20:31 to Gibeah in the field, about t men of Israel. 7970
20:39 kill of the men of Israel about t persons: 7970
1Sa 4:10 for there fell of Israel t thousand footmen. 7970
9:22 were bidden, which *were* about t persons. 7970
11: 8 and the men of Judah t thousand. 7970
13: 5 t thousand chariots, and six thousand 7970
2Sa 5: 4 David *was* t years old when he *began* to 7970
5: 5 in Jerusalem he reigned t and three years 7970
6: 1 all the chosen *men* of Israel, t thousand. 7970
23:13 three of the t chief went down, and came to 7970
23:23 He was more honourable than the t, but 7970
23:24 Asahel the brother of Joab *was* one of the t; 7970
23:39 Uriah the Hittite: t and seven *in* all. 7970
1Ki 2:11 t and three years reigned he in Jerusalem. 7970
4:22 Solomon's provision for one day was t 7970
5:13 all Israel; and the levy was t thousand men. 7970
6: 2 and the height thereof t cubits. 7970
7: 2 fifty cubits, and the height thereof t cubits, 7970
7: 6 and the breadth thereof t cubits: 7970
7:23 a line of t cubits did compass it round 7970
16:23 In the t and first year of Asa king of Judah 7970
16:29 in the t and eighth year of Asa king of 7970
20: 1 *there were* t and two kings with him, and 7970
20:15 and they were two hundred and t two: 7970
20:16 the t and two kings that helped him. 7970
22:31 the king of Syria commanded his t and 7970
22:42 Jehoshaphat *was* t and five years old when 7970
2Ki 8:17 T and two years old was he when he *began* 7970
13:10 In the t and seventh year of Joash king of 7970
15: 8 In the t and eighth year of Azariah king of 7970
18:14 talents of silver and t talents of gold. 7970
22: 1 he reigned t and one years in Jerusalem. 7970
1Ch 3: 4 in Jerusalem he reigned t and three years. 7970
7: 4 t thousand *men:* for they had many wives 7970
7: 7 and two thousand and t and four. 7970
11:15 Now three of the t captains went down to 7970
11:25 he was honourable among the t, but 7970
11:42 a captain of the Reubenites, and t with him, 7970
12: 4 a mighty *man* among the t, and over 7970
12: 4 *man* among the thirty, and over the t; 7970
12:34 with shield and spear t and seven thousand. 7970
15: 7 and his brethren an hundred and t: 7970
19: 7 So they hired t and two thousand chariots, 7970
23: 3 were numbered from the age of t years 7970
23: 3 man by man, was t and eight thousand. 7970
27: 6 *who was* mighty among the t, and 7970
27: 6 mighty among the thirty, and above the t: 7970
29:27 t and three *years* reigned he in Jerusalem. 7970
2Ch 3:15 he made before the house two pillars of t 7970
4: 2 a line of t cubits did compass it round 7970
16:12 Asa in the t and ninth year of his reign was 7970
20:31 *he was* t and five years old when he *began* 7970
21: 5 Jehoram *was* t and two years old when he 7970
21:20 T and two *years* old was he when he *began* 7970
24:15 and t years old *was he* when he died. 7970
34: 1 he reigned in Jerusalem one and t years. 7970
35: 7 to the number of t thousand, and 7970
Ezr 1: 9 t chargers of gold, a thousand chargers of 7970
1:10 T basons of gold, silver basons of a second 7970
2:35 three thousand and six hundred and t. 7970
2:42 of Shobai, *in* all an hundred t and nine. 7970
2:65 *there were* seven thousand three hundred t 7970
2:66 Their horses *were* seven hundred t and six; 7970

Ezr 2:67 Their camels, four hundred t and five; 7970
Ne 7:38 three thousand nine hundred and t. 7970
7:45 children of Shobai, an hundred t and eight. 7970
7:67 there were seven thousand three hundred t 7970
7:68 Their horses, seven hundred t and six: 7970
7:69 Their camels, four hundred t and five: 7970
7:70 five hundred and t priests' garments. 7970
Est 4:11 to come in unto the king these t days. 7970
Jer 38:10 Take from hence t men with thee, and 7970
52:29 captive from Jerusalem eight hundred t 7970
Eze 40:17 t chambers were upon the pavement. 7970
41: 6 one over another, and t in order; 7970
46:22 joined of forty cubits long and t broad: 7970
Da 6: 7 ask a petition of any God or man for t days, 8533
6:12 a petition of any God or man within t days, 8533
12:12 thousand three hundred and five and t days. 7970
Zec 11:12 So they weighed for my price t pieces of 7970
11:13 I took the t pieces of silver, and cast them 7970
Mt 13:23 some an hundredfold, some sixty, some t. 5144
26:15 And they covenanted with him for t pieces 5144
27: 3 brought again the t pieces of silver to 5144
27: 9 saying, And they took the t pieces of silver, 5144
Mk 4: 8 some t, and some sixty, and some an 5144
Lk 3:23 And Jesus himself began to be about t 5144
Jn 5: 5 which had an infirmity t and eight years. 5144
6:19 rowed about five and twenty or t furlongs, 5144
Gal 3:17 which was four hundred and t years after, 5144

THIRTYFOLD (2) [THIRTY]

Mt 13: 8 hundredfold, some sixtyfold, some t. 5144
Mk 4:20 some t, some sixty, and some an 5144

THIS (2786) [THESE]

Ge 2:23 T is now bone of my bones, and flesh of 2063
3:13 the woman, What is t that thou hast done? 2088
3:14 Because thou hast done t, thou art cursed 2088
4:14 thou hast driven me out t day from the face NIH
5: 1 T is the book of the generations of Adam. 2088
5:29 T same shall comfort us concerning our 2088
6:15 t is the fashion which thou shalt make it of: 2088
7: 1 I seen righteous before me in t generation. 2088
9:12 T is the token of the covenant which I 2088
9:17 unto Noah, T is the token of the covenant, 2088
11: 6 all one language; and t they begin to do: 2088
12: 7 and said, Unto thy seed will I give t land: 2063
12:12 see thee, that they shall say, T is his wife: 2088
12:18 said, What is t that thou hast done unto me? 2088
15: 2 the steward of my house is t Eliezer of 1931
15: 4 unto him, saying, T shall not be thine heir; 2088
15: 7 to give thee t land to inherit it. 2088
15:18 saying, Unto thy seed have I given t land, 2088
17:10 T is my covenant, which ye shall keep, 2088
17:21 which Sarah shall bear unto thee at t set 2088
18:25 That be far from thee to do after t manner, 2088
18:32 be angry, and I will speak yet but t once: NIH
19: 5 the men which came in to thee t night? 1886.1
19: 9 they said again, T one fellow came in to NIH
19:12 hast in the city, bring them out of t place: NIH
19:13 For we will destroy t place, because the cry 2088
19:14 and said, Up, get ye out of t place; 2088
19:14 for the LORD will destroy t city. 1886.1
19:20 t city is near to flee unto, and it is a little 2088
19:21 I have accepted thee concerning t thing, 2088
19:21 that I will not overthrow t city, for NIH
19:34 let us make him drink wine t night also; 1886.1
19:37 the same is the father of the Moabites unto t NIH
19:38 father of the children of Ammon unto t day. NIH
20: 5 and innocency of my hands have I done t. 2088
20: 6 I know that thou didst t in the integrity of 2088
20:10 sawest thou, that thou hast done t thing? 2088
20:11 Surely the fear of God is not in t place; 2088
20:13 T is thy kindness which thou shalt shew 2088
21:10 Cast out t bondwoman and her son: 2088
21:10 for the son of t bondwoman shall not be 2088
21:26 I wot not who hath done t thing: 2088
21:30 witness unto me, that I have digged t well. 2088
22:14 as it is said to t day, In the mount of NIH
22:16 for because thou hast done t thing, and 2088
23:19 after t, Abraham buried Sarah his wife in 3651
24: 5 will not be willing to follow me unto t land: 2088
24: 7 saying, Unto thy seed will I give t land; 2088
24: 8 then thou shalt be clear from t my oath: 2088
24:12 send me good speed t day, and NIH
24:41 shalt thou be clear from t my oath, NIH
24:42 I came t day unto the well, and said, 1886.1
24:58 and said unto her, Wilt thou go with t man? 2088
24:65 What man is t that walketh in the field to 1976
25:31 And Jacob said, Sell me t day thy birthright. NIH
25:32 and what profit shall t birthright do to me? 2088
25:33 Jacob said, Swear to me t day; and he sware NIH
26: 3 Sojourn in t land, and I will be with thee, 2088
26:10 What is t thou hast done unto us? 2088
26:11 He that toucheth t man or his wife shall 2088
26:33 the name of the city is Beer-sheba unto t 2088
28:15 and will bring thee again into t land; 2088
28:16 he said, Surely the LORD is in t place; 2088
28:17 and said, How dreadful is t place! 2088
28:17 t is none other but the house of God, and 2088
28:17 house of God, and t is the gate of heaven. 2088
28:20 will keep me in t way that I go, and 2088
28:22 t stone, which I have set for a pillar, 2088
29:25 What is t thou hast done unto me? 2088
29:27 we will give thee t also for the service 2063
29:33 he hath therefore given me t son also: 2088
29:34 Now t time will my husband be joined unto NIH
30:31 if thou wilt do t thing for me, I will again 2088
31: 1 of our father's hath he gotten all t glory. 2088
31:13 get thee out from t land, and return unto 2088
31:38 T twenty years have I been with thee; 2088
31:43 what can I do t day unto these my NIH
31:48 T heap is a witness between me and thee 2088
31:48 is a witness between me and thee t day. NIH
31:51 Behold t heap, and behold this pillar, 2088
31:51 Behold this heap, and behold t pillar, NIH
31:52 T heap be witness, and this pillar be 2088
Ge 31:52 heap be witness, and t pillar be witness, NIH
31:52 that I will not pass over t heap to thee, and 2088
31:52 that thou shalt not pass over t heap and 2088
31:52 not pass over this heap and t pillar unto me, 2088
32: 2 Jacob saw them, he said, T is God's host: 2088
32:10 for with my staff I passed over t Jordan; 2088
32:19 On t manner shall you speak unto Esau, 2088
32:32 is upon the hollow of the thigh, unto t day: 2088
33: 8 What meanest thou by all t drove which I 2088
34: 4 saying, Get me t damsel to wife. 2088
34:14 they said unto them, We cannot do t thing, 2088
34:15 in t will we consent unto you: If ye will be 2063
35:17 Fear not; thou shalt have t son also. 2088
35:20 that is the pillar of Rachel's grave unto t NIH
36:24 t was that Anah that found the mules in 1931
37: 6 I pray you, t dream which I have dreamed: 2088
37:10 What is t dream that thou hast dreamed? 2088
37:19 one to another, Behold, t dreamer cometh. 1976
37:22 cast him into t pit that is in the wilderness, 2088
37:32 to their father; and said, T have we found: 2088
38:21 they said, There was no harlot in t place. 2088
38:22 that there was no harlot in t place. 2088
38:23 I sent t kid, and thou hast not found her. 2088
38:28 a scarlet thread, saying, T came out first. 2088
38:29 t breach be upon thee: therefore his name NIH
39: 9 There is none greater in t house than I; 2088
39: 9 how then can I do t great wickedness, and 2088
39:11 it came to pass about t time, that Joseph 2088
39:19 saying, After t manner did thy servant to me; 428
40:12 said unto him, T is the interpretation of it: 2088
40:14 unto Pharaoh, and bring me out of t house: 2088
40:18 and said, T is the interpretation thereof: 2088
41: 9 I do remember my faults t day: NIH
41:24 I told t unto the magicians; but there was NIH
41:28 T is the thing which I have spoken unto 1931
41:34 Let Pharaoh do t, and let him appoint NIH
41:38 Can we find such a one as t is, a man in 2088
41:39 Forasmuch as God hath shewed thee all t, 2088
42:13 the youngest is t day with our father, and NIH
42:18 said unto them the third day, T do, and live; 2088
42:21 therefore is t distress come upon us. 2088
42:28 What is t that God hath done unto us? 2088
42:32 the youngest is t day with our father in NIH
43:10 surely now we had returned t second time. 2088
43:11 said unto them, If it must be so now, do t; 2088
43:29 and said, Is t your younger brother, 2088
44: 5 Is not t it in which my lord drinketh, and 2088
44: 7 thy servants should do according to t thing. 2088
44:15 What deed is t that ye have done? 2088
44:29 if ye take t also from me, and 2088
45:17 Say unto thy brethren, T do ye; 2088
45:19 Now thou art commanded, t do ye; 2088
45:23 to his father he sent after t manner; 2063
47:23 I have bought you t day and your land for NIH
47:26 it a law over the land of Egypt unto t day, 2088
48: 4 will give t land to thy seed after thee for an 2088
48: 9 whom God hath given me in t place. And 2088
48:15 which fed me all my life long unto t day, 2088
48:18 for t is the firstborn; put thy right hand 2088
49:28 t is it that their father spake unto them, and 2088
50:11 T is a grievous mourning to the Egyptians: 2088
50:20 it unto good, to bring to pass, as it is t day, 2088
50:24 bring you out of t land unto the land which 2088
Ex 1:18 Why have ye done t thing, and have saved 2088
2: 6 and said, T is one of the Hebrews' children. 2088
2: 9 Take t child away, and nurse it for me, and 2088
2:12 he looked t way and that way, and when he 3541
2:14 and said, Surely t thing is known. NIH
2:15 Now when Pharaoh heard t thing, he 2088
3: 3 I will now turn aside, and see t great sight, 2088
3:12 t shall be a token unto thee, that I have sent 2088
3:12 ye shall serve God upon t mountain. 2088
3:15 t is my name for ever, and this is my 2088
3:15 and t is my memorial unto all generations. 2088
3:21 I will give t people favour in the sight of 2088
4:17 thou shalt take t rod in thine hand, 2088
5:22 hast thou so evil entreated t people? 2088
5:23 in thy name, he hath done evil to t people; 2088
7:17 In t thou shalt know that I am the LORD: 2088
7:23 neither did he set his heart to t also. 2063
8:19 said unto Pharaoh, T is the finger of God: 1931
8:23 and thy people: to morrow shall t sign be. 2088
8:32 Pharaoh hardened his heart at t time also, 2088
9: 5 To morrow the LORD shall do t thing in 2088
9:14 For I will at t time send all my plagues 2088
9:16 in very deed for t cause have I raised thee 2088
9:18 to morrow about t time I will cause it to rain NIH
9:27 and said unto them, I have sinned t time: NIH
10: 6 that they were upon the earth unto t day. 2088
10: 7 How long shall t man be a snare unto us? 2088
10:17 my sin only t once, and intreat the LORD NIH
10:17 that he may take away from me t death 2088
12: 2 T month shall be unto you the beginning of 2088
12: 3 In the tenth day of t month they shall take 2088
12:12 For I will pass through the land of Egypt t 2088
12:14 And t day shall be unto you for a memorial; 2088
12:17 for in t selfsame day have I brought your 2088
12:17 shall ye observe t day in your generations 2088
12:24 ye shall observe t thing for an ordinance to 2088
12:25 hath promised, that ye shall keep t service. 2088
12:26 say unto you, What mean you by t service? 2088
12:42 t is that night of the LORD to be observed 2088
12:43 Aaron, T is the ordinance of the passover. 2088
13: 3 said unto the people, Remember t day, 2088
13: 3 t place: there shall no leavened bread be 2088
13: 4 T day came ye out in the month Abib. NIH
13: 5 that thou shalt keep t service in this month. 2088
13: 5 that thou shalt keep this service in t month. 2088
13: 8 T is done because of that which the LORD NIH
13:10 keep t ordinance in his season from year to 2088
13:14 thee in time to come, saying, What is t? 2088
14: 5 they said, Why have we done t, that we 2088
14:12 Is not t the word that we did tell thee in 2088
15: 1 the children of Israel t song unto 2088
16: 3 for ye have brought us forth into t 2088
Ex 16: 3 to kill t whole assembly with hunger. 2088
16: 8 T shall be, when the LORD shall give you NIH
16:15 T is the bread which the LORD hath 1931
16:16 T is the thing which the LORD hath 2088
16:23 T is that which the LORD hath said, 1931
16:32 T is the thing which the LORD 2088
17: 3 Wherefore is t that thou hast brought us up 2088
17: 4 What shall I do unto t people? 2088
17:14 Write t for a memorial in a book, and 2088
18:14 What is t thing that thou doest to 2088
18:18 both thou, and t people that is with thee: 2088
18:18 for t thing is too heavy for thee; thou art not NIH
18:23 If thou shalt do t thing, and God command 2088
18:23 all t people shall also go to their place in 2088
21:31 according to t judgment shall it be done 2088
25: 3 t is the offering which ye shall take of 2088
26:13 over the sides of the tabernacle on t side 2088
28:17 and a carbuncle: t shall be the first row. NIH
29: 1 t is the thing that thou shalt do unto them to 2088
29:38 Now t is that which thou shalt offer upon 2088
29:42 T shall be a continual burnt offering NIH
30:13 T they shall give, every one that passeth 2088
30:31 T shall be a holy anointing oil unto me 2088
32: 1 for as for t Moses, the man that brought us 2088
32: 9 I have seen t people, and behold, it is a 2088
32:12 and repent of t evil against thy people. NIH
32:13 all t land that I have spoken of will I give 2088
32:21 What did t people unto thee, that thou hast 2088
32:23 for as for t Moses, the man that brought us 2088
32:24 it into the fire, and there came out t calf. 2088
32:29 that he may bestow upon you a blessing t NIH
32:31 t people have sinned a great sin, and 2088
33:12 thou sayest unto me, Bring up t people: 2088
33:13 and consider that t nation is thy people. 2088
33:17 I will do t thing also that thou hast spoken: 2088
34:11 Observe thou that which I command thee t NIH
35: 4 T is the thing which the LORD 2088
37: 8 One cherub on the end on t side, and 2088
38:15 on t hand and that hand, were hangings of 2088
38:21 T is the sum of the tabernacle, even of 428
39:10 a topaz, and a carbuncle: t was the first row. NIH
Lev 4:20 for a sin offering, so shall he do with t: 2050.2
6: 9 T is the law of the burnt offering: 2088
6:14 t is the law of the meat offering: the sons of 2088
6:20 T is the offering of Aaron and of his sons, 2088
6:25 T is the law of the sin offering: 2088
7: 1 Likewise t is the law of the trespass 2088
7:11 t is the law of the sacrifice of peace 2088
7:35 T is the portion of the anointing of Aaron, 2088
7:37 T is the law of the burnt offering, of 2088
8: 5 T is the thing which the LORD 2088
8:34 As he hath done t day, so the LORD hath 2088
9: 6 T is the thing which the LORD 2088
10: 3 T is it that the LORD spake, saying, 1931
10:19 t day have they offered their sin offering NIH
11:46 T is the law of the beasts, and of the fowl, 2088
12: 7 T is the law for her that hath born a male or 2088
13:59 T is the law of the plague of leprosy in a 2088
14: 2 T shall be the law of the leper in the day of 2088
14:32 T is the law of him in whom is the plague 2088
14:54 T is the law for all manner of plague of 2088
14:57 and when it is clean: t is the law of leprosy. 2088
15: 3 t shall be his uncleanness in his issue: 2088
15:32 T is the law of him that hath an issue, and 2088
16:29 t shall be a statute for ever unto you: that in NIH
16:34 t shall be an everlasting statute unto you, 2088
17: 2 T is the thing which the LORD hath 2088
17: 7 T shall be a statute for ever unto them 2088
23:27 Also on the tenth day of t seventh month 2088
23:34 The fifteenth day of t seventh month shall 2088
24:10 t son of the Israelitish woman and a man of NIH
25:13 In the year of t jubile ye shall return every 2088
26:16 I also will do t unto you; I will even 2088
26:18 if ye will not yet for all t hearken unto me, 428
26:27 And if ye will not for all t hearken unto me, 2088
Nu 4: 4 T shall be the service of the sons of Kohath 2088
4:24 T is the service of the families of 2088
4:28 T is the service of the families of the sons 2088
4:31 t is the charge of their burden, according to 2088
4:33 T is the service of the families of the sons 2088
5:19 be thou free from t bitter water that causeth 428
5:22 t water that causeth the curse shall go into 428
5:29 T is the law of jealousies, when a wife 2088
5:30 the priest shall execute upon her all t law. 2088
5:31 and t woman shall bear her iniquity. 1931
6:13 t is the law of the Nazarite, when the days 2088
6:20 t is holy for the priest, with the wave breast 1931
6:21 T is the law of the Nazarite who hath 2088
6:23 On t wise ye shall bless the children of 3541
7:17 t was the offering of Nahshon the son of 2088
7:23 t was the offering of Nethaneel the son of 2088
7:29 t was the offering of Eliab the son of 2088
7:35 t was the offering of Elizur the son of 2088
7:41 t was the offering of Shelumiel the son of 2088
7:47 t was the offering of Eliasaph the son of 2088
7:53 t was the offering of Elishama the son of 2088
7:59 t was the offering of Gamaliel the son of 2088
7:65 t was the offering of Abidan the son of 2088
7:71 t was the offering of Ahiezer the son of 2088
7:77 t was the offering of Pagiel the son of 2088
7:83 t was the offering of Ahira the son of Enan. 2088
7:84 T was the dedication of the altar, in the day 2088
7:88 T was the dedication of the altar, after that 2088
8: 4 t work of the candlestick was of beaten 2088
8:24 T is it that belongeth unto the Levites: 2088
9: 3 In the fourteenth day of t month, at even, 2088
11: 6 at all, beside t manna, before our eyes. NIH
11:11 that thou layest the burden of all t people 2088
11:12 Have I conceived all t people? have I 2088
11:13 I have flesh to give unto all t people? 2088
11:14 I am not able to bear all t people alone, 2088
11:31 as it were a day's journey on t side, and 3541
13:17 Get you up t way southward, and go up 2088
13:27 with milk and honey; and t is the fruit of it. 2088
14: 2 or would God we had died in t wilderness! 2088

T

Nu 14: 3 hath the LORD brought us unto t land, 2088
14: 8 he will bring us into t land, and give it us; 2088
14:11 How long will t people provoke me? 2088
14:13 t people in thy might from among them;) 2088
14:14 they will tell it to the inhabitants of t land: 2088
14:14 heard that thou LORD art among t people, 2088
14:15 Now if thou shalt kill all t people as one 2088
14:16 Because the LORD was not able to bring t 2088
14:19 the iniquity of t people according unto 2088
14:19 as thou hast forgiven t people, from Egypt 2088
14:27 How long shall I bear with t evil 2088
14:29 Your carcases shall fall in t wilderness; and 2088
14:32 they shall fall in t wilderness. 2088
14:35 I will surely do it unto all t evil 2088
14:35 in t wilderness they shall be consumed, and 2088
15:13 shall do these things after t manner, 3602
16: 6 T do; Take you censers, Korah, and all his 2088
16:21 Separate yourselves from among t 2088
16:45 Get you up from among t congregation, 2088
18: 9 T shall be thine of the most holy things, 2088
18:11 t is thine; the heave offering of their gift, 2088
18:27 t your heave offering shall be reckoned unto NIH
19: 2 T is the ordinance of the law which 2088
19:14 T is the law, when a man dieth in a tent: 2088
20: 4 of the LORD into t wilderness, 2088
20: 5 of Egypt, to bring us in unto t evil place? 2088
20:10 must we fetch you water out of t rock? 2088
20:12 ye shall not bring t congregation into 2088
20:13 T is the water of Meribah; because 1992
21: 2 If thou wilt indeed deliver t people into my 2088
21: 5 and our soul loatheth t light bread. NIH
21:17 Israel sang t song, Spring up, O well; 2088
22: 1 pitched in the plains of Moab on t side NIH
22: 4 Now shall t company lick up all that are NIH
22: 6 I pray thee, curse me t people; 2088
22: 8 Lodge here t night, and I will bring you NIH
22:17 I pray thee, curse me t people. 2088
22:19 I pray you, tarry ye also here t night, NIH
22:24 a wall being on t side, and a wall on that 2088
22:30 ridden ever since I was thine unto t day? 2088
23:23 according to t time it shall be said of Jacob NIH
24:14 I will advertise thee what t people shall do 2088
24:23 Alas, who shall live when God doeth t! 2050.2
26: 9 T is that Dathan and Abiram, which were 1931
27:12 Get thee up into t mount Abarim, and 2088
28: 3 T is the offering made by fire which ye 2088
28:10 T is the burnt offering of every sabbath, NIH
28:14 t is the burnt offering of every month 2088
28:17 in the fifteenth day of t month is the feast: 2088
28:24 After t manner ye shall offer daily, 428
29: 7 ye shall have on the tenth day of t seventh 2088
30: 1 T is the thing which the LORD hath 2088
31:21 T is the ordinance of the law which 2088
32: 5 let t land be given unto thy servants for a 2088
32:15 and ye shall destroy all t people. 2088
32:19 our inheritance is fallen to us on t side NIH
32:20 Moses said unto them, If ye will do t thing, 2088
32:22 t land shall be your possession before 2088
32:32 that the possession of our inheritance on t NIH
34: 2 (t is the land that shall fall unto you for an 2088
34: 6 for a border: t shall be your west border. 2088
34: 7 t shall be your north border: from the great 2088
34: 9 at Hazar-enan: t shall be your north border. 2088
34:12 t shall be your land with the coasts thereof 2088
34:13 T is the land which ye shall inherit by lot, 2088
34:15 on t side Jordan near Jericho eastward, NIH
35: 5 t shall be to them the suburbs of the cities. 2088
35:14 Ye shall give three cities on t side Jordan, NIH
36: 6 T is the thing which the LORD doth 2088
Dt 1: 1 all Israel on t side Jordan in the wilderness, NIH
1: 5 On t side Jordan, in the land of Moab, NIH
1: 5 began Moses to declare t law, saying, 2088
1: 6 Ye have dwelt long enough in t mount: 2088
1:10 you are t day as the stars of heaven for NIH
1:31 that ye went, until ye came into t place. 2088
1:32 Yet in t thing ye did not believe 2088
1:35 Surely there shall not one of these men of t 2088
2: 3 Ye have compassed t mountain long 2088
2: 7 he knoweth thy walking through t great 2088
2:18 over through Ar, the coast of Moab, t day: NIH
2:22 and dwelt in their stead even unto t day: 2088
2:25 T day will I begin to put the dread of thee 2088
2:30 him into thy hand, as appeareth t day. 2088
3: 8 Amorites the land that was on t side Jordan, NIH
3:12 t land, which we possessed at that time, 2088
3:14 own name, Bashan-havoth-jair, unto t day. 2088
3:18 The LORD your God hath given you t 2088
3:26 speak no more unto me of t matter. 2088
3:27 for thou shalt not go over t Jordan. 2088
3:28 for he shall go over before t people, and 2088
4: 4 your God are alive every one of you t day. NIH
4: 6 and do them; for t is your wisdom and 1931
4: 6 Surely t great nation is a wise and 2088
4: 8 and judgments so righteous as all t law, 2088
4: 8 as all this law, which I set before you t day? NIH
4:20 him a people of inheritance, as ye are t day. 2088
4:22 I must die in t land, I must not go over 2088
4:26 and earth to witness against you t day, NIH
4:32 whether there hath been any such thing as t 2088
4:38 their land for an inheritance, as it is t day. 2088
4:39 Know therefore t day, and consider it in NIH
4:40 which I command thee t day, NIH
4:41 Moses severed three cities on t side Jordan NIH
4:44 t is the law which Moses set before 2088
4:46 On t side Jordan, in the valley over against NIH
4:47 which were on t side Jordan toward NIH
4:49 all the plain on t side Jordan eastward, even NIH
5: 1 judgments which I speak in your ears t day, NIH
5: 3 The LORD made not t covenant with our 2088
5: 3 even us, who are all of us here alive t day. NIH
5:24 we have seen t day that God doth talk with 2088
5:25 for t great fire will consume us: if we hear 2088
5:28 I have heard the voice of the words of t 2088
6: 6 these words, which I command thee t day, NIH
6:24 he might preserve us alive, as it is at t day. 2088

Dt 7:11 which I command thee t day, to do them. NIH
8: 1 command thee t day shall ye observe to do, NIH
8:11 his statutes, which I command thee t day: NIH
8:17 the might of mine hand hath gotten me t 2088
8:18 he sware unto thy fathers, as it is t day. 2088
8:19 I testify against you t day that ye shall NIH
9: 1 Thou art to pass over Jordan t day, to go in NIH
9: 3 Understand therefore t day, that the LORD NIH
9: 4 hath brought me in to possess t land: 2088
9: 6 that the LORD thy God giveth thee not t 2088
9: 7 until ye came unto t place, ye have been 2088
9:13 saying, I have seen t people, and behold, 2088
9:27 look not unto the stubbornness of t people, 2088
10: 8 and to bless in his name, unto t day. 2088
10:13 which I command thee t day for thy good? NIH
10:15 even you above all people, as it is t day. 2088
11: 2 know you t day: for I speak not with your NIH
11: 4 LORD hath destroyed them unto t day; 2088
11: 5 the wilderness, until ye came into t place; 2088
11: 8 which I command you t day, NIH
11:13 which I command you t day, NIH
11:26 I set before you t day a blessing and a curse; NIH
11:27 your God, which I command you t day: NIH
11:28 out of the way which I command you t day, NIH
11:32 and judgments which I set before you t day. NIH
12: 8 do after all the things that we do here t day, NIH
13:11 shall do no more any such wickedness as t 2088
13:18 which I command thee t day, NIH
15: 2 t is the manner of the release: 2088
15: 5 which I command thee t day. NIH
15:10 that for t thing the LORD thy God shall 2088
15:15 I command thee t thing to day. 2088
17:18 that he shall write him a copy of t law in a 2088
17:19 to keep all the words of t law and 2088
18: 3 t shall be the priest's due from the people, 2088
18:16 neither let me see t great fire any more, 2088
19: 4 t is the case of the slayer, which shall flee 2088
19: 9 which I command thee t day, to love NIH
20: 3 you approach t day unto battle against your NIH
21: 7 and say, Our hands have not shed t blood, 2088
21:20 T our son is stubborn and rebellious, 2088
22:14 I took t woman, and when I came to her, 2088
22:16 I gave my daughter unto t man to wife, and 2088
22:20 if t thing be true, and the tokens of virginity 2088
22:26 and slayeth him, even so is t matter: 2088
24:18 I command thee to do t thing. 2088
24:22 I command thee to do t thing. 2088
26: 3 I profess t day unto the LORD thy God, NIH
26: 9 he hath brought us into t place, and 2088
26: 9 hath given us t land, even a land that 2088
26:16 T day the LORD thy God hath 2088
26:17 Thou hast avouched the LORD t day to be NIH
26:18 the LORD hath avouched thee t day to be NIH
27: 1 which I command you t day. NIH
27: 3 shalt write upon them all the words of t 2088
27: 4 which I command you t day, in mount Ebal, NIH
27: 8 stones all the words of t law very plainly. 2088
27: 9 t day thou art become the people of 2088
27:10 his statutes, which I command thee t day. NIH
27:26 not all the words of t law to do them. 2088
28: 1 which I command thee t day, NIH
28:13 which I command thee t day, to observe and NIH
28:14 of the words which I command thee t day, NIH
28:15 his statutes which I command thee t day; NIH
28:58 words of t law that are written in this book, 2088
28:58 words of this law that are written in t book, 2088
28:58 that thou mayest fear t glorious and fearful 2088
28:61 which is not written in the book of t law, 2088
29: 4 eyes to see, and ears to hear, unto t day. 2088
29: 7 when ye came unto t place, Sihon the king 2088
29: 9 Keep therefore the words of t covenant, 2088
29:10 Ye stand t day all of you before the LORD NIH
29:12 LORD thy God maketh with thee t day: NIH
29:14 Neither with you only do I make t covenant 2088
29:14 only do I make this covenant and t oath; 2088
29:15 with him that standeth here with us t day NIH
29:15 also with him that is not here with us t day: NIH
29:18 whose heart turneth away t day from NIH
29:19 when he heareth the words of t curse, 2088
29:20 all the curses that are written in t book shall 2088
29:21 that are written in t book of the law: 2088
29:24 hath the LORD done thus unto t land? 2088
29:24 what meaneth the heat of t great anger? 2088
29:27 of the LORD was kindled against t land, 1931
29:27 it all the curses that are written in t book: 2088
29:28 cast them into another land, as it is t day. 2088
29:29 that we may do all the words of t law. 2088
30: 2 according to all that I command thee t day, NIH
30: 8 which I command thee t day. NIH
30:10 his statutes which are written in t book of 2088
30:11 For t commandment which I command thee 2088
30:11 which I command thee t day, NIH
30:15 I have set before thee t day life and good, NIH
30:16 In that I command thee t day to love NIH
30:18 I denounce unto you t day, that ye shall NIH
30:19 and earth to record t day against you, NIH
31: 2 I am an hundred and twenty years old t day; NIH
31: 2 unto me, Thou shalt not go over t Jordan. 2088
31: 7 for thou must go with t people unto 2088
31: 9 Moses wrote t law, and delivered it unto 2088
31:11 thou shalt read t law before all Israel in 2088
31:12 and observe to do all the words of t law: 2088
31:16 t people will rise up, and go a whoring after 2088
31:19 Now therefore write ye t song for you, 2088
31:19 that t song may be a witness for me against 2088
31:21 that t song shall testify against them as a 2088
31:22 Moses therefore wrote t song the same day, 2088
31:24 end of writing the words of t law in a book, 2088
31:26 Take t book of the law, and put it in 2088
31:27 behold, while I am yet alive with you t day, NIH
31:30 congregation of Israel the words of t song, 2088
32:27 is high, and the LORD hath not done all t. 2088
32:29 that they were wise, that they understood t, 2088
32:34 Is not t laid up in store with me, and 1931
32:44 spake all the words of t song in the ears of 2088

Dt 32:46 the words which I testify among you t day, NIH
32:46 to observe to do, all the words of t law. 2088
32:47 through t thing ye shall prolong your days 2088
32:49 Get thee up into t mountain Abarim, 2088
33: 1 t is the blessing, wherewith Moses the man 2088
33: 7 t is the blessing of Judah: and he said, 2088
34: 4 T is the land which I sware unto Abraham, 2088
34: 6 no man knoweth of his sepulchre unto t 2088
Jos 1: 2 go over t Jordan, thou, and all this people, 2088
1: 2 go over this Jordan, thou, and all t people, 2088
1: 4 and t Lebanon even unto the great river, 2088
1: 6 for unto t people shalt thou divide for an 2088
1: 8 T book of the law shall not depart out of 2088
1:11 for within three days ye shall pass over t 2088
1:13 given you rest, and hath given you t land. 2088
1:14 which Moses gave you on t side Jordan; NIH
1:15 you on t side Jordan toward the sunrising. NIH
2:14 life for yours, if ye utter not t our business. 2088
2:17 We will be blameless of t thine oath which 2088
2:18 thou shalt bind t line of scarlet thread in 2088
2:20 if thou utter t our business, then we will be 2088
3: 4 for ye have not passed t way heretofore. NIH
3: 7 T day will I begin to magnify thee in 2088
4: 3 where you shall lodge t night. NIH
4: 6 That t may be a sign among you, that when 2088
4: 9 and they are there unto t day. 2088
4:22 Israel came over t Jordan on dry land. 2088
5: 4 t is the cause why Joshua did circumcise: 2088
5: 9 T day have I rolled away the reproach of NIH
5: 9 of the place is called Gilgal unto t day. 2088
6:25 she dwelleth in Israel even unto t day; 2088
6:26 that riseth up and buildeth t city Jericho: 2088
7: 7 wherefore hast thou at all brought t people 2088
7:25 the LORD shall trouble thee t day. And all 2088
7:26 over him a great heap of stones unto t day. 2088
7:26 was called, The valley of Achor, unto t day. 2088
8:20 they had no power to flee t way or 2008
8:22 some on t side, and some on that side: 2088
8:28 heap for ever, even a desolation unto t day. 2088
8:29 heap of stones, that remaineth unto t day. 2088
8:33 stood on t side the ark and on that side 2088
9: 1 when all the kings which were on t side NIH
9:12 T our bread we took hot for our provision 2088
9:20 T we will do to them; we will even let them 2088
9:24 because of you, and have done t thing. 2088
9:27 the altar of the LORD, even unto t day, 2088
10:13 Is not t written in the book of Jasher? 1931
10:27 which remain until t very day. 2088
11: 6 for to morrow about t time will I deliver 2088
12: 7 the children of Israel smote on t side Jordan NIH
13: 2 T is the land that yet remaineth: all 2088
13: 7 divide t land for an inheritance unto 2088
13:13 dwell among the Israelites until t day.) 2088
13:23 the border thereof. T was the inheritance of 2088
13:28 T is the inheritance of the children of Gad 2088
13:29 t was the possession of the half tribe of NIH
14:10 even since the LORD spake t word unto 2088
14:10 I am t day fourscore and five years old. NIH
14:11 As yet I am as strong t day as I was in NIH
14:12 Now therefore give me t mountain, 2088
14:14 son of Jephunneh the Kenezite unto t day, 2088
15: 1 T then was the lot of the tribe of NIH
15: 4 were at the sea: t shall be your south coast. 2088
15:12 the coast thereof. T is the coast of 2088
15:20 T is the inheritance of the tribe of 2088
15:63 children of Judah at Jerusalem unto t day. 2088
16: 8 T is the inheritance of the tribe of 2088
16:10 dwell among the Ephraimites unto t day, 2088
18:14 children of Judah: t was the west quarter. 2088
18:19 south end of Jordan: t was the south coast. 2088
18:20 T was the inheritance of the children of 2088
18:28 T is the inheritance of the children of 2088
19: 8 T is the inheritance of the tribe of 2088
19:16 T is the inheritance of the children of 2088
19:23 T is the inheritance of the tribe of 2088
19:31 T is the inheritance of the tribe of 2088
19:39 T is the inheritance of the tribe of 2088
19:48 T is the inheritance of the tribe of 2088
22: 3 your brethren these many days unto t day, 2088
22: 7 their brethren on t side Jordan westward. NIH
22:16 What trespass is t that ye have committed 2088
22:16 to turn away t day from following NIH
22:16 that ye might rebel t day against NIH
22:17 from which we are not cleansed until t day, 2088
22:18 that ye must turn away t day from following NIH
22:22 against the LORD, (save us not t day,) 2088
22:24 if we have not rather done it for fear of t NIH
22:29 turn t day from following the LORD, NIH
22:31 T day we perceive that the LORD is NIH
22:31 ye have not committed t trespass against 2088
23: 8 your God, as ye have done unto t day. 2088
23: 9 been able to stand before you unto t day. 2088
23:13 until ye perish from off t good land which 2088
23:14 t day I am going the way of all the earth: NIH
23:15 until he have destroyed you from off t good 2088
24:15 choose you t day whom you will serve; NIH
24:27 Behold, t stone shall be a witness unto us; 2088
Jdg 1:21 of Benjamin in Jerusalem unto t day. 2088
1:26 which is the name thereof unto t day. 2088
2: 2 no league with the inhabitants of t land; 2088
2: 2 not obeyed my voice: why have ye done t? 2088
2:20 Because that t people hath transgressed my 2088
4:14 for t is the day in which the LORD hath 2088
6:13 be with us, why then is all t befallen us? 2088
6:14 Go in t thy might, and thou shalt save Israel 2088
6:20 and lay them upon t rock, 1975
6:24 unto t day it is yet in Ophrah of 2088
6:26 the LORD thy God upon the top of t rock, 2088
6:29 said one to another, Who hath done t thing? 2088
6:29 Gideon the son of Joash hath done t thing. 2088
6:39 hot against me, and I will speak but t once: NIH
6:39 I pray thee, but t once with the fleece; NIH
7: 4 T shall go with thee, the same shall go with 2088
7: 4 T shall not go with thee, the same shall not 2088
7:14 T is nothing else save the sword of Gideon 2088

Jdg 8: 9 again in peace, I will break down t tower. 2088
9:18 ye are risen up against my father's house t NIH
9:19 with Jerubbaal and with his house t day, 2088
9:29 would to God t people were under my 2088
9:38 is not t the people that thou hast despised? 2088
10: 4 which are called Havoth-jair unto t day, 2088
10:15 deliver us only, we pray thee, t day. 2088
11:27 the LORD the Judge be judge t day NIH
11:37 unto her father, Let t thing be done for me: 2088
12: 3 are ye come up unto me t day, 2088
13:23 at t time have told us such things as these. NIH
15: 6 the Philistines said, Who hath done t? 2088
15: 7 Though ye have done t, yet will I be 2063
15:11 what is t that thou hast done unto us? 2088
15:18 Thou hast given t great deliverance into 2088
15:19 which is in Lehi unto t day. 2088
16:18 saying, Come up t once, for he hath shewed NIH
16:28 I pray thee, only t once, O God, 2088
18: 3 what makest thou in t place? and what hast 2088
18:12 called that place Mahaneh-dan unto t day: 2088
18:24 what is t that ye say unto me, What aileth 2088
19:11 and let us turn in into t city of the Jebusites, 2088
19:23 seeing that t man is come into mine house, 2088
19:23 is come into mine house, do not t folly. 2088
19:24 but unto t man do not so vile a thing. 2088
19:30 up out of the land of Egypt unto t day: 2088
20: 3 of Israel, Tell us, how was t wickedness? 2088
20: 9 now t shall be the thing which we will do 2088
20:12 What wickedness is t that is done among 2088
20:16 Among all t people there were seven 2088
21: 3 of Israel, why is t come to pass in Israel, 2088
21: 6 There is one tribe cut off from Israel t day. NIH
21:11 t is the thing that ye shall do, Ye shall 2088
21:22 for ye did not give unto them at t time, NIH
Ru 1:19 about them, and they said, Is t Naomi? 2088
2: 5 set over the reapers, Whose damsel is t? 2088
3:13 Tarry t night, and it shall be in the morning, NIH
3:18 until he have finished the thing t day. NIH
4: 7 Now t was the manner in former time in 2088
4: 7 and t was a testimony in Israel. 2088
4: 9 unto all the people, Ye are witnesses t day, NIH
4:10 the gate of his place: ye are witnesses t day. NIH
4:12 LORD shall give thee of t young woman. 2088
4:14 which hath not left thee t day without a NIH
1Sa 1: 3 t man went up out of his city yearly to 1931
1:27 For t child I prayed; and the LORD hath 2088
2:20 The LORD give thee seed of t woman for 2088
2:23 for I hear of your evil dealings by all t 428
2:34 t shall be a sign unto thee, that shall come 2088
4: 6 What meaneth the noise of t great shout in 2088
4:14 What meaneth the noise of t tumult? 2088
5: 5 threshold of Dagon in Ashdod unto t day. 2088
6: 9 then he hath done us t great evil: 2088
6:18 which stone remaineth unto t day in 2088
6:20 Who is able to stand before t holy LORD 2088
8: 8 them up out of Egypt even unto t day, 2088
8:11 T will be the manner of the king that shall 2088
9: 6 there is in t city a man of God, and he is an 2088
9:13 you up; for about t time ye shall find him. NIH
9:16 To morrow about t time I will send thee a NIH
9:17 thee of: t same shall reign over my people. 2088
9:24 for unto t time hath it been kept for thee NIH
10:11 What is t that is come unto the son of Kish? 2088
10:19 ye have t day rejected your God, NIH
10:27 of Belial said, How shall t man save us? 2088
11: 2 On t condition will I make a covenant with 2063
11:13 There shall not a man be put to death t day: 2088
12: 2 before you from my childhood unto t day. 2088
12: 5 and his anointed is witness t day, 2088
12: 8 of Egypt, and made them dwell in t place. 2088
12:16 Now therefore stand and see t great thing, 2088
12:19 for we have added unto all our sins t evil, NIH
12:20 ye have done all t wickedness: yet turn not 2088
14:10 into our hand: and t shall be a sign unto us. 2088
14:28 Cursed be the man that eateth any food t NIH
14:29 because I tasted a little of t honey. 2088
14:33 roll a great stone unto me t day. NIH
14:38 and see wherein t sin hath been this day. 2088
14:38 and see wherein this sin hath been t day. NIH
14:45 who hath wrought t great salvation in 2088
14:45 for he hath wrought with God t day. 2088
15:14 then t bleating of the sheep in mine ears, 2088
15:16 what the LORD hath said to me t night. NIH
15:28 rent the kingdom of Israel from thee t day, NIH
16: 8 he said, Neither hath the LORD chosen t. 2088
16: 9 he said, Neither hath the LORD chosen t. 2088
16:12 LORD said, Arise, anoint him: for t is he. 2088
17:10 I defy the armies of Israel t day; 2088
17:17 Take now for thy brethren an ephah of t 2088
17:25 Have ye seen t man that is come up? 2088
17:26 What shall be done to the man that killeth t 1975
17:26 for who is t uncircumcised Philistine, that 2088
17:27 the people answered him after t manner, 2088
17:32 servant will go and fight with t Philistine. 2088
17:33 Thou art not able to go against t Philistine 2088
17:36 t uncircumcised Philistine shall be as one 2088
17:37 he will deliver me out of the hand of t 2088
17:46 T day will the LORD deliver thee into 2088
17:46 Philistines t day unto the fowls of the air, 2088
17:47 all t assembly shall know that the LORD 2088
17:55 of the host, Abner, whose son is t youth? 2088
18:21 Thou shalt t day be my son in law in the one NIH
18:24 told him, saying, On t manner spake David. 428
20: 2 why should my father hide t thing from 2088
20: 3 he saith, Let not Jonathan know t, lest he be 2088
20:21 Behold, the arrows are on t side of thee, 2008
21: 5 though it were sanctified t day in the vessel. NIH
21:11 Is not t David the king of the land? 2088
21:15 that ye have brought t fellow to play 2088
21:15 shall t fellow come into my house? 2088
22: 8 against me, to lie in wait, as at t day? 2088
22:13 rise against me, to lie in wait, as at t day? 2088
22:15 for thy servant knew nothing of all t, less or 2088
23:26 Saul went on t side of the mountain, and 2088
24: 6 The LORD forbid that I should do t thing 2088
1Sa 24:10 t day thine eyes have seen how that 2088
24:16 that Saul said, Is t thy voice, my son 2088
24:18 thou hast shewed t day how that thou hast NIH
24:19 good for that thou hast done unto me t day. 2088
25:21 Surely in vain have I kept all that t fellow 2088
25:24 upon me let t iniquity be: and let thine NIH
25:25 I pray thee, regard t man of Belial, 2088
25:27 now t blessing which thine handmaid hath 2088
25:31 That t shall be no grief unto thee, 2088
25:32 of Israel, which sent thee t day to meet me: 2088
25:33 which hast kept me t day from coming to 2088
26: 8 delivered thine enemy into thine hand t day: NIH
26:16 T thing is not good that thou hast done. 2088
26:17 and said, Is t thy voice, my son David? 2088
26:19 for they have driven me out t day from NIH
26:21 my soul was precious in thine eyes t day: 2088
26:24 as thy life was much set by t day in mine 2088
27: 6 unto the kings of Judah unto t day. 2088
28:10 no punishment happen to thee for t thing. 2088
28:18 hath the LORD done t thing unto thee this 2088
28:18 hath the LORD done this thing unto thee t 2088
29: 3 Is not t David, the servant of Saul the king 2088
29: 3 in him since he fell unto me unto t day? 2088
29: 4 Make t fellow return, that he may go again NIH
29: 5 Is not t David, of whom they sang one to 2088
29: 6 the day of thy coming unto me unto t day: 2088
29: 8 so long as I have been with thee unto t day, 2088
30: 8 Shall I pursue after t troop? 2088
30:15 Canst thou bring me down to t company? 2088
30:15 and I will bring thee down to t company. 2088
30:20 other cattle, and said, T is David's spoil. 2088
30:24 For who will hearken unto you in t matter? 2088
30:25 and an ordinance for Israel unto t day. 2088
2Sa 1:17 David lamented with t lamentation over 2088
2: 1 it came to pass after t, that David inquired 3651
2: 5 that ye have shewed t kindness unto your 2088
2: 6 I also will requite you t kindness, because 2088
2: 6 this kindness, because ye have done t thing. 2088
3: 8 which against Judah do shew kindness t day NIH
3: 8 me to day with a fault concerning t woman? NIH
3:38 and a great man fallen t day in Israel? 2088
3:39 And I am t day weak, though anointed king; NIH
4: 3 and were sojourners there until t day.) 2088
4: 8 LORD hath avenged my lord the king t 2088
6: 8 the name of the place Perez-uzzah to t day. 2088
7: 6 even to t day, but have walked in a tent and 2088
7:17 according to all t vision, so did Nathan 2088
7:19 t was yet a small thing in thy sight, O Lord 2088
7:19 is t the manner of man, O Lord GOD? 2088
7:27 hath thy servant found in his heart to pray t 2088
7:28 thou hast promised t goodness unto thy 2088
8: 1 after t it came to pass, that David smote 3651
10: 1 it came to pass after t, that the king of 3651
11: 3 one said, Is not t Bath-sheba, the daughter 2088
11:11 and as thy soul liveth, I will not do t thing. 2088
11:25 unto Joab, Let not t thing displease thee, 2088
12: 5 the man that hath done t thing shall surely 2088
12: 6 because he did t thing, and because he had 2088
12:11 he shall lie with thy wives in the sight of t 2088
12:12 I will do t thing before all Israel, and 2088
12:14 by t deed thou hast given great occasion to 2088
12:21 What thing is t that thou hast done? 2088
13: 1 it came to pass after t, that Absalom the son 3651
13:12 to be done in Israel: do not thou t folly. 2088
13:16 t evil in sending me away is greater than 1886.1
13:17 Put now t woman out from me, and bolt 2088
13:20 he is thy brother; regard not t thing. So 2088
13:32 for by the appointment of Absalom t hath NIH
14: 3 the king, and speak on t manner unto him. 2088
14:13 for the king doth speak t thing as one which 2088
14:15 that I am come to speak of t thing unto my 2088
14:19 Is not the hand of Joab with thee in all t? 2088
14:20 To fetch about t form of speech hath thy NIH
14:20 speech hath thy servant Joab done t thing: 2088
14:21 unto Joab, Behold now, I have done t thing: 2088
15: 1 it came to pass after t, that Absalom 3651
15: 6 on t manner did Absalom to all Israel that 2088
15:20 should I t day make thee go up and NIH
16: 9 Why should t dead dog curse my lord 2088
16:11 how much more now may t Benjamite do NIH
16:12 will requite me good for his cursing t day. 2088
16:17 to Hushai, Is t thy kindness to thy friend? 2088
16:18 t people, and all the men of Israel, choose, 2088
17: 1 I will arise and pursue after David t night: NIH
17: 6 Ahithophel hath spoken after t manner: 2088
17: 7 Ahithophel hath given is not good at t time. 2088
17:16 Lodge not t night in the plains of NIH
18:18 and it is called unto t day, Absalom's place. 2088
18:20 Thou shalt not bear tidings t day, but 2088
18:20 but t day thou shalt bear no tidings, because 2088
18:31 for the LORD hath avenged thee t day of NIH
19: 5 Thou hast shamed t day the faces of all thy NIH
19: 5 which t day have saved thy life, and NIH
19: 6 for thou hast declared t day, that thou NIH
19: 6 for t day I perceive, that if Absalom had NIH
19: 6 all we had died t day, then it had pleased NIH
19: 7 there will not tarry one with thee t night: NIH
19:14 so that they sent t word unto the king, NIH
19:20 I am come the first t day of all the house of NIH
19:21 said, Shall not Shimei be put to death for t, 2088
19:22 that ye should t day be adversaries unto me? NIH
19:22 shall there any man be put to death t day in NIH
19:22 for do not I know that I am t day king over NIH
19:35 I am t day fourscore years old: and can I NIH
19:42 wherefore then be ye angry for t matter? 2088
21:18 it came to pass after t, that there was again 3651
22: 1 spake unto the LORD the words of t 2088
23: 5 for t is all my salvation, and all my desire, NIH
23:17 far from me, O LORD, that I should do t: 2088
23:17 is not t the blood of the men that went in NIH
24: 3 why doth my lord the king delight in t 2088
1Ki 1:25 For he is gone down t day, and hath slain NIH
1:27 Is t thing done by my lord the king, and 2088
1:30 my stead; even so will I certainly do t day. 2088
1:41 Wherefore is t noise of the city being in an NIH
2Sa 1:45 T is the noise that ye have heard. 1931
1:48 which hath given one to sit on my throne t NIH
2:23 if Adonijah have not spoken t word against 2088
2:24 Adonijah shall be put to death t day. NIH
2:26 I will not at t time put thee to death, 2088
3: 6 thou hast kept for him t great kindness, that 2088
3: 6 him a son to sit on his throne, as it is t day. 2088
3: 9 for who is able to judge t thy so great a 2088
3:10 the Lord, that Solomon had asked t thing. 2088
3:11 Because thou hast asked t thing, and 2088
3:17 my lord, I and t woman dwell in one house; 2088
3:18 that t woman was delivered also: 2088
3:19 t woman's child died in the night; because 2088
3:22 t said, No; but the dead is thy son, and 2088
3:23 T is my son that liveth, and thy son is 2088
4:24 For he had dominion over all the region on t NIH
4:24 over all the kings on t side the river: NIH
5: 7 and said, Blessed be the LORD t day, NIH
5: 7 unto David a wise son over t great people. 2088
6:12 Concerning t house which thou art in 2088
7: 8 whom he had taken to wife, like unto t 2088
7:28 the work of the bases was on t manner: 2088
7:37 After t manner he made the ten bases: all of 2088
8: 8 seen without: and there they are unto t day. 2088
8:24 fulfilled it with thine hand, as it is t day. 2088
8:27 how much less t house that I have builded? 2088
8:29 That thine eyes may be open toward t 2088
8:29 thy servant shall make towards t place. 2088
8:30 when they shall pray towards t place: 2088
8:31 the oath come before thine altar in t house: 2088
8:33 and make supplication unto thee in t house: 2088
8:35 if they pray towards t place, and 2088
8:38 and spread forth his hands towards t house: 2088
8:42 he shall come and pray towards t house; 2088
8:43 that they may know that t house, which I 2088
8:54 had made an end of praying all t prayer 2088
8:61 and to keep his commandments, as at t day. 2088
9: 3 I have hallowed t house, which thou hast 2088
9: 7 t house, which I have hallowed for my NIH
9: 8 at t house, which is high, every one that 2088
9: 8 Why hath the LORD done thus unto t 2088
9: 8 done thus unto this land, and to t house? 2088
9: 9 hath the LORD brought upon them all t 2088
9:13 he called them the land of Cabul unto t day. 2088
9:15 t is the reason of the levy which king 2088
9:21 levy a tribute of bondservice unto t day. 2088
10:12 such almug trees, nor were seen unto t day. 2088
11:10 had commanded him concerning t thing, 2088
11:11 Forasmuch as t is done of thee, and 2088
11:27 t was the cause that he lift up his hand 2088
11:39 I will for t afflict the seed of David, but 2088
12: 6 How do you advise that I may answer t 2088
12: 7 If thou wilt be a servant unto t people this 2088
12: 7 If thou wilt be a servant unto this people t NIH
12: 9 What counsel give ye that we may answer t 2088
12:10 Thus shalt thou speak unto t people that 2088
12:19 against the house of David unto t day. 2088
12:24 man to his house; for t thing is from me. 2088
12:27 If t people go up to do sacrifice in 2088
12:27 shall the heart of t people turn again unto 2088
12:30 t thing became a sin: for the people went to 2088
13: 3 T is the sign which the LORD hath 2088
13: 8 neither will I eat bread nor drink water in t 2088
13:16 bread nor drink water with thee in t place: 2088
13:33 After t thing Jeroboam returned not from 2088
13:34 t thing became sin unto the house of 2088
14: 2 which told me that I should be king over t 2088
14:15 he shall root up Israel out of t good land, 2088
17:21 let t child's soul come into him again. 2088
17:24 Now by t I know that thou art a man of 2088
18:36 let it be known t day that thou art God in NIH
18:37 that t people may know that thou art 2088
19: 2 of one of them by to morrow about t time. NIH
20: 6 servants unto thee to morrow about t time, NIH
20: 7 and see how t man seeketh mischief: 2088
20: 9 t thing I may not do. And the messengers 2088
20:12 when Ben-hadad heard t message, as he 2088
20:13 Hast thou seen all t great multitude? 2088
20:13 I will deliver it into thine hand t day; NIH
20:24 do t thing, Take the kings away, every man 2088
20:28 will I deliver all t great multitude into thine 2088
20:34 said Ahab, I will send thee away with t NIH
20:39 a man unto me, and said, Keep t man: 2088
22:20 one said on t manner, and another said on 3541
22:27 Put t fellow in the prison, and feed him 2088
2Ki 1: 2 Ekron whether I shall recover of t disease. 2088
2:19 I pray thee, the situation of t city is pleasant, NIH
2:22 So the waters were healed unto t day, 2088
3:16 the LORD, Make t valley full of ditches. 2088
3:18 t is but a light thing in the sight of 2088
3:23 they said, T is blood: the kings are surely 2088
4: 9 I perceive that t is a holy man of God, 1931
4:12 to Gehazi his servant, Call t Shunammite. 2088
4:13 thou hast been careful for us with all t care; 2088
4:16 he said, About t season, according to 2088
4:36 called Gehazi, and said, Call t Shunammite. 2088
4:43 should I set t before an hundred men? 2088
5: 6 Now when t letter is come unto thee, 2088
5: 7 that t man doth send unto me to recover a 2088
5:18 In t thing the LORD pardon thy servant, 2088
5:18 the LORD pardon thy servant in t thing. 2088
5:20 my master hath spared Naaman t Syrian, 2088
6:11 king of Syria was sore troubled for t thing; 2088
6:18 said, Smite t people, I pray thee, 2088
6:19 T is not the way, neither is this the city: 2088
6:19 This is not the way, neither is t the city: 2090
6:24 it came to pass after t, that Ben-hadad king 3651
6:28 T woman said unto me, Give thy son, 2088
6:31 the son of Shaphat shall stand on him t day. NIH
6:32 See ye how t son of a murderer hath sent to 2088
6:33 he said, Behold, t evil is of the LORD; 2088
7: 1 To morrow about t time shall a measure of NIH
7: 2 make windows in heaven, might t thing be? 2088
7: 9 t day is a day of good tidings, and we hold 2088
7:18 shall be to morrow about t time in the gate NIH

T

Book	Ref	Text	Strong's
2Ki	8: 5	O king, t *is* the woman, and this *is* her son,	2088
	8: 5	O king, this *is* the woman, and t *is* her son,	2088
	8: 8	by him, saying, Shall I recover of t disease?	2088
	8: 9	to thee, saying, Shall I recover of t disease?	2088
	8:13	a dog, that he should do t great thing?	2088
	8:22	from under the hand of Judah unto t day.	2088
	9: 1	take t box of oil in thine hand, and go *to*	2088
	9:11	wherefore came t mad *fellow* to thee?	2088
	9:25	the LORD laid t burden upon him;	2088
	9:26	I will requite thee in t plat, saith	2088
	9:27	when Ahaziah the king of Judah saw *t*, he	NIH
	9:34	Go, see now t cursed *woman*, and bury her:	2088
	9:36	he said, T *is* the word of the LORD,	1931
	9:37	*so* that they shall not say, T *is* Jezebel.	2088
	10: 2	Now as soon as t letter cometh to you,	2088
	10: 6	come to me to Jezreel by to morrow *t* time.	NIH
	10:27	and made it a draught house unto *t* day.	NIH
	11: 5	saying, T *is* the thing that ye shall do;	2088
	14: 7	called the name of it Joktheel unto t day.	2088
	14:10	glory *of t*, and tarry at home: for why	NIH
	15:12	T *was* the word of the LORD which he	1931
	16: 6	came *to* Elath, and dwelt there unto t day.	2088
	17:12	had said unto them, Ye shall not do t thing.	2088
	17:23	out of their own land to Assyria unto t day.	2088
	17:34	Unto t day they do after the former	2088
	17:41	as did their fathers, *so* do they unto t day.	2088
	18:19	What confidence *is* t where*in* thou trustest?	2088
	18:21	thou trustest upon the staff of t bruised	2088
	18:22	Ye shall worship before t altar in	2088
	18:25	the LORD against t place to destroy it?	2088
	18:25	to me, Go up against t land, and destroy it.	2088
	18:30	t city shall not be delivered into the hand of	2088
	19: 3	T day *is* a day of trouble, and of rebuke,	2088
	19:21	T *is* the word that the LORD hath spoken	2088
	19:29	t *shall be* a sign unto thee, Ye shall eat *this*	2088
	19:29	Ye shall eat *t* year such things as grow of	NIH
	19:31	the zeal of the LORD *of hosts* shall do t.	2088
	19:32	He shall not come into t city, nor shoot an	2088
	19:33	into t city, saith the LORD.	2088
	19:34	For I will defend t city, to save it, for mine	2088
	20: 6	t city out of the hand of the king of	2088
	20: 6	I will defend t city for mine own sake, and	2088
	20: 9	T sign shalt thou have of the LORD,	2088
	20:17	thy fathers have laid up in store unto t day,	2088
	21: 7	his son, In t house, and in Jerusalem,	2088
	21:15	came forth out of Egypt, even unto t day.	2088
	22:13	concerning the words of t book that is	2088
	22:13	not hearkened unto the words of t book,	2088
	22:16	I will bring evil upon t place, and upon	2088
	22:17	my wrath shall be kindled against t place,	2088
	22:19	when thou heardest what I spake against t	2088
	22:20	all the evil which I will bring upon t place.	2088
	23: 3	to perform the words of t covenant that	2088
	23: 3	of this covenant that were written in t book.	2088
	23:21	as it is written in the book of t covenant.	2088
	23:23	*wherein* t passover was holden to	2088
	23:27	will cast off t city Jerusalem which I have	2088
	24: 3	of the LORD came *t* upon Judah,	NIH
1Ch	4:41	destroyed them utterly unto t day, and	2088
	4:43	were escaped, and dwelt there unto t day.	2088
	5:26	Hara, and to the river Gozan, unto t day.	2088
	11:11	t *is* the number of the mighty *men* whom	428
	11:19	that *I* should do t *thing*: shall I drink	2063
	13:11	that place is called Perez-uzza to t	2088
	16: 7	on that day David delivered first *t psalm* to	NIH
	17: 5	the day that I brought up Israel unto t day;	2088
	17:15	according to all t vision, so did Nathan	2088
	17:17	*yet* t was a small thing in thine eyes,	2088
	17:19	own heart, hast thou done all t greatness,	2088
	17:26	hast promised t goodness unto thy servant:	2088
	18: 1	Now after t it came to pass, that David	3651
	19: 1	Now it came to pass after t, that Nahash	3651
	20: 4	it came to pass after t, that there arose war	3651
	21: 3	doth my lord require t *thing*? why will he	2088
	21: 7	God was displeased with t thing; therefore	2088
	21: 8	sinned greatly, because I have done t thing:	2088
	21:22	Grant me the place of *t* threshingfloor,	NIH
	22: 1	T *is* the house of the LORD God, and	2088
	22: 1	t *is* the altar of the burnt offering for Israel.	2088
	26:30	*were* officers among them of Israel on *t* side	NIH
	27: 6	T *is that* Benaiah, *who was* mighty among	1931
	28: 7	and my judgments, as at t day.	2088
	28: 8	that ye may possess *t* good land, and	NIH
	28:19	All *t*, *said David*, the LORD made me	NIH
	28:19	upon me, *even* all the works of *t* pattern.	NIH
	29: 5	is willing to consecrate his service *t* day	NIH
	29:14	willingly after t *sort*? for all *things come* of	2088
	29:16	all t store that we have prepared to build	2088
	29:18	keep t for ever in the imagination of	2088
2Ch	1:10	I may go out and come in before t people:	2088
	1:10	for who can judge t thy people, *that is so*	2088
	1:11	Because t was in thine heart, and thou hast	2088
	2: 4	T *is an ordinance* for ever to Israel.	2088
	5: 9	not seen without. And there it is unto t day.	2088
	6:15	fulfilled *it* with thine hand, as *it is* t day.	2088
	6:18	how much less t house which I have built?	2088
	6:20	That thine eyes may be open upon t house	2088
	6:20	which thy servant prayeth towards t place.	2088
	6:21	which they shall make towards t place:	2088
	6:22	the oath come before thine altar in t house;	2088
	6:24	make supplication before thee in t house;	2088
	6:26	*yet* if they pray towards t place,	2088
	6:29	and shall spread forth his hands in t house:	2088
	6:32	out arm; if they come and pray in t house;	2088
	6:33	may know that t house which I have built is	2088
	6:34	they pray unto thee toward t city which	2088
	6:40	unto the prayer *that is made* in t place.	2088
	7:12	have chosen t place to myself for a house	2088
	7:15	unto the prayer *that is made* in t place.	2088
	7:16	now have I chosen and sanctified t house,	2088
	7:20	t house, which I have sanctified for my	2088
	7:21	t house, which is high, shall be an	2088
	7:21	Why hath the LORD done thus unto t	2088
	7:21	done thus unto this land, and unto t house?	2088
	7:22	hath he brought all t evil upon them.	2088
2Ch	8: 8	did Solomon make to pay tribute until t	2088
	10: 6	give ye *me* to return answer to t people?	2088
	10: 7	If thou be kind to t people, and	2088
	10: 9	ye that we may return answer to t people,	2088
	10:19	against the house of David unto t day.	2088
	11: 4	man to his house, for t thing is done of me.	2088
	14:11	and in thy name we go against t multitude.	2088
	16:10	of t *thing*. And Asa oppressed *some* of	2088
	18:19	one spake saying **after t manner**, and	3602
	18:26	Put t *fellow in* the prison, and feed him	2088
	19:10	t do, and ye shall not trespass.	3541
	20: 1	It came to pass after t also, *that* the children	3651
	20: 2	thee from beyond the sea on t side Syria;	NIH
	20: 7	who didst drive out the inhabitants of t land	2088
	20: 9	we stand before t house, and in thy	2088
	20: 9	thy presence, (for thy name *is* in t house,)	2088
	20:12	for we have no might against t great	2088
	20:15	Be not afraid nor dismayed by reason of t	2088
	20:17	Ye shall not need to fight in t *battle*: set	2063
	20:26	The valley of Berachah, unto *t* day.	NIH
	20:35	after t did Jehoshaphat king of Judah join	3651
	21:10	from under the hand of Judah unto t day.	2088
	21:18	after all t the LORD smote him in his	2088
	23: 4	T *is* the thing that ye shall do; A third *part*	2088
	24: 4	it came to pass after t, *that* Joash was	3651
	24:18	and Jerusalem for t their trespass.	2088
	25: 9	is able to give thee much more than t.	2088
	25:16	because thou hast done t, and hast not	2088
	28:22	against the LORD: t *is that* king Ahaz.	1931
	29: 9	and our wives *are* in captivity for t.	2088
	29:28	all *t continued* until the burnt offering was	NIH
	30: 9	so that *they shall* come again into t land:	2088
	31: 1	Now when all t was finished, all Israel that	2088
	31:10	and that which is left *is* t great store.	2088
	32: 9	After t did Sennacherib king of Assyria	2088
	32:15	nor persuade you on t *manner*, neither yet	2088
	32:20	for t *cause* Hezekiah the king, and	2088
	32:30	**T same** Hezekiah also stopped the upper	1931
	33: 7	his son, In t house, and in Jerusalem,	2088
	33:14	Now after t he built a wall without the city	3651
	34:21	to do after all that is written in t book.	2088
	34:24	I will bring evil upon t place, and upon	2088
	34:25	my wrath shall be poured out upon t place,	2088
	34:27	when thou heardest his words against t	2088
	34:28	all the evil that I will bring upon t place,	2088
	34:31	of the covenant which are written in t book.	2088
	35:19	of the reign of Josiah was t passover kept.	2088
	35:20	After all t, when Josiah had prepared	2088
	35:21	*I come* not against thee *t* day, but	NIH
	35:25	of Josiah in their lamentations to *t* day,	NIH
Ezr	1: 9	t *is* the number of them: thirty chargers of	428
	3:12	when the foundation of t house was laid	2088
	4: 8	Jerusalem to Artaxerxes the king **in t sort**:	3660
	4:10	the rest *that are on t* side the river, and	NIH
	4:11	T *is* the copy of the letter that they sent	1836
	4:11	Thy servants the men *on t* side the river,	NIH
	4:13	if t city be builded, and the walls set up	1791
	4:15	and know that t city *is* a rebellious city, and	1791
	4:15	for which *cause* was t city destroyed.	1791
	4:16	if t city be builded *again*, and the walls	1791
	4:16	by t means thou shalt have no portion on	1836
	4:16	shalt have no portion on *t* side the river.	NIH
	4:19	it is found that t city of old time hath made	1791
	4:21	*that* t city be not builded, until *another*	1791
	4:22	Take heed now that ye fail not to do t: why	1836
	5: 3	governor on *t* side the river, and	NIH
	5: 3	Who hath commanded you to build t house,	1836
	5: 3	to build this house, and to make up t wall?	1836
	5: 4	said we unto them **after t manner**,	3660
	5: 4	What are the names of the men that make t	1836
	5: 5	they returned answer by letter concerning t	1836
	5: 6	governor on *t* side the river, and	NIH
	5: 6	which *were* on *t* side the river, sent unto	NIH
	5: 8	t work goeth fast on, and prospereth in their	1791
	5: 9	Who commanded you to build t house, and to	1836
	5:12	who destroyed t house, and carried	1836
	5:13	made a decree to build t house of God.	1836
	5:17	king to build t house of God at Jerusalem,	1791
	5:17	send his pleasure to us concerning t *matter*.	1836
	6: 7	Let the work of t house of God alone;	1791
	6: 7	the elders of the Jews build t house of God	1791
	6: 8	Jews for the building of t house of God:	1791
	6:11	a decree, that whosoever shall alter t word,	1836
	6:11	let his house be made a dunghill for t.	1836
	6:12	to destroy t house of God which *is* at	1791
	6:13	Tatnai, governor on *t* side the river,	NIH
	6:15	t house was finished on the third day of	1836
	6:16	kept the dedication of t house of God with	1836
	6:17	offered at the dedication of t house of God	1836
	7: 6	T Ezra went up from Babylon; and he *was*	1931
	7:11	Now t *is* the copy of the letter that the king	2088
	7:17	That thou mayest buy speedily with t	1836
	7:24	or ministers of t house of God,	1836
	7:27	which hath put *such a thing* as t in	2088
	8: 1	t *is* the genealogy of them that went up with	NIH
	8:23	So we fasted and besought our God for t:	2088
	8:35	all *t was* a burnt offering unto the LORD.	NIH
	8:36	and *to* the governors on *t* side the river:	NIH
	9: 2	and rulers hath been chief in t trespass.	2088
	9: 3	when I heard t thing, I rent my garment	2088
	9: 7	*have* we *been* in a great trespass unto t day;	2088
	9: 7	and to confusion of face, as *it is* t day.	2088
	9:10	O our God, what shall we say after t?	2088
	9:13	and hast given us *such* deliverance as t;	2088
	9:15	for we remain *yet* escaped, as *it is* t day:	2088
	9:15	*we* cannot stand before thee because of t.	2088
	10: 2	yet now there is hope in Israel concerning t	2088
	10: 4	Arise; for *t* matter *belongeth* unto thee:	NIH
	10: 5	to swear that *they* should do according to t	2088
	10: 9	trembling because of *t* matter, and for	NIH
	10:13	neither *is t* a work of one day or two:	NIH
	10:13	for we are many that have transgressed in t	2088
	10:14	until the fierce wrath of our God for t	2088
	10:15	of Tikvah were employed about t *matter*:	2088
Ne	1:11	thy servant *t* day, and grant him mercy in	NIH
Ne	1:11	and grant him mercy in the sight of t man.	2088
	2: 2	t *is* nothing *else* but sorrow of heart. Then I	2088
	2:18	So they strengthened their hands for *t* good	NIH
	2:19	and said, What *is* t thing that ye do?	2088
	3: 7	unto the throne of the governor on *t* side	NIH
	5:10	corn: I pray you, let us leave off t usury.	2088
	5:11	Restore, I pray you, to them, even *t* day,	NIH
	5:12	that *they* should do according to t promise.	2088
	5:13	his labour, that performeth not t promise,	2088
	5:13	And the people did according to t promise.	2088
	5:16	Yea also I continued in the work of t wall,	2088
	5:18	yet for *all* t required not I the bread of	2088
	5:18	the bondage was heavy upon t people.	2088
	5:19	*according to* all that I have done for t	2088
	6: 4	Yet they sent unto me four times after t	2088
	6:12	*that* he pronounced *t* prophecy against me:	NIH
	6:16	for they perceived that t work was wrought	2088
	7: 7	of the men of the people of Israel *was t*:	NIH
	8: 9	*T* day *is* holy unto the LORD your God;	NIH
	8:10	for *t* day *is* holy unto our Lord: neither be	NIH
	9: 1	fourth day of t month the children of Israel	2088
	9:10	So didst thou get thee a name, as *it is* t day.	2088
	9:18	T *is* thy God that brought thee up out of	2088
	9:32	since the time of the kings of Assyria unto t	2088
	9:36	we *are* servants *t* day, and *for* the land that	NIH
	9:38	because of all t we make a sure covenant,	2088
	13: 4	before t, Eliashib the priest, having	2088
	13: 6	in all t *time* was not I at Jerusalem: for in	2088
	13:14	concerning t, and wipe not out my good	2088
	13:17	What evil thing *is* t that ye do, and	2088
	13:18	*did not* our God bring all t evil upon us,	2088
	13:18	bring all this evil upon us, and upon t city?	2088
	13:22	*concerning* t also, and spare me according	2088
	13:27	then hearken unto you to do all t great evil,	2088
Est	1: 1	(t *is* Ahasuerus which reigned, from India	1931
	1:17	For *t* deed of the queen shall come abroad	NIH
	1:18	Media say t day unto all the king's princes,	2088
	4:14	For if thou altogether holdest thy peace at t	2088
	4:14	come to the kingdom for *such* a time as t?	2088
	4:15	Esther bade *them* return Mordecai *t*	NIH
	5: 4	Haman come *t* day unto the banquet that I	NIH
	5:13	Yet all t availeth me nothing, so long as I	2088
	6: 3	dignity hath been done to Mordecai for t?	2088
	6: 9	let *t* apparel and horse be delivered to	NIH
	7: 6	and enemy *is* t wicked Haman.	2088
	9: 4	for *t* man Mordecai waxed greater and	NIH
	9:13	morrow also according unto *t* day's decree,	NIH
	9:21	To stablish *t* among them, that they should	NIH
	9:26	Therefore for all the words of t letter, and	2088
	9:26	*of that* which they had seen concerning t	3602
	9:29	to confirm t second letter of Purim.	2088
Job	1: 3	that t man was the greatest of all the men of	1931
	1:22	In all t Job sinned not, nor charged God	2088
	2:10	In all t did not Job sin with his lips.	2088
	2:11	Now when Job's three friends heard of all t	2088
	3: 1	After t opened Job his mouth, and	3651
	4: 6	*Is* not *t* thy fear, thy confidence, thy hope;	NIH
	5:27	Lo t, we have searched it, so it *is*; hear it,	2088
	8:19	t *is* the joy of his way, and out of the earth	1931
	9:22	T *is* one *thing*, therefore I said *it*, He	1931
	10:13	hid in thine heart: I know that t *is* with thee.	2088
	12: 9	the hand of the LORD hath wrought t?	2088
	13: 1	mine eye hath seen all *t*, mine ear hath	NIH
	17: 8	Upright *men* shall be astonied at t, and	2088
	18:21	t *is* the place *of him that* knoweth not God.	2088
	19:26	*though* after my skin *worms* destroy t *body*,	2088
	20: 2	cause me to answer, and for *t* I make haste.	NIH
	20: 4	Knowest thou *not* t of old, since man was	2088
	20:29	T *is* the portion of a wicked man from God,	2088
	21: 2	my speech, and let t be your consolations.	2088
	27:13	T *is* the portion of a wicked man with God,	2088
	31:11	For t *is* a heinous crime; yea, it *is* an	1931
	31:28	T also *were* an iniquity *to be punished by*	1931
	33:12	Behold, *in* t thou art not just: I will answer	2088
	34:16	If now *thou hast* understanding, hear t:	2088
	35: 2	Thinkest thou t to be right, *that* thou saidst,	2088
	36:21	for t hast thou chosen rather than affliction.	2088
	37: 1	At t also my heart trembleth, and is moved	2063
	37:14	Hearken unto t, O Job: stand still, and	2088
	38: 2	Who *is* t that darkeneth counsel by words	2088
	42:16	After t lived Job an hundred and	2088
Ps	2: 7	*art* my Son; *t* day have I begotten thee.	NIH
	7: 3	O LORD my God, if I have done t;	2088
	11: 6	t *shall be* the portion of their cup.	NIH
	12: 7	thou shalt preserve them from t generation	2098
	17:14	*which have* their portion in *t* life, and	NIH
	18: T	who spake unto the LORD the words of t	2088
	22:31	that *shall be* born, that he hath done *t*.	NIH
	24: 6	T *is* the generation of them that seek him,	2088
	24: 8	Who *is* t King of glory? The LORD strong	2088
	24:10	Who is t King of glory? The LORD of	2088
	27: 3	rise against me, in t *will* I *be* confident.	2088
	32: 6	For t shall every one *that is* godly pray unto	2088
	34: 6	T poor *man* cried, and the LORD heard	2088
	35:22	*T* thou hast seen, O LORD: keep not	NIH
	41:11	By t I know that thou favourest me,	2088
	44:17	All t is come upon us; yet have we not	2088
	44:21	Shall not God search t out? for he knoweth	2088
	48:14	For t God *is* our God for ever and ever:	2088
	49: 1	Hear t, all ye people; give ear, all ye	2088
	49:13	T their way *is* their folly: yet their posterity	2088
	50:22	Now consider t, ye that forget God, lest I	2088
	51: 4	have I sinned, and done *t* evil in thy sight:	NIH
	52: 7	t *is* the man *that* made not God his strength;	NIH
	56: 9	turn back: t I know; for God *is* for me.	2088
	62:11	hath spoken once; twice have I heard t;	2098
	68:16	t *is* the hill *which* God desireth to dwell in;	NIH
	69:31	*T* also shall please the LORD better than	NIH
	69:32	The humble shall see *t*, *and* be glad: and	NIH
	71:18	until I have shewed thy strength unto *t*	NIH
	73:16	When I thought to know t, it *was* too	2088
	74: 2	t mount Zion, wherein thou hast dwelt.	2088
	74:18	Remember t, *that* the enemy hath	2088
	77:10	I said, T *is* my infirmity: *but I will*	1931
	78:21	Therefore the LORD heard *t*, and	NIH

Ps 78:32 For all t they sinned still, and believed not 2088
78:54 *even to* t mountain, *which* his right hand 2088
78:59 When God heard *t*, he was wroth, and NIH
80:14 from heaven, and behold, and visit t vine; 2088
81: 4 For t *was* a statute for Israel, *and* a law of 1931
81: 5 T he ordained in Joseph *for* a testimony, NIH
87: 4 Tyre, with Ethiopia; t *man* was born there. 2088
87: 5 be said, T[S] and that man was born in her: 376
87: 6 *up* the people, *that* t *man* was born there. 2088
92: 6 neither doth a fool understand t. 2088
95:10 Forty years long was I grieved with *t* NIH
102:18 T shall be written for the generation to 2088
104:25 *So is* t great and wide sea, wherein *are* 2088
109:20 *Let* t *be* the reward of mine adversaries 2088
109:27 That they may know that t *is* thy hand; 2088
113: 2 the name of the LORD from **t time forth** 6258
115:18 we will bless the LORD from **t time forth** 6258
118:20 T gate of the LORD, into which 2088
118:23 T is the LORD'S doing; it is marvellous 2088
118:24 T *is* the day *which* the LORD hath made; 2088
119:50 T *is* my comfort in my affliction: for thy 2088
119:56 T I had, because I kept thy precepts. 2088
119:91 They continue *t* day according to thine NIH
121: 8 and thy coming in from **t time forth**, 6258
132:14 T *is* my rest for ever: here will I dwell; for I 2088
149: 9 t honour have all his saints. Praise ye 1931
Pr 6: 3 Do t now, my son, and deliver thyself, 2088
7:14 with me; *t* day have I payed my vows. NIH
22:19 I have made known to thee *t* day, even *to* NIH
Ecc 1:10 thing whereof it may be said, See, t *is* new? 2088
1:13 t sore travail hath God given to the sons of 1931
1:17 I perceived that t also *is* vexation of spirit. 2088
2: 1 enjoy pleasure: and behold, t also *is* vanity. 1931
2:10 and t was my portion of all my labour. 2088
2:15 I said in my heart, that t also *is* vanity. 2088
2:19 myself wise under the sun. T *is* also vanity. 2088
2:21 T also *is* vanity and a great evil. 2088
2:23 taketh not rest in the night. T *is* also vanity. 2088
2:24 T also I saw, that it *was* from the hand of 2090
2:26 T also *is* vanity and vexation of spirit. 2088
4: 4 that for t a man is envied of his neighbour. 1931
4: 4 T *is* also vanity and vexation of spirit. 2088
4: 8 T *is* also vanity, yea, it *is* a sore travail. 2088
4:16 Surely t also *is* vanity and vexation of 2088
5:10 abundance *with* increase: t *is* also vanity. 2088
5:16 t also *is* a sore evil, *that* in all points as he 2090
5:19 to rejoice in his labour; t *is* the gift of God. 2090
6: 2 t *is* vanity, and it *is* an evil disease. 2088
6: 5 nor known *any thing:* t hath more rest than 2088
6: 9 t *is* also vanity and vexation of spirit. 2088
6:12 For who knoweth what *is* good for man in *t* NIH
7: 6 *is* the laughter of the fool: t also *is* vanity. 2088
7:10 thou dost not inquire wisely concerning t. 2088
7:18 *It is* good that thou shouldest take hold of t; 2088
7:18 yea, also from t withdraw not thine hand: 2088
7:23 All t have I proved by wisdom: I said, 2090
7:27 Behold, t have I found, saith the Preacher, 2088
7:29 Lo, t only have I found, that God hath 2088
8: 9 All t have I seen, and applied my heart unto 2088
8:10 where they had so done: t *is* also vanity. 2088
8:14 of the righteous: I said that t also *is* vanity. 2088
9: 1 For all t I considered in my heart even to 2088
9: 1 considered in my heart even to declare all t, 2088
9: 3 T *is* an evil among all *things* that are done 2088
9: 9 for that *is* thy portion in *t* life, and in thy NIH
9:13 T wisdom have I seen also under the sun, 2090
11: 6 either t or that, or whether they both *shall* 2088
12:13 for t *is* the whole *duty of* man. 2088
SS 3: 6 Who *is* t that cometh out of the wilderness 2088
5:16 T *is* my beloved, and this *is* my friend, 2088
5:16 This *is* my beloved, and t *is* my friend, 2088
7: 7 T thy stature is like to a palm tree, and 2088
8: 5 Who *is* t that cometh up from 2088
Isa 1:12 who hath required t at your hand, to tread 2088
3: 6 our ruler, and *let* t ruin *be* under thy hand: 2088
5:25 For all t his anger is not turned away, but 2088
6: 7 and said, Lo, t hath touched thy lips; 2088
6: 9 he said, Go, and tell t people, Hear ye 2088
6:10 Make the heart of t people fat, and 2088
8: 6 Forsomuch as t people refuseth the waters 2088
8:11 *I* should not walk in the way of t people, 2088
8:12 to all *them to* whom t people shall say, 2088
8:20 if they speak not according to t word, *it is* 2088
9: 5 but *t* shall be with burning *and* fuel of fire. NIH
9: 7 zeal of the LORD of hosts will perform t. 2088
9:12 For all t his anger is not turned away, but 2088
9:16 For the leaders of t people cause *them* to 2088
9:17 For all t his anger is not turned away, but 2088
9:21 For all t his anger is not turned away, but 2088
10: 4 For all t his anger is not turned away, but 2088
12: 5 excellent things: t *is* known in all the earth. 2088
14: 4 That thou shalt take up t proverb against 2088
14:16 *saying, Is* t the man that made the earth to 2088
14:26 T *is* the purpose that is purposed upon 2088
14:26 t *is* the hand that is stretched out upon all 2088
14:28 In the year that king Ahaz died was t 2088
16:13 T *is* the word that the LORD hath spoken 2088
17:14 T *is* the portion of them that spoil us, and 2088
20: 6 the inhabitant of t isle shall say in that day, 2088
22:14 Surely t iniquity shall not be purged from 2088
22:15 Go, get thee unto t treasurer, *even* unto 2088
23: 7 *Is* t your joyous *city,* whose antiquity *is* of 2088
23: 8 Who hath taken t counsel against Tyre, 2088
23:13 t people was not, *till* the Assyrian founded 2088
24: 3 for the LORD hath spoken t word. 2088
25: 6 in t mountain shall the LORD of hosts 2088
25: 7 he will destroy in t mountain the face of 2088
25: 9 it shall be said in that day, Lo, t *is* our God; 2088
25: 9 t *is* the LORD; we have waited for him, 2088
25:10 For in t mountain shall the hand of 2088
26: 1 In that day shall t song be sung in the land 2088
27: 9 By t therefore shall the iniquity of Jacob be 2063
27: 9 and t *is* all the fruit to take away his sin; 2088
28:11 another tongue will he speak to t people. 2088
28:12 T *is* the rest *wherewith* ye may cause 2088
Isa 28:12 the weary to rest; and t *is* the refreshing: 2088
28:14 that rule t people which *is* in Jerusalem. 2088
28:29 T also cometh forth from the LORD of 2088
29:11 that is learned, saying, Read t, I pray thee: 2088
29:12 is not learned, saying, Read t, I pray thee: 2088
29:13 Forasmuch as t people draw near *me* with 2088
29:14 to do a marvellous work amongst t people, 2088
30: 7 therefore have I cried concerning t, 2063
30: 9 That t *is* a rebellious people, lying children, 1931
30:12 Because ye despise t word, and trust in 2088
30:13 Therefore t iniquity shall be to you as a 2088
30:21 saying, T *is* the way, walk ye in it, when ye 2088
36: 4 What confidence *is* t where*in* thou trustest? 2088
36: 6 thou trustest in the staff of t broken reed, 2088
36: 7 Ye shall worship before t altar? 2088
36:10 the LORD against t land to destroy it? 2088
36:10 Go up against t land, and destroy it. 2088
36:15 t city shall not be delivered into the hand of 2088
37: 3 T day *is* a day of trouble, and of rebuke, 2088
37:22 T *is* the word which the LORD hath 2088
37:30 t *shall be* a sign unto thee, Ye shall eat *this* 2088
37:30 Ye shall eat *t* year such as groweth of itself; NIH
37:32 the zeal of the LORD of hosts shall do t. 2088
37:33 He shall not come into t city, nor shoot an 2088
37:34 shall not come into t city, saith the LORD. 2088
37:35 For I will defend t city to save it for mine 2088
38: 6 t city out of the hand of the king of 2088
38: 6 the king of Assyria: and I will defend t city. 2088
38: 7 t *shall be* a sign unto thee from 2088
38: 7 that the LORD will do t thing that he hath 2088
38:19 the living, he shall praise thee, as I *do t* day: NIH
39: 6 thy fathers have laid up in store until t day, 2088
41:20 that the hand of the LORD hath done t, 2088
42:22 t *is* a people robbed and spoiled; *they are* 1931
42:23 Who among you will give ear to t? 2088
43: 9 who among them can declare t, and 2088
43:21 T people have I formed for myself; 2098
45:21 who hath declared t from ancient time? 2088
46: 8 Remember t, and shew yourselves men: 2088
47: 8 Therefore hear now t, *thou that art* given to 2088
48: 1 Hear ye t, O house of Jacob, which are 2088
48: 6 Thou hast heard, see all t; and will not ye 1886.3
48: 6 I have shewed thee new *things* from **t time**, 6258
48:16 Come ye near unto me, hear ye t; I have not 2088
48:20 with a voice of singing declare ye, tell t, 2088
50:11 T shall ye have of mine hand; ye shall lie 2088
51:21 Therefore hear now t, thou afflicted, and 2088
54: 9 For t *is as* the waters of Noah unto me: 2088
54:17 T *is* the heritage of the servants of 2088
56: 2 Blessed *is* the man *that* doeth t, and the son 2088
56:12 to morrow shall be as t day, *and* 2088
58: 4 ye shall not fast as *ye do t* day, to make NIH
58: 5 and ashes *under him?* wilt thou call t a fast, 2088
58: 6 *Is* not t the fast that I have chosen? to loose 2088
59:21 As for me, t *is* my covenant with them, 2088
63: 1 Who *is* t *that* cometh from Edom, 2088
63: 1 t *that is* glorious in his apparel, travelling in 2088
66: 2 to t *man* will I look, *even* to *him that is* 2088
66:14 when ye see *t*, your heart shall rejoice, and NIH
Jer 1:10 I have t day set thee over the nations and 2088
1:18 I have made thee *t* day a defenced city, and NIH
2:12 O ye heavens, at t, and be horribly afraid, 2088
2:17 Hast thou not procured t unto thyself, 2088
3: 4 Wilt thou not from **t time** cry unto me, 6258
3:10 yet for all t her treacherous sister Judah 2088
3:25 from our youth even unto t day, and 2088
4: 8 For t gird you with sackcloth, lament and 2088
4:10 surely thou hast greatly deceived t people 2088
4:11 At that time shall it be said to t people and 2088
4:18 t *is* thy wickedness, because *it is* bitter, 2088
4:28 For t shall the earth mourn, and the heavens 2088
5: 7 How shall I pardon thee for t? thy children 2063
5: 9 my soul be avenged on such a nation as t? 2088
5:14 Because ye speak t word, behold, I will 2088
5:14 t people wood, and it shall devour them. 2088
5:20 Declare t in the house of Jacob, and 2088
5:21 Hear now t, O foolish people, and 2088
5:23 t people hath a revolting and a rebellious 2088
5:29 my soul be avenged on such a nation as t? 2088
6: 6 t is the city to be visited; she *is* wholly 1931
6:19 behold, I will bring evil upon t people, 2088
6:21 I will lay stumblingblocks before t people, 2088
7: 2 proclaim there t word, and say, Hear 2088
7: 3 and I will cause you to dwell in t place. 2088
7: 6 and shed not innocent blood in t place, 2088
7: 7 will I cause you to dwell in t place, in 2088
7:10 come and stand before me in t house, 2088
7:11 Is t house, which is called by my name, 2088
7:14 Therefore will I do unto *t* house, which is NIH
7:16 Therefore pray not thou for t people, 2088
7:20 my fury *shall be* poured out upon t place, 2088
7:23 t thing commanded I them, saying, 2088
7:25 forth out of the land of Egypt unto t day, 2088
7:28 T *is* a nation that obeyeth not the voice of 2088
7:33 the carcases of t people shall be meat for 2088
8: 3 residue of them that remain of t evil family, 2088
8: 5 is t people of Jerusalem slidden back *by* a 2088
9: 9 my soul be avenged on such a nation as t? 2088
9:12 *is* the wise man, that may understand t? 2088
9:15 Behold, I *will* feed them, *even* t people, 2088
9:24 let him that glorieth glory in t, that *he* 2088
10:18 will sling out the inhabitants of the land at t 2088
10:19 I said, Truly t *is* a grief, and I must bear it. 2088
11: 2 Hear ye the words of t covenant, and 2088
11: 3 that obeyeth not the words of t covenant, 2088
11: 5 flowing with milk and honey, as *it is* t day. 2088
11: 6 Hear ye the words of t covenant, and 2088
11: 7 *even* unto t day, rising early and protesting, 2088
11: 8 I will bring upon them all the words of t 2088
11:14 Therefore pray not thou for t people, 2088
13: 9 **After t manner** will I mar the pride of 3602
13:10 T evil people, which refuse to hear my 2088
13:10 to worship them, shall even be as t girdle, 2088
13:12 Therefore thou shalt speak unto them t 2088
13:13 I *will* fill all the inhabitants of t land, 2088
Jer 13:25 T *is* thy lot, the portion of thy measures 2088
14:10 Thus saith the LORD unto t people, Thus 2088
14:11 Pray not for t people for *their* good. 2088
14:13 but I will give you assured peace in t place. 2088
14:15 Sword and famine shall not be in t land; 2088
14:17 Therefore thou shalt say t word unto them; 2088
15: 1 *yet* my mind *could* not *be* toward t people: 2088
15:20 I will make thee unto t people a fenced 2088
16: 2 thou have sons nor daughters in t place. 2088
16: 3 concerning the daughters that are born in t 2088
16: 3 concerning their fathers that begat them in t 2088
16: 5 for I have taken away my peace from t 2088
16: 6 the great and the small shall die in t land: 2088
16: 9 I will cause to cease out of t place in your 2088
16:10 when thou shalt shew t people all these 2088
16:10 hath the LORD pronounced all t 2088
16:13 Therefore will I cast you out of t land into a 2088
16:21 I *will* t once cause them to know, 2088
17:24 to bring in no burden through the gates of t 2088
17:25 shall there enter into the gates of t city 2088
17:25 and t city shall remain for ever. 2088
18: 6 of Israel, cannot I do with you as t potter? 2088
19: 3 Behold, I *will* bring evil upon t place, 2088
19: 4 have estranged t place, and have burnt 2088
19: 4 have filled t place *with* the blood of 2088
19: 6 that t place shall no more be called Tophet, 2088
19: 7 counsel of Judah and Jerusalem in t place; 2088
19: 8 I will make t city desolate, and a hissing; 2088
19:11 Even so will I break t people and this city, 2088
19:11 Even so will I break this people and t city, 2088
19:12 Thus will I do unto t place, saith 2088
19:12 and *even* make t city as Tophet: 2088
19:15 I will bring upon t city and upon all her 2088
20: 5 Moreover I will deliver all the strength of t 2088
21: 4 I will assemble them into the midst of t 2088
21: 6 I will smite the inhabitants of t city, both 2088
21: 7 such as are left in t city from the pestilence, 2088
21: 8 unto t people thou shalt say, Thus saith 2088
21: 9 He that abideth in t city shall die by 2088
21:10 For I have set my face against t city for 2088
22: 1 the king of Judah, and speak there t word, 2088
22: 3 neither shed innocent blood in t place. 2088
22: 4 For if ye do t thing indeed, then shall there 2088
22: 4 shall there enter in by the gates of t house 2088
22: 5 that t house shall become a desolation. 2088
22: 8 many nations shall pass by t city, and 2088
22: 8 the LORD done thus unto t great city? 2088
22:11 his father, which went forth out of t place; 2088
22:12 him captive, and shall see t land no more. 2088
22:16 it was well *with him: was* not t to know 1931
22:21 T *hath been* thy manner from thy youth, 2088
22:28 *Is* t man Coniah a despised broken idol? 2088
22:30 saith the LORD, Write ye t man childless, 2088
23: 6 t *is* his name whereby he shall be called, 2088
23:26 How long shall *t* be in the heart of NIH
23:32 they shall not profit t people at all, 2088
23:33 when t people, or the prophet, or a priest, 2088
23:38 Because you say t word, The burden of 2088
24: 5 whom I have sent out of t place *into* 2088
24: 6 and I will bring them again to t land: 2088
24: 8 that remain in t land, and them that dwell in 2088
25: 3 even unto t day, that *is* the three and 2088
25: 9 will bring them against t land, and 2088
25:11 t whole land shall be a desolation, *and* 2088
25:13 *even* all that is written in t book, which 2088
25:15 Take the wine cup of t fury at mine hand, 2088
25:18 a hissing, and a curse; as *it is* t day; 2088
26: 1 of Judah came t word from the LORD, 2088
26: 6 will I make t house like Shiloh, and will 2088
26: 6 will make t city a curse to all the nations of 2088
26: 9 T house shall be like Shiloh, and this city 2088
26: 9 t city shall be desolate without an 2088
26:11 the people, saying, T man *is* worthy to die; 2088
26:11 for he hath prophesied against t city, as ye 2088
26:12 The LORD sent me to prophesy against t 2088
26:12 against t city all the words that ye have 2088
26:15 upon t city, and upon the inhabitants 2088
26:16 to the prophets; T man *is* not worthy to die: 2088
26:20 who prophesied against t city and 2088
26:20 against t land according to all the words of 2088
27: 1 t word unto Jeremiah from the LORD, 2088
27:16 I spake to the priests and to all t people, 2088
27:17 live: wherefore should t city be laid waste? 2088
27:19 residue of the vessels that remain in t city, 2088
27:22 I bring them up, and restore them to t place. 2088
28: 3 two full years *will* I bring again into t 2088
28: 3 king of Babylon took away from t place, 2088
28: 4 I *will* bring again to t place Jeconiah 2088
28: 6 away captive, from Babylon into t place. 2088
28: 7 Nevertheless hear thou now t word that I 2088
28:15 but thou makest t people to trust in a lie. 2088
28:16 *t* year thou *shalt* die, because thou hast NIH
29:10 in causing you to return to t place. 2088
29:16 of all the people that dwelleth in t city, 2088
29:28 us *in* Babylon, saying, T *captivity is* long: 1931
29:29 Zephaniah the priest read t letter in the ears 2088
29:32 he shall not have a man to dwell among t 2088
30:17 called thee an Outcast, *saying,* T *is* Zion, 1931
30:21 for who *is* t that engaged his heart to 1931
31:23 As yet they shall use t speech in the land of 2088
31:26 Upon t I awaked, and beheld; and my sleep 2088
31:33 t *shall be* the covenant that I will make with 2088
32: 3 I *will* give t city into the hand of the king of 2088
32: 8 I knew that t *was* the word of the LORD. 1931
32:14 t evidence of the purchase, both which is 2088
32:14 is sealed, and t evidence which is open; 2088
32:15 vineyards shall be possessed again in t 2088
32:20 *even* unto t day, and in Israel, and 2088
32:20 and hast made thee a name, as *at* t day; 2088
32:22 hast given them t land, which thou didst 2088
32:23 thou hast caused all t evil to come upon 2088
32:28 I *will* give t city into the hand of 2088
32:29 that fight against t city, shall come and 2088
32:29 shall come and set fire on t city, and burn it 2088
32:31 For t city hath been to me *as* a provocation 2088

Jer 32:31 the day that they built it even unto t day; 2088
32:35 that they should do t abomination, to cause 2088
32:36 of Israel, concerning t city, whereof ye say, 2088
32:37 I will bring them again unto t place, 2088
32:41 I will plant them in t land assuredly with 2088
32:42 Like as I have brought all t great evil upon 2088
32:42 brought all this great evil upon t people, 2088
32:43 fields shall be bought in t land, whereof ye 2088
33: 4 concerning the houses of t city, 2088
33: 5 wickedness I have hid my face from t city. 2088
33:10 Again there shall be heard in t place, which 2088
33:12 Again in t place, which is desolate without 2088
33:16 t is the name wherewith she shall be called, 2088
33:24 Considerest thou not what t people have 2088
34: 2 I will give t city into the hand of the king of 2088
34: 8 T is the word that came unto Jeremiah from NIH
34:22 and cause them to return to t city; 2088
35:14 for unto t day they drink none, but 2088
35:16 but t people hath not hearkened unto me: 2088
36: 1 that t word came unto Jeremiah from 2088
36: 2 from the days of Josiah, even unto t day. 2088
36: 7 LORD hath pronounced against t people. 2088
36:29 Thou hast burnt t roll, saying, Why hast 2088
36:29 shall certainly come and destroy t land, 2088
37: 8 fight against t city, and take it, and burn it 2088
37:10 man in his tent, and burn t city with fire. 2088
37:18 or against thy servants, or against t people, 2088
37:19 not come against you, nor against t land? 2088
38: 2 He that remaineth in t city shall die by 2088
38: 3 T city shall surely be given into the hand of 2088
38: 4 We beseech thee, let t man be put to death: 2088
38: 4 of the men of war that remain in t city, 2088
38: 4 for t man seeketh not the welfare of this 2088
38: 4 for this man seeketh not the welfare of t 2088
38:16 As the LORD liveth, that made us t soul, 2088
38:17 and t city shall not be burnt with fire; 2088
38:18 shall t city be given into the hand of 2088
38:21 t is the word that the LORD hath shewed 2088
38:23 thou shalt cause t city to be burnt with fire. 2088
39:16 I will bring my words upon t city for evil, 2088
40: 2 The LORD thy God hath pronounced t 2088
40: 2 God hath pronounced this evil upon t place. 2088
40: 3 therefore t thing is come upon you. 2088
40: 4 I loose thee t day from the chains which NIH
40:16 son of Kareah, Thou shalt not do t thing: 2088
42: 2 LORD thy God, even for all t remnant; 2088
42:10 If ye will still abide in t land, then will I 2088
42:13 if ye say, We will not dwell in t land, 2088
42:18 and ye shall see t place no more. 2088
42:19 certainly that I have admonished you t NIH
42:21 And now I have t day declared it to you; but NIH
44: 2 t day they are a desolation, and no man 2088
44: 4 Oh, do not t abominable thing that I hate. 2088
44: 6 they are wasted and desolate, as at t day. 2088
44: 7 Wherefore commit ye t great evil against NIH
44:10 They are not humbled even unto t day, 2088
44:22 a curse, without an inhabitant, as at t day. 2088
44:23 therefore t evil is happened unto you, as at 2088
44:23 this evil is happened unto you, as at t day. 2088
44:29 t shall be a sign unto you, saith 2088
44:29 that I will punish you in t place, 2088
45: 4 planted I will pluck up, even t whole land. 1931
46: 7 Who is t that cometh up as a flood, 2088
46:10 For t is the day of the Lord GOD of hosts, 1931
50:17 last t Nebuchadrezzar king of Babylon hath 2088
50:25 for t is the work of the Lord GOD of hosts 1931
51: 6 for t is the time of the LORD'S 1931
51:59 his reign. And t Seraiah was a quiet prince. NIH
51:62 thou hast spoken against t place, 2088
51:63 when thou hast made an end of reading t 2088
52:28 T is the people whom Nebuchadrezzar 2088
La 2:15 saying, Is t the city that men call The 2088
2:16 certainly t is the day that we looked for; we 2088
2:20 and consider to whom thou hast done t. 3541
3:21 T I recall to my mind, therefore have I 2088
5:17 For t our heart is faint; for these things our 2088
Eze 1: 5 t was their appearance; they had 2088
1:23 which covered on t side, and every one had 2007
1:28 T was the appearance of the likeness of 1931
2: 3 against me, even unto t very day. 2088
3: 1 eat t roll, and go speak unto the house of 2088
3: 3 fill thy bowels with t roll that I give thee. 2088
4: 3 T shall be a sign to the house of Israel. 1931
5: 5 Thus saith the Lord GOD; T is Jerusalem: 2088
6:10 that I have not said in vain that I would do t 2088
8: 5 northward at the gate of the altar t image of 2088
8:15 he unto me, Hast thou seen t, O son of man? NIH
8:17 unto me, Hast thou seen t, O son of man? NIH
10:15 T is the living creature that I saw by 1931
10:20 T is the living creature that I saw under 1931
11: 2 and give wicked counsel in t city: 2088
11: 3 t city is the caldron, and we be the flesh. 1931
11: 6 Ye have multiplied your slain in t city, 2088
11: 7 they are the flesh, and t city is the caldron: 1931
11:11 T city shall not be your caldron, 1931
11:15 unto us is t land given in possession. 1931
12:10 T burden concerneth the prince in 2088
12:23 I will make t proverb to cease, and 2088
16:20 Is t of thy whoredoms a small matter, NIH
16:43 thou shalt not commit t lewdness above all NIH
16:44 every one that useth proverbs shall use t NIH
16:49 t was the iniquity of thy sister Sodom, 2088
17: 7 t vine did bend her roots toward him, and 2088
18: 2 that ye use t proverb concerning the land of 2088
18: 3 shall not have occasion any more to use t 2088
19:14 T is a lamentation, and shall be for a 1931
20:27 Yet in t your fathers have blasphemed me, 2088
20:29 the name thereof is called Bamah unto t 2088
20:31 with all your idols, even unto t day: NIH
21:11 t sword is sharpened, and it is furbished, 1931
21:26 t shall not be the same: exalt him that is 2063
23:11 when her sister Aholibah saw t, she was NIH
23:38 Moreover t they have done unto me: 2088
24: 2 the name of the day, even of t same day: 2088
24: 2 set himself against Jerusalem t same day. 2088

Eze 24:24 when t cometh, ye shall know that I am 1886.3
31:18 T is Pharaoh and all his multitude, saith 1931
32:16 T is the lamentation wherewith they shall 1931
33:33 when t cometh to pass, (lo, it will come) 1886.3
36:22 I do not t for your sakes, O house of Israel, NIH
36:32 Not for your sakes do I t, saith the Lord NIH
36:35 T land that was desolate is become like 1977
36:37 I will yet for t be inquired of by the house 2088
39: 8 t is the day whereof I have spoken. 1931
40:10 of the gate eastward were three on t side, 6311
40:10 the posts had one measure on t side and 6311
40:12 the little chambers was one cubit on t side, NIH
40:12 little chambers were six cubits on t side, 6311
40:21 little chambers thereof were three on t side 6311
40:26 one on t side, and another on that side, 6311
40:34 posts thereof, on t side, and on that side: 6311
40:37 posts thereof, on t side, and on that side: 6311
40:39 porch of the gate were two tables on t side, 6311
40:41 Four tables were on t side, and four tables 6311
40:45 he said unto me, T chamber, 2090
40:48 five cubits on t side, and five cubits on that 6311
40:48 of the gate was three cubits on t side, 6311
40:49 one on t side, and another on that side. 6311
41: 4 he said unto me, T is the most holy place. 2088
41:22 T is the table that is before the LORD. 2088
43:12 T is the law of the house; Upon the top of 2088
43:12 Behold, t is the law of the house. 2088
43:13 and t shall be the higher place of the altar. 2088
44: 2 T gate shall be shut, it shall not be opened, 2088
45: 1 T shall be holy in all the borders thereof 1931
45: 2 Of t there shall be for the sanctuary five 2088
45: 3 of t measure shalt thou measure the length 2088
45:13 T is the oblation that ye shall offer; 2088
45:16 All the people of the land shall give t 2088
46: 3 of t gate before the LORD in the sabbaths 1931
46:20 T is the place where the priests shall boil 2088
47: 6 hast thou seen t? Then he brought me, and NIH
47:12 on t side and on that side, shall grow all 2088
47:13 T shall be the border, whereby ye shall 1454
47:14 t land shall fall unto you for inheritance. 2088
47:15 t shall be the border of the land toward 2088
47:17 border of Hamath. And t is the north side. NIH
47:18 unto the east sea. And t is the east side. NIH
47:19 great sea. And t is the south side southward. NIH
47:20 over against Hamath. T is the west side. 2088
47:21 So shall ye divide t land unto you 2088
48:10 even for the priests, shall be t holy oblation; NIH
48:12 t oblation of the land that is offered shall be NIH
48:29 T is the land which ye shall divide by lot 2088
Da 1:14 So he consented to them in t matter, and 2088
2:12 For t cause the king was 1836+3606+6903
2:18 of the God of heaven concerning t secret; 1836
2:30 t secret is not revealed to me for any 1836
2:31 T great image, whose brightness was 1797
2:32 T image's head was of fine gold, his breast 0.2
2:36 T is the dream; and we will tell 1836
2:38 ruler over them all. Thou art t head of gold. 1932
2:47 seeing thou couldest reveal t secret. 1836
3:16 we are not careful to answer thee in t 1836
3:29 there is no other God that can deliver after t 1836
4:17 T matter is by the decree of the watchers, NIH
4:18 T dream I king Nebuchadnezzar have seen. 1836
4:24 T is the interpretation, O king, and this is 1836
4:24 and t is the decree of the most High, 1932
4:28 All t came upon the king Nebuchadnezzar. 0.2
4:30 king spake, and said, Is not t great Babylon, 1668
5: 7 Whosoever shall read t writing, and 1836
5:15 that they should read t writing, and 1836
5:22 thine heart, though thou knewest all t; 1836
5:24 sent from him; and t writing was written. 1836
5:25 t is the writing that was written, MENE, 1836
5:26 T is the interpretation of the thing: MENE; 1836
6: 3 t Daniel was preferred above the presidents 1836
6: 5 We shall not find any occasion against t 1836
6:28 So t Daniel prospered in the reign of 1836
7: 6 After t I beheld, and lo another, like a 1836
7: 7 After t I saw in the night visions, and 1836
7: 8 in t horn were eyes like the eyes of man, 1668
7:16 stood by, and asked him the truth of all t. 1836
7:24 the ten horns out of t kingdom are ten 1886.7
8:16 make t man to understand the vision. 1975
9: 7 but unto us confusion of faces, as at t day; 2088
9:13 law of Moses, all t evil is come upon us: 2088
9:15 and hast gotten thee renown, as at t day; 2088
10: 8 saw t great vision, and there remained no 2088
10:11 when he had spoken t word unto me, I 2088
10:17 For how can the servant of t my lord talk 2088
10:17 servant of this my lord talk with t my lord? 2088
11:18 After t shall he turn his face unto 2050.1
12: 5 the one on t side of the bank of the river, 2008
Hos 5: 1 Hear ye t, O priests; and hearken, ye house 2088
7:10 LORD their God, nor seek him for all t. 2088
7:16 t shall be their derision in the land of 2097
Joel 1: 2 Hear t, ye old men, and give ear, all ye 2088
1: 2 Hath t been in your days, or even in 2088
3: 9 Proclaim ye t among the Gentiles; 2088
Am 3: 1 Hear t word that the LORD hath spoken 2088
4: 1 Hear t word, ye kine of Bashan, that are in 2088
4: 5 for t liketh you, O ye children of Israel, 3651
4:12 and because I will do t unto thee, prepare to 2088
5: 1 Hear ye t word which I take up against you, 2088
7: 3 The LORD repented for t: It shall not be, 2088
7: 6 The LORD repented for t: This also shall 2088
7: 6 T also shall not be, saith the Lord GOD. 1931
8: 4 Hear t, O ye that swallow up the needy, 2088
8: 8 Shall not the land tremble for t, and 2088
9:12 by my name, saith the LORD that doeth t. 2088
Ob 1:20 the captivity of t host of the children of 2088
Jnh 1: 7 that we may know for whose cause t evil is 2088
1: 8 pray thee, for whose cause t evil is upon us; 2088
1:10 said unto him, Why hast thou done t? 2088
1:12 for I know that for my sake t great tempest 2088
1:14 let us not perish for t man's life, and lay not 2088
4: 2 pray thee, O LORD, was not t my saying, 2088
Mic 1: 5 For the transgression of Jacob is all t, and 2088

Mic 2: 3 Behold, against t family do I devise an evil, 2088
2: 3 shall ye go haughtily: for t time is evil. 1931
2:10 Arise ye, and depart; for t is not your rest: 2088
2:11 he shall even be the prophet of t people. 2088
3: 9 Hear t, I pray you, ye heads of the house of 2088
5: 5 t man shall be the peace, when the Assyrian 2088
Hab 1:11 offend, imputing t his power unto his god. 2098
Zep 1: 4 I will cut off the remnant of Baal from t 2088
2:10 T shall they have for their pride, because 2088
2:15 T is the rejoicing city that dwelt carelessly, 2088
Hag 1: 2 T people say, The time is not come, 2088
1: 4 your cieled houses, and t house lie waste? 2088
2: 3 Who is left among you that saw t house in 2088
2: 7 I will fill t house with glory, saith 2088
2: 9 The glory of t latter house shall be greater 2088
2: 9 in t place will I give peace, saith 2088
2:14 So is t people, and so is this nation before 2088
2:14 is this people, and so is t nation before me, 2088
2:15 pray you, consider from t day and upward, 2088
2:18 Consider now from t day and upward, from 2088
2:19 brought forth: from t day will I bless you. 2088
Zec 2: 4 Run, speak to t young man, saying, 1975
3: 2 is not t a brand pluckt out of the fire? 2088
4: 6 T is the word of the LORD unto 2088
4: 9 have laid the foundation of t house; 2088
5: 3 T is the curse that goeth forth over the face 2088
5: 3 shall be cut off as on t side according to it; 2088
5: 5 and see what is t that goeth forth. 2088
5: 6 he said, T is an ephah that goeth forth. 2088
5: 6 T is their resemblance through all the earth. 2088
5: 7 t is a woman that sitteth in the midst of 2088
5: 8 he said, T is wickedness. And he cast it into 2088
6:15 t shall come to pass, if ye will diligently NIH
8: 6 of the remnant of t people in these days, 2088
8:11 now I will not be unto the residue of t 2088
8:12 I will cause the remnant of t people to 2088
14:12 t shall be the plague wherewith the LORD 2088
14:15 that shall be in these tents, as t plague. 2088
14:19 T shall be the punishment of Egypt, and 2088
Mal 1: 9 t hath been by your means: will he regard 2088
1:13 should I accept t of your hand? saith 1886.3
2: 1 O ye priests, t commandment is for you. 2088
2: 4 ye shall know that I have sent t 2088
2:12 LORD will cut off the man that doth t, 5089.1
2:13 t have ye done again, covering the altar of 2088
3: 9 ye have robbed me, even t whole nation. 1886.1
4: 3 that I shall do t, saith the LORD of hosts. NIH
Mt 1:18 the birth of Jesus Christ was on t wise: 3779
1:22 Now all t was done, that it might be 3778
3: 3 For t is he that was spoken of by 3778
3:17 saying, T is my beloved Son, in whom I am 3778
6: 9 After t manner therefore pray ye: 3779
6:11 Give us t day our daily bread. 4594
7:12 to them: for t is the law and the prophets. 3778
8: 9 and I say to t man, Go, and he goeth; and 3778
8: 9 and to my servant, Do t, and he doeth it. 3778
8:27 saying, What manner of man is t, that even 3778
9: 3 within themselves, T man blasphemeth. 3778
9:28 Believe ye that I am able to do t? 3778
10:23 But when they persecute you in t city, 3778
11:10 For t is he, of whom it is written, Behold, 3778
11:14 And if ye will receive it, t is Elias, 846
11:16 But whereunto shall I liken t generation? 3778
11:23 it would have remained until t day. 4594
12: 6 That in t place is one greater than 5602
12: 7 But if ye had known what t meaneth, I will NIG
12:23 and said, Is t the son of David? 3778
12:24 T fellow doth not cast out devils, but by 3778
12:32 not be forgiven him, neither in t world, 3778
12:41 shall rise in judgment with t generation, 3778
12:42 rise up in the judgment with t generation, 3778
12:45 so shall it be also unto t wicked generation. 3778
13:15 For t people's heart is waxed gross, and 3778
13:19 T is he which received seed by the way 3778
13:22 and the care of t world, and 3778
13:28 He said unto them, An enemy hath done t. 3778
13:40 the fire; so shall it be in the end of t world. 3778
13:54 Whence hath t man this wisdom, and 3778
13:54 Whence hath this man t wisdom, and 3778
13:55 Is not t the carpenter's son? is not his 3778
13:56 Whence then hath t man all these things? 3778
14: 2 unto his servants, T is John the Baptist; 3778
14:15 T is a desert place, and the time is now past; NIG
15: 8 T people draweth nigh unto me with their 3778
15:11 cometh out of the mouth, t defileth a man. 3778
15:12 were offended, after they heard t saying? NIG
15:15 said unto him, Declare unto us t parable. 3778
16:18 and upon t rock I will build my church; 3778
16:22 far from thee, Lord: t shall not be unto thee. 3778
17: 5 which said, T is my beloved Son, in whom 3778
17:20 ye shall say unto t mountain, 3778
17:21 Howbeit t kind goeth not out but by prayer 3778
18: 4 shall humble himself as t little child, 3778
19: 5 For t cause shall a man leave father 1752+3778
19:11 unto them, All men cannot receive t saying, 3778
19:26 said unto them, With men t is unpossible; 3778
20:14 I will give unto t last, even as unto thee. 3778
21: 4 All t was done, that it might be fulfilled 3778
21:10 all the city was moved, saying, Who is t? 3778
21:11 T is Jesus the prophet of Nazareth of 3778
21:21 ye shall not only do t which is done to 3588
21:21 but also if ye shall say unto t mountain, 3778
21:23 and who gave thee t authority? 3778
21:38 they said among themselves, T is the heir; 3778
21:42 t is the Lord's doing, and it is marvellous in 3778
21:44 And whosoever shall fall on t stone shall be 3778
22:20 Whose is t image and superscription? 3778
22:33 And when the multitude heard t, they were NIG
22:38 T is the first and great commandment. 3778
23:36 All these things shall come upon t 3778
24:14 And t gospel of the kingdom shall be 3778
24:21 the beginning of the world to t time, 3568+3588
24:34 I say unto you, T generation shall not pass, 3778
24:43 But know t, that if the goodman of 1565
26: 8 saying, To what purpose is t waste? 3778

T

Mt 26: 9 For t ointment might have been sold for 3778
26:12 For in that she hath poured t ointment on 3778
26:13 Wheresoever t gospel shall be preached in 3778
26:13 *there* shall also t, that this *woman* hath NIG
26:13 *there* shall also *this,* that t *woman* hath 3778
26:26 and said, Take, eat; t is my body. 3778
26:28 For t is my blood of the new testament, 3778
26:29 I will not drink henceforth of t fruit of 3778
26:31 ye shall be offended because of me t night: 3778
26:34 That t night, before *the* cock crow, 3778
26:39 if it be possible, let t cup pass from me: 3778
26:42 if t cup may not pass away from me, 3778
26:56 But all t was done, that the scriptures of 3778
26:61 And said, T *fellow* said, I am able to 3778
26:71 T *fellow* was also with Jesus of Nazareth. 3778
27: 8 called, The field of blood, unto **t day**. 4594
27:19 have suffered many *things* **t day** in a dream 4594
27:24 I am innocent of the blood of t just *person:* 3778
27:37 T IS JESUS THE KING OF THE JEWS. 3778
27:47 heard *that,* said, T *man* calleth for Elias. 3778
27:54 saying, Truly t was the Son of God. 3778
28:14 And if t come to the governor's ears, 3778
28:15 t saying is commonly reported among 3778
28:15 reported among the Jews until **t day**. 4594
Mk 1:27 among themselves, saying, What *thing* is t? 3778
1:27 what new doctrine *is* t? for with authority 3778
2: 7 Why doth t *man* thus speak blasphemies? 3778
2:12 saying, We never saw *it* **on t fashion**. 3779
4:13 he said unto them, Know ye not t parable? 3778
4:19 And the cares of t world, and 3778
4:41 What *manner of* man is t, that even 3778
5:32 about to see her that had done t *thing.* 3778
5:39 unto them, Why make ye t ado, and weep? NIG
6: 2 From whence hath t *man* these *things?* and 3778
6: 2 what wisdom *is* t which is given unto him, NIG
6: 3 Is not t the carpenter, the son of Mary, 3778
6:35 *T* is a desert place, and now the time *is* far NIG
7: 6 T people honoureth me with *their* lips, but 3778
7:29 he said unto her, For t saying go thy way; 3778
8:12 Why doth t generation seek after a sign? 3778
8:12 There shall no sign be given unto t 3778
8:38 and of my words in t adulterous and 3778
9: 7 of the cloud, saying, T is my beloved Son: 3778
9:21 How long is it ago since t came unto him? 3778
9:29 T kind can come forth by nothing, but by 3778
10: 5 of your heart he wrote you t precept. 3778
10: 7 **For t cause** shall a man leave his 1752+3778
10:30 he shall receive an hundredfold now in t 3778
11: 3 And if any *man* say unto you, Why do ye t? 3778
11:23 That whosoever shall say unto t mountain, 3778
11:28 who gave thee t authority to do these 3778
12: 7 said amongst themselves, T is the heir; 3778
12:10 And have ye not read t scripture; The stone 3778
12:11 T was the Lord's doing, and it is 3778
12:16 Whose *is* t image and superscription? 3778
12:30 all thy strength: t *is* the first commandment. 3778
12:31 And the second *is* like, *namely* t, 3778
12:43 That t poor widow hath cast more in, 3778
13:19 which God created unto **t time**, 3568+3588
13:30 unto you, that t generation shall not pass, 3778
14: 4 Why was t waste of the ointment made? 3778
14: 9 Wheresoever t gospel shall be preached 3778
14: 9 *t* also that she hath done shall be spoken of NIG
14:22 to them, and said, Take, eat: t is my body. 3778
14:24 T is my blood of the new testament, 3778
14:27 ye shall be offended because of me t night: 3778
14:30 unto thee, That **t day**, *even* in this night, 4594
14:30 say unto thee, That this day, *even* in t night, 3778
14:36 unto thee; take away t cup from me: 3778
14:58 I will destroy t temple that is made with 3778
14:69 say to them that stood by, T is *one* of them. 3778
14:71 *saying,* I know not t man of whom ye 3778
15:39 he said, Truly t man was the Son of God. 3778
Lk 1:18 unto the angel, Whereby shall I know t? 3778
1:29 what manner of salutation t should be. 3778
1:34 How shall t be, seeing I know not a man? 3778
1:36 and t is the sixth month with her, who was 3778
1:43 And whence *is* t to me, that the mother of 3778
1:61 of thy kindred that is called by t name. 3778
1:66 saying, What *manner of* child shall t be! 3778
2: 2 (*And* t taxing was first made when 3778
2:11 For unto you is born **t day** in the city of 4594
2:12 And t *shall be* a sign unto you; Ye shall 3778
2:15 and see t thing which is come to pass, 3778
2:17 which was told them concerning t child. 3778
2:34 t *child* is set for the fall and rising again of 3778
3:20 Added yet t above all, that he shut up John 3778
4: 3 command t stone that it be made bread. 3778
4: 6 All t power will I give thee, and the glory 3778
4:21 **T day** is this scripture fulfilled in your ears. 4594
4:21 This day is t scripture fulfilled in your ears. 3778
4:22 And they said, Is not t Joseph's son? 3778
4:23 Ye will surely say unto me t proverb, 3778
4:36 saying, What a word *is* t! 3778
5: 6 And when they had t done, they inclosed a 3778
5:21 Who is t which speaketh blasphemies? 3778
6: 3 Have ye not read so much as t, what David 3778
7: 4 he was worthy for whom he should do t: 3778
7: 8 and to my servant, Do t, and he doeth *it.* 3778
7:17 And t rumour of him went forth throughout 3778
7:27 T is *he,* of whom it is written, Behold, 3778
7:31 then shall I liken the men of t generation? 3778
7:39 saying, T *man,* if he were a prophet, 3778
7:39 what manner of woman *t is* that toucheth NIG
7:44 and said unto Simon, Seest thou t woman? 3778
7:45 t *woman* since the time I came in hath not 3778
7:46 t *woman* hath anointed my feet with 3778
7:49 Who is t that forgiveth sins also? 3778
8: 9 saying, What might t parable be? 3778
8:11 Now the parable is t: The seed is the word 3778
8:14 with cares and riches and pleasures of *t* life, NIG
8:25 one to another, What *manner of* man is t? 3778
9: 9 but who is t, of whom I hear such *things?* 3778
9:13 we should go and buy meat for all t people. 3778
9:35 of the cloud, saying, T is my beloved Son: 3778
Lk 9:45 But they understood not t saying, and 3778
9:48 Whosoever shall receive t child in my 3778
9:54 disciples James and John saw *t,* they said, NIG
10: 5 ye enter, first say, Peace *be* to t house. 3778
10:11 notwithstanding be ye sure of t, that 3778
10:20 Notwithstanding in t rejoice not, that 3778
10:28 answered right: t do, and thou shalt live. 3778
11:29 he began to say, T is an evil generation: 3778
11:30 shall also the Son of man be to t 3778
11:31 the judgment with the men of t generation, 3778
11:32 rise up in the judgment with t generation, 3778
11:50 the world, may be required of t generation; 3778
11:51 It shall be required of t generation. 3778
12:18 And he said, T will I do: I will pull down 3778
12:20 t night thy soul shall be required of thee: 3778
12:39 And t know, that if the goodman of 3778
12:41 speakest thou t parable unto us, or even to 3778
12:56 but how *is it that* ye do not discern t time? 3778
13: 6 He spake also t parable; A certain *man* had 3778
13: 7 *these* three years I come seeking fruit on t 3778
13: 8 Lord, let it alone t year also, till I shall dig 3778
13:16 And ought not t *woman,* being a daughter 3778
13:16 be loosed from t bond on the sabbath day? 3778
14: 9 and say to thee, Give t *man* place; 3778
14:30 T man began to build, and was not able to 3778
15: 2 T *man* receiveth sinners, and eateth with 3778
15: 3 And he spake t parable unto them, saying, 3778
15:24 For t my son was dead, and is alive again; 3778
15:30 But as soon as t thy son was come, 3778
15:32 for t thy brother was dead, and is alive 3778
16: 2 unto him, How *is it that* I hear t of thee? 3778
16: 8 for the children of t world are in their 3778
16:24 my tongue; for I am tormented in t flame. 3778
16:26 And besides all t, between us and you there 3778
16:28 lest they also come into t place of torment. 3778
17: 6 ye might say unto t sycamine tree, Be thou 3778
17:18 to give glory to God, save t stranger. 3778
17:25 and be rejected of t generation. 3778
18: 1 And he spake a parable unto them *to t end,* NIG
18: 5 Yet because t widow troubleth me, I will 3778
18: 9 And he spake t parable unto certain which 3778
18:11 unjust, adulterers, or even as t publican. 3778
18:14 t man went down to his house justified 3778
18:23 And when he heard t, he was very 3778
18:30 Who shall not receive manifold more in t 3778
18:34 and t saying was hid from them, 3778
19: 9 **T day** is salvation come to this house, 4594
19: 9 This day is salvation come to t house, 3778
19:14 We will not have t *man* to reign over us. 3778
19:42 even thou, at least in t thy day, 3778
20: 2 or who is he that gave thee t authority? 3778
20: 9 Then began he to speak to the people t 3778
20:14 among themselves, saying, T is the heir: 3778
20:17 and said, What is t then that is written, 3778
20:19 for they perceived that he had spoken t 3778
20:34 The children of t world marry, and 3778
21: 3 that t poor widow hath cast in more than 3778
21:23 in the land, and wrath upon t people. 3778
21:32 T generation shall not pass away, till all be 3778
21:34 and cares of *t* life, and *so* that day come NIG
22:15 With desire I have desired to eat t passover 3778
22:17 Take t, and divide *it* among yourselves: 3778
22:19 T is my body which is given for you: 3778
22:19 given for you: t do in remembrance of me. 3778
22:20 T cup *is* the new testament in my blood, 3778
22:23 which of them it was that should do t 3778
22:34 Peter, *the* cock shall not crow **t day**, 4594
22:37 that t that is written must yet be 3778
22:42 if thou be willing, remove t cup from me: 3778
22:53 but t is your hour, and the power of 3778
22:56 and said, T *man* was also with him. 3778
22:59 Of a truth t *fellow* also was with him: 3778
23: 2 We found t *fellow* perverting the nation, 3778
23: 4 and *to* the people, I find no fault in t man. 3778
23: 5 beginning from Galilee to **t place**. 5602
23:14 unto them, Ye have brought t man unto me, 3778
23:14 have found no fault in t man *touching those* 3778
23:18 Away with t *man,* and release unto us 3778
23:38 Hebrew, T IS THE KING OF THE JEWS. 3778
23:41 but t *man* hath done nothing amiss. 3778
23:47 saying, Certainly t was a righteous man. 3778
23:52 T *man* went unto Pilate, and begged 3778
24:21 and beside all t, to day is the third day since 3778
Jn 1:15 cried, saying, T was he of whom I spake, 3778
1:19 And t is the record of John, when the Jews 3778
1:30 T is he of whom I said, After me cometh a 3778
1:34 and bare record that t is the Son of God. 3778
2:11 T beginning of miracles did Jesus in Cana 3778
2:12 After t he went down to Capernaum, he, 3778
2:19 Destroy t temple, and in three days I will 3778
2:20 and six years was t temple in building, 3778
2:22 his disciples remembered that he had said t 3778
3:19 And t is the condemnation, that light is 3778
3:29 t my joy therefore is fulfilled. 3778
4:13 Whosoever drinketh of t water shall thirst 3778
4:15 Sir, give me t water, that I thirst not, 3778
4:20 Our fathers worshipped in t mountain; and 3778
4:21 when ye shall neither in t mountain, 3778
4:27 And upon t came his disciples, and 3778
4:29 all *things* that ever I did: is not t the Christ? 3778
4:42 and know that t is indeed the Christ, 3778
4:54 T *is* again the second miracle *that* Jesus 3778
5: 1 After t there was a feast of the Jews; and 3778
5:28 Marvel not at t: for the hour is coming, 3778
6: 6 And t he said to prove him: for he himself 3778
6:14 T is of a truth *that* prophet that should 3778
6:29 and said unto them, T is the work of God, 3778
6:34 unto him, Lord, evermore give us t bread. 3778
6:39 And t is the Father's will which hath sent 3778
6:40 And t is the will of him that sent me, 3778
6:42 And they said, Is not t Jesus, the son of 3778
6:50 T is the bread which cometh down from 3778
6:51 if any *man* eat of t bread, he shall live for 3778
6:52 How can t *man* give us *his* flesh to eat? 3778
6:58 T is *that* bread which came down from 3778
Jn 6:58 he that eateth *of* t bread shall live for ever. 3778
6:60 of his disciples, when they had heard *t,* said, NIG
6:60 had heard *this,* said, T is a hard saying; 3778
6:61 at it, he said unto them, Doth t offend you? 3778
7: 8 Go ye up unto t feast: I go not up yet unto 3778
7: 8 I go not up yet unto t feast; for my time is 3778
7:15 saying, How knoweth t *man* letters, 3778
7:25 Is not t he, whom they seek to kill? 3778
7:26 Do the rulers know indeed that t is the very 3778
7:27 Howbeit we know t *man* whence he is: but 3778
7:31 will he do moe miracles than these which t 3778
7:36 What *manner of* saying is t that he said, 3778
7:39 (But t spake he of the Spirit, which they 3778
7:40 when they heard *t* saying, said, Of a truth NIG
7:40 *this* saying, said, Of a truth t is the Prophet. 3778
7:41 Others said, T is the Christ. But some said, 3778
7:46 Never man spake like t man. 3778
7:49 But t people who knoweth not the law are 3778
8: 4 Master, t woman was taken in adultery, in 3778
8: 6 T they said, tempting him, that they might 3778
8:23 ye are of t world; I am not of this world. 3778
8:23 ye are of this world; I am not of t world. 3778
8:40 I have heard of God: t did not Abraham. 3778
9: 2 Master, who did sin, t *man,* or his parents, 3778
9: 3 Neither hath t *man* sinned, nor his parents: 3778
9: 8 said, Is not t he that sat and begged? 3778
9: 9 Some said, T is he: others *said,* He is like 3778
9:16 T man is not of God, because he keepeth 3778
9:19 And they asked them, saying, Is t your son, 3778
9:20 We know that t is our son, and that he was 3778
9:24 the praise: we know that t man is a sinner. 3778
9:29 *as for t fellow,* we know not from whence 3778
9:33 If t *man* were not of God, he could do 3778
9:39 For judgment I am come into t world, 3778
10: 6 T parable spake Jesus unto them: but 3778
10:16 other sheep I have, which are not of t fold: 3778
10:18 T commandment have I received of my 3778
10:41 all *things* that John spake of t *man* were 3778
11: 4 T sickness is not unto death, but for 3778
11: 9 because he seeth the light of t world. 3778
11:26 in me shall never die. Believest thou t? 3778
11:37 Could not t *man,* which opened the eyes of 3778
11:37 have caused that even t *man* should not 3778
11:39 saith unto him, Lord, **by t time** he stinketh: 2235
11:47 do we? for t man doeth many miracles. 3778
11:51 And t spake he not of himself: but 3778
12: 5 Why was not t ointment sold for three 3778
12: 6 T he said, not that he cared for the poor; 3778
12: 7 the day of my burying hath she kept **t.** 846
12:18 **For t cause** the people also met him, 1223+3778
12:18 for that they heard that he had done t 3778
12:25 he that hateth his life in t world shall keep 3778
12:27 Father, save me from t hour: but for this 3778
12:27 but **for t cause** came I unto this hour. 1223+3778
12:27 but for this cause came I unto t hour. 3778
12:30 T voice came not because of me, but 3778
12:31 Now is the judgment of t world: now shall 3778
12:31 now shall the prince of t world be cast out. 3778
12:33 T he said, signifying what death he should 3778
12:34 man must be lift up? who is t Son of man? 3778
13: 1 depart out of t world unto the Father, 3778
13:28 knew for what intent he spake t unto him. 3778
13:35 By t shall all *men* know that ye are my 3778
14:30 for the prince of t world cometh, and 3778
15:12 T is my commandment, That ye love one 3778
15:13 Greater love hath no *man* than t, that a man 3778
15:25 But *t cometh to pass,* that the word might be NIG
16:11 because the prince of t world is judged. 3778
16:17 What is t that he saith unto us, A little 3778
16:18 What is t that he saith, A little while? 3778
16:30 by t we believe that thou camest forth from 3778
17: 3 And t is life eternal, that they might know 3778
18:17 Art not thou also *one* of t man's disciples? 3778
18:29 What accusation bring you against t man? 3778
18:34 Sayest thou t *thing* of thyself, 3778
18:36 My kingdom is not of t world: 3778
18:36 this world: if my kingdom were of t world, 3778
18:37 To t end was I born, and for this cause 3778
18:37 **for t cause** came I into the world, 1519+3778
18:38 And when he had said t, he went out again 3778
18:40 all again, saying, Not t *man,* but Barabbas. 3778
19:12 Jews cried out, saying, If thou let t *man* go, 3778
19:20 T title then read many of the Jews: for 3778
19:28 After t, Jesus knowing that all *things* were 3778
19:38 And after t Joseph of Arimathea, being a 3778
20:22 And when he had said t, he breathed on 3778
20:30 which are not written in t book: 3778
21: 1 and **on t wise** shewed he *himself.* 3779
21:14 T *is* now the third time *that* Jesus shewed 3778
21:19 T spake he, signifying by what death he 3778
21:19 And when he had spoken t, he saith unto 3778
21:21 to Jesus, Lord, and what *shall* t *man do?* 3778
21:23 Then went t saying abroad among 3778
21:24 T is the disciple which testifieth of these 3778
Ac 1: 6 wilt thou at t time restore again 3778
1:11 t *same* Jesus, which is taken up from you 3778
1:16 t scripture must needs have been fulfilled, 3778
1:17 with us, and had obtained part of t ministry. 3778
1:18 Now t *man* purchased a field with 3778
1:25 That *he* may take part of t ministry and 3778
2: 6 Now when t was noised abroad, 3778
2:12 saying one to another, What meaneth t? 3778
2:14 be t known unto you, and hearken to my 3778
2:16 But t is that which was spoken by 3778
2:29 and his sepulchre is with us unto t day. 3778
2:31 He seeing *t* before, spake of the resurrection NIG
2:32 T Jesus hath God raised up, whereof we all 3778
2:33 he hath shed forth t, which ye now see and 3778
2:37 Now when they heard *t,* they were pricked NIG
2:40 Save yourselves from t untoward 3778
3:12 Ye men of Israel, why marvel ye at t? 3778
3:12 or holiness we had made t *man* to walk? 846
3:16 faith in his name hath made t *man* strong, 3778
3:16 the faith which is by him hath given him t 3778
4: 7 or by what name, have ye done t? 3778

Ac 4: 9 If we t day be examined of the good deed 4594
4:10 even by him doth t man stand here before 3778
4:11 T is the stone which was set at nought of 3778
4:17 that they speak henceforth to no man in t 3778
4:22 on whom t miracle of healing was shewed. 3778
5: 4 why hast thou conceived t thing in thine 3778
5:20 temple to the people all the words of t life. 3778
5:24 they doubted of them whereunto t would 3778
5:28 you that you should not teach in t name? 3778
5:28 and intend to bring t man's blood upon us. 3778
5:37 After t man rose up Judas of Galilee in 3778
5:38 for if t counsel or this work be of men, 3778
5:38 for if this counsel or t work be of men, 3778
6: 3 whom we may appoint over t business. 3778
6:13 T man ceaseth not to speak blasphemous 3778
6:13 blasphemous words against t holy place, 3778
6:14 that t Jesus of Nazareth shall destroy this 3778
6:14 that this Jesus of Nazareth shall destroy t 3778
7: 4 he removed him into t land, wherein ye 3778
7: 6 And God spake on t wise, That his seed 3779
7: 7 they come forth, and serve me in t place. 3778
7:29 Then fled Moses at t saying, and was a 3778
7:35 T Moses whom they refused, saying, 3778
7:37 T is that Moses, which said unto 3778
7:38 T is he, that was in the church in 3778
7:40 for as for t Moses, which brought us out of 3778
7:60 Lord, lay not t sin to their charge. 3778
7:60 And when he had said t, he fell asleep. 3778
8:10 saying, T man is the great power of God. 3778
8:19 Saying, Give me also t power, that on 3778
8:21 Thou hast neither part nor lot in t matter: 3778
8:22 Repent therefore of t thy wickedness, and 3778
8:29 Go near, and join thyself to t chariot. 3778
8:32 place of the scripture which he read was t, 3778
8:34 pray thee, of whom speaketh the prophet t? 3778
9: 2 that if he found any of t way, whether they NIG
9:13 Lord, I have heard by many of t man, 3778
9:21 Is not t he that destroyed them which called 3778
9:21 them which called on t name in Jerusalem, 3778
9:22 at Damascus, proving that t is very Christ. 3778
9:36 t woman was full of good works and 3778
10:16 T was done thrice: and the vessel was 3778
10:17 Now while Peter doubted in himself what t NIG
10:30 Four days ago I was fasting until t hour; 3778
11:10 And t was done three times: and all were 3778
13:17 The God of t people of Israel chose our 3778
13:23 Of t man's seed hath God according to his 3778
13:26 to you is the word of t salvation sent. 3778
13:33 art my Son, t day have I begotten thee. 4594
13:34 to return to corruption, he said on t wise, 3779
13:38 that through t man is preached unto you 3778
13:48 And when the Gentiles heard t, they were NIG
15: 2 the apostles and elders about t question. 3778
15: 6 elders came together for to consider of t 3778
15:15 And to t agree the words of the prophets; 3778
15:16 After t I will return, and will build again 3778
15:23 they wrote letters by them after t manner; 3592
16:18 And t did she many days. But Paul, 3778
16:36 And the keeper of the prison told t saying 3778
17: 3 and that t Jesus, whom I preach unto you, 3778
17:18 And some said, What will t babbler say? 3778
17:19 saying, May we know what t new doctrine, 3778
17:23 I found an altar with t inscription, 3739
17:30 And the times of t ignorance God winked NIG
17:32 We will hear thee again of t matter. 3778
18:10 hurt thee: for I have much people in t city. 3778
18:13 T fellow persuadeth men to worship God 3778
18:18 And Paul after t tarried there yet a good NIG
18:21 I must by all means keep t feast that cometh NIG
18:25 T man was instructed in the way of 3778
19: 5 When they heard t, they were baptized in NIG
19:10 And t continued by the space of two years; 3778
19:17 And t was known to all the Jews and 3778
19:25 ye know that by t craft we have our wealth. 3778
19:26 t Paul hath persuaded and turned away 3778
19:27 So that not only t our craft is in danger to 3778
19:40 to be called in question for t day's uproar, 4594
19:40 we may give an account of t concourse. 3778
20:26 Wherefore I take you to record t day, 2250+4594
20:29 For I know t, that after my departing shall 3778
21:11 Jerusalem bind the man that oweth t girdle, 3778
21:23 Do therefore t that we say to thee: We have 3778
21:28 T is the man, that teacheth all men every 3778
21:28 against the people, and the law, and t place: 3778
21:28 the temple, and hath polluted t holy place. 3778
22: 3 yet brought up in t city at the feet of 3778
22: 3 zealous towards God, as ye all are t day. 4594
22: 4 And I persecuted t way unto the death, 3778
22:22 And they gave him audience unto t word, 3778
22:26 what thou doest: for t man is a Roman. 3778
22:28 With a great sum obtained I t freedom. 3778
23: 1 all good conscience before God until t day. 3778
23: 9 strove, saying, We find no evil in t man: 3778
23:13 than forty which had made t conspiracy. 3778
23:17 Bring t young man unto the chief captain: 3778
23:18 prayed me to bring t young man unto thee, 3778
23:25 And he wrote a letter after t manner: 3778
23:27 T man was taken of the Jews, and 3778
24: 2 that very worthy deeds are done unto t 3778
24: 5 For we have found t man a pestilent fellow, 3778
24:10 been of many years a judge unto t nation, 3778
24:14 But t I confess unto thee, that after the way 3778
24:21 Except it be for t one voice, that I cried 3778
24:21 dead I am called in question by you t day. 4594
24:25 and answered, Go thy way for t time; NIG
25: 5 go down with me, and accuse t man, 3778
25:24 ye see t man, about whom all the multitude 3778
26: 2 I shall answer for myself t day before thee 4594
26:16 for I have appeared unto thee for t purpose, 3778
26:22 obtained help of God, I continue unto t day, 3778
26:26 for t thing was not done in a corner. 3778
26:29 but also all that hear me t day, were both 4594
26:31 T man doeth nothing worthy of death or 3778
26:32 T man might have been set at liberty, 3778
27:10 I perceive that t voyage will be with hurt NIG
Ac 27:21 and to have gained t harm and loss. 3778
27:23 For there stood by me t night the angel of 3778
27:33 T day is the fourteenth day that ye have 4594
27:34 for t is for your health: for there shall not a 3778
28: 4 No doubt t man is a murderer, whom, 3778
28: 9 So when t was done, others also, which had 3778
28:20 For t cause therefore have I called for you, 3778
28:20 that for the hope of Israel I am bound with t 3778
28:22 for as concerning t sect, we know that 3778
28:26 Saying, Go unto t people, and say, 3778
28:27 For the heart of t people is waxed gross, 3778
Ro 1:26 For t cause God gave them up unto 1223+3778
2: 3 And thinkest thou t, O man, that judgest 3778
3:26 I say, at t time his righteousness: 3568+3588
4: 9 Cometh t blessedness then upon 3778
5: 2 whom also we have access by faith into t 3778
6: 6 Knowing t, that our old man is crucified 3778
7:24 who shall deliver me from the body of t 3778
8:18 For I reckon that the sufferings of t present NIG
9: 9 For t is the word of promise, At this time 3778
9: 9 At t time will I come, and Sara shall have a 3778
9:10 And not only t; but when Rebecca also had NIG
9:17 Even for t same purpose have I raised thee 3778
10: 6 which is of faith speaketh on t wise, 3779
11: 5 at t present time also there is a remnant NIG
11: 8 they should not hear;) unto t day. 2250+4594
11:25 that ye should be ignorant of t mystery, 3778
11:27 For t is my covenant unto them, when I 3778
12: 2 And be not conformed to t world: but be ye 3778
13: 6 For for t cause pay you tribute also: 1223+3778
13: 6 attending continually upon t very thing. 3778
13: 9 For t, Thou shalt not commit adultery, NIG
13: 9 it is briefly comprehended in t saying, 3778
14: 9 For to t end Christ both died, and 1519+3778
14:13 but judge t rather, that no man put a 3778
15: 9 For t cause I will confess to thee 1223+3778
15:28 When therefore I have performed t, and 3778
15:28 and have sealed to them t fruit, 3778
16:22 I Tertius, who wrote t epistle, salute you in NIG
1Co 1:12 Now t I say, that every one of you saith, I 3778
1:20 where is the disputer of t world? hath not 3778
1:20 hath not God made foolish the wisdom of t 3778
2: 6 yet not the wisdom of t world, nor of 3778
2: 6 nor of the princes of t world, that come to 3778
2: 8 Which none of the princes of t world knew: 3778
3:12 Now if any man build upon t foundation 3778
3:18 among you seemeth to be wise in t world, 3778
3:19 For the wisdom of t world is foolishness 3778
4:11 Even unto t present hour we both hunger, 3588
4:13 are the offscouring of all things unto t day. 737
4:17 For t cause have I sent unto you 1223+3778
5: 2 that he that hath done t deed might be taken 3778
5: 3 concerning him that hath so done t deed, 3778
5:10 Yet not altogether with the fornicators of t 3778
6: 3 how much more things that pertain to t life? NIG
6: 4 ye have judgments of things pertaining to t NIG
7: 6 But I speak t by permission, and not of 3778
7: 7 his proper gift of God, one after t manner, 3779
7:26 that t is good for the present distress, 3778
7:29 But t I say, brethren, the time is short: 3778
7:31 And they that use t world, as not abusing it: 3778
7:31 as not abusing it: for the fashion of t world 3778
7:35 And t I speak for your own profit; not that I 3778
8: 7 with conscience of the idol unto t hour, 737
8: 9 But take heed lest by any means t liberty of 3778
9: 3 answer to them that do examine me is t: 3778
9:10 For our sakes, no doubt, t is written: that he NIG
9:12 If others be partakers of t power over you, NIG
9:12 Nevertheless we have not used t power; but 3778
9:17 For if I do t thing willingly, I have a 3778
9:23 And t I do for the gospel's sake, that I 3778
10:28 T is offered in sacrifice unto idols, 3778
11:10 For t cause ought the woman to 1223+3778
11:17 Now in t that I declare unto you I praise 3778
11:20 one place, t is not to eat the Lord's supper. NIG
11:22 shall I praise you in t? I praise you not. 3778
11:24 t is my body, which is broken for you: 3778
11:24 broken for you: t do in remembrance of me. 3778
11:25 T cup is the new testament in my blood: 3778
11:25 t do ye, as oft as ye drink it, in 3778
11:26 For as often as ye eat t bread, and drink this 3778
11:26 often as ye eat this bread, and drink t cup, 3778
11:27 Wherefore whosoever shall eat t bread, and 3778
11:27 and drink t cup of the Lord unworthily, NIG
11:30 For t cause many are weak and 1223+3778
14:21 and other lips will I speak unto t people; 3778
15: 6 the greater part remain unto t present, 737
15:19 If in t life only we have hope in Christ, 3778
15:34 knowledge of God: I speak t to your shame. NIG
15:50 Now t I say, brethren, that flesh and 3778
15:53 For t corruptible must put on incorruption, 3778
15:53 and t mortal must put on immortality. 3778
15:54 So when t corruptible shall have put on 3778
15:54 and t mortal shall have put on immortality, 3778
16:12 but his will was not at all to come at t time; 3568
2Co 1:12 For our rejoicing is t, the testimony of our 3778
1:15 And in t confidence I was minded to come 3778
2: 1 But I determined t with myself, that I 3778
2: 3 And I wrote t same unto you, lest, when I 3778
2: 6 Sufficient to such a man is t punishment, 3778
2: 9 For to t end also did I write, that I 1519+3778
3:10 made glorious had no glory in t respect, 3778
3:14 for until t day remaineth the same 2250+4594
3:15 But even unto t day, when Moses is read, 4594
4: 1 Therefore seeing we have t ministry, as we 3778
4: 4 In whom the god of t world hath blinded 3778
4: 7 But we have t treasure in earthen vessels, 3778
5: 1 For we know that if our earthly house of t NIG
5: 2 For in t we groan, earnestly desiring to be 3778
5: 4 For we that are in t tabernacle do groan, NIG
7: 3 I speak not t to condemn you: for I have NIG
7:11 For behold t selfsame thing, that ye 3778
7:11 approved yourselves to be clear in t matter. NIG
8: 5 And t they did, not as we hoped, but NIG
8: 7 to us, see that ye abound in t grace also. 3778
2Co 8:10 for t is expedient for you, who have begun 3778
8:14 that now at t time your abundance may be a NIG
8:19 the churches to travel with us with t grace, 3778
8:20 Avoiding t, that no man should blame us in 3778
8:20 that no man should blame us in t 3778
9: 3 of you should be in vain in t behalf; 3778
9: 4 should be ashamed in t same confident 3778
9: 6 But t I say, He which soweth sparingly 3778
9:12 For the administration of t service not only 3778
9:13 Whiles by the experiment of t ministration 3778
10: 7 let him of himself think t again, that, as he 3778
10:11 Let such a one think t, that, such as we are 3778
11:10 no man shall stop me of t boasting in 3778
11:17 were foolishly, in t confidence of boasting. 3778
12: 8 For t thing I besought the Lord thrice, 3778
12:13 burdensome to you? forgive me t wrong. 3778
13: 1 T is the third time I am coming to you. 3778
13: 9 and t also we wish, even your perfection. 3778
Gal 1: 4 that he might deliver us from t present evil NIG
3: 2 T only would I learn of you, Received ye 3778
3:17 And t I say, that the covenant, that was 3778
4:25 For t Agar is mount Sinai in Arabia, and NIG
5: 8 T persuasion cometh not of him that calleth NIG
5:14 even in t; Thou shalt love thy neighbour as NIG
5:16 T I say then, Walk in the Spirit, and ye shall NIG
6:16 And as many as walk according to t rule, 3778
Eph 1:21 not only in t world, but also in that which is 3778
2: 2 walked according to the course of t world, 3778
3: 1 For t cause I Paul, the prisoner of Jesus 3778
3: 8 than the least of all saints, is t grace given, 3778
3:14 For t cause I bow my knees unto the Father 3778
4:17 T I say therefore, and testify in the Lord, 3778
5: 5 For t ye know, that no whoremonger, 3778
5:31 For t cause shall a man leave his father and 3778
5:32 T is a great mystery: but I speak 3778
6: 1 obey your parents in the Lord: for t is right. 3778
6:12 against the rulers of the darkness of t 3778
Php 1: 6 Being confident of t very thing, that he 3778
1: 7 Even as it is meet for me to think t of you 3778
1: 9 And t I pray, that your love may abound 3778
1:19 For I know that t shall turn to my salvation 3778
1:22 live in the flesh, t is the fruit of my labour: 3778
1:25 And having t confidence, I know that I 3778
2: 5 Let t mind be in you, which was also in 3778
3:13 t one thing I do, forgetting those things NIG
3:15 God shall reveal even t unto you. 3778
Col 1: 9 For t cause we also, since the day 1223+3778
1:27 the glory of t mystery among the Gentiles; 3778
2: 4 And t I say, lest any man should beguile 3778
3:20 obey your parents in all things: for t is well 3778
4:16 And when t epistle is read amongst you, NIG
1Th 2:13 For t cause also thank we God 1223+3778
3: 5 For t cause, when I could no longer 1223+3778
4: 3 For t is the will of God, even your 3778
4:15 For t we say unto you by the word of 3778
5:18 for t is the will of God in Christ Jesus 3778
5:27 I charge you by the Lord that t epistle be NIG
2Th 1:11 that our God would count you worthy of t NIG
2:11 And for t cause God shall send them 1223+3778
3:10 t we commanded you, that if any would not 3778
3:14 And if any man obey not our word by t NIG
1Ti 1: 9 Knowing t, that the law is not made for a 3778
1:15 T is a faithful saying, and worthy of all NIG
1:16 Howbeit for t cause I obtained 1223+3778
1:18 T charge I commit unto thee, son Timothy, 3778
2: 3 For t is good and acceptable in the sight of 3778
3: 1 T is a true saying, If a man desire the office NIG
4: 9 T is a faithful saying and worthy of all NIG
4:16 for in doing t thou shalt both save thyself, 3778
6: 7 For we brought nothing into t world, and NIG
6:14 That thou keep t commandment without NIG
6:17 Charge them that are rich in t world, 3568
2Ti 1:15 T thou knowest, that all they which are in 3778
2: 4 entangleth himself with the affairs of t life; NIG
2:19 having t seal, The Lord knoweth them that 3778
3: 1 T know also, that in the last days perilous 3778
3: 6 For of t sort are they which creep into 3778
4:10 having loved t present world, and NIG
Tit 1: 5 For t cause left I thee in Crete, that thou 3778
1:13 T witness is true. Wherefore rebuke them 3778
2:12 and godly, in t present world; NIG
3: 8 T is a faithful saying, and these things I will NIG
Heb 1: 5 art my Son, t day have I begotten thee? 4594
3: 3 For t man was counted worthy of more 3778
4: 4 a certain place of the seventh day on t wise, 3779
4: 5 And in t place again, If they shall enter into 3778
5: 4 And no man taketh t honour unto himself, NIG
6: 3 And t will we do, if God permit. 3778
7: 1 For t Melchisedec, king of Salem, priest of 3778
7: 4 Now consider how great t man was, unto 3778
7:21 t with an oath by him that said unto him, 3588
7:24 But t man, because he continueth ever, hath 846
7:27 for t he did once, when he offered up 3778
8: 1 Now of the things which we have spoken t NIG
8: 3 wherefore it is of necessity that t man have 3778
8:10 For t is the covenant that I will make with 3778
9: 8 The Holy Ghost t signifying, that the way 3778
9:11 with hands, that is to say, not of t building, 3778
9:15 And for t cause he is the mediator of 1223+3778
9:20 T is the blood of the testament which God 3778
9:27 men once to die, but after t the judgment: 3778
10:12 But t man, after he had offered one sacrifice 846
10:16 T is the covenant that I will make with 3778
11: 5 for before his translation he had t testimony, NIG
12:27 And t word, Yet once more, signifieth 3588
13:19 But I beseech you the rather to do t, that I 3778
Jas 1: 3 Knowing t, that the trying of your faith NIG
1:25 t man shall be blessed in his deed. 3778
1:26 his own heart, t man's religion is vain. 3778
1:27 undefiled before God and the Father is t, 3778
2: 5 Hath not God chosen the poor of t world 3778
3:15 T wisdom descendeth not from above, but 3778
4:15 Lord will, we shall live, and do t, or that. 3778
1Pe 1:25 And t is the word which by the gospel is 3778
2:19 For t is thankworthy, if a man for 3778

1Pe 2:20 take it patiently, t *is* acceptable with God. 3778
3: 5 For after t manner in the old time the holy 3779
4: 6 For for t cause was the gospel 1519+3778
4:16 but let him glorify God on t behalf. 3778
5:12 testifying that t is the true grace of God 3778
2Pe 1: 5 And beside t, giving all diligence, add to 3778
1:13 it meet, as long as I am in t tabernacle, 3778
1:14 Knowing that shortly *I* must put off t my NIG
1:17 T is my beloved Son, in whom I am well 3778
1:18 And t voice which came from heaven we 3778
1:20 Knowing t first, that no prophecy of 3778
3: 1 T second epistle, beloved, I now write unto 3778
3: 3 Knowing t first, that there shall come in 3778
3: 5 For t they willingly are ignorant of, that by 3778
3: 8 be not ignorant of t one *thing,* that one day 3778
1Jn 1: 5 T then is the message which we have heard 3778
2:25 And t is the promise that he hath promised 3778
3: 3 And every *man* that hath t hope in him 3778
3: 8 For t purpose the Son of God was 3778
3:10 In t the children of God are manifest, and 3778
3:11 For t is the message that ye heard from 3778
3:17 But whoso hath t world's good, and NIG
3:23 And t is his commandment, That we should 3778
4: 3 and t is *that spirit* of antichrist, whereof you 3778
4: 9 In t was manifested the love of God 3778
4:17 because as he is, so are we in t world. 3778
4:21 And t commandment have we from him, 3778
5: 2 By t we know that we love the children of 3778
5: 3 For t is the love of God, that we keep his 3778
5: 4 t is the victory that overcometh the world, 3778
5: 6 T is he that came by water and blood, 3778
5: 9 for t is the witness of God which he hath 3778
5:11 And t is the record, that God hath given to 3778
5:11 to us eternal life, and t life is in his Son. 3778
5:14 And t is the confidence that we have in 3778
5:20 T is the true God, and eternal life. 3778
2Jn 1: 6 And t is love, that we walk after his 3778
1: 6 T is the commandment, That, as ye have 3778
1: 7 the flesh. T is a deceiver and an antichrist. 3778
1:10 any unto you, and bring not t doctrine, 3778
Jude 1: 4 who were before of old ordained to t 3778
1: 5 though ye once knew t, how that the Lord, 3778
Rev 1: 3 and they that hear the words of t prophecy, NIG
2: 6 But t thou hast, that thou hatest the deeds 3778
2:24 as many as have not t doctrine, and 3778
4: 1 After t I looked, and behold, a door *was* 3778
7: 9 After t I beheld, and lo, a great multitude, 3778
11: 5 hurt them, he must in t manner be killed. 3779
11:15 The kingdoms of t world are become NIG
18:18 saying, What *city is* like unto t great city? NIG
20: 5 were finished. T *is* the first resurrection. 3778
20:14 into the lake of fire. T is the second death. 3778
22: 7 the sayings of the prophecy of t book. 3778
22: 9 of them which keep the sayings of t book: 3778
22:10 Seal not the sayings of the prophecy of t 3778
22:18 the words of the prophecy of t book, 3778
22:18 him the plagues that are written in t book: 3778
22:19 from the words of the book of t prophecy, 3778
22:19 *from* the *things* which are written in t book. 3778

THISTLE (5) [THISTLES]

2Ki 14: 9 The t that *was* in Lebanon sent to the cedar 2336
14: 9 that *was* in Lebanon, and trode down the t. 2336
2Ch 25:18 The t that *was* in Lebanon sent to the cedar 2336
25:18 that *was* in Lebanon, and trode down the t. 2336
Hos 10: 8 and the t shall come up on their altars; 1863

THISTLES (3) [THISTLE]

Ge 3:18 and t shall it bring forth to thee; 1863
Job 31:40 Let t grow instead of wheat, and 2336
Mt 7:16 *men* gather grapes of thorns, or figs of t? 5146

THITHER (95) [THITHERWARD]

Ge 19:20 Oh, let me escape t, (*is* it not a 8033+1886.5
19:22 Haste thee, escape t; for I cannot 8033+1886.5
19:22 do any thing till thou be come t. 8033+1886.5
24: 6 that thou bring not my son t again. 8033+1886.5
24: 8 only bring not my son t again. 8033+1886.5
29: 3 t were all the flocks gathered: and 8033+1886.5
39: 1 which had brought him down t. 8033+1886.5
42: 2 get you down t, and buy for us 8033+1886.5
Ex 10:26 serve the LORD, until we come t. 8033+1886.5
26:33 that thou mayest bring in t within 8033+1886.5
Nu 35: 6 the manslayer, that he may flee t: 8033+1886.5
35:11 that the slayer may flee t, which 8033+1886.5
35:15 *any* person unawares may flee t. 8033+1886.5
Dt 1:37 saying, Thou also shalt not go in t. 8033
1:38 before thee, he shall go in t: 8033+1886.5
1:39 they shall go in t, and unto them 8033+1886.5
4:42 That the slayer might flee t, which 8033+1886.5
12: 5 ye seek, and t thou shalt come: 8033+1886.5
12: 6 t ye shall bring your burnt 8033+1886.5
12:11 t shall ye bring all that I command 8033+1886.5
19: 3 that every slayer may flee t. 8033+1886.5
19: 4 which shall flee t, that he may live: 8033+1886.5
32:52 thou shalt not go t unto the land 8033+1886.5
34: 4 but thou shalt not go over t. 8033+1886.5
Jos 7: 3 make not all the people to labour t; 8033+1886.5
7: 4 So there went up t of the people 8033+1886.5
20: 3 *and* unwittingly may flee t: 8033+1886.5
20: 9 person at unawares might flee t, 8033+1886.5
Jdg 8:27 all Israel went t a whoring after it: 8033
9:51 t fled all the men and women, 8033+1886.5
18: 3 they turned in t, and said unto him, 8033
18:17 *and* came in t, *and* took the graven 8033+1886.5
19:15 they turned aside t, to go in *and* to lodge in 8033
21:10 the congregation sent t twelve thousand 8033
1Sa 2:14 in Shiloh unto all the Israelites that came t. 8033
5: 8 carried the ark of the God of Israel about t. NIH
9: 6 now let us go t; peradventure he can shew 8033
10: 5 to pass, when thou art come t to the city, 8033
10:10 when they came t to the hill, behold, 8033
10:22 if the man should yet come t. 1988
19:23 he went t to Naioth in Ramah: and the spirit 8033
1Sa 22: 1 heard *it*, they went down t to him. 8033+1886.5
30: 7 Abiathar brought t the ephod to David. 5066
2Sa 2: 2 So David went up t, and his two wives also, 8033
4: 6 they came t into the midst of the house, 2007
1Ki 6: 7 *of* stone made ready *before it was* brought t: NIH
19: 9 he came t unto a cave, and lodged there; 8033
2Ki 2: 8 they were divided hither and t, so that they 2008
2:14 smitten the waters, they parted hither and t: 2008
4: 8 he turned in t to eat bread. 8033+1886.5
4:10 cometh to us, *that* he shall turn in t. 8033+1886.5
4:11 that he came t, and he turned into 8033+1886.5
6: 6 he cut down a stick, and cast *it* in t; 8033+1886.5
6: 9 a place; for t the Syrians are come down. 8033
6:14 Therefore sent he t horses, and 8033+1886.5
9: 2 when thou comest t, look out there 8033+1886.5
17:27 Carry t one of the priests whom ye 8033+1886.5
2Ch 1: 6 Solomon went up t to the brasen altar 8033
Ezr 10: 6 *when* he came t, he did eat no bread, 8033
Ne 4:20 of the trumpet, resort ye t unto us: 8033+1886.5
5:16 all my servants *were* gathered t unto 8033
13: 9 t brought I again the vessels of the house of 8033
Job 1:21 and naked shall I return t: 8033+1886.5
6:20 they came t, and were ashamed. 5704+1886.3
Ecc 1: 7 whence the rivers come, t they return again. 8033
Isa 7:24 and with bows shall *men* come t; 8033+1886.5
7:25 there shall not come t the fear of 8033+1886.5
32:20 that send forth t the feet of the ox and NIH
55:10 returneth not t, but watereth 8033+1886.5
57: 7 even t wentest thou up to offer sacrifice. 8033
Jer 22:11 this place; He shall not return t any more: 8033
22:27 to return, t shall they not return. 8033+1886.5
31: 8 a great company shall return t. 2008
40: 4 and convenient for thee to go, t go. 8033+1886.5
Eze 1:20 they went, t *was their* spirit to go; 8033+1886.5
11:18 they shall come t, and they shall 8033+1886.5
40: 1 was upon me, and brought me t. 8033+1886.5
40: 3 he brought me t, and behold, 8033+1886.5
47: 9 because these waters shall come t: 8033+1886.5
Joel 3:11 t cause thy mighty ones to come 8033+1886.5
Mt 2:22 of his father Herod, he was afraid to go t: 1563
Mk 6:33 and ran afoot t out of all cities, and 1563
Lk 17:37 Wheresoever the body *is*, t will the eagles 1563
21: 2 a certain poor widow casting in t two mites. 1563
Jn 7:34 find *me:* and where I am, t ye cannot come. NIG
7:36 *me:* and where I am, t ye cannot come? NIG
11: 8 to stone thee; and goest thou t again? 1563
18: 2 for Jesus ofttimes resorted t with his 1563
18: 3 cometh t with lanterns and torches and 1563
Ac 8:30 And Philip ran t to *him,* and heard him read NIG
14:19 And there came t *certain* Jews from 1904
16:13 spake unto the women which resorted t. NIG
17:10 who coming t went into the synagogue of NIG
17:13 they came t also, and stirred up the people. 2546
25: 4 and that he himself would depart shortly t. NIG

THITHERWARD (3) [THITHER]

Jdg 18:15 they turned t, and came to 8033+1886.5
Jer 50: 5 shall ask the way *to* Zion with their faces t, 2008
Ro 15:24 and to be brought on my way t by you, 1563

THOMAS (12)

Mt 10: 3 T, and Matthew the publican; 2381
Mk 3:18 and T, and James the *son* of Alpheus, and 2381
Lk 6:15 Matthew and T, James the *son* of Alpheus, 2381
Jn 11:16 Then said T, which is called Didymus, 2381
14: 5 T saith unto him, Lord, we know not 2381
20:24 But T, one of the twelve, called Didymus, 2381
20:26 his disciples were within, and T with them: 2381
20:27 Then saith he to T, Reach hither thy finger, 2381
20:28 And T answered and said unto him, 2381
20:29 T, because thou hast seen me, thou hast 2381
21: 2 and T called Didymus, and Nathanael of 2381
Ac 1:13 and John, and Andrew, Philip, and T, 2381

THONG; THONGS See LATCHET; SHOELATCHET; WITHS

THONGS (1)

Ac 22:25 And as they bound him with t, Paul said 2438

THORN (7) [THORNS]

Job 41: 2 his nose? or bore his jaw through with a t? 2336
Pr 26: 9 *As* a t goeth up into the hand of a drunkard, 2336
Isa 55:13 Instead of the t shall come up the fir tree, 5285
Eze 28:24 nor *any* grieving t of all *that are* round 6975
Hos 10: 8 the t and the thistle shall come up on their 6975
Mic 7: 4 the *most* upright *is sharper* than a t hedge: 4534
2Co 12: 7 there was given to me a t in the flesh, 4647

THORNBUSH See BRAMBLE

THORNS (50) [THORN]

Ge 3:18 T also and thistles shall it bring forth to 6975
Ex 22: 6 catch in t, so that the stacks of corn, or 6975
Nu 33:55 t in your sides, and shall vex you in 6796
Jos 23:13 scourges in your sides, and t in your eyes, 6796
Jdg 2: 3 they shall be *as* t in your sides, and NIH
8: 7 I will tear your flesh with the t of 6975
8:16 t of the wilderness and briers, and 6975
2Sa 23: 6 *the sons of* Belial *shall be* all of them as t 6975
2Ch 33:11 which took Manasseh among the t, and 2336
Job 5: 5 taketh it *even* out of the t, and the robber 6791
Ps 58: 9 Before your pots can feel the t, he shall take 329
118:12 like bees; they are quenched as the fire of t: 6975
Pr 15:19 way of the slothful *man is* as a hedge of t: 2312
22: 5 T and snares *are* in the way of the froward: 6791
24:31 it was all grown over *with* t, *and* nettles had 7063
Ecc 7: 6 For as the crackling of t under a pot, so 5518
SS 2: 2 As the lily among t, so *is* my love among 2336
Isa 5: 6 but there shall come up briers and t: 7898
7:19 and upon all t, and upon all bushes. 5285
7:23 it shall *even* be for briers and t. 7898
7:24 all the land shall become briers and t. 7898
7:25 not come thither the fear of briers and t: 7898
Isa 9:18 it shall devour the briers and t, and 7898
10:17 it shall burn and devour his t and his briers 7898
27: 4 set the briers *and* t against me in battle? 7898
32:13 Upon the land of my people shall come up t 6975
33:12 *as* t cut up shall they be burnt in the fire. 6975
34:13 t shall come up *in* her palaces, nettles and 5518
Jer 4: 3 your fallow ground, and sow not among t. 6975
12:13 They have sown wheat, but shall reap t: 6975
Eze 2: 6 though briers and t *be* with thee, and 5544
Hos 2: 6 I will hedge up thy way with t, and make a 5518
9: 6 possess them: t *shall be* in their tabernacles. 2336
Na 1:10 For while *they be* folden together *as* t, and 5518
Mt 7:16 Do *men* gather grapes of t, or figs of 173
13: 7 And some fell among t; and the thorns 173
13: 7 and the t sprung up, and choked them: 173
13:22 He also that received seed among the t is he 173
27:29 And when they had platted a crown of t, 173
Mk 4: 7 And some fell among t, and the thorns grew 173
4: 7 and the t grew up, and choked it, and 173
4:18 And these are they which are sown among t; 173
15:17 and platted a crown of t, and put *it* about his 174
Lk 6:44 For of t *men* do not gather figs, nor of a 173
8: 7 And some fell among t; and the thorns 173
8: 7 and the t sprang up with *it,* and choked it. 173
8:14 And that which fell among t are they, which, 173
Jn 19: 2 And the soldiers platted a crown of t, and 173
19: 5 wearing the crown of t, and the purple robe. 174
Heb 6: 8 But that which beareth t and briers *is* 173

THOROUGHLY (2) [THROUGHLY]

Ge 11: 3 and burn *them* t. 8313+8316+3807.1
Ex 21:19 and shall cause *him* to be t healed. 7495+7495

THOSE (465) [THAT]

Ge 6: 4 There were giants in the earth in t days; and 1992
15:17 a burning lamp that passed between t pieces. 428
19:25 he overthrew t cities, and all the plain, and 411
24:60 let thy seed possess the gate of t which hate NIH
33: 5 the children; and said, Who *are* t with thee? 428
41:35 let them gather all the food of t good years 428
42: 5 the sons of Israel came to buy *corn* among t NIH
50: 3 are fulfilled the days of t which are NIH
Ex 2:11 it came to pass in t days, when Moses was 1992
4:21 see that thou do all t wonders before NIH
29:33 they shall eat t *things* wherewith 3963.1
35:35 and of t that devise cunning work. 2803+4284
Lev 11:27 that go on *all* four, t *are* unclean unto you: 1992
14:11 t *things,* before the LORD, *at* the door 3963.1
14:42 and put *them* in the place of t stones; NIH
15:10 he that beareth *any of* t *things* shall wash 3963.1
15:27 whosoever toucheth t *things* shall be 3963.1
22: 2 that they profane not my holy name *in* t NIH
Nu 1:21 T that were numbered of them, *even* of NIH
1:22 their fathers, t that were numbered of them, NIH
1:23 T that were numbered of them, *even* of NIH
1:25 T that were numbered of them, *even* of NIH
1:27 T that were numbered of them, *even* of NIH
1:29 T that were numbered of them, *even* of NIH
1:31 T that were numbered of them, *even* of NIH
1:33 T that were numbered of them, *even* of NIH
1:35 T that were numbered of them, *even* of NIH
1:37 T that were numbered of them, *even* of NIH
1:39 T that were numbered of them, *even* of NIH
1:41 T that were numbered of them, *even* of NIH
1:43 T that were numbered of them, *even* of NIH
1:44 These *are* t that were numbered, NIH
1:45 So were all t that were numbered of NIH
2: 4 his host, and t that were numbered of them, NIH
2: 5 t that do pitch next unto him *shall be* NIH
2: 6 and t that were numbered thereof, *were* fifty NIH
2: 8 and t that were numbered thereof, *were* fifty NIH
2:11 t that were numbered thereof, *were* forty NIH
2:12 t which pitch by him *shall be* the tribe of 1886.1
2:13 t that were numbered of them, *were* fifty NIH
2:15 t that were numbered of them, *were* forty NIH
2:19 his host, and t that were numbered of them, NIH
2:21 t that were numbered of them, *were* thirty NIH
2:23 t that were numbered of them, *were* thirty NIH
2:26 his host, and t that were numbered of them, NIH
2:27 t that encamp by him *shall be* the tribe of NIH
2:28 t that were numbered of them, *were* forty NIH
2:30 t that were numbered of them, *were* fifty NIH
2:32 These *are* t which were numbered of NIH
2:32 all t that were numbered of the camps NIH
3:22 T that were numbered of them, according to NIH
3:22 *even* t that were numbered of them *were* NIH
3:34 t that were numbered of them, according to NIH
3:38 t that encamp before the tabernacle toward NIH
3:43 upward, of t that were numbered of them, NIH
3:46 for t that are *to be* redeemed of the two 6302
4:36 t that were numbered of them by their NIH
4:38 t that were numbered of the sons of NIH
4:40 Even t that were numbered of them, NIH
4:42 t that were numbered of the families of NIH
4:44 Even t that were numbered of them after NIH
4:45 These *be* t that were numbered of NIH
4:46 All t that were numbered of the Levites, NIH
4:48 Even t that were numbered of them, NIH
9: 7 t men said unto him, We *are* defiled by 1992
13: 3 all t men *were* heads of the children of 3963.1
14:22 Because all t men which have seen my NIH
14:37 Even t men that did bring up the evil report NIH
18:16 t that are *to be* redeemed from a month 2050.2
25: 9 t that died in the plague were twenty and NIH
26:18 according to t that were numbered of them, NIH
26:22 according to t that were numbered of them, NIH
26:25 according to t that were numbered of them, NIH
26:27 according to t that were numbered of them, NIH
26:34 t that were numbered of them, fifty and NIH
26:37 according to t that were numbered of them, NIH
26:43 according to t that were numbered of them, NIH
26:47 according to t that were numbered of them; NIH
26:54 according to t that were numbered of him. NIH
26:62 t that were numbered of them were twenty NIH
33:55 *that* t which ye let remain of them *shall be* NIH

Dt 7:22 the LORD thy God will put out t nations 411
17: 9 unto the judge that shall be in t days, 1992
18: 9 to do after the abominations of t nations. 1992
19: 5 he shall flee unto one of t cities, and live: 428
19:17 and the judges, which shall be in t days; 1992
19:20 t which remain shall hear, and fear, and 1886.1
26: 3 shalt go unto the priest that shall be in t 1992
29: 3 have seen, the signs, and t great miracles: 1992
29:29 *t things* which are revealed *belong* unto us NIH
32:21 I will move them to jealousy with *t which* NIH
Jos 3:16 t that came down toward the sea of 1886.1
4:20 t twelve stones, which they took out of 1886.1
10:22 bring out t five kings unto me out of 428
10:23 brought forth t five kings unto him out of 428
10:24 when they brought out t kings unto Joshua, 428
11: 1 when Jabin king of Hazor had heard *t* NIH
11:10 for Hazor beforetime *was* the head of all t 428
11:12 all the cities of t kings, and all the kings of 428
11:18 Joshua made war a long time with all t 428
17:12 could not drive out *the inhabitants of* t cities; 428
20: 4 when he that doth flee unto one of t cities 428
20: 6 of the high priest that shall be in t days: 1992
21:16 her suburbs; nine cities out of t two tribes. 428
24:17 and which did t great signs in our sight, and 428
Jdg 2:16 which delivered them out of the hand of t NIH
2:23 Therefore the LORD left t nations, without 428
7: 8 his tent, and retained *t* three hundred men: NIH
11:13 therefore restore t *lands* again peaceably. 2006.1
12: 5 that when t Ephraimites which were NIH
17: 6 In t days *there was* no king in Israel, *but* 1992
18: 1 In t days *there was* no king in Israel: and 1992
18: 1 in t days the tribe of the Danites sought 1992
19: 1 it came to pass in t days, when *there was* no 1992
20:27 of the covenant of God *was* there in t days, 1992
20:28 the son of Aaron, stood before it in t days,) 1992
21:25 In t days *there was* no king in Israel: 1992
1Sa 3: 1 the word of the LORD was precious in t 1992
7:16 and Mizpeh, and judged Israel in all t places. 428
10: 9 and all t signs came to pass that day. 428
11: 6 came upon Saul when he heard t tidings, 428
17:11 and all Israel heard t words of the Philistine, 428
17:28 with whom hast thou left t few sheep in 2007
18:23 Saul's servants spake t words in the ears of 428
19: 7 and Jonathan shewed him all t things. 428
25: 9 they spake to Nabal according to all t words 428
25:12 and came and told him all t sayings. 428
27: 8 for t *nations were* of old the inhabitants of 2007
28: 1 it came to pass in t days, that the Philistines 1992
28: 3 Saul had put away t that had familiar spirits, NIH
28: 9 how he hath cut off t that have familiar 1886.1
30: 9 where t that were left behind stayed. NIH
30:20 *which* they drave before t *other* cattle, and 1931
30:22 of t[S] that went with David, and said, 376
2Sa 5:14 these *be* the names of t that were born unto NIH
16:23 which he counselled in t days, 1992
1Ki 2: 7 and let them be of *t* that eat at thy table: NIH
3: 2 unto the name of the LORD, until t days. 1992
4:27 t officers provided victual for king Solomon, 428
8: 4 even t did the priests and the Levites 3963.1
9:21 upon t did Solomon levy a tribute of 3963.1
21:27 it came to pass, when Ahab heard t words, 428
2Ki 4: 4 shalt pour out into all t vessels, and 428
6:22 *t* whom thou hast taken captive with thy NIH
10:32 In t days the LORD began to cut Israel 1992
15:37 In t days the LORD began to send against 1992
17: 9 the children of Israel did secretly *t* things NIH
18: 4 for unto t days the children of Israel did 1992
20: 1 In t days was Hezekiah sick unto death. 1992
24:15 *t* carried he *into* captivity from Jerusalem to NIH
1Ch 4:23 and t that dwelt amongst plants and hedges: NIH
16:42 and cymbals for t that should make a sound, NIH
2Ch 14: 6 land had rest, and he had no war in t years; 428
15: 5 in t times *there was* no peace to him that 1992
17:19 besides *t* whom the king put in the fenced NIH
20:29 the fear of God was on all the kingdoms of *t* NIH
32:13 were the gods of the nations of *t* lands any NIH
32:14 Who *was there* among all the gods of t 428
32:24 In t days Hezekiah was sick to the death, 1992
Ezr 1: 8 Even t did Cyrus king of Persia bring forth NIH
2: 1 *of* t which had been **carried away**, 1473
2:62 These sought their register *among* t that 1886.1
3: 3 because of the people of *t* countries: NIH
5: 9 asked we t elders, *and* said unto them thus, 479
5:14 t did Cyrus the king take out of the temple 1994
7:19 *t* deliver thou before the God of Jerusalem. NIH
8:35 *Also* the children of t that had been carried NIH
9: 2 themselves with the people of *t* lands: NIH
9: 4 of the transgression of t that had been NIH
10: 3 of t that tremble at the commandment of our NIH
10: 8 of t that had been **carried away**. 1473
Ne 4:17 they that bare burdens, *with* t that laded, 871.1
5:17 besides t[S] that came unto us from among 376
6:17 Moreover in t days the nobles of Judah sent 1992
7: 6 *of* t that had been **carried away**, 1473
7:64 These sought their register *among* t that NIH
8: 3 and the women, and t that could understand; NIH
10: 1 Now t that sealed *were*, Nehemiah, NIH
13:15 In t days saw I in Judah *some* treading wine 1992
13:23 In t days also saw I Jews *that* had married 1992
Est 1: 2 *That* in t days, when the king Ahasuerus sat 1992
2:21 In t days, while Mordecai sat in the king's 1992
2:21 and Teresh, of t which kept the door, NIH
3: 9 of t that have the charge of the business, NIH
9: 5 did what they would unto t that hated them. NIH
9:11 On that day the number of t that were 1886.1
Job 5:11 To set up on high t that be low; that those NIH
5:11 that t which mourn may be exalted *to* NIH
21:22 seeing he judgeth t that are high. NIH
24:13 They are of t that rebel against the light; 1992
24:19 *so doth* the grave *t which* have sinned. NIH
27:15 T that remain of him shall be buried in NIH
Ps 5:11 let all t that put their trust in thee rejoice: NIH
13: 4 t that trouble me rejoice when I am moved. NIH
17: 7 *in thee* from t that rise up *against them*. NIH
18:30 he *is* a buckler to all t that trust in him. NIH

Ps 18:39 thou hast subdued under me t that rose up NIH
18:48 thou liftest me up above t that rise up NIH
21: 8 thy right hand shall find out t that hate thee. NIH
37: 9 t that wait upon the LORD, they shall NIH
40:16 Let all t that seek thee rejoice and be glad in NIH
50: 5 t that have made a covenant with me by NIH
61: 5 thou hast given *me* the heritage of t that fear NIH
63: 9 t *that* seek my soul, to destroy *it*, shall go 1992
68: 6 he bringeth out t which are bound with NIH
68:11 great *was* the company of t that 1886.1
69: 6 let not t that seek thee be confounded for NIH
69:26 they talk to the grief of t whom thou hast NIH
70: 4 Let all t that seek thee rejoice and be glad in NIH
74:23 the tumult of t that rise up against thee NIH
79:11 preserve thou t that are appointed to die; NIH
92:13 T that be planted in the house of NIH
102:20 to loose t that are appointed to death; NIH
103:18 to t that remember his commandments to do NIH
106:46 He made them also to be pitied of all t that NIH
109:31 to save *him* from t that condemn his soul. NIH
119:79 Let t that fear thee turn unto me, and NIH
119:79 and t that have known thy testimonies. NIH
119:132 as thou usest to do unto t that love thy NIH
123: 4 filled *with* the scorning of t that are at ease, NIH
125: 4 unto *t that be* good, and to *them that are* NIH
139:21 am not I grieved with t that rise up against NIH
140: 9 *As for* the head of t that compass me about, NIH
143: 3 in darkness, as t that have been long dead. NIH
145:14 and raiseth up all t that be bowed down. 1886.1
147:11 that fear him, in t that hope in his mercy. NIH
Pr 1:12 and whole, as t that go down into the pit: NIH
4:22 For they *are* life unto t that find them, and NIH
8:17 and t that seek me early shall find me. NIH
8:21 That *I* may cause t that love me to inherit NIH
22:23 and spoil the soul of t that spoiled them. NIH
24:11 unto death, and *t that are* ready to be slain; NIH
26:28 A lying tongue hateth *t that are* afflicted by NIH
31: 6 and wine unto t that be of heavy hearts. NIH
Ecc 1:11 that are to come with *t* that shall come after. NIH
5:14 t riches perish by evil travail: and 1931
7:28 but a woman among all t have I not found. 428
8: 8 wickedness deliver **t that are given to** it. 1167
12: 3 t that look out of the windows be darkened, NIH
SS 7: 9 causing the lips of *t that are* asleep to speak. NIH
8:12 t that keep the fruit thereof two hundred. NIH
Isa 14:19 *and as* the raiment of t that are slain, NIH
27: 7 smitten him, as he smote t that smote him? NIH
35: 8 shall not pass over it; but it *shall be* for t: 4123.1
38: 1 In t days was Hezekiah sick unto death. 1992
40:11 *and* shall gently lead t that are with young. NIH
56: 8 to him, besides t that are gathered unto him. NIH
60:12 yea, *t* nations shall be utterly wasted. NIH
64: 5 *t that* remember thee in thy ways: NIH
64: 5 in t is continuance, and we shall be saved. 1992.1
66: 2 For all t *things* hath mine hand made, and 428
66: 2 and all t *things* have been, saith the LORD: 428
66:19 I will send t that escape of them unto NIH
Jer 3:16 in the land, in t days, saith the LORD, 1992
3:18 In t days the house of Judah shall walk with 1992
4:12 *Even* a full wind from t *places* shall come 428
5:18 Nevertheless in t days, saith the LORD, 1992
8:16 that is in it; the city, and t that dwell therein. NIH
14:15 and famine shall t prophets be consumed. 1992
21: 7 and into the hand of t that seek their life: NIH
27:11 t will I let remain still in their own land, 2050.2
31:29 In t days they shall say no more, 1992
31:33 After t days, saith the LORD, I will put 1992
31:36 If t ordinances depart from before me, 428
33:15 In t days, and at that time, will I cause 1992
33:16 In t days shall Judah be saved, and 1992
38:22 *t women shall* say, Thy friends have set 2007
39: 9 t that fell away, that fell to him, with NIH
46:26 I will deliver them into the hand of t that NIH
49: 5 of hosts, from all t that be about thee; NIH
49:36 and will scatter them towards all t winds; 428
50: 4 In t days, and in that time, saith 1992
50:20 In t days, and in that time, saith 1992
52:15 t that fell away, that fell to the king of NIH
La 2:22 t that I have swaddled and brought up hath 834
3:62 The lips of t that rose up against me, and NIH
Eze 1:21 When t went, *these* went; and when those 3963.1
1:21 when t stood, *these* stood; and 3963.1
1:21 when t were lifted up from the earth, 3963.1
18:11 that doeth not any of t *duties*, but even hath 428
22: 5 *T that be* near, and *those that be* far from NIH
22: 5 and *t that be* far from thee, shall mock thee, NIH
28:26 when I have executed judgments upon all t NIH
33:24 they that inhabit t wastes of the land of Israel 428
34:27 delivered them out of the hand of t that NIH
38:17 which prophesied in t days *many* years, 1992
39:10 they shall spoil t that spoiled them, and NIH
39:10 rob t that robbed them, saith the Lord NIH
39:14 t that remain upon the face of the earth, NIH
40:25 arches thereof round about, like t windows: 428
42:14 shall approach to *t things* which *are* for NIH
Da 3:22 the flame of the fire slew t men that took up 479
4:37 and t that walk in pride he *is* able to abase. 1768
6:24 they brought t men which had accused 479
10: 2 In t days I Daniel was mourning three full 1992
11: 4 shall be pluckt up, even for others besides t. 428
11:14 in t times there shall many stand up against 1992
Joel 2:16 the children, and **t that suck** the breasts: 3243
2:29 upon the handmaids in t days will I pour 1992
3: 1 For behold, in t days, and in that time, 1992
Ob 1:14 to cut off t of his that did escape; NIH
1:14 neither shouldest thou have delivered up t NIH
Zep 1: 6 *t* that have not sought the LORD, nor NIH
1: 9 In the same day also will I punish all t that NIH
Hag 2:16 Since t *days* were, when *one* came to a 3963.1
2:22 the chariots, and t that ride in them; NIH
Zec 3: 4 and spake unto t that stood before him, 1886.1
4:10 in the hand of Zerubbabel *with* t seven; 428
7: 5 and seventh *month*, even t seventy years, 2088
8:23 In t days *it shall come to pass*, that ten men 1992
11:16 *which* shall not visit t that be cut off, NIH

Zec 13: 6 *T with* which I was wounded *in* the house NIH
14: 3 go forth, and fight against t nations, 1992
Mal 3: 5 against t that oppress the hireling in *his* NIH
Mt 3: 1 In t days came John the Baptist, *1565*
4:24 and t which were possessed with devils, and NIG
4:24 and t which were lunatick, and those that NIG
4:24 were lunatick, and t that had the palsy; NIG
11: 4 shew John again *t things* which ye do hear NIG
13:17 righteous *men* have desired to see *t things* NIG
13:17 and to hear *t things* which ye hear, NIG
15:18 But *t things* which proceed out of *3588*
15:30 having with them *t that were* lame, blind, NIG
16:23 *things* that be of God, but *t* that be of men. NIG
21:40 what will he do unto t husbandmen? *1565*
21:41 He will miserably destroy t wicked *men*, and *846*
22: 7 and destroyed t murderers, and burnt up *1565*
22:10 So t servants went out into the *high*ways, *1565*
24:19 and to them that give suck in t days. *1565*
24:22 And except t days should be shortened, *1565*
24:22 for the elect's sake t days shall be *1565*
24:29 Immediately after the tribulation of t days *1565*
25: 7 Then all t virgins arose, and trimmed their *1565*
25:19 After a long time the lord of t servants *1565*
27:54 and *t things* that were done, they feared NIG
Mk 1: 9 And it came to pass in t days, *that* Jesus *1565*
1:44 offer for thy cleansing *t things* which Moses NIG
2:20 and then shall they fast in t days. *1565*
6:55 began to carry about in beds t that were *3588*
7:15 out of him, t are they that defile the man. *1565*
8: 1 In t days the multitude being very great, *1565*
10:13 *his* disciples rebuked t that brought *them*. *3588*
11:23 shall believe that *t things* which he saith NIG
12: 7 But t husbandmen said amongst *1565*
13:17 and to them that give suck in t days. *1565*
13:19 For *in* t days shall be affliction, such as was *1565*
13:20 And except that the Lord had shortened *t* NIG
13:24 But in t days, after that tribulation, the sun *1565*
Lk 1: 1 t things which are most surely believed *3588*
1: 4 That thou mightest know the certainty of *t* NIG
1:24 And after t days his wife Elisabeth *3778*
1:39 And Mary arose in t days, and went into *3778*
1:45 for there shall be a performance of t *things* *3588*
2: 1 And it came to pass in t days, *that* there *1565*
2:18 And all they that heard *it* wondered at t *3588*
2:33 his mother marvelled at t *things* which *3588*
4: 2 And in t days he did eat nothing: and *1565*
5:35 and then shall they fast in t days. *1565*
6:12 And it came to pass in t days, *that* he went *3778*
6:32 for sinners also love t that love them. *3588*
7:28 Among *t that are* born of women there is NIG
8:12 T by the way side are they that hear; then *3588*
9:36 told no *man* in t days any of *those things* *1565*
9:36 told no *man* in those days any of *t things* NIG
10:24 kings have desired to see *t things* which ye NIG
10:24 and to hear *t things* which ye hear, NIG
12:20 then whose shall *t things* be, which thou NIG
12:37 Blessed *are* t servants, whom the lord when *1565*
12:38 and find *them* so, blessed are t servants. *1565*
13: 4 Or t eighteen, upon whom the tower in *1565*
14: 7 And he put forth a parable to t which were *3588*
14:24 That none of t men which were bidden *1565*
17:10 when ye shall have done all t *things* which *3588*
19:27 But t mine enemies, which would not that I *1565*
20: 1 And it came to pass, *that* on one of t days, *1565*
21:23 and to them that give suck, in t days, *1565*
21:26 *for* looking after t *things* which are coming *3588*
23:14 have found no fault in this man *touching t* NIG
Jn 2:14 And found in the temple t that sold oxen *3588*
6:14 Then *t* men, when they had seen the miracle NIG
8:10 Woman, where are t thine accusers? *1565*
8:26 I speak to the world t *things* which I have *3778*
8:29 for I do always *t things* that please him. *3588*
8:31 Then said Jesus to t Jews which believed *3588*
10:32 for which of t works do ye stone me? *846*
13:29 Buy *t things* that we have need of against NIG
17:11 keep through thine own name t whom thou *846*
17:12 *t* that thou gavest me I have kept, and NIG
Ac 1:15 And in t days Peter stood up in the midst of *3778*
2:18 on my handmaidens I will pour out in t *1565*
3:18 But *t things*, which God before had shewed NIG
3:24 from Samuel and t that follow after, *3588*
6: 1 And in t days, when the number of *3778*
7:41 And they made a calf in t days, and *1565*
8: 6 gave heed unto t *things* which Philip spake, *3588*
9:37 And it came to pass in t days, that she was *1565*
13:45 spake against t *things* which were spoken *3588*
16: 3 of the Jews which were in t quarters: *1565*
16:35 sent the sergeants, saying, Let t men go. *1565*
17:11 These were more noble than t in *3588*
17:11 scriptures daily, whether t *things* were so. *3778*
18:17 And Gallio cared for none of t *things*. *3778*
20: 2 And when he had gone over t parts, and *1565*
21: 5 And when we had accomplished *t* days, NIG
21:15 And after t days we took up our carriages, *3778*
21:24 all may know that *t things*, whereof they NIG
26:16 *of t things* in the which I will appear unto NIG
26:22 saying none other *things* than t which NIG
27:11 more than t *things* which were spoken by *3588*
28:31 teaching t *things* which concern the Lord *3588*
Ro 1:28 to do t *things* which are not convenient; *3588*
4:17 calleth t *things* which be not as though they *3588*
6:13 as *t that are* alive from the dead, and NIG
6:21 *in t things* whereof ye are now ashamed? NIG
6:21 for the end of t *things is* death. *1565*
10: 5 That the man which doeth t *things* shall live *846*
15:17 *I* may glory through Jesus Christ *in t* NIG
15:18 For I will not dare to speak of any of t NIG
1Co 8: 4 the eating of t things that are offered in *3588*
8:10 to eat t things which are offered to idols; *3588*
12:22 Nay, much more t members of the body, NIG
12:23 And t *members* of the body, which we *3739*
14:23 and there come in t *that are* unlearned, or NIG
2Co 7: 6 that comforteth *t that are* cast down, NIG
11:28 Besides t *things* that are without, *3588*
Eph 5:12 For it is a shame even to speak of t *things* *3588*

T

Php 3: 7 were gain to me, t I counted loss for Christ. 3778
3:13 this one thing I do, forgetting t things 3588
3:13 reaching forth unto t things which are 3588
4: 3 help t women which laboured with me in 846
4: 9 T things, which ye have both learned, and 3778
Col 2:18 intruding into t things which he hath not NIG
3: 1 with Christ, seek t things which are above, 3588
1Ti 4:10 of all men, specially of t that believe. NIG
5: 8 and specially for t of his own house, he hath NIG
2Ti 2:25 In meekness instructing t that oppose 3588
3: 3 fierce, despisers of t that are good, NIG
Heb 3: 5 for a testimony of t things which were to be 3588
5:14 even t who by reason of use have their NIG
6: 4 For it is impossible for t who were once 3588
7:21 (For t priests were made without an oath; 3588
7:27 as t high priests, to offer up sacrifice, NIG
8:10 make with the house of Israel after t days, 1565
10: 1 can never with t sacrifices which they 846
10: 3 But in t sacrifices there is a remembrance 846
10:16 that I will make with them after t days, 1565
12:27 the removing of t things that are shaken, 3588
12:27 that t things which cannot be shaken may 3588
13:11 For the bodies of t beasts, whose blood is 3778
Jas 2:16 notwithstanding ye give them not t things 3588
2Pe 2: 6 unto t that after should live ungodly; 764
2:18 t that were clean escaped from them who 3588
1Jn 3:22 do t things that are pleasing in his sight. 3588
2Jn 1: 8 that we lose not t things which we have NIG
Jude 1:10 But these speak evil of t things which they NIG
1:10 in t things they corrupt themselves. 3778
Rev 1: 3 and keep t things which are written therein: 3588
2:10 Fear none of t things which thou shalt NIG
2:13 even in t days wherein Antipas was my NIG
4: 9 And when t beasts give glory and honour NIG
9: 4 only t men which have not the seal of God NIG
9: 6 And in t days shall men seek death, and 1565
10: 4 Seal up t things which the seven thunders NIG
13:14 t miracles which he had power to do in NIG
20:12 the dead were judged out of t things which 3588

THOU (5474) [THEE, THEE-WARD, THINE, THY, THYSELF, YOU] See Index of Articles, Etc.

THOUGH (233) [ALTHOUGH]

Ge 31:30 t thou wouldest needs be gone, because NIH
33:10 as t I had seen the face of God, and 3509.1
40:10 it was as t it budded, and her blossoms 3509.1
Lev 5:17 t he wist it not, yet is he guilty, and 2050.1
11: 7 t he divide the hoof, and be clovenfooted, 3588
25:35 yea, t he be a stranger, or a sojourner; NIH
Nu 18:27 as t it were the corn of the threshingfloor, 3509.1
Dt 29:19 t I walk in the imagination of mine heart, 3588
Jos 17:18 t they have iron chariots, and though they 3588
17:18 have iron chariots, and t they be strong. 3588
Jdg 13:16 T thou detain me, I will not eat of thy bread: 518
15: 3 t I do them a displeasure. 3588+5973
15: 7 T ye have done this, yet will I be avenged of 518
Ru 2:13 t I be not like unto one of thy 2050.1
1Sa 14:39 t it be in Jonathan my son, he shall 518+3588
20:20 on the side thereof, as t I shot at a mark. NIH
21: 5 t it were sanctified this day in 637+3588
2Sa 1:21 as t he had not been anointed with oil. NIH
3:39 I am this day weak, t anointed king; and 2050.1
4: 6 as t they would have fetched wheat; NIH
18:12 T I should receive a thousand 3863+2050.1
1Ki 2:28 t he turned not after Absalom. 2050.1
1Ch 5: 1 the chief, (for t he was not the firstborn, NIH
2Ch 30:19 t he be not cleansed according to 2050.1
Ne 1: 9 t there were of you cast out unto 518
6: 1 (t at that time I had not set up the doors 1571
Est 9: 1 (t it was turned to the contrary, that 2050.1
Job 8: 7 T thy beginning was small, yet thy latter 2050.1
9:15 Whom, t I were righteous, yet would I not 518
9:21 T I were perfect, yet would I not know my NIH
10:19 I should have been as t I had not 834+3509.1
11:12 t man be born like a wild ass's colt. 2050.1
13:15 T he slay me, yet will I trust in him: but 2005
14: 8 T the root thereof wax old in the earth, and 518
16: 6 T I speak, my grief is not asswaged: and 518
16: 6 and t I forbear, what am I eased? NIH
19:17 t I intreated for the children's sake of 2050.1
19:26 t after my skin worms destroy this body, yet NIH
19:27 t my reins be consumed within me. NIH
20: 6 T his excellency mount up to the heavens, 518
20:12 T wickedness be sweet in his mouth, 518
20:12 in his mouth, t he hide it under his tongue; NIH
20:13 T he spare it, and forsake it not; but keep it NIH
24:23 T it be given him to be in safety, NIH
27: 8 t he hath gained, when God taketh away his 3588
27:16 T he heap up silver as the dust, and 518
30:24 to the grave, t they cry in his destruction. 518
39:16 her young ones, as t they were not hers: 3807.1
Ps 23: 4 t I walk through the valley of the shadow of 3588
27: 3 T a host should encamp against me, 518
27: 3 t war should rise against me, in this will I be 518
35:14 I behaved myself as t he had been my 3509.1
37:24 T he fall, he shall not be utterly cast down: 3588
44:19 T thou hast sore broken us in the place of 3588
46: 2 t the earth be removed, and though 871.1
46: 2 t the mountains be carried into the midst of 871.1
46: 3 T the waters thereof roar and be troubled, NIH
46: 3 t the mountains shake with the swelling NIH
49:18 T whiles he lived he blessed his soul: and 3588
68:13 T ye have lien among the pots, yet shall ye 518
78:23 T he had commanded the clouds from 2050.1
99: 8 t thou tookest vengeance of their 2050.1
138: 6 T the LORD be high, yet hath he respect 3588
138: 7 T I walk in the midst of trouble, thou wilt 518
Pr 6:35 he rest content, t thou givest many gifts. 3588
11:21 T hand join in hand, the wicked shall not be NIH
16: 5 t hand join in hand, he shall not be NIH
27:22 T thou shouldest bray a fool in a mortar 518
28: 6 that is perverse in his ways, t he be rich. 2050.1
Pr 29:19 for t he understand he will not answer. 2050.1
Ecc 6: 6 t he live a thousand years twice told, yet 432
8:12 T a sinner do evil an hundred times, and his 834
8:17 because t a man labour to seek it 834+3807.1
8:17 t a wise man think to know it, yet shall he 518
Isa 1:18 t your sins be as scarlet, they shall be as 518
1:18 t they be red like crimson, they shall be as 518
10:22 For t thy people Israel be as the sand 518+3588
12: 1 t thou wast angry with me, thine anger is 3588
30:20 t the Lord give you the bread of adversity, NIH
35: 8 the wayfaring men, t fools, shall not err 2050.1
45: 4 surnamed thee, t thou hast not known me. 2050.1
45: 5 I girded thee t thou hast not known me: 2050.1
49: 5 again to him, T Israel be not gathered, 2050.1
63:16 t Abraham be ignorant of us, and 3588
Jer 2:22 For t thou wash thee with nitre, and 518
4:30 T thou clothest thyself with crimson, 3588
4:30 t thou deckest thee with ornaments of gold, 3588
4:30 t thou rentest thy face with painting, in vain 3588
5: 2 t they say, The LORD liveth; surely they 518
5:22 and t the waves thereof toss themselves, 2050.1
5:22 t they roar, yet can they not pass over it? 2050.1
11:11 and t they shall cry unto me, I will not 2050.1
12: 6 them not, t they speak fair words unto thee. 3588
14: 7 O LORD, t our iniquities testify against us, 518
15: 1 T Moses and Samuel stood before me, 518
22:24 t Coniah the son of Jehoiakim king of 518+3588
30:11 t I make a full end of all nations whither I 3588
32: 5 t ye fight with the Chaldeans, ye shall not 3588
32:33 t I taught them, rising up early and 2050.1
37:10 For t ye had smitten the whole army of 518
46:23 saith the LORD, t it cannot be searched; 3588
49:16 t thou shouldest make thy nest as high as 3588
51: 5 t their land was filled with sin against 3588
51:53 T Babylon should mount up to heaven, and 3588
51:53 t she should fortify the height of her 3588
La 3:32 t he cause grief, yet will he have compassion 518
Eze 2: 6 t briers and thorns be with thee, and 3588
2: 6 at their looks, t they be a rebellious house. 3588
3: 9 at their looks, t they be a rebellious house. 3588
8:18 and t they cry in mine ears with a loud 2050.1
12: 3 will consider, t they be a rebellious house. 3588
12:13 yet shall he not see it, t he shall die there. 2050.1
14:14 T these three men, Noah, Daniel, and 2050.1
14:16 T these three men were in it, as I live, NIH
14:18 T these three men were in it, as I live, 2050.1
14:20 T Noah, Daniel, and Job, were in it, as I 2050.1
26:21 shalt be no more: t thou be sought for, 2050.1
28: 2 t thou set thine heart as the heart of God: 2050.1
32:25 t their terror was caused in the land of 3588
32:26 t they caused their terror in the land of 3588
32:27 t they were the terror of the mighty in 3588
Da 5:22 t thou knewest all this; 1768+3606+6903
9: 9 t we have rebelled against him; 3588
Hos 4:15 T thou, Israel, play the harlot, yet let not 518
5: 2 t I have been a rebuker of them all. 2050.1
7:13 t I have redeemed them, yet they have 2050.1
7:15 T I have bound and strengthened their 2050.1
8:10 Yea, t they have hired among the nations, 3588
9:12 T they bring up their children, yet will 518+3588
9:16 yea, t they bring forth, yet will I slay even 3588
11: 7 t they called them to the most High, 2050.1
13:15 T he be fruitful among his brethren, an east 3588
Am 5:22 T ye offer me burnt offerings and 518+3588
9: 2 T they dig into hell, thence shall mine hand 518
9: 2 t they climb up to heaven, 518+2050.1
9: 3 t they hide themselves in the top of Carmel, 518
9: 3 t they be hid from my sight in the bottom of 518
9: 4 t they go into captivity before their enemies, 518
Ob 1: 4 T thou exalt thyself as the eagle, and 518
1: 4 t thou set thy nest among the stars, 518
1:16 and they shall be as t they had not been. 3509.1
Mic 5: 2 t thou be little among the thousands of NIH
Na 1:12 T they be quiet, and likewise many, yet thus 518
1:12 T I have afflicted thee, I will afflict thee 2050.1
Hab 1: 5 which ye will not believe, t it be told you. 3588
2: 3 t it tarry, wait for it; because it will surely 518
Zec 9: 2 and Zidon, t it be very wise. 3588
10: 6 shall be as t I had not cast them off: 834+3509.1
12: 3 t all the people of the earth be gathered 2050.1
Mt 26:33 T all men shall be offended because 1400
26:35 said unto him, T I should die with thee, 2579
26:60 yea, t many false witnesses came, yet found 2532
Lk 9:53 his face was as t he would go to Jerusalem. NIG
11: 8 T he will not rise and give him, because he 1499
16:31 be persuaded, t one rose from the dead. 1437
18: 4 T I fear not God, nor regard man; 1499
18: 7 night unto him, t he bear long with them? 2532
24:28 he made as t he would have gone further. 4364
Jn 4: 2 (T Jesus himself baptized not, but 2544
8: 6 on the ground, as t he heard them not. NIG
8:14 said unto them, T I bear record of myself, 2579
10:38 But if I do, t ye believe not me, believe 2579
11:25 in me, t he were dead, yet shall he live: 2579
12:37 But t he had done so many miracles before 1161
Ac 3:12 as t by our own power or holiness we had 5613
13:28 And t they found no cause of death in him, NIG
13:41 wise believe, t a man declare it unto you. 1437
17:25 as t he needed any thing, seeing he giveth to NIG
17:27 find him, t he be not far from every one of 2544
23:15 as t ye would inquire something more 5613
23:20 as t they would inquire somewhat of him 5613
27:30 under colour as t they would have cast 5613
28: 4 whom, t he hath escaped the sea, NIG
28:17 t I have committed nothing against NIG
Ro 4:11 that believe, t they be not circumcised; 1223
4:17 calleth those things which be not as t they 5613
7: 3 t she be married to another man. NIG
9: 6 Not as t the word of God hath taken none 3754
9:27 T the number of the children of Israel be as 1437
1Co 4:15 For t you have ten thousand instructors in 1437
4:18 puffed up, as t I would not come to you. 5613
5: 3 have judged already, as t I were present, 5613
7:29 that both they that have wives be as t they 5613
7:30 And they that weep, as t they wept not; and 5613
1Co 7:30 and they that rejoice, as t they rejoiced not; 5613
7:30 and they that buy, as t they possessed not; 5613
8: 5 For t there be that are called gods, 1512+2532
9:16 For t I preach the gospel, I have nothing to 1437
9:19 For t I be free from all men, yet have I NIG
13: 1 T I speak with the tongues of men and 1437
13: 2 And t I have the gift of prophecy, and 1437
13: 2 and t I have all faith, so that I could remove 1437
13: 3 And t I bestow all my goods to feed 2579
13: 3 and t I give my body to be burned, 1437
2Co 4:16 but t our outward man perish, yet 1499
5:16 yea, t we have known Christ after the flesh, 1499
5:20 for Christ, as t God did beseech you by us: 5613
7: 8 For t I made you sorry with a letter, I do 1499
7: 8 with a letter, I do not repent, t I did repent: 1499
7: 8 made you sorry, t it were but for a season. 1499
7:12 Wherefore, t I wrote unto you, I did it not 1499
8: 9 that, t he was rich, yet for your sakes he NIG
10: 3 For t we walk in the flesh, we do not war NIG
10: 8 For t I should boast somewhat more of our 1437
10:14 our measure, as t we reached not unto you: 5613
11: 6 But t I be rude in speech, 1161+1487+2532
11:21 as t we had been weak. 3754
12: 6 For t I would desire to glory, I shall not be 1437
12:11 the very chiefest apostles, t I be nothing. 1499
12:15 t the more abundantly I love you, the less I 1499
13: 4 For t he was crucified through weakness, 2532
13: 7 that which is honest, t we be as reprobates. 1161
Gal 1: 8 But t we, or an angel from heaven, 1437+2532
3:15 T it be but a man's covenant, yet if it be 3676
4: 1 nothing from a servant, t he be lord of all; NIG
Php 3: 4 T I might also have confidence in the flesh. 2539
3:12 Not as t I had already attained, either were 3754
Col 2: 5 For t I be absent in the flesh, yet am 1487+2532
2:20 why, as t living in the world, are ye subject 5613
Phm 1: 8 t I might be much bold in Christ to enjoin NIG
Heb 5: 8 T he were a Son, yet learned he obedience 2539
6: 9 that accompany salvation, t we thus speak. 1499
7: 5 t they come out of the loins of Abraham: 2539
12:17 t he sought it carefully with tears. 2539
Jas 2:14 t a man say he hath faith, and have not 1437
3: 4 which t they be so great, and are driven of NIG
1Pe 1: 6 t now for a season, if need be, NIG
1: 7 t it be tried with fire, might be found unto 1161
1: 8 in whom, t now ye see him not, NIG
4:12 as t some strange thing happened unto you: 5613
2Pe 1:12 of these things, t ye know them, 2539
2Jn 1: 5 not as t I wrote a new commandment unto 5613
Jude 1: 5 t ye once knew this, how that the Lord, NIG

THOUGHT (81) [THINK]

Ge 20:11 Abraham said, Because I t, Surely the fear of 559
38:15 Judah saw her, he t her to be a harlot; 2803
48:11 said unto Joseph, I had not t to see thy face: 6419
50:20 as for you, ye t evil against me; but 2803
Ex 32:14 the LORD repented of the evil which he t 1696
Nu 24:11 I t to promote thee unto great honour; but lo, 559
33:56 I shall do unto you, as I t to do unto them. 1819
Dt 15: 9 Beware that there be not a t in thy wicked 1697
19:19 as he had t to have done unto his brother: 2161
Jdg 15: 2 verily t that thou hadst utterly hated 559+559
20: 5 upon me by night, and t to have slain me: 1819
Ru 4: 4 I t to advertise thee, saying, Buy it before 559
1Sa 1:13 therefore Eli t she had been drunken. 2803
9: 5 leave caring for the asses, and take t for us. 1672
18:25 Saul t to make David fall by the hand of 2803
20:26 for he t, Something hath befallen him, he is 559
2Sa 4:10 who t that I would have given him a reward NIH
13: 2 Amnon t it hard for him to do any 5869+871.1
14:13 hast thou t such a thing against the people 2803
19:18 and to do what he t good. 5869+871.1
21:16 he being girded with a new sword, t to have 559
2Ki 5:11 and went away, and said, Behold, I t, 559
2Ch 11:22 his brethren: for he t to make him king. NIH
32: 1 fenced cities, and t to win them for himself. 559
Ne 6: 2 plain of Ono. But they t to do me mischief. 2803
Est 3: 6 he t scorn to lay hands on Mordecai 5869+871.1
6: 6 Now Haman t in his heart, To whom would 559
Job 12: 5 lamp despised in the t of him that is at ease. 6248
42: 2 and that no t can be withholden from thee. 4209
Ps 48: 9 We have t of thy lovingkindness, O God, 1819
49:11 Their inward t is, that their houses shall NIH
64: 6 both the inward t of every one of them, and NIH
73:16 When I t to know this, it was too painful 2803
119:59 I t on my ways, and turned my feet unto 2803
139: 2 thou understandest my t afar off. 7454
Pr 24: 9 The t of foolishness is sin: and the scorner 2154
30:32 or if thou hast t evil, lay thine hand upon 2161
Ecc 10:20 Curse not the king, no not in thy t; and 4093
Isa 14:24 Surely as I have t, so shall it come to pass; 1819
Jer 18: 8 I will repent of the evil that I t to do unto 2803
Eze 38:10 thy mind, and thou shalt think an evil t: 4284
Da 4: 2 I t it good to shew the signs and 6925
6: 3 the king t to set him over the whole realm. 6246
Am 4:13 and declareth unto man what is his t, 7808
Zec 1: 6 Like as the LORD of hosts t to do unto us, 2161
8:14 As I t to punish you, when your fathers 2161
8:15 So again have I t in these days to do well 2161
Mal 3:16 the LORD, and that t upon his name. 2803
Mt 1:20 But while he t on these things, behold, 1760
6:25 Take no t for your life, what ye shall eat, 3309
6:27 Which of you by taking t can add one cubit 3309
6:28 And why take ye t for raiment? 3309
6:31 Therefore take no t, saying, What shall we 3309
6:34 Take therefore no t for the morrow: for 3309
6:34 for the morrow shall take t for the things of 3309
10:19 take no t how or what ye shall speak: 3309
Mk 13:11 take no t beforehand what ye shall speak, 4305
14:72 me thrice. And when he t thereon, he wept. 1911
Lk 7: 7 Wherefore neither t I myself worthy to 515
9:47 And Jesus, perceiving the t of their heart, 1261
12:11 take ye no t how or what thing ye shall 3309
12:17 And he t within himself, saying, What shall 1260
12:22 Take no t for your life, what ye shall eat; 3309
12:25 And which of you with taking t can add to 3309

T

Lk 12:26 *which is* least, why **take** ye **t** for the rest? *3309*
19:11 they **t** that the kingdom of God should *1380*
Jn 11:13 they **t** that he had spoken of taking of rest *1380*
13:29 For some *of them* **t**, because Judas had *1380*
Ac 8:20 thou hast **t** that the gift of God may be *3543*
8:22 if perhaps the **t** of thine heart may be *1963*
10:19 While Peter **t** on the vision, the Spirit said *1760*
12: 9 done by the angel; but **t** he saw a vision. *1380*
15:38 But Paul **t** not **good** to take him with *them,* *515*
26: 8 Why should it be **t** *a thing* incredible with *2919*
26: 9 I verily **t** with myself, that *I* ought to do *1380*
1Co 13:11 I understood as a child, I **t** as a child: *3049*
2Co 9: 5 Therefore I **t** it necessary to exhort *2233*
10: 5 bringing into captivity every **t** to *3540*
Php 2: 6 **t** it not robbery to be equal with God: *2233*
1Th 3: 1 we **t** it **good** to be left at Athens alone; *2106*
Heb 10:29 suppose ye, shall he be **t worthy**, *515*

THOUGHTEST (1) [THINK]

Ps 50:21 thou **t** that I was altogether *such a one* as 1819

THOUGHTS (57) [THINK]

Ge 6: 5 *that* every imagination of the **t** of his heart 4284
Jdg 5:15 of Reuben *there were* great **t** of heart. 2711
1Ch 28: 9 understandeth all the imaginations of the **t**: 4284
29:18 of the **t** of the heart of thy people, 4284
Job 4:13 In **t** from the visions of the night, 5587
17:11 are broken off, *even* the **t** of my heart. 4180
20: 2 Therefore do my **t** cause me to answer, and 5587
21:27 I know your **t**, and the devices *which* ye 4284
Ps 10: 4 not seek *after God:* God *is* not *in* all his **t**. 4209
33:11 for ever, the **t** of his heart to all generations. 4284
40: 5 hast done, and thy **t** *which are* to us-ward: 4284
56: 5 all their **t** *are* against me for evil. 4284
92: 5 are thy works! *and* thy **t** are very deep. 4284
94:11 The LORD knoweth the **t** of man, 4284
94:19 In the multitude of my **t** within me thy 8312
119:113 I hate *vain* **t**: but thy law do I love. 5588
139:17 How precious also are thy **t** unto me, 7454
139:23 know my heart: try me, and know my **t**: 8312
146: 4 to his earth; in that *very* day his **t** perish. 6250
Pr 12: 5 The **t** of the righteous *are* right: *but* 4284
15:26 The **t** of the wicked *are* an abomination to 4284
16: 3 the LORD, and thy **t** shall be established. 4284
21: 5 The **t** of the diligent *tend* only to 4284
Isa 55: 7 his way, and the unrighteous man his **t**: 4284
55: 8 For my **t** *are* not your thoughts, neither *are* 4284
55: 8 For my thoughts *are* not your **t**, neither *are* 4284
55: 9 your ways, and my **t** than your thoughts. 4284
55: 9 your ways, and my thoughts than your **t**. 4284
59: 7 their **t** *are* thoughts of iniquity; wasting and 4284
59: 7 their thoughts *are* **t** of iniquity; wasting and 4284
65: 2 a way *that was* not good, after their own **t**; 4284
66:18 For I *know* their works and their **t**: it shall 4284
Jer 4:14 How long shall thy vain **t** lodge within 4284
6:19 *even* the fruit of their **t**, because they have 4284
23:20 till he have performed the **t** of his heart: 4209
29:11 For I know the **t** that I think towards you, 4284
29:11 the LORD, **t** of peace, and not of evil, 4284
Da 2:29 thy **t** came *into thy mind* upon thy bed, 7476
2:30 *that* thou mightest know the **t** of thy heart. 7476
4: 5 the **t** upon my bed and the visions of my 2031
4:19 for one hour, and his **t** troubled him. 7476
5: 6 his **t** troubled him, so that the joints of his 7476
5:10 let not thy **t** trouble thee, nor let thy 7476
Mic 4:12 they know not the **t** of the LORD, 4284
Mt 9: 4 And Jesus knowing their **t** said, *1761*
12:25 And Jesus knew their **t**, and said unto them, *1761*
15:19 For out of the heart proceed evil **t**, murders, *1261*
Mk 7:21 proceed evil **t**, adulteries, fornications, *1261*
Lk 2:35 that the **t** of many hearts may be revealed. *1261*
5:22 But when Jesus perceived their **t**, *1261*
6: 8 But he knew their **t**, and said to the man *1261*
11:17 But he, knowing their **t**, said unto them, *1270*
24:38 and why do **t** arise in your hearts? *1261*
Ro 2:15 and *their* **t** the mean while accusing or *3053*
1Co 3:20 The Lord knoweth the **t** of the wise, *1261*
Heb 4:12 and *is* a discerner of the **t** and intents of *1761*
Jas 2: 4 and are become judges of evil **t**? *1261*

THOUSAND (521) [THOUSANDS]

Ge 20:16 I have given thy brother a **t** *pieces* of silver: 505
Ex 12:37 about six hundred **t** on foot *that were* men, 505
32:28 there fell of the people that day about three **t** 505
38:25 a **t** seven hundred and threescore and 505
38:26 for six hundred **t** and three thousand and 505
38:26 and three **t** and five hundred and fifty *men.* 505
38:28 of the **t** seven hundred seventy and 505
38:29 and **two t** and four hundred shekels. 505
Lev 26: 8 an hundred of you shall put **ten t** to flight: 7233
Nu 1:21 *were* forty and six **t** and five hundred. 505
1:23 *were* fifty and nine **t** and three hundred. 505
1:25 *were* forty and five **t** six hundred and fifty. 505
1:27 and fourteen **t** and six hundred. 505
1:29 *were* fifty and four **t** and four hundred. 505
1:31 *were* fifty and seven **t** and four hundred. 505
1:33 of Ephraim, *were* forty **t** and five hundred. 505
1:35 *were* thirty and two **t** and two hundred. 505
1:37 *were* thirty and five **t** and four hundred. 505
1:39 and two **t** and seven hundred. 505
1:41 *were* forty and one **t** and five hundred. 505
1:43 *were* fifty and three **t** and four hundred. 505
1:46 they that were numbered were six hundred **t** 505
1:46 and three **t** and five hundred and fifty. 505
2: 4 and fourteen **t** and six hundred. 505
2: 6 *were* fifty and four **t** and four hundred. 505
2: 8 *were* fifty and seven **t** and four hundred. 505
2: 9 in the camp of Judah *were* an hundred **t** 505
2: 9 fourscore **t** and six thousand and 505
2: 9 and six **t** and four hundred, 505
2:11 *were* forty and six **t** and five hundred. 505
2:13 *were* fifty and nine **t** and three hundred. 505
2:15 *were* forty and five **t** and six hundred and 505
2:16 in the camp of Reuben *were* an hundred **t** 505
Nu 2:16 fifty and one **t** and four hundred and fifty, 505
2:19 of them, *were* forty **t** and five hundred. 505
2:21 *were* thirty and two **t** and two hundred. 505
2:23 *were* thirty and five **t** and four hundred. 505
2:24 of the camp of Ephraim *were* an hundred **t** 505
2:24 and eight **t** and an hundred, 505
2:26 and two **t** and seven hundred. 505
2:28 *were* forty and one **t** and five hundred. 505
2:30 *were* fifty and three **t** and four hundred. 505
2:31 in the camp of Dan *were* an hundred **t** 505
2:31 and fifty and seven **t** and six hundred. 505
2:32 throughout their hosts *were* six hundred **t** 505
2:32 and three **t** and five hundred and fifty. 505
3:22 that were numbered of them *were* seven **t** 505
3:28 and upward, *were* eight **t** and six hundred, 505
3:34 and upward, *were* six **t** and two hundred. 505
3:39 and upward, *were* twenty and two **t**. 505
3:43 two **t** two hundred and threescore and 505
3:50 a **t** three hundred and threescore and 505
4:36 by their families were **two t** seven hundred 505
4:40 were **two t** and six hundred and thirty. 505
4:44 their families, were three **t** and two hundred. 505
4:48 were eight **t** and five hundred and fourscore. 505
7:85 all the silver vessels *weighed* **two t** and 505
11:21 amongst whom I *am, are* six hundred **t** 505
16:49 they that died in the plague were fourteen **t** 505
25: 9 died in the plague were twenty and four **t**. 505
26: 7 and three **t** and seven hundred and thirty. 505
26:14 twenty and two **t** and two hundred. 505
26:18 numbered of them, forty **t** and five hundred. 505
26:22 threescore and sixteen **t** and five hundred. 505
26:25 threescore and four **t** and three hundred. 505
26:27 of them, threescore **t** and five hundred. 505
26:34 of them, fifty and two **t** and seven hundred. 505
26:37 of them, thirty and two **t** and five hundred. 505
26:41 them *were* forty and five **t** and six hundred. 505
26:43 *were* threescore and four **t** and four hundred. 505
26:47 *who were* fifty and three **t** and four hundred. 505
26:50 them *were* forty and five **t** and four hundred. 505
26:51 six hundred **t** and a thousand seven hundred 505
26:51 and a **t** seven hundred and thirty. 505
26:62 numbered of them were twenty and three **t**, 505
31: 4 Of every tribe a **t**, throughout all the tribes of 505
31: 5 a **t** of *every* tribe, twelve thousand armed for 505
31: 5 of *every* tribe, twelve **t** armed for war. 505
31: 6 a **t** of *every* tribe, them and Phinehas the son 505
31:32 was six hundred **t** and seventy thousand and 505
31:32 and seventy **t** and five thousand sheep, 505
31:32 and seventy thousand and five **t** sheep, 505
31:33 And threescore and twelve **t** beeves, 505
31:34 And threescore and one **t** asses, 505
31:35 thirty and two **t** persons in all, of women that 505
31:36 was *in* number three hundred **t** and seven 505
31:36 seven and thirty **t** and five hundred sheep: 505
31:38 the beeves *were* thirty and six **t**; of which 505
31:39 And the asses *were* thirty **t** and five hundred; 505
31:40 the persons *were* sixteen **t**; of which 505
31:43 unto the congregation was three hundred **t** 505
31:43 thirty **t** *and* seven thousand and five hundred 505
31:43 thirty thousand *and* seven **t** and five hundred 505
31:44 And thirty and six **t** beeves, 505
31:45 And thirty **t** asses and five hundred, 505
31:46 And sixteen **t** persons;) 505
31:52 was sixteen **t** seven hundred and 505
35: 4 the city and outward a **t** cubits round about. 505
35: 5 without the city *on* the east side **two t** cubits, 505
35: 5 *on* the south side **two t** cubits, and *on* 505
35: 5 *on* the west side **two t** cubits, and *on* 505
35: 5 and *on* the north side **two t** cubits; 505
Dt 1:11 God of your fathers make you a **t** times 505
7: 9 keep his commandments to a **t** generations; 505
32:30 How should one chase a **t**, and two put ten 505
32:30 two put **ten t** to flight, except their Rock 7233
Jos 3: 4 and it, about **two t** cubits by measure: 505
4:13 About forty **t** prepared for war passed over 505
7: 3 *but* let about **two** or three **t** men go up 505
7: 4 up thither of the people about three **t** men: 505
8: 3 Joshua chose out thirty **t** mighty *men* of 505
8:12 he took about five **t** men, and set them to lie 505
8:25 both of men and women, *were* twelve **t**, 505
23:10 One man of you shall chase a **t**: for 505
Jdg 1: 4 and they slew *of* them in Bezek ten **t** men. 505
3:29 they slew *of* Moab at that time about ten **t** 505
4: 6 take with thee ten **t** men of the children of 505
4:10 and he went up with ten **t** men at his feet: 505
4:14 from mount Tabor, and ten **t** men after him. 505
5: 8 or spear seen among forty **t** in Israel? 505
7: 3 returned of the people twenty and two **t**; 505
7: 3 and two thousand; and there remained ten **t**. 505
8:10 about fifteen **t** *men,* all that were left of all 505
8:10 and twenty **t** men that drew sword. 505
8:26 the golden earrings that he requested was a **t** 505
9:49 died also, about a **t** men and women. 505
12: 6 that time of the Ephraimites forty and two **t**. 505
15:11 three **t** men of Judah went to the top of 505
15:15 and took it, and slew a **t** men therewith. 505
15:16 with the jaw of an ass have I slain a **t** men. 505
16:27 *there were* upon the roof about three **t** men 505
20: 2 four hundred **t** footmen that drew sword. 505
20:10 an hundred of a **t**, and a thousand out of ten 505
20:10 of a thousand, and a **t** out of ten thousand, 505
20:10 of a thousand, and a thousand out of **ten t**, 7233
20:15 cities twenty and six **t** men that drew sword, 505
20:17 were numbered four hundred **t** men that 505
20:21 the Israelites that day twenty and two **t** men. 505
20:25 the children of Israel again eighteen **t** men; 505
20:34 there came against Gibeah ten **t** chosen men 505
20:35 day twenty and five **t** and an hundred men: 505
20:44 there fell of Benjamin eighteen **t** men; all 505
20:45 they gleaned of them in the highways five **t** 505
20:45 unto Gidom, and slew **two t** men of them. 505
20:46 and five **t** men that drew the sword; 505
21:10 the congregation sent thither twelve **t** men of 505
1Sa 4: 2 of the army in the field about four **t** men. 505
4:10 for there fell of Israel thirty **t** footmen. 505
1Sa 6:19 even he smote of the people fifty **t** 505
11: 8 the children of Israel were three hundred **t**, 505
11: 8 and the men of Judah thirty **t**. 505
13: 2 Saul chose him three **t** *men* of Israel; 505
13: 2 *whereof* **two t** were with Saul in Michmash 505
13: 2 a **t** were with Jonathan in Gibeah of 505
13: 5 thirty **t** chariots, and six thousand horsemen, 505
13: 5 six **t** horsemen, and people as the sand which 505
15: 4 two hundred **t** footmen, and ten thousand 505
15: 4 thousand footmen, and ten **t** men of Judah. 505
17: 5 the weight of the coat *was* five **t** shekels *of* 505
17:18 these ten cheeses unto the captain of *their* **t**, 505
18:13 from him, and made him his captain over a **t**; 505
24: 2 Saul took three **t** chosen men out of all 505
25: 2 he had three **t** sheep, and a thousand goats: 505
25: 2 he had three thousand sheep, and a **t** goats: 505
26: 2 having three **t** chosen men of Israel with 505
2Sa 6: 1 together all the chosen *men* of Israel, thirty **t**. 505
8: 4 David took from him a **t** *chariots,* and 505
8: 4 hundred horsemen, and twenty **t** footmen: 505
8: 5 slew of the Syrians two and twenty **t** men. 505
8:13 in the valley of salt, *being* eighteen **t** *men.* 505
10: 6 twenty **t** footmen, and of king Maacah a 505
10: 6 of king Maacah a **t** men, and of Ish-tob 505
10: 6 thousand men, and of Ish-tob twelve **t** men. 505
10:18 forty **t** horsemen, and smote Shobach 505
17: 1 Let me now choose out twelve **t** men, and 505
18: 3 but now *thou art* worth ten **t** of us: therefore 505
18: 7 a great slaughter that day *of* twenty **t** *men.* 505
18:12 Though I should receive a **t** *shekels of* silver 505
19:17 *there were* a **t** men of Benjamin with him, 505
24: 9 there were in Israel eight hundred **t** valiant 505
24: 9 the men of Judah *were* five hundred **t** men. 505
24:15 from Dan even to Beer-sheba seventy **t** men. 505
1Ki 3: 4 a **t** burnt offerings did Solomon offer up on 505
4:26 Solomon had forty **t** stalls of horses for his 505
4:26 for his chariots, and twelve **t** horsemen. 505
4:32 he spake three **t** proverbs: and his songs 505
4:32 and his songs were a **t** and five. 505
5:11 Solomon gave Hiram twenty **t** measures of 505
5:13 of all Israel; and the levy was thirty **t** men. 505
5:14 them to Lebanon, ten **t** a month *by* courses: 505
5:15 had threescore and ten **t** that bare burdens, 505
5:15 and fourscore **t** hewers in the mountains; 505
5:16 three **t** and three hundred, which ruled over 505
7:26 flowers of lilies: it contained **two t** baths. 505
8:63 two and twenty **t** oxen, and an hundred and 505
8:63 and an hundred and twenty **t** sheep. 505
10:26 he had a **t** and four hundred chariots, and 505
10:26 hundred chariots, and twelve **t** horsemen, 505
12:21 fourscore **t** chosen *men,* which were 505
19:18 Yet I have left *me* seven **t** in Israel, all 505
20:15 *even* all the children of Israel, *being* seven **t**. 505
20:29 the Syrians an hundred **t** footmen in one day. 505
20:30 and seven **t** of the men that were left. 505
2Ki 3: 4 rendered unto the king of Israel an hundred **t** 505
3: 4 and an hundred **t** rams, *with* the wool. 505
5: 5 six **t** *pieces* of gold, and ten changes of 505
13: 7 and ten chariots, and ten **t** footmen; 505
14: 7 He slew *of* Edom in the valley of salt ten **t**, 505
15:19 Menahem gave Pul a **t** talents of silver, 505
18:23 and I will deliver thee **two t** horses, 505
19:35 Assyrians an hundred fourscore and five **t**: 505
24:14 even ten **t** captives, and all the craftsmen and 505
24:16 *even* seven **t**, and craftsmen and smiths a 505
24:16 craftsmen and smiths a **t**, all *that were* strong 505
1Ch 5:18 *were* four and forty **t** seven hundred and 505
5:21 *of* their camels fifty **t**, and *of* sheep two 505
5:21 *of* sheep two hundred and fifty **t**, and 505
5:21 *of* asses **two t**, and *of* men an hundred 505
5:21 two thousand, and *of* men an hundred **t**. 505
7: 2 of David two and twenty **t** and six hundred. 505
7: 4 thirty **t** *men:* for they had many wives and 505
7: 5 by their genealogies fourscore and seven **t**. 505
7: 7 and two **t** and thirty and four. 505
7: 9 of valour, *was* twenty **t** and two hundred. 505
7:11 *were* seventeen **t** and two hundred *soldiers,* 505
7:40 *and* to battle *was* twenty and six **t** men. 505
9:13 a **t** and seven hundred and threescore; 505
12:14 over an hundred, and the greatest over a **t**. 505
12:24 and spear *were* six **t** and eight hundred, 505
12:25 valour for the war, seven **t** and one hundred. 505
12:26 Of the children of Levi four **t** and 505
12:27 with him *were* three **t** and seven hundred; 505
12:29 of Benjamin, the kindred of Saul, three **t**: 505
12:30 And of the children of Ephraim twenty **t** and 505
12:31 And of the half tribe of Manasseh eighteen **t**, 505
12:33 of war, fifty **t**, which could keep rank: 505
12:34 of Naphtali a **t** captains, and with them with 505
12:34 with shield and spear thirty and seven **t**. 505
12:35 in war twenty and eight **t** and six hundred. 505
12:36 as went forth to battle, expert in war, forty **t**. 505
12:37 war for the battle, an hundred and twenty **t**. 505
16:15 the word *which* he commanded to a **t** 505
18: 4 David took from him a **t** chariots, and 505
18: 4 seven **t** horsemen, and twenty thousand 505
18: 4 thousand horsemen, and twenty **t** footmen: 505
18: 5 slew of the Syrians two and twenty **t** men. 505
18:12 the Edomites in the valley of salt eighteen **t**. 505
19: 6 the children of Ammon sent a **t** talents of 505
19: 7 So they hired thirty and two **t** chariots, and 505
19:18 David slew of the Syrians seven **t** *men* 505
19:18 forty **t** footmen, and killed Shophach 505
21: 5 And all *they of* Israel were a **t** thousand and 505
21: 5 And all *they of* Israel were a thousand **t** and 505
21: 5 and an hundred **t** men that drew sword: 505
21: 5 and ten **t** men that drew sword. 505
21:14 and there fell of Israel seventy **t** men. 505
22:14 of the LORD an hundred **t** talents *of* gold, 505
22:14 *of* gold, and a **t** thousand talents *of* silver; 505
22:14 *of* gold, and a thousand **t** talents *of* silver; 505
23: 3 man by man, was thirty and eight **t**. 505
23: 4 four **t** *were* to set forward the work of 505
23: 4 and six **t** *were* officers and judges: 505
23: 5 Moreover four **t** *were* porters; and 505

1Ch 23: 5 four **t** praised the LORD with 505
26:30 men of valour, a **t** and seven hundred, 505
26:32 *were* **two t** and seven hundred chief fathers, 505
27: 1 *of* every course *were* twenty and four **t**. 505
27: 2 and in his course *were* twenty and four **t**. 505
27: 4 his course likewise *were* twenty and four **t**. 505
27: 5 and in his course *were* twenty and four **t**. 505
27: 7 and in his course *were* twenty and four **t**. 505
27: 8 and in his course *were* twenty and four **t**. 505
27: 9 and in his course *were* twenty and four **t**. 505
27:10 and in his course *were* twenty and four **t**. 505
27:11 and in his course *were* twenty and four **t**. 505
27:12 and in his course *were* twenty and four **t**. 505
27:13 and in his course *were* twenty and four **t**. 505
27:14 and in his course *were* twenty and four **t**. 505
27:15 and in his course *were* twenty and four **t**. 505
29: 4 *Even* three **t** talents of gold, of the gold of 505
29: 4 and seven **t** talents of refined silver, 505
29: 7 of the house of God *of* gold five **t** talents 505
29: 7 gold five thousand talents and **ten t** drams, 7239
29: 7 *of* silver ten **t** talents, and *of* brass eighteen 505
29: 7 *of* brass **eighteen t** 505+7239+8083+2050.1
29: 7 and one hundred **t** talents *of* iron. 505
29:21 *even* a **t** bullocks, a thousand rams, *and* 505
29:21 a **t** rams, *and* a thousand lambs, with their 505
29:21 a thousand rams, *and* a **t** lambs, with their 505
2Ch 1: 6 and offered a **t** burnt offerings upon it. 505
1:14 he had a **t** and four hundred chariots, and 505
1:14 hundred chariots, and twelve **t** horsemen, 505
2: 2 out threescore and ten **t** men to bear burdens, 505
2: 2 fourscore **t** to hew in the mountain, and 505
2: 2 and three **t** and six hundred to oversee them. 505
2:10 twenty **t** measures of beaten wheat, and 505
2:10 twenty **t** measures of barley, and 505
2:10 twenty **t** baths of wine, and twenty thousand 505
2:10 baths of wine, and twenty **t** baths of oil. 505
2:17 fifty **t** and three thousand and six hundred. 505
2:17 fifty thousand and three **t** and six hundred. 505
2:18 and ten **t** of them *to be* bearers of burdens, 505
2:18 fourscore **t** *to be* hewers in the mountain, 505
2:18 three **t** and six hundred overseers to set 505
4: 5 *and* it received and held three **t** baths. 505
7: 5 offered a sacrifice of twenty and two **t** oxen, 505
7: 5 and an hundred and twenty **t** sheep: 505
9:25 And Solomon had four **t** stalls for horses and 505
9:25 and chariots, and twelve **t** horsemen; 505
11: 1 fourscore **t** chosen *men,* which were 505
12: 3 hundred chariots, and threescore **t** horsemen: 505
13: 3 of war, *even* four hundred **t** chosen men: 505
13: 3 him with eight hundred **t** chosen men, 505
13:17 there fell down slain of Israel five hundred **t** 505
14: 8 and spears, out of Judah three hundred **t**; 505
14: 8 drew bows, two hundred and fourscore **t**: 505
14: 9 the Ethiopian with a host of a **t** thousand, 505
14: 9 the Ethiopian with a host of a thousand **t**, 505
15:11 seven hundred oxen and seven **t** sheep. 505
17:11 seven **t** and seven hundred rams, and 505
17:11 and seven **t** and seven hundred he goats. 505
17:14 him mighty *men* of valour three hundred **t**. 505
17:15 and with him two hundred and fourscore **t**. 505
17:16 with him two hundred **t** mighty *men* of 505
17:17 *men* with bow and shield two hundred **t**. 505
17:18 and fourscore **t** ready prepared for the war. 505
25: 5 found them three hundred **t** choice *men, able* 505
25: 6 He hired also an hundred **t** mighty *men* of 505
25:11 and smote *of* the children of Seir ten **t**. 505
25:12 *other* ten **t** *left* alive did the children of Judah 505
25:13 smote three **t** of them, and took much spoil. 505
26:12 of the mighty *men* of valour *were* **two t** 505
26:13 three hundred **t** and seven thousand and 505
26:13 and seven **t** and five hundred, 505
27: 5 ten **t** measures of wheat, and ten thousand of 505
27: 5 measures of wheat, and ten **t** of barley. 505
28: 6 in Judah an hundred and twenty **t** in one day, 505
28: 8 captive of their brethren two hundred **t**, 505
29:33 *were* six hundred oxen and three **t** sheep. 505
30:24 did give to the congregation a **t** bullocks 505
30:24 a thousand bullocks and seven **t** sheep; 505
30:24 the princes gave to the congregation a **t** 505
30:24 a thousand bullocks and ten **t** sheep: 505
35: 7 to the number of thirty **t**, and three thousand 505
35: 7 of thirty thousand, and three **t** bullocks: 505
35: 8 the priests for the passover *offerings* **two t** 505
35: 9 for passover *offerings* five **t** *small cattle,* 505
Ezr 1: 9 a **t** chargers of silver, nine and 505
1:10 four hundred and ten, *and* other vessels a **t**. 505
1:11 and of silver *were* five **t** and four hundred. 505
2: 3 **two t** an hundred seventy and two. 505
2: 6 *and* Joab, **two t** eight hundred and twelve. 505
2: 7 of Elam, a **t** two hundred fifty and four. 505
2:12 of Azgad, a **t** two hundred twenty and two. 505
2:14 The children of Bigvai, **two t** fifty and six. 505
2:31 other Elam, a **t** two hundred fifty and four. 505
2:35 of Senaah, three **t** and six hundred and thirty. 505
2:37 The children of Immer, a **t** fifty and two. 505
2:38 of Pashur, a **t** two hundred forty and seven. 505
2:39 The children of Harim, a **t** and seventeen. 505
2:64 together *was* **forty** *and* **two t** 505+702+7239
2:65 of whom *there were* seven **t** three hundred 505
2:67 *their* asses, six **t** seven hundred and twenty. 505
2:69 **threescore and one t** 505+7239+8337+2050.1
2:69 five **t** pound *of* silver, and one hundred 505
8:27 Also twenty basons of gold, of a **t** drams; 505
Ne 3:13 and a **t** cubits on the wall unto the dung gate. 505
7: 8 **two t** an hundred seventy and two. 505
7:11 Joab, **two t** and eight hundred *and* eighteen. 505
7:12 of Elam, a **t** two hundred fifty and four. 505
7:17 **two t** three hundred twenty and two. 505
7:19 of Bigvai, **two t** threescore and seven. 505
7:34 other Elam, a **t** two hundred fifty and four. 505
7:38 of Senaah, three **t** nine hundred and thirty. 505
7:40 The children of Immer, a **t** fifty and two. 505
7:41 of Pashur, a **t** two hundred forty and seven. 505
7:42 The children of Harim, a **t** *and* seventeen. 505
7:66 together *was* **forty** *and* **two t** 505+702+7239
Ne 7:67 of whom *there were* seven **t** three hundred 505
7:69 five: six **t** seven hundred and twenty asses. 505
7:70 The Tirshatha gave to the treasure a **t** drams 505
7:71 of the work twenty **t** drams *of* gold, 7239
7:71 and **two t** and two hundred pound *of* silver. 505
7:72 people gave *was* twenty **t** drams *of* gold, 7239
7:72 **two t** pound *of* silver, and threescore and 505
Est 3: 9 I will pay ten **t** talents of silver to the hands 505
9:16 and slew of their foes seventy and five **t**, but 505
Job 1: 3 His substance also was seven **t** sheep, and 505
1: 3 three **t** camels, and five hundred yoke of 505
9: 3 with him, he cannot answer him one of a **t**. 505
33:23 with him, an interpreter, one among a **t**, 505
42:12 for he had fourteen **t** sheep, and six thousand 505
42:12 six **t** camels, and a thousand yoke of oxen, 505
42:12 a **t** yoke of oxen, and a thousand she asses. 505
42:12 a thousand yoke of oxen, and a **t** she asses. 505
Ps 50:10 forest *is* mine, *and* the cattle upon a **t** hills. 505
60: T smote of Edom in the valley of salt twelve **t**. 505
68:17 The chariots of God *are* **twenty t**, 7239
84:10 For a day in thy courts *is* better than a **t**. 505
90: 4 For a **t** years in thy sight *are but* as yesterday 505
91: 7 A **t** shall fall at thy side, and ten thousand at 505
91: 7 fall at thy side, and **ten t** at thy right hand; 7233
105: 8 the word *which* he commanded to a **t** 505
Ecc 6: 6 though he live a **t** years twice *told,* yet hath 505
7:28 one man among a **t** have I found; but 505
SS 4: 4 whereon there hang a **t** bucklers, all shields 505
5:10 and ruddy, the chiefest among **ten t**. 7233
8:11 fruit thereof was to bring a **t** *pieces* of silver. 505
8:12 *must have* a **t**, and those that keep the fruit 505
Isa 7:23 where there were a **t** vines at a thousand 505
7:23 where there were a thousand vines at a **t** 505
30:17 One **t** *shall flee* at the rebuke of one; at 505
36: 8 of Assyria, and I will give thee **two t** horses, 505
37:36 an hundred and fourscore and five **t**: 505
60:22 A little one shall become a **t**, and a small one 505
Jer 52:28 in the seventh year three **t** Jews and three 505
52:30 all the persons *were* four **t** and six hundred. 505
Eze 45: 1 twenty **t** *reeds,* and the breadth *shall be* ten 505
45: 1 and the breadth *shall be* ten **t**. 505
45: 3 thou measure the length of five and twenty **t**, 505
45: 3 twenty thousand, and the breadth of ten **t**: 505
45: 5 *the* five and twenty **t** of length, and *the* ten 505
45: 5 *the* ten **t** of breadth, shall also the Levites, 505
45: 6 the possession of the city five **t** broad, 505
45: 6 thousand broad, and five and twenty **t** long, 505
47: 3 went forth east*ward,* he measured a **t** cubits, 505
47: 4 Again he measured a **t**, and brought me 505
47: 4 Again he measured a **t**, and brought me 505
47: 5 Afterward he measured a **t**; *and it was* a river 505
48: 8 offer *of* five and twenty **t** *reeds in* breadth, 505
48: 9 *shall be of* five and twenty **t** *in* length, 505
48: 9 thousand *in* length, and *of* ten **t** *in* breadth. 505
48:10 the north five and twenty **t** *in length,* and 505
48:10 and toward the west ten **t** *in* breadth, 505
48:10 toward the east ten **t** *in* breadth, and 505
48:10 toward the south five and twenty **t** *in* length: 505
48:13 *shall have* five and twenty **t** *in* length, 505
48:13 thousand *in* length, and ten **t** *in* breadth: 505
48:13 all the length *shall be* five and twenty **t**, and 505
48:13 and twenty thousand, and the breadth ten **t**. 505
48:15 the five **t**, that are left in the breadth over 505
48:15 breadth over against the five and twenty **t**, 505
48:16 the north side four **t** and five hundred, and 505
48:16 the south side four **t** and five hundred, and 702
48:16 and on the east side four **t** and five hundred, 505
48:16 and the west side four **t** and five hundred. 505
48:18 of the holy *portion shall be* ten **t** eastward, 505
48:18 ten thousand eastward, and ten **t** westward: 505
48:20 and twenty **t** by five and twenty thousand: 505
48:20 and twenty thousand by five and twenty **t**: 505
48:21 twenty **t** of the oblation toward the east 505
48:21 the five and twenty **t** toward the west border, 505
48:30 north side, four **t** and five hundred measures. 505
48:32 And at the east side four **t** and five hundred: 505
48:33 *at* the south side four **t** and five hundred 505
48:34 *At* the west side four **t** and five hundred, 505
48:35 *It was* round about eighteen **t** *measures:* and 505
Da 5: 1 Belshazzar the king made a great feast to a **t** 506
5: 1 of his lords, and drank wine before the **t**. 506
7:10 **t** thousands ministered unto him, and 506
7:10 **ten t** times ten thousand stood before him: 7240
7:10 ten thousand times **ten t** stood before him: 7240
8:14 unto me, Unto **two t** and three hundred days; 505
12:11 *there shall be* a **t** two hundred and 505
12:12 cometh to the **t** three hundred *and* five and 505
Am 5: 3 The city that went out *by* a **t** shall leave an 505
Jnh 4:11 wherein are more than sixscore **t** persons 7239
Mt 14:21 And they that had eaten were about **five t** 4000
15:38 And they that did eat were **four t** men, 5070
16: 9 remember the five loaves of the **five t**, 4000
16:10 Neither the seven loaves of the **four t**, and 5070
18:24 unto him, which ought him **ten t** talents. 3463
Mk 5:13 place into the sea, (they were about **two t**,) 1367
6:44 did eat *of* the loaves were about **five t** men. 4000
8: 9 And they that had eaten were about **four t**: 5070
8:19 When I brake the five loaves among **five t**, 4000
8:20 And when the seven among **four t**, 5070
Lk 9:14 For they were about **five t** men. And he 4000
14:31 consulteth whether he be able with ten **t** to 5505
14:31 him that cometh against him with twenty **t**? 5505
Jn 6:10 the men sat down, *in* number about **five t**. 4000
Ac 2:41 were added *unto them* about **three t** souls. 5153
4: 4 the number of the men was about five **t**. 5505
19:19 and found *it* **fifty t** *pieces* of silver. 3461+4002
21:38 leddest out into the wilderness **four t** men 5070
Ro 11: 4 I have reserved to myself **seven t** men, 2035
1Co 4:15 For though you have **ten t** instructors in 3463
10: 8 and fell in one day three and twenty **t**. 5505
14:19 than **ten t** words in an *unknown* tongue. 3463
2Pe 3: 8 that one day *is* with the Lord as a **t** years, 5507
3: 8 a thousand years, and a **t** years as one day. 5507
Rev 5:11 the number of them was **ten t** times ten 3461
5:11 of them was ten thousand times **ten t**, 3461
Rev 7: 4 four **t** of all the tribes of the children of 5505
7: 5 Of the tribe of Juda *were* sealed twelve **t**. 5505
7: 5 the tribe of Reuben *were* sealed twelve **t**. 5505
7: 5 Of the tribe of Gad *were* sealed twelve **t**. 5505
7: 6 Of the tribe of Aser *were* sealed twelve **t**. 5505
7: 6 tribe of Nephthalim *were* sealed twelve **t**. 5505
7: 6 the tribe of Manasses *were* sealed twelve **t**. 5505
7: 7 the tribe of Simeon *were* sealed twelve **t**. 5505
7: 7 Of the tribe of Levi *were* sealed twelve **t**. 5505
7: 7 Of the tribe of Isachar *were* sealed twelve **t**. 5505
7: 8 the tribe of Zabulon *were* sealed twelve **t**. 5505
7: 8 Of the tribe of Joseph *were* sealed twelve **t**. 5505
7: 8 the tribe of Benjamin *were* sealed twelve **t**. 5505
9:16 *were* **two hundred t thousand**: 1417+3461
9:16 *were* **two hundred thousand t**: 1417+3461
11: 3 they shall prophesy a **t** two hundred *and* 5507
11:13 the earthquake were slain of men seven **t**: 5505
12: 6 that they should feed her there a **t** two 5507
14: 1 and with him an hundred forty *and* four **t**, 5505
14: 3 but the hundred *and* forty *and* four **t**, 5505
14:20 by the space of a **t** *and* six hundred 5507
20: 2 and Satan, and bound him a **t** years, 5507
20: 3 no more, till the **t** years should be fulfilled: 5507
20: 4 they lived and reigned with Christ a **t** years. 5507
20: 5 not again until the **t** years were finished. 5507
20: 6 and shall reign with him a **t** years. 5507
20: 7 And when the **t** years are expired, Satan 5507
21:16 the city with the reed, twelve **t** furlongs. 5505

THOUSANDS (62) [THOUSAND]

Ge 24:60 be thou *the mother* of **t** of millions, and 505
Ex 18:21 *to be* rulers of **t**, *and* rulers of hundreds, 505
18:25 rulers of **t**, rulers of hundreds, rulers of 505
20: 6 shewing mercy unto **t** of them that love me, 505
34: 7 Keeping mercy for **t**, forgiving iniquity and 505
Nu 1:16 the tribes of their fathers, heads of **t** in Israel. 505
10: 4 *which are* heads of the **t** of Israel, 505
10:36 Return, O LORD, *unto* the many **t** of Israel. 505
31: 5 So there were delivered out of the **t** of Israel, 505
31:14 *with* the captains over **t**, and captains over 505
31:48 the officers which *were* over **t** of the host, 505
31:48 the captains of **t**, and captains of hundreds, 505
31:52 of the captains of **t**, and of the captains of 505
31:54 the priest took the gold of the captains of **t** 505
Dt 1:15 captains over **t**, and captains over hundreds, 505
5:10 shewing mercy unto **t** of them that love me 505
33: 2 and he came with **ten t** of saints: 7233
33:17 they *are* the **ten t** of Ephraim, and they *are* 7233
33:17 of Ephraim, and they *are* the **t** of Manasseh. 505
Jos 22:14 house of their fathers among the **t** of Israel. 505
22:21 and said unto the heads of the **t** of Israel, 505
22:30 heads of the **t** of Israel which *were* with him, 505
1Sa 8:12 And he will appoint him captains over **t**, and 505
10:19 the LORD by your tribes, and by your **t**. 505
18: 7 Saul hath slain his **t**, and David his ten 505
18: 7 slain his thousands, and David his **ten t**. 7233
18: 8 They have ascribed unto David **ten t**, and 7233
18: 8 and to me they have ascribed *but* **t**: 505
21:11 Saul hath slain his **t**, and David his ten 505
21:11 slain his thousands, and David his **ten t**? 7233
22: 7 *and* make you all captains of **t**, and 505
23:23 that I will **search him** out throughout all the **t** 505
29: 2 Philistines passed on by hundreds, and by **t**: 505
29: 5 Saul slew his **t**, and David his ten thousands? 505
29: 5 slew his thousands, and David his **ten t**? 7233
2Sa 18: 1 set captains of **t** and captains of hundreds 505
18: 4 the people came out by hundreds and by **t**. 505
1Ch 12:20 captains of the **t** that *were* of Manasseh. 505
13: 1 David consulted with the captains of **t** and 505
15:25 the elders of Israel, and the captains over **t**, 505
26:26 the captains over **t** and hundreds, and 505
27: 1 chief fathers and captains of **t** and hundreds, 505
28: 1 the captains over the **t**, and captains over 505
29: 6 and the captains of **t** and of hundreds, 505
2Ch 1: 2 to the captains of **t** and of hundreds, and 505
17:14 Of Judah, the captains of **t**; Adnah the chief, 505
25: 5 made them captains over **t**, and captains over 505
Ps 3: 6 I will not be afraid of **ten t** of people, 7233
68:17 God *are* twenty thousand, *even* **t** of angels: 505
119:72 of thy mouth *is* better unto me than **t** of gold 505
144:13 *that* our sheep may **bring forth t** and 503
144:13 forth thousands and **ten t** in our streets: 7231
Jer 32:18 Thou shewest lovingkindness unto **t**, and 505
Da 7:10 thousand **t** ministered unto him, and 506
11:12 and he shall cast down *many* **ten t**: 7239
Mic 5: 2 *though thou* be little among the **t** of Judah, 505
6: 7 Will the LORD be pleased with **t** of rams, 505
6: 7 of rams, *or* with **ten t** of rivers of oil? 7233
Ac 21:20 how many **t** of Jews there are which 3461
Jude 1:14 the Lord cometh with **ten t** of his saints, 3461
Rev 5:11 times ten thousand, and **t** of thousands; 5505
5:11 times ten thousand, and thousands of **t**; 5505

THREAD (7)

Ge 14:23 That I will not *take* from a **t** even to a 2339
38:28 and bound upon his hand a **scarlet t**, 8144
38:30 that had the **scarlet t** upon his hand: 8144
Jos 2:18 thou shalt bind this line of scarlet **t** in 2339
Jdg 16: 9 as a **t** of tow is broken when it toucheth 6616
16:12 he brake them from off his arms like a **t**. 2339
SS 4: 3 Thy lips *are* like a **t** of scarlet, and 2339

THREATEN (1) [THREATENED, THREATENING, THREATENINGS]

Ac 4:17 among the people, let us **straitly t** them, 546

THREATENED (2) [THREATEN]

Ac 4:21 So when they had **further t** *them,* they let 4324
1Pe 2:23 when he suffered, he **t** not; but 546

THREATENING (1) [THREATEN]

Eph 6: 9 do the same *things* unto them, forbearing **t**: 547

THREATENINGS (2) [THREATEN]

Ac 4:29 And now, Lord, behold their **t**: and *547*
9: 1 yet breathing out **t** and slaughter against *547*

THREE (485) [THIRD, THIRDLY, THREEFOLD, THRICE]

Ge 5:22 after he begat Methuselah **t** hundred years, 7969
5:23 all the days of Enoch were **t** hundred sixty 7969
6:10 Noah begat **t** sons, Shem, Ham, and 7969
6:15 length of the ark *shall be* **t** hundred cubits, 7969
7:13 the **t** wives of his sons with them, into 7969
9:19 These *are* the **t** sons of Noah: and of them 7969
9:28 Noah lived after the flood **t** hundred and 7969
11:13 he begat Salah four hundred and **t** years, 7969
11:15 he begat Eber four hundred and **t** years, 7969
14:14 **t** hundred and eighteen, and pursued *them* 7969
15: 9 Take me a heifer of **t years old**, and a she 8027
15: 9 a she goat of **t years old**, and a ram of three 8027
15: 9 a ram of **t years old**, and a turtle-dove, and 8027
18: 2 and looked, and lo, **t** men stood by him: 7969
18: 6 Make ready quickly **t** measures of fine 7969
29: 2 lo, there *were* **t** flocks of sheep lying by it; 7969
29:34 unto me, because I have born him **t** sons: 7969
30:36 he set **t** days' journey betwixt himself and 7969
38:24 it came to pass about **t** months after, that it 7969
40:10 in the vine *were* **t** branches: and it *was* as 7969
40:12 of it: The **t** branches *are* three days: 7969
40:12 of it: The three branches *are* **t** days: 7969
40:13 Yet within **t** days shall Pharaoh lift up thine 7969
40:16 behold, *I had* **t** white baskets on my head: 7969
40:18 The **t** baskets *are* three days: 7969
40:18 The three baskets *are* **t** days: 7969
40:19 Yet within **t** days shall Pharaoh lift up thy 7969
42:17 he put them all together into ward **t** days. 7969
45:22 to Benjamin he gave **t** hundred *pieces* of 7969
46:15 his sons and his daughters *were* thirty and **t**. 7969
Ex 2: 2 *was a* goodly *child*, she hid him **t** months. 7969
3:18 **t** days' journey into the wilderness, 7969
5: 3 **t** days' journey into the desert, and 7969
6:18 Kohath *were* an hundred thirty and **t** years. 7969
7: 7 Aaron fourscore and **t** years old, when they 7969
8:27 We will go **t** days' journey into 7969
10:22 darkness in all the land of Egypt **t** days: 7969
10:23 neither rose any from his place for **t** days: 7969
15:22 they went **t** days in the wilderness, and 7969
21:11 if he do not these **t** unto her, then shall she 7969
23:14 **T** times thou shalt keep a feast unto me in 7969
23:17 **T** times in the year all thy males shall 7969
25:32 **t** branches of the candlestick out of the one 7969
25:32 **t** branches of the candlestick out of 7969
25:33 **T** bowls made like unto almonds, *with* a 7969
25:33 **t** bowls made like almonds in the other 7969
27: 1 and the height thereof *shall be* **t** cubits. 7969
27:14 their pillars **t**, and their sockets three. 7969
27:14 their pillars three, and their sockets **t**. 7969
27:15 fifteen *cubits*: their pillars **t**, and 7969
27:15 their pillars three, and their sockets **t**. 7969
32:28 there fell of the people that day about **t** 7969
37:18 **t** branches of the candlestick out of the one 7969
37:18 **t** branches of the candlestick out of 7969
37:19 **T** bowls made after the fashion of almonds 7969
37:19 **t** bowls made like almonds in another 7969
38: 1 and **t** cubits the height thereof. 7969
38:14 their pillars **t**, and their sockets three. 7969
38:14 their pillars three, and their sockets **t**. 7969
38:15 their pillars **t**, and their sockets three. 7969
38:15 their pillars three, and their sockets **t**. 7969
38:26 **t** thousand and five hundred and fifty *men*. 7969
Lev 12: 4 continue in the blood of her purifying **t** and 7969
14:10 **t tenth deals** of fine flour *for* a meat 6241+7969
19:23 **t** years shall it be as uncircumcised unto 7969
25:21 it shall bring forth fruit for **t** years. 7969
27: 6 for the female thy estimation *shall be* **t** 7969
Nu 1:23 *were* fifty and nine thousand and **t** hundred. 7969
1:43 *were* fifty and **t** thousand and four hundred. 7969
1:46 and **t** thousand and five hundred and fifty. 7969
2:13 *were* fifty and nine thousand and **t** hundred. 7969
2:30 *were* fifty and **t** thousand and four hundred. 7969
2:32 and **t** thousand and five hundred and fifty. 7969
3:50 a thousand **t** hundred and threescore and 7969
4:44 were **t** thousand and two hundred. 7969
10:33 the mount of the LORD **t** days' journey: 7969
10:33 went before them *in* the **t** days' journey, 7969
12: 4 Come out ye **t** unto the tabernacle of 7969
12: 4 of the congregation. And they **t** came out. 7969
15: 9 **t** tenth deals *of* flour mingled with half a 7969
22:28 that thou hast smitten me these **t** times? 7969
22:32 hast thou smitten thine ass these **t** times? 7969
22:33 saw me, and turned from me these **t** times: 7969
24:10 thou hast altogether blessed *them* these **t** 7969
26: 7 **t** thousand and seven hundred and thirty. 7969
26:25 and four thousand and **t** hundred. 7969
26:47 *were* fifty and **t** thousand and four hundred. 7969
26:62 of them were twenty and **t** thousand, 7969
28:12 **t** tenth deals *of* flour *for* a meat offering, 7969
28:20 **t** tenth deals shall ye offer for a bullock, 7969
28:28 **t** tenth deals unto one bullock, two tenth 7969
29: 3 **t** tenth deals for a bullock, *and* two tenth 7969
29: 9 **t** tenth deals to a bullock, *and* two tenth 7969
29:14 **t** tenth deals unto every bullock of 7969
31:36 was *in* number **t** hundred thousand and 7969
31:43 the congregation was **t** hundred thousand 7969
33: 8 went **t** days' journey in the wilderness of 7969
33:39 and **t** years old when he died in mount Hor. 7969
35:14 Ye shall give **t** cities on *this* side Jordan, 7969
35:14 **t** cities shall ye give in the land of Canaan, 7969
Dt 4:41 Moses severed **t** cities on *this* side Jordan 7969
14:28 At the end of **t** years thou shalt bring forth 7969
16:16 **T** times in a year shall all thy males appear 7969
17: 6 the mouth of two witnesses, or **t** witnesses, 7969
19: 2 Thou shalt separate **t** cities for thee in 7969
19: 3 **divide** the coasts of thy land, which the LORD thy God giveth thee to inherit, **into t parts**, 8027
19: 7 Thou shalt separate **t** cities for thee. 7969
Dt 19: 9 shalt thou add **t** cities moe for thee, 7969
19: 9 add three cities moe for thee, beside these **t**: 7969
19:15 or at the mouth of **t** witnesses, shall 7969
Jos 1:11 for within **t** days ye shall pass over this 7969
2:16 hide yourselves there **t** days, until 7969
2:22 unto the mountain, and abode there **t** days, 7969
3: 2 it came to pass after **t** days, that the officers 7969
7: 3 or **t** thousand men go up and smite Ai; 7969
7: 4 thither of the people about **t** thousand men: 7969
9:16 it came to pass at the end of **t** days after 7969
15:14 And Caleb drove thence the **t** sons of Anak, 7969
17:11 and her towns, *even* **t** countries. 7969
18: 4 Give out from among you **t** men for *each* 7969
21:32 and Kartan with her suburbs; **t** cities. 7969
Jdg 1:20 and he expelled thence the **t** sons of Anak. 7969
7: 6 hand to their mouth, were **t** hundred men: 7969
7: 7 By the **t** hundred men that lapped will I 7969
7: 8 his tent, and retained *those* **t** hundred men: 7969
7:16 he divided the **t** hundred men *into* three 7969
7:16 he divided the three hundred men *into* **t** 7969
7:20 the **t** companies blew the trumpets, and 7969
7:22 the **t** hundred blew the trumpets, and 7969
8: 4 and the **t** hundred men that *were* with him, 7969
9:22 When Abimelech had reigned **t** years over 7969
9:43 divided them into **t** companies, and 7969
10: 2 he judged Israel twenty and **t** years, and 7969
11:26 by the coasts of Arnon, **t** hundred years? 7969
14:14 they could not *in* **t** days expound the riddle. 7969
15: 4 Samson went and caught **t** hundred foxes, 7969
15:11 **t** thousand men of Judah went to the top of 7969
16:15 thou hast mocked me these **t** times, and 7969
16:27 *there were* upon the roof about **t** thousand 7969
19: 4 and he abode with him **t** days: 7969
1Sa 1:24 with **t** bullocks, and one ephah of flour, and 7969
2:13 with a fleshhook of **t** teeth in his hand; 7969
2:21 and bare **t** sons and two daughters. 7969
9:20 as for thine asses that were lost **t** days ago, 7969
10: 3 there shall meet thee **t** men going up to God 7969
10: 3 one carrying **t** kids, and another carrying 7969
10: 3 another carrying **t** loaves of bread, and 7969
11: 8 the children of Israel were **t** hundred 7969
11:11 that Saul put the people *in* **t** companies; 7969
13: 2 Saul chose him **t** thousand *men* of Israel; 7969
13:17 the camp of the Philistines *in* **t** companies: 7969
17:13 the **t** eldest sons of Jesse went *and* 7969
17:13 the names of his **t** sons that went to 7969
17:14 and the **t** eldest followed Saul. 7969
20:19 *when* thou hast **stayed t days**, *then* 8027
20:20 I will shoot **t** arrows on the side *thereof*, as 7969
20:41 to the ground, and bowed himself **t** times: 7969
21: 5 kept from us about **these t days**, 8032+8543
24: 2 Saul took **t** thousand chosen men out of all 7969
25: 2 he had **t** thousand sheep, and a thousand 7969
26: 2 having **t** thousand chosen men of Israel 7969
30:12 drunk *any* water, **t** days and three nights. 7969
30:12 drunk *any* water, three days and **t** nights. 7969
30:13 left me, because **t** days agone I fell sick. 7969
31: 6 his **t** sons, and his armourbearer, and all his 7969
31: 8 and his **t** sons fallen in mount Gilboa. 7969
2Sa 2:18 there were **t** sons of Zeruiah there, Joab, 7969
2:31 *so that* **t** hundred and threescore men died. 7969
5: 5 and **t** years over all Israel and Judah. 7969
6:11 house of Obed-edom the Gittite **t** months: 7969
13:38 and went to Geshur, and was there **t** years. 7969
14:27 unto Absalom there were born **t** sons, and 7969
18:14 he took **t** darts in his hand, and thrust them 7969
20: 4 Assemble me the men of Judah *within* **t** 7969
21: 1 there was a famine in the days of David **t** 7969
21:16 the weight of whose spear *weighed* **t** 7969
23: 9 *one* of the **t** mighty *men* with David, 7969
23:13 **t** of the thirty chief went down, and came to 7969
23:16 the **t** mighty *men* brake through the host of 7969
23:17 These *things* did *these* **t** mighty *men*. 7969
23:18 the son of Zeruiah, *was* chief among **t**. 7969
23:18 he lift up his spear against **t** hundred, and 7969
23:18 and slew them, and had the name among **t**. 7969
23:19 Was he not most honourable of **t**? therefore 7969
23:19 howbeit he attained not unto the *first* **t**. 7969
23:22 and had the name among **t** mighty *men*. 7969
23:23 the thirty, but he attained not to the *first* **t**. 7969
24:12 I offer thee **t** *things;* choose thee one of 7969
24:13 wilt thou flee **t** months before thine 7969
24:13 that there be **t** days' pestilence in thy land? 7969
1Ki 2:11 thirty and **t** years reigned he in Jerusalem. 7969
2:39 it came to pass at the end of **t** years, 7969
4:32 he spake **t** thousand proverbs: and his songs 7969
5:16 **t** thousand and three hundred, which ruled 7969
5:16 three thousand and **t** hundred, which ruled 7969
6:36 he built the inner court *with* **t** rows of 7969
7: 4 *there were* windows *in* **t** rows, and 7969
7: 4 and light *was* against light *in* **t** ranks. 7969
7: 5 and light *was* against light *in* **t** ranks. 7969
7:12 the great court round about *was with* **t** rows 7969
7:25 **t** looking toward the north, and 7969
7:25 **t** looking toward the west, and 7969
7:25 **t** looking toward the south, and 7969
7:25 the south, and **t** looking toward the east: 7969
7:27 and **t** cubits the height of it. 7969
9:25 **t** times in a year did Solomon offer burnt 7969
10:17 *he made* **t** hundred shields *of* beaten gold; 7969
10:17 **t** pound *of* gold went to one shield: 7969
10:22 once in **t** years came the navy of Tharshish, 7969
11: 3 princesses, and **t** hundred concubines: 7969
12: 5 Depart yet *for* **t** days, then come again to 7969
15: 2 **T** years reigned he in Jerusalem. And his 7969
17:21 he stretched himself upon the child **t** times, 7969
22: 1 they continued **t** years without war between 7969
2Ki 2:17 and they sought **t** days, but found him not. 7969
3:10 that the LORD hath called these **t** kings 7969
3:13 for the LORD hath called these **t** kings 7969
9:32 there looked out to him two *or* **t** eunuchs. 7969
12: 6 it was *so, that* in the **t** and twentieth year of 7969
13: 1 In the **t** and twentieth year of Joash the son 7969
13:25 **T** times did Joash beat him, and 7969
17: 5 went up *to* Samaria, and besieged it **t** years. 7969
2Ki 18:10 at the end of **t** years they took it: *even* in 7969
18:14 king of Judah **t** hundred talents of silver 7969
23:31 and **t** years old when he *began* to reign; 7969
23:31 and he reigned **t** months in Jerusalem. 7969
24: 1 and Jehoiakim became his servant **t** years: 7969
24: 8 and he reigned in Jerusalem **t** months. 7969
25:17 the height of the chapiter **t** cubits; and 7969
25:18 second priest, and the **t** keepers of the door: 7969
1Ch 2: 3 *which* **t** were born unto him of the daughter 7969
2:16 Abishai, and Joab, and Asahel, **t**. 7969
2:22 who had **t** and twenty cities in the land of 7969
3: 4 in Jerusalem he reigned thirty and **t** years. 7969
3:23 Elioenai, and Hezekiah, and Azrikam, **t**. 7969
7: 6 Bela, and Becher, and Jediael, **t**. 7969
10: 6 his **t** sons, and all his house died together. 7969
11:11 he lift up his spear against **t** hundred slain 7969
11:12 the Ahohite, who *was one* of the **t** mighties. 7969
11:15 Now **t** of the thirty captains went down to 7969
11:18 the **t** brake through the host of 7969
11:19 drink it. These *things* did *these* **t** mightiest. 7969
11:20 the brother of Joab, he was chief of the **t**: 7969
11:20 for lifting up his spear against **t** hundred, 7969
11:20 he slew *them*, and had a name among the **t**. 7969
11:21 Of the **t**, he was more honourable than 7969
11:21 howbeit he attained not to the *first* **t**. 7969
11:24 and had the name among the **t** mighties. 7969
11:25 the thirty, but attained not to the *first* **t**: 7969
12:27 with him *were* **t** thousand and 7969
12:29 the kindred of Saul, **t** thousand: 7969
12:39 there they were with David **t** days, eating 7969
13:14 of Obed-edom in his house **t** months. 7969
21:10 I offer thee **t** *things:* choose thee one of 7969
21:12 Either **t** years' famine; or three months to 7969
21:12 or **t** months to be destroyed before thy foes, 7969
21:12 or else **t** days the sword of the LORD, 7969
23: 8 chief *was* Jehiel, and Zetham, and Joel, **t**. 7969
23: 9 Shelomith, and Haziel, and Haran, **t**. 7969
23:23 of Mushi; Mahli, and Eder, and Jeremoth, **t**. 7969
24:18 The **t** and twentieth to Delaiah, the four and 7969
25: 5 to Heman fourteen sons and **t** daughters. 7969
25:30 The **t** and twentieth to Mahazioth, *he*, his 7969
29: 4 *Even* **t** thousand talents of gold, of the gold 7969
29:27 thirty and **t** *years* reigned he in Jerusalem. 7969
2Ch 2: 2 **t** thousand and six hundred to oversee 7969
2:17 and **t** thousand and six hundred. 7969
2:18 **t** thousand and six hundred overseers to set 7969
4: 4 **t** looking toward the north, and 7969
4: 4 **t** looking toward the west, and 7969
4: 4 **t** looking toward the south, and 7969
4: 4 the south, and **t** looking toward the east: 7969
4: 5 *and* it received and held **t** thousand baths. 7969
6:13 **t** cubits high, and had set it in the midst of 7969
7:10 on the **t** and twentieth day of the seventh 7969
8:13 on the solemn feasts, **t** times in the year, 7969
9:16 **t** hundred shields *made he of* beaten gold: 7969
9:16 **t** hundred *shekels* of gold went to one 7969
9:21 every **t** years once came the ships of 7969
10: 5 Come again unto me after **t** days. 7969
11:17 the son of Solomon strong, **t** years: 7969
11:17 for **t** years they walked in the way of David 7969
13: 2 He reigned **t** years in Jerusalem. 7969
14: 8 spears, out of Judah **t** hundred thousand; 7969
14: 9 thousand thousand, and **t** hundred chariots; 7969
17:14 with him mighty *men* of valour **t** hundred 7969
20:25 they were **t** days in gathering of the spoil, 7969
25: 5 found them **t** hundred thousand choice 7969
25:13 smote **t** thousand of them, and took much 7969
26:13 **t** hundred thousand and seven thousand and 7969
29:33 six hundred oxen and **t** thousand sheep. 7969
31:16 of males, from **t** years old and upward, 7969
35: 7 of thirty thousand, and **t** thousand bullocks: 7969
35: 8 hundred *small cattle*, and **t** hundred oxen. 7969
36: 2 and **t** years old when he *began* to reign, 7969
36: 2 and he reigned **t** months in Jerusalem. 7969
36: 9 he reigned **t** months and ten days in 7969
Ezr 2: 4 of Shephatiah, **t** hundred seventy and two. 7969
2:11 of Bebai, six hundred twenty and **t**. 7969
2:17 of Bezai, **t** hundred twenty and three. 7969
2:17 of Bezai, three hundred twenty and **t**. 7969
2:19 of Hashum, two hundred twenty and **t**. 7969
2:21 of Beth-lehem, an hundred twenty and **t**. 7969
2:25 and Beeroth, seven hundred and forty and **t**. 7969
2:28 and Ai, two hundred twenty and **t**. 7969
2:32 children of Harim, **t** hundred and twenty. 7969
2:34 of Jericho, **t** hundred forty and five. 7969
2:35 **t** thousand and six hundred and thirty. 7969
2:36 of Jeshua, nine hundred seventy and **t**. 7969
2:58 *were* **t** hundred ninety and two. 7969
2:64 *and* two thousand **t** hundred *and* threescore, 7969
2:65 of whom *there were* seven thousand **t** 7969
6: 4 *With* **t** rows of great stones, and a row of 8532
8: 5 of Jahaziel, and with him **t** hundred males. 7969
8:15 and there abode we in tents **t** days: 7969
8:32 came *to* Jerusalem, and abode there **t** days. 7969
10: 8 *that* whosoever would not come within **t** 7969
10: 9 together *unto* Jerusalem within **t** days. 7969
Ne 2:11 I came to Jerusalem, and was there **t** days. 7969
7: 9 of Shephatiah, **t** hundred seventy and two. 7969
7:17 two thousand **t** hundred twenty and two. 7969
7:22 of Hashum, **t** hundred twenty and eight. 7969
7:23 of Bezai, **t** hundred twenty and four. 7969
7:29 and Beeroth, seven hundred forty and **t**. 7969
7:32 of Beth-el and Ai, an hundred twenty and **t**. 7969
7:35 children of Harim, **t** hundred and twenty. 7969
7:36 of Jericho, **t** hundred forty and five. 7969
7:38 **t** thousand nine hundred and thirty. 7969
7:39 of Jeshua, nine hundred seventy and **t**. 7969
7:60 *were* **t** hundred ninety and two. 7969
7:66 two thousand **t** hundred and threescore, 7969
7:67 of whom *there were* seven thousand **t** 7969
Est 4:16 neither eat nor drink **t** days, night or day; 7969
8: 9 on the **t** and twentieth *day* thereof; 7969
9:15 and slew **t** hundred men at Shushan; 7969
Job 1: 2 born unto him seven sons and **t** daughters. 7969
1: 3 **t** thousand camels, and five hundred yoke 7969

Job 1: 4 sent and called for their t sisters to eat and 7969
1:17 The Chaldeans made out t bands, and 7969
2:11 Now when Job's t friends heard of all this 7969
32: 1 So these t men ceased to answer Job, 7969
32: 3 Also against his t friends was his wrath 7969
32: 5 *was* no answer in the mouth of *these* t men, 7969
42:13 He had also seven sons and t daughters. 7969
Pr 30:15 There are t *things that* are never satisfied, 7969
30:18 There be t *things which* are too wonderful 7969
30:21 For t *things* the earth is disquieted, and 7969
30:29 There be t *things* which go well, yea, 7969
Isa 15: 5 *shall flee* unto Zoar, a heifer of **t years old**: 7992
16:14 saying, Within t years, as the years of a 7969
17: 6 t berries in the top of the uppermost bough, 7969
20: 3 barefoot t years *for* a sign and wonder upon 7969
Jer 25: 3 this day, that *is* the t and twentieth year, 7969
36:23 *that* when Jehudi had read t or four leaves, 7969
48:34 unto Horonaim, *as* a heifer of **t years old**: 7992
52:24 second priest, and the t keepers of the door: 7969
52:28 in the seventh year t thousand Jews and 7969
52:28 year three thousand Jews and t and twenty: 7969
52:30 In the t and twentieth year of 7969
Eze 4: 5 of the days, t hundred and ninety days: 7969
4: 9 t hundred and ninety days shalt thou eat 7969
14:14 Though these t men, Noah, Daniel, and 7969
14:16 *Though* these t men *were* in it, *as* I live, 7969
14:18 Though these t men *were* in it, *as* I live, 7969
40:10 of the gate eastward *were* t on this side, 7969
40:10 *were* three on this side, and t on that side; 7969
40:10 on that side; they t *were* of one measure: 7969
40:21 the little chambers thereof *were* t on this 7969
40:21 *were* three on this side and t on that side; 7969
40:48 the breadth of the gate *was* t cubits on this 7969
40:48 cubits on this side, and t cubits on that side. 7969
41: 6 the side chambers *were* t, one over another, 7969
41:16 the galleries round about on their t *stories*, 7969
41:22 The altar *of* wood *was* t cubits high, and 7969
42: 3 *was* gallery against gallery in t *stories*. 7992
42: 6 For they *were* in t *stories*, but had not 8027
48:31 t gates northward; one gate of Reuben, 7969
48:32 t gates; and one gate of Joseph, one gate of 7969
48:33 t gates; one gate of Simeon, one gate of 7969
48:34 and five hundred, *with* their t gates; 7969
Da 1: 5 so nourishing them t years, that at the end 7969
3:23 these t men, Shadrach, Meshach, and 8532
3:24 Did not we cast t men bound into the midst 8532
6: 2 over these t presidents; of whom Daniel 8532
6:10 he kneeled upon his knees t times a day, 8532
6:13 but maketh his petition t times a day. 8532
7: 5 *it had* t ribs in the mouth of it between 8532
7: 8 before whom there were t of the first horns 8532
7:20 which came up, and before whom t fell; 8532
7:24 from the first, and he shall subdue t kings. 8532
8:14 Unto two thousand and t hundred days; 7969
10: 2 In those days I Daniel was mourning t full 7969
10: 3 at all, till t whole weeks were fulfilled. 7969
11: 2 there *shall* stand up yet t kings in Persia; 7969
12:12 cometh to the thousand t hundred *and* five 7969
Am 1: 3 For t transgressions of Damascus, and 7969
1: 6 For t transgressions of Gaza, and for four, 7969
1: 9 For t transgressions of Tyrus, and for four, 7969
1:11 For t transgressions of Edom, and for four, 7969
1:13 For t transgressions of the children of 7969
2: 1 For t transgressions of Moab, and for four, 7969
2: 4 For t transgressions of Judah, and for four, 7969
2: 6 For t transgressions of Israel, and for four, 7969
4: 4 *and* your tithes after t years: 7969
4: 7 when *there were* yet t months to 7969
4: 8 So two *or* t cities wandered unto one city, 7969
Jnh 1:17 Jonah was in the belly of the fish t days 7969
1:17 the belly of the fish three days and t nights. 7969
3: 3 an exceeding great city of t days' journey. 7969
Zec 11: 8 **T** shepherds also I cut off in one month; 7969
Mt 12:40 For as Jonas was t days and three nights in *5140*
12:40 three days and t nights in the whale's belly; *5140*
12:40 so shall the Son of man be t days and *5140*
12:40 and t nights in the heart of the earth. *5140*
13:33 woman took, and hid in t measures of meal, *5140*
15:32 because they continue with me now t days, *5140*
17: 4 if thou wilt, let us make here t tabernacles: *5140*
18:16 t witnesses every word may be established. *5140*
18:20 or t are gathered together in my name, *5140*
26:61 the temple of God, and to build it in t days. *5140*
27:40 and buildest *it* in t days, save thyself. *5140*
27:63 was yet alive, After t days I will rise *again*. *5140*
Mk 8: 2 they have now been with me t days, *5140*
8:31 and be killed, and after t days rise again. *5140*
9: 5 and let us make t tabernacles; one for thee, *5140*
14: 5 been sold for more than t **hundred** pence, *5145*
14:58 within t days I will build another made *5140*
15:29 the temple, and buildest *it* in t days, *5140*
Lk 1:56 And Mary abode with her about t months, *5140*
2:46 *that* after t days they found him in *5140*
4:25 when the heaven was shut up t years and *5140*
9:33 and let us make t tabernacles; one for thee, *5140*
10:36 Which now of these t, thinkest thou, *5140*
11: 5 and say unto him, Friend, lend me t loaves; *5140*
12:52 t against two, and two against three. *5140*
12:52 three against two, and two against t. *5140*
13: 7 *these* t years I come seeking fruit on this fig *5140*
13:21 woman took and hid in t measures of meal, *5140*
Jn 2: 6 the Jews, containing two or t firkins apiece. *5140*
2:19 this temple, and in t days I will raise it up. *5140*
2:20 and wilt thou rear it up in t days? *5140*
12: 5 not this ointment sold for t **hundred** pence, *5145*
21:11 of great fishes, an hundred and fifty *and* t: *5140*
Ac 2:41 added *unto them* about t **thousand** souls. *5153*
5: 7 And it was about the space of t hours after, *5140*
7:20 nourished up in his father's house t months: *5140*
9: 9 And he was t days without sight, and *5140*
10:19 said unto him, Behold, t men seek thee: *5140*
11:10 And this was done t **times**: and *1909+5151*
11:11 immediately there were t men already *5140*
17: 2 t sabbath days reasoned with them out of *5140*
19: 8 and spake boldly for the space of t months, *5140*
Ac 20: 3 And *there* abode t months: and when *5140*
20:31 that *by the space of* t **years** I ceased not to *5148*
25: 1 after t days he ascended from Cesarea to *5140*
28: 7 and lodged *us* t days courteously. *5140*
28:11 And after t months we departed in a ship of *5140*
28:12 landing at Syracuse, we tarried *there* t days. *5140*
28:15 us as far as Appii forum, and The t taverns: *5140*
28:17 that after t days Paul called the chief of *5140*
1Co 10: 8 and fell in one day t and twenty thousand. *5140*
13:13 now abideth faith, hope, charity, these t; *5140*
14:27 or at the most *by* t, and *that* by course; *5140*
14:29 Let the prophets speak two or t, and let *5140*
2Co 13: 1 t witnesses shall every word be established. *5140*
Gal 1:18 Then after t years I went up to Jerusalem to *5140*
1Ti 5:19 but before two or t witnesses. *5140*
Heb 10:28 without mercy under two or t witnesses: *5140*
11:23 was hid t **months** of his parents, because *5150*
Jas 5:17 it rained not on the earth *by the space of* t *5140*
1Jn 5: 7 For there are t that bear record in heaven, *5140*
5: 7 and the Holy Ghost: and these t are one. *5140*
5: 8 And there are t that bear witness in earth, *5140*
5: 8 and the blood: and *these* t agree in one. *5140*
Rev 6: 6 and t measures of barley for a penny; *5140*
8:13 other voices of the trumpet of the t angels, *5140*
9:18 By these t was the third *part* of men killed, *5140*
11: 9 nations shall see their dead bodies t days *5140*
11:11 And after t days and a half the spirit of life *5140*
16:13 And I saw t unclean spirits like frogs *come* *5140*
16:19 And the great city was *divided* into t parts, *5140*
21:13 On the east t gates; on the north three gates; *5140*
21:13 On the east three gates; on the north t gates; *5140*
21:13 on the south t gates; and on the west three *5140*
21:13 south three gates; and on the west t gates. *5140*

THREEFOLD (1) [THREE]

Ecc 4:12 and a t cord is not quickly broken. 8027

THREESCORE (93) [SIXTY]

Ge 25: 7 hundred **t and fifteen** years. 2568+7657+2050.1
25:26 Isaac *was* t years old when she bare them. 8346
46:26 sons' wives, all the souls *were* t and six; 8346
46:27 which came into Egypt, *were* **t and ten**. 7657
50: 3 the Egyptians mourned for him **t and ten** 7657
Ex 15:27 wells of water, and **t and ten** palm trees: 7657
38:25 **t and fifteen** 2568+7657+2050.1+2050.1
Lev 12: 5 continue in the blood of her purifying t 8346
Nu 1:27 *were* **t and fourteen** thousand 702+7657+2050.1
1:39 *were* t and two thousand and 8346
2: 4 *were* **t and fourteen** thousand 702+7657+2050.1
2:26 *were* t and two thousand and 8346
3:43 and **t and thirteen**. 7657+7969+2050.1
3:46 **t and thirteen** of 7657+7969+1886.1+2050.1
3:50 a thousand three hundred and t and 8346
26:22 **t and sixteen** thousand and 7657+8337+2050.1
26:25 t and four thousand and three hundred. 8346
26:27 of them, t thousand and five hundred. 8346
26:43 *were* t and four thousand and four hundred. 8346
31:33 **t and twelve** thousand 7657+8147+2050.1
31:34 And t and one thousand asses, 8346
31:37 *and* **t and fifteen**. 2568+7657+2050.1
31:38 tribute *was* **t and twelve**. 7657+8147+2050.1
31:39 tribute *was* **t and one**. 259+8346+2050.1
33: 9 of water, and **t and ten** palm trees; 7657
Dt 3: 4 t cities, all the region of Argob, 8346
10:22 went down into Egypt with **t and ten** 7657
Jos 13:30 towns of Jair, which *are* in Bashan, t cities: 8346
Jdg 1: 7 **T and ten** kings, having their thumbs 7657
8:14 *even* **t and seventeen** men. 7651+7657+2050.1
8:30 Gideon had **t and ten** sons of his body 7657
9: 2 *which are* **t and ten** persons, reign over 7657
9: 4 they gave him **t and ten** *pieces* of silver out 7657
9: 5 *being* **t and ten** persons, upon one stone: 7657
9:18 **t and ten** persons, upon one stone, and 7657
9:24 That the cruelty *done* to the **t and ten** sons 7657
12:14 that rode on **t and ten** ass colts: 7651
1Sa 6:19 people fifty thousand and **t and ten** men: 7657
2Sa 2:31 *so that* three hundred and t men died. 8346
1Ki 4:13 t great cities *with* walls and brasen bars: 8346
4:22 of fine flour, and t measures of meal, 8346
5:15 Solomon had **t and ten** thousand that bare 7657
6: 2 the length thereof *was* t cubits, and 8346
10:14 to Solomon in one year was six hundred t 8346
2Ki 25:19 t men of the people of the land that were 8346
1Ch 2:21 whom he married when he *was* t years old; 8346
2:23 and the towns thereof, *even* t cities. 8346
5:18 and forty thousand seven hundred and t, 8346
9:13 a thousand and seven hundred and t; 8346
16:38 Obed-edom with their brethren, t and eight; 8346
21: 5 Judah *was* four hundred **t and ten** thousand 7657
26: 8 the service, *were* t and two of Obed-edom. 8346
2Ch 2: 2 Solomon told out **t and ten** thousand men 7657
2:18 he set **t and ten** thousand of them *to be* 7657
3: 3 cubits after the first measure *was* t cubits, 8346
9:13 six hundred and t and six talents of gold; 8346
11:21 he took eighteen wives, and t concubines; 8346
11:21 and eight sons, and t daughters.) 8346
12: 3 hundred chariots, and t thousand horsemen: 8346
29:32 was **t and ten** bullocks, an hundred rams, 7657
36:21 she kept sabbath, to fulfil **t and ten** years. 7657
Ezr 2: 9 children of Zaccai, seven hundred and t. 8346
2:64 *and* two thousand three hundred *and* t, 8346
2:69 **t and one thousand** 505+7239+8337+2050.1
6: 3 the height thereof t cubits, *and* the breadth 8361
6: 3 *and* the breadth thereof t cubits; 8361
8:10 and with him an hundred and t males. 8346
8:13 and Shemaiah, and with them t males. 8346
Ne 7:14 children of Zaccai, seven hundred and t. 8346
7:18 of Adonikam, six hundred t and seven. 8346
7:19 of Bigvai, two thousand t and seven. 8346
7:66 *and* two thousand three hundred and t, 8346
7:72 *of* silver, and t and seven priests' garments. 8346
11: 6 that dwelt at Jerusalem *were* four hundred t 8346
Ps 90:10 The days of our years *are* t years **and ten**; 7657
SS 3: 7 t valiant *men are* about it, of the valiant of 8346
6: 8 There *are* t queens, and 8346
Isa 7: 8 within t and five years shall Ephraim be 8346
Jer 52:25 t men of the people of the land, that were 8346
Eze 40:14 He made also posts *of* t cubits, even unto 8346
Da 3: 1 whose height *was* t cubits, *and* the breadth 8361
5:31 *being* about t and two year old. 8361
9:25 *shall be* seven weeks, and t and two weeks: 8346
9:26 after t and two weeks shall Messiah be cut 8346
Zec 1:12 thou hast had indignation these **t and ten** 7657
Lk 24:13 which was from Jerusalem *about* t furlongs. *1835*
Ac 7:14 all his kindred, **t and fifteen** souls. *1440+4002*
23:23 and horsemen t *and* **ten**, and spearmen two *1440*
27:37 in the ship two hundred t *and* **sixteen** *1440+1803*
1Ti 5: 9 be taken into the number under t years old, *1835*
Rev 11: 3 a thousand two hundred *and* t days, *1835*
12: 6 there a thousand two hundred *and* t days. *1835*
13:18 and his number *is* **Six hundred** t *and* **six**. *5516*

THRESH (4) [THRESHED, THRESHETH, THRESHING, THRESHINGFLOOR, THRESHINGFLOORS, THRESHINGPLACE]

Isa 41:15 thou shalt t the mountains, and beat *them* 1758
Jer 51:33 *is* like a threshingfloor, *it is* time to t her: 1869
Mic 4:13 Arise and t, O daughter of Zion: for I will 1758
Hab 3:12 thou didst t the heathen in anger. 1758

THRESHED (3) [THRESH]

Jdg 6:11 his son Gideon t wheat by the winepress, 2251
Isa 28:27 For the fitches are not t with a threshing 1758
Am 1: 3 they have t Gilead with threshing 1758

THRESHETH (1) [THRESH]

1Co 9:10 that he that t in hope should be partaker of *248*

THRESHING (10) [THRESH]

Lev 26: 5 And your t shall reach unto the vintage, and 1786
2Sa 24:22 **t instruments** and *other* instruments of 4173
2Ki 13: 7 and had made them like the dust by t. 1758
1Ch 21:20 hid themselves. Now Ornan was t wheat. 1758
21:23 the **t instruments** for wood, and the wheat 4173
Isa 21:10 O my t, and the corn of my floor: 4098
28:27 For the fitches are not threshed with a t 2742
28:28 because he will not ever be t it, 156+156
41:15 I will make thee a new sharp **t instrument** 4173
Am 1: 3 they have threshed Gilead with t 2742

THRESHINGFLOOR (17) [FLOOR, THRESH]

Ge 50:10 they came to the t of Atad, which *is* beyond 1637
Nu 15:20 as *ye do* the heave offering of the t, so 1637
18:27 as though it were the corn of the t, and 1637
18:30 unto the Levites as the increase of the t, 1637
Ru 3: 2 he winnoweth barley to night in the t. 1637
2Sa 6: 6 when they came to Nachon's t, Uzzah put 1637
24:18 rear an altar unto the LORD in the t of 1637
24:21 David said, To buy the t of thee, to build an 1637
24:24 So David bought the t and the oxen for fifty 1637
1Ch 13: 9 when they came unto the t of Chidon, Uzza 1637
21:15 the angel of the LORD stood by the t of 1637
21:18 set up an altar unto the LORD in the t of 1637
21:21 went out of the t, and bowed himself to 1637
21:22 said to Ornan, Grant me the place of *this* t, 1637
21:28 him in the t of Ornan the Jebusite, 1637
2Ch 3: 1 in the place that David had prepared in the t 1637
Jer 51:33 The daughter of Babylon *is* like a t, *it is* 1637

THRESHINGFLOORS (2) [FLOOR, THRESH]

1Sa 23: 1 fight against Keilah, and they rob the t. 1637
Da 2:35 and became like the chaff of the summer t; 147

THRESHINGPLACE (1) [PLACE, THRESH]

2Sa 24:16 the angel of the LORD was by the t of 1637

THRESHOLD (14) [THRESHOLDS]

Jdg 19:27 the house, and her hands *were* upon the t. 5592
1Sa 5: 4 palms of his hands *were* cut off upon the t; 4670
5: 5 tread on the t of Dagon in Ashdod unto this 4670
1Ki 14:17 *and* when she came to the t of the door, 5592
Eze 9: 3 whereupon he was, to the t of the house. 4670
10: 4 *and stood* over the t of the house; 4670
10:18 departed from off the t of the house, 4670
40: 6 and measured the t of the gate, 5592
40: 6 the other t *of the gate, which was* one reed 5592
40: 7 the t of the gate by the porch of the gate 5592
43: 8 In their setting of their t by my thresholds, 5592
46: 2 and he shall worship at the t of the gate: 4670
47: 1 waters issued out from under the t of 4670
Zep 1: 9 will I punish all those that leap on the t, 4670

THRESHOLDS (3) [THRESHOLD]

Ne 12:25 *were* porters keeping the ward at the t of 624
Eze 43: 8 In their setting of their threshold by my t, 5592
Zep 2:14 in the windows; desolation *shall be* in the t: 5592

THREW (6) [THROW]

2Sa 16:13 he went, and t stones at him, and cast dust. 5619
2Ki 9:33 So they t her **down**: and *some* of her blood 8058
2Ch 31: 1 **t down** the high places and the altars out of 5422
Mk 12:42 and she t in two mites, which make a *906*
Lk 9:42 the devil t him **down**, and tare *him*. And *4486*
Ac 22:23 cast *off their* clothes, and t dust into the air, *906*

THREWEST (1) [THROW]

Ne 9:11 and their persecutors thou t into the deeps, 7993

THRICE (15) [THREE]

Ex 34:23 **T** in the year shall all your men 6471+7969
34:24 the LORD thy God t in the year. 6471+7969
2Ki 13:18 And he smote t, and stayed. 6471+7969
13:19 now thou shalt smite Syria *but* t. 6471+7969
Mt 26:34 before *the* cock crow, thou shalt deny me **t**. *5151*
26:75 Before *the* cock crow, thou shalt deny me **t**. *5151*
Mk 14:30 *the* cock crow twice, thou shalt deny me **t**. *5151*
14:72 *the* cock crow twice, thou shalt deny me **t**. *5151*
Lk 22:34 before that thou shalt **t** deny that *thou* *5151*

T

Lk 22:61 Before *the* cock crow, thou shalt deny me t. 5151
Jn 13:38 shall not crow, till thou hast denied me t. 5151
Ac 10:16 This was done t: and the vessel was 1909+5151
2Co 11:25 T was I beaten with rods, once was I 5151
11:25 t I suffered shipwrack, a night and a day I 5151
12: 8 For this *thing* I besought the Lord t, that it 5151

THROAT (7)

Ps 5: 9 their t *is* an open sepulchre; they flatter 1627
69: 3 my t is dried: mine eyes fail while *I* wait 1627
115: 7 walk not: neither speak they through their t. 1627
Pr 23: 2 put a knife to thy t, if thou *be* a man given 3930
Jer 2:25 from being unshod, and thy t from thirst: 1627
Mt 18:28 on him, and **took** *him* **by the** t, saying, 4155
Ro 3:13 Their t *is* an open sepulchre; with their 2995

THRONE (176) [THRONES]

Ge 41:40 only *in* the t will I be greater than thou. 3678
Ex 11: 5 firstborn of Pharaoh that sitteth upon his t, 3678
12:29 t unto the firstborn of the captive that *was* 3678
Dt 17:18 when he sitteth upon the t of his kingdom, 3678
1Sa 2: 8 and to make them inherit the t of glory: 3678
2Sa 3:10 to set up the t of David over Israel and 3678
7:13 I will stablish the t of his kingdom for ever. 3678
7:16 thy t shall be stablished for ever. 3678
14: 9 and the king and his t *be* guiltless. 3678
1Ki 1:13 reign after me, and he shall sit upon my t? 3678
1:17 reign after me, and he shall sit upon my t. 3678
1:20 sit on the t of my lord the king after him. 3678
1:24 reign after me, and he shall sit upon my t? 3678
1:27 who should sit on the t of my lord the king 3678
1:30 and he shall sit upon my t in my stead; 3678
1:35 that he may come and sit upon my t; 3678
1:37 make his t greater than the throne of my 3678
1:37 make his throne greater than the t of my 3678
1:46 also Solomon sitteth on the t of 3678
1:47 and make his t greater than thy throne. 3678
1:47 and make his throne greater than thy t. 3678
1:48 which hath given *one* to sit on my t *this* 3678
2: 4 fail thee (said he) a man on the t of Israel. 3678
2:12 sat Solomon upon the t of David his father; 3678
2:19 sat down on his t, and caused a seat to be 3678
2:24 set me on the t of David my father, and 3678
2:33 and upon his house, and upon his t, 3678
2:45 the t of David shall be established before 3678
3: 6 thou hast given him a son to sit on his t, 3678
5: 5 whom I will set upon thy t in thy room, 3678
7: 7 he made a porch for the t where he might 3678
8:20 sit on the t of Israel, as the LORD 3678
8:25 a man in my sight to sit on the t of Israel; 3678
9: 5 I will establish the t of thy kingdom upon 3678
9: 5 There shall not fail thee a man upon the t of 3678
10: 9 in thee, to set thee on the t of Israel: 3678
10:18 Moreover the king made a great t of ivory, 3678
10:19 The t had six steps, and the top of 3678
10:19 and the top of the t *was* round behind: 3678
16:11 he *began* to reign, as soon as he sat on his t, 3678
22:10 the king of Judah sat each on his t, 3678
22:19 I saw the LORD sitting on his t, and 3678
2Ki 10: 3 set *him* on his father's t, and fight for your 3678
10:30 fourth *generation* shall sit on the t of Israel. 3678
11:19 And he sat on the t of the kings. 3678
13:13 his fathers; and Jeroboam sat upon his t: 3678
15:12 Thy sons shall sit on the t of Israel unto 3678
25:28 set his t above the throne of the kings that 3678
25:28 set his throne above the t of the kings that 3678
1Ch 17:12 a house, and I will stablish his t for ever. 3678
17:14 and his t shall be established for evermore. 3678
22:10 I will establish the t of his kingdom over 3678
28: 5 t of the kingdom of the LORD over Israel. 3678
29:23 Solomon sat on the t of the LORD as king 3678
2Ch 6:10 am set on the t of Israel, as the LORD 3678
6:16 a man in my sight to sit upon the t of Israel; 3678
7:18 will I stablish the t of thy kingdom, 3678
9: 8 which delighted in thee to set thee on his t, 3678
9:17 Moreover the king made a great t of ivory, 3678
9:18 *there were* six steps to the t, with a 3678
9:18 *which were* fastened to the t, and stays on 3678
18: 9 king of Judah sat either of them on his t, 3678
18:18 I saw the LORD sitting upon his t, and 3678
23:20 and set the king upon the t of the kingdom. 3678
Ne 3: 7 unto the t of the governor on *this* side 3678
Est 1: 2 when the king Ahasuerus sat on the t of his 3678
5: 1 the king sat upon his royal t in the royal 3678
Job 26: 9 He holdeth back the face of *his* t, *and* 3678
36: 7 with kings *are they* on the t; yea, he doth 3678
Ps 9: 4 my cause; thou satest in the t judging right. 3678
9: 7 he hath prepared his t for judgment. 3678
11: 4 holy temple, the LORD'S t *is* in heaven: 3678
45: 6 Thy t, O God, *is* for ever and ever: 3678
47: 8 God sitteth upon the t of his holiness. 3678
89: 4 and build up thy t to all generations. 3678
89:14 and judgment *are* the habitation of thy t: 3678
89:29 for ever, and his t as the days of heaven. 3678
89:36 for ever, and his t as the sun before me. 3678
89:44 to cease, and cast his t down to the ground. 3678
93: 2 Thy t is established of old: thou *art* from 3678
94:20 Shall the t of iniquity have fellowship *with* 3678
97: 2 and judgment *are* the habitation of his t. 3678
103:19 The LORD hath prepared his t in 3678
132:11 the fruit of thy body will I set upon thy t. 3678
132:12 their children also shall sit upon thy t for 3678
Pr 16:12 for the t is established by righteousness. 3678
20: 8 A king that sitteth in the t of judgment 3678
20:28 the king: and his t is upholden by mercy. 3678
25: 5 his t shall be established in righteousness. 3678
29:14 the poor, his t shall be established for ever. 3678
Isa 6: 1 died I saw also the Lord sitting upon a t, 3678
9: 7 upon the t of David, and upon his kingdom, 3678
14:13 I will exalt my t above the stars of God: 3678
16: 5 And in mercy shall the t be established: and 3678
22:23 he shall be for a glorious t to his father's 3678
47: 1 *there is* no t, O daughter of the Chaldeans; 3678
66: 1 The heaven *is* my t, and the earth *is* my 3678
Jer 1:15 they shall set every one his t *at* the entering 3678
3:17 At that time they shall call Jerusalem the t 3678
13:13 even the kings that sit upon David's t, 3678
14:21 do not disgrace the t of thy glory: 3678
17:12 A glorious high t from the beginning *is* 3678
17:25 and princes sitting upon the t of David, 3678
22: 2 that sittest upon the t of David, thou, and 3678
22: 4 this house kings sitting upon the t of David, 3678
22:30 sitting upon the t of David, and ruling any 3678
29:16 of the king that sitteth upon the t of David, 3678
33:17 man to sit upon the t of the house of Israel; 3678
33:21 should not have a son to reign upon his t; 3678
36:30 He shall have none to sit upon the t of 3678
43:10 will set his t upon these stones that I have 3678
49:38 I will set my t in Elam, and will destroy 3678
52:32 set his t above the throne of the kings that 3678
52:32 set his throne above the t of the kings that 3678
La 5:19 thy t from generation to generation. 3678
Eze 1:26 *was* over their heads *was* the likeness of a t, 3678
1:26 upon the likeness of the t *was* the likeness 3678
10: 1 as the appearance of the likeness of a t. 3678
43: 7 the place of my t, and the place of the soles 3678
Da 5:20 he was deposed from his kingly t, and 3764
7: 9 his t *was like* the fiery flame, *and* 3764
Jnh 3: 6 he arose from his t, and he laid his robe 3678
Hag 2:22 I will overthrow the t of kingdoms, and 3678
Zec 6:13 the glory, and shall sit and rule upon his t: 3678
6:13 he shall be a priest upon his t: and 3678
Mt 5:34 at all; neither by heaven; for it is God's t: 2362
19:28 when the Son of man shall sit in the t of his 2362
23:22 sweareth by the t of God, and by him that 2362
25:31 then shall he sit upon the t of his glory: 2362
Lk 1:32 the Lord God shall give unto him the t of 2362
Ac 2:30 *he* would raise up Christ to sit on his t; 2362
7:49 Heaven *is* my t, and earth *is* my footstool: 2362
12:21 sat upon his t, and made an oration unto 968
Heb 1: 8 But unto the Son *he saith*, Thy t, O God, 2362
4:16 therefore come boldly unto the t of grace, 2362
8: 1 who is set on the right hand of the t of 2362
12: 2 is set down at the right hand of the t of 2362
Rev 1: 4 the seven spirits which are before his t; 2362
3:21 will I grant to sit with me in my t, 2362
3:21 and am set down with my Father in his t. 2362
4: 2 a t was set in heaven, and one sat on 2362
4: 2 was set in heaven, and one sat on the t. 2362
4: 3 and *there was* a rainbow round about the t, 2362
4: 4 And round about the t *were* four and 2362
4: 5 And out of the t proceeded lightnings and 2362
4: 5 seven lamps of fire burning before the t, 2362
4: 6 And before the t *there was* a sea of glass 2362
4: 6 and in the midst of the t, and round about 2362
4: 6 midst of the throne, and round about the t, 2362
4: 9 honour and thanks to him that sat on the t, 2362
4:10 fall down before him that sat on the t, 2362
4:10 and ever, and cast their crowns before the t, 2362
5: 1 him that sat on the t a book written within 2362
5: 6 in the midst of the t and of the four beasts, 2362
5: 7 of the right hand of him that sat upon the t. 2362
5:11 the voice of many angels round about the t 2362
5:13 *be* unto him that sitteth upon the t, and 2362
6:16 us from the face of him that sitteth on the t, 2362
7: 9 stood before the t, and before the Lamb, 2362
7:10 to our God which sitteth upon the t, 2362
7:11 And all the angels stood round about the t, 2362
7:11 and fell before the t on their faces, and 2362
7:15 Therefore are they before the t of God, and 2362
7:15 he that sitteth on the t shall dwell among 2362
7:17 For the Lamb which is in the midst of the t 2362
8: 3 the golden altar which was before the t. 2362
12: 5 child was caught up unto God, and *to* his t. 2362
14: 3 sung as *it were* a new song before the t, 2362
14: 5 for they are without fault before the t of 2362
16:17 of heaven, from the t, saying, It is done. 2362
19: 4 and worshipped God that sat on the t, 2362
19: 5 And a voice came out of the t, saying, 2362
20:11 And I saw a great white t, and him that sat 2362
21: 5 And he that sat upon the t said, Behold, 2362
22: 1 proceeding out of the t of God and of 2362
22: 3 but the t of God and of the Lamb shall be in 2362

THRONES (9) [THRONE]

Ps 122: 5 For there are set t of judgment, the thrones 3678
122: 5 of judgment, the t of the house of David. 3678
Isa 14: 9 it hath raised up from their t all the kings of 3678
Eze 26:16 of the sea shall come down from their t, 3678
Da 7: 9 I beheld till the t were cast *down*, and 3764
Mt 19:28 ye also shall sit upon twelve t, judging 2362
Lk 22:30 sit on t judging the twelve tribes of Israel. 2362
Col 1:16 whether *they be* t, or dominions, or 2362
Rev 20: 4 And I saw t, and they sat upon them, and 2362

THRONG (2) [THRONGED, THRONGING]

Mk 3: 9 of the multitude, lest they should t him. 2346
Lk 8:45 the multitude t thee and press *thee*, and 4912

THRONGED (2) [THRONG]

Mk 5:24 and much people followed him, and t him. 4918
Lk 8:42 a dying. (But as he went the people t him. 4846

THRONGING (1) [THRONG]

Mk 5:31 Thou seest the multitude t thee, and 4918

THROUGH (463) [THROUGHOUT]

Ge 6:13 for the earth is filled *with* violence t 4480+6440
12: 6 Abram passed t the land unto the place of 871.1
13:17 walk t the land in the length of it and in 871.1
30:32 I will pass t all thy flock to day, 871.1
41:36 that the land perish not t the famine. 871.1
Ex 10:15 herbs of the field, t all the land of Egypt. 871.1
12:12 For I will pass t the land of Egypt this 871.1
12:23 For the LORD will **pass** t to smite 5674
13:17 that God led them not *t* the way of the land NIH
13:18 *t* the way of the wilderness of the Red sea: NIH
14:16 go on dry *ground* t the midst of the sea. 871.1
14:24 the host of the Egyptians t the pillar of fire 871.1
19:13 he shall surely be stoned, or **shot** t; 3384+3384
19:21 lest they **break** t unto the LORD to gaze, 2040
19:24 the people **break** t to come up unto 2040
21: 6 his master shall **bore** his ear t with an aul; 7527
36:33 he made the middle bar to shoot t 8432+871.1
Lev 4: 2 If a soul shall sin t ignorance against any 871.1
4:13 congregation of Israel **sin** t **ignorance**, 7686
4:22 done somewhat t ignorance against any of 871.1
4:27 if any one of the common people sin t 871.1
5:15 commit a trespass, and sin t ignorance, 871.1
18:21 thou shalt not let *any* of thy seed **pass** t 5674
26: 6 neither shall the sword go t your land. 871.1
Nu 13:32 t which we have gone to search it, 871.1
14: 7 The land, which we passed t to search it, 871.1
15:27 if any soul sin t ignorance, then he shall 871.1
15:29 him that **sinneth** t **ignorance**, 6213+7684+871.1
20:17 Let us pass, I pray thee, t thy country: 871.1
20:17 we will not pass t the fields, or through 871.1
20:17 pass through the fields, or t the vineyards, 871.1
20:19 without *doing any* thing *else*, **go** t on my 5674
20:20 he said, Thou shalt not **go** t. And Edom 5674
20:21 Thus Edom refused to give Israel passage t 871.1
21:22 Let me pass t thy land: we will not turn 871.1
21:23 Sihon would not suffer Israel to pass t his 871.1
24: 8 and **pierce** *them* t *with* his arrows. 4272
25: 8 **thrust** both of them t, the man of Israel, 1856
25: 8 the man of Israel, and the woman t her belly. 413
31:16 children of Israel, t the counsel of Balaam, 871.1
31:23 ye shall **make** *it* **go** t the fire, and it shall be 5674
31:23 not the fire ye shall **make go** t the water. 5674
33: 8 **passed** t the midst of the sea into 5674
Dt 1:19 we went *t* all that great and terrible NIH
2: 4 Ye are to pass t the coast of your brethren 871.1
2: 7 he knoweth thy walking *t* this great NIH
2: 8 t the way of the plain from Elath, and 4480
2:18 Thou art to pass over *t* Ar, the coast of NIH
2:27 Let me pass t thy land: I will go along by 871.1
2:28 I may drink: only I will **pass** t on my feet; 5674
5:15 brought thee out thence t a mighty hand 871.1
8:15 Who led thee t *that* great and terrible 871.1
9:26 which thou hast redeemed t thy greatness, 871.1
15:17 thrust *it* t his ear unto the door, and 871.1
18:10 **maketh** his son or his daughter **to pass** t 5674
29:16 how we came t the nations which ye 7130+871.1
31:29 to provoke him to anger t the work of your 871.1
32:47 t this thing ye shall prolong *your* days in 871.1
33:11 smite t the loins of them that rise against NIH
Jos 1:11 Pass t the host, and command 7130+871.1
2:15 she let them down by a cord t the window: 1157
3: 2 that the officers went t the host; 7130+871.1
18: 4 go t the land, and describe it according to 871.1
18: 8 Go and walk t the land, and describe it, 871.1
18: 9 the men went and **passed** t the land, and 5674
18:12 and went up t the mountains westward; 871.1
24:17 all the people t whom we passed: 7130+871.1
Jdg 2:22 That t them I may prove Israel, 871.1
3:23 Ehud went forth t the porch, and shut 1886.5
5: 6 and the travellers walked *t* byways. NIH
5:26 she had pierced and **stricken** t his temples. 2498
5:28 cried t the lattice, Why is his chariot *so* 1157
9:54 his young man **thrust** him t, and he died. 1856
11:16 walked t the wilderness unto the Red sea, 871.1
11:17 Let me, I pray thee, pass t thy land: 871.1
11:18 they went along t the wilderness, and 871.1
11:19 we pray thee, t thy land into my place. 871.1
11:20 Sihon trusted not Israel to pass t his coast: 871.1
20:12 the tribes of Israel sent men t all the tribe 871.1
1Sa 9: 4 he passed t mount Ephraim, and 871.1
9: 4 passed t the land of Shalisha, but 871.1
9: 4 they passed t the land of Shalim, and 871.1
9: 4 he passed t the land of the Benjamites, but 871.1
19:12 So Michal let David down t a window: and 1157
31: 4 thy sword, and **thrust** me t therewith; 1856
31: 4 these uncircumcised come and **thrust** me t, 1856
2Sa 2:29 his men walked all that night t the plain, 871.1
2:29 went *t* all Bithron, and they came *to* NIH
4: 7 and gat them away t the plain all night. 1870
6:16 Michal Saul's daughter looked t a window, 1157
12:31 and made them pass t the brickkiln: 871.1
18:14 and thrust them t the heart of Absalom, 871.1
20:14 he **went** t all the tribes of Israel unto Abel, 5674
22:13 T the brightness before him were coals of 4480
22:30 For by thee I have run *t* a troop: by my God NIH
23:16 the three mighty *men* brake t the host of 871.1
24: 2 with him, Go now t all the tribes of Israel, 871.1
24: 8 So when they had gone t all the land, they 871.1
2Ki 1: 2 Ahaziah fell down t a lattice in his upper 1157
3: 8 The way t the wilderness of Edom. NIH
3:26 to **break** t *even* unto the king of Edom: 1234
10:21 Jehu sent t all Israel: and all 871.1
16: 3 yea, and made his son to pass t the fire, 871.1
17:17 and their daughters to pass t the fire, 871.1
21: 6 he made his son pass t the fire, and 871.1
23:10 or his daughter to pass t the fire to Molech. 871.1
24:20 For t the anger of the LORD it came to 5921
1Ch 10: 4 thy sword, and **thrust** me t therewith; 1856
11:18 the three brake t the host of the Philistines, 871.1
2Ch 19: 4 he went out again t the people from 871.1
23:20 they came t the high gate *into* 8432+871.1
24: 9 they made a proclamation t Judah and 871.1
30:10 So the posts passed from city to city t 871.1
31:18 their daughters, t all the congregation: 3807.1
32: 4 the brook that ran t the midst of the land, 871.1
33: 6 he caused his children to pass t the fire in 871.1
Ezr 6:14 they prospered t the prophesying of 871.2
Ne 9:11 that they **went** t the midst of the sea on 5674
Est 6: 9 bring him on horseback t the street of 871.1
6:11 brought him on horseback t the street of 871.1
Job 7:14 me with dreams, and terrifiest me t visions: 4480
14: 9 *Yet* t the sent of water it will bud, and 4480
20:24 and the bow of steel shall **strike** him t. 2498
22:13 God know? can he judge t the dark *cloud?* 1157
24:16 In the dark *they* dig *t* houses, *which* they NIH
26:12 by his understanding he **smiteth** t 4272
29: 3 *and when* by his light I walked *t* darkness; NIH

T

Job 29: 7 When I went out *to* the gate **t** the city, 5921
40:24 it with his eyes: *his* nose pierceth **t** snares. 871.1
41: 2 his nose? or **bore** his jaw **t** with a thorn? 5344
Ps 8: 8 *whatsoever* passeth **t** the paths of the seas. NIH
10: 4 The wicked, **t** the pride of his 3509.1
18:29 For by thee I have run **t** a troop; and by my NIH
19: 4 Their line is gone out **t** all the earth, and 871.1
21: 7 **t** the mercy of the most High he shall not 871.1
23: 4 though I walk **t** the valley of the shadow of 871.1
32: 3 my bones waxed old **t** my roaring all 871.1
44: 5 **T** thee will we push down our enemies: 871.1
44: 5 **t** thy name will we tread them under that 871.1
60:12 **T** God we shall do valiantly: for he *it is* 871.1
66: 3 **t** the greatness of thy power shall thine 871.1
66: 6 dry *land:* they went **t** the flood on foot: 871.1
66:12 we went **t** fire and through water: 871.1
66:12 we went through fire and **t** water: 871.1
68: 7 when thou didst march **t** the wilderness; 871.1
73: 9 and their tongue walketh **t** the earth. 871.1
78:13 divided the sea, and **caused** them **to pass t**; 5674
81: 5 when he went out **t** the land of Egypt: 5921
84: 6 *Who* passing **t** the valley of Baca make it a 871.1
92: 4 LORD, hast made me glad **t** thy work: 871.1
106: 9 so he led them **t** the depths, as *through* 871.1
106: 9 through the depths, as **t** the wilderness. NIH
107:39 are minished and brought low **t** oppression, 4480
108:13 **T** God we shall do valiantly: for he *it is* 871.1
109:24 My knees are weak **t** fasting; and my flesh 4480
110: 5 The Lord at thy right hand shall **strike t** 4272
115: 7 walk not: neither speak they **t** their throat. 871.1
119:98 Thou **t** thy commandments hast made me NIH
119:104 **T** thy precepts I get understanding: 4480
136:14 **made** Israel **to pass t** the midst of it: for his 5674
136:16 To him which led his people **t** 871.1
Pr 7: 6 For at the window of my house I looked **t** 1157
7: 8 Passing **t** the street near her corner; and 871.1
7:23 Till a dart **strike t** his liver; as a bird 6398
11: 9 but **t** knowledge shall the just be delivered. 871.1
18: 1 **T** desire a man, having separated himself, 3807.1
24: 3 **T** wisdom is a house builded; and 871.1
Ecc 5: 3 For a dream cometh **t** the multitude of 871.1
10:18 **t** idleness of the hands the house droppeth 871.1
10:18 idleness of the hands the house **droppeth t**. 1811
SS 2: 9 the windows, shewing himself **t** the lattice. 4480
Isa 8: 8 he shall pass **t** Judah; he shall overflow 871.1
8:21 they shall pass **t** it, hardly bestead and 871.1
9:19 **T** the wrath of the LORD of hosts is 871.1
13:15 Every one that is found shall be **thrust t**; 1856
14:19 **thrust t** with a sword, that go down to 2944
16: 8 unto Jazer, they wandered **t** the wilderness: NIH
21: 1 As whirlwinds in the south **pass t**; *so* 2498
23:10 **Pass t** thy land as a river, O daughter of 5674
27: 4 I would go **t** them, I would burn them 871.1
28: 7 they also have erred **t** wine, and 871.1
28: 7 and **t** strong drink are out of the way; 871.1
28: 7 and the prophet have erred **t** strong drink, 871.1
28: 7 they are out of the way **t** strong drink; 4480
28:15 when the overflowing scourge shall **pass t**, 5674
28:18 when the overflowing scourge shall **pass t**, 5674
30:31 For **t** the voice of the LORD shall 4480
34:10 none shall pass **t** it for ever and ever. 871.1
43: 2 When thou passest **t** the waters, I *will be* 871.1
43: 2 **t** the rivers, they shall not overflow thee: 871.1
43: 2 when thou walkest **t** the fire, thou shalt not 1119
48:21 they thirsted not *when* he led them **t** 871.1
60:15 that no man **went t** *thee,* I will make thee 5674
62:10 **Go t**, go through the gates; prepare you 5674
62:10 Go through, **go t** the gates; prepare you 5674
63:13 That led them **t** the deep, as a horse in 871.1
Jer 2: 6 that led us **t** the wilderness, through a land 871.1
2: 6 **t** a land of deserts and of pits, through a 871.1
2: 6 **t** a land of drought, and of the shadow of 871.1
2: 6 **t** a land that no man passed through, 871.1
2: 6 through a land that no man passed **t**, 871.1
3: 9 it came to pass **t** the lightness of her 4480
5: 1 Run ye to and fro **t** the streets of 871.1
9: 6 **t** deceit they refuse to know me, saith 871.1
9:10 that none can **pass t** *them;* neither can *men* 5674
9:12 up like a wilderness, that none **passeth t**? 5674
12:12 come upon all high places **t** the wilderness: 871.1
17:24 to bring in no burden **t** the gates of this city 871.1
32:35 **cause** their sons and their daughters **to pass t** 5674
51: 4 and *they that are* **thrust t** in her streets. 1856
51:52 and **t** all her land the wounded shall groan. 871.1
52: 3 For **t** the anger of the LORD it came to 5921
La 3:44 a cloud, that *our* prayer should not **pass t**. 5674
4: 9 **stricken t** for *want of* the fruits of the field. 1856
4:21 of Uz; the cup also shall **pass t** unto thee: 5674
Eze 5:17 pestilence and blood shall **pass t** thee; and 871.1
6: 8 when ye shall be scattered **t** the countries. 871.1
9: 4 **Go t** the midst of the city through the midst 5674
9: 4 Go through the midst of the city **t** 871.1
9: 5 Go ye after him **t** the city, and smite: 871.1
12: 5 Dig thou **t** the wall in their sight, and 871.1
12: 7 in the even I digged **t** the wall with mine 871.1
12:12 they shall dig **t** the wall to carry out 871.1
14: 5 they are all estranged from me **t** their idols. 871.1
14:15 If I cause noisome beasts to pass **t** the land, 871.1
14:15 that no man may **pass t** because of 5674
14:17 that land, and say, Sword, go **t** the land; 871.1
16:14 for it *was* perfect **t** my comeliness, which I 871.1
16:21 delivered them to **cause** them **to pass t** 5674
16:36 thy nakedness discovered **t** thy whoredoms 871.1
16:40 and **thrust** thee **t** with their swords. 1333
20:23 and disperse them **t** the countries; 871.1
20:26 in that they **caused to pass t** *the fire* all that 5674
20:31 when *ye* make your sons to pass **t** the fire, 871.1
23:37 **caused** their sons, whom they bare unto me,
to pass for them **t** 5674
29:11 No foot of man shall pass **t** it, nor foot of 871.1
29:11 through it, nor foot of beast shall pass **t** it, 871.1
29:12 and will disperse them **t** the countries. 871.1
30:23 and will disperse them **t** the countries. 871.1
33:28 shall be desolate, that none shall **pass t**. 5674
34: 6 My sheep wandered **t** all the mountains, 871.1
Eze 36:19 and they were dispersed **t** the countries: 871.1
39:14 **passing t** the land to bury with 5674
39:15 the passengers *that* **pass t** the land, 5674
41:19 *it was* made **t** all the house round about. 413
46:19 After, he brought me **t** the entry, 871.1
47: 3 and he brought me **t** the waters; 871.1
47: 4 a thousand, and brought me **t** the waters; 871.1
47: 4 he measured a thousand, and **brought** me **t**; 5674
Da 8:25 **t** his policy also he shall cause craft to 5921
9: 7 **t** all the countries whither thou hast driven 871.1
11: 2 by his strength **t** his riches he shall stir up 871.1
11:10 certainly come, and overflow, and **pass t**: 5674
Joel 3:17 there shall no strangers pass **t** her any 871.1
Am 2:10 led you forty years **t** the wilderness, 871.1
5:17 I will pass **t** thee, saith the LORD. 7130+871.1
Jnh 3: 7 published **t** Nineveh by the decree of 871.1
Mic 2:13 have **passed t** the gate, and are gone out by 5674
5: 8 who, if he **go t**, both treadeth down, and 5674
Na 1:12 they be cut down, when he shall **pass t**. 5674
1:15 for the wicked shall no more pass **t** thee; 871.1
3: 4 that selleth nations **t** her whoredoms, and 871.1
3: 4 and families **t** her witchcrafts. 871.1
Hab 1: 6 *shall* march **t** the breadth of the land, 3807.1
3:12 Thou didst **march t** the land in indignation, 6805
3:14 Thou didst **strike t** with his staves the head 5344
3:15 Thou didst walk **t** the sea *with* thine 871.1
3:15 *with* thine horses, **t** the heap of great waters. NIH
Zec 1:10 hath sent to walk to and fro **t** the earth. 871.1
1:11 We have walked to and fro **t** the earth, and 871.1
1:17 My cities **t** prosperity shall yet be spread 4480
4:10 which run to and fro **t** the whole earth. 871.1
4:12 **t** the two golden pipes empty 3027+871.1
5: 6 This *is* their resemblance **t** all the earth. 871.1
6: 7 that *they* might walk to and fro **t** the earth: 871.1
6: 7 Get ye *hence,* walk to and fro **t** the earth. 871.1
6: 7 So they walked to and fro **t** the earth. 871.1
7:14 that no man **passed t** nor returned: 5674
9: 8 no oppressor shall pass **t** them any more: 5921
9:15 they shall drink, *and* make a noise as **t** wine; NIH
10: 7 and their heart shall rejoice as **t** wine: NIH
10:11 he shall pass **t** the sea *with* affliction, and 871.1
13: 3 shall **thrust** him **t** when he prophesieth. 1856
13: 9 I will bring the third *part* **t** the fire, and 871.1
Mt 6:19 and where thieves **break t** and steal: *1358*
6:20 and where thieves do not **break t** nor steal: *1358*
9:34 He casteth out the devils **t** the prince of *1722*
12: 1 Jesus went on the sabbath day **t** the corn; *1223*
12:43 he **walketh t** dry places, seeking rest, *1330*
19:24 It is easier for a camel to **go t** the eye *1330*
Mk 2:23 that he went **t** the corn fields on the sabbath *1223*
6:55 And **ran t** that whole region round about, *4063*
7:13 Making the word of God of none effect **t** NIG
7:31 **t** the midst of the coasts of Decapolis. *303*
9:30 they departed thence, and passed **t** Galilee; *1223*
10:25 It is easier for a camel to **go t** the eye of a *1330*
11:16 *man* should carry *any* vessel **t** the temple. *1223*
Lk 1:78 **T** the tender mercy of our God; *1223*
2:35 a sword shall **pierce t** thy own soul also,) *1330*
4:14 there went out a fame of him **t** all *2596*
4:30 But he **passing t** the midst of them *1330*
5:19 let him down **t** the tiling with *his* couch into *1223*
6: 1 that he **went t** the corn fields; *1279*
9: 6 And they departed, and **went t** the towns, *1330*
10:17 even the devils are subject unto us **t** thy *1722*
11:15 He casteth out devils **t** Beelzebub the chief *1722*
11:18 ye say that I cast out devils **t** Beelzebub. *1722*
11:24 **walketh t** dry places, seeking rest; *1330*
12:39 not have suffered his house to be **broken t**. *1358*
13:22 And he went **t** the cities and villages, *2596*
17: 1 but woe *unto him,* **t** whom they come. *1223*
17:11 that he **passed t** the midst of Samaria *1330*
18:25 For it is easier for a camel to go **t** a needle's *1223*
19: 1 And *Jesus* entered and **passed t** Jericho. *1330*
Jn 1: 7 the Light, that all *men* **t** him might believe. *1223*
3:17 but that the world **t** him might be saved. *1223*
4: 4 And he must needs **go t** Samaria. *1330*
8:59 going **t** the midst of them, and so *1223*
15: 3 Now ye are clean **t** the word which I have *1223*
17:11 keep **t** thine own name those whom thou *1722*
17:17 Sanctify them **t** thy truth: thy word is truth. *1722*
17:19 that they also might be sanctified **t** *1722*
17:20 for them also which shall believe on me **t** *1223*
20:31 that believing ye might have life **t** his *1722*
Ac 1: 2 after that he **t** the Holy Ghost had given *1223*
3:16 And his name **t** faith in his name hath made *1909*
3:17 I wot that **t** ignorance ye did *it,* as *did* also *2596*
4: 2 preached **t** Jesus the resurrection from *1722*
8:18 And when Simon saw that **t** laying on of *1223*
8:40 and **passing t** he preached in all the cities, *1330*
10:43 that **t** his name whosoever believeth in him *1223*
12:10 they went out, and passed on **t** one street; NIG
13: 6 And when they had **gone t** the isle unto *1330*
13:38 that **t** this *man* is preached unto you *1223*
14:22 that we must **t** much tribulation enter into *1223*
15: 3 they **passed t** Phenice and Samaria, *1330*
15:11 But we believe that **t** the grace of the Lord *1223*
15:41 And he **went t** Syria and Cilicia, *1330*
16: 4 And as they **went t** the cities, *1279*
17: 1 Now when they had **passed t** Amphipolis *1353*
18:27 helped them much which had believed **t** *1223*
19: 1 Paul having **passed t** the upper coasts came *1330*
19:21 when he had **passed t** Macedonia and *1330*
20: 3 he purposed to return **t** Macedonia. *1223*
21: 4 who said to Paul **t** the Spirit, that *he* should *1223*
Ro 1: 8 I thank my God **t** Jesus Christ for you all, *1223*
1:24 uncleanness **t** the lusts of their own hearts, *1722*
2:23 **t** breaking the law dishonourest thou God? *1223*
2:24 is blasphemed among the Gentiles **t** you, *1223*
3: 7 *more* abounded **t** my lie unto his glory; *1722*
3:24 Being justified freely by his grace **t** *1223*
3:25 *to be* a propitiation **t** faith in his blood, *1223*
3:25 sins that are past, **t** the forbearance of God; *1722*
3:30 by faith, and uncircumcision **t** faith. *1223*
3:31 Do we then make void the law **t** faith? *1223*
4:13 **t** the law, but through the righteousness of *1223*
Ro 4:13 the law, but **t** the righteousness of faith. *1223*
4:20 He staggered not at the promise of God **t** NIG
5: 1 we have peace with God **t** our Lord Jesus *1223*
5: 9 we shall be saved from wrath **t** him. *1223*
5:11 we also joy in God **t** our Lord Jesus Christ, *1223*
5:15 For if **t** the offence of one many be dead, NIG
5:21 might grace reign **t** righteousness unto *1223*
6:11 but alive unto God **t** Jesus Christ our Lord. *1722*
6:23 the gift of God *is* eternal life **t** Jesus Christ *1722*
7:25 I thank God **t** Jesus Christ our Lord. So *1223*
8: 3 could not do, in that it was weak **t** the flesh, *1223*
8:13 if ye **t** the Spirit do mortify the deeds of NIG
8:37 more than conquerors **t** him that loved us. *1223*
11:11 *rather* **t** their fall salvation *is come* unto NIG
11:30 yet have now obtained mercy **t** their NIG
11:31 that **t** your mercy they also may obtain NIG
11:36 For of him, and **t** him, and to him, *are* all *1223*
12: 3 For I say, **t** the grace given unto me, *1223*
15: 4 that we **t** patience and comfort of *1223*
15:13 in hope, **t** the power of the Holy Ghost. *1722*
15:17 whereof *I* may glory **t** Jesus Christ *in those* *1722*
15:19 **T** mighty signs and wonders, by the power *1722*
16:27 only wise, *be* glory **t** Jesus Christ for ever. *1223*
1Co 1: 1 called *to be* an apostle of Jesus Christ **t** *1223*
4:15 for in Christ Jesus I have begotten you **t** *1223*
8:11 And **t** thy knowledge shall the weak brother *1909*
10: 1 under the cloud, and all passed **t** the sea; *1223*
13:12 For now we see **t** a glass, darkly; *1223*
15:57 which giveth us the victory **t** our Lord *1223*
16: 5 unto you, when I shall **pass t** Macedonia: *1330*
16: 5 for I do **pass t** Macedonia. *1330*
2Co 3: 4 And such trust have we **t** Christ to *1223*
4:15 that the abundant grace might **t** *1223*
8: 9 that ye **t** his poverty might be rich. NIG
9:11 which causeth **t** us thanksgiving to God. *1223*
10: 4 mighty **t** God to the pulling down of strong NIG
11: 3 as the serpent beguiled Eve **t** his subtilty, so *1722*
11:33 And **t** a window in a basket was I let down *1223*
12: 7 measure **t** the abundance of the revelations, NIG
13: 4 For though he was crucified **t** weakness, *1537*
Gal 2:19 For I **t** the law am dead to the law, that I *1223*
3: 8 that God would justify the heathen **t** faith, *1537*
3:14 might come on the Gentiles **t** Jesus Christ; *1722*
3:14 receive the promise of the Spirit **t** faith. *1223*
4: 7 and if a son, then an heir of God **t** Christ. *1223*
4:13 Ye know how **t** infirmity of the flesh I *1223*
5: 5 For we **t** the Spirit wait for the hope of NIG
5:10 I have confidence in you **t** the Lord, *1722*
Eph 1: 7 In whom we have redemption **t** his blood, *1223*
2: 7 in *his* kindness towards us **t** Christ Jesus. *1722*
2: 8 For by grace are ye saved **t** faith; and *1223*
2:18 For **t** him we both have access by one Spirit *1223*
2:22 together for a habitation of God **t** the Spirit. *1722*
4: 6 who *is* above all, and **t** all, and in you all. *1223*
4:18 being alienated from the life of God **t** *1223*
Php 1:19 this shall turn to my salvation **t** your prayer, *1223*
2: 3 *Let* nothing *be done* **t** strife or vainglory; *2596*
3: 9 but that which is **t** the faith of Christ, *1223*
4: 7 keep your hearts and minds **t** Christ Jesus. *1722*
4:13 I can do all *things* **t** Christ which *1722*
Col 1:14 In whom we have redemption **t** his blood, *1223*
1:20 having made peace **t** the blood of his cross, *1223*
1:22 In the body of his flesh **t** death, to present *1223*
2: 8 Beware lest any *man* spoil you **t** philosophy *1223*
2:12 wherein also you are risen with *him* **t** *1223*
2Th 2:13 to salvation **t** sanctification of the Spirit *1722*
2:16 and good hope **t** grace, *1722*
1Ti 6:10 **pierced** themselves **t** with many sorrows. *4044*
2Ti 1:10 and immortality to light **t** the gospel: *1223*
3:15 salvation **t** faith which is in Christ Jesus. *1223*
Tit 1: 3 But hath in due times manifested his word **t** *1722*
3: 6 Which he shed on us abundantly **t** Jesus *1223*
Phm 1:22 for I trust that **t** your prayers I shall be *1223*
Heb 2:10 of their salvation perfect **t** sufferings. *1223*
2:14 that **t** death he might destroy him that had *1223*
2:15 And deliver them who **t** fear of death were *1223*
3:13 lest any of you be hardened **t** NIG
6:12 but followers of them who **t** faith and *1223*
9:14 who **t** the eternal Spirit offered himself *1223*
10:10 By the which will we are sanctified **t** *1223*
10:20 for us, **t** the vail, that is to say, his flesh; *1223*
11: 3 **T** faith we understand that the worlds were NIG
11:11 **T** faith also Sara herself received strength to NIG
11:28 **T** faith he kept the passover, and NIG
11:29 By faith they **passed t** the Red sea as by *1224*
11:33 Who **t** faith subdued kingdoms, *1223*
11:39 having obtained a good report **t** faith, *1223*
12:20 it shall be stoned, or **thrust t** with a dart: *2700*
13:20 **t** the blood of the everlasting covenant, *1722*
13:21 *is* well pleasing in his sight, **t** Jesus Christ; *1223*
1Pe 1: 2 **t** sanctification of the Spirit, unto obedience *1722*
1: 5 Who are kept by the power of God **t** faith *1223*
1: 6 ye are in heaviness **t** manifold temptations: *1722*
1:22 **t** the Spirit unto unfeigned love of *1223*
4:11 that God in all *things* may be glorified **t** *1223*
2Pe 1: 1 faith with us **t** the righteousness of God *1722*
1: 2 peace be multiplied unto you **t** *1722*
1: 3 **t** the knowledge of him that hath called us *1223*
1: 4 the corruption that is in the world **t** lust: *1722*
2: 3 And **t** covetousness shall they with feigned *1722*
2:18 they allure **t** the lusts of the flesh, *1722*
2:18 the lusts of the flesh, **t** much wantonness, *1722*
2:20 of the world **t** the knowledge of the Lord *1722*
1Jn 4: 9 into the world, that we might live **t** him. *1223*
Rev 8:13 heard an angel flying **t** the midst of heaven, *1722*
18: 3 the merchants of the earth are waxed rich **t** *1537*
22:14 and may **enter in t** the gates into the city. *1525*

THROUGHLY (12) [THOROUGHLY]

2Ki 11:18 and his images brake they in pieces **t**, 3190
Job 6: 2 Oh that my grief were **t weighed**, 8254+8254
Ps 51: 2 Wash me **t** from mine iniquity, and 7235
Jer 6: 9 They shall **t glean** the remnant of 5953+5953
7: 5 For if you **t amend** your ways and 3190+3190
7: 5 If you **t execute** judgment between a 6213+6213

Jer 50:34 he shall t **plead** their cause, that he 7378+7378
Eze 16: 9 I t **washed away** thy blood from thee, and 7857
Mt 3:12 and he will t **purge** his floor, and gather his *1245*
Lk 3:17 and he will t **purge** his floor, and *1245*
2Co 11: 6 we *have been* t made manifest *1722+3956*
2Ti 3:17 t **furnished** unto all good works. *1822*

THROUGHOUT (162) [THROUGH]

Ge 41:29 there come seven years of great plenty t all 871.1
41:46 and **went** t all the land of Egypt. 5674+871.1
45: 8 and a ruler t all the land of Egypt. 871.1
Ex 5:12 So the people were scattered abroad t all 871.1
7:19 *that* there may be blood t all the land of 871.1
7:21 and there was blood t all the land of Egypt. 871.1
8:16 that it may become lice t all the land of 871.1
8:17 all the dust of the land became lice t all 871.1
9: 9 and upon beast, t all the land of Egypt. 871.1
9:16 that my name may be declared t all 871.1
9:22 every herb of the field, t the land of Egypt. 871.1
9:25 the hail smote t all the land of Egypt all 871.1
11: 6 there shall be a great cry t all the land of 871.1
12:14 you shall keep it a feast to the LORD t 3807.1
29:42 *This shall be* a continual burnt offering t 3807.1
30: 8 a perpetual incense before the LORD t 3807.1
30:10 atonement upon it t your generations: 3807.1
30:21 to him and to his seed t their generations. 3807.1
30:31 anointing oil unto me t your generations. 3807.1
31:13 between me and you t your generations; 3807.1
31:16 to observe the sabbath t their generations, 3807.1
32:27 go in and out from gate to gate t the camp, 871.1
34: 3 neither let any man be seen t all the mount; 871.1
35: 3 Ye shall kindle no fire t your 3605+871.1
36: 6 they caused it to be proclaimed t the camp, 871.1
37:19 t the six branches going out of 3807.1
40:15 everlasting priesthood t their generations. 3807.1
40:38 all the house of Israel, t all their journeys. 3807.1
Lev 3:17 generations t all your dwellings, 3605+871.1
7:36 *by* a statute for **ever** t their generations. 5769
10: 9 *it shall be* a statute for **ever** t your 5769
17: 7 for ever unto them t their generations. 3807.1
23:14 *it shall be* a statute for ever t your 3807.1
23:21 in all your dwellings t your generations. 3807.1
23:31 *it shall be* a statute for ever t your 3807.1
25: 9 ye make the trumpet sound t all your land. 871.1
25:10 proclaim liberty t *all* the land unto all 871.1
25:30 to him that bought it t his generations: 3807.1
Nu 1:42 *t* their generations, after their families, NIH
1:52 man by his own standard, t their hosts. 3807.1
2: 3 of the camp of Judah pitch t their armies: 3807.1
2: 9 and four hundred, t their armies. 3807.1
2:16 and four hundred and fifty, t their armies. 3807.1
2:24 and an hundred, t their armies. 3807.1
2:32 t their hosts *were* six hundred thousand 3807.1
3:39 t their families, all the males from a 3807.1
4:22 t the houses of their fathers, by their 3807.1
4:38 t their families, and by the house of their 3807.1
4:40 t their families, by the house of their 3807.1
4:42 t their families, by the house of their 3807.1
10: 8 an ordinance for ever t your generations. 3807.1
10:25 *which was* the rereward of all the camps t 3807.1
11:10 Moses heard the people weep t their 3807.1
15:38 of their garments t their generations, 3807.1
18:23 *it shall be* a statute for ever t your 3807.1
26: 2 and upward, t their fathers' house, 3807.1
28:14 this *is* the burnt offering of every month t 3807.1
28:21 offer for every lamb, t the seven lambs; 3807.1
28:24 ye shall offer daily, *t* the seven days, NIH
28:29 deal unto one lamb, t the seven lambs; 3807.1
29: 4 deal for one lamb, t the seven lambs: 3807.1
29:10 deal for one lamb, t the seven lambs: 3807.1
31: 4 t all the tribes of Israel, shall ye send to 3807.1
35:29 t your generations in all your dwellings. 3807.1
Dt 16:18 LORD thy God giveth thee, t thy tribes: 3807.1
28:40 Thou shalt have olive trees t all thy coasts, 871.1
28:52 wherein thou trustedst, t all thy land: 871.1
28:52 he shall besiege thee in all thy gates t all 871.1
Jos 2:22 the pursuers sought *them* t all the way, but 871.1
6:27 and his fame was *noised* t all the country. 871.1
16: 1 goeth up from Jericho t mount Beth-el, 871.1
22:14 of each chief house a prince t all 3807.1
24: 3 led him t all the land of Canaan, and 871.1
Jdg 6:35 he sent messengers t all Manasseh; who 871.1
7:22 against his fellow, even t all the host: 871.1
7:24 Gideon sent messengers t all mount 871.1
20: 6 sent her t all the country of the inheritance 871.1
20:10 we will take ten men of an hundred t all 3807.1
1Sa 5:11 for there was a deadly destruction t all 871.1
11: 7 sent *them* t all the coasts of Israel by 871.1
13: 3 And Saul blew the trumpet t all the land, 871.1
13:19 Now there was no smith found t all 871.1
23:23 that I will search him out t all 871.1
2Sa 8:14 t all Edom put he garrisons, and all they of 871.1
15:10 Absalom sent spies t all the tribes of Israel, 871.1
19: 9 all the people were at strife t all the tribes 871.1
1Ki 1: 3 So they sought for a fair damsel t all 871.1
6:38 was the house finished t all the parts 3807.1
15:22 king Asa made a proclamation **t all** Judah; 3605
18: 6 divided the land between them to pass t it: 871.1
22:36 there went a proclamation t the host about 871.1
2Ki 17: 5 the king of Assyria came up t all the land, 871.1
1Ch 5:10 they dwelt in their tents t all the east 5921+6440
6:54 Now these *are* their dwelling places t 3807.1
6:60 All their cities t their families *were* 871.1
6:62 to the sons of Gershom t their families 3807.1
6:63 t their families, out of the tribe of 3807.1
7:40 the number t the **genealogy** of them *that* 3187
9:34 the Levites *were* chief t their generations; 3807.1
12:30 famous t the house of their fathers. 3807.1
21: 4 went t all Israel, and came *to* Jerusalem. 871.1
21:12 the angel of the LORD destroying t all 871.1
22: 5 of fame and of glory t all countries: 3807.1
26: 6 that ruled t the house of their father: 3807.1
27: 1 went out month by month t all the months 3807.1
2Ch 8: 6 and t all the land of his dominion. 871.1
11:23 dispersed of all his children t all 3807.1
2Ch 16: 9 LORD run to and fro t the whole earth, 871.1
17: 9 went about t all the cities of Judah, and 871.1
17:19 the king put in the fenced cities t all Judah. 871.1
19: 5 he set judges in the land t all the fenced 871.1
20: 3 and proclaimed a fast t all Judah. 5921
25: 5 of *their* fathers, t all Judah and Benjamin: 3807.1
26:14 Uzziah prepared for them t all the host 3807.1
30: 5 a decree to make proclamation t all Israel, 871.1
30: 6 and his princes t all Israel and Judah, 871.1
30:22 they did eat t the feast seven days, NIH
31:20 thus did Hezekiah t all Judah, and 871.1
34: 7 cut down all the idols t all the land of 871.1
36:22 that he made a proclamation t all his 871.1
Ezr 1: 1 that he made a proclamation t all his 871.1
10: 7 they made proclamation t Judah and 871.1
Est 1:20 make shall be published t all his empire, 871.1
3: 6 *were* t the whole kingdom of Ahasuerus, 871.1
9: 2 t all the provinces of the king Ahasuerus, 871.1
9: 4 and his fame went out t all the provinces: 871.1
9:28 and kept t every generation, 871.1
Ps 72: 5 and moon endure, **t all generations**. 1755+1755
102:24 of my days: thy years *are* t all generations. 871.1
135:13 O LORD, t all generations. 3807.1
145:13 thy dominion *endureth* t all generations. 871.1
Jer 17: 3 thy high places for sin, t all thy borders. 871.1
Eze 38:21 I will call *for* a sword against him t all 3807.1
Mt 4:24 And his fame went t all Syria: and *1519*
Mk 1:28 t all the region round about Galilee. *1519+3837*
1:39 And he preached in their synagogues t all *1519*
14: 9 gospel shall be preached t the whole world, *1519*
Lk 1:65 all these sayings were noised abroad t all *1722*
4:25 when great famine was t all the land; *1909*
7:17 And this rumour of him went forth t all *1722*
7:17 all Judea, and t all the region round about. *1722*
8: 1 that he **went** t every city and village, *1353*
8:39 published t the whole city how great *things* *2596*
23: 5 stirreth up the people, teaching t all Jewry, *2596*
Jn 19:23 without seam, woven from the top t. *1223+3650*
Ac 8: 1 they were all scattered abroad t the regions *2596*
9:31 Then had the churches rest t all Judea and *2596*
9:32 as Peter passed t all *quarters*, he came *1223*
9:42 And it was known t all Joppa; and *2596*
10:37 which was published t all Judea, and *2596*
11:28 there should be great dearth t all the world: *1909*
13:49 And the word of the Lord was published t *1223*
14:24 And after they had **passed** t Pisidia, *1330*
16: 6 Now when they had **gone** t Phrygia and *1330*
19:26 but almost t all Asia, this Paul hath NIG
24: 5 a mover of sedition among all the Jews t *2596*
26:20 and t all the coasts of Judea, and *then* to *1519*
Ro 1: 8 that your faith is spoken of t the whole *1722*
9:17 that my name might be declared t all *1722*
2Co 8:18 whose praise *is* in the gospel t all *1223*
Eph 3:21 in the church by Christ Jesus t all ages, *1519*
1Pe 1: 1 to the strangers **scattered** t Pontus, Galatia, *1290*

THROW (9) [OVERTHROW, THREWEST, THROWING, THROWN]

Jdg 2: 2 of this land; you shall t **down** their altars: 5422
6:25 **t down** the altar of Baal that thy father 2040
2Sa 20:15 with Joab battered the wall, to t *it* **down**. 5307
2Ki 9:33 he said, **T** her **down**. So they threw her 8058
Jer 1:10 and to t **down**, to build, and to plant. 2040
31:28 to t **down**, and to destroy, and to afflict; 2040
Eze 16:39 they shall t **down** thine eminent place, and 2040
Mic 5:11 thy land, and t **down** all thy strong holds: 2040
Mal 1: 4 They shall build, but I will t **down**; 2040

THROWING (1) [THROW]

Nu 35:17 if he smite him with t a stone, 3027

THROWN (19) [THROW]

Ex 15: 1 and his rider hath he t into the sea. 7411
15:21 and his rider hath he t into the sea. 7411
Jdg 6:32 because he hath t **down** his altar. 5422
2Sa 20:21 his head *shall be* t to thee over the wall. 7993
1Ki 19:10 **t down** thine altars, and slain thy prophets 2040
19:14 **t down** thine altars, and slain thy prophets 2040
Jer 31:40 plucked up, nor t **down** any more for ever. 2040
33: 4 which are t **down** by the mounts, and 5422
50:15 are fallen, her walls are t **down**: 2040
La 2: 2 he hath t **down** in his wrath the strong 2040
2:17 he hath t **down**, and hath not pitied: and 2040
Eze 29: 5 I will leave thee *t* into the wilderness, thee NIH
38:20 the mountains shall be t **down**, and 2040
Na 1: 6 like fire, and the rocks are t **down** by him. 5422
Mt 24: 2 upon another, that shall not be **t down**. *2647*
Mk 13: 2 upon another, that shall not be **t down**. *2647*
Lk 4:35 And when the devil had t him in the midst, *4496*
21: 6 upon another, that shall not be **t down**. *2647*
Rev 18:21 shall *that* great city Babylon be t down, *906*

THRUST (50) [THRUSTETH]

Ex 11: 1 **surely** t you **out** hence altogether. 1644+1644
12:39 because they were t **out** of Egypt, and 1644
Nu 22:25 she t herself unto the wall, and 3905
25: 8 t both of them **through**, the man of Israel, 1856
35:20 if he t him of hatred, or hurl at him by 1920
35:22 if he t him suddenly without enmity, or 1920
Dt 13: 5 to t thee out of the way which the LORD 5080
13:10 he hath sought to t thee **away** from the 5080
15:17 t *it* through his ear unto the door, and 5414
33:27 he shall t **out** the enemy from before thee; 1644
Jdg 3:21 from his right thigh, and t it into his belly: 8628
6:38 t the fleece **together**, and wringed the dew 2115
9:41 Zebul t **out** Gaal and his brethren, that *they* 1644
9:54 his young man t him **through**, and he died. 1856
11: 2 and they t **out** Jephthah, and said unto him, 1644
1Sa 11: 2 that *I* may t **out** all your right eyes, and 5365
31: 4 thy sword, and t me **through** therewith; 1856
31: 4 uncircumcised come and t me **through**, 1856
2Sa 2:16 and *t* his sword in his fellow's side; NIH
18:14 and t them through the heart of Absalom, 8628
23: 6 Belial *shall be* all of them as thorns t **away**, 5074
1Ki 2:27 So Solomon t **out** Abiathar from being 1644
2Ki 4:27 Gehazi came near to t her **away**. And 1920
1Ch 10: 4 thy sword, and t me **through** therewith; 1856
2Ch 26:20 and they t him **out** from thence; 926
Ps 118:13 Thou hast **t sore** at me that *I* might 1760+1760
Isa 13:15 Every one that is found shall be **t through**; 1856
14:19 **t through** with a sword, that go down to 2944
Jer 51: 4 and *they that are* **t through** in her streets. 1856
Eze 16:40 and **t** thee **through** with their swords. 1333
34:21 Because ye have t with side and 1920
46:18 by oppression to t them out of their NIH
Joel 2: 8 Neither shall one t another; they shall walk 1766
Zec 13: 3 shall t him **through** when he prophesieth. 1856
Lk 4:29 and t him **out** of the city, and led him unto *1544*
5: 3 prayed him that *he* would **t out** a little from *1877*
10:15 exalted to heaven, shalt be **t down** to hell. *2601*
13:28 kingdom of God, and you yourselves **t out**. *1544*
Jn 20:25 and t my hand into his side, I will not *906*
20:27 reach *hither* thy hand, and t *it* into my side: *906*
Ac 7:27 he that did his neighbour wrong t him **away**, *683*
7:39 but t *him* **from** *them*, and in their hearts *683*
16:24 t them into the inner prison, and made their *906*
16:37 and now do they t us **out** privily? *1544*
27:39 if it were possible, to **t in** the ship. *1856*
Heb 12:20 it shall be stoned, or **t through** with a dart: *2700*
Rev 14:15 sat on the cloud, **T in** thy sickle, and reap: *3992*
14:16 And he that sat on the cloud **t in** his sickle *906*
14:18 **T in** thy sharp sickle, and gather *3992*
14:19 And the angel **t in** his sickle into the earth, *906*

THRUSTETH (1) [THRUST]

Job 32:13 out wisdom: God t him **down**, not man. 5086

THUMB (6) [THUMBS]

Ex 29:20 upon the t of their right hand, and upon 931
Lev 8:23 upon the t of his right hand, and upon 931
14:14 upon the t of his right hand, and upon 931
14:17 upon the t of his right hand, and upon 931
14:25 upon the t of his right hand, and upon 931
14:28 upon the t of his right hand, and upon 931

THUMBS (3) [THUMB]

Lev 8:24 upon the t of their right hands, and upon 931
Jdg 1: 6 and cut off his t and his great toes. 931+3027
1: 7 their t and their great toes cut off, 931+3027

THUMMIM (5)

Ex 28:30 of judgment the Urim and the **T**; 8550
Lev 8: 8 put in the breastplate the Urim and the **T**. 8550
Dt 33: 8 *Let* thy **T** and thy Urim *be* with thy holy 8550
Ezr 2:63 stood *up* a priest with Urim and with **T**. 8550
Ne 7:65 till there stood *up* a priest with Urim and **T**. 8550

THUNDER (19) [THUNDERBOLTS, THUNDERED, THUNDERETH, THUNDERINGS, THUNDERS]

Ex 9:23 the LORD sent t and hail, and the fire ran 6963
9:29 *and* the t shall cease, neither shall there be 6963
1Sa 2:10 out of heaven shall he t upon them: 7481
7:10 the LORD thundered with a great t on that 6963
12:17 the LORD, and he shall send t and rain; 6963
12:18 and the LORD sent t and rain that day: 6963
Job 26:14 but the t of his power who can understand? 7482
28:26 and a way for the lightning of the t: 6963
38:25 of waters, or a way for the lightning of t; 6963
39:19 hast thou clothed his neck with t? 7483
39:25 the t of the captains, and the shouting. 7482
40: 9 or, canst thou t with a voice like him? 7481
Ps 77:18 The voice of thy t *was* in the heaven: 7482
81: 7 I answered thee in the secret place of t: 7482
104: 7 at the voice of thy t they hasted away. 7482
Isa 29: 6 be visited of the LORD of hosts with t, 7482
Mk 3:17 them Boanerges, which is, The sons of t:) *1027*
Rev 6: 1 and I heard, as *it were* the noise of t, one of *1027*
14: 2 many waters, and as the voice of a great t: *1027*

THUNDERBOLTS (1) [THUNDER]

Ps 78:48 also to the hail, and their flocks to **hot t**. 7565

THUNDERED (4) [THUNDER]

1Sa 7:10 the LORD t with a great thunder on that 7481
2Sa 22:14 The LORD t from heaven, and the most 7481
Ps 18:13 The LORD also t in the heavens, and 7481
Jn 12:29 stood *by*, and heard *it*, said that it t: *1027+1096*

THUNDERETH (3) [THUNDER]

Job 37: 4 he t with the voice of his excellency; and 7481
37: 5 God t marvellously with his voice; 7481
Ps 29: 3 the God of glory t: the LORD *is* upon 7481

THUNDERINGS (6) [THUNDER]

Ex 9:28 that there be no *more* mighty t and hail; and 6963
20:18 all the people saw the t, and the lightnings, 6963
Rev 4: 5 proceeded lightnings and t and voices: *1027*
8: 5 and t, and lightnings, and an earthquake. *1027*
11:19 and t, and an earthquake, and great hail. *1027*
19: 6 and as the voice of mighty t, saying, *1027*

THUNDERS (7) [THUNDER]

Ex 9:33 the t and hail ceased, and the rain was not 6963
9:34 the rain and the hail and the t were ceased, 6963
19:16 that there were t and lightnings, and a thick 6963
Rev 10: 3 he had cried, seven t uttered their voices. *1027*
10: 4 And when the seven t had uttered their *1027*
10: 4 Seal *up those things* which the seven t *1027*
16:18 there were voices, and t, and lightnings; *1027*

THUS (737)

Ge 2: 1 **T** the heavens and the earth were 2050.1
6:22 **T** did Noah; according to all that God 2050.1
19:36 **T** were both the daughters of Lot with 2050.1
20:16 and with all *other*: t she was reproved. 2050.1
21:32 **T** they made a covenant at Beer-sheba: 2050.1
24:30 his sister, saying, **T** spake the man unto me; 3541

Ge 25:22 and she said, If it be so, why am I t? 2088
25:34 his way: t Esau despised his birthright. 2050.1
31: 8 If he said t, The speckled shall be thy 3541
31: 8 if he said t, The ringstraked shall be thy 3541
31: 9 T God hath taken away the cattle of your 2050.1
31:40 T I was in the day, the drought consumed NIH
31:41 T have I been twenty years in thy house; 2088
32: 4 saying, T shall ye speak unto my lord Esau; 3541
32: 4 Thy servant Jacob saith t, I have sojourned 3541
36: 8 T dwelt Esau in mount Seir: Esau is 2050.1
37:35 son mourning. T his father wept for him. 2050.1
42:25 for the way: and t did he unto them. 3651
45: 9 and say unto him, T saith thy son Joseph, 3541
Ex 3:14 T shalt thou say unto the children of Israel, 3541
3:15 T shalt thou say unto the children of Israel, 3541
4:22 T saith the LORD, Israel is my son, 3541
5: 1 T saith the LORD God of Israel, 3541
5:10 to the people, saying, T saith Pharaoh, 3541
5:15 Wherefore dealest thou t with thy servants? 3541
7:17 T saith the LORD, In this thou shalt know 3541
8: 1 and say unto him, T saith the LORD, 3541
8:20 say unto him, T saith the LORD, Let my 3541
9: 1 T saith the LORD God of the Hebrews, 3541
9:13 T saith the LORD God of the Hebrews, 3541
10: 3 T saith the LORD God of the Hebrews, 3541
11: 4 Moses said, T saith the LORD, 3541
12:11 And t shall ye eat it; with your loins girded, 3602
12:50 T did all the children of Israel; as 2050.1
14:11 wherefore hast thou dealt t with us, to carry 2063
14:30 T the LORD saved Israel that day out of 2050.1
19: 3 T shalt thou say to the house of Jacob, and 3541
20:22 T thou shalt say unto the children of Israel, 3541
26:17 t shalt thou make for all the boards of 3651
26:24 t shall it be for them both; they shall be for 3651
29:35 t shalt thou do unto Aaron, and to his sons, NIH
32:27 T saith the LORD God of Israel, 3541
36:22 t did he make for all the boards of 3651
36:29 t he did to both of them in both the corners. 3651
39:32 T was all the work of the tabernacle of 2050.1
40:16 T did Moses: according to all that 2050.1
Lev 15:31 T shall ye separate the children of Israel 2050.1
16: 3 T shall Aaron come into the holy 2063+871.1
Nu 4:19 t do unto them, that they may live, and 2088
4:49 t were they numbered of him, as 2050.1
8: 7 t shalt thou do unto them, to cleanse them: 3541
8:14 T shalt thou separate the Levites from 2050.1
8:26 T shalt thou do unto the Levites touching 3602
10:28 T were the journeyings of the children of 428
11:15 if thou deal t with me, kill me, I pray thee, 3602
15:11 T shall it be done for one bullock, or 3602
18:26 T speak unto the Levites, and say unto 2050.1
18:28 T you also shall offer a heave offering unto 3651
20:14 T saith thy brother Israel, Thou knowest all 3541
20:21 T Edom refused to give Israel passage 2050.1
21:31 T Israel dwelt in the land of 2050.1
22:16 to him, T saith Balak the son of Zippor, 3541
23: 5 Return unto Balak, and t thou shalt speak. 3541
23:16 and said, Go again unto Balak, and say t. 3541
32: 8 T did your fathers, when I sent them from 3541
Dt 7: 5 t shall ye deal with them; ye shall destroy 3541
9:25 T I fell down before the LORD forty 2050.1
20:15 T shalt thou do unto all the cities which are 3651
29:24 Wherefore hath the LORD done t unto 3602
32: 6 Do ye t requite the LORD, O foolish 2088
Jos 2: 4 hid them, and said t, There came men unto 3651
6: 3 the city once. T shalt thou do six days. 3541
7:10 wherefore liest thou t upon thy face? 2088
7:13 for t saith the LORD God of Israel, 3541
7:20 and t and thus have I done: 2088+3509.1
7:20 and thus and t have I done: 2088+3509.1
10:25 for t shall the LORD do to all your 3602
16: 5 t even the border of their inheritance on NIH
21:13 T they gave to the children of Aaron 2050.1
21:42 round about them: t were all these cities. 3651
22:16 T saith the whole congregation of 3541
24: 2 T saith the LORD God of Israel, 3541
Jdg 6: 8 T saith the LORD God of Israel, 3541
8: 1 thou served us t, 1697+2088+1886.1+1886.1
8:28 T was Midian subdued before 2050.1
9:56 T God rendered the wickedness of 2050.1
11:15 said unto him, T saith Jephthah, Israel took 3541
11:33 T the children of Ammon were subdued 2050.1
13:18 Why askest thou t after my name, seeing it 2088
18: 4 T and thus dealeth Micah with me, 2090+3509.1
18: 4 Thus and t dealeth Micah with me, 2088+3509.1
20:43 T they inclosed the Benjamites round about, NIH
1Sa 2:27 and said unto him, T saith the LORD, 3541
9: 9 t he spake, Come, and let us go to the seer: 3541
10:18 T saith the LORD God of Israel, I brought 3541
11: 9 T shall ye say unto the men of 3541
14: 9 If they say t unto us, Tarry until we come 3541
14:10 if they say t, Come up unto us; then we will 3541
15: 2 T saith the LORD of hosts, I remember 3541
18:25 Saul said, T shall ye say to David, The king 3541
20: 7 If he say t, It is well; thy servant shall have 3541
20:22 if I say t unto the young man, Behold, 3541
25: 6 t shall ye say to him that liveth in 3541
26:18 Wherefore doth my lord t pursue after his 2088
2Sa 6:22 I will yet be more vile than t, and will be 2063
7: 5 tell my servant David, T saith the LORD, 3541
7: 8 T saith the LORD of hosts, I took thee 3541
11:25 T shalt thou say unto Joab, Let not this 3541
12: 7 T saith the LORD God of Israel, 3541
12:11 T saith the LORD, Behold, I will raise up 3541
12:31 t did he unto all the cities of the children of 3651
15:26 if he t say, I have no delight in thee; 3541
16: 7 t said Shimei when he cursed, Come out, 3541
17:15 T and thus did Ahithophel counsel 2088+3509.1
17:15 t did Ahithophel counsel Absalom 2088+3509.1
17:15 and t and thus have I counselled. 2088+3509.1
17:15 and thus and t have I counselled. 2088+3509.1
17:21 for t hath Ahithophel counselled against 3602
18:14 said Joab, I may not tarry t with thee. 3651
18:33 as he went, t he said, O my son Absalom, 3541
24:12 and say unto David, T saith the LORD, 3541
1Ki 1:48 also t said the king, Blessed be the LORD 3602
2:30 said unto him, T saith the king, Come forth. 3541
2:30 T said Joab, and thus he answered me. 3541
2:30 Thus said Joab, and t he answered me. 3541
3:22 is my son. T they spake before the king. 2050.1
5:11 t gave Solomon to Hiram year by year. 3541
9: 8 Why hath the LORD done t unto this land, 3602
11:31 for t saith the LORD, the God of Israel, 3541
12:10 T shalt thou speak unto this people that 3541
12:10 t shalt thou say unto them, My little finger 3541
12:24 T saith the LORD, Ye shall not go up, 3541
13: 2 and said, O altar, altar, t saith the LORD; 3541
13:21 from Judah, saying, T saith the LORD, 3541
14: 5 for he is sick: t and thus shalt thou 2090+3509.1
14: 5 thus and t shalt thou say unto her: 2090+3509.1
14: 7 T saith the LORD God of Israel, 3541
16:12 T did Zimri destroy all the house of 2050.1
17:14 For t saith the LORD God of Israel, 3541
20: 2 and said unto him, T saith Ben-hadad, 3541
20: 5 said, T speaketh Ben-hadad, saying, 3541
20:13 saying, T saith the LORD, Hast thou seen 3541
20:14 he said, T saith the LORD, Even by 3541
20:28 of Israel, and said, T saith the LORD, 3541
20:42 he said unto him, T saith the LORD, 3541
21:19 saying, T saith the LORD, Hast thou 3541
21:19 unto him, saying, T saith the LORD, 3541
22:11 he said, T saith the LORD, With these 3541
22:27 say, T saith the king, Put this fellow in 3541
2Ki 1: 4 Now therefore t saith the LORD, 3541
1: 6 T saith the LORD, Is it not because 3541
1:11 O man of God, t hath the king said, 3541
1:16 he said unto him, T saith the LORD, 3541
2:21 salt in there, and said, T saith the LORD, 3541
3:16 he said, T saith the LORD, Make this 3541
3:17 For t saith the LORD, Ye shall not see 3541
4:43 for t saith the LORD, They shall eat, and 3541
5: 4 T and thus said the maid that is of 2088+3509.1
5: 4 t said the maid that is of the land of 2088+3509.1
7: 1 T saith the LORD, To morrow about this 3541
9: 3 it on his head, and say, T saith the LORD, 3541
9: 6 T saith the LORD God of Israel, 3541
9:12 T and thus spake he to me, saying, 2088+3509.1
9:12 Thus and t spake he to me, saying, 2088+3509.1
9:12 spake he to me, saying, T saith the LORD, 3541
9:18 and said, T saith the king, Is it peace? 3541
9:19 and said, T saith the king, Is it peace? 3541
10:28 T Jehu destroyed Baal out of Israel. 2050.1
16:16 T did Urijah the priest, according to all 2050.1
18:19 T saith the great king, the king of Assyria, 3541
18:29 T saith the king, Let not Hezekiah deceive 3541
18:31 for t saith the king of Assyria, Make an 3541
19: 3 they said unto him, T saith Hezekiah, 3541
19: 6 T shall ye say to your master, Thus saith 3541
19: 6 ye say to your master, T saith the LORD, 3541
19:10 T shall ye speak to Hezekiah king of Judah, 3541
19:20 T saith the LORD God of Israel, 3541
19:32 Therefore t saith the LORD concerning 3541
20: 1 said unto him, T saith the LORD, 3541
20: 5 T saith the LORD, the God of David thy 3541
21:12 Therefore t saith the LORD God of Israel, 3541
22:15 T saith the LORD God of Israel, 3541
22:16 T saith the LORD, Behold, I will bring 3541
22:18 t shall ye say to him, Thus saith 3541
22:18 to him, T saith the LORD God of Israel, 3541
1Ch 15:28 T all Israel brought up the ark of 2050.1
17: 4 tell David my servant, T saith the LORD, 3541
17: 7 t shalt thou say unto my servant David, 3541
17: 7 T saith the LORD of hosts, I took thee 3541
18: 6 T the LORD preserved David 2050.1
18:13 T the LORD preserved David 2050.1
21:10 and tell David, saying, T saith the LORD, 3541
21:11 unto him, T saith the LORD, Choose thee 3541
24: 4 sons of Ithamar; and t were they divided. NIH
24: 5 T were they divided by lot, one sort with 2050.1
29:26 T David the son of Jesse reigned over all 2050.1
2Ch 4:18 T Solomon made all these vessels in 2050.1
5: 1 T all the work that Solomon made for 2050.1
7:11 T Solomon finished the house of 2050.1
7:21 Why hath the LORD done t unto this land, 3602
10:10 T shalt thou answer the people that spake 3541
10:10 t shalt thou say unto them, My little finger 3541
11: 4 T saith the LORD, Ye shall not go up, 3541
12: 5 and said unto them, T saith the LORD, 3541
13:18 T the children of Israel were brought 2050.1
18:10 said, T saith the LORD, With these thou 3541
18:26 say, T saith the king, Put this fellow in 3541
19: 9 T shall ye do in the fear of the LORD, 3541
20:15 T saith the LORD unto you, 3541
21:12 T saith the LORD God of David thy 3541
24:11 T they did day by day, and gathered money 3541
24:20 and said unto them, T saith God, 3541
24:22 T Joash the king remembered not 2050.1
31:20 t did Hezekiah throughout all 2088+3509.1
32:10 T saith Sennacherib king of Assyria, 3541
32:22 T the LORD saved Hezekiah and 2050.1
34:23 T saith the LORD God of Israel, 3541
34:24 T saith the LORD, Behold, I will bring 3541
34:26 T saith the LORD God of Israel 3541
36:23 T saith Cyrus king of Persia, All 3541
Ezr 1: 2 T saith Cyrus king of Persia, The LORD 3541
5: 3 and their companions, and said t unto them, 3652
5: 7 unto him, wherein was written t: 1836+3509.4
5: 9 we those elders, and said unto them t, 3660
5:11 t they returned us answer, saying, We are 3660
6: 2 a roll, and therein was a record t written: 3652
Ne 5:13 even t be he shaken out, and emptied. 3602
13:18 Did not your fathers t, and did not our God 3541
13:30 T cleansed I them from all strangers, and 2050.1
Est 1:18 T shall there arise too much contempt 2050.1
2:13 t came every maiden unto the king; 2088+871.1
6: 9 T shall it be done to the man whom 3602
6:11 T shall it be done unto the man whom 3602
9: 5 T the Jews smote all their enemies with 2050.1
Job 1: 5 God in their hearts. T did Job continually. 3602
27:12 seen it; why then are ye t altogether vain? 2088
Ps 38:14 T I was as a man that heareth not, and 2050.1
63: 4 T will I bless thee while I live: I will lift up 3651
73:15 If I say, I will speak t; behold, I should 3644
73:21 T my heart was grieved, and I was pricked 3588
106:20 T they changed their glory into 2050.1
106:29 T they provoked him to anger with their 2050.1
106:39 T were they defiled with their own 2050.1
128: 4 that t shall the man be blessed that feareth 3651
Isa 7: 7 T saith the Lord GOD, It shall not stand, 3541
8:11 For the LORD spake t to me with a strong 3541
10:24 Therefore t saith the Lord GOD of hosts, 3541
21: 6 For t hath the Lord said unto me, Go, set a 3541
21:16 For t hath the Lord said unto me, Within a 3541
22:15 T saith the Lord GOD of hosts, Go, 3541
24:13 When t it shall be in the midst of the land 3541
28:16 Therefore t saith the Lord GOD, Behold, 3541
29:22 Therefore t saith the LORD, 3541
30:12 Wherefore t saith the Holy One of Israel, 3541
30:15 For t saith the Lord GOD, the Holy One 3541
31: 4 For t hath the LORD spoken unto me, 3541
36: 4 T saith the great king, the king of Assyria, 3541
36:14 T saith the king, Let not Hezekiah deceive 3541
36:16 for t saith the king of Assyria, Make an 3541
37: 3 they said unto him, T saith Hezekiah, 3541
37: 6 T shall ye say unto your master, Thus saith 3541
37: 6 say unto your master, T saith the LORD, 3541
37:10 T shall ye speak to Hezekiah king of Judah, 3541
37:21 T saith the LORD God of Israel, 3541
37:33 Therefore t saith the LORD concerning 3541
38: 1 said unto him, T saith the LORD, 3541
38: 5 and say to Hezekiah, T saith the LORD, 3541
42: 5 T saith God the LORD, he that created 3541
43: 1 now t saith the LORD that created thee, 3541
43:14 T saith the LORD, your redeemer, 3541
43:16 T saith the LORD, which maketh a way in 3541
44: 2 T saith the LORD that made thee, and 3541
44: 6 T saith the LORD the King of Israel, and 3541
44:24 T saith the LORD, thy redeemer, and 3541
45: 1 T saith the LORD to his anointed, 3541
45:11 T saith the LORD, the Holy One of Israel, 3541
45:14 T saith the LORD, The labour of Egypt, 3541
45:18 For t saith the LORD that created 3541
47:15 T shall they be unto thee with whom thou 3651
48:17 T saith the LORD, thy redeemer, the Holy 3541
49: 7 T saith the LORD, the redeemer of Israel, 3541
49: 8 T saith the LORD, In an acceptable time 3541
49:22 T saith the Lord GOD, Behold, I will lift 3541
49:25 t saith the LORD, Even the captives of 3541
50: 1 T saith the LORD, Where is the bill of 3541
51:22 T saith thy Lord the LORD, and thy God 3541
52: 3 For t saith the LORD, Ye have sold 3541
52: 4 For t saith the Lord GOD, My people 3541
56: 1 T saith the LORD, Keep ye judgment, and 3541
56: 4 For t saith the LORD unto the eunuchs 3541
57:15 For t saith the high and lofty One that 3541
65: 8 T saith the LORD, As the new wine is 3541
65:13 Therefore t saith the Lord GOD, Behold, 3541
66: 1 T saith the LORD, The heaven is my 3541
66:12 For t saith the LORD, Behold, I will 3541
Jer 2: 2 of Jerusalem, saying, T saith the LORD; 3541
2: 5 T saith the LORD, What iniquity have 3541
4: 3 For t saith the LORD to the men of Judah 3541
4:27 For t hath the LORD said, The whole land 3541
5:13 is not in them: t shall it be done unto them. 3541
5:14 Wherefore t saith the LORD God of hosts, 3541
6: 6 For t hath the LORD of hosts said, 3541
6: 9 T saith the LORD of hosts, They shall 3541
6:16 T saith the LORD, Stand ye in the ways, 3541
6:21 Therefore t saith the LORD, Behold, 3541
6:22 T saith the LORD, Behold, a people 3541
7: 3 T saith the LORD of hosts, the God of 3541
7:20 Therefore t saith the Lord GOD; Behold, 3541
7:21 T saith the LORD of hosts, the God of 3541
8: 4 shalt say unto them, T saith the LORD; 3541
9: 7 Therefore t saith the LORD of hosts, 3541
9:15 Therefore t saith the LORD of hosts, 3541
9:17 T saith the LORD of hosts, Consider ye, 3541
9:22 Speak, T saith the LORD, Even 3541
9:23 T saith the LORD, Let not the wise man 3541
10: 2 T saith the LORD, Learn not the way of 3541
10:11 T shall ye say unto them, The gods 1836+3509.4
10:18 For t saith the LORD, Behold, I will sling 3541
11: 3 T saith the LORD God of Israel; 3541
11:11 Therefore t saith the LORD, Behold, 3541
11:21 Therefore t saith the LORD of the men of 3541
11:22 Therefore t saith the LORD of hosts, 3541
12:14 T saith the LORD against all mine evil 3541
13: 1 T saith the LORD unto me, Go and 3541
13: 9 T saith the LORD, After this manner will 3541
13:12 T saith the LORD God of Israel, 3541
13:13 say unto them, T saith the LORD, Behold, 3541
14:10 T saith the LORD unto this people, Thus 3541
14:10 T have they loved to wander, they have not 3651
14:15 Therefore t saith the LORD concerning 3541
15: 2 thou shalt tell them, T saith the LORD; 3541
15:19 Therefore t saith the LORD, If thou 3541
16: 3 For t saith the LORD concerning the sons 3541
16: 5 For t saith the LORD, Enter not into 3541
16: 9 For t saith the LORD of hosts, the God of 3541
17: 5 T saith the LORD; Cursed be the man that 3541
17:19 T said the LORD unto me; Go and 3541
17:21 T saith the LORD; Take heed to 3541
18:11 of Jerusalem, saying, T saith the LORD; 3541
18:13 Therefore t saith the LORD; Ask ye now 3541
18:23 deal t with them in the time of thine anger. NIH
19: 1 T saith the LORD, Go and get a potter's 3541
19: 3 T saith the LORD of hosts, the God of 3541
19:11 say unto them, T saith the LORD of hosts; 3541
19:12 T will I do unto this place, saith 3651
19:15 T saith the LORD of hosts, the God of 3541
20: 4 For t saith the LORD, Behold, I will make 3541
21: 3 unto them, T shall ye say to Zedekiah: 3541
21: 4 T saith the LORD God of Israel; Behold, 3541
21: 8 people thou shalt say, T saith the LORD; 3541
21:12 O house of David, t saith the LORD; 3541

T

Jer 22: 1 **T** saith the LORD; Go down *to* the house 3541
22: 3 **T** saith the LORD; Execute ye judgment 3541
22: 6 For **t** saith the LORD unto the king's 3541
22: 8 Wherefore hath the LORD done **t** unto 3602
22:11 For **t** saith the LORD touching Shallum 3541
22:18 Therefore **t** saith the LORD concerning 3541
22:30 **T** saith the LORD, Write ye this man 3541
23: 2 Therefore **t** saith the LORD God of Israel 3541
23:15 Therefore **t** saith the LORD of hosts 3541
23:16 **T** saith the LORD of hosts, Hearken not 3541
23:35 **T** shall ye say every one to his neighbour, 3541
23:37 **T** shalt thou say to the prophet, What hath 3541
23:38 the LORD; therefore **t** saith the LORD; 3541
24: 5 **T** saith the LORD, the God of Israel; 3541
24: 8 surely **t** saith the LORD, So will I give 3541
25: 8 Therefore **t** saith the LORD of hosts; 3541
25:15 For **t** saith the LORD God of Israel unto 3541
25:27 **T** saith the LORD of hosts, the God of 3541
25:28 say unto them, **T** saith the LORD of hosts; 3541
25:32 **T** saith the LORD of hosts, Behold, 3541
26: 2 **T** saith the LORD; Stand in the court of 3541
26: 4 shalt say unto them, **T** saith the LORD; 3541
26:18 saying, **T** saith the LORD of hosts; 3541
26:19 **T** *might* we procure great evil against our 2050.1
27: 2 **T** saith the LORD to me; Make thee 3541
27: 4 **T** saith the LORD of hosts, the God of 3541
27: 4 of Israel; **T** shall ye say unto your masters; 3541
27:16 all this people, saying, **T** saith the LORD; 3541
27:19 For **t** saith the LORD of hosts concerning 3541
27:21 Yea, **t** saith the LORD of hosts, the God 3541
28: 2 **T** speaketh the LORD of hosts, the God of 3541
28:11 all the people, saying, **T** saith the LORD; 3541
28:13 tell Hananiah, saying, **T** saith the LORD; 3541
28:14 For **t** saith the LORD of hosts, the God of 3541
28:16 Therefore **t** saith the LORD; Behold, 3541
29: 4 **T** saith the LORD of hosts, the God of 3541
29: 8 For **t** saith the LORD of hosts, the God of 3541
29:10 For **t** saith the LORD, That after seventy 3541
29:16 *Know* that **t** saith the LORD of the king 3541
29:17 **T** saith the LORD of hosts; Behold, I will 3541
29:21 **T** saith the LORD of hosts, the God of 3541
29:24 *T* shalt thou also speak to Shemaiah NIH
29:25 **T** speaketh the LORD of hosts, the God of 3541
29:31 **T** saith the LORD concerning Shemaiah 3541
29:32 Therefore **t** saith the LORD; Behold, 3541
30: 2 **T** speaketh the LORD God of Israel, 3541
30: 5 For **t** saith the LORD; We have heard a 3541
30:12 For **t** saith the LORD, Thy bruise *is* 3541
30:18 **T** saith the LORD: Behold, I *will* bring 3541
31: 2 **T** saith the LORD, The people which 3541
31: 7 For **t** saith the LORD; Sing with gladness 3541
31:15 **T** saith the LORD; A voice was heard in 3541
31:16 **T** saith the LORD, Refrain thy voice from 3541
31:18 himself *t*; Thou hast chastised me, NIH
31:23 **T** saith the LORD of hosts, the God of 3541
31:35 **T** saith the LORD, which giveth the sun 3541
31:37 **T** saith the LORD; If heaven above can be 3541
32: 3 and say, **T** saith the LORD, Behold, 3541
32:14 **T** saith the LORD of hosts, the God of 3541
32:15 For **t** saith the LORD of hosts, the God of 3541
32:28 Therefore **t** saith the LORD; Behold, 3541
32:36 now therefore **t** saith the LORD, the God 3541
32:42 For **t** saith the LORD; Like as I have 3541
33: 2 **T** saith the LORD the maker thereof, 3541
33: 4 For **t** saith the LORD, the God of Israel, 3541
33:10 **T** saith the LORD; Again there shall be 3541
33:12 **T** saith the LORD of hosts, Again in this 3541
33:17 For **t** saith the LORD; David shall never 3541
33:20 **T** saith the LORD; If you can break my 3541
33:24 **t** they have despised my people, that *they* 2050.1
33:25 **T** saith the LORD; If my covenant *be* not 3541
34: 2 **T** saith the LORD, the God of Israel; Go 3541
34: 2 of Judah, and tell him, **T** saith the LORD; 3541
34: 4 **T** saith the LORD of thee, Thou shalt not 3541
34:13 **T** saith the LORD, the God of Israel; 3541
34:17 Therefore **t** saith the LORD; Ye have not 3541
35: 8 **T** have we obeyed the voice of Jonadab 2050.1
35:13 **T** saith the LORD of hosts, the God of 3541
35:17 Therefore **t** saith the LORD God of hosts, 3541
35:18 **T** saith the LORD of hosts, the God of 3541
35:19 Therefore **t** saith the LORD of hosts, 3541
36:29 king of Judah, **T** saith the LORD; 3541
36:30 Therefore **t** saith the LORD of Jehoiakim 3541
37: 7 **T** saith the LORD, the God of Israel; 3541
37: 7 **T** shall ye say to the king of Judah, 3541
37: 9 **T** saith the LORD; Deceive not 3541
37:21 **T** Jeremiah remained in the court of 2050.1
38: 2 **T** saith the LORD, He that remaineth in 3541
38: 3 **T** saith the LORD, This city shall surely 3541
38: 4 for **t** he weakeneth the hands of the men of 3651
38:17 **T** saith the LORD, the God of hosts, 3541
39:16 saying, **T** saith the LORD of hosts, 3541
42: 9 **T** saith the LORD, the God of Israel, 3541
42:15 **T** saith the LORD of hosts, the God of 3541
42:18 For **t** saith the LORD of hosts, the God of 3541
43: 7 **t** came they *even* to Tahpanhes. 2050.1
43:10 **T** saith the LORD of hosts, the God of 3541
44: 2 **T** saith the LORD of hosts, the God of 3541
44: 7 Therefore now **t** saith the LORD, the God 3541
44:11 Therefore **t** saith the LORD of hosts, 3541
44:25 **T** saith the LORD of hosts, the God of 3541
44:30 **T** saith the LORD; Behold, I *will* give 3541
45: 2 **T** saith the LORD, the God of Israel, 3541
45: 4 **T** shalt thou say unto him, The LORD 3541
45: 4 thou say unto him, The LORD saith **t**; 3541
47: 2 **T** saith the LORD; Behold, waters rise up 3541
48: 1 Against Moab **t** saith the LORD of hosts, 3541
48:40 For **t** saith the LORD; Behold, he shall fly 3541
48:47 **T far** *is* the judgment of Moab. 2008+5704
49: 1 the Ammonites, **t** saith the LORD; 3541
49: 7 **t** saith the LORD of hosts; 3541
49:12 For **t** saith the LORD; Behold, they whose 3541
49:28 of Babylon shall smite, **t** saith the LORD; 3541
49:35 **T** saith the LORD of hosts; Behold, I *will* 3541
50:18 Therefore **t** saith the LORD of hosts, 3541

Jer 50:33 **T** saith the LORD of hosts; The children 3541
51: 1 **T** saith the LORD; Behold, I *will* raise up 3541
51: 4 **T** the slain shall fall in the land of 2050.1
51:33 For **t** saith the LORD of hosts, the God of 3541
51:36 Therefore **t** saith the LORD; Behold, 3541
51:58 **T** saith the LORD of hosts; The broad 3541
51:64 **T** shall Babylon sink, and shall not rise 3602
51:64 **T far** *are* the words of Jeremiah. 2008+5704
52:27 **T** Judah was carried away captive out of 2050.1
Eze 1:11 **T** *were* their faces: and their wings *were* 2050.1
2: 4 say unto them, **T** saith the Lord GOD. 3541
3:11 and tell them, **T** saith the Lord GOD; 3541
3:27 say unto them, **T** saith the Lord GOD; 3541
4:13 **Even t** shall the children of Israel eat their 3602
5: 5 **T** saith the Lord GOD; This *is* Jerusalem: 3541
5: 7 Therefore **t** saith the Lord GOD; 3541
5: 8 Therefore **t** saith the Lord GOD; Behold, 3541
5:13 **T** shall mine anger be accomplished, and 2050.1
6: 3 **T** saith the Lord GOD to the mountains, 3541
6:11 **T** saith the Lord GOD; Smite with thine 3541
6:12 **t** will I accomplish my fury upon them. 2050.1
7: 2 **t** saith the Lord GOD unto the land of 3541
7: 5 **T** saith the Lord GOD; An evil, an only 3541
11: 5 said unto me, Speak; **T** saith the LORD; 3541
11: 5 **T** have ye said, O house of Israel: 3651
11: 7 Therefore **t** saith the Lord GOD; 3541
11:16 Therefore say, **T** saith the Lord GOD; 3541
11:17 Therefore say, **T** saith the Lord GOD; 3541
12:10 thou unto them, **T** saith the Lord GOD; 3541
12:19 **T** saith the Lord GOD, of the inhabitants 3541
12:23 them therefore, **T** saith the Lord GOD; 3541
12:28 say unto them, **T** saith the Lord GOD; 3541
13: 3 **T** saith the Lord GOD; Woe unto 3541
13: 8 Therefore **t** saith the Lord GOD; 3541
13:13 Therefore **t** saith the Lord GOD; I will 3541
13:15 **T** will I accomplish my wrath upon 2050.1
13:18 say, **T** saith the Lord GOD; Woe to 3541
13:20 Wherefore **t** saith the Lord GOD; Behold, 3541
14: 4 and say unto them, **T** saith the Lord GOD; 3541
14: 6 the house of Israel, **T** saith the Lord GOD; 3541
14:21 For **t** saith the Lord GOD; How much 3541
15: 6 Therefore **t** saith the Lord GOD; As 3541
16: 3 **T** saith the Lord GOD unto Jerusalem; 3541
16:13 **T** wast thou decked *with* gold and silver; 2050.1
16:19 and *t* it was, saith the Lord GOD. NIH
16:36 **T** saith the Lord GOD; Because thy 3541
16:59 For **t** saith the Lord GOD; I will even deal 3541
17: 3 say, **T** saith the Lord GOD; A great eagle 3541
17: 9 Say thou, **T** saith the Lord GOD; Shall it 3541
17:19 Therefore **t** saith the Lord GOD; *As* I live, 3541
17:22 **T** saith the Lord GOD; I will also take of 3541
20: 3 and say unto them, **T** saith the Lord GOD; 3541
20: 5 say unto them, **T** saith the Lord GOD; 3541
20:27 and say unto them, **T** saith the Lord GOD; 3541
20:30 the house of Israel, **T** saith the Lord GOD; 3541
20:39 O house of Israel, **t** saith the Lord GOD; 3541
20:47 **T** saith the Lord GOD; Behold, I *will* 3541
21: 3 to the land of Israel, **T** saith the LORD; 3541
21: 9 prophesy, and say, **T** saith the LORD; 3541
21:24 Therefore **t** saith the Lord GOD; 3541
21:26 **T** saith the Lord GOD; Remove 3541
21:28 **T** saith the Lord GOD concerning 3541
22: 3 say thou, **T** saith the Lord GOD, The city 3541
22:19 Therefore **t** saith the Lord GOD; 3541
22:28 unto them, saying, **T** saith the Lord GOD, 3541
23: 4 **T** *were* their names; Samaria *is* Aholah, 2050.1
23: 7 **T** she committed her whoredoms with 2050.1
23:21 **T** thou calledst to remembrance 2050.1
23:22 O Aholibah, **t** saith the Lord GOD; 3541
23:27 **T** will I make thy lewdness to cease from 2050.1
23:28 For **t** saith the Lord GOD; Behold, I *will* 3541
23:32 **T** saith the Lord GOD; Thou shalt drink 3541
23:35 Therefore **t** saith the Lord GOD; 3541
23:39 **t** have they done in the midst of mine 3541
23:46 For **t** saith the Lord GOD; *I will* bring up 3541
23:48 **T** will I cause lewdness to cease out of 2050.1
24: 3 and say unto them, **T** saith the Lord GOD; 3541
24: 6 Wherefore **t** saith the Lord GOD; Woe to 3541
24: 9 Therefore **t** saith the Lord GOD; Woe to 3541
24:21 the house of Israel, **T** saith the Lord GOD; 3541
24:24 **T** Ezekiel is unto you a sign: according to 2050.1
25: 3 **T** saith the Lord GOD; Because thou 3541
25: 6 For **t** saith the Lord GOD; Because thou 3541
25: 8 **T** saith the Lord GOD; Because that Moab 3541
25:12 **T** saith the Lord GOD; Because that 3541
25:13 Therefore **t** saith the Lord GOD; I will 3541
25:15 **T** saith the Lord GOD; Because 3541
25:16 Therefore **t** saith the Lord GOD; Behold, 3541
26: 3 Therefore **t** saith the Lord GOD; Behold, 3541
26: 7 For **t** saith the Lord GOD; Behold, I *will* 3541
26:15 **T** saith the Lord GOD to Tyrus; Shall not 3541
26:19 For **t** saith the Lord GOD; When I shall 3541
27: 3 for many isles, **T** saith the Lord GOD; 3541
28: 2 prince of Tyrus, **T** saith the Lord GOD; 3541
28: 6 Therefore **t** saith the Lord GOD; 3541
28:12 and say unto him, **T** saith the Lord GOD; 3541
28:22 say, **T** saith the Lord GOD; Behold, I *am* 3541
28:25 **T** saith the Lord GOD; When I shall have 3541
29: 3 Speak, and say, **T** saith the Lord GOD; 3541
29: 8 Therefore **t** saith the Lord GOD; Behold, 3541
29:13 Yet **t** saith the Lord GOD; At the end of 3541
29:19 Therefore **t** saith the Lord GOD; Behold, 3541
30: 2 prophesy and say, **T** saith the Lord GOD; 3541
30: 6 **T** saith the LORD; They also that uphold 3541
30:10 **T** saith the Lord GOD; I will also make 3541
30:13 **T** saith the Lord GOD; I will also destroy 3541
30:19 **T** will I execute judgments in Egypt: and 2050.1
30:22 Therefore **t** saith the Lord GOD; Behold, 3541
31: 7 **T** was he fair in his greatness, in 2050.1
31:10 Therefore **t** saith the Lord GOD; 3541
31:15 **T** saith the Lord GOD; In the day when he 3541
31:18 To whom art thou **t** like in glory and 3602
32: 3 **T** saith the Lord GOD; I will therefore 3541
32:11 For **t** saith the Lord GOD; The sword of 3541
33:10 **T** ye speak, saying, If our transgressions 3651

Eze 33:25 say unto them, **T** saith the Lord GOD; 3541
33:27 Say thou **t** unto them, Thus saith the Lord 3541
33:27 thus unto them, **T** saith the Lord GOD; 3541
34: 2 **T** saith the Lord GOD unto the shepherds; 3541
34:10 **T** saith the Lord GOD; Behold, I *am* 3541
34:11 For **t** saith the Lord GOD; Behold, I, 3541
34:17 O my flock, **t** saith the Lord GOD; 3541
34:20 Therefore **t** saith the Lord GOD unto 3541
34:30 **T** shall they know that I the LORD their 2050.1
35: 3 say unto it, **T** saith the Lord GOD; 3541
35: 7 **T** will I make mount Seir most desolate, 2050.1
35:13 **T** with your mouth ye have boasted 2050.1
35:14 **T** saith the Lord GOD; When the whole 3541
36: 2 **T** saith the Lord GOD; Because 3541
36: 3 and say, **T** saith the Lord GOD; 3541
36: 4 **T** saith the Lord GOD to the mountains, 3541
36: 5 Therefore **t** saith the Lord GOD; Surely in 3541
36: 6 and to the valleys, **T** saith the Lord GOD; 3541
36: 7 Therefore **t** saith the Lord GOD; I have 3541
36:13 **T** saith the Lord GOD; Because they say 3541
36:22 the house of Israel, **T** saith the Lord GOD; 3541
36:33 **T** saith the Lord GOD; In the day that I 3541
36:37 **T** saith the Lord GOD; I will yet *for* this 3541
37: 5 **T** saith the Lord GOD unto these bones; 3541
37: 9 say to the wind, **T** saith the Lord GOD; 3541
37:12 and say unto them, **T** saith the Lord GOD; 3541
37:19 Say unto them, **T** saith the Lord GOD; 3541
37:21 say unto them, **T** saith the Lord GOD; 3541
38: 3 say, **T** saith the Lord GOD; Behold, I *am* 3541
38:10 **T** saith the Lord GOD; It shall also come 3541
38:14 and say unto Gog, **T** saith the Lord GOD; 3541
38:17 **T** saith the Lord GOD; *Art* thou he of 3541
38:23 **T** will I magnify myself, and 2050.1
39: 1 and say, **T** saith the Lord GOD; 3541
39:16 **T** shall they cleanse the land. 2050.1
39:17 thou son of man, **t** saith the Lord GOD; 3541
39:20 **T** ye shall be filled at my table *with* 2050.1
39:25 Therefore **t** saith the Lord GOD; Now will 3541
43:18 Son of man, **t** saith the Lord GOD; 3541
43:20 **t** shalt thou cleanse and purge it. 2050.1
44: 6 the house of Israel, **T** saith the Lord GOD; 3541
44: 9 **T** saith the Lord GOD; No stranger, 3541
45: 9 **T** saith the Lord GOD; Let it suffice you, 3541
45:18 **T** saith the Lord GOD; In the first *month,* 3541
46: 1 **T** saith the Lord GOD; The gate of 3541
46:15 **T** shall they prepare the lamb, and 2050.1
46:16 **T** saith the Lord GOD; If the prince give a 3541
47:13 **T** saith the Lord GOD; This *shall be* 3541
Da 1:16 **T** Melzar took away the portion of their 2050.1
2:24 he went and said **t** unto him; Destroy not 3652
2:25 said **t** unto him, I have found a man of 3652
4:10 **T** *were* the visions of mine head in my 2050.3
4:14 He cried aloud, and said **t**, Hew down 3652
6: 6 said **t** unto him, King Darius, live for ever. 3652
7: 5 they said **t** unto it, Arise, devour much 3652
7:23 **T** he said, The fourth beast shall be 3652
11:17 and upright ones with him; **t** shall he do: 2050.1
11:39 **T** shall he do in the most strong holds 2050.1
Hos 10: 4 **t** judgment springeth up as hemlock in 2050.1
Am 1: 3 **T** saith the LORD; For three 3541
1: 6 **T** saith the LORD; For three 3541
1: 9 **T** saith the LORD; For three 3541
1:11 **T** saith the LORD; For three 3541
1:13 **T** saith the LORD; For three 3541
2: 1 **T** saith the LORD; For three 3541
2: 4 **T** saith the LORD; For three 3541
2: 6 **T** saith the LORD; For three 3541
2:11 *Is it* not even **t**, O ye children of Israel? 2088
3:11 Therefore **t** saith the Lord GOD; 3541
3:12 **T** saith the LORD; As the shepherd taketh 3541
4:12 Therefore **t** will I do unto thee, O Israel: 3541
5: 3 For **t** saith the Lord GOD; The city that 3541
5: 4 For **t** saith the LORD unto the house of 3541
5:16 the God of hosts, the Lord, saith **t**; 3541
7: 1 **T** hath the Lord GOD shewed unto me; 3541
7: 4 **T** hath the Lord GOD shewed unto me: 3541
7: 7 **T** he shewed me: and behold, the Lord 3541
7:11 For **t** Amos saith, Jeroboam shall die by 3541
7:17 Therefore **t** saith the LORD; Thy wife 3541
8: 1 **T** hath the Lord GOD shewed unto me: 3541
Ob 1: 1 **T** saith the Lord GOD concerning Edom; 3541
Mic 2: 3 Therefore **t** saith the LORD; Behold, 3541
3: 5 **T** saith the LORD concerning 3541
5: 6 **t** shall he deliver *us* from the Assyrian, 2050.1
Na 1:12 **T** saith the LORD; Though *they be* quiet, 3541
1:12 yet **t** shall they be cut down, 3651
Hag 1: 2 **T** speaketh the LORD of hosts, saying, 3541
1: 5 Now therefore **t** saith the LORD of hosts; 3541
1: 7 **T** saith the LORD of hosts; Consider your 3541
2: 6 For **t** saith the LORD of hosts; Yet once, 3541
2:11 **T** saith the LORD of hosts; Ask now 3541
Zec 1: 3 unto them, **T** saith the LORD of hosts; 3541
1: 4 saying, **T** saith the LORD of hosts; 3541
1:14 saying, **T** saith the LORD of hosts; 3541
1:16 Therefore **t** saith the LORD; I am returned 3541
1:17 saying, **T** saith the LORD of hosts; 3541
2: 8 For **t** saith the LORD of hosts; After 3541
3: 7 **T** saith the LORD of hosts; If thou wilt 3541
6:12 **T** speaketh the LORD of hosts, saying, 3541
7: 9 **T** speaketh the LORD of hosts, saying, 3541
7:14 **t** the land was desolate after them, that no 2050.1
8: 2 **T** saith the LORD of hosts; I was jealous 3541
8: 3 **T** saith the LORD; I am returned unto 3541
8: 4 **T** saith the LORD of hosts; There shall 3541
8: 6 **T** saith the LORD of hosts; If it be 3541
8: 7 **T** saith the LORD of hosts; Behold, I *will* 3541
8: 9 **T** saith the LORD of hosts; Let your 3541
8:14 For **t** saith the LORD of hosts; As I 3541
8:19 **T** saith the LORD of hosts; The fast of 3541
8:20 **T** saith the LORD of hosts; *It shall* yet 3541
8:23 **T** saith the LORD of hosts; In those days 3541
11: 4 **T** saith the LORD my God; Feed the flock 3541
Mal 1: 4 **t** saith the LORD of hosts, They shall 3541
1:13 and the sick; **t** ye brought an offering: 2050.1
Mt 2: 5 of Judea: for **t** it is written by the prophet, *3779*

Mt 3:15 for t it becometh us to fulfil all 3779
15: 6 he shall be free. T have ye made 2532
26:54 the scriptures be fulfilled, that t it must be? 3779
Mk 2: 7 Why doth this man t speak blasphemies? 3779
Lk 1:25 T hath the Lord dealt with me in the days 3779
2:48 Son, why hast thou t dealt with us? 3779
9:34 While he t spake, there came a cloud, and 3778
11:45 Master, t saying thou reproachest us also. 3778
17:30 Even t shall it be in the day when 2596+5024
18:11 Pharisee stood and prayed t with himself, 3778
19:28 And when he had t spoken, he went before, 3778
19:31 Why do ye loose him? t shall ye say unto 3779
22:51 and said, Suffer ye t far. 2193+3778
23:46 and having said t, he gave up the ghost. 3778
24:36 And as they t spake, Jesus himself stood in 3778
24:40 And when he had t spoken, he shewed 3778
24:46 T it is written, and thus it behoved Christ to 3779
24:46 and t it behoved Christ to suffer, and to rise 3779
Jn 4: 6 wearied with his journey, sat t on the well: 3779
9: 6 When he had t spoken, he spat on 3778
11:43 And when he t had spoken, he cried with a 3778
11:48 If we let him t alone, all men will believe 3779
13:21 When Jesus had t said, he was troubled in 3778
18:22 And when he had t spoken, one of 3778
20:14 And when she had t said, she turned herself 3778
Ac 19:41 And when he had t spoken, he dismissed 3778
20:36 And when he had t spoken, he kneeled 3778
21:11 and feet, and said, T saith the Holy Ghost, 3592
26:24 And as he t spake for himself, Festus said 3778
26:30 And when he had t spoken, the king rose 3778
27:35 And when he had t spoken, he took bread, 3778
Ro 9:20 that formed it, Why hast thou made me t? 3779
1Co 14:25 And t are the secrets of his heart made 3779
2Co 1:17 When I therefore was t minded, did I use 3778
5:14 because we t judge, that if one died for all, 3778
Php 3:15 as many as be perfect, be t minded: 3778
Heb 6: 9 accompany salvation, though we t speak. 3779
9: 6 Now when these things were t ordained, 3779
Rev 9:17 And t I saw the horses in the vision, and 3779
16: 5 and shalt be, because thou hast judged t. 3778
18:21 T with violence shall that great city 3779

THWART See DISANNUL; DISANNULLED

THWARTED See NOUGHT

THY (4607) [THOU] See Index of Articles, Etc.

THYATIRA (4)
Ac 16:14 a seller of purple, of the city of T, 2363
Rev 1:11 and unto T, and unto Sardis, and 2363
2:18 And unto the angel of the church in T 2363
2:24 But unto you I say, and unto the rest in T, 2363

THYINE (1)
Rev 18:12 and all t wood, and all manner vessels of 2367

THYSELF (215) [SELF, THOU]
Ge 13: 9 separate t, I pray thee, from me: if thou wilt NIH
14:21 me the persons, and take the goods to t. 3509.2
16: 9 thy mistress, and submit t under her hands. NIH
33: 9 my brother; keep that thou hast unto t. 3509.2
Ex 9:17 As yet exaltest thou t against my people, NIH
10: 3 How long wilt thou refuse to humble t NIH
10:28 Get thee from me, take heed to t, see my 3509.2
18:14 why sittest thou t alone, and all the people 859
18:18 thou art not able to perform it t alone. 3509.2
18:22 so shall it be easier for t, and they shall 3509.2
20: 5 Thou shalt not bow down t to them, NIH
34: 2 present t there to me in the top of NIH
34:12 Take heed to t, lest thou make a covenant 3509.2
Lev 9: 7 make an atonement for t, and for 3509.2
18:20 thy neighbour's wife, to defile t with her. NIH
18:23 thou lie with any beast to defile t therewith: NIH
19:18 but thou shalt love thy neighbour as t: 3509.2
19:34 and thou shalt love him as t; 3509.2
Nu 11:17 with thee, that thou bear it not t alone. 3509.2
16:13 except thou make t altogether a prince over NIH
Dt 4: 9 Only take heed to t, and keep thy soul 3509.2
5: 9 Thou shalt not bow down t unto them, NIH
9: 1 nations greater and mightier than t, 3509.2
12:13 Take heed to t that thou offer not thy 3509.2
12:19 Take heed to t that thou forsake not 3509.2
12:30 Take heed to t that thou be not snared by 3509.2
20:14 the spoil thereof, shalt thou take unto t; 3509.2
22: 1 his sheep go astray, and hide t from them: NIH
22: 3 thou do likewise: thou mayest not hide t. NIH
22: 4 fall down by the way, and hide t from them: NIH
22:12 of thy vesture, wherewith thou coverest t. NIH
23:13 it shall be, when thou wilt ease t abroad, 3509.2
28:40 but thou shalt not anoint t with the oil; NIH
Jos 17:15 cut down for t there in the land of 3509.2
Ru 3: 3 Wash t therefore, and anoint thee, and NIH
3: 3 but make not t known unto the man, until he NIH
4: 6 redeem thou my right to t; for I cannot 3509.2
1Sa 19: 2 take heed to t until the morning, and NIH
19: 2 and abide in a secret place, and hide t: NIH
20: 8 if there be in me iniquity, slay me t; 859
20:19 come to the place where thou didst hide t NIH
25:26 from avenging t with thine own 3509.2+3807.1
2Sa 5:24 mulberry trees, that then thou shalt bestir t: NIH
7:24 For thou hast confirmed to t thy people 3509.2
13: 5 Lay thee down on thy bed, and make t sick: NIH
14: 2 feign t to be a mourner, and put on now NIH
14: 2 anoint not t with oil, but be as a woman that NIH
18:13 thou t wouldest have set thyself against me. 859
18:13 thou thyself wouldest have set t against me. NIH
22:26 With the merciful thou wilt shew t merciful, NIH
22:26 with the upright man thou wilt shew t NIH
22:27 With the pure thou wilt shew t pure; and NIH
22:27 with the froward thou wilt shew t NIH
1Ki 2: 2 be thou strong therefore, and shew t a man; NIH
2: 3 and whithersoever thou turnest t: NIH
3:11 and hast not asked for t long life; 3509.2
3:11 neither hast asked riches for t, nor hast 3509.2
1Ki 3:11 hast asked for t understanding to discern 3509.2
13: 7 and refresh t, and I will give thee a reward. NIH
14: 2 his wife, Arise, I pray thee, and disguise t, NIH
14: 6 why feignest thou t to be another? NIH
17: 3 and hide t by the brook Cherith, NIH
18: 1 third year, saying, Go, shew t unto Ahab; NIH
20:22 strengthen t, and mark, and see what thou NIH
20:40 So shall thy judgment be; t hast decided it. 859
21:20 thou hast sold t to work evil in the sight 3509.2
22:25 shalt go into an inner chamber to hide t. NIH
2Ki 22:19 and thou hast humbled t before the LORD, NIH
1Ch 21:12 advise t what word I shall bring again to NIH
2Ch 1:11 hast asked wisdom and knowledge for t, 3509.2
18:24 shalt go into an inner chamber to hide t. NIH
20:37 Because thou hast joined t with Ahaziah, 3509.2
21:13 father's house, which were better than t: 3509.2
34:27 and thou didst humble t before God, NIH
34:27 humbledst t before me, and didst rend thy NIH
Est 4:13 Think not with t that thou shalt 5315+3509.3
Job 8: 8 and prepare t to the search of their fathers: NIH
10:16 again thou shewest t marvellous upon me. NIH
15: 8 and dost thou restrain wisdom to t? 3509.2
22:21 Acquaint now t with him, and be at peace: NIH
30:21 with thy strong hand thou opposest t against NIH
40:10 Deck t now with majesty and excellency; NIH
40:10 and array t with glory and beauty. NIH
Ps 7: 6 lift up t because of the rage of mine NIH
10: 1 why hidest thou t in times of trouble? NIH
18:25 With the merciful thou wilt shew t merciful; NIH
18:25 with an upright man thou wilt shew t NIH
18:26 With the pure thou wilt shew t pure; and NIH
18:26 with the froward thou wilt shew t froward. NIH
35:23 Stir up t, and awake to my judgment, NIH
37: 1 Fret not t because of evildoers, neither be NIH
37: 4 Delight t also in the LORD; and he shall NIH
37: 7 fret not t because of him who prospereth in NIH
37: 8 fret not t in any wise to do evil. NIH
49:18 praise thee, when thou doest well to t. 3509.2
50:21 that I was altogether such a one as t: 3509.2
52: 1 Why boastest thou t in mischief, O mighty NIH
55: 1 and hide not t from my supplication. NIH
60: 1 hast been displeased; O turn t to us again. NIH
80:15 the branch that thou madest strong for t. 3509.2
80:17 of man whom thou madest strong for t. 3509.2
85: 3 thou hast turned t from the fierceness of NIH
89:46 wilt thou hide t, for ever? shall thy wrath NIH
94: 1 to whom vengeance belongeth, shew t. NIH
94: 2 Lift up t, thou judge of the earth: render a NIH
104: 2 Who coverest t with light as with a NIH
Pr 6: 3 Do this now, my son, and deliver t, NIH
6: 3 go, humble t, and make sure thy friend. NIH
6: 5 Deliver t as a roe from the hand of NIH
9:12 If thou be wise, thou shalt be wise for t: 3509.2
24:19 Fret not t because of evil men, neither be NIH
24:27 and make it fit for t in the field; 3509.2
25: 6 Put not forth t in the presence of the king, NIH
27: 1 Boast not t of to morrow; for thou knowest NIH
30:32 If thou hast done foolishly in lifting up t, or NIH
Ecc 7:16 over much; neither make t over wise: NIH
7:16 over wise: why shouldest thou destroy t? NIH
7:22 that thou t likewise hast cursed others. 859
Isa 26:20 hide t as it were for a little moment, NIH
33: 3 at the lifting up of t the nations were 3509.2
45:15 Verily thou art a God that hidest t, O God of NIH
52: 2 Shake t from the dust; arise, and sit down, NIH
52: 2 loose t from the bands of thy neck, NIH
57: 8 for thou hast discovered t to another than NIH
57: 9 far off, and didst debase t even unto hell. NIH
58: 7 that thou hide not t from thine own flesh? NIH
58:14 Then shalt thou delight t in the LORD; and NIH
63:14 thy people, to make t a glorious name. 3509.2
64:12 Wilt thou refrain t for these things, O NIH
65: 5 Which say, Stand by t, come not near to 3509.2
Jer 2:17 Hast thou not procured this unto t, in that 3509.3
4:30 Though thou clothest t with crimson, NIH
4:30 with painting, in vain shalt thou make t fair; NIH
6:26 thee with sackcloth, and wallow t in ashes: NIH
17: 4 thou, even t, shalt discontinue from thine 3509.2
20: 4 I will make thee a terror to t, and to all 3509.2
22:15 thou reign, because thou closest t in cedar? NIH
32: 8 and the redemption is thine; buy it for t. 3509.2
45: 5 seekest thou great things for t? seek them 3509.2
46:19 in Egypt, furnish t to go into captivity: 3509.3
47: 5 of their valley: how long wilt thou cut t? NIH
47: 6 put up t into thy scabbard, rest, and be still. NIH
La 2:18 give t no rest; let not the apple of thine 3509.2
3:44 Thou hast covered t with a cloud, that our 3509.2
4:21 shalt be drunken, and shalt make t naked. NIH
Eze 3:24 said unto me, Go, shut t within thine house. NIH
16:17 madest to t images of men, and 3509.2
22: 4 hast defiled t in thine idols which thou hast NIH
22:16 thou shalt take thine inheritance in t in 3509.3
23:40 for whom thou didst wash t, paintedst thy NIH
23:40 thy eyes, and deckedst t with ornaments, NIH
31:10 Because thou hast lifted up t in height, and NIH
38: 7 prepare for t, thou, and all thy company 3509.2
Da 5:17 Let thy gifts be to t, and give thy rewards 3509.5
5:23 hast lifted up t against the Lord of heaven; NIH
10:12 to chasten t before thy God, thy words were NIH
Hos 13: 9 O Israel, thou hast destroyed t; but in me 3509.2
Ob 1: 4 Though thou exalt t as the eagle, and NIH
Mic 1:10 in the house of Aphrah roll t in the dust. NIH
5: 1 Now gather t in troops, O daughter of NIH
Na 3:15 make t many as the cankerworm, NIH
3:15 make t many as the locusts. NIH
Zec 2: 7 Deliver t, O Zion, that dwellest with NIH
Mt 4: 6 If thou be the Son of God, cast t down: 4572
5:33 Thou shalt not forswear t, but shalt perform NIG
8: 4 shew t to the priest, and offer the gift that 4572
19:19 and, Thou shalt love thy neighbour as t. 4572
22:39 unto it, Thou shalt love thy neighbour as t. 4572
27:40 and buildest it in three days, save t. 4572
Mk 1:44 shew t to the priest, and offer for thy 4572
12:31 Thou shalt love thy neighbour as t. 4572
15:30 Save t, and come down from the cross. 4572
Lk 4: 9 be the Son of God, cast t down from hence: 4572
4:23 say unto me this proverb, Physician, heal t: 4572
5:14 no man: but go, and shew t to the priest, 4572
6:42 when thou t beholdest not the beam that is in 846
7: 6 to him, saying unto him, Lord, trouble not t: NIG
10:27 with all thy mind; and thy neighbour as t. 4572
17: 8 and gird t, and serve me, till I have eaten NIG
23:37 If thou be the King of the Jews, save t. 4572
23:39 saying, If thou be Christ, save t and us. 4572
Jn 1:22 to them that sent us. What sayest thou of t? 4572
7: 4 If thou do these things, shew t to the world. 4572
8:13 said unto him, Thou bearest record of t; 4572
8:53 prophets are dead: whom makest thou t? 4572
10:33 that thou, being a man, makest t God. 4572
14:22 how is it that thou wilt manifest t unto us, 4572
18:34 answered him, Sayest thou this thing of t, 1438
21:18 thou girdedst t, and walkedst whither thou 4572
Ac 8:29 Go near, and join t to this chariot. NIG
12: 8 unto him, Gird t, and bind on thy sandals. NIG
16:28 with a loud voice, saying, Do t no harm: 4572
21:24 and purify t with them, and be at charges NIG
21:24 but that thou t also walkest orderly, and 846
24: 8 by examining of whom t mayest take 846
26: 1 Thou art permitted to speak for t. 4572
26:24 with a loud voice, Paul, thou art beside t; 3105
Ro 2: 1 thou judgest another, thou condemnest t; 4572
2: 5 impenitent heart treasurest up unto t wrath 4572
2:19 And art confident that thou t art a guide of 4572
2:21 which teachest another, teachest thou not t? 4572
13: 9 namely, Thou shalt love thy neighbour as t. 4572
14:22 have it to t before God. Happy is he that 4572
Gal 5:14 in this; Thou shalt love thy neighbour as t. 4572
6: 1 considering t, lest thou also be tempted. 4572
1Ti 3:15 oughtest to behave t in the house of God, NIG
4: 7 and exercise t rather unto godliness. 4572
4:15 Meditate upon these things; give t wholly to NIG
4:16 Take heed unto t, and unto the doctrine; 4572
4:16 for in doing this thou shalt both save t, and 4572
5:22 partaker of other men's sins: keep t pure. 4572
6: 5 gain is godliness: from such withdraw t. NIG
2Ti 2:15 Study to shew t approved unto God, 4572
Tit 2: 7 In all things shewing t a pattern of good 4572
Jas 2: 8 Thou shalt love thy neighbour as t, ye do 4572

TIBERIAS (3)
Jn 6: 1 the sea of Galilee, which is the sea of T. 5085
6:23 (Howbeit there came other boats from T 5085
21: 1 again to the disciples at the sea of T; 5085

TIBERIUS (1)
Lk 3: 1 Now in the fifteenth year of the reign of T 5086

TIBHATH (1)
1Ch 18: 8 Likewise from T, and from Chun, cities of 2880

TIBNI (3)
1Ki 16:21 half of the people followed T the son of 8402
16:22 people that followed T the son of Ginath: 8402
16:22 son of Ginath: so T died, and Omri reigned. 8402

TIDAL (2)
Ge 14: 1 king of Elam, and T king of nations; 8413
14: 9 with T king of nations, and Amraphel king 8413

TIDINGS (46)
Ge 29:13 when Laban heard the t of Jacob his sister's 8088
Ex 33: 4 when the people heard these evil t, they 1697
1Sa 4:19 when she heard the t that the ark of God 8052
11: 4 and told the t in the ears of the people: 1697
11: 5 they told him the t of the men of Jabesh. 1697
11: 6 came upon Saul when he heard those t, 1697
27:11 to bring t to Gath, saying, Lest they should NIH
2Sa 4: 4 was five years old when the t came of Saul 8052
4:10 is dead, thinking to have brought good t, 1319
4:10 I would have given him a reward for his t: 1309
13:30 in the way, that t came to David, saying, 8052
18:19 Let me now run, and bear the king t, 1319
18:20 Thou shalt not bear t this day, but 1309
18:20 this day, but thou shalt bear t another day: 1319
18:20 this day thou shalt bear no t, because 1319
18:22 my son, seeing that thou hast no t ready? 1309
18:25 If he be alone, there is t in his mouth. 1309
18:26 And the king said, He also bringeth t. 1319
18:27 He is a good man, and cometh with good t. 1309
18:31 and Cushi said, T, my lord the king: 1319
1Ki 1:42 thou art a valiant man, and bringest good t. 1319
2:28 t came to Joab: for Joab had turned after 8052
14: 6 for I am sent to thee with heavy t. NIH
2Ki 7: 9 this day is a day of good t, and we hold our 1309
1Ch 10: 9 to carry t unto their idols, and to 1319
Ps 112: 7 He shall not be afraid of evil t: his heart is 8052
Isa 40: 9 O Zion, that bringest good t, get thee up 1319
40: 9 O Jerusalem, that bringest good t, lift up 1319
41:27 give to Jerusalem one that bringeth good t. 1319
52: 7 are the feet of him that bringeth good t, 1319
52: 7 that bringeth good t of good, 1319
61: 1 me to preach good t unto the meek; 1319
Jer 20:15 Cursed be the man who brought t to my 1319
37: 5 that besieged Jerusalem heard t of them, 8088
49:23 for they have heard evil t: they are 8052
Eze 21: 7 that thou shalt answer, For the t; because 8052
Da 11:44 t out of the east and out of the north shall 8052
Na 1:15 the feet of him that bringeth good t, 1319
Lk 1:19 unto thee, and to shew thee these glad t. 2097
2:10 for behold, I bring you good t of great joy, 2097
8: 1 shewing the glad t of the kingdom of God: 2097
Ac 11:22 Then t of these things came unto the ears of 3056
13:32 And we declare unto you glad t, how that 2097
21:31 t came unto the chief captain of the band, 5334
Ro 10:15 of peace, and bring glad t of good things! 2097
1Th 3: 6 and brought us good t of your faith and 2097

TIE (2) [TIED]
1Sa 6: 7 t the kine to the cart, and bring their calves 631

T

Pr 6:21 thine heart, *and* t them about thy neck. 6029

TIED (8) [TIE]
Ex 39:31 they t unto it a lace of blue, to fasten *it* on 5414
1Sa 6:10 t them to the cart, and shut up their calves at 631
2Ki 7:10 horses t, and asses tied, and the tents as they 631
7:10 and asses t, and the tents as they *were.* 631
Mt 21: 2 and straightway ye shall find an ass t, and *1210*
Mk 11: 2 ye shall find a colt t, whereon never man *1210*
11: 4 found the colt t by the door without in a *1210*
Lk 19:30 which at your entering ye shall find a colt t, *1210*

TIGLATH-PILESER (3) [PUL, TILGATH-PILNESER]
2Ki 15:29 In the days of Pekah king of Israel came T 8407
16: 7 So Ahaz sent messengers to T king of 8407
16:10 king Ahaz went *to* Damascus to meet T 8407

TIGRIS See HIDDEKEL

TIKVAH (2) [TIKVATH]
2Ki 22:14 the wife of Shallum the son of T, the son of 8616
Ezr 10:15 Jahaziah the son of T were employed about 8616

TIKVATH (1) [TIKVAH]
2Ch 34:22 the wife of Shallum the son of T, the son of 8616

TILE (1) [TILING]
Eze 4: 1 take thee a t, and lay it before thee, and 3843

TILGATH-PILNESER (3) [TIGLATH-PILESER]
1Ch 5: 6 whom T king of Assyria carried away 8407
5:26 the spirit of T king of Assyria, and 8407
2Ch 28:20 T king of Assyria came unto him, and 8407

TILING (1) [TILE]
Lk 5:19 let him down through the t with *his* couch *2766*

TILL (169) [TILLAGE, TILLED, TILLER, TILLEST, TILLETH]
Ge 2: 5 and *there was* not a man to t the ground. 5647
3:19 eat bread, t thou return unto the ground; 5704
3:23 to t the ground from whence he was taken. 5647
19:22 for I cannot do any thing t thou be come 5704
29: 8 *t* they roll the stone from the well's mouth; NIH
38:11 father's house, t Shelah my son be grown: 5704
38:17 Wilt thou give *me* a pledge, t thou send *it?* 5704
Ex 15:16 t thy people pass over, O LORD, till 5704
15:16 O LORD, t the people pass over, 5704
16:19 Let no man leave of it t the morning. 5704
16:24 they laid it up t the morning, as Moses 5704
34:33 *t* Moses had done speaking with them, he NIH
40:37 they journeyed not t the day that it was 5704
Nu 12:15 the people journeyed not t Miriam was 5704
Dt 17: 5 and shalt stone them with stones, t they die. NIH
28:45 and overtake thee, t thou be destroyed; 5704
Jos 5: 6 t all the people *that were* men of war, 5704
5: 8 their places in the camp, t they were whole. 5704
8: 6 t we have drawn them from the city; 5704
10:20 t they were consumed, that the rest *which* 5704
Jdg 3:25 they tarried t *they* were ashamed: and 5704
6: 4 t thou come *unto* Gaza, and left no 5704
11:33 even t thou come *to* Minnith, *even* twenty 5704
16: 3 Samson lay t midnight, and arose at 5704
19:26 house where her lord *was,* t it was light. 5704
21: 2 abode there t even before God, and lift up 5704
Ru 1:13 Would ye tarry for them t they were 834+5704
1Sa 10: 8 t I come to thee, and shew thee what thou 5704
16:11 for we will not sit down t he come hither. 5704
22: 3 t I know what God will do for me. 834+5704
2Sa 3:35 or ought else, t the sun be down. 6440+3807.1
9:10 shall t the land for him, and thou shalt 5647
1Ki 14:10 as *a man* taketh away dung, t it be all gone. 5704
18:28 t the blood gushed out upon them. 5704
2Ki 2:17 when they urged him t *he* was ashamed, 5704
4:20 he sat on her knees t noon, and *then* died. 5704
7: 9 if we tarry t the morning light, 5704
10:17 t *he* had destroyed him, according to 5704
13:17 in Aphek, t *thou* have consumed *them.* 5704
13:19 hadst thou smitten Syria t *thou* hadst 5704
21:16 t he had filled Jerusalem from one end 834+5704
2Ch 26:15 marvellously helped, t he was strong. 3588+5704
29:34 t the work was ended, and until the *other* 5704
36:16 against his people, t *there was* no remedy. 5704
Ezr 2:63 *things* t there stood *up* a priest with Urim 5704
5: 5 them to cease, t the matter came to Darius: 5705
9:14 wouldest thou not be angry with us t *thou* 5704
Ne 2: 7 that they may convey me over t I 834+5704
4:11 t we come in the midst among them, 834+5704
4:21 rising of the morning t the stars appeared. 5704
7:65 *things,* t there stood *up* a priest with Urim 5704
13:19 charged that they should not be opened t 5704
Job 7:19 nor let me alone t I swallow down my 5704
8:21 T he fill thy mouth *with* laughing, and 5704
14: 6 t he shall accomplish, as a hireling, his day. 5704
14:12 t the heavens *be* no more, they shall not 5704
14:14 time will I wait, t my change come. 5704
27: 5 t I die I will not remove my integrity from 5704
32: 4 Now Elihu had waited t Job had spoken, 871.1
Ps 10:15 the evil *man:* seek out his wickedness *t* thou NIH
18:37 neither did I turn again t they were 5704
68:30 *t every one* submit himself with pieces of NIH
Pr 7:23 T a dart strike through his liver; as a bird 5704
29:11 but a wise *man* keepeth it in *t* afterwards. NIH
Ecc 2: 3 t I might see what *was* that good for 834+5704
SS 2: 7 nor awake *my* love, t he please. 5704+7945
3: 5 nor awake *my* love, t he please. 5704+7945
Isa 5: 8 *that* lay field to field, t *there be* no place, 5704
5:11 continue until night, *t* wine inflame them! NIH
22:14 shall not be purged from you t ye die, 5704
23:13 *t* the Assyrian founded it for them that NIH
30:17 t ye be left as a beacon upon the top of 518+5704
38:13 I reckoned t morning, *that,* as a lion, so 5704
42: 4 t he have set judgment in the earth: 5704
62: 7 t he establish, and till he make Jerusalem a 5704
Isa 62: 7 t he make Jerusalem a praise in the earth. 5704
Jer 7:32 shall bury in Tophet, t there be no place. 4480
9:16 sword after them, t I have consumed them. 5704
19:11 *them* in Tophet, t *there be* no place to bury. 4480
23:20 t he have performed the thoughts of his 5704
24:10 t they be consumed from off the land that I 5704
27:11 and they shall t it, and dwell therein. 5647
49: 9 they will destroy t they have enough. NIH
49:37 sword after them, t I have consumed them: 5704
52: 3 t he had cast them out from his presence, 5704
52:11 and put him in prison t the day of his death. 5704
La 3:50 T the LORD look down, and behold from 5704
Eze 4: 8 t thou hast ended the days of thy siege. 5704
4:14 for from my youth up even t now have I 5704
24:13 t I have caused my fury to rest upon thee. 5704
28:15 wast created, t iniquity was found in thee. 5704
34:21 t ye have scattered them abroad; 834+5704
39:15 t the buriers have buried it in the valley of 5704
39:19 ye shall eat fat t *ye* be full, and 3807.1
39:19 be full, and drink blood t *ye* be drunken, 3807.1
47:20 t *a man* come over against Hamath. 5704
Da 2: 9 before me, t the time be changed: 1768+5705
2:34 Thou sawest t that a stone was cut out 5705
4:23 t seven times pass over him; 1768+5705
4:25 t thou know that the most High 1768+5705
4:33 t his hairs were grown like eagles' 1768+5705
5:21 t he knew that the most high God 1768+5705
6:14 he laboured t the going down of the sun to 5705
7: 4 I beheld t the wings thereof were 1768+5705
7: 9 I beheld t the thrones were cast 1768+5705
7:11 I beheld *even* t the beast *was* slain, 1768+5705
10: 3 at all, t three whole weeks were fulfilled. 5704
11:36 shall prosper t the indignation be 5704
12: 9 closed up and sealed t the time of the end. 5704
12:13 go thou thy way t the end *be:* for thou 3807.1
Hos 5:15 t they acknowledge their offence, and 834+5704
10:12 t he come and rain righteousness upon you. 5704
Ob 1: 5 would they not have stolen t they had NIH
Jnh 4: 5 t he might see what would become of 834+5704
Zep 3: 3 they gnaw not the bones t the morrow. 3807.1
Mt 1:25 And knew her not t she had brought *2193+3739*
2: 9 t it came and stood over where the young *2193*
5:18 T heaven and earth pass, one jot or *302+2193*
5:18 pass from the law, t all be fulfilled. *302+2193*
5:26 t thou hast paid the uttermost farthing. *302+2193*
10:11 and there abide t ye go thence. *302+2193*
10:23 of Israel, t the Son of man be come. *302+2193*
12:20 t he send forth judgment unto victory. *302+2193*
13:33 of meal, t the whole was leavened. *2193+3739*
16:28 t they see the Son of man coming in *302+2193*
18:21 and I forgive him? t seven times? *2193*
18:30 him into prison, t he should pay the debt. *2193*
18:34 t he should pay all that was due unto *2193+3739*
22:44 t I make thine enemies thy footstool? *302+2193*
23:39 not see me henceforth, t ye shall say, *302+2193*
24:34 not pass, t all these *things* be fulfilled. *302+2193*
Mk 6:10 there abide t ye depart from that place. *302+2193*
9: 1 t they have seen the kingdom of God *302+2193*
9: 9 t the Son of man were risen from *1508+3752*
12:36 t I make thine enemies thy footstool. *302+2193*
13:30 not pass, t all these *things* be done. *3360+3739*
Lk 1:80 was in the deserts t the day of his shewing *2193*
9:27 t they see the kingdom of God. *302+2193*
12:50 am I straitened t it be accomplished! *2193+3748*
12:59 t thou hast paid the very last mite. *2193*
13: 8 t I shall dig about it, and dung *it:* *2193+3748*
13:21 of meal, t the whole was leavened. *2193+3739*
15: 8 and seek diligently t she find *it?* *2193+3739*
17: 8 and serve me, t I have eaten and drunken; *2193*
19:13 and said unto them, Occupy t I come. *2193*
20:43 T I make thine enemies thy footstool. *302+2193*
21:32 shall not pass away, t all be fulfilled. *302+2193*
Jn 13:38 t thou hast denied me thrice. *2193+3739*
21:22 If I will that he tarry t I come, what *is that* *2193*
21:23 but, If I will that he tarry t I come, what *is* *2193*
Ac 7:18 T another king arose, which knew not *891+3739*
8:40 in all the cities, t he came to Cesarea. *2193*
20:11 *even* t break of day, so he departed. *891*
21: 5 and children, t *we were* out of the city: *2193*
23:12 eat nor drink t they had killed Paul. *2193+3739*
23:21 that *they* will neither eat nor drink t *2193+3739*
25:21 I commanded him to be kept t I *2193+3739*
28:23 *of* the prophets, from morning t evening. *2193*
1Co 11:26 do shew the Lord's death t he come. *891+3739*
15:25 t he hath put all enemies under his *891+3739*
Gal 3:19 t the seed should come to whom *891+3739*
Eph 4:13 T we all come in the unity of the faith, and *3360*
Php 1:10 and without offence t the day of Christ; *1519*
1Ti 4:13 T I come, give attendance to reading, *2193*
Heb 10:13 From henceforth expecting t his enemies be *2193*
Rev 2:25 have *already* hold fast t I come. *302+891+3739*
7: 3 t we have sealed the servants of our God in *891*
15: 8 t the seven plagues of the seven angels were *891*
20: 3 t the thousand years should be fulfilled: *891*

TILLAGE (3) [TILL]
1Ch 27:26 t of the ground *was* Ezri the son of Chelub: 5656
Ne 10:37 have the tithes in all the cities of our t. 5656
Pr 13:23 Much food *is in* the t of the poor: but 5215

TILLED (2) [TILL]
Eze 36: 9 turn unto you, and ye shall be t and sown: 5647
36:34 the desolate land shall be t, whereas it lay 5647

TILLER (1) [TILL]
Ge 4: 2 of sheep, but Cain was a t of the ground. 5647

TILLEST (1) [TILL]
Ge 4:12 When thou t the ground, it shall not 5647

TILLETH (2) [TILL]
Pr 12:11 He that t his land shall be satisfied *with* 5647
28:19 He that t his land shall have plenty *of* 5647

TILON (1)
1Ch 4:20 and Rinnah, Ben-hanan, and T. 8436

TIMBER (26)
Ex 31: 5 of stones, to set *them,* and in carving of t, 6086
Lev 14:45 the t thereof, and all the morter of 6086
1Ki 5: 6 can skill to hew t like unto the Sidonians. 6086
5: 8 I will do all thy desire concerning t of 6086
5: 8 timber of cedar, and concerning t of fir. 6086
5:18 so they prepared t and stones to build 6086
6:10 they rested on the house with t of cedar. 6086
15:22 the t thereof, where*with* Baasha had 6086
2Ki 12:12 to buy t and hewed stone to repair 6086
22: 6 to buy t and hewn stone to repair the house. 6086
1Ch 14: 1 t of cedars, with masons and carpenters, 6086
22:14 t also and stone have I prepared; and 6086
22:15 hewers and workers of stone and t, and 6086
2Ch 2: 8 thy servants can skill to cut t in Lebanon; 6086
2: 9 Even to prepare me t in abundance: for 6086
2:10 give to thy servants, the hewers that cut t, 6086
2:14 in silver, in brass, in iron, in stone, and in t, 6086
16: 6 the t thereof, where*with* Baasha was a 6086
34:11 t for couplings, and to floor the houses 6086
Ezr 5: 8 t *is* laid in the walls, and this work goeth fast 636
6: 4 rows of great stones, and a row of new t: 636
6:11 let t be pulled down from his house, and 636
Ne 2: 8 that he may give me t to make beams for 6086
Eze 26:12 they shall lay thy stones and thy t and 6086
Hab 2:11 and the beam out of the t shall answer it. 6086
Zec 5: 4 shall consume it with the t thereof and 6086

TIMBREL (5) [TIMBRELS]
Ex 15:20 the sister of Aaron, took a t in her hand; 8596
Job 21:12 They take the t and harp, and rejoice at 8596
Ps 81: 2 Take a psalm, and bring hither the t, 8596
149: 3 let them sing *praises* unto him with the t 8596
150: 4 Praise him with the t and dance: praise him 8596

TIMBRELS (5) [TIMBREL]
Ex 15:20 all the women went out after her with t and 8596
Jdg 11:34 his daughter came out to meet him with t 8596
2Sa 6: 5 and on t, and on cornets, and on cymbals. 8596
1Ch 13: 8 with t, and with cymbals, and 8596
Ps 68:25 *them were* the damsels **playing** with t. 8608

TIME (619) [BEFORETIME, BETIMES, DAYTIME, LIFETIME, MEALTIME, OFTENTIMES, OFTTIMES, SEEDTIME, SOMETIME, SOMETIMES, TIMES, UNTIMELY]
Ge 4: 3 in process of t it came to pass, that Cain 3117
17:21 bear unto thee at this **set** t in the next year. 4150
18:10 return unto thee according to the t of life; 6256
18:14 At the t **appointed** I will return unto thee, 4150
18:14 according to the t of life, and Sarah shall 6256
21: 2 at the **set** t of which God had spoken to 4150
21:22 it came to pass at that t, that Abimelech 6256
22:15 unto Abraham out of heaven the **second** t, 8145
24:11 by a well of water at the t of the evening, 6256
24:11 *even* the t that *women* go out to draw 6256
26: 8 to pass, when he had been there a long t, 3117
29: 7 neither *is it* t that the cattle should be 6256
29:34 Now *this* t will my husband be joined unto 6471
30:33 righteousness answer for me in t to come, 3117
31:10 it came to pass at the t that the cattle 6256
38: 1 it came to pass at that t, that Judah went 6256
38:12 **in process of** t the daughter 3117+7235+1886.1
38:27 it came to pass in the t of her travail, that, 6256
39: 5 it came to pass from the t *that* he had made 227
39:11 it came to pass about this t, that *Joseph* 3117
41: 5 he slept and dreamed the **second** t: and 8145
43:10 surely now we had returned this **second** t. 6471
43:18 in our sacks at the **first** t *are* we brought in; 8462
43:20 we came indeed down at the **first** t to buy 8462
47:29 the t drew nigh that Israel must die: and 3117
Ex 2:23 pass in **process of** t, 3117+7227+1886.1+1886.1
8:32 Pharaoh hardened his heart at this t also, 6471
9: 5 the LORD appointed a **set** t, saying, 4150
9:14 For I will at this t send all my plagues upon 6471
9:18 to morrow about *this* t I will cause it to rain 6256
9:27 and said unto them, I have sinned *this* t: 6471
13:14 be when thy son asketh thee **in** t **to come,** 4279
21:19 only he shall pay *for* the **loss of** his t, and 7674
21:29 to push with his horn **in** t **past,** 4480+8032+8543
21:36 ox *hath* used to push **in** t **past,** 4480+8032+8543
23:15 in the t **appointed** of the month Abib; 4150
34:18 in the t of the month Abib: 4150
34:21 in **earing** t and in harvest thou shalt rest. 2758
Lev 13:58 it shall be washed the **second** t, and 8145
15:25 many days out of the t of her separation, 6256
15:25 or if it run beyond the t of her separation; NIH
18:18 besides the other in her life *t.* NIH
25:32 may the Levites redeem at **any** t. 5769
25:50 according to the t of a hired servant shall it 3117
26: 5 the vintage shall reach unto the **sowing** t: 2233
Nu 10: 6 When you blow an alarm the **second** t, then 8145
13:20 Now the t *was* the time of the first ripe 3117
13:20 Now the time *was* the t of the first ripe 3117
14:14 **by day** t in a pillar of a cloud, and in a 3119
20:15 and we have dwelt in Egypt a long t; 3117
22: 4 Zippor *was* king of the Moabites at that t. 6256
23:23 according to *this* t it shall be said of Jacob 6256
26:10 **what** t the fire devoured two hundred and 871.1
32:10 LORD'S anger was kindled the same t, 3117
35:26 if the slayer shall **at any** t **come** 3318+3318
Dt 1: 9 I spake unto you at that t, saying, I am not 6256
1:16 I charged your judges at that t, saying, 6256
1:18 I commanded you at that t all the things 6256
2:20 giants dwelt therein **in old** t; and 6440+3807.1
2:34 we took all his cities at that t, and 6256
3: 4 we took all his cities at that t, there was not 6256
3: 8 we took at that t out of the hand of the two 6256
3:12 *which* we possessed at that t, from Aroer, 6256
3:18 I commanded you at that t, saying, 6256

Dt 3:21 I commanded Joshua at that **t**, saying, 6256
3:23 I besought the LORD at that **t**, saying, 6256
4:14 the LORD commanded me at that **t** to 6256
5: 5 between the LORD and you at that **t**, 6256
6:20 *And* when thy son asketh thee **in t to come**, 4279
9:19 the LORD hearkened unto me at that **t** 6471
9:20 and I prayed for Aaron also the same **t**. 6256
10: 1 At that **t** the LORD said unto me, 6256
10: 8 At that **t** the LORD separated the tribe of 6256
10:10 according to the first **t**, forty days and 3117
10:10 the LORD hearkened unto me at that **t** 6471
16: 9 *t as thou* beginnest *to put* the sickle to NIH
19: 4 whom he hated not **in t past**; 4480+8032+8543
19: 6 as he hated him not **in t past**. 4480+8032+8543
19:14 which they of **old t** have set in thine 7223
20:19 When thou shalt besiege a city a long **t**, 3117
32:35 recompence; their foot shall slide in *due* **t**: 6256
Jos 2: 5 it came to pass *about the* **t** of shutting of NIH
3:15 all his banks all the **t** of harvest,) 3117
4: 6 your children ask *their fathers* **in t to come**, 4279
4:21 children shall ask their fathers **in t to come**, 4279
5: 2 At that **t** the LORD said unto Joshua, 6256
5: 2 again the children of Israel the **second t**. 8145
6:16 it came to pass at the seventh **t**, when 6471
6:26 Joshua adjured *them* at that **t**, saying, 6256
8:14 he and all his people, at a **t appointed**, 4150
10:27 it came to pass at the **t** of the going down of 6256
10:42 and their land did Joshua take *at* one **t**, 6471
11: 6 for to morrow about this **t** will I deliver 6256
11:10 Joshua at that **t** turned back, and 6256
11:18 Joshua made war a long **t** with all those 3117
11:21 at that **t** came Joshua, and cut off 6256
22:24 **In t to come** your children might speak 4279
22:27 may not say to our children **in t to come**, 4279
22:28 say to us or to our generations **in t to come**, 4279
23: 1 it came to pass a long **t** after that 3117
24: 2 dwelt on the *other* side of the flood in **old t**, 5769
Jdg 3:29 they slew *of* Moab at that **t** about ten 6256
4: 4 wife of Lapidoth, she judged Israel at that **t**. 6256
9: 8 The trees **went forth on a t** to anoint 1980+1980
10:14 let them deliver you in the **t** of your 6256
11: 4 it came to pass **in process of t**, 3117+4480
11:26 did ye not recover *them* within that **t**? 6256
12: 6 there fell at that **t** of the Ephraimites forty 6256
13:23 as *at this* **t** have told us *such things* as these. 6256
14: 4 for at that **t** the Philistines had dominion 6256
14: 8 after a **t** he returned to take her, and 3117
15: 1 in the **t** of wheat harvest, that Samson 3117
18:31 all the **t** that the house of God was in 3117
20:15 numbered at that **t** out of the cities twenty 3117
21:14 Benjamin came again at that **t**; and 6256
21:22 for ye did not give unto them at *this* **t**, 6256
21:24 children of Israel departed thence at that **t**, 6256
Ru 4: 7 **in former t** in Israel concerning 6440+3807.1
1Sa 1: 4 when the **t** was that Elkanah offered, he 3117
1:20 when the **t** was come about after Hannah 3117
3: 2 it came to pass at that **t**, when Eli *was* laid 3117
3: 8 LORD called Samuel again the **third t**. 7992
4:20 about the **t** of her death the *women* that 6256
7: 2 abode in Kirjath-jearim, that the **t** was long: 3117
9:13 you up; for about *this* **t** ye shall find him. 3117
9:16 To morrow about *this* **t** I will send thee a 6256
9:24 for unto *this* **t** *hath it* been kept for thee 4150
11: 9 To morrow, by *that* **t** the sun be hot, ye shall NIH
13: 8 according to the **set t** that Samuel *had* 4150
14:18 For the ark of God was at that **t** with 3117
14:21 the Philistines **before that t**, 865+8032+3509.1
18:19 it came to pass at the **t** when Merab Saul's 6256
19:21 Saul sent messengers again the **third t**, 7992
20:12 sounded my father about to morrow *any* **t**, 6256
20:35 the field at the **t appointed** with David, 4150
26: 8 and I will not *smite* him the **second t**. 8138
27: 7 the **t** that David dwelt in the country 3117+4557
2Sa 2:11 the **t** that David was king in Hebron 3117+4557
5: 2 Also **in t past**, when Saul was 865+1571+8032
7: 6 **t** that I brought up the children of Israel out 3117
7:11 *as* since the **t** that I commanded judges *to* 3117
11: 1 at the **t** when kings go forth *to battle*, that 6256
14: 2 be as a woman *that had* a long **t** mourned 3117
14:29 when he sent again the **second t**, he would 8145
17: 7 Ahithophel hath given *is* not good at this **t**. 6471
20: 5 he tarried longer than the **set t** which he 4150
20:18 They were wont to speak in **old t**, saying, 7223
23: 8 eight hundred, whom he slew at one **t**. 6471
23:13 came to David in the **harvest t** unto 7105
23:20 slew a lion in the midst of a pit in **t** of 3117
24:15 from the morning even to the **t** appointed: 6256
1Ki 1: 6 his father had not displeased him at **any t** in 3117
2:26 I will not at this **t** put thee to death, because 3117
8:65 at that **t** Solomon held a feast, and all Israel 6256
9: 2 LORD appeared to Solomon the **second t**, 8145
11:29 it came to pass at that **t** when Jeroboam 6256
11:42 the **t** that Solomon reigned in Jerusalem 3117
14: 1 At that **t** Abijah the son of Jeroboam fell 6256
15:23 Nevertheless in the **t** of his old age he was 6256
18:29 they prophesied until *the* **t** of the offering of NIH
18:34 he said, **Do** *it* **the second t**. And they did *it* 8138
18:34 they **did** *it* **the second t**. And he said, Do *it* 8138
18:34 he said, **Do** *it* **the third t**. And they did *it* 8027
18:34 the third time. And they **did** *it* **the third t**. 8027
18:36 it came to pass at *the* **t** *of* the offering of NIH
18:44 it came to pass at the seventh **t**, that he said, NIH
19: 2 of one of them *by* to morrow about *this* **t**. 6256
19: 7 of the LORD came again the **second t**, 8145
20: 6 servants unto thee to morrow about *this* **t**, 6256
2Ki 3: 6 Jehoram went out of Samaria the same **t**, 3117
4:16 About this season, according to the **t** of life, 6256
4:17 had said unto her, according to the **t** of life. 6256
5:26 *Is it* a **t** to receive money, and to receive 6256
7: 1 To morrow about *this* **t** *shall* a measure of 6256
7:18 shall be to morrow about *this* **t** in the gate 6256
8:22 Then Libnah revolted at the same **t**. 6256
10: 6 Then he wrote a letter the **second t** to them, 8145
10: 6 come to me to Jezreel by to morrow *this* **t**. 6256
10:36 the **t** that Jehu reigned over Israel in 3117
2Ki 16: 6 At that **t** Rezin king of Syria recovered 6256
18:16 At that **t** did Hezekiah cut off *the gold from* 6256
20:12 At that **t** Berodach-baladan, the son of 6256
24:10 At that **t** the servants of Nebuchadnezzar 6256
1Ch 9:20 was the ruler over them **in t past**, 6440+3807.1
9:25 *were* to come after seven days from **t** to 6256
9:25 after seven days from time to **t** with them. 6256
11: 2 *And* moreover **in t past**, even when 8032+8543
11:11 against three hundred slain *by him* at one **t**. 6471
12:22 For at *that* **t** day by day there came to 6256
17:10 since the **t** that I commanded judges *to be* 3117
20: 1 at the **t** that kings go out *to battle*, Joab led 6256
20: 4 **at which t** Sibbechai the Hushathite slew 227
21:28 At that **t** when David saw that the LORD 6256
29:22 the son of David king the **second t**, 8145
29:27 the **t** that he reigned over Israel *was* forty 3117
2Ch 7: 8 Also at the same **t** Solomon kept the feast 6256
13:18 of Israel were brought under at that **t**, 6256
15:11 they offered unto the LORD the same **t**, 3117
16: 7 at that **t** Hanani the seer came to Asa king 6256
16:10 oppressed *some* of the people the same **t**. 6256
18:34 about the **t** of the sun going down he died. 6256
21:10 The same **t** also did Libnah revolt from 6256
21:19 that **in process of t**, 3117+3117+4480+3807.1
24:11 that at *what* **t** the chest was brought unto 6256
25:27 Now after the **t** that Amaziah did turn away 6256
28:16 At that **t** did king Ahaz send unto the kings 6256
28:22 in the **t** of his distress did he trespass yet 6256
30: 3 For they could not keep it at that **t**, because 6256
30: 5 For they had not done *it* of a long *t in such* NIH
30:26 for since the **t** of Solomon the son of David 3117
35:17 that were present kept the passover at that **t**, 6256
Ezr 4:10 *are on this* side the river, and at **such a t**. 3706
4:11 men *on this* side the river, and **at such a t**. 3706
4:15 moved sedition within the same of old **t**: 3118
4:17 beyond the river: Peace, and **at such a t**. 3706
4:19 it is found that this city of old **t** *hath* made 3118
5: 3 At the same **t** came to them Tatnai, 2166
5:16 since **that t** even until now *hath it been* in 116
7:12 of heaven, perfect *peace*, and **at such a t**. 3706
8:34 and all the weight was written at that **t**. 6256
10:13 *it is* a **t** of much rain, and *we are* not able to 6256
Ne 2: 6 the king to send me; and I set him a **t**. 2165
4:16 it came to pass from that **t** forth, *that* 3117
4:22 Likewise at the same **t** said I unto 6256
5:14 Moreover from the **t** that I was appointed to 3117
6: 1 (though at that **t** I had not set up the doors 6256
6: 5 the fifth **t** with an open letter in his hand; 6471
9:27 in the **t** of their trouble, when they cried 6256
9:32 since the **t** of the kings of Assyria unto this 3117
12:44 at that **t** were some appointed over 3117
13: 6 in all this *t* was not I at Jerusalem: for in NIH
13:21 From that **t** forth came they no *more* on 6256
Est 2:19 were gathered together the **second t**, 8145
4:14 if thou altogether holdest thy peace at this **t**, 6256
4:14 come to the kingdom for *such* a **t** as this? 6256
8: 9 were the king's scribes called at that **t** in 6256
9:27 according to their *appointed* **t** every year; 2165
Job 6:17 What **t** they wax warm, they vanish: 6256
7: 1 *Is there* not an **appointed t** to man upon 6635
9:19 of judgment, who shall **set** me **a t** *to plead?* 3259
14:13 that thou wouldest appoint me a **set t**, and 2706
14:14 all the days of my **appointed t** will I wait, 6635
15:32 It shall be accomplished before his **t**, and 3117
22:16 Which were cut down out of **t**, 6256
30: 3 flying *into* the wilderness **in former t** 570
38:23 Which I have reserved against the **t** of 6256
39: 1 Knowest thou the **t** when the wild goats of 6256
39: 2 knowest thou the **t** when they bring forth? 6256
39:18 What **t** she lifteth up herself on high, 6256
Ps 4: 7 more than *in* the **t** *that* their corn and 6256
21: 9 them as a fiery oven in the **t** of thine anger: 6256
27: 5 For in the **t** of trouble he shall hide me in 3117
32: 6 unto thee in a **t** when thou mayest be found: 6256
37:19 They shall not be ashamed in the evil **t**: and 6256
37:39 *he is* their strength in the **t** of trouble. 6256
41: 1 the LORD will deliver him in **t** of trouble. 3117
56: 3 *What* **t** I am afraid, I will trust in thee. 3117
69:13 *is* unto thee, O LORD, *in* an acceptable **t**: 6256
71: 9 Cast me not off in the **t** of old age; 6256
78:38 **many a t** turned he his anger away, and 7235
81: 3 in the **t appointed**, on our solemn feast 3677
81:15 but their **t** should have endured for ever. 6256
89:47 Remember how **short** my **t** is: 2465
102:13 for the **t** to favour her, yea, the set time, 6256
102:13 time to favour her, yea, the **set t**, is come. 4150
105:19 Until the **t** that his word came: the word of 6256
113: 2 the name of the LORD from **this t forth** 6258
115:18 we will bless the LORD from **this t forth** 6258
119:126 *It is* **t** *for thee*, LORD, to work: *for* they 6256
121: 8 and thy coming in from **this t forth**, 6258
129: 1 **Many a t** have they afflicted me from my 7227
129: 2 **Many a t** have they afflicted me from my 7227
Pr 25:13 As the cold of snow in the **t** of harvest, *so* 3117
25:19 Confidence in an unfaithful *man* in **t** of 3117
31:25 and she shall rejoice in **t** to come. 3117
Ecc 1:10 it hath been already of **old t**, 5769+3807.1
3: 1 and a **t** to every purpose under the heaven: 6256
3: 2 A **t** to be born, and a time to die; a time to 6256
3: 2 A time to be born, and a **t** to die; a time to 6256
3: 2 a **t** to plant, and a time to pluck up *that* 6256
3: 2 and a **t** to pluck up *that which is* planted; 6256
3: 3 A **t** to kill, and a time to heal; a time to 6256
3: 3 A time to kill, and a **t** to heal; a time to build 6256
3: 3 a **t** to break down, and a time to build *up;* 6256
3: 3 a time to break down, and a **t** to build *up;* 6256
3: 4 A **t** to weep, and a time to laugh; a time to 6256
3: 4 A time to weep, and a **t** to laugh; a time to 6256
3: 4 to laugh; a **t** to mourn, and a time to dance; 6256
3: 4 to laugh; a time to mourn, and a **t** to dance; 6256
3: 5 A **t** to cast away stones, and a time to 6256
3: 5 and a **t** to gather stones together; 6256
3: 5 a **t** to embrace, and a time to refrain from 6256
3: 5 and a **t** to refrain from embracing; 6256
3: 6 A **t** to get, and a time to lose; a time to 6256
Ecc 3: 6 A time to get, and a **t** to lose; a time to 6256
3: 6 to lose; a **t** to keep, and a time to cast away; 6256
3: 6 to lose; a time to keep, and a **t** to cast away; 6256
3: 7 A **t** to rent, and a time to sew; a time to 6256
3: 7 A time to rent, and a **t** to sew; a time to 6256
3: 7 a **t** to keep silence, and a time to speak; 6256
3: 7 a time to keep silence, and a **t** to speak; 6256
3: 8 A **t** to love, and a time to hate; a time of 6256
3: 8 A time to love, and a **t** to hate; a time of 6256
3: 8 to hate; a **t** of war, and a time of peace. 6256
3: 8 to hate; a time of war, and a **t** of peace. 6256
3:11 He hath made every *thing* beautiful in his **t**: 6256
3:17 for *there is* a **t** there for every purpose and 6256
7:17 why shouldest thou die before thy **t**? 6256
8: 5 a wise *man's* heart discerneth *both* **t** and 6256
8: 6 Because to every purpose there is **t** and 6256
8: 9 *there is* a **t** wherein one man ruleth over 6256
9:11 but **t** and chance happeneth to them all. 6256
9:12 For man also knoweth not his **t**: as 6256
9:12 so *are* the sons of men snared in an evil **t**, 6256
SS 2:12 the **t** of the singing *of birds* is come, and 6256
Isa 11:11 **second t** to recover the remnant of his 8145
13:22 her **t** *is* near to come, and her days shall not 6256
16:13 hath spoken concerning Moab since that **t**. 227
18: 7 In that **t** shall the present be brought unto 6256
20: 2 At the same **t** spake the LORD by Isaiah 6256
26:17 *that* **draweth near the t** of her delivery, 7126
28:19 From the **t** that it goeth forth it shall take 1767
30: 8 that it may be for the **t** to come for ever and 3117
33: 2 our salvation also in the **t** of trouble. 6256
39: 1 At that **t** Merodach-baladan, the son of 6256
42:14 I have **long t** holden my peace; I have been 5769
42:23 *who* will hearken and hear for the **t to come**? 268
44: 8 have not I told thee from **that t**, and 227
45:21 who hath declared this from **ancient t**? 6924
45:21 *who* hath told it from **that t**? *have* not I 227
48: 6 I have shewed thee new *things* from **this t**, 6258
48: 8 from **that t** *that* thine ear was not opened: 227
48:16 from the **t** that it was, there *am* I: 6256
49: 8 In an acceptable **t** have I heard thee, and 6256
60:22 I the LORD will hasten it in his **t**. 6256
Jer 1:13 of the LORD came unto me the **second t**, 8145
2:20 For **of old t** I have broken thy yoke, 4480+5769
2:27 in the **t** of their trouble they will say, Arise, 6256
2:28 if they can save thee in the **t** of thy trouble: 6256
3: 4 Wilt thou not from **this t** cry unto me, 6258
3:17 At that **t** they shall call Jerusalem 6256
4:11 At that **t** shall it be said to this people and 6256
6:15 at the **t** *that* I visit them they shall be cast 6256
8: 1 At that **t**, saith the LORD, they shall bring 6256
8: 7 the swallow observe the **t** of their coming; 6256
8:12 in the **t** of their visitation they shall be cast 6256
8:15 but no good *came; and* for a **t** of health, and 6256
10:15 in the **t** of their visitation they shall perish. 6256
11:12 they shall not save them at all in the **t** of 6256
11:14 for I will not hear *them* in the **t** that they 6256
13: 3 of the LORD came unto me the **second t**, 8145
14: 8 of Israel, the saviour thereof in **t** of trouble, 6256
14:19 and for the **t** of healing, and behold trouble. 6256
15:11 enemy to entreat thee *well* in the **t** of evil, 6256
15:11 in the time of evil, and in the **t** of affliction. 6256
18:23 deal *thus* with them in the **t** of thine anger. 6256
27: 7 son's son, until the very **t** of his land come: 6256
30: 7 it *is* even the **t** of Jacob's trouble; but 6256
31: 1 At the same **t**, saith the LORD, will I be 6256
33: 1 LORD came unto Jeremiah the **second t**, 8145
33:15 In those days, and at that **t**, will I cause 6256
39:10 them vineyards and fields at the same **t**. 3117
46:17 *but* a noise; he hath passed the **t appointed**. 4150
46:21 upon them, *and* the **t** of their visitation. 6256
49: 8 of Esau upon him, the **t** *that* I will visit him. 6256
49:19 who will **appoint** me **the t**? and who *is* that 3259
50: 4 In those days, and in that **t**, saith 6256
50:16 him that handleth the sickle in the **t** of 6256
50:20 In those days, and in that **t**, saith 6256
50:27 their day is come, the **t** of their visitation. 6256
50:31 thy day is come, the **t** *that* I will visit thee. 6256
50:44 who will **appoint** me **the t**? and who *is* that 3259
51: 6 for this *is* the **t** of the LORD'S vengeance; 6256
51:18 in the **t** of their visitation they shall perish. 6256
51:33 *is* like a threshingfloor, *it is* **t** to thresh her: 6256
51:33 and the **t** of her harvest shall come. 6256
La 5:20 forget us for ever, *and* forsake us so long **t**? 3117
Eze 4:10 a day: from **t** to time shalt thou eat it. 6256
4:10 a day: from time to **t** shalt thou eat it. 6256
4:11 of a hin: from **t** to time shalt thou drink. 6256
4:11 of a hin: from time to **t** shalt thou drink. 6256
7: 7 the **t** is come, the day of trouble *is* near, and 6256
7:12 The **t** is come, the day draweth near: let not 6256
16: 8 behold, thy **t** *was* the time of love; 6256
16: 8 behold, thy time *was* the **t** of love; 6256
16:57 as *at* the **t** of *thy* reproach of the daughters 6256
21:14 let the sword be doubled the **third t**, 7992
22: 3 that her **t** may come, and maketh idols 6256
26:20 with the people of **old t**, and shall set thee 5769
27:34 *In* the **t** when *thou shalt be* broken by 6256
30: 3 cloudy day; it shall be the **t** of the heathen. 6256
35: 5 force of the sword in the **t** of their calamity, 6256
35: 5 in the **t** *that their* iniquity *had* an end: 6256
38:10 *that* at the same **t** shall things come into thy 3117
38:17 *Art* thou he of whom I have spoken in old **t** 3117
38:18 it shall come to pass at the same **t** when 3117
Da 2: 8 know of certainty that ye would gain the **t**, 5732
2: 9 to speak before me, till the **t** be changed: 5732
2:16 of the king that he would give him **t**, 2166
3: 5 *That* **at what t** ye hear 0.2+1768+5732+871.2
3: 7 Therefore at that **t**, when all the people 2166
3: 8 Wherefore at that **t** certain Chaldeans came 2166
3:15 Now if ye be ready that at what **t** ye hear 5732
4:36 At the same **t** my reason returned unto me; 2166
7:12 lives were prolonged for a season and **t**. 5732
7:22 the **t** came that the saints possessed 2166
7:25 they shall be given into his hand until a **t** 5732
7:25 until a time and times and the dividing of **t**. 5732
8:17 for at the **t** of the end *shall be* the vision. 6256

Da 8:19 for at the **t appointed** the end *shall be.* 4150
8:23 in the **latter t** of their kingdom, when 319
9:21 touched me about the **t** of the evening 6256
10: 1 *was* true, but the **t appointed** *was* long: 6635
11:24 against the strong holds, even for a **t.** 6256
11:27 for yet the end *shall be* at the **t appointed.** 4150
11:29 At the **t appointed** he shall return, and 4150
11:35 make *them* white, *even* to the **t** of the end: 6256
11:35 the end: because *it is* yet for a **t appointed.** 4150
11:40 at the **t** of the end shall the king of 6256
12: 1 at that **t** shall Michael stand up, the great 6256
12: 1 there shall be a **t** of trouble, such as never 6256
12: 1 there was a nation *even* to that same **t:** 6256
12: 1 at that **t** thy people shall be delivered, 6256
12: 4 and seal the book, *even* to the **t** of the end: 6256
12: 7 that liveth for ever that *it shall be* for a **t,** 4150
12: 9 closed up and sealed till the **t** of the end. 6256
12:11 from the **t** *that* the daily *sacrifice* shall be 6256
Hos 2: 9 take *away* my corn in the **t** thereof, and 6256
9:10 as the firstripe in the fig tree at her **first t:** 7225
10:12 for *it is* **t** to seek the LORD, till he come 6256
Joel 3: 1 For behold, in those days, and in that **t,** 6256
Am 5:13 the prudent shall keep silence in that **t;** 6256
5:13 keep silence in that time; for it *is* an evil **t.** 6256
Jnh 3: 1 the LORD came unto Jonah the **second t,** 8145
Mic 2: 3 shall ye go haughtily: for this **t** *is* evil. 6256
3: 4 will even hide his face from them at that **t,** 6256
5: 3 until the **t** *that* she which travaileth hath 6256
Na 1: 9 affliction shall not rise up the **second t.** 6471
Hab 2: 3 For the vision *is* yet for an **appointed t,** but 4150
Zep 1:12 it shall come to pass at that **t,** *that* I will 6256
3:19 at that **t** I *will* undo all that afflict thee: 6256
3:20 At that **t** will I bring you *again,* even in 6256
3:20 you *again,* even in the **t** that I gather you: 6256
Hag 1: 2 This people say, The **t** is not come, 6256
1: 2 the **t** that the LORD'S house should be 6256
1: 4 *Is it* **t** for you, O ye, to dwell in your cieled 6256
Zec 10: 1 Ask ye of the LORD rain in the **t** of 6256
14: 7 to pass, *that* at evening **t** it shall be light. 6256
Mal 3:11 vine **cast** her **fruit before the t** in the field, 7921
Mt 1:11 **about the t** they were carried away to *1909*
2: 7 inquired of them diligently what **t** the star *5550*
2:16 according to the **t** which he had diligently *5550*
4: 6 **lest at any t** thou dash thy foot against a *3379*
4:17 From **that t** Jesus began to preach, and *5119*
5:21 have heard that it was said by them **of old t,** *744*
5:25 **lest at any t** the adversary deliver thee to *3379*
5:27 have heard that it was said by them **of old t,** *744*
5:33 heard that it hath been said by them **of old t,** *744*
8:29 come hither to torment us before the **t?** *2540*
11:25 At that **t** Jesus answered and said, I thank *2540*
12: 1 At that **t** Jesus went on the sabbath day *2540*
13:15 **lest at any t** they should see with *their* *3379*
13:30 in the **t** of harvest I will say to the reapers, *2540*
14: 1 At that **t** Herod the tetrarch heard of *2540*
14:15 *This* is a desert place, and the **t** is now past; *5610*
16:21 From **that t forth** began Jesus to shew unto *5119*
18: 1 At the same **t** came the disciples unto Jesus, *5610*
21:34 And when the **t** of the fruit drew near, *2540*
24:21 the beginning of the world to **this t,** *3568+3588*
25:19 After a long **t** the lord of those servants *5550*
26:16 And from that **t** he sought opportunity to *5119*
26:18 The Master saith, My **t** is at hand; *2540*
26:42 He went away again the **second t,** *1208+1537*
26:44 away again, and prayed the **third t,** *1537+5154*
Mk 1:15 And saying, The **t** is fulfilled, *2540*
4:12 **lest at any t** they should be converted, and *3379*
4:17 in themselves, and so endure but **for a t;** *4340*
6:35 a desert place, and now the **t** *is* far passed: *5610*
10:30 shall receive an hundredfold now in this **t,** *2540*
11:13 but leaves; for the **t** of figs was not *yet.* *2540*
13:19 which God created unto **this t,** *3568+3588*
13:33 and pray: for ye know not when the **t** is. *2540*
14:41 And he cometh the **third t,** and saith unto *5154*
14:72 And the **second t** *the* cock crew. *1208+1537*
Lk 1:10 were praying without at the **t** of incense. *5610*
1:57 Now Elisabeth's full **t** came that she should *5550*
4: 5 kingdoms of the world in a moment of **t.** *5550*
4:11 **lest at any t** thou dash thy foot against a *3379*
4:27 And many lepers were in Israel **in the t of** *1909*
7:45 this *woman* **since the t** I came in hath *575+3739*
8:13 and in **t** of temptation fall away. *2540*
8:27 which had devils long **t,** and ware no *5550*
9:51 when the **t** was come that he should be *2250*
12: 1 **In the mean t,** when there were *1722+3739*
12:56 but how *is it that* ye do not discern this **t?** *2540*
13:35 see me, until *the* **t** come when ye shall say, NIG
14:17 And sent his servant at supper **t** to say to *5610*
15:29 **neither** transgressed I **at any t** thy *2532+3763*
16:16 since **that t** the kingdom of God is *5119*
18:30 not receive manifold more in this *present* **t,** *2540*
19:44 thou knewest not the **t** of thy visitation. *2540*
20: 9 and went into a far country for a long **t.** *5550*
21: 8 saying, I am *Christ;* and the **t** draweth near: *2540*
21:34 **lest at any t** your hearts be overcharged *3379*
21:37 And in the **day t** he was teaching in *2250*
23: 7 who himself also was at Jerusalem at that **t.** *2250*
23:22 And he said unto them the **third t,** Why, *5154*
Jn 1:18 No *man* hath seen God **at any t;** the only *4455*
3: 4 can he enter the **second t** into his mother's *1208*
5: 6 knew that he had been now a long **t** *in that* *5550*
5:37 Ye have neither heard his voice **at any t,** *4455*
6:66 From that **t** many of his disciples went back, NIG
7: 6 Jesus said unto them, My **t** is not yet come: *2540*
7: 6 is not yet come: but your **t** is alway ready. *2540*
7: 8 this feast; for my **t** is not yet full come. *2540*
11:39 saith unto him, Lord, **by this t** he stinketh: *2235*
14: 9 Have I been so long **t** with you, and *5550*
16: 2 yea, the **t** cometh, that whosoever killeth *5610*
16: 4 have I told you, that when the **t** shall come, *5610*
16:25 but the **t** cometh, when I shall no more *5610*
21:14 This *is* now the **third t** *that* Jesus shewed *5154*
21:16 He saith to him again the **second t,** Simon, *1208*
21:17 He saith unto him the **third t,** Simon, *5154*
21:17 because he said unto him the **third t,** *5154*

Ac 1: 6 wilt thou at this **t** restore again the kingdom *5550*
1:21 with us all the **t** that the Lord Jesus went in *5550*
7:13 And at the second **t** Joseph was made NIG
7:17 But when the **t** of the promise drew nigh, *5550*
7:20 In which **t** Moses was born, and *2540*
8: 1 And at that **t** there was a great persecution *2250*
8:11 that of long **t** *he* had bewitched them with *5550*
10:15 *spake* unto him again the **second t,** *1208+1537*
11: 8 **nothing** common or unclean hath
at any t *3763+3956*
12: 1 Now about that **t** Herod the king stretched *2540*
13:18 And about the **t** of forty years suffered he *5550*
14: 3 Long **t** therefore abode they speaking *5550*
14:28 And there they abode long **t** with *5550*
15:21 For Moses of old **t** hath in every city them *1074*
17:21 strangers which were there **spent** their **t** in *2119*
18:20 When they desired *him* to tarry longer **t** *5550*
18:23 And after he had spent some **t** *there,* he *5550*
19:23 And the same **t** there arose no small stir *2540*
20:16 because he would not **spend** the **t** in Asia: *5551*
24:25 and answered, Go *thy way* for *this* **t;** *3568*
27: 9 Now when much **t** was spent, and *5550*
Ro 3:26 To declare, *I say,* at this **t** his righteousness: *2540*
5: 6 in due **t** Christ died for the ungodly. *2540*
8:18 **t** *are* not worthy to be compared with *2540*
9: 9 At this **t** will I come, and Sara shall have a *2540*
11: 5 at *this* present **t** also there is a remnant *2540*
13:11 And that, knowing the **t,** that now *it is* high *2540*
13:11 **now** *it is* **high t** to awake out of *2235+5610*
1Co 4: 5 Therefore judge nothing before the **t,** *2540*
7: 5 the other, except *it be* with consent for a **t,** *2540*
7:29 But this I say, brethren, the **t** *is* short: *2540*
9: 7 Who goeth a warfare **any t** at his own *4218*
15: 8 of me also, as of one **born out of due t.** *1626*
16:12 but *his* will was not at all to come **at this t;** *3568*
16:12 come when he shall **have convenient t.** *2119*
2Co 6: 2 I have heard thee in a **t** accepted, and in *2540*
6: 2 behold, now *is* the accepted **t;** behold, *2540*
8:14 *that* now at *this* **t** your abundance *may be* a *2540*
12:14 the third **t** I am ready to come to you; NIG
13: 1 This *is* the third **t** I am coming to you. In NIG
13: 2 *you,* as if I were present the second **t;** NIG
Gal 1:13 conversation **in t past** in the Jews' religion, *4218*
4: 2 governors until the **t appointed** of *4287*
4: 4 But when the fulness of the **t** was come, *5550*
5:21 as I have also **told** *you* **in t past,** *4302*
Eph 2: 2 Wherein **in t past** ye walked according to *4218*
2:11 that ye *being* **in t passed** Gentiles in *4218*
2:12 That at that **t** ye were without Christ, *2540*
5:16 Redeeming the **t,** because the days are evil. *2540*
Col 4: 5 them that are without, redeeming the **t.** *2540*
1Th 2: 5 For neither **at any t** used we flattering *4218*
2:17 being taken from you for a short **t** in *2540*
2Th 2: 6 that he might be revealed in his **t.** *2540*
1Ti 2: 6 a ransom for all, to be testified in due **t.** *2540*
6:19 a good foundation against the **t to come,** *3195*
2Ti 4: 3 For the **t** will come when they will not *2540*
4: 6 and the **t** of my departure is at hand. *2540*
4: S Paul was brought before Nero the second **t.** NIG
Phm 1:11 Which **in t past** was to thee unprofitable, *4218*
Heb 1: 1 **in t** past unto the fathers by **the** prophets, *3588*
1: 5 unto which of the angels said he **at any t,** *4218*
1:13 But to which of the angels said he **at any t,** *4218*
2: 1 **lest at any t** we should let *them* slip. *3379*
4: 7 saying in David, To day, after so long a **t;** *5550*
4:16 and find grace to help in **t of need.** *2121*
5:12 For when for the **t** ye ought to be teachers, *5550*
9: 9 Which *was* a figure for the **t** *then* present, *2540*
9:10 imposed *on them* until the **t** of reformation. *2540*
9:28 **second t** without sin unto salvation. *1208+1537*
11:32 for the **t** would fail me to tell of Gedeon, *5550*
Jas 4:14 that appeareth for a little **t,** and then NIG
1Pe 1: 5 salvation ready to be revealed in the last **t.** *2540*
1:11 what manner of **t** the Spirit of Christ which *2540*
1:17 pass the **t** of your sojourning *here* in fear: *5550*
2:10 Which **in t past** *were* not a people, but *4218*
3: 5 For after this manner **in the old t** the holy *4218*
4: 2 rest of *his* **t** in the flesh to the lusts of men, *5550*
4: 3 For the **t** past of *our* life may suffice us to *5550*
4:17 For the **t** *is come* that judgment must begin *2540*
5: 6 of God, that he may exalt you in **due t:** *2540*
2Pe 1:21 For the prophecy came not **in old t** by *4218*
2: 3 whose judgment now **of a long t** lingereth *1597*
2:13 that count it pleasure to riot in the day **t.** NIG
1Jn 2:18 Little children, it is the last **t:** and as ye *5610*
2:18 whereby we know that it is the last **t.** *5610*
4:12 No *man* hath seen God **at any t.** If we love *4455*
Jude 1:18 you there should be mockers in the last **t,** *5550*
Rev 1: 3 are written therein: for the **t** *is* at hand. *2540*
10: 6 are therein, that there should be **t** no longer: *5550*
11:18 thy wrath is come, and the **t** of the dead, *2540*
12:12 he knoweth that he hath *but* a short **t.** *2540*
12:14 where she is nourished for a **t,** and times, *2540*
12:14 and times, and half a **t,** from the face of *2540*
14:15 for the **t** is come for thee to reap; for *5610*
22:10 prophecy of this book: for the **t** is at hand. *2540*

TIMES (146) [TIME]

Ge 27:36 for he hath supplanted me these **two t:** he 6471
31: 7 deceived me, and changed my wages ten **t;** 4489
31:41 and thou hast changed my wages ten **t.** 4489
33: 3 and bowed himself to the ground seven **t,** 6471
43:34 Benjamin's mess was five **t** so much as any 3027
Ex 23:14 Three **t** thou shalt keep a feast unto me in 7272
23:17 Three **t** in the year all thy males shall 6471
Lev 4: 6 sprinkle of the blood seven **t** before 6471
4:17 sprinkle *it* seven **t** before the LORD, 6471
8:11 he sprinkled thereof upon the altar seven **t,** 6471
14: 7 is to be cleansed from the leprosy seven **t,** 6471
14:16 with his finger seven **t** before the LORD: 6471
14:27 in his left hand seven **t** before the LORD: 6471
14:51 and sprinkle the house seven **t:** 6471
16: 2 that he come not at all **t** into the holy *place* 6256
16:14 of the blood with his finger seven **t.** 6471
16:19 of the blood upon it with his finger seven **t,** 6471

Lev 19:26 shall ye use enchantment, nor **observe t.** 6049
25: 8 of years unto thee, seven **t** seven years; 6471
26:18 I will punish you seven **t** more for your sins. NIH
26:21 I will bring seven **t** moe plagues upon you NIH
26:24 will punish you yet seven **t** for your sins. NIH
26:28 will chastise you seven **t** for your sins. NIH
Nu 14:22 have tempted me *now* these ten **t,** and 6471
19: 4 the tabernacle of the congregation seven **t:** 6471
22:28 that thou hast smitten me these three **t?** 7272
22:32 hast thou smitten thine ass these three **t?** 7272
22:33 saw me, and turned from me these three **t:** 7272
24: 1 he went not, as **at other t,** to 6471+6471+871.1
24:10 hast altogether blessed *them* these three **t.** 6471
Dt 1:11 God of your fathers make you a thousand **t** 6471
2:10 Emims dwelt therein **in t past,** 6440+3807.1
4:42 hated him not **in t past;** 4480+8032+8543
16:16 Three **t** in a year shall all thy males appear 6471
18:10 *or* an **observer of t,** or an enchanter, or 6049
18:14 hearkened unto **observers of t,** and 6049
Jos 6: 4 day ye shall compass the city seven **t,** 6471
6:15 the city after the same manner seven **t:** 6471
6:15 that day they compassed the city seven **t.** 6471
Jdg 13:25 began to **move** him **at t** in the camp of Dan, 6470
16:15 thou hast mocked me these three **t,** and 6471
16:20 I will go out as **at other t** 6471+6471+871.1
20:30 against Gibeah, as **at other t.** 6471+6471+871.1
20:31 as **at other t,** in the highways, 6471+6471+871.1
1Sa 3:10 and called as **at other t,** 6471+6471+871.1
18:10 with his hand, as **at other t:** 3117+3117+871.1
19: 7 he was in his presence, as **in t past.** 865+8032
20:25 **at other t,** *even* upon a seat 6471+6471+871.1
20:41 to the ground, and bowed himself three **t:** 6471
2Sa 3:17 **in t past** to be king over 1571+1571+8032+8543
1Ki 8:59 of his people Israel **at all t,** 3117+3117+871.1
9:25 three **t** in a year did Solomon offer burnt 6471
17:21 he stretched himself upon the child three **t,** 6471
18:43 *is* nothing. And he said, Go again seven **t.** 6471
22:16 How many **t** shall I adjure thee that thou 6471
2Ki 4:35 the child neesed seven **t,** and the child 6471
5:10 Go and wash in Jordan seven **t,** and 6471
5:14 and dipped *himself* seven **t** in Jordan, 6471
13:19 *Thou* shouldest have smitten five or six **t;** 6471
13:25 Three **t** did Joash beat him, and 6471
19:25 *and* of ancient **t** that I have formed it? 3117
21: 6 **observed t,** and used enchantments, and 6049
1Ch 12:32 *were men* that had understanding of the **t,** 6256
21: 3 The LORD make his people an hundred **t** 6471
29:30 the **t** that went over him, and over Israel, 6256
2Ch 8:13 on the solemn feasts, three **t** in the year, 6471
15: 5 in those **t** *there was* no peace to him that 6256
18:15 How many **t** shall I adjure thee that thou 6471
33: 6 also he **observed t,** and used enchantments, 6049
Ezr 10:14 wives in our cities come at appointed **t,** 6256
Ne 4:12 by them came, they said unto us ten **t,** 6471
6: 4 Yet they sent unto me four **t** after this sort; 6471
9:28 many **t** didst thou deliver them according to 6256
10:34 of our fathers, at **t** appointed year by year, 6256
13:31 at **t** appointed, and for the firstfruits. 6256
Est 1:13 said to the wise *men,* which knew the **t,** 6256
9:31 To confirm these days of Purim in their **t** 2165
Job 19: 3 These ten **t** have ye reproached me: you are 6471
24: 1 seeing **t** are not hidden from the Almighty, 6256
Ps 9: 9 for the oppressed, a refuge in **t** of trouble. 6256
10: 1 *why* hidest thou *thyself* in **t** of trouble? 6256
12: 6 tried in a furnace of earth, purified **seven t.** 7659
31:15 My **t** *are* in thy hand: deliver me from 6256
34: 1 I will bless the LORD at all **t:** his praise 6256
44: 1 thou didst in their days, in the **t** of old. 3117
62: 8 Trust in him at all **t;** ye people, pour out 6256
77: 5 the days of old, the years of **ancient t.** 5769
106: 3 *and* he that doeth righteousness at all **t.** 6256
106:43 Many **t** did he deliver them; but 6471
119:20 *that it hath* unto thy judgments at all **t.** 6256
119:164 Seven **t** a day do I praise thee because NIH
Pr 5:19 let her breasts satisfy thee at all **t;** and 6256
17:17 A friend loveth at all **t,** and a brother is 6256
24:16 For a just *man* falleth seven **t,** and riseth up NIH
Ecc 8:12 Though a sinner do evil an hundred **t,** and NIH
Isa 14:31 and none *shall be* alone in his **appointed t.** 4151
33: 6 knowledge shall be the stability of thy **t,** 6256
37:26 *and* of ancient **t,** that I have formed it? 3117
46:10 from **ancient t** *the things* that are not *yet* 6924
Jer 8: 7 in the heaven knoweth her **appointed t;** 4150
Eze 12:27 and he prophesieth of the **t** *that are* far off. 6256
Da 1:20 he found them ten **t** better than all 3027
2:21 he changeth the **t** and the seasons: 5732
3:19 seven **t** more than *it was* wont to be heat. NIH
4:16 unto him; and let seven **t** pass over him. 5732
4:23 of the field, till seven **t** pass over him; 5732
4:25 of heaven, and seven **t** shall pass over thee, 5732
4:32 as oxen, and seven **t** shall pass over thee, 5732
6:10 he kneeled upon his knees three **t** a day, 2166
6:13 but maketh his petition three **t** a day. 2166
7:10 ten thousand **t** ten thousand stood before NIH
7:25 most High, and think to change **t** and laws: 2166
7:25 until a time and **t** and the dividing of time. 5732
9:25 and the wall, even in troublous **t.** 6256
11: 6 and he that strengthened her in *these* **t.** 6256
11:14 in those **t** there shall many stand up against 6256
12: 7 ever that *it shall be* for a time, **t,** and a half; 4150
Mt 16: 3 but can ye not *discern* the signs of the **t?** *2540*
18:21 against me, and I forgive him? till **seven t?** *2034*
18:22 unto him, I say not unto thee, Until **seven t:** *2034*
18:22 seven times: but, Until **seventy t** seven. *1441*
Lk 17: 4 And if he trespass against thee **seven t** in a *2034*
17: 4 and **seven t** in a day turn again to thee, *2034*
21:24 until the **t** of the Gentiles be fulfilled. *2540*
Ac 1: 7 It is not for you to know *the* **t** or *5550*
3:19 when *the* **t** of refreshing shall come from *2540*
3:21 Whom the heaven must receive until the **t** *5550*
11:10 And this was done **three t:** and *1909+5151*
14:16 Who in **t** past suffered all nations to walk in *1074*
17:26 and hath determined the **t** before appointed, *2540*
17:30 And the **t** of *this* ignorance God winked at; *5550*
Ro 11:30 For as ye **in t past** have not believed God, *4218*

T

2Co 11:24 Of the Jews **five t** received I forty *stripes* 3999
Gal 1:23 That he which persecuted us **in t past** now 4218
4:10 observe days, and months, and **t**, and years. 2540
Eph 1:10 That in the dispensation of the fulness of **t** 2540
2: 3 **in t past** in the lusts of our flesh, 4218
1Th 5: 1 But of the **t** and the seasons, brethren, 5550
1Ti 4: 1 that in the latter **t** some shall depart from 2540
6:15 Which in his **t** he shall shew, *who is* 2540
2Ti 3: 1 that in the last days perilous **t** shall come. 2540
Tit 1: 3 But hath in due **t** manifested his word 2540
Heb 1: 1 who at sundry **t** and in divers manners 4181
1Pe 1:20 but was manifest in *these* last **t** for you, 5550
Rev 5:11 the number of them was ten thousand **t** ten NIG
12:14 and **t**, and half a time, from the face of 2540

TIMEUS (1)
Mk 10:46 of people, blind Bartimeus, the son of **T**, 5090

TIMNA (4)
Ge 36:12 **T** was concubine to Eliphaz Esau's son; 8555
36:22 and Hemam; and Lotan's sister *was* **T**. 8555
1Ch 1:36 and Gatam, Kenaz, and **T**, and Amalek. 8555
1:39 and Homam: and **T** *was* Lotan's sister. 8555

TIMNAH (5)
Ge 36:40 duke **T**, duke Alvah, duke Jetheth, 8555
Jos 15:10 down *to* Beth-shemesh, and passed on *to* **T**: 8553
15:57 Cain, Gibeah, and **T**; ten cities with their 8553
1Ch 1:51 duke **T**, duke Aliah, duke Jetheth, 8555
2Ch 28:18 **T** with the villages thereof, Gimzo also and 8553

TIMNATH (8)
Ge 38:12 and went up unto his sheepshearers to **T**, he 8553
38:13 Behold thy father in law goeth up to **T** to 8553
38:14 in an open place, which *is* by the way to **T**; 8553
Jdg 14: 1 Samson went down *to* **T**, and saw a woman 8553
14: 1 saw a woman in **T** of the daughters of 8553
14: 2 I have seen a woman in **T** of the daughters 8553
14: 5 *to* **T**, and came to the vineyards of 8553
14: 5 and came to the vineyards of **T**: 8553

TIMNATH-HERES (1) [TIMNATH-SERAH]
Jdg 2: 9 him in the border of his inheritance in **T**, 8556

TIMNATH-SERAH (2) [TIMNATH-HERES]
Jos 19:50 which he asked, *even* **T** in mount Ephraim: 8556
24:30 him in the border of his inheritance in **T**, 8556

TIMNITE (1)
Jdg 15: 6 the son in law of the **T**, because he had 8554

TIMON (1)
Ac 6: 5 and **T**, and Parmenas, and Nicolas a 5096

TIMOTHEUS (19) [TIMOTHY]
Ac 16: 1 named **T**, the son of a certain woman, 5095
17:14 to the sea: but Silas and **T** abode there still. 5095
17:15 and **T** for to come to him with all speed, 5095
18: 5 and **T** were come from Macedonia, 5095
19:22 that ministered unto him, **T** and Erastus; 5095
20: 4 and Gaius of Derbe, and **T**; and of Asia, 5095
Ro 16:21 **T** my workfellow, and Lucius, and Jason, 5095
1Co 4:17 For this cause have I sent unto you **T**, 5095
16:10 Now if **T** come, see that he may be with 5095
16: S and Fortunatus, and Achaicus, and **T**. 5095
2Co 1:19 *even* by me and Silvanus and **T**, was not 5095
Php 1: 1 Paul and **T**, the servants of Jesus Christ, 5095
2:19 But I trust in the Lord Jesus to send **T** 5095
Col 1: 1 by the will of God, and **T** *our* brother, 5095
1Th 1: 1 Paul, and Silvanus, and **T**, unto the church 5095
3: 2 And sent **T**, our brother, and minister of 5095
3: 6 But now when **T** came from you unto us, 5095
2Th 1: 1 Paul, and Silvanus, and **T**, unto the church 5095
2Ti 4: S The second *epistle* unto **T**, ordained 5095

TIMOTHY (9) [TIMOTHEUS]
2Co 1: 1 and **T** *our* brother, unto the church of God 5095
1Ti 1: 2 Unto **T**, *my* own son in the faith: Grace, 5095
1:18 This charge I commit unto thee, son **T**, 5095
6:20 O **T**, keep that which is committed to *thy* 5095
6: S The first to **T** was written from Laodicea, 5095
2Ti 1: 2 To **T**, *my* dearly beloved son: Grace, 5095
Phm 1: 1 prisoner of Jesus Christ, and **T** *our* brother, 5095
Heb 13:23 Know ye that *our* brother **T** is set at liberty; 5095
13: S Written to the Hebrews from Italy by **T**. 5095

TIN (5)
Nu 31:22 the brass, the iron, the **t**, and the lead, 913
Isa 1:25 away thy dross, and take away all thy **t**: 913
Eze 22:18 all they *are* brass, and **t**, and iron, and lead, 913
22:20 and brass, and iron, and lead, and **t**, 913
27:12 with silver, iron, **t**, and lead, they traded in 913

TINDER See TOW

TINGLE (3)
1Sa 3:11 the ears of every one that heareth it shall **t**. 6750
2Ki 21:12 heareth of it, both his ears shall **t**. 6750
Jer 19: 3 which whosoever heareth, his ears shall **t**. 6750

TINKLING (3)
Isa 3:16 *as* they go, and **making a t** with their feet: 5913
3:18 of *their* **t ornaments** *about their feet,* 5914
1Co 13: 1 am become *as* sounding brass, or a **t** cymbal. 214

TIP (9)
Ex 29:20 put *it* upon the **t** of the *right* ear of Aaron, 8571
29:20 upon the **t** of the right ear of his sons, and 8571
Lev 8:23 put *it* upon the **t** of Aaron's right ear, and 8571
8:24 Moses put of the blood upon the **t** of their 8571
14:14 the priest shall put *it* upon the **t** of the right 8571
14:17 **t** of the right ear of him that is to be 8571
14:25 put *it* upon the **t** of the right ear of him that 8571
Lev 14:28 **t** of the right ear of him that is to be 8571
Lk 16:24 that he may dip the **t** of his finger in water, 206

TIPHSAH (2)
1Ki 4:24 from **T** even to Azzah, over all the kings on 8607
2Ki 15:16 Menahem smote **T**, and all that *were* 8607

TIRAS (2)
Ge 10: 2 and Javan, and Tubal, and Meshech, and **T**. 8494
1Ch 1: 5 and Javan, and Tubal, and Meshech, and **T**. 8494

TIRATHITES (1)
1Ch 2:55 the **T**, the Shimeathites, *and* Suchathites. 8654

TIRE (1) [TIRED, TIRES]
Eze 24:17 bind the **t of** thine **head** upon thee, and 6287

TIRED (1) [TIRE]
2Ki 9:30 and **t** her head, and looked out at a window. 3190

TIRES (2) [TIRE]
Isa 3:18 and *their* **round t like the moon**, 7720
Eze 24:23 your **t** *shall be* upon your heads, and 6287

TIRHAKAH (2)
2Ki 19: 9 when he heard say of **T** king of Ethiopia, 8640
Isa 37: 9 he heard say concerning **T** king of 8640

TIRHANAH (1)
1Ch 2:48 Caleb's concubine, bare Sheber, and **T**. 8647

TIRIA (1)
1Ch 4:16 Ziph, and Ziphah, **T**, and Asareel. 8493

TIRSHATHA (5)
Ezr 2:63 the **T** said unto them, that they should not 8660
Ne 7:65 the **T** said unto them, that they should not 8660
7:70 The **T** gave to the treasure a thousand 8660
8: 9 which *is* the **T**, and Ezra the priest 8660
10: 1 the **T**, the son of Hachaliah, and Zidkijah, 8660

TIRZAH (18)
Nu 26:33 and Noah, Hoglah, Milcah, and **T**. 8656
27: 1 Noah, and Hoglah, and Milcah, and **T**. 8656
36:11 **T**, and Hoglah, and Milcah, and Noah, 8656
Jos 12:24 The king of **T**, one: all the kings thirty and 8656
17: 3 Mahlah, and Noah, Hoglah, Milcah, and **T**. 8656
1Ki 14:17 wife arose, and departed, and came to **T**: 8656
15:21 left off building of Ramah, and dwelt in **T**. 8656
15:33 son of Ahijah to reign over all Israel in **T**, 8656
16: 6 slept with his fathers, and was buried in **T**: 8656
16: 8 the son of Baasha to reign over Israel in **T**, 8656
16: 9 conspired against him, as he *was* in **T**, 8656
16: 9 house of Arza steward of *his* house in **T**. 8656
16:15 of Judah did Zimri reign seven days in **T**. 8656
16:17 all Israel with him, and they besieged **T**. 8656
16:23 twelve years: six years reigned he in **T**. 8656
2Ki 15:14 Menahem the son of Gadi went up from **T**, 8656
15:16 *were* therein, and the coasts thereof from **T**: 8656
SS 6: 4 Thou *art* beautiful, O my love, as **T**, 8656

TISHBITE (6)
1Ki 17: 1 Elijah the **T**, *who was* of the inhabitants of 8664
21:17 word of the LORD came to Elijah the **T**, 8664
21:28 word of the LORD came to Elijah the **T**, 8664
2Ki 1: 3 angel of the LORD said to Elijah the **T**, 8664
1: 8 his loins. And he said, It *is* Elijah the **T**. 8664
9:36 which he spake by his servant Elijah the **T**, 8664

TITHE (14) [TITHES, TITHING]
Lev 27:30 all the **t** of the land, *whether* of the seed of 4643
27:32 *concerning* the **t** of the herd, or of the flock, 4643
Nu 18:26 it for the LORD, *even* a tenth *part* of the **t**. 4643
Dt 12:17 Thou mayest not eat within thy gates the **t** 4643
14:22 Thou shalt **truly t** all the increase of 6237+6237
14:23 the **t** of thy corn, of thy wine, and of thine 4643
14:28 all the **t** of thine increase the same year, 4643
2Ch 31: 5 the **t** of all *things* brought they in 4643
31: 6 they also brought in the **t** of oxen and 4643
31: 6 the **t** of holy *things* which were consecrated 4643
Ne 10:38 the Levites shall bring up the **t** of the tithes 4643
13:12 Then brought all Judah the **t** of the corn and 4643
Mt 23:23 for ye **pay t** of mint and anise and cummin, 586
Lk 11:42 for ye **t** mint and rue and all *manner of* 586

TITHES (24) [TITHE]
Ge 14:20 into thy hand. And he gave him **t** of all. 4643
Lev 27:31 if a man will at all redeem *ought* of his **t**, 4643
Nu 18:24 the **t** of the children of Israel, which they 4643
18:26 When ye take of the children of Israel the **t** 4643
18:28 offering unto the LORD of all your **t**, 4643
Dt 12: 6 your **t**, and heave offerings of your hand, 4643
12:11 your **t**, and the heave offering of your hand, 4643
26:12 all the **t** of thine increase the third year, 4643
2Ch 31:12 brought in the offerings and the **t** and 4643
Ne 10:37 the **t** of our ground unto the Levites, 4643
10:37 that the same Levites *might* have the **t** in all 6237
10:38 with the Levites, when the Levites **take t**: 6237
10:38 the Levites shall bring up the tithe of the **t** 4643
12:44 for the firstfruits, and for the **t**, 4643
13: 5 the vessels, and the **t** of the corn, the new 4643
Am 4: 4 *every* morning, *and* your **t** after three years: 4643
Mal 3: 8 have we robbed thee? *In* **t** and offerings. 4643
3:10 Bring ye all the **t** into the storehouse, that 4643
Lk 18:12 in the week, I **give t** of all that I possess. 586
Heb 7: 5 to **take t** of the people according to the law, 586
7: 6 counted from them **received t** of Abraham, 1183
7: 8 And here men that die receive **t**; but 1181
7: 9 as *I* may so say, Levi also, who receiveth **t**, 1181
7: 9 who receiveth tithes, **payed t** in Abraham. 1183

TITHING (2) [TITHE]
Dt 26:12 When thou hast made an end of **t** all 6237
Dt 26:12 *which is* the year of **t**, and hast given *it* unto 4643

TITLE (3) [TITLES]
2Ki 23:17 he said, What **t** *is* that that I see? And 6725
Jn 19:19 And Pilate wrote a **t**, and put *it* on 5102
19:20 This **t** then read many of the Jews: for 5102

TITLES (2) [TITLE]
Job 32:21 neither let me **give flattering t** unto man. 3655
32:22 For I know not to **give flattering t**; *in so* 3655

TITTLE (2)
Mt 5:18 or one **t** shall in no wise pass from the law, 2762
Lk 16:17 earth to pass, than one **t** of the law to fail. 2762

TITUS (15)
2Co 2:13 because I found not **T** my brother: 5103
7: 6 comforted us by the coming of **T**; 5103
7:13 the more joyed we for the joy of **T**, 5103
7:14 so our boasting, which *I made* before **T**, 5103
8: 6 Insomuch that we desired **T**, that as he had 5103
8:16 earnest care into the heart of **T** for you. 5103
8:23 Whether *any do inquire* of **T**, *he is* my 5103
12:18 I desired **T**, and with *him* I sent a brother. 5103
12:18 Did **T** make a gain of you? walked we not 5103
13: S *a city* of Macedonia, by **T** and Lucas. 5103
Gal 2: 1 with Barnabas, and took **T** with *me* also. 5103
2: 3 But neither **T**, who was with me, being a 5103
2Ti 4:10 Crescens to Galatia, **T** unto Dalmatia. 5103
Tit 1: 4 To **T**, *mine* own son after the common 5103
3: S It was written to **T**, ordained the first 5103

TIZITE (1)
1Ch 11:45 son of Shimri, and Joha his brother, the **T**, 8491

TO (13641) [HERETOFORE, HITHERTO, INTO, THERETO, WHERETO] See Index of Articles, Etc.

TOAH (1)
1Ch 6:34 of Jeroham, the son of Eliel, the son of **T**, 8430

TOB (2)
Jdg 11: 3 his brethren, and dwelt in the land of **T**: 2897
11: 5 went to fetch Jephthah out of the land of **T**: 2897

TOB-ADONIJAH (1)
2Ch 17: 8 and Adonijah, and Tobijah, and **T**, Levites; 2899

TOBIAH (15)
Ezr 2:60 the children of **T**, the children of Nekoda, 2900
Ne 2:10 and **T** the servant, the Ammonite, 2900
2:19 **T** the servant, the Ammonite, and 2900
4: 3 Now **T** the Ammonite *was* by him, and 2900
4: 7 **T**, and the Arabians, and the Ammonites, 2900
6: 1 **T**, and Geshem the Arabian, and the rest of 2900
6:12 for **T** and Sanballat had hired him. 2900
6:14 think thou upon **T** and Sanballat according 2900
6:17 nobles of Judah sent many letters unto **T**, 2900
6:17 and *the letters* of **T** came unto them. 2900
6:19 to him. *And* **T** sent letters to put me in fear. 2900
7:62 the children of **T**, the children of Nekoda, 2900
13: 4 of the house of our God, *was* allied unto **T**: 2900
13: 7 of the evil that Eliashib did for **T**, 2900
13: 8 I cast forth all the household stuff of **T** out 2900

TOBIJAH (3)
2Ch 17: 8 and **T**, and Tob-adonijah, Levites; 2900
Zec 6:10 *even* of Heldai, of **T**, and of Jedaiah, 2900
6:14 to **T**, and to Jedaiah, and to Hen the son of 2900

TOCHEN (1)
1Ch 4:32 Ain, Rimmon, and **T**, and Ashan, 8507

TODAY See TO DAY

TOE (6) [TOES]
Ex 29:20 upon the **great t** of their right foot, and 931
Lev 8:23 and upon the **great t** of his right foot. 931
14:14 and upon the **great t** of his right foot: 931
14:17 and upon the **great t** of his right foot, 931
14:25 and upon the **great t** of his right foot: 931
14:28 and upon the **great t** of his right foot, 931

TOES (7) [TOE]
Lev 8:24 and upon the **great t** of their right feet: 931
Jdg 1: 6 and cut off his thumbs and his **great t**. 7272
1: 7 their thumbs and their **great t** cut off, 7272
2Sa 21:20 on every foot six **t**, four and twenty *in* 676
1Ch 20: 6 whose **fingers and t** *were* four and twenty, 676
Da 2:41 whereas thou sawest the feet and **t**, part of 677
2:42 And *as* the **t** of the feet *were* part of iron, and 677

TOGARMAH (4)
Ge 10: 3 of Gomer; Ashkenaz, and Riphath, and **T**. 8425
1Ch 1: 6 of Gomer; Ashchenaz, and Riphath, and **T**. 8425
Eze 27:14 They of the house of **T** traded in thy fairs 8425
38: 6 the house of **T** *of* the north quarters, and all 8425

TOGETHER (484) [ALTOGETHER]
Ge 1: 9 the heaven be **gathered t** unto one place, 6960
1:10 the **gathering t** of the waters called he 4723
3: 7 they **sewed** fig leaves **t**, and 8609
13: 6 able to bear them, that they might dwell **t**: 3162
13: 6 was great, so that they could not dwell **t**. 3162
14: 3 All these were **joined t** in the vale of 2266
22: 6 a knife; and they went both of them **t**. 3162
22: 8 burnt offering: so they went both of them **t**. 3162
22:19 and they rose up and went **t** to Beer-sheba; 3162
25:22 the children **struggled t** within her; and 7533
29: 7 *it* time that the cattle should be **gathered t**: 622
29: 8 until all the flocks be **gathered t**, and 622

Ge 29:22 Laban **gathered t** all the men of the place, 622
34:30 they shall **gather** themselves **t** against me, 622
36: 7 were more than that they might dwell **t**; 3162
42:17 And he **put** them **all t** into ward three days. 622
49: 1 unto his sons, and said, **Gather** yourselves **t**, 622
49: 2 **Gather** yourselves **t**, and hear, ye sons of 6908
Ex 2:13 two men of the Hebrews **strove t**: 5327
3:16 **gather** the elders of Israel **t**, and say unto 622
4:29 **gathered t** all the elders of the children of 622
8:14 they **gathered** them **t** upon heaps: and 6651
15: 8 of thy nostrils the waters were **gathered t**, 6192
19: 8 all the people answered **t**, and said, All that 3162
21:18 if men **strive t**, and one smite another with 7378
26: 3 The five curtains shall be **coupled t** one to 2266
26: 6 the curtains **t** with the taches: 269+413+802
26:11 and **couple** the tent **t**, that it may be one. 2266
26:24 they shall be **coupled t** beneath, and 8382
26:24 they shall be **coupled t** above 3162+8535
28: 7 edges thereof; and *so* it shall be **joined t**. 2266
30:35 the apothecary, **tempered t**, pure *and* holy: 4414
32: 1 the people **gathered** themselves **t** unto 6950
32:26 all the sons of Levi **gathered** themselves **t** 622
35: 1 **gathered** all the congregation of the children of Israel **t**, 6950
36:18 fifty taches of brass to **couple** the tent **t**, 2266
36:29 coupled **t** at the head thereof, to one ring: 3162
39: 4 made shoulderpieces for it, to **couple** *it* **t**: 2266
39: 4 by the two edges was it **coupled t**. 2266
Lev 8: 3 **gather** thou all the congregation **t** unto 6950
8: 4 the assembly was **gathered t** unto the door 6950
24:10 and a man of Israel **strove t** in the camp; 5327
26:25 when ye are **gathered t** within your cities, 622
Nu 1:18 they **assembled** all the congregation **t** on 6950
8: 9 **gather** the whole assembly of the children of Israel **t**: 6950
10: 7 when the congregation is to be **gathered t**, 6950
11:22 shall all the fish of the sea be **gathered t** for 622
14:35 that are **gathered t** against me: 3259
16: 3 they **gathered** themselves **t** against Moses 6950
16:11 all thy company *are* **gathered t** against 3259
20: 2 they **gathered** themselves **t** against Moses 6950
20: 8 **gather** thou the assembly **t**, thou, and 6950
20:10 Aaron **gathered** the congregation **t** before 6950
21:16 **Gather** the people **t**, and I will give them 622
21:23 Sihon **gathered** all his people **t**, and 622
24:10 against Balaam, and he **smote** his hands **t**: 5606
26:10 swallowed them up **t with** Korah, 2050.1
27: 3 **gathered** themselves **t** against the LORD 3259
Dt 4:10 **Gather** me the people **t**, and I will make 6950
22:10 shalt not plow with an ox and an ass **t**. 3162
22:11 of divers sorts, *as* of woollen and linen **t**. 3162
25: 5 If brethren dwell **t**, and one of them die, 3162
25:11 When men strive **t** one with another, 3162
31:12 **Gather** the people **t**, men, and women, and 6950
33: 5 *and* the tribes of Israel were gathered **t**. 3162
33:17 with them he shall push the people **t** *to* 3162
Jos 8:16 all the people that *were* in Ai were called ***t*** NIH
9: 2 That they gathered themselves **t**, to fight 3162
10: 5 **gathered** themselves **t**, and went up, they 622
10: 6 in the mountains are **gathered t** against us. 6908
11: 5 when all these kings were **met t**, they came 3259
11: 5 and pitched **t** at the waters of Merom, 3162
17:10 they **met t** in Asher on the north, and 6293
18: 1 children of Israel **assembled t** *at* Shiloh, 6950
22:12 of Israel **gathered** themselves **t** *at* Shiloh, 6950
Jdg 4:13 Sisera **gathered t** all his chariots, *even* nine 2199
6:33 and the children of the east were gathered **t**, 3162
6:38 **thrust** the fleece **t**, and wringed the dew 2115
7:23 the men of Israel **gathered** themselves **t** out 6817
7:24 the men of Ephraim **gathered** themselves **t**, 6817
9: 6 And all the men of Shechem **gathered t**, and 622
9:47 of the tower of Shechem were **gathered t**. 6908
10:17 the children of Ammon were **gathered t**, 6817
10:17 children of Israel **assembled** themselves **t**, 622
11:20 Sihon **gathered** all his people **t**, and 622
12: 1 men of Ephraim **gathered themselves t**, 6817
12: 4 Jephthah **gathered t** all the men of Gilead, 6908
16:23 the lords of the Philistines **gathered** them **t** 622
18:22 near to Micah's house were **gathered t**, 2199
19: 6 and did eat and drink both of them **t**: 3162
19:29 divided her, ***t*** with her bones, into twelve NIH
20: 1 the congregation was **gathered t** as one 6950
20:11 gathered against the city, **knit t** as one man. 2270
20:14 **gathered** themselves **t** out of the cities unto 622
1Sa 5:11 **gathered t** all the lords of the Philistines, 622
7: 6 they **gathered t** to Mizpeh, and drew water, 6908
7: 7 of Israel were **gathered t** to Mizpeh, 6908
8: 4 the elders of Israel **gathered** themselves **t**, 6908
10:17 Samuel **called** the people **t** unto 6817
11:11 so that two of them were not left **t**. 3162
13: 4 the people were **called t** after Saul *to* 6817
13: 5 the Philistines **gathered** themselves **t** to 622
13:11 *that* the Philistines **gathered** themselves **t** *at* 622
15: 4 Saul **gathered** the people **t**, and 8085
17: 1 Now the Philistines **gathered t** their armies 622
17: 1 were **gathered t** *at* Shochoh, 622
17: 2 and the men of Israel were **gathered t**, 622
17:10 give me a man, that we may fight **t**. 3162
23: 8 Saul **called** all the people **t** to war, to go 8085
25: 1 all the Israelites were **gathered t**, and 6908
28: 1 that the Philistines **gathered** their armies **t** 6908
28: 4 the Philistines **gathered** themselves **t**, and 6908
28: 4 Saul **gathered** all Israel **t**, and they pitched 6908
28:23 **t with** the woman, compelled him; 1571+2050.1
29: 1 Now the Philistines **gathered t** all their 6908
31: 6 all his men, that *same* day **t**. 3162
2Sa 2:13 went out, and met **t** by the pool of Gibeon: 3162
2:16 in his fellow's side; so they fell down **t**: 3162
2:25 **gathered** themselves **t** after Abner, 6908
2:30 when he had **gathered** all the people **t**, 6908
6: 1 David **gathered t** all the chosen *men* of 622
10:15 before Israel, they gathered themselves **t**. 3162
10:17 he **gathered** all Israel **t**, and passed over 622
12: 3 it grew up **t** with him, and with his 3162
12:28 therefore **gather** the rest of the people **t**, 622

2Sa 12:29 David **gathered** all the people **t**, and went to 622
14: 6 they two **strove t** in the field, and *there was* 5327
14:16 and my son **t** out of the inheritance of God. 3162
20:14 they were **gathered t**, and went also after 6950
21: 9 they fell *all* seven **t**, and were put to death 3162
23: 9 *that* were there **gathered t** to battle, 622
23:11 the Philistines were **gathered t** into a troop, 622
1Ki 3:18 we *were* **t**; *there was* no stranger with us in 3162
5:12 and they two made a league ***t***. NIH
10:26 Solomon **gathered t** chariots and horsemen: 622
11: 1 **t with** the daughter of Pharaoh, *women of* 2050.1
18:20 **gathered** the prophets **t** unto mount 6908
20: 1 the king of Syria **gathered** all his host **t**: 6908
22: 6 the king of Israel **gathered** the prophets **t**, 6908
2Ki 2: 8 **wrapt** *it* **t**, and smote the waters, and 1563
3:10 ***t***, to deliver them into the hand of Moab. NIH
3:13 ***t***, to deliver them into the hand of Moab. NIH
9:25 and thou rode **t** after Ahab his father, 6776
10:18 Jehu **gathered** all the people **t**, and 6908
1Ch 10: 6 and his three sons, and all his house died **t**. 3162
11:13 there the Philistines were **gathered t** to 622
13: 5 So David **gathered** all Israel **t**, from Shihor 6950
15: 3 David **gathered** all Israel **t** to Jerusalem, 6950
16:35 **gather** us **t**, and deliver us from 6908
19: 7 **gathered** themselves **t** from their cities, 622
22: 2 David commanded to **gather t** the strangers 3664
23: 2 he **gathered t** all the princes of Israel, 622
2Ch 12: 5 that were **gathered t** to Jerusalem because 622
15:10 So they **gathered** themselves **t** *at* Jerusalem 6908
18: 5 Therefore the king of Israel **gathered t** *of* 6908
20: 4 Judah **gathered** themselves **t**, to ask *help* of 6908
24: 5 he **gathered t** the priests and the Levites, 6908
25: 5 Moreover Amaziah **gathered** Judah **t**, and 6908
28:24 Ahaz **gathered t** the vessels of the house of 622
29: 4 and **gathered** them **t** into the east street, 622
30: 3 people **gathered** themselves **t** to Jerusalem. 622
32: 4 So there was **gathered** much people **t**, 6908
32: 6 **gathered** them **t** to him in the street of 6908
34:17 they have **gathered t** the money that was 5413
34:29 **gathered t** all the elders of Judah and 622
Ezr 2:64 The whole congregation **t** *was* forty 259+3509.1
3: 1 the people **gathered** themselves **t** as one 622
3: 9 and his sons, the sons of Judah, **t**, 259+3509.1
3:11 they sung **t** by course in praising and giving NIH
4: 3 we ourselves **t** will build unto the LORD 3162
6:20 and the Levites were purified **t**, 259+3509.1
7:28 I **gathered t** out of Israel chief *men* to go 6908
8:15 I **gathered** them **t** to the river that runneth 6908
10: 7 that *they* should **gather** themselves **t** *unto* 6908
10: 9 Benjamin **gathered** themselves **t** *unto* 6908
Ne 4: 6 all the wall was **joined t** unto the half 7194
4: 8 conspired all of them **t** to come *and* to fight 3162
6: 2 let us meet **t** in *some one of* the villages in 3162
6: 7 now therefore, and let us take counsel **t**. 3162
6:10 he said, Let us **meet t** in the house of God, 3259
7: 5 my God put into mine heart to **gather t** 6908
7:66 The whole congregation **t** *was* forty 259+3509.1
8: 1 all the people **gathered** themselves **t** as one 622
8:13 on the second day were **gathered t** the chief 622
12:28 sons of the singers **gathered** themselves **t**, 622
13:11 I **gathered** them **t**, and set them in their 6908
Est 2: 3 that they may **gather t** all the fair young 6908
2: 8 when many maidens were **gathered t** unto 6908
2:19 when the virgins were **gathered t** 6908
4:16 **gather t** all the Jews that are present in 3664
8:11 *were* in every city to **gather** themselves **t**, 6950
9: 2 The Jews **gathered** themselves **t** in their 6950
9:15 **gathered** themselves **t** on the fourteenth 6950
9:16 king's provinces **gathered** themselves **t**, 6950
9:18 the Jews that *were* at Shushan **assembled t** 6950
Job 2:11 for they had made an appointment **t** to 3162
3:18 *There* the prisoners rest **t**; they hear not 3162
6: 2 my calamity laid in the balances **t**! 3162
9:32 *and* we should come **t** in judgment. 3162
10: 8 made me and fashioned me **t** round about; 3162
11:10 or **gather t**, then who can hinder him? 6950
16:10 they have gathered themselves **t** against 3162
17:16 of the pit, when *our* rest **t** *is* in the dust. 3162
19:12 His troops come **t**, and raise up their way 3162
24: 4 the poor of the earth hide themselves **t**. 3162
30: 7 under the nettles they were **gathered t**. 5596
34:15 All flesh shall perish **t**, and man shall turn 3162
38: 7 When the morning stars sang **t**, and all 3162
38:38 into hardness, and the clods **cleave fast t**? 1692
40:13 Hide them in the dust **t**; *and* bind their faces 3162
40:17 the sinews of his stones are **wrapt t**. 8276
41:15 *are his* pride, shut up ***t*** *as with* a close seal. NIH
41:17 they **stick t**, that they cannot be sundered. 3920
41:23 The flakes of his flesh are **joined t**: they are 1692
Ps 2: 2 the rulers take counsel **t**, against 3162
14: 3 all gone aside, they are *all* **t** become filthy: 3162
31:13 while they took counsel **t** against me, 3162
33: 7 He **gathereth** the waters of the sea **t** as a 3664
34: 3 with me, and let us exalt his name **t**. 3162
35:15 they rejoiced, and **gathered** themselves **t**: 622
35:15 *yea,* the abjects **gathered** themselves **t** 622
35:26 brought to confusion **t** that rejoice at mine 3162
37:38 the transgressors shall be destroyed **t**: 3162
40:14 confounded **t** that seek after my soul to 3162
41: 7 All that hate me whisper **t** against me: 3162
47: 9 The princes of the people are **gathered t**, 622
48: 4 the kings were assembled, they passed by **t**. 3162
49: 2 Both low and high, rich and poor, **t**. 3162
50: 5 Gather my saints **t** unto me; those that have NIH
55:14 We took sweet counsel **t**, *and* walked unto 3162
56: 6 They **gather** themselves **t**, they hide 1481
71:10 that lay wait for my soul take counsel **t**, 3162
74: 8 said in their hearts, Let us destroy them **t**: 3162
83: 5 For they have consulted **t** *with one* consent: 3162
85:10 Mercy and truth are **met t**; righteousness 6298
88:17 like water; they compassed me about **t**. 3162
94:21 They **gather** themselves **t** against the soul 1413
98: 8 clap *their* hands: let the hills be joyful **t** 3162
102:22 When the people are gathered **t**, and 3162
104:22 they **gather** themselves **t**, and lay them 622

Ps 122: 3 *is* builded as a city that is compact **t**: 3162
133: 1 *it is* for brethren to dwell **t in unity**. 3162
140: 2 continually are they **gathered t** *for* war. 1481
147: 2 he **gathereth t** the outcasts of Israel. 3664
Pr 22: 2 The rich and poor **meet t**: the LORD *is* 6298
29:13 The poor and the deceitful man **meet t**: 6298
Ecc 3: 5 away stones, and a time to **gather** stones **t**; 3664
4: 5 The fool **foldeth** his hands **t**, and eateth his 2263
4:11 Again, if two **lie t**, then they have heat: but 7901
Isa 1:18 Come now, and let us **reason t**, saith 3198
1:28 and of the sinners *shall be* **t**, 3162
1:31 they shall both burn **t**, and none shall 3162
8:10 **Take counsel t**, and it shall come to 5779+6098
9:11 Rezin against him, and **join** his enemies **t**; 5526
9:21 *and* they **t** *shall be* against Judah. For all 3162
11: 6 the calf and the young lion and the fatling **t**; 3162
11: 7 their young ones shall lie down **t**: 3162
11:12 **gather t** the dispersed of Judah from 6908
11:14 the west; they shall spoil them of the east **t**: 3162
13: 4 noise of the kingdoms of nations **gathered t**: 622
18: 6 They shall be left **t** unto the fowls of 3162
22: 3 All thy rulers are fled **t**, they are bound by 3162
22: 3 all that are found in thee are bound **t**, 3162
22: 9 ye **gathered t** the waters of the lower pool. 6908
24:22 they shall be **gathered t**, *as* prisoners 622+626
25:11 he shall bring down their pride **t with** 5973
26:19 ***t*** *with* my dead body shall they arise. NIH
27: 4 go through them, I would burn them **t**. 3162
31: 3 shall fall down, and they all shall fail **t**. 3162
34: 4 the heavens shall be **rolled t** as a scrole: 1556
40: 5 shall be revealed, and all flesh shall see *it* **t**: 3162
41: 1 them speak: let us come near **t** to judgment. 3162
41:19 the fir tree, *and* the pine, and the box tree **t**: 3162
41:20 and know, and consider, and understand **t**, 3162
41:23 that we may be dismayed, and behold *it* **t**. 3162
43: 9 Let all the nations be gathered **t**, and let 3162
43:17 they shall lie down **t**, they shall not rise: 3162
43:26 let us plead **t**: declare thou, that thou 3162
44:11 let them all be **gathered t**, let them stand 6908
44:11 they shall fear, *and* they shall be ashamed **t**. 3162
45: 8 and let righteousness spring up **t**; 3162
45:16 they shall go to confusion **t** *that are* makers 3162
45:20 draw near **t**, ye *that are* escaped of 3162
45:21 *them* near; yea, let them take counsel **t**: 3162
46: 2 They stoop, they bow down **t**; they could 3162
48:13 *when* I call unto them, they stand *up* **t**. 3162
49:18 all these **gather** themselves **t**, *and* come to 6908
50: 8 let us stand **t**: who *is* mine adversary? let 3162
52: 8 the voice; *with* the voice **t** shall they sing: 3162
52: 9 Break forth into joy, sing **t**, ye waste places 3162
54:15 shall **surely gather t**, *but* not by me: 1481+1481
54:15 whosoever shall **gather t** against thee shall 1481
60: 4 all they **gather** themselves **t**, they come to 6908
60: 5 flow ***t***, and thine heart shall fear, and NIH
60: 7 All the flocks of Kedar shall be **gathered t** 6908
60:13 the fir tree, the pine tree, and the box **t**, 3162
62: 9 they that have **brought** it **t** shall drink it in 6908
65: 7 and the iniquities of your fathers **t**, 3162
65:25 The wolf and the lamb shall feed **t**, 259+3509.1
66:17 and the mouse, shall be consumed **t**, 3162
Jer 3:18 they shall come **t** out of the land of 3162
4: 5 cry, **gather t**, and say, 4390
6:11 and upon the assembly of young men **t**: 3162
6:12 unto others, *with their* fields and wives **t**: 3162
6:21 and the sons **t** shall fall upon them; 3162
13:14 even the fathers and the sons **t**, saith 3162
31: 8 and her that travaileth with child **t**: 3162
31:12 shall flow ***t*** to the goodness of the LORD, NIH
31:13 in the dance, both young men and old **t**: 3162
31:24 *in* all the cities thereof **t**, husbandmen, and 3162
41: 1 and there they did eat bread **t** in Mizpah. 3162
46:12 the mighty, *and* they are fallen both **t**. 3162
46:21 also are turned back, *and* are fled away **t**; 3162
48: 7 captivity *with* his priests and his princes **t**. 3162
49: 3 *and* his priests and his princes **t**. 3162
49:14 *saying,* **Gather** ye **t**, and come against her, 6908
50: 4 they and the children of Judah **t**, going and 3162
50:29 **Call t** the archers against Babylon: all ye 8085
50:33 and the children of Judah *were* oppressed **t**: 3162
51:27 **call t** against her the kingdoms of Ararat, 8085
51:38 They shall roar **t** like lions: they shall yell 3162
51:44 the nations shall not flow ***t*** any more unto NIH
La 2: 8 and the wall to lament; they languished **t**. 3162
Eze 21:14 smite *thine* **hands t**, and let 413+3709+3709
21:17 I will also smite mine **hands t**, 413+3709+3709
29: 5 thou shalt not be brought **t**, nor gathered: 622
37: 7 and the bones **came t**, bone to his bone. 7126
Da 2:35 broken to pieces **t**, and became like 2298+3509.4
3: 2 Nebuchadnezzar the king sent to **gather t** 3673
3: 3 were **gathered t** unto the dedication of 3673
3:27 being **gathered t**, saw these men, 3673
6: 6 princes assembled ***t*** to the king, NIH
6: 7 have **consulted t** to establish a royal 3272
11: 6 end of years they shall **join** themselves **t**; 2266
Hos 1:11 and the children of Israel be gathered **t**, 3162
11: 8 within me, my repentings are kindled **t**. 3162
Joel 3:11 and **gather** yourselves **t** round about: 6908
Am 1:15 he and his princes **t**, saith the LORD. 3162
3: 3 Can two walk **t**, except they be agreed? 3162
Mic 2:12 I will put them **t** as the sheep of Bozrah, 3162
Na 1:10 For while *they be* **folden t** *as* thorns, and 5440
2:10 the knees **smite t**, and much pain *is* in all 6375
Zep 2: 1 **Gather** yourselves **t**, yea, gather together, 7197
2: 1 yea, **gather t**, O nation not desired; 7197
Zec 10: 4 battle bow, out of him every oppressor **t**. 3162
12: 3 people of the earth be **gathered t** against it. 622
14:14 the heathen round about shall be **gathered t**, 622
Mt 1:18 before they **came t**, she was found with *4905*
2: 4 **gathered** all the chief priests and scribes of the people **t**, *4863*
13: 2 And great multitudes were **gathered t** unto *4863*
13:30 Let both **grow t** until the harvest: and in *4885*
13:30 **Gather** ye **t** first the tares, and bind them in *4816*
18:20 or three are **gathered t** in my name, *4863*
19: 6 What therefore God hath **joined t**, let not *4801*

Mt 22:10 and gathered t all as many as they found, 4863
22:34 to silence, they were gathered t. 846+1909+3588
22:41 While the Pharisees were gathered t, Jesus 4863
23:37 often would I have gathered thy children t, 1996
24:28 there will the eagles be gathered t. 4863
24:31 they shall gather t his elect from the four 1996
26: 3 Then assembled t the chief priests, and 4863
27:17 Therefore when they were gathered t, 4863
27:62 and Pharisees came t unto Pilate, 4863
Mk 1:33 And all the city was gathered t at the door. 1996
2: 2 And straightway many were gathered t, 4863
2:15 and sinners sat also t with Jesus and 4873
3:20 And *the* multitude cometh t again, so 4905
6:30 And the apostles gathered themselves t 4863
6:33 and outwent them, and came t unto him. 4905
7: 1 Then came t unto him the Pharisees, and 4863
9:25 Jesus saw that the people came running t, 1998
10: 9 What therefore God hath joined t, let not 4801
12:28 and having heard them reasoning t, and 4802
13:27 shall gather t his elect from the four winds, 1996
14:56 but *their* witness agreed not t. 1510+2470
14:59 so did their witness agree t. 1510+2470
15:16 and they call t the whole band. 4779
Lk 5:15 and great multitudes came t to hear, and 4905
6:38 and shaken *t*, and running over, NIG
8: 4 And when much people were gathered t, 4896
9: 1 Then he called his twelve disciples t, and 4779
11:29 when the people were gathered thick t, 1865
12: 1 when there were gathered t an 1996
13:11 and was bowed t, and could in no wise lift 4794
13:34 often would I have gathered thy children t, 1996
15: 6 he calleth t *his* friends and neighbours, 4779
15: 9 calleth *her* friends and *her* neighbours t, 4779
15:13 days after the younger son gathered all t, 4863
17:35 Two *women* shall be grinding t; 846+1909+3588
17:37 *is*, thither will the eagles be gathered t. 4863
22:55 and were set down t, Peter sat down among 4776
22:66 and the chief priests and the scribes came t, 4863
23:12 Pilate and Herod were made friends t: 240+3326
23:13 when he had called t the chief priests and 4779
23:48 And all the people that came t to that sight, 4836
24:14 And they talked t of all these *things* 240+4314
24:15 that while they communed *t* and reasoned, NIG
24:33 and found the eleven gathered t, and 4867
Jn 4:36 and he that reapeth may rejoice t. 3674
6:13 Therefore they gathered *them* t, and 4863
11:52 that also he should gather t in one 4863
11:53 they took counsel t for to put him to death. 4823
20: 4 So they ran both t: and the other disciple 3674
20: 7 but wrapped t in a place by itself. 1794
21: 2 There were t Simon Peter, and 3674
Ac 1: 4 And, being assembled t with them, 4871
1: 6 When they therefore were come t, 4905
1:15 (the number of names t were 846+1909+3588
2: 6 the multitude came t, and 4905
2:44 And all that believed were t, 846+1909+3588
3: 1 John went up t into the temple 846+1909+3588
3:11 all the people ran t unto them in the porch 4936
4: 6 high priest, were gathered t at Jerusalem. 4863
4:26 gathered t against the Lord, 846+1909+3588
4:27 and the people of Israel, were gathered t, 4863
4:31 was shaken where they were assembled t; 4863
5: 9 How *is it* that ye have agreed t to tempt 4856
5:21 and called the council t, and all the senate 4779
10:24 and had called t his kinsmen and near 4779
10:27 went in, and found many *that were* come t. 4905
12:12 where many were gathered t praying. 4867
13:44 came almost the whole city t to hear 4863
14: 1 that they went *both* t into 846+2596+3588
14:27 were come, and had gathered the church t, 4863
15: 6 elders came t for to consider of this matter. 4863
15:30 when they had gathered the multitude t, 4863
16:22 And the multitude rose up t against them: 4911
19:19 used curious arts brought their books t, 4851
19:25 Whom he called t with the workmen of 4867
19:32 part knew not wherefore they were come t. 4905
20: 7 when the disciples came t to break bread, 4863
20: 8 where they were gathered t. 4863
21:22 the multitude must needs come t: for they 4905
21:30 was moved, and the people ran t: 1096+4890
23:12 certain of the Jews banded t, 4160+4963
28:17 days Paul called the chief of the Jews t: 4779
28:17 and when they were come t, he said unto 4905
Ro 1:12 that *I* may be comforted t with you by 4837
3:12 of the way, they are t become unprofitable; 260
6: 5 For if we have been planted t in 4854
8:17 with *him*, that we may be also glorified t. 4888
8:22 and travaileth in pain t until now. 4944
8:28 And we know that all *things* work t for 4903
15:30 that *ye* strive t with me in *your* prayers to 4865
1Co 1:10 *that* ye be perfectly joined t in the same 2675
3: 9 For we are labourers t with God: ye are 4904
5: 4 when ye are gathered t, and my spirit, 4863
7: 5 and prayer, and come t again, 846+1909+3588
11:17 that you come t not for the better, but 4905
11:18 first of all, when ye come t in the church, 4905
11:20 When ye come t therefore into one place, 4905
11:33 my brethren, when ye come t to eat, 4905
11:34 that ye come not t unto condemnation. 4905
12:24 but God hath tempered the body t, 4786
14:23 the whole church be come t into one place, 4905
14:26 when ye come t, every one of you hath a 4905
2Co 1:11 You also helping t by prayer for us, 4943
6: 1 *as* workers t *with him*, beseech *you* also 4903
6:14 Be ye not unequally yoked t with 2086
Eph 1:10 *he* might gather t in one all *things* in Christ, 346
2: 5 hath quickened *us* t with Christ, (by grace 4806
2: 6 And hath raised *us* up t, and made *us* sit 4891
2: 6 made *us* sit t in heavenly *places* in Christ 4776
2:21 In whom all the building fitly framed t 4883
2:22 In whom you also are builded t for a 4925
4:16 From whom the whole body fitly joined t 4883
Php 1:27 with one mind striving t for the faith of 4866
3:17 be followers t of me, and mark them which 4831
Col 2: 2 being knit t in love, and unto all riches of 4822
Col 2:13 your flesh, hath he quickened t with him, 4806
2:19 and knit t, increaseth *with* the increase of 4822
1Th 4:17 remain shall be caught up t with them in 260
5:10 we wake or sleep, we should live t with him. 260
5:11 Wherefore comfort yourselves t, and 240
2Th 2: 1 and *by* our gathering t unto him, 1997
Heb 10:25 forsaking the assembling of ourselves t, 1997
Jas 5: 3 ye have heaped treasure t for the last 2343
1Pe 3: 7 and as *being* heirs t of the grace of life; 4789
5:13 elected t with *you*, saluteth you; 4899
Rev 6:14 departed as a scrole when it is rolled t; 1507
16:16 And he gathered them t into a place called 4863
19:17 gather yourselves t unto the supper of 4863
19:19 gathered t to make war against him that sat 4863
20: 8 and Magog, to gather them t to battle: 4863

TOHU (1)
1Sa 1: 1 the son of T, the son of Zuph, 8459

TOI (3) [TOU]
2Sa 8: 9 When T king of Hamath heard that David 8583
8:10 Then T sent Joram his son unto king David, 8583
8:10 for Hadadezer had wars with T. And *Joram* 8583

TOIL (4) [TOILED, TOILING]
Ge 5:29 us concerning our work and t of our hands, 6093
41:51 *said he*, hath made me forget all my t, and 5999
Mt 6:28 they grow; they t not, neither do they spin: 2872
Lk 12:27 they t not, they spin not; and yet I say unto 2872

TOILED (1) [TOIL]
Lk 5: 5 we have t all the night, and have taken 2872

TOILING (1) [TOIL]
Mk 6:48 And he saw them t in rowing; for the wind 928

TOKEN (14) [TOKENS]
Ge 9:12 This *is* the t of the covenant which I make 226
9:13 it shall be for a t of a covenant between me 226
9:17 said unto Noah, This *is* the t of the covenant, 226
17:11 it shall be a t of the covenant betwixt me and 226
Ex 3:12 this *shall be* a t unto thee, that I have sent 226
12:13 the blood shall be to you for a t upon 226
13:16 it shall be for a t upon thine hand, and 226
Nu 17:10 to be kept for a t against the rebels; 226
Jos 2:12 unto my father's house, and give me a true t: 226
Ps 86:17 Shew me a t for good; that they which hate 226
Mk 14:44 he that betrayed him had given them a t, 4953
Php 1:28 which is to them an evident t of perdition, 1732
2Th 1: 5 *Which is* a manifest t of the righteous 1730
3:17 own hand, which is the t in every epistle: 4592

TOKENS (7) [TOKEN]
Dt 22:15 bring forth *the t of* the damsel's virginity NIH
22:17 *yet* these *are the t of* my daughter's NIH
22:20 *the t of* virginity be not found for NIH
Job 21:29 go by the way? and do ye not know their t, 226
Ps 65: 8 in the uttermost parts are afraid at thy t: 226
135: 9 *Who* sent t and wonders into the midst of 226
Isa 44:25 That frustrateth the t of the liars, and 226

TOKHATH See TIKVATH

TOLA (6) [TOLAITES]
Ge 46:13 T, and Phuvah, and Job, and Shimron. 8439
Nu 26:23 *of* T, the family of the Tolaites: of Pua, 8439
Jdg 10: 1 arose to defend Israel T the son of Puah, 8439
1Ch 7: 1 Now the sons of Issachar *were*, T, and 8439
7: 2 And the sons of T; Uzzi, and Rephaiah, and 8439
7: 2 heads of their fathers' house, *to wit*, of T: 8439

TOLAD (1)
1Ch 4:29 And at Bilhah, and at Ezem, and at T, 8434

TOLAITES (1) [TOLA]
Nu 26:23 *of* Tola, the family of the T: of Pua, 8440

TOLD (283) [TELL]
Ge 3:11 he said, Who t thee that thou *wast* naked? 5046
9:22 his father, and t his two brethren without 5046
14:13 that had escaped, and t Abram the Hebrew; 5046
20: 8 and t all these things in their ears: 1696
22: 3 went unto the place of which God had t him. 559
22: 9 they came to the place which God had t him 559
22:20 that it was t Abraham, saying, Behold, 5046
24:28 t *them of* her mother's house these things. 5046
24:33 I will not eat, until I have t mine errand. 1696
24:66 the servant t Isaac all things that he had 5608
26:32 t him concerning the well which they had 5046
27:42 these words of Esau her elder son were t to 5046
29:12 Jacob t Rachel that he *was* her father's 5046
29:12 Rebekah's son: and she ran and t her father. 5046
29:13 his house. And he t Laban all these things. 5608
31:20 the Syrian, in that he t him not that he fled. 5046
31:22 it was t Laban on the third day that Jacob 5046
37: 5 dreamed a dream, and he t *it* his brethren: 5046
37: 9 t it his brethren, and said, Behold, I have 5608
37:10 And he t *it* to his father, and to his brethren: 5608
38:13 it was t Tamar, saying, Behold thy father in 5046
38:24 months after, that it was t Judah, saying, 5046
40: 9 the chief butler t his dream to Joseph, and 5608
41: 8 Pharaoh t them his dream; but *there was* 5608
41:12 we t him, and he interpreted to us our 5608
41:24 I t *this* unto the magicians; but *there was* 559
42:29 and t him all that befell unto them; 5046
43: 7 we t him according to the tenor of these 5046
44:24 my father, we t him the words of my lord. 5046
45:26 t him, saying, Joseph *is* yet alive, and he *is* 5046
45:27 they t him all the words of Joseph, 1696
47: 1 Joseph came and t Pharaoh, and said, 5046
48: 1 that *one* t Joseph, Behold, thy father *is* sick: 559
48: 2 *one* t Jacob, and said, Behold, thy son 5046
Ex 4:28 Moses t Aaron all the words of the LORD 5046
5: 1 and Aaron went in, and t Pharaoh, 559
Ex 14: 5 it was t the king of Egypt that the people 5046
16:22 of the congregation came and t Moses. 5046
18: 8 Moses t his father in law all that 5608
19: 9 Moses t the words of the people unto 5046
24: 3 t the people all the words of the LORD, 5608
Lev 21:24 Moses t *it* unto Aaron, and to his sons, and 1696
Nu 11:24 t the people the words of the LORD, and 1696
11:27 t Moses, and said, Eldad and Medad do 5046
13:27 they t him, and said, We came unto 5608
14:39 Moses t these sayings unto all the children 1696
23:26 and said unto Balak, T not I thee, saying, 1696
29:40 Moses t the children of Israel according to 559
Dt 17: 4 it be t thee, and thou hast heard *of it*, and 5046
Jos 2: 2 it was t the king of Jericho, saying, Behold, 559
2:23 and t him all *things* that befell them: 5608
9:24 it was certainly t thy servants, 5046+5046
10:17 it was t Joshua, saying, The five kings are 5046
Jdg 6:13 *be* all his miracles which our fathers t 5608
7:13 *there was* a man that t a dream unto his 5608
9: 7 when they t *it* to Jotham, he went and 5046
9:25 *that* way by them: and it was t Abimelech. 5046
9:42 out *into* the field; and they t Abimelech. 5046
9:47 it was t Abimelech, that all the men of 5046
13: 6 the woman came and t her husband, saying, 559
13: 6 I asked him not whence he *was*, neither t he 5046
13:23 *at this* time have t us *such things* as these. 8085
14: 2 and t his father and his mother, and said, 5046
14: 6 he t not his father or his mother what he 5046
14: 9 he t not them that he had taken the honey 5046
14:16 children of my people, and hast not t *it* me. 5046
14:16 I have not t *it* my father nor my mother, 5046
14:17 that he t her, because she lay sore upon 5046
14:17 she t the riddle to the children of her 5046
16: 2 *And it was* t the Gazites, saying, Samson is NIH
16:10 thou hast mocked me, and t me lies: 1696
16:13 thou hast mocked me, and t me lies: 1696
16:15 hast not t me wherein thy great strength 5046
16:17 That he t her all his heart, and said unto 5046
16:18 when Delilah saw that he had t her all his 5046
Ru 3:16 she t her all that the man had done to her. 5046
1Sa 3:13 For I have t him that I will judge his house 5046
3:18 Samuel t him every whit, and hid nothing 5046
4:13 into the city, and t *it*, all the city cried out. 5046
4:14 And the man came in hastily, and t Eli. 5046
8:10 Samuel t all the words of the LORD unto 559
9:15 Now the LORD had t Samuel in his ear a 1540
10:16 t us plainly that the asses were 5046+5046
10:16 whereof Samuel spake, he t him not. 5046
10:25 Samuel t the people the manner of 1696
11: 4 and t the tidings in the ears of the people: 1696
11: 5 they t him the tidings of the men of Jabesh. 5608
14: 1 *is* on the other side. But he t not his father. 5046
14:33 they t Saul, saying, Behold, the people sin 5046
14:43 Jonathan t him, and said, I did but taste a 5046
15:12 it was t Samuel, saying, Saul came to 5046
18:20 and they t Saul, and the thing pleased him. 5046
18:24 the servants of Saul t him, saying, On this 5046
18:26 when his servants t David these words, 5046
19: 2 Jonathan t David, saying, Saul my father 5046
19:11 Michal David's wife t him, saying, If thou 5046
19:18 and t him all that Saul had done to him. 5046
19:19 it was t Saul, saying, Behold, David *is* at 5046
19:21 when it was t Saul, he sent other 5046
23: 1 they t David, saying, Behold, 5046
23: 7 it was t Saul that David was come *to* 5046
23:13 it was t Saul that David was escaped from 5046
23:22 for it is t me *that* he dealeth very subtilly. 559
23:25 his men went to seek *him*. And they t 5046
24: 1 that it was t him, saying, Behold, David *is* 5046
25:12 and came and t him all those sayings. 5046
25:14 one of the young men t Abigail, 5046
25:19 after you. But she t not her husband Nabal. 5046
25:36 wherefore she t him nothing, less or more, 5046
25:37 his wife had t him these things, that his 5046
27: 4 it was t Saul that David was fled *to* Gath: 5046
2Sa 1: 5 David said unto the young man that t him, 5046
1: 6 the young man that t him said, As I 5046
1:13 David said unto the young man that t him, 5046
2: 4 they t David, saying, *That* the men of 5046
3:23 they t Joab, saying, Abner the son of Ner 5046
4:10 When one t me, saying, Behold, Saul is 5046
6:12 it was t king David, saying, The LORD 5046
10: 5 When they t *it* unto David, he sent to meet 5046
10:17 when it was t David, he gathered all Israel 5046
11: 5 sent and t David, and said, I *am* with child. 5046
11:10 when they had t David, saying, Uriah went 5046
11:18 t David all the things concerning the war; 5046
14:33 So Joab came to the king, and t him: and 5046
15:31 *one* t David, saying, Ahithophel *is* among 5046
17:17 a wench went and t them; and they went 5046
17:17 told them; and they went and t king David. 5046
17:18 a lad saw them, and t Absalom: 5046
17:21 went and t king David, and said unto 5046
18:10 a certain man saw *it*, and t Joab, and said, 5046
18:11 Joab said unto the man that t him, 5046
18:25 the watchman cried, and t the king. And 5046
19: 1 it was t Joab, Behold, the king weepeth 5046
19: 8 they t unto all the people, saying, Behold, 5046
21:11 it was t David what Rizpah the daughter of 5046
24:13 to David, and t him, and said unto him, 5046
1Ki 1:23 they t the king, saying, Behold Nathan 5046
1:51 it was t Solomon, saying, Behold, 5046
2:29 it was t king Solomon that Joab was fled 5046
2:39 they t Shimei, saying, Behold, thy servants 5046
2:41 it was t Solomon that Shimei had gone 5046
8: 5 that could not be t nor numbered for 5608
10: 3 Solomon t her all her questions: there was 5046
10: 3 thing hid from the king, which he t her not. 5046
10: 7 seen *it*: and behold, the half was not t me: 5046
13:11 t him all the works that the man of God had 5608
13:11 the king, them they t also to their father. 5608
13:25 t *it* in the city where the old prophet dwelt. 1696
14: 2 which t me that I should be king over this 1696
18:13 Was it not t my lord what I did when 5046
18:16 So Obadiah went to meet Ahab, and t him: 5046

1Ki 19: 1 Ahab **t** Jezebel all that Elijah had done, 5046
20:17 Ben-hadad sent out, and they **t** him, saying, 5046
2Ki 1: 7 up to meet you, and **t** you these words? 1696
4: 7 She came and **t** the man of God. And he 5046
4:27 hath hid *it* from me, and hath not **t** me. 5046
4:31 and **t** him, saying, The child is not awaked. 5046
5: 4 **t** his lord, saying, Thus and thus said 5046
6:10 sent to the place which the man of God **t** him 559
6:13 it was **t** him, saying, Behold, *he is* in 5046
7:10 they **t** them, saying, We came to the camp 5046
7:11 and they **t** *it to* the king's house within. 5046
7:15 the messengers returned, and **t** the king. 5046
8: 6 when the king asked the woman, she **t** him. 5608
8: 7 it was **t** him, saying, The man of God is 5046
8:14 He **t** me *that* thou shouldest surely recover. 559
9:18 the watchman **t**, saying, The messenger 5046
9:20 the watchman **t**, saying, He came even unto 5046
9:36 Wherefore they came again, and **t** him. 5046
10: 8 there came a messenger, and **t** him, saying, 5046
12:10 **t** the money that was found *in* the house of 4487
12:11 they gave the money, being **t**, into 8505
18:37 and **t** him the words of Rab-shakeh. 5046
23:17 the men of the city **t** him, *It is* the sepulchre 559
1Ch 17:25 hast **t** thy servant that *thou* wilt build 241+1540
19: 5 and **t** David how the men were served. 5046
19:17 it was **t** David; and he gathered all Israel, 5046
2Ch 2: 2 Solomon **t out** threescore and ten thousand 5608
5: 6 which could not be **t** nor numbered for 5608
9: 2 Solomon **t** her all her questions: and 5046
9: 2 hid from Solomon which he **t** her not. 5046
9: 6 the greatness of thy wisdom was not **t** me: 5046
20: 2 there came *some* that **t** Jehoshaphat, saying, 5046
34:18 Shaphan the scribe **t** the king, saying, 5046
Ezr 8:17 **t** them what they should say 6310+7760+871.1
Ne 2:12 neither **t** I *any* man what my God had put in 5046
2:16 neither had I as yet **t** *it* to the Jews, nor to 5046
2:18 I **t** them of the hand of my God which was 5046
Est 2:22 who **t** *it* unto Esther the queen; 5046
3: 4 not unto them, that they **t** Haman, 5046
3: 4 for he had **t** them that he *was* a Jew. 5046
4: 4 and her chamberlains came and **t** *it* her. 5046
4: 7 Mordecai **t** him of all that had happened 5046
4: 9 and **t** Esther the words of Mordecai. 5046
4:12 And they **t** to Mordecai Esther's words. 5046
5:11 Haman **t** them of the glory of his riches, 5608
6: 2 that Mordecai had **t** of Bigthana and 5046
6:13 Haman **t** Zeresh his wife and all his friends 5608
8: 1 for Esther had **t** what he *was* unto her. 5046
Job 15:18 Which wise *men* have **t** from their fathers, 5046
37:20 Shall it be **t** him that I speak? if a man 5608
Ps 44: 1 with our ears, O God, our fathers have **t** us, 5608
52: T when Doeg the Edomite came and **t** Saul, 5046
78: 3 and known, and our fathers have **t** us. 5608
90: 9 we spend our years as a tale *that is t*. NIH
Ecc 6: 6 though he live a thousand years twice *t*, yet NIH
Isa 7: 2 it was **t** the house of David, saying, Syria is 5046
36:22 and **t** him the words of Rabshakeh. 5046
40:21 hath it not been **t** you from the beginning? 5046
44: 8 have not I **t** thee from that time, and 8085
45:21 *who* hath **t** it from that time? *have* not I 5046
52:15 for *that* which had not been **t** them shall 5608
Jer 36:20 and **t** all the words in the ears of the king. 5046
38:27 he **t** them according to all these words that 5046
Da 4: 7 I **t** the dream before them; but they *did* not 560
4: 8 and before him I **t** the dream, *saying,* 560
7: 1 the dream, *and* **t** the sum of the matters. 560
7:16 So he **t** me, and made me know 560
8:26 and the morning which was **t** *is* true: 559
Jnh 1:10 of the LORD, because he had **t** them. 5046
Hab 1: 5 ye will not believe, though it be **t** *you.* 5608
Zec 10: 2 have seen a lie, and have **t** false dreams; 1696
Mt 8:33 and **t** every *thing,* and what was befallen to *518*
12:48 he answered and said unto him that **t** him, *3004*
14:12 and buried it, and went and **t** Jesus. *518*
18:31 and **t** unto their lord all that was done. *1285*
24:25 Behold, I have **t** you **before**. *4302*
26:13 hath done, be **t** for a memorial of her. *2980*
28: 7 there shall ye see him: lo, I have **t** you. *3004*
Mk 5:14 and **t** *it* in the city, and in the country. *312*
5:16 And they that saw *it* **t** them how it befell to *1334*
5:33 down before him, and **t** him all the truth. *3004*
6:30 **t** him all *things,* both what they had done, *518*
9:12 And he answered and **t** them, Elias verily *3004*
16:10 she went and **t** them that had been with him, *518*
16:13 And they went and **t** *it* unto the residue: *518*
Lk 1:45 *things* which were **t** her from the Lord. *2980*
2:17 which was **t** them concerning this child. *2980*
2:18 *things* which were **t** them by the shepherds. *2980*
2:20 had heard and seen, as it was **t** unto them. *2980*
8:20 And it was **t** him *by certain* which said, *518*
8:34 and went and **t** *it* in the city and in *518*
8:36 They also which saw *it* **t** them by what *518*
9:10 were returned, **t** him all that they had done. *1334*
9:36 **t** no *man* in those days any of *those things* *518*
13: 1 There were present at that season some that **t** *518*
18:37 And they **t** him, that Jesus of Nazareth *518*
24: 9 and **t** all these *things* unto the eleven, and *518*
24:10 which **t** these *things* unto the apostles. *3004*
24:35 And they **t** what *things were done* in *1834*
Jn 3:12 If I have **t** you earthly *things,* and *3004*
4:29 a man, which **t** me all *things* that ever I did: *3004*
4:39 which testified, He **t** me all that ever I did. *3004*
4:51 met him, and **t** *him,* saying, Thy son liveth. *518*
5:15 and **t** the Jews that it was Jesus, *312*
8:40 a man that hath **t** you the truth, which I *2980*
9:27 I have **t** you already, and ye did not hear: *3004*
10:25 answered them, I **t** you, and ye believe not: *3004*
11:46 and **t** them what *things* Jesus had done. *3004*
14: 2 if *it were* not *so,* I would have **t** you. I go to *3004*
14:29 And now I have **t** you before it come to *3004*
16: 4 But these *things* have I **t** you, that when *2980*
16: 4 ye may remember that I **t** you of them. *3004*
18: 8 I have **t** you that I am *he:* if therefore *3004*
20:18 **t** the disciples that she had seen the Lord, *518*
Ac 5:22 them not in the prison, they returned, and **t**, *518*
5:25 Then came one and **t** them, saying, Behold, *518*
9: 6 and it shall be **t** thee what thou must do. *2980*
12:14 ran in, and **t how** Peter stood before the gate. *518*
16:36 And the keeper of the prison **t** this saying to *518*
16:38 And the sergeants **t** these words unto *312*
22:10 there it shall be **t** thee of all *things* which *2980*
22:26 heard *that,* he went and **t** the chief captain, *518*
23:16 and entered into the castle, and **t** Paul. *518*
23:30 And when it was **t** me how that the Jews *3377*
27:25 that it shall be even as it was **t** me. *2980*
2Co 7: 7 when he **t** us your earnest desire, your *312*
13: 2 I **t** *you* **before**, and foretell *you,* as if I were *4302*
Gal 5:21 as I have also **t** *you* **in time past**, *4302*
Php 3:18 of whom I have **t** you often, and now tell *3004*
1Th 3: 4 we **t** you **before** that we should suffer *4302*
2Th 2: 5 I was yet with you, I **t** you these *things?* *3004*
Jude 1:18 How that they **t** you there should be *3004*

TOLERABLE (6)

Mt 10:15 It shall be **more t** for the land of Sodom and *414*
11:22 It shall be **more t** for Tyre and Sidon at *414*
11:24 that it shall be **more t** for the land of Sodom *414*
Mk 6:11 It shall be **more t** for Sodom and *414*
Lk 10:12 that it shall be **more t** in that day for Sodom, *414*
10:14 But it shall be **more t** for Tyre and Sidon at *414*

TOLL (3)

Ezr 4:13 walls set up *again, then* will they not pay **t**, 4061
4:20 **t**, tribute, and custom, *was* paid unto them. 4061
7:24 it *shall* not *be* lawful to impose **t**, tribute, or 4061

TOMB (3) [TOMBS]

Job 21:32 to the grave, and shall remain in the **t**. 1430
Mt 27:60 And laid it in his own new **t**, which he had *3419*
Mk 6:29 and took up his corpse, and laid it in a **t**. *3419*

TOMBS (6) [TOMB]

Mt 8:28 coming out of the **t**, exceeding fierce, so *3419*
23:29 because ye build the **t** of the prophets, and *5028*
Mk 5: 2 immediately there met him out of the **t** a *3419*
5: 3 Who had *his* dwelling among the **t**; *3419*
5: 5 and in the **t**, crying, and cutting himself *3418*
Lk 8:27 neither abode in *any* house, but in the **t**. *3418*

TOMORROW See TO MORROW

TONGS (6)

Ex 25:38 the **t** thereof, and the snuffdishes thereof, 4457
Nu 4: 9 his **t**, and his snuffdishes, and all the oil 4457
1Ki 7:49 and the lamps, and the **t** *of* gold, 4457
2Ch 4:21 the flowers, and the lamps, and the **t**, 4457
Isa 6: 6 *which* he had taken with the **t** from off 4457
44:12 The smith *with* the **t** both worketh in 4621

TONGUE (129) [DOUBLETONGUED, TONGUES]

Ge 10: 5 every one after his **t**, after their families, 3956
Ex 4:10 but I *am* slow of speech, and of a slow **t**. 3956
11: 7 of Israel shall not a dog move his **t**, 3956
Dt 28:49 a nation whose **t** thou shalt not understand; 3956
Jos 10:21 none moved his **t** against any of 3956
Jdg 7: 5 one that lappeth of the water with his **t**, 3956
2Sa 23: 2 spake by me, and his word *was* in my **t**. 3956
Ezr 4: 7 of the letter *was* written **in the Syrian t**, 762
4: 7 and interpreted **in the** Syrian **t**. 762
Est 7: 4 and bondwomen, I had **held** my **t**, 2790
Job 5:21 Thou shalt be hid from the scourge of the **t**: 3956
6:24 Teach me, and I will **hold** my **t**: and 2790
6:30 Is there iniquity in my **t**? cannot my taste 3956
13:19 for now, if I **hold** my **t**, I shall give up 2790
15: 5 and thou choosest the **t** of the crafty. 3956
20:12 in his mouth, *though* he hide it under his **t**; 3956
20:16 poison of asps: the viper's **t** shall slay him. 3956
27: 4 not speak wickedness, nor my **t** utter deceit. 3956
29:10 their **t** cleaved to the roof of their mouth. 3956
33: 2 my mouth, my **t** hath spoken in my mouth. 3956
41: 1 his **t** with a cord *which* thou lettest down? 3956
Ps 5: 9 an open sepulchre; they flatter with their **t**. 3956
10: 7 fraud: under his **t** *is* mischief and vanity. 3956
12: 3 *and* the **t** that speaketh proud *things:* 3956
12: 4 Who have said, With our **t** will we prevail; 3956
15: 3 *He that* backbiteth not with his **t**, nor doeth 3956
22:15 my **t** cleaveth *to* my jaws; and thou hast 3956
34:13 Keep thy **t** from evil, and thy lips from 3956
35:28 my **t** shall speak of thy righteousness *and* 3956
37:30 and his **t** talketh of judgment. 3956
39: 1 heed to my ways, that *I* sin not with my **t**: 3956
39: 3 the fire burned: *then* spake I with my **t**, 3956
45: 1 *the* king: my **t** *is* the pen of a ready writer. 3956
50:19 thy mouth to evil, and thy **t** frameth deceit. 3956
51:14 my **t** shall sing aloud of thy righteousness. 3956
52: 2 Thy **t** deviseth mischiefs; like a sharp rasor, 3956
52: 4 all devouring words, O thou deceitful **t**. 3956
57: 4 and arrows, and their **t** a sharp sword. 3956
64: 3 Who whet their **t** like a sword, *and* 3956
64: 8 So they shall make their own **t** to fall upon 3956
66:17 my mouth, and *he was* extolled with my **t**. 3956
68:23 *and* the **t** of thy dogs in the same. 3956
71:24 My **t** also shall talk of thy righteousness all 3956
73: 9 and their **t** walketh through the earth. 3956
109: 2 they have spoken against me *with* a lying **t**. 3956
119:172 My **t** shall speak of thy word: for all thy 3956
120: 2 from lying lips, *and* from a deceitful **t**. 3956
120: 3 what shall be done unto thee, thou false **t**? 3956
126: 2 filled *with* laughter, and our **t** *with* singing: 3956
137: 6 let my **t** cleave to the roof of my mouth; 3956
139: 4 For *there is* not a word in my **t**, *but* lo, 3956
Pr 6:17 a lying **t**, and hands that shed innocent 3956
6:24 from the flattery of the **t** of a strange 3956
10:20 The **t** of the just *is as* choice silver: 3956
10:31 but the froward **t** shall be cut out. 3956
12:18 of a sword: but the **t** of the wise *is* health. 3956
12:19 for ever: but a lying **t** *is* but for a moment. 3956
15: 2 The **t** of the wise useth knowledge aright: 3956
15: 4 A wholesome **t** *is* a tree of life: but 3956
Pr 16: 1 the answer of the **t**, *is* from the LORD. 3956
17: 4 *and* a liar giveth ear to a naughty **t**. 3956
17:20 he that hath a perverse **t** falleth into 3956
18:21 Death and life *are* in the power of the **t**: and 3956
21: 6 The getting of treasures by a lying **t** *is* a 3956
21:23 and his **t** keepeth his soul from troubles. 3956
25:15 and a soft **t** breaketh the bone. 3956
25:23 *doth* an angry countenance a backbiting **t**. 3956
26:28 A lying **t** hateth *those that are* afflicted by 3956
28:23 favour than he that flattereth with the **t**. 3956
31:26 and in her **t** *is* the law of kindness. 3956
SS 4:11 honey and milk *are* under thy **t**; and 3956
Isa 3: 8 because their **t** and their doings *are* against 3956
11:15 the LORD shall utterly destroy the **t** of 3956
28:11 and another **t** will he speak to this people. 3956
30:27 *of* indignation, and his **t** as a devouring fire: 3956
32: 4 the **t** of the stammerers shall be ready to 3956
33:19 of a stammering **t**, *that thou canst* not 3956
35: 6 leap as a hart, and the **t** of the dumb sing: 3956
41:17 *there is* none, *and* their **t** faileth for thirst, 3956
45:23 every knee shall bow, every **t** shall swear. 3956
50: 4 The Lord GOD hath given me the **t** of 3956
54:17 every **t** *that* shall rise against thee in 3956
57: 4 make ye a wide mouth, *and* draw out the **t**? 3956
59: 3 your **t** hath muttered perverseness. 3956
Jer 9: 5 they have taught their **t** to speak lies, *and* 3956
9: 8 Their **t** *is as* an arrow shot out; it speaketh 3956
18:18 let us smite him with the **t**, and let us not 3956
La 4: 4 The **t** of the sucking child cleaveth to 3956
Eze 3:26 I will make thy **t** cleave to the roof of thy 3956
Da 1: 4 the learning and the **t** of the Chaldeans. 3956
Hos 7:16 fall by the sword for the rage of their **t**: 3956
Am 6:10 shall he say, **Hold** thy **t**: for *we may* not 2013
Mic 6:12 and their **t** *is* deceitful in their mouth. 3956
Hab 1:13 **holdest** thy **t** when the wicked devoureth 2790
Zep 3:13 neither shall a deceitful **t** be found in their 3956
Zec 14:12 their **t** shall consume away in their mouth. 3956
Mk 7:33 into his ears, and he spit, and touched his **t**; *1100*
7:35 and the string of his **t** was loosed, and *1100*
Lk 1:64 and his **t** *loosed,* and he spake, and *1100*
16:24 the tip of his finger in water, and cool my **t**; *1100*
Jn 5: 2 which is called **in the Hebrew t** Bethesda, *1447*
Ac 1:19 as that field is called in their proper **t**, *1258*
2: 8 And how hear we every man in our own **t**, *1258*
2:26 did my heart rejoice, and my **t** was glad; *1100*
21:40 he spake unto *them* in the Hebrew **t**, *1258*
22: 2 that he spake in the Hebrew **t** to them, *1258*
26:14 and saying in the Hebrew **t**, Saul, Saul, *1258*
Ro 14:11 to me, and every **t** shall confess to God. *1100*
1Co 14: 2 For he that speaketh in an *unknown* **t** *1100*
14: 4 He that speaketh in an *unknown* **t** edifieth *1100*
14: 9 except ye utter by the **t** words easy to be *1100*
14:13 in an *unknown* **t** pray that he may interpret. *1100*
14:14 For if I pray in an *unknown* **t**, my spirit *1100*
14:19 than ten thousand words in an *unknown* **t**. *1100*
14:26 hath a doctrine, hath a **t**, hath a revelation, *1100*
14:27 If any *man* speak in an *unknown* **t**, *let it be* *1100*
Php 2:11 And *that* every **t** should confess that Jesus *1100*
Jas 1:26 and bridleth not his **t**, but deceiveth his own *1100*
3: 5 Even so the **t** is a little member, and *1100*
3: 6 And the **t** *is* a fire, a world of iniquity: so *1100*
3: 6 so is the **t** amongst our members, that it *1100*
3: 8 But the **t** can no man tame; *it is* an unruly *1100*
1Pe 3:10 let him refrain his **t** from evil, and his lips *1100*
1Jn 3:18 let us not love in word, neither in **t**; *1100*
Rev 5: 9 and **t**, and people, and nation; *1100*
9:11 whose name **in the Hebrew t** *is* Abaddon, *1447*
9:11 but in the Greek *t* hath *his* name Apollyon. NIG
14: 6 and kindred, and **t**, and people, *1100*
16:16 place called **in the Hebrew t** Armageddon. *1447*

TONGUES (36) [TONGUE]

Ge 10:20 after their **t**, in their countries, *and* in their 3956
10:31 after their **t**, in their lands, after their 3956
Ps 31:20 secretly in a pavilion from the strife of **t**. 3956
55: 9 Destroy, O Lord, *and* divide their **t**: for I 3956
78:36 and they lied unto him with their **t**. 3956
140: 3 They have sharpened their **t** like a serpent; 3956
Isa 66:18 that *I* will gather all nations and **t**; 3956
Jer 9: 3 they bend their **t** *like* their bow *for* lies: 3956
23:31 that use their **t**, and say, He saith. 3956
Mk 16:17 cast out devils; they shall speak with new **t**; *1100*
Ac 2: 3 And there appeared unto them cloven **t** like *1100*
2: 4 and began to speak with other **t**, as *1100*
2:11 we do hear them speak in our **t** *1100*
10:46 For they heard them speak with **t**, and *1100*
19: 6 and they spake with **t**, and prophesied. *1100*
Ro 3:13 with their **t** they have used deceit; *1100*
1Co 12:10 of spirits; to another *divers* kinds of **t**; *1100*
12:10 to another the interpretation of **t**: *1100*
12:28 helps, governments, diversities of **t**. *1100*
12:30 do all speak with **t**? do all interpret? *1100*
13: 1 Though I speak with the **t** of men and *1100*
13: 8 whether *there be* **t**, they shall cease; *1100*
14: 5 I would that ye all spake with **t**, but rather *1100*
14: 5 prophesieth than he that speaketh with **t**, *1100*
14: 6 if I come unto you speaking with **t**, *1100*
14:18 my God, I speak with **t** more than you all: *1100*
14:21 With *men* of **other t** and other lips will I *2084*
14:22 Wherefore **t** are for a sign, not to them that *1100*
14:23 and all speak with **t**, and there come in *1100*
14:39 to prophesy, and forbid not to speak with **t**. *1100*
Rev 7: 9 all nations, and kindreds, and people, and **t**, *1100*
10:11 and nations, and **t**, and kings. *1100*
11: 9 *they* of the people and kindreds and **t** and *1100*
13: 7 him over all kindreds, and **t**, and nations. *1100*
16:10 and they gnawed their **t** for pain, *1100*
17:15 and multitudes, and nations, and **t**. *1100*

TOO (51)

Ge 18:14 Is any thing **t** hard for the LORD? At 4480
Ex 12: 4 if the household be **t** little for the lamb, 4480
18:18 for *this* thing *is* **t** heavy for thee; thou art 4480
36: 7 for all the work to make it, and **t much**. 3498
Nu 11:14 people alone, because *it is* **t** heavy for me. 4480

Nu 16: 3 said unto them, *Ye take* **t much** upon you, 7227
16: 7 *ye take* **t much** upon you, ye sons of Levi. 7227
22: 6 this people; for they *are* t mighty for me: 4480
Dt 1:17 the cause that is t hard for you, bring *it* unto 4480
2:36 there was not one city t strong for us: 4480
12:21 to put his name there be t far from thee, 4480
14:24 if the way be t long for thee, so that thou 4480
14:24 *or* if the place be t far from thee, which NIH
17: 8 If there arise a matter t hard for thee in 4480
Jos 17:15 if mount Ephraim be t narrow for thee. 3588
19: 9 the children of Judah was **t much** for them: 7227
19:47 the coast of the children of Dan went out *t* NIH
22:17 *Is* the iniquity of Peor *t* little for us, from NIH
Jdg 7: 2 The people that *are* with thee *are* **t many** 7227
7: 4 unto Gideon, The people *are* yet t many; NIH
18:26 when Micah saw that they *were* t strong for 4480
Ru 1:12 go *your way;* for I am t old to have a 4480
2Sa 3:39 these men the sons of Zeruiah *be* t hard for 4480
10:11 If the Syrians be t strong for me, then 4480
10:11 if the children of Ammon be t strong for 4480
12: 8 if *that had been t* little, I would moreover NIH
22:18 hated me: for they were t strong for me. 4480
1Ki 1:36 LORD God of my lord the king say so *t*. NIH
8:64 *was* t little to receive the burnt offerings, 4480
12:28 *It is* t much for you to go up *to* Jerusalem: 4480
19: 7 eat; because the journey *is* t great for thee. 4480
2Ki 3:26 saw that the battle was **t** sore **for** him, 4480
6: 1 the place where we dwell with thee is t 4480
1Ch 19:12 If the Syrians be t strong for me, then thou 4480
19:12 if the children of Ammon be t strong for 4480
2Ch 29:34 the priests were *t* few, so that they could not NIH
Est 1:18 Thus *shall there arise* t much contempt 3509.1
Job 42: 3 *things* t wonderful for me, which I knew 4480
Ps 18:17 hated me: for they were t strong for me. 4480
35:10 which deliverest the poor from him that is t 4480
38: 4 as a heavy burden they are t heavy for me. 4480
73:16 to know this, it *was* t painful for me; NIH
131: 1 in great *matters,* or in *things* t high for me. 4480
139: 6 *Such* knowledge *is* t wonderful for me; it is 4480
Pr 24: 7 Wisdom *is t* high for a fool: he openeth not NIH
30:18 There be three *things which* are t wonderful 4480
Isa 49:19 shall even now be t narrow by reason of NIH
49:20 in thine ears, The place *is* t strait for me: NIH
Jer 32:17 *and* there is nothing t hard for thee: 4480
32:27 all flesh: is there any thing t hard for me? 4480
Ac 17:22 that in all *things* ye are **t superstitious**. *1174*

TOOK (752) [TAKE]

Ge 2:15 the LORD God t the man, and put him 3947
2:21 he t one of his ribs, and closed up the flesh 3947
3: 6 she t of the fruit thereof, and did eat, and 3947
4:19 Lamech t unto him two wives: the name of 3947
5:24 with God: and he *was* not; for God t him. 3947
6: 2 they t them wives of all which they chose. 3947
8: 9 t her, and pulled her in unto him into 3947
8:20 t of every clean beast, and of every clean 3947
9:23 Shem and Japheth t a garment, and laid *it* 3947
11:29 Abram and Nahor t them wives: the name 3947
11:31 Terah t Abram his son, and Lot the son of 3947
12: 5 Abram t Sarai his wife, and Lot his 3947
14:11 they t all the goods of Sodom and 3947
14:12 they t Lot, Abram's brother's son, 3947
15:10 he t unto him all these, and divided them in 3947
16: 3 Sarai Abram's wife t Hagar her maid 3947
17:23 Abraham t Ishmael his son, and all that 3947
18: 8 he t butter, and milk, and the calf which he 3947
20: 2 Abimelech king of Gerar sent, and t Sarah. 3947
20:14 Abimelech t sheep, and oxen, and 3947
21:14 t bread, and a bottle of water, and gave *it* 3947
21:21 his mother t him a wife out of the land of 3947
21:27 Abraham t sheep and oxen, and gave *them* 3947
22: 3 t two of his young men with him, and Isaac 3947
22: 6 Abraham t the wood of the burnt offering, 3947
22: 6 he t the fire in his hand, and a knife; and 3947
22:10 his hand, and t the knife to slay his son. 3947
22:13 Abraham went and t the ram, and 3947
24: 7 which t me from my father's house, and 3947
24:10 the servant t ten camels of the camels of his 3947
24:22 that the man t a golden earring of half a 3947
24:61 the servant t Rebekah, and went his way. 3947
24:65 therefore she t a vail, and covered herself. 3947
24:67 and t Rebekah, and she became his wife; 3947
25: 1 again Abraham t a wife, and her name *was* 3947
25:20 Isaac was forty years old when he t 3947
25:26 and his hand **t hold** on Esau's heel; 270
26:34 Esau was forty years old when he t to wife 3947
27:15 Rebekah t goodly raiment of her eldest son 3947
27:36 he **t away** my birthright; and behold, 3947
28: 9 t unto the wives which he had Mahalath 3947
28:11 he t of the stones of *that* place, and 3947
28:18 t the stone that he had put *for* his pillows, 3947
29:23 that he t Leah his daughter, and brought her 3947
30: 9 she t Zilpah her maid, and gave her Jacob 3947
30:37 Jacob t him rods of green poplar, and of 3947
31:23 he t his brethren with him, and 3947
31:45 Jacob t a stone, and set it up *for* a pillar. 3947
31:46 and they t stones, and made a heap: 3947
32:13 t of that which came to his hand a present 3947
32:22 t his two wives, and his two 3947
32:23 he t them, and sent them over the brook, 3947
33:11 And he urged him, and he t *it*. 3947
34: 2 he t her, and lay with her, and defiled her. 3947
34:25 t each man his sword, and came upon 3947
34:26 t Dinah out of Shechem's house, and 3947
34:28 They t their sheep, and their oxen, and their 3947
34:29 their wives t they **captive**, and spoiled even 7617
36: 2 Esau t his wives of the daughters of 3947
36: 6 Esau t his wives, and his sons, and his 3947
37:24 they t him, and cast him into a pit: and 3947
37:31 they t Joseph's coat, and killed a kid of 3947
38: 2 and he t her, and went in unto her. 3947
38: 6 Judah t a wife for Er his firstborn, 3947
38:28 the midwife t and bound upon his hand a 3947
39:20 Joseph's master t him, and put him into 3947
40:11 I t the grapes, and pressed them into 3947

Ge 41:42 Pharaoh **t off** his ring from his hand, and 5493
42:24 t from them Simeon, and bound him before 3947
42:30 to us, and t us for spies of the country. 5414
43:15 the men t that present, and they took double 3947
43:15 they t double money in their hand, and 3947
43:34 he t *and sent* messes unto them from before 5375
44:11 they speedily **t down** every man his sack to 3381
46: 1 Israel t his **journey** with all that he had, 5265
46: 6 they t their cattle, and their goods, 3947
47: 2 he t some of his brethren, *even* five men, 3947
48: 1 he t with him his two sons, Manasseh and 3947
48:13 Joseph t them both, Ephraim in his right 3947
48:22 which I t out of the hand of the Amorite 3947
50:25 Joseph **t an oath** of the children of Israel, 7650
Ex 2: 1 of Levi, and t *to wife* a daughter of Levi. 3947
2: 3 she t for him an ark of bulrushes, and 3947
2: 9 And the woman t the child, and nursed it. 3947
4: 6 when he t it **out**, behold, his hand *was* 3318
4:20 Moses t his wife and his sons, and set them 3947
4:20 and Moses t the rod of God in his hand. 3947
4:25 Zipporah t a sharp stone, and cut off 3947
6:20 Amram t him Jochebed his father's sister to 3947
6:23 Aaron t him Elisheba, daughter of 3947
6:25 Eleazar Aaron's son t him *one* of 3947
9:10 they t ashes of the furnace, and 3947
10:19 which **t away** the locusts, and cast them 5375
12:34 the people t their dough before it was 5375
13:19 Moses t the bones of Joseph with him: 3947
13:20 And they t their **journey** from Succoth, and 5265
13:22 He t not **away** the pillar of the cloud by 4185
14: 6 his chariot, and t his people with him: 3947
14: 7 he t six hundred chosen chariots, and all 3947
14:25 **t off** their chariot wheels, that they drave 5493
15:20 the sister of Aaron, t a timbrel in her hand; 3947
16: 1 they t their **journey** from Elim, and all 5265
17:12 they t a stone, and put *it* under him, and 3947
18: 2 father in law, t Zipporah, Moses' wife, 3947
18:12 t a burnt offering and sacrifices for God: 3947
24: 6 Moses t half of the blood, and put *it* in 3947
24: 7 he t the book of the covenant, and read in 3947
24: 8 Moses t the blood, and sprinkled *it* on 3947
32:20 he t the calf which they had made, and 3947
33: 7 Moses t the tabernacle, and pitched it 3947
34: 4 and t in his hand the two tables of stone. 3947
34:34 he **t** the vail **off**, until he came out. 5493
40:20 he t and put the Testimony into the ark, 3947
Lev 6: 4 that which he **t violently away**, 1497+1500
8:10 Moses t the anointing oil, and anointed 3947
8:15 he slew *it;* and Moses t the blood, and put *it* 3947
8:16 he t all the fat that *was* upon the inwards, 3947
8:23 he slew *it;* and Moses t of the blood of it, 3947
8:25 he t the fat, and the rump, and all the fat 3947
8:26 he t one unleavened cake, and a cake of 3947
8:28 Moses t them from off their hands, and 3947
8:29 Moses t the breast, and waved it *for* a wave 3947
8:30 Moses t of the anointing oil, and of 3947
9:15 the people's offering, and t the goat, 3947
9:17 **t a handful** thereof, and burnt *it* 3709+4390
10: 1 t either of them his censer, and put fire 3947
Nu 1:17 Aaron t these men which are expressed by 3947
3:49 Moses t the redemption money of them that 3947
3:50 Of the firstborn of the children of Israel t 3947
7: 6 Moses t the wagons and the oxen, and 3947
10:12 the children of Israel t their journeys out of 5265
10:13 they first t their **journey** according to 5265
11:25 t of the spirit that *was* upon him, and gave *it* 680
16: 1 the son of Peleth, sons of Reuben, t *men:* 3947
16:18 they t every man his censer, and put fire in 3947
16:39 Eleazar the priest t the brasen censers, 3947
16:47 Aaron t as Moses commanded, and ran into 3947
17: 9 and they looked, and t every man his rod. 3947
20: 9 Moses t the rod from before the LORD, 3947
21: 1 and t *some* of them **prisoners**. 7617+7628
21:25 Israel t all these cities: and Israel dwelt in 3947
21:32 they t the villages thereof, and drove out 3920
22:41 that Balak t Balaam, and brought him up 3947
23: 7 he **t up** his parable, and said, Balak 5375
23:11 I t thee to curse mine enemies, and behold, 3947
23:18 he **t up** his parable, and said, Rise up, 5375
24: 3 he **t up** his parable, and said, Balaam 5375
24:15 he **t up** his parable, and said, Balaam 5375
24:20 on Amalek, he **t up** his parable, and said, 5375
24:21 **t up** his parable, and said, Strong *is* thy 5375
24:23 he **t up** his parable, and said, Alas, 5375
25: 7 and t a javelin in his hand; 3947
27:22 he t Joshua, and set him before Eleazar 3947
31: 9 Israel t *all* the women of Midian **captives**, 7617
31: 9 t the **spoil** of all their cattle, and all their 962
31:11 they t all the spoil, and all the prey, *both* of 3947
31:27 between them that t the war upon them, 8610
31:47 Moses t one portion of fifty, *both* of man 3947
31:51 and Eleazar the priest t the gold of them, 3947
31:54 Eleazar the priest t the gold of the captains 3947
32:39 t it, and dispossessed the Amorite which 3920
32:41 and t the small towns thereof, 3920
32:42 Nobah went and t Kenath, and the villages 3920
33:12 they t their **journey** out of the wilderness 5265
Dt 1:15 So I t the chief of your tribes, wise men, 3947
1:23 I t twelve men of you, one of a tribe: 3947
1:25 they t of the fruit of the land in their hands, 3947
2: 1 t our **journey** into the wilderness *by* 5265
2:34 we t all his cities at that time, and 3920
2:35 Only the cattle we **t for a prey** unto 962
2:35 and the spoil of the cities which we t. 3920
3: 4 we t all his cities at that time, there was not 3920
3: 4 there was not a city which we t not from 3947
3: 7 of the cities, we **t for a prey** to ourselves. 962
3: 8 we t at that time out of the hand of the two 3947
3:14 Jair the son of Manasseh t all the country of 3947
9:17 I t the two tables, and cast them out of my 8610
9:21 I t your sin, the calf which ye had made, 3947
10: 6 the children of Israel t their **journey** from 5265
22:14 I t this woman, and when I came to her, 3947
24: 3 husband die, which t her *to be* his wife; 3947
29: 8 we t their land, and gave it for an 3947

Jos 2: 4 the woman t the two men, and hid them, 3947
3: 6 they **t up** the ark of the covenant, and 5375
4: 8 **t up** twelve stones out of the midst of 5375
4:20 twelve stones, which they t out of Jordan, 3947
6:12 and the priests **t up** the ark of the LORD. 5375
6:20 man straight before him, and they t the city. 3920
7: 1 the tribe of Judah, t of the accursed thing: 3947
7:17 and he t the family of the Zarhites: 3920
7:21 then I coveted them, and t them; 3947
7:23 they t them out of the midst of the tent, 3947
7:24 t Achan the son of Zerah, and the silver, 3947
8:12 he t about five thousand men, and set them 3947
8:19 and t it, and hasted and set the city on fire. 3920
8:23 the king of Ai they t alive, and brought him 8610
8:27 the spoil of that city Israel **t for a prey** unto 962
9: 4 t old sacks upon their asses, and 3947
9:12 This our bread we t hot for our **provision** 6679
9:14 the men t of their victuals, and asked not 3947
10:27 they t them **down** off the trees, and 3381
10:28 that day Joshua t Makkedah, and smote it 3920
10:32 which t it on the second day, and smote it 3920
10:35 they t it on that day, and smote it with 3920
10:37 they t it, and smote it with the edge of 3920
10:39 he t it, and the king thereof, and all 3920
11:10 t Hazor, and smote the king thereof with 3920
11:14 the children of Israel **t for a prey** unto 962
11:16 So Joshua t all that land, the hills, and all 3947
11:17 all their kings he t, and smote them, and 3920
11:19 of Gibeon: all *other* they t in battle. 3947
11:23 So Joshua t the whole land, according to all 3947
15:17 the son of Kenaz, the brother of Caleb, t it: 3920
16: 4 and Ephraim, t their **inheritance**. 5157
19:47 t it, and smote it with the edge of 3920
24: 3 I t your father Abraham from the *other* side 3947
24:26 t a great stone, and set it up there under an 3947
Jdg 1:13 son of Kenaz, Caleb's younger brother, t it: 3920
1:18 Also Judah t Gaza with the coast thereof, 3920
3: 6 they t their daughters to be their wives, 3947
3:21 t the dagger from his right thigh, and 3947
3:25 therefore they t a key, and opened *them:* 3947
3:28 t the fords of Jordan toward Moab, and 3920
4:21 Jael Heber's wife t a nail of the tent, and 3947
4:21 t a hammer in her hand, and went softly 7760
5:19 of Megiddo; they t no gain of money. 3947
6:27 Gideon t ten men of his servants, and did as 3947
7: 8 So the people t victuals in their hand, and 3947
7:24 t the waters unto Beth-barah and Jordan. 3920
7:25 they t two princes of the Midianites, Oreb 3920
8:12 t the two kings of Midian, Zebah and 3920
8:16 he t the elders of the city, and thorns of 3947
8:21 **t away** the ornaments that *were* on their 3947
9:43 he t the people, and divided them into three 3947
9:45 he t the city, and slew the people that *was* 3920
9:48 Abimelech t an axe in his hand, and 3947
9:48 t it, and laid *it* on his shoulder, and 5375
9:50 and encamped against Thebez, and t it. 3920
11:13 Because Israel **t away** my land, when they 3947
11:15 Israel t not **away** the land of Moab, 3947
12: 5 the Gileadites t the passages of Jordan 3920
12: 6 they t him, and slew him at the passages of 270
12: 9 **t in** thirty daughters from abroad for his 935
13:19 So Manoah t a kid with a meat offering, 3947
14: 9 he t thereof in his hands, and went on 7287
14:19 t their spoil, and gave change *of garments* 3947
15: 4 t firebrands, and turned tail to tail, and 3947
15:15 t it, and slew a thousand men therewith. 3947
16: 3 t the doors of the gate of the city, and 270
16:12 Delilah therefore t new ropes, and 3947
16:21 the Philistines t him, and put out his eyes, 270
16:29 Samson **t hold** of the two middle pillars 3943
16:31 t him, and brought *him* up, and buried him 5375
17: 2 behold, the silver *is* with me; I t it. 3947
17: 4 his mother t two hundred *shekels* of silver, 3947
18:17 *and* t the graven image, and the ephod, and 3947
18:20 he t the ephod, and the teraphim, and 3947
18:27 they t *the things* which Micah had made, 3947
19: 1 who t to him a concubine out of 3947
19:15 for *there was* no man that t them into *his* 622
19:25 so the man t his concubine, and brought *her* 2388
19:28 the man t her *up* upon an ass, and the man 3947
19:29 he t a knife, and laid hold on his concubine, 3947
20: 6 And I t my concubine, and cut her in pieces, 270
21:23 t *them* wives, according to their number, 5375
Ru 1: 4 they t them wives of the women of Moab; 5375
2:18 she t *it* **up**, and went *into* the city: and 5375
4: 2 he t ten men of the elders of the city, and 3947
4:13 So Boaz t Ruth, and she was his wife: and 3947
4:16 Naomi t the child, and laid it in her bosom, 3947
1Sa 1:24 she t him **up** with her, with three bullocks, 5927
2:14 all that the fleshhook brought up the priest t 3947
5: 1 the Philistines t the ark of God, and 3947
5: 2 When the Philistines t the ark of God, they 3947
5: 3 they t Dagon, and set him in his place 3947
6:10 t two milch kine, and tied them to the cart, 3947
6:12 the kine t the **straight** way to the way of 3474
6:15 the Levites **t down** the ark of the LORD, 3381
7: 9 Samuel t a sucking lamb, and offered it *for* 3947
7:12 Samuel t a stone, and set *it* between 3947
8: 3 and t bribes, and perverted judgment. 3947
9:22 Samuel t Saul and his servant, and 3947
9:24 the cook **t up** the shoulder, and *that* which 7311
10: 1 Samuel t a vial of oil, and poured *it* upon 3947
11: 7 he t a yoke of oxen, and hewed them in 3947
14:32 t sheep, and oxen, and calves, and 3947
14:47 So Saul t the kingdom over Israel, and 3920
14:52 or any valiant man, he t him unto him. 622
15: 8 he t Agag the king of the Amalekites alive, 8610
15:21 the people t of the spoil, sheep and oxen, 3947
16:13 Samuel t the horn of oil, and anointed him 3947
16:20 Jesse t an ass *laden* with bread, and a bottle 3947
16:23 that David t a harp, and played with his 3947
17:20 the sheep with a keeper, and t, and went, 5375
17:34 and a bear, and t a lamb out of the flock: 5375
17:40 he t his staff in his hand, and chose him 3947
17:49 t thence a stone, and slang *it,* and smote 3947

T

1Sa 17:51 t his sword, and drew it out of the sheath 3947
17:54 David t the head of the Philistine, and 3947
17:57 Abner t him, and brought him before Saul 3947
18: 2 Saul t him that day, and would let him go 3947
19:13 Michal t an image, and laid it in the bed, 3947
24: 2 Saul t three thousand chosen men out of all 3947
25:18 t two hundred loaves, and two bottles of 3947
25:43 David also t Ahinoam of Jezreel; and 3947
26:12 So David t the spear and the cruse of water 3947
27: 9 t away the sheep, and the oxen, and 3947
28:24 t flour, and kneaded it, and did bake 3947
30:20 David t all the flocks and the herds, 3947
31: 4 therefore Saul t a sword, and fell upon it. 3947
31:12 t the body of Saul and the bodies of his 3947
31:13 they t their bones, and buried them under a 3947
2Sa 1:10 I t the crown that was upon his head, and 3947
1:11 David t hold on his clothes, and rent them; 2388
2: 8 t Ish-bosheth the son of Saul, and 3947
2:32 they t up Asahel, and buried him in 5375
3:15 and t her from her husband, 3947
3:27 Joab t him aside in the gate to speak with 5186
3:36 all the people t notice of it, and it pleased 5234
4: 4 of Jezreel, and his nurse t him up, and fled: 5375
4: 7 t his head, and gat them away through 3947
4:10 I t hold of him, and slew him in Ziklag, 270
4:12 they t the head of Ish-bosheth, and buried it 3947
5: 7 Nevertheless David t the strong hold of 3920
5:13 David t him mo concubines and wives out 3947
6: 6 his hand to the ark of God, and t hold of it; 270
7: 8 I t thee from the sheepcote, from following 3947
7:15 as I t it from Saul, whom I put away before 5493
8: 1 David t Metheg-ammah out of the hand of 3947
8: 4 David t from him a thousand chariots, and 3920
8: 7 David t the shields of gold that were on 3947
8: 8 king David t exceeding much brass. 3947
10: 4 Wherefore Hanun t David's servants, and 3947
11: 4 David sent messengers, and t her; and 3947
12: 4 t the poor man's lamb, and dressed it for 3947
12:26 children of Ammon, and t the royal city. 3920
12:29 to Rabbah, and fought against it, and t it. 3920
12:30 he t their king's crown from off his head, 3947
13: 8 she t flour, and kneaded it, and made cakes 3947
13: 9 she t a pan, and poured them out before 3947
13:10 Tamar t the cakes which she had made, 3947
13:11 he t hold of her, and said unto her, 2388
15: 5 forth his hand, and t him, and kissed him. 2388
17:19 the woman t and spread a covering over 3947
18:14 he t three darts in his hand, and thrust them 3947
18:17 they t Absalom, and cast him into a great 3947
20: 3 the king t the ten women his concubines, 3947
20: 9 Joab t Amasa by the beard with the right 270
20:10 Amasa t no heed to the sword that was in 8104
21: 8 the king t the two sons of Rizpah 3947
21:10 Rizpah the daughter of Aiah t sackcloth, 3947
21:12 David went and t the bones of Saul and 3947
22:17 He sent from above, he t me; he drew me 3947
23:16 the gate, and t it, and brought it to David: 5375
1Ki 1:39 Zadok the priest t a horn of oil out of 3947
3: 1 t Pharaoh's daughter, and brought her into 3947
3:20 at midnight, and t my son from beside me, 3947
4:15 he also t Basmath the daughter of Solomon 3947
8: 3 of Israel came, and the priests t up the ark. 5375
11:18 they t men with them out of Paran, and 3947
12:28 Whereupon the king t counsel, and 3289
13:29 the prophet t up the carcase of the man of 5375
14:26 he t away the treasures of the house of 3947
14:26 of the king's house; he even t away all: 3947
14:26 he t away all the shields of gold which 3947
15:12 he t away the sodomites out of the land, 5674
15:18 Asa t all the silver and the gold that were 3947
15:22 they t away the stones of Ramah, and 5375
16:31 that he t to wife Jezebel the daughter of 3947
17:19 he t him out of her bosom, and carried him 3947
17:23 Elijah t the child, and brought him down 3947
18: 4 that Obadiah t an hundred prophets, and 3947
18:10 He is not there; he t an oath of 7650
18:26 they t the bullock which was given them, 3947
18:31 Elijah t twelve stones, according to 3947
18:40 they t them: and Elijah brought them down 8610
19:21 t a yoke of oxen, and slew them, and boiled 3947
20:34 which my father t from thy father, 3947
20:41 and t the ashes away from his face; 5493
22:46 days of his father Asa, he t out of the land. 1197
2Ki 2: 8 Elijah t his mantle, and wrapt it together, 3947
2:12 he t hold of his own clothes, and rent them 2388
2:13 He t up also the mantle of Elijah that fell 7311
2:14 he t the mantle of Elijah that fell from him, 3947
3:26 he t with him seven hundred men that drew 3947
3:27 he t his eldest son that should have reigned 3947
4:37 the ground, and t up her son, and went out. 5375
5: 5 t with him ten talents of silver, and 3947
5:24 he t them from their hand, and 3947
6: 7 to thee. And he put out his hand, and t it. 3947
6: 8 t counsel with his servants, saying, In such 3289
7:14 They t therefore two chariot horses; and 3947
8: 9 went to meet him, and t a present with him, 3947
8:15 that he t a thick cloth, and dipt it in water, 3947
9:13 t every man his garment, and put it under 3947
10: 7 that they t the king's sons, and 3947
10:14 they t them alive, and slew them at the pit 8610
10:15 and he t him up to him into the chariot. 5927
10:31 Jehu t no heed to walk in the law of 8104
11: 2 t Joash the son of Ahaziah, and stale him 3947
11: 4 t an oath of them in the house of 7650
11: 9 they t every man his men that were to come 3947
11:19 he t the rulers over hundreds, and 3947
12: 9 Jehoiada the priest t a chest, and bored a 3947
12:17 went up, and fought against Gath, and t it: 3920
12:18 Jehoash king of Judah t all the hallowed 3947
13:15 arrows. And he t unto him bow and arrows. 3947
13:18 he t them. And he said unto the king of 3947
13:25 Jehoash the son of Jehoahaz t again out of 3947
14: 7 t Selah by war, and called the name of it 8610
14:13 Jehoash king of Israel t Amaziah king of 8610
14:14 he t all the gold and silver, and all 3947

2Ki 14:21 all the people of Judah t Azariah, which 3947
15:29 t Ijon, and Abel-beth-maachah, and Janoah, 3947
16: 8 Ahaz t the silver and gold that was found in 3947
16: 9 t it, and carried the people of it captive to 8610
16:17 t down the sea from off the brasen oxen 3381
17: 6 the king of Assyria t Samaria, and 3920
18:10 at the end of three years they t it: even in 3920
18:13 all the fenced cities of Judah, and t them. 8610
20: 7 they t and laid it on the boil, and 3947
23:11 he t away the horses that the kings of Judah 7673
23:16 t the bones out of the sepulchres, and 3947
23:19 Josiah t away, and did to them according to 5493
23:30 the people of the land t Jehoahaz the son of 3947
23:34 t Jehoahaz away: and he came to Egypt, 3947
24:12 the king of Babylon t him in the eighth year 3947
25: 6 So they t the king, and brought him up to 8610
25:14 wherewith they ministered, t they away. 3947
25:15 in silver, the captain of the guard t away. 3947
25:18 the captain of the guard t Seraiah the chief 3947
25:19 out of the city he t an officer that was set 3947
25:20 Nebuzar-adan captain of the guard t these, 3947
1Ch 2:19 Caleb t unto him Ephrath, which bare him 3947
2:23 he t Geshur, and Aram, with the towns of 3947
4:18 the daughter of Pharaoh, which Mered t. 3947
5:21 they t away their cattle; of their camels 7617
7:15 Machir t to wife the sister of Huppim and 3947
10: 4 So Saul t a sword, and fell upon it. 3947
10: 9 they t his head, and his armour, and 5375
10:12 t away the body of Saul, and the bodies of 5375
11: 5 Nevertheless David t the castle of Zion, 3920
11:18 the gate, and t it, and brought it to David: 5375
14: 3 David t moe wives at Jerusalem: and 3947
17: 7 I t thee from the sheepcote, even from 3947
17:13 as I t it from him that was before thee: 5493
18: 1 t Gath and her towns out of the hand of 3947
18: 4 David t from him a thousand chariots, and 3920
18: 7 David t the shields of gold that were on 3947
19: 4 Wherefore Hanun t David's servants, and 3947
20: 2 David t the crown of their king from off his 3947
23:22 and their brethren the sons of Kish t them. 5375
27:23 David t not the number of them from 5375
2Ch 5: 4 of Israel came; and the Levites t up the ark. 5375
8:18 t thence four hundred and fifty talents of 3947
10: 6 king Rehoboam t counsel with the old men 3289
10: 8 t counsel with the young men that were 3289
11:18 Rehoboam t him Mahalath the daughter of 3947
11:20 after her he t Maachah the daughter of 3947
11:21 (for he t eighteen wives, and 5375
12: 4 he t the fenced cities which pertained to 3920
12: 9 t away the treasures of the house of 3947
12: 9 the treasures of the king's house; he t all: 3947
13:19 t cities from him, Beth-el with the towns 3920
14: 3 For he t away the altars of the strange 5493
14: 5 Also he t away out of all the cities of Judah 5493
15: 8 he t courage, and put away the abominable 2388
16: 6 Asa the king t all Judah; and they carried 3947
17: 6 moreover he t away the high places and 5493
22:11 t Joash the son of Ahaziah, and stole him 3947
23: 1 t the captains of hundreds, Azariah the son 3947
23: 8 t every man his men that were to come in 3947
23:20 he t the captains of hundreds, and 3947
24: 3 Jehoiada t for him two wives; and he begat 5375
24:11 and t it, and carried it to his place again. 5375
25:13 three thousand of them, and t much spoil. 962
25:17 Amaziah king of Judah t advice, and 3289
25:23 Joash the king of Israel t Amaziah king of 8610
25:24 he t all the gold and the silver, and all NIH
26: 1 all the people of Judah t Uzziah, who was 3947
28: 8 t also away much spoil from them, and 962
28:15 t the captives, and with the spoil clothed all 2388
28:21 For Ahaz t away a portion out of 2505
29:16 the Levites t it, to carry it out abroad into 6901
30:14 t away the altars that were in Jerusalem, 5493
30:14 all the altars for incense t they away, and 5493
30:23 the whole assembly t counsel to keep other 3289
32: 3 He t counsel with his princes and 3289
33:11 which t Manasseh among the thorns, and 3920
33:15 he t away the strange gods, and the idol out 5493
34:33 Josiah t away all the abominations out of 5493
35:24 therefore t him out of that chariot, 5674
36: 1 the people of the land t Jehoahaz the son of 3947
36: 4 Necho t Jehoahaz his brother, and 3947
Ezr 2:61 which t a wife of the daughters of Barzillai 3947
5:14 which Nebuchadnezzar t out of the temple 5312
6: 5 which Nebuchadnezzar t forth out of 5312
8:30 So t the priests and the Levites the weight 6901
Ne 2: 1 I t up the wine, and gave it unto the king. 5375
4: 1 t great indignation, and mocked the Jews. 3707
5:12 I called the priests, and t an oath of them, 7650
7:63 which t one of the daughters of Barzillai 3947
9:25 they t strong cities, and a fat land, and 3920
Est 2: 7 mother were dead, t for his own daughter. 3947
3:10 the king t his ring from his hand, and 5493
6:11 t Haman the apparel and the horse, and 3947
8: 2 the king t off his ring, which he had taken 5493
9:27 t upon them, and upon their seed, and 6901
Job 1:15 Sabeans fell upon them, and t them away; 3947
2: 8 he t him a potsherd to scrape himself 3947
Ps 18:16 He sent from above, he t me, he drew me 3947
22: 9 thou art he that t me out of the womb: 1518
31:13 while they t counsel together against me, 3245
48: 6 Fear t hold upon them there, and pain, as of 270
55:14 We t sweet counsel together, and 4985
56: T of David, when the Philistines t him in Gath. 270
69: 4 then I restored that which I t not away. NIH
71: 6 thou art he that t me out of my mother's 1491
78:70 his servant, and t him from the sheepfolds: 3947
Pr 12:27 roasteth not that which he t in hunting: 6718
Ecc 2:20 of all the labour which I t under the sun. 5998
SS 5: 7 the keepers of the walls t away my vail 5375
Isa 8: 2 I t unto me faithful witnesses to record, 5749
20: 1 and fought against Ashdod, and t it; 3920
36: 1 all the defenced cities of Judah, and t them. 8610
40:14 With whom t he counsel, and 3289
Jer 13: 7 t the girdle from the place where I had hid 3947

Jer 25:17 t I the cup at the LORD'S hand, and 3947
26: 8 and the prophets and all the people t him, 8610
27:20 Which Nebuchadnezzar king of Babylon t 3947
28: 3 king of Babylon t away from this place, 3947
28:10 Hananiah the prophet t the yoke from off 3947
31:32 fathers in the day that I t them by the hand, 2388
32:10 sealed it, and t witnesses, 5707+5749
32:11 So I t the evidence of the purchase, both 3947
35: 3 I t Jaazaniah the son of Jeremiah, the son of 3947
36:14 So Baruch the son of Neriah t the roll in his 3947
36:21 he t it out of Elishama the scribe's 3947
36:32 t Jeremiah another roll, and gave it to 3947
37:13 he t Jeremiah the prophet, saying, 8610
37:14 so Irijah t Jeremiah, and brought him to 8610
37:17 t him out: and the king asked him secretly 3947
38: 6 t they Jeremiah, and cast him into 3947
38:11 So Ebed-melech t the men with him, and 3947
38:11 t thence old cast clouts and old rotten rags, 3947
38:13 and t him up out of the dungeon: 5927
38:14 t Jeremiah the prophet unto him into 3947
39:14 t Jeremiah out of the court of the prison, 3947
40: 2 the captain of the guard t Jeremiah, and 3947
41:12 they t all the men, and went to fight with 3947
41:16 t Johanan the son of Kareah, and all 3947
43: 5 of the forces, t all the remnant of Judah, 3947
50:33 all that t them captives held them fast; 7617
50:43 anguish t hold of him, and pangs as of a 2388
52: 9 they t the king, and carried him up unto 8610
52:18 wherewith they ministered, t they away. 3947
52:19 in silver, t the captain of the guard away. 3947
52:24 the captain of the guard t Seraiah the chief 3947
52:25 He t also out of the city an eunuch, 3947
52:26 So Nebuzar-adan the captain of the guard t 3947
La 5:13 They t the young men to grind, and 5375
Eze 3:12 the spirit t me up, and I heard behind me a 5375
3:14 t me away, and I went in bitterness, in 3947
8: 3 of a hand, and t me by a lock of mine head; 3947
10: 7 t thereof, and put it into the hands of him 5375
10: 7 clothed with linen: who t it, and went out. 3947
11:24 Afterwards the spirit t me up, and 5375
16:50 therefore I t them away as I saw good. 5493
17: 3 and t the highest branch of the cedar: 3947
17: 5 He t also of the seed of the land, and 3947
19: 5 she t another of her whelps, and made him 3947
23:10 they t her sons and her daughters, and slew 3947
23:13 she was defiled, that they t both one way, 3807.1
29: 7 When they t hold of thee by thy hand, 8610
33: 5 sound of the trumpet, and t not warning; 2094
43: 5 So the spirit t me up, and brought me into 5375
Da 1:16 Thus Melzar t away the portion of their 5375
3:22 the fire slew those men that t up Shadrach, 5267
5:20 and they t his glory from him: 5709
5:31 Darius the Median t the kingdom, 6902
Hos 1: 3 and t Gomer the daughter of Diblaim; 3947
12: 3 He t his brother by the heel in the womb, 6117
13:11 in mine anger, and t him away in my wrath. 3947
Am 7:15 the LORD t me as I followed the flock, 3947
Jnh 1:15 So they t up Jonah, and cast him forth into 5375
Zec 11: 7 I t unto me two staves; the one I called 3947
11:10 I t my staff, even Beauty, and cut it 3947
11:13 I t the thirty pieces of silver, and cast them 3947
Mt 1:24 had bidden him, and t unto him his wife: 3880
2:14 he t the young child and his mother by 3880
2:21 and t the young child and his mother, and 3880
8:17 saying Himself t our infirmities, and 2983
9:25 and t her by the hand, and the maid arose. 2902
13:31 which a man t, and sowed in his field: 2983
13:33 which a woman t, and hid in three 2983
14:12 And his disciples came, and t up the body, 142
14:19 and t the five loaves, and the two fishes, 2983
14:20 they t up of the fragments that remained 142
15:36 And he t the seven loaves and the fishes, 2983
15:37 they t up of the broken meat that was left 142
15:39 and t ship, and came into the coasts of 1684
16: 9 and how many baskets ye t up? 2983
16:10 and how many baskets ye t up? 2983
16:22 Then Peter t him, and began to rebuke him, 4355
18:28 on him, and t him by the throat, saying, 4155
20:17 And Jesus going up to Jerusalem t 3880
21:35 And the husbandmen t his servants, and 2983
21:46 because they t him for a prophet. 2192
22: 6 And the remnant t his servants, and 2902
22:15 t counsel how they might entangle him in 2983
24:39 until the flood came, and t them all away; 142
25: 1 which t their lamps, and went forth to meet 2983
25: 3 They that were foolish t their lamps, and 2983
25: 3 took their lamps, and t no oil with them: 2983
25: 4 But the wise t oil in their vessels with their 2983
25:15 and straightway t his journey. 589
25:35 me drink: I was a stranger, and ye t me in: 4863
25:38 saw we thee a stranger, and t thee in? 4863
25:43 I was a stranger, and ye t me not in: naked, 4863
26:26 Jesus t bread, and blessed it, and brake it, 2983
26:27 And he t the cup, and gave thanks, and 2983
26:37 And he t with him Peter and the two sons 3880
26:50 and laid hands on Jesus, and t him. 2902
27: 1 elders of the people t counsel against Jesus 2983
27: 6 And the chief priests t the silver pieces, and 2983
27: 7 And they t counsel, and bought with them 2983
27: 9 And they t the thirty pieces of silver, 2983
27:24 he t water, and washed his hands before 2983
27:27 Then the soldiers of the governor t Jesus 3880
27:30 and t the reed, and smote him on the head. 2983
27:31 they t the robe off from him, and put his 1562
27:48 and t a spunge, and filled it with vinegar, 2983
28:15 So they t the money, and did as they were 2983
Mk 1:31 And he came and t her by the hand, and 2902
2:12 t up the bed, and went forth before them all; 142
3: 6 straightway t counsel with the Herodians 4160
4:36 they t him even as he was in the ship. 3880
5:41 And he t the damsel by the hand, and 2902
6:29 heard of it, they came and t up his corpse, 142
6:43 And they t up twelve baskets full of 142
7:33 And he t him aside from the multitude, and 618
8: 6 and he t the seven loaves, and gave thanks, 2983

T

Mk 8: 8 they **t up** of the broken *meat* that was left 142
8:19 how many baskets full of fragments **t** ye **up**? 142
8:20 how many baskets full of fragments **t** ye **up**? 142
8:23 And he **t** the blind man by the hand, and led 1949
8:32 And Peter **t** him, and began to rebuke him. 4355
9:27 But Jesus **t** him by the hand, and lifted him 2902
9:36 And he **t** a child, and set him in the midst 2983
10:16 And he **t** them **up in** his **arms**, put *his* 1723
10:32 And he **t** again the twelve, and began to tell 3880
12: 8 And they **t** him, and killed *him,* and 2983
12:20 and the first **t** a wife, and dying left no 2983
12:21 And the second **t** her, and died, neither left 2983
14:22 Jesus **t** bread, and blessed, and brake *it,* and 2983
14:23 And he **t** the cup, and when he had given 2983
14:46 they laid their hands on him, and **t** him. 2902
14:49 in the temple teaching, and ye **t** me not: 2902
15:20 they **t off** the purple **from** him, and put his 1562
15:46 and **t** him **down**, and wrapped *him* in 2507
Lk 2:28 Then **t** he him *up* in his arms, and 1209
5:25 and **t up** *that* whereon he lay, and 142
8:54 and **t** her by the hand, and called, saying, 2902
9:10 And he **t** them, and went aside privately 3880
9:16 Then he **t** the five loaves and the two 2983
9:28 he **t** Peter and John and James, and went up 3880
9:47 of their heart, **t** a child, and set him by him, 1949
10:34 brought him to an inn, and **t care of** him. 1959
10:35 he **t out** two pence, and gave *them* to 1544
13:19 which a man **t**, and cast into his garden; 2983
13:21 which a woman **t** and hid in three measures 2983
14: 4 And he **t** *him,* and healed him, and let *him* 1949
15:13 and **t** his **journey** into a far country, and 589
18:31 Then he **t unto** *him* the twelve, and 3880
20:29 and the first **t** a wife, and died without 2983
20:30 And the second **t** her to wife, and he died 2983
20:31 And the third **t** her; and in like manner 2983
22:17 And he **t** *the* cup, and gave thanks, and 1209
22:19 And he **t** bread, and gave thanks, and 2983
22:54 Then **t** they him, and led *him,* and 4815
23:53 And he **t** it **down**, and wrapped it in linen, 2507
24:30 he **t** bread, and blessed *it,* and brake, and 2983
24:43 And he **t** *it,* and did eat before them. 2983
Jn 5: 9 made whole, and **t up** his bed, and walked: 142
6:11 And Jesus **t** the loaves; and when he had 2983
6:24 they also **t shipping**, 1519+1684+3588+4143
8:59 Then **t** they **up** stones to cast at him: but 142
10:31 Then the Jews **t up** stones again to stone 941
11:41 Then they **t away** the stone *from the place* 142
11:53 **t counsel together** for to put him to death 4823
12: 3 Then **t** Mary a pound of ointment of 2983
12:13 **T** branches of palm trees, and went forth to 2983
13: 4 and **t** a towel, and girded himself. 2983
18:12 the captain and officers of the Jews **t** Jesus, 4815
19: 1 Then Pilate therefore **t** Jesus, and 2983
19:16 And they **t** Jesus, and led *him* away. 3880
19:23 **t** his garments, and made four parts, 2983
19:27 And from that hour *that* disciple **t** her unto 2983
19:38 He came therefore, and **t** the body of Jesus. 142
19:40 Then **t** they the body of Jesus, and wound it 2983
Ac 1:16 which was guide to them that **t** Jesus. 4815
3: 7 And he **t** him by the right hand, and lift *him* 4084
4:13 and they **t knowledge** of them, that they 1921
5:33 cut *to the heart,* and **t counsel** to slay them. 1011
7:21 Pharaoh's daughter **t** him **up**, and 337
7:43 ye **t up** the tabernacle of Moloch, and 353
9:23 the Jews **t counsel** to kill him: 4823
9:25 Then the disciples **t** him by night, and 2983
9:27 But Barnabas **t** him, and brought *him* to 1949
10:26 But Peter **t** him **up**, saying, Stand up; 1453
12:25 and **t with** *them* John, whose surname was 4838
13:29 they **t** *him* **down** from the tree, and 2507
15:39 and *so* Barnabas **t** Mark, and sailed unto 3880
16: 3 and **t** and circumcised him because of 2983
16:33 And he **t** them the same hour of the night, 3880
17: 5 **t unto** *them* certain lewd fellows of 4355
17:19 And they **t** him, and brought him unto 1949
18:17 Then all the Greeks **t** Sosthenes, the *chief* 1949
18:18 and then **t** his **leave** of the brethren, and 657
18:26 they **t** him unto *them,* and expounded unto 4355
19:13 **t upon** them to call over them which had 2021
20:14 at Assos, we **t** him **in**, and came to Mitylene. 353
21: 6 taken our leave one of another, we **t** ship; 1910
21:11 he **t** Paul's girdle, and bound his *own* hands 142
21:15 And after those days we **t up** our **carriages**, 643
21:26 Then Paul **t** the men, and the next day 3880
21:30 and they **t** Paul, and drew him out of 1949
21:32 Who immediately **t** soldiers and centurions, 3880
21:33 and **t** him, and commanded *him* to be 1949
23:18 So he **t** him, and brought *him* to the chief 3880
23:19 Then the chief captain **t** him by the hand, 1949
23:31 **t** Paul, and brought *him* by night to 353
24: 6 whom we **t**, and would have judged 2902
24: 7 with great violence **t** *him* **away** out of our 520
27:35 he **t** bread, and gave thanks to God in 2983
27:36 of good cheer, and they also **t** *some* meat. 4355
28:15 Paul saw, he thanked God, and **t** courage. 2983
1Co 11:23 night in which he was betrayed **t** bread: 2983
11:25 After the same manner also *he t* the cup, NIG
Gal 2: 1 with Barnabas, and **t** Titus **with** *me* also. 4838
Php 2: 7 and **t** *upon him* the form of a servant, and 2983
Col 2:14 and **t** it out of the way, nailing it to *his* cross; 142
Heb 2:14 he also himself likewise **t part** of the same; 3348
2:16 For verily he **t** not **on** *him the nature of* 1949
2:16 but he **t on** *him* the seed of Abraham. 1949
8: 9 **t** them by the hand to lead them out of 1949
9:19 he **t** the blood of calves and of goats, 2983
10:34 and **t** joyfully the spoiling of your goods, 4327
Rev 5: 7 **t** the book out of the right hand of him that 2983
8: 5 And the angel **t** the censer, and filled it 2983
10:10 And I **t** the little book out of the angel's 2983
18:21 And a mighty angel **t up** a stone like a great 142

TOOKEST (2) [TAKE]

Ps 99: 8 though thou **t vengeance** of their 5358
Eze 16:18 **t** thy broidered garments, and 3947

TOOL (4)

Ex 20:25 for if thou lift up thy **t** upon it, thou hast 2719
32: 4 fashioned it with a **graving t**, after he had 2747
Dt 27: 5 thou shalt not lift up *any* iron *t* upon them. NIH
1Ki 6: 7 nor axe *nor* any **t** of iron heard in the house, 3627

TOOTH (11) [CHEEK-TEETH, TEETH, TOOTH'S]

Ex 21:24 Eye for eye, **t** for tooth, hand for hand, 8127
21:24 Eye for eye, tooth for **t**, hand for hand, 8127
21:27 if he smite out his manservant's **t**, or 8127
21:27 manservant's tooth, or his maidservant's **t**; 8127
Lev 24:20 Breach for breach, eye for eye, **t** for tooth: 8127
24:20 Breach for breach, eye for eye, tooth for **t**: 8127
Dt 19:21 eye for eye, **t** for tooth, hand for hand, 8127
19:21 eye for eye, tooth for **t**, hand for hand, 8127
Pr 25:19 *man* in time of trouble *is like* a broken **t**, 8127
Mt 5:38 An eye for an eye, and a **t** for a tooth: 3599
5:38 An eye for an eye, and a tooth for a **t**: 3599

TOOTH'S (1) [TOOTH]

Ex 21:27 he shall let him go free for his **t** sake. 8127

TOP (90) [HOUSETOP, HOUSETOPS, TOPS]

Ge 11: 4 a tower, whose **t** *may reach* unto heaven; 7218
28:12 the earth, and the **t** of it reached to heaven: 7218
28:18 *for* a pillar, and poured oil upon the **t** of it. 7218
Ex 17: 9 to morrow I will stand on the **t** of the hill 7218
17:10 Aaron, and Hur went up *to* the **t** of the hill. 7218
19:20 upon mount Sinai, on the **t** of the mount: 7218
19:20 the LORD called Moses *up* to the **t** of 7218
24:17 **t** of the mount in the eyes of the children of 7218
28:32 there shall be a hole in the **t** of it, in 7218
30: 3 the **t** thereof, and the sides thereof round 1406
34: 2 present thyself there to me in the **t** of 7218
37:26 *both* the **t** of it, and the sides thereof round 1406
Nu 14:40 gat them up into the **t** of the mountain, 7218
14:44 they presumed to go up unto the hill **t**: 7218
20:28 and Aaron died there in the **t** of the mount: 7218
21:20 in the country of Moab, *to* the **t** of Pisgah, 7218
23: 9 For from the **t** of the rocks I see him, and 7218
23:14 to the **t** of Pisgah, and built seven altars, 7218
23:28 Balak brought Balaam *unto* the **t** of Peor, 7218
Dt 3:27 Get thee up *into* the **t** of Pisgah, and lift up 7218
28:35 the sole of thy foot unto the **t of** thy **head**. 6936
33:16 upon the **t of the head** of him *that was* 6936
34: 1 *to* the **t** of Pisgah, that *is* over against 7218
Jos 15: 8 the border went up to the **t** of the mountain 7218
15: 9 the border was drawn from the **t** of the hill 7218
Jdg 6:26 the LORD thy God upon the **t** of this rock, 7218
9: 7 and stood in the **t** of mount Gerizim, 7218
9:25 in wait for him in the **t** of the mountains, 7218
9:36 there come people down from the **t** of 7218
9:51 and gat them up to the **t** of the tower. 1406
15: 8 and dwelt in the **t** of the rock Etam. 5585
15:11 three thousand men of Judah went to the **t** 5585
16: 3 carried them up to the **t** of a hill that *is* 7218
1Sa 9:25 with Saul upon the **t of** the **house**. 1406
9:26 Samuel called Saul to the **t of** the **house**, 1406
26:13 and stood on the **t** of a hill afar off; 7218
2Sa 2:25 one troop, and stood on the **t** of a hill. 7218
15:32 that *when* David was come to the **t** *of* 7218
16: 1 when David was a little past the **t** *of* 7218
16:22 Absalom a tent upon the **t of** the **house**; 1406
1Ki 7:17 for the chapiters which *were* upon the **t** of 7218
7:18 to cover the chapiters that *were* upon the **t**, 7218
7:19 (And the chapiters that *were* upon the **t** of 7218
7:22 upon the **t** of the pillars *was* lily work: so 7218
7:35 in the **t** of the base *was there* a round 7218
7:35 on the **t** of the base the ledges thereof and 7218
7:41 that *were* on the **t** of the *two* pillars; 7218
7:41 which *were* upon the **t** of the pillars; 7218
10:19 and the **t** of the throne *was* round behind: 7218
18:42 Elijah went up to the **t** of Carmel; and 7218
2Ki 1: 9 behold, he sat on the **t** of a hill. And he 7218
9:13 put *it* under him on the **t** of the stairs, and 1634
23:12 the altars that *were* on the **t** of the upper 1406
2Ch 3:15 the chapiter that *was* on the **t** *of each* of 7218
4:13 the chapiters *which were* on the **t** of the two 7218
4:12 chapiters which *were* on the **t** of the pillars; 7218
25:12 brought them unto the **t** of the rock, and 7218
25:12 cast them down from the **t** of the rock, 7218
Est 5: 2 drew near, and touched the **t** of the sceptre. 7218
Ps 72:16 in the earth upon the **t** of the mountains; 7218
Pr 8: 2 She standeth in the **t** of high places by 7218
23:34 or as he that lieth upon the **t** of a mast. 7218
SS 4: 8 look from the **t** of Amana, from the top of 7218
4: 8 from the **t** of Shenir and Hermon, from 7218
Isa 2: 2 be established in the **t** of the mountains, 7218
17: 6 three berries in the **t** of the uppermost 7218
30:17 till ye be left as a beacon upon the **t** of a 7218
42:11 let them shout from the **t** of the mountains. 7218
La 2:19 that faint for hunger in the **t** of every street. 7218
4: 1 are poured out in the **t** of every street. 7218
Eze 17: 4 He cropt off the **t** of his young twigs, and 7218
17:22 will set *it;* I will crop off from the **t** of his 7218
24: 7 she set it upon the **t** of a rock; she poured it 6706
24: 8 I have set her blood upon the **t** of a rock, 6706
26: 4 from her, and make her like the **t** of a rock. 6706
26:14 I will make thee like the **t** of a rock: 6706
31: 3 and his **t** was among the thick boughs. 6788
31:10 he hath shot up his **t** among the thick 6788
31:14 neither shoot up their **t** among the thick 6788
43:12 Upon the **t** of the mountain the whole limit 7218
Am 1: 2 and the **t** of Carmel shall wither. 7218
9: 3 though they hide themselves in the **t** of 7218
Mic 4: 1 be established in the **t** of the mountains, 7218
Na 3:10 dashed in pieces at the **t** of all the streets: 7218
Zec 4: 2 with a bowl upon the **t** of it, and his seven 7218
4: 2 which *were* upon the **t** thereof: 7218
Mt 27:51 was rent in twain from the **t** to the bottom; 509
Mk 15:38 was rent in twain from the **t** to the bottom. 509
Jn 19:23 without seam, woven from the **t** throughout. 509
Heb 11:21 worshipped, *leaning* upon the **t** of his staff. 206

TOPAZ (5)

Ex 28:17 row *shall be* a sardius, a **t**, and a carbuncle: 6357
39:10 *first* row *was* a sardius, a **t**, and a carbuncle: 6357
Job 28:19 The **t** of Ethiopia shall not equal it, 6357
Eze 28:13 **t**, and the diamond, the beryl, the onyx, and 6357
Rev 21:20 the eighth, beryl; the ninth, a **t**; the tenth, 5116

TOPHEL (1)

Dt 1: 1 **T**, and Laban, and Hazeroth, and Dizahab. 8603

TOPHET (9) [TOPHETH]

Isa 30:33 For **T** *is* ordained of old; yea, for the king it 8613
Jer 7:31 they have built the high places of **T**, 8612
7:32 that it shall no more be called **T**, 8612
7:32 for they shall bury in **T**, till there be no 8612
19: 6 that this place shall no more be called **T**, 8612
19:11 they shall bury *them* in **T**, till *there be* no 8612
19:12 and *even* make this city as **T**: 8612
19:13 shall be defiled as the place of **T**, because 8612
19:14 came Jeremiah from **T**, whither the LORD 8612

TOPHETH (1) [TOPHET]

2Ki 23:10 he defiled **T**, which *is* in the valley of 8612

TOPMOST See OUTMOST; UPPERMOST

TOPS (10) [TOP]

Ge 8: 5 were the **t** of the mountains seen. 7218
2Sa 5:24 of a going in the **t** of the mulberry trees, 7218
1Ki 7:16 to set upon the **t** of the pillars: 7218
1Ch 14:15 of going in the **t** of the mulberry trees, 7218
Job 24:24 and cut off as the **t** of the ears of corn. 7218
Isa 2:21 into the **t** of the ragged rocks, for fear of 5585
15: 3 on the **t of** their **houses**, and in their streets, 1406
Eze 6:13 in all the **t** of the mountains, and 7218
Hos 4:13 They sacrifice upon the **t** of the mountains, 7218
Joel 2: 5 Like the noise of chariots on the **t** of 7218

TORCH (1) [TORCHES]

Zec 12: 6 the wood, and like a **t** of fire in a sheaf; 3940

TORCHES (3) [TORCH]

Na 2: 3 the chariots *shall be* with flaming **t** in 6393
2: 4 they shall seem like **t**, they shall run like 3940
Jn 18: 3 thither with lanterns and **t** and weapons. 2985

TORMENT (11) [TORMENTED, TORMENTORS, TORMENTS]

Mt 8:29 art thou come hither to **t** us before the time? 928
Mk 5: 7 I adjure thee by God, that thou **t** me not. 928
Lk 8:28 of God most high? I beseech thee, **t** me not. 928
16:28 lest they also come into this place of **t**. 931
1Jn 4:18 because fear hath **t**. He that feareth is not 2851
Rev 9: 5 and their **t** *was* as the torment of a scorpion, 929
9: 5 and their torment *was* as the **t** of a scorpion, 929
14:11 And the smoke of their **t** ascendeth up for 929
18: 7 so much **t** and sorrow give her: 929
18:10 Standing afar off for the fear of her **t**, saying, 929
18:15 shall stand afar off for the fear of her **t**, 929

TORMENTED (8) [TORMENT]

Mt 8: 6 lieth at home sick of the palsy, grievously **t**. 928
Lk 16:24 cool my tongue; for I am **t** in this flame. 3600
16:25 but now he is comforted, and thou art **t**. 3600
Heb 11:37 and goatskins; being destitute, afflicted, **t**; 2558
Rev 9: 5 but that they should be **t** five months: 928
11:10 these two prophets **t** them that dwelt on 928
14:10 and he shall be **t** with fire and brimstone in 928
20:10 and shall be **t** day and night for ever and 928

TORMENTORS (1) [TORMENT]

Mt 18:34 lord was wroth, and delivered him to the **t**, 930

TORMENTS (2) [TORMENT]

Mt 4:24 that were taken with divers diseases and **t**, 931
Lk 16:23 being in **t**, and seeth Abraham afar off, and 931

TORN (17) [TEAR]

Ge 31:39 **That which was t** *of beasts* I brought not 2966
44:28 and I said, Surely he is **t in pieces**; 2963+2963
Ex 22:13 If it be **t in pieces**, *then* let him bring 2963+2963
22:13 he shall not make good that which was **t**. 2966
22:31 neither shall ye eat *any* flesh *that is* **t** *of* 2966
Lev 7:24 the fat of **that which is t** *with beasts,* may 2966
17:15 **that which was t** *with beasts, whether it be* 2966
22: 8 is **t** *with beasts,* he shall not eat to defile 2966
1Ki 13:26 which hath **t** him, and slain him, 7665
13:28 lion had not eaten the carcase, nor **t** the ass. 7665
Isa 5:25 their carcases were **t** in the midst of 5478
Jer 5: 6 that goeth out thence shall be **t in pieces**: 2963
Eze 4:14 that which dieth of itself, or is **t in pieces**; 2966
44:31 of itself, or **t**, whether it be fowl or beast. 2966
Hos 6: 1 for he hath **t**, and he will heal us; he hath 2963
Mal 1:13 ye brought *that which was* **t**, and the lame, 1497
Mk 1:26 And when the unclean spirit had **t** him, and 4682

TORTOISE (1)

Lev 11:29 and the mouse, and the **t** after his kind, 6632

TORTURED (1)

Heb 11:35 and others were **t**, not accepting 5178

TOSS (2) [TOSSED, TOSSINGS]

Isa 22:18 **surely violently turn and t** 6801+6801+6802
Jer 5:22 though the waves thereof **t** themselves, 1607

TOSSED (7) [TOSS]

Ps 109:23 I am **t up and down** as the locust. 5287
Pr 21: 6 by a lying tongue *is* a vanity **t to and fro** 5086
Isa 54:11 **t with tempest**, *and* not comforted, behold, 5590
Mt 14:24 now in the midst of the sea, **t** with waves: 928
Ac 27:18 we being exceedingly **t with a tempest**, 5492
Eph 4:14 **t to and fro**, and carried about with every 2831

Jas 1: 6 wave of the sea driven with the wind and t. 4494

TOSSINGS (1) [TOSS]

Job 7: 4 I am full of t to and fro unto the dawning 5076

TOTTERING (1)

Ps 62: 3 a bowing wall shall ye be, and as a t fence. 1760

TOU (2) [TOI]

1Ch 18: 9 Now when T king of Hamath heard how 8583
18:10 (for Hadarezer had war with T;) and 8583

TOUCH (48) [TOUCHED, TOUCHETH, TOUCHING]

Ge 3: 3 not eat of it, neither shall ye t it, lest ye die. 5060
20: 6 therefore suffered I thee not to t her. 5060
Ex 19:12 not up into the mount, or t the border of it: 5060
19:13 There shall not a hand t it, but he shall 5060
Lev 5: 2 Or if a soul t any unclean thing, whether it 5060
5: 3 Or if he t the uncleanness of man, 5060
6:27 Whatsoever shall t the flesh thereof shall be 5060
7:21 Moreover the soul that shall t any unclean 5060
11: 8 ye not eat, and their carcase shall ye not t; 5060
11:31 whosoever doth t them, when they be dead, 5060
12: 4 she shall t no hallowed thing, nor come into 5060
Nu 4:15 they shall not t any holy thing, lest they die. 5060
16:26 these wicked men, and t nothing of theirs, 5060
Dt 14: 8 eat of their flesh, nor t their dead carcase. 5060
Jos 9:19 of Israel: now therefore we may not t them. 5060
Ru 2: 9 the young men that they shall not t thee? 5060
2Sa 14:10 to me, and he shall not t thee any more. 5060
18:12 Beware that none t the young man NIH
23: 7 the man that shall t them must be fenced 5060
1Ch 16:22 Saying, T not mine anointed, and do my 5060
Job 1:11 t all that he hath, and he will curse thee to 5060
2: 5 t his bone and his flesh, and he will curse 5060
5:19 yea, in seven there shall no evil t thee. 5060
6: 7 The things that my soul refused to t are as 5060
Ps 105:15 Saying, T not mine anointed, and do my 5060
144: 5 t the mountains, and they shall smoke. 5060
Isa 52:11 t no unclean thing; go ye out of the midst 5060
Jer 12:14 that t the inheritance which I have caused 5060
La 4:14 so that men could not t their garments. 5060
4:15 depart, depart, t not, when they fled away 5060
Hag 2:12 with his skirt do t bread, or pottage, or 5060
2:13 If one that is unclean by a dead body t any 5060
Mt 9:21 If I may but t his garment, I shall be whole. 681
14:36 And besought him that they might only t 681
Mk 3:10 insomuch that they pressed upon him for to t 681
5:28 For she said, If I may t but his clothes, 681
6:56 besought him that they might t if it were but 681
8:22 man unto him, and besought him to t him. 681
10:13 young children to him, that he should t them: 681
Lk 6:19 And the whole multitude sought to t him: 681
11:46 ye yourselves t not the burdens with one of 4379
18:15 unto him also infants, that he would t them: 681
Jn 20:17 Jesus saith unto her, T me not; for I am not 681
1Co 7: 1 It is good for a man not to t a woman. 681
2Co 6:17 and t not the unclean thing; and I will 681
Col 2:21 (T not; taste not; handle not; 681
Heb 11:28 lest he that destroyed the firstborn should t 2345
12:20 And if so much as a beast t the mountain, 2345

TOUCHED (49) [TOUCH]

Ge 26:29 as we have not t thee, and as we have done 5060
32:25 against him, he t the hollow of his thigh; 5060
32:32 he t the hollow of Jacob's thigh in 5060
Lev 22: 6 The soul which hath t any such shall be 5060
Nu 19:18 upon him that t a bone, or one slain, or one 5060
31:19 whosoever hath t any slain, purify both 5060
Jdg 6:21 t the flesh and the unleavened cakes; and 5060
1Sa 10:26 a band of men, whose hearts God had t. 5060
1Ki 6:27 so that the wing of the one t the one wall, 5060
6:27 the wing of the other cherub t the other 5060
6:27 their wings t one another in the midst of 5060
19: 5 an angel t him, and said unto him, Arise 5060
19: 7 and t him, and said, Arise and eat; 5060
2Ki 13:21 t the bones of Elisha, he revived, and 5060
Est 5: 2 drew near, and t the top of the sceptre. 5060
Job 19:21 my friends; for the hand of God hath t me. 5060
Isa 6: 7 my mouth, and said, Lo, this hath t thy lips; 5060
Jer 1: 9 put forth his hand, and t my mouth. 5060
Eze 3:13 of the living creatures that t one another, 5401
Da 8: 5 of the whole earth, and t not the ground: 5060
8:18 the ground: but he t me, and set me upright. 5060
9:21 t me about the time of the evening oblation. 5060
10:10 behold, a hand t me, which set me upon my 5060
10:16 one like the similitude of the sons of men t 5060
10:18 and t me one like the appearance of a man, 5060
Mt 8: 3 put forth his hand, and t him, saying, I will; 681
8:15 And he t her hand, and the fever left her: and 681
9:20 behind him, and t the hem of his garment: 681
9:29 Then t he their eyes, saying, According to 681
14:36 and as many as t were made perfectly whole. 681
17: 7 And Jesus came and t them, and said, Arise, 681
20:34 had compassion on them, and t their eyes: 681
Mk 1:41 and t him, and saith unto him, I will; 681
5:27 came in the press behind, and t his garment. 681
5:30 in the press, and said, Who t my clothes? 681
5:31 thronging thee, and sayest thou, Who t me? 681
6:56 and as many as t him were made whole. 681
7:33 into his ears, and he spit, and t his tongue; 681
Lk 5:13 put forth his hand, and t him, saying, I will: 681
7:14 And he came and t the bier: and they that 681
8:44 behind him, and t the border of his garment: 681
8:45 And Jesus said, Who t me? When all denied, 681
8:45 and press thee, and sayest thou, Who t me? 681
8:46 And Jesus said, Somebody hath t me: for I 681
8:47 all the people for what cause she had t him, 681
22:51 ye thus far. And he t his ear, and healed him. 681
Ac 27: 3 And the next day we t at Sidon. And Julius 2609
Heb 4:15 be t with the feeling of our infirmities; 4834
12:18 not come unto the mount that might be t, 5584

TOUCHETH (40) [TOUCH]

Ge 26:11 He that t this man or his wife shall surely 5060
Ex 19:12 whosoever t the mount shall be surely put 5060
29:37 whatsoever t the altar shall be holy. 5060
30:29 most holy: whatsoever t them shall be holy. 5060
Lev 6:18 by fire: every one that t them shall be holy. 5060
7:19 the flesh that t any unclean thing shall not 5060
11:24 whosoever t the carcase of them shall be 5060
11:26 every one that t them shall be unclean. 5060
11:27 whoso t their carcase shall be unclean until 5060
11:36 that which t their carcase shall be unclean. 5060
11:39 he that t the carcase thereof shall be 5060
15: 5 whosoever t his bed shall wash his clothes, 5060
15: 7 he that t the flesh of him that hath the issue 5060
15:10 whosoever t any thing that was under him 5060
15:11 whomsoever he t that hath the issue, and 5060
15:12 that he t which hath the issue, shall be 5060
15:19 whosoever t her shall be unclean until 5060
15:21 whosoever t her bed shall wash his clothes, 5060
15:22 whosoever t any thing that she sat upon 5060
15:23 any thing whereon she sitteth, when he t it, 5060
15:27 whosoever t those things shall be unclean, 5060
22: 4 whoso t any thing that is unclean by 5060
22: 5 Or whosoever t any creeping thing, 5060
Nu 19:11 He that t the dead body of any man shall be 5060
19:13 Whosoever t the dead body of any man that 5060
19:16 whosoever t one that is slain with a sword 5060
19:21 he that t the water of separation shall be 5060
19:22 whatsoever the unclean person t shall be 5060
19:22 the soul that t it shall be unclean until even. 5060
Jdg 16: 9 as a thread of tow is broken when it t 7306
Job 4: 5 it t thee, and thou art troubled. 5060
Ps 104:32 it trembleth: he t the hills, and they smoke. 5060
Pr 6:29 whosoever t her shall not be innocent. 5060
Eze 17:10 not utterly wither, when the east wind t it? 5060
Hos 4: 2 they break out, and blood t blood. 5060
Am 9: 5 the Lord GOD of hosts is he that t 5060
Zec 2: 8 for he that t you toucheth the apple of his 5060
2: 8 for he that toucheth you t the apple of his 5060
Lk 7:39 what manner of woman this is that t him: 681
1Jn 5:18 and that wicked one t him not. 681

TOUCHING (30) [TOUCH]

Ge 27:42 Behold, thy brother Esau, as t thee, 3807.1
Lev 5:13 as t his sin that he hath sinned in one of 5921
Nu 8:26 Thus shalt thou do unto the Levites t their 871.1
1Sa 20:23 as t the matter which thou and I have NIH
2Ki 22:18 As t the words which thou hast heard; NIH
Ezr 7:24 that t any of the priests and Levites, singers, NIH
Job 37:23 T the Almighty, we cannot find him out: NIH
Ps 45: 1 I speak of the things which I have made t 3807.1
Isa 5: 1 a song of my beloved t his vineyard. 3807.1
Jer 1:16 I will utter my judgments against them t all 5921
21:11 t the house of the king of Judah, 3807.1
22:11 For thus saith the LORD t Shallum the son 413
Eze 7:13 for the vision is t the whole multitude 413
Mt 18:19 That if two of you shall agree on earth as t 4012
22:31 But as t the resurrection of the dead, 4012
Mk 12:26 And as t the dead, that they rise: have ye 4012
Lk 23:14 have found no fault in this man t those NIG
Ac 5:35 what ye intend to do as t these men. 1909
21:25 As t the Gentiles which believe, we have 4012
24:21 T the resurrection of the dead I am called in 4012
26: 2 t all the things whereof I am accused of 4012
Ro 11:28 but as t the election, they are beloved for 2596
1Co 8: 1 Now as t things offered unto idols, 4012
16:12 As t our brother Apollos, I greatly desired 4012
2Co 9: 1 For as t the ministering to the saints, it is 4012
Php 3: 5 of the Hebrews; as t the law, a Pharisee; 2596
3: 6 t the righteousness which is in the law, 2596
Col 4:10 (t whom ye received commandments: 4012
1Th 4: 9 But as t brotherly love ye need not that I 4012
2Th 3: 4 And we have confidence in the Lord t you, 1909

TOW (3)

Jdg 16: 9 as a thread of t is broken when it toucheth 5296
Isa 1:31 the strong shall be as t, and the maker of it 5296
43:17 they are extinct, they are quenched as t. 6594

TOWARD (265) [TOWARDS]

Ge 2:14 that is it which goeth t the east of Assyria. 6926
12: 9 going on still t the south. 1886.5
13:12 of the plain, and pitched his tent t Sodom. 5704
18: 2 and bowed himself t the ground, 1886.5
18:16 up from thence, and looked t Sodom: 5921+6440
18:22 faces from thence, and went t Sodom: 1886.5
19: 1 he bowed himself with his face t 1886.5
19:28 he looked t Sodom and Gomorrah, 5921+6440
19:28 t all the land of the plain, and beheld, 5921+6440
20: 1 Abraham journeyed from thence t 1886.5
28:10 out from Beer-sheba, and went t Haran. 1886.5
30:40 set the faces of the flocks t the ringstraked, 413
31: 2 and behold, it was not t him as before. 5973
31: 5 that it is not t me as before; 413
31:21 and set his face t the mount Gilead. NIH
48:13 Ephraim in his right hand t Israel's left 4480
Ex 9:10 Moses sprinkled it up t heaven; and 1886.5
9:22 Stretch forth thine hand t heaven, 5921
9:23 And Moses stretched forth his rod t heaven: 5921
10:21 Stretch out thine hand t heaven, 5921
10:22 Moses stretched forth his hand t heaven; 5921
16:10 that they looked t the wilderness, and 413
25:20 t the mercy seat shall the faces of 413
26:35 on the side of the tabernacle t the south: 1886.5
34: 8 bowed his head t the earth, and 1886.5
36:25 which is t the north corner, he made 3807.1
39:20 t the forepart of it, over against the other 4480
Lev 13:41 off from the part of his head t his face, NIH
Nu 2: 3 on the east side t the rising of the sun 1886.5
3:38 those that encamp before the tabernacle t 1886.5
16:42 that they looked t the tabernacle of 413
21:11 which is before Moab, t the sunrising. 4480
21:20 of Pisgah, which looketh t Jeshimon. 5921+6440
23:28 top of Peor, that looketh t Jeshimon. 5921+6440
Nu 24: 1 but he set his face t the wilderness. 413
32:14 yet the fierce anger of the LORD t Israel. 413
34:15 near Jericho eastward, t the sunrising. 1886.5
Dt 4:41 cities on this side Jordan t the sunrising; 1886.5
4:47 which were on this side Jordan t NIH
28:54 his eye shall be evil t his brother, and 871.1
28:54 t the wife of his bosom, and towards 871.1
Jos 1: 4 unto the great sea t the going down of NIH
1:15 gave you on this side Jordan t the sunrising. NIH
3:16 those that came down t the sea of the plain, 5921
8:18 Stretch out the spear that is in thy hand t Ai; 413
8:18 the spear that he had in his hand t the city. 413
12: 1 other side Jordan t the rising of the sun, 1886.5
13: 5 and all Lebanon, t the sunrising, NIH
15: 4 From thence it passed t Azmon, and 1886.5
15: 7 the border went up t Debir from 1886.5
15: 7 so northward, looking t Gilgal, that is before 413
15:21 t the coast of Edom southward were 413
16: 6 the border went out t the sea to 1886.5
18:13 the border went over from thence t Luz, 1886.5
18:17 to En-shemesh, and went forth t Geliloth, 413
18:18 passed along t the side over against Arabah 413
19:11 their border went up t the sea, and 1886.5
19:12 turned from Sarid eastward t the sunrising NIH
19:18 their border was t Jezreel, and 1886.5
19:27 turneth t the sunrising to Beth-dagon, and NIH
19:27 to the valley of Jiphthah-el t the north 1886.5
19:34 and to Judah upon Jordan t the sunrising. NIH
Jdg 3:28 took the fords of Jordan t Moab, and 3807.1
4: 6 saying, Go and draw t mount Tabor, and 871.1
5: 9 My heart is t the governors of Israel, 3807.1
8: 3 their anger was abated t him, 4480+5921
13:20 when the flame went up t heaven from 1886.5
19:18 We are passing from Beth-lehem-judah t 5704
20:43 ease over against Gibeah t the sunrising. 4480
20:45 fled t the wilderness unto the rock of 1886.5
1Sa 13:18 to the valley of Zeboim t the wilderness. 1886.5
17:48 and ran t the army to meet the Philistine. NIH
20:12 if there be good t David, and I then send not 413
20:41 David arose out of a place t the south, and 681
2Sa 14: 1 that the king's heart was t Absalom. 5921
15:23 t the way of the wilderness. 5921+6440
24: 5 in the midst of the river of Gad, and t Jazer: 413
24:20 the king and his servants coming on t him: 5921
1Ki 7: 9 and so on the outside t the great court. 5704
7:25 three looking t the north, and 1886.5
7:25 three looking t the west, and 1886.5
7:25 three looking t the south, and 1886.5
7:25 the south, and three looking t the east: 1886.5
8:22 and spread forth his hands t heaven: NIH
8:29 That thine eyes may be open t this house 413
8:29 day, even t the place of which thou hast said, 413
8:44 shall pray unto the LORD t the city which 1870
8:44 t the house that I have built for thy name: NIH
8:48 and pray unto thee t their land, 1870
14:13 in him there is found some good thing t 413
18:43 to his servant, Go up now, look t the sea. 1870
2Ki 3:14 I would not look t thee, nor see thee. 413
25: 4 and the king went the way t the plain. NIH
1Ch 9:24 t the east, west, north, and south. 1886.5
12:15 both t the east, and toward the west. 3807.1
12:15 both toward the east, and t the west. 3807.1
26:17 four a day, and t Asuppim two and two. 3807.1
2Ch 4: 4 three looking t the north, and 1886.5
4: 4 three looking t the west, and 1886.5
4: 4 three looking t the south, and 1886.5
4: 4 the south, and three looking t the east: 1886.5
6:34 they pray unto thee t this city which thou 1870
6:38 pray t their land, which thou gavest unto 1870
6:38 t the city which thou hast chosen, and NIH
6:38 t the house which I have built for thy 3807.1
20:24 when Judah came t the watch tower in 5921
31:14 of Imnah the Levite, the porter t the east, 1886.5
Ne 3:26 over against the water gate t the east, 3807.1
12:31 right hand upon the wall t the dung gate: 3807.1
Est 8: 4 the king held out the golden sceptre t 3807.1
Job 2:12 sprinkled dust upon their heads t heaven. 1886.5
11:13 and stretch out thine hands t him; 413
39:26 and stretch her wings t the south? 3807.1
Ps 5: 7 in thy fear will I worship t thy holy temple. 413
28: 2 when I lift up my hands t thy holy oracle. 413
66: 5 he is terrible in his doing t the children of 5921
86:13 For great is thy mercy t me: and thou hast 5921
98: 3 and his truth t the house of Israel: 3807.1
103:11 so great is his mercy t them that fear him. 5921
117: 2 For his merciful kindness is great t us: and 5921
138: 2 I will worship t thy holy temple, and 413
Pr 14:35 The king's favour is t a wise servant: but 3807.1
23: 5 they fly away as an eagle t heaven. NIH
Ecc 1: 6 The wind goeth t the south, and 413
11: 3 if the tree fall t the south, or toward 871.1
11: 3 tree fall toward the south, or t the north, 871.1
SS 7: 4 of Lebanon which looketh t Damascus. 6440
Isa 11:14 the shoulders of the Philistines t the west; 1886.5
38: 2 Hezekiah turned his face t the wall, and 413
49:23 bow down to thee with their face t the earth, NIH
Jer 3:12 Go and proclaim these words t the north, 1886.5
4: 6 Set up the standard t Zion: retire, 1886.5
4:11 the wilderness t the daughter of my people, 1870
15: 1 yet my mind could not be t this people: 413
31:21 set thine heart t the highway, even 3807.1
46: 6 and fall t the north by the river Euphrates. 1886.5
La 2:19 lift up thy hands t him for the life of thy 413
Eze 1:23 were their wings straight, the one t the other: 413
4: 7 Therefore thou shalt set thy face t the siege 413
6:14 more desolate than the wilderness t 1886.5
8: 3 to the door of the inner gate that looketh t 1886.5
8: 5 So I lift up mine eyes the way t the north, 1886.5
8:16 with their backs t the temple of the LORD, 413
9: 2 which lieth t the north, and every man a 1886.5
12:14 I will scatter t every wind all that are 3807.1
16:63 when I am pacified t thee for all that thou 3807.1
17: 6 whose branches turned t him, and the roots 413
17: 7 this vine did bend her roots t him, and 5921
17: 7 and shot forth her branches t him, 3807.1

Eze 20:46 set thy face **t** the south, and drop *thy word* 1870
20:46 drop *thy word* **t** the south, and 413
21: 2 set thy face **t** Jerusalem, and drop *thy word* 413
21: 2 drop *thy word* **t** the holy places, and 413
33:25 lift up your eyes **t** your idols, and 413
40: 6 came he unto the gate which looketh **t** 1870
40:20 the gate of the outward court that looked **t** 1870
40:23 *was* over against the gate **t** the north, 3807.1
40:23 the gate toward the north, and **t** the east; 3807.1
40:24 After that he brought me **t** the south, and 1870
40:24 the south, and behold a gate **t** the south: 1870
40:27 *there was* a gate in the inner court **t** 1870
40:27 he measured from gate to gate **t** the south 1870
40:31 And the arches thereof *were* **t** the utter court; 413
40:32 he brought me into the inner court **t** 1870
40:34 the arches thereof *were* **t** the outward 3807.1
40:37 the posts thereof *were* **t** the utter court; 3807.1
40:44 and their prospect *was* **t** the south: 1870
40:44 east gate *having* the prospect **t** the north. 1870
40:45 whose prospect *is* **t** the south, 1870
40:46 the chamber whose prospect *is* **t** the north 1870
41:11 the doors of the side chambers *were* **t** 3807.1
41:11 one door **t** the north, and another door 1870
41:11 the north, and another door **t** the south: 3807.1
41:12 end **t** the west *was* seventy cubits broad; 1870
41:14 of the separate place **t** the east, 3807.1
41:19 So that the face of a man *was* **t** the palm tree 413
41:19 the face of a young lion **t** the palm tree on 413
42: 1 into the utter court, the way **t** the north: 1870
42: 1 which *was* before the building **t** the north. 413
42: 4 of one cubit; and their doors **t** the north. 3807.1
42:10 thickness of the wall of the court **t** the east, 1870
42:11 of the chambers which *were* **t** the north, 1870
42:12 **t** the south *was* a door in the head of 1870
42:12 *even* the way directly before the wall **t** 1870
42:15 he brought me forth **t** the gate whose 1870
42:15 the gate whose prospect *is* **t** the east, 1870
43: 1 *even* the gate that looketh **t** the east: 1870
43: 4 of the gate whose prospect *is* **t** the east. 1870
43:17 and his stairs *shall* **look t** the east. 6437
44: 1 outward sanctuary which looketh ***t*** the east; NIH
46: 1 The gate of the inner court that looketh ***t*** NIH
46:12 open him the gate that looketh ***t*** the east, NIH
46:19 of the priests, which **looked t** the north: 6437
47: 1 for the forefront of the house *stood* ***t*** NIH
47: 8 These waters issue out **t** the east country, 413
47:15 this *shall be* the border of the land **t** 3807.1
48:10 **t** the north five and twenty thousand *in* 1886.5
48:10 and **t** the west ten thousand *in* breadth, 1886.5
48:10 **t** the east ten thousand *in* breadth, and 1886.5
48:10 **t** the south five and twenty thousand *in* 1886.5
48:17 the suburbs of the city shall be **t** the north 1886.5
48:17 **t** the south two hundred and fifty, and 1886.5
48:17 **t** the east two hundred and fifty, and 1886.5
48:17 and **t** the west two hundred and fifty. 1886.5
48:21 twenty thousand of the oblation **t** the east 5704
48:21 and twenty thousand **t** the west border, 5921
48:28 *in* Kadesh, *and to the* river **t** the great sea. 5921
Da 4: 2 wonders that the high God hath wrought **t** 5974
6:10 his windows being open in his chamber **t** 5049
8: 8 for it came up four notable ones **t** the four 3807.1
8: 9 **t** the south, and toward the east, and 413
8: 9 and **t** the east, and toward the pleasant *land.* 413
8: 9 and toward the east, and **t** the pleasant *land.* 413
8:18 I was in a deep sleep on my face **t** 1886.5
10: 9 on my face, and my face **t** the ground. 1886.5
10:15 I set my face **t** the ground, and I became 1886.5
11: 4 be divided **t** the four winds of heaven; 3807.1
11:29 he shall return, and come **t** the south; 871.1
Hos 3: 1 according to the love of the LORD **t** NIH
5: 1 for judgment *is* **t** you, because ye have 3807.1
Joel 2:20 with his face **t** the east sea, and his hinder 413
Jnh 2: 4 yet I will look again **t** thy holy temple. 413
Zec 6: 6 and the grisled go forth **t** the south country. 413
6: 8 these that go **t** the north country have 413
9: 1 the tribes of Israel, *shall be* **t** the LORD. 3807.1
14: 4 shall cleave in the midst thereof **t** the east 1886.5
14: 4 thereof toward the east and **t** the west, 1886.5
14: 4 half of the mountain shall remove **t** 1886.5
14: 4 the north, and half of it **t** the south. 1886.5
14: 8 half of them **t** the former sea, and half of 413
14: 8 former sea, and half of them **t** the hinder sea: 413
Mt 12:49 And he stretched forth his hand **t** his *1909*
14:14 and was moved with compassion **t** them, *1909*
Mk 6:34 and was moved with compassion **t** them, *1909*
Ac 1:10 And while they looked stedfastly **t** heaven *1519*
8:26 go **t** the south unto the way that goeth down *2596*
20:21 repentance **t** God, and faith toward our *1519*
20:21 and faith **t** our Lord Jesus Christ. *1519*
24:16 always a conscience void of offence **t** God, *4314*
24:16 void of offence toward God, and ***t*** men. NIG
27:12 and lieth **t** the south west and north west. *2596*
27:40 the mainsail to the wind, and made **t** shore. *1519*
28:14 them seven days: and so we went **t** Rome. *1519*
Ro 5: 8 But God commendeth his love **t** us, in that, *1519*
11:22 but **t** thee, goodness, if thou continue in *his* *1909*
1Co 7:36 *he* behaveth himself uncomely **t** his virgin, *1909*
2Co 1:16 of you to be brought on *my* way **t** Judea. *1519*
1:18 *is* true, our word **t** you was not yea and nay. *4314*
7: 4 Great *is* my boldness of speech **t** you, *4314*
7: 7 your mourning, your fervent mind **t** me; *5228*
7:15 inward affection is more abundant **t** you, *1519*
10: 1 but being absent am bold **t** you: *1519*
13: 4 live with him by the power of God **t** you. *1519*
Eph 1: 8 Wherein he hath abounded **t** us in all *1519*
Php 2:30 *his* life, to supply your lack of service **t** me. *4314*
3:14 I press **t** the mark for the prize of the high *2596*
Col 4: 5 Walk in wisdom **t** them that are without, *4314*
1Th 4:12 That ye may walk honestly **t** them that are *4314*
5:14 support the weak, be patient **t** all *men.* *4314*
Tit 3: 4 **love** of God our Saviour **t man** appeared, *5363*
Phm 1: 5 which thou hast **t** the Lord Jesus, and *4314*
1: 5 hast toward the Lord Jesus, and **t** all saints; *1519*
Heb 6:10 of love, which ye have shewed **t** his name, *1519*
1Pe 2:19 if a man for conscience **t** God endure grief, NIG
1Pe 3:21 the answer of a good conscience **t** God,) *1519*

TOWARDS (81) [TOWARD]

Ge 15: 5 Look now **t** heaven, and tell the stars, 1886.5
25:18 *is* before Egypt, as thou goest **t** Assyria: 1886.5
48:13 Manasseh in his left hand **t** Israel's right 4480
Ex 9: 8 let Moses sprinkle it **t** the heaven in 1886.5
28:27 **t** the forepart thereof, over against 4136+4480
Lev 9:22 And Aaron lift up his hand **t** the people, and 413
Dt 28:54 **t** the remnant of his children which he 871.1
28:56 her eye shall be evil **t** the husband of her 871.1
28:56 and **t** her son, and towards her daughter, 871.1
28:56 and towards her son, and **t** her daughter, 871.1
28:57 **t** her young one that cometh out from 871.1
28:57 and **t** her children which she shall bear: 871.1
Jos 15: 7 the border passed **t** the waters of 413
Jdg 5:11 *even* the righteous acts ***t the inhabitants*** of NIH
19: 9 Behold now, the day draweth **t** evening, 3807.1
1Sa 17:30 he turned from him **t** another, and 413+4136
1Ki 8:29 which thy servant shall make **t** this place. 413
8:30 when they shall pray **t** this place: 413
8:35 if they pray **t** this place, and confess thy 413
8:38 and spread forth his hands **t** this house: 413
8:42 when he shall come and pray **t** this house; 413
2Ch 6:13 and spread forth his hands **t** heaven, 1886.5
6:20 prayer which thy servant prayeth **t** this place. 413
6:21 which they shall make **t** this place: 413
6:26 *yet* if they pray **t** this place, and confess thy 413
16: 9 behalf of *them* whose heart *is* perfect **t** him. 413
24:16 both **t** God, and *towards* his house. 5973
24:16 in Israel, both towards God, and ***t*** his house. NIH
Ezr 3:11 for his mercy *endureth* for ever **t** Israel. 5921
Est 1:13 king's manner **t** all that knew law 6440+3807.1
Ps 25:15 Mine eyes *are* ever **t** the LORD; for he 413
85: 4 and cause thine anger **t** us to cease. 5973
116:12 unto the LORD *for* all his benefits **t** me? 5921
SS 7:10 I *am* my beloved's, and his desire *is* **t** me. 5921
Isa 7: 1 went up ***t*** Jerusalem to war against it, but NIH
29:13 their fear **t** me is taught *by* the precept of NIH
63: 7 the great goodness **t** the house of Israel, 3807.1
63:15 of thy bowels and of thy mercies **t** me? 413
66:14 the hand of the LORD shall be known **t** his NIH
66:14 and *his* indignation **t** his enemies. NIH
Jer 1:13 and the face thereof *is* **t** the north. 4480+6440
12: 3 hast seen me, and tried mine heart **t** thee: 854
29:10 perform my good word **t** you, in causing 5921
29:11 For I know the thoughts that I think **t** you, 5921
31:40 unto the corner of the horse gate **t** 1886.5
49:36 and will scatter them **t** all those winds; 3807.1
Eze 6: 2 set thy face **t** the mountains of Israel, and 413
8: 5 lift up thine eyes now the way **t** the north. 1886.5
8:14 LORD'S house which *was* **t** the north; 1886.5
8:16 of the LORD, and their faces **t** the east; 1886.5
8:16 and they worshipped the sun **t** the east. 1886.5
16:42 So will I make my fury **t** thee to rest, and 871.1
17:21 they that remain shall be scattered **t** all 3807.1
24:23 for your iniquities, and mourn one **t** another. 413
40:22 measure of the gate that looketh **t** the east; 1870
42: 7 **t** the utter court on the forepart of 1870
Da 11:19 he shall turn his face **t** the fort of his own 3807.1
Joel 2:20 his hinder part **t** the utmost sea, and his stink 413
Mt 28: 1 as it began to dawn **t** the first *day* of *1519*
Lk 2:14 and on earth peace, good will **t** men. *1722*
12:21 treasure for himself, and is not rich **t** God. *1519*
13:22 teaching, and journeying **t** Jerusalem. *1519*
24:29 for it is **t** evening, and the day is far spent. *4314*
Jn 6:17 a ship, and went over the sea **t** Capernaum. *1519*
Ac 22: 3 and was zealous **t** God, as ye all are this NIG
24:15 And have hope **t** God, which they *1519*
Ro 1:27 burned in their lust one **t** another; *1519*
12:16 *Be* of the same mind one **t** another. *1519*
15: 5 one **t** another according to Christ Jesus: *1722*
2Co 2: 8 that *you* would confirm *your* love **t** him. *1519*
9: 8 And God *is* able to make all grace abound **t** *1519*
Gal 2: 8 *the same* was mighty in me **t** the Gentiles:) *1519*
Eph 2: 7 in *his* kindness **t** us through Christ Jesus. *1909*
1Th 3:12 and abound in love one **t** another, *1519*
3:12 and **t** all *men,* even as we *do* towards you: *1519*
3:12 and towards all *men,* even as we *do* **t** you: *1519*
4:10 And indeed ye do it **t** all the brethren which *1519*
2Th 1: 3 the charity of every one of you all **t** each *1519*
Heb 6: 1 from dead works, and of faith **t** God, *1909*
1Jn 3:21 us not, *then* have we confidence **t** God. *4314*
4: 9 In this was manifested the love of God **t** us, *1722*

TOWEL (2)

Jn 13: 4 and took a **t**, and girded himself. *3012*
13: 5 to wipe *them* with the **t** wherewith he was *3012*

TOWER (48) [TOWERS, WATCHTOWER]

Ge 11: 4 Go to, let us build us a city and a **t**, 4026
11: 5 came down to see the city and the **t**, 4026
35:21 and spread his tent beyond the **t** of Edar. 4026
Jdg 8: 9 again in peace, I will break down this **t**. 4026
8:17 he beat down the **t** of Penuel, and slew 4026
9:46 when all the men of the **t** of Shechem heard 4026
9:47 that all the men of the **t** of Shechem were 4026
9:49 that all the men of the **t** of Shechem died 4026
9:51 But there was a strong **t** within the city, and 4026
9:51 to them, and gat them up to the top of the **t**. 4026
9:52 Abimelech came unto the **t**, and 4026
9:52 went hard unto the door of the **t** to burn it 4026
2Sa 22: 3 my **high t**, and my refuge, my saviour; 4869
22:51 *He is* the **t** of salvation for his king: and 4024
2Ki 5:24 when he came to the **t**, he took *them* from 6076
9:17 there stood a watchman on the **t** in Jezreel, 4026
17: 9 from the **t** of the watchmen to the fenced 4026
18: 8 from the **t** of the watchmen to the fenced 4026
2Ch 20:24 when Judah came toward the **watch t** in 4707
Ne 3: 1 even unto the **t** of Meah they sanctified it, 4026
3: 1 they sanctified it, unto the **t** of Hananeel. 4026
3:11 the other piece, and the **t** of the furnaces. 4026
3:25 the **t** which lieth out from the king's high 4026
3:26 gate toward the east, and the **t** that lieth out. 4026
Ne 3:27 over against the great **t** that lieth out, 4026
12:38 from beyond the **t** of the furnaces even unto 4026
12:39 the **t** of Hananeel, and the tower of Meah, 4026
12:39 the tower of Hananeel, and the **t** of Meah, 4026
Ps 18: 2 the horn of my salvation, *and* my **high t**. 4869
61: 3 for me, *and* a strong **t** from the enemy. 4026
144: 2 my **high t**, and my deliverer; my shield, 4869
Pr 18:10 The name of the LORD *is* a strong **t**: 4026
SS 4: 4 Thy neck *is* like the **t** of David builded for 4026
7: 4 Thy neck *is* as a **t** of ivory; thine eyes *like* 4026
7: 4 thy nose *is* as the **t** of Lebanon which 4026
Isa 2:15 upon every high **t**, and upon every fenced 4026
5: 2 built a **t** in the midst of it, and also made a 4026
Jer 6:27 I have set thee *for* a **t** *and* a fortress among 969
31:38 **t** of Hananeel unto the gate of the corner. 4026
Eze 29:10 from the **t** of Syene even unto the border of 4024
30: 6 from the **t** of Syene shall they fall in it by 4024
Mic 4: 8 thou, O **t** of the flock, the strong hold of 4026
Hab 2: 1 set me upon the **t**, and will watch to see 4692
Zec 14:10 *from* the **t** of Hananeel unto the king's 4026
Mt 21:33 and built a **t**, and let it out to husbandmen, *4444*
Mk 12: 1 and built a **t**, and let it out to husbandmen, *4444*
Lk 13: 4 upon whom the **t** in Siloam fell, and *4444*
14:28 For which of you, intending to build a **t**, *4444*

TOWERS (17) [TOWER]

2Ch 14: 7 about *them* walls, and **t**, gates, and bars, 4026
26: 9 Moreover Uzziah built **t** in Jerusalem at 4026
26:10 Also he built **t** in the desert, and 4026
26:15 invented by cunning *men,* to be on the **t** 4026
27: 4 and in the forests he built castles and **t**. 4026
32: 5 raised *it* up to the **t**, and another wall 4026
Ps 48:12 and go round about her: tell the **t** thereof. 4026
SS 8:10 I *am* a wall, and my breasts like **t**: then 4026
Isa 23:13 they set up the **t** thereof, they raised up 971
30:25 day of the great slaughter, when the **t** fall. 4026
32:14 the forts and **t** shall be for dens for ever, 975
33:18 where *is* he that counted the **t**? 4026
Eze 26: 4 the walls of Tyrus, and break down her **t**: 4026
26: 9 and with his axes he shall break down thy **t**. 4026
27:11 and the Gammadims were in thy **t**: 4026
Zep 1:16 the fenced cities, and against the high **t**. 6438
3: 6 their **t** are desolate; I made their streets 6438

TOWN (13) [TOWNCLERK, TOWNS]

Jos 2:15 for her house *was* upon the **t** wall, and 7023
1Sa 16: 4 the elders of the **t** trembled at his coming, 5892
23: 7 by entering into a **t** that hath gates and bars. 5892
27: 5 let them give me a place in some **t** in 5892
Hab 2:12 Woe to him that buildeth a **t** with blood, 5892
Mt 10:11 And into whatsoever city or **t** ye shall enter, *2968*
Mk 8:23 man by the hand, and led him out of the **t**; *2968*
8:26 saying, Neither go into the **t**, nor tell *it* to *2968*
8:26 go into the town, nor tell *it* to any in the **t**. *2968*
Lk 5:17 which were come out of every **t** of Galilee, *2968*
Jn 7:42 and out of the **t** of Bethlehem, where David *2968*
11: 1 the **t** of Mary and her sister Martha. *2968*
11:30 Now Jesus was not yet come into the **t**, but *2968*

TOWNCLERK (1) [TOWN]

Ac 19:35 And when the **t** had appeased the people, *1122*

TOWNS (45) [TOWN]

Ge 25:16 their names, by their **t**, and by their castles; 2691
Nu 32:41 and took the **small t** thereof, 2333
Dt 3: 5 and bars; beside unwalled **t** a great many. 5892
Jos 13:30 all the **t** of Jair, which *are* in Bashan, 2333
15:45 Ekron, with her **t** and her villages: 1323
15:47 Ashdod *with* her **t** and her villages, 1323
15:47 Gaza *with* her **t** and her villages, 1323
17:11 and in Asher Beth-shean and her **t**, 1323
17:11 Ibleam and her **t**, and the inhabitants of Dor 1323
17:11 the inhabitants of Dor and her **t**, and 1323
17:11 the inhabitants of Endor and her **t**, and 1323
17:11 the inhabitants of Taanach and her **t**, and 1323
17:11 and the inhabitants of Megiddo and her **t**, 1323
17:16 *both they* who *are* of Beth-shean and her **t**, 1323
Jdg 1:27 out *the inhabitants of* Beth-shean and her **t**, 1323
1:27 and her towns, nor Taanach and her **t**, 1323
1:27 nor the inhabitants of Dor and her **t**, 1323
1:27 nor the inhabitants of Ibleam and her **t**, 1323
1:27 nor the inhabitants of Megiddo and her **t**: 1323
11:26 While Israel dwelt in Heshbon and her **t**, 1323
11:26 in Aroer and her **t**, and in all the cities that 1323
1Ki 4:13 to him *pertained* the **t** of Jair the son of 2333
1Ch 2:23 Aram, with the **t** of Jair, from them, 2333
2:23 from them, with Kenath, and the **t** thereof, 1323
5:16 in her **t**, and in all the suburbs of Sharon, 1323
7:28 habitations *were,* Beth-el and the **t** thereof, 1323
7:28 and westward Gezer, with the **t** thereof; 1323
7:28 Shechem also and the **t** thereof, unto Gaza 1323
7:28 towns thereof, unto Gaza and the **t** thereof: 1323
7:29 Beth-shean and her **t**, Taanach and 1323
7:29 Taanach and her **t**, Megiddo and her towns, 1323
7:29 Megiddo and her **t**, Dor and her towns. 1323
7:29 Megiddo and her towns, Dor and her **t**. 1323
8:12 who built Ono, and Lod, with the **t** thereof: 1323
18: 1 and her **t** out of the hand of the Philistines. 1323
2Ch 13:19 Beth-el with the **t** thereof, and Jeshanah 1323
13:19 Jeshanah with the **t** thereof, and Ephrain 1323
13:19 and Ephrain with the **t** thereof. 1323
Est 9:19 of the villages, that dwelt in the unwalled **t**, 5892
Jer 19:15 upon all her **t** all the evil that I have 5892
Zec 2: 4 *as* **t without walls** for the multitude of men 6519
Mk 1:38 he said unto them, Let us go into the next **t**, *2969*
8:27 his disciples, into the **t** of Cesarea Philippi: *2968*
Lk 9: 6 And they departed, and went through the **t**, *2968*
9:12 that they may go into the **t** and *2968*

TRACHONITIS (1)

Lk 3: 1 tetrarch of Iturea and of the region of **T**, *5139*

TRACONITIS See TRACHONITIS

TRADE (5) [TRADED, TRADING]
Ge 34:10 dwell and t you therein, and get you 5503
34:21 let them dwell in the land, and t therein; 5503
46:32 for their t hath been **to feed cattle**; 376+4735
46:34 Thy servants' t hath been **about cattle** 376+4735
Rev 18:17 and sailers, and as many as t by sea, *2038*

TRADED (5) [TRADE]
Eze 27:12 iron, tin, and lead, they t in thy fairs. 5414
27:13 they t the persons of men and vessels of 5414
27:14 They of the house of Togarmah t in thy 5414
27:17 they t in thy market wheat of Minnith, and 5414
Mt 25:16 the five talents went and t with the same, *2038*

TRADERS See TRAFFICK; TRAFFICKERS

TRADING (1) [TRADE]
Lk 19:15 how much every *man* had **gained by** t. *1281*

TRADITION (11) [TRADITIONS]
Mt 15: 2 Why do thy disciples transgress the t of *3862*
15: 3 the commandment of God by your t? *3862*
15: 6 of God of none effect by your t. *3862*
Mk 7: 3 eat not, holding the t of the elders. *3862*
7: 5 disciples according to the t of the elders, *3862*
7: 8 ye hold the t of men, *as* the washing of pots *3862*
7: 9 of God, that ye may keep your own t. *3862*
7:13 word of God of none effect through your t, *3862*
Col 2: 8 and vain deceit, after the t of men, *3862*
2Th 3: 6 and not after the t which he received of us. *3862*
1Pe 1:18 **received by t from** your **fathers**; *3970*

TRADITIONS (2) [TRADITION]
Gal 1:14 being more exceedingly zealous of the t of *3862*
2Th 2:15 and hold the t which ye have been taught, *3862*

TRAFFICK (5) [TRAFFICKERS]
Ge 42:34 you your brother, and ye shall t in the land. 5503
1Ki 10:15 *of* the t of the *spice* merchants, and *of* all 4536
Eze 17: 4 young twigs, and carried it into a land of t; 3667
28: 5 *and* by thy t hast thou increased thy riches, 7404
28:18 of thine iniquities, by the iniquity of thy t; 7404

TRAFFICKERS (1) [TRAFFICK]
Isa 23: 8 whose t *are* the honourable of the earth? 3667

TRAIN (3) [TRAINED]
1Ki 10: 2 she came to Jerusalem with a very great t, 2428
Pr 22: 6 **T up** a child in the way he should go: and 2596
Isa 6: 1 and lifted up, and his t filled the temple. 7757

TRAINED (1) [TRAIN]
Ge 14:14 he armed his t *servants*, born in his own 2593

TRAITOR (1) [TRAITORS, TREASON]
Lk 6:16 and Judas Iscariot, which also was the t. *4273*

TRAITORS (1) [TRAITOR]
2Ti 3: 4 T, heady, highminded, lovers of pleasures *4273*

TRAMPLE (3)
Ps 91:13 and the dragon shalt thou **t under feet**. 7429
Isa 63: 3 them in mine anger, and t them in my fury; 7429
Mt 7: 6 lest they t them under their feet, and *2662*

TRANCE (5)
Nu 24: 4 falling *into a t*, but having his eyes open: NIH
24:16 falling *into a t*, but having his eyes open: NIH
Ac 10:10 but while they made ready, he fell into a t, *1611*
11: 5 and in a t I saw a vision, A certain vessel *1611*
22:17 while I prayed in the temple, I was in a t; *1611*

TRANQUILLITY (1)
Da 4:27 the poor; if it may be a lengthening of thy t. 7963

TRANSFER See TRANSLATE

TRANSFERRED (1)
1Co 4: 6 I have **in a figure** t to myself and *3345*

TRANSFIGURED (2)
Mt 17: 2 And was t before them: and his face did *3339*
Mk 9: 2 by themselves: and he was t before them. *3339*

TRANSFORMED (3) [TRANSFORMING]
Ro 12: 2 but be ye t by the renewing of your mind, *3339*
2Co 11:14 for Satan himself is t into an angel of light. *3345*
11:15 also be t as the ministers of righteousness; *3345*

TRANSFORMING (1) [TRANSFORMED]
2Co 11:13 t themselves into the apostles of Christ. *3345*

TRANSGRESS (14) [TRANSGRESSED, TRANSGRESSEST, TRANSGRESSETH, TRANSGRESSING, TRANSGRESSION, TRANSGRESSIONS, TRANSGRESSOR, TRANSGRESSORS]
Nu 14:41 Wherefore now do ye t the commandment 5674
1Sa 2:24 I hear: *ye* **make** the LORD'S people **to t**. 5674
2Ch 24:20 Why t ye the commandments of 5674
Ne 1: 8 saying, *If* ye t, I will scatter you abroad 4603
13:27 to t against our God in marrying strange 4603
Ps 17: 3 I am purposed *that* my mouth shall not t. 5674
25: 3 let them be ashamed which t without cause. 898
Pr 28:21 for for a piece of bread *that* man will t. 6586
Jer 2:20 thy bands; and thou saidst, I will not t; 5674
Eze 20:38 you the rebels, and them that t against me: 6586
Am 4: 4 Come *to* Beth-el, and t; *at* Gilgal multiply 6586
Mt 15: 2 Why do thy disciples t the tradition of *3845*
15: 3 Why do you also t the commandment of *3845*
Ro 2:27 the letter and circumcision dost t the law? *3848*

TRANSGRESSED (34) [TRANSGRESS]
Dt 26:13 I have not t thy commandments, 5674
Jos 7:11 they have also t my covenant which I 5674
7:15 he hath t the covenant of the LORD, 5674
23:16 When ye have t the covenant of 5674
Jdg 2:20 Because that this people hath t my 5674
1Sa 14:33 he said, Ye have t: roll a great stone unto me 898
15:24 for I have t the commandment of 5674
1Ki 8:50 all their transgressions wherein they have t 6586
2Ki 18:12 t his covenant, *and* all that Moses 5674
1Ch 2: 7 of Israel, who t in the thing accursed. 4603
5:25 they t against the God of their fathers, and 4603
2Ch 12: 2 because they had t against the LORD, 4603
26:16 for he t against the LORD his God, and 4603
28:19 and t **sore** against the LORD. 4603+4604
36:14 t very **much** after all 4603+4604
Ezr 10:10 Ye have t, and have taken strange wives, 4603
10:13 for we are many that have t in this thing. 6586
Isa 24: 5 because they have t the laws, changed 5674
43:27 and thy teachers have t against me. 6586
66:24 carcases of the men that have t against me: 6586
Jer 2: 8 the pastors also t against me, and 6586
2:29 ye all have t against me, saith the LORD. 6586
3:13 that thou hast t against the LORD thy 6586
33: 8 whereby they have t against me. 6586
34:18 I will give the men that have t my 5674
La 3:42 We have t and have rebelled: thou hast not 6586
Eze 2: 3 they and their fathers have t against me, 6586
18:31 all your transgressions, whereby ye have t; 6586
Da 9:11 Yea, all Israel have t thy law, even by 5674
Hos 6: 7 they like men have t the covenant: 5674
7:13 because they have t against me: though I 6586
8: 1 because they have t my covenant, and 5674
Zep 3:11 thy doings, wherein thou hast t against me: 6586
Lk 15:29 neither t I at any time thy commandment: *3928*

TRANSGRESSEST (1) [TRANSGRESS]
Est 3: 3 Why t thou the king's commandment? 5674

TRANSGRESSETH (4) [TRANSGRESS]
Pr 16:10 of the king: his mouth t not in judgment. 4603
Hab 2: 5 Yea also, because he t *by* wine, *he is* a proud 898
1Jn 3: 4 committeth sin t also the **law**: *458+4160*
2Jn 1: 9 Whosoever t, *3845*

TRANSGRESSING (2) [TRANSGRESS]
Dt 17: 2 of the LORD thy God, in t his covenant, 5674
Isa 59:13 In t and lying against the LORD, and 6586

TRANSGRESSION (51) [TRANSGRESS]
Ex 34: 7 forgiving iniquity and t and sin, and 6588
Nu 14:18 forgiving iniquity and t, and by no means 6588
Jos 22:22 in rebellion, or if in t against the LORD, 4604
1Sa 24:11 see that *there is* neither evil nor t in mine 6588
1Ch 9: 1 were carried away to Babylon for their t. 4604
10:13 t which he **committed** against 4603+4604
2Ch 29:19 Ahaz in his reign did cast away in his t, 4604
Ezr 9: 4 of the t of those that had been carried away; 4604
10: 6 of the t of them that had been carried away. 4604
Job 7:21 why dost thou not pardon my t, and 6588
8: 4 and he have cast them away for their t; 6588
13:23 sins? make me to know my t and my sin. 6588
14:17 My t *is* sealed up in a bag, and thou sewest 6588
33: 9 I am clean without t, I *am* innocent; 6588
34: 6 my right? my wound *is* incurable without t. 6588
Ps 19:13 and I shall be innocent from *the* great t. 6588
32: 1 Blessed *is he whose* t *is* forgiven, 6588
36: 1 The t of the wicked saith within my heart, 6588
59: 3 not *for* my t, nor *for* my sin, O LORD. 6588
89:32 will I visit their t with the rod, and 6588
107:17 Fools because of their t, and because 1870+6588
Pr 12:13 The wicked is snared by the t of *his* lips: 6588
17: 9 He that covereth a t seeketh love; but 6588
17:19 He loveth t that loveth strife: *and* he that 6588
19:11 and *it is* his glory to pass over a t. 6588
28: 2 For the t of a land many *are* the princes 6588
28:24 his father or his mother, and saith, *It is* no t; 6588
29: 6 In the t of an evil man *there is* a snare: but 6588
29:16 the wicked are multiplied, t increaseth: 6588
29:22 up strife, and a furious man aboundeth in t. 6588
Isa 24:20 and the t thereof shall be heavy upon it; and 6588
53: 8 for the t of my people was he stricken. 6588
57: 4 *are* ye not children of t, a seed of falsehood, 6588
58: 1 shew my people their t, and the house of 6588
59:20 unto them that turn from t in Jacob, 6588
Eze 33:12 shall not deliver him in the day of his t: 6588
Da 8:12 against the daily *sacrifice* by reason of t, 6588
8:13 the daily *sacrifice*, and the t of desolation, 6588
9:24 to finish the t, and to make an end of sins, 6588
Am 4: 4 *at* Gilgal multiply t; and bring your 6586
Mic 1: 5 For the t of Jacob *is* all this, and for the sins 6588
1: 5 What *is* the t of Jacob? *is it* not Samaria? 6588
3: 8 to declare unto Jacob his t, and to Israel his 6588
6: 7 shall I give my firstborn *for* my t, the fruit 6588
7:18 passeth by the t of the remnant of his 6588
Ac 1:25 and apostleship, from which Judas **by t fell**, *3845*
Ro 4:15 for where no law is, *there is* no t. *3847*
5:14 not sinned after the similitude of Adam's t, *3847*
1Ti 2:14 but the woman being deceived was in the t. *3847*
Heb 2: 2 and every t and disobedience received a *3847*
1Jn 3: 4 also the law: for sin is the **t of** the **law**. *458*

TRANSGRESSIONS (48) [TRANSGRESS]
Ex 23:21 him not; for he will not pardon your t: 6588
Lev 16:16 and because of their t in all their sins: 6588
16:21 all their t in all their sins, putting them 6588
Jos 24:19 he will not forgive your t nor your sins. 6588
1Ki 8:50 all their t wherein they have transgressed 6588
Job 31:33 If I covered my t as Adam, by hiding mine 6588
35: 6 or *if* thy t be multiplied, what doest thou 6588
36: 9 and their t that they have exceeded. 6588
Ps 5:10 cast them out in the multitude of their t; 6588
25: 7 not the sins of my youth, nor my t: 6588
32: 5 I said, I will confess my t unto the LORD; 6588
39: 8 Deliver me from all my t: make me not 6588
51: 1 of thy tender mercies blot out my t. 6588
51: 3 For I acknowledge my t: and my sin *is* ever 6588
65: 3 *as for* our t, thou shalt purge them away. 6588
103:12 *so* far hath he removed our t from us. 6588
Isa 43:25 *am* he that blotteth out thy t for mine own 6588
44:22 thick cloud, thy t, and, as a cloud, thy sins: 6588
50: 1 and for your t *is* your mother put away. 6588
53: 5 he *was* wounded for our t, *he was* bruised 6588
59:12 For our t are multiplied before thee, and 6588
59:12 for our t *are* with us; and *as for* our 6588
Jer 5: 6 because their t are many, *and* 6588
La 1: 5 hath afflicted her for the multitude of her t: 6588
1:14 The yoke of my t is bound by his hand: 6588
1:22 as thou hast done unto me for all my t: 6588
Eze 14:11 be polluted any more with all their t; 6588
18:22 All his t that he hath committed, they shall 6588
18:28 turneth away from all his t that he hath 6588
18:30 Repent, and turn *yourselves* from all your t; 6588
18:31 Cast away from you all your t, whereby ye 6588
21:24 in that your t are discovered, so that in all 6588
33:10 If our t and our sins *be* upon us, and 6588
37:23 detestable things, nor with any of their t: 6588
39:24 according to their t have I done unto them, 6588
Am 1: 3 For three t of Damascus, and for four, I will 6588
1: 6 For three t of Gaza, and for four, I will not 6588
1: 9 For three t of Tyrus, and for four, I will not 6588
1:11 For three t of Edom, and for four, I will not 6588
1:13 For three t of the children of Ammon, and 6588
2: 1 For three t of Moab, and for four, I will not 6588
2: 4 For three t of Judah, and for four, I will not 6588
2: 6 For three t of Israel, and for four, I will not 6588
3:14 That in the day that I shall visit the t of 6588
5:12 For I know your manifold t and 6588
Mic 1:13 for the t of Israel were found in thee. 6588
Gal 3:19 It was added because of t, till the seed *3847*
Heb 9:15 for the redemption of the t that were under *3847*

TRANSGRESSOR (5) [TRANSGRESS]
Pr 21:18 for the righteous, and the t for the upright. 898
22:12 and he overthroweth the words of the t. 898
Isa 48: 8 wast called a t from the womb. 6586
Gal 2:18 which I destroyed, I make myself a t. *3848*
Jas 2:11 *if* thou kill, thou art become a t of the law. *3848*

TRANSGRESSORS (20) [TRANSGRESS]
Ps 37:38 the t shall be destroyed together: the end of 6586
51:13 *Then* will I teach t thy ways; and 6586
59: 5 be not merciful to any wicked t. Selah. 898
119:158 I beheld the t, and was grieved; because 898
Pr 2:22 the earth, and the t shall be rooted out of it. 898
11: 3 but the perverseness of t shall destroy them. 898
11: 6 but t shall be taken in their own naughtiness. 898
13: 2 but the soul of the t *shall eat* violence. 898
13:15 giveth favour: but the way of t *is* hard. 898
23:28 *for* a prey, and increaseth the t among men. 898
26:10 both rewardeth the fool, and rewardeth t. 5674
Isa 1:28 the destruction of the t and of the sinners 6586
46: 8 bring *it* again to mind, O ye t. 6586
53:12 he was numbered with the t; and he bare 6586
53:12 of many, and made intercession for the t. 6586
Da 8:23 when the t are come to the full, a king of 6586
Hos 14: 9 walk in them: but the t shall fall therein. 6586
Mk 15:28 And he was numbered with the t. *459*
Lk 22:37 in me, And he was reckoned among the t: *459*
Jas 2: 9 and are convinced of the law as t. *3848*

TRANSLATE (1) [TRANSLATED, TRANSLATION]
2Sa 3:10 To t the kingdom from the house of Saul, 5674

TRANSLATED (3) [TRANSLATE]
Col 1:13 hath t *us* into the kingdom of his dear Son: *3179*
Heb 11: 5 By faith Enoch was t that *he* should not see *3346*
11: 5 and was not found, because God had t him: *3346*

TRANSLATION (1) [TRANSLATE]
Heb 11: 5 for before his t he had this testimony, *3331*

TRANSPARENT (1)
Rev 21:21 of the city *was* pure gold, as *it were* t glass. *1307*

TRAP (4) [TRAPS]
Job 18:10 in the ground, and a t for him in the way. 4434
Ps 69:22 *been* for *their* welfare, *let it become* a t. 4170
Jer 5:26 setteth snares; they set a t, they catch men. 4889
Ro 11: 9 and a t, and a stumblingblock, and a *2339*

TRAPS (1) [TRAP]
Jos 23:13 they shall be snares and t unto you, and 4170

TRAVAIL (31) [TRAVAILED, TRAVAILEST, TRAVAILETH, TRAVAILING]
Ge 38:27 it came to pass in the time of her t, that, 3205
Ex 18: 8 all the t that had come upon them by 8513
Nu 20:14 Thou knowest all the t that hath befallen 8513
Ps 48: 6 them there, *and* pain, as of a woman **in t**. 3205
Ecc 1:13 this sore t hath God given to the sons of 6045
2:23 For all his days *are* sorrows, and his t grief; 6045
2:26 to the sinner he giveth t, to gather and 6045
3:10 I have seen the t, which God hath given to 6045
4: 4 I considered all t, and every right work, 5999
4: 6 than both the hands full *with* t and 5999
4: 8 This *is* also vanity, yea, it *is* a sore t. 6045
5:14 those riches perish by evil t: and 6045
Isa 23: 4 saying, I t not, nor bring forth children, 2342
53:11 He shall see of the t of his soul, *and* 5999
54: 1 cry aloud, thou *that* didst not **t with child**: 2342
Jer 4:31 I have heard a voice as of a woman **in t**, 2470
6:24 hold of us, *and* pain, as of a woman **in t**. 3205
13:21 not sorrows take thee, as a woman **in t**? 3205
22:23 upon thee, the pain as of a woman **in t**. 3205
30: 6 and see whether a man doth **t with child**? 3205
30: 6 as a woman **in t**, and all faces are turned 3205
49:24 sorrows have taken her as a woman **in t**. 3205

Jer 50:43 hold of him, *and* pangs as of a woman **in t**. 3205
La 3: 5 and compassed *me* with gall and **t**. 8513
Mic 4: 9 for pangs have taken thee as a woman **in t**. 3205
4:10 O daughter of Zion, like a woman **in t**: 3205
Jn 16:21 A woman when she is **in t** hath sorrow, *5088*
Gal 4:19 of whom I **t in birth** again until Christ be *5605*
1Th 2: 9 ye remember, brethren, our labour and **t**: *3449*
5: 3 upon them, as **t** upon a *woman* with child; *5604*
2Th 3: 8 wrought with labour and **t** night and day, *3449*

TRAVAILED (5) [TRAVAIL]
Ge 35:16 and Rachel **t**, and she had hard labour. 3205
38:28 it came to pass, when she **t**, that *the one* put 3205
1Sa 4:19 were dead, she bowed herself and **t**; 3205
Isa 66: 7 Before she **t**, she brought forth; before her 2342
66: 8 for as soon as Zion **t**, she brought forth her 2342

TRAVAILEST (1) [TRAVAIL]
Gal 4:27 break forth and cry, thou that **t** not: *5605*

TRAVAILETH (7) [TRAVAIL]
Job 15:20 The wicked *man* **t with pain** all his days, 2342
Ps 7:14 he **t** with iniquity, and hath conceived 2254
Isa 13: 8 they shall be in pain as a woman that **t**: 3205
21: 3 upon me, as the pangs of a woman that **t**: 3205
Jer 31: 8 and her that **t with child** together: 3205
Mic 5: 3 until the time *that* she which **t** hath brought 3205
Ro 8:22 and **t in pain together** until now. *4944*

TRAVAILING (3) [TRAVAIL]
Isa 42:14 *now* will I cry like a **t woman**; I will 3205
Hos 13:13 The sorrows of a **t** *woman* shall come upon 3205
Rev 12: 2 **t in birth**, and pained to be delivered. *5605*

TRAVEL (2) [TRAVELLED, TRAVELLER, TRAVELLERS, TRAVELLETH, TRAVELLING]
Ac 19:29 of Macedonia, Paul's **companions in t**, *4898*
2Co 8:19 of the churches to **t with** us with this grace, *4898*

TRAVELLED (1) [TRAVEL]
Ac 11:19 that arose about Stephen **t** as far as Phenice, *1330*

TRAVELLER (2) [TRAVEL]
2Sa 12: 4 there came a **t** unto the rich man, and 1982
Job 31:32 in the street: *but* I opened my doors to the **t**. 734

TRAVELLERS (1) [TRAVEL]
Jdg 5: 6 and the **t** walked *through* byways. 1980+5410

TRAVELLETH (2) [TRAVEL]
Pr 6:11 So shall thy poverty come as one that **t**, and 1980
24:34 So shall thy poverty come *as* one that **t**; and 1980

TRAVELLING (3) [TRAVEL]
Isa 21:13 ye lodge, O ye **t companies** of Dedanim. 736
63: 1 **t** in the greatness of his strength? 6808
Mt 25:14 *of heaven is* as a man **t into a far country**, *589*

TRAVERSING (1)
Jer 2:23 *thou art* a swift dromedary **t** her ways; 8308

TRAYS See SNUFFDISHES

TREACHEROUS (9) [TREACHERY]
Isa 21: 2 the **t dealer** dealeth treacherously, and 898
24:16 the **t dealers** have dealt treacherously; yea, 898
24:16 the **t dealers** have dealt very treacherously. 898
Jer 3: 7 returned not. And her **t** sister Judah saw *it*. 901
3: 8 yet her **t** sister Judah feared not, but went 898
3:10 yet for all this her **t** sister Judah hath not 901
3:11 hath justified herself more than **t** Judah. 898
9: 2 they *be* all adulterers, an assembly of **t** *men*. 898
Zep 3: 4 Her prophets *are* light *and* **t** persons: 900

TREACHEROUSLY (23) [TREACHERY]
Jdg 9:23 the men of Shechem **dealt t** with Abimelech: 898
Isa 21: 2 the treacherous dealer **dealeth t**, and 898
24:16 the treacherous dealers have **dealt t**; yea, 898
24:16 treacherous dealers have **dealt very t**. 898+899
33: 1 **dealest t**, and they dealt not treacherously 898
33: 1 and they **dealt** not **t** with thee! 898
33: 1 *and* when thou shalt make an end to **deal t**, 898
33: 1 they shall **deal t** with thee. 898
48: 8 I knew *that* thou wouldest **deal very t**, 898+898
Jer 3:20 Surely *as* a wife **t** departeth from her 898
3:20 so have you **dealt t** with me, O house of 898
5:11 the house of Judah have **dealt very t** 898+898
12: 1 are all they happy that **deal very t**? 898+899
12: 6 thy father, even they have **dealt t** with thee; 898
La 1: 2 *her:* all her friends have **dealt t** with her, 898
Hos 5: 7 They have **dealt t** against the LORD: 898
6: 7 there have they **dealt t** against me. 898
Hab 1:13 lookest thou upon them that **deal t**, 898
Mal 2:10 why do we **deal t** every man against his 898
2:11 Judah hath **dealt t**, and an abomination is 898
2:14 of thy youth, against whom thou hast **dealt t**: 898
2:15 let none **deal t** against the wife of his youth. 898
2:16 take heed to your spirit, that ye **deal** not **t**. 898

TREACHERY (1) [TREACHEROUS, TREACHEROUSLY]
2Ki 9:23 and said to Ahaziah, *There is* **t**, O Ahaziah. 4820

TREAD (33) [TREADER, TREADERS, TREADETH, TREADING, TRODDEN, TRODE]
Dt 11:24 the soles of your feet shall **t** shall be yours: 1869
11:25 you upon all the land that ye shall **t** upon, 1869
33:29 and thou shalt **t** upon their high places. 1869
Jos 1: 3 that the sole of your foot shall **t upon**, 1869
1Sa 5: 5 **t** on the threshold of Dagon in Ashdod unto 1869
Job 24:11 *and* **t** *their* winepresses, and suffer thirst. 1869
40:12 and **t down** the wicked in their place. 1915
Ps 7: 5 let him **t down** my life upon the earth, and 7429
44: 5 through thy name will we **t** them **under** that 947
60:12 for he *it is that* shall **t down** our enemies. 947
91:13 Thou shalt **t** upon the lion and adder: 1869
108:13 for he *it is that* shall **t down** our enemies. 947
Isa 1:12 required this at your hand, to **t** my courts? 7429
10: 6 **t** them **down** like the mire of 4823+7760
14:25 and upon my mountains **t** him **under foot**: 947
16:10 the treaders shall **t out** no wine in *their* 1869
26: 6 The foot shall **t** it **down**, *even* the feet of 7429
63: 3 for I will **t** them in mine anger, and 1869
63: 6 And I will **t down** the people in mine anger, 947
Jer 25:30 as they that **t** *the grapes,* against all 1869
48:33 none shall **t** *with* shouting; *their* shouting 1869
Eze 26:11 the hoofs of his horses shall he **t down** 7429
34:18 ye must **t down** with your feet the residue 7429
Da 7:23 and shall **t** it **down**, and break it in pieces. 1759
Hos 10:11 *and* loveth to **t out** *the corn;* but I passed 1758
Mic 1: 3 and **t** upon the high places of the earth. 1869
5: 5 when he shall **t** in our palaces, then 1869
6:15 thou shalt **t** the olives, but thou shalt not 1869
Na 3:14 go into clay, and **t** the morter, make strong 7429
Zec 10: 5 they shall be as mighty *men,* which **t down** 947
Mal 4: 3 ye shall **t down** the wicked; for they shall 6072
Lk 10:19 I give unto you power to **t** on serpents and *3961*
Rev 11: 2 the holy city shall they **t under foot** forty *3961*

TREADER (1) [TREAD]
Am 9:13 and the **t** of grapes him that soweth seed; 1869

TREADERS (1) [TREAD]
Isa 16:10 the **t** shall tread out no wine in *their* 1869

TREADETH (10) [TREAD]
Dt 25: 4 not muzzle the ox when he **t out** *the corn.* 1758
Job 9: 8 and **t** upon the waves of the sea. 1869
Isa 41:25 as *upon* morter, and as the potter **t** clay. 7429
63: 2 thy garments like him that **t** in the winefat? 1869
Am 4:13 **t** upon the high places of the earth, 1869
Mic 5: 6 our land, and when he **t** within our borders. 1869
5: 8 both **t down**, and teareth in pieces, and 7429
1Co 9: 9 the mouth of the ox that **t out the corn**. *248*
1Ti 5:18 shalt not muzzle the ox that **t out the corn**. *248*
Rev 19:15 and he **t** the winepress of the fierceness and *3961*

TREADING (4) [TREAD]
Ne 13:15 In those days saw I in Judah *some* **t** wine 1869
Isa 7:25 forth of oxen, and for the **t** of lesser cattle. 4823
22: 5 of **t down**, and of perplexity by the Lord 4001
Am 5:11 as your **t** *is* upon the poor, 1318

TREASON (5) [TRAITOR]
1Ki 16:20 the acts of Zimri, and his **t** that he wrought, 7195
2Ki 11:14 rent her clothes, and cried, **T**, Treason. 7195
11:14 rent her clothes, and cried, Treason, **T**. 7195
2Ch 23:13 rent her clothes, and said, **T**, Treason. 7195
23:13 rent her clothes, and said, Treason, **T**. 7195

TREASURE (37) [TREASURED, TREASURER, TREASURERS, TREASURES, TREASUREST, TREASURIES, TREASURY]
Ge 43:23 your father, hath given you **t** in your sacks: 4301
Ex 1:11 they built for Pharaoh **t** cities, Pithom and 4543
19: 5 ye shall be a **peculiar t** unto me above all 5459
Dt 28:12 The LORD shall open unto thee his good **t**, 214
1Ch 29: 8 *them* to the **t** of the house of the LORD, 214
Ezr 2:69 They gave after their ability unto the **t** of 214
5:17 let there be search made in the king's **t** 1596
7:20 bestow *it* out of the king's **t** house. 1596
Ne 7:70 The Tirshatha gave to the **t** a thousand drams 214
7:71 *some* of the chief of the fathers gave to the **t** 214
10:38 our God, to the chambers, into the **t** house. 214
Ps 17:14 whose belly thou fillest *with* thy hid **t**: they NIH
135: 4 unto himself, *and* Israel for his **peculiar t**. 5459
Pr 15: 6 *In* the house of the righteous *is* much **t**: but 2633
15:16 little with the fear of the LORD than great **t** 214
21:20 *There is* **t** to be desired and oil in 214
Ecc 2: 8 the **peculiar t** of kings and of 5459
Isa 33: 6 of salvation: the fear of the LORD *is* his **t**. 214
Eze 22:25 they have taken the **t** and precious things; 2633
Da 1: 2 he brought the vessels *into* the **t** house of his 214
Hos 13:15 he shall spoil the **t** of all pleasant vessels. 214
Mt 6:21 For where your **t** is, there will your heart be *2344*
12:35 A good man out of the good **t** of the heart *2344*
12:35 an evil man out of the evil **t** bringeth forth *2344*
13:44 the kingdom of heaven is like unto **t** hid in *2344*
13:52 which bringeth forth out of his **t** *things* *2344*
19:21 to the poor, and thou shalt have **t** in heaven: *2344*
Mk 10:21 to the poor, and thou shalt have **t** in heaven: *2344*
Lk 6:45 A good man out of the good **t** of his heart *2344*
6:45 an evil man out of the evil **t** of his heart *2344*
12:21 So *is* he that **layeth up t** for himself, and *2343*
12:33 a **t** in the heavens that faileth not, where no *2344*
12:34 For where your **t** is, there will your heart be *2344*
18:22 the poor, and thou shalt have **t** in heaven: *2344*
Ac 8:27 who had the charge of all her **t**, and had *1047*
2Co 4: 7 But we have this **t** in earthen vessels, *2344*
Jas 5: 3 ye have **heaped t together** for the last *2343*

TREASURED (1) [TREASURE]
Isa 23:18 it shall not be **t** nor laid up; for her 686

TREASURER (2) [TREASURE]
Ezr 1: 8 bring forth by the hand of Mithredath the **t**, 1489
Isa 22:15 Go, get thee unto this **t**, *even* unto Shebna, 5532

TREASURERS (4) [TREASURE]
Ezr 7:21 do make a decree to all the **t** which *are* 1490
Ne 13:13 I **made t** over the treasuries, Shelemiah 686
Da 3: 2 and the captains, the judges, the **t**, 1411
3: 3 and captains, the judges, the **t**, 1411

TREASURES (62) [TREASURE]
Dt 32:34 in store with me, *and* sealed up among my **t**? 214
33:19 of the seas, and *of* **t** hid in the sand. 8226
1Ki 7:51 did he put among the **t** of the house of 214
14:26 he took away the **t** of the house of 214
14:26 of the LORD, and the **t** of the king's house; 214
15:18 the gold that were left in the **t** of the house of 214
15:18 the **t** of the king's house, and delivered them 214
2Ki 12:18 all the gold that was found in the **t** of 214
14:14 in the **t** of the king's house, and hostages, 214
16: 8 in the **t** of the king's house, and sent *it for* a 214
18:15 the LORD, and in the **t** of the king's house. 214
20:13 of his armour, and all that was found in his **t**: 214
20:15 there is nothing among my **t** that I have not 214
24:13 he carried out thence all the **t** of the house of 214
24:13 the **t** of the king's house, and cut in pieces 214
1Ch 26:20 Ahijah *was* over the **t** of the house of God, 214
26:20 and over the **t** of the dedicate *things.* 214
26:22 *which were* over the **t** of the house of 214
26:24 the son of Moses, *was* ruler of the **t**. 214
26:26 his brethren *were* over all the **t** of 214
27:25 over the king's **t** *was* Azmaveth the son of 214
2Ch 5: 1 put he among the **t** of the house of God. 214
8:15 concerning any matter, or concerning the **t**. 214
12: 9 took away the **t** of the house of the LORD, 214
12: 9 of the LORD, and the **t** of the king's house; 214
16: 2 gold out of the **t** of the house of the LORD 214
25:24 the **t** of the king's house, the hostages also, 214
36:18 the **t** of the house of the LORD, and 214
36:18 and the **t** of the king, and of his princes; 214
Ezr 6: 1 where the **t** were laid up in Babylon. 1596
Ne 12:44 some appointed over the chambers for the **t**, 214
Job 3:21 and dig for it more than for **hid t**; 4301
38:22 Hast thou entered into the **t** of the snow? or 214
38:22 the snow? or hast thou seen the **t** of the hail, 214
Pr 2: 4 as silver, and searchest for her as *for* **hid t**; 4301
8:21 me to inherit substance; and I will fill their **t**. 214
10: 2 **T** of wickedness profit nothing: but 214
21: 6 The getting of **t** by a lying tongue *is* a vanity 214
Isa 2: 7 and gold, neither *is there any* end of their **t**; 214
10:13 have robbed their **t**, and I have put down 6259
30: 6 their **t** upon the bunches of camels, to a 214
39: 2 of his armour, and all that was found in his **t**: 214
39: 4 there is nothing among my **t** that I have not 214
45: 3 I will give thee the **t** of darkness, and 214
Jer 10:13 and bringeth forth the wind out of his **t**. 214
15:13 thy **t** will I give to the spoil without price, 214
17: 3 give thy substance *and* all thy **t** to the spoil, 214
20: 5 all the **t** of the kings of Judah will I give into 214
41: 8 for we have **t** in the field, *of* wheat, and 4301
48: 7 thou hast trusted in thy works and in thy **t**, 214
49: 4 that trusted in her **t**, *saying,* Who shall come 214
50:37 a sword *is* upon her **t**; and they shall be 214
51:13 abundant in **t**, thine end is come, *and* 214
51:16 and bringeth forth the wind out of his **t**. 214
Eze 28: 4 and hast gotten gold and silver into thy **t**: 214
Da 11:43 he shall have power over the **t** of gold and 4362
Mic 6:10 Are there yet the **t** of wickedness *in* 214
Mt 2:11 and when they had opened their **t**, *2344*
6:19 Lay not up for yourselves **t** upon earth, *2344*
6:20 But lay up for yourselves **t** in heaven, *2344*
Col 2: 3 In whom are hid all the **t** of wisdom and *2344*
Heb 11:26 of Christ greater riches than the **t** in Egypt: *2344*

TREASUREST (1) [TREASURE]
Ro 2: 5 impenitent heart **t up** unto thyself wrath *2343*

TREASURIES (10) [TREASURE]
1Ch 9:26 over the chambers and **t** of the house of God. 214
28:11 of the **t** thereof, and of the upper chambers 1597
28:12 of the **t** of the house of God, and of 214
28:12 of God, and of the **t** of the dedicate *things:* 214
2Ch 32:27 he made himself **t** for silver, and for gold, 214
Ne 13:12 and the new wine and the oil unto the **t**. 214
13:13 I made treasurers over the **t**, Shelemiah 214
Est 3: 9 of the business, to bring *it* into the king's **t**. 1595
4: 7 to pay to the king's **t** for the Jews, 1595
Ps 135: 7 for the rain; he bringeth the wind out of his **t**. 214

TREASURY (9) [TREASURE]
Jos 6:19 they shall come *into* the **t** of the LORD. 214
6:24 they put *into* the **t** of the house of 214
Jer 38:11 went *into* the house of the king under the **t**, 214
Mt 27: 6 It is not lawful for to put them into the **t**, *2878*
Mk 12:41 And Jesus sat over against the **t**, and *1049*
12:41 how the people cast money into the **t**: *1049*
12:43 than all they which have cast into the **t**: *1049*
Lk 21: 1 the rich *men* casting their gifts into the **t**. *1049*
Jn 8:20 These words spake Jesus in the **t**, as he *1049*

TREATISE (1)
Ac 1: 1 The former **t** have I made, O Theophilus, *3056*

TREATY See LEAGUE

TREE (201) [TREES]
Ge 1:11 *and* the fruit **t** yielding fruit after his kind, 6086
1:12 the **t** yielding fruit, whose seed *was* in 6086
1:29 upon the face of all the earth, and every **t**, 6086
1:29 in the which *is* the fruit of a **t** yielding seed; 6086
2: 9 to grow every **t** that is pleasant to the sight, 6086
2: 9 the **t** of life also in the midst of the garden, 6086
2: 9 and the **t** of knowledge of good and evil. 6086
2:16 Of every **t** of the garden thou mayest freely 6086
2:17 of the **t** of the knowledge of good and evil, 6086
3: 1 Ye shall not eat of every **t** of the garden? 6086
3: 3 of the fruit of the **t** which *is* in the midst of 6086
3: 6 when the woman saw that the **t** *was* good 6086
3: 6 a **t** to be desired to make *one* wise, she took 6086
3:11 Hast thou eaten of the **t**, whereof I 6086
3:12 with me, she gave me of the **t**, and I did eat. 6086
3:17 hast eaten of the **t**, of which I commanded 6086
3:22 take also of the **t** of life, and eat, and 6086
3:24 every way, to keep the way of the **t** of life. 6086
18: 4 your feet, and rest yourselves under the **t**: 6086
18: 8 he stood by them under the **t**, and they did 6086

Ge 30:37 and of the hazel and **chesnut t**; 6196
40:19 from off thee, and shall hang thee on a **t**; 6086
Ex 9:25 of the field, and brake every **t** of the field. 6086
10: 5 a **t** and shall eat every **t** which groweth for you out 6086
15:25 the LORD shewed him a **t**, *which* when he 6086
Lev 27:30 *or* of the fruit of the **t**, *is* the LORD'S: 6086
Nu 6: 4 he eat nothing that is made of the vine **t**, 1612
Dt 12: 2 and upon the hills, and under every green **t**: 6086
19: 5 a stroke with the axe to cut down the **t**, 6086
20:19 thou shalt not cut them down (for the **t** of 6086
21:22 *be* put to death, and thou hang him on a **t**: 6086
21:23 body shall not remain all night upon the **t**, 6086
22: 6 to be before thee in the way in any **t**, 6086
24:20 When thou beatest thine **olive t**, thou shalt 2132
Jos 8:29 the king of Ai he hanged on a **t** until 6086
8:29 should take his carcase down from the **t**, 6086
Jdg 4: 5 she dwelt under the **palm t** of Deborah 8560
9: 8 they said unto the **olive t**, Reign thou over 2132
9: 9 the **olive t** said unto them, Should I leave 2132
9:10 the trees said to the **fig t**, Come thou, *and* 8384
9:11 the **fig t** said unto them, Should I forsake 8384
1Sa 14: 2 under a **pomegranate t** which *is* in Migron: 7416
22: 6 (now Saul abode in Gibeah under a **t** in 815
31:13 buried *them* under a **t** at Jabesh, and 815
1Ki 4:25 man under his vine and under his **fig t**, 8384
4:33 from the **cedar t** that *is* in Lebanon even 730
6:23 oracle he made two cherubims *of* olive **t**, 6086
6:31 of the oracle he made doors of olive **t**: 6086
6:32 The two doors also *were* of olive **t**; and 6086
6:33 for the door of the temple posts of olive **t**, 6086
6:34 the two doors *were* of fir **t**: the two leaves 6086
14:23 on every high hill, and under every green **t**. 6086
19: 4 and came and sat down under a **juniper t**: 7574
19: 5 as he lay and slept under a **juniper t**, 7574
2Ki 3:19 shall fell every good **t**, and stop all wells of 6086
16: 4 and on the hills, and under every green **t**. 6086
17:10 in every high hill, and under every green **t**: 6086
18:31 every one of his **fig t**, and drink ye every 8384
2Ch 3: 5 the greater house he cieled with fir **t**, 6086
28: 4 and on the hills, and under every green **t**. 6086
Est 2:23 therefore they were both hanged on a **t**: 6086
Job 14: 7 For there is hope of a **t**, if it be cut down, 6086
19:10 and mine hope hath he removed like a **t**. 6086
24:20 and wickedness shall be broken as a **t**. 6086
Ps 1: 3 he shall be like a **t** planted by the rivers of 6086
37:35 and spreading himself like a green **bay t**. 249
52: 8 I *am* like a green **olive t** in the house of 2132
92:12 The righteous shall flourish like the **palm t**: 8558
Pr 3:18 She *is* a **t** of life to them that lay hold upon 6086
11:30 The fruit of the righteous *is* a **t** of life; and 6086
13:12 but *when* the desire cometh, *it is* a **t** of life. 6086
15: 4 A wholesome tongue *is* a **t** of life: but 6086
27:18 Whoso keepeth the **fig t** shall eat the fruit 8384
Ecc 11: 3 if the **t** fall toward the south, or toward 6086
11: 3 *in* the place where the **t** falleth, there it 6086
12: 5 the **almond t** shall flourish, and 8247
SS 2: 3 As the **apple t** among the trees of 8598
2:13 The **fig t** putteth forth her green figs, and 8384
7: 7 This thy stature is like to a **palm t**, and 8558
7: 8 I said, I will go up to the **palm t**, I will take 8558
8: 5 I raised thee up under the **apple t**: there thy 8598
Isa 6:13 as a **teil t**, and as an oak, whose substance *is* 424
17: 6 as the shaking of an **olive t**, two *or* 2132
24:13 *there shall be* as the shaking of an **olive t**, 2132
34: 4 the vine, and as a falling *fig* from the **fig t**. 8384
36:16 every one *of* his **fig t**, and drink ye every 8384
40:20 no oblation chooseth a **t** *that* will not rot; 6086
41:19 the **shittah t**, and the myrtle, and the oil 7848
41:19 shittah tree, and the myrtle, and the oil **t**; 6086
41:19 I will set in the desert the **fir t**, *and* 1265
41:19 *and* the pine, and the **box t** together: 8391
44:19 shall I fall down to the stock of a **t**? 6086
44:23 ye mountains, O forest, and every **t** therein: 6086
55:13 Instead of the thorn shall come up the **fir t**, 1265
55:13 of the brier shall come up the **myrtle t**: 1918
56: 3 let the eunuch say, Behold, I *am* a dry **t**. 6086
57: 5 yourselves with idols under every green **t**, 6086
60:13 the **fir t**, the pine tree, and the box together, 1265
60:13 the fir tree, the **pine t**, and the box together, 8410
65:22 for as the days of a **t** *are* the days of my 6086
66:17 in the gardens behind one **t** in the midst, NIH
Jer 1:11 And I said, I see a rod of an **almond t**. 8247
2:20 and under every green **t** thou wanderest, 6086
3: 6 high mountain and under every green **t**, 6086
3:13 ways to the strangers under every green **t**, 6086
8:13 nor figs on the **fig t**, and the leaf shall fade; 8384
10: 3 for *one* cutteth a **t** out of the forest, 6086
10: 5 They *are* upright as the **palm t**, but 8560
11:16 A green **olive t**, fair, *and* of goodly fruit: 2132
11:19 saying, Let us destroy the **t** with the fruit 6086
17: 8 For he shall be as a **t** planted by the waters, 6086
Eze 6:13 under every green **t**, and under every thick 6086
15: 2 What is the vine **t** more than any tree, *or* 6086
15: 2 What is the vine tree more than any **t**, *or* 6086
15: 6 As the vine **t** among the trees of the forest, 6086
17: 5 *it* by great waters, *and* set it *as* a **willow t**. 6851
17:24 I the LORD have brought down the high **t**, 6086
17:24 have exalted the low **t**, have dried up 6086
17:24 have dried up the green **t**, and have made 6086
17:24 and have made the dry **t** to flourish: 6086
20:47 it shall devour every green **t** in thee, and 6086
20:47 every green tree in thee, and every dry **t**: 6086
21:10 it contemneth the rod of my son, *as* every **t**. 6086
31: 8 nor any **t** in the garden of God was like 6086
34:27 the **t** of the field shall yield her fruit, and 6086
36:30 I will multiply the fruit of the **t**, and 6086
41:18 so that a **palm t** *was* between a cherub and 8561
41:19 man *was* toward the **palm t** on the one side, 8561
41:19 the face of a young lion toward the **palm t** 8561
Da 4:10 a **t** in the midst of the earth, and the height 363
4:11 The **t** grew, and was strong, and the height 363
4:14 Hew down the **t**, and cut off his branches, 363
4:20 The **t** that thou sawest, which grew, and 363
4:23 saying, Hew the **t** down, and destroy it; 363
4:26 to leave the stump of the **t** roots; 363

Hos 9:10 as the firstripe in the **fig t** at her first time: 8384
14: 6 his beauty shall be as the **olive t**, and his 2132
14: 8 I *am* like a green **fir t**. From me is thy fruit 1265
Joel 1: 7 laid my vine waste, and barked my **fig t**: 8384
1:12 vine is dried up, and the **fig t** languisheth; 8384
1:12 the **pomegranate t**, the palm tree also, and 7416
1:12 the **palm t** also, and the apple tree, 8558
1:12 the palm tree also, and the **apple t**, 8598
2:22 for the **t** beareth her fruit, the fig tree and 6086
2:22 the **fig t** and the vine do yield their 8384
Mic 4: 4 man under his vine and under his **fig t**; 8384
Hab 3:17 Although the **fig t** shall not blossom, 8384
Hag 2:19 the **fig t**, and the pomegranate, and 8384
2:19 and the pomegranate, and the olive **t**, 6086
Zec 3:10 under the vine and under the **fig t**. 8384
11: 2 Howl, **fir t**; for the cedar is fallen; because 1265
Mt 3:10 every **t** which bringeth not forth good fruit *1186*
7:17 so every good **t** bringeth forth good fruit; *1186*
7:17 but a corrupt **t** bringeth forth evil fruit. *1186*
7:18 A good **t** cannot bring forth evil fruit, *1186*
7:18 neither *can* a corrupt **t** bring forth good *1186*
7:19 Every **t** that bringeth not forth good fruit is *1186*
12:33 Either make the **t** good, and his fruit good; *1186*
12:33 or else make the **t** corrupt, and his fruit *1186*
12:33 fruit corrupt: for the **t** is known by *his* fruit. *1186*
13:32 and becometh a **t**, so that the birds of the air *1186*
21:19 And when he saw a **fig t** in the way, *4808*
21:19 And presently the **fig t** withered away. *4808*
21:20 How soon is the **fig t** withered away! *4808*
21:21 not only do this which is done to the **fig t**, *4808*
24:32 Now learn a parable of the **fig t**; When his *4808*
Mk 11:13 And seeing a **fig t** afar off having leaves, *4808*
11:20 they saw the **fig t** dried up from the roots. *4808*
11:21 the **fig t** which thou cursedst is withered *4808*
13:28 Now learn a parable of the **fig t**; When her *4808*
Lk 3: 9 every **t** therefore which bringeth not forth *1186*
6:43 For a good **t** bringeth not forth corrupt *1186*
6:43 neither doth a corrupt **t** bring forth good *1186*
6:44 For every **t** is known by his own fruit. *1186*
13: 6 A certain *man* had a **fig t** planted in his *4808*
13: 7 years I come seeking fruit on this **fig t**, *4808*
13:19 and it grew, and waxed a great **t**; and *1186*
17: 6 ye might say unto this **sycamine t**, Be thou *4807*
19: 4 climbed up into a **sycomore t** to see him: *4809*
21:29 a parable; Behold the **fig t**, and all the trees; *4808*
23:31 For if they do these *things* in a green **t**, *3586*
Jn 1:48 when thou wast under the **fig t**, I saw thee. *4808*
1:50 I saw thee under the **fig t**, believest thou? *4808*
Ac 5:30 up Jesus, whom ye slew and hanged on a **t**. *3586*
10:39 whom they slew and hanged on a **t**: *3586*
13:29 they took *him* down from the **t**, and *3586*
Ro 11:17 and thou, being a **wild olive t**, wert graffed in *65*
11:17 of the root and fatness of the **olive t**; *1636*
11:24 cut out of the **olive t which is wild** by nature, *65*
11:24 contrary to nature into a **good olive t**: *2565*
11:24 *branches*, be graffed into their own **olive t**? *1636*
Gal 3:13 Cursed *is* every one that hangeth on a **t**: *3586*
Jas 3:12 Can the **fig t**, my brethren, bear olive *4808*
1Pe 2:24 self bare our sins in his own body on the **t**, *3586*
Rev 2: 7 overcometh will I give to eat of the **t** of life, *3586*
6:13 *even* as a **fig t** casteth her untimely figs, *4808*
7: 1 on the earth, nor on the sea, nor on any **t**. *1186*
9: 4 neither any green *thing*, neither any **t**; *1186*
22: 2 side of the river, *was there* the **t** of life, *3586*
22: 2 the leaves of the **t** *were* for the healing of *3586*
22:14 that they may have right to the **t** of life, and *3586*

TREES (157) [TREE]

Ge 3: 2 We may eat of the fruit of the **t** of 6086
3: 8 LORD God amongst the **t** of the garden. 6086
23:17 and all the **t** that *were* in the field, 6086
Ex 10:15 all the fruit of the **t** which the hail had left: 6086
10:15 there remained not any green thing in the **t**, 6086
15:27 of water, and threescore and ten **palm t**: 8558
Lev 19:23 shall have planted all *manner of* **t** for food, 6086
23:40 you on the first day the boughs of goodly **t**, 6086
23:40 branches of **palm t**, and the boughs of thick 8558
23:40 the boughs of thick **t**, and willows of 6086
26: 4 and the **t** of the field shall yield their fruit. 6086
26:20 neither shall the **t** of the land yield their 6086
Nu 24: 6 as the **t of lign aloes** *which* the LORD hath 174
24: 6 *and* as **cedar t** beside the waters. 730
33: 9 of water, and threescore and ten **palm t**; 8558
Dt 6:11 thou diggedst not, vineyards and **olive t**, 2132
8: 8 and vines, and **fig t**, and pomegranates; 8384
16:21 Thou shalt not plant thee a grove *of* any **t** 6086
20:19 thou shalt not destroy the **t** thereof by 6086
20:20 Only the **t** which thou knowest that they *be* 6086
20:20 thou knowest that they *be* not **t** for meat, 6086
28:40 Thou shalt have **olive t** throughout all thy 2132
28:42 All thy **t** and fruit of thy land shall 6086
34: 3 of Jericho, the city of **palm t**, unto Zoar. 8558
Jos 10:26 and slew them, and hanged them on five **t**: 6086
10:26 they were hanging upon the **t** until 6086
10:27 they took them down off the **t**, and 6086
Jdg 1:16 went up out of the city of **palm t** with 8558
3:13 and possessed the city of **palm t**. 8558
9: 8 The **t** went forth on a time to anoint a king 6086
9: 9 and man, and go to be promoted over the **t**? 6086
9:10 the **t** said to the fig tree, Come thou, *and* 6086
9:11 and go to be promoted over the **t**? 6086
9:12 said the **t** unto the vine, Come thou, *and* 6086
9:13 and man, and go to be promoted over the **t**? 6086
9:14 said all the **t** unto the bramble, Come thou, 6086
9:15 the bramble said unto the **t**, If in truth ye 6086
9:48 cut down a bough from the **t**, and took it, 6086
2Sa 5:11 and cedar **t**, and carpenters, and masons: 6086
5:23 upon them over against the **mulberry t**. 1057
5:24 of a going in the tops of the **mulberry t**, 1057
1Ki 4:33 he spake of **t**, from the cedar tree that *is* in 6086
5: 6 command thou that they hew me **cedar t** out 730
5:10 So Hiram gave Solomon cedar **t** and 6086
5:10 and fir **t** *according to* all his desire. 6086
6:29 of cherubims and **palm t** and open flowers, 8561
6:32 of cherubims and **palm t** and open flowers, 8561

1Ki 6:32 upon the cherubims, and upon the **palm t**. 8561
6:35 and **palm t** and open flowers: 8561
7:36 he graved cherubims, lions, and **palm t**, 8561
9:11 of Tyre had furnished Solomon with cedar **t** 6086
9:11 Solomon with cedar trees and fir **t**, 6086
10:11 in from Ophir great plenty of almug **t**, 6086
10:12 the king made *of* the almug **t** pillars for 6086
10:12 there came no such almug **t**, nor were seen 6086
10:27 cedars made he *to be* as the **sycomore t** that 8256
2Ki 3:25 the wells of water, and felled all the good **t**: 6086
19:23 will cut down the tall **cedar t** thereof, *and* 730
19:23 trees thereof, *and* the choice **fir t** thereof: 1265
1Ch 14:14 upon them over against the **mulberry t**. 1057
14:15 of going in the tops of the **mulberry t**, 1057
16:33 shall the **t** of the wood sing out at 6086
22: 4 Also cedar **t** in abundance: for 6086
27:28 over the **olive t** and the sycomore trees that 2132
27:28 the **sycomore t** that *were* in the low plains 8256
2Ch 1:15 **cedar t** made he as the sycomore trees that 730
1:15 cedar trees made he as the **sycomore t** that 8256
2: 8 Send me also cedar **t**, fir trees, and 6086
2: 8 **fir t**, and algum trees, out of Lebanon: 1265
2: 8 fir trees, and **algum t**, out of Lebanon: 418
3: 5 and set thereon **palm t** and chains. 8561
9:10 brought algum **t** and precious stones. 6086
9:11 the king made *of* the algum **t** terraces to 6086
9:27 **cedar t** made he as the sycomore trees that 730
9:27 cedar trees made he as the **sycomore t** that 8256
28:15 the city of **palm t**, to their brethren: 8558
Ezr 3: 7 to bring cedar **t** from Lebanon to the sea of 6086
Ne 8:15 palm branches, and branches of thick **t**, 6086
9:25 and oliveyards, and fruit **t** in abundance: 6086
10:35 the firstfruits of all fruit of all **t**, year by 6086
10:37 the fruit of all *manner of* **t**, of wine and 6086
Job 40:21 He lieth under the **shady t**, in the covert of 6628
40:22 The **shady t** cover him *with* their shadow; 6628
Ps 74: 5 as he had lifted up axes upon the thick **t**. 6086
78:47 with hail, and their **sycomore t** with frost. 8256
96:12 shall all the **t** of the wood rejoice 6086
104:16 The **t** of the LORD are full *of sap;* 6086
104:17 *as for* the stork, the **fir t** *are* her house. 1265
105:33 He smote their vines also and their **fig t**; 8384
105:33 fig trees; and brake the **t** of their coasts. 6086
148: 9 all hills; fruitful **t**, and all cedars: 6086
Ecc 2: 5 and I planted **t** in them of all *kind of* fruits: 6086
2: 6 therewith the wood that bringeth forth **t**: 6086
SS 2: 3 As the apple tree among the **t** of the wood, 6086
4:14 and cinnamon, with all **t** of frankincense; 6086
Isa 7: 2 as the **t** of the wood are moved with 6086
10:19 the rest of the **t** of his forest shall be few, 6086
14: 8 the **fir t** rejoice at thee, *and* the cedars of 1265
37:24 cedars thereof, *and* the choice **fir t** thereof: 1265
44:14 for himself among the **t** of the forest: 6086
55:12 all the **t** of the field shall clap *their* hands. 6086
61: 3 that they might be called **t** of righteousness, 352
Jer 5:17 they shall eat up thy vines and thy **fig t**: 8384
6: 6 Hew ye down **t**, and cast a mount against 6097
7:20 upon the **t** of the field, and upon the fruit of 6086
17: 2 their groves by the green **t** upon the high 6086
Eze 15: 2 *than* a branch which is among the **t** of 6086
15: 6 As the vine tree among the **t** of the forest, 6086
17:24 all the **t** of the field shall know that I 6086
20:28 all the thick **t**, and they offered there their 6086
27: 5 They have made all thy *ship* boards of **fir t** 1265
31: 4 sent out her little rivers unto all the **t** of 6086
31: 5 was exalted above all the **t** of the field, 6086
31: 8 the **fir t** were not like his boughs, and 1265
31: 8 the **chesnut t** were not like his branches; 6196
31: 9 so that all the **t** of Eden, that *were* in 6086
31:14 To the end that none of all the **t** by 6086
31:14 neither their **t** stand up in their height, 352
31:15 and all the **t** of the field fainted for him. 6086
31:16 all the **t** of Eden, the choice and best of 6086
31:18 and in greatness among the **t** of Eden? 6086
31:18 yet shalt thou be brought down with the **t** of 6086
40:16 and upon *each* post *were* **palm t**. 8561
40:22 and their arches, and their **palm t**, 8561
40:26 it had **palm t**, one on this side, and 8561
40:31 and **palm t** *were* upon the posts thereof: 8561
40:34 **palm t** *were* upon the posts thereof, on this 8561
40:37 **palm t** *were* upon the posts thereof, on this 8561
41:18 *it was* made *with* cherubims and **palm t**, 8561
41:20 the door *were* cherubims and **palm t** made, 8561
41:25 doors of the temple, cherubims and **palm t**, 8561
41:26 **palm t** on the one side and on the other 8561
47: 7 at the bank of the river *were* very many **t** 6086
47:12 and on that side, shall grow all **t** for meat, 6086
Hos 2:12 I will destroy her vines and her **fig t**, 8384
Joel 1:12 *even* all the **t** of the field, are withered: 6086
1:19 the flame hath burnt all the **t** of the field. 6086
Am 4: 9 and your vineyards and your **fig t** and 8384
4: 9 your fig trees and your **olive t** increased, 2132
Na 2: 3 and the **fir t** shall be terribly shaken. 1265
3:12 All thy strong holds *shall be like* **fig t** with 8384
Zec 1: 8 he stood among the **myrtle t** that *were* in 1918
1:10 the man that stood among the **myrtle t** 1918
1:11 the LORD that stood among the **myrtle t**, 1918
4: 3 two **olive t** by it, one upon the right *side* of 2132
4:11 What *are* these two **olive t** upon the right 2132
Mt 3:10 also the axe is laid unto the root of the **t**: *1186*
21: 8 others cut down branches from the **t**, and *1186*
Mk 8:24 and said, I see men as **t**, walking. *1186*
11: 8 and others cut down branches off the **t**, *1186*
Lk 3: 9 also the axe is laid unto the root of the **t**: *1186*
21:29 a parable; Behold the fig tree, and all the **t**; *1186*
Jn 12:13 Took branches of **palm t**, and went forth to *5404*
Jude 1:12 **t** whose fruit withereth, without fruit, *1186*
Rev 7: 3 Hurt not the earth, neither the sea, nor the **t**, *1186*
8: 7 and the third *part* of **t** was burnt up, and all *1186*
11: 4 These are the two **olive t**, and the two *1636*

TREMBLE (29) [TREMBLED, TREMBLETH, TREMBLING]

Dt 2:25 shall **t**, and be in anguish because of thee. 7264
20: 3 fear not, and do not **t**, neither be ye terrified 2648

T

Ezr 10: 3 of those that **t** at the commandment of our 2730
Job 9: 6 out of her place, and the pillars thereof **t**. 6426
26:11 The pillars of heaven **t** and are astonished 7322
Ps 60: 2 Thou hast **made** the earth **to t**; thou hast 7493
99: 1 The LORD reigneth; let the people **t**: 7264
114: 7 **T**, thou earth, at the presence of the Lord, 2342
Ecc 12: 3 day when the keepers of the house shall **t**, 2111
Isa 5:25 the hills did **t**, and their carcases were torn 7264
14:16 *Is* this the man that **made** the earth **to t**, 7264
32:11 **T**, ye *women* that are at ease; be troubled, 2729
64: 2 *that* the nations may **t** at thy presence. 7264
66: 5 word of the LORD, ye that **t** at his word; 2730
Jer 5:22 will ye not **t** at my presence, which have 2342
10:10 at his wrath the earth shall **t**, and 7493
33: 9 shall fear and **t** for all the goodness and 7264
51:29 the land shall **t** and sorrow: for every 7493
Eze 26:16 shall **t** at every moment, and be astonished 2729
26:18 Now shall the isles **t** *in* the day of thy fall; 2729
32:10 they shall **t** at every moment, every man for 2729
Da 6:26 in every dominion of my kingdom *men* **t** 2112
Hos 11:10 then the children shall **t** from the west. 2729
11:11 They shall **t** as a bird out of Egypt, and as a 2729
Joel 2: 1 let all the inhabitants of the land **t**: for 7264
2:10 quake before them; the heavens shall **t**: 7493
Am 8: 8 Shall not the land **t** for this, and every one 7264
Hab 3: 7 *and* the curtains of the land of Midian did **t**. 7264
Jas 2:19 doest well: the devils also believe, and **t**. *5425*

TREMBLED (21) [TREMBLE]

Ge 27:33 Isaac **t** very exceedingly, and said, 2729+2731
Ex 19:16 so that all the people that *was* in the camp **t**. 2729
Jdg 5: 4 the earth **t**, and the heavens dropped, 7493
1Sa 4:13 for his heart **t** for the ark of God. 1961+2730
14:15 they also **t**, and the earth quaked: 2729
16: 4 the elders of the town **t** at his coming, and 2729
28: 5 he was afraid, and his heart greatly **t**. 2729
2Sa 22: 8 the earth shook and **t**; the foundations of 7493
Ezr 9: 4 were assembled unto me every one that **t** at 2730
Ps 18: 7 the earth shook and **t**; the foundations also 7493
77:18 lightened the world: the earth **t** and shook. 7264
97: 4 enlightened the world: the earth saw, and **t**. 2342
Jer 4:24 lo, they **t**, and all the hills moved lightly. 7493
8:16 the whole land **t** at the sound of 7493
Da 5:19 languages, **t** and feared before him: 2112
Hab 3:10 The mountains saw thee, *and* they **t**: 2342
3:16 When I heard, my belly **t**; my lips quivered 7264
3:16 entered into my bones, and I **t** in myself, 7264
Mk 16: 8 for they **t** and were amazed: *2192+5156*
Ac 7:32 and the God of Jacob. Then Moses **t**, *1096+1790*
24:25 and judgment to come, Felix **t**, *1096+1719*

TREMBLETH (4) [TREMBLE]

Job 37: 1 At this also my heart **t**, and is moved out of 2729
Ps 104:32 He looketh on the earth, and it **t**: 7460
119:120 My flesh **t** for fear of thee; and I am afraid 5568
Isa 66: 2 and of a contrite spirit, and **t** at my word. 2730

TREMBLING (26) [TREMBLE]

Ex 15:15 men of Moab, **t** shall take hold upon them; 7461
Dt 28:65 the LORD shall give thee there a **t** heart, 7268
1Sa 13: 7 in Gilgal, and all the people followed him **t**. 2729
14:15 And there was **t** in the host, in the field, and 2731
14:15 the earth quaked: so it was a very great **t**. 2731
Ezr 10: 9 **t** because of *this* matter, and for the great 7460
Job 4:14 Fear came upon me, and **t**, which made all 7461
21: 6 I am afraid, and **t** taketh hold on my flesh. 6427
Ps 2:11 the LORD with fear, and rejoice with **t**. 7461
55: 5 Fearfulness and **t** are come upon me, and 7461
Isa 51:17 thou hast drunken the dregs of the cup of **t**, 8653
51:22 I have taken out of thine hand the cup of **t**, 8653
Jer 30: 5 We have heard a voice of **t**, of fear, and 2731
Eze 12:18 drink thy water with **t** and with carefulness; 7269
26:16 they shall clothe themselves with **t**; 2731
Da 10:11 he had spoken this word unto me, I stood **t**. 7460
Hos 13: 1 When Ephraim spake **t**, he exalted *himself* 7578
Zec 12: 2 I *will* make Jerusalem a cup of **t** unto all 7478
Mk 5:33 But the woman fearing and **t**, *5141*
Lk 8:47 she came **t**, and falling down before him, *5141*
Ac 9: 6 And he **t** and astonished said, Lord, *5141*
16:29 and came **t**, and fell down before Paul and *1790*
1Co 2: 3 in weakness, and in fear, and in much **t**. *5156*
2Co 7:15 how with fear and **t** you received him. *5156*
Eph 6: 5 with fear and **t**, in singleness of your heart, *5156*
Php 2:12 out your own salvation with fear and **t**. *5156*

TRENCH (8)

1Sa 17:20 he came to the **t**, as the host was going 4570
26: 5 Saul lay in the **t**, and the people pitched 4570
26: 7 Saul lay sleeping within the **t**, and his spear 4570
2Sa 20:15 a bank against the city, and it stood in the **t**: 2426
1Ki 18:32 he made a **t** about the altar, as great as 8585
18:35 the altar; and he filled the **t** also *with* water. 8585
18:38 and licked up the water that *was* in the **t**. 8585
Lk 19:43 that thine enemies shall cast a **t** about thee, *5482*

TRESPASS (82) [TRESPASSED, TRESPASSES, TRESPASSING]

Ge 31:36 and said to Laban, What *is* my **t**? 6588
50:17 the **t** of thy brethren, and their sin; 6588
50:17 forgive the **t** of the servants of the God of 6588
Ex 22: 9 For all manner of **t**, *whether it be* for ox, 6588
Lev 5: 6 he shall bring his **t offering** unto the LORD 817
5: 7 he shall bring for his **t**, which he hath 817
5:15 If a soul **commit a t**, and sin through 4603+4604
5:15 he shall bring for his **t** unto the LORD a 817
5:15 the shekel of the sanctuary, for a **t offering**: 817
5:16 for him with the ram of the **t offering**, 817
5:18 for a **t offering**, unto the priest: 817
5:19 It *is* a **t offering**: he hath certainly trespassed 817
6: 2 **commit a t** against the LORD, and 4603+4604
6: 5 it appertaineth, in the day of his **t offering**. 819
6: 6 he shall bring his **t offering** unto 817
6: 6 for a **t offering**, unto the priest: 817
6:17 as *is* the sin offering, and as the **t offering**. 817
7: 1 Likewise this *is* the law of the **t offering**: 817
7: 2 burnt offering shall they kill the **t offering**: 817
7: 5 by fire unto the LORD: it *is* a **t offering**. 817
7: 7 As the sin offering *is*, so *is* the **t offering**: 817
7:37 of the **t offering**, and of the consecrations, 817
14:12 offer him for a **t offering**, and the log of oil, 817
14:13 offering *is* the priest's, *so is* the **t offering**: 817
14:14 take *some* of the blood of the **t offering**, 817
14:17 right foot, upon the blood of the **t offering**: 817
14:21 he shall take one lamb *for* a **t offering** to be 817
14:24 priest shall take the lamb of the **t offering**, 817
14:25 he shall kill the lamb of the **t offering**, and 817
14:25 take *some* of the blood of the **t offering**, 817
14:28 upon the place of the blood of the **t offering**: 817
19:21 he shall bring his **t offering** unto 817
19:21 *even* a ram for a **t offering**. 817
19:22 **t offering** before the LORD for his sin 817
22:16 Or suffer them to bear the iniquity of **t**, 819
26:40 with their **t** which they trespassed against 4604
Nu 5: 6 to **do a t** against the LORD, and 4603+4604
5: 7 he shall recompense his **t** with the principal 817
5: 8 have no kinsman to recompense the **t** unto, 817
5: 8 *let* the **t** *be* recompensed unto the LORD, 817
5:12 and **commit a t** against him, 4603+4604
5:27 and have **done t** against her husband, 4603+4604
6:12 bring a lamb of the first year for a **t offering**: 817
18: 9 of theirs, and every **t offering** of theirs, 817
31:16 to commit **t** against the LORD in 4604
Jos 7: 1 the children of Israel **committed a t** 4603+4604
22:16 What **t** *is* this that ye have committed 4604
22:20 **commit a t** in the accursed thing, 4603+4604
22:31 ye have not **committed** this **t** against 4603+4604
1Sa 6: 3 but in any wise return him a **t offering**: 817
6: 4 What *shall be* the **t offering** which we shall 817
6: 8 of gold, which ye return him *for* a **t offering**, 817
6:17 returned *for* a **t offering** unto the LORD; 817
25:28 I pray thee, forgive the **t** of thine handmaid: 6588
1Ki 8:31 If any man **t** against his neighbour, and 2398
2Ki 12:16 The **t** money and sin money was not brought 817
1Ch 21: 3 *thing?* why will he be a **cause of t** to Israel? 819
2Ch 19:10 ye shall even warn them that they **t** not 816
19:10 your brethren: this do, and ye shall not **t**. 816
24:18 upon Judah and Jerusalem for this their **t**. 819
28:13 intend to add *more* to our sins and to our **t**: 819
28:13 for our **t** is great, and *there is* fierce wrath 819
28:22 in the time of his distress did he **t** yet more 4603
33:19 his **t**, and the places wherein he built high 4604
Ezr 9: 2 and rulers hath been chief in this **t**. 4604
9: 6 and our **t** is grown up unto the heavens. 819
9: 7 *have* we *been* in a great **t** unto this day; 819
9:13 us for our evil deeds, and for our great **t**, 819
10:10 strange wives, to increase the **t** of Israel. 819
10:19 *they offered* a ram of the flock for their **t**. 819
Eze 15: 8 because they have **committed a t**, 4603+4604
17:20 will plead with him there *for* his **t** that he 4604
18:24 in his **t** that he hath trespassed, and in his 4604
20:27 in that they have **committed a t** 4603+4604
40:39 and the sin offering and the **t offering**. 817
42:13 and the sin offering, and the **t offering**; 817
44:29 and the sin offering, and the **t offering**; 817
46:20 where the priests shall boil the **t offering** 817
Da 9: 7 of their **t** that they have trespassed against 4604
Mt 18:15 Moreover if thy brother shall **t** against thee, *264*
Lk 17: 3 If thy brother **t** against thee, rebuke him; and *264*
17: 4 And if he **t** against thee seven times in a day, *264*

TRESPASSED (15) [TRESPASS]

Lev 5:19 he hath **certainly t** against the LORD. 816+816
26:40 with their trespass which they **t** against me, 4603
Nu 5: 7 give *it* unto *him* against whom he **hath t**. 816
Dt 32:51 Because ye **t** against me among 4603
2Ch 26:18 go out of the sanctuary; for thou hast **t**; 4603
29: 6 For our fathers have **t**, and done *that* which 4603
30: 7 which **t** against the LORD God of their 4603
33:23 but Amon **t** more and more. 819
Ezr 10: 2 We have **t** against our God, and have taken 4603
Eze 17:20 *for* his trespass that he hath **t** against me. 4603
18:24 in his trespass that he hath **t**, and in his sin 4603
39:23 because they **t** against me, therefore hid I 4603
39:26 all their trespasses whereby they have **t** 4603
Da 9: 7 of their trespass that they have **t** against 4603
Hos 8: 1 my covenant, and **t** against my law. 6586

TRESPASSES (12) [TRESPASS]

Ezr 9:15 behold, we *are* before thee in our **t**: for *we* 819
Ps 68:21 scalp of such a one as goeth on still in his **t**. 817
Eze 39:26 all their **t** whereby they have trespassed 4604
Mt 6:14 For if ye forgive men their **t**, your heavenly *3900*
6:15 But if ye forgive not men their **t**, *3900*
6:15 neither will your Father forgive your **t**. *3900*
18:35 forgive not every one his brother their **t**. *3900*
Mk 11:25 which is in heaven may forgive you your **t**. *3900*
11:26 Father which is in heaven forgive your **t**. *3900*
2Co 5:19 not imputing their **t** unto them; *3900*
Eph 2: 1 you *hath he quickened*, who were dead in **t** *3900*
Col 2:13 with him, having forgiven you all **t**; *3900*

TRESPASSING (2) [TRESPASS]

Lev 6: 7 any *thing* of all that he hath done in **t** therein. 819
Eze 14:13 sinneth against me by **t grievously**, 4603+4604

TRIAL (6) [TRY]

Job 9:23 he will laugh at the **t** of the innocent. 4531
Eze 21:13 Because *it is* a **t**, and what if *the sword* 974
2Co 8: 2 How that in a great **t** of affliction *1382*
Heb 11:36 And others had **t** of *cruel* mockings and *3984*
1Pe 1: 7 That the **t** of your faith, *being* much more *1383*
4:12 think it not strange concerning the **fiery t** *4451*

TRIBE (242) [TRIBES]

Ex 31: 2 of Uri, the son of Hur, of the **t** of Judah: 4294
31: 6 the son of Ahisamach, of the **t** of Dan: 4294
35:30 of Uri, the son of Hur, of the **t** of Judah; 4294
35:34 the son of Ahisamach, of the **t** of Dan. 4294
38:22 of Uri, the son of Hur, of the **t** of Judah, 4294
38:23 of the **t** of Dan, an engraver, and a cunning 4294
Lev 24:11 the daughter of Dibri, of the **t** of Dan:) 4294
Nu 1: 4 with you there shall be a man of every **t**; 4294
1: 5 of *the* **t** *of* Reuben; Elizur the son of NIH
1:21 *even* of the **t** of Reuben, *were* forty and 4294
1:23 *even* of the **t** of Simeon, *were* fifty and 4294
1:25 *even* of the **t** of Gad, *were* forty and 4294
1:27 *even* of the **t** of Judah, *were* threescore and 4294
1:29 *even* of the **t** of Issachar, *were* fifty and 4294
1:31 *even* of the **t** of Zebulun, *were* fifty and 4294
1:33 *even* of the **t** of Ephraim, *were* forty 4294
1:35 *even* of the **t** of Manasseh, *were* thirty and 4294
1:37 *even* of the **t** of Benjamin, *were* thirty and 4294
1:39 *even* of the **t** of Dan, *were* threescore and 4294
1:41 *even* of the **t** of Asher, *were* forty and 4294
1:43 *even* of the **t** of Naphtali, *were* fifty and 4294
1:47 the Levites after the **t** of their fathers were 4294
1:49 Only thou shalt not number the **t** of Levi, 4294
2: 5 next unto him *shall be* the **t** of Issachar: 4294
2: 7 *Then* the **t** of Zebulun: and Eliab the son of 4294
2:12 those which pitch by him *shall be* the **t** of 4294
2:14 the **t** of Gad: and the captain of the sons of 4294
2:20 by him *shall be* the **t** of Manasseh: and 4294
2:22 the **t** of Benjamin: and the captain of 4294
2:27 those that encamp by him *shall be* the **t** of 4294
2:29 the **t** of Naphtali: and the captain of 4294
3: 6 Bring the **t** of Levi near, and present them 4294
4:18 Cut ye not off the **t** of the families of 7626
7:12 the son of Amminadab, of the **t** of Judah: 4294
10:15 over the host of the **t** of the children of 4294
10:16 over the host of the **t** of the children of 4294
10:19 over the host of the **t** of the children of 4294
10:20 over the host of the **t** of the children of Gad 4294
10:23 over the host of the **t** of the children of 4294
10:24 over the host of the **t** of the children of 4294
10:26 over the host of the **t** of the children of 4294
10:27 over the host of the **t** of the children of 4294
13: 2 of every **t** of their fathers shall ye send a 4294
13: 4 of the **t** of Reuben, Shammua the son of 4294
13: 5 Of the **t** of Simeon, Shaphat the son of 4294
13: 6 Of the **t** of Judah, Caleb the son of 4294
13: 7 Of the **t** of Issachar, Igal the son of Joseph. 4294
13: 8 Of the **t** of Ephraim, Oshea the son of Nun. 4294
13: 9 Of the **t** of Benjamin, Palti the son of 4294
13:10 Of the **t** of Zebulun, Gaddiel the son of 4294
13:11 Of the **t** of Joseph, *namely*, of the tribe of 4294
13:11 *namely*, of the **t** of Manasseh, Gaddi 4294
13:12 Of the **t** of Dan, Ammiel the son of 4294
13:13 Of the **t** of Asher, Sethur the son of 4294
13:14 Of the **t** of Naphtali, Nahbi the son of 4294
13:15 Of the **t** of Gad, Geuel the son of Machi. 4294
18: 2 thy brethren also *of* the **t** of Levi, the tribe 4294
18: 2 the **t** of thy father, bring thou with thee, 7626
31: 4 Of every **t** a thousand, throughout all 4294
31: 5 a thousand of *every* **t**, twelve thousand 4294
31: 6 a thousand of *every* **t**, them and Phinehas 4294
32:33 unto half the **t** of Manasseh the son of 7626
34:13 give unto the nine tribes, and *to* the half **t**: 4294
34:14 For the **t** of the children of Reuben 4294
34:14 the **t** of the children of Gad according to 4294
34:14 half the **t** of Manasseh have received their 4294
34:15 the half **t** have received their inheritance on 4294
34:18 ye shall take one prince of every **t**, 4294
34:19 Of the **t** of Judah, Caleb the son of 4294
34:20 of the **t** of the children of Simeon, 4294
34:21 Of the **t** of Benjamin, Elidad the son of 4294
34:22 the prince of the **t** of the children of Dan, 4294
34:23 for the **t** of the children of Manasseh, 4294
34:24 the prince of the **t** of the children of 4294
34:25 the prince of the **t** of the children of 4294
34:26 the prince of the **t** of the children of 4294
34:27 the prince of the **t** of the children of Asher, 4294
34:28 the prince of the **t** of the children of 4294
36: 3 shall be put to the inheritance of the **t** 4294
36: 4 of the **t** whereunto they are received: 4294
36: 4 from the inheritance of the **t** of our fathers. 4294
36: 5 The **t** of the sons of Joseph hath said well. 4294
36: 6 only to the family of the **t** of their father 4294
36: 7 children of Israel remove from **t** to tribe: 4294
36: 7 children of Israel remove from tribe to **t**: 4294
36: 7 to the inheritance of the **t** of his fathers. 4294
36: 8 that possesseth an inheritance in any **t** of 4294
36: 8 shall be wife unto one of the family of the **t** 4294
36: 9 remove from *one* **t** to another tribe; 4294
36: 9 remove from *one* tribe to another **t**; 4294
36:12 their inheritance remained in the **t** of 4294
Dt 1:23 I took twelve men of you, one of a **t**: 7626
3:13 of Og, gave I unto the half **t** of Manasseh; 7626
10: 8 At that time the LORD separated the **t** of 7626
18: 1 priests the Levites, *and* all the **t** of Levi, 7626
29: 8 the Gadites, and to the half **t** of Manasseh. 7626
29:18 among you man, or woman, or family, or **t**, 7626
Jos 1:12 to half the **t** of Manasseh, spake Joshua, 7626
3:12 of the tribes of Israel, out of every **t** a man. 7626
4: 2 men out of the people, out of every **t** a man, 7626
4: 4 the children of Israel, out of every **t** a man: 7626
4:12 of Gad, and half the **t** of Manasseh, 7626
7: 1 the son of Zerah, of the **t** of Judah, 4294
7:14 *that* the **t** which the LORD taketh shall 7626
7:16 their tribes; and the **t** of Judah was taken: 7626
7:18 son of Zerah, of the **t** of Judah, was taken. 4294
12: 6 the Gadites, and the half **t** of Manasseh. 7626
13: 7 the nine tribes, and the half **t** of Manasseh, 7626
13:14 Only unto the **t** of Levi he gave none 7626
13:15 Moses gave unto the **t** of the children of 4294
13:24 Moses gave *inheritance* unto the **t** of Gad, 4294
13:29 Moses gave *inheritance* unto the half **t** of 7626
13:29 *this* was *the possession* of the half **t** of 4294
13:33 unto the **t** of Levi Moses gave not *any* 7626
14: 2 for the nine tribes, and *for* the half **t**. 4294
14: 3 and a half **t** on the *other* side Jordan: 4294
15: 1 was the lot of the **t** of the children of Judah 4294
15:20 This *is* the inheritance of the **t** of 4294
15:21 the uttermost cities of the **t** of the children 4294

T

Jos 16: 8 This *is* the inheritance of the t of 4294
17: 1 There was also a lot for the t of Manasseh; 4294
18: 4 out from among you three men for *each* t: 7626
18: 7 and Reuben, and half the t of Manasseh, 7626
18:11 the lot of the t of the children of Benjamin 4294
18:21 Now the cities of the t of the children of 4294
19: 1 *even* for the t of the children of Simeon 4294
19: 8 This *is* the inheritance of the t of 4294
19:23 This *is* the inheritance of the t of 4294
19:24 the fifth lot came out for the t of 4294
19:31 This *is* the inheritance of the t of 4294
19:39 This *is* the inheritance of the t of 4294
19:40 *And* the seventh lot came out for the t of 4294
19:48 This *is* the inheritance of the t of 4294
20: 8 upon the plain out of the t of Reuben, 4294
20: 8 Ramoth in Gilead out of the t of Gad, and 4294
20: 8 Golan in Bashan out of the t of Manasseh. 4294
21: 4 had by lot out of the t of Judah, and out of 4294
21: 4 out of the t of Simeon, and out of the tribe 4294
21: 4 and out of the t of Benjamin, thirteen cities. 4294
21: 5 lot out of the families of the t of Ephraim, 4294
21: 5 out of the t of Dan, and out of the half tribe 4294
21: 5 and out of the half t of Manasseh, ten cities. 4294
21: 6 lot out of the families of the t of Issachar, 4294
21: 6 out of the t of Asher, and out of the tribe of 4294
21: 6 out of the t of Naphtali, and out of the half 4294
21: 6 out of the half t of Manasseh in Bashan, 4294
21: 7 by their families *had* out of the t of Reuben, 4294
21: 7 out of the t of Gad, and out of the tribe of 4294
21: 7 and out of the t of Zebulun, twelve cities. 4294
21: 9 they gave out of the t of the children of 4294
21: 9 out of the t of the children of Simeon, these 4294
21:17 out of the t of Benjamin, Gibeon with her 4294
21:20 cities of their lot out of the t of Ephraim. 4294
21:23 out of the t of Dan, Eltekeh with her 4294
21:25 out of the half t of Manasseh, Tanach with 4294
21:27 out of the *other* half t of Manasseh *they* 4294
21:28 out of the t of Issachar, Kishon with her 4294
21:30 out of the t of Asher, Mishal with her 4294
21:32 out of the t of Naphtali, Kedesh in Galilee 4294
21:34 rest of the Levites, out of the t of Zebulun, 4294
21:36 out of the t of Reuben, Bezer with her 4294
21:38 out of the t of Gad, Ramoth in Gilead with 4294
22: 1 the Gadites, and the half t of Manasseh, 4294
22: 7 Now to the *one* half of the t of Manasseh 7626
22: 9 of Gad and the half t of Manasseh returned, 7626
22:10 the half t of Manasseh built there an altar 7626
22:11 the half t of Manasseh have built an altar 7626
22:13 of Gad, and to the half t of Manasseh, 7626
22:15 of Gad, and to the half t of Manasseh, 7626
22:21 and the half t of Manasseh answered, 7626
Jdg 18: 1 in those days the t of the Danites sought 7626
18:19 or that thou be a priest unto a t and a family 7626
18:30 his sons were priests to the t of Dan until 7626
20:12 sent men through all the t of Benjamin, 7626
21: 3 that there should be to day one t lacking in 7626
21: 6 There is one t cut off from Israel *this* day. 7626
21:17 that a t be not destroyed out of Israel. 7626
21:24 every man to his t and to his family, and 7626
1Sa 9:21 of all the families of the t of Benjamin? 7626
10:20 to come near, the t of Benjamin was taken. 7626
10:21 When he had caused the t of Benjamin to 7626
1Ki 7:14 He *was* a widow's son of the t of Naphtali, 4294
11:13 will give one t to thy son for David my 7626
11:32 (But he shall have one t for my servant 7626
11:36 unto his son will I give one t, that David 7626
12:20 the house of David, but the t of Judah only. 7626
12:21 with the t of Benjamin, an hundred and 7626
2Ki 17:18 there was none left but the t of Judah only. 7626
1Ch 5:18 the Gadites, and half the t of Manasseh, 7626
5:23 the children of the half t of Manasseh dwelt 7626
5:26 the half t of Manasseh, and brought them 7626
6:60 out of the t of Benjamin; Geba with her 4294
6:61 which were left of the family of *that* t, 4294
6:61 *were cities given* out of the half t, 4294
6:61 *namely, out of* the half t of Manasseh, NIH
6:62 their families out of the t of Issachar, 4294
6:62 out of the t of Asher, and out of the tribe of 4294
6:62 out of the t of Naphtali, and out of the tribe 4294
6:62 out of the t of Manasseh in Bashan, 4294
6:63 out of the t of Reuben, and out of the tribe 4294
6:63 out of the t of Gad, and out of the tribe of 4294
6:63 and out of the t of Zebulun, twelve cities. 4294
6:65 they gave by lot out of the t of the children 4294
6:65 out of the t of the children of Simeon, and 4294
6:65 out of the t of the children of Benjamin, 4294
6:66 of their coasts out of the t of Ephraim. 4294
6:70 out of the half t of Manasseh; Aner with 4294
6:71 out of the family of the half t of Manasseh, 4294
6:72 out of the t of Issachar; Kedesh with her 4294
6:74 out of the t of Asher; Mashal with her 4294
6:76 out of the t of Naphtali; Kedesh in Galilee 4294
6:77 Merari *were given* out of the t of Zebulun, 4294
6:78 *were given them* out of the t of Reuben, 4294
6:80 out of the t of Gad; Ramoth in Gilead with 4294
12:31 of the half t of Manasseh eighteen 4294
12:37 the Gadites, and of the half t of Manasseh, 7626
23:14 his sons were named of the t of Levi. 7626
26:32 the Gadites, and the half t of Manasseh, 7626
27:20 of the half t of Manasseh, Joel the son of 7626
27:21 Of the half t of Manasseh in Gilead, NIH
Ps 78:67 of Joseph, and chose not the t of Ephraim: 7626
78:68 chose the t of Judah, the mount Zion which 7626
Eze 47:23 *that* in what t the stranger sojourneth, 7626
Lk 2:36 the daughter of Phanuel, of the t of Aser: *5443*
Ac 13:21 a man of the t of Benjamin, *by the space of* *5443*
Ro 11: 1 the seed of Abraham, *of* the t of Benjamin. *5443*
Php 3: 5 of the stock of Israel, of the t of Benjamin, *5443*
Heb 7:13 *things* are spoken pertaineth to another t, *5443*
7:14 of which t Moses spake nothing concerning *5443*
Rev 5: 5 behold, the Lion of the t of Juda, the root of *5443*
7: 5 Of the t of Juda *were* sealed twelve *5443*
7: 5 Of the t of Reuben *were* sealed twelve *5443*
7: 5 Of the t of Gad *were* sealed twelve *5443*
7: 6 Of the t of Aser *were* sealed twelve *5443*
Rev 7: 6 Of the t of Nephthalim *were* sealed twelve *5443*
7: 6 Of the t of Manasses *were* sealed twelve *5443*
7: 7 Of the t of Simeon *were* sealed twelve *5443*
7: 7 Of the t of Levi *were* sealed twelve *5443*
7: 7 Of the t of Isachar *were* sealed twelve *5443*
7: 8 Of the t of Zabulon *were* sealed twelve *5443*
7: 8 Of the t of Joseph *were* sealed twelve *5443*
7: 8 Of the t of Benjamin *were* sealed twelve *5443*

TRIBES (112) [TRIBE]

Ge 49:16 judge his people, as one of the t of Israel. 7626
49:28 All these *are* the twelve t of Israel: and 7626
Ex 24: 4 according to the twelve t of Israel. 7626
28:21 shall they be according to the twelve t. 7626
39:14 with his name, according to the twelve t. 7626
Nu 1:16 princes of the t of their fathers, heads of 4294
7: 2 who *were* the princes of the t, and were 4294
24: 2 abiding *in his tents* according to their t; 7626
26:55 according to the names of the t of their 4294
30: 1 Moses spake unto the heads of the t 4294
31: 4 throughout all the t of Israel, shall ye send 4294
32:28 the chief fathers of the t of the children of 4294
33:54 according to the t of your fathers ye shall 4294
34:13 commanded to give unto the nine t, 4294
34:15 The two t and the half tribe have received 4294
36: 3 sons of the *other* t of the children of Israel, 7626
36: 9 every one of the t of the children of Israel 4294
Dt 1:13 known among your t, and I will make them 7626
1:15 So I took the chief of your t, wise men, and 7626
1:15 over tens, and officers among your t. 7626
5:23 *even* all the heads of your t, and 7626
12: 5 out of all your t to put his name there, 7626
12:14 the LORD shall choose in one of thy t, 7626
16:18 thy God giveth thee, throughout thy t: 7626
18: 5 thy God hath chosen him out of all thy t, 7626
29:10 your captains of your t, your elders, and 7626
29:21 him unto evil out of all the t of Israel, 7626
31:28 Gather unto me all the elders of your t, and 7626
33: 5 *and* the t of Israel were gathered together. 7626
Jos 3:12 take ye twelve men out of the t of Israel, 7626
4: 5 according unto the number of the t of 7626
4: 8 according to the number of the t of 7626
7:14 ye shall be brought according to your t: 7626
7:16 the morning, and brought Israel by their t; 7626
11:23 Israel according to their divisions by their t. 7626
12: 7 which Joshua gave unto the t of Israel *for* a 7626
13: 7 this land for an inheritance unto the nine t, 7626
14: 1 the heads of the fathers of the t of 4294
14: 2 for the nine t, and *for* the half tribe. 4294
14: 3 Moses had given the inheritance of two t 4294
14: 4 For the children of Joseph were two t, 4294
18: 2 among the children of Israel seven t, 7626
19:51 the heads of the fathers of the t of 4294
21: 1 unto the heads of the fathers of the t of 4294
21:16 her suburbs; nine cities out of those two t. 7626
22:14 house a prince throughout all the t of Israel; 4294
23: 4 to be an inheritance for your t, from Jordan, 7626
24: 1 Joshua gathered all the t of Israel to 7626
Jdg 18: 1 not fallen unto them among the t of Israel. 7626
20: 2 of all the people, *even* of all the t of Israel, 7626
20:10 of an hundred throughout all the t of Israel, 7626
20:12 the t of Israel sent men through all the tribe 7626
21: 5 Who *is there* among all the t of Israel that 7626
21: 8 What one *is there* of the t of Israel that 7626
21:15 that the LORD had made a breach in the t 7626
1Sa 2:28 did I choose him out of all the t of Israel to 7626
9:21 of the smallest of the t of Israel? 7626
10:19 yourselves before the LORD by your t, 7626
10:20 when Samuel had caused all the t of Israel 7626
15:17 *wast* thou not *made* the head of the t of 7626
2Sa 5: 1 came all the t of Israel to David unto 7626
7: 7 spake I a word with any of the t of Israel, 7626
15: 2 Thy servant *is* of one of the t of Israel. 7626
15:10 Absalom sent spies throughout all the t of 7626
19: 9 were at strife throughout all the t of Israel, 7626
20:14 he went through all the t of Israel unto 7626
24: 2 Go now through all the t of Israel, 7626
1Ki 8: 1 elders of Israel, and all the heads of the t, 4294
8:16 I chose no city out of all the t of Israel to 7626
11:31 of Solomon, and will give ten t to thee: 7626
11:32 the city which I have chosen out of all the t 7626
11:35 and will give it unto thee, *even* ten t. 7626
14:21 LORD did choose out of all the t of Israel, 7626
18:31 according to the number of the t of the sons 7626
2Ki 21: 7 which I have chosen out of all t of Israel, 7626
1Ch 27:16 Furthermore over the t of Israel: the ruler 7626
27:22 These *were* the princes of the t of Israel. 7626
28: 1 the princes of the t, and the captains of 7626
29: 6 of the fathers and princes of the t of Israel, 7626
2Ch 5: 2 elders of Israel, and all the heads of the t, 4294
6: 5 t of Israel to build a house *in*, that my name 7626
11:16 after them out of all the t of Israel such as 7626
12:13 had chosen out of all the t of Israel, 7626
33: 7 which I have chosen before all the t of 7626
Ezr 6:17 according to the number of the t of Israel. 7625
Ps 78:55 made the t of Israel to dwell in their tents. 7626
105:37 *was* not *one* feeble *person* among their t. 7626
122: 4 Whither the t go up, the tribes of 7626
122: 4 the tribes go up, the t of the LORD, 7626
Isa 19:13 *even they that are* the stay of the t thereof. 7626
49: 6 be my servant to raise up the t of Jacob, 7626
63:17 servants' sake, the t of thine inheritance. 7626
Eze 37:19 the t of Israel his fellows, and will put them 7626
45: 8 to the house of Israel according to their t. 7626
47:13 the land according to the twelve t of Israel: 7626
47:21 land unto you according to the t of Israel. 7626
47:22 inheritance with you among the t of Israel. 7626
48: 1 Now these *are* the names of the t. From 7626
48:19 city shall serve it out of all the t of Israel. 7626
48:23 As for the rest of the t, from the east side 7626
48:29 *by lot* unto the t of Israel for inheritance, 7626
48:31 *shall be* after the names of the t of Israel: 7626
Hos 5: 9 among the t of Israel have I made known 7626
Hab 3: 9 *according to* the oaths of the t, *even thy* 4294
Zec 9: 1 the eyes of man, as of all the t of Israel, 7626
Mt 19:28 judging the twelve t of Israel. *5443*
24:30 and then shall all the t of the earth mourn, *5443*
Lk 22:30 sit on thrones judging the twelve t of Israel. *5443*
Ac 26: 7 Unto which *promise* our **twelve t**, *1429*
Jas 1: 1 to the twelve t which are scattered abroad, *5443*
Rev 7: 4 four thousand of all the t of the children of *5443*
21:12 which are *the names* of the twelve t of *5443*

TRIBULATION (22) [TRIBULATIONS]

Dt 4:30 When thou art in t, and all these things are 6862
Jdg 10:14 let them deliver you in the time of your t. 6869
1Sa 26:24 and let him deliver me out of all t. 6869
Mt 13:21 for when t or persecution ariseth because *2347*
24:21 For then shall be great t, such as was not *2347*
24:29 Immediately after the t of those days shall *2347*
Mk 13:24 But in those days, after that t, the sun shall *2347*
Jn 16:33 In the world ye shall have t: but be of good *2347*
Ac 14:22 that we must through much t enter into *2347*
Ro 2: 9 T and anguish, upon every soul of man that *2347*
5: 3 knowing that t worketh patience; *2347*
8:35 *shall* t, or distress, or persecution, or *2347*
12:12 Rejoicing in hope; patient in t; *2347*
2Co 1: 4 Who comforteth us in all our t, that we may *2347*
7: 4 I am exceeding joyful in all our t. *2347*
1Th 3: 4 we told you before that we should **suffer** t; *2346*
2Th 1: 6 to recompense t to them that trouble you; *2347*
Rev 1: 9 and companion in t, and in the kingdom *2347*
2: 9 and t, and poverty, (but thou art rich) *2347*
2:10 may be tried; and ye shall have t ten days: *2347*
2:22 that commit adultery with her into great t, *2347*
7:14 These are they which came out of great t, *2347*

TRIBULATIONS (4) [TRIBULATION]

1Sa 10:19 you out of all your adversities and your t; 6869
Ro 5: 3 And not only *so*, but we glory in t also: *2347*
Eph 3:13 Wherefore I desire that *ye* faint not at my t *2347*
2Th 1: 4 all your persecutions and t that ye endure: *2347*

TRIBUTARIES (4) [TRIBUTE]

Dt 20:11 that is found therein shall be t unto thee, 4522
Jdg 1:30 dwelt among them, and became t. 4522
1:33 and of Beth-anath became t unto them. 4522
1:35 of Joseph prevailed, so that they became t. 4522

TRIBUTARY (1) [TRIBUTE]

La 1: 1 among the provinces, *how* is she become t! 4522

TRIBUTE (37) [TRIBUTARIES, TRIBUTARY]

Ge 49:15 to bear, and became a servant unto t. 4522
Nu 31:28 levy a t unto the LORD of the men of war 4371
31:37 the LORD'S t of the sheep was six 4371
31:38 of which the LORD'S t *was* threescore 4371
31:39 of which the LORD'S t *was* threescore 4371
31:40 of which the LORD'S t *was* thirty and 4371
31:41 Moses gave the t, *which was* the LORD'S 4371
Dt 16:10 *with* a t of a freewill offering of thine hand, 4530
Jos 16:10 unto this day, and serve under t. 4522
17:13 that they put the Canaanites to t; 4522
Jdg 1:28 that they put the Canaanites to t, and 4522
2Sa 20:24 Adoram *was* over the t: and 4522
1Ki 4: 6 Adoniram the son of Abda *was* over the t. 4522
9:21 upon those did Solomon levy a t of 4522
12:18 sent Adoram, who *was* over the t; 4522
2Ki 23:33 put the land to a t of an hundred talents of 6066
2Ch 8: 8 them did Solomon make to pay t until this 4522
10:18 sent Hadoram that *was* over the t; 4522
17:11 brought Jehoshaphat presents, and t silver; 4853
Ezr 4:13 t, and custom, and *so* thou shalt endamage 1093
4:20 and toll, t, and custom, *was* paid unto them. 1093
6: 8 *even* of the t beyond the river, 4061
7:24 to impose toll, t, or custom, upon them. 1093
Ne 5: 4 We have borrowed money for the king's t, 4060
Est 10: 1 the king Ahasuerus laid a t upon the land, 4522
Pr 12:24 bear rule: but the slothful shall be under t. 4522
Mt 17:24 they that received **t money** came to Peter, *1323*
17:24 and said, Doth not your master pay t? *1323*
17:25 do the kings of the earth take custom or t? *2778*
22:17 Is it lawful to give t unto Cesar, or not? *2778*
22:19 Shew me the t money. And they brought *2778*
Mk 12:14 Is it lawful to give t to Cesar, or not? *2778*
Lk 20:22 Is it lawful for us to give t unto Cesar, or *5411*
23: 2 and forbidding to give t to Cesar, saying *5411*
Ro 13: 6 For for this cause pay you t also: for they *5411*
13: 7 t to whom tribute *is due;* custom to whom *5411*
13: 7 tribute to whom t *is due;* custom to whom *5411*

TRICKERY See GUILE

TRICKLETH (1)

La 3:49 Mine eye **t down**, and ceaseth not, without 5064

TRIED (20) [TRY]

Dt 21: 5 every controversy and every stroke be *t*: NIH
2Sa 22:31 way *is* perfect; the word of the LORD *is* t: 6884
Job 23:10 *when* he hath t me, I shall come forth as 974
34:36 My desire *is that* Job may be t unto the end 974
Ps 12: 6 *as* silver t in a furnace of earth, 6884
17: 3 thou hast t me, *and* shalt find nothing; 6884
18:30 the word of the LORD is t: he *is* a buckler 6884
66:10 proved us: thou hast t us, as silver is tried. 6884
66:10 proved us: thou hast tried us, as silver is t. 6884
105:19 word came: the word of the LORD t him. 6884
Isa 28:16 in Zion for a foundation a stone, a t stone, 976
Jer 12: 3 hast seen me, and t mine heart towards thee: 974
Da 12:10 shall be purified, and made white, and t; 6884
Zec 13: 9 is refined, and will try them as gold is t: 974
Heb 11:17 when he was t, offered up Isaac: *3985*
Jas 1:12 for when he is t, he shall receive the crown *1384*
1Pe 1: 7 though it be t with fire, might be found *1381*
Rev 2: 2 thou hast t them which say *they are* *3985*
2:10 *some* of you into prison, that ye may be t; *3985*
3:18 I counsel thee to buy of me gold t in *4448*

T

TRIEST (3) [TRY]
1Ch 29:17 that thou t the heart, and hast pleasure in 974
Jer 11:20 that t the reins and the heart, 974
20:12 that t the righteous, and seest the reins and 974

TRIETH (5) [TRY]
Job 34: 3 For the ear t words, as the mouth tasteth 974
Ps 7: 9 for the righteous God t the hearts and reins. 974
11: 5 The LORD t the righteous: but the wicked 974
Pr 17: 3 for gold: but the LORD t the hearts. 974
1Th 2: 4 pleasing men, but God, which t our hearts. 1381

TRIMMED (2) [TRIMMEST]
2Sa 19:24 nor t his beard, nor washed his clothes, 6213
Mt 25: 7 all those virgins arose, and t their lamps. 2885

TRIMMEST (1) [TRIMMED]
Jer 2:33 Why t thou thy way to seek love? therefore 3190

TRIPOLIS See TARPELITES

TRIUMPH (10) [TRIUMPHED, TRIUMPHING]
2Sa 1:20 lest the daughters of the uncircumcised t. 5937
Ps 25: 2 let not mine enemies t over me. 5970
41:11 because mine enemy doth not t over me. 7321
47: 1 shout unto God with the voice of t. 7440
60: 8 my shoe: Philistia, t thou because of me. 7321
92: 4 thy work: I will t in the works of thy hands. 7442
94: 3 the wicked, how long shall the wicked t? 5937
106:47 unto thy holy name, and to t in thy praise. 7623
108: 9 I cast out my shoe; over Philistia will I t. 7321
2Co 2:14 which always causeth us to t in Christ, and 2358

TRIUMPHED (2) [TRIUMPH]
Ex 15: 1 the LORD, for he hath t gloriously: 1342+1342
15:21 the LORD, for he hath t gloriously; 1342+1342

TRIUMPHING (2) [TRIUMPH]
Job 20: 5 That the t of the wicked is short, and 7445
Col 2:15 a shew of them openly, t over them in it. 2358

TROAS (6)
Ac 16: 8 they passing by Mysia came down to T. 5174
16:11 Therefore loosing from T, we came with a 5174
20: 5 These going before tarried for us at T. 5174
20: 6 and came unto them to T in five days; 5174
2Co 2:12 when I came to T to preach Christ's gospel, 5174
2Ti 4:13 The cloke that I left at T with Carpus, 5174

TRODDEN (27) [TREAD]
Dt 1:36 to him will I give the land that he hath t 1869
Jos 14: 9 Surely the land whereon thy feet have t 1869
Jdg 5:21 O my soul, thou hast t down strength. 1869
Job 22:15 the old way which wicked men have t? 1869
28: 8 The lion's whelps have not t it, nor 1869
Ps 119:118 Thou hast t down all them that err from thy 5541
Isa 5: 5 the wall thereof, and it shall be t down: 4823
14:19 stones of the pit; as a carcase t under feet. 947
18: 2 a nation meted out and t down, whose land 4001
18: 7 a nation meted out and t under foot, 4001
25:10 Moab shall be t down under him, even as 1758
25:10 even as straw is t down for the dunghill. 1758
28: 3 drunkards of Ephraim, shall be t under feet: 7429
28:18 pass through, then ye shall be t down by it. 4823
63: 3 I have t the winepress alone; and of 1869
63:18 our adversaries have t down thy sanctuary. 947
Jer 12:10 they have t my portion under foot, 947
La 1:15 The Lord hath t under foot all my mighty 5541
1:15 the Lord hath t the virgin, the daughter of 1869
Eze 34:19 they eat that which ye have t with your 4823
Da 8:13 and the host to be t under foot? 4823
Mic 7:10 now shall she be t down as the mire of 4823
Mt 5:13 be cast out, and to be t under foot of men. 2662
Lk 8: 5 and it was t down, and the fowls of the air 2662
21:24 Jerusalem shall be t down of the Gentiles, 3961
Heb 10:29 who hath t under foot the Son of God, and 2662
Rev 14:20 And the winepress was t without the city, 3961

TRODE (8) [TREAD]
Jdg 9:27 t the grapes, and made merry, and 1869
20:43 t them down with ease over against Gibeah 1869
2Ki 7:17 the people t upon him in the gate, and 7429
7:20 for the people t upon him in the gate, and 7429
9:33 and on the horses: and he t her under foot. 7429
14: 9 was in Lebanon, and t down the thistle. 7429
2Ch 25:18 was in Lebanon, and t down the thistle. 7429
Lk 12: 1 insomuch that they t one upon another, 2662

TROGYLLIUM (1)
Ac 20:15 day we arrived at Samos, and tarried at T; 5175

TROOP (13) [TROOPS]
Ge 30:11 Leah said, A t cometh: and she called his 1409
49:19 Gad, a t shall overcome him: but he shall 1416
1Sa 30: 8 saying, Shall I pursue after this t? 1416
2Sa 2:25 became one t, and stood on the top of a hill. 92
3:22 of David and Joab came from pursuing a t, 1416
22:30 For by thee I have run through a t: by my 1416
23:11 Philistines were gathered together into a t, 2416
23:13 the t of the Philistines pitched in the valley 2416
Ps 18:29 For by thee I have run through a t; and 1416
Isa 65:11 that prepare a table for that t, and 1409
Jer 18:22 when thou shalt bring a t suddenly upon 1416
Hos 7: 1 and the t of robbers spoileth without. 1416
Am 9: 6 and hath founded his t in the earth; 92

TROOPS (7) [TROOP]
Job 6:19 The t of Tema looked, the companies of 734
19:12 His t come together, and raise up their way 1416
Jer 5: 7 assembled themselves by t in the harlots' 1413
Hos 6: 9 as t of robbers wait for a man, so 1416
Mic 5: 1 Now gather thyself in t, O daughter of 1413
5: 1 gather thyself in troops, O daughter of t: 1416

Hab 3:16 the people, he will invade them with his t. 1464

TROPHIMUS (3)
Ac 20: 4 Timotheus; and of Asia, Tychicus and T. 5161
21:29 before with him in the city T an Ephesian, 5161
2Ti 4:20 but T have I left at Miletum sick. 5161

TROUBLE (110) [TROUBLED, TROUBLEDST, TROUBLER, TROUBLES, TROUBLEST, TROUBLETH, TROUBLING, TROUBLOUS]
Jos 6:18 make the camp of Israel a curse, and t it. 5916
7:25 the LORD shall t thee this day. And all 5916
Jdg 11:35 and thou art one of them that t me: 5916
2Ki 19: 3 This day is a day of t, and of rebuke, and 6869
1Ch 22:14 in my t I have prepared for the house of 6040
2Ch 15: 4 when they in their t did turn unto 6862
29: 8 Jerusalem, and he hath delivered them to t, 2189
32:18 on the wall, to affright them, and to t them; 926
Ne 9:27 in the time of their t, when they cried unto 6869
9:32 let not all the t seem little before thee, 8513
Job 3:26 had I rest, neither was I quiet; yet t came. 7267
5: 6 neither doth t spring out of the ground; 5999
5: 7 Yet man is born unto t, as the sparks fly 5999
14: 1 of a woman is of few days, and full of t. 7267
15:24 T and anguish shall make him afraid; 6862
27: 9 Will God hear his cry when t cometh upon 6869
30:25 Did not I weep for him that was in t? 3117+7186
34:29 he giveth quietness, who then can make t? 7561
38:23 Which I have reserved against the time of t, 6862
Ps 3: 1 LORD, how are they increased that t me! 6862
9: 9 for the oppressed, a refuge in times of t. 6869
9:13 consider my t which I suffer of them that 6040
10: 1 why hidest thou thyself in times of t? 6869
13: 4 those that t me rejoice when I am moved. 6862
20: 1 The LORD hear thee in the day of t; 6869
22:11 Be not far from me; for t is near; for there 6869
27: 5 For in the time of t he shall hide me in his 7451
31: 7 for thou hast considered my t; thou hast 6040
31: 9 mercy upon me, O LORD, for I am in t: 6887
32: 7 hiding place; thou shalt preserve me from t; 6862
37:39 he is their strength in the time of t. 6869
41: 1 the LORD will deliver him in time of t. 7451
46: 1 and strength, a very present help in t. 6869
50:15 call upon me in the day of t: I will deliver 6869
54: 7 For he hath delivered me out of all t: and 6869
59:16 my defence and refuge in the day of my t. 6862
60:11 Give us help from t: for vain is the help of 6862
66:14 my mouth hath spoken, when I was in t. 6862
69:17 not thy face from thy servant; for I am in t: 6887
73: 5 They are not in t as other men; neither are 5999
77: 2 In the day of my t I sought the Lord: 6869
78:33 he consume in vanity, and their years in t. 928
78:49 wrath, and indignation, and t, by sending 6869
81: 7 Thou calledst in t, and I delivered thee; 6869
86: 7 In the day of my t I will call upon thee: 6869
91:15 I will be with him in t; I will deliver him, 6869
102: 2 thy face from me in the day when I am in t; 6862
107: 6 they cried unto the LORD in their t, and 6862
107:13 they cried unto the LORD in their t, and 6862
107:19 they cry unto the LORD in their t, 6862
107:26 the depths: their soul is melted because of t. 7451
107:28 they cry unto the LORD in their t, and 6862
108:12 Give us help from t: for vain is the help of 6862
116: 3 gat hold upon me: I found t and sorrow. 6869
119:143 T and anguish have taken hold on me: 6862
138: 7 Though I walk in the midst of t, thou wilt 6869
142: 2 before him; I shewed before him my t. 6869
143:11 righteousness' sake bring my soul out of t. 6869
Pr 11: 8 The righteous is delivered out of t, and 6869
12:13 of his lips: but the just shall come out of t. 6869
15: 6 but in the revenues of the wicked is t. 5916
15:16 LORD than great treasure and t therewith. 4103
25:19 man in time of t is like a broken tooth, 6869
Isa 1:14 they are a t unto me; I am weary to bear 2960
8:22 behold t and darkness, dimness of anguish; 6869
17:14 behold at eveningtide t; and before 1091
22: 5 For it is a day of t, and of treading down, 4103
26:16 LORD, in t have they visited thee, 6862
30: 6 into the land of t and anguish, from whence 6869
33: 2 our salvation also in the time of t. 6869
37: 3 This day is a day of t, and of rebuke, and 6869
46: 7 he not answer, nor save him out of his t. 6869
65:23 shall not labour in vain, nor bring forth for t; 928
Jer 2:27 in the time of their t they will say, Arise, 7451
2:28 if they can save thee in the time of thy t: 7451
8:15 and for a time of health, and behold t. 1205
11:12 not save them at all in the time of their t. 7451
11:14 in the time that they cry unto me for their t. 7451
14: 8 of Israel, the saviour thereof in time of t, 6869
14:19 and for the time of healing, and behold t. 1205
30: 7 it is even the time of Jacob's t; but he shall 6869
51: 2 for in the day of t they shall be against her 7451
La 1:21 all mine enemies have heard of my t; 7451
Eze 7: 7 the day of t is near, and not the sounding 4103
32:13 neither shall the foot of man t them any 1804
32:13 any more, nor the hoofs of beasts t them. 1804
Da 4:19 or the interpretation thereof, t thee. 927
5:10 let not thy thoughts t thee, nor let thy 927
11:44 of the east and out of the north shall t him: 926
12: 1 there shall be a time of t, such as never was 6869
Na 1: 7 is good, a strong hold in the day of t; 6869
Hab 3:16 in myself, that I might rest in the day of t: 6869
Zep 1:15 a day of t and distress, a day of wasteness 6869
Mt 26:10 unto them, Why t ye the woman? 2873+3930
Mk 14: 6 Let her alone; why t you her? 2873+3930
Lk 7: 6 to him, saying unto him, Lord, t not thyself: 4660
8:49 Thy daughter is dead; t not the Master. 4660
11: 7 shall answer and say, T me not: 2873+3930
Ac 15:19 my sentence is, that we t not them, 3926
16:20 being Jews, do exceedingly t our city, 1613
20:10 and embracing him said, T not yourselves; 2350
1Co 7:28 Nevertheless such shall have t in the flesh: 2347
2Co 1: 4 be able to comfort them which are in any t, 2347
1: 8 have you ignorant of our t which came to 2347

Gal 1: 7 but there be some that t you, and 5015
5:12 I would they were even cut off which t you. 387
6:17 From henceforth let no man t me: 2873+3930
2Th 1: 6 recompense tribulation to them that t you; 2346
2Ti 2: 9 Wherein I suffer t, as an evil doer, 2553
Heb 12:15 lest any root of bitterness springing up t 1776

TROUBLED (68) [TROUBLE]
Ge 34:30 Ye have t me to make me to stink among 5916
41: 8 to pass in the morning that his spirit was t; 6470
45: 3 answer him; for they were t at his presence. 926
Ex 14:24 the cloud, and t the host of the Egyptians, 2000
Jos 7:25 Joshua said, Why hast thou t us? 5916
1Sa 14:29 said Jonathan, My father hath t the land: 5916
16:14 and an evil spirit from the LORD t him. 1204
28:21 saw that he was sore t, and said unto him, 926
2Sa 4: 1 were feeble, and all the Israelites were t. 926
1Ki 18:18 he answered, I have not t Israel; but thou, 5916
2Ki 6:11 the king of Syria was sore t for this thing; 5590
Ezr 4: 4 the people of Judah, and t them in building, 926
Job 4: 5 thou faintest; it toucheth thee, and thou art t. 926
21: 4 if it were so, why should not my spirit be t? 7114
23:15 Therefore am I t at his presence: when I 926
34:20 the people shall be t at midnight, and 1607
Ps 30: 7 thou didst hide thy face, and I was t. 926
38: 6 I am t; I am bowed down greatly; I go 5753
46: 3 Though the waters thereof roar and be t, 2560
48: 5 they were t, and hasted away. 926
77: 3 I remembered God, and was t: 1993
77: 4 eyes waking: I am so t that I cannot speak. 6470
77:16 they were afraid: the depths also were t. 7264
83:17 Let them be confounded and t for ever; yea, 926
90: 7 by thine anger, and by thy wrath are we t. 926
104:29 Thou hidest thy face, they are t: thou takest 926
Pr 25:26 down before the wicked is as a t fountain, 7515
Isa 32:10 Many days and years shall ye be t, 7264
32:11 that are at ease; be t, ye careless ones: 7264
57:20 the wicked are like the t sea, when it cannot 1644
Jer 31:20 therefore my bowels are t for him; I will 1993
La 1:20 my bowels are t; mine heart is turned 2560
2:11 eyes do fail with tears, my bowels are t, 2560
Eze 7:27 the hands of the people of the land shall be t: 926
26:18 the isles that are in the sea shall be t at thy 926
27:35 they shall be t in their countenance. 7481
Da 2: 1 wherewith his spirit was t, and his sleep 6470
2: 3 and my spirit was t to know the dream. 6470
4: 5 my bed and the visions of my head t me. 927
4:19 for one hour, and his thoughts t him. 927
5: 6 his thoughts t him, so that the joints of his 927
5: 9 was king Belshazzar greatly t, and 927
7:15 my body, and the visions of my head t me. 927
7:28 my cogitations much t me, and 927
Zec 10: 2 they were t, because there was no shepherd. 6031
Mt 2: 3 the king had heard these things, he was t, 5015
14:26 on the sea, they were t, saying, It is a spirit; 5015
24: 6 see that ye be not t: for all these things 2360
Mk 6:50 For they all saw him, and were t. 5015
13: 7 of wars and rumours of wars, be ye not t: 2360
Lk 1:12 And when Zacharias saw him, he was t, 5015
1:29 And when she saw him, she was t at his 1298
10:41 thou art careful and t about many things: 5182
24:38 And he said unto them, Why are ye t? and 5015
Jn 5: 4 season into the pool, and t the water: 5015
5: 7 Sir, I have no man, when the water is t, 5015
11:33 he groaned in the spirit, and was t, 5015
12:27 Now is my soul t; and what shall I say? 5015
13:21 he was t in spirit, and testified, and said, 5015
14: 1 Let not your heart be t: ye believe in God, 5015
14:27 Let not your heart be t, neither let it be 5015
Ac 15:24 that certain which went out from us have t 5015
17: 8 And they t the people and the rulers of 5015
2Co 4: 8 We are t on every side, yet not distressed; 2346
7: 5 we were t on every side; without were 2346
2Th 1: 7 And to you who are t rest with us, when 2346
2: 2 or be t, neither by spirit, nor by word, 2360
1Pe 3:14 be not afraid of their terror, neither be t; 5015

TROUBLEDST (1) [TROUBLE]
Eze 32: 2 t the waters with thy feet, and fouledst their 1804

TROUBLEMAKER See PESTILENT

TROUBLER (1) [TROUBLE]
1Ch 2: 7 Achar, the t of Israel, who transgressed in 5916

TROUBLES (12) [TROUBLE]
Dt 31:17 and many evils and t shall befall them; 6869
31:21 when many evils and t are befallen them, 6869
Job 5:19 He shall deliver thee in six t: yea, in seven 6869
Ps 25:17 The t of my heart are enlarged: O bring 6869
25:22 Redeem Israel, O God, out of all his t. 6869
34: 6 heard him, and saved him out of all his t. 6869
34:17 and delivereth them out of all their t. 6869
71:20 which hast shewed me great and sore t, 6869
88: 3 For my soul is full of t: and my life 7451
Pr 21:23 and his tongue keepeth his soul from t. 6869
Isa 65:16 because the former t are forgotten, and 6869
Mk 13: 8 and there shall be famines and t: 5016

TROUBLEST (1) [TROUBLE]
Mk 5:35 is dead: why t thou the Master any further? 4660

TROUBLETH (10) [TROUBLE]
1Sa 16:15 Behold now, an evil spirit from God t thee. 1204
1Ki 18:17 said unto him, Art thou he that t Israel? 5916
Job 22:10 are round about thee, and sudden fear t thee; 926
23:16 my heart soft, and the Almighty t me: 926
Pr 11:17 but he that is cruel t his own flesh. 5916
11:29 He that t his own house shall inherit 5916
15:27 He that is greedy of gain t his own house; 5916
Da 4: 9 the holy gods is in thee, and no secret t thee, 598
Lk 18: 5 Yet because this widow t me, I will 2873+3930
Gal 5:10 but he that t you shall bear his judgment, 5015

T

TROUBLING (2) [TROUBLE]
Job 3:17 There the wicked cease *from* t; and 7267
Jn 5: 4 then first after the t of the water stepped in, *5016*

TROUBLOUS (1) [TROUBLE]
Da 9:25 be built again, and the wall, even in t times. 6695

TROUGH (1) [KNEADINGTROUGHS, TROUGHS]
Ge 24:20 emptied her pitcher into the t, and ran again 8268

TROUGHS (2) [TROUGH]
Ge 30:38 watering t when the flocks came to drink, 8268
Ex 2:16 and filled the t to water their father's flock. 7298

TROUSERS See HOSEN

TROW (1)
Lk 17: 9 *things* that were commanded him? I t not. *1380*

TRUCEBREAKERS (1) [BREAK]
2Ti 3: 3 t, false accusers, incontinent, fierce, *786*

TRUE (81) [TRUTH]
Ge 42:11 we *are* t *men,* thy servants are no spies. 3651
42:19 If ye *be* t *men,* let one of your brethren be 3651
42:31 unto him, We *are* t *men;* we are no spies: 3651
42:33 Hereby shall I know that ye *are* t *men;* 3651
42:34 *that* ye *are* t *men: so* will I deliver you your 3651
Dt 17: 4 and behold, *it is* t, *and* the thing certain, 571
22:20 if this thing be t, *and the tokens of* virginity 571
Jos 2:12 my father's house, and give me a t token: 571
Ru 3:12 now it is t that I *am thy* near kinsman: 551
2Sa 7:28 thy words be t, and thou hast promised this 571
1Ki 10: 6 It was a t report that I heard in mine own 571
22:16 *that which is* t in the name of the LORD? 571
2Ch 9: 5 *It was* a t report which I heard in mine own 571
15: 3 season Israel *hath been* without the t God, 571
Ne 9:13 t laws, good statutes and commandments: 571
Ps 19: 9 the judgments of the LORD *are* t *and* 571
119:160 Thy word *is* t *from* the beginning: and 571
Pr 14:25 A t witness delivereth souls: but a deceitful 571
Jer 10:10 the LORD *is* the t God, he *is* the living 571
42: 5 The LORD be a t and faithful witness 571
Eze 18: 8 hath executed t judgment between man and 571
Da 3:14 *Is it* t, O Shadrach, Meshach, and 6656
3:24 and said unto the king, T, O king. 3330
6:12 The king answered and said, The thing *is* t, 3330
8:26 and the morning which was told *is* t: 571
10: 1 the thing *was* t, but the time appointed *was* 571
Zec 7: 9 Execute t judgment, and shew mercy and 571
Mt 22:16 we know that thou art t, and teachest *227*
Mk 12:14 we know that thou art t, and carest for no *227*
Lk 16:11 who will commit to your trust the t *riches?* *228*
Jn 1: 9 *That* was the t Light, which lighteth every *228*
3:33 testimony hath set to *his* seal that God is t. *227*
4:23 when the t worshippers shall worship *228*
4:37 And herein is *that* saying t, One soweth, *228*
5:31 I bear witness of myself, my witness is not t. *227*
5:32 the witness which he witnesseth of me is t. *227*
6:32 my Father giveth you the t bread from *228*
7:18 the same is t, and no unrighteousness is in *227*
7:28 but he that sent me is t, whom ye know not. *228*
8:13 bearest record of thyself; thy record is not t. *227*
8:14 I bear record of myself, *yet* my record is t: *227*
8:16 And yet if I judge, my judgment is t: for I *227*
8:17 your law, that the testimony of two men is t. *227*
8:26 but he that sent me is t; and I speak to *227*
10:41 all *things* that John spake of this *man* were t. *227*
15: 1 I am the t vine, and my Father is *228*
17: 3 that they might know thee the only t God, *228*
19:35 he that saw *it* bare record, and his record is t: *228*
19:35 and he knoweth that he saith t, that ye might *227*
21:24 and we know that his testimony is t. *227*
Ac 12: 9 wist not that it was t which was done by *227*
Ro 3: 4 yea, let God be t, but every man a liar; as it *227*
2Co 1:18 But *as* God *is* t, our word toward you was *4103*
6: 8 and good report: as deceivers, and *yet* t; *227*
Eph 4:24 is created in righteousness and t holiness. *225*
Php 4: 3 And I intreat thee also, t yokefellow, *1103*
4: 8 Finally, brethren, whatsoever *things* are t, *227*
1Th 1: 9 God from idols to serve the living and t God, *228*
1Ti 3: 1 *This is* a t saying, If a man desire the office *4103*
Tit 1:13 This witness is t. Wherefore rebuke them *227*
Heb 8: 2 and of the t tabernacle, which the Lord *228*
9:24 with hands, *which are* the figures of the t; *228*
10:22 Let us draw near with a t heart in full *228*
1Pe 5:12 testifying that this is the t grace of God *227*
2Pe 2:22 unto them according to the t proverb, *227*
1Jn 2: 8 unto you, which *thing* is t in him and in you: *227*
2: 8 darkness is past, and the t light now shineth. *228*
5:20 that we may know him *that is* t, and we are *228*
5:20 and we are in him *that is* t, *even* in his Son *228*
5:20 This is the t God, and eternal life. *228*
3Jn 1:12 bear record; and ye know that our record is t. *227*
Rev 3: 7 he *that is* t, he that hath the key of David, *228*
3:14 saith the Amen, the faithful and t witness, *228*
6:10 saying, How long, O Lord, holy and t, *228*
15: 3 just and t *are* thy ways, thou King of saints. *228*
16: 7 t and righteous *are* thy judgments. *228*
19: 2 For t and righteous *are* his judgments: for he *228*
19: 9 unto me, These are the t sayings of God. *228*
19:11 that sat upon him *was* called Faithful and T, *228*
21: 5 Write: for these words are t and faithful. *228*
22: 6 unto me, These sayings *are* faithful and t: *228*

TRULY (42) [TRUTH]
Ge 4:24 t Lamech seventy and sevenfold. 2050.1
24:49 if ye will deal kindly and t with my master, 571
47:29 my thigh, and deal kindly and t with me; 571
48:19 t his younger brother shall be greater than 199
Nu 14:21 *as* t *as* I live, all the earth shall be filled *with* 199
14:28 Say unto them, *As* t *as* I live, saith NIH
Dt 14:22 Thou shalt t **tithe** all the increase of 6237+6237
Jos 2:14 that we will deal kindly and t with thee. 571
Jos 2:24 T the LORD hath delivered into our hands 3588
Jdg 9:16 if ye have done t and sincerely, 571+871.1
9:19 If ye then have dealt t and sincerely 571+871.1
1Sa 20: 3 t *as* the LORD liveth, and *as* thy soul 199
Job 36: 4 For t my words *shall* not *be* false: *he that is* 551
Ps 62: 1 T my soul waiteth upon God: from him 389
73: 1 T God *is* good to Israel, *even* to such as are 389
116:16 Oh LORD, t I *am* thy servant; I *am* thy 3588
Pr 12:22 but they that deal t *are* his delight. 530
Ecc 11: 7 T the light *is* sweet, and a pleasant *thing* 2050.1
Jer 3:23 T in vain *is salvation hoped for* from 403
3:23 t in the LORD our God *is* the salvation of 403
10:19 but I said, T this *is* a grief, and I must bear it. 389
28: 9 that the LORD hath t sent him. 571+871.1
Eze 18: 9 and hath kept my judgments, to deal t; 571
Mic 3: 8 t I am full *of* power by the spirit of 199
Mt 9:37 The harvest t *is* plenteous, but the labourers *3303*
17:11 Elias t shall first come, and restore all *3303*
27:54 saying, T this was the Son of God. *230*
Mk 14:38 The spirit t *is* ready, but the flesh *is* weak. *3303*
15:39 he said, T this man was the Son of God. *230*
Lk 10: 2 The harvest t *is* great, but the labourers *are* *3303*
11:48 T ye bear witness that ye allow the deeds of *686*
20:21 *of any,* but teachest the way of God t: *225+1909*
22:22 And t the Son of man goeth, as it was *3303*
Jn 4:18 hast is not thy husband: *in* that saidst thou t. *227*
20:30 And many other signs t did Jesus in *3303*
Ac 1: 5 For John t baptized with water; but ye shall *3303*
3:22 For Moses t said unto the fathers, *3303*
5:23 The prison t found we shut with all safety, *3303*
2Co 12:12 T the signs of an apostle were wrought *3303*
Heb 7:23 And they t were many priests, because *3303*
11:15 And t, if they had been mindful of that *3303*
1Jn 1: 3 and t our fellowship *is* with the Father, and NIG

TRUMP (2) [TRUMPET]
1Co 15:52 in the twinkling of an eye, at the last t: *4536*
1Th 4:16 of the archangel, and with the t of God: *4536*

TRUMPET (61) [TRUMP, TRUMPETERS, TRUMPETS]
Ex 19:13 when the t soundeth long, they shall come 3104
19:16 and the voice of the t exceeding loud; 7782
19:19 when the voice of the t sounded long, and 7782
20:18 the noise of the t, and the mountain 7782
Lev 25: 9 shalt thou cause the t of the jubile to sound 7782
25: 9 in the day of atonement shall ye make the t 7782
Nu 10: 4 if they blow *but* with one *t,* then the princes, NIH
Jos 6: 5 *and* when ye hear the sound of the t, all 7782
6:20 when the people heard the sound of the t, 7782
Jdg 3:27 that he blew a t in the mountain of 7782
6:34 came upon Gideon, and he blew a t; 7782
7:16 he put a t in every man's hand, with empty 7782
7:18 When I blow with a t, I and all that *are* with 7782
1Sa 13: 3 And Saul blew the t throughout all the land, 7782
2Sa 2:28 So Joab blew a t, and all the people stood 7782
6:15 with shouting, and with the sound of the t. 7782
15:10 As soon as ye hear the sound of the t, then 7782
18:16 Joab blew the t, and the people returned 7782
20: 1 he blew a t, and said, We have no part in 7782
20:22 he blew a t, and they retired from the city, 7782
1Ki 1:34 blow ye with the t, and say, God save king 7782
1:39 they blew the t; and all the people said, 7782
1:41 when Joab heard the sound of the t, he said, 7782
Ne 4:18 And he that sounded the t *was* by me. 7782
4:20 *therefore* ye hear the sound of the t, 7782
Job 39:24 believeth he that *it is* the sound of the t. 7782
Ps 47: 5 a shout, the LORD with the sound of a t. 7782
81: 3 Blow up the t in the new moon, in the time 7782
150: 3 Praise him with the sound of the t: 7782
Isa 18: 3 and when *he* bloweth a t, hear ye. 7782
27:13 *that* the great t shall be blown, and 7782
58: 1 lift up thy voice like a t, and shew my 7782
Jer 4: 5 and say, Blow ye the t in the land: 7782
4:19 hast heard, O my soul, the sound of the t, 7782
4:21 the standard, *and* hear the sound of the t? 7782
6: 1 blow the t in Tekoa, and set up a sign of 7782
6:17 *saying,* Hearken to the sound of the t. 7782
42:14 nor hear the sound of the t, nor have hunger 7782
51:27 blow the t among the nations, prepare 7782
Eze 7:14 They have blown the t, even to make all 8619
33: 3 he blow the t, and warn the people; 7782
33: 4 whosoever heareth the sound of the t, and 7782
33: 5 He heard the sound of the t, and took not 7782
33: 6 blow not the t, and the people be not 7782
Hos 5: 8 the cornet in Gibeah, *and* the t in Ramah: 2689
8: 1 *Set* the t to thy mouth. *He shall come* as an 7782
Joel 2: 1 Blow ye the t in Zion, and sound an alarm 7782
2:15 Blow the t in Zion, sanctify a fast, call a 7782
Am 2: 2 with shouting, *and* with the sound of the t: 7782
3: 6 Shall a t be blown in the city, and 7782
Zep 1:16 A day of the t and alarm against the fenced 7782
Zec 9:14 the Lord GOD shall blow the t, and 7782
Mt 6: 2 *thine* alms, do not **sound a** t before thee, *4537*
24:31 send his angels with a great sound of a t, *4536*
1Co 14: 8 For if the t give an uncertain sound, *4536*
15:52 for the t shall **sound**, and the dead shall be *4537*
Heb 12:19 And the sound of a t, and the voice of *4536*
Rev 1:10 heard behind me a great voice, as of a t, *4536*
4: 1 heard *was* as *it were* of a t talking with me; *4536*
8:13 the other voices of the t of the three angels, *4536*
9:14 Saying to the sixth angel which had the t, *4536*

TRUMPETERS (4) [TRUMPET]
2Ki 11:14 and the princes and the t by the king, 2689
2Ch 5:13 to pass, as the t and singers *were* as one, 2690
29:28 and the singers sang, and the t sounded: 2689
Rev 18:22 and musicians, and of pipers, and t, *4538*

TRUMPETS (51) [TRUMPET]
Lev 23:24 a memorial of **blowing of** t, a holy 8643
Nu 10: 2 Make thee two t of silver; of a whole piece 2689
10: 8 of Aaron, the priests, shall blow with the t; 2689
10: 9 then ye shall blow an alarm with the t; 2689
Nu 10:10 ye shall blow with the t over your burnt 2689
29: 1 it is a day of **blowing** the t unto you. 8643
31: 6 and the t to blow in his hand. 2689
Jos 6: 4 bear before the ark seven t of rams' horns: 7782
6: 4 and the priests shall blow with the t. 7782
6: 6 let seven priests bear seven t of rams' horns 7782
6: 8 that the seven priests bearing the seven t of 7782
6: 8 on before the LORD, and blew with the t: 7782
6: 9 went before the priests that blew *with* the t, 7782
6: 9 *priests* going on, and blowing with the t. 7782
6:13 seven priests bearing seven t of rams' horns 7782
6:13 went on continually, and blew with the t: 7782
6:13 *priests* going on, and blowing with the t. 7782
6:16 when the priests blew with the t, Joshua 7782
6:20 shouted when *the priests* blew with the t: 7782
Jdg 7: 8 took victuals in their hand, and their t: 7782
7:18 blow ye the t also on every side of all 7782
7:19 they blew the t, and brake the pitchers that 7782
7:20 the three companies blew the t, and 7782
7:20 the t in their right hands to blow *withal:* 7782
7:22 the three hundred blew the t, and 7782
2Ki 9:13 and blew with t, saying, Jehu is king. 7782
11:14 of the land rejoiced, and blew with t: 2689
12:13 snuffers, basons, t, any vessels of gold, or 2689
1Ch 13: 8 and with cymbals, and with t. 2689
15:24 did blow with the t before the ark of God: 2689
15:28 of the cornet, and with t, and with cymbals, 2689
16: 6 Jahaziel the priests with t continually 2689
16:42 with them Heman and Jeduthun *with* t and 2689
2Ch 5:12 and twenty priests sounding with t:) 2689
5:13 when *they* lift up *their* voice with the t and 2689
7: 6 the priests **sounded** t before them, and 2690
13:12 his priests with sounding t to cry alarm 2689
13:14 and the priests sounded with the t. 2689
15:14 with shouting, and with t, and with cornets. 2689
20:28 and t unto the house of the LORD. 2689
23:13 and the princes and the t by the king: 2689
23:13 of the land rejoiced, and sounded with t, 2689
29:26 of David, and the priests with the t. 2689
29:27 song of the LORD began *also* with the t, 2689
Ezr 3:10 they set the priests in their apparel with t, 2689
Ne 12:35 *certain* of the priests' sons with t; 2689
12:41 Elioenai, Zechariah, *and* Hananiah, with t; 2689
Job 39:25 He saith among the t, Ha, ha; and 7782
Ps 98: 6 With t and sound of cornet make a joyful 2689
Rev 8: 2 and to them were given seven t. *4536*
8: 6 And the seven angels which had the seven t *4536*

TRUST (134) [TRUSTED, TRUSTEDST, TRUSTEST, TRUSTETH, TRUSTING, TRUSTY]
Jdg 9:15 *then* come *and* **put** your t in my shadow: 2620
Ru 2:12 under whose wings thou art come to t. 2620
2Sa 22: 3 The God of my rock; in him will I t: *he is* 2620
22:31 he *is* a buckler to all them that t in him. 2620
2Ki 18:20 Now on whom dost thou t, that thou 982
18:21 *is* Pharaoh king of Egypt unto all that t on 982
18:22 say unto me, We t in the LORD our God: 982
18:24 **put** thy t on Egypt for chariots and 982
18:30 Neither let Hezekiah **make** you t in 982
1Ch 5:20 of them; because they **put** their t in him. 982
2Ch 32:10 Whereon do ye t, that ye abide in the siege 982
Job 4:18 Behold, he **put** no t in his servants; and his 539
8:14 cut off, and whose t *shall be* a spider's web. 4009
13:15 Though he slay me, *yet* will I t in him: but 3176
15:15 Behold, he **putteth** no t in his saints; yea, 539
15:31 Let not him that is deceived t in vanity: 539
35:14 *is* before him; therefore t thou in him. 2342
39:11 Wilt thou t him, because his strength *is* 982
Ps 2:12 blessed *are* all they that **put** their t in him. 2620
4: 5 and **put** your t in the LORD. 982
5:11 let all those that **put** their t in thee rejoice: 2620
7: 1 O LORD my God, in thee do I **put** my t: 2620
9:10 they that know thy name will **put** their t in 982
11: 1 In the LORD **put** I my t: how say ye to 2620
16: 1 O God: for in thee do I **put** my t. 2620
17: 7 **put** their t *in thee* from those that rise up 2620
18: 2 my God, my strength, in whom I will t; 2620
18:30 he *is* a buckler to all those that t in him. 2620
20: 7 Some *t* in chariots, and some in horses: but NIH
25: 2 O my God, I t in thee: let me not be 982
25:20 me not be ashamed; for I **put** my t in thee. 2620
31: 1 In thee, O LORD, do I **put** my t; let me 2620
31: 6 regard lying vanities: but I t in the LORD. 982
31:19 *which* thou hast wrought for them that t in 2620
34:22 none of them that t in him shall be desolate. 2620
36: 7 the children of men **put** their t under 2620
37: 3 T in the LORD, and do good; *so* shalt thou 982
37: 5 t also in him; and he shall bring *it* to pass. 982
37:40 and save them, because they t in him. 2620
40: 3 see *it,* and fear, and shall t in the LORD. 982
40: 4 *is that* man that maketh the LORD his t, 4009
44: 6 For I will not t in my bow, neither shall my 982
49: 6 They that t in their wealth, and 982
52: 8 I t in the mercy of God for ever and ever. 982
55:23 live out half their days; but I will t in thee. 982
56: 3 *What* time I am afraid, I will t in thee. 982
56: 4 will praise his word, in God I have **put** my t; 982
56:11 In God have I **put** my t: I will not be afraid 982
61: 4 I will t in the covert of thy wings. Selah. 2620
62: 8 T in him at all times; ye people, pour out 982
62:10 T not in oppression, and become not vain in 982
64:10 be glad in the LORD, and shall t in him; 2620
71: 1 In thee, O LORD, do I **put** my t: let me 2620
71: 5 Lord GOD: *thou art* my t from my youth. 4009
73:28 I have put my t in the Lord GOD, that *I* 4268
91: 2 and my fortress: my God; in him will I t. 982
91: 4 and under his wings shalt thou t: 2620
115: 9 O Israel, t thou in the LORD: he *is* their 982
115:10 O house of Aaron, t in the LORD: he *is* 982
115:11 Ye that fear the LORD, t in the LORD: 982
118: 8 *It is* better to t in the LORD than to put 2620
118: 9 *It is* better to t in the LORD than to put 2620
119:42 him that reproacheth me: for I t in thy word. 982
125: 1 They that t in the LORD *shall be* as mount 982
141: 8 in thee is my t; leave not my soul destitute. 2620

Ps 143: 8 in the morning; for in thee do I **t**: 982
144: 2 my shield, and *he* in whom I **t**; 2620
146: 3 **Put** not your **t** in princes, *nor* in the son of 982
Pr 3: 5 **T** in the LORD with all thine heart; and 982
22:19 That thy **t** may be in the LORD, I have 4009
28:25 he that **putteth** his **t** in the LORD shall be 982
29:25 whoso **putteth** his **t** in the LORD shall be 982
30: 5 he *is* a shield unto them that **put** their **t** in 2620
31:11 The heart of her husband doth *safely* **t** in her, 982
Isa 12: 2 *is* my salvation; I will **t**, and not be afraid: 982
14:32 and the poor of his people shall **t** in it. 2620
26: 4 **T** ye in the LORD for ever: for in 982
30: 2 and to **t** in the shadow of Egypt. 2620
30: 3 the **t** in the shadow of Egypt *your* 2622
30:12 **t** in oppression and perverseness, and 982
31: 1 and **t** in chariots, because *they are* many; 982
36: 5 now on whom dost thou **t**, that thou rebellest 982
36: 6 *is* Pharaoh king of Egypt to all that **t** in him. 982
36: 7 say to me, We **t** in the LORD our God: 982
36: 9 **put** thy **t** on Egypt for chariots and 982
36:15 Neither let Hezekiah **make** you **t** in 982
42:17 that **t** in graven images, that say to 982
50:10 let him **t** in the name of the LORD, and 982
51: 5 upon me, and on mine arm shall they **t**. 3176
57:13 he that **putteth** his **t** in me shall possess 2620
59: 4 *they* **t** in vanity, and speak lies; 982
Jer 7: 4 **T** ye not in lying words, saying, The temple 982
7: 8 Behold, ye **t** in lying words, *that* cannot 982
7:14 wherein ye **t**, and unto the place which I 982
9: 4 of his neighbour, and **t** ye not in any brother: 982
28:15 but thou **makest** this people **to t** in a lie. 982
29:31 sent him not, and he **caused** you **to t** in a lie: 982
39:18 because thou hast **put** thy **t** in me, saith 982
46:25 even Pharaoh, and *all* them that **t** in him: 982
49:11 *them* alive; and let thy widows **t** in me. 982
Eze 16:15 thou didst **t** in thine own beauty, and 982
33:13 if he **t** to his own righteousness, and 982
Hos 10:13 because thou didst **t** in thy way, in 982
Am 6: 1 in Zion, and **t** in the mountain of Samaria, 982
Mic 7: 5 **T** ye not in a friend, put ye not confidence in 539
Na 1: 7 and he knoweth them that **t** in him. 2620
Zep 3:12 and they shall **t** in the name of the LORD. 2620
Mt 12:21 And in his name shall the Gentiles **t**. *1679*
Mk 10:24 how hard is it for them that **t** in riches to *3982*
Lk 16:11 who will **commit to** your **t** the true *riches?* *4100*
Jn 5:45 accuseth you, *even* Moses, in whom ye **t**. *1679*
Ro 15:12 the Gentiles; in him shall the Gentiles **t**. *1679*
15:24 for I **t** to see you in my journey, and to be *1679*
1Co 16: 7 but I **t** to tarry a while with you, if the Lord *1679*
2Co 1: 9 that we should not **t** in ourselves, but *3982*
1:10 in whom we **t** that he will yet deliver *us;* *1679*
1:13 I **t** you shall acknowledge even to the end; *1679*
3: 4 And such **t** have we through Christ to *4006*
5:11 I **t** also are made manifest in your *1679*
10: 7 If any *man* **t** to himself that *he* is Christ's, *3982*
13: 6 But I **t** that ye shall know that we are not *1679*
Php 2:19 But I **t** in the Lord Jesus to send Timotheus *1679*
2:24 But I **t** in the Lord that I also myself shall *3982*
3: 4 that *he hath whereof he* might **t** in the flesh, *3982*
1Th 2: 4 of God to be **put in t** with the gospel, *4100*
1Ti 1:11 which was **committed to** my **t**. *4100*
4:10 because we **t** in the living God, *1679*
6:17 nor **t** in uncertain riches, but in the living *1679*
6:20 keep that which is **committed to** *thy* **t**, *3872*
Phm 1:22 for I **t** that through your prayers I shall be *1679*
Heb 2:13 And again, I will **put** my **t** in him. *3982*
13:18 for we **t** we have a good conscience, in all *3982*
2Jn 1:12 but I **t** to come unto you, and speak face to *1679*
3Jn 1:14 But I **t** *I* shall shortly see thee, and we shall *1679*

TRUSTED (29) [TRUST]

Dt 32:37 *are* their gods, *their* rock in whom they **t**, 2620
Jdg 11:20 Sihon **t** not Israel to pass through his coast: 539
20:36 they **t** unto the liers in wait which they had 982
2Ki 18: 5 He **t** in the LORD God of Israel; so 982
Ps 13: 5 I have **t** in thy mercy; my heart shall rejoice 982
22: 4 Our fathers **t** in thee: they trusted, and 982
22: 4 in thee: they **t**, and thou didst deliver them. 982
22: 5 they **t** in thee, and were not confounded. 982
22: 8 He **t** on the LORD *that* he would deliver 1556
26: 1 I have **t** also in the LORD; *therefore* I shall 982
28: 7 my heart **t** in him, and I am helped: 982
31:14 I **t** in thee, O LORD: I said, Thou *art* my 982
33:21 in him, because we have **t** in his holy name. 982
41: 9 Yea, mine own familiar friend, in whom I **t**, 982
52: 7 **t** in the abundance of his riches, *and* 982
78:22 not in God, and **t** not in his salvation: 982
Isa 47:10 For thou hast **t** in thy wickedness: thou hast 982
Jer 13:25 thou hast forgotten me, and **t** in falsehood. 982
48: 7 For because thou hast **t** in thy works and 982
49: 4 that **t** in her treasures, *saying,* Who shall 982
Da 3:28 delivered his servants that **t** in him, and 7365
Zep 3: 2 not correction; she **t** not in the LORD; 982
Mt 27:43 He **t** in God; let him deliver him now, if he *3982*
Lk 11:22 *from him* all his armour wherein he **t**, *3982*
18: 9 **t** in themselves that they were righteous, *3982*
24:21 But we **t** that it had been he which should *1679*
Eph 1:12 the praise of his glory, who **first t** in Christ: *4276*
1:13 In whom ye also *t*, after that ye heard NIG
1Pe 3: 5 who **t** in God, adorned themselves, being in *1679*

TRUSTEDST (3) [TRUST]

Dt 28:52 wherein thou **t**, throughout all thy land: 982
Jer 5:17 fenced cities, wherein thou **t**, with the sword. 982
12: 5 *wherein* thou **t**, *they wearied thee,* then 982

TRUSTEST (6) [TRUST]

2Ki 18:19 What confidence *is* this where*in* thou **t**? 982
18:21 thou **t** upon the staff of this bruised reed, 982
19:10 Let not thy God in whom thou **t** deceive 982
Isa 36: 4 What confidence *is* this where*in* thou **t**? 982
36: 6 Lo, thou **t** in the staff of this broken reed, on 982
37:10 in whom thou **t**, deceive thee, saying, 982

TRUSTETH (17) [TRUST]

Job 40:23 he **t** that he can draw up Jordan into his 982
Ps 21: 7 For the king **t** in the LORD, and 982
32:10 he that **t** in the LORD, mercy shall compass 982
34: 8 *is* good: blessed *is* the man *that* **t** in him. 2620
57: 1 for my soul **t** in thee: yea, in the shadow of 2620
84:12 of hosts, blessed *is* the man that **t** in thee. 982
86: 2 thou my God, save thy servant that **t** in thee. 982
115: 8 unto them; *so is* every one that **t** in them. 982
135:18 unto them: *so is* every one that **t** in them. 982
Pr 11:28 He that **t** in his riches shall fall: but 982
16:20 and whoso **t** in the LORD, happy *is* he. 982
28:26 He that **t** in his own heart *is* a fool: but 982
Isa 26: 3 mind *is* stayed *on thee:* because he **t** in thee. 982
Jer 17: 5 Cursed *be* the man that **t** in man, and 982
17: 7 Blessed *is* the man that **t** in the LORD, and 982
Hab 2:18 of lies, that the maker of his work **t** therein, 982
1Ti 5: 5 **t** in God, and continueth in supplications *1679*

TRUSTING (1) [TRUST]

Ps 112: 7 his heart is fixed, **t** in the LORD. 982

TRUSTY (1) [TRUST]

Job 12:20 He removeth away the speech of the **t**, and 539

TRUTH (235) [TRUE, TRULY, TRUTH'S]

Ge 24:27 destitute my master of his mercy and his **t**: 571
32:10 of all the **t**, which thou hast shewed unto thy 571
42:16 be proved, whether *there be any* **t** in you: 571
Ex 18:21 such as fear God, men of **t**, 571
34: 6 abundant in goodness and **t**, 571
Dt 13:14 behold, *if it be* **t**, *and* the thing certain, *that* 571
32: 4 a God of **t** and without iniquity, just and 530
Jos 24:14 and serve him in sincerity and in **t**: 571
Jdg 9:15 If in **t** ye anoint me king over you, *then* 571
1Sa 12:24 and serve him in **t** with all your heart: 571
21: 5 **Of a t** women *have been* kept from us 518+3588
2Sa 2: 6 the LORD shew kindness and **t** unto you: 571
15:20 back thy brethren: mercy and **t** *be* with thee. 571
1Ki 2: 4 to walk before me in **t** with all their heart 571
3: 6 according as he walked before thee in **t**, and 571
17:24 the word of the LORD in thy mouth *is* **t**. 571
2Ki 19:17 **Of a t**, LORD, the kings of Assyria have 551
20: 3 now how I have walked before thee in **t** 571
20:19 *Is it* not *good,* if peace and **t** be in my days? 571
2Ch 18:15 but the **t** to me in the name of the LORD? 571
31:20 and right and **t** before the LORD his God. 571
Est 9:30 of Ahasuerus, *with* words of peace and **t**, 571
Job 9: 2 I know *it is* so **of a t**: but how should man be 551
Ps 15: 2 and speaketh the **t** in his heart. 571
25: 5 Lead me in thy **t**, and teach me: for thou *art* 571
25:10 **t** unto such as keep his covenant and 571
26: 3 before mine eyes: and I have walked in thy **t**. 571
30: 9 the dust praise thee? shall it declare thy **t**? 571
31: 5 thou hast redeemed me, O LORD God of **t**. 571
33: 4 *is* right; and all his works *are done* in **t**. 530
40:10 and thy **t** from the great congregation. 571
40:11 and thy **t** continually preserve me. 571
43: 3 O send out thy light and thy **t**: let them lead 571
45: 4 because of **t** and meekness *and* 571
51: 6 Behold, thou desirest **t** in the inward parts: 571
54: 5 unto mine enemies: cut them off in thy **t**. 571
57: 3 God shall send forth his mercy and his **t**. 571
57:10 unto the heavens, and thy **t** unto the clouds. 571
60: 4 that *it* may be displayed because of the **t**. 7189
61: 7 O prepare mercy and **t**, *which* may preserve 571
69:13 thy mercy hear me, in the **t** of thy salvation. 571
71:22 thee with the psaltery, *even* thy **t**, O my God: 571
85:10 Mercy and **t** are met together; righteousness 571
85:11 **T** shall spring out of the earth; and 571
86:11 me thy way, O LORD; I will walk in thy **t**: 571
86:15 longsuffering, and plenteous in mercy and **t**. 571
89:14 mercy and **t** shall go before thy face. 571
89:49 *which* thou swarest unto David in thy **t**? 530
91: 4 his **t** *shall be thy* shield and buckler. 571
96:13 with righteousness, and the people with his **t**. 530
98: 3 and his **t** toward the house of Israel: 530
100: 5 his **t** *endureth* to all generations. 530
108: 4 and thy **t** *reacheth* unto the clouds. 571
111: 8 and ever, *and are* done in **t** and uprightness. 571
117: 2 the **t** of the LORD *endureth* for ever. 571
119:30 I have chosen the way of **t**: thy judgments 530
119:43 take not the word of **t** utterly out of my 571
119:142 and thy law *is* the **t**. 571
119:151 O LORD; and all thy commandments *are* **t**. 571
132:11 The LORD hath sworn *in* **t** unto David; 571
138: 2 name for thy lovingkindness and for thy **t**: 571
145:18 call upon him, to all that call upon him in **t**. 571
146: 6 all that therein is: which keepeth **t** for ever: 571
Pr 3: 3 Let not mercy and **t** forsake thee: bind them 571
8: 7 For my mouth shall speak **t**; and 571
12:17 *He that* speaketh **t** sheweth forth 530
12:19 The lip of **t** shall be established for ever: but 571
14:22 and **t** *shall be to* them that devise good. 571
16: 6 By mercy and **t** iniquity is purged: and 571
20:28 Mercy and **t** preserve the king: and 571
22:21 thee know the certainty of the words of **t**; 571
22:21 that *thou* mightest answer the words *of* **t** to 571
23:23 Buy the **t**, and sell *it* not; *also* wisdom, and 571
Ecc 12:10 *was* written *was* upright, *even* words of **t**. 571
Isa 5: 9 **Of a t** many houses shall be desolate, 518+3808
10:20 the LORD, the Holy One of Israel, in **t**. 571
16: 5 he shall sit upon it in **t** in the tabernacle of 571
25: 1 *thy* counsels of old *are* faithfulness *and* **t**. 544
26: 2 that the righteous nation which keepeth the **t** 529
37:18 **Of a t**, LORD, the kings of Assyria have 551
38: 3 how I have walked before thee in **t** and 571
38:18 go down into the pit cannot hope for thy **t**. 571
38:19 to the children shall make known thy **t**. 571
39: 8 For there shall be peace and **t** in my days. 571
42: 3 he shall bring forth judgment unto **t**. 571
43: 9 be justified: or let them hear, and say, *It is* **t**. 571
48: 1 of Israel, *but* not in **t**, nor in righteousness. 571
59: 4 calleth for justice, nor any pleadeth for **t**: 530
59:14 for **t** is fallen in the street, and equity cannot 571
59:15 Yea, **t** faileth; and he *that* departeth from evil 571
61: 8 I will direct their work in **t**, and I will make 571
65:16 the earth shall bless himself in the God of **t**; 543
65:16 in the earth shall swear by the God of **t**; 543
Jer 4: 2 in **t**, in judgment, and in righteousness; 571
5: 1 that executeth judgment, that seeketh the **t**; 530
5: 3 O LORD, *are* not thine eyes upon the **t**? 530
7:28 **t** is perished, and is cut off from their mouth. 530
9: 3 they are not valiant for the **t** upon the earth; 530
9: 5 one his neighbour, and will not speak the **t**: 571
26:15 for of a **t** the LORD hath sent me unto you 571
33: 6 unto them the abundance of peace and **t**. 571
Da 2:47 **Of a t** *it is,* that your God *is* a God of 4481+7187
4:37 all whose works *are* **t**, and his ways 7187
7:16 stood *by,* and asked him the **t** of all this. 3330
7:19 I would **know the t** of the fourth beast, 3321
8:12 and it cast down the **t** to the ground; 571
9:13 from our iniquities, and understand thy **t**. 571
10:21 thee that which is noted in the scripture of **t**: 571
11: 2 now will I shew thee the **t**. Behold, 571
Hos 4: 1 because *there is* no **t**, nor mercy, 571
Mic 7:20 Thou wilt perform the **t** to Jacob, *and* 571
Zec 8: 3 and Jerusalem shall be called a city of **t**; and 571
8: 8 I will be their God, in **t** and in righteousness. 571
8:16 Speak ye every man the **t** to his neighbour; 571
8:16 execute the judgment of **t** and peace in your 571
8:19 therefore love the **t** and peace. 571
Mal 2: 6 The law of **t** was in his mouth, and 571
Mt 14:33 saying, **Of a t** thou art the Son of God. *230*
15:27 And she said, **T**, Lord: yet the dogs eat of *3483*
22:16 art true, and teachest the way of God in **t**, *225*
Mk 5:33 fell down before him, and told him all the **t**. *225*
12:14 of men, but teachest the way of God in **t**: *225*
12:32 unto him, Well, Master, thou hast said the **t**: *225*
Lk 4:25 But I tell you of a **t**, many widows were in *225*
9:27 But I tell you **of a t**, there be some standing *230*
12:44 **Of a t** I say unto you, that he will make him *230*
21: 3 And he said, **Of a t** I say unto you, that this *230*
22:59 **Of a t** this *fellow* also was with him: *225+1909*
Jn 1:14 begotten of the Father,) full of grace and **t**. *225*
1:17 *but* grace and **t** came by Jesus Christ. *225*
3:21 But he that doeth **t** cometh to the light, *225*
4:23 shall worship the Father in spirit and *in* **t**: *225*
4:24 him must worship *him* in spirit and *in* **t**. *225*
5:33 unto John, and he bare witness unto the **t**. *225*
6:14 This is **of a t** *that* prophet that should come *230*
7:40 *this* saying, said, **Of a t** this is the Prophet. *230*
8:32 And ye shall know the **t**, and the truth shall *225*
8:32 the truth, and the **t** shall make you free *225*
8:40 a man that hath told you the **t**, which I have *225*
8:44 and abode not in the **t**, because there is no *225*
8:44 not in the truth, because there is no **t** in him. *225*
8:45 And because I tell *you* the **t**, ye believe me *225*
8:46 And if I say the **t**, why do ye not believe me? *225*
14: 6 unto him, I am the way, the **t**, and the life: *225*
14:17 *Even* the Spirit of **t**; whom the world cannot *225*
15:26 *even* the Spirit of **t**, which proceedeth from *225*
16: 7 Nevertheless I tell you the **t**; It is expedient *225*
16:13 Howbeit when he, the Spirit of **t**, is come, *225*
16:13 of truth, is come, he will guide you into all **t**: *225*
17:17 Sanctify them through thy **t**: thy word is *225*
17:17 them through thy truth: thy word is **t**. *225*
17:19 they also might be sanctified through the **t**. *225*
18:37 that I should bear witness unto the **t**. *225*
18:37 Every one that is of the **t** heareth my voice. *225*
18:38 Pilate saith unto him, What is **t**? And when *225*
Ac 4:27 For **of a t** against thy holy child Jesus, *225+1909*
10:34 **Of a t** I perceive that God is no *225+1909*
26:25 but speak forth *the* words of **t** and *225*
Ro 1:18 of men, who hold the **t** in unrighteousness; *225*
1:25 Who changed the **t** of God into a lie, and *225*
2: 2 to **t** against them which commit such *things.* *225*
2: 8 and do not obey the **t**, but *225*
2:20 form of knowledge and of the **t** in the law. *225*
3: 7 For if the **t** of God hath *more* abounded *225*
9: 1 I say the **t** in Christ, I lie not, my conscience *225*
15: 8 minister of the circumcision for the **t** of God, *225*
1Co 5: 8 with the unleavened bread of sincerity and **t**. *225*
13: 6 not in iniquity, but rejoiceth in the **t**; *225*
14:25 and report that God is in you **of a t**. *3689*
2Co 4: 2 by manifestation of the **t** commending *225*
6: 7 By the word of **t**, by the power of God, *225*
7:14 but as we spake all *things* to you in **t**, even *225*
7:14 which *I made* before Titus, is found a **t**. *225*
11:10 *As* the **t** of Christ is in me, no *man* shall stop *225*
12: 6 I shall not be a fool; for I will say the **t**: *225*
13: 8 For we can do nothing against the **t**, but *225*
13: 8 do nothing against the truth, but for the **t**. *225*
Gal 2: 5 that the **t** of the gospel might continue with *225*
2:14 uprightly according to the **t** of the gospel, *225*
3: 1 that *you* should not obey the **t**, *225*
4:16 your enemy, because I **tell** you **the t**? *226*
5: 7 did hinder you that *ye* should not obey the **t**? *225*
Eph 1:13 also *trusted,* after that ye heard the word of **t**, *225*
4:15 But **speaking the t** in love, may grow *up* *226*
4:21 have been taught by him, as the **t** is in Jesus: *225*
4:25 speak every man **t** with his neighbour: *225*
5: 9 *is* in all goodness and righteousness and **t**;) *225*
6:14 having your loins girt about with **t**, and *225*
Php 1:18 in pretence, or in **t**, Christ is preached; *225*
Col 1: 5 whereof ye heard before in the word of the **t** *225*
1: 6 heard of *it,* and knew the grace of God in **t**: *225*
1Th 2:13 of men, but as it is **in t**, the word of God, *230*
2Th 2:10 because they received not the love of the **t**, *225*
2:12 all might be damned who believed not the **t**, *225*
2:13 sanctification of the Spirit and belief of the **t**: *225*
1Ti 2: 4 and to come unto the knowledge of the **t**. *225*
2: 7 (I speak the **t** in Christ, *and* lie not;) *225*
3:15 the living God, the pillar and ground of the **t**. *225*
4: 3 of them which believe and know the **t**. *225*
6: 5 and destitute of the **t**, supposing that gain is *225*
2Ti 2:15 be ashamed, rightly dividing the word of **t**. *225*
2:18 Who concerning the **t** have erred, saying that *225*
2:25 repentance to the acknowledging of the **t**; *225*

2Ti 3: 7 able to come to the knowledge of the t. 225
3: 8 so do these also resist the t: 225
4: 4 they shall turn away *their* ears from the t, 225
Tit 1: 1 the acknowledging of the t which is after 225
1:14 commandments of men, that turn from the t. 225
Heb 10:26 *we* have received the knowledge of the t, 225
Jas 1:18 his own will begat he us with the word of t, 225
3:14 glory not, and lie *not* against the t. 225
5:19 if any of you do err from the t, and 225
1Pe 1:22 t through the Spirit unto unfeigned love of 225
2Pe 1:12 and be stablished in the present t. 225
2: 2 by reason of whom the way of t shall be evil 225
1Jn 1: 6 walk in darkness, we lie, and do not the t: 225
1: 8 we deceive ourselves, and the t is not in us. 225
2: 4 is a liar, and the t is not in him. 225
2:21 written unto you because ye know not the t, 225
2:21 ye know it, and that no lie is of the t. 225
2:27 anointing teacheth you of all *things*, and is t, 227
3:18 neither in tongue; but in deed and in t. 225
3:19 And hereby we know that we are of the t, 225
4: 6 Hereby know we the spirit of t, and the spirit 225
5: 6 that beareth witness, because the Spirit is t. 225
2Jn 1: 1 and her children, whom I love in the t; 225
1: 1 but also all they that have known the t; 225
1: 3 the Son of the Father, in t and love. 225
1: 4 that I found of thy children walking in t, 225
3Jn 1: 1 the wellbeloved Gaius, whom I love in the t. 225
1: 3 and testified of the t *that is* in thee, 225
1: 3 *that is* in thee, even as thou walkest in the t. 225
1: 4 joy than to hear that my children walk in t. 225
1: 8 that we might be fellowhelpers to the t. 225
1:12 good report of all *men*, and of the t itself: 225

TRUTH'S (2) [TRUTH]
Ps 115: 1 give glory, for thy mercy, *and* for thy t sake. 571
2Jn 1: 2 For the t sake, which dwelleth in us, and 225

TRY (17) [TRIAL, TRIED, TRIEST, TRIETH, TRYING]
Jdg 7: 4 the water, and I will t them for thee there: 6884
2Ch 32:31 God left him, to t him, that *he* might know 5254
Job 7:18 every morning, *and* t him every moment? 974
12:11 Doth not the ear t words? and the mouth 974
Ps 11: 4 his eyes behold, his eyelids t, the children of 974
26: 2 and prove me; t my reins and my heart. 6884
139:23 my heart: t me, and know my thoughts: 974
Jer 6:27 that thou mayest know and t their way. 974
9: 7 Behold, I will melt them, and t them; 974
17:10 I the LORD search the heart, *I* t the reins, 974
La 3:40 Let us search and t our ways, and 2713
Da 11:35 to t them, and to purge, and to make *them* 6884
Zec 13: 9 is refined, and will t them as gold is tried: 974
1Co 3:13 the fire shall t every man's work of what 1381
1Pe 4:12 concerning the fiery trial which is to t you, 3986
1Jn 4: 1 but t the spirits whether they are of God: 1381
Rev 3:10 to t them that dwell upon the earth. 3985

TRYING (1) [TRY]
Jas 1: 3 Knowing *this*, that the t of your faith 1383

TRYPHENA (1)
Ro 16:12 Salute T and Tryphosa, who labour in 5170

TRYPHOSA (1)
Ro 16:12 Salute Tryphena and T, who labour in 5173

TUBAL (8)
Ge 10: 2 and Javan, and T, and Meshech, and Tiras. 8422
1Ch 1: 5 and Javan, and T, and Meshech, and Tiras. 8422
Isa 66:19 Lud, that draw the bow, *to* T, and Javan, 8422
Eze 27:13 Javan, T, and Meshech, they *were* thy 8422
32:26 There *is* Meshech, T, and all her multitude: 8422
38: 2 the chief prince of Meshech and T, and 8422
38: 3 O Gog, the chief prince of Meshech and T: 8422
39: 1 O Gog, the chief prince of Meshech and T: 8422

TUBAL-CAIN (2)
Ge 4:22 Zillah, she also bare T, an instructor of 8423
4:22 and iron: and the sister of T *was* Naamah. 8423

TUCKED INTO BELT See GIRDED

TUMBLED (1)
Jdg 7:13 a cake of barley bread t into the host of 2015

TUMORS See EMERODS

TUMULT (16) [TUMULTS, TUMULTUOUS]
1Sa 4:14 he said, What *meaneth* the noise of this t? 1995
2Sa 18:29 I saw a great t, but I knew not what *it was*. 1995
2Ki 19:28 and thy t is come up into mine ears, 7600
Ps 65: 7 of their waves, and the t of the people. 1995
74:23 the t of those that rise up against thee 7588
83: 2 For lo, thine enemies **make a** t: and 1993
Isa 33: 3 At the noise of the t the people fled; at 1995
37:29 thy t, is come up into mine ears, therefore 7600
Jer 11:16 with the noise of a great t he hath kindled 1999
Hos 10:14 Therefore shall a t arise among thy people, 7588
Am 2: 2 Moab shall die with t, with shouting, *and* 7588
Zec 14:13 *that* a great t from the LORD shall be 4103
Mt 27:24 but *that* rather a t was made, he took water, 2351
Mk 5:38 and seeth *the* t, and them that wept and 2351
Ac 21:34 he could not know the certainty for the t, 2351
24:18 neither with multitude, nor with t. 2351

TUMULTS (3) [TUMULT]
Am 3: 9 behold the great t in the midst thereof, and 4103
2Co 6: 5 in t, in labours, in watchings, in fastings; 181
12:20 backbitings, whisperings, swellings, t: 181

TUMULTUOUS (3) [TUMULT]
Isa 13: 4 a t noise of the kingdoms of nations 7588
22: 2 *that art* full of stirs, a t city, a joyous city: 1993
Jer 48:45 and the crown of the head of the t ones. 7588

TUNNEL See CONDUIT

TURBAN See MITRE

TURBANS See BONNETS; TIRES

TURN (283) [OVERTURN, TURNED, TURNEST, TURNETH, TURNING]
Ge 19: 2 Behold now, my lords, **t in**, I pray you, 5493
24:49 that I may t to the right hand, or to the left. 6437
27:44 a few days, until thy brother's fury **t away**; 7725
27:45 Until thy brother's anger **t away** from thee, 7725
Ex 3: 3 I will now **t aside**, and see this great sight, 5493
14: 2 that they t and encamp before Pi-hahiroth, 7725
23:27 I will make all thine enemies t their **backs** 6203
32:12 T from thy fierce wrath, and repent of *this* 7725
Lev 13:16 Or if the raw flesh **t again**, and be changed 7725
19: 4 T ye not unto idols, nor make to yourselves 6437
Nu 14:25 To morrow t you, and get you *into* 6437
20:17 we will not t *to* the right hand nor *to* 5186
21:22 we will not t into the fields, or into 5186
22:23 Balaam smote the ass, to t her *into* the way. 5186
22:26 where *was* no way to t *either to* the right 5186
32:15 For if ye **t away** from after him, he will yet 7725
34: 4 your border shall t from the south to 5437
Dt 1: 7 T you, and take your journey, and go *to* 6437
1:40 t ye, and take your journey into 6437
2: 3 mountain long enough: t you northward. 6437
2:27 I will neither t *unto* the right hand nor *to* 5493
4:30 if thou t to the LORD thy God, and 7725
5:32 ye shall not **t aside** *to* the right hand or 5493
7: 4 For they will **t away** thy son from 5493
11:16 ye **t aside**, and serve other gods, and 5493
11:28 **t aside** out of the way which I command 5493
13: 5 he hath spoken to t *you* **away** from 5627
13:17 that the LORD may t from the fierceness 7725
14:25 shalt thou t *it* into money, and bind up 5414
16: 7 thou shalt t in the morning, and go unto thy 6437
17:17 wives to himself, that his heart t not **away**: 5493
17:20 that *he* t not **aside** from the commandment, 5493
23:13 shalt **t back** and cover that which cometh 7725
23:14 thing in thee, and **t away** from thee. 7725
30: 3 the LORD thy God will t thy captivity, 7725
30:10 if thou t unto the LORD thy God with all 7725
30:17 if thine heart **t away**, so that thou wilt not 6437
31:20 will they t unto other gods, and serve them, 6437
31:29 **t aside** from the way which I have 5493
Jos 1: 7 t not from it *to* the right hand or *to* the left, 5493
22:16 to **t away** *this* day from following 7725
22:18 that ye must **t away** *this* day from 7725
22:23 That we have built us an altar to t from 7725
22:29 t *this* day from following the LORD, 7725
23: 6 that *ye* t not **aside** therefrom *to* the right 5493
24:20 he will t and do you hurt, and 7725
Jdg 4:18 said unto him, **T in**, my lord, turn in to me; 5493
4:18 said unto him, Turn in, my lord, **t in** to me; 5493
11: 8 Therefore we **t again** to thee now, that thou 7725
19:11 let us **t in** into this city of the Jebusites, and 5493
19:12 We will not **t aside** hither into the city of a 5493
20: 8 neither will we any *of us* t into his house. 5493
Ru 1:11 Naomi said, **T again**, my daughters: why 7725
1:12 **T again**, my daughters, go *your way*; for I 7725
4: 1 *Ho*, such a one, **t aside**, sit down here. 5493
1Sa 12:20 yet t not **aside** from following the LORD, 5493
12:21 t ye not **aside**: for *then should ye go* after 5493
14: 7 t thee; behold, I *am* with thee according to 5186
15:25 pardon my sin, and **t again** with me, 7725
15:30 and before Israel, and **t again** with me, 7725
22:17 T, and slay the priests of the LORD; 5437
22:18 to Doeg, T thou, and fall upon the priests. 5437
2Sa 2:21 T thee **aside** to thy right hand or to thy left, 5186
2:21 Asahel would not **t aside** from following of 5493
2:22 to Asahel, T thee **aside** from following me: 5493
2:23 Howbeit he refused to **t aside**: 5493
14:19 none can **t to the right hand** or to the left 3231
14:24 Let him t to his own house, and let him not 5437
15:31 t the counsel of Ahithophel **into foolishness**. 5528
18:30 the king said *unto him*, **T aside**, *and* 5437
19:37 Let thy servant, I pray thee, **t back again**, 7725
1Ki 8:33 shall **t again** to thee, and confess thy name, 7725
8:35 confess thy name, and t from their sin, 7725
9: 6 *But* if you shall **at all** t from following me, 7725
11: 2 *for* surely they will **t away** your heart after 5186
12:27 shall the heart of this people **t again** unto 7725
13: 9 nor **t again** by the *same* way that thou 7725
13:17 nor **t again** to go by the way that thou 7725
17: 3 t thee eastward, and hide thyself by 6437
22:34 T thine hand, and carry me out of the host; 2015
2Ki 1: 6 **t again** unto the king that sent you, and 7725
4:10 he cometh to us, *that* he shall **t in** thither. 5493
9:18 t thee behind me. And the watchman told, 5437
9:19 thou to do with peace? t thee behind me. 5437
17:13 T ye from your evil ways, and keep my 7725
18:24 wilt thou **t away** the face of one captain of 7725
19:28 I will t thee **back** by the way by which thou 7725
20: 5 **T again**, and tell Hezekiah the captain of 7725
1Ch 12:23 to Hebron, to t the kingdom of Saul to him, 5437
14:14 **t away** from them, and come upon them 5437
2Ch 6:26 confess thy name, *and* t from their sin, 7725
6:37 t and pray unto thee in the land of their 7725
6:42 t not **away** the face of thine anointed: 7725
7:14 my face, and t from their wicked ways; 7725
7:19 if ye **t away**, and forsake my statutes and 7725
15: 4 when they in their trouble did t unto 7725
18:33 he said to *his* chariot man, T thine hand, 2015
25:27 after the time that Amaziah did **t away** 5493
29:10 that his fierce wrath may **t away** from us. 7725
30: 6 **t again** unto the LORD God of Abraham, 7725
30: 8 that the fierceness of his wrath may **t away** 7725
30: 9 For if ye **t again** unto the LORD, 7725
30: 9 and will not **t away** *his* face from you, 5493
35:22 Nevertheless Josiah would not t his face 5437
Ne 1: 9 *if* ye t unto me, and keep my 7725
4: 4 t their reproach upon their own head, and 7725
9:26 testified against them to t them to thee, 7725
Est 2:12 Now when every maid's t was come to go 8447
2:15 Now when the t of Esther, the daughter of 8447
Job 5: 1 and to which of the saints wilt thou t? 6437
14: 6 T from him, that he may rest, till he shall 8159
23:13 he *is* in one *mind*, and who can t him? and 7725
24: 4 They t the needy out of the way: the poor 5186
34:15 and man shall **t again** unto dust. 7725
Ps 4: 2 how long *will ye* t my glory into shame? NIH
7:12 If he t not, he will whet his sword; he hath 7725
18:37 neither did I **t again** till they were 7725
21:12 Therefore shalt thou **make** them t their 7896
22:27 shall remember and t unto the LORD: 7725
25:16 T thee unto me, and have mercy upon me; 6437
40: 4 not the proud, nor such as **t aside** to lies. 7750
44:10 Thou **makest** us **to** t back from the enemy: 7725
56: 9 *unto thee*, then shall mine enemies t back: 7725
60: 1 been displeased; O t thyself to us **again**. 7725
69:16 t unto me according to the multitude of thy 6437
80: 3 T us **again**, O God, and cause thy face to 7725
80: 7 T us **again**, O God *of* hosts, and cause thy 7725
80:19 T us **again**, O LORD God *of* hosts, 7725
85: 4 T us, O God of our salvation, and 7725
85: 8 his saints: but let them not t *again* to folly. 7725
86:16 O t unto me, and have mercy upon me; 6437
101: 3 I hate the work of them that **t aside**; *it* shall 7750
104: 9 *that* they t not **again** to cover the earth. 7725
106:23 to **t away** his wrath, lest *he* should destroy 7725
119:37 **T away** mine eyes from beholding vanity; 5674
119:39 **T away** my reproach which I fear: for thy 5674
119:79 Let those that fear thee t unto me, and 7725
125: 5 As for such as **t aside** *unto* their crooked 5186
126: 4 **T again** our captivity, O LORD, as 7725
132:10 For thy servant David's sake t not **away** 7725
132:11 *in* truth unto David; he will not t from it; 7725
Pr 1:23 T you at my reproof: behold, I will pour 7725
4:15 pass not by it, t from it, and pass away. 7847
4:27 T not *to* the right hand nor *to* the left: 5186
9: 4 Whoso *is* simple, let him **t in** hither: *as for* 5493
9:16 Whoso *is* simple, let him **t in** hither: and 5493
24:18 and he **t away** his wrath from him. 7725
25:10 to shame, and thine infamy t not **away**. 7725
29: 8 into a snare: but wise *men* **t away** wrath. 7725
Ecc 3:20 all are of the dust, and all t to dust **again**. 7725
SS 2:17 t, my beloved, and be thou like a roe or a 5437
6: 5 **T away** thine eyes from me, for they have 5437
Isa 1:25 I will t my hand upon thee, and purely 7725
10: 2 To **t aside** the needy from judgment, and 5186
13:14 they shall every man t to his own people, 6437
14:27 *is* stretched out, and who shall t it **back**? 7725
19: 6 they shall t the rivers **far away**; *and* 2186
22:18 **surely violently t and toss** 6801+6801+6802
23:17 she shall t to her hire, and shall commit 7725
28: 6 for strength to them that t the battle to 7725
29:21 and **t aside** the just for a thing of nought. 5186
30:11 ye out of the way, **t aside** out of the path, 5186
30:21 when ye **t to the right hand**, and when ye 541
30:21 to the right hand, and when ye **t to the left**. 8041
31: 6 T ye unto *him from* whom the children of 7725
36: 9 wilt thou **t away** the face of one captain of 7725
37:29 I will t thee **back** by the way by which thou 7725
58:13 If thou **t away** thy foot from the sabbath, 7725
59:20 unto them that t **from** transgression in 7725
Jer 2:24 *in* her occasion who can t her **away**? 7725
2:35 surely his anger shall t from me. 7725
3: 7 I said after she had done all these *things*, T 7725
3:14 T, O backsliding children, saith 7725
3:19 My father; and shalt not **t away** from me. 7725
4:28 not repent, neither will I **t back** from it. 7725
6: 9 **t back** thine hand as a grapegatherer into 7725
8: 4 not arise? shall he **t away**, and not return? 7725
13:16 he t it into the shadow of death, *and* make *it* 7760
18: 8 whom I have pronounced, t from their evil, 7725
18:20 *and* to **t away** thy wrath from them. 7725
21: 4 I *will* **t back** the weapons of war that *are* in 5437
25: 5 T ye **again** now every one from his evil 7725
26: 3 and t every man from his evil way, 7725
29:14 I will **t away** your captivity, and I will 7725
31:13 for I will t their mourning into joy, and 2015
31:18 as a bullock unaccustomed *to the yoke*; t 7725
31:21 t **again**, O virgin of Israel, turn again to 7725
31:21 virgin of Israel, **t again** to these thy cities, 7725
32:40 that I will not **t away** from them, to do 7725
44: 5 nor inclined their ear to t from their 7725
49: 8 Flee ye, **t back**, dwell deep, O inhabitants 6437
50:16 for fear of the oppressing sword they shall t 6437
La 2:14 thine iniquity, to **t away** thy captivity; 7725
3:35 To **t aside** the right of a man before 5186
3:40 try our ways, and **t again** to the LORD. 7725
5:21 T thou us unto thee, O LORD, and 7725
Eze 3:19 he t not from his wickedness, nor from his 7725
3:20 When a righteous *man* doth t from his 7725
4: 8 thou shalt not t thee from one side to 2015
7:22 My face will I t also from them, and 5437
8: 6 t thee yet **again**, *and* thou shalt see great*er* 7725
8:13 T thee yet **again**, *and* thou shalt see great*er* 7725
8:15 t thee yet **again**, *and* thou shalt see greater 7725
14: 6 Repent, and t *yourselves* from your idols; 7725
14: 6 **t away** your faces from all your 7725
18:21 if the wicked will t from all his sins that he 7725
18:30 t *yourselves* from all your transgressions; 7725
18:32 wherefore t *yourselves*, and live ye. 7725
33: 9 if thou warn the wicked of his way to t 7725
33: 9 if he do not t from his way, he shall die in 7725
33:11 but that the wicked t from his way and live: 7725
33:11 t ye, turn ye from your evil ways; for why 7725
33:11 turn ye, t ye from your evil ways; for why 7725
33:14 if he t from his sin, and do that which is 7725
33:19 if the wicked t from his wickedness, and 7725
36: 9 I will t unto you, and ye shall be tilled and 6437
38: 4 I will t thee **back**, and put hooks into thy 7725
38:12 to t thine hand upon the desolate places *that* 7725
39: 2 I will t thee **back**, and leave but the sixth 7725
Da 9:13 that *we* might t from our iniquities, and 7725
11:18 After this shall he t his face unto the isles, 7725

Da 11:18 reproach he shall **cause** *it* **to t** upon him. 7725
11:19 he shall **t** his face towards the fort of his 7725
12: 3 they that **t** many **to righteousness** as 6663
Hos 5: 4 They will not frame their doings to **t** unto 7725
12: 6 Therefore **t** thou to thy God: keep mercy 7725
14: 2 Take with you words, and **t** to the LORD: 7725
Joel 2:12 **t** ye *even* to me with all your heart, and 7725
2:13 and **t** unto the LORD your God: 7725
Am 1: 3 I will not **t away** *the punishment* thereof; 7725
1: 6 I will not **t away** *the punishment* thereof; 7725
1: 8 and I will **t** mine hand against Ekron: 7725
1: 9 I will not **t away** *the punishment* thereof; 7725
1:11 I will not **t away** *the punishment* thereof; 7725
1:13 I will not **t away** *the punishment* thereof; 7725
2: 1 I will not **t away** *the punishment* thereof; 7725
2: 4 I will not **t away** *the punishment* thereof; 7725
2: 6 I will not **t away** *the punishment* thereof; 7725
2: 7 the poor, and **t aside** the way of the meek: 5186
5: 7 *Ye* who **t** judgment to wormwood, and 2015
5:12 they **t aside** the poor in the gate *from their* 5186
8:10 I will **t** your feasts into mourning, and 2015
Jnh 3: 8 let them **t** every one from his evil way, and 7725
3: 9 Who can tell *if* God will **t** and repent, and 7725
3: 9 repent, and **t away** from his fierce anger, 7725
Mic 7:19 He will **t again**, he will have compassion 7725
Zep 2: 7 shall visit them, and **t away** their captivity. 7725
3: 9 then will I **t** to the people a pure language, 2015
3:20 when I **t back** your captivity before your 7725
Zec 1: 3 **T** ye unto me, saith the LORD of hosts, 7725
1: 3 I will **t** unto you, saith the LORD of hosts. 7725
1: 4 **T** ye now from your evil ways, and 7725
9:12 **T** ye to the strong hold, ye prisoners of 7725
10: 9 shall live with their children, and **t again**. 7725
13: 7 and I will **t** mine hand upon the little ones. 7725
Mal 2: 6 and did **t** many **away** from iniquity. 7725
3: 5 that **t aside** the stranger *from his right*, and 5186
4: 6 he shall **t** the heart of the fathers to 7725
Mt 5:39 on thy right cheek, **t** to him the other also. *4762*
5:42 that would borrow of thee **t** not thou **away**. *654*
7: 6 under their feet, and **t** *again* and rent you. *4762*
Mk 13:16 And let him that is in the field not **t back** *1994*
Lk 1:16 shall he **t to** the Lord their God. *1994*
1:17 to **t** the hearts of the fathers **to** *1994*
10: 6 rest upon it: if not, it shall **t** to you **again**. *344*
17: 4 and seven times in a day **t again** to thee, *1994*
21:13 And it shall **t to** you for a testimony. *576*
Ac 13: 8 seeking to **t** away the deputy from the faith. *1294*
13:46 of everlasting life, lo, we **t** to the Gentiles. *4762*
14:15 **t** from these vanities **unto** the living *1994*
26:18 *and* to **t** *them* from darkness to light, and *1994*
26:20 that *they* should repent and **t to** God, *1994*
Ro 11:26 and shall **t away** ungodliness from Jacob: *654*
2Co 3:16 Nevertheless when *it* shall **t** to the Lord, *1994*
Gal 4: 9 how **t** ye again to the weak and *1994*
Php 1:19 For I know that this shall **t** to my salvation *576*
2Ti 3: 5 the power thereof: **from** such **t away**. *665*
4: 4 And they shall **t away** *their* ears from *654*
Tit 1:14 of men, that **t from** the truth. *654*
Heb 12:25 **t away from** him that *speaketh* from heaven: *654*
Jas 3: 3 obey us; and we **t about** their whole body. *3329*
2Pe 2:21 after they have known *it*, to **t** from the holy *1994*
Rev 11: 6 have power over waters to **t** them to blood, *4762*

TURNED (287) [TURN]

Ge 3:24 a flaming sword which **t every way**, 2015
18:22 the men **t** their **faces** from thence, and 6437
19: 3 they **t in** unto him, and entered into his 5493
38: 1 **t in** to a certain Adullamite, whose name 5186
38:16 he **t** unto her by the way, and said, Go to, 5186
42:24 he **t** himself **about** from them, and wept; 5437
Ex 3: 4 when the LORD saw that he **t aside** to 5493
4: 7 behold, it was **t again** as his *other* flesh. 7725
7:15 the rod which was **t** to a serpent shalt thou 2015
7:17 *are* in the river, and they shall be **t** to blood. 2015
7:20 all the waters that *were* in the river were **t** 2015
7:23 Pharaoh **t** and went into his house, 6437
10: 6 he **t** himself, and went out from Pharaoh. 6437
10:19 the LORD **t** a mighty strong west wind, 2015
14: 5 and of his servants was **t** against the people, 2015
32: 8 They have **t aside** quickly out of the way 5493
32:15 Moses **t**, and went down from the mount, 6437
33:11 he **t again** into the camp: but his servant 7725
Lev 13: 3 *when* the hair in the plague is **t** white, and 2015
13: 4 the skin, and the hair thereof be not **t** white; 2015
13:10 it have **t** the hair white, and *there be* quick 2015
13:13 *hath* the plague: it is all **t** white: he *is* clean. 2015
13:17 behold, *if* the plague be **t** into white; then 2015
13:20 the skin, and the hair thereof be **t** white; 2015
13:25 *if* the hair in the bright spot be **t** white, and 2015
Nu 14:43 because ye are **t away** from the LORD, 7725
20:21 wherefore Israel **t** away from him. 5186
21:33 they **t** and went up *by* the way of Bashan: 6437
22:23 the ass **t aside** out of the way, and 5186
22:33 saw me, and **t** from me these three times: 5186
22:33 unless she had **t** from me, surely now also I 5186
25: 4 of the LORD may be **t away** from Israel. 7725
25:11 hath **t** my wrath **away** from the children of 7725
33: 7 **t again** unto Pi-hahiroth, which *is* before 7725
Dt 1:24 they **t** and went up into the mountain, and 6437
2: 1 we **t**, and took our journey into 6437
2: 8 we **t** and passed *by* the way of 6437
3: 1 we **t**, and went up the way to Bashan: and 6437
9:12 **t aside** out of the way which I commanded 5493
9:15 So I **t** and came down from the mount, and 6437
9:16 ye had **t aside** quickly out of the way which 5493
10: 5 I **t** myself and came down from the mount, 6437
23: 5 the LORD thy God **t** the curse into a 2015
31:18 in that they are **t** unto other gods. 6437
Jos 7:12 *but* **t** *their* backs before their enemies, 6437
7:26 So the LORD **t** from the fierceness of his 7725
8:20 *to* the wilderness **t back** upon the pursuers. 2015
8:21 then they **t again**, and slew the men of Ai. 7725
11:10 Joshua at that time **t back**, and took Hazor, 7725
19:12 **t** from Sarid eastward *toward* the sunrising 7725
Jdg 2:17 they **t** quickly out of the way which their 5493

Jdg 3:19 he himself **t again** from the quarries that 7725
4:18 And when he had **t in** unto her into the tent, 5493
8:33 that the children of Israel **t again**, and 7725
14: 8 and he **t aside** to see the carcase of the lion: 5493
15: 4 **t** tail to tail, and put a firebrand in the midst 6437
18: 3 they **t in** thither, and said unto him, 5493
18:15 they **t** thitherward, and came to the house 5493
18:21 So they **t** and departed, and put the little 6437
18:23 And they **t** their faces, and said unto Micah, 5437
18:26 for him, he **t** and went back unto his house. 6437
19:15 they **t aside** thither, to go in *and* to lodge in 5493
20:41 when the men of Israel **t** *again*, the men of 2015
20:42 Therefore they **t** *their backs* before the men 6437
20:45 they **t** and fled toward the wilderness unto 6437
20:47 six hundred men **t** and fled to 6437
20:48 the men of Israel **t again** upon the children 7725
Ru 3: 8 that the man was afraid, and **t** himself: 3943
4: 1 down here. And he **t aside**, and sat down. 5493
1Sa 6:12 **t** not **aside** *to* the right hand or *to* the left; 5493
8: 3 **t aside** after lucre, and took bribes, and 5186
10: 6 with them, and shalt be **t** into another man. 2015
10: 9 that when he had **t** his back to go from 6437
13:17 one company **t** unto the way that leadeth to 6437
13:18 another company **t** the way to Beth horon: 6437
13:18 another company **t** *to* the way of the border 6437
14:21 even they also **t** to be with the Israelites that NIH
14:47 whithersoever he **t** himself, he vexed *them*. 6437
15:11 for he is **t back** from following me, and 7725
15:27 as Samuel **t about** to go away, he laid hold 5437
15:31 So Samuel **t again** after Saul; and 7725
17:30 he **t** from him towards another, and 5437
22:18 Doeg the Edomite **t**, and he fell upon 5437
25:12 So David's young men **t** their way, and 2015
2Sa 1:22 the bow of Jonathan **t** not back, and 7734
2:19 in going he **t** not to the right hand nor to 5186
18:30 stand here. And he **t aside**, and stood still. 5437
19: 2 the victory that day was **t** into mourning NIH
22:38 and **t** not **again** until I had consumed them. 7725
1Ki 2:15 howbeit the kingdom is **t about**, and 5437
2:28 for Joab had **t** after Adonijah, though he 5186
2:28 though he **t** not after Absalom. 5186
8:14 the king **t** his face **about**, and blessed all 5437
10:13 So she **t** and went to her own country, she 6437
11: 3 and his wives **t away** his heart. 5186
11: 4 *that* his wives **t away** his heart after other 5186
11: 9 his heart was **t** from the LORD God of 5186
15: 5 **t** not **aside** from any *thing* that he 5493
18:37 and *that* thou hast **t** their heart **back** again. 5437
20:39 a man **t aside**, and brought a man unto me, 5493
21: 4 **t away** his face, and would eat no bread. 5437
22:32 they **t aside** to fight against him: and 5493
22:33 that they **t back** from pursuing him. 7725
22:43 he **t** not **aside** from it, doing *that* which *was* 5493
2Ki 1: 5 when the messengers **t back** unto him, 7725
1: 5 he said unto them, Why are ye now **t back**? 7725
2:24 he **t** back, and looked on them, and 6437
4: 8 as he passed by, he **t in** thither to eat bread. 5493
4:11 he **t** into the chamber, and lay there. 5493
5:12 be clean? So he **t** and went away in a rage. 6437
5:26 man **t** *again* from his chariot to meet thee? 2015
9:23 Joram **t** his hands, and fled, and said to 2015
15:20 So the king of Assyria **t back**, and 7725
16:18 **t** he *from* the house of the LORD for 5437
20: 2 he **t** his face to the wall, and prayed unto 5437
22: 2 **t** not **aside** to the right hand or *to* the left. 5493
23:16 as Josiah **t** himself, he spied the sepulchres 6437
23:25 that **t** to the LORD with all his heart, and 7725
23:26 Notwithstanding the LORD **t** not from 7725
23:34 **t** his name *to* Jehoiakim, and took Jehoahaz 5437
24: 1 then he **t** and rebelled against him. 7725
1Ch 10:14 **t** the kingdom unto David the son of Jesse. 5437
21:20 Ornan **t back**, and saw the angel; and 7725
2Ch 6: 3 the king **t** his face, and blessed the whole 5437
9:12 So she **t**, and went away to her own land, 2015
12:12 the wrath of the LORD **t** from him, 7725
18:32 they **t back** *again* from pursuing him. 7725
20:10 they **t** from them, and destroyed them not; 5493
29: 6 have **t away** their faces from the habitation 5437
29: 6 habitation of the LORD, and **t** *their* backs. 5414
36: 4 Jerusalem, and **t** his name to Jehoiakim. 5437
Ezr 6:22 **t** the heart of the king of Assyria unto them, 5437
10:14 of our God for this matter be **t** from us. 7725
Ne 2:15 **t back**, and entered by the gate of 7725
9:35 neither **t** they from their wicked works. 7725
13: 2 howbeit our God **t** the curse into a blessing. 2015
Est 9: 1 (though it was **t** *to the contrary*, that 2015
9:22 the month which was **t** unto them from 2015
Job 6:18 The paths of their way are **t aside**; they go 3943
16:11 and **t** me **over** into the hands of the wicked. 3399
19:19 and they whom I loved are **t** against me. 2015
20:14 *Yet* his meat in his bowels is **t**, *it is* the gall 2015
28: 5 and under it is **t up** as it were fire. 2015
30:15 Terrors are **t** upon me: they pursue my soul 2015
30:31 My harp also is **t** to mourning, and NIH
31: 7 If my step hath **t** out of the way, and 5186
34:27 Because they **t back** from him, and 5493
37:12 it is **t** round about by his counsels: that they 2015
38:14 It is **t** as clay *to* the seal; and they stand as a 2015
41:22 and sorrow is **t into joy** before him. 1750
41:28 slingstones are **t** with him **into** stubble. 2015
42:10 the LORD **t** the captivity of Job, when he 7725
Ps 9: 3 When mine enemies are **t** back, they shall 7725
9:17 The wicked shall be **t** into hell, *and* all 7725
30:11 Thou hast **t** for me my mourning into 2015
32: 4 my moisture is **t** into the drought of 2015
35: 4 let them be **t** back and brought to confusion 5472
44:18 Our heart is not **t** back, neither have our 5472
66: 6 He **t** the sea into dry *land*: they went 2015
66:20 *be* God, which hath not **t away** my prayer, 5493
70: 2 let them be **t** backward, and put to 5472
70: 3 Let them be **t back** for a reward of their 7725
78: 9 carrying bows, **t** *back* in the day of battle. 2015
78:38 many a time **t** he his anger **away**, and 7725
78:41 they **t** *back* and tempted God, and 7725
78:44 had **t** their rivers into blood; and 2015

Ps 78:57 **t** *back*, and dealt unfaithfully like their 5472
78:57 they were **t aside** like a deceitful bow. 2015
81:14 and **t** my hand against their adversaries. 7725
85: 3 thou hast **t** *thyself* from the fierceness of 7725
89:43 Thou hast also **t** the edge of his sword, and 7725
105:25 He **t** their heart to hate his people, to deal 2015
105:29 He **t** their waters into blood, and slew their 2015
114: 8 Which **t** the rock *into* a standing water, 2015
119:59 and **t** my feet unto thy testimonies. 7725
126: 1 When the LORD **t again** the captivity of 7725
129: 5 be confounded and **t** back that hate Zion. 5472
Ecc 2:12 I **t** myself to behold wisdom, and madness, 6437
SS 6: 1 whither is thy beloved **t aside**? that we may 6437
Isa 5:25 For all this his anger is not **t away**, but 7725
9:12 For all this his anger is not **t away**, but 7725
9:17 For all this his anger is not **t away**, but 7725
9:21 For all this his anger is not **t away**, but 7725
10: 4 For all this his anger is not **t away**, but 7725
12: 1 thine anger is **t away**, and thou comfortedst 7725
21: 4 the night of my pleasure hath he **t** into fear 7760
28:27 is a cart wheel **t about** upon the cummin; 5437
29:17 Lebanon shall be **t** into a fruitful field, and 7725
34: 9 the streams thereof shall be **t** into pitch, 2015
38: 2 Hezekiah **t** his face toward the wall, and 5437
42:17 They shall be **t** back, they shall be greatly 5472
44:20 a deceived heart hath **t** him **aside**, that he 5186
50: 5 I was not rebellious, neither **t away** back. 5472
53: 6 we have **t** every one to his own way; and 6437
59:14 judgment is **t away** backward, and 5253
63:10 therefore he was **t** to be their enemy, *and* 2015
Jer 2:21 art thou **t** *into* the degenerate plant of a 2015
2:27 for they have **t** *their* back unto me, and 6437
3:10 hath not **t** unto me with her whole heart, 7725
4: 8 anger of the LORD is not **t back** from us. 7725
5:25 Your iniquities have **t away** these *things*, 5186
6:12 their houses shall be **t** unto others, 5437
8: 6 every one **t** to his course, as the horse 7725
11:10 They are **t back** to the iniquities of their 7725
23:22 they should have **t** them from their evil 7725
30: 6 in travail, and all faces are **t** into paleness? 2015
31:18 *to the yoke*; turn thou me, and I shall be **t**; 7725
31:19 Surely after that I was **t**, I repented; and 7725
32:33 they have **t** unto me the back, and not 6437
34:11 afterwards they **t**, and caused the servants 7725
34:15 ye were now **t**, and had done right in my 7725
34:16 ye **t** and polluted my name, and 7725
38:22 sunk in the mire, *and* they are **t away** back. 5472
46: 5 I seen them dismayed *and* **t away** back? 5472
46:21 for they also are **t back**, *and* are fled away 6437
48:39 how hath Moab **t** the back with shame! so 6437
50: 6 they have **t** them **away** *on* the mountains: 7725
La 1:13 spread a net for my feet, he hath **t** me back; 7725
1:20 are troubled; mine heart is **t** within me; 2015
3: 3 Surely against me is he **t**; he turneth his 7725
3:11 He hath **t aside** my ways, and pulled me in 5493
5: 2 Our inheritance is **t** to strangers, our houses 2015
5:15 is ceased; our dance is **t** into mourning. 2015
5:21 us unto thee, O LORD, and we shall be **t**; 7725
Eze 1: 9 they **t** not when they went; they went every 5437
1:12 they went; *and* they **t** not when they went. 5437
1:17 four sides: *and* they **t** not when they went. 5437
10:11 they **t** not as they went, but *to* the place 5437
10:11 they followed it; they **t** not as they went. 5437
10:16 the same wheels also **t** not from beside 5437
17: 6 whose branches **t** toward him, and the roots 6437
26: 2 she is **t** unto me: I shall be replenished, 5437
42:19 He **t about** to the west side, *and* 5437
Da 9:16 thy fury be **t away** from thy city Jerusalem, 7725
10: 8 for my comeliness was **t** in me into 2015
10:16 by the vision my sorrows are **t** upon me, 2015
Hos 7: 8 among the people; Ephraim is a cake not **t**. 2015
11: 8 mine heart is **t** within me, my repentings 2015
14: 4 for mine anger is **t away** from him. 7725
Joel 2:31 The sun shall be **t** into darkness, and 2015
Am 6:12 for ye have **t** judgment into gall, and 2015
Jnh 3:10 their works, that they **t** from their evil way; 7725
Na 2: 2 For the LORD hath **t** *away* the excellency 7725
Hab 2:16 LORD'S right hand shall be **t** unto thee, 5437
Zep 1: 6 And them that are **t back** from the LORD; 5472
Hag 2:17 yet ye **t** not to me, saith the LORD. NIH
Zec 5: 1 I **t**, and lift up mine eyes, and looked, and 7725
6: 1 I **t**, and lift up mine eyes, and looked, and 7725
14:10 All the land shall be **t** as a plain from Geba 5437
Mt 2:22 a dream, he **t aside** into the parts of Galilee: *402*
9:22 But Jesus **t** him **about**, and when he saw *1994*
16:23 But he **t**, and said unto Peter, Get thee *4762*
Mk 5:30 **t** him **about** in the press, and said, *1994*
8:33 But when he had **t about** and looked on his *1994*
Lk 2:45 they **t back again** to Jerusalem, *5290*
7: 9 and **t** him *about*, and said unto the people *4762*
7:44 And he **t** to the woman, and said unto *4762*
9:55 But he **t**, and rebuked them, and said, *4762*
10:23 And he **t** him unto *his* disciples, and *4762*
14:25 with him: and he **t**, and said unto them, *4762*
17:15 **t back**, and with a loud voice glorified *5290*
22:61 And the Lord **t**, and looked upon Peter. *4762*
Jn 1:38 Then Jesus **t**, *4762*
16:20 but your sorrow shall be **t** into joy *1096*
20:14 when she had thus said, she **t** herself back, *4762*
20:16 She **t** herself, and saith unto him, Rabboni; *4762*
Ac 2:20 The sun shall be **t** into darkness, and *3344*
7:39 and in their hearts **t** *back again* into Egypt, *4762*
7:42 Then God **t**, and gave them up to worship *4762*
9:35 Saron saw him, and **t to** the Lord. *1994*
11:21 and **t unto** the Lord. *1994*
15:19 among the Gentiles are **t to** God: *1994*
16:18 being grieved, **t** and said to the spirit, *1994*
17: 6 These that have **t** the world **upside down** are *387*
19:26 hath persuaded and **t away** much people, *3179*
1Th 1: 9 how ye **t** to God from idols to serve *1994*
1Ti 1: 6 swerved have **t aside** unto vain jangling; *1624*
5:15 For some are already **t aside** after Satan. *1624*
2Ti 1:15 they which are in Asia be **t away from** me; *654*
4: 4 from the truth, and shall be **t** unto fables. *1624*
Heb 11:34 in fight, **t to flight** the armies of the aliens. *2827*

T

Heb 12:13 lest *that which is* lame be **t out of the way**; *1624*
Jas 3: 4 *yet* are they **t about** with a very small *3329*
4: 9 let your laughter be **t** to mourning, and *3344*
2Pe 2:22 The dog *is* **t** to his own vomit **again**; *1994*
Rev 1:12 And I **t** to see the voice that spake with me. *1994*
1:12 And being **t**, I saw seven golden *1994*

TURNEST (3) [TURN]

1Ki 2: 3 and whithersoever thou **t** thyself: 6437
Job 15:13 That thou **t** thy spirit against God, and 7725
Ps 90: 3 Thou **t** man to destruction; and sayest, 7725

TURNETH (33) [TURN]

Lev 20: 6 the soul that **t** after such as have familiar 6437
Dt 29:18 whose heart **t away** *this* day from 6437
Jos 7: 8 when Israel **t** *their* backs before their 2015
19:27 **t** *toward* the sunrising *to* Beth-dagon, and 7725
19:29 *then* the coast **t** *to* Ramah, and to the strong 7725
19:29 the coast **t** *to* Hosah; and the outgoings 7725
19:34 *then* the coast **t** westward *to* Aznoth-tabor, 7725
Job 39:22 neither **t** he **back** from the sword. 7725
Ps 107:33 He **t** rivers into a wilderness, and 7760
107:35 He **t** the wilderness into a standing water, 7760
146: 9 the way of the wicked he **t upside down**. 5791
Pr 15: 1 A soft answer **t away** wrath: but 7725
17: 8 hath it: whithersoever it **t**, it prospereth. 6437
21: 1 of water: he **t** it whithersoever he will. 5186
26:14 *As* the door **t** upon his hinges, so *doth* 5437
28: 9 He that **t away** his ear from hearing 5493
30:30 among beasts, and **t** not **away** for any; 7725
Ecc 1: 6 the south, and **t about** unto the north; 5437
SS 1: 7 for why should I be as one that **t aside** by 5844
Isa 9:13 For the people **t** not unto him that smiteth 7725
24: 1 **t** it upside down, and scattereth abroad 5753
44:25 that **t** wise *men* backward, and maketh their 7725
Jer 14: 8 as a wayfaring man *that* **t aside** to tarry for 5186
49:24 *and* **t** herself to flee, and fear hath seized on 6437
La 1: 8 yea, she sigheth, and **t** backward. 7725
3: 3 he **t** his hand *against me* all the day. 2015
Eze 18:24 when the righteous **t away** from his 7725
18:26 When a righteous *man* **t away** from his 7725
18:27 when the wicked *man* **t away** from his 7725
18:28 **t away** from all his transgressions that he 7725
33:12 he shall not fall thereby in the day that he **t** 7725
33:18 When the righteous **t** from his 7725
Am 5: 8 **t** the shadow of death into the morning, and 2015

TURNING (18) [TURN]

2Ki 21:13 a dish, wiping *it*, and **t** *it* upside down. 2015
2Ch 26: 9 and at the **t** *of the wall*, and fortified them. 4740
36:13 hardened his heart from **t** unto the LORD 7725
Ne 3:19 up to the armoury *at* the **t** *of the wall*. 4740
3:20 from the **t** *of the wall* unto the door of 4740
3:24 from the house of Azariah unto the **t** *of* 4740
3:25 over against the **t** *of the wall*, and the tower 4740
Pr 1:32 For the **t away** of the simple shall slay 4878
Isa 29:16 Surely your **t** *of things* **upside down** shall 2017
Eze 41:24 the doors had two leaves *apiece*, two **t** 5437
Mic 2: 4 from me! **t away** he hath divided our fields. 7725
Lk 23:28 But Jesus **t** unto them, said, Daughters of *4762*
Jn 21:20 Then Peter, **t about**, seeth the disciple *1994*
Ac 3:26 in **t away** every one of you from *his* *654*
9:40 and **t** *him* to the body said, Tabitha, arise. *1994*
Jas 1:17 is no variableness, neither shadow of **t**. *5157*
2Pe 2: 6 **t** the cities of Sodom and Gomorrha **into ashes** *5077*
Jude 1: 4 ungodly *men*, **t** the grace of our God into *3346*

TURTLE (2) [TURTLEDOVE, TURTLE-DOVE, TURTLEDOVES, TURTLES]

SS 2:12 and the voice of the **t** is heard in our land; 8449
Jer 8: 7 the **t** and the crane and the swallow observe 8449

TURTLEDOVE, TURTLE-DOVE (3) [TURTLE]

Ge 15: 9 years old, and a **t**, and a young pigeon. 8449
Lev 12: 6 a young pigeon, or a **t**, for a sin offering, 8449
Ps 74:19 O deliver not the soul of thy **t** unto 8449

TURTLEDOVES (7) [TURTLE]

Lev 1:14 he shall bring his offering of **t**, or of young 8449
5: 7 two **t**, or two young pigeons, unto 8449
5:11 if he be not able to bring two **t**, or two 8449
14:22 two **t**, or two young pigeons, such as he is 8449
14:30 he shall offer the one of the **t**, or of 8449
15:14 on the eighth day he shall take to him two **t**, 8449
Lk 2:24 the Lord, A pair of **t**, or two young pigeons. *5167*

TURTLES (3) [TURTLE]

Lev 12: 8 she shall bring two **t**, or two young 8449
15:29 the eighth day she shall take unto her two **t**, 8449
Nu 6:10 on the eighth day he shall bring two **t**, or 8449

TUTORS (1)

Gal 4: 2 But is under **t** and governors until the time *2012*

TWAIN (17) [TWO]

1Sa 18:21 day be my son in law in *the one of* the **t**. 8147
2Ki 4:33 shut the door upon them **t**, and prayed unto 8147
Isa 6: 2 with **t** he covered his face, and with twain 8147
6: 2 with **t** he covered his feet, and with twain 8147
6: 2 he covered his feet, and with **t** he did fly. 8147
Jer 34:18 when they cut the calf in **t**, and 8147
Eze 21:19 **both t** shall come forth out of one land: and 8147
Mt 5:41 compel thee to go a mile, go with him **t**. *1417*
19: 5 to his wife: and they **t** shall be one flesh? *1417*
19: 6 Wherefore they are no more **t**, but *1417*
21:31 Whether of *them* **t** did the will of *his* *1417*
27:21 Whether of the **t** will ye *that* I release unto *1417*
27:51 the vail of the temple was rent in **t** from *1417*
Mk 10: 8 And they **t** shall be one flesh: so then *1417*
10: 8 so then they are no more **t**, but one flesh. *1417*
15:38 And the vail of the temple was rent in **t** *1417*
Eph 2:15 for to make in himself of **t** one new man, *so* *1417*

TWELFTH (23) [TWELVE]

Nu 7:78 On the **t** day Ahira the son of Enan, 6240+8147
1Ki 19:19 *oxen* before him, and he with the **t**: 6240+8147
2Ki 8:25 In the **t** year of Joram the son of 6240+8147
17: 1 In the **t** year of Ahaz king of Judah 6240+8147
25:27 in the **t** month, on the seven and 6240+8147
1Ch 24:12 eleventh to Eliashib, the **t** to Jakim, 6240+8147
25:19 The **t** to Hashabiah, *he*, his sons, and 6240+8147
27:15 The **t** *captain* for the twelfth month 6240+8147
27:15 The twelfth *captain* for the **t** month 6240+8147
2Ch 34: 3 **t** year he began to purge Judah and 6240+8147
Ezr 8:31 on the **t** *day* of the first month, 6240+8147
Est 3: 7 in the **t** year of king Ahasuerus, 6240+8147
3: 7 the **t** *month*, that *is*, the month Adar. 6240+8147
3:13 *even* upon the thirteenth *day* of the **t** 6240+8147
8:12 the thirteenth *day* of the **t** month, 6240+8147
9: 1 Now in the **t** month, that *is*, 6240+8147
Jer 52:31 in the **t** month, in the five and 6240+8147
Eze 29: 1 in the tenth *month*, in the **t** *day* of 6240+8147
32: 1 it came to pass in the **t** year, in 6240+8147
32: 1 in the **t** month, in the first *day* of 6240+8147
32:17 It came to pass also in the **t** year, 6240+8147
33:21 it came to pass in the **t** year of our 6240+8147
Rev 21:20 the eleventh, a jacinth; the **t**, an amethyst. *1428*

TWELVE (189) [TWELFTH]

Ge 5: 8 Seth were nine hundred and **t** years: 6240+8147
14: 4 **T** years they served Chedorlaomer, 6240+8147
17:20 **t** princes shall he beget, and I will 6240+8147
25:16 **t** princes according to their nations. 6240+8147
35:22 *it*. Now the sons of Jacob were **t**: 6240+8147
42:13 they said, Thy servants *are* **t** 6240+8147
42:32 We *be* **t** brethren, sons of our father; 6240+8147
49:28 All these *are* the **t** tribes of Israel: 6240+8147
Ex 15:27 where *were* **t** wells of water, and 6240+8147
24: 4 an altar under the hill, and **t** pillars, 6240+8147
24: 4 according to the **t** tribes of Israel. 6240+8147
28:21 **t**, according to their names, *like* 6240+8147
28:21 they be according to the **t** tribes. 6240+8147
39:14 **t**, according to their names, *like* 6240+8147
39:14 his name, according to the **t** tribes. 6240+8147
Lev 24: 5 fine flour, and bake **t** cakes thereof: 6240+8147
Nu 1:44 the princes of Israel, *being* **t** men: 6240+8147
7: 3 six covered wagons, and **t** oxen; 6240+8147
7:84 **t** chargers of silver, twelve silver 6240+8147
7:84 **t** silver bowls, twelve spoons of 6240+8147
7:84 silver bowls, **t** spoons of gold: 6240+8147
7:86 The golden spoons *were* **t**, full *of* 6240+8147
7:87 the burnt offering *were* **t** bullocks, 6240+8147
7:87 the rams **t**, the lambs of the first year 6240+8147
7:87 the lambs of the first year **t**, 6240+8147
7:87 kids of the goats for sin offering **t**. 6240+8147
17: 2 to the house of their fathers **t** rods: 6240+8147
17: 6 to their fathers' houses, *even* **t** rods: 6240+8147
29:17 on the second day *ye shall offer* **t** 6240+8147
31: 5 **t** thousand armed for war. 6240+8147
31:33 **threescore and t** thousand 7657+8147+2050.1
31:38 *was* **threescore and t**. 7657+8147+2050.1
33: 9 in Elim *were* **t** fountains of water, 6240+8147
Dt 1:23 I took **t** men of you, one of a tribe: 6240+8147
Jos 3:12 ye **t** men out of the tribes of Israel, 6240+8147
4: 2 Take you **t** men out of the people, 6240+8147
4: 3 **t** stones, and ye shall carry them over 6240+8147
4: 4 Joshua called the **t** men, whom he 6240+8147
4: 8 **t** stones out of the midst of Jordan, 6240+8147
4: 9 Joshua set up **t** stones in the midst of 6240+8147
4:20 those **t** stones, which they took out of 6240+8147
8:25 both of men and women, *were* **t** 6240+8147
18:24 and Gaba; **t** cities with their villages. 6240+8147
19:15 **t** cities with their villages. 6240+8147
21: 7 out of the tribe of Zebulun, **t** cities. 6240+8147
21:40 the Levites, were *by* their lot **t** cities. 6240+8147
Jdg 19:29 into **t** pieces, and sent her into all 6240+8147
21:10 the congregation sent thither **t** 6240+8147
2Sa 2:15 went over by number **t** of Benjamin, 6240+8147
2:15 and **t** of the servants of David. 6240+8147
10: 6 and of Ish-tob **t** thousand men. 6240+8147
17: 1 Let me now choose out **t** thousand 6240+8147
1Ki 4: 7 Solomon had **t** officers over all 6240+8147
4:26 and **t** thousand horsemen. 6240+8147
7:15 a line of **t** cubits did compass either 6240+8147
7:25 It stood upon **t** oxen, three looking 6240+8147
7:44 one sea, and **t** oxen under the sea; 6240+8147
10:20 **t** lions stood there on the one side 6240+8147
10:26 and **t** thousand horsemen, 6240+8147
11:30 *was* on him, and rent it *in* **t** pieces: 6240+8147
16:23 Omri to reign over Israel, **t** years: 6240+8147
18:31 Elijah took **t** stones, according to 6240+8147
19:19 who *was* plowing *with* **t** yoke *of* 6240+8147
2Ki 3: 1 king of Judah, and reigned **t** years. 6240+8147
21: 1 Manasseh *was* **t** years old when he 6240+8147
1Ch 6:63 out of the tribe of Zebulun, **t** cities. 6240+8147
9:22 in the gates *were* two hundred and **t**. 6240+8147
15:10 and his brethren an hundred and **t**. 6240+8147
25: 9 with his brethren and sons *were* **t**: 6240+8147
25:10 *he*, his sons, and his brethren, *were* **t**: 6240+8147
25:11 *he*, his sons, and his brethren, *were* **t**: 6240+8147
25:12 *he*, his sons, and his brethren, *were* **t**: 6240+8147
25:13 *he*, his sons, and his brethren, *were* **t**: 6240+8147
25:14 *he*, his sons, and his brethren, *were* **t**: 6240+8147
25:15 *he*, his sons, and his brethren, *were* **t**: 6240+8147
25:16 *he*, his sons, and his brethren, *were* **t**: 6240+8147
25:17 *he*, his sons, and his brethren, *were* **t**: 6240+8147
25:18 *he*, his sons, and his brethren, *were* **t**: 6240+8147
25:19 *he*, his sons, and his brethren, *were* **t**: 6240+8147
25:20 *he*, his sons, and his brethren, *were* **t**: 6240+8147
25:21 *he*, his sons, and his brethren, *were* **t**: 6240+8147
25:22 *he*, his sons, and his brethren, *were* **t**: 6240+8147
25:23 *he*, his sons, and his brethren, *were* **t**: 6240+8147
25:24 *he*, his sons, and his brethren, *were* **t**: 6240+8147
25:25 *he*, his sons, and his brethren, *were* **t**: 6240+8147
25:26 *he*, his sons, and his brethren, *were* **t**: 6240+8147
25:27 *he*, his sons, and his brethren, *were* **t**: 6240+8147
25:28 *he*, his sons, and his brethren, *were* **t**: 6240+8147
25:29 *he*, his sons, and his brethren, *were* **t**: 6240+8147
25:30 *he*, his sons, and his brethren, *were* **t**: 6240+8147
25:31 *he*, his sons, and his brethren, *were* **t**. 6240+8147
2Ch 1:14 and **t** thousand horsemen, 6240+8147
4: 4 It stood upon **t** oxen, three looking 6240+8147
4:15 One sea, and **t** oxen under it. 6240+8147
9:19 **t** lions stood there on the one side 6240+8147
9:25 chariots, and **t** thousand horsemen; 6240+8147
12: 3 With **t hundred** chariots, and 505+3967+2050.1
33: 1 Manasseh *was* **t** years old when he 6240+8147
Ezr 2: 6 two thousand eight hundred and **t**. 6240+8147
2:18 children of Jorah, an hundred and **t**. 6240+8147
6:17 sin offering for all Israel, **t** he goats, 6236+8648
8:24 I separated **t** of the chief of 6240+8147
8:35 **t** bullocks for all Israel, ninety and 6240+8147
8:35 **t** he goats *for* a sin offering: 6240+8147
Ne 5:14 *that is*, **t** years, I and my brethren 6240+8147
7:24 children of Hariph, an hundred *and* **t**. 6240+8147
Est 2:12 after that she had been **t** months, 6240+8147
Ps 60: T smote of Edom in the valley of salt **t** 6240+8147
Jer 52:20 **t** brasen bulls that *were* under 6240+8147
52:21 a fillet of **t** cubits did compass it; and 6240+8147
Eze 43:16 the altar *shall be* **t** *cubits* long, twelve 6240+8147
43:16 **t** broad, square in the four squares 6240+8147
47:13 according to the **t** tribes of Israel: 6240+8147
Da 4:29 At the end of **t** months he walked in 6236+8648
Mt 9:20 which was diseased with an issue of blood **t** *1427*
10: 1 And when he had called unto *him* his **t** *1427*
10: 2 Now the names of the **t** apostles are these; *1427*
10: 5 These **t** Jesus sent forth, and *1427*
11: 1 an end of commanding his **t** disciples, *1427*
14:20 the fragments that remained **t** baskets full. *1427*
19:28 ye also shall sit upon **t** thrones, judging *1427*
19:28 judging the **t** tribes of Israel. *1427*
20:17 And Jesus going up to Jerusalem took the **t** *1427*
26:14 Then one of the **t**, called Judas Iscariot, *1427*
26:20 the even was come, he sat down with the **t**. *1427*
26:47 one of the **t**, came, and with him a great *1427*
26:53 he shall presently give me more than **t** *1427*
Mk 3:14 And he ordained **t**, that they should be with *1427*
4:10 they that were about him with the **t** asked *1427*
5:25 which had an issue of blood **t** years, *1427*
5:42 walked; for she was *of the age* of **t** years. *1427*
6: 7 And he calleth unto *him* the **t**, and began to *1427*
6:43 And they took up **t** baskets full of *1427*
8:19 took ye up? They say unto him, **T**. *1427*
9:35 and called the **t**, and saith unto them, *1427*
10:32 And he took again the **t**, and began to tell *1427*
11:11 he went out unto Bethany with the **t**. *1427*
14:10 And Judas Iscariot, one of the **t**, went unto *1427*
14:17 And in the evening he cometh with the **t**. *1427*
14:20 and said unto them, *It is* one of the **t**, *1427*
14:43 one of the **t**, and with him a great multitude *1427*
Lk 2:42 And when he was **t** years old, they went up *1427*
6:13 and of them he chose **t**, whom also he *1427*
8: 1 kingdom of God: and the **t** *were* with him, *1427*
8:42 about **t** years of age, and she lay a dying. *1427*
8:43 And a woman having an issue of blood **t** *1427*
9: 1 Then he called his **t** disciples together, and *1427*
9:12 then came the **t**, and said unto him, *1427*
9:17 fragments that remained to them **t** baskets. *1427*
18:31 Then he took unto *him* the **t**, and said unto *1427*
22: 3 being of the number of the **t**. *1427*
22:14 he sat down, and the **t** apostles with him. *1427*
22:30 sit on thrones judging the **t** tribes of Israel. *1427*
22:47 one of the **t**, went before them, and *1427*
Jn 6:13 filled **t** baskets with the fragments of *1427*
6:67 Then said Jesus unto the **t**, Will ye also go *1427*
6:70 Have not I chosen you **t**, and one of you is *1427*
6:71 *that* should betray him, being one of the **t**. *1427*
11: 9 Are there not **t** hours in the day? *1427*
20:24 But Thomas, one of the **t**, called Didymus, *1427*
Ac 6: 2 Then the **t** called the multitude of *1427*
7: 8 and Jacob *begat* the **t** patriarchs. *1427*
19: 7 And all the men were about **t**. *1177*
24:11 **t** days since I went up to Jerusalem for to *1177*
26: 7 Unto which *promise* our **t tribes**, *1429*
1Co 15: 5 that he was seen of Cephas, then of the **t**: *1427*
Jas 1: 1 to the **t** tribes which are scattered abroad, *1427*
Rev 7: 5 Of the tribe of Juda *were* sealed **t** thousand. *1427*
7: 5 Of the tribe of Reuben *were* sealed **t** *1427*
7: 5 Of the tribe of Gad *were* sealed **t** thousand. *1427*
7: 6 Of the tribe of Aser *were* sealed **t** thousand. *1427*
7: 6 Of the tribe of Nephthalim *were* sealed **t** *1427*
7: 6 Of the tribe of Manasses *were* sealed **t** *1427*
7: 7 Of the tribe of Simeon *were* sealed **t** *1427*
7: 7 Of the tribe of Levi *were* sealed **t** thousand. *1427*
7: 7 Of the tribe of Isachar *were* sealed **t** *1427*
7: 8 Of the tribe of Zabulon *were* sealed **t** *1427*
7: 8 Of the tribe of Joseph *were* sealed **t** *1427*
7: 8 Of the tribe of Benjamin *were* sealed **t** *1427*
12: 1 and upon her head a crown of **t** stars: *1427*
21:12 and had **t** gates, and at the gates twelve *1427*
21:12 and at the gates **t** angels, and names written *1427*
21:12 which are *the names* of the **t** tribes of *1427*
21:14 And the wall of the city had **t** foundations, *1427*
21:14 in them the names of the **t** apostles of *1427*
21:16 the city with the reed, **t** thousand furlongs. *1427*
21:21 And the **t** gates *were* twelve pearls; *1427*
21:21 And the twelve gates *were* **t** pearls; *1427*
22: 2 which bare **t** *manner of* fruits, *and* *1427*

TWENTIETH (36) [TWENTY]

Ge 8:14 on the seven and **t** day of the month, 6242
Ex 12:18 the one and **t** day of the month at even. 6242
Nu 10:11 it came to pass on the **t** *day* of the second 6242
1Ki 15: 9 in the **t** year of Jeroboam king of Israel 6242
2Ki 12: 6 **t** year of king Jehoash the priests had not 6242
13: 1 **t** year of Joash the son of Ahaziah king of 6242
15:30 in the **t** year of Jotham the son of Uzziah. 6242
25:27 on the seven and **t** *day* of the month, 6242
1Ch 24:16 nineteenth to Pethahiah, the **t** to Jehezekel, 6242
24:17 The one and **t** to Jachin, the two and 6242
24:17 twentieth to Jachin, the two and **t** to Gamul, 6242
24:18 The three and **t** to Delaiah, the four and 6242

1Ch 24:18 to Delaiah, the four and t to Maaziah. 6242
25:27 The t to Eliathah, he, his sons, and 6242
25:28 The one and t to Hothir, he, his sons, and 6242
25:29 The two and t to Giddalti, he, his sons, and 6242
25:30 The three and t to Mahazioth, he, his sons, 6242
25:31 The four and t to Romamti-ezer, he, his 6242
2Ch 7:10 t day of the seventh month he sent 6242
Ezr 10: 9 the ninth month, on the t day of the month; 6242
Ne 1: 1 in the t year, as I was in Shushan 6242
2: 1 in the t year of Artaxerxes the king, 6242
5:14 from the t year even unto the two 6242
Est 8: 9 on the three and t day thereof; 6242
Jer 25: 3 unto this day, that is the three and t year, 6242
52:30 t year of Nebuchadrezzar Nebuzar-adan 6242
52:31 in the five and t day of the month, 6242
Eze 29:17 it came to pass in the seven and t year, 6242
40: 1 In the five and t year of our captivity, in 6242
Da 10: 4 And in the four and t day of the first month, 6242
Hag 1:15 In the four and t day of the sixth month, 6242
2: 1 month, in the one and t day of the month, 6242
2:10 t day of the ninth month, in the second year 6242
2:18 t day of the ninth month, even from the day 6242
2:20 Haggai in the four and t day of the month, 6242
Zec 1: 7 the four and t day of the eleventh month, 6242

TWENTY (293) [TWENTIETH, TWENTY'S]

Ge 6: 3 his days shall be an hundred and t years. 6242
11:24 Nahor lived nine and t years, and 6242
18:31 Peradventure there shall be t found there. 6242
23: 1 was an hundred and seven and t years old: 6242
31:38 This t years have I been with thee; thy ewes 6242
31:41 Thus have I been t years in thy house; 6242
32:14 t he goats, two hundred ewes, and 6242
32:14 he goats, two hundred ewes, and t rams, 6242
32:15 and ten bulls, t she asses, and ten foals. 6242
37:28 sold Joseph to the Ishmeelites for t pieces 6242
Ex 26: 2 of one curtain shall be eight and t cubits, 6242
26:18 t boards on the south side southward. 6242
26:19 forty sockets of silver under the t boards; 6242
26:20 on the north side there shall be t boards: 6242
27:10 the t pillars thereof and their twenty sockets 6242
27:10 and their t sockets shall be of brass; 6242
27:11 his t pillars and their twenty sockets of 6242
27:11 twenty pillars and their t sockets of brass; 6242
27:16 of the court shall be a hanging of t cubits, 6242
30:13 (a shekel is t gerahs:) a half shekel shall be 6242
30:14 from t years old and above, shall give an 6242
36: 9 The length of one curtain was t and 6242
36:23 t boards for the south side southward: 6242
36:24 forty sockets of silver he made under the t 6242
36:25 toward the north corner, he made t boards, 6242
38:10 Their pillars were t, and their brasen 6242
38:10 were twenty, and their brasen sockets t; 6242
38:11 their pillars were t, and their sockets of 6242
38:11 were twenty, and their sockets of brass t; 6242
38:18 t cubits was the length, and the height in 6242
38:24 was t and nine talents, and seven hundred 6242
38:26 from t years old and upward, for six 6242
Lev 27: 3 of the male from t years old even unto sixty 6242
27: 5 if it be from five years old even unto t 6242
27: 5 thy estimation shall be of the male t 6242
27:25 the sanctuary: t gerahs shall be the shekel. 6242
Nu 1: 3 From t years old and upward, all that are 6242
1:18 from t years old and upward, by their polls. 6242
1:20 every male from t years old and upward, 6242
1:22 every male from t years old and upward, 6242
1:24 from t years old and upward, all that were 6242
1:26 from t years old and upward, all that were 6242
1:28 from t years old and upward, all that were 6242
1:30 from t years old and upward, all that were 6242
1:32 from t years old and upward, all that were 6242
1:34 from t years old and upward, all that were 6242
1:36 from t years old and upward, all that were 6242
1:38 from t years old and upward, all that were 6242
1:40 from t years old and upward, all that were 6242
1:42 from t years old and upward, all that were 6242
1:45 their fathers, from t years old and upward, 6242
3:39 and upward, were t and two thousand. 6242
3:43 were t and two thousand two hundred and 6242
3:47 thou take them: (the shekel is t gerahs:) 6242
7:86 the spoons was an hundred and t shekels. 6242
7:88 the sacrifice of the peace offerings were t 6242
8:24 from t and five years old and upward they 6242
11:19 nor five days, neither ten days, nor t days; 6242
14:29 from t years old and upward, 6242
18:16 shekel of the sanctuary, which is t gerahs. 6242
25: 9 those that died in the plague were t and 6242
26: 2 from t years old and upward, throughout 6242
26: 4 Take the sum of the people, from t years 6242
26:14 t and two thousand and two hundred. 6242
26:62 those that were numbered of them were t 6242
32:11 from t years old and upward, shall see 6242
33:39 Aaron was an hundred and t and 6242
Dt 31: 2 I am an hundred and t years old this day; 6242
34: 7 an hundred and t years old when he died: 6242
Jos 15:32 all the cities are t and nine, with their 6242
19:30 Rehob: t and two cities with their villages. 6242
Jdg 4: 3 t years he mightily oppressed the children 6242
7: 3 there returned of the people t and 6242
8:10 and t thousand men that drew sword. 6242
10: 2 he judged Israel t and three years, and died, 6242
10: 3 and judged Israel t and two years. 6242
11:33 even t cities, and unto the plain of 6242
15:20 Israel in the days of the Philistines t years. 6242
16:31 his father. And he judged Israel t years. 6242
20:15 numbered at that time out of the cities t 6242
20:21 to the ground of the Israelites that day t 6242
20:35 destroyed of the Benjamites that day t 6242
20:46 all which fell that day of Benjamin were t 6242
1Sa 7: 2 for it was t years: and all the house of Israel 6242
14:14 his armourbearer made, was about t men, 6242
2Sa 3:20 to David to Hebron, and t men with him. 6242
8: 4 and t thousand footmen: 6242
8: 5 of the Syrians two and t thousand men. 6242
9:10 Now Ziba had fifteen sons and t servants. 6242
2Sa 10: 6 t thousand footmen, and of king Maacah a 6242
18: 7 great slaughter that day of t thousand men. 6242
19:17 his fifteen sons and his t servants with him; 6242
21:20 every foot six toes, four and t in number; 6242
24: 8 at the end of nine months and t days. 6242
1Ki 4:23 t oxen out of the pastures, and an hundred 6242
5:11 Solomon gave Hiram t thousand measures 6242
5:11 his household, and t measures of pure oil: 6242
6: 2 the breadth thereof t cubits, and the height 6242
6: 3 t cubits was the length thereof, according to 6242
6:16 he built t cubits on the sides of the house, 6242
6:20 the oracle in the forepart was t cubits in 6242
6:20 t cubits in breadth, and twenty cubits in 6242
6:20 and t cubits in the height thereof: 6242
8:63 two and t thousand oxen, and an hundred 6242
8:63 and an hundred and t thousand sheep. 6242
9:10 it came to pass at the end of t years, 6242
9:11 king Solomon gave Hiram t cities in 6242
9:28 four hundred and t talents, and brought it to 6242
10:10 the king an hundred and t talents of gold, 6242
14:20 Jeroboam reigned were two and t years: 6242
15:33 over all Israel in Tirzah, t and four years. 6242
16: 8 In the t and sixth year of Asa king of Judah 6242
16:10 in the t and seventh year of Asa king of 6242
16:15 In the t and seventh year of Asa king of 6242
16:29 of Omri reigned over Israel in Samaria t 6242
20:30 there a wall fell upon t and seven thousand 6242
22:42 he reigned t and five years in Jerusalem. 6242
2Ki 4:42 t loaves of barley, and full ears of corn in 6242
8:26 t years old was Ahaziah when he began to 6242
10:36 Jehu reigned over Israel in Samaria was t 6242
14: 2 He was t and five years old when he began 6242
14: 2 and reigned t and nine years in Jerusalem. 6242
15: 1 In the t and seventh year of Jeroboam king 6242
15:27 over Israel in Samaria, and reigned t years. 6242
15:33 t years old was he when he began to reign, 6242
16: 2 T years old was Ahaz when he began to 6242
18: 2 T and five years old was he when he began 6242
18: 2 he reigned t and nine years in Jerusalem. 6242
21:19 Amon was t and two years old when he 6242
23:31 Jehoahaz was t and three years old when he 6242
23:36 Jehoiakim was t and five year old when he 6242
24:18 Zedekiah was t and one years old when he 6242
1Ch 2:22 had three and t cities in the land of Gilead. 6242
7: 2 David two and t thousand and six hundred. 6242
7: 7 were reckoned by their genealogies t and 6242
7: 9 of valour, was t thousand and two hundred. 6242
7:40 and to battle was t and six thousand men. 6242
12:28 of his father's house t and two captains. 6242
12:30 of the children of Ephraim t thousand and 6242
12:35 of the Danites expert in war t and 6242
12:37 for the battle, an hundred and t thousand. 6242
15: 5 and his brethren an hundred and t: 6242
15: 6 and his brethren two hundred and t: 6242
18: 4 and t thousand footmen: 6242
18: 5 of the Syrians two and t thousand men. 6242
20: 6 whose fingers and toes were four and t, 6242
23: 4 t and four thousand were to set forward 6242
23:24 from the age of t years and upward. 6242
23:27 the Levites were numbered from t years old 6242
27: 1 of every course were t and four thousand. 6242
27: 2 and in his course were t and four thousand. 6242
27: 4 in his course likewise were t and 6242
27: 5 and in his course were t and four thousand. 6242
27: 7 and in his course were t and four thousand. 6242
27: 8 and in his course were t and four thousand. 6242
27: 9 and in his course were t and four thousand. 6242
27:10 and in his course were t and four thousand. 6242
27:11 and in his course were t and four thousand. 6242
27:12 and in his course were t and four thousand. 6242
27:13 and in his course were t and four thousand. 6242
27:14 and in his course were t and four thousand. 6242
27:15 and in his course were t and four thousand. 6242
27:23 David took not the number of them from t 6242
2Ch 2:10 t thousand measures of beaten wheat, and 6242
2:10 t thousand measures of barley, and 6242
2:10 t thousand baths of wine, and 6242
2:10 baths of wine, and t thousand baths of oil. 6242
3: 3 threescore cubits, and the breadth t cubits. 6242
3: 4 t cubits, and the height was an hundred and 6242
3: 4 and the height was an hundred and t: 6242
3: 8 t cubits, and the breadth thereof twenty 6242
3: 8 and the breadth thereof t cubits: 6242
3:11 the wings of the cherubims were t cubits 6242
3:13 cherubims spread themselves forth t cubits: 6242
4: 1 t cubits the length thereof, and 6242
4: 1 t cubits the breadth thereof, and ten cubits 6242
5:12 and t priests sounding with trumpets:) 6242
7: 5 king Solomon offered a sacrifice of t and 6242
7: 5 and an hundred and t thousand sheep: 6242
8: 1 it came to pass at the end of t years, 6242
9: 9 the king an hundred and t talents of gold, 6242
11:21 begat t and eight sons, and 6242
13:21 begat t and two sons, and 6242
20:31 he reigned t and five years in Jerusalem. 6242
25: 1 Amaziah was t and five years old when he 6242
25: 1 he reigned t and nine years in Jerusalem. 6242
25: 5 and he numbered them from t years old and 6242
27: 1 Jotham was t and five years old when he 6242
27: 8 and t years old when he began to reign, 6242
28: 1 Ahaz was t years old when he began to 6242
28: 6 an hundred and t thousand in one day, 6242
29: 1 to reign when he was five and t years old, 6242
29: 1 he reigned nine and t years in Jerusalem. 6242
31:17 the Levites from t years old and upward, 6242
33:21 and t years old when he began to reign, 6242
36: 2 Jehoahaz was t and three years old when he 6242
36: 5 Jehoiakim was t and five years old when he 6242
36:11 and t years old when he began to reign, 6242
Ezr 1: 9 chargers of silver, nine and t knives, 6242
2:11 children of Bebai, six hundred t and three. 6242
2:12 a thousand two hundred t and two. 6242
2:17 of Bezai, three hundred t and three. 6242
2:19 of Hashum, two hundred t and three. 6242
2:21 of Beth-lehem, an hundred t and three. 6242
Ezr 2:23 men of Anathoth, an hundred t and eight. 6242
2:26 of Ramah and Gaba, six hundred t and one. 6242
2:27 men of Michmas, an hundred t and two. 6242
2:28 of Beth-el and Ai, two hundred t and three. 6242
2:32 The children of Harim, three hundred and t. 6242
2:33 Hadid, and Ono, seven hundred t and five. 6242
2:41 children of Asaph, an hundred t and eight. 6242
2:67 six thousand seven hundred and t. 6242
3: 8 appointed the Levites from t years old and 6242
8:11 of Bebai, and with him t and eight males. 6242
8:19 of Merari, his brethren and their sons, t; 6242
8:20 the Levites, two hundred and t Nethinims: 6242
8:27 Also t basons of gold, of a thousand drams; 6242
Ne 6:15 So the wall was finished in the t and 6242
7:16 children of Bebai, six hundred t and eight. 6242
7:17 two thousand three hundred t and two. 6242
7:22 of Hashum, three hundred t and eight. 6242
7:23 children of Bezai, three hundred t and four. 6242
7:27 men of Anathoth, an hundred t and eight. 6242
7:30 of Ramah and Geba, six hundred t and one. 6242
7:31 of Michmas, an hundred and t and two. 6242
7:32 of Beth-el and Ai, an hundred t and three. 6242
7:35 The children of Harim, three hundred and t. 6242
7:37 Hadid, and Ono, seven hundred t and one. 6242
7:69 six thousand seven hundred and t asses. 6242
7:71 of the work t thousand drams of gold, 8147
7:72 that which the rest of the people gave was t 8147
9: 1 Now in the t and fourth day of this month 6242
11: 8 Sallai, nine hundred t and eight. 6242
11:12 the work of the house were eight hundred t 6242
11:14 men of valour, an hundred t and eight: 6242
Est 1: 1 an hundred and seven and t provinces:) 6242
8: 9 an hundred t and seven provinces, 6242
9:30 to the hundred t and seven provinces of 6242
Ps 68:17 The chariots of God are t **thousand**, 7239
Jer 52: 1 and t year old when he began to reign, 6242
52:28 year three thousand Jews and three and t: 6242
Eze 4:10 shalt eat shall be by weight, t shekels a day: 6242
8:16 and the altar, were about five and t men, 6242
11: 1 at the door of the gate five and t men; 6242
40:13 the breadth was five and t cubits, 6242
40:21 and the breadth five and t cubits. 6242
40:25 and the breadth five and t cubits. 6242
40:29 cubits long, and five and t cubits broad. 6242
40:30 round about were five and t cubits long, 6242
40:33 cubits long, and five and t cubits broad. 6242
40:36 and the breadth five and t cubits. 6242
40:49 The length of the porch was t cubits, and 6242
41: 2 forty cubits: and the breadth, t cubits. 6242
41: 4 So he measured the length thereof, t cubits; 6242
41: 4 and the breadth, t cubits, before the temple: 6242
41:10 the chambers was the wideness of t 6242
42: 3 Over against the t cubits which were for 6242
45: 1 t thousand reeds, and the breadth shall be 6242
45: 3 measure the length of five and t thousand, 6242
45: 5 the five and t thousand of length, and 6242
45: 5 for a possession for t chambers. 6242
45: 6 and five and t thousand long, 6242
45:12 the shekel shall be t gerahs: twenty shekels, 6242
45:12 t shekels, five and twenty shekels, 6242
45:12 five and t shekels, fifteen shekels, 6242
48: 8 of five and t thousand reeds in breadth, 6242
48: 9 shall be of five and t thousand in length, 6242
48:10 the north five and t thousand in length, and 6242
48:10 the south five and t thousand in length: 6242
48:13 shall have five and t thousand in length, 6242
48:13 all the length shall be five and t thousand, 6242
48:15 over against the five and t thousand, 6242
48:20 t thousand by five and twenty thousand: 6242
48:20 twenty thousand by five and t thousand: 6242
48:21 t thousand of the oblation toward the east 6242
48:21 and t thousand toward the west border, 6242
Da 6: 1 over the kingdom an hundred and t princes, 6243
10:13 of Persia withstood me one and t days: 6242
Hag 2:16 when one came to a heap of t measures, 6242
2:16 vessels out of the press, there were but t. 6242
Zec 5: 2 the length thereof is t cubits, and 6242
Lk 14:31 that cometh against him with t thousand? 1501
Jn 6:19 rowed about five and t or thirty furlongs, 1501
Ac 1:15 together were about an hundred and t,) 1501
27:28 And sounded, and found it t fathoms: and 1501
1Co 10: 8 and fell in one day three and t thousand. 1501
Rev 4: 4 about the throne were four and t seats: 1501
4: 4 the seats I saw four and t elders sitting, 1501
4:10 t elders fall down before him that sat on 1501
5: 8 and t elders fell down before the Lamb, 1501
5:14 And the four and t elders fell down and 1501
11:16 And the four and t elders, which sat before 1501
19: 4 And the four and t elders and the four 1501

TWENTY'S (1) [TWENTY]

Ge 18:31 And he said, I will not destroy it for t sake. 6242

TWICE (17) [TWO]

Ge 41:32 that the dream was doubled unto Pharaoh t; 6471
Ex 16: 5 it shall be t as much as they gather daily. 4932
16:22 sixth day they gathered t **as much** bread, 4932
Nu 20:11 and with his rod he smote the rock t: 6471
1Sa 18:11 it. And David avoided out of his presence t. 6471
1Ki 11: 9 of Israel, which had appeared unto him t, 6471
2Ki 6:10 and saved himself there, not once nor t. 8147
Ne 13:20 ware lodged without Jerusalem once or t. 8147
Job 33:14 For God speaketh once, yea t, 8147+871.1
40: 5 yea, t; but I will proceed no further. 8147
42:10 also the LORD gave Job t as much as he 4932
Ps 62:11 God hath spoken once; t have I heard this; 8147
Ecc 6: 6 though he live a thousand years t told, yet 6471
Mk 14:30 even in this night, before the cock crow t, 1364
14:72 Before the cock crow t, thou shalt deny me 1364
Lk 18:12 I fast t in the week, I give tithes of all that I 1364
Jude 1:12 without fruit, t dead, plucked up by 1364

TWIGS (2)

Eze 17: 4 He cropt off the top of his **young** t, and 3242

Eze 17:22 from the top of his **young t** a tender one, 3127

TWILIGHT (9)

1Sa 30:17 David smote them from the **t** even unto 5399
2Ki 7: 5 they rose up in the **t**, to go unto the camp of 5399
7: 7 Wherefore they arose and fled in the **t**, and 5399
Job 3: 9 Let the stars of the **t** thereof be dark; let it 5399
24:15 eye also of the adulterer waiteth for the **t**, 5399
Pr 7: 9 In the **t**, in the evening, in the black and 5399
Eze 12: 6 *thy* shoulders, *and* carry *it* forth in the **t**: 5939
12: 7 I brought *it* forth in the **t**, *and* I bare *it* upon 5939
12:12 them shall bear upon *his* shoulder in the **t**, 5939

TWINED (21)

Ex 26: 1 tabernacle *with* ten curtains *of* fine **t** linen, 7806
26:31 scarlet, and fine **t** linen *of* cunning work: 7806
26:36 and purple, and scarlet, and fine **t** linen, 7806
27: 9 **t** linen of an hundred cubits long for one 7806
27:16 and purple, and scarlet, and fine **t** linen, 7806
27:18 the height five cubits *of* fine **t** linen, and 7806
28: 6 and *of* purple, *of* scarlet, and fine **t** linen, 7806
28: 8 and purple, and scarlet, and fine **t** linen. 7806
28:15 *of* purple, and *of* scarlet, and *of* fine **t** linen, 7806
36: 8 tabernacle made ten curtains *of* fine **t** linen, 7806
36:35 and purple, and scarlet, and fine **t** linen: 7806
36:37 purple, and scarlet, and fine **t** linen, 7806
38: 9 hangings of the court *were of* fine **t** linen, 7806
38:16 the court round about *were of* fine **t** linen. 7806
38:18 and purple, and scarlet, and fine **t** linen: 7806
39: 2 and purple, and scarlet, and fine **t** linen. 7806
39: 5 and purple, and scarlet, and fine **t** linen; 7806
39: 8 and purple, and scarlet, and fine **t** linen. 7806
39:24 and purple, and scarlet, *and* **t** *linen.* 7806
39:28 and linen breeches *of* fine **t** linen, 7806
39:29 a girdle *of* fine **t** linen, and blue, and 7806

TWINKLING (1)

1Co 15:52 In a moment, in the **t** of an eye, at the last *4493*

TWINS (6)

Ge 25:24 behold, *there were* **t** in her womb. 8380
38:27 that, behold, **t** *were* in her womb. 8380
SS 4: 2 whereof every one **beareth t**, and none *is* 8382
4: 5 breasts *are* like two young roes *that are* **t**, 8380
6: 6 whereof every one **beareth t**, and *there is* 8382
7: 3 breasts *are* like two young roes *that are* **t**. 8380

TWIST See WREST

TWISTED See PLATTED; TWINED

TWO (835) [SECOND, TWAIN, TWICE, TWOEDGED, TWOFOLD]

Ge 1:16 God made **t** great lights; the greater light to 8147
4:19 Lamech took unto him **t** wives: the name of 8147
5:18 Jared lived an hundred sixty and **t** years, 8147
5:20 Jared were nine hundred sixty and **t** years: 8147
5:26 Lamech seven hundred eighty and **t** years, 8147
5:28 lived an hundred eighty and **t** years, 8147
6:19 **t** of every *sort* shalt thou bring into the ark, 8147
6:20 **t** of every *sort* shall come unto thee, to keep 8147
7: 2 of beasts that *are* not clean by **t**, the male 8147
7: 9 There went in **t** and two unto Noah into 8147
7: 9 went in two and **t** unto Noah into the ark, 8147
7:15 **t** and two of all flesh, wherein *is* the breath 8147
7:15 two and **t** of all flesh, wherein *is* the breath 8147
9:22 his father, and told his **t** brethren without. 8147
10:25 unto Eber were born **t** sons: the name of 8147
11:10 and begat Arphaxad **t years** after the flood: 8141
11:19 Peleg lived after he begat Reu **t hundred** 3967
11:20 Reu lived **t** and thirty years, and 8147
11:21 Reu lived after he begat Serug **t hundred** 3967
11:23 Serug lived after he begat Nahor **t hundred** 3967
11:32 the days of Terah were **t hundred** and 3967
19: 1 there came **t** angels to Sodom at even; and 8147
19: 8 I have **t** daughters which have not known 8147
19:15 Arise, take thy wife, and thy **t** daughters, 8147
19:16 and upon the hand of his **t** daughters; 8147
19:30 the mountain, and his **t** daughters with him; 8147
19:30 he dwelt in a cave, he and his **t** daughters. 8147
22: 3 took **t** of his young men with him, and 8147
24:22 **t** bracelets for her hands of ten *shekels* 8147
25:23 **T** nations *are* in thy womb, and two manner 8147
25:23 **t** manner of people shall be separated from 8147
27: 9 fetch me from thence **t** good kids of 8147
27:36 for he hath supplanted me these **t times**: he 6471
29:16 Laban had **t** daughters: the name of 8147
31:33 and into the **t** maidservants' tents; 8147
31:41 I served thee fourteen years for thy **t** 8147
32: 7 and herds, and the camels, into **t** bands; 8147
32:10 this Jordan; and now I am become **t** bands. 8147
32:14 **T hundred** she goats, and twenty he goats, 3967
32:14 **t hundred** ewes, and twenty rams, 3967
32:22 took his **t** wives, and his two 8147
32:22 his **t** womenservants, and his eleven sons, 8147
33: 1 and unto Rachel, and unto the **t** handmaids. 8147
34:25 that **t** of the sons of Jacob, Simeon and 8147
40: 2 Pharaoh was wroth against **t** *of* his officers, 8147
41: 1 to pass at the end of **t full years**, 3117+8141
41:50 unto Joseph were born **t** sons before 8147
42:37 saying, Slay my **t** sons, if I bring him not to 8147
44:27 Ye know that my wife bare me **t** *sons:* 8147
45: 6 For these **t years** *hath* the famine *been* in 8141
46:27 were born him in Egypt, *were* **t** souls: 8147
48: 1 he took with him his **t** sons, Manasseh and 8147
48: 5 now thy **t** sons, Ephraim and Manasseh, 8147
49:14 ass couching down between **t burdens**: 4942
Ex 2:13 **t** men of the Hebrews strove together: 8147
4: 9 if they will not believe also these **t** signs, 8147
12: 7 strike *it* on the **t** side posts and on the upper 8147
12:22 the **t** side posts with the blood that *is* in 8147
12:23 on the **t** side posts, the LORD will pass 8147
16:22 **t** omers for one *man:* and all the rulers of 8147
16:29 you on the sixth day the bread of **t days**; 3117
18: 3 her **t** sons; of which the name of the one 8147
18: 6 and thy wife, and her **t** sons with her. 8147
21:21 Notwithstanding, if he continue a day or **t**, 3117
25:10 **t cubits** and a half *shall be* the length 520
25:12 and **t** rings *shall be* in the one side of it, and 8147
25:12 side of it, and **t** rings in the other side of it. 8147
25:17 **t cubits** and a half *shall be* the length 520
25:18 thou shalt make **t** cherubims *of* gold, 8147
25:18 make them, in the **t** ends of the mercy seat. 8147
25:19 make the cherubims on the **t** ends thereof. 8147
25:22 from between the **t** cherubims which *are* 8147
25:23 **t cubits** *shall be* the length thereof, and 520
25:35 *there shall be* a knop under **t** branches of 8147
25:35 a knop under **t** branches of the same, and 8147
25:35 and a knop under **t** branches of the same, 8147
26:17 **T** tenons *shall there be* in one board, set in 8147
26:19 **t** sockets under one board for his two 8147
26:19 two sockets under one board for his **t** 8147
26:19 **t** sockets under another board for his two 8147
26:19 two sockets under another board for his **t** 8147
26:21 **t** sockets under one board, and two sockets 8147
26:21 and **t** sockets under another board. 8147
26:23 **t** boards shalt thou make for the corners of 8147
26:23 the corners of the tabernacle in the **t sides**. 3411
26:24 them both; they shall be for the **t** corners. 8147
26:25 **t** sockets under one board, and two sockets 8147
26:25 and **t** sockets under another board. 8147
26:27 of the tabernacle, for the **t sides** westward. 3411
27: 7 the staves shall be upon the **t** sides of 8147
28: 7 It shall have the **t** shoulderpieces *thereof* 8147
28: 7 *thereof* joined at the **t** edges thereof; 8147
28: 9 thou shalt take **t** onyx stones, and grave on 8147
28:11 shalt thou engrave the **t** stones with 8147
28:12 thou shalt put the **t** stones upon 8147
28:12 upon his **t** shoulders for a memorial. 8147
28:14 **t** chains *of* pure gold at the ends; 8147
28:23 thou shalt make upon the breastplate **t** rings 8147
28:23 shalt put the **t** rings on the two ends of 8147
28:23 shalt put the two rings on the **t** ends of 8147
28:24 thou shalt put the **t** wreathen *chains of* gold 8147
28:24 **t** rings *which are* on the ends of 8147
28:25 *the other* **t** ends of the two wreathen *chains* 8147
28:25 *the other* two ends of the **t** wreathen *chains* 8147
28:25 *chains* thou shalt fasten in the **t** ouches, 8147
28:26 thou shalt make **t** rings of gold, and 8147
28:26 thou shalt put them upon the **t** ends of 8147
28:27 **t** *other* rings of gold thou shalt make, and 8147
28:27 shalt put them on the **t** sides of the ephod 8147
29: 1 young bullock, and **t** rams without blemish, 8147
29: 3 the basket, with the bullock and the **t** rams. 8147
29:13 the **t** kidneys, and the fat that *is* upon them, 8147
29:22 the **t** kidneys, and the fat that *is* upon them, 8147
29:38 **t** lambs of the first year day by day 8147
30: 2 **t cubits** *shall be* the height thereof: the horns 520
30: 4 **t** golden rings shalt thou make to it under 8147
30: 4 by the **t** corners thereof, upon the two sides 8147
30: 4 upon the **t** sides of it shalt thou make *it;* and 8147
30:23 *even* **t hundred** and fifty *shekels,* and 3967
30:23 and of sweet calamus **t hundred** and 3967
31:18 **t** tables of Testimony, tables of stone, 8147
32:15 the **t** tables of the Testimony *were* in his 8147
34: 1 Hew thee **t** tables of stone like unto 8147
34: 4 he hewed **t** tables of stone like unto 8147
34: 4 and took in his hand the **t** tables of stone. 8147
34:29 the **t** tables of Testimony in Moses' hand, 8147
36:22 One board had **t** tenons, equally distant one 8147
36:24 **t** sockets under one board for his two 8147
36:24 two sockets under one board for his **t** 8147
36:24 **t** sockets under another board for his two 8147
36:24 two sockets under another board for his **t** 8147
36:26 **t** sockets under one board, and two sockets 8147
36:26 and **t** sockets under another board. 8147
36:28 **t** boards made he for the corners of 8147
36:28 the corners of the tabernacle in the **t sides**. 3411
36:30 *of* silver, under every board **t** sockets. 8147
37: 1 **t cubits** and a half *was* the length of it, and 520
37: 3 even **t** rings upon the one side of it, and 8147
37: 3 of it, and **t** rings upon the other side of it. 8147
37: 6 **t cubits** and a half *was* the length thereof, 520
37: 7 he made **t** cherubims *of* gold, beaten out of 8147
37: 7 he them, on the **t** ends of the mercy seat; 8147
37: 8 he the cherubims on the **t** ends thereof. 8147
37:10 **t cubits** *was* the length thereof, and a cubit 520
37:21 a knop under **t** branches of the same, and 8147
37:21 a knop under **t** branches of the same, and 8147
37:21 and a knop under **t** branches of the same, 8147
37:25 and **t cubits** *was* the height of it; 520
37:27 he made **t** rings of gold for it under 8147
37:27 by the **t** corners of it, upon the two sides 8147
37:27 two corners of it, upon the **t** sides thereof, 8147
38:29 and **t thousand** and four hundred shekels. 505
39: 4 by the **t** edges was it coupled together. 8147
39:16 they made **t** ouches *of* gold, and two gold 8147
39:16 made two ouches *of* gold, and **t** gold rings; 8147
39:16 put the **t** rings in the two ends of 8147
39:16 put the two rings in the **t** ends of 8147
39:17 they put the **t** wreathen *chains of* gold in 8147
39:17 in the **t** rings on the ends of the breastplate. 8147
39:18 the **t** ends of the two wreathen *chains* they 8147
39:18 the two ends of the **t** wreathen *chains* they 8147
39:18 *chains* they fastened in the **t** ouches, 8147
39:19 they made **t** rings of gold, and put *them* on 8147
39:19 put *them* on the **t** ends of the breastplate, 8147
39:20 they made **t** *other* golden rings, and 8147
39:20 put them on the **t** sides of the ephod 8147
Lev 3: 4 the **t** kidneys, and the fat that *is* on them, 8147
3:10 the **t** kidneys, and the fat that *is* upon them, 8147
3:15 the **t** kidneys, and the fat that *is* upon them, 8147
4: 9 the **t** kidneys, and the fat that *is* upon them, 8147
5: 7 **t** turtledoves, or two young pigeons, 8147
5: 7 two turtledoves, or **t** young pigeons, 8147
5:11 if he be not able to bring **t** turtledoves, or 8147
5:11 or **t** young pigeons, then he that sinned 8147
7: 4 the **t** kidneys, and the fat that *is* on them, 8147
8: 2 **t** rams, and a basket of unleavened bread; 8147
8:16 the **t** kidneys, and their fat, and 8147
8:25 the **t** kidneys, and their fat, and the right 8147
12: 5 she shall be unclean **t weeks**, as *in* her 7620
12: 8 she shall bring **t** turtles, or two young 8147
12: 8 shall bring two turtles, or **t** young pigeons; 8147
14: 4 for him that is to be cleansed **t** birds alive 8147
14:10 on the eighth day he shall take **t** he lambs 8147
14:22 **t** turtledoves, or two young pigeons, 8147
14:22 two turtledoves, or **t** young pigeons, 8147
14:49 he shall take to cleanse the house **t** birds, 8147
15:14 on the eighth day he shall take to him **t** 8147
15:14 or **t** young pigeons, and come before 8147
15:29 on the eighth day she shall take unto her **t** 8147
15:29 or **t** young pigeons, and bring them unto 8147
16: 1 after the death of the **t** sons of Aaron, 8147
16: 5 Israel **t** kids of the goats for a sin offering, 8147
16: 7 he shall take the **t** goats, and present them 8147
16: 8 Aaron shall cast lots upon the **t** goats; 8147
23:13 the meat offering thereof *shall be* **t** tenth 8147
23:17 Ye shall bring out of your habitations **t** 8147
23:17 two wave loaves of **t** tenth deals: 8147
23:18 and one young bullock, and **t** rams: 8147
23:19 **t** lambs of the first year for a sacrifice of 8147
23:20 before the LORD, with the **t** lambs: 8147
24: 5 **t** tenth deals shall be *in* one cake. 8147
24: 6 thou shalt set them *in* **t** rows, six on a row, 8147
Nu 1:35 *were* thirty and **t** thousand and 8147
1:35 and two thousand and **t hundred.** 3967
1:39 and **t** thousand and seven hundred. 8147
2:21 *were* thirty and **t** thousand and 8147
2:21 and two thousand and **t hundred.** 3967
2:26 and **t** thousand and seven hundred. 8147
3:34 upward, *were* six thousand and **t hundred.** 3967
3:39 and upward, *were* twenty and **t** thousand. 8147
3:43 **t** thousand two hundred and threescore and 8147
3:43 two thousand **t hundred** and threescore 3967
3:46 that are *to be* redeemed of the **t hundred** 3967
4:36 families were **t thousand** seven hundred 505
4:40 were **t thousand** and six hundred and thirty. 505
4:44 were three thousand and **t hundred.** 3967
6:10 on the eighth day he shall bring **t** turtles, 8147
6:10 or **t** young pigeons, to the priest, 8147
7: 3 a wagon for **t** of the princes, and for *each* 8147
7: 7 **T** wagons and four oxen he gave unto 8147
7:17 **t** oxen, five rams, five he goats, five lambs 8147
7:23 **t** oxen, five rams, five he goats, five lambs 8147
7:29 **t** oxen, five rams, five he goats, five lambs 8147
7:35 **t** oxen, five rams, five he goats, five lambs 8147
7:41 **t** oxen, five rams, five he goats, five lambs 8147
7:47 **t** oxen, five rams, five he goats, five lambs 8147
7:53 **t** oxen, five rams, five he goats, five lambs 8147
7:59 **t** oxen, five rams, five he goats, five lambs 8147
7:65 **t** oxen, five rams, five he goats, five lambs 8147
7:71 **t** oxen, five rams, five he goats, five lambs 8147
7:77 **t** oxen, five rams, five he goats, five lambs 8147
7:83 **t** oxen, five rams, five he goats, five lambs 8147
7:85 all the silver vessels *weighed* **t thousand** 505
7:89 from between the **t** cherubims: 8147
9:22 Or *whether it were* **t days**, or a month, or 3117
10: 2 Make thee **t** trumpets of silver; of a whole 8147
11:19 nor **t days**, nor five days, neither ten days, 3117
11:26 there remained **t** *of the* men in the camp, 8147
11:31 as it were **t cubits** *high* upon the face of 520
13:23 and they bare it between **t** upon a staff; 8147
15: 6 thou shalt prepare *for* a meat offering **t** 8147
16: 2 **t hundred** and fifty princes of 3967
16:17 his censer, **t hundred** and fifty censers; 3967
16:35 consumed the **t hundred** and fifty men that 3967
22:22 his ass, and his **t** servants *were* with him. 8147
26:10 what time the fire devoured **t hundred** and 3967
26:14 twenty and **t** thousand and two hundred. 8147
26:14 twenty and two thousand and **t hundred.** 3967
26:34 fifty and **t** thousand and seven hundred. 8147
26:37 thirty and **t** thousand and five hundred. 8147
28: 3 **t** lambs of the first year without spot day by 8147
28: 9 on the sabbath day **t** lambs of the first year 8147
28: 9 **t** tenth deals *of* flour *for* a meat offering, 8147
28:11 **t** young bullocks, and one ram, seven lambs 8147
28:12 **t** tenth deals *of* flour *for* a meat offering, 8147
28:19 **t** young bullocks, and one ram, and 8147
28:20 for a bullock, and **t** tenth deals for a ram; 8147
28:27 **t** young bullocks, one ram, seven lambs of 8147
28:28 one bullock, **t** tenth deals unto one ram, 8147
29: 3 for a bullock, *and* **t** tenth deals for a ram, 8147
29: 9 to a bullock, *and* **t** tenth deals to one ram, 8147
29:13 **t** rams, *and* fourteen lambs of the first year; 8147
29:14 **t** tenth deals to each ram of the two rams, 8147
29:14 two tenth deals to each ram of the **t** rams, 8147
29:17 **t** rams, fourteen lambs of the first year 8147
29:20 on the third day eleven bullocks, **t** rams, 8147
29:23 **t** rams, *and* fourteen lambs of the first year 8147
29:26 **t** rams, *and* fourteen lambs of the first year 8147
29:29 **t** rams, *and* fourteen lambs of the first year 8147
29:32 **t** rams, *and* fourteen lambs of the first year 8147
31:27 **divide** the prey **into t parts**; between them 2673
31:35 thirty and **t** thousand persons in all, 8147
31:40 LORD'S tribute *was* thirty and **t** persons. 8147
34:15 The **t** tribes and the half tribe have received 8147
35: 5 the city *on* the east side **t thousand** cubits, 505
35: 5 and *on* the south side **t thousand** cubits, and 505
35: 5 *on* the west side **t thousand** cubits, and 505
35: 5 and *on* the north side **t thousand** cubits; 505
35: 6 to them ye shall add forty and **t** cities. 8147
Dt 3: 8 we took at that time out of the hand of the **t** 8147
3:21 your God hath done unto these **t** kings: 8147
4:13 and he wrote them upon **t** tables of stone. 8147
4:47 Og king of Bashan, **t** kings of the Amorites, 8147
5:22 he wrote them in **t** tables of stone, and 8147
9:10 the LORD delivered unto me **t** tables of 8147
9:11 *that* the LORD gave me the **t** tables of 8147
9:15 the **t** tables of the covenant *were* in my two 8147
9:15 the two tables of the covenant *were* in my **t** 8147
9:17 I took the **t** tables, and cast them out of my 8147
9:17 cast them out of my **t** hands, and 8147
10: 1 Hew thee **t** tables of stone like unto 8147

T

Dt 10: 3 hewed **t** tables of stone like unto the first, 8147
10: 3 having the **t** tables in mine hand. 8147
14: 6 cleaveth the cleft *into* **t** claws, *and* 8147
17: 6 At the mouth of **t** witnesses, or 8147
18: 3 and the **t cheeks**, and the maw. 3895
19:15 at the mouth of **t** witnesses, or at the mouth 8147
21:15 If a man have **t** wives, one beloved, and 8147
32:30 **t** put ten thousand to flight, except their 8147
Jos 2: 1 Joshua the son of Nun sent out of Shittim **t** 8147
2: 4 the woman took the **t** men, and hid them, 8147
2:10 what you did unto the **t** kings of 8147
2:23 So the **t** men returned, and descended from 8147
3: 4 and it, about **t thousand** cubits by measure: 505
6:22 Joshua had said unto the **t** men that had 8147
7: 3 *but* let about **t** or three **thousand** men go up 505
7:21 **t hundred** shekels *of* silver, and a wedge of 3967
9:10 all that he did to the **t** kings of 8147
14: 3 For Moses had given the inheritance of **t** 8147
14: 4 For the children of Joseph were **t** tribes, 8147
15:60 and Rabbah; **t** cities with their villages. 8147
19:30 twenty and **t** cities with their villages. 8147
21:16 her suburbs; nine cities out of those **t** tribes. 8147
21:25 and Gath-rimmon with her suburbs; **t** cities. 8147
21:27 and Beeshterah with her suburbs; **t** cities. 8147
24:12 *even* the **t** kings of the Amorites; 8147
Jdg 3:16 Ehud made him a dagger which had **t** 8147
5:30 the prey; to every man a damsel *or* **t**S; 7361
7: 3 of the people twenty and **t** thousand; 8147
7:25 they took **t** princes of the Midianites, Oreb 8147
8:12 took the **t** kings of Midian, Zebah and 8147
9:44 the **t** *other* companies ran upon all 8147
10: 3 and judged Israel twenty and **t** years. 8147
11:37 let me alone **t** months, that I may go up and 8147
11:38 he sent her away *for* **t** months: and 8147
11:39 it came to pass at the end of **t** months, 8147
12: 6 of the Ephraimites forty and **t** thousand. 8147
15: 4 put a firebrand in the midst between **t** tails. 8147
15:13 they bound him with **t** new cords, and 8147
16: 3 the **t** posts, and went away with them, bar 8147
16:28 avenged of the Philistines for my **t** eyes. 8147
16:29 Samson took hold of the **t** middle pillars 8147
17: 4 his mother took **t hundred** *shekels* of 3967
19:10 *there were* with him **t** asses saddled, 6776
20:21 that day twenty and **t** thousand men. 8147
20:45 and slew **t thousand** men of them. 505
Ru 1: 1 of Moab, he, and his wife, and his **t** sons. 8147
1: 2 the name of his **t** sons Mahlon and Chilion, 8147
1: 3 and she was left, and her **t** sons. 8147
1: 5 the woman was left of her **t** sons and 8147
1: 7 and her **t** daughters in law with her; 8147
1: 8 Naomi said unto her **t** daughters in law, 8147
1:19 So they **t** went until they came *to* 8147
4:11 which **t** did build the house of Israel: 8147
1Sa 1: 2 he had **t** wives; the name of the one *was* 8147
1: 3 the **t** sons of Eli, Hophni and Phinehas, 8147
2:21 and bare three sons and **t** daughters. 8147
2:34 that shall come upon thy **t** sons, on Hophni 8147
4: 4 the **t** sons of Eli, Hophni and Phinehas, 8147
4:11 the **t** sons of Eli, Hophni and Phinehas, 8147
4:17 thy **t** sons also, Hophni and Phinehas, 8147
6: 7 make a new cart, and take **t** milch kine, 8147
6:10 took **t** milch kine, and tied them to the cart, 8147
10: 2 thou shalt find **t** men by Rachel's sepulchre 8147
10: 4 salute thee, and give thee **t** *loaves* of bread; 8147
11:11 so that **t** of them were not left together. 8147
13: 1 when he had reigned **t** years over Israel, 8147
13: 2 *whereof* **t thousand** were with Saul in 505
14:49 the names of his **t** daughters *were these;* 8147
15: 4 **t hundred** thousand footmen, and 3967
18:27 and slew of the Philistines **t hundred** men; 3967
23:18 they **t** made a covenant before the LORD: 8147
25:13 and **t hundred** abode by the stuff. 3967
25:18 took **t hundred** loaves, and two bottles of 3967
25:18 **t** bottles of wine, and five sheep ready 8147
25:18 **t hundred** cakes *of figs*, and laid *them* on 3967
27: 3 *even* David with his **t** wives, Ahinoam 8147
28: 8 **t** men with him, and they came to 8147
30: 5 David's **t** wives were taken captives, 8147
30:10 for **t hundred** abode *behind*, which were so 3967
30:12 of a cake *of figs*, and **t** clusters of raisins: 8147
30:18 and David rescued his **t** wives. 8147
30:21 David came to the **t hundred** men, 3967
2Sa 1: 1 and David had abode **t** days in Ziklag; 8147
2: 2 his **t** wives also, Ahinoam the Jezreelitess, 8147
2:10 to reign over Israel, and reigned **t** years. 8147
4: 2 Saul's son had **t** men *that were* captains of 8147
8: 2 even *with* **t** lines measured he to put to 8147
8: 5 David slew of the Syrians **t** and 8147
12: 1 unto him, There were **t** men in one city; 8147
13:23 it came to pass after **t full years**, 3117+8141
14: 6 thy handmaid had **t** sons, and they two 8147
14: 6 they **t** strove together in the field, and 8147
14:26 **t hundred** shekels after the king's weight. 3967
14:28 So Absalom dwelt **t full years** in 3117+8141
15:11 with Absalom went **t hundred** men out of 3967
15:27 your **t** sons with you, Ahimaaz thy son, and 8147
15:36 *they have* there with them their **t** sons, 8147
16: 1 upon them **t hundred** *loaves of* bread, and 3967
18:24 David sat between the **t** gates: and 8147
21: 8 the king took the **t** sons of Rizpah 8147
23:20 he slew **t** lionlike men of Moab: 8147
1Ki 2: 5 what he did to the **t** captains of the hosts of 8147
2:32 who fell upon **t** men more righteous and 8147
2:39 that **t** of the servants of Shimei ran away 8147
3:16 came there **t** women, *that were* harlots, 8147
3:18 us in the house, save we **t** in the house. 8147
3:25 Divide the living child in **t**, and give half to 8147
5:12 and they **t** made a league *together.* 8147
5:14 were in Lebanon, *and* **t** months at home: 8147
6:23 within the oracle he made **t** cherubims *of* 8147
6:32 The **t** doors also *were of* olive tree; and 8147
6:34 the **t** doors *were of* fir tree: the two leaves 8147
6:34 the **t** leaves of the one door *were* folding, 8147
6:34 the **t** leaves of the other door *were* folding. 8147
7:15 For he cast **t** pillars *of* brass, of eighteen 8147

1Ki 7:16 he made **t** chapiters *of* molten brass, to set 8147
7:18 **t** rows round about upon the one network, 8147
7:20 the chapiters upon the **t** pillars *had* 8147
7:20 the pomegranates *were* **t hundred** *in* rows 3967
7:24 the knops *were* cast *in* **t** rows, when it was 8147
7:26 of lilies: it contained **t thousand** baths. 505
7:41 The **t** pillars, and the two bowls of 8147
7:41 the **t** bowls of the chapiters that *were* on 8147
7:41 that *were* on the top of the **t** pillars; NIH
7:41 the **t** networks, to cover the two bowls of 8147
7:41 to cover the **t** bowls of the chapiters which 8147
7:42 four hundred pomegranates for the **t** 8147
7:42 *even* **t** rows *of* pomegranates for one 8147
7:42 to cover the **t** bowls of the chapiters that 8147
8: 7 forth *their* **t wings** over the place of the ark, 3671
8: 9 *There was* nothing in the ark save the **t** 8147
8:63 **t** and twenty thousand oxen, and 8147
9:10 when Solomon had built the **t** houses, 8147
10:16 king Solomon made **t hundred** targets *of* 3967
10:19 the seat, and **t** lions stood beside the stays. 8147
11:29 and they **t** *were* alone in the field: 8147
12:28 made **t** calves of gold, and said unto them, 8147
14:20 the days which Jeroboam reigned *were* **t** 8147
15:25 of Judah, and reigned over Israel **t years.** 8141
16: 8 to reign over Israel in Tirzah, **t years.** 8141
16:21 the people of Israel divided into **t parts:** 2677
16:24 Samaria of Shemer for **t talents** of silver, 3603
16:29 over Israel in Samaria twenty and **t** years. 8147
17:12 behold, I *am* gathering **t** sticks, that I may 8147
18:21 said, How long halt ye between **t** opinions? 8147
18:23 Let them therefore give us **t** bullocks; and 8147
18:32 as great as would contain **t measures** of 5429
20: 1 *there were* thirty and **t** kings with him, and 8147
20:15 and they were **t hundred** and thirty two: 3967
20:15 and they were two hundred and thirty **t**: 8147
20:16 the thirty and **t** kings that helped him. 8147
20:27 before them like **t** little flocks of kids; 8147
21:10 set **t** men, sons of Belial, before him, to 8147
21:13 there came in **t** men, children of Belial, 8147
22:31 **t** captains that had rule over *his* chariots, 8147
22:51 of Judah, and reigned **t years** over Israel. 8141
2Ki 1:14 burnt up the **t** captains of the former fifties 8147
2: 6 I will not leave thee. And they **t** went on. 8147
2: 7 to view afar off: and they **t** stood by Jordan. 8147
2: 8 so that they **t** went over on dry *ground.* 8147
2:12 his own clothes, and rent them in **t** pieces. 8147
2:24 there came forth **t** she bears out of 8147
2:24 and tare forty and **t** children of them. 8147
4: 1 the creditor is come to take unto him my **t** 8147
5:17 be given to thy servant **t** mules' burden of 6776
5:22 **t** young men of the sons of the prophets: 8147
5:22 talent of silver, and **t** changes of garments. 8147
5:23 Naaman said, Be content, take **t talents.** 3603
5:23 and bound **t talents** of silver in two bags, 3603
5:23 and bound two talents of silver in **t** bags, 8147
5:23 with **t** changes of garments, and laid *them* 8147
5:23 and laid *them* upon **t** of his servants; 8147
7: 1 **t measures** of barley for a shekel, in 5429
7:14 They took therefore **t** chariot horses; and 8147
7:16 **t measures** of barley for a shekel, 5429
7:18 **T measures** of barley for a shekel, and 5429
8:17 **t** years old was he when he *began* to reign; 8147
8:26 **T** and twenty years old *was* Ahaziah when 8147
9:32 there looked out to him **t** *or* three eunuchs. 8147
10: 4 said, Behold, **t** kings stood not before him: 8147
10: 8 Lay ye them *in* **t** heaps *at* the entering in of 8147
10:14 the shearing house, *even* **t** and forty men; 8147
11: 7 **t** parts of all you that go forth on 8147
15: 2 he reigned **t** and fifty years in Jerusalem. 8147
15:23 over Israel in Samaria, *and reigned* **t years.** 8141
15:27 In the **t** and fiftieth year of Azariah king of 8147
17:16 *even* **t** calves, and made a grove, and 8147
18:23 and I will deliver thee **t thousand** horses, 505
21: 5 in the **t** courts of the house of the LORD. 8147
21:19 and **t** years old when he *began* to reign, 8147
21:19 and he reigned **t** years in Jerusalem. 8147
23:12 in the **t** courts of the house of the LORD, 8147
25: 4 *by* the way of the gate between **t walls,** 2346
25:16 The **t** pillars, one sea, and the bases which 8147
1Ch 1:19 unto Eber were born **t** sons: the name of 8147
4: 5 Ashur the father of Tekoa had **t** wives, 8147
5:21 *of* sheep **t hundred** and fifty thousand, and 3967
5:21 *of* asses **t thousand**, and *of* men an hundred 505
7: 2 whose number *was* in the days of David **t** 8147
7: 7 and **t** thousand and thirty and four. 8147
7: 9 *was* twenty thousand and **t hundred.** 3967
7:11 **t hundred** *soldiers, fit* to go out *for* war 3967
9:22 to be porters in the gates *were* **t hundred** 3967
11:21 he was more honourable than the **t**; 8147
11:22 many acts; he slew **t** lionlike men of Moab: 8147
12:28 *of* his father's house twenty and **t** captains. 8147
12:32 the heads of them *were* **t hundred**; and 3967
15: 6 and his brethren **t hundred** and twenty: 3967
15: 8 the chief, and his brethren **t hundred**: 3967
18: 5 David slew of the Syrians **t** and 8147
19: 7 So they hired thirty and **t** thousand chariots, 8147
24:17 to Jachin, the **t** and twentieth to Gamul, 8147
25: 7 was **t hundred** fourscore and eight. 3967
25:29 The **t** and twentieth to Giddalti, *he,* his 8147
26: 8 *were* threescore and **t** of Obed-edom. 8147
26:17 four a day, and toward Asuppim **t** *and* two. 8147
26:17 four a day, and toward Asuppim two *and* **t**. 8147
26:18 four at the causeway, *and* **t** at Parbar. 8147
26:32 *were* **t thousand** and seven hundred chief 505
2Ch 3:10 in the most holy house he made **t** 8147
3:15 Also he made before the house **t** pillars of 8147
4: 3 **T** rows *of* oxen *were* cast, when it was cast. 8147
4:12 *To wit,* the **t** pillars, and the pommels, and 8147
4:12 the chapiters *which were* on the top of the **t** 8147
4:12 the **t** wreaths to cover the two pommels of 8147
4:12 the two wreaths to cover the **t** pommels of 8147
4:13 four hundred pomegranates on the **t** 8147
4:13 **t** rows *of* pomegranates on each wreath, to 8147
4:13 to cover the **t** pommels of the chapiters 8147
5:10 *There was* nothing in the ark save the **t** 8147

2Ch 7: 5 a sacrifice of twenty and **t** thousand oxen, 8147
8:10 *even* **t hundred** and fifty, that bare rule 3967
9:15 king Solomon made **t hundred** targets *of* 3967
9:18 and **t** lions standing by the stays: 8147
13:21 begat twenty and **t** sons, and 8147
14: 8 **t hundred** and fourscore thousand: 3967
17:15 with him **t hundred** and 3967
17:16 with him **t hundred** thousand mighty *men* 3967
17:17 with bow and shield **t hundred** thousand. 3967
21: 5 and **t** years old when he *began* to reign, 8147
21:19 in process of time, after the end of **t** years, 8147
21:20 **t** *years* old was he when he *began* to reign, 8147
22: 2 **t** years old *was* Ahaziah when he *began* to 8147
24: 3 Jehoiada took for him **t** wives; and he begat 8147
26: 3 he reigned fifty and **t** years in Jerusalem. 8147
26:12 the mighty *men* of valour *were* **t thousand** 505
28: 8 of their brethren **t hundred** thousand, 3967
29:32 an hundred rams, *and* **t hundred** lambs: 3967
33: 5 in the **t** courts of the house of the LORD. 8147
33:21 Amon *was* **t** and twenty years old when he 8147
33:21 to reign, and reigned **t** years in Jerusalem. 8147
35: 8 priests for the passover *offerings* **t thousand** 505
Ezr 2: 3 **t thousand** an hundred seventy and two. 505
2: 3 two thousand an hundred seventy and **t.** 8147
2: 4 of Shephatiah, three hundred seventy and **t.** 8147
2: 6 Joab, **t thousand** eight hundred and twelve. 505
2: 7 a thousand **t hundred** fifty and four. 3967
2:10 children of Bani, six hundred forty and **t.** 8147
2:12 a thousand **t hundred** twenty and two. 3967
2:12 a thousand two hundred twenty and **t.** 8147
2:14 children of Bigvai, **t thousand** fifty and six. 505
2:19 of Hashum, **t hundred** twenty and three. 3967
2:24 The children of Azmaveth, forty and **t.** 8147
2:27 men of Michmas, an hundred twenty and **t.** 8147
2:28 and Ai, **t hundred** twenty and three. 3967
2:29 The children of Nebo, fifty and **t.** 8147
2:31 a thousand **t hundred** fifty and four. 3967
2:37 children of Immer, a thousand fifty and **t.** 8147
2:38 a thousand **t hundred** forty and seven. 3967
2:58 *were* three hundred ninety and **t.** 8147
2:60 children of Nekoda, six hundred fifty and **t.** 8147
2:64 *was* **forty** *and* **t thousand** 505+702+7239
2:65 *there were* among them **t hundred** singing 3967
2:66 six; their mules, **t hundred** forty and five; 3967
6:17 **t hundred** rams, four hundred lambs; 3969
8: 4 and with him **t hundred** males. 3967
8: 9 with him **t hundred** and eighteen males. 3967
8:20 **t hundred** and twenty Nethinims: 3967
8:27 **t** vessels of fine copper, precious as gold. 8147
10:13 neither *is this* a work of one day or **t**: 8147
Ne 5:14 from the twentieth year even unto the **t** 8147
6:15 *day of the month* Elul, in fifty and **t** days. 8147
7: 8 **t thousand** an hundred seventy and two. 505
7: 8 two thousand an hundred seventy and **t.** 8147
7: 9 of Shephatiah, three hundred seventy and **t.** 8147
7:10 children of Arah, six hundred fifty and **t.** 8147
7:11 **t thousand** and eight hundred *and* eighteen. 505
7:12 a thousand **t hundred** fifty and four. 3967
7:17 **t thousand** three hundred twenty and two. 505
7:17 two thousand three hundred twenty and **t.** 8147
7:19 of Bigvai, **t thousand** threescore and seven. 505
7:28 The men of Beth-azmaveth, forty and **t.** 8147
7:31 of Michmas, an hundred and twenty and **t.** 8147
7:33 The men of the other Nebo, fifty and **t.** 8147
7:34 a thousand **t hundred** fifty and four. 3967
7:40 children of Immer, a thousand fifty and **t.** 8147
7:41 a thousand **t hundred** forty and seven. 3967
7:60 *were* three hundred ninety and **t.** 8147
7:62 of Nekoda, six hundred forty and **t.** 8147
7:66 *was* **forty** *and* **t thousand** 505+702+7239
7:67 they had **t hundred** forty and five singing 3967
7:68 six: their mules, **t hundred** forty and five: 3967
7:71 **t thousand** and two hundred pound *of* silver. 505
7:71 and **t hundred** pound *of* silver. 3967
7:72 **t thousand** pound *of* silver, and threescore 505
11:12 the house *were* eight hundred twenty and **t**: 8147
11:13 of the fathers, **t hundred** forty and two: 3967
11:13 of the fathers, two hundred forty and **t**: 8147
11:18 in the holy city *were* **t hundred** fourscore 3967
11:19 the gates, *were* an hundred seventy and **t.** 8147
12:31 appointed **t** great *companies of them that* 8147
12:40 So stood the **t** *companies of them that gave* 8147
13: 6 for in the **t** and thirtieth year of Artaxerxes 8147
Est 2:21 **t** of the king's chamberlains, Bigthan and 8147
6: 2 and Teresh, **t** of the king's chamberlains, 8147
9:27 that they would keep these **t** days according 8147
Job 13:20 Only do not **t** *things* unto me: then will I 8147
42: 7 against thee, and against thy **t** friends: 8147
Pr 30: 7 **T** *things* have I required of thee; deny me 8147
30:15 The horseleach hath **t** daughters, 8147
Ecc 4: 9 **T** *are* better than one; because they have a 8147
4:11 Again, if **t** lie together, then they have heat: 8147
4:12 prevail against him, **t** shall withstand him; 8147
SS 4: 5 Thy **t** breasts *are* like two young roes *that* 8147
4: 5 Thy two breasts *are* like **t** young roes *that* 8147
6:13 As it were the company of **t armies.** 4264
7: 3 Thy **t** breasts *are* like two young roes *that* 8147
7: 3 Thy two breasts *are* like **t** young roes *that* 8147
8:12 those that keep the fruit thereof **t hundred.** 3967
Isa 7: 4 neither be fainthearted for the **t** tails of 8147
7:21 shall nourish a young cow, and **t** sheep; 8147
17: 6 **t** *or* three berries in the top of 8147
22:11 Ye made also a ditch between the **t walls** 2346
36: 8 and I will give thee **t thousand** horses, 505
45: 1 to open before him the **t leaved gates;** 1817
47: 9 these **t** *things* shall come to thee *in* a 8147
51:19 These **t** *things* are come unto thee; 8147
Jer 2:13 For my people have committed **t** evils; 8147
3:14 **t** of a family, and I will bring you to Zion: 8147
24: 1 **t** baskets of figs *were* set before the temple 8147
28: 3 Within **t full years** *will* I bring again 3117+8141
28:11 within the space of **t full years.** 3117+8141
33:24 The **t** families which the LORD hath 8147
39: 4 by the gate betwixt the **t walls:** 2346
52: 7 *by* the way of the gate between the **t walls,** 2346

Jer 52:20 The t pillars, one sea, and twelve brasen 8147
52:29 eight hundred thirty and t persons: 8147
Eze 1:11 t *wings* of every one *were* joined one to 8147
1:11 one to another, and t covered their bodies. 8147
1:23 every one had t, which covered on this 8147
1:23 covered on this *side*, and every one had t, 8147
21:19 Also, thou son of man, appoint thee t ways, 8147
21:21 at the head of the t ways, to use divination: 8147
23: 2 Son of man, there were t women, 8147
35:10 These t nations and these two countries 8147
35:10 and these t countries shall be mine, 8147
37:22 they shall be no more t nations, 8147
37:22 neither shall they be divided into t 8147
40: 9 the posts thereof, t cubits; and the porch of 8147
40:39 in the porch of the gate *were* t tables on this 8147
40:39 t tables on that side, to slay thereon 8147
40:40 to the entry of the north gate, *were* t tables; 8147
40:40 *was* at the porch of the gate, *were* t tables. 8147
41: 3 measured the post of the door, t cubits; 8147
41:18 and a cherub; and *every* cherub had t faces; 8147
41:22 cubits high, and the length thereof t cubits; 8147
41:23 the temple and the sanctuary had t doors. 8147
41:24 the doors had t leaves *apiece*, two turning 8147
41:24 the doors had two leaves *apiece*, t turning 8147
41:24 t *leaves* for the one door, and two leaves 8147
41:24 one door, and t leaves for the other *door*. 8147
43:14 *even* to the lower settle *shall be* t cubits, 8147
45:15 lamb out of the flock, out of **t hundred**, 3967
46:19 there *was* a place on the **t sides** westward. 3411
47:13 tribes of Israel: Joseph *shall have* **t** portions. NIH
48:17 city shall be toward the north **t hundred** 3967
48:17 toward the south **t hundred** and fifty, and 3967
48:17 toward the east **t hundred** and fifty, and 3967
48:17 and toward the west **t hundred** and fifty. 3967
Da 5:31 *being* about threescore and t year old. 8648
8: 3 before the river a ram which had **t horns**: 7161
8: 3 the **t horns** *were* high; but one *was* higher 7161
8: 6 he came to the ram that had **t horns**, 7161
8: 7 and smote the ram, and brake his t horns: 8147
8:14 Unto **t thousand** and three hundred days; 505
8:20 The ram which thou sawest having **t horns** 7161
9:25 seven weeks, and threescore and t weeks: 8147
9:26 and t weeks shall Messiah be cut off, 8147
12: 5 and behold, there stood other t, 8147
12:11 *there shall be* a thousand **t hundred** and 3967
Hos 6: 2 After **t days** will he revive us: in the third 3117
10:10 when *they* shall bind themselves in their t 8147
Am 1: 1 king of Israel, **t year** before the earthquake. 8141
3: 3 Can t walk together, except they be agreed? 8147
3:12 taketh out of the mouth of the lion t legs, 8147
4: 8 So t *or* three cities wandered unto one city, 8147
Zec 4: 3 t olive trees by it, one upon the right *side* of 8147
4:11 What *are* these t olive trees upon the right 8147
4:12 What *be these* t olive branches which 8147
4:12 t golden pipes empty the golden *oil* out of 8147
4:14 Then said he, These *are* the t anointed ones, 8147
5: 9 there came out t women, and the wind *was* 8147
6: 1 there came four chariots out from between t 8147
11: 7 I took unto me t staves; the one I called 8147
13: 8 t parts therein shall be cut off *and* die; 8147
Mt 2:16 coasts thereof, from **t years old** and under, *1332*
4:18 saw t brethren, Simon called Peter, and *1417*
4:21 he saw other t brethren, James the *son* of *1417*
6:24 No *man* can serve t masters: for either he *1417*
8:28 there met him t possessed with devils, *1417*
9:27 t blind men followed him, crying, and *1417*
10:10 neither t coats, neither shoes, nor yet *1417*
10:29 Are not t sparrows sold for a farthing? and *1417*
11: 2 works of Christ, he sent t of his disciples, *1417*
14:17 We have here but five loaves, and t fishes. *1417*
14:19 and the t fishes, and looking up to heaven, *1417*
18: 8 rather than having t hands or two feet to be *1417*
18: 8 or t feet to be cast into everlasting fire. *1417*
18: 9 rather than having t eyes to be cast into hell *1417*
18:16 *then* take with thee one or t more, *1417*
18:16 that in the mouth of t or three witnesses *1417*
18:19 That if t of you shall agree on earth as *1417*
18:20 For where t or three are gathered together *1417*
20:21 Grant that these my t sons may sit, *1417*
20:24 with indignation against the t brethren. *1417*
20:30 t blind men sitting by the way side, *1417*
21: 1 mount of Olives, then sent Jesus t disciples, *1417*
21:28 A *certain* man had t sons; and he came to *1417*
22:40 On these t commandments hang all the law *1417*
24:40 Then shall t be in the field; the one shall be *1417*
24:41 **T** *women shall be* grinding at the mill; *1417*
25:15 to another t, and to another one; *1417*
25:17 And likewise he that *had received* t, he also *1417*
25:17 *had received* two, he also gained other **t**. *1417*
25:22 He also that had received t talents came *1417*
25:22 Lord, thou deliveredst unto me t talents: *1417*
25:22 I have gained t other talents besides them. *1417*
26: 2 Ye know that after t days is *the feast of* *1417*
26:37 with *him* Peter and the t sons of Zebedee, *1417*
26:60 At the last came t false witnesses, *1417*
27:38 Then were there t thieves crucified with *1417*
Mk 5:13 into the sea, (they were about **t thousand**,) *1367*
6: 7 and began to send them forth by t and two; *1417*
6: 7 and began to send them forth by two and **t**; *1417*
6: 9 shod with sandals; and not put on t coats. *1417*
6:37 and buy **t hundred** pennyworth of bread, *1250*
6:38 they knew, they say, Five, and t fishes. *1417*
6:41 had taken the five loaves and the t fishes, *1417*
6:41 and the t fishes divided he among *them* all. *1417*
9:43 than having t hands to go into hell, into *1417*
9:45 than having t feet to be cast into hell, *1417*
9:47 than having t eyes to be cast into hell fire: *1417*
11: 1 he sendeth forth t of his disciples, *1417*
11: 4 door without in a place where t ways met; NIG
12:42 and she threw in t mites, which make a *1417*
14: 1 After t days was *the feast of* the passover, *1417*
14:13 And he sendeth forth t of his disciples, and *1417*
15:27 And with him they crucify t thieves; *1417*
16:12 he appeared in another form unto t of them, *1417*
Lk 2:24 A pair of turtledoves, or t young pigeons. *1417*
3:11 and saith unto them, He that hath t coats, *1417*
5: 2 And saw t ships standing by the lake: but *1417*
7:19 And John calling unto *him* t of his disciples *1417*
7:41 There was a certain creditor which had t *1417*
9: 3 neither money; neither have t coats apiece. *1417*
9:13 have no more but five loaves and t fishes; *1417*
9:16 he took the five loaves and the t fishes, *1417*
9:30 And behold, there talked with him t men, *1417*
9:32 and the t men that stood with him. *1417*
10: 1 and sent them t and two before his face into *1417*
10: 1 and t before his face into every city and *1417*
10:35 he took out t pence, and gave *them* to *1417*
12: 6 Are not five sparrows sold for t farthings, *1417*
12:52 three against t, and two against three. *1417*
12:52 three against two, and t against three. *1417*
15:11 And he said, A certain man had t sons: *1417*
16:13 No servant can serve t masters: for either *1417*
17:34 in that night there shall be t *men* in one *1417*
17:35 **T** *women* shall be grinding together; *1417*
17:36 **T** *men* shall be in the field; the one shall be *1417*
18:10 **T** men went up into the temple to pray; *1417*
19:29 *mount* of Olives, he sent t of his disciples, *1417*
21: 2 poor widow casting in thither t mites. *1417*
22:38 they said, Lord, behold, here *are* t swords. *1417*
23:32 And there were also t other, malefactors, *1417*
24: 4 t men stood by them in shining garments: *1417*
24:13 t of them went *that* same day to a village *1417*
Jn 1:35 day *after* John stood, and t of his disciples; *1417*
1:37 And the t disciples heard him speak, and *1417*
1:40 One of the t which heard John speak, and *1417*
2: 6 containing t or three firkins apiece. *1417*
4:40 tarry with them: and he abode there t days. *1417*
4:43 Now after t days he departed thence, and *1417*
6: 7 **T hundred** pennyworth of bread is not *1250*
6: 9 hath five barley loaves, and t small fishes: *1417*
8:17 that the testimony of t men is true. *1417*
11: 6 he abode t days *still* in the *same* place *1417*
19:18 and t other with him, on either side one, *1417*
20:12 And seeth t angels in white sitting, the one *1417*
21: 2 of Zebedee, and t other of his disciples. *1417*
21: 8 from land, but as it were **t hundred** cubits,) *1250*
Ac 1:10 t men stood by them in white apparel; *1417*
1:23 And they appointed t, Joseph called *1417*
1:24 shew whether of these t thou hast chosen, *1417*
7:29 the land of Madian, where he begat t sons. *1417*
9:38 Peter was there, they sent unto him t men, *1417*
10: 7 he called t of his household servants, and *1417*
12: 6 night Peter was sleeping between t soldiers, *1417*
12: 6 between two soldiers, bound with t chains: *1417*
19:10 And this continued by the space of t years; *1417*
19:22 So he sent into Macedonia t of them that *1417*
19:34 all with one voice about the space of t *1417*
21:33 commanded *him* to be bound with t chains; *1417*
23:23 And he called unto *him* t centurions, *1417*
23:23 Make ready **t hundred** soldiers to go to *1250*
23:23 *and* ten, and spearmen **t hundred**, *1250*
24:27 But after **t years** Porcius Festus came into *1333*
27:37 And we were in all in the ship **t hundred** *1250*
27:41 And falling into a place **where t seas met**, *1337*
28:30 And Paul dwelt t whole **years** in his own *1333*
1Co 6:16 one body? for t, saith *he*, shall be one flesh. *1417*
14:27 *let it be* by t, or at the most *by* three, and *1417*
14:29 Let the prophets speak t or three, and *1417*
2Co 13: 1 In the mouth of t or three witnesses shall *1417*
Gal 4:22 For it is written, that Abraham had t sons, *1417*
4:24 for these are the t covenants; the one from *1417*
Eph 5:31 unto his wife, and they t shall be one flesh. *1417*
Php 1:23 For I am in a strait betwixt t, having a *1417*
1Ti 5:19 but before t or three witnesses. *1417*
Heb 6:18 That by t immutable things, in which *it was* *1417*
10:28 Moses' law died without mercy under t *1417*
Rev 2:12 which hath the sharp sword **with t edges**; *1366*
9:12 behold, there come t woes more hereafter. *1417*
9:16 **t hundred thousand thousand**: *1417+3461*
11: 2 they tread under foot forty *and* t months. *1417*
11: 3 And I will give *power* unto my t witnesses, *1417*
11: 3 they shall prophesy a thousand **t hundred** *1250*
11: 4 These are the t olive trees, and the two *1417*
11: 4 the t candlesticks standing before the God *1417*
11:10 these t prophets tormented them that dwelt *1417*
12: 6 should feed her there a thousand **t hundred** *1250*
12:14 And to the woman were given t wings of a *1417*
13: 5 unto him to continue forty *and* t months. *1417*
13:11 and he had t horns like a lamb, and *1417*

TWOEDGED (4) [EDGE, TWO]

Ps 149: 6 in their mouth, and a t sword in their hand; 6374
Pr 5: 4 is bitter as wormwood, sharp as a t sword. 6310
Heb 4:12 powerful, and sharper than any t sword, *1366*
Rev 1:16 and out of his mouth went a sharp t sword: *1366*

TWOFOLD (1) [TWO]

Mt 23:15 ye make him **t more** *the* child of hell **than** *1362*

TYCHICUS (7)

Ac 20: 4 Timotheus; and of Asia, **T** and Trophimus. *5190*
Eph 6:21 *and* how I do, T, a beloved brother and *5190*
6: S from Rome unto the Ephesians by T. *5190*
Col 4: 7 All my state shall T declare unto you, *5190*
4: S Written from Rome to the Colossians by **T** *5190*
2Ti 4:12 And **T** have I sent to Ephesus. *5190*
Tit 3:12 When I shall send Artemas unto thee, or T, *5190*

TYRANNUS (1)

Ac 19: 9 disputing daily in the school of one **T**. *5181*

TYRE (37) [TYRUS]

Jos 19:29 turneth *to* Ramah, and to the strong city **T**; 6865
2Sa 5:11 Hiram king of **T** sent messengers to David, 6865
24: 7 came *to* the strong hold of T, and *to* all 6865
1Ki 5: 1 Hiram king of **T** sent his servants unto 6865
7:13 king Solomon sent and fet Hiram out of **T**. 6865
7:14 his father *was* a man of **T**, a worker in 6876
9:11 (*Now* Hiram the king of **T** had furnished 6865
1Ki 9:12 Hiram came out from **T** to see the cities 6865
1Ch 14: 1 Now Hiram king of **T** sent messengers to 6865
22: 4 they **of T** brought much cedar wood to 6876
2Ch 2: 3 Solomon sent to Huram the king of **T**, 6865
2:11 Huram the king of **T** answered in writing, 6865
2:14 his father *was* a man of **T**, skilful to work 6876
Ezr 3: 7 oil, unto them of Zidon, and to them of **T**, 6876
Ne 13:16 There dwelt **men of T** also therein, which 6876
Ps 45:12 the daughter of **T** *shall be there* with a gift; 6865
83: 7 the Philistines with the inhabitants of **T**; 6865
87: 4 behold Philistia, and **T**, with Ethiopia; 6865
Isa 23: 1 The burden of **T**. Howl, ye ships of 6865
23: 5 they be sorely pained *at* the report of **T**. 6865
23: 8 Who hath taken this counsel against **T**, 6865
23:15 that **T** shall be forgotten seventy years, 6865
23:15 after the end of seventy years shall **T** sing 6865
23:17 *that* the LORD will visit **T**, and she shall 6865
Joel 3: 4 O **T**, and Zidon, and all the coasts of 6865
Mt 11:21 had been done in **T** and Sidon they would *5184*
11:22 It shall be more tolerable for **T** and Sidon at *5184*
15:21 and departed into the coasts of **T** and *5184*
Mk 3: 8 and they about **T** and Sidon, a great *5184*
7:24 and went into the borders of **T** and Sidon, *5184*
7:31 departing from the coasts of **T** and Sidon, *5184*
Lk 6:17 and *from* the sea coast of **T** and Sidon, *5184*
10:13 for if the mighty works had been done in **T** *5184*
10:14 But it shall be more tolerable for **T** and *5184*
Ac 12:20 was highly displeased with them **of T** *5183*
21: 3 and sailed into Syria, and landed at **T**: *5184*
21: 7 when we had finished *our* course from **T**, *5184*

TYRUS (22) [TYRE]

Jer 25:22 all the kings of **T**, and all the kings of 6865
27: 3 to the king of **T**, and to the king of Zidon, 6865
47: 4 *and* to cut off from **T** and Zidon every 6865
Eze 26: 2 because that **T** hath said against Jerusalem, 6865
26: 3 O **T**, and will cause many nations to come 6865
26: 4 they shall destroy the walls of **T**, and 6865
26: 7 I *will* bring upon **T** Nebuchadrezzar king of 6865
26:15 Thus saith the Lord GOD to **T**; Shall not 6865
27: 2 son of man, take up a lamentation for **T**; 6865
27: 3 say unto **T**, O thou that art situate at 6865
27: 3 O **T**, thou hast said, I *am* of perfect beauty. 6865
27: 8 thy wise *men*, O **T**, *that* were in thee, 6865
27:32 over thee, *saying*, What *city is* like **T**, 6865
28: 2 Son of man, say unto the prince of **T**, 6865
28:12 take up a lamentation upon the king of **T**, 6865
29:18 his army to serve a great service against **T**: 6865
29:18 yet had he no wages, nor his army, for **T**, 6865
Hos 9:13 Ephraim, as I saw **T**, *is* planted in a 6865
Am 1: 9 For three transgressions of **T**, and for four, 6865
1:10 I will send a fire on the wall of **T**, 6865
Zec 9: 2 **T**, and Zidon, though it be very wise. 6865
9: 3 **T** did build herself a strong hold, and 6865

U

UCAL (1)

Pr 30: 1 spake unto Ithiel, even unto Ithiel and **U**. 401

UEL (1)

Ezr 10:34 Of the sons of Bani; Maadai, Amram, and **U**, 177

UGLY See NOISOME

ULAI (2)

Da 8: 2 I saw in a vision, and I was by the river of **U**. 195
8:16 heard a man's voice between *the banks of* **U**, 195

ULAM (4)

1Ch 7:16 and his sons *were* **U** and Rakem. 198
7:17 the sons of **U**; Bedan. These *were* the sons of 198
8:39 the sons of Eshek his brother *were*, **U** his 198
8:40 the sons of **U** were mighty men of valour, 198

ULLA (1)

1Ch 7:39 the sons of **U**; Arah, and Haniel, and Rezia. 5925

UMMAH (1)

Jos 19:30 **U** also, and Aphek, and Rehob: twenty and 5981

UNACCUSTOMED (1) [ACCUSTOMED]

Jer 31:18 as a bullock **u** *to the yoke;* turn thou 3808+3925

UNADVISEDLY (1) [ADVISE]

Ps 106:33 his spirit, so that he **spake u** with his lips. 981

UNAWARES (12) [AWARE]

Ge 31:20 Jacob **stale away u** to Laban 1589+3820
31:26 that thou hast **stolen away u** to me, 1589+3824
Nu 35:11 flee thither, which killeth *any* person at **u**. 7684
35:15 *any* person **u** may flee thither. 7684+871.1
Dt 4:42 should kill his neighbour **u**, 1097+1847+871.1
Jos 20: 3 the slayer that killeth *any* person **u** 7684+871.1
20: 9 that whosoever killeth *any* person at **u** 7684
Ps 35: 8 Let destruction come upon him at **u**; 3045+3808
Lk 21:34 *this* life, and *so* that day come upon you **u**. *160*
Gal 2: 4 because of false brethren **u brought in**, *3920*
Heb 13: 2 for thereby some have entertained angels **u**. *2990*
Jude 1: 4 For there are certain men **crept in u**, *3921*

UNBELIEF (16) [BELIEVE, UNBELIEVERS, UNBELIEVING]
Mt 13:58 mighty works there, because of their **u**. 570
17:20 Jesus said unto them, Because of your **u**: 570
Mk 6: 6 And he marvelled because of their **u**. And he 570
9:24 with tears, Lord, I believe; help thou mine **u**. 570
16:14 and upbraided them with their **u** and 570
Ro 3: 3 shall their **u** make the faith of God without 570
4:20 not at the promise of God through **u**; 570
11:20 because of **u** they were broken off, and 570
11:23 And they also, if they bide not still in **u**, 570
11:30 have now obtained mercy through their **u**: 543
11:32 For God hath concluded *them* all in **u**, 543
1Ti 1:13 because I did *it* ignorantly in **u**. 570
Heb 3:12 lest there be in any of you an evil heart of **u**, 570
3:19 see that they could not enter in because of **u**. 570
4: 6 first preached entered not in because of **u**, 543
4:11 any *man* fall after the same example of **u**. 543

UNBELIEVER See INFIDEL

UNBELIEVERS (4) [UNBELIEF]
Lk 12:46 and will appoint *him* his portion with the **u**. 571
1Co 6: 6 to law with brother, and that before the **u**. 571
14:23 or **u**, will they not say that ye are mad? 571
2Co 6:14 Be ye not unequally yoked together with **u**: 571

UNBELIEVING (6) [UNBELIEF]
Ac 14: 2 But the **u** Jews stirred up the Gentiles, and 544
1Co 7:14 For the **u** husband is sanctified by the wife, 571
7:14 and the **u** wife is sanctified by the husband: 571
7:15 But if the **u** depart, let him depart. A brother 571
Tit 1:15 them that are defiled and **u** *is* nothing pure; 571
Rev 21: 8 and **u**, and the abominable, and murderers, 571

UNBLAMEABLE (2) [BLAME, UNBLAMEABLY]
Col 1:22 to present you holy and **u** and 299
1Th 3:13 To the end *he* may stablish your hearts **u** in 273

UNBLAMEABLY (1) [UNBLAMEABLE]
1Th 2:10 **u** we behaved ourselves among you that 274

UNCERTAIN (2) [CERTAIN, UNCERTAINLY]
1Co 14: 8 For if the trumpet give an **u** sound, who shall 82
1Ti 6:17 nor trust in **u** riches, but in the living God, 83

UNCERTAINLY (1) [UNCERTAIN]
1Co 9:26 I therefore so run, not as **u**; so fight I, not as 84

UNCHANGEABLE (1) [CHANGE]
Heb 7:24 he continueth ever, hath an **u** priesthood. 531

UNCIRCUMCISED (43) [CIRCUMCISE, UNCIRCUMCISION]
Ge 17:14 the **u** man *child* whose flesh of his foreskin 6189
34:14 this thing, to give our sister to one that is **u**; 6190
Ex 6:12 shall Pharaoh hear me, who *am* of **u** lips? 6189
6:30 I *am* of **u** lips, and how shall Pharaoh 6189
12:48 the land: for no **u person** shall eat thereof. 6189
Lev 19:23 ye shall **count** the fruit thereof **as u**: 6188+6190
19:23 three years shall it be as **u** unto you: it shall 6189
26:41 if then their **u** hearts be humbled, and they 6189
Jos 5: 7 for they were **u**, because they had not 6189
Jdg 14: 3 that thou goest to take a wife of the **u** 6189
15:18 for thirst, and fall into the hand of the **u**? 6189
1Sa 14: 6 let us go over unto the garrison of these **u**: 6189
17:26 for who *is* this **u** Philistine, that he should 6189
17:36 this **u** Philistine shall be as one of them, 6189
31: 4 lest these **u** come and thrust me through, 6189
2Sa 1:20 lest the daughters of the **u** triumph. 6189
1Ch 10: 4 lest these **u** come and abuse me. 6189
Isa 52: 1 there shall no more come into thee the **u** 6189
Jer 6:10 their ear *is* **u**, and they cannot hearken: 6189
9:25 all *them which are* circumcised with the **u**; 6190
9:26 for all *these* nations *are* **u**, and all the house 6189
9:26 and all the house of Israel *are* **u** in the heart. 6189
Eze 28:10 Thou shalt die the deaths of the **u** by 6189
31:18 thou shalt lie in the midst of the **u** with 6189
32:19 go down, and be thou laid with the **u**. 6189
32:21 gone down, they lie **u**, slain by the sword. 6189
32:24 which are gone down **u** into the nether 6189
32:25 all of them **u**, slain by the sword: 6189
32:26 all of them **u**, slain by the sword, 6189
32:27 lie with the mighty *that are* fallen of the **u**, 6189
32:28 thou shalt be broken in the midst of the **u**, 6189
32:29 they shall lie with the **u**, and with them that 6189
32:30 they lie **u** with *them that be* slain by 6189
32:32 he shall be laid in the midst of the **u** with 6189
44: 7 **u** in heart, and uncircumcised in flesh, to be 6189
44: 7 **u** in flesh, to be in my sanctuary, to pollute 6189
44: 9 No stranger, **u** in heart, nor uncircumcised 6189
44: 9 uncircumcised in heart, nor **u** in flesh, 6189
Ac 7:51 Ye stiffnecked and **u** in heart and ears, ye do 564
11: 3 Saying, Thou wentest in to men **u**, 203+2192
Ro 4:11 of the faith which he had *yet* being **u**: 203
4:12 which he had being *yet* **u**. 203+1722
1Co 7:18 let him not **become u**. Is any called in 1986

UNCIRCUMCISION (16) [UNCIRCUMCISED]
Ro 2:25 of the law, thy circumcision is made **u**. 203
2:26 Therefore if the **u** keep the righteousness of 203
2:26 shall not his **u** be counted for circumcision? 203
2:27 And shall not **u** which is by nature, if it fulfil 203
3:30 circumcision by faith, and **u** through faith. 203
4: 9 the circumcision *only*, or upon the **u** also? 203
4:10 when he was in circumcision, or in **u**? Not in 203
4:10 Not in circumcision, but in **u**. 203
1Co 7:18 Is any called in **u**? let him not be 203
7:19 and **u** is nothing, but the keeping of 203
Gal 2: 7 when they saw that the gospel of the **u** was 203
5: 6 circumcision availeth any *thing*, nor **u**; 203
6:15 circumcision availeth any *thing*, nor **u**, 203
Eph 2:11 who are called **U** by that which is called 203
Col 2:13 dead in *your* sins and the **u** of your flesh, 203
3:11 circumcision nor **u**, barbarian, Scythian, 203

UNCLE (10) [UNCLE'S]
Lev 10: 4 the sons of Uzziel the **u** of Aaron, and 1730
25:49 Either his **u**, or his uncle's son, 1730
1Sa 10:14 Saul's **u** said unto him and to his servant, 1730
10:15 Saul's **u** said, Tell me, I pray thee, 1730
10:16 Saul said unto his **u**, He told us plainly that 1730
14:50 host *was* Abner, the son of Ner, Saul's **u**. 1730
1Ch 27:32 Also Jonathan David's **u** *was* a counseller, 1730
Est 2:15 the daughter of Abihail the **u** of Mordecai, 1730
Jer 32: 7 Hanameel the son of Shallum thine **u** *shall* 1730
Am 6:10 a man's **u** shall take him up, and he that 1730

UNCLE'S (7) [UNCLE]
Lev 20:20 if a man shall lie with his **u wife**, he hath 1733
20:20 he hath uncovered his **u** nakedness: 1730
25:49 Either his uncle, or his **u** son, may redeem 1730
Est 2: 7 up Hadassah, that *is*, Esther, his **u** daughter: 1730
Jer 32: 8 So Hanameel mine **u** son came to me in 1730
32: 9 I bought the field of Hanameel my **u** son, 1730
32:12 in the sight of Hanameel mine **u** *son*, and 1730

UNCLEAN (194) [CLEAN, UNCLEANNESS, UNCLEANNESSES]
Lev 5: 2 Or if a soul touch any **u** thing, whether *it be* 2931
5: 2 whether *it be* a carcase of an **u** beast, or a 2931
5: 2 or a carcase of **u** cattle, or the carcase of 2931
5: 2 or the carcase of **u** creeping things, and *if* it 2931
5: 2 from him; he also shall be **u**, and guilty. 2931
7:19 the flesh that toucheth any **u** *thing* shall not 2931
7:21 Moreover the soul that shall touch any **u** 2931
7:21 or *any* **u** beast, or any abominable unclean 2931
7:21 or any abominable **u** *thing*, and eat of 2931
10:10 and unholy, and between **u** and clean; 2931
11: 4 but divideth not the hoof; he *is* **u** unto you. 2931
11: 5 but divideth not the hoof; he *is* **u** unto you. 2931
11: 6 but divideth not the hoof; he *is* **u** unto you. 2931
11: 7 yet he cheweth not the cud; he *is* **u** to you. 2931
11: 8 shall ye not touch; they *are* **u** to you. 2931
11:24 for these ye shall be **u**: whosoever toucheth 2930
11:24 carcase of them shall be **u** until the even. 2930
11:25 wash his clothes, and be **u** until the even. 2930
11:26 nor cheweth the cud, *are* **u** unto you: 2931
11:26 every one that toucheth them shall be **u**. 2930
11:27 that go on *all* four, those *are* **u** unto you: 2931
11:27 whoso toucheth their carcase shall be **u** 2930
11:28 wash his clothes, and be **u** until the even: 2930
11:28 unclean until the even: they *are* **u** unto you. 2931
11:29 These also *shall be* **u** unto you among 2931
11:31 These *are* **u** to you among all that creep: 2931
11:31 they be dead, shall be **u** until the even. 2930
11:32 when they are dead, doth fall, it shall be **u**; 2930
11:32 into water, and it shall be **u** until the even; 2930
11:33 them falleth, whatsoever *is* in it shall be **u**; 2930
11:34 on which *such* water cometh shall be **u**: 2930
11:34 be drunk in every *such* vessel shall be **u**. 2930
11:35 *any part* of their carcase falleth shall be **u**; 2930
11:35 *for* they *are* **u**, and shall be unclean unto 2931
11:35 they *are* unclean, and shall be **u** unto you. 2931
11:36 that which toucheth their carcase shall be **u**. 2930
11:38 carcase fall thereon, it *shall be* **u** unto you. 2931
11:39 the carcase thereof shall be **u** until the even. 2930
11:40 wash his clothes, and be **u** until the even: 2930
11:40 wash his clothes, and be **u** until the even. 2930
11:43 neither shall ye **make** yourselves **u** with 2933
11:47 To make a difference between the **u** and 2931
12: 2 she shall be **u** seven days; according to 2930
12: 2 separation for her infirmity shall she be **u**. 2930
12: 5 she shall be **u** two weeks, as *in* her 2930
13: 3 shall look on him, and **pronounce** him **u**. 2930
13: 8 then the priest shall **pronounce** him **u**: 2930
13:11 the priest shall **pronounce** him **u**, *and* 2930
13:11 *and* shall not shut him up: for he *is* **u**. 2931
13:14 raw flesh appeareth in him, he shall be **u**. 2930
13:15 the raw flesh, and **pronounce** him to be **u**: 2930
13:15 *for* the raw flesh *is* **u**: it *is* a leprosy. 2931
13:20 the priest shall **pronounce** him **u**: 2930
13:22 then the priest shall **pronounce** him **u**: 2930
13:25 the priest shall **pronounce** him **u**: 2930
13:27 then the priest shall **pronounce** him **u**: 2930
13:30 then the priest shall **pronounce** him **u**: 2930
13:36 priest shall not seek for yellow hair: he *is* **u**. 2931
13:44 He *is* a leprous man, he *is* **u**: the priest shall 2931
13:44 shall **pronounce** him **utterly u**, 2930+2930
13:45 *his* upper lip, and shall cry, **U**, unclean. 2931
13:45 *his* upper lip, and shall cry, Unclean, **u**. 2931
13:46 *shall be* in him he shall be defiled; he *is* **u**: 2931
13:51 the plague *is* a fretting leprosy; it *is* **u**. 2931
13:55 and the plague be not spread; it *is* **u**; 2931
13:59 to pronounce it clean, or to **pronounce** it **u**. 2930
14:36 that all that *is* in the house be not *made* **u**: 2930
14:40 they shall cast them into an **u** place without 2931
14:41 scrape off without the city into an **u** place: 2931
14:44 it *is* a fretting leprosy in the house: it *is* **u**. 2931
14:45 *them* forth out of the city into an **u** place. 2931
14:46 that it is shut up shall be **u** until the even. 2930
14:57 To teach when *it is* **u**, and when *it is* clean: 2931
15: 2 out of his flesh, *because of* his issue he *is* **u**. 2931
15: 4 whereon he lieth that hath the issue, is **u**: 2930
15: 4 every thing, whereon he sitteth, shall be **u**. 2930
15: 5 *himself* in water, and be **u** until the even. 2930
15: 6 *himself* in water, and be **u** until the even. 2930
15: 7 *himself* in water, and be **u** until the even. 2930
15: 8 *himself* in water, and be **u** until the even. 2930
15: 9 rideth upon that hath the issue shall be **u**. 2930
15:10 was under him shall be **u** until the even: 2930
15:10 *himself* in water, and be **u** until the even. 2930
15:11 *himself* in water, and be **u** until the even. 2930
15:16 his flesh in water, and be **u** until the even. 2930
15:17 washed with water, and be **u** until the even. 2930
15:18 in water, and be **u** until the even. 2930
15:19 whosoever toucheth her shall be **u** until 2930
Lev 15:20 she lieth upon in her separation shall be **u**: 2930
15:20 *thing* also that she sitteth upon shall be **u**. 2930
15:21 *himself* in water, and be **u** until the even. 2930
15:22 *himself* in water, and be **u** until the even. 2930
15:23 he toucheth it, he shall be **u** until the even. 2930
15:24 be upon him, he shall be **u** seven days; 2930
15:24 and all the bed whereon he lieth shall be **u**. 2930
15:25 the days of her separation: she *shall be* **u**. 2931
15:26 whatsoever she sitteth upon shall be **u**, 2931
15:27 whosoever toucheth those *things* shall be **u**, 2930
15:27 *himself* in water, and be **u** until the even. 2930
15:33 and of him that lieth with her which is **u**. 2931
17:15 *himself* in water, and be **u** until the even: 2930
20:21 take his brother's wife, it *is* an **u thing**: 5079
20:25 put difference between clean beasts and **u**, 2931
20:25 and between **u** fowls and clean: 2931
20:25 which I have separated from you as **u**. 2930
22: 4 whoso toucheth any *thing that is* **u** *by* 2931
22: 5 whereby he may be **made u**, or a man of 2930
22: 6 hath touched *any* such shall be **u** until even, 2930
27:11 if *it be* any **u** beast, of which they do not 2931
27:27 if *it be* of an **u** beast, then he shall redeem *it* 2931
Nu 6: 7 He shall not **make** himself **u** for his father, 2930
9:10 of your posterity shall be **u** by reason of a 2931
18:15 the firstling of **u** beasts shalt thou redeem. 2931
19: 7 and the priest shall be **u** until the even. 2930
19: 8 flesh in water, and shall be **u** until the even. 2930
19:10 wash his clothes, and be **u** until the even: 2930
19:11 *body* of any man shall be **u** seven days. 2930
19:13 was not sprinkled upon him, he shall be **u**; 2931
19:14 all that *is* in the tent, shall be **u** seven days. 2930
19:15 which hath no covering bound upon it, *is* **u**. 2931
19:16 of a man, or a grave, shall be **u** seven days. 2930
19:17 for an **u** *person* they shall take of the ashes 2931
19:19 the clean *person* shall sprinkle upon the **u** 2931
19:20 the man that shall be **u**, and shall not purify 2930
19:20 hath not been sprinkled upon him; he *is* **u**. 2931
19:21 water of separation shall be **u** until even. 2930
19:22 whatsoever the **u** *person* toucheth shall be 2931
19:22 the unclean *person* toucheth shall be **u**; 2930
19:22 the soul that toucheth *it* shall be **u** until 2930
Dt 12:15 the **u** and the clean may eat thereof, as of 2931
12:22 the **u** and the clean shall eat of them alike. 2931
14: 7 not the hoof; *therefore* they *are* **u** unto you. 2931
14: 8 yet *cheweth* not the cud, it *is* **u** unto you: 2931
14:10 and scales ye may not eat; it *is* **u** unto you. 2931
14:19 every creeping thing that flieth *is* **u** unto 2931
15:22 the **u** and the clean *person shall eat it* alike, 2931
23:14 that he see no **u** thing in thee, and 6172
26:14 **u** *use*, nor given *ought* thereof for the dead: 2931
Jos 22:19 if the land of your possession *be* **u**, *then* 2931
Jdg 13: 4 nor strong drink, and eat not any **u** *thing*: 2931
13: 7 neither eat any **u** *thing*: for the child shall 2932
13:14 nor eat any **u** *thing*: all that I commanded 2932
2Ch 23:19 that none *which was* **u** in any thing should 2931
Ezr 9:11 *is* an **u** land with the filthiness of the people 5079
Job 14: 4 Who can bring a clean *thing* out of an **u**? 2931
36:14 die in youth, and their life *is* among the **u**. 6945
Ecc 9: 2 to the good and to the clean, and to the **u**; 2931
Isa 6: 5 because I *am* a man of **u** lips, and I dwell in 2931
6: 5 I dwell in the midst of a people of **u** lips: 2931
35: 8 the **u** shall not pass over it; but it *shall be* 2931
52: 1 into thee the uncircumcised and the **u**. 2931
52:11 touch no **u** *thing*; go ye out of the midst of 2931
64: 6 we are all as an **u** *thing*, and all our 2931
La 4:15 *it is* **u**; depart, depart, touch not, when they 2931
Eze 22:26 have they shewed *difference* between the **u** 2931
44:23 cause them to discern between the **u** and 2931
Hos 9: 3 and they shall eat **u** *things* in Assyria. 2931
Hag 2:13 If *one that is* **u** *by* a dead body touch any of 2931
2:13 dead body touch any of these, shall it be **u**? 2930
2:13 the priests answered and said, It shall be **u**. 2930
2:14 and *that* which they offer there *is* **u**. 2931
Zec 13: 2 and the **u** spirit to pass out of the land. 2932
Mt 10: 1 he gave them power against **u** spirits, to cast 169
12:43 When the **u** spirit is gone out of a man, 169
Mk 1:23 in their synagogue a man with an **u** spirit; 169
1:26 And when the **u** spirit had torn him, and 169
1:27 for with authority commandeth he even the **u** 169
3:11 And **u** spirits, when they saw him, fell down 169
3:30 Because they said, He hath an **u** spirit. 169
5: 2 him out of the tombs a man with an **u** spirit, 169
5: 8 Come out of the man, *thou* **u** spirit. 169
5:13 And the **u** spirits went out, and entered into 169
6: 7 two; and gave them power over **u** spirits; 169
7:25 whose young daughter had an **u** spirit, 169
Lk 4:33 which had a spirit of an **u** devil, and 169
4:36 and power he commandeth the **u** spirits, 169
6:18 And they that were vexed with **u** spirits: and 169
8:29 (For he had commanded the **u** spirit to come 169
9:42 and tare *him*. And Jesus rebuked the **u** spirit, 169
11:24 When the **u** spirit is gone out of a man, 169
Ac 5:16 and *them which were* vexed with **u** spirits: 169
8: 7 For **u** spirits, crying with loud voice, 169
10:14 never eaten any *thing that is* common or **u**. 169
10:28 that *I* should not call any man common or **u**. 169
11: 8 or **u** hath at any time entered into my mouth. 169
Ro 14:14 Lord Jesus, that *there is* nothing **u** of itself: 2839
14:14 but to him that esteemeth any *thing* to be **u**, 2839
14:14 any *thing* to be unclean, to him *it is* **u**. 2839
1Co 7:14 else were your children **u**; but now are they 169
2Co 6:17 and touch not the **u** *thing*; and I will receive 169
Eph 5: 5 nor **u** *person*, nor covetous man who is an 169
Heb 9:13 and the ashes of a heifer sprinkling the **u**, 2840
Rev 16:13 And I saw three **u** spirits like frogs *come* out 169
18: 2 and a cage of every **u** and hateful bird. 169

UNCLEANNESS (40) [UNCLEAN]
Lev 5: 3 Or if he touch the **u** of man, 2932
5: 3 whatsoever **u** *it be* that a man shall be 2932
7:20 unto the LORD, having his **u** upon him, 2932
7:21 touch any unclean *thing*, *as* the **u** of man, 2932
14:19 for him that is to be cleansed from his **u**; 2932
15: 3 this shall be his **u** in his issue: *whether* his 2932
15: 3 flesh be stopped from his issue, it *is* his **u**. 2932

Lev 15:25 all the days of the issue of her **u** shall be as 2932
15:26 shall be unclean, as the **u** of her separation. 2932
15:30 before the LORD for the issue of her **u**. 2932
15:31 separate the children of Israel from their **u**; 2932
15:31 that they die not in their **u**, when they defile 2932
16:16 because of the **u** of the children of Israel, 2932
16:16 among them in the midst of their **u**. 2932
16:19 hallow it from the **u** of the children of 2932
18:19 as long as she is put apart for her **u**. 2932
22: 3 having his **u** upon him, that soul shall be 2932
22: 5 or a man of whom he may **take u**, 2930
22: 5 take uncleanness, whatsoever **u** he hath; 2932
Nu 5:19 if thou hast not gone aside *to* **u** *with* 2932
19:13 he shall be unclean; his **u** *is* yet upon him. 2932
Dt 23:10 that is not clean by reason of **u** that NIH
24: 1 because he hath found some **u** in her: 6172
2Sa 11: 4 with her; for she was purified from her **u**: 2932
2Ch 29:16 brought out all the **u** that they found in 2932
Ezr 9:11 it from one end to another with their **u**. 2932
Eze 36:17 their way was before me as the **u** of a 2932
39:24 According to their **u** and according to their 2932
Zec 13: 1 inhabitants of Jerusalem for sin and for **u**. 5079
Mt 23:27 within full of dead *men's* bones, and of all **u**. *167*
Ro 1:24 Wherefore God also gave them up to **u** *167*
6:19 ye have yielded your members servants to **u** *167*
2Co 12:21 and have not repented of the **u** and *167*
Gal 5:19 fornication, **u**, lasciviousness, *167*
Eph 4:19 to work all **u** with greediness. *167*
5: 3 But fornication, and all **u**, or covetousness, *167*
Col 3: 5 fornication, **u**, inordinate affection, *167*
1Th 2: 3 *was* not of deceit, nor of **u**, nor in guile: *167*
4: 7 For God hath not called us unto **u**, but *167*
2Pe 2:10 that walk after the flesh in the lust of **u**, *3394*

UNCLEANNESSES (1) [UNCLEAN]

Eze 36:29 I will also save you from all your **u**: and 2932

UNCLOTHED (1) [CLOTHE]

2Co 5: 4 not for that we would be **u**, but *1562*

UNCOMELY (2) [COMELINESS]

1Co 7:36 *he* **behaveth** himself **u** toward his virgin, *807*
12:23 our **u** *parts* have more abundant comeliness. *809*

UNCONDEMNED (2) [CONDEMN]

Ac 16:37 They have beaten us openly **u**, *178*
22:25 to scourge a man *that is* a Roman, and **u**? *178*

UNCORRUPTIBLE (1) [CORRUPT, UNCORRUPTNESS]

Ro 1:23 And changed the glory of the **u** God into an *862*

UNCORRUPTNESS (1) [UNCORRUPTIBLE]

Tit 2: 7 in doctrine *shewing* **u**, gravity, sincerity, *90*

UNCOVER (26) [COVER, UNCOVERED, UNCOVERETH]

Lev 10: 6 unto Ithamar his sons, **U** not your heads, 6544
18: 6 is near of kin to him, to **u** *their* nakedness: 1540
18: 7 nakedness of thy mother, shalt thou not **u**: 1540
18: 7 thy mother; thou shalt not **u** her nakedness. 1540
18: 8 of thy father's wife shalt thou not **u**: 1540
18: 9 *even* their nakedness thou shalt not **u**. 1540
18:10 *even* their nakedness thou shalt not **u**: 1540
18:11 *is* thy sister, thou shalt not **u** her nakedness. 1540
18:12 Thou shalt not **u** the nakedness of thy 1540
18:13 Thou shalt not **u** the nakedness of thy 1540
18:14 Thou shalt not **u** the nakedness of thy 1540
18:15 Thou shalt not **u** the nakedness of thy 1540
18:15 son's wife; thou shalt not **u** her nakedness. 1540
18:16 Thou shalt not **u** the nakedness of thy 1540
18:17 Thou shalt not **u** the nakedness of a woman 1540
18:17 daughter's daughter, to **u** her nakedness; 1540
18:18 to vex *her*, to **u** her nakedness, besides 1540
18:19 approach unto a woman to **u** her nakedness, 1540
20:18 her sickness, and shall **u** her nakedness; 1540
20:19 thou shalt not **u** the nakedness of thy 1540
21:10 shall not **u** his head, nor rend his clothes; 6544
Nu 5:18 **u** the woman's head, and put the offering of 6544
Ru 3: 4 go in, and **u** his feet, and lay thee down; 1540
Isa 47: 2 **u** thy locks, make bare the leg, uncover 1540
47: 2 thy locks, make bare the leg, **u** the thigh, 1540
Zep 2:14 for he shall **u** the cedar work. 6168

UNCOVERED (17) [UNCOVER]

Ge 9:21 was drunken; and he was **u** within his tent. 1540
Lev 20:11 father's wife hath **u** his father's nakedness: 1540
20:17 he hath **u** his sister's nakedness; he shall 1540
20:18 and she hath **u** the fountain of her blood: 1540
20:20 he hath **u** his uncle's nakedness: 1540
20:21 he hath **u** his brother's nakedness; 1540
Ru 3: 7 and **u** his feet, and laid her down. 1540
2Sa 6:20 who **u** himself to day in the eyes of 1540
Isa 20: 4 and barefoot, even with *their* buttocks **u**, 2834
22: 6 of men *and* horsemen, and Kir **u** the shield. 6168
47: 3 Thy nakedness shall be **u**, yea, thy shame 1540
Jer 49:10 I have **u** his secret places, and he shall not 1540
Eze 4: 7 thine arm *shall be* **u**, and thou shalt 2834
Hab 2:16 drink thou also, and let thy **foreskin** be **u**: 6188
Mk 2: 4 for the press, they **u** the roof where he was: *648*
1Co 11: 5 prophesieth with *her* head **u** dishonoureth *177*
11:13 is it comely that a woman pray unto God **u**? *177*

UNCOVERETH (3) [UNCOVER]

Lev 20:19 for he **u** his near kin: they shall bear their 6168
Dt 27:20 because he **u** his father's skirt. 1540
2Sa 6:20 as one of the vain *fellows* **shamelessly u** 1540

UNCTION (1)

1Jn 2:20 But ye have an **u** from the Holy One, and *5545*

UNDEFILED (7) [DEFILE]

Ps 119: 1 Blessed *are* the **u** in the way, who walk in 8549
SS 5: 2 to me, my sister, my love, my dove, my **u**: 8535
6: 9 My dove, my **u** *is but* one; she *is* the *only* 8535
Heb 7:26 *who is* holy, harmless, **u**, separate from *283*
13: 4 Marriage *is* honourable in all, and the bed **u**: *283*
Jas 1:27 Pure religion and **u** before God and *283*
1Pe 1: 4 and **u**, and that fadeth not away, reserved in *283*

UNDER (392)

Ge 1: 7 divided the waters which *were* **u** 4480+8478
1: 9 Let the waters **u** the heaven be 4480+8478
6:17 *is* the breath of life, from **u** heaven; 8478
7:19 that *were* **u** the whole heaven, 8478
16: 9 and submit thyself **u** her hands. 8478
18: 4 your feet, and rest yourselves **u** the tree: 8478
18: 8 he stood by them **u** the tree, and they did 8478
19: 8 came they **u** the shadow of my roof. 871.1
21:15 and she cast the child **u** one of the shrubs. 8478
24: 2 Put, I pray thee, thy hand **u** my thigh: 8478
24: 9 the servant put his hand **u** the thigh of 8478
35: 4 Jacob hid them **u** the oak which *was* by 8478
35: 8 she was buried beneath Beth-el **u** an oak: 8478
39:23 not to any thing *that was* **u** his hand; 871.1
41:35 lay up corn **u** the hand of Pharaoh, and 8478
47:29 thy hand **u** my thigh, and deal kindly and 8478
49:25 blessings of the deep that lieth **u**, 8478
Ex 6: 6 I will bring you out from **u** the burdens of 8478
6: 7 which bringeth you out from **u** the burdens 8478
17:12 and put *it* **u** him, and he sat thereon; 8478
17:14 remembrance of Amalek from **u** heaven. 8478
18:10 who hath delivered the people from **u** 8478
20: 4 or that *is* in the water **u** the earth: 4480+8478
21:20 his maid, with a rod, and he die **u** his hand; 8478
23: 5 of him that hateth thee lying **u** his burden, 8478
24: 4 builded an altar **u** the hill, and 8478
24:10 *there was* **u** his feet as it were a paved work 8478
25:35 *there shall be* a knop **u** two branches of 8478
25:35 and a knop **u** two branches of the same, and 8478
25:35 and a knop **u** two branches of the same, 8478
26:19 thou shalt make forty sockets of silver **u** 8478
26:19 two sockets **u** one board for his two tenons, 8478
26:19 two sockets **u** another board for his two 8478
26:21 two sockets **u** one board, and two sockets 8478
26:21 and two sockets **u** another board. 8478
26:25 two sockets **u** one board, and two sockets 8478
26:25 and two sockets **u** another board. 8478
26:33 thou shalt hang up the vail **u** the taches, 8478
27: 5 thou shalt put it **u** the compass of the altar 8478
30: 4 thou make to it **u** the crown of it, 4480+8478
36:24 forty sockets of silver he made **u** the twenty 8478
36:24 two sockets **u** one board for his two tenons, 8478
36:24 two sockets **u** another board for his two 8478
36:26 two sockets **u** one board, and two sockets 8478
36:26 and two sockets **u** another board. 8478
36:30 *of* silver, **u** every board two sockets. 8478
37:21 a knop **u** two branches of the same, and 8478
37:21 and a knop **u** two branches of the same, and 8478
37:21 and a knop **u** two branches of the same, 8478
37:27 he made two rings of gold for it **u** 4480+8478
38: 4 **u** the compass thereof beneath unto 8478
Lev 15:10 whosoever toucheth any *thing* that was **u** 8478
22:27 then it shall be seven days **u** the dam; 8478
27:32 *even of* whatsoever passeth **u** the rod, 8478
Nu 3:36 **u** the custody and charge of the sons of NIH
4:28 their charge *shall be* **u** the hand of Ithamar 871.1
4:33 **u** the hand of Ithamar the son of Aaron 871.1
6:18 put *it* in the fire which *is* **u** the sacrifice of 8478
7: 8 **u** the hand of Ithamar the son of Aaron 871.1
16:31 that the ground clave asunder that *was* **u** 8478
22:27 of the LORD, she fell down **u** Balaam: 8478
31:49 of the men of war which *are* **u** our charge, 871.1
33: 1 with their armies **u** the hand of Moses 871.1
Dt 2:25 the fear of thee upon the nations *that are* **u** 8478
3:17 the salt sea, **u** Ashdoth-pisgah eastward. 8478
4:11 ye came near and stood **u** the mountain; 8478
4:19 unto all nations **u** the whole heaven. 8478
4:49 the sea of the plain, **u** the springs of Pisgah. 8478
7:24 thou shalt destroy their name from **u** 8478
9:14 and blot out their name from **u** heaven: 8478
12: 2 and upon the hills, and **u** every green tree: 8478
25:19 remembrance of Amalek from **u** heaven; 8478
28:23 and the earth that *is* **u** thee *shall be* iron. 8478
29:20 the LORD shall blot out his name from **u** 8478
Jos 7:21 in the midst of my tent, and the silver **u** it. 8478
7:22 *it was* hid in his tent, and the silver **u** it. 8478
11: 3 *to* the Hivite **u** Hermon in the land of 8478
11:17 in the valley of Lebanon **u** mount Hermon: 8478
12: 3 and from the south, **u** Ashdoth-pisgah: 8478
13: 5 from Baal-gad **u** mount Hermon unto 8478
16:10 unto this day, and serve **u** tribute. 3807.1
24:26 a great stone, and set it up there **u** an oak, 8478
Jdg 1: 7 toes cut off, gathered *their meat* **u** my table: 8478
3:16 he did gird it **u** his raiment upon his 4480+8478
3:30 So Moab was subdued that day **u** the hand 8478
4: 5 she dwelt **u** the palm tree of Deborah 8478
6:11 sat **u** an oak which *was* in Ophrah, 8478
6:19 brought *it* out unto him **u** the oak, and 413+8478
9:29 would to God this people were **u** my hand; 871.1
Ru 2:12 **u** whose wings thou art come to trust. 8478
1Sa 7:11 until *they came* **u** Beth-car. 4480+8478
14: 2 **u** a pomegranate tree which *is* in Migron: 8478
21: 3 Now therefore what is **u** thine hand? 8478
21: 4 *There is* no common bread **u** mine 413+8478
21: 8 is there not here **u** thine hand spear or 8478
22: 6 (now Saul abode in Gibeah **u** a tree in 8478
31:13 buried *them* **u** a tree at Jabesh, and 8478
2Sa 2:23 **u** the fifth *rib*, that the spear came out behind 413
3:27 smote him there **u** the fifth *rib*, that he died, NIH
4: 6 they smote him **u** the fifth *rib*: and Rechab 413
12:31 put *them* **u** saws, and under harrows of 871.1
12:31 **u** harrows of iron, and under axes of iron, 871.1
12:31 **u** axes of iron, and made them pass 871.1
18: 2 third part of the people **u** the hand of Joab, 871.1
18: 2 a third part **u** the hand of Abishai the son 871.1
18: 2 a third part **u** the hand of Ittai the Gittite. 871.1
18: 9 the mule went **u** the thick boughs of a great 8478
2Sa 18: 9 and the mule that *was* **u** him went away. 8478
22:10 came down; and darkness *was* **u** his feet. 8478
22:37 Thou hast enlarged my steps **u** me; so 8478
22:39 not arise: yea, they are fallen **u** my feet. 8478
22:40 rose up against me hast thou subdued **u** me. 8478
22:48 and that bringeth down the people **u** me, 8478
1Ki 4:25 every man **u** his vine and under his fig tree, 8478
4:25 every man under his vine and **u** his fig tree, 8478
5: 3 until the LORD put them **u** the soles of his 8478
7:24 **u** the brim of it round about *there* 4480+8478
7:30 corners thereof had undersetters: **u** 4480+8478
7:32 **u** the borders *were* four wheels; and 4480+8478
7:44 And one sea, and twelve oxen **u** the sea; 8478
8: 6 to the most holy *place*, even **u** 413+8478
13:14 of God, and found him sitting **u** an oak: 8478
14:23 on every high hill, and **u** every green tree. 8478
18:23 put no fire **u**: and I will dress the other NIH
18:23 and lay *it* on wood, and put no fire **u**: NIH
18:25 on the name of your gods, but put no fire **u**. NIH
19: 4 and came and sat down **u** a juniper tree: 8478
19: 5 as he lay and slept **u** a juniper tree, 8478
2Ki 8:20 In his days Edom revolted from **u** the hand 8478
8:22 Yet Edom revolted from **u** the hand of 8478
9:13 and put *it* **u** him on the top of the stairs, and 8478
9:33 and on the horses: and he **trode** her **u foot**. 7429
13: 5 that they went out from **u** the hand of 8478
14:27 blot out the name of Israel from **u** heaven: 8478
16: 4 and on the hills, and **u** every green tree. 8478
16:17 sea from off the brasen oxen that *were* **u** it, 8478
17: 7 from **u** the hand of Pharaoh king of Egypt, 8478
17:10 in every high hill, and **u** every green tree: 8478
1Ch 10:12 buried their bones **u** the oak in Jabesh, and 8478
17: 1 of the LORD *remaineth* **u** curtains. 8478
24:19 their manner, **u** Aaron their father, 3027+871.1
25: 2 the sons of Asaph **u** the hands of Asaph, 5921
25: 3 six, **u** the hands of their father Jeduthun, 5921
25: 6 All these *were* **u** the hands of their father 5921
26:28 whosoever had dedicated *anything, it was* **u** 5921
27:23 of them from twenty years old and **u**: 4295
2Ch 4: 3 **u** it *was* the similitude of oxen, which did 8478
4:15 One sea, and twelve oxen **u** it. 8478
5: 7 into the most holy *place*, even **u** the wings 8478
13:18 Thus the children of Israel were **brought u** 3665
21: 8 In his days the Edomites revolted from **u** 8478
21:10 So the Edomites revolted from **u** the hand 8478
21:10 also did Libnah revolt from **u** his hand; 8478
26:11 Maaseiah the ruler, **u** the hand of Hananiah, 5921
26:13 **u** their hand *was* an army, three hundred 5921
28: 4 and on the hills, and **u** every green tree. 8478
28:10 now ye purpose to **keep u** the children of 3533
31:13 *were* overseers **u** the hand of Cononiah and 4480
Ne 2:14 *there was* no place for the beast *that was* **u** 8478
8:17 made booths, and sat **u** the booths: 871.1
Job 9:13 the proud helpers do stoop **u** him. 8478
20:12 his mouth, *though* he hide it **u** his tongue; 8478
26: 5 Dead *things* are formed from **u** the waters, 8478
26: 8 and the cloud is not rent **u** them. 8478
28: 5 and **u** it is turned up as it were fire. 8478
28:24 of the earth, *and* seeth **u** the whole heaven; 8478
30: 7 **u** the nettles they were gathered together. 8478
37: 3 He directeth it **u** the whole heaven, and 8478
40:21 He lieth **u** the shady trees, in the covert of 8478
41:11 that I should repay *him? whatsoever is* **u** 8478
41:30 Sharp stones *are* **u** him: he spreadeth sharp 8478
Ps 8: 6 thou hast put all *things* **u** his feet: 8478
10: 7 fraud: **u** his tongue *is* mischief and vanity. 8478
17: 8 hide me **u** the shadow of thy wings, 871.1
18: 9 came down: and darkness *was* **u** his feet. 8478
18:36 Thou hast enlarged my steps **u** me, that my 8478
18:38 not able to rise: they are fallen **u** my feet. 8478
18:39 thou hast subdued **u** me those that rose up 8478
18:47 and subdueth the people **u** me. 8478
36: 7 the children of men put their trust **u** 871.1
44: 5 through thy name will we **tread** them **u** that 947
45: 5 *whereby* the people fall **u** thee. 8478
47: 3 He shall subdue the people **u** us, and 8478
47: 3 people under us, and the nations **u** our feet. 8478
91: 1 shall abide **u** the shadow of the Almighty. 871.1
91: 4 and **u** his wings shalt thou trust: 8478
91:13 and the dragon shalt thou **trample u feet**. 7429
106:42 they were brought into subjection **u** their 8478
140: 3 like a serpent; adder's poison *is* **u** their lips. 8478
144: 2 I trust; who subdueth my people **u** me. 8478
Pr 12:24 but the slothful shall be **u** tribute. 3807.1
22:27 why should he take away thy bed from **u** 8478
Ecc 1: 3 of all his labour which he taketh **u** the sun? 8478
1: 9 and *there is* no new *thing* **u** the sun. 8478
1:13 all *things* that are done **u** heaven: 8478
1:14 I have seen all the works that are done **u** 8478
2: 3 which they should do **u** the heaven all 8478
2:11 of spirit, and *there was* no profit **u** the sun. 8478
2:17 the work that is wrought **u** the sun *is* 8478
2:18 I hated all my labour which I *had* taken **u** 8478
2:19 where*in* I have shewed myself wise **u** 8478
2:20 of all the labour which I took **u** the sun. 8478
2:22 wherein he *hath* laboured **u** the sun? 8478
3: 1 and a time to every purpose **u** the heaven: 8478
3:16 moreover I saw **u** the sun the place of 8478
4: 1 all the oppressions that *are* done **u** the sun: 8478
4: 3 seen the evil work that is done **u** the sun. 8478
4: 7 Then I returned, and I saw vanity **u** the sun. 8478
4:15 I considered all the living which walk **u** 8478
5:13 There is a sore evil *which* I have seen **u** 8478
5:18 he taketh **u** the sun all the days of his life, 8478
6: 1 There is an evil which I have seen **u** 8478
6:12 a man what shall be after him **u** the sun? 8478
7: 6 For as the crackling of thorns **u** a pot, so 8478
8: 9 unto every work that is done **u** the sun: 8478
8:15 a man hath no better *thing* **u** the sun, 8478
8:15 of his life, which God giveth him **u** the sun. 8478
8:17 find out the work that is done **u** the sun: 8478
9: 3 among all *things* that are done **u** the sun, 8478
9: 6 for ever in any *thing* that is done **u** the sun. 8478
9: 9 which he hath given thee **u** the sun, all 8478
9: 9 in thy labour which thou takest **u** the sun. 8478

U

Ecc 9:11 I returned, and saw **u** the sun, that the race 8478
9:13 This wisdom have I seen also **u** the sun, 8478
10: 5 There is an evil *which* I have seen **u** 8478
SS 2: 3 I sat down **u** his shadow with great delight, 871.1
2: 6 His left hand *is* **u** my head, and his right 8478
4:11 honey and milk *are* **u** thy tongue; and 8478
8: 3 His left hand *should be* **u** my head, and 8478
8: 5 I raised thee up **u** the apple tree: there thy 8478
Isa 3: 6 our ruler, and *let* this ruin *be* **u** thy hand: 8478
10: 4 Without me they shall bow down **u** 8478
10: 4 the prisoners, and they shall fall **u** the slain. 8478
10:16 **u** his glory he shall kindle a burning like 8478
14:11 the worm is spread **u** thee, and the worms 8478
14:19 of the pit; as a carcase **trodden u feet**. 947
14:25 and upon my mountains **tread** him **u foot**: 947
18: 7 a nation meted out and **trodden u foot**, 4001
24: 5 The earth also is defiled **u** the inhabitants 8478
25:10 Moab shall be trodden down **u** him, *even* as 8478
28: 3 of Ephraim, shall be trodden **u** feet: 871.1
28:15 and **u** falsehood have we hid ourselves: 871.1
34:15 lay, and hatch, and gather **u** her shadow: 871.1
57: 5 Inflaming yourselves with idols **u** every 8478
57: 5 slaying the children in the valleys **u** 8478
58: 5 and ashes **u** *him?* wilt thou call this a fast, NIH
Jer 2:20 and **u** every green tree thou wanderest, 8478
3: 6 high mountain and **u** every green tree, 8478
3:13 hast scattered thy ways to the strangers **u** 8478
10:11 from the earth, and from **u** these heavens. 8460
12:10 they have **trodden** my portion **u foot**, 947
27: 8 that will not put their neck **u** the yoke of 871.1
27:11 the nations that bring their neck **u** the yoke 871.1
27:12 Bring your necks **u** the yoke of the king of 871.1
33:13 shall the flocks pass again **u** the hands of 5921
38:11 went *into* the house of the king **u** 413+8478
38:12 rotten rags **u** thine armholes under 8478
38:12 rotten rags under thine armholes **u** 4480+8478
48:45 They that fled stood **u** the shadow of 871.1
52:20 twelve brasen bulls that *were* **u** the bases, 8478
La 1:15 The Lord hath **trodden u foot** all my 5541
3:34 To crush **u** his feet all the prisoners of 8478
3:66 destroy them in anger from **u** the heavens 8478
4:20 **U** his shadow we shall live among 871.1
5: 5 Our necks *are* **u** persecution: we labour, 5921
5:13 to grind, and the children fell **u** the wood. 871.1
Eze 1: 8 *they had* the hands of a man **u** their 4480+8478
1:23 **u** the firmament *were* their wings straight, 8478
6:13 **u** every green tree, and under every thick 8478
6:13 every green tree, and **u** every thick oak, 8478
10: 2 *even* **u** the cherub, and fill thine hand *with* 8478
10: 8 the form of a man's hand **u** their wings. 8478
10:20 This *is* the living creature that I saw **u** 8478
10:21 the likeness of the hands of a man *was* **u** 8478
17: 6 and the roots thereof were **u** him: 8478
17:23 **u** it shall dwell all fowl of every wing; 8478
20:37 I will cause you to pass **u** the rod, and I will 8478
24: 5 burn also the bones **u** it, *and* make it boil 8478
31: 6 **u** his branches did all the beasts of the field 8478
31: 6 and **u** his shadow dwelt all great nations. 871.1
31:17 *that* dwelt **u** his shadow in the midst of 871.1
32:27 they have laid their swords **u** their heads, 8478
42: 9 from **u** these chambers *was* the entry on 8478
46:23 *it was* made *with* boiling places **u** 4480+8478
47: 1 waters issued out from **u** the threshold of 8478
47: 1 the waters came down from **u** from 8478
Da 4:12 the beasts of the field had shadow **u** it, and 8460
4:14 let the beasts get away from **u** it, and 8479
4:21 **u** which the beasts of the field dwelt, and 8460
7:27 the greatness of the kingdom **u** the whole 8460
8:13 and the host to be **trodden u foot**? 4823
9:12 for **u** the whole heaven hath not been done 8478
Hos 4:12 they have gone a whoring from **u** their 8478
4:13 **u** oaks and poplars and elms, because 8478
14: 7 They that dwell **u** his shadow shall return; 871.1
Joel 1:17 The seed is rotten **u** their clods, the garners 8478
Am 2:13 Behold, I am pressed **u** you, as a cart is 8478
Ob 1: 7 *they that eat* thy bread have laid a wound **u** 8478
Jnh 4: 5 him a booth, and sat **u** it in the shadow, 8478
Mic 1: 4 the mountains shall be molten **u** him, and 8478
4: 4 they shall sit every man **u** his vine and 8478
4: 4 every man under his vine and **u** his fig tree; 8478
Zec 3:10 **u** the vine and under the fig tree. 8478
3:10 under the vine and **u** the fig tree. 8478
Mal 4: 3 for they shall be ashes **u** the soles of your 8478
Mt 2:16 coasts thereof, from two years old and **u**, *2736*
5:13 cast out, and to be **trodden u foot** of men. *2662*
5:15 and put it **u** a bushel, but on a candlestick; *5259*
7: 6 lest they trample them **u** their feet, and *1722*
8: 8 I am not worthy that thou shouldest come **u** *5259*
8: 9 For I am a man **u** authority, having soldiers *5259*
8: 9 man under authority, having soldiers **u** me: *5259*
23:37 even as a hen gathereth her chickens **u** *her* *5259*
Mk 4:21 Is a candle brought to be put **u** a bushel, or *5259*
4:21 to be put under a bushel, or **u** a bed? *5259*
4:32 that the fowls of the air may lodge **u** *5259*
6:11 shake off the dust **u** your feet for a *5270*
7:28 yet the dogs **u** the table eat of the children's *5270*
Lk 7: 6 worthy that thou shouldest enter **u** my roof: *5259*
7: 8 For I also am a man set **u** authority, *5259*
7: 8 having **u** me soldiers, and I say unto one, *5259*
8:16 it with a vessel, or putteth *it* **u** a bed; *5270*
11:33 neither **u** a bushel, but on a candlestick, *5259*
13:34 as a hen *doth gather* her brood **u** *her* wings, *5259*
17:24 that lighteneth out of the one *part* **u** heaven, *5259*
17:24 shineth unto the other *part* **u** heaven; *5259*
Jn 1:48 when thou wast **u** the fig tree, I saw thee. *5259*
1:50 I saw thee **u** the fig tree, believest thou? *5270*
Ac 2: 5 devout men, out of every nation **u** heaven. *5259*
4:12 for there is none other name **u** heaven *5259*
8:27 an eunuch of great authority **u** Candace NIG
23:12 and **bound** themselves **u a curse**, *332*
23:14 have **bound** ourselves **u a great curse**, *331+332*
27: 4 we **sailed u** Cyprus, because the winds *5284*
27: 7 we **sailed u** Crete, over against Salmone; *5284*
27:16 And **running u** a certain island *which is* *5295*
27:30 **u colour** as though they would have cast *4392*

Ro 3: 9 and Gentiles, that *they* are all **u** sin; *5259*
3:13 the poison of asps *is* **u** their lips: *5259*
3:19 it saith to them who are **u** the law: *1722*
6:14 for ye are not **u** the law, but under grace. *5259*
6:14 for ye are not under the law, but **u** grace. *5259*
6:15 because we are not **u** the law, but *5259*
6:15 we are not under the law, but **u** grace? *5259*
7:14 law is spiritual: but I am carnal, sold **u** sin. *5259*
16:20 And the God of peace shall bruise Satan **u** *5259*
1Co 6:12 I will not be **brought u** the **power** of any. *1850*
7:15 or a sister is not **u bondage** in such *cases:* *1402*
9:20 to them that are **u** the law, as under the law, *5259*
9:20 to them that are under the law, as **u** the law, *5259*
9:20 that I might gain them that are **u** the law; *5259*
9:21 law to God, but **u** the **law** to Christ,) *1772*
9:27 But I **keep u** my body, and bring *it* into *5299*
10: 1 how that all our fathers were **u** the cloud, *5259*
14:34 *they are commanded* to be **u obedience**, *5293*
15:25 till he hath put all enemies **u** his feet. *5259*
15:27 For he hath put all *things* **u** his feet. *5259*
15:27 all *things* are **put u** *him, it is* manifest that *5293*
15:27 is excepted, which did **put** all *things* **u** him. *5293*
15:28 subject unto him that **put** all *things* **u** him, *5293*
2Co 11:32 In Damascus the governor **u** Aretas the king NIG
Gal 3:10 are of the works of the law are **u** the curse: *5259*
3:22 But the scripture hath concluded all **u** sin, *5259*
3:23 before faith came, we were kept **u** the law, *5259*
3:25 is come, we are no longer **u** a schoolmaster. *5259*
4: 2 But is **u** tutors and governors until the time *5259*
4: 3 were in bondage **u** the elements of *5259*
4: 4 his Son, made of a woman, made **u** the law, *5259*
4: 5 To redeem them that were **u** the law, *5259*
4:21 Tell me, ye that desire to be **u** the law, *5259*
5:18 ye be led of the Spirit, ye are not **u** the law. *5259*
Eph 1:22 And hath put all *things* **u** his feet, and *5259*
Php 2:10 and *things* in earth, and *things* **u the earth**; *2709*
Col 1:23 to every creature which is **u** heaven; *5259*
1Ti 5: 9 Let not a widow be taken into the number **u** *1640*
6: 1 Let as many servants as are **u** the yoke *5259*
Heb 2: 8 Thou hast put all *things* in subjection **u** his *5270*
2: 8 For in that *he* **put** all **in subjection u** him, *5293*
2: 8 he left nothing *that is* **not put u** him. *506*
2: 8 But now we see not yet all *things* **put u** *5293*
7:11 (for **u** it the people received the law,) *1909*
9:15 that were **u** the first testament, *1909*
10:28 Moses' law died without mercy **u** two *1909*
10:29 who hath **trodden u foot** the Son of God, *2662*
Jas 2: 3 Stand thou there, or sit here **u** my footstool: *5259*
1Pe 5: 6 therefore **u** the mighty hand of God, *5259*
Jude 1: 6 he hath reserved in everlasting chains **u** *5259*
Rev 5: 3 in heaven, nor in earth, neither **u** the earth, *5270*
5:13 and **u** the earth, and such as are in the sea, *5270*
6: 9 I saw **u** the altar the souls of them that were *5270*
11: 2 the holy city shall they **tread u foot** forty *3961*
12: 1 and the moon **u** her feet, and upon her head *5270*

UNDERGARMENT See BREECHES

UNDERGIRDING (1) [GIRD]

Ac 27:17 had taken up, they used helps, **u** the ship; *5269*

UNDERNEATH (3)

Ex 28:27 the two sides of the ephod **u**, 4295+4480+3807.1
39:20 the two sides of the ephod **u**, 4295+4480+3807.1
Dt 33:27 and **u** *are* the everlasting arms: 4480+8478

UNDERSETTERS (4)

1Ki 7:30 the four corners thereof had **u**: under 3802
7:30 under the laver *were* **u** molten, at the side 3802
7:34 *there were* four **u** to the four corners of one 3802
7:34 *and* the **u** *were* of the *very* base itself. 3802

UNDERSTAND (91) [UNDERSTANDEST, UNDERSTANDETH, UNDERSTANDING, UNDERSTOOD]

Ge 11: 7 that they may not **u** one another's speech. 8085
41:15 *that* thou canst **u** a dream to interpret it. 8085
Nu 16:30 ye shall **u** that these men have provoked 3045
Dt 9: 3 **U** therefore *this* day, that the LORD thy 3045
9: 6 **U** therefore, that the LORD thy God 3045
28:49 a nation whose tongue thou shalt not **u**; 8085
2Ki 18:26 for we **u** *it:* and talk not with us in 8085
1Ch 28:19 **made** me **u** in writing by *his* hand upon 7919
Ne 8: 3 and the women, and those that could **u**; 995
8: 7 the Levites, **caused** the people **to u** the law: 995
8: 8 the sense, and **caused** *them* **to u** the reading. 995
8:13 the scribe, even to **u** the words of the law. 7919
Job 6:24 and **cause** me **to u** wherein I have erred. 995
23: 5 and **u** what he would say unto me. 995
26:14 but the thunder of his power who can **u**? 995
32: 9 neither do the aged **u** judgment. 995
36:29 Also can *any* **u** the spreadings of the clouds, 995
Ps 14: 2 to see if there were *any* that did **u**, *and* 7919
19:12 Who can **u** *his* errors? cleanse thou me from 995
53: 2 to see if there were *any* that did **u**, that did 7919
82: 5 They know not, neither will they **u**; 995
92: 6 man knoweth not; neither doth a fool **u** this. 995
94: 8 **U**, ye brutish among the people: and 995
107:43 will observe these *things*, even they shall **u** 995
119:27 **Make** me **to u** the way of thy precepts: so 995
119:100 I **u** more than the ancients, because I keep 995
Pr 1: 6 To **u** a proverb, and the interpretation; 995
2: 5 shalt thou **u** the fear of the LORD, and 995
2: 9 shalt thou **u** righteousness, and judgment, 995
8: 5 O ye simple, **u** wisdom: and, ye fools, be ye 995
14: 8 The wisdom of the prudent *is* to **u** his way: 995
19:25 *and* he will **u** knowledge. 995
20:24 how can a man then **u** his own way? 995
28: 5 Evil men **u** not judgment: but they that seek 995
28: 5 but they that seek the LORD **u** all *things*. 995
29:19 for though he **u** he will not answer. 995
Isa 6: 9 tell this people, Hear ye indeed, but **u** not; 995
6:10 **u** *with* their heart, and convert, and 995
28: 9 whom shall he **make to u** doctrine? 995

Isa 28:19 it shall be a vexation only *to* **u** the report. 995
32: 4 The heart also of the rash shall **u** knowledge, 995
33:19 a stammering tongue, *that thou canst* not **u**. 998
36:11 for we **u** *it:* and speak not to us in the Jews' 8085
41:20 and know, and consider, and **u** together, 7919
43:10 and believe me, and **u** that I *am* he: 995
44:18 *and* their hearts, that *they* cannot **u**. 7919
56:11 and they *are* shepherds *that* cannot **u**: 995+3045
Jer 9:12 Who *is* the wise man, that may **u** this? and 995
Eze 3: 6 whose words thou canst not **u**. 8085
Da 8:16 said, Gabriel, **make** this *man* **to u** the vision. 995
8:17 he said unto me, **U**, O son of man: for at 995
9:13 turn from our iniquities, and **u** thy truth. 7919
9:23 therefore **u** the matter, and consider 995
9:25 Know therefore and **u**, *that* from the going 7919
10:11 **u** the words that I speak unto thee, and 995
10:12 first day that thou didst set thine heart to **u**, 995
10:14 Now I am come to **make** thee **u** what shall 995
11:33 they that **u** among the people shall instruct 7919
12:10 none of the wicked shall **u**; but the wise shall 995
12:10 shall understand; but the wise shall **u**. 995
Hos 4:14 therefore the people *that* doth not **u** shall fall. 995
14: 9 he shall **u** these *things?* prudent, and he shall 995
Mic 4:12 of the LORD, neither **u** they his counsel: 995
Mt 13:13 hearing they hear not, neither do they **u**. *4920*
13:14 By hearing ye shall hear, and shall not **u**; *4920*
13:15 and should **u** with *their* heart, and *4920*
15:10 and said unto them, Hear, and **u**: *4920*
15:17 Do not ye yet **u**, that whatsoever entereth in *3539*
16: 9 Do ye not yet **u**, neither remember the five *3539*
16:11 How *is it that* ye do not **u** that I spake *it* not *3539*
24:15 the holy place, (whoso readeth, let him **u**:) *3539*
Mk 4:12 and hearing they may hear, and not **u**; *4920*
7:14 Hearken unto me every one of you, and **u**: *4920*
8:17 perceive ye not yet, neither **u**? have ye your *4920*
8:21 said unto them, How *is it that* ye do not **u**? *4920*
13:14 where it ought not, (let him that readeth **u**,) *3539*
14:68 I know not, neither **u** I what thou sayest. *1987*
Lk 8:10 not see, and hearing they might not **u**. *4920*
24:45 that *they* might **u** the scriptures, *4920*
Jn 8:43 Why do ye not **u** my speech? *even* because *1097*
12:40 nor **u** with *their* heart, and be converted, *3539*
Ac 24:11 Because that thou mayest **u**, that there are *1097*
28:26 say, Hearing ye shall hear, and shall not **u**; *4920*
28:27 and **u** with *their* heart, and should be *4920*
Ro 15:21 and they that have not heard shall **u**. *4920*
1Co 12: 3 Wherefore I **give** you **to u**, that no *man* *1107*
13: 2 and **u** all mysteries, and all knowledge; *1492*
Eph 3: 4 ye may **u** my knowledge in the mystery of *3539*
Php 1:12 But I would ye should **u**, brethren, that *1097*
Heb 11: 3 Through faith we **u** that the worlds were *3539*
2Pe 2:12 speak evil of *the things* that they **u not**; *50*

UNDERSTANDEST (4) [UNDERSTAND]

Job 15: 9 know not? *what* **u** thou, which *is* not in us? 995
Ps 139: 2 mine uprising, thou **u** my thought afar off. 995
Jer 5:15 thou knowest not, neither **u** what they say. 8085
Ac 8:30 and said, **U** thou what thou readest? *1097*

UNDERSTANDETH (11) [UNDERSTAND]

1Ch 28: 9 and **u** all the imaginations of the thoughts: 995
Job 28:23 God **u** the way thereof, and he knoweth 995
Ps 49:20 Man *that is* in honour, and **u** not, is like 995
Pr 8: 9 They *are* all plain to him that **u**, and right to 995
14: 6 but knowledge *is* easy unto him that **u**. 995
Jer 9:24 glory in this, that *he* **u** and knoweth me, 7919
Mt 13:19 and **u** *it* not, then cometh the wicked one, *4920*
13:23 and **u** *it;* which also beareth fruit, and *4920*
Ro 3:11 There is none that **u**, there is none that *4920*
1Co 14: 2 for no *man* **u** *him;* howbeit in the spirit he *191*
14:16 seeing he **u** not what thou sayest? *1492*

UNDERSTANDING (160) [UNDERSTAND]

Ex 31: 3 in **u**, and in knowledge, and in all *manner* 8394
35:31 in **u**, and in knowledge, and in all *manner* 8394
36: 1 **u** to know how to work all *manner of* work 8394
Dt 1:13 **u**, and known among your tribes, and I will 995
4: 6 and your **u** in the sight of the nations, 998
4: 6 this great nation *is* a wise and **u** people. 995
32:28 of counsel, neither *is there any* **u** in them. 8394
1Sa 25: 3 *she was* a woman of good **u**, and of a 7922
1Ki 3: 9 thy servant an **u** heart to judge thy people, 8085
3:11 hast asked for thyself **u** to discern judgment; 995
3:12 lo, I have given thee a wise and an **u** heart; 995
4:29 Solomon wisdom and **u** exceeding much, 8394
7:14 **u**, and cunning to work all works in brass. 8394
1Ch 12:32 *were men* that **had u** of the times, 998+3045
22:12 Only the LORD give thee wisdom and **u**, 998
2Ch 2:12 endued with prudence and **u**, that might 998
2:13 endued with **u**, of Huram my father's, 998
26: 5 who **had u** in the visions of God: 995
Ezr 8:16 also for Joiarib, and for Elnathan, *men* of **u**. 995
8:18 God upon us they brought us a man of **u**, 7922
Ne 8: 2 and women, and all that could hear with **u**, 995
10:28 every one having knowledge, *and* **having u**; 995
Job 12: 3 I have **u** as well as you; I *am* not inferior to 3824
12:12 ancient *is* wisdom; and *in* length of days **u**. 8394
12:13 and strength, he hath counsel and **u**. 8394
12:20 and taketh *away* the **u** of the aged. 2940
17: 4 For thou hast hid their heart from **u**: 7922
20: 3 and the spirit of my **u** causeth me to answer. 998
26:12 and by his **u** he smiteth through the proud. 8394
28:12 be found? and where *is* the place of **u**? 998
28:20 and where *is* the place of **u**? 998
28:28 that *is* wisdom; and to depart from evil *is* **u**. 998
32: 8 inspiration of the Almighty **giveth** them **u**. 995
34:10 Therefore hearken unto me, ye men of **u**: 3824
34:16 If now *thou hast* **u**, hear this: hearken to 998
34:34 Let men of **u** tell me, and let a wise man 3824
38: 4 of the earth? declare, if thou hast **u**. 998
38:36 or who hath given **u** to the heart? 998
39:17 neither hath he imparted to her **u**. 998
Ps 32: 9 the horse, *or* as the mule, *which have* no **u**: 995
47: 7 King of all the earth: sing ye *praises* with **u**. 7919

U

Ps 49: 3 the meditation of my heart shall be of u. 8394
111:10 a good u have all they that do his 7922
119:34 Give me u, and I shall keep thy law; yea, 995
119:73 give me u, that I may learn thy 995
119:99 I have more u than all my teachers: for thy 7919
119:104 Through thy precepts I get u: therefore I hate 995
119:125 give me u, that I may know thy testimonies. 995
119:130 giveth light; it giveth u unto the simple. 995
119:144 is everlasting: give me u, and I shall live. 995
119:169 O LORD: give me u according to thy word. 995
147: 5 and of great power: his u is infinite. 8394
Pr 1: 2 and instruction; to perceive the words of u; 998
1: 5 a man of u shall attain unto wise counsels: 995
2: 2 unto wisdom, and apply thine heart to u; 8394
2: 3 and liftest up thy voice for u; 8394
2: 6 out of his mouth cometh knowledge and u. 8394
2:11 shall preserve thee, u shall keep thee: 8394
3: 4 and good u in the sight of God and man. 7922
3: 5 thine heart; and lean not unto thine own u. 998
3:13 findeth wisdom, and the man that getteth u. 8394
3:19 by u hath he established the heavens. 8394
4: 1 instruction of a father, and attend to know u. 998
4: 5 Get wisdom, get u: forget it not; 998
4: 7 get wisdom: and with all thy getting get u. 998
5: 1 my wisdom, and bow thine ear to my u: 8394
6:32 adultery with a woman lacketh u: 3820
7: 4 art my sister; and call u thy kinswoman: 998
7: 7 among the youths, a young man void of u, 3820
8: 1 not wisdom cry? and u put forth her voice? 8394
8: 5 and, ye fools, be ye of an u heart. 995
8:14 and sound wisdom: I am u; I have strength. 998
9: 4 as for him that wanteth u, she saith to him, 3820
9: 6 the foolish, and live; and go in the way of u. 998
9:10 and the knowledge of the holy is u. 998
9:16 as for him that wanteth u, she saith to him, 3820
10:13 In the lips of him that hath u wisdom is 995
10:13 rod is for the back of him that is void of u. 3820
10:23 do mischief: but a man of u hath wisdom. 8394
11:12 but a man of u holdeth his peace. 8394
12:11 he that followeth vain persons is void of u. 3820
13:15 Good u giveth favour: but the way of 7922
14:29 He that is slow to wrath is of great u: but 8394
14:33 resteth in the heart of him that hath u: 995
15:14 The heart of him that hath u seeketh 995
15:21 but a man of u walketh uprightly. 8394
15:32 but he that heareth reproof getteth u. 3820
16:16 and to get u rather to be chosen than silver! 998
16:22 U is a wellspring of life unto him that hath 7922
17:18 A man void of u striketh hands, and 3820
17:24 Wisdom is before him that hath u; but 995
17:27 and a man of u is of an excellent spirit. 8394
17:28 that shutteth his lips is esteemed a man of u. 995
18: 2 A fool hath no delight in u, but that his 8394
19: 8 own soul: he that keepeth u shall find good. 8394
19:25 reprove one that hath u, and he will 995
20: 5 deep water; but a man of u will draw it out. 8394
21:16 The man that wandereth out of the way of u 7919
21:30 There is no wisdom nor u nor counsel 8394
23:23 it not; also wisdom, and instruction, and u. 998
24: 3 a house builded; and by u it is established: 8394
24:30 by the vineyard of the man void of u; 3820
28: 2 by a man of u and knowledge the state 995
28:11 but the poor that hath u searcheth him out. 995
28:16 The prince that wanteth u is also a great 8394
30: 2 than any man, and have not the u of a man. 998
Ecc 9:11 bread to the wise, nor yet riches to men of u, 995
Isa 11: 2 the spirit of wisdom and u, the spirit of 998
11: 3 shall make him of quick u in the fear of 7306
27:11 for it is a people of no u: therefore he that 998
29:14 and the u of their prudent men shall be hid. 998
29:16 say of him that framed it, He had no u? 995
29:24 that erred in spirit shall come to u, 998+3045
40:14 and shewed to him the way of u? 8394
40:28 is weary? there is no searching of his u. 8394
44:19 neither is there knowledge nor u to say, 8394
Jer 3:15 shall feed you with knowledge and u. 7919
4:22 are sottish children, and they have none u: 995
5:21 now this, O foolish people, and without u; 3820
51:15 and hath stretched out the heaven by his u. 8394
Eze 28: 4 with thine u thou hast gotten thee riches, 8394
Da 1: 4 u science, and such as had ability in them to 995
1:17 and Daniel had u in all visions and dreams. 995
1:20 in all matters of wisdom and u, that the king 998
2:21 and knowledge to them that know u: 999
4:34 mine u returned unto me, and I blessed 4486
5:11 days of thy father light and u and wisdom, 7924
5:12 knowledge, and u, interpreting of dreams, 7924
5:14 that light and u and excellent wisdom is 7924
8:23 and u dark sentences, shall stand up. 995
9:22 I am now come forth to give thee skill and u. 998
10: 1 the thing, and had u of the vision. 998
11:35 some of them of u shall fall, to try them, 7919
Hos 13: 2 and idols according to their own u, all of it 8394
Ob 1: 7 a wound under thee: there is none u in him. 8394
1: 8 of Edom, and u out of the mount of Esau? 8394
Mt 15:16 And Jesus said, Are ye also yet without u? 801
Mk 7:18 saith unto them, Are ye so without u also? 801
12:33 and with all the u, and with all the soul, and 4907
Lk 1: 3 having had perfect u of all things from 3877
2:47 all that heard him were astonished at his u 4907
24:45 Then opened he their u, that they might 3563
Ro 1:31 Without u, covenant-breakers, 801
1Co 1:19 will bring to nothing the u of the prudent. 4907
14:14 my spirit prayeth, but my u is unfruitful. 3563
14:15 the spirit, and will pray with the u also: 3563
14:15 the spirit, and I will sing with the u also. 3563
14:19 I had rather speak five words with my u, 3563
14:20 Brethren, be not children in u: howbeit in 5424
14:20 in malice be ye children, but in u be men. 5424
Eph 1:18 The eyes of your u being enlightened; 1271
4:18 Having the u darkened, being alienated 1271
5:17 but u what the will of the Lord is. 4920
Php 4: 7 which passeth all u, shall keep your hearts 3563
Col 1: 9 of his will in all wisdom and spiritual u; 4907
2: 2 unto all riches of the full assurance of u, 4907
1Ti 1: 7 u neither what they say, nor whereof they 3539
2Ti 2: 7 and the Lord give thee u in all things. 4907
1Jn 5:20 and hath given us an u, that we may know 1271
Rev 13:18 Let him that hath u count the number of 3563

UNDERSTOOD (37) [UNDERSTAND]

Ge 42:23 they knew not that Joseph u them; for he 8085
Dt 32:29 O that they were wise, that they u this, 7919
1Sa 4: 6 they u that the ark of the LORD was come 3045
26: 4 and u that Saul was come in very deed. 3045
2Sa 3:37 all Israel u that day that it was not of 3045
Ne 8:12 they had u the words that were declared unto 995
13: 7 u of the evil that Eliashib did for Tobiah, 995
Job 13: 1 seen all this, mine ear hath heard and u it. 995
42: 3 therefore have I uttered that I u not; 995
Ps 73:17 into the sanctuary of God; then u I their end. 995
81: 5 where I heard a language that I u not. 3045
106: 7 Our fathers u not thy wonders in Egypt; 7919
Isa 40:21 have ye not u from the foundations of 995
44:18 They have not known nor u: for he hath shut 995
Da 8:27 I was astonished at the vision, but none u it. 995
9: 2 In the first year of his reign I Daniel u by 995
10: 1 he u the thing, and had understanding of 995
12: 8 I heard, but I u not: then said I, O my lord, 995
Mt 13:51 Have ye u all these things? They say unto 4920
16:12 Then u they how that he bade them not 4920
17:13 Then the disciples u that he spake unto 4920
26:10 When Jesus u it, he said unto them, 1097
Mk 9:32 But they u not that saying, and were afraid to 50
Lk 2:50 And they u not the saying which he spake 4920
9:45 But they u not this saying, and it was hid 50
18:34 And they u none of these things: and 4920
Jn 8:27 They u not that he spake to them of 1097
10: 6 they u not what things they were which he 1097
12:16 These things u not his disciples at the first: 1097
Ac 7:25 For he supposed his brethren would have u 4920
7:25 hand would deliver them: but they u not. 4920
23:27 having u that he was a Roman. 3129
23:34 and when he u that he was of Cilicia; 4441
Ro 1:20 being u by the things that are made, 3539
1Co 13:11 I spake as a child, I u as a child, I thought 5426
14: 9 ye utter by the tongue words easy to be u, 2154
2Pe 3:16 in which are some things hard to be u, 1425

UNDERTAKE (1) [UNDERTOOK]

Isa 38:14 O LORD, I am oppressed; u for me. 6148

UNDERTOOK (1) [UNDERTAKE]

Est 9:23 the Jews u to do as they had begun, and 6901

UNDO (2) [DO, UNDONE]

Isa 58: 6 to u the heavy burdens, and to let 5425
Zep 3:19 that time I will u all that afflict thee: 854+6213

UNDONE (5) [UNDO]

Nu 21:29 thou art u, O people of Chemosh: he hath given 6
Jos 11:15 he left nothing u of all that the LORD 5493
Isa 6: 5 for I am u; because I am a man of unclean 1820
Mt 23:23 ye to have done, and not to leave the other u. 863
Lk 11:42 ye to have done, and not to leave the other u. 863

UNDRESSED (2) [DRESS]

Lev 25: 5 neither gather the grapes of thy vine u: 5139
25:11 nor gather the grapes in it of thy vine u. 5139

UNEQUAL (2) [EQUAL, UNEQUALLY]

Eze 18:25 my way equal? are not your ways u? 3808+8505
18:29 ways equal? are not your ways u? 3808+8505

UNEQUALLY (1) [UNEQUAL]

2Co 6:14 Be ye not u yoked together with 2086

UNFAILING LOVE See LOVINGKINDNESS

UNFAITHFUL (1) [FAITH, UNFAITHFULLY]

Pr 25:19 Confidence in an u man in time of trouble is 898

UNFAITHFULLY (1) [UNFAITHFUL]

Ps 78:57 turned back, and dealt u like their fathers: 898

UNFAITHFULNESS See WHOREDOM

UNFEIGNED (4) [FEIGN]

2Co 6: 6 by kindness, by the Holy Ghost, by love u, 505
1Ti 1: 5 and of a good conscience, and of faith u: 505
2Ti 1: 5 When I call to remembrance the u faith that 505
1Pe 1:22 the Spirit unto u love of the brethren, 505

UNFIT See REPROBATE; REPROBATES

UNFORGIVING See TRUCEBREAKERS

UNFORMED See UNPERFECT

UNFRUITFUL (6) [FRUIT]

Mt 13:22 choke the word, and he becometh u. 175
Mk 4:19 choke the word, and it becometh u. 175
1Co 14:14 my spirit prayeth, but my understanding is u. 175
Eph 5:11 And have no fellowship with the u works of 175
Tit 3:14 works for necessary uses, that they be not u. 175
2Pe 1: 8 u in the knowledge of our Lord Jesus Christ. 175

UNGIRDED (1) [GIRD]

Ge 24:32 he u his camels, and gave straw and 6605

UNGODLINESS (4) [GOD, UNGODLY]

Ro 1:18 of God is revealed from heaven against all u 763
11:26 and shall turn away u from Jacob: 763
2Ti 2:16 for they will increase unto more u. 763
Tit 2:12 Teaching us that denying u and worldly lusts 763

UNGODLY (27) [UNGODLINESS]

2Sa 22: 5 the floods of u men made me afraid; 1100
2Ch 19: 2 Shouldest thou help the u, and love them 7563
Job 16:11 God hath delivered me to the u, and 5760
34:18 Thou art wicked? and to princes, Ye are u? 7563
Ps 1: 1 that walketh not in the counsel of the u, 7563
1: 4 The u are not so: but are like the chaff 7563
1: 5 Therefore the u shall not stand in 7563
1: 6 but the way of the u shall perish. 7563
3: 7 thou hast broken the teeth of the u. 7563
18: 4 and the floods of u men made me afraid. 1100
43: 1 plead my cause against an u nation: 2623+3808
73:12 Behold, these are the u, who prosper in 7563
Pr 16:27 An u man diggeth up evil: and in his lips 1100
19:28 An u witness scorneth judgment: and 1100
Ro 4: 5 but believeth on him that justifieth the u, 765
5: 6 in due time Christ died for the u. 765
1Ti 1: 9 for the u and for sinners, for unholy and 765
1Pe 4:18 where shall the u and the sinner appear? 765
2Pe 2: 5 in the flood upon the world of the u; 765
2: 6 ensample unto those that after should live u; 764
3: 7 the day of judgment and perdition of u men. 765
Jude 1: 4 u men, turning the grace of our God into 765
1:15 to convince all that are u among them of all 765
1:15 u deeds which they have ungodly 763
1:15 deeds which they have u committed, 764
1:15 of all their hard speeches which u sinners 765
1:18 who should walk after their own u lusts. 763

UNGRATEFUL See UNTHANKFUL

UNHOLY (4) [HOLY]

Lev 10:10 ye may put difference between holy and u, 2455
1Ti 1: 9 and for sinners, for u and profane, 462
2Ti 3: 2 disobedient to parents, unthankful, u, 462
Heb 10:29 an u thing, and hath done despite unto 2839

UNICORN (6) [UNICORNS]

Nu 23:22 he hath as it were the strength of an u. 7214
24: 8 he hath as it were the strength of an u: 7214
Job 39: 9 Will the u be willing to serve thee, or 7214
39:10 Canst thou bind the u with his band in 7214
Ps 29: 6 a calf; Lebanon and Sirion like a young u. 7214
92:10 horn shalt thou exalt like the horn of an u: 7214

UNICORNS (3) [UNICORN]

Dt 33:17 and his horns are like the horns of u: 7214
Ps 22:21 thou hast heard me from the horns of the u. 7214
Isa 34: 7 the u shall come down with them, and 7214

UNINTENTIONALLY See UNAWARES

UNITE (1) [UNITED, UNITY]

Ps 86:11 in thy truth: u my heart to fear thy name. 3161

UNITED (1) [UNITE]

Ge 49: 6 their assembly, mine honour, be not thou u: 3161

UNITY (3) [UNITE]

Ps 133: 1 it is for brethren to dwell together in u. 3162
Eph 4: 3 Endeavouring to keep the u of the Spirit in 1775
4:13 Till we all come in the u of the faith, and 1775

UNJUST (17) [JUST, UNJUSTLY]

Ps 43: 1 O deliver me from the deceitful and u man. 5766
Pr 11: 7 and the hope of u men perisheth. 205
28: 8 and u gain increaseth his substance, 8636
29:27 An u man is an abomination to the just: and 5766
Zep 3: 5 he faileth not; but the u knoweth no shame. 5767
Mt 5:45 and sendeth rain on the just and on the u. 94
Lk 16: 8 And the lord commended the u steward, 93
16:10 he that is u in the least is unjust also in much. 94
16:10 he that is unjust in the least is u also in much. 94
18: 6 the Lord said, Hear what the u judge saith. 93
18:11 u, adulterers, or even as this publican. 94
Ac 24:15 of the dead, both of the just and u. 94
1Co 6: 1 go to law before the u, and not before 94
1Pe 3:18 the just for the u, that he might bring us to 94
2Pe 2: 9 to reserve the u unto the day of judgment to 94
Rev 22:11 He that is u, let him be unjust still: and 91
22:11 He that is unjust, let him be u still: and 91

UNJUSTLY (2) [UNJUST]

Ps 82: 2 How long will ye judge u, and accept 5766
Isa 26:10 in the land of uprightness will he deal u, 5765

UNKNOWN (9) [KNOW]

Ac 17:23 altar with this inscription, TO THE U GOD. 57
1Co 14: 2 For he that speaketh in an u tongue NIG
14: 4 He that speaketh in an u tongue edifieth NIG
14:13 Wherefore let him that speaketh in an u NIG
14:14 For if I pray in an u tongue, my spirit NIG
14:19 than ten thousand words in an u tongue. NIG
14:27 If any man speak in an u tongue, let it be by NIG
2Co 6: 9 As u, and yet well known; as dying, and 50
Gal 1:22 And was u by face unto the churches of Judea 50

UNLADE (1) [LADE]

Ac 21: 3 for there the ship was to u her burden. 670

UNLAWFUL (2) [LAW]

Ac 10:28 Ye know how that it is an u thing for a man 111
2Pe 2: 8 soul from day to day with their u deeds;) 459

UNLEARNED (6) [LEARN]

Ac 4:13 and perceived that they were u and 62
1Co 14:16 of the u say Amen at thy giving of thanks, 2399
14:23 and there come in those that are u, or 2399
14:24 or one u, he is convinced of all, he is 2399
2Ti 2:23 But foolish and u questions avoid, 521
2Pe 3:16 which they that are u and unstable wrest, 261

UNLEAVENED (61) [LEAVEN]

Ge 19: 3 and did bake u bread, and they did eat. 4682
Ex 12: 8 in that night, roast with fire, and u bread; 4682

U

Ex 12:15 Seven days shall ye eat **u bread**; even 4682
12:17 ye shall observe the *feast of* **u bread**; for in 4682
12:18 ye shall eat **u bread**, until the one and 4682
12:20 in all your habitations shall ye eat **u bread**. 4682
12:39 they baked **u** cakes of the dough which 4682
13: 6 Seven days thou shalt eat **u bread**, and 4682
13: 7 **U bread** shall be eaten seven days; and 4682
23:15 Thou shalt keep the feast of **u bread**: 4682
23:15 thou shalt eat **u bread** seven days, as I 4682
29: 2 **u** bread, and cakes unleavened tempered 4682
29: 2 cakes **u** tempered with oil, and 4682
29: 2 with oil, and wafers **u** anointed with oil: 4682
29:23 one wafer out of the basket of the **u bread** 4682
34:18 The feast of **u bread** shalt thou keep: 4682
34:18 seven days thou shalt eat **u bread**, as I 4682
Lev 2: 4 *it shall be* **u** cakes of fine flour mingled 4682
2: 4 with oil, or **u** wafers anointed with oil. 4682
2: 5 it shall be *of* fine flour **u**, mingled with oil. 4682
6:16 *with* **u bread** shall it be eaten in the holy 4682
7:12 of thanksgiving **u** cakes mingled with oil, 4682
7:12 **u** wafers anointed with oil, and 4682
8: 2 and two rams, and a basket of **u bread**; 4682
8:26 out of the basket of **u bread**, that *was* 4682
8:26 he took one **u** cake, and a cake of oiled 4682
23: 6 *is* the feast of **u bread** unto the LORD: 4682
23: 6 seven days ye must eat **u bread**. 4682
Nu 6:15 a basket of **u bread**, cakes *of* fine flour 4682
6:15 wafers of **u bread** anointed with oil, and 4682
6:17 the LORD, with the basket of **u bread**: 4682
6:19 one **u** cake out of the basket, and 4682
6:19 one **u** wafer, and shall put *them* upon 4682
9:11 *and* eat it with **u bread** and bitter *herbs*. 4682
28:17 seven days shall **u bread** be eaten. 4682
Dt 16: 3 seven days shalt thou eat **u bread** 4682
16: 8 Six days thou shalt eat **u bread**: and on 4682
16:16 in the feast of **u bread**, and in the feast of 4682
Jos 5:11 **u** *cakes*, and parched *corn* in the selfsame 4682
Jdg 6:19 a kid, and **u** *cakes of* an ephah of flour: 4682
6:20 Take the flesh and the **u** *cakes*, and 4682
6:21 touched the flesh and the **u** *cakes*; and 4682
6:21 the **u** *cakes*. Then the angel of the LORD 4682
1Sa 28:24 kneaded *it*, and did bake **u bread** thereof: 4682
2Ki 23: 9 they did eat of the **u bread** among their 4682
1Ch 23:29 for the **u** cakes, and for *that which is baked* 4682
2Ch 8:13 *even* in the feast of **u bread**, and in 4682
30:13 the feast of **u bread** in the second month, 4682
30:21 of **u bread** seven days with great gladness: 4682
35:17 and the feast of **u bread** seven days. 4682
Ezr 6:22 kept the feast of **u bread** seven days with 4682
Eze 45:21 feast of seven days; **u bread** shall be eaten. 4682
Mt 26:17 Now the first *day* of the *feast of* **u bread** *106*
Mk 14: 1 *the feast of* the passover, and *of* **u bread**: *106*
14:12 And the first day of **u bread**, when they *106*
Lk 22: 1 Now the feast of **u bread** drew nigh, *106*
22: 7 Then came the day of **u bread**, when *106*
Ac 12: 3 Peter also. (Then were the days of **u bread**.) *106*
20: 6 from Philippi after the days of **u bread**, *106*
1Co 5: 7 that ye may be a new lump, as ye are **u**. *106*
5: 8 but with the **u bread** of sincerity and truth. *106*

UNLESS (8)

Lev 22: 6 shall not eat of the holy *things*, **u** he 518+3588
Nu 22:33 **u** she had turned from me, surely now also I 194
2Sa 2:27 **u** thou hadst spoken, surely then 3588+3884
Ps 27:13 *I had fainted*, **u** I had believed to see 3884
94:17 **U** the LORD *had been* my help, my soul 3884
119:92 **U** thy law *had been* my delights, I should 3884
Pr 4:16 taken away, **u** they cause *some* to fall. 518+3808
1Co 15: 2 **u** ye have believed in vain. *1487+1622+3361*

UNLOAD See UNLADE

UNLOADED See UNGIRDED

UNLOOSE (3) [LOOSE]

Mk 1: 7 shoes I am not worthy to stoop down and **u**. *3089*
Lk 3:16 of whose shoes I am not worthy to **u**: *3089*
Jn 1:27 whose shoe's latchet I am not worthy to **u**. *3089*

UNMARRIED (4) [MARRY]

1Co 7: 8 I say therefore to the **u** and widows, It is good *22*
7:11 let her remain **u**, or be reconciled to *her* *22*
7:32 He *that is* **u** careth for the *things* that belong *22*
7:34 The **u** *woman* careth for the *things* of *22*

UNMERCIFUL (1) [MERCY]

Ro 1:31 without natural affection, implacable, **u**: *415*

UNMINDFUL (1) [MIND]

Dt 32:18 Of the Rock *that* begat thee thou art **u**, and 7876

UNMOVEABLE (2) [MOVE]

Ac 27:41 and remained **u**, but the hinder part was *761*
1Co 15:58 my beloved brethren, be ye stedfast, **u**, *277*

UNNI (3)

1Ch 15:18 **U**, Eliab, and Benaiah, and Maaseiah, and 6042
15:20 **U**, and Eliab, and Maaseiah, and Benaiah, 6042
Ne 12: 9 Also Bakbukiah and **U**, their brethren, *were* 6042

UNOCCUPIED (1) [OCCUPY]

Jdg 5: 6 the highways were **u**, and the travellers 2308

UNPERFECT (1) [PERFECT]

Ps 139:16 eyes did see my **substance**, **yet being u**; 1564

UNPLOWED See FALLOW

UNPOSSIBLE (4) [IMPOSSIBLE, POSSIBLE]

Mt 17:20 and nothing shall be **u** unto you. *101*
19:26 and said unto them, With men this is **u**; *102*
Lk 1:37 For with God nothing shall be **u**. *101*
18:27 The *things which are* **u** with men are *102*

UNPREPARED (1) [PREPARE]

2Co 9: 4 and find you **u**, we (that we say not, you) *532*

UNPRESENTABLE See UNCOMELY

UNPROFITABLE (7) [PROFIT, UNPROFITABLENESS]

Job 15: 3 Should he reason *with* **u** talk? or 3808
Mt 25:30 And cast ye the **u** servant into outer *888*
Lk 17:10 are commanded you, say, We are **u** servants: *888*
Ro 3:12 out of the way, they are together become **u**; *889*
Tit 3: 9 about the law; for they are **u** and vain. *512*
Phm 1:11 Which in time past was to thee **u**, but *890*
Heb 13:17 and not with grief: for that *is* **u** for you. *255*

UNPROFITABLENESS (1) [UNPROFITABLE]

Heb 7:18 going before for the weakness and **u** thereof. *512*

UNPUNISHED (11) [PUNISH]

Pr 11:21 *join* in hand, the wicked shall not be **u**: 5352
16: 5 *though* hand *join* in hand, he shall not be **u**. 5352
17: 5 he that is glad at calamities shall not be **u**. 5352
19: 5 A false witness shall not be **u**, and *he that* 5352
19: 9 A false witness shall not be **u**, and *he that* 5352
Jer 25:29 and should ye be **utterly u**? 5352+5352
25:29 Ye shall not be **u**: for I *will* call for a sword 5352
30:11 and will not **leave** thee **altogether u**. 5352+5352
46:28 yet will I not **leave** thee **wholly u**. 5352+5352
49:12 thou he *that* shall **altogether go u**? 5352+5352
49:12 thou shalt not **go u**, but thou shalt surely 5352

UNQUENCHABLE (2) [QUENCH]

Mt 3:12 but will burn up the chaff with **u** fire. *762*
Lk 3:17 but the chaff he will burn with fire **u**. *762*

UNREASONABLE (2) [REASON]

Ac 25:27 For it seemeth to me **u** to send a prisoner, *249*
2Th 3: 2 And that we may be delivered from **u** and *824*

UNREBUKEABLE (1) [REBUKE]

1Ti 6:14 **u**, until the appearing of our Lord Jesus *423*

UNREPENTANT See IMPENITENT

UNREPROVEABLE (1) [REPROVE]

Col 1:22 you holy and unblameable and **u** in his sight: *410*

UNRIGHTEOUS (9) [RIGHT, UNRIGHTEOUSLY, UNRIGHTEOUSNESS]

Ex 23: 1 hand with the wicked to be an **u** witness. 2555
Job 27: 7 and he that riseth up against me as the **u**. 5767
Ps 71: 4 out of the hand of the **u** and cruel *man*. 5765
Isa 10: 1 Woe unto them that decree **u** decrees, and 205
55: 7 forsake his way, and the **u** man his thoughts: 205
Lk 16:11 ye have not been faithful in the **u** mammon, *94*
Ro 3: 5 *Is* God **u** who taketh vengeance? (I speak as a *94*
1Co 6: 9 Know ye not that the **u** shall not inherit *94*
Heb 6:10 For God *is* not **u** to forget your work and *94*

UNRIGHTEOUSLY (1) [UNRIGHTEOUS]

Dt 25:16 all that do such *things, and* all that do **u**, 5766

UNRIGHTEOUSNESS (21) [UNRIGHTEOUS]

Lev 19:15 Ye shall do no **u** in judgment: thou shalt 5766
19:35 Ye shall do no **u** in judgment, in meteyard, 5766
Ps 92:15 *he is* my rock, and *there is* no **u** in him. 5766
Jer 22:13 him that buildeth his house by **u**, 3808+6664
Lk 16: 9 to yourselves friends of the mammon of **u**; *93*
Jn 7:18 sent him, the same is true, and no **u** is in him. *93*
Ro 1:18 heaven against all ungodliness and **u** of men, *93*
1:18 of men, who hold the truth in **u**; *93*
1:29 Being filled with all **u**, fornication, *93*
2: 8 the truth, but obey **u**, indignation and wrath, *93*
3: 5 But if our **u** commend the righteousness of *93*
6:13 ye your members *as* instruments of **u** unto sin: *93*
9:14 we say then? *Is there* **u** with God? God forbid. *93*
2Co 6:14 what fellowship hath righteousness with **u**? *458*
2Th 2:10 And with all deceivableness of **u** in them that *93*
2:12 believed not the truth, but had pleasure in **u**. *93*
Heb 8:12 For I will be merciful to their **u**, and their sins *93*
2Pe 2:13 And shall receive the reward of **u**, *as* they that *93*
2:15 *the son* of Bosor, who loved the wages of **u**; *93*
1Jn 1: 9 us *our* sins, and to cleanse us from all **u**. *93*
5:17 All **u** is sin: and there is a sin not unto death. *93*

UNRIPE (1) [RIPE]

Job 15:33 He shall shake off his **u grape** as the vine, 1154

UNRULY (4)

1Th 5:14 exhort you, brethren, warn *them that are* **u**, *813*
Tit 1: 6 faithful children not accused of riot or **u**. *506*
1:10 For there are many **u** and vain talkers and *506*
Jas 3: 8 *it is* an **u** evil, full of deadly poison. *183*

UNSANDALED See SHOE; SHOE'S; SHOES

UNSATIABLE (1) [SATIATE]

Eze 16:28 the Assyrians, because thou wast **u**; 1115+7654

UNSAVOURY (2) [SAVOUR]

2Sa 22:27 with the froward thou wilt **shew** thyself **u**. 6617
Job 6: 6 Can **that which is u** be eaten without salt? 8602

UNSCHOOLED See UNLEARNED

UNSEARCHABLE (5) [SEARCH]

Job 5: 9 Which doeth great *things* and **u**; 369+2714
Ps 145: 3 to be praised; and his greatness *is* **u**. 369+2714
Pr 25: 3 for depth, and the heart of kings *is* **u**. 369+2714
Ro 11:33 how **u** *are* his judgments, and his ways past *419*
Eph 3: 8 *I* should preach among the Gentiles the **u** *421*

UNSEEMLY (2) [SEEM]

Ro 1:27 men with men working that which is **u**, and *808*
1Co 13: 5 Doth not **behave** itself **u**, seeketh not her *807*

UNSHOD (1) [SHOD]

Jer 2:25 Withhold thy foot from being **u**, and 3182

UNSKILFUL (1) [SKILL]

Heb 5:13 For every one that useth milk *is* **u** in *552*

UNSPEAKABLE (3) [SPEAK]

2Co 9:15 Thanks *be* unto God for his **u** gift. *411*
12: 4 and heard **u** words, which *it is* not lawful for *731*
1Pe 1: 8 ye rejoice with joy **u** and full of glory: *412*

UNSPIRITUAL See CARNAL

UNSPOTTED (1) [SPOT]

Jas 1:27 *and* to keep himself **u** from the world. *784*

UNSTABLE (4) [STABLE]

Ge 49: 4 **U** as water, thou shalt not excel; because 6349
Jas 1: 8 A double minded man *is* **u** in all his ways. *182*
2Pe 2:14 cannot cease from sin; beguiling **u** souls: *793*
3:16 which *they that are* unlearned and **u** wrest, *793*

UNSTOPPED (1) [STOP]

Isa 35: 5 and the ears of the deaf shall be **u**. 6605

UNTAKEN (1) [TAKE]

2Co 3:14 **u away** in the reading of the old *343+3361*

UNTEMPERED (5) [TEMPER]

Eze 13:10 and lo, others daubed it *with* **u** *morter:* 8602
13:11 Say unto them which daub *it with* **u** *morter,* 8602
13:14 the wall that ye have daubed *with* **u** *morter,* 8602
13:15 upon them that have daubed it *with* **u** 8602
22:28 her prophets have daubed them *with* **u** 8602

UNTENDED See UNDRESSED

UNTHANKFUL (2) [THANK]

Lk 6:35 for he is kind unto the **u** and *to the* evil. *884*
2Ti 3: 2 disobedient to parents, **u**, unholy, *884*

UNTIL (366)

Ge 8: 5 the waters decreased continually **u** 5704+2050.1
8: 7 **u** the waters were dried up from off 5704
24:19 **u** they have done drinking. 518+5704
24:33 will not eat, **u** I have told mine errand. 518+5704
26:13 grew **u** he became very great: 3588+5704
27:44 **u** thy brother's fury turn away; 834+5704
27:45 **U** thy brother's anger turn away from thee, 5704
28:15 **u** I have done *that* which I have 518+834+5704
29: 8 **u** all the flocks be gathered together, 834+5704
32: 4 with Laban, and stayed *there* **u** now: 5704
32:24 there wrestled a man with him **u** 5704
33: 3 seven times, **u** he came near to his brother. 5704
33:14 **u** I come unto my lord unto Seir. 834+5704
34: 5 and Jacob held his peace **u** they were come. 5704
39:16 his garment by her, **u** his lord came home. 5704
41:49 very much, **u** he left numbering; 3588+5704
46:34 about cattle from our youth even **u** now, 5704
49:10 between his feet, **u** Shiloh come; 3588+5704
Ex 9:18 since the foundation thereof even **u** now. 5704
10:26 must serve the LORD, **u** we come thither. 5704
12: 6 ye shall keep it *up* **u** the fourteenth day of 5704
12:10 ye shall let nothing of it remain **u** 5704
12:10 that which remaineth of it **u** the morning ye 5704
12:15 bread from the first day **u** the seventh day, 5704
12:18 **u** the one and twentieth day of the month at 5704
12:22 out at the door of his house **u** the morning. 5704
16:20 some of them left of it **u** the morning, and 5704
16:23 lay up for you to be kept **u** the morning. 5704
16:35 **u** they came to a land inhabited; 5704
16:35 **u** they came unto the borders of the land of 5704
17:12 his hands were steady **u** the going down of 5704
23:18 fat of my sacrifice remain **u** the morning. 5704
23:30 **u** thou be increased, and inherit 834+5704
24:14 for us, **u** we come again unto you: 834+5704
33: 8 **u** he was gone into the tabernacle. 5704
34:34 he took the vail off, **u** he came out. 5704
34:35 face again, **u** he went in to speak with him. 5704
Lev 7:15 he shall not leave *any* of it **u** the morning. 5704
8:33 **u** the days of your consecration be at an 5704
11:24 of them shall be unclean **u** the even. 5704
11:25 his clothes, and be unclean **u** the even. 5704
11:27 their carcase shall be unclean **u** the even. 5704
11:28 his clothes, and be unclean **u** the even: 5704
11:31 they be dead, shall be unclean **u** the even. 5704
11:32 and it shall be unclean **u** the even; 5704
11:39 carcase thereof shall be unclean **u** the even. 5704
11:40 his clothes, and be unclean **u** the even: 5704
11:40 his clothes, and be unclean **u** the even. 5704
12: 4 **u** the days of her purifying be fulfilled. 5704
14:46 it is shut up shall be unclean **u** the even. 5704
15: 5 in water, and be unclean **u** the even. 5704
15: 6 in water, and be unclean **u** the even. 5704
15: 7 in water, and be unclean **u** the even. 5704
15: 8 in water, and be unclean **u** the even. 5704
15:10 was under him shall be unclean **u** the even: 5704
15:10 in water, and be unclean **u** the even. 5704
15:11 in water, and be unclean **u** the even. 5704
15:16 flesh in water, and be unclean **u** the even. 5704
15:17 with water, and be unclean **u** the even. 5704
15:18 in water, and be unclean **u** the even. 5704
15:19 whosoever toucheth her shall be unclean **u** 5704
15:21 in water, and be unclean **u** the even. 5704
15:22 in water, and be unclean **u** the even. 5704
15:23 toucheth it, he shall be unclean **u** the even. 5704
15:27 in water, and be unclean **u** the even. 5704
16:17 atonement in the holy *place*, **u** he come out, 5704
17:15 in water, and be unclean **u** the even: 5704

U

Lev 19: 6 if ought remain **u** the third day, it shall be 5704
19:13 not abide with thee all night **u** the morning. 5704
22: 4 he shall not eat of the holy *things,* **u** 834+5704
22: 6 touched *any* such shall be unclean **u** even, 5704
22:30 ye shall leave none of it **u** the morrow: 5704
23:14 **u** the selfsame day that ye have brought an 5704
25:22 and eat *yet* of old fruit **u** the ninth year; 5704
25:22 **u** her fruits come in ye shall eat *of* the old 5704
25:28 him that hath bought it **u** the year of jubile: 5704
Nu 4: 3 and upward even **u** fifty years old, 5704
4:23 upward **u** fifty years old shalt thou number 5704
6: 5 **u** the days be fulfilled, *in* the which he 5704
9:15 were the appearance of fire, **u** the morning. 5704
11:20 **u** it come out at your nostrils, and it be 834+5704
14:19 this people, from Egypt even **u** now. 5704
14:33 **u** your carcases be wasted in 5704
19: 7 and the priest shall be unclean **u** the even. 5704
19: 8 in water, and shall be unclean **u** the even. 5704
19:10 his clothes, and be unclean **u** the even: 5704
19:21 water of separation shall be unclean **u** even. 5704
19:22 the soul that toucheth *it* shall be unclean **u** 5704
20:17 the left, **u** we have passed thy borders. 834+5704
21:22 *high* way, **u** we be past thy borders. 834+5704
21:35 his people, **u** there was none left him alive: 5704
23:24 he shall not lie down **u** he eat *of* the prey, 5704
24:22 **u** Asshur shall carry thee away 4100+5704
32:13 **u** all the generation, that had done evil in 5704
32:17 **u** we have brought them unto 518+834+5704
32:18 **u** the children of Israel have inherited every 5704
32:21 **u** he hath driven out his enemies from 5704
35:12 **u** he stand before the congregation in 5704
35:28 of his refuge **u** the death of the high priest: 5704
35:32 dwell in the land, **u** the death of the priest. 5704
Dt 1:31 way that ye went, **u** ye came into this place. 5704
2:14 **u** we were come over the brook Zered, 834+5704
2:14 **u** all the generation of the men of war were 5704
2:15 among the host, **u** they were consumed. 5704
2:29 **u** I shall pass over Jordan into the land 834+5704
3: 3 we smote him **u** none was left to him 5704
3:20 **U** the LORD have given rest unto 834+5704
3:20 *u* they also possess the land which NIH
7:20 **u** they that are left, and hide themselves 5704
7:23 a mighty destruction, **u** they be destroyed. 5704
7:24 before thee, **u** thou have destroyed them. 5704
9: 7 **u** ye came unto this place, ye have been 5704
9:21 *even* **u** *it was as* small as dust: 834+5704
11: 5 in the wilderness, **u** ye came into this place; 5704
16: 4 at even, remain all night **u** the morning. 3807.1
20:20 that maketh war with thee, **u** it be subdued. 5704
22: 2 it shall be with thee **u** thy brother seek after 5704
28:20 **u** thou be destroyed, and until thou perish 5704
28:20 be destroyed, and **u** thou perish quickly; 5704
28:21 **u** he have consumed thee from off the land, 5704
28:22 and they shall pursue thee **u** thou perish. 5704
28:24 come down upon thee, **u** thou be destroyed. 5704
28:48 upon thy neck, **u** he have destroyed thee. 5704
28:51 the fruit of thy land, **u** thou be destroyed: 5704
28:51 of thy sheep, **u** he have destroyed thee. 5704
28:52 **u** thy high and fenced walls come down, 5704
28:61 bring upon thee, **u** thou be destroyed. 5704
31:24 of this law in a book, **u** they were finished, 5704
31:30 the words of this song, **u** they were ended. 5704
Jos 1:15 **U** the LORD have given your 834+5704
2:16 there three days, **u** the pursuers be returned: 5704
2:22 three days, **u** the pursuers were returned: 5704
3:17 **u** all the people were passed clean 834+5704
4:10 **u** every thing was finished that the LORD 5704
4:23 **u** ye were passed over, as the LORD your 5704
4:23 up from before us, **u** we were gone over: 5704
5: 1 **u** we were passed over, that their heart 5704
6:10 of your mouth, **u** the day I bid you shout; 5704
7: 6 the ark of the LORD **u** the eventide, 5704
7:13 **u** ye take away the accursed thing from 5704
8:24 **u** they were consumed, that all 5704
8:26 **u** *he* had utterly destroyed all 834+5704
8:29 the king of Ai he hanged on a tree **u** 5704
10:13 **u** the people had avenged themselves upon 5704
10:26 they were hanging upon the trees **u** 5704
10:27 *which remain* **u** this very day. 5704
10:33 **u** *he* had left him none remaining. 5704
11: 8 **u** *they* left them none remaining. 5704
11:14 **u** they had destroyed them, neither left they 5704
13:13 dwell among the Israelites **u** this day.) 5704
20: 6 **u** he stand before the congregation for 5704
20: 6 **u** the death of the high priest that shall be 5704
20: 9 **u** he stood before the congregation. 5704
22:17 from which we are not cleansed **u** this day, 5704
23:13 **u** ye perish from off this good land which 5704
23:15 **u** he have destroyed you from off this good 5704
Jdg 4:24 **u** they had destroyed Jabin king of 834+5704
5: 7 ceased in Israel, **u** that I Deborah arose, 5704
6:18 **u** I come unto thee, and bring forth my 5704
6:18 And he said, I will tarry **u** thou come again. 5704
13:15 **u** we shall have made ready a kid for 2050.1
18:30 his sons were priests to the tribe of Dan **u** 5704
19: 8 they tarried **u** afternoon, and they did eat 5704
19:25 and abused her all the night **u** the morning: 5704
20:23 and wept before the LORD **u** even, 5704
20:26 fasted that day **u** even, and offered burnt 5704
Ru 1:19 So they two went **u** they came *to* 5704
2: 7 even from the morning **u** now, 5704+2050.1
2:17 So she gleaned in the field **u** even, and 5704
2:21 **u** they have ended all my harvest. 518+5704
3: 3 **u** he shall have done eating and drinking. 5704
3:13 the LORD liveth: lie down **u** the morning. 5704
3:14 she lay *at* his feet **u** the morning: and 5704
3:18 **u** thou know how the matter will fall: 834+5704
3:18 **u** he have finished the thing *this* day. 518+3588
1Sa 1:22 *I will not go up* **u** the child be weaned, and 5704
1:23 thee good; tarry **u** thou have weaned him; 5704
1:23 and gave her son suck **u** she weaned him. 5704
3:15 Samuel lay **u** the morning, and opened 5704
7:11 smote them, **u** *they came* under Beth-car. 5704
9:13 for the people will not eat **u** he come, 5704
11:11 slew the Ammonites **u** the heat of the day: 5704
1Sa 14: 9 say thus unto us, Tarry **u** we come to you; 5704
14:24 Cursed *be* the man that eateth *any* food **u** 5704
14:36 spoil them **u** the morning light, and let us 5704
15: 7 Saul smote the Amalekites from Havilah *u* NIH
15:18 and fight against them **u** they be consumed. 5704
15:35 Samuel came no more to see Saul **u** the day 5704
17:52 **u** thou come *to* the valley, and to the gates 5704
19: 2 take heed to thyself **u** the morning, and 871.1
19:23 prophesied, **u** he came to Naioth in Ramah. 5704
20:41 wept one with another, **u** David exceeded. 5704
25:36 less or more, **u** the morning light. 5704
30: 4 **u** they had no more power to weep. 834+5704
2Sa 1:12 wept, and fasted **u** even, for Saul, and 5704
4: 3 and were sojourners there **u** this day.) 5704
5:25 smote the Philistines from Geba **u** thou 5704
10: 5 Tarry at Jericho **u** your beards be grown, 5704
15:24 **u** all the people had done passing out of 5704
15:28 **u** there come word from you to certify me. 5704
17:13 **u** there be not one small stone found 834+5704
19: 7 evil that befell thee from thy youth **u** now. 5704
19:24 from the day the king departed **u** the day he 5704
21:10 from the beginning of harvest **u** water 5704
22:38 turned not again **u** I had consumed them. 5704
23:10 the Philistines **u** his hand was weary, 3588+5704
1Ki 3: 1 **u** he had made an end of building his own 5704
3: 2 unto the name of the LORD, **u** those days. 5704
5: 3 **u** the LORD put them under the soles of 5704
6:22 with gold, **u** *he* had finished all the house: 5704
10: 7 **u** I came, and mine eyes had seen *it:* 834+5704
11:16 **u** he had cut off every male in Edom:) 5704
11:40 and was in Egypt **u** the death of Solomon. 5704
15:29 **u** *he* had destroyed him, according unto 5704
17:14 **u** the day *that* the LORD sendeth rain 5704
18:26 name of Baal from morning even **u** noon, 5704
18:29 they prophesied **u** *the time* of the offering 5704
22:11 the Syrians, **u** *thou* have consumed them. 5704
22:27 with water of affliction, **u** I come in peace. 5704
2Ki 6:25 **u** an ass's head was *sold* for fourscore 5704
7: 3 one to another, Why sit we here **u** we die? 5704
8: 6 the day that she left the land, even **u** now. 5704
8:11 countenance stedfastly, **u** *he* was ashamed: 5704
10: 8 *at* the entering in of the gate **u** the morning. 5704
10:11 his priests, **u** *he* left him none remaining. 5704
17:20 **u** *he* had cast them out of his sight. 834+5704
17:23 **U** the LORD removed Israel out of 834+5704
18:32 **U** I come and take you away to a land like 5704
24:20 **u** he had cast them out from his presence, 5704
1Ch 5:22 they dwelt in their steads **u** the captivity. 5704
6:32 **u** Solomon had built the house of 5704
12:22 **u** it was a great host, like the host of God. 5704
19: 5 Tarry at Jericho **u** your beards be 834+5704
28:20 **u** *thou* hast finished all the work for 5704
2Ch 8: 8 them did Solomon make to pay tribute **u** 5704
8:16 house of the LORD, and **u** it was finished. 5704
9: 6 **u** I came, and mine eyes had seen *it:* 834+5704
16:12 **u** his disease *was* exceeding *great:* yet in 5704
18:10 With these thou shalt push Syria **u** they be 5704
18:26 with water of affliction, **u** I return in peace. 5704
18:34 *his* chariot against the Syrians **u** the even: 5704
21:15 **u** thy bowels fall out by reason of 5704
24:10 cast into the chest, **u** *they* had made an end. 5704
29:28 all *this continued* **u** the burnt offering was 5704
29:34 **u** the *other* priests had sanctified 5704
31: 1 **u** *they* had utterly destroyed *them all.* Then 5704
35:14 of burnt offerings and the fat **u** night; 5704
36:16 **u** the wrath of the LORD arose against his 5704
36:20 his sons **u** the reign of the kingdom of 5704
36:21 **u** the land had enjoyed her sabbaths: 5704
Ezr 4: 5 even **u** the reign of Darius king of Persia. 5704
4:21 **u** *another* commandment shall be given 5705
5:16 since that time even **u** now *hath it been* in 5705
8:29 keep *them,* **u** ye weigh *them* before 5704
9: 4 and I sat astonied **u** the evening sacrifice. 5704
10:14 **u** the fierce wrath of our God for this 5704
Ne 7: 3 Let not the gates of Jerusalem be opened **u** 5704
8: 3 the water gate from the morning **u** midday, 5704
12:23 even **u** the days of Johanan the son of 5704
Job 14:13 keep me secret, **u** thy wrath be past, 5704
26:10 **u** the day and night come to an end. 5704
Ps 36: 2 **u** his iniquity be found to be hateful. NIH
57: 1 my refuge, **u** *these* calamities be overpast. 5704
71:18 **u** I have shewed thy strength unto *this* 5704
73:17 **U** I went into the sanctuary of God; *then* 5704
94:13 **u** the pit be digged for the wicked. 5704
104:23 his work and to his labour **u** the evening. 5704
105:19 **U** the time that his word came: the word of 5704
110: 1 **u** I make thine enemies thy footstool. 5704
112: 8 **u** he see *his desire* upon his enemies. 834+5704
123: 2 our God, **u** that he have mercy upon us. 5704
132: 5 **U** I find out a place for the LORD, 5704
Pr 7:18 let us take our fill of love **u** the morning: 5704
SS 2:17 **U** the day break, and the shadows 5704+7945
3: 4 **u** I had brought him into my 5704+7945
4: 6 **U** the day break, and the shadows 5704+7945
8: 4 nor awake *my* love, **u** he please. 5704+7945
Isa 5:11 that continue **u** night, *till* wine inflame 871.1
6:11 **U** the cities be wasted without 518+834+5704
26:20 **u** the indignation be overpast. 5704
32:15 **U** the spirit be poured upon us from on 5704
36:17 **U** I come and take you away to a land like 5704
39: 6 thy fathers have laid up in store **u** this day, 5704
62: 1 **u** the righteousness thereof go forth as 5704
Jer 23:20 **u** he have executed, and till he have 5704
27: 7 son's son, **u** the very time of his land come: 5704
27: 8 **u** I have consumed them by his hand. 5704
27:22 there shall they be **u** the day that I visit 5704
30:24 **u** he have done *it,* and until he have 5704
30:24 **u** he have performed the intents of his 5704
32: 5 there shall he be **u** I visit him, saith 5704
36:23 **u** all the roll was consumed in the fire that 5704
37:21 **u** all the bread in the city were spent. 5704
38:28 prison **u** the day that Jerusalem was taken: 5704
44:27 by the famine, **u** there be an end of them. 5704
52:34 every day a portion **u** the day of his death, 5704
Eze 21:27 it shall be no *more,* **u** he come whose right 5704
Eze 33:22 **u** *he* came to me in the morning; 5704
46: 2 but the gate shall not be shut **u** the evening. 5704
Da 4:32 **u** thou know that the most High 1768+5705
7:22 **U** the Ancient of days came, and 1768+5705
7:25 they shall be given into his hand **u** a time 5705
9:27 even **u** the consummation, and 5704
Hos 7: 4 hath kneaded the dough, **u** it be leavened. 5704
Mic 5: 3 **u** the time *that* she which travaileth hath 5704
7: 9 **u** he plead my cause, and 834+5704
Zep 3: 8 **u** the day that I rise up to the prey: 3807.1
Mt 1:17 from David **u** the carrying away into *2193*
2:13 and be thou there **u** I bring thee word: *302+2193*
2:15 And was there **u** the death of Herod: that it *2193*
11:12 And from the days of John the Baptist **u** *2193*
11:13 and the law prophesied **u** John. *2193*
11:23 it would have remained **u** this day. *3360*
13:30 Let both grow together **u** the harvest: and *3360*
17: 9 Tell the vision to no *man,* **u** the Son *2193+3739*
18:22 I say not unto thee, **U** seven times: *2193*
18:22 seven times: but, **U** seventy times seven. *2193*
24:38 **u** the day that Noe entered into the ark, *891*
24:39 And knew not **u** the flood came, and *2193*
26:29 **u** that day when I drink it new with you in *2193*
27:64 that the sepulchre be made sure **u** the third *2193*
28:15 reported among the Jews **u** this day. *3360*
Mk 14:25 **u** that day that I drink it new in *2193*
15:33 there was darkness over the whole land **u** *2193*
Lk 1:20 **u** the day that these *things* shall be *891*
13:35 see me, **u** *the time* come when ye shall say, *2193*
15: 4 and go after that which is lost, **u** he find it? *2193*
16:16 The law and the prophets *were* **u** John: *2193*
17:27 **u** the day that Noe entered into *891+3739*
21:24 **u** the times of the Gentiles be fulfilled. *891+3739*
22:16 **u** it be fulfilled in the kingdom of *2193+3748*
22:18 **u** the kingdom of God shall come. *2193+3739*
23:44 there was a darkness over all the earth **u** *2193*
24:49 **u** ye be endued with power from on *2193+3739*
Jn 2:10 *but* thou hast kept the good wine **u** now. *2193*
9:18 **u** they called the parents of him that *2193+3748*
Ac 1: 2 **U** the day *in* which he was taken up, *891*
2:35 **U** I make thy foes thy footstool. *302+2193*
3:21 Whom the heaven must receive **u** the times *891*
10:30 Four days ago I was fasting **u** this hour; *3360*
13:20 and fifty years, **u** Samuel the prophet. *2193*
20: 7 and continued *his* speech **u** midnight. *3360*
21:26 **u** that an offering should be offered for *2193*
23: 1 all good conscience before God **u** this day. *891*
23:14 that *we* will eat nothing **u** we have *2193+3739*
Ro 5:13 For **u** the law sin was in the world: but sin is *891*
8:22 and travaileth in pain together **u** now. *891*
11:25 **u** the fulness of the Gentiles be come *891+3739*
1Co 4: 5 before the time, **u** the Lord come, *302+2193*
16: 8 But I will tarry at Ephesus **u** Pentecost. *2193*
2Co 3:14 for **u** this day remaineth the same vail *891*
Gal 4: 2 governors **u** the time appointed of the father. *891*
4:19 of whom I travail in birth again **u** *891+3739*
Eph 1:14 **u** the redemption of the purchased *1519*
Php 1: 5 in the gospel from the first day **u** now; *891*
1: 6 you will perform *it* **u** the day of Jesus Christ: *891*
2Th 2: 7 only he who now letteth *will let,* **u** he be *2193*
1Ti 6:14 **u** the appearing of our Lord Jesus Christ: *3360*
Heb 1:13 **u** I make thine enemies thy footstool? *302+2193*
9:10 imposed *on them* **u** the time of reformation. *3360*
Jas 5: 7 **u** he receive the early and latter rain. *302+2193*
2Pe 1:19 **u** the day dawn, and the day star *2193+3739*
1Jn 2: 9 his brother, is in darkness *even* **u** now. *2193*
Rev 6:11 **u** their fellowservants also and their *2193*
17:17 **u** the words of God shall be fulfilled. *891*
20: 5 But the rest of the dead lived not again **u** *2193*

UNTIMELY (4) [TIME]

Job 3:16 Or as a hidden **u birth** I had not been; 5309
Ps 58: 8 *like* the **u birth** of a woman, *that* they may 5309
Ecc 6: 3 I say, *that* an **u birth** *is* better than he. 5309
Rev 6:13 *even* as a fig tree casteth her **u figs,** when *3653*

UNTO (9005) [HEREUNTO, THEREUNTO, WHEREUNTO] See Index of Articles, Etc.

UNTOWARD (1)

Ac 2:40 Save yourselves from this **u** generation. *4646*

UNWALLED (3) [WALL]

Dt 3: 5 and bars; beside **u** towns a great many. 6521
Est 9:19 of the villages, that dwelt in the **u** towns, 6519
Eze 38:11 I will go up to the land of **u villages;** 6519

UNWASHEN (3) [WASH]

Mt 15:20 but to eat with **u** hands defileth not a man. *449*
Mk 7: 2 that is to say, with **u,** hands, they found fault. *449*
7: 5 of the elders, but eat bread with **u** hands? *449*

UNWEIGHED (1) [WEIGH]

1Ki 7:47 Solomon left all the vessels *u,* because NIH

UNWISE (4) [WISDOM]

Dt 32: 6 the LORD, O foolish people and **u**? 2450+3808
Hos 13:13 he *is* an **u** son; for he should not stay 2450+3808
Ro 1:14 the barbarians; both to the wise, and to the **u**. *453*
Eph 5:17 Wherefore be ye not **u**, but *878*

UNWITTINGLY (3) [WIT]

Lev 22:14 if a man eat *of* the holy *thing* **u**, then 7684+871.1
Jos 20: 3 *and* **u** may flee thither: 1097+1847+871.1
20: 5 he smote his neighbour **u**, 1097+1847+871.1

UNWORTHILY (2) [UNWORTHY]

1Co 11:27 and drink *this* cup of the Lord **u**, shall be *371*
11:29 For he that eateth and drinketh **u**, eateth and *371*

UNWORTHY (2) [UNWORTHILY, WORTH]

Ac 13:46 judge yourselves **u** of everlasting life, *514+3756*
1Co 6: 2 are ye **u** to judge the smallest matters? *370*

U

UP (2381) [UPON, UPPER, UPPERMOST, UPSIDE, UPWARD] See Index of Articles, Etc.

UPBRAID (2) [UPBRAIDED, UPBRAIDETH]
Jdg 8:15 Zalmunna, with whom ye did **u** me, saying, 2778
Mt 11:20 Then began he to **u** the cities wherein most *3679*

UPBRAIDED (1) [UPBRAID]
Mk 16:14 and **u** them with their unbelief and *3679*

UPBRAIDETH (1) [UPBRAID]
Jas 1: 5 that giveth to all *men* liberally, and **u** not; *3679*

UPHARSIN (1)
Da 5:25 MENE, MENE, TEKEL, **U**. 6537+2050.3

UPHAZ (2)
Jer 10: 9 and gold from **U**, the work of the workman, 210
Da 10: 5 whose loins *were* girded with fine gold of **U**: 210

UPHELD (1) [UPHOLD]
Isa 63: 5 salvation unto me; and my fury, it **u** me. 5564

UPHOLD (8) [UPHELD, UPHOLDEN, UPHOLDEST, UPHOLDETH, UPHOLDING]
Ps 51:12 thy salvation; and **u** me *with thy* free spirit. 5564
54: 4 the Lord *is* with them that **u** my soul. 5564
119:116 **U** me according unto thy word, that I may 5564
Pr 29:23 but honour shall **u** the humble in spirit. 8551
Isa 41:10 I will **u** thee with the right hand of my 8551
42: 1 Behold my servant, whom I **u**; mine elect, 8551
63: 5 and I wondered that *there was* none to **u**: 5564
Eze 30: 6 They also that **u** Egypt shall fall; and 5564

UPHOLDEN (2) [UPHOLD]
Job 4: 4 Thy words have **u** him that was falling, and 6965
Pr 20:28 the king: and his throne is **u** by mercy. 5582

UPHOLDEST (1) [UPHOLD]
Ps 41:12 thou **u** me in mine integrity, and settest me 8551

UPHOLDETH (4) [UPHOLD]
Ps 37:17 be broken: but the LORD **u** the righteous. 5564
37:24 for the LORD **u** *him with* his hand. 5564
63: 8 hard after thee: thy right hand **u** me. 8551
145:14 The LORD **u** all that fall, and raiseth up 5564

UPHOLDING (1) [UPHOLD]
Heb 1: 3 and **u** all *things* by the word of his power, *5342*

UPON (2763) [THEREUPON, UP, WHEREUPON] See Index of Articles, Etc.

UPPER (25) [UP]
Ex 12: 7 and on the **u door post** of the houses, 4947
Lev 13:45 he shall put a covering upon *his* **u lip**, and 8222
Dt 24: 6 the nether or the **u millstone** to pledge: 7393
Jos 15:19 he gave her the **u** springs, and the nether 5942
16: 5 was Ataroth-addar, unto Beth-horon the **u**; 5945
Jdg 1:15 Caleb gave her the **u** springs and the nether 5942
2Ki 1: 2 in his **u chamber** that *was* in Samaria, 5944
18:17 and stood by the conduit of the **u** pool, 5945
23:12 *were* on the top of the **u chamber** of Ahaz, 5944
1Ch 7:24 the nether, and the **u**, and Uzzen-sherah.) 5945
28:11 of the **u chambers** thereof, and of the inner 5944
2Ch 3: 9 And he overlaid the **u chambers** with gold. 5944
8: 5 Also he built Beth-horon the **u**, and 5945
32:30 This same Hezekiah also stopped the **u** 5945
Isa 7: 3 at the end of the conduit of the **u** pool in 5945
36: 2 he stood by the conduit of the **u** pool in 5945
Eze 42: 5 Now the **u** chambers *were* shorter: for 5945
Zep 2:14 the bittern shall lodge in the **u lintels** of it; 3730
Mk 14:15 And he will shew you a large **u room** *508*
Lk 22:12 And he shall shew you a large **u room** *508*
Ac 1:13 they went up into an **u room**, where abode *5253*
9:37 had washed, they laid *her* in an **u chamber**. *5253*
9:39 they brought him into the **u chamber**: *5253*
19: 1 Paul having passed through the **u** coasts *510*
20: 8 there were many lights in the **u chamber**, *5253*

UPPERMOST (6) [UP]
Ge 40:17 in the **u** basket *there was* of all *manner of* 5945
Isa 17: 6 *or* three berries in the top of the **u bough**, 534
17: 9 an **u** branch, which they left because of NIH
Mt 23: 6 And love the **u rooms** at feasts, and *4411*
Mk 12:39 the synagogues, and the **u rooms** at feasts: *4411*
Lk 11:43 for ye love the **u seats** in the synagogues, *4410*

UPRIGHT (68) [UPRIGHTNESS]
Ge 37: 7 and lo, my sheaf arose, and also **stood u**; 5324
Ex 15: 8 the floods **stood u** as a heap, *and* the depths 5324
Lev 26:13 the bands of your yoke, and made you go **u**. 6968
1Sa 29: 6 thou *hast been* **u**, and thy going out and 3477
2Sa 22:24 I was also **u** before him, and have kept 8549
22:26 with the **u** man thou wilt shew thyself 8549
22:26 the upright man thou wilt **shew** thyself **u**. 8552
2Ch 29:34 for the Levites *were* more **u** in heart to 3477
Job 1: 1 that man was perfect and **u**, and one that 3477
1: 8 a perfect and an **u** man, one that feareth 3477
2: 3 a perfect and an **u** man, one that feareth 3477
8: 6 If thou *wert* pure and **u**; surely now he 3477
12: 4 the just **u** *man is* laughed to scorn. 8549
17: 8 **U** *men* shall be astonied at this, and 3477
Ps 7:10 *is* of God, which saveth the **u** in heart. 3477
11: 2 that *they* may privily shoot at the **u** in heart. 3477
11: 7 his countenance doth behold the **u**. 3477
18:23 I was also **u** before him, and I kept myself 8549
18:25 with an **u** man thou wilt shew thyself 8549
18:25 an upright man thou wilt **shew** thyself **u**; 8552
19:13 shall I be **u**, and I shall be innocent from 8552
Ps 20: 8 and fallen: but we are risen, and **stand u**. 5749
25: 8 Good and **u** *is* the LORD: therefore 3477
32:11 and shout for joy, all *ye that are* **u** in heart. 3477
33: 1 ye righteous: *for* praise is comely for the **u**. 3477
36:10 and thy righteousness to the **u** in heart. 3477
37:14 *and* to slay such as be of **u** conversation. 3477
37:18 The LORD knoweth the days of the **u**: 8549
37:37 Mark the perfect *man*, and behold the **u**: 3477
49:14 the **u** shall have dominion over them in 3477
64:10 in him; and all the **u** in heart shall glory. 3477
92:15 To shew that the LORD *is* **u**: *he is* my 3477
94:15 and all the **u** in heart shall follow it. 3477
97:11 and gladness for the **u** in heart. 3477
111: 1 in the assembly of the **u**, and *in* 3477
112: 2 the generation of the **u** shall be blessed. 3477
112: 4 Unto the **u** there ariseth light in 3477
119:137 O LORD, and **u** *are* thy judgments. 3477
125: 4 and to *them that are* **u** in their hearts. 3477
140:13 thy name: the **u** shall dwell in thy presence. 3477
Pr 2:21 For the **u** shall dwell *in* the land, and 3477
10:29 The way of the LORD *is* strength to the **u**: 8537
11: 3 The integrity of the **u** shall guide them: but 3477
11: 6 The righteousness of the **u** shall deliver 3477
11:11 By the blessing of the **u** the city is exalted: 3477
11:20 *such as are* **u** in *their* way *are* his delight. 8549
12: 6 but the mouth of the **u** shall deliver them. 3477
13: 6 Righteousness keepeth *him that is* **u** in 8537
14:11 but the tabernacle of the **u** shall flourish. 3477
15: 8 but the prayer of the **u** *is* his delight. 3477
16:17 The highway of the **u** *is* to depart from evil: 3477
21:18 and the transgressor for the **u**. 3477
21:29 but *as for* the **u**, he directeth his way. 3477
28:10 the **u** shall have good *things* in possession. 8549
29:10 The bloodthirsty hate the **u**: but the just 8535
29:27 *he that is* **u** in the way *is* abomination to 3477
Ecc 7:29 have I found, that God hath made man **u**; 3477
12:10 *that which was* written *was* **u**, *even* words 3476
SS 1: 4 thy love more than wine: the **u** love thee. 4339
Isa 26: 7 thou, **most u**, dost weigh the path of 3477
Jer 10: 5 They *are* **u** as the palm tree, but speak not: 4749
Da 8:18 but he touched me, and set me **u**. 5921+5977
10:11 that I speak unto thee, and stand **u**: 5921+5977
11:17 his whole kingdom, and **u ones** with him; 3477
Mic 7: 2 *there is* none **u** among men: they all lie in 3477
7: 4 the *most* **u** *is sharper* than a thorn hedge: 3477
Hab 2: 4 his soul *which* is lifted up is not **u** in him: 3474
Ac 14:10 Said with a loud voice, Stand **u** on thy feet. *3717*

UPRIGHTLY (12) [UPRIGHTNESS]
Ps 15: 2 He that walketh **u**, and 8549
58: 1 do ye judge **u**, O ye sons of men? 4339
75: 2 receive the congregation I will judge **u**. 4339
84:11 he withhold from them that walk **u**. 8549+871.1
Pr 2: 7 *he is* a buckler to them that walk **u**. 8537
10: 9 He that walketh **u** walketh surely: 8537+871.1
15:21 but a man of understanding walketh **u**. 3474
28:18 Whoso walketh **u** shall be saved: but 8549
Isa 33:15 that walketh righteously, and speaketh **u**; 4339
Am 5:10 and they abhor him that speaketh **u**. 8549
Mic 2: 7 my words do good to him that walketh **u**? 3477
Gal 2:14 But when I saw that they **walked** not **u** *3716*

UPRIGHTNESS (19) [UPRIGHT, UPRIGHTLY]
Dt 9: 5 or for the **u** of thine heart, 3476
1Ki 3: 6 and in **u** of heart with thee; 3483
9: 4 in integrity of heart, and in **u**, 3476
1Ch 29:17 thou triest the heart, and hast pleasure in **u**. 4339
29:17 in the **u** of mine heart I have willingly 3476
Job 4: 6 thy hope; and the **u** of thy ways? 8537
33: 3 My words *shall be of* the **u** of my heart: 3476
33:23 among a thousand, to shew unto man his **u**: 3476
Ps 9: 8 shall minister judgment to the people in **u**. 4339
25:21 Let integrity and **u** preserve me; for I wait 3476
111: 8 and ever, *and are* done in truth and **u**. 3477
119: 7 I will praise thee with **u** of heart, when I 3476
143:10 spirit *is* good; lead me into the land of **u**. 4334
Pr 2:13 Who leave the paths of **u**, to walk in 3476
14: 2 He that walketh in his **u** feareth 3476
28: 6 Better *is* the poor that walketh in his **u**, 8537
Isa 26: 7 The way of the just *is* **u**: thou, most upright, 4339
26:10 in the land of **u** will he deal unjustly, and 5229
57: 2 in their beds, *each one* walking *in* his **u**. 5228

UPRISING (1)
Ps 139: 2 Thou knowest my downsitting and mine **u**, 6965

UPROAR (8)
1Ki 1:41 *is this* noise of the city being **in an u**? 1993
Mt 26: 5 Not on the feast *day*, lest there be an **u** *2351*
Mk 14: 2 Not on the feast *day*, lest there be an **u** of *2351*
Ac 17: 5 and **set** all the city **on an u**, and assaulted *2350*
19:40 to be called in question for this day's **u**, *4714*
20: 1 And after the **u** was ceased, Paul called *2351*
21:31 of the band, that all Jerusalem was **in an u**. *4797*
21:38 which before these days **madest an u**, and *387*

UPSIDE (5) [UP]
2Ki 21:13 wiping *it*, and turning *it* **u down**. 5921+6440
Ps 146: 9 the way of the wicked he **turneth u down**. 5791
Isa 24: 1 turneth it **u down**, and scattereth abroad 6440
29:16 Surely your **turning** *of things* **u down** shall 2017
Ac 17: 6 These that have **turned** the world **u down** *387*

UPWARD (61) [UP]
Ge 7:20 Fifteen cubits **u** did 4480+4605+1886.5+3807.1
Ex 38:26 from twenty years old and **u**, for 4605+1886.5
Nu 1: 3 From twenty years old and **u**, all 4605+1886.5
1:18 years old and **u**, by their polls. 4605+1886.5
1:20 male from twenty years old and **u**, 4605+1886.5
1:22 male from twenty years old and **u**, 4605+1886.5
1:24 from twenty years old and **u**, all 4605+1886.5
1:26 from twenty years old and **u**, all 4605+1886.5
1:28 from twenty years old and **u**, all 4605+1886.5
1:30 from twenty years old and **u**, all 4605+1886.5
Nu 1:32 from twenty years old and **u**, all 4605+1886.5
1:34 from twenty years old and **u**, all 4605+1886.5
1:36 from twenty years old and **u**, all 4605+1886.5
1:38 from twenty years old and **u**, all 4605+1886.5
1:40 from twenty years old and **u**, all 4605+1886.5
1:42 from twenty years old and **u**, all 4605+1886.5
1:45 from twenty years old and **u**, 4605+1886.5
3:15 and **u** shalt thou number them. 4605+1886.5
3:22 the males, from a month old and **u**, 4605+1886.5
3:28 from a month old and **u**, *were* eight 4605+1886.5
3:34 from a month old and **u**, *were* six 4605+1886.5
3:39 the males from a month old and **u**, 4605+1886.5
3:40 of Israel from a month old and **u**, 4605+1886.5
3:43 from a month old and **u**, of those 4605+1886.5
4: 3 and **u** even until fifty years old, 4605+1886.5
4:23 **u** until fifty years old shalt thou 4605+1886.5
4:30 **u** even unto fifty years old shalt 4605+1886.5
4:35 and **u** even unto fifty years old, 4605+1886.5
4:39 and **u** even unto fifty years old, 4605+1886.5
4:43 and **u** even unto fifty years old, 4605+1886.5
4:47 and **u** even unto fifty years old, 4605+1886.5
8:24 **u** they shall go in to wait upon 4605+1886.5
14:29 from twenty years old and **u**, 4605+1886.5
26: 2 from twenty years old and **u**, 4605+1886.5
26: 4 from twenty years old and **u**; 4605+1886.5
26:62 all males from a month old and **u**: 4605+1886.5
32:11 from twenty years old and **u**, shall 4605+1886.5
Jdg 1:36 to Akrabbim, from the rock, and **u**. 4605+1886.5
1Sa 9: 2 **u** *he was* higher than any of 4605+1886.5
10:23 people from his shoulders and **u**. 4605+1886.5
2Ki 3:21 **u**, and stood in the border. 4605+1886.5
19:30 and bear fruit **u**. 4605+1886.5+3807.1
1Ch 23: 3 from the age of thirty years and **u**: 4605+1886.5
23:24 from the age of twenty years and **u**. 4605+1886.5
2Ch 31:16 from three years old and **u**, 4605+1886.5+3807.1
31:17 twenty years old and **u**, 4605+1886.5+3807.1
Ezr 3: 8 from twenty years old and **u**, 4605+1886.5
Job 5: 7 is born unto trouble, as the sparks fly **u**. 1361
Ecc 3:21 spirit of man that goeth **u**, 4605+1886.5+3807.1
Isa 8:21 and their God, and look **u**. 4605+1886.5+3807.1
37:31 and bear fruit **u**. 4605+1886.5+3807.1
38:14 mine eyes fail *with looking* **u**: O LORD, 4791
Eze 1:11 *were* stretched **u**; 4480+4605+1886.5+3807.1
1:27 of his loins even **u**, 4605+1886.5+3807.1
8: 2 from his loins even **u**, as 4605+1886.5+3807.1
41: 7 a winding about still **u** to 4605+1886.5+3807.1
41: 7 **u** round about the house: 4605+1886.5+3807.1
41: 7 of the house *was still* **u**, 4605+1886.5+3807.1
43:15 and **u** *shall be* four horns. 4605+1886.5+3807.1
Hag 2:15 consider from this day and **u**, 4605+1886.5
2:18 Consider now from this day and **u**, 4605+1886.5

UR (5)
Ge 11:28 the land of his nativity, in **U** of the Chaldees. 218
11:31 they went forth with them from **U** of 218
15: 7 I *am* the LORD that brought thee out of **U** 218
1Ch 11:35 of Sacar the Hararite, Eliphal the son of **U**, 218
Ne 9: 7 broughtest him forth out of **U** of 218

URBAN (1)
Ro 16: 9 Salute **U** our helper in Christ, and *3773*

URBANUS See URBAN

URGE (1) [URGED]
Lk 11:53 the Pharisees began to **u** *him* vehemently, *1758*

URGED (6) [URGE]
Ge 33:11 have enough. And he **u** him, and he took *it*. 6484
Jdg 16:16 **u** him, *so* that his soul was vexed unto death; 509
19: 7 rose up to depart, his father in law **u** him: 6484
2Ki 2:17 when they **u** him till *he* was ashamed, he 6484
5:16 And he **u** him to take *it*; but he refused. 6484
5:23 he **u** him, and bound two talents of silver in 6555

URGENT (2)
Ex 12:33 the Egyptians were **u** upon the people, that 2388
Da 3:22 the king's commandment *was* **u**, 2685

URI (8)
Ex 31: 2 I have called by name Bezaleel the son of **U**, 221
35:30 hath called by name Bezaleel the son of **U**, 221
38:22 Bezaleel the son of **U**, the son of Hur, of 221
1Ki 4:19 Geber the son of **U** *was* in the country of 221
1Ch 2:20 And Hur begat **U**, and Uri begat Bezaleel. 221
2:20 And Hur begat Uri, and **U** begat Bezaleel. 221
2Ch 1: 5 that Bezaleel the son of **U**, the son of Hur, 221
Ezr 10:24 of the porters; Shallum, and Telem, and **U**. 221

URIAH (26) [URIAH'S, URIAS, URIJAH]
2Sa 11: 3 daughter of Eliam, the wife of **U** the Hittite? 223
11: 6 sent to Joab, *saying*, Send me **U** the Hittite. 223
11: 6 Uriah the Hittite. And Joab sent **U** to David. 223
11: 7 when **U** was come unto him, David 223
11: 8 And David said to **U**, Go down to thy house, 223
11: 8 And **U** departed out of the king's house, and 223
11: 9 **U** slept *at* the door of the king's house with 223
11:10 saying, **U** went not down unto his house, 223
11:10 David said unto **U**, Camest thou not from *thy* 223
11:11 And **U** said unto David, The ark, and Israel, 223
11:12 And David said to **U**, Tarry here to day also, 223
11:12 So **U** abode in Jerusalem that day, and 223
11:14 a letter to Joab, and sent *it* by the hand of **U**. 223
11:15 Set ye **U** in the forefront of the hottest battle, 223
11:16 that he assigned **U** unto a place where he 223
11:17 of David; and **U** the Hittite died also. 223
11:21 Thy servant **U** the Hittite is dead also. 223
11:24 and thy servant **U** the Hittite is dead also. 223
11:26 when the wife of **U** heard that Uriah her 223
11:26 when the wife of Uriah heard that **U** her 223
12: 9 thou hast killed **U** the Hittite with the sword, 223
12:10 hast taken the wife of **U** the Hittite to be thy 223
23:39 **U** the Hittite: thirty and seven *in* all. 223
1Ch 11:41 **U** the Hittite, Zabad the son of Ahlai, 223

Ezr 8:33 hand of Meremoth the son of **U** the priest; 223
Isa 8: 2 **U** the priest, and Zechariah the son of 223

URIAH'S (1) [URIAH]
2Sa 12:15 the LORD strake the child that **U** wife bare 223

URIAS (1) [URIAH]
Mt 1: 6 of *her that had been* the *wife* of **U**; *3774*

URIEL (4)
1Ch 6:24 Tahath his son, **U** his son, Uzziah his son, 222
15: 5 **U** the chief, and his brethren an hundred and 222
15:11 for **U**, Asaiah, and Joel, Shemaiah, and Eliel, 222
2Ch 13: 2 *was* Michaiah the daughter of **U** of Gibeah. 222

URIJAH (12) [URIAH]
1Ki 15: 5 save only in the matter of **U** the Hittite. 223
2Ki 16:10 king Ahaz sent to **U** the priest the fashion of 223
16:11 **U** the priest built an altar according to all 223
16:11 **U** the priest made *it* against king Ahaz came 223
16:15 king Ahaz commanded **U** the priest, saying, 223
16:16 Thus did **U** the priest, according to all that 223
Ne 3: 4 unto them repaired Meremoth the son of **U**, 223
3:21 After him repaired Meremoth the son of **U** 223
8: 4 Anaiah, and **U**, and Hilkiah, and Maaseiah, 223
Jer 26:20 **U** the son of Shemaiah of Kirjath-jearim, 223
26:21 but when **U** heard *it*, he was afraid, and fled, 223
26:23 they fet forth **U** out of Egypt, and 223

URIM (7)
Ex 28:30 shalt put in the breastplate of judgment the **U** 224
Lev 8: 8 also he put in the breastplate the **U** and 224
Nu 27:21 after the judgment of **U** before the LORD: 224
Dt 33: 8 and thy **U** *be* with thy holy one, 224
1Sa 28: 6 by dreams, nor by **U**, nor by prophets. 224
Ezr 2:63 holy *things* till there stood *up* a priest with **U** 224
Ne 7:65 *things*, till there stood *up* a priest with **U** 224

URINE See PISS

US (1449) [WE] See Index of Articles, Etc.

USE (35) [USED, USES, USEST, USETH, USING]
Lev 7:24 *with beasts*, may be used in any *other* **u**: 4399
19:26 neither shall ye **u enchantment**, 5172
Nu 10: 2 that thou mayest **u** them for 1961+3807.1
15:39 own eyes, after which ye **u** to go a whoring: NIH
Dt 26:14 **u**, nor given *ought* thereof for the dead: NIH
2Sa 1:18 the children of Judah the **u** *of the* bow: NIH
1Ch 12: 2 could **u** both **the right hand** and the left in 3231
28:15 according to the **u** of every candlestick. 5656
Jer 23:31 that **u** their tongues, and say, He saith. 3947
31:23 As yet they shall **u**[S] this speech in the land 559
46:11 in vain shalt thou **u many** medicines; *for* 7235
Eze 12:23 they shall no more **u** it **as a proverb** in 4911
16:44 proverbs shall **u** *this* **proverb** against thee, 4911
18: 2 that ye **u** this **proverb** concerning 4911+4912
18: 3 any more to **u** this **proverb** in Israel. 4911+4912
21:21 of the two ways, to **u divination**: 7080+7081
Mt 5:44 pray for them which **despitefully u** you, *1908*
6: 7 But when ye pray, **u** not **vain repetitions**, *945*
Lk 6:28 pray for them which **despitefully u** you. *1908*
Ac 14: 5 to **u** *them* **despitefully**, and to stone them, *5195*
Ro 1:26 natural **u** into that which is against nature: *5540*
1:27 leaving the natural **u** of the woman, *5540*
1Co 7:21 if thou mayest be made free, **u** *it* rather. *5530*
7:31 And they that **u** this world, as not abusing *5530*
2Co 1:17 was thus minded, did I **u** lightness? *5530*
3:12 such hope, we **u** great plainness of speech: *5530*
13:10 lest being present I should **u** sharpness, *5530*
Gal 5:13 only ***u*** not liberty for an occasion to NIG
Eph 4:29 but that which *is* good to the **u** of edifying, *5532*
1Ti 1: 8 that the law *is* good, if a man **u** it lawfully; *5530*
3:10 then let them **u the office of a deacon**, *1247*
5:23 but **u** a little wine for thy stomach's sake *5530*
2Ti 2:21 and **meet for** the master's **u**, *and* *2173*
Heb 5:14 *even* those who by reason of **u** have their *1838*
1Pe 4: 9 **U** hospitality one to another without NIG

USED (22) [USE]
Ex 21:36 Or *if* it be known that the ox *hath* **u to push** 5056
Lev 7:24 torn *with beasts*, may be **u** in any *other* use: 6213
Jdg 14:10 there a feast; for so **u** the young men **to do**. 6213
14:20 whom he had **u as** his friend. 3807.1
2Ki 17:17 **u divination** and enchantments, and 7080+7081
21: 6 **u enchantments**, and dealt with familiar 5172
2Ch 33: 6 **u enchantments**, and used witchcraft, and 5172
33: 6 **u witchcraft**, and dealt with a familiar 3784
Jer 2:24 A wild ass **u to** the wilderness, 3928
Eze 22:29 of the land have **u oppression**, 6231+6233
35:11 according to thine envy which thou hast **u** 6213
Hos 12:10 **u similitudes** by the ministry of 1819
Mk 2:18 of John and of the Pharisees **u** to fast: *1510*
Ac 8: 9 beforetime in the *same* city **u sorcery**, *3096*
19:19 Many also of them which **u** curious arts *4238*
27:17 they **u** helps, undergirding the ship; *5530*
Ro 3:13 with their tongues they have **u deceit**; *1387*
1Co 9:12 Nevertheless we have not **u** this power; but *5530*
9:15 But I have **u** none of these *things*: neither *5530*
1Th 2: 5 For neither at any time **u** we flattering *1096*
1Ti 3:13 For they that have **u the office of a deacon** *1247*
Heb 10:33 became companions of them that were so **u**. *390*

USELESS See NOUGHT

USES (1) [USE]
Tit 3:14 to maintain good works for necessary **u**, *5532*

USEST (1) [USE]
Ps 119:132 as thou **u to do** unto those that love thy 4941

USETH (7) [USE]
Dt 18:10 *or* that **u divination**, *or* an observer 7080+7081
Est 6: 8 be brought which the king **u** to wear, NIH
Pr 15: 2 tongue of the wise **u** knowledge **aright**: 3190
18:23 The poor **u intreaties**; but the rich 8469
Jer 22:13 *that* **u** his neighbour's **service** without 5647
Eze 16:44 every one that **u proverbs** shall use *this* 4911
Heb 5:13 For every one that **u** milk *is* unskilful in *3348*

USING (2) [USE]
Col 2:22 Which all are to perish with the **u**;) after *671*
1Pe 2:16 not **u** *your* liberty for a cloke of *2192*

USUAL See WONT

USURER (1) [USURY]
Ex 22:25 thou shalt not be to him as an **u**, 5383

USURP (1)
1Ti 2:12 nor to **u authority over** the man, but to be in *831*

USURY (24) [USURER]
Ex 22:25 neither shalt thou lay upon him **u**. 5392
Lev 25:36 Take thou no **u** of him, or increase: but 5392
25:37 Thou shalt not give him thy money upon **u**, 5392
Dt 23:19 Thou shalt not **lend upon u** to thy brother; 5391
23:19 **u** of money, usury of victuals, usury of any 5392
23:19 usury of money, **u** of victuals, usury of any 5392
23:19 **u** of any thing that is lent upon usury: 5392
23:19 usury of any thing that is **lent upon u**: 5391
23:20 Unto a stranger thou mayest **lend upon u**; 5391
23:20 thy brother thou shalt not **lend upon u**: 5391
Ne 5: 7 the rulers, and said unto them, You exact **u**, 4855
5:10 and corn: I pray you, let us leave off this **u**. 4855
Ps 15: 5 *He that* putteth not out his money to **u**, 5392
Pr 28: 8 He that by **u** and unjust gain increaseth his 5392
Isa 24: 2 as *with* the **taker of u**, so *with* the giver of 5378
24: 2 of usury, so *with* the **giver of u** to him. 5383
Jer 15:10 I have neither **lent on u**, nor *men* have lent 5383
15:10 on usury, nor *men* have **lent** to me **on u**; 5383
Eze 18: 8 He *that* hath not given forth upon **u**, 5392
18:13 Hath given forth upon **u**, and hath taken 5392
18:17 *that* hath not received **u** nor increase, 5392
22:12 thou hast taken **u** and increase, and 5392
Mt 25:27 I should have received mine own with **u**. *5110*
Lk 19:23 I might have required *mine own* with **u**? *5110*

US-WARD (3) [WE]
Ps 40: 5 and thy thoughts *which are* to **u**: 413+5105.1
Eph 1:19 greatness of his power to **u** who believe, *1473*
2Pe 3: 9 but is longsuffering to **u**, not willing that *1473*

UTENSILS See FURNITURE

UTHAI (2)
1Ch 9: 4 **U** the son of Ammihud, the son of Omri, 5793
Ezr 8:14 **U**, and Zabbud, and with them seventy 5793

UTMOST (11) [UTTER]
Ge 49:26 unto the **u bound** of the everlasting hills: 8379
Nu 22:36 border of Arnon, which *is* in the **u** coast. 7097
22:41 that thence he might see the **u part** of 7097
23:13 thou shalt see but the **u part** of them, and 7097
Dt 34: 2 and all the land of Judah, unto the **u** sea, 314
Jer 9:26 and Moab, and all *that are* **in the u** corners, 7112
25:23 and Buz, and all *that are* **in the u** corners, 7112
49:32 all winds them *that are* **in the u** corners; 7112
50:26 Come against her from the **u border**, 7093
Joel 2:20 his hinder part towards the **u** sea, and 314
Lk 11:31 for she came from the **u parts** of the earth *4009*

UTTER (46) [UTMOST, UTTERANCE, UTTERED, UTTERETH, UTTERING, UTTERLY, UTTERMOST]
Lev 5: 1 or known *of it*; if he do not **u** *it*, then 5046
Jos 2:14 life for yours, if ye **u** not this our business. 5046
2:20 if thou **u** this our business, then we will be 5046
Jdg 5:12 awake, awake, **u** a song: arise, Barak, and 1696
1Ki 20:42 a man whom I **appointed to u destruction**, 2764
Job 8:10 tell thee, and **u** words out of their heart? 3318
15: 2 Should a wise *man* **u** vain knowledge, and 6030
27: 4 speak wickedness, nor my tongue **u** deceit. 1897
33: 3 and my lips shall **u** knowledge clearly. 4448
Ps 78: 2 in a parable: I will **u** dark sayings of old: 5042
94: 4 *How long* shall they **u** *and* speak hard 5042
106: 2 Who can **u** the mighty acts of the LORD? 4448
119:171 My lips shall **u** praise, when thou hast 5042
145: 7 They shall **abundantly u** the memory of 5042
Pr 14: 5 will not lie: but a false witness will **u** lies. 6315
23:33 and thine heart shall **u** perverse things. 1696
Ecc 1: 8 man cannot **u** *it*: the eye is not satisfied 1696
5: 2 let not thine heart be hasty to **u** *any* thing 3318
Isa 32: 6 and to **u** error against the LORD, 1696
48:20 tell this, **u** it *even* to the end of the earth; 3318
Jer 1:16 I will **u** my judgments against them 1696
25:30 and **u** his voice from his holy habitation; 5414
Eze 10: 5 wings was heard *even* to the **u** court, 2435
24: 3 **u** a parable unto the rebellious house, and 4911
40:31 the arches thereof *were* toward the **u** court; 2435
40:37 the posts thereof *were* toward the **u** court; 2435
42: 1 he brought me forth into the **u** court, 2435
42: 3 the pavement which *was* for the **u** court, 2435
42: 7 towards the **u** court on the forepart of 2435
42: 8 that *were* in the **u** court *was* fifty cubits: 2435
42: 9 as one goeth into them from the **u** court. 2435
42:14 go out of the holy *place* into the **u** court, 2435
44:19 when they go forth into the **u** court, 2435
44:19 *even* into the **u** court to the people, 2435
46:20 that *they* bear *them* not out into the **u** court, 2435
46:21 he brought me forth into the **u** court, 2435
47: 2 led me about the way without unto the **u** 2351
Joel 2:11 the LORD shall **u** his voice before his 5414
3:16 of Zion, and **u** his voice from Jerusalem; 5414
Am 1: 2 from Zion, and **u** his voice from Jerusalem; 5414
Na 1: 8 he will make an **u end** of the place thereof, 3617
1: 9 he *will* make an **u end**: affliction shall not 3617
Zec 14:11 and there shall be no more **u destruction**; 2764
Mt 13:35 I will **u** *things which have been* kept secret *2044*
1Co 14: 9 except ye **u** by the tongue words easy to be *1325*
2Co 12: 4 which *it is* not lawful for a man to **u**. *2980*

UTTERANCE (5) [UTTER]
Ac 2: 4 other tongues, as the Spirit gave them **u**. *669*
1Co 1: 5 by him, in all **u**, and *in* all knowledge; *3056*
2Co 8: 7 and **u**, and knowledge, and *in* all diligence, *3056*
Eph 6:19 And for me, that **u** may be given unto me, *3056*
Col 4: 3 that God would open unto us a door of **u**, *3056*

UTTERED (17) [UTTER]
Nu 30: 6 she vowed, or **u ought out** of her lips, 4008
30: 8 **that which** she **u** with her lips, 4008
Jdg 11:11 Jephthah **u** all his words before the LORD 1696
2Sa 22:14 and the most High **u** his voice. 5414
Ne 6:19 deeds before me, and **u** my words to him. 3318
Job 26: 4 To whom hast thou **u** words? and 5046
42: 3 therefore have I **u** that I understood not; 5046
Ps 46: 6 he **u** his voice, the earth melted. 5414
66:14 Which my lips have **u**, and my mouth hath 6475
Jer 48:34 *even* unto Jahaz, have they **u** their voice, 5414
51:55 like great waters, a noise of their voice is **u**: 5414
Hab 3:10 the deep **u** his voice, *and* lift up his hands 5414
Ro 8:26 for us with groanings which **cannot be u**. *215*
Heb 5:11 and hard to be **u**, seeing ye are dull of *3004*
Rev 10: 3 he had cried, seven thunders **u** their voices. *2980*
10: 4 And when the seven thunders had **u** their *2980*
10: 4 *up those things* which the seven thunders **u**, *2980*

UTTERETH (9) [UTTER]
Job 15: 5 For thy mouth **u** thine iniquity, and 502
Ps 19: 2 Day unto day **u** speech, and night unto 5042
Pr 1:20 she **u** her voice in the streets: 5414
1:21 in the city she **u** her words, *saying*, 559
10:18 lying lips, and he that **u** a slander, *is* a fool. 3318
29:11 A fool **u** all his mind: but a wise *man* 3318
Jer 10:13 When he **u** his voice, *there is* a multitude of 5414
51:16 When he **u** *his* voice, *there is* a multitude of 5414
Mic 7: 3 the great *man*, he **u** his mischievous desire: 1696

UTTERING (1) [UTTER]
Isa 59:13 and **u** from the heart words of falsehood. 1897

UTTERLY (101) [UTTER]
Ex 17:14 for I will **u put out** the remembrance 4229+4229
22:17 If her father **u refuse** to give her unto 3985+3985
22:20 the LORD only, he shall be **u destroyed**. 2763
23:24 thou shalt **u overthrow** them, and 2040+2040
Lev 13:44 shall **pronounce** him **u unclean**, 2930+2930
26:44 to **destroy** them **u**, and to break my 3615
Nu 15:31 that soul shall **u** be **cut off**; 3772+3772
21: 2 my hand, then I will **u destroy** their cities. 2763
21: 3 and they **u destroyed** them and their cities: 2763
30:12 **u made** them **void** on the day he 6565+6565
Dt 2:34 **u destroyed** the men, and the women, and 2763
3: 6 we **u destroyed** them, as we did unto Sihon 2763
3: 6 **u destroying** the men, women, and 2763
4:26 that ye shall soon **u perish** from off the land 6+6
4:26 *your* days upon it, but shall **u** be destroyed. NIH
7: 2 thou shalt smite them, *and* **u destroy** 2763+2763
7:26 *but* thou shalt **u detest** it, and 8262+8262
7:26 detest it, and thou shalt **u abhor** it; 8581+8581
12: 2 Ye shall **u destroy** all the places, 6+6
13:15 **destroying** it **u**, and all that *is* therein, 2763
20:17 thou shalt **u destroy** them; 2763+2763
31:29 death ye will **u corrupt** *yourselves*, 7843+7843
Jos 2:10 and Og, whom ye **u destroyed**. 2763
6:21 they **u destroyed** all that *was* in the city, 2763
8:26 until *he* had **u destroyed** all the inhabitants 2763
10: 1 had taken Ai, and had **u destroyed** it; 2763
10:28 the king thereof he **u destroyed**, them, 2763
10:35 that *were* therein he **u destroyed** that day, 2763
10:37 **destroyed** it **u**, and all the souls that *were* 2763
10:39 **u destroyed** all the souls that *were* therein; 2763
10:40 but **u destroyed** all that breathed, 2763
11:11 **u destroying** *them*: there was not any left 2763
11:12 of the sword, *and* he **u destroyed** them, 2763
11:20 that *he* might **destroy** them **u**, *and* that they 2763
11:21 Joshua **destroyed** them **u** with their cities. 2763
17:13 but did not **u drive** them **out**. 3423+3423
Jdg 1:17 that inhabited Zephath, and **u destroyed** it: 2763
1:28 and did not **u drive** them **out**. 3423+3423
15: 2 thought that thou hadst **u hated** her; 8130+8130
21:11 Ye shall **u destroy** every male, and 2763
1Sa 15: 3 **u destroy** all that they have, and 2763
15: 8 **u destroyed** all the people with the edge of 2763
15: 9 *was* good, and would not **u destroy** them: 2763
15: 9 *was* vile and refuse, that they **destroyed u**. 2763
15:15 thy God; and the rest we have **u destroyed**. 2763
15:18 and **u destroy** the sinners the Amalekites, 2763
15:20 and have **u destroyed** the Amalekites. 2763
15:21 **things** which should have been **u destroyed**, 2764
27:12 **made** his people Israel **u to abhor** him; 887+887
2Sa 17:10 *is* as the heart of a lion, shall **u melt**: 4549+4549
23: 7 they shall be **u burnt** with fire in 8313+8313
1Ki 9:21 of Israel also were not able **u to destroy**, 2763
2Ki 19:11 done to all lands, by **destroying** them **u**: 2763
1Ch 4:41 **destroyed** them **u** unto this day, and 2763
2Ch 20:23 **u to slay** and destroy *them*: and when they 2763
31: 1 until *they* had **u destroyed** *them all*. Then 3615
32:14 those nations that my fathers **u destroyed**, 2763
Ne 9:31 sake thou didst not **u consume** them, 3617
Ps 37:24 he fall, he shall not be **u cast down**: 2904
73:19 they are **u** consumed with terrors. 8552
89:33 lovingkindness will I not **u take** from him, 6331
119: 8 thy statutes: O forsake me not **u**. 3966+5704
119:43 take not the word of truth **u** out of 3966+5704
SS 8: 7 for love, it would **u** be **contemned**. 936+936
Isa 2:18 And the idols he shall **u** abolish. 3632
6:11 without man, and the land be **u** desolate, 8077
11:15 the LORD shall **u destroy** the tongue of 2763
24: 3 The land shall be **u emptied**, 1238+1238
24: 3 shall be utterly emptied, and **u spoiled**: 962+962
24:19 The earth is **u broken down**, 7489+7489

U

Isa 34: 2 he hath **u destroyed** them, he hath 2763
37:11 done to all lands by **destroying** them **u**; 2763
40:30 and the young men shall **u fall**: 3782+3782
56: 3 The LORD hath **u separated** me from 914+914
60:12 yea, *those* nations shall be **u wasted**. 2717+2717
Jer 9: 4 for every brother will **u supplant**, 6117+6117
12:17 I will **u pluck up** and destroy that 5428+5428
14:19 Hast thou **u rejected** Judah? hath thy 3988+3988
23:39 will **u forget** you, and I will forsake 5377+5382
25: 9 will **u destroy** them, and make them an 2763
25:29 and should ye be **u unpunished**? 5352+5352
50:21 waste and **u destroy** after them, saith 2763
50:26 cast her up as heaps, and **destroy** her **u**: 2763
51: 3 her young men; **destroy** ye **u** all her host. 2763
51:58 walls of Babylon shall be **u broken**, 6209+6209
La 5:22 thou hast **u rejected** us; thou art very 3988+3988
Eze 9: 6 Slay **u** old *and* young, both maids, 4889+3807.1
17:10 shall it not **u wither**, when the east 3001+3001
27:31 they shall **make** themselves **u bald** 7139+7139
29:10 make the land of Egypt **u waste** *and* 2721+2723
Da 11:44 fury to destroy, and **u** to **make away** many. 2763
Hos 1: 6 but I will **u take** them **away**. 5375+5375
10:15 shall the king of Israel **u** be **cut off**. 1820+1820
Am 9: 8 saving that I will not **u destroy** 8045+8045
Mic 2: 4 *and* say, We be **u spoiled**: 7703+7703
Na 1:15 no more pass through thee; he is **u** cut off. 3605
Zep 1: 2 I will **u** consume all *things* from off the land, 622
Zec 11:17 his right eye shall be **u darkened**. 3543+3543
1Co 6: 7 therefore there is **u** a fault among you, *3654*
2Pe 2:12 and shall **u perish** in their own corruption; *2704*
Rev 18: 8 famine; and she shall be **u burnt** with fire: *2618*

UTTERMOST (28) [UTTER]

Ex 26: 4 likewise shalt thou make in the **u** edge of 7020
36:11 likewise he made in the **u** side of *another* 7020
36:17 he made fifty loops upon the **u** edge of 7020
Nu 11: 1 consumed *them that were* in the **u parts** of 7097
20:16 *are* in Kadesh, a city in the **u** of thy border: 7097
Dt 11:24 even unto the **u** sea shall your coast be. 314
Jos 15: 1 *was* the **u part** of the south *coast*. 4480+7097
15: 5 the bay of the sea at the **u part** of Jordan: 7097
15:21 the **u** cities of the tribe of 4480+7097
1Sa 14: 2 Saul tarried in the **u part** of Gibeah under a 7097
1Ki 6:24 from the **u part** of the one wing unto 7098
6:24 unto the **u part** of the other *were* ten cubits. 7098
2Ki 7: 5 when they were come to the **u part** of 7097
7: 8 when these lepers came to the **u part** of 7097
Ne 1: 9 you cast out unto the **u part** of the heaven, 7097
Ps 2: 8 the **u parts** of the earth *for* thy possession. 657
65: 8 They also that dwell in the **u parts** are 7099
139: 9 *and* dwell in the **u parts** of the sea; 319
Isa 7:18 that *is* in the **u part** of the rivers of Egypt, 7097
24:16 From the **u part** of the earth have we heard 3671
Mt 5:26 out thence, till thou hast paid the **u** farthing. *2078*
12:42 for she came from the **u parts** of the earth *4009*
Mk 13:27 from the **u part** of the earth to the uttermost *206*
13:27 part of the earth to the **u part** of heaven. *206*
Ac 1: 8 and unto the **u part** of the earth. *2078*
24:22 I will **know the u** of your matter. *1231*
1Th 2:16 for the wrath is come upon them to the **u**. *5056*
Heb 7:25 them to the **u** that come unto God by him, *3838*

UZ (7)

Ge 10:23 **U**, and Hul, and Gether, and Mash. 5780
36:28 children of Dishan *are* these; **U**, and Aran. 5780
1Ch 1:17 and **U**, and Hul, and Gether, and Meshech. 5780
1:42 Jakan. The sons of Dishan; **U**, and Aran. 5780
Job 1: 1 There was a man in the land of **U**, 5780
Jer 25:20 all the kings of the land of **U**, and all 5780
La 4:21 of Edom, that dwellest in the land of **U**; 5780

UZAI (1)

Ne 3:25 Palal the son of **U**, over against the turning 186

UZAL (2)

Ge 10:27 And Hadoram, and **U**, and Diklah, 187
1Ch 1:21 Hadoram also, and **U**, and Diklah, 187

UZZA (10) [UZZAH]

2Ki 21:18 of his own house, in the garden of **U**: 5798
21:26 buried in his sepulchre in the garden of **U**: 5798
1Ch 6:29 Libni his son, Shimei his son, **U** his son, 5798
8: 7 removed them, and begat **U**, and Ahihud. 5798
13: 7 and **U** and Ahio drave the cart. 5798
13: 9 **U** put forth his hand to hold the ark; 5798
13:10 of the LORD was kindled against **U**, 5798
13:11 the LORD had made a breach upon **U**: 5798
Ezr 2:49 The children of **U**, the children of Paseah, 5798
Ne 7:51 the children of **U**, the children of Phaseah, 5798

UZZAH (4) [PEREZ-UZZA, PEREZ-UZZAH, UZZA]

2Sa 6: 3 **U** and Ahio, the sons of Abinadab, 5798
6: 6 **U** put forth *his hand* to the ark of God, and 5798
6: 7 of the LORD was kindled against **U**; 5798
6: 8 the LORD had made a breach upon **U**: 5798

UZZEN SHEERAH See UZZEN-SHERAH

UZZEN-SHERAH (1)

1Ch 7:24 the nether, and the upper, and **U**.) 242

UZZI (11)

1Ch 6: 5 Abishua begat Bukki, and Bukki begat **U**, 5813
6: 6 **U** begat Zerahiah, and Zerahiah begat 5813
6:51 Bukki his son, **U** his son, Zerahiah his son, 5813
7: 2 **U**, and Rephaiah, and Jeriel, and Jahmai, 5813
7: 3 the sons of **U**; Izrahiah: and the sons of 5813
7: 7 **U**, and Uzziel, and Jerimoth, and Iri, five; 5813
9: 8 Elah the son of **U**, the son of Michri, and 5813
Ezr 7: 4 of Zerahiah, the son of **U**, the son of Bukki, 5813
Ne 11:22 Levites at Jerusalem *was* **U** the son of Bani, 5813
12:19 And of Joiarib, Mattenai; of Jedaiah, **U**; 5813
12:42 **U**, and Jehohanan, and Malchijah, and 5813

UZZIA (1)

1Ch 11:44 **U** the Ashterathite, Shama and Jehiel 5814

UZZIAH (27) [AZARIAH]

2Ki 15:13 and thirtieth year of **U** king of Judah; 5818
15:30 the twentieth year of Jotham the son of **U**. 5818
15:32 Jotham the son of **U** king of Judah to reign. 5818
15:34 he did according to all that his father **U** had 5818
1Ch 6:24 Uriel his son, **U** his son, and Shaul his son. 5818
27:25 in the castles, *was* Jehonathan the son of **U**: 5818
2Ch 26: 1 all the people of Judah took **U**, who *was* 5818
26: 3 Sixteen years old *was* **U** when he *began* to 5818
26: 8 the Ammonites gave gifts to **U**: and 5818
26: 9 Moreover **U** built towers in Jerusalem at 5818
26:11 Moreover **U** had a host of fighting *men*, 5818
26:14 **U** prepared for them throughout all the host 5818
26:18 they withstood **U** the king, and said unto 5818
26:18 unto him, *It pertaineth* not unto thee, **U**, 5818
26:19 **U** was wroth, and *had* a censer in his hand 5818
26:21 **U** the king was a leper unto the day of his 5818
26:22 Now the rest of the acts of **U**, first and last, 5818
26:23 So **U** slept with his fathers, and they buried 5818
27: 2 according to all that his father **U** did: 5818
Ezr 10:21 Elijah, and Shemaiah, and Jehiel, and **U**. 5818
Ne 11: 4 Athaiah the son of **U**, the son of Zechariah, 5818
Isa 1: 1 and Jerusalem in the days of **U**, 5818
6: 1 In the year that king **U** died I saw also 5818
7: 1 the son of **U** king of Judah, *that* Rezin 5818
Hos 1: 1 in the days of **U**, Jotham, Ahaz, *and* 5818
Am 1: 1 Israel in the days of **U** king of Judah, 5818
Zec 14: 5 earthquake in the days of **U** king of Judah: 5818

UZZIEL (16) [UZZIELITES]

Ex 6:18 Amram, and Izhar, and Hebron, and **U**: 5816
6:22 the sons of **U**; Mishael, and Elzaphan, and 5816
Lev 10: 4 the sons of **U** the uncle of Aaron, and 5816
Nu 3:19 Amram, and Izehar, Hebron, and **U**. 5816
3:30 Kohathites *shall be* Elizaphan the son of **U**. 5816
1Ch 4:42 Neariah, and Rephaiah, and **U**, the sons of 5816
6: 2 Amram, Izhar, and Hebron, and **U**. 5816
6:18 and Izhar, and Hebron, and **U**. 5816
7: 7 Uzzi, and **U**, and Jerimoth, and Iri, five; 5816
15:10 Of the sons of **U**; Amminadab the chief, 5816
23:12 Amram, Izhar, Hebron, and **U**, four. 5816
23:20 *Of* the sons of **U**; Michah the first, and 5816
24:24 *Of* the sons of **U**; Michah: of the sons of 5816
25: 4 **U**, Shebuel, and Jerimoth, Hananiah, 5816
2Ch 29:14 of the sons of Jeduthun; Shemaiah, and **U**. 5816
Ne 3: 8 Next unto him repaired **U** the son of 5816

UZZIELITES (2) [UZZIEL]

Nu 3:27 of the Hebronites, and the family of the **U**: 5817
1Ch 26:23 the Izharites, the Hebronites, *and* the **U**: 5817

V

VAGABOND (3) [VAGABONDS]

Ge 4:12 a fugitive and a **v** shalt thou be in the earth. 5110
4:14 and I shall be a fugitive and a **v** in the earth; 5110
Ac 19:13 Then certain of the **v** Jews, exorcists, *4022*

VAGABONDS (1) [VAGABOND]

Ps 109:10 Let his children be **continually v**, 5128+5128

VAIL (45) [VAILS]

Ge 24:65 therefore she took a **v**, and covered herself. 6809
38:14 covered her with a **v**, and wrapped herself, 6809
38:19 laid by her **v** from her, and put on 6809
Ex 26:31 thou shalt make a **v** *of* blue, and purple, 6532
26:33 thou shalt hang up the **v** under the taches, 6532
26:33 within the **v** the ark of the Testimony: 6532
26:33 the **v** shall divide unto you between 6532
26:35 thou shalt set the table without the **v**, and 6532
27:21 of the congregation without the **v**, 6532
30: 6 thou shalt put it before the **v** that *is* by 6532
34:33 speaking with them, he put a **v** on his face. 4533
34:34 he took the **v** off, until he came out. 4533
34:35 Moses put the **v** upon his face again, 4533
35:12 the mercy seat, and the **v** of the covering, 6532
36:35 he made a **v** *of* blue, and purple, and 6532
38:27 of the sanctuary, and the sockets of the **v**; 6532
39:34 of badgers' skins, and the **v** of the covering, 6532
40: 3 and cover the ark with the **v**. 6532
40:21 set up the **v** of the covering, and 6532
40:22 of the tabernacle northward, without the **v**. 6532
40:26 in the tent of the congregation before the **v**: 6532
Lev 4: 6 the LORD, before the **v** of the sanctuary. 6532
4:17 times before the LORD, *even* before the **v**. 6532
16: 2 *place* within the **v** before the mercy seat, 6532
16:12 beaten small, and bring *it* within the **v**: 6532
16:15 bring his blood within the **v**, and do with 6532
21:23 Only he shall not go in unto the **v**, 6532
24: 3 Without the **v** of the Testimony, in 6532
Nu 4: 5 they shall take down the covering **v**, and 6532
18: 7 every thing of the altar, and within the **v**; 6532
Ru 3:15 Bring the **v** that *thou hast* upon thee, and 4304
2Ch 3:14 he made the **v** *of* blue, and purple, and 6532
SS 5: 7 the keepers of the walls took away my **v** 7289
Isa 25: 7 and the **v** that is spread over all nations. 4541
Mt 27:51 the **v** of the temple was rent in twain from *2665*
Mk 15:38 And the **v** of the temple was rent in twain *2665*
Lk 23:45 the **v** of the temple was rent in the midst. *2665*
2Co 3:13 not as Moses, *which* put a **v** over his face, *2571*
3:14 for until this day remaineth the same **v** *2571*
3:14 which **v** is done away in Christ. NIG
3:15 Moses is read, the **v** is upon their heart. *2571*
3:16 turn to the Lord, the **v** shall be taken away. *2571*
Heb 6:19 and which entereth into that within the **v**; *2665*
9: 3 And after the second **v**, the tabernacle *2665*
10:20 through the **v**, that is to say, his flesh; *2665*

VAILS (1) [VAIL]

Isa 3:23 and the fine linen, and the hoods, and the **v**. 7289

VAIN (112) [VAINGLORY, VAINLY, VANITIES, VANITY]

Ex 5: 9 and let them not regard **v** words. 8267
20: 7 take the name of the LORD thy God in **v**; 7723
20: 7 hold him guiltless that taketh his name in **v**. 7723
Lev 26:16 ye shall sow your seed in **v**, for your 7385
26:20 your strength shall be spent in **v**: for your 7385
Dt 5:11 take the name of the LORD thy God in **v**: 7723
5:11 hold *him* guiltless that taketh his name in **v**. 7723
32:47 For it *is* not a **v** thing for you; because it *is* 7386
Jdg 9: 4 wherewith Abimelech hired **v** and 7386
11: 3 there were gathered **v** men to Jephthah, and 7386
1Sa 12:21 *should ye go* after **v** *things*, which cannot 8414
12:21 cannot profit nor deliver; for they *are* **v**. 8414
25:21 Surely **in v** have I kept all 8267+1886.1+3807.1
2Sa 6:20 as one of the **v** *fellows* shamelessly 7386
2Ki 17:15 became **v**, and *went* after the heathen that 1891
18:20 Thou sayest, (but *they are but* **v** words,) 8193
2Ch 13: 7 there are gathered unto him **v** men, 7386
Job 9:29 *If* I be wicked, why then labour I **in v**? 1892
11:11 For he knoweth **v** men: he seeth 7723
11:12 For **v** man would be wise, though man be 5014
15: 2 Should a wise *man* utter **v** knowledge, and 7307
16: 3 Shall **v** words have an end? or 7307
21:34 How then comfort ye me **in v**, seeing *in* 1892
27:12 seen *it*; why then are ye thus **altogether v**? 1892
35:16 Therefore doth Job open his mouth **in v**; 1892
39:16 not hers: her labour *is* in **v** without fear; 7385
41: 9 Behold, the hope of him is **in v**: shall *not* 3576
Ps 2: 1 and the people imagine a **v** *thing?* 7385
26: 4 I have not sat with **v** persons, neither will I 7723
33:17 A horse *is* a **v thing** for safety: neither shall 8267
39: 6 Surely every man walketh **in a v shew**: 6754
39: 6 surely they are disquieted **in v**: he heapeth 1892
60:11 help from trouble: for **v** *is* the help of man. 7723
62:10 and become not **v** in robbery: 1891
73:13 Verily I have cleansed my heart **in v**, and 7385
89:47 wherefore hast thou made all men **in v**? 7723
108:12 help from trouble: for **v** *is* the help of man. 7723
119:113 I hate **v** thoughts: but thy law do I love. NIH
127: 1 the house, they labour **in v** that build it: 7723
127: 1 the city, the watchman waketh *but* **in v**. 7723
127: 2 *It is* **v** for you to rise up early, to sit up late, 7723
139:20 *and* thine enemies take *thy name* in **v**. 7723
Pr 1:17 Surely **in v** the net *is* spread in the sight of 2600
12:11 he that followeth **v** *persons is* void of 7386
28:19 he that followeth after **v** *persons* shall have 7386
30: 9 steal, and take the name of my God *in v*. NIH
31:30 Favour *is* deceitful, and beauty *is* **v**: *but* 1892
Ecc 6:12 all the days of his **v** life which he spendeth 1892
Isa 1:13 Bring no more **v** oblations; incense *is* an 7723
30: 7 For the Egyptians shall help **in v**, and to no 1892
36: 5 *sayest thou*, (but *they are but* **v** words) 8193
45:18 he hath established it, he created it not **in v**, 8414
45:19 unto the seed of Jacob, Seek ye me **in v**: 8414
49: 4 I said, I have laboured in **v**, I have spent my 7385
49: 4 spent my strength for nought, and **in v**: 1892
65:23 They shall not labour in **v**, nor bring forth 7385
Jer 2: 5 walked after vanity, and are **become v**? 1891
2:30 **In v** have I smitten your 7723+1886.1+3807.1
3:23 Truly in **v** *is salvation hoped for* from 8267
4:14 How long shall thy **v** thoughts lodge within 205
4:30 in **v** shalt thou make thyself fair; 7723
6:29 the founder melteth **in v**: 7723+1886.1+3807.1
8: 8 certainly **in v** made he *it*; the pen of 8267
8: 8 made he *it*; the pen of the scribes *is* in **v**. 8267
10: 3 For the customs of the people *are* **v**: for *one* 1892
23:16 they **make** you **v**: they speak a vision of 1891
46:11 in **v** shalt thou use many medicines; *for* 7723
50: 9 a mighty expert *man*; none shall return **in v**. 7387
51:58 the people shall labour in **v**, and the folk in 7385
La 2:14 Thy prophets have seen **v** and 7723
4:17 for us, our eyes as yet failed for our **v** help: 1892
Eze 6:10 *that* I have not said in **v** that *I* would do this 2600
12:24 For there shall be no more any **v** vision nor 7723
13: 7 Have ye not seen a **v** vision, and have ye 7723
Zec 10: 2 have told false dreams; they comfort **in v**: 1892
Mal 3:14 Ye have said, It *is* **v** to serve God: and 7723
Mt 6: 7 But when ye pray, **use not v repetitions**, *945*
15: 9 But **in v** they do worship me, teaching for *3155*
Mk 7: 7 Howbeit **in v** do they worship me, *3155*
Ac 4:25 and the people imagine **v** *things?* *2756*
Ro 1:21 but became **v** in their imaginations, and *3154*
13: 4 be afraid; for he beareth not the sword **in v**: *1500*
1Co 3:20 the thoughts of the wise, that they are **v**. *3152*
15: 2 unto you, unless ye have believed **in v**. *1500*
15:10 which was *bestowed* upon me was not **in v**; *2756*
15:14 then *is* our preaching **v**, and your faith *is* *2756*
15:14 our preaching vain, and your faith *is* also **v**. *2756*
15:17 And if Christ be not raised, your faith *is* **v**; *3152*
15:58 that your labour is not in **v** in the Lord. *2756*
2Co 6: 1 that ye receive not the grace of God in **v**. *2756*
9: 3 lest our boasting of you should be **in v** in *2758*
Gal 2: 2 by any means I should run, or had run, in **v**. *2756*
2:21 *come* by the law, then Christ is dead **in v**. *1432*
3: 4 Have ye suffered so many *things* in **v**? if *it* *1500*
3: 4 so many *things* in vain? if *it be* yet **in v**. *1500*
4:11 lest I have bestowed upon you labour **in v**. *1500*
5:26 Let us not be desirous of **v glory**, *2755*
Eph 5: 6 Let no *man* deceive you with **v** words: for *2756*
Php 2:16 that I have not run in **v**, neither laboured in *2756*
2:16 have not run in vain, neither laboured in **v**. *2756*
Col 2: 8 spoil you through philosophy and **v** deceit, *2756*

1Th 2: 1 entrance in unto you, that it was not in v: 2756
3: 5 have tempted you, and our labour be in v. 2756
1Ti 1: 6 swerved have turned aside unto v jangling; 3150
6:20 avoiding profane and v babblings, and 2757
2Ti 2:16 But shun profane and v babblings: for they 2757
Tit 1:10 many unruly and v talkers and deceivers, 3151
3: 9 the law; for they are unprofitable and v. 3152
Jas 1:26 his own heart, this man's religion is v. 3152
2:20 But wilt thou know, O v man, that faith 2756
4: 5 Do ye think that the scripture saith in v, 2761
1Pe 1:18 from your v conversation received by 3152

VAINGLORY (1) [GLORY, VAIN]
Php 2: 3 Let nothing be done through strife or v; but 2754

VAINLY (1) [VAIN]
Col 2:18 hath not seen, v puft up by his fleshly mind, 1500

VAIZATHA See VAJEZATHA

VAJEZATHA (1)
Est 9: 9 and Arisai, and Aridai, and V, 2055

VALE (9) [VALLEY]
Ge 14: 3 All these were joined together in the v of 6010
14: 8 they joined battle with them in the v of 6010
14:10 the v of Siddim was full of slimepits; 6010
37:14 So he sent him out of the v of Hebron, and 6010
Dt 1: 7 in the v, and in the south, and by the sea 8219
Jos 10:40 of the v, and of the springs, and all their 8219
1Ki 10:27 to be as the sycomore trees that are in the v, 8219
2Ch 1:15 trees that are in the v for abundance. 8219
Jer 33:13 in the cities of the v, and in the cities of 8219

VALIANT (31) [VALOUR]
1Sa 14:52 or any v man, he took him unto him. 2428
16:18 a mighty v man, and a man of war, and 2428
18:17 only be thou v for me, and fight 1121+2428
26:15 David said to Abner, Art not thou a v man? NIH
31:12 All the v men arose, and went all night, and 2428
2Sa 2: 7 hands be strengthened, and be ye v: 1121+2428
11:16 a place where he knew that v men were. 2428
13:28 be courageous, and be v. 1121+2428
17:10 he also that is v, whose heart is as 1121+2428
17:10 and they which be with him are v men. 2428
23:20 the son of a v man, of Kabzeel, who had 2428
24: 9 thousand v men that drew the sword; 2428
1Ki 1:42 for thou art a v man, and bringest good 2428
1Ch 5:18 of v men, men able to bear buckler and 2428
7: 2 they were v men of might in their 1368
10:12 all the v men, and took away the body of 2428
11:22 the son of a v man of Kabzeel, who had 2428
11:26 Also the v men of the armies were, Asahel 1368
28: 1 the mighty men, and with all the v men, 2428
2Ch 13: 3 in array with an army of v men of war, 1368
26:17 priests of the LORD, that were v men: 2428
28: 6 thousand in one day, which were all v men; 2428
Ne 11: 6 four hundred threescore and eight v men. 2428
SS 3: 7 threescore v men are about it, of the valiant 1368
3: 7 valiant men are about it, of the v of Israel. 1368
Isa 10:13 I have put down the inhabitants like a v man: 47
33: 7 Behold, their v ones shall cry without: 691
Jer 9: 3 they are not v for the truth upon the earth; 1396
46:15 Why are thy v men swept away? they stood 47
Na 2: 3 men is made red, the v men are in scarlet: 2428
Heb 11:34 were made strong, waxed v in fight, 2478

VALIANTEST (1) [VALOUR]
Jdg 21:10 thither twelve thousand men of the v, 1121+2428

VALIANTLY (6) [VALOUR]
Nu 24:18 for his enemies; and Israel shall do v. 2428
1Ch 19:13 let us behave ourselves v for our people, 2388
Ps 60:12 Through God we shall do v: for he it is that 2428
108:13 Through God we shall do v: for he it is that 2428
118:15 the right hand of the LORD doeth v. 2428
118:16 the right hand of the LORD doeth v. 2428

VALLEY (140) [VALE, VALLEYS]
Ge 14:17 at the v of Shaveh, which is the king's dale. 6010
26:17 pitched his tent in the v of Gerar, and 5158
26:19 Isaac's servants digged in the v, and 5158
Nu 14:25 and the Canaanites dwelt in the v.) 6010
21:12 and pitched in the v of Zared. 5158
21:20 from Bamoth in the v, that is in the country 1516
32: 9 For when they went up unto the v of 5158
Dt 1:24 came unto the v of Eshcol, and searched it 5158
3:16 half the v, and the border, even unto 5158
3:29 So we abode in the v over against 1516
4:46 in the v over against Beth-peor, 1516
21: 4 shall bring down the heifer unto a rough v, 5158
21: 4 strike off the heifer's neck there in the v: 5158
21: 6 over the heifer that is beheaded in the v: 5158
34: 3 the south, and the plain of the v of Jericho, 1237
34: 6 he buried him in a v in the land of Moab, 1516
Jos 7:24 and they brought them unto the v of Achor. 6010
7:26 was called, The v of Achor, unto this day. 6010
8:11 now there was a v between them and Ai. 1516
8:13 went that night into the midst of the v. 6010
10:12 and thou, Moon, in the v of Ajalon. 6010
11: 2 in the v, and in the borders of Dor on 8219
11: 8 and unto the v of Mizpeh eastward; 1237
11:16 the v, and the plain, and the mountain of 8219
11:16 mountain of Israel, and the v of the same; 8219
11:17 even unto Baal-gad in the v of Lebanon 1237
12: 7 from Baal-gad in the v of Lebanon even 1237
13:19 and Zareth-shahar in the mount of the v, 6010
13:27 in the v, Beth-aram, and Beth-nimrah, and 6010
15: 7 the border went up toward Debir from the v 6010
15: 8 the border went up by the v of the son of 1516
15: 8 that lieth before the v of Hinnom westward, 1516
15: 8 which is at the end of the v of the giants 6010
15:33 And in the v, Eshtaol, and Zoreah, and 8219
17:16 in the land of the v have chariots of iron, 6010
Jos 17:16 and they who are of the v of Jezreel. 6010
18:16 lieth before the v of the son of Hinnom, 1516
18:16 which is in the v of the giants on the north, 6010
18:16 descended to the v of Hinnom, to the side 1516
18:21 and Beth-hoglah, and the v of Keziz, 6010
19:14 the outgoings thereof are in the v of 1516
19:27 to the v of Jiphthah-el toward the north side 1516
Jdg 1: 9 the mountain, and in the south, and in the v. 8219
1:19 could not drive out the inhabitants of the v, 6010
1:34 not suffer them to come down to the v: 6010
5:15 he was sent on foot into the v. For 6010
6:33 went over, and pitched in the v of Jezreel. 6010
7: 1 side of them, by the hill of Moreh, in the v. 6010
7: 8 host of Midian was beneath him in the v. 6010
7:12 all the children of the east lay along in the v 6010
16: 4 that he loved a woman in the v of Sorek, 5158
18:28 and it was in the v that lieth by Beth-rehob. 6010
1Sa 6:13 were reaping their wheat harvest in the v: 6010
13:18 to the v of Zeboim toward the wilderness. 1516
15: 5 to a city of Amalek, and laid wait in the v. 5158
17: 2 pitched by the v of Elah, and set the battle 6010
17: 3 other side: and there was a v between them. 1516
17:19 all the men of Israel, were in the v of Elah, 6010
17:52 until thou come to the v, and to the gates of 1516
21: 9 whom thou slewest in the v of Elah, 6010
31: 7 Israel that were on the other side of the v, 6010
2Sa 5:18 and spread themselves in the v of Rephaim. 6010
5:22 and spread themselves in the v of Rephaim. 6010
8:13 from smiting of the Syrians in the v of salt, 1516
23:13 the troop of the Philistines pitched in the v 6010
2Ki 2:16 him upon some mountain, or into some v. 1516
3:16 the LORD, Make this v full of ditches. 5158
3:17 yet that v shall be filled with water, that ye 5158
14: 7 He slew of Edom in the v of salt ten 1516
23:10 which is in the v of the children of Hinnom, 1516
1Ch 4:14 the father of the v of Charashim; 1516
4:39 even unto the east side of the v, to seek 1516
10: 7 Israel that were in the v saw that they fled, 6010
11:15 Philistines encamped in the v of Rephaim. 6010
14: 9 and spread themselves in the v of Rephaim. 6010
14:13 again spread themselves abroad in the v. 6010
18:12 Edomites in the v of salt eighteen thousand. 1516
2Ch 14:10 they set the battle in array in the v of 1516
20:26 assembled themselves in the v of Berachah; 6010
20:26 The v of Berachah, unto this day. 6010
25:11 went to the v of salt, and smote of 1516
26: 9 at the v gate, and at the turning of the wall, 1516
28: 3 Moreover he burnt incense in the v of 1516
33: 6 the fire in the v of the son of Hinnom: 1516
33:14 on the west side of Gihon, in the v, even to 5158
35:22 and came to fight in the v of Megiddo. 1237
Ne 2:13 I went out by night by the gate of the v, 1516
2:15 entered by the gate of the v, and so 1516
3:13 The v gate repaired Hanun, and 1516
11:30 they dwelt from Beer-sheba unto the v of 1516
11:35 Lod, and Ono, the v of craftsmen. 1516
Job 21:33 The clods of the v shall be sweet unto him, 5158
39:21 He paweth in the v, and rejoiceth in his 6010
Ps 23: 4 though I walk through the v of the shadow 1516
60: T smote of Edom in the v of salt twelve 1516
60: 6 and mete out the v of Succoth. 6010
84: 6 Who passing through the v of Baca make it 6010
108: 7 and mete out the v of Succoth. 6010
Pr 30:17 the ravens of the v shall pick it out, and 5158
SS 6:11 the garden of nuts to see the fruits of the v, 5158
Isa 17: 5 it shall be as he that gathereth ears in the v 6010
22: 1 The burden of the v of vision. What aileth 1516
22: 5 the Lord GOD of hosts in the v of vision, 1516
28: 4 which is on the head of the fat v, shall be a 1516
28:21 he shall be wroth as in the v of Gibeon, 6010
40: 4 Every v shall be exalted, and 1516
63:14 As a beast goeth down into the v, the Spirit 1237
65:10 the v of Achor a place for the herds to lie 6010
Jer 2:23 see thy way in the v, know what thou hast 1516
7:31 which is in the v of the son of Hinnom, 1516
7:32 nor the v of the son of Hinnom, but 1516
7:32 the son of Hinnom, but the v of slaughter: 1516
19: 2 go forth unto the v of the son of Hinnom, 1516
19: 6 nor The v of the son of Hinnom, but The 1516
19: 6 the son of Hinnom, but The v of slaughter. 1516
21:13 O inhabitant of the v, and rock of the plain, 6010
31:40 the whole v of the dead bodies, and of 6010
32:35 which are in the v of the son of Hinnom, 1516
32:44 in the cities of the v, and in the cities of 8219
47: 5 is cut off with the remnant of their v: 6010
48: 8 the v also shall perish, and the plain shall 6010
49: 4 thy flowing v, O backsliding daughter? 6010
Eze 37: 1 set me down in the midst of the v which 1237
37: 2 there were very many in the open v; 1237
39:11 the v of the passengers on the east of 1516
39:11 and they shall call it The v of Hamon-gog. 1516
39:15 till the buriers have buried it in the v of 1516
Hos 1: 5 that I will break the bow of Israel in the v 6010
2:15 and the v of Achor for a door of hope: 6010
Joel 3: 2 will bring them down into the v of 6010
3:12 and come up to the v of Jehoshaphat: 6010
3:14 Multitudes, multitudes in the v of decision: 6010
3:14 for the day of the LORD is near in the v of 6010
3:18 and shall water the v of Shittim. 5158
Mic 1: 6 pour down the stones thereof into the v, 1516
Zec 12:11 as the mourning of Hadadrimmon in the v 1237
14: 4 the west, and there shall be a very great v; 1516
14: 5 ye shall flee to the v of the mountains; 1516
14: 5 for the v of the mountains shall reach unto 1516
Lk 3: 5 Every v shall be filled, and every mountain 5327

VALLEYS (28) [VALLEY]
Nu 24: 6 As the v are they spread forth, as gardens 5158
Dt 8: 7 and depths that spring out of the v and hills; 1237
11:11 is a land of hills and v, and drinketh water 1237
Jos 9: 1 in the v, and in all the coasts of the great 8219
12: 8 in the v, and in the plains, and in 8219
1Ki 20:28 he is not God of the v, therefore will I 6010
1Ch 12:15 they put to flight all them of the v, 6010
27:29 over the herds that were in the v was 6010
Job 30: 6 To dwell in the clifts of the v, in caves of 5158
39:10 or will he harrow the v after thee? 6010
Ps 65:13 the v also are covered over with corn; 6010
104: 8 they go down by the v unto the place which 1237
104:10 He sendeth the springs into the v, 5158
SS 2: 1 am the rose of Sharon, and the lily of the v. 6010
Isa 7:19 shall rest all of them in the desolate v, and 5158
22: 7 that thy choicest v shall be full of chariots, 6010
28: 1 which are on the head of the fat v of them 1516
41:18 and fountains in the midst of the v: 1237
57: 5 slaying the children in the v under the clifts 5158
Jer 49: 4 Wherefore gloriest thou in the v, 6010
Eze 6: 3 and to the hills, to the rivers, and to the v; 1516
7:16 be on the mountains like doves of the v, 1516
31:12 and in all the v his branches are fallen, 1516
32: 5 and fill the v with thy height. 1516
35: 8 in thy v, and in all thy rivers, shall they fall 1516
36: 4 to the hills, to the rivers, and to the v, to 1516
36: 6 and to the hills, to the rivers, and to the v, 1516
Mic 1: 4 the v shall be cleft, as wax before the fire, 6010

VALOUR (37) [VALIANT, VALIANTEST, VALIANTLY]
Jos 1:14 all the mighty men of v, and help them; 2428
6: 2 the king thereof, and the mighty men of v. 2428
8: 3 chose out thirty thousand mighty men of v, 2428
10: 7 war with him, and all the mighty men of v. 2428
Jdg 3:29 thousand men, all lusty, and all men of v; 2428
6:12 LORD is with thee, thou mighty man of v. 2428
11: 1 the Gileadite was a mighty man of v, 2428
18: 2 men of v, from Zorah and from Eshtaol, 2428
20:44 thousand men; all these were men of v. 2428
20:46 drew the sword; all these were men of v. 2428
1Ki 11:28 the man Jeroboam was a mighty man of v: 2428
2Ki 5: 1 he was also a mighty man in v, but he was 2428
24:14 all the princes, and all the mighty men of v, 2428
1Ch 5:24 Hodaviah, and Jahdiel, mighty men of v, 2428
7: 7 the house of their fathers, mighty men of v; 2428
7: 9 mighty men of v, was twenty thousand and 2428
7:11 mighty men of v, were seventeen thousand 2428
7:40 choice and mighty men of v, chief of 2428
8:40 the sons of Ulam were mighty men of v, 2428
12:21 rovers: for they were all mighty men of v, 2428
12:25 mighty men of v for the war, 2428
12:28 a young man mighty of v, and of his 2428
12:30 and eight hundred, mighty men of v, 2428
26: 6 their father: for they were mighty men of v. 2428
26:30 men of v, a thousand and seven hundred, 2428
26:31 them mighty men of v at Jazer of Gilead. 2428
26:32 his brethren, men of v, were two thousand 2428
2Ch 13: 3 chosen men, being mighty men of v. 2428
14: 8 all these were mighty men of v. 2428
17:13 the men of war, mighty men of v, were in 2428
17:14 with him mighty men of v three hundred 2428
17:16 two hundred thousand mighty men of v. 2428
17:17 Eliada a mighty man of v, and with him 2428
25: 6 v out of Israel for an hundred talents of 2428
26:12 of the mighty men of v were two thousand 2428
32:21 which cut off all the mighty men of v, and 2428
Ne 11:14 mighty men of v, an hundred twenty and 2428

VALUE (7) [VALUED, VALUEST]
Lev 27: 8 before the priest, and the priest shall v him; 6186
27: 8 his ability that vowed shall the priest v him. 6186
27:12 the priest shall v it, whether it be good or 6186
Job 13: 4 forgers of lies, ye are all physicians of no v. 457
Mt 10:31 ye are of more v than many sparrows. 1308
27: 9 whom they of the children of Israel did v; 5091
Lk 12: 7 ye are of more v than many sparrows. 1308

VALUED (4) [VALUE]
Lev 27:16 a homer of barley seed shall be v at fifty NIH
Job 28:16 It cannot be v with the gold of Ophir, 5541
28:19 equal it, neither shall it be v with pure gold. 5541
Mt 27: 9 pieces of silver, the price of him that was v, 5091

VALUEST (1) [VALUE]
Lev 27:12 as thou v it, who art the priest, so shall it 6187

VANIAH (1)
Ezr 10:36 V, Meremoth, Eliashib, 2057

VANISH (4) [VANISHED, VANISHETH]
Job 6:17 What time they wax warm, they v: when it 6789
Isa 51: 6 for the heavens shall v away like smoke, 4414
1Co 13: 8 there be knowledge, it shall v away. 2673
Heb 8:13 and waxeth old is ready to v away. 854

VANISHED (2) [VANISH]
Jer 49: 7 from the prudent? is their wisdom v? 5628
Lk 24:31 knew him; and he v out of their sight. 855+1096

VANISHETH (2) [VANISH]
Job 7: 9 As the cloud is consumed and v away: so 1980
Jas 4:14 appeareth for a little time, and then v away. 853

VANITIES (13) [VAIN]
Dt 32:21 have provoked me to anger with their v: 1892
1Ki 16:13 LORD God of Israel to anger with their v. 1892
16:26 LORD God of Israel to anger with their v. 1892
Ps 31: 6 I have hated them that regard lying v: but 1892
Ecc 1: 2 Vanity of v, saith the Preacher, vanity of 1892
1: 2 of vanities, saith the Preacher, vanity of v; 1892
5: 7 and many words there are also divers v: 1892
12: 8 Vanity of v, saith the Preacher; all is 1892
Jer 8:19 their graven images, and with strange v? 1892
10: 8 and foolish: the stock is a doctrine of v. 1892
14:22 Are there any among the v of the Gentiles 1892
Jnh 2: 8 They that observe lying v forsake their own 1892
Ac 14:15 turn from these v unto the living God, 3152

VANITY (86) [VAIN]
2Ki 17:15 they followed v, and became vain, and 1892
Job 7: 3 So am I made to possess months of v, and 7723

Job 7:16 live alway: let me alone; for my days *are* **v**. 1892
15:31 Let not him that is deceived trust in **v**: 7723
15:31 in vanity: for **v** shall be his recompence. 7723
15:35 bring forth **v**, and their belly prepareth 205
31: 5 If I have walked with **v**, or *if* my foot hath 7723
35:13 Surely God will not hear **v**, neither will 7723
Ps 4: 2 *how long* will ye love **v**, *and* seek after 7385
10: 7 fraud: under his tongue *is* mischief and **v**. 205
12: 2 They speak **v** every one with his neighbour: 7723
24: 4 who hath not lift up his soul unto **v**, 7723
39: 5 every man at his best state *is* altogether **v**. 1892
39:11 like a moth: surely every man *is* **v**. Selah. 1892
41: 6 if he come to see *me*, he speaketh **v**: 7723
62: 9 Surely men of low degree *are* **v**, *and* men of 1892
62: 9 they *are* altogether *lighter* than **v**. 1892
78:33 Therefore their days did he consume in **v**, 1892
94:11 the thoughts of man, that they *are* **v**. 1892
119:37 Turn away mine eyes from beholding **v**; 7723
144: 4 Man is like to **v**: his days *are* as a shadow 1892
144: 8 Whose mouth speaketh **v**, and their right 7723
144:11 whose mouth speaketh **v**, and their right 7723
Pr 13:11 Wealth *gotten* by **v** shall be diminished: but 1892
21: 6 treasures by a lying tongue *is* a **v** tossed to 1892
22: 8 He that soweth iniquity shall reap **v**: and 205
30: 8 Remove far from me **v** and lies: give me 7723
Ecc 1: 2 **V** of vanities, saith the Preacher, vanity of 1892
1: 2 of vanities, saith the Preacher, **v** of vanities; 1892
1: 2 the Preacher, vanity of vanities; all *is* **v**. 1892
1:14 and behold, all *is* **v** and vexation of spirit. 1892
2: 1 enjoy pleasure: and behold, this also *is* **v**. 1892
2:11 all *was* **v** and vexation of spirit, and 1892
2:15 Then I said in my heart, that this also *is* **v**. 1892
2:17 unto me: for all *is* **v** and vexation of spirit. 1892
2:19 myself wise under the sun. This *is* also **v**. 1892
2:21 his portion. This also *is* **v** and a great evil. 1892
2:23 taketh not rest in the night. This *is* also **v**. 1892
2:26 This also *is* **v** and vexation of spirit. 1892
3:19 no preeminence above a beast: for all *is* **v**. 1892
4: 4 This *is* also **v** and vexation of spirit. 1892
4: 7 Then I returned, and I saw **v** under the sun. 1892
4: 8 This *is* also **v**, yea, it *is* a sore travail. 1892
4:16 Surely this also *is* **v** and vexation of spirit. 1892
5:10 abundance *with* increase: this *is* also **v**. 1892
6: 2 eateth it: this *is* **v**, and it *is* an evil disease. 1892
6: 4 For he cometh in with **v**, and departeth in 1892
6: 9 this *is* also **v** and vexation of spirit. 1892
6:11 there be many things that increase **v**, 1892
7: 6 so *is* the laughter of the fool: this also *is* **v**. 1892
7:15 All *things* have I seen in the days of my **v**: 1892
8:10 city where they had so done: this *is* also **v**. 1892
8:14 There is a **v** which is done upon the earth; 1892
8:14 of the righteous: I said that this also *is* **v**. 1892
9: 9 thou lovest all the days of the life of thy **v**, 1892
9: 9 thee under the sun, all the days of thy **v**: 1892
11: 8 for they shall be many. All that cometh *is* **v**. 1892
11:10 thy flesh: for childhood and youth *are* **v**. 1892
12: 8 **V** of vanities, saith the Preacher; all *is* 1892
12: 8 of vanities, saith the Preacher; all *is* **v**. 1892
Isa 5:18 them that draw iniquity with cords of **v**, 7723
30:28 to sift the nations with the sieve of **v**: 7723
40:17 are counted to him less than nothing, and **v**. 8414
40:23 he maketh the judges of the earth as **v**. 8414
41:29 Behold, they *are* all **v**; their works *are* 205
44: 9 that make a graven image *are* all of them **v**; 8414
57:13 **v** shall take *them*: but he that putteth his 1892
58: 9 putting forth of the finger, and speaking **v**; 205
59: 4 *they* trust in **v**, and speak lies; 8414
Jer 2: 5 have walked after **v**, and are become vain? 1892
10:15 They *are* **v**, *and* the work of errors: in 1892
16:19 **v**, and *things* wherein *there is* no profit. 1892
18:15 they have burnt incense to **v**, and they have 7723
51:18 They *are* **v**, the work of errors: in the time 1892
Eze 13: 6 They have seen **v** and lying divination, 7723
13: 8 Because ye have spoken **v**, and seen lies, 7723
13: 9 hand shall be upon the prophets that see **v**, 7723
13:23 Therefore ye shall see no more **v**, 7723
21:29 Whiles *they* see **v** unto thee, whiles *they* 7723
22:28 them *with* untempered *morter*, seeing **v**, 7723
Hos 12:11 surely they are **v**: they sacrifice bullocks in 7723
Hab 2:13 people shall weary themselves for very **v**? 7385
Zec 10: 2 For the idols have spoken **v**, and the diviners 205
Ro 8:20 For the creature was made subject to **v**, *3153*
Eph 4:17 other Gentiles walk, in the **v** of their mind, *3153*
2Pe 2:18 when they speak great swelling *words* of **v**, *3153*

VAPOUR (5) [VAPOURS]
Job 36:27 they pour down rain according to the **v** 108
36:33 the cattle also concerning the **v**. 5927
Ps 148: 8 Fire, and hail; snow, and **v**; stormy wind 7008
Ac 2:19 blood, and fire, and **v** of smoke: *822*
Jas 4:14 It is even a **v**, that appeareth for a little *time*, *822*

VAPOURS (3) [VAPOUR]
Ps 135: 7 He causeth the **v** to ascend from the ends of 5387
Jer 10:13 he causeth the **v** to ascend from the ends of 5387
51:16 he causeth the **v** to ascend from the ends of 5387

VARIABLENESS (1) [VARIANCE]
Jas 1:17 with whom is no **v**, neither shadow of *3883*

VARIANCE (2) [VARIABLENESS]
Mt 10:35 For I am come to **set** a man **at v** against his *1369*
Gal 5:20 Idolatry, witchcraft, hatred, **v**, emulations, *2054*

VARIED See DIVERS; DIVERSE

VASHNI (1)
1Ch 6:28 sons of Samuel; the firstborn **V**, and Abiah. 2059

VASHTI (10)
Est 1: 9 Also **V** the queen made a feast for 2060
1:11 To bring **V** the queen before the king with 2060
1:12 the queen **V** refused to come at the king's 2060
1:15 What shall *we* do unto the queen **V** 2060
Est 1:16 **V** the queen hath not done wrong to 2060
1:17 The king Ahasuerus commanded **V** 2060
1:19 That **V** come no *more* before king 2060
2: 1 he remembered **V**, and what she had done, 2060
2: 4 pleaseth the king be queen instead of **V**. 2060
2:17 her head, and made her queen instead of **V**. 2060

VAT; VATS See CELLARS; FATS; LIQUORS; PRESSES

VAUNT (1) [VAUNTETH]
Jdg 7: 2 lest Israel **v** themselves against me, saying, 6286

VAUNTETH (1) [VAUNT]
1Co 13: 4 charity **v** not itself, is not puffed up, *4068*

VEGETABLES See PULSE

VEHEMENT (3) [VEHEMENTLY]
SS 8: 6 coals of fire, *which hath* a **most v flame**. 7957
Jnh 4: 8 did arise, that God prepared a **v** east wind; 2759
2Co 7:11 yea, *what* fear, yea, *what* **v desire**, yea, *1972*

VEHEMENTLY (5) [VEHEMENT]
Mk 14:31 But he spake the more **v**, If I should *1537+4053*
Lk 6:48 the stream **beat v upon** that house, and *4366*
6:49 **against** which the stream did **beat v**, and *4366*
11:53 and the Pharisees began to urge *him* **v**, *1171*
23:10 and scribes stood and **v** accused him. *2159*

VEIL, VEILS See KERCHIEFS; LOCKS; MUFFLERS; VAIL; VAILS

VEIN (1)
Job 28: 1 Surely there is a **v** for the silver, and 4161

VENGEANCE (45) [AVENGE, AVENGED, AVENGER, AVENGETH, AVENGING, REVENGE, REVENGED, REVENGER, REVENGERS, REVENGES, REVENGETH, REVENGING]
Ge 4:15 **v** shall be **taken** on him sevenfold. 5358
Dt 32:35 To me *belongeth* **v**, and recompence; 5359
32:41 I will render **v** to mine enemies, and 5359
32:43 will render **v** to his adversaries, and will be 5359
Jdg 11:36 forasmuch as the LORD hath taken **v** for 5360
Ps 58:10 righteous shall rejoice when he seeth the **v**: 5359
94: 1 O LORD God, to whom **v** belongeth; 5360
94: 1 O God, to whom **v** belongeth, shew thyself. 5360
99: 8 though thou **tookest v** of their inventions. 5358
149: 7 To execute **v** upon the heathen, *and* 5360
Pr 6:34 therefore he will not spare in the day of **v**. 5359
Isa 34: 8 For *it is* the day of the LORD'S **v**, *and* 5359
35: 4 behold, your God will come *with* **v**, 5359
47: 3 I will take **v**, and I will not meet *thee as* a 5359
59:17 he put on the garments of **v** *for* clothing, 5359
61: 2 the LORD, and the day of **v** of our God; 5359
63: 4 For the day of **v** *is* in mine heart, and 5359
Jer 11:20 and the heart, let me see thy **v** on them: 5360
20:12 and the heart, let me see thy **v** on them: 5360
46:10 a day of **v**, that *he* may avenge him of his 5360
50:15 for it *is* the **v** of the LORD: 5360
50:15 **take v** upon her; as she hath done, do unto 5358
50:28 to declare in Zion the **v** of the LORD our 5360
50:28 of the LORD our God, the **v** of his temple. 5360
51: 6 for this *is* the time of the LORD'S **v**; 5360
51:11 because it *is* the **v** of the LORD, 5360
51:11 of the LORD, the **v** of his temple. 5360
51:36 plead thy cause, and **take v** for thee; 5358+5360
La 3:60 Thou hast seen all their **v** *and* all their 5360
Eze 24: 8 cause fury to come up to **take v**; 5358+5359
25:12 the house of Judah by **taking v**, 5358+5359
25:14 I will lay my **v** upon Edom by the hand of 5360
25:14 they shall know my **v**, saith the Lord 5360
25:15 have **taken v** with a despiteful heart, 5358+5359
25:17 I will execute great **v** upon them with 5360
25:17 when I shall lay my **v** upon them. 5360
Mic 5:15 I will execute **v** in anger and fury upon 5359
Na 1: 2 the LORD will **take v** on his adversaries, 5358
Lk 21:22 For these be *the* days of **v**, that all *things* *1557*
Ac 28: 4 escaped the sea, yet **V** suffereth not to live. *1349*
Ro 3: 5 *Is* God unrighteous who taketh **v**? (I speak *3709*
12:19 for it is written, **V** *is* mine; I will repay, *1557*
2Th 1: 8 taking **v** on them that know not God, and *1557*
Heb 10:30 **V** *belongeth* unto me, I will recompense, *1557*
Jude 1: 7 an example, suffering the **v** of eternal fire. *1349*

VENISON (8)
Ge 25:28 loved Esau, because he did eat of *his* **v**: 6718
27: 3 and go out to the field, and take me *some* **v**; 6718
27: 5 Esau went to the field to hunt for **v**, *and* 6718
27: 7 Bring me **v**, and make me savoury meat, 6718
27:19 arise, I pray thee, sit and eat of my **v**, that 6718
27:25 *it* near to me, and I will eat of my son's **v**, 6718
27:31 Let my father arise, and eat of his son's **v**, 6718
27:33 where *is* he that hath taken **v**, and brought *it* 6718

VENOM (1) [VENOMOUS]
Dt 32:33 poison of dragons, and the cruel **v** of asps. 7219

VENOMOUS (1) [VENOM]
Ac 28: 4 And when the barbarians saw the **v** beast NIG

VENT (1)
Job 32:19 my belly *is* as wine *which* hath no **v**; 6605

VENTURE (2)
1Ki 22:34 a *certain* man drew a bow at a **v**, and 8537
2Ch 18:33 a *certain* man drew a bow at a **v**, and 8537

VERIFIED (3) [VERITY]
Ge 42:20 so shall your words be **v**, and ye shall not 539
1Ki 8:26 God of Israel, let thy word, I pray thee, be **v**, 539
2Ch 6:17 O LORD God of Israel, let thy word be **v**, 539

VERILY (140) [VERITY]
Ge 42:21 We *are* **v** guilty concerning our brother, 61
Ex 31:13 saying, **V** my sabbaths ye shall keep: 389
Jdg 15: 2 I **v thought** that thou hadst utterly 559+559
1Ki 1:43 **V** our lord king David hath made Solomon 61
2Ki 4:14 **V** she hath no child, and her husband is old. 61
1Ch 21:24 but I will **v buy** *it* for the full price: 7069+7069
Job 19:13 mine acquaintance are **v** estranged from me. 389
Ps 37: 3 dwell in the land, and **v** thou shalt be fed. 530
39: 5 **v** every man at his best state *is* altogether 389
58:11 **V** *there is* a reward for the righteous: 389
58:11 **v** he is a God that judgeth in the earth. 389
66:19 *But* **v** God hath heard *me*; he hath attended 403
73:13 **V** I have cleansed my heart *in* vain, and 389
Isa 45:15 **V** thou *art* a God that hidest thyself, O God 403
Jer 15:11 **V** it shall be well with thy remnant; 518+3808
15:11 **v** I will cause the enemy to entreat 518+3808
Mt 5:18 For **v** I say unto you, Till heaven and earth *281*
5:26 **V** I say unto thee, Thou shalt by no means *281*
6: 2 **V** I say unto you, They have their reward. *281*
6: 5 **V** I say unto you, They have their reward. *281*
6:16 **V** I say unto you, They have their reward. *281*
8:10 **V** I say unto you, I have not found so *281*
10:15 **V** I say unto you, It shall be more tolerable *281*
10:23 for **v** I say unto you, Ye shall not have gone *281*
10:42 **v** I say unto you, he shall in no wise lose his *281*
11:11 **V** I say unto you, Among *them that are* born *281*
13:17 For **v** I say unto you, That many prophets *281*
16:28 **V** I say unto you, There be some standing *281*
17:20 for **v** I say unto you, If ye have faith as a *281*
18: 3 And said, **V** I say unto you, Except ye be *281*
18:13 And if so be that he find it, **v** I say unto you, *281*
18:18 **V** I say unto you, Whatsoever ye shall bind *281*
19:23 Jesus unto his disciples, **V** I say unto you, *281*
19:28 And Jesus said unto them, **V** I say unto you, *281*
21:21 and said unto them, **V** I say unto you, *281*
21:31 **V** I say unto you, That the publicans and *281*
23:36 **V** I say unto you, All these *things* shall come *281*
24: 2 See ye not all these *things?* **v** I say unto you, *281*
24:34 **V** I say unto you, This generation shall not *281*
24:47 **V** I say unto you, That he shall make him *281*
25:12 But he answered and said, **V** I say unto you, *281*
25:40 and say unto them, **V** I say unto you, *281*
25:45 he answer them, saying, **V** I say unto you, *281*
26:13 **V** I say unto you, Wheresoever this gospel *281*
26:21 as they did eat, he said, **V** I say unto you, *281*
26:34 unto him, **V** I say unto thee, That this night, *281*
Mk 3:28 **V** I say unto you, All sins shall be forgiven *281*
6:11 **V** I say unto you, It shall be more tolerable *281*
8:12 **v** I say unto you, There shall no sign be *281*
9: 1 And he said unto them, **V** I say unto you, *281*
9:12 Elias **v** cometh first, and restoreth all *3303*
9:41 ye belong to Christ, **v** I say unto you, *281*
10:15 **V** I say unto you, Whosoever shall not *281*
10:29 Jesus answered and said, **V** I say unto you, *281*
11:23 For **v** I say unto you, That whosoever shall *281*
12:43 and saith unto them, **V** I say unto you, *281*
13:30 **V** I say unto you, that this generation shall *281*
14: 9 **V** I say unto you, Wheresoever this gospel *281*
14:18 and did eat, Jesus said, **V** I say unto you, *281*
14:25 **V** I say unto you, I will drink no more of *281*
14:30 **V** I say unto thee, That this day, *even* in this *281*
Lk 4:24 And he said, **V** I say unto you, No prophet is *281*
11:51 **v** I say unto you, It shall be required of this *3483*
12:37 **v** I say unto you, that he shall gird himself, *281*
13:35 and **v** I say unto you, Ye shall not see me, *281*
18:17 **V** I say unto you, Whosoever shall not *281*
18:29 And he said unto them, **V** I say unto you, *281*
21:32 **V** I say unto you, This generation shall not *281*
23:43 And Jesus said unto him, **V** I say unto thee, *281*
Jn 1:51 he saith unto him, **V**, verily, I say unto you, *281*
1:51 he saith unto him, Verily, **v**, I say unto you, *281*
3: 3 Jesus answered and said unto him, **V**, verily, *281*
3: 3 Jesus answered and said unto him, Verily, **v**, *281*
3: 5 Jesus answered, **V**, verily, I say unto thee, *281*
3: 5 Jesus answered, Verily, **v**, I say unto thee, *281*
3:11 **V**, verily, I say unto thee, We speak that we *281*
3:11 Verily, **v**, I say unto thee, We speak that we *281*
5:19 and said unto them, **V**, verily, I say unto you, *281*
5:19 and said unto them, Verily, **v**, I say unto you, *281*
5:24 **V**, verily, I say unto you, He that heareth my *281*
5:24 Verily, **v**, I say unto you, He that heareth my *281*
5:25 **V**, verily, I say unto you, The hour is *281*
5:25 Verily, **v**, I say unto you, The hour is *281*
6:26 Jesus answered them and said, **V**, verily, *281*
6:26 Jesus answered them and said, Verily, **v**, *281*
6:32 said unto them, **V**, verily, I say unto you, *281*
6:32 said unto them, Verily, **v**, I say unto you, *281*
6:47 **V**, verily, I say unto you, He that believeth *281*
6:47 Verily, **v**, I say unto you, He that believeth *281*
6:53 said unto them, **V**, verily, I say unto you, *281*
6:53 said unto them, Verily, **v**, I say unto you, *281*
8:34 answered them, **V**, verily, I say unto you, *281*
8:34 answered them, Verily, **v**, I say unto you, *281*
8:51 **V**, verily, I say unto you, If a man keep my *281*
8:51 Verily, **v**, I say unto you, If a man keep my *281*
8:58 said unto them, **V**, verily, I say unto you, *281*
8:58 said unto them, Verily, **v**, I say unto you, *281*
10: 1 **V**, verily, I say unto you, He that entereth *281*
10: 1 Verily, **v**, I say unto you, He that entereth *281*
10: 7 **V**, verily, I say unto you, I am the door of *281*
10: 7 Verily, **v**, I say unto you, I am the door of *281*
12:24 **V**, verily, I say unto you, Except a corn of *281*
12:24 Verily, **v**, I say unto you, Except a corn of *281*
13:16 **V**, verily, I say unto you, The servant is not *281*
13:16 Verily, **v**, I say unto you, The servant is not *281*
13:20 **V**, verily, I say unto you, He that receiveth *281*
13:20 Verily, **v**, I say unto you, He that receiveth *281*
13:21 and testified, and said, **V**, verily, I say unto *281*
13:21 and testified, and said, Verily, **v**, I say unto *281*
13:38 **V**, verily, I say unto thee, *The* cock shall not *281*
13:38 Verily, **v**, I say unto thee, *The* cock shall not *281*
14:12 **V**, verily, I say unto you, He that believeth *281*

Jn 14:12 Verily, v, I say unto you, He that believeth 281
16:20 V, verily, I say unto you, That ye shall weep 281
16:20 Verily, v, I say unto you, That ye shall weep 281
16:23 V, verily, I say unto you, Whatsoever ye 281
16:23 Verily, v, I say unto you, Whatsoever ye 281
21:18 V, verily, I say unto thee, When thou wast 281
21:18 Verily, v, I say unto thee, When thou wast 281
Ac 16:37 nay v; but let them come themselves and 1063
19: 4 John v baptized *with* the baptism of 3303
22: 3 I am v a man *which am* a Jew, born in 3303
26: 9 I v thought with myself, that *I* ought to do 3303
Ro 2:25 For circumcision v profiteth, if thou keep 3303
10:18 **Yes** v, their sound went into all the earth, 3304
15:27 It hath pleased them v; and their debtors 1063
1Co 5: 3 For I v, as absent in body, but present in 3303
9:18 *V* that, when I preach the gospel, I may NIG
14:17 For thou v givest thanks well, but the other 3303
Gal 3:21 v righteousness should have been by 3689
1Th 3: 4 For v, when we were with you, we told you 2532
Heb 2:16 For v he took not on *him the nature of* 1222
3: 5 And Moses v *was* faithful in all his house, 3303
6:16 For men v swear by the greater: and an oath 3303
7: 5 And v they that are of the sons of Levi who 3303
7:18 For there is v a disannulling of 3303
9: 1 Then v the first *covenant* had also 3303
12:10 For they v for a few days chastened *us* after 3303
1Pe 1:20 Who v was foreordained before 3303
1Jn 2: 5 in him v is the love of God perfected: 230

VERITY (2) [VERIFIED, VERILY]

Ps 111: 7 The works of his hands *are* v and judgment; 571
1Ti 2: 7 a teacher of the Gentiles in faith and v. 225

VERMILION (2)

Jer 22:14 *it is* cieled with cedar, and painted with v. 8350
Eze 23:14 images of the Chaldeans pourtrayed with v, 8350

VERY (257)

Ge 1:31 he had made, and behold, *it was* v good. 3966
4: 5 Cain was v wroth, and his countenance fell. 3966
12:14 beheld the woman that she *was* v fair. 3966
13: 2 Abram *was* v rich in cattle, in silver, and 3966
18:20 is great, and because their sin is v grievous; 3966
21:11 the thing was v grievous in Abraham's 3966
24:16 the damsel *was* v fair to look upon, 3966
26:13 and grew until he became v great: 3966
27:21 whether thou **be** my v son Esau or not. 2088
27:24 he said, *Art* thou my v son Esau? And he 2088
27:33 Isaac trembled v exceedingly, and 3966+5704
34: 7 they were v wroth, because he had wrought 3966
41:19 poor and v ill favoured and leanfleshed, 3966
41:31 famine following; for it *shall be* v grievous. 3966
41:49 of the sea, v much, until he left numbering; 3966
47:13 for the famine *was* v sore, so that the land 3966
50: 9 horsemen: and it was a v great company. 3966
50:10 with a great and v sore lamentation: 3966
Ex 1:20 the people multiplied, and waxed v mighty. 3966
8:28 only you shall not go v **far away**: 7368+7368
9: 3 *there shall be* a v grievous murrain. 3966
9:16 **in** v **deed** for this cause have I raised thee 199
9:18 time I will cause it to rain a v grievous hail, 3966
9:24 and fire mingled with the hail, v grievous, 3966
10:14 v grievous *were they;* before them there 3966
11: 3 Moreover the man Moses *was* v great in 3966
12:38 and flocks, and herds, *even* v much cattle. 3966
16:36 thou shalt beat *some* of it v **small**, and 1854
Nu 6: 9 if any man die v **suddenly** by 6597+6621+871.1
11:33 the LORD smote the people *with* a v great 3966
12: 3 (Now the man Moses *was* v meek, 3966
13:28 and the cities *are* walled, *and* v great: 3966
16:15 Moses was v wroth, and said unto 3966
22:17 For I will promote thee unto v **great** 3966
32: 1 the children of Gad had a v great multitude 3966
Dt 9:20 the LORD was v angry with Aaron to 3966
9:21 and stamped it, *and* **ground** *it* v **small**, 2912
20:15 all the cities *which are* v far off from thee, 3966
27: 8 stones all the words of this law v plainly. 3190
28:43 above thee v **high**; 4605+4605+1886.5+1886.5
28:43 thou shalt come down v **low**. 4295+4295
28:54 v delicate, his eye shall be evil toward his 3966
30:14 the word *is* v nigh unto thee, in thy mouth, 3966
32:20 *be:* for they *are* a v **froward** generation, 8419
Jos 1: 7 Only be thou strong and v courageous, 3966
3:16 above stood *and* rose up *upon* a heap v far, 3966
8: 4 go not v far from the city, but be ye all 3966
9: 9 From a v far country thy servants are come 3966
9:13 our shoes are become old by reason of the v 3966
9:22 beguiled us, saying, We *are* v far from you; 3966
10:20 of slaying them *with* a v great slaughter, 3966
10:27 *which remain* until this v day. 6106
11: 4 with horses and chariots v many. 3966
13: 1 there remaineth *yet* v much land to be 3966
22: 8 with v much cattle, with silver, and 3966
22: 8 and with iron, and with v much raiment: 3966
23: 6 Be ye therefore v courageous to keep and 3966
Jdg 3:17 king of Moab: and Eglon *was* a v fat man. 3966
11:33 of the vineyards, *with* a v great slaughter. 3966
11:35 thou hast **brought** me v **low**, 3766+3766
13: 6 countenance of an angel of God, v terrible: 3966
18: 9 have seen the land, and behold, it *is* v good: 3966
Ru 1:20 for the Almighty hath dealt v bitterly with 3966
1Sa 2:17 Wherefore the sin of the young men was v 3966
2:22 Now Eli was v old, and heard all that his 3966
4:10 there was a v great slaughter; for there fell 3966
5: 9 against the city *with* a v great destruction: 3966
5:11 the hand of God was v heavy there. 3966
14:15 earth quaked: so it was a v **great** trembling. 430
14:20 *and there was* a v great discomfiture. 3966
14:31 to Aijalon: and the people were v faint. 3966
18: 8 Saul was v wroth, and the saying 3966
18:15 Saul saw that he behaved himself v wisely, 3966
19: 4 his works *have been* to thee-ward v good: 3966
20: 7 if he be v **wroth**, *then* be sure that 2734+2734
23:22 is told me *that* he **dealeth** v **subtilly**. 6191+6191

1Sa 25: 2 the man *was* v great, and he had three 3966
25:15 the men *were* v good unto us, and we were 3966
25:34 For **in** v **deed**, *as* the LORD God of Israel 199
25:36 within him, for he *was* v drunken: 3966+5704
26: 4 understood that Saul was come in v **deed**. 3559
2Sa 1:26 v pleasant hast thou been unto me: thy love 3966
2:17 there was a v sore battle that day; 3966+5704
3: 8 was Abner v wroth for the words of 3966
11: 2 the woman *was* v beautiful to look upon. 3966
12:15 wife bare unto David, and it was v **sick**. 605
13: 3 and Jonadab *was* a v subtil man. 3966
13:21 heard of all these things, he was v wroth. 3966
13:36 and all his servants wept v sore. 1419+3966
18:17 and laid a v great heap of stones upon him: 3966
19:32 Now Barzillai was a v aged man, 3966
19:32 lay at Mahanaim; for he *was* a v great man. 3966
24:10 of thy servant; for I have done v foolishly. 3966
1Ki 1: 4 the damsel *was* v fair, and 3966+5704
1: 6 he also *was* a v goodly *man;* and *his mother* 3966
1:15 the king was v old; and Abishag 3966
7:34 the undersetters *were* of the v base itself. NIH
10: 2 she came to Jerusalem with a v great train, 3966
10: 2 and v much gold, and precious stones: 3966
10:10 of spices v great store, and precious stones: 3966
19:10 I have been v **jealous** for the LORD 7065+7065
19:14 I have been v **jealous** for the LORD 7065+7065
21:26 he did v abominably in following idols, 3966
2Ki 14:26 the affliction of Israel, *that it was* v bitter: 3966
17:18 Therefore the LORD was v angry with 3966
21:16 Moreover Manasseh shed innocent blood v 3966
1Ch 9:13 v **able** men *for* the work of the service of 2428
18: 8 of Hadarezer, brought David v much brass, 3966
21: 8 of thy servant; for I have done v foolishly. 3966
21:13 of the LORD; for v great *are* his mercies: 3966
23:17 of Rehabiah were v many. 4605+1886.5+3807.1
2Ch 6:18 will God **in** v **deed** dwell with men on 552
7: 8 all Israel with him, a v great congregation, 3966
9: 1 with a v great company, and camels that 3966
14:13 and they carried away v much spoil. 3966
16: 8 with v many chariots and horsemen? 3966
16:14 a v great burning for him. 3966+5704+3807.1
20:35 king of Israel, who did v **wickedly**: 7561
24:24 the LORD delivered a v great host into 3966
30:13 the second month, a v great congregation. 3966
32:29 for God had given him substance v much. 3966
33:14 raised it up a v great height, and 3966
36:14 transgressed v much after all 7235
Ezr 10: 1 there assembled unto him out of Israel a v 3966
10: 1 and children: for the people wept v sore. 7235
Ne 1: 7 We have **dealt** v **corruptly** against 2254+2254
2: 2 sorrow of heart. Then I was v sore afraid, 3966
4: 7 to be stopped, then they were v wroth, 3966
5: 6 I was v angry when I heard their cry and 3966
8:17 done so. And there was v great gladness. 3966
Est 1:12 therefore was the king v wroth, and 3966
Job 1: 3 hundred she asses, and a v great household; 3966
2:13 for they saw that *his* grief was v great. 3966
15:10 *are* both the grayheaded and v **aged men**, 3453
32: 6 and said, I *am* young, and ye *are* v **old**; 3453
Ps 5: 9 their inward *part is* v wickedness; NIH
35: 8 into that *v* destruction let him fall. NIH
46: 1 and strength, a v present help in trouble. 3966
50: 3 it shall be v tempestuous round about him. 3966
71:19 righteousness also, O God, *is* v **high**, 4791+5704
79: 8 prevent us: for we are brought v low. 3966
89: 2 thy faithfulness shalt thou establish in the v NIH
92: 5 are thy works! *and* thy thoughts are v deep. 3966
93: 5 Thy testimonies are v sure: 3966
104: 1 O LORD my God, thou art v great; 3966
105:12 in number; yea, v few, and strangers in it. NIH
119:107 I am afflicted v **much**: quicken me, 3966+5704
119:138 commanded *are* righteous and v faithful. 3966
119:140 Thy word *is* v pure: therefore thy servant 3966
142: 6 unto my cry; for I am brought v low: 3966
146: 4 his earth; in that *v* day his thoughts perish. NIH
147:15 his word runneth v **swiftly**. 4120+5704
Pr 17: 9 that repeateth a matter separateth v **friends**. 441
27:15 A continual dropping in a v **rainy** day and 5464
Isa 1: 9 had left unto us a v **small** remnant, 4592+3509.1
5: 1 hath a vineyard in a v **fruitful** hill: 1121+8081
10:25 For yet a v **little while**, and 4213+4592
16: 6 heard of the pride of Moab; *he is* v proud: 3966
16:14 and the remnant *shall be* v small *and* feeble. 4592
24:16 dealers have **dealt** v **treacherously**. 898+899
29:17 *Is* it not yet a v **little while**, 4213+4592
30:19 he will be v **gracious** unto thee at 2603+2603
31: 1 and in horsemen, because they are v strong; 3966
33:17 they shall behold the land that is v **far off**. 4801
40:15 he taketh up the isles as a v **little thing**. 1851
47: 6 upon the ancient hast thou v heavily laid 3966
48: 8 thou wouldest **deal** v **treacherously**, 898+898
52:13 shall be exalted and extolled, and be v high. 3966
64: 9 Be not wroth v **sore**, O LORD, 3966+5704
64:12 hold thy peace, and afflict us v **sore**? 3966+5704
Jer 2:12 be ye v desolate, saith the LORD. 3966
4:19 I am pained *at* my v **heart**; my heart 3820+7023
5:11 have **dealt** v **treacherously** against me, 898+898
12: 1 they happy that **deal** v **treacherously**? 898+899
14:17 *with* a great breach, *with* a v grievous blow. 3966
18:13 virgin of Israel hath done a v horrible thing. 3966
20:15 born unto thee; **making** him v **glad**. 8055+8055
24: 2 One basket *had* v good figs, *even* like 3966
24: 2 the other basket *had* v naughty figs, 3966
24: 3 the good figs, v good; and the evil, 3966
24: 3 the evil, v evil, that cannot be eaten, 3966
27: 7 son's son, until the v time of his land come: 1931
40:12 gathered wine and summer fruits v much. 3966
46:20 Egypt *is like* a v **fair** heifer, *but* 3304
La 5:22 thou art v wroth against us. 3966+5704
Eze 2: 3 against me, *even* unto this v day. 6106
16:47 as *if that were* a v **little** *thing,* thou 4592+6985
27:25 made v glorious in the midst of the seas. 3966
33:32 thou *art* unto them as a v **lovely** song *of* one 5690
37: 2 *there were* v many in the open valley; 3966
37: 2 in the open valley; and lo, *they were* v dry. 3966

Eze 40: 2 set me upon a v high mountain, by which 3966
47: 7 at the bank of the river *were* v many trees 3966
47: 9 there shall be a v great multitude of fish, 3966
Da 2:12 this cause the king was angry and v furious, 7690
6:19 the king arose v **early** in the morning, and 8238
7:20 a mouth that spake v **great** *things,* whose 7229
8: 8 Therefore the he goat waxed v great: 3966+5704
11:25 be stirred up to battle with a v great 3966+5704
Joel 2:11 for his camp *is* v great: for *he is* strong that 3966
2:11 day of the LORD *is* great and v terrible; 3966
Am 5:20 even v **dark**, and no brightness in it? 651
Jnh 4: 1 Jonah exceedingly, and he was v **angry**. 2734
Hab 2:13 that the people shall labour in the v fire, 1767
2:13 the people shall weary themselves for v 1767
Zec 1:15 I am v sore displeased with the heathen *that* 1419
8: 4 every man with his staff in his hand for v 7230
9: 2 and Zidon, though it be v wise. 3966
9: 5 Gaza also *shall see it,* and be v sorrowful, 3966
14: 4 the west, *and there shall be* a v great valley; 3966
Mt 10:30 But the v hairs of your head are all 2532
15:28 daughter was made whole from that *v* hour. NIG
17:18 and the child was cured from that *v* hour. NIG
18:31 they were v sorry, and came and told unto 4970
21: 8 And a v **great** multitude spread their 4183
24:24 *they shall* deceive the v elect. 2532
26: 7 an alabaster box of v **precious** ointment, 927
26:37 and began to be sorrowful and v **heavy**. 85
Mk 8: 1 In those days the multitude being v **great**, 3827
14: 3 box of ointment of spikenard v **precious**; 4185
14:33 began to be sore amazed, and to be v **heavy**; 85
16: 2 And v early in the morning the first *day* of 3029
16: 4 stone was rolled away: for it was v great. 4970
Lk 1: 3 understanding of all *things* **from the** v **first**, 509
9: 5 shake off the v dust from your feet for a 2532
10:11 Even the *v* dust of your city, which cleaveth NIG
12: 7 But even the *v* hairs of your head are all NIG
12:59 till thou hast paid the v last mite. NIG
18:23 when he heard this, he was v **sorrowful**: 4036
18:23 for he was v rich. 4970
18:24 when Jesus saw that he was v **sorrowful**, 4036
19:17 because thou hast been faithful in a v **little**, 1646
19:48 for all the people were v **attentive** to hear 1582
24: 1 v **early in the morning**, they came 901+3722
Jn 7:26 Do the rulers know indeed that this is the v 230
8: 4 woman was taken in adultery, **in the** v **act**. 1888
12: 3 v **costly**, and anointed the feet of Jesus, and 4186
14:11 or else believe me for the v works' sake. 846
Ac 9:22 at Damascus, proving that this is *v* Christ. NIG
10:10 And he became v hungry, and would have NIG
24: 2 that v **worthy deeds** are done unto this 2735
25:10 I done no wrong, as thou v **well** knowest. 2573
Ro 10:20 But Esaias is v **bold**, and saith, I was found 662
13: 6 attending continually upon this v *thing.* 846
1Co 4: 3 But with me it is a v **small** *thing* that I 1646
2Co 9: 2 and your zeal hath provoked v **many**. 4183
11: 5 For I suppose *I* was not a whit behind the v 5228
12:11 for *in* nothing am I behind the v chiefest 5228
12:15 And I will v **gladly** spend and be spent for 2236
Php 1: 6 Being confident of this v *thing,* that he 846
1Th 5:13 And to esteem them v highly in love for 5228
5:23 And **the** v God of peace sanctify you 846
2Ti 1:17 in Rome, he sought me out v **diligently**, 4706
1:18 *unto me* at Ephesus, thou knowest v **well**. 957
Heb 10: 1 to come, *and* not the v image of the things, 846
Jas 3: 4 *yet* are they turned about with a v **small** 1646
5:11 that the Lord is v **pitiful**, and of tender 4184

VESSEL (46) [VESSELS]

Lev 6:28 the earthen v wherein it is sodden shall be 3627
11:32 whether *it be* any v of wood, or raiment, or 3627
11:32 whatsoever v *it be,* wherein *any* work is 3627
11:33 every earthen v, whereinto *any* of them 3627
11:34 all drink that may be drunk in every *such* v 3627
14: 5 killed in an earthen v over running water: 3627
14:50 birds in an earthen v over running water: 3627
15:12 the v of earth, that he toucheth which hath 3627
15:12 every v of wood shall be rinsed in water. 3627
Nu 5:17 priest shall take holy water in an earthen v; 3627
19:15 every open v, which hath no covering 3627
19:17 running water shall be put thereto in a v: 3627
Dt 23:24 but thou shalt not put *any* in thy v. 3627
1Sa 21: 5 though it were sanctified *this* day in the v. 3627
1Ki 17:10 Fetch me, I pray thee, a little water in a v, 3627
2Ki 4: 6 that she said unto her son, Bring me yet a v. 3627
4: 6 he said unto her, *There is* not a v more. 3627
Ps 2: 9 shalt dash them in pieces like a potter's v. 3627
31:12 dead man out of mind: I am like a broken v. 3627
Pr 25: 4 and there shall come forth a v for the finer. 3627
Isa 30:14 of the potters' v that is broken in pieces; 5035
66:20 in a clean v *into* the house of the LORD. 3627
Jer 18: 4 the v that he made of clay was marred in 3627
18: 4 so he made it again another v, as seemed 3627
19:11 this city, as *one* breaketh a potter's v, 3627
22:28 *is he* a v wherein *is* no pleasure? 3627
25:34 And ye shall fall like a pleasant v. 3627
32:14 put them in an earthen v, that they may 3627
48:11 and hath not been emptied from v to vessel, 3627
48:11 and hath not been emptied from vessel to v, 3627
48:38 for I have broken Moab like a v wherein *is* 3627
51:34 crushed me, he hath made me an empty v, 3627
Eze 4: 9 put them in one v, and make thee bread 3627
15: 3 will *men* take a pin of it to hang any v 3627
Hos 8: 8 now shall they be among the Gentiles as a v 3627
Mk 11:16 *man* should carry *any* v through the temple. 4632
Lk 8:16 covereth it with a v, or putteth *it* under a 4632
Jn 19:29 Now there was set a v full of vinegar: and 4632
Ac 9:15 Go *thy way:* for he is a chosen v unto me, 4632
10:11 and a certain v descending unto him, 4632
10:16 the v was received up again into heaven. 4632
11: 5 a trance I saw a vision, A certain v descend, 4632
Ro 9:21 of the same lump to make one v unto 4632
1Th 4: 4 know how to possess his v in sanctification 4632
2Ti 2:21 he shall be a v unto honour, sanctified, and 4632
1Pe 3: 7 as unto the weaker v, and as *being* heirs 4632

VESSELS (154) [VESSEL]
Ge 43:11 take of the best fruits in the land in your **v**, 3627
Ex 7:19 both in **v** *of* wood, and in *vessels of* stone. NIH
7:19 both in *vessels of* wood, and in **v** *of* stone. NIH
25:39 pure gold shall he make it, with all these **v**. 3627
27: 3 all the **v** thereof thou shalt make *of* brass. 3627
27:19 All the **v** of the tabernacle in all the service 3627
30:27 the table and all his **v**, and the candlestick 3627
30:27 the candlestick and his **v**, and the altar of 3627
30:28 the altar of burnt offering with all his **v**, 3627
35:13 his staves, and all his **v**, and the shewbread, 3627
35:16 and all his **v**, the laver and his foot, 3627
37:16 he made the **v** which *were* upon the table, 3627
37:24 pure gold made he it, and all the **v** thereof. 3627
38: 3 he made all the **v** of the altar, the pots, and 3627
38: 3 all the **v** thereof made he *of* brass. 3627
38:30 brasen grate for it, and all the **v** of the altar, 3627
39:36 all the **v** thereof, and the shewbread, 3627
39:37 and all the **v** thereof, and the oil for light, 3627
39:39 and all his **v**, the laver and his foot, 3627
39:40 all the **v** of the service of the tabernacle, 3627
40: 9 shalt hallow it, and all the **v** thereof: 3627
40:10 and all his **v**, and sanctify the altar: 3627
Lev 8:11 anointed the altar and all his **v**, both 3627
Nu 1:50 over all the **v** thereof, and over all *things* 3627
1:50 bear the tabernacle, and all the **v** thereof; 3627
3:31 the **v** of the sanctuary wherewith they 3627
3:36 all the **v** thereof, and all that serveth 3627
4: 9 his snuffdishes, and all the oil **v** thereof, 3627
4:10 all the **v** thereof within a covering of 3627
4:14 they shall put upon it all the **v** thereof, 3627
4:14 and the basons, all the **v** of the altar; 3627
4:15 all the **v** of the sanctuary, as the camp is to 3627
4:16 *is*, in the sanctuary, and in the **v** thereof. 3627
7: 1 both the altar and all the **v** thereof, and 3627
7:85 all the silver **v** *weighed* two thousand and 3627
18: 3 only they shall not come nigh the **v** of 3627
19:18 upon all the **v**, and upon the persons that 3627
Jos 6:19 the silver, and gold, and **v** of brass and iron, 3627
6:24 and the gold, and the **v** of brass and of iron, 3627
Ru 2: 9 go unto the **v**, and drink of *that* which 3627
1Sa 9: 7 for the bread is spent in our **v**, and *there is* 3627
21: 5 the **v** of the young men are holy, and 3627
2Sa 8:10 *Joram* brought with him **v** of silver, and 3627
8:10 and **v** of gold, and vessels of brass: 3627
8:10 and vessels of gold, and **v** of brass: 3627
17:28 earthen **v**, and wheat, and barley, and flour, 3627
1Ki 7:45 all these **v**, which Hiram made to king 3627
7:47 Solomon left all the **v** *unweighed*, because 3627
7:48 Solomon made all the **v** that *pertained* unto 3627
7:51 *even* the silver, and the gold, and the **v**, 3627
8: 4 all the holy **v** that *were* in the tabernacle, 3627
10:21 all king Solomon's drinking **v** *were of* gold, 3627
10:21 all the **v** of the house of the forest of 3627
10:25 **v** of silver, and vessels of gold, and 3627
10:25 **v** of gold, and garments, and armour, and 3627
15:15 of the LORD, silver, and gold, and **v**. 3627
2Ki 4: 3 borrow thee **v** abroad of all thy neighbours, 3627
4: 3 abroad of all thy neighbours, *even* empty **v**; 3627
4: 4 shalt pour out into all those **v**, and 3627
4: 5 upon her sons, who brought *the* **v** to her; NIH
4: 6 it came to pass, when the **v** were full, 3627
7:15 lo, all the way *was* full *of* garments and **v**, 3627
12:13 trumpets, any **v** of gold, or vessels of silver, 3627
12:13 trumpets, any vessels of gold, or **v** of silver, 3627
14:14 all the **v** that were found *in* the house of 3627
23: 4 LORD all the **v** that were made for Baal, 3627
24:13 cut in pieces all the **v** of gold which 3627
25:14 all the **v** of brass wherewith they 3627
25:16 the brass of all these **v** was without weight. 3627
1Ch 9:28 of them had the charge of the ministering **v**, 3627
9:29 them also *were* appointed to oversee the **v**, 3627
18: 8 and the pillars, and the **v** of brass. 3627
18:10 *with him* all *manner of* **v** of gold and silver 3627
22:19 of the LORD, and the holy **v** of God, 3627
23:26 nor any **v** of it for the service thereof. 3627
28:13 for all the **v** of service in the house of 3627
2Ch 4:18 Thus Solomon made all these **v** in great 3627
4:19 Solomon made all the **v** that *were for* 3627
5: 5 all the holy **v** that *were* in the tabernacle, 3627
9:20 all the drinking **v** of king Solomon *were of* 3627
9:20 all the **v** of the house of the forest of 3627
9:24 **v** of silver, and vessels of gold, and 3627
9:24 **v** of gold, and raiment, harness, and spices, 3627
15:18 had dedicated, silver, and gold, and **v**. 3627
24:14 whereof were made **v** for the house of 3627
24:14 *even* **v** to minister, and to offer *withal*, and 3627
24:14 and spoons, and **v** of gold and silver. 3627
25:24 all the **v** that were found in the house of 3627
28:24 Ahaz gathered together the **v** of the house 3627
28:24 cut in pieces the **v** of the house of God, and 3627
29:18 with all the **v** thereof, and the shewbread 3627
29:18 the shewbread table, with all the **v** thereof. 3627
29:19 Moreover all the **v**, which king Ahaz in his 3627
36: 7 Nebuchadnezzar also carried of the **v** of 3627
36:10 with the goodly **v** of the house of 3627
36:18 And all the **v** of the house of God, great and 3627
36:19 and destroyed all the goodly **v** thereof. 3627
Ezr 1: 6 strengthened their hands with **v** of silver, 3627
1: 7 Also Cyrus the king brought forth the **v** of 3627
1:10 and ten, *and* other **v** a thousand. 3627
1:11 All the **v** of gold and of silver *were* five 3627
5:14 the **v** also of gold and silver of the house of 3984
5:15 said unto him, Take these **v**, go, carry them 3984
6: 5 the golden and silver **v** of the house of God, 3984
7:19 The **v** also that *are* given thee for 3984
8:25 them the silver, and the gold, and the **v**, 3627
8:26 silver **v** an hundred talents, *and of* gold an 3627
8:27 and two **v** of fine copper, precious as gold. 3627
8:28 the **v** *are* holy also; and the silver and 3627
8:30 of the silver, and the gold, and the **v**, 3627
8:33 the **v** weighed in the house of our God by 3627
Ne 10:39 where *are* the **v** of the sanctuary, and 3627
13: 5 the **v**, and the tithes of the corn, the new 3627
13: 9 thither brought I again the **v** of the house of 3627
Est 1: 7 *they* gave *them* drink in **v** of gold, 3627
1: 7 (the **v** being diverse one from another,) 3627
Isa 18: 2 even in **v** of bulrushes upon the waters, 3627
22:24 and the issue, all **v** of small quantity, 3627
22:24 of small quantity, from the **v** of cups, 3627
22:24 vessels of cups, even to all the **v** of flagons. 3627
52:11 be ye clean, that bear the **v** of the LORD. 3627
65: 4 and broth of abominable *things is in* their **v**; 3627
Jer 14: 3 no water; they returned *with* their **v** empty; 3627
27:16 the **v** of the LORD'S house *shall* now 3627
27:18 that the **v** which are left in the house of 3627
27:19 concerning the residue of the **v** that remain 3627
27:21 concerning the **v** that remain *in* the house 3627
28: 3 this place all the **v** of the LORD'S house, 3627
28: 6 to bring again the **v** of the LORD'S house, 3627
40:10 oil, and put *them* in your **v**, and dwell in 3627
48:12 shall empty his **v**, and break their bottles. 3627
49:29 and all their **v**, and their camels; 3627
52:18 all the **v** of brass wherewith they 3627
52:20 the brass of all these **v** was without weight. 3627
Eze 27:13 of men and **v** of brass in thy market. 3627
Da 1: 2 with part of the **v** of the house of God: 3627
1: 2 he brought the **v** *into* the treasure house of 3627
5: 2 silver **v** which his father Nebuchadnezzar 3984
5: 3 they brought the golden **v** that were taken 3984
5:23 they have brought the **v** of his house before 3984
11: 8 *and* with their precious **v** *of* silver and 3627
Hos 13:15 he shall spoil the treasure of all pleasant **v**. 3627
Hag 2:16 for to draw out fifty **v** *out of* the press, NIH
Mt 13:48 and gathered the good into **v**, but cast the bad 30
25: 4 But the wise took oil in their **v** with their 30
Mk 7: 4 of cups, and pots, **brasen v**, and of tables. 5473
Ro 9:22 endured with much longsuffering *the* **v** of 4632
9:23 the riches of his glory on the **v** of mercy, 4632
2Co 4: 7 But we have this treasure in earthen **v**, 4632
2Ti 2:20 But in a great house there are not only **v** of 4632
Heb 9:21 the tabernacle, and all the **v** of the ministry. 4632
Rev 2:27 as the **v** of a potter *shall* they be broken to 4632
18:12 and all *manner* **v** of ivory, and all *manner* 4632
18:12 and all *manner* **v** of most precious wood, 4632

VESTMENTS (2) [VESTURE]
2Ki 10:22 Bring forth **v** for all the worshippers of 3830
10:22 of Baal. And he brought them forth **v**. 4403

VESTRY (1) [VESTURE]
2Ki 10:22 he said unto *him* that *was* over the **v**, 4458

VESTURE (8) [VESTMENTS, VESTRY, VESTURES]
Dt 22:12 thee fringes upon the four quarters of thy **v**, 3682
Ps 22:18 among them, and cast lots upon my **v**. 3830
102:26 as a **v** shalt thou change them, and 3830
Mt 27:35 and upon my **v** did they cast lots. 2441
Jn 19:24 and for my **v** they did cast lots. 2441
Heb 1:12 And as a **v** shalt thou fold them up, and 4018
Rev 19:13 And he *was* clothed with a **v** dipt in blood: 2440
19:16 And he hath on *his* **v** and on his thigh a 2440

VESTURES (1) [VESTURE]
Ge 41:42 arrayed him in **v** of fine linen, and put a gold 899

VEX (15) [VEXATION, VEXATIONS, VEXED]
Ex 22:21 Thou shalt neither **v** a stranger, nor oppress 3238
Lev 18:18 to **v** *her*, to uncover her nakedness, 6887
19:33 with thee in your land, ye shall not **v** him. 3238
Nu 25:17 **V** the Midianites, and smite them: 6887
25:18 For they **v** you with their wiles, 6887
33:55 shall **v** you in the land wherein ye dwell. 6887
2Sa 12:18 how will he then **v** himself, if we tell 6213+7451
2Ch 15: 6 for God did **v** them with all adversity. 2000
Job 19: 2 How long will ye **v** my soul, and break me 3013
Ps 2: 5 his wrath, and **v** them in his sore displeasure. 926
Isa 7: 6 **v** it, and let us make a breach therein for us, 6973
11:13 envy Judah, and Judah shall not **v** Ephraim. 6887
Eze 32: 9 I will also **v** the hearts of many people, 3707
Hab 2: 7 awake that *shall* **v** thee, and thou shalt be 2111
Ac 12: 1 forth *his* hands to **v** certain of the church. 2559

VEXATION (14) [VEX]
Dt 28:20 shall send upon thee cursing, **v**, and rebuke, 4103
Ecc 1:14 and behold, all *is* vanity and **v** of spirit. 7469
1:17 folly: I perceived that this also *is* **v** of spirit. 7475
2:11 all *was* vanity and **v** of spirit, and *there was* 7469
2:17 unto me: for all *is* vanity and **v** of spirit. 7469
2:22 of all his labour, and of the **v** of his heart, 7475
2:26 This also *is* vanity and **v** of spirit. 7469
4: 4 This *is* also vanity and **v** of spirit. 7469
4: 6 the hands full *with* travail and **v** of spirit. 7469
4:16 Surely this also *is* vanity and **v** of spirit. 7475
6: 9 the desire: this *is* also vanity and **v** of spirit. 7469
Isa 9: 1 dimness *shall* not *be* such as *was* in her **v**, 4164
28:19 it shall be a **v** only to understand the report. 2113
65:14 of heart, and shall howl for **v** of spirit. 7667

VEXATIONS (1) [VEX]
2Ch 15: 5 great **v** *were* upon all the inhabitants of 4103

VEXED (22) [VEX]
Nu 20:15 and the Egyptians **v** us, and our fathers: 7489
Jdg 2:18 of them that oppressed them and **v** them. 1766
10: 8 that year they **v** and oppressed the children 7492
16:16 *so* that his soul was **v** unto death; 7114
1Sa 14:47 he turned himself, he **v** *them*. 7561
2Sa 13: 2 Amnon was *so* **v**, that he fell sick for his 3334
2Ki 4:27 Let her alone; for her soul *is* **v** within her: 4843
Ne 9:27 into the hand of their enemies, who **v** them: 6887
Job 27: 2 and the Almighty, *who* hath **v** my soul; 4843
Ps 6: 2 O LORD, heal me; for my bones are **v**. 926
6: 3 My soul is also sore **v**: but thou, O LORD, 926
6:10 Let all mine enemies be ashamed and sore **v**: 926
Isa 63:10 they rebelled, and **v** his holy Spirit: 6087
Eze 22: 5 mock thee, *which art* infamous *and* much **v**. 4103
22: 7 in thee have they **v** the fatherless and 3238
22:29 and have **v** the poor and needy: 3238
Mt 15:22 my daughter is grievously **v with a devil**. 1139
17:15 for he is lunatick, and sore **v**: for ofttimes 3958
Lk 6:18 And they that were **v** with unclean spirits: 3791
Ac 5:16 *them which were* **v** with unclean spirits: 3791
2Pe 2: 7 **v** with the filthy conversation of 2669
2: 8 **v** *his* righteous soul from day to day with 928

VIAL (8) [VIALS]
1Sa 10: 1 Samuel took a **v** of oil, and poured *it* upon 6378
Rev 16: 2 and poured out his **v** upon the earth; 5357
16: 3 And the second angel poured out his **v** 5357
16: 4 And the third angel poured out his **v** upon 5357
16: 8 And the fourth angel poured out his **v** upon 5357
16:10 And the fifth angel poured out his **v** upon 5357
16:12 And the sixth angel poured out his **v** upon 5357
16:17 And the seventh angel poured out his **v** into 5357

VIALS (5) [VIAL]
Rev 5: 8 and golden **v** full of odours, which are 5357
15: 7 seven golden **v** full of the wrath of God, 5357
16: 1 pour out the **v** of the wrath of God upon 5357
17: 1 of the seven angels which had the seven **v**, 5357
21: 9 the seven **v** full of the seven last plagues, 5357

VICTORY (12)
2Sa 19: 2 the **v** that day was *turned* into mourning 8668
23:10 the LORD wrought a great **v** that day; 8668
23:12 and the LORD wrought a great **v**. 8668
1Ch 29:11 and the glory, and the **v**, and the majesty: 5331
Ps 98: 1 and his holy arm, hath **gotten** him the **v**. 3467
Isa 25: 8 He will swallow up death in **v**; and 5331
Mt 12:20 till he send forth judgment unto **v**. 3534
1Co 15:54 that is written, Death is swallowed up in **v**. 3534
15:55 where *is* thy sting? O grave, where *is* thy **v**? 3534
15:57 which giveth us the **v** through our Lord 3534
1Jn 5: 4 and this is the **v** that overcometh the world, 3529
Rev 15: 2 them that had **gotten the v** over the beast, 3528

VICTUAL (5) [VICTUALS]
Ex 12:39 had they prepared for themselves *any* **v**. 6720
Jdg 20:10 to fetch **v** for the people, that *they* may do, 6720
1Ki 4:27 those officers **provided v** for king 3557
2Ch 11:11 in them, and store of **v**, and *of* oil and wine. 3978
11:23 he gave them **v** in abundance. And he 4202

VICTUALS (17) [VICTUAL]
Ge 14:11 and all their **v**, and went their way. 400
Lev 25:37 upon usury, nor lend him thy **v** for increase. 400
Dt 23:19 usury of money, usury of **v**, usury of any 400
Jos 1:11 the people, saying, Prepare you **v**; 6720
9:11 Take **v** with you for the journey, and go to 6720
9:14 the men took of their **v**, and asked not 6718
Jdg 7: 8 So the people took **v** in their hand, and their 6720
17:10 by the year, and a suit of apparel, and thy **v**. 4241
1Sa 22:10 gave him **v**, and gave him the sword of 6720
1Ki 4: 7 which **provided v** for the king and his 3557
11:18 and appointed him **v**, and gave him land. 3899
Ne 10:31 or any **v** on the sabbath day to sell, 7668
13:15 *them* in the day wherein they sold **v**. 6718
Jer 40: 5 So the captain of the guard gave him **v** and 737
44:17 for *then* had we plenty of **v**, and were well, 3899
Mt 14:15 go into the villages, and buy themselves **v**. 1033
Lk 9:12 country round about, and lodge, and get **v**: 1979

VIEW (4) [VIEWED]
Jos 2: 1 Go **v** the land, even Jericho. 7200
7: 2 unto them, saying, Go up and **v** the country. 7270
2Ki 2: 7 and stood to **v** afar off: 4480+5048
2:15 which *were* to **v** at Jericho saw him, 4480+5048

VIEWED (4) [VIEW]
Jos 7: 2 the country. And the men went up and **v** Ai. 7270
Ezr 8:15 I **v** the people, and the priests, and 995
Ne 2:13 the dung port, and **v** the walls of Jerusalem, 7663
2:15 **v** the wall, and turned back, and entered by 7663

VIGILANT (2)
1Ti 3: 2 **v**, sober, of good behaviour, given to 3524
1Pe 5: 8 Be sober, be **v**; because your adversary 1127

VIGOROUS See LIVELY

VIGOROUSLY See THROUGHLY

VILE (19) [VILELY, VILER, VILEST]
Dt 25: 3 then thy brother should seem **v** unto thee. 7034
Jdg 19:24 but unto this man do not so **v** a thing. 5039
1Sa 3:13 because his sons **made** themselves **v**, 7043
15: 9 every thing *that was* **v** and refuse, that they 5240
2Sa 6:22 I will yet be more **v** than thus, and will be 7043
Job 18: 3 as beasts, *and* **reputed v** in your sight? 2933
40: 4 Behold, I am **v**; what shall I answer thee? 7043
Ps 15: 4 In whose eyes a **v** *person* is contemned; but 3988
Isa 32: 5 The **v person** shall be no more called 5036
32: 6 For the **v person** will speak villany, and 5036
Jer 15:19 if thou take forth the precious from the **v**, 2151
29:17 and will make them like **v** figs, 8182
La 1:11 and consider; for I am become **v**. 2151
Da 11:21 in his estate shall stand up a **v person**, to 959
Na 1:14 I will make thy grave; for thou art **v**. 7043
3: 6 **make** thee **v**, and will set thee as a 5034
Ro 1:26 For this cause God gave them up unto **v** 819
Php 3:21 Who shall change our **v** body, that it may 5014
Jas 2: 2 there come in also a poor *man* in **v** raiment; 4508

VILELY (1) [VILE]
2Sa 1:21 the shield of the mighty is **v cast away**, 1602

VILER (1) [VILE]
Job 30: 8 of base men: they were **v** than the earth. 5217

VILEST (1) [VILE]
Ps 12: 8 on every side, when the **v** men are exalted. 2149

VILLAGE (10) [VILLAGES]
Mt 21: 2 Go into the **v** over against you, and *2968*
Mk 11: 2 Go your way into the **v** over against you: *2968*
Lk 8: 1 that he went throughout every city and **v**, *2968*
9:52 and entered into a **v** of the Samaritans, *2968*
9:56 to save *them.* And they went to another **v**. *2968*
10:38 they went, that he entered into a certain **v**: *2968*
17:12 And as he entered into a certain **v**, *2968*
19:30 Go ye into the **v** over against *you;* in *2968*
24:13 two of them went *that* same day to a **v** *2968*
24:28 And they drew nigh unto the **v**, *2968*

VILLAGES (75) [VILLAGE]
Ex 8:13 out of the **v**, and out of the fields. 2691
Lev 25:31 the houses of the **v** which have no wall 2691
Nu 21:25 in Heshbon, and in all the **v** thereof. 1323
21:32 they took the **v** thereof, and drove out 1323
32:42 and the **v** thereof, and called it Nobah, 1323
Jos 13:23 after their families, the cities and **v** thereof. 2691
13:28 after their families, the cities, and their **v**. 2691
15:32 the cities *are* twenty and nine, with their **v**. 2691
15:36 Gederothaim; fourteen cities with their **v**. 2691
15:41 and Makkedah; sixteen cities with their **v**. 2691
15:44 and Mareshah; nine cities with their **v**. 2691
15:45 Ekron, with her towns and her **v**: 2691
15:46 all that *lay* near Ashdod, with their **v**: 2691
15:47 Ashdod *with* her towns and her **v**, 2691
15:47 Gaza *with* her towns and her **v**, 2691
15:51 Holon, and Giloh; eleven cities with their **v**. 2691
15:54 *is* Hebron, and Zior; nine cities with their **v**. 2691
15:57 Gibeah, and Timnah; ten cities with their **v**. 2691
15:59 and Eltekon; six cities with their **v**. 2691
15:60 and Rabbah; two cities with their **v**. 2691
15:62 of salt, and En-gedi; six cities with their **v**. 2691
16: 9 of Manasseh, all the cities with their **v**. 2691
18:24 and Gaba; twelve cities with their **v**. 2691
18:28 *and* Kirjath; fourteen cities with their **v**. 2691
19: 6 and Sharuhen; thirteen cities and their **v**: 2691
19: 7 Ether, and Ashan; four cities and their **v**: 2691
19: 8 all the **v** that *were* round about these cities 2691
19:15 and Beth-lehem: twelve cities with their **v**. 2691
19:16 to their families, these cities with their **v**. 2691
19:22 were *at* Jordan: sixteen cities with their **v**. 2691
19:23 to their families, the cities and their **v**. 2691
19:30 Rehob: twenty and two cities with their **v**. 2691
19:31 to their families, these cities with their **v**. 2691
19:38 Beth-shemesh; nineteen cities with their **v**. 2691
19:39 to their families, the cities and their **v**. 2691
19:48 to their families, these cities with their **v**. 2691
21:12 the fields of the city, and the **v** thereof, 2691
Jdg 5: 7 *The inhabitants of* the **v** ceased, they ceased 6520
5:11 *towards the inhabitants* of his **v** in Israel: 6520
1Sa 6:18 *both* of fenced cities, and of country **v**, 3724
1Ch 4:32 their **v** *were,* Etam, and Ain, Rimmon, and 2691
4:33 all their **v** that *were* round about the same 2691
6:56 the fields of the city, and the **v** thereof, 2691
9:16 that dwelt in the **v** of the Netophathites. 2691
9:22 reckoned by their genealogy in their **v**, 2691
9:25 their brethren, *which were* in their **v**, 2691
27:25 in the cities, and in the **v**, and in the castles, 3723
2Ch 28:18 Shocho with the **v** thereof, and Timnah 1323
28:18 Timnah with the **v** thereof, Gimzo also and 1323
28:18 Gimzo also and the **v** thereof: 1323
Ne 6: 2 let us meet together in *some one of* the **v** in 3715
11:25 for the **v**, with their fields, *some of* 2691
11:25 *in* the **v** thereof, and at Dibon, and *in* 1323
11:25 *in* the **v** thereof, and at Jekabzeel, and *in* 1323
11:25 and at Jekabzeel, and *in* the **v** thereof, 2691
11:27 and at Beer-sheba, and *in* the **v** thereof, 1323
11:28 and at Mekonah, and in the **v** thereof, 1323
11:30 Zanoah, Adullam, and *in* their **v**, 2691
11:30 *at* Azekah, and *in* the **v** thereof. 1323
11:31 and Aija, and Beth-el, and *in* their **v**, 1323
12:28 and from the **v** of Netophathi; 2691
12:29 for the singers had builded them **v** round 2691
Est 9:19 Therefore the Jews of the **v**, that dwelt in 6521
Ps 10: 8 He sitteth in the lurking places of the **v**: 2691
SS 7:11 go forth *into* the field; let us lodge in the **v**. 3723
Isa 42:11 the cities thereof lift up *their voice,* the **v** 2691
Eze 38:11 I will go up to the land of **unwalled v**; 6519
Hab 3:14 through with his staves the head of his **v**: 6518
Mt 9:35 And Jesus went about all the cities and **v**, *2968*
14:15 that they may go into the **v**, and *2968*
Mk 6: 6 And he went round about the **v**, teaching. *2968*
6:36 and *into* the **v**, and buy themselves bread: *2968*
6:56 he entered, into **v**, or cities, or country, *2968*
Lk 13:22 And he went through the cities and **v**, *2968*
Ac 8:25 preached the gospel in many **v** of *2968*

VILLANY (2)
Isa 32: 6 For the vile person will speak **v**, and 5039
Jer 29:23 Because they have committed **v** in Israel, 5039

VINE (61) [VINEDRESSERS, VINES, VINEYARD, VINEYARDS, VINTAGE]
Ge 40: 9 In my dream, behold, a **v** *was* before me; 1612
40:10 in the **v** *were* three branches: and it *was* as 1612
49:11 Binding his foal unto the **v**, and his ass's 1612
49:11 and his ass's colt unto the **choice v**; 8322
Lev 25: 5 gather the grapes of thy **v undressed**: 5139
25:11 gather *the grapes* in it of thy **v undressed**. 5139
Nu 6: 4 he eat nothing that is made of the **v** tree, 3196
Dt 32:32 For their **v** *is* of the vine of Sodom, and 1612
32:32 For their vine *is* of the **v** of Sodom, and 1612
Jdg 9:12 said the trees unto the **v**, Come thou, *and* 1612
9:13 the **v** said unto them, Should I leave my 1612
13:14 eat of any *thing* that cometh of the **v**, 1612+3196
1Ki 4:25 every man under his **v** and under his fig 1612
2Ki 4:39 found a wild **v**, and gathered thereof wild 1612
18:31 *then* eat ye every man of his own **v**, and 1612
Job 15:33 He shall shake off his unripe grape as the **v**, 1612
Ps 80: 8 Thou hast brought a **v** out of Egypt: 1612
80:14 from heaven, and behold, and visit this **v**; 1612
128: 3 Thy wife *shall be* as a fruitful **v** by the sides 1612
SS 6:11 *and* to see whether the **v** flourished, *and* 1612
7: 8 also thy breasts shall be as clusters of the **v**, 1612
7:12 let us see if the **v** flourish, *whether* 1612
Isa 5: 2 planted it *with* the **choicest v**, and built a 8321
16: 8 of Heshbon languish, *and* the **v** of Sibmah: 1612
16: 9 with the weeping of Jazer the **v** of Sibmah: 1612
24: 7 The new wine mourneth, the **v** languisheth, 1612
32:12 for the pleasant fields, for the fruitful **v**. 1612
34: 4 as the leaf falleth off from the **v**, and as a 1612
36:16 eat ye every one *of* his **v**, and every one *of* 1612
Jer 2:21 Yet I had planted thee a **noble v**, wholly a 8321
2:21 degenerate **plant of** a strange **v** unto me? 1612
6: 9 glean the remnant of Israel as a **v**: 1612
8:13 *there shall be* no grapes on the **v**, nor figs 1612
48:32 O **v** of Sibmah, I will weep for thee with 1612
Eze 15: 2 What is the **v** tree more than any tree, *or* 1612
15: 6 As the **v** tree among the trees of the forest, 1612
17: 6 and became a spreading **v** of low stature, 1612
17: 6 so it became a **v**, and brought forth 1612
17: 7 this **v** did bend her roots toward him, and 1612
17: 8 might bear fruit, that *it* might be a goodly **v**. 1612
19:10 Thy mother *is* like a **v** in thy blood, 1612
Hos 10: 1 Israel *is* an empty **v**, he bringeth forth fruit 1612
14: 7 shall revive *as* the corn, and grow as the **v**: 1612
Joel 1: 7 He hath laid my **v** waste, and barked my fig 1612
1:12 The **v** is dried up, and the fig tree 1612
2:22 the fig tree and the **v** do yield their strength. 1612
Mic 4: 4 But they shall sit every man under his **v** and 1612
Na 2: 2 them out, and marred their **v branches**. 2156
Hag 2:19 as yet the **v**, and the fig tree, and 1612
Zec 3:10 under the **v** and under the fig tree. 1612
8:12 the **v** shall give her fruit, and the ground 1612
Mal 3:11 neither shall your **v** cast her fruit before 1612
Mt 26:29 not drink henceforth of this fruit of the **v**, *288*
Mk 14:25 I will drink no more of the fruit of the **v**, *288*
Lk 22:18 I will not drink of the fruit of the **v**, *288*
Jn 15: 1 I am the true **v**, and my Father is *288*
15: 4 bear fruit of itself, except it abide in the **v**; *288*
15: 5 I am the **v**, ye *are* the branches: He that *288*
Jas 3:12 either a **v**, figs? so *can* no fountain *both* yield *288*
Rev 14:18 and gather the clusters of the **v** of the earth; *288*
14:19 and gathered the **v** of the earth, and cast *it* *288*

VINE GROWERS See VINEDRESSERS

VINEDRESSERS (5) [VINE]
2Ki 25:12 the guard left of the poor of the land to be **v** 3755
2Ch 26:10 husbandmen *also,* and **v** in the mountains, 3755
Isa 61: 5 the alien *shall be* your plowmen and your **v**. 3755
Jer 52:16 left *certain* of the poor of the land for **v** 3755
Joel 1:11 howl, O ye **v**, for the wheat and for 3755

VINEGAR (13)
Nu 6: 3 *and* shall drink no **v** of wine, or vinegar of 2558
6: 3 no vinegar of wine, or **v** of strong drink, 2558
Ru 2:14 of the bread, and dip thy morsel in the **v**. 2558
Ps 69:21 and in my thirst they gave me **v** to drink. 2558
Pr 10:26 As **v** to the teeth, and as smoke to the eyes, 2558
25:20 *and as* **v** upon nitre, so *is* he that singeth 2558
Mt 27:34 They gave him **v** to drink mingled with *3690*
27:48 and filled *it* with **v**, and put *it* on a reed, and *3690*
Mk 15:36 And one ran and filled a spunge *full* of **v**, *3690*
Lk 23:36 coming to *him,* and offering him **v**, *3690*
Jn 19:29 Now there was set a vessel full of **v**: and *3690*
19:29 and they filled a spunge with **v**, and put *it* *3690*
19:30 When Jesus therefore had received the **v**, *3690*

VINES (12) [VINE]
Nu 20: 5 or of figs, or **v**, or of pomegranates; 1612
Dt 8: 8 and **v**, and fig trees, and pomegranates; 1612
Ps 78:47 He destroyed their **v** with hail, and 1612
105:33 He smote their **v** also and their fig trees; 1612
SS 2:13 the **v** *with* the tender grape give a *good* 1612
2:15 the foxes, the little foxes, that spoil the **v**: 3754
2:15 the vines: for our **v** *have* tender grapes. 3754
Isa 7:23 where there were a thousand **v** at a 1612
Jer 5:17 they shall eat up thy **v** and thy fig trees: 1612
31: 5 Thou shalt yet plant **v** upon the mountains 3754
Hos 2:12 I will destroy her **v** and her fig trees, 1612
Hab 3:17 not blossom, neither *shall* fruit *be* in the **v**; 1612

VINEYARD (69) [VINE]
Ge 9:20 *to be* a husbandman, and he planted a **v**: 3754
Ex 22: 5 If a man shall cause a field or **v** to be eaten, 3754
22: 5 of the best of his own **v**, shall he make 3754
23:11 In like manner thou shalt deal with thy **v**, 3754
Lev 19:10 thou shalt not glean thy **v**, neither shalt thou 3754
19:10 shalt thou gather *every* grape of thy **v**; 3754
25: 3 six years thou shalt prune thy **v**, and 3754
25: 4 shalt neither sow thy field, nor prune thy **v**. 3754
Dt 20: 6 what man *is he* that hath planted a **v**, and 3754
22: 9 Thou shalt not sow thy **v** with divers seeds: 3754
22: 9 hast sown, and the fruit of thy **v**, be defiled. 3754
23:24 When thou comest into thy neighbour's **v**, 3754
24:21 When thou gatherest the grapes of thy **v**, 3754
28:30 thou shalt plant a **v**, and shalt not gather 3754
1Ki 21: 1 *that* Naboth the Jezreelite had a **v**, 3754
21: 2 spake unto Naboth, saying, Give me thy **v**, 3754
21: 2 I will give thee for it a better **v** than it; *or,* 3754
21: 6 said unto him, Give me thy **v** for money; 3754
21: 6 please thee, I will give thee *another* **v** for it: 3754
21: 6 and he answered, I will not give thee my **v**. 3754
21: 7 I will give thee the **v** of Naboth 3754
21:15 take possession of the **v** of Naboth 3754
21:16 that Ahab rose up to go down to the **v** of 3754
21:18 behold, *he is* in the **v** of Naboth, whither he 3754
Ps 80:15 the **v** which thy right hand hath planted, 3657
Pr 24:30 by the **v** of the man void of understanding; 3754
31:16 with the fruit of her hands she planteth a **v**. 3754
SS 1: 6 *but* mine own **v** have I not kept. 3754
8:11 Solomon had a **v** at Baal-hamon; he let out 3754
8:11 he let out the **v** unto keepers; 3754
8:12 My **v**, which *is* mine, *is* before me: thou, 3754
Isa 1: 8 daughter of Zion is left as a cottage in a **v**, 3754
3:14 for ye have eaten up the **v**; the spoil of 3754
5: 1 a song of my beloved touching his **v**. 3754
5: 1 My wellbeloved hath a **v** in a very fruitful 3754
5: 3 judge, I pray you, betwixt me and my **v**. 3754
5: 4 What could have been done more to my **v**, 3754
5: 5 go to, I will tell you what I *will* do to my **v**: 3754
5: 7 For the **v** of the LORD of hosts *is* 3754
5:10 ten acres of **v** shall yield one bath, and 3754
27: 2 that day sing ye unto her, A **v** of red wine. 3754
Jer 12:10 Many pastors have destroyed my **v**, 3754
35: 7 nor plant **v**, nor have *any:* but all your days 3754
35: 9 neither have we **v**, nor field, nor seed: 3754
Mic 1: 6 a heap of the field, *and* as plantings of a **v**: 3754
Mt 20: 1 in the morning to hire labourers into his **v**. *290*
20: 2 for a penny a day, he sent them into his **v**. *290*
20: 4 Go ye also into the **v**, and whatsoever is *290*
20: 7 He saith unto them, Go ye also into the **v**; *290*
20: 8 the lord of the **v** saith unto his steward, *290*
21:28 and said, Son, go work to day in my **v**. *290*
21:33 which planted a **v**, and hedged it round *290*
21:39 and cast *him* out of the **v**, and slew *him.* *290*
21:40 When the lord therefore of the **v** cometh, *290*
21:41 and will let out *his* **v** unto other husbandmen, *290*
Mk 12: 1 A *certain* man planted a **v**, and set a hedge *290*
12: 2 from the husbandmen of the fruit of the **v**. *290*
12: 8 and killed *him,* and cast *him* out of the **v**. *290*
12: 9 What shall therefore the lord of the **v** do? *290*
12: 9 and will give the **v** unto others. *290*
Lk 13: 6 A certain *man* had a fig tree planted in his **v**; *290*
13: 7 Then said he unto the **dresser of** his **v**, *289*
20: 9 A certain man planted a **v**, and let it forth to *290*
20:10 they should give him of the fruit of the **v**: *290*
20:13 Then said the lord of the **v**, What shall I do? *290*
20:15 So they cast him out of the **v**, and killed *him.* *290*
20:15 shall the lord of the **v** do unto them? *290*
20:16 and shall give the **v** to others. *290*
1Co 9: 7 who planteth a **v**, and eateth not of the fruit *290*

VINEYARDS (45) [VINE]
Nu 16:14 or given us inheritance of fields and **v**: 3754
20:17 pass through the fields, or through the **v**, 3754
21:22 will not turn into the fields, or into the **v**; 3754
22:24 of the LORD stood in a path of the **v**, 3754
Dt 6:11 which thou diggedst not, **v** and olive trees, 3754
28:39 Thou shalt plant **v**, and dress *them,* but 3754
Jos 24:13 of the **v** and oliveyards which ye planted 3754
Jdg 9:27 gathered their **v**, and trode *the grapes,* and 3754
11:33 twenty cities, and unto the plain of the **v**, 3754
14: 5 *to* Timnath, and came to the **v** of Timnath: 3754
15: 5 the standing corn, with the **v** *and* olives. 3754
21:20 Go and lie in wait in the **v**; 3754
21:21 come ye out of the **v**, and catch you every 3754
1Sa 8:14 your **v**, and your oliveyards, *even* the best 3754
8:15 of your **v**, and give to his officers, and 3754
22: 7 of Jesse give every one of you fields and **v**, 3754
2Ki 5:26 **v**, and sheep, and oxen, and menservants, 3754
18:32 of corn and wine, a land of bread and **v**, 3754
19:29 reap, and plant **v**, and eat the fruits thereof. 3754
1Ch 27:27 over the **v** *was* Shimei the Ramathite: over 3754
27:27 over the increase of the **v** for the wine 3754
Ne 5: 3 **v**, and houses, that we might buy corn, 3754
5: 4 *and that upon* our lands and **v**. 3754
5: 5 *them;* for other men have our lands and **v**. 3754
5:11 to them, even *this* day, their lands, their **v**, 3754
9:25 **v**, and oliveyards, and fruit trees in 3754
Job 24:18 he beholdeth not the way of the **v**. 3754
Ps 107:37 sow the fields, and plant **v**, which may 3754
Ecc 2: 4 I builded me houses; I planted me **v**: 3754
SS 1: 6 they made me the keeper of the **v**; *but* 3754
1:14 *as* a cluster of camphire in the **v** of En-gedi. 3754
7:12 Let us get up early to the **v**; let us see if 3754
Isa 16:10 in the **v** there shall be no singing, 3754
36:17 of corn and wine, a land of bread and **v**. 3754
37:30 reap, and plant **v**, and eat the fruit thereof. 3754
65:21 inhabit *them;* and they shall plant **v**, and 3754
Jer 32:15 and **v** shall be possessed again in this land. 3754
39:10 gave them **v** and fields at the same time. 3754
Eze 28:26 and shall build houses, and plant **v**; 3754
Hos 2:15 I will give her her **v** from thence, and 3754
Am 4: 9 and your **v** and your fig trees and 3754
5:11 ye have planted pleasant **v**, but ye shall not 3754
5:17 in all **v** *shall be* wailing: for I will pass 3754
9:14 inhabit *them;* and they shall plant **v**, and 3754
Zep 1:13 not inhabit *them;* and they shall plant **v**, but 3754

VINTAGE (10) [VINE]
Lev 26: 5 your threshing shall reach unto the **v**, and 1210
26: 5 and the **v** shall reach unto the sowing time: 1210
Jdg 8: 2 of Ephraim better than the **v** of Abi-ezer? 1210
Job 24: 6 and they gather the **v** of the wicked. 3754
Isa 16:10 I have made *their* **v** shouting to cease. NIH
24:13 as the gleaning grapes when the **v** is done. 1210
32:10 ye careless *women:* for the **v** shall fail, 1210
Jer 48:32 upon thy summer fruits and upon thy **v**. 1210
Mic 7: 1 as the grapegleanings of the **v**: 1210
Zec 11: 2 for the forest of the **v** is come down. 1210

VIOL (2) [VIOLS]
Isa 5:12 and the **v**, the tabret, and pipe, and wine, 5035
Am 6: 5 That chant to the sound of the **v**, *and* 5035

VIOLATED (1)
Eze 22:26 Her priests have **v** my law, and 2554

VIOLENCE (57) [VIOLENT, VIOLENTLY]
Ge 6:11 before God, and the earth was filled *with* **v**. 2555
6:13 for the earth is filled *with* **v** through them; 2555
Lev 6: 2 or in a **thing taken away by v**, or 1498
2Sa 22: 3 my saviour; thou savest me from **v**. 2555
Ps 11: 5 and him that loveth **v** his soul hateth. 2555
55: 9 for I have seen **v** and strife in the city. 2555
58: 2 you weigh the **v** of your hands in the earth. 2555
72:14 shall redeem their soul from deceit and **v**: 2555
73: 6 as a chain; **v** covereth them *as* a garment. 2555

V

Pr 4:17 of wickedness, and drink the wine of v. 2555
10:6 but v covereth the mouth of the wicked. 2555
10:11 but v covereth the mouth of the wicked. 2555
13:2 but the soul of the transgressors *shall eat* v. 2555
28:17 A man that **doeth** v to the blood of *any* 6231
Isa 53:9 because he had done no v, neither *was any* 2555
59:6 and the act of v *is* in their hands. 2555
60:18 V shall no more be heard in thy land, 2555
Jer 6:7 v and spoil is heard in her; before me 2555
20:8 I spake, I cried out, I cried v and spoil; 2555
22:3 do no wrong, **do** no v, to the stranger, 2554
22:17 and for oppression, and for v, to do *it*. 4835
51:35 The v done to me and *to* my flesh *be* upon 2555
51:46 and v in the land, ruler against ruler. 2555
Eze 7:11 V is risen up into a rod of wickedness: 2555
7:23 *of* bloody crimes, and the city is full *of* v. 2555
8:17 for they have filled the land *with* v, and 2555
12:19 of the v of all them that dwell therein. 2555
18:7 hath spoiled none by v, hath given his 1500
18:12 the poor and needy, hath spoiled by v, 1500
18:16 neither hath spoiled by v, *but* hath given his 1500
18:18 spoiled *his* brother by v, and did *that* which 1499
28:16 they have filled the midst of thee *with* v, 2555
45:9 remove v and spoil, and execute judgment 2555
Joel 3:19 for the v against the children of Judah, 2555
Am 3:10 who store up v and robbery in their palaces. 2555
6:3 and cause the seat of v to come near; 2555
Ob 1:10 For *thy* v against thy brother Jacob shame 2555
Jnh 3:8 and from the v that *is* in their hands. 2555
Mic 2:2 they covet fields, and **take** *them* **by** v; and 1497
6:12 For the rich *men* thereof are full of v, and 2555
Hab 1:2 *even* cry out unto thee *of* v, and thou wilt 2555
1:3 for spoiling and v *are* before me: and 2555
1:9 They shall come all for v: their faces shall 2555
2:8 *for* the v of the land, *of* the city, and *of* all 2555
2:17 For the v of Lebanon shall cover thee, and 2555
2:17 *for* the v of the land, *of* the city, and *of* all 2555
Zep 1:9 which fill their masters' houses *with* v and 2555
3:4 the sanctuary, they have **done** v to the law. 2554
Mal 2:16 for *one* covereth v with his garment, 2555
Mt 11:12 now the kingdom of heaven **suffereth** v, 971
Lk 3:14 And he said unto them, Do v to no man, 1286
Ac 5:26 the officers, and brought them without v: 970
21:35 that he was borne of the soldiers for the v of 970
24:7 with great v took *him* away out of our hands, 970
27:41 the hinder part was broken with the v of 970
Heb 11:34 Quenched the v of fire, escaped the edge of 1411
Rev 18:21 Thus with v shall *that* great city Babylon be 3731

VIOLENT (10) [VIOLENCE]

2Sa 22:49 thou hast delivered me from the v man. 2555
Ps 7:16 his v **dealing** shall come down upon his 2555
18:48 thou hast delivered me from the v man. 2555
86:14 the assemblies of v *men* have sought after 6184
140:1 the evil man: preserve me from the v man; 2555
140:4 of the wicked; preserve me from the v man; 2555
140:11 evil shall hunt the v man to overthrow *him*. 2555
Pr 16:29 A v man enticeth his neighbour, and 2555
Ecc 5:8 v **perverting** of judgment and justice in a 1499
Mt 11:12 suffereth violence, and the v take it by force. 973

VIOLENTLY (10) [VIOLENCE]

Ge 21:25 Abimelech's servants had v **taken away**. 1497
Lev 6:4 restore that which he **took** v **away**, 1497+1500
Dt 28:31 thine ass *shall be* v **taken away** from 1497
Job 20:19 he hath v **taken away** a house which he 1497
24:2 they v **take away** flocks, and feed *thereof*. 1497
Isa 22:18 He will **surely** v **turn and toss** 6801+6801+6802
La 2:6 he hath v **taken away** his tabernacle, as *if it* 2554
Mt 8:32 the whole herd of swine **ran** v down a steep 3729
Mk 5:13 the herd **ran** v down a steep place into 3729
Lk 8:33 the herd **ran** v down a steep place into 3729

VIOLS (2) [VIOL]

Isa 14:11 down *to* the grave, *and* the noise of thy v: 5035
Am 5:23 for I will not hear the melody of thy v. 5035

VIPER (3) [VIPER'S, VIPERS]

Isa 30:6 and old lion, the v and fiery flying serpent, 660
59:5 that which is crushed breaketh out *into* a v. 660
Ac 28:3 there came a v out of the heat, and 2191

VIPER'S (1) [VIPER]

Job 20:16 poison of asps: the v tongue shall slay him. 660

VIPERS (4) [VIPER]

Mt 3:7 he said unto them, O generation of v, 2191
12:34 O generation of v, how can ye, being evil, 2191
23:33 *Ye* serpents, *ye* generation of v, how can ye 2191
Lk 3:7 O generation of v, who hath warned you to 2191

VIRGIN (33) [VIRGIN'S, VIRGINITY, VIRGINS]

Ge 24:16 a v, neither had any man known her: 1330
24:43 *that when* the v cometh forth to draw *water*, 5959
Lev 21:3 for his sister a v, that is nigh unto him, 1330
21:14 he shall take a v of his own people to wife. 1330
Dt 22:19 he hath brought up an evil name upon a v 1330
22:23 If a damsel *that is* a v be betrothed unto a 1330
22:28 If a man find a damsel *that is* a v, which is 1330
32:25 shall destroy both the young man and the v, 1330
2Sa 13:2 for she *was* a v; and Amnon thought it hard 1330
1Ki 1:2 be sought for my lord the king a young v: 1330
2Ki 19:21 The v the daughter of Zion hath despised 1330
Isa 7:14 a V shall conceive, and bear a Son, and 5959
23:12 O thou oppressed v, daughter of Zidon: 1330
37:22 The v, the daughter of Zion, hath despised 1330
47:1 sit in the dust, O v daughter of Babylon, 1330
62:5 For *as* a young man marrieth a v, *so* 1330
Jer 14:17 for the v daughter of my people is broken 1330
18:13 who hath heard such *things*: the v of Israel 1330
31:4 and thou shalt be built, O v of Israel: 1330
31:13 shall the v rejoice in the dance, both young 1330
31:21 turn again, O v of Israel, turn again to these 1330
46:11 Go up *into* Gilead, and take balm, O v, 1330

La 1:15 the Lord hath trodden the v, the daughter of 1330
2:13 I may comfort thee, O v daughter of Zion? 1330
Joel 1:8 Lament like a v girded with sackcloth for 1330
Am 5:2 The v of Israel is fallen; she shall no more 1330
Mt 1:23 a v shall be with child, and shall bring forth 3933
Lk 1:27 To a v espoused to a man whose name was 3933
1Co 7:28 and if a v marry, she hath not sinned. 3933
7:34 is difference *also* between a wife and a v. 3933
7:36 behaveth himself uncomely toward his v, 3933
7:37 decreed in his heart that *he* will keep his v, 3933
2Co 11:2 that *I* may present *you as* a chaste v to 3933

VIRGIN'S (1) [VIRGIN]

Lk 1:27 house of David; and the v name *was* Mary. 3933

VIRGINITY (9) [VIRGIN]

Lev 21:13 And he shall take a wife in her v. 1331
Dt 22:15 bring forth *the tokens of* the damsel's v 1331
22:17 *yet* these *are the tokens of* my daughter's v. 1331
22:20 *the tokens of* v be not found for the damsel: 1331
Jdg 11:37 and bewail my v, I and my fellows. 1331
11:38 and bewailed her v upon the mountains. 1331
Eze 23:3 and there they bruised the teats of their v. 1331
23:8 they bruised the breasts of her v, and 1331
Lk 2:36 with a husband seven years from her v; 3932

VIRGINS (22) [VIRGIN]

Ex 22:17 pay money according to the dowry of v. 1330
Jdg 21:12 of Jabesh-gilead four hundred young v, 1330
2Sa 13:18 the king's daughters *that were* v apparelled. 1330
Est 2:2 Let there be fair young v sought for 1330
2:3 the fair young v unto Shushan the palace, 1330
2:17 and favour in his sight more than all the v; 1330
2:19 when the v were gathered together 1330
Ps 45:14 the v her companions that follow her *shall* 1330
SS 1:3 poured forth, therefore do the v love thee. 5959
6:8 and v without number. 5959
Isa 23:4 do I nourish up young men, *nor* bring up v. 1330
La 1:4 her v *are* afflicted, and she *is* in bitterness. 1330
1:18 my v and my young men are gone into 1330
2:10 the v of Jerusalem hang down their heads 1330
2:21 my v and my young men are fallen by 1330
Am 8:13 In that day shall the fair v and young men 1330
Mt 25:1 kingdom of heaven be likened unto ten v, 3933
25:7 Then all those v arose, and trimmed their 3933
25:11 Afterward came also the other v, saying, 3933
Ac 21:9 had four daughters, v, which did prophesy. 3933
1Co 7:25 Now concerning v I have no commandment 3933
Rev 14:4 not defiled with women; for they are v. 3933

VIRTUE (7) [VIRTUOUS, VIRTUOUSLY]

Mk 5:30 in himself that v had gone out of him, 1411
Lk 6:19 for there went v out of him, and 1411
8:46 for I perceive that v is gone out of me. 1411
Php 4:8 if *there be* any v, and if *there be* any praise, 703
2Pe 1:3 of him that hath called us to glory and v: 703
1:5 giving all diligence, add to your faith v; 703
1:5 add to your faith virtue; and to v knowledge; 703

VIRTUOUS (3) [VIRTUE]

Ru 3:11 people doth know that thou *art* a v woman. 2428
Pr 12:4 A v woman *is* a crown to her husband: but 2428
31:10 Who can find a v woman? for her price *is* 2428

VIRTUOUSLY (1) [VIRTUE]

Pr 31:29 Many daughters have done v, but 2428

VISAGE (3) [VISION]

Isa 52:14 his v *was* so marred more than *any* man, 4758
La 4:8 Their v is blacker than a coal; they are not 8389
Da 3:19 the form of his v was changed against 600

VISIBLE (1) [VISION]

Col 1:16 and that are in earth, v and invisible, 3707

VISION (79) [VISAGE, VISIBLE, VISIONS]

Ge 15:1 of the LORD came unto Abram in a v, 4236
Nu 12:6 will make myself known unto him in a v, 4759
24:4 which saw the v of the Almighty, 4236
24:16 *which* saw the v of the Almighty, 4236
1Sa 3:1 in those days; *there was* no open v. 2377
3:15 And Samuel feared to shew Eli the v. 4759
2Sa 7:17 according to all this v, so did Nathan speak 2384
1Ch 17:15 according to all this v, so did Nathan speak 2377
2Ch 32:32 they *are* written in the v of Isaiah 2377
Job 20:8 he shall be chased away as a v of the night. 2384
33:15 In a dream, *in* a v of the night, when deep 2384
Ps 89:19 thou spakest in v to thy holy one, and 2377
Pr 29:18 Where *there is* no v, the people perish: but 2377
Isa 1:1 The v of Isaiah the son of Amoz, which he 2377
21:2 A grievous v is declared unto me; 2380
22:1 The burden of the valley of v. What aileth 2384
22:5 the Lord GOD of hosts in the valley of v, 2384
28:7 they err in v, they stumble *in* judgment. 7203
29:7 shall be as a dream of a night v. 2377
29:11 the v of all is become unto you as 2380
Jer 14:14 they prophesy unto you a false v and 2377
23:16 they speak a v of their own heart, *and* 2377
La 2:9 prophets also find no v from the LORD. 2377
Eze 7:13 for the v *is* touching the whole multitude 2377
7:26 shall they seek a v of the prophet; but 2377
8:4 according to the v that I saw in the plain. 4758
11:24 brought me in v by the Spirit of God into 4758
11:24 So the v that I had seen went up from me. 4758
12:22 days are prolonged, and every v faileth? 2377
12:23 days are at hand, and the effect of every v. 2377
12:24 For there shall be no more any vain v nor 2377
12:27 The v that he seeth *is* for many days *to* 2377
13:7 Have ye not seen a vain v, and have ye not 4236
43:3 *it was* according to the appearance of the v 4758
43:3 *even* according to the v that I saw when I 4758
43:3 the visions *were* like the v that I saw by 4758
Da 2:19 the secret revealed unto Daniel in a night v. 2376
7:2 said, I saw in my v by night, and behold, 2376

Da 8:1 of king Belshazzar a v appeared unto me, 2377
8:2 I saw in a v; and it came to pass, when I 2377
8:2 I saw in a v, and I was by the river of Ulai. 2377
8:13 How long *shall be* the v *concerning* 2377
8:15 had seen the v, and sought for the meaning, 2377
8:16 Gabriel, make this *man* to understand the v. 4758
8:17 for at the time of the end *shall be* the v. 2377
8:26 the v of the evening and the morning which 4758
8:26 wherefore shut thou up the v; for *it shall be* 2377
8:27 I was astonished at the v, but 4758
9:21 whom I had seen in the v at the beginning, 2377
9:23 understand the matter, and consider the v. 4758
9:24 to seal up the v and prophecy, and to anoint 2377
10:1 the thing, and had understanding of the v. 4758
10:7 I Daniel alone saw the v: for the men that 4759
10:7 the men that were with me saw not the v; 4759
10:8 saw this great v, and there remained no 4759
10:14 latter days: for yet the v *is* for *many* days. 2377
10:16 by the v my sorrows are turned upon me, 4759
11:14 shall exalt themselves to establish the v; 2377
Ob 1:1 The v of Obadiah. Thus saith the Lord 2377
Mic 3:6 *shall be* unto you, that *ye* shall not have a v; 2377
Na 1:1 The book of the v of Nahum the Elkoshite. 2377
Hab 2:2 Write the v, and make *it* plain upon tables, 2377
2:3 For the v *is* yet for an appointed time, but 2377
Zec 13:4 shall be ashamed every one of his v, 2384
Mt 17:9 Tell the v to no *man*, until the Son of man 3705
Lk 1:22 they perceived that he had seen a v in 3701
24:23 that *they* had also seen a v of angels, 3701
Ac 9:10 and to him said the Lord in a v, Ananias. 3705
9:12 And hath seen in a v a man named Ananias 3705
10:3 He saw in a v evidently, about the ninth 3705
10:17 what *this* v which he had seen should mean, 3705
10:19 While Peter thought on the v, the Spirit said 3705
11:5 and in a trance I saw a v, A certain vessel 3705
12:9 done by the angel; but thought he saw a v. 3705
16:9 And a v appeared to Paul in the night; 3705
16:10 And after he had seen the v, 3705
18:9 spake the Lord to Paul in the night by a v, 3705
26:19 I was not disobedient unto the heavenly v: 3701
Rev 9:17 And thus I saw the horses in the v, and 3706

VISIONS (24) [VISION]

Ge 46:2 God spake unto Israel in the v of the night, 4759
2Ch 9:29 in the v of Iddo the seer against Jeroboam 2378
26:5 who had understanding in the v of God: 7200
Job 4:13 In thoughts from the v of the night, 2384
7:14 with dreams, and terrifiest me through v: 2384
Eze 1:1 heavens were opened, and I saw v of God. 4759
8:3 brought me in the v of God to Jerusalem, 4759
13:16 which see v of peace for her, and *there is* 2377
40:2 In the v of God brought he me into the land 4759
43:3 the v *were* like the vision that I saw by 4759
Da 1:17 Daniel had understanding in all v and 2377
2:28 the v of thy head upon thy bed, *are* these; 2376
4:5 my bed and the v of my head troubled me. 2376
4:9 tell *me* the v of my dream that I have seen, 2376
4:10 Thus *were* the v of mine head in my bed; 2376
4:13 I saw in the v of my head upon my bed, and 2376
7:1 a dream and v of his head upon his bed: 2376
7:7 After this I saw in the night v, and behold, 2376
7:13 I saw in the night v, and behold, *one* like 2376
7:15 and the v of my head troubled me. 2376
Hos 12:10 I have multiplied v, and used similitudes by 2377
Joel 2:28 dream dreams, your young men shall see v: 2384
Ac 2:17 and your young men shall see v, and 3706
2Co 12:1 I will come to v and revelations of 3701

VISIT (38) [VISITATION, VISITED, VISITEST, VISITETH, VISITING]

Ge 50:24 God will **surely** v you, and bring you 6485+6485
50:25 God will **surely** v you, and ye shall 6485+6485
Ex 13:19 saying, God will **surely** v you; 6485+6485
32:34 nevertheless in the day when I v, I will visit 6485
32:34 when I visit, I will v their sin upon them. 6485
Lev 18:25 therefore I do v the iniquity thereof upon it, 6485
Job 5:24 thou shalt v thy habitation, and shalt not 6485
7:18 *that* thou shouldest v him every morning, 6485
Ps 59:5 God of Israel, awake to v all the heathen: 6485
80:14 from heaven, and behold, and v this vine; 6485
89:32 will I v their transgression with the rod, 6485
106:4 unto thy people: O v me with thy salvation; 6485
Isa 23:17 *that* the LORD will v Tyre, and she shall 6485
Jer 3:16 neither shall they v *it*; neither shall *that* be 6485
5:9 Shall I not v for these *things?* saith 6485
5:29 Shall I not v for these *things?* saith 6485
6:15 at the time *that* I v them they shall be cast 6485
9:9 Shall I not v them for these *things?* saith 6485
14:10 remember their iniquity, and v their sins. 6485
15:15 v me, and revenge me of my persecutors; 6485
23:2 I will v upon you the evil of your doings, 6485
27:22 there shall they be until the day that I v 6485
29:10 be accomplished at Babylon I will v you, 6485
32:5 there shall he be until I v him, saith 6485
49:8 Esau upon him, the time *that* I will v him. 6485
50:31 thy day is come, the time *that* I will v thee. 6485
La 4:22 he will v thine iniquity, O daughter of 6485
Hos 2:13 I will v upon her the days of Baalim, 6485
8:13 he remember their iniquity, and v their sins: 6485
9:9 their iniquity, he will v their sins. 6485
Am 3:14 That in the day that I shall v 6485
3:14 upon him I will also v the altars of Beth-el: 6485
Zep 2:7 for the LORD their God shall v them, and 6485
Zec 11:16 *which* shall not v those that be cut off, 6485
Ac 7:23 it came into his heart to v his brethren 1980
15:14 how God at the first did v the Gentiles, 1980
15:36 v our brethren in every city where we have 1980
Jas 1:27 To v the fatherless and widows in their 1980

VISITATION (15) [VISIT]

Nu 16:29 or if they be visited after the v of all men; 6486
Job 10:12 favour, and thy v hath preserved my spirit. 6486
Isa 10:3 what will ye do in the day of v, and in 6486
Jer 8:12 in the time of their v they shall be cast 6486

Jer 10:15 in the time of their **v** they shall perish. 6486
11:23 men of Anathoth, *even* the year of their **v**. 6486
23:12 *even* the year of their **v**, saith the LORD. 6486
46:21 come upon them, *and* the time of their **v**. 6486
48:44 *even* upon Moab, the year of their **v**, 6486
50:27 for their day is come, the time of their **v**. 6486
51:18 in the time of their **v** they shall perish. 6486
Hos 9: 7 The days of **v** are come, the days of 6486
Mic 7: 4 the day of thy watchmen *and* thy **v** cometh; 6486
Lk 19:44 because thou knewest not the time of thy **v**. *1984*
1Pe 2:12 shall behold, glorify God in the day of **v**. *1984*

VISITED (23) [VISIT]

Ge 21: 1 the LORD **v** Sarah as he had said, and 6485
Ex 3:16 I have **surely v** you, and *seen* that 6485+6485
4:31 when they heard that the LORD had **v** 6485
Nu 16:29 if they be **v** after the visitation of all men; 6485
Jdg 15: 1 that Samson **v** his wife with a kid; 6485
Ru 1: 6 had **v** his people in giving them bread. 6485
1Sa 2:21 the LORD **v** Hannah, so that she 6485
Job 35:15 because *it is* not *so,* he hath **v** *in* his anger; 6485
Ps 17: 3 thou hast **v** *me* in the night; thou hast tried 6485
Pr 19:23 abide satisfied; he shall not be **v** *with* evil. 6485
Isa 24:22 and after many days shall they be **v**. 6485
26:14 therefore hast thou **v** and destroyed them, 6485
26:16 LORD, in trouble have they **v** thee, 6485
29: 6 Thou shalt be **v** of the LORD of hosts 6485
Jer 6: 6 this is the city to be **v**; she *is* wholly 6485
23: 2 driven them away, and have not **v** them: 6485
Eze 38: 8 After many days thou shalt be **v**: in 6485
Zec 10: 3 for the LORD of hosts hath **v** his flock 6485
Mt 25:36 I was sick, and ye **v** me: I was in prison, *1980*
25:43 sick, and in prison, and ye **v** me not. *1980*
Lk 1:68 for he hath **v** and redeemed his people, *1980*
1:78 whereby the dayspring from on high hath **v** *1980*
7:16 among us; and, That God hath **v** his people. *1980*

VISITEST (3) [VISIT]

Ps 8: 4 and the son of man, that thou **v** him? 6485
65: 9 Thou **v** the earth, and waterest it: 6485
Heb 2: 6 of him? or the son of man, that thou **v** him? *1980*

VISITETH (1) [VISIT]

Job 31:14 and when he **v**, what shall I answer him? 6485

VISITING (4) [VISIT]

Ex 20: 5 **v** the iniquity of the fathers upon 6485
34: 7 *that* will by no means clear *the guilty;* **v** 6485
Nu 14:18 by no means clearing *the guilty,* **v** 6485
Dt 5: 9 **v** the iniquity of the fathers upon 6485

VOCATION (1)

Eph 4: 1 beseech you that *ye* walk worthy of the **v** *2821*

VOICE (505) [VOICES]

Ge 3: 8 they heard the **v** of the LORD God 6963
3:10 I heard thy **v** in the garden, and I was 6963
3:17 Because thou hast hearkened unto the **v** of 6963
4:10 the **v** of thy brother's blood crieth unto me 6963
4:23 his wives, Adah and Zillah, Hear my **v**; 6963
16: 2 And Abram hearkened to the **v** of Sarai. 6963
21:12 hath said unto thee, hearken unto her **v**; 6963
21:16 she sat over against *him,* and lift up her **v**, 6963
21:17 God heard the **v** of the lad; and the angel of 6963
21:17 God hath heard the **v** of the lad where 6963
22:18 be blessed; because thou hast obeyed my **v**. 6963
26: 5 Because that Abraham obeyed my **v**, and 6963
27: 8 obey my **v** according to *that* which I 6963
27:13 only obey my **v**, and go fetch me *them.* 6963
27:22 The **v** *is* Jacob's voice, but the hands *are* 6963
27:22 The voice *is* Jacob's **v**, but the hands *are* 6963
27:38 my father. And Esau lift up his **v**, and wept. 6963
27:43 Now therefore, my son, obey my **v**; and 6963
29:11 and lifted up his **v**, and wept. 6963
30: 6 hath also heard my **v**, and hath given me a 6963
39:14 me to lie with me, and I cried with a loud **v**: 6963
39:15 when he heard that I lifted up my **v** and 6963
39:18 it came to pass, as I lift up my **v** and cried, 6963
Ex 3:18 they shall hearken to thy **v**: and thou shalt 6963
4: 1 will not believe me, nor hearken unto my **v**: 6963
4: 8 neither hearken to the **v** of the first sign, 6963
4: 8 that they will believe the **v** of the latter 6963
4: 9 these two signs, neither hearken unto thy **v**, 6963
5: 2 that I should obey his **v** to let Israel go? 6963
15:26 If thou wilt diligently hearken to the **v** of 6963
18:19 Hearken now unto my **v**, I will give thee 6963
18:24 So Moses hearkened to the **v** of his father 6963
19: 5 if ye will obey my **v** indeed, and keep my 6963
19:16 and the **v** of the trumpet exceeding loud; 6963
19:19 when the **v** of the trumpet sounded long, 6963
19:19 and God answered him by a **v**. 6963
23:21 Beware of him, and obey his **v**, 6963
23:22 if thou shalt indeed obey his **v**, and do all 6963
24: 3 and all the people answered *with* one **v**, and 6963
32:18 *It is* not the **v** of *them that* shout for 6963
32:18 neither *is it* the **v** of *them that* cry for being 6963
Lev 5: 1 hear the **v** of swearing, and *is* a witness, 6963
Nu 7:89 he heard the **v** of one speaking unto him 6963
14: 1 all the congregation lifted up their **v**, and 6963
14:22 ten times, and have not hearkened to my **v**; 6963
20:16 he heard our **v**, and sent an angel, and 6963
21: 3 the LORD hearkened to the **v** of Israel, 6963
Dt 1:34 the LORD heard the **v** of your words, and 6963
1:45 the LORD would not hearken to your **v**, 6963
4:12 ye heard the **v** of the words, but saw no 6963
4:12 but saw no similitude; only *ye heard* a **v**. 6963
4:30 thy God, and shalt be obedient unto his **v**; 6963
4:33 Did *ever* people hear the **v** of God speaking 6963
4:36 Out of heaven he made thee to hear his **v**, 6963
5:22 and of the thick darkness, *with* a great **v**: 6963
5:23 when ye heard the **v** out of the midst of 6963
5:24 we have heard his **v** out of the midst of 6963
5:25 if we hear the **v** of the LORD our God any 6963
5:26 that hath heard the **v** of the living God 6963
Dt 5:28 the LORD heard the **v** of your words, 6963
5:28 I have heard the **v** of the words of this 6963
8:20 ye would not be obedient unto the **v** of 6963
9:23 ye believed him not, nor hearkened to his **v**. 6963
13: 4 obey his **v**, and you shall serve him, and 6963
13:18 When thou shalt hearken to the **v** of 6963
15: 5 Only if thou carefully hearken unto the **v** of 6963
18:16 Let me not hear again the **v** of the LORD 6963
21:18 which will not obey the **v** of his father, or 6963
21:18 or the **v** of his mother, and *that,* when they 6963
21:20 and rebellious, he will not obey our **v**; 6963
26: 7 the LORD heard our **v**, and looked on our 6963
26:14 I have hearkened to the **v** of the LORD 6963
26:17 his judgments, and to hearken unto his **v**: 6963
27:10 obey the **v** of the LORD thy God, 6963
27:14 say unto all the men of Israel *with* a loud **v**, 6963
28: 1 if thou shalt hearken diligently unto the **v** 6963
28: 2 if thou shalt hearken unto the **v** of 6963
28:15 if thou wilt not hearken unto the **v** of 6963
28:45 thou hearkenedst not unto the **v** of 6963
28:62 thou wouldest not obey the **v** of 6963
30: 2 shalt obey his **v** according to all that I 6963
30: 8 shalt return and obey the **v** of the LORD, 6963
30:10 If thou shalt hearken unto the **v** of 6963
30:20 *and* that thou mayest obey his **v**, and 6963
33: 7 the **v** of Judah, and bring him unto his 6963
Jos 5: 6 they obeyed not the **v** of the LORD: 6963
6:10 not shout, nor make any noise with your **v**, 6963
10:14 that the LORD hearkened unto the **v** of a 6963
22: 2 have obeyed my **v** in all that I commanded 6963
24:24 God will we serve, and his **v** will we obey. 6963
Jdg 2: 2 ye have not obeyed my **v**: why have ye 6963
2: 4 that the people lift up their **v**, and wept. 6963
2:20 and have not hearkened unto my **v**; 6963
6:10 ye dwell: but ye have not obeyed my **v**. 6963
9: 7 lift up his **v**, and cried, and said unto them, 6963
13: 9 God hearkened to the **v** of Manoah; and 6963
18: 3 they knew the **v** of the young man 6963
18:25 Let not thy **v** be heard among us, lest angry 6963
20:13 the **v** of their brethren the children of Israel: 6963
Ru 1: 9 and they lift up their **v**, and wept. 6963
1:14 they lift up their **v**, and wept again: and 6963
1Sa 1:13 her lips moved, but her **v** was not heard: 6963
2:25 hearkened not unto the **v** of their father, 6963
8: 7 Hearken unto the **v** of the people in all that 6963
8: 9 Now therefore hearken unto their **v**: 6963
8:19 the people refused to obey the **v** of Samuel; 6963
8:22 Hearken unto their **v**, and make them a 6963
12: 1 I have hearkened unto your **v** in all that ye 6963
12:14 obey his **v**, and not rebel against 6963
12:15 But if ye will not obey the **v** of the LORD, 6963
15: 1 hearken thou unto the **v** of the words of 6963
15:19 didst thou not obey the **v** of the LORD, 6963
15:20 I have obeyed the **v** of the LORD, and 6963
15:22 as in obeying the **v** of the LORD? 6963
15:24 I feared the people, and obeyed their **v**. 6963
19: 6 And Saul hearkened unto the **v** of Jonathan: 6963
24:16 that Saul said, *Is* this thy **v**, my son David? 6963
24:16 And Saul lift up his **v**, and wept. 6963
25:35 I have hearkened to thy **v**, and 6963
26:17 Saul knew David's **v**, and said, *Is* this thy 6963
26:17 and said, *Is* this thy **v**, my son David? 6963
26:17 David said, *It is* my **v**, my lord, O king. 6963
28:12 saw Samuel, she cried with a loud **v**: 6963
28:18 Because thou obeyedst not the **v** of 6963
28:21 thine handmaid hath obeyed thy **v**, and 6963
28:22 hearken thou also unto the **v** of thine 6963
28:23 and he hearkened unto their **v**. 6963
30: 4 the people that *were* with him lift up their **v** 6963
2Sa 3:32 the king lift up his **v**, and wept at the grave 6963
12:18 and he would not hearken unto our **v**: 6963
13:14 Howbeit he would not hearken unto her **v**: 6963
13:36 sons came, and lift up their **v** and wept: 6963
15:23 all the country wept *with* a loud **v**, and 6963
19: 4 the king cried *with* a loud **v**, O my son 6963
19:35 can I hear any more the **v** of singing *men* 6963
22: 7 he did hear my **v** out of his temple, and 6963
22:14 and the most High uttered his **v**. 6963
1Ki 8:55 all the congregation of Israel *with* a loud **v**, 6963
17:22 the LORD heard the **v** of Elijah; and 6963
18:26 *there was* no **v**, nor any that answered. 6963
18:29 that *there was* neither **v**, nor any to answer, 6963
19:12 in the fire: and after the fire a still small **v**. 6963
19:13 *there came* a **v** unto him, and said, 6963
20:25 And he hearkened unto their **v**, and did so. 6963
20:36 Because thou hast not obeyed the **v** of 6963
2Ki 4:31 but *there was* neither **v**, nor hearing. 6963
7:10 neither **v** of man, but horses tied, and asses 6963
10: 6 *be* mine, and *if* ye will hearken unto my **v**, 6963
18:12 Because they obeyed not the **v** of 6963
18:28 cried with a loud **v** in the Jews' language, 6963
19:22 against whom hast thou exalted *thy* **v**, and 6963
1Ch 15:16 sounding, by lifting up the **v** with joy. 6963
2Ch 5:13 when *they* lift up *their* **v** with the trumpets 6963
15:14 they sware unto the LORD with a loud **v**, 6963
20:19 God of Israel with a loud **v** on high. 6963
30:27 their **v** was heard, and their prayer came *up* 6963
32:18 they cried with a loud **v** in the Jews' speech 6963
Ezr 3:12 laid before their eyes, wept with a loud **v**; 6963
10:12 and said *with* a loud **v**, 6963
Ne 9: 4 cried with a loud **v** unto the LORD their 6963
Job 2:12 him not, they lifted up their **v**, and wept; 6963
3: 7 be solitary, let no **joyful v** come therein. 7445
3:18 they hear not the **v** of the oppressor. 6963
4:10 the **v** of the fierce lion, and the teeth of 6963
4:16 *there was* silence, and I heard a **v**, *saying,* 6963
9:16 believe that he had hearkened unto my **v**. 6963
30:31 and my organ into the **v** of them that weep. 6963
33: 8 I have heard the **v** of *thy* words, 6963
34:16 hear this: hearken to the **v** of my words. 6963
37: 2 Hear attentively the noise of his **v**, and 6963
37: 4 After it a **v** roareth: he thundereth with 6963
37: 4 he thundereth with the **v** of his excellency; 6963
37: 4 he will not stay them when his **v** is heard. 6963
37: 5 God thundereth marvellously with his **v**; 6963
Job 38:34 Canst thou lift up thy **v** to the clouds, 6963
40: 9 or, canst thou thunder with a **v** like him? 6963
Ps 3: 4 I cried unto the LORD *with* my **v**, and 6963
5: 2 Hearken unto the **v** of my cry, my King, 6963
5: 3 My **v** shalt thou hear *in* the morning, 6963
6: 8 for the LORD hath heard the **v** of my 6963
18: 6 he heard my **v** out of his temple, and 6963
18:13 in the heavens, and the Highest gave his **v**; 6963
19: 3 nor language, *where* their **v** is not heard. 6963
26: 7 That *I* may publish with the **v** of 6963
27: 7 Hear, O LORD, *when* I cry *with* my **v**: 6963
28: 2 Hear the **v** of my supplications, when I cry 6963
28: 6 he hath heard the **v** of my supplications. 6963
29: 3 The **v** of the LORD *is* upon the waters: 6963
29: 4 The **v** of the LORD *is* powerful; the voice 6963
29: 4 the **v** of the LORD *is* full of majesty. 6963
29: 5 The **v** of the LORD breaketh the cedars; 6963
29: 7 The **v** of the LORD divideth the flames of 6963
29: 8 The **v** of the LORD shaketh 6963
29: 9 The **v** of the LORD maketh the hinds to 6963
31:22 nevertheless thou heardest the **v** of my 6963
42: 4 with the **v** of joy and praise, *with* a 6963
44:16 For the **v** of him that reproacheth and 6963
46: 6 he uttered his **v**, the earth melted. 6963
47: 1 shout unto God with the **v** of triumph. 6963
55: 3 Because of the **v** of the enemy, because 6963
55:17 and cry aloud: and he shall hear my **v**. 6963
58: 5 Which will not hearken to the **v** of 6963
64: 1 Hear my **v**, O God, in my prayer: 6963
66: 8 and make the **v** of his praise to be heard: 6963
66:19 *me;* he hath attended to the **v** of my prayer. 6963
68:33 lo, he doth send out his **v**, *and that* a mighty 6963
68:33 send out his voice, *and that* a mighty **v**. 6963
74:23 Forget not the **v** of thine enemies: 6963
77: 1 I cried unto God *with* my **v**, *even* unto God 6963
77: 1 *with* my voice, *even* unto God *with* my **v**; 6963
77:18 The **v** of thy thunder *was* in the heaven: 6963
81:11 my people would not hearken to my **v**; and 6963
86: 6 and attend to the **v** of my supplications. 6963
93: 3 O LORD, the floods have lifted up their **v**; 6963
95: 7 of his hand. To day if ye will hear his **v**, 6963
98: 5 with the harp, and the **v** of a psalm. 6963
102: 5 By reason of the **v** of my groaning my 6963
103:20 hearkening unto the **v** of his word. 6963
104: 7 at the **v** of thy thunder they hasted away. 6963
106:25 hearkened not unto the **v** of the LORD. 6963
116: 1 because he hath heard my **v** *and* 6963
118:15 The **v** of rejoicing and salvation *is* in 6963
119:149 Hear my **v** according unto thy 6963
130: 2 Lord, hear my **v**: let thine ears be attentive 6963
130: 2 let thine ears be attentive to the **v** of my 6963
140: 6 hear the **v** of my supplications, O LORD. 6963
141: 1 give ear unto my **v**, when I cry unto thee. 6963
142: 1 I cried unto the LORD *with* my **v**; 6963
142: 1 *with* my **v** unto the LORD did I make my 6963
Pr 1:20 she uttereth her **v** in the streets: 6963
2: 3 *and* liftest up thy **v** for understanding; 6963
5:13 have not obeyed the **v** of my teachers, 6963
8: 1 and understanding put forth her **v**? 6963
8: 4 I call; and my **v** *is* to the sons of man. 6963
27:14 He that blesseth his friend with a loud **v**, 6963
Ecc 5: 3 a fool's **v** *is known* by multitude of words. 6963
5: 6 wherefore should God be angry at thy **v**, 6963
10:20 for a bird of the air shall carry the **v**, and 6963
12: 4 he shall rise up at the **v** of the bird, and 6963
SS 2: 8 The **v** of my beloved! behold, he cometh 6963
2:12 and the **v** of the turtle is heard in our land; 6963
2:14 me see thy countenance, let me hear thy **v**; 6963
2:14 for sweet *is* thy **v**, and thy countenance *is* 6963
5: 2 *it is* the **v** of my beloved that knocketh 6963
8:13 the companions hearken to thy **v**: 6963
Isa 6: 4 the posts of the door moved at the **v** of him 6963
6: 8 Also I heard the **v** of the Lord, saying, 6963
10:30 Lift up thy **v**, O daughter of Gallim: 6963
13: 2 exalt the **v** unto them, shake the hand, 6963
15: 4 their **v** shall be heard *even* unto Jahaz: 6963
24:14 They shall lift up their **v**, they shall sing, 6963
28:23 Give ye ear, and hear my **v**; hearken, and 6963
29: 4 thy **v** shall be, as of one that hath a familiar 6963
30:19 he will be very gracious unto thee at the **v** 6963
30:30 the LORD shall cause his glorious **v** to be 6963
30:31 For through the **v** of the LORD shall 6963
31: 4 he will not be afraid of their **v**, nor abase 6963
32: 9 ye women that are at ease, hear my **v**; 6963
36:13 cried with a loud **v** in the Jews' language, 6963
37:23 against whom hast thou exalted *thy* **v**, and 6963
40: 3 The **v** of him that crieth in the wilderness, 6963
40: 6 The **v** said, Cry. And he said, What shall I 6963
40: 9 good tidings, lift up thy **v** with strength; 6963
42: 2 nor cause his **v** to be heard in the street. 6963
42:11 the cities thereof lift up *their* **v**, the villages NIH
48:20 with a **v** of singing declare ye, tell this, 6963
50:10 that obeyeth the **v** of his servant, 6963
51: 3 thanksgiving, and the **v** of melody. 6963
52: 8 Thy watchmen shall lift up the **v**; *with* 6963
52: 8 *with* the **v** together shall they sing: 6963
58: 1 lift up thy **v** like a trumpet, and shew my 6963
58: 4 to make your **v** to be heard on high. 6963
65:19 the **v** of weeping shall be no more heard in 6963
65:19 no more heard in her, nor the **v** of crying. 6963
66: 6 A **v** of noise from the city, a voice from 6963
66: 6 of noise from the city, a **v** from the temple, 6963
66: 6 a **v** of the LORD that rendereth 6963
Jer 3:13 ye have not obeyed my **v**, saith 6963
3:21 A **v** was heard upon the high places, 6963
3:25 have not obeyed the **v** of the LORD our 6963
4:15 For a **v** declareth from Dan, and 6963
4:16 give out their **v** against the cities of Judah. 6963
4:31 For I have heard a **v** as of a woman in 6963
4:31 the **v** of the daughter of Zion, 6963
6:23 their **v** roareth like the sea; and they ride 6963
7:23 Obey my **v**, and I will be your God, and 6963
7:28 This *is* a nation that obeyeth not the **v** of 6963
7:34 the **v** of mirth, and the voice of gladness, 6963
7:34 the voice of mirth, and the **v** of gladness, 6963

Jer 7:34 the **v** of the bridegroom, and the voice of 6963
7:34 of the bridegroom, and the **v** of the bride: 6963
8:19 Behold the **v** of the cry of the daughter of 6963
9:10 neither can *men* hear the **v** of the cattle; 6963
9:13 have not obeyed my **v**, neither walked 6963
9:19 For a **v** of wailing is heard out of Zion, 6963
10:13 When he uttereth his **v**, *there is* a multitude 6963
11: 4 saying, Obey my **v**, and do them, 6963
11: 7 and protesting, saying, Obey my **v**. 6963
16: 9 the **v** of mirth, and the voice of gladness, 6963
16: 9 the voice of mirth, and the **v** of gladness, 6963
16: 9 the **v** of the bridegroom, and the voice of 6963
16: 9 of the bridegroom, and the **v** of the bride. 6963
18:10 that *it* obey not my **v**, then I will repent of 6963
18:19 hearken to the **v** of them that contend with 6963
22:20 lift up thy **v** in Bashan, and cry from 6963
22:21 thy youth, that thou obeyedst not my **v**. 6963
25:10 Moreover I will take from them the **v** of 6963
25:10 the **v** of gladness, the voice of 6963
25:10 the **v** of the bridegroom, and the voice of 6963
25:10 the **v** of the bride, the sound of 6963
25:30 and utter his **v** from his holy habitation; 6963
25:36 A **v** of the cry of the shepherds, and 6963
26:13 and obey the **v** of the LORD your God; 6963
30: 5 We have heard a **v** of trembling, of fear, 6963
30:19 and the **v** of them that make merry: 6963
31:15 A **v** was heard in Ramah, lamentation, *and* 6963
31:16 Refrain thy **v** from weeping, and thine eyes 6963
32:23 they obeyed not thy **v**, neither walked in 6963
33:11 The **v** of joy, and the voice of gladness, 6963
33:11 The voice of joy, and the **v** of gladness, 6963
33:11 the **v** of the bridegroom, and the voice of 6963
33:11 of the bridegroom, and the **v** of the bride, 6963
33:11 of the bride, the **v** of them that shall say, 6963
35: 8 Thus have we obeyed the **v** of Jonadab 6963
38:20 I beseech thee, the **v** of the LORD, which 6963
40: 3 have not obeyed his **v**, therefore this thing 6963
42: 6 we will obey the **v** of the LORD our God, 6963
42: 6 when we obey the **v** of the LORD our 6963
42:13 neither obey the **v** of the LORD your God, 6963
42:21 ye have not obeyed the **v** of the LORD 6963
43: 4 the people, obeyed not the **v** of the LORD, 6963
43: 7 for they obeyed not the **v** of the LORD: 6963
44:23 have not obeyed the **v** of the LORD, 6963
46:22 The **v** thereof shall go like a serpent; 6963
48: 3 A **v** of crying *shall be* from Horonaim, 6963
48:34 *even* unto Jahaz, have they uttered their **v**, 6963
50:28 The **v** of them that flee and escape out of 6963
50:42 their **v** shall roar like the sea, and they shall 6963
51:16 When he uttereth *his* **v**, *there is* a multitude 6963
51:55 and destroyed out of her the great **v**; 6963
51:55 great waters, a noise of their **v** is uttered: 6963
La 3:56 Thou hast heard my **v**: hide not thine ear at 6963
Eze 1:24 as the **v** of the Almighty, the voice of 6963
1:24 the **v** of speech, as the noise of a host: 6963
1:25 there was a **v** from the firmament that *was* 6963
1:28 my face, and I heard a **v** of one that spake. 6963
3:12 I heard behind me a **v** of a great rushing, 6963
8:18 though they cry in mine ears *with* a loud **v**, 6963
9: 1 He cried also in mine ears *with* a loud **v**, 6963
10: 5 as the **v** of the Almighty God when he 6963
11:13 cried *with* a loud **v**, and said, Ah Lord 6963
19: 9 that his **v** should no more be heard upon 6963
21:22 the slaughter, to lift up the **v** with shouting, 6963
23:42 a **v** of a multitude being at ease *was* with 6963
27:30 shall cause their **v** to be heard against thee, 6963
33:32 lovely song *of* one that hath a pleasant **v**, 6963
43: 2 his **v** *was* like a noise of many waters: and 6963
Da 4:31 there fell a **v** from heaven, *saying*, O king 7032
6:20 he cried with a lamentable **v** unto Daniel: 7032
7:11 of the **v** of the great words which the horn 7032
8:16 I heard a man's **v** between *the banks of* 6963
9:10 Neither have we obeyed the **v** of 6963
9:11 that *they* might not obey thy **v**; 6963
9:14 which he doeth: for we obeyed not his **v**. 6963
10: 6 the **v** of his words like the voice of a 6963
10: 6 the voice of his words like the **v** of a 6963
10: 9 Yet heard I the **v** of his words: and when I 6963
10: 9 when I heard the **v** of his words, then was I 6963
Joel 2:11 the LORD shall utter his **v** before his 6963
3:16 out of Zion, and utter his **v** from Jerusalem; 6963
Am 1: 2 from Zion, and utter his **v** from Jerusalem; 6963
Jnh 2: 2 of hell cried I, *and* thou heardest my **v**. 6963
2: 9 I will sacrifice unto thee with the **v** of 6963
Mic 6: 1 the mountains, and let the hills hear thy **v**. 6963
6: 9 The LORD'S **v** crieth unto the city, and 6963
Na 2: 7 her maids *shall* lead *her* as *with* the **v** of 6963
2:13 the **v** of thy messengers shall no more be 6963
Hab 3:10 the deep uttered his **v**, *and* lift up his hands 6963
3:16 belly trembled; my lips quivered at the **v**: 6963
Zep 1:14 *even* the **v** of the day of the LORD: 6963
2:14 *their* **v** shall sing in the windows; 6963
3: 2 She obeyed not the **v**; she received not 6963
Hag 1:12 obeyed the **v** of the LORD their God, and 6963
Zec 6:15 if ye will diligently obey the **v** of 6963
11: 3 *There is* a **v** of the howling of 6963
11: 3 a **v** of the roaring of young lions; for 6963
Mt 2:18 In Rama was there a **v** heard, lamentation, 5456
3: 3 The **v** of one crying in the wilderness, 5456
3:17 And lo a **v** from heaven, saying, This is my 5456
12:19 neither shall any *man* hear his **v** in 5456
17: 5 and behold a **v** out of the cloud, which said, 5456
27:46 the ninth hour Jesus cried with a loud **v**, 5456
27:50 when he had cried again with a loud **v**, 5456
Mk 1: 3 The **v** of one crying in the wilderness, 5456
1:11 And there came a **v** from heaven, 5456
1:26 and cried with a loud **v**, he came out of 5456
5: 7 And cried with a loud **v**, and said, 5456
9: 7 and a **v** came out of the cloud, saying, 5456
15:34 at the ninth hour Jesus cried with a loud **v**, 5456
15:37 And Jesus cried with a loud **v**, and gave up 5456
Lk 1:42 And she spake out with a loud **v**, 5456
1:44 as soon as the **v** of thy salutation sounded 5456
3: 4 The **v** of one crying in the wilderness, 5456
3:22 and a **v** came from heaven, which said, 5456
Lk 4:33 unclean devil, and cried out with a loud **v**, 5456
8:28 down before him, and with a loud **v** said, 5456
9:35 And there came a **v** out of the cloud, 5456
9:36 And when the **v** was past, Jesus was found 5456
11:27 certain woman of the company lift up her **v**, 5456
17:15 and with a loud **v** glorified God, 5456
19:37 praise God with a loud **v** for all the mighty 5456
23:46 And when Jesus had cried with a loud **v**, 5456
Jn 1:23 I *am* the **v** of one crying in the wilderness, 5456
3:29 because of the bridegroom's **v**: 5456
5:25 when the dead shall hear the **v** of the Son of 5456
5:28 all that are in the graves shall hear his **v**, 5456
5:37 Ye have neither heard his **v** at any time, 5456
10: 3 porter openeth; and the sheep hear his **v**: 5456
10: 4 the sheep follow him: for they know his **v**. 5456
10: 5 for they know not the **v** of strangers. 5456
10:16 also I must bring, and they shall hear my **v**; 5456
10:27 My sheep hear my **v**, and I know them, and 5456
11:43 he cried with a loud **v**, Lazarus, come forth. 5456
12:28 Then came there a **v** from heaven, *saying*, I 5456
12:30 This **v** came not because of me, but 5456
18:37 Every one that is of the truth heareth my **v**. 5456
Ac 2:14 lift up his **v**, and said unto them, Ye men of 5456
4:24 they lift up their **v** to God with one accord, 5456
7:31 as he drew near to behold *it*, the **v** of 5456
7:57 Then they cried out with a loud **v**, and 5456
7:60 and cried with a loud **v**, Lord, 5456
8: 7 For unclean spirits, crying with loud **v**, 5456
9: 4 and heard a **v** saying unto him, Saul, Saul, 5456
9: 7 hearing a **v**, but seeing no *man*. 5456
10:13 And there came a **v** to him, Rise, Peter; kill, 5456
10:15 And *the* **v** *spake* unto him again the second 5456
11: 7 And I heard a **v** saying unto me, Arise, 5456
11: 9 But *the* **v** answered me again from heaven, 5456
12:14 And when she knew Peter's **v**, she opened 5456
12:22 *saying, It is* the **v** of a god, and not of a 5456
14:10 Said with a loud **v**, Stand upright on thy 5456
16:28 But Paul cried with a loud **v**, saying, 5456
19:34 all with one **v** about the space of two hours 5456
22: 7 and heard a **v** saying unto me, Saul, Saul, 5456
22: 9 they heard not the **v** of him that spake to 5456
22:14 and shouldest hear the **v** of his mouth. 5456
24:21 Except *it be* for this one **v**, that I cried 5456
26:10 put to death, I gave my **v** **against** *them*. 5586
26:14 I heard a **v** speaking unto me, and saying in 5456
26:24 Festus said with a loud **v**, Paul, thou art 5456
1Co 14:11 if I know not the meaning of the **v**, 5456
14:19 that *by my* **v** I might teach others also, NIG
Gal 4:20 present with you now, and to change my **v**; 5456
1Th 4:16 with the **v** of the archangel, and with 5456
Heb 3: 7 Ghost saith, To day if ye will hear his **v**, 5456
3:15 it is said, To day if ye will hear his **v**, 5456
4: 7 as it is said, To day if ye will hear his **v**, 5456
12:19 the sound of a trumpet, and the **v** of words; 5456
12:19 which **v** they that heard intreated that NIG
12:26 Whose **v** then shook the earth: but now he 5456
2Pe 1:17 when there came such a **v** to him from 5456
1:18 And this **v** which came from heaven we 5456
2:16 the dumb ass speaking with man's **v** forbad 5456
Rev 1:10 and heard behind me a great **v**, as of a 5456
1:12 And I turned to see the **v** that spake with 5456
1:15 and his **v** as the sound of many waters. 5456
3:20 if any *man* hear my **v**, and open the door, I 5456
4: 1 the first **v** which I heard *was* as *it were* of a 5456
5: 2 a strong angel proclaiming with a loud **v**, 5456
5:11 I heard the **v** of many angels round about 5456
5:12 Saying with a loud **v**, Worthy is the Lamb 5456
6: 6 And I heard a **v** in the midst of the four 5456
6: 7 I heard the **v** of the fourth beast say, Come 5456
6:10 And they cried with a loud **v**, saying, 5456
7: 2 he cried with a loud **v** to the four angels, 5456
7:10 And cried with a loud **v**, saying, Salvation 5456
8:13 saying with a loud **v**, Woe, woe, woe, 5456
9:13 I heard a **v** from the four horns of 5456
10: 3 And cried with a loud **v**, as *when* a lion 5456
10: 4 I heard a **v** from heaven saying unto me, 5456
10: 7 But in the days of the **v** of the seventh 5456
10: 8 And the **v** which I heard from heaven spake 5456
11:12 And they heard a great **v** from heaven 5456
12:10 And I heard a loud **v** saying in heaven, 5456
14: 2 And I heard a **v** from heaven, as the voice 5456
14: 2 as the **v** of many waters, and as the voice of 5456
14: 2 and as the **v** of a great thunder: 5456
14: 2 I heard the **v** of harpers harping with their 5456
14: 7 Saying with a loud **v**, Fear God, and 5456
14: 9 saying with a loud **v**, If any *man* worship 5456
14:13 And I heard a **v** from heaven saying unto 5456
14:15 crying with a loud **v** to him that sat on 5456
16: 1 And I heard a great **v** out of the temple 5456
16:17 there came a great **v** out of the temple of 5456
18: 2 And he cried mightily with a strong **v**, 5456
18: 4 And I heard another **v** from heaven, saying, 5456
18:22 And the **v** of harpers, and musicians, and 5456
18:23 and the **v** of the bridegroom and of 5456
19: 1 And after these *things* I heard a great **v** of 5456
19: 5 And a **v** came out of the throne, saying, 5456
19: 6 And I heard as *it were* the **v** of a great 5456
19: 6 and as the **v** of many waters, and as 5456
19: 6 and as the **v** of mighty thunderings, saying, 5456
19:17 and he cried with a loud **v**, saying to all 5456
21: 3 And I heard a great **v** out of heaven saying, 5456

VOICES (17) [VOICE]

Jdg 21: 2 and lift up their **v**, and wept sore; 6963
1Sa 11: 4 and all the people lift up their **v**, and wept. 6963
Lk 17:13 And they lifted up *their* **v**, and said, Jesus, 5456
23:23 And they were instant with loud **v**, 5456
23:23 And the **v** of them and of the chief priests 5456
Ac 13:27 nor *yet* the **v** of the prophets which are read 5456
14:11 they lift up their **v**, saying in the speech of 5456
22:22 and *then* lift up their **v**, and said, 5456
1Co 14:10 so many kinds of **v** in the world, and 5456
Rev 4: 5 and thunderings and **v**: 5456
8: 5 and there were **v**, and thunderings, and 5456
8:13 other **v** of the trumpet of the three angels, 5456
Rev 10: 3 he had cried, seven thunders uttered their **v**. 5456
10: 4 the seven thunders had uttered their **v**, 5456
11:15 and there were great **v** in heaven, saying, 5456
11:19 and **v**, and thunderings, and an earthquake, 5456
16:18 And there were **v**, and thunders, and 5456

VOID (24)

Ge 1: 2 the earth was without form, and **v**; and 922
Nu 30:12 **utterly made** them **v** on the day he 6565+6565
30:12 her husband hath **made** them **v**; and 6565
30:13 establish it, or her husband may **make** it **v**. 6565
30:15 if he shall **any ways make** them **v** 6565+6565
Dt 32:28 For they *are* a nation **v** of counsel, neither *is* 6
1Ki 22:10 in a **v place** *in* the entrance of the gate of 1637
2Ch 18: 9 they sat in a **v place** *at* the entering in of 1637
Ps 89:39 Thou hast **made v** the covenant of thy 5010
119:126 to work: *for* they have **made v** thy law. 6565
Pr 7: 7 a young man **v** of understanding, 2638
10:13 a rod *is* for the back of him that is **v** of 2638
11:12 He that is **v** of wisdom despiseth his 2638
12:11 he that followeth vain *persons is* **v** of 2638
17:18 A man **v** of understanding striketh hands, 2638
24:30 by the vineyard of the man **v** of 2638
Isa 55:11 it shall not return unto me **v**, but it shall 7387
Jer 4:23 the earth, and lo, *it was* without form, and **v**; 922
19: 7 And I will **make v** the counsel of Judah and 1238
Na 2:10 She *is* empty, and **v**, and waste: and 4003
Ac 24:16 to have always a conscience **v of offence** 677
Ro 3:31 Do we then **make v** the law through faith? 2673
4:14 faith is **made v**, and the promise made of 2758
1Co 9:15 that any *man* should **make** my glorying **v**. 2758

VOLUME (2)

Ps 40: 7 in the **v** of the book *it is* written of me, 4039
Heb 10: 7 I come (in the **v** of the book it is written of 2777

VOLUNTARILY (1) [VOLUNTARY]

Eze 46:12 or peace offerings **v** unto the LORD, 5071

VOLUNTARY (4) [VOLUNTARILY]

Lev 1: 3 he shall offer it of his own **v will** at 7522
7:16 of his offering *be* a vow, or a **v offering**, 5071
Eze 46:12 Now when the prince shall prepare a **v** 5071
Col 2:18 beguile you of your reward in a **v** humility 2309

VOMIT (8) [VOMITED, VOMITETH]

Job 20:15 down riches, and he shall **v** them **up** again: 6958
Pr 23: 8 *which* thou hast eaten shalt thou **v up**, 6958
25:16 lest thou be filled there*with*, and **v** it. 6958
26:11 As a dog returneth to his **v**, *so* a fool 6892
Isa 19:14 as a drunken *man* staggereth in his **v**. 6892
28: 8 For all tables are full *of* **v** *and* filthiness, *so* 6892
Jer 48:26 Moab also shall wallow in his **v**, and 6892
2Pe 2:22 The dog *is* turned to his own **v** again; 1829

VOMITED (1) [VOMIT]

Jnh 2:10 and it **v out** Jonah upon the dry *land*. 6958

VOMITETH (1) [VOMIT]

Lev 18:25 and the land *itself* **v out** her inhabitants. 6958

VOPHSI (1)

Nu 13:14 the tribe of Naphtali, Nahbi the son of **V**. 2058

VOW (41) [VOWED, VOWEDST, VOWEST, VOWETH, VOWS]

Ge 28:20 Jacob vowed a **v**, saying, If God will be 5088
31:13 *and* where thou vowedst a **v** unto me: 5088
Lev 7:16 if the sacrifice of his offering *be* a **v**, or 5088
22:21 unto the LORD to accomplish *his* **v**, 5088
22:23 but for a **v** it shall not be accepted. 5088
27: 2 a man shall **make a singular v**, 5088+6381
Nu 6: 2 woman shall separate *themselves* to **v** a 5087
6: 2 *themselves* to vow a **v** of a Nazarite, 5088
6: 5 All the days of the **v** of his separation there 5088
6:21 according to the **v** which he vowed, so 5088
15: 3 or a sacrifice in performing a **v**, or in a 5088
15: 8 or *for* a sacrifice in performing a **v**, or 5088
21: 2 Israel vowed a **v** unto the LORD, and 5088
30: 2 If a man **v** a vow unto the LORD, or 5087
30: 2 If a man vow a **v** unto the LORD, or 5088
30: 3 If a woman also **v** a vow unto the LORD, 5087
30: 3 If a woman also vow a **v** unto the LORD, 5088
30: 4 her father hear her **v**, and her bond 5088
30: 8 then he shall make her **v** which she vowed, 5088
30: 9 every **v** of a widow, and of her that is 5088
30:13 Every **v**, and every binding oath to afflict 5088
Dt 12:11 all your choice vows which ye **v** unto 5087
23:18 the house of the LORD thy God for any **v**: 5088
23:21 When thou shalt **v** a vow unto the LORD 5087
23:21 When thou shalt vow a **v** unto the LORD 5088
23:22 if thou shalt forbear to **v**, it shall be no sin 5087
Jdg 11:30 Jephthah vowed a **v** unto the LORD, and 5088
11:39 who did with her *according to* his **v** which 5088
1Sa 1:11 she vowed a **v**, and said, O LORD of 5088
1:21 the LORD the yearly sacrifice, and his **v**. 5088
2Sa 15: 7 I pray thee, let me go and pay my **v**, 5088
15: 8 For thy servant vowed a **v** while I abode at 5088
Ps 65: 1 and unto thee shall the **v** be performed. 5088
76:11 **V**, and pay unto the LORD your God: 5087
Ecc 5: 4 When thou vowest a **v** unto God, defer not 5088
5: 5 Better *is it* that thou shouldest not **v**, 5087
5: 5 than that thou shouldest **v** and not pay. 5087
Isa 19:21 they shall **v** a vow unto the LORD, and 5087
19:21 they shall vow a **v** unto the LORD, and 5088
Ac 18:18 shorn *his* head in Cenchrea: for he had a **v**. 2171
21:23 We have four men which have a **v** on them; 2171

VOWED (18) [VOW]

Ge 28:20 Jacob **v** a vow, saying, If God will be with 5087
Lev 27: 8 according to his ability that **v** shall 5087
Nu 6:21 This *is* the law of the Nazarite who hath **v**, 5087
6:21 according to the vow which he **v**, so 5087
21: 2 Israel **v** a vow unto the LORD, and said, 5087

V

Nu 30: 6 when she **v**, or uttered ought out of her lips, 5088
30: 8 then he shall make her vow which she **v**S, 5921
30:10 if she **v** *in* her husband's house, or 5087
Dt 23:23 according as thou hast **v** unto the LORD 5087
Jdg 11:30 Jephthah **v** a vow unto the LORD, and 5087
11:39 her *according to* his vow which he had **v**: 5087
1Sa 1:11 she **v** a vow, and said, O LORD of hosts, 5087
2Sa 15: 7 which I have **v** unto the LORD, 5087
15: 8 For thy servant **v** a vow while I abode at 5087
Ps 132: 2 *and* **v** unto the mighty *God* of Jacob; 5087
Ecc 5: 4 in fools: pay that which thou hast **v**. 5087
Jer 44:25 surely perform our vows that we have **v**, 5087
Jnh 2: 9 I will pay *that* that I have **v**. 5087

VOWEDST (1) [VOW]
Ge 31:13 the pillar, *and* where thou **v** a vow unto me: 5087

VOWEST (2) [VOW]
Dt 12:17 nor any of thy vows which thou **v**, 5087
Ecc 5: 4 When thou **v** a vow unto God, defer not to 5087

VOWETH (1) [VOW]
Mal 1:14 **v**, and sacrificeth unto the Lord a corrupt 5087

VOWS (30) [VOW]
Lev 22:18 that will offer his oblation for all his **v**, and 5088
23:38 beside all your **v**, and beside all your 5088
Nu 29:39 besides your **v**, and your freewill offerings, 5088
30: 4 all her **v** shall stand, and every bond 5088
30: 5 not any of her **v**, or of her bonds wherewith 5088
30: 7 day that he heard *it:* then her **v** shall stand, 5088
30:11 all her **v** shall stand, and every bond 5088
30:12 proceeded out of her lips concerning her **v**, 5088
30:14 he establisheth all her **v**, or all her bonds, 5088
Dt 12: 6 your **v**, and your freewill offerings, and 5088
12:11 all your choice **v** which ye vow unto 5088
12:17 nor any of thy **v** which thou vowest, 5088
12:26 thy **v**, thou shalt take, and go unto the place 5088
Job 22:27 he shall hear thee, and thou shalt pay thy **v**. 5088
Ps 22:25 I will pay my **v** before them that fear him. 5088
50:14 and pay thy **v** unto the most High: 5088
56:12 Thy **v** *are* upon me, O God: I will render 5088
61: 5 For thou, O God, hast heard my **v**: 5088
61: 8 for ever, that I may daily perform my **v**. 5088
66:13 with burnt offerings: I will pay thee my **v**, 5088
116:14 I will pay my **v** unto the LORD now in 5088
116:18 I will pay my **v** unto the LORD now in 5088
Pr 7:14 with me; *this* day have I payed my **v**. 5088
20:25 *which is* holy, and after **v** to make inquiry. 5088
31: 2 of my womb? and what, the son of my **v**? 5088
Jer 44:25 We will surely perform our **v** that we have 5088
44:25 ye will surely accomplish your **v**, and 5088
44:25 your vows, and surely perform your **v**. 5088
Jnh 1:16 a sacrifice unto the LORD, and made **v**. 5088
Na 1:15 keep thy solemn feasts, perform thy **v**: 5088

VOYAGE (1)
Ac 27:10 I perceive that *this* **v** will be with hurt and *4144*

VULTURE (2) [VULTURE'S, VULTURES]
Lev 11:14 And the **v**, and the kite after his kind; 1676
Dt 14:13 and the kite, and the **v** after his kind, 1772

VULTURE'S (1) [VULTURE]
Job 28: 7 and which the **v** eye hath not seen: 344

VULTURES (1) [VULTURE]
Isa 34:15 there shall the **v** also be gathered, every one 1772

W

WADI See BROOKS

WAFER (3) [WAFERS]
Ex 29:23 one **w** out of the basket of the unleavened 7550
Lev 8:26 one **w**, and put *them* on the fat, and 7550
Nu 6:19 one unleavened **w**, and shall put *them* upon 7550

WAFERS (5) [WAFER]
Ex 16:31 the taste of it *was* like **w** *made* with honey. 6838
29: 2 and **w** unleavened anointed with oil: 7550
Lev 2: 4 with oil, or unleavened **w** anointed with oil. 7550
7:12 unleavened **w** anointed with oil, and 7550
Nu 6:15 **w** of unleavened bread anointed with oil, 7550

WAG (3) [WAGGING]
Jer 18:16 thereby shall be astonished, and **w** his head. 5110
La 2:15 **w** their head at the daughter of Jerusalem, 5128
Zep 2:15 passeth by her shall hiss, *and* **w** his hand. 5128

WAGES (18)
Ge 29:15 for nought? tell me, what *shall* thy **w** *be?* 4909
30:28 Appoint me thy **w**, and I will give *it.* 7939
31: 7 deceived me, and changed my **w** ten times; 4909
31: 8 If he said thus, The speckled shall be thy **w**; 7939
31:41 and thou hast changed my **w** ten times. 4909
Ex 2: 9 nurse it for me, and I will give *thee* thy **w**. 7939
Lev 19:13 neither rob *him:* the **w** of him that is hired 6468
Jer 22:13 useth his neighbour's service **without w**, 2600
Eze 29:18 yet had he no **w**, nor his army, for Tyrus, 7939
29:19 her prey; and it shall be the **w** for his army. 7939
Hag 1: 6 he that **earneth w** earneth wages *to put it* 7936
1: 6 he that earneth wages **earneth w** *to put it* 7936
Mal 3: 5 those that oppress the hireling in *his* **w**, 7939
Lk 3:14 *any* falsely; and be content with your **w**. *3800*
Jn 4:36 And he that reapeth receiveth **w**, and *3408*
Ro 6:23 For the **w** of sin *is* death; but the gift of *3800*
2Co 11: 8 taking **w** *of them,* to do you service. *3800*
2Pe 2:15 who loved the **w** of unrighteousness; *3408*

WAGGING (2) [WAG]
Mt 27:39 that passed by, reviled him, **w** their heads, *2795*
Mk 15:29 **w** their heads, and saying, Ah, *thou* that *2795*

WAGON (1) [WAGONS]
Nu 7: 3 a **w** for two of the princes, and for *each* one 5699

WAGONS (9) [WAGON]
Ge 45:19 take you **w** out of the land of Egypt for 5699
45:21 Joseph gave them **w**, according to 5699
45:27 when he saw the **w** which Joseph had sent 5699
46: 5 in the **w** which Pharaoh had sent to carry 5699
Nu 7: 3 six covered **w**, and twelve oxen; 5699
7: 6 Moses took the **w** and the oxen, and 5699
7: 7 Two **w** and four oxen he gave unto the sons 5699
7: 8 four **w** and eight oxen he gave unto 5699
Eze 23:24 **w**, and wheels, and with an assembly of 7393

WAIL (3) [WAILED, WAILING]
Eze 32:18 **w** for the multitude of Egypt, and cast them 5091
Mic 1: 8 Therefore I will **w** and howl, I will go stript 5594
Rev 1: 7 and all kindreds of the earth shall **w** *2875*

WAILED (1) [WAIL]
Mk 5:38 and them that wept and **w** greatly. *214*

WAILING (16) [WAIL]
Est 4: 3 the Jews, and fasting, and weeping, and **w**; 4553
Jer 9:10 mountains will I take up a weeping and **w**, 5092
9:18 let them make haste, and take up a **w** for us, 5092
9:19 For a voice of **w** is heard out of Zion, 5092
9:20 teach your daughters **w**, and every one her 5092
Eze 7:11 of theirs: neither *shall there be* **w** for them. 5089
27:31 thee with bitterness of heart *and* bitter **w**. 4553
27:32 in their **w** they shall take up a lamentation 5204
Am 5:16 **W** *shall be* in all streets; and they shall say 4553
5:16 and such as are skilful of lamentation to **w**. 4553
5:17 in all vineyards *shall be* **w**: for I will pass 4553
Mic 1: 8 I will make a **w** like the dragons, and 4553
Mt 13:42 there shall be **w** and gnashing of teeth. *2805*
13:50 there shall be **w** and gnashing of teeth. *2805*
Rev 18:15 for the fear of her torment, weeping and **w**, *3996*
18:19 and cried, weeping and **w**, saying, Alas, *3996*

WAIT (106) [AWAIT, WAITED, WAITETH, WAITING]
Ex 21:13 if a man **lie** not **in w**, but God deliver *him* 6658
Nu 3:10 and they shall **w on** their priest's office: 8104
8:24 upward they shall go in to **w** upon 6633+6635
35:20 or hurl at him by **laying of w**, that he die; 6660
35:22 upon him any thing without **laying of w**, 6660
Dt 19:11 and **lie in w** for him, and rise up against him, 693
Jos 8: 4 Behold, ye shall **lie in w against** the city, 693
8:13 and their **liers in w** on the west of the city, 6119
Jdg 9:25 the men of Shechem set **liers in w** for him in 693
9:32 that *is* with thee, *and* **lie in w** in the field: 693
9:34 they **laid w** against Shechem *in* four 693
9:35 people that *were* with him, from **lying in w**. 3993
9:43 **laid w** in the field, and looked, and behold, 693
16: 2 **laid w** for him all night in the gate of 693
16: 9 Now *there were* men **lying in w**, 693
16:12 *there were* **liers in w** abiding in the chamber. 693
20:29 Israel set **liers in w** round about Gibeah. 693
20:33 the **liers in w** of Israel came forth out of 693
20:36 they trusted unto the **liers in w** which they 693
20:37 the **liers in w** hasted, and rushed upon 693
20:37 the **liers in w** drew *themselves* along, and 693
20:38 between the men of Israel and the **liers in w**, 693
21:20 Go and **lie in w** in the vineyards; 693
1Sa 15: 2 how he laid *w* for him in the way, when he NIH
15: 5 a city of Amalek, and **laid w** in the valley. 7378
22: 8 against me, to **lie in w**, as at this day? 693
22:13 rise against me, to **lie in w**, as at this day? 693
2Ki 6:33 what should I **w** for the LORD any 3176
1Ch 23:28 Because their office *was* to **w on** the sons 3027
2Ch 5:11 *and* did not *then* **w** by course: 8104
13:10 and the Levites *w* upon *their* business: NIH
Ezr 8:31 and of such as **lay in w** by the way. 693
Job 14:14 all the days of my appointed time will I **w**, 3176
17:13 If I **w**, the grave *is* mine house: I have made 6960
31: 9 or *if* I have **laid w** at my neighbour's door; 693
38:40 *and* abide in the covert to **lie in w**? 695
Ps 10: 9 He **lieth in w** secretly as a lion in his den: 693
10: 9 he **lieth in w** to catch the poor: he doth catch 693
25: 3 Yea, let none that **w on** thee be ashamed: 6960
25: 5 of my salvation; on thee do I **w** all the day. 6960
25:21 uprightness preserve me; for I **w on** thee. 6960
27:14 **W** on the LORD: be of good courage, and 6960
27:14 thine heart: **w**, I say, on the LORD. 6960
37: 7 in the LORD, and **w patiently** for him: 2342
37: 9 those that **w upon** the LORD, they shall 6960
37:34 **W** on the LORD, and keep his way, and 6960
39: 7 now, Lord, what **w** I **for**? my hope *is* in 6960
52: 9 thou hast done *it:* and I will **w on** thy name; 6960
56: 6 mark my steps, when they **w for** my soul. 6960
59: 3 For lo, they **lie in w** for my soul: the mighty 693
59: 9 *Because of* his strength will I **w** upon thee: 8104
62: 5 My soul, **w** thou only upon God; for my 1826
69: 3 mine eyes fail while *I* **w** for my God. 3176
69: 6 Let not them that **w on** thee, O Lord GOD 6960
71:10 they that **lay w** for my soul take counsel 8104
104:27 These **w** all upon thee; that *thou* mayest 7663
123: 2 so our eyes *w* upon the LORD our God, NIH
130: 5 I **w** for the LORD, my soul doth wait, and 6960
130: 5 my soul doth **w**, and in his word do I hope. 6960
145:15 The eyes of all **w** upon thee; and 7663
Pr 1:11 Come with us, let us **lay w** for blood, 693
1:18 they **lay w** for their own blood; they lurk 693
7:12 in the streets, and **lieth in w** at every corner.) 693
12: 6 The words of the wicked *are* to **lie in w** *for* 693
20:22 *but* **w** on the LORD, and he shall save 6960
23:28 She also **lieth in w** as *for* a prey, and 693
24:15 **Lay** not **w**, O wicked *man,* against 693
Isa 8:17 I will **w** upon the LORD, that hideth his 2442
30:18 therefore will the LORD **w**, that *he* may 2442
30:18 blessed *are* all they that **w** for him. 2442
40:31 they that **w upon** the LORD shall renew 6960
42: 4 the earth: and the isles shall **w** for his law. 3176
49:23 for they shall not be ashamed that **w for** 6960
51: 5 the isles shall **w** upon me, and on mine arm 6960
59: 9 we **w** for light, but behold obscurity; 6960
60: 9 Surely the isles shall **w** for me, and 6960
Jer 5:26 people are found wicked *men:* they **lay w**, 7789
9: 8 with his mouth, but in heart he layeth his **w**. 696
14:22 therefore we will **w** upon thee: for thou 6960
La 3:10 He *was* unto me *as* a bear **lying in w**, *and* 693
3:25 The LORD *is* good unto them that **w** for 6960
3:26 **quietly w** for the salvation of the LORD. 1748
4:19 they **laid w** for us in the wilderness. 693
Hos 6: 9 as troops *of robbers* **w for** a man, *so* 2442
7: 6 their heart like an oven, whiles they **lie in w**: 693
12: 6 judgment, and **w** on thy God continually. 6960
Mic 7: 2 they all **lie in w** for blood; they hunt every 693
7: 7 I will **w** for the God of my salvation: 3176
Hab 2: 3 though it tarry, **w** for it; because it will 2442
Zep 3: 8 Therefore **w** ye upon me, saith the LORD, 2442
Mk 3: 9 that a small ship should **w on** him because *4342*
Lk 11:54 **Laying w for** him, and seeking to catch *1748*
12:36 And ye yourselves like unto men that **w for** *4327*
Ac 1: 4 but **w for** the promise of the Father, which, *4037*
20: 3 and when the Jews **laid w for** him, *1096+1917*
20:19 which befell me by the **lying in w** of *1917*
23:16 Paul's sister's son heard of *their* **lying in w**, *1747*
23:21 for there **lie in w for** him of them moe *than* *1748*
23:30 me how that the Jews **laid w** for the man, *1917*
25: 3 **laying w** in the way to kill him. *1747+4160*
Ro 8:25 see not, *then* do we with patience **w for** *it.* *553*
12: 7 Or ministry, *let us* **w** on *our* ministering: or NIG
1Co 9:13 they which **w at** the altar are partakers with *4332*
Gal 5: 5 For we through the Spirit **w for** the hope of *553*
Eph 4:14 whereby they **lie in w** to deceive; *3180*
1Th 1:10 And to **w for** his Son from heaven, whom he *362*

WAITED (35) [WAIT]
Ge 49:18 I have **w** for thy salvation, O LORD. 6960
1Ki 20:38 **w** for the king by the way, and 5975
2Ki 5: 2 she **w on** Naaman's wife. 1961+6440+3807.1
1Ch 6:32 they **w** on their office according to their 5975
6:33 these *are* they that **w** with their children. 5975
9:18 Who hitherto *w* in the king's gate eastward: NIH
2Ch 7: 6 the priests **w on** their offices: the Levites 5975
17:19 These **w on** the king, besides *those* whom 8334
35:15 king's seer; and the porters *w* at every gate; NIH
Ne 12:44 for the priests and for the Levites that **w**. 5975
Job 6:19 the companies of Sheba **w** for them. 6960
15:22 of darkness, and he *is* **w** for of the sword. 6822
29:21 and **w**, and kept silence at my counsel. 3176
29:23 they **w** for me as for the rain; and 3176
30:26 evil came *unto me:* and when I **w** for light, 3176
32: 4 Now Elihu had **w** till Job had spoken, 2442
32:11 Behold, I **w** for your words; I gave ear to 3176
32:16 When I had **w**, (for they spake not, but 3176
Ps 40: 1 I **w patiently for** the LORD; and 6960+6960
106:13 his works; they **w** not for his counsel: 2442
119:95 The wicked have **w** for me to destroy me: 6960
Isa 25: 9 we have **w** for him, and he will save us: 6960
25: 9 we have **w** for him, we will be glad and 6960
26: 8 O LORD, have we **w for** thee; 6960
33: 2 be gracious unto us; we have **w** for thee: 6960
Eze 19: 5 Now when she saw that she had **w**, *and* 3176
Mic 1:12 For the inhabitant of Maroth **w carefully** 2342
Zec 11:11 the poor of the flock that **w** upon me knew 8104
Mk 15:43 which also **w** for the kingdom of God, *4327*
Lk 1:21 And the people **w for** Zacharias, and *4328*
23:51 who also himself **w for** the kingdom of *4327*
Ac 10: 7 soldier of them that **w on** him **continually**; *4342*
10:24 And Cornelius **w for** them, and had called *4328*
17:16 Now while Paul **w for** them at Athens, his *1551*
1Pe 3:20 when once the longsuffering of God **w** in *1551*

WAITETH (11) [WAIT]
Job 24:15 The eye also of the adulterer **w** for 8104
Ps 33:20 Our soul **w** for the LORD: he *is* our help 2442
62: 1 Truly my soul **w** upon God: from him 1747
65: 1 Praise **w** for thee, O God, in Zion: and 1747
130: 6 My soul *w* for the Lord more than they that NIH
Pr 27:18 he that **w on** his master shall be honoured. 8104
Isa 64: 4 *what* he hath prepared for him that **w** for 2442
Da 12:12 Blessed *is* he that **w**, and cometh to 2442
Mic 5: 7 not for man, nor **w** for the sons of men. 3176
Ro 8:19 **w for** the manifestation of the sons of God. *553*
Jas 5: 7 the husbandman **w for** the precious fruit of *1551*

WAITING (8) [WAIT]
Nu 8:25 they shall cease **w upon** the service *thereof,* 6635
Pr 8:34 at my gates, **w** at the posts of my doors. 8104
Lk 2:25 and devout, **w for** the consolation of Israel: *4327*
8:40 received him: for they were all **w for** him. *4328*
Jn 5: 3 withered, **w for** the moving of the water. *1551*
Ro 8:23 **w for** the adoption, *to wit,* the redemption of *553*
1Co 1: 7 **w for** the coming of our Lord Jesus Christ: *553*
2Th 3: 5 of God, and into the **patient w** for Christ. *5281*

WAKE (4) [AWAKE, AWAKED, AWAKEST, AWAKETH, AWAKING, AWOKE, WAKED, WAKENED, WAKENETH, WAKETH, WAKING]
Jer 51:39 and not **w**, saith the LORD. 6974
51:57 a perpetual sleep, and not **w**, saith the King, 6974
Joel 3: 9 **w up** the mighty *men,* let all the men of 5782
1Th 5:10 died for us, that, whether we **w** or sleep, *1127*

WAKED (1) [WAKE]
Zec 4: 1 **w** me, as a man that is wakened out of his 5782

WAKENED (2) [WAKE]
Joel 3:12 Let the heathen be **w**, and come up to 5782
Zec 4: 1 as a man that is **w** out of his sleep, 5782

WAKENETH (2) [WAKE]
Isa 50: 4 he **w** morning by morning, he wakeneth 5782
50: 4 he **w** mine ear to hear as the learned. 5782

WAKETH (2) [WAKE]
Ps 127: 1 keep the city, the watchman **w** *but* in vain. 8245
SS 5: 2 I sleep, but my heart **w**: *it is* the voice of 5782

WAKING (1) [WAKE]
Ps 77: 4 Thou holdest mine eyes **w**: I am *so* 8109

WALK (212) [WALKED, WALKEDST, WALKEST, WALKETH, WALKING]
Ge 13:17 **w** through the land in the length of it and 1980
17: 1 **w** before me, and be thou perfect. 1980
24:40 unto me, The LORD, before whom I **w**, 1980
48:15 my fathers Abraham and Isaac did **w**, 1980
Ex 16: 4 whether they will **w** in my law, or no. 1980
18:20 shew them the way *wherein* they must **w**, 1980
21:19 **w** abroad upon his staff, then shall he that 1980
Lev 18: 3 neither shall ye **w** in their ordinances. 1980
18: 4 and keep mine ordinances, to **w** therein: 1980
20:23 ye shall not **w** in the manners of the nation, 1980
26: 3 If ye **w** in my statutes, and keep my 1980
26:12 I will **w** among you, and will be your God, 1980
26:21 if ye **w** contrary unto me, and will not 1980
26:23 these *things,* but will **w** contrary unto me; 1980
26:24 will I also **w** contrary unto you, and 1980
26:27 hearken unto me, but **w** contrary unto me; 1980
26:28 I will **w** contrary unto you also in fury; 1980
Dt 5:33 You shall **w** in all the ways which 1980
8: 6 thy God, to **w** in his ways, and to fear him. 1980
8:19 **w** after other gods, and serve them, and 1980
10:12 to **w** in all his ways, and to love him, and 1980
11:22 to **w** in all his ways, and to cleave unto 1980
13: 4 Ye shall **w** after the LORD your God, and 1980
13: 5 LORD thy God commanded thee to **w** in. 1980
19: 9 thy God, and to **w** ever in his ways; 1980
26:17 to **w** in his ways, and to keep his statutes, 1980
28: 9 of the LORD thy God, and **w** in his ways. 1980
29:19 though I **w** in the imagination of mine 1980
30:16 to **w** in his ways, and to keep his 1980
Jos 18: 8 Go and **w** through the land, and describe it, 1980
22: 5 to **w** in all his ways, and to keep his 1980
Jdg 2:22 keep the way of the LORD to **w** therein, 1980
5:10 ye that sit in judgment, and **w** by the way. 1980
1Sa 2:30 of thy father, should **w** before me for ever: 1980
2:35 he shall **w** before mine anointed for ever. 1980
8: 5 art old, and thy sons **w** not in thy ways: 1980
1Ki 2: 3 to **w** in his ways, to keep his statutes, *and* 1980
2: 4 to **w** before me in truth with all their heart 1980
3:14 if thou wilt **w** in my ways, to keep my 1980
3:14 as thy father David did **w**, then I will 1980
6:12 if thou wilt **w** in my statutes, and execute 1980
6:12 keep all my commandments to **w** in them; 1980
8:23 mercy with thy servants that **w** before thee 1980
8:25 that they **w** before me as thou hast walked 1980
8:36 them the good way wherein they should **w**, 1980
8:58 to **w** in all his ways, and to keep his 1980
8:61 to **w** in his statutes, and to keep his 1980
9: 4 if thou wilt **w** before me, as David thy 1980
11:38 wilt **w** in my ways, and do that *is* right in 1980
16:31 as if it had been a light thing for him to **w** 1980
2Ki 10:31 Jehu took no heed to **w** in the law of 1980
23: 3 to **w** after the LORD, and to keep his 1980
2Ch 6:14 that **w** before thee with all their hearts: 1980
6:16 take heed to their way to **w** in my law, 1980
6:27 them the good way, wherein they should **w**; 1980
6:31 to **w** in thy ways, so long as they live in 1980
7:17 *as for* thee, if thou wilt **w** before me, 1980
34:31 to **w** after the LORD, and to keep his 1980
Ne 5: 9 ought ye not to **w** in the fear of our God 1980
10:29 and into an oath, to **w** in God's law, 1980
Ps 12: 8 The wicked **w** on every side, when 1980
23: 4 though I **w** through the valley of 1980
26:11 *as for* me, I will **w** in mine integrity: 1980
48:12 **W about** Zion, and go round about her: 5437
56:13 that *I* may **w** before God in the light of 1980
78:10 of God, and refused to **w** in his law; 1980
82: 5 they understand; they **w on** in darkness: 1980
84:11 he withhold from them that **w** uprightly. 1980
86:11 thy way, O LORD; I will **w** in thy truth: 1980
89:15 they shall **w**, O LORD, in the light of thy 1980
89:30 my law, and **w** not in my judgments; 1980
101: 2 I will **w** within my house with a perfect 1980
115: 7 feet *have* they, but they **w** not: 1980
116: 9 I will **w** before the LORD in the land of 1980
119: 1 the way, who **w** in the law of the LORD. 1980
119: 3 also do no iniquity: they **w** in his ways. 1980
119:45 I will **w** at liberty: for I seek thy precepts. 1980
138: 7 Though I **w** in the midst of trouble, 1980
143: 8 me to know the way wherein I should **w**; 1980
Pr 1:15 My son, **w** not thou in the way with them; 1980
2: 7 *he is* a buckler to them that **w** uprightly. 1980
2:13 to **w** in the ways of darkness; 1980
2:20 That thou mayest **w** in the way of good 1980
3:23 shalt thou **w** *in* thy way safely, and thy foot 1980
Ecc 4:15 I considered all the living which **w** under 1980
6: 8 that knoweth to **w** before the living? 1980
11: 9 **w** in the ways of thine heart, and in 1980
Isa 2: 3 us of his ways, and we will **w** in his paths: 1980
2: 5 and let us **w** in the light of the LORD. 1980
3:16 **w** with stretched forth necks and 1980
8:11 instructed me that *I* should not **w** in the way 1980
30: 2 That **w** to go down *into* Egypt, and 1980
30:21 saying, This *is* the way, **w** ye in it, when ye 1980
35: 9 but the redeemed shall **w** *there:* 1980
40:31 be weary; *and* they shall **w**, and not faint. 1980
42: 5 upon it, and spirit to them that **w** therein: 1980
42:24 for they would not **w** in his ways, 1980
50:11 **w** in the light of your fire, and in the sparks 1980
59: 9 for brightness, *but* we **w** in darkness. 1980
Jer 3:17 neither shall they **w** any more after 1980
3:18 In those days the house of Judah shall **w** 1980
6:16 **w** therein, and ye shall find rest for your 1980
6:16 But they said, We will not **w** *therein.* 1980
6:25 not forth *into* the field, nor **w** by the way; 1980
7: 6 neither **w** after other gods to your hurt: 1980
7: 9 and **w** after other gods whom ye know not; 1980
7:23 **w** ye in all the ways that I have commanded 1980
9: 4 every neighbour will **w** *with* slanders. 1980
13:10 which **w** in the imagination of their heart, 1980
13:10 **w** after other gods, to serve them, and 1980
16:12 ye **w** every one after the imagination of his 1980
18:12 we will **w** after our own devices, and 1980
18:15 to **w** *in* paths, *in* a way not cast up; 1980
23:14 *they* commit adultery, and **w** in lies: 1980
26: 4 to **w** in my law, which I have set before 1980
31: 9 I will **cause** them to **w** by the rivers of 1980
42: 3 may shew us the way wherein we may **w**, 1980
La 5:18 which is desolate, the foxes **w** upon it. 1980
Eze 11:20 That they may **w** in my statutes, and keep 1980
20:18 **W** ye not in the statutes of your fathers, 1980
20:19 **w** in my statutes, and keep my judgments, 1980
33:15 **w** in the statutes of life, without committing 1980
36:12 Yea, I will **cause** men **to w** upon you, 1980
36:27 cause you to **w** in my statutes, and ye shall 1980
37:24 they shall also **w** in my judgments, and 1980
42: 4 before the chambers *was* a **w** of ten cubits 4109
Da 4:37 those that **w** in pride he *is* able to abase. 1981
9:10 to **w** in his laws, which he set before us by 1980
Hos 11:10 They shall **w** after the LORD: he shall 1980
14: 9 *are* right, and the just shall **w** in them: 1980
Joel 2: 8 they shall **w** every one in his path: 1980
Am 3: 3 Can two **w** together, except they be agreed? 1980
Mic 4: 2 us of his ways, and we will **w** in his paths: 1980
4: 5 For all people will **w** every one in the name 1980
4: 5 we will **w** in the name of the LORD our 1980
6: 8 and to **w** humbly with thy God? 1980
6:16 house of Ahab, and ye **w** in their counsels; 1980
Na 2: 5 they shall stumble in their **w**; they shall 1979
Hab 3:15 Thou didst **w** through the sea *with* thine 1869
3:19 he will **make** me **to w** upon mine high 1869
Zep 1:17 that they shall **w** like blind *men,* because 1980
Zec 1:10 the LORD hath sent to **w to and fro** 1980
3: 7 If thou wilt **w** in my ways, and if thou wilt 1980
3: 7 I will give thee **places to w** among these 4108
6: 7 sought to go that *they* might **w to and fro** 1980
6: 7 Get ye *hence,* **w to and fro** through 1980
10:12 they shall **w up and down** in his name, 1980
Mt 9: 5 be forgiven thee; or to say, Arise, and **w**? *4043*
11: 5 and the lame **w**, the lepers are cleansed, and *4043*
15:31 the lame to **w**, and the blind to see: *4043*
Mk 2: 9 to say, Arise, and take up thy bed, and **w**? *4043*
7: 5 Why **w** not thy disciples according to *4043*
Lk 5:23 be forgiven thee; or to say, Rise up and **w**? *4043*
7:22 how that the blind see, the lame **w**, *4043*
11:44 the men that **w** over *them* are not aware *of* *4043*
13:33 Nevertheless I must **w** to day, and *4198*
20:46 which desire to **w** in long robes, and *4043*
24:17 have one to another, as ye **w**, and are sad? *4043*
Jn 5: 8 unto him, Rise, take up thy bed, and **w**. *4043*
5:11 same said unto me, Take up thy bed, and **w**. *4043*
5:12 said unto thee, Take up thy bed, and **w**? *4043*
7: 1 for he would not **w** in Jewry, because *4043*
8:12 he that followeth me shall not **w** in *4043*
11: 9 If any *man* **w** in the day, he stumbleth not, *4043*
11:10 But if a man **w** in the night, he stumbleth, *4043*
12:35 **W** while ye have the light, lest darkness *4043*
Ac 3: 6 of Jesus Christ of Nazareth rise up and **w**. *4043*
3:12 or holiness we had made this *man* to **w**? *4043*
14:16 Who in times past suffered all nations to **w** *4198*
21:21 neither to **w** after the customs. *4043*
Ro 4:12 who also **w** in the steps of *that* faith of our *4748*
6: 4 so we also should **w** in newness of life. *4043*
8: 1 in Christ Jesus who **w** not after the flesh, *4043*
8: 4 who **w** not after the flesh, but after *4043*
13:13 Let us **w** honestly, as in the day; not in *4043*
1Co 3: 3 divisions, are ye not carnal, and **w** as men? *4043*
7:17 Lord hath called every one, so let him **w**. *4043*
2Co 5: 7 (For we **w** by faith, not by sight:) *4043*
6:16 and **w in** *them;* and I will be their God, and *1704*
10: 3 For though we **w** in the flesh, we do not *4043*
Gal 5:16 **W** in the Spirit, and ye shall not fulfil *4043*
5:25 live in the Spirit, let us also **w** in the Spirit. *4748*
6:16 And as many as **w** according to this rule, *4748*
Eph 2:10 before ordained that we should **w** in them. *4043*
4: 1 beseech you that *ye* **w** worthy of *4043*
4:17 that ye henceforth **w** not as other Gentiles *4043*
4:17 ye henceforth walk not as other Gentiles **w**, *4043*
5: 2 And **w** in love, as Christ also hath loved us, *4043*
5: 8 *ye* light in the Lord: **w** as children of light: *4043*
5:15 See then that ye **w** circumspectly, not as *4043*
Php 3:16 *let us* **w** by the same rule, *let us* mind *4748*
3:17 and mark them which **w** so as ye have us *4043*
3:18 (For many **w**, of whom I have told you *4043*
Col 1:10 That ye might **w** worthy of the Lord unto *4043*
2: 6 Christ Jesus the Lord, *so* **w** ye in him: *4043*
4: 5 **W** in wisdom toward them that are without, *4043*
1Th 2:12 That ye would **w** worthy of God, who hath *4043*
4: 1 ye have received of us how ye ought to **w** *4043*
4:12 That ye may **w** honestly toward them that *4043*
2Th 3:11 For we hear that *there are* some which **w** *4043*
2Pe 2:10 But chiefly them that **w** after the flesh in *4198*
1Jn 1: 6 and **w** in darkness, we lie, and do not *4043*
1: 7 But if we **w** in the light, as he is in the light, *4043*
2: 6 abideth in him ought himself also so to **w**, *4043*
2Jn 1: 6 is love, that we **w** after his commandments. *4043*
1: 6 heard from the beginning, ye should **w** in it. *4043*
3Jn 1: 4 joy than to hear that my children **w** in truth. *4043*
Jude 1:18 who should **w** after their own ungodly *4198*
Rev 3: 4 and they shall **w** with me in white: *4043*
9:20 which neither can see, nor hear, nor **w**: *4043*
16:15 lest he **w** naked, and they see his shame. *4043*
21:24 which are saved shall **w** in the light of it: *4043*

WALKED (122) [WALK]
Ge 5:22 Enoch **w** with God after he begat 1980
5:24 Enoch **w** with God: and he *was* not; 1980
6: 9 in his generations, *and* Noah **w** with God. 1980
Ex 2: 5 her maidens **w** along by the river's side; 1980
14:29 the children of Israel **w** upon dry *land* in 1980
Lev 26:40 and that also they have **w** contrary unto me; 1980
26:41 *And that* I also have **w** contrary unto them, 1980
Jos 5: 6 For the children of Israel **w** forty years in 1980
Jdg 2:17 out of the way which their fathers **w** in, 1980
5: 6 and the travellers **w** *through* byways. 1980
11:16 **w** through the wilderness unto the Red sea, 1980
1Sa 8: 3 his sons **w** not in his ways, but turned aside 1980
12: 2 I have **w** before you from my childhood 1980
2Sa 2:29 his men **w** all that night through the plain, 1980
7: 6 but have **w** in a tent and in a tabernacle. 1980
7: 7 In all *the places* wherein I have **w** with all 1980
11: 2 and **w** upon the roof of the king's house: 1980
1Ki 3: 6 according as he **w** before thee in truth, and 1980
8:25 that they walk before me as thou hast **w** 1980
9: 4 as David thy father **w**, in integrity of heart, 1980
11:33 have not **w** in my ways, to do *that* which *is* 1980
15: 3 he **w** in all the sins of his father, which he 1980
15:26 **w** in the way of his father, and in his sin 1980
15:34 **w** in the way of Jeroboam and in his sin 1980
16: 2 thou hast **w** in the way of Jeroboam, and 1980
16:26 For he **w** in all the way of Jeroboam the son 1980
22:43 he **w** in all the ways of Asa his father; 1980
22:52 **w** in the way of his father, and in the way 1980
2Ki 4:35 he returned, and **w** in the house to and fro; 1980
8:18 he **w** in the way of the kings of Israel, 1980
8:27 he **w** in the way of the house of Ahab, and 1980
13: 6 who made Israel sin, *but* **w** therein: 1980
13:11 who made Israel sin: *but* he **w** therein. 1980
16: 3 he **w** in the way of the kings of Israel, yea, 1980
17: 8 **w** in the statutes of the heathen, whom 1980
17:19 **w** in the statutes of Israel which they made. 1980
17:22 For the children of Israel **w** in all the sins of 1980
20: 3 remember now how I have **w** before thee in 1980
21:21 he **w** in all the way that his father walked 1980
21:21 he walked in all the way that his father **w** 1980
21:22 and **w** not in the way of the LORD. 1980
22: 2 **w** in all the way of David his father, and 1980
1Ch 17: 6 Wheresoever I have **w** with all Israel, spake 1980
17: 8 been with thee whithersoever thou hast **w**, 1980
2Ch 6:16 walk in my law, as thou hast **w** before me. 1980
7:17 as David thy father **w**, and do according to 1980
11:17 for three years they **w** in the way of David 1980
17: 3 he **w** in the first ways of his father David, 1980
17: 4 **w** in his commandments, and not after 1980
20:32 he **w** in the way of Asa his father, and 1980
21: 6 he **w** in the way of the kings of Israel, 1980
21:12 Because thou hast not **w** in the ways of 1980
21:13 hast **w** in the way of the kings of Israel, and 1980
22: 3 He also **w** in the ways of the house of 1980
22: 5 He **w** also after their counsel, and 1980
28: 2 For he **w** in the ways of the kings of Israel, 1980
34: 2 **w** in the ways of David his father, and 1980
Est 2:11 Mordecai **w** every day before the court of 1980
Job 29: 3 *and when* by his light I **w** *through* darkness; 1980
31: 5 If I have **w** with vanity, or *if* my foot hath 1980
31: 7 mine heart **w** after mine eyes, and *if any* 1980
38:16 or hast thou **w** in the search of the depth? 1980
Ps 26: 1 O LORD; for I have **w** in mine integrity: 1980
26: 3 before mine eyes: and I have **w** in thy truth. 1980
55:14 *and* **w** unto the house of God in company. 1980
81:12 *and* they **w** in their own counsels. 1980
81:13 unto me, *and* Israel had **w** in my ways! 1980
142: 3 In the way wherein I **w** have they privily 1980
Isa 9: 2 The people that **w** in darkness have seen a 1980
20: 3 Like as my servant Isaiah hath **w** naked and 1980
38: 3 how I have **w** before thee in truth and 1980
Jer 2: 5 have **w** after vanity, and are become vain? 1980
2: 8 and **w** after *things that* do not profit. 1980
7:24 **w** in the counsels *and* in the imagination of 1980
8: 2 after whom they have **w**, and whom they 1980
9:13 not obeyed my voice, neither **w** therein; 1980
9:14 have **w** after the imagination of their own 1980
11: 8 **w** every one in the imagination of their evil 1980
16:11 have **w** after other gods, and have served 1980
32:23 obeyed not thy voice, neither **w** in thy law; 1980
44:10 nor **w** in my law, nor in my statutes, that I 1980
44:23 nor **w** in his law, nor in his statutes, nor in 1980
Eze 5: 6 and my statutes, they have not **w** in them. 1980
5: 7 *and* have not **w** in my statutes, neither have 1980
11:12 for ye have not **w** in my statutes, 1980
16:47 Yet hast thou not **w** after their ways, 1980
18: 9 Hath **w** in my statutes, and hath kept my 1980
18:17 my judgments, hath **w** in my statutes; 1980
20:13 they **w** not in my statutes, and they 1980
20:16 **w** not in my statutes, but polluted my 1980
20:21 they **w** not in my statutes, neither kept my 1980
23:31 Thou hast **w** in the way of thy sister; 1980
28:14 thou hast **w up and down** in the midst of 1980
Da 4:29 At the end of twelve months he **w** in 1981
Hos 5:11 he willingly **w** after the commandment. 1980
Am 2: 4 to err, after the which their fathers have **w**: 1980
Na 2:11 **w**, *and* the lion's whelp, and none made 1980
Zec 1:11 We have **w to and fro** through the earth, 1980
6: 7 So they **w to and fro** through the earth. 1980
Mal 2: 6 he **w** with me in peace and equity, and 1980
3:14 that we have **w** mournfully before 1980
Mt 14:29 the ship, he **w** on the water, to go to Jesus. *4043*
Mk 1:16 Now as he **w** by the sea of Galilee, he saw *4043*
5:42 And straightway the damsel arose, and **w**; *4043*
16:12 as they **w**, and went into the country. *4043*
Jn 1:36 And looking upon Jesus as he **w**, he saith, *4043*
5: 9 made whole, and took up his bed, and **w**: *4043*
6:66 went back, and **w** no more with him. *4043*
7: 1 After these *things* Jesus **w** in Galilee: for he *4043*
10:23 And Jesus **w** in the temple in Solomon's *4043*

Jn 11:54 w no more openly among the Jews; 4043
Ac 3: 8 and w, and entered with them into 4043
14: 8 from his mother's womb, who never had w: 4043
14:10 upright on thy feet. And he leaped and w. 4043
2Co 10: 2 which think of us as if we w according to 4043
12:18 w we not in the same spirit? walked we not 4043
12:18 the same spirit? w we not in the same steps? NIG
Gal 2:14 But when I saw that they w not uprightly 3716
Eph 2: 2 Wherein in time past ye w according to 4043
Col 3: 7 In the which ye also w sometime, when ye 4043
1Pe 4: 3 when we w in lasciviousness, lusts, 4198
1Jn 2: 6 himself also so to walk, even as he w. 4043

WALKEDST (1) [WALK]
Jn 21:18 and w whither thou wouldest: 4043

WALKEST (7) [WALK]
Dt 6: 7 when thou w by the way, and when thou 1980
11:19 when thou w by the way, when thou liest 1980
1Ki 2:42 w abroad any whither, that thou shalt surely 1980
Isa 43: 2 when thou w through the fire, thou shalt not 1980
Ac 21:24 but that thou thyself also w orderly, and 4748
Ro 14:15 with thy meat, now w thou not charitably. 4043
3Jn 1: 3 that is in thee, even as thou w in the truth. 4043

WALKETH (41) [WALK]
Ge 24:65 What man is this that w in the field to meet 1980
Dt 23:14 For the LORD thy God w in the midst of 1980
1Sa 12: 2 now behold, the king w before you: and 1980
Job 18: 8 net by his own feet, and he w upon a snare. 1980
22:14 seeth not; and he w in the circuit of heaven. 1980
34: 8 of iniquity, and w with wicked men. 1980
Ps 1: 1 Blessed is the man that w not in the counsel 1980
15: 2 He that w uprightly, and 1980
39: 6 Surely every man w in a vain shew: 1980
73: 9 and their tongue w through the earth. 1980
91: 6 Nor for the pestilence that w in darkness; 1980
101: 6 he that w in a perfect way, he shall serve 1980
104: 3 who w upon the wings of the wind: 1980
128: 1 that feareth the LORD; that w in his ways. 1980
Pr 6:12 a wicked man, w with a froward mouth. 1980
10: 9 He that w uprightly walketh surely: but 1980
10: 9 He that walketh uprightly w surely: but 1980
13:20 He that w with wise men shall be wise: but 1980
14: 2 He that w in his uprightness feareth 1980
15:21 but a man of understanding w uprightly. 1980
19: 1 Better is the poor that w in his integrity, 1980
20: 7 The just man w in his integrity: his children 1980
28: 6 Better is the poor that w in his uprightness, 1980
28:18 Whoso w uprightly shall be saved: but 1980
28:26 but whoso w wisely, he shall be delivered. 1980
Ecc 2:14 are in his head; but the fool w in darkness: 1980
10: 3 when he that is a fool w by the way, 1980
Isa 33:15 He that w righteously, and 1980
50:10 that w in darkness, and hath no light? 1980
65: 2 which w in a way that was not good, 1980
Jer 10:23 it is not in man that w to direct his steps. 1980
23:17 they say unto every one that w after 1980
Eze 11:21 as for them whose heart w after the heart of 1980
Mic 2: 7 do not my words do good to him that w 1980
Mt 12:43 he w through dry places, 1330
Lk 11:24 w through dry places, seeking rest; 1330
Jn 12:35 for he that w in darkness knoweth not 4043
2Th 3: 6 from every brother that w disorderly, 4043
1Pe 5: 8 the devil, as a roaring lion, w about, 4043
1Jn 2:11 and w in darkness, and knoweth not 4043
Rev 2: 1 who w in the midst of the seven golden 4043

WALKING (30) [WALK]
Ge 3: 8 they heard the voice of the LORD God w 1980
Dt 2: 7 he knoweth thy w through this great 1980
1Ki 3: 3 w in the statutes of David his father: 1980
16:19 in w in the way of Jeroboam, and in his sin 1980
Job 1: 7 in the earth, and from w up and down in it. 1980
2: 2 in the earth, and from w up and down in it. 1980
31:26 it shined, or the moon w in brightness; 1980
Ecc 10: 7 and princes w as servants upon the earth. 1980
Isa 3:16 w and mincing as they go, and making a 1980
20: 2 And he did so, w naked and barefoot. 1980
57: 2 in their beds, each one w in his uprightness. 1980
Jer 6:28 are all grievous revolters, w with slanders: 1980
Da 3:25 w in the midst of the fire, and they have no 1981
Mic 2:11 If a man w in the spirit and falsehood do 1980
Mt 4:18 And Jesus, w by the sea of Galilee, saw two 4043
14:25 night Jesus went unto them, w on the sea. 4043
14:26 And when the disciples saw him w on 4043
Mk 6:48 w upon the sea, and would have passed by 4043
6:49 But when they saw him w upon the sea, 4043
8:24 looked up, and said, I see men as trees, w. 4043
11:27 and as he was w in the temple, there come 4043
Lk 1: 6 w in all the commandments and 4198
Jn 6:19 they see Jesus w on the sea, and drawing 4043
Ac 3: 8 w, and leaping, and praising God. 4043
3: 9 And all the people saw him w and 4043
9:31 and w in the fear of the Lord, and in 4198
2Co 4: 2 not w in craftiness, nor handling the word 4043
2Pe 3: 3 last days scoffers, w after their own lusts, 4198
2Jn 1: 4 that I found of thy children w in truth, 4043
Jude 1:16 complainers, w after their own lusts; 4198

WALL (179) [UNWALLED, WALLED, WALLS]
Ge 49: 6 and in their selfwill they digged down a w. 7794
49:22 by a well; whose branches run over the w. 7791
Ex 14:22 the waters were a w unto them on their 2346
14:29 the waters were a w unto them on their 2346
Lev 14:37 which in sight are lower than the w; 7023
25:31 the houses of the villages which have no w 2346
Nu 22:24 a w being on this side, and a wall on that 1447
22:24 being on this side, and a w on that side. 1447
22:25 she thrust herself unto the w, and 7023
22:25 and crusht Balaam's foot against the w: 7023
35: 4 shall reach from the w of the city and 7023
Jos 2:15 for her house was upon the town w, and 2346
2:15 the town wall, and she dwelt upon the w. 2346
Jos 6: 5 the w of the city shall fall down flat, 2346
6:20 that the w fell down flat, so that the people 2346
1Sa 18:11 I will smite David even to the w with it. 7023
19:10 Saul sought to smite David even to the w 7023
19:10 and he smote the javelin into the w: 7023
20:25 at other times, even upon a seat by the w: 7023
25:16 They were a w unto us both by night and 2346
25:22 light any that pisseth against the w. 7023
25:34 light any that pisseth against the w. 7023
31:10 they fastened his body to the w of 2346
31:12 the bodies of his sons from the w of 2346
2Sa 11:20 ye not that they would shoot from the w? 2346
11:21 a piece of a millstone upon him from the w, 2346
11:21 why went ye nigh the w? then say thou, 2346
11:24 the shooters shot from off the w upon thy 2346
18:24 up to the roof over the gate unto the w, 2346
20:15 people that were with Joab battered the w, 2346
20:21 his head shall be thrown to thee over the w. 2346
22:30 a troop: by my God have I leaped over a w. 7791
1Ki 3: 1 and the w of Jerusalem round about. 2346
4:33 unto the hyssop that springeth out of the w: 7023
6: 5 against the w of the house he built 7023
6: 6 for without in the w of the house he made NIH
6:27 that the wing of the one touched the one w, 7023
6:27 of the other cherub touched the other w; 7023
6:31 and side posts were a fifth part of the w. NIH
6:33 posts of olive tree, a fourth part of the w. NIH
9:15 the w of Jerusalem, and Hazor, and 2346
14:10 Jeroboam him that pisseth against the w, 7023
16:11 he left him not one that pisseth against a w, 7023
20:30 there a w fell upon twenty and 2346
21:21 from Ahab him that pisseth against the w, 7023
21:23 The dogs shall eat Jezebel by the w of 2426
2Ki 3:27 offered him for a burnt offering upon the w. 2346
4:10 a little chamber, I pray thee, on the w; 7023
6:26 king of Israel was passing by upon the w, 2346
6:30 he passed by upon the w, and the people 2346
9: 8 from Ahab him that pisseth against the w, 7023
9:33 some of her blood was sprinkled on the w, 7023
14:13 brake down the w of Jerusalem from 2346
18:26 in the ears of the people that are on the w. 2346
18:27 not sent me to the men which sit on the w, 2346
20: 2 he turned his face to the w, and prayed unto 7023
2Ch 3:11 five cubits, reaching to the w of the house: 7023
3:12 five cubits, reaching to the w of the house: 7023
25:23 brake down the w of Jerusalem from 2346
26: 6 brake down the w of Gath, and the wall of 2346
26: 6 the w of Jabneh, and the wall of Ashdod, 2346
26: 6 the w of Ashdod, and built cities about 2346
26: 9 at the turning of the w, and fortified them. NIH
27: 3 and on the w of Ophel he built much. 2346
32: 5 built up all the w that was broken, and 2346
32: 5 another w without, and repaired Millo in 2346
32:18 the people of Jerusalem that were on the w, 2346
33:14 Now after this he built a w without the city 2346
36:19 brake down the w of Jerusalem, and 2346
Ezr 5: 3 to build this house, and to make up this w? 846
9: 9 to give us a w in Judah and in Jerusalem. 1447
Ne 1: 3 the w of Jerusalem also is broken down, 2346
2: 8 for the w of the city, and for the house that 2346
2:15 viewed the w, and turned back, and 2346
2:17 and let us build up the w of Jerusalem, 2346
3: 8 they fortified Jerusalem unto the broad w. 2346
3:13 a thousand cubits on the w unto the dung 2346
3:15 the w of the pool of Siloah by the king's 2346
3:19 up to the armoury at the turning of the w. NIH
3:20 from the turning of the w unto the door of NIH
3:24 the turning of the w, even unto the corner. NIH
3:25 over against the turning of the w, and NIH
3:27 that lieth out, even unto the w of Ophel. 2346
4: 1 Sanballat heard that we builded the w, 2346
4: 3 he shall even break down their stone w. 2346
4: 6 So built we the w; and all the wall was 2346
4: 6 all the w was joined together unto the half 2346
4:10 so that we are not able to build the w. 2346
4:13 set I in the lower places behind the w, 2346
4:15 that we returned all of us to the w, 2346
4:17 They which builded on the w, and they that 2346
4:19 and large, and we are separated upon the w, 2346
5:16 Yea also I continued in the work of this w, 2346
6: 1 heard that I had builded the w, and 2346
6: 6 for which cause thou buildest the w, 2346
6:15 So the w was finished in the twenty and 2346
7: 1 when the w was built, and I had set up 2346
12:27 at the dedication of the w of Jerusalem they 2346
12:30 the people, and the gates, and the w. 2346
12:31 brought up the princes of Judah upon the w, 2346
12:31 hand upon the w toward the dung gate: 2346
12:37 at the going up of the w, above the house of 2346
12:38 and the half of the people upon the w, 2346
12:38 of the furnaces even unto the broad w; 2346
13:21 said unto them, Why lodge ye about the w? 2346
Ps 18:29 and by my God have I leaped over a w. 7791
62: 3 as a bowing w shall ye be, and as a 7023
Pr 18:11 and as a high w in his own conceit. 2346
24:31 and the stone w thereof was broken down. 1444
SS 2: 9 behold, he standeth behind our w, 3796
8: 9 If she be a w, we will build upon her a 2346
8:10 I am a w, and my breasts like towers: then 2346
Isa 2:15 every high tower, and upon every fenced w, 2346
5: 5 and break down the w thereof, and it shall 1447
22:10 have ye broken down to fortify the w. 2346
25: 4 the terrible ones is as a storm against the w. 7023
30:13 swelling out in a high w, whose breaking 2346
36:11 in the ears of the people that are on the w. 2346
36:12 not sent me to the men that sit upon the w, 2346
38: 2 Hezekiah turned his face toward the w, 7023
59:10 We grope for the w like the blind, and 7023
Jer 15:20 thee unto this people a fenced brasen w: 2346
49:27 I will kindle a fire in the w of Damascus, 2346
51:44 unto him: yea, the w of Babylon shall fall. 2346
La 2: 8 The LORD hath purposed to destroy the w 2346
2: 8 he made the rampart and the w to lament; 2346
2:18 unto the Lord, O w of the daughter of Zion, 2346
Eze 4: 3 set it for a w of iron between thee and 7023
Eze 8: 7 and when I looked, behold a hole in the w. 7023
8: 8 he unto me, Son of man, dig now in the w: 7023
8: 8 when I had digged in the w, behold a door. 7023
8:10 pourtrayed upon the w round about. 7023
12: 5 Dig thou through the w in their sight, and 7023
12: 7 in the even I digged through the w with 7023
12:12 they shall dig through the w to carry out 7023
13:10 one built up a w, and lo, others daubed it 2434
13:12 Lo, when the w is fallen, shall it not be said 7023
13:14 So will I break down the w that ye have 7023
13:15 will I accomplish my wrath upon the w, 7023
13:15 The w is no more, neither they that daubed 7023
23:14 when she saw men pourtrayed upon the w, 7023
38:20 and every w shall fall to the ground. 2346
40: 5 behold a w on the outside of the house 2346
41: 5 After he measured the w of the house, 7023
41: 6 they entered into the w which was of 7023
41: 6 but they had not hold in the w of the house. 7023
41: 9 The thickness of the w, which was for 7023
41:12 the w of the building was five cubits thick 7023
41:17 by all the w round about within 7023
41:20 trees made, and on the w of the temple. 7023
42: 7 the w that was without over against 1447
42:10 of the w of the court toward the east, 1444
42:12 even the way directly before the w toward 1448
42:20 it had a w round about, five hundred reeds 2346
43: 8 my posts, and the w between me and them, 7023
Da 5: 5 the plaister of the w of the king's palace: 3797
9:25 and the w, even in troublous times. 2742
Hos 2: 6 make a w, that she shall not find her 1443+1447
Joel 2: 7 they shall climb the w like men of war; 2346
2: 9 they shall run upon the w, they shall climb 2346
Am 1: 7 I will send a fire on the w of Gaza, 2346
1:10 I will send a fire on the w of Tyrus, 2346
1:14 I will kindle a fire in the w of Rabbah, and 2346
5:19 leaned his hand on the w, and a serpent bit 7023
7: 7 the Lord stood upon a w made by a 2346
Na 2: 5 they shall make haste to the w thereof, and 2346
3: 8 was the sea, and her w was from the sea? 2346
Hab 2:11 For the stone shall cry out of the w, and 7023
Zec 2: 5 will be unto her a w of fire round about, 2346
Ac 9:25 and let him down by the w in a basket. 5038
23: 3 God shall smite thee, thou whited w: 5109
2Co 11:33 in a basket was I let down by the w, 5038
Eph 2:14 hath broken down the middle w of 3320
Rev 21:12 And had a w great and high, and 5038
21:14 And the w of the city had twelve 5038
21:15 and the gates thereof, and the w thereof. 5038
21:17 And he measured the w thereof, an hundred 5038
21:18 And the building of the w of it was of 5038
21:19 And the foundations of the w of the city 5038

WALLED (4) [WALL]
Lev 25:29 if a man sell a dwelling house in a w city, 2346
25:30 the house that is in the w city shall be 2346
Nu 13:28 and the cities are w, and very great: 1219
Dt 1:28 the cities are great and w up to heaven; and 1219

WALLOW (4) [WALLOWED, WALLOWING]
Jer 6:26 thee with sackcloth, and w thyself in ashes: 6428
25:34 w yourselves in the ashes, ye principal of 6428
48:26 Moab also shall w in his vomit, and he also 5606
Eze 27:30 they shall w themselves in the ashes: 6428

WALLOWED (2) [WALLOW]
2Sa 20:12 Amasa w in blood in the midst of 1556
Mk 9:20 and he fell on the ground, and w foaming. 2947

WALLOWING (1) [WALLOW]
2Pe 2:22 The sow that was washed to her w in 2946

WALLS (66) [WALL]
Lev 14:37 if the plague be in the w of the house with 7023
14:39 if the plague be spread in the w of 7023
Dt 3: 5 All these cities were fenced with high w, 2346
28:52 until thy high and fenced w come down, 2346
1Ki 4:13 threescore great cities with w and 2346
6: 5 against the w of the house round about, 7023
6: 6 not be fastened in the w of the house. 7023
6:15 he built the w of the house within with 7023
6:15 floor of the house, and the w of the cieling: 7023
6:16 the floor and the w with boards of cedar: 7023
6:29 he carved all the w of the house round 7023
2Ki 25: 4 by the way of the gate between two w, 2346
25:10 brake down the w of Jerusalem round 2346
1Ch 29: 4 to overlay the w of the houses withal: 7023
2Ch 3: 7 and the w thereof, and the doors thereof, 7023
3: 7 with gold; and graved cherubims on the w. 7023
8: 5 fenced cities, with w, gates, and bars; 2346
14: 7 make about them w, and towers, gates, and 2346
Ezr 4:12 have set up the w thereof, and joined 7792
4:13 the w set up again, then will they not pay 7792
4:16 be builded again, and the w thereof set up, 7792
5: 8 timber is laid in the w, and this work goeth 3797
5: 9 to build this house, and to make up these w? 846
Ne 2:13 dung port, and viewed the w of Jerusalem, 2346
4: 7 heard that the w of Jerusalem were made 2346
Job 24:11 Which make oil within their w, and 7791
Ps 51:18 unto Zion: build thou the w of Jerusalem. 2346
55:10 night they go about it upon the w thereof: 2346
122: 7 Peace be within thy w, and 2426
Pr 25:28 a city that is broken down, and without w. 2346
SS 5: 7 the keepers of the w took away my vail 2346
Isa 22: 5 breaking down the w, and of crying to 7023
22:11 Ye made also a ditch between the two w 2346
25:12 the fortress of the high fort of thy w shall 2346
26: 1 salvation will God appoint for w and 2346
49:16 my hands; thy w are continually before me. 2346
56: 5 within my w a place and a name better than 2346
60:10 the sons of strangers shall build up thy w, 2346
60:18 thou shalt call thy w Salvation, and 2346
62: 6 I have set watchmen upon thy w, 2346
Jer 1:15 against all the w thereof round about, and 2346
1:18 and brasen w against the whole land, 2346

W

Jer 5:10 Go ye up upon her **w**, and destroy; but 8284
21: 4 which besiege you without the **w**, and I will 2346
39: 4 by the gate betwixt the **two w**: 2346
39: 8 and brake down the **w** of Jerusalem. 2346
50:15 are fallen, her **w** are thrown down: 2346
51:12 Set up the standard upon the **w** of Babylon, 2346
51:58 The broad **w** of Babylon shall be utterly 2346
52: 7 *by* the way of the gate between the **two w**, 2346
52:14 brake down all the **w** of Jerusalem round 2346
La 2: 7 the hand of the enemy the **w** of her palaces; 2346
Eze 26: 4 they shall destroy the **w** of Tyrus, and 2346
26: 9 he shall set engines of war against thy **w**, 2346
26:10 thy **w** shall shake at the noise of 2346
26:12 they shall break down thy **w**, and 2346
27:11 thine army *were* upon thy **w** round about, 2346
27:11 they hanged their shields upon thy **w** round 2346
33:30 still are talking against thee by the **w** 7023
38:11 all of them dwelling without **w**, and 2346
41:13 and the building, with the **w** thereof, 7023
41:22 and the **w** thereof, *were of* wood: 7023
41:25 palm trees, like as *were* made upon the **w**; 7023
Mic 7:11 *In* the day that thy **w** are *to be* built, *in* that 1447
Zec 2: 4 **towns without w** for the multitude of men 6519
Heb 11:30 By faith the **w** of Jericho fell down, *5038*

WANDER (14) [WANDERED, WANDERERS, WANDEREST, WANDERETH, WANDERING, WANDERINGS]

Ge 20:13 when God **caused** me **to w** from my 8582
Nu 14:33 your children shall **w** in the wilderness 7462
32:13 he **made** them **w** in the wilderness forty 5128
Dt 27:18 Cursed *be* he that **maketh** the blind **to w** 7686
Job 12:24 **causeth** them **to w** in a wilderness *where* 8582
38:41 ones cry unto God, they **w** for lack of meat. 8582
Ps 55: 7 Lo, *then* would I **w** far off, *and* remain in 5074
59:15 Let them **w up and down** for meat, and 5128
107:40 **causeth** them **to w** in the wilderness, 8582
119:10 O let me not **w** from thy commandments. 7686
Isa 47:15 they shall **w** every one to his quarter; 8582
Jer 14:10 Thus have they loved to **w**, they have not 5128
48:12 that shall **cause** him **to w**, and shall empty 6808
Am 8:12 they shall **w** from sea to sea, and from 5128

WANDERED (10) [WANDER]

Ge 21:14 and **w** in the wilderness of Beer-sheba. 8582
Jos 14:10 while *the children of* Israel **w** in 1980
Ps 107: 4 They **w** in the wilderness in a solitary way; 8582
Isa 16: 8 unto Jazer, they **w** *through* the wilderness: 8582
La 4:14 They have **w** *as* blind *men* in the streets, 5128
4:15 touch not, when they fled away and **w**: 5128
Eze 34: 6 My sheep **w** through all the mountains, and 7686
Am 4: 8 So two *or* three cities **w** unto one city, 5128
Heb 11:37 they **w about** in sheepskins and goatskins; *4022*
11:38 they **w** in deserts, and *in* mountains, and *4105*

WANDERERS (2) [WANDER]

Jer 48:12 the LORD, that I will send unto him **w**, 6808
Hos 9:17 and they shall be **w** among the nations. 5074

WANDEREST (1) [WANDER]

Jer 2:20 high hill and under every green tree thou **w**, 6808

WANDERETH (6) [WANDER]

Job 15:23 He **w abroad** for bread, *saying,* Where *is* 5074
Pr 21:16 The man that **w** out of the way of 8582
27: 8 As a bird that **w** from her nest, so *is* a man 5074
27: 8 her nest, so *is* a man that **w** from his place. 5074
Isa 16: 3 hide the outcasts; bewray not him that **w**. 5074
Jer 49: 5 and none shall gather up him that **w**. 5074

WANDERING (6) [WANDER]

Ge 37:15 and behold, *he was* **w** in the field: 8582
Pr 26: 2 As the bird by **w**, as the swallow by flying, 5110
Ecc 6: 9 Better *is* the sight of the eyes than the **w** of 1980
Isa 16: 2 *that,* as a **w** bird cast out of the nest, *so* 5074
1Ti 5:13 *to be* idle, **w about** from house to house; *4022*
Jude 1:13 **w** stars, to whom is reserved the blackness *4107*

WANDERINGS (1) [WANDER]

Ps 56: 8 Thou tellest my **w**: put thou my tears into 5112

WANT (31) [WANTED, WANTETH, WANTING, WANTS]

Dt 28:48 in **w** of all *things:* and he shall put a yoke of 2640
28:57 for she shall eat them for **w** of all *things* 2640
Jdg 18:10 a place where *there is* no **w** of any thing 4270
19:19 thy servants: *there is* no **w** of any thing. 4270
Job 24: 8 embrace the rock **for w of** a shelter. 1097+4480
30: 3 For **w** and famine *they were* solitary; flying 2639
31:19 If I have seen *any* perish for **w** of clothing, 1097
Ps 23: 1 The LORD *is* my shepherd; I shall not **w**. 2637
34: 9 for *there is* no **w** to them that fear him. 4270
34:10 they that seek the LORD shall not **w** any 2637
Pr 6:11 that travelleth, and thy **w** as an armed man. 4270
10:21 feed many: but fools die for **w** of wisdom. 2638
13:23 there is *that is* destroyed for **w of** judgment. 3808
13:25 but the belly of the wicked shall **w**. 2637
14:28 in the **w** of people *is* the destruction of 657
21: 5 but *of* every one that is hasty only to **w**. 4270
22:16 giveth to the rich, *shall* surely *come* to **w**. 4270
24:34 that travelleth; and thy **w** as an armed man. 4270
Isa 34:16 of these shall fail, none shall **w** her mate: 6485
Jer 33:17 David shall never **w** a man to sit upon 3772
33:18 Neither shall the priests the Levites **w** a 3772
35:19 Jonadab the son of Rechab shall not **w** a 3772
La 4: 9 stricken through for **w** *of* the fruits of NIH
Eze 4:17 That they may **w** bread and water, and 2637
Am 4: 6 and **w** of bread in all your places: 2640
Mk 12:44 but she of her **w** did cast in all that she had, *5304*
Lk 15:14 in that land; and he began to be **in w**. *5302*
2Co 8:14 abundance *may be a supply* for their **w**, *5303*
8:14 also may be *a supply* for your **w**: *5303*
9:12 not only supplieth the **w** of the saints, *5303*
Php 4:11 Not that I speak in respect of **w**: for I have *5304*

WANTED (3) [WANT]

Jer 44:18 we have **w** all *things,* and have been 2637
Jn 2: 3 And when they **w** wine, the mother of Jesus *5302*
2Co 11: 9 And when I was present with you, and **w**, *5302*

WANTETH (7) [WANT]

Dt 15: 8 sufficient for his need, *in that* which he **w**. 2637
Pr 9: 4 *as for* him that **w** understanding, she saith 2638
9:16 *as for* him that **w** understanding, she saith 2638
10:19 In the multitude of words there **w** not sin: 2308
28:16 The prince that **w** understanding *is* also a 2638
Ecc 6: 2 that he **w** nothing for his soul of all that he 2638
SS 7: 2 *is like* a round goblet, *which* **w** not liquor: 2637

WANTING (8) [WANT]

2Ki 10:19 and all his priests; let none be **w**: 6485
10:19 whosoever shall be **w**, he shall not live. 6485
Pr 19: 7 *them with* words, *yet* they *are* **w** *to him.* 3808
Ecc 1:15 and **that which is w** cannot be numbered. 2642
Da 5:27 weighed in the balances, and art found **w**. 2627
Tit 1: 5 shouldest set in order the *things* that are **w**, *3007*
3:13 that nothing be **w** unto them. *3007*
Jas 1: 4 ye may be perfect and entire, **w** nothing. *3007*

WANTON (3) [WANTONNESS]

Isa 3:16 walk with stretched forth necks and **w** eyes, 8265
1Ti 5:11 when they have *begun to* **wax w against** *2691*
Jas 5: 5 lived in pleasure on the earth, and been **w**; *4684*

WANTONNESS (2) [WANTON]

Ro 13:13 not in chambering and **w**, not in strife and *766*
2Pe 2:18 the lusts of the flesh, through much **w**, *766*

WANTS (2) [WANT]

Jdg 19:20 howsoever *let* all thy **w** *lie* upon me; 4270
Php 2:25 and he that ministered to my **w**. *5532*

WAR (225) [WARFARE, WARRED, WARRETH, WARRING, WARRIOR, WARRIORS, WARS]

Ge 14: 2 *That these* made **w** with Bera king of 4421
Ex 1:10 to pass, that, when there falleth out any **w**, 4421
13:17 the people repent when they see **w**, 4421
15: 3 The LORD *is* a man of **w**: the LORD *is* 4421
17:16 **w** with Amalek from generation *to* 4421
32:17 *There is* a noise of **w** in the camp. 4421
Nu 1: 3 all that *are able to* go forth *to* **w** in Israel: 6635
1:20 upward, all that *were able to* go forth *to* **w**; 6635
1:22 upward, all that *were able to* go forth *to* **w**; 6635
1:24 upward, all that *were able to* go forth *to* **w**; 6635
1:26 upward, all that *were able to* go forth *to* **w**; 6635
1:28 upward, all that *were able to* go forth *to* **w**; 6635
1:30 upward, all that *were able to* go forth *to* **w**; 6635
1:32 upward, all that *were able to* go forth *to* **w**; 6635
1:34 upward, all that *were able to* go forth *to* **w**; 6635
1:36 upward, all that *were able to* go forth *to* **w**; 6635
1:38 upward, all that *were able to* go forth *to* **w**; 6635
1:40 upward, all that *were able to* go forth *to* **w**; 6635
1:42 upward, all that *were able to* go forth *to* **w**; 6635
1:45 all that *were able to* go forth *to* **w** in Israel; 6635
10: 9 if ye go *to* **w** in your land against 4421
26: 2 all that *are able to* go *to* **w** in Israel. 6635
31: 3 Arm some of yourselves unto the **w**, and 6635
31: 4 the tribes of Israel, shall ye send to the **w**. 6635
31: 5 *every* tribe, twelve thousand armed for **w**. 6635
31: 6 Moses sent them to the **w**, a thousand of 6635
31: 6 to the **w**, with the holy instruments, and 6635
31:21 Eleazar the priest said unto the men of **w** 6635
31:27 between them that took the **w** upon them, 4421
31:28 of the men of **w** which went out to battle: 4421
31:32 of the prey which the men of **w** had caught, 6635
31:36 *was* the portion of them that went out to **w**, 6635
31:49 the men of **w** which *are* under our charge, 4421
31:53 (*For* the men of **w** had taken spoil, 6635
32: 6 Shall your brethren go to **w**, and shall ye sit 4421
32:20 ye will go armed before the LORD to **w**, 4421
32:27 every man armed for **w**, before the LORD 6635
Dt 1:41 had girded on every man his weapons of **w**, 4421
2:14 until all the generation of the men of **w** 4421
2:16 when all the men of **w** were consumed and 4421
3:18 of Israel, all *that are* **meet for the w**. 1121+2428
4:34 by **w**, and by a mighty hand, and by a 4421
20:12 will make **w** against thee, then thou shalt 4421
20:19 long time, in **making w** against it to take it, 3898
20:20 against the city that maketh **w** with thee, 4421
21:10 When thou goest forth to **w** against thine 4421
24: 5 taken a new wife, he shall not go out to **w**, 6635
Jos 4:13 About forty thousand prepared for **w** 6635
5: 4 *that were* males, *even* all the men of **w**, 4421
5: 6 till all the people *that were* men of **w**, 4421
6: 3 all *ye* men of **w**, *and* go round about 4421
8: 1 take all the people of **w** with thee, 4421
8: 3 So Joshua arose, and all the people of **w**, 4421
8:11 *even the people* of **w** that *were* with him, 4421
10: 5 before Gibeon, and **made w** against it. 3898
10: 7 he, and all the people of **w** with him, and 4421
10:24 said unto the captains of the men of **w** 4421
11: 7 and all the people of **w** with him, 4421
11:18 Joshua made **w** a long time with all those 4421
11:23 by their tribes. And the land rested from **w**. 4421
14:11 for **w**, both to go out, and to come in. 4421
14:15 the Anakims. And the land had rest from **w**. 4421
17: 1 because he was a man of **w**, therefore 4421
22:12 *at* Shiloh, to go up to **w** against them. 6635
Jdg 3: 2 to teach them **w**, at the least such as before 4421
3:10 and he judged Israel, and went out to **w**: 4421
5: 8 chose new gods; then *was* **w** in the gates: 3901
11: 4 that the children of Ammon **made w** 3898
11: 5 that when the children of Ammon **made w** 3898
11:27 but thou doest me wrong to **w** against me: 3898
18:11 hundred men appointed *with* weapons of **w**. 4421
18:16 men appointed *with* their weapons of **w**, 4421
18:17 that were appointed *with* weapons of **w**. 4421
Jdg 20:17 that drew sword: all these *were* men of **w**. 4421
21:22 reserved not to each man his wife in the **w**: 4421
1Sa 8:12 to make his instruments of **w**, and 4421
14:52 there was sore **w** against the Philistines all 4421
16:18 a mighty valiant *man,* and a man of **w**, and 4421
17:33 a youth, and he a man of **w** from his youth. 4421
18: 5 Saul set him over the men of **w**, and he was 4421
19: 8 there was **w** again: and David went out, 4421
23: 8 Saul called all the people together to **w**, 4421
28:15 for the Philistines **make w** against me, and 3898
2Sa 1:27 and the weapons of **w** perished! 4421
3: 1 Now there was long **w** between the house 4421
3: 6 while there was **w** between the house of 4421
11: 7 the people did, and how the **w** prospered. 4421
11:18 told David all the things concerning the **w**; 4421
11:19 telling the matters of the **w** unto the king, 4421
17: 8 thy father *is* a man of **w**, and will not lodge 4421
21:15 Moreover the Philistines had yet **w** again 4421
22:35 He teacheth my hands to **w**; so that a bow 4421
1Ki 2: 5 shed the blood of **w** in peace, and put 4421
2: 5 put the blood of **w** upon his girdle that *was* 4421
9:22 they *were* men of **w**, and his servants, and 4421
14:30 there was **w** between Rehoboam and 4421
15: 6 there was **w** between Rehoboam and 4421
15: 7 there was **w** between Abijam and 4421
15:16 there was **w** between Asa and Baasha king 4421
15:32 there was **w** between Asa and Baasha king 4421
20:18 or whether they be come out for **w**, 4421
22: 1 they continued three years without **w** 4421
2Ki 8:28 **w** against Hazael king of Syria in 4421
13:25 out of the hand of Jehoahaz his father by **w**. 4421
14: 7 took Selah by **w**, and called the name of it 4421
16: 5 king of Israel came up *to* Jerusalem to **w**: 4421
18:20 *I have* counsel and strength for the **w**. 4421
24:16 all *that were* strong *and* apt for **w**, 4421
25: 4 all the men of **w** *fled* by night *by* the way of 4421
25:19 an officer that was set over the men of **w**, 4421
1Ch 5:10 in the days of Saul they made **w** with 4421
5:18 skilful in **w**, *were* four and forty thousand 4421
5:18 and threescore, that went out *to* the **w**. 6635
5:19 they made **w** with the Hagarites, with Jetur, 4421
5:22 many slain, because the **w** *was* of God. 4421
7: 4 *were* bands of soldiers for **w**, six and 4421
7:11 two hundred *soldiers, fit to* go out *for* **w** 6635
7:40 genealogy of them *that were apt* to the **w** 6635
12: 1 among the mighty *men,* helpers of the **w**. 4421
12: 8 *and* men of **w** *fit* for the battle, that could 6635
12:23 the bands that were ready armed to the **w**, 6635
12:24 and eight hundred, ready armed to the **w**. 6635
12:25 mighty *men* of valour for the **w**, 6635
12:33 expert in **w**, with all instruments of war, 4421
12:33 expert in war, with all instruments of **w**, 4421
12:35 of the Danites expert in **w** twenty and 4421
12:36 forth to battle, expert in **w**, forty thousand. 4421
12:37 with all *manner of* instruments of **w** for 6635
12:38 All these men of **w**, that could keep rank, 4421
18:10 (for Hadarezer **had w with** 376+1961+4421
20: 4 that there arose **w** at Gezer with 4421
20: 5 there was **w** again with the Philistines; and 4421
20: 6 yet again there was **w** at Gath, where was a 4421
28: 3 because thou *hast been* a man of **w**, and 4421
2Ch 6:34 If thy people go out to **w** against their 4421
8: 9 they *were* men of **w**, and chief of his 4421
13: 2 there was **w** between Abijah and Jeroboam. 4421
13: 3 in array with an army of valiant *men* of **w**, 4421
14: 6 had rest, and he had no **w** in those years; 4421
15:19 there was no *more* **w** unto the five and 4421
17:10 that they **made** no **w** against Jehoshaphat. 3898
17:13 the men of **w**, mighty *men* of valour, 4421
17:18 thousand ready prepared for the **w**. 6635
18: 3 and *we will be* with thee in the **w**. 4421
22: 5 **w** against Hazael king of Syria at 4421
25: 5 thousand choice *men, able to* go forth *to* **w**, 6635
26:11 fighting *men,* that went out to **w** by bands, 6635
26:13 that made **w** with mighty power, 4421
28:12 up against them that came from the **w**, 6635
32: 6 he set captains of **w** over the people, and 4421
33:14 put captains of **w** in all the fenced cities of 2428
35:21 but against the house wherewith I have **w**: 4421
Job 5:20 and in **w** from the power of the sword. 4421
10:17 upon me; changes and **w** *are* against me. 6635
38:23 of trouble, against the day of battle and **w**? 4421
Ps 18:34 He teacheth my hands to **w**, so that a bow 4421
27: 3 though **w** should rise against me, in this 4421
55:21 than butter, but **w** *was* in his heart: 7128
68:30 scatter thou the people *that* delight in **w**. 7128
120: 7 *for* peace: but when I speak, they *are* for **w**. 4421
140: 2 are they gathered together *for* **w**. 4421
144: 1 which teacheth my hands to **w**, *and* 7128
Pr 20:18 by counsel: and with good advice make **w**. 4421
24: 6 For by wise counsel thou shalt make thy **w**: 4421
Ecc 3: 8 to hate; a time of **w**, and a time of peace. 4421
8: 8 *there is* no discharge in *that* **w**; neither shall 4421
9:18 Wisdom *is* better than weapons of **w**: but 7128
SS 3: 8 They all hold swords, *being* expert in **w**: 4421
Isa 2: 4 neither shall they learn **w** any more. 4421
3: 2 The mighty *man,* and the man of **w**, 4421
3:25 fall by the sword, and thy mighty in the **w**. 4421
7: 1 went up *towards* Jerusalem to **w** against it, 4421
21:15 bent bow, and from the grievousness of **w**. 4421
36: 5 *I have* counsel and strength for **w**: 4421
37: 9 He is come forth to **make w** with thee. 3898
41:12 they that **w** against thee shall be as nothing, 4421
42:13 he shall stir up jealousy like a man of **w**: 4421
Jer 4:19 the sound of the trumpet, the alarm of **w**. 4421
6: 4 Prepare ye **w** against her; arise, and let us 4421
6:23 set in array as men for **w** against thee, 4421
21: 2 king of Babylon **maketh w** against us; 3898
21: 4 I *will* turn back the weapons of **w** that *are* 4421
28: 8 of **w**, and of evil, and of pestilence. 4421
38: 4 of the men of **w** that remain in this city, 4421
39: 4 all the men of **w**, then they fled, and 4421
41: 3 that were found there, *and* the men of **w**. 4421
41:16 *even* mighty men of **w**, and the women, and 4421
42:14 the land of Egypt, where we shall see no **w**, 4421

Jer 48:14 We *are* mighty and strong men for the w? 4421
49: 2 that I will cause an alarm of w to be heard 4421
49:26 all the men of w shall be cut off in that day, 4421
50:30 all her men of w shall be cut off in that day, 4421
51:20 Thou *art* my battle axe *and* weapons of w: 4421
51:32 with fire, and the men of w are affrighted. 4421
52: 7 all the men of w fled, and went forth out of 4421
52:25 which had the charge of the men of w; 4421
Eze 17:17 and great company make for him in the w, 4421
26: 9 he shall set engines of w against thy walls, 6904
27:10 of Phut were in thine army, thy men of w: 4421
27:27 all thy men of w, that *are* in thee, and in all 4421
32:27 gone down *to* hell with their weapons of w: 4421
39:20 with mighty *men,* and *with* all men of w, 4421
Da 7:21 the same horn made w with the saints, and 7129
9:26 unto the end of the w desolations *are* 4421
Joel 2: 7 they shall climb the wall like men of w; 4421
3: 9 Prepare w, wake up the mighty *men,* let all 4421
3: 9 mighty *men,* let all the men of w draw near; 4421
Mic 2: 8 that pass by securely *as men* averse from w. 4421
3: 5 they even prepare w against him. 4421
4: 3 neither shall they learn w any more. 4421
Lk 14:31 **make w against** another king, *1519+4171+4820*
23:11 And Herod with his **men of w** set him at *4753*
2Co 10: 3 in the flesh, we do not w after the flesh: *4754*
1Ti 1:18 that thou by them mightest w a good *4754*
Jas 4: 1 *even* of your lusts that w in your members? *4754*
4: 2 ye fight and w, yet ye have not, because ye *4170*
1Pe 2:11 fleshly lusts, which w against the soul; *4754*
Rev 11: 7 bottomless *pit* shall make w against them, *4171*
12: 7 And there was w in heaven: Michael and *4171*
12:17 went to make w with the remnant of her *4171*
13: 4 who is able to **make** w with him? *4170*
13: 7 And it was given unto him to make w with *4171*
17:14 These shall **make** w with the Lamb, and *4170*
19:11 righteousness he doth judge and **make** w. *4170*
19:19 gathered together to make w against him *4171*

WARD (22) [WARDS]

Ge 40: 3 he put them in w *in* the house of the captain 4929
40: 4 and they continued a season in w. 4929
40: 7 *were* with him in the w of his lord's house, 4929
41:10 put me in w *in* the captain of the guard's 4929
42:17 he put them all together into w three days. 4929
Lev 24:12 they put him in w, that the mind of 4929
Nu 15:34 they put him in w, because it was not 4929
2Sa 20: 3 put them *in* w, and fed them, but 1004+4931
1Ch 12:29 them had kept the w of the house of Saul. 4931
25: 8 w against *ward,* as well the small as 4931
25: 8 ward against w, as well the small as NIH
26:16 causeway of the going up, w against ward. 4929
26:16 causeway of the going up, ward against w. 4929
Ne 12:24 the man of God, w over against ward, 4929
12:24 the man of God, ward over against w, 4929
12:25 *were* porters keeping the w at 4929
12:45 and the porters kept the w of their God, 4931
12:45 of their God, and the w of the purification, 4931
Isa 21: 8 and I *am* set in my w whole nights: 4931
Jer 37:13 a captain of the w *was* there, whose name 6488
Eze 19: 9 they put him in w in chains, and 5474
Ac 12:10 they were past the first and the second w, *5438*

WARDROBE (2)

2Ki 22:14 the son of Harhas, keeper of the w; 899
2Ch 34:22 the son of Hasrah, keeper of the w; 899

WARDS (3) [WARD]

1Ch 9:23 *namely,* the house of the tabernacle, by w. 4931
26:12 chief men, *having* w one against another, 4931
Ne 13:30 appointed the w of the priests and 4931

WARE (8) [AWARE, WARES, WEAR]

Ne 10:31 *if* the people of the land bring w or 4728
13:16 all *manner of* w, and sold on the sabbath 4377
13:20 sellers of all *kind of* w lodged without 4465
Mt 24:50 for *him,* and in an hour that he is not w of, *1097*
Lk 8:27 and w no clothes, neither abode in *any* *1737*
12:46 for *him,* and at an hour when he is not w, *1097*
Ac 14: 6 They were w of *it,* and fled unto Lystra and *4894*
2Ti 4:15 Of whom **be** thou w also; for he hath *5442*

WARES (5) [WARE]

Jer 10:17 Gather up thy w out of the land, 3666
Eze 27:16 of the multitude of the **w of** thy **making**: 4639
27:18 in the multitude of the **w of** thy **making**, 4639
27:33 When thy w went forth out of the seas, 5801
Jnh 1: 5 cast forth the w that *were* in the ship into 3627

WARFARE (5) [WAR]

1Sa 28: 1 gathered their armies together for w, 6635
Isa 40: 2 cry unto her, that her w is accomplished, 6635
1Co 9: 7 Who **goeth a** w any time at his own *4754*
2Co 10: 4 (For the weapons of our w *are* not carnal, *4752*
1Ti 1:18 that thou by them mightest war a good w; *4752*

WARM (8) [LUKEWARM]

2Ki 4:34 and the flesh of the child **waxed** w. 2552
Job 6:17 What time they **wax** w, they vanish: 2215
37:17 How thy garments *are* w, when he quieteth 2525
Ecc 4:11 have heat: but how can one be w *alone?* 3179
Isa 44:15 for he will take thereof, and w himself; yea, 2552
44:16 and saith, Aha, I am w, I have seen the fire: 2552
47:14 *there shall* not *be* a coal to w at, *nor* fire to 2552
Hag 1: 6 *ye* clothe you, but there is none w; and he 2527

WARMED (6) [WARMETH, WARMING]

Job 31:20 *if* he were *not* w with the fleece of my 2552
Mk 14:54 with the servants, and w himself at the fire. *2328*
Jn 18:18 and they w themselves: and Peter stood *2328*
18:18 and Peter stood with them, and w himself. *2328*
18:25 And Simon Peter stood and w himself. *2328*
Jas 2:16 Depart in peace, be you w and filled; *2328*

WARMETH (2) [WARMED]

Job 39:14 her eggs in the earth, and w them in dust, 2552
Isa 44:16 yea, he w himself, and saith, Aha, I am 2552

WARMING (1) [WARMED]

Mk 14:67 And when she saw Peter w himself, *2328*

WARN (11) [FOREWARN, FOREWARNED, WARNED, WARNING]

2Ch 19:10 ye shall even w them that they trespass not 2094
Eze 3:18 nor speakest to w the wicked from his 2094
3:19 Yet if thou w the wicked, and he turn not 2094
3:21 Nevertheless if thou w the righteous *man,* 2094
33: 3 he blow the trumpet, and w the people; 2094
33: 7 word at my mouth, and w them from me. 2094
33: 8 if thou dost not speak to w the wicked from 2094
33: 9 if thou w the wicked of his way to turn 2094
Ac 20:31 years I ceased not to w every one night *3560*
1Co 4:14 but as my beloved sons I w *you.* *3560*
1Th 5:14 brethren, w *them that are* unruly, *3560*

WARNED (10) [WARN]

2Ki 6:10 the man of God told him and w him of, 2094
Ps 19:11 Moreover by them *is* thy servant w: *and* 2094
Eze 3:21 he shall surely live, because he is w; 2094
33: 6 not the trumpet, and the people be not w; 2094
Mt 2:12 And being **w of God** in a dream that *they* *5537*
2:22 being **w of God** in a dream, *5537*
3: 7 who hath w you to flee from the wrath to *5263*
Lk 3: 7 who hath w you to flee from the wrath to *5263*
Ac 10:22 was **w from God** by a holy angel to send *5537*
Heb 11: 7 being **w of God** of *things* not seen as yet, *5537*

WARNING (8) [WARN]

Jer 6:10 I speak, and **give** w, that they may hear? 5749
Eze 3:17 at my mouth, and **give** them w from me. 2094
3:18 and thou **givest** him not w, 2094
3:20 because thou hast not **given** him w, he shall 2094
33: 4 the sound of the trumpet, and **taketh** not w; 2094
33: 5 the sound of the trumpet, and **took** not w; 2094
33: 5 But he that **taketh** w shall deliver his soul. 2094
Col 1:28 w every man, and teaching every man in all *3560*

WARP (9)

Lev 13:48 Whether *it be* in the w, or woof; of linen, or 8359
13:49 either in the w, or in the woof, or in any 8359
13:51 either in the w, or in the woof, or in a skin, 8359
13:52 whether w or woof, in woollen or in linen, 8359
13:53 either in the w, or in the woof, or in any 8359
13:56 the skin, or out of the w, or out of the woof: 8359
13:57 either in the w, or in the woof, or in any 8359
13:58 either w, or woof, or whatsoever thing of 8359
13:59 either *in* the w, or woof, or any thing of 8359

WARRED (9) [WAR]

Nu 31: 7 they w against the Midianites, as 6633
31:42 which Moses divided from the men that w, 6633
Jos 24: 9 arose and w against Israel, and sent and 3898
1Ki 14:19 how he w, and how he reigned, 3898
20: 1 and besieged Samaria, and w against it. 3898
22:45 his might that he shewed, and how he w, 3898
2Ki 6: 8 the king of Syria w against Israel, and 3898
14:28 how he w, and how he recovered 3898
2Ch 26: 6 he went forth and w against the Philistines, 3898

WARRETH (1) [WAR]

2Ti 2: 4 No *man* that w entangleth himself with *4754*

WARRING (3) [WAR]

2Ki 19: 8 found the king of Assyria w against 3898
Isa 37: 8 found the king of Assyria w against 3898
Ro 7:23 **w against** the law of my mind, and *497*

WARRIOR (1) [WAR]

Isa 9: 5 For every battle of the w *is* with confused 5431

WARRIORS (2) [WAR]

1Ki 12:21 thousand chosen *men,* which were w, 4421+6213
2Ch 11: 1 thousand chosen *men,* which were w, 4421+6213

WARS (15) [WAR]

Nu 21:14 Wherefore it is said in the book of the w of 4421
Jdg 3: 1 as had not known all the w of Canaan; 4421
2Sa 8:10 for Hadadezer **had** w **with** Toi. 376+1961+4421
1Ki 5: 3 the w which were about him on every side, 4421
1Ch 22: 8 blood abundantly, and hast made great w: 4421
2Ch 12:15 *there were* w between Rehoboam and 4421
16: 9 from henceforth thou shalt have w. 4421
27: 7 acts of Jotham, and all his w, and his ways, 4421
Ps 46: 9 He maketh w to cease unto the end of 4421
Mt 24: 6 And ye shall hear of w and rumours of *4171*
24: 6 ye shall hear of w and rumours of w: *4171*
Mk 13: 7 And when ye shall hear of w and *4171*
13: 7 ye shall hear of wars and rumours of w, *4171*
Lk 21: 9 But when ye shall hear of w and *4171*
Jas 4: 1 From whence *come* w and fightings among *4171*

WART See WEN

WAS (4531) [BE] See Index of Articles, Etc.

WASH (89) [UNWASHEN, WASHED, WASHEST, WASHING, WASHINGS, WASHPOT]

Ge 18: 4 w your feet, and rest yourselves under 7364
19: 2 w your feet, and ye shall rise up early, and 7364
24:32 water to w his feet, and the men's feet that 7364
Ex 2: 5 the daughter of Pharaoh came down to w 7364
19:10 to morrow, and let them w their clothes, 3526
29: 4 and shalt w them with water. 7364
29:17 w the inwards of him, and his legs, and 7364
30:18 to w *withal:* and thou shalt put it between 7364
30:19 and his sons shall w their hands and 7364
30:20 they shall w *with* water, that they die not; 7364
Ex 30:21 So they shall w their hands and their feet, 7364
40:12 the congregation, and w them with water. 7364
40:30 the altar, and put water there, to w *withal.* 7364
Lev 1: 9 and his legs shall he w in water: 7364
1:13 he shall w the inwards and the legs with 7364
6:27 thou shalt w that whereon it was sprinkled 3526
9:14 he did w the inwards and the legs, and 7364
11:25 of the carcase of them shall w his clothes, 3526
11:28 he that beareth the carcase of them shall w 3526
11:40 he that eateth of the carcase of it shall w his 3526
11:40 he also that beareth the carcase of it shall w 3526
13: 6 and he shall w his clothes, and be clean. 3526
13:34 and he shall w his clothes, and be clean. 3526
13:54 the priest shall command that they w 3526
13:58 thing of skin *it be,* which thou shalt w, 3526
14: 8 he that is to be cleansed shall w his clothes, 3526
14: 8 off all his hair, and w *himself* in water, 7364
14: 9 he shall w his clothes, also he shall wash 3526
14: 9 also he shall w his flesh in water, and 7364
14:47 he that lieth in the house shall w his 3526
14:47 he that eateth in the house shall w his 3526
15: 5 whosoever toucheth his bed shall w his 3526
15: 6 sat that hath the issue shall w his clothes, 3526
15: 7 him that hath the issue shall w his clothes, 3526
15: 8 he shall w his clothes, and bathe *himself* in 3526
15:10 he that beareth *any of* those *things* shall w 3526
15:11 he shall w his clothes, and bathe *himself* in 3526
15:13 w his clothes, and bathe his flesh in running 3526
15:16 he shall w all his flesh in water, and 7364
15:21 whosoever toucheth her bed shall w his 3526
15:22 thing that she sat upon shall w his clothes, 3526
15:27 shall w his clothes, and bathe *himself* in 3526
16: 4 therefore shall he w his flesh in water, and 7364
16:24 he shall w his flesh with water in the holy 7364
16:26 goat for the scapegoat shall w his clothes, 3526
16:28 he that burneth them shall w his clothes, 3526
17:15 he shall both w his clothes, and 3526
17:16 if he w *them* not, nor bathe his flesh; then 3526
22: 6 shall not eat of the holy *things,* unless he w 7364
Nu 8: 7 let them w their clothes, and *so* 3526
19: 7 the priest shall w his clothes, and he shall 3526
19: 8 he that burneth her shall w his clothes in 3526
19:10 the ashes of the heifer shall w his clothes, 3526
19:19 he shall purify him*self,* and w his clothes, 3526
19:21 the water of separation shall w his clothes; 3526
31:24 ye shall w your clothes on the seventh day, 3526
Dt 21: 6 *that are* next unto the slain *man,* shall w 7364
23:11 cometh on, he shall w *himself* with water: 7364
Ru 3: 3 W *thyself* therefore, and anoint thee, and 7364
1Sa 25:41 *let* thine handmaid *be* a servant to w 7364
2Sa 11: 8 Go down to thy house, and w thy feet. 7364
2Ki 5:10 Go and w in Jordan seven times, and 7364
5:12 may I not w in them, and be clean? So he 7364
5:13 when he saith to thee, W, and be clean? 7364
2Ch 4: 6 and five on the left, to w in them: 7364
4: 6 but the sea *was* for the priests to w in. 7364
Job 9:30 If I w myself with snow water, and 7364
Ps 26: 6 I will w mine hands in innocency: so will I 7364
51: 2 W me throughly from mine iniquity, and 3526
51: 7 w me, and I shall be whiter than snow. 3526
58:10 he shall w his feet in the blood of 7364
Isa 1:16 W ye, make you clean; put away the evil of 7364
Jer 2:22 For though thou w thee with nitre, and 3526
4:14 w thine heart from wickedness, 3526
Eze 23:40 for whom thou didst w *thyself,* paintedst 7364
Mt 6:17 anoint thine head, and w thy face; *3538*
15: 2 for they w not their hands when they eat *3538*
Mk 7: 3 except they w *their* hands oft, eat not, *3538*
7: 4 from the market, except they w, they eat not. *907*
Lk 7:38 and began to w his feet with tears, and *1026*
Jn 9: 7 said unto him, Go, w in the pool of Siloam, *3538*
9:11 unto me, Go to the pool of Siloam, and w: *3538*
13: 5 and began to w the disciples' feet, and *3538*
13: 6 saith unto him, Lord, dost thou w my feet? *3538*
13: 8 saith unto him, Thou shalt never w my feet. *3538*
13: 8 Jesus answered him, If I w thee not, *3538*
13:10 He that is washed needeth not save to w *his* *3538*
13:14 ye also ought to w one another's feet. *3538*
Ac 22:16 arise, and be baptized, and **w away** thy sins, *628*

WASHBASIN See WASHPOT

WASHED (45) [WASH]

Ge 43:24 and gave *them* water, and they w their feet; 7364
43:31 he w his face, and went out, and 7364
49:11 he w his garments in wine, and his clothes 3526
Ex 19:14 the people; and they w their clothes. 3526
40:31 and Aaron and his sons w their hands and 7364
40:32 when they came near unto the altar, they w; 7364
Lev 8: 6 and his sons, and w them with water. 7364
8:21 And he w the inwards and the legs in water; 7364
13:55 shall look on the plague, after *that* it is w: 3526
13:58 it shall be w the second time, and shall be 3526
15:17 shall be w with water, and be unclean until 3526
Nu 8:21 were purified, and they w their clothes; 3526
Jdg 19:21 and they w their feet, and did eat and drink. 7364
2Sa 12:20 w, and anointed *himself,* and changed his 7364
19:24 nor trimmed his beard, nor w his clothes, 3526
1Ki 22:38 *one* w the chariot in the pool of Samaria; 7857
22:38 licked up his blood; and they w his armour; 7364
2Ch 4: 6 for the burnt offering they w in them; 1740
Job 29: 6 When *I* w my steps with butter, and 7364
Ps 73:13 *in* vain, and w my hands in innocency. 7364
Pr 30:12 and *yet* is not w from their filthiness. 7364
SS 5: 3 I have w my feet; how shall I defile them? 7364
5:12 rivers of waters, w with milk, *and* fitly set. 7364
Isa 4: 4 When the Lord shall have **w away** the filth 7364
Eze 16: 4 neither wast thou w in water to supple *thee;* 7364
16: 9 w I thee with water; yea, I throughly 7364
16: 9 I **throughly w away** thy blood from thee, 7857
40:38 the gates, where they w the burnt offering. 1740
Mt 27:24 and w *his* hands before the multitude, *633*
Lk 7:44 but she hath w my feet with tears, and *1026*
11:38 that he had not first w before dinner. *907*
Jn 9: 7 his way therefore, and w, and came seeing. *3538*

Jn 9:11 and I went and **w**, and I received sight. *3538*
9:15 He put clay upon mine eyes, and I **w**, *3538*
13:10 He that is **w** needeth not save to wash *his* *3068*
13:12 So after he had **w** their feet, and had taken *3538*
13:14 *your* Lord and Master, have **w** your feet; *3538*
Ac 9:37 whom when they had **w**, they laid *her* in an *3068*
16:33 same hour of the night, and **w** *their* stripes; *3068*
1Co 6:11 but ye are **w**, but ye are sanctified, but ye are *628*
1Ti 5:10 if she have **w** the saints' feet, *3538*
Heb 10:22 and *our* bodies **w** with pure water. *3068*
2Pe 2:22 The sow that was **w** to *her* wallowing in *3068*
Rev 1: 5 and **w** us from our sins in his own blood, *3068*
7:14 and have **w** their robes, and made them *4150*

WASHERMAN'S See FULLER'S

WASHEST (1) [WASH]
Job 14:19 thou **w away** the things which grow out of 7857

WASHING (10) [WASH]
Lev 13:56 the plague *be* somewhat dark after the **w** of 3526
2Sa 11: 2 from the roof he saw a woman **w** *herself;* 7364
Ne 4:23 *saving that* every one put them off *for* **w**. 4325
SS 4: 2 *are* even shorn, which came up from the **w**; 7367
6: 6 as a flock of sheep which go up from the **w**, 7367
Mk 7: 4 *as* the **w** of cups, and pots, brasen vessels, *909*
7: 8 tradition of men, *as* the **w** of pots and cups: *909*
Lk 5: 2 gone out of them, and were **w** *their* nets. *637*
Eph 5:26 cleanse *it* with the **w** of water by the word, *3067*
Tit 3: 5 by the **w** of regeneration, and renewing of *3067*

WASHINGS (1) [WASH]
Heb 9:10 drinks, and divers **w**, and carnal ordinances, *909*

WASHPOT (2) [POT, WASH]
Ps 60: 8 Moab *is* my **w**; over Edom will I cast 5518+7366
108: 9 Moab *is* my **w**; over Edom will I cast 5518+7366

WAST (66) [BE]
Ge 3:11 he said, Who told thee that thou *w* naked? NIH
3:19 unto the ground; for out of it **w** thou taken: NIH
33:10 face of God, and thou **w** pleased with me. NIH
40:13 after the former manner when thou **w** his 1961
Dt 5:15 remember that thou **w** a servant in the land 1961
15:15 thou shalt remember that thou **w** a 1961
16:12 thou shalt remember that thou **w** a 1961
23: 7 because thou **w** a stranger in his land. 1961
24:18 thou shalt remember that thou **w** a 1961
24:22 thou shalt remember that thou **w** a 1961
25:18 behind thee, when thou *w* faint and weary; NIH
28:60 diseases of Egypt, which thou **w** afraid of; NIH
Ru 3: 2 our kindred, with whose maidens thou **w**? 1961
1Sa 15:17 When thou *w* little in thine own sight, NIH
15:17 *w* thou not *made* the head of the tribes of NIH
2Sa 1:14 How **w** thou not afraid to stretch forth thine NIH
1:25 *thou w* slain in thine high places. NIH
5: 2 thou **w** he that leddest out and broughtest in 1961
1Ch 11: 2 thou *w* he that leddest out and broughtest in NIH
Job 15: 7 was born? or **w** thou made before the hills? NIH
38: 4 Where **w** thou when I laid the foundations 1961
38:21 Knowest thou *it,* because thou **w** then born? NIH
Ps 99: 8 thou **w** a God that forgavest them, 1961
114: 5 thou Jordan, *that* thou **w** driven back? NIH
Isa 12: 1 though thou **w** angry with me, thine anger is NIH
14: 3 from the hard bondage wherein thou **w** NIH
33: 1 to thee that spoilest, and thou *w* not spoiled; NIH
43: 4 Since thou **w** precious in my sight, thou hast NIH
48: 8 and **w** called a transgressor from the womb. NIH
54: 6 when thou **w** refused, saith thy God. NIH
57:10 of thine hand; therefore thou **w** not grieved. NIH
Jer 2:36 of Egypt, as thou **w** ashamed of Assyria. NIH
50:24 O Babylon, and thou **w** not aware: NIH
Eze 16: 4 in the day thou **w** born thy navel was not NIH
16: 4 neither **w** thou washed in water to supple NIH
16: 4 to supple *thee;* thou **w** not salted at all, NIH
16: 5 thou **w** cast out in the open field, to NIH
16: 5 of thy person, in the day that thou **w** born. NIH
16: 6 I said unto thee *when thou w* in thy blood, NIH
16: 6 I said unto thee *when thou w* in thy blood, NIH
16: 7 is grown, whereas thou *w* naked and bare. NIH
16:13 Thus **w** thou decked *with* gold and silver; NIH
16:13 thou **w** exceeding beautiful, and thou didst NIH
16:22 when thou **w** naked and bare, *and* 1961
16:22 and bare, *and* **w** polluted in thy blood. 1961
16:28 the Assyrians, because thou **w** unsatiable; NIH
16:29 and yet thou **w** not satisfied herewith. NIH
16:47 as *if that were* a very little *thing,* thou **w** NIH
21:30 I will judge thee in the place where thou **w** NIH
24:13 I have purged thee, and thou **w** not purged, NIH
26:17 *that* *w* inhabited of seafaring men, NIH
26:17 which **w** strong in the sea, she and 1961
27:25 thou **w** replenished, and made very glorious NIH
28:13 in thee in the day that thou **w** created. NIH
28:14 *so:* thou **w** upon the holy mountain of God; 1961
28:15 Thou *w* perfect in thy ways from the day NIH
28:15 thy ways from the day that thou **w** created, NIH
Ob 1:11 even thou *w* as one of them. NIH
Mt 26:69 saying, Thou also **w** with Jesus of Galilee. *1510*
Mk 14:67 *And* thou also **w** with Jesus of Nazareth. *1510*
Jn 1:48 when thou **w** under the fig tree, I saw thee. *1510*
9:34 Thou **w** altogether born in sins, and NIG
21:18 verily, I say unto thee, When thou **w** young, *1510*
Rev 5: 9 for thou **w** slain, and hast redeemed us to NIG
11:17 which art, and **w**, and art to come; *1510*
16: 5 O Lord, which art, and **w**, and shalt be, *1510*

WASTE (64) [WASTED, WASTENESS, WASTER, WASTES, WASTETH, WASTING]
Lev 26:31 I will make your cities **w**, and bring your 2723
26:33 land shall be desolate, and your cities **w**. 2723
Nu 21:30 we have **laid** *them* **w** even unto Nophah, 8074
Dt 32:10 and in the **w** howling wilderness; 8414
1Ki 17:14 The barrel of meal shall not **w**, neither shall 3615
2Ki 19:25 that thou shouldest be to **lay w** fenced cities 7582
1Ch 17: 9 neither shall the children of wickedness **w** 1086
Ne 2: 3 *lieth* **w**, and the gates thereof are consumed 2720
2:17 how Jerusalem *lieth* **w**, and the gates 2720
Job 30: 3 wilderness in former time desolate and **w**. 4875
38:27 To satisfy the desolate and **w** *ground;* and 4875
Ps 79: 7 and **laid w** his dwelling place. 8074
80:13 The boar out of the wood doth **w** it, and 3765
Isa 5: 6 I will lay it **w**: it shall not be pruned, nor 1326
5:17 the **w places** of the fat ones shall strangers 2723
15: 1 Because in the night Ar of Moab is **laid w**, 7703
15: 1 because in the night Kir of Moab is **laid w**, 7703
23: 1 for it is **laid w**, so that *there is* no house, 7703
23:14 of Tarshish: for your strength is **laid w**. 7703
24: 1 **maketh** it **w**, and turneth it upside down, 1110
33: 8 The highways **lie w**, the wayfaring man 8074
34:10 from generation to generation it shall **lie w**; 2717
37:18 the kings of Assyria have **laid w** all 2717
37:26 that thou shouldest be to **lay w** defenced 7582
42:15 I will **make w** mountains and hills, and 2717
49:17 they that **made** thee **w** shall go forth of 2717
49:19 For thy **w** and thy desolate places, and 2723
51: 3 he will comfort all her **w places;** and 2723
52: 9 sing together, ye **w places** of Jerusalem: 2723
58:12 *be* of thee shall build the old **w places:** 2723
61: 4 they shall repair the **w** cities, 2721
64:11 and all our pleasant things are **laid w**. 2723
Jer 2:15 *and* yelled, and they made his land **w**: 8047
4: 7 *and* thy cities shall be **laid w**, without an 5327
27:17 live: wherefore should this city be **laid w**? 2723
46:19 for Noph shall be **w** and desolate without 8047
49:13 a desolation, a reproach, a **w**, and a curse; 2721
50:21 **w** and utterly destroy after them, saith 2717
Eze 5:14 Moreover I will make thee **w**, and 2723
6: 6 dwelling places the cities shall be **laid w**, 2717
6: 6 that your altars may be **laid w** and 2717
12:20 the cities that are inhabited shall be **laid w**, 2717
19: 7 desolate palaces, and he **laid w** their cities; 2717
26: 2 I shall be replenished, *now* she is **laid w**: 2717
29: 9 the land of Egypt shall be desolate and **w**; 2723
29:10 make the land of Egypt **utterly w** 2721+2723
29:12 her cities among the cities *that are* **laid w** 2717
30:12 I will **make** the land **w**, and all that is 8074
35: 4 I will lay thy cities **w**, and thou shalt be 2723
36:35 the **w** and desolate and ruined cities *are* 2720
36:38 shall the **w** cities be filled *with* flocks of 2720
38: 8 of Israel, which have been always **w**: 2723
Joel 1: 7 He hath laid my vine **w**, and barked my fig 8047
Am 7: 9 the sanctuaries of Israel shall be **laid w**; 2717
9:14 they shall build the **w** cities, and 8074
Mic 5: 6 they shall **w** the land of Assyria with 7462
Na 2:10 She *is* empty, and void, and **w**: and 1110
3: 7 flee from thee, and say, Nineveh is **laid w**: 7703
Zep 3: 6 I **made** their streets **w**, that none passeth 2717
Hag 1: 4 in your cieled houses, and this house *lie* **w**? 2720
1: 9 Because of mine house that *is* **w**, and 2720
Mal 1: 3 his heritage **w** for the dragons of 8077
Mt 26: 8 saying, To what purpose *is* this **w**? *684*
Mk 14: 4 said, Why was this **w** of the ointment made? *684*

WASTED (16) [WASTE]
Nu 14:33 until your carcases be **w** in the wilderness. 8552
24:22 Nevertheless the Kenite shall be **w**, 1197
Dt 2:14 of war were **w** out from among the host, 8552
1Ki 17:16 *And* the barrel of meal **w** not, neither did 3615
1Ch 20: 1 **w** the country of the children of Ammon, 7843
Ps 137: 3 they that **w** us *required of us* mirth, 8437
Isa 6:11 Until the cities be **w** without inhabitant, and 7582
19: 5 and the river shall be **w** and dried up. 2717
60:12 yea, *those* nations shall be **utterly w**. 2717+2717
Jer 44: 6 and they are **w** *and* desolate, as *at* this day. 2723
Eze 30: 7 shall be in the midst of the cities *that are* **w**. 2717
Joel 1:10 The field is **w**, the land mourneth; for 7703
1:10 for the corn is **w**, the new wine is dried up, 7703
Lk 15:13 there **w** his substance with riotous living. *1287*
16: 1 accused unto him that he had **w** his goods. *1287*
Gal 1:13 I persecuted the church of God, and **w** it: *4199*

WASTENESS (1) [WASTE]
Zep 1:15 and distress, a day of **w** and desolation, 7722

WASTER (2) [WASTE]
Pr 18: 9 his work *is* brother to him that is a great **w**. 7843
Isa 54:16 and I have created the **w** to destroy. 7843

WASTES (7) [WASTE]
Isa 61: 4 they shall build the old **w**, they shall raise 2723
Jer 49:13 all the cities thereof shall be perpetual **w**. 2723
Eze 33:24 they that inhabit those **w** of the land of 2723
33:27 surely *they* that *are* in the **w** shall fall by 2723
36: 4 to the desolate **w**, and to the cities that are 2723
36:10 be inhabited, and the **w** shall be builded: 2723
36:33 in the cities, and the **w** shall be builded. 2723

WASTETH (3) [WASTE]
Job 14:10 man dieth, and **w away**: yea, man giveth up 2522
Ps 91: 6 *nor* for the destruction *that* **w** at noonday. 7736
Pr 19:26 He that **w** *his* father, *and* chaseth away *his* 7703

WASTING (2) [WASTE]
Isa 59: 7 **w** and destruction are in their paths. 7701
60:18 **w** nor destruction within thy borders; 7701

WATCH (61) [WATCHED, WATCHER, WATCHERS, WATCHES, WATCHETH, WATCHFUL, WATCHING, WATCHINGS, WATCHMAN, WATCHMAN'S, WATCHMEN, WATCHT, WATCHTOWER]
Ge 31:49 The LORD **w** between me and thee, 6822
Ex 14:24 that in the morning **w** the LORD looked 821
Jdg 7:19 the camp *in* the beginning of the middle **w**; 821
7:19 *and* they had but newly set the **w**: 8104
1Sa 11:11 into the midst of the host in the morning **w**, 821
19:11 to **w** him, and to slay him in the morning: 8104
2Sa 13:34 the young man that **kept** the **w** lift up his 6822
2Ki 11: 5 be keepers of the **w** of the king's house; 4931
11: 6 so shall ye keep the **w** of the house, that it 4931
11: 7 even they shall keep the **w** of the house of 4931
2Ch 20:24 when Judah came toward the **w tower** in 4707
23: 6 all the people shall keep the **w** of 4931
Ezr 8:29 **W** ye, and keep *them,* until ye weigh *them* 8245
Ne 4: 9 set a **w** against them day and night, because 4929
7: 3 every one in his **w**, and every one *to be* 4929
Job 7:12 or a whale, that thou settest a **w** over me? 4929
14:16 my steps: dost thou not **w** over my sin? 8104
Ps 90: 4 when it is past, and *as* a **w** in the night. 821
102: 7 I **w**, and am as a sparrow alone upon 8245
130: 6 more than they that **w** for the morning: 8104
130: 6 *I say, more than* they that **w** for 8104
141: 3 Set a **w**, O LORD, before my mouth; 8108
Isa 21: 5 the table, **w** *in* the watchtower, eat, drink: 6822
29:20 and all that **w** for iniquity are cut off: 8245
Jer 5: 6 a leopard shall **w** over their cities: 8245
31:28 so will I **w** over them, to build, and to plant, 8245
44:27 I *will* **w** over them for evil, and not for 8245
51:12 make the **w** strong, set up the watchmen, 4929
Na 2: 1 keep the munition, **w** the way, make *thy* 6822
Hab 2: 1 I will stand upon my **w**, and set me upon 4931
2: 1 will **w** to see what he will say unto me, and 6822
Mt 14:25 And in the fourth **w** of the night Jesus went *5438*
24:42 **W** therefore: for ye know not what hour *1127*
24:43 had known in what **w** the thief would come, *5438*
25:13 **W** therefore, for ye know neither the day *1127*
26:38 unto death: tarry ye here, and **w** with me. *1127*
26:40 What, could ye not **w** with me one hour? *1127*
26:41 **W** and pray, that ye enter not into *1127*
27:65 Pilate said unto them, Ye have a **w**: go your *2892*
27:66 sealing the stone, and setting a **w**. *2892*
28:11 some of the **w** came into the city, and *2892*
Mk 6:48 about the fourth **w** of the night he cometh *5438*
13:33 Take ye heed, **w** and pray: for ye know not *69*
13:34 his work, and commanded the porter to **w**. *1127*
13:35 **W** ye therefore: for ye know not when *1127*
13:37 And what I say unto you I say unto all, **W**. *1127*
14:34 sorrowful unto death: tarry ye here, and **w**. *1127*
14:37 couldest not thou **w** one hour? *1127*
14:38 **W** ye and pray, lest ye enter into *1127*
Lk 2: 8 **keeping w** over their flock by night. *5438+5442*
12:38 And if he shall come in the second **w**, or *5438*
12:38 or come in the third **w**, and find *them* so, *5438*
21:36 **W** ye therefore, and pray always, that ye may *69*
Ac 20:31 Therefore **w**, and remember, that *by* *1127*
1Co 16:13 **W** ye, stand fast in the faith, quit you like *1127*
Col 4: 2 and **w** in the same with thanksgiving; *1127*
1Th 5: 6 as *do* others; but let us **w** and be sober. *1127*
2Ti 4: 5 But **w** thou in all *things,* endure afflictions, *3525*
Heb 13:17 for they **w** for your souls, as they that must *69*
1Pe 4: 7 be ye therefore sober, and **w** unto prayer. *3525*
Rev 3: 3 If therefore thou shalt not **w**, I will come on *1127*

WATCHED (12) [WATCH]
Jer 20:10 All my familiars **w** for my halting, 8104
31:28 *that* like as I have **w** over them, to pluck up, 8245
La 4:17 in our watching we have **w** for a nation 6822
Da 9:14 Therefore hath the LORD **w** upon the evil, 8245
Mt 24:43 he would have **w**, and would not have *1127*
27:36 And sitting down they **w** him there; *5083*
Mk 3: 2 And they **w** him, whether he would heal *3906*
Lk 6: 7 And the scribes and Pharisees **w** him, *3906*
12:39 he would have **w**, and not have suffered his *1127*
14: 1 bread on the sabbath day, that they **w** him. *3906*
20:20 And they **w** *him,* and sent forth spies, *3906*
Ac 9:24 And they **w** the gates day and night to kill *3906*

WATCHER (2) [WATCH]
Da 4:13 a **w** and a holy one came down from 5894
4:23 whereas the king saw a **w** and a holy one 5894

WATCHERS (2) [WATCH]
Jer 4:16 *that* **w** come from a far country, and 5341
Da 4:17 *This* matter *is* by the decree of the **w**, and 5894

WATCHES (5) [WATCH]
Ne 7: 3 appoint **w** of the inhabitants of Jerusalem, 4931
12: 9 *were* over against them in the **w**. 4931
Ps 63: 6 my bed, *and* meditate on thee in the *night* **w**. 821
119:148 Mine eyes prevent the *night* **w**, that *I* might 821
La 2:19 in the beginning of the **w**, pour out thine 821

WATCHETH (3) [WATCH]
Ps 37:32 The wicked **w** the righteous, and seeketh to 6822
Eze 7: 6 is come: it **w** for thee; behold, it is come. 6974
Rev 16:15 Blessed *is* he that **w**, and keepeth his *1127*

WATCHFUL (1) [WATCH]
Rev 3: 2 Be **w**, and strengthen the *things* which *1127*

WATCHING (6) [WATCH]
1Sa 4:13 Eli sat upon a seat *by* the wayside **w**: 6822
Pr 8:34 **w** daily at my gates, waiting at the posts of 8245
La 4:17 in our **w** we have watched for a nation *that* 6836
Mt 27:54 **w** Jesus, saw the earthquake, and *5083*
Lk 12:37 the lord when he cometh shall find **w**: *1127*
Eph 6:18 and **w** thereunto with all perseverance and *69*

WATCHINGS (2) [WATCH]
2Co 6: 5 in tumults, in labours, in **w**, in fastings; *70*
11:27 painfulness, in **w** often, in hunger and thirst, *70*

WATCHMAN (18) [WATCH]
2Sa 18:24 the **w** went *up* to the roof over the gate unto 6822
18:25 the **w** cried, and told the king. And the king 6822
18:26 the **w** saw another man running: and 6822
18:26 the **w** called unto the porter, and said, 6822
18:27 the **w** said, Me thinketh the running of 6822
2Ki 9:17 there stood a **w** on the tower in Jezreel, 6822
9:18 the **w** told, saying, The messenger came to 6822
9:20 the **w** told, saying, He came even unto 6822

Ps 127: 1 keep the city, the **w** waketh *but* in vain. 8104
Isa 21: 6 Go, set a **w**, let him declare what he seeth. 6822
21:11 to me out of Seir, **W**, what of the night? 8104
21:11 what of the night? **W**, what of the night? 8104
21:12 The **w** said, The morning cometh, and 8104
Eze 3:17 I have made thee a **w** unto the house of 6822
33: 2 man of their coasts, and set him for their **w**: 6822
33: 6 if the **w** see the sword come, and blow not 6822
33: 7 I have set thee a **w** unto the house of Israel; 6822
Hos 9: 8 The **w** of Ephraim *was* with my God: *but* 6822

WATCHMAN'S (1) [WATCH]

Eze 33: 6 but his blood will I require at the **w** hand. 6822

WATCHMEN (12) [WATCH]

1Sa 14:16 the **w** of Saul in Gibeah of Benjamin 6822
2Ki 17: 9 from the tower of the **w** to the fenced city. 5341
18: 8 from the tower of the **w** to the fenced city. 5341
SS 3: 3 The **w** that go about the city found me: 8104
5: 7 The **w** that went about the city found me, 8104
Isa 52: 8 Thy **w** shall lift up the voice; *with* the voice 6822
56:10 His **w** *are* blind: they are all ignorant, they 6822
62: 6 I have set **w** upon thy walls, O Jerusalem, 8104
Jer 6:17 Also I set **w** over you, *saying,* Hearken to 6822
31: 6 *that* the **w** upon the mount Ephraim shall 5341
51:12 set up the **w**, prepare the ambushes: 8104
Mic 7: 4 the day of thy **w** *and* thy visitation cometh; 6822

WATCHT (1) [WATCH]

Ps 59: T Saul sent, and they **w** the house to kill him. 8104

WATCHTOWER (2) [TOWER, WATCH]

Isa 21: 5 the table, watch *in* the **w**, eat, drink: 6844
21: 8 I stand continually upon the **w** in 4707

WATER (396) [WATERCOURSE, WATERED, WATEREDST, WATEREST, WATERETH, WATERFLOOD, WATERING, WATERPOT, WATERPOTS, WATERS, WATERSPOUTS, WATERSPRINGS]

Ge 2:10 a river went out of Eden to **w** the garden; 8248
16: 7 her by a fountain of **w** in the wilderness, 4325
18: 4 Let a little **w**, I pray you, be fetched, and 4325
21:14 and a bottle of **w**, and gave *it* unto Hagar, 4325
21:15 the **w** was spent in the bottle, and she cast 4325
21:19 opened her eyes, and she saw a well of **w**; 4325
21:19 filled the bottle *with* **w**, and gave the lad 4325
21:25 because of a well of **w**, 4325
24:11 by a well of **w** at the time of the evening, 4325
24:11 the time that *women* go out to draw ***w***. NIH
24:13 Behold, I stand *here* by the well of **w**; and 4325
24:13 of the men of the city come out to draw **w**: 4325
24:17 I pray thee, drink a little **w** of thy pitcher. 4325
24:19 she said, I will draw ***w*** for thy camels also, NIH
24:20 ran again unto the well to draw ***w***, and NIH
24:32 **w** to wash his feet, and the men's feet that 4325
24:43 Behold, I stand by the well of **w**; and 4325
24:43 *when* the virgin cometh forth to draw ***w***, NIH
24:43 I pray thee, a little **w** of thy pitcher to drink; 4325
24:45 drew ***w***: and I said unto her, Let me drink, NIH
26:18 Isaac digged again the wells of **w**, 4325
26:19 and found there a well of springing **w**. 4325
26:20 Isaac's herdmen, saying, The **w** *is* ours: 4325
26:32 and said unto him, We have found **w**. 4325
29: 7 **w** ye the sheep, and go *and* feed *them.* 8248
29: 8 the well's mouth; then we **w** the sheep. 8248
37:24 and the pit *was* empty, *there was* no **w** in it. 4325
43:24 gave *them* **w**, and they washed their feet; 4325
49: 4 Unstable as **w**, thou shalt not excel; 4325
Ex 2:10 she said, Because I drew him out of the **w**. 4325
2:16 they came and **drew w**, and filled 1802
2:16 filled the troughs to **w** their father's flock. 8248
2:19 also **drew w enough** for us, and 1802+1802
4: 9 that thou shalt take of the **w** of the river, 4325
4: 9 the **w** which thou takest out of the river 4325
7:15 lo, he goeth out unto the **w**; and thou shalt 4325
7:18 the Egyptians shall lothe to drink of the **w** 4325
7:19 their ponds, and upon all their pools of **w**, 4325
7:21 the Egyptians could not drink of the **w** of 4325
7:24 digged round about the river *for* **w** to drink; 4325
7:24 for they could not drink of the **w** of 4325
8:20 lo, he cometh forth to the **w**; and say unto 4325
12: 9 nor sodden at all with **w**, but roast with fire; 4325
15:22 days in the wilderness, and found no **w**. 4325
15:27 where *were* twelve wells of **w**, and 4325
17: 1 and *there was* no **w** for the people to drink. 4325
17: 2 and said, Give us **w** that we may drink. 4325
17: 3 the people thirsted there for **w**; and 4325
17: 6 the rock, and there shall come **w** out of it, 4325
20: 4 or that *is* in the **w** under the earth: 4325
23:25 and he shall bless thy bread, and thy **w**; 4325
29: 4 and shalt wash them with **w**. 4325
30:18 and the altar, and thou shalt put **w** therein. 4325
30:20 they shall wash *with* **w**, that they die not; 4325
32:20 strawed *it* upon the **w**, and made 4325
34:28 he did neither eat bread, nor drink **w**. 4325
40: 7 and the altar, and shalt put **w** therein. 4325
40:12 of the congregation, and wash them with **w**. 4325
40:30 and the altar, and put **w** there, 4325
Lev 1: 9 his inwards and his legs shall he wash in **w**: 4325
1:13 shall wash the inwards and the legs with **w**: 4325
6:28 it shall be both scoured, and rinsed in **w**. 4325
8: 6 and his sons, and washed them with **w**. 4325
8:21 he washed the inwards and the legs in **w**; 4325
11:32 it must be put into **w**, and it shall be 4325
11:34 *that* on which *such* **w** cometh shall be 4325
11:36 or pit, *wherein there is* plenty of **w**, 4325
11:38 if *any* **w** be put upon the seed, and *any part* 4325
14: 5 killed in an earthen vessel over running **w**: 4325
14: 6 the bird *that was* killed over the running **w**: 4325
14: 8 off all his hair, and wash *himself* in **w**, 4325
14: 9 also he shall wash his flesh in **w**, and 4325
14:50 birds in an earthen vessel over running **w**: 4325
14:51 in the running **w**, and sprinkle the house 4325
Lev 14:52 with the running **w**, and with the living 4325
15: 5 bathe *himself* in **w**, and be unclean until 4325
15: 6 bathe *himself* in **w**, and be unclean until 4325
15: 7 bathe *himself* in **w**, and be unclean until 4325
15: 8 bathe *himself* in **w**, and be unclean until 4325
15:10 bathe *himself* in **w**, and be unclean until 4325
15:11 hath not rinsed his hands in **w**, he shall 4325
15:11 bathe *himself* in **w**, and be unclean until 4325
15:12 every vessel of wood shall be rinsed in **w**. 4325
15:13 bathe his flesh in running **w**, and shall be 4325
15:16 he shall wash all his flesh in **w**, and 4325
15:17 shall be washed with **w**, and be unclean 4325
15:18 they shall *both* bathe *themselves* in **w**, and 4325
15:21 bathe *himself* in **w**, and be unclean until 4325
15:22 bathe *himself* in **w**, and be unclean until 4325
15:27 bathe *himself* in **w**, and be unclean until 4325
16: 4 therefore shall he wash his flesh in **w**, and 4325
16:24 he shall wash his flesh with **w** in the holy 4325
16:26 bathe his flesh in **w**, and afterward come 4325
16:28 bathe his flesh in **w**, and afterward he shall 4325
17:15 bathe *himself* in **w**, and be unclean until 4325
22: 6 *things,* unless he wash his flesh with **w**. 4325
Nu 5:17 the priest shall take holy **w** in an earthen 4325
5:17 the priest shall take, and put *it* into the **w**: 4325
5:18 the priest shall have in his hand the bitter **w** 4325
5:19 be thou free from this bitter **w** that causeth 4325
5:22 this **w** that causeth the curse shall go into 4325
5:23 and he shall blot *them* out with the bitter **w**: 4325
5:24 to drink the bitter **w** that causeth the curse: 4325
5:24 the **w** that causeth the curse shall enter into 4325
5:26 shall cause the woman to drink the **w**. 4325
5:27 when he hath made her to drink the **w**, then 4325
5:27 that the **w** that causeth the curse shall enter 4325
8: 7 Sprinkle **w** of purifying upon them, and 4325
19: 7 he shall bathe his flesh in **w**, and 4325
19: 8 that burneth her shall wash his clothes in **w**, 4325
19: 8 bathe his flesh in **w**, and shall be unclean 4325
19: 9 the children of Israel for a **w** of separation: 4325
19:13 the **w** of separation was not sprinkled upon 4325
19:17 running **w** shall be put thereto in a vessel: 4325
19:18 dip *it* in the **w**, and sprinkle *it* upon the tent, 4325
19:19 bathe *himself* in **w**, and shall be clean at 4325
19:20 the **w** of separation hath not been sprinkled 4325
19:21 that he that sprinkleth the **w** of separation 4325
19:21 he that toucheth the **w** of separation shall 4325
20: 2 there was no **w** for the congregation: and 4325
20: 5 neither *is there any* **w** to drink. 4325
20: 8 it shall give forth his **w**, and thou shalt 4325
20: 8 thou shalt bring forth to them **w** out of 4325
20:10 must we fetch you **w** out of this rock? 4325
20:11 the **w** came out abundantly, and 4325
20:13 This *is* the **w** of Meribah; because 4325
20:17 neither will we drink *of* the **w** of the wells: 4325
20:19 if I and my cattle drink *of* thy **w**, then I will 4325
20:24 ye rebelled against my word at the **w** of 4325
21: 5 for *there is* no bread, neither *is there any* **w**; 4325
21:16 the people together, and I will give them **w**. 4325
24: 7 He shall pour the **w** out of his buckets, and 4325
27:14 to sanctify me at the **w** before their eyes: 4325
27:14 that *is* the **w** of Meribah in Kadesh *in* 4325
31:23 nevertheless it shall be purified with the **w** 4325
31:23 not the fire ye shall make go through the **w**. 4325
33: 9 in Elim *were* twelve fountains of **w**, and 4325
33:14 where was no **w** for the people to drink. 4325
Dt 2: 6 ye shall also buy **w** of them for money, 4325
2:28 and give me **w** for money, that I may drink: 4325
8: 7 a land of brooks of **w**, of fountains and 4325
8:15 and drought, where *there was* no **w**; 4325
8:15 who brought thee forth **w** out of the rock of 4325
9: 9 I neither did eat bread nor drink **w**: 4325
9:18 nor drink **w**, because of all your sins which 4325
11: 4 how he made the **w** of the Red sea to 4325
11:11 *and* drinketh **w** of the rain of heaven: 4325
12:16 ye shall pour it upon the earth as **w**. 4325
12:24 eat it; thou shalt pour it upon the earth as **w**. 4325
15:23 thou shalt pour it upon the ground as **w**. 4325
23: 4 you not with bread and with **w** in the way, 4325
23:11 cometh on, he shall wash *himself* with **w**: 4325
29:11 of thy wood unto the drawer of thy **w**: 4325
Jos 2:10 dried up the **w** of the Red sea for you, 4325
3: 8 When ye are come to the brink of the **w** of 4325
3:15 the ark were dipped in the brim of the **w**, 4325
7: 5 of the people melted, and became as **w**. 4325
9:21 and drawers of **w** unto all the congregation; 4325
9:23 and drawers of **w** for the house of my God. 4325
9:27 and drawers of **w** for the congregation, 4325
15: 9 hill unto the fountain of the **w** of Nephtoah, 4325
15:19 me a south land; give me also springs of **w**. 4325
16: 1 unto the **w** of Jericho on the east, 4325
Jdg 1:15 me a south land; give me also springs of **w**. 4325
4:19 Give me, I pray thee, a little **w** to drink; 4325
5: 4 the clouds also dropped **w**. 4325
5:11 ***w***, there shall they rehearse the righteous NIH
5:25 He asked **w**, *and* she gave *him* milk; 4325
6:38 the dew out of the fleece, a bowl full *of* **w**. 4325
7: 4 bring them down unto the **w**, and I will try 4325
7: 5 So he brought down the people unto the **w**: 4325
7: 5 Every one that lappeth of the **w** with his 4325
7: 6 bowed down upon their knees to drink **w**. 4325
15:19 *was* in the jaw, and there came **w** thereout; 4325
1Sa 7: 6 drew **w**, and poured *it* out before 4325
9:11 found young maidens going out to draw **w**, 4325
25:11 my **w**, and my flesh that I have killed for 4325
26:11 and the cruse of **w**, and let us go. 4325
26:12 and the cruse of **w** from Saul's bolster; 4325
26:16 and the cruse of **w** that *was at* his bolster. 4325
30:11 and he did eat; and they made him drink **w**; 4325
30:12 nor drunk *any* **w**, three days and 4325
2Sa 14:14 needs die, and *are* as **w** spilt on the ground, 4325
17:20 They be gone over the brook of **w**. 4325
17:21 Arise, and pass quickly over the **w**: 4325
21:10 from the beginning of harvest until **w** 4325
23:15 Oh that one would give me drink *of* the **w** of 4325
23:16 drew **w** out of the well of Beth-lehem, 4325
1Ki 13: 8 neither will I eat bread nor drink **w** in this 4325
1Ki 13: 9 saying, Eat no bread, nor drink **w**, 4325
13:16 neither will I eat bread nor drink **w** with 4325
13:17 Thou shalt eat no bread nor drink **w** there, 4325
13:18 that he may eat bread and drink **w**. 4325
13:19 and did eat bread in his house, and drank **w**. 4325
13:22 hast eaten bread and drunk **w** in the place, 4325
13:22 say to thee, Eat no bread, and drink no **w**; 4325
14:15 as a reed is shaken in the **w**, and he shall 4325
17:10 Fetch me, I pray thee, a little **w** in a vessel, 4325
18: 4 in a cave, and fed them *with* bread and **w**.) 4325
18: 5 unto all fountains of **w**, and unto all brooks: 4325
18:13 in a cave, and fed them *with* bread and **w**? 4325
18:33 Fill four barrels *with* **w**, and pour *it* on 4325
18:35 the **w** ran round about the altar; and 4325
18:35 and he filled the trench also *with* **w**. 4325
18:38 and licked up the **w** that *was* in the trench. 4325
19: 6 on the coals, and a cruse of **w** *at* his head. 4325
22:27 bread of affliction and with **w** of affliction, 4325
2Ki 2:19 but the **w** *is* naught, and the ground barren. 4325
3: 9 there was no **w** for the host, and for 4325
3:11 which poured **w** on the hands of Elijah. 4325
3:17 yet that valley shall be filled *with* **w**, that ye 4325
3:19 stop all wells of **w**, and mar every good 4325
3:20 there came **w** by the way of Edom, and 4325
3:20 and the country was filled with **w**. 4325
3:22 the sun shone upon the **w**, and the Moabites 4325
3:22 the Moabites saw the **w** on the other side *as* 4325
3:25 they stopped all the wells of **w**, and 4325
6: 5 felling a beam, the axe head fell into the **w**: 4325
6:22 set bread and **w** before them, that they may 4325
8:15 dipt *it* in **w**, and spread *it* on his face, so 4325
20:20 and a conduit, and brought **w** into the city, 4325
1Ch 11:17 Oh that one would give me drink *of* the **w** 4325
11:18 drew **w** out of the well of Beth-lehem, 4325
2Ch 18:26 bread of affliction and with **w** of affliction, 4325
32: 4 kings of Assyria come, and find much **w**? 4325
Ezr 10: 6 he did eat no bread, nor drink **w**: 4325
Ne 3:26 unto *the place* over against the **w** gate 4325
8: 1 into the street that *was* before the **w** gate; 4325
8: 3 the **w** gate from the morning until midday, 4325
8:16 in the street of the **w** gate, and in the street 4325
9:15 broughtest forth **w** for them out of the rock 4325
9:20 and gavest them **w** for their thirst. 4325
12:37 of David, even unto the **w** gate east*ward.* 4325
13: 2 children of Israel with bread and with **w**, 4325
Job 8:11 without mire? can the flag grow without **w**? 4325
9:30 If I wash myself with snow **w**, and 4325
14: 9 *Yet* through the scent of **w** it will bud, and 4325
15:16 *is* man, which drinketh iniquity like **w**? 4325
22: 7 Thou hast not given **w** to the weary to 4325
34: 7 like Job, *who* drinketh up scorning like **w**? 4325
36:27 For he maketh small the drops of **w**: 4325
Ps 1: 3 be like a tree planted by the rivers of **w**, 4325
6: 6 bed to swim; I **w** my couch with my tears. 4529
22:14 I am poured out like **w**, and all my bones 4325
42: 1 As the hart panteth after the **w** brooks, so 4325
63: 1 in a dry and thirsty land, where no **w** is; 4325
65: 9 it *with* the river of God, *which* is full *of* **w**: 4325
66:12 we went through fire and through **w**: 4325
72: 6 mown grass: as showers that **w** the earth. 2222
77:17 The clouds poured out **w**: the skies sent out 4325
79: 3 Their blood have they shed like **w** round 4325
88:17 They came round about me daily like **w**; 4325
107:35 turneth the wilderness into a standing **w**, 4325
109:18 so let it come into his bowels like **w**, and 4325
114: 8 Which turned the rock *into* a standing **w**, 4325
Pr 8:24 *there were* no fountains abounding with **w**. 4325
17:14 of strife *is as* when one letteth out **w**: 4325
20: 5 Counsel in the heart of man *is like* deep **w**; 4325
21: 1 the hand of the LORD, *as* the rivers of **w**: 4325
25:21 and if he *be* thirsty, give him **w** to drink: 4325
27:19 As *in* **w** face *answereth* to face, so the heart 4325
30:16 the earth *that* is not filled *with* **w**; and 4325
Ecc 2: 6 I made me pools of **w**, to water therewith 4325
2: 6 to **w** therewith the wood that bringeth forth 8248
Isa 1:22 is become dross, thy wine mixt with **w**: 4325
1:30 leaf fadeth, and as a garden that hath no **w**. 4325
3: 1 stay of bread, and the whole stay of **w**, 4325
12: 3 Therefore with joy shall ye draw **w** out of 4325
14:23 a possession for the bittern, and pools of **w**: 4325
16: 9 I will **w** thee *with* my tears, O Heshbon, 7301
21:14 of Tema brought **w** to him that was thirsty, 4325
22:11 the two walls for the **w** of the old pool: 4325
27: 3 do keep it; I will **w** it every moment: 8248
30:14 or to take **w** *withal* out of the pit. 4325
30:20 bread of adversity, and the **w** of affliction, 4325
32: 2 as rivers of **w** in a dry place, as the shadow 4325
35: 7 a pool, and the thirsty land springs of **w**: 4325
37:25 I have digged, and drunk **w**; and with 4325
41:17 *When* the poor and needy seek **w**, and 4325
41:18 I will make the wilderness a pool of **w**, and 4325
41:18 of water, and the dry land springs of **w**. 4325
44: 3 For I will pour **w** upon *him that is* thirsty, 4325
44: 4 the grass, as willows by the **w** courses. 4325
44:12 he drinketh no **w**, and is faint. 4325
49:10 even by the springs of **w** shall he guide 4325
50: 2 because *there is* no **w**, and dieth for thirst. 4325
58:11 like a spring of **w**, whose waters fail not. 4325
63:12 dividing the **w** before them, to make 4325
Jer 2:13 broken cisterns, that can hold no **w**. 4325
8:14 given us **w** of gall to drink, because 4325
9:15 and give them **w** of gall to drink. 4325
13: 1 put it upon thy loins, and put it not in **w**. 4325
14: 3 they came to the pits, *and* found no **w**; 4325
23:15 and make them drink the **w** of gall: 4325
38: 6 in the dungeon *there was* no **w**, but mire: 4325
La 1:16 mine eye runneth down *with* **w**, because 4325
2:19 pour out thine heart like **w** before the face 4325
3:48 Mine eye runneth down *with* rivers of **w** for 4325
5: 4 We have drunken our **w** for money; 4325
Eze 4:11 Thou shalt drink also **w** by measure, 4325
4:16 they shall drink **w** by measure, and 4325
4:17 That they may want bread and **w**, and 4325
7:17 be feeble, and all knees shall be weak *as* **w**. 4325
12:18 drink thy **w** with trembling and 4325

W

Eze 12:19 and drink their **w** with astonishment, 4325
16: 4 neither wast thou washed in **w** to supple 4325
16: 9 washed I thee with **w**; yea, I throughly 4325
17: 7 that *he* might **w** it by the furrows of her 8248
21: 7 and all knees shall be weak *as* **w**: 4325
24: 3 on a pot, set *it* on, and also pour **w** into it: 4325
26:12 and thy dust in the midst of the **w**. 4325
31:14 stand up in their height, all that drink **w**: 4325
31:16 and best of Lebanon, all that drink **w**, 4325
32: 6 I will also **w** with thy blood the land 8248
36:25 will I sprinkle clean **w** upon you, and 4325
Da 1:12 them give us pulse to eat, and **w** to drink. 4325
Hos 2: 5 that give *me* my bread and my **w**, my wool 4325
5:10 I will pour out my wrath upon them like **w**. 4325
10: 7 her king is cut off as the foam upon the **w**. 4325
Joel 3:18 and shall **w** the valley of Shittim. 8248
Am 4: 8 cities wandered unto one city, to drink **w**; 4325
8:11 nor a thirst for **w**, but of hearing the words 4325
Jnh 3: 7 any thing: let them not feed, nor drink **w**: 4325
Na 2: 8 Nineveh *is* of old like a pool of **w**: yet they 4325
Hab 3:10 the overflowing of the **w** passed by: 4325
Zec 9:11 thy prisoners out of the pit wherein *is* no **w**. 4325
Mt 3:11 I indeed baptize you with **w** unto *5204*
3:16 went up straightway out of the **w**: *5204*
10:42 cup of cold ***w*** only in the name of a disciple, NIG
14:28 it be thou, bid me come unto thee on the **w**. *5204*
14:29 the ship, he walked on the **w**, to go to Jesus. *5204*
17:15 he falleth into the fire, and oft into the **w**. *5204*
27:24 he took **w**, and washed *his* hands before *5204*
Mk 1: 8 I indeed have baptized you with **w**: but *5204*
1:10 And straightway coming up out of the **w**, *5204*
9:41 For whosoever shall give you a cup of **w** to *5204*
14:13 meet you a man bearing a pitcher of **w**: *5204*
Lk 3:16 unto *them* all, I indeed baptize you with **w**; *5204*
7:44 thou gavest me no **w** for my feet: *5204*
8:23 and they were filled *with* ***w***, and were in NIG
8:24 rebuked the wind and the raging of the **w**: *5204*
8:25 for he commandeth even the winds and **w**, *5204*
16:24 that he may dip the tip of his finger in **w**, *5204*
22:10 a man meet you, bearing a pitcher of **w**; *5204*
Jn 1:26 answered them, saying, I baptize with **w**: *5204*
1:31 therefore am I come baptizing with **w**. *5204*
1:33 but he that sent me to baptize with **w**, *5204*
2: 7 saith unto them, Fill the waterpots with **w**. *5204*
2: 9 When the ruler of the feast had tasted the **w** *5204*
2: 9 (but the servants which drew the **w** knew;) *5204*
3: 5 Except a man be born of **w** and *of* *5204*
3:23 to Salim, because there was much **w** there: *5204*
4: 7 cometh a woman of Samaria to draw **w**: *5204*
4:10 and he would have given thee living **w**. *5204*
4:11 from whence then hast thou *that* living **w**? *5204*
4:13 Whosoever drinketh of this **w** shall thirst *5204*
4:14 But whosoever drinketh of the **w** that I *5204*
4:14 the **w** that I shall give him shall be in him a *5204*
4:14 well of **w** springing up into everlasting life. *5204*
4:15 Sir, give me this **w**, that I thirst not, *5204*
4:46 of Galilee, where he made the **w** wine. *5204*
5: 3 withered, waiting for the moving of the **w**. *5204*
5: 4 season into the pool, and troubled the **w**: *5204*
5: 4 first after the troubling of the **w** stepped in, *5204*
5: 7 Sir, I have no man, when the **w** is troubled, *5204*
7:38 of his belly shall flow rivers of living **w**. *5204*
13: 5 he poureth **w** into a bason, and began to *5204*
19:34 and forthwith came there out blood and **w**. *5204*
Ac 1: 5 For John truly baptized with **w**; but ye shall *5204*
8:36 on *their* way, they came unto a certain **w**: *5204*
8:36 and the eunuch said, See, *here is* **w**; *5204*
8:38 and they went down both into the **w**, *5204*
8:39 And when they were come up out of the **w**, *5204*
10:47 Can any *man* forbid **w**, that these should *5204*
11:16 that he said, John indeed baptized with **w**; *5204*
Eph 5:26 cleanse *it* with the washing of **w** by *5204*
1Ti 5:23 **Drink** no longer **w**, but use a little wine for *5202*
Heb 9:19 with **w**, and scarlet wool, and hyssop, and *5204*
10:22 and *our* bodies washed with pure **w**. *5204*
Jas 3:11 send forth at the same place sweet ***w*** NIG
3:12 so *can* no fountain *both* yield salt **w** and *5204*
1Pe 3:20 that is, eight souls were saved by **w**. *5204*
2Pe 2:17 These are wells **without w**, clouds that are *504*
3: 5 and the earth standing out of the **w** and *5204*
3: 5 standing out of the water and in the **w**: *5204*
3: 6 then was, being overflowed with **w**, *5204*
1Jn 5: 6 This is he that came by **w** and blood, *5204*
5: 6 not by **w** only, but by water and blood. *5204*
5: 6 not by water only, but by **w** and blood. *5204*
5: 8 the Spirit, and the **w**, and the blood: *5204*
Jude 1:12 clouds *they are* **without w**, carried about of *504*
Rev 12:15 And the serpent cast out of his mouth **w** as *5204*
16:12 and the **w** thereof was dried up, that *5204*
21: 6 of the fountain of the **w** of life freely. *5204*
22: 1 And he shewed me a pure river of **w** of life, *5204*
22:17 let him take the **w** of life freely. *5204*

WATERCOURSE (2) [WATER]

2Ch 32:30 also stopped the upper **w** of Gihon, 4161+4325
Job 38:25 Who hath divided a **w** for the overflowing 8585

WATERED (11) [WATER]

Ge 2: 6 and **w** the whole face of the ground. 8248
13:10 of Jordan, that it *was* **well w** every where, 4945
29: 2 by it; for out of that well they **w** the flocks. 8248
29: 3 **w** the sheep, and put the stone again upon 8248
29:10 **w** the flock of Laban his mother's brother. 8248
Ex 2:17 and helped them, and **w** their flock. 8248
2:19 drew water enough for us, and **w** the flock. 8248
Pr 11:25 he that watereth shall be **w** also himself. 3384
Isa 58:11 thou shalt be like a **w** garden, and like a 7302
Jer 31:12 their soul shall be as a **w** garden; and 7302
1Co 3: 6 I have planted, Apollos **w**; but God gave *4222*

WATEREDST (1) [WATER]

Dt 11:10 and **w** *it* with thy foot, as a garden of herbs: 8248

WATEREST (2) [WATER]

Ps 65: 9 Thou visitest the earth, and **w** it: 7783
65:10 *Thou* **w** the ridges thereof **abundantly**: 7301

WATERETH (5) [WATER]

Ps 104:13 He **w** the hills from his chambers: the earth 8248
Pr 11:25 and he that **w** shall be watered also himself. 7301
Isa 55:10 **w** the earth, and maketh it bring forth and 7301
1Co 3: 7 that planteth any *thing*, neither he that **w**; *4222*
3: 8 Now he that planteth and he that **w** are one: *4222*

WATERFALLS See WATERSPOUTS

WATERFLOOD (1) [FLOOD, WATER]

Ps 69:15 Let not the **w** overflow me, 4325+7641

WATERING (3) [WATER]

Ge 30:38 **w** troughs when the flocks came to drink, 4325
Job 37:11 Also by **w** he wearieth the thick cloud: 7377
Lk 13:15 ass from the stall, and lead *him* away to **w**? *4222*

WATERPOT (1) [POT, WATER]

Jn 4:28 The woman then left her **w**, and went her *5201*

WATERPOTS (2) [POT, WATER]

Jn 2: 6 And there were set there six **w** of stone, *5201*
2: 7 saith unto them, Fill the **w** with water. *5201*

WATERS (287) [WATER]

Ge 1: 2 of God moved upon the face of the **w**. 4325
1: 6 there be a firmament in the midst of the **w**, 4325
1: 6 let it divide the **w** from the waters. 4325
1: 6 let it divide the waters from the **w**. 4325
1: 7 divided the **w** which *were* under 4325
1: 7 the **w** which *were* above the firmament: 4325
1: 9 Let the **w** under the heaven be gathered 4325
1:10 the gathering together of the **w** called he 4325
1:20 Let the **w** bring forth abundantly 4325
1:21 which the **w** brought forth abundantly, 4325
1:22 fill the **w** in the seas, and let fowl multiply 4325
6:17 do bring a flood of **w** upon the earth, 4325
7: 6 when the flood of **w** was upon the earth. 4325
7: 7 into the ark, because of the **w** of the flood. 4325
7:10 that the **w** of the flood were upon the earth. 4325
7:17 the **w** increased, and bare up the ark, and 4325
7:18 the **w** prevailed, and were increased greatly 4325
7:18 and the ark went upon the face of the **w**. 4325
7:19 the **w** prevailed exceedingly upon the earth; 4325
7:20 Fifteen cubits upward did the **w** prevail; 4325
7:24 the **w** prevailed upon the earth an hundred 4325
8: 1 to pass over the earth, and the **w** asswaged; 4325
8: 3 the **w** returned from off the earth 4325
8: 3 and fifty days the **w** were abated. 4325
8: 5 the **w** decreased continually until the tenth 4325
8: 7 until the **w** were dried up from off 4325
8: 8 to see if the **w** were abated from off 4325
8: 9 for the **w** *were* on the face of the whole 4325
8:11 Noah knew that the **w** were abated from off 4325
8:13 the **w** were dried up from off the earth: 4325
9:11 be cut off any more by the **w** of a flood; 4325
9:15 the **w** shall no more become a flood to 4325
Ex 7:17 hand upon the **w** which *are* in the river, 4325
7:19 stretch out thine hand upon the **w** of Egypt, 4325
7:20 and smote the **w** that *were* in the river, 4325
7:20 all the **w** that *were* in the river were turned 4325
8: 6 Aaron stretched out his hand over the **w** of 4325
14:21 the sea dry *land*, and the **w** were divided. 4325
14:22 the **w** *were* a wall unto them on their right 4325
14:26 that the **w** may come again upon 4325
14:28 the **w** returned, and covered the chariots, 4325
14:29 the **w** *were* a wall unto them on their right 4325
15: 8 with the blast of thy nostrils the **w** were 4325
15:10 they sank as lead in the mighty **w**. 4325
15:19 the LORD brought again the **w** of the sea 4325
15:23 they could not drink of the **w** of Marah, 4325
15:25 *which* when he had cast into the **w**, 4325
15:25 into the waters, the **w** were made sweet: 4325
15:27 and they encamped there by the **w**. 4325
Lev 11: 9 These shall ye eat of all that *are* in the **w**: 4325
11: 9 whatsoever hath fins and scales in the **w**, 4325
11:10 of all that move in the **w**, and of any living 4325
11:10 and of any living thing which *is* in the **w**, 4325
11:12 hath no fins nor scales in the **w**, 4325
11:46 every living creature that moveth in the **w**, 4325
Nu 21:22 we will not drink *of* the **w** of the well: 4325
24: 6 *and* as cedar trees beside the **w**. 4325
24: 7 his seed *shall be* in many **w**, and his king 4325
Dt 4:18 the likeness of any fish that *is* in the **w** 4325
5: 8 or that *is* in the **w** beneath the earth: 4325
10: 7 Gudgodah to Jotbath, a land of rivers of **w**. 4325
14: 9 These ye shall eat of all that *are* in the **w**: 4325
32:51 of Israel at the **w** of Meribah-Kadesh, 4325
33: 8 *with* whom thou didst strive at the **w** of 4325
Jos 3:13 all the earth, shall rest in the **w** of Jordan, 4325
3:13 *that* the **w** of Jordan shall be cut off *from* 4325
3:13 off *from* the **w** that come down from above; 4325
3:16 That the **w** which came down from above 4325
4: 7 That the **w** of Jordan were cut off before 4325
4: 7 over Jordan, the **w** of Jordan were cut off: 4325
4:18 the **w** of Jordan returned unto their place, 4325
4:23 For the LORD your God dried up the **w** of 4325
5: 1 heard that the LORD had dried up the **w** 4325
11: 5 and pitched together at the **w** of Merom, 4325
11: 7 against them by the **w** of Merom suddenly; 4325
15: 7 the border passed towards the **w** of 4325
18:15 and went out to the well of **w** of Nephtoah: 4325
Jdg 5:19 Canaan in Taanach by the **w** of Megiddo; 4325
7:24 take before them the **w** unto Beth-barah and 4325
7:24 and took the **w** unto Beth-barah and Jordan. 4325
2Sa 5:20 enemies before me, as the breach of **w**. 4325
12:27 and have taken the city of **w**. 4325
22:12 dark **w**, *and* thick clouds of the skies. 4325
22:17 he took me; he drew me out of many **w**; 4325
2Ki 2: 8 smote the **w**, and they were divided hither 4325
2Ki 2:14 smote the **w**, and said, Where *is* 4325
2:14 when he also had smitten the **w**, they parted 4325
2:21 he went forth unto the spring of the **w**, and 4325
2:21 saith the LORD, I have healed these **w**; 4325
2:22 So the **w** were healed unto this day, 4325
5:12 better than all the **w** of Israel? 4325
18:31 and drink ye every one the **w** of his cistern: 4325
19:24 I have digged and drunk strange **w**, and 4325
1Ch 14:11 by mine hand like the breaking forth of **w**: 4325
2Ch 32: 3 his mighty *men* to stop the **w** of 4325
Ne 9:11 into the deeps, as a stone into the mighty **w**. 4325
Job 3:24 and my roarings are poured out like the **w**. 4325
5:10 the earth, and sendeth **w** upon the fields: 4325
11:16 *and* remember *it* as **w** *that* pass away: 4325
12:15 he withholdeth the **w**, and they dry up: 4325
14:11 *As* the **w** fail from the sea, and the flood 4325
14:19 The **w** wear the stones: thou washest away 4325
22:11 not see; and abundance of **w** cover thee. 4325
24:18 He *is* swift as the **w**; their portion is cursed 4325
24:19 Drought and heat consume the snow **w**: *so* 4325
26: 5 Dead *things* are formed from under the **w**, 4325
26: 8 He bindeth up the **w** in his thick clouds; 4325
26:10 He hath compassed the **w** with bounds, 4325
27:20 Terrors take hold on him as **w**, a tempest 4325
28: 4 *even the* ***w*** forgotten of the foot: NIH
28:25 and he weigheth the **w** by measure. 4325
29:19 My root *was* spread out by the **w**, and 4325
30:14 ***w***: in the desolation they rolled themselves NIH
37:10 and the breadth of the **w** is straitened. 4325
38:25 a watercourse for the **overflowing of w**, 7858
38:30 The **w** are hid as *with* a stone, and the face 4325
38:34 that abundance of **w** may cover thee? 4325
Ps 18:11 his pavilion round about him *were* dark **w** 4325
18:15 the channels of **w** were seen, and 4325
18:16 he took me, he drew me out of many **w**. 4325
23: 2 he leadeth me beside the still **w**. 4325
29: 3 The voice of the LORD *is* upon the **w**: 4325
29: 3 the LORD *is* upon many **w**. 4325
32: 6 surely in the floods of great **w** they shall 4325
33: 7 He gathereth the **w** of the sea together as a 4325
46: 3 *Though* the **w** thereof roar *and* be troubled, 4325
58: 7 Let them melt away as **w** *which* run 4325
69: 1 O God; for the **w** are come in unto *my* soul. 4325
69: 2 I am come into deep **w**, where the floods 4325
69:14 them that hate me, and out of the deep **w**. 4325
73:10 and **w** of a full *cup* are wrung out to them. 4325
74:13 brakest the heads of the dragons in the **w**. 4325
77:16 The **w** saw thee, O God, the waters saw 4325
77:16 waters saw thee, O God, the **w** saw thee; 4325
77:19 thy path in the great **w**, and thy footsteps 4325
78:13 and he made the **w** to stand as a heap. 4325
78:16 and caused **w** to run down like rivers. 4325
78:20 that the **w** gushed out, and the streams 4325
81: 7 I proved thee at the **w** of Meribah. Selah. 4325
93: 4 high *is* mightier than the noise of many **w**, 4325
104: 3 layeth the beams of his chambers in the **w**: 4325
104: 6 the **w** stood above the mountains. 4325
105:29 He turned their **w** into blood, and slew their 4325
105:41 He opened the rock, and the **w** gushed out; 4325
106:11 the **w** covered their enemies: there was not 4325
106:32 They angered *him* also at the **w** of strife, so 4325
107:23 the sea in ships, that do business in great **w**; 4325
114: 8 the flint into a fountain of **w**. 4325
119:136 Rivers of **w** run down mine eyes, because 4325
124: 4 the **w** had overwhelmed us, the stream had 4325
124: 5 Then the proud **w** had gone over our soul. 4325
136: 6 that stretched out the earth above the **w**: 4325
144: 7 rid me, and deliver me out of great **w**, 4325
147:18 causeth his wind to blow, *and* the **w** flow. 4325
148: 4 and ye **w** that *be* above the heavens. 4325
Pr 5:15 Drink **w** out of thine own cistern, and 4325
5:15 and **running w** out of thine own well. 5140
5:16 *and* rivers of **w** in the streets. 4325
8:29 that the **w** should not pass his 4325
9:17 Stolen **w** are sweet, and bread *eaten* in 4325
18: 4 The words of a man's mouth *are as* deep **w**, 4325
25:25 *As* cold **w** to a thirsty soul, so *is* good news 4325
30: 4 who hath bound the **w** in a garment? 4325
Ecc 11: 1 Cast thy bread upon the **w**: for thou shalt 4325
SS 4:15 a well of living **w**, and streams from 4325
5:12 *are as the eyes of* doves by the rivers of **w**, 4325
8: 7 Many **w** cannot quench love, neither can 4325
Isa 8: 6 Forsomuch as this people refuseth the **w** of 4325
8: 7 the Lord bringeth up upon them the **w** of 4325
11: 9 of the LORD, as the **w** cover the sea. 4325
15: 6 For the **w** of Nimrim shall be desolate: 4325
15: 9 For the **w** of Dimon shall be full *of* blood: 4325
17:12 a rushing like the rushing of mighty **w**. 4325
17:13 shall rush like the rushing of many **w**: 4325
18: 2 even in vessels of bulrushes upon the **w**, 4325
19: 5 the **w** shall fail from the sea, and the river 4325
19: 8 they that spread nets upon the **w** shall 4325
22: 9 ye gathered together the **w** of the lower 4325
23: 3 by great **w** the seed of Sihor, the harvest of 4325
28: 2 as a flood of mighty **w** overflowing, 4325
28:17 and the **w** shall overflow the hiding place. 4325
30:25 streams of **w** in the day of the great 4325
32:20 Blessed *are* ye that sow beside all **w**, 4325
33:16 *shall be* given him; his **w** *shall be* sure. 4325
35: 6 for in the wilderness shall **w** break out, and 4325
36:16 drink ye every one the **w** of his own cistern; 4325
40:12 Who hath measured the **w** in the hollow of 4325
43: 2 When thou passest through the **w**, I *will be* 4325
43:16 way in the sea, and a path in the mighty **w**; 4325
43:20 because I give **w** in the wilderness, *and* 4325
48: 1 and are come forth out of the **w** of Judah, 4325
48:21 he caused the **w** to flow out of the rock for 4325
48:21 clave the rock also, and the **w** gushed out. 4325
51:10 hath dried the sea, the **w** of the great deep; 4325
54: 9 For this *is as* the **w** of Noah unto me: for *as* 4325
54: 9 for *as* I have sworn that the **w** of Noah 4325
55: 1 come ye to the **w**, and he that hath no 4325
57:20 cannot rest, whose **w** cast up mire and dirt. 4325
58:11 and like a spring of water, whose **w** fail not. 4325
64: 2 fire burneth, the fire causeth the **w** to boil, 4325

Jer 2:13 have forsaken me the fountain of living **w**, 4325
2:18 the way of Egypt, to drink the **w** of Sihor? 4325
2:18 way of Assyria, to drink the **w** of the river? 4325
6: 7 As a fountain casteth out her **w**, so 4325
9: 1 O that my head were **w**, and mine eyes a 4325
9:18 *with* tears, and our eyelids gush out with **w**. 4325
10:13 *there is* a multitude of **w** in the heavens, 4325
14: 3 nobles have sent their little ones to the **w**: 4325
15:18 unto me as a liar, *and as* **w** *that* fail? 4325
17: 8 For he shall be as a tree planted by the **w**, 4325
17:13 the LORD, the fountain of living **w**. 4325
18:14 shall the cold flowing **w** that come from 4325
31: 9 I will cause them to walk by the rivers of **w** 4325
41:12 found him by the great **w** that *are* in 4325
46: 7 a flood, whose **w** are moved as the rivers? 4325
46: 8 and *his* **w** are moved like the rivers; 4325
47: 2 **w** rise up out of the north, and shall be an 4325
48:34 for the **w** also of Nimrim shall be desolate. 4325
50:38 A drought *is* upon her **w**; and they shall be 4325
51:13 O thou that dwellest upon many **w**, 4325
51:16 *there is* a multitude of **w** in the heavens; 4325
51:55 when her waves do roar like great **w**, 4325
La 3:54 **W** flowed over mine head; *then* I said, I am 4325
Eze 1:24 like the noise of great **w**, as the voice of 4325
17: 5 he placed *it* by great **w**, *and* set it *as* a 4325
17: 8 It *was* planted in a good soil by great **w**, 4325
19:10 *is* like a vine in thy blood, planted by the **w**: 4325
19:10 and full of branches by reason of many **w**. 4325
26:19 upon thee, and great **w** shall cover thee; 4325
27:26 Thy rowers have brought thee into great **w**: 4325
27:34 broken by the seas in the depths of the **w**, 4325
31: 4 The **w** made him great, the deep set him up 4325
31: 5 became long because of the multitude of **w**, 4325
31: 7 of his branches: for his root was by great **w**. 4325
31:14 by the **w** exalt themselves for their height, 4325
31:15 floods thereof, and the great **w** were stayed: 4325
32: 2 troubledst the **w** with thy feet, and 4325
32:13 the beasts thereof from besides the great **w**; 4325
32:14 will I make their **w** deep, and cause their 4325
34:18 to have drunk of the deep **w**, but ye must 4325
43: 2 his voice *was* like a noise of many **w**: and 4325
47: 1 **w** issued out from under the threshold of 4325
47: 1 the **w** came down from under from the right 4325
47: 2 behold, there ran out **w** on the right side. 4325
47: 3 and he brought me through the **w**; 4325
47: 3 the waters; the **w** *were* to the ankles. 4325
47: 4 a thousand, and brought me through the **w**; 4325
47: 4 the waters; the **w** *were* to the knees. 4325
47: 4 me through; the **w** *were* to the loins. 4325
47: 5 for the **w** were risen, waters to swim in, 4325
47: 5 for the waters were risen, **w** to swim in, 4325
47: 8 These **w** issue out toward the east country, 4325
47: 8 forth into the sea, the **w** shall be healed. 4325
47: 9 of fish, because these **w** shall come thither: 4325
47:12 their **w** they issued out of the sanctuary: 4325
47:19 from Tamar *even* to the **w** of strife *in* 4325
48:28 from Tamar *unto* the **w** of strife *in* Kadesh, 4325
Da 12: 6 in linen, which *was* upon the **w** of the river, 4325
12: 7 which *was* upon the **w** of the river, when he 4325
Joel 1:20 for the rivers of **w** are dried up, and the fire 4325
3:18 all the rivers of Judah shall flow *with* **w**, 4325
Am 5: 8 that calleth for the **w** of the sea, and 4325
5:24 let judgment run down as **w**, and 4325
9: 6 he that calleth for the **w** of the sea, and 4325
Jnh 2: 5 The **w** compassed me about, *even* to 4325
Mic 1: 4 as the **w** *that are* poured down a steep 4325
Na 3: 8 *that had* the **w** round about it, 4325
3:14 Draw thee **w** for the siege, fortify thy 4325
Hab 2:14 of the LORD, as the **w** cover the sea. 4325
3:15 thine horses, *through* the heap of great **w**. 4325
Zec 14: 8 *that* living **w** shall go out from Jerusalem: 4325
Mt 8:32 place into the sea, and perished in the **w**. *5204*
Mk 9:22 into the fire, and into the **w**, to destroy him: *5204*
2Co 11:26 *in* perils of **w**, *in* perils of robbers, *4215*
Rev 1:15 and his voice as the sound of many **w**. *5204*
7:17 shall lead them unto living fountains of **w**: *5204*
8:10 of the rivers, and upon the fountains of **w**; *5204*
8:11 the third *part* of the **w** became wormwood; *5204*
8:11 and many men died of the **w**, because *5204*
11: 6 have power over **w** to turn them to blood, *5204*
14: 2 as the voice of many **w**, and as the voice of *5204*
14: 7 and the sea, and the fountains of **w**. *5204*
16: 4 his vial upon the rivers and fountains of **w**; *5204*
16: 5 And I heard the angel of the **w** say, *5204*
17: 1 the great whore that sitteth upon many **w**: *5204*
17:15 he saith unto me, The **w** which thou sawest, *5204*
19: 6 and as the voice of many **w**, and as *5204*

WATERSPOUTS (1) [WATER]

Ps 42: 7 calleth unto deep at the noise of thy **w**: 6794

WATERSPRINGS (2) [SPRING, WATER]

Ps 107:33 and the **w** into dry ground; 4161+4325
107:35 and dry ground into **w**; 4161+4325

WAVE (32) [WAVED, WAVES]

Ex 29:24 shalt **w** them *for* a wave offering before 5130
29:24 shalt wave them *for* a **w offering** before 8573
29:26 **w** it *for* a wave offering before the LORD: 5130
29:26 wave it *for* a **w offering** before 8573
29:27 shalt sanctify the breast of the **w offering**, 8573
Lev 7:30 waved *for* a **w offering** before the LORD. 8573
7:34 For the **w** breast and the heave shoulder 8573
8:27 waved them *for* a **w offering** before 8573
8:29 waved it *for* a **w offering** before 8573
9:21 waved *for* a **w offering** before the LORD; 8573
10:14 the **w** breast and heave shoulder shall ye eat 8573
10:15 the **w** breast shall they bring with 8573
10:15 to **w** *it for* a wave offering before 5130
10:15 to wave *it for* a **w offering** before 8573
14:12 **w** them *for* a wave offering before 5130
14:12 wave them *for* a **w offering** before 8573
14:24 the priest shall **w** them *for* a wave offering 5130
14:24 the priest shall wave them *for* a **w offering** 8573
Lev 23:11 he shall **w** the sheaf before the LORD, 5130
23:11 after the sabbath the priest shall **w** it. 5130
23:12 ye shall offer that day when ye **w** the sheaf 5130
23:15 that ye brought the sheaf of the **w offering**; 8573
23:17 habitations two **w** loaves of two tenth deals: 8573
23:20 the priest shall **w** them with the bread of 5130
23:20 *for* a **w offering** before the LORD, 8573
Nu 5:25 and shall **w** the offering before the LORD, 5130
6:20 the priest shall **w** them *for* a wave offering 5130
6:20 the priest shall wave them *for* a **w offering** 8573
6:20 with the **w** breast and heave shoulder: 8573
18:11 with all the **w offerings** of the children of 8573
18:18 as the **w** breast and as the right shoulder are 8573
Jas 1: 6 for he that wavereth is like a **w** of the sea *2830*

WAVED (6) [WAVE]

Ex 29:27 which is **w**, and which is heaved up, of 5130
Lev 7:30 that the breast may be **w** *for* a wave 5130
8:27 **w** them *for* a wave offering before 5130
8:29 **w** it *for* a wave offering before the LORD: 5130
9:21 the right shoulder Aaron **w** *for* a wave 5130
14:21 one lamb *for* a trespass offering to be **w**, 8573

WAVERETH (1) [WAVERING]

Jas 1: 6 for he that **w** is like a wave of the sea *1252*

WAVERING (2) [WAVERETH]

Heb 10:23 fast the profession of *our* hope **without w**; *186*
Jas 1: 6 But let him ask in faith, nothing **w**: for he *1252*

WAVES (26) [WAVE]

2Sa 22: 5 When the **w** of death compassed me, 4867
Job 9: 8 and treadeth upon the **w** of the sea. 1116
38:11 and here shall thy proud **w** be stayed? 1530
Ps 42: 7 all thy **w** and thy billows are gone over me. 4867
65: 7 the noise of their **w**, and the tumult of 1530
88: 7 and thou hast afflicted *me with* all thy **w**. 4867
89: 9 when the **w** thereof arise, thou stillest them. 1530
93: 3 up their voice; the floods lift up their **w**. 1796
93: 4 *yea, than* the mighty **w** of the sea. 4867
107:25 which lifteth up the **w** thereof. 1530
107:29 storm a calm, so that the **w** thereof are still. 1530
Isa 48:18 and thy righteousness as the **w** of the sea: 1530
51:15 that divided the sea, whose **w** roared: 1530
Jer 5:22 though the **w** thereof toss themselves, 1530
31:35 which divideth the sea when the **w** thereof 1530
51:42 she is covered with the multitude of the **w** 1530
51:55 when her **w** do roar like great waters, 1530
Eze 26: 3 as the sea causeth his **w** to come up. 1530
Jnh 2: 3 all thy billows and thy **w** passed over me. 1530
Zec 10:11 shall smite the **w** in the sea, and all 1530
Mt 8:24 that the ship was covered with the **w**: *2949*
14:24 now in the midst of the sea, tossed with **w**: *2949*
Mk 4:37 and the **w** beat into the ship, so that it was *2949*
Lk 21:25 with perplexity; the sea and the **w** roaring; *4535*
Ac 27:41 part was broken with the violence of the **w**. *2949*
Jude 1:13 Raging **w** of the sea, foaming out their own *2949*

WAVY See BUSHY

WAX (24) [WAXED, WAXEN, WAXETH, WAXING]

Ex 22:24 my wrath shall **w hot**, and I will kill you 2734
32:10 that my wrath may **w hot** against them, and 2734
32:11 why doth thy wrath **w hot** against thy 2734
32:22 Let not the anger of my lord **w hot**: 2734
Lev 25:47 or stranger **w rich** by thee, 3027+5381
25:47 thy brother *that dwelleth* by him **w poor**, 4134
1Sa 3: 2 his eyes began *to* **w** dim, *that* he could not NIH
Job 6:17 What time they **w warm**, they vanish: 2215
14: 8 Though the root thereof **w old** in the earth, 2204
Ps 22:14 my heart is like **w**; it is melted in the midst 1749
68: 2 as **w** melteth before the fire, *so* let 1749
97: 5 The hills melted like **w** at the presence of 1749
102:26 yea, all of them shall **w old** like a garment; 1086
Isa 17: 4 and the fatness of his flesh shall **w lean**. 7329
29:22 neither shall his face now **w pale**. 2357
50: 9 lo, they all shall **w old** as a garment; 1086
51: 6 the earth shall **w old** like a garment, and 1086
Jer 6:24 our hands **w feeble**: anguish hath taken 7503
Mic 1: 4 as **w** before the fire, *and* as the waters *that* 1749
Mt 24:12 the love of many shall **w cold**. *5594*
Lk 12:33 provide yourselves bags which **w** not **old**, *3822*
1Ti 5:11 have *begun to* **w wanton against** Christ, *2691*
2Ti 3:13 and seducers shall **w** worse and worse, *4298*
Heb 1:11 and they all shall **w old** as *doth* a garment; *3822*

WAXED (38) [WAX]

Ge 18:12 After I am **w old** shall I have pleasure, 1086
26:13 the man **w great**, and went forward, 1431
41:56 and the famine **w sore** in the land of Egypt. 2388
Ex 1: 7 and multiplied, and **w** exceeding **mighty**; 6105
1:20 the people multiplied, and **w** very **mighty**. 6105
16:21 and when the sun **w hot**, it melted. 2552
19:19 **w louder and louder**, Moses spake, 2390+3966
32:19 Moses' anger **w hot**, and he cast the tables 2734
Nu 11:23 Is the LORD'S hand **w short**? 7114
Dt 8: 4 Thy raiment **w** not **old** upon thee, 1086
32:15 Jeshurun **w fat**, and kicked: thou art waxed 8080
32:15 thou art **w fat**, thou art grown thick, 8080
Jos 23: 1 that Joshua **w old** *and* stricken in age. 2204
1Sa 2: 5 and she that hath many children is **w feeble**. 535
2Sa 3: 1 David **w stronger** and stronger, and 1980
3: 1 the house of Saul **w weaker** and weaker. 1980
21:15 against the Philistines: and David **w faint**. 5774
2Ki 4:34 and the flesh of the child **w warm**. 2552
1Ch 11: 9 So David **w greater** and greater: 1980+1980
2Ch 13:21 Abijah **w mighty**, and married fourteen 2388
17:12 Jehoshaphat **w** great exceedingly; and 1980
24:15 Jehoiada **w old**, and was full *of* days when 2204
Ne 9:21 their clothes **w** not **old**, and their feet 1086
Est 9: 4 for *this* man Mordecai **w greater** and 1980
Ps 32: 3 my bones **w old** through my roaring all 1086
Jer 49:24 Damascus is **w feeble**, *and* turneth herself 7503
50:43 the report of them, and his hands **w feeble**: 7503
Da 8: 8 Therefore the he goat **w** very **great**: and 1431
8: 9 which **w** exceeding great, toward the south, 4480
8:10 it **w great**, *even* to the host of heaven; and 1431
Mt 13:15 For this people's heart is **w gross**, and *their* *3975*
Lk 1:80 and **w strong** in spirit, and was in *2901*
2:40 and **w strong** in spirit, filled with wisdom: *2901*
13:19 and it grew, and **w** a great tree; and *1096+1519*
Ac 13:46 Then Paul and Barnabas **w bold**, and said, *3955*
28:27 For the heart of this people is **w gross**, and *3975*
Heb 11:34 were made strong, **w** valiant in fight, *1096*
Rev 18: 3 the merchants of the earth are **w rich** *4147*

WAXEN (11) [WAX]

Ge 19:13 the cry of them is **w great** before the face 1431
Lev 25:25 If thy brother be **w poor**, and hath sold 4134
25:35 if thy brother be **w poor**, and fallen in 4134
25:39 brother *that dwelleth* by thee be **w poor**, 4134
Dt 29: 5 your clothes are not **w old** upon you, and 1086
29: 5 and thy shoe is not **w old** upon thy foot. 1086
31:20 and filled *themselves*, and **w fat**; 1878
Jos 17:13 when the children of Israel were **w strong**, 2388
Jer 5:27 they are become great, and **w rich**. 6238
5:28 They are **w fat**, they shine: yea, 8080
Eze 16: 7 thou hast increased and **w great**, and 1431

WAXETH (2) [WAX]

Ps 6: 7 it **w old** because of all mine enemies. 6275
Heb 8:13 and **w old** *is* ready to vanish away. *1095*

WAXING (1) [WAX]

Php 1:14 in the Lord, **w confident** by my bonds, *3982*

WAY (665) [BYWAYS, HIGHWAY, HIGHWAYS, WAYFARING, WAYMARKS, WAYS, WAYSIDE]

Ge 3:24 a flaming sword which **turned every w**, 2015
3:24 every way, to keep the **w** of the tree of life. 1870
6:12 for all flesh had corrupted his **w** upon 1870
12:19 behold thy wife, take *her*, and go thy **w**. NIH
14:11 and all their victuals, and went their **w**. NIH
16: 7 by the fountain in the **w** to Shur. 1870
18:16 went with them to **bring** them **on** the **w**. 7971
18:19 they shall keep the **w** of the LORD, to do 1870
18:33 the LORD went his **w**, as soon as he had NIH
21:16 her down over against *him* a **good w off**, 7368
24:27 I *being* in the **w**, the LORD led me to 1870
24:40 send his angel with thee, and prosper thy **w**; 1870
24:42 if now thou do prosper my **w** which I go: 1870
24:48 which had led me in the right **w** to take my 1870
24:56 seeing the LORD hath prospered my **w**; 1870
24:61 the servant took Rebekah, and went his **w**. NIH
24:62 Isaac came from the **w** of the well Lahai-roi; 935
25:34 and drink, and rose up, and went his **w**: NIH
28:20 will keep me in this **w** that I go, and 1870
32: 1 Jacob went on his **w**, and the angels of God 1870
33:16 So Esau returned that day on his **w** unto 1870
35: 3 and was with me in the **w** which I went. 1870
35:16 a **little w** to come to Ephrath: 776+3530+1886.1
35:19 and was buried in the **w** to Ephrath, 1870
38:14 open place, which *is* by the **w** to Timnath; 1870
38:16 he turned unto her by the **w**, and said, 1870
38:21 *is* the harlot, that *was* openly by the **w side**? 1870
42:25 and to give them provision for the **w**: 1870
42:38 if mischief befall him by the **w** in the which 1870
45:21 and gave them provision for the **w**. 1870
45:23 and bread and meat for his father by the **w**. 1870
45:24 unto them, See that ye fall not out by the **w**. 1870
48: 7 died by me in the land of Canaan in the **w**, 1870
48: 7 but a little **w** to come unto Ephrath: 776
48: 7 I buried her there in the **w** of Ephrath; 1870
49:17 Dan shall be a serpent by the **w**, an adder in 1870
Ex 2:12 he looked **this w** and that way, and 3541
2:12 he looked this way and **that w**, and 3541
4:24 it came to pass by the **w** in the inn, that 1870
5:20 and Aaron, who stood **in the w**, 7125+3807.1
13:17 that God led them not *through* the **w** of 1870
13:18 *through* the **w** of the wilderness of the Red 1870
13:21 in a pillar of a cloud, to lead them the **w**; 1870
18: 8 travail that had come upon them by the **w**, 1870
18:20 shalt shew them the **w** *wherein* they must 1870
18:27 and he **went** his **w** into his own land. 1980
23:20 to keep thee in the **w**, and to bring thee into 1870
32: 8 out of the **w** which I commanded them: 1870
33: 3 lest I consume thee in the **w**. 1870
33:13 shew me now thy **w**, that I may know thee, 1870
Nu 13:17 Get you up this **w** southward, and go up into NIH
14:25 get you *into* the wilderness *by* the **w** of 1870
20:17 we will go *by* the king's *high* **w**, we will 1870
20:19 said unto him, We will go by the **high w**: 4546
21: 1 heard *tell* that Israel came *by* the **w** of 1870
21: 4 they journeyed from mount Hor *by* the **w** of 1870
21: 4 was much discouraged because of the **w**. 1870
21:22 *but* we will go along by the king's *high* **w**, 1870
21:33 and went up *by* the **w** of Bashan: 1870
22:22 the angel of the LORD stood in the **w** for 1870
22:23 the angel of the LORD standing in the **w**, 1870
22:23 the ass turned aside out of the **w**, and 1870
22:23 smote the ass, to turn her *into* the **w**. 1870
22:26 where *was* no **w** to turn *either to* the right 1870
22:31 the angel of the LORD standing in the **w**, 1870
22:32 because *thy* **w** is perverse before me: 1870
22:34 for I knew not that thou stoodest in the **w** 1870
24:25 to his place: and Balak also went his **w**. 1870
Dt 1: 2 the **w** of mount Seir unto Kadesh-barnea.) 1870
1:19 which you saw *by* the **w** of the mountain of 1870
1:22 bring us word again by what **w** we must go 1870
1:31 doth bear his son, in all the **w** that ye went, 1870
1:33 Who went in the **w** before you, to search 1870
1:33 to shew you by what **w** ye should go, and 1870
1:40 into the wilderness *by* the **w** of the Red sea. 1870
2: 1 into the wilderness *by* the **w** of the Red sea, 1870
2: 8 through the **w** of the plain from Elath, and 1870
2: 8 passed *by* the **w** of the wilderness of Moab. 1870
2:27 I will go along by the **high w**, I will neither 1870
3: 1 we turned, and went up the **w** to Bashan: 1870

W

Dt 6: 7 when thou walkest by the w, and when thou 1870
8: 2 thou shalt remember all the w which 1870
9:12 out of the w which I commanded them; 1870
9:16 ye had turned aside quickly out of the w 1870
11:19 when thou walkest by the w, when thou 1870
11:28 turn aside out of the w which I command 1870
11:30 by the w where the sun goeth down, in 1870
13: 5 to thrust thee out of the w which 1870
14:24 if the w be too long for thee, so that thou 1870
17:16 Ye shall henceforth return no more that w. 1870
19: 3 Thou shalt prepare thee a w, and divide 1870
19: 6 because the w is long, and slay him; 1870
22: 4 brother's ass or his ox fall down by the w, 1870
22: 6 to be before thee in the w in any tree, 1870
23: 4 you not with bread and with water in the w, 1870
24: 9 LORD thy God did unto Miriam by the w, 1870
25:17 what Amalek did unto thee by the w, 1870
25:18 How he met thee by the w, and smote 1870
27:18 maketh the blind to wander out of the w. 1870
28: 7 they shall come out against thee one w, and 1870
28:25 thou shalt go out one w against them, and 1870
28:68 by the w where *of* I spake unto thee, 1870
31:29 turn aside from the w which I have 1870
Jos 1: 8 for then thou shalt make thy w prosperous, 1870
2: 7 the men pursued after them the w to Jordan 1870
2:16 and afterward may ye go your w. 1870
2:22 pursuers sought *them* throughout all the w, 1870
3: 4 that ye may know the w by which ye must 1870
3: 4 for ye have not passed *this* w heretofore. 1870
5: 4 of war, died in the wilderness by the w, 1870
5: 5 by the w as they came forth out of Egypt, 1870
5: 7 they had not circumcised them by the w. 1870
8:15 and fled *by* the w of the wilderness. 1870
8:20 they had no power to flee this w or that w: 2008
8:20 had no power to flee this way or that w: 2008
10:10 chased them *along* the w that goeth up to 1870
12: 3 sea on the east, the w to Beth-jeshimoth; 1870
23:14 *this* day I am going the w of all the earth: 1870
24:17 preserved us in all the w wherein we went, 1870
Jdg 2:17 they turned quickly out of the w which 1870
2:19 own doings, nor from their stubborn w. 1870
2:22 whether they will keep the w of 1870
5:10 ye that sit in judgment, and walk by the w. 1870
8:11 Gideon went up *by* the w of them that 1870
9:25 they robbed all that came along *that* w by 1870
18: 5 that we may know whether our w which we 1870
18: 6 before the LORD *is* your w wherein ye 1870
18:22 *And* when they were a good w from 7368
18:26 the children of Dan went their w: and 1870
19: 5 a morsel of bread, and afterward go your w. NIH
19: 9 to morrow get you early on your w, that 1870
19:14 they passed on and went *their* w; and NIH
19:27 of the house, and went out to go his w: 1870
20:42 men of Israel unto the w of the wilderness; 1870
Ru 1: 7 they went on the w to return unto the land 1870
1:12 go *your* w; for I am too old to have a NIH
1Sa 1:18 So the woman went her w, and did eat, and 1870
6: 9 if it goeth up *by* the w of his own coast *to* 1870
6:12 the kine took the straight w to the way of 1870
6:12 the kine took the straight way to the w of 1870
9: 6 peradventure he can shew us our w that we 1870
9: 8 I give to the man of God, to tell us our w. 1870
12:23 I will teach you the good and the right w: 1870
13:17 one company turned unto the w that leadeth 1870
13:18 another company turned the w to 1870
13:18 another company turned *to* the w of 1870
15: 2 how he laid *wait* for him in the w, when he 1870
15:20 have gone the w which the LORD sent 1870
17:52 Philistines fell down by the w to Shaaraim, 1870
20:22 go *thy* w: for the LORD hath sent thee NIH
24: 3 he came to the sheepcotes by the w, where 1870
24: 7 rose up out of the cave, and went on *his* w. 1870
25:12 So David's young men turned their w, and 1870
26: 3 which *is* before Jeshimon, by the w. 1870
26:25 So David went on his w, and Saul returned 1870
28:22 have strength, when thou goest on *thy* w. 1870
30: 2 carried *them* away, and went on their w. 1870
2Sa 2:24 that *lieth* before Giah *by* the w of 1870
13:30 it came to pass, while they *were* in the w, 1870
13:34 there came much people by the w of the hill 1870
15: 2 and stood beside the w of the gate: 1870
15:23 toward the w of the wilderness. 1870
16:13 as David and his men went by the w, 1870
18:23 Ahimaaz ran *by* the w of the plain, and 1870
19:36 Thy servant will go a little *w* over Jordan NIH
22:31 *As for* God, his w *is* perfect; the word of 1870
22:33 *and* power: and he maketh my w perfect. 1870
1Ki 1:49 and rose up, and went every man his w. 1870
2: 2 I go the w of all the earth: be thou strong 1870
2: 4 saying, If thy children take heed to their w, 1870
8:25 so that thy children take heed to their w, 1870
8:32 the wicked, to bring his w upon his head; 1870
8:36 that thou teach them the good w wherein 1870
11:29 Ahijah the Shilonite found him in the w; 1870
13: 9 nor turn again by the *same* w that thou 1870
13:10 So he went another w, and returned not by 1870
13:10 returned not by the w that he came to 1870
13:12 father said unto them, What w went he? 1870
13:12 For his sons had seen what w the man of 1870
13:17 nor turn again to go by the w that thou 1870
13:24 a lion met him by the w, and slew him: 1870
13:24 his carcase was cast in the w, and the ass 1870
13:25 saw the carcase cast in the w, and the lion 1870
13:26 him back from the w heard *thereof,* he said, 1870
13:28 he went and found his carcase cast in the w, 1870
13:33 Jeroboam returned not from his evil w, 1870
15:26 walked in the w of his father, and in his sin 1870
15:34 walked in the w of Jeroboam and in his sin 1870
16: 2 thou hast walked in the w of Jeroboam, and 1870
16:19 in walking in the w of Jeroboam, and in his 1870
16:26 For he walked in all the w of Jeroboam 1870
18: 6 Ahab went one w by himself, and 1870
18: 6 Obadiah went another w by himself. 1870
18: 7 as Obadiah was in the w, behold Elijah met 1870
19:15 return on thy w to the wilderness of 1870
1Ki 20:38 waited for the king by the w, and 1870
22:24 Which w went the spirit of 335+2088
22:52 walked in the w of his father, and in 1870
22:52 in the w of his mother, and in the way of 1870
22:52 in the w of Jeroboam the son of Nebat, 1870
2Ki 2:23 as he was going up by the w, there came 1870
3: 8 he said, Which w shall we go up? And he 1870
3: 8 The w through the wilderness of Edom. 1870
3:20 there came water by the w of Edom, and 1870
4:29 go *thy* w: if thou meet any man, salute him NIH
5:19 in peace. So he departed from him a little w. 776
6:19 This *is* not the w, neither *is* this the city: 1870
7:15 all the w *was* full *of* garments and vessels, 1870
8:18 he walked in the w of the kings of Israel, 1870
8:27 he walked in the w of the house of Ahab, 1870
9:27 *this,* he fled *by* the w of the garden house. 1870
10:12 as he *was at* the shearing house in the w, 1870
11:16 she went *by* the w by the which the horses 1870
11:19 came *by* the w of the gate of the guard *to* 1870
16: 3 he walked in the w of the kings of Israel, 1870
19:28 I will turn thee back by the w by which 1870
19:33 By the w that he came, *by the same* shall he 1870
21:21 he walked in all the w that his father 1870
21:22 and walked not in the w of the LORD. 1870
22: 2 walked in all the w of David his father, and 1870
25: 4 all the men of war *fled* by night *by* the w of 1870
25: 4 and *the king* went the w toward the plain. 1870
2Ch 6:16 that thy children take heed to their w to 1870
6:23 by recompensing his w upon his own head; 1870
6:27 when thou hast taught them the good w, 1870
6:34 enemies by the w that thou shalt send them, 1870
11:17 for three years they walked in the w of 1870
18:23 Which w went the spirit of the LORD 1870
20:32 he walked in the w of Asa his father, and 1870
21: 6 he walked in the w of the kings of Israel, 1870
21:13 hast walked in the w of the kings of Israel, 1870
Ezr 8:21 to seek of him a right w for us, and for our 1870
8:22 to help us against the enemy in the w: 1870
8:31 and of such as lay in wait by the w. 1870
Ne 8:10 Go *your* w, eat the fat, and drink the sweet, NIH
8:12 all the people went *their* w to eat, and NIH
9:12 to give them light in the w wherein they 1870
9:19 from them by day, to lead them in the w; 1870
9:19 and the w wherein they should go. 1870
Est 4:17 So Mordecai went his w, and did according NIH
Job 3:23 *Why is light given* to a man whose w is hid, 1870
6:18 The paths of their w are turned aside; 1870
8:19 this *is* the joy of his w, and out of the earth 1870
12:24 wander in a wilderness *where there is* no w. 1870
16:22 I shall go the w *whence* I shall not return. 734
17: 9 The righteous also shall hold on his w, and 1870
18:10 in the ground, and a trap for him in the w. 5410
19: 8 He hath fenced up my w that I cannot pass, 734
19:12 raise up their w against me, and 1870
21:29 Have ye not asked them that go by the w? 1870
21:31 Who shall declare his w to his face? and 1870
22:15 Hast thou marked the old w which wicked 734
23:10 he knoweth the w that I take: *when* he hath 1870
23:11 his w have I kept, and not declined. 1870
24: 4 They turn the needy out of the w: the poor 1870
24:18 he beholdeth not the w of the vineyards. 1870
24:24 they are taken out of the w as all *other,* 7092
28:23 God understandeth the w thereof, and 1870
28:26 and a w for the lightning of the thunder: 1870
29:25 I chose out their w, and sat chief, and 1870
31: 7 If my step hath turned out of the w, and 1870
36:23 Who hath enjoined him his w? or who can 1870
38:19 Where *is* the w *where* light dwelleth? and 1870
38:24 By what w is the light parted, 1870
38:25 or a w for the lightning of thunder; 1870
Ps 1: 1 nor standeth in the w of sinners, nor sitteth 1870
1: 6 For the LORD knoweth the w of 1870
1: 6 but the w of the ungodly shall perish. 1870
2:12 lest he be angry, and ye perish *from* the w, 1870
5: 8 make thy w straight before my face. 1870
18:30 *As for* God, his w *is* perfect: the word of 1870
18:32 *with* strength, and maketh my w perfect. 1870
25: 8 will he teach sinners in the w. 1870
25: 9 and the meek will he teach his w. 1870
25:12 him shall he teach in the w *that* he shall 1870
27:11 Teach me thy w, O LORD, and lead me in 1870
32: 8 and teach thee in the w which thou shalt go: 1870
35: 3 stop *the* w against them that persecute me. NIH
35: 6 Let their w be dark and slippery: and let 1870
36: 4 he setteth himself in a w *that is* not good; 1870
37: 5 Commit thy w unto the LORD; trust also 1870
37: 7 because of him who prospereth *in* his w, 1870
37:23 by the LORD: and he delighteth in his w. 1870
37:34 keep his w, and he shall exalt thee to inherit 1870
44:18 neither have our steps declined from thy w; 734
49:13 This their w *is* their folly: yet their posterity 1870
67: 2 That thy w may be known upon earth, 1870
77:13 Thy w, O God, *is* in the sanctuary: who *is* 1870
77:19 Thy w *is* in the sea, and thy path in 1870
78:50 He made a w to his anger; he spared not 5410
80:12 that all they which pass by the w do pluck 1870
85:13 and shall set *us* in the w of his steps. 1870
86:11 Teach me thy w, O LORD; I will walk in 1870
89:41 All that pass by the w spoil him: he is a 1870
101: 2 I will behave myself wisely in a perfect w. 1870
101: 6 he that walketh in a perfect w, he shall 1870
102:23 He weakened my strength in the w; 1870
107: 4 wandered in the wilderness in a solitary w; 1870
107: 7 he led them forth by the right w, that *they* 1870
107:40 in the wilderness, *where there is* no w. 1870
110: 7 He shall drink of the brook in the w: 1870
119: 1 Blessed *are* the undefiled in the w, 1870
119: 9 shall a young man cleanse his w? 734
119:14 I have rejoiced in the w of thy testimonies, 1870
119:27 Make me to understand the w of thy 1870
119:29 Remove from me the w of lying: and 1870
119:30 I have chosen the w of truth: 1870
119:32 I will run the w of thy commandments, 1870
119:33 Teach me, O LORD, the w of thy statutes; 1870
119:37 *and* quicken thou me in thy w. 1870
Ps 119:101 I have refrained my feet from every evil w, 734
119:104 I hate every false w. 734
119:128 *things* to be right; *and* I hate every false w. 734
139:24 see if *there be any* wicked w in me, and 1870
139:24 and lead me in the w everlasting. 1870
140: 5 they have spread a net by the w side; 3027+4570
142: 3 In the w wherein I walked have they privily 734
143: 8 cause me to know the w wherein I should 1870
146: 9 the w of the wicked he turneth upside 1870
Pr 1:15 My son, walk not thou in the w with them; 1870
1:31 shall they eat of the fruit of their own w, 1870
2: 8 and preserveth the w of his saints. 1870
2:12 To deliver thee from the w of the evil *man,* 1870
2:20 That thou mayest walk in the w of good 1870
3:23 shalt thou walk *in* thy w safely, and 1870
4:11 I have taught thee in the w of wisdom; 1870
4:14 and go not in the w of evil *men.* 1870
4:19 The w of the wicked *is* as darkness: 1870
5: 8 Remove thy w far from her, and come not 1870
6:23 and reproofs of instruction *are* the w of life: 1870
7: 8 her corner; and he went the w to her house, 1870
7:27 Her house *is* the w to hell, going down to 1870
8: 2 standeth in the top of high places by the w, 1870
8:13 the evil w, and the froward mouth, do I 1870
8:20 I lead in the w of righteousness, in the midst 734
8:22 possessed me *in* the beginning of his w, 1870
9: 6 and live; and go in the w of understanding. 1870
10:17 He *is in* the w of life that keepeth 734
10:29 The w of the LORD *is* strength to 1870
11: 5 of the perfect shall direct his w: 1870
11:20 *such as are* upright in *their* w *are* his 1870
12:15 The w of a fool *is* right in his own eyes: but 1870
12:26 but the w of the wicked seduceth them. 1870
12:28 In the w of righteousness *is* life; and *in* 734
13: 6 keepeth *him that is* upright in the w: 1870
13:15 but the w of transgressors *is* hard. 1870
14: 8 of the prudent *is* to understand his w: 1870
14:12 There is a w which seemeth right unto a 1870
15: 9 The w of the wicked *is* an abomination 1870
15:10 *is* grievous unto him that forsaketh the w: 734
15:19 The w of the slothful *man is* as a hedge of 1870
15:19 but the w of the righteous *is* made plain. 734
15:24 The w of life *is* above to the wise, that *he* 734
16: 9 A man's heart deviseth his w: but 1870
16:17 he that keepeth his w preserveth his soul. 1870
16:25 There is a w that seemeth right unto a man, 1870
16:29 and leadeth him into the w *that is* not good. 1870
16:31 *if* it be found in the w of righteousness. 1870
19: 3 The foolishness of man perverteth his w: 1870
20:14 but when he is gone his w, then he boasteth. 235
20:24 how can a man then understand his own w? 1870
21: 2 Every w of a man *is* right in his own eyes: 1870
21: 8 The w of man *is* froward and strange: but 1870
21:16 The man that wandereth out of the w of 1870
21:29 but *as for* the upright, he directeth his w. 1870
22: 5 *and* snares *are* in the w of the froward: 1870
22: 6 a child in the w he should go: 1870+5921+6310
23:19 and be wise, and guide thine heart in the w. 1870
26:13 slothful *man* saith, *There is* a lion in the w; 1870
28:10 the righteous to go astray in an evil w, 1870
29:27 *he that is* upright in the w *is* abomination to 1870
30:19 The w of an eagle in the air; the way of a 1870
30:19 in the air; the w of a serpent upon a rock; 1870
30:19 the w of a ship in the midst of the sea; and 1870
30:19 of the sea; and the w of a man with a maid. 1870
30:20 Such *is* the w of an adulterous woman; 1870
Ecc 9: 7 Go *thy* w, eat thy bread with joy, and NIH
10: 3 when he that is a fool walketh by the w, 1870
11: 5 As thou knowest not what *is* the w of 1870
12: 5 fears *shall be* in the w, and the almond tree 1870
SS 1: 8 go thy w forth by the footsteps of 3318
Isa 3:12 *thee* to err, and destroy the w of thy paths. 1870
8:11 *I* should not walk in the w of this people, 1870
9: 1 grievously afflict *her by* the w of the sea, 1870
15: 5 for *in* the w of Horonaim they shall raise up 1870
26: 7 The w of the just *is* uprightness: thou, 734
26: 8 Yea, *in* the w of thy judgments, O LORD, 734
28: 7 and through strong drink are out of the w; 8582
28: 7 they are out of the w through strong drink; 8582
30:11 Get ye out of the w, turn aside out of 1870
30:21 saying, This *is* the w, walk ye in it, when ye 1870
35: 8 a w, and it shall be called The way of 1870
35: 8 and it shall be called The w of holiness; 1870
37:29 I will turn thee back by the w by which 1870
37:34 By the w that he came, *by the same* shall he 1870
40: 3 Prepare ye the w of the LORD, 1870
40:14 and shewed to him the w of understanding? 1870
40:27 My w is hid from the LORD, and 1870
41: 3 *even by* the w *that* he had not gone with his 734
42:16 I will bring the blind by a w *that* they knew 1870
43:16 which maketh a w in the sea, and a path in 1870
43:19 I will even make a w in the wilderness, *and* 1870
48:15 and he shall make his w prosperous. 1870
48:17 which leadeth thee by the w *that* thou 1870
49:11 I will make all my mountains a w, and 1870
51:10 that hath made the depths of the sea a w for 1870
53: 6 we have turned every one to his own w; 1870
55: 7 Let the wicked forsake his w, and 1870
56:11 they all look to their own w, every one for 1870
57:10 Thou art wearied in the greatness of thy w; 1870
57:14 Cast ye up, cast ye up, prepare the w, 1870
57:14 take up the stumblingblock out of the w of 1870
57:17 he went on frowardly in the w of his heart. 1870
59: 8 The w of peace they know not; and *there is* 1870
62:10 prepare you the w of the people; cast up, 1870
65: 2 which walketh *in* a w *that was* not good, 1870
Jer 2:17 thy God, when he led thee by the w? 1870
2:18 now what hast thou to do in the w of Egypt, 1870
2:18 or what hast thou to do in the w of Assyria, 1870
2:23 see thy w in the valley, know what thou 1870
2:33 Why trimmest thou thy w to seek love? 1870
2:36 thou about *so* much to change thy w? 1870
3:21 for they have perverted their w, *and* 1870
4: 7 the destroyer of the Gentiles is on his w; 5265
4:18 Thy w and thy doings have procured these 1870

Jer 5: 4 for they know not the **w** of the LORD, 1870
5: 5 for they have known the **w** of the LORD, 1870
6:16 where *is* the good **w**, and walk therein, 1870
6:25 not forth *into* the field, nor walk by the **w**; 1870
6:27 that thou mayest know and try their **w**. 1870
10: 2 Learn not the **w** of the heathen, and be not 1870
10:23 I know that the **w** of man *is* not in himself: 1870
12: 1 Wherefore doth the **w** of the wicked 1870
18:11 return ye now every one from his evil **w**, 1870
18:15 to walk *in* paths, *in* a **w** not cast up; 1870
21: 8 I set before you the **w** of life, and the way 1870
21: 8 you the way of life, and the **w** of death. 1870
23:12 Wherefore their **w** shall be unto them as 1870
23:22 should have turned them from their evil **w**, 1870
25: 5 ye again now every one from his evil **w**, 1870
25:35 the shepherds shall have no **w to flee**, 4498
26: 3 and turn every man from his evil **w**, 1870
28:11 And the prophet Jeremiah went his **w**. 1870
31: 9 walk by the rivers of waters in a straight **w**, 1870
31:21 *even* the **w** *which* thou wentest: 1870
32:39 one **w**, that *they* may fear me for ever, for 1870
35:15 Return ye now every man from his evil **w**, 1870
36: 3 they may return every man from his evil **w**; 1870
36: 7 and will return every one from his evil **w**: 1870
39: 4 *by* the **w** of the king's garden, by the gate 1870
39: 4 and he went out the **w** of the plain. 1870
42: 3 may shew us the **w** wherein we may walk, 1870
48:19 of Aroer, stand by the **w** and espy; 1870
50: 5 They shall ask the **w** *to* Zion with their 1870
52: 7 went forth out of the city by night *by* the **w** 1870
52: 7 and they went *by* the **w** of the plain. 1870
Eze 3:18 to warn the wicked from his wicked **w**, 1870
3:19 nor from his wicked **w**, he shall die in his 1870
7:27 I will do unto them after their **w**, and 1870
8: 5 lift up thine eyes now the **w** towards 1870
8: 5 So I lift up mine eyes the **w** toward 1870
9: 2 six men came from the **w** of the higher 1870
9:10 I will recompense their **w** upon their head. 1870
11:21 I will recompense their **w** upon their own 1870
13:22 *he* should not return from his wicked **w**, 1870
14:22 and ye shall see their **w** and their doings: 1870
16:25 built thy high place at every head of the **w**, 1870
16:27 which are ashamed of thy lewd **w**. 1870
16:31 thine eminent place in the head of every **w**, 1870
16:43 I also will recompense thy **w** upon *thine* 1870
18:25 Yet ye say, The **w** of the Lord is not equal. 1870
18:25 O house of Israel; Is not my **w** equal? 1870
18:29 of Israel, The **w** of the Lord is not equal. 1870
21:16 **Go thee one w or other**, *either* on the right 258
21:19 choose *it*, at the head of the **w** to the city. 1870
21:20 Appoint a **w**, that the sword may come to 1870
21:21 of Babylon stood at the parting of the **w**, 1870
22:31 their own **w** have I recompensed upon their 1870
23:13 she was defiled, *that* they took both one **w**, 1870
23:31 Thou hast walked in the **w** of thy sister; 1870
33: 8 not speak to warn the wicked from his **w**, 1870
33: 9 if thou warn the wicked of his **w** to turn 1870
33: 9 if he do not turn from his **w**, he shall die in 1870
33:11 that the wicked turn from his **w** and live: 1870
33:17 people say, The **w** of the Lord is not equal: 1870
33:17 but *as for* them, their **w** is not equal. 1870
33:20 Yet ye say, The **w** of the Lord is not equal. 1870
36:17 they defiled it by their own **w** and by their 1870
36:17 their **w** was before me as the uncleanness 1870
36:19 according to their **w** and according to their 1870
42: 1 into the utter court, the **w** toward the north: 1870
42: 4 ten cubits breadth inward, a **w** of one cubit; 1870
42:11 the **w** before them *was* like the appearance 1870
42:12 the south *was* a door in the head of the **w**, 1870
42:12 *even* the **w** directly before the wall toward 1870
43: 2 God of Israel came from the **w** of the east: 1870
43: 4 **w** of the gate whose prospect *is* toward 1870
44: 1 he brought me back the **w** of the gate of 1870
44: 3 he shall enter by the **w** of the porch of *that* 1870
44: 3 and shall go out by the **w** of the same. 1870
44: 4 brought he me the **w** of the north gate 1870
46: 2 the prince shall enter by the **w** of the porch 1870
46: 8 he shall go in *by* the **w** of the porch of *that* 1870
46: 8 and he shall go forth by the **w** thereof. 1870
46: 9 he that entereth in *by* the **w** of the north 1870
46: 9 shall go out *by* the **w** of the south gate; 1870
46: 9 he that entereth *by* the **w** of the south gate 1870
46: 9 shall go forth *by* the **w** of the north gate: 1870
46: 9 he shall not return *by* the **w** of the gate 1870
47: 2 brought he me out *of* the **w** of the gate 1870
47: 2 led me about the **w** without unto the utter 1870
47: 2 utter gate *by* the **w** that looketh east*ward;* 1870
47:15 from the great sea, the **w** of Hethlon, as 1870
48: 1 From the north end to the coast of the **w** of 1870
Da 12: 9 he said, Go thy **w**, Daniel: for the words *are* NIH
12:13 go thou thy **w** till the end *be:* for thou shalt NIH
Hos 2: 6 I will hedge up thy **w** with thorns, and 1870
6: 9 the company of priests murder *in* the **w** by 1870
10:13 because thou didst trust in thy **w**, in 1870
13: 7 as a leopard by the **w** will I observe *them:* 1870
Am 2: 7 the poor, and turn aside the **w** of the meek: 1870
Jnh 3: 8 let them turn every one from his evil **w**, and 1870
3:10 that they turned from their evil **w**; 1870
Na 1: 3 the LORD *hath* his **w** in the whirlwind 1870
2: 1 keep the munition, watch the **w**, make *thy* 1870
Zec 10: 2 therefore they went their **w** as a flock, NIH
Mal 2: 8 ye are departed out of the **w**; ye have 1870
3: 1 and he shall prepare the **w** before me: 1870
Mt 2:12 departed into their own country another **w**. 3598
3: 3 Prepare ye the **w** of the Lord, make his 3598
4:15 *by* the **w** of the sea, beyond Jordan, 3598
5:24 there thy gift before the altar, and go thy **w**; NIG
5:25 whiles thou art in the **w** with him; 3598
7:13 for wide *is* the gate, and broad *is* the **w**, 3598
7:14 and narrow *is* the **w**, which leadeth unto 3598
8: 4 See thou tell no *man;* but go thy **w**, NIG
8:13 Jesus said unto the centurion, Go thy **w**; NIG
8:28 so that no *man* might pass by that **w**. 3598
8:30 And there was a **good w off** from them a 3112
10: 5 Go not into the **w** of the Gentiles, and 3598
Mt 11:10 which shall prepare thy **w** before thee. 3598
13: 4 some *seeds* fell by the **w** side, and the fowls 3598
13:19 This is he which received seed by the **w** 3598
13:25 tares among the wheat, and went his **w**. NIG
15:32 them away fasting, lest they faint in the **w**. 3598
20: 4 right I will give you. And they **went** their **w**. 565
20:14 Take *that* thine *is*, and go thy **w**: I will give NIG
20:17 took the twelve disciples apart in the **w**, 3598
20:30 two blind men sitting by the **w** side, 3598
21: 8 multitude spread their garments in the **w**; 3598
21: 8 from the trees, and strawed *them* in the **w**. 3598
21:19 And when he saw a fig tree in the **w**, 3598
21:32 For John came unto you in the **w** of 3598
22:16 art true, and teachest the **w** of God in truth, 3598
22:22 and left him, and went their **w**. NIG
27:65 go your **w**, make *it* as sure as you can. NIG
Mk 1: 2 which shall prepare thy **w** before thee. 3598
1: 3 Prepare ye the **w** of the Lord, make his 3598
1:44 thou say nothing to any *man:* but go thy **w**, NIG
2:11 up thy bed, and go thy **w** into thine house. NIG
4: 4 some fell by the **w side**, and the fowls of 3598
4:15 And these are they by the **w side**, where 3598
7:29 he said unto her, For this saying go thy **w**; NIG
8: 3 their own houses, they will faint by the **w**: 3598
8:27 and by the **w** he asked his disciples, 3598
9:33 ye disputed among yourselves by the **w**? 3598
9:34 for by the **w** they had disputed among 3598
10:17 And when he was gone forth into the **w**, 3598
10:21 go thy **w**, sell whatsoever thou hast, and NIG
10:32 And they were in the **w** going up to 3598
10:52 And Jesus said unto him, Go thy **w**; NIG
10:52 his sight, and followed Jesus in the **w**. 3598
11: 2 Go your **w** into the village over against you: NIG
11: 4 And they went their **w**, and found the colt NIG
11: 8 And many spread their garments in the **w**: 3598
11: 8 off the trees, and strawed *them* in the **w**. 3598
12:12 and they left him, and went their **w**. NIG
12:14 of men, but teachest the **w** of God in truth: 3598
16: 7 But go your **w**, tell his disciples and Peter NIG
Lk 1:79 to guide our feet into the **w** of peace. 3598
3: 4 Prepare ye the **w** of the Lord, make his 3598
4:30 through the midst of them went *his w*, NIG
5:19 And when they could not find by what *w* NIG
7:22 Go *your w*, and tell John what *things* ye NIG
7:27 which shall prepare thy **w** before thee. 3598
8: 5 and as he sowed, some fell by the **w side**; 3598
8:12 Those by the **w side** are they that hear; then 3598
8:39 And he went his **w**, and NIG
9:57 it came to pass *that*, as they went in the **w**, 3598
10: 4 nor shoes: and salute no *man* by the **w**. 3598
10:31 there came down a certain priest that **w**: 3598
12:58 *as thou art* in the **w**, give diligence that *thou* 3598
14:32 Or else, while the other is yet a **great w off**, 4206
15:20 But when he was yet a **great w** off, 3112
17:19 go *thy w*: thy faith hath made thee whole. NIG
18:35 a certain blind man sat by the **w side** 3598
19: 4 tree to see him: for he was to pass that *w*. NIG
19:32 And they that were sent went their **w**, and NIG
19:36 he went, they spread their clothes in the **w**. 3598
20:21 *of any*, but teachest the **w** of God truly: 3598
22: 4 And he went his **w**, and communed with NIG
24:32 while he talked with us by the **w**, and 3598
24:35 they told what *things were done* in the **w**, 3598
Jn 1:23 Make straight the **w** of the Lord, as said 3598
4:28 and went her **w** into the city, and saith to NIG
4:50 saith unto him, Go *thy w*; thy son liveth. NIG
4:50 had spoken unto him, and he went *his w*. NIG
8:21 I go my **w**, and ye shall seek me, and NIG
9: 7 He went his **w** therefore, and washed, and NIG
10: 1 but climbeth up **some other w**, the same is a 237
11:28 she went her **w**, and called Mary her sister NIG
14: 4 whither I go ye know, and the **w** ye know. 3598
14: 5 thou goest; and how can we know the **w**? 3598
14: 6 unto him, I am the **w**, the truth, and the life: 3598
16: 5 But now I go my **w** to him that sent me; and NIG
18: 8 therefore ye seek me, let these go their **w**: NIG
Ac 8:26 go toward the south unto the **w** that goeth 3598
8:36 And as they went on *their* **w**, they came 3598
8:39 no more: and he went *on* his **w** rejoicing. 3598
9: 2 that if he found any of *this* **w**, whether they 3598
9:15 Go *thy w*: for he is a chosen vessel unto me, NIG
9:17 And Ananias went his **w**, and entered into NIG
9:17 that appeared unto thee in the **w** as thou 3598
9:27 them how he had seen the Lord in the **w**, 3598
15: 3 And being **brought on** their **w** by 4311
16:17 which shew unto us the **w** of salvation. 3598
18:25 This *man* was instructed in the **w** of 3598
18:26 expounded unto him the **w** of God more 3598
19: 9 spake evil of *that* **w** before the multitude, 3598
19:23 time there arose no small stir about *that* **w**. 3598
21: 5 we departed and went *our w*; and *they* all NIG
21: 5 *our way;* and *they* all brought us on our **w**, NIG
22: 4 And I persecuted this **w** unto the death, 3598
24:14 that after the **w** which they call heresy, so 3598
24:22 having more perfect knowledge of *that* **w**, 3598
24:25 and answered, Go *thy w* for *this* time; NIG
25: 3 laying wait in the **w** to kill him. 3598
26:13 O king, I saw in the **w** a light from heaven, 3598
Ro 3: 2 Much every **w**: chiefly, because that unto 5158
3:12 They are all **gone out of the w**, they are 1578
3:17 And the **w** of peace have they not known: 3598
14:13 **put** a stumblingblock or an occasion to fall
in *his* brother's **w**. 5087
15:24 to be **brought on** my **w** thitherward by you, 4311
1Co 10:13 the temptation also make a **w to escape**, 1545
12:31 yet shew I unto you a more excellent **w**. 3598
16: 7 For I will not see you now by the **w**; but I 3938
2Co 1:16 of you to be **brought on** *my* **w** toward 4311
Php 1:18 notwithstanding, every **w**, whether in 5158
Col 2:14 and took it out of the **w**, nailing it to *his* 3319
1Th 3:11 Lord Jesus Christ, direct our **w** unto you. 3598
2Th 2: 7 *will let*, until he be taken out of the **w**. 3319
Heb 5: 2 and on them that are **out of the w**; 4105
9: 8 that the **w** into the holiest *of all* was not yet 3598
10:20 *By* a new and living **w**, which he hath 3598
Heb 12:13 *that which is* lame be **turned out of the w**; 1624
Jas 1:24 and **goeth** his **w**, and straightway forgetteth 565
2:25 and had sent *them* out another **w**? 3598
5:20 error of his **w** shall save a soul from death, 3598
2Pe 2: 2 by reason of whom the **w** of truth shall be 3598
2:15 Which have forsaken the right **w**, and 3598
2:15 following the **w** of Balaam *the son* of 3598
2:21 not to have known the **w** of righteousness, 3598
3: 1 up your pure minds **by w of** remembrance: 1722
Jude 1:11 for they have gone in the **w** of Cain, and 3598
Rev 16:12 that the **w** of the kings of the east might be 3598

WAYFARING (6) [FARE, WAY]

Jdg 19:17 he saw a **w** man in the street of the city: 732
2Sa 12: 4 to dress for the **w man** that was come unto 732
Isa 33: 8 lie waste, the **w man** ceaseth: 734+5674
35: 8 the **w men**, though fools, shall not 1870+1980
Jer 9: 2 in the wilderness a lodging place of **w men**; 732
14: 8 as a **w man** *that* turneth aside to tarry for a 732

WAYMARKS (1) [MARK, WAY]

Jer 31:21 Set thee up **w**, make thee high heaps: 6725

WAYS (205) [WAY]

Ge 19: 2 ye shall rise up early, and go on your **w**. 1870
Lev 20: 4 **any w hide** their eyes from the man, 5956+5956
26:22 and your *high* **w** shall be desolate. 1870
Nu 30:15 if he shall **any w make** them **void** 6565+6565
Dt 5:33 You shall walk in all the **w** which 1870
8: 6 thy God, to walk in his **w**, and to fear him. 1870
10:12 to walk in all his **w**, and to love him, and 1870
11:22 to walk in all his **w**, and to cleave unto him; 1870
19: 9 LORD thy God, and to walk ever in his **w**; 1870
26:17 to walk in his **w**, and to keep his statutes, 1870
28: 7 thee one way, and flee before thee seven **w**. 1870
28: 9 of the LORD thy God, and walk in his **w**. 1870
28:25 and flee seven **w** before them: 1870
28:29 and thou shalt not prosper in thy **w**: 1870
30:16 to walk in his **w**, and to keep his 1870
32: 4 for all his **w** *are* judgment: a God of truth 1870
Jos 22: 5 to walk in all his **w**, and to keep his 1870
1Sa 8: 3 his sons walked not in his **w**, but 1870
8: 5 art old, and thy sons walk not in thy **w**: 1870
18:14 David behaved himself wisely in all his **w**; 1870
2Sa 22:22 For I have kept the **w** of the LORD, and 1870
1Ki 2: 3 to walk in his **w**, to keep his statutes, *and* 1870
3:14 if thou wilt walk in my **w**, to keep my 1870
8:39 and give to every man according to his **w**, 1870
8:58 to walk in all his **w**, and to keep his 1870
11:33 have not walked in my **w**, to do *that* which 1870
11:38 wilt walk in my **w**, and do that *is* right in 1870
22:43 walked in all the **w** of Asa his father; 1870
2Ki 17:13 Turn ye from your evil **w**, and keep my 1870
2Ch 6:30 unto every man according unto all his **w**, 1870
6:31 to walk in thy **w**, so long as they live in 1870
7:14 my face, and turn from their wicked **w**; 1870
13:22 acts of Abijah, and his **w**, and his sayings, 1870
17: 3 he walked in the first **w** of his father David, 1870
17: 6 his heart was lift up in the **w** of 1870
21:12 Because thou hast not walked in the **w** of 1870
21:12 nor in the **w** of Asa king of Judah, 1870
22: 3 He also walked in the **w** of the house of 1870
27: 6 he prepared his **w** before the LORD his 1870
27: 7 acts of Jotham, and all his wars, and his **w**, 1870
28: 2 For he walked in the **w** of the kings of 1870
28:26 Now the rest of his acts and of all his **w**, 1870
32:13 **any w able** to deliver their lands out 3201+3201
34: 2 walked in the **w** of David his father, and 1870
Job 4: 6 thy hope; and the uprightness of thy **w**? 1870
13:15 but I will maintain mine own **w** before him. 1870
21:14 for we desire not the knowledge of thy **w**. 1870
22: 3 *is it* gain *to him*, that thou makest thy **w** 1870
22:28 and the light shall shine upon thy **w**. 1870
24:13 they know not the **w** thereof, nor abide in 1870
24:23 he resteth; yet his eyes *are* upon their **w**. 1870
26:14 Lo, these *are* parts of his **w**: but how little a 1870
30:12 they raise up against me the **w** of their 734
31: 4 Doth not he see my **w**, and count all my 1870
34:11 cause every man to find according to *his* **w**. 734
34:21 For his eyes *are* upon the **w** of man, and 1870
34:27 and would not consider any of his **w**: 1870
40:19 He *is* the chief of the **w** of God: he that 1870
Ps 10: 5 His **w** are always grievous; thy judgments 1870
18:21 For I have kept the **w** of the LORD, and 1870
25: 4 Shew me thy **w**, O LORD; teach me thy 1870
39: 1 I said, I will take heed to my **w**, that *I* sin 1870
51:13 *Then* will I teach transgressors thy **w**; and 1870
81:13 unto me, *and* Israel had walked in my **w**! 1870
84: 5 in thee; in whose heart *are* the **w** *of them.* 4546
91:11 charge over thee, to keep thee in all thy **w**. 1870
95:10 *their* heart, and they have not known my **w**: 1870
103: 7 He made known his **w** unto Moses, his acts 1870
119: 3 also do no iniquity: they walk in his **w**. 1870
119: 5 O that my **w** were directed to keep thy 1870
119:15 in thy precepts, and have respect unto thy **w**. 734
119:26 I have declared my **w**, and thou heardest 1870
119:59 I thought on my **w**, and turned my feet unto 1870
119:168 for all my **w** *are* before thee. 1870
125: 5 for such as turn aside *unto* their **crooked w**, 6128
128: 1 feareth the LORD; that walketh in his **w**. 1870
138: 5 they shall sing in the **w** of the LORD: 1870
139: 3 and art acquainted *with* all my **w**. 1870
145:17 The LORD *is* righteous in all his **w**, and 1870
Pr 1:19 So *are* the **w** of every one that is greedy of 734
2:13 to walk in the **w** of darkness; 1870
2:15 Whose **w** *are* crooked, and *they* froward in 734
3: 6 In all thy **w** acknowledge him, and he shall 1870
3:17 Her **w** *are* ways of pleasantness, and all her 1870
3:17 Her ways *are* **w** of pleasantness, and all her 1870
3:31 the oppressor, and choose none of his **w**. 1870
4:26 of thy feet, and let all thy **w** be established. 1870
5: 6 her **w** are moveable, *that* thou canst not 4570
5:21 For the **w** of man *are* before the eyes of 1870
6: 6 thou sluggard; consider her **w**, and be wise: 1870

Ps 7:25 Let not thine heart decline to her **w**, go not 1870
8:32 for blessed *are they that* keep my **w**. 1870
9:15 To call passengers who go right *on* their **w**: 734
10: 9 but he that perverteth his **w** shall be known. 1870
14: 2 he that is perverse in his **w** despiseth him. 1870
14:12 but the end thereof *are* the **w** of death. 1870
14:14 in heart shall be filled with his own **w**: 1870
16: 2 All the **w** of a man *are* clean in his own 1870
16: 7 When a man's **w** please the LORD, 1870
16:25 but the end thereof *are* the **w** of death. 1870
17:23 of the bosom to pervert the **w** of judgment. 734
19:16 *but* he that despiseth his **w** shall die. 1870
22:25 Lest thou learn his **w**, and get a snare to thy 734
23:26 and let thine eyes observe my **w**. 1870
28: 6 than *he that is* perverse in *his* **w**, though he 1870
28:18 *he that is* perverse in *his* **w** shall fall at 1870
31: 3 nor thy **w** to *that which* destroyeth kings. 1870
31:27 She looketh well to the **w** of her household, 1979
Ecc 11: 9 walk in the **w** of thine heart, and in 1870
SS 3: 2 the city in the streets and in the **broad w**, 7339
Isa 2: 3 he will teach us of his **w**, and we will walk 1870
42:24 for they would not walk in his **w**, 1870
45:13 in righteousness, and I will direct all his **w**: 1870
49: 9 They shall feed in the **w**, and their pastures 1870
55: 8 neither *are* your **w** my ways, saith 1870
55: 8 neither *are* your ways my **w**, saith 1870
55: 9 so are my **w** higher than your ways, and 1870
55: 9 so are my ways higher than your **w**, and 1870
57:18 I have seen his **w**, and will heal him: I will 1870
58: 2 seek me daily, and delight to know my **w**, 1870
58:13 shalt honour him, not doing thine own **w**, 1870
63:17 why hast thou made us to err from thy **w**, 1870
64: 5 *those that* remember thee in thy **w**: 1870
66: 3 they have chosen their own **w**, and 1870
Jer 2:23 *art* a swift dromedary traversing her **w**; 1870
2:33 thou also taught the wicked ones thy **w**. 1870
3: 2 In the **w** hast thou sat for them, as 1870
3:13 hast scattered thy **w** to the strangers under 1870
6:16 Stand ye in the **w**, and see, and ask for 1870
7: 3 Amend your **w** and your doings, and I will 1870
7: 5 For if you throughly amend your **w** and 1870
7:23 walk ye in all the **w** that I have commanded 1870
12:16 if they will diligently learn the **w** of my 1870
15: 7 *sith* they return not from their **w**. 1870
16:17 For mine eyes *are* upon all their **w**: they are 1870
17:10 even to give every man according to his **w**, 1870
18:11 and make your **w** and your doings good. 1870
18:15 stumble in their **w** *from* the ancient paths, 1870
23:12 be unto them as slippery *w* in the darkness: NIH
26:13 Therefore now amend your **w** and 1870
32:19 for thine eyes *are* open upon all the **w** of 1870
32:19 to give every one according to his **w**, and 1870
La 1: 4 The **w** of Zion do mourn, because 1870
3: 9 He hath inclosed my **w** with hewn stone, 1870
3:11 He hath turned aside my **w**, and pulled me 1870
3:40 Let us search and try our **w**, and turn again 1870
Eze 7: 3 will judge thee according to thy **w**, and 1870
7: 4 I will recompense thy **w** upon thee, and 1870
7: 8 I will judge thee according to thy **w**, and 1870
7: 9 I will recompense thee according to thy **w** 1870
14:23 when ye see their **w** and their doings: 1870
16:47 Yet hast thou not walked after their **w**, 1870
16:47 wast corrupted more than they in all thy **w**. 1870
16:61 thou shalt remember thy **w**, and 1870
18:23 *and* not that he should return from his **w**, 1870
18:25 not my way equal? are not your **w** unequal? 1870
18:29 O house of Israel, are not my **w** equal? 1870
18:29 my ways equal? are not your **w** unequal? 1870
18:30 of Israel, every one according to his **w**, 1870
20:43 there shall ye remember your **w**, and all 1870
20:44 not according to your wicked **w**, 1870
21:19 Also, thou son of man, appoint thee two **w**, 1870
21:21 at the head of the two **w**, to use divination: 1870
24:14 according to thy **w**, and according to thy 1870
28:15 Thou *wast* perfect in thy **w** from the day 1870
33:11 turn ye, turn ye from your evil **w**; for why 1870
33:20 I will judge you every one after his **w**. 1870
36:31 shall ye remember your own evil **w**, and 1870
36:32 and confounded for your own **w**, 1870
Da 4:37 whose works *are* truth, and his **w** judgment: 735
5:23 hand thy breath *is*, and whose *are* all thy **w**, 735
Hos 4: 9 I will punish them for their **w**, and 1870
9: 8 prophet *is* a snare of a fowler in all his **w**, 1870
12: 2 and *will* punish Jacob according to his **w**; 1870
14: 9 for the **w** of the LORD *are* right, and 1870
Joel 2: 7 they shall march every one on his **w**, and 1870
Mic 4: 2 he will teach us of his **w**, and we will walk 1870
Na 2: 4 justle one against another in the **broad w**: 7339
Hab 3: 6 hills did bow: his **w** *are* everlasting. 1979
Hag 1: 5 the LORD of hosts; Consider your **w**. 1870
1: 7 the LORD of hosts; Consider your **w**. 1870
Zec 1: 4 Turn ye now from your evil **w**, and 1870
1: 6 according to our **w**, and according to our 1870
3: 7 If thou wilt walk in my **w**, and if thou wilt 1870
Mal 2: 9 according as ye have not kept my **w**, but 1870
Mt 8:33 and went their **w** into the city, and NIG
22: 5 But they made light of *it*, and went their **w**, NIG
Mk 11: 4 door without in a place where two **w** met; NIG
Lk 1:76 the face of the Lord to prepare his **w**; *3598*
3: 5 and the rough **w** *shall be* made smooth; *3598*
10: 3 Go your **w**: behold, I send you forth as NIG
10:10 go *your* **w** out into the streets of the same, NIG
Jn 11:46 But some of them went their **w** to NIG
Ac 2:28 Thou hast made known to me the **w** of life; *3598*
13:10 wilt thou not cease to pervert the right **w** of *3598*
14:16 suffered all nations to walk in their own **w**. *3598*
Ro 3:16 Destruction and misery *are* in their **w**: *3598*
11:33 his judgments, and his **w** past finding out! *3598*
1Co 4:17 remembrance of my **w** which be in Christ, *3598*
Heb 3:10 *their* heart; and they have not known my **w**. *3598*
Jas 1: 8 double minded man *is* unstable in all his **w**. *3598*
1:11 also shall the rich *man* fade away in his **w**. *4197*
2Pe 2: 2 And many shall follow their **pernicious w**; *684*
Rev 15: 3 just and true *are* thy **w**, thou King of saints. *3598*
16: 1 Go your **w**, and pour out the vials of NIG

WAYSIDE (1) [SIDE, WAY]
1Sa 4:13 sat upon a seat *by* the **w** watching: 1870+3027

WAYWARDNESS See BACKSLIDERS; BACKSLIDING

WE (1844) [OUR, OURS, OURSELVES, US, US-WARD] See Index of Articles, Etc.

WEAK (46) [WEAKEN, WEAKENED, WEAKENETH, WEAKER, WEAKNESS]
Nu 13:18 whether they *be* strong or **w**, few or many; 7504
Jdg 16: 7 then shall I be **w**, and be as another man. 2470
16:11 shall I be **w**, and be as another man. 2470
16:17 I shall become **w**, and be like any *other* 2470
2Sa 3:39 I *am this* day **w**, though anointed king; and 7390
17: 2 upon him while he *is* weary and **w** handed, 7504
2Ch 15: 7 and let not your hands be **w**: 7503
Job 4: 3 and thou hast strengthened the **w** hands. 7504
Ps 6: 2 mercy upon me, O LORD; for I *am* **w**: 536
109:24 My knees are **w** through fasting; and 3782
Isa 14:10 unto thee, Art thou also **become w** as we? 2470
35: 3 Strengthen ye the **w** hands, and confirm 7504
Eze 7:17 be feeble, and all knees shall be **w** *as* water. 1980
16:30 How **w** is thine heart, saith the Lord GOD, 535
21: 7 and all knees shall be **w** *as* water: 1980
Joel 3:10 into spears: let the **w** say, I *am* strong. 2523
Mt 26:41 the spirit indeed *is* willing, but the flesh *is* **w**. *772*
Mk 14:38 The spirit truly *is* ready, but the flesh *is* **w**. *772*
Ac 20:35 so labouring *ye* ought to support the **w**, *770*
Ro 4:19 And being not **w** in faith, he considered not *770*
8: 3 not do, in that it was **w** through the flesh, *770*
14: 1 Him that is **w** in the faith receive you, *but* *770*
14: 2 all *things:* another, who is **w**, eateth herbs. *770*
14:21 or is offended, or is *made* **w**. *770*
15: 1 strong ought to bear the infirmities of the **w**, *102*
1Co 1:27 God hath chosen the **w** *things* of the world to *772*
4:10 we *are* **w**, but ye *are* strong; ye *are* *772*
8: 7 and their conscience being **w** is defiled. *772*
8: 9 become a stumblingblock to them that are **w**. *770*
8:10 shall not the conscience of him which is **w** *772*
8:11 And through thy knowledge shall the **w** *770*
8:12 the brethren, and wound their **w** conscience, *770*
9:22 To the **w** became I as weak, that I might gain *772*
9:22 To the weak became I as **w**, that I might gain *772*
9:22 became I as weak, that I might gain the **w**: *772*
11:30 For this cause many *are* **w** and sickly among *772*
2Co 10:10 but *his* bodily presence *is* **w**, and *his* speech *772*
11:21 as though we had been **w**. *770*
11:29 Who is **w**, and I am not weak? who is *770*
11:29 Who is weak, and I am not **w**? who is *770*
12:10 for when I am **w**, then am I strong. *770*
13: 3 which to you-ward is not **w**, but is mighty in *770*
13: 4 For we also are **w** in him, but we shall live *770*
13: 9 are glad, when we are **w**, and ye are strong: *770*
Gal 4: 9 how turn ye again to the **w** and *772*
1Th 5:14 comfort the feebleminded, support the **w**, *772*

WEAK-WILLED See SILLY

WEAKEN (1) [WEAK]
Isa 14:12 to the ground, which didst **w** the nations! 2522

WEAKENED (3) [WEAK]
Ezr 4: 4 the people of the land **w** the hands of 7503
Ne 6: 9 Their hands shall be **w** from the work, 7503
Ps 102:23 He **w** my strength in the way; he shortened 6031

WEAKENETH (2) [WEAK]
Job 12:21 and **w** the strength of the mighty. 7503
Jer 38: 4 for thus he **w** the hands of the men of war 7503

WEAKER (3) [WEAK]
2Sa 3: 1 the house of Saul **waxed w** and weaker. 1980
3: 1 and the house of Saul waxed weaker and **w**. 1800
1Pe 3: 7 as unto the **w** vessel, and as *being* heirs *772*

WEAKNESS (7) [WEAK]
1Co 1:25 and the **w** of God is stronger than men. *772*
2: 3 And I was with you in **w**, and in fear, and *769*
15:43 it is sown in **w**; it is raised in power: *769*
2Co 12: 9 for my strength is made perfect in **w**. *769*
13: 4 For though he was crucified through **w**, *769*
Heb 7:18 of the commandment going before for the **w** *772*
11:34 out of **w** were made strong, waxed valiant in *769*

WEALTH (27) [WEALTHY]
Ge 34:29 all their **w**, and all their little ones, and their 2428
Dt 8:17 might of mine hand hath gotten me this **w**. 2428
8:18 for *it is* he that giveth thee power to get **w**, 2428
Ru 2: 1 a mighty man of **w**, of the family of 2428
1Sa 2:32 in all *the* **w** which *God* shall give Israel: NIH
2Ki 15:20 *even* of all the mighty *men* of **w**, of each 2428
2Ch 1:11 thou hast not asked riches, **w**, or honour, 5233
1:12 I will give thee riches, and **w**, and honour, 5233
Ezr 9:12 nor seek their peace or their **w** for ever: 2896
Est 10: 3 seeking the **w** of his people, and 2896
Job 21:13 They spend their days in **w**, and in a 2896
31:25 If I rejoiced because my **w** *was* great, and 2428
Ps 44:12 and dost not increase *thy* **w** by their price. NIH
49: 6 They that trust in their **w**, and 2428
49:10 person perish, and leave their **w** to others. 2428
112: 3 **W** and riches *shall be* in his house: and 1952
Pr 5:10 Lest strangers be filled *with* thy **w**; and 3581
10:15 The rich *man's* **w** *is* his strong city: 1952
13:11 **W** *gotten* by vanity shall be diminished: but 1952
13:22 the **w** of the sinner *is* laid up for the just. 2428
18:11 The rich *man's* **w** *is* his strong city, and as a 1952
19: 4 **W** maketh many friends; but the poor is 1952
Ecc 5:19 also to whom God hath given riches and **w**, 5233
6: 2 **w**, and honour, so that he wanteth nothing 5233
Zec 14:14 the **w** of all the heathen round about shall 2428
Ac 19:25 ye know that by this craft we have our **w**. *2142*
1Co 10:24 seek his own, but every man another's *w*. NIG

WEALTHY (2) [WEALTH]
Ps 66:12 but thou broughtest us out into a **w** *place*. 7310
Jer 49:31 Arise, get you up unto the **w** nation, 7961

WEANED (12)
Ge 21: 8 the child grew, and was **w**: and 1580
21: 8 a great feast the *same* day that Isaac was **w**. 1580
1Sa 1:22 *I will not go up* until the child be **w**, and 1580
1:23 thee good; tarry until thou have **w** him; 1580
1:23 and gave her son suck until she **w** him. 1580
1:24 when she had **w** him, she took him up with 1580
1Ki 11:20 whom Tahpenes **w** in Pharaoh's house: 1580
Ps 131: 2 as a **child** that is **w** of his mother: 1580
131: 2 of his mother: my soul *is even* as a **w child**. 1580
Isa 11: 8 the **w child** shall put his hand on 1580
28: 9 them that are **w** from the milk, *and* 1580
Hos 1: 8 Now when she had **w** Lo-ruhamah, 1580

WEAPON (8) [WEAPONS]
Nu 35:18 Or *if* he smite him with a hand **w** of wood, 3627
Dt 23:13 thou shalt have a paddle upon thy **w**; and 240
2Ch 23:10 every man having his **w** in his hand, 7973
Ne 4:17 the work, and with the other *hand* held a **w**. 7973
Job 20:24 He shall flee from the iron **w**, *and* the bow 5402
Isa 54:17 No **w** *that is* formed against thee shall 3627
Eze 9: 1 even every man *with* his destroying **w** in 3627
9: 2 and every man a slaughter **w** in his hand; 3627

WEAPONS (21) [WEAPON]
Ge 27: 3 thy **w**, thy quiver and thy bow, and go out 3627
Dt 1:41 when ye had girded on every man his **w** of 3627
Jdg 18:11 six hundred men appointed *with* **w** of war. 3627
18:16 the six hundred men appointed *with* their **w** 3627
18:17 men that were appointed *with* **w** of war. 3627
1Sa 21: 8 brought my sword nor my **w** with me, 3627
2Sa 1:27 mighty fallen, and the **w** of war perished! 3627
2Ki 11: 8 every man with his **w** in his hand: 3627
11:11 every man with his **w** in his hand, 3627
2Ch 23: 7 every man with his **w** in his hand; 3627
Ecc 9:18 Wisdom *is* better than **w** of war: but 3627
Isa 13: 5 the LORD, and the **w** of his indignation, 3627
Jer 21: 4 I *will* turn back the **w** of war that *are* in 3627
22: 7 against thee, every one with his **w**: 3627
50:25 hath brought forth the **w** of his indignation: 3627
51:20 Thou *art* my battle axe *and* **w** of war: 3627
Eze 32:27 which are gone down *to* hell with their **w** of 3627
39: 9 shall set on fire and burn the **w**, both 5402
39:10 for they shall burn the **w** with fire: 5402
Jn 18: 3 thither with lanterns and torches and **w**. *3696*
2Co 10: 4 (For the **w** of our warfare *are* not carnal, *3696*

WEAR (12) [WARE, WEARETH, WEARING]
Ex 18:18 Thou wilt **surely w away**, both thou, 5034+5034
Dt 22: 5 The woman shall not **w** that which 1961+5921
22:11 Thou shalt not **w** a garment of divers sorts, 3847
1Sa 2:28 to burn incense, to **w** an ephod before me? 5375
22:18 and five persons that did **w** a linen ephod. 5375
Est 6: 8 be brought which the king *useth* to **w**, 3847
Job 14:19 The waters **w** the stones: thou washest 7833
Isa 4: 1 eat our own bread, and **w** our own apparel: 3847
Da 7:25 shall **w out** the saints of the most High, and 1080
Zec 13: 4 neither shall they **w** a rough garment to 3847
Mt 11: 8 they that **w** soft *clothing* are in kings' *5409*
Lk 9:12 And *when* the day began to **w away**, then *2827*

WEARETH (1) [WEAR]
Jas 2: 3 And ye have respect to him that **w** the gay *5409*

WEARIED (14) [WEARY]
Ge 19:11 so that they **w** themselves to find the door. 3811
Isa 43:23 with an offering, nor **w** thee with incense. 3021
43:24 thou hast **w** me with thine iniquities. 3021
47:13 Thou art **w** in the multitude of thy counsels. 3811
57:10 Thou art **w** in the greatness of thy way; 3021
Jer 4:31 for my soul *is* **w** because of murderers. 5888
12: 5 they have **w** thee, then how canst thou 3811
12: 5 *they* **w** *thee,* then how wilt thou do in NIH
Eze 24:12 She hath **w** *herself with* lies, and her great 3811
Mic 6: 3 wherein have I **w** thee? testify against me. 3811
Mal 2:17 Ye have **w** the LORD with your words. 3021
2:17 Wherein have we **w** *him?* When ye say, 3021
Jn 4: 6 Jesus therefore, being **w** with *his* journey, *2872*
Heb 12: 3 lest ye be **w** and faint in your minds. *2577*

WEARIETH (2) [WEARY]
Job 37:11 Also by watering he **w** the thick cloud: 2959
Ecc 10:15 The labour of the foolish **w** every one of 3021

WEARINESS (3) [WEARY]
Ecc 12:12 no end; and much study *is* a **w** of the flesh. 3024
Mal 1:13 what a **w** *is it!* and ye have snuffed at it, 4972
2Co 11:27 In **w** and painfulness, in watchings often, *2873*

WEARING (3) [WEAR]
1Sa 14: 3 the LORD'S priest in Shiloh, **w** an ephod. 5375
Jn 19: 5 **w** the crown of thorns, and the purple robe. *5409*
1Pe 3: 3 and of **w** of gold, or of putting on of *4025*

WEARISOME (1) [WEARY]
Job 7: 3 and **w** nights are appointed to me. 5999

WEARY (42) [WEARIED, WEARIETH, WEARINESS, WEARISOME]
Ge 27:46 I am **w** of my life because of the daughters 6973
Dt 25:18 behind thee, when thou *wast* faint and **w**; 3023
Jdg 4:21 for he was fast asleep and **w**. So he died. 5774
8:15 should give bread unto thy men *that are* **w**? 3287
2Sa 16:14 came **w**, and refreshed themselves there. 5889
17: 2 I will come upon him while he *is* **w** and 3023
17:29 and **w**, and thirsty, in the wilderness. 5889
23:10 smote the Philistines until his hand was **w**, 3021

Job 3:17 and there the **w** be at rest. 3019+3581
10: 1 My soul is **w** of my life; I will leave my 5354
16: 7 now he hath **made** me **w**: thou hast made 3811
22: 7 Thou hast not given water to the **w** to drink, 5889
Ps 6: 6 I am **w** with my groaning; all the night 3021
68: 9 confirm thine inheritance, when it was **w**. 3811
69: 3 I am **w** of my crying: my throat is dried: 3021
Pr 3:11 the LORD; neither be **w** of his correction: 6973
25:17 lest he be **w** *of* thee, and *so* hate thee. 7646
Isa 1:14 are a trouble unto me; I am **w** to bear *them.* 3811
5:27 None *shall be* **w** nor stumble amongst 5889
7:13 *Is it* a small thing for you to **w** men, but 3811
7:13 to weary men, but will ye **w** my God also? 3811
16:12 when it is seen that Moab is **w** on the high 3811
28:12 rest *wherewith* ye may cause the **w** to rest; 5889
32: 2 as the shadow of a great rock in a **w** land. 5889
40:28 ends of the earth, fainteth not, neither is **w**? 3021
40:30 Even the youths shall faint and be **w**, and 3021
40:31 they shall run, and not be **w**; *and* they shall 3021
43:22 but thou hast been **w** of me, O Israel. 3021
46: 1 *they are* a burden to the **w** *beast.* 5889
50: 4 to speak a word in season to *him that is* **w**: 3287
Jer 2:24 all they that seek her will not **w** themselves; 3286
6:11 of the LORD; I am **w** with holding in: 3811
9: 5 *and* **w** themselves to commit iniquity. 3811
15: 6 and destroy thee; I am **w** with repenting. 3811
20: 9 I was **w** with forbearing, and I could not 3811
31:25 For I have satiated the **w** soul, and I have 5889
51:58 and the folk in the fire, and they shall be **w**. 3286
51:64 they shall be **w**. Thus far *are* the words of 3286
Hab 2:13 the people shall **w** themselves for very 3286
Lk 18: 5 lest by her continual coming she **w** me. *5299*
Gal 6: 9 And let us not be **w** in well doing: for in *1573*
2Th 3:13 But ye, brethren, be not **w** in well doing. *1573*

WEASEL (1)
Lev 11:29 the **w**, and the mouse, and the tortoise after 2467

WEATHER (4)
Job 37:22 **Fair w** cometh out of the north: with God 2091
Pr 25:20 *As* he that taketh away a garment in cold **w**, 3117
Mt 16: 2 it is evening, ye say, *It will be* **fair w**: *2105*
16: 3 in the morning, *It will be* **foul w** to day: *5494*

WEAVE (2) [WEAVER, WEAVER'S, WEAVEST, WOVE, WOVEN]
Isa 19: 9 they that **w** networks, shall be confounded. 707
59: 5 cockatrice' eggs, and **w** the spider's web: 707

WEAVER (2) [WEAVE]
Ex 35:35 in scarlet, and in fine linen, and of the **w**, 707
Isa 38:12 I have cut off like a **w** my life: he will cut 707

WEAVER'S (5) [WEAVE]
1Sa 17: 7 And the staff of his spear *was* like a **w** beam; 707
2Sa 21:19 the staff of whose spear *was* like a **w** beam. 707
1Ch 11:23 in the Egyptian's hand *was* a spear like a **w** 707
20: 5 whose spear staff *was* like a **w** beam. 707
Job 7: 6 My days are swifter than a **w shuttle**, and 708

WEAVEST (1) [WEAVE]
Jdg 16:13 If thou **w** the seven locks of my head with 707

WEB (4) [WEBS]
Jdg 16:13 the seven locks of my head with the **w**. 4545
16:14 with the pin of the beam, and with the **w**. 4545
Job 8:14 and whose trust *shall be* a spider's **w**. 1004
Isa 59: 5 cockatrice' eggs, and weave the spider's **w**: 6980

WEBS (1) [WEB]
Isa 59: 6 Their **w** shall not become garments, 6980

WEDDING (7) [WEDLOCK]
Mt 22: 3 to call them that were bidden to the **w**: *1062*
22: 8 The **w** is ready, but they which were bidden *1062*
22:10 good: and the **w** was furnished with guests. *1062*
22:11 he saw there a man which had not on a **w** *1062*
22:12 how camest thou in hither not having a **w** *1062*
Lk 12:36 their lord, when he will return from the **w**; *1062*
14: 8 When thou art bidden of any *man* to a **w**, *1062*

WEDGE (3)
Jos 7:21 a **w** of gold of fifty shekels weight, then 3956
7:24 the **w** of gold, and his sons, and his 3956
Isa 13:12 even a man than the **golden w** of Ophir. 3800

WEDLOCK (1) [WEDDING]
Eze 16:38 as *women* that **break w** and shed blood are 5003

WEED See COCKLE

WEEDS (1)
Jnh 2: 5 the **w** *were* wrapt about my head. 5488

WEEK (13) [WEEKS]
Ge 29:27 Fulfil her **w**, and we will give thee this also 7620
29:28 Jacob did so, and fulfilled her **w**: and 7620
Da 9:27 confirm the covenant with many *for* one **w**: 7620
9:27 *in* the midst of the **w** he shall cause 7620
Mt 28: 1 to dawn towards the first *day* of the **w**, *4521*
Mk 16: 2 early in the morning the first *day* of the **w**, *4521*
16: 9 *Jesus* was risen early the first *day* of the **w**, *4521*
Lk 18:12 I fast twice in the **w**, I give tithes of all that *4521*
24: 1 Now upon the first *day* of the **w**, very early *4521*
Jn 20: 1 The first *day* of the **w** cometh Mary *4521*
20:19 day at evening, being the first *day* of the **w**, *4521*
Ac 20: 7 And upon the first *day* of the **w**, when *4521*
1Co 16: 2 Upon the first *day* of the **w** let every one of *4521*

WEEKS (15) [WEEK]
Ex 34:22 thou shalt observe the feast of **w**, of 7620
Lev 12: 5 she shall be unclean **two w**, as *in* her 7620
Nu 28:26 after your **w** *be out*, ye shall have a holy 7620
Dt 16: 9 Seven **w** shalt thou number unto thee: 7620
16: 9 begin to number the seven **w** from *such* 7620
16:10 thou shalt keep the feast of **w** unto 7620
16:16 in the feast of **w**, and in the feast of 7620
2Ch 8:13 in the feast of **w**, and in the feast of 7620
Jer 5:24 he reserveth unto us the appointed **w** of 7620
Da 9:24 Seventy **w** are determined upon thy people 7620
9:25 the Messiah the Prince *shall be* seven **w**, 7620
9:25 *be* seven weeks, and threescore and two **w**: 7620
9:26 and two **w** shall Messiah be cut off, 7620
10: 2 I Daniel was mourning three **full w**. 3117+7620
10: 3 till three **whole w** were fulfilled. 3117+7620

WEEP (49) [WEEPEST, WEEPETH, WEEPING, WEPT]
Ge 23: 2 came to mourn for Sarah, and to **w** for her. 1058
43:30 he sought *where* to **w**; and he entered into 1058
Nu 11:10 Moses heard the people **w** throughout their 1058
11:13 for they **w** unto me, saying, Give us flesh, 1058
1Sa 11: 5 What aileth the people that they **w**? 1058
30: 4 wept, until they had no more power to **w**. 1058
2Sa 1:24 Ye daughters of Israel, **w** over Saul, 1058
12:21 thou didst fast and **w** for the child, *while it* 1058
2Ch 34:27 didst rend thy clothes, and **w** before me; 1058
Ne 8: 9 the LORD your God; mourn not, nor **w**. 1058
Job 27:15 in death: and his widows shall not **w**. 1058
30:25 Did not I **w** for him that was in trouble? 1058
30:31 and my organ into the voice of them that **w**. 1058
Ecc 3: 4 A time to **w**, and a time to laugh; a time to 1058
Isa 15: 2 and *to* Dibon, the high places, to **w**: 1065
22: 4 I will **w** bitterly, labour not to comfort me, 1065
30:19 thou shalt **w** no **more**: he will be 1058+1058
33: 7 the ambassadors of peace shall **w** bitterly. 1058
Jer 9: 1 that I might **w** day and night for the slain of 1058
13:17 my soul shall **w** in secret places for *your* 1058
13:17 mine eye shall **w sore**, and run down 1830+1830
22:10 **W** ye not for the dead, neither bemoan him: 1058
22:10 *but* **w sore** for him that goeth away: 1058+1058
48:32 I will **w** for thee with the weeping of Jazer: 1058
La 1:16 For these *things* I **w**; mine eye, mine eye 1058
Eze 24:16 yet neither shalt thou mourn nor **w**, 1058
24:23 ye shall not mourn nor **w**; but ye shall pine 1058
27:31 they shall **w** for thee with bitterness of 1058
Joel 1: 5 Awake, ye drunkards, and **w**; and howl, 1058
2:17 **w** between the porch and the altar, and 1058
Mic 1:10 ye *it* not at Gath, **w** ye not **at all**: 1058+1058
Zec 7: 3 Should I **w** in the fifth month, 1058
Mk 5:39 unto them, Why make ye *this* ado, and **w**? *2799*
Lk 6:21 Blessed *are ye* that **w** now: for ye shall *2799*
6:25 that laugh now: for ye shall mourn and **w**. *2799*
7:13 on her, and said unto her, **W** not. *2799*
8:52 but he said, **W** not; she is not dead, but *2799*
23:28 **w** not for me, but weep for yourselves, and *2799*
23:28 but **w** for yourselves, and for your children. *2799*
Jn 11:31 saying, She goeth unto the grave to **w** there. *2799*
16:20 That ye shall **w** and lament, but the world *2799*
Ac 21:13 What mean ye to **w** and to break *2799+4160*
Ro 12:15 that do rejoice, and **w** with them that weep. *2799*
12:15 that do rejoice, and weep with them that **w**. *2799*
1Co 7:30 And they that **w**, as though they wept not; *2799*
Jas 4: 9 Be afflicted, and mourn, and **w**: let your *2799*
5: 1 ye rich *men*, **w** and howl for your miseries *2799*
Rev 5: 5 And one of the elders saith unto me, **W** not: *2799*
18:11 And the merchants of the earth *shall* **w** and *2799*

WEEPEST (3) [WEEP]
1Sa 1: 8 her husband to her, Hannah, why **w** thou? 1058
Jn 20:13 they say unto her, Woman, why **w** thou? *2799*
20:15 Jesus saith unto her, Woman, why **w** thou? *2799*

WEEPETH (4) [WEEP]
2Sa 19: 1 the king **w** and mourneth for Absalom. 1058
2Ki 8:12 Hazael said, Why **w** my lord? And he 1058
Ps 126: 6 He that goeth forth and **w**, bearing precious 1058
La 1: 2 She **w sore** in the night, and her tears 1058+1058

WEEPING (44) [WEEP]
Nu 25: 6 who *were* **w** *before* the door of 1058
Dt 34: 8 so the days of **w** *and* mourning for Moses 1065
2Sa 3:16 her husband went with her along **w** behind 1058
15:30 and they went up, **w** as they went up. 1058
Ezr 3:13 joy from the noise of the **w** of the people: 1065
10: 1 **w** and casting himself down before 1058
Est 4: 3 the Jews, and fasting, and **w**, and wailing; 1065
Job 16:16 My face is foul with **w**, and on mine 1065
Ps 6: 8 the LORD hath heard the voice of my **w**. 1065
30: 5 **w** may endure for a night, but joy *cometh* 1065
102: 9 like bread, and mingled my drink with **w**, 1065
Isa 15: 3 every one shall howl, **w** abundantly. 1065
15: 5 for *by* the mounting up of Luhith with **w** 1065
16: 9 Therefore I will bewail with the **w** of Jazer 1065
22:12 day did the Lord GOD of hosts call to **w**, 1065
65:19 the voice of **w** shall be no more heard in 1065
Jer 3:21 **w** *and* supplications of the children of 1065
9:10 For the mountains will I take up a **w** and 1065
31: 9 They shall come with **w**, and 1065
31:15 heard in Ramah, lamentation, *and* bitter **w**; 1065
31:15 Rahel **w** for her children refused to be 1058
31:16 Refrain thy voice from **w**, and thine eyes 1065
41: 6 to meet them, **w** all along as he went: 1058
48: 5 of Luhith **continual w** shall go up; 1065+1065
48:32 I will weep for thee with the **w** of Jazer: 1065
50: 4 children of Judah together, going and **w**: 1058
Eze 8:14 behold, there sat women **w** for Tammuz. 1058
Joel 2:12 and with **w**, and with mourning: 1065
Mal 2:13 *with* tears, *with* **w**, and *with* crying out, 1065
Mt 2:18 lamentation, and **w**, and great mourning, *2805*
2:18 Rachel **w** for her children, and would not *2799*
8:12 there shall be **w** and gnashing of teeth. *2805*
22:13 there shall be **w** and gnashing of teeth. *2805*
24:51 there shall be **w** and gnashing of teeth. *2805*
25:30 there shall be **w** and gnashing of teeth. *2805*
Lk 7:38 And stood at his feet behind *him* **w**, and *2799*
13:28 There shall be **w** and gnashing of teeth, *2805*
Jn 11:33 When Jesus therefore saw her **w**, and *2799*
11:33 and the Jews also **w** which came with her, *2799*
20:11 But Mary stood without at the sepulchre **w**: *2799*
Ac 9:39 and all the widows stood by him **w**, and *2799*
Php 3:18 told you often, and now tell *you* even **w**, *2799*
Rev 18:15 for the fear of her torment, **w** and wailing, *2799*
18:19 and cried, **w** and wailing, saying, Alas, *2799*

WEIGH (6) [UNWEIGHED, WEIGHED, WEIGHETH, WEIGHING, WEIGHT, WEIGHTIER, WEIGHTS, WEIGHTY]
1Ch 20: 2 found it to **w** a talent of gold, and 4948
Ezr 8:29 keep *them*, until ye **w** *them* before the chief 8254
Ps 58: 2 you **w** the violence of your hands in 6424
Isa 26: 7 most upright, dost **w** the path of the just. 6424
46: 6 **w** silver in the balance, *and* hire a 8254
Eze 5: 1 take thee balances to **w**, and divide 4948

WEIGHED (17) [WEIGH]
Ge 23:16 Abraham **w** to Ephron the silver, which he 8254
Nu 7:85 all the silver vessels **w** two thousand and NIH
1Sa 2: 3 of knowledge, and by him actions are **w**. 8505
17: 7 his spear's head **w** six hundred shekels *of* NIH
2Sa 14:26 he **w** the hair of his head *at* two hundred 8254
21:16 the weight of whose spear **w** three hundred NIH
Ezr 8:25 **w** unto them the silver, and the gold, and 8254
8:26 I even **w** unto their hand six hundred and 8254
8:33 the vessels **w** in the house of our God by 8254
Job 6: 2 Oh that my grief were **throughly w**, 8254+8254
28:15 neither shall silver be **w** *for* the price 8254
31: 6 Let me be **w** in an even balance, that God 8254
Isa 40:12 **w** the mountains in scales, and the hills in a 8254
Jer 32: 9 *was* in Anathoth, and **w** him the money, 8254
32:10 **w** *him* the money in the balances. 8254
Da 5:27 Thou art **w** in the balances, and art found 8625
Zec 11:12 So they **w** *for* my price thirty *pieces* of 8254

WEIGHETH (2) [WEIGH]
Job 28:25 the winds; and he **w** the waters by measure. 8505
Pr 16: 2 his own eyes; but the LORD **w** the spirits. 8505

WEIGHING (2) [WEIGH]
Nu 7:85 Each charger of silver **w** an hundred and NIH
7:86 full *of* incense, **w** ten *shekels* apiece, NIH

WEIGHT (58) [WEIGH]
Ge 24:22 took a golden earring of half a shekel **w**, 4948
24:22 two bracelets for her hands of ten *shekels* **w** 4948
43:21 the mouth of his sack, our money in **full w**: 4948
Ex 30:34 of each shall there be a like **w**: NIH
Lev 19:35 in meteyard, in **w**, or in measure. 4948
26:26 shall deliver *you* your bread again by **w**: 4948
Nu 7:13 the **w** thereof *was* an hundred and 4948
7:19 the **w** whereof *was* an hundred and 4948
7:25 the **w** whereof *was* an hundred and 4948
7:31 one silver charger of the **w** of an hundred 4948
7:37 the **w** whereof *was* an hundred and 4948
7:43 one silver charger of the **w** of an hundred 4948
7:49 the **w** whereof *was* an hundred and 4948
7:55 one silver charger of the **w** of an hundred 4948
7:61 the **w** whereof *was* an hundred and 4948
7:67 the **w** whereof *was* an hundred and 4948
7:73 the **w** whereof *was* an hundred and 4948
7:79 the **w** whereof *was* an hundred and 4948
Dt 25:15 *But* thou shalt have a perfect and just **w**, 68
Jos 7:21 and a wedge of gold of fifty shekels **w**, then 4948
Jdg 8:26 the **w** of the golden earrings that he 4948
1Sa 17: 5 the **w** of the coat *was* five thousand shekels 4948
2Sa 12:30 the **w** whereof *was* a talent of gold with 4948
14:26 *at* two hundred shekels after the king's **w**. 68
21:16 the **w** of whose spear *weighed* three 4948
21:16 three hundred *shekels* of brass in **w**, 4948
1Ki 7:47 neither was the **w** of the brass found out. 4948
10:14 Now the **w** of gold that came to Solomon in 4948
2Ki 25:16 the brass of all these vessels was without **w**. 4948
1Ch 21:25 the place six hundred shekels of gold *by* **w**. 4948
22: 3 and brass in abundance without **w**; 4948
22:14 of brass and iron without **w**; for it is in 4948
28:14 *He gave* of gold by **w** for *things of* gold, 4948
28:14 *also* for all instruments of silver by **w**, 4948
28:15 Even the **w** for the candlesticks of gold, and 4948
28:15 by **w** for every candlestick, and *for* 4948
28:15 for the candlesticks of silver by **w**, *both* for 4948
28:16 *by* **w** *he gave* gold for the tables of 4948
28:17 for the golden basons *he gave gold* by **w** for 4948
28:17 *likewise silver* by **w** for every bason of 4948
28:18 for the altar of incense refined gold by **w**; 4948
2Ch 3: 9 the **w** of the nails *was* fifty shekels of gold. 4948
4:18 for the **w** of the brass could not be found 4948
9:13 Now the **w** of gold that came to Solomon in 4948
Ezr 8:30 and the Levites the **w** of the silver, 4948
8:34 By number *and* by **w** of every one: and 4948
8:34 and all the **w** was written at that time. 4948
Job 28:25 To make the **w** for the winds; and 4948
Pr 11: 1 to the LORD: but a just **w** *is* his delight. 68
16:11 A just **w** and balance *are* the LORD'S: 6425
Jer 52:20 the brass of all these vessels was without **w**. 4948
Eze 4:10 thy meat which thou shalt eat *shall be* by **w**, 4946
4:16 they shall eat bread by **w**, and with care; 4948
Zec 5: 8 he cast the **w** of lead upon the mouth thereof. 68
Jn 19:39 and aloes, about an hundred pound **w**. NIG
2Co 4:17 a far more exceeding *and* eternal **w** of glory; *922*
Heb 12: 1 let us lay aside every **w**, and the sin which *3591*
Rev 16:21 *every stone* about the **w of a talent**: *5006*

WEIGHTIER (1) [WEIGH]
Mt 23:23 and have omitted the **w** *matters* of the law, *926*

WEIGHTS (6) [WEIGH]
Lev 19:36 just **w**, a just ephah, and a just hin, shall ye 68
Dt 25:13 not have in thy bag **divers w**, 68+68+2050.1
Pr 16:11 all the **w** of the bag *are* his work. 68
20:10 **Divers w**, *and* divers measures, 68+68+2050.1
20:23 **Divers w** *are* an abomination unto 68+68+2050.1
Mic 6:11 and with the bag of deceitful **w**? 68

WEIGHTY (2) [WEIGH]
Pr 27: 3 A stone *is* heavy, and the sand **w**; but 5192
2Co 10:10 For *his* letters, say they, *are* **w** and powerful; *926*

WELDING See SODERING

WELFARE (7) [WELL]
Ge 43:27 he asked them of *their* **w**, and said, *Is* your 7965
Ex 18: 7 they asked each other of *their* **w**; and 7965
1Ch 18:10 to inquire of his **w**, and to congratulate him, 7965
Ne 2:10 man to seek the **w** of the children of Israel. 2896
Job 30:15 and my **w** passeth away as a cloud. 3444
Ps 69:22 *that which should have been* for *their* **w**, 7965
Jer 38: 4 for this man seeketh not the **w** of this 7965

WELL (258) [BEER-LAHAI-ROI, WELFARE, WELL'S, WELLBELOVED, WELL-BELOVED, WELLFAVOURED, WELLS, WELLSPRING]
Ge 4: 7 If thou doest **w**, *shalt thou* not be accepted? 3190
4: 7 if thou doest not **w**, sin lieth at the door. 3190
12:13 that it may be **w** with me for thy sake; and 3190
12:16 he **entreated** Abram **w** for her sake: and 3190
13:10 that it *was* **w watered** every where, 4945
16:14 Wherefore the **w** was called Beer-lahai-roi; 875
18:11 and Sarah *were* old *and* **w stricken** in age; 935
21:19 opened her eyes, and she saw a **w** of water; 875
21:25 because of a **w** of water, 875
21:30 a witness unto me, that I have digged this **w**. 875
24: 1 Abraham was old, *and* **w stricken** in age: 935
24:11 by a **w** of water at the time of the evening, 875
24:13 Behold, I stand *here* by the **w** of water; and 5869
24:16 she went down to the **w**, and filled her 5869
24:20 and ran again unto the **w** to draw *water,* and 875
24:29 Laban ran out unto the man, unto the **w**. 5869
24:30 behold, he stood by the camels at the **w**. 5869
24:42 I came this day unto the **w**, and said, 5869
24:43 Behold, I stand by the **w** of water; and 5869
24:45 she went down unto the **w**, and drew *water:* 5869
24:62 came from the way of the **w Lahai-roi**; 883
25:11 and Isaac dwelt by the **w Lahai-roi**. 883
26:19 and found there a **w** of springing water. 875
26:20 he called the name of the **w** Esek; because 875
26:21 they digged another **w**, and strove for that 875
26:22 removed from thence, and digged another **w**; 875
26:25 and there Isaac's servants digged a **w**. 875
26:32 told him concerning the **w** which they had 875
29: 2 and behold a **w** in the field, and lo, 875
29: 2 for out of that **w** they watered the flocks: 875
29: 6 he said unto them, *Is* he **w**? And they said, 7965
29: 6 they said, *He is* **w**: and behold, Rachel his 7965
29:17 but Rachel was beautiful and **w** favoured. 3303
32: 9 to thy kindred, and I will **deal w** with thee: 3190
37:14 see whether it be **w** with thy brethren, and 7965
37:14 with thy brethren, and **w** with the flocks; 7965
39: 6 was a goodly *person,* and **w** favoured. 3303
40:14 think on me when it shall be **w** with thee, 3190
41: 2 there came up out of the river seven **w** 3303
41: 4 leanfleshed kine did eat up the seven **w** 3303
41:18 river seven kine, fatfleshed and **w** favoured; 3303
43:27 said, *Is* your father **w**, the old man of whom 7965
45:16 **pleased** Pharaoh **w**, and his 3190+5869+871.1
49:22 *even* a fruitful bough by a **w**; 5869
Ex 1:20 Therefore God **dealt w** with the midwives: 3190
2:15 the land of Midian: and he sat down by a **w**. 875
4:14 I know that he can **speak w**. And 1696+1696
10:29 Moses said, Thou hast spoken **w**, I will see 3651
Lev 24:16 **as w** the stranger, as he that is born in 3509.1
24:22 **as w for** the stranger, as for one of your 3509.1
Nu 11:18 for *it was* **w** with us in Egypt: therefore 2895
13:30 for we are **w able to overcome** it. 3201+3201
21:16 that *is* the **w** whereof the LORD spake unto 875
21:17 Israel sang this song, Spring up, O **w**; 875
21:18 The princes digged the **w**, the nobles of 875
21:22 we will not drink *of* the waters of the **w**: 875
36: 5 The tribe of the sons of Joseph hath said **w**. 3651
Dt 1:17 you shall hear the small **as w** as the great; 3509.1
1:23 the saying **pleased** me **w**: 3190+5869+871.1
3:20 **as w as** *unto* you, and *until* they also 3509.1
4:40 that it may **go w** with thee, and with thy 3190
5:14 and thy maidservant may rest **as w as** thou. 3644
5:16 and that it may **go w** with thee, 3190
5:28 they have **w** *said* all that they have spoken. 3190
5:29 that it might be **w** with them, and with their 3190
5:33 *that it may be* **w** with you, and *that* ye may 2895
6: 3 observe to do *it;* that it may be **w** with thee, 3190
6:18 that it may be **w** with thee, and *that* thou 3190
7:18 shalt **w remember** what the LORD 2142+2142
12:25 that it may **go w** with thee, and with thy 3190
12:28 that it may **go w** with thee, and with thy 3190
15:16 and thine house, because he is **w** with thee; 2895
18:17 They have **w** *spoken that* which they have 3190
19:13 from Israel, that *it may go* **w** with thee. 2895
20: 8 lest his brethren's heart faint **as w as** his 3509.1
22: 7 that it may be **w** with thee, and *that* thou 3190
Jos 8:33 **as w** the stranger, as he that was born 3509.1
18:15 went out to the **w** of waters of Nephtoah: 4599
Jdg 7: 1 and pitched beside the **w** of Harod: 5869
9:16 if ye have dealt **w** with Jerubbaal and his 2896
14: 3 her for me; for she **pleaseth** me **w**. 3474+5869+871.1
14: 7 and she **pleased** Samson **w**. 3474+5869+871.1
20:48 **as w** the men of *every* city, as the beast, 4480
Ru 3: 1 rest for thee, that it may be **w** with thee? 3190
3:13 perform unto thee the part of a kinsman, **w**; 2896
1Sa 9:10 said Saul to his servant, **W** said; come, 2896
16:16 play with his hand, and thou shalt be **w**. 2895
16:17 Provide me now a man that can play **w**, and 3190
16:23 was **w**, and the evil spirit departed from 2895
18:26 it **pleased** David **w** to be 3474+5869+871.1
19:22 and came to a great **w** that *is* in Sechu: 953
20: 7 If he say thus, *It is* **w**; thy servant shall have 2896
24:18 day how that thou hast dealt **w** with me: 2896
24:19 find his enemy, will he let him go **w** away? 2896
24:20 I **know w** that thou shalt surely be king, 3045
25:31 when the LORD shall have **dealt w** with 3190
2Sa 3:13 he said, **W**; I will make a league with thee: 2896
3:26 which brought him again from the **w** of 953
6:19 **as w** to the women as men, 4480+3807.1
11:25 for the sword devoureth one **as w** as 3509.1
17: 4 saying **pleased** Absalom **w**, 3474+5869+871.1
17:18 in Bahurim, which had a **w** in his court; 875
17:21 that they came up out of the **w**, and went and 875
18:28 and said unto the king, **All is w**. 7965
19: 6 then it had **pleased** thee **w**. 3477+5869+871.1
23:15 drink *of* the water of the **w** of Beth-lehem, 953
23:16 drew water out of the **w** of Beth-lehem, 953
1Ki 2:18 Bath-sheba said, **W**; I will speak for thee 2896
8:18 thou **didst w** that it was in thine heart. 2895
18:24 people answered and said, It is **w** spoken. 2896
2Ki 4:23 nor sabbath. And she said, *It shall be* **w**. 7965
4:26 and say unto her, *Is it* **w** with thee? 7965
4:26 *is it* **w** with thy husband? *is it* well with 7965
4:26 *is it* **w** with the child? And she answered, 7965
4:26 with the child? And she answered, *It is* **w**. 7965
5:21 the chariot to meet him, and said, *Is all* **w**? 7965
5:22 he said, *All is* **w**. My master hath sent me, 7965
7: 9 they said one to another, We do not **w**: 3651
9:11 *one* said unto him, *Is all* **w**? 7965
10:30 Because thou hast **done w** in executing *that* 2895
25:24 of Babylon; and it shall be **w** with you. 3190
1Ch 11:17 drink *of* the water of the **w** of Beth-lehem, 953
11:18 drew water out of the **w** of Beth-lehem, 953
25: 8 ward against *ward,* **as w** the small as 3509.1
26:13 they cast lots, **as w** the small as the great, 3509.1
2Ch 6: 8 thou **didst w** *in* that it was in thine heart: 2895
12:12 and also in Judah things went **w**. 2896
31:15 **as w** *to* the great as *to* the small: 3509.1
Ne 2:13 even before the dragon **w**, and to the dung 5869
Job 12: 3 I have understanding **as w as** you; I *am* not 3644
33:31 **Mark w**, O Job, hearken unto me: hold thy 7181
Ps 48:13 Mark ye **w** her bulwarks, consider her 3820
49:18 praise thee, when thou **doest w** to thyself. 3190
73: 2 my steps had **w nigh** slipt. 369+3509.1
78:29 So they did eat, and were **w** filled: for he 3966
84: 6 through the valley of Baca make it a **w**; 4599
87: 7 **As w** the singers as the players on 2050.1
119:65 Thou hast dealt **w** with thy servant, 2896
128: 2 *shalt* thou *be,* and *it shall be* **w** with thee. 2896
139:14 and *that* my soul knoweth **right w**. 3966
Pr 5:15 and running waters out of thine own **w**. 875
10:11 The mouth of a righteous *man is* a **w** of 4726
11:10 When it **goeth w** with the righteous, 2898
13:10 but with the **w advised** *is* wisdom. 3289
14:15 but the prudent *man* **looketh w** to his going. 995
24:32 I saw, *and* considered *it* **w**: I looked upon *it,* NIH
27:23 state of thy flocks, *and* look **w** to thy herds. 3820
30:29 There be three *things* which go **w**, yea, 2895
31:27 She **looketh w** to the ways of her 6822
Ecc 8:12 yet surely I know that it shall be **w** with 2896
8:13 it shall not be **w** with the wicked, 2896
SS 4:15 a **w** of living waters, and streams from 875
Isa 1:17 Learn to **do w**; seek judgment, relieve 3190
3:10 that *it shall be* **w** *with him:* for they shall 2896
3:24 instead of **w set hair** baldness; and 4639+4748
25: 6 of marrow, of wines on the lees **w refined**. 2212
33:23 they could not **w** strengthen their mast, 3653
42:21 The LORD is **w pleased** for his 2654
Jer 1:12 the LORD unto me, Thou hast **w** seen: 3190
7:23 that it may be **w** unto you. 3190
15:11 Verily it shall be **w** with thy remnant; 2896
15:11 enemy to entreat thee *w* in the time of evil, NIH
22:15 and justice, *and* then *it was* **w** with him? 2896
22:16 *it was* **w** *with him: was* not this to know 2896
38:20 so it shall be **w** unto thee, and thy soul shall 3190
39:12 **look w** to him, and do him no harm; 5869+7760
40: 4 come; and I will **look w** unto thee: 5869+7760
40: 9 king of Babylon, and it shall be **w** with you. 3190
42: 6 that it may be **w** with us, when we obey 3190
44:17 of victuals, and were **w**, and saw no evil. 2896
Eze 24: 5 *and* **make** it **boil w**, and let them 7570+7571
24:10 and spice it **w**, and let the bones be burnt. 4841
33:32 and can play **w** on an instrument: 2895
44: 5 **mark w**, and behold with thine eyes, 3820+7760
44: 5 **mark w** the entering in of the house, 3820+7760
47:14 ye shall inherit it, one **as w as** another: 3509.1
Da 1: 4 **w** favoured, and skilful in all wisdom, and 2896
3:15 **w**: but if ye worship not, ye shall be cast NIH
Jnh 4: 4 said the LORD, Doest thou **w** to be angry? 3190
4: 9 Doest thou **w** to be angry for the gourd? 3190
4: 9 he said, I **do w** to be angry, *even* unto 3190
Zec 8:15 in these days to **do w** unto Jerusalem 3190
Mt 3:17 my beloved Son, in whom I am **w pleased**. *2106*
12:12 Wherefore it is lawful to do **w** on *2573*
12:18 in whom my soul is **w pleased**: *2106*
15: 7 **w** did Esaias prophesy of you, saying, *2573*
17: 5 my beloved Son, in whom I am **w pleased**; *2106*
25:21 **W** *done, thou* good and faithful servant: *2095*
25:23 **W** *done,* good and faithful servant; *2095*
Mk 1:11 my beloved Son, in whom I am **w pleased**. *2106*
7: 6 **W** hath Esaias prophesied of you *2573*
7: 9 **Full w** ye reject the commandment of God, *2573*
7:37 saying, He hath done all *things* **w**: *2573*
12:28 perceiving that he had answered them **w**, *2573*
12:32 **W**, Master, thou hast said the truth: *2573*
Lk 1: 7 they both were *now* **w stricken** in years. *4260*
1:18 old man, and my wife **w stricken** in years. *4260*
3:22 my beloved Son; in thee I am **w pleased**. *2106*
6:26 when all men shall speak **w** of you: *2573*
13: 9 **w**: and if not, *then* after that thou shalt cut it NIG
19:17 he said unto him, **W**, *thou* good servant: *2095*
20:39 answering said, Master, thou hast **w** said. *2573*
Jn 2:10 and when *men* have **w drunk**, then *3182*
4: 6 Now Jacob's **w** was there. Jesus therefore, *4077*
4: 6 wearied with *his* journey, sat thus on the **w**: *4077*
4:11 nothing to draw with, and the **w** is deep: *5421*
4:12 which gave us the **w**, and drank thereof *5421*
4:14 **w** of water springing up into everlasting *4077*
4:17 Thou hast **w** said, I have no husband: *2573*
8:48 Say we not **w** that thou art a Samaritan, and *2573*
11:12 Lord, if he sleep, he shall **do w**. *4982*
13:13 and Lord: and ye say **w**; for *so* I am. *2573*
18:23 of the evil: but if **w**, why smitest thou me? *2573*
Ac 10:33 and thou hast **w** done that thou art come. *2573*
10:47 have received the Holy Ghost **as w as** *2531*
15:29 which if ye keep yourselves, ye shall do **w**. *2095*
15:29 ye shall do well. **Fare** ye **w**. *4517*
16: 2 Which was **w reported of** by the brethren *3140*
25:10 I done no wrong, as thou **very w** knowest. *2573*
28:25 **W** spake the Holy Ghost by Esaias *2573*
Ro 2: 7 To them who by patient continuance in **w** *18*
11:20 **W**; because of unbelief they were broken *2573*
1Co 7:37 heart that *he* will keep his virgin, doeth **w**. *2573*
7:38 then he that giveth *her* in marriage doeth **w**; *2573*
9: 5 **as w** as other apostles, and *as* the brethren *2532*
10: 5 with many of them God was not **w pleased**: *2106*
14:17 For thou verily givest thanks **w**, but *2573*
2Co 6: 9 As unknown, and *yet* **w known**; as dying, *1921*
11: 4 not accepted, ye might **w** bear with *him.* *2573*
Gal 4:17 They zealously affect you, *but* not **w**; yea, *2573*
5: 7 Ye did run **w**; who did hinder you that *ye* *2573*
6: 9 And let us not be weary in **w** doing: for in *2570*
Eph 6: 3 That it may be **w** with thee, and *2095*
Php 4:14 Notwithstanding ye have **w** done, that ye *2573*
4:18 a sacrifice acceptable, **w pleasing** to God. *2101*
Col 3:20 *things:* for this is **w pleasing** unto the Lord. *2101*
2Th 3:13 But ye, brethren, be not weary in **w doing**. *2569*
1Ti 3: 4 One that ruleth **w** his own house, having *his* *2573*
3:12 *their* children and their own houses **w**. *2573*
3:13 **w** purchase to themselves a good degree, *2573*
5:10 **W reported** of for good works; if she have *3140*
5:17 Let the elders that rule **w** be counted *2573*
2Ti 1:18 *unto me* at Ephesus, thou knowest **very w**. *957*
Tit 2: 9 to **please** *them* **w** in all *things;* not *1510+2101*
Heb 4: 2 the gospel preached, **as w** as unto them: *2509*
13:16 for with such sacrifices God is **w pleased**. *2100*
13:21 working in you *that which is* **w pleasing** in *2101*
Jas 2: 8 love thy neighbour as thyself, ye do **w**: *2573*
2:19 that there is one God; thou doest **w**: *2573*
1Pe 2:14 and *for* the praise of them that **do w**. *17*
2:15 that with **w doing** *ye* may put to silence *15*
2:20 but if, when ye **do w**, and suffer *for it,* ye take *15*
3: 6 as long as ye **do w**, and are not afraid with *15*
3:17 that *ye* suffer for **w doing**, than for evil doing. *15*
4:19 the keeping of their souls *to him* in **w doing**, *16*
2Pe 1:17 my beloved Son, in whom I am **w pleased**. *2106*
1:19 whereunto ye do **w** that ye take heed, *2573*
3Jn 1: 6 journey after a godly sort, thou shalt do **w**: *2573*

WELL'S (6) [WELL]
Ge 29: 2 and a great stone *was* upon the **w** mouth. 875
29: 3 and they rolled the stone from the **w** mouth, 875
29: 3 put the stone again upon the **w** mouth in his 875
29: 8 and *till* they roll the stone from the **w** mouth; 875
29:10 rolled the stone from the **w** mouth, and 875
2Sa 17:19 and spread a covering over the **w** mouth, 875

WELL-BUILT See GOODLIER; GOODLIEST; GOODLY

WELLBELOVED, WELL-BELOVED (6) [LOVE, WELL]
SS 1:13 A bundle of myrrh *is* my **w** unto me; 1730
Isa 5: 1 Now will I sing to my **w** a song of my 3039
5: 1 My **w** hath a vineyard in a very fruitful hill: 3039
Mk 12: 6 Having yet therefore one son, his **w**, he sent *27*
Ro 16: 5 Salute my **w** Epenetus, who is the firstfruits of *27*
3Jn 1: 1 The elder unto the **w** Gaius, whom I love in *27*

WELLFAVOURED (1) [FAVOUR, WELL]
Na 3: 4 of the whoredoms of the **w** harlot, 2580+2896

WELLS (11) [WELL]
Ge 26:15 For all the **w** which his father's servants had 875
26:18 Isaac digged again the **w** of water, 875
Ex 15:27 where *were* twelve **w** of water, and 5869
Nu 20:17 neither will we drink *of* the water of the **w**: 875
Dt 6:11 **w** digged, which thou diggedst not, 953
2Ki 3:19 stop all **w** of water, and mar every good 4599
3:25 they stopped all the **w** of water, and 4599
2Ch 26:10 towers in the desert, and digged many **w**: 953
Ne 9:25 **w** digged, vineyards, and oliveyards, and 953
Isa 12: 3 ye draw water out of the **w** of salvation. 4599
2Pe 2:17 These are **w** without water, clouds that are *4077*

WELLSPRING (2) [SPRING, WELL]
Pr 16:22 Understanding *is* a **w** of life unto him that 4726
18: 4 *and* the **w** of wisdom *as* a flowing brook. 4726

WEN (1)
Lev 22:22 or **having a w**, or scurvy, or scabbed, 2990

WENCH (1)
2Sa 17:17 a **w** went and told them; and they went and 8198

WENT (1400) [GO]
Ge 2: 6 there **w up** a mist from the earth, and 5927
2:10 a river **w out** of Eden to water the garden; 3318
4:16 Cain **w out** from the presence of 3318
7: 7 Noah **w in**, and his sons, and his wife, and 935
7: 9 There **w in** two and two unto Noah into 935
7:15 they **w in** unto Noah into the ark, two and 935
7:16 they that **w in**, went in male and female of 935
7:16 went in, **w in** male and female of all flesh, 935
7:18 and the ark **w** upon the face of the waters. 1980
8: 7 forth a raven, which **w forth** to and fro, 3318
8:18 Noah **w forth**, and his sons, and his wife, 3318
8:19 after their kinds, **w forth** out of the ark. 3318
9:18 that **w forth** of the ark, were Shem, and 3318
9:23 **w** backward, and covered the nakedness of 1980
10:11 Out of that land **w forth** Asshur, and 3318
11:31 they **w forth** with them from Ur of 3318
12: 4 had spoken unto him; and Lot **w** with him: 1980
12: 5 they **w forth** to go into the land of Canaan; 3318

Ge 12:10 Abram **w down** into Egypt to sojourn there; 3381
13: 1 Abram **w up** out of Egypt, he, and his wife, 5927
13: 3 he **w** on his journeys from the south even to 1980
13: 5 which **w** with Abram, had flocks, and 1980
14: 8 there **w out** the king of Sodom, and 3318
14:11 and all their victuals, and **w** their way. 1980
14:17 the king of Sodom **w out** to meet him after 3318
14:24 the portion of the men which **w** with me, 1980
15:17 that, when the sun **w down**, and it was dark, 935
16: 4 And he **w in** unto Hagar, and she conceived: 935
17:22 with him, and God **w up** from Abraham. 5927
18:16 Abraham **w** with them to bring them on 1980
18:22 faces from thence, and **w** toward Sodom: 1980
18:33 the LORD **w** his way, as soon as he had 1980
19: 6 Lot **w out** at the door unto them, and 3318
19:14 Lot **w out**, and spake unto his sons in law, 3318
19:28 the smoke of the country **w up** as 5927
19:30 Lot **w up** out of Zoar, and dwelt in 5927
19:33 the firstborn **w in**, and lay with her father; 935
21:16 she **w**, and sat her down over against *him* a 1980
21:19 she **w**, and filled the bottle *with* water, and 1980
22: 3 **w** unto the place of which God had told 1980
22: 6 a knife; and they **w** both of them together. 1980
22: 8 so they **w** both of them together. 1980
22:13 Abraham **w** and took the ram, and 1980
22:19 they rose up and **w** together to Beer-sheba; 1980
23:10 *even* of all that **w in** *at* the gate of his city, 935
23:18 before all that **w in** *at* the gate of his city. 935
24:10 he arose, and **w** to Mesopotamia, unto 1980
24:16 she **w down** to the well, and filled her 3381
24:45 she **w down** unto the well, and drew *water*: 3381
24:61 the servant took Rebekah, and **w** his way. 1980
24:63 Isaac **w out** to meditate in the field at 3318
25:22 And she **w** to inquire of the LORD. 1980
25:34 and drink, and rose up, and **w** his way: 1980
26: 1 Isaac **w** unto Abimelech king of 1980
26:13 **w forward**, and grew until he became very 1980
26:23 And he **w up** from thence to Beer-sheba. 5927
26:26 Abimelech **w** to him from Gerar, and 1980
27: 5 And Esau **w** to the field to hunt for venison, 1980
27:14 he **w**, and fetched, and brought *them* to his 1980
27:22 Jacob **w near** unto Isaac his father; and 5066
28: 5 he **w** to Padan-aram unto Laban, son of 1980
28: 9 **w** Esau unto Ishmael, and took unto 1980
28:10 Jacob **w out** from Beer-sheba, and 3318
28:10 out from Beer-sheba, and **w** toward Haran. 1980
29: 1 Jacob **w on** his **journey**, and 5375+7272
29:10 that Jacob **w near**, and rolled the stone 5066
29:23 brought her to him; and he **w in** unto her. 935
29:30 he **w in** also unto Rachel, and he loved also 935
30: 4 handmaid to wife: and Jacob **w in** unto her. 935
30:14 Reuben **w** in the days of wheat harvest, 1980
30:16 Leah **w out** to meet him, and said, 3318
31:19 Laban **w** to shear his sheep: and Rachel had 1980
31:33 Laban **w** into Jacob's tent, and into Leah's 935
31:33 **w** he **out** of Leah's tent, and entered into 3318
32: 1 Jacob **w** on his way, and the angels of God 1980
32:21 So **w** the present **over** before him: and 5674
34: 1 **w out** to see the daughters of the land. 3318
34: 6 Hamor the father of Shechem **w out** unto 3318
34:24 all that **w out** of the gate of his city; 3318
34:24 all that **w out** of the gate of his city. 3318
34:26 Dinah out of Shechem's house, and **w out**. 3318
35: 3 and was with me in the way which I **w**. 1980
35:13 God **w up** from him in the place where he 5927
35:22 that Reuben **w** and lay with Bilhah his 1980
36: 6 **w** into the country from the face of his 1980
37:12 his brethren **w** to feed their father's flock in 1980
37:17 Joseph **w** after his brethren, and found them 1980
38: 1 that Judah **w down** from his brethren, and 3381
38: 2 and he took her, and **w in** unto her. 935
38: 9 when he **w in** unto his brother's wife, 935
38:11 as his brethren *did*. And Tamar **w** and 1980
38:12 **w up** unto his sheepshearers to Timnath, 5927
38:19 **w away**, and laid by her vail from her, and 1980
39:11 that *Joseph* **w** into the house to do his 935
41:45 Joseph **w out** over *all* the land of Egypt. 3318
41:46 Joseph **w out** from the presence of 3318
41:46 **w throughout** all the land of Egypt. 5674+871.1
42: 3 Joseph's ten brethren **w down** to buy corn 3381
43:15 **w down** *to* Egypt, and stood before Joseph. 3381
43:31 **w out**, and refrained himself, and said, 3318
44:28 the one **w out** from me, and I said, 3318
45:25 they **w up** out of Egypt, and came *into* 5927
46:29 **w up** to meet Israel his father, to Goshen, 5927
47:10 and **w out** from before Pharaoh. 3318
49: 4 then defiledst thou *it*: he **w up** to my couch. 5927
50: 7 Joseph **w up** to bury his father: and 5927
50: 7 with him **w up** all the servants of Pharaoh, 5927
50: 9 there **w up** with him both chariots and 5927
50:14 all that **w up** with him to bury his father, 5927
50:18 his brethren also **w** and fell down before his 1980
Ex 2: 1 there **w** a man of the house of Levi, and 1980
2: 8 the maid **w** and called the child's mother. 1980
2:11 that he **w out** unto his brethren, and 3318
2:13 when he **w out** the second day, behold, 3318
4:18 Moses **w** and returned to Jethro his father 1980
4:27 he **w**, and met him in the mount of God, 1980
4:29 Moses and Aaron **w** and gathered together 1980
5: 1 afterward Moses and Aaron **w in**, and 935
5:10 the taskmasters of the people **w out**, and 3318
7:10 Moses and Aaron **w in** unto Pharaoh, and 935
7:23 Pharaoh turned and **w** into his house, 935
8:12 and Aaron **w out** from Pharaoh: 3318
8:30 Moses **w out** from Pharaoh, and 3318
9:33 Moses **w out** of the city from Pharaoh, 3318
10: 6 he turned himself, and **w out** from Pharaoh. 3318
10:14 the locusts **w up** over all the land of Egypt, 5927
10:18 he **w out** from Pharaoh, and intreated 3318
11: 8 he **w out** from Pharaoh in a great anger. 3318
12:28 the children of Israel **w away**, and did as 1980
12:38 a mixed multitude **w up** also with them; 5927
12:41 *that* all the hosts of the LORD **w out** from 3318
13:18 the children of Israel **w up** harnessed out of 5927
13:21 the LORD **w** before them by day in a 1980

Ex 14: 8 the children of Israel **w out** with a high 3318
14:19 which **w** before the camp of Israel, 1980
14:19 of Israel, removed and **w** behind them; 1980
14:19 the pillar of the cloud **w** from before their 5265
14:22 the children of Israel **w** into the midst of 935
14:23 **w in** after them to the midst of the sea, 935
15:19 For the horse of Pharaoh **w in** with his 935
15:19 the children of Israel **w** on dry *land* in 1980
15:20 all the women **w out** after her with timbrels 3318
15:22 and they **w out** into the wilderness of Shur; 3318
15:22 they **w** three days in the wilderness, and 1980
16:27 *that* there **w out** *some* of the people on 3318
17:10 Aaron, and Hur **w up** *to* the top of the hill. 5927
18: 7 Moses **w out** to meet his father in law, and 3318
18:27 and he **w** his **way** into his own land. 1980
19: 3 Moses **w up** unto God, and the LORD 5927
19:14 Moses **w down** from the mount unto 3381
19:20 to the top of the mount; and Moses **w up**. 5927
19:25 So Moses **w down** unto the people, and 3381
24: 9 **w up** Moses, and Aaron, Nadab, and 5927
24:13 and Moses **w up** into the mount of God. 5927
24:15 Moses **w up** into the mount, and a cloud 5927
24:18 Moses **w** into the midst of the cloud, and 935
32:15 **w down** from the mount, and the two tables 3381
33: 7 **w out** unto the Tabernacle of 3318
33: 8 when Moses **w out** unto the tabernacle, 3318
34: 4 in the morning, and **w up** unto mount Sinai, 5927
34:34 when Moses **w in** before the LORD to 935
34:35 face again, until he **w in** to speak with him. 935
38:26 for every one that **w** to be numbered, 5674
40:32 When they **w** into the tent of 935
40:36 the children of Israel **w onward** in all their 5265
Lev 9: 8 Aaron therefore **w** unto the altar, and 7126
9:23 Aaron **w** into the tabernacle of 935
10: 2 there **w out** fire from the LORD, and 3318
10: 5 So they **w near**, and carried them in their 7126
16:23 which he put on when he **w** into the holy 935
24:10 **w out** among the children of Israel: 3318
Nu 8:22 after that **w** the Levites **in** to do their service 935
10:14 In the first *place* **w** the standard of the camp 5265
10:33 the ark of the covenant of the LORD **w** 5265
10:34 them by day, when they **w out** of the camp. 5265
11: 8 *And* the people **w about**, and gathered *it*, 7751
11:24 Moses **w out**, and told the people the words 3318
11:26 but **w** not **out** unto the tabernacle: 3318
11:31 there **w forth** a wind from the LORD, 5265
13:21 So they **w up**, and searched the land from 5927
13:26 they **w** and came to Moses, and to Aaron, 1980
13:31 the men that **w up** with him said, We be not 5927
14:24 will I bring into the land whereinto he **w**; 935
14:38 *which were* of the men that **w** to search 1980
16:25 rose up and **w** unto Dathan and Abiram; 1980
16:33 **w down** alive into the pit, and the earth 3381
17: 8 that on the morrow Moses **w** into 935
20: 6 Aaron **w** from the presence of the assembly 935
20:15 How our fathers **w down** into Egypt, and 3381
20:27 they **w up** into mount Hor in the sight of all 5927
21:16 from thence *they* **w** to Beer: that *is* the well NIH
21:18 from the wilderness *they* **w** *to* Mattanah: NIH
21:23 **w out** against Israel into the wilderness: 3318
21:33 and **w up** *by* the way of Bashan: 5927
21:33 Og the king of Bashan **w out** against them, 3318
22:14 they **w** unto Balak, and said, 935
22:21 his ass, and **w** with the princes of Moab. 1980
22:22 God's anger was kindled because he **w**: 1980
22:23 aside out of the way, and **w** into the field: 1980
22:26 And the angel of the LORD **w** further, and 5674
22:32 behold, I **w out** to withstand thee, because 3318
22:35 So Balaam **w** with the princes of Balak. 1980
22:36 he **w out** to meet him unto a city of Moab, 3318
22:39 Balaam **w** with Balak, and they came *unto* 1980
23: 3 I will tell thee. And he **w** to a high place. 1980
24: 1 he **w** not, as at other times, to seek for 1980
24:25 rose up, and **w** and returned to his place: 1980
24:25 to his place: and Balak also **w** his way. 1980
25: 8 he **w** after the man of Israel into the tent, 935
26: 4 which **w forth** out of the land of Egypt. 3318
31:13 **w forth** to meet them without the camp. 3318
31:21 unto the men of war which **w** to the battle, 935
31:27 who **w out** to battle, and between all 3318
31:28 of the men of war which **w out** to battle: 3318
31:36 *which was* the portion of them that **w out** to 3318
32: 9 For when they **w up** unto the valley of 5927
32:39 of Machir the son of Manasseh **w** to Gilead, 1980
32:41 Jair the son of Manasseh **w** and took 1980
32:42 Nobah **w** and took Kenath, and the villages 1980
33: 1 which **w forth** out of the land of Egypt 3318
33: 3 **w out** with a high hand in the sight of all 3318
33: 8 **w** three days' journey in the wilderness of 1980
33:23 they **w** from Kehelathah, and pitched in 5265
33:29 they **w** from Mithcah, and pitched in 5265
33:33 they **w** from Hor-hagidgad, and pitched in 5265
33:38 Aaron the priest **w up** into mount Hor at 5927
Dt 1:19 we **w** *through* all that great and terrible 1980
1:24 they turned and **w up** into the mountain, 5927
1:31 doth bear his son, in all the way that ye **w**, 1980
1:33 Who **w** in the way before you, to search 1980
1:43 and **w** presumptuously **up** into the hill. 5927
2:13 And we **w over** the brook Zered. 5674
3: 1 we turned, and **w up** the way to Bashan: 5927
5: 5 of the fire, and **w** not **up** into the mount;) 5927
10: 3 **w up** into the mount, having the two tables 5927
10:22 Thy fathers **w down** into Egypt with 3381
26: 5 he **w down** into Egypt, and sojourned there 3381
29:26 For they **w** and served other gods, and 1980
31: 1 Moses **w** and spake these words unto all 1980
31:14 Moses and Joshua **w**, and 1980
33: 2 from his right hand **w** a fiery law for them. NIH
34: 1 Moses **w up** from the plains of Moab unto 5927
Jos 2: 1 they **w**, and came *into* a harlot's house, 1980
2: 5 when it was dark, that the men **w out**: 3318
2: 5 whither the men **w** I wot not: pursue after 1980
2:22 they **w**, and came unto the mountain, and 1980
3: 2 that the officers **w** through the host; 5674
3: 6 of the covenant, and **w** before the people. 1980

Jos 5:13 Joshua **w** unto him, and said unto him, 1980
6: 1 of Israel: none **w out**, and none came in. 3318
6: 9 the armed men **w** before the priests that 1980
6:13 ark of the LORD **w on continually**, 1980+1980
6:13 the armed men **w** before them; but 1980
6:20 so that the people **w up** into the city, 5927
6:23 the young men that were spies **w in**, and 935
7: 2 And the men **w up** and viewed Ai. 5927
7: 4 So there **w up** thither of the people about 5927
8: 9 they **w** to lie in ambush, and abode between 1980
8:10 and **w up**, he and the elders of Israel, 5927
8:11 **w up**, and drew nigh, and came before 5927
8:13 Joshua **w** that night into the midst of 1980
8:14 the men of the city **w out** against Israel to 3318
8:17 in Ai or Beth-el, that **w** not **out** after Israel: 3318
9: 4 **w** and made as if they had been 1980
9: 6 they **w** to Joshua unto the camp *at* Gilgal, 1980
10: 5 **w up**, they and all their hosts, and 5927
10: 9 *and* **w up** from Gilgal all night. 5927
10:24 of the men of war which **w** with him, 1980
10:36 Joshua **w up** from Eglon, and all Israel with 5927
11: 4 they **w out**, they and all their hosts with 3318
14: 8 Nevertheless my brethren that **w up** with 5927
15: 3 it **w out** to the south side to 3318
15: 3 **w up** to Adar, and fetched a compass to 5927
15: 4 and **w out** *unto* the river of Egypt; 3318
15: 6 the border **w up** *to* Beth-hogla, and 5927
15: 6 the border **w up** *to* the stone of Bohan 5927
15: 7 the border **w up** toward Debir from 5927
15: 8 the border **w up** *by* the valley of the son of 5927
15: 8 the border **w up** to the top of the mountain 5927
15: 9 and **w out** to the cities of mount Ephron; 3318
15:10 **w down** *to* Beth-shemesh, and passed on *to* 3381
15:11 the border **w out** unto the side of Ekron 3318
15:11 *to* mount Baalah, and **w out** *unto* Jabneel; 3318
15:15 he **w up** thence to the inhabitants of Debir: 5927
16: 6 the border **w out** toward the sea *to* 3318
16: 6 the border **w about** eastward *unto* 5437
16: 7 it **w down** from Janohah *to* Ataroth, and 3381
16: 7 and came to Jericho, and **w out** *at* Jordan. 3318
16: 8 The border **w** *out* from Tappuah westward 1980
17: 7 the border **w** *along* on the right hand unto 1980
18: 8 the men arose, and **w away**: and 1980
18: 8 Joshua charged them that **w** to describe 1980
18: 9 the men **w** and passed through the land, 1980
18:12 the border **w up** to the side of Jericho on 5927
18:12 and **w up** through the mountains westward; 5927
18:13 the border **w over** from thence toward Luz, 5674
18:15 the border **w out** on the west, and went out 3318
18:15 **w out** to the well of waters of Nephtoah: 3318
18:17 **w forth** *to* En-shemesh, and went forth 3318
18:17 and **w forth** toward Geliloth, 3318
18:18 and **w down** unto Arabah: 3381
19:11 their border **w up** toward the sea, and 5927
19:47 the coast of the children of Dan **w out** *too* 3318
19:47 the children of Dan **w up** to fight against 5927
22: 6 them away: and they **w** unto their tents. 1980
24: 4 Jacob and his children **w down** *into* Egypt. 3381
24:11 ye **w over** Jordan, and came unto Jericho: 5674
24:17 preserved us in all the way wherein we **w**, 1980
Jdg 1: 3 thee into thy lot. So Simeon **w** with him. 1980
1: 4 Judah **w up**; and the LORD delivered 5927
1: 9 afterward the children of Judah **w down** to 3381
1:10 Judah **w** against the Canaanites that dwelt 1980
1:11 from thence he **w** against the inhabitants of 1980
1:16 **w up** out of the city of palm trees with 5927
1:16 and they **w** and dwelt among the people. 1980
1:17 Judah **w** with Simeon his brother, and 1980
1:22 of Joseph, they also **w up** *against* Beth-el: 5927
1:26 the man **w** *into* the land of the Hittites, and 1980
2: 6 the children of Israel **w** every man unto his 1980
2:15 Whithersoever they **w out**, the hand of 3318
2:17 they **w a whoring** after other gods, and 2181
3:10 and he judged Israel, and **w out** to war: 3318
3:13 **w** and smote Israel, and possessed the city 1980
3:19 And all that stood by him **w out** from him. 3318
3:22 the haft also **w in** after the blade; and the fat 935
3:23 Ehud **w forth** through the porch, and 3318
3:27 the children of Israel **w down** with him 3381
3:28 they **w down** after him, and took the fords 3381
4: 9 and **w** with Barak to Kedesh. 1980
4:10 he **w up** with ten thousand men at his feet: 5927
4:10 at his feet: and Deborah **w up** with him. 5927
4:14 So Barak **w down** from mount Tabor, and 3381
4:18 Jael **w out** to meet Sisera, and said unto 3318
4:21 **w** softly unto him, and smote the nail into 935
6:19 And Gideon **w in**, and made ready a kid, and 935
6:33 **w over**, and pitched in the valley of Jezreel. 5674
7:11 **w** he **down** with Phurah his servant unto 3381
8: 8 he **w up** thence *to* Penuel, and spake unto 5927
8:11 Gideon **w up** *by* the way of them that dwelt 5927
8:27 all Israel **w** thither **a whoring** after it: 2181
8:29 Jerubbaal the son of Joash **w** and dwelt in 1980
8:33 **w a whoring** after Baalim, and 2181
9: 1 Abimelech the son of Jerubbaal **w** to 1980
9: 5 And he **w** unto his father's house at Ophrah, 935
9: 6 of Millo, and **w**, and made Abimelech king, 1980
9: 7 he **w** and stood in the top of mount 1980
9: 8 The trees **w forth on a time** to 1980+1980
9:21 and fled, and **w** to Beer, and dwelt there, 1980
9:26 with his brethren, and **w over** to Shechem: 5674
9:27 they **w out** *into* the fields, and 3318
9:27 and **w** *into* the house of their god, and did eat 935
9:35 Gaal the son of Ebed **w out**, and stood *in* 3318
9:39 Gaal **w out** before the men of Shechem, 3318
9:42 that the people **w out** *into* the field; 3318
9:50 **w** Abimelech to Thebez, and 1980
9:52 **w hard** unto the door of the tower to burn 5066
11: 3 vain men to Jephthah, and **w out** with him. 3318
11: 5 the elders of Gilead **w** to fetch Jephthah out 1980
11:11 Jephthah **w** with the elders of Gilead, and 1980
11:18 they **w along** through the wilderness, and 1980
11:38 she **w** with her companions, and 1980
11:40 *That* the daughters of Israel **w** yearly to 1980
12: 1 and **w** northward, and said unto Jephthah, 5674

Jdg 13:11 **w** after his wife, and came to the man, and 1980
13:20 when the flame **w up** toward heaven from 5927
14: 1 Samson **w down** *to* Timnath, and saw a 3381
14: 5 **w** Samson **down**, and his father and 3381
14: 7 he **w down**, and talked with the woman; 3381
14: 9 **w on** eating, and came to his father 1980+1980
14:10 So his father **w down** unto the woman: and 3381
14:18 on the seventh day before the sun **w down**, 935
14:19 he **w down** *to* Ashkelon, and slew thirty 3381
14:19 and he **w up** *to* his father's house. 5927
15: 4 Samson **w** and caught three hundred foxes, 1980
15: 8 he **w down** and dwelt in the top of the rock 3381
15: 9 the Philistines **w up**, and pitched in Judah, 5927
15:11 three thousand men of Judah **w** to the top of 3381
16: 1 **w** Samson to Gaza, and saw there a harlot, 1980
16: 1 and saw there a harlot, and **w in** unto her. 935
16: 3 **w away** with them, bar and all, and 5265
16:14 **w away** with the pin of the beam, and 5265
16:19 to afflict him, and his strength **w** from him. 5493
17:10 and thy victuals. So the Levite **w** *in*. 1980
18:11 there **w** from thence of the family of 5265
18:12 they **w up**, and pitched in Kirjath-jearim, 5927
18:14 answered the five men that **w** to spy out 1980
18:17 the five men that **w** to spy out the land went 1980
18:17 men that went to spy out the land **w up**, 5927
18:18 these **w** *into* Micah's house, and fetched 935
18:20 and **w** in the midst of the people. 935
18:26 the children of Dan **w** their way: and 1980
18:26 he turned and **w back** unto his house. 7725
19: 2 **w away** from him unto her father's house 1980
19: 3 her husband arose, and **w** after her, to speak 1980
19:14 they passed on and **w** *their way;* and 1980
19:14 the sun **w down** upon them *when they were* 935
19:15 when he **w in**, he sat him down in a street of 935
19:18 I **w** to Beth-lehem-judah, but I am *now* 1980
19:23 **w out** unto them, and said unto them, Nay, 3318
19:27 of the house, and **w out** to go his way: 3318
20: 1 all the children of Israel **w out**, and 3318
20:18 **w up** *to* the house of God, and 5927
20:20 the men of Israel **w out** to battle against 3318
20:23 (And the children of Israel **w up** and 5927
20:25 Benjamin **w forth** against them out of 3318
20:26 **w up**, and came *unto* the house of God, and 5927
20:30 the children of Israel **w up** against 5927
20:31 the children of Benjamin **w out** against 3318
21:23 they **w** and returned unto their inheritance, 1980
21:24 they **w out** from thence every man to his 3318
Ru 1: 1 a *certain* man of Beth-lehem-judah **w** to 1980
1: 7 Wherefore she **w forth** out of the place 3318
1: 7 they **w** on the way to return unto the land of 1980
1:19 So they two **w** until they came *to* 1980
1:21 I **w out** full, and the LORD hath brought 1980
2: 3 she **w**, and came, and gleaned in the field 1980
2:18 she took *it* up, and **w** *into* the city: and 935
3: 6 she **w down** *unto* the floor, and 3381
3: 7 he **w** to lie down at the end of the heap *of* 935
3:15 and laid *it* on her: and he **w** *into* the city. 935
4: 1 **w** Boaz **up** *to* the gate, and sat him down 5927
4:13 when he **w in** unto her, the LORD gave her 935
1Sa 1: 3 this man **w up** out of his city yearly to 5927
1: 7 when she **w up** to the house of the LORD, 5927
1:18 So the woman **w** her way, and did eat, and 1980
1:21 **w up** to offer unto the LORD the yearly 5927
1:22 Hannah **w** not **up**; for she said unto her 5927
2:11 Elkanah **w** to Ramah to his house. And 1980
2:20 And they **w** unto their own home. 1980
3: 3 ere the lamp of God **w out** in the temple of 3518
3: 5 lie down again. And he **w** and lay down. 1980
3: 6 Samuel arose and **w** to Eli, and said, 1980
3: 8 he arose and **w** to Eli, and said, Here *am* I; 1980
3: 9 So Samuel **w** and lay down in his place. 1980
4: 1 Now Israel **w out** against the Philistines to 3318
5:12 and the cry of the city **w up** *to* heaven. 5927
6:12 *and* **w along** the highway, lowing as they 1980
6:12 lowing as they **w**, and turned not aside *to* 1980
6:12 the lords of the Philistines **w** after them 1980
7: 7 the lords of the Philistines **w up** against 5927
7:11 the men of Israel **w out** of Mizpeh, and 3318
7:16 he **w** from year to year in circuit *to* Beth-el, 1980
9: 9 when a man **w** to inquire of God, thus he 1980
9:10 So they **w** unto the city where the man of 1980
9:11 *And* as they **w up** the hill to the city, they 5927
9:14 they **w up** *into* the city: *and* when they 5927
9:26 they **w out** both of them, he and Samuel, 3318
10:14 unto him and to his servant, Whither **w** ye? 1980
10:26 Saul also **w** home to Gibeah; and 1980
10:26 there **w** with him a band of men, 1980
11:15 all the people **w** *to* Gilgal; and there they 1980
13: 7 *some of the* Hebrews **w over** Jordan *to* 5674
13:10 Saul **w out** to meet him, that he might 3318
13:20 all the Israelites **w down** *to* the Philistines, 3381
13:23 the garrison of the Philistines **w out** to 3318
14:16 and they **w on** beating down *one another.* 1980
14:19 in the host of the Philistines **w on** 1980+1980
14:21 which **w up** with them into the camp *from* 5927
14:46 Saul **w up** from following the Philistines: 5927
14:46 and the Philistines **w** to their own place. 1980
15:34 Samuel **w** to Ramah; and Saul went up to 1980
15:34 Saul **w up** to his house *to* Gibeah of Saul. 5927
16:13 So Samuel rose up, and **w** to Ramah. 1980
17: 4 there **w out** a champion out of the camp of 3318
17: 7 and one bearing a shield **w** before him. 1980
17:12 the man **w** among men *for* an old man in 935
17:13 the three eldest sons of Jesse **w** *and* 1980
17:13 the names of his three sons that **w** to 1980
17:15 David **w** and returned from Saul to feed his 1980
17:20 the sheep with a keeper, and took, and **w**, 1980
17:35 I **w out** after him, and smote him, and 3318
17:41 the man that bare the shield *w* before him. NIH
18: 5 David **w out** whithersoever Saul sent him, 3318
18:13 he **w out** and came in before the people. 3318
18:16 because he **w out** and came in before them. 3318
18:27 Wherefore David arose and **w**, he and 1980
18:30 the princes of the Philistines **w forth**: and 3318
18:30 it came to pass, after they **w forth**, 3318

1Sa 19: 8 David **w out**, and fought with 3318
19:12 a window: and he **w**, and fled, and escaped. 1980
19:18 And he and Samuel **w** and dwelt in Naioth. 1980
19:22 **w** he also to Ramah, and came to a great 1980
19:23 he **w** thither to Naioth in Ramah: and 1980
19:23 he **w on**, and prophesied, until he 1980+1980
20:11 And they **w out** both of them *into* the field. 3318
20:35 that Jonathan **w out** *into* the field at 3318
20:42 and departed: and Jonathan **w** *into* the city. 935
21:10 of Saul, and **w** to Achish the king of Gath. 935
22: 1 all his father's house heard *it*, they **w down** 3381
22: 3 David **w** thence *to* Mizpeh of Moab: and 1980
23: 5 So David and his men **w** *to* Keilah, and 1980
23:13 and **w** whithersoever they could go. 1980
23:16 **w** to David *into* the wood, and 1980
23:18 in the wood, and Jonathan **w** to his house. 1980
23:24 they arose, and **w** to Ziph before Saul: but 1980
23:25 his men **w** to seek *him*. And they told 1980
23:26 Saul **w** on this side of the mountain, and 1980
23:28 after David, and **w** against the Philistines: 1980
23:29 David **w up** from thence, and dwelt in 5927
24: 2 **w** to seek David and his men upon 1980
24: 3 *was* a cave; and Saul **w in** to cover his feet: 935
24: 7 rose up out of the cave, and **w** on *his* way. 1980
24: 8 **w out** of the cave, and cried after Saul, 3318
24:22 Saul **w** home; but David and his men gat 1980
25: 1 and **w down** to the wilderness of Paran. 3381
25:12 **w again**, and came and told him all those 7725
25:13 there **w up** after David about four hundred 5927
25:42 with five damsels of hers that **w** after her; 1980
25:42 she **w** after the messengers of David, and 1980
26: 2 and **w down** to the wilderness of Ziph, 3381
26:13 David **w over** *to* the *other* side, and 5674
26:25 So David **w** on his way, and Saul returned 1980
27: 8 David and his men **w up**, and invaded 5927
28: 8 he **w**, and two men with him, and 1980
28:25 Then they arose up, and **w away** that night. 1980
29:11 And the Philistines **w up** *to* Jezreel. 5927
30: 2 but carried *them* away, and **w** on their way. 1980
30: 9 So David **w**, he and the six hundred men 1980
30:21 they **w forth** to meet David, and to meet 3318
30:22 of those that **w** with David, and said, 1980
30:22 and said, Because they **w** not with us, 1980
31: 3 the battle **w sore** against Saul, and 3513
31:12 **w** all night, and took the body of Saul and 1980
2Sa 1: 4 David said unto him, How **w** the matter? 1961
2: 2 So David **w up** thither, and his two wives 5927
2:12 of Saul, **w out** from Mahanaim to Gibeon. 3318
2:13 **w out**, and met together by the pool of 3318
2:15 and **w over** by number twelve of Benjamin, 5674
2:24 the sun **w down** when they were come to 935
2:29 **w** *through* all Bithron, and they came *to* 1980
2:32 Joab and his men **w** all night, and they 1980
3:16 her husband **w** with her along weeping 1980
3:19 Abner **w** also to speak in the ears of David 1980
3:21 David sent Abner away; and he **w** in peace. 1980
4: 5 **w**, and came about the heat of the day to 1980
5: 6 his men **w** *to* Jerusalem unto the Jebusites, 1980
5:10 David **w on**, and grew great, and 1980
5:17 David heard *of it*, and **w down** to the hold. 3381
6: 2 **w** with all the people that *were* with him 1980
6: 4 the ark of God: and Ahio **w** before the ark. 1980
6:12 So David **w** and brought up the ark of God 1980
7:18 **w** king David **in**, and sat before the LORD, 935
7:23 whom God **w** to redeem for a people to 1980
8: 3 as he **w** to recover his border at the river 1980
8: 6 preserved David whithersoever he **w**. 1980
8:14 preserved David whithersoever he **w**. 1980
10:16 of the host of Hadarezer *w* before them. NIH
11: 9 of his lord, and **w** not **down** to his house. 3381
11:10 saying, Uriah **w** not **down** unto his house, 3381
11:13 at even he **w out** to lie on his bed with 3318
11:13 of his lord, but **w** not **down** to his house. 3381
11:17 the men of the city **w out**, and fought with 3318
11:21 why **w** ye **nigh** the wall? then say 5066
11:22 So the messenger **w**, and came and 1980
12:16 and **w in**, and lay all night upon the earth. 935
12:17 *and* **w** to him, to raise him up from NIH
12:24 his wife, and **w in** unto her, and lay with her: 935
12:29 **w** to Rabbah, and fought against it, and 1980
13: 8 So Tamar **w** *to* her brother Amnon's house; 1980
13: 9 And they **w out** every man from him. 3318
13:19 laid her hand on her head, and **w on** crying. 1980
13:37 Absalom fled, and **w** to Talmai, the son of 1980
13:38 and **w** to Geshur, and was there three years. 1980
14:23 So Joab arose and **w** to Geshur, and 1980
15: 9 Go in peace. So he arose, and **w** to Hebron. 1980
15:11 with Absalom **w** two hundred men out of 1980
15:11 they **w** in their simplicity, and they knew 1980
15:16 the king **w forth**, and all his household 3318
15:17 the king **w forth**, and all the people after 3318
15:24 Abiathar **w up**, until all the people had 5927
15:30 David **w up** by the ascent of *mount* Olivet, 5927
15:30 wept as he **w up**, and had his head covered, 5927
15:30 had his head covered, and he **w** barefoot: 1980
15:30 and they **w up**, weeping as they went up. 5927
15:30 and they went up, weeping as they **w up**. 5927
16:13 as David and his men **w** by the way, Shimei 1980
16:13 Shimei **w along** on the hill's side over 1980
16:13 cursed as he **w**, and threw stones at him, 1980
16:22 Absalom **w in** unto his father's concubines 935
17:17 a wench **w** and told them; and they went 1980
17:17 told them; and they **w** and told king David. 1980
17:18 they **w** both of them **away** quickly, and 1980
17:18 a well in his court; whither they **w down**. 3381
17:21 **w** and told king David, and said unto 1980
17:25 that **w in** to Abigail the daughter of Nahash, 935
18: 6 So the people **w out** *into* the field against 3318
18: 9 the mule **w** under the thick boughs of a great 935
18: 9 and the mule that *was* under him **w away**. 5674
18:24 the watchman **w** *up* to the roof over 1980
18:33 **w up** to the chamber over the gate, and 5927
18:33 as he **w**, thus he said, O my son Absalom, 1980
19:17 and they **w over** Jordan before the king. 6743
19:18 there **w over** a ferry boat to carry over 5674

2Sa 19:19 that my lord the king **w out** of Jerusalem, 3318
19:31 **w over** Jordan with the king, to conduct 5674
19:39 all the people **w over** Jordan. And when 5674
19:40 the king **w on** to Gilgal, and 5674
19:40 on to Gilgal, and Chimham **w on** with him: 5674
20: 2 So every man of Israel **w up** from after 5927
20: 3 and fed them, but **w** not **in** unto them. 935
20: 5 So Amasa **w** to assemble *the men of* Judah: 1980
20: 7 there **w out** after him Joab's men, and 3318
20: 7 mighty *men:* and they **w out** of Jerusalem, 3318
20: 8 which *is* in Gibeon, Amasa **w** before them. 935
20: 8 sheath thereof; and as he **w forth** it fell out. 3318
20:13 all the people **w on** after Joab, to pursue 5674
20:14 he **w through** all the tribes of Israel unto 5674
20:14 were gathered together, and **w** also after him. 935
20:22 the woman **w** unto all the people in her 935
21:12 David **w** and took the bones of Saul and 1980
21:15 David **w down**, and his servants with him, 3381
22: 9 There **w up** a smoke out of his nostrils, and 5927
23:13 three of the thirty chief **w down**, and 3381
23:17 *is not this* the blood of the men that **w** in 1980
23:20 he **w down** also and slew a lion in 3381
23:21 he **w down** to him with a staff, and 3381
24: 4 the captains of the host **w out** from 3318
24: 7 they **w out** to the south of Judah, *even to* 3318
24:19 of Gad, **w up** as the LORD commanded. 5927
24:20 Araunah **w out**, and bowed himself before 3318
1Ki 1:15 Bath-sheba **w in** unto the king into 935
1:38 **w down**, and caused Solomon to ride upon 3381
1:49 and rose up, and **w** every man his way. 1980
1:50 **w**, and caught hold on the horns of 1980
2: 8 curse in the day when I **w** *to* Mahanaim: 1980
2:19 Bath-sheba therefore **w** unto king Solomon, 935
2:34 So Benaiah the son of Jehoiada **w up**, and 5927
2:40 **w** to Gath to Achish to seek his servants: 1980
2:40 Shimei **w**, and brought his servants from 1980
2:46 which **w out**, and fell upon him, that he 3318
3: 4 the king **w** to Gibeon to sacrifice there; 1980
6: 8 they **w up** with winding stairs into 5927
8:66 **w** unto their tents joyful and glad of heart 1980
10: 5 his ascent *by* which he **w up** *unto* the house 5927
10:13 So she turned and **w** to her own country, 1980
10:16 six hundred *shekels* of gold **w** to one target. 5927
10:17 three pound *of* gold **w** to one shield: 5927
10:29 **w out** of Egypt for six hundred *shekels* of 3318
11: 5 For Solomon **w** after Ashtoreth the goddess 1980
11: 6 **w** not **fully** after the LORD, as *did* David 4390
11:24 them *of Zobah:* and they **w** *to* Damascus, 1980
11:29 time when Jeroboam **w out** of Jerusalem, 3318
12: 1 Rehoboam **w** *to* Shechem: for all Israel 1980
12:25 **w out** from thence, and built Penuel. 3318
12:30 for the people **w** *to worship* before the one, 1980
13:10 So he **w** another way, and returned not by 1980
13:12 father said unto them, What way **w** he? 1980
13:12 sons had seen what way the man of God **w**, 1980
13:14 **w** after the man of God, and found him 1980
13:19 So he **w back** with him, and did eat bread 7725
13:28 he **w** and found his carcase cast in the way, 1980
14: 4 **w** *to* Shiloh, and came *to* the house of 1980
14:28 when the king **w** *into* the house of 935
15:17 Baasha king of Israel **w up** against Judah, 5927
16:10 Zimri **w in** and smote him, and killed him, 935
16:17 Omri **w up** from Gibbethon, and all Israel 5927
16:18 that he **w** into the palace of the king's house, 935
16:31 and **w** and served Baal, and worshipped him. 1980
17: 5 So he **w** and did according unto the word of 1980
17: 5 for he **w** and dwelt by the brook Cherith, 1980
17:10 So he arose and **w** to Zarephath. And when 1980
17:15 she **w** and did according to the saying of 1980
18: 2 Elijah **w** to shew himself unto Ahab. 1980
18: 6 Ahab **w** one way by himself, and 1980
18: 6 Obadiah **w** another way by himself. 1980
18:16 So Obadiah **w** to meet Ahab, and told him: 1980
18:16 and told him: and Ahab **w** to meet Elijah. 1980
18:42 So Ahab **w up** to eat and to drink. 5927
18:42 Elijah **w up** to the top of Carmel; and 5927
18:43 he **w up**, and looked, and said, *There is* 5927
18:45 And Ahab rode, and **w** to Jezreel. 1980
19: 3 **w** for his life, and came *to* Beer-sheba, 1980
19: 4 he himself **w** a day's journey into 1980
19: 8 **w** in the strength of that meat forty days 1980
19:13 **w out**, and stood *in* the entering in of 3318
19:21 **w** after Elijah, and ministered unto him. 1980
20: 1 he **w up** and besieged Samaria, and 5927
20:16 they **w out** at noon. But Ben-hadad *was* 3318
20:17 of the princes of the provinces **w out** first; 3318
20:21 the king of Israel **w out**, and smote 3318
20:26 and **w up** to Aphek, to fight against Israel. 5927
20:27 and were all present, and **w** against them: 1980
20:39 Thy servant **w out** into the midst of 3318
20:43 the king of Israel **w** to his house heavy and 1980
21:27 fasted, and lay in sackcloth, and **w** softly. 1980
22:24 Zedekiah the son of Chenaanah **w near**, 5066
22:24 Which way **w** the spirit of the LORD from 5674
22:29 Jehoshaphat the king of Judah **w up** *to* 5927
22:30 disguised himself, and **w** into the battle. 935
22:36 there **w** a proclamation throughout the host 5674
22:48 they **w** not; for the ships were broken at 1980
2Ki 1: 9 he **w up** to him: and behold, he sat on 5927
1:13 the third captain of fifty **w up**, and came 5927
1:15 and **w down** with him unto the king. 3381
2: 1 that Elijah **w** with Elisha from Gilgal. 1980
2: 2 not leave thee. So they **w down** *to* Beth-el. 3381
2: 6 I will not leave thee. And they two **w on**. 1980
2: 7 fifty men of the sons of the prophets **w**, 1980
2: 8 so that they two **w over** on dry *ground.* 5674
2:11 **still w on**, and talked, that behold, 1980+1980
2:11 Elijah **w up** by a whirlwind *into* heaven. 5927
2:13 **w back**, and stood by the bank of Jordan; 7725
2:14 and thither: and Elisha **w over**. 5674
2:21 he **w forth** unto the spring of the waters, 3318
2:23 And he **w up** from thence *unto* Beth-el: and 5927
2:25 he **w** from thence to mount Carmel, and 1980
3: 6 king Jehoram **w out** of Samaria the same 3318
3: 7 he **w** and sent to Jehoshaphat the king of 1980

2Ki 3: 9 So the king of Israel **w**, and the king of 1980
3:12 and the king of Edom **w down** to him. 3381
3:24 they **w forward** smiting the Moabites, 935
3:25 howbeit the slingers **w about** *it,* and 5437
4: 5 So she **w** from him, and shut the door upon 1980
4:18 that he **w out** to his father to the reapers. 3318
4:21 she **w up**, and laid him on the bed of 5927
4:21 and shut *the door* upon him, and **w out.** 3318
4:25 So she **w** and came unto the man of God to 1980
4:31 Wherefore he **w again** to meet him, and 7725
4:33 He **w in** therefore, and shut the door upon 935
4:34 he **w up**, and lay upon the child, and put his 5927
4:35 **w up**, and stretched himself upon him: 5927
4:37 she **w in**, and fell at his feet, and 935
4:37 the ground, and took up her son, and **w out.** 3318
4:39 one **w out** into the field to gather herbs, 3318
5: 4 *one* **w in**, and told his lord, saying, Thus 935
5:11 and **w away**, and said, Behold, I thought, 1980
5:12 So he turned and **w away** in a rage. 1980
5:14 **w** he **down**, and dipped *himself* seven 3381
5:25 he **w in**, and stood before his master. 935
5:25 And he said, Thy servant **w** no whither. 1980
5:26 **W** not mine heart *with thee,* when the man 1980
5:27 he **w out** from his presence a leper *as white* 3318
6: 4 So he **w** with them. And when they came to 1980
6:23 sent them away, and they **w** to their master. 1980
6:24 his host, and **w up**, and besieged Samaria. 5927
7: 8 they **w** into one tent, and did eat and drink, 935
7: 8 and **w** and hid *it;* and came again, and 1980
7: 8 and carried thence *also,* and **w** and hid *it.* 1980
7:15 they **w** after them unto Jordan: and lo, 1980
7:16 the people **w out**, and spoiled the tents of 3318
8: 2 she **w** with her household, and sojourned in 1980
8: 3 she **w forth** to cry unto the king for her 3318
8: 9 So Hazael **w** to meet him, and took a 1980
8:21 So Joram **w over** to Zair, and all 5674
8:28 he **w** with Joram the son of Ahab to the war 1980
8:29 king Joram **w back** to be healed in Jezreel 7725
8:29 **w down** to see Joram the son of Ahab in 3381
9: 4 man the prophet, **w** *to* Ramoth-gilead. 1980
9: 6 he arose, and **w** into the house; and 935
9:16 So Jehu rode *in a chariot,* and **w** to Jezreel; 1980
9:18 So there **w** one on horseback to meet him, 1980
9:21 of Israel and Ahaziah king of Judah **w out,** 3318
9:21 they **w** out against Jehu, and met him in 3318
9:24 the arrow **w out** at his heart, and he sunk 3318
9:35 they **w** to bury her: but they found no more 1980
10: 9 that he **w out**, and stood, and said to all 3318
10:23 Jehu **w**, and Jehonadab the son of Rechab, 935
10:24 when they **w in** to offer sacrifices and 935
10:25 and **w** to the city of the house of Baal. 1980
11:16 she **w** *by* the way by the which the horses 935
11:18 all the people of the land **w** *into* the house of 935
12:17 Hazael king of Syria **w up**, and 5927
12:18 of Syria: and he **w away** from Jerusalem. 5927
13: 5 that they **w out** from under the hand of 3318
14:11 Therefore Jehoash king of Israel **w up**; and 5927
15:14 For Menahem the son of Gadi **w up** from 5927
16: 9 for the king of Assyria **w up** against 5927
16:10 king Ahaz **w** *to* Damascus to meet 1980
17: 5 **w up** *to* Samaria, and besieged it three 5927
17:15 **w** after the heathen that *were* round about NIH
18: 7 he prospered whithersoever he **w forth**: 3318
18:17 they **w up** and came *to* Jerusalem. 5927
19: 1 and **w** *into* the house of the LORD. 935
19:14 Hezekiah **w up** *into* the house of 5927
19:35 that the angel of the LORD **w out**, and 3318
19:36 and **w** and returned, and dwelt at Nineveh. 1980
22:14 Asahiah, **w** unto Huldah the prophetess, 1980
23: 2 the king **w up** *into* the house of 5927
23:29 **w up** against the king of Assyria to 5927
23:29 king Josiah **w** against him; and he slew him 1980
24:12 Jehoiachin the king of Judah **w out** to 3318
25: 4 and *the king* **w** the way toward the plain. 1980
1Ch 2:21 afterward Hezron **w in** to the daughter of 935
4:39 they **w** to the entrance of Gedor, *even* unto 1980
4:42 five hundred men, **w** to mount Seir, 1980
5:18 and threescore, that **w out** *to* the war. 3318
5:25 **w a whoring** after the gods of the people of 2181
6:15 Jehozadak **w** *into captivity,* when 1980
7:23 when he **w in** to his wife, she conceived, 935
7:23 because it **w** evil with his house. 1961
10: 3 the battle **w sore** against Saul, and 3513
11: 4 David and all Israel **w** *to* Jerusalem, 1980
11: 6 So Joab the son of Zeruiah **w** first **up**, and 5927
11:15 Now three of the thirty captains **w down** to 3381
11:22 also he **w down** and slew a lion in a pit in a 3381
11:23 he **w down** to him with a staff, and 3381
12:15 These *are* they that **w over** Jordan in 5674
12:17 David **w out** to meet them, and answered 3318
12:20 As he **w** to Ziklag, there fell to him of 1980
12:33 Of Zebulun, such as **w forth** to battle, 3318
12:36 such as **w forth** to battle, expert in war, 3318
13: 6 David **w up**, and all Israel, to Baalah, 5927
14: 8 all the Philistines **w up** to seek David. 5927
14: 8 David heard *of it,* and **w out** against them. 3318
14:17 And the fame of David **w out** into all lands; 3318
15:25 **w** to bring up the ark of the covenant of 1980
16:20 *when* they **w** from nation to nation, and 1980
17:21 whom God **w** to redeem *to be* his own 1980
18: 3 as he **w** to stablish his dominion by 1980
18: 6 preserved David whithersoever he **w**. 1980
18:13 preserved David whithersoever he **w**. 1980
19: 5 there **w** *certain,* and told David how 1980
19:16 of the host of Hadarezer **w** before them. NIH
21: 4 **w** throughout all Israel, and came *to* 1980
21:19 David **w up** at the saying of Gad, which he 5927
21:21 **w out** of the threshingfloor, and 3318
27: 1 **w out** month by month throughout all 3318
29:30 the times that **w** over him, and over Israel, 5674
2Ch 1: 3 **w** to the high place that *was* at Gibeon; 1980
1: 6 Solomon **w up** thither to the brasen altar 5927
8: 3 Solomon **w** *to* Hamath-zobah, and 1980
8:17 **w** Solomon to Ezion-geber, and to Eloth, 1980
8:18 they **w** with the servants of Solomon to 935
2Ch 9: 4 his ascent *by* which he **w up** *into* the house 5927
9:12 **w away** to her own land, she and 1980
9:15 six hundred *shekels* of beaten gold **w** to one 5927
9:16 three hundred *shekels* of gold **w** to one 5927
9:21 For the king's ships **w** *to* Tarshish with 1980
10: 1 Rehoboam **w** to Shechem: for *to* Shechem 1980
10:16 own house. So all Israel **w** to their tents. 1980
12:12 and also in Judah things **w** well. 1961
14:10 Asa **w out** against him, and they set 3318
15: 2 he **w out** to meet Asa, and said unto him, 3318
15: 5 times *there was* no peace to him that **w out,** 3318
17: 9 **w about** throughout all the cities of Judah, 5437
18: 2 after *certain* years he **w down** to Ahab to 3381
18:12 the messenger that **w** to call Micaiah spake 1980
18:23 Which way **w** the spirit of the LORD from 5674
18:28 Jehoshaphat the king of Judah **w up** to 5927
18:29 disguised himself; and they **w** to the battle. 935
19: 2 Jehu the son of Hanani the seer **w out** to 3318
19: 4 he **w out** again through the people from 3318
20:20 and **w forth** into the wilderness of Tekoa: 3318
20:20 as they **w forth**, Jehoshaphat stood and 3318
20:21 as *they* **w out** before the army, and to say, 3318
21: 9 Jehoram **w forth** with his princes, and 5674
22: 5 **w** with Jehoram the son of Ahab king of 1980
22: 6 **w down** to see Jehoram the son of Ahab at 3381
22: 7 he **w out** with Jehoram against Jehu the son 3318
23: 2 they **w about** in Judah, and gathered 5437
23:17 all the people **w** *to* the house of Baal, and 935
25:11 **w** *to* the valley of salt, and smote *of* 1980
25:21 So Joash the king of Israel **w up**; and 5927
26: 6 he **w forth** and warred against 3318
26:11 fighting *men,* that **w out** to war by bands, 3318
26:16 **w** into the temple of the LORD to burn 935
26:17 Azariah the priest **w in** after him, and 935
28: 9 he **w out** before the host that came to 3318
29:16 the priests **w** into the inner part *of* the house 935
29:18 they **w** in to Hezekiah the king, and said, 935
29:20 and **w up** *to* the house of the LORD. 5927
30: 6 So the posts **w** with the letters from 1980
31: 1 all Israel that were present **w out** to 3318
34:22 *they* that the king *had appointed,* **w** to 1980
34:30 the king **w up** *into* the house of 5927
35:20 and Josiah **w out** against him. 3318
Ezr 2: 1 the province that **w up** out of the captivity, 5927
2:59 these *were* they which **w up** from 5927
4:23 they **w up** in haste to Jerusalem unto 236
5: 8 that we **w** into the province of Judea, 236
7: 6 This Ezra **w up** from Babylon; and he *was* 5927
7: 7 there **w up** *some* of the children of Israel, 5927
8: 1 *this is* the genealogy of them that **w up** 5927
10: 6 **w** into the chamber of Johanan the son of 1980
Ne 2:13 I **w out** by night by the gate of the valley, 3318
2:14 I **w on** to the gate of the fountain, and 5674
2:15 **w** I **up** in the night by the brook, and 5927
2:16 the rulers knew not whither I **w**, or what I 1980
7: 6 that **w up** out of the captivity, *of* those that 5927
7:61 these *were* they which **w up** *also* from 5927
8:12 all the people **w** *their way* to eat, and 1980
8:16 So the people **w forth**, and brought *them,* 3318
9:11 that they **w through** the midst of the sea on 5674
9:24 So the children **w in** and possessed the land, 935
12: 1 the Levites that **w up** with Zerubbabel 5927
12:31 whereof *one* **w** on the right hand upon 8418
12:32 after them **w** Hoshaiah, and half of 1980
12:37 they **w up** by the stairs of the city of David, 5927
12:38 *them that gave* thanks **w** over against *them,* 1980
Est 2:14 In the evening she **w**, and on the morrow she 935
3:15 The posts **w out**, being hastened by 3318
4: 1 **w out** into the midst of the city, and 3318
4: 6 So Hatach **w forth** to Mordecai unto 3318
4:17 So Mordecai **w** his way, and did according 5674
5: 9 **w** Haman **forth** that day joyful and with a 3318
7: 7 wine in his wrath **w** *into* the palace garden: NIH
7: 8 As the word **w out** of the king's mouth, 3318
8:14 that rode upon mules *and* camels **w out,** 3318
8:15 Mordecai **w out** from the presence of 3318
9: 4 his fame **w out** throughout all 1980
Job 1: 4 his sons **w** and feasted *in their* houses, 1980
1:12 So Satan **w forth** from the presence of 3318
2: 7 So **w** Satan **forth** from the presence of 3318
18:20 as **they that w before** were affrighted. 6931
29: 7 When I **w out** *to* the gate through the city, 3318
30:28 I **w** mourning without the sun: I stood up, 1980
31:34 I kept silence, *and* **w** not **out** *of* the door? 3318
42: 9 the Shuhite *and* Zophar the Naamathite **w**, 1980
Ps 18: 8 There **w up** a smoke out of his nostrils, and 5927
42: 4 I **w with** them to the house of God, with 1718
66: 6 He turned the sea into dry *land:* they **w** 5674
66:12 we **w** through fire and through water: 935
68:25 The singers **w before**, the players on 6923
73:17 Until I **w** into the sanctuary of God; *then* 935
77:17 out a sound: thine arrows also **w abroad**. 1980
81: 5 when he **w out** through the land of Egypt: 3318
105:13 When they **w** from one nation to another, 1980
106:32 so that it **w** ill with Moses for their sakes: NIH
106:39 **w a whoring** with their own inventions. 2181
114: 1 When Israel **w out** of Egypt, the house of 3318
119:67 Before I was afflicted I **w astray**: but 7683
133: 2 that **w down** to the skirts of his garments; 3381
Pr 7: 8 her corner; and he **w** the way to her house, 6805
24:30 I **w** by the field of the slothful, and by 5674
Ecc 2:20 Therefore I **w about** to cause my heart to 5437
SS 5: 7 The watchmen that **w about** the city found 5437
6:11 I **w down** into the garden of nuts to see 3381
Isa 7: 1 **w up** *towards* Jerusalem to war against it, 5927
8: 3 I **w** unto the prophetess; and she conceived, 7126
37: 1 and **w** *into* the house of the LORD. 935
37:14 Hezekiah **w up** *unto* the house of 5927
37:36 the angel of the LORD **w forth**, and 3318
37:37 and **w** and returned, and dwelt at Nineveh. 1980
48: 3 they **w forth** out of my mouth, and 3318
51:23 and as the street, to them that **w over**. 5674
52: 4 My people **w down** aforetime *into* Egypt to 3381
57:17 he **w on** frowardly in the way of his heart. 1980
60:15 that no man **w through** *thee,* I will make 5674
Jer 3: 8 feared not, but **w** and played the harlot also. 1980
7:24 and **w** backward, and not forward. 1961
11:10 and they **w** after other gods to serve them: 1980
13: 5 So I **w**, and hid it by Euphrates, as 1980
13: 7 I **w** to Euphrates, and digged, and took 1980
18: 3 I **w down** *to* the potter's house, and behold, 3381
22:11 his father, which **w forth** out of this place; 3318
26:21 *it,* he was afraid, and fled, and **w** *into* Egypt; 935
28: 4 that **w** into Babylon, saith the LORD: 935
28:11 And the prophet Jeremiah **w** his way. 1980
31: 2 *even* Israel when *I* **w** to cause him to rest. 1980
36:12 he **w down** *into* the king's house, into 3381
36:20 And they **w in** to the king into the court, but 935
37: 4 came in and **w out** among the people: 3318
37:12 Jeremiah **w forth** out of Jerusalem to go 3318
38: 8 Ebed-melech **w forth** out of the king's 3318
38:11 **w** *into* the house of the king under 935
39: 4 and **w forth** out of the city by night, 3318
39: 4 and he **w out** the way of the plain. 3318
40: 6 **w** Jeremiah unto Gedaliah the son of 935
41: 6 Ishmael the son of Nethaniah **w forth** from 3318
41: 6 weeping **all along as** he **w**: 1980+1980
41:12 **w** to fight with Ishmael the son of 1980
41:14 and **w** unto Johanan the son of Kareah. 1980
41:15 with eight men, and **w** to the Ammonites. 1980
44: 3 in that *they* **w** to burn incense, *and* to serve 1980
51:59 when he **w** with Zedekiah the king of Judah 1980
52: 7 **w forth** out of the city by night *by* the way 3318
52: 7 and they **w** *by* the way of the plain. 1980
Eze 1: 9 they turned not when they **w**; they went 1980
1: 9 they **w** every one straight forward. 1980
1:12 they **w** every one straight forward: whither 1980
1:12 whither the spirit was to go, they **w**; *and* 1980
1:12 *and* they turned not when they **w**. 1980
1:13 it **w up and down** among the living 1980
1:13 and out of the fire **w forth** lightning. 3318
1:17 When they **w**, they went upon their four 1980
1:17 they went, they **w** upon their four sides: 1980
1:17 *and* they turned not when they **w**. 1980
1:19 when the living creatures **w**, the wheels 1980
1:19 creatures went, the wheels **w** by them: 1980
1:20 to go, they **w**, thither *was their* spirit to go; 1980
1:21 When those **w**, *these* went; and when those 1980
1:21 When those went, *these* **w**; and when those 1980
1:24 when they **w**, I heard the noise of their 1980
3:14 took me away, and I **w** in bitterness, in 1980
3:23 I arose, and **w forth** into the plain: and 3318
8:10 So I **w in** and saw; and behold every form of 935
8:11 and a thick cloud of incense **w up**. 5927
9: 2 they **w in**, and stood beside the brasen altar. 935
9: 7 And they **w forth**, and slew in the city. 3318
10: 2 *them* over the city. And he **w in** in my sight. 935
10: 3 right side of the house, when the man **w in**; 935
10: 4 the glory of the LORD **w up** from 7311
10: 6 then he **w in**, and stood beside the wheels. 935
10: 7 clothed with linen: who took *it,* and **w out**. 3318
10:11 When they **w**, they went upon their four 1980
10:11 they went, they **w** upon their four sides; 1980
10:11 they turned not as they **w**, but *to* the place 1980
10:11 they followed it; they turned not as they **w**. 1980
10:16 when the cherubims **w**, the wheels went by 1980
10:16 the cherubims went, the wheels **w** by them: 1980
10:19 when they **w out**, the wheels also *were* 3318
10:22 they **w** every one straight forward. 1980
11:23 the glory of the LORD **w up** from 5927
11:24 So the vision that I had seen **w up** from me. 5927
16:14 thy renown **w forth** among the heathen for 3318
19: 6 he **w up and down** among the lions, 1980
20:16 for their heart **w** after their idols. 1980
23:44 Yet they **w in** unto her, as *they* go in unto a 935
23:44 so **w** they **in** unto Aholah and unto Aholibah, 935
24:12 and her great scum **w** not **forth** out of her: 3318
25: 3 house of Judah, when they **w** into captivity; 1980
27:33 When thy wares **w forth** out of the seas, 3318
31:15 In the day when he **w down** to the grave I 3381
31:17 They also **w down** into hell with him unto 3381
36:20 whither they **w**, they profaned my holy 935
36:21 among the heathen, whither they **w**. 935
36:22 profaned among the heathen, whither ye **w**. 935
39:23 of Israel **w into captivity** for their iniquity: 1540
40: 6 **w up** the stairs thereof, and measured 5927
40:22 they **w up** unto it by seven steps; and 5927
40:49 *me* by the steps whereby they **w up** to it: 5927
41: 3 **w** he inward, and measured the post of 935
41: 7 for the winding about of the house **w** still NIH
44:10 away far from me, when Israel **w astray,** 8582
44:10 which **w astray** away from me after their 8582
44:15 the children of Israel **w astray** from me, 8582
47: 3 **w forth** east*ward,* he measured a thousand 3318
48:11 which **w** not **astray** when the children of 8582
48:11 astray when the children of Israel **w astray,** 8582
48:11 Israel went astray, as the Levites **w astray**. 8582
Da 2:13 the decree **w forth** that the wise *men* 5312
2:16 Daniel **w in**, and desired of the king that he 5954
2:17 Daniel **w** to his house, and made the thing 236
2:24 Therefore Daniel **w in** unto Arioch, 5954
2:24 he **w** and said thus unto him; Destroy not 236
6:10 the writing *was* signed, he **w** into his house; 5954
6:18 the king **w** to his palace, and passed 236
6:18 before him: and his sleep **w** from him. 5075
6:19 and **w** in haste unto the den of lions. 236
Hos 1: 3 So he **w** and took Gomer the daughter of 1980
2:13 and she **w** after her lovers, and forgat me, 1980
5:13 **w** Ephraim to the Assyrian, and sent to king 1980
9:10 *but* they **w** to Baal-peor, and 935
11: 2 *As* they called them, so they **w** from them: 1980
Am 5: 3 The city that **w out** *by* a thousand shall 3318
5: 3 that which **w forth** *by* an hundred shall 3318
5:19 or **w** *into* the house, and leaned his hand on 935
Jnh 1: 3 of the LORD, and **w down** *to* Joppa; 3381
1: 3 paid the fare thereof, and **w down** into it, 3381
2: 6 I **w down** to the bottoms of the mountains; 3381
3: 3 So Jonah arose, and **w** unto Nineveh, 1980
4: 5 So Jonah **w out** of the city, and sat on 3318
Na 3:10 *was* she carried away, she **w** into captivity: 1980

Hab 3: 5 Before him **w** the pestilence, and 1980
3: 5 and burning coals **w forth** at his feet. 3318
3:11 at the light of thine arrows they **w**, *and* 1980
Zec 2: 3 the angel that talked with me **w forth**, and 3318
2: 3 and another angel **w out** to meet him, 3318
5: 5 Then the angel that talked with me **w forth**, 3318
6: 7 the bay **w forth**, and sought to go that *they* 3318
8:10 *was there any* peace to him that **w out** 3318
10: 2 therefore they **w** their way as a flock, 5265
Mt 2: 9 **w before** them, till it came and stood over *4254*
3: 5 Then **w out** to him Jerusalem, and *1607*
3:16 **w up** straightway out of the water: *305*
4:23 And Jesus **w about** all Galilee, teaching in *4013*
4:24 And his fame **w** throughout all Syria: and *565*
5: 1 the multitudes, he **w up** into a mountain: *305*
8:32 come out, they **w** into the herd of swine: *565*
8:33 and **w** their ways into the city, and told every *565*
9:25 he **w in**, and took her by the hand, and *1525*
9:26 And the fame hereof **w abroad** into all that *1831*
9:32 As they **w out**, behold, they brought to him *1831*
9:35 And Jesus **w about** all the cities and *4013*
11: 7 What **w** ye **out** into the wilderness to see? *1831*
11: 8 But what **w** ye **out** for to see? A man *1831*
11: 9 But what **w** ye **out** for to see? A prophet? *1831*
12: 1 At that time Jesus **w** on the sabbath day *4198*
12: 9 departed thence, he **w** into their synagogue: *2064*
12:14 Then the Pharisees **w out**, and held a *1831*
13: 1 The same day **w** Jesus **out** of the house, *1831*
13: 2 unto him, so that he **w** into a ship, and sat; *1684*
13: 3 saying, Behold, a sower **w forth** to sow; *1831*
13:25 tares among the wheat, and **w** his way. *565*
13:36 the multitude away, and **w** into the house: *2064*
13:46 **w** and sold all that he had, and bought it. *565*
14:12 and buried it, and **w** and told Jesus. *2064*
14:14 And Jesus **w forth**, and saw a great *1831*
14:23 he **w up** into a mountain apart to pray: *305*
14:25 And in the fourth watch of the night Jesus **w** *565*
15:21 Then Jesus **w** thence, and departed into *1831*
15:29 and **w up** into a mountain, and sat down *305*
18:13 of the ninety and nine which **w** not **astray**. *4105*
18:28 But the same servant **w out**, and found one *1831*
18:30 but **w** and cast him into prison, till he should *565*
19:22 heard *that* saying, he **w away** sorrowful: *565*
20: 1 which **w out** early in the morning to hire *1831*
20: 3 And he **w out** about the third hour, and *1831*
20: 4 right I will give you. And they **w** their **way**. *565*
20: 5 Again he **w out** about the sixth and *1831*
20: 6 And about the eleventh hour he **w out**, and *1831*
21: 6 And the disciples **w**, and did as Jesus *4198*
21: 9 And the multitudes that **w before**, *4254*
21:12 And Jesus **w into** the temple of God, *1525*
21:17 and **w out** of the city into Bethany; *1831*
21:29 I will not: but afterward he repented, and **w**. *565*
21:30 he answered and said, I *go*, sir: and **w** not. *565*
21:33 to husbandmen, and **w into a far country**: *589*
22: 5 But they made light of *it*, and **w** their ways, *565*
22:10 So those servants **w out** into the *high*ways, *1831*
22:15 Then **w** the Pharisees, and took counsel *4198*
22:22 and left him, and **w** their way. *565*
24: 1 And Jesus **w out**, and departed from *1831*
25: 1 and **w forth** to meet the bridegroom. *1831*
25:10 And while they **w** to buy, the bridegroom *565*
25:10 they *that were* ready **w in** with him to *1525*
25:16 he that had received the five talents **w** *4198*
25:18 But he that had received one **w** and digged in *565*
25:25 and **w** and hid thy talent in the earth: *565*
26:14 Judas Iscariot, **w** unto the chief priests, *4198*
26:30 they **w out** into the mount of Olives. *1831*
26:39 And he **w** a little **further**, and fell on his *4281*
26:42 He **w away** again the second time, and *565*
26:44 and **w away** again, and prayed the third *565*
26:58 off unto the high priest's palace, and **w in**, *1525*
26:75 thou shalt deny me thrice. And he **w out**, *1831*
27: 5 and departed, and **w** and hanged himself. *565*
27:53 and **w into** the holy city, and *1525*
27:58 He **w** to Pilate, and begged the body of *4334*
27:66 So they **w**, and made the sepulchre sure, *4198*
28: 9 And as they **w** to tell his disciples, behold, *4198*
28:16 Then the eleven disciples **w** *away* into *4198*
Mk 1: 5 And there **w out** unto him all the land of *1607*
1:20 ship with the hired servants, and **w** after him. *565*
1:21 And they **w into** Capernaum; and *1531*
1:35 he **w out**, and departed into a solitary place, *1831*
1:45 But he **w out**, and began to publish *it* much, *1831*
2:12 up the bed, and **w forth** before *them* all; *1715*
2:13 And he **w forth** again by the sea side; and *1831*
2:23 that he **w** through the corn fields on *3899*
2:23 and his disciples began, **as** they **w**, to *3598+4160*
2:26 How he **w into** the house of God in *1525*
3: 6 And the Pharisees **w forth**, and *1831*
3:19 betrayed him. And they **w** into a house. *2064*
3:21 heard *of it*, they **w out** to lay hold on him: *1831*
4: 3 Behold, there **w out** a sower to sow: *1831*
5:13 And the unclean spirits **w out**, and *1831*
5:14 And they **w out** to see what it was that was *1831*
5:24 And *Jesus* **w** with him; and much people *565*
6: 1 And he **w out** from thence, and came into *1831*
6: 6 And he **w** round about the villages, *4013*
6:12 And they **w out**, and preached that *men* *1831*
6:24 And she **w forth**, and said unto her mother, *1831*
6:27 and he **w** and beheaded him in the prison, *565*
6:51 And he **w up** unto them into the ship; and *305*
7:24 and **w** into the borders of Tyre and Sidon, *565*
8:27 And Jesus **w out**, and his disciples, into *1831*
10:22 was sad at *that* saying, and **w away** grieved: *565*
10:32 up to Jerusalem; and Jesus **w before** them: *4254*
10:46 as he **w out** of Jericho with his disciples *1607*
11: 4 And they **w** their way, and found the colt *565*
11: 9 And they that **w before**, and they that *4254*
11:11 he **w out** unto Bethany with the twelve. *1831*
11:15 and Jesus **w into** the temple, and began to *1525*
11:19 when even was come, he **w out** of the city. *1607*
12: 1 to husbandmen, and **w into a far country**. *589*
12:12 and they left him, and **w** their way. *565*
13: 1 And as he **w out** of the temple, one of his *1607*
Mk 14:10 one of the twelve, **w** unto the chief priests, *565*
14:16 And his disciples **w forth**, and came into *1831*
14:26 they **w out** into the mount of Olives. *1831*
14:35 And he **w forward** a little, and fell on *4281*
14:39 And again he **w away**, and prayed, and *565*
14:68 And he **w out** into the porch; and *the* cock *1831*
15:43 and **w in** boldly unto Pilate, and craved *1525*
16: 8 And they **w out** quickly, and fled from *1831*
16:10 *And* she **w** and told them that had been *4198*
16:12 as they walked, and **w** into the country. *4198*
16:13 And they **w** and told *it* unto the residue: *565*
16:20 And they **w forth**, and preached every *1831*
Lk 1: 9 he **w into** the temple of the Lord. *1525*
1:39 and **w** into the hill country with haste, *4198*
2: 1 *that* there **w out** a decree from Cesar *1831*
2: 3 And all **w** to be taxed, every one into his *4198*
2: 4 And Joseph also **w up** from Galilee, out of *305*
2:41 Now his parents **w** to Jerusalem every year *4198*
2:42 they **w up** to Jerusalem after the custom of *305*
2:44 been in the company, **w** a day's journey; *2064*
2:51 And he **w down** with them, and came to *2597*
4:14 there **w out** a fame of him through all *1831*
4:16 he **w into** the synagogue on *1525*
4:30 through the midst of them **w** *his way*, *4198*
4:37 And the fame of him **w out** into every place *1607*
4:42 he departed and **w** into a desert place: *4198*
5:15 *much* the more **w** there a fame **abroad** of *1330*
5:19 they **w upon** the housetop, and let him down *305*
5:27 And after these *things* he **w forth**, and *1831*
6: 1 that he **w through** the corn fields; *1279*
6: 4 How he **w into** the house of God, *1525*
6:12 *that* he **w out** into a mountain to pray, and *1831*
6:19 for there **w** virtue **out** of him, and *1831*
7: 6 Then Jesus **w** with them. And when he was *4198*
7:11 *day* after, *that* he **w** into a city called Nain; *4198*
7:11 and many of his disciples **w with** him, and *4848*
7:17 And this rumour of him **w forth** throughout *1831*
7:24 What **w** ye **out** into the wilderness for to *1831*
7:25 But what **w** ye **out** for to see? A man *1831*
7:26 But what **w** ye **out** for to see? A prophet? *1831*
7:36 And he **w into** the Pharisee's house, *1525*
8: 1 that he **w throughout** every city and *1353*
8: 2 out of whom **w** seven devils, *1831*
8: 5 A sower **w out** to sow his seed: and as he *1831*
8:22 that he **w** into a ship with his disciples: *1684*
8:27 And when he **w forth** to land, there met *1831*
8:33 Then **w** the devils **out** of the man, and *1831*
8:34 and **w** and told *it* in the city and in *565*
8:35 Then they **w out** to see what was done; and *1831*
8:37 and he **w** *up* into the ship, and *1684*
8:39 And he **w** his way, and published throughout *565*
8:42 (But as he **w** the people thronged him. *5217*
9: 6 they departed, and **w through** the towns, *1330*
9:10 **w aside** privately into a desert place *5298*
9:28 James, and **w up** into a mountain to pray. *305*
9:52 and they **w**, and entered into a village of *4198*
9:56 to save *them*. And they **w** to another *4198*
9:57 And it came to pass *that*, as they **w** in *4198*
10:30 A certain man **w down** from Jerusalem to *2597*
10:34 And **w to** *him*, and bound up his wounds, *4334*
10:38 Now it came to pass, as they **w**, that he *4198*
11:37 and he **w in**, and sat down to meat. *1525*
13:22 And he **w** through the cities and villages, *1279*
14: 1 as he **w** into the house of one of the chief *2064*
14:25 And there **w** great multitudes **with** him: and *4848*
15:15 And he **w** and joined himself to a citizen of *4198*
16:30 but if one **w** unto them from the dead, *4198*
17:11 And it came to pass, as he **w** to Jerusalem, *4198*
17:14 And it came to pass *that*, as they **w**, *5217*
17:29 But the *same* day that Lot **w out** of Sodom *1831*
18:10 Two men **w up** into the temple to pray; *305*
18:14 this man **w down** to his house justified *2597*
18:39 And they which **w before** rebuked him, *4254*
19:12 A certain nobleman **w** into a far country to *4198*
19:28 he **w** before, ascending up to Jerusalem. *4198*
19:32 And they that were sent **w** their way, and *565*
19:36 And as he **w**, they spread their clothes in *4198*
19:45 And he **w into** the temple, and *1525*
20: 9 and **w into a far country** for a long time. *589*
21:37 and at night he **w out**, and abode in *1831*
22: 4 And he **w** his way, and communed with *565*
22:13 And they **w**, and found as he had said unto *565*
22:39 And he came out, and **w**, as he was wont, to *4198*
22:47 **w before** them, and drew near unto Jesus to *4281*
22:62 And Peter **w out**, *1831*
23:52 This *man* **w unto** Pilate, and begged *4334*
24:13 two of them **w** *that* same day to a village *4198*
24:15 Jesus himself drew near, and **w with** them. *4848*
24:24 And certain of them which were with us **w** to *565*
24:28 drew nigh unto the village, whither they **w**: *4198*
24:29 is far spent. And he **w in** to tarry with them. *1525*
Jn 2:12 After this he **w down** to Capernaum, he, *2597*
2:13 was at hand, and Jesus **w up** to Jerusalem, *305*
4:28 and **w** her way into the city, and saith to *565*
4:30 Then they **w out** of the city, and came unto *1831*
4:43 days he departed thence, and **w** into Galilee. *565*
4:45 at the feast: for they also **w** unto the feast. *2064*
4:47 he **w** unto him, and besought him that he *565*
4:50 had spoken unto him, and he **w** *his way*. *4198*
5: 1 of the Jews; and Jesus **w up** to Jerusalem. *305*
5: 4 For an angel **w down** at a *certain* season *2597*
6: 1 After these *things* Jesus **w** over the sea of *565*
6: 3 And Jesus **w up** into a mountain, and *424*
6:16 his disciples **w down** unto the sea, *2597*
6:17 and **w** over the sea towards Capernaum. *2064*
6:21 the ship was at the land whither they **w**. *5217*
6:22 that Jesus **w** not **with** his disciples into *4897*
6:66 of his disciples **w back**, *565+1519+3588+3694*
7:10 then **w** he also **up** unto the feast, not openly, *305*
7:14 Now about the midst of the feast Jesus **w up** *305*
7:53 And every man **w** unto his own house. *4198*
8: 1 Jesus **w** unto the mount of Olives. *4198*
8: 9 **w out** one by one, beginning at the eldest, *1831*
8:59 Jesus hid himself, and **w out** of the temple, *1831*
9: 7 He **w** his way therefore, and washed, and *565*
Jn 9:11 and I **w** and washed, and I received sight. *565*
10:40 And **w away** again beyond Jordan into *565*
11:20 that Jesus was coming, **w and met** him: *5221*
11:28 she **w** her way, and called Mary her sister *565*
11:31 that she rose up hastily and **w out**, *1831*
11:46 But some of them **w** their ways to *565*
11:54 **w** thence unto a country near to *565*
11:55 many **w** out of the country **up** to Jerusalem *305*
12:11 reason of him many of the Jews **w away**, *5217*
12:13 and **w forth** to meet him, and cried, *1831*
13: 3 that he was come from God, and **w** to God; *5217*
13:30 received the sop **w** immediately **out**: *1831*
18: 1 **w forth** with his disciples over the brook *1831*
18: 4 **w forth**, and said unto them, Whom seek *1831*
18: 6 said unto them, I am *he*, they **w** backward, *565*
18:15 **w in with** Jesus into the palace of the high *4897*
18:16 Then **w out** *that* other disciple, which was *1831*
18:28 they themselves **w** not into the judgment *1525*
18:29 Pilate then **w out** unto them, and said, *1831*
18:38 he **w out** again unto the Jews, and *1831*
19: 4 Pilate therefore **w** forth again, and *1831*
19: 9 And **w** again **into** the judgment hall, and *1525*
19:17 And he bearing his cross **w forth** into a *1831*
20: 3 Peter therefore **w forth**, and *that* other *1831*
20: 5 saw the linen clothes lying; yet **w** he not **in**. *1525*
20: 6 and **w into** the sepulchre, and seeth *1525*
20: 8 Then **w in** also *that* other disciple, *1525*
20:10 Then the disciples **w away** again unto their *565*
21: 3 They **w forth**, and entered into a ship *1831*
21:11 Simon Peter **w up**, and drew the net to land *305*
21:23 Then **w** this saying **abroad** among *1831*
Ac 1:10 toward heaven as he **w** *up*, behold, *4198*
1:13 they **w up** into an upper room, where abode *305*
1:21 with us all the time that the Lord Jesus **w in** *1525*
3: 1 John **w up** together into the temple at *305*
4:23 they **w** to their own *company*, and *2064*
5:26 Then **w** the captain with the officers, and *565*
7:15 So Jacob **w down** into Egypt, and died, he, *2597*
8: 4 abroad **w every where** preaching the word. *1330*
8: 5 Then Philip **w down** to the city of Samaria, *2718*
8:27 And he arose and **w**: and behold, a man of *4198*
8:36 And as they **w** on *their* way, they came *4198*
8:38 and they **w down** both into the water, *2597*
8:39 no more: and he **w** *on* his way rejoicing. *4198*
9: 1 of the Lord, **w unto** the high priest, *4334*
9:17 And Ananias **w** his way, and entered into *565*
9:29 the Grecians: but they **w about** to slay him. *2021*
9:39 Then Peter arose and **w with** them. *4905*
10: 9 as they **w on** their **journey**, and drew nigh *3596*
10: 9 Peter **w up** upon the house to pray about *305*
10:21 Then Peter **w down** to the men which were *2597*
10:23 on the morrow Peter **w away** with them, *1831*
10:27 he **w in**, and found many *that were* come *1525*
10:38 who **w about** doing good, and healing all *1330*
12: 9 And he **w out**, and followed him; and *1831*
12:10 and they **w out**, and passed on through one *1831*
12:17 And he departed, and **w** into another place. *4198*
12:19 And he **w down** from Judea to Cesarea, and *2718*
13:11 he **w about** seeking *some* to lead him by *4013*
13:14 **w into** the synagogue on the sabbath *1525*
14: 1 that they **w** *both* together **into** *1525*
14:25 word in Perga, they **w down** into Attalia: *2597*
15:24 that certain which **w out** from us have *1831*
15:38 and **w** not with them to the work. *4905*
15:41 And he **w through** Syria and Cilicia, *1330*
16: 4 And as they **w through** the cities, *1279*
16:13 And on the sabbath we **w out** of the city by *1831*
16:16 And it came to pass, as we **w** to prayer, *4198*
16:40 And they **w out** of the prison, and *1831*
17: 2 **w in** unto them, and three sabbath days *1525*
17:10 who coming *thither* **w** into the synagogue of *549*
18:22 saluted the church, he **w down** to Antioch. *2597*
18:23 and **w over** *all* the country of Galatia and *1330*
19: 8 And he **w into** the synagogue, and *1525*
19:12 and the evil spirits **w out** of them. *1831*
20:10 And Paul **w down**, and fell on him, and *2597*
20:13 And we **w before** to ship, and sailed unto *4281*
21: 2 unto Phenicia, we **w aboard**, and set forth. *1910*
21: 5 we departed and **w** *our way*; and *they* all *4198*
21:15 up our carriages, and **w up** to Jerusalem. *305*
21:16 There **w with** us also *certain* of *4905*
21:18 And the *day* following Paul **w in** with us *1524*
21:31 And as *they* **w about** to kill him, *2212*
22: 5 and **w** to Damascus, to bring them which *4198*
22:26 When the centurion heard *that*, he **w** and *4334*
23:16 he **w** and entered into the castle, and *3854*
23:19 by the hand, and **w** *with him* **aside** privately, *402*
24:11 twelve days since I **w up** to Jerusalem for to *305*
25: 6 than ten days, he **w down** unto Cesarea; *2597*
26:12 Whereupon as I **w** to Damascus with *4198*
26:21 me in the temple, and **w about** to kill *me*. *3987*
28:14 seven days: and so we **w** toward Rome. *2064*
Ro 10:18 their sound **w** into all the earth, and *1831*
2Co 2:13 of them, I **w from** *thence* into Macedonia. *1831*
8:17 of his own accord he **w** unto you. *1831*
Gal 1:17 Neither **w** I **up** to Jerusalem to them which *424*
1:17 but I **w** into Arabia, and returned again unto *565*
1:18 Then after three years I **w up** to Jerusalem to *424*
2: 1 Then fourteen years after I **w up** again to *305*
2: 2 And I **w up** by revelation, and *305*
1Ti 1: 3 *still* at Ephesus, when I **w** into Macedonia, *4198*
1:18 to the prophecies which **w before** on thee, *4254*
Heb 9: 6 the priests **w** always into the first *1524*
9: 7 But into the second **w** the high priest alone NIG
11: 8 and he **w out**, not knowing whither he *1831*
11: 8 he went out, not knowing whither he **w**. *2064*
1Pe 3:19 By which also he **w** and preached unto *4198*
1Jn 2:19 They **w out** from us, but they were not of *1831*
2:19 *they* **w** *out*, that they might be made NIG
3Jn 1: 7 that for his name's sake they **w forth**, *1831*
Rev 1:16 out of his mouth **w** a sharp twoedged *1607*
6: 2 and he **w forth** conquering, and to conquer. *1831*
6: 4 And there **w out** another horse *that was* *1831*
10: 9 And I **w** unto the angel, and said unto him, *565*
12:17 **w** to make war with the remnant of her seed, *565*

Rev 16: 2 And the first **w**, and poured out his vial upon *565*
20: 9 And they **w up** on the breadth of the earth, *305*

WENTEST (14) [GO]

Ge 49: 4 because thou **w up** to thy father's bed; then 5927
Jdg 5: 4 LORD, when thou **w out** of Seir, 3318
8: 1 when thou **w** to fight with the Midianites? 1980
1Sa 10: 2 The asses which thou **w** to seek are found: 1980
2Sa 7: 9 I was with thee whithersoever thou **w**, and 1980
16:17 thy friend? why **w** thou not with thy friend? 1980
19:25 Wherefore **w** not thou with me, 1980
Ps 68: 7 when thou **w forth** before thy people, 3318
Isa 57: 7 even thither **w** thou **up** to offer sacrifice. 5927
57: 9 thou **w** to the king with ointment, and 7788
Jer 2: 2 when thou **w** after me in the wilderness, 1980
31:21 the highway, *even* the way *which* thou **w**: 1980
Hab 3:13 Thou **w forth** for the salvation of thy 3318
Ac 11: 3 Saying, Thou **w in** to men uncircumcised, *1525*

WEPT (71) [WEEP]

Ge 21:16 against *him,* and lift up her voice, and **w**. 1058
27:38 And Esau lift up his voice, and **w**. 1058
29:11 and lifted up his voice, and **w**. 1058
33: 4 on his neck, and kissed him: and they **w**. 1058
37:35 son mourning. Thus his father **w** for him. 1058
42:24 he turned himself about from them, and **w**; 1058
43:30 he entered into *his* chamber, and **w** there. 1058
45: 2 he **w aloud**: and 1065+5414+6963+871.1
45:14 upon his brother Benjamin's neck, and **w**; 1058
45:14 and wept; and Benjamin **w** upon his neck. 1058
45:15 kissed all his brethren, and **w** upon them: 1058
46:29 his neck, and **w** on his neck a good while. 1058
50: 1 and **w** upon him, and kissed him. 1058
50:17 And Joseph **w** when they spake unto him. 1058
Ex 2: 6 behold, the babe **w**. And she had 1058
Nu 11: 4 the children of Israel also **w** again, and 1058
11:18 for you have **w** in the ears of the LORD, 1058
11:20 have **w** before him, saying, Why came we 1058
14: 1 and cried; and the people **w** that night. 1058
Dt 1:45 ye returned and **w** before the LORD; but 1058
34: 8 the children of Israel **w** for Moses in 1058
Jdg 2: 4 that the people lift up their voice, and **w**. 1058
14:16 And Samson's wife **w** before him, and said, 1058
14:17 she **w** before him the seven days, 1058
20:23 and **w** before the LORD until even, 1058
20:26 **w**, and sat there before the LORD, and 1058
21: 2 up their voices, and **w sore**; 1058+1065+1419
Ru 1: 9 and they lift up their voice, and **w**. 1058
1:14 they lift up their voice, and **w** again: and 1058
1Sa 1: 7 therefore she **w**, and did not eat. 1058
1:10 prayed unto the LORD, and **w sore**. 1058+1058
11: 4 all the people lift up their voices, and **w**. 1058
20:41 **w** one with another, until David exceeded. 1058
24:16 And Saul lift up his voice, and **w**. 1058
30: 4 *were* with him lift up their voice and **w**, 1058
2Sa 1:12 **w**, and fasted until even, for Saul, and 1058
3:32 up his voice, and **w** at the grave of Abner; 1058
3:32 at the grave of Abner; and all the people **w**. 1058
3:34 And all the people **w** again over him. 1058
12:22 the child *was* yet alive, I fasted and **w**: 1058
13:36 sons came, and lift up their voice and **w**: 1058
13:36 and all his servants **w** very **sore**. 1058+1065
15:23 all the country **w** *with* a loud voice, and 1058
15:30 **w** as he went up, and had his head covered, 1058
18:33 up to the chamber over the gate, and **w**: 1058
2Ki 8:11 *he* was ashamed: and the man of God **w**. 1058
13:14 **w** over his face, and said, O my father, 1058
20: 3 And Hezekiah **w sore**. 1058+1065+1419
22:19 and hast rent thy clothes, and **w** before me; 1058
Ezr 3:12 laid before their eyes, **w** with a loud voice; 1058
10: 1 children: for the people **w** very **sore**. 1058+1059
Ne 1: 4 *that* I sat down and **w**, and mourned *certain* 1058
8: 9 For all the people **w**, when they heard 1058
Job 2:12 him not, they lifted up their voice, and **w**; 1058
Ps 69:10 When I **w**, *and chastened* my soul with 1058
137: 1 of Babylon, there we sat down, yea, we **w**, 1058
Isa 38: 3 And Hezekiah **w sore**. 1058+1065+1419
Hos 12: 4 he **w**, and made supplication unto him: 1058
Mt 26:75 me thrice. And he went out, and **w** bitterly. *2799*
Mk 5:38 and them that **w** and wailed greatly. *2799*
14:72 And when he thought thereon, he **w**. *2799*
16:10 had been with him, as they mourned and **w**. *2799*
Lk 7:32 have mourned to you, and ye have not **w**. *2799*
8:52 And all **w**, and bewailed her: but he said, *2799*
19:41 he beheld the city, and **w** over it, *2799*
22:62 And Peter went out, and **w** bitterly. *2799*
Jn 11:35 Jesus **w**. *1145*
20:11 and as she **w**, she stooped down, and *2799*
Ac 20:37 And *they* all **w** sore, and fell on *1096+2805*
1Co 7:30 And they that weep, as though they **w** not; *2799*
Rev 5: 4 And I **w** much, because no *man* was found *2799*

WERE (2776) [BE] See Index of Articles, Etc.

WERT (6) [BE]

Job 8: 6 If thou **w** pure and upright; surely now he NIH
SS 8: 1 O that thou **w** as my brother, that sucked NIH
Ro 11:17 **w** graffed in amongst them, and with *them* NIG
11:24 For if thou **w** cut out of the olive tree which NIG
11:24 **w** graffed contrary to nature into a good NIG
Rev 3:15 cold nor hot: I would thou **w** cold or hot. *1510*

WEST (69) [WESTERN, WESTWARD]

Ge 12: 8 *having* Beth-el on the **w**, and Hai on 3220
28:14 thou shalt spread abroad to the **w**, and 3220
Ex 10:19 the LORD turned a mighty strong **w** wind, 3220
27:12 *for* the breadth of the court on the **w** side 3220
38:12 for the **w** side *were* hangings of fifty cubits, 3220
Nu 2:18 On the **w side** *shall be* the standard of 3220
34: 6 for a border: this shall be your **w** border. 3220
35: 5 *on* the **w** side two thousand cubits, and 3220
Dt 33:23 possess thou the **w** and the south. 3220
Jos 8: 9 and Ai, on the **w side** of Ai: 3220
8:12 and Ai, on the **w side** of the city. 3220
8:13 and their liers in wait on the **w** of the city, 3220
11: 2 and in the borders of Dor on the **w**, 3220
11: 3 *to* the Canaanite on the east and on the **w**, 3220
12: 7 Israel smote on *this* side Jordan on the **w**, 3220
15:12 the **w** border *was* to the great sea, and 3220
18:14 children of Judah: this *was* the **w** quarter. 3220
18:15 the border went out on the **w**, and went out 3220
19:34 reacheth to Asher on the **w** side, and 3220
1Ki 7:25 three looking toward the **w**, and 3220
1Ch 9:24 toward the east, **w**, north, and south. 3220
12:15 *both* toward the east, and toward the **w**. 4628
2Ch 4: 4 three looking toward the **w**, and 3220
32:30 brought it straight down to the **w** *side* of 4628
33:14 on the **w** *side* of Gihon, in the valley, 4628
Ps 75: 6 nor from the **w**, nor from the south. 4628
103:12 As far as the east is from the **w**, *so* far hath 4628
107: 3 from the east, and from the **w**, from 4628
Isa 11:14 shoulders of the Philistines toward the **w**; 3220
43: 5 from the east, and gather thee from the **w**; 4628
45: 6 from the **w**, that *there is* none besides me. 4628
49:12 lo, these from the north and from the **w**; 3220
59:19 fear the name of the LORD from the **w**, 4628
Eze 41:12 end toward the **w** *was* seventy cubits broad; 3220
42:19 He turned about to the **w** side, *and* 3220
45: 7 from the **w** side westward, and from 3220
45: 7 from the **w** border unto the east border. 3220
47:20 The **w** side also *shall be* the great sea from 3220
47:20 over against Hamath. This *is* the **w** side. 3220
48: 1 for these are his sides east *and* **w**; a *portion* 3220
48: 2 from the east side unto the **w** side, 3220+1886.5
48: 3 from the east side even unto the **w** 3220+1886.5
48: 4 from the east side unto the **w** side, 3220+1886.5
48: 5 from the east side unto the **w** side, 3220+1886.5
48: 6 from the east side even unto the **w** 3220+1886.5
48: 7 from the east side unto the **w** side, 3220+1886.5
48: 8 from the east side unto the **w** side, 3220+1886.5
48: 8 from the east side unto the **w** side: 3220+1886.5
48:10 and toward the **w** ten thousand *in* breadth, 3220
48:16 the **w** side four thousand and 3220+1886.5
48:17 and toward the **w** two hundred and fifty. 3220
48:21 thousand toward the **w** border, 3220+1886.5
48:23 from the east side unto the **w** side, 3220+1886.5
48:24 from the east side unto the **w** side, 3220+1886.5
48:25 from the east side unto the **w** side, 3220+1886.5
48:26 from the east side unto the **w** side, 3220+1886.5
48:27 from the east side unto the **w** side, 3220+1886.5
48:34 *At* the **w** side four thousand and 3220
Da 8: 5 a he goat came from the **w** on the face of 4628
Hos 11:10 then the children shall tremble from the **w**. 3220
Zec 8: 7 and from **the w** country; 3996+8121+1886.1
14: 4 thereof toward the east and toward the **w**, 3220
Mt 8:11 That many shall come from the east and **w**, *1424*
24:27 of the east, and shineth *even* unto the **w**; *1424*
Lk 12:54 When ye see a cloud rise out of the **w**, *1424*
13:29 and *from* the **w**, and from the north, and *1424*
Ac 27:12 and lieth toward the **south w** and *3047*
27:12 lieth toward the south west and **north w**. *5566*
Rev 21:13 south three gates; and on the **w** three gates. *1424*

WESTERN (1) [WEST]

Nu 34: 6 *as for* the **w** border, you shall even have 3220

WESTWARD (26) [WEST]

Ge 13:14 southward, and eastward, and **w**: 3220+1886.5
Ex 26:22 for the sides of the tabernacle **w** 3220+1886.5
26:27 the tabernacle, for the two sides **w**. 3220+1886.5
36:27 for the sides of the tabernacle **w** he 3220+1886.5
36:32 of the tabernacle for the sides **w**. 3220+1886.5
Nu 3:23 shall pitch behind the tabernacle **w**. 3220+1886.5
Dt 3:27 lift up thine eyes **w**, and northward, 3220+1886.5
Jos 5: 1 *were* on the side of Jordan **w**, 3220+1886.5
15: 8 before the valley of Hinnom **w**, 3220+1886.5
15:10 from Baalah **w** unto mount Seir, 3220+1886.5
16: 3 goeth down **w** to the coast of 3220+1886.5
16: 8 Tappuah **w** *unto* the river Kanah; 3220+1886.5
18:12 went up through the mountains **w**; 3220+1886.5
19:26 reacheth to Carmel **w**, and 3220+1886.5
19:34 coast turneth **w** *to* Aznoth-tabor, 3220+1886.5
22: 7 brethren on *this* side Jordan **w**. 3220+1886.5
23: 4 even *unto* the great sea **w**. 3996+8121+1886.1
1Ch 7:28 and **w** Gezer, 4628+1886.1+3807.1
26:16 and Hosah *the lot came forth* **w**, 4628
26:18 At Parbar **w**, four at the causeway, *and* 4628
26:30 **w** in all the business of 4628+1886.5
Eze 45: 7 from the west side **w**, and from 3220+1886.5
46:19 *was* a place on the two sides **w**. 3220+1886.5
48:18 and ten thousand **w**: 3220+1886.5
48:21 **w** over against the five and 3220+1886.5
Da 8: 4 I saw the ram pushing **w**, 3220+1886.5

WET (6)

Job 24: 8 They are **w** with the showers of 7372
Da 4:15 let it be **w** with the dew of heaven, and 6647
4:23 let it be **w** with the dew of heaven, and 6647
4:25 they *shall* **w** thee with the dew of heaven, 6647
4:33 his body was **w** with the dew of heaven, 6647
5:21 his body was **w** with the dew of heaven; 6647

WHALE (2) [WHALE'S, WHALES]

Job 7:12 *Am* I a sea, or a **w**, that thou settest a watch 8577
Eze 32: 2 the nations, and thou *art* as a **w** in the seas: 8577

WHALE'S (1) [WHALE]

Mt 12:40 three days and three nights in the **w** belly; *2785*

WHALES (1) [WHALE]

Ge 1:21 God created great **w**, and every living 8577

WHAT (984) [SOMEWHAT, WHATSOEVER]

Ge 2:19 brought *them* unto Adam to see **w** he would 4100
3:13 the woman, **W** *is* this *that* thou hast done? 4100
4:10 he said, **W** hast thou done? the voice of thy 4100
9:24 knew **w** his younger son had done unto him. 834
12:18 said, **W** *is* this *that* thou hast done unto me? 4100
15: 2 Lord GOD, **w** wilt thou give me, 4100
20: 9 said unto him, **W** hast thou done unto us? 4100
20: 9 **w** have I offended thee, that thou hast 4100
20:10 **W** sawest thou, that thou hast done this 4100
21:17 unto her, **W aileth** thee, Hagar? 4100+3807.1
21:29 **W** *mean* these seven ewe lambs which thou 4100
23:15 of silver; **w** *is* that betwixt me and thee? 4100
24:65 **W** man *is* this that walketh in the field to 4310
25:32 **w profit** shall this birthright do to 4100+3807.1
26:10 **W** *is* this thou hast done unto us? 4100
27:37 and **w** shall I do now unto thee, my son? 4100
27:46 the daughters of the land, **w good** 4100+3807.1
29:15 for nought? tell me, **w** *shall* thy wages *be?* 4100
29:25 **W** *is* this thou hast done unto me? 4100
30:31 he said, **W** shall I give thee? And Jacob 4100
31:26 Laban said to Jacob, **W** hast thou done, 4100
31:32 before our brethren discern thou **w** *is* thine 4100
31:36 and said to Laban, **W** *is* my trespass? 4100
31:36 **w** *is* my sin, that thou hast *so* hotly pursued 4100
31:37 **w** hast thou found of all thy household 4100
31:43 **w** can I do *this* day unto these my 4100
32:27 he said unto him, **W** *is* thy name? And he 4100
33: 8 **W** meanest thou by all this drove which I 4310
33:15 he said, **W** needeth it? let me find 4100+3807.1
34:11 and **w** ye shall say unto me I will give. 834
37:10 **W** *is* this dream that thou hast dreamed? 4100
37:15 man asked him, saying, **W** seekest thou? 4100
37:20 we shall see **w** will become of his dreams. 4100
37:26 **W** profit *is it* if we slay our brother, and 4100
38:16 she said, **W** wilt thou give me, that thou 4100
38:18 he said, **W** pledge shall I give thee? 4100
39: 8 my master wotteth not **w** *is* with me in 4100
41:25 God hath shewed Pharaoh **w** he *is* about to 834
41:28 **W** God *is* about to do he sheweth unto 834
41:55 Go unto Joseph; **w** he saith to you, do. 834
42:28 saying one to another, **W** *is* this 4100+3807.1
44:15 **W** deed *is* this that ye have done? 4100
44:16 Judah said, **W** shall we say unto my lord? 4100
44:16 **w** shall we speak? or how shall we clear 4100
46:33 and shall say, **W** *is* your occupation? 4100
47: 3 unto his brethren, **W** *is* your occupation? 4100
Ex 2: 4 afar off, to wit **w** would be done to him. 4100
3:13 and they shall say to me, **W** *is* his name? 4100
3:13 What *is* his name? **w** shall I say unto them? 4100
4: 2 said unto him, **W** *is* that in thine hand? 4100
4:12 thy mouth, and teach thee **w** thou shalt say. 834
4:15 his mouth, and will teach you **w** ye shall do. 834
6: 1 Now shalt thou see **w** I will do to Pharaoh: 834
10: 2 **w things** I have wrought in Egypt, and my 834
10:26 we know not with **w** we must serve 4100
12:26 say unto you, **W** mean you by this service? 4100
13:14 thee in time to come, saying, **W** *is* this? 4100
15:24 against Moses, saying, **W** shall we drink? 4100
16: 7 and **w** *are* we, that ye murmur against us? 4100
16: 8 **w** *are* we? your murmurings *are* not against 4100
16:15 for they wist not **w** it *was*. And Moses said 4100
17: 4 **W** shall I do unto this people? 4100
18:14 **W** *is* this thing that thou doest to 4100
19: 4 Ye have seen **w** I did unto the Egyptians, 834
23:11 **w** they leave the beasts of the field shall eat. NIH
32: 1 of Egypt, we wot not **w** is become of him. 4100
32:21 **W** did this people unto thee, that thou hast 4100
32:23 of Egypt, we wot not **w** is become of him. 4100
33: 5 that I may know **w** to do unto thee. 4100
Lev 15: 9 **w** saddle **soever** he rideth upon that 834+3605
17: 3 **W man soever** *there be* of the house of 376+376
22: 4 **W man soever** of the seed of Aaron *is* 376+376
25:20 shall say, **W** shall we eat the seventh year? 4100
Nu 9: 8 I will hear **w** the LORD will command 4100
10:32 *that* **w** goodness the LORD shall do 834+1931
13:18 **w** it *is;* and the people that dwelleth therein, 4100
13:19 **w** the land *is* that they dwell in, whether it 4100
13:19 **w** cities *they be* that they dwell in, whether 4100
13:20 **w** the land *is,* whether it *be* fat or lean, 4100
15:34 it was not declared **w** should be done to 4100
16:11 **w** *is* Aaron, that ye murmur against him? 4100
21:14 **W he did** in the Red sea, and *in* the brooks 2052
22: 9 and said, **W** men *are* these with thee? 4310
22:19 that I may know **w** the LORD will say 4100
22:28 said unto Balaam, **W** have I done unto thee, 4100
23:11 unto Balaam, **W** hast thou done unto me? 4100
23:17 said unto him, **W** hath the LORD spoken? 4100
23:23 and of Israel, **W** hath God wrought! 4100
24:13 *but* **w** the LORD saith, that will I speak? 834
24:14 I will advertise thee **w** this people shall do to 834
26:10 **w time** the fire devoured two hundred and 871.1
31:50 **w** every man hath gotten, *of* jewels of gold, 834
Dt 1:22 bring us word again by **w** way we must go 834
1:22 go up, and into **w** cities we shall come. 1886.3
1:33 to shew you by **w** way ye should go, and in a 834
3:24 for **w** God *is there* in heaven or in earth, 4310
4: 3 Your eyes have seen **w** the LORD did 834
4: 7 For **w** nation *is there so* great, who hath 4310
4: 8 **w** nation *is there so* great, that hath statutes 4310
6:20 **W** *mean* the testimonies, and the statutes, 4100
7:18 shalt well remember **w** the LORD thy God 834
8: 2 to prove thee, to know **w** *was* in thine heart, 834
10:12 **w** doth the LORD thy God require of thee, 4100
11: 4 **w** he did unto the army of Egypt, unto their 834
11: 5 **w** he did unto you in the wilderness, until ye 834
11: 6 **w** he did unto Dathan and Abiram, the sons 834
12:32 **W** thing **soever** I command you, 834+3605
20: 5 **W** man *is there* that hath built a new house, 4310
20: 6 **w** man *is he* that hath planted a vineyard, 4310
20: 7 **w** man *is there* that hath betrothed a wife, 4310
20: 8 **W** man *is there that is* fearful and 4310
24: 9 Remember **w** the LORD thy God did unto 834
25:17 Remember **w** Amalek did unto thee by 834
29:24 **w** *meaneth* the heat of this great anger? 4100
32:20 I will see **w** their end *shall be:* for they *are* a 4100
Jos 2:10 **w** you did unto the two kings of 834
4: 6 **W** mean you by these stones? 4100
4:21 to come, saying, **W** *mean* these stones? 4100
5:14 **W** saith my lord unto his servant? 4100
7: 8 O Lord, **w** shall I say, when Israel turneth 4100

W

Jos 7: 9 and w wilt thou do unto thy great name? 4100
7:19 tell me now w thou hast done; hide it not 4100
9: 3 when the inhabitants of Gibeon heard w 834
15:18 and Caleb said unto her, W wouldest thou? 4100
22:16 W trespass is this that ye have committed 4100
22:24 W have you to do with the LORD God of 4100
24: 7 your eyes have seen w I have done in Egypt: 834
Jdg 1:14 and Caleb said unto her, W wilt thou? 4100
7:11 thou shalt hear w they say; and 4100
8: 2 W have I done now in comparison of you? 4100
8: 3 w was I able to do in comparison of you? 4100
8:18 W manner of men were they whom ye slew 375
9:48 W ye have seen me do, make haste, and 4100
10:18 W man is he that will begin to fight against 4310
11:12 saying, W hast thou to do with me, 4100
13: 8 teach us w we shall do unto the child that 4100
13:17 the angel of the LORD, W is thy name, 4310
14: 6 not his father or his mother w he had done. 834
14:18 sun went down, W is sweeter than honey? 4100
14:18 w is stronger than a lion? And he said unto 4100
15:11 w is this that thou hast done unto us? 4100
16: 5 by w means we may prevail against him, 4100
18: 3 w makest thou in this place? and what hast 4100
18: 3 thou in this place? and w hast thou here? 4100
18: 8 their brethren said unto them, W say ye? 4100
18:14 now therefore consider w ye have to do. 4100
18:18 Then said the priest unto them, W do ye? 4100
18:23 and said unto Micah, W aileth thee, 4100
18:24 w have I more? and what is this that ye say 4100
18:24 w is this that ye say unto me, What aileth 4100
18:24 is this that ye say unto me, W aileth thee? 4100
19:24 do with them w seemeth good unto you: 1886.1
20:12 W wickedness is this that is done among 4100
21: 8 W one is there of the tribes of Israel that 4310
Ru 2:18 her mother in law saw w she had gleaned: 834
3: 4 and he will tell thee w thou shalt do. 834
4: 5 W day thou buyest the field of the hand of NIH
1Sa 1:23 said unto her, Do w seemeth thee good; 1886.1
3:17 W is the thing that the LORD hath said 4100
3:18 let him do w seemeth him good. 1886.1
4: 6 W meaneth the noise of this great shout in 4100
4:14 W meaneth the noise of this tumult? 4100
4:16 W is there done, my son? 1697+4100+1886.1
5: 8 W shall we do with the ark of the God of 4100
6: 2 W shall we do to the ark of the LORD? 4100
6: 4 W shall be the trespass offering which we 4100
9: 7 if we go, w shall we bring the man? 4100
9: 7 to bring to the man of God: w have we? 4100
10: 2 for you, saying, W shall I do for my son? 4100
10: 8 come to thee, and shew thee w thou shalt do. 834
10:11 W is this that is come unto the son of Kish? 4100
10:15 I pray thee, w Samuel said unto you. 4100
11: 5 W aileth the people that they weep? 4100
13:11 Samuel said, W hast thou done? And Saul 4100
14:40 unto Saul, Do w seemeth good unto thee. 1886.1
14:43 said to Jonathan, Tell me w thou hast done. 4100
15:14 W meaneth then this bleating of the sheep 4100
15:16 I will tell thee w the LORD hath said to me 834
16: 3 and I will shew thee w thou shalt do: 834
17:26 W shall be done to the man that killeth this 4100
17:29 David said, W have I now done? Is there 4100
18: 8 and w can he have more but the kingdom? NIH
18:18 W is my life, or my father's family in Israel, 4310
19: 3 of thee; and w I see, that I will tell thee. 4100
20: 1 and said before Jonathan, W have I done? 4100
20: 1 w is mine iniquity? and what is my sin 4100
20: 1 w is my sin before thy father, that he 4100
20:10 or w if thy father answer thee roughly? 4100
20:32 shall he be slain? w hath he done? 4100
21: 2 I send thee, and w I have commanded thee: 834
21: 3 Now therefore w is under thine hand? 4100
21: 3 bread in mine hand, or w there is present. 1886.1
22: 3 with you, till I know w God will do for me. 4100
25:17 know and consider w thou wilt do; 4100
26:18 for w have I done? or what evil is in mine 4100
26:18 have I done? or w evil is in mine hand? 4100
28: 2 Surely thou shalt know w thy servant can do. 834
28: 9 Behold, thou knowest w Saul hath done, 834
28:13 for w sawest thou? And the woman said 4100
28:14 he said unto her, W form is he of? And she 4100
28:15 that thou mayest make known unto me w I 4100
29: 3 W do these Hebrews here? And Achish 4100
29: 8 said unto Achish, But w have I done? 4100
29: 8 w hast thou found in thy servant so long as 4100
2Sa 3:24 to the king, and said, W hast thou done? 4100
7:18 w is my house, that thou hast brought me 4310
7:20 w can David say more unto thee? for thou, 4100
7:23 w one nation in the earth is like thy people, 4310
9: 8 bowed himself, and said, W is thy servant, 4100
12:21 W thing is this that thou hast done? 4100
14: 5 the king said unto her, W aileth thee? 4100
15: 2 and said, Of w city art thou? 335+2088+4480
15:21 surely in w place my lord the king shall be, 834
15:35 that w thing soever thou shalt hear out 834+3605
16: 2 said unto Ziba, W meanest thou by these? 4100
16:10 the king said, W have I to do with you, 4100
16:20 Give counsel among you w we shall do. 4100
17: 5 and let us hear likewise w he saith. 4100
18: 4 unto them, W seemeth you best I will do. 834
18:21 to Cushi, Go tell the king w thou hast seen. 834
18:29 a great tumult, but I knew not w it was. 4100
18:29 and to do w he thought good. 1886.1
19:22 David said, W have I to do with you, 4100
19:27 do therefore w is good in thine eyes. 1886.1
19:28 W right therefore have I yet to cry any 4100
19:35 can thy servant taste w I eat or what I drink? 834
19:35 can thy servant taste what I eat or w I drink? 834
19:37 and do to him w shall seem good unto thee. 834
21: 3 unto the Gibeonites, W shall I do for you? 4100
21: 4 he said, W you shall say, that will I do for 4100
21:11 it was told David w Rizpah the daughter of 834
24:13 see w answer I shall return to him that sent 4100
24:17 these sheep, w have they done? let thine 4100
24:22 and offer up w seemeth good unto him: 1886.1
1Ki 1:16 And the king said, W wouldest thou? 4100
2: 5 Moreover thou knowest also w Joab the son 834
2: 5 w he did to the two captains of the hosts of 834
2: 9 and knowest w thou oughtest to do unto him; 834
3: 5 and God said, Ask w I shall give thee. 4100
8:38 W prayer and supplication soever be made 3605
9:13 W cities are these which thou hast given 4100
11:22 w hast thou lacked with me, that behold, 4100
12: 9 W counsel give ye that we may answer this 4100
12:16 saying, W portion have we in David? 4100
13:12 said unto them, W way went he? 335+2088
13:12 For his sons had seen w way the man of 1886.1
14: 3 he shall tell thee w shall become of 4100
14:14 of Jeroboam that day: but w? even now. 4100
16: 5 acts of Baasha, and w he did, and his might, 834
17:18 W have I to do with thee, O thou man of 4100
18: 9 he said, W have I sinned, that thou 4100
18:13 Was it not told my lord w I did when Jezebel 834
19: 9 said unto him, W dotest thou here, Elijah? 4100
19:13 and said, W doest thou here, Elijah? 4100
19:20 Go back again: for w have I done to thee? 4100
20:22 and mark, and see w thou doest: 834
22:14 w the LORD saith unto me, that will I 834
2Ki 1: 7 W manner of man was he which came up 4100
2: 9 said unto Elisha, Ask w I shall do for thee, 4100
3:13 king of Israel, W have I to do with thee? 4100
4: 2 Elisha said unto her, W shall I do for thee? 4100
4: 2 tell me, w hast thou in the house? And she 4100
4:13 with all this care; w is to be done for thee? 4100
4:14 he said, W then is to be done for her? 4100
4:43 his servitor said, W, should I set this before 4100
6:28 the king said unto her, W aileth thee? 4100
6:33 w should I wait for the LORD any longer? 4100
7:12 I will now shew you w the Syrians have 834
8:13 Hazael said, But w, is thy servant a dog, 4100
8:14 who said to him, W said Elisha to thee? 4100
9:18 Jehu said, W hast thou to do with peace? 4100
9:19 W hast thou to do with peace? 4100
9:22 W peace, so long as the whoredoms of thy 4100
18:19 W confidence is this wherein thou trustest? 4100
19:11 thou hast heard w the kings of Assyria have 834
20: 8 W shall be the sign that the LORD will 4100
20:14 and said unto him, W said these men? 4100
20:15 he said, W have they seen in thine house? 4100
22:19 when thou heardest w I spake against this 834
23:17 he said, W title is that that I see? And 4100
1Ch 12:32 of the times, to know w Israel ought to do; 4100
17:16 am I, O LORD God, and w is mine house, 4310
17:18 W can David speak more to thee for 4100
17:21 w one nation in the earth is like thy people 4310
21:12 advise thyself w word I shall bring again to 4100
21:17 as for these sheep, w have they done? 4100
29:14 who am I, and w is my people, that we 4310
2Ch 1: 7 and said unto him, Ask w I shall give thee. 4100
6:29 Then w prayer or what supplication soever 3605
6:29 w supplication soever shall be made of any 3605
10: 6 W counsel give ye me to return answer to 349
10: 9 W advice give ye that we may return 4100
10:16 saying, W portion have we in David? 4100
18:13 even w my God saith, that will I speak. 834
19: 6 said to the judges, Take heed w ye do: 4100
19:10 w cause soever shall come to you of 834+3605
20:12 against us; neither know we w to do: 4100
24:11 that at w time the chest was brought unto NIH
25: 9 w shall we do for the hundred talents which 4100
32:13 Know ye not w I and my fathers have done 4100
35:21 saying, W have I to do with thee, thou king 4100
Ezr 5: 4 W are the names of the men that make this 4479
6: 8 Moreover I make a decree w 1768+3964+3807.2
8:17 I told them w they should say unto Iddo, 1697
9:10 O our God, w shall we say after this? 4100
Ne 2: 4 For w dost thou make request? 2088+4100
2:12 neither told I any man w my God had put in 4100
2:16 rulers knew not whither I went, or w I did; 4100
2:19 and said, W is this thing that ye do? 4100
4: 2 and said, W do these feeble Jews? 4100
4:20 In w place therefore ye hear the sound of 834
13:17 W evil thing is this that ye do, and 4100
Est 1:15 W shall we do unto the queen Vashti 4100
2: 1 w she had done, and what was decreed 834
2: 1 had done, and w was decreed against her. 834
2:11 Esther did, and w should become of her. 4100
2:15 but w Hegai the king's chamberlain, 834
4: 5 to know w it was, and why it was. 4100
5: 3 king unto her, W wilt thou, queen Esther? 4100
5: 3 w is thy request? it shall be even given thee 4100
5: 6 at the banquet of wine, W is thy petition? 4100
5: 6 w is thy request? even to the half of 4100
6: 3 W honour and dignity hath been done to 4100
6: 6 W shall be done unto the man whom 4100
7: 2 of wine, W is thy petition, queen Esther? 4100
7: 2 w is thy request? and it shall be performed, 4100
8: 1 for Esther had told w he was unto her. 4100
9: 5 did w they would unto those that hated 3509.1
9:12 w have they done in the rest of the king's 4100
9:12 now w is thy petition? and it shall be 4100
9:12 or w is thy request further? and it shall be 4100
Job 2:10 W? shall we receive good at the hand of 1571
6:11 W is my strength, that I should hope? and 4100
6:11 w is mine end, that I should prolong my 4100
6:17 W time they wax warm, they vanish: 871.1
6:25 but w doth your arguing reprove? 4100
7:17 W is man, that thou shouldest magnify 4100
7:20 w shall I do unto thee, O thou preserver of 4100
9:12 who will say unto him, W doest thou? 4100
11: 8 It is as high as heaven; w canst thou do? 4100
11: 8 deeper than hell; w canst thou know? 4100
13: 2 W ye know, the same do I know also. 3509.1
13:13 I may speak, and let come on me w will. 4100
15: 9 W knowest thou, that we know not? 4100
15: 9 w understandest thou, which is not in us? NIH
15:12 thee away? and w do thine eyes wink at, 4100
15:14 W is man, that he should be clean? and 4100
16: 3 or w emboldeneth thee that thou answerest? 4100
16: 6 and though I forbear, w am I eased? 4100
21:15 W is the Almighty, that we should serve 4100
Job 21:15 w profit should we have, if we pray unto 4100
21:21 For w pleasure hath he in his house after 4100
21:31 and who shall repay him w he hath done? NIH
22:17 and w can the Almighty do for them? 4100
23: 5 and understand w he would say unto me. 4100
23:13 and w his soul desireth, even that he doeth. NIH
27: 8 For w is the hope of the hypocrite, 4100
31: 2 For w portion of God is there from above? 4100
31: 2 w inheritance of the Almighty from on NIH
31:14 W then shall I do when God riseth up? and 4100
31:14 and when he visiteth, w shall I answer him? 4100
32:11 whilst you searched out w to say. 4405
34: 4 let us know among ourselves w is good. 4100
34: 7 W man is like Job, who drinketh up 4310
34:33 and not I: therefore speak w thou knowest. 4100
35: 3 W advantage will it be unto thee? 4100
35: 3 and, W profit shall I have, if I be cleansed 4100
35: 6 If thou sinnest, w doest thou against him? 4100
35: 6 be multiplied, w doest thou unto him? 4100
35: 7 If thou be righteous, w givest thou him? or 4100
35: 7 thou him? or w receiveth he of thine hand? 4100
37:19 Teach us w we shall say unto him; for we 4100
38:24 By w way is the light parted, 335+2088
39:18 W time she lifteth up herself on high, 3509.1
40: 4 Behold, I am vile; w shall I answer thee? 4100
Ps 8: 4 W is man, that thou art mindful of him? 4100
11: 3 be destroyed, w can the righteous do? 4100
25:12 W man is he that feareth 2088+4310
30: 9 W profit is there in my blood, when I go 4100
34:12 W man is he that desireth life, and 4310
39: 4 w it is; that I may know how frail I am. 4100
39: 7 now, Lord, w wait I for? my hope is in 4100
44: 1 w work thou didst in their days, in the times NIH
46: 8 w desolations he hath made in the earth. 834
50:16 W hast thou to do to declare my statutes, or 4100
56: 3 W time I am afraid, I will trust in thee. NIH
56: 4 I will not fear w flesh can do unto me. 4100
56:11 I will not be afraid w man can do unto me. 4100
66:16 I will declare w he hath done for my soul. 834
85: 8 I will hear w God the LORD will speak: 4100
89:48 W man is he that liveth, and shall not see 4310
114: 5 W ailed thee, O thou sea, that thou 4100
116:12 W shall I render unto the LORD for all his 4100
118: 6 I will not fear: w can man do unto me? 4100
120: 3 W shall be given unto thee? or what shall 4100
120: 3 or w shall be done unto thee, thou false 4100
144: 3 LORD, w is man, that thou takest 4100
Pr 4:19 they know not at w they stumble. 4100
10:32 The lips of the righteous know w is NIH
23: 1 a ruler, consider diligently w is before thee: 834
25: 8 lest thou know not w to do in the end 4100
27: 1 for thou knowest not w a day may bring 4100
30: 4 w is his name, and what is his son's name, 4100
30: 4 and w is his son's name, if thou canst tell? 4100
31: 2 W, my son? and what, the son of my 4100
31: 2 w, the son of my womb? and what, the son 4100
31: 2 of my womb? and w, the son of my vows? 4100
Ecc 1: 3 W profit hath a man of all his labour which 4100
2: 2 It is mad: and of mirth, W doeth it? 4100
2: 3 till I might see w was that good for the sons 335
2:12 for w can the man do that cometh after 4100
2:22 For w hath man of all his labour, and of 4100
3: 9 W profit hath he that worketh in that 4100
3:22 for who shall bring him to see w shall be 4100
5:11 w good is there to the owners thereof, 4100
5:16 w profit hath he that hath laboured for 4100
6: 8 For w hath the wise more than the fool? 4100
6: 8 w hath the poor, that knoweth to walk 4100
6:11 that increase vanity, w is man the better? 4100
6:12 For who knoweth w is good for man in this 4100
6:12 for who can tell a man w shall be after him 4100
7:10 W is the cause that the former days were 4100
8: 4 and who may say unto him, W doest thou? 4100
10:14 a man cannot tell w shall be; and what shall 4100
10:14 and w shall be after him, who can tell him? 834
11: 2 for thou knowest not w evil shall be upon 4100
11: 5 As thou knowest not w is the way of 4100
SS 5: 9 W is thy beloved more than another 4100
5: 9 W is thy beloved more than another 4100
6:13 W will ye see in the Shulamite? As it were 4100
8: 8 w shall we do for our sister in the day when 4100
Isa 1:11 To w purpose is the multitude of your 4100
3:15 W mean ye that ye beat my people to 4100
5: 4 W could have been done more to my 4100
5: 5 I will tell you w I will do to my vineyard: 834
10: 3 w will ye do in the day of visitation, and 4100
14:32 W shall one then answer the messengers of 4100
19:12 let them know w the LORD of hosts hath 4100
21: 6 set a watchman, let him declare w he seeth. 834
21:11 me out of Seir, Watchman, w of the night? 4100
21:11 of the night? Watchman, w of the night? 4100
22: 1 W aileth thee now, that thou art wholly 4100
22:16 W hast thou here? and whom hast thou 4100
33:13 Hear, ye that are far off, w I have done; and 834
36: 4 W confidence is this wherein thou trustest? 4100
37:11 thou hast heard w the kings of Assyria have 834
38:15 W shall I say? he hath both spoken unto 4100
38:22 W is the sign that I shall go up to the house 4100
39: 3 and said unto him, W said these men? 4100
39: 4 said he, W have they seen in thine house? 4100
40: 6 he said, W shall I cry? All flesh is grass, 4100
40:18 or w likeness will ye compare unto him? 4100
41:22 them forth, and shew us w shall happen: 834
41:22 let them shew the former things, w they be, 4100
45: 9 to him that fashioneth it, W makest thou? 4100
45:10 that saith unto his father, W begettest thou? 4100
45:10 to the woman, W hast thou brought forth? 4100
52: 5 Now therefore, w have I here, saith 4100
64: 4 w he hath prepared for him that waiteth for NIH
Jer 1:11 unto me, saying, Jeremiah, w seest thou? 4100
1:13 me the second time, saying, W seest thou? 4100
2: 5 W iniquity have your fathers found in me, 4100
2:18 now w hast thou to do in the way of Egypt, 4100
2:18 or w hast thou to do in the way of Assyria, 4100
2:23 way in the valley, know w thou hast done: 4100

Jer 4:30 when thou art spoiled, w wilt thou do? 4100
5:15 neither understandest w they say. 4100
5:31 it so: and w will ye do in the end thereof? 4100
6:18 know, O congregation, w is among them. 834
6:20 To w purpose cometh there to me incense 4100
7:12 see w I did to it for the wickedness of my 834
7:17 Seest thou not w they do in the cities of 4100
8: 6 of his wickedness, saying, W have I done? 4100
8: 9 of the LORD; and w wisdom is in them? 4100
9:12 for w the land perisheth and is burnt up like 4100
11:15 W hath my beloved to do in mine house, 4100
13:21 W wilt thou say when he shall punish thee? 4100
16:10 or w is our iniquity? or what is our sin that 4100
16:10 w is our sin that we have committed against 4100
18: 7 At w instant I shall speak concerning a NIH
18: 9 at w instant I shall speak concerning a NIH
23:25 I have heard w the prophets said, 834
23:28 W is the chaff to the wheat? saith 4100
23:33 W is the burden of the LORD? 4100
23:33 thou shalt then say unto them, W burden? 4100
23:35 his brother, W hath the LORD answered? 4100
23:35 and, W hath the LORD spoken? 4100
23:37 W hath the LORD answered thee? 4100
23:37 and, W hath the LORD spoken? 4100
24: 3 LORD unto me, W seest thou, Jeremiah? 4100
32:24 and w thou hast spoken is come to pass; and 834
33:24 Considerest thou not w this people have 4100
37:18 W have I offended against thee, or 4100
38:25 Declare unto us now w thou hast said unto 4100
38:25 to death; also w the king said unto thee: 4100
48:19 and her that escapeth, and say, W is done? 4100
La 2:13 W thing shall I take to witness for thee? 4100
2:13 w thing shall I liken to thee, O daughter of 4100
2:13 w shall I equal to thee, that I may comfort 4100
5: 1 Remember, O LORD, w is come upon us: 4100
Eze 2: 8 But thou, son of man, hear w I say unto thee; 834
8: 6 unto me, Son of man, seest thou w they do? 4100
8:12 hast thou seen w the ancients of the house of 834
12: 9 said unto thee, W doest thou? 4100
12:22 w is that proverb that ye have in the land of 4100
15: 2 W is the vine tree more than any tree, or 4100
17:12 Know ye not w these things mean? tell 4100
18: 2 W mean ye, that ye use this proverb 4100
19: 2 say, W is thy mother? A lioness: she lay 4100
20:29 W is the high place whereunto ye go? 4100
21:13 and w if the sword contemn even the rod? 4100
24:19 Wilt thou not tell us w these things are to 4100
27:32 over thee, saying, W city is like Tyrus, 4310
33:30 hear w is the word that cometh forth from 4100
37:18 Wilt thou not shew us w thou meanest by 4100
47:23 that in w tribe the stranger sojourneth, 834
Da 2:22 secret things: he knoweth w is in 4101
2:23 hast made known unto me now w we 1768
2:28 w shall be in the latter days. 4101
2:29 thy bed, w should come to pass hereafter: 4101
2:29 known to thee w shall come to pass. 4101
2:45 to the king w shall come to pass hereafter: 4101
3: 5 That at w time ye hear 0.2+1768+5732+871.2
3:15 Now if ye be ready that at w time ye hear 1768
4:35 his hand, or say unto him, W doest thou? 4101
8:19 I will make thee know w shall be in the last 834
10:14 Now I am come to make thee understand w 834
12: 8 w shall be the end of these things? 4100
Hos 6: 4 O Ephraim, w shall I do unto thee? 4100
6: 4 O Judah, w shall I do unto thee? for your 4100
9: 5 W will ye do in the solemn day, and in 4100
9:14 w wilt thou give? give them a miscarrying 4100
10: 3 the LORD; w then should a king do to us? 4100
14: 8 Ephraim shall say, W have I to do any 4100
Joel 3: 4 Yea, and w have ye to do with me, O Tyre, 4100
Am 4:13 and declareth unto man w is his thought, 4100
5:18 to w end is it for you? the day of 4100+3807.1
7: 8 LORD said unto me, Amos, w seest thou? 4100
8: 2 he said, Amos, w seest thou? And I said, 4100
Jnh 1: 6 said unto him, W meanest thou, O sleeper? 4100
1: 8 this evil is upon us; W is thine occupation? 4100
1: 8 w is thy country? and of what people art 4100
1: 8 is thy country? and of w people art thou? 2088
1:11 they unto him, W shall we do unto thee, 4100
4: 5 till he might see w would become of 4100
Mic 1: 5 W is the transgression of Jacob? is it not 4310
1: 5 w are the high places of Judah? are they not 4310
6: 1 Hear ye now w the LORD saith; Arise, 834
6: 3 O my people, w have I done unto thee? and 4100
6: 5 remember now w Balak king of Moab 4100
6: 5 w Balaam the son of Beor answered him; 4100
6: 8 He hath shewed thee, O man, w is good; 4100
6: 8 w doth the LORD require of thee, but to 4100
Na 1: 9 W do ye imagine against the LORD? 4100
Hab 2: 1 will watch to see w he will say unto me, 4100
2: 1 and w I shall answer when I am reproved. 4100
2:18 W profiteth the graven image that 4100
Zec 1: 9 said I, O my lord, w are these? And 4100
1: 9 said unto me, I will shew thee w these be. 4100
1:19 the angel that talked with me, W be these? 4100
1:21 said I, W come these to do? And he spake, 4100
2: 2 to see w is the breadth thereof, and 4100+3509.1
2: 2 and w is the length thereof. 4100+3509.1
4: 2 said unto me, W seest thou? And I said, 4100
4: 4 with me, saying, W are these, my lord? 4100
4: 5 Knowest thou not w these be? And I said, 4100
4:11 W are these two olive trees upon the right 4100
4:12 W be these two olive branches which 4100
4:13 Knowest thou not w these be? And I said, 4100
5: 2 he said unto me, W seest thou? And I 4100
5: 5 and see w is this that goeth forth. 4100
5: 6 I said, W is it? And he said, This is an 4100
6: 4 that talked with me, W are these, my lord? 4100
13: 6 W are these wounds in thine hands? 4100
Mal 1:13 w a weariness is it! and ye have snuffed at 4100
3:13 W have we spoken so much against thee? 4100
3:14 w profit is it that we have kept his 4100
Mt 2: 7 inquired of them diligently w time the star 3588
5:46 them which love you, w reward have ye? 5101
5:47 w do ye more than others? do not even 5101
Mt 6: 3 let not thy left hand know w thy right hand 5101
6: 8 for your Father knoweth w things ye have 3739
6:25 w ye shall eat, or what ye shall drink; 5101
6:25 what ye shall eat, or w ye shall drink; 5101
6:25 nor yet for your body, w ye shall put on. 5101
6:31 take no thought, saying, W shall we eat? 5101
6:31 or, W shall we drink? or, Wherewithal shall 5101
7: 2 For with w judgment ye judge, ye shall be 3739
7: 2 and with w measure ye mete, it shall be 3739
7: 9 Or w man is there of you, whom if his son 5101
8:27 saying, W manner of man is this, 4217
8:29 saying, W have we to do with thee, Jesus, 5101
8:33 w was befallen to the possessed of 3588
9:13 But go ye and learn w that meaneth, I will 5101
10:19 take no thought how or w ye shall speak: 5101
10:19 you in that same hour w ye shall speak. 5101
10:27 W I tell you in darkness, that speak ye in 3739
10:27 and w ye hear in the ear, that preach ye 3739
11: 7 W went ye out into the wilderness to see? 5101
11: 8 But w went ye out for to see? A man 5101
11: 9 But w went ye out for to see? A prophet? 5101
12: 3 unto them, Have ye not read w David did, 5101
12: 7 But if ye had known w this meaneth, I will 5101
12:11 W man shall there be among you, 5101
16:26 For w is a man profited, if he shall gain 5101
16:26 w shall a man give in exchange for his 5101
17:25 saying, W thinkest thou, Simon? 5101
18:31 So when his fellowservants saw w was 3588
19: 6 W therefore God hath joined together, 3739
19:16 Good Master, w good thing shall I do, 5101
19:20 I kept from my youth up: w lack I yet? 5101
19:27 followed thee; w shall we have therefore? 5101
20:15 Is it not lawful for me to do w I will with 3739
20:21 And he said unto her, W wilt thou? 5101
20:22 and said, Ye know not w ye ask. 5101
20:32 said, W will ye that I shall do unto you? 5101
21:16 said unto him, Hearest thou w these say? 5101
21:23 By w authority doest thou these things? and 4169
21:24 I in like wise will tell you by w authority I 4169
21:27 Neither tell I you by w authority I do these 4169
21:28 But w think you? A certain man had two 5101
21:40 w will he do unto those husbandmen? 5101
22:17 Tell us therefore, W thinkest thou? Is it 5101
22:42 Saying, W think ye of Christ? whose son is 5101
24: 3 and w shall be the sign of thy coming, and 5101
24:42 for ye know not w hour your Lord doth 4169
24:43 known in w watch the thief would come, 4169
26: 8 saying, To w purpose is this waste? 5101
26:15 And said unto them, W will ye give me, 5101
26:40 them asleep, and saith unto Peter, W, 3779
26:62 w is it which these witness against thee? 5101
26:65 w further need have we of witnesses? 5101
26:66 W think ye? They answered and said, He is 5101
26:70 them all, saying, I know not w thou sayest. 5101
27: 4 And they said, W is that to us? see thou to 5101
27:22 W shall I do then with Jesus which is called 5101
27:23 governor said, Why, w evil hath he done? 5101
Mk 1:24 w have we to do with thee, thou Jesus of 5101
1:27 among themselves, saying, W thing is this? 5101
1:27 w new doctrine is this? for with authority 5101
2:25 Have ye never read w David did, when he 5101
3: 8 when they had heard w great things he did, 3745
4:24 he said unto them, Take heed w ye hear: 5101
4:24 with w measure ye mete, it shall be 3739
4:30 or with w comparison shall we compare it? 4169
4:41 W manner of man is this, that even 687+5101
5: 7 and said, W have I to do with thee, Jesus, 5101
5: 9 And he asked him, W is thy name? And he 5101
5:14 And they went out to see w it was that was 5101
5:33 knowing w was done in her, came and 3739
6: 2 w wisdom is this which is given unto him, 5101
6:10 In w place soever ye enter into a 1437+3699
6:24 and said unto her mother, W shall I ask? 5101
6:30 told him all things, both w they had done, 3745
6:30 what they had done, and w they had taught. 3745
8:36 For w shall it profit a man, if he shall gain 5101
8:37 Or w shall a man give in exchange for his 5101
9: 6 For he wist not w to say; for they were sore 5101
9: 9 should tell no man w things they had seen, 3739
9:10 questioning one with another w the rising 5101
9:16 the scribes, W question ye with them? 5101
9:33 W was it that ye disputed among 5101
10: 3 unto them, W did Moses command you? 5101
10: 9 W therefore God hath joined together, 3739
10:17 w shall I do that I may inherit eternal life? 5101
10:32 began to tell them w things should happen 3588
10:36 W would ye that I should do for you? 5101
10:38 said unto them, Ye know not w ye ask: 5101
10:51 W wilt thou that I should do unto thee? 5101
11: 5 said unto them, W do ye, loosing the colt? 5101
11:24 W things soever ye desire, when ye pray, 3745
11:28 By w authority doest thou these things? and 4169
11:29 I will tell you by w authority I do these 4169
11:33 Neither do I tell you by w authority I do 4169
12: 9 W shall therefore the lord of the vineyard 5101
13: 1 see w manner of stones and 4217
13: 1 manner of stones and w buildings are here. 4217
13: 4 w shall be the sign when all these things 5101
13:11 take no thought beforehand w ye shall 5101
13:37 And w I say unto you I say unto all, Watch. 3739
14: 8 She hath done w she could: she is come 3739
14:36 not that I will, but w thou wilt. 5101
14:40 neither wist they w to answer him. 5101
14:60 w is it which these witness against thee? 5101
14:63 saith, W need we any further witnesses? 5101
14:64 w think ye? And they all condemned him to 5101
14:68 neither understand I w thou sayest. 5101
15:12 W will ye then that I shall do unto him 5101
15:14 said unto them, Why, w evil hath he done? 5101
15:24 lots upon them, w every man should take. 5101
Lk 1:29 cast in her mind w manner of salutation 4217
1:66 W manner of child shall this be! 687+5101
3:10 asked him, saying, W shall we do then? 5101
3:12 and said unto him, Master, w shall we do? 5101
3:14 of him, saying, And w shall we do? 5101
Lk 4:34 w have we to do with thee, thou Jesus of 5101
4:36 saying, W a word is this! 5101
5:19 And when they could not find by w way 4169
5:22 unto them, W reason ye in your hearts? 5101
6: 3 ye not read so much as this, w David did, 3739
6:11 communed one with another w they might 5101
6:32 them which love you, w thank have ye? 4169
6:33 which do good to you, w thank have ye? 4169
6:34 whom ye hope to receive, w thank have ye? 4169
7:22 and tell John w things ye have seen and 3739
7:24 W went ye out into the wilderness for to 5101
7:25 But w went ye out for to see? A man 5101
7:26 But w went ye out for to see? A prophet? 5101
7:31 of this generation? and to w are they like? 5101
7:39 w manner of woman this is that toucheth 4217
8: 9 saying, W might this parable be? 5101
8:25 to another, W manner of man is this? 687+5101
8:28 voice said, W have I to do with thee, Jesus, 5101
8:30 Jesus asked him, saying, W is thy name? 5101
8:34 When they that fed them saw w was done, 3588
8:35 Then they went out to see w was done; and 3588
8:36 by w means he that was possessed of 4459
8:47 people for w cause she had touched him, 3739
8:56 that they should tell no man w was done. 3588
9:25 For w is a man advantaged, if he gain 5101
9:33 and one for Elias: not knowing w he said. 3739
9:55 Ye know not w manner of spirit ye are of. 3634
10:25 Master, w shall I do to inherit eternal life? 5101
10:26 He said unto him, W is written in the law? 5101
12:11 no thought how or w thing ye shall answer, 5101
12:11 thing ye shall answer, or w ye shall say: 5101
12:12 you in the same hour w ye ought to say. 3739
12:17 saying, W shall I do, because I have no 5101
12:22 no thought for your life, w ye shall eat; 5101
12:22 neither for the body, w ye shall put on. 5101
12:29 And seek not ye w ye shall eat, or what ye 5101
12:29 or w ye shall drink, neither be ye of 5101
12:39 had known w hour the thief would come, 4169
12:49 and w will I, if it be already kindled? 5101
12:57 why even of yourselves judge ye not w is 3588
13:18 Unto w is the kingdom of God like? 5101
14:31 Or w king, going to make war against 5101
15: 4 W man of you, having an hundred sheep, 5101
15: 8 Either w woman having ten pieces of 5101
15:26 and asked w these things meant. 5101
16: 3 steward said within himself, W shall I do? 5101
16: 4 I am resolved w to do, that, when I am put 5101
18: 6 Lord said, Hear w the unjust judge saith. 5101
18:18 w shall I do to inherit eternal life? 5101
18:36 the multitude pass by, he asked w it meant. 5101
18:41 W wilt thou that I shall do unto thee? 5101
19:48 And could not find w they might do: for all 5101
20: 2 by w authority doest thou these things? or 4169
20: 8 Neither tell I you by w authority I do these 4169
20:13 said the lord of the vineyard, W shall I do? 5101
20:15 and killed him. W therefore shall the lord 5101
20:17 and said, W is this then that is written, 5101
21: 7 w sign will there be when these things shall 5101
21:14 not to meditate before w ye shall answer: NIG
22:49 When they which were about him saw w 3588
22:60 Peter said, Man, I know not w thou sayest. 3739
22:71 they said, W need we any further witness? 5101
23:22 the third time, Why, w evil hath he done? 5101
23:31 in a green tree, w shall be done in the dry? 5101
23:34 forgive them; for they know not w they do. 5101
23:47 Now when the centurion saw w was done, 3588
24:17 W manner of communications are these 5101
24:19 W things? And they said unto him, 4169
24:35 And they told w things were done in 3588
Jn 1:21 And they asked him, W then? Art thou 5101
1:22 them that sent us. W sayest thou of thyself? 5101
1:38 and saith unto them, W seek ye? 5101
2: 4 unto her, Woman, w have I to do with thee? 5101
2:18 unto him, W sign shewest thou unto us, 5101
2:25 testify of man: for he knew w was in man. 5101
3:32 And w he hath seen and heard, that he 3739
4:22 Ye worship ye know not w: we know what 3739
4:22 we know w we worship: for salvation is of 3739
4:27 yet no man said, W seekest thou? or, 5101
5:12 W man is that which said unto thee, 5101
5:19 of himself, but w he seeth the Father do: 5100
5:19 for w things soever he doeth, these also 5100
6: 6 for he himself knew w he would do. 5101
6: 9 but w are they among so many? 5101
6:28 Then said they unto him, W shall we do, 5101
6:30 unto him, W sign shewest thou then, 5101
6:30 and believe thee? w dost thou work? 5101
6:62 W and if ye shall see the Son of man ascend NIG
7:36 W manner of saying is this that he said, 5101
7:51 before it hear him, and know w he doeth? 5101
8: 5 such should be stoned: but w sayest thou? 5101
9:17 W sayest thou of him, that he hath opened 5101
9:21 But by w means he now seeth, we know 4459
9:26 said they to him again, W did he to thee? 5101
10: 6 they understood not w things they were 5101
11:46 and told them w things Jesus had done. 3739
11:47 the Pharisees a council, and said, W do we? 5101
11:56 as they stood in the temple, W think ye, 5101
12: 6 had the bag, and bare w was put therein. 3588
12:27 Now is my soul troubled; and w shall I say? 5101
12:33 he said, signifying w death he should die. 4169
12:49 w I should say, and what I should speak. 5101
12:49 what I should say, and w I should speak. 5101
13: 7 unto him, W I do thou knowest not now; 3739
13:12 unto them, Know ye w I have done to you? 5101
13:28 Now no man at the table knew for w intent 5101
15: 7 ye shall ask w ye will, and it shall be 1437+3739
15:15 for the servant knoweth not w his lord 5101
16:17 W is this that he saith unto us, A little 5101
16:18 W is this that he saith, A little while? 5101
16:18 A little while? we cannot tell w he saith. 5101
18:21 ask them which heard me, w I have said 5101
18:21 said unto them: behold, they know w I said. 3739
18:29 W accusation bring you against this man? 5101
18:32 he spake, signifying w death he should die. 4169

W

Jn 18:35 delivered thee unto me: **w** hast thou done? 5101
18:38 Pilate saith unto him, **W** is truth? 5101
19:22 **W** I have written I have written. 3739
21:19 signifying by **w** death he should glorify 4169
21:21 to Jesus, Lord, and **w** *shall* this *man do?* 5101
21:22 that he tarry till I come, **w** *is that* to thee? 5101
21:23 that he tarry till I come, **w** *is that* to thee? 5101
Ac 2:12 saying one to another, **W** meaneth this? 5101
2:37 Men *and* brethren, **w** shall we do? 5101
4: 7 they asked, By **w** power, or by what name, 4169
4: 7 they asked, By what power, or by **w** name, 4169
4: 9 by **w** *means* he is made whole; 5101
4:16 Saying, **W** shall we do to these men? 5101
5: 7 his wife, not knowing **w** was done, came in. 3588
5:35 take heed to yourselves **w** ye intend to do 5101
7:40 of Egypt, we wot not **w** is become of him. 5101
7:49 **w** house will ye build me? saith the Lord: 4169
7:49 saith the Lord: or **w** *is* the place of my rest? 5101
8:30 said, Understandest thou **w** thou readest? 3739
8:36 *is* water; **w** doth hinder me to be baptized? 5101
9: 6 Lord, **w** wilt thou have me to do? 5101
9: 6 it shall be told thee **w** thou must do. 3739+5101
10: 4 he was afraid, and said, **W** is it, Lord? 5101
10: 6 he shall tell thee **w** thou oughtest to do. 5101
10:15 **W** God hath cleansed, *that* call not thou 3739
10:17 Now while Peter doubted in himself **w** 302+5101
10:21 **w** *is* the cause wherefore ye are come? 5101
10:29 therefore for **w** intent ye have sent for me? 5101
11: 9 **W** God hath cleansed, *that* call not thou 3739
11:17 **w** was I, that I could withstand God? 5101
12:18 among the soldiers, **w** was become of Peter. 5101
13:12 when he saw **w** was done, believed, 3588
14:11 And when the people saw **w** Paul had done, 3739
15:12 declaring **w** miracles and wonders God had 3745
16:30 and said, Sirs, **w** must I do to be saved? 5101
17:18 And some said, **W** will this babbler 302+5101
17:19 saying, May we know **w** this new doctrine, 5101
17:20 therefore **w** these *things* mean. 302+5101
19: 3 unto them, Unto **w** then were ye baptized? 5101
19:35 **w** man is there that knoweth not how that 5101
20:18 **after w manner** I have been with you at all 4459
21:13 **W mean** ye to weep and to break mine 5101
21:19 he declared particularly **w** *things* God had 3739
21:22 **W** is it therefore? the multitude must needs 5101
21:33 demanded who he was, and **w** he had done. 5101
22:10 And I said, **W** shall I do, Lord? And 5101
22:15 witness unto all men of **w** thou hast seen 3739
22:26 saying, Take heed **w** thou doest: 5101
23:19 asked *him,* **W** is that thou hast to tell me? 5101
23:30 to say before thee **w** *they had* against him. 3588
23:34 *the letter,* he asked of **w** province he was: 4169
28:22 But we desire to hear of thee **w** thou 3739
Ro 3: 1 **W** advantage then hath the Jew? or 5101
3: 1 or **w** profit *is there* of circumcision? 5101
3: 3 For **w** if some did not believe? shall their 5101
3: 5 the righteousness of God, **w** shall we say? 5101
3: 9 **W** then? are we better *than they?* No, in no 5101
3:19 Now we know that **w** *things* **soever** the law 3745
3:27 By **w** law? of works? Nay: but by the law 4169
4: 1 **W** shall we say then that Abraham our 5101
4: 3 For **w** saith the scripture? 5101
4:21 **w** he had promised, he was able also to 3739
6: 1 **W** shall we say then? Shall we continue in 5101
6:15 **W** then? shall we sin, because we are not 5101
6:21 **W** fruit had ye then *in those things* whereof 5101
7: 7 **W** shall we say then? *Is* the law sin? 5101
7:15 for **w** I would, that do I not; but what I hate, 3739
7:15 that do I not; but **w** I hate, that do I. 3739
8: 3 For **w** the law could not do, in that it was NIG
8:24 for **w** a man seeth, why doth he yet hope 3739
8:26 for we know not **w** we should pray for as 5101
8:27 And he that searcheth the hearts knoweth **w** 5101
8:31 **W** shall we then say to these *things?* If God 5101
9:14 **W** shall we say then? *Is there* 5101
9:22 **W if** God, willing to shew *his* wrath, and 1487
9:30 **W** shall we say then? That the Gentiles, 5101
10: 8 But **w** saith it? The word is nigh thee, 5101
11: 2 Wot ye not **w** the scripture saith of Elias? 5101
11: 4 But **w** saith the answer of God unto him? 5101
11: 7 **W** then? Israel hath not obtained that which 5101
11:15 **w** *shall* the receiving *of them be,* but life 5101
12: 2 that ye may prove **w** *is that* good, and 5101
1Co 2:11 For **w** man knoweth the *things* of a man, 5101
3:13 shall try every man's work of **w sort** it is. 3697
4: 7 and **w** hast thou that thou didst not receive? 5101
4:21 **W** will ye? shall I come unto you with a 5101
5:12 For **w have I to do** to judge them 1473+5101
6:16 **W?** know ye not that he which is joined to 2228
6:19 **W?** know ye not that your body is 2228
7:16 For **w** knowest thou, O wife, whether thou 5101
7:36 and need so require, let him do **w** he will, 3739
9:18 **W** is my reward then? *Verily* that, when I 5101
10:15 I speak as to wise *men;* judge ye **w** I say. 3739
10:19 **W** say I then? that the idol is any *thing,* or 5101
11:22 **W?** have ye not houses to eat and to drink NIG
11:22 **W** shall I say to you? shall I praise you in 5101
14: 6 speaking with tongues, **w** shall I profit you, 5101
14: 7 how shall it be known **w** is piped or 3588
14: 9 how shall it be known **w** is spoken? 3588
14:15 **W** is it then? I will pray with the spirit, and 5101
14:16 seeing he understandeth not **w** thou sayest? 5101
14:36 **W?** came the word of God out from you? 2228
15: 2 if ye keep in memory **w** I preached unto 5101
15:10 But by the grace of God I am **w** I am: and 3739
15:29 Else **w** shall they do which are baptized for 5101
15:32 **w** advantageth it me, if the dead rise not? 5101
15:35 raised up? and with **w** body do they come? 4169
2Co 1:13 unto you, than **w** ye read or acknowledge; 3739
6:14 for **w** fellowship hath righteousness with 5101
6:14 **w** communion hath light with darkness? 5101
6:15 And **w** concord hath Christ with Belial? or 5101
6:15 **w** part hath he that believeth with an 5101
6:16 And **w** agreement hath the temple of God 5101
7:11 **w** carefulness it wrought in you, yea, 4214
7:11 yea, **w** clearing of yourselves, yea, NIG
2Co 7:11 yea, **w** indignation, yea, *what* fear, yea, NIG
7:11 yea, *what* indignation, yea, **w** fear, yea, NIG
7:11 yea, *what* fear, yea, **w** vehement desire, yea, NIG
7:11 yea, **w** zeal, yea, *what* revenge! NIG
7:11 yea, *what* zeal, yea, **w** revenge! NIG
11:12 But **w** I do, that I will do, that I may cut off 3739
12:13 For **w** is it wherein ye were inferior to other 5101
Gal 4:30 Nevertheless **w** saith the scripture? Cast out 5101
Eph 1:18 that ye may know **w** is the hope of his 5101
1:18 **w** the riches of the glory of his inheritance 5101
1:19 And **w** *is* the exceeding greatness of his 5101
3: 9 And to make all *men* see **w** *is* 5101
3:18 with all saints **w** *is* the breadth, 5101
4: 9 **w** is it but that he also descended first into 5101
5:10 Proving **w** is acceptable unto the Lord. 5101
5:17 understanding **w** the will of the Lord *is.* 5101
Php 1:18 **W** then? notwithstanding, every way, 5101
1:22 my labour: yet **w** I shall choose I wot not. 5101
3: 7 But **w** *things* were gain to me, those I 3748
Col 1:27 To whom God would make known **w** *is* 5101
2: 1 For I would that ye knew **w great** conflict I 2245
1Th 1: 5 as ye know **w manner** of *men* we were 3634
1: 9 **w manner** of entering in we had unto you, 3697
2:19 For **w** *is* our hope, or joy, or crown of 5101
3: 9 For **w** thanks can we render to God again 5101
4: 2 For ye know **w** commandments we gave 5101
2Th 2: 6 And now ye know **w** withholdeth that he 3588
1Ti 1: 7 understanding neither **w** they say, 3739
2Ti 2: 7 Consider **w** I say; and the Lord give thee 3739
3:11 at Lystra; **w** persecutions I endured: 3634
Heb 2: 6 saying, **W** is man, that thou art mindful of 5101
7:11 **w** further need *was there* that another priest 5101
11:32 And **w** shall I more say? for the time would 5101
12: 7 for **w** son is *he* whom the father chasteneth 5101
13: 6 and I will not fear **w** man shall do unto me. 5101
Jas 1:24 straightway forgetteth **w manner of** *man* 3697
2:14 **W** *doth it* profit, my brethren, though a 5101
2:16 *are* needful to the body; **w** *doth it* profit? 5101
4:14 Whereas ye know not **w** *shall be* on 3588
4:14 for **w** *is* your life? It is even a vapour, 4169
1Pe 1:11 Searching **w**, or what manner of time 5101
1:11 **w manner** of time the Spirit of Christ 4169
2:20 For **w** glory *is it,* if, when ye be buffeted 4169
4:17 **w** *shall* the end *be* of them that obey not 5101
2Pe 3:11 **w manner** *of persons* ought ye to be in all 4217
1Jn 3: 1 **w manner** of love the Father hath 4217
3: 2 and it doth not yet appear **w** we shall be: 5101
Jude 1:10 but **w** they know naturally, as brute beasts, 3745
Rev 1:11 and, **W** thou seest, write in a book, and 3739
2: 7 let him hear **w** the Spirit saith unto 5101
2:11 let him hear **w** the Spirit saith unto 5101
2:17 let him hear **w** the Spirit saith unto 5101
2:29 let him hear **w** the Spirit saith unto 5101
3: 3 thou shalt not know **w** hour I will come 4169
3: 6 let him hear **w** the Spirit saith unto 5101
3:13 let him hear **w** the Spirit saith unto 5101
3:22 let him hear **w** the Spirit saith unto 5101
7:13 **W** are these which are arrayed in white 5101
18:18 saying, **W** *city is* like unto *this* great city? 5101

WHATSOEVER (152) [EVER, SO, WHAT]

Ge 2:19 **w** Adam called every living creature, 834+3605
8:19 every fowl, *and* **w** creepeth upon the earth, 3605
19:12 and **w** thou hast in the city, 834+3605
31:16 **w** God hath said unto thee, do. 834+3605
39:22 **w** they did there, he was the doer *of* 834+3605
Ex 13: 2 **w** openeth the womb among the children of 3605
21:30 of his life **w** is laid upon him. 834+3605+3509.1
29:37 **w** toucheth the altar shall be holy. 3605
30:29 most holy: **w** toucheth them shall be holy. 3605
Lev 5: 3 **w** uncleanness *it be* that a man 3605+3807.1
5: 4 **w** *it be* that a man shall pronounce 3605+3807.1
6:27 **W** shall touch the flesh thereof shall 834+3605
7:27 **W** soul *it be* that eateth any *manner of* 3605
11: 3 **W** parteth the hoof, and *is* clovenfooted, 3605
11: 9 **w** hath fins and scales in the waters, 834+3605
11:12 **W** hath no fins nor scales in 834+3605
11:27 **w** goeth upon his paws, among all *manner* 3605
11:32 upon **w** *any* of them, when they are 834+3605
11:32 **w** vessel *it be,* wherein *any* work is 834+3605
11:33 **w** *is* in it shall be unclean; 834+3605
11:42 **W** goeth upon the belly, and 3605
11:42 **w** goeth upon *all* four, or whatsoever hath 3605
11:42 **w** hath more feet among all creeping things 3605
13:58 **w** thing of skin *it be,* which thou shalt 3605
15:26 **w** she sitteth upon shall be 3605+3627+1886.1
17: 8 **W man** *there be* of the house of Israel, 376+376
17:10 **w man** *there be* of the house of Israel, 376+376
17:13 **w man** *there be* of the children of 376+376
21:18 For **w** man *he be* that hath a blemish, 834+3605
22: 5 take uncleanness, **w** uncleanness he hath; 3605
22:18 **W** *he be* of the house of Israel, or of 376
22:20 *But* **w** hath a blemish, *that* shall ye not 834+3605
23:29 For **w** soul *it be* that shall not be afflicted in 3605
23:30 **w** soul *it be* that doeth any work in that 3605
27:32 *even of* **w** passeth under the rod, 834+3605
Nu 5:10 **w** any man giveth the priest, it shall be his. 834
18:13 *And* **w** is first ripe in the land, 834+3605
19:22 **w** the unclean *person* toucheth shall be 834+3605
22:17 I will do **w** thou sayest unto me: 834+3605
23: 3 **w** he sheweth me I will tell thee. 1697+4100
30:12 **w** proceeded out of her lips concerning her 3605
Dt 2:37 **w** the LORD our God forbad *us.* 834+3605
12: 8 every man **w** *is* right in his own eyes. 3605
12:15 all thy gates, **w** thy soul lusteth after, 3605+871.1
12:20 eat flesh, **w** thy soul lusteth after. 3605+871.1
12:21 thou shalt eat in thy gates **w** thy soul 3605+871.1
14:10 **w** hath not fins and scales ye may not 834+3605
14:26 thou shalt bestow *that* money for **w** 834+3605
14:26 or for **w** thy soul desireth: 834+3605
Jdg 10:15 do thou unto us **w** seemeth good 3605+3509.1
11:31 that **w** cometh forth of the doors of my house 834
1Sa 14:36 they said, Do **w** seemeth good unto thee. 3605
20: 4 **W** thy soul desireth, I will even do *it* for 4100
25: 8 **w** cometh to thine hand unto thy servants, 834
2Sa 3:36 **w** the king did, pleased all the people. 834+3605
15:15 thy servants *are ready to do* **w** 834+3605+3509.1
19:38 **w** thou shalt require of me, *that* will I 834+3605
1Ki 8:37 **w** plague, whatsoever sickness *there be;* 3605
8:37 whatsoever plague, **w** sickness *there be;* 3605
10:13 **w** she asked, besides *that* which 834
20: 6 it shall be, *that* **w** *is* pleasant in thine eyes, 3605
2Ch 6:28 **w** sore or whatsoever sickness *there be:* 3605
6:28 whatsoever sore or **w** sickness *there be:* 3605
9:12 **w** she asked, besides *that* which she 834
Ezr 7:18 **w** shall seem good to thee, and to thy 1768+4101
7:20 **w** more *shall be* needful for the house of thy NIH
7:21 that **w** Ezra the priest, 1768+1768+3606
7:23 **W** *is* commanded by the God of 1768+3606
Est 2:13 **w** she desired was given her to go 834+3605
Job 37:12 that they may do **w** he commandeth 834+3605
41:11 that I should repay *him?* **w** *is* under NIH
Ps 1: 3 and **w** he doeth shall prosper. 834+3605
8: 8 *and* **w** passeth *through* the paths of the seas. NIH
115: 3 he hath done **w** he pleased. 834+3605
135: 6 **W** the LORD pleased, *that* did he in 834+3605
Ecc 2:10 **w** mine eyes desired I kept not from 834+3605
3:14 I know that, **w** God doeth, it shall be 834+3605
8: 3 for he doeth **w** pleaseth him. 834+3605
9:10 **W** thy hand findeth to do, do *it* with 834+3605
Jer 1: 7 **w** I command thee thou shalt speak. 834+3605
42: 4 *that* **w** thing the LORD shall answer you, 3605
44:17 we will certainly do **w** thing goeth 834+3605
Mt 5:37 for **w** is more than these cometh of evil. 3588
7:12 Therefore all *things* **w** ye would that 302+3745
10:11 And into **w** city or town ye shall enter, 302+3739
14: 7 an oath to give her **w** she would ask. 1437+3739
15: 5 **w** thou mightest be profited by me; 1437+3739
15:17 that **w** entereth in at the mouth goeth into 3956
16:19 **w** thou shalt bind on earth shall be 1437+3739
16:19 **w** thou shalt loose on earth shall be 1437+3739
17:12 but have done unto him **w** they listed. 3745
18:18 **W** ye shall bind on earth shall be 1437+3745
18:18 **w** ye shall loose on earth shall be 1437+3745
20: 4 and **w** is right I will give you. 1437+3739
20: 7 and **w** is right, *that* shall ye receive. 1437+3739
21:22 And all *things,* **w** ye shall ask in 302+3745
23: 3 All therefore **w** they bid you observe, 302+3745
28:20 Teaching them to observe all *things* **w** I 3745
Mk 6:22 Ask of me **w** thou wilt, and I will 1437+3739
6:23 **W** thou shalt ask of me, I will give *it* 1437+3739
7:11 **w** thou mightest be profited by me; 1437+3739
7:18 that **w** *thing* from without entereth into 3956
9:13 and they have done unto him **w** they listed, 3745
10:21 sell **w** thou hast, and give to the poor, and 3745
10:35 shouldest do for us **w** we shall desire. 1437+3739
11:23 to pass; he shall have **w** he saith. 1437+3739
13:11 but **w** shall be given you in that hour, 1437+3739
Lk 4:23 **w** we have heard done in Capernaum, 3745
9: 4 And **w** house ye enter into, 302+3739
10: 5 And into **w** house ye enter, first say, 302+3739
10: 8 And into **w** city ye enter, and 302+3739
10:10 But into **w** city ye enter, and 302+3739
10:35 and **w** thou spendest more, when I 302+3748
12: 3 Therefore **w** ye have spoken in darkness 3745
Jn 2: 5 **W** he saith unto you, do *it.* 302+3739+5100
5: 4 was made whole of **w** disease he had. 3739
11:22 even now, **w** thou wilt ask of God, 302+3745
12:50 **w** I speak therefore, even as the Father said 3739
14:13 And **w** ye shall ask in my name, 302+3739+5100
14:26 **w** I have said unto you. 3739
15:14 are my friends, if ye do **w** I command you. 3745
15:16 that **w** ye shall ask of the Father 302+3739+5100
16:13 but **w** he shall hear, *that* shall he speak: 3745
16:23 **W** ye shall ask the Father in my name, 302+3745
17: 7 Now they have known that all *things* **w** 3745
Ac 3:22 him shall ye hear in all *things* **w** he 302+3745
4:28 For to do **w** thy hand and thy counsel 3745
Ro 14:23 of faith: for **w** *is* not of faith is sin. 3739+3956
15: 4 For **w** *things* were written aforetime were 3745
16: 2 *that* ye assist her in **w** business she 302+3739
1Co 10:25 **W** is sold in the shambles, *that* eat, 3956
10:27 **w** is set before you, eat, asking no question 3956
10:31 therefore ye eat, or drink, or **w** ye do, 5100
Gal 2: 6 (**w** they were, it maketh no matter to me: 3697
6: 7 **w** a man soweth, that shall he also 1437+3739
Eph 3:13 the light: for **w** doth make manifest is light. 3956
6: 8 Knowing that **w** good *thing* 1437+3739+5100
Php 4: 8 Finally, brethren, **w** *things* are true, 3745
4: 8 **w** *things are* honest, whatsoever *things are* 3745
4: 8 **w** *things are* just, whatsoever *things are* 3745
4: 8 *things are* just, **w** *things are* pure, 3745
4: 8 *things are* pure, **w** *things are* lovely, 3745
4: 8 *are* lovely, **w** *things are* of good report; 3745
4:11 for I have learned, in **w** *state* I am, 3739
Col 3:17 And **w** ye do in word or 302+302+3739+5100
3:23 And **w** ye do, do *it* 1437+3748+3956+5100
1Jn 3:22 And **w** we ask, we receive of him, 1437+3739
5: 4 For **w** is born of God overcometh 3956
5:15 And if we know that he hear us, **w** we 302+3739
3Jn 1: 5 thou doest faithfully **w** thou doest to 1437+3739
Rev 18:22 of **w** craft *he be,* shall be found any more in 3956
21:27 neither **w** worketh abomination, or *maketh* a NIG

WHEAT (51) [WHEATEN]

Ge 30:14 Reuben went in the days of **w** harvest, and 2406
Ex 9:32 the **w** and the rye were not smitten: for they 2406
34:22 of the firstfruits of **w** harvest, and the feast 2406
Nu 18:12 and all the best of the wine, and of the **w**, 1715
Dt 8: 8 A land of **w**, and barley, and vines, and 2406
32:14 and goats, with the fat of kidneys of **w**; 2406
Jdg 6:11 his son Gideon threshed **w** by 2406
15: 1 in the time of **w** harvest, that Samson 2406
Ru 2:23 the end of barley harvest and of **w** harvest; 2406
1Sa 6:13 *they of* Beth-shemesh *were* reaping their **w** 2406
12:17 *Is it* not **w** harvest to day? I will call unto 2406
2Sa 4: 6 *as though* they would have fetched **w**; 2406
17:28 **w**, and barley, and flour, and parched *corn,* 2406
1Ki 5:11 measures of **w** *for* food to his household, 2406
1Ch 21:20 Now Ornan was threshing **w**. 2406

1Ch 21:23 for wood, and the **w** for the meat offering; 2406
2Ch 2:10 twenty thousand measures of beaten **w**, and 2406
2:15 Now therefore the **w**, and the barley, 2406
27: 5 ten thousand measures of **w**, and 2406
Ezr 6: 9 of the God of heaven, **w**, salt, wine, and oil, 2591
7:22 to an hundred measures *of* **w**, and to an 2591
Job 31:40 Let thistles grow instead of **w**, and 2406
Ps 81:16 have fed them also with the finest of the **w**: 2406
147:14 *and* filleth thee *with* the finest of the **w**. 2406
Pr 27:22 a fool in a mortar among **w** with a pestle, 7383
SS 7: 2 thy belly *is like* a heap of **w** set about with 2406
Isa 28:25 cast in the principal **w** and the appointed 2406
Jer 12:13 They have sown **w**, but shall reap thorns: 2406
23:28 What *is* the chaff to the **w**? saith 1250
31:12 for **w**, and for wine, and for oil, and for 1715
41: 8 *of* **w**, and *of* barley, and *of* oil, and 2406
Eze 4: 9 Take thou also unto thee **w**, and barley, and 2406
27:17 they traded in thy market **w** of Minnith, and 2406
45:13 the sixth *part* of an ephah of a homer of **w**, 2406
Joel 1:11 for the **w** and for the barley; 2406
2:24 the floors shall be full *of* **w**, and the fats 1250
Am 5:11 and ye take from him burdens of **w**: 1250
8: 5 the sabbath, that we may set forth **w**, 1250
8: 6 of shoes; *yea*, and sell the refuse of the **w**? 1250
Mt 3:12 his floor, and gather his **w** into the garner; *4621*
13:25 enemy came and sowed tares among the **w**, *4621*
13:29 the tares, ye root up also the **w** with them. *4621*
13:30 burn them: but gather the **w** into my barn. *4621*
Lk 3:17 and will gather the **w** into his garner; *4621*
16: 7 And he said, An hundred measures of **w**. *4621*
22:31 *to have* you, that *he* may sift *you* as **w**: *4621*
Jn 12:24 Except a corn of **w** fall into the ground and *4621*
Ac 27:38 the ship, and cast out the **w** into the sea. *4621*
1Co 15:37 it may chance of **w**, or of some other *grain:* *4621*
Rev 6: 6 A measure of **w** for a penny, and *4621*
18:13 and **w**, and beasts, and sheep, and horses, *4621*

WHEATEN (1) [WHEAT]

Ex 29: 2 with oil: *of* **w** flour shalt thou make them. 2406

WHEEL (15) [WHEELS]

1Ki 7:32 the height of a **w** *was* a cubit and half a 212
7:33 the wheels *was* like the work of a chariot **w**: 212
Ps 83:13 O my God, make them like a **w**; as 1534
Pr 20:26 the wicked, and bringeth the **w** over them. 212
Ecc 12: 6 the fountain, or the **w** broken at the cistern. 1534
Isa 28:27 is a cart **w** turned about upon the cummin; 212
28:28 nor break *it with* the **w** of his cart, 1536
Eze 1:15 behold one **w** upon the earth by the living 212
1:16 their work *was* as it were a **w** in the middle 212
1:16 *was* as it were a wheel in the middle of a **w**. 212
10: 9 one **w** by one cherub, and another wheel by 212
10: 9 and another **w** by another cherub: 212
10:10 as if a **w** had been in the midst of a wheel. 212
10:10 as if a wheel had been in the midst of a **w**. 212
10:13 it was cried unto them in my hearing, O **w**. 1534

WHEELS (33) [WHEEL]

Ex 14:25 took off their chariot **w**, that they drave them 212
Jdg 5:28 in coming? why tarry the **w** of his chariots? 6471
1Ki 7:30 every base had four brasen **w**, and plates of 212
7:32 under the borders *were* four **w**; and 212
7:32 the axletrees of the **w** *were* joined to 212
7:33 the work of the **w** *was* like the work of a 212
Isa 5:28 like flint, and their **w** like a whirlwind: 1534
Jer 18: 3 and behold, he wrought a work on the **w**. 70
47: 3 *and at* the rumbling of his **w**, the fathers 1534
Eze 1:16 The appearance of the **w** and their work *was* 212
1:19 living creatures went, the **w** went by them: 212
1:19 lift up from the earth, the **w** were lift up. 212
1:20 and the **w** were lifted up over against them: 212
1:20 the spirit of the living creature *was* in the **w**. 212
1:21 the **w** were lifted up over against them: 212
1:21 the spirit of the living creature *was* in the **w**. 212
3:13 the noise of the **w** over against them, and 212
10: 2 said, Go in between the **w**, *even* under 1534
10: 6 saying, Take fire from between the **w**, 1534
10: 6 then he went in, and stood beside the **w**. 212
10: 9 behold the four **w** by the cherubims, 212
10: 9 the appearance of the **w** *was* as the colour of 212
10:12 and their hands, and their wings, and the **w**, 212
10:12 round about, *even* the **w** that they four had. 212
10:13 As for the **w**, it was cried unto them in my 212
10:16 the cherubims went, the **w** went by them: 212
10:16 the same **w** also turned not from beside 212
10:19 the **w** also *were* besides them, and *every one* 212
11:22 lift up their wings, and the **w** besides them; 212
23:24 and **w**, and with an assembly of people, 1534
26:10 of the **w**, and of the chariots, when he shall 1534
Da 7: 9 the fiery flame, *and* his **w** *as* burning fire. 1535
Na 3: 2 the noise of the rattling of the **w**, and of 212

WHELP (3) [WHELPS]

Ge 49: 9 Judah *is* a lion's **w**: from the prey, my son, 1482
Dt 33:22 of Dan he said, Dan *is* a lion's **w**: he shall 1482
Na 2:11 *and* the lion's **w**, and none made *them* 1482

WHELPS (10) [WHELP]

2Sa 17: 8 as a bear **robbed of** her **w** in the field: 7909
Job 4:11 and the stout lion's **w** are scattered abroad. 1121
28: 8 The lion's **w** have not trodden it, nor 1121
Pr 17:12 *Let* a bear robbed of her **w** meet a man, NIH
Jer 51:38 like lions: they shall yell as lions' **w**. 1484
Eze 19: 2 she nourished her **w** among young lions. 1482
19: 3 she brought up one of her **w**: it became a 1482
19: 5 she took another of her **w**, *and* made him a 1482
Hos 13: 8 them as a bear *that is* **bereaved of** her **w**, 7909
Na 2:12 lion did tear in pieces enough for his **w**, 1484

WHEN (2848) [WHENSOEVER]

Ge 2: 4 and of the earth **w** they were created, 871.1
3: 6 **And w** the woman saw that the tree *was* 2050.1
4: 8 it came to pass, **w** they were in the field, 871.1
4:12 **W** thou tillest the ground, it shall not 3588

Ge 5: 2 in the day **w** they were created. NIH
6: 1 **w** men began to multiply on the face of 3588
6: 4 **w** the sons of God came in unto 834
7: 6 Noah *was* six hundred years old **w** 2050.1
9:14 to pass, **w** I bring a cloud over the earth, 871.1
12: 4 five years old **w** he departed out of Haran. 871.1
12:11 **w** he was come near to enter into 834+3509.1
12:12 **w** the Egyptians shall see thee, that they 3588
12:14 that, **w** Abram was come into Egypt, 3509.1
14:14 **And w** Abram heard that his brother was 2050.1
15:11 **And w** the fowls came down upon 2050.1
15:12 **And w** the sun was going down, a deep 2050.1
15:17 that, **w** the sun went down, and it was dark, NIH
16: 4 **and w** she saw that she had conceived, 2050.1
16: 5 **and w** she saw that she had conceived, I 2050.1
16: 6 **And w** Sarai dealt hardly with her, 2050.1
16:16 years old, **w** Hagar bare Ishmael to Abram. 871.1
17: 1 **And w** Abram was ninety years old and 2050.1
17:24 **w** he was circumcised *in* the flesh of his 871.1
17:25 **w** he was circumcised in the flesh of his 871.1
18: 2 **and w** he saw *them*, he ran to meet them 2050.1
19:15 **w** the morning arose, then the angels 3644
19:17 **w** they had brought them forth abroad, 3509.1
19:23 The sun was risen upon the earth **w** Lot 2050.1
19:29 **w** God destroyed the cities of the plain, 871.1
19:29 **w** he overthrew the cities in the which Lot 871.1
19:33 he perceived not **w** she lay down, 871.1
19:33 not when she lay down, nor **w** she arose. 871.1
19:35 he perceived not **w** she lay down, 871.1
19:35 not when she lay down, nor **w** she arose. 871.1
20:13 **w** God caused me to wander from 834+3509.1
21: 5 **w** his son Isaac was born unto him. 871.1
24:19 **And w** she had done giving him drink, 2050.1
24:30 **w** he saw the earring and bracelets upon 3509.1
24:30 **w** he heard the words of Rebekah his 3509.1
24:36 wife bare a son to my master **w** she was old: 310
24:41 *this* my oath, **w** thou comest to my kindred; 3588
24:43 *that* **w** the virgin cometh forth to draw NIH
24:52 **w** Abraham's servant heard their 834+3509.1
24:64 **and w** she saw Isaac, she lighted off 2050.1
25:20 Isaac was forty years old **w** he took 871.1
25:24 **And w** her days to be delivered were 2050.1
25:26 Isaac *was* threescore years old **w** she bare 871.1
26: 8 to pass, **w** he had been there a long time, 3588
26:34 Esau was forty years old **w** he took to 2050.1
27: 1 that **w** Isaac was old, and his eyes were dim, NIH
27: 5 Rebekah heard **w** Isaac spake to Esau his 871.1
27:34 **w** Esau heard the words of his father, he 3509.1
27:40 it shall come to pass **w** thou shalt 834+3509.1
28: 6 **W** Esau saw that Isaac had blessed Jacob, 2050.1
29:10 **w** Jacob saw Rachel the daughter of 834+3509.1
29:13 **w** Laban heard the tidings of Jacob his 3509.1
29:31 **And w** the LORD saw that Leah *was* 2050.1
30: 1 **And w** Rachel saw that she bare Jacob no 2050.1
30: 9 **W** Leah saw that she had left bearing, she 2050.1
30:25 to pass, **w** Rachel had born Joseph, 834+3509.1
30:30 now **w** shall I provide for mine own house 4970
30:33 **w** it shall come for my hire before thy face: 3588
30:38 watering troughs **w** the flocks came to drink, 834
30:38 that they should conceive **w** they came to 871.1
30:42 **w** the cattle were feeble, he put *them* not 871.1
31:49 **w** we are absent one from another. 3588
32: 2 **w** Jacob saw them, he said, This *is* 834+3509.1
32:17 **W** Esau my brother meeteth thee, and 3588
32:19 shall you speak unto Esau, **w** you find him. 871.1
32:25 **And w** he saw that he prevailed not 2050.1
33:18 of Canaan, **w** he came from Padan-aram; 871.1
34: 2 **And w** Shechem the son of Hamor 2050.1
34: 7 the sons of Jacob came out of the field **w** 3509.1
34:25 **w** they were sore, that two of the sons of 871.1
35: 1 that appeared unto thee **w** thou fleddest 871.1
35: 7 **w** he fled from the face of his brother. 871.1
35: 9 **w** he came out of Padan-aram, and 871.1
35:17 it came to pass, **w** she was in hard labour, 871.1
35:22 **w** Israel dwelt in that land, that Reuben 871.1
37: 4 **And w** his brethren saw that their father 2050.1
37:18 **And w** they saw him afar off, even before 2050.1
37:23 **w** Joseph was come unto his 834+3509.1
38: 5 and he was at Chezib, **w** she bare him. 871.1
38: 9 to pass, **w** he went in unto his brother's wife, 518
38:15 **W** Judah saw her, he thought her to be a 2050.1
38:25 **W** she *was* brought forth, she sent to her 2050.1
38:28 it came to pass, **w** she travailed, that 871.1
39:13 **w** she saw that he had left his garment in 3509.1
39:15 **w** he heard that I lifted up my voice and 3509.1
39:19 **w** his master heard the words of his wife, 3509.1
40:13 after the former manner **w** thou wast his 834
40:14 think on me **w** it shall be well with 834+3509.1
40:16 **W** the chief baker saw that 2050.1
41:21 **And w** they had eaten them up, it could 2050.1
41:46 Joseph *was* thirty years old **w** he stood 871.1
41:55 **And w** all the land of Egypt was 2050.1
42: 1 **Now w** Jacob saw that there was corn in 2050.1
42:21 **w** he besought us, and we would not hear; 871.1
42:35 **and w** *both* they and their father saw 2050.1
43: 2 **w** they had eaten up the corn which 834+3509.1
43:16 **And w** Joseph saw Benjamin with them, 2050.1
43:21 it came to pass, **w** we came to the inn, 3588
43:26 **And w** Joseph came home, they brought 2050.1
44: 4 *And* **w** they were gone out of the city, *and* NIH
44: 4 **and w** thou dost overtake them, say unto 2050.1
44:24 it came to pass **w** we came up unto thy 3588
44:30 **w** I come to thy servant my father, 2050.1
44:31 **w** he seeth that the lad *is* not *with us*, that 2050.1
45:27 **and w** he saw the wagons which Joseph 2050.1
46:33 **w** Pharaoh shall call you, and shall say, 3588
47:15 **And w** money failed in the land of Egypt, 2050.1
47:18 **W** that year was ended, they came unto 2050.1
48: 7 as for me, **w** I came from Padan, 871.1
48: 7 **w** yet *there was* but a little way to come 871.1
48:17 **And w** Joseph saw that his father laid his 2050.1
49:33 **And w** Jacob had made an end of 2050.1
50: 4 **And w** the days of his mourning were 2050.1
50:11 **And w** the inhabitants of the land, 2050.1
50:15 **And w** Joseph's brethren saw that their 2050.1

Ge 50:17 And Joseph wept **w** they spake unto him. 871.1
Ex 1:10 to pass, that, **w** there falleth out any war, 2050.1
1:16 **W** ye do the office of a midwife to 871.1
2: 2 **and w** she saw him that he *was* a goodly 2050.1
2: 3 **And w** she could not longer hide him, she 2050.1
2: 5 **and w** she saw the ark among the flags, 2050.1
2: 6 **And w** she had opened *it*, she saw 2050.1
2:11 pass in those days, **w** Moses was grown, 2050.1
2:12 **and w** he saw that *there was* no man, 2050.1
2:13 **And w** he went out the second day, 2050.1
2:15 **Now w** Pharaoh heard this thing, he 2050.1
2:18 **And w** they came to Reuel their father, 2050.1
3: 4 **And w** the LORD saw that he turned 2050.1
3:12 **W** thou hast brought forth the people out 871.1
3:13 **w** I come unto the children of Israel, and NIH
3:21 it shall come to pass, that, **w** ye go, ye shall 3588
4: 6 **and w** he took it out, behold, his hand 2050.1
4:14 **and w** he seeth thee, he will be glad in 2050.1
4:21 **W** thou goest to return into Egypt, 871.1
4:31 **and w** they heard that the LORD had 2050.1
5:13 *your* daily tasks, as **w** there was straw. 871.1
6:28 it came to pass on the day **w** the LORD NIH
7: 5 **w** I stretch forth mine hand upon Egypt, 871.1
7: 7 years old, **w** they spake unto Pharaoh. 871.1
7: 9 **W** Pharaoh shall speak unto you, saying, 3588
8: 9 Glory over me: **w** shall I intreat for 4970+3807.1
8:15 **But w** Pharaoh saw that there was respite, 2050.1
9:34 **And w** Pharaoh saw that the rain and 2050.1
10:13 *and* **w** it was morning, the east wind 2050.1
11: 1 **w** he shall let *you* go, he shall surely 3509.1
12:13 where ye *are*: **and w** I see the blood, 2050.1
12:13 destroy *you*, **w** I smite the land of Egypt. 871.1
12:23 **and w** he seeth the blood upon the lintel, 2050.1
12:25 **w** ye be come to the land which 3588
12:26 to pass, **w** your children shall say unto you, 3588
12:27 **w** he smote the Egyptians, and delivered 871.1
12:44 **w** thou hast circumcised him, then 2050.1
12:48 **w** a stranger shall sojourn with thee, and 3588
13: 5 it shall be **w** the LORD shall bring thee 3588
13: 8 of that *which* the LORD did unto me **w** I 871.1
13:11 it shall be **w** the LORD shall bring thee 3588
13:14 it shall be **w** thy son asketh thee in time to 3588
13:15 to pass, **w** Pharaoh would hardly let us go, 3588
13:17 to pass, **w** Pharaoh had let the people go, 871.1
13:17 Lest peradventure the people repent **w** they 871.1
14:10 **And w** Pharaoh drew nigh, the children 2050.1
14:18 **w** I have gotten me honour upon Pharaoh, 871.1
14:27 strength **w** the morning **appeared**; 6437+3807.1
15:23 **And w** they came to Marah, they could 2050.1
15:25 *which* **w** he had cast into the waters, 2050.1
16: 3 **w** we sat by the flesh pots, *and* when we 871.1
16: 3 *and* **w** we did eat bread to the full; 871.1
16: 8 *This shall be*, **w** the LORD shall give you 871.1
16:14 **And w** the dew that lay was gone up, 2050.1
16:15 **And w** the children of Israel saw *it*, they 2050.1
16:18 **And w** they did mete *it* with an omer, he 2050.1
16:21 **and w** the sun waxed hot, it melted. 2050.1
16:32 **w** I brought you forth from the land of 871.1
17:11 to pass, **w** Moses held up his hand, 834+3509.1
17:11 **w** he let down his hand, 834+3509.1
18: 1 **W** Jethro, the priest of Midian, 2050.1
18:14 **And w** Moses' father in law saw all that 2050.1
18:16 **W** they have a matter, they come unto me; 3588
19: 1 **w** the children of Israel were gone forth out NIH
19: 9 that the people may hear **w** I speak with 871.1
19:13 **w** the trumpet soundeth long, they shall 871.1
19:19 **w** the voice of the trumpet sounded long, NIH
20:18 **and w** the people saw *it*, they removed, 2050.1
22:27 **w** he crieth unto me, that I will hear; 3588
23:16 **w** thou hast gathered in thy labours out of 871.1
28:29 **w** he goeth in unto the holy *place*, for a 871.1
28:30 **w** he goeth in before the LORD: 871.1
28:35 his sound shall be heard **w** he goeth in unto 871.1
28:35 and **w** he cometh out, that he die not. 871.1
28:43 **w** they come in unto the tabernacle of 871.1
28:43 **w** they come near unto the altar to minister 871.1
29:30 **w** he cometh into the tabernacle of 834
29:36 **w** thou hast made an atonement for it, and 871.1
30: 7 **w** he dresseth the lamps, he shall burn 871.1
30: 8 **w** Aaron lighteth the lamps at even, 871.1
30:12 **W** thou takest the sum of the children of 3588
30:12 unto the LORD, **w** *thou* numberest them; 871.1
30:12 amongst them, **w** *thou* numberest them. 871.1
30:15 **w** *they* give an offering unto the LORD, 3807.1
30:20 **W** they go into the tabernacle of 871.1
30:20 **w** they come near to the altar to minister, 871.1
31:18 **w** he had made an end of communing 3509.1
32: 1 **And w** the people saw that Moses 2050.1
32: 5 **And w** Aaron saw *it*, he built an altar 2050.1
32:17 **And w** Joshua heard the noise of 2050.1
32:25 **And w** Moses saw that the people *were* 2050.1
32:34 nevertheless in the day **w** I visit, I will 2050.1
33: 4 **And w** the people heard these evil 2050.1
33: 8 **w** Moses went out unto the tabernacle, 3509.1
34:24 **w** thou shalt go up to appear before 871.1
34:29 **w** Moses came down from mount Sinai 871.1
34:29 **w** he came down from the mount, 871.1
34:30 **And w** Aaron and all the children of 2050.1
34:34 **w** Moses went in before the LORD to 871.1
40:32 **W** they went into the tent of 871.1
40:32 **w** they came near unto the altar, 871.1
40:36 **w** the cloud was taken up from over 871.1
Lev 2: 1 **w** any will offer a meat offering unto 3588
2: 8 **and w** it is presented unto the priest, he 2050.1
4:14 **W** the sin, which they have sinned 2050.1
4:22 **W** a ruler hath sinned, and done somewhat 834
5: 3 **w** he knoweth *of it*, then he shall be 2050.1
5: 4 **w** he knoweth *of it*, then he shall be guilty 2050.1
5: 5 **w** he shall be guilty in one of these *things*, 3588
6:20 the LORD in the day **w** he is anointed; NIH
6:21 *and* **w** *it is* baken, thou shalt bring it in: NIH
6:27 **and w** there is sprinkled of the blood 2050.1
7:35 in the day **w** he presented them to minister NIH
9:24 *which* **w** all the people saw, they shouted, 2050.1
10: 9 **w** ye go into the tabernacle of 871.1

W

Lev 10:20 **And w** Moses heard *that,* he was content. 2050.1
11:31 doth touch them, **w** they be dead, 871.1
11:32 **w** they are dead, doth fall, it shall be 871.1
12: 6 **w** the days of her purifying are fulfilled, 871.1
13: 2 **W** a man shall have in the skin of his flesh 3588
13: 3 and **w** the hair in the plague is turned white, NIH
13: 9 **W** the plague of leprosy is in a man, then 3588
13:14 **w** raw flesh appeareth in him, 3117+871.1
13:20 if, **w** the priest seeth it, behold, it *be* in sight NIH
14:34 **W** ye be come into the land of Canaan, 3588
14:57 To teach **w** *it is* unclean, and when *it* 3117+871.1
14:57 when *it is* unclean, and **w** *it is* clean: 3117+871.1
15: 2 **W** any man hath a running issue out of his 3588
15:13 **w** he that hath an issue is cleansed of his 3588
15:23 thing whereon she sitteth, **w** he toucheth it, 871.1
15:31 **w** they defile my tabernacle that *is* among 871.1
16: 1 **w** they offered before the LORD, and 871.1
16:17 **w** he goeth in to make an atonement in 871.1
16:20 **And w** he hath made an end of 2050.1
16:23 which he put on **w** he went into the holy 871.1
18:28 land spue not you out also, **w** ye defile it, 871.1
19: 9 **w** ye reap the harvest of your land, 871.1
19:23 **w** ye shall come into the land, and 3588
20: 4 **w** he giveth of his seed unto Molech, and 871.1
22: 7 **And w** the sun is down, he shall be clean, 2050.1
22:16 **w** they eat their holy *things:* for I 871.1
22:27 **W** a bullock, or a sheep, or a goat, 3588
22:29 **w** ye will offer a sacrifice of thanksgiving 3588
23:10 **W** ye be come into the land which I give 3588
23:12 ye shall offer that day **w** ye wave the sheaf 871.1
23:22 **w** ye reap the harvest of your land, 871.1
23:22 of the corners of thy field **w** thou reapest, 871.1
23:39 **w** ye have gathered in the fruit of the land, 871.1
23:43 **w** I brought them out of the land of Egypt: 871.1
24:16 **w** he blasphemeth the name *of* 871.1
25: 2 **W** ye come into the land which I give you, 3588
26:17 and ye shall flee **w** none pursueth you. 2050.1
26:25 **and w** ye are gathered together within 2050.1
26:26 *And* **w** I have broken the staff of your 871.1
26:35 rest in your sabbaths, **w** ye dwelt upon it. 871.1
26:36 and they shall fall **w** none pursueth. 2050.1
26:37 it were before a sword, **w** none pursueth: 2050.1
26:44 **w** they be in the land of their enemies, 871.1
27: 2 **W** a man shall make a singular vow, 3588
27:14 **w** a man shall sanctify his house *to be* holy 3588
27:21 the field, **w** it goeth out in the jubile, 871.1
Nu 1:51 **w** the tabernacle setteth forward, 871.1
1:51 **w** the tabernacle is to be pitched, 871.1
3: 4 **w** they offered strange fire before 871.1
4: 5 **w** the camp setteth forward, Aaron shall 871.1
4:15 **And w** Aaron and his sons have made an 2050.1
4:19 **w** they approach unto the most holy *things:* 871.1
4:20 they shall not go in to see **w** the holy 3509.1
5: 6 **W** a man or woman shall commit any sin 3588
5:21 **w** the LORD doth make thy thigh to rot, 871.1
5:27 **And w** he hath made her to drink 2050.1
5:29 **w** a wife goeth aside *to another* instead of 834
5:30 Or **w** the spirit of jealousy cometh upon him, 834
6: 2 **W** either man or woman shall separate 3588
6: 7 for his brother, or for his sister, **w** they die: 871.1
6:13 **w** the days of his separation are 3117+871.1
7:84 in the day **w** it was anointed, by the princes NIH
7:89 **w** Moses was gone into the tabernacle of 871.1
8: 2 say unto him, **W** thou lightest the lamps, 871.1
8:19 **w** the children of Israel come nigh unto 871.1
9:17 **w** the cloud was taken up from 6310+3807.1
9:19 **w** the cloud tarried long upon 871.1
9:20 **w** the cloud was a few days upon 834
9:21 **w** the cloud abode from even unto NIH
9:22 but **w** it was taken up, they journeyed. 871.1
10: 3 **And w** they shall blow with them, all 2050.1
10: 5 **W** ye blow an alarm, then the camps that 2050.1
10: 6 **W** you blow an alarm the second time, 2050.1
10: 7 **w** the congregation is to be gathered 871.1
10:28 to their armies, **w** they set forward. 2050.1
10:34 them by day, **w** they went out of the camp. 871.1
10:35 **w** the ark set forward, that Moses said, 871.1
10:36 **w** it rested, he said, Return, O LORD, 871.1
11: 1 **w** the people complained, it displeased NIH
11: 2 **and w** Moses prayed unto the LORD, 2050.1
11: 9 **w** the dew fell upon the camp in the night, 871.1
11:25 that **w** the spirit rested upon them, 3509.1
12:12 of whom the flesh is half consumed **w** he 871.1
15: 2 **W** ye be come into the land of your 3588
15: 8 **w** thou preparest a bullock *for* a burnt 3588
15:18 **W** ye come into the land whither I bring 871.1
15:19 *that* **w** ye eat of the bread of the land, 871.1
15:28 **w** he sinneth by ignorance before 871.1
16: 4 **And w** Moses heard *it,* he fell upon his 2050.1
16:42 **w** the congregation was gathered against 871.1
18:26 **W** ye take of the children of Israel 3588
18:30 **W** ye have heaved the best thereof from it, 871.1
18:32 **w** ye have heaved from it the best of it: 871.1
19:14 This *is* the law, **w** a man dieth in a tent: 3588
20: 3 Would God that we had died **w** our 871.1
20:16 **And w** we cried unto the LORD, he 2050.1
20:29 **And w** all the congregation saw that 2050.1
21: 1 **w** king Arad the Canaanite, which dwelt *in* NIH
21: 8 is bitten, **w** he looketh upon it, shall live. 2050.1
21: 9 **w** he beheld the serpent of brass, he lived. 2050.1
22:25 **And w** the ass saw the angel of 2050.1
22:27 **And w** the ass saw the angel of 2050.1
22:36 **And w** Balak heard that Balaam was 2050.1
23:17 **And w** he came to him, behold, he stood 2050.1
24: 1 **And w** Balaam saw that it pleased 2050.1
24:20 **And w** he looked on Amalek, he took up 2050.1
24:23 said, Alas, who shall live **w** God doeth this! 4480
25: 7 **And w** Phinehas, the son of Eleazar, 2050.1
26: 9 **w** they strove against the LORD: 871.1
26:10 **w** that company died, what time the fire 871.1
26:61 **w** they offered strange fire before 871.1
26:64 **w** they numbered the children of Israel in 834
27:13 **And w** thou hast seen it, thou also shalt 2050.1
28:26 **w** ye bring a new meat offering unto 871.1
30: 6 **w** she vowed, or uttered ought out of her 2050.1

Nu 32: 1 **and w** they saw the land of Jazer, and 2050.1
32: 8 **w** I sent them from Kadesh-barnea to see 871.1
32: 9 **For w** they went up unto the valley of 2050.1
33:39 three years old **w** he died in mount Hor. 871.1
33:51 **W** ye are passed over Jordan into the land 3588
34: 2 **W** ye come into the land of Canaan; 3588
35:10 **W** ye be come over Jordan into the land of 3588
35:19 **w** he meeteth him, he shall slay him. 871.1
35:21 shall slay the murderer, **w** he meeteth him. 871.1
36: 4 **w** the jubile of the children of Israel shall be, 518
Dt 1:19 **And w** we departed from Horeb, we went 2050.1
1:41 **And w** ye had girded on every man his 2050.1
2: 8 **And w** we passed by from our brethren 2050.1
2:12 **w** they had destroyed them from before 2050.1
2:16 **w** all the men of war were consumed 834+3509.1
2:19 **w** thou comest nigh over against NIH
2:22 **w** he destroyed the Horims from before 834
4:10 **w** the LORD said unto me, Gather me 871.1
4:19 **and w** thou seest the sun, and the moon, 2050.1
4:25 **W** thou shalt beget children, and 3588
4:30 **W** thou art in tribulation, and all these 3807.1
5:23 **w** ye heard the voice out of the midst of 3509.1
5:28 voice of your words, **w** ye spake unto me; 871.1
6: 7 shalt talk of them **w** thou sittest in thine 871.1
6: 7 **w** thou walkest by the way, and when thou 871.1
6: 7 **w** thou liest down, and when thou risest 871.1
6: 7 thou liest down, and **w** thou risest up. 871.1
6:10 **w** the LORD thy God shall have brought 3588
6:11 **w** thou shalt have eaten and be full; 2050.1
6:20 *And* **w** thy son asketh thee in time to come, 3588
7: 1 **W** the LORD thy God shall bring thee 3588
7: 2 **And w** the LORD thy God shall deliver 2050.1
8:10 **W** thou hast eaten and art full, then 2050.1
8:12 Lest **w** thou hast eaten and art full, and NIH
8:13 **w** thy herds and thy flocks multiply, and NIH
9: 9 **W** I was gone up into the mount to receive 871.1
9:23 Likewise **w** the LORD sent you from 871.1
11:19 speaking of them **w** thou sittest in thine 871.1
11:19 **w** thou walkest by the way, when thou liest 871.1
11:19 **w** thou liest down, and when thou risest 871.1
11:19 thou liest down, and **w** thou risest up. 871.1
11:29 **w** the LORD thy God hath brought thee in 3588
12:10 **w** ye go over Jordan and dwell in the land NIH
12:10 **w** he giveth you rest from all your enemies NIH
12:20 **W** the LORD thy God shall enlarge thy 3588
12:25 **w** thou shalt do *that which is* right in 3588
12:28 **w** thou doest *that which is* good and right in 3588
12:29 **W** the LORD thy God shall cut off 3588
13:18 **W** thou shalt hearken to the voice of 3588
14:24 **w** the LORD thy God hath blessed thee: 3588
15: 4 Save **w** there shall be no poor among you; 3588
15:10 thine heart shall not be grieved **w** thou 871.1
15:13 **w** thou sendest him out free from thee, 3588
15:18 **w** thou sendest him away free from thee; 871.1
16: 3 that thou mayest remember the day **w** thou NIH
17:14 **W** thou art come unto the land which 3588
17:18 **w** he sitteth upon the throne of his 3509.1
18: 9 **W** thou art come into the land which 3588
18:22 **W** a prophet speaketh in the name of 834
19: 1 **W** the LORD thy God hath cut off 3588
19: 5 **As w** *a man* goeth into the wood with his 2050.1
20: 1 **W** thou goest out to battle against thine 3588
20: 2 **w** ye are come nigh unto the battle, 3509.1
20: 9 **w** the officers have made an end of 3509.1
20:10 **W** thou comest nigh unto a city to fight 3588
20:13 **And w** the LORD thy God hath 2050.1
20:19 **W** thou shalt besiege a city a long time, 3588
21: 9 **w** thou shalt do *that which is* right in 3588
21:10 **W** thou goest forth to war against thine 3588
21:16 **w** he maketh his sons to inherit *that* 3117+871.1
21:18 and *that,* **w** they have chastened him, NIH
22: 8 **W** thou buildest a new house, then 3588
22:14 I took this woman, **and w** I came to her, 2050.1
22:26 for **as w** a man riseth against his 834+3509.1
23: 4 in the way, **w** ye came forth out of Egypt; 871.1
23: 9 **W** the host goeth forth against thine 3588
23:11 it shall be, **w** evening cometh on, he shall NIH
23:11 **w** the sun is down, he shall come into 3509.1
23:13 it shall be, **w** thou wilt ease thyself abroad, 871.1
23:21 **W** thou shalt vow a vow unto the LORD 3588
23:24 **W** thou comest into thy neighbour's 3588
23:25 **W** thou comest into the standing corn of 3588
24: 1 **W** a man hath taken a wife, and 3588
24: 2 **And w** she is departed out of his house, 2050.1
24: 5 **W** a man hath taken a new wife, he shall 3588
24:10 **W** thou dost lend thy brother any thing, 3588
24:13 the pledge again **w** the sun goeth down, 3509.1
24:19 **W** thou cuttest down thine harvest in thy 3588
24:20 **W** thou beatest thine olive tree, thou shalt 3588
24:21 **W** thou gatherest the grapes of thy 3588
25: 4 Thou shalt not muzzle the ox **w** he 871.1
25:11 **W** men strive together one with another, 3588
25:17 **w** ye were come forth out of Egypt; 871.1
25:18 behind thee, **w** thou *wast* faint and weary; 2050.1
25:19 **w** the LORD thy God hath given thee rest 871.1
26: 1 **w** thou art come in unto the land which 3588
26: 7 **And w** we cried unto the LORD God of 2050.1
26:12 **W** thou hast made an end of tithing all 3588
27: 2 it shall be on the day **w** you shall pass over 834
27: 3 words of this law, **w** thou art passed over, 871.1
27: 4 Therefore it shall be **w** ye be gone over 871.1
27:12 the people, **w** ye are come over Jordan; 871.1
28: 6 Blessed *shalt* thou *be* **w** thou comest in, 871.1
28: 6 and blessed *shalt* thou *be* **w** thou goest out. 871.1
28:19 Cursed *shalt* thou *be* **w** thou comest in, and 871.1
28:19 and cursed *shalt* thou *be* **w** thou goest out. 871.1
29: 7 **And w** ye came unto this place, Sihon 2050.1
29:19 **w** he heareth the words of this curse, 871.1
29:22 **w** they see the plagues of that land, 2050.1
29:25 which he made with them **w** he brought 871.1
30: 1 **w** all these things are come upon thee, 3588
31:11 **W** all Israel is come to appear before 871.1
31:20 *For* **w** I shall have brought them into 3588
31:21 **w** many evils and troubles are befallen 3588
31:24 **w** Moses had made an end of writing 3509.1

Dt 32: 8 **W** the most High divided to the nations 871.1
32: 8 **w** he separated the sons of Adam, 871.1
32:19 **And w** the LORD saw *it,* he abhorred 2050.1
32:36 **w** he seeth that *their* power is gone, and 3588
33: 5 **w** the heads of the people *and* the tribes of 871.1
34: 7 and twenty years old **w** he died: 871.1
Jos 2: 5 **w** it was dark, that the men went out: 871.1
2:10 Red sea for you, **w** you came out of Egypt; 871.1
2:14 **w** the LORD hath given us the land, 871.1
2:18 Behold, **w** we come into the land, thou shalt NIH
3: 3 **W** ye see the ark of the covenant of 3509.1
3: 8 **W** ye are come to the brink of the water 3509.1
3:14 **w** the people removed from their tents, 871.1
4: 1 **w** all the people were clean passed 834+3509.1
4: 6 *that* **w** your children ask *their fathers* in 3588
4: 7 **w** it passed over Jordan, the waters of 871.1
4:11 **w** all the people were clean passed 834+3509.1
4:18 **w** the priests that bare the ark of 3509.1
4:21 **W** your children shall ask their fathers in 834
5: 1 to pass, **w** all the kings of the Amorites, 3509.1
5: 8 **w** they had done circumcising all 834+3509.1
5:13 it came to pass, **w** Joshua was by Jericho, 871.1
6: 5 *that* **w** *they* make a long blast with 871.1
6: 5 *and* **w** ye hear the sound of the trumpet, 3509.1
6: 8 **w** Joshua had spoken unto the people, 3509.1
6:16 **w** the priests blew with the trumpets, Joshua NIH
6:18 **w** ye take of the accursed thing, and 2050.1
6:20 So the people shouted **w** *the priests* blew 2050.1
6:20 **w** the people heard the sound of 2050.1
7: 8 **w** Israel turneth *their* backs before their 310+834
7:21 **W** I saw among the spoils a goodly 2050.1
8: 5 **w** they come out against us, as at the first, 3588
8: 8 it shall be, **w** ye have taken the city, 3509.1
8:13 **And w** they had set the people, *even* all 2050.1
8:14 **w** the king of Ai saw *it,* that they hasted 3509.1
8:20 **And w** the men of Ai looked behind 2050.1
8:21 **And w** Joshua and all Israel saw that 2050.1
8:24 **w** Israel had made an end of slaying all 3509.1
8:24 **w** they were all fallen on the edge of NIH
9: 1 **w** all the kings which *were* on *this* side 3509.1
9: 3 **w** the inhabitants of Gibeon heard what NIH
9:22 very far from you; **w** ye dwell among us? 2050.1
10: 1 **w** Adoni-zedek king of Jerusalem had 3509.1
10:12 spake Joshua to the LORD in the day **w** NIH
10:20 **w** Joshua and the children of Israel had 3509.1
10:24 **w** they brought out those kings unto 3509.1
11: 1 **w** Jabin king of Hazor had heard *those* 3509.1
11: 5 **And w** all these kings were met together, 2050.1
14: 7 Forty years old *was* I **w** Moses the servant 871.1
17:13 **w** the children of Israel were waxen strong, 3588
19:49 **W** they had made an end of dividing 2050.1
20: 4 **And w** he that doth flee unto one of those 2050.1
22: 7 **w** Joshua sent them away also unto their 3588
22:10 **And w** they came unto the borders of 2050.1
22:12 **And w** the children of Israel heard *of it,* 2050.1
22:28 **w** they should *so* say to us or to our 3588
22:30 **And w** Phinehas the priest, and 2050.1
23:16 **W** ye have transgressed the covenant of 871.1
24: 7 **And w** they cried unto the LORD, he 2050.1
Jdg 1:14 **w** she came *to him,* that she moved him to 871.1
1:25 **And w** he shewed them the entrance into 2050.1
1:28 it came to pass, **w** Israel was strong, 3588
2: 4 **w** the angel of the LORD spake these 3509.1
2: 6 **And w** Joshua had let the people go, 2050.1
2:18 **w** the LORD raised them up judges, then 3588
2:19 **w** the judge was dead, *that* they returned, 871.1
2:21 the nations which Joshua left **w** he died: 2050.1
3: 9 **And w** the children of Israel cried unto 2050.1
3:15 **But w** the children of Israel cried unto 2050.1
3:18 **w** he had made an end to offer 834+3509.1
3:24 **W** he was gone out, his servants came; 2050.1
3:24 **and w** they saw that behold, the doors of 2050.1
3:27 it came to pass, **w** he was come, that he 871.1
4: 1 sight of the LORD, **w** Ehud was dead. 2050.1
4:18 **And w** he had turned in unto her into 2050.1
4:20 **w** any man doth come and inquire of thee, 518
4:22 **And w** he came into her *tent,* behold, 2050.1
5: 2 **w** the people willingly offered themselves. 871.1
5: 4 LORD, **w** thou wentest out of Seir, 871.1
5: 4 **w** thou marchedst out of the field of Edom, 871.1
5:26 **w** she had pierced and stricken through 2050.1
5:31 *let* them that love him *be* as the sun **w** he NIH
6: 3 *so* it was, **w** Israel had sown, that 518
6: 7 **w** the children of Israel cried unto 3588
6:22 **And w** Gideon perceived that he *was* an 2050.1
6:28 **And w** the men of the city arose early in 2050.1
6:29 **And w** they inquired and asked, they 2050.1
7:13 **And w** Gideon was come, behold, 2050.1
7:15 **w** Gideon heard the telling of the dream, 3509.1
7:17 behold, **w** I come to the outside of the camp, NIH
7:18 **W** I blow with a trumpet, I and all that 2050.1
8: 1 **w** thou wentest to fight with 3588
8: 3 was abated toward him, **w** he had said that. 871.1
8: 7 Therefore **w** the LORD hath delivered 871.1
8: 9 saying, **W** I come again in peace, I will 871.1
8:12 **And w** Zebah and Zalmunna fled, 2050.1
9: 7 **And w** they told *it* to Jotham, he went 2050.1
9:22 **W** Abimelech had reigned three years 2050.1
9:30 **And w** Zebul the ruler of the city heard 2050.1
9:33 **w** he and the people that *is* with him come NIH
9:36 **And w** Gaal saw the people, he said to 2050.1
9:46 **And w** all the men of the tower of 2050.1
9:55 **And w** the men of Israel saw that 2050.1
11: 5 **that w** the children of Ammon made 834+3509.1
11: 7 why are ye come unto me now **w** ye 834+3509.1
11:13 **w** they came up out of Egypt, from Arnon 871.1
11:16 **w** Israel came up from Egypt, and 871.1
11:31 **w** I return in peace from the children of 871.1
11:35 it came to pass, **w** he saw her, that he rent 3509.1
12: 2 **and w** I called you, ye delivered me not 2050.1
12: 3 **And w** I saw that ye delivered *me* not, I 2050.1
12: 5 that **w** those Ephraimites which were NIH
13:17 that **w** thy sayings come to pass we may do NIH
13:20 **w** the flame went up toward heaven from 871.1
14:11 it came to pass, **w** they saw him, that they 3509.1

Jdg 15: 5 **And w** he had set the brands on fire, 2050.1
15:14 *And* **w** he came unto Lehi, the Philistines NIH
15:17 **w** he had made an end of speaking, 3509.1
15:19 **and w** he had drunk, his spirit came 2050.1
16: 2 saying, In the morning, **w** it is day, 2050.1
16: 9 as a thread of tow is broken **w** it toucheth 871.1
16:15 I love thee, **w** thine heart *is* not with me? 2050.1
16:16 **w** she pressed him daily with her words, 3588
16:18 **And w** Delilah saw that he had told her 2050.1
16:24 **And w** the people saw him, they praised 2050.1
16:25 **w** their hearts were merry, that they said, 3509.1
17: 3 **And w** he had restored the eleven 2050.1
18: 2 who **w** they came *to* mount Ephraim, 2050.1
18: 3 **W** they *were* by the house of Micah, they NIH
18:10 **W** ye go, ye shall come unto a people 3509.1
18:22 *And* **w** they were a good way from NIH
18:26 **and w** Micah saw that they *were* too 2050.1
19: 1 those days, **w** *there was* no king in Israel, 2050.1
19: 3 **and w** the father of the damsel saw him, 2050.1
19: 5 **w** they arose early in the morning, that he 2050.1
19: 7 **And w** the man rose up to depart, his 2050.1
19: 9 **And w** the man rose up to depart, he, and 2050.1
19:11 *And* **w** they *were* by Jebus, the day was far NIH
19:14 the sun went down upon them *w they were* NIH
19:15 **and w** he went in, he sat him down in a 2050.1
19:17 **And w** he had lift up his eyes, he saw a 2050.1
19:25 **w** the day began to spring, they let her go. 3509.1
19:29 **And w** he was come into his house, 2050.1
20:10 **w** they come to Gibeah of Benjamin, 3807.1
20:39 **And w** the men of Israel retired in 2050.1
20:40 **But w** the flame began to arise up out of 2050.1
20:41 **And w** the men of Israel turned *again,* 2050.1
21:22 **w** their fathers or their brethren come unto 3588
Ru 1: 1 Now it came to pass in the days **w** NIH
1:18 **W** she saw that she *was* stedfastly 2050.1
1:19 to pass, **w** they were come *to* Beth-lehem, 3509.1
2: 9 **and w** thou art athirst, go unto 2050.1
2:15 **And w** she was risen up to glean, Boaz 2050.1
3: 4 it shall be, **w** he lieth down, that thou shalt 871.1
3: 7 **And w** Boaz had eaten and drunk, and 2050.1
3:15 **And w** she held it, he measured six 2050.1
3:16 **And w** she came to her mother in law, 2050.1
4:13 **and w** he went in unto her, the LORD 2050.1
1Sa 1: 4 **And w** the time was that Elkanah offered, 2050.1
1: 7 **w** she went up to the house of 1767+4480
1:20 **w** the time was come about after Hannah NIH
1:24 **w** she had weaned him, she took 834+3509.1
2:13 *was, that* **w** any man offered sacrifice, NIH
2:19 **w** she came up with her husband to offer 871.1
2:27 **w** they were in Egypt in Pharaoh's house? 871.1
3: 2 **w** Eli *was* laid down in his place, and 2050.1
3:12 **w** I begin, I will also make an end. NIH
4: 2 **and w** they joined battle, Israel was 2050.1
4: 3 **And w** the people were come into 2050.1
4: 3 that **w** it cometh among us, it may save us 2050.1
4: 5 **w** the ark of the covenant of the LORD 3509.1
4: 6 **And w** the Philistines heard the noise of 2050.1
4:13 **And w** he came, lo, Eli sat upon a seat *by* 2050.1
4:13 **And w** the man came into the city, and 2050.1
4:14 **And w** Eli heard the noise of the crying, 2050.1
4:18 **w** he made mention of the ark of God, 3509.1
4:19 **and w** she heard the tidings that the ark 2050.1
5: 2 **W** the Philistines took the ark of God, 2050.1
5: 3 **And w** they of Ashdod arose early on 2050.1
5: 4 **And w** they arose early on the morrow 2050.1
5: 7 **And w** the men of Ashdod saw that *it* 2050.1
6: 6 **w** he had wrought wonderfully 834+3509.1
6:16 **And w** the five lords of the Philistines 2050.1
7: 7 **And w** the Philistines heard that 2050.1
7: 7 **And w** the children of Israel heard *it,* 2050.1
8: 1 it came to pass, **w** Samuel was old, 834+3509.1
8: 6 **w** they said, Give us a king to judge 834+3509.1
9: 5 *And* **w** they were come to the land of Zuph, NIH
9: 9 **w** a man went to inquire of God, thus he NIH
9:14 *and* **w** they were come into the city, 2050.1
9:17 **And w** Samuel saw Saul, the LORD 2050.1
9:25 **And w** they were come down from 2050.1
10: 2 **W** thou art departed from me to day, then 871.1
10: 5 **w** thou art come thither *to* the city, 3509.1
10: 7 let it be, **w** these signs are come unto thee, 3588
10: 9 that **w** he had turned his back to go from 3509.1
10:10 **And w** they came thither to the hill, 2050.1
10:11 **w** all that knew him beforetime saw that 2050.1
10:13 **And w** he had made an end of 2050.1
10:14 **and w** we saw that *they were* no where, 2050.1
10:20 **And w** Samuel had caused all the tribes 2050.1
10:21 **W** he had caused the tribe of Benjamin to 2050.1
10:21 **and w** they sought him, he could not be 2050.1
10:23 **and w** he stood among the people, he was 2050.1
11: 6 the spirit of God came upon Saul **w** he 3509.1
11: 8 **And w** he numbered them in Bezek, 2050.1
12: 8 **W** Jacob was come *into* Egypt, and 834+3509.1
12: 9 **And w** they forgat the LORD their God, 2050.1
12:12 **And w** ye saw that Nahash the king of 2050.1
12:12 **w** the LORD your God *was* your king. 2050.1
13: 1 **w** he had reigned two years over Israel, 871.1
13: 6 **W** the men of Israel saw that they were in 2050.1
14:17 **And w** they had numbered, behold 2050.1
14:22 *w* they heard that the Philistines fled, NIH
14:26 **And w** the people were come into 2050.1
14:27 Jonathan heard not **w** his father charged 871.1
14:52 **and w** Saul saw any strong man, or 2050.1
15: 2 him in the way, **w** he came up from Egypt. 871.1
15: 6 of Israel, **w** they came up out of Egypt. 871.1
15:12 **And w** Samuel rose early to meet Saul in 2050.1
15:17 **W** thou *wast* little in thine own sight, 518
16: 6 it came to pass, **w** they were come, that he 871.1
16:16 **w** the evil spirit from God is upon thee, 871.1
16:23 **w** the *evil* spirit from God was upon Saul, 871.1
17:11 **W** Saul and all Israel heard those words 2050.1
17:24 **w** they saw the man, fled from him, and 871.1
17:28 Eliab his eldest brother heard **w** he spake 871.1
17:31 **And w** the words were heard which 2050.1
17:35 **w** he arose against me, I caught *him* by 2050.1
17:42 **And w** the Philistine looked about, and 2050.1

1Sa 17:48 **w** the Philistine arose, and came and 3588
17:51 **And w** the Philistines saw their champion 2050.1
17:55 **w** Saul saw David go forth against 3509.1
18: 1 **w** he made an end of speaking unto Saul, 3509.1
18: 6 **w** David was returned from the slaughter 871.1
18:15 **Wherefore w** Saul saw that he behaved 2050.1
18:19 it came to pass at the time **w** Merab Saul's NIH
18:26 **And w** his servants told David these 2050.1
19:14 **And w** Saul sent messengers to take 2050.1
19:16 **And w** the messengers were come in, 2050.1
19:20 **and w** they saw the company of 2050.1
19:21 **And w** it was told Saul, he sent other 2050.1
20:12 **w** I have sounded my father about to 3588
20:15 not **w** the LORD hath cut off the enemies 871.1
20:19 *w* thou hast stayed three days, *then* NIH
20:19 thyself **w** the business was *in hand,* 3117+871.1
20:24 **and w** the new moon was come, the king 2050.1
20:37 **And w** the lad was come to the place of 2050.1
21: 6 to put hot bread in the day **w** it was taken NIH
22: 1 **and w** his brethren and all his father's 2050.1
22: 6 **W** Saul heard that David was discovered, 2050.1
22:17 because they knew **w** he fled, and did not 3588
22:22 *it* that day, **w** Doeg the Edomite *was* there, 3588
23: 6 **w** Abiathar the son of Ahimelech fled to 871.1
23:25 **And w** Saul heard *that,* he pursued after 2050.1
24: 1 **w** Saul was returned from following 834+3509.1
24: 8 **And w** Saul looked behind him, David 2050.1
24:16 **w** David had made an end of speaking 3509.1
24:18 **forasmuch as w** the LORD had delivered 834
25: 9 **And w** David's young men came, they 2050.1
25:15 with them, **w** we were in the fields: 871.1
25:23 **And w** Abigail saw David, she hasted, 2050.1
25:30 **w** the LORD shall have done to my lord 3588
25:31 **but w** the LORD shall have dealt well 2050.1
25:37 **w** the wine was gone out of Nabal, and 871.1
25:39 **And w** David heard that Nabal was dead, 2050.1
25:40 **And w** the servants of David were come 2050.1
26:20 **as w** *one* doth hunt a partridge in 834+3509.1
28: 5 **And w** Saul saw the host of 2050.1
28: 6 **And w** Saul inquired of the LORD, 2050.1
28:12 **And w** the woman saw Samuel, she cried 2050.1
28:22 have strength, **w** thou goest on *thy* way. 3588
30: 1 **w** David and his men were come *to* Ziklag 871.1
30:12 **and w** he had eaten, his spirit came again 2050.1
30:16 **And w** he had brought him down, behold 2050.1
30:21 **and w** David came near to the people, he 2050.1
30:26 **And w** David came to Ziklag, he sent of 2050.1
31: 5 **And w** his armourbearer saw that Saul 2050.1
31: 7 **And w** the men of Israel that *were* on 2050.1
31: 8 **w** the Philistines came to strip the slain, 2050.1
31:11 **And w** the inhabitants of Jabesh-gilead 2050.1
2Sa 1: 1 **w** David was returned from the slaughter 2050.1
1: 2 *so* it was, **w** he came to David, that he fell 871.1
1: 7 **And w** he looked behind him, he saw me, 2050.1
2:10 years old **w** he *began* to reign over Israel, 871.1
2:24 the sun went down **w** they were come to 2050.1
2:30 **and w** he had gathered all the people 2050.1
3:13 **w** thou comest to see my face. 871.1
3:23 **W** Joab and all the host that *was* with him 2050.1
3:26 **And w** Joab was come out from David, 2050.1
3:27 **And w** Abner was returned *to* Hebron, 2050.1
3:28 afterward **w** David heard *it,* he said, I and 2050.1
3:35 **And w** all the people came to cause 2050.1
4: 1 **And w** Saul's son heard that Abner was 2050.1
4: 4 was five years old **w** the tidings came of 871.1
4: 7 **For w** they came *into* the house, he lay 2050.1
4:10 **W** one told me, saying, Behold, Saul is 3588
4:11 **w** wicked men have slain a righteous 3588
5: 2 Also in time past, **w** Saul was king over us, 871.1
5: 4 David *was* thirty years old **w** he *began* to 871.1
5:17 **But w** the Philistines heard that they had 2050.1
5:23 **And w** David inquired of the LORD, he 2050.1
5:24 **w** thou hearest the sound of a going in 3509.1
6: 6 **And w** they came to Nachon's 2050.1
6:13 that **w** they that bare the ark of the LORD 3588
7: 1 **w** the king sat in his house, and the LORD 3588
7:12 **And w** thy days be fulfilled, and thou shalt 3588
8: 5 **And w** the Syrians of Damascus came to 2050.1
8: 9 **W** Toi king of Hamath heard that David 2050.1
8:13 David gat *him* a name **w** he returned from 871.1
9: 2 **And w** they had called him unto David, 2050.1
9: 6 **Now w** Mephibosheth, the son of 2050.1
10: 5 **W** they told *it* unto David, he sent to meet 2050.1
10: 6 **And w** the children of Ammon saw that 2050.1
10: 7 **And w** David heard *of it,* he sent Joab, 2050.1
10: 9 **W** Joab saw that the front of the battle 2050.1
10:14 **And w** the children of Ammon saw that 2050.1
10:15 **And w** the Syrians saw that they were 2050.1
10:17 **And w** it was told David, he gathered all 2050.1
10:19 **And w** all the kings *that were* servants to 2050.1
11: 1 at the time **w** kings go forth *to battle,* that NIH
11: 7 **And w** Uriah was come unto him, David 2050.1
11:10 **And w** they had told David, saying, 2050.1
11:13 **And w** David had called him, he did eat 2050.1
11:16 it came to pass, **w** Joab observed the city, 871.1
11:19 **W** thou hast made an end of telling 3509.1
11:20 *so* nigh unto the city **w** *ye* did fight? 3807.1
11:26 **And w** the wife of Uriah heard that Uriah 2050.1
11:27 **And w** the mourning was past, 2050.1
12:19 **But w** David saw that his servants 2050.1
12:20 **and w** he required, they set bread before 2050.1
12:21 **w** the child was dead, thou didst rise 834+3509.1
13: 5 **and w** thy father cometh to see thee, say 2050.1
13: 6 **and w** the king was come to see him, 2050.1
13:11 **And w** she had brought *them* unto him to 2050.1
13:21 **But w** king David heard of all these 2050.1
13:28 Mark ye now **w** Amnon's heart is merry 3509.1
13:28 **and w** I say unto you, Smite Amnon; 2050.1
14: 4 **And w** the woman of Tekoah spake to 2050.1
14:26 **w** he polled his head, (for it was at every 871.1
14:29 **and w** he sent again the second time, he 2050.1
14:33 **and w** he had called for Absalom, he 2050.1
15: 2 *that* **w** any man that had a controversy came NIH
15: 5 that **w** any man came nigh *to him* to do 871.1
15:32 that **w** David was come to the top *of* NIH

2Sa 16: 1 **And w** David was a little past the top *of* 2050.1
16: 5 **And w** king David came to Bahurim, 2050.1
16: 7 thus said Shimei **w** he cursed, Come out, 871.1
16:16 **w** Hushai the Archite, 834+3509.1
17: 6 **And w** Hushai was come to Absalom, 2050.1
17: 9 **w** *some* of them be overthrown at 3509.1
17:20 **And w** Absalom's servants came to 2050.1
17:20 **And w** they had sought and could not 2050.1
17:23 **And w** Ahithophel saw that his counsel 2050.1
17:27 to pass, **w** David was come to Mahanaim, 3509.1
18: 5 all the people heard **w** the king gave all 871.1
18:29 **W** Joab sent the king's servant, and *me* thy NIH
19: 3 as people being ashamed steal away **w** 871.1
19:25 **w** he was come *to* Jerusalem to meet 3588
19:39 **And w** the king was come over, the king 2050.1
20: 8 **W** they *were* at the great stone which *is* in NIH
20:12 **And w** the man saw that all the people 2050.1
20:12 **w** he saw that every one that came 834+3509.1
20:13 **W** he was removed out of 834+3509.1
20:17 **And w** he was come near unto her, 2050.1
21:12 **w** the Philistines had slain Saul in 3117+871.1
21:21 **And w** he defied Israel, Jonathan the son 2050.1
22: 5 **W** the waves of death compassed me, 3588
23: 4 *w* the sun riseth, *even* a morning without NIH
23: 9 **w** they defied the Philistines *that* were 871.1
24: 8 **So w** they had gone through all the land, 2050.1
24:11 **For w** David was up in the morning, 2050.1
24:16 **And w** the angel stretched out his hand 2050.1
24:17 David spake unto the LORD **w** he saw 871.1
1Ki 1:21 **w** my lord the king shall sleep with his 3509.1
1:23 **And w** he was come in before the king, 2050.1
1:41 **And w** Joab heard the sound of 2050.1
2: 7 for so they came to me **w** I fled because of 871.1
2: 8 curse in the day **w** I went *to* Mahanaim: NIH
3:21 **And w** I rose in the morning to give my 2050.1
3:21 **but w** I had considered it in the morning, 2050.1
5: 7 **w** Hiram heard the words of Solomon, 3509.1
6: 7 the house, **w** it was in building, was built 871.1
7:24 knops *were* cast *in* two rows, **w** it was cast. 871.1
8: 9 **w** the LORD made *a covenant* with 834
8: 9 **w** they came out of the land of Egypt. 871.1
8:10 **w** the priests were come out of the holy 871.1
8:21 **w** he brought them out of the land of 871.1
8:30 **w** they shall pray towards this place: 834
8:30 and **w** thou hearest, forgive. 2050.1
8:33 **W** thy people Israel be smitten down 871.1
8:35 **W** heaven is shut up, and there is no rain, 871.1
8:35 turn from their sin, **w** thou afflictest them: 3588
8:42 **w** he shall come and pray towards this 2050.1
8:53 **w** thou broughtest our fathers out of Egypt, 871.1
8:54 *that* **w** Solomon had made an end of 3509.1
9: 1 **w** Solomon had finished the building of 3509.1
9:10 **w** Solomon had built the two houses, 834
10: 1 **And w** the queen of Sheba heard of 2050.1
10: 2 **and w** she was come to Solomon, she 2050.1
10: 4 **And w** the queen of Sheba had seen all 2050.1
11: 4 For it came to pass, **w** Solomon 6256+3807.1
11:15 **w** David was in Edom, and Joab 871.1
11:21 **And w** Hadad heard in Egypt that David 2050.1
11:24 **w** David slew them *of Zobah:* and 871.1
11:29 it came to pass at that time **w** Jeroboam 2050.1
12: 2 to pass, **w** Jeroboam the son of Nebat, 3509.1
12:16 **So w** all Israel saw that the king 2050.1
12:20 **w** all Israel heard that Jeroboam was 3509.1
12:21 **And w** Rehoboam was come *to* 2050.1
13: 4 **w** king Jeroboam heard the saying of 3509.1
13:24 **And w** he was gone, a lion met him by 2050.1
13:26 **And w** the prophet that brought him back 2050.1
13:31 **W** I am dead, then bury me in 871.1
14: 5 for it shall be, **w** she cometh in, that she 3509.1
14: 6 *so,* **w** Ahijah heard the sound of her feet, 3509.1
14:12 *and* **w** thy feet enter into the city, the child 871.1
14:17 *and* **w** she came to the threshold of the door, NIH
14:21 and one years old **w** he *began* to reign, 871.1
14:28 *so,* **w** the king went *into* the house of 1767+4480
15:21 **w** Baasha heard *thereof,* that he left off 3509.1
15:29 it came to pass, **w** he reigned, *that* he 3509.1
16:11 it came to pass, **w** he *began* to reign, 871.1
16:18 **w** Zimri saw that the city was taken, 3509.1
17:10 **And w** he came to the gate of the city, 2050.1
18: 4 **w** Jezebel cut off the prophets of 871.1
18:10 **and w** they said, *He is* not *there;* he took 2050.1
18:12 **and** *so* **w** I come and tell Ahab, and 2050.1
18:13 Was it not told my lord what I did **w** 871.1
18:17 it came to pass, **w** Ahab saw Elijah, 3509.1
18:29 **w** midday was past, and they prophesied 3509.1
18:39 **And w** all the people saw *it,* they fell on 2050.1
19: 3 **And w** he saw *that,* he arose, and 2050.1
19:13 **w** Elijah heard *it,* that he wrapped his 3509.1
19:15 **and w** thou comest, anoint Hazael to be 2050.1
20:12 **w** *Ben-hadad* heard this message, as he 3509.1
21:15 **w** Jezebel heard that Naboth was stoned, 3509.1
21:16 **w** Ahab heard that Naboth was dead, 3509.1
21:27 came to pass, **w** Ahab heard those words, 3509.1
22:25 **w** thou shalt go into an inner chamber to 834
22:32 **w** the captains of the chariots saw 3509.1
22:33 **w** the captains of the chariots perceived 3509.1
22:42 and five years old **w** he *began* to reign; 871.1
2Ki 1: 5 **And w** the messengers turned back unto 2050.1
2: 1 **w** the LORD would take up Elijah *into* 871.1
2: 9 it came to pass, **w** they were gone over, 3509.1
2:10 *nevertheless,* if thou see me *w I am* taken NIH
2:14 **and w** he also had smitten the waters, they 637
2:15 **And w** the sons of the prophets which 2050.1
2:17 **And w** they urged him till *he* was 2050.1
2:18 **And w** they came again to him, (for he 2050.1
3: 5 it came to pass, **w** Ahab was dead, 3509.1
3:15 it came to pass, **w** the minstrel played, 3509.1
3:20 **w** the meat offering was offered, 3509.1
3:21 **And w** all the Moabites heard that 2050.1
3:24 **And w** they came to the camp of Israel, 2050.1
3:26 **And w** the king of Moab saw that 2050.1
4: 4 **And w** thou art come in, thou shalt shut 2050.1
4: 6 it came to pass, **w** the vessels were full, 3509.1
4:10 it shall be, **w** he cometh to us, *that* he shall 871.1

Book	Ref	Context	Number
2Ki	4:12	**And w** he had called her, she stood	2050.1
	4:15	**And w** he had called her, she stood in	2050.1
	4:18	**And w** the child was grown, it fell on a	2050.1
	4:20	**And w** he had taken him, and	2050.1
	4:25	**w** the man of God saw her afar off,	3509.1
	4:27	**And w** she came to the man of God to	2050.1
	4:32	**And w** Elisha was come into the house,	2050.1
	4:36	**And w** she was come in unto him, he	2050.1
	5: 6	Now **w** this letter is come unto thee,	3509.1
	5: 7	**w** the king of Israel had read the letter,	3509.1
	5: 8	**w** Elisha the man of God had heard that	3509.1
	5:13	**w** he saith to thee, Wash, and be clean?	3588
	5:18	*that* **w** my master goeth *into* the house of	871.1
	5:18	**w** I bow down myself *in* the house of	871.1
	5:21	**And w** Naaman saw *him* running after	2050.1
	5:24	**And w** he came to the tower, he took	2050.1
	5:26	Went not mine heart *with thee,* **w**	834+3509.1
	6: 4	**And w** they came to Jordan, they cut	2050.1
	6:15	**And w** the servant of the man of God was	2050.1
	6:18	**And w** they came down to him, Elisha	2050.1
	6:20	**w** they were come *into* Samaria,	3509.1
	6:21	unto Elisha, **w** he saw them, My father,	3509.1
	6:23	**and w** they had eaten and drunk, he sent	2050.1
	6:30	**w** the king heard the words of	3509.1
	6:32	look, **w** the messenger cometh, shut	3509.1
	7: 5	**and w** they were come to the uttermost	2050.1
	7: 8	**And w** these lepers came to the uttermost	2050.1
	7:12	saying, **W** they come out of the city, we	3588
	7:17	who spake **w** the king came down to him.	871.1
	8: 6	**And w** the king asked the woman, she	2050.1
	8:17	two years old was he **w** he *began* to reign;	871.1
	8:26	twenty years old *was* Ahaziah **w** he *began*	871.1
	8:29	**w** he fought against Hazael king of Syria.	871.1
	9: 2	**And w** thou comest thither, look out there	2050.1
	9: 5	**And w** he came, behold, the captains of	2050.1
	9:15	**w** he fought with Hazael king of Syria.)	871.1
	9:22	**w** Joram saw Jehu, that he said, *Is it*	3509.1
	9:25	**w** I and thou rode together after Ahab his	NIH
	9:27	**But w** Ahaziah the king of Judah saw	2050.1
	9:30	**And w** Jehu was come to Jezreel, Jezebel	2050.1
	9:34	**And w** he was come in, he did eat and	2050.1
	10: 7	it came to pass, **w** the letter came to them,	3509.1
	10:15	**And w** he was departed thence, he lighted	2050.1
	10:17	**And w** he came *to* Samaria, he slew all	2050.1
	10:24	**And w** they went in to offer sacrifices	2050.1
	11: 1	**And w** Athaliah the mother of Ahaziah	2050.1
	11:13	**And w** Athaliah heard the noise of	2050.1
	11:14	**And w** she looked, behold, the king stood	2050.1
	11:21	Seven years old *was* Jehoash **w** he *began*	871.1
	12:10	**w** they saw that *there was* much money in	3509.1
	13:21	**and w** the man was let down, and	2050.1
	14: 2	and five years old **w** he *began* to reign,	871.1
	15: 2	Sixteen years old was he **w** he *began*	871.1
	15:33	twenty years old was he **w** he *began* to	871.1
	16: 2	Twenty years old *was* Ahaz **w** he *began* to	871.1
	16:12	**And w** the king was come from	2050.1
	18: 2	five years old was he **w** he *began* to reign;	871.1
	18:17	**And w** they were come up, they came	2050.1
	18:18	**And w** they had called to the king, there	2050.1
	18:32	**w** he persuadeth you, saying,	3588
	19: 1	**w** king Hezekiah heard *it,* that he rent his	3509.1
	19: 9	**And w** he heard say of Tirhakah king of	2050.1
	19:35	**and w** they arose early in the morning,	2050.1
	21: 1	Manasseh *was* twelve years old **w** he	871.1
	21:19	and two years old **w** he *began* to reign,	871.1
	22: 1	Josiah *was* eight years old **w** he *began* to	871.1
	22:11	**w** the king had heard the words of	3509.1
	22:19	**w** thou heardest what I spake against this	871.1
	23:29	slew him at Megiddo, **w** he had seen him.	3509.1
	23:31	and three years old **w** he *began* to reign;	871.1
	23:36	and five year old **w** he *began* to reign;	871.1
	24: 8	Jehoiachin *was* eighteen years old **w** he	871.1
	24:18	and one years old **w** he *began* to reign,	871.1
	25:23	**And w** all the captains of the armies, they	2050.1
1Ch	1:44	**And w** Bela was dead, Jobab the son of	2050.1
	1:45	**And w** Jobab was dead, Husham of	2050.1
	1:46	**And w** Husham was dead, Hadad the son	2050.1
	1:47	**And w** Hadad was dead, Samlah of	2050.1
	1:48	**And w** Samlah was dead, Shaul of	2050.1
	1:49	**And w** Shaul was dead, Baal-hanan	2050.1
	1:50	**And w** Baal-hanan was dead,	2050.1
	2:19	**And w** Azubah was dead, Caleb took	2050.1
	2:21	whom he married **w** he *was* threescore	2050.1
	5: 7	**w** the genealogy of their generations was	871.1
	6:15	Jehozadak went *into captivity,* **w**	871.1
	7:23	**And w** he went in to his wife,	2050.1
	10: 5	**And w** his armourbearer saw that Saul	2050.1
	10: 7	**And w** all the men of Israel that *were* in	2050.1
	10: 8	**w** the Philistines came to strip the slain,	2050.1
	10: 9	**And w** they had stripped him, they took	2050.1
	10:11	**And w** all Jabesh-gilead heard all that	2050.1
	11: 2	in time past, even **w** Saul was king,	871.1
	12:15	**w** it had overflown all his banks;	2050.1
	12:19	**w** he came with the Philistines against Saul	871.1
	13: 9	**And w** they came unto the threshingfloor	2050.1
	14: 8	**And w** the Philistines heard that David	2050.1
	14:12	**And w** they had left their gods there,	2050.1
	14:15	**w** thou shalt hear a sound of going in	3509.1
	15:26	**w** God helped the Levites that bare the ark	871.1
	16: 2	**And w** David had made an end of	2050.1
	16:19	**W** ye were *but* few, even a few, and	871.1
	16:20	And **w** they went from nation to nation, and	NIH
	17:11	**w** thy days be expired that *thou* must go *to*	3588
	18: 5	**And w** the Syrians of Damascus came to	2050.1
	18: 9	**Now w** Tou king of Hamath heard how	2050.1
	19: 6	**And w** the children of Ammon saw that	2050.1
	19: 8	**And w** David heard *of it,* he sent Joab,	2050.1
	19:10	**Now w** Joab saw that the battle was set	2050.1
	19:15	**And w** the children of Ammon saw that	2050.1
	19:16	**And w** the Syrians saw that they were put	2050.1
	19:17	**So w** David had put the battle in array	2050.1
	19:19	**And w** the servants of Hadarezer saw that	2050.1
	20: 7	**But w** he defied Israel, Jonathan the son	2050.1
	21:28	At that time **w** David saw that the LORD	871.1
	23: 1	**So w** David was old and full *of* days,	2050.1
2Ch	4: 3	Two rows *of* oxen *were* cast, **w** it was cast.	871.1
	5:10	**w** the LORD made *a covenant* with	834
	5:10	of Israel, **w** they came out of Egypt.	871.1
	5:11	**w** the priests were come out of the holy	871.1
	5:13	**w** *they* lift up *their* voice with	3509.1
	6:21	**and w** thou hearest, forgive.	2050.1
	6:26	**W** the heaven is shut up, and there is no	871.1
	6:26	from their sin, **w** thou dost afflict them;	3588
	6:27	**w** thou hast taught them the good way,	3588
	6:29	**w** every one shall know his own sore and	834
	7: 1	Now **w** Solomon had made an end of	3509.1
	7: 3	**And w** all the children of Israel saw how	2050.1
	7: 6	**w** David praised by their ministry;	871.1
	9: 1	**And w** the queen of Sheba heard of	2050.1
	9: 1	**and w** she was come to Solomon, she	2050.1
	9: 3	**And w** the queen of Sheba had seen	2050.1
	10: 2	**w** Jeroboam the son of Nebat, who *was* in	3509.1
	10:16	**And w** all Israel saw that the king would	2050.1
	11: 1	**And w** Rehoboam was come *to*	2050.1
	12: 1	**w** Rehoboam had established	3509.1
	12: 7	**w** the LORD saw that they humbled	871.1
	12:11	**w** the king entered *into* the house of	1767+4480
	12:12	**w** he humbled himself, the wrath of	871.1
	12:13	and forty years old **w** he *began* to reign,	871.1
	13: 7	**w** Rehoboam was young and	2050.1
	13:14	**And w** Judah looked back, behold,	2050.1
	15: 4	**But w** they in their trouble did turn unto	2050.1
	15: 8	**w** Asa heard these words, and	3509.1
	15: 9	**w** they saw that the LORD his God *was*	871.1
	16: 5	**w** Baasha heard *it,* that he left off	3509.1
	18:14	**And w** he was come to the king, the king	2050.1
	18:24	thou shalt see on that day **w** thou shalt go	834
	18:31	**w** the captains of the chariots saw	3509.1
	18:32	that **w** the captains of the chariots	3509.1
	19: 8	**w** they returned *to* Jerusalem.	2050.1
	20: 9	If, **w** evil cometh upon us, *as* the sword,	NIH
	20:10	**w** they came out of the land of Egypt, but	871.1
	20:21	**And w** he had consulted with the people,	2050.1
	20:22	**w** they began to sing and to praise,	6256+871.1
	20:23	**w** they had made an end of	3509.1
	20:24	**And w** Judah came toward the watch	2050.1
	20:25	**And w** Jehoshaphat and his people came	2050.1
	20:29	**w** they had heard that the LORD fought	871.1
	20:31	and five years old **w** he *began* to reign,	871.1
	21: 4	**Now w** Jehoram was risen up to	2050.1
	21: 5	and two years old **w** he *began* to reign,	871.1
	21:20	two *years* old was he **w** he *began* to reign,	871.1
	22: 2	two years old *was* Ahaziah **w** he *began* to	871.1
	22: 6	**w** he fought with Hazael king of Syria.	871.1
	22: 7	for **w** he was come, he went out with	871.1
	22: 8	that **w** Jehu was executing judgment upon	3509.1
	22: 9	**and w** they had slain him, they buried	2050.1
	22:10	**But w** Athaliah the mother of Ahaziah	2050.1
	23: 7	be you with the king **w** he cometh in, and	871.1
	23: 7	when he cometh in, and **w** he goeth out.	871.1
	23:12	**Now w** Athaliah heard the noise of	2050.1
	23:15	**and w** she was come to the entering of	2050.1
	24: 1	Joash *was* seven years old **w** he *began* to	871.1
	24:11	**w** they saw that *there was* much money,	3509.1
	24:14	**w** they had finished *it,* they brought	3509.1
	24:15	and was full *of* days **w** he died;	2050.1
	24:15	and thirty years old *was he* **w** he died.	871.1
	24:22	**w** he died, he said, The LORD look	3509.1
	24:25	**w** they were departed from him, (for they	871.1
	25: 1	and five years old **w** he *began* to reign,	NIH
	25: 3	**w** the kingdom was established to	834+3509.1
	26: 3	Sixteen years old *was* Uzziah **w** he *began*	871.1
	26:16	**w** he was strong, his heart was lifted up to	3509.1
	27: 1	and five years old **w** he *began* to reign,	871.1
	27: 8	and twenty years old **w** he *began* to reign,	871.1
	28: 1	Ahaz *was* twenty years old **w** he *began* to	871.1
	29: 1	Hezekiah *began* to reign **w** *he was* five and	NIH
	29:22	**likewise, w** they had killed the rams, they	2050.1
	29:27	**w** the burnt offering began, the song	6256+871.1
	29:29	**w** *they* had made an end of offering,	3509.1
	31: 1	Now **w** all this was finished, all Israel	3509.1
	31: 8	**And w** Hezekiah and the princes came	2050.1
	32: 2	**And w** Hezekiah saw that Sennacherib	2050.1
	32:21	**And w** he was come *into* the house of his	2050.1
	33: 1	Manasseh *was* twelve years old **w** he	871.1
	33:12	**And w** he was in affliction, he besought	2050.1
	33:21	and twenty years old **w** he *began* to reign,	871.1
	34: 1	Josiah *was* eight years old **w** he *began* to	871.1
	34: 7	**And w** he had broken down the altars and	2050.1
	34: 8	**w** he had purged the land, and the house,	3807.1
	34: 9	**And w** they came to Hilkiah the high	2050.1
	34:14	**w** they brought out the money that was	871.1
	34:19	**w** the king had heard the words of	3509.1
	34:27	**w** thou heardest his words against this	871.1
	35:20	all this, **w** Josiah had prepared the temple,	834
	36: 2	and three years old **w** he *began* to reign,	871.1
	36: 5	and five years old **w** he *began* to reign,	871.1
	36: 9	Jehoiachin *was* eight years old **w** he *began*	871.1
	36:10	**And w** the year was expired, king	2050.1
	36:11	and twenty years old **w** he *began* to reign,	871.1
Ezr	2:68	**w** they came to the house of the LORD	871.1
	3: 1	**And w** the seventh month was come, and	2050.1
	3:10	**And w** the builders laid the foundation of	2050.1
	3:11	**w** they praised the LORD, because	871.1
	3:12	**w** the foundation of this house was laid	871.1
	4: 1	Now **w** the adversaries of Judah and	NIH
	4:23	Now **w** the copy of king Artaxerxes' letter	4481
	9: 1	Now **w** these *things* were done,	3509.1
	9: 3	**w** I heard this thing, I rent my garment	3509.1
	10: 1	Now **w** Ezra had prayed, and when he	3509.1
	10: 1	**w** he had confessed, weeping and	3509.1
	10: 6	**w** he came thither, he did eat no bread,	NIH
Ne	1: 4	**w** I heard these words, *that* I sat down	3509.1
	2: 3	**w** the city, the place of my fathers'	834
	2: 6	**w** wilt thou return? So it pleased the king to	4970
	2:10	**W** Sanballat the Horonite, and Tobiah	2050.1
	2:19	**But w** Sanballat the Horonite, and	2050.1
	4: 1	**that w** Sanballat heard that we	834+3509.1
	4: 7	*that* **w** Sanballat, and Tobiah, and	834+3509.1
	4:12	**that w** the Jews which dwelt by	834+3509.1
Ne	4:15	**w** our enemies heard that it was	834+3509.1
	5: 6	I was very angry **w** I heard their cry	834+3509.1
	6: 1	**w** Sanballat, and Tobiah, and	834+3509.1
	6:16	**that w** all our enemies heard	834+3509.1
	7: 1	**w** the wall was built, and I had set	834+3509.1
	7:73	**w** the seventh month came, the children	2050.1
	8: 5	**w** he opened *it,* all the people stood *up:*	3509.1
	8: 9	**w** they heard the words of the law.	3509.1
	9:18	**w** they had made them a molten calf, and	3588
	9:27	time of their trouble, **w** they cried unto thee,	NIH
	9:28	**yet w** they returned, and cried unto thee,	2050.1
	10:38	with the Levites, **w** the Levites take tithes:	871.1
	13: 3	it came to pass, **w** they had heard the law,	3509.1
	13:19	that **w** the gates of Jerusalem began to be	834
Est	1: 2	**w** the king Ahasuerus sat on the throne of	3509.1
	1: 4	**W** he shewed the riches of his glorious	871.1
	1: 5	**w** these days were expired, the king made	871.1
	1:10	**w** the heart of the king was merry with	3509.1
	1:17	in their eyes, **w** it shall be reported,	871.1
	1:20	**And w** the king's decree which he shall	2050.1
	2: 1	**w** the wrath of king Ahasuerus was	3509.1
	2: 7	**w** her father and mother were dead,	871.1
	2: 8	**w** the king's commandment and his decree	871.1
	2: 8	**w** many maidens were gathered together	871.1
	2:12	Now **w** every maid's turn was come to go	871.1
	2:15	Now **w** the turn of Esther, the daughter of	871.1
	2:19	**w** the virgins were gathered together	871.1
	2:20	**like as w** she was brought up with	834+3509.1
	2:23	**And w** inquisition was made of	2050.1
	3: 4	**w** they spake daily unto him, and	3509.1
	3: 5	**And w** Haman saw that Mordecai bowed	2050.1
	4: 1	**W** Mordecai perceived all that was done,	2050.1
	5: 2	**w** the king saw Esther the queen standing	3509.1
	5: 9	**w** Haman saw Mordecai in the king's	3509.1
	5:10	**and w** he came home, he sent and	2050.1
	9: 1	**w** the king's commandment and his decree	834
	9:25	**w** *Esther* came before the king,	871.1
Job	1: 5	**w** the days of *their* feasting were gone	NIH
	1: 6	Now there was a day **w** the sons of God	2050.1
	1:13	there was a day **w** his sons and	2050.1
	2: 1	Again there was a day **w** the sons of God	2050.1
	2:11	**Now w** Job's three friends heard of all	2050.1
	2:12	**And w** they lift up their eyes afar off, and	2050.1
	3:11	*why* did I *not* give up the ghost **w** I came	2050.1
	3:22	are glad, **w** they can find the grave?	3588
	4:13	of the night, **w** deep sleep falleth on men.	871.1
	5:21	neither shalt thou be afraid of destruction **w**	3588
	6: 5	Doth the wild ass bray **w** he hath grass? or	5921
	6:17	**w** it is hot, they are consumed out of their	871.1
	7: 4	**W** I lie down, I say, When shall I arise, and	518
	7: 4	**W** shall I arise, and the night be gone?	4970
	7:13	**W** I say, My bed shall comfort me,	3588
	11: 3	**and w** thou mockest, shall no man make	2050.1
	16:22	**W** a few years are come, then I shall go	3588
	17:16	of the pit, **w** *our* rest together *is* in the dust.	518
	20:23	**W** he is about to fill his belly, *God* shall	NIH
	21: 6	Even **w** I remember I am afraid, and	518
	21:21	**w** the number of his months is cut off in	2050.1
	22:29	**W** *men* are cast down, then thou shalt say,	3588
	23:10	**w** he hath tried me, I shall come forth as	NIH
	23:15	**w** I consider, I am afraid of him.	NIH
	27: 8	hath gained, **w** God taketh away his soul?	3588
	27: 9	Will God hear his cry **w** trouble cometh	3588
	28:26	**W** he made a decree for the rain, and	871.1
	29: 2	as *in* the days **w** God preserved me;	NIH
	29: 3	**W** his candle shined upon my head, *and*	871.1
	29: 3	**w** by his light I walked *through* darkness;	NIH
	29: 4	**w** the secret of God *was* upon my	871.1
	29: 5	**W** the Almighty *was* yet with me,	871.1
	29: 5	yet with me, **w** my children *were* about me;	NIH
	29: 6	**W** *I* washed my steps with butter, and	871.1
	29: 7	**W** I went out *to* the gate through the city,	871.1
	29: 7	the city, **w** I prepared my seat in the street;	NIH
	29:11	**W** the ear heard *me,* then it blessed me; and	3588
	29:11	**and w** the eye saw *me,* it gave witness to	2050.1
	30:26	**W** I looked for good, then evil came *unto*	3588
	30:26	came *unto me:* **and w** I waited for light,	2050.1
	31:13	**w** they contended with me;	871.1
	31:14	What then shall I do **w** God riseth up? and	3588
	31:14	and **w** he visiteth, what shall I answer him?	3588
	31:21	the fatherless, **w** I saw my help in the gate:	3588
	31:26	If I beheld the sun **w** it shined, or the moon	3588
	31:29	or lift up myself **w** evil found him:	3588
	32: 5	**W** Elihu saw that *there was* no answer in	2050.1
	32:16	**W** I had waited, (for they spake not, but	2050.1
	33:15	the night, **w** deep sleep falleth upon men,	871.1
	34:29	**W** he giveth quietness, who then	2050.1
	34:29	**and w** he hideth *his* face, who then	2050.1
	36:13	up wrath: they cry not **w** he bindeth them.	3588
	36:20	**w** people are cut off in their place.	3807.1
	37: 4	he will not stay them **w** his voice is heard.	3588
	37:15	Dost thou know **w** God disposed them, and	871.1
	37:17	**w** he quieteth the earth by the south *wind?*	871.1
	38: 4	Where wast thou **w** I laid the foundations	871.1
	38: 7	**W** the morning stars sang together, and	871.1
	38: 8	up the sea with doors, **w** it brake forth,	871.1
	38: 9	**W** I made the cloud the garment thereof,	871.1
	38:38	**W** the dust groweth into hardness, and	871.1
	38:40	**W** they couch in *their* dens, *and* abide in	3588
	38:41	**w** his young ones cry unto God,	3588
	39: 1	Knowest thou the time **w** the wild goats of	NIH
	39: 1	*or* canst thou mark **w** the hinds do calve?	NIH
	39: 2	knowest thou the time **w** they bring forth?	NIH
	41:25	**W** he raiseth up *himself,* the mighty are	4480
	42:10	of Job, **w** he prayed for his friends:	871.1
Ps	2:12	the way, **w** his wrath is kindled but a little.	3588
	3: T	of David, **w** he fled from Absalom his son.	871.1
	4: 1	Hear me **w** I call, O God of my	871.1
	4: 1	thou hast enlarged me **w** *I was* in distress;	NIH
	4: 3	the LORD will hear **w** I call unto him.	871.1
	8: 3	**W** I consider thy heavens, the work of thy	3588
	9: 3	**W** mine enemies are turned back,	871.1
	9:12	**W** he maketh inquisition for blood, he	3588
	10: 9	the poor, **w** he draweth him into his net.	871.1
	12: 8	every side, **w** the vilest men are exalted.	3509.1

Ps 13: 4 those that trouble me rejoice **w** I am 3588
14: 7 **w** the LORD bringeth back the captivity 871.1
17:15 be satisfied, **w** *I* awake, *with* thy likeness. 871.1
20: 9 let the king hear us **w** we call. 3117+871.1
21:12 **w** thou shalt make ready *thine arrows* upon NIH
22: 9 thou didst make me hope **w** *I was* upon my NIH
22:24 but **w** he cried unto him, he heard. 871.1
27: 2 **W** the wicked, *even* mine enemies and 871.1
27: 7 Hear, O LORD, **w** I cry *with* my voice: NIH
27: 8 **W** *thou saidst,* Seek ye my face; my heart NIH
27:10 **W** my father and my mother forsake me, 3588
28: 2 of my supplications, **w** I cry unto thee, 871.1
28: 2 **w** I lift up my hands toward thy holy 871.1
30: 9 *there* in my blood, **w** I go down to the pit? 871.1
31:22 of my supplications **w** I cried unto thee. 871.1
32: 3 **W** I kept silence, my bones waxed old 3588
32: 6 unto thee in a time **w** thou mayest be found: NIH
34: T **w** he changed his behaviour before 871.1
35:13 *as for* me, **w** they were sick, my clothing 871.1
37:33 his hand, nor condemn him **w** he is judged. 871.1
37:34 **w** the wicked are cut off, thou shalt see *it.* 871.1
38:16 **w** my foot slippeth, they magnify 871.1
39:11 **W** thou with rebukes dost correct man for 871.1
41: 5 of me, **W** shall he die, and his name perish? 4970
41: 6 to itself; **w** he goeth abroad, he telleth *it.* NIH
42: 2 **w** shall I come and appear before God? 4970
42: 4 **W** I remember these *things,* I pour out 2050.1
49: 5 **w** the iniquity of my heels shall compass me NIH
49:16 Be not thou afraid **w** one is made rich, 3588
49:16 **w** the glory of his house is increased; 3588
49:17 For **w** he dieth he shall carry nothing 871.1
49:18 praise thee, **w** thou doest well to thyself. 3588
50:18 **W** thou sawest a thief, then thou consentedst 518
51: T **w** Nathan the prophet came unto him, 871.1
51: 4 that thou mightest be justified **w** thou 871.1
51: 4 thou speakest, *and* be clear **w** thou judgest. 871.1
52: T **w** Doeg the Edomite came and told Saul, 871.1
53: 6 **W** God bringeth back the captivity of his 871.1
54: T **w** the Ziphims came and said to Saul, 871.1
56: T **w** the Philistines took him in Gath. 871.1
56: 6 my steps, **w** they wait for my soul. 834+3509.1
56: 9 **W** I cry *unto thee,* then shall mine 3117+871.1
57: T of David, **w** he fled from Saul in the cave. 871.1
58: 7 **w** he bendeth *his bow to shoot* his arrows, NIH
58:10 The righteous shall rejoice **w** he seeth 3588
59: T **w** Saul sent, and they watcht the house to 871.1
60: T **w** he strove with Aram-naharaim and 871.1
60: T **w** Joab returned, and smote of Edom in 2050.1
61: 2 cry unto thee, **w** my heart is overwhelmed: 871.1
63: T **w** he was in the wilderness of Judah. 871.1
63: 6 **W** I remember thee upon my bed, *and* 518
65: 9 them corn, **w** thou hast so provided for it. 3588
66:14 mouth hath spoken, **w** I was in trouble. 3807.1
68: 7 **w** thou wentest forth before thy people, 871.1
68: 7 **w** thou didst march through the wilderness; 871.1
68: 9 thine inheritance, **w** it was weary. 2050.1
68:14 **W** the Almighty scattered kings in it, 871.1
69:10 **W** I wept, *and chastened* my soul with 2050.1
71: 9 forsake me not **w** my strength faileth. 3509.1
71:18 Now also **w** I am old and grayheaded, 5704
71:23 My lips shall greatly rejoice **w** I sing unto 3588
72:12 For he shall deliver the needy **w** he crieth; NIH
73: 3 **w** I saw the prosperity of the wicked. NIH
73:16 **W** I thought to know this, it *was* too 2050.1
73:20 As a dream **w** *one* awaketh; *so,* O Lord, 4480
73:20 *so,* O Lord, **w** *thou* awakest, thou shalt 871.1
75: 2 **W** I shall receive the congregation I will 3588
76: 7 who may stand in thy sight **w once** 227+4480
76: 9 **W** God arose to judgment, to save all 871.1
78:34 **W** he slew them, then they sought him: and 518
78:42 *nor* the day **w** he delivered them from 834
78:59 **W** God heard *this,* he was wroth, and 2050.1
81: 5 **w** he went out through the land of Egypt: 871.1
87: 6 shall count, **w** he writeth *up* the people, 871.1
89: 9 **w** the waves thereof arise, thou stillest 871.1
90: 4 in thy sight *are but* as yesterday **w** it is past, 3588
92: 7 **W** the wicked spring as the grass, and 871.1
92: 7 **and w** all the workers of iniquity do 2050.1
94: 8 the people: and ye fools, **w** will ye be wise? 4970
94:18 **W** I said, My foot slippeth; thy mercy, 518
95: 9 **W** your fathers tempted me, proved me, and 834
101: 2 O **w** wilt thou come unto me? I will walk 4970
102: T **w** he is overwhelmed, and poureth out his 3588
102: 2 Hide not thy face from me in the day **w** I am NIH
102: 2 in the day **w** I call answer me speedily. NIH
102:16 **W** the LORD shall build up Zion, he shall 3588
102:22 **W** the people are gathered together, and 871.1
105:12 **W** they were *but a few* men in number; 871.1
105:13 **W** they went from one nation to another, 2050.1
105:38 Egypt was glad **w** they departed: for 871.1
106:44 their affliction, **w** he heard their cry: 871.1
109: 7 **W** he shall be judged, let him be 871.1
109:23 I am gone like the shadow **w** it declineth: 3509.1
109:25 **w** they looked upon me they shaked their NIH
109:28 **w** they arise, let them be ashamed; but NIH
114: 1 **W** Israel went out of Egypt, the house of 871.1
119: 6 **w** I have respect unto all thy 871.1
119: 7 **w** I shall have learned thy righteous 871.1
119:32 **w** thou shalt enlarge my heart. 3588
119:74 They that fear thee will be glad **w** they see NIH
119:82 thy word, saying, **W** wilt thou comfort me? 4970
119:84 **w** wilt thou execute judgment on them that 4970
119:171 **w** thou hast taught me thy statutes. 3588
120: 7 *for* peace: but **w** I speak, they *are* for war. 3588
122: 1 I was glad **w** they said unto me, Let us go 871.1
124: 2 was on our side, **w** men rose up against us: 871.1
124: 3 **w** their wrath was kindled against us: 871.1
126: 1 **W** the LORD turned again the captivity 871.1
137: 1 yea, we wept, **w** we remembered Zion. 871.1
138: 3 In the day **w** I cried thou answeredst me, NIH
138: 4 **w** they hear the words of thy mouth. 3588
139:15 **w** I was made in secret, *and* 834
139:16 **w** *as yet there was* none of them. 2050.1
139:18 the sand: **w** I awake, I am still with thee. NIH
141: 1 give ear unto my voice, **w** I cry unto thee. 871.1

Ps 141: 6 **W** their judges are overthrown in stony NIH
141: 7 as **w** one cutteth and cleaveth *wood* upon NIH
142: T of David; A Prayer **w** he was in the cave. 871.1
142: 3 **W** my spirit was overwhelmed within me, 871.1
Pr 1:26 I will mock **w** your fear cometh; 871.1
1:27 **W** your fear cometh as desolation, and 871.1
1:27 **w** distress and anguish cometh upon you: 871.1
2:10 **W** wisdom entereth into thine heart, and 3588
3:24 **W** thou liest down, thou shalt not be afraid: 518
3:25 the desolation of the wicked, **w** it cometh. 3588
3:27 **w** it is in the power of thine hand to do *it.* 871.1
3:28 I will give; **w** thou hast it by thee. 2050.1
4: 8 thee to honour, **w** thou dost embrace her. 3588
4:12 **W** thou goest thy steps shall not be 871.1
4:12 and **w** thou runnest, thou shalt not stumble. 518
5:11 **w** thy flesh and thy body are consumed, 871.1
6: 3 **w** thou art come into the hand of thy friend; 3588
6: 9 **w** wilt thou arise out of thy sleep? 4970
6:22 **W** thou goest, it shall lead thee; when thou 871.1
6:22 **w** thou sleepest, it shall keep thee; and 871.1
6:22 and **w** thou awakest, it shall talk *with* thee. NIH
6:30 if he steal to satisfy his soul **w** he is hungry; 3588
8:24 **W** *there were* no depths, I was brought 871.1
8:24 **w** *there were* no fountains abounding with 871.1
8:27 **W** he prepared the heavens, I *was* there: 871.1
8:27 **w** he set a compass upon the face of 871.1
8:28 **W** he established the clouds above: 871.1
8:28 **w** *he* strengthened the fountains of 871.1
8:29 **W** he gave to the sea his decree, that 871.1
8:29 **w** he appointed the foundations of 871.1
11: 2 **W** pride cometh, then cometh shame: but NIH
11: 7 **W** a wicked man dieth, *his* expectation 871.1
11:10 **W** it goeth well with the righteous, the city 871.1
11:10 and **w** the wicked perish, *there is* shouting. 871.1
13:12 but **w** the desire cometh, *it is* a tree of life. NIH
14: 7 **w** thou perceivest not *in him* the lips of 2050.1
16: 7 **W** a man's ways please the LORD, 871.1
17:14 The beginning of strife *is as* **w** one letteth NIH
17:28 Even a fool, **w** he holdeth his peace, NIH
18: 3 **W** the wicked cometh, *then* cometh also 871.1
20:14 **but w** he is gone his way, then 2050.1
21:11 **W** the scorner is punished, the simple is 871.1
21:11 **w** the wise is instructed, he receiveth 871.1
21:27 **w** he bringeth it with a wicked mind? NIH
22: 6 and **w** he is old, he will not depart from it. 3588
23: 1 **W** thou sittest to eat with a ruler, 3588
23:16 shall rejoice, **w** thy lips speak right things. 871.1
23:22 and despise not thy mother **w** she is old. 3588
23:31 Look not thou upon the wine **w** it is red, 3588
23:31 **w** it giveth his colour in the cup, *when* it 3588
23:31 colour in the cup, **w** it moveth itself aright. NIH
23:35 **w** shall I awake? I will seek it yet again. 4970
24:14 **w** thou hast found *it,* then there shall be a 518
24:17 Rejoice not **w** thine enemy falleth, and 871.1
24:17 let not thine heart be glad **w** he stumbleth: 871.1
25: 8 **w** thy neighbour hath put thee to shame. 871.1
26:25 **W** he speaketh fair, believe him not: 3588
28: 1 The wicked flee **w** no man pursueth: but 2050.1
28:12 **W** righteous *men* do rejoice, *there is* great 871.1
28:12 but **w** the wicked rise, a man is hidden. 871.1
28:28 **W** the wicked rise, men hide themselves: 871.1
28:28 but **w** they perish, the righteous increase. 871.1
29: 2 **W** the righteous are in authority, 871.1
29: 2 **w** the wicked beareth rule, the people 871.1
29:16 **W** the wicked are multiplied, 871.1
30:22 For a servant **w** he reigneth; and a fool 3588
30:22 and a fool **w** he is filled *with* meat; 3588
30:23 For an odious *woman* **w** she is married; and 3588
31:23 **w** he sitteth among the elders of the land. 871.1
Ecc 4:10 woe to him *that is* alone **w** he falleth; for *he* 7945
5: 1 Keep thy foot **w** thou goest to 834+3509.1
5: 4 **W** thou vowest a vow unto God, 834+3509.1
5:11 **W** goods increase, they are increased that 871.1
8: 7 for who can tell him **w** it shall be? 834+3509.1
8:16 **W** I applied mine heart to know 834+3509.1
9:12 **w** it falleth suddenly upon them. 7945+3509.1
10: 3 **w** he that is a fool walketh by the way, 3509.1
10:16 **w** thy king *is* a child, and thy princes eat in 7945
10:17 **w** thy king *is* the son of nobles, and 7945
12: 1 nor the years draw nigh, **w** thou shalt say, 834
12: 3 In the day **w** the keepers of the house shall 7945
12: 4 **w** the sound of the grinding is low, and 871.1
12: 5 Also **w** they shall be afraid of *that which is* NIH
SS 5: 6 my soul failed **w** he spake: I sought him, 871.1
8: 1 **w** I should find thee without, I would kiss NIH
8: 8 what shall we do for our sister in the day **w** 7945
Isa 1:12 **W** ye come to appear before me, who hath 3588
1:15 **w** ye spread forth your hands, I will hide 871.1
1:15 yea, **w** ye make many prayers, I will not 3588
2:19 **w** he ariseth to shake terribly the earth. 871.1
2:21 **w** he ariseth to shake terribly the earth. 871.1
3: 6 **W** a man shall take hold of his brother *of* 3588
4: 4 **W** the Lord shall have washed away the filth 518
5: 4 **w** I looked that *it* should bring forth grapes, NIH
6:13 **w** they cast *their leaves: so* the holy seed 871.1
8:19 **w** they shall say unto you, Seek unto them 3588
8:21 come to pass, **that w** they shall be hungry, 3588
9: 1 **w** at the first he lightly afflicted the land of 6256
9: 3 *and* as *men* rejoice **w** they divide the spoil. 871.1
10:12 *that* **w** the Lord hath performed his whole 3588
10:18 they shall be as **w** a standard-bearer NIH
13:19 shall be as **w** God overthrew Sodom and NIH
16:12 **w** it is seen that Moab is weary on the high 3588
17: 5 it shall be as **w** the harvestman gathereth NIH
18: 3 **w** *he* lifteth up an ensign *on* 3509.1
18: 3 and **w** *he* bloweth a trumpet, hear ye. 3509.1
18: 5 **w** the bud is perfect, and the sour grape is 3509.1
20: 1 (**W** Sargon the king of Assyria sent him,) 871.1
24:13 **W** thus it shall be in the midst of the land 3588
24:13 as the gleaning grapes **w** the vintage is done. 518
24:23 **w** the LORD of hosts shall reign in mount 3588
25: 4 **w** the blast of the terrible ones *is* as a storm 3588
26: 9 for **w** thy judgments *are* in the earth, 834+3509.1
26:11 LORD, **w** thy hand is lifted up, they will NIH
26:16 they poured out a prayer **w** thy chastening NIH

Isa 27: 8 In measure, **w** it shooteth forth, thou wilt 871.1
27: 9 **w** he maketh all the stones of the altar as 871.1
27:11 **W** the boughs thereof are withered, 871.1
28: 4 which **w** he that looketh upon it seeth, NIH
28:15 **w** the overflowing scourge shall pass 3588
28:18 **w** the overflowing scourge shall pass 3588
28:25 **W** he hath made plain the face thereof, 518
29: 8 It shall even be **as w** a hungry *man* 834+3509.1
29: 8 or **as w** a thirsty *man* dreameth, and 834+3509.1
29:23 **w** he seeth his children, the work of mine 871.1
30:19 **w** *he* shall hear it, he will answer thee. 3509.1
30:21 **w** ye turn to the right hand, and when ye 3588
30:21 to the right hand, and **w** ye turn to the left. 3588
30:25 of the great slaughter, **w** the towers fall. 871.1
30:29 as *in* the night **w** a holy solemnity is kept; NIH
30:29 as **w** one goeth with a pipe to come into NIH
31: 3 **W** the LORD shall stretch out his hand, 2050.1
31: 4 **w** a multitude of shepherds is called forth 834
32: 7 even **w** the needy speaketh right. 871.1
32:19 **W** it shall hail, coming down *on* 2050.1
33: 1 **w** thou shalt cease to spoil, thou shalt be 3509.1
33: 1 **w** thou shalt make an end to deal 3509.1
37: 1 **w** king Hezekiah heard *it,* that he rent his 3509.1
37: 9 **And w** he heard *it,* he sent messengers to 2050.1
37:36 **and w** they arose early in the morning, 2050.1
38: 9 **w** he had been sick, and was recovered of 871.1
41:17 **W** the poor and needy seek water, and NIH
41:28 that, **w** I asked of them, could answer a NIH
43: 2 **W** thou passest through the waters, I *will* 3588
43: 2 **w** thou walkest through the fire, thou shalt 3588
43:12 **w** *there was* no strange *god* among you: 2050.1
48: 7 even before the day **w** thou heardest them 2050.1
48:13 **w** I call unto them, they stand *up* together. NIH
48:21 they thirsted not **w** he led them through NIH
50: 2 Wherefore, **w** I came, *was there* no man? NIH
50: 2 **w** I called, *was there* none to answer? Is my NIH
52: 8 **w** the LORD shall bring again Zion. NIH
53: 2 **and w** we shall see him, *there is* no 2050.1
53:10 **w** thou shalt make his soul an offering for 518
54: 6 **w** thou wast refused, saith thy God. 3588
57:13 **W** thou criest, let thy companies deliver 871.1
57:20 **w** it cannot rest, whose waters cast up mire 3588
58: 7 **w** thou seest the naked, that thou cover 3588
59:19 **W** the enemy shall come in like a flood, 3588
64: 2 As **w** the melting fire burneth, the fire NIH
64: 3 **W** thou didst terrible things *which* we 871.1
65:12 because **w** I called, ye did not answer; NIH
65:12 **w** I spake, ye did not hear; but did evil NIH
66: 4 because **w** I called, none did answer; when I NIH
66: 4 did answer; **w** I spake, they did not hear: NIH
66:14 **And w** ye see *this,* your heart shall 2050.1
Jer 2: 2 **w** thou wentest after me in the wilderness, NIH
2: 7 **but w** ye entered, ye defiled my land, and 2050.1
2:17 thy God, **w** he led thee by the way? 6256+871.1
2:20 **w** upon every high hill and under every 3588
2:26 As the thief is ashamed **w** he is found, so 3588
3: 8 **w** for all the causes whereby backsliding 3588
3:16 **w** ye be multiplied and increased in 3588
4:30 **w** thou art spoiled, what wilt thou do? NIH
5: 7 **w** I had fed them to the full, they then 2050.1
5:19 it shall come to pass, **w** ye shall say, 3588
6:14 Peace, peace; **w** *there is* no peace. 2050.1
6:15 Were they ashamed **w** they had committed 3588
8:11 Peace, peace; **w** *there is* no peace. 2050.1
8:12 Were they ashamed **w** they had committed 3588
8:18 **W** I would comfort myself against sorrow, NIH
10:13 **W** he uttereth his voice, *there is* a 3807.1
11:15 **W** thou doest evil, then thou rejoicest. 3588
12: 1 *art* thou, O LORD, **w** I plead with thee: 3588
13:21 What wilt thou say **w** he shall punish thee? 3588
13:27 be made clean? **w** *shall it* once *be?* 310+4970
14:12 **W** they fast, I will not hear their cry; and 3588
14:12 **w** they offer burnt offering and an oblation, 3588
16:10 **w** thou shalt shew this people all these 3588
17: 6 and shall not see **w** good cometh; 3588
17: 8 shall not see **w** heat cometh, but her leaf 3588
18:22 **w** thou shalt bring a troop suddenly upon 3588
21: 1 **w** king Zedekiah sent unto him Pashur 871.1
22:23 how gracious shalt thou be **w** pangs come 871.1
23:33 **w** this people, or the prophet, or a priest, 3588
25:12 **w** seventy years are accomplished, 3509.1
26: 8 **w** Jeremiah had made an end of speaking 3509.1
26:10 **W** the princes of Judah heard these 2050.1
26:21 **And w** Jehoiakim the king, with all his 2050.1
26:21 **but w** Urijah heard *it,* he was afraid, and 2050.1
27:20 **w** he carried away captive Jeconiah the son 871.1
28: 9 **w** the word of the prophet shall come to 871.1
29:13 find *me,* **w** ye shall search for me with all 3588
31: 2 *even* Israel, **w** *I* went to cause him to rest. NIH
31:23 **w** I shall bring again their captivity; 871.1
31:35 which divideth the sea **w** the waves 2050.1
32:16 Now **w** I had delivered the evidence of 310
34: 1 **w** Nebuchadnezzar king of Babylon, and 2050.1
34: 7 **W** the king of Babylon's army fought 2050.1
34:10 *Now* **w** all the princes, and all the people, 2050.1
34:14 **and w** he hath served thee six years, thou 2050.1
34:18 **w** they cut the calf in twain, and 834
35:11 **w** Nebuchadrezzar king of Babylon came 871.1
36:11 **W** Michaiah the son of Gemariah, the son 2050.1
36:13 **w** Baruch read the book in the ears of 871.1
36:16 Now it came to pass **w** they had heard all 3509.1
36:23 **w** Jehudi had read three or four leaves, 3509.1
37: 5 **and w** the Chaldeans that besieged 2050.1
37:11 *that* **w** the army of the Chaldeans was 871.1
37:13 **And w** he was in the gate of Benjamin, 2050.1
37:16 **W** Jeremiah was entered into the dungeon, 3588
38: 7 **Now w** Ebed-melech the Ethiopian, 2050.1
38:28 he was *there* **w** Jerusalem was taken. 834+3509.1
39: 4 *that* **w** Zedekiah the king of Judah 834+3509.1
39: 5 **and w** they had taken him, they brought 2050.1
40: 1 **w** he had taken him being bound in chains 871.1
40: 7 *Now* **w** all the captains of the forces 2050.1
40:11 Likewise **w** all the Jews that *were* in 2050.1
41: 7 *so,* **w** they came into the midst of the city, 3509.1
41:11 **But w** Johanan the son of Kareah, and 2050.1

Jer 41:13 *that* **w** all the people which *were* with 3509.1
42: 6 **w** we obey the voice of the LORD our 3588
42:18 upon you, **w** ye shall enter *into* Egypt: 871.1
42:20 **w** ye sent me unto the LORD your God, 3588
43: 1 *that* **w** Jeremiah had made an end of 3509.1
43:11 **And w** he cometh, he shall smite the land 2050.1
44:19 **w** we burnt incense to the queen of heaven, 3588
45: 1 **w** he had written these words in a book at 871.1
51:16 **W** he uttereth *his* voice, *there is* a 3807.1
51:55 **w** her waves do roar like great waters, 2050.1
51:59 **w** he went with Zedekiah the king of Judah 871.1
51:61 **W** thou comest *to* Babylon, and shalt see, 3509.1
51:63 **w** thou hast made an end of reading this 3509.1
52: 1 and twenty year old **w** he *began* to reign, 871.1
La 1: 7 **w** her people fell into the hand of 871.1
2:12 **w** they swooned as the wounded in 871.1
2:12 **w** their soul was poured out into their 871.1
3: 8 Also **w** I cry and shout, he shutteth out my 3588
3:37 to pass, **w** the Lord commandeth *it* not? NIH
4:15 touch not, **w** they fled away and wandered: 3588
Eze 1: 9 they turned not **w** they went; they went 871.1
1:12 *and* they turned not **w** they went. 871.1
1:17 **W** they went, they went upon their four 871.1
1:17 *and* they turned not **w** they went. 871.1
1:19 **w** the living creatures went, the wheels 871.1
1:19 **w** the living creatures were lift up from 871.1
1:21 **W** those went, *these* went; and when those 871.1
1:21 **w** those stood, *these* stood; and when those 871.1
1:21 **w** those were lifted up from the earth, 871.1
1:24 **w** they went, I heard the noise of their 871.1
1:24 **w** they stood, they let down their wings. 871.1
1:25 **w** they stood, *and* had let down their 871.1
1:28 **And w** I saw *it,* I fell upon my face, and 2050.1
2: 2 the spirit entered into me **w** he spake 834+3509.1
2: 9 **And w** I looked, behold, a hand *was* sent 2050.1
3:18 **W** I say unto the wicked, Thou shalt surely 871.1
3:20 **W** a righteous *man* doth turn from his 871.1
3:27 **w** I speak with thee, I will open thy mouth, 871.1
4: 6 **And w** thou hast accomplished them, lie 2050.1
5: 2 **w** the days of the siege are fulfilled: 3509.1
5:13 **w** I have accomplished my fury in them. 871.1
5:15 **w** I shall execute judgments in thee in 871.1
5:16 **W** I shall send upon them the evil arrows 871.1
6: 8 **w** ye shall be scattered through 871.1
6:13 **w** their slain *men* shall be among their 871.1
8: 7 **and w** I looked, behold a hole in the wall. 2050.1
8: 8 **and w** I had digged in the wall, behold a 2050.1
10: 3 right side of the house, **w** the man went in; 871.1
10: 5 as the voice of the Almighty God **w** he 871.1
10: 6 *that* **w** he had commanded the man clothed 871.1
10: 9 **And w** I looked, behold the four wheels 2050.1
10:11 **W** they went, they went upon their four 871.1
10:16 **w** the cherubims went, the wheels went by 871.1
10:16 **w** the cherubims lift up their wings to 871.1
10:17 **W** they stood, *these* stood; and when they 871.1
10:17 **w** they were lifted up, *these* lift up 871.1
10:19 **w** they went out, the wheels also *were* 871.1
11:13 it came to pass, **w** I prophesied, 3509.1
12:15 **w** I shall scatter them among the nations, 871.1
13:12 Lo, **w** the wall is fallen, shall it not be 2050.1
14: 9 if the prophet be deceived **w** he hath 2050.1
14:13 **w** the land sinneth against me by 3588
14:21 How much more **w** I send my four sore NIH
14:23 **w** ye see their ways and their doings: 3588
15: 5 Behold, **w** it was whole, it was meet for no 871.1
15: 5 **w** the fire hath devoured it, and it is 2050.1
15: 7 the LORD, **w** I set my face against them. 871.1
16: 6 **And w** I passed by thee, and saw thee 2050.1
16: 6 I said unto thee **w** *thou wast* in thy blood, NIH
16: 6 I said unto thee **w** *thou wast* in thy blood, NIH
16: 8 **Now w** I passed by thee, and looked upon 2050.1
16:22 **w** thou wast naked and bare, *and* 871.1
16:53 **W** I shall bring again their captivity, 2050.1
16:55 **W** thy sisters, Sodom and her daughters, 2050.1
16:61 **w** thou shalt receive thy sisters, thine elder 871.1
16:63 **w** I am pacified toward thee for all that 871.1
17:10 **w** the east wind toucheth it? 3509.1
17:18 **w** lo, he had given his hand, and 2050.1
18:19 **W** the son hath done that which is lawful 2050.1
18:24 **But w** the righteous turneth away from 2050.1
18:26 **W** a righteous *man* turneth away from his 871.1
18:27 **w** the wicked *man* turneth away from his 871.1
19: 5 **Now w** she saw that she had waited, *and* 2050.1
20: 5 In the day **w** I chose Israel, and lifted up 871.1
20: 5 **w** I lifted up mine hand unto them, 2050.1
20:28 *For* **w** I had brought them into the land, 2050.1
20:31 For **w** *ye* offer your gifts, when *ye* make 871.1
20:31 **w** *ye* make your sons to pass through 871.1
20:41 **w** I bring you out from the people, and 871.1
20:42 **w** I shall bring you into the land of Israel, 871.1
20:44 **w** I have wrought with you for my name's 871.1
21: 7 it shall be, **w** they say unto thee, Wherefore 3588
21:25 **w** iniquity *shall have* an end, 6256+871.1
21:29 **w** *their* iniquity *shall have* an end. 6256+871.1
22:28 **w** the LORD hath not spoken. 2050.1
23: 5 Aholah played the harlot **w** she was mine; NIH
23:11 **And w** her sister Aholibah saw *this,* she 2050.1
23:14 **for w** she saw men pourtrayed upon 2050.1
23:39 For **w** they had slain their children to their 871.1
24:24 **w** this cometh, ye shall know that I *am* 871.1
24:25 *shall it not be* in the day **w** I take from them NIH
25: 3 against my sanctuary, **w** it was profaned; 3588
25: 3 against the land of Israel, **w** it was desolate; 3588
25: 3 house of Judah, **w** they went into captivity; 3588
25:17 **w** I shall lay my vengeance upon them. 871.1
26:10 the chariots, **w** he shall enter into thy gates, 871.1
26:15 the sound of thy fall, **w** the wounded cry, 871.1
26:15 **w** the slaughter is made in the midst of 871.1
26:19 **W** I shall make thee a desolate city, 871.1
26:19 **w** *I* shall bring up the deep upon thee, 871.1
26:20 **W** I shall bring thee down with them that 2050.1
27:33 **W** thy wares went forth out of the seas, 871.1
27:34 *In* the time **w** *thou shalt be* broken by NIH
28:22 **w** I shall have executed judgments in her, 871.1
28:25 **W** I shall have gathered the house of Israel 871.1
Eze 28:26 **w** I have executed judgments upon all 871.1
29: 7 **W** they took hold of thee by thy hand, 871.1
29: 7 **w** they leaned upon thee, thou brakest, and 871.1
29:16 **w** they shall look after them: 871.1
30: 4 **w** the slain shall fall in Egypt, and 871.1
30: 8 **w** I have set a fire in Egypt, and *when* all 871.1
30: 8 and **w** all her helpers shall be destroyed. NIH
30:18 **w** I shall break there the yokes of Egypt: 871.1
30:25 **w** I shall put my sword into the hand of 871.1
31: 5 of the multitude of waters, **w** he shot forth. 871.1
31:15 In the day **w** he went down to the grave I NIH
31:16 **w** I cast him down to hell with them that 871.1
32: 7 **w** *I* shall put thee out, I will cover 871.1
32: 9 **w** I shall bring thy destruction among 871.1
32:10 **w** I shall brandish my sword before them; 871.1
32:15 **W** I shall make the land of Egypt desolate, 871.1
32:15 **w** I shall smite all them that dwell therein, 871.1
33: 2 **W** I bring the sword upon a land, 3588
33: 3 *If* **w** he seeth the sword come upon 2050.1
33: 8 **W** I say unto the wicked, O wicked *man,* 871.1
33:13 **W** I shall say to the righteous, *that* he shall 871.1
33:14 Again, **w** I say unto the wicked, Thou shalt 871.1
33:18 **W** the righteous turneth from his 871.1
33:29 **w** I have laid the land most desolate 871.1
33:33 **w** this cometh to pass, (lo, it will come) 871.1
34: 5 beasts of the field, **w** they were scattered. 2050.1
34:27 **w** I have broken the bands of their yoke, 871.1
35:11 amongst them, **w** I have judged thee. 834+3509.1
35:14 **W** the whole earth rejoiceth, I will make 3509.1
36:17 **w** the house of Israel dwelt in their own NIH
36:20 **And w** they entered unto the heathen, 2050.1
36:20 my holy name, **w** *they* said to them, 871.1
36:23 **w** I shall be sanctified in you before their 871.1
37: 8 **And w** I beheld, lo, the sinews and 2050.1
37:13 **w** I have opened your graves, O my 871.1
37:18 **w** the children of thy people shall 834+3509.1
37:28 **w** my sanctuary shall be in the midst of 871.1
38:14 In that day **w** my people of Israel dwelleth 871.1
38:16 **w** I shall be sanctified in thee, O Gog, 871.1
38:18 **w** Gog shall come against the land 3117+871.1
39:15 **w** *any* seeth a man's bone, then shall he 2050.1
39:26 **w** they dwelt safely in their land, and 871.1
39:27 **W** I have brought them again from 871.1
42:14 **W** the priests enter *therein,* then shall they 871.1
42:15 **Now w** he had made an end of measuring 2050.1
43: 3 *even* according to the vision that I saw **w** I 871.1
43:18 of the altar in the day **w** *they* shall make it, NIH
43:23 **W** thou hast made an end of cleansing *it,* 871.1
43:27 **And w** *these* days are expired, it shall be 2050.1
44: 7 **w** ye offer my bread, the fat and the blood, 871.1
44:10 away far from me, **w** Israel went astray, 871.1
44:15 that kept the charge of my sanctuary **w** 871.1
44:17 *that* **w** they enter in at the gates of the inner 871.1
44:19 **w** they go forth into the utter court, 871.1
44:21 **w** they enter into the inner court. 871.1
45: 1 **w** ye shall divide *by lot* the land for 871.1
46: 8 **w** the prince shall enter, he shall go in *by* 871.1
46: 9 **w** the people of the land shall come before 871.1
46:10 midst of them, **w** they go in, shall go in; 871.1
46:10 go in; and **w** they go forth, shall go forth. 871.1
46:12 Now **w** the prince shall prepare a voluntary 3588
47: 3 **w** the man that had the line in his hand 871.1
47: 7 Now **w** I had returned, behold, at the bank 871.1
48:11 which went not astray **w** the children of 871.1
Da 3: 7 **w** all the people heard the sound of 1768+3509.4
5:20 **w** his heart was lifted up, and 1768+3509.4
6:10 Now **w** Daniel knew that 1768+3509.4
6:14 the king, **w** he heard *these* words, 1768+3509.4
6:20 **w** he came to the den, he cried with a 3509.4
8: 2 it came to pass, **w** I saw, that I *was* at 871.1
8: 8 **w** he was strong, the great horn was 3509.1
8:15 **w** I, *even* I Daniel, had seen the vision, and 871.1
8:17 **w** he came, I was afraid, and fell upon my 871.1
8:23 **w** the transgressors are come to the full, 3509.1
10: 9 **w** I heard the voice of his words, then 3509.1
10:11 **w** he had spoken this word unto me, I 871.1
10:15 **w** he had spoken such words unto me, I set 871.1
10:19 **w** he had spoken unto me, I was 3509.1
10:20 **and w** I am gone forth, lo, the prince of 2050.1
11: 4 **w** he shall stand up, his kingdom shall be 3509.1
11:12 *And* **w** he hath taken away the multitude, 2050.1
11:34 Now **w** they shall fall, they shall be holpen 871.1
12: 7 **w** he held up his right hand and his left 2050.1
12: 7 **w** *he* shall have accomplished to scatter 3509.1
Hos 1: 8 **Now w** she had weaned Lo-ruhamah, 2050.1
2:15 as *in* the day **w** she came up out of the land NIH
4:14 I will not punish your daughters **w** they 3588
4:14 nor your spouses **w** they commit adultery: 3588
5:13 **W** Ephraim saw his sickness, and 2050.1
6:11 **w** I returned the captivity of my people. 871.1
7: 1 **W** I *would have* healed Israel, then 3509.1
7:12 **W** they shall go, I will spread my 834+3509.1
7:14 their heart, **w** they howled upon their beds: 3588
9:12 woe also to them **w** I depart from them! 871.1
10:10 **w** *they* shall bind themselves in their two 871.1
11: 1 **W** Israel *was* a child, then I loved him, and 3588
11:10 **w** he shall roar, then the children shall 3588
13: 1 **W** Ephraim spake trembling, he exalted 3509.1
13: 1 **but w** he offended in Baal, he died. 2050.1
Joel 2: 8 **w** they fall upon the sword, they shall not be NIH
3: 1 **w** I shall bring again the captivity of Judah 834
Am 3: 4 lion roar in the forest, **w** he hath no prey? 2050.1
4: 7 **w** *there were* yet three months to 871.1
4: 9 **w** your gardens and your vineyards and 871.1
7: 2 *that* **w** they had made an end of eating 518
8: 5 Saying, **W** will the new moon be gone, 4970
Jnh 2: 7 **W** my soul fainted within me I 871.1
4: 2 this my saying, **w** I was yet in my country? NIH
4: 7 God prepared a worm **w** the morning rose 871.1
4: 8 it came to pass, **w** the sun did arise, 3509.1
Mic 2: 1 **w** the morning is light, they practise it, 871.1
5: 5 **w** the Assyrian shall come into our land: 3588
5: 5 **w** he shall tread in our palaces, then 3588
5: 6 **w** he cometh into our land, and when he 3588
5: 6 and **w** he treadeth within our borders. 3588
Mic 7: 1 for I am as **w** they have gathered NIH
7: 8 **w** I fall, I shall arise; when I sit in darkness, 3588
7: 8 **w** I sit in darkness, the LORD *shall be* a 3588
Na 1:12 be cut down, **w** he shall pass through. 2050.1
3:17 *but* **w** the sun ariseth they flee away, and 2050.1
Hab 1:13 holdest thy tongue **w** the wicked devoureth 871.1
2: 1 and what I shall answer **w** I am reproved. 5921
3:16 **W** I heard, my belly trembled; my lips 2050.1
3:16 **w** *he* cometh up unto the people, he will 3807.1
Zep 3:20 **w** I turn back your captivity before your 871.1
Hag 1: 9 **and w** ye brought *it* home, I did blow 2050.1
2: 5 with you **w** ye came out of Egypt, 871.1
2:16 **w** *one* came to a heap of twenty *measures,* NIH
2:16 **w** *one* came to the pressfat for to draw out NIH
Zec 7: 2 **W** they had sent *unto* the house of God 2050.1
7: 5 **W** ye fasted and mourned in the fifth and 3588
7: 6 **w** ye did eat, and when ye did drink, did 3588
7: 6 when ye did eat, and **w** ye did drink, did 3588
7: 7 **w** Jerusalem was inhabited and 871.1
7: 7 **w** *men* inhabited the south and the plain? 2050.1
8:14 **w** your fathers provoked me to wrath, 871.1
9: 1 **w** the eyes of man, as of all the tribes of 3588
9:13 **W** I have bent Judah for me, filled the bow 3588
12: 2 **w** they shall be in the siege both against NIH
13: 3 *that* **w** any shall yet prophesy, then 3588
13: 3 shall thrust him through **w** he prophesieth. 871.1
13: 4 one of his vision, **w** he hath prophesied; 871.1
14: 3 as **w** he fought in the day of battle. 3117
Mal 2:17 Wherein have we wearied *him?* **W** ye say, 871.1
3: 2 who *shall* stand **w** he appeareth? for he *is* 871.1
3:17 of hosts, in that day **w** I make *up my* jewels; 834
Mt 1:18 **W** as his mother Mary was espoused to NIG
2: 1 Now **w** Jesus was born in Bethlehem of NIG
2: 3 **W** Herod the king had heard *these things,* *1161*
2: 4 And **w** he had gathered all the chief priests NIG
2: 7 **w** he had privily called the wise men, NIG
2: 8 **w** ye have found *him,* bring me word again, *1875*
2: 9 **W** they had heard the king, they departed; *1161*
2:10 **W** they saw the star, they rejoiced *with* *1161*
2:11 And **w** they were come into the house, NIG
2:11 and **w** they had opened their treasures, NIG
2:13 And **w** they were departed, behold, NIG
2:14 **W** he arose, he took the young child and *1161*
2:16 **w** he saw that he was mocked of the wise NIG
2:19 But **w** Herod was dead, behold, an angel of NIG
2:22 But **w** he heard that Archelaus did reign in NIG
3: 7 But **w** he saw many of the Pharisees and NIG
3:16 And Jesus, **w** he was baptized, went up NIG
4: 2 And **w** he had fasted forty days and NIG
4: 3 And **w** the tempter came to him, he said, NIG
4:12 Now **w** Jesus had heard that John was cast NIG
5: 1 and **w** he was set, his disciples came unto NIG
5:11 **w** *men* shall revile you, and persecute *you,* *3752*
6: 2 Therefore **w** thou doest *thine* alms, do not *3752*
6: 3 But **w** thou doest alms, let not thy left hand NIG
6: 5 And **w** thou prayest, thou shalt not be as *3752*
6: 6 But thou, **w** thou prayest, enter into thy *3752*
6: 6 thy closet, and **w** thou hast shut thy door, NIG
6: 7 But **w** ye pray, use not vain repetitions, NIG
6:16 Moreover **w** ye fast, be not as *3752*
6:17 But thou, **w** thou fastest, anoint thine head, NIG
7:28 to pass, **w** Jesus had ended these sayings, *3753*
8: 1 **W** he was come down from the mountain, *1161*
8: 5 And **w** Jesus was entered into Capernaum, NIG
8:10 **W** Jesus heard *it,* he marvelled, and said to *1161*
8:14 And **w** Jesus was come into Peter's house, NIG
8:16 **W** the even was come, they brought unto *1161*
8:18 Now **w** Jesus saw great multitudes about NIG
8:23 And **w** he was entered into a ship, NIG
8:28 And **w** he was come to the other side into NIG
8:32 And **w** they were come out, they went into NIG
8:34 and **w** they saw him, they besought *him* that NIG
9: 8 But **w** the multitudes saw *it,* they marvelled, NIG
9:11 And **w** the Pharisees saw *it,* they said unto NIG
9:12 But **w** Jesus heard *that,* he said unto them, NIG
9:15 **w** the bridegroom shall be taken from them, *3752*
9:22 and **w** he saw her, he said, Daughter, be of NIG
9:23 And **w** Jesus came into the ruler's house, NIG
9:25 But **w** the people were put forth, he went *3753*
9:27 And **w** Jesus departed thence, two blind NIG
9:28 And **w** he was come into the house, NIG
9:31 But they, **w** they were departed, NIG
9:33 And **w** the devil was cast out, the dumb NIG
9:36 But **w** he saw the multitudes, he was moved NIG
10: 1 And **w** he had called unto *him* his twelve NIG
10:12 And **w** ye come into a house salute it. NIG
10:14 **w** ye depart out of that house or city, NIG
10:19 But **w** they deliver you up, take no thought *3752*
10:23 But **w** they persecute you in this city, *3752*
11: 1 **w** Jesus had made an end of commanding *3753*
11: 2 Now **w** John had heard in the prison NIG
12: 2 But **w** the Pharisees saw *it,* they said unto NIG
12: 3 **w** he was a hungred, and they that were *3753*
12: 9 And **w** he was departed thence, he went into NIG
12:15 But **w** Jesus knew *it,* he withdrew himself NIG
12:24 But **w** the Pharisees heard *it,* they said, NIG
12:43 **W** the unclean spirit is gone out of a man, *3752*
12:44 and **w** he is come, he findeth *it* empty, NIG
13: 4 And **w** he sowed, some *seeds* fell by *1722+3588*
13: 6 And **w** the sun was up, they were scorched; NIG
13:19 **W** any one heareth the word of NIG
13:21 for **w** tribulation or persecution ariseth NIG
13:26 But **w** the blade was sprung up, and *3753*
13:32 but **w** it is grown, it is the greatest among *3752*
13:44 the which **w** a man hath found, he hideth, NIG
13:46 **w** he had found one pearl of great price, NIG
13:48 Which, **w** it was full, they drew to shore, *3753*
13:53 *that* **w** Jesus had finished these parables, *3753*
13:54 And **w** he was come into his own country, NIG
14: 5 And **w** he would have put him to death, NIG
14: 6 But **w** Herod's birthday was kept, NIG
14:13 **W** Jesus heard *of it,* he departed thence by *2532*
14:13 **w** the people had heard *thereof,* they NIG
14:15 And **w** it was evening, his disciples came to NIG
14:23 And **w** he had sent the multitudes away, NIG

Mt 14:23 and **w** the evening was come, he was there NIG
14:26 And **w** the disciples saw him walking on NIG
14:29 And **w** Peter was come down out of NIG
14:30 But **w** he saw the wind boysterous, he was NIG
14:32 And **w** they were come into the ship, NIG
14:34 And **w** they were gone over, they came into NIG
14:35 And **w** the men of that place had knowledge NIG
15: 2 for they wash not their hands **w** they eat *3752*
15:31 **w** they saw the dumb to speak, the maimed NIG
16: 2 and said unto them, **W** it is evening, ye say, NIG
16: 5 And **w** his disciples were come to the other NIG
16: 8 *Which* **w** Jesus perceived, he said unto *1161*
16:13 **W** Jesus came into the coasts of Cesarea *1161*
17: 6 And **w** the disciples heard *it,* they fell on NIG
17: 8 And **w** they had lift up their eyes, they saw NIG
17:14 And **w** they were come to the multitude, NIG
17:24 And **w** they were come to Capernaum, NIG
17:25 And **w** he was come into the house, *3753*
17:27 and **w** thou hast opened his mouth, NIG
18:24 And **w** he had begun to reckon, one was NIG
18:31 So **w** his fellowservants saw what was *3767*
19: 1 *that* **w** Jesus had finished these sayings, *3753*
19:22 But **w** the young man heard *that* saying, NIG
19:25 **W** his disciples heard *it,* they were *1161*
19:28 **w** the Son of man shall sit in the throne of *3752*
20: 2 And **w** he had agreed with the labourers for NIG
20: 8 So **w** even was come, the lord of NIG
20: 9 And **w** they came that *were hired* about NIG
20:10 But **w** the first came, they supposed that NIG
20:11 And **w** they had received *it,* they murmured NIG
20:24 And **w** the ten heard *it,* they were moved NIG
20:30 **w** they heard that Jesus passed by, cried out, NIG
21: 1 And **w** they drew nigh unto Jerusalem, and *3753*
21:10 And **w** he was come into Jerusalem, all NIG
21:15 And **w** the chief priests and scribes saw NIG
21:19 And **w** he saw a fig tree in the way, he came NIG
21:20 And **w** the disciples saw *it,* they marvelled, NIG
21:23 And **w** he was come into the temple, NIG
21:32 ye, **w** ye had seen *it,* repented not afterward, NIG
21:34 And **w** the time of the fruit drew near, *3753*
21:38 But **w** the husbandmen saw the son, NIG
21:40 **W** the lord therefore of the vineyard *3752*
21:45 And **w** the chief priests and Pharisees had NIG
21:46 But **w** they sought to lay hands on him, NIG
22: 7 But **w** the king heard *thereof,* he was wroth: NIG
22:11 And **w** the king came in to see the guests, NIG
22:22 **W** they had heard *these words,* they *2532*
22:25 **w** he had married *a wife,* deceased, and, NIG
22:33 And **w** the multitude heard *this,* they were NIG
22:34 But **w** the Pharisees had heard that he had NIG
23:15 to make one proselyte, and **w** he is made, *3752*
24: 3 Tell us, **w** shall these *things* be? *4219*
24:15 **W** ye therefore shall see the abomination of *3752*
24:32 **W** his branch is yet tender, and *3752*
24:33 **w** ye shall see all these *things,* know that it *3752*
24:46 whom his lord **w** he cometh shall find so NIG
24:50 come in a day **w** he looketh not for *him,* *3739*
25:31 **W** the Son of man shall come in his glory, *3752*
25:37 **w** saw we thee a hungred, and fed *thee?* or *4219*
25:38 **W** saw we thee a stranger, and took *thee* *4219*
25:39 Or **w** saw we thee sick, *4219*
25:44 **w** saw we thee a hungred, or athirst, or *4219*
26: 1 **w** Jesus had finished all these sayings, *3753*
26: 6 Now **w** Jesus was in Bethany, in the house NIG
26: 8 But **w** his disciples saw *it,* they had NIG
26:10 **W** Jesus understood *it,* he said unto them, *1161*
26:20 Now **w** the even was come, he sat down NIG
26:29 until that day **w** I drink it new with you in *3752*
26:30 And **w** they had sung a hymn, they went out NIG
26:71 And **w** he was gone out into the porch, NIG
27: 1 **W** the morning was come, all the chief *1161*
27: 2 And **w** they had bound him, they led *him* NIG
27: 3 **w** he saw that he was condemned, NIG
27:12 And **w** he was accused of the chief *1722+3588*
27:17 Therefore **w** they were gathered together, NIG
27:19 **W** he was set down on the judgment seat, *1161*
27:24 **W** Pilate saw that he could prevail nothing, *1161*
27:26 and **w** he had scourged Jesus, he delivered NIG
27:29 And **w** they had platted a crown of thorns, NIG
27:33 And **w** they were come unto a place called NIG
27:34 **w** he had tasted *thereof,* he would not drink. NIG
27:47 **w** they heard *that,* said, This *man* calleth for NIG
27:50 **w** he had cried again with a loud voice, NIG
27:54 Now **w** the centurion, and they that were NIG
27:57 **W** the even was come, there came a rich *1161*
27:59 And **w** Joseph had taken the body, NIG
28:11 Now **w** they were going, behold, some of NIG
28:12 And **w** they were assembled with the elders, NIG
28:17 And **w** they saw him, they worshipped him: NIG
Mk 1:19 And **w** he had gone a little further thence, NIG
1:26 And **w** the unclean spirit had torn him, and NIG
1:29 **w** they were come out of the synagogue, NIG
1:32 And at even, **w** the sun did set, *3753*
1:37 And **w** they had found him, they said unto *2532*
2: 4 And **w** they could not come nigh unto him NIG
2: 4 and **w** they had broken *it* up, they let down NIG
2: 5 **W** Jesus saw their faith, he said unto *1161*
2: 8 **w** Jesus perceived in his spirit that they so NIG
2:16 And **w** the scribes and Pharisees saw him NIG
2:17 **W** Jesus heard *it,* he saith unto them, They *2532*
2:20 **w** the bridegroom shall be taken away from *3752*
2:25 **w** he had need, and was a hungred, he, and *3753*
3: 5 And **w** he had looked round about on them NIG
3: 8 **w** they had heard what great *things* he did, NIG
3:11 And unclean spirits, **w** they saw him, *3752*
3:21 And **w** his friends heard *of it,* they went out NIG
4: 6 But **w** the sun was up, it was scorched; and *3753*
4:10 And **w** he was alone, they that were about *3753*
4:15 but **w** they have heard, Satan cometh *3752*
4:16 who, **w** they have heard the word, *3752*
4:17 **w** affliction or persecution ariseth for NIG
4:29 But **w** the fruit is brought forth, *3752*
4:31 which, **w** it is sown in the earth, *3752*
4:32 But **w** it is sown, it groweth up, and *3752*
4:34 and **w** *they were* alone, he expounded all NIG

Mk 4:35 And the same day, **w** the even was come, NIG
4:36 And **w** they had sent away the multitude, NIG
5: 2 And **w** he was come out of the ship, NIG
5: 6 But **w** he saw Jesus afar off, he ran and NIG
5:18 And **w** he was come into the ship, he that NIG
5:21 And **w** Jesus was passed over again by ship NIG
5:22 and **w** he saw him, he fell at his feet, NIG
5:27 **W** she had heard of Jesus, came in the press NIG
5:39 And **w** he was come in, he saith unto them, NIG
5:40 But **w** he had put *them* all out, he taketh NIG
6: 2 And **w** the sabbath day was come, he began NIG
6:11 nor hear you, **w** ye depart thence, NIG
6:16 But **w** Herod heard *thereof,* he said, It is NIG
6:20 and **w** he heard him, he did many *things,* NIG
6:21 And **w** a convenient day was come, NIG
6:22 And **w** the daughter of the said Herodias *2532*
6:29 And **w** his disciples heard *of it,* they came NIG
6:34 And Jesus, **w** he came out, saw much NIG
6:35 And **w** the day was now far spent, NIG
6:38 And **w** they knew, they say, Five, and NIG
6:41 And **w** he had taken the five loaves and NIG
6:46 And **w** he had sent them away, he departed NIG
6:47 And **w** even was come, the ship was in NIG
6:49 But **w** they saw him walking upon the sea, NIG
6:53 And **w** they had passed over, they came into NIG
6:54 And **w** they were come out of the ship, NIG
7: 2 And **w** they saw some of his disciples eat NIG
7: 4 And **w** *they come* from the market, NIG
7:14 And **w** he had called all the people unto NIG
7:17 And **w** he was entered into *the* house from *3753*
7:30 And **w** she was come to her house, NIG
8:17 And **w** Jesus knew *it,* he saith unto them, NIG
8:19 **W** I brake the five loaves among five *3753*
8:20 And **w** the seven among four thousand, *3753*
8:23 and **w** he had spit on his eyes, and put *his* NIG
8:33 But **w** he had turned about and looked on NIG
8:34 And **w** he had called the people unto *him* NIG
8:38 **w** he cometh in the glory of his Father with *3752*
9: 8 **w** they had looked round about, NIG
9:14 And **w** he came to *his* disciples, he saw a NIG
9:15 **w** they beheld him, were greatly amazed, NIG
9:20 and **w** he saw him, straightway the spirit NIG
9:25 **W** Jesus saw that the people came running *1161*
9:28 And **w** he was come into *the* house, NIG
9:36 and **w** he had taken him in his arms, he said NIG
10:14 But **w** Jesus saw *it,* he was much displeased, NIG
10:17 And **w** he was gone forth into the way, NIG
10:41 And **w** the ten heard *it,* they began to be NIG
10:47 And **w** he heard that it was Jesus of NIG
11: 1 And **w** they came nigh to Jerusalem, *3753*
11:11 **w** he had looked round about upon all NIG
11:12 **w** they were come from Bethany, he was NIG
11:13 and **w** he came to it, he found nothing but NIG
11:19 And **w** even was come, he went out of *3753*
11:24 **w** ye pray, believe that ye receive *them,* and NIG
11:25 And **w** ye stand praying, forgive, if ye have *3752*
12:14 And **w** they were come, they say unto him, NIG
12:23 the resurrection therefore, **w** they shall rise, *3752*
12:25 For **w** they shall rise from the dead, *3752*
12:34 And **w** Jesus saw that he answered NIG
13: 4 Tell us, **w** shall these *things* be? and *4219*
13: 4 what *shall be* the sign **w** all these *things* *3752*
13: 7 And **w** ye shall hear of wars and rumours of *3752*
13:11 But **w** they shall lead *you,* and deliver you *3752*
13:14 But **w** ye shall see the abomination of *3752*
13:28 **W** her branch is yet tender, and *3752*
13:29 **w** ye shall see these *things* come to pass, *3752*
13:33 and pray: for ye know not **w** the time is. *4219*
13:35 for ye know not **w** the master of the house *4219*
14:11 And **w** they heard *it,* they were glad, and NIG
14:12 **w** they killed the passover, his disciples *3753*
14:23 and **w** he had given thanks, he gave *it* to NIG
14:26 And **w** they had sung a hymn, they went out NIG
14:40 And **w** he returned, he found them asleep NIG
14:67 And **w** she saw Peter warming himself, NIG
14:72 And **w** he thought thereon, he wept. NIG
15:15 **w** he had scourged *him,* to be crucified. NIG
15:20 And **w** they had mocked him, they took off *3753*
15:24 And **w** they had crucified him, they parted NIG
15:33 And **w** the sixth hour was come, there was NIG
15:35 **w** they heard *it,* said, Behold, he calleth NIG
15:39 And **w** the centurion, which stood over NIG
15:41 (Who also, **w** he was in Galilee, *3753*
15:42 And now **w** the even was come, because NIG
15:45 And **w** he knew *it* of the centurion, he gave NIG
16: 1 And **w** the sabbath was past, NIG
16: 4 And **w** they looked, they saw that the stone NIG
16: 9 Now **w** *Jesus* was risen early the first *day* of NIG
16:11 **w** they had heard that he was alive, and NIG
Lk 1: 9 his lot was to burn incense **w** he went into NIG
1:12 And **w** Zacharias saw *him,* he was troubled, NIG
1:22 And **w** he came out, he could not speak unto NIG
1:29 And **w** she saw *him,* she was troubled at his NIG
1:41 And it came to pass *that,* **w** Elisabeth heard *5613*
2: 2 (*And* this taxing was first made **w** Cyrenius NIG
2:17 And **w** they had seen *it,* they made known NIG
2:21 And **w** eight days were accomplished for *3753*
2:22 And **w** the days of her purification *3753*
2:27 **w** the parents brought in the child *1722+3588*
2:39 And **w** they had performed all *things* *5613*
2:42 And **w** he was twelve years old, they went *3753*
2:43 And **w** they had fulfilled the days, as they NIG
2:45 And **w** they found him not, they turned back NIG
2:48 And **w** they saw him, they were amazed: NIG
3:21 Now **w** all the people were baptized, *1722+3588*
4: 2 and **w** they were ended, he afterward NIG
4:13 And **w** the devil had ended all NIG
4:17 And **w** he had opened the book, he found NIG
4:25 **w** the heaven was shut up three years and *3753*
4:25 **w** great famine was throughout all the land; *5613*
4:28 **w** they heard these *things,* were filled with NIG
4:35 And **w** the devil had thrown him in NIG
4:40 Now **w** the sun was setting, all they that had NIG
4:42 And **w** it was day, he departed and NIG
5: 4 Now **w** he had left speaking, he said unto *5613*

Lk 5: 6 And **w** they had this done, they inclosed a NIG
5: 8 **W** Simon Peter saw *it,* he fell down at *1161*
5:11 And **w** they had brought *their* ships to land, NIG
5:12 to pass, **w** he was in a certain city, *1722+3588*
5:19 And **w** they could not find by what *way* NIG
5:20 And **w** he saw their faith, he said unto him, NIG
5:22 But **w** Jesus perceived their thoughts, NIG
5:35 **w** the bridegroom shall be taken away from *3752*
6: 3 **w** himself was a hungred, and they which *3698*
6:13 And **w** it was day, he called unto *him* his *3753*
6:22 **w** men shall hate you, and when they shall *3752*
6:22 **w** they shall separate you *from their* *3752*
6:26 **w** all men shall speak well of you: *3752*
6:42 **w** thou thyself beholdest not the beam that NIG
6:48 and **w** the flood arose, the stream beat NIG
7: 1 Now **w** he had ended all his sayings in *1893*
7: 3 And **w** he heard of Jesus, he sent unto him NIG
7: 4 And **w** they came to Jesus, they besought NIG
7: 6 And **w** he was now not far from the house, NIG
7: 9 **W** Jesus heard these *things,* he marvelled at *1161*
7:12 Now **w** he came nigh to the gate of the city, *5613*
7:13 And **w** the Lord saw her, he had compassion NIG
7:20 **W** the men were come unto him, they said, *1161*
7:24 And **w** the messengers of John were NIG
7:37 **w** she knew that *Jesus* sat at meat in NIG
7:39 Now **w** the Pharisee which had bidden him NIG
7:42 And **w** they had nothing to pay, he frankly NIG
8: 4 And **w** much people were gathered together, NIG
8: 8 And **w** he had said these *things,* he cried, NIG
8:13 **w** they hear, receive the word with joy; *3752*
8:14 which, **w** they have heard, go *forth,* and NIG
8:16 No *man,* **w** he hath lighted a candle, NIG
8:27 And **w** he went forth to land, there met him NIG
8:28 **W** he saw Jesus, he cried out, and fell down *1161*
8:34 **W** they that fed *them* saw what was done, *1161*
8:40 to pass that, **w** Jesus was returned, *1722+3588*
8:45 **W** all denied, Peter and they that were with *1161*
8:47 And **w** the woman saw that she was not hid, NIG
8:50 But **w** Jesus heard *it,* he answered him, NIG
8:51 And **w** he came into the house, he suffered NIG
9: 5 not receive you, **w** ye go out of that city, NIG
9:10 And the apostles, **w** they were returned, NIG
9:11 the people, **w** they knew *it,* followed him: NIG
9:12 And **w** the day began to wear away, then NIG
9:26 **w** he shall come in his own glory, and *in* *3752*
9:32 and **w** they were awake, they saw his glory, NIG
9:36 And **w** the voice was past, Jesus was *1722+3588*
9:37 **w** they were come down from the hill, NIG
9:51 **w** the time was come that he should *1722+3588*
9:54 And **w** his disciples James and John saw NIG
10:31 and **w** he saw him, he passed by on NIG
10:32 **w** he was at the place, came and looked *on* NIG
10:33 and **w** he saw him, he had compassion *on* NIG
10:35 And on the morrow **w** he departed, he took NIG
10:35 **w** I come again, I will repay thee. *1722+3588*
11: 1 **w** he ceased, one of his disciples said unto *5613*
11: 2 And he said unto them, **W** ye pray, say, *3752*
11:14 **w** the devil was gone out, the dumb spake; NIG
11:21 **W** a strong *man* armed keepeth his palace, *3752*
11:22 But **w** a stronger than he shall come upon *1875*
11:24 **W** the unclean spirit is gone out of a man, *3752*
11:25 And **w** he cometh, he findeth *it* swept and NIG
11:29 And **w** the people were gathered thick NIG
11:33 No *man,* **w** he hath lighted a candle, NIG
11:34 therefore **w** thine eye is single, thy whole *3752*
11:34 but **w** *thine eye* is evil, thy body also *is* full *1875*
11:36 as **w** the bright shining of a candle doth *3752*
11:38 And **w** the Pharisee saw *it,* he marvelled NIG
12: 1 **w** there were gathered together an NIG
12:11 And **w** they bring you unto the synagogues, *3752*
12:36 **w** he will return from the wedding; *4219*
12:36 that **w** *he* cometh and knocketh, they may NIG
12:37 whom the lord **w** he cometh shall find NIG
12:40 for the Son of man cometh at an hour **w** ye *3739*
12:43 whom his lord **w** he cometh shall find so NIG
12:46 come in a day **w** he looketh not for *him,* *3739*
12:46 for *him,* and at an hour **w** he is not ware, *3739*
12:54 **W** ye see a cloud rise out of the west, *3752*
12:55 And **w** *ye see* the south wind blow, ye say, *3752*
12:58 **W** thou goest with thine adversary to *1063+5613*
13:12 And **w** Jesus saw her, he called *her* to *him,* NIG
13:17 And **w** he had said these *things,* all his NIG
13:25 **W** once the master of the house is risen up, NIG
13:28 **w** ye shall see Abraham, and Isaac, and *3752*
13:35 see me, until *the time* come **w** ye shall say, *3753*
14: 7 **w** he marked how they chose out the chief NIG
14: 8 **W** thou art bidden of any *man* to a *3752*
14:10 But **w** thou art bidden, go and sit down in *3752*
14:10 that **w** he that bade thee cometh, he may *3752*
14:12 **W** thou makest a dinner or a supper, *3752*
14:13 But **w** thou makest a feast, call the poor, *3752*
14:15 And **w** one of them that sat at meat with NIG
15: 5 And **w** he hath found *it,* he layeth *it* on his NIG
15: 6 And **w** he cometh home, he calleth together NIG
15: 9 And **w** she hath found *it,* she calleth *her* NIG
15:14 And **w** he had spent all, there arose a NIG
15:17 And **w** he came to himself, he said, How NIG
15:20 But **w** he was yet a great way off, his father NIG
16: 4 that, **w** I am put out of the stewardship, *3752*
16: 9 that, **w** ye fail, they may receive you into *3752*
17: 7 **w** he is come from the field, Go and NIG
17:10 **w** ye shall have done all those *things* which *3752*
17:14 And **w** he saw *them,* he said unto them, NIG
17:15 **w** he saw that he was healed, turned back, NIG
17:20 And **w** he was demanded of the Pharisees, NIG
17:20 **w** the kingdom of God should come, *4219*
17:22 **w** ye shall desire to see one of the days of *3753*
17:30 Even thus shall it be in the day **w** the Son of NIG
18: 8 Nevertheless **w** the Son of man cometh, NIG
18:15 **w** *his* disciples saw *it,* they rebuked them. NIG
18:22 Now **w** Jesus heard these *things,* he said NIG
18:23 And **w** he heard this, he was very sorrowful: NIG
18:24 And **w** Jesus saw that he was very NIG
18:40 and **w** he was come near, he asked him, NIG
18:43 **w** they saw *it,* gave praise unto God. NIG

Lk 19: 5 And **w** Jesus came to the place, he looked *5613*
19: 7 And **w** they saw *it,* they all murmured, NIG
19:15 came to pass, that **w** he was returned, *1722+3588*
19:28 And **w** he had thus spoken, he went before, NIG
19:29 **w** he was come nigh to Bethphage and *5613*
19:37 And **w** he was come nigh, *even* now at NIG
19:41 And **w** he was come near, he beheld *5613*
20:13 it may be they will reverence *him* **w** they NIG
20:14 But **w** the husbandmen saw him, NIG
20:16 And **w** they heard *it,* they said, God forbid. NIG
20:37 **w** he calleth the Lord the God of Abraham, *5613*
21: 7 Master, but **w** shall these *things* be? *4219*
21: 7 what sign *will there be* **w** these *things* shall *3752*
21: 9 But **w** ye shall hear of wars and *3752*
21:20 And **w** ye shall see Jerusalem compassed *3752*
21:28 And **w** these *things* begin to come to pass, NIG
21:30 **W** they now shoot forth, ye see and *3752*
21:31 **w** ye see these *things* come to pass, *3752*
22: 7 **w** the passover must be killed. *1722+3739*
22:10 Behold, **w** ye are entered into the city, NIG
22:14 And **w** the hour was come, he sat down, *3753*
22:32 and **w** thou art converted, strengthen thy *4218*
22:35 **W** I sent you without purse, and scrip, and *3753*
22:40 And **w** he was at the place, he said unto NIG
22:45 And **w** he rose up from prayer, and NIG
22:49 **W** they which were about him saw what *1161*
22:53 **W** I was daily with you in the temple, NIG
22:55 And **w** they had kindled a fire in the midst NIG
22:64 And **w** they had blindfolded him, NIG
23: 6 **W** Pilate heard of Galilee, he asked *1161*
23: 8 And **w** Herod saw Jesus, he was exceeding NIG
23:13 **w** he had called together the chief priests NIG
23:33 And **w** they were come to the place, *3753*
23:42 remember me **w** thou comest into thy *3752*
23:46 And **w** Jesus had cried with a loud voice, NIG
23:47 Now **w** the centurion saw what was done, NIG
24: 6 remember how he spake unto you **w** he was NIG
24:23 And **w** they found not his body, they came, NIG
24:40 And **w** he had thus spoken, he shewed them NIG
Jn 1:19 **w** the Jews sent priests and Levites from *3753*
1:42 And **w** Jesus beheld him, he said, Thou art NIG
1:48 **w** thou wast under the fig tree, I saw thee. NIG
2: 3 And **w** they wanted wine, the mother of NIG
2: 9 **W** the ruler of the feast had tasted *1161+5613*
2:10 and **w** *men* have well drunk, then *3752*
2:15 And **w** he had made a scourge of small NIG
2:22 **W** therefore he was risen from the dead, *3753*
2:23 Now **w** he was in Jerusalem at *5613*
2:23 **w** they saw the miracles which he did. NIG
3: 4 How can a man be born **w** he is old? NIG
4: 1 **W** therefore the Lord knew how *5613*
4:21 **w** ye shall neither in this mountain, *3753*
4:23 **w** the true worshippers shall worship *3753*
4:25 **w** he is come, he will tell us all *things.* *3752*
4:40 So **w** the Samaritans were come unto him, *5613*
4:45 Then **w** he was come into Galilee, *3753*
4:47 **W** he heard that Jesus was come out of NIG
4:52 Then inquired he of them the hour **w** *1722+3739*
4:54 **w** he was come out of Judea into Galilee. NIG
5: 6 **W** Jesus saw him lie, and knew that he had NIG
5: 7 Sir, I have no man, **w** the water is troubled, *3752*
5:25 **w** the dead shall hear the voice of the Son *3753*
6: 5 **W** Jesus then lift up *his* eyes, NIG
6:11 and **w** he had given thanks, he distributed to NIG
6:12 **W** they were filled, he said unto his *5613*
6:14 **w** they had seen the miracle that Jesus did, NIG
6:15 **W** Jesus therefore perceived that they NIG
6:16 And **w** even was *now* come, his disciples *5613*
6:19 So **w** they had rowed about five and twenty *5613*
6:22 **w** the people which stood on the other side NIG
6:24 **W** the people therefore saw that Jesus was *3753*
6:25 And **w** they had found him on the other side NIG
6:25 unto him, Rabbi, **w** camest thou hither? *4219*
6:60 of his disciples, **w** they had heard *this,* said, NIG
6:61 **W** Jesus knew in himself that his disciples *1161*
7: 9 **W** he had said these *words* unto them, *1161*
7:10 But **w** his brethren were gone up, then *5613*
7:27 but **w** Christ cometh, no *man* knoweth *3752*
7:31 on him, and said, **W** Christ cometh, *3752*
7:40 **w** they heard *this* saying, said, Of a truth NIG
8: 3 and **w** they had set her in the midst, NIG
8: 7 So **w** they continued asking him, he lift up *5613*
8:10 **W** Jesus had lift up *himself,* and saw none *1161*
8:28 **W** ye have lift up the Son of man, then *3752*
8:44 **W** he speaketh a lie, he speaketh of his *3752*
9: 4 the night cometh, **w** no *man* can work. *3753*
9: 6 **W** he had thus spoken, he spat on NIG
9:14 And it was the sabbath day **w** Jesus made *3753*
9:35 and **w** he had found him, he said unto him, NIG
10: 4 And **w** he putteth forth his own sheep, he *3752*
11: 4 **W** Jesus heard *that,* he said, This sickness *1161*
11: 6 **W** he had heard therefore that he was sick, *5613*
11:17 Then **w** Jesus came, he found that he had NIG
11:28 And **w** she had so said, she went her way, NIG
11:31 and comforted her, **w** they saw Mary, NIG
11:32 Then **w** Mary was come where Jesus was, *5613*
11:33 **W** Jesus therefore saw her weeping, and *5613*
11:43 And **w** he thus had spoken, he cried with a NIG
12:12 **w** they heard that Jesus was coming to NIG
12:14 And Jesus, **w** he had found a young ass, NIG
12:16 but **w** Jesus was glorified, then *3753*
12:17 that was with him **w** he called Lazarus out *3753*
12:41 **w** he saw his glory, and spake of him. *3753*
13: 1 **w** Jesus knew that his hour was come that NIG
13:19 that, **w** it is come to pass, ye may believe *3752*
13:21 **W** Jesus had thus said, he was troubled in NIG
13:26 **w** I have dipped *it.* And when he had dipped NIG
13:26 when I have dipped *it.* And **w** he had dipped NIG
13:31 Therefore, **w** he was gone out, Jesus said, *3753*
14:29 that, **w** it is come to pass, ye might believe. *3752*
15:26 But **w** the Comforter is come, whom I will *3752*
16: 4 have I told you, that **w** the time shall come, *3752*
16: 8 And **w** he is come, he will reprove NIG
16:13 Howbeit **w** he, the Spirit of truth, is come, *3752*
16:21 A woman **w** she is in travail hath sorrow, *3752*
16:25 **w** I shall no more speak unto you in *3753*
18: 1 **W** Jesus had spoken these *words,* he went NIG
18:22 And **w** he had thus spoken, one of NIG
18:38 And **w** he had said this, he went out again NIG
19: 6 **W** the chief priests therefore and officers *3753*
19: 8 **W** Pilate therefore heard that saying, *3753*
19:13 **W** Pilate therefore heard that saying, NIG
19:23 the soldiers, **w** they had crucified Jesus, *3753*
19:26 **W** Jesus therefore saw *his* mother, and NIG
19:30 **W** Jesus therefore had received the vinegar, *3753*
19:33 But **w** they came to Jesus, and saw that he NIG
20: 1 **w** it was yet dark, unto the sepulchre, and NIG
20:14 And **w** she had thus said, she turned herself NIG
20:19 **w** the doors were shut where the disciples NIG
20:20 And **w** he had so said, he shewed unto them NIG
20:20 the disciples glad, **w** they saw the Lord. NIG
20:22 And **w** he had said this, he breathed on NIG
20:24 was not with them **w** Jesus came. *3753*
21: 4 But **w** the morning was now come, NIG
21: 7 Now **w** Simon Peter heard that it was NIG
21:15 So **w** they had dined, Jesus saith to Simon *3753*
21:18 verily, I say unto thee, **W** thou wast young, *3753*
21:18 but **w** thou shalt be old, thou shalt stretch *3752*
21:19 And **w** he had spoken this, he saith unto NIG
Ac 1: 6 **W** they therefore were come together, NIG
1: 9 And **w** he had spoken these *things,* while NIG
1:13 And **w** they were come in, they went up *3753*
2: 1 And **w** the day of Pentecost was fully *1722+3588*
2: 6 Now **w** this was noised abroad, NIG
2:37 Now **w** they heard *this,* they were pricked in NIG
3:12 And **w** Peter saw *it,* he answered unto NIG
3:13 **w** he was determined to let *him* go. NIG
3:19 **w** *the* times of refreshing shall come *302+3704*
4: 7 And **w** they had set them in the midst, NIG
4:13 Now **w** they saw the boldness of Peter and NIG
4:15 But **w** they had commanded them to go NIG
4:21 So **w** they had further threatened *them,* they NIG
4:24 And **w** they heard *that,* they lift up their NIG
4:31 And **w** they had prayed, the place was NIG
5: 7 **w** his wife, not knowing what was done, *2532*
5:21 And **w** they heard *that,* they entered into NIG
5:22 But **w** the officers came, and found them NIG
5:23 but **w** we had opened, we found no *man* NIG
5:24 Now **w** the *high* priest and the captain of *5613*
5:27 And **w** they had brought them, they set *them* NIG
5:33 **W** they heard *that,* they were cut *to* *1161*
5:40 and **w** they had called the apostles, and NIG
6: 1 **w** the number of the disciples was NIG
6: 6 and **w** they had prayed, they laid *their* hands NIG
7: 2 **w** he was in Mesopotamia, before he dwelt NIG
7: 4 and from thence, **w** his father was dead, *3326*
7: 5 his seed after him, **w** *as yet* he had no child. NIG
7:12 But **w** Jacob heard that there was corn in NIG
7:17 But **w** the time of the promise drew nigh, *2531*
7:21 And **w** he was cast out, Pharaoh's daughter NIG
7:23 And **w** he was full forty years old, it came *5613*
7:30 And **w** forty years were expired, NIG
7:31 **W** Moses saw *it,* he wondered at the sight: *1161*
7:54 **W** they heard these *things,* they were cut to *1161*
7:60 And **w** he had said this, he fell asleep. NIG
8:12 But **w** they believed Philip preaching *3753*
8:13 and **w** he was baptized, he continued with NIG
8:14 Now **w** the apostles which were at NIG
8:15 Who, **w** they were come down, prayed for NIG
8:18 And **w** Simon saw that through laying on of NIG
8:25 **w** they had testified and preached the word *3767*
8:39 And **w** they were come up out of the water, *3753*
9: 8 and **w** his eyes were opened, he saw no NIG
9:19 And **w** he had received meat, he was NIG
9:26 And **w** Saul was come to Jerusalem, NIG
9:30 Which **w** the brethren knew, they brought NIG
9:37 whom **w** they had washed, they laid *her* in *1161*
9:39 **W** he was come, they brought him into NIG
9:40 her eyes: and **w** she saw Peter, she sat up. NIG
9:41 and **w** he had called the saints and widows, NIG
10: 4 And **w** he looked on him, he was afraid, and NIG
10: 7 And **w** the angel which spake unto *5613*
10: 8 And **w** he had declared all *these things* unto NIG
10:32 who, **w** he cometh, shall speak unto thee. NIG
11: 2 And **w** Peter was come up to Jerusalem, *3753*
11: 6 Upon the which **w** I had fastened mine eyes, NIG
11:18 **W** they heard these *things,* they held their *1161*
11:20 which, **w** they were come to Antioch, NIG
11:23 **w** he came, and had seen the grace of God, NIG
11:26 And **w** he had found him, he brought him NIG
12: 4 And **w** he had apprehended him, he put *him* NIG
12: 6 And **w** Herod would have brought him *3753*
12:10 **W** they were past the first and the second *1161*
12:11 And **w** Peter was come to himself, he said, NIG
12:12 And **w** he had considered *the thing,* he came NIG
12:14 And **w** she knew Peter's voice, she opened NIG
12:16 and **w** they had opened *the door,* and NIG
12:19 And **w** Herod had sought for him, and NIG
12:25 **w** they had fulfilled *their* ministry, and NIG
13: 3 And **w** they had fasted and prayed, and *5119*
13: 5 And **w** they were at Salamis, they preached NIG
13: 6 And **w** they had gone through the isle unto NIG
13:12 **w** he saw what was done, believed, NIG
13:13 Now **w** Paul and his company loosed from NIG
13:14 But **w** they departed from Perga, they came NIG
13:17 exalted the people **w** *they* dwelt as *1722*
13:19 And **w** he had destroyed seven nations in NIG
13:22 And **w** he had removed him, he raised up NIG
13:24 **W** John had first preached before his NIG
13:29 And **w** they had fulfilled all that was *5613*
13:42 And **w** the Jews were gone out of NIG
13:43 Now **w** the congregation was broken up, NIG
13:45 But **w** the Jews saw the multitudes, NIG
13:48 And **w** the Gentiles heard *this,* they were NIG
14: 5 And **w** there was an assault made both of *5613*
14:11 And **w** the people saw what Paul had done, NIG
14:14 *Which* **w** the apostles, Barnabas and Paul, *1161*
14:21 And **w** they had preached the gospel to that NIG
14:23 And **w** they had ordained them elders in NIG
14:25 And **w** they had preached the word in Perga, NIG
Ac 14:27 And **w** they were come, and had gathered NIG
15: 2 **W** therefore Paul and Barnabas had no NIG
15: 4 And **w** they were come to Jerusalem, NIG
15: 7 And **w** there had been much disputing, Peter NIG
15:30 So **w** they were dismissed, they came to NIG
15:30 **w** they had gathered the multitude together, NIG
15:31 *Which* **w** they had read, they rejoiced for *1161*
16: 6 Now **w** they had gone throughout Phrygia NIG
16:15 And **w** she was baptized, and *5613*
16:19 And **w** her masters saw that the hope of NIG
16:23 And **w** they had laid many stripes upon NIG
16:34 And **w** he had brought them into his house, NIG
16:35 And **w** it was day, the magistrates sent NIG
16:38 **w** they heard that they were Romans, NIG
16:40 and **w** they had seen the brethren, NIG
17: 1 Now **w** they had passed through NIG
17: 6 And **w** they found them not, they drew NIG
17: 8 rulers of the city, **w** they heard these *things.* NIG
17: 9 And **w** they had taken security of Jason, and NIG
17:13 But **w** the Jews of Thessalonica had *5613*
17:16 **w** he saw the city wholly given to idolatry. NIG
17:32 And **w** they heard of the resurrection of NIG
18: 5 And **w** Silas and Timotheus were come *5613*
18: 6 And **w** they opposed themselves, and NIG
18:12 And **w** Gallio was the deputy of Achaia, NIG
18:14 And **w** Paul was *now* about to open *his* NIG
18:20 **W** they desired *him* to tarry longer time *1161*
18:22 And **w** he had landed at Cesarea, and NIG
18:26 whom **w** Aquila and Priscilla had heard, NIG
18:27 And **w** he was disposed to pass into Achaia, NIG
18:27 who, **w** he was come, helped them much NIG
19: 5 **W** they heard *this,* they were baptized in *1161*
19: 6 And **w** Paul had laid *his* hands upon them, NIG
19: 9 But **w** divers were hardened, and *5613*
19:21 **w** he had passed through Macedonia and NIG
19:28 And **w** they heard *these sayings,* they were NIG
19:30 And **w** Paul would have entered in unto NIG
19:34 But **w** *they* knew that he was a Jew, all with NIG
19:35 And **w** the townclerk had appeased NIG
19:41 And **w** he had thus spoken, he dismissed NIG
20: 2 And **w** he had gone over those parts, and NIG
20: 3 and **w** the Jews laid wait for him, as he was NIG
20: 7 **w** the disciples came together to break NIG
20:11 **W** he therefore was come up *again,* and NIG
20:14 And **w** he met with us at Assos, we took *5613*
20:18 And **w** they were come to him, he said unto *5613*
20:36 And **w** he had thus spoken, he kneeled NIG
21: 3 Now **w** we had discovered Cyprus, we left it NIG
21: 5 And **w** we had accomplished *those* days, *3753*
21: 6 And **w** we had taken our leave one of NIG
21: 7 And **w** we had finished *our* course from NIG
21:11 And **w** he was come unto us, he took Paul's NIG
21:12 And **w** we heard these *things,* both we, and *5613*
21:14 And **w** he would not be persuaded, NIG
21:17 And **w** we were come to Jerusalem, NIG
21:19 And **w** he had saluted them, he declared NIG
21:20 And **w** they heard *it,* they glorified the Lord, NIG
21:27 And **w** the seven days were almost ended, *5613*
21:27 **w** they saw him in the temple, stirred up all NIG
21:32 and **w** they saw the chief captain and NIG
21:34 **w** he could not know the certainty for NIG
21:35 And **w** he came upon the stairs, so it was, *3753*
21:40 And **w** he had given *him* licence, Paul stood NIG
21:40 And **w** there was made a great silence, NIG
22: 2 (And **w** they heard that he spake in NIG
22:11 And **w** I could not see for the glory of that *5613*
22:17 pass that, **w** I was come again to Jerusalem, NIG
22:20 And **w** the blood of thy martyr Stephen was *3753*
22:26 **W** the centurion heard *that,* he went and NIG
23: 6 But **w** Paul perceived that the one part were NIG
23: 7 And **w** he had so said, there arose a NIG
23:10 And **w** there arose a great dissension, NIG
23:12 And **w** it was day, certain of the Jews NIG
23:16 And **w** Paul's sister's son heard of *their* NIG
23:28 And **w** I would have known the cause NIG
23:30 And **w** it was told me how that the Jews laid NIG
23:33 **w** they came to Cesarea, and delivered NIG
23:34 And **w** the governor had read *the letter,* he NIG
23:34 And **w** he understood that *he was* of Cilicia; NIG
23:35 said he, **w** thine accusers are also come. *3752*
24: 2 And **w** he was called *forth,* Tertullus began NIG
24:22 And **w** Felix heard these *things,* having NIG
24:22 **W** Lysias the chief captain shall come *3752*
24:24 **w** Felix came with his wife Drusilla, NIG
24:25 **w** I have a convenient season, I will call for *1161*
25: 1 Now **w** Festus was come into the province, NIG
25: 6 And **w** he had tarried among them more NIG
25: 7 And **w** he was come, the Jews which came NIG
25:12 **w** he had conferred with the council, NIG
25:14 And **w** they had been there many days, *5613*
25:15 About whom, **w** I was at Jerusalem, NIG
25:17 Therefore, **w** they were come hither, NIG
25:18 Against whom **w** the accusers stood *up,* NIG
25:21 But **w** Paul had appealed to be reserved NIG
25:23 **w** Agrippa was come, and Bernice, NIG
25:25 But **w** I found that he had committed NIG
26:10 and **w** they were put to death, I gave my NIG
26:14 And **w** we were all fallen to the earth, NIG
26:30 And **w** he had thus spoken, the king rose up, NIG
26:31 And **w** they were gone aside, they talked NIG
27: 1 And **w** it was determined that we should *5613*
27: 4 And **w** we had launched from thence, NIG
27: 5 And **w** we had sailed over the sea of Cilicia NIG
27: 7 And **w** we had sailed slowly many days, and NIG
27: 9 Now **w** much time was spent, and NIG
27: 9 and **w** sailing was now dangerous, because NIG
27:13 And **w** the south wind blew softly, NIG
27:15 And **w** the ship was caught, and could not NIG
27:17 Which **w** they had taken up, they used NIG
27:20 And **w** neither sun nor stars in many days NIG
27:27 But **w** the fourteenth night was come, as we *5613*
27:28 and **w** they had gone a little further, NIG
27:30 **w** they had let down the boat into the sea, *2532*
27:35 And **w** he had thus spoken, he took bread, NIG
27:35 and **w** he had broken *it,* he began to eat. NIG

Ac 27:38 And **w** they had eaten enough, NIG
27:39 And **w** it was day, they knew not the land: *3753*
27:40 And **w** they had taken up the anchors, NIG
28: 1 And **w** they were escaped, then they knew NIG
28: 3 And **w** Paul had gathered a bundle of sticks, NIG
28: 4 And **w** the barbarians saw the *venomous* *5613*
28: 6 Howbeit they looked **w** he should have NIG
28: 9 So **w** this was done, others also, which had NIG
28:10 and **w** we departed, they laded *us* with such NIG
28:15 from thence, **w** the brethren heard of us, NIG
28:15 whom **w** Paul saw, he thanked God, and NIG
28:16 And **w** we came to Rome, the centurion *3753*
28:17 and **w** they were come together, he said NIG
28:18 Who, **w** they had examined me, would have NIG
28:19 But **w** the Jews spake against *it,* I was NIG
28:23 And **w** they had appointed him a day, NIG
28:25 And **w** they agreed not among themselves, NIG
28:29 And **w** he had said these *words,* the Jews NIG
Ro 1:21 Because that, **w** they knew God, NIG
2:14 For **w** *the* Gentiles, which have not the law, *3752*
2:16 In the day **w** God shall judge the secrets of *3753*
3: 4 overcome **w** thou art judged. *1722+3588*
4:10 **w** he was in circumcision, or NIG
4:19 **w** he was about an hundred year old, NIG
5: 6 For **w** we were yet without strength, in due NIG
5:10 For if, **w** we were enemies, we were NIG
5:13 but sin is not imputed **w** there is no law. NIG
6:20 For **w** ye were the servants of sin, ye were *3753*
7: 5 For **w** we were in the flesh, the motions of *3753*
7: 9 but **w** the commandment came, sin revived, NIG
7:21 I find then a law, that, **w** I would do good, NIG
9:10 but **w** Rebecca also had conceived by one, NIG
11:27 unto them, **w** I shall take away their sins. *3752*
13:11 for now *is* our salvation nearer than **w** we *3753*
15:28 **W** therefore I have performed this, and NIG
15:29 And I am sure that, **w** I come unto you, NIG
1Co 2: 1 And I, brethren, **w** I came to you, came not NIG
5: 4 **w** ye are gathered together, and my spirit, NIG
8:12 But **w** ye sin so against the brethren, and NIG
9:18 *Verily* that, **w** I preach the gospel, I may NIG
9:27 by any means, **w** I have preached to others, NIG
11:18 of all, **w** ye come together in the church, NIG
11:20 **W** ye come together therefore into one NIG
11:24 And **w** he had given thanks, he brake *it,* and NIG
11:25 **w** *he* had supped, saying, This cup is *3326+3588*
11:32 But **w** we are judged, we are chastened of NIG
11:33 my brethren, **w** ye come together to eat, NIG
11:34 the rest will I set in order **w** I come. *302+5613*
13:10 But **w** *that which is* perfect is come, then *3752*
13:11 **W** I was a child, I spake as a child, *3753*
13:11 but **w** I became a man, I put away childish *3753*
14:16 Else **w** thou shalt bless with the spirit, *1437*
14:26 **w** ye come together, every one of you hath *3752*
15:24 **w** he shall have delivered up the kingdom *3752*
15:24 **w** he shall have put down all rule and *3752*
15:27 But **w** *he* saith, all *things* are put under *him,* *3752*
15:28 And **w** all *things* shall be subdued unto *3752*
15:54 So **w** this corruptible shall have put on *3752*
16: 2 that there be no gatherings **w** I come. *3752*
16: 3 And **w** I come, whomsoever you shall *3752*
16: 5 **w** I shall pass through Macedonia: *3752*
16:12 he will come **w** he shall have convenient *3752*
2Co 1:17 **W** I therefore was thus minded, did I use NIG
2: 3 I wrote this same unto you, lest, **w** I came, NIG
2:12 **w** I came to Troas to *preach* Christ's gospel, NIG
3:15 But *even* unto this day, **w** Moses is *302+2259*
3:16 Nevertheless **w** *it* shall turn to *302+2259*
7: 5 For, **w** we were come into Macedonia, NIG
7: 7 **w** he told us your earnest desire, your NIG
10: 2 But I beseech *you,* that I may not be bold **w** NIG
10: 6 **w** your obedience is fulfilled. *3752*
10:11 such as we are in word by letters **w** we are NIG
10:11 such *will we be* also in deed **w** we are NIG
10:15 but having hope, **w** your faith is increased, NIG
11: 9 And **w** I was present with you, and wanted, NIG
12:10 for **w** I am weak, then am I strong. *3752*
12:20 For I fear, lest, **w** I come, I shall not find NIG
12:21 *And* lest, **w** I come again, my God will NIG
13: 9 are glad, **w** we are weak, and ye are strong: *3752*
Gal 1:15 But **w** it pleased God, who separated me *3753*
2: 7 **w** they saw that the gospel of NIG
2: 9 And **w** James, Cephas, and John, NIG
2:11 But **w** Peter was come to Antioch, *3753*
2:12 but **w** they were come, he withdrew and *3753*
2:14 But **w** I saw that they walked not uprightly *3753*
4: 3 Even so we, **w** we were children, were in *3753*
4: 4 But **w** the fulness of the time was come, *3753*
4: 8 Howbeit then, **w** ye knew not God, ye did NIG
4:18 and not only **w** I am present with you. *1722*
6: 3 **w** he is nothing, he deceiveth himself. NIG
Eph 1:20 **w** he raised him from the dead, and set *him* NIG
2: 5 Even **w** we were dead in sins, NIG
3: 4 Whereby, **w** ye read, ye may understand my NIG
4: 8 *he* saith, **W** he ascended up on high, NIG
Php 2:19 be of good comfort, **w** I know your state. NIG
2:28 that, **w** ye see him again, ye may rejoice, NIG
4:15 the gospel, **w** I departed from Macedonia, *3753*
Col 3: 4 **W** Christ, *who is* our life, shall appear, then *3752*
3: 7 also walked sometime, **w** ye lived in them. *3753*
4:16 And **w** *this* epistle is read amongst you, *3752*
1Th 2: 6 **w** we might have been burdensome, NIG
2:13 **w** ye received the word of God which *ye* NIG
3: 1 Wherefore **w** we could no longer forbear, NIG
3: 4 For verily, **w** we were with you, we told *3753*
3: 5 For this cause, **w** I could no longer forbear, *2504*
3: 6 But now **w** Timotheus came from you unto NIG
5: 3 For **w** they shall say, Peace and safety; then *3752*
2Th 1: 7 **w** the Lord Jesus shall be revealed from *1722*
1:10 **W** he shall come to be glorified in his *3752*
2: 5 ye not, that, **w** I was yet with you, NIG
3:10 For even **w** we were with you, this we *3753*
1Ti 1: 3 *still* at Ephesus, **w** I went into Macedonia, NIG
5:11 for **w** they have *begun to* wax wanton *3752*
2Ti 1: 5 **W** I call to remembrance the unfeigned faith NIG
1:17 But, **w** he was in Rome, he sought me out NIG

2Ti 4: 3 For the time will come **w** they will not *3753*
4:13 **w** thou comest, bring *with thee,* and NIG
4: S **w** Paul was brought before Nero the second *3753*
Tit 3:12 **W** I shall send Artemas unto thee, or *3752*
Heb 1: 3 **w** he had by himself purged our sins, NIG
1: 6 **w** he bringeth in the firstbegotten into *3752*
3: 9 **W** your fathers tempted me, proved me, *3757*
3:16 For some, **w** they had heard, did provoke: NIG
5: 7 **w** he had offered up prayers and NIG
5:12 For **w** for the time ye ought to be teachers, *2532*
6:13 For **w** God made promise to Abraham, NIG
7:10 loins of his father, **w** Melchisedec met him. *3753*
7:27 this he did once, **w** he offered up himself. NIG
8: 5 God **w** he was about to make the tabernacle: NIG
8: 8 **w** I will make a new covenant with *2532*
8: 9 **w** I took them by the hand to lead them out NIG
9: 6 Now **w** these *things* were thus ordained, NIG
9:19 For **w** Moses had spoken every precept to NIG
10: 5 Wherefore **w** he cometh into the world, NIG
10: 8 Above **w** he said, Sacrifice and offering and NIG
11: 8 **w** he was called to go out into a place which NIG
11:11 was delivered of a child **w** *she* was past age, NIG
11:17 **w** he was tried, offered up Isaac: NIG
11:21 By faith Jacob, **w** he was a dying, NIG
11:22 By faith Joseph, **w** he died, made mention NIG
11:23 By faith Moses, **w** he was born, was hid NIG
11:24 By faith Moses, **w** he was come to years, NIG
11:31 **w** she had received the spies with peace. NIG
12: 5 nor faint **w** thou art rebuked of him: NIG
12:17 **w** he would have inherited the blessing, NIG
Jas 1: 2 count *it* all joy **w** ye fall into divers *3752*
1:12 for **w** he is tried, he shall receive the crown NIG
1:13 Let no *man* say **w** he is tempted, I am NIG
1:14 **w** he is drawn away of his own lust, and NIG
1:15 Then **w** lust hath conceived, it bringeth NIG
1:15 and sin, **w** it is finished, bringeth forth NIG
2:21 **w** he had offered Isaac his son upon NIG
2:25 **w** she had received the messengers, and NIG
1Pe 1:11 **w** it testified beforehand the sufferings of NIG
2:20 *is it,* if, **w** ye be buffeted for your faults, *2532*
2:20 but if, **w** ye do well, and suffer *for it,* ye NIG
2:23 Who, **w** he was reviled, reviled not again; NIG
2:23 **w** he suffered, he threatened not; but NIG
3:20 **w** once the longsuffering of God waited in *3753*
4: 3 **w** we walked in lasciviousness, lusts, NIG
4:13 that, **w** his glory shall be revealed, ye may *1722*
5: 4 And **w** the chief Shepherd shall appear, NIG
2Pe 1:16 **w** we made known unto you the power and NIG
1:17 **w** there came such a voice to him from NIG
1:18 **w** we were with him in the holy mount. NIG
2:18 For **w** they speak great swelling *words* of NIG
1Jn 2:28 that, **w** he shall appear, we may have *3752*
3: 2 but we know that, **w** he shall appear, *1437*
5: 2 **w** we love God, and keep his *3752*
3Jn 1: 3 **w** *the* brethren came and testified of NIG
Jude 1: 3 **w** I gave all diligence to write unto you of NIG
1: 9 **w** contending with the devil he disputed *3753*
1:12 These are spots in your feasts of charity **w** NIG
Rev 1:17 And **w** I saw him, I fell at his feet as dead. *3753*
4: 9 And **w** *those* beasts give glory and honour *3752*
5: 8 And **w** he had taken the book, the four *3753*
6: 1 And I saw **w** the Lamb opened one of *3753*
6: 3 And **w** he had opened the second seal, *3753*
6: 5 And **w** he had opened the third seal, I heard *3753*
6: 7 And **w** he had opened the fourth seal, *3753*
6: 9 And **w** he had opened the fifth seal, I saw *3753*
6:12 And I beheld **w** he had opened the sixth *3753*
6:13 **w** she is shaken of a mighty wind. NIG
6:14 And the heaven departed as a scrole **w** it is NIG
8: 1 And **w** he had opened the seventh seal, *3753*
9: 5 torment of a scorpion, **w** he striketh a man. *3752*
10: 3 cried with a loud voice, as **w** a lion roareth: NIG
10: 3 and **w** he had cried, seven thunders uttered *3753*
10: 4 And **w** the seven thunders had uttered their *3753*
10: 7 **w** he shall begin to sound, the mystery of *3752*
11: 7 And **w** they shall have finished their *3752*
12:13 And **w** the dragon saw that he was cast unto *3753*
17: 6 and **w** I saw her, I wondered *with* great NIG
17: 8 **w** they behold the beast that was, and is not, NIG
17:10 and **w** he cometh, he must continue a short *3752*
18: 9 **w** they shall see the smoke of her burning, *3752*
18:18 And cried **w** they saw the smoke of her NIG
20: 7 And **w** the thousand years are expired, *3752*
22: 8 and heard *them.* And **w** I had heard and *3753*

WHENCE (72)

Ge 3:23 till the ground from **w** he was taken. 834+8033
16: 8 Sarai's maid, **w** camest thou? 335+2088+4480
24: 5 again unto the land from **w** thou camest? 8033
29: 4 said unto them, My brethren, **w** *be* ye? 370+4480
42: 7 and he said unto them, **W** come ye? 370+4480
Nu 11:13 **W** should I have flesh to give unto all 370+4480
23:13 from **w** thou mayest see them: 8033
Dt 9:28 Lest the land **w** thou broughtest 834+4480+8033
11:10 land of Egypt, from **w** ye came out, 834+8033
Jos 2: 4 unto me, but I wist not **w** they *were:* 370+4480
9: 8 Who *are* ye? and from **w** come ye? 370
20: 6 own house, unto the city from **w** he fled. 8033
Jdg 13: 6 I asked him not **w** he *was,* 335+2088+4480
17: 9 Micah said unto him, **W** comest thou? 370+4480
19:17 goest thou? and **w** comest thou? 370+4480
1Sa 25:11 whom I know not **w** they *be?* 335+2088+4480
30:13 **w** *art* thou? And he said, I *am* a 335+2088+4480
2Sa 1: 3 **From w** comest thou? 335+2088+4480
1:13 man that told him, **W** *art* thou? 335+2088+4480
2Ki 5:25 unto him, **W** *comest thou,* Gehazi? 370+4480
6:27 *If* the LORD do not help thee, **w** 370+4480
20:14 from **w** came they unto thee? And Hezekiah 370
Ne 4:12 From all places **w** ye shall return unto us 834
Job 1: 7 said unto Satan, **W** comest thou? 370+4480
2: 2 **From w** comest thou? 335+2088+4480
10:21 Before I go **w** I shall not return, *even* to NIH
16:22 then I shall go the way **w** I shall not return. NIH
28:20 **W** then cometh wisdom? and where *is* 370+4480
Ps 121: 1 eyes unto the hills, from **w** cometh my help. 370

Ecc 1: 7 unto the place **from w** the rivers come, 7945
Isa 30: 6 from **w** *come* the young and old lion, 1992.1
39: 3 from **w** came they unto thee? And Hezekiah 370
47:11 thou shalt not know from **w** it riseth: NIH
51: 1 look unto the rock **w** ye are hewn, and to NIH
51: 1 and to the hole of the pit **w** ye are digged. NIH
Jer 29:14 **w** I caused you to be carried 834+4480+8033
Jnh 1: 8 **w** comest thou? what *is* thy country? 370+4480
Na 3: 7 **w** shall I seek comforters for thee? 370+4480
Mt 12:44 I will return into my house **from w** I came *3606*
13:27 seed in thy field? **from w** then hath it tares? *4159*
13:54 **W** hath this *man* this wisdom, and *4159*
13:56 **W** then hath this *man* all these *things?* *4159*
15:33 **W** should we have so much bread in *4159*
21:25 The baptism of John, **w** was it? *4159*
Mk 6: 2 **From w** hath this *man* these *things?* and *4159*
8: 4 **From w** can a man satisfy these *men* with *4159*
12:37 calleth him Lord; and **w** is he *then* his son? *4159*
Lk 1:43 And **w** *is* this to me, that the mother of my *4159*
11:24 I will return unto my house **w** I came out. *3606*
13:25 say unto you, I know you not **w** you are: *4159*
13:27 I tell you, I know you not **w** you are; *4159*
20: 7 that *they* could not tell **w** *it was.* *4159*
Jn 1:48 saith unto him, **W** knowest thou me? *4159*
2: 9 *was* made wine, and knew not **w** it was: *4159*
3: 8 but canst not tell **w** it cometh, and *4159*
4:11 **from w** then hast thou *that* living water? *4159*
6: 5 **W** shall we buy bread, that these may eat? *4159*
7:27 Howbeit we know this *man* **w** he is: but *4159*
7:27 Christ cometh, no *man* knoweth **w** he is. *4159*
7:28 Ye both know me, and ye know **w** I am: *4159*
8:14 for I know **w** I came, and whither I go; but *4159*
8:14 but ye cannot tell **w** I come, and whither I *4159*
9:29 *as for* this *fellow,* we know not **from w** he *4159*
9:30 *thing,* that ye know not **from w** he is, *4159*
19: 9 and saith unto Jesus, **W** art thou? *4159*
Ac 14:26 **from w** they had been recommended to *3606*
Php 3:20 from **w** also we look for the Saviour, *3757*
Heb 11:15 of that *country* from **w** they came out, *3739*
11:19 from **w** also he received him in a figure. *3606*
Jas 4: 1 **From w** *come* wars and fightings among *4159*
Rev 2: 5 therefore **from w** thou art fallen, *4159*
7:13 arrayed in white robes? and **w** came they? *4159*

WHENSOEVER (3) [EVER, SO, WHEN]

Ge 30:41 **w** the stronger cattle did conceive, 3605+871.1
Mk 14: 7 and **w** ye will ye may do them good: *3752*
Ro 15:24 **W** I take my journey into Spain, *1437+5613*

WHERE (401)

Ge 2:11 land of Havilah, **w** *there is* gold; 834+8033
3: 9 unto Adam, and said unto him, **W** *art* thou? 335
4: 9 said unto Cain, **W** *is* Abel thy brother? 335
13: 3 unto the place **w** his tent had been at 8033
13:10 of Jordan, that it *was* well watered **every w**, 3605
13:14 from the place **w** thou *art* northward, 834+8033
18: 9 they said unto him, **W** *is* Sarah thy wife? 346
19: 5 **W** *are* the men which came in to thee this 346
19:27 place **w** he stood before the LORD: 834+8033
20:15 *is* before thee: dwell **w** it pleaseth thee. 871.1
21:17 the voice of the lad **w** he *is.* 834+8033+871.1
22: 7 but **w** *is* the lamb for a burnt offering? 346
27:33 **w** *is* he that hath taken venison, and 645
31:13 **w** thou anointedst the pillar, *and* 834+8033
31:13 *and* **w** thou vowedst a vow unto me: 834+8033
33:19 of a field, **w** he had spread his tent, 834+8033
35:13 God went up from him in the place **w** he 834
35:14 Jacob set up a pillar in the place **w** he talked 834
35:15 Jacob called the name of the place **w** 834+8033
35:27 **w** Abraham and Isaac sojourned. 834+8033
37:16 tell me, I pray thee, **w** they feed *their flocks.* 375
38:21 saying, **W** *is* the harlot, that *was* openly by 346
39:20 a place **w** the king's prisoners *were* bound: 834
40: 3 the place **w** Joseph *was* bound. 834+8033
43:30 he sought **w** to weep; and he entered into *his* NIH
Ex 2:20 he said unto his daughters, And **w** *is* he? 335
5:11 get you straw **w** you can find *it:* yet 834+4480
9:26 **w** the children of Israel *were,* was 834+8033
12:13 for a token upon the houses **w** you *are:* 834+8033
12:30 for *there was* not a house **w** *there was* 834+8033
15:27 **w** *were* twelve wells of water, and 8033
18: 5 **w** he encamped *at* the mount of God: 834
20:21 unto the thick darkness **w** God *was.* 834+8033
20:24 in all places **w** I record my name I will come 834
27:18 breadth **fifty every w**, 2572+2572+871.1+1886.1
29:42 **w** I will meet with you, to speak 834+8033+1886.5
30: 6 **w** I will meet with thee. 834+8033+1886.5
30:36 **w** I will meet with thee: 834+8033+1886.5
Lev 4:12 **w** the ashes are poured out, and burn him on NIH
4:12 **w** the ashes are poured out shall he be 5921
4:24 kill it in the place **w** they kill the burnt 834
4:33 slay it for a sin offering in the place **w** they 834
6:25 In the place **w** the burnt offering is killed 834
7: 2 In the place **w** they kill the burnt offering 834
14:13 he shall slay the lamb in the place **w** he shall 834
Nu 9:17 in the place **w** the cloud abode, 834+8033
13:22 **w** Ahiman, Sheshai, and Talmai, 8033
17: 4 **w** I will meet with you. 834+8033+1886.5
22:26 **w** *was* no way to turn *either to* the right hand 834
33:14 **w** was no water for the people to drink. 8033
33:54 shall be in the **place w** his lot falleth; 8033
Dt 1:31 **w** thou hast seen how that the LORD thy 834
8:15 and drought, **w** *there was* no water; 834
11:10 **w** thou sowedst thy seed, and wateredst *it* 834
11:30 by the way **w** the sun goeth down, in NIH
18: 6 **w** he sojourned, and come with all 834+8033
23:16 in one of thy gates, **w** it liketh him best: NIH
32:37 he shall say, **W** *are* their gods, *their* rock in 335
Jos 4: 3 out of the place **w** the priests' feet stood NIH
4: 3 lodging place, **w** you shall lodge *this* night. 834
4: 8 with them unto the **place w** they **lodged**, 4411
4: 9 in the place **w** the feet of the priests which NIH
Jdg 5:27 **w** he bowed, there he fell down dead. 834+871.1
6:13 **w** *be* all his miracles which our fathers told 346
9:38 **W** *is* now thy mouth, wherewith thou saidst, 346

W

Jdg 17: 8 to sojourn w he could find *a place:* 834+871.1
17: 9 I go to sojourn w I may find *a place.* 834+871.1
18:10 a place w *there is* no want of any thing 834+8033
19:26 house w her lord *was,* till it was light. 834+8033
20:22 w they put *themselves* in array 834+8033
Ru 1: 7 out of the place w she was, 834+8033+1886.5
1:16 and w thou lodgest, I will lodge: 834+871.1
1:17 W thou diest, will I die, and 834+871.1
2:19 said unto her, W hast thou gleaned to day? 375
2:19 w wroughtest thou? blessed be he 575+1886.5
3: 4 that thou shalt mark the place w he 834+8033
1Sa 3: 3 w the ark of God *was,* and 834+8033
6:14 stood there, w *there was* a great stone: 8033
9:10 So they went unto the city w the man 834+8033
9:18 I pray thee, w the seer's house *is.* 335+2088
10: 5 w *is* the garrison of the Philistines: 834+8033
10:14 when we saw that *they were* **no w**, we came 369
14:11 the holes w they had hid themselves. 834+8033
19: 3 stand beside my father in the field w 834+8033
19:22 he asked and said, W *are* Samuel and David? 375
20:19 come to the place w thou didst hide 834+8033
23:22 know and see his place w his haunt is, *and* 834
23:23 lurking places w he hideth himself, 834+8033
24: 3 to the sheepcotes by the way, w *was* a cave; 8033
26: 5 came to the place w Saul had pitched: 834+8033
26: 5 David beheld the place w Saul lay, 834+8033
26:16 now see w the king's spear *is,* and the cruse 335
30: 9 w those that were left behind stayed. 2050.1
30:31 to all the places w David himself and 834+8033
2Sa 2:23 that as many as came to the place w 834+8033
9: 4 the king said unto him, W *is* he? And Ziba 375
11:16 that he assigned Uriah unto a place w 834+8033
15:32 *of the mount,* w he worshipped God, 834+8033
16: 3 the king said, And w *is* thy master's son? 346
17:12 in some place w he shall be found, 834+8033
17:20 they said, W *is* Ahimaaz and Jonathan? 346
18: 7 W the people of Israel were slain before 8033
21:12 w the Philistines had hanged them, 834+8033
21:19 w Elhanan the son of Jaare-oregim, NIH
21:20 w was a man of *great* stature, that had on NIH
23:11 w was a piece of ground full *of* lentiles: 8033
1Ki 4:28 unto the place w *the officers* were, 834+8033
7: 7 he made a porch for the throne w he 834+8033
7: 8 his house w he dwelt *had* another 834+8033
13:25 told *it* in the city w the old prophet dwelt. 834
17:19 w he abode, and laid him upon his 834+8033
21:19 In the place w dogs licked the blood of 834
2Ki 2:14 and said, W *is* the LORD God of Elijah? 346
4: 8 passed to Shunem, w *was* a great woman; 8033
6: 1 the place w we dwell with thee is too 834+8033
6: 2 us make us a place there, w we may dwell. 8033
6: 6 the man of God said, W fell it? 575+1886.5
6:13 Go and spy w he *is,* that I may send and 351
18:34 W *are* the gods of Hamath, and of Arpad? 346
18:34 w *are* the gods of Sepharvaim, Hena, and 346
19:13 W *is* the king of Hamath, and the king of 335
23: 7 w the women wove hangings for 834+8033
23: 8 defiled the high places w, 834+8033+1886.5
1Ch 11: 4 w the Jebusites *were,* the inhabitants of 8033
11:13 w was a parcel of ground full *of* barley; 8033
13: 2 us send **abroad** unto our brethren **every w**, 6555
20: 6 w was a man of *great* stature, whose fingers NIH
2Ch 3: 1 w *the LORD* appeared unto David his 834
25: 4 w the LORD commanded, saying, 834
36:20 w they were servants to him and his sons NIH
Ezr 1: 4 whosoever remaineth in any place w 834+8033
6: 1 w the treasures were laid up in Babylon. 8536
6: 3 the place w they offered sacrifices, and 1768
Ne 10:39 w *are* the vessels of the sanctuary, and 8033
13: 5 w aforetime they laid the meat offerings, 8033
Est 1: 6 *W were* white, green, and blue *hangings,* NIH
7: 5 the queen, Who *is* he, and w *is* he, 335+2088
Job 4: 7 or w were the righteous cut off? 375
9:24 the judges thereof; if not, w, *and* who *is* he? 645
10:22 any order, and w the light is as darkness. NIH
12:24 causeth them to wander in a wilderness w NIH
14:10 yea, man giveth up the ghost, and w *is* he? 335
15:23 *saying,* W *is it?* he knoweth that the day of 346
17:15 w *is* now my hope? as for my hope, 346
20: 7 which have seen him shall say, W *is* he? 335
21:28 For ye say, W *is* the house of the prince? and 346
21:28 and w *are* the dwelling places of the wicked? 346
23: 3 O that I knew w I might find him! *that* I NIH
23: 9 w he doth work, but I cannot behold *him:* 871.1
28: 1 and a place for gold w they fine *it.* NIH
28:12 w shall wisdom be found? and 370+4480
28:12 and w *is* the place of understanding? 335+2088
28:20 and w *is* the place of understanding? 335+2088
34:22 w the workers of iniquity may hide 8033
35:10 none saith, W *is* God my Maker, who giveth 346
36:16 w *there is* no straitness; 8478+1886.3
38: 4 W wast thou when I laid the foundations of 375
38:19 W *is* the way *where* light dwelleth? 335+2088
38:19 Where *is* the way w light dwelleth? and NIH
38:19 *as for* darkness, w *is* the place thereof, 335+2088
38:26 w no man *is; on* the wilderness, NIH
39:30 and w the slain *are,* there *is* she. 834+871.1
40:20 forth food, w all the beasts of the field play. 8033
Ps 19: 3 nor language, w their voice is not heard. NIH
26: 8 and the place w thine honour **dwelleth.** 4908
42: 3 *they* continually say unto me, W *is* thy God? 346
42:10 while they say daily unto me, W *is* thy God? 346
53: 5 were they in great fear, w no fear was: NIH
63: 1 in a dry and thirsty land, w no water is; NIH
69: 2 I sink in deep mire, w *there is* no standing: NIH
69: 2 into deep waters, w the floods overflow me. NIH
79:10 should the heathen say, W *is* their God? 346
81: 5 w I heard a language *that* I understood not. NIH
84: 3 w she may lay her young, *even* thine altars, 834
89:49 Lord, w *are* thy former lovingkindnesses, 346
104:17 W the birds make their nests: *as for* 834+8033
107:40 wander in the wilderness, w *there is* no way. NIH
115: 2 should the heathen say, W *is* now their God? 346
Pr 11:14 W no counsel *is,* the people fall: but in 871.1
14: 4 W no oxen *are,* the crib *is* clean: but 871.1

Pr 15:17 Better *is* a dinner of herbs w love is, than a 8033
26:20 W no wood is, *there* the fire goeth out: so 871.1
26:20 so w *there is* no talebearer, the strife 871.1
29:18 W *there is* no vision, the people perish: but 871.1
Ecc 1: 5 and hasteth to his place w he arose. 8033
8: 4 W the word of a king *is, there is* 834+871.1
8:10 they were forgotten in the city w they had so 834
11: 3 *in* the place w the tree falleth, there it shall 7945
SS 1: 7 thou whom my soul loveth, w thou feedest, 349
1: 7 w thou makest *thy flock* to rest at noon: 349
Isa 7:23 w there were a thousand vines at a 834+8033
10: 3 and w will ye leave your glory? 575+1886.5
19:12 W *are* they? where *are* thy wise *men?* and 335
19:12 w *are* thy wise *men?* and let them tell thee 645
29: 1 to Ariel, to Ariel, the city w David dwelt! NIH
30:32 *in* every *place* w the grounded staff shall NIH
33:18 W *is* the scribe? where *is* the receiver? 346
33:18 w *is* the receiver? where *is* he that counted 346
33:18 w *is* he that counted the towers? 346
35: 7 w each **lay,** *shall be* grass with reeds and 7258
36:19 W *are* the gods of Hamath and Arphad? 346
36:19 w *are* the gods of Sepharvaim? and have 346
37:13 W *is* the king of Hamath, and the king of 346
49:21 I was left alone; these, w *had* they *been?* 375
50: 1 W *is* the bill of your mother's 335+2088
51:13 and w *is* the fury of the oppressor? 346
57: 8 thou lovedst their bed w thou sawest *it.* 3027
63:11 *saying,* W *is* he that brought them up out of 346
63:11 w *is* he that put his holy Spirit within him? 346
63:15 w *is* thy zeal and thy strength, the sounding 346
64:11 beautiful house, w our fathers praised thee, 834
66: 1 w *is* the house that ye build unto me? 335+2088
66: 1 and w *is* the place of my rest? 335+2088
Jer 2: 6 W *is* the LORD that brought us up out of 346
2: 6 man passed through, and w no man dwelt? 8033
2: 8 The priests said not, W *is* the LORD? and 346
2:28 But w *are* thy gods that thou hast made thee? 346
3: 2 and see w thou hast not been lien with. 375
6:16 w *is* the good way, and walk therein, 335+2088
7:12 w I set my name at the first, and 834+8033
13: 7 from the place w I had hid it: 834+8033+1886.5
13:20 w *is* the flock *that* was given thee, 346
16:13 and night; w I will not shew you favour. 834
17:15 say unto me, W *is* the word of the LORD? 346
22:26 another country, w ye were not born; 834+8033
35: 7 days in the land w ye *be* strangers. 834+8033
36:19 and Jeremiah; and let no man know w ye *be.* 375
37:19 W *are* now your prophets which prophesied 346
38: 9 he is like to die for hunger **in the place w** 8478
39: 5 of Hamath, w he gave judgment upon him. NIH
42:14 the land of Egypt, w we shall see no war, 834
52: 9 of Hamath; w he gave judgment upon him. NIH
La 2:12 say to their mothers, W *is* corn and wine? 346
Eze 3:15 I sat w they sat, and remained there 8033
6:13 the place w they did offer sweet 834+8033
8: 3 w *was* the seat of the image of 834+8033
11:16 in the countries w they shall come. 834+8033
11:17 w ye have been scattered, 834+871.1+1992.1
13:12 W *is* the daubing where*with* ye have daubed 346
17:10 it shall wither in the furrows w it grew. NIH
17:16 surely in the place w the king *dwelleth* that NIH
20:38 I will bring them forth out of the country w NIH
21:30 I will judge thee in the place w thou wast 834
34:12 will deliver them out of all places w 834+8033
40:38 the gates, w they washed the burnt offering. 8033
42:13 w the priests that approach unto 834+8033
43: 7 w I will dwell in the midst of 834+8033
46:20 This *is* the place w the priests shall 834+8033
46:20 w they shall bake the meat offering; 834
46:24 w the ministers of the house shall boil 834+8033
Da 8:17 So he came near w I **stood:** and when he 5977
Hos 1:10 *that* in the place w it was said unto them, 834
13:10 w *is any other* that may save thee in all 165+645
Joel 2:17 they say among the people, W *is* their God? 346
Am 3: 5 snare upon the earth, w no gin *is* for him? 2050.1
Mic 7:10 said unto me, W is the LORD thy God? 335
Na 2:11 W *is* the dwelling of the lions, and 346
2:11 w the lion, *even* the old lion, walked, *and* 8033
3:17 and their place is not known w they *are.* 335
Zep 3:19 fame in every land w they have been put to NIH
Zec 1: 5 Your fathers, w *are* they? and the prophets, 346
Mal 1: 6 if then I *be* a father, w *is* mine honour? and 346
1: 6 if I *be* a master, w *is* my fear? saith 346
2:17 in them; or, W *is* the God of judgment? 346
Mt 2: 2 W is he that is born King of the Jews? *4226*
2: 4 he demanded of them w Christ should be *4226*
2: 9 and stood over w the young child was. *3757*
6:19 w moth and rust doth corrupt, and *3699*
6:19 and w thieves break through and steal: *3699*
6:20 w neither moth nor rust doth corrupt, and *3699*
6:20 w thieves do not break through nor steal: *3699*
6:21 For w your treasure is, there will your heart *3699*
8:20 the Son of man hath not w to lay *his* head. *4226*
13: 5 Some fell upon stony *places,* w they had *3699*
18:20 For w two or three are gathered together in *3757*
25:24 reaping w thou hast not sown, and *3699*
25:24 and gathering w thou hast not strawed: *3606*
25:26 thou knewest that I reap w I sowed not, and *3699*
25:26 and gather w I have not strawed: *3606*
26:17 W wilt thou *that* we prepare for thee to eat *4226*
26:57 w the scribes and the elders were *3699*
28: 6 Come, see the place w the Lord lay. *3699*
28:16 into a mountain w Jesus had appointed *3757*
Mk 2: 4 they uncovered the roof w he was: *3699*
4: 5 on stony ground, w it had not much earth; *3699*
4:15 they by the way side, w the word is sown; *3699*
5:40 and entereth in w the damsel was lying. *3699*
6:55 those that were sick, w they heard he was. *3699*
9:44 W their worm dieth not, and the fire is not *3699*
9:46 W their worm dieth not, and the fire is not *3699*
9:48 W their worm dieth not, and the fire is not *3699*
11: 4 the door without in a place w two ways met; NIG
13:14 Daniel the prophet, standing w it ought not, *3699*
14:12 W wilt thou *that* we go and prepare that *4226*
14:14 The Master saith, W is the guestchamber, *4226*

Mk 14:14 w I shall eat the passover with my *3699*
15:47 Mary *the mother* of Joses beheld w he was *4226*
16: 6 not here: behold the place w they laid him. *3699*
16:20 they went forth, and preached **every w**, *3837*
Lk 4:16 to Nazareth, w he had been brought up: *3757*
4:17 he found the place w it was written, *3757*
8:25 And he said unto them, W is your faith? *4226*
9: 6 preaching the gospel, and healing **every w**. *3837*
9:58 the Son of man hath not w to lay *his* head. *4226*
10:33 as he journeyed, came w he was: *2596*
12:17 I have no room w to bestow my fruits? *4226*
12:33 w no thief approacheth, neither moth *3699*
12:34 For w your treasure is, there will your heart *3699*
17:17 there not ten cleansed? but w *are* the nine? *4226*
17:37 they answered and said unto him, W, Lord? *4226*
22: 9 unto him, W wilt thou *that* we prepare? *4226*
22:10 follow him into the house w he entereth in. *3757*
22:11 saith unto thee, W is the guestchamber, *4226*
22:11 w I shall eat the passover with my *3699*
Jn 1:28 beyond Jordan, w John was baptizing. *3699*
1:38 Master,) w dwellest thou? *4226*
1:39 They came and saw w he dwelt, and *4226*
3: 8 The wind bloweth w it listeth, and *3699*
4:20 that in Jerusalem is the place w *men* ought *3699*
4:46 Cana of Galilee, w he made the water wine. *3699*
6:23 nigh unto the place w they did eat bread, *3699*
6:62 if ye shall see the Son of man ascend up w *3699*
7:11 sought him at the feast, and said, W is he? *4226*
7:34 and shall not find *me:* and w I am, *3699*
7:36 and shall not find *me:* and w I am, *3699*
7:42 of the town of Bethlehem, w David was? *3699*
8:10 Woman, w are those thine accusers? *4226*
8:19 Then said they unto him, W is thy Father? *4226*
9:12 Then said they unto him, W is he? He said, *4226*
10:40 into the place w John at first baptized; *3699*
11: 6 he abode two days *still* in the *same* place w *3739*
11:30 but was in *that* place w Martha met him. *3699*
11:32 Then when Mary was come w Jesus was, *3699*
11:34 And said, W have ye laid him? They say *4226*
11:41 stone *from the place* w the dead was laid. *3757*
11:57 that, if any *man* knew w he were, *4226*
12: 1 w Lazarus was which had been dead, *3699*
12:26 and w I am, there shall also my servant be: *3699*
14: 3 that w I am, *there* ye may be also. *3699*
17:24 thou hast given me, be with me w I am; *3699*
18: 1 w was a garden, into the which he entered, *3699*
19:18 W they crucified him, and two other with *3699*
19:20 for the place w Jesus was crucified was *3699*
19:41 Now in the place w he was crucified there *3699*
20: 2 and we know not w they have laid him. *4226*
20:12 at the feet, w the body of Jesus had lain. *3699*
20:13 and I know not w they have laid him. *4226*
20:15 if thou have borne him *hence,* tell me w *4226*
20:19 when the doors were shut w the disciples *3699*
Ac 1:13 w abode both Peter, and James, and John, *3757*
2: 2 it filled all the house w they were sitting. *3757*
4:31 the place was shaken w they were *1722+3739*
7:29 in the land of Madian, w he begat two sons. *3757*
7:33 for the place w thou standest is holy *1722+3739*
8: 4 abroad **went every w** preaching the word. *1330*
11:11 come unto the house w I was, *1722+3739*
12:12 w many were gathered together praying. *3757*
15:36 visit our brethren in every city w we *1722+3739*
16:13 a river side, w prayer was wont to be made; *3757*
17: 1 w was a synagogue of the Jews: *3699*
17:30 now commandeth all men **every w** to *3837*
20: 6 Troas in five days; w we abode seven days. *3757*
20: 8 w they were gathered together. *3757*
21:28 that teacheth all *men* **every w** against *3837*
25:10 judgment seat, w I ought to be judged: *3757*
27:41 And falling into a place **w two seas met**, *1337*
28:14 W we found brethren, and were desired to *3757*
28:22 we know that **every w** it is spoken against. *3837*
Ro 3:27 W *is* boasting then? It is excluded. By what *4226*
4:15 for w no law is, *there is* no transgression. *3757*
5:20 But w sin abounded, grace did much more *3757*
9:26 *that* in the place w it was said unto them, *3757*
15:20 preach the gospel, not w Christ was named, *3699*
1Co 1:20 W *is* the wise? where *is* the scribe? *4226*
1:20 w *is* the scribe? where *is* the disputer of this *4226*
1:20 w *is* the disputer of this world? hath not *4226*
4:17 as I teach **every w** in every church. *3837*
12:17 body *were* an eye, w *were* the hearing? *4226*
12:17 whole *were* hearing, w *were* the smelling? *4226*
12:19 were all one member, w *were* the body? *4226*
15:55 O death, w *is* thy sting? O grave, where *is* *4226*
15:55 *is* thy sting? O grave, w *is* thy victory? *4226*
2Co 3:17 w the Spirit of the Lord *is,* there *is* liberty. *3757*
Gal 4:15 W is then the blessedness you spake of? for *5101*
Php 4:12 **every w** and in all *things* I am instructed *3956*
Col 3: 1 w Christ sitteth on the right hand of God. *3757*
3:11 W there is neither Greek nor Jew, *3699*
1Ti 2: 8 I will therefore that men pray **every w**, *5117*
Heb 9:16 For w a testament *is,* there must also of *3699*
10:18 Now w remission of these *is, there is* no *3699*
Jas 3:16 For w envying and strife *is,* there *is* *3699*
1Pe 4:18 w shall the ungodly and the sinner appear? *4226*
2Pe 3: 4 W is the promise of his coming? *4226*
Rev 2:13 I know thy works, and w thou dwellest, *4226*
2:13 *even* w Satan's seat *is:* and thou holdest *3699*
2:13 was slain among you, w Satan dwelleth. *3699*
11: 8 and Egypt, w also our Lord was crucified. *3699*
12: 6 w she hath a place prepared of God, *3699*
12:14 w she is nourished for a time, and times, *3699*
17:15 w the whore sitteth, are peoples, and *3757*
20:10 w the beast and the false prophet *are,* and *3699*

WHEREABOUT (1) [ABOUT]

1Sa 21: 2 any thing of the business w I send thee, 834

WHEREAS (33) [AS]

Ge 31:37 W thou hast searched all my stuff, 3588
Dt 19: 6 w he *was* not worthy of death, 2050.1
28:62 w ye were as the stars of heaven for 834
1Sa 24:17 me good, w I have rewarded thee evil. 2050.1

2Sa 7: 6 W I have not dwelt in *any* house since 3588
15:20 W thou camest *but* yesterday, should I *this* NIH
1Ki 8:18 W it was in thine heart to build a 834+3282
12:11 now w my father did lade you with a 2050.1
2Ki 13:19 *it:* w now thou shalt smite Syria 2050.1
2Ch 10:11 For w my father put a heavy yoke upon 6258
28:13 for w we have offended against 3807.1
Job 22:20 W our substance is not cut down, but 518
Ecc 4:14 w also *he that is* born in his kingdom 3588
Isa 37:21 W thou hast prayed to me against 834
60:15 W thou hast been forsaken and hated, so 8478
Jer 4:10 w the sword reacheth unto the soul). 2050.1
Eze 13: 7 not spoken a lying divination, w ye say, 2050.1
16: 7 is grown, w thou *wast* naked and bare. 2050.1
16:34 w none followeth thee to commit 2050.1
35:10 will possess it; w the LORD was there: 2050.1
36:34 w it lay desolate in the sight of all that 834+8478
Da 2:41 w thou sawest the feet and toes, part of 1768
2:43 w thou sawest iron mixt with miry clay, 1768
4:23 w the king saw a watcher and a holy one 1768
4:26 w they commanded to leave the stump of 1768
8:22 that being broken, w four stood up for it, 2050.1
Mal 1: 4 W Edom saith, We are impoverished, but 3588
Jn 9:25 *thing* I know, that, w I was blind, now I see. NIG
1Co 3: 3 for w *there is* among you envying, and *3699*
Jas 4:14 W ye know not what *shall be* on *3748*
1Pe 2:12 that, w they speak against you as *1722+3739*
3:16 that, w they speak evil of you, as of *1722+3739*
2Pe 2:11 W angels, which are greater in power and *3699*

WHEREBY (39) [BY]

Ge 15: 8 Lord GOD, w shall I know that I 4100+871.1
44: 5 and w indeed he divineth? 871.1+2050.2
Lev 22: 5 w he may be made unclean, or a man of 834
Nu 5: 8 w an atonement shall be 834+871.1+2050.2
17: 5 of Israel, w they murmur against you. 834+1992
Dt 7:19 w the LORD thy God brought thee out: 834
28:20 of thy doings, w thou hast forsaken me. 834
1Sa 20:33 w Jonathan knew that it was determined 2050.1
Ps 45: 5 *w* the people fall under thee. NIH
45: 8 *w*by they have made thee glad. 4482
68: 9 w thou didst confirm thine inheritance, 1886.3
Jer 3: 8 when for all the causes w backsliding Israel 834
17:19 w the kings of Judah come 834+871.1+2050.2
23: 6 this *is* his name w he shall be called, 834
33: 8 w they have sinned against me, and I will 834
33: 8 w they have sinned, and whereby they have 834
33: 8 w they have transgressed against me. 834
Eze 18:31 w ye have transgressed; 834+871.1
20:25 judgments w they should not live; 871.1+1992.1
39:26 all their trespasses w they have trespassed 834
40:49 *he brought me* by the steps w they went up 834
46: 9 way of the gate w he came in, 834+871.1+2050.2
47:13 w ye shall inherit the land according to 834
Zep 2: 8 w they have reproached my people, and 834
Lk 1:18 unto the angel, W shall I know this? *2596+5101*
1:78 w the dayspring from on high hath *1722+3739*
Ac 4:12 among men, w we must be saved. *1722+3739*
11:14 w thou and all thy house shall be *1722+3739*
19:40 there being no cause w we may give *3739+4012*
Ro 8:15 of adoption, w we cry, Abba, Father. *1722+3739*
14:21 nor *any thing* w thy brother *1722+3739*
Eph 3: 4 W, when ye read, ye may understand *3739+4314*
4:14 w they lie in wait to deceive; *4314*
4:30 w ye are sealed unto the day of *1722+3739*
Php 3:21 according to the working w he is able even NIG
Heb 12:28 w we may serve God acceptably with *1223+3739*
2Pe 1: 4 W are given unto us exceeding great *1223+3739*
3: 6 W the world that then was, *1223+3739*
1Jn 2:18 w we know that it is the last time. *3606*

WHEREFORE (348)

Ge 10: 9 mighty hunter before the LORD: w 3651+5921
16:14 W the well was called 3651+5921
18:13 said unto Abraham, W 2088+4100+3807.1
21:10 W she said unto Abraham, Cast out this 2050.1
21:31 W he called that place Beer-sheba; 3651+5921
24:31 thou blessed of the LORD; w 4100+3807.1
26:27 W come ye to me, seeing ye hate me, and 4069
29:25 not I serve with thee for Rachel? w 4100+3807.1
31:27 W didst thou flee away secretly, 4100+3807.1
31:30 after thy father's house, *yet* w 4100+3807.1
32:29 he said, W *is* it *that* thou dost ask 4100+3807.1
38:10 the LORD: w he slew him also. 2050.1
40: 7 saying, W look ye *so* sadly to day? 4069
43: 6 Israel said, W dealt ye *so* ill with 4100+3807.1
44: 4 say unto them, W have ye 4100+3807.1
44: 7 they said unto him, W saith my 4100+3807.1
47:19 W shall we die before thine eyes, 4100+3807.1
47:22 portion which Pharaoh gave them: w 3651+5921
50:11 mourning to the Egyptians: w 3651+5921
Ex 2:13 said to him that did the wrong, W 4100+3807.1
5: 4 king of Egypt said unto them, W 4100+3807.1
5:14 W have ye not fulfilled your task in making 4069
5:15 saying, W dealest thou thus with 4100+3807.1
5:22 Lord, w hast thou *so* evil entreated 4100+3807.1
6: 6 W say unto the children of Israel, 3651+3807.1
14:11 w hast thou dealt thus with us, to carry us 4100
14:15 said unto Moses, W criest thou unto me? 4100
17: 2 W the people did chide with Moses, and 2050.1
17: 2 you with me? w do ye tempt the LORD? 4100
17: 3 said, W *is* this *that* thou hast 4100+3807.1
20:11 w the LORD blessed the sabbath 3651+5921
31:16 W the children of Israel shall keep 2050.1
32:12 W should the Egyptians speak, and 4100+3807.1
Lev 10:17 W have ye not eaten the sin offering in 4069
13:25 w the priest shall pronounce him unclean: 2050.1
25:18 W ye shall do my statutes, and keep my 2050.1
Nu 9: 7 by the dead body of a man: w 4100+3807.1
11:11 Moses said unto the LORD, W 4100+3807.1
11:11 w have I not found favour in thy 4100+3807.1
12: 8 w then were ye not afraid to speak against 4069
14: 3 w *hath* the LORD brought us unto 4100+3807.1
14:41 Moses said, W now do ye 4100+3807.1
16: 3 w then lift you up yourselves above 4069
Nu 20: 5 w have ye made us to come up out 4100+3807.1
20:21 w Israel turned away from him. 2050.1
21: 5 against Moses, W have ye brought 4100+3807.1
21:14 W it is said in the book of the wars 3651+5921
21:27 W they that speak in proverbs say, 3651+5921
22:32 of the LORD said unto him, W 4100+5921
22:37 send unto thee to call thee? w 4100+3807.1
25:12 W say, Behold, I give unto him my 3651+3807.1
32: 5 W, said they, if we have found grace in 2050.1
32: 7 w discourage ye the heart of 4100+3807.1
Dt 7:12 W it shall come to pass, if ye hearken to 2050.1
10: 9 W Levi hath no part nor inheritance 3651+5921
19: 7 W I command thee, saying, 3651+5921
29:24 Even all nations shall say, W hath 4100+5921
Jos 5: 9 W the name of the place is called Gilgal 2050.1
7: 5 w the hearts of the people melted, and 2050.1
7: 7 w hast thou at all brought this 4100+3807.1
7:10 w liest thou thus upon thy face? 4100+3807.1
7:26 W the name of that place was called, 3651+5921
9:11 W our elders and all the inhabitants of 2050.1
9:22 W have ye beguiled us, saying, 4100+3807.1
10: 3 W Adoni-zedek king of Jerusalem sent 2050.1
Jdg 2: 3 W I also said, I will not drive them out 2050.1
10:13 w I will deliver you no more. 3651+3807.1
11:27 W I have not sinned against thee, but 2050.1
12: 1 W passedst thou over to fight against 4069
12: 3 w then are ye come up unto me this 4100+3807.1
15:19 w he called the name thereof 3651+5921
18:12 w they called that place 3651+5921
Ru 1: 7 W she went forth out of the place where 2050.1
1Sa 1:20 W it came to pass, when the time was 2050.1
2:17 W the sin of the young men was very 2050.1
2:29 W kick ye at my sacrifice and 4100+3807.1
2:30 W the LORD God of Israel saith, 3651+3807.1
4: 3 the elders of Israel said, W hath 4100+3807.1
6: 5 W ye shall make images of your 2050.1
6: 6 W then do ye harden your hearts, 4100+3807.1
9:21 of the tribe of Benjamin? w 4100+3807.1
14:27 w he put forth the end of the rod that *was* 2050.1
15:19 W then didst thou not obey 4100+3807.1
16:19 W Saul sent messengers unto Jesse, and 2050.1
18:15 W **when** Saul saw that he behaved 2050.1
18:21 W Saul said to David, Thou shalt *this* day 2050.1
18:27 W David arose and went, he and his men, 2050.1
19: 5 thou sawest *it,* and didst rejoice: w 4100+3807.1
19:24 W they say, *Is* Saul also among 3651+5921
20:27 W cometh not the son of Jesse to meat, 4069
20:31 W now send and fetch him unto me, 2050.1
20:32 said unto him, W shall he be slain? 4100+3807.1
21:14 you see the man *is* mad: w *then* 4100+3807.1
23:25 w he came down *into* a rock, and 2050.1
23:28 W Saul returned from pursuing after 2050.1
24: 9 David said to Saul, W hearest thou 4100+3807.1
24:19 w the LORD reward thee good for that 2050.1
25: 8 W let the young men find favour in thine 2050.1
25:36 w she told him nothing, less or more, 2050.1
26:15 who *is* like to thee in Israel? w then 4100+3807.1
26:18 W doth my lord thus pursue after 4100+3807.1
27: 6 gave him Ziklag that day: w 3651+3807.1
28: 9 out of the land: w then layest thou 4100+3807.1
28:16 said Samuel, W then dost thou ask 4100+3807.1
29: 7 W now return, and go in peace, that thou 2050.1
29:10 W now rise up early in the morning with 2050.1
2Sa 2:16 w that place was called 2050.1
2:22 thee aside from following me: w 4100+3807.1
2:23 w Abner with the hinder end of the spear 2050.1
3: 7 W hast thou gone in unto my father's 4069
5: 8 *he shall be chief and captain.* W they 3651+5921
7:22 W thou art great, O LORD God: 3651+5921
10: 4 W Hanun took David's servants, and 2050.1
11:20 W approached ye *so* nigh unto the city 4069
12: 9 W hast thou despised the commandment of 4069
12:23 now he is dead, w should I fast? 4100+3807.1
14:13 the woman said, W then hast thou 4100+3807.1
14:31 said unto him, W have thy servants 4100+3807.1
14:32 to say, W am I come from Geshur? 4100+3807.1
15:19 said the king to Ittai the Gittite, W 4100+3807.1
16:10 Who shall then say, W hast thou done so? 4069
18:22 Joab said, W wilt thou run, 2088+4100+3807.1
19:12 ye *are* my bones and my flesh: w 4100+3807.1
19:25 that the king said unto him, W 4100+3807.1
19:35 and singing *women?* w then 4100+3807.1
19:42 the king *is* near of kin to us: w 4100+3807.1
21: 3 W David said unto the Gibeonites, 2050.1
24:21 W is my lord the king come to his servant? 4069
1Ki 1: 2 W his servants said unto him, Let there 2050.1
1:11 W Nathan spake unto Bath-sheba 2050.1
1:41 W *is this* noise of the city being in an 4069
11:11 W the LORD said unto Solomon, 2050.1
12:15 W the king hearkened not unto 2050.1
16:16 w all Israel made Omri, the captain of 2050.1
20: 9 W he said unto the messengers of 2050.1
22:34 w he said unto the driver of his chariot, 2050.1
2Ki 4:23 he said, W wilt thou go to him to day? *it is* 4069
4:31 W he went again to meet him, and 2050.1
5: 7 w consider, I pray you, and see how 389+3588
5: 8 W hast thou rent thy clothes? 4100+3807.1
7: 7 W they arose and fled in the twilight, and 2050.1
9:11 w came this mad *fellow* to thee? And he 4069
9:36 W they came again, and told him. And he 2050.1
17:26 W they spake to the king of Assyria, 2050.1
19: 4 w lift up *thy* prayer for the remnant that 2050.1
1Ch 13:11 w that place is called Perez-uzza to this 2050.1
19: 4 W Hanun took David's servants, and 2050.1
21: 4 W Joab departed, and went throughout all 2050.1
29:10 W David blessed the LORD before all 2050.1
2Ch 5: 3 W all the men of Israel assembled 2050.1
19: 7 W now let the fear of the LORD be 2050.1
22: 4 W he did evil in the sight of the LORD, 2050.1
25:10 to go home *again:* w their anger was 2050.1
25:15 W the anger of the LORD was kindled 2050.1
28: 5 W the LORD his God delivered him 2050.1
29: 8 W the wrath of the LORD was upon 2050.1
29:34 w their brethren the Levites did help 2050.1
33:11 W the LORD brought upon them 2050.1
Ne 2: 2 W the king said unto me, Why *is* thy 2050.1
Est 3: 6 w Haman sought to destroy all the Jews 2050.1
9:26 W they called these days Purim after 3651+5921
Job 3:20 W is light given to him that is in 4100+3807.1
10: 2 shew me w thou contendest with me. 4100+5921
10:18 W then hast thou brought me forth 4100+3807.1
13:14 W do I take my flesh in my teeth, 4100+5921
13:24 W hidest thou thy face, and 4100+3807.1
18: 3 W are we counted as beasts, *and* 4069
21: 7 W do the wicked live, become old, yea, 4069
32: 6 w I was afraid, and durst not shew 3651+5921
33: 1 W, Job, I pray thee, hear my 199+2050.1
42: 6 W I abhor *myself,* and repent in dust 3651+5921
Ps 10:13 W doth the wicked contemn God? 4100+5921
44:24 W hidest thou thy face, *and* 4100+3807.1
49: 5 W should I fear in the days of evil, 4100+3807.1
79:10 W should the heathen say, 4100+3807.1
89:47 w hast thou made all men in vain? 4100+5921
115: 2 W should the heathen say, 4100+3807.1
Pr 17:16 W *is there* a price in 2088+4100+3807.1
Ecc 3:22 W I perceive that *there is* nothing better, 2050.1
4: 2 W I praised the dead which are already 2050.1
5: 6 that it *was* an error: w should God 4100+3807.1
Isa 5: 4 w, when I looked that *it* should bring forth 4069
10:12 W it shall come to pass, *that* when 2050.1
16:11 W my bowels shall sound like a harp 3651+5921
24:15 W glorify ye the LORD in the fires, 3651+5921
28:14 W hear the word of the LORD, 3651+3807.1
29:13 W the Lord said, Forasmuch as this 2050.1
30:12 W thus saith the Holy One of 3651+3807.1
37: 4 w lift up *thy* prayer for the remnant that is 2050.1
50: 2 W, when I came, *was there* no man? when I 4069
55: 2 W do ye spend money for *that* 4100+3807.1
58: 3 W have we fasted, *say they,* and 4100+3807.1
58: 3 *w* have we afflicted our soul, and NIH
63: 2 W *art thou* red in thine apparel, and 4069
Jer 2: 9 W I will yet plead with you, 3651+3807.1
2:29 W will ye plead with me? ye all 4100+3807.1
2:31 w say my people, We are lords; we will 4069
5: 6 W a lion out of the forest shall slay 3651+5921
5:14 W thus saith the LORD God of 3651+3807.1
5:19 W doth the LORD our God all 4100+8478
12: 1 W doth the way of the wicked prosper? 4069
12: 1 *w* are all they happy that deal very NIH
13:22 thine heart, W come these *things* upon me? 4069
16:10 they shall say unto thee, W hath 4100+5921
20:18 W came I forth out of 2088+4100+3807.1
22: 8 say every man to his neighbour, W 4100+5921
22:28 w are they cast out, he and his seed, and 4069
23:12 W their way shall be unto them as 3651+3807.1
27:17 w should this city be laid waste? 4100+3807.1
30: 6 w do I see every man *with* his hands on his 4069
32: 3 saying, W dost thou prophesy, and say, 4069
37:15 W the princes were wroth with Jeremiah, 2050.1
40:15 no man shall know *it:* w should he 4100+3807.1
44: 6 W my fury and mine anger was poured 2050.1
44: 7 the God of Israel; W commit ye 4100+3807.1
46: 5 W have I seen them dismayed *and* 4069
49: 4 W gloriest thou in the valleys, thy flowing 4100
51:52 W behold, the days come, saith 3651+3807.1
La 3:39 W doth a living man complain, a man for 4100
5:20 W dost thou forget us for ever, *and* 4100+3807.1
Eze 5:11 W, *as* I live, saith the Lord GOD; 3651+3807.1
7:24 W I will bring the worst of the heathen, 2050.1
13:20 W thus saith the Lord GOD; 3651+3807.1
16:35 W, O harlot, hear the word of 3651+3807.1
18:32 w turn *yourselves,* and live ye. 2050.1
20:10 W I caused them to go forth out of 2050.1
20:25 W I gave them also statutes *that were* not 2050.1
20:30 W say unto the house of Israel, 3651+3807.1
21: 7 they say unto thee, W sighest thou? 4100+5921
23: 9 W I have delivered her into 3651+3807.1
24: 6 W thus saith the Lord GOD; 3651+3807.1
33:25 W say unto them, Thus saith 3651+3807.1
36:18 W I poured my fury upon them for 2050.1
43: 8 w I have consumed them in mine anger. 2050.1
Da 3: 8 W at that time certain 1836+3606+6903
4:27 W, O king, let my counsel be acceptable 3861
6: 9 W king Darius signed 1836+3606+6903
8:26 w shut thou up the vision; for *it shall be* 2050.1
10:20 Knowest thou w I come unto thee? 4100+3807.1
Joel 2:17 w should they say among 4100+3807.1
Jnh 1:14 W they cried unto the LORD, and said, 2050.1
Hab 1:13 w lookest thou upon them that deal 4100+3807.1
Mal 2:14 Yet ye say, W? Because the LORD 4100+5921
2:15 w one? That he might seek a godly seed. 4100
Mt 6:30 W, if God so clothe the grass of the field, *1161*
7:20 W by their fruits ye shall know them. *686+1065*
9: 4 W think ye evil in your hearts? *2444*
12:12 W it is lawful to do well on the sabbath *5620*
12:31 W I say unto you, All *manner of* sin *1223+3778*
14:31 of little faith, w didst thou doubt? *1519+5101*
18: 8 W if thy hand or thy foot offend thee, *1161*
19: 6 W they are no more twain, but one flesh. *5620*
23:31 W ye be witnesses unto yourselves, that ye *5620*
23:34 W, behold, I send unto you prophets, *1223+3778*
24:26 W if they shall say unto you, Behold, he is *3767*
26:50 unto him, Friend, w art thou come? *1909+3739*
27: 8 W that field was called, The field of blood, *1352*
Lk 7: 7 W neither thought I myself worthy to come *1352*
7:47 W I say unto thee, Her sins, *3739+5484*
19:23 W then gavest not thou my money into *1302*
Jn 9:27 w would you hear *it* again? will ye also be *5101*
Ac 1:21 W of these men which have companied *3767*
6: 3 W, brethren, look ye out among you seven *3767*
10:21 what *is* the cause w ye are come? *1223+3739*
13:35 W he saith also in another *psalm,* Thou *1352*
15:19 W my sentence is, that *we* trouble not *1352*
19:32 the more part knew not w they were *1752+5101*
19:38 W if Demetrius, and the craftsmen which *3767*
20:26 W I take you to record this day, that I *am* *1352*
22:24 that he might know w they cried *156+1223+3739*
22:30 he would have known the certainty w he *5101*
23:28 the cause w they accused him, *1223+3739*
24:26 w he sent for him the oftener, and *1352+2532*

Ac 25:26 **W** I have brought him forth before you, and *1352*
26: 3 **w** I beseech thee to hear me patiently. *1352*
27:25 **W**, sirs, be of good cheer: for I believe *1352*
27:34 **W** I pray you to take *some* meat: for this is *1352*
Ro 1:24 **W** God also gave them up to uncleanness *1352*
5:12 **W**, as by one man sin entered into *1223+3778*
7: 4 **W**, my brethren, ye also are become dead *5620*
7:12 **W** the law *is* holy, and the commandment *5620*
9:32 **W**? Because *they sought it* not by faith, but *1302*
13: 5 **W** *ye* must needs be subject, not only for *1352*
15: 7 **W** receive ye one another, as Christ also *1352*
1Co 4:16 **W** I beseech you, be ye followers of me. *3767*
8:13 **W**, if meat make my brother to offend, *1355*
10:12 **W** let him that thinketh he standeth take *5620*
10:14 **W**, my dearly beloved, flee from idolatry. *1355*
11:27 **W** whosoever shall eat this bread, and *5620*
11:33 **W**, my brethren, when ye come together to *5620*
12: 3 **W** I give you to understand, that no *man* *1352*
14:13 **W** let him that speaketh in an *unknown* *1355*
14:22 **W** tongues are for a sign, not to them that *5620*
14:39 **W**, brethren, covet to prophesy, and *5620*
2Co 2: 8 **W** I beseech you that *you* would confirm *1352*
5: 9 **W** we labour, that, whether present or *1352*
5:16 **W** henceforth know we no *man* after *5620*
6:17 **W** come out from among them, and be ye *1352*
7:12 **W**, though I wrote unto you, *I did it* not for *686*
8:24 **W** shew ye to them, and before *3767*
11:11 **W**? because I love you not? God knoweth. *1302*
Gal 3:19 **W** then *serveth* the law? It was added *5101*
3:24 **W** the law was our schoolmaster *to bring* *5620*
4: 7 **W** thou art no more a servant, but a son; *5620*
Eph 1:15 **W** I also, after I heard of your faith *1223+3778*
2:11 **W** remember, that ye *being* in time passed *1352*
3:13 **W** I desire that ye faint not at my *1352*
4: 8 **W** *he* saith, When he ascended up on high, *1352*
4:25 **W** putting away lying, speak every man *1352*
5:14 **W** *he* saith, Awake thou that sleepest, and *1352*
5:17 **W** be ye not unwise, but *1223+3778*
6:13 **W** take unto *you* the whole armour *1223+3778*
Php 2: 9 **W** God also hath highly exalted him, and *1352*
2:12 **W**, my beloved, as ye have always obeyed, *5620*
Col 2:20 **W** if ye be dead with Christ from *3767*
1Th 2:18 **W** we would have come unto you, even I *1352*
3: 1 **W** when we could no longer forbear, *1352*
4:18 **W** comfort one another with these words. *5620*
5:11 **W** comfort yourselves together, and *1352*
2Th 1:11 **W** also we pray always for you, *1519+3739*
2Ti 1: 6 **W** I put thee in remembrance *156+1223+3739*
Tit 1:13 **W** rebuke them sharply, *156+1223+3739*
Phm 1: 8 **W**, though I might be much bold in Christ *1352*
Heb 2:17 **W** in all *things* it behoved him to be made *3606*
3: 1 **W**, holy brethren, partakers of the heavenly *3606*
3: 7 **W**, as the Holy Ghost saith, To day if ye *1352*
3:10 **W** I was grieved with that generation, and *1352*
7:25 **W** he is able also to save them to *3606*
8: 3 **w** *it is* of necessity that this *man* have *3606*
10: 5 **W** when he cometh into the world, he saith, *1352*
11:16 **W** God is not ashamed to be called their *1352*
12: 1 **W seeing** we also are compassed about *5105*
12:12 **W** lift up the hands which hang down, and *1352*
12:28 **W** we receiving a kingdom which cannot *1352*
13:12 **W** Jesus also, that he might sanctify *1352*
Jas 1:19 **W**, my beloved brethren, let every man be *5620*
1:21 **W** lay apart all filthiness and superfluity of *1352*
4: 6 **W** *he* saith, God resisteth the proud, but *1352*
1Pe 1:13 **W** gird up the loins of your mind, be sober, *1352*
2: 1 **W** laying aside all malice, and all guile, *3767*
2: 6 **W** also it is contained in the scripture, *1352*
4:19 **W** let them that suffer according to *2532+5620*
2Pe 1:10 **W** the rather, brethren, give diligence to *1352*
1:12 **W** I will not be negligent to put you always *1352*
3:14 **W**, beloved, **seeing that** ye look for such *1352*
1Jn 3:12 And **w** slew he him? Because his *5101+5484*
3Jn 1:10 **W**, if I come, I will remember his *1223+3778*
Rev 17: 7 angel said unto me, **W** didst thou marvel? *1302*

WHEREIN (167) [IN]

Ge 1:30 **w** *there is* life, *I have given* every 834+871.1
6:17 to destroy all flesh, **w** *is* the breath of 834+871.1
7:15 of all flesh, **w** *is* the breath of life. 834+871.1
17: 8 after thee, the land **w** thou art a stranger, NIH
21:23 land **w** thou hast sojourned. 834+871.1+1886.3
28: 4 that thou mayest inherit the land **w** thou art NIH
36: 7 the land **w** they were strangers could not NIH
37: 1 Jacob dwelt in the land **w** his father was a NIH
Ex 1:14 all their service, **w** they made them 834+871.1
6: 4 **w** they were strangers. 834+871.1+1886.3
12: 7 post of the houses, **w** they shall eat it. 834+871.1
18:11 for in the thing **w** they dealt proudly *he was* 834
18:20 shalt shew them the way **w** they must walk, NIH
22:27 **w** shall he sleep? and it shall 4100+871.1+1886.1
33:16 For **w** shall it be known here that I 4100+871.1
Lev 4:23 Or if his sin, **w** he hath 834+871.1+1886.3
5:18 for him concerning his ignorance **w** he erred 834
6:28 the earthen vessel **w** it is sodden shall 834+871.1
11:32 whatsoever vessel *it be,* **w** *any* 871.1+1992.1
11:36 a fountain or pit, **w** *there is* plenty of water, NIH
13:46 All the days **w** the plague *shall be* in him he 834
13:52 thing of skin, **w** the plague is: 834+871.1+2050.2
13:54 *the thing* **w** the plague *is,* 834+871.1+2050.2
13:57 burn that **w** the plague *is* with fire. 871.1+2050.2
18: 3 **w** ye dwelt, shall ye not do: 834+871.1+1886.3
Nu 12:11 **w** we have done foolishly, and wherein we 834
12:11 have done foolishly, and **w** we have sinned. 834
19: 2 **w** *is* no blemish, *and* 834+871.1+1886.3
31:10 they burnt all their cities **w** they dwelt, and 871.1
33:55 you in the land **w** ye dwell. 834+871.1+1886.3
35:33 So ye shall not pollute the land **w** ye 834+871.1
35:34 ye shall inhabit, **w** I dwell: 834+8432+871.1
Dt 8: 9 A land **w** thou shalt eat bread without 834+871.1
8:15 **w** *were* fiery serpents, and scorpions, and NIH
12: 2 **w** the nations which ye shall possess 834+8033
12: 7 **w** the LORD thy God hath blessed thee. 834
17: 1 **w** is blemish, *or* any evil 834+871.1
28:52 **w** thou trustedst, throughout all thy 834+871.1
Jos 8:24 in the wilderness **w** they 834+871.1+2050.2
10:27 cast them into the cave **w** they had 834+8033
22:19 **w** the LORD'S tabernacle dwelleth, 834+8033
22:33 to destroy the land **w** the children of Reuben 834
24:17 preserved us in all the way **w** we 834+871.1+1886.3
Jdg 16: 5 see **w** his great strength *lieth,* and 4100+871.1
16: 6 **w** thy great strength *lieth,* and 4100+871.1
16:15 told me **w** thy great strength *lieth.* 4100+871.1
18: 6 LORD *is* your way **w** ye go. 834+871.1+1886.3
1Sa 6:15 **w** the jewels of gold *were,* 834+871.1+2050.2
14:38 see **w** this sin hath been *this* day. 4100+871.1
2Sa 7: 7 In all *the places* **w** I have walked with all 834
1Ki 2:26 thou hast been afflicted in all **w** my father 834
8:21 **w** *is* the covenant of the LORD, 834+8033
8:36 that thou teach them the good way **w** 834+871.1
8:50 all their transgressions **w** they have 834
13:31 bury me in the sepulchre **w** the man 834+871.1
2Ki 12: 2 days **w** Jehoiada the priest instructed him. 834
14: 6 **w** the LORD commanded, saying, 834
17:29 nation in their cities **w** they dwelt. 834+8033
18:19 What confidence *is* this **w** thou trustest? 834
23:23 **w** this passover was holden to the LORD NIH
2Ch 3: 3 Now these *are the things* **w** Solomon was NIH
6:11 **w** *is* the covenant of the LORD, 834+8033
6:27 **w** they should walk; 834+871.1+1886.3
8: 1 **w** Solomon had built the house of 834
33:19 the places **w** he built high 834+871.1+1992.1
Ezr 5: 7 letter unto him, **w** *was* written thus: 1459+871.2
Ne 6: 6 **W** *was* written, *It is* reported 871.1+1886.3
9:12 in the way **w** they should go. 834+871.1+1886.3
9:19 the way **w** they should go. 834+871.1+1886.3
13:15 I testified *against them* in the day **w** they 3963.1
Est 5:11 all *the things* **w** the king had promoted 834
8:11 **W** the king granted the Jews which *were* 834
9:22 As the days **w** the Jews rested from their 834
Job 3: 3 Let the day perish **w** I was born, 871.1+2050.2
6:16 of the ice, *and* **w** the snow is hid: 5921+4123.1
6:24 and cause me to understand **w** I have erred. 4100
38:26 the wilderness, **w** *there is* no man; 871.1+2050.2
Ps 74: 2 mount Zion, **w** thou hast dwelt. 871.1+2050.2
90:15 Make us glad according to the days **w** thou NIH
90:15 *and* the years **w** we have seen evil. NIH
104:20 **w** all the beasts of the forest do 871.1+2050.2
104:25 **w** *are* things creeping innumerable, 8033
142: 3 In the way **w** I walked have they privily 2098
143: 8 cause me to know the way **w** I should walk; 2098
Ecc 2:19 over all my labour **w** I have laboured, 7945
2:19 **w** I have shewed myself wise under 7945
2:22 **w** he *hath* laboured under the sun? 7945
3: 9 What profit *hath* he that worketh in *that* **w** 834
8: 9 *there is* a time **w** one man ruleth over 834
Isa 2:22 for **w** is he *to be* accounted of? 4100+871.1
14: 3 from the hard bondage **w** thou wast made to 834
33:21 **w** shall go no galley with oars, 871.1+2050.2
36: 4 What confidence *is* this **w** thou trustest? 834
47:12 **w** thou hast laboured from thy youth; 834+871.1
65:12 and did choose *that* **w** I delighted not. 871.1
Jer 5:17 **w** thou trustedst, with 834+2007+871.1
7:14 **w** ye trust, and unto the place which I 834+871.1
12: 5 **w** thou trustedst, *they wearied thee,* then NIH
16:19 and *things* **w** *there is* no profit. 871.1+3963.1
20:14 Cursed *be* the day **w** I was born: 834+871.1
20:14 let not the day **w** my mother bare me be 834
22:28 *is he* a vessel **w** *is* no pleasure? 871.1+2050.2
31: 9 **w** they shall not stumble: 871.1+1886.3
36:14 Take in thine hand the roll **w** 834+871.1+1886.3
41: 9 Now the pit **w** Ishmael had cast all 834+8033
42: 3 us the way **w** we may walk, 834+871.1+1886.3
48:38 like a vessel **w** *is* no pleasure, 871.1+2050.2
51:43 a land **w** no man dwelleth, 871.1+2006.1
Eze 20:34 countries **w** ye are scattered, 834+871.1+3963.1
20:41 **w** ye have been scattered; 834+871.1+3963.1
20:43 **w** ye have been defiled; 834+871.1+3963.1
23:19 **w** she had played the harlot in the land of 834
26:10 as men enter into a city **w** is made a breach. NIH
32: 6 I will also water with thy blood the land **w** NIH
37:23 **w** they have sinned, and 834+871.1+1992.1
37:25 **w** your fathers have dwelt; 834+871.1+1886.3
42:14 garments **w** they minister; 834+871.1+2006.1
44:19 garments **w** they ministered, 834+871.1+3963.1
Hos 2:13 **w** she burnt incense to them, and 834
8: 8 as a vessel **w** *is* no pleasure. 871.1+2050.2
Jnh 4:11 **w** are more than sixscore thousand 871.1+1886.3
Mic 6: 3 **w** have I wearied thee? testify against me. 4100
Zep 3:11 **w** thou hast transgressed against me: 834
Zec 9:11 out of the pit **w** *is* no water. 871.1+2050.2
Mal 1: 2 Yet ye say, **W** hast thou loved us? 4100+871.1
1: 6 **W** have we despised thy name? 4100+871.1
1: 7 ye say, **W** have we polluted thee? 4100+871.1
2:17 **W** have we wearied *him?* When ye 4100+871.1
3: 7 But ye said, **W** shall we return? 4100+871.1
3: 8 ye say, **W** have we robbed thee? 4100+871.1
Mt 11:20 began he to upbraid the cities **w** *1722+3739*
25:13 the hour **w** the Son of man cometh. *1722+3739*
Mk 2: 4 they let down the bed **w** the sick of *1909+3739*
Lk 1: 4 **w** thou hast been instructed. *3739+4012*
1:25 **w** he looked on *me,* to take away my *3739*
11:22 he taketh *from him* all his armour **w** *1909+3739*
23:53 in stone, **w** never man before was laid. *3757*
Jn 19:41 **w** was never man yet laid. *1722+3739*
Ac 2: 8 in our own tongue, **w** we were born? *1722+3739*
7: 4 him into this land, **w** ye now dwell. *1519+3739*
10:12 **W** were all *manner of* fourfooted *1722+3739*
Ro 2: 1 for **w** thou judgest another, *1722+3739*
5: 2 by faith into this grace **w** we stand, *1722+3739*
7: 6 *that* being dead **w** we were held; *1722+3739*
1Co 7:20 same calling **w** he was called. *1722+3739+3778*
7:24 Brethren, let every man, **w** he is *1722+3739*
15: 1 you have received, and **w** ye stand; *1722+3739*
2Co 11:12 that **w** they glory, they may be found *1722+3739*
12:13 For what is it **w** ye were inferior to other *3739*
Eph 1: 6 **W** he hath made us accepted in *1722+3739*
1: 8 **W** he hath abounded toward us in all *3739*
2: 2 **W** in time past ye walked according *1722+3739*
5:18 And be not drunk with wine, **w** is *1722+3739*
Php 4:10 **w** ye were also careful, but ye lacked *1909+3739*
Col 2:12 **w** also you are risen with *him* *1722+3739*
2Ti 2: 9 **W** I suffer trouble, as an evil doer, *1722+3739*
Heb 6:17 **W** God, willing more abundantly to *1722+3739*
9: 2 **w** *was* the candlestick, and the table, and *1722*
9: 4 **w** *was* the golden pot that had *1722+3739*
1Pe 1: 6 **W** ye greatly rejoice, though now for *1722+3739*
3:20 ark was a preparing, **w** few, that is, *1519+3739*
4: 4 **W** they think it strange that you run *1722+3739*
5:12 is the true grace of God **w** ye stand. *1519+3739*
2Pe 3:12 **w** the heavens being on fire shall be *1223+3739*
3:13 new earth, **w** dwelleth righteousness. *1722+3739*
Rev 2:13 even in *those* days **w** Antipas *was* *1722+3739*
18:19 **w** were made rich all that had ships *1722+3739*

WHEREINSOEVER (1) [EVER, IN, SO]

2Co 11:21 **Howbeit w** any is bold, *302+1161+1722+3739*

WHEREINTO (4) [INTO]

Lev 11:33 earthen vessel, **w** *any* of them falleth, 413+8432
Nu 14:24 bring into the land **w** he went; 834+8033+1886.5
36: 3 shall be put to the inheritance of the tribe **w** 834
Jn 6:22 save that one **w** his disciples were *1519+3739*

WHEREOF (71) [OF]

Ge 3:11 **w** I commanded thee that thou shouldest not 834
Lev 6:30 **w** *any* of the blood is brought into 834
13:24 in the skin **w** *there is* a hot burning, and 2050.2
27: 9 **w** *men* bring an offering unto the LORD, 834
Nu 5: 3 their camps, in the midst **w** I dwell. 834+3963.1
7:19 the weight **w** *was* an hundred and 1886.3
7:25 the weight **w** *was* an hundred and 1886.3
7:37 the weight **w** *was* an hundred and 1886.3
7:49 the weight **w** *was* an hundred and 1886.3
7:61 the weight **w** *was* an hundred and 1886.3
7:67 the weight **w** *was* an hundred and 1886.3
7:73 the weight **w** *was* an hundred and 1886.3
7:79 the weight **w** *was* an hundred and 1886.3
21:16 that *is* the well **w** the LORD spake unto 834
Dt 13: 2 come to pass, **w** he spake unto thee, saying, 834
28:27 with the itch, **w** thou canst not be healed. 834
28:68 by the way **w** I spake unto thee, Thou shalt 834
Jos 14:12 **w** the LORD spake in that day; 834
20: 2 **w** I spake unto you by the hand of Moses: 834
22: 9 of their possession, **w** they were possessed, 834
1Sa 10:16 **w** Samuel spake, he told him not. 834
13: 2 **w** two thousand were with Saul in NIH
2Sa 12:30 the weight **w** *was* a talent of gold with 1886.3
2Ki 13:14 of his sickness **w** he died. 834+871.1+2050.2
17:12 **w** the LORD had said unto them, 834
2Ch 3: 8 the length **w** *was* according to the breadth 2050.2
6:20 upon the place **w** thou hast said that *thou* 834
24:14 **w** were made vessels for the house of 1930.2
33: 4 **w** the LORD had said, In Jerusalem shall 834
Ne 12:31 **w** *one* went on the right hand upon the wall NIH
Job 6: 4 the poison **w** drinketh up my spirit: 3963.1
Ps 46: 4 the streams **w** shall make glad the city of 2050.2
57: 6 into the midst **w** they are fallen 1886.3
126: 3 hath done great things for us; **w** we are glad. NIH
Ecc 1:10 Is there *any* thing **w** it may be said, See, 7945
SS 4: 2 **w** every one beareth twins, and none *is* 7945
6: 6 **w** every one beareth twins, and *there is* not 7945
Jer 32:36 God of Israel, concerning this city, **w** ye say, 834
32:43 **w** ye say, *It is* desolate without man or beast; 834
42:16 the famine, **w** ye were afraid, 834+4480
Eze 32:15 the country shall be destitute of that **w** it 4480
39: 8 Lord GOD; this *is* the day **w** I have spoken. 834
Da 9: 2 **w** the word of the LORD came to 834
Hos 2:12 her vines and her fig trees, **w** she hath said, 834
Lk 23:14 *touching those things* **w** ye accuse him: *3739*
Ac 2:32 hath God raised up, **w** we all are witnesses. *3739*
3:15 raised from the dead; **w** we are witnesses. *3739*
17:19 this new doctrine, **w** thou speakest, *is?* *5259*
17:31 **w** he hath given assurance unto all *men,* in *NIG*
21:24 all may know that *those things,* **w** they *3739*
24: 8 of all these *things,* **w** we accuse him. *3739*
24:13 Neither can they prove *the things* **w** *3739+4012*
25:11 if there be none *of these things* **w** these *3739*
26: 2 all *the things* **w** I am accused of the Jews: *3739*
Ro 4: 2 were justified by works, he hath **w** to glory; *NIG*
6:21 *in those things* **w** ye are now ashamed? *3739*
15:17 **w** *I* may glory through Jesus Christ *in those* *NIG*
1Co 7: 1 Now concerning *the things* **w** ye wrote unto *3739*
2Co 9: 5 **w** *ye* had notice before, that the same might *NIG*
Eph 3: 7 **W** I was made a minister, according to *3739*
Php 3: 4 If any other *man* thinketh that *he hath* **w** *he* *NIG*
Col 1: 5 **w** ye heard before in the word of the truth *3739*
1:23 **w** I Paul am made a minister; *3739*
1:25 **W** I am made a minister, according to *3739*
1Ti 1: 7 what they say, nor **w** they affirm. *4012+5101*
6: 4 **w** cometh envy, strife, railings, *1537*
Heb 2: 5 the world to come, **w** we speak: *3739+4012*
10:15 **W** the Holy Ghost also is a witness to us: *NIG*
12: 8 **w** all are partakers, then are ye bastards, *3739*
13:10 **w** they have no right to eat which *1537+3739*
1Jn 4: 3 **w** you have heard that it should come; *3739*

WHEREON (27) [ON]

Ge 28:13 the land **w** thou liest, to thee will I give it, 834
Ex 3: 5 for the place **w** thou standest *is* holy ground. 834
8:21 also the ground **w** they *are.* 834+5921+1886.3
Lev 6:27 thou shalt wash that **w** it was 834+5921
15: 4 **w** he lieth that hath the issue, 834+5921
15: 4 every thing, **w** he sitteth, shall be 834+5921
15: 6 he that sitteth on *any* thing **w** he sat 834+5921
15:17 **w** is the seed of copulation, 834+5921
15:23 or on *any* thing **w** she sitteth, when he 834+5921
15:24 all the bed **w** he lieth shall be unclean. 834+5921
15:26 Every bed **w** she lieth all the days of 834+5921
Dt 11:24 Every place **w** the soles of your feet 834+871.1
Jos 5:15 for the place **w** thou standest *is* holy. 834+5921
14: 9 Surely the land **w** thy feet have trodden shall 834
1Sa 6:18 **w** they set down the ark of 834+5921+1886.3
2Ch 4:19 tables **w** the shewbread *was set;* 5921+1992.1

W

2Ch 32:10 W do ye trust, that ye abide in 4100+5921
Est 7: 8 W Esther was. Then said 834+5921+1886.3
Job 24:23 be given him to be in safety, w he resteth; 2050.1
SS 4: 4 w there hang a thousand bucklers, 5921+2050.2
Isa 36: 6 w if a man lean, it will go into his 834+5921
Eze 37:20 the sticks w thou writest shall 834+5921+1992.1
Mk 11: 2 find a colt tied, w never man sat; 1909+3739
Lk 4:29 led him unto the brow of the hill w 1909+3739
5:25 and took up that w he lay, and 1909+3739
19:30 find a colt tied, w yet never man sat: 1909+3739
Jn 4:38 I sent you to reap that w ye bestowed no 3739

WHERESOEVER (12) [EVER, SO]

Lev 13:12 from his head even to his foot, w 3605+3807.1
2Ki 8: 1 and sojourn w thou canst sojourn: 834+871.1
12: 5 w any breach shall be found. 834+3605+8033
1Ch 17: 6 W I have walked with all 834+3605+871.1
Jer 40: 5 w it seemeth convenient unto thee to 413+3605
Da 2:38 w the children of men dwell, 1768+3606+871.2
Mt 24:28 For w the carcase is, there will 1437+3699
26:13 W this gospel shall be preached in 1437+3699
Mk 9:18 And w he taketh him, he teareth him: 302+3699
14: 9 W this gospel shall be preached 302+3699
14:14 And w he shall go in, say ye to 1437+3699
Lk 17:37 W the body is, thither will the eagles be 3699

WHERETO (3) [TO]

Job 30: 2 Yea, w might the strength of their 4100+3807.1
Isa 55:11 and it shall prosper in the thing w I sent it. 834
Php 3:16 Nevertheless, w we have already 1519+3739

WHEREUNTO (26) [UNTO]

Nu 36: 4 inheritance of the tribe w they are received: 834
Dt 4:26 w you go over Jordan to 834+8033+1886.5
2Ch 8:11 w the ark of the LORD hath come. 413+834
Est 10: 2 of Mordecai, w the king advanced him, 834
Ps 71: 3 w I may continually resort: NIH
Jer 22:27 to the land w they desire to return, 834+8033
Eze 5: 9 w I will not do any more the like, because 834
20:29 What is the high place w ye go? 834+8033
Mt 11:16 But w shall I liken this generation? It is like 5101
Mk 4:30 W shall we liken the kingdom of God? 5101
Lk 7:31 W then shall I liken the men of this 5101
13:18 of God like? and w shall I resemble it? 5101
13:20 W shall I liken the kingdom of God? 5101
Ac 5:24 doubted of them w this would grow. 302+5101
13: 2 and Saul for the work w I have called them. 3739
27: 8 fair havens; nigh w was the city of Lasea. 3739
Gal 4: 9 w ye desire again to be in bondage? 3739+3825
Col 1:29 W I also labour, striving according 1519+3739
2Th 2:14 W he called you by our gospel, 1519+3739
1Ti 2: 7 W I am ordained a preacher, and 1519+3739
4: 6 and of good doctrine, w thou hast attained. 3739
6:12 w thou art also called, and 1519+3739
2Ti 1:11 W I am appointed a preacher, and 1519+3739
1Pe 2: 8 w also they were appointed. 1519+3739
3:21 The like figure w even baptism doth also 3739
2Pe 1:19 w ye do well that ye take heed, as unto a 3739

WHEREUPON (17) [UPON]

Lev 11:35 every thing w any part of their carcase 834
Jdg 16:26 Suffer me that I may feel the pillars w 834
1Ki 7:48 table of gold, w the shewbread was, 834+5921
12:28 W the king took counsel, and made two 2050.1
2Ch 12: 6 W the princes of Israel and the king 2050.1
Job 38: 6 W are the foundations thereof 4100+5921
Eze 9: 3 w he was, to the threshold of 834+5921
23:41 w thou hast set mine incense and 5921+1886.3
24:25 that w they set their minds, their sons and NIH
40:41 w they slew their sacrifices. 413+1992.1
40:42 w also they laid the instruments 413+1992.1
Am 4: 7 and the piece w it rained not withered. 834
Mt 14: 7 W he promised with an oath to give her 3606
Ac 24:18 W certain Jews from Asia found me 1722+3739
26:12 W as I went to Damascus with 1722+3739
26:19 W, O king Agrippa, I was not disobedient 3606
Heb 9:18 W neither the first testament was dedicated 3606

WHEREWITH (110) [WITH]

Ge 27:41 of the blessing w his father blessed him: 834
Ex 3: 9 I have also seen the oppression w 834
4:17 w thou shalt do signs. 834+871.1+2050.2
16:32 that they may see the bread w I have fed you 834
17: 5 thy rod, w thou smotest 834+871.1+2050.2
29:33 they shall eat those things w 834+871.1+1992.1
Nu 3:31 the vessels of the sanctuary w they 834+871.1
3:48 w the odd number of them is to be NIH
4: 9 w they minister unto it: 834+871.1
4:12 w they minister in the sanctuary, and 834+871.1
4:14 w they minister about it, even 834+871.1
16:39 w they that were burnt had offered; 834
25:18 w they have beguiled you in the matter of 834
30: 4 her bond w she hath bound her soul, 834+5921
30: 4 every bond w she hath bound her soul 834+5921
30: 5 or of her bonds w she hath bound her 834+5921
30: 6 out of her lips, w she bound her soul; 834+5921
30: 7 w she bound her soul shall stand. 834+5921
30: 8 w she bound her soul, of none effect: 834+5921
30: 9 w they have bound their souls, 834+5921
30:11 every bond w she bound her soul shall 834+5921
35:17 w he may die, and he die, he is a 834+871.1
35:18 w he may die, and he die, he is a 834+871.1
35:23 w a man may die, seeing him not, and 834+871.1
Dt 9:19 w the LORD was wroth against you to 834
15:14 of that w the LORD thy God hath 834
22:12 thy vesture, w thou coverest thyself. 834+871.1
28:53 w thine enemies shall distress thee: 834
28:55 w thine enemies shall distress thee in all thy 834
28:57 w thine enemy shall distress thee in thy 834
28:67 for the fear of thine heart w thou shalt 834
33: 1 w Moses the man of God blessed 834
Jos 8:26 w he stretched out the spear, 834+871.1
Jdg 6:15 O my Lord, w shall I save Israel? 4100+871.1
9: 4 w Abimelech hired vain 871.1+1992.1+2050.1

Jdg 9: 9 w by me they honour God and man, and 871.1
9:38 w thou saidst, Who is Abimelech, 834
16: 6 w thou mightest be bound to afflict 4100+871.1
16:10 w thou mightest be bound. 4100+871.1
16:13 tell me w thou mightest be bound. 4100+871.1
1Sa 6: 2 us w we shall send it to his place. 4100+871.1
8: 8 w they have forsaken me, and 2050.1
29: 4 for w should he reconcile himself 4100+871.1
2Sa 13:15 that the hatred w he hated her was greater 834
13:15 greater than the love w he had loved her. 834
21: 3 w shall I make the atonement, 4100+871.1
1Ki 8:59 w I have made supplication before 834
15:22 timber thereof, w Baasha had builded; 834
15:26 and in his sin w he made Israel to sin. 834
15:30 by his provocation w he provoked 834
15:34 and in his sin w he made Israel to sin. 834
16:26 and in his sin w he made Israel to sin, 834
21:22 for the provocation w thou hast provoked me 834
22:22 the LORD said unto him, W? And 4100+871.1
2Ki 13:12 his might w he fought against Amaziah 834
21:16 beside his sin w he made Judah to sin, 834
23:26 w his anger was kindled against Judah, 834
25:14 vessels of brass w they ministered, 834+871.1
1Ch 18: 8 w Solomon made the brasen sea, 871.1+1886.3
2Ch 2:17 after the numbering w David his father 834
16: 6 w Baasha was a building; 834
18:20 And the LORD said unto him, W? 4100+871.1
35:21 this day, but against the house w I have war: NIH
Ne 9:34 w thou didst testify against them. 834
Job 15: 3 speeches w he can do no good? 871.1+3963.1
Ps 79:12 w they have reproached thee, O Lord. 834
89:51 W thine enemies have reproached, 834
89:51 w they have reproached the footsteps of 834
93: 1 with strength, w he hath girded himself: NIH
109:19 a girdle w he is girded continually. 1886.3
119:42 So shall I have w to answer him that 1697
129: 7 W the mower filleth not his hand; 7945
SS 3:11 king Solomon with the crown w 7945
Isa 28:12 This is the rest w ye may cause the weary to NIH
37: 6 w the servants of the king of Assyria 834
Jer 18:10 of the good, w I said I would benefit them. 834
19: 9 w their enemies, and they that seek their 834
21: 4 w ye fight against the king of 834+871.1
33:16 this is the name w she shall be called, The 834
52:18 of brass w they ministered, 834+871.1+1992.1
La 1:12 w the LORD hath afflicted me in the day of 834
Eze 13:12 Where is the daubing w ye have daubed 834
13:20 w ye there hunt the souls to make them 834
16:19 fine flour, and oil, and honey, w I fed thee, NIH
29:20 Egypt for his labour w he served against it, 834
32:16 This is the lamentation w they shall 2050.1
36:18 and for their idols w they had polluted it: NIH
40:42 w they slew the burnt 834+871.1+3963.1
Da 2: 1 w his spirit was troubled, and his sleep 2050.1
Mic 6: 6 W shall I come before the LORD, 4100+871.1
Zec 14:12 this shall be the plague w the LORD 834
14:18 w the LORD will smite the heathen 834
Mal 2: 5 I gave them to him for the fear w he 2050.1
Mt 5:13 lost his savour, w shall it be salted? 1722+5101
Mk 3:28 blasphemies w soever they shall 302+3745
9:50 his saltness, w will you season it? 1722+5101
Lk 14:34 his savour, w shall it be seasoned? 1722+5101
17: 8 Make ready w I may sup, and gird thyself, 5101
Jn 13: 5 to wipe them with the towel w he was 3739
17:26 will declare it: that the love w thou 3739
Ro 14:19 and things w one may edify another. 1519
2Co 1: 4 by the comfort w we ourselves are 3739
7: 7 by the consolation w he was comforted in 3739
10: 2 w I think to be bold against some, 3739
Gal 5: 1 in the liberty w Christ hath made us free, 3739
Eph 2: 4 in mercy, for his great love w he loved us, 3739
4: 1 worthy of the vocation w ye are called, 3739
6:16 w ye shall be able to quench all 1722+3739
1Th 3: 9 for all the joy w we joy for your sakes 3739
Heb 10:29 w he was sanctified, an unholy thing, 1722+3739

WHEREWITHAL (2) [WITHAL]

Ps 119: 9 W shall a young man cleanse his 4100+871.1
Mt 6:31 shall we drink? or, W shall we be clothed? 5101

WHET (4)

Dt 32:41 If I w my glittering sword, and mine hand 8150
Ps 7:12 If he turn not, he will w his sword; he hath 3913
64: 3 Who w their tongue like a sword, and 8150
Ecc 10:10 he do not w the edge, then must he put to 7043

WHETHER (171)

Ge 18:21 see w they have done altogether 1886.2
24:21 to wit w the LORD had made his 1886.2
27:21 w thou be my very son Esau or not. 1886.2
31:39 w stolen by day, or stolen by night. NIH
37:14 see w it be well with thy brethren, and well NIH
37:32 know now w it be thy son's coat or no. 518
42:16 be proved, w there be any truth in you: 1886.2
43: 6 as to tell the man w ye had yet a brother? 1886.2
Ex 4:18 are in Egypt, and see w they be yet alive. 1886.2
12:19 w he be a stranger, or born in the land. 871.1
16: 4 w they will walk in my law, or no. 1886.2
19:13 w it be beast or man, it shall not live: 518
21:31 W he have gored a son, or have gored a 176
22: 4 his hand alive, w it be ox, or ass, or sheep; 4480
22: 8 to see w he have put his hand unto his 518+3808
22: 9 w it be for ox, for ass, for sheep, NIH
34:19 thy cattle, w ox or sheep, that is male. NIH
Lev 3: 1 w it be a male or female, he shall offer it 518
5: 1 w he hath seen or known of it; if he do not 176
5: 2 w it be a carcase of an unclean beast, or a 176
7:26 w it be of fowl or of beast, in any of your NIH
11:32 w it be any vessel of wood, or raiment, or 4480
11:35 w it be oven, or ranges for pots, they shall NIH
13:47 w it be a woollen garment, or a linen NIH
13:48 W it be in the warp, or woof; of linen, or of 176
13:48 w in a skin, or in any thing made of skin; 176
13:52 w warp or woof, in woollen or in linen, or 176

Lev 13:55 fret inward, w it be bare within or without. NIH
15: 3 w his flesh run with his issue, or his flesh be NIH
16:29 do no work at all, w it be one of your own NIH
17:15 that which was torn with beasts, w it be one NIH
18: 9 w she be born at home, or born abroad, NIH
22:28 w it be cow or ewe, ye shall not kill it and NIH
27:12 the priest shall value it, w it be good or bad: 996
27:14 priest shall estimate it, w it be good or bad: 996
27:26 no man shall sanctify it; w it be ox, or sheep: 518
27:30 w of the seed of the land, or of the fruit of NIH
27:33 He shall not search w it be good or bad, 996
Nu 9:21 w it was by day or by night that the cloud 176
9:22 Or w it were two days, or a month, or NIH
11:23 thou shalt see now w my word shall come 1886.2
13:18 w they be strong or weak, few or many; 1886.2
13:19 is that they dwell in, w it be good or bad; 1886.2
13:19 dwell in, w in tents, or in strong holds; 1886.2
13:20 what the land is, w it be fat or lean, 1886.2
13:20 or lean, w there be wood therein, or not. 1886.2
15:30 w he be born in the land, or a stranger, NIH
18:15 w it be of men or beasts, shall be thine: NIH
Dt 4:32 w there hath been any such thing as this 1886.2
8: 2 w thou wouldest keep his 1886.2
13: 3 to know w you love the LORD your 1886.2
18: 3 that offer a sacrifice, w it be ox or sheep; 518
22: 6 w they be young ones, or eggs, and the dam NIH
24:14 w he be of thy brethren, or of thy strangers NIH
Jos 24:15 w the gods which your fathers served that 518
Jdg 2:22 w they will keep the way of the LORD 1886.2
3: 4 to know w they would hearken unto 1886.2
9: 2 W is better for you, either that all the sons 4100
18: 5 that we may know w our way which we 1886.2
Ru 3:10 followedst not young men, w poor or rich. 518
2Sa 12:22 Who can tell w GOD will be gracious to NIH
15:21 w in death or life, even there also will thy 518
1Ki 20:18 And he said, W they be come out for peace, 518
20:18 or w they be come out for war, take them 518
20:33 Now the men did diligently observe w 1886.2
2Ki 1: 2 inquire of Baal-zebub the god of Ekron w I 518
2Ch 14:11 w with many, or with them that have no NIH
15:13 w small or great, whether man or 4480+3807.1
15:13 or great, w man or woman. 4480+3807.1
Ezr 2:59 and their seed, w they were of Israel: 518+4480
5:17 w it be so, that a decree was made of Cyrus 2006
7:26 w it be unto death, or to banishment, or 2006
Ne 7:61 nor their seed, w they were of Israel. 518
Est 3: 4 to see w Mordecai's matters would stand: 1886.2
4:11 do know, that whosoever, w man or woman, NIH
4:14 who knoweth w thou art come to 518
Job 34:29 w it be done against a nation, or against a 2050.1
34:33 w thou refuse, or whether thou choose; 3588
34:33 whether thou refuse, or w thou choose; 3588
37:13 w for correction, or for his land, or 518
Pr 20:11 w his work be pure, and whether it be right. 518
20:11 whether his work be pure, and w it be right. 518
29: 9 w he rage or laugh, there is no rest. 2050.1
Ecc 2:19 who knoweth w he shall be a wise man 1886.2
5:12 man is sweet, w he eat little or much: 518
11: 6 for thou knowest not w shall prosper, 335+2088
11: 6 or that, or w they both shall be alike good. 518
12:14 with every secret thing, w it be good, or 518
12:14 thing, whether it be good, or w it be evil. 518
SS 6:11 and to see w the vine flourished, and 1886.2
7:12 w the tender grape appear, and NIH
Jer 30: 6 and see w a man doth travail with child? 518
42: 6 W it be good, or whether it be evil, we will 518
42: 6 Whether it be good, or w it be evil, we will 518
Eze 2: 5 w they will hear, or whether they will 518
2: 5 they will hear, or w they will forbear, 518
2: 7 w they will hear, or whether they will 518
2: 7 they will hear, or w they will forbear: 518
3:11 w they will hear, or whether they will 518
3:11 they will hear, or w they will forbear. 518
44:31 dead of itself, or torn, w it be fowl or beast. 4480
Mt 9: 5 For w is easier, to say, Thy sins be forgiven 5101
21:31 W of them twain did the will of his father? 5101
23:17 for w is greater, the gold, or the temple that 5101
23:19 for w is greater, the gift, or the altar that 5101
26:63 that thou tell us w thou be the Christ, 1487
27:21 W of the twain will ye that I release unto 5101
27:49 let us see w Elias will come to save him. 1487
Mk 2: 9 W is it easier to say to the sick of the palsy, 5101
3: 2 w he would heal him on the sabbath day; 1487
15:36 let us see w Elias will come to take him 1487
15:44 he asked him w he had been any while 1487
Lk 3:15 of John, w he were the Christ, or not; 3379
5:23 W is easier, to say, Thy sins be forgiven 5101
6: 7 w he would heal on the sabbath day; 1487
14:28 the cost, w he have sufficient to finish it? 1487
14:31 consulteth w he be able with ten thousand 1487
22:27 For w is greater, he that sitteth at meat, or 5101
23: 6 he asked w the man were a Galilean. 1487
Jn 7:17 w it be of God, or whether I speak of 4220
7:17 it be of God, or w I speak of myself. NIG
9:25 said, W he be a sinner or no, I know not: 1487
Ac 1:24 w of these two thou hast chosen, 1520+3739
4:19 W it be right in the sight of God to hearken 1487
5: 8 Tell me w ye sold the land for so much? 1487
9: 2 of this way, w they were men or women, 5037
10:18 And called, and asked w Simon, which was 1487
17:11 the scriptures daily, w those things were so. 1487
19: 2 much as heard w there be any Holy Ghost. 1487
25:20 I asked him w he would go to Jerusalem, 1487
Ro 6:16 w of sin unto death, or of obedience unto 2273
12: 6 w prophecy, let us prophesy according to 1535
14: 8 For w we live, we live unto the Lord; 1437+5037
14: 8 and w we die, we die unto the Lord: 1437+5037
14: 8 w we live therefore, or die, we are 1437+5037
1Co 1:16 besides, I know not w I baptized any other. 1536
3:22 W Paul, or Apollos, or Cephas, or 1535
7:16 O wife, w thou shalt save thy husband? 1487
7:16 O man, w thou shalt save thy wife? 1487
8: 5 w in heaven or in earth, (as there be gods 1535
10:31 W therefore ye eat, or drink, or 1535
12:13 w we be Jews or Gentiles, whether we be 1535

1Co 12:13 *be* Jews or Gentiles, w *we be* bond or free; *1535*
12:26 And w one member suffer, all the members *1535*
13: 8 but w *there be* prophecies, they shall fail; *1535*
13: 8 w *there be* tongues, they shall cease; *1535*
13: 8 w *there be* knowledge, it shall vanish away. *1535*
14: 7 without life giving sound, w pipe or harp, *1535*
15:11 Therefore w *it were* I or they, so we preach, *1535*
2Co 1: 6 And w we be afflicted, *it is* for your *1535*
1: 6 **or w** we be comforted, *it is* for your *1535*
2: 9 of you, w ye be obedient in all *things.* *1487*
5: 9 we labour, that, w present or absent, *1535*
5:10 to that he hath done, w *it be* good or bad. *1535*
5:13 For w we be beside ourselves, *it is* to God: *1535*
5:13 **or w** we be sober, *it is* for your cause. *1535*
8:23 W *any do inquire* of Titus, *he is* my partner *1535*
12: 2 years ago, (w in the body, I cannot tell; *1535*
12: 2 **or w** out of the body, I cannot tell: *1535*
12: 3 (w in the body, or out of the body, I cannot *1535*
13: 5 Examine yourselves, w ye be in the faith; *1487*
Eph 6: 8 receive of the Lord, w *he be* bond or free. *1535*
Php 1:18 every way, w in pretence, or in truth, *1535*
1:20 in my body, w *it be* by life, or by death. *1535*
1:27 that w I come and see you, or *else* be *1535*
Col 1:16 w *they be* thrones, or dominions, or *1535*
1:20 *I say,* w *they be things* in earth, or *things* in *1535*
1Th 5:10 Who died for us, that, w we wake or sleep, *1535*
2Th 2:15 been taught, w by word, or by our epistle. *1535*
1Pe 2:13 w *it be* to the king, as supreme; *1535*
1Jn 4: 1 but try the spirits w they are of God: *1487*

WHICH (4419)

Ge 1: 7 divided the waters w *were* under 834
1: 7 the waters w *were* above the firmament: 834
1:21 w the waters brought forth abundantly, 834
1:29 w *is* upon the face of all the earth, and every 834
1:29 in the w *is* the fruit of a tree yielding seed; 834
2: 2 on the seventh day God ended his work w he 834
2: 2 day from all his work w he had made. 834
2: 3 that in it he had rested from all his work w 834
2:11 that *is it* w compasseth the whole land of 1886.1
2:14 that *is it* w goeth toward the east of 1886.1
2:22 w the LORD God had taken from man, 834
3: 1 of the field w the LORD God had made. 834
3: 3 of the fruit of the tree w *is* in the midst of 834
3:17 of the tree, of w I commanded thee, saying, 834
3:24 a flaming sword w turned every way, 1886.1
4:11 w hath opened her mouth to receive thy 834
5:29 of the ground w the LORD hath cursed. 834
6: 2 they took them wives of all w they chose. 834
6: 4 the same *became* mighty *men* w *were* of old, 834
6:15 this *is the fashion* w thou shalt make it *of:* 834
7:23 every living substance was destroyed w *was* 834
8: 6 that Noah opened the window of the ark w 834
8: 7 forth a raven, w went forth to and fro, 2050.1
8:12 w returned not again unto him any more. 2050.1
9: 4 w *is* the blood thereof, shall you not eat. NIH
9:12 This *is* the token of the covenant w I make 834
9:15 w *is* between me and you and every living 834
9:17 w I have established between me and all 834
11: 5 the tower, w the children of men builded. 834
11: 6 from them, w they have imagined to do. 834
13: 4 of the altar, w he had made there at the first: 834
13: 5 w went with Abram, had flocks, and 1886.1
13:15 For all the land w thou seest, to thee will I 834
13:18 w *is* in Hebron, and built there an altar unto 834
14: 2 and the king of Bela, w *is* Zoar. 1931
14: 3 in the vale of Siddim, w *is* the salt sea. 1931
14: 6 unto El-paran, w *is* by the wilderness. 834
14: 7 w *is* Kadesh, and smote all the country of 1931
14:15 w *is* on the left hand of Damascus. 834
14:17 the valley of Shaveh, w *is* the king's dale. 1931
14:20 w hath delivered thine enemies into thy 834
14:24 Save only that w the young men have eaten, 834
14:24 and the portion of the men w went with me, 834
16:15 his son's name, w Hagar bare, Ishmael. 834
17:10 w ye shall keep, between me and you and 834
17:12 money of any stranger, w *is* not of thy seed. 834
17:21 w Sarah shall bear unto thee at this set time 834
18: 8 the calf w he had dressed, and set *it* before 834
18:10 heard *it in* the tent door, w *was* behind him. 1931
18:13 Shall I of a surety bear *a child,* w am old? NIH
18:17 Shall I hide from Abraham *that thing* w I do; 834
18:19 upon Abraham that w he hath spoken of him. 834
18:21 to the cry of it, w is come unto me; 1886.1
18:27 unto the Lord, w *am but* dust and ashes: 2050.1
19: 5 Where *are* the men w came in to thee this 834
19: 8 I have two daughters w have not known 834
19:14 w married his daughters, and said, Up, NIH
19:15 and thy two daughters, w are here; 1886.1
19:19 w thou hast shewed unto me in saving my 834
19:21 *this* city, for the w thou hast spoken. 834
19:25 and **that w grew** upon the ground. 6780
19:29 when he overthrew the cities in the w Lot 834
20: 3 dead man, for the woman w thou hast taken; 834
20:13 This *is* thy kindness w thou shalt shew unto 834
21: 2 at the set time of w God had spoken to him. 834
21: 9 w she had born unto Abraham, mocking. 834
21:25 w Abimelech's servants had violently taken 834
21:29 What *mean* these seven ewe lambs w thou 834
22: 2 one of the mountains w I will tell thee of. 834
22: 3 went unto the place of w God had told him. 834
22: 9 they came to the place w God had told him 834
22:17 and as the sand w *is* upon the sea shore; 834
23: 9 w he hath, which *is* in the end of his field; 834
23: 9 which he hath, w *is* in the end of his field; 834
23:16 w he had named in the audience of the sons 834
23:17 the field of Ephron, w *was* in Machpelah, 834
23:17 w *was* before Mamre, the field, and the cave 834
23:17 the cave w *was* therein, and all the trees that 834
24: 7 w took me from my father's house, and 834
24: 7 w spake unto me, and that sware unto me, 834
24:24 the son of Milcah, w she bare unto Nahor. 834
24:42 if now thou do prosper my way w I go: 834
24:48 w had led me in the right way to take my 834
24:60 let thy seed possess the gate of those w hate NIH

Ge 25: 6 w Abraham had, Abraham gave gifts, and 834
25: 7 of the years of Abraham's life w he lived, 834
25: 9 son of Zohar the Hittite, w *is* before Mamre; 834
25:10 The field w Abraham purchased of the sons 834
26: 2 dwell in the land w I shall tell thee of: 834
26: 3 I will perform the oath w I sware unto 834
26:15 For all the wells w his father's servants had 834
26:18 w they had digged in the days of Abraham 834
26:18 he called their names after the names by w 834
26:32 told him concerning the well w they had 834
26:35 W were a grief of mind unto Isaac and 2050.1
27: 8 obey my voice according to *that* w I 834
27:15 w *were* with her in the house, and put them 834
27:17 and the bread, w she had prepared, 834
27:27 smell of a field w the LORD hath blessed: 834
27:45 and he forget *that* w thou hast done to him: 834
27:46 such as these w *are* of the daughters of NIH
28: 4 art a stranger, w God gave unto Abraham. 834
28: 9 took unto the wives w he had Mahalath NIH
28:15 until I have done *that* w I have spoken to 834
28:22 this stone, w I have set *for* a pillar, shall be 834
29:27 we will give thee this also for the service w 834
30:26 for thou knowest my service w I have done 834
30:30 For *it was* little w thou hadst before I *came,* 834
30:37 made the white appear w *was* in the rods. 834
30:38 he set the rods w he had pilled before 834
31: 1 of *that* w *was* of our father's hath he gotten 834
31:10 the rams w leaped upon the cattle *were* 1886.1
31:12 all the rams w leap upon the cattle *are* 1886.1
31:16 For all the riches w God hath taken from our 834
31:18 all his goods w he had gotten, the cattle of 834
31:18 his getting, w he had gotten in Padan-aram, 834
31:39 **That w was torn** *of beasts* I brought not 2966
31:43 or unto their children w they have born? 834
31:51 w I have cast betwixt me and thee; 834
32: 8 the *other* company w is left shall escape. 1886.1
32: 9 the LORD w saidst unto me, 1886.1
32:10 w thou hast shewed unto thy servant; 834
32:12 the sea, w cannot be numbered for multitude. 834
32:13 took of that w came to his hand a present NIH
32:32 of Israel eat not *of* the sinew w shrank, 834
32:32 w *is* upon the hollow of the thigh, unto this NIH
33: 5 The children w God hath graciously given 834
33: 8 What meanest thou by all this drove w I 834
33:18 city of Shechem, w *is* in the land of Canaan, 834
34: 1 the daughter of Leah, w she bare unto Jacob, 834
34: 7 **w thing** ought not to be done. 3651
34:28 that w *was* in the city, and that which *was* in 834
34:28 *was* in the city, and that w *was* in the field, 834
35: 3 and was with me in the way w I went. 834
35: 4 they gave unto Jacob all the strange gods w 834
35: 4 and *all their* earrings w *were* in their ears; 834
35: 4 Jacob hid them under the oak w *was* by 834
35: 6 w *is* in the land of Canaan, that *is,* Beth-el, 834
35:12 the land w I gave Abraham and Isaac, to thee 834
35:19 in the way to Ephrath, w *is* Beth-lehem. 1931
35:26 of Jacob, w were born to him in Padan-aram. 834
35:27 w *is* Hebron, where Abraham and 1931
36: 5 w were born unto him in the land of Canaan. 834
36: 6 w he had got in the land of Canaan; 834
37: 6 I pray you, this dream w I have dreamed: 834
38:10 *the thing* w he did displeased the LORD: 834
38:14 an open place, w *is* by the way to Timnath; 834
39: 1 w had brought him down thither. 834
39: 6 ought he had, save the bread w he did eat. 834
39:17 w thou hast brought unto us, 834
39:19 w she spake unto him, saying, After this 834
39:23 the LORD *was* with him, and *that* w he did, 834
40: 5 king of Egypt, w *were* bound in the prison. 834
40:20 the third day, w *was* Pharaoh's birthday, NIH
41:28 This *is* the thing w I have spoken unto 834
41:36 of famine, w shall be in the land of Egypt; 834
41:43 he made him to ride in the second chariot w 834
41:48 w were in the land of Egypt, and laid up 834
41:48 of the field, w *was* round about every city, 834
41:50 w Asenath the daughter of Poti-pherah priest 834
42: 9 Joseph remembered the dreams w he 834
42:38 if mischief befall him by the way in the w ye 834
43: 2 when they had eaten up the corn w they had 834
43:26 they brought him the present w *was* in their 834
43:32 w did eat with him, by themselves: 1886.1
44: 5 *Is* not this *it* in w my lord drinketh, and 834
44: 8 w we found in our sacks' mouths, 834
45: 6 *in the* w *there shall* neither *be* earing nor 834
45:27 words of Joseph, w he had said unto them: 834
45:27 when he saw the wagons w Joseph had sent 834
46: 5 in the wagons w Pharaoh had sent to carry 834
46: 6 w they had gotten in the land of Canaan, and 834
46: 8 w came into Egypt, Jacob and his sons: 1886.1
46:15 w she bare unto Jacob in Padan-aram, 834
46:20 w Asenath the daughter of Poti-pherah priest 834
46:22 the sons of Rachel, w were born to Jacob: 834
46:25 w Laban gave unto Rachel his daughter, and 834
46:26 w came out of his loins, besides Jacob's NIH
46:27 w were born him in Egypt, *were* two souls: 834
46:27 w came into Egypt, *were* threescore and 1886.1
46:31 w *were* in the land of Canaan, are come unto 834
47:14 land of Canaan, for the corn w they bought: 834
47:22 did eat their portion w Pharaoh gave them: 834
47:26 of the priests only, w became not Pharaoh's. NIH
48: 5 w were born unto thee in the land of 1886.1
48: 6 w thou begettest after them, shall be thine, 834
48:15 the God w fed me all my life long unto 1886.1
48:16 The Angel w redeemed me from all evil, 1886.1
48:22 w I took out of the hand of the Amorite with 834
49: 1 that I may tell you *that* w shall befall you in 834
49:30 w *is* before Mamre, in the land of Canaan, 834
49:30 w Abraham bought with the field of Ephron 834
50: 3 are fulfilled the days of those w are NIH
50: 5 in my grave w I have digged for me in 834
50:10 w *is* beyond Jordan, and there they mourned 834
50:11 called Abel-mizraim, w *is* beyond Jordan. 834
50:13 w Abraham bought with the field for a 834
50:15 will certainly requite us all the evil w we did 834
50:24 bring you out of this land unto the land w he 834

Ex 1: 1 the children of Israel, w came into Egypt; 1886.1
1: 8 a new king over Egypt, w knew not Joseph. 834
1:15 of w the name of the one *was* Shiphrah, and 834
3: 7 the affliction of my people w *are* in Egypt, 834
3:16 and *seen* that w is done to you in Egypt: NIH
3:20 smite Egypt with all my wonders w I will do 834
4: 9 the water w thou takest out of the river shall 834
4:18 and return unto my brethren w *are* in Egypt, 834
4:19 for all the men are dead w sought thy life. 1886.1
4:21 before Pharaoh, w I have put in thine hand: 834
4:28 and all the signs w he had commanded him. 834
4:30 Aaron spake all the words w the LORD had 834
5: 8 w they did make heretofore, you shall lay 834
5:14 w Pharaoh's taskmasters had set over them, 834
6: 7 w bringeth you out from under 1886.1
6: 8 *concerning* the w I did swear to give it to 834
6:27 *These are* they w spake to Pharaoh king 1886.1
7:15 the rod w was turned to a serpent shalt thou 834
7:17 hand upon the waters w *are* in the river, 834
8: 3 w shall go up and come into thine house, 2050.1
8:12 of the frogs w he had brought against 834
8:22 in w my people dwell, that no swarms *of* 1886.3
9: 3 the hand of the LORD is upon thy cattle w 834
9:19 and beast w shall be found in the field, 834
10: 2 and my signs w I have done amongst them; 834
10: 5 **w is escaped** which remaineth unto you 6413
10: 5 w remaineth unto you from the hail, 1886.1
10: 5 shall eat every tree w groweth for you out 1886.1
10: 6 w neither thy fathers, nor thy fathers' fathers 834
10:15 all the fruit of the trees w the hail had left: 834
10:19 w took away the locusts, and cast them 2050.1
10:21 land of Egypt, even darkness w may be felt. NIH
12:10 that w remaineth of it until the morning ye NIH
12:16 save *that* w every man must eat, that only 834
12:19 for whosoever eateth **that w is leavened,** 2556
12:25 when ye be come to the land w the LORD 834
12:39 they baked unleavened cakes of the dough w 834
13: 3 this day, *in* w ye came out from Egypt, 834
13: 5 w he sware unto thy fathers to give thee, 834
13: 8 of that w the LORD did unto me when I NIH
13:12 every firstling that cometh of a beast w thou 834
14:13 of the LORD, w he will shew to you to day: 834
14:19 w went before the camp of Israel, 1886.1
14:31 Israel saw *that* great work w the LORD did 834
15: 7 thy wrath, w consumed them as stubble. NIH
15:13 led forth the people w thou hast redeemed: NIH
15:16 the people pass over, w thou hast purchased. NIH
15:17 w thou hast made for thee to dwell in, NIH
15:17 O Lord, w thy hands have established. NIH
15:25 w when he had cast into the waters, NIH
15:26 wilt do that w is right in his sight, and NIH
15:26 w I have brought upon the Egyptians: 834
16: 1 of Sin, w *is* between Elim and Sinai, 834
16: 5 day they shall prepare *that* w they bring in; 834
16: 8 your murmurings w ye murmur against him: 834
16:15 This *is* the bread w the LORD hath given 834
16:16 This *is* the thing w the LORD hath 834
16:16 take ye every man for *them* w *are* in his 834
16:23 This *is that* w the LORD hath said, 834
16:23 bake *that* w you will bake *to day,* and seethe 834
16:23 that w remaineth over lay up for you to 1886.1
16:26 on the seventh day, w *is* the sabbath, in it NIH
16:32 This *is* the thing, w the LORD commandeth, 834
18: 3 of w the name of the one *was* Gershom; 834
18: 9 Jethro rejoiced for all the goodness w 834
19: 6 These *are* the words w thou shalt speak unto 834
19: 7 laid before their faces all these words w 834
19:22 w come near to the LORD, 1886.1
20: 2 w have brought thee out of the land of 834
20:12 that thy days may be long upon the land w 834
21: 1 Now these *are* the judgments w thou shalt 834
22: 9 for any manner of lost *thing,* w *another* 834
22:13 *and* he shall not make good that w was torn. NIH
23:16 of thy labours, w thou hast sown in the field: 834
23:16 of ingathering, w *is* in the end of the year, NIH
23:20 to bring thee into the place w I have 834
23:28 w shall drive out the Hivite, 2050.1
24: 3 All the words w the LORD hath said will 834
24: 5 w offered burnt offerings, and 2050.1
24: 8 w the LORD hath made with you 834
24:12 a law, and commandments w I have written; 834
25: 3 this *is* the offering w ye shall take of them; 834
25:16 thou shalt put into the ark the Testimony w I 834
25:22 from between the two cherubims w *are* upon 834
25:22 of all *things* w I will give thee in 834
25:40 w was shewed thee in the mount. 834
26:10 fifty loops in the edge of the curtain w 1886.1
26:13 a cubit on the other side of **that w** 1886.1
26:30 thereof w was shewed thee in the mount. 834
27:21 w *is* before the Testimony, Aaron and 834
28: 4 these *are* the garments w they shall make; 834
28: 8 w *is* upon it, shall be of the same, 834
28:24 rings w *are* on the ends of the breastplate. NIH
28:26 w *is* in the side of the ephod inward. 834
28:38 w the children of Israel shall hallow in all 834
29:27 w is waved, and which is heaved up, of 834
29:27 which is waved, and w is heaved up, of 834
29:27 *even* of *that* w *is* for Aaron, and of *that* 834
29:27 *is* for Aaron, and of *that* w *is* for his sons: 834
29:35 according to all *things* w I have commanded 834
29:38 Now this *is that* w thou shalt offer upon 834
30:37 *as for* the perfume w thou shalt make, 834
32: 1 Up, make us gods, w shall go before us; 834
32: 2 w *are* in the ears of your wives, of your sons, 834
32: 3 off the golden earrings w *were* in their ears, 834
32: 4 w brought thee up out of the land of Egypt. 834
32: 7 w thou broughtest out of the land of Egypt, 834
32: 8 out of the way w I commanded them: 834
32: 8 w have brought thee up out of the land of 834
32:11 w thou hast brought forth out of the land of 834
32:14 the LORD repented of the evil w he 834
32:20 he took the calf w they had made, and 834
32:23 Make us gods, w shall go before us: 834
32:32 out of thy book w thou hast written. 834
32:34 lead the people unto *the place* of w I have 834

W

Ex 32:35 because they made the calf, **w** Aaron made. 834
33: 1 the people **w** thou hast brought up out of 834
33: 1 unto the land **w** I sware unto Abraham, 834
33: 7 *that* every one **w** sought the LORD went NIH
33: 7 the Congregation, **w** *was* without the camp. 834
34: 1 that were in the first tables, **w** thou brakest. 834
34:10 all the people among **w** thou *art* shall see 834
34:11 Observe thou that **w** I command thee *this* 834
34:34 spake unto the children of Israel *that* **w** he 834
35: 1 These *are* the words **w** the LORD hath 834
35: 4 This *is* the thing **w** the LORD commanded, 834
35:25 brought that **w** they had spun, *both* of blue, NIH
35:29 **w** the LORD had commanded to be made 834
36: 3 **w** the children of Israel had brought for 834
36: 4 came every man from his work **w** they 834
36: 5 **w** the LORD commanded to make. 834
36:12 curtain **w** *was* in the coupling of the second: 834
36:17 of the curtain **w** coupleth the second. 1886.1
36:25 **w** *is* toward the north corner, he made NIH
37:16 he made the vessels **w** *were* upon the table, 834
38: 8 **w** assembled *at* the door of the tabernacle of 834
39:19 of it, **w** *was* on the side of the ephod inward. 834
Lev 1: 8 in order upon the wood that *is* on the fire **w** 834
1:12 wood that *is* on the fire **w** *is* upon the altar: 834
2:10 that **w** is left of the meat offering *shall be* NIH
2:11 **w** ye shall bring unto the LORD, 834
3: 4 **w** *is* by the flanks, and the caul above 834
3: 5 **w** *is* upon the wood that *is* on the fire: 834
3:10 **w** *is* by the flanks, and the caul above 834
3:15 **w** *is* by the flanks, and the caul above 834
4: 2 (*concerning things* **w** ought not to be done), 834
4: 3 let him bring for his sin, **w** he hath sinned, 834
4: 7 **w** *is* in the tabernacle of the congregation; 834
4: 7 **w** *is at* the door of the tabernacle of 834
4: 9 **w** *is* by the flanks, and the caul above 834
4:13 *concerning things* **w** should not be done, 834
4:14 **w** they have sinned against it, is known, then 834
4:18 horns of the altar **w** *is* before the LORD, 834
4:18 **w** *is at* the door of the tabernacle of 834
4:22 *concerning things* **w** should not be done, 834
4:27 *concerning things* **w** ought not to be done, 834
4:28 Or if his sin, **w** he hath sinned, come to his 834
4:28 for his sin **w** he hath sinned. 834
5: 6 the LORD for his sin **w** he hath sinned, 834
5: 7 **w** he hath committed, two turtledoves, or 834
5: 8 who shall offer *that* **w** *is* for the sin offering 834
5:10 for him for his sin **w** he had sinned, 834
5:17 commit any *of these things* **w** are forbidden 834
6: 2 in **that w was delivered** him **to keep**, 6487
6: 3 Or have found **that w was lost**, and 9
6: 4 that he shall restore that **w** he took violently 834
6: 4 or the thing **w** he hath deceitfully gotten, 834
6: 4 or that **w** was delivered him to keep, or 834
6: 4 him to keep, or the lost *thing* **w** he found, 834
6: 5 Or all *that* about **w** he hath sworn falsely; 834
6:10 take up the ashes **w** the fire hath consumed 834
6:15 all the frankincense **w** *is* upon the meat 834
6:20 **w** they shall offer unto the LORD in 834
7: 4 **w** *is* by the flanks, and the caul *that is* above 834
7: 8 skin of the burnt offering **w** he hath offered. 834
7:11 **w** he shall offer unto the LORD. 834
7:21 **w** *pertain* unto the LORD, even that soul 834
7:24 the fat of **that w is torn** *with beasts,* may 2966
7:25 of **w** *men* offer an offering made by fire unto 834
7:36 **W** the LORD commanded to be given them 834
7:38 **W** the LORD commanded Moses in mount 834
8: 5 This *is* the thing **w** the LORD commanded 834
8:30 of the blood **w** *was* upon the altar, and 834
8:32 that **w** remaineth of the flesh and of NIH
8:36 his sons did all things **w** the LORD 834
9: 5 they brought *that* **w** Moses commanded 834
9: 6 This *is* the thing **w** the LORD commanded 834
9: 8 calf of the sin offering, **w** *was* for himself. 834
9:12 **w** he sprinkled round about upon 2050.1
9:15 **w** *was* the sin offering for the people, and 834
9:18 of peace offerings, **w** *was* for the people: 834
9:18 **w** he sprinkled upon the altar round 1930.2
9:19 that **w** covereth *the inwards,* and NIH
9:24 **w** when all the people saw, they shouted, NIH
10: 1 the LORD, **w** he commanded them not. 834
10: 6 bewail the burning **w** the LORD hath 834
10:11 **w** the LORD hath spoken unto them by 834
10:14 **w** are given out of the sacrifices of peace NIH
10:16 Ithamar the sons of Aaron **w** were left 1886.1
11: 2 These *are* the beasts **w** ye shall eat among all 834
11:10 and of any living thing **w** *is* in the waters, 834
11:13 these *are they* **w** ye shall have in NIH
11:21 **w** have legs above their feet, to leap withal 834
11:23 **w** have four feet, *shall be* an abomination 834
11:26 *The carcases* of every beast **w** divideth 834
11:34 Of all meat **w** may be eaten, *that* on which 834
11:34 *that* on **w** *such* water cometh shall be 834
11:36 that **w** toucheth their carcase shall be NIH
11:37 fall upon any sowing seed **w** is to be sown, 834
11:39 if any beast, of **w** ye may eat, die; he that 834
13:18 The flesh also, in **w**, *even* in the skin 2050.2
13:58 whatsoever thing of skin *it be,* **w** thou shalt 834
14:32 whose hand is not able to get *that* **w** NIH
14:34 **w** I give to you for a possession, and I put 834
14:37 **w** in sight *are* lower than the wall; 2050.1
14:40 they take away the stones in **w** the plague *is,* 834
15:12 that he toucheth **w** hath the issue, shall be 2050.2
15:33 and of him that lieth with her **w** is unclean. NIH
16: 2 vail before the mercy seat, **w** *is* upon the ark; 834
16: 6 **w** *is* for himself, and make an atonement for 834
16: 9 Aaron shall bring the goat upon **w** 834
16:10 on **w** the lot fell to be the scapegoat, 834
16:11 **w** *is* for himself, and shall make an 834
16:11 shall kill the bullock of the sin offering **w** *is* 834
16:23 **w** he put on when he went into the holy 834
17: 2 This *is* the thing **w** the LORD hath 834
17: 5 **w** they offer in the open field, even that they 834
17: 8 or of the strangers **w** sojourn among you, 834
17:13 **w** hunteth and catcheth *any* beast or 834
17:15 every soul that eateth **that w died of itself,** 5038

Lev 17:15 **that w was torn** *with beasts, whether it be* 2966
18: 5 **w** if a man do, he shall live in them: I *am* 834
18:24 nations are defiled **w** I cast out before you: 834
18:27 **w** *were* before you, and the land is defiled;) 834
18:30 **w** were committed before you, and that ye 834
19:22 the LORD for his sin **w** he hath done: 834
19:22 the sin **w** he hath done shall be forgiven him. 834
19:36 **w** brought you out of the land of Egypt. 834
20: 8 do them: I *am* the LORD **w** sanctify you. NIH
20:23 of the nation, **w** I cast out before you: 834
20:24 **w** have separated you from *other* people. 834
20:25 **w** I have separated from you as unclean. 834
21: 3 is nigh unto him, **w** hath had no husband; 834
21: 8 for I the LORD, **w** sanctify you, *am* holy. NIH
22: 2 name *in those things* **w** they hallow unto me: 834
22: 3 that goeth unto the holy *things* **w** 834
22: 6 The soul **w** hath touched *any* such shall be 834
22: 8 **That w dieth of itself,** or is torn *with* 5038
22:15 of Israel, **w** they offer unto the LORD; 834
22:18 **w** they will offer unto the LORD for a 834
22:24 Ye shall not offer unto the LORD that **w** is NIH
22:32 of Israel: I *am* the LORD **w** hallow you, NIH
23: 2 **w** ye shall proclaim *to be* holy convocations, 834
23: 4 **w** ye shall proclaim in their seasons. 834
23:10 When ye be come into the land **w** I give unto 834
23:37 **w** ye shall proclaim *to be* holy convocations, 834
23:38 **w** ye give unto the LORD. 834
25: 2 When ye come into the land **w** I give you, 834
25: 5 **That w groweth of it own accord** of thy 5599
25:11 neither reap **that w groweth of itself** in it, 5599
25:25 shall he redeem **that w** his brother **sold**. 4465
25:28 **that w is sold** shall remain in the hand of 4465
25:31 the houses of the villages **w** have no wall 834
25:38 **w** brought you forth out of the land of Egypt, 834
25:42 **w** I brought forth out of the land of Egypt: 834
25:44 and thy bondmaids, **w** thou shalt have, 834
25:45 that *are* with you, **w** they begat in your land: 834
26:13 **w** brought you forth out of the land of Egypt, 834
26:22 **w** shall rob you of your children, and 2050.1
26:32 your enemies **w** dwell therein shall be 1886.1
26:40 with their trespass **w** they trespassed against 834
26:46 **w** the LORD made between him and 834
27:11 of **w** they do not offer a sacrifice unto 834
27:22 if *a man* sanctify unto the LORD a field **w** NIH
27:22 **w** *is* not of the fields of his possession; 834
27:26 **w** should be the LORD'S firstling, no man 834
27:29 None devoted, **w** shall be devoted of men, 834
27:34 **w** the LORD commanded Moses for 834
Nu 1:17 Aaron took these men **w** are expressed by 834
1:44 **w** Moses and Aaron numbered, and 834
2:12 those **w** pitch by him *shall be* the tribe of NIH
2:32 These *are* those **w** were numbered of NIH
3: 3 of Aaron, the priests **w** were anointed, 1886.1
3:26 **w** *is* by the tabernacle, and by the altar round 834
3:39 **w** Moses and Aaron numbered at 834
3:46 of Israel, **w** are more than the Levites; 1886.1
4:26 **w** *is* by the tabernacle and by the altar round 834
4:37 **w** Moses and Aaron did number according to 834
5: 7 they shall confess their sin **w** they have 834
5: 9 **w** they bring unto the priest, shall be his. 834
5:18 in her hands, **w** *is* the jealousy offering: 1931
6: 5 *in the* **w** he separateth *himself* unto 834
6:18 put *it* in the fire **w** *is* under the sacrifice of 834
6:21 according to the vow **w** he vowed, so 834
8: 4 according unto the pattern **w** the LORD had 834
10: 4 **w** *are* heads of the thousands of Israel, NIH
10:25 **w** *was* the rereward of all the camps NIH
10:29 We *are* journeying unto the place of **w** 834
11: 5 the fish, **w** we did eat in Egypt freely; 834
11:12 unto the land **w** thou swarest unto their 834
11:17 I will take of the spirit **w** *is* upon thee, and 834
11:20 that ye have despised the LORD **w** *is* 834
12: 3 above all the men **w** *were* upon the face of 834
13: 2 **w** I give unto the children of Israel: 834
13:16 These *are* the names of the men **w** Moses 834
13:24 of the cluster of grapes **w** the children of 834
13:32 they brought up an evil report of the land **w** 834
13:32 through **w** we have gone to search it, 834
13:33 the sons of Anak, **w** *come* of the giants: NIH
14: 6 **w** *were* of them that searched the land, NIH
14: 7 The land, **w** we passed through to search it, 834
14: 8 it us; a land **w** floweth with milk and honey. 834
14:11 for all the signs **w** I have shewed among 834
14:15 the nations **w** have heard the fame of thee 834
14:16 people into the land **w** he sware unto them, 834
14:22 Because all *those* men **w** have seen my 1886.1
14:22 **w** I did in Egypt and in the wilderness, and 834
14:23 Surely they shall not see the land **w** I sware 834
14:27 evil congregation, **w** murmur against me? 834
14:27 of Israel, **w** they murmur against me. 834
14:29 and upward, **w** have murmured against me, 834
14:30 *concerning* **w** I sware to make you dwell 834
14:31 your little ones, **w** ye said should be a prey, 834
14:31 they shall know the land **w** ye have despised. 834
14:34 After the number of the days *in* **w** ye 834
14:36 the men, **w** Moses sent to search the land, 834
14:38 **w** *were* of the men that went to search NIH
14:40 will go up unto the place **w** the LORD hath 834
14:45 the Canaanites **w** dwelt in that hill, 1886.1
15: 2 land of your habitations, **w** I give unto you, 834
15:22 **w** the LORD hath spoken unto Moses, 834
15:39 own eyes, after **w** ye use to go a whoring: 834
15:41 **w** brought you out of the land of Egypt, to be 834
16:11 **For w cause** *both* thou and all thy 3651+3807.1
16:12 of Eliab: **w** said, We will not come up: 2050.1
16:40 no stranger, **w** *is* not of the seed of Aaron, 834
18: 9 **w** they shall render unto me, *shall be* most 834
18:12 the firstfruits of them **w** they shall offer unto 834
18:13 **w** they shall bring unto the LORD, shall be 834
18:15 **w** they bring unto the LORD, *whether it be* 834
18:16 shekel of the sanctuary, **w** *is* twenty gerahs. 1931
18:19 All the heave offerings of the holy *things,* **w** 834
18:21 for their service **w** they serve, *even* 834
18:24 **w** they offer *as* a heave offering unto 834
18:26 **w** I have given you from them for your 834

Nu 18:28 **w** ye receive of the children of Israel; 834
19: 2 This *is* the ordinance of the law **w** 834
19: 2 *is* no blemish, *and* upon **w** never came yoke: 834
19:15 **w** hath no covering bound upon it, 834
20:12 into the land **w** I have given them. 834
20:24 for he shall not enter into the land **w** I have 834
21: 1 Arad the Canaanite, **w** dwelt *in* the south, NIH
21:11 in the wilderness **w** *is* before Moab, 834
21:13 **w** *is* in the wilderness that cometh out of 834
21:20 of Pisgah, **w** looketh toward Jeshimon. 2050.1
21:30 even unto Nophah, **w** *reacheth* unto Medeba. 834
21:34 king of the Amorites, **w** dwelt at Heshbon. 834
22: 5 **w** *is* by the river *of* the land of the children 834
22:11 **w** covereth the face of the earth: 2050.1
22:20 yet the word **w** I shall say unto thee, 834
22:30 upon **w** thou hast ridden ever since *I was* 834
22:36 **w** *is* in the border of Arnon, which *is* in 834
22:36 border of Arnon, **w** *is* in the utmost coast. 834
23:12 Must I not take heed to speak that **w** 834
24: 4 He hath said, **w** heard the words of God, NIH
24: 4 **w** saw the vision of the Almighty, 834
24: 6 as the trees of lign aloes **w** the LORD hath NIH
24:12 Spake I not also to thy messengers **w** thou 834
24:16 **w** heard the words of God, and knew NIH
24:16 **w** saw the vision of the Almighty, NIH
25:18 **w** was slain in the day of the plague for 1886.1
26: 4 **w** went forth out of the land of Egypt. 1886.1
26: 9 **w** *were* famous in the congregation, NIH
27:12 see the land **w** I have given unto the children 834
27:17 **W** may go out before them, and which may 834
27:17 **w** may go in before them, and which may 834
27:17 **w** may lead them out, and which may bring 834
27:17 lead them out, and **w** may bring them in; 834
27:17 LORD be not as sheep **w** have no shepherd. 834
28: 3 This *is* the offering made by fire **w** ye shall 834
28: 6 **w** was ordained in mount Sinai for a 1886.1
28:23 **w** *is* for a continual burnt offering. 834
30: 1 This *is* the thing **w** the LORD hath 834
30: 8 then he shall make her vow **w** she vowed, 834
30: 8 **that w** she **uttered** with her lips, 4008
30:14 her vows, or all her bonds, **w** *are* upon her: 834
30:16 **w** the LORD commanded Moses, 834
31:12 of Moab, **w** *are* by Jordan *near* Jericho. 834
31:14 over hundreds, **w** came from the battle. 1886.1
31:21 unto the men of war **w** went to the battle, 1886.1
31:21 This *is* the ordinance of the law **w** 834
31:28 of the men of war **w** went out to battle: 1886.1
31:30 **w** keep the charge of the tabernacle of NIH
31:32 *being* the rest of the prey **w** the men of war 834
31:36 **w** *was* the portion of them that went out to NIH
31:38 of **w** the LORD'S tribute *was* threescore 3963.1
31:39 of **w** the LORD'S tribute *was* threescore 3963.1
31:40 of **w** the LORD'S tribute *was* thirty and 3963.1
31:41 **w** *was* the LORD'S heave offering, NIH
31:42 **w** Moses divided from the men that warred, 834
31:47 **w** kept the charge of the tabernacle of NIH
31:48 the officers **w** *were* over thousands of 834
31:49 of the men of war **w** *are* under our charge, 834
32: 4 *Even* the country **w** the LORD smote 834
32: 7 into the land **w** the LORD hath given them? 834
32: 9 that *they* should not go into the land **w** 834
32:11 shall see the land **w** I sware unto Abraham, 834
32:24 do that **w** hath proceeded out of your mouth. NIH
32:38 gave other names unto the cities **w** they 834
32:39 and dispossessed the Amorite **w** *was* in it. 834
33: 1 **w** went forth out of the land of Egypt with 834
33: 4 **w** the LORD had smitten among them: 834
33: 6 in Etham, **w** *is* in the edge of the wilderness. 834
33: 7 unto Pi-hahiroth, **w** *is* before Baal-zephon: 834
33:36 in the wilderness of Zin, **w** *is* Kadesh. 1931
33:40 **w** dwelt in the south in the land of Canaan, 1931
33:55 *that those* **w** ye let remain of them *shall be* 834
34:13 This *is* the land **w** ye shall inherit by lot, 834
34:13 **w** the LORD commanded to give unto 834
34:17 These *are* the names of the men **w** shall 834
35: 4 the cities, **w** ye shall give unto the Levites, 834
35: 6 *among* the cities **w** ye shall give unto 834
35: 6 **w** ye shall appoint for the manslayer, that he 834
35: 7 *So* all the cities **w** ye shall give to 834
35: 8 the cities **w** ye shall give *shall be* of 834
35: 8 according to his inheritance **w** he inheriteth. 834
35:11 **w** killeth *any* person at unawares. NIH
35:13 *of these* cities **w** ye shall give six cities shall 834
35:14 land of Canaan, **w** shall be cities of refuge. NIH
35:25 high priest, **w** was anointed with the holy oil. 834
35:31 the life of a murderer, **w** *is* guilty of death: 834
35:34 therefore the land **w** ye shall inhabit, 834
36: 6 This *is* the thing **w** the LORD doth 834
36:13 **w** the LORD commanded by the hand of 834
Dt 1: 1 These *be* the words **w** Moses spake unto all 834
1: 4 **w** dwelt in Heshbon, and Og the king of 834
1: 4 of Bashan, **w** dwelt at Astaroth in Edrei: 834
1: 8 possess the land **w** the LORD sware unto 834
1:14 The thing **w** thou hast spoken *is* good *for us* 834
1:18 at that time all the things **w** ye should do. 834
1:19 **w** you saw *by* the way of the mountain of 834
1:20 **w** the LORD our God doth give unto us. 834
1:25 *It is* a good land **w** the LORD our God doth 834
1:30 The LORD your God **w** goeth before 1886.1
1:35 **w** I sware to give unto your fathers, 834
1:38 **w** standeth before thee, he shall go in 1886.1
1:39 **w** ye said should be a prey, and 834
1:39 **w** *in that* day had no knowledge between 834
1:44 the Amorites, **w** dwelt in that mountain, 1886.1
2: 4 the children of Esau, **w** dwell in Seir; 1886.1
2: 8 **w** dwelt in Seir, through the way of 1886.1
2:11 **W** also were accounted giants, as 1992
2:12 **w** the LORD gave unto them.) 834
2:14 the space in **w** we came from 834
2:22 to the children of Esau, **w** dwelt in Seir, 1886.1
2:23 the Avims **w** dwelt in Hazerim, *even* unto 1886.1
2:23 **w** came forth out of Caphtor, 1886.1
2:29 (As the children of Esau **w** dwell in Seir, 1886.1
2:29 the Moabites **w** dwell in Ar, did unto 1886.1
2:29 until I shall pass over Jordan into the land **w** 834

Dt	2:35	and the spoil of the cities w we took.	834
	2:36	w *is* by the brink of the river of Arnon, and	834
	3: 2	king of the Amorites, w dwelt at Heshbon.	834
	3: 4	there was not a city w we took not from	834
	3: 9	(W Hermon the Sidonians call Sirion; and	NIH
	3:12	w we possessed at that time, from Aroer,	NIH
	3:12	w *is* by the river Arnon, and half mount	834
	3:13	all Bashan, w was called the land of giants.	1931
	3:16	w *is* the border of the children of Ammon;	NIH
	3:19	shall abide in your cities w I have given you;	834
	3:20	*until* they also possess the land w	834
	3:20	unto his possession, w I have given you.	834
	3:28	he shall cause them to inherit the land w	834
	4: 1	and unto the judgments, w I teach you,	834
	4: 1	possess the land w the LORD God of your	834
	4: 2	Ye shall not add unto the word w I command	834
	4: 2	of the LORD your God w I command you.	834
	4: 6	w shall hear all these statutes, and say,	834
	4: 8	as all this law, w I set before you *this* day?	834
	4: 9	lest thou forget the things w thine eyes have	834
	4:13	w he commanded you to perform, *even* ten	834
	4:19	w the LORD thy God hath divided unto all	834
	4:21	w the LORD thy God giveth thee *for* an	834
	4:23	w he made with you, and make you a graven	834
	4:23	the likeness of any *thing,* w the LORD thy	834
	4:28	wood and stone, w neither see, nor hear,	834
	4:31	nor forget the covenant of thy fathers w he	834
	4:32	of the days that are past, w were before thee,	834
	4:40	w I command thee *this* day,	834
	4:40	w the LORD thy God giveth thee, for ever.	834
	4:42	w should kill his neighbour unawares,	834
	4:44	this *is* the law w Moses set before	834
	4:45	w Moses spake unto the children of Israel,	834
	4:47	w *were* on *this* side Jordan *toward*	834
	4:48	w *is* by the bank of the river Arnon,	834
	4:48	even unto mount Sion, w *is* Hermon,	1931
	5: 1	judgments w I speak in your ears *this* day,	834
	5: 6	w brought thee out of the land of Egypt,	834
	5:16	in the land w the LORD thy God giveth	834
	5:28	of this people, w they have spoken unto thee:	834
	5:31	and the judgments, w thou shalt teach them,	834
	5:31	that they may do *them* in the land w I give	834
	5:33	You shall walk in all the ways w the LORD	834
	5:33	*that* ye may prolong *your* days in the land w	834
	6: 1	w the LORD your God commanded to	834
	6: 2	w I command thee, thou, and thy son, and	834
	6: 6	these words, w I command thee *this* day,	834
	6:10	into the land w he sware unto thy fathers,	834
	6:10	and goodly cities, w thou buildedst not,	834
	6:11	houses full *of* all good *things,* w thou filledst	834
	6:11	w thou diggedst not, vineyards and	834
	6:11	and olive trees, w thou plantedst not;	834
	6:12	w brought thee forth out of the land of	834
	6:14	of the gods of the people w *are* round about	834
	6:17	and his statutes, w he hath commanded thee.	834
	6:18	thou shalt do *that* w *is* right and good in	NIH
	6:18	possess the good land w the LORD sware	834
	6:20	w the LORD our God hath commanded	834
	6:23	to give us the land w he sware unto our	834
	7: 8	he would keep the oath w he had sworn unto	834
	7: 9	w keepeth covenant and mercy with them	NIH
	7:11	w I command thee *this* day, to do them.	834
	7:12	and the mercy w he sware unto thy fathers:	834
	7:13	in the land w he sware unto thy fathers to	834
	7:15	of Egypt, w thou knowest, upon thee;	834
	7:16	thou shalt consume all the people w	834
	7:19	The great temptations w thine eyes saw, and	834
	8: 1	All the commandments w I command thee	834
	8: 1	possess the land w the LORD sware unto	834
	8: 2	thou shalt remember all the way w	834
	8: 3	fed thee with manna, w thou knewest not,	834
	8:10	God for the good land w he hath given thee.	834
	8:11	and his statutes, w I command thee *this* day:	834
	8:14	w brought thee forth out of the land of	1886.1
	8:16	w thy fathers knew not, that he might	834
	8:18	that he may establish his covenant w he	834
	8:20	As the nations w the LORD destroyeth	834
	9: 3	that the LORD thy God *is* he w goeth	1886.1
	9: 5	that he may perform the word w the LORD	834
	9: 9	*even* the tables of the covenant w	834
	9:10	w the LORD spake with you in the mount	834
	9:12	for thy people w thou hast brought forth out	834
	9:12	aside out of the way w I commanded them;	834
	9:16	ye had turned aside quickly out of the way w	834
	9:18	because of all your sins w ye sinned,	834
	9:21	the calf w ye had made, and burnt it with	834
	9:23	and possess the land w I have given you;	834
	9:26	w thou hast redeemed through thy greatness,	834
	9:26	w thou hast brought forth out of Egypt with	834
	9:28	them into the land w he promised them,	834
	9:29	w thou broughtest out by thy mighty power	834
	10: 2	that were in the first tables w thou brakest,	834
	10: 4	w the LORD spake unto you in the mount	834
	10: 5	and put the tables in the ark w I had made;	834
	10:11	w I sware unto their fathers to give unto	834
	10:13	w I command thee *this* day for thy good?	834
	10:17	and a terrible, w regardeth not persons,	834
	10:21	and terrible *things,* w thine eyes have seen.	834
	11: 2	for *I speak* not with your children w have not	834
	11: 2	w have not seen the chastisement of	834
	11: 3	w he did in the midst of Egypt unto Pharaoh	834
	11: 7	all the great acts of the LORD w he did.	834
	11: 8	commandments w I command you *this* day,	834
	11: 9	w the LORD sware unto your fathers to	834
	11:12	A land w the LORD thy God careth for:	834
	11:13	commandments w I command you *this* day,	834
	11:17	off the good land w the LORD giveth you.	834
	11:21	in the land w the LORD sware unto your	834
	11:22	all these commandments w I command you,	834
	11:27	your God, w I command you *this* day:	834
	11:28	turn aside out of the way w I command you	834
	11:28	to go after other gods, w ye have not known.	834
	11:30	w dwell in the champaign over against	1886.1
	11:31	the land w the LORD your God giveth you,	834
	11:32	and judgments w I set before you *this* day.	834
Dt	12: 1	w ye shall observe to do in the land,	834
	12: 1	w the LORD God of thy fathers giveth thee	834
	12: 2	wherein the nations w ye shall possess	834
	12: 5	unto the place w the LORD your God shall	834
	12: 9	w the LORD your God giveth you.	834
	12:10	dwell in the land w the LORD your God	834
	12:11	there shall be a place w the LORD your	834
	12:11	all your choice vows w ye vow unto	834
	12:14	in the place w the LORD shall choose in	834
	12:15	of the LORD thy God w he hath given thee:	834
	12:17	nor any of thy vows w thou vowest,	834
	12:18	place w the LORD thy God shall choose,	834
	12:21	If the place w the LORD thy God hath	834
	12:21	of thy flock, w the LORD hath given thee,	834
	12:25	when thou shalt do *that* w *is* right in	NIH
	12:26	Only thy holy *things* w thou hast, and	834
	12:26	go unto the place w the LORD shall	834
	12:28	and hear all these words w I command thee,	834
	12:28	when thou doest *that* w *is* good and right in	NIH
	12:31	w he hateth, have they done unto their gods;	834
	13: 2	w thou hast not known, and let us serve	834
	13: 5	w brought you out of the land of Egypt,	1886.1
	13: 5	to thrust thee out of the way w the LORD	834
	13: 6	or thy friend, w *is* as thine own soul,	834
	13: 6	w thou hast not known, thou, nor thy fathers;	834
	13: 7	*Namely,* of the gods of the people w *are*	834
	13:10	w brought thee out of the land of Egypt,	1886.1
	13:12	w the LORD thy God hath given thee to	834
	13:13	and serve other gods, w ye have not known;	834
	13:18	to keep all his commandments w I command	834
	13:18	to do *that* w *is* right in the eyes of	NIH
	14: 4	These *are* the beasts w ye shall eat: the ox,	834
	14:12	these *are they* of w ye shall not eat:	834
	14:23	in the place w he shall choose to place his	834
	14:24	w the LORD thy God shall choose to set	834
	14:25	shalt go unto the place w the LORD thy	834
	14:29	the widow, w *are* within thy gates,	834
	14:29	in all the work of thine hand w thou doest.	834
	15: 3	*that* w is thine with thy brother thine hand	834
	15: 4	w the LORD thy God giveth thee *for* an	834
	15: 5	to observe to do all these commandments w	834
	15: 7	thy land w the LORD thy God giveth thee,	834
	15: 8	sufficient for his need, *in that* w he wanteth.	834
	15:20	year in the place w the LORD shall choose,	834
	16: 2	in the place w the LORD shall choose to	834
	16: 4	w thou sacrificedst the first day at even,	834
	16: 5	w the LORD thy God giveth thee:	834
	16: 6	at the place w the LORD thy God shall	834
	16: 7	eat *it* in the place w the LORD thy God	834
	16:10	w thou shalt give *unto the LORD thy God,*	834
	16:11	in the place w the LORD thy God hath	834
	16:15	God in the place w the LORD shall choose:	834
	16:16	thy God in the place w he shall choose;	834
	16:17	of the LORD thy God w he hath given thee.	834
	16:18	w the LORD thy God giveth thee,	834
	16:20	That w is altogether just shalt thou follow,	NIH
	16:20	inherit the land w the LORD thy God	834
	16:21	LORD thy God, w thou shalt make thee.	834
	16:22	up *any* image; w the LORD thy God hateth.	834
	17: 2	within any of thy gates w the LORD thy	834
	17: 3	host of heaven, w I have not commanded;	834
	17: 5	w have committed that wicked thing,	834
	17: 8	get thee up into the place w the LORD thy	834
	17:10	w *they* of that place which the LORD shall	834
	17:10	which *they* of that place w the LORD shall	834
	17:11	According to the sentence of the law w they	834
	17:11	according to the judgment w they shall tell	834
	17:11	thou shalt not decline from the sentence w	834
	17:14	When thou art come unto the land w	834
	17:15	set a stranger over thee, w *is* not thy brother.	834
	17:18	of *that* w *is* before the priests the Levites:	NIH
	18: 6	unto the place w the LORD shall choose;	834
	18: 7	as all his brethren the Levites *do,* w stand	NIH
	18: 8	beside **that w cometh** of the **sale** of his	4465
	18: 9	When thou art come into the land w	834
	18:14	For these nations, w thou shalt possess,	834
	18:17	They have well *spoken that* w they have	834
	18:19	unto my words w he shall speak in my name,	834
	18:20	w shall presume to speak a word in my	834
	18:20	w I have not commanded him to speak, or	834
	18:21	How shall we know the word w the LORD	834
	18:22	that *is* the thing w the LORD hath not	834
	19: 2	w the LORD thy God giveth thee to	834
	19: 3	w the LORD thy God giveth thee to inherit,	834
	19: 4	w shall flee thither, that he may live:	834
	19: 8	give thee all the land w he promised to give	834
	19: 9	w I command thee *this* day, to love	834
	19:10	w the LORD thy God giveth thee *for* an	834
	19:14	w they of old time have set in thine	834
	19:14	w thou shalt inherit in the land that	834
	19:16	man to testify against him *that* w *is* wrong;	NIH
	19:17	and the judges, w shall be in those days;	834
	19:20	those w remain shall hear, and fear, and	NIH
	20: 1	w brought thee up out of the land of	1886.1
	20:14	w the LORD thy God hath given thee.	834
	20:15	Thus shalt thou do unto all the cities w *are*	NIH
	20:15	w *are* not of the cities of these nations.	834
	20:16	w the LORD thy God doth give thee *for* an	834
	20:18	w they have done unto their gods;	834
	20:20	Only the trees w thou knowest that they *be*	834
	21: 1	If *one* be found slain in the land w	834
	21: 2	they shall measure unto the cities w *are*	834
	21: 3	*that* the city w *is* next unto the slain *man,*	NIH
	21: 3	w hath not been wrought with, *and*	834
	21: 3	*and* w hath not drawn in the yoke;	834
	21: 4	w is neither eared nor sown, and shall strike	834
	21: 9	when thou shalt do *that* w *is* right in	NIH
	21:16	when he maketh his sons to inherit *that* w he	834
	21:16	son of the hated, w *is indeed* the firstborn:	NIH
	21:18	w will not obey the voice of his father, or	5105.2
	21:23	w the LORD thy God giveth thee *for* an	834
	22: 3	w he hath lost, and thou hast found, shalt	834
	22: 5	not wear **that w pertaineth** unto a man,	3627
	22: 9	lest the fruit of *thy* seed w thou hast sown,	834
	22:28	w is not betrothed, and lay hold on her, and	834
Dt	23:13	and cover that w cometh from thee:	NIH
	23:15	w is escaped from his master unto thee:	834
	23:16	in *that* place w he shall choose in one of thy	834
	23:23	**That w is gone out** of thy lips thou shalt	4161
	23:23	w thou hast promised with thy mouth.	834
	24: 3	latter husband die, w took her *to be* his wife;	834
	24: 4	Her former husband, w sent her away,	834
	24: 4	w the LORD thy God giveth thee *for* an	834
	24: 5	and shall cheer up his wife w he hath taken.	834
	25: 6	*that* the firstborn w she beareth shall succeed	834
	25: 6	in the name of his brother w is dead,	1886.1
	25:15	the land w the LORD thy God giveth thee.	834
	25:19	in the land w the LORD thy God giveth	834
	26: 1	when thou art come in unto the land w	834
	26: 2	w thou shalt bring of thy land that	834
	26: 2	shalt go unto the place w the LORD thy	834
	26: 3	that I am come unto the country w	834
	26:10	the land, w thou, O LORD, hast given me.	834
	26:11	thou shalt rejoice in every good *thing* w	834
	26:12	w *is* the year of tithing, and hast given *it*	NIH
	26:13	according to all thy commandments w thou	834
	26:15	and the land w thou hast given us,	834
	26:19	to make thee high above all nations w he	834
	27: 1	Keep all the commandments w I command	834
	27: 2	the land w the LORD thy God giveth thee,	834
	27: 3	that thou mayest go in unto the land w	834
	27: 4	w I command you *this* day, in mount Ebal,	834
	27:10	and his statutes, w I command thee *this* day.	834
	28: 1	to do all his commandments w I command	834
	28: 8	he shall bless thee in the land w the LORD	834
	28:11	in the land w the LORD sware unto thy	834
	28:13	w I command thee *this* day, to observe and	834
	28:14	any of the words w I command thee *this* day,	834
	28:15	and his statutes w I command thee *this* day;	834
	28:33	shall a nation w thou knowest not eat up;	834
	28:34	for the sight of thine eyes w thou shalt see.	834
	28:36	and thy king w thou shalt set over thee,	834
	28:36	unto a nation w neither thou nor thy fathers	834
	28:45	and his statutes w he commanded thee:	834
	28:48	Therefore shalt thou serve thine enemies w	834
	28:50	w shall not regard the person of the old,	834
	28:51	w *also* shall not leave thee *either* corn, wine,	834
	28:52	w the LORD thy God hath given thee.	834
	28:53	w the LORD thy God hath given thee,	834
	28:54	towards the remnant of his children w he	834
	28:56	w would not adventure to set the sole of her	834
	28:57	and towards her children w she shall bear:	834
	28:60	the diseases of Egypt, w thou wast afraid of;	834
	28:61	w *is* not written in the book of this law,	834
	28:64	w neither thou nor thy fathers have known,	834
	28:67	for the sight of thine eyes w thou shalt see.	834
	29: 1	w the LORD commanded Moses to make	834
	29: 1	beside the covenant w he made with them in	834
	29: 3	The great temptations w thine eyes have	834
	29:12	w the LORD thy God maketh with thee *this*	834
	29:16	how we came through the nations w ye	834
	29:17	stone, silver and gold, w *were* among them:)	834
	29:22	the sicknesses w the LORD hath laid upon	834
	29:23	w the LORD overthrew in his anger, and	834
	29:25	w he made with them when he brought them	834
	29:29	*things* w are revealed *belong* unto us	1886.1
	30: 1	w I have set before thee, and thou shalt call	834
	30: 5	thee into the land w thy fathers possessed,	834
	30: 7	on them that hate thee, w persecuted thee.	834
	30: 8	do all his commandments w I command thee	834
	30:10	his statutes w are written in this book of	1886.1
	30:11	For this commandment w I command thee	834
	30:20	that thou mayest dwell in the land w	834
	31: 5	commandments w I have commanded you.	834
	31: 7	w the LORD hath sworn unto their fathers	834
	31: 9	w bare the ark of the covenant of	1886.1
	31:11	thy God in the place w he shall choose,	834
	31:13	w have not known *any thing,* may hear, and	834
	31:16	break my covenant w I have made with	834
	31:18	for all the evils w they shall have wrought,	834
	31:20	into the land w I sware unto their fathers,	834
	31:21	for I know their imagination w they go	834
	31:21	before I have brought them into the land w I	834
	31:23	of Israel into the land w I sware unto them:	834
	31:25	w bare the ark of the covenant of	NIH
	31:29	turn aside from the way w I have	834
	32:15	then he forsook God w made him,	NIH
	32:21	me to jealousy with *that* w *is* not God;	NIH
	32:21	I will move them to jealousy with *those* w	NIH
	32:38	W did eat the fat of their sacrifices, *and*	834
	32:46	Set your hearts unto all the words w I testify	834
	32:46	w ye shall command your children to	834
	32:49	*unto* mount Nebo, w *is* in the land of Moab,	834
	32:49	w I give unto the children of Israel for a	834
	32:52	thou shalt not go thither unto the land w I	834
	34: 4	This *is* the land w I sware unto Abraham,	834
	34:11	w the LORD sent him to do in the land of	834
	34:12	in all the great terror w Moses shewed in	834
Jos	1: 2	unto the land w I do give to them,	834
	1: 6	w I sware unto their fathers to give them.	834
	1: 7	w Moses my servant commanded thee:	834
	1:11	w the LORD your God giveth you to	834
	1:13	Remember the word w Moses the servant of	834
	1:14	shall remain in the land w Moses gave you	834
	1:15	they also have possessed the land w	834
	1:15	w Moses the LORD'S servant gave you on	834
	2: 3	come to thee, w are entered into thine house:	834
	2: 6	w she had laid in order upon the roof.	NIH
	2: 7	as soon as they w pursued after them were	NIH
	2:17	We *will be* blameless of this thine oath w	834
	2:18	in the window w thou didst let us down by:	834
	2:20	we will be quit of thine oath w thou hast	834
	3: 4	that ye may know the way by w ye must go:	834
	3:16	That the waters w came down from above	1886.1
	4: 9	in the place where the feet of the priests w	NIH
	4:10	For the priests w bare the ark stood in	NIH
	4:20	twelve stones, w they took out of Jordan,	834
	4:23	w he dried up from before us,	834+3509.1
	5: 1	w *were* on the side of Jordan westward, and	834
	5: 1	kings of the Canaanites, w *were* by the sea,	834

Jos 5: 6 **w** came out of Egypt, were consumed, 1886.1
5: 6 **w** the LORD sware unto their fathers that 834
6:25 **w** Joshua sent to spy out Jericho. 834
7: 2 **w** *is* beside Beth-aven, on the east side of 834
7:11 they have also transgressed my covenant **w** I 834
7:14 *that* the tribe **w** the LORD taketh shall 834
7:14 the family **w** the LORD shall take shall 834
7:14 the household **w** the LORD shall take shall 834
8:27 according unto the word of the LORD **w** he 834
8:31 over **w** no *man* hath lift up *any* iron: 834
8:32 **w** he wrote in the presence of the children of 834
8:33 **w** bare the ark of the covenant of NIH
8:35 **w** Joshua read not before all 834
9: 1 when all the kings **w** *were* on *this* side 834
9:10 to Og king of Bashan, **w** *was* at Ashtaroth. 834
9:13 these bottles of wine, **w** we filled, *were* new; 834
9:20 because of the oath **w** we sware unto them. 834
9:27 this day, in the place **w** he should choose. 834
10:11 *they were* moe **w** died with hailstones than 834
10:20 that the rest **w** remained of them entered NIH
10:24 of the men of war **w** went with him, 1886.1
10:27 cave's mouth, **w** *remain* until this very day. NIH
10:32 **w** took it on the second day, and smote it 2050.1
12: 1 **w** the children of Israel smote, and 834
12: 2 **w** *is* upon the bank of the river of Arnon, and 834
12: 2 **w** *is* the border of the children of Ammon; NIH
12: 4 **w** *was* of the remnant of the giants, NIH
12: 7 these *are* the kings of the country **w** Joshua 834
12: 7 **w** Joshua gave unto the tribes of Israel *for* 2050.1
12: 9 one; the king of Ai, **w** *is* beside Beth-el, one; 834
13: 3 From Sihor, **w** *is* before Egypt, even unto 834
13: 3 **w** is counted to the Canaanite: NIH
13: 8 **w** Moses gave them, beyond Jordan 834
13:10 **w** reigned in Heshbon, unto the border of 834
13:12 **w** reigned in Ashtaroth and in Edrei, 834
13:21 king of the Amorites, **w** reigned in Heshbon, 834
13:21 Hur, and Reba, **w** *were* dukes of Sihon, NIH
13:30 of Jair, **w** *are* in Bashan, threescore cities: 834
13:32 These *are the countries* **w** Moses did 834
14: 1 these *are the countries* **w** the children of 834
14: 1 **w** Eleazar the priest, and Joshua the son of 834
14:15 **w** *Arba was* a great man among NIH
15: 7 **w** *is* on the south side of the river: 834
15: 8 **w** *is* at the end of the valley of the giants 834
15: 9 was drawn *to* Baalah, **w** *is* Kirjath-jearim: 1931
15:10 **w** *is* Chesalon, on the north side, 1931
15:13 Arba the father of Anak, **w** *city is* Hebron. 1931
15:25 and Kerioth, *and* Hezron, **w** *is* Hazor, 1931
15:49 and Kirjath-sannah, **w** *is* Debir, 1931
15:54 and Kirjath-arba, **w** *is* Hebron, and Zior; 1931
15:60 **w** *is* Kirjath-jearim, and Rabbah; 1931
17: 5 **w** *were* on the *other* side Jordan; 834
18: 2 **w** had not *yet* received their inheritance. 834
18: 3 **w** the LORD God of your fathers hath 834
18: 7 **w** Moses the servant of the LORD gave 834
18:13 to the side of Luz, **w** *is* Beth-el, southward; 1931
18:14 **w** *is* Kirjath-jearim, a city of the children of 1931
18:16 **w** *is* in the valley of the giants on the north, 834
18:17 **w** *is* over against the going up of Adummim, 834
18:28 Eleph, and Jebusi, **w** *is* Jerusalem, Gibeath, 1931
19:50 LORD they gave him the city **w** he asked, 834
19:51 **w** Eleazar the priest, and Joshua the son of 834
20: 7 Kirjath-arba, **w** *is* Hebron, in the mountain 1931
21: 4 of Aaron the priest, **w** *were* of the Levites, NIH
21: 9 these cities **w** are *here* mentioned by name, 834
21:10 **W** the children of Aaron, *being* of 2050.1
21:11 **w** *city is* Hebron, in the hill *country* of 1931
21:20 the Levites **w** remained of the children of 1886.1
21:40 **w** were remaining of the families of 1886.1
21:43 the LORD gave unto Israel all the land **w** 834
21:45 There failed not ought of any good thing **w** 834
22: 4 **w** Moses the servant of the LORD gave 834
22: 5 **w** Moses the servant of the LORD charged 834
22: 9 **w** *is* in the land of Canaan, to go unto 834
22:17 from **w** we are not cleansed until this day, 834
22:28 **w** our fathers made, not for burnt offerings, 834
22:30 heads of the thousands of Israel **w** *were* with 834
23:13 until ye perish from off this good land **w** 834
23:14 **w** the LORD your God spake concerning 834
23:15 **w** the LORD your God promised you; 834
23:15 **w** the LORD your God hath given you. 834
23:16 **w** he commanded you, and have gone and 834
23:16 off the good land **w** he hath given unto you. 834
24: 5 according to *that* **w** I did amongst them: 834
24: 8 **w** dwelt on the *other* side Jordan; 1886.1
24:12 **w** drave them out from before you, 2050.1
24:13 I have given you a land for **w** ye did not 834
24:13 cities **w** ye built not, and ye dwell in them; 834
24:13 and oliveyards **w** ye planted not do ye eat. 834
24:14 put away the gods **w** your fathers served on 834
24:15 whether the gods **w** your fathers served that 834
24:17 and **w** did those great signs in our sight, and 834
24:18 even the Amorites **w** dwelt in the land: NIH
24:23 *said he,* the strange gods **w** *are* among you, 834
24:27 the words of the LORD **w** he spake unto us: 834
24:30 **w** *is* in mount Ephraim, on the north side of 834
24:31 **w** had known all the works of the LORD, 834
24:32 **w** the children of Israel brought up out of 834
24:32 in a parcel of ground **w** Jacob bought of 834
24:33 his son, **w** was given him in mount Ephraim. 834
Jdg 1:16 of Judah, **w** *lieth* in the south of Arad; 834
1:26 **w** *is* the name thereof unto this day. 1931
2: 1 have brought you unto the land **w** I sware 834
2:10 after them, **w** knew not the LORD, 834
2:10 nor yet the works **w** he had done for Israel. 834
2:12 **w** brought them out of the land of Egypt, 1886.1
2:16 **w** delivered them out of the hand of those 2050.1
2:17 they turned quickly out of the way **w** their 834
2:20 my covenant **w** I commanded their fathers, 834
2:21 of the nations **w** Joshua left when he died: 834
3: 1 Now these *are* the nations **w** the LORD left, 834
3: 4 **w** he commanded their fathers by the hand 834
3:16 Ehud made him a dagger **w** had two 2050.1
3:20 summer parlour, **w** he had for himself alone. 834
3:31 **w** slew *of* the Philistines six hundred men 2050.1
4: 2 **w** dwelt in Harosheth of the Gentiles. 1931
4:11 **w** *was* of the children of Hobab the father in NIH
4:11 unto the plain of Zaanaim, **w** *is* by Kedesh. 834
4:14 for this *is* the day in **w** the LORD hath 834
6: 2 made them the dens **w** *are* in the mountains, 834
6: 8 **w** said unto them, Thus saith the LORD 2050.1
6:11 sat under an oak **w** *was* in Ophrah, 834
6:13 where *be* all his miracles **w** our fathers told 834
6:26 wood of the grove **w** thou shalt cut down. 834
8:27 **w** *thing* became a snare unto Gideon, and NIH
8:35 according to all the goodness **w** he had 834
9: 2 **w** *are* threescore and ten persons, reign over NIH
9: 4 and light persons, **w** followed him. 2050.1
9:13 **w** cheereth God and man, and go to be 1886.1
9:24 upon Abimelech their brother, **w** slew them; 834
9:24 **w** aided him in the killing of his brethren. 834
9:56 **w** he did unto his father, in slaying his 834
10: 4 **w** are called Havoth-jair unto this day, NIH
10: 4 unto this day, **w** *are* in the land of Gilead. 834
10: 8 in the land of the Amorites, **w** *is* in Gilead. 834
10:14 Go and cry unto the gods **w** ye have chosen; 834
11:24 Wilt not thou possess that **w** Chemosh thy 834
11:28 unto the words of Jephthah **w** he sent him. 834
11:36 do to me according to that **w** hath proceeded 834
11:39 who did with her *according to* his vow **w** he 834
12: 5 that when those Ephraimites **w** were NIH
13: 8 let the man of God **w** thou didst send come 834
14:19 gave change of *garments* unto them **w** NIH
15:19 **w** *is* in Lehi unto this day. 834
16: 8 her seven green withs **w** had not been dried, 834
16:24 destroyer of our country, **w** slew many of us. 834
16:29 two middle pillars upon **w** the house stood, 834
16:29 on **w** it was borne up, of the one with his 1992.1
16:30 So the dead **w** he slew at his death were moe 834
16:30 were moe than *they* **w** he slew in his life. 834
17: 2 about **w** thou cursedst, and spakest of also NIH
17: 6 every man did *that* **w** *was* right in his own 1886.1
18: 5 that we may know whether our way **w** we go 834
18:16 **w** *were* of the children of Dan, stood *by* 834
18:24 Ye have taken away my gods **w** I made, and 834
18:27 And they took *the things* **w** Micah had made, 834
18:27 the priest **w** he had, and came unto Laish, 834
18:31 them up Micah's graven image, **w** he made, 834
19:10 came over against Jebus, **w** *is* Jerusalem; 1931
19:14 *were* by Gibeah, **w** *belongeth* to Benjamin. 834
19:16 at even, **w** *was* also of mount Ephraim; 2050.1
19:19 for the young man **w** *is* with thy servants: NIH
20: 9 now this *shall be* the thing **w** we will do to 834
20:13 the children of Belial, **w** *are* in Gibeah, 834
20:15 **w** were numbered seven hundred chosen NIH
20:18 **W** of us shall go up first to the battle 4310
20:31 *of* **w** one goeth up *to* the house of God, and 834
20:36 they trusted unto the liers in wait **w** they had 834
20:42 them **w** *came* out of the cities they destroyed 834
20:46 So that all **w** fell that day of Benjamin 1886.1
21:12 camp *to* Shiloh, **w** *is* in the land of Canaan. 834
21:14 they gave them wives **w** they had saved alive 834
21:19 *in a place* **w** *is* on the north side of Beth-el, 834
21:25 every man did *that* **w** *was* right in his own 1886.1
Ru 1:22 **w** returned out of the country of Moab: 1886.1
2: 9 drink of *that* **w** the young men have drawn. 834
2:11 art come unto a people **w** thou knewest not 834
4: 3 of land, **w** *was* our brother Elimelech's: 834
4:11 **w** two did build the house of Israel: 834
4:12 of the seed **w** the LORD shall give thee of 834
4:14 **w** hath not left thee *this* day without a 834
4:15 for thy daughter in law, **w** loveth thee, 834
4:15 **w** *is* better to thee than seven sons, hath born 834
1Sa 1:27 the LORD hath given me my petition **w** I 834
2:20 woman for the loan **w** is lent to the LORD. 834
2:29 **w** I have commanded *in my* habitation; 834
2:32 in all *the wealth* **w** *God* shall give Israel: 834
2:35 *that* shall do according to *that* **w** *is* in my 834
3:11 *at* **w** both the ears of every one that heareth it 834
3:12 **w** I have spoken concerning his house: 834
3:13 for ever for the iniquity **w** he knoweth; 834
4: 4 of hosts, **w** dwelleth *between* the cherubims: NIH
6: 4 What *shall be* the trespass offering **w** we 834
6: 7 on **w** there hath come no yoke, and tie 1992.1
6: 8 **w** ye return him *for* a trespass offering, 834
6:17 these *are* the golden emerods **w** 834
6:18 **w** *stone remaineth* unto this day in the field NIH
7:14 the cities **w** the Philistines had taken from 834
8: 8 According to all the works **w** they have done 834
8:18 of your king **w** ye shall have chosen you; 834
9:22 were bidden, **w** *were* about thirty persons. 2050.1
9:23 Bring the portion **w** I gave thee, of which I 834
9:23 of **w** I said unto thee, Set it by thee. 834
9:24 *that* **w** *was* upon it, and set *it* before Saul. 1886.1
9:24 *Samuel* said, Behold that **w** is left; set *it* NIH
10: 2 The asses **w** thou wentest to seek are found: 834
10: 4 **w** thou shalt receive of their hands. 2050.1
11:11 that they **w** remained were scattered, so NIH
12: 7 **w** he did to you and to your fathers. 834
12: 8 **w** brought forth your fathers out of Egypt, NIH
12:16 **w** the LORD will do before your eyes. 834
12:17 **w** ye have done in the sight of the LORD, 834
12:21 *should ye go* after vain *things,* **w** cannot 834
13: 5 people as the sand **w** *is* on the sea shore in 834
13:13 the LORD thy God, **w** he commanded thee: 834
13:14 thou hast not kept *that* **w** the LORD 834
14: 2 under a pomegranate tree **w** *is* in Migron: 834
14: 4 *by* **w** Jonathan sought to go over unto 834
14:14 **w** Jonathan and his armourbearer made, was 834
14:14 acre of land, **w** a yoke *of oxen might plow.* NIH
14:21 **w** went up with them into the camp *from* 834
14:22 Likewise all the men of Israel **w** had hid 1886.1
14:30 of the spoil of their enemies **w** they found? 834
14:39 For, *as* the LORD liveth, **w** saveth 1886.1
15: 2 I remember *that* **w** Amalek did to Israel, 834
15:14 and the lowing of the oxen **w** I hear? 834
15:20 have gone the way **w** the LORD sent me, 834
15:21 the chief of the things **w** should have been NIH
16: 4 Samuel did *that* **w** the LORD spake, and 834
16:16 Let our lord now command thy servants **w** NIH
1Sa 16:19 Send me David thy son, **w** *is* with the sheep. 834
17: 1 **w** *belongeth* to Judah, and pitched between 834
17:31 when the words were heard **w** David spake, 834
17:40 put them in a shepherd's bag **w** he had, 834
20:23 *as touching* the matter **w** thou and I have 834
20:27 **w** *was* the second *day* of the month, NIH
20:36 Run, find out now the arrows **w** I shoot. 834
20:37 the place of the arrow **w** Jonathan had shot, 834
22: 9 **w** *was* set over the servants of Saul, and 1931
22:14 **w** *is* the king's son in law, and goeth at 2050.1
23:13 **w** *were* about six hundred, arose and NIH
23:19 of Hachilah, **w** *is* on the south of Jeshimon? 834
24: 4 Behold the day of **w** the LORD said unto 834
25: 7 now thy shepherds **w** were with us, we hurt 834
25:27 now this blessing **w** thine handmaid hath 834
25:32 of Israel, **w** sent thee this day to meet me: 834
25:33 **w** hast kept me this day from coming to *shed* 834
25:34 **w** hath kept me back from hurting thee, 834
25:35 So David received of her hand *that* **w** she 834
25:44 to Phalti the son of Laish, **w** *was* of Gallim. 834
26: 1 the hill of Hachilah, **w** *is* before Jeshimon? NIH
26: 3 **w** *is* before Jeshimon, by the way. 834
28:21 have hearkened unto thy words **w** thou 834
29: 1 the Israelites pitched by a fountain **w** *is* in 834
29: 3 **w** hath been with me these days, or 834
29: 4 **w** thou hast appointed him, and let him not 834
30:10 for two hundred abode *behind,* **w** were so 834
30:14 upon *the coast* **w** *belongeth* to Judah, and 834
30:17 young men, **w** rode upon camels, and fled. 834
30:20 **w** they drave before those *other* cattle, and NIH
30:21 **w** were so faint that they could not follow 834
30:23 with *that* **w** the LORD hath given us, 834
30:27 To *them* **w** *were* in Beth-el, and to *them* 834
30:27 to *them* **w** *were* in south Ramoth, and 834
30:27 south Ramoth, and to *them* **w** *were* in Jattir, 834
30:28 to *them* **w** *were* in Aroer, and to *them* which 834
30:28 to *them* **w** *were* in Siphmoth, and to *them* 834
30:28 and to *them* **w** *were* in Eshtemoa, 834
30:29 to *them* **w** *were* in Rachal, and to *them* 834
30:29 to *them* **w** *were* in the cities of 834
30:29 to *them* **w** *were* in the cities of the Kenites, 834
30:30 to *them* **w** *were* in Hormah, and to *them* 834
30:30 to *them* **w** *were* in Chor-ashan, and to *them* 834
30:30 and to *them* **w** *were* in Athach, 834
30:31 to *them* **w** *were* in Hebron, and to all 834
31:11 of that **w** the Philistines had done to Saul, 834
2Sa 2:15 **w** *pertained* to Ish-bosheth the son of 2050.1
2:16 called Helkath-hazzurim, **w** *is* in Gibeon. 834
2:32 of his father, **w** *was* in Beth-lehem. 834
3: 8 **w** against Judah do shew kindness *this* day 834
3:14 **w** I espoused to me for an hundred foreskins 834
3:26 **w** brought him again from the well of Sirah: NIH
4: 8 son of Saul thine enemy, **w** sought thy life; 834
5: 6 **w** spake unto David, saying, Except thou NIH
6: 4 of the house of Abinadab **w** *was* at Gibeah, 834
6:21 **w** chose me before thy father, and before all 834
6:22 of the maidservants **w** thou hast spoken of, 834
7:12 **w** shall proceed out of thy bowels, and I will 834
7:23 **w** thou redeemedst to thee from Egypt, 834
8:11 **W** also king David did dedicate unto 3963.1
8:11 gold that he had dedicated of all nations **w** 834
9: 3 hath yet a son, **w** *is* lame on *his* feet. NIH
10:12 the LORD do that **w** seemeth him good. NIH
12: 3 **w** he had bought and nourished up: 834
13:10 Tamar took the cakes **w** she had made, and 834
13:23 in Baal-hazor, **w** *is* beside Ephraim: 834
14: 7 *so* they shall quench my coal **w** is left, and 834
14:13 king doth speak this thing as one **w is faulty**, 818
14:14 **w** cannot be gathered up *again;* neither doth 834
15: 4 that every man **w** hath *any* suit or 834
15: 7 **w** I have vowed unto the LORD, 834
15:16 **w** *were* concubines, to keep the house. NIH
15:18 six hundred men **w** came after him from 834
16:11 Behold, my son, **w** came forth of my bowels, 834
16:21 **w** he hath left to keep the house; 834
16:23 **w** he counselled in those days, 834
17:10 and *they* **w** *be* with him *are* valiant men. 834
17:18 in Bahurim, **w** had a well in his court; 2050.2
17:25 **w** Amasa *was* a man's son, whose name 2050.1
18:18 for himself a pillar, **w** *is* in the king's dale: 834
18:28 **w** hath delivered up the men that lift up their 834
19: 5 **w** *this* day have saved thy life, and the lives NIH
19:16 **w** *was* of Bahurim, hasted and came down 834
19:19 neither do thou remember *that* **w** thy servant 834
19:38 I will do to him *that* **w** shall seem good 1886.1
20: 5 he tarried longer than the set time **w** he had 834
20: 8 When they *were* at the great stone **w** *is* in 834
21:12 **w** had stolen them from the street of 834
21:16 **w** *was* of the sons of the giant, 834
21:18 slew Saph, **w** *was* of the sons of the giant. 834
22:44 a people **w** I knew not shall serve me. NIH
23:15 of the well of Beth-lehem, **w** *is* by the gate. 834
24: 2 **w** *was* with him, Go now through all 834
24:24 my God of that **w** doth cost me nothing. NIH
1Ki 1: 8 and the mighty *men* **w** *belonged* to David, 834
1: 9 **w** *is* by En-rogel, and called all his brethren 834
1:48 **w** hath given *one* to sit on my throne *this* 834
2: 4 That the LORD may continue his word **w** 834
2: 8 **w** cursed me *with* a grievous curse in 1931
2:24 **w** hath established me, and set me on 834
2:27 **w** he spake concerning the house of Eli in 834
2:31 **w** Joab shed, from me, and from the house of 834
2:44 Thou knowest all the wickedness **w** thine 834
2:46 **w** went out, and fell upon him, that he 2050.1
3: 8 thy servant *is* in the midst of thy people **w** 834
3:13 I have also given thee *that* **w** thou hast not 834
3:21 it was not my son, **w** I did bear. 834
3:28 all Israel heard of the judgment **w** the king 834
4: 2 these *were* the princes **w** he had; Azariah 834
4: 7 **w** provided victuals for the king and his NIH
4:11 **w** had Taphath the daughter of Solomon to NIH
4:12 **w** *is* by Zartanah beneath Jezreel, 834
4:13 of Jair the son of Manasseh, **w** *are* in Gilead; 834
4:13 **w** *is* in Bashan, threescore great cities *with* 834
4:19 *he was* the only officer **w** *was* in the land. 834

W

1Ki 4:20 as the sand **w** *is* by the sea in multitude, 834
4:34 of the earth, **w** had heard of his wisdom. 834
5: 3 for the wars **w** were about him on every side, 834
5: 7 **w** hath given unto David a wise son over this 834
5: 8 I have considered *the things* **w** thou sentest 834
5:16 Besides the chief of Solomon's officers **w** 834
5:16 **w** ruled over the people that wrought in 1886.1
6: 1 in the month Zif, **w** *is* the second month, 1931
6: 2 the house **w** king Solomon built for 834
6:12 *Concerning* this house **w** thou art in 834
6:12 with thee, **w** I spake unto David thy father: 834
6:20 and *so* covered the altar *w was of* cedar. NIH
6:38 in the month Bul, **w** *is* the eighth month, 1931
7: 8 within the porch, *w* was of the like work. NIH
7:17 for the chapiters **w** *were* upon the top of 834
7:20 over against the belly **w** *was* by the network: 834
7:41 to cover the two bowls of the chapiters **w** 834
7:45 **w** Hiram made to king Solomon *for* 834
7:51 Solomon brought in the *things* **w** David his NIH
8: 1 LORD out of the city of David, **w** *is* Zion. 1931
8: 2 month Ethanim, **w** *is* the seventh month. 1931
8: 9 tables of stone, **w** Moses put there at Horeb, 834
8:15 **w** spake with his mouth unto David my 834
8:21 of the LORD, **w** he made with our fathers, 834
8:26 **w** thou spakest unto thy servant David my 834
8:28 **w** thy servant prayeth before thee to day: 834
8:29 *even* toward the place of **w** thou hast said, 834
8:29 that *thou* mayest hearken unto the prayer **w** 834
8:34 bring them again unto the land **w** thou gavest 834
8:36 **w** thou hast given to thy people for an 834
8:38 **w** shall know every man the plague of his 834
8:40 in the land **w** thou gavest unto our fathers. 834
8:43 **w** I have builded, is called by thy name. 834
8:44 LORD toward the city **w** thou hast chosen, 834
8:48 **w** led them away captive, and pray unto thee 834
8:48 **w** thou gavest unto their fathers, the city 834
8:48 the city **w** thou hast chosen, and the house 834
8:48 and the house **w** I have built for thy name: 834
8:51 **w** thou broughtest forth out of Egypt, 834
8:56 **w** he promised by the hand of Moses his 834
8:58 his judgments, **w** he commanded our fathers. 834
8:63 **w** he offered unto the LORD, two and 834
9: 1 all Solomon's desire **w** he was pleased to do, 834
9: 3 have hallowed this house, **w** thou hast built, 834
9: 6 *and* my statutes **w** I have set before you, 834
9: 7 will I cut off Israel out of the land **w** I have 834
9: 7 *this* house, **w** I have hallowed for my name, 834
9: 8 *at* this house, *w* is high, every one that NIH
9:12 came out from Tyre to see the cities **w** 834
9:13 What cities *are* these **w** thou hast given me, 834
9:15 this *is* the reason of the levy **w** king Solomon 834
9:19 that **w** Solomon desired to build in 834
9:20 **w** *were* not of the children of Israel, 834
9:23 **w** bare rule over the people that wrought 1886.1
9:24 unto her house **w** *Solomon* had built for her: 834
9:25 peace offerings upon the altar **w** he built 834
9:26 **w** *is* beside Eloth, on the shore of the Red 834
10: 3 thing hid from the king, **w** he told her not. 834
10: 5 his ascent *by* **w** he went up *unto* the house of 834
10: 7 and prosperity exceedeth the fame **w** I heard. 834
10: 8 **w** stand continually before thee, *and* 1886.1
10: 9 be the LORD thy God, **w** delighted in thee, 834
10:10 **w** the queen of Sheba gave to king Solomon. 834
10:13 besides *that* **w** Solomon gave her of his royal 834
10:24 hear his wisdom, **w** God had put in his heart. 834
11: 2 Of the nations *concerning* **w** the LORD 834
11: 8 **w** burnt incense and sacrificed unto their NIH
11: 9 of Israel, **w** had appeared unto him twice, 1886.1
11:10 he kept not *that* **w** the LORD commanded. 834
11:11 and my statutes, **w** I have commanded thee, 834
11:13 and for Jerusalem's sake, **w** I have chosen. 834
11:18 **w** gave him a house, and appointed him NIH
11:23 **w** fled from his lord Hadadezer king of 834
11:32 the city **w** I have chosen out of all the tribes 834
11:33 to do *that* **w** *is* right in mine eyes, 1886.1
11:36 the city **w** I have chosen me to put my name 834
12: 4 his heavy yoke **w** he put upon us, lighter, 834
12: 8 **w** they had given him, and consulted with 834
12: 8 grown up with him, *and* **w** stood before him: 834
12: 9 Make the yoke **w** thy father did put upon us 834
12:15 **w** the LORD spake by Ahijah the Shilonite 834
12:17 *as for* the children of Israel **w** dwelt in 1886.1
12:21 fourscore thousand chosen *men*, **w** were NIH
12:28 **w** brought thee up out of the land of Egypt. 834
12:31 the people, **w** were not of the sons of Levi. 834
12:32 the priests of the high places **w** he had made. 834
12:33 So he offered upon the altar **w** he had made 834
12:33 *even* in the month **w** he had devised of his 834
13: 3 This *is* the sign **w** the LORD hath spoken; 834
13: 4 **w** had cried against the altar in Beth-el, 834
13: 4 **w** he put forth against him, dried up, so 834
13: 5 according to the sign **w** the man of God had 834
13:11 the words **w** he had spoken unto the king, 834
13:12 the man of God went, **w** came from Judah. 834
13:21 hast not kept the commandment **w** 834
13:22 of the **w** *the LORD* did say to thee, Eat no 834
13:26 **w** hath torn him, and slain him, according to NIH
13:26 word of the LORD, **w** he spake unto him. 834
13:32 For the saying **w** he cried by the word of 834
13:32 against all the houses of the high places **w** 834
14: 2 **w** told me that I should be king over this 1931
14: 8 to do *that* only **w** *was* right in mine eyes; 1886.1
14:15 **w** he gave to their fathers, and shall scatter 834
14:18 **w** he spake by the hand of his servant Ahijah 834
14:20 And the days **w** Jeroboam reigned *were* two 834
14:21 the city **w** the LORD did choose out of all 834
14:22 with their sins **w** they had committed, 834
14:24 **w** the LORD cast out before the children of 834
14:26 he took away all the shields of gold **w** 834
14:27 **w** kept the door of the king's house. 1886.1
15: 3 sins of his father, **w** he had done before him: 834
15: 5 Because David did *that* **w** *was* right in 1886.1
15:11 Asa did *that* **w** *was* right in the eyes of 1886.1
15:15 he brought in *the things* **w** his father had NIH
15:15 *the things* **w** himself had dedicated, *into* NIH
1Ki 15:20 sent the captains of the hosts **w** he had 834
15:23 and all that he did, and the cities **w** he built, 834
15:27 at Gibbethon, **w** *belongeth* to the Philistines; 834
15:29 **w** he spake by his servant Ahijah 834
15:30 Because of the sins of Jeroboam **w** he 834
15:30 which he sinned, and **w** he made Israel sin, 834
16:12 **w** he spake against Baasha by Jehu 834
16:13 *by* **w** they sinned, and *by* which they made 834
16:13 and *by* **w** they made Israel to sin, 834
16:15 **w** *belonged* to the Philistines. 834
16:19 For his sins **w** he sinned in doing evil in 834
16:19 and in his sin **w** he did, to make Israel sin. 834
16:24 and called the name of the city **w** he built, 834
16:27 Now the rest of the acts of Omri **w** he did, 834
16:32 the house of Baal, **w** he had built in Samaria. 834
16:34 **w** he spake by Joshua the son of Nun. 834
17: 9 **w** *belongeth* to Zidon, and dwell there: 834
17:16 word of the LORD, **w** he spake by Elijah. 834
18: 3 **w** *was* the governor of *his* house. 834
18:19 four hundred, **w** eat *at* Jezebel's table. NIH
18:26 they took the bullock **w** was given them, 834
18:26 And they leapt upon the altar **w** was made. 834
19: 3 **w** *belongeth* to Judah, and left his servant 834
19:18 all the knees **w** have not bowed unto Baal, 834
19:18 and every mouth **w** hath not kissed him. 834
20:19 of the city, and the army **w** followed them. 834
20:34 The cities, **w** my father took from thy father, 834
21: 1 Jezreelite had a vineyard, **w** *was* in Jezreel, 834
21: 4 of the word **w** Naboth the Jezreelite had 834
21:11 as *it was* written in the letters **w** she had sent 834
21:15 **w** he refused to give thee for money: 834
21:18 to meet Ahab king of Israel, **w** *is* in Samaria: 834
21:25 **w** did sell himself to work wickedness in 834
22:13 of one of them, and speak *that* **w** *is* good. NIH
22:16 *that* **w** *is* true in the name of the LORD? NIH
22:24 **W way** went the spirit of the LORD 335+2088
22:38 according unto the word of the LORD **w** he 834
22:39 the ivory house **w** he made, and all the cities 834
22:43 doing *that* **w** *was* right in the eyes of 1886.1
22:46 **w** remained in the days of his father Asa, 834
2Ki 1: 4 down from *that* bed on **w** thou art gone up, 834
1: 6 shalt not come down from *that* bed on **w** 834
1: 7 What manner of man *was he* **w** came up to 834
1:16 thou shalt not come down off *that* bed on **w** 834
1:17 word of the LORD **w** Elijah had spoken. 834
1:18 Now the rest of the acts of Ahaziah **w** he did, 834
2:15 when the sons of the prophets **w** *were* to 834
2:22 according to the saying of Elisha **w** he spake. 834
3: 3 the son of Nebat, **w** made Israel to sin; 834
3: 8 he said, **W** way shall we go up? 335+2088
3:11 **w** poured water on the hands of Elijah. 834
4: 4 and thou shalt set aside *that* **w** *is* full. 1886.1
4: 9 man of God, **w** passeth by us continually. NIH
5:20 in not receiving at his hands *that* **w** he 834
6:10 the king of Israel sent to the place **w** the man 834
6:11 Will ye not shew me **w** of us *is* for the king 4310
7:13 that remain, **w** are left in the city, (behold, 834
7:15 **w** the Syrians had cast away in their haste. 834
8:21 smote the Edomites **w** compassed him 1886.1
8:29 **w** the Syrians had given him at Ramah, 834
9: 5 Jehu said, Unto **w** of all us? And he said, 4310
9:15 of the wounds **w** the Syrians had given him, 834
9:19 **w** came to them, and said, Thus saith NIH
9:27 *so* at the going up to Gur, **w** *is* by Ibleam. 834
9:36 **w** he spake by his servant Elijah 834
10: 5 do thou *that* **w** *is* good in thine eyes. 1886.1
10: 6 great *men* of the city, **w** brought them up. NIH
10:10 **w** the LORD spake concerning the house of 834
10:10 for the LORD hath done *that* **w** he spake by 834
10:17 saying of the LORD, **w** he spake to Elijah. 834
10:30 in executing *that* **w** *is* right in mine eyes, 1886.1
10:31 the sins of Jeroboam, **w** made Israel to sin. 834
10:33 from Aroer, **w** *is* by the river Arnon, 834
11: 2 stale him from among the king's sons **w** 1886.1
11:16 she went *by* the way by the **w** the horses NIH
12: 2 Jehoash did *that* **w** *was* right in the sight 1886.1
12:20 house of Millo, **w** goeth down *to* Silla. 1886.1
13: 2 he did *that* **w** *was* evil in the sight of 1886.1
13: 2 the son of Nebat, **w** made Israel to sin; 834
13:11 he did *that* **w** *was* evil in the sight of 1886.1
13:25 **w** he had taken out of the hand of Jehoahaz 834
14: 3 he did *that* **w** *was* right in the sight of 1886.1
14: 5 that he slew his servants **w** had slain 1886.1
14: 6 according unto that **w** is written in the book NIH
14:11 face at Beth-shemesh, **w** *belongeth* to Judah. 834
14:15 Now the rest of the acts of Jehoash **w** he did, 834
14:21 **w** *was* sixteen years old, and made him 1931
14:24 he did *that* **w** *was* evil in the sight of 1886.1
14:25 **w** he spake by the hand of his servant Jonah, 834
14:25 the prophet, **w** *was* of Gath-hepher. 834
14:28 Hamath, *w belonged* to Judah, for Israel, NIH
15: 3 he did *that* **w** *was* right in the sight of 1886.1
15: 9 he did *that* **w** *was* evil in the sight of 1886.1
15:12 This *was* the word of the LORD **w** he spake 834
15:15 and his conspiracy **w** he made, behold, 834
15:18 he did *that* **w** *was* evil in the sight of 1886.1
15:24 he did *that* **w** *was* evil in the sight of 1886.1
15:28 he did *that* **w** *was* evil in the sight of 1886.1
15:34 he did *that* **w** *was* right in the sight of 1886.1
16: 2 did not *that* **w** *was* right in the sight of 1886.1
16: 7 the king of Israel, **w** rise up against me. 1886.1
16:14 **w** *was* before the LORD, from the forefront 834
16:19 Now the rest of the acts of Ahaz **w** he did, 834
17: 2 he did *that* **w** *was* evil in the sight of 1886.1
17: 7 **w** had brought them up out of the land of 1886.1
17: 8 and of the kings of Israel, **w** they had made. 834
17:13 according to all the law **w** I commanded 834
17:13 **w** I sent to you by my servants the prophets. 834
17:15 his testimonies **w** he testified against them; 834
17:19 walked in the statutes of Israel **w** they made. 834
17:22 walked in all the sins of Jeroboam **w** he did; 834
17:25 lions among them, **w** slew *some* of them. NIH
17:26 The nations **w** thou hast removed, and 834
17:29 put *them* in the houses of the high places **w** 834
17:32 **w** sacrificed for them in the houses of NIH
2Ki 17:34 commandment **w** the LORD commanded 834
17:37 and the commandment, **w** he wrote for you, 834
18: 3 he did *that* **w** *was* right in the sight of 1886.1
18: 6 **w** the LORD commanded Moses. 834
18: 9 **w** *was* the seventh year of Hoshea son of 1931
18:14 *that* **w** thou puttest on me will I bear. 834
18:16 *from* the pillars **w** Hezekiah king of Judah 834
18:17 **w** *is* in the highway of the fuller's field. 834
18:18 **w** *was* over the household, and Shebna 834
18:21 *even* upon Egypt, on **w** if a man lean, it will 834
18:27 *hath he* not *sent me* to the men **w** sit on 1886.1
18:37 **w** *was* over the household, and Shebna 834
19: 2 **w** was over the household, and Shebna 834
19: 4 will reprove the words **w** the LORD thy 834
19: 6 Be not afraid of the words **w** thou hast heard, 834
19: 6 *with* **w** the servants of the king of Assyria 834
19:12 delivered them **w** my fathers have destroyed; 834
19:12 the children of Eden **w** *were* in Thelasar? 834
19:15 **w** dwellest *between* the cherubims, thou *art* NIH
19:16 **w** hath sent him to reproach the living God. 834
19:20 *That* **w** thou hast prayed to me against 834
19:28 I will turn thee back by the way by **w** thou 834
19:29 second year **that w springeth of the same**; 7823
20: 3 and have done *that* **w** *is* good in thy sight. 1886.1
20:11 by **w** it had gone down in the dial of Ahaz. 834
20:17 *that* **w** thy fathers have laid up in store unto 834
20:18 **w** thou shalt beget, shall they take *away*; and 834
20:19 Good *is* the word of the LORD **w** thou hast 834
21: 2 he did *that* **w** *was* evil in the sight of 1886.1
21: 3 For he built *up* again the high places **w** 834
21: 4 of **w** the LORD said, In Jerusalem will I 834
21: 7 of **w** the LORD said to David, and 834
21: 7 **w** I have chosen out of all tribes of Israel, 834
21: 8 more out of the land **w** I gave their fathers; 834
21:11 **w** *were* before him, and hath made Judah 834
21:15 Because they have done *that* **w** *was* evil 1886.1
21:16 in doing *that* **w** *was* evil in the sight of 1886.1
21:20 he did *that* **w** *was* evil in the sight of 1886.1
21:25 Now the rest of the acts of Amon **w** he did, 834
22: 2 he did *that* **w** *was* right in the sight of 1886.1
22: 4 that he may sum the silver **w** is brought 1886.1
22: 4 **w** the keepers of the door have gathered of 834
22: 5 let them give it to the doers of the work **w** *is* 834
22:13 to do according unto all that **w** is written NIH
22:16 *even* all the words of the book **w** the king of 834
22:18 to the king of Judah **w** sent you to inquire 1886.1
22:18 *As touching* the words **w** thou hast heard; 834
22:20 thine eyes shall not see all the evil **w** I will 834
23: 2 **w** was found in the house of the LORD. 1886.1
23: 8 **w** *were* on a man's left hand at the gate of 834
23:10 **w** *is* in the valley of the children of Hinnom, 834
23:11 **w** *was* in the suburbs, and burnt the chariots 834
23:12 **w** the kings of Judah had made, and 834
23:12 the altars **w** Manasseh had made in the two 834
23:13 **w** *were* on the right hand of the mount of 834
23:13 **w** Solomon the king of Israel had builded for 834
23:15 the high place **w** Jeroboam the son of Nebat, 834
23:16 according to the word of the LORD **w** 834
23:17 **w** came from Judah, and proclaimed these 834
23:19 **w** the kings of Israel had made to provoke 834
23:24 **w** were written in the book that Hilkiah 1886.1
23:27 will cast off this city Jerusalem **w** I have 834
23:27 the house of **w** I said, My name shall be 834
23:32 he did *that* **w** *was* evil in the sight of 1886.1
23:37 he did *that* **w** *was* evil in the sight of 1886.1
24: 2 **w** he spake by his servants the prophets. 834
24: 4 **w** the LORD would not pardon. NIH
24: 9 he did *that* **w** *was* evil in the sight of 1886.1
24:13 cut in pieces all the vessels of gold **w** 834
24:19 he did *that* **w** *was* evil in the sight of 1886.1
25: 4 two walls, **w** *is* by the king's garden: 834
25: 8 **w** *is* the nineteenth year of king 1931
25:16 the bases **w** Solomon had made for the house 834
25:19 **w** were found in the city, and the principal 834
25:19 **w** mustered the people of the land, and 1886.1
1Ch 1:46 **w** smote Midian in the field of Moab, 1886.1
2: 3 *w* three were born unto him of the daughter NIH
2:19 took unto him Ephrath, **w** bare him Hur. NIH
2:42 his firstborn, **w** *was* the father of Ziph; 1931
2:55 the families of the scribes **w** dwelt at Jabez; NIH
3: 1 of David, **w** were born unto him in Hebron; 834
4:10 And God granted *him that* **w** he requested. 834
4:11 begat Mehir, **w** *was* the father of Eshton. 1931
4:18 the daughter of Pharaoh, **w** Mered took. 834
6:61 **w** were left of the family of *that* tribe, 1886.1
6:65 these cities, **w** are called by *their* names. 834
9:22 All these **w** were chosen to be porters in 1886.1
9:25 And their brethren, *w were* in their villages, NIH
10:13 So Saul died for his transgression **w** he 834
10:13 **w** he kept not, and also for asking *counsel* of 834
11: 4 and all Israel went *to* Jerusalem, **w** *is* Jebus; 1931
11: 5 the castle of Zion, **w** *is* the city of David. 1931
12:31 **w** were expressed by name, to come and 834
12:32 *w were men* that had understanding of NIH
12:33 of war, fifty thousand, **w** could keep rank: NIH
13: 2 Levites *w are* in their cities *and* suburbs, NIH
13: 6 *is*, to Kirjath-jearim, **w** *belonged* to Judah, 834
14: 4 Now these *are* the names of *his* children **w** 834
15: 3 unto his place, **w** he had prepared for it. 834
16:15 the word **w** he commanded to a thousand NIH
16:16 *Even of the covenant* **w** he made with 834
16:40 law of the LORD, **w** he commanded Israel; 834
17:11 up thy seed after thee, **w** shall be of thy sons; 834
19:13 let the LORD do *that* **w** *is* good in his 1886.1
19:18 seven thousand **w** *men fought in* chariots, NIH
20: 4 **at w time** Sibbechai the Hushathite slew 227
21:19 **w** he spake in the name of the LORD. 834
21:23 let my lord the king do *that* **w** *is* good in 1886.1
21:24 for I will not take *that* **w** *is* thine for 834
21:29 **w** Moses made in the wilderness, and 834
22:13 judgments **w** the LORD charged Moses 834
23: 4 Of **w**, twenty and four thousand *were* to set 428
23: 5 the LORD with the instruments **w** I made, 834
23:29 for *that* **w** *is baked in* the pan, and for that NIH
23:29 for that **w** is fried, and for all *manner of* NIH

1Ch 25: 2 **w** prophesied according to the order of 1886.1
26:22 ***w*** *were* over the treasures of the house of NIH
26:26 **W** Shelomith and his brethren *were* over all 1931
26:26 of the dedicate *things,* **w** David the king, 834
27: 1 **w** came in and went out month by month 1886.1
27:31 All these *were* the rulers of the substance **w** 834
29: 3 ***w*** I have given to the house of my God, NIH
29:17 **w** are present here, to offer willingly unto 1886.1
29:19 the palace, *for* the **w** I have made provision. 834
2Ch 1: 3 **w** Moses the servant of the LORD had 834
1: 4 to *the place* **w** David had prepared for it: NIH
1: 6 **w** *was* at the tabernacle of the congregation, 834
1:14 **w** he placed in the chariot cities, and 3963.1
2: 5 the house **w** I build *is* great: for great *is* our 834
2: 9 for the house **w** I am about to build *shall be* 834
2:11 **w** he sent to Solomon, Because the LORD NIH
2:14 to find out every device **w** shall be put to 834
2:15 and the wine, **w** my lord hath spoken of, 834
3: 5 **w** he overlaid with fine gold, and 1930.2
4: 3 of oxen, **w** did compass it round about: NIH
4:12 the chapiters ***w*** *were* on the top of the two NIH
4:12 the chapiters **w** *were* on the top of the pillars; 834
4:13 to cover the two pommels of the chapiters **w** 834
5: 2 LORD out of the city of David, **w** *is* Zion. 1931
5: 3 in the feast **w** *was in* the seventh month. 1931
5: 6 **w** could not be told nor numbered for 834
5:10 the two tables **w** Moses put *therein* at Horeb, 834
5:12 Also the Levites ***w*** *were* the singers, all of NIH
6: 4 who hath with his hands fulfilled *that* **w** he 834
6: 9 son **w** shall come forth out of thy loins, 1886.1
6:14 **w** keepest covenant, and *shewest* mercy NIH
6:15 Thou **w** hast kept with thy servant David my 834
6:15 my father *that* **w** thou hast promised him; 834
6:16 with thy servant David my father *that* **w** 834
6:17 **w** thou hast spoken unto thy servant David. 834
6:18 how much less this house **w** I have built? 834
6:19 the prayer **w** thy servant prayeth before thee: 834
6:20 to hearken unto the prayer **w** thy servant 834
6:21 **w** they shall make towards this place: 834
6:25 bring them again unto the land **w** thou gavest 834
6:27 **w** thou hast given unto thy people for an 834
6:31 long as they live in the land **w** thou gavest 834
6:32 **w** *is* not of thy people Israel, but is come 834
6:33 may know that this house **w** I have built is 834
6:34 they pray unto thee toward this city **w** thou 834
6:34 the house **w** I have built for thy name; 834
6:36 (for *there is* no man **w** sinneth not,) 834
6:38 **w** thou gavest unto their fathers, and 834
6:38 and *toward* the city **w** thou hast chosen, and 834
6:38 toward the house **w** I have built for thy 834
6:39 forgive thy people **w** have sinned against 834
7: 6 **w** David the king had made to praise 834
7: 7 the brasen altar **w** Solomon had made was 834
7:14 If my people, **w** are called by my name, 834
7:19 **w** I have set before you, and shall go and 834
7:20 roots out of my land **w** I have given them; 834
7:20 this house, **w** I have sanctified for my name, 834
7:21 this house, **w** is high, shall be an 834
7:22 **w** brought them forth out of the land of 834
8: 2 That the cities **w** Huram had restored to 834
8: 4 and all the store cities, **w** he built in Hamath. 834
8: 7 and the Jebusites, **w** *were* not of Israel, 834
8:12 the LORD, **w** he had built before the porch, 834
9: 2 there was nothing hid from Solomon **w** he 834
9: 4 his ascent *by* **w** he went up *into* the house of 834
9: 5 *It was* a true report **w** I heard in mine own 834
9: 7 **w** stand continually before thee, and 1886.1
9: 8 **w** delighted in thee to set thee on his throne, 834
9:10 **w** brought gold from Ophir, brought algum 834
9:12 besides *that* **w** she had brought unto the king. 834
9:14 Besides *that* ***w*** chapmen and merchants NIH
9:18 ***w*** *were* fastened to the throne, and stays on NIH
10: 8 he forsook the counsel **w** the old men gave 834
10: 9 **w** have spoken to me, saying, 834
10:15 **w** he spake by the hand of Ahijah 834
11: 1 fourscore thousand chosen *men,* **w** were NIH
11:10 **w** *are* in Judah and in Benjamin, 834
11:15 the devils, and for the calves **w** he had made. 834
11:19 **W** bare him children; Jeush, and Shamariah, NIH
11:20 **w** bare him Abijah, and Attai, and Ziza, 2050.1
12: 4 he took the fenced cities **w** *pertained* to 834
12: 9 he carried away also the shields of gold **w** 834
12:10 Instead of **w** king Rehoboam made 1992.1
12:13 the city **w** the LORD had chosen out of all 834
13: 4 **w** *is* in mount Ephraim, and said, Hear me, 834
13: 8 **w** Jeroboam made you for gods. 834
13:10 and the priests, **w** minister unto the LORD, NIH
14: 2 Asa did *that* **w** *was* good and right in 1886.1
15: 8 out of the cities **w** he had taken from mount 834
15:11 of the spoil ***w*** they had brought, NIH
16:14 **w** he had made for himself in the city of 834
16:14 laid him in the bed **w** was filled *with* sweet 834
17: 2 of Ephraim, **w** Asa his father had taken. 834
18:23 **W** way went the spirit of the LORD 335+2088
20: 2 they *be* in Hazazon-tamar, **w** *is* En-gedi. 1931
20:11 **w** thou hast given us to inherit. 834
20:22 mount Seir, **w** were come against Judah; 1886.1
20:25 **w** they stript off for themselves, 2050.1
20:32 doing *that* **w** *was* right in the sight of 1886.1
21: 6 he wrought *that* **w** *was* evil in the eyes of 1886.1
21: 9 smote the Edomites **w** compassed him in, 1886.1
21:13 father's house, **w** *were* better than thyself: NIH

22: 6 of the wounds **w** were given him at Ramah, 834
23: 9 king David's, **w** *were in* the house of God. 834
23:19 that none ***w*** *was* unclean in any thing should NIH
24: 2 Joash did *that* **w** *was* right in the sight of 1886.1
24:20 **w** stood above the people, and said unto NIH
24:22 **w** Jehoiada his father had done to him, 834
25: 2 he did *that* **w** *was* right in the sight of 1886.1
25: 9 what *shall we* do for the hundred talents **w** I 834
25:13 the soldiers of the army **w** Amaziah sent 834
25:15 he sent unto him a prophet, **w** said unto him, NIH
25:15 **w** could not deliver their own people out of 834
25:21 at Beth-shemesh, **w** *belongeth* to Judah. 834
26: 4 he did *that* **w** *was* right in the sight of 1886.1

2Ch 26:23 field of the burial **w** *belonged* to the kings; 834
27: 2 he did *that* **w** *was* right in the sight of 1886.1
28: 1 he did not *that* **w** *was* right in the sight of 1886.1
28: 6 in one day, ***w*** *were* all valiant men; NIH
28:11 **w** ye have taken captive of your brethren: 834
28:15 the men **w** were expressed by name rose up, 834
28:23 unto the gods of Damascus, **w** smote him: 1886.1
29: 2 he did *that* **w** *was* right in the sight of 1886.1
29: 6 done *that* **w** *was* evil in the eyes of 1886.1
29:19 **w** king Ahaz in his reign did cast away in his 834
29:32 **w** the congregation brought, was threescore 834
30: 7 **w** trespassed against the LORD God of 834
30: 8 his sanctuary, **w** he hath sanctified for ever: 834
30:16 ***w*** *they received* of the hand of the Levites. NIH
31: 6 the tithe of holy *things* **w** were 1886.1
31:10 and that **w** is left *is* this great store. NIH
31:12 over **w** Cononiah the Levite *was* ruler, 1992.1
31:19 ***w*** *were* in the fields of the suburbs of their NIH
31:20 wrought *that* **w** *was* good and right and 1886.1
32: 3 of the fountains **w** *were* without the city: 834
32:19 ***w*** *were* the work of the hands of man. NIH
32:21 **w** cut off all the mighty *men* of valour, and NIH
33: 2 did *that* **w** *was* evil in the sight of 1886.1
33: 3 For he built again the high places **w** 834
33: 7 the idol **w** he had made, in the house of God, 834
33: 7 of **w** God had said to David and to Solomon 834
33: 7 **w** I have chosen before all the tribes of 834
33: 8 the land **w** I have appointed for your fathers; 834
33:11 **w** took Manasseh among the thorns, and 834
33:22 he did *that* **w** *was* evil in the sight of 1886.1
33:22 images **w** Manasseh his father had made, 834
34: 2 he did *that* **w** *was* right in the sight of 1886.1
34: 9 **w** the Levites that kept the doors had 834
34:11 to floor the houses **w** the kings of Judah had 834
34:24 **w** they have read before the king of Judah: 834
34:26 *concerning* the words **w** thou hast heard; 834
34:31 to perform the words of the covenant **w** 1886.1
35: 3 all Israel, **w** were holy unto the LORD, 1886.1
35: 3 Put the holy ark in the house **w** Solomon 834
35:26 according to that **w** was written in the law 1886.1
36: 5 he did *that* **w** *was* evil in the sight of 1886.1
36: 8 his abominations **w** he did, and that which 834
36: 8 and that **w** was found in him, behold, NIH
36: 9 he did *that* **w** *was* evil in the sight of 1886.1
36:12 he did *that* **w** *was* evil in the sight of 1886.1
36:14 polluted the house of the LORD **w** he had 834
36:23 him a house in Jerusalem, **w** *is* in Judah. 834
Ezr 1: 2 him a house at Jerusalem, **w** *is* in Judah. 834
1: 3 **w** *is* in Judah, and build the house of 834
1: 3 of Israel, (he *is* the God,) **w** *is* in Jerusalem. 834
1: 5 to go up to build the house of the LORD **w** 834
1: 7 **w** Nebuchadnezzar had brought forth out of 834
2: 1 *of* those **w** had been carried away, 1886.1
2: 2 **W** came with Zerubbabel: Jeshua, 834
2:59 these *were* they **w** went up from 1886.1
2:61 **w** took a wife of the daughters of Barzillai 834
2:68 the house of the LORD **w** *is* at Jerusalem, 834
4: 2 king of Assur, **w** brought us up hither. 1886.1
4:12 that the Jews **w** came up from thee to us are 1768
4:15 for **w** *cause* was this city destroyed. 1836
4:18 The letter **w** ye sent unto us *hath been* 1768
4:20 **w** have ruled over all *countries* beyond NIH
4:24 ceased the work of the house of the God **w** 1768
5: 2 began to build the house of God **w** *is* at 1768
5: 6 **w** *were* on *this* side the river, sent unto 1768
5: 8 **w** *is* builded *with* great stones, and 2050.3
5:11 **w** a great king of Israel builded and 1958.2
5:14 **w** Nebuchadnezzar took out of the temple 1768
5:16 laid the foundation of the house of God **w** 1768
5:17 **w** *is* there at Babylon, whether it be *so,* 1768
6: 5 **w** Nebuchadnezzar took forth out of 1768
6: 5 forth out of the temple **w** *is* at Jerusalem, 1768
6: 5 brought *again* unto the temple **w** *is* at 1768
6: 6 **w** *are* beyond the river, be ye far from 1768
6: 9 **that w** *they* have need of, both young 4101
6: 9 of the priests **w** *are* at Jerusalem, 1768
6:12 to destroy this house of God **w** *is* at 1768
6:13 according to **that w** Darius the king had 1768
6:15 **w** *was in* the sixth year of the reign of 1768
6:18 for the service of God, **w** *is* at Jerusalem; 1768
6:21 **w** were come again out of captivity, and 1886.1
7: 6 **w** the LORD God of Israel had given: 834
7: 8 **w** *was in* the seventh year of the king. 1931
7:13 **w** *are* minded of their own freewill to go *up* NIH
7:14 according to the law of thy God **w** *is* in 1768
7:15 **w** the king and his counsellers have freely 1768
7:16 the house of their God **w** *is* in Jerusalem: 1768
7:17 of the house of your God **w** *is* in Jerusalem. 1768
7:20 **w** thou shalt have occasion to bestow, 1768
7:21 do make a decree to all the treasurers **w** *are* 1768
7:25 **w** may judge all the people that *are* beyond 1768
7:27 **w** hath put *such a thing* as this in the king's 834
7:27 to beautify the house of the LORD **w** *is* in 834
8:25 **w** the king, and his counsellers, and NIH
8:35 **w** were come out of the captivity, 1886.1
9:11 **W** thou hast commanded by thy servants 834
9:11 saying, The land, *unto* **w** ye go to possess it, 834
9:11 **w** have filled it from one end to another with 834
10:14 let all *them* **w** have taken strange wives in 834
Ne 1: 2 **w** were left of the captivity, and 834
1: 6 **w** I pray before thee now, day and night, 834
1: 6 of Israel, **w** we have sinned against thee: 834
1: 7 **w** thou commandedst thy servant Moses. 834
2: 8 of the palace **w** *appertained* to the house, 834
2:13 **w** were broken down, and the gates thereof 834
2:18 I told them of the hand of my God **w** was 834
3:25 the tower **w** lieth out from the king's high 1886.1
4: 2 out of the heaps of the rubbish **w** are burnt? 1992
4: 3 he said, Even *that* **w** they build, if a fox go 834
4:12 when the Jews **w** dwelt by them came, 1886.1
4:14 **w** *is* great and terrible, and fight for your NIH
4:17 They **w** builded on the wall, and they that 1886.1
4:23 nor the men of the guard **w** followed me, 834
5: 8 the Jews, **w** were sold unto the heathen; 1886.1
5:18 Now *that* **w** was prepared *for me* daily *was* 834

Ne 6: 6 **for w cause** thou buildest the wall, 3651+5921
7: 5 genealogy of them **w** came up at the first, 1886.1
7:61 these *were* they **w** went up *also* from 1886.1
7:63 **w** took *one* of the daughters of Barzillai 834
7:72 *that* **w** the rest of the people gave *was* twenty 834
8: 1 **w** the LORD had commanded to Israel. 834
8: 4 of wood, **w** they had made for the purpose; 834
8: 9 **w** *is* the Tirshatha, and Ezra the priest 1931
8:14 they found written in the law **w** the LORD 834
9: 5 **w** *is* exalted above all blessing and praise. 2050.1
9:15 the land **w** thou hadst sworn to give them. 834
9:23 *concerning* **w** thou hadst promised to their 834
9:26 slew thy prophets **w** testified against them to 834
9:29 (**w** if a man do, he shall live in them;) 834
9:35 and fat land **w** thou gavest before them, 834
10:29 **w** was given by Moses the servant of God, 834
12: 8 ***w*** *was* over the thanksgiving, he and NIH
12:37 fountain gate, **w** *was* over against them, 2050.1
13: 5 **w** was commanded *to be given* to NIH
13:15 **w** they brought *into* Jerusalem on 2050.1
13:16 **w** brought fish, and all *manner of* ware, and NIH
Est 1: 1 (this *is* Ahasuerus **w** reigned, from India 1886.1
1: 2 his kingdom, **w** *was* in Shushan the palace, 834
1: 9 royal house **w** *belonged* to king Ahasuerus. 834
1:13 the king said to the wise *men,* **w** knew NIH
1:14 **w** saw the king's face, *and* which sat NIH
1:14 *and* **w** sat the first in the kingdom;) 1886.1
1:18 **w** have heard of the deed of the queen. 834
1:20 when the king's decree **w** he shall make 834
2: 4 let the maiden **w** pleaseth the king be queen 834
2: 6 **w** had been carried away with Jeconiah king 834
2: 9 ***w*** *were* meet to be given her, NIH
2:14 king's chamberlain, **w** kept the concubines: NIH
2:16 **w** *is* the month Tebeth, in the seventh year 1931
2:21 and Teresh, of those **w** kept the door, NIH
3: 3 **w** *were* in the king's gate, said unto 834
3:13 **w** *is* the month Adar, and *to take* the spoil 1931
4: 6 of the city, **w** *was* before the king's gate. 834
4:16 unto the king, **w** *is* not according to the law: 834
6: 8 Let the royal apparel be brought **w** the king 834
6: 8 the crown royal **w** is set upon his head: 834
7: 9 **w** Haman had made for Mordecai, 834
8: 2 **w** he had taken from Haman, and gave it 834
8: 5 **w** he wrote to destroy the Jews which *are* in 834
8: 5 which he wrote to destroy the Jews **w** *are* in 834
8: 8 for the writing **w** *is* written in the king's 834
8: 9 rulers of the provinces **w** *are* from India unto 834
8:11 Where*in* the king granted the Jews **w** *were* in 834
8:12 of the twelfth month, **w** *is* the month Adar. 1931
9:13 let it be granted to the Jews **w** *are* in Shushan 834
9:22 the month **w** was turned unto them from 834
9:25 **w** he devised against the Jews, should return 834
9:26 *of that* **w** they had seen concerning this 4100
9:26 this *matter,* and **w** had come unto them, 4100
Job 3: 3 the night *in* **w** *it was* said, There is a man NIH
3:14 **w** built desolate places for themselves; 1886.1
3:16 I had not been; as infants ***w*** never saw light. NIH
3:21 **W** long for death, but it *cometh* not; and 1886.1
3:22 **W** rejoice exceedingly, *and* are glad, 1886.1
3:25 For the thing **w** I greatly feared is come NIH
3:25 and *that* **w** I was afraid of is come unto me. 834
4:14 trembling, **w** made all my bones to shake. 2050.1
4:19 the dust, **w** are crushed before the moth? 3963.1
4:21 Doth not their excellency **w** *is* in them go NIH
5: 1 and to **w** of the saints wilt thou turn? 4310
5: 9 **W** doeth great *things* and unsearchable; NIH
5:11 that those **w** mourn may be exalted *to* NIH
6: 6 Can **that w is unsavoury** be eaten without 8602
6:16 **W** are blackish by reason of the ice, *and* 1886.1
6:26 of one that is desperate, ***w*** *are* as wind? NIH
9: 5 **W** removeth the mountains, and 1886.1
9: 5 know not: **w** overturneth them in his anger. 834
9: 6 **W** shaketh the earth out of her place, and 1886.1
9: 7 **W** commandeth the sun, and it riseth not; 1886.1
9: 8 **W** alone spreadeth out the heavens, and NIH
9: 9 **W** maketh Arcturus, Orion, and Pleiades, NIH
9:10 **W** doeth great *things* past finding out; yea, NIH
11: 6 that *they are* double to **that w is.** 8454
14:19 thou washest away the **things w grow** out 5599
15: 9 *what* understandest thou, **w** *is* not in us? 2050.1
15:14 *he* **w** *is* born of a woman, that he should be NIH
15:16 *is* man, **w** drinketh iniquity like water? NIH
15:17 and that **w** I have seen I will declare; NIH
15:18 **W** wise *men* have told from their fathers, 834
15:28 *and* in houses **w** no man 3807.1+4123.1
15:28 **w** are ready to become heaps. 834
16: 8 **w** is a witness *against me:* and my leanness NIH
20: 7 they **w** have seen him shall say, Where *is* NIH
20: 9 The eye also **w** saw him shall *see him* no NIH
20:11 **w** shall lie down with him in the dust. 2050.1
20:18 **That w** he **laboured for** shall he restore, 3022
20:19 he hath violently taken away a house **w** 2050.1
20:20 he shall not save of that **w** he desired. NIH
21:27 the devices ***w*** ye wrongfully imagine NIH
22:15 Hast thou marked the old way **w** wicked 834
22:16 **W** were cut down out of time, 834
22:17 **W** said unto God, Depart from us: and 1886.1
23: 5 I would know the words ***w*** he would answer NIH
24:11 **W** make oil within their walls, *and* NIH
24:16 ***w*** they had marked for themselves in NIH
24:19 *so doth* the grave *those* ***w*** have sinned. NIH
25: 6 a worm? and the son of man, ***w*** *is* a worm? NIH
27:11 *that* **w** *is* with the Almighty will I not 834
27:13 ***w*** they shall receive of the Almighty. NIH
28: 7 *There is* a path **w** no fowl knoweth, and 2050.2
28: 7 and **w** the vulture's eye hath not seen: 2050.2
29:16 and the cause **w** I knew not I searched out. NIH
32:19 Behold, my belly *is* as wine ***w*** hath no vent; NIH
33:27 perverted *that* ***w*** *was* right, and it profited NIH
34: 8 **W** goeth in company with the workers of 2050.1
34:32 *That* ***w*** I see not teach thou me: if I have NIH
35: 5 behold the clouds ***w*** are higher than thou. NIH
36:16 **that w** should **be set on** thy table *should be* 5183
36:24 that thou magnify his work, **w** men behold. 834
36:28 **W** the clouds do drop *and* distil upon man 834

Job 37: 5 doeth he, w we cannot comprehend. 2050.1
37:16 the wondrous works of *him* w *is* perfect in NIH
37:18 *w is* strong, *and* as a molten looking glass? NIH
37:21 now *men* see not the bright light w *is* in 1931
38:23 W I have reserved against the time of 834
38:24 *w* scattereth the east wind upon the earth? NIH
39:14 W leaveth her eggs in the earth, and 3588
40:15 Behold now behemoth, w I made with thee; 834
41: 1 his tongue with a cord w thou lettest down? NIH
42: 3 too wonderful for me, w I knew not. 2050.1
42: 8 in that ye have not spoken of me *the thing* w NIH
Ps 1: 4 *are* like the chaff w the wind driveth away. 834
3: 2 Many *there be* w say of my soul, *There is* NIH
7: T of David, w he sang unto the LORD, 834
7:10 *is* of God, w saveth the upright in heart. NIH
7:15 and is fallen into the ditch *w* he made. NIH
8: 3 and the stars, w thou hast ordained; 834
9:11 *praises* to the LORD, w dwelleth in Zion: NIH
9:13 consider my trouble *w I suffer* of them that NIH
9:15 in the net w they hid is their own foot 2098
9:16 The LORD is known *by* the judgment *w* NIH
17: 7 O thou that savest by thy right hand them w NIH
17:13 my soul from the wicked, *w is* thy sword: NIH
17:14 From men *w are* thy hand, O LORD, NIH
17:14 *w have* their portion in *this* life, and NIH
18:17 strong enemy, and from them w hated me: NIH
19: 5 W *is* as a bridegroom coming out of his 1931
21:11 *w* they are not able *to perform.* NIH
25: 3 let them be ashamed w transgress without 1886.1
28: 3 w speak peace to their neighbours, but NIH
31:18 w speak grievous things proudly and 1886.1
31:19 w thou hast laid up for them that fear thee; 834
31:19 *w* thou hast wrought for them that trust in NIH
32: 8 and teach thee in the way w thou shalt go: 2098
32: 9 *or* as the mule, *w have* no understanding: NIH
35: 7 *w* without cause they have digged for my NIH
35:10 w deliverest the poor from him that is too NIH
35:27 w hath pleasure in the prosperity of his 1886.1
40: 5 *are* thy wonderful works *w* thou hast done, NIH
40: 5 and thy thoughts *w are* to us-ward: NIH
41: 9 in whom I trusted, w did eat *of* my bread, 2050.2
44:10 and they w hate us spoil for themselves. NIH
45: 1 I speak of the things w I have made NIH
51: 8 *that* the bones *w* thou hast broken may NIH
58: 5 W will not hearken to the voice of charmers, 834
58: 7 Let them melt away as waters *w* run NIH
58: 8 As a snail *w* melteth, let *every one of them* NIH
59:12 and for cursing and lying *w* they speak. NIH
60:10 *Wilt* not thou, O God, *w* hadst cast us off? NIH
60:10 O God, *w* didst not go out with our armies? NIH
61: 7 and truth, *w* may preserve him. NIH
65: 6 W by his strength setteth fast NIH
65: 7 W stilleth the noise of the seas, the noise of NIH
65: 9 it *with* the river of God, w is full *of* water: NIH
66: 9 W holdeth our soul in life, and 1886.1
66:14 W my lips have uttered, and my mouth hath 834
66:20 *be* God, w hath not turned away my prayer, 834
68: 6 he bringeth out those w are bound with NIH
68:16 *this is* the hill *w* God desireth to dwell in; NIH
68:28 O God, **that w** thou hast wrought for us. 2098
68:33 upon the heavens of heavens, *w were* of old; NIH
69: 4 then I restored *that* w I took not away. 834
69:22 *that w should have been* for *their* welfare, NIH
71:20 *Thou,* w hast shewed me great and 834
71:23 and my soul, w thou hast redeemed. 834
74: 2 *w* thou hast purchased of old; NIH
74: 2 of thine inheritance, *w* thou hast redeemed; NIH
78: 3 W we have heard and known, and 834
78: 5 a law in Israel, w he commanded our fathers, 834
78: 6 *them, even* the children *w* should be born; NIH
78:45 *of flies* among them, w devoured them; 2050.1
78:45 and frogs, w destroyed them. 2050.1
78:54 *w* his right hand had purchased. NIH
78:60 of Shiloh, the tent *w* he placed among men; NIH
78:68 tribe of Judah, the mount Zion w he loved. 834
78:69 the earth w he hath established for ever. 1886.3
79:10 of the blood of thy servants w is shed. 1886.1
80:12 that all they w pass by the way do pluck NIH
80:15 the vineyard w thy right hand hath planted, 834
81:10 W brought thee out of the land of Egypt: 1886.1
83:10 W perished at En-dor: they became *as* dung NIH
85:12 Yea, the LORD shall give *that w is* good; NIH
86:17 that they w hate me may see *it,* and NIH
89:49 *w* thou swarest unto David in thy truth? NIH
90: 5 in the morning *they are* like grass *w* NIH
91: 9 *w is* my refuge, *even* the most High, NIH
94:20 *with* thee, w frameth mischief by a law? NIH
102:18 the people w *shall be* created shall praise NIH
104: 8 the place w thou hast founded for them. 2088
104:10 into the valleys, *w* run among the hills. NIH
104:12 their habitation, *w* sing among the branches. NIH
104:15 and bread *w* strengtheneth man's heart. NIH
104:16 the cedars of Lebanon, w he hath planted; 834
105: 8 the word *w* he commanded to a thousand NIH
105: 9 W *covenant* he made with Abraham, and 834
106:21 w had done great *things* in Egypt; NIH
106:36 their idols: w were a snare unto them. NIH
107:25 stormy wind, w lifteth up the waves thereof. NIH
107:37 w may yield fruits of increase. NIH
109:19 Let it be unto him as the garment *w* NIH
114: 8 W turned the rock *into* a standing water, 1886.1
115:15 You *are* blessed of the LORD w made NIH
118:20 into w the righteous shall enter. 2050.2
118:22 The stone *w* the builders refused is become NIH
118:24 This *is* the day *w* the LORD hath made; NIH
118:27 *is* the LORD, w hath shewed us light: 2050.1
119:21 w do err from thy commandments. 1886.1
119:39 Turn away my reproach w I fear: for thy 834
119:47 in thy commandments, w I have loved. 834
119:48 up unto thy commandments, w I have loved; 834
119:49 upon w thou hast caused me to hope. 834
119:85 digged pits for me, w *are* not after thy law. 834
119:165 Great peace have they w love thy law: and NIH
121: 2 from the LORD, w made heaven and earth. NIH
125: 1 *w* cannot be removed, *but* abideth for ever. NIH
Ps 129: 6 w withereth afore it groweth up: 7945
129: 8 Neither do they w go by say, 1886.1
134: 1 w by night stand in the house of 1886.1
135:21 out of Zion, w dwelleth *at* Jerusalem. NIH
136:13 To him w divided the Red sea into parts: NIH
136:16 To him w led his people through NIH
136:17 To him w smote great kings: for his mercy NIH
138: 8 The LORD will perfect that w concerneth NIH
139:16 *w* in continuance were fashioned, when *as* NIH
140: 2 W imagine mischiefs in *their* heart; 834
141: 5 an excellent oil, *w* shall not break my head: NIH
141: 9 Keep me from the snare *w* they have laid NIH
144: 1 w teacheth my hands to war, *and* 1886.1
146: 6 W made heaven, and earth, the sea, and all NIH
146: 6 that therein is: w keepeth truth for ever: 1886.1
146: 7 W executeth judgment for the oppressed: NIH
146: 7 W giveth food to the hungry. The LORD NIH
147: 9 his food, *and* to the young ravens w cry. 834
148: 6 he hath made a decree w shall not pass. 2050.1
Pr 1:19 *w* taketh away the life of the owners NIH
2:16 *even* from the stranger *w* flattereth with her NIH
2:17 W forsaketh the guide of her youth, and 1886.1
6: 7 W having no guide, overseer, or ruler, 834
7: 5 from the stranger *w* flattereth with her NIH
9: 5 and drink of the wine *w* I have mingled. NIH
11:22 *so is* a fair woman w is without discretion. NIH
12:27 The slothful *man* roasteth not that w he took NIH
14:12 There is a way w seemeth right unto a man, NIH
14:33 *that w is* in the midst of fools is made NIH
19:17 that w he hath given will he pay him again. NIH
20:25 to the man *who* devoureth *that w is* holy, NIH
22:28 the ancient landmark, w thy fathers have set. 834
23: 5 Wilt thou set thine eyes upon that w is 2050.1
23: 8 The morsel *w* thou hast eaten shalt thou NIH
24:13 and the honeycomb, *w is* sweet to thy taste: NIH
25: 1 w the men of Hezekiah king of Judah copied 834
27:16 of his right hand, w bewrayeth *itself.* NIH
28: 3 *is like* a sweeping rain w leaveth no food. 2050.1
30:18 There be three *things w* are too wonderful NIH
30:18 wonderful for me, yea, four w I know not: NIH
30:21 is disquieted, and for four *w* it cannot bear: NIH
30:24 There be four *things w are* little upon NIH
30:29 There be three *things w* go well, yea, NIH
30:30 A lion *w is* strongest among beasts, and NIH
31: 3 nor thy ways to *that w* destroyeth kings. NIH
Ecc 1: 3 What profit hath a man of all his labour w 7945
1: 9 thing that hath been, *it is* that w shall be; 7945
1: 9 that w is done *is* that which shall be done: 7945
1: 9 that which is done *is* that w shall be done: 7945
1:10 been already of old time, w was before us. 834
1:15 *That w is* crooked cannot be made straight: NIH
1:15 **that w is wanting** cannot be numbered. 2642
2: 3 w they should do under the heaven all 834
2:12 *even* that w hath been already done. 1930.2
2:16 seeing *that* w now *is, in* the days to come 7945
2:18 I hated all my labour w I *had* taken under 7945
2:20 of all the labour w I took under the sun. 7945
3: 2 and a time to pluck up *that w is* planted; NIH
3:10 w God hath given to the sons of men to be 834
3:15 That w hath been, *is* now; and *that* which *is* 7945
3:15 *that w is* to be hath already been; and God 834
3:15 and God requireth that w is past. NIH
3:19 For that w befalleth the sons of men NIH
4: 2 Wherefore I praised the dead w are already 7945
4: 2 dead more than the living w are yet alive. 834
4: 3 *is he* than both they, w hath not yet been, 834
4:15 I considered all the living w walk under 1886.1
5: 4 in fools: pay that w thou hast vowed. 834
5:13 There is a sore evil *w* I have seen under NIH
5:15 w he may carry away in his hand. 7945
5:18 Behold *that* w I have seen: *it is* good and 834
5:18 all the days of his life, w God giveth him: 834
6: 1 There is an evil w I have seen under the sun, 834
6:10 That w hath been is named already, and 7945
6:12 all the days of his vain life w he spendeth 2050.1
7:13 make *that* straight, w he hath made crooked? 834
7:19 more than ten mighty *men* w are in the city. 834
7:24 That w is far off, and exceeding deep, who 7945
7:28 W yet my soul seeketh, but I find not: 834
8: 7 For he knoweth not that w shall be: for who 7945
8:12 with them that fear God, w fear before him: 834
8:13 he prolong *his* days, *w are* as a shadow; NIH
8:14 There is a vanity w is done upon the earth; 834
8:15 of his life, w God giveth him under the sun. 834
9: 9 w he hath given thee under the sun, all 834
9: 9 in thy labour w thou takest under the sun. 834
10: 5 There is an evil w I have seen under the sun, NIH
10: 5 as an error *w* proceedeth from the ruler: NIH
10:20 and **that w hath** wings shall tell the matter. 1167
12: 5 Also *when* they shall be afraid of *that w is* NIH
12:10 *that w was* written *was* upright, *even* words NIH
12:11 *w* are given from one shepherd. NIH
SS 1: 1 The song of songs, *w is* Solomon's. 834
3: 7 Behold his bed, *w is* Solomon's; 7945
4: 2 even shorn, w came up from the washing; 7945
4: 5 *that are* twins, w feed among the lilies. 1886.1
6: 6 Thy teeth *are* as a flock of sheep w go up 7945
7: 2 *is like* a round goblet, *w* wanteth not liquor: NIH
7: 4 thy nose *is* as the tower of Lebanon w NIH
7:13 and old, *w* I have laid up for thee, NIH
8: 6 coals of fire, *w hath* a most vehement flame. NIH
8:12 My vineyard, *w is* mine, *is* before me: thou, 7945
Isa 1: 1 w he saw concerning Judah and Jerusalem in 834
1:29 For they shall be ashamed of the oaks w ye 834
2: 8 *that* w their own fingers have made: 834
2:20 w they made *each one* for himself to 834
3:12 they w lead thee cause *thee* to err, and NIH
5:23 W justify the wicked for reward, and NIH
6: 6 *w* he had taken with the tongs from off NIH
8:18 of hosts, w dwelleth in mount Zion. 1886.1
10: 1 that write grievousness *w* they have NIH
10: 3 in the desolation *w* shall come from far? NIH
11:10 w shall stand for an ensign of the people; 834
11:11 w shall be left from Assyria, and 834
11:16 of his people, w shall be left from Assyria; 834
Isa 13: 1 w Isaiah the son of Amoz did see. 834
13:17 against them, w shall not regard silver; 834
14:12 to the ground, w didst weaken the nations! NIH
15: 7 have gotten, and that w they have laid up, NIH
17: 2 w shall lie down, and none shall make *them* NIH
17: 8 neither shall respect *that* w his fingers have 834
17: 9 w they left because of the children of Israel: 834
17:12 *w* make a noise like the noise of the seas; NIH
18: 1 w *is* beyond the rivers of Ethiopia: 834
19:15 w the head or tail, branch or rush, may do. 834
19:16 of the LORD of hosts, w he shaketh over it. 834
19:17 of hosts, w he hath determined against it. 834
21:10 that w I have heard of the LORD of hosts, 834
22: 3 are bound together, *w* have fled from far. NIH
22:15 unto Shebna, *w is* over the house, *and say,* 834
26: 2 that the righteous nation w keepeth the truth NIH
27:13 they shall come w were ready to perish in 1886.1
28: 1 w *are* on the head of the fat valleys of them 834
28: 2 *w* as a tempest of hail *and* a destroying NIH
28: 4 w *is* on the head of the fat valley, shall be a 834
28: 4 w *when* he that looketh upon it seeth, 834
28:14 that rule this people w *is* in Jerusalem. 834
28:29 w is wonderful in counsel, *and* excellent in NIH
29:11 w *men* deliver to one that is learned, saying, 834
30:10 W say to the seers, See not; and to 834
30:24 w hath been winnowed with the shovel and 834
30:31 be beaten down, *w* smote with a rod. NIH
30:32 w the LORD shall lay upon him, *it* shall be 834
31: 7 w your own hands have made unto you *for* a 834
36: 3 w *was* over the house, and Shebna 834
37: 4 will reprove the words w the LORD thy 834
37:12 delivered them w my fathers have destroyed, 834
37:12 and the children of Eden w *were* in Telassar? 834
37:17 w hath sent to reproach the living God. 834
37:22 This *is* the word w the LORD hath spoken 834
37:29 I will turn thee back by the way by w thou 834
37:30 second year **that w springeth of the same**: 7823
38: 3 and have done *that* w *is* good in thy sight. 1886.1
38: 8 w is gone down in the sun dial of Ahaz, 834
38: 8 ten degrees, by w degrees it was gone down. 834
39: 6 *that* w thy fathers have laid up in store until 834
39: 7 w thou shalt beget, shall they take away; 834
39: 8 Good *is* the word of the LORD w thou hast 834
42: 5 the earth, and **that w cometh out** of it; 6631
43:16 w maketh a way in the sea, and a path in 1886.1
43:17 W bringeth forth the chariot and horse, 1886.1
44: 2 thee from the womb, *w* will help thee; NIH
44:14 w he strengtheneth for himself among 2050.1
45: 3 the LORD, w call *thee* by thy name, 1886.1
46: 3 w are borne *by me* from the belly, 1886.1
46: 3 the belly, w are carried from the womb: 1886.1
47:11 upon thee suddenly, *w* thou shalt not know. NIH
48: 1 w are called by the name of Israel, and 1886.1
48: 1 w swear by the name of the LORD, and 1886.1
48:14 w among them hath declared these *things?* 4310
48:17 I *am* the LORD thy God w teacheth thee to NIH
48:17 w leadeth thee by the way *that* thou NIH
49:20 The children w thou shalt have, after thou NIH
50: 1 w of my creditors *is it* to whom I have sold 4310
51:10 *Art* thou not it w hath dried the sea, 1886.1
51:12 of the son of man *w* shall be made *as* grass; NIH
51:17 w hast drunk at the hand of the LORD 834
51:23 w have said to thy soul, Bow down, that we 834
52:15 for *that* w had not been told them shall they 834
52:15 *that* w they had not heard shall they 834
55: 2 Wherefore do ye spend money for *that w is* NIH
55: 2 your labour for *that w* satisfieth not? NIH
55: 2 eat ye *that* w *is* good, and let your soul NIH
55:11 it shall accomplish that w I please, and 834
56: 8 The Lord GOD w gathereth the outcasts of NIH
56:11 *they are* greedy dogs w can never have NIH
57:16 fail before me, and the souls *w* I have made. NIH
59: 5 that w is crushed breaketh out *into* a viper. NIH
59:21 and my words w I have put in thy mouth, 834
61: 9 that they *are* the seed *w* the LORD hath NIH
62: 2 w the mouth of the LORD shall name. 834
62: 6 *w* shall never hold their peace day nor NIH
62: 8 drink thy wine, for the w thou hast laboured: 834
63: 7 w he hath bestowed on them according to his 834
64: 3 When thou didst terrible things *w* we looked NIH
65: 2 w walketh *in* a way *that was* not good, 1886.1
65: 4 W remain among the graves, and lodge in 1886.1
65: 4 w eat swine's flesh, and broth of 1886.1
65: 5 W say, Stand by thyself, come not near to 1886.1
65: 7 w have burnt incense upon the mountains, 834
65:18 and rejoice for ever *in that* w I create: 834
66: 4 and chose *that* in w I delighted not. 834
66:22 and the new earth, w I *will* make, 834
Jer 2:11 changed *their* gods, w *are* yet no gods? 1992
2:11 their glory for *that* w doth not profit. NIH
3: 6 Hast thou seen *that* w backsliding Israel hath 834
3:15 w shall feed you with knowledge and NIH
5:17 *w* thy sons and thy daughters should eat: NIH
5:21 w have eyes, and see not; which have 1992.1
5:21 and see not; w have ears, and hear not: 1992.1
5:22 w have placed the sand *for* the bound of 834
7:10 this house, w is called by my name, and say, 834
7:11 Is this house, w is called by my name, 834
7:12 go ye now unto my place w *was* in Shiloh, 834
7:14 w is called by my name, wherein ye trust, 834
7:14 unto the place w I gave to you and to your 834
7:30 in the house w is called by my name, 834
7:31 w *is* in the valley of the son of Hinnom, 834
7:31 w I commanded *them* not, neither came it 834
8: 3 w remain in all the places whither I have 834
8:17 w *will* not *be* charmed, and they shall bite 834
9:13 Because they have forsaken my law w I set 834
9:14 after Baalim, w their fathers taught them: 834
9:24 that I *am* the LORD w exercise NIH
9:25 that I will punish all *them w are* NIH
10: 1 Hear ye the word w the LORD speaketh 834
11: 4 W I commanded your fathers in the day that 834
11: 4 do them, according to all w I command you: 834
11: 5 That *I* may perform the oath w I have sworn 834
11: 8 this covenant, w I commanded *them* to do; 834

Jer 11:10 **w** refused to hear my words; 834
11:10 my covenant **w** I made with their fathers. 834
11:11 **w** they shall not be able to escape; 834
11:17 **w** they have done against themselves to 834
12:14 that touch the inheritance **w** I have caused 834
13: 4 **w** *is* upon thy loins, and arise, go to 834
13: 6 **w** I commanded thee to hide there. 834
13:10 evil people, **w** refuse to hear my words, 1886.1
13:10 **w** walk in the imagination of their heart, 1886.1
13:10 even be as this girdle, **w** is good for nothing. 834
15: 4 king of Judah, for *that* **w** he did in Jerusalem. 834
15:14 enemies into a land **w** thou knowest not: NIH
15:14 in mine anger, ***w*** shall burn upon you. NIH
15:18 wound incurable, ***w*** refuseth to be healed? NIH
17: 4 enemies in the land **w** thou knowest not: 834
17: 4 a fire in mine anger, ***w*** shall burn for ever. NIH
17:16 **that w came out of** my lips was right 4161
17:19 by the **w** they go out, and in all the gates of 834
18: 1 The word **w** came to Jeremiah from 834
18:14 Will *a man* leave the snow of Lebanon ***w*** NIH
19: 2 **w** *is by* the entry of the east gate, and 834
19: 3 the **w** whosoever heareth, his ears shall 834
19: 5 **w** I commanded not, nor spake *it,* neither 834
20: 2 **w** *was* by the house of the LORD. 834
20: 5 **w** shall spoil them, and take them, and 2050.1
20:16 let that man be as the cities **w** the LORD 834
21: 1 The word **w** came unto Jeremiah from 834
21: 4 **w** besiege you without the walls, and 1886.1
21:13 **w** say, Who shall come down against us? 1886.1
22: 6 a wilderness *and* cities ***w*** are not inhabited. NIH
22:11 **w** reigned instead of Josiah his father, 1886.1
22:11 his father, **w** went forth out of this place; 834
22:28 and are cast into a land **w** they know not? 834
23: 4 I will set up shepherds over them **w** shall NIH
23: 7 **w** brought up the children of Israel out of 834
23: 8 **w** brought up and which led the seed of 834
23: 8 **w** led the seed of the house of Israel out of 834
23:27 **W** think to cause my people to forget my 1886.1
23:27 **w** they tell every man to his neighbour, 834
23:40 a perpetual shame, **w** shall not be forgotten. 834
24: 2 **w** could not be eaten, they were so bad. 834
24: 8 evil figs, **w** cannot be eaten, they are so evil; 834
25: 2 The **w** Jeremiah the prophet spake unto all 834
25:13 I will bring upon that land all my words **w** I 834
25:13 **w** Jeremiah hath prophesied against all 834
25:22 the kings of the isles **w** *are* beyond the sea, 834
25:26 the world, **w** *are* upon the face of the earth: 834
25:27 of the sword **w** I will send among you. 834
25:29 I begin to bring evil on the city **w** is called 834
26: 2 **w** come to worship *in* the LORD'S 1886.1
26: 3 **w** I purpose to do unto them because of 834
26: 4 to walk in my law, **w** I have set before you, 834
26:19 the LORD repented him of the evil **w** he 834
27: 3 by the hand of the messengers **w** come *to* 1886.1
27: 8 kingdom **w** will not serve the same 834
27: 9 to your sorcerers, **w** speak unto you, saying, 834
27:18 that the vessels **w** are left in the house of 1886.1
27:20 **W** Nebuchadnezzar king of Babylon took 834
28: 1 son of Azur the prophet, **w** *was* of Gibeon, 834
28: 6 the LORD perform thy words **w** thou hast 834
28: 9 The prophet **w** prophesieth of peace, 834
29: 1 the elders **w** were carried away captives, 1886.1
29: 8 neither hearken to your dreams **w** ye cause 834
29:19 **w** I sent unto them by my servants 834
29:21 **w** prophesy a lie unto you in my name; 1886.1
29:22 all the captivity of Judah **w** *are* in Babylon, 834
29:23 in my name, **w** I have not commanded them; 834
29:27 **w** maketh himself a prophet to you? 1886.1
31: 2 The people **w** were left of the sword found NIH
31:21 the highway, *even* the way ***w*** thou wentest: NIH
31:32 **w** my covenant they brake, although I was a 834
31:35 **w** giveth the sun for a light by day, *and* NIH
31:35 **w** divideth the sea when the waves thereof NIH
32: 1 **w** *was* the eighteenth year of 1931
32: 2 **w** *was in* the king of Judah's house. 834
32: 8 **w** *is* in the country of Benjamin: 834
32:11 *both* that **w** was sealed *according to* the law NIH
32:11 *to* the law and custom, and that **w** was open: NIH
32:14 both **w** is sealed, and this evidence which 1886.1
32:14 is sealed, and this evidence **w** is open; 1886.1
32:20 **W** hast set signs and wonders in the land of 834
32:22 **w** thou didst swear to their fathers to give 834
32:32 **w** they have done to provoke me to anger, 834
32:34 **w** is called by my name, to defile it. 834
32:35 **w** *are* in the valley of the son of Hinnom, 834
32:35 **w** I commanded them not, neither came it 834
33: 3 and mighty *things,* **w** thou knowest not. NIH
33: 4 **w** are thrown down by the mounts, and 1886.1
33: 9 **w** shall hear all the good that I do unto them: 834
33:10 **w** ye say *shall be* desolate without man and 834
33:12 ***w*** *is* desolate without man and NIH
33:14 that I will perform *that* good thing **w** I have 834
33:24 The two families **w** the LORD hath chosen, 834
34: 1 The word **w** came unto Jeremiah from 834
34: 5 the former kings **w** were before thee, so 834
34: 8 with all the people **w** *were* at Jerusalem, 834
34:10 the people, **w** had entered into the covenant, 834
34:14 a Hebrew, **w** hath been sold unto thee; 834
34:15 me in the house **w** is called by my name. 834
34:18 **w** have not performed the words of 834
34:18 of the covenant **w** they had made before me, 834
34:19 **w** passed between the parts of the calf; 1886.1
34:21 Babylon's army, **w** are gone up from you. 1886.1
35: 1 The word **w** came unto Jeremiah from 834
35: 4 **w** *was* by the chamber of the princes, 834
35: 4 **w** *was* above the chamber of Maaseiah 834
35:15 ye shall dwell in the land **w** I have given to 834
35:16 of their father, **w** he commanded them; 834
36: 3 hear all the evil **w** I purpose to do unto them; 834
36: 4 **w** he had spoken unto him, upon a roll of a 834
36: 6 the roll, **w** thou hast written from my mouth, 834
36:21 in the ears of all the princes **w** stood 1886.1
36:27 the words **w** Baruch wrote at the mouth of 834
36:28 **w** Jehoiakim the king of Judah hath burnt. 834
36:32 **w** Jehoiakim king of Judah had burnt in 834

Jer 37: 2 **w** he spake by the prophet Jeremiah. 834
37: 7 **w** is come forth to help you, 1886.1
37:19 Where *are* now your prophets **w** prophesied 834
38: 3 king of Babylon's army, **w** shall take it. 2050.1
38: 7 one of the eunuchs **w** *was* in the king's 1931
38:20 voice of the LORD, **w** I speak unto thee: 834
39:10 **w** had nothing, in the land of Judah, and 834
40: 1 The word **w** came to Jeremiah from 834
40: 1 **w** were carried away captive unto 1886.1
40: 4 I loose thee *this* day from the chains **w** *were* 834
40: 7 *Now* when all the captains of the forces **w** 834
40:10 to serve the Chaldeans, **w** will come unto us: 834
40:15 that all the Jews **w** are gathered unto thee 1886.1
41: 9 *was* it **w** Asa the king had made for fear of 834
41:13 *that* when all the people **w** *were* with 834
41:17 **w** *is* by Beth-lehem, to go to enter *into* 834
42: 5 **w** the LORD thy God shall send thee to us. 834
42: 8 all the captains of the forces **w** *were* with 834
42:16 come to pass, *that* the sword, **w** ye feared, 834
42:21 nor any *thing* for the **w** he hath sent me unto 834
43: 1 *for* **w** the LORD their God had sent him to 834
43: 9 **w** *is* at the entry of Pharaoh's house in 834
44: 1 all the Jews **w** dwell in the land of Egypt, 1886.1
44: 1 **w** dwell at Migdol, and at Tahpanhes, and 1886.1
44: 3 Because of their wickedness **w** they have 834
44: 9 **w** they have committed in the land of Judah, 834
44:14 **w** are gone into the land of Egypt to 1886.1
44:14 to the **w** they have a desire to return to dwell 834
44:15 all the men **w** knew that their wives had 1886.1
44:20 to all the people **w** had given him *that* 1886.1
44:22 of the abominations **w** ye have committed; 834
45: 4 *that* **w** I have built *will* I break down, and 834
45: 4 *that* **w** I have planted I *will* pluck up, 834
46: 1 The word of the LORD **w** came to 834
46: 2 **w** was by the river Euphrates in Carchemish, 834
46: 2 **w** Nebuchadrezzar king of Babylon smote in 834
49:28 **w** Nebuchadrezzar king of Babylon shall 834
49:31 **w** have neither gates nor bars, 2050.2
49:31 have neither gates nor bars, ***w*** dwell alone. NIH
50: 3 **w** shall make her land desolate, and 1931
51:12 done that **w** he spake against the inhabitants 834
51:25 the LORD, **w** destroyest all the earth: 1886.1
51:44 I will bring forth out of his mouth that **w** he NIH
51:59 The word **w** Jeremiah the prophet 834
52: 2 he did *that* **w** *was* evil in the eyes of 1886.1
52: 7 the two walls, **w** *was* by the king's garden; 834
52:12 **w** *was* the nineteenth year of 1931
52:12 ***w*** served the king of Babylon, NIH
52:19 *that* **w** *was of* gold *in* gold, and *that* which 834
52:19 *in* gold, and *that* **w** *was of* silver *in* silver, 834
52:20 **w** king Solomon had made in the house of 834
52:25 **w** had the charge of the men of war; 834
52:25 the king's person, **w** were found in the city; 834
La 1:12 like unto my sorrow, **w** is done unto me, 834
2: 3 a flaming fire, ***w*** devoureth round about. NIH
2:17 The LORD hath done *that* **w** he had 834
5:18 **w** is desolate, the foxes walk upon it. 7945
Eze 1: 2 **w** *was* the fifth year of king Jehoiachin's 1931
1:23 **w** covered on this *side,* and every one had NIH
1:23 **w** covered on that *side,* their bodies. NIH
3:20 his righteousness **w** he hath done shall not be 834
3:23 as the glory **w** I saw by the river of Chebar: 834
4:10 thy meat **w** thou shalt eat *shall be* by weight, 834
4:14 have I not eaten *of* that **w** dieth of itself, NIH
5: 9 And I will do in thee that **w** I have not done, 834
5:16 **w** shall be for *their* destruction, *and* which I 834
5:16 *and* **w** I will send to destroy you: 834
6: 9 **w** hath departed from me, and with their 834
6: 9 **w** go a whoring after their idols: 1886.1
6: 9 they shall lothe themselves for the evils **w** 834
7:13 For the seller shall not return to that **w** is NIH
7:13 whole multitude thereof, ***w*** shall not return; NIH
8: 3 of jealousy, **w** provoketh to jealousy. 1886.1
8:14 LORD'S house **w** *was* towards the north; 834
8:17 the abominations **w** they commit here? 834
9: 2 **w** lieth toward the north, and every man a 834
9: 3 **w** *had* the writer's inkhorn by his side; 834
9: 6 they began at the ancient men **w** *were* before 834
9:11 **w** *had* the inkhorn by his side, reported 834
10:22 same faces **w** I saw by the river of Chebar, 834
11: 1 the LORD'S house, **w** looketh eastward: 1886.1
11: 3 **W** say, *It is* not near; *let us* build houses: 1886.1
11:23 stood upon the mountain **w** *is* on the east 834
12: 2 **w** have eyes to see, and see not; 834
12:28 but the word **w** I have spoken shall be done, 834
13:11 Say unto them **w** daub *it with* untempered NIH
13:16 *To wit,* the prophets of Israel **w** prophesy 1886.1
13:16 **w** see visions of peace for her, and 1886.1
13:17 **w** prophesy out of their own heart; 1886.1
14: 7 **w** separateth himself from me, and NIH
15: 2 *than* a branch **w** is among the trees of 834
15: 6 **w** I have given to the fire for fuel, so will I 834
16:14 **w** I had put upon thee, saith the Lord GOD. 834
16:17 **w** I had given thee, and madest to thyself 834
16:19 My meat also **w** I gave thee, fine flour, and 834
16:27 **w** are ashamed of thy lewd way. 1886.1
16:32 ***w*** taketh strangers instead of her husband. NIH
16:36 of thy children, **w** thou didst give unto them; 834
16:45 **w** lothed their husbands and their children: 834
16:51 in all thine abominations **w** thou hast done. 834
16:52 Thou also, **w** hast judged thy sisters, 834
16:57 **w** despise thee round about. 1886.1
16:59 **w** hast despised the oath in breaking 834
17: 3 full *of* feathers, **w** had divers colours, 834
18: 5 be just, and do **that w is lawful** and right, 4941
18:14 that seeth all his father's sins **w** he hath 834
18:18 and did *that* **w** *is* not good among his people, 834
18:19 When the son hath done **that w is lawful** 4941
18:21 do **that w is lawful** and right, he shall 4941
18:27 doeth **that w is lawful** and right, he shall 4941
19:14 ***w*** hath devoured her fruit, so that she hath NIH
20: 6 and honey, **w** *is* the glory of all lands: 1931
20:11 **w** *if* a man do, he shall even live in them. 834
20:13 **w** *if* a man do, he shall even live in them; 834
20:15 that *I* would not bring them into the land **w** I 834

Eze 20:15 and honey, **w** *is* the glory of all lands; 1931
20:21 **w** *if* a man do, he shall even live in them; 834
20:28 *for* the **w** I lifted up mine hand to give it to 834
20:32 that **w** cometh into your mind shall not be at NIH
20:42 into the country *for* the **w** I lifted up mine 834
21:14 **w** entereth into their privy chambers. 1886.1
22: 4 hast defiled *thyself* in thine idols **w** thou hast 834
22: 5 mock thee, **w** *art* infamous *and* much vexed. NIH
22:13 hand at thy dishonest gain **w** thou hast made, 834
22:13 at thy blood **w** hath been in the midst of thee. 834
23: 6 ***W*** *were* clothed with blue, captains and NIH
23:24 ***w*** shall set against thee buckler and shield NIH
23:42 **w** put bracelets upon their hands, and 2050.1
24:21 of your eyes, and that **w** your soul pitieth; NIH
24:27 thy mouth be opened to him **w** is escaped, NIH
25: 9 from his cities **w** *are* on his frontiers, NIH
26: 6 her daughters **w** *are* in the field shall be slain 834
26:17 **w** wast strong in the sea, she and 834
26:17 **w** cause their terror *to be* on all that haunt it. 834
27: 3 **w** *art* a merchant of the people for many NIH
27: 7 that **w** thou **spreadest forth** to be thy sail; 4666
27: 7 purple from the isles of Elishah was that **w** NIH
27:27 in all thy company **w** *is* in the midst of thee, 834
29: 3 **w** hath said, My river *is* mine own, and 834
29:16 **w** bringeth *their* iniquity to remembrance, NIH
30:22 his arms, the strong, and that **w** was broken; NIH
32: 9 into the countries **w** thou hast not known. 834
32:23 **w** caused terror in the land of the living. 834
32:24 **w** are gone down uncircumcised into 834
32:24 **w** caused their terror in the land of 834
32:27 **w** are gone down *to* hell with their weapons 834
32:29 **w** with their might are laid by *them that were* 834
32:30 **w** are gone down with the slain; 834
33:14 his sin, and do **that w is lawful** and right; 4941
33:16 he hath done **that w is lawful** and right; 4941
33:19 do **that w is lawful** and right, he shall live 4941
33:29 of all their abominations **w** they have 834
34: 4 neither have ye healed that **w** was sick, NIH
34: 4 neither have ye bound up that **w** was NIH
34: 4 neither have ye brought again that **w** was NIH
34: 4 neither have ye sought that **w** was lost; NIH
34:16 I will seek that **w** was lost, and bring again NIH
34:16 bring again that **w** was driven away, and NIH
34:16 will bind up that **w** was broken, and NIH
34:16 and will strengthen that **w** was sick: NIH
34:19 they eat **that w** ye have **trodden** with your 4823
34:19 they drink **that w** ye have **fouled** with your 4833
35:11 according to thine envy **w** thou hast used out 834
35:12 *that* I have heard all thy blasphemies **w** thou 834
36: 4 **w** became a prey and derision to the residue 834
36: 5 **w** have appointed my land into their 834
36:21 **w** the house of Israel had profaned among 834
36:22 **w** ye have profaned among the heathen, 834
36:23 **w** was profaned among the heathen, 1886.1
36:23 **w** ye have profaned in the midst of them; 834
37: 1 set me down in the midst of the valley **w** 1931
37:19 **w** *is* in the hand of Ephraim, and the tribes of 834
38: 8 of Israel, **w** have been always waste: 834
38:12 **w** have gotten cattle and goods, that dwell NIH
38:17 **w** prophesied in those days *many* years, 1886.1
39:19 of my sacrifice **w** I have sacrificed for you. 834
39:28 **w** caused them to be led into captivity NIH
40: 2 by **w** *was* as the frame of a city on 2050.2
40: 6 came he unto the gate **w** looketh toward 834
40: 6 threshold of the gate, ***w*** *was* one reed broad; NIH
40: 6 the other threshold *of the gate,* ***w*** *was* one NIH
40:40 **w** *was* at the porch of the gate, *were* two 834
40:44 **w** *was* at the side of the north gate; 834
40:46 **w** come near to the LORD to minister 1886.1
41: 1 **w** *was* the breadth of the tabernacle. NIH
41: 6 they entered into the wall **w** *was* of the house 834
41: 9 **w** *was* for the side chamber without, *was* 834
41: 9 *that* **w** *was* left *was* the place of the side 834
41:15 against the separate place **w** *was* behind it, 834
42: 1 **w** *was* before the building toward the north. 834
42: 3 Over against the twenty *cubits* **w** *were* for 834
42: 3 over against the pavement **w** *was* for 834
42:11 of the chambers **w** *were* toward the north, 834
42:13 **w** *are* before the separate place, 834
42:14 shall approach to *those things* **w** *are* for 834
43: 3 to the appearance of the vision **w** I saw, 834
43:19 **w** approach unto me, to minister unto me, 1886.1
44: 1 sanctuary **w** looketh *toward* the east; 1886.1
44:10 **w** went astray away from me after their 834
44:13 their abominations **w** they have committed. 834
45: 4 **w** shall come near to minister unto 1886.1
45:14 out of the cor, **w** *is* a homer of ten baths; NIH
46:19 the entry, **w** *was* at the side of the gate, 834
46:19 of the priests, **w** looked toward the north: 1886.1
47: 8 ***w*** being brought forth into the sea, NIH
47: 9 *that* every thing that liveth, **w** moveth, 834
47:14 *concerning* the **w** I lifted up mine hand to 834
47:16 **w** *is* between the border of Damascus and 834
47:16 Hazar-hatticon, **w** *is* by the coast of Hauran. 834
47:22 **w** shall beget children among you: 834
48: 8 shall be the offering **w** ye shall offer *of* five 834
48:11 **w** have kept my charge, which went not 834
48:11 **w** went not astray when the children of Israel 834
48:22 *being* in the midst *of that* **w** is the prince's, 834
48:29 This *is* the land **w** ye shall divide *by lot* unto 834
Da 1: 2 **w** he carried *into* the land of Shinar *to* 2050.1
1: 5 king's meat, and of the wine **w** he drank: NIH
1: 8 king's meat, nor with the wine **w** he drank: NIH
1:10 liking than the children **w** *are* of your sort? 834
1:15 fatter in flesh than all the children **w** did 1886.1
2:14 **w** was gone forth to slay the wise *men* of 1768
2:26 known unto me the dream **w** I have seen, 1768
2:27 The secret **w** the king hath demanded 1768
2:34 **w** smote the image upon his feet *that* 2050.3
2:39 of brass, **w** shall bear rule over all the earth. 1768
2:44 up a kingdom, **w** shall never be destroyed: 1768
3: 2 to come to the dedication of the image **w** 1768
3:12 nor worship the golden image **w** thou hast 1768
3:14 nor worship the golden image **w** I have set 1768
3:15 and worship the image **w** I have made; 1768

W

Da 3:18 nor worship the golden image w thou hast 1768
3:29 w speak any thing amiss against the God of 1768
4: 5 I saw a dream w made me afraid, and 2050.3
4:20 that thou sawest, w grew, and was strong, 1768
4:21 under w the beasts of the field dwelt, and 1958.2
4:24 w is come upon my lord the king: 1768
5: 2 silver vessels w his father Nebuchadnezzar 1768
5: 2 taken out of the temple w was in Jerusalem; 1768
5: 3 of the house of God w was at Jerusalem; 1768
5:13 w art of the children of the captivity of 1768
5:23 of brass, iron, wood, and stone, w see not, 1768
6: 1 w should be over the whole kingdom; 1768
6: 8 of the Medes and Persians, w altereth not. 1768
6:12 of the Medes and Persians, w altereth not. 1768
6:13 w is of the children of the captivity of 1768
6:15 Persians is, That no decree nor statute w 1768
6:24 they brought those men w had accused 1768
6:26 his kingdom that w shall not be destroyed, 1768
7: 6 w had upon the back of it four wings of a 2050.3
7:11 of the voice of the great words w the horn 1768
7:14 w shall not pass away, and his kingdom 1768
7:14 his kingdom that w shall not be destroyed. 1768
7:17 great beasts, w are four, are four kings, 581
7:17 are four kings, w shall arise out of the earth. NIH
7:19 w was diverse from all the others, 1768
7:19 w devoured, brake in pieces, and NIH
7:20 of the other w came up, and before whom 1768
7:23 w shall be diverse from all kingdoms, 1768
8: 1 after that w appeared unto me at the first. NIH
8: 2 in the palace, w is in the province of Elam; 834
8: 3 there stood before the river a ram w had 2050.1
8: 6 w I had seen standing before the river, and 834
8: 9 w waxed exceeding great, toward 2050.1
8:13 saint said unto that certain saint w spake, 1886.1
8:16 w called, and said, Gabriel, make this 2050.1
8:20 The ram w thou sawest having two horns are 834
8:26 and the morning w was told is true: 834
9: 1 w was made king over the realm of 834
9: 6 w spake in thy name to our kings, 834
9:10 w he set before us by his servants 834
9:12 w he spake against us, and against our 834
9:14 God is righteous in all his works w he doeth: 834
9:18 and the city w is called by thy name: 834
10: 4 the side of the great river, w is Hiddekel; 1931
10:10 w set me upon my knees and upon 2050.1
10:21 I will shew thee that w is noted in NIH
11: 4 nor according to his dominion w he ruled: 834
11: 7 w shall come with an army, and 2050.1
11:10 w by his hand shall be consumed. 2050.1
11:24 he shall do that w his fathers have not done, 834
12: 1 the great prince w standeth for 1886.1
12: 6 in linen, w was upon the waters of the river, 834
12: 7 w was upon the waters of the river, when he 834
Hos 1: 3 w conceived, and bare him a son. 2050.1
1:10 w cannot be measured nor numbered; 834
2: 8 and gold, w they prepared for Baal. NIH
2:23 I will say to them w were not my people, NIH
5: 9 have I made known that w shall surely be. NIH
Joel 1: 4 That w the palmerworm hath left hath NIH
1: 4 that w the locust hath left hath NIH
1: 4 that w the cankerworm hath left hath NIH
2:25 my great army w I sent among you. 834
Am 1: 1 w he saw concerning Israel in the days of 834
1: 4 w shall devour the palaces of Ben-hadad. 2050.1
1: 7 w shall devour the palaces thereof: 2050.1
1:10 w shall devour the palaces thereof. 2050.1
1:12 w shall devour the palaces of Bozrah. 2050.1
2: 4 to err, after the w their fathers have walked: 834
3: 1 against the whole family w I brought up 834
4: 1 w oppress the poor, which crush 1886.1
4: 1 which oppress the poor, w crush 1886.1
4: 1 w say to their masters, Bring, and let us 1886.1
4: 3 every cow at that w is before her; NIH
5: 1 Hear ye this word w I take up against you, 834
5: 3 that w went forth by an hundred shall leave NIH
5:26 star of your god, w ye made to yourselves. 834
6: 1 w are named chief of the nations, NIH
6:13 Ye w rejoice in a thing of nought, 1886.1
6:13 which rejoice in a thing of nought, w say, 1886.1
9:10 w say, The evil shall not overtake nor 1886.1
9:12 of all the heathen, w are called by my name, 834
9:15 up out of their land w I have given them, 834
Ob 1:20 the captivity of Jerusalem, w is in Sepharad, 834
Jnh 1: 9 w hath made the sea and the dry land. 834
4:10 for the w thou hast not laboured, neither 834
4:10 w came up in a night, and perished in a 7945
Mic 1: 1 w he saw concerning Samaria and 834
2: 3 from w[S] ye shall not remove your necks; 8033
5: 3 until the time that she w travaileth hath NIH
6:14 that w thou deliverest will I give up to 834
7:10 shame shall cover her w said unto me, 1886.1
7:14 w dwell solitarily in the wood, in the midst NIH
7:20 w thou hast sworn unto our fathers from 834
Na 3:17 w camp in the hedges in the cold day, but 1886.1
Hab 1: 1 The burden w Habakkuk the prophet did see. 834
1: 5 w ye will not believe, though it be told you. NIH
1: 6 w shall march through the breadth of 1886.1
2: 4 his soul w is lifted up is not upright in him: NIH
2: 6 Woe to him that increaseth that w is not his! NIH
2:17 w made them afraid, because of men's NIH
Zep 1: 1 The word of the LORD w came unto 834
1: 9 w fill their masters' houses with violence 1886.1
2: 3 of the earth, w have wrought his judgment; 834
Hag 1:11 upon that w the ground bringeth forth, and 834
2:14 and that w they offer there is unclean. 834
Zec 1: 6 w I commanded my servants the prophets, 834
1: 7 w is the month Sebat, in the second year of 1931
1:12 against w thou hast had indignation these 834
1:19 These are the horns w have scattered Judah, 834
1:21 These are the horns w have scattered Judah, 834
1:21 w lift up their horn over the land of Judah 1886.1
2: 8 sent me unto the nations w spoiled you: 1886.1
4: 2 seven lamps, w were upon the top thereof: 834
4:10 w run to and fro through the whole earth. NIH
4:12 What be these two olive branches w through 834

Zec 6: 5 w go forth from standing before the Lord of NIH
6: 6 The black horses w are therein go forth into 834
6:10 w are come from Babylon, and come thou 834
7: 3 And to speak unto the priests w were in 834
7: 7 Should ye not hear the words w the LORD 834
7:12 the words w the LORD of hosts hath sent in 834
8: 9 w were in the day that the foundation of 834
10: 5 they shall be as mighty men, w tread down NIH
11:10 that I might break my covenant w I had 834
11:16 w shall not visit those that be cut off, NIH
12: 1 w stretcheth forth the heavens, and NIH
13: 6 Those with w I was wounded in the house of 834
14: 4 w is before Jerusalem on the east, and 834
14: 7 it shall be one day w shall be known to NIH
14:16 w came against Jerusalem shall even go 1886.1
Mal 1:13 ye brought that w was torn, and the lame, NIH
1:14 w hath in his flock a male, and voweth, 2050.1
2:11 the holiness of the LORD w he loved, 834
4: 4 w I commanded unto him in Horeb for all 834
Mt 1:20 for that w is conceived in her is of the Holy NIG
1:22 that it might be fulfilled w was spoken of 3588
1:23 w being interpreted is, God with us. 3739
2: 9 and lo, the star, w they saw in the east, 3739
2:15 that it might be fulfilled w was spoken of 3588
2:16 according to the time w he had diligently 3739
2:17 Then was fulfilled that w was spoken by NIG
2:20 for they are dead w sought the young 3588
2:23 that it might be fulfilled w was spoken by 3588
3:10 every tree w bringeth not forth good fruit is NIG
4:13 in Capernaum, w is upon the sea coast, 3588
4:14 That it might be fulfilled w was spoken by 3588
4:16 The people w sat in darkness saw great 3588
4:16 and to them w sat in the region and NIG
4:24 and those w were possessed with devils, and NIG
4:24 and those w were lunatick, and those that NIG
5: 6 Blessed are they w do hunger and NIG
5:10 Blessed are they w are persecuted for NIG
5:12 persecuted they the prophets w were before 3588
5:16 and glorify your Father w is in heaven. 3588
5:44 and pray for them w despitefully use you, NIG
5:45 the children of your Father w is in heaven: 3588
5:46 For if ye love them w love you, NIG
5:48 even as your Father w is in heaven is 3588
6: 1 no reward of your Father w is in heaven. 3588
6: 4 thy Father w seeth in secret himself shall 3588
6: 6 thy door, pray to thy Father w is in secret; 3588
6: 6 thy Father w seeth in secret shall reward 3588
6: 9 Our Father w art in heaven, Hallowed be 3588
6:18 to fast, but unto thy Father w is in secret: 3588
6:18 and thy Father, w seeth in secret, 3588
6:27 W of you by taking thought can add one 5101
6:30 w to day is, and to morrow is cast into NIG
7: 6 Give not that w is holy unto the dogs, NIG
7:11 how much more shall your Father w is in 3588
7:13 and many there be w go in thereat: 3588
7:14 w leadeth unto life, and few there be that 3588
7:15 w come to you in sheep's clothing, but 3748
7:21 he that doeth the will of my Father w is in 3588
7:24 a wise man, w built his house upon a rock: 3748
7:26 w built his house upon the sand: 3748
8:17 That it might be fulfilled w was spoken by 3588
9: 8 w had given such power unto men. 3588
9:16 for that w is put in to fill it up taketh from NIG
9:20 w was diseased with an issue of blood NIG
10:20 the Spirit of your Father w speaketh in you. 3588
10:28 And fear not them w kill the body, but 3588
10:28 rather fear him w is able to destroy both NIG
10:32 him will I confess also before my Father w 3588
10:33 him will I also deny before my Father w is 3588
11: 4 shew John again those things w ye do hear 3739
11:10 w shall prepare thy way before thee. 3739
11:14 receive it, this is Elias, w was for to come. 3588
11:21 for if the mighty works w were done in 3588
11:23 Capernaum, w art exalted unto heaven, 3588
11:23 mighty works, w have been done in thee, 3588
12: 2 thy disciples do that w is not lawful to do 3739
12: 4 w was not lawful for him to eat, 3739
12: 4 neither for them w were with him, but only NIG
12:10 there was a man w had his hand withered. NIG
12:17 That it might be fulfilled w was spoken by 3588
12:50 do the will of my Father w is in heaven, 3588
13:14 w saith, By hearing ye shall hear, and 3588
13:17 have desired to see those things w ye see, 3739
13:17 and to hear those things w ye hear, 3739
13:19 catcheth away that w was sown in his heart. NIG
13:19 This is he w received seed by the way side. NIG
13:23 and understandeth it; w also beareth fruit, 3739
13:24 unto a man w sowed good seed in his field: NIG
13:31 w a man took, and sowed in his field: 3739
13:32 W indeed is the least of all seeds: but 3739
13:33 w a woman took, and hid in three measures 3739
13:35 That it might be fulfilled w was spoken by 3588
13:35 I will utter things w have been kept secret NIG
13:41 things that offend, and them w do iniquity; NIG
13:44 the w when a man hath found, he hideth, 3739
13:48 W, when it was full, they drew to shore, 3739
13:52 Therefore every scribe w is instructed unto NIG
13:52 w bringeth forth out of his treasure things 3748
14: 9 and them w sat with him at meat, NIG
15: 1 and Pharisees, w were of Jerusalem, saying, 3588
15:11 Not that w goeth into the mouth defileth a NIG
15:11 but that w cometh out of the mouth, NIG
15:13 w my heavenly Father hath not planted, 3739
15:18 But those things w proceed out of the mouth NIG
15:20 These are the things w defile a man: but 3588
15:27 yet the dogs eat of the crumbs w fall from 3588
16: 8 W when Jesus perceived, he said unto them, NIG
16:17 it unto thee, but my Father w is in heaven. 3588
16:28 standing here, w shall not taste of death, 3748
17: 5 w said, This is my beloved Son, in whom I NIG
18: 6 one of these little ones w believe in me, 3588
18:10 the face of my Father w is in heaven. 3588
18:11 For the Son of man is come to save that w NIG
18:12 and seeketh that w is gone astray? NIG
18:13 of the ninety and nine w went not astray. 3588

Mt 18:14 it is not the will of your Father w is in 3588
18:19 it shall be done for them of my Father w is 3588
18:23 w would take account of his servants. 3739
18:24 unto him, w ought him ten thousand talents. NIG
18:28 w ought him an hundred pence: 3739
19: 4 that he w made them at the beginning made NIG
19: 9 whoso marrieth her w is put away doth NIG
19:12 w were so born from their mother's womb: 3748
19:12 w were made eunuchs of men: 3748
19:12 w have made themselves eunuchs for 3748
19:18 He saith unto him, W? Jesus said, 4169
19:28 That ye w have followed me, in 3588
20: 1 w went out early in the morning to hire 3748
20:12 w have borne the burden and heat of 3588
21: 4 that it might be fulfilled w was spoken by 3588
21:21 ye shall not only do this w is done to the fig NIG
21:24 also will ask you one thing, w if ye tell me, 3739
21:33 w planted a vineyard, and hedged it round 3748
21:41 w shall render him the fruits in their 3748
21:42 The stone w the builders rejected, 3739
22: 2 w made a marriage for his son, 3748
22: 4 saying, Tell them w are bidden, Behold, NIG
22: 8 but they w were bidden were not worthy. NIG
22:11 he saw there a man w had not on a wedding NIG
22:21 unto Cesar the things w are Cesar's; NIG
22:23 w say that there is no resurrection, and NIG
22:31 have ye not read that w was spoken unto NIG
22:35 Then one of them, w was a lawyer, NIG
22:36 w is the great commandment in the law? 4169
23: 9 for one is your Father, w is in heaven. 3588
23:16 Woe unto you, ye blind guides, w say, 3588
23:24 w strain out a gnat, and swallow a camel. 3588
23:26 cleanse first that w is within the cup and NIG
23:27 w indeed appear beautiful outward, but 3748
23:31 that ye are the children of them w killed NIG
23:37 and stonest them w are sent unto thee, NIG
24:16 Then let them w be in Judea flee into NIG
24:17 Let him w is on the housetop not come NIG
24:18 Neither let him w is in the field return back NIG
25: 1 w took their lamps, and went forth to meet 3748
25:24 Then he w had received the one talent came NIG
25:28 and give it unto him w hath ten talents. NIG
25:29 shall be taken away even that w he hath. 3739
26:25 w betrayed him, answered and said, Master, 3588
26:28 w is shed for many for the remission of 3588
26:51 one of them w were with Jesus stretched out NIG
26:62 what is it w these witness against thee? NIG
26:75 w said unto him, Before the cock crow, NIG
27: 3 Then Judas, w had betrayed him, when he 3588
27: 9 Then was fulfilled that w was spoken by NIG
27:17 Barabbas, or Jesus w is called Christ? 3588
27:22 I do then with Jesus w is called Christ? 3588
27:35 that it might be fulfilled w was spoken by NIG
27:44 thieves also, w were crucified with him, 3588
27:52 and many bodies of saints w slept arose, 3588
27:55 w followed Jesus from Galilee, 3748
27:56 Among w was Mary Magdalene, and 3739
27:60 new tomb, w he had hewn out in the rock: 3739
28: 5 I know that ye seek Jesus, w was crucified. 3588
Mk 1: 2 w shall prepare thy way before thee. 3739
1:44 offer for thy cleansing those things w 3739
2: 3 one sick of the palsy, w was borne of four. NIG
2:24 why do they on the sabbath day that w is 3739
2:26 w is not lawful to eat but for the priests, 3739
2:26 and gave also to them w were with him? NIG
3: 1 there was a man there w had a withered NIG
3: 3 And he saith unto the man w had 3588
3:17 w is, The sons of thunder:) 3739
3:19 And Judas Iscariot, w also betrayed him. 3739
3:22 And the scribes w came down from 3588
3:34 And he looked round about on them w sat NIG
4:16 And these are they likewise w are sown on NIG
4:18 And these are they w are sown among NIG
4:20 And these are they w are sown on good NIG
4:22 is nothing hid, w shall not be manifested; 3739
4:25 from him shall be taken even that w he 3739
4:31 w, when it is sown in the earth, 3739
5:25 w had an issue of blood twelve years, NIG
5:35 of the synagogue's house certain w said, NIG
5:41 w is, being interpreted, Damsel (I say unto 3739
6: 2 what wisdom is this w is given unto him, 3588
6:26 for their sakes w sat with him, he would not NIG
7: 1 of the scribes, w came from Jerusalem. NIG
7: 4 w they have received to hold, as 3739
7:13 your tradition, w ye have delivered: 3739
7:15 but the things w come out of him, those are NIG
7:20 And he said, That w cometh out of the man, NIG
9: 1 that stand here, w shall not taste of death, 3748
9:17 unto thee my son, w hath a dumb spirit; NIG
9:39 for there is no man w shall do a miracle in 3739
10:42 Ye know that they w are accounted to rule NIG
11:21 the fig tree w thou cursedst is withered 3739
11:23 shall believe that those things w he saith 3739
11:25 that your Father also w is in heaven may 3588
11:26 neither will your Father w is in heaven 3588
12:10 The stone w the builders rejected is become 3739
12:18 w say there is no resurrection; 3748
12:25 but are as the angels w are in heaven. NIG
12:28 W is the first commandment of all? 4169
12:38 w love to go in long clothing, and 3588
12:40 W devour widows' houses, and for a 3588
12:42 she threw in two mites, w make a farthing. 3739
12:43 than all they w have cast into the treasury: NIG
13:19 the creation w God created unto this time, 3739
13:32 not the angels w are in heaven, neither 3588
14:18 One of you w eateth with me shall betray 3588
14:24 of the new testament, w is shed for many. 3588
14:32 And they came to a place w was named 3739
14:60 what is it w these witness against thee? NIG
15: 7 w lay bound with them that had made NIG
15:22 w is, being interpreted, The place of a skull. 3739
15:28 And the scripture was fulfilled, w saith, 3588
15:34 w is, being interpreted, My God, my God, 3739
15:39 w stood over against him, saw that he so 3588
15:41 many other women w came up with him 3588

Mk 15:43 **w** also waited for the kingdom of God, 3739
15:46 laid him in a sepulchre **w** was hewn out of 3739
16: 6 seek Jesus of Nazareth, **w** was crucified: 3588
16:14 they believed not them **w** had seen him after NIG
Lk 1: 1 things **w** are most surely believed among us, NIG
1: 2 **w** from the beginning were eyewitnesses, 3588
1:20 **w** shall be fulfilled in their season. 3748
1:35 also *that* holy thing **w** shall be born of thee NIG
1:45 those *things* **w** were told her from the Lord. NIG
1:70 **w** have been since the world began:) NIG
1:73 The oath **w** he sware to our father 3739
2: 4 the city of David, **w** is called Bethlehem; 3748
2:10 tidings of great joy, **w** shall be to all people. 3748
2:11 of David a Saviour, **w** is Christ the Lord. 3739
2:15 and see this thing **w** is come to pass, 3588
2:15 **w** the Lord hath made known unto us. 3739
2:17 **w** was told them concerning this child. 3588
2:18 *things* **w** were told them by the shepherds. NIG
2:21 **w** was *so* named of the angel before he was 3588
2:24 And to offer a sacrifice according to that **w** NIG
2:31 **W** thou hast prepared before the face of all 3739
2:33 his mother marvelled at those *things* **w** were NIG
2:34 and for a sign **w** shall be spoken against; NIG
2:37 **w** departed not from the temple, but 3739
2:50 And they understood not the saying **w** he 3739
3: 9 **w** bringeth not forth good fruit is hewn NIG
3:13 Exact no more than that **w** is appointed you. NIG
3:19 and for all the evils **w** Herod had done, 3739
3:22 **w** said, Thou art my beloved Son; NIG
3:23 the son of Joseph, **w** was *the son* of Heli, NIG
3:24 **W** was *the son* of Matthat, which was NIG
3:24 **w** was *the son* of Levi, which was *the son* of NIG
3:24 *the son* of Levi, **w** was *the son* of Melchi, NIG
3:24 **w** was *the son* of Janna, which was *the son* NIG
3:24 *the son* of Janna, **w** was *the son* of Joseph, NIG
3:25 **W** was *the son* of Mattathias, which was NIG
3:25 **w** was *the son* of Amos, which was *the son* NIG
3:25 **w** was *the son* of Naum, which was *the son* NIG
3:25 was *the son* of Naum, **w** was *the son* of Esli, NIG
3:25 *the son* of Esli, **w** was *the son* of Nagge, NIG
3:26 **W** was *the son* of Maath, which was *the son* NIG
3:26 **w** was *the son* of Mattathias, which was NIG
3:26 **w** was *the son* of Semei, which was *the son* NIG
3:26 **w** was *the son* of Joseph, which was *the son* NIG
3:26 *the son* of Joseph, **w** was *the son* of Juda, NIG
3:27 **W** was *the son* of Joanna, which was NIG
3:27 *the son* of Joanna, **w** was *the son* of Rhesa, NIG
3:27 *son* of Rhesa, **w** was *the son* of Zorobabel, NIG
3:27 **w** was *the son* of Salathiel, which was NIG
3:27 *the son* of Salathiel, **w** was *the son* of Neri, NIG
3:28 **W** was *the son* of Melchi, which was NIG
3:28 **w** was *the son* of Addi, which was *the son* NIG
3:28 *the son* of Addi, **w** was *the son* of Cosam, NIG
3:28 **w** was *the son* of Elmodam, which was NIG
3:28 *the son* of Elmodam, **w** was *the son* of Er, NIG
3:29 **W** was *the son* of Jose, which was *the son* NIG
3:29 *the son* of Jose, **w** was *the son* of Eliezer, NIG
3:29 *the son* of Eliezer, **w** was *the son* of Jorim, NIG
3:29 **w** was *the son* of Matthat, which was NIG
3:29 *the son* of Matthat, **w** was *the son* of Levi, NIG
3:30 **W** was *the son* of Simeon, which was NIG
3:30 **w** was *the son* of Juda, which was *the son* of NIG
3:30 *the son* of Juda, **w** was *the son* of Joseph, NIG
3:30 *the son* of Joseph, **w** was *the son* of Jonan, NIG
3:30 *the son* of Jonan, **w** was *the son* of Eliakim, NIG
3:31 **W** was *the son* of Melea, which was *the son* NIG
3:31 *the son* of Melea, **w** was *the son* of Menan, NIG
3:31 *son* of Menan, **w** was *the son* of Mattatha, NIG
3:31 **w** was *the son* of Nathan, which was *the son* NIG
3:31 *the son* of Nathan, **w** was *the son* of David, NIG
3:32 **W** was *the son* of Jesse, which was *the son* NIG
3:32 **w** was *the son* of Obed, which was *the son* NIG
3:32 *the son* of Obed, **w** was *the son* of Booz, NIG
3:32 *the son* of Booz, **w** was *the son* of Salmon, NIG
3:32 *son* of Salmon, **w** was *the son* of Naasson, NIG
3:33 **W** was *the son* of Aminadab, which was NIG
3:33 **w** was *the son* of Aram, which was *the son* NIG
3:33 *the son* of Aram, **w** was *the son* of Esrom, NIG
3:33 **w** was *the son* of Phares, which was *the son* NIG
3:33 *the son* of Phares, **w** was *the son* of Juda, NIG
3:34 **W** was *the son* of Jacob, which was *the son* NIG
3:34 *the son* of Jacob, **w** was *the son* of Isaac, NIG
3:34 *the son* of Isaac, **w** was *the son* of Abraham, NIG
3:34 **w** was *the son* of Thara, which was *the son* NIG
3:34 *the son* of Thara, **w** was *the son* of Nachor, NIG
3:35 **W** was *the son* of Saruch, which was NIG
3:35 **w** was *the son* of Ragau, which was *the son* NIG
3:35 **w** was *the son* of Phalec, which was *the son* NIG
3:35 **w** was *the son* of Heber, which was *the son* NIG
3:35 *the son* of Heber, **w** was *the son* of Sala, NIG
3:36 **W** was *the son* of Cainan, which was NIG
3:36 **w** was *the son* of Arphaxad, which was NIG
3:36 **w** was *the son* of Sem, which was *the son* of NIG
3:36 was *the son* of Sem, **w** was *the son* of Noe, NIG
3:36 *the son* of Noe, **w** was *the son* of Lamech, NIG
3:37 **W** was *the son* of Mathusala, which was NIG
3:37 **w** was *the son* of Enoch, which was *the son* NIG
3:37 *the son* of Enoch, **w** was *the son* of Jared, NIG
3:37 *the son* of Jared, **w** was *the son* of Maleleel, NIG
3:37 *son* of Maleleel, **w** was *the son* of Cainan, NIG
3:38 **W** was *the son* of Enos, which was *the son* NIG
3:38 was *the son* of Enos, **w** was *the son* of Seth, NIG
3:38 **w** was *the son* of Adam, which was *the son* NIG
3:38 *the son* of Adam, **w** was *the son* of God. NIG
4:22 wondered at the gracious words **w** 3588
4:33 **w** had a spirit of an unclean devil, and NIG
5: 3 **w** was Simon's, and prayed him that he 3739
5: 7 **w** were in the other ship, that *they* should NIG
5: 9 at the draught of the fishes **w** they had 3739
5:10 of Zebedee, **w** were partners with Simon. 3739
5:17 doctors of the law sitting *by,* **w** were come 3739
5:18 men brought in a bed a man **w** was taken 3739
5:21 Who is this **w** speaketh blasphemies? 3739
6: 2 Why do ye *that* **w** is not lawful to do on 3739
6: 3 was a hungred, and they **w** were with him; NIG

Lk 6: 4 **w** it is not lawful to eat but for the priests 3739
6: 8 said to the man **w** had the withered hand, NIG
6:16 and Judas Iscariot, **w** also was the traitor. 3739
6:17 **w** came to hear him, and to be healed of 3739
6:27 But I say unto you **w** hear, Love your 3588
6:27 your enemies, do good to them **w** hate you, NIG
6:28 and pray for them **w** despitefully use you. NIG
6:32 For if ye love them **w** love you, what thank NIG
6:33 And if ye do good to them **w** do good to NIG
6:45 of his heart bringeth forth that **w** is good; NIG
6:45 of his heart bringeth forth that **w** is evil: NIG
6:46 Lord, Lord, and do not *the things* **w** I say? 3739
6:48 He is like a man **w** built a house, and 3739
6:49 against **w** the stream did beat vehemently, 3739
7:25 they **w** are gorgeously apparelled, and NIG
7:27 **w** shall prepare thy way before thee. 3739
7:37 a woman in the city, **w** was a sinner, 3748
7:39 Now when the Pharisee **w** had bidden him 3588
7:41 There was a certain creditor **w** had two NIG
7:42 **w** of them will love him most? 5101
7:47 Her sins, **w** are many, are forgiven; 3588
8: 2 **w** had been healed of evil spirits and 3739
8: 3 **w** ministered unto him of their substance. 3748
8:13 They on the rock *are they,* **w**, when they 3739
8:13 **w** for a while believe, and in time of 3739
8:14 And that **w** fell among thorns are they, NIG
8:14 **w**, when they have heard, go *forth,* and NIG
8:15 **w** in an honest and good heart, 3748
8:16 that they **w** enter in may see the light. NIG
8:18 from him shall be taken even *that* **w** he 3739
8:20 And it was told him *by certain* **w** said, NIG
8:21 my brethren are these **w** hear the word of 3588
8:26 of the Gadarenes, **w** is over against Galilee. 3748
8:27 **w** had devils long time, and ware no 3739
8:36 They also **w** saw *it* told them by what means NIG
8:43 **w** had spent all *her* living upon physicians, 3748
9:27 standing here, **w** shall not taste of death, 3739
9:30 him two men, **w** were Moses and Elias: 3748
9:31 spake of his decease **w** he should 3739
9:36 days any of *those things* **w** they had seen. 3739
9:43 every one at all *things* **w** Jesus did, 3739
9:46 **w** of them should be greatest. 302+5101
9:61 them farewell, **w** are *at home* in my house. NIG
10:11 **w** cleaveth on us, we do wipe off against 3588
10:13 and Sidon, **w** have been done in you, NIG
10:15 Capernaum, **w** art exalted to heaven, NIG
10:23 Blessed *are* the eyes **w** see *the things* that 3588
10:24 kings have desired to see *those things* **w** ye 3739
10:24 and to hear *those things* **w** ye hear, 3739
10:30 **w** stripped him of his raiment, and 3739
10:36 **W** now of these three, thinkest thou, 5101
10:39 **w** also sat at Jesus' feet, and heard his 3739
10:42 **w** shall not be taken away from her. 3748
11: 2 ye pray, say, Our Father **w** art in heaven, 3588
11: 5 **W** of you shall have a friend, and shall go 5101
11:27 bare thee, and the paps **w** thou hast sucked. 3739
11:33 that they **w** come in may see the light. NIG
11:35 that the light **w** is in thee be not darkness. 3588
11:40 did not he that made that *w is* without make NIG
11:40 *is* without make that *w is* within also? NIG
11:44 for ye are as graves **w** appear not, and 3588
11:50 **w** was shed from the foundation of 3588
11:51 **w** perished between the altar and 3588
12: 1 the leaven of the Pharisees, **w** is hypocrisy. 3748
12: 3 *that* **w** ye have spoken in the ear in closets 3739
12: 5 **w** after *he* hath killed hath power to cast NIG
12:15 abundance of the *things* **w** he possesseth. 3588
12:20 shall *those things* be, **w** thou hast provided? 3739
12:24 **w** neither have storehouse nor barn; and 3739
12:25 And **w** of you with taking thought can add 5101
12:26 then be not able *to do that thing* *w is* least, NIG
12:28 **w** is to day in the field, and to morrow is NIG
12:33 provide yourselves bags **w** wax not old, NIG
12:47 **w** knew his lord's will, and prepared not 3588
13:11 there was a woman **w** had a spirit of NIG
13:14 There are six days in **w** *men* ought to work: 3739
13:19 **w** a man took, and cast into his garden; 3739
13:21 **w** a woman took and hid in three measures 3739
13:30 there are last **w** shall be first, and there are 3739
13:30 be first, and there are first **w** shall be last. 3739
13:34 **w** killest the prophets, and stonest them that 3588
14: 2 a certain man before him, **w** had the dropsy. NIG
14: 5 **W** of you shall have an ass or an ox fallen 5101
14: 7 And he put forth a parable to those **w** were NIG
14:24 That none of those men **w** were bidden 3588
14:28 For **w** of you, intending to build a tower, 5101
15: 4 and go after that **w** is lost, until he find it? NIG
15: 6 for I have found my sheep **w** was lost. 3588
15: 7 nine just *persons* **w** need no repentance. 3748
15: 9 for I have found the piece **w** I had lost. 3739
15:30 **w** hath devoured thy living with harlots, 3588
16: 1 was a certain rich man, **w** had a steward; 3739
16:10 He that is faithful in *that* *w is* least is NIG
16:12 And if ye have not been faithful in that **w** is NIG
16:12 who shall give you that **w** is your own? NIG
16:15 Ye are they **w** justify yourselves before NIG
16:15 for that **w** is highly esteemed amongst men NIG
16:19 **w** was clothed in purple and fine linen, and 2532
16:20 **w** was laid at his gate, full of sores, 3739
16:21 And desiring to be fed with the crumbs **w** 3588
16:26 that they **w** would pass from hence to you NIG
17: 7 But **w** of you, having a servant plowing or 5101
17:10 when ye shall have done all those *things* **w** NIG
17:10 we have done *that* **w** was our duty to do. NIG
17:12 ten men *that were* lepers, **w** stood afar off: 3739
17:31 he **w** shall be upon the housetop, and 3739
18: 2 **w** feared not God, neither regarded man: NIG
18: 7 **w** cry day and night unto him, though he 3588
18: 9 And he spake this parable unto certain **w** 3588
18:27 The *things* *w are* unpossible with men are NIG
18:34 neither knew they the *things* **w** were NIG
18:39 And they **w** went before rebuked him, NIG
19: 2 **w** was *the* chief among the publicans, and 846
19:10 is come to seek and to save that **w** was lost. NIG
19:20 **w** I have kept laid up in a napkin: 3739

Lk 19:26 That unto every one **w** hath shall be given; 3588
19:27 **w** would not that I should reign over them, 3588
19:30 **w** at your entering ye shall find a colt tied, 3739
19:42 thy day, the *things* **w** belong unto thy peace! NIG
20:17 The stone **w** the builders rejected, 3739
20:20 **w** *should* feign themselves just *men,* that NIG
20:25 unto Cesar the *things* **w** be Cesar's, NIG
20:25 and unto God the *things* **w** be God's. NIG
20:27 **w** deny that there is any resurrection; 3588
20:35 But they **w** shall be accounted worthy to NIG
20:46 **w** desire to walk in long robes, and 3588
20:47 **W** devour widows' houses, and for a shew 3739
21: 6 *As for* these *things* **w** ye behold, the days 3739
21: 6 in the **w** there shall not be left one stone 3739
21:15 **w** all your adversaries shall not be able to 3739
21:21 Then let them **w** are in Judea flee to NIG
21:21 let them **w** are in the midst of it depart out; NIG
21:22 that all *things* **w** are written may be 3588
21:26 *for* looking after those *things* **w** are coming NIG
22: 1 bread drew nigh, **w** is called the Passover. 3588
22:19 saying, This is my body **w** is given for you: 3588
22:20 testament in my blood, **w** is shed for you. 3588
22:23 **w** of them it was that should do this *thing.* 5101
22:24 **w** of them should be accounted the greatest. 5101
22:28 Ye are they **w** have continued with me in NIG
22:49 When they **w** were about him saw what NIG
22:52 and the elders, **w** were come to him, Be ye NIG
23:27 **w** also bewailed and lamented him. 3739
23:29 days are coming, in the **w** they shall say, 3739
23:29 and the paps **w** never gave suck. 3739
23:33 **w** is called Calvary, there they crucified 3588
23:39 And one of the malefactors **w** were hanged NIG
23:48 beholding the *things* **w** were done, NIG
23:55 **w** came with him from Galilee, 3748
24: 1 bringing the spices **w** they had prepared, 3739
24:10 **w** told these *things* unto the apostles. 3739
24:12 wondering in himself at that **w** was come to NIG
24:13 **w** was from Jerusalem *about* threescore 3739
24:14 of all these *things* **w** had happened. 3588
24:18 hast not known the *things* **w** are come to NIG
24:19 **w** was a prophet mighty in deed and 3739
24:21 But we trusted that it had been he **w** should 3588
24:22 **w** were early at the sepulchre; NIG
24:23 a vision of angels, **w** said that he was alive. 3739
24:24 And certain of them **w** were with us went to NIG
24:44 These *are* the words **w** I spake unto you, 3739
24:44 **w** were written in the law of Moses, and 3588
Jn 1: 9 **w** lighteth every man *that* cometh into 3739
1:13 **W** were born, not of blood, nor of the will 3739
1:18 **w** is in the bosom of the Father, he hath 3588
1:24 And they **w** were sent were of the Pharisees. NIG
1:29 of God, **w** taketh away the sin of the world. 3588
1:30 After me cometh a man **w** is preferred 3739
1:33 the same is he **w** baptizeth with the Holy NIG
1:38 Rabbi, (**w** is to say, being interpreted, 3739
1:40 One of the two **w** heard John speak, and 3588
1:41 **w** is, being interpreted, the Christ. 3739
1:42 **w** is by interpretation, A stone. 3739
2: 9 (but the servants **w** drew the water knew;) 3588
2:10 *men* have well drunk, then that **w** is worse: NIG
2:22 and the word **w** Jesus had said. 3739
2:23 when they saw the miracles **w** he did. 3739
3: 6 That **w** is born of the flesh is flesh; and NIG
3: 6 and that **w** is born of the Spirit is spirit. NIG
3:13 *even* the Son of man **w** is in heaven. 3588
3:29 **w** standeth and heareth him, 3588
4: 5 he to a city of Samaria, **w** is called Sychar, NIG
4: 9 drink of me, **w** am a woman of Samaria? NIG
4:12 **w** gave us the well, and drank thereof 3739
4:25 that Messias cometh, **w** is called Christ: 3588
4:29 a man, **w** told me all *things* that ever I did: 3739
4:39 **w** testified, He told me all that ever I did. NIG
4:53 in the **w** Jesus said unto him, Thy son 3739
5: 2 **w** is called in the Hebrew tongue Bethesda, 3588
5: 5 **w** had an infirmity thirty *and* eight years. NIG
5:12 What man is that **w** said unto thee, Take up NIG
5:15 that it was Jesus, **w** had made him whole. 3588
5:23 honoureth not the Father **w** hath sent him. 3588
5:28 in the **w** all that are in the graves shall hear 3739
5:30 but the will of the Father **w** hath sent me. 3588
5:32 I know that the witness **w** he witnesseth of 3739
5:36 for the works **w** the Father hath given me to 3739
5:37 And the Father himself, **w** hath sent me, NIG
5:39 and they are they **w** testify of me. NIG
5:44 **w** receive honour one of another, and NIG
6: 1 the sea of Galilee, *w is* the *sea* of Tiberias. NIG
6: 2 they saw his miracles **w** he did on them that 3739
6: 9 **w** hath five barley loaves, and two small 3739
6:13 **w** remained over and above unto them that 3739
6:22 when the people **w** stood on the other side 3588
6:27 Labour not for the meat **w** perisheth, but 3588
6:27 for *that* meat **w** endureth unto everlasting 3588
6:27 **w** the Son of man shall give unto you: 3739
6:33 For the bread of God is he **w** cometh down 3588
6:39 And this is the Father's will **w** hath sent 3588
6:39 that of all **w** he hath given me I should lose 3739
6:40 that every one **w** seeth the Son, and 3588
6:41 I am the bread **w** came down from heaven. 3588
6:44 except the Father **w** hath sent me draw him: 3588
6:46 save he **w** is of God, he hath seen NIG
6:50 This is the bread **w** cometh down from 3588
6:51 I am the living bread **w** came down from 3588
6:51 **w** I will give for the life of the world. 3739
6:58 This is *that* bread **w** came down from 3588
7:31 will he do moe miracles than these **w** this 3739
7:39 **w** they that believe on him should receive: 3739
8: 9 And they **w** heard *it,* being convicted by NIG
8:26 I speak to the world those *things* **w** I have 3739
8:31 Then said Jesus to those Jews **w** believed on NIG
8:38 I speak *that* **w** I have seen with my Father: 3739
8:38 ye do *that* **w** ye have seen with your father. 3739
8:40 told you the truth, **w** I have heard of God: 3739
8:46 **W** of you convinceth me of sin? And if I 5101
8:53 than our father Abraham, **w** is dead? 3748
9: 1 he saw a man *w was* blind from *his* birth. NIG

Book	Ref	Context	No.
Jn	9: 7	of Siloam, (**w** is by interpretation, Sent.)	3739
	9: 8	they **w** before had seen him that he was	3588
	9:39	this world, that they **w** see not might see;	NIG
	9:39	and that they **w** see might be made blind.	NIG
	9:40	And *some* of the Pharisees **w** were with	3588
	10: 6	*things* they were **w** he spake unto them.	3739
	10:16	other sheep I have, **w** are not of this fold:	3739
	10:29	My Father, **w** gave *them* me, is greater than	3739
	10:32	for **w** of those works do ye stone me?	4169
	11: 2	(It was *that* Mary **w** anointed the Lord with	3588
	11:16	Then said Thomas, **w** is called Didymus,	3588
	11:27	Son of God, **w** should come into the world.	3588
	11:31	then **w** were with her in the house,	3588
	11:33	and the Jews also weeping **w** came with her,	NIG
	11:37	Could not this *man*, **w** opened the eyes of	3588
	11:42	of the people **w** stand by I said *it*, that they	3588
	11:45	Then many of the Jews **w** came to Mary,	3588
	11:45	and had seen *the things* **w** Jesus did,	3739
	12: 1	where Lazarus was **w** had been dead,	3588
	12: 4	Simon's *son*, **w** should betray him,	3588
	12:21	**w** was of Bethsaida of Galilee, and	3588
	12:38	**w** he spake, Lord, who hath believed our	3739
	12:49	but the Father **w** sent me, he gave me a	3588
	13: 1	having loved his own **w** were in the world,	3588
	14:24	and the word **w** you hear is not mine, but	3739
	14:24	hear is not mine, but the Father's **w** sent me.	NIG
	14:26	But the Comforter, **w** *is* the Holy Ghost,	NIG
	15: 3	Now ye are clean through the word **w** I	3739
	15:24	If I had not done among them the works **w**	3739
	15:26	**w** proceedeth from the Father, he shall	3739
	17: 4	I have finished the work **w** thou gavest me	3739
	17: 5	**w** I had with thee before the world was.	3739
	17: 6	I have manifested thy name unto the men **w**	3739
	17: 8	For I have given unto them the words **w**	3739
	17: 9	but for *them* **w** thou hast given me;	3739
	17:20	for them also **w** shall believe on me through	NIG
	17:22	And the glory **w** thou gavest me I have	3739
	17:24	behold my glory, **w** thou hast given me:	3739
	18: 1	into the **w** he entered, and his disciples.	3739
	18: 2	Judas also, **w** betrayed him, knew the place:	3588
	18: 5	**w** betrayed him, stood with them.	3588
	18: 9	the saying might be fulfilled, **w** he spake,	3739
	18: 9	Of them **w** thou gavest me have I lost none.	3739
	18:11	the cup **w** my Father hath given me, shall I	3739
	18:13	**w** was the high priest that *same* year.	3739
	18:14	was he, **w** gave counsel to the Jews,	3588
	18:16	**w** was known unto the high priest, and	3739
	18:21	ask them **w** heard *me*, what I have said unto	NIG
	18:22	one of the officers **w** stood by stroke Jesus	NIG
	18:32	**w** he spake, signifying what death he	3739
	19:17	a skull, **w** is called in the Hebrew Golgotha:	3739
	19:24	that the scripture might be fulfilled, **w** saith,	3588
	19:32	and of the other **w** was crucified with him.	3588
	19:39	**w** at the first came to Jesus by night, and	3588
	20: 8	**w** came first to the sepulchre, and he saw,	3588
	20:16	unto him, Rabboni; **w** is to say, Master.	3739
	20:30	his disciples, **w** are not written in this book:	3739
	21:10	Bring of the fish **w** ye have now caught.	3739
	21:20	**w** also leaned on his breast at supper, and	3739
	21:20	and said, Lord, **w** is he that betrayeth thee?	5101
	21:24	This is the disciple **w** testifieth of these	3588
	21:25	And there are also many other *things* **w**	3745
	21:25	the **w**, if they should be written every one,	3748
Ac	1: 2	Until the day *in* **w** he was taken up,	3739
	1: 4	**w**, *saith he*, ye have heard of me.	3739
	1: 7	**w** the Father hath put in his own power.	3739
	1:11	**W** also said, Ye men of Galilee, why stand	3739
	1:11	**w** is taken up from you into heaven, shall	3588
	1:12	**w** is from Jerusalem a sabbath day's	3739
	1:16	**w** the Holy Ghost by the mouth of David	3739
	1:16	**w** was guide to them that took Jesus.	3739
	1:21	Wherefore of these men **w** have companied	3588
	1:24	**w** knowest the hearts of all *men*, shew	NIG
	1:25	from **w** Judas by transgression fell,	3739
	2: 7	are not all these **w** speak Galileans?	3588
	2:16	But this is that **w** was spoken by the prophet	NIG
	2:22	**w** God did by him in the midst of you,	3739
	2:33	hath shed forth this, **w** ye now see and hear.	3739
	3: 2	the gate of the temple **w** is called Beautiful,	3588
	3:10	And they knew that it was he **w** sat for alms	3588
	3:10	amazement at that **w** had happened unto	NIG
	3:11	And as the lame *man* **w** was healed held	NIG
	3:16	the faith **w** is by him hath given him this	3588
	3:18	But *those things*, **w** God before had shewed	3739
	3:20	**w** before was preached unto you:	NIG
	3:21	**w** God hath spoken by the mouth of all his	3739
	3:23	**w** will not hear that prophet,	302+3748
	3:25	of the covenant **w** God made with our	3739
	4: 4	Howbeit many of them **w** heard the word	NIG
	4:11	This is the stone **w** was set at nought of you	3588
	4:11	**w** is become the head of the corner.	3588
	4:14	And beholding the man **w** was healed	3588
	4:20	but speak *the things* **w** we have seen and	3739
	4:21	for all *men* glorified God for that **w** was	NIG
	4:24	**w** hast made heaven, and earth, and the sea,	3588
	4:32	of the *things* **w** he possessed was his own;	NIG
	4:36	(**w** is, being interpreted, The son of	3739
	5: 9	the feet of them **w** have buried thy husband	NIG
	5:16	*them* **w** *were* vexed with unclean spirits:	NIG
	5:17	with him, (**w** is the sect of the Sadducees,)	3588
	6: 9	**w** is called *the synagogue* of the Libertines,	3588
	6:10	the wisdom and the spirit by **w** he spake.	3739
	6:11	Then they suborned men, **w** said, We have	NIG
	6:13	And set up false witnesses, **w** said,	NIG
	6:14	shall change the customs **w** Moses	3739
	7: 3	and come into the land **w** I shall shew thee.	3739
	7:17	**w** God had sworn to Abraham, the people	3739
	7:18	Till another king arose, **w** knew not Joseph.	3739
	7:20	In **w** time Moses was born, and	3739
	7:34	I have seen the affliction of my people **w** is	3588
	7:35	a deliverer by the hand of the angel **w**	3588
	7:37	**w** said unto the children of Israel,	3588
	7:38	the angel **w** spake to him in the mount Sina,	3588
	7:40	**w** brought us out of the land of Egypt,	3739
	7:43	figures **w** ye made to worship them:	3739
Ac	7:45	**W** also our fathers that came after brought	3739
	7:52	**W** of the prophets have not your fathers	5101
	7:52	they have slain them **w** shewed before of	3588
	8: 1	against the church **w** was at Jerusalem;	3588
	8: 6	gave heed unto those *things* **w** Philip spake,	NIG
	8: 6	hearing and seeing the miracles **w** he did.	3739
	8: 9	**w** beforetime in the *same* city used sorcery,	NIG
	8:13	*the* miracles and signs **w** *were* done.	NIG
	8:14	Now when the apostles **w** were at Jerusalem	NIG
	8:24	that none of *these things* **w** ye have spoken	3739
	8:26	from Jerusalem unto Gaza, **w** is desert.	3778
	8:32	The place of the scripture **w** he read was	3739
	9: 7	And the men **w** journeyed with him stood	3588
	9:11	and go into the street **w** is called Straight,	3588
	9:19	with the disciples **w** were at Damascus.	NIG
	9:21	Is not this he that destroyed them **w** called	NIG
	9:22	confounded the Jews **w** dwelt at Damascus,	3588
	9:30	**W** when the brethren knew, they brought	NIG
	9:32	down also to the saints **w** dwelt at Lydda.	3588
	9:33	**w** had kept his bed eight years, and was sick	NIG
	9:36	**w** by interpretation is called Dorcas:	3739
	9:36	of good works and almsdeeds **w** she did.	3739
	9:39	the coats and garments **w** Dorcas made,	3745
	10: 2	**w** gave much alms to the people, and	NIG
	10: 7	And when the angel **w** spake unto	3588
	10:17	*this* vision **w** he had seen should mean,	3739
	10:17	the men **w** were sent from Cornelius had	3588
	10:18	**w** was surnamed Peter, were lodged there.	3588
	10:21	Then Peter went down to the men **w** were	NIG
	10:36	The word **w** *God* sent unto the children of	3739
	10:37	**w** was published throughout all Judea, and	NIG
	10:37	after the baptism **w** John preached;	3739
	10:39	And we are witnesses of all *things* **w** he did	3739
	10:42	to testify that it is he **w** was ordained of	3588
	10:44	the Holy Ghost fell on all them **w** heard	NIG
	10:45	And they of the circumcision **w** believed	NIG
	10:47	**w** have received the Holy Ghost as well as	3748
	11: 6	Upon the **w** when I had fastened mine eyes,	3739
	11:13	**w** stood and said unto him, Send men to	NIG
	11:19	Now they **w** were scattered abroad upon	NIG
	11:20	them were men of Cyprus and Cyrene, **w**,	3748
	11:22	the ears of the church **w** was in Jerusalem:	3588
	11:28	**w** came to pass in the days of Claudius	3748
	11:29	to send relief unto the brethren **w**	NIG
	11:30	**W** also they did, and sent it to the elders by	3739
	12: 9	wist not that it was true **w** was done by	3588
	12:10	**w** opened to them of his own accord:	3748
	13: 1	**w** had been brought up with Herod	NIG
	13: 7	**W** was with the deputy *of the country*,	3739
	13:22	mine own heart, **w** shall fulfil all my will.	3739
	13:27	nor *yet* the voices of the prophets **w** are	3588
	13:31	And he was seen many days of them **w**	NIG
	13:32	how that the promise **w** was made unto	NIG
	13:39	**w** ye could not be justified by the law of	3739
	13:40	upon you, **w** is spoken of in the prophets;	NIG
	13:41	a work **w** you shall in no wise believe,	3739
	13:45	spake against those *things* **w** were spoken	NIG
	14: 3	**w** gave testimony unto the word of his	3588
	14:13	**w** was before their city, brought oxen and	3588
	14:14	***W*** when the apostles, Barnabas and Paul,	NIG
	14:15	**w** made heaven, and earth, and the sea, and	3739
	14:26	grace of God for the work **w** they fulfilled.	3739
	15: 1	And certain *men* **w** came down from Judea	NIG
	15: 5	of the sect of the Pharisees **w** believed,	3588
	15: 8	And God, **w** knoweth the hearts, bare them	NIG
	15:10	**w** neither our fathers nor we were able to	3739
	15:16	the tabernacle of David, **w** is fallen down;	3588
	15:19	**w** from among the Gentiles are turned to	NIG
	15:23	brethren *send* greeting unto the brethren **w**	3588
	15:24	that certain **w** went out from us have	NIG
	15:29	from **w** if ye keep yourselves, ye shall do	3739
	15:31	***W*** when they had read, they rejoiced for	NIG
	16: 1	**w** *was* a Jewess, and believed;	NIG
	16: 2	**W** was well reported of by the brethren that	3739
	16: 3	of the Jews **w** were in those quarters:	3588
	16: 4	and elders **w** were at Jerusalem.	3588
	16:12	**w** is the chief city of *that* part of	3748
	16:13	spake unto the women **w** resorted *thither*.	NIG
	16:14	of the city of Thyatira, **w** worshipped God,	NIG
	16:14	that *she* attended unto the *things* **w** were	NIG
	16:16	**w** brought her masters much gain by	3748
	16:17	**w** shew unto us the way of salvation.	3748
	16:21	**w** are not lawful for us to receive, neither to	3739
	17: 5	But the Jews **w** believed not, moved with	NIG
	17:12	also of honourable women **w** were Greeks,	3588
	17:21	strangers **w** were there spent their time in	3588
	17:31	in the **w** he will judge the world in	3739
	17:34	among the **w** *was* Dionysius	3739
	18:27	helped them much **w** had believed through	NIG
	19: 4	that they should believe on him **w** should	NIG
	19:10	that all they **w** dwelt in Asia heard the word	NIG
	19:13	took upon them to call over them **w** had evil	NIG
	19:14	a Jew, *and* chief of the priests, **w** did so.	NIG
	19:19	Many also of them **w** used curious arts	NIG
	19:24	**w** made silver shrines for Diana,	NIG
	19:26	they be no gods, **w** are made with hands:	NIG
	19:31	of Asia, **w** were his friends, sent unto him,	NIG
	19:35	and of the *image* **w** fell down from Jupiter?	NIG
	19:37	**w** *are* neither robbers of churches, nor yet	NIG
	19:38	and the craftsmen **w** are with him,	NIG
	20:19	**w** befell me by the lying in wait of	3588
	20:24	**w** I have received of the Lord Jesus,	3739
	20:28	over the **w** the Holy Ghost hath made you	3739
	20:28	**w** he hath purchased with his own blood.	3739
	20:32	**w** is able to build *you* up, and to give you	3588
	20:32	inheritance among all them **w** are sanctified.	NIG
	20:38	Sorrowing most *of all* for the words **w** he	3739
	21: 8	the evangelist, **w** was *one* of the seven;	NIG
	21: 9	had four daughters, virgins, **w** did prophesy.	NIG
	21:20	how many thousands of Jews there are **w**	3588
	21:21	that thou teachest all the Jews **w** are among	3588
	21:23	We have four men **w** have a vow on them;	NIG
	21:25	As touching the Gentiles **w** believe,	NIG
	21:27	the Jews **w** were of Asia, when they saw	NIG
	21:38	**w** before these days madest an uproar, and	3588
Ac	21:39	Paul said, I am a man **w** *am* a Jew of Tarsus,	NIG
	22: 1	hear ye my defence **w** *I make* now unto you.	NIG
	22: 3	I am verily a man **w** *am* a Jew, born in	NIG
	22: 5	to Damascus, to bring them **w** were there,	NIG
	22:10	there it shall be told thee of all *things* **w** are	3739
	22:12	having a good report of all the Jews **w**	NIG
	22:29	from him **w** should have examined him:	3588
	23:13	And they were more *than* forty **w** had made	3588
	23:21	**w** have bound themselves with an oath,	3748
	24:14	that after the way **w** they call heresy, so	3739
	24:14	believing all *things* **w** are written in the law	3588
	24:15	**w** they themselves also allow,	3739
	24:24	**w** was a Jewess, he sent for Paul, and	NIG
	25: 5	said he, **w** among you are able, go down	NIG
	25: 7	the Jews **w** came down from Jerusalem	NIG
	25: 7	against Paul, **w** they could not prove.	3739
	25:16	before that he **w** is accused have	NIG
	25:19	and of one Jesus, **w** *was* dead, whom Paul	NIG
	25:24	and all men **w** are here present with us,	3588
	26: 3	and questions **w** are among the Jews:	NIG
	26: 4	**w** was at the first among mine own nation	3588
	26: 5	**W** knew me from the beginning, if they	NIG
	26: 7	Unto **w** *promise* our twelve tribes,	3739
	26: 7	For **w** hope's sake, king Agrippa, I am	3739
	26:10	**W** *thing* I also did in Jerusalem: and	3739
	26:13	about me and them **w** journeyed with me.	NIG
	26:16	a witness both of *these things* **w** thou hast	3739
	26:16	*of those things* in the **w** I will appear unto	3739
	26:18	inheritance among them **w** are sanctified by	NIG
	26:22	saying none other *things* than those **w**	3739
	27: 8	came unto a place **w** *is* called The fair	NIG
	27:11	more than those *things* **w** were spoken by	NIG
	27:12	**w** *is* a haven of Crete, and lieth toward	NIG
	27:16	And running under a certain island **w** *is*	NIG
	27:17	**W** when they had taken up, they used	3739
	27:39	into the **w** they were minded, if it were	3739
	27:43	commanded that they **w** could swim should	NIG
	28: 9	**w** had diseases in the island, came, and	3588
	28:11	**w** had wintered in the isle, *whose* sign *was*	NIG
	28:24	And some believed the *things* **w** were	NIG
	28:31	teaching those *things* **w** concern the Lord	NIG
Ro	1: 2	(**W** he had promised afore by his prophets	3739
	1: 3	**w** was made of the seed of David according	3588
	1:19	Because that **w** may be known of God is	NIG
	1:26	the natural use into that **w** is against nature:	NIG
	1:27	men with men working that **w** is unseemly,	NIG
	1:27	*that* recompence of their error **w** was meet.	3739
	1:28	to do those *things* **w** are not convenient;	NIG
	1:32	that they **w** commit such *things* are worthy	NIG
	2: 2	to truth against them **w** commit such *things*.	NIG
	2: 3	that judgest them **w** do such *things*, and	NIG
	2:14	For when *the* Gentiles, **w** have not the law,	3588
	2:15	**W** shew the work of the law written in their	3748
	2:19	the blind, a light of them **w** are in darkness,	NIG
	2:20	**w** hast the form of knowledge and of	NIG
	2:21	Thou therefore **w** teachest another,	3588
	2:27	And shall not uncircumcision **w** is by	3588
	2:28	For he is not a Jew, **w** is one outwardly;	3588
	2:28	*that* circumcision, **w** is outward in the flesh:	NIG
	2:29	But he *is* a Jew, **w** is one inwardly;	NIG
	3:22	Even the righteousness of God **w** *is* by faith	NIG
	3:26	and the justifier of him **w** believeth in Jesus.	NIG
	3:30	**w** shall justify the circumcision by faith,	3739
	4:11	a seal of the righteousness of the faith **w** he	3588
	4:12	**w** he had being *yet* uncircumcised.	NIG
	4:14	For if they **w** are of the law *be* heirs, faith is	NIG
	4:16	not to that only **w** is of the law, but to that	NIG
	4:16	but to that also **w** is of the faith of Abraham;	NIG
	4:17	calleth those *things* **w** be not as though they	NIG
	4:18	according to that **w** was spoken, So shall thy	NIG
	5: 5	by the Holy Ghost **w** is given unto us.	3588
	5:15	gift by grace, **w** is by one man, Jesus Christ,	NIG
	5:17	much more they **w** receive abundance of	NIG
	6:17	*that* form of doctrine **w** was delivered you.	3739
	7: 2	For the woman **w** hath a husband is bound	NIG
	7: 5	the motions of sins, **w** were by the law,	3588
	7:10	the commandment, **w** was *ordained* to life,	3588
	7:13	then **that w** is good made death unto me?	3588
	7:13	working death in me by **that w** is good;	3588
	7:15	For *that* **w** I do I allow not: for what I	3739
	7:16	If then I do that **w** I would not, I consent	3739
	7:18	*how* to perform **that w** is good I find not.	3588
	7:19	do not: but the evil **w** I would not, that I do.	3739
	7:23	to the law of sin **w** is in my members.	3588
	8: 1	now no condemnation to them **w** *are* in	NIG
	8:18	with the glory **w** shall be revealed in us.	NIG
	8:23	**w** have the firstfruits of the Spirit,	NIG
	8:26	for us with groanings **w** cannot be uttered.	NIG
	8:39	love of God, **w** is in Christ Jesus our Lord.	3588
	9: 6	For they *are* not all Israel, **w** are of Israel:	3588
	9: 8	That is, *They* **w** *are* the children of the flesh,	NIG
	9:23	**w** he had afore prepared unto glory,	3739
	9:25	*them* my people, **w** were not my people;	3588
	9:25	and her beloved, **w** was not beloved.	NIG
	9:30	**w** followed not *after* righteousness,	3588
	9:30	even the righteousness **w** is of faith.	3588
	9:31	**w** followed *after* the law of righteousness,	NIG
	10: 5	For Moses describeth the righteousness **w**	3588
	10: 5	That the man **w** doeth those *things* shall live	NIG
	10: 6	But the righteousness **w** is of faith speaketh	3588
	10: 8	that is, the word of faith, **w** we preach;	3739
	11: 2	God hath not cast away his people **w** he	3739
	11: 7	Israel hath not obtained that **w** he seeketh	3739
	11:14	provoke to emulation *them* **w** *are* my flesh,	NIG
	11:22	on them **w** fell, severity; but toward thee,	NIG
	11:24	cut out of the **olive tree w is wild** by nature,	65
	11:24	**w** be the natural *branches*, be graffed into	NIG
	12: 1	unto God, **w** *is* your reasonable service.	NIG
	12: 9	Abhor *that* **w** *is* evil; cleave to *that which is*	NIG
	12: 9	*that which is* evil; cleave to *that* **w** *is* good.	NIG
	12:14	Bless them **w** persecute you: bless, and	NIG
	13: 3	do *that* **w** *is* good, and thou shalt have praise	NIG
	13: 4	But if thou do *that* **w** *is* evil, be afraid;	NIG
	14: 3	let not him **w** eateth not judge him that	NIG
	14:19	follow *after* the *things* **w** make for peace,	3588

Ro 14:22 not himself in *that thing* **w** he alloweth. 3739
15:17 Christ *in those things* **w** pertain to God. NIG
15:18 *things* **w** Christ hath not wrought by me, 3739
15:22 **For w cause** also I have been much 1352
15:26 for the poor saints **w** are at Jerusalem. 3588
15:31 that my service **w** I have for Jerusalem may 3588
16: 1 **w** is a servant of the church which is at NIG
16: 1 which is a servant of the church **w** is at 3588
16:10 Salute them **w** are of Aristobulus' NIG
16:11 *household* of Narcissus, **w** are in the Lord. 3588
16:12 **w** laboured much in the Lord. 3748
16:14 Hermes, and the brethren **w** are with them. NIG
16:15 Olympas, and all the saints **w** are with them. NIG
16:17 mark them **w** cause divisions and offences NIG
16:17 offences contrary to the doctrine **w** ye have 3739
16:19 *yet* I would have you wise unto *that* **w** *is* NIG
16:25 **w** was kept secret since the world began, NIG
1Co 1: 2 Unto the church of God **w** is at Corinth, NIG
1: 4 for the grace of God **w** is given you by 3588
1:11 by them **w** are of the *house* of Chloe, NIG
1:18 unto us **w** are saved it is the power of God. 3588
1:24 But unto them **w** are called, both Jews and 3588
1:27 world to confound the *things* **w** *are* mighty; NIG
1:28 and *things* **w** are despised, hath God chosen, NIG
1:28 hath God chosen, *yea,* and *things* **w** are not, NIG
2: 7 *even* the hidden *wisdom,* **w** God ordained 3739
2: 8 **W** none of the princes of this world knew: 3739
2: 9 *the things* **w** God hath prepared for them 3739
2:11 a man, save the spirit of man **w** is in him? 3588
2:12 of the world, but the Spirit **w** is of God; 3588
2:13 **W** *things* also we speak, not in the words 3739
2:13 not in the words **w** man's wisdom teacheth, NIG
2:13 but **w** the Holy Ghost teacheth; NIG
3:10 According to the grace of God **w** is given 3588
3:11 *man* lay than that is laid, **w** is Jesus Christ. 3739
3:14 If any *man's* work abide **w** he hath built 3739
3:17 the temple of God is holy, **w** *temple* ye are. 3748
4: 6 not to think *of men* above *that* **w** is written, 3739
4:17 remembrance of my ways **w** be in Christ, 3588
4:19 not the speech of them **w** are puffed up, but NIG
6:16 know ye not that he **w** is joined to a harlot is NIG
6:19 is the temple of the Holy Ghost **w** is in you, NIG
6:19 **w** ye have of God, and ye are not your 3739
6:20 your body, and in your spirit, **w** are God's. 3748
7:13 And the woman **w** hath a husband that 3748
7:35 but for *that* **w** *is* comely, and that you may NIG
8:10 For if any *man* see thee **w** hast knowledge 3588
8:10 shall not the conscience of him **w** is weak NIG
8:10 to eat those things **w** are offered to idols; NIG
9:13 Do ye not know that they **w** minister about NIG
9:13 they **w** wait at the altar are partakers with NIG
9:14 hath the Lord ordained that they **w** preach NIG
9:24 Know ye not that they **w** run in a race run NIG
10:16 The cup of blessing **w** we bless, is it not 3739
10:16 The bread **w** we break, is it not 3739
10:18 are not they **w** eat *of* the sacrifices partakers NIG
10:19 that **w** is offered in sacrifice to idols is any NIG
10:20 But *I say,* that *the things* **w** the Gentiles 3739
10:30 why am I evil spoken of for *that for* **w** I 3739
11:19 that they **w** *are* approved may be made NIG
11:23 For I have received of the Lord *that* **w** also 3739
11:23 That the Lord Jesus the *same* night in **w** he 3739
11:24 this is my body, **w** is broken for you: 3588
12: 6 but it is the same God **w** worketh all in all. 3588
12:22 **w** seem to be more feeble, are necessary: 3588
12:23 the body, **w** we think to be less honourable, NIG
12:24 more abundant honour to that *part* **w** lacked: NIG
13:10 But when *that* **w** *is* perfect is come, then NIG
13:10 then that **w** is in part shall be done away. NIG
14:22 that believe not, but for them **w** believe. NIG
15: 1 I declare unto you the gospel **w** I preached 3739
15: 1 **w** also you have received, and wherein ye 3739
15: 2 By **w** also ye are saved, if ye keep in 3739
15: 3 For I delivered unto you first *of all* that **w** I 3739
15:10 his grace **w** was *bestowed* upon me was not 3588
15:10 not I, but the grace of God **w** was with me. 3588
15:18 Then they also **w** are fallen asleep in Christ NIG
15:27 is excepted, **w** did put all *things* under him. 3588
15:29 Else what shall they do **w** are baptized for NIG
15:31 I protest by your rejoicing **w** I have in 3739
15:36 *that* **w** thou sowest is not quickened, 3739
15:37 And *that* **w** thou sowest, thou sowest not 3739
15:46 Howbeit *that was* not first **w** *is* spiritual, but NIG
15:46 first *which is* spiritual, but *that* **w** *is* natural; NIG
15:46 *is* natural; *and* afterward *that* **w** *is* spiritual. NIG
15:57 **w** giveth us the victory through our Lord 3588
16:17 for that **w** was lacking on your part they NIG
2Co 1: 1 unto the church of God **w** is at Corinth, 3588
1: 1 with all the saints **w** are in all Achaia: 3588
1: 4 that we may be able to comfort them **w** are NIG
1: 6 **w** is effectual in the enduring of the same 3588
1: 6 of the same sufferings **w** we also suffer: 3739
1: 8 have you ignorant of our trouble **w** came to 3588
1: 9 in ourselves, but in God **w** raiseth the dead: 3588
1:21 Now he **w** stablisheth us with you in Christ, NIG
2: 2 but *the same* **w** is made sorry by me? NIG
2: 4 that ye might know the love **w** I have more 3739
2: 6 this punishment, **w** *was inflicted* of many. 3588
2:14 **w** always causeth us to triumph in Christ, 3588
2:17 are not as many, **w** corrupt the word of God: NIG
3: 7 **w** *glory* was to be done away: 3588
3:10 For even that **w** was made glorious had no NIG
3:11 For if that **w** is done away *was* glorious, NIG
3:11 much more that **w** remaineth *is* glorious. NIG
3:13 not as Moses, **w** put a vail over his face, NIG
3:13 look to the end of that **w** is abolished: NIG
3:14 **w** *vail* is done away in Christ. 3748
4: 4 blinded the minds of them **w** believe not, NIG
4:11 For we **w** live are alway delivered unto 3588
4:14 Knowing that he **w** raised up the Lord Jesus NIG
4:16 **For w cause** we faint not; but though our 1352
4:17 our light affliction, **w** is but for a moment, NIG
4:18 While we look not at the *things* **w** are seen, NIG
4:18 are seen, but at the *things* **w** are not seen: NIG
4:18 for the *things* **w** are seen *are* temporal; but NIG

2Co 4:18 but the *things* **w** are not seen *are* eternal. NIG
5: 2 upon with our house **w** is from heaven: 3588
5:12 to *answer* them **w** glory in appearance, NIG
5:15 that they **w** live should not henceforth live NIG
5:15 but unto him **w** died for them, and NIG
7:14 so our boasting, **w** *I made* before Titus, 3588
8:11 a performance also out of that **w** *you* have. NIG
8:16 **w** put the same earnest care into the heart 3588
8:19 **w** is administered by us to the glory of 3588
8:20 in this abundance **w** is administered by us: 3588
8:22 upon the great confidence **w** *I have* in you. 3588
9: 2 for **w** I boast of you to them of Macedonia, 3739
9: 6 But this *I say,* He **w** soweth sparingly shall 3588
9: 6 he **w** soweth bountifully shall reap also NIG
9:11 **w** causeth through us thanksgiving to God. 3748
9:14 **w** long after you for the exceeding grace of NIG
10: 2 **w** think of us as if we walked according to 3588
10: 8 **w** the Lord hath given us for edification, 3739
10:13 according to the measure of the rule **w** God 3739
11: 4 **w** ye have not received, or another gospel, 3739
11: 4 or another gospel, **w** ye have not accepted, 3739
11: 9 I was chargeable to no *man:* for that **w** was NIG
11: 9 brethren **w** came from Macedonia supplied: NIG
11:12 that I may cut off occasion from them **w** NIG
11:17 *That* **w** I speak, I speak *it* not after 3739
11:28 that **w** cometh upon me daily, the care of all NIG
11:30 I will glory of the *things* **w** concern mine 3588
11:31 **w** is blessed for evermore, knoweth that I 3588
12: 4 **w** *it is* not lawful for a man to utter. 3739
12: 6 think of me above *that* **w** he seeth me *to be,* 3739
12:21 *that* I shall bewail many **w** have sinned 3588
12:21 and lasciviousness **w** they have committed. 3739
13: 2 being absent now I write to them **w** NIG
13: 3 **w** to you-ward is not weak, but is mighty in 3739
13: 7 but that ye should do *that* **w** *is* honest, NIG
13:10 according to the power **w** the Lord hath 3739
Gal 1: 2 And all the brethren **w** are with me, unto NIG
1: 7 **W** is not another; but there be some that 3739
1: 8 than *that* **w** we have preached unto you, 3739
1:11 that the gospel **w** was preached of me is not 3588
1:17 Neither went I up to Jerusalem to them **w** NIG
1:20 Now *the things* **w** I write unto you, behold, 3739
1:22 the churches of Judea **w** were in Christ: 3588
1:23 That he **w** persecuted us in times past now NIG
1:23 preacheth the faith **w** once he destroyed. 3739
2: 2 communicated unto them *that* gospel **w** I 3739
2: 2 but privately to them **w** were of reputation, NIG
2: 4 out our liberty **w** we have in Christ Jesus, 3739
2:10 the same **w** I also was forward to do. 3739
2:12 fearing them **w** were of the circumcision. NIG
2:18 For if I build again the *things* **w** I 3739
2:20 *the life* **w** I now live in the flesh I live by 3739
3: 7 Know ye therefore that they **w** are of faith, NIG
3: 9 they **w** be of faith are blessed with faithful NIG
3:10 **w** are written in the book of the law to do 3588
3:16 but as of one, And to thy seed, **w** is Christ. 3739
3:17 **w** was four hundred and thirty years after, NIG
3:21 for if there had been a law given **w** could 3588
3:23 shut up unto the faith **w** should afterwards NIG
4: 8 ye did service unto them **w** by nature are no NIG
4:14 And my temptation **w** was in my flesh ye NIG
4:24 **W** *things* are an allegory: for these are 3748
4:24 **w** gendereth to bondage, which is Agar. NIG
4:24 which gendereth to bondage, **w** is Agar. 3748
4:25 and answereth to Jerusalem **w** now is, and 3588
4:26 But Jerusalem **w** is above is free, which is 3588
4:26 is above is free, **w** is the mother of us all. 3748
4:27 moe children than she **w** hath a husband. NIG
5: 6 but faith **w** worketh by love. NIG
5:12 I would they were even cut off **w** trouble NIG
5:19 **w** are *these;* Adultery, fornication, 3748
5:21 of the **w** I tell you before, as I have also 3739
5:21 that they **w** do such *things* shall not inherit NIG
6: 1 be overtaken in a fault, ye **w** are spiritual, 3588
Eph 1: 1 to the saints **w** are at Ephesus, and to 3588
1: 9 according to his good pleasure **w** he had 3739
1:10 both **w** are in heaven, and which are on 3588
1:10 which are in heaven, and **w** are on earth; 3588
1:14 **W** is the earnest of our inheritance, 3739
1:20 **W** he wrought in Christ, when he raised 3739
1:21 in this world, but also in that **w** is to come: 3588
1:23 **W** is his body, the fulness of him that 3748
2:10 **w** God hath before ordained that we should 3739
2:11 who are called Uncircumcision by that **w** is NIG
2:17 and preached peace to you **w** were afar off, 3588
3: 2 grace of God **w** is given me to you-ward: 3588
3: 5 **W** in other ages was not made known unto 3739
3: 9 **w** from the beginning of the world hath 3588
3:11 According to the eternal purpose **w** he 3739
3:13 at my tribulations for you, **w** is your glory. 3748
3:19 the love of Christ, **w** passeth knowledge, NIG
4:15 may grow *up* into him *in* all *things,* **w** is 3739
4:16 compacted by that **w** every joint supplieth, NIG
4:22 **w** is corrupt according to the deceitful lusts; 3588
4:24 **w** after God is created in righteousness and 3588
4:28 working with *his* hands the *thing* **w** *is* good, NIG
4:29 but **that w** *is* good to the use of edifying, 1536
5: 4 nor jesting, **w** are not convenient: 3588
5:12 of those *things* **w** are done of them in secret. NIG
6: 2 (**w** is the first commandment with 3748
6:17 sword of the Spirit, **w** is the word of God: 3739
6:20 For **w** I am an ambassador in bonds: 3739
Php 1: 1 to all the saints in Christ Jesus **w** are at 3588
1: 6 Being confident of this very *thing,* that he **w** NIG
1:11 **w** are by Jesus Christ unto the glory and 3588
1:12 that the *things* **w** *happened* unto me have NIG
1:23 and to be with Christ; **w** *is* far better: NIG
1:28 **w** is to them an evident token of perdition, 3748
1:30 Having the same conflict **w** ye saw in me, 3634
2: 5 mind be in you, **w** *was* also in Christ Jesus: 3739
2: 9 given him a name **w** is above every name: 3588
2:13 For it is God **w** worketh in you both to will 3588
2:21 not the *things* **w** *are* Jesus Christ's. NIG
3: 3 **w** worship God in the spirit, and rejoice in 3588
3: 6 touching the righteousness **w** is in the law, 3588

Php 3: 9 **w** is of the law, but that which is through 3588
3: 9 but that **w** is through the faith of Christ, NIG
3: 9 the righteousness **w** is of God by faith: 3588
3:12 **w** also I am apprehended of Christ Jesus. 3739
3:13 *this* one *thing I do,* forgetting those *things* **w** NIG
3:13 reaching forth unto those *things* **w** *are* NIG
3:17 and mark them **w** walk so as ye have us for NIG
4: 3 help those *women* **w** laboured with me in 3748
4: 7 **w** passeth all understanding, shall keep 3588
4: 9 Those *things,* **w** ye have both learned, and 3739
4:13 I can do all *things* through Christ **w** 3588
4:18 the *things* **w** *were sent* from you, NIG
4:21 The brethren **w** are with me greet you. NIG
Col 1: 2 faithful brethren in Christ **w** are at Colosse: NIG
1: 4 and of the love **w** *ye have* to all the saints, 3588
1: 5 For the hope **w** is laid up for you in heaven, 3588
1: 6 **W** is come unto you, as *it is* in all 3588
1:12 **w** hath made us meet to be partakers of 3588
1:23 **w** ye have heard, *and* which was preached 3739
1:23 **w** was preached to every creature which is 3588
1:23 which was preached to every creature **w** is 3588
1:24 fill up that **w** is behind of the afflictions of NIG
1:24 flesh for his body's sake, **w** is the church: 3739
1:25 according to the dispensation of God **w** is 3588
1:26 *Even* the mystery **w** hath been hid from 3588
1:27 **w** is Christ in you, the hope of glory: 3739
1:29 to his working, **w** worketh in me mightily. 3588
2:10 **w** is the head of all principality and power: 3739
2:14 **w** was contrary to us, and took it out of 3739
2:17 **W** are a shadow of *things* to come; but 3739
2:18 intruding into *those things* **w** he hath not 3739
2:19 from **w** all the body by joints and 3739
2:22 **W** all are to perish with the using;) after 3739
2:23 **W** *things* have indeed a shew of wisdom in 3748
3: 1 with Christ, seek those *things* **w** are above, NIG
3: 5 your members **w** are upon the earth; 3588
3: 5 and covetousness, **w** is idolatry: 3748
3: 6 For **w** *things'* sake the wrath of God 3739
3: 7 In the **w** ye also walked sometime, when ye 3739
3:10 And have put on the new *man,* **w** is 3588
3:14 *put on* charity, **w** is the bond of perfectness. 3739
3:15 to the **w** also ye are called in one body; 3739
3:25 shall receive *for* the wrong **w** he hath done: 3739
4: 1 give unto *your* servants that **w** is just and NIG
4: 3 mystery of Christ, for **w** I am also in bonds: 3739
4: 9 known unto you all *things* **w** *are done* here. 3588
4:11 And Jesus, **w** is called Justus, who are of 3588
4:11 of God, **w** have been a comfort unto me. 3748
4:15 Salute the brethren **w** are in Laodicea, and NIG
4:15 Nymphas, and the church **w** is in his house. NIG
4:17 Take heed to the ministry **w** thou hast 3739
1Th 1: 1 unto the church of the Thessalonians **w** *is* in NIG
1:10 **w** delivered us from the wrath to come. 3588
2: 4 pleasing men, but God, **w** trieth our hearts. 3588
2:13 when ye received the word of God **w** *ye* NIG
2:13 **w** effectually worketh also in you that 3739
2:14 became followers of the churches of God **w** NIG
3:10 might perfect that **w** is lacking in your NIG
4: 5 even as the Gentiles **w** know not God: 3588
4:10 all the brethren **w** are in all Macedonia: 3588
4:13 brethren, concerning them **w** are asleep, NIG
4:13 sorrow not, even as others **w** have no hope. 3588
4:14 them also **w** sleep in Jesus will God bring 3588
4:15 that we **w** are alive *and* remain unto 3588
4:15 Lord shall not prevent them **w** are asleep. NIG
4:17 Then we **w** are alive *and* remain shall be 3588
5:12 to know them **w** labour among you, and NIG
5:15 any *man;* but ever follow *that* **w** *is* good, NIG
5:21 Prove all *things;* hold fast *that* **w** *is* good. NIG
2Th 1: 5 **W** *is* a manifest token of the righteous NIG
1: 5 the kingdom of God, for **w** ye also suffer: 3739
2:15 hold the traditions **w** ye have been taught, 3739
2:16 **w** hath loved us, and hath given *us* 3588
3: 4 and will do the *things* **w** we command you. 3739
3: 6 not after the tradition **w** he received of us. 3739
3:11 For we hear that *there are* some **w** walk NIG
3:17 own hand, **w** is the token in every epistle: 3739
1Ti 1: 1 and Lord Jesus Christ, **w** *is* our hope; NIG
1: 4 endless genealogies, **w** minister questions, 3748
1: 4 rather than godly edifying **w** is in faith: 3588
1: 6 From **w** some having swerved have turned 3739
1:11 blessed God, **w** was committed to my trust. 3739
1:14 with faith and love **w** is in Christ Jesus. 3588
1:16 for a pattern to them **w** should hereafter NIG
1:18 according to the prophecies **w** went before NIG
1:19 **w** some having put away, concerning faith 3739
2:10 But (**w** becometh women professing 3739
3: 7 have a good report of them **w** are without; NIG
3:13 great boldness in the faith **w** is in Christ 3588
3:15 **w** is the church of the living God, the pillar 3748
4: 3 **w** God hath created to be received with 3739
4: 3 with thanksgiving of them **w** believe NIG
4: 8 life that now is, and of that **w** is to come. 3588
4:14 is in thee, **w** was given thee by prophecy, 3739
5:13 speaking *things* **w** they ought not. 3588
6: 3 to the doctrine **w** is according to godliness; 3588
6: 9 **w** drown men in destruction and perdition. 3748
6:10 **w** while some coveted after, they have 3739
6:15 **W** in his times he shall shew, *who is* 3739
6:16 in the light **w no** *man* **can approach unto;** 676
6:20 keep that **w** is committed to *thy* trust, 3739
6:21 **W** some professing have erred concerning 3739
6: S **w** is the chiefest city of Phrygia Pacatiana. 3748
2Ti 1: 1 according to the promise of life **w** is in 3588
1: 5 **w** dwelt first in thy grandmother Lois, and 3748
1: 6 **w** is in thee by the putting on of my hands. 3739
1: 9 **w** was given us in Christ Jesus before 3588
1:12 For the **w** cause I also suffer these *things:* 3739
1:12 am persuaded that he is able to keep that **w** 3588
1:13 **w** thou hast heard of me, in faith and 3739
1:13 of me, in faith and love **w** is in Christ Jesus. 3588
1:14 *That* good thing **w** was committed unto *thee* NIG
1:14 keep by the Holy Ghost **w** dwelleth in us. 3588
1:15 that all they **w** are in Asia be turned away NIG
2:10 that they may also obtain the salvation **w** is 3588

2Ti 3: 6 For of this sort are they **w** creep into houses, NIG
3:11 afflictions, **w** came unto me at Antioch, *3634*
3:14 But continue thou in *the things* **w** thou hast *3739*
3:15 **w** are able to make thee wise unto salvation *3588*
3:15 salvation through faith **w** is in Christ Jesus. *3588*
4: 8 **w** the Lord, the righteous judge, shall give *3739*
Tit 1: 1 the acknowledging of the truth **w** is after *3588*
1: 2 hope of eternal life, **w** God, that cannot lie, *3739*
1: 3 **w** is committed unto me according to *3739*
1:11 teaching *things* **w** *they* ought not, for filthy *3739*
2: 1 But speak thou *the things* **w** become sound *3739*
3: 5 Not by works of righteousness **w** we have *3739*
3: 6 **W** he shed on us abundantly through Jesus *3739*
3: 8 that they **w** have believed in God might be NIG
Phm 1: 5 **w** thou hast toward the Lord Jesus, and *3739*
1: 6 good *thing* **w** is in you in Christ Jesus. *3588*
1: 8 in Christ to enjoin thee that **w** is convenient, NIG
1:11 **W** in time past was to thee unprofitable, but *3588*
Heb 1: 5 For unto **w** of the angels said he at any *5101*
1:13 But to **w** of the angels said he at any time, *5101*
2: 1 earnest heed to the *things* **w** we have heard, NIG
2: 3 **w** at the first began to be spoken by *3748*
2:11 for **w** cause he is not ashamed to call them *3739*
2:13 I, and the children **w** God hath given me. *3739*
3: 5 for a testimony of those *things* **w** were to be NIG
4: 3 For we **w** have believed do enter into rest, NIG
4:15 For we have not a high priest **w** cannot be NIG
5: 8 *yet* learned he obedience by *the things* **w** he *3739*
5:12 ye have need that *one* teach you again **w** *be* *5101*
6: 7 For the earth **w** drinketh *in* the rain that *3588*
6: 8 But that **w** beareth thorns and briers *is* NIG
6:10 **w** ye have shewed toward his name, *3739*
6:18 in **w** *it was* impossible for God to lie, *3739*
6:19 **W** *hope* we have as an anchor of the soul, *3739*
6:19 and **w** entereth into that within the vail; NIG
7: 2 also King of Salem, **w** is, King of peace; *3739*
7:13 of **w** no *man* gave attendance at the altar. *3739*
7:14 of **w** tribe Moses spake nothing concerning *3739*
7:19 hope *did;* by the **w** we draw nigh unto God. *3739*
7:28 For the law maketh men high priests **w** have NIG
7:28 **w** was since the law, *maketh* the Son, *3588*
8: 1 Now of the *things* **w** we have spoken *this is* NIG
8: 2 **w** the Lord pitched, and not man. *3739*
8: 6 **w** was established upon better promises. *3748*
8:13 Now that **w** decayeth and waxeth old *is* *3588*
9: 2 the shewbread; **w** is called the sanctuary. *3748*
9: 3 the tabernacle **w** is called the holiest of all; *3588*
9: 4 **W** had the golden censer, and the ark of NIG
9: 5 of **w** *we* cannot now speak particularly. *3739*
9: 7 **w** he offered for himself, and *for* the errors *3739*
9: 9 **W** *was* a figure for the time *then* present, *3748*
9: 9 in **w** were offered both gifts and sacrifices, *3739*
9:10 **W** *stood* only in meats and drinks, and NIG
9:15 they **w** are called might receive the promise NIG
9:20 This *is* the blood of the testament **w** God *3739*
9:24 with hands, **w** *are* the figures of the true; NIG
10: 1 can never with those sacrifices **w** they *3739*
10: 8 neither hadst pleasure *therein;* **w** are *3748*
10:10 By the **w** will we are sanctified through *3739*
10:11 **w** can never take away sins: *3748*
10:20 living way, **w** he hath consecrated for us, *3739*
10:27 **w** shall devour the adversaries. NIG
10:32 in **w**, after ye were illuminated, ye endured *3739*
10:35 **w** hath great recompence of reward. *3748*
11: 3 that *things* **w** are seen were not made of NIG
11: 3 seen were not made of *things* **w** do appear. NIG
11: 4 by **w** he obtained witness that he was *3739*
11: 7 by the **w** he condemned the world, and *3739*
11: 7 became heir of the righteousness **w** is by NIG
11: 8 when he was called to go out into a place **w** *3739*
11:10 For he looked for a city **w** hath foundations, NIG
11:12 as the sand **w** is by the sea shore *3588*
11:29 **w** the Egyptians assaying to do were *3739*
12: 1 and the sin **w** doth so easily beset *us,* and NIG
12: 5 And ye have forgotten the exhortation **w** *3748*
12: 9 have had fathers of our flesh **w** corrected *us,* NIG
12:11 unto them **w** are exercised thereby. NIG
12:12 Wherefore lift up the hands **w** hang down, NIG
12:13 lest *that* **w** *is* lame be turned out of the way; NIG
12:14 without **w** no *man* shall see the Lord: *3739*
12:19 **w** *voice* they that heard intreated that *3739*
12:20 (For they could not endure that **w** was NIG
12:23 **w** are written in heaven, and to God NIG
12:27 that those *things* **w** cannot be shaken may NIG
12:28 Wherefore we receiving a kingdom **w** NIG
13: 3 with *them; and* them **w** suffer adversity, NIG
13: 7 Remember them **w** have the rule over you, NIG
13: 9 **w** have not profited them that have been *3739*
13:10 whereof they have no right to eat **w** serve NIG
13:21 working in you *that* **w** *is* well pleasing in his NIG
Jas 1: 1 to the twelve tribes **w** are scattered abroad, *3588*
1:12 **w** the Lord hath promised to them that love *3739*
1:21 **w** is able to save your souls. *3588*
2: 5 heirs of the kingdom **w** he hath promised to *3739*
2: 7 *that* worthy name by the **w** ye are called? NIG
2:16 not those *things* **w** *are* needful to the body; NIG
2:23 And the scripture was fulfilled **w** saith, *3588*
3: 4 **w** though they be so great, and are driven of NIG
3: 9 **w** are made after the similitude of God. *3588*
5: 4 the hire of the labourers **w** have reaped *3588*
5: 4 **w** is of you kept back by fraud, crieth: NIG
5: 4 the cries of them **w** have reaped are entered NIG
5:11 Behold, we count them happy **w** endure. NIG
5:20 that he **w** converteth the sinner from NIG
1Pe 1: 3 **w** according to his abundant mercy hath *3588*
1:10 Of **w** salvation the prophets have inquired *3739*
1:11 what manner of time the Spirit of Christ **w** *3588*
1:12 **w** are now reported unto you by them that *3739*
1:12 **w** *things the* angels desire to look into. *3739*
1:15 But as he **w** hath called you is holy, so be ye NIG
1:23 word of God, **w** liveth and abideth for ever. NIG
1:25 And this is the word **w** by the gospel is NIG
2: 7 therefore **w** believe *he is* precious: *3588*
2: 7 but unto them **w** be disobedient, the stone NIG
2: 7 the stone **w** the builders disallowed, *3739*

1Pe 2: 8 *even to them* **w** stumble at the word, *3739*
2:10 **W** in time past *were* not a people, but *3588*
2:10 **w** had not obtained mercy, but now have *3588*
2:11 from fleshly lusts, **w** war against the soul; *3748*
2:12 by *your* good works, **w** they shall behold, NIG
3: 4 in *that* **w** *is* not corruptible, *even* NIG
3: 4 **w** is in the sight of God of great price. *3739*
3:13 if ye be followers of *that* **w** *is* good? NIG
3:19 By **w** also he went and preached unto *3739*
3:20 **W** sometime were disobedient, when once NIG
4:11 *let him do it* as of the ability **w** God giveth: *3739*
4:12 concerning the fiery trial **w** is to try you, NIG
5: 1 The elders **w** are among you I exhort, NIG
5: 2 Feed the flock of God **w** is among you, NIG
2Pe 1:18 And this voice **w** came from heaven we NIG
2:11 **w** are greater in power and might, NIG
2:15 **W** have forsaken the right way, and NIG
3: 1 in both **w** I stir up your pure minds by way *3739*
3: 2 That *ye* may be mindful of the words **w** NIG
3: 7 But the heavens and the earth, **w** are now, NIG
3:10 in the **w** the heavens shall pass away with a *3739*
3:16 speaking in them of these *things;* in **w** are *3739*
3:16 **w** *they that are* unlearned and *3739*
1Jn 1: 1 *That* **w** was from the beginning, which we *3739*
1: 1 **w** we have heard, which we have seen with *3739*
1: 1 have heard, **w** we have seen with our eyes, *3739*
1: 1 **w** we have looked upon, and our hands *3739*
1: 2 **w** was with the Father, and was manifested *3748*
1: 3 *That* **w** we have seen and heard declare we *3739*
1: 5 is the message **w** we have heard of him, *3739*
2: 7 an old commandment **w** ye had from *3739*
2: 7 The old commandment is the word **w** ye *3739*
2: 8 unto you, **w** *thing* is true in him and in you: *3739*
2:24 **w** ye have heard from the beginning. *3739*
2:24 If *that* **w** ye have heard from the beginning *3739*
2:27 But the anointing **w** ye have received of *3739*
2:29 ye know that every one **w** doeth *3588*
3:24 in us, by the Spirit **w** he hath given us. *3739*
5: 9 for this is the witness of God **w** he hath *3739*
5:16 If any *man* see his brother sin a sin **w** *is* not NIG
2Jn 1: 2 **w** dwelleth in us, and shall be with us for *3588*
1: 5 but *that* **w** we had from the beginning, *3739*
1: 8 that we lose not *those things* **w** we have *3739*
3Jn 1: 6 **W** have borne witness of thy charity before *3739*
1:10 I will remember his deeds **w** he doeth, *3739*
1:11 follow not *that* **w** *is* evil, but *that which is* NIG
1:11 not *that which is* evil, but *that* **w** *is* good. NIG
Jude 1: 3 faith **w** was once delivered unto the saints. NIG
1: 6 And the angels **w** kept not their first estate, NIG
1:10 But these speak evil of those *things* **w** they *3745*
1:15 deeds **w** they have ungodly committed, *3739*
1:15 of all *their* hard *speeches* **w** ungodly sinners *3739*
1:17 remember ye the words **w** were spoken NIG
Rev 1: 1 of Jesus Christ, **w** God gave unto him, *3739*
1: 1 to shew unto his servants *things* **w** must *3739*
1: 3 and keep those *things* **w** are written therein: NIG
1: 4 John to the seven churches **w** are in Asia: *3588*
1: 4 from him **w** is, and which was, and *3588*
1: 4 which is, and **w** was, and which is to come; *3588*
1: 4 which is, and which was, and **w** is to come; *3588*
1: 4 from the seven spirits **w** are before his *3739*
1: 7 shall see him, and they *also* **w** pierced him: *3748*
1: 8 **w** is, and which was, and which is to come, *3588*
1: 8 which is, and **w** was, and which is to come, *3588*
1: 8 which is, and which was, and **w** is to come, *3588*
1:11 send *it* unto the seven churches **w** are in *3588*
1:19 Write *the things* **w** thou hast seen, and *3739*
1:19 and *the things* **w** are, and *the things* which *3739*
1:19 and *the things* **w** shall be hereafter; *3739*
1:20 The mystery of the seven stars **w** thou *3739*
1:20 the seven candlesticks **w** thou sawest are *3739*
2: 2 how thou canst not bear *them* **w** *are* evil: NIG
2: 2 thou hast tried them **w** say *they* are apostles, NIG
2: 6 the deeds of the Nicolaitans, **w** I also hate. *3739*
2: 7 **w** is in the midst of the paradise of God. *3739*
2: 8 and the last, **w** was dead, and is alive; *3739*
2: 9 *I know* the blasphemy of them **w** say they NIG
2:10 Fear none *of those things* **w** thou shalt *3739*
2:12 These *things* saith he **w** hath the sharp NIG
2:15 doctrine of the Nicolaitans, **w** *thing* I hate. *3739*
2:17 **w** no *man* knoweth saving he that *3739*
2:20 **w** calleth herself a prophetess, to teach and *3588*
2:23 all the churches shall know that I am he **w** NIG
2:24 and **w** have not known the depths of Satan, *3748*
2:25 But *that* **w** ye have *already* hold fast till I *3739*
3: 2 and strengthen the *things* **w** remain, NIG
3: 4 **w** have not defiled their garments; *3739*
3: 9 **w** say they are Jews, and are not, but do lie; *3588*
3:10 **w** shall come upon all the world, to try *3588*
3:11 hold *that* fast **w** thou hast, that no *man* take *3739*
3:12 of the city of my God, **w** *is* new Jerusalem, NIG
3:12 **w** cometh down out of heaven from my *3588*
4: 1 the first voice **w** I heard *was* as *it were* of a *3739*
4: 1 **w** said, Come up hither, and I will shew NIG
4: 1 I will shew thee *things* **w** must be hereafter. *3739*
4: 5 the throne, **w** are the seven spirits of God. *3739*
4: 8 **w** was, and is, and is to come. *3588*
5: 6 **w** are the seven spirits of God sent forth *3739*
5: 8 full of odours, **w** are the prayers of saints. *3739*
5:13 And every creature **w** is in heaven, and *3739*
6: 9 of God, and for the testimony **w** they held: *3739*
7: 4 And I heard the number of them **w** were NIG
7: 9 **w** no *man* could number, of all nations, and *3739*
7:10 Salvation to our God **w** sitteth upon *3588*
7:13 What are these **w** are arrayed in white *3588*
7:14 These are they **w** came out of great NIG
7:17 For the Lamb **w** is in the midst of *3588*
8: 2 And I saw the seven angels **w** stood before *3739*
8: 3 the golden altar **w** was before the throne. *3588*
8: 4 **w** *came* with the prayers of the saints, NIG
8: 6 And the seven angels **w** had the seven *3588*
8: 9 And the third *part* of the creatures **w** were in NIG
8:13 of the three angels, **w** are yet to sound. NIG
9: 4 only *those* men **w** have not the seal of God *3748*
9:11 **w** *is* the angel of the bottomless *pit,* whose NIG

Rev 9:13 horns of the golden altar **w** is before God, *3588*
9:14 Saying to the sixth angel **w** had *3739*
9:14 Loose the four angels **w** are bound in *3588*
9:15 **w** were prepared for an hour, and a day, *3588*
9:18 the brimstone, **w** issued out of their mouths. *3588*
9:20 And the rest of the men **w** were not killed *3739*
9:20 **w** neither can see, nor hear, nor walk: *3739*
10: 4 Seal *up those things* **w** the seven thunders *3739*
10: 5 And the angel **w** I saw stand upon the sea *3739*
10: 6 and the sea, and the *things* **w** are therein, NIG
10: 8 And the voice **w** I heard from heaven spake *3739*
10: 8 take the little book **w** is open in the hand of *3588*
10: 8 hand of the angel **w** standeth upon the sea *3588*
11: 2 But the court **w** is without the temple leave *3588*
11: 8 **w** spiritually is called Sodom and Egypt, *3748*
11:11 and great fear fell upon them **w** saw them. NIG
11:16 **w** sat before God on their seats, *3588*
11:17 **w** art, and wast, and art to come; *3588*
11:18 shouldest destroy them **w** destroy the earth. NIG
12: 4 the dragon stood before the woman **w** was *3588*
12: 9 and Satan, **w** deceiveth the whole world: *3588*
12:10 **w** accused them before our God day and *3588*
12:13 he persecuted the woman **w** brought forth *3748*
12:16 swallowed up the flood **w** the dragon cast *3739*
12:17 **w** keep the commandments of God, and *3588*
13: 2 And the beast **w** I saw was like unto a *3739*
13: 4 And they worshipped the dragon **w** gave *3739*
13:12 them **w** dwell therein to worship the first NIG
13:14 **w** he had power to do in the sight of *3739*
13:14 **w** had the wound by a sword, and did live. *3739*
14: 3 **w** were redeemed from the earth. *3588*
14: 4 These are they **w** were not defiled with *3739*
14: 4 These are they **w** follow the Lamb NIG
14:10 **w** is poured out without mixture into *3588*
14:13 Blessed *are* the dead **w** die in the Lord from *3588*
14:17 another angel came out of the temple **w** *3588*
14:18 out from the altar, **w** had power over fire; *3588*
16: 2 grievous sore upon the men **w** had the mark *3588*
16: 2 and *upon* them **w** worshipped his image. NIG
16: 5 O Lord, **w** art, and wast, and shalt be, *3588*
16: 9 of God, **w** hath power over these plagues: *3588*
16:14 **w** go forth unto the kings of the earth and *3739*
17: 1 And there came one of the seven angels **w** *3588*
17: 7 **w** hath the seven heads and ten horns. *3588*
17: 9 *And* here *is* the mind **w** hath wisdom. *3588*
17: 9 seven mountains, on **w** the woman sitteth. *846*
17:12 And the ten horns **w** thou sawest are ten *3739*
17:12 **w** have received no kingdom as yet; *3748*
17:15 saith unto me, The waters **w** thou sawest, *3739*
17:16 And the ten horns **w** thou sawest upon *3739*
17:18 And the woman **w** thou sawest is *that* great *3739*
17:18 **w** reigneth over the kings of the earth. *3588*
18: 6 in the cup **w** she hath filled fill to her *3739*
18:14 and all *things* **w** *were* dainty and goodly are NIG
18:15 The merchants of these *things,* **w** were *3588*
19: 2 **w** did corrupt the earth with her fornication, *3748*
19: 9 Blessed *are* they **w** are called unto NIG
19:14 And the armies **w** were in heaven followed NIG
19:20 with **w** he deceived them that had received *3739*
19:21 **w** *sword* proceeded out of his mouth: *3588*
20: 2 **w** is the devil, and Satan, and bound him a *3739*
20: 4 and **w** had not worshipped the beast, *3748*
20: 8 And shall go out to deceive the nations **w** *3588*
20:12 book was opened, **w** is *the book* of life: *3739*
20:12 the dead were judged out of those *things* **w** NIG
20:13 And the sea gave up the dead **w** were in it; *3588*
20:13 hell delivered up the dead **w** were in them: *3588*
21: 8 shall have their part in the lake **w** burneth *3588*
21: 8 and brimstone: **w** is the second death. *3739*
21: 9 **w** had the seven vials full of the seven last *3588*
21:12 **w** are *the names* of the twelve tribes of *3739*
21:24 And the nations of them **w** are saved shall NIG
21:27 they **w** are written in the Lamb's book of NIG
22: 2 **w** bare twelve *manner of* fruits, *and* NIG
22: 6 servants *the things* **w** must shortly be done. *3739*
22: 8 of the angel **w** shewed me these *things.* *3588*
22: 9 of them **w** keep the sayings of this book: NIG
22:11 and he **w** is filthy, let him be filthy still: and NIG
22:19 *from* the *things* **w** are written in this book. NIG
22:20 He **w** testifieth these *things* saith, Surely I NIG

WHILE (210) [WHILES, WHILST]

Ge 8:22 **W** the earth remaineth, seedtime and 3605+5750
19:16 **And w** he lingered, the men laid hold 2050.1
25: 6 **w** he yet lived, eastward, unto the east 871.1
29: 9 **w** he **yet** spake with them, Rachel came 5750
45: 1 **w** Joseph made himself known unto his 871.1
46:29 his neck, and wept on his neck a **good w.** 5750
Ex 33:22 shall come to pass, **w** my glory passeth by, 871.1
33:22 will cover thee with my hand **w** I pass by: 5704
34:29 of his face shone **w** he talked with him. 871.1
Lev 4:27 **w** he doeth somewhat against *any of* 871.1
14:46 **w** that it is shut up shall be unclean until 3117
26:43 **w** she lieth desolate without them: 871.1
Nu 11:33 **w** the flesh *was* **yet** between their teeth, 5750
15:32 **And w** the children of Israel were in 2050.1
23:15 **W** I meet *the* LORD yonder. 2050.1
25:11 **w** he was zealous for my sake among 871.1
Dt 19: 6 **w** his heart is hot, and overtake him, 3588
31:27 behold, **w** I am yet alive with you *this* day, 871.1
Jos 14:10 **w** *the children of* Israel wandered in 834
Jdg 3:26 Ehud escaped **w** they tarried, and passed 5704
11:26 **W** Israel dwelt in Heshbon and her towns, 871.1
14:17 him the seven days, **w** their feast lasted: 834
15: 1 it came to pass **within a w after,** 3117+4480
16:27 women, that beheld **w** Samson made sport. 871.1
1Sa 2:13 servant came, **w** the flesh was in seething, 3509.1
7: 2 **w** the ark abode in Kirjath-jearim, 3117+4480
9:27 stand thou still a **w**, that I 3117+1886.1+3509.1
14:19 came to pass, **w** Saul talked unto the priest, 5704
20:14 thou shalt not only **w yet** I live shew me 5750
22: 4 they dwelt with him all the **w** that David 3117
25: 7 unto them, all the **w** they were in Carmel. 3117
25:16 all the **w** we were with them keeping 3117
27:11 *will be* his manner all the **w** he dwelleth in 3117

W

2Sa 3: 6 **w** there was war between the house of Saul 871.1
3:35 cause David to eat meat **w** it was yet day, 871.1
7:19 house for a **great w to come**. 4480+7350
12:18 Behold, **w** the child was *yet* alive, 871.1
12:21 and weep for the child, ***w** it was* alive; NIH
12:22 **W** the child *was* yet alive, I fasted and 871.1
13:30 it came to pass, **w** they *were* in the way, NIH
15: 8 For thy servant vowed a vow **w** I abode at 871.1
15:12 *even* from Giloh, **w** he offered sacrifices. 871.1
17: 2 I will come upon him **w** he *is* weary and 2050.1
18:14 **w** he *was* **yet** alive in the midst of the oak. 5750
19:32 he had provided the king of sustenance **w** 871.1
24:13 before thine enemies, **w** they pursue thee? 2050.1
1Ki 1:14 **w** thou **yet** talkest there with the king, 5750
1:22 lo, **w** she **yet** talked with the king, 5750
1:42 **w** he **yet** spake, behold, Jonathan the son of 5750
3:20 **w** thine handmaid slept, and laid it in her 2050.1
6: 7 heard in the house, **w** it was in building. 871.1
12: 6 that stood before Solomon his father **w** he 871.1
17: 7 it came to pass after a **w**, that the brook 3117
18:45 **in the mean w**, 3541+3541+5704+5704+2050.1
2Ki 6:33 **w** he **yet** talked with them, behold, 5750
1Ch 12: 1 **w** he **yet** kept himself close because of Saul 5750
17:17 house for a **great w to come**, 4480+7350
21:12 **w** that the sword of thine enemies 2050.1
2Ch 10: 6 before Solomon his father **w** he *yet* lived, 871.1
14: 7 gates, and bars, ***w*** the land *is* yet before us; NIH
15: 2 The LORD *is* with you, **w** ye be with 871.1
26:19 **w** he was wroth with the priests, 871.1
34: 3 year of his reign, **w** he was yet young, 2050.1
Ne 7: 3 **w** they stand by, let them shut the doors, 5704
Est 2:21 **w** Mordecai sat in the king's gate, 2050.1
6:14 **w** they *were* **yet** talking with him, came 5750
Job 1:16 **W** he *was* **yet** speaking, there came also 5750
1:17 **W** he *was* **yet** speaking, there came also 5750
1:18 **W** he *was* **yet** speaking, there came also 5704
20:23 and shall rain *it* upon him **w** he is eating. 871.1
24:24 They are exalted for a **little w**, but are gone 4592
27: 3 All the **w** my breath *is* in me, and the spirit 5750
Ps 7: 2 *it* in pieces, **w** *there is* none to deliver. 2050.1
31:13 **w** they took counsel together against me, 871.1
37:10 For yet a **little w**, and the wicked *shall* not 4592
39: 1 will keep my mouth with a bridle, **w** 5750+871.1
39: 3 within me, **w** I was musing the fire burned: 871.1
42: 3 and night, **w** *they* continually say unto me, 871.1
42:10 **w** they say daily unto me, Where *is* thy 871.1
63: 4 Thus will I bless thee **w** I live: I will lift up 871.1
69: 3 is dried: mine eyes fail **w** *I* wait for my God. NIH
78:30 But **w** their meat *was* **yet** in their mouths, 5750
88:15 ready to die from *my* youth *up:* **w** I suffer NIH
104:33 to my God **w** I **have** my **being**. 5750+871.1
146: 2 **W** I live will I praise the LORD: I will 871.1
146: 2 unto my God **w** I **have** *any* **being**. 5750+871.1
Pr 8:26 **W as yet** he had not made the earth, nor 5704
19:18 Chasten thy son **w** there is hope, and let not 3588
31:15 She riseth also **w** *it is* yet night, and 871.1
Ecc 9: 3 madness *is* in their heart **w** they live, and 871.1
12: 1 **w** the evil days come not, nor 834+5704
12: 2 **W** the sun, or the light, or the moon, 834+5704
SS 1:12 **W** the king *sitteth* at his table, 5704+7945
Isa 10:25 For yet a **very little w**, and 4213+4592
28: 4 **w** it is yet in his hand he eateth it up. 871.1
29:17 *Is* it not yet a **very little w**, 4213+4592
55: 6 Seek ye the LORD **w** he may be found, 871.1
55: 6 be found, call ye upon him **w** he is near: 871.1
63:18 holiness have possessed *it* but a **little w**: 4705
Jer 13:16 and, **w** ye look for light, he turn it into NIH
15: 9 her sun is gone down **w** *it was* yet day: 871.1
33: 1 **w** he was yet shut up in the court of 2050.1
39:15 **w** he was shut up in the court of the prison, 871.1
40: 5 Now **w** he was not yet gone back, *he said,* NIH
51:33 yet a **little w**, and the time of her harvest 4592
La 1:19 **w** they sought their meat, to relieve their 3588
Eze 9: 8 **w** they were slaying them, and I *was* left, 3509.1
Da 4:31 **W** the word *was* in the king's mouth, 5751
Hos 1: 4 for yet a little ***w***, and I will avenge the blood NIH
Na 1:10 For **w** *they be* folden together *as* thorns, and NIH
1:10 **w** they be drunken *as* drunkards, 3509.1
Hag 2: 6 it *is* a **little w**, and I *will* shake the heavens, 4592
Zec 14:12 Their flesh *shall* consume away **w** they 2050.1
Mt 1:20 But **w** he thought on these *things*, behold, NIG
9:18 **W** he spake these *things* unto them, behold, NIG
12:46 **W** he **yet** talked to the people, behold, *2089*
13:21 he not root in himself, but dureth **for a w**: *4340*
13:25 But **w** men slept, his enemy came *1722+3588*
13:29 lest **w** ye gather up the tares, ye root up also NIG
14:22 **w** he sent the multitudes away. *2193+3739*
17: 5 **W** he yet spake, behold, a bright cloud NIG
17:22 And **w** they abode in Galilee, Jesus said NIG
22:41 **W** the Pharisees were gathered together, *1161*
25: 5 **W** the bridegroom tarried, they all *1161*
25:10 And **w** they went to buy, the bridegroom NIG
26:36 Sit ye here, **w** I go and pray yonder. *2193+3739*
26:47 And **w** he **yet** spake, lo, Judas, one of *2089*
26:73 And after a **w** came unto *him* they that *3398*
27:63 **w** he was **yet** alive, After three days I will *2089*
28:13 by night, and stole him *away* **w** we slept. NIG
Mk 1:35 rising up a **great w** before day, he went out, *3029*
2:19 **w** the bridegroom is with them? *1722+3739*
5:35 **W** he **yet** spake, there came from the ruler *2089*
6:31 apart into a desert place, and rest a **w**: *3641*
6:45 unto Bethsaida, **w** he sent away the people. *2193*
12:35 and said, **w** he taught in the temple, NIG
14:32 to his disciples, Sit ye here, **w** I shall pray. *2193*
14:43 **w** he **yet** spake, cometh Judas, one of *2089*
15:44 he asked him whether he had been **any w** *3819*
Lk 1: 8 *that* **w** he executed the priest's office *1722+3588*
2: 6 And so it was *that*, **w** they *1510+1722+3588*
5:34 **w** the bridegroom is with them? *1722+3739*
8:13 which for a **w** believe, and in time of *2540*
8:49 **W** he yet spake, there cometh one from NIG
9:34 **W** he thus spake, there came a cloud, and *1161*
9:43 But **w** they wondered every one at all *things* NIG
10:13 they had a **great w ago** repented, sitting in *3819*
14:32 Or else, **w** the other is yet a great way off, NIG
Lk 18: 4 And he would not for a **w**: but afterward he *5550*
22:47 And **w** he yet spake, behold a multitude, NIG
22:58 And after a **little w** another saw him, and *1024*
22:60 **w** he **yet** spake, the cock crew. *2089*
24:15 that **w** they communed *together* and *1722+3588*
24:32 **w** he talked with us by the way, and *5613*
24:32 and **w** he opened to us the scriptures? *5613*
24:41 And **w** they **yet** believed not for joy, and *2089*
24:44 **w** I was yet with you, that all *things* must be NIG
24:51 And it came to pass, **w** he blessed *1722+3588*
Jn 4:31 In the **mean w** *his* disciples prayed him, *3342*
5: 7 but **w** I am coming, another steppeth *1722+3739*
7:33 Yet a little **w** am I with you, and *then* I go *5550*
9: 4 the works of him that sent me, **w** it is day: *2193*
12:35 Yet a little **w** is the light with you. *5550*
12:35 Walk **w** ye have the light, lest darkness *2193*
12:36 **W** ye have light, believe in the light, that ye *2193*
13:33 Little children, yet a **little w** I am with you. *3398*
14:19 **Yet a** little **w**, and the world seeth me no *2089*
16:16 A **little w**, and ye shall not see me: and *3398*
16:16 and again, a **little w**, and ye shall see me, *3398*
16:17 unto us, A **little w**, and ye shall not see me: *3398*
16:17 and again, a **little w**, and ye shall see me: *3398*
16:18 What is this that he saith, A **little w**? *3398*
16:19 I said, A **little w**, and ye shall not see me: *3398*
16:19 and again, a **little w**, and ye shall see me? *3398*
17:12 **W** I was with them in the world, I kept *3753*
Ac 1: 9 And when he had spoken these *things*, **w** NIG
1:10 And **w** they looked stedfastly toward *5613*
9:39 which Dorcas made, **w** she was with them. NIG
10:10 but **w** they made ready, he fell into a trance, NIG
10:17 Now **w** Peter doubted in himself what *this* *5613*
10:19 **W** Peter thought on the vision, the Spirit *1161*
10:44 **W** Peter yet spake these words, the Holy NIG
15: 7 ye know how that **a good w ago** *575+744+2250*
17:16 Now **w** Paul waited for them at Athens, his NIG
18:18 *after this* tarried *there* yet a **good w**, *2250+2425*
19: 1 pass that, **w** Apollos was at Corinth, *1722+3588*
20:11 and eaten, and talked a **long w**, *1909+2425*
22:17 even **w** I prayed in the temple, I was in a NIG
24:20 doing in me, **w** I stood before the council, NIG
25: 8 **W** he answered for himself, Neither against NIG
27:33 And **w** the day was coming on, Paul *891+3739*
28: 6 but after they had looked a **great w**, *1909+4183*
Ro 2:15 and *their* thoughts the mean **w** accusing or NIG
5: 8 in that, **w** we were yet sinners, Christ died NIG
7: 3 So then if, **w** *her* husband liveth, she be NIG
1Co 3: 4 For **w** one saith, I am of Paul; and another, *3752*
8:13 I will eat no flesh **w** the world **standeth**, *1519*
16: 7 but I trust to tarry a **w** with you, if the Lord *5550*
2Co 4:18 **W** we look not at the *things* which are seen, NIG
Gal 2:17 But if, **w** we seek to be justified by Christ, NIG
1Ti 5: 6 But she that liveth in pleasure is dead **w** she NIG
6:10 which **w** some coveted after, they have NIG
Heb 3:13 another daily, **w** it is called To day; *891+3739*
9: 8 **w as** the first tabernacle was **yet** standing: *2089*
10:37 For yet a **little w**, *3398+3745+3745*
1Pe 3: 2 **W** they behold your chaste conversation NIG
3:20 **w** the ark was a preparing, wherein few, NIG
5:10 after that ye have suffered a **w**, make you *3641*
2Pe 2:13 their own deceivings **w** they feast with you; NIG
2:19 **W** they promise them liberty, NIG

WHILES (12) [WHILE]

Ps 49:18 Though **w** he lived he blessed his soul: and 871.1
Isa 65:24 and **w** they are yet speaking, I will hear. NIH
Eze 21:29 **W** *they* see vanity unto thee; whiles *they* 871.1
21:29 unto thee, **w** *they* divine a lie unto thee, 871.1
44:17 **w** they minister in the gates of the inner 871.1
Da 5: 2 Belshazzar, **w** *he* tasted the wine, 871.2
9:20 **w** I *was* speaking, and praying, and 5750
9:21 Yea, **w** I *was* speaking in prayer, even 5750
Hos 7: 6 their heart like an oven, **w** they lie in wait: 871.1
Mt 5:25 **w** thou art in the way with him; *2193+3748*
Ac 5: 4 **W** it remained, was it not thine own? and NIG
2Co 9:13 **W** by the experiment of this ministration NIG

WHILST (12) [WHILE]

Jdg 6:31 let him be put to death **w** *it is yet* morning: 5704
Ne 6: 3 **w** I leave it, and come down to you? 834+3509.1
Job 8:12 **W** it *is* **yet** in his greenness, *and* not cut 5750
32:11 **w** you searched out what to say. 5704
Ps 141:10 into their own nets, **w** that I withal escape. 5704
Jer 17: 2 **W** their children remember their altars 3509.1
2Co 5: 6 knowing that, **w** we are at home in the body, NIG
7:15 **w** he remembereth the obedience of you all, NIG
Heb 3:15 **W** it is said, To day if ye will hear *1722+3588*
9:17 otherwise it is of no strength at all **w** *3753*
10:33 **w** ye were made a gazingstock both by NIG
10:33 **w** ye became companions of them that were NIG

WHIP (2) [WHIPS]

Pr 26: 3 A **w** for the horse, a bridle for the ass, and 7752
Na 3: 2 The noise of a **w**, and the noise of 7752

WHIPS (4) [WHIP]

1Ki 12:11 my father hath chastised you with **w**, but 7752
12:14 my father *also* chastised you with **w**, but 7752
2Ch 10:11 my father chastised you with **w**, but I *will* 7752
10:14 my father chastised you with **w**, but I *will* 7752

WHIRLETH (1) [WHIRLWIND, WHIRLWINDS]

Ecc 1: 6 it **w about continually**, and 1980+5437+5437

WHIRLWIND (27) [WHIRLETH, WIND]

2Ki 2: 1 would take up Elijah *into* heaven by a **w**, 5591
2:11 and Elijah went up by a **w** *into* heaven. 5591
Job 37: 9 Out of the south cometh the **w**: and cold out 5492
38: 1 the LORD answered Job out of the **w**, 5591
40: 6 the LORD unto Job out of the **w**, 5591
Ps 58: 9 he shall **take** them **away as with a w**, 8175
Pr 1:27 and your destruction cometh as a **w**; 5492
10:25 As the **w** passeth, so *is* the wicked no *more:* 5492
Isa 5:28 counted like flint, and their wheels like a **w**: 5492
Isa 17:13 and like a rolling thing before the **w**. 5492
40:24 and the **w** shall take them away as stubble. 5591
41:16 them away, and the **w** shall scatter them: 5591
66:15 with his chariots like a **w**, to render his 5492
Jer 4:13 as clouds, and his chariots *shall be* as a **w**: 5492
23:19 a **w** of the LORD is gone forth *in* fury, 5591
23:19 is gone forth *in* fury, even a grievous **w**: 5591
25:32 a great **w** shall be raised up from the coasts 5591
30:23 the **w** of the LORD goeth forth *with* fury, 5591
30:23 goeth forth *with* fury, a continuing **w**: 5591
Eze 1: 4 behold, a **w** came out of the north, 5591+7307
Da 11:40 the north shall **come** against him **like a w**, 8175
Hos 8: 7 sown the wind, and they shall reap the **w**: 5492
13: 3 as the chaff *that* is **driven with a w** out of 5590
Am 1:14 with a tempest in the day of the **w**: 5492
Na 1: 3 *wicked:* the LORD *hath* his way in the **w** 5492
Hab 3:14 they **came out as a w** to scatter me: 5590
Zec 7:14 I **scattered** them **with a w** among all 5590

WHIRLWINDS (2) [WHIRLETH, WIND]

Isa 21: 1 As **w** in the south pass through; *so* 5492
Zec 9:14 and shall go with **w** of the south. 5591

WHISPER (2) [WHISPERED, WHISPERER, WHISPERERS, WHISPERINGS]

Ps 41: 7 All that hate me **w** together against me: 3907
Isa 29: 4 and thy speech shall **w** out of the dust. 6850

WHISPERED (1) [WHISPER]

2Sa 12:19 when David saw that his servants **w**, David 3907

WHISPERER (1) [WHISPER]

Pr 16:28 and a **w** separateth chief friends. 5372

WHISPERERS (1) [WHISPER]

Ro 1:29 murder, debate, deceit, malignity; **w**, *5588*

WHISPERINGS (1) [WHISPER]

2Co 12:20 strifes, backbitings, **w**, swellings, tumults: *5587*

WHIT (5)

Dt 13:16 all the spoil thereof **every w**, for 3632
1Sa 3:18 Samuel told him every **w**, and hid nothing 1697
Jn 7:23 I have made a man **every w** whole on *3650*
13:10 save to wash *his* feet, but is clean **every w**: *3650*
2Co 11: 5 For I suppose *I* was **not a w** behind *3367*

WHITE (75) [WHITED, WHITER]

Ge 30:35 *and* every one that had *some* **w** in it, and 3836
30:37 pilled **w** strakes in them, and made 3836
30:37 made the **w** appear which *was* in the rods. 3836
40:16 behold, *I had* three **w** baskets on my head: 2751
49:12 *be* red with wine, and *his* teeth **w** with milk. 3836
Ex 16:31 it *was* like coriander seed, **w**; and the taste 3836
Lev 13: 3 and *when* the hair in the plague is turned **w**, 3836
13: 4 If the bright spot *be* **w** in the skin of his 3836
13: 4 and the hair thereof be not turned **w**; 3836
13:10 *if* the rising *be* **w** in the skin, and it have 3836
13:10 it have turned the hair **w**, and *there be* 3836
13:13 the plague: it is all turned **w**: he *is* clean. 3836
13:16 be changed unto **w**, he shall come unto 3836
13:17 behold, *if* the plague be turned into **w**; then 3836
13:19 in the place of the boil there be a **w** rising, 3836
13:19 **w**, *and* somewhat reddish, and it be shewed 3836
13:20 the skin, and the hair thereof be turned **w**; 3836
13:21 *there be* no **w** hairs therein, and *if* it *be* not 3836
13:24 the quick *flesh* that burneth have a **w** bright 3836
13:24 white bright spot, somewhat reddish, or **w**; 3836
13:25 *if* the hair in the bright spot be turned **w**, 3836
13:26 *there be* no **w** hair in the bright spot, and 3836
13:38 their flesh bright spots, *even* **w** bright spots; 3836
13:39 spots in the skin of their flesh *be* darkish **w**; 3836
13:42 or bald forehead, a **w** reddish sore; 3836
13:43 *if* the rising of the sore *be* **w** reddish in his 3836
Nu 12:10 behold, Miriam *became* leprous, ***w*** as snow: NIH
Jdg 5:10 Speak, ye that ride on **w** asses, ye that sit in 6715
2Ki 5:27 he went out from his presence a leper *as **w*** NIH
2Ch 5:12 and their brethren, *being* arrayed in **w linen**, 948
Est 1: 6 *Where were* **w**, green, and blue *hangings*, 2353
1: 6 of red, and blue, and **w**, and black marble. 1858
8:15 of the king in royal apparel *of* blue and **w**, 2353
Job 6: 6 or is there *any* taste in the **w** of an egg? 7388
Ps 68:14 kings in it, it was ***w*** as snow in Salmon. NIH
Ecc 9: 8 Let thy garments be always **w**; and let thy 3836
SS 5:10 My beloved *is* **w** and ruddy, the chiefest 6703
Isa 1:18 be as scarlet, they shall be as **w** as snow; 3835
Eze 27:18 in the wine of Helbon, and **w** wool. 6713
Da 7: 9 whose garment *was* **w** as snow, and the hair 2358
11:35 and to purge, and to **make** *them* **w**, 3835
12:10 shall be purified, and **made w**, and tried; 3835
Joel 1: 7 *it* away; the branches thereof are **made w**. 3835
Zec 1: 8 him *were there* red horses, speckled, and **w**. 3836
6: 3 in the third chariot **w** horses; and in 3836
6: 6 the **w** go forth after them; and the grisled 3836
Mt 5:36 thou canst not make one hair **w** or black. *3022*
17: 2 the sun, and his raiment was **w** as the light. *3022*
28: 3 like lightning, and his raiment **w** as snow: *3022*
Mk 9: 3 became shining, exceeding **w** as snow; *3022*
9: 3 so as no fuller on earth can **w** *them.* *3021*
16: 5 the right side, clothed in a long **w** garment; *3022*
Lk 9:29 and his raiment *was* **w** *and* glistering. *3022*
Jn 4:35 the fields; for they are **w** already to harvest. *3022*
20:12 And seeth two angels in **w** sitting, the one *3022*
Ac 1:10 two men stood by them in **w** apparel; *3022*
Rev 1:14 His head and *his* hairs *were* **w** like wool, *3022*
1:14 hairs were white like wool, *as* **w** as snow; *3022*
2:17 and will give him a **w** stone, and in *3022*
3: 4 and they shall walk with me in **w**: *3022*
3: 5 the same shall be clothed in **w** raiment; *3022*
3:18 and **w** raiment, that thou mayest be clothed, *3022*
4: 4 twenty elders sitting, clothed in **w** raiment; *3022*
6: 2 And I saw, and behold a **w** horse: and *3022*
6:11 And **w** robes were given unto every one of *3022*
7: 9 clothed with **w** robes, and palms in their *3022*

Rev 7:13 What are these which are arrayed in **w** *3022*
7:14 **made** them **w** in the blood of the Lamb. *3021*
14:14 and behold a **w** cloud, and upon the cloud *3022*
15: 6 clothed in pure and **w** linen, and *2986*
19: 8 be arrayed in fine linen, clean and **w**: *2986*
19:11 saw heaven opened, and behold a **w** horse; *3022*
19:14 in heaven followed him upon **w** horses, *3022*
19:14 clothed in fine linen, **w** and clean. *3022*
20:11 And I saw a great **w** throne, and him that *3022*

WHITED (2) [WHITE]

Mt 23:27 for ye are like unto **w** sepulchres, *2867*
Ac 23: 3 God shall smite thee, *thou* **w** wall: *2867*

WHITER (2) [WHITE]

Ps 51: 7 wash me, and I shall be **w** than snow. 3835
La 4: 7 purer than snow, they were **w** than milk, 6705

WHITEWASH See MORTER

WHITHER (124) [WHITHERSOEVER]

Ge 16: 8 **w** wilt thou go? And she said, I flee 575+1886.5
20:13 at every place **w** we shall 834+8033+1886.5
28:15 and will keep thee in all *places* **w** thou goest, 834
32:17 **w** goest thou? and whose *are* these 575+1886.5
37:30 The child *is* not; and I, **w** shall I go? 575+1886.5
Ex 21:13 thee a place **w** he shall flee. 834+8033+1886.5
34:12 inhabitants of the land **w** thou goest, 834+5921
Lev 18: 3 **w** I bring you, shall ye not do: 834+8033+1886.5
20:22 **w** I bring you to dwell therein, 834+8033+1886.5
Nu 13:27 We came unto the land **w** thou sentest us, 834
15:18 into the land **w** I bring you, 834+8033+1886.5
35:25 of his refuge, **w** he was fled: 834+8033+1886.5
35:26 of his refuge, **w** he was fled; 834+8033+1886.5
Dt 1:28 **W** shall we go up? our brethren 575+1886.5
3:21 the kingdoms **w** thou passest. 834+8033+1886.5
4: 5 the land **w** ye go to possess it. 834+8033+1886.5
4:14 **w** ye go over to possess it. 834+8033+1886.5
4:27 **w** the LORD shall lead you. 834+8033+1886.5
6: 1 the land **w** ye go to possess it: 834+8033+1886.5
7: 1 **w** thou goest to possess it, 834+8033+1886.5
11: 8 **w** ye go to possess it; 834+8033+1886.5
11:10 For the land, **w** thou goest in 834+8033+1886.5
11:11 the land, **w** ye go to possess it, 834+8033+1886.5
11:29 **w** thou goest to possess it, 834+8033+1886.5
12:29 **w** thou goest to possess them, 834+8033+1886.5
21:14 then thou shalt let her go **w** she will; 3807.1
23:12 **w** thou shalt go forth abroad: 8033+1886.5
23:20 **w** thou goest to possess it. 834+8033+1886.5
28:21 **w** thou goest to possess it. 834+8033+1886.5
28:37 among all nations **w** 834+8033+1886.5
28:63 **w** thou goest to possess it. 834+8033+1886.5
30: 1 **w** the LORD thy God hath 834+8033+1886.5
30: 3 **w** the LORD thy God hath 834+8033+1886.5
30:16 **w** thou goest to possess it. 834+8033+1886.5
30:18 **w** thou passest over Jordan to 834+8033+1886.5
31:13 long as ye live in the land **w** 834+8033+1886.5
31:16 **w** they go *to be* amongst 834+8033+1886.5
32:47 **w** ye go over Jordan to 834+8033+1886.5
32:50 die in the mount **w** thou goest 834+8033+1886.5
Jos 2: 5 **w** the men went I wot not: 575+1886.5
Jdg 19:17 the old man said, **W** goest thou? and 575+1886.5
Ru 1:16 for **w** thou goest, I will go; and 413+834
1Sa 10:14 said unto him and to his servant, **W** went ye? 575
27:10 Achish said, **W** have ye made a road to day? 408
2Sa 2: 1 David said, **W** shall I go up? And he 575+1886.5
13:13 I, **w** shall I cause my shame to go? 575+1886.5
15:20 seeing I go **w** I may, return thou, and 834+5921
17:18 had a well in his court; **w** they went down. 8033
1Ki 2:36 thence **any w**. 575+575+1886.5+1886.5+2050.1
2:42 *abroad* **any w**, 575+575+1886.5+1886.5+2050.1
8:47 the land **w** they were carried captives, 834+8033
18:10 **w** my lord hath not sent to seek thee: 834+8033
18:12 LORD shall carry thee **w** I know not; 834+5921
21:18 **w** he is gone down to possess it. 834+8033
2Ki 5:25 went no **w**. 575+575+1886.5+1886.5+2050.1
2Ch 6:37 in the land **w** they are carried captive, 834+8033
6:38 **w** they have carried them captives, and 834
10: 2 **w** he had fled from the presence of Solomon 834
Ne 2:16 the rulers knew not **w** I went, or 575+1886.5
Ps 122: 4 **W** the tribes go up, the tribes of 7945+8033
139: 7 **W** shall I go from thy spirit? or 575+1886.5
139: 7 or **w** shall I flee from thy presence? 575+1886.5
Ecc 9:10 in the grave, **w** thou goest. 834+8033+1886.5
SS 6: 1 **W** is thy beloved gone, O thou 575+1886.5
6: 1 **w** is thy beloved turned aside? 575+1886.5
Isa 20: 6 **w** we flee for help to be delivered 834+8033
Jer 8: 3 which remain in all the places **w** I have 8033
15: 2 say unto thee, **W** shall we go forth? 575+1886.5
16:15 lands **w** he had driven them: 834+8033+1886.5
19:14 **w** the LORD had sent him to 834+8033
22:12 he shall die in the place **w** they have 834+8033
23: 3 of all countries **w** I have driven them, 834+8033
23: 8 all countries **w** I had driven them; 834+8033
24: 9 in all places **w** I shall drive them. 834+8033
29: 7 seek the peace of the city **w** I 834+8033+1886.5
29:14 all the places **w** I have driven you, 834+8033
29:18 among all the nations **w** I have driven 834+8033
30:11 of all nations **w** I have scattered thee, 834+8033
32:37 **w** I have driven them in mine anger, 834+8033
40: 4 **w** it seemeth good and convenient for thee to 413
40:12 out of all places **w** they were driven, 834+8033
42:22 in the place **w** ye desire to go *and* 834+8033
43: 5 **w** they had been driven, to dwell in 834+8033
44: 8 **w** ye be gone to dwell, that ye might 834+8033
45: 5 for a prey in all places **w** thou goest. 834+8033
46:28 nations **w** I have driven thee: 834+8033+1886.5
49:36 there shall be no nation **w** the outcasts 834+8033
Eze 1:12 **w** the spirit was to go, they went; 8033+1886.5
4:13 the Gentiles, **w** I will drive them. 834+8033
6: 9 **w** they shall be carried captives, 834+8033
10:11 *to* the place **w** the head looked they followed 834
12:16 among the heathen **w** they come; 834+8033
29:13 people **w** they were scattered: 834+8033+1886.5
Eze 36:20 **w** they went, they profaned my holy 834+8033
36:21 the heathen, **w** they went. 834+8033+1886.5
36:22 among the heathen, **w** ye went. 834+8033
37:21 **w** they be gone, and will gather them 834+8033
47: 9 shall live **w** the river cometh. 834+8033+1886.5
Da 9: 7 through all the countries **w** thou hast 834+8033
Joel 3: 7 place **w** ye have sold them, 834+8033+1886.5
Zec 2: 2 said I, **W** goest thou? And he said 575+1886.5
5:10 **W** do these bear the ephah? 575+1886.5
Lk 10: 1 and place, **w** he himself would come. *3757*
24:28 drew nigh unto the village, **w** they went: *3757*
Jn 3: 8 not tell whence it cometh, and **w** it goeth: *4226*
6:21 the ship was at the land **w** they went. *1519+3739*
7:35 **W** will he go, that we shall not find him? *4226*
8:14 for I know whence I came, and **w** I go; but *4226*
8:14 ye cannot tell whence I come, and **w** I go. *4226*
8:21 die in your sins: **w** I go, ye cannot come. *3699*
8:22 because he saith, **W** I go, ye cannot come. *3699*
12:35 in darkness knoweth not **w** he goeth. *4226*
13:33 unto the Jews, **W** I go, ye cannot come; *3699*
13:36 Peter said unto him, Lord, **w** goest thou? *4226*
13:36 Jesus answered him, **W** I go, thou canst not *3699*
14: 4 And **w** I go ye know, and the way ye know. *3699*
14: 5 unto him, Lord, we know not **w** thou goest; *4226*
16: 5 and none of you asketh me, **W** goest thou? *4226*
18:20 in the temple, **w** the Jews always resort; *3699*
21:18 and walkedst **w** thou wouldest: *3699*
21:18 and carry *thee* **w** thou wouldest not. *3699*
Heb 6:20 **W** the forerunner is for us entered, *3699*
11: 8 and he went out, not knowing **w** he went. *4226*
1Jn 2:11 and knoweth not **w** he goeth, because *4226*

WHITHERSOEVER (29) [EVER, SO, WHITHER]

Jos 1: 7 mayest prosper **w** thou goest. 834+3605+871.1
1: 9 God *is* with thee **w** thou goest. 834+3605+871.1
1:16 **w** thou sendest us, we will go. 413+834+3605
Jdg 2:15 **W** they went out, the hand of 834+3605+871.1
1Sa 14:47 **w** he turned himself, he vexed 834+3605+871.1
18: 5 David went out **w** Saul sent 834+3605+871.1
23:13 of Keilah, and went **w** they could go. 834+871.1
2Sa 7: 9 I was with thee **w** thou wentest, 834+3605+871.1
8: 6 the LORD preserved David **w** 834+3605+871.1
8:14 the LORD preserved David **w** 834+3605+871.1
1Ki 2: 3 and **w** thou turnest thyself: 834+3605+8033
8:44 **w** thou shalt send 834+1870+871.1+1886.5
2Ki 18: 7 he prospered **w** he went forth: 834+3605+871.1
1Ch 17: 8 I have been with thee **w** thou 834+3605+871.1
18: 6 preserved David **w** he went. 834+3605+871.1
18:13 preserved David **w** he went. 834+3605+871.1
Est 4: 3 **w** the king's commandment and 834+4725
8:17 **w** the king's commandment and 834+4725
Pr 17: 8 hath it: **w** it turneth, it prospereth. 413+834+3605
21: 1 of water: he turneth it **w** he will. 834+3605+5921
Eze 1:20 **W** the spirit was to go, 834+5921+8033
21:16 on the left, **w** thy face *is* set. 575+1886.5
47: 9 **w** the rivers shall come, 413+834+3605
Mt 8:19 I will follow thee **w** thou goest. *1437+3699*
Mk 6:56 And **w** he entered, into villages, or *302+3699*
Lk 9:57 Lord, I will follow thee **w** thou goest. *302+3699*
1Co 16: 6 may bring me on my journey **w** I go. *1437+3757*
Jas 3: 4 small helm, **w** the governor listeth. *302+3699*
Rev 14: 4 which follow the Lamb **w** he goeth. *302+3699*

WHO (969) [WHOM, WHOMSOEVER, WHOSE, WHOSO, WHOSOEVER]

Ge 3:11 he said, **W** told thee that thou *wast* naked? 4310
12: 7 unto the LORD, **w** appeared unto him. 1886.1
14:12 **w** dwelt in Sodom, and his goods, and 1931
21: 7 **W** would have said unto Abraham, 4310
21:26 I wot not **w** hath done this thing: 4310
24:15 **w** was born to Bethuel, son of Milcah, 834
24:27 **w** hath not left destitute my master of his 834
27:18 and he said, Here *am* I; **w** *art* thou, my son? 4310
27:32 Isaac his father said unto him, **W** *art* thou? 4310
27:33 trembled very exceedingly, and said, **W**? 4310
30: 2 **w** hath withheld from thee the fruit of 834
33: 5 and said, **W** *are* those with thee? 4310
35: 3 **w** answered me in the day of my distress, 1886.1
36: 1 *are* the generations of Esau, **w** *is* Edom. 1931
36:19 **w** *is* Edom, and these *are* their dukes. 1931
36:20 of Seir the Horite, **w** inhabited the land; NIH
36:35 **w** smote Midian in the field of Moab, 1886.1
42:30 The man, **w** *is* the lord of the land, NIH
43:22 we cannot tell **w** put our money in our 4310
48: 8 Joseph's sons, and said, **W** *are* these? 4310
48:14 **w** *was* the younger, and his left hand upon 1931
49: 9 and as an old lion; **w** shall rouse him up? 4310
49:25 by the God of thy father, **w** shall help thee; NIH
49:25 **w** shall bless thee *with* blessings of heaven NIH
Ex 2:14 **W** made thee a prince and a judge over us? 4310
3:11 Moses said unto God, **W** *am* I, that I should 4310
4:11 said unto him, **W** hath made man's mouth? 4310
4:11 or **w** maketh the dumb, or deaf, or 4310
4:28 all the words of the LORD **w** had sent him, 834
5: 2 Pharaoh said, **W** *is* the LORD, that I 4310
5:20 met Moses and Aaron, **w** stood in the way, NIH
6:12 hear me, **w** *am* of uncircumcised lips? 589
10: 8 your God: *but* **w** *are* they that shall go? 4310
12:27 **w** passed over the houses of the children of 834
12:40 **w** dwelt in Egypt, *was* four hundred and 834
15:11 **W** *is* like unto thee, O LORD, among 4310
15:11 **w** *is* like thee, glorious in holiness, 4310
18:10 **w** hath delivered you out of the hand of 834
18:10 **w** hath delivered the people from under 834
21: 8 **w** hath betrothed her to himself, then shall he 834
32:26 and said, **W** *is* on the LORD'S side? 4310
Lev 5: 8 **w** shall offer *that* which *is* for the sin 2050.1
12: 7 **W** shall offer it before the LORD, and NIH
27:12 valuest it, **w** *art* the priest, so shall it be. NIH
Nu 6:21 This *is* the law of the Nazarite **w** hath 834
7: 2 **w** *were* the princes of the tribes, and were 1992
9: 6 **w** were defiled by the dead body of a man, 834
11: 4 and said, **W** shall give us flesh to eat? 4310
11:18 **W** shall give us flesh to eat? 4310
Nu 12: 7 *is* not so, **w** *is* faithful in all mine house. 1931
14:36 **w** returned, and made all the congregation NIH
16: 5 Even to morrow the LORD will shew **w** *are* 834
16: 5 will shew who *are* his, and **w** *is* holy; NIH
21:26 **w** had fought against the former king of 1931
23:10 **W** can count the dust of Jacob, and 4310
24: 9 **w** shall stir him up? Blessed *is* he that 4310
24:23 Alas, **w** shall live when God doeth this! 4310
25: 6 **w** *were* weeping *before* the door of 1992
26: 9 **w** strove against Moses and against Aaron in 834
26:47 **w** *were* fifty and three thousand and NIH
26:63 **w** numbered the children of Israel in 834
27:21 **w** shall ask *counsel* for him after NIH
31:27 **w** went out to battle, and between all 1886.1
Dt 1:33 **W** went in the way before you, to search 1886.1
2:25 **w** shall hear report of thee, and 834
4: 7 *so* great, **w** hath God *so* nigh unto them, 834
4:46 **w** dwelt at Heshbon, whom Moses and 834
5: 3 *even* us, **w** *are* all of us here alive *this* day. 428
5:26 For **w** *is there of* all flesh, that hath heard 4310
8:15 **W** led thee through *that* great and terrible 1886.1
8:15 **w** brought thee forth water out of the rock 1886.1
8:16 **W** fed thee in the wilderness with manna, 1886.1
9: 2 *of whom* thou hast heard *say*, **W** can stand 4310
21: 1 *and* it be not known **w** hath slain him: 4310
30:12 **W** shall go up for us to heaven, and bring it 4310
30:13 **W** shall go over the sea for us, and bring it 4310
33: 9 **W** said unto his father and to his mother, 1886.1
33:26 **w** rideth *upon* the heaven in thy help, and NIH
33:29 **w** *is* like unto thee, O people saved by 4310
33:29 and **w** *is* the sword of thy excellency! 834
Jos 9: 8 Joshua said unto them, **W** *are* ye? and 4310
11: 8 **w** smote them, and chased them unto great NIH
12: 2 **w** dwelt in Heshbon, *and* ruled from 1886.1
13:12 **w** remained of the remnant of the giants: 1931
15:19 **W** answered, Give me a blessing; 2050.1
17:16 *both they* **w** *are* of Beth-shean and 834
17:16 and *they* **w** *are* of the valley of Jezreel. 834
21:10 *w were* of the children of Levi, had: NIH
Jdg 1: 1 **W** shall go up for us against the Canaanites 4310
2: 7 **w** had seen all the great works of 834
3: 9 **w** delivered them, *even* Othniel the son of NIH
3:19 **w** said, Keep silence. And all that stood by NIH
6:29 one to another, **W** hath done this thing? 4310
6:35 **w** also was gathered after him: 1931
7: 1 **w** *is* Gideon, and all the people that *were* 1931
8:34 **w** had delivered them out of the hands of 1886.1
9:28 **W** *is* Abimelech, and who *is* Shechem, 4310
9:28 Who *is* Abimelech, and **w** *is* Shechem, 4310
9:38 wherewith thou saidst, **W** *is* Abimelech, 4310
11:39 **w** did with her *according to* his vow which NIH
15: 6 the Philistines said, **W** hath done this? 4310
17: 4 **w** made thereof a graven image and NIH
17: 5 one of his sons, **w** became his priest. NIH
17: 7 **w** *was* a Levite, and he sojourned there. 1931
18: 2 **w** when they came *to* mount Ephraim, to NIH
18: 3 and said unto him, **W** brought thee hither? 4310
18:29 of Dan their father, **w** was born unto Israel: 834
19: 1 **w** took to him a concubine out of NIH
21: 5 **W** *is there* among all the tribes of Israel 4310
Ru 2: 3 **w** *was* of the kindred of Elimelech. 834
2:20 **w** hath not left off his kindness to the living 834
3: 9 he said, **W** *art* thou? And she answered, 4310
3:16 in law, she said, **W** *art* thou, my daughter? 4310
1Sa 2:25 the LORD, **w** shall intreat for him? 4310
4: 8 **w** shall deliver us out of the hand of these 4310
6:20 **W** is able to stand before this holy LORD 4310
10:12 and said, But **w** *is* their father? 4310
10:19 **w** himself saved you out of all your 834
11:12 **W** *is* he that said, Shall Saul reign over us? 4310
14:17 Number now, and see **w** is gone from us. 4310
14:45 **w** hath wrought this great salvation in Israel? 834
16:16 out a man, **w** *is* a cunning player on a harp: NIH
17:25 it shall be, *that* the man **w** killeth him, 834
17:26 for **w** *is* this uncircumcised Philistine, that 4310
18:18 David said unto Saul, **W** *am* I? and what *is* 4310
20:10 said David to Jonathan, **W** shall tell me? 4310
22:14 **w** *is so* faithful among all thy servants as 4310
23:22 his haunt is, *and* **w** hath seen him there: 4310
25:10 David's servants, and said, **W** *is* David? 4310
25:10 **w** *is* the son of Jesse? there be many 4310
26: 6 **W** will go down with me to Saul to 4310
26: 9 for **w** can stretch forth his hand against 4310
26:14 and said, **W** *art* thou *that* criest to the king? 4310
26:15 **w** *is* like to thee in Israel? wherefore then 4310
30:23 **w** hath preserved us, and delivered NIH
30:24 For **w** will hearken unto you in this matter? 4310
2Sa 1: 8 he said unto me, **W** *art* thou? And I 4310
1:24 weep over Saul, **w** clothed you in scarlet, 1886.1
1:24 **w** put on ornaments of gold upon your 1886.1
4: 5 of Ish-bosheth, **w** lay on a bed at noon. 1931
4: 9 **w** hath redeemed my soul out of all 834
4:10 **w** *thought* that I would have given him a 834
6:20 **w** uncovered himself to day in the eyes of 834
7:18 and he said, **W** *am* I, O Lord GOD? 4310
10:18 the captain of their host, **w** died there. NIH
11:21 **W** smote Abimelech the son of 4310
12:22 **W** can tell *whether* GOD will be gracious 4310
16:10 **W** shall then say, Wherefore hast thou done 4310
22: 4 on the LORD, **w** is *worthy* to be praised: NIH
22:32 For **w** *is* God, save the LORD? and who *is* 4310
22:32 and **w** *is* a rock, save our God? 4310
23: 1 and the man **w** was raised up on high, NIH
23:20 of Kabzeel, **w** had done many acts, NIH
1Ki 1:20 that *thou* shouldest tell them **w** shall sit on 4310
1:27 **w** should sit on the throne of my lord 4310
2:24 **w** hath made me a house, as he promised, 834
2:32 **w** fell upon two men more righteous and 834
3: 9 for **w** is able to judge this thy *so* great a 4310
8:23 **w** keepest covenant and mercy with thy NIH
8:24 **W** hast kept with thy servant David my 834
8:50 give them compassion before them **w** NIH
9: 9 **w** brought forth their fathers out of the land 834
12: 2 the son of Nebat, **w** was yet in Egypt, 1931
12: 9 this people, **w** have spoken to me, saying, 834

1Ki 12:18 sent Adoram, w was over the tribute; 834
13:26 w was disobedient unto the word of 834
14: 8 w kept my commandments, and 834
14: 8 and w followed me with all his heart, 834
14:14 w shall cut off the house of Jeroboam that 834
14:16 w did sin, and who made Israel to sin. 834
14:16 who did sin, and w made Israel to sin. 834
17: 1 w was of the inhabitants of Gilead, NIH
19:19 w was plowing with twelve yoke of oxen 1931
20:14 he said, W shall order the battle? And he 4310
21:11 the nobles w were the inhabitants in his city, 834
22:20 W shall persuade Ahab, that he may go up 4310
22:52 the son of Nebat, w made Israel to sin: 834
2Ki 4: 5 upon her sons, w brought the vessels to her; 1992
7:17 w spake when the king came down to him. 834
8:14 w said to him, What said Elisha to thee? NIH
9:31 Had Zimri peace, w slew his master? NIH
9:32 to the window, and said, W is on my side? 4310
9:32 w? And there looked out to him two or 4310
10: 9 and slew him: but w slew all these? 4310
10:13 Ahaziah king of Judah, and said, W are ye? 4310
10:29 w made Israel to sin, Jehu departed not from 834
13: 6 w made Israel sin, but walked therein: 834
13:11 the son of Nebat, w made Israel sin: 834
14:24 the son of Nebat, w made Israel to sin. 834
15: 9 the son of Nebat, w made Israel to sin. 834
15:18 the son of Nebat, w made Israel to sin. 834
15:24 the son of Nebat, w made Israel to sin. 834
15:28 the son of Nebat, w made Israel to sin. 834
17:36 w brought you up out of the land of Egypt 834
18:35 W are they among all the gods of 4310
23:15 w made Israel to sin, had made, both that 834
23:16 God proclaimed, w proclaimed these words. 834
1Ch 2: 7 w transgressed in the thing accursed. 834
2:22 w had three and twenty cities in the land 2050.2
4:22 w had the dominion in Moab, and 834
5: 8 the son of Joel, w dwelt in Aroer, even unto 1931
5:10 war with the Hagarites, w fell by their hand: NIH
6:39 brother Asaph, w stood on his right hand, 1886.1
7:24 w built Beth-horon the nether, and NIH
7:31 and Malchiel, w is the father of Birzavith. 1931
8:12 and Shamed, w built Ono, and Lod, 1931
8:13 w were heads of the fathers of 1992
8:13 w drove away the inhabitants of Gath: 1992
9: 1 w were carried away to Babylon for their NIH
9:18 W hitherto waited in the king's gate NIH
9:31 w was the firstborn of Shallum 1931
9:33 w remaining in the chambers were free: NIH
11:10 w strengthened themselves with him in 1886.1
11:12 w was one of the three mighties. 1931
11:22 man of Kabzeel, w had done many acts; NIH
12:18 w was chief of the captains, and he said, NIH
16:41 were chosen, w were expressed by name, 834
17:16 said, W am I, O LORD God, and what is 4310
19: 7 w came and pitched before Medeba. NIH
21:16 the elders of Israel, w were clothed in NIH
22: 9 be born to thee, w shall be a man of rest; 1931
24:28 Of Mahli came Eleazar, w had no sons. 2050.2
25: 1 w should prophesy with harps, 1886.1
25: 3 w prophesied with a harp, to give thanks 1886.1
25: 9 w with his brethren and sons were twelve: 1931
27: 6 w was mighty among the thirty, and NIH
29: 5 w then is willing to consecrate his service 4310
29:14 w am I, and what is my people, that we 4310
2Ch 1:10 for w can judge this thy people, that is so 4310
2: 6 w is able to build him a house, seeing 4310
2: 6 w am I then, that I should build him a 4310
2:12 w hath given to David the king a wise son, 834
6: 4 w hath with his hands fulfilled that which NIH
8: 8 w were left after them in the land, 834
10: 2 Jeroboam the son of Nebat, w was in Egypt, NIH
17:16 w willingly offered himself unto 1886.1
18:19 W shall entice Ahab king of Israel, that he 4310
19: 6 the LORD, w is with you in the judgment. NIH
20: 7 w didst drive out the inhabitants of this land NIH
20:34 w is mentioned in the book of the kings of 834
20:35 king of Israel, w did very wickedly: 1931
22: 9 w sought the LORD with all his heart. 834
26: 1 w was sixteen years old, and made him 1931
26: 5 w had understanding in the visions of 1886.1
28: 5 w smote him with a great slaughter. NIH
30: 7 w therefore gave them up to desolation, NIH
32: 4 w stopt all the fountains, and the brook that NIH
32:14 W was there among all the gods of those 4310
32:31 w sent unto him to inquire of the wonder 1886.1
34:26 w sent you to inquire of the LORD, so 1886.1
35:21 w is with me, that he destroy thee not. 834
36:13 w had made him swear by God: 834
36:17 w slew their young men with the sword in NIH
36:23 W is there among you of all his people? 4310
Ezr 1: 3 W is there among you of all his people? 4310
3:12 w were ancient men that had seen the first NIH
5: 3 W hath commanded you to build this 4479
5: 9 W commanded you to build this house, and 4479
5:12 w destroyed this house, and carried NIH
Ne 1:11 of thy servants, w desire to fear thy name: 1886.1
3: 3 w also laid the beams thereof, and set up 1992
6:10 the son of Mehetabeel, w was shut up; 1931
6:11 w is there, that, being as I am, would go 4310
7: 7 W came with Zerubbabel, Jeshua, 1886.1
9: 7 w didst choose Abram, and broughtest him 834
9:27 the hand of their enemies, w vexed them: NIH
9:27 w saved them out of the hand of their NIH
9:32 w keepest covenant and mercy, NIH
13:26 w was beloved of his God, and God made 2050.1
Est 2: 6 W had been carried away from Jerusalem 834
2:15 w had taken her for his daughter, was come 834
2:22 w told it unto Esther the queen; NIH
4:11 w is not called, there is one law of his to put 834
4:14 w knoweth whether thou art come to 4310
6: 2 w sought to lay hand on the king Ahasuerus. 834
6: 4 the king said, W is in the court? 4310
7: 5 Esther the queen, W is he, and where is he, 4310
7: 9 w had spoken good for the king, standeth in 834
Job 3: 8 w are ready to raise up their mourning. 1886.1
3:15 w filled their houses with silver: 1886.1
4: 2 but w can withhold himself from speaking? 4310
4: 7 Remember, I pray thee, w ever perished, 4310
5:10 W giveth rain upon the earth, and 1886.1
9: 4 w hath hardened himself against him, and 4310
9:12 Behold, he taketh away, w can hinder him? 4310
9:12 w will say unto him, What doest thou? 4310
9:19 w shall set me a time to plead? 4310
9:24 judges thereof; if not, where, and w is he? 4310
11:10 or gather together, then w can hinder him? 4310
12: 3 yea, w knoweth not such things as these? 4310
12: 4 w calleth upon God, and he answereth him: NIH
12: 9 W knoweth not in all these that the hand of 4310
13:19 W is he that will plead with me? for now, 4310
14: 4 W can bring a clean thing out of an 4310
16: 9 He teareth me in his wrath, w hateth me: NIH
17: 3 w is he that will strike hands with me? 4310
17:15 my hope? as for my hope, w shall see it? 4310
21:31 W shall declare his way to his face? and 4310
21:31 and w shall repay him what he hath done? 4310
23:13 he is in one mind, and w can turn him? and 4310
24:25 w will make me a liar, and make my speech 4310
26:14 the thunder of his power w can understand? 4310
27: 2 w hath taken away my judgment; NIH
27: 2 and the Almighty, w hath vexed my soul; NIH
30: 4 W cut up mallows by the bushes, and 1886.1
34: 7 like Job, w drinketh up scorning like water? NIH
34:13 W hath given him a charge over the earth? 4310
34:13 or w hath disposed the whole world? 4310
34:29 giveth quietness, w then can make trouble? 4310
34:29 he hideth his face, w then can behold him? 4310
35:10 God my Maker, w giveth songs in the night; NIH
35:11 W teacheth us more than the beasts of NIH
36:22 exalteth by his power: w teacheth like him? 4310
36:23 W hath enjoined him his way? or who can 4310
36:23 or w can say, Thou hast wrought iniquity? 4310
38: 2 W is this that darkeneth counsel by words 4310
38: 5 W hath laid the measures thereof, if thou 4310
38: 5 or w hath stretched the line upon it? 4310
38: 6 or w laid the corner stone thereof; 4310
38: 8 Or w shut up the sea with doors, when it NIH
38:25 W hath divided a watercourse for 4310
38:28 or w hath begotten the drops of dew? 4310
38:29 hoary frost of heaven, w hath gendered it? 4310
38:36 W hath put wisdom in the inward parts? or 4310
38:36 or w hath given understanding to the heart? 4310
38:37 W can number the clouds in wisdom? or 4310
38:37 or w can stay the bottles of heaven, 4310
38:41 W provideth for the raven his food? 4310
39: 5 W hath sent out the wild ass free? or 4310
39: 5 or w hath loosed the bands of the wild ass? 4310
41:10 him up: w then is able to stand before me? 4310
41:11 W hath prevented me, that I should repay 4310
41:13 W can discover the face of his garment? or 4310
41:13 w can come to him with his double bridle? 4310
41:14 W can open the doors of his face? his teeth 4310
41:33 is not his like, w is made without fear. 1886.1
42: 3 W is he that hideth counsel without 4310
Ps 4: 6 many that say, W will shew us any good? 4310
6: 5 in the grave w shall give thee thanks? 4310
8: 1 w hast set thy glory above the heavens. 834
12: 4 W have said, With our tongue will we 834
12: 4 our lips are our own: w is lord over us? 4310
14: 4 w eat up my people as they eat bread, and NIH
15: 1 LORD, w shall abide in thy tabernacle? 4310
15: 1 w shall dwell in thy holy hill? 4310
16: 7 bless the LORD, w hath given me counsel: 834
17: 9 my deadly enemies, w compass me about. NIH
18: T w spake unto the LORD the words of this 834
18: 3 upon the LORD, w is worthy to be praised: NIH
18:31 For w is God save the LORD? or who is a 4310
18:31 the LORD? or w is a rock save our God? 4310
19:12 W can understand his errors? cleanse thou 4310
24: 3 W shall ascend into the hill of the LORD? 4310
24: 3 and w shall stand in his holy place? 4310
24: 4 w hath not lift up his soul unto vanity, 834
24: 8 W is this King of glory? the LORD strong 4310
24:10 W is this King of glory? The LORD of 4310
34: T w drove him away, and he departed. NIH
35:10 shall say, LORD, w is like unto thee, 4310
37: 7 because of him w prospereth in his way, NIH
37: 7 of the man w bringeth wicked devices to NIH
39: 6 and knoweth not w shall gather them. 4310
42:11 w is the health of my countenance, and NIH
43: 5 w is the health of my countenance, and NIH
53: 4 w eat up my people as they eat bread: NIH
59: 7 are in their lips: for w, say they, doth hear? 4310
60: 9 W will bring me into the strong city? 4310
60: 9 the strong city? w will lead me into Edom? 4310
64: 3 W whet their tongue like a sword, and 834
64: 5 snares privily; they say, W shall see them? 4310
65: 5 w art the confidence of all the ends of NIH
68:19 w daily loadeth us with benefits, even NIH
71:19 very high, w hast done great things: O God, 834
71:19 great things: O God, w is like unto thee! 4310
72:18 of Israel, w only doeth wondrous things. 2050.2
73:12 are the ungodly, w prosper in the world; NIH
76: 7 w may stand in thy sight when once thou 4310
77:13 w is so great a God as our God? 4310
78: 6 w should arise and declare them to their NIH
83:12 W said, Let us take to ourselves the houses 834
84: 6 W passing through the valley of Baca make NIH
89: 6 For w in the heaven can be compared unto 4310
89: 6 w among the sons of the mighty can be NIH
89: 8 w is a strong LORD like unto thee? 4310
90:11 W knoweth the power of thine anger? 4310
94:16 W will rise up for me against the evildoers? 4310
94:16 w will stand up for me against the workers 4310
103: 3 W forgiveth all thine iniquities; 1886.1
103: 3 w healeth all thy diseases; 1886.1
103: 4 W redeemeth thy life from destruction; 1886.1
103: 4 W crowneth thee with lovingkindness and 1886.1
103: 5 W satisfieth thy mouth with good things; 1886.1
104: 2 W coverest thyself with light as with a NIH
104: 2 w stretchest out the heavens like a curtain: NIH
Ps 104: 3 W layeth the beams of his chambers in 1886.1
104: 3 w maketh the clouds his chariot: 1886.1
104: 3 w walketh upon the wings of the wind: 1886.1
104: 4 W maketh his angels spirits; his ministers a NIH
104: 5 W laid the foundations of the earth, that it NIH
105:17 even Joseph, w was sold for a servant: NIH
106: 2 W can utter the mighty acts of the LORD? 4310
106: 2 w can shew forth all his praise? NIH
108:10 W will bring me into the strong city? 4310
108:10 the strong city? w will lead me into Edom? 4310
108:11 Wilt not thou, O God, w hast cast us off? NIH
113: 5 W is like unto the LORD our God, who 4310
113: 5 the LORD our God, w dwelleth on high, NIH
113: 6 W humbleth himself to behold the things 1886.1
119: 1 w walk in the law of the LORD. 1886.1
119:38 unto thy servant, w is devoted to thy fear. 834
124: 1 If it had not been the LORD w was on our 7945
124: 2 If it had not been the LORD w was on our 7945
124: 6 w hath not given us as a prey to their teeth. 7945
124: 8 of the LORD, w made heaven and earth. NIH
130: 3 mark iniquities, O Lord, w shall stand? 4310
135: 8 W smote the firstborn of Egypt, both of 7945
135: 9 W sent tokens and wonders into the midst NIH
135:10 W smote great nations, and slew mighty 7945
136: 4 To him w alone doeth great wonders: for his NIH
136:23 W remembered us in our low estate: for his 7945
136:25 W giveth food to all flesh: for his mercy NIH
137: 7 w said, Rase it, rase it, even to 1886.1
137: 8 of Babylon, w art to be destroyed; 1886.1
140: 4 w have purposed to overthrow my goings. 834
144: 2 I trust; w subdueth my people under me. 1886.1
144:10 w delivereth David his servant from 1886.1
147: 8 W covereth the heaven with clouds, 1886.1
147: 8 w prepareth rain for the earth, 1886.1
147: 8 w maketh grass to grow upon 1886.1
147:17 like morsels: w can stand before his cold? 4310
Pr 2:13 W leave the paths of uprightness, to walk 1886.1
2:14 W rejoice to do evil, and delight in 1886.1
9:15 To call passengers w go right on their 1886.1
18:14 but a wounded spirit w can bear? 4310
20: 6 but a faithful man w can find? 4310
20: 9 W can say, I have made my heart clean, 4310
20:25 It is a snare to the man w devoureth that NIH
21:24 is his name, w dealeth in proud wrath. NIH
23:29 W hath woe? who hath sorrow? who hath 4310
23:29 w hath sorrow? who hath contentions? 4310
23:29 w hath contentions? who hath babbling? 4310
23:29 w hath babbling? who hath wounds without 4310
23:29 w hath wounds without cause? who hath 4310
23:29 without cause? w hath redness of eyes? 4310
24:22 and w knoweth the ruin of them both? 4310
26:18 As a mad man w casteth firebrands, 1886.1
27: 4 but w is able to stand before envy? 4310
30: 4 W hath ascended up into heaven, or 4310
30: 4 w hath gathered the wind in his fists? 4310
30: 4 w hath bound the waters in a garment? 4310
30: 4 w hath established all the ends of the earth? 4310
30: 9 and deny thee, and say, W is the LORD? 4310
31:10 W can find a virtuous woman? for her price 4310
Ecc 2:19 w knoweth whether he shall be a wise man 4310
2:25 For w can eat, or who else can hasten 4310
2:25 or w else can hasten hereunto, more than I? 4310
3:21 W knoweth the spirit of man that goeth 4310
3:22 for w shall bring him to see what shall be 4310
4: 3 w hath not seen the evil work that is done 834
4:13 foolish king, w will no more be admonished. 834
6:12 For w knoweth what is good for man in this 4310
6:12 for w can tell a man what shall be after him 4310
7:13 for w can make that straight, which he hath 4310
7:24 and exceeding deep, w can find it out? 4310
8: 1 W is as the wise man? and who knoweth 4310
8: 1 w knoweth the interpretation of a thing? 4310
8: 4 and w may say unto him, What doest thou? 4310
8: 7 for w can tell him when it shall be? 4310
8:10 w had come and gone from the place of NIH
10:14 and what shall be after him, w can tell him? 4310
11: 5 thou knowest not the works of God w 834
12: 7 the spirit shall return unto God w gave it. 834
SS 3: 6 W is this that cometh out of the wilderness 4310
6:10 W is she that looketh forth as the morning, 4310
8: 2 my mother's house, w would instruct me: NIH
8: 5 W is this that cometh up from 4310
Isa 1:12 w hath required this at your hand, to tread 4310
6: 8 Whom shall I send, and w will go for us? 4310
14: 6 He w smote the people in wrath with a NIH
14:27 w shall disannul it? and his hand is 4310
14:27 is stretched out, and w shall turn it back? 4310
23: 8 W hath taken this counsel against Tyre, 4310
24:18 that he w fleeth from the noise of the fear 1886.1
27: 4 w would set the briers and thorns against 4310
29:15 are in the dark, and they say, W seeth us? 4310
29:15 they say, Who seeth us? and w knoweth us? 4310
29:22 w redeemed Abraham, concerning the house 834
33:14 W among us shall dwell with the devouring 4310
33:14 w amongst us shall dwell with everlasting 4310
36:20 W are they amongst all the gods of these 4310
37: 2 w was over the household, and Shebna 834
40:12 W hath measured the waters in the hollow 4310
40:13 W hath directed the spirit of the LORD, or 4310
40:14 w instructed him, and taught him in the path NIH
40:26 behold w hath created these things, that 4310
41: 2 W raised up the righteous man from 4310
41: 4 W hath wrought and done it, calling 4310
41:26 W hath declared from the beginning, 4310
42:19 W is blind, but my servant? or deaf, as my 4310
42:19 w is blind as he that is perfect, and blind as 4310
42:23 W among you will give ear to this? 4310
42:23 w will hearken and hear for the time to NIH
42:24 W gave Jacob for a spoil, and Israel to 4310
43: 9 w among them can declare this, and 4310
43:13 of my hand: I will work, and w shall let it? 4310
44: 7 w, as I, shall call, and shall declare it, and 4310
44:10 W hath formed a god, or molten a graven 4310
45:21 w hath declared this from ancient time? 4310
45:21 w hath told it from that time? have not I NIH

Isa 49:21 **W** hath begotten me these, seeing I have 4310
49:21 **w** hath brought up these? Behold, I was left 4310
50: 8 that justifieth me; **w** will contend with me? 4310
50: 8 **w** *is* mine adversary? let him come near to 4310
50: 9 help me; **w** *is* he *that* shall condemn me? 4310
50:10 **W** *is* among you that feareth the LORD, 4310
51:12 **w** *art* thou, that thou shouldest be afraid of 4310
51:19 come unto thee; **w** shall be sorry for thee? 4310
53: 1 **W** hath believed our report? and to whom 4310
53: 8 **w** shall declare his generation? for he was 4310
60: 8 **W** *are* these *that* fly as a cloud, and as 4310
63: 1 **W** *is* this *that* cometh from Edom, 4310
65:16 That he **w** blesseth himself in the earth 1886.1
66: 8 **W** hath heard such *a thing?* who hath seen 4310
66: 8 Who hath heard such *a thing?* **w** hath seen 4310
Jer 1:16 **w** have forsaken me, and have burnt incense 834
2:24 *in* her occasion **w** can turn her away? 4310
9:12 **W** *is* the wise man, that may understand 4310
9:12 **w** *is he* to whom the mouth of the LORD NIH
10: 7 **W** would not fear thee, O King of nations? 4310
15: 5 For **w** shall have pity upon thee, 4310
15: 5 or **w** shall bemoan thee? or who shall go 4310
15: 5 or **w** shall go aside to ask how thou doest? 4310
17: 9 and desperately wicked: **w** can know it? 4310
18:13 **w** hath heard such *things:* the virgin of 4310
20: 1 **w** *was* also chief governor in the house of 1931
20:15 Cursed *be* the man **w** brought tidings to my 834
21:13 which say, **W** shall come down against us? 4310
21:13 or **w** shall enter into our habitations? 4310
23:18 For **w** hath stood in the counsel of 4310
23:18 **w** hath marked his word, and heard *it?* 4310
26:20 **w** prophesied against this city and 1886.1
26:23 **w** slew him with the sword, and cast his NIH
30:21 for **w** *is* this that engaged his heart to 4310
36:32 **w** wrote therein from the mouth of Jeremiah NIH
46: 7 **W** *is* this *that* cometh up as a flood, 4310
49: 4 *saying,* **W** shall come unto me? 4310
49:19 **w** *is* a chosen *man, that* I may appoint over 4310
49:19 for **w** *is* like me? and who will appoint me 4310
49:19 **w** will appoint me the time? and who *is* that 4310
49:19 **w** *is* that shepherd that will stand before 4310
50:44 **w** *is* a chosen *man, that* I may appoint over 4310
50:44 for **w** *is* like me? and who will appoint me 4310
50:44 **w** will appoint me the time? and who *is* that 4310
50:44 **w** *is* that shepherd that will stand before 4310
52:25 **w** mustered the people of the land; 1886.1
La 2:13 *is* great like the sea: **w** can heal thee? 4310
3:37 **W** *is* he *that* saith, and it cometh to pass, 4310
Eze 10: 7 clothed with linen: **w** took *it,* and went out. NIH
Da 1:10 **w** hath appointed your meat and your drink: 834
2:23 **w** hast given me wisdom and might, 1768
3:15 **w** *is* that God that shall deliver you out of 4479
3:28 **w** hath sent his angel, and delivered his 1768
6:27 **w** hath delivered Daniel from the power of 1768
Hos 3: 1 **w** look to other gods, and love flagons of 1992
7: 4 **w** ceaseth from raising after *he* hath NIH
14: 9 **W** *is* wise, and he shall understand these 4310
Joel 2:11 and very terrible; and **w** can abide it? 4310
2:14 **W** knoweth *if* he will return and repent, and 4310
Am 1: 1 **w** was among the herdmen of Tekoa, 834
3: 8 The lion hath roared, **w** will not fear? 4310
3: 8 GOD hath spoken, **w** can but prophesy? 4310
3:10 **w** store up violence and robbery in their 1886.1
5: 7 *Ye* **w** turn judgment to wormwood, and 1886.1
Ob 1: 3 **W** shall bring me down *to* the ground? 4310
Jnh 3: 9 **W** can tell *if* God will turn and repent, and 4310
Mic 3: 2 **W** hate the good, and love the evil; NIH
3: 2 **w** pluck off their skin from off them, and NIH
3: 3 **W** also eat the flesh of my people, and 834
5: 8 **w**, if he go through, both treadeth down, and 834
6: 9 hear ye the rod, and **w** hath appointed it. 4310
7:18 **W** *is* a God like unto thee, that pardoneth 4310
Na 1: 6 **W** can stand before his indignation? and 4310
1: 6 **w** can abide in the fierceness of his anger? 4310
3: 7 **w** will bemoan her? whence shall I seek 4310
Hab 2: 5 **w** enlargeth his desire as hell, and *is* as 834
Zep 3:18 **w** are of thee, *to whom* the reproach of it NIH
Hag 2: 3 **W** *is* left among you that saw this house in 4310
Zec 4: 7 **W** *art* thou, O great mountain? 4310
4:10 For **w** hath despised the day of small 4310
Mal 1:10 **W** *is there* even among you that would shut 4310
3: 2 **w** *may* abide the day of his coming? and 4310
3: 2 **w** *shall* stand when he appeareth? for he *is* 4310
Mt 1:16 of whom was born Jesus, **w** is called Christ. 3588
3: 7 **w** hath warned you to flee from the wrath 5101
10: 2 **w** is called Peter, and Andrew his brother; 3588
10: 4 and Judas Iscariot, **w** also betrayed him. 3588
10:11 ye shall enter, inquire **w** in it is worthy; 5101
12:48 unto him that told him, **W** is my mother? 5101
12:48 is my mother? and **w** are my brethren? 5101
13: 9 **W** hath ears to hear, let him hear. 3588
13:43 **W** hath ears to hear, let him hear. 3588
13:46 **W**, when he had found one pearl of great 3739
18: 1 **W** is the greatest in the kingdom of 5101
19:25 saying, **W** then can be saved? 5101
21:10 all the city was moved, saying, **W** is this? 5101
21:23 and **w** gave thee this authority? 5101
24:45 **W** then is a faithful and wise servant, 5101
25:14 **w** called his own servants, and NIG
26: 3 of the high priest, **w** was called Caiaphas, 3588
26:68 *thou* Christ, **W** is he that smote thee? 5101
27:57 **w** also himself was Jesus' disciple: 3739
Mk 1:19 **w** also *were* in the ship mending *their* nets. 846
1:24 I know thee **w** thou art, the Holy One of 5101
2: 7 **w** can forgive sins but God only? 5101
3:33 saying, **W** is my mother, or my brethren? 5101
4:16 **w**, when they have heard the word, 3739
5: 3 **W** had *his* dwelling among the tombs; 3739
5:30 the press, and said, **W** touched my clothes? 5101
5:31 and sayest thou, **W** touched me? 5101
9:34 **w** *should be* the greatest. 5101
10:26 among themselves, **W** then can be saved? 5101
11:28 **w** gave thee this authority to do these 5101
13:34 **w** left his house, and gave authority to his NIG
15: 7 **w** had committed murder in 3748
Mk 15:21 **w** passed by, coming out of the country, NIG
15:41 (**W** also, when he was in Galilee, 3739
16: 3 **W** shall roll us away the stone from 5101
Lk 1:36 sixth month with her, **w** was called barren. 3588
3: 7 **w** hath warned you to flee from the wrath 5101
4:34 I know thee **w** thou art, the Holy One of 5101
5:12 **w** seeing Jesus fell on *his* face, and NIG
5:21 **W** is this which speaketh blasphemies? 5101
5:21 **W** can forgive sins, but God alone? 5101
7: 2 **w** was dear unto him, was sick, and 3739
7:39 would have known **w** and what manner of 5101
7:49 **W** is this that forgiveth sins also? 5101
8:45 And Jesus said, **W** touched me? When all 5101
8:45 press *thee,* and sayest thou, **W** touched me? 5101
9: 9 but **w** is this, of whom I hear such *things?* 5101
9:31 **W** appeared in glory, and spake of his 3739
10:22 and no *man* knoweth **w** the Son is, but 5101
10:22 and **w** the Father is, but the Son, and *he* to 5101
10:29 said unto Jesus, And **w** is my neighbour? 5101
12:14 **w** made me a judge or a divider over you? 5101
12:42 **W** then is *that* faithful and wise steward, 5101
16:11 **w** will commit to your trust the true *riches?* 5101
16:12 **w** shall give you that which is your own? 5101
16:14 **w** were covetous, heard all these *things:* and NIG
18:26 that heard *it* said, **W** then can be saved? 5101
18:30 **W** shall not receive manifold more in this 3739
19: 3 And he sought to see Jesus **w** he was; and 5101
20: 2 or **w** is he that gave thee this authority? 5101
22:64 saying, Prophesy, **w** is it that smote thee? 5101
23: 7 **w** himself also was at Jerusalem at that NIG
23:19 (**W** for a certain sedition made in the city, 3748
23:51 **w** also himself waited for the kingdom of 3739
Jn 1:19 from Jerusalem to ask him, **W** art thou? 5101
1:22 Then said they unto him, **W** art thou? 5101
1:27 **w** coming after me is preferred before me, 3588
4:10 and **w** it is that saith to thee, Give me to 5101
5:13 And he that was healed wist not **w** it was: 5101
6:60 This is a hard saying; **w** can hear it? 5101
6:64 For Jesus knew from the beginning **w** they 5101
6:64 that believed not, and **w** should betray him. 5101
7:20 hast a devil: **w** goeth about to kill thee? 5101
7:49 But this people **w** knoweth not the law are 3588
8:25 Then said they unto him, **W** art thou? 5101
9: 2 saying, Master, **w** did sin, this *man,* or 5101
9:19 Is this your son, **w** ye say was born blind? 3739
9:21 or **w** hath opened his eyes, we know not: 5101
9:36 He answered and said, **W** is he, Lord, that I 5101
12:34 man must be lift up? **w** is this Son of man? 5101
12:38 he spake, Lord, **w** hath believed our report? 5101
13:11 For he knew **w** should betray him; therefore 3588
13:24 that *he* should ask **w** it should be of 302+5101
13:25 Jesus' breast saith unto him, Lord, **w** is it? 5101
18:18 officers stood *there,* **w** had made a fire of NIG
21:12 of the disciples durst ask him, **W** art thou? 5101
Ac 1:23 **w** was surnamed Justus, and Matthias. 3739
3: 3 **W** seeing Peter and John about to go into 3739
4:25 **W** by the mouth of thy servant David hast 3588
4:36 **w** by the apostles was surnamed Barnabas, 3588
5:36 **w** was slain; and all, as many as obeyed 3739
7:27 **W** made thee a ruler and a judge over us? 5101
7:35 saying, **W** made thee a ruler and a judge? 5101
7:38 **w** received *the* lively oracles to give unto 3739
7:46 **W** found favour before God, and desired to 3739
7:53 **W** have received the law by the disposition 3748
8:15 **W**, when they were come down, prayed for 3748
8:27 **w** had the charge of all her treasure, and 3739
8:33 and **w** shall declare his generation? for his 5101
9: 5 And he said, **W** art thou, Lord? And 5101
10:32 **w**, when he cometh, shall speak unto thee. 3739
10:38 **w** went about doing good, and healing all 3739
10:41 **w** did eat and drink with him after he rose 3748
11:14 **W** shall tell thee words, whereby thou and 3739
11:17 **w** believed on the Lord Jesus Christ; NIG
11:23 **W**, when he came, and had seen the grace 3739
13: 7 **w** called for Barnabas and Saul, and 3778
13: 9 Then Saul, (**w** also *is called* Paul,) 3588
13:31 **w** are his witnesses unto the people. 3748
13:43 **w**, speaking to them, persuaded them to 3748
14: 8 his mother's womb, **w** never had walked: 3739
14: 9 **w** stedfastly beholding him, and 3739
14:16 **W** in times past suffered all nations to walk 3739
14:19 and Iconium, **w** persuaded the people, and, NIG
15:17 saith the Lord, **w** doeth all these *things.* 3588
15:27 **w** shall also tell *you* the same *things* by 846
15:38 **w** departed from them from Pamphylia, NIG
16:24 **W**, having received such a charge, 3739
17:10 **w** coming *thither* went into the synagogue 3748
18:27 **w**, when he was come, helped them much 3739
19:15 I know, and Paul I know; but **w** are ye? 5101
21: 4 **w** said to Paul through the Spirit, that *he* 3748
21:32 **W** immediately took soldiers and 3739
21:33 and demanded **w** he was, and what he had 5101
21:37 **W** said, Canst thou speak Greek? 1161+3588
22: 8 And I answered, **W** art thou, Lord? And he 5101
23:18 **w** hath something to say unto thee. NIG
23:33 **W**, when they came to Cesarea, and 3748
24: 1 **w** informed the governor against Paul. 3748
24: 6 **W** also hath gone about to profane 3739
24:19 **W** ought to have been here before thee, and 3739
26:15 And I said, **W** art thou, Lord? And he said, 5101
28: 7 **w** received us, and lodged *us* three days 3739
28:10 **W** also honoured us with many honours; 3739
28:18 **W**, when they had examined me, 3748
Ro 1:18 **w** hold the truth in unrighteousness; 3588
1:25 **W** changed the truth of God into a lie, and 3748
1:25 than the Creator, **w** is blessed for ever. 3739
1:32 **W** knowing the judgment of God, that they 3748
2: 6 **W** will render to every *man* according to 3739
2: 7 To them **w** by patient continuance in well NIG
2:27 **w** by the letter and circumcision dost 3588
3: 5 *Is* God unrighteous **w** taketh vengeance? 3588
3:19 it saith to them **w** are under the law: NIG
4:12 And the father of circumcision to them **w** NIG
4:12 **w** also walk in the steps of *that* faith of our 3588
4:16 faith of Abraham; **w** is the father of us all, 3739
Ro 4:17 **w** quickeneth the dead, and calleth those 3588
4:18 **W** against hope believed in hope, that he 3739
4:25 **W** was delivered for our offences, and 3739
5:14 **w** is the figure of *him* that was to come. 3739
7: 4 *even* to him **w** is raised from the dead, NIG
7:24 **w** shall deliver me from the body of this 5101
8: 1 in Christ Jesus **w** walk not after the flesh, NIG
8: 4 **w** walk not after the flesh, but after 3588
8:20 by reason of him **w** hath subjected *the same,* NIG
8:28 to them **w** are *the* called according to *his* NIG
8:31 If God *be* for us, **w** *can be* against us? 5101
8:33 **W** shall lay any thing to the charge of 5101
8:34 **W** *is* he that condemneth? *It is* Christ that 5101
8:34 that is risen *again,* **w** is even at the right 3739
8:34 of God, **w** also maketh intercession for us. 3739
8:35 **W** shall separate us from the love of 5101
9: 4 **W** are Israelites; to whom pertaineth 3748
9: 5 the flesh Christ *came,* **w** is over all, 3588
9:19 yet find fault? For **w** hath resisted his will? 5101
9:20 **w** art thou that repliest against God? 5101
10: 6 in thine heart, **W** shall ascend into heaven? 5101
10: 7 Or, **W** shall descend into the deep? (that is, 5101
10:16 Lord, **w** hath believed our report? 5101
11: 4 **w** have not bowed the knee to *the image of* 3748
11:34 For **w** hath known the mind of the Lord? or 5101
11:34 of the Lord? or **w** hath been his counseller? 5101
11:35 Or **w** hath first given to him, and it shall be 5101
14: 2 all *things:* another, **w** is weak, eateth herbs. NIG
14: 4 **W** art thou that judgest another *man's* 5101
14:20 *it is* evil for *that* man **w** eateth with offence. NIG
16: 4 **W** have for my life laid down their own 3748
16: 5 **w** is the firstfruits of Achaia unto Christ. 3739
16: 6 **w** bestowed much labour on us. 3748
16: 7 **w** are of note among the apostles, 3748
16: 7 **w** also were in Christ before me. 3739
16:12 and Tryphosa, **w** labour in the Lord. 3588
16:22 I Tertius, **w** wrote *this* epistle, salute you in 3588
1Co 1: 8 **W** shall also confirm you unto the end, 3739
1:30 **w** of God is made unto us wisdom, and 3739
2:16 For **w** hath known the mind of the Lord, 5101
3: 5 **W** then is Paul, and who *is* Apollos, but 5101
3: 5 and **w** *is* Apollos, but ministers by whom 5101
4: 5 **w** both will bring to light the hidden *things* 3739
4: 7 For **w** maketh thee to differ *from another?* 5101
4:17 **w** is my beloved son, and faithful in 3739
4:17 **w** shall bring you into remembrance of my 3739
6: 4 set them to judge **w** are least esteemed in 3588
9: 7 **W** goeth a warfare any time at his own 5101
9: 7 **w** planteth a vineyard, and eateth not of 5101
9: 7 or **w** feedeth a flock, and eateth not of 5101
10:13 **w** will not suffer you to be tempted above 3739
14: 8 **w** shall prepare himself to the battle? 5101
2Co 1: 4 **W** comforteth us in all our tribulation, 3588
1:10 **W** delivered us from so great a death, and 3739
1:19 **w** was preached among you by us, *even* by 3588
1:22 **W** hath also sealed us, and given 3588
2: 2 **w** is he then that maketh me glad, but 5101
2:16 And **w** *is* sufficient for these *things?* 5101
3: 6 **W** also hath made us able ministers of 3739
4: 4 **w** is the image of God, should shine unto 3739
4: 6 **w** commanded the light to shine out of 3588
5: 5 **w** also hath given unto us the earnest of 3588
5:18 **w** hath reconciled us to himself by Jesus 3588
5:21 made him *to be* sin for us, **w** knew no sin; 3588
8:10 **w** have begun before, not only to do, but 3748
8:19 **w** was also chosen of the churches to travel NIG
10: 1 **w** in presence *am* base among you, but 3739
11:29 **W** is weak, and I am not weak? who is 5101
11:29 not weak? **w** is offended, and I burn not? 5101
Gal 1: 1 the Father, **w** raised him from the dead;) 3588
1: 4 **W** gave himself for our sins, that he might 3588
1:15 **w** separated me from my mother's womb, 3588
2: 3 **w** was with me, being a Greek, 3588
2: 4 **w** came in privily to spy out our liberty 3748
2: 6 But of these **w** seemed to be somewhat, NIG
2: 6 for they **w** seemed *to be somewhat* in NIG
2: 9 Cephas, and John, **w** seemed to be pillars, 3588
2:15 We **w** *are* Jews by nature, and not sinners of NIG
2:20 **w** loved me, and gave himself for me. 3588
3: 1 O foolish Galatians, **w** hath bewitched you, 5101
4:23 But he **w** was of the bondwoman was born NIG
5: 7 **w** did hinder you that *ye* should not obey 5101
6:10 unto them **w** are of the household of faith. NIG
6:13 For neither they themselves **w** are NIG
Eph 1: 3 **w** hath blessed us with all spiritual 3588
1:11 **w** worketh all *things* after the counsel of his NIG
1:12 praise of his glory, **w** first trusted in Christ: 3588
1:19 of his power to us-ward **w** believe, 3588
2: 1 And you *hath he quickened,* **w** were dead in NIG
2: 4 But God, **w** is rich in mercy, for his great NIG
2:11 **w** are called Uncircumcision by that which 3588
2:13 But now in Christ Jesus ye **w** sometimes 3588
2:14 **w** hath made both one, and hath broken 3588
3: 8 **w** *am* less than the least of all saints, NIG
3: 9 **w** created all *things* by Jesus Christ: 3588
4: 6 **w** *is* above all, and through all, and in you 3588
4:19 **W** being past feeling have given 3748
5: 5 nor unclean *person,* nor covetous man **w** is 3739
Php 2: 6 **W**, being in the form of God, thought it not 3739
2:20 **w** will naturally care for your state. 3748
3:19 *is* in their shame, **w** mind earthly *things.*) 3588
3:21 **W** shall change our vile body, that it may 3739
Col 1: 7 **w** is for you a faithful minister of Christ; 3739
1: 8 **W** also declared unto us your love in 3588
1:13 **W** hath delivered us from the power of 3739
1:15 **W** is the image of the invisible God, 3739
1:18 **w** is the beginning, the firstborn from 3739
1:24 **W** now rejoice in my sufferings for you, 3739
2:12 of God, **w** hath raised him from the dead. 3588
3: 4 **w** *is* our life, shall appear, then shall ye also NIG
4: 7 **w** *is* a beloved brother, and a faithful NIG
4: 9 and beloved brother, **w** is *one* of you. 3739
4:11 is called Justus, **w** are of the circumcision. 3588
4:12 Epaphras, **w** is *one* of you, a servant of 3588
1Th 2:12 **w** hath called you unto his kingdom and 3588

1Th 2:15 **W** both killed the Lord Jesus, and their own *3588*
4: 8 **w** hath also given unto us his holy Spirit. *3588*
5: 8 But let us, **w** are of the day, be sober, NIG
5:10 **W** died for us, that, whether we wake or *3588*
5:24 *is* he that calleth you, **w** also will do *it*. *3739*
2Th 1: 7 And to you **w** are troubled rest with us, *3588*
1: 9 **W** shall be punished *with* everlasting *3748*
2: 4 **W** opposeth and exalteth himself above all *3588*
2: 7 only he **w** now letteth *will let*, until he be NIG
2:12 That they all might be damned **w** believed *3588*
3: 3 **w** shall stablish you, and keep *you* from *3739*
1Ti 1:12 **w** hath enabled me, for that he counted me *3588*
1:13 **W** was before a blasphemer, and NIG
2: 4 **W** will have all men to be saved, and *3739*
2: 6 **W** gave himself a ransom for all, to be *3588*
4:10 the living God, **w** is the Saviour of all men, *3739*
5:17 especially they **w** labour in the word and NIG
6:13 **w** quickeneth all *things*, and *before* Christ *3588*
6:13 **w** before Pontius Pilate witnessed a good *3588*
6:15 **w** *is* the blessed and only Potentate, NIG
6:16 **W** only hath immortality, dwelling in *3588*
6:17 **w** giveth us richly all *things* to enjoy; *3588*
2Ti 1: 9 **W** hath saved us, and called *us* with a holy *3588*
1:10 **w** hath abolished death, and hath brought NIG
2: 2 **w** shall be able to teach others also. *3748*
2: 4 that he may please him **w** hath chosen *him* NIG
2:18 **W** concerning the truth have erred, *3748*
2:26 **w** *are* taken captive by him at his will. NIG
4: 1 **w** shall judge the quick and the dead at his *3588*
Tit 1:11 must be stopped, **w** subvert whole houses, *3748*
2:14 **W** gave himself for us, that he might *3739*
Heb 1: 1 **w** at sundry times and in divers manners NIG
1: 3 **W** being the brightness of *his* glory, and *3739*
1: 7 **W** maketh his angels spirits, and *3588*
1:14 sent forth to minister for them **w** shall be *3588*
2: 9 **w** was made a little lower than the angels, *3588*
2:11 and they **w** are sanctified *are* all of one: NIG
2:15 And deliver them **w** through fear of death *3745*
3: 2 **W** was faithful to him that appointed him, NIG
3: 3 inasmuch as he **w** hath builded the house NIG
5: 2 **W** can have compassion on the ignorant, NIG
5: 7 **W** in the days of his flesh, when he had *3739*
5:14 *even* those **w** by reason of use have their *3588*
6: 4 For *it is* impossible for those **w** were once NIG
6:12 but followers of them **w** through faith and NIG
6:18 **w** have fled for refuge to lay hold upon *3588*
7: 1 **w** met Abraham returning from *3588*
7: 5 **w** receive the office of the priesthood have *3588*
7: 9 *I* may so say, Levi also, **w** receiveth tithes, *3588*
7:16 **W** is made, not after the law of a carnal *3739*
7:26 **w** *is* holy, harmless, undefiled, NIG
7:27 **W** needeth not daily, as *those* high priests, *3739*
7:28 the Son, **w** is consecrated for evermore. NIG
8: 1 **w** is set on the right hand of the throne of *3739*
8: 5 **W** serve unto the example and shadow of *3748*
9:14 **w** through the eternal Spirit offered himself *3739*
10:29 **w** hath trodden under foot the Son of God, *3588*
10:39 But we are not of *them* **w** draw back unto NIG
11:11 she judged him faithful **w** had promised. NIG
11:27 for he endured, as seeing *him* **w** *is* invisible. NIG
11:33 **W** through faith subdued kingdoms, *3739*
12: 2 **w** for the joy that was set before him *3739*
12:16 **w** for one morsel of meat sold his *3739*
12:25 for if they escaped not **w** refused him that NIG
13: 7 **w** have spoken unto you the word of God: *3748*
Jas 3:13 **W** *is* a wise *man* and endued with *5101*
4:12 **w** is able to save and to destroy: *3588*
4:12 to destroy: **w** art thou that judgest another? *5101*
5:10 **w** have spoken in the name of the Lord, *3739*
1Pe 1: 5 **W** are kept by the power of God through *3588*
1:10 **w** prophesied of the grace *that should come* *3588*
1:17 **w** without respect of persons judgeth *3588*
1:20 **W** verily was foreordained before NIG
1:21 **W** by him do believe in God, that raised *3588*
2: 9 **w** hath called you out of darkness into his NIG
2:22 **W** did no sin, neither was guile found in his *3739*
2:23 **W**, when he was reviled, reviled not again; *3739*
2:24 **W** his own self bare our sins in his own *3739*
3: 5 **w** trusted in God, adorned themselves, *3588*
3:13 And **w** *is* he that will harm you, if ye be *5101*
3:22 **W** is gone into heaven, and is on the right *3739*
4: 5 **W** shall give account to him that is ready to *3739*
5: 1 **w** am also an elder, and a witness of *3588*
5:10 **w** hath called us into his eternal glory by *3588*
2Pe 2: 1 **w** privily shall bring in damnable heresies, *3748*
2:15 **w** loved the wages of unrighteousness; *3739*
2:18 those that were clean escaped from them **w** NIG
1Jn 2:22 **W** is a liar but he that denieth that Jesus is *5101*
3:12 **w** was of *that* wicked one, and slew his NIG
4:21 That he **w** loveth God love his brother also. NIG
5: 5 **W** is he that overcometh the world, but he *5101*
2Jn 1: 7 **w** confess not that Jesus Christ is come in *3588*
3Jn 1: 9 **w** loveth to have the preeminence among *3588*
Jude 1: 4 **w** were before of old ordained to this *3588*
1:18 **w** should walk after their own ungodly NIG
1:19 These be they **w** separate themselves, NIG
Rev 1: 2 **W** bare record of the word of God, and *3739*
1: 5 **w** *is* the faithful witness, *and* the first NIG
1: 9 **w** also am your brother, and companion in *3588*
2: 1 **w** walketh in the midst of the seven golden *3588*
2:13 **w** was slain among you, where Satan *3739*
2:14 **w** taught Balac to cast a stumblingblock *3739*
2:18 **w** hath his eyes like unto a flame of fire, *3588*
4: 9 on the throne, **w** liveth for ever and ever, *3588*
5: 2 **W** is worthy to open the book, and to loose *5101*
6:17 is come; and **w** shall be able to stand? *5101*
10: 6 **w** created heaven, and the *things* that *3739*
12: 5 **w** was to rule all nations with a rod of iron: *3739*
13: 4 the beast, saying, **W** *is* like unto the beast? *5101*
13: 4 the beast? **w** is able to make war with him? *5101*
14:11 **w** worship the beast and his image, and *3588*
15: 4 **W** shall not fear thee, O Lord, and *5101*
15: 7 wrath of God, **w** liveth for ever and ever. *3588*
18: 8 for strong *is* the Lord God **w** judgeth her. *3588*
18: 9 **w** have committed fornication and *3588*

WHOLE (250) [WHOLESOME, WHOLLY]

Ge 2: 6 and watered the **w** face of the ground. 3605
2:11 that *is it* which compasseth the **w** land of 3605
2:13 the same *is it* that compasseth the **w** land of 3605
7:19 that *were* under the **w** heaven, 3605
8: 9 for the waters *were* on the face of the **w** 3605
9:19 and of them was the **w** earth overspread. 3605
11: 1 the **w** earth was *of* one language, and 3605
11: 4 abroad upon the face of the **w** earth. 3605
13: 9 *Is* not the **w** land before thee? 3605
47:28 so the **w age** of Jacob was an 2416+3117+8141
Ex 10:15 For they covered the face of the **w** earth, so 3605
12: 6 the **w** assembly of the congregation of 3605
16: 2 the **w** congregation of the children of Israel 3605
16: 3 to kill this **w** assembly with hunger. 3605
16:10 as Aaron spake unto the **w** congregation of 3605
19:18 a furnace, and the **w** mount quaked greatly. 3605
29:18 thou shalt burn the **w** ram upon the altar: 3605
Lev 3: 9 the fat thereof, *and* the **w** rump, it shall he 8549
4:12 Even the **w** bullock shall he carry forth 3605
4:13 if the **w** congregation of Israel sin through 3605
7:14 of it he shall offer one out of the **w** oblation 3605
8:21 and Moses burnt the **w** ram upon the altar: 3605
10: 6 let your brethren, the **w** house of Israel, 3605
25:29 he may redeem it within a **w** year after it is 8552
Nu 3: 7 the charge of the **w** congregation before 3605
8: 9 thou shalt gather the **w** assembly of 3605
10: 2 of a **w piece** thou shalt make them: 4749
11:20 *But* even a **w** month, until it come out at 3117
11:21 them flesh, that they may eat a **w** month. 3117
14: 2 the **w** congregation said unto them, 3605
14:29 according to your **w** number, from twenty 3605
20: 1 children of Israel, *even* the **w** congregation, 3605
20:22 *even* the **w** congregation, journeyed from 3605
Dt 2:25 the nations *that are* under the **w** heaven, 3605
4:19 unto all nations under the **w** heaven. 3605
27: 6 altar of the LORD thy God *of* **w** stones: 8003
29:23 *And that* the **w** land thereof *is* brimstone, 3605
33:10 and **w** *burnt sacrifice* upon thine altar. 3632
Jos 5: 8 in their places in the camp, till they were **w**. 2421
8:31 an altar of **w** stones, over which no *man* 8003
10:13 and hasted not to go down about a **w** day. 8549
11:23 So Joshua took the **w** land, according to all 3605
18: 1 the **w** congregation of the children of Israel 3605
22:12 **w** congregation of the children of Israel 3605
22:16 Thus saith the **w** congregation of 3605
22:18 that to morrow he will be wroth with the **w** 3605
Jdg 19: 2 was there four **w** months. 3117
21:13 the **w** congregation sent *some* to speak to 3605
2Sa 1: 9 upon me, because my life *is* yet **w** in me. 3605
3:19 that seemed *good* to the **w** house of 3605
6:19 *even* among the **w** multitude of Israel, 3605
14: 7 the **w** family is risen against thine 3605
1Ki 6:22 the **w** house he overlaid with gold, until *he* 3605
6:22 also the **w** altar that *was* by the oracle he 3605
11:34 Howbeit I will not take the **w** kingdom out 3605
2Ki 9: 8 For the **w** house of Ahab shall perish: and 3605
2Ch 6: 3 and blessed the **w** congregation of Israel: 3605
15:15 and sought him with their **w** desire; 3605
16: 9 run to and fro throughout the **w** earth, 3605
26:12 The **w** number of the chief of the fathers of 3605
30:23 the **w** assembly took counsel to keep other 3605
33: 8 according to the **w** law and the statutes and 3605
Ezr 2:64 The **w** congregation together *was* forty *and* 3605
Ne 7:66 The **w** congregation together *was* forty 3605
Est 3: 6 throughout the **w** kingdom of Ahasuerus, 3605
Job 5:18 he woundeth, and his hands **make w**. 7495
28:24 of the earth, *and* seeth under the **w** heaven; 3605
34:13 or who hath disposed the **w** world? 3605
37: 3 He directeth it under the **w** heaven, and 3605
41:11 *whatsoever is* under the **w** heaven *is* mine. 3605
Ps 9: 1 praise *thee*, O LORD, with my **w** heart; 3605
48: 2 the joy of the **w** earth, *is* mount Zion, 3605
51:19 burnt offering and **w** *burnt offering:* then 3632
72:19 let the **w** earth be filled *with* his glory; 3605
97: 5 at the presence of the Lord of the **w** earth. 3605
105:16 the land: he brake the **w** staff of bread. 3605
111: 1 I will praise the LORD with *my* **w** heart, 3605
119: 2 *and that* seek him with the **w** heart. 3605
119:10 With my **w** heart have I sought thee: O let 3605
119:34 yea, I shall observe it with *my* **w** heart. 3605
119:58 I intreated thy favour with *my* **w** heart: 3605
119:69 I will keep thy precepts with *my* **w** heart. 3605
119:145 I cried with *my* **w** heart; hear me, 3605
138: 1 I will praise thee with my **w** heart: 3605
Pr 1:12 and **w**, as those that go down into the pit: 8549
16:33 the **w** disposing thereof *is* of the LORD. 3605
26:26 shall be shewed before the **w** congregation. NIH
Ecc 12:13 Let us hear the conclusion of the **w** matter: 3605
12:13 for this *is* the **w** *duty of* man. 3605
Isa 1: 5 the **w** head *is* sick, and the whole heart 3605
1: 5 whole head *is* sick, and the **w** heart faint. 3605
3: 1 the **w** stay of bread, and the whole stay of 3605
3: 1 stay of bread, and the **w** stay of water, 3605
6: 3 of hosts: the **w** earth *is* full of his glory. 3605
10:12 *that* when the Lord hath performed his **w** 3605
13: 5 of his indignation, to destroy the **w** land. 3605
14: 7 The **w** earth is at rest, *and* is quiet: 3605
14:26 purpose that is purposed upon the **w** earth: 3605
14:29 **w** Palestina, because the rod of him that 3605
14:31 cry, O city; thou, **w** Palestina, *art* dissolved: 3605
21: 8 and I *am* set in my ward **w** nights: 3605
28:22 even determined upon the **w** earth. 3605
54: 5 The God of the **w** earth shall he be called. 3605
Jer 1:18 and brasen walls against the **w** land, 3605
3:10 hath not turned unto me with her **w** heart, 3605
4:20 is cried; for the **w** land is spoiled: 3605
4:27 LORD said, The **w** land shall be desolate; 3605
4:29 The **w** city shall flee for the noise of 3605
7:15 your brethren, *even* the **w** seed of Ephraim. 3605
8:16 the **w** land trembled at the sound of 3605
12:11 the **w** land is made desolate, because 3605
13:11 have I caused to cleave unto me the **w** 3605
13:11 house of Israel and the **w** house of Judah, 3605
Jer 15:10 and a man of contention to the **w** earth! 3605
19:11 that cannot be **made w** again: 7495
24: 7 for they shall return unto me with their **w** 3605
25:11 this **w** land shall be a desolation, *and* 3605
31:40 the **w** valley of the dead bodies, and of 3605
32:41 them in this land assuredly with my **w** heart 3605
32:41 with my whole heart and with my **w** soul. 3605
35: 3 and the **w** house of the Rechabites; 3605
37:10 For though ye had smitten the **w** army of 3605
45: 4 planted I *will* pluck up, even this **w** land. 3605
50:23 How is the hammer of the **w** earth cut 3605
51:41 *how* is the praise of the **w** earth surprised! 3605
51:47 her **w** land shall be confounded, and all her 3605
La 2:15 of beauty, The joy of the **w** earth? 3605
Eze 5:10 the **w** remnant of thee will I scatter into all 3605
7:13 for the vision *is* touching the **w** multitude 3605
10:12 their **w** body, and their backs, and 3605
15: 5 Behold, when it was **w**, it was meet for no 8549
32: 4 I will fill the beasts of the **w** earth with 3605
35:14 When the **w** earth rejoiceth, I will make 3605
37:11 these bones *are* the **w** house of Israel: 3605
39:25 have mercy upon the **w** house of Israel, and 3605
43:11 that they may keep the **w** form thereof, and 3605
43:12 Upon the top of the mountain the **w** limit 3605
45: 6 *portion:* it shall be for the **w** house of Israel. 3605
Da 2:35 a great mountain, and filled the **w** earth. 3606
2:48 made him ruler over the **w** province of 3606
6: 1 which should be over the **w** kingdom; 3606
6: 3 the king thought to set him over the **w** 3606
7:23 shall devour the **w** earth, and shall tread it 3606
7:27 the greatness of the kingdom under the **w** 3606
8: 5 from the west on the face of the **w** earth, 3605
9:12 for under the **w** heaven hath not been done 3605
10: 3 till three **w weeks** were fulfilled. 3117+7620
11:17 to enter with the strength of his **w** kingdom, 3605
Am 1: 6 they carried away captive the **w** captivity, 8003
1: 9 they delivered up the **w** captivity to Edom, 8003
3: 1 against the **w** family which I brought up 3605
Mic 4:13 their substance unto the Lord of the **w** 3605
Zep 1:18 the **w** land shall be devoured by the fire of 3605
Zec 4:10 which run to and fro through the **w** earth. 3605
4:14 that stand by the Lord of the **w** earth. 3605
5: 3 goeth forth over the face of the **w** earth: 3605
Mal 3: 9 for ye *have* robbed me, *even* this **w** nation. 3605
Mt 5:29 not *that* thy **w** body should be cast into hell. *3650*
5:30 not *that* thy **w** body should be cast into hell. *3650*
6:22 be single, thy **w** body shall be full of light. *3650*
6:23 thy **w** body shall be full of darkness. *3650*
8:32 the **w** herd of swine ran violently down a *3956*
8:34 the **w** city came out to meet Jesus: *3956*
9:12 They that be **w** need not a physician, but *2480*
9:21 If I may but touch his garment, I shall be **w**. *4982*
9:22 good comfort; thy faith hath **made** thee **w**. *4982*
9:22 And the woman was **made w** from that *4982*
12:13 and it was restored **w**, *like* as the other. *5199*
13: 2 sat; and the **w** multitude stood on the shore. *3956*
13:33 measures of meal, till the **w** was leavened. *3650*
14:36 many as touched were **made perfectly w**. *1295*
15:28 And her daughter was **made w** from that *2390*
15:31 the maimed *to be* **w**, the lame to walk, and *5199*
16:26 if he shall gain the **w** world, and lose his *3650*
26:13 gospel shall be preached in the **w** world, *3650*
27:27 gathered unto him the **w** band *of soldiers*. *3650*
Mk 2:17 They that are **w** have no need of *2480*
3: 5 and his hand was restored **w** as the other. *5199*
4: 1 the **w** multitude was by the sea on the land. *3956*
5:28 If I may touch but his clothes, I shall be **w**. *4982*
5:34 Daughter, thy faith hath **made** thee **w**; *4982*
5:34 go in peace, and be **w** of thy plague. *5199*
6:55 And ran through that **w** region round about, *3650*
6:56 and as many as touched him were **made w**. *4982*
8:36 if he shall gain the **w** world, and lose his *3650*
10:52 Go thy way; thy faith hath **made** thee **w**. *4982*
12:33 is more than all **w burnt offerings** and *3646*
14: 9 shall be preached throughout the **w** world, *3650*
15: 1 the elders and scribes and the **w** council, *3650*
15:16 and they call together the **w** band. *3650*
15:33 there was darkness over the **w** land until *3650*
Lk 1:10 And the **w** multitude of the people were *3956*
5:31 They that are **w** need not a physician; *5198*
6:10 and his hand was restored **w** as the other. *5199*
6:19 And the **w** multitude sought to touch him: *3956*
7:10 found the servant **w** that had been sick. *5198*
8:37 Then the **w** multitude of the country of *537*
8:39 published throughout the **w** city how great *3650*
8:48 thy faith hath **made** thee **w**; go in peace.) *4982*
8:50 believe only, and she shall be **made w**. *4982*
9:25 if he gain the **w** world, and lose himself, or *3650*
11:34 is single, thy **w** body also is full of light; *3650*
11:36 If thy **w** body therefore *be* full of light, *3650*
11:36 no part dark, the **w** shall be full of light, *3650*
13:21 measures of meal, till the **w** was leavened. *3650*
17:19 go *thy way:* thy faith hath **made** thee **w**. *4982*
19:37 the **w** multitude of the disciples began to *537*
21:35 them that dwell on the face of the **w** earth. *3956*
23: 1 And the **w** multitude of them arose, and *537*
Jn 4:53 and himself believed, and his **w** house. *3650*
5: 4 was made **w** of whatsoever disease he had. *5199*
5: 6 he saith unto him, Wilt thou be made **w**? *5199*
5: 9 And immediately the man was made **w**, and *5199*
5:11 He answered them, He that made me **w**, *5199*
5:14 said unto him, Behold, thou art made **w**: *5199*
5:15 that it was Jesus, which had made him **w**. *5199*
7:23 I have made a man every whit **w** on *5199*
11:50 the people, and *that* the **w** nation perish not. *3650*
Ac 4: 9 by what *means* he is **made w**; *4982*
4:10 him doth this *man* stand here before you **w**. *5199*
6: 5 And the saying pleased the **w** multitude: *3956*
9:34 Aeneas, Jesus Christ **maketh** thee **w**: *2390*
11:26 that a **w** year they assembled themselves *3650*
13:44 the **w** city together to hear the word of God. *3956*
15:22 the apostles and elders, with the **w** church, *3650*
19:29 And the **w** city was filled with confusion: *3650*
28:30 And Paul dwelt two **w** years in his own *3650*
Ro 1: 8 faith is spoken of throughout the **w** world. *3650*

Ro 8:22 For we know that the **w** creation groaneth *3956*
16:23 and of the **w** church, saluteth you. *3650*
1Co 5: 6 that a little leaven leaveneth the **w** lump? *3650*
12:17 If the **w** body *were* an eye, where *were* *3650*
12:17 If the **w** *were* hearing, where *were* *3650*
14:23 the **w** church be come together into one *3650*
Gal 5: 3 that he is a debtor to do the **w** law. *3650*
5: 9 A little leaven leaveneth the **w** lump. *3650*
Eph 3:15 Of whom the **w** family in heaven and earth *3956*
4:16 From whom the **w** body fitly joined *3956*
6:11 Put on the **w armour** of God, that ye may *3833*
6:13 Wherefore take unto *you* the **w armour** of *3833*
1Th 5:23 and *I pray God* your **w** spirit and soul and *3648*
Tit 1:11 must be stopped, who subvert **w** houses, *3650*
Jas 2:10 For whosoever shall keep the **w** law, and *3650*
3: 2 *and* able also to bridle the **w** body. *3650*
3: 3 obey us; and we turn about their **w** body. *3650*
3: 6 that it defileth the **w** body, and setteth on *3650*
1Jn 2: 2 but also for *the sins of* the **w** world. *3650*
5:19 and the **w** world lieth in wickedness. *3650*
Rev 12: 9 and Satan, which deceiveth the **w** world: *3650*
16:14 the kings of the earth and of the **w** world, *3650*

WHOLESOME (2) [WHOLE]

Pr 15: 4 A **w** tongue *is* a tree of life: but 4832
1Ti 6: 3 and consent not to **w** words, *5198*

WHOLLY (29) [WHOLE]

Lev 6:22 ever unto the LORD; it shall be **w** burnt. 3632
6:23 priest shall be **w** *burnt:* it shall not be eaten. 3632
19: 9 thou shalt not **w reap** the corners 3615+3807.1
Nu 3: 9 they *are* **w given** unto him out of 5414+5414
4: 6 shall spread over *it* a cloth **w** of blue, and 3632
8:16 For they *are* **w given** unto me from 5414+5414
32:11 because they have not **w** followed me: 4390
32:12 for they have **w** followed the LORD. 4390
Dt 1:36 because he hath **w** followed the LORD. 4390
Jos 14: 8 I **w** followed the LORD my God. 4390
14: 9 thou hast **w** followed the LORD my God. 4390
14:14 that he **w** followed the LORD God of 4390
Jdg 17: 3 I had **w dedicated** the silver unto 6942+6942
1Sa 7: 9 offered it *for* a burnt offering **w** unto 3632
1Ch 28:21 all the people *will be* **w** at thy 3605
Job 21:23 his full strength, *being* **w** at ease and quiet. 3605
Isa 22: 1 that thou art **w** gone up to the housetops? 3605
Jer 2:21 planted thee a noble vine, **w** a right seed: 3605
6: 6 she *is* **w** oppression in the midst of her. 3605
13:19 all of it, it shall be **w** carried away captive. 7965
42:15 If ye **w set** your faces to enter *into* 7760+7760
46:28 will I not **leave** thee **w unpunished**. 5352+5352
50:13 not be inhabited, but it shall be **w** desolate: 3605
Eze 11:15 thy kindred, and all the house of Israel **w**, 3605
Am 8: 8 it shall rise up **w** as a flood; and it shall be 3605
9: 5 it shall rise up **w** like a flood; and shall be 3605
Ac 17:16 he saw the city **w given to idolatry**. *1510+2712*
1Th 5:23 And the very God of peace sanctify you **w**; *3651*
1Ti 4:15 upon these *things;* give thyself **w to** them; *1722*

WHOM (763) [WHO]

Ge 2: 8 and there he put the man **w** he had formed. 834
3:12 The woman **w** thou gavest *to be* with me, 834
4:25 another seed instead of Abel, **w** Cain slew. 3588
6: 7 I will destroy man **w** I have created from 834
10:14 and Casluhim, (out of **w**[s] came Philistim) 8033
15:14 that nation, **w** they shall serve, will I judge: 834
21: 3 born unto him, **w** Sarah bare to him, Isaac. 834
22: 2 **w** thou lovest, and get thee into the land of 834
24: 3 of the Canaanites, amongst **w** I dwell: 834
24:14 *that* the damsel to **w** I shall say, Let down 1886.3
24:40 said unto me, The LORD, before **w** I walk, 834
24:44 *let* the same *be* the woman **w** the LORD 834
24:47 Nahor's son, **w** Milcah bare unto him: 834
25:12 Abraham's son, **w** Hagar the Egyptian, 834
30:26 for **w** I have served thee, and let me go: 834
41:38 *is,* a man in **w** the spirit of God *is?* 834+2050.2
43:27 your father well, the old man of **w** ye spake? 834
43:29 younger brother, of **w** ye spake unto me? 834
44:10 he with **w** it is found shall be my servant; 2050.2
44:16 and *he* also with **w** the cup is found. 834
45: 4 Joseph your brother, **w** ye sold into Egypt. 834
46:18 **w** Laban gave to Leah his daughter, and 834
48: 9 **w** God hath given me in this *place.* 834+1992
48:15 before **w** my fathers Abraham and Isaac did 834
49: 8 thou *art he* **w** thy brethren shall praise: NIH
Ex 4:13 by the hand *of him* **w** thou wilt send. NIH
6: 5 of Israel, **w** the Egyptians keep in bondage; 834
6:26 and Moses, to **w** the LORD said, 1992.1
14:13 for the Egyptians **w** ye have seen to day, 834
18: 9 **w** he had delivered out of the hand of 834
22: 9 *and* **w** the judges shall condemn, he shall pay 834
23:27 will destroy all the people to **w** thou shalt 1992.1
28: 3 **w** I have filled with the spirit of wisdom, 834
32:13 to **w** thou swarest by thine own self, and 1992.1
33:12 thou hast not let me know **w** thou wilt send 834
33:19 and will be gracious to **w** I will be gracious, 834
33:19 will shew mercy on **w** I will shew mercy. 834
35:21 and every one **w** his spirit made willing, *and* 834
35:23 with **w** was found blue, and purple, and 2050.2
35:24 with **w** was found shittim wood for any 2050.2
36: 1 in **w** the LORD put wisdom and 1992
Lev 6: 5 *and* give it unto him to **w** it appertaineth, 834
13:45 the leper in **w** the plague *is,* his clothes 2050.2
14:32 This *is* the law *of him* in **w** *is* the plague 2050.2
15:18 The woman also with **w** man shall lie 1886.3
16:32 **w** he shall anoint, and whom he shall 834
16:32 **w** he shall consecrate to minister in 834
17: 7 after **w** they have gone a whoring. 1992.1
22: 5 or a man of **w** he may take uncleanness, 834
25:27 restore the overplus unto the man to **w** he 834
25:55 they *are* my servants **w** I brought forth out of 834
26:45 **w** I brought forth out of the land of Egypt 3963.1
27:24 shall return unto him of **w** it was bought, 834
27:24 *even* to him to **w** the possession of the land 834
Nu 3: 3 **w** he consecrated to minister in the priest's 834
4:41 **w** Moses and Aaron did number according to 834
4:45 **w** Moses and Aaron numbered according to 834
4:46 **w** Moses and Aaron and the chief of Israel 834
5: 7 give *it* unto *him* against **w** he hath 834
11:16 **w** thou knowest to be the elders of 834+1992
11:21 amongst **w** I *am, are* six hundred 834+2050.2
12: 1 of the Ethiopian woman **w** he had married: 834
12:12 of **w** the flesh is half consumed when he 834
16: 5 even *him* **w** he hath chosen 834+871.1+2050.2
16: 7 it shall be *that* the man **w** the LORD doth 834
17: 5 **w** I shall choose, shall 834+871.1+2050.2
22: 6 for I wot that *he* **w** thou blessest *is* blessed, 834
22: 6 *is* blessed, and *he* **w** thou cursest is cursed. 834
23: 8 How shall I curse, **w** God hath not cursed? NIH
23: 8 shall I defy, *w* the LORD hath not defied? NIH
26: 5 *of* **w** *cometh* the family of the Hanochites: NIH
26:59 of Levi, **w** *her mother* bare to Levi in Egypt: 834
26:64 among these there was not a man of them **w** NIH
27:18 a man in **w** *is* the spirit, and 834+2050.2
34:29 These *are they* **w** the LORD commanded to 834
36: 6 Let them marry to **w** they think best; 1886.1
Dt 4:46 **w** Moses and the children of Israel smote, 834
7:19 do unto all the people of **w** thou *art* afraid. 834
9: 2 **w** thou knowest, and *of whom* thou hast 834
9: 2 *of* **w** thou hast heard *say,* Who can stand NIH
17:15 **w** the LORD thy God shall choose: 834
19: 4 **w** he hated not in time past; 1931
19:17 between **w** the controversy *is,* shall stand 834
21: 8 **w** thou hast redeemed, and lay not innocent 834
24:11 the man to **w** thou dost lend shall bring out 834
28:55 of the flesh of his children **w** he shall eat: 834
29:26 gods **w** they knew not, and *whom* he had not 834
29:26 and *w* he had not given unto them: NIH
31: 4 and unto the land of them, **w** he destroyed. 834
32:17 *to* gods **w** they knew not, *to* new *gods* 3963.1
32:17 newly up, **w** your fathers feared not. 3963.1
32:20 children in **w** *is* no faith. 3963.1
32:37 their gods, *their* rock in **w** they trusted, 2050.2
33: 8 **w** thou didst prove at Massah, *and* 834
33: 8 *with* **w** thou didst strive at the waters of 1930.2
34:10 **w** the LORD knew face to face, 834
Jos 2:10 and Og, **w** ye utterly destroyed. 834
4: 4 **w** he had prepared of the children of Israel, 834
5: 6 unto **w** the LORD sware that *he* would not 834
5: 7 their children, *w* he raised up in their stead, NIH
10:11 **w** the children of Israel slew with the sword. 834
10:25 do to all your enemies against **w** ye fight. 3963.1
13: 8 With **w** the Reubenites and the Gadites 2050.2
13:21 **w** Moses smote with the princes of Midian, 834
24:15 choose you *this* day **w** you will serve; 4310
24:17 among all the people through **w** we passed: 834
Jdg 4:22 and I will shew thee the man **w** thou seekest. 834
7: 4 it shall be, *that* of **w** I say unto thee, 834
8:15 with **w** ye did upbraid me, saying, 834
8:18 What manner of men *were they* **w** ye slew at 834
12: 9 *w* he sent abroad, and took in thirty NIH
14:20 his companion, **w** he had used as his friend. 834
21:23 of them that danced, **w** they caught: 834
Ru 2:19 she shewed her mother in law with **w** she 2050.2
2:19 The man's name with **w** I wrought to day 2050.2
4: 1 the kinsman of **w** Boaz spake came by, 834
4: 1 unto **w** he said, *Ho,* such a one, turn aside, NIH
4:12 house of Pharez, **w** Tamar bare unto Judah, 834
1Sa 2:33 **w** I shall not cut off from mine altar, NIH
6:20 and to **w** shall he go up from us? 4310
9:17 Behold the man **w** I spake to thee of: 834
9:20 on **w** *is* all the desire of Israel? *Is it* not on 4310
10:24 See ye him **w** the LORD hath chosen, 834
12: 3 or **w** have I defrauded? whom have I 4310
12: 3 **w** have I oppressed? or of whose hand have 4310
12:13 therefore behold the king **w** ye have chosen, 834
12:13 ye have chosen, *and* **w** ye have desired: 834
16: 3 thou shalt anoint unto me *him* **w** I name unto 834
17:28 with **w** hast thou left those few sheep in 4310
17:45 of the armies of Israel, **w** thou hast defied. 834
21: 9 **w** thou slewest in the valley of Elah, behold, 834
24:14 After **w** is the king of Israel come out? 4310
24:14 after **w** dost thou pursue? after a dead dog, 4310
25:11 *it* unto men, **w** I know not whence they *be?* 834
25:25 young men of my lord, **w** thou didst send. 834
28: 8 bring me *him* up, **w** I shall name unto thee. 834
28:11 the woman, **W** shall I bring up unto thee? 4310
29: 5 of **w** they sang one to another in dances, 834
30:13 David said unto him, To **w** *belongest* thou? 4310
30:21 **w** they had made also to abide at 3963.1
2Sa 7: 7 **w** I commanded to feed my people Israel, 834
7:15 I took *it* from Saul, **w** I put away before thee. 834
7:23 **w** God went to redeem for a people to 834
14: 7 kill him, for the life of his brother **w** he slew; 834
15:33 Unto **w** David said, If thou passest on 2050.2
16:18 **w** the LORD, and this people, and all 834
16:19 again, **w** should I serve? *should I* not *serve* 4310
17: 3 the man **w** thou seekest *is* as if all returned: 834
19:10 Absalom, **w** we anointed over us, is dead in 834
20: 3 **w** he had left to keep the house, and 834
21: 6 Gibeah of Saul, **w** the LORD did choose. NIH
21: 8 **w** she bare unto Saul, Armoni and 834
21: 8 **w** she brought up for Adriel the son of 834
23: 8 These *be* the names of the mighty *men* **w** 834
23: 8 eight hundred, **w** he slew at one time. NIH
1Ki 2: 5 **w** he slew, and shed the blood of war in 3963.1
5: 5 **w** I will set upon thy throne in thy room, 834
7: 8 **w** he had taken *to wife,* like unto this porch. 834
9:21 **w** the children of Israel also were not able 834
10:26 **w** he bestowed in the cities for chariots, 3963.1
11:20 **w** Tahpenes weaned in Pharaoh's house: 1930.2
11:34 **w** I chose, because he kept my 834
13:23 *to wit,* for the prophet **w** he had brought 834
17: 1 God of Israel liveth, before **w** I stand, 834
17:20 evil upon the widow with **w** I sojourn, 1886.3
18:15 the LORD of hosts liveth, before **w** I stand, 834
18:31 unto **w** the word of the LORD came, 834
20:14 Ahab said, By **w**? And he said, Thus saith 4310
20:42 a man **w** I appointed to utter destruction, NIH
21:25 of the LORD, **w** Jezebel his wife stirred up. 834
1Ki 21:26 **w** the LORD cast out before the children of 834
22: 8 by **w** *we* may inquire of the LORD: 2050.2
2Ki 3:14 of hosts liveth, before **w** I stand, surely, 834
5:16 before **w** I stand, I will receive none. 834
6:19 and I will bring you to the man **w** ye seek. 834
6:22 **w** thou hast taken captive with thy sword 834
8: 5 and this *is* her son, **w** Elisha restored to life. 834
10:24 *If* any of the men **w** I *have* brought into your 834
16: 3 **w** the LORD cast out from before 834
17: 8 **w** the LORD cast out from before 834
17:11 as *did* the heathen **w** the LORD carried 834
17:15 *concerning* **w** the LORD had charged them, 834
17:27 Carry thither one of the priests **w** ye brought 834
17:28 one of the priests **w** they had carried away 834
17:33 after the manner of the nations **w** they 834
17:34 the children of Jacob, **w** he named Israel; 834
17:35 With **w** the LORD had made a covenant, 3963.1
18:20 Now on **w** dost thou trust, that thou 4310
19: 4 **w** the king of Assyria his master hath sent to 834
19:10 Let not thy God in **w** thou trustest deceive 834
19:22 **W** hast thou reproached and blasphemed? 4310
19:22 against **w** hast thou exalted *thy* voice, and 4310
21: 2 **w** the LORD cast out before the children of 834
21: 9 **w** the LORD destroyed before the children 834
23: 5 **w** the kings of Judah had ordained to burn 834
25:22 **w** Nebuchadnezzar king of Babylon had left, 834
1Ch 1:12 (of **w** came the Philistines,) 834+8033
2:21 **w** he married when he *was* threescore 1886.3
5: 6 **w** Tilgath-pilneser king of Assyria carried 834
5:25 of the land, **w** God destroyed before them. 834
6:31 these *are they* **w** David set over the service 834
7:14 The sons of Manasseh; Ashriel, **w** she bare: 834
7:21 **w** the men of Gath that were born in *that* 3963.1
9:22 **w** David and Samuel the seer did ordain in 1992
11:10 These also *are* the chief of the mighty *men* **w** 834
11:11 this *is* the number of the mighty *men* **w** 834
17: 6 **w** I commanded to feed my people, saying, 834
17:21 **w** God went to redeem *to be* his own people, 834
17:21 **w** thou hast redeemed out of Egypt? 834
26:32 **w** king David made rulers over 3963.1
29: 1 **w** alone God hath chosen, *is yet* young 2050.2
29: 8 they with **w** *precious* stones were found 2050.2
2Ch 1:11 my people, over **w** I have made thee king: 834
2: 7 **w** David my father did provide. 834
8: 8 **w** the children of Israel consumed not, 834
9:25 **w** he bestowed in the chariot cities, and 3963.1
17:19 besides *those* **w** the king put in the fenced 834
18: 7 by **w** *we* may inquire of the LORD: 2050.2
20:10 **w** thou wouldest not let Israel invade, 834
22: 7 **w** the LORD had anointed to cut off 834
23:18 **w** David had distributed in the house of 834
28: 3 **w** the LORD had cast out before 834
33: 2 **w** the LORD had cast out before 834
33: 9 **w** the LORD had destroyed before 834
Ezr 2: 1 **w** Nebuchadnezzar the king of Babylon had 834
2:65 of **w** *there were* seven thousand three 428
4:10 the rest of the nations **w** the great and 1768
5:14 *was* Sheshbazzar, **w** he had made governor; 1768
8:20 **w** David and the princes had appointed for 7945
10:44 *some* of them had wives by *w* they had NIH
Ne 1:10 **w** thou hast redeemed by thy great power, 834
7: 6 **w** Nebuchadnezzar the king of Babylon had 834
7:67 of **w** *there were* seven thousand three 428
8:10 send portions unto *them* for **w** nothing is 2050.2
9:37 it yieldeth much increase unto the kings **w** 834
Est 2: 6 **w** Nebuchadnezzar the king of Babylon had 834
2: 7 **w** Mordecai, when her father and NIH
4: 5 **w** he had appointed to attend upon her, and 834
4:11 except such to **w** the king shall hold out 2050.2
6: 6 What shall be done unto the man **w** the king 834
6: 6 To **w** would the king delight to do honour 4310
6: 7 *For* the man **w** the king delighteth to honour, 834
6: 9 that they may array the man *withal* **w** 834
6: 9 Thus shall it be done to the man **w** the king 834
6:11 Thus shall it be done unto the man **w** 834
6:13 before **w** thou hast begun to fall, thou shalt 834
Job 3:23 way is hid, and **w** God hath hedged in? 2050.2
5:17 happy *is* the man **w** God correcteth: 5105.2
9:15 **W**, though I were righteous, *yet* would I not 834
15:19 Unto **w** alone the earth was given, and 1992.1
19:19 and they **w** I loved are turned against me. NIH
19:27 **W** I shall see for myself, and mine eyes shall 834
25: 3 and upon **w** doth not his light arise? 4310
26: 4 To **w** hast thou uttered words? and 4310
30: 2 profit me, in **w** old age was perished? 4123.1
Ps 10: 3 the covetous, **w** the LORD abhorreth. NIH
16: 3 *to* the excellent, in **w** *is* all my delight. 3963.1
18: 2 my God, my strength, in **w** I will trust; 2050.2
18:43 a people **w** I have not known shall serve me. NIH
27: 1 *is* my light and my salvation; **w** shall I fear? 4310
27: 1 strength of my life; of **w** shall I be afraid? 4310
32: 2 Blessed *is* the man unto **w** the LORD 2050.2
33:12 the people *w* he hath chosen for his own NIH
41: 9 mine own familiar friend, in **w** I trusted, 834
45:16 **w** thou mayest make princes in all 4123.1
47: 4 for us, the excellency of Jacob **w** he loved. 834
65: 4 Blessed *is the man* **w** thou choosest, and NIH
69:26 For they persecute *him* **w** thou hast smitten; 834
69:26 they talk to the grief of those **w** thou hast NIH
73:25 **W** have I in heaven *but thee? and there is* 4310
80:17 upon the son of man *w* thou madest strong NIH
86: 9 All nations **w** thou hast made shall come and 834
88: 5 in the grave, **w** thou rememberest no more: 834
89:21 With **w** my hand shall be established. 834
94: 1 O LORD God, to **w** vengeance belongeth; NIH
94: 1 O God, to **w** vengeance belongeth, NIH
94:12 Blessed *is* the man **w** thou 834+5105.2
95:11 *Unto* **w** I sware in my wrath that they should 834
104:26 **w** thou hast made to play therein. NIH
105:26 his servant; *and* Aaron **w** he had chosen. 834
106:34 *concerning* **w** the LORD commanded them: 834
106:38 **w** they sacrificed unto the idols of Canaan: 834
107: 2 **w** he hath redeemed from the hand of 834
144: 2 my shield, and *he* in **w** I trust; 2050.2
146: 3 *nor* in the son of man, in **w** *there is* no help. 7945

Pr 3:12 For w the LORD loveth he correcteth; 834
3:12 even as a father the son *in* w he delighteth. NIH
3:27 not good from them to w it is due, 1167
25: 7 of the prince w thine eyes have seen. 834
30:31 a king, against w *there is* no rising up. 2050.2
Ecc 4: 8 neither *saith he,* For w do I labour, and 4310
5:19 Every man also to w God hath given riches 834
6: 2 A man to w God hath given riches, wealth, 834
8:14 that there be just *men,* unto w it happeneth 834
8:14 there be wicked *men,* to w it happeneth 1992.1
9: 9 Live joyfully with the wife w thou lovest all 834
SS 1: 7 Tell me, O thou w my soul loveth, 7945
3: 1 By night on my bed I sought *him* w my 7945
3: 2 I will seek *him* w my soul loveth: 7945
3: 3 *to* w *I said,* Saw ye *him* whom my soul NIH
3: 3 *to whom I said,* Saw ye *him* w my soul 7945
3: 4 But I found *him* w my soul loveth: 7945
Isa 6: 8 W shall I send, and who will go for us? 4310
8:12 to all *them to* w this people shall say, 834
8:18 the children w the LORD hath given me *are* 834
10: 3 to w will ye flee for help? and where will 4310
19:25 W the LORD of hosts shall bless, saying, 834
22:16 w hast thou here, that thou hast hewed thee 4310
23: 2 thou w the merchants of Zidon, that pass 3509.3
28: 9 W shall he teach knowledge? and whom 4310
28: 9 w shall he make to understand doctrine? 4310
28:12 To w he said, This *is* the rest *wherewith* ye 834
31: 6 Turn ye unto *him from* w the children of 834
36: 5 now on w dost thou trust, that thou rebellest 4310
37: 4 w the king of Assyria his master hath sent to 834
37:10 in w thou trustest, deceive thee, saying, 834
37:23 W hast thou reproached and blasphemed? 4310
37:23 against w hast thou exalted *thy* voice, and 4310
40:14 With w took he counsel, and 4310
40:18 To w then will ye liken God? or 4310
40:25 To w then will ye liken me, or shall I be 4310
41: 8 *art* my servant, Jacob w I have chosen, 834
41: 9 *Thou* w I have taken from the ends of 834
42: 1 Behold my servant, w I uphold; mine 2050.2
42: 1 mine elect, *in* w my soul delighteth; NIH
42:24 the LORD, he against w we have sinned? 2098
43:10 and my servant w I have chosen: 834
44: 1 my servant; and Israel, w I have chosen: 2050.2
44: 2 and *thou,* Jeshurun, w I have chosen. 2050.2
46: 5 To w will ye liken me, and make *me* equal, 4310
47:15 Thus shall they be unto thee *with* w thou 834
49: 3 my servant, O Israel, in w I will be glorified. 834
49: 7 *and* his Holy One, to him w man despiseth, NIH
49: 7 to him w the nation abhorreth, to a servant NIH
50: 1 mother's divorcement, w I have put away? 834
50: 1 which of my creditors *is it* to w I have sold 834
51:18 all the sons w she hath brought forth; NIH
51:19 and the sword: *by* w shall I comfort thee? 4310
53: 1 to w is the arm of the LORD revealed? 4310
57: 4 Against w do ye sport yourselves? 4310
57: 4 against w make ye a wide mouth, *and* 4310
57:11 of w hast thou been afraid or feared, 4310
66:13 As one w his mother comforteth, so will I 834
Jer 1: 2 To w the word of the LORD came in 834
6:10 To w shall I speak, and give warning, 4310
7: 9 and walk after other gods w ye know not; 834
8: 2 w they have loved, and whom they 834+3963.1
8: 2 w they have served, and after whom 834+3963.1
8: 2 after w they have walked, and 834+1992.1
8: 2 w they have sought, and whom they 834+3963.1
8: 2 and w they have worshipped: 834+1992.1
9:12 *who is he* to w the mouth of the LORD 834
9:16 w neither they nor their fathers have known: 834
11:12 cry unto the gods unto w they offer 834+1992.1
14:16 the people to w they prophesy shall be cast 834
18: 8 If that nation, against w I have pronounced, 834
19: 4 w neither they nor their fathers have known, 834
20: 6 thy friends, to w thou hast prophesied lies. 834
23: 9 like a man w wine hath overcome, 2050.2
24: 5 w I have sent out of this place *into* the land 834
25:15 all the nations, to w I send thee, to drink it. 834
25:17 to drink, unto w the LORD had sent me: 834
26: 5 w I sent unto you, both rising up early, and 834
27: 5 have given it unto w it seemed meet unto 834
29: 1 to all the people w Nebuchadnezzar had 834
29: 3 w Zedekiah king of Judah sent unto Babylon 834
29: 4 w I have caused to be carried away from 834
29:20 w I have sent from Jerusalem to Babylon: 834
29:22 w the king of Babylon roasted in the fire; 834
30: 9 David their king, w I will raise up unto them. 834
30:17 This *is* Zion, w no man seeketh after. 1886.3
33: 5 w I have slain in mine anger and in my fury, 834
34:11 w they had let go free, to return, and 834
34:16 w ye had set at liberty at their pleasure, 834
37: 1 w Nebuchadrezzar king of Babylon made 834
38: 9 w they have cast into the dungeon; 834
39:17 into the hand of the men of w thou *art* afraid. 834
40: 5 w the king of Babylon hath made governor 834
41: 2 w the king of Babylon had made governor 834
41: 9 the men, w he had slain because of Gedaliah, 834
41:10 w Nebuzar-adan the captain of the guard had 834
41:16 all the remnant of the people w he had 834
41:16 w he had brought again from Gibeon: 834
41:18 w the king of Babylon made governor in 834
42: 6 of the LORD our God, to w we send thee; 834
42: 9 unto w ye sent me to present your 834
42:11 of Babylon, of w ye *are* afraid; 834+4480+6440
44: 3 w they knew not, *neither* they, you, nor your 834
50:20 be found: for I will pardon them w I reserve. 834
52:28 This *is* the people w Nebuchadrezzar carried 834
La 1:10 w thou didst command *that* they should not 834
1:14 *their* hands, *from* w I am not able to rise up. NIH
2:20 and consider to w thou hast done this. 4310
4:20 was taken in their pits, *of* w we said, 834
Eze 9: 6 come not near any man upon w *is* the mark; 834
11: 1 among w I saw Jaazaniah the son of 3963.1
11: 7 Your slain w ye have laid in the midst of it, 834
11:15 *are* they unto w the inhabitants of Jerusalem 834
13:22 the righteous sad, w I have not made sad; 2050.2
16:20 w thou hast borne unto me, and these hast 834

Eze 16:37 with w thou hast taken pleasure, and all *them* 834
20: 9 among w they *were,* in whose sight I made 834
23: 7 men of Assyria, and with all *on* w she doted: 834
23: 9 the hand of the Assyrians, upon w she doted. 834
23:22 from w thy mind is alienated, and I will 834
23:28 I *will* deliver thee into the hand *of them* w 834
23:28 into the hand *of them* from w thy mind is 834
23:37 also caused their sons, w they bare unto me, 834
23:40 come from far, unto w a messenger *was* sent; 834
23:40 for w thou didst wash *thyself,* paintedst thy 834
24:21 your daughters w ye have left shall fall by 834
28:25 from the people among w they are scattered, 834
31: 2 W art thou like in thy greatness? 4310
31:18 To w art thou thus like in glory and 4310
32:19 W dost thou pass in beauty? go down, and 4310
38:17 *Art* thou he of w I have spoken in old time 834
Da 1: 4 Children in w *was* no blemish, but 834
1: 4 w *they* might teach the learning and NIH
1: 7 Unto w the prince of the eunuchs gave 1992.1
1:11 w the prince of the eunuchs had set over 834
2:24 w the king had ordained to destroy the wise 1768
3:12 There are certain Jews w thou hast set over 1768
3:17 our God w we serve *is* able to deliver us 1768
4: 8 and in w *is* the spirit of the holy gods: 1886.8
5:11 in w *is* the spirit of the holy gods; 1886.8
5:11 w the king Nebuchadnezzar thy father, NIH
5:12 w the king named Belteshazzar: 1768
5:13 w the king my father brought out of Jewry? 1768
5:19 w he would he slew; and whom he would 1768
5:19 w he would he kept alive; and whom he 1768
5:19 w he would he set up; and whom he would 1768
5:19 he set up; and w he would he put down. 1768
6: 2 three presidents; of w Daniel *was* first: 1952.1
6:16 Thy God w thou servest continually, 1768
6:20 is thy God, w thou servest continually, 1768
7: 8 before w there were three of the first 1886.9
7:20 which came up, and before w three fell; 1886.9
9:21 w I had seen in the vision at the beginning, 834
11:21 to w they shall not give the honour of 2050.2
11:38 a god w his fathers knew not shall he honour 834
11:39 w he shall acknowledge *and* increase *with* 834
Hos 13:10 thy judges *of* w thou saidst, Give me a king 834
Joel 2:32 and in the remnant w the LORD *shall* call. 834
3: 2 w they have scattered among the nations, 834
Am 6: 1 to w the house of Israel came! 1992.1
7: 2 *by* w shall Jacob arise? for he *is* small. 4310
7: 5 *by* w shall Jacob arise? for he *is* small. 4310
Na 3:19 for upon w hath not thy wickedness passed 4310
Zep 3:18 *to* w the reproach of it *was* a burden. NIH
Zec 1: 4 unto w the former prophets have cried, 834
1:10 These *are they* w the LORD hath sent to 834
7:14 among all the nations w they knew not: 834
12:10 they shall look upon me w they have 834
Mal 1: 4 The people *against* w the LORD hath 834
2:14 against w thou hast dealt treacherously: 834
3: 1 the LORD, w ye seek, shall suddenly come 834
3: 1 messenger of the covenant, w ye delight in: 834
Mt 1:16 of w was born Jesus, who is called Christ. 3739
3:17 is my beloved Son, in w I am well pleased. 3739
7: 9 w if his son ask bread, will he give him a 3739
11:10 For this is *he,* of w it is written, Behold, 3739
12:18 Behold my servant, w I have chosen; my 3739
12:18 my beloved, in w my soul is well pleased: 3739
12:27 by w do your children cast *them* out? 5101
16:13 W do men say that I the Son of man am? 5101
16:15 He saith unto them, But w say ye that I am? 5101
17: 5 is my beloved Son, in w I am well pleased; 3739
17:25 of w do the kings of the earth take custom 5101
18: 7 woe to that man by w the offence cometh. 3739
19:11 this saying, save *they* to w it is given. 3739
20:23 *it shall be given to them* for w it is prepared 3739
23:35 w ye slew between the temple and the altar. 3739
24:45 w his lord hath made ruler over his 3739
24:46 w his lord when he cometh shall find so 3739
26:24 woe unto that man by w the Son of man is 3739
27: 9 w they of the children of Israel did value; 3739
27:15 unto the people a prisoner, w they would. 3739
27:17 W will ye *that* I release unto you? 5101
Mk 1:11 art my beloved Son, in w I am well pleased. 3739
3:13 and calleth unto *him* w he would: 3739
6:16 *thereof,* he said, It is John, w I beheaded: 3739
8:27 saying unto them, W do men say that I am? 5101
8:29 he saith unto them, But w say ye that I am? 5101
10:40 *it shall be given to them* for w it is 3739
13:20 but for the elect's sake, w he hath chosen, 3739
14:21 woe to that man by w the Son of man is 3739
14:71 *saying,* I know not this man of w ye speak. 3739
15:12 *that* I shall do *unto him* w ye call the King 3739
15:40 among w was Mary Magdalene, and 3739
16: 9 out of w he had cast seven devils. 3739
Lk 6:13 he chose twelve, w also he named apostles; 3739
6:14 Simon, (w he also named Peter,) and 3739
6:34 And if ye lend *to them of* w ye hope to 3739
6:47 doeth them, I will shew you to w he is like: 5101
7: 4 That he was worthy for w he should do 3739
7:27 This is *he,* of w it is written, Behold, I send 3739
7:43 I suppose that *he,* to w he forgave most. 3739
7:47 but to w little is forgiven, *the same* loveth 3739
8: 2 out of w went seven devils, 3739
8:35 the man, out of w the devils were departed, 3739
8:38 Now the man out of w the devils were 3739
9: 9 of w I hear such *things?* And he desired to 3739
9:18 saying, W say the people that I am? 5101
9:20 He said unto them, But w say ye that I am? 5101
10:22 and *he* to w the Son will reveal *him.* 1437+3739
11:19 by w do your sons cast *them* out? 5101
12: 5 But I will *forewarn* you w ye shall fear: 5101
12:37 w the lord when he cometh shall find 3739
12:42 w *his* lord shall make ruler over his 3739
12:43 w his lord when he cometh shall find so 3739
12:48 and to w *men* have committed much, 3739
13: 4 upon w the tower in Siloam fell, and 3739
13:16 w Satan hath bound, lo *these* eighteen 3739
17: 1 but woe *unto him,* through w they come. 3739
19:15 unto him, to w he had given the money, 3739

Lk 22:22 but woe unto that man by w he is betrayed. 3739
23:25 was cast into prison, w they had desired; 3739
Jn 1:15 and cried, saying, This was he of w I spake, 3739
1:26 standeth one among you, w ye know not; 3739
1:30 This is he of w I said, After me cometh a 3739
1:33 Upon w thou shalt see the Spirit 302+3739
1:45 of w Moses in the law, and the prophets, 3739
1:47 Behold an Israelite indeed, in w is no guile. 3739
3:26 to w thou barest witness, behold, the same 3739
3:34 For he w God hath sent speaketh the words 3739
4:18 and he w thou now hast is not thy husband: 3739
5:21 so the Son quickeneth w he will. 3739
5:38 for w he hath sent, him ye believe not. 3739
5:45 accuseth you, *even* Moses, in w ye trust. 3739
6:29 that ye believe on *him* w he hath sent. 3739
6:68 answered him, Lord, to w shall we go? 5101
7:25 Is not this he, w they seek to kill? 3739
7:28 but he that sent me is true, w ye know not. 3739
8:53 prophets are dead: w makest thou thyself? 5101
8:54 of w ye say, that he is your God: 3739
10:35 unto w the word of God came, and 3739
10:36 Say ye *of him,* w the Father hath sanctified, 3739
11: 3 Lord, behold, he w thou lovest is sick. 3739
12: 1 had been dead, w he raised from the dead. 3739
12: 9 w he had raised from the dead. 3739
12:38 to w hath the arm of the Lord been 5101
13:18 I know w I have chosen: but that 3739
13:22 one on another, doubting of w he spake. 5101
13:23 bosom one of his disciples, w Jesus loved. 3739
13:24 that *he* should ask who it should be of w he 3739
13:26 He it is, to w I shall give a sop, 3739
14:17 w the world cannot receive, because 3739
14:26 w the Father will send in my name, 3739
15:26 w I will send unto you from the Father, 3739
17: 3 and Jesus Christ, w thou hast sent. 3739
17:11 keep through thine own name those w thou 3739
17:24 I will that they also, w thou hast given me, 3739
18: 4 went forth, and said unto them, W seek ye? 5101
18: 7 Then asked he them again, W seek ye? 5101
19:26 and the disciple standing by, w he loved, 3739
19:37 They shall look on *him* w they pierced. 3739
20: 2 w Jesus loved, and saith unto them, 3739
20:15 w seekest thou? She, supposing him to be 5101
21: 7 Therefore that disciple w Jesus loved saith 3739
21:20 seeth the disciple w Jesus loved following; 3739
Ac 1: 2 unto the Apostles w he had chosen: 3739
1: 3 To w also he shewed himself alive after his 3739
2:24 W God hath raised up, having loosed 3739
2:36 w ye have crucified, both Lord and Christ. 3739
3: 2 w they laid daily at the gate of the temple 3739
3:13 w ye delivered up, and denied him in 3739
3:15 of life, w God hath raised from the dead; 3739
3:16 made this *man* strong, w ye see and know: 3739
3:21 W the heaven must receive until the times 3739
4:10 w ye crucified, whom God raised from 3739
4:10 ye crucified, w God raised from the dead, 3739
4:22 on w this miracle of healing was shewed. 3739
4:27 w thou hast anointed, both Herod, and 3739
5:25 the men w ye put in prison are standing in 3739
5:30 up Jesus, w ye slew and hanged on a tree. 3739
5:32 w God hath given to them that obey him. 3739
5:36 to w a number of men, about four hundred, 3739
6: 3 w we may appoint over this business. 3739
6: 6 W they set before the apostles: and 3739
7: 7 And the nation to w they shall be in 1437+3739
7:35 This Moses w they refused, saying, 3739
7:39 To w our fathers would not obey, 3739
7:45 w God drave out before the face of our 3739
7:52 of w ye have been now the betrayers and 3739
8:10 To w they all gave heed, from the least to 3739
8:34 I pray thee, of w speaketh the prophet this? 5101
9: 5 Lord said, I am Jesus w thou persecutest: 3739
9:37 w when they had washed, they laid *her* in an NIG
10:21 and said, Behold, I am he w ye seek: 3739
10:39 w they slew and hanged on a tree: 3739
13:22 to w also he gave testimony, and said, 3739
13:25 *his* course, he said, W think ye that I am? 5101
13:37 w God raised *again,* saw no corruption. 3739
14:23 them to the Lord, on w they believed. 3739
15:17 upon w my name is called, saith the Lord, 3739
15:24 to w we gave no *such* commandment: 3739
17: 3 this Jesus, w I preach unto you, is Christ. 3739
17: 7 W Jason hath received: and these all do 3739
17:23 W therefore ye ignorantly worship, 3739
17:31 by *that* man w he hath ordained; 3739
18:26 w when Aquila and Priscilla had heard, 846
19:13 We adjure you by Jesus w Paul preacheth. 3739
19:16 And the man in w the evil spirit was leapt 3739
19:25 W he called together with the workmen of 3739
19:27 w all Asia and the world worshippeth. 3739
20:25 among w I have gone preaching 3739
21:16 an old disciple, with w we should lodge. 3739
21:29 w they supposed that Paul had brought into 3739
22: 5 from w also I received letters unto 3739
22: 8 I am Jesus of Nazareth, w thou persecutest. 3739
23:29 W I perceived to be accused of questions of 3739
24: 6 w we took, and would have judged 3739
24: 8 by examining of w thyself mayest take 3739
25:15 About w, when I was at Jerusalem, 3739
25:16 To w I answered, It is not the manner of 3739
25:18 Against w when the accusers stood *up,* they 3739
25:19 *was* dead, w Paul affirmed to be alive. 3739
25:24 ye see this *man,* about w all the multitude 3739
25:26 Of w I have no certain *thing* to write unto 3739
26:15 And he said, I am Jesus w thou persecutest. 3739
26:17 *from* the Gentiles, unto w now I send thee, 3739
26:26 these *things,* before w also I speak freely: 3739
27:23 angel of God, whose I am, and w I serve, 3739
28: 4 w, though he hath escaped the sea, 3739
28: 8 to w Paul entered in, and prayed, and 3739
28:15 w when Paul saw, he thanked God, and 3739
28:23 to w he expounded and testified 3739
Ro 1: 5 By w we have received grace and 3739
1: 6 Among w are ye also *the* called of Jesus 3739
1: 9 w I serve with my spirit in the gospel of his 3739

W

Ro 3:25 W God hath set forth *to be* a propitiation 3739
4: 6 unto w God imputeth righteousness without 3739
4: 8 Blessed *is* the man to w the Lord will not 3739
4:17 before *him* w he believed, *even* God, 3739
4:24 But for us also, to w it shall be imputed, 3739
5: 2 By w also we have access by faith into this 3739
5:11 by w we have now received the atonement. 3739
6:16 that to w ye yield yourselves servants to 3739
6:16 to obey, *his* servants ye are to w ye obey; 3739
8:29 For w he did foreknow, he also did 3739
8:30 Moreover w he did predestinate, them he 3739
8:30 and w he called, them he also justified: and 3739
8:30 and w he justified, them he also glorified. 3739
9: 4 to w pertaineth the adoption, and the glory, 3739
9: 5 of w as concerning the flesh Christ *came,* 3739
9:15 I will have mercy on w I will have 302+3739
9:15 I will have compassion on w I will 302+3739
9:18 Therefore hath he mercy on w he will *have* 3739
9:18 *have mercy,* and w he will he hardeneth. 3739
9:24 Even us, w he hath called, not of the Jews 3739
10:14 shall they call on *him* in w they have not 3739
10:14 how shall they believe *in him* of w they 3739
11:36 to him, *are* all *things:* to w *be* glory for ever. 846
13: 7 tribute to w tribute *is due;* custom to whom 3588
13: 7 tribute to whom tribute *is due;* custom to w 3588
13: 7 fear to w fear; honour to whom honour. 3588
13: 7 fear to whom fear; honour to w honour. 3588
14:15 not him with thy meat, for w Christ died. 3739
15:21 To w he was not spoken of, they shall see: 3739
16: 4 unto w not only I give thanks, but also all 3739
1Co 1: 9 by w ye were called unto the fellowship of 3739
3: 5 *is* Apollos, but ministers by w ye believed, 3739
7:39 she is at liberty to be married to w she will; 3739
8: 6 of w *are* all *things,* and we in him; 3739
8: 6 by w *are* all *things,* and we by him. 3739
8:11 the weak brother perish, for w Christ died? 3739
10:11 upon w the ends of the world are come. 3739
15: 6 of w the greater part remain unto this 3739
15:15 w he raised not up, if so be that the dead 3739
2Co 1:10 in w we trust that he will yet deliver *us;* 3739
2: 3 I should have sorrow from *them of* w I 3739
2:10 To w ye forgive any *thing,* I *forgive* also: 3739
2:10 for if I forgave any *thing,* to w I forgave *it,* 3739
4: 4 In w the god of this world hath blinded 3739
8:22 w we have oftentimes proved diligent in 3739
10:18 is approved, but w the Lord commendeth. 3739
11: 4 w we have not preached, or *if* ye receive 3739
12:17 Did I make a gain of you by any of them w 3739
Gal 1: 5 To w *be* glory for ever and ever. Amen. 3739
2: 5 To w we gave place by subjection, no, 3739
3:19 till the seed should come to w the promise 3739
4:19 of w I travail in birth again until Christ be 3739
6:14 by w the world is crucified unto me, and I 3739
Eph 1: 7 In w we have redemption through his 3739
1:11 In w also we have obtained an inheritance, 3739
1:13 In w ye also *trusted,* after that ye heard 3739
1:13 in w also after that ye believed, ye were 3739
2: 3 Among w also we all had our conversation 3739
2:21 In w all the building fitly framed together 3739
2:22 In w you also are builded together for a 3739
3:12 In w we have boldness and access with 3739
3:15 Of w the whole family in heaven and earth 3739
4:16 From w the whole body fitly joined 3739
6:22 W I have sent unto you for the same 3739
Php 2:15 among w ye shine as lights in the world; 3739
3: 8 for w I have suffered the loss of all *things,* 3739
3:18 of w I have told you often, and now tell *you* 3739
Col 1:14 In w we have redemption through his 3739
1:27 To w God would make known what *is* 3739
1:28 W we preach, warning every man, and 3739
2: 3 In w are hid all the treasures of wisdom and 3739
2:11 In w also ye are circumcised with 3739
4: 8 W I have sent unto you for the same 3739
4:10 (touching w ye received commandments: 3739
1Th 1:10 w he raised from the dead, *even* Jesus, 3739
2Th 2: 8 w the Lord shall consume with the spirit of 3739
1Ti 1:15 the world to save sinners; of w I am chief. 3739
1:20 Of w is Hymeneus and Alexander; whom I 3739
1:20 w I have delivered unto Satan, that they 3739
6:16 w no man hath seen, nor can see: 3739
6:16 to w *be* honour and power everlasting. 3739
2Ti 1: 3 w I serve from *my* forefathers with pure 3739
1:12 for I know w I have believed, and I am 3739
1:15 of w are Phygellus and Hermogenes. 3739
2:17 a canker: of w is Hymeneus and Philetus; 3739
3:14 knowing of w thou hast learned *them;* 5101
4:15 Of w be thou ware also; for he hath greatly 3739
4:18 to w *be* glory for ever and ever. Amen. 3739
Phm 1:10 w I have begotten in my bonds: 3739
1:12 W I have sent again: thou therefore 3739
1:13 W I would have retained with me, that in 3739
Heb 1: 2 w he hath appointed heir of all *things,* by 3739
1: 2 of all *things,* by w also he made the worlds; 3739
2:10 for w *are* all *things,* and by whom *are* all 3739
2:10 by w *are* all *things,* in bringing many sons 3739
3:17 But with w was he grieved forty years? 5101
3:18 And to w sware he that *they* should not 5101
4: 6 they to w it was first preached entered not in NIG
4:13 opened unto the eyes of him with w we 3739
5:11 Of w we have many things to say, and 3739
6: 7 bringeth forth herbs meet for them by w it 3739
7: 2 To w also Abraham gave a tenth *part* of all; 3739
7: 4 w even the patriarch Abraham gave 3739
7: 8 there he *receiveth them,* of w it is witnessed NIG
7:13 For he of w these *things* are spoken 3739
11:18 Of w it was said, That in Isaac shall thy 3739
11:38 (Of w the world was not worthy:) 3739
12: 6 For w the Lord loveth he chasteneth, and 3739
12: 6 and scourgeth every son w he receiveth. 3739
12: 7 for what son is *he* w the father chasteneth 3739
13:21 to w *be* glory for ever and ever. 3739
13:23 with w, if he come shortly, I will see you. 3739
Jas 1:17 with w is no variableness, neither shadow 3739
1Pe 1: 8 W having not seen, ye love; in whom, 3739
1: 8 in w, though now ye see *him* not, 3739
1Pe 1:12 Unto w it was revealed, that not unto 3739
2: 4 To w coming, *as unto* a living stone, 3739
4:11 to w be praise and dominion for ever and 3739
5: 8 walketh about, seeking w he may devour: 5101
5: 9 W resist stedfast in the faith, knowing that 3739
2Pe 1:17 is my beloved Son, in w I am well pleased. 3739
2: 2 by reason of w the way of truth shall be 3739
2:17 to w the mist of darkness is reserved for 3739
2:19 for of w a man is overcome, of the same is 3739
1Jn 4:20 for he that loveth not his brother w he hath 3739
4:20 how can he love God w he hath not seen? 3739
2Jn 1: 1 and her children, w I love in the truth; 3739
3Jn 1: 1 wellbeloved Gaius, w I love in the truth. 3739
1: 6 w if thou bring forward on their journey 3739
Jude 1:13 to w is reserved the blackness of darkness 3739
Rev 7: 2 to w it was given to hurt the earth and 3739
17: 2 With w the kings of the earth have 3739
20: 8 the number of w *is* as the sand of the sea. 3739

WHOMSOEVER (20) [EVER, SO, WHO]

Ge 31:32 With w thou findest thy gods, let him not 834
44: 9 With w of thy servants it be found, 834
Lev 15:11 w he toucheth that hath the issue, and 834+3605
Jdg 7: 4 of w I say unto thee, This shall not go 834+3605
11:24 So w the LORD our God shall drive 834+3605
Da 4:17 giveth it to w he will, and setteth up 1768+4479
4:25 of men, and giveth it to w he will. 1768+4479
4:32 of men, and giveth it to w he will. 1768+4479
5:21 *that* he appointeth over it w he will. 1768+4479
Mt 11:27 and *he* to w the Son will reveal *him.* 1437+3739
21:44 but on w it shall fall, it will grind him 302+3739
26:48 saying, W I shall kiss, that *same* is he: 302+3739
Mk 14:44 saying, W I shall kiss, *that* same is he; 302+3739
15: 6 unto them one prisoner, w they desired. 3746
Lk 4: 6 unto me; and to w I will I give it. 1437+3739
12:48 *stripes.* For unto w much is given, 3739+3956
20:18 but on w it shall fall, it will grind him 302+3739
Jn 13:20 that receiveth w I send receiveth me; 1437+5100
Ac 8:19 this power, that on w I lay hands, 1437+3739
1Co 16: 3 w you shall approve by *your* letters, 1437+3739

WHORE (14) [WHORE'S, WHOREDOM, WHOREDOMS, WHOREMONGER, WHOREMONGERS, WHORES, WHORING, WHORISH]

Lev 19:29 thy daughter, to **cause** her **to be a** w; 2181
21: 7 They shall not take a wife *that is* a w, or 2181
21: 9 if she profane herself by **playing the** w, she 2181
Dt 22:21 to **play the** w *in* her father's house: 2181
23:17 There shall be no w of the daughters of 6945
23:18 Thou shalt not bring the hire of a w, or 2181
Jdg 19: 2 his concubine **played the** w against him, 2181
Pr 23:27 For a w *is* a deep ditch; and a strange 2181
Isa 57: 3 the seed of the adulterer and the w. 2181
Eze 16:28 Thou hast **played the** w also with 2181
Rev 17: 1 the great w that sitteth upon many waters: 4204
17:15 where the w sitteth, are peoples, and 4204
17:16 these shall hate the w, and shall make her 4204
19: 2 for he hath judged the great w, which did 4204

WHORE'S (1) [WHORE]

Jer 3: 3 thou hadst a w forehead, 802+2181

WHOREDOM (22) [WHORE]

Ge 38:24 and also, behold, she *is* with child by w. 2183
Lev 19:29 lest the land **fall to** w, and the land become 2181
20: 5 to commit w with Molech, from among 2181
Nu 25: 1 the people begun to **commit** w with 2181
Jer 3: 9 came to pass through the lightness of her w, 2184
13:27 the lewdness of thy w, *and* 2184
Eze 16:17 of men, and didst **commit** w with them, 2181
16:33 come unto thee on every side for thy w. 8457
20:30 and **commit** ye w after their abominations? 2181
23: 8 her virginity, and poured their w upon her. 8457
23:17 they defiled her with their w, and she was 8457
23:27 and thy w *brought* from the land of Egypt: 2184
43: 7 *neither* they, nor their kings, by their w, 2184
43: 9 Now let them put away their w, and 2184
Hos 1: 2 the land hath **committed great** w, 2181+2181
4:10 they shall **commit** w, and shall not 2181
4:11 W and wine and new wine take *away* 2184
4:13 therefore your daughters shall **commit** w, 2181
4:14 your daughters when they **commit** w, 2181
4:18 they have **committed** w **continually**: 2181+2181
5: 3 thou **committest** w, *and* Israel is defiled. 2181
6:10 there *is* the w of Ephraim, Israel is defiled. 2184

WHOREDOMS (32) [WHORE]

Nu 14:33 bear your w, until your carcases be wasted 2184
2Ki 9:22 so long as the w of thy mother Jezebel and 2183
2Ch 21:13 like to the w of the house of Ahab, and 2181
Jer 3: 2 thou hast polluted the land with thy w and 2184
Eze 16:20 be devoured. *Is this* of thy w a small matter, 8457
16:22 thy w thou hast not remembered the days of 8457
16:25 one that passed by, and multiplied thy w. 8457
16:26 hast increased thy w, to provoke me to 8457
16:34 is in thee from *other* women in thy w, 8457
16:34 whereas none followeth thee to **commit** w: 2181
16:36 thy nakedness discovered through thy w 8457
23: 3 they **committed** w in Egypt; 2181
23: 3 in Egypt; they **committed** w in their youth: 2181
23: 7 Thus she committed her w with them, 8457
23: 8 Neither left she her w *brought* from Egypt: 8457
23:11 in her w more than her sister in *her* 8457
23:11 whoredoms more than her sister in *her* w. 2183
23:14 *that* she increased her w: for when she saw 8457
23:18 So she discovered her w, and 8457
23:19 Yet she multiplied her w, in calling to 8457
23:29 the nakedness of thy w shall be discovered, 2183
23:29 both thy lewdness and thy w. 8457
23:35 bear thou also thy lewdness and thy w. 8457
23:43 Will they now **commit** w with her, 2181+8457
Hos 1: 2 take unto thee a wife of w and children of 2183
1: 2 a wife of whoredoms and children of w: 2183
Hos 2: 2 therefore put away her w out of her sight, 2183
2: 4 her children; for they *be the* children of w. 2183
4:12 for the spirit of w hath caused *them* to err, 2183
5: 4 for the spirit of w *is* in the midst of them, 2183
Na 3: 4 Because of the multitude of the w of 2183
3: 4 that selleth nations through her w, and 2183

WHOREMONGER (1) [WHORE]

Eph 5: 5 For this ye know, that no w, nor unclean 4205

WHOREMONGERS (4) [WHORE]

1Ti 1:10 For w, for them that defile themselves with 4205
Heb 13: 4 but w and adulterers God will judge. 4205
Rev 21: 8 and w, and sorcerers, and idolaters, 4205
22:15 and w, and murderers, and idolaters, and 4205

WHORES (2) [WHORE]

Eze 16:33 They give gifts to all w: but thou givest thy 2181
Hos 4:14 for themselves are separated with w, and 2181

WHORING (19) [WHORE]

Ex 34:15 they **go a** w after their gods, and 2181
34:16 their daughters **go a** w after their gods, and 2181
34:16 and **make** thy sons **go a** w after their gods. 2181
Lev 17: 7 after whom they have **gone a** w. 2181
20: 5 cut him off, and all that **go a** w after him, 2181
20: 6 after wizards, to **go a** w after them, I will 2181
Nu 15:39 own eyes, after which ye use to **go a** w: 2181
Dt 31:16 **go a** w after the gods of the strangers of 2181
Jdg 2:17 they **went a** w after other gods, and 2181
8:27 all Israel **went** thither **a** w after it: 2181
8:33 **went a** w after Baalim, and 2181
1Ch 5:25 **went a** w after the gods of the people of 2181
2Ch 21:13 **made** Judah and the inhabitants of Jerusalem **to go a** w, 2181
Ps 73:27 thou hast destroyed all them that **go a** w 2181
106:39 and **went a** w with their own inventions. 2181
Eze 6: 9 their eyes, which **go a** w after their idols: 2181
23:30 thou hast **gone a** w after the heathen, 2181
Hos 4:12 they have **gone a** w from under their God. 2181
9: 1 for thou hast **gone a** w from thy God, 2181

WHORISH (3) [WHORE]

Pr 6:26 For by means of a w woman *a man is* 2181
Eze 6: 9 because I am broken with their w heart, 2181
16:30 *things,* the work of an imperious w woman; 2181

WHOSE (314) [WHO]

Ge 1:11 his kind, w seed *is* in itself, upon the earth: 834
1:12 w seed *was* in itself, after his kind: 834
7:22 All in w nostrils *was* the breath of life, 2050.2
11: 4 a tower, w top *may reach* unto heaven; 2050.2
16: 1 an Egyptian, w name *was* Hagar. 1886.3
17:14 the uncircumcised man *child* w flesh of his 834
22:24 his concubine, w name *was* Reumah, she 1886.3
24:23 said, W daughter *art* thou? tell me, I pray 4310
24:37 of the Canaanites, in w land I dwell: 834
24:47 I asked her, and said, W daughter *art* thou? 4310
32:17 asketh thee, saying, W *art* thou? 4310+3807.1
32:17 and w *are* these before thee? 4310+3807.1
38: 1 a certain Adullamite, w name *was* Hirah. 2050.2
38: 2 a certain Canaanite, w name *was* Shuah; 2050.2
38: 6 for Er his firstborn, w name *was* Tamar. 1886.3
38:25 w these *are,* *am* I with child: 834+2050.2+3807.1
38:25 Discern, I pray thee, w *are* these, 4310+3807.1
44:17 *but* the man in w hand the cup is 834+2050.2
49:22 by a well; w branches run over the wall. NIH
Ex 34:14 for the LORD, w name *is* Jealous, *is* a 2050.2
35:21 every one w heart stirred him up, and 834
35:26 all the women w heart stirred them up in 834
35:29 w heart made them willing to bring for all 834
36: 2 in w heart the LORD had put wisdom, 2050.2
36: 2 *even* every one w heart stirred him up to 834
Lev 13:40 the man w hair is fallen off his head, he *is* 3588
14:32 w hand is not able to get *that which* 2050.2
15:32 *of him* w seed goeth from him, and is defiled 834
16:27 w blood was brought in to make 3963.1
21:10 upon w head the anointing oil was 2050.2
22: 4 the dead, or a man w seed goeth from him; 834
24:10 w father *was* an Egyptian, 1031
Nu 24: 3 and the man w eyes are open hath said: 1886.1
24:15 and the man w eyes are open hath said: 1886.1
Dt 8: 9 a land w stones *are* iron, and out of whose 834
8: 9 and out of w hills thou mayest dig brass. 1886.3
19: 1 w land the LORD thy God giveth thee, and 834
28:49 a nation w tongue thou shalt not understand; 834
29:18 w heart turneth away *this* day from 834
Jos 24:15 the gods of the Amorites, in w land ye dwell: 834
Jdg 4: 2 the captain of w host *was* Sisera, which 2050.2
6:10 gods of the Amorites, in w land ye dwell: 3963.1
8:31 him a son, w name he called Abimelech. 2050.2
13: 2 of the Danites, w name *was* Manoah; 2050.2
16: 4 the valley of Sorek, w name *was* Delilah. 1886.3
17: 1 of mount Ephraim, w name *was* Micah. 2050.2
Ru 2: 2 glean ears of corn after *him* in w sight I 2050.2
2: 5 that was set over the reapers, W 4310+3807.1
2:12 under w wings thou art come to trust. 2050.2
3: 2 our kindred, with w maidens thou wast? 2050.2
1Sa 9: 1 w name *was* Kish, the son of Abiel, 2050.2
9: 2 he had a son, w name *was* Saul, a choice 2050.2
10:26 a band of men, w hearts God had touched. 834
12: 3 w ox have I taken? or whose ass have I 4310
12: 3 or w ass have I taken? or whom have I 4310
12: 3 of w hand have I received *any* bribe to 4310
17: 4 w height *was* six cubits and a span. 2050.2
17:12 of Beth-lehem-judah, w name *was* Jesse; 2050.2
17:55 of the host, Abner, w son *is* this youth? 4310
17:56 Inquire thou w son the stripling *is.* 4310
17:58 to him, W son *art* thou, *thou* young man? 4310
25: 2 in Maon, w possessions *were* in Carmel; 1930.2
2Sa 3: 7 w name *was* Rizpah, the daughter of 1886.3
3:12 his behalf, saying, W *is* the land? 4310+3807.1
6: 2 w name is called *by* the name of the LORD 834
9: 2 house of Saul a servant w name *was* Ziba. 2050.2

2Sa 9:12 had a young son, w name was Micha. 2050.2
13: 1 had a fair sister, w name was Tamar; 1886.3
13: 3 had a friend, w name was Jonadab, 2050.2
14:27 and one daughter, w name was Tamar: 1886.3
16: 5 w name was Shimei, the son of Gera: 2050.2
16: 8 of Saul, in w stead thou hast reigned; 2050.2
17:10 w heart is as the heart of a lion, shall utterly 834
17:25 man's son, w name was Ithra an Israelite, 2050.2
20: 1 w name was Sheba, the son of Bichri, 2050.2
21:16 the weight of w spear weighed three 2050.2
21:19 the staff of w spear was like a weaver's 2050.2
1Ki 3:26 spake the woman w the living child was unto 834
8:39 to his ways, w heart thou knowest; 834+2050.2
11:26 w mother's name was Zeruah, a widow 2050.2
2Ki 7: 2 a lord on w hand the king leaned answered 834
7:17 the king appointed the lord on w hand he 834
8: 1 w son he had restored to life, saying, Arise, 834
8: 5 the woman, w son he had restored to life, 834
12:15 into w hand they delivered the money to be 834
18: 4 w high places and whose altars 834+2050.2
18:22 and w altars Hezekiah hath taken away, 2050.2
1Ch 2:16 W sisters were Zeruiah, and Abigail. 1992.1
2:26 also another wife, w name was Atarah; 1886.3
2:34 an Egyptian, w name was Jarha. 2050.2
7: 2 w number was in the days of David two 3963.1
7:15 w sister's name was Maachah;) 2050.2
8:29 of Gibeon; w wife's name was Maachah: 2050.2
8:38 w names are these, Azrikam, Bocheru, 3963.1
9:35 Jehiel, w wife's name was Maachah: 2050.2
9:44 w names are these, Azrikam, Bocheru, 3963.1
12: 8 w faces were like the faces of lions, and 1992.1
13: 6 the cherubims, w name is called on it. 834
20: 5 w spear staff was like a weaver's beam. 2050.2
20: 6 w fingers and toes were four and twenty, 2050.2
26: 7 w brethren were strong men, Elihu, and 2050.2
2Ch 6:30 unto all his ways, w heart thou knowest; 834
16: 9 of them w heart is perfect towards him. 3963.1
28: 9 LORD was there, w name was Oded: 2050.2
Ezr 1: 5 with all them w spirit God had raised, 2050.2
5:14 they were delivered unto one, w name 1886.8
7:15 God of Israel, w habitation is in Jerusalem, 1768
8:13 w names are these, Eliphelet, Jeiel, and 3963.1
Est 2: 5 w name was Mordecai, the son of Jair, 2050.2
Job 1: 1 a man in the land of Uz, w name was Job; 2050.2
3:23 Why is light given to a man w way is hid, 834
4:19 w foundation is in the dust, which are 834
5: 5 W harvest the hungry eateth up, and taketh it 834
8:14 W hope shall be cut off, and whose trust 2050.2
8:14 and w trust shall be a spider's web. 2050.2
12: 6 into w hand God bringeth abundantly. 2050.2
12:10 In w hand is the soul of every living 2050.2
22:16 w foundation was overflown with a flood: 3963.1
26: 4 and w spirit came from thee? 4310
30: 1 w fathers I would have disdained to have 3963.1
38:29 Out of w womb came the ice? and 4310
39: 6 W house I have made the wilderness, and 834
Ps 15: 4 In w eyes a vile person is contemned; but 2050.2
17:14 w belly thou fillest with thy hid treasure: 3963.1
26:10 In w hands is mischief, and their right hand 834
32: 1 Blessed is he w transgression is forgiven, NIH
32: 1 transgression is forgiven, w sin is covered. NIH
32: 2 and in w spirit there is no guile. 2050.2
32: 9 w mouth must be held in with bit and 2050.2
33:12 Blessed is the nation w God is the LORD; 834
38:14 and in w mouth are no reproofs. 2050.2
57: 4 w teeth are spears and arrows, and 1992.1
78: 8 and w spirit was not stedfast with God. 2050.2
83:18 that thou, w name alone is JEHOVAH, 3509.2
84: 5 Blessed is the man w strength is 2050.2+3807.1
84: 5 in thee; in w heart are the ways of them. 3963.1
105:18 W feet they hurt with fetters: he was laid 2050.2
144: 8 W mouth speaketh vanity, and their right 834
144:11 w mouth speaketh vanity, and their right 834
144:15 happy is that people, w God is the LORD. 7945
146: 5 w hope is in the LORD his God: 2050.2
Pr 2:15 W ways are crooked, and they froward in 834
26:26 W hatred is covered by deceit, NIH
30:14 w teeth are as swords, and their jaw teeth 2050.2
Ecc 2:21 For there is a man w labour is in 7945+2050.2
7:26 w heart is snares and nets, and her hands as 834
Isa 1:30 For ye shall be as an oak w leaf fadeth, 1886.3
2:22 ye from man, w breath is in his nostrils: 834
5:28 W arrows are sharp, and all their bows bent, 834
6:13 and as an oak, w substance is in them, 834
10:10 w graven images did excel them of 1992.1
14: 2 take them captives, w captives they were; NIH
18: 2 w land the rivers have spoiled. 834
18: 7 under foot, w land the rivers have spoiled, 834
23: 7 Is this your joyous city, w antiquity is of 1886.3
23: 8 the crowning city, w merchants are princes, 834
23: 8 w traffickers are the honourable of 1886.3
26: 3 w mind is stayed on thee: because NIH
28: 1 w glorious beauty is a fading flower, 2050.2
30:13 w breaking cometh suddenly at an instant. 834
31: 9 w fire is in Zion, and his furnace 2050.2+3807.1
36: 7 w high places and whose altars Hezekiah 834
36: 7 and w altars Hezekiah hath taken away, 2050.2
43:14 and the Chaldeans, w cry is in the ships. 3963.1
45: 1 to Cyrus, w right hand I have holden, to 834
51: 7 the people in w heart is my law; 3963.1
51:15 that divided the sea, w waves roared: 2050.2
57:15 that inhabiteth eternity, w name is Holy; 2050.2
57:20 w waters cast up mire and dirt. 2050.2
58:11 and like a spring of water, w waters fail not. 834
Jer 5:15 a nation w language thou knowest not, 2050.2
17: 5 and w heart departeth from the LORD. 2050.2
17: 7 the LORD, and w hope the LORD is. 2050.2
19:13 of all the houses upon w roofs they have 834
22:25 into the hand of them w face thou fearest, 834
32:29 upon w roofs they have offered incense unto 834
33: 5 for all w wickedness I have hid my face 834
37:13 w name was Irijah, the son of Shelemiah, 2050.2
44:28 shall know w words shall stand, mine, or 4310
46: 7 w waters are moved as the rivers? 2050.2
46:18 the King, w name is the LORD of hosts, 2050.2
Jer 48:15 the King, w name is the LORD of hosts. 2050.2
49:12 they w judgment was not to drink of the cup 834
51:57 the King, w name is the LORD of hosts. 2050.2
Eze 3: 6 w words thou canst not understand. 834
11:21 as for them w heart walketh after 3963.1
17: 6 w branches turned toward him, and 2050.2
17:16 w oath he despised, and whose covenant he 834
17:16 oath he despised, and w covenant he brake, 834
20: 9 among whom they were, in w sight I made 834
20:14 the heathen, in w sight I brought them out. 834
20:22 the heathen, in w sight I brought them forth. 834
21:25 wicked prince of Israel, w day is come, 834
21:27 until he come w right it is; 834+2050.2+3807.1
21:29 w day is come, when their iniquity shall 834
23:20 w flesh is as the flesh of asses, and 834
23:20 and w issue is like the issue of horses. 3963.1
24: 6 to the pot w scum is therein, and 834
24: 6 and w scum is not gone out of it! 1886.3
32:23 W graves are set in the sides of the pit, and 834
40: 3 w appearance was like the appearance of 1930.2
40:45 w prospect is toward the south, 834
40:46 the chamber w prospect is toward the north 834
42:15 he brought me forth toward the gate w 834
43: 4 of the gate w prospect is toward the east. 834
47:12 all trees for meat, w leaf shall not fade, 1930.2
Da 2:11 the gods, w dwelling is not with flesh. 1768
2:26 said to Daniel, w name was Belteshazzar, 1768
2:31 great image, w brightness was excellent, 1886.8
3: 1 w height was threescore cubits, and 1886.8
3:27 upon w bodies the fire had no power, 1952.1
4: 8 w name was Belteshazzar, according to 1768
4:19 Daniel, w name was Belteshazzar, 1886.8
4:20 w height reached unto the heaven, and 1886.8
4:21 W leaves were fair, and the fruit thereof 1886.8
4:21 upon w branches the fowls of the heaven 1958.2
4:34 w dominion is an everlasting dominion, 1886.8
4:37 all w works are truth, and his ways 1958.2
5:23 the God in w hand thy breath is, and 1886.8
5:23 thy breath is, and w are all thy ways, 1886.8
7: 9 w garment was white as snow, and 1886.8
7:19 w teeth were of iron, and his nails of 1886.9
7:20 a mouth that spake very great things, w 1886.9
7:27 w kingdom is an everlasting kingdom, 1886.8
10: 1 w name was called Belteshazzar; 834
10: 5 w loins were girded with fine gold of 2050.2
Joel 1: 6 w teeth are the teeth of a lion, 2050.2+3807.1
Am 2: 9 w height was like the height of the cedars, 834
5:27 the LORD, w name is The God of hosts. 2050.2
Ob 1: 3 clefts of the rock, w habitation is high; 2050.2
Jnh 1: 7 that we may know for w cause this 4310+3807.1
1: 8 for w cause this evil is upon us; 4310+3807.1
Mic 5: 2 w goings forth have been from of old, 2050.2
Na 3: 8 w rampart was the sea, and 1886.3+3807.1
Zec 6:12 the man w name is The BRANCH; 2050.2
11: 5 W possessors slay them, and 834
Mt 3:11 than I, w shoes I am not worthy to bear: 3739
3:12 W fan is in his hand, and he will throughly 3739
10: 3 and Lebbeus, w surname was Thaddeus; NIG
22:20 W is this image and superscription? 5101
22:28 Therefore in the resurrection w wife shall 5101
22:42 w son is he? They say unto him, The Son of 5101
Mk 1: 7 the latchet of w shoes I am not worthy to 3739
7:25 w young daughter had an unclean spirit, 3739
12:16 W is this image and superscription? 5101
12:23 they shall rise, w wife shall she be of them? 5101
Lk 1:27 To a virgin espoused to a man w name was 3739
2:25 a man in Jerusalem, w name was Simeon; 3739
3:16 the latchet of w shoes I am not worthy to 3739
3:17 W fan is in his hand, and he will throughly 3739
6: 6 there was a man w right hand was withered. 846
12:20 then w shall those things be, which thou 5101
13: 1 w blood Pilate had mingled with their 3739
20:24 W image and superscription hath it? 5101
20:33 Therefore in the resurrection w wife of 5101
24:18 And the one of them, w name was Cleopas, 3739
Jn 1: 6 was a man sent from God, w name was John. 846
1:27 w shoe's latchet I am not worthy to 3739
4:46 w son was sick at Capernaum. 3739
6:42 of Joseph, w father and mother we know? 3739
10:12 not the shepherd, w own the sheep are not, 3739
11: 2 with her hair, w brother Lazarus was sick.) 3739
18:26 being his kinsman w ear Peter cut off, saith, 3739
19:24 not rent it, but cast lots for it, w it shall be: 5101
20:23 W soever sins ye remit, they are remitted 5100
20:23 and w soever sins ye retain, they are 5100
Ac 7:58 at a young man's feet, w name was Saul. NIG
10: 5 and call for one Simon, w surname is Peter: 3739
10: 6 Simon a tanner, w house is by the sea side: 3739
10:32 and call hither Simon, w surname is Peter; 3739
11:13 and call for Simon, w surname is Peter; 3588
12:12 the mother of John, w surname was Mark; 3588
12:25 took with them John, w surname was Mark. 3588
13: 6 a Jew, w name was Bar-jesus: 3739
13:25 w shoes of his feet I am not worthy to 3739
15:37 take with them John, w surname was Mark. 3588
16:14 heard us: w heart the Lord opened, 3739
18: 7 w house joined hard to the synagogue. 3739
27:23 angel of God, w I am, and whom I serve, 3739
28: 7 man of the island, w name was Publius; NIG
28:11 in the isle, w sign was Castor and Pollux. NIG
Ro 2:29 w praise is not of men, but of God. 3739
3: 8 that good may come? w damnation is just. 3739
3:14 W mouth is full of cursing and bitterness: 3739
4: 7 Saying, Blessed are they w iniquities are 3739
4: 7 are forgiven, and w sins are covered. 3739
9: 5 W are the fathers, and of whom as 3739
2Co 8:18 w praise is in the gospel throughout all 3739
11:15 w end shall be according to their works. 3739
Gal 3: 1 before w eyes Jesus Christ hath been 3739
Php 3:19 W end is destruction, whose God is their 3739
3:19 w God is their belly, and whose glory is in 3739
3:19 is their belly, and w glory is in their shame, NIG
4: 3 w names are in the book of life. 3739
2Th 2: 9 Even him, w coming is after the working of 3739
Tit 1:11 W mouths must be stopped, who subvert 3739
Heb 3: 6 w house are we, if we hold fast 3739
3:17 w carcases fell in the wilderness? 3739
6: 8 is nigh unto cursing; w end is to be burned. 3739
7: 6 But he w descent is not counted from them 3588
11:10 w builder and maker is God. 3739
12:26 W voice then shook the earth: but now he 3739
13: 7 w faith follow, considering the end of their 3739
13:11 w blood is brought into the sanctuary by 3739
1Pe 2:24 by w stripes ye were healed. 3739
3: 3 W adorning let it not be that outward 3739
3: 6 w daughters ye are, as long as ye do well, 3739
2Pe 2: 3 w judgment now of a long time lingereth 3739
Jude 1:12 trees w fruit withereth, without fruit, NIG
Rev 9:11 which is the angel of the bottomless pit, w 846
13: 8 w names are not written in the book of life 3739
13:12 the first beast, w deadly wound was healed. 3739
17: 8 w names were not written in the book of 3739
20:11 from w face the earth and the heaven fled 3739

WHOSO (54) [SO, WHO]

Ge 9: 6 W sheddeth man's blood, by man shall his NIH
Lev 11:27 w toucheth their carcase shall be unclean 3605
22: 4 w toucheth any thing that is unclean by 1886.1
Nu 35:30 W killeth any person, the murderer shall be 3605
Dt 19: 4 W killeth his neighbour ignorantly, whom he 834
2Ch 23:14 w followeth her, let him be slain with 1886.1
Ps 50:23 W offereth praise glorifieth me: and to him NIH
101: 5 W privily slandereth his neighbour, him NIH
107:43 W is wise, and will observe these things, 4310
Pr 1:33 w hearkeneth unto me shall dwell safely, NIH
6:32 But w committeth adultery with a woman NIH
8:35 For w findeth me findeth life, and NIH
9: 4 W is simple, let him turn in hither: as for 4310
9:16 W is simple, let him turn in hither: and 4310
12: 1 W loveth instruction loveth knowledge: but NIH
13:13 W despiseth the word shall be destroyed: NIH
16:20 and w trusteth in the LORD, happy is he. NIH
17: 5 W mocketh the poor reproacheth his Maker: NIH
17:13 W rewardeth evil for good, evil shall not NIH
18:22 W findeth a wife findeth a good thing, and NIH
20: 2 w provoketh him to anger sinneth against NIH
20:20 W curseth his father or his mother, his lamp NIH
21:13 W stoppeth his ears at the cry of the poor, NIH
21:23 W keepeth his mouth and his tongue NIH
25:14 W boasteth himself of a false gift is like 376
26:27 W diggeth a pit shall fall therein: and NIH
27:18 W keepeth the fig tree shall eat the fruit NIH
28: 7 W keepeth the law is a wise son: but he that NIH
28:10 W causeth the righteous to go astray in an NIH
28:13 w confesseth and forsaketh them shall have NIH
28:18 W walketh uprightly shall be saved: but NIH
28:24 W robbeth his father or his mother, and NIH
28:26 but w walketh wisely, he shall be delivered. NIH
29: 3 W loveth wisdom rejoiceth his father: but 376
29:24 W is partner with a thief hateth his own NIH
29:25 w putteth his trust in the LORD shall be NIH
Ecc 7:26 w pleaseth God shall escape from her; but NIH
8: 5 W keepeth the commandment shall feel no NIH
10: 8 w breaketh a hedge, a serpent shall bite him. NIH
10: 9 W removeth stones shall be hurt therewith; NIH
Da 3: 6 w falleth not down and 1768+4479
3:11 w falleth not down and worshippeth, 1768+4479
Zec 14:17 that w will not come up of all the families of 834
Mt 18: 5 And w shall receive one such little 1437+3739
18: 6 But w shall offend one of these little 302+3739
19: 9 w marrieth her which is put away doth 3588
23:20 W therefore shall swear by the altar, 3588
23:21 And w shall swear by the temple, 3588
24:15 holy place, (w readeth, let him understand:) 3588
Mk 7:10 and, W curseth father or mother, let him 3588
Jn 6:54 W eateth my flesh, and drinketh my blood, 3588
Jas 1:25 But w looketh into the perfect law of 3588
1Jn 2: 5 But w keepeth his word, in him verily 302+3739
3:17 But w hath this world's good, and 302+3739

WHOSOEVER (183) [EVER, SO, WHO]

Ge 4:15 said unto him, Therefore w slayeth Cain, 3605
Ex 12:15 for w eateth leavened bread from the first 3605
12:19 for w eateth that which is leavened, 3605
19:12 w toucheth the mount shall be surely put to 3605
22:19 W lieth with a beast shall surely be put to 3605
30:33 W compoundeth any like it, or 376+834
30:33 like it, or w putteth any of it upon a stranger, 834
30:38 W shall make like unto that, to smell 376+834
31:14 for w doeth any work therein, that soul 3605
31:15 w doeth any work in the sabbath day, 3605
32:24 W hath any gold, let them break it off. 4310
32:33 W hath sinned against me, him will I 834+4310
35: 2 w doeth work therein shall be put to death. 3605
35: 5 w is of a willing heart, let him 3605+2050.2
Lev 7:25 For w eateth the fat of the beast, of which 3605
11:24 w toucheth the carcase of them shall be 3605
11:25 w beareth ought of the carcase of them 3605
11:31 w doth touch them, when they be dead, 3605
15: 5 w toucheth his bed shall wash his 376+834
15:10 w toucheth any thing that was under him 3605
15:19 w toucheth her shall be unclean until 3605
15:21 w toucheth her bed shall wash his clothes, 3605
15:22 w toucheth any thing that she sat upon shall 3605
15:27 w toucheth those things shall be unclean, 3605
17:14 blood thereof: w eateth it shall be cut off. 3605
18:29 For w shall commit any of these 834+3605
19:20 w lieth carnally with a woman that is a 376
20: 2 W he be of the children of Israel, or of 376
21:17 W he be of thy seed in their generations that 376
22: 3 W he be of all your seed among 376+834+3605
22: 5 Or w toucheth any creeping thing, 376+834
22:21 w offereth a sacrifice of peace offerings unto 376
24:15 W curseth his God shall bear his sin. 376+376
Nu 5: 2 hath an issue, and w is defiled by the dead: 3605
15:14 or w be among you in your generations, and 834
17:13 W cometh any thing near unto 1886.1
19:13 W toucheth the dead body of any man that 3605
19:16 w toucheth one that is slain with a 834+3605
31:19 w hath killed any person, and 3605

Nu 31:19 w hath touched *any* slain, purify *both* 3605
Dt 18:19 *that* w will not hearken unto my words 376+834
Jos 1:18 W *he be* that doth rebel against thy 376+3605
2:19 *that* w shall go out of the doors of thy 834+3605
2:19 w shall be with thee in the house, 834+3605
20: 9 that w killeth *any* person at unawares might 3605
Jdg 7: 3 saying, W *is* fearful and afraid, let him 4310
1Sa 11: 7 W cometh not forth after Saul and 834+5105.2
2Sa 5: 8 W getteth up to the gutter, and smiteth 3605
14:10 W saith *ought* unto thee, bring him to me, 1886.1
17: 9 at the first, that w heareth *it* will say, 1886.1
1Ki 13:33 w would, he consecrated him, and 1886.1
2Ki 10:19 w shall be wanting, he shall not live. 834+3605
21:12 and Judah, that w heareth of it, 3605
1Ch 11: 6 W smiteth the Jebusites first shall be chief 3605
26:28 w had dedicated *anything, it was* under 3605
2Ch 13: 9 that w cometh to consecrate himself with a 3605
15:13 That w would not seek the LORD 834+3605
23: 7 w *else* cometh into the house, he shall be 1886.1
Ezr 1: 4 w remaineth in any place where he 3605
6:11 a decree, that w shall alter this word, 606+3606
7:26 w will not do the law of thy God, and 1768+3606
10: 8 *that* w would not come within three 834+3605
Est 4:11 do know, that w, *whether* man or woman, 3605
Pr 6:29 w toucheth her shall not be innocent. 3605
20: 1 and w is deceived thereby is not wise. 3605
27:16 W hideth her, hideth the wind, and NIH
Isa 54:15 w shall gather together against thee shall 4310
59: 8 w goeth therein shall not know peace. 3605
Jer 19: 3 the which w heareth, his ears shall tingle. 3605
Eze 33: 4 w heareth the sound of the trumpet, and 1886.1
Da 5: 7 W shall read this writing, 606+1768+1768+3606
6: 7 that w shall ask a petition of any God 1768+3606
Joel 2:32 *that* w shall call on the name of 834+3605
Mt 5:19 W therefore shall break one of these 1437+3739
5:19 but w shall do and teach *them,* 302+3739
5:21 w shall kill shall be in danger of 302+3739
5:22 That w is angry with his brother without a 3956
5:22 and w shall say to his brother, Raca, 302+3739
5:22 but w shall say, *Thou* fool, shall be in 302+3739
5:28 That w looketh on a woman to lust after her 3956
5:31 been said, W shall put away his wife, 302+3739
5:32 That w shall put away his wife, 302+3739
5:32 w shall marry her that is divorced 1437+3739
5:39 but w shall smite thee on thy right cheek, 3748
5:41 And w shall compel thee to go a mile, 3748
7:24 Therefore w heareth these sayings of 3748+3956
10:14 And w shall not receive you, 1437+3739
10:32 W therefore shall confess me before 3748+3956
10:33 But w shall deny me before men, 302+3748
10:42 And w shall give to drink unto one of 1437+3739
11: 6 And blessed is *he,* w shall not be 1437+3739
12:32 And w speaketh a word against 302+3739
12:32 but w speaketh against the Holy 302+3739
12:50 For w shall do the will of my Father 302+3748
13:12 For w hath, to him shall be given, and 3748
13:12 but w hath not, from him shall be taken 3748
15: 5 W shall say to *his* father or 302+3739
16:25 For w will save his life shall lose it: 302+3739
16:25 w will lose his life for my sake shall 302+3739
18: 4 W therefore shall humble himself as this 3748
19: 9 unto you, W shall put away his wife, 302+3739
20:26 but w will be great among you, 1437+3739
20:27 And w will be chief among you, 1437+3739
21:44 And w shall fall on this stone shall be 3588
23:12 And w shall exalt himself shall be abased; 3748
23:16 which say, W shall swear by 302+3739
23:16 w shall swear by the gold of 302+3739
23:18 And, W shall swear by the altar, it is 1437+3739
23:18 but w sweareth by the gift that is upon 302+3739
Mk 3:35 For w shall do the will of God, 302+3739
6:11 And w shall not receive you, nor hear 302+3745
8:34 he said unto them, W will come after me, 3748
8:35 For w will save his life shall lose it; 302+3739
8:35 but w shall lose his life for my sake 302+3739
8:38 W therefore shall be ashamed of me 302+3739
9:37 W shall receive one of such children 1437+3739
9:37 and w shall receive me, receiveth not 1437+3739
9:41 For w shall give you a cup of water to 302+3739
9:42 And w shall offend one of *these* little 302+3739
10:11 W shall put away his wife, and 1437+3739
10:15 W shall not receive the kingdom of 1437+3739
10:43 but w will be great among you, 1437+3739
10:44 And w of you will be the chiefest, 302+3739
11:23 That w shall say unto this mountain, 302+3739
Lk 6:47 W cometh to me, and heareth my sayings, 3956
7:23 And blessed is *he,* w shall not be 1437+3739
8:18 for w hath, to him shall be given; and 302+3739
8:18 and w hath not, from him shall be 302+3739
9: 5 And w will not receive you, when ye 302+3745
9:24 For w will save his life shall lose it: 302+3739
9:24 but w will lose his life for my sake, 302+3739
9:26 For w shall be ashamed of me and 302+3739
9:48 W shall receive this child in my 1437+3739
9:48 w shall receive me receiveth him that 1437+3739
12: 8 W shall confess me before men, 302+3739+3956
12:10 And w shall speak a word against 3739+3956
14:11 For w exalteth himself shall be abased; and 3956
14:27 And w doth not bear his cross, and 3748
14:33 w *he be* of you that forsaketh not all that he 3956
16:18 W putteth away his wife, and 3956
16:18 w marrieth her that is put away from *her* 3956
17:33 W shall seek to save his life shall 1437+3739
17:33 w shall lose *his life* shall preserve it. 1437+3739
18:17 W shall not receive the kingdom of 1437+3739
20:18 W shall fall upon that stone shall be 3956
Jn 3:15 That w believeth in him should not perish, 3956
3:16 that w believeth in him should not perish, 3956
4:13 W drinketh of this water shall thirst again: 3956
4:14 But w drinketh of the water that I shall 302+3739
5: 4 w then first after the troubling of the water NIG
8:34 W committeth sin is the servant of sin. 3956
11:26 And w liveth and believeth in me shall 3956
12:46 that w believeth on me should not abide in 3956
16: 2 that w killeth you will think that he doeth 3956
Jn 19:12 w maketh himself a king speaketh against 3956
Ac 2:21 *that* w shall call on the name of 302+3739+3956
10:43 that through his name w believeth in him 3956
13:26 and w among you feareth God, 3588
Ro 2: 1 O man, w thou art that judgest: 3956
9:33 w believeth on him shall not be ashamed. 3956
10:11 W believeth on him shall not be ashamed. 3956
10:13 For w shall call upon the name 302+3739+3956
13: 2 W therefore resisteth the power, 3588
1Co 11:27 Wherefore w shall eat this bread, and 302+3739
Gal 5: 4 unto you, w of you are justified by the law; 3748
5:10 you shall bear *his* judgment, w he be. 302+3748
Jas 2:10 For w shall keep the whole law, and 3748
4: 4 w therefore will be a friend of 302+3739
1Jn 2:23 W denieth the Son, the same hath not 3956
3: 4 W committeth sin transgresseth also 3956
3: 6 W abideth in him sinneth not: 3956
3: 6 w sinneth hath not seen him, neither known 3956
3: 9 W is born of God doth not commit sin; 3956
3:10 w doeth not righteousness is not of God, 3956
3:15 W hateth his brother is a murderer: and 3956
4:15 W shall confess that Jesus is the Son 302+3739
5: 1 W believeth that Jesus is the Christ is born 3956
5:18 We know that w is born of God sinneth not; 3956
2Jn 1: 9 W transgresseth, 3956
Rev 14:11 and w receiveth the mark of his name. 1536
20:15 And w was not found written in the book of 1536
22:15 and w loveth and maketh a lie. 3956
22:17 And w will, let him take the water of life 3588

WHY (282)

Ge 4: 6 the LORD said unto Cain, W art 4100+3807.1
4: 6 w is thy countenance fallen? 4100+3807.1
12:18 this *that* thou hast done unto me? w 4100+3807.1
12:19 W saidst thou, She *is* my sister? so 4100+3807.1
25:22 she said, If *it be* so, w *am* I thus? 4100+3807.1
27:45 fetch thee from thence: w should I 4100+3807.1
42: 1 Jacob said unto his sons, W do ye 4100+3807.1
47:15 for w should we die in thy 4100+3807.1
Ex 1:18 W have ye done this thing, and have saved 4069
2:20 where *is* he? w *is* it *that* ye have 4100+3807.1
3: 3 see this great sight, w the bush is not burnt. 4069
5:22 evil entreated this people? w *is* it 4100+3807.1
14: 5 they said, W have we done this, that we 4100
17: 2 said unto them, W chide you with me? 4100
18:14 w sittest thou thyself alone, and all 4069
32:11 LORD, w doth thy wrath wax hot 4100+3807.1
Nu 11:20 W came we forth out of Egypt? 4100+3807.1
20: 4 w have ye brought up 4100+3807.1
27: 4 W should the name of our father be 4100+3807.1
Dt 5:25 Now therefore w should we die? 4100+3807.1
Jos 5: 4 this *is* the cause w Joshua did circumcise: 834
7:25 Joshua said, W hast thou troubled us? 4100
17:14 W hast thou given me *but* one lot and 4069
Jdg 2: 2 not obeyed my voice: w have ye done this? 4100
5:16 W abodest thou among 4100+3807.1
5:17 w did Dan remain *in* ships? 4100+3807.1
5:28 W *is* his chariot *so* long in coming? 4069
5:28 w tarry the wheels of his chariots? 4069
6:13 if the LORD be with us, w then 4100+3807.1
8: 1 W hast thou served us thus, that *thou* 4100
9:28 of Shechem: for w should we serve him? 4069
11: 7 w are ye come unto me now when ye are in 4069
11:26 w therefore did ye not recover *them* within 4069
13:18 of the LORD said unto him, W 4100+3807.1
15:10 the men of Judah said, W are ye 4100+3807.1
21: 3 w is this come to pass in Israel, 4100+3807.1
Ru 1:11 w will you go with me? 4100+3807.1
1:21 brought me *home* again empty: w 4100+3807.1
2:10 W have I found grace in thine eyes, 4069
1Sa 1: 8 to her, Hannah, w weepest thou? 4100+3807.1
1: 8 w eatest thou not? and why is thy 4100+3807.1
1: 8 w is thy heart grieved? *am* not I 4100+3807.1
2:23 he said unto them, W do ye such 4100+3807.1
6: 3 it shall be known to you w his hand 4100+3807.1
17: 8 said unto them, W are ye come out 4100+3807.1
17:28 W camest thou down hither? 4100+3807.1
19:17 Saul said unto Michal, W hast thou 4100+3807.1
19:17 Let me go; w should I kill thee? 4100+3807.1
20: 2 w should my father hide this thing from 4069
20: 8 for w shouldest thou bring me to 4100+3807.1
21: 1 W *art* thou alone, and no man with thee? 4069
22:13 Saul said unto him, W have ye 4100+3807.1
27: 5 for w should thy servant dwell in the royal 4100
28:12 W hast thou deceived me? 4100+3807.1
28:15 Samuel said to Saul, W hast thou 4100+3807.1
2Sa 3:24 Abner came unto thee; w *is* it *that* 4100+3807.1
7: 7 saying, W build ye not me a house 4100+3807.1
11:10 w *then* didst thou not go down unto thine 4069
11:21 that he died in Thebez? w went ye 4100+3807.1
13: 4 W *art* thou, *being* the king's son, lean from 4069
13:26 the king said unto him, W should 4100+3807.1
16: 9 son of Zeruiah unto the king, W 4100+3807.1
16:17 this thy kindness to thy friend? w 4100+3807.1
18:11 w didst thou not smite him there to 4069
19:10 therefore w speak ye not a word of 4100+3807.1
19:11 saying, W are ye the last to bring 4100+3807.1
19:29 the king said unto him, W speakest 4100+3807.1
19:36 w should the king recompense *it* 4100+3807.1
19:41 W have our brethren the men of Judah 4069
19:43 w then did ye despise us, that our advice 4069
20:19 a mother in Israel: w wilt thou 4100+3807.1
24: 3 w doth my lord the king delight in 4100+3807.1
1Ki 1: 6 at any time in saying, W hast thou done so? 4069
1:13 my throne? w then doth Adonijah reign? 4069
2:22 w dost thou ask Abishag 4100+3807.1
2:43 W then hast thou not kept the oath of 4069
9: 8 they shall say, W hath the LORD 4100+5921
14: 6 thou wife of Jeroboam; w 2088+4100+3807.1
21: 5 said unto him, W is thy spirit so sad, 4100
2Ki 1: 5 said unto them, W are ye now turned back? 4100
7: 3 one to another, W sit we here until we die? 4100
8:12 Hazael said, W weepeth my lord? And he 4069
12: 7 W repair ye not the breaches of the house? 4069
14:10 for w shouldest thou meddle to *thy* 4100+3807.1
1Ch 17: 6 saying, W have ye not built me a 4100+3807.1
21: 3 they not all my lord's servants? w 4100+3807.1
21: 3 doth my lord require this *thing?* w 4100+3807.1
2Ch 7:21 that he shall say, W hath 4100+871.1
24: 6 W hast thou not required of the Levites to 4069
24:20 Thus saith God, W transgress ye 4100+3807.1
25:15 which said unto him, W hast thou 4100+3807.1
25:16 forbear; w shouldest thou be 4100+3807.1
25:19 abide now at home; w shouldest 4100+3807.1
32: 4 saying, W should the kings of 4100+3807.1
Ezr 4:22 now that ye fail not to do this: w 4101+3807.2
7:23 for w should there be wrath against 4101+3807.2
Ne 2: 2 W *is* thy countenance sad, seeing thou *art* 4069
2: 3 w should not my countenance be sad, 4069
6: 3 that I cannot come down: w should 4100+3807.1
13:11 and said, W is the house of God forsaken? 4069
13:21 said unto them, W lodge ye about the wall? 4069
Est 3: 3 W transgressest thou the king's 4069
4: 5 to know what it *was,* and w it *was.* 4100
Job 3:11 W died I not from the womb? 4100+3807.1
3:11 *w* did I *not* give up the ghost when I came NIH
3:12 W did the knees prevent me? or why 4069
3:12 or w the breasts that I should suck? 4100
3:23 *W is light given* to a man whose way is hid, NIH
7:20 O thou preserver of men? w hast 4100+3807.1
7:21 w dost thou not pardon my transgression, 4100
9:29 *If* I be wicked, w then 2088+4100+3807.1
15:12 W doth thine heart carry thee away? and 4100
19:22 W do ye persecute me as God, and 4100+3807.1
19:28 ye should say, W persecute we him? 4100
21: 4 *so,* w should not my spirit be troubled? 4069
24: 1 W, seeing times are not hidden from 4069
27:12 all ye yourselves have seen *it;* w 4100+3807.1
31: 1 w then should I think upon a maid? 4100
33:13 W dost thou strive against him? for he 4069
Ps 2: 1 W do the heathen rage, and 4100+3807.1
10: 1 W standest thou afar off, 4100+3807.1
10: 1 *w* hidest thou *thyself* in times of trouble? NIH
22: 1 my God, w hast thou forsaken me? 4100+3807.1
22: 1 *w art thou so* far from helping me, *and* NIH
42: 5 W art thou cast down, O my soul? and 4100
42: 5 *w* art thou disquieted in me? hope thou in NIH
42: 9 I will say unto God my rock, W 4100+3807.1
42: 9 Why hast thou forgotten me? w go 4100+3807.1
42:11 W art thou cast down, O my soul? and 4100
42:11 w art thou disquieted within me? hope thou 4100
43: 2 thou *art* the God of my strength: w 4100+3807.1
43: 2 why dost thou cast me off? w go I 4100+3807.1
43: 5 W art thou cast down, O my soul? and 4100
43: 5 w art thou disquieted within me? hope in 4100
44:23 Awake, w sleepest thou, O Lord? 4100+3807.1
52: 1 W boastest thou thyself in mischief, O 4100
68:16 W leap ye, ye high hills? *this is* 4100+3807.1
74: 1 O God, w hast thou cast *us* off for 4100+3807.1
74: 1 *w* doth thine anger smoke against the sheep NIH
74:11 W withdrawest thou thy hand, 4100+3807.1
80:12 W hast thou *then* broken down her 4100+3807.1
88:14 LORD, w castest thou off my 4100+3807.1
88:14 my soul? *w* hidest thou thy face from me? NIH
Pr 5:20 w wilt thou, my son, be ravisht 4100+3807.1
22:27 w should he take away thy bed 4100+3807.1
Ecc 2:15 and w was I then more wise? 4100+3807.1
7:16 neither make thyself over wise: w 4100+3807.1
7:17 neither be thou foolish: w 4100+3807.1
SS 1: 7 for w should I be as one that 4100+3807.1
Isa 1: 5 W should ye be stricken any more? 4100+5921
40:27 W sayest thou, O Jacob, and 4100+3807.1
63:17 O LORD, w hast thou made us to 4100+3807.1
Jer 2:14 *is* he a homeborn *slave?* w is he spoiled? 4069
2:33 W trimmest thou thy way to seek love? 4100
2:36 W gaddest thou about *so* much to change 4100
8: 5 W *then* is this people of Jerusalem slidden 4069
8:14 W do we sit still? 4100+5921
8:19 W have they provoked me to anger with 4069
8:22 w then is not the health of the daughter of 4069
14: 8 thereof in time of trouble, w 4100+3807.1
14: 9 W shouldest thou be as a man 4100+3807.1
14:19 w hast thou smitten us, and *there is* no 4069
15:18 W is my pain perpetual, and 4100+3807.1
26: 9 W hast thou prophesied in the name of 4069
27:13 W will ye die, thou and thy people, 4100+3807.1
29:27 therefore w hast thou not reproved 4100+3807.1
30:15 W criest thou for thine affliction? 4100
36:29 W hast thou written therein, saying, 4069
46:15 W are thy valiant *men* swept away? 4069
49: 1 w *then* doth their king inherit Gad, and 4069
Eze 18:19 Yet say ye, W? doth not the son bear 4069
18:31 for w will ye die, O house of Israel? 4100
33:11 for w will ye die, O house of Israel? 4100
Da 1:10 for w should he see your faces 4100+3807.1
2:15 said to Arioch the king's captain, W 4101+5922
Jnh 1:10 said unto him, W hast thou done this? 4100
Mic 4: 9 Now w dost thou cry out aloud? *is* 4100+3807.1
Hab 1: 3 W dost thou shew me iniquity, and 4100+3807.1
Hag 1: 9 W? saith the LORD of hosts. Because of 4100
Mal 2:10 w do we deal treacherously every man 4069
Mt 6:28 And w take ye thought for raiment? 5101
7: 3 And w beholdest thou the mote that is in 5101
8:26 W are ye fearful, O ye of little faith? 5101
9:11 W eateth your Master with publicans and 1302
9:14 W do we and the Pharisees fast oft, but 1302
13:10 W speakest thou unto them in parables? 1302
15: 2 W do thy disciples transgress the tradition 1302
15: 3 W do you also transgress 1302
16: 8 w reason ye among yourselves, because 5101
17:10 W then say the scribes that Elias must first 5101
17:19 and said, W could not we cast him out? 1302
19: 7 W did Moses then command to give a 5101
19:17 he said unto him, W callest thou me good? 5101
20: 6 W stand ye here all the day idle? 5101
21:25 unto us, W did ye not then believe him? 1302
22:18 and said, W tempt ye me, *ye* hypocrites? 5101
26:10 said unto them, W trouble ye the woman? 5101
27:23 And the governor said, W, what evil hath 1063
27:46 my God, w hast thou forsaken me? 2444

Mk 2: 7 W doth this man thus speak blasphemies? 5101
2: 8 W reason ye these things in your hearts? 5101
2:18 W do the disciples of John and of 1302
2:24 w do they on the sabbath day that which is 5101
4:40 he said unto them, W are ye so fearful? 5101
5:35 w troublest thou the Master any further? 5101
5:39 unto them, W make ye this ado, and weep? 5101
7: 5 W walk not thy disciples according to 1302
8:12 W doth this generation seek after a sign? 5101
8:17 W reason ye, because ye have no bread? 5101
9:11 W say the scribes that Elias must first NIG
9:28 W could not we cast him out? 3754
10:18 said unto him, W callest thou me good? 5101
11: 3 if any man say unto you, W do ye this? 5101
11:31 will say, W then did ye not believe him? 1302
12:15 said unto them, W tempt ye me? 5101
14: 4 W was this waste of the ointment 1519+5101
14: 6 Let her alone; w trouble you her? 5101
15:14 said unto them, W, what evil hath he done? 1063
15:34 my God, w hast thou forsaken me? 1519+5101
Lk 2:48 Son, w hast thou thus dealt with us? 5101
5:30 W do ye eat and drink with publicans and 1302
5:33 W do the disciples of John fast often, and 1302
6: 2 W do ye that which is not lawful to do on 5101
6:41 And w beholdest thou the mote that is in 5101
6:46 And w call ye me, Lord, Lord, and do not 5101
12:26 is least, w take ye thought for the rest? 5101
12:57 w even of yourselves judge ye not what is 5101
13: 7 cut it down; w cumbereth it the ground? 2444
18:19 said unto him, W callest thou me good? 5101
19:31 W do ye loose him? thus shall ye say unto 1302
19:33 said unto them, W loose ye the colt? 5101
20: 5 he will say, W then believed ye him not? 1302
20:23 and said unto them, W tempt ye me? 5101
22:46 And said unto them, W sleep ye? rise and 5101
23:22 the third time, W, what evil hath he done? 1063
24: 5 W seek ye the living among the dead? 5101
24:38 And he said unto them, W are ye troubled? 5101
24:38 and w do thoughts arise in your hearts? 1302
Jn 1:25 and said unto him, W baptizest thou then, 5101
4:27 seekest thou? or, W talkest thou with her? 5101
7:19 keepeth the law? W go ye about to kill me? 5101
7:45 unto them, W have ye not brought him? 1302
8:43 W do ye not understand my speech? even 1302
8:46 if I say the truth, w do ye not believe me? 1302
9:30 W herein is a marvellous thing, that ye 1063
10:20 He hath a devil, and is mad; w hear ye him? 5101
12: 5 W was not this ointment sold for three 1302
13:37 Lord, w cannot I follow thee now? 1302
18:21 W askest thou me? ask them which heard 5101
18:23 of the evil: but if well, w smitest thou me? 5101
20:13 say unto her, Woman, w weepest thou? 5101
20:15 saith unto her, Woman, w weepest thou? 5101
Ac 1:11 w stand ye gazing up into heaven? 5101
3:12 Ye men of Israel, w marvel ye at this? 5101
3:12 or w look ye so earnestly on us, as though 5101
4:25 W did the heathen rage, and the people 2444
5: 3 w hath Satan filled thine heart to lie to 1302
5: 4 w hast thou conceived this thing in thine 5101
7:26 w do ye wrong one to another? 2444
9: 4 Saul, Saul, w persecutest thou me? 5101
14:15 w do ye these things? We also are men of 5101
15:10 Now therefore w tempt ye God, to put a 5101
22: 7 Saul, Saul, w persecutest thou me? 5101
22:16 And now w tarriest thou? arise, and 5101
26: 8 W should it be thought a thing incredible 5101
26:14 Saul, Saul, w persecutest thou me? 5101
Ro 3: 7 w yet am I also judged as a sinner? 5101
8:24 what a man seeth, w doth he yet hope for? 5101
9:19 then unto me, W doth he yet find fault? 5101
9:20 that formed it, W hast thou made me thus? 5101
14:10 But w dost thou judge thy brother? or why 5101
14:10 or w dost thou set at nought thy brother? 5101
1Co 4: 7 now if thou didst receive it, w dost thou 5101
6: 7 W do ye not rather take wrong? why do ye 1302
6: 7 w do ye not rather suffer yourselves to be 1302
10:29 for w is my liberty judged of another man's 2444
10:30 w am I evil spoken of for that for which I 5101
15:29 w are they then baptized for the dead? 5101
15:30 And w stand we in jeopardy every hour? 5101
Gal 2:14 w compellest thou the Gentiles to live as do 5101
5:11 w do I yet suffer persecution? 5101
Col 2:20 w, as though living in the world, are ye 5101

WICK See TOW

WICK TRIMMERS See SNUFFERS

WICKED (344) [WICKEDLY, WICKEDNESS]

Ge 13:13 the men of Sodom were w and 7451
18:23 thou also destroy the righteous with the w? 7563
18:25 to slay the righteous with the w: 7563
18:25 that the righteous should be as the w, 7563
38: 7 was w in the sight of the LORD; 7451
Ex 9:27 is righteous, and I and my people are w. 7563
23: 1 put not thine hand with the w to be an 7563
23: 7 slay thou not: for I will not justify the w. 7563
Lev 20:17 it is a w thing; and they shall be cut off in 2617
Nu 16:26 from the tents of these w men, and 7563
Dt 15: 9 Beware that there be not a thought in thy w 1100
17: 5 which have committed that w thing, 7451
23: 9 then keep thee from every w thing. 7451
25: 1 justify the righteous, and condemn the w. 7563
25: 2 if the w man be worthy to be beaten, 7563
1Sa 2: 9 and the w shall be silent in darkness; 7563
24:13 Wickedness proceedeth from the w: 7563
30:22 answered all the w men and men of Belial, 7451
2Sa 3:34 as a man falleth before w men, so 5766
4:11 when w men have slain a righteous person 7563
1Ki 8:32 and judge thy servants, condemning the w, 7563
2Ki 17:11 wrought w things to provoke the LORD to 7451
2Ch 6:23 and judge thy servants, by requiting the w, 7563
7:14 seek my face, and turn from their w ways; 7451
24: 7 For the sons of Athaliah, that w woman, 4849
Ne 9:35 neither turned they from their w works. 7451

Est 7: 6 The adversary and enemy is this w Haman. 7451
9:25 he commanded by letters that his w device, 7451
Job 3:17 There the w cease from troubling; and 7563
8:22 the dwelling place of the w shall come to 7563
9:22 said it, He destroyeth the perfect and the w. 7563
9:24 The earth is given into the hand of the w: 7563
9:29 If I be w, why then labour I in vain? 7561
10: 3 and shine upon the counsel of the w? 7563
10: 7 Thou knowest that I am not w; and there is 7561
10:15 If I be w, woe unto me; and if I be 7561
11:20 the eyes of the w shall fail, and they shall 7563
15:20 The w man travaileth with pain all his days, 7563
16:11 and turned me over into the hands of the w. 7563
18: 5 the light of the w shall be put out, and 7563
18:21 Surely such are the dwellings of the w, and 5767
20: 5 That the triumphing of the w is short, and 7563
20:22 every hand of the w shall come upon him. 6001
20:29 This is the portion of a w man from God, 7563
21: 7 Wherefore do the w live, become old, yea, 7563
21:16 the counsel of the w is far from me. 7563
21:17 How oft is the candle of the w put out! and 7563
21:28 and where are the dwelling places of the w? 7563
21:30 That the w is reserved to the day of 7451
22:15 Hast thou marked the old way which w men 205
22:18 but the counsel of the w is far from me. 7563
24: 6 and they gather the vintage of the w. 7563
27: 7 Let mine enemy be as the w, and he that 7563
27:13 This is the portion of a w man with God, 7563
29:17 I brake the jaws of the w, and pluckt 5767
31: 3 Is not destruction to the w? and a strange 5767
34: 8 of iniquity, and walketh with w men. 7562
34:18 Is it fit to say to a king, Thou art w? and 1100
34:26 He striketh them as w men in the open sight 7563
34:36 the end because of his answers for w men. 205
36: 6 He preserveth not the life of the w: but 7563
36:17 thou hast fulfilled the judgment of the w: 7563
38:13 that the w might be shaken out of it? 7563
38:15 from the w their light is withholden, and 7563
40:12 and tread down the w in their place. 7563
Ps 7: 9 O let the wickedness of the w come to an 7563
7:11 and God is angry with the w every day. NIH
9: 5 the heathen, thou hast destroyed the w, 7563
9:16 the w is snared in the work of his own 7563
9:17 The w shall be turned into hell, and all 7563
10: 2 The w in his pride doth persecute the poor: 7563
10: 3 For the w boasteth of his heart's desire, and 7563
10: 4 The w, through the pride of his 7563
10:13 Wherefore doth the w contemn God? 7563
10:15 Break thou the arm of the w and the evil 7563
11: 2 For lo, the w bend their bow, they make 7563
11: 5 the w and him that loveth violence his soul 7563
11: 6 Upon the w he shall rain snares, fire and 7563
12: 8 The w walk on every side, when the vilest 7563
17: 9 From the w that oppress me, from my 7563
17:13 deliver my soul from the w, which is thy 7563
22:16 the assembly of the w have inclosed me: 7489
26: 5 of evildoers; and will not sit with the w. 7563
27: 2 When the w, even mine enemies and 7489
28: 3 Draw me not away with the w, and with 7563
31:17 let the w be ashamed, and let them be silent 7563
32:10 Many sorrows shall be to the w: but he that 7563
34:21 Evil shall slay the w: and they that hate 7563
36: 1 The transgression of the w saith within my 7563
36:11 and let not the hand of the w remove me. 7563
37: 7 of the man who bringeth w devices to pass. 4209
37:10 a little while, and the w shall not be: yea, 7563
37:12 The w plotteth against the just, and 7563
37:14 The w have drawn out the sword, and 7563
37:16 hath is better than the riches of many w. 7563
37:17 For the arms of the w shall be broken: but 7563
37:20 the w shall perish, and the enemies of 7563
37:21 The w borroweth, and payeth not again: but 7563
37:28 but the seed of the w shall be cut off. 7563
37:32 The w watcheth the righteous, and 7563
37:34 when the w are cut off, thou shalt see it. 7563
37:35 I have seen the w in great power, and 7563
37:38 the end of the w shall be cut off. 7563
37:40 he shall deliver them from the w, and 7563
39: 1 with a bridle, while the w is before me. 7563
50:16 unto the w God saith, What hast thou to do 7563
55: 3 because of the oppression of the w: 7563
58: 3 The w are estranged from the womb: 7563
58:10 he shall wash his feet in the blood of the w. 7563
59: 5 be not merciful to any w transgressors. 205
64: 2 Hide me from the secret counsel of the w; 7489
68: 2 so let the w perish at the presence of God. 7563
71: 4 O my God, out of the hand of the w, 7563
73: 3 when I saw the prosperity of the w. 7563
74:19 w: forget not the congregation of thy poor NIH
75: 4 and to the w, Lift not up the horn: 7563
75: 8 all the w of the earth shall wring them out, 7563
75:10 All the horns of the w also will I cut off; 7563
82: 2 and accept the persons of the w? 7563
82: 4 needy: rid them out of the hand of the w. 7563
91: 8 thou behold and see the reward of the w. 7563
92: 7 When the w spring as the grass, and 7563
92:11 mine ears shall hear my desire of the w that 7489
94: 3 LORD, how long shall the w, how long 7563
94: 3 the wicked, how long shall the w triumph? 7563
94:13 until the pit be digged for the w. 7563
97:10 he delivereth them out of the hand of the w. 7563
101: 3 I will set no w thing before mine eyes: 1100
101: 4 from me: I will not know a w person. 7451
101: 8 I will early destroy all the w of the land; 7563
101: 8 that I may cut off all w doers from the city of 205
104:35 out of the earth, and let the w be no more. 7563
106:18 in their company; the flame burnt up the w. 7563
109: 2 For the mouth of the w and the mouth of 7563
109: 6 Set thou a w man over him: and let Satan 7563
112:10 The w shall see it, and be grieved; he shall 7563
112:10 melt away: the desire of the w shall perish. 7563
119:53 because of the w that forsake thy law. 7563
119:61 The bands of the w have robbed me: but 7563
119:95 The w have waited for me to destroy me: 7563
119:110 The w have laid a snare for me: yet I erred 7563

Ps 119:119 Thou puttest away all the w of the earth 7563
119:155 Salvation is far from the w: for they seek 7563
125: 3 For the rod of the w shall not rest upon 7562
129: 4 he hath cut asunder the cords of the w. 7563
139:19 Surely thou wilt slay the w, O God: 7563
139:24 see if there be any w way in me, and 6090
140: 4 O LORD, from the hands of the w; 7563
140: 8 Grant not, O LORD, the desires of the w: 7563
140: 8 further not his w device; lest they exalt 2162
141: 4 to practise w works with men that work 7562
141:10 Let the w fall into their own nets, 7563
145:20 that love him: but all the w will he destroy. 7563
146: 9 the way of the w he turneth upside down. 7563
147: 6 he casteth the w down to the ground. 7563
Pr 2:14 and delight in the frowardness of the w; 7451
2:22 the w shall be cut off from the earth, and 7563
3:25 neither of the desolation of the w, when it 7563
3:33 of the LORD is in the house of the w: 7563
4:14 Enter not into the path of the w, and go not 7563
4:19 The way of the w is as darkness: they know 7563
5:22 His own iniquities shall take the w himself, 7563
6:12 A naughty person, a w man, walketh with a 205
6:18 A heart that deviseth w imaginations, 205
9: 7 he that rebuketh a w man getteth himself a 7563
10: 3 but he casteth away the substance of the w. 7563
10: 6 but violence covereth the mouth of the w. 7563
10: 7 is blessed: but the name of the w shall rot. 7563
10:11 but violence covereth the mouth of the w. 7563
10:16 tendeth to life: the fruit of the w to sin. 7563
10:20 the heart of the w is little worth. 7563
10:24 The fear of the w, it shall come upon him: 7563
10:25 so is the w no more: but the righteous is an 7563
10:27 but the years of the w shall be shortened. 7563
10:28 but the expectation of the w shall perish. 7563
10:30 but the w shall not inhabit the earth. 7563
10:32 the mouth of the w speaketh frowardness. 7563
11: 5 but the w shall fall by his own wickedness. 7563
11: 7 When a w man dieth, his expectation shall 7563
11: 8 of trouble, and the w cometh in his stead. 7563
11:10 and when the w perish, there is shouting. 7563
11:11 but it is overthrown by the mouth of the w. 7563
11:18 The w worketh a deceitful work: but to him 7563
11:21 join in hand, the w shall not be unpunished: 7451
11:23 but the expectation of the w is wrath. 7563
11:31 the earth: much more the w and the sinner. 7563
12: 2 but a man of w devices will he condemn. 4209
12: 5 but the counsels of the w are deceit. 7563
12: 6 The words of the w are to lie in wait for 7563
12: 7 The w are overthrown, and are not: but 7563
12:10 but the tender mercies of the w are cruel. 7563
12:12 The w desireth the net of evil men: but 7563
12:13 The w is snared by the transgression of his 7451
12:21 but the w shall be filled with mischief. 7563
12:26 but the way of the w seduceth them. 7563
13: 5 a w man is loathsome, and cometh to 7563
13: 9 but the lamp of the w shall be put out. 7563
13:17 A w messenger falleth into mischief: but 7563
13:25 his soul: but the belly of the w shall want. 7563
14:11 The house of the w shall be overthrown: 7563
14:17 and a man of w devices is hated. 4209
14:19 and the w at the gates of the righteous. 7563
14:32 The w is driven away in his wickedness: 7563
15: 6 but in the revenues of the w is trouble. 7563
15: 8 The sacrifice of the w is an abomination to 7563
15: 9 The way of the w is an abomination unto 7563
15:26 The thoughts of the w are an abomination 7451
15:28 the mouth of the w poureth out evil things. 7563
15:29 The LORD is far from the w: but 7563
16: 4 yea, even the w for the day of evil. 7563
17: 4 A w doer giveth heed to false lips; and 7489
17:15 He that justifieth the w, and he that 7563
17:23 A w man taketh a gift out of the bosom to 7563
18: 3 When the w cometh, then cometh also 7563
18: 5 It is not good to accept the person of the w, 7563
19:28 and the mouth of the w devoureth iniquity. 7563
20:26 A wise king scattereth the w, and 7563
21: 4 and the plowing of the w, is sin. 7563
21: 7 The robbery of the w shall destroy them; 7563
21:10 The soul of the w desireth evil: 7563
21:12 man wisely considereth the house of the w: 7563
21:12 God overthroweth the w for their 7563
21:18 The w shall be a ransom for the righteous, 7563
21:27 The sacrifice of the w is abomination: 7563
21:27 when he bringeth it with a w mind? 2154
21:29 A w man hardeneth his face: but as for 7563
24:15 O w man, against the dwelling of 7563
24:16 up again: but the w shall fall into mischief. 7563
24:19 evil men, neither be thou envious at the w; 7563
24:20 man; the candle of the w shall be put out. 7563
24:24 He that saith unto the w, Thou art 7563
25: 5 Take away the w from before the king, and 7563
25:26 A righteous man falling down before the w 7563
26:23 a w heart are like a potsherd covered with 7451
28: 1 The w flee when no man pursueth: but 7563
28: 4 They that forsake the law praise the w: but 7563
28:12 but when the w rise, a man is hidden. 7563
28:15 so is a w ruler over the poor people. 7563
28:28 When the w rise, men hide themselves: but 7563
29: 2 when the w beareth rule, the people mourn. 7563
29: 7 but the w regardeth not to know it. 7563
29:12 ruler hearken to lies, all his servants are w. 7563
29:16 When the w are multiplied, 7563
29:27 upright in the way is abomination to the w. 7563
Ecc 3:17 God shall judge the righteous and the w: 7563
7:15 there is a w man that prolongeth his life in 7563
7:17 Be not over much w, neither be thou 7561
8:10 so I saw the w buried, who had come and 7563
8:13 it shall not be well with the w, neither shall 7563
8:14 happeneth according to the work of the w; 7563
8:14 there be w men, to whom it happeneth 7563
9: 2 is one event to the righteous, and to the w; 7563
Isa 3:11 Woe unto the w! it shall be ill with him: for 7563
5:23 Which justify the w for reward, and 7563
11: 4 the breath of his lips shall he slay the w. 7563
13:11 for their evil, and the w for their iniquity; 7563

Isa 14: 5 The LORD hath broken the staff of the w, 7563
26:10 Let favour be shewed to the w, yet will he 7563
32: 7 he deviseth w devices to destroy the poor 2154
48:22 is no peace, saith the LORD, unto the w. 7563
53: 9 he made his grave with the w, and with 7563
55: 7 Let the w forsake his way, and 7563
57:20 the w are like the troubled sea, when it 7563
57:21 There is no peace, saith my God, to the w. 7563
Jer 2:33 hast thou also taught the w ones thy ways. 7451
5:26 For among my people are found w men: 7563
5:28 yea, they overpass the deeds of the w: 7451
6:29 in vain: for the w are not plucked away. 7451
12: 1 Wherefore doth the way of the w prosper? 7563
15:21 I will deliver thee out of the hand of the w, 7451
17: 9 above all things, and desperately w: 605
23:19 shall fall grievously upon the head of the w. 7563
25:31 he will give them that are w to the sword, 7563
30:23 shall fall with pain upon the head of the w. 7563
Eze 3:18 When I say unto the w, Thou shalt surely 7563
3:18 nor speakest to warn the w from his wicked 7563
3:18 nor speakest to warn the wicked from his w 7563
3:18 the same w man shall die in his iniquity; 7563
3:19 Yet if thou warn the w, and he turn not 7563
3:19 nor from his w way, he shall die in his 7563
7:21 a prey, and to the w of the earth for a spoil; 7563
8: 9 behold the w abominations that they do 7451
11: 2 and give w counsel in this city: 7451
13:22 strengthened the hands of the w, that he 7451
13:22 that he should not return from his w way, 7563
18:20 the wickedness of the w shall be upon him. 7563
18:21 if the w will turn from all his sins that he 7563
18:23 Have I any pleasure at all that the w should 7563
18:24 all the abominations that the w man doeth, 7563
18:27 when the w man turneth away from his 7563
20:44 not according to your w ways, 7451
21: 3 cut off from thee the righteous and the w. 7563
21: 4 cut off from thee the righteous and the w, 7563
21:25 thou, profane w prince of Israel, whose day 7563
21:29 the necks of them that are slain of the w, 7563
30:12 and sell the land into the hand of the w: 7451
33: 8 When I say unto the w, O wicked man, 7563
33: 8 the wicked, O w man, thou shalt surely die; 7563
33: 8 if thou dost not speak to warn the w from 7563
33: 8 that w man shall die in his iniquity; 7563
33: 9 if thou warn the w of his way to turn from 7563
33:11 I have no pleasure in the death of the w; 7563
33:11 but that the w turn from his way and live: 7563
33:12 as for the wickedness of the w, he shall not 7563
33:14 Again, when I say unto the w, Thou shalt 7563
33:15 If the w restore the pledge, give again that 7563
33:19 if the w turn from his wickedness, and 7563
Da 12:10 and tried; but the w shall do wickedly: 7563
12:10 none of the w shall understand; but 7563
Mic 6:10 of wickedness in the house of the w, 7563
6:11 Shall I count them pure with the w 7562
Na 1: 3 will not at all acquit the w: the LORD hath NIH
1:11 evil against the LORD, a w counseller. 1100
1:15 for the w shall no more pass through thee; 1100
Hab 1: 4 for the w doth compass about the righteous; 7563
1:13 holdest thy tongue when the w devoureth 7563
3:13 the head out of the house of the w, 7563
Zep 1: 3 and the stumblingblocks with the w; 7563
Mal 3:18 discern between the righteous and the w, 7563
4: 3 ye shall tread down the w; for they shall be 7563
Mt 12:45 seven other spirits more w than himself, 4191
12:45 so shall it be also unto this w generation. 4190
13:19 then cometh the w one, and catcheth away 4190
13:38 but the tares are the children of the w one; 4190
13:49 and sever the w from among the just, 4190
16: 4 A w and adulterous generation seeketh 4190
18:32 said unto him, O thou w servant, I forgave 4190
21:41 He will miserably destroy those w men, 2556
25:26 said unto him, Thou w and slothful servant, 4190
Lk 11:26 seven other spirits more w than himself; 4191
19:22 mouth will I judge thee, thou w servant. 4190
Ac 2:23 and by w hands have crucified and slain: 459
18:14 If it were a matter of wrong or w lewdness, 4190
1Co 5:13 from among yourselves that w person. 4190
Eph 6:16 able to quench all the fiery darts of the w. 4190
Col 1:21 and enemies in your mind by w works, 4190
2Th 2: 8 And then shall that W be revealed, 459
3: 2 be delivered from unreasonable and w men: 4190
2Pe 2: 7 vexed with the filthy conversation of the w: 113
3:17 being led away with the error of the w, 113
1Jn 2:13 because you have overcome the w one. 4190
2:14 in you, and ye have overcome the w one. 4190
3:12 who was of that w one, and slew his 4190
5:18 and that w one toucheth him not. 4190

WICKEDLY (23) [WICKED]

Ge 19: 7 And said, I pray you, brethren, do not so w. 7489
Dt 9:18 in doing w in the sight of the LORD, 7451
Jdg 19:23 my brethren, nay, I pray you, do not so w; 7489
1Sa 12:25 if ye shall still do w, ye shall be 7489+7489
2Sa 22:22 and have not w departed from my God. 7561
24:17 said, Lo, I have sinned, and I have done w: 5753
2Ki 21:11 hath done w above all that the Amorites 7489
2Ch 6:37 we have done amiss, and have dealt w; 7561
20:35 Ahaziah king of Israel, who did very w: 7561
22: 3 for his mother was his counseller to do w. 7561
Ne 9:33 thou hast done right, but we have done w: 7561
Job 13: 7 Will you speak w for God? and 5766
34:12 Yea, surely God will not do w, neither will 7561
Ps 18:21 and have not w departed from my God. 7561
73: 8 and speak w concerning oppression: 7451+871.1
74: 3 even all that the enemy hath done w in 7489
106: 6 have committed iniquity, we have done w. 7561
139:20 For they speak against thee w, and 4209+3807.1
Da 9: 5 and have done w, and have rebelled, 7561
9:15 this day; we have sinned, we have done w. 7561
11:32 such as do w against the covenant shall he 7561
12:10 and tried; but the wicked shall do w: 7561
Mal 4: 1 all the proud, yea, and all that do w, 7564

WICKEDNESS (127) [WICKED]

Ge 6: 5 GOD saw that the w of man was great in 7451
39: 9 how then can I do this great w, and 7451
Lev 18:17 for they are her near kinswomen: it is w. 2154
19:29 and the land become full of w. 2154
20:14 if a man take a wife and her mother, it is w: 2154
20:14 and they; that there be no w among you. 2154
Dt 9: 4 for the w of these nations the LORD doth 7564
9: 5 for the w of these nations the LORD thy 7564
9:27 this people, nor to their w, nor to their sin: 7562
13:11 shall do no more any such w as this is 7451
17: 2 that hath wrought w in the sight of 7451
28:20 because of the w of thy doings, 7455
Jdg 9:56 Thus God rendered the w of Abimelech, 7451
20: 3 children of Israel, Tell us, how was this w? 7451
20:12 What w is this that is done among you? 7451
1Sa 12:17 may perceive and see that your w is great, 7451
12:20 ye have done all this w: yet turn not aside 7451
24:13 W proceedeth from the wicked: 7562
25:39 for the LORD hath returned the w of 7451
2Sa 3:39 reward the doer of evil according to his w. 7451
7:10 neither shall the children of w afflict them 5766
1Ki 1:52 but if w shall be found in him, he shall die. 7451
2:44 Thou knowest all the w which thine heart is 7451
2:44 the LORD shall return thy w upon thine 7451
8:47 done perversely, we have committed w; 7561
21:25 which did sell himself to work w in 7451
2Ki 21: 6 he wrought much w in the sight of 7451
1Ch 17: 9 neither shall the children of w waste them 5766
Job 4: 8 plow iniquity, and sow w, reap the same. 5999
11:11 he seeth w also; will he not then consider it? 205
11:14 and let not w dwell in thy tabernacles. 5766
20:12 Though w be sweet in his mouth, though he 7451
22: 5 Is not thy w great? and thine iniquities 7451
24:20 and w shall be broken as a tree. 5766
27: 4 My lips shall not speak w, nor my tongue 5766
34:10 far be it from God, that he should do w; and 7562
35: 8 Thy w may hurt a man as thou art; and thy 7562
Ps 5: 4 thou art not a God that hath pleasure in w: 7562
5: 9 their inward part is very w; their throat is 1942
7: 9 O let the w of the wicked come to an end; 7451
10:15 the evil man: seek out his w till thou find 7562
28: 4 and according to the w of their endeavours: 7455
45: 7 Thou lovest righteousness, and hatest w: 7562
52: 7 and strengthened himself in his w. 1942
55:11 W is in the midst thereof: deceit and 1942
55:15 for w is in their dwellings, and 7451
58: 2 Yea, in heart ye work w; ye weigh 5766
84:10 of my God, than to dwell in the tents of w. 7562
89:22 upon him; nor the son of w afflict him. 5766
94:23 and shall cut them off in their own w; 7451
107:34 for the w of them that dwell therein. 7451
Pr 4:17 For they eat the bread of w, and drink 7562
8: 7 and w is an abomination to my lips. 7562
10: 2 Treasures of w profit nothing: but 7562
11: 5 but the wicked shall fall by his own w. 7564
12: 3 A man shall not be established by w: but 7562
13: 6 in the way: but w overthroweth the sinner. 7564
14:32 The wicked is driven away in his w: but 7451
16:12 It is an abomination to kings to commit w: 7562
21:12 God overthroweth the wicked for their w. 7451
26:26 his w shall be shewed before the whole 7451
30:20 her mouth, and saith, I have done no w. 205
Ecc 3:16 the place of judgment, that w was there; 7562
7:15 man that prolongeth his life in his w. 7451
7:25 of things, and to know the w of folly, 7562
8: 8 neither shall w deliver those that are given 7562
Isa 9:18 For w burneth as the fire: it shall devour 7564
47:10 For thou hast trusted in thy w: thou hast 7451
58: 4 and debate, and to smite with the fist of w: 7562
58: 6 to loose the bands of w, to undo the heavy 7562
Jer 1:16 against them touching all their w, 7451
2:19 Thine own w shall correct thee, and 7451
3: 2 land with thy whoredoms and with thy w. 7451
4:14 O Jerusalem, wash thine heart from w, that 7451
4:18 this is thy w, because it is bitter, because 7451
6: 7 out her waters, so she casteth out her w: 7451
7:12 see what I did to it for the w of my people 7451
8: 6 no man repented him of his w, saying, 7451
12: 4 for the w of them that dwell therein? 7451
14:16 for I will pour their w upon them. 7451
14:20 our w, and the iniquity of our fathers: 7562
22:22 be ashamed and confounded for all thy w. 7451
23:11 yea, in my house have I found their w, 7451
23:14 that none doth return from his w: 7451
33: 5 for all whose w I have hid my face from 7451
44: 3 Because of their w which they have 7451
44: 5 nor inclined their ear to turn from their w, 7451
44: 9 Have ye forgotten the w of your fathers, 7451
44: 9 the w of the kings of Judah, and 7451
44: 9 the w of their wives, and your own 7451
44: 9 your own w, and the wickedness of your 7451
44: 9 own wickedness, and the w of your wives, 7451
La 1:22 Let all their w come before thee; and 7451
Eze 3:19 he turn not from his w, nor from his wicked 7562
5: 6 she hath changed my judgments into w 7564
7:11 Violence is risen up into a rod of w: 7562
16:23 it came to pass after all thy w, (woe, 7451
16:57 Before thy w was discovered, as at the time 7451
18:20 and the w of the wicked shall be upon him. 7564
18:27 away from his w that he hath committed, 7564
31:11 with him: I have driven him out for his w. 7562
33:12 as for the w of the wicked, he shall not fall 7564
33:12 in the day that he turneth from his w; 7562
33:19 if the wicked turn from his w, and do that 7564
Hos 7: 1 was discovered, and the w of Samaria: 7451
7: 2 in their hearts that I remember all their w: 7451
7: 3 They make the king glad with their w, and 7451
9:15 All their w is in Gilgal, for there I hated 7451
9:15 for the w of their doings I will drive them 7455
10:13 Ye have plowed w, ye have reaped 7562
10:15 unto you because of your great w; 7451+7465
Joel 3:13 the fats overflow; for their w is great. 7451
Jnh 1: 2 against it; for their w is come up before me. 7451
Mic 6:10 Are there yet the treasures of w in 7562
Na 3:19 for upon whom hath not thy w passed 7451
Zec 5: 8 he said, This is w. And he cast it into 7564
Mal 1: 4 they shall call them, The border of w, and, 7564
3:15 yea, they that work w are set up; yea, 7564
Mt 22:18 But Jesus perceived their w, and said, 4189
Mk 7:22 Thefts, covetousness, w, deceit, 4189
Lk 11:39 your inward part is full of ravening and w. 4189
Ac 8:22 Repent therefore of this thy w, and 2549
25: 5 accuse this man, if there be any w in him. NIG
Ro 1:29 fornication, w, covetousness, 4189
1Co 5: 8 neither with the leaven of malice and w; 4189
Eph 6:12 against spiritual w in high places. 4189
1Jn 5:19 are of God, and the whole world lieth in w. 4190

WIDE (15) [WIDENESS]

Dt 15: 8 thou shalt open thine hand w unto 6605+6605
15:11 Thou shalt open thine hand w unto 6605+6605
1Ch 4:40 the land was w, and quiet, and 3027+7342
Job 29:23 they opened their mouth w as for the latter 6473
30:14 They came upon me as a w breaking in of 7342
Ps 35:21 they opened their mouth w against me, and 7337
81:10 open thy mouth w, and I will fill it. 7337
104:25 So is this great and w sea, 3027+7342
Pr 13: 3 he that openeth w his lips shall have 6589
21: 9 than with a brawling woman in a w house. 2267
25:24 with a brawling woman and in a w house. 2267
Isa 57: 4 against whom make ye a w mouth, and 7337
Jer 22:14 I will build me a w house and 4060
Na 3:13 the gates of thy land shall be set w open 6605
Mt 7:13 for w is the gate, and broad is the way, 4116

WIDENESS (1) [WIDE]

Eze 41:10 between the chambers was the w of twenty 7341

WIDOW (50) [WIDOW'S, WIDOWHOOD, WIDOWS, WIDOWS']

Ge 38:11 Remain a w at thy father's house, till Shelah 490
Ex 22:22 Ye shall not afflict any w, or fatherless child. 490
Lev 21:14 A w, or a divorced woman, or profane, or 490
22:13 if the priest's daughter be a w, or divorced, 490
Nu 30: 9 every vow of a w, and of her that is 490
Dt 10:18 the judgment of the fatherless and w, 490
14:29 the stranger, and the fatherless, and the w, 490
16:11 the stranger, and the fatherless, and the w, 490
16:14 the stranger, and the fatherless, and the w, 490
24:19 the stranger, for the fatherless, and for the w: 490
24:20 the stranger, for the fatherless, and for the w. 490
24:21 the stranger, for the fatherless, and for the w. 490
26:12 the stranger, the fatherless, and the w, 490
26:13 the stranger, to the fatherless, and to the w, 490
27:19 judgment of the stranger, fatherless, and w. 490
2Sa 14: 5 I am indeed a w woman, and mine husband 490
1Ki 11:26 mother's name was Zeruah, a w woman, 490
17: 9 I have commanded a w woman there to 490
17:10 the w woman was there gathering of sticks: 490
17:20 hast thou also brought evil upon the w with 490
Job 24:21 beareth not: and doeth not good to the w. 490
31:16 or have caused the eyes of the w to fail; 490
Ps 94: 6 They slay the w and the stranger, and 490
109: 9 his children be fatherless, and his wife a w. 490
146: 9 he relieveth the fatherless and w: 490
Pr 15:25 but he will establish the border of the w. 490
Isa 1:17 judge the fatherless, plead for the w. 490
1:23 neither doth the cause of the w come unto 490
47: 8 I shall not sit as a w, neither shall I know 490
Jer 7: 6 the w, and shed not innocent blood in this 490
22: 3 to the stranger, the fatherless, nor the w, 490
La 1: 1 how is she become as a w! she that was great 490
Eze 22: 7 have they vexed the fatherless and the w. 490
44:22 Neither shall they take for their wives a w, 490
44:22 of Israel, or a w that had a priest before. 490
Zec 7:10 oppress not the w, nor the fatherless, 490
Mal 3: 5 the w, and the fatherless, and that turn aside 490
Mk 12:42 And there came a certain poor w, and 5503
12:43 That this poor w hath cast more in, 5503
Lk 2:37 And she was a w of about fourscore and 5503
4:26 a city of Sidon, unto a woman that was a w. 5503
7:12 only son of his mother, and she was a w: 5503
18: 3 And there was a w in that city; and 5503
18: 5 Yet because this w troubleth me, I will 5503
21: 2 And he saw also a certain poor w casting in 5503
21: 3 that this poor w hath cast in more than they 5503
1Ti 5: 4 But if any w have children or nephews, 5503
5: 5 Now she that is a w indeed, and desolate, 5503
5: 9 Let not a w be taken into the number under 5503
Rev 18: 7 and am no w, and shall see no sorrow. 5503

WIDOW'S (5) [WIDOW]

Ge 38:14 she put her w garments off from her, and 491
Dt 24:17 nor take a w raiment to pledge: 490
1Ki 7:14 He was a w son of the tribe of Naphtali, 490+802
Job 24: 3 they take the w ox for a pledge. 490
29:13 and I caused the w heart to sing for joy. 490

WIDOWHOOD (4) [WIDOW]

Ge 38:19 from her, and put on the garments of her w. 491
2Sa 20: 3 up unto the day of their death, living in w. 491
Isa 47: 9 in one day, the loss of children, and w: 489
54: 4 shalt not remember the reproach of thy w 491

WIDOWS (23) [WIDOW]

Ex 22:24 your wives shall be w, and your children 490
Job 22: 9 Thou hast sent w away empty, and the arms 490
27:15 be buried in death: and his w shall not weep. 490
Ps 68: 5 father of the fatherless, and a judge of the w, 490
78:64 the sword; and their w made no lamentation. 490
Isa 9:17 shall have mercy on their fatherless and w: 490
10: 2 that w may be their prey, and that they may 490
Jer 15: 8 Their w are increased to me above the sand 490
18:21 be bereaved of their children, and be w; 490
49:11 them alive; and let thy w trust in me. 490
La 5: 3 and fatherless, our mothers are as w. 490
Eze 22:25 they have made her many w in the midst 490

Lk 4:25 many **w** were in Israel in the days of Elias, *5503*
Ac 6: 1 their **w** were neglected in the daily *5503*
9:39 and all the **w** stood by him weeping, and *5503*
9:41 and when he had called the saints and **w**, *5503*
1Co 7: 8 I say therefore to the unmarried and **w**, It is *5503*
1Ti 5: 3 Honour **w** that are widows indeed. *5503*
5: 3 Honour widows that are **w** indeed. *5503*
5:11 But the younger **w** refuse: for when they *5503*
5:16 any man or woman that believeth have **w**, *5503*
5:16 that it may relieve them that are **w** indeed. *5503*
Jas 1:27 visit the fatherless and **w** in their affliction, *5503*

WIDOWS' (3) [WIDOW]

Mt 23:14 for ye devour **w** houses, and for a pretence *5503*
Mk 12:40 Which devour **w** houses, and for a pretence *5503*
Lk 20:47 Which devour **w** houses, and for a shew *5503*

WIFE (396) [WIFE'S, WIVES, WIVES']

Ge 2:24 and his mother, and shall cleave unto his **w**: 802
2:25 the man and his **w**, and were not ashamed. 802
3: 8 his **w** hid themselves from the presence of 802
3:17 thou hast hearkened unto the voice of thy **w**, 802
3:21 to his **w** did the LORD God make coats of 802
4: 1 Adam knew Eve his **w**; and she conceived, 802
4:17 Cain knew his **w**; and she conceived, and 802
4:25 Adam knew his **w** again; and she bare a son, 802
6:18 and thy **w**, and thy sons' wives with thee. 802
7: 7 and his **w**, and his sons' wives with him, 802
7:13 Noah's **w**, and the three wives of his sons 802
8:16 thy **w**, and thy sons, and thy sons' wives 802
8:18 and his **w**, and his sons' wives with him: 802
11:29 the name of Abram's **w** *was* Sarai; and 802
11:29 the name of Nahor's **w**, Milcah, the daughter 802
11:31 his daughter in law, his son Abram's **w**; 802
12: 5 Abram took Sarai his **w**, and Lot his 802
12:11 that he said unto Sarai his **w**, Behold now, 802
12:12 see thee, that they shall say, This *is* his **w**: 802
12:17 great plagues because of Sarai Abram's **w**. 802
12:18 didst thou not tell me that she *was* thy **w**? 802
12:19 so I might have taken her to me to **w**: now 802
12:19 now therefore behold thy **w**, take *her,* and 802
12:20 him away, and his **w**, and all that he had. 802
13: 1 he, and his **w**, and all that he had, and 802
16: 1 Now Sarai Abram's **w** bare him no *children:* 802
16: 3 Sarai Abram's **w** took Hagar her maid 802
16: 3 gave her to her husband Abram to be his **w**. 802
17:15 God said unto Abraham, *As for* Sarai thy **w**, 802
17:19 Sarah thy **w** shall bear thee a son indeed; 802
18: 9 they said unto him, Where *is* Sarah thy **w**? 802
18:10 of life; and lo, Sarah thy **w** shall have a son. 802
19:15 Arise, take thy **w**, and thy two daughters, 802
19:16 upon the hand of his **w**, and upon the hand of 802
19:26 But his **w** looked back from behind him, and 802
20: 2 Abraham said of Sarah his **w**, She *is* my 802
20: 3 which thou hast taken; for she *is* a man's **w**. 1166
20: 7 Now therefore restore the man *his* **w**; for he 802
20:12 of my mother; and she became my **w**. 802
20:14 and restored him Sarah his **w**. 802
20:17 and his **w**, and his maidservants; 802
20:18 because of Sarah Abraham's **w**. 802
21:21 his mother took him a **w** out of the land of 802
23:19 Abraham buried Sarah his **w** in the cave of 802
24: 3 that thou shalt not take a **w** unto my son of 802
24: 4 my kindred, and take a **w** unto my son Isaac. 802
24: 7 thou shalt take a **w** unto my son from thence. 802
24:15 son of Milcah, the **w** of Nahor, 802
24:36 Sarah my master's **w** bare a son to my 802
24:37 Thou shalt not take a **w** to my son of 802
24:38 to my kindred, and take a **w** unto my son. 802
24:40 thou shalt take a **w** for my son of my 802
24:51 and go, and let her be thy master's son's **w**, 802
24:67 and took Rebekah, and she became his **w**; 802
25: 1 again Abraham took a **w**, and her name *was* 802
25:10 there was Abraham buried, and Sarah his **w**. 802
25:20 forty years old when he took Rebekah to **w**, 802
25:21 Isaac intreated the LORD for his **w**, 802
25:21 of him, and Rebekah his **w** conceived. 802
26: 7 the men of the place asked *him* of his **w**; 802
26: 7 for he feared to say, *She is* my **w**; lest, 802
26: 8 Isaac *was* sporting with Rebekah his **w**. 802
26: 9 and said, Behold, of a surety she *is* thy **w**: 802
26:10 people might lightly have lien with thy **w**, 802
26:11 or his **w** shall surely be put to death. 802
26:34 Esau was forty years old when he took to **w** 802
27:46 if Jacob take a **w** of the daughters of Heth, 802
28: 1 Thou shalt not take a **w** of the daughters of 802
28: 2 take thee a **w** from thence of the daughters of 802
28: 6 to Padan-aram, to take him a **w** from thence; 802
28: 6 Thou shalt not take a **w** of the daughters of 802
28: 9 the sister of Nebajoth, to be his **w**. 802
29:21 Give *me* my **w**, for my days are fulfilled, 802
29:28 he gave him Rachel his daughter to **w** *also.* 802
30: 4 she gave him Bilhah her handmaid to **w**: 802
30: 9 Zilpah her maid, and gave her Jacob to **w**. 802
34: 4 saying, Get me this damsel to **w**. 802
34: 8 your daughter: I pray you give her him to **w**. 802
34:12 say unto me: but give me the damsel to **w**. 802
36:10 Eliphaz the son of Adah the **w** of Esau, 802
36:10 Reuel the son of Bashemath the **w** of Esau. 802
36:12 these *were* the sons of Adah Esau's **w**. 802
36:13 these were the sons of Bashemath Esau's **w**. 802
36:14 of Anah, daughter of Zibeon, Esau's **w**: 802
36:17 these *are* the sons of Bashemath Esau's **w**. 802
36:18 these *are* the sons of Aholibamah Esau's **w**: 802
36:18 Aholibamah the daughter of Anah, Esau's **w**. 802
38: 6 Judah took a **w** for Er his firstborn, 802
38: 8 Go in unto thy brother's **w**, and marry her, 802
38: 9 when he went in unto his brother's **w**, 802
38:12 time the daughter of Shuah Judah's **w** died; 802
38:14 and she was not given unto him to **w**. 802
39: 7 that his master's **w** cast her eyes upon 802
39: 8 and said unto his master's **w**, Behold, 802
39: 9 from me but thee, because thou *art* his **w**: 802
39:19 when his master heard the words of his **w**, 802
41:45 he gave him to **w** Asenath the daughter of 802

Ge 44:27 Ye know that my **w** bare me two *sons:* 802
46:19 The sons of Rachel Jacob's **w**; Joseph, and 802
49:31 There they buried Abraham and Sarah his **w**; 802
49:31 there they buried Isaac and Rebekah his **w**; 802
Ex 2: 1 of Levi, and took *to* **w** a daughter of Levi. NIH
4:20 Moses took his **w** and his sons, and set them 802
6:20 took him Jochebed his father's sister to **w**; 802
6:23 of Amminadab, sister of Naashon, to **w**; 802
6:25 took him *one* of the daughters of Putiel to **w**; 802
18: 2 father in law, took Zipporah, Moses' **w**, 802
18: 5 and his **w** unto Moses into the wilderness, 802
18: 6 and thy **w**, and her two sons with her. 802
20:17 thou shalt not covet thy neighbour's **w**, 802
21: 3 then his **w** shall go out with him. 802
21: 4 If his master have given him a **w**, and 802
21: 4 the **w** and her children shall be her master's, 802
21: 5 I love my master, my **w**, and my children; 802
21:10 If he take him another *w;* her food, NIH
22:16 he shall surely endow her to be his **w**. 802
Lev 18: 8 The nakedness of thy father's **w** shalt thou 802
18:14 thou shalt not approach to his **w**: 802
18:15 she *is* thy son's **w**; thou shalt not uncover her 802
18:16 uncover the nakedness of thy brother's **w**: 802
18:18 Neither shalt thou take a **w** to her sister, 802
18:20 shalt not lie carnally with thy neighbour's **w**, 802
20:10 committeth adultery with *another* man's **w**, 802
20:10 committeth adultery with his neighbour's **w**, 802
20:11 the man that lieth with his father's **w** hath 802
20:14 if a man take a **w** and her mother, it *is* 802
20:20 if a man shall lie with his **uncle's** **w**, 1733
20:21 if a man shall take his brother's **w**, it *is* an 802
21: 7 They shall not take a **w** *that is* a whore, or 802
21:13 And he shall take a **w** in her virginity. 802
21:14 he shall take a virgin of his own people to **w**. 802
Nu 5:12 If any man's **w** go aside, and commit a 802
5:14 he be jealous of his **w**, and she be defiled: 802
5:14 he be jealous of his **w**, and she be not 802
5:15 shall the man bring his **w** unto the priest, 802
5:29 when a **w** goeth aside *to another* instead of 802
5:30 he be jealous over his **w**, and shall set 802
26:59 And the name of Amram's **w** *was* Jochebed, 802
30:16 between a man and his **w**, between the father 802
36: 8 shall be **w** unto one of the family of 802+3807.1
Dt 5:21 Neither shalt thou desire thy neighbour's **w**, 802
13: 6 or the **w** of thy bosom, or thy friend, 802
20: 7 what man *is there* that hath betrothed a **w**, 802
21:11 that thou wouldest have *her* to thy **w**; 802
21:13 and be her husband, and she shall be thy **w**. 802
22:13 If any man take a **w**, and go in unto her, and 802
22:16 I gave my daughter unto this man to **w**, and 802
22:19 she shall be his **w**; he may not put her away 802
22:24 because he hath humbled his neighbour's **w**: 802
22:29 fifty *shekels* of silver, and she shall be his **w**; 802
22:30 A man shall not take his father's **w**, 802
24: 1 When a man hath taken a **w**, and 802
24: 2 she may go and be another man's *w.* NIH
24: 3 husband die, which took her *to be* his **w**; 802
24: 4 may not take her again to be his **w**, 802
24: 5 When a man hath taken a new **w**, he shall 802
24: 5 shall cheer up his **w** which he hath taken. 802
25: 5 the **w** of the dead shall not marry without 802
25: 5 take her to him to **w**, and perform the duty of 802
25: 7 if the man like not to take his **brother's** **w**, 2994
25: 7 let his **brother's** **w** go up to the gate unto 2994
25: 9 shall his **brother's** **w** come unto him in 2994
25:11 the **w** of the one draweth near for to deliver 802
27:20 Cursed *be* he that lieth with his father's **w**; 802
28:30 Thou shalt betroth a **w**, and another man 802
28:54 toward the **w** of his bosom, and towards 802
Jos 15:16 to him will I give Achsah my daughter to **w**. 802
15:17 and he gave him Achsah his daughter to **w**. 802
Jdg 1:12 to him will I give Achsah my daughter to **w**. 802
1:13 and he gave him Achsah his daughter to **w**. 802
4: 4 a prophetess, the **w** of Lapidoth, 802
4:17 to the tent of Jael the **w** of Heber the Kenite: 802
4:21 Jael Heber's **w** took a nail of the tent, and 802
5:24 Blessed above women shall Jael the **w** of 802
11: 2 Gilead's **w** bare him sons; and *his* wife's 802
13: 2 and his **w** *was* barren, and bare not. 802
13:11 went after his **w**, and came to the man, and 802
13:19 and Manoah and his **w** looked on. 802
13:20 Manoah and his **w** looked on *it,* and fell on 802
13:21 did no more appear to Manoah and to his **w**. 802
13:22 Manoah said unto his **w**, We shall surely die, 802
13:23 his **w** said unto him, If the LORD were 802
14: 2 therefore get her for me to **w**. 802
14: 3 that thou goest to take a **w** of 802
14:15 that they said unto Samson's **w**, Entice thy 802
14:16 And Samson's **w** wept before him, and said, 802
14:20 Samson's **w** was *given* to his companion, 802
15: 1 that Samson visited his **w** with a kid; 802
15: 1 I will go in to my **w** into the chamber. 802
15: 6 because he had taken his **w**, and given her to 802
21: 1 of us give his daughter unto Benjamin to **w**. 802
21:18 Cursed *be* he that giveth a **w** to Benjamin. 802
21:21 catch you every man his **w** of the daughters 802
21:22 we reserved not to each man his **w** in 802
Ru 1: 1 of Moab, he, and his **w**, and his two sons. 802
1: 2 the name of his **w** Naomi, and the name of 802
4: 5 of Ruth the Moabitess, the **w** of the dead, 802
4:10 Ruth the Moabitess, the **w** of Mahlon, 802
4:10 of Mahlon, have I purchased to be my **w**, 802
4:13 So Boaz took Ruth, and she was his **w**: and 802
1Sa 1: 4 he gave to Peninnah his **w**, and to all her 802
1:19 Elkanah knew Hannah his **w**; and 802
2:20 And Eli blessed Elkanah and his **w**, and said, 802
4:19 Phinehas' **w**, was with child, *near* to be 802
14:50 the name of Saul's **w** *was* Ahinoam, 802
18:17 daughter Merab, her will I give thee to **w**: 802
18:19 was given unto Adriel the Meholathite to **w**. 802
18:27 Saul gave him Michal his daughter to **w**. 802
19:11 Michal David's **w** told him, saying, If thou 802
25: 3 *was* Nabal; and the name of his **w** Abigail: 802
25:14 told Abigail, Nabal's **w**, saying, Behold, 802
25:37 his **w** had told him these things, that his 802

1Sa 25:39 with Abigail, to take her to him to **w**. 802
25:40 sent us unto thee, to take thee to him to **w**. 802
25:42 the messengers of David, and became his **w**. 802
25:44 David's **w**, to Phalti the son of Laish, 802
27: 3 and Abigail the Carmelitess, Nabal's **w**. 802
30: 5 and Abigail the **w** of Nabal the Carmelite. 802
30:22 save *to* every man his **w** and his children, 802
2Sa 2: 2 and Abigail Nabal's **w** the Carmelite. 802
3: 3 of Abigail the **w** of Nabal the Carmelite; 802
3: 5 And the sixth, Ithream, by Eglah David's **w**. 802
3:14 Saul's son, saying, Deliver *me* my **w** Michal, 802
11: 3 of Eliam, the **w** of Uriah the Hittite? 802
11:11 to eat and to drink, and to lie with my **w**? 802
11:26 when the **w** of Uriah heard that Uriah her 802
11:27 and she became his **w**, and bare him a son. 802
12: 9 hast taken his **w** to be thy wife, and hast 802
12: 9 hast taken his wife to be thy **w**, and hast 802
12:10 hast taken the **w** of Uriah the Hittite to be 802
12:10 the wife of Uriah the Hittite to be thy **w**. 802
12:15 the LORD strake the child that Uriah's **w** 802
12:24 And David comforted Bath-sheba his **w**, and 802
1Ki 2:17 he give me Abishag the Shunammite to **w**. 802
2:21 be given to Adonijah thy brother to **w**. 802
4:11 had Taphath the daughter of Solomon to **w**: 802
4:15 took Basmath the daughter of Solomon to **w**: 802
7: 8 whom he had taken *to* **w**, like unto this NIH
9:16 a present unto his daughter, Solomon's **w**. 802
11:19 that he gave him *to* **w** the sister of his own 802
11:19 he gave him *to* wife the sister of his own **w**, 802
14: 2 Jeroboam said to his **w**, Arise, I pray thee, 802
14: 2 that thou be not known to be the **w** of 802
14: 4 Jeroboam's **w** did so, and arose, and went *to* 802
14: 5 the **w** of Jeroboam cometh to ask a thing of 802
14: 6 that he said, Come in, thou **w** of Jeroboam; 802
14:17 Jeroboam's **w** arose, and departed, and 802
16:31 that he took *to* **w** Jezebel the daughter of 802
21: 5 Jezebel his **w** came to him, and said unto 802
21: 7 Jezebel his **w** said unto him, Dost thou now 802
21:25 the LORD, whom Jezebel his **w** stirred up. 802
2Ki 5: 2 a little maid; and she waited on Naaman's **w**. 802
8:18 for the daughter of Ahab was his **w**: and 802
14: 9 Give thy daughter to my son to **w**: 802
22:14 the **w** of Shallum the son of Tikvah, the son 802
1Ch 2:18 of Hezron begat *children* of Azubah *his* **w**, 802
2:24 Abiah Hezron's **w** bare him Ashur the father 802
2:26 Jerahmeel had also another **w**, whose name 802
2:29 the name of the **w** of Abishur *was* Abihail, 802
2:35 gave his daughter to Jarha his servant to **w**; 802
3: 3 of Abital: the sixth, Ithream by Eglah his **w**. 802
4:18 his **w** Jehudijah bare Jered the father of 802
4:19 the sons of *his* **w** Hodiah the sister of 802
7:15 Machir took to **w** *the sister* of Huppim and 802
7:16 Maachah the **w** of Machir bare a son, and 802
7:23 when he went in to his **w**, she conceived, 802
8: 9 he begat of Hodesh his **w**, Jobab, and Zibia, 802
2Ch 8:11 My **w** shall not dwell in the house of David 802
11:18 daughter of Jerimoth the son of David *to* **w**, 802
21: 6 for he had the daughter of Ahab to **w**: and 802
22:11 king Jehoram, the **w** of Jehoiada the priest, 802
25:18 Give thy daughter to my son to **w**: 802
34:22 the **w** of Shallum the son of Tikvath, the son 802
Ezr 2:61 which took a **w** of the daughters of Barzillai 802
Ne 7:63 the daughters of Barzillai the Gileadite *to* **w**, 802
Est 5:10 and called for his friends, and Zeresh his **w**. 802
5:14 said Zeresh his **w** and all his friends unto 802
6:13 Haman told Zeresh his **w** and all his friends 802
6:13 his wise *men* and Zeresh his **w** unto him, 802
Job 2: 9 said his **w** unto him, Dost thou still retain 802
19:17 My breath is strange to my **w**, though I 802
31:10 *Then* let my **w** grind unto another, and 802
Ps 109: 9 children be fatherless, and his **w** a widow. 802
128: 3 Thy **w** *shall be* as a fruitful vine by the sides 802
Pr 5:18 and rejoice with the **w** of thy youth. 802
6:29 So he that goeth in to his neighbour's **w**; 802
18:22 *Whoso* findeth a **w** findeth a good *thing,* and 802
19:13 the contentions of a **w** *are* a continual 802
19:14 and a prudent **w** *is* from the LORD. 802
Ecc 9: 9 Live joyfully with the **w** whom thou lovest 802
Isa 54: 1 than the children of the **married** **w**, 1166
54: 6 and grieved in spirit, and a **w** of youth, 802
Jer 3: 1 If a man put away his **w**, and she go from 802
3:20 Surely *as* a **w** treacherously departeth from 802
5: 8 every one neighed after his neighbour's **w**. 802
6:11 for even the husband with the **w** shall be 802
16: 2 Thou shalt not take thee a **w**, neither shalt 802
Eze 16:32 *But as* a **w** that committeth adultery, 802
18: 6 neither hath defiled his neighbour's **w**, 802
18:11 and defiled his neighbour's **w**, 802
18:15 of Israel, hath not defiled his neighbour's **w**, 802
22:11 abomination with his neighbour's **w**; 802
24:18 at even my **w** died; and I did in the morning 802
33:26 and ye defile every one his neighbour's **w**: 802
Hos 1: 2 take unto thee a **w** of whoredoms and 802
2: 2 for she *is* not my **w**, neither *am* I her 802
12:12 Israel served for a **w**, and for a wife he kept 802
12:12 served for a wife, and for a **w** he kept *sheep.* 802
Am 7:17 Thy **w** shall be a harlot in the city, and 802
Mal 2:14 witness between thee and the **w** of thy youth, 802
2:14 thy companion, and the **w** of thy covenant. 802
2:15 let none deal treacherously against the **w** of 802
Mt 1: 6 of *her that had been* the *w* of Urias; NIG
1:20 fear not to take unto thee Mary thy **w**: *1135*
1:24 had bidden him, and took unto *him* his **w**: *1135*
5:31 been said, Whosoever shall put away his **w**, *1135*
5:32 That whosoever shall put away his **w**, *1135*
14: 3 for Herodias' sake, his brother Philip's **w**. *1135*
18:25 and his **w**, and children, and all that he had, *1135*
19: 3 Is it lawful for a man to put away his **w** for *1135*
19: 5 and mother, and shall cleave to his **w**: *1135*
19: 9 unto you, Whosoever shall put away his **w**, *1135*
19:10 If the case of the man be so with *his* **w**, it is *1135*
19:29 or mother, or **w**, or children, or lands, *1135*
22:24 his brother shall marry his **w**, and raise up *1135*
22:25 when he had married *a* **w**, deceased, and, NIG
22:25 having no issue, left his **w** unto his brother: *1135*

W

Mt 22:28 Therefore in the resurrection whose **w** shall *1135*
27:19 judgment seat, his **w** sent unto him, saying, *1135*
Mk 6:17 for Herodias' sake, his brother Philip's **w**: *1135*
6:18 not lawful for thee to have thy brother's **w**. *1135*
10: 2 Is it lawful for a man to put away *his* **w**? *1135*
10: 7 his father and mother, and cleave to his **w**; *1135*
10:11 Whosoever shall put away his **w**, and *1135*
10:29 or mother, or **w**, or children, or lands, *1135*
12:19 and leave *his* **w** *behind him,* and leave no *1135*
12:19 that his brother should take his **w**, and *1135*
12:20 and the first took a **w**, and dying left no *1135*
12:23 shall rise, whose **w** shall she be of them? *1135*
12:23 she be of them? for the seven had her to **w**. *1135*
Lk 1: 5 and his **w** *was* of the daughters of Aaron, *1135*
1:13 and thy **w** Elisabeth shall bear thee a son, *1135*
1:18 old man, and my **w** well stricken in years. *1135*
1:24 And after those days his **w** Elisabeth *1135*
2: 5 To be taxed with Mary his espoused **w**, *1135*
3:19 by him for Herodias his brother Philip's **w**, *1135*
8: 3 And Joanna the **w** of Chuza Herod's *1135*
14:20 I have married a **w**, and therefore I cannot *1135*
14:26 and **w**, and children, and brethren, and *1135*
16:18 Whosoever putteth away his **w**, and *1135*
17:32 Remember Lot's **w**. *1135*
18:29 or parents, or brethren, or **w**, or children, *1135*
20:28 having a **w**, and he die without children, *1135*
20:28 that his brother should take *his* **w**, and *1135*
20:29 and the first took a **w**, and died without *1135*
20:30 And the second took her to **w**, and he died *1135*
20:33 Therefore in the resurrection whose **w** of *1135*
20:33 wife of them is she? for seven had her to **w**. *1135*
Jn 19:25 Mary the *w* of Cleophas, and NIG
Ac 5: 1 with Sapphira his **w**, sold a possession, *1135*
5: 2 his **w** also being privy *to it,* and brought a *1135*
5: 7 when his **w**, not knowing what was done, *1135*
18: 2 lately come from Italy, with his **w** Priscilla; *1135*
24:24 when Felix came with his **w** Drusilla, *1135*
1Co 5: 1 that one should have *his* father's **w**. *1135*
7: 2 let every man have his own **w**, and *1135*
7: 3 Let the husband render unto the **w** due *1135*
7: 3 and likewise also the **w** unto the husband. *1135*
7: 4 The **w** hath not power of her own body, but *1135*
7: 4 hath not power of his own body, but the **w**. *1135*
7:10 Let not the **w** depart from *her* husband: *1135*
7:11 and let not the husband put away *his* **w**. *1135*
7:12 If any brother hath a **w** that believeth not, *1135*
7:14 unbelieving husband is sanctified by the **w**, *1135*
7:14 the unbelieving **w** is sanctified by *1135*
7:16 For what knowest thou, O **w**, whether thou *1135*
7:16 O man, whether thou shalt save *thy* **w**? *1135*
7:27 Art thou bound unto a **w**? seek not to be *1135*
7:27 Art thou loosed from a **w**? seek not a wife. *1135*
7:27 Art thou loosed from a wife? seek not a **w**. *1135*
7:33 *are* of the world, how he may please *his* **w**. *1135*
7:34 There is difference *also* between a **w** and a *1135*
7:39 The **w** is bound by the law as long as her *1135*
9: 5 a **w**, as well as other apostles, and *as* *1135*
Eph 5:23 For the husband is the head of the **w**, *1135*
5:28 He that loveth his **w** loveth himself. *1135*
5:31 and shall be joined unto his **w**, and *1135*
5:33 in particular so love his **w** even as himself; *1135*
5:33 the **w** *see* that she reverence *her* husband. *1135*
1Ti 3: 2 the husband of one **w**, vigilant, sober, *1135*
3:12 Let the deacons be the husbands of one **w**, *1135*
5: 9 years old, having been the **w** of one man, *1135*
Tit 1: 6 If any be blameless, the husband of one **w**, *1135*
1Pe 3: 7 giving honour unto the **w**, as unto *1134*
Rev 19: 7 is come, and his **w** hath made herself ready. *1135*
21: 9 I will shew thee the bride, the Lamb's **w**. *1135*

WIFE'S (11) [WIFE]

Ge 3:20 Adam called his **w** name Eve; because 802
20:11 and they will slay me for my **w** sake. 802
36:39 his **w** name *was* Mehetabel, the daughter of 802
Lev 18:11 The nakedness of thy father's **w** daughter, 802
Jdg 11: 2 *his* **w** sons grew up, and they thrust out 802
1Ch 1:50 his **w** name *was* Mehetabel, the daughter of 802
8:29 of Gibeon; whose **w** name *was* Maachah: 802
9:35 Jehiel, whose **w** name *was* Maachah: 802
Mt 8:14 he saw his **w mother** laid, and sick of a *3994*
Mk 1:30 But Simon's **w mother** lay sick of a fever, *3994*
Lk 4:38 And Simon's **w mother** was taken with a *3994*

WILD (44) [WILDERNESS]

Ge 16:12 he will be a **w** man; his hand *will be* against 6501
Lev 26:22 I will also send **w** beasts among you, which 7704
Dt 14: 5 the **w goat**, and the pygarg, and the wild ox, 689
14: 5 the pygarg, and the **w ox**, and the chamois. 8377
1Sa 17:46 of the air, and to the **w beasts** of the earth; 2416
24: 2 and his men upon the rocks of the **w goats**. 3277
2Sa 2:18 *as* light of foot as a **w** roe. 7704+871.1+1886.1
2Ki 4:39 found a **w** vine, and gathered thereof wild 7704
4:39 gathered thereof **w** gourds his lap full, and 7704
14: 9 there passed by a **w** beast that *was* in 7704
2Ch 25:18 there passed by a **w** beast that *was* in 7704
Job 6: 5 Doth the **w ass** bray when he hath grass? or 6501
11:12 though man be born *like* a **w ass's** colt. 6501
24: 5 Behold, *as* **w asses** in the desert, go they 6501
39: 1 Knowest thou the time when the **w goats** of 3277
39: 5 Who hath sent out the **w ass** free? or 6501
39: 5 or who hath loosed the bands of the **w ass**? 6171
39:15 or *that* the **w** beast may break them. 7704
Ps 50:11 and the **w beasts** of the field *are* mine. 2123
80:13 and the **w beast** of the field doth devour it. 2123
104:11 of the field: the **w asses** quench their thirst. 6501
104:18 The high hills *are* a refuge for the **w goats**; 3277
Isa 5: 2 forth grapes, and it brought forth **w grapes**. 891
5: 4 forth grapes, brought it forth **w grapes**? 891
13:21 **w beasts of the desert** shall lie there; and 6728
13:22 the **w beasts of the islands** shall cry in their 338
32:14 a joy of **w asses**, a pasture of flocks; 6501
34:14 The **w beasts of the desert** shall also meet 6728
34:14 also meet with the **w beasts of the island**, 338
51:20 head of all the streets, as a **w bull** *in* a net: 8377
Jer 2:24 A **w ass** used to the wilderness, 6501
14: 6 the **w asses** did stand in the high places, 6501
50:39 Therefore the **w beasts of the desert** with 6728
50:39 the **w beasts of the islands** shall dwell *there,* 338
Da 5:21 and his dwelling *was* with the **w asses**: 6167
Hos 8: 9 up *to* Assyria, a **w ass** alone by himself: 6501
13: 8 like a lion: the **w** beast shall tear them. 7704
Mt 3: 4 and his meat was locusts and **w** honey. *66*
Mk 1: 6 his loins; and he did eat locusts and **w** honey; *66*
1:13 and was with the **w beasts**; and the angels *2342*
Ac 10:12 and **w beasts**, and creeping things, and *2342*
11: 6 and **w beasts**, and creeping things, and *2342*
Ro 11:17 and thou, being a **w olive tree**, wert graffed in *65*
11:24 cut out of the **olive tree which is w** by nature, *65*

WILD GOATS See SATYRS

WILD OX, OXEN See UNICORN; UNICORNS

WILDERNESS (305) [WILD]

Ge 14: 6 unto El-paran, which *is* by the **w**. 4057
16: 7 found her by a fountain of water in the **w**, 4057
21:14 and wandered in the **w** of Beer-sheba. 4057
21:20 and dwelt in the **w**, and became an archer. 4057
21:21 he dwelt in the **w** of Paran: and his mother 4057
36:24 *that* Anah that found the mules in the **w**, 4057
37:22 *but* cast him into this pit that *is* in the **w**, 4057
Ex 3:18 three days' journey into the **w**, 4057
4:27 to Aaron, Go into the **w** to meet Moses. 4057
5: 1 that they may hold a feast unto me in the **w**. 4057
7:16 people go, that they may serve me in the **w**: 4057
8:27 We will go three days' journey into the **w**, 4057
8:28 sacrifice to the LORD your God in the **w**; 4057
13:18 *through* the way of the **w** of the Red sea: 4057
13:20 encamped in Etham, in the edge of the **w**. 4057
14: 3 in the land, the **w** hath shut them in. 4057
14:11 hast thou taken us away to die in the **w**? 4057
14:12 than that we should die in the **w**. 4057
15:22 and they went out into the **w** of Shur; 4057
15:22 they went three days in the **w**, and found no 4057
16: 1 children of Israel came unto the **w** of Sin, 4057
16: 2 against Moses and Aaron in the **w**: 4057
16: 3 for ye have brought us forth into this **w**, to 4057
16:10 that they looked toward the **w**, and behold, 4057
16:14 upon the face of the **w** *there lay* a small 4057
16:32 bread wherewith I have fed you in the **w**, 4057
17: 1 of Israel journeyed from the **w** of Sin, 4057
18: 5 and his wife unto Moses into the **w**, 4057
19: 1 the same day came they *into* the **w** of Sinai. 4057
19: 2 desert of Sinai, and had pitched in the **w**; 4057
Lev 7:38 unto the LORD, in the **w** of Sinai. 4057
16:10 *and* to let him go for a scapegoat into the **w**. 4057
16:21 away by the hand of a fit man into the **w**: 4057
16:22 and he shall let go the goat in the **w**. 4057
Nu 1: 1 the LORD spake unto Moses in the **w** of 4057
1:19 so he numbered them in the **w** of Sinai. 4057
3: 4 in the **w** of Sinai, and they had no children: 4057
3:14 the LORD spake unto Moses in the **w** of 4057
9: 1 the LORD spake unto Moses in the **w** of 4057
9: 5 of the first month at even in the **w** of Sinai: 4057
10:12 took their journeys out of the **w** of Sinai; 4057
10:12 and the cloud rested in the **w** of Paran. 4057
10:31 knowest how we are to encamp in the **w**, 4057
12:16 and pitched in the **w** of Paran. 4057
13: 3 the LORD sent them from the **w** of Paran: 4057
13:21 searched the land from the **w** of Zin unto 4057
13:26 of Israel, unto the **w** of Paran, to Kadesh; 4057
14: 2 or would God we had died in this **w**! 4057
14:16 therefore he hath slain them in the **w**. 4057
14:22 which I did in Egypt and in the **w**, and 4057
14:25 get you *into* the **w** *by* the way of the Red 4057
14:29 Your carcases shall fall in this **w**; and 4057
14:32 your carcases, they shall fall in this **w**. 4057
14:33 your children shall wander in the **w** forty 4057
14:33 until your carcases be wasted in the **w**. 4057
14:35 in this **w** they shall be consumed, and 4057
15:32 while the children of Israel were in the **w**, 4057
16:13 with milk and honey, to kill us in the **w**, 4057
20: 4 the congregation of the LORD into this **w**, 4057
21: 5 brought us up out of Egypt to die in the **w**? 4057
21:11 in the **w** which *is* before Moab, toward 4057
21:13 which *is* in the **w** that cometh out of 4057
21:18 And from the **w** *they went* to Mattanah: 4057
21:23 and went out against Israel into the **w**: 4057
24: 1 but he set his face toward the **w**. 4057
26:64 the children of Israel in the **w** of Sinai. 4057
26:65 said of them, They shall surely die in the **w**. 4057
27: 3 Our father died in the **w**, and he was not in 4057
27:14 of Meribah in Kadesh *in* the **w** of Zin. 4057
32:13 he made them wander in the **w** forty years, 4057
32:15 he will yet again leave them in the **w**; 4057
33: 6 in Etham, which *is* in the edge of the **w**. 4057
33: 8 through the midst of the sea into the **w**, 4057
33: 8 went three days' journey in the **w** of Etham, 4057
33:11 the Red sea, and encamped in the **w** of Sin. 4057
33:12 they took their journey out of the **w** of Sin, 4057
33:15 and pitched in the **w** of Sinai. 4057
33:36 pitched in the **w** of Zin, which *is* Kadesh. 4057
34: 3 your south quarter shall be from the **w** of 4057
Dt 1: 1 unto all Israel on *this* side Jordan in the **w**, 4057
1:19 went *through* all that great and terrible **w**, 4057
1:31 in the **w**, where thou hast seen how that 4057
1:40 take your journey into the **w** *by* the way of 4057
2: 1 took our journey into the **w** *by* the way of 4057
2: 7 knoweth thy walking *through* this great **w**. 4057
2: 8 and passed *by* the way of the **w** of Moab. 4057
2:26 I sent messengers out of the **w** of 4057
4:43 *Namely,* Bezer in the **w**, in the plain 4057
8: 2 thy God led thee these forty years in the **w**, 4057
8:15 led thee through *that* great and terrible **w**, 4057
8:16 Who fed thee in the **w** with manna, 4057
9: 7 the LORD thy God to wrath in the **w**; 4057
9:28 brought them out to slay them in the **w**. 4057
11: 5 what he did unto you in the **w**, until ye 4057
11:24 from the **w** and Lebanon, from the river, 4057
29: 5 I have led you forty years in the **w**: 4057
32:10 a desert land, and in the waste howling **w**; 3452
32:51 waters of Meribah-Kadesh, *in* the **w** of Zin; 4057
Jos 1: 4 From the **w** and this Lebanon even unto 4057
5: 4 the men of war, died in the **w** by the way, 4057
5: 5 all the people *that were* born in the **w** by 4057
5: 6 of Israel walked forty years in the **w**, 4057
8:15 before them, and fled *by* the way of the **w**. 4057
8:20 the people that fled *to* the **w** turned back 4057
8:24 in the **w** wherein they chased them, and 4057
12: 8 in the **w**, and in the south *country;* 4057
14:10 *the children of* Israel wandered in the **w**: 4057
15: 1 the **w** of Zin southward *was* the uttermost 4057
15:61 In the **w**, Beth-arabah, Middin, and 4057
16: 1 *to* the **w** that goeth up from Jericho 4057
18:12 the goings out thereof were at the **w** of 4057
20: 8 they assigned Bezer in the **w** upon the plain 4057
24: 7 and ye dwelt in the **w** a long season. 4057
Jdg 1:16 the children of Judah *into* the **w** of Judah, 4057
8: 7 will tear your flesh with the thorns of the **w** 4057
8:16 thorns of the **w** and briers, and with them 4057
11:16 and walked through the **w** unto the Red sea, 4057
11:18 they went along through the **w**, and 4057
11:22 and from the **w** even unto Jordan. 4057
20:42 the men of Israel unto the way of the **w**; 4057
20:45 fled toward the **w** unto the rock of 4057
20:47 and fled to the **w** unto the rock Rimmon, 4057
1Sa 4: 8 the Egyptians with all the plagues in the **w**. 4057
13:18 to the valley of Zeboim toward the **w**. 4057
17:28 hast thou left those few sheep in the **w**? 4057
23:14 David abode in the **w** in strong holds, and 4057
23:14 remained in a mountain in the **w** of Ziph. 4057
23:15 and David *was* in the **w** of Ziph in a wood. 4057
23:24 David and his men *were* in the **w** of Maon, 4057
23:25 *into* a rock, and abode in the **w** of Maon. 4057
23:25 he pursued after David *in* the **w** of Maon. 4057
24: 1 Behold, David *is* in the **w** of En-gedi. 4057
25: 1 and went down to the **w** of Paran. 4057
25: 4 David heard in the **w** that Nabal did shear 4057
25:14 David sent messengers out of the **w** to 4057
25:21 I kept all that this *fellow* hath in the **w**, 4057
26: 2 and went down to the **w** of Ziph, 4057
26: 2 with him, to seek David in the **w** of Ziph. 4057
26: 3 David abode in the **w**, and he saw that Saul 4057
26: 3 he saw that Saul came after him into the **w**. 4057
2Sa 2:24 that *lieth* before Giah *by* the way of the **w** 4057
15:23 passed over, toward the way of the **w**. 4057
15:28 See, I will tarry in the plain of the **w**, 4057
16: 2 that such as be faint in the **w** may drink. 4057
17:16 Lodge not *this* night in the plains of the **w**, 4057
17:29 *is* hungry, and weary, and thirsty, in the **w**. 4057
1Ki 2:34 he was buried in his own house in the **w**. 4057
9:18 and Tadmor in the **w**, in the land, 4057
19: 4 he himself went a day's journey into the **w**, 4057
19:15 return on thy way to the **w** of Damascus: 4057
2Ki 3: 8 The way through the **w** of Edom. 4057
1Ch 5: 9 in of the **w** from the river Euphrates: 4057
6:78 Bezer in the **w** with her suburbs, and 4057
12: 8 David into the hold to the **w** men of might, 4057
21:29 which Moses made in the **w**, and the altar 4057
2Ch 1: 3 servant of the LORD had made in the **w**. 4057
8: 4 he built Tadmor in the **w**, and all the store 4057
20:16 the end of the brook, before the **w** of Jeruel. 4057
20:20 and went forth into the **w** of Tekoa: 4057
20:24 came toward the watch tower in the **w**, 4057
24: 9 servant of God laid upon Israel in the **w**. 4057
Ne 9:19 mercies forsookest them not in the **w**: 4057
9:21 forty years didst thou sustain them in the **w**, 4057
Job 1:19 there came a great wind from the **w**, and 4057
12:24 causeth them to wander in a **w** *where there* 8414
24: 5 the **w** *yieldeth* food for them *and* for *their* 6160
30: 3 flying *into* the **w** in former time desolate 6723
38:26 *where* no man *is; on* the **w**, wherein *there is* 4057
39: 6 Whose house I have made the **w**, and 6160
Ps 29: 8 The voice of the LORD shaketh the **w**; 4057
29: 8 the LORD shaketh the **w** of Kadesh. 4057
55: 7 I wander far off, *and* remain in the **w**. 4057
63: T of David, when he was in the **w** of Judah. 4057
65:12 They drop *upon* the pastures of the **w**: and 4057
68: 7 when thou didst march through the **w**; 3452
72: 9 They **that dwell in the w** shall bow before 6728
74:14 *to be* meat to the people **inhabiting the w**. 6728
78:15 He clave the rocks in the **w**, and gave *them* 4057
78:17 him by provoking the most High in the **w**. 6723
78:19 they said, Can God furnish a table in the **w**? 4057
78:40 How oft did they provoke him in the **w**, *and* 4057
78:52 and guided them in the **w** like a flock. 4057
95: 8 *and* as *in* the day of temptation in the **w**: 4057
102: 6 I am like a pelican of the **w**: I am like an 4057
106: 9 them through the depths, as *through* the **w**. 4057
106:14 lusted exceedingly in the **w**, and 4057
106:26 against them, to overthrow them in the **w**: 4057
107: 4 They wandered in the **w** in a solitary way; 4057
107:33 He turneth rivers into a **w**, and 4057
107:35 He turneth the **w** into a standing water, and 4057
107:40 causeth them to wander in the **w**, 8414
136:16 To him which led his people through the **w**: 4057
Pr 21:19 *It is* better to dwell in the **w**, than with 776+4057
SS 3: 6 Who *is* this that cometh out of the **w** like 4057
8: 5 Who *is* this that cometh up from the **w**, 4057
Isa 14:17 *That* made the world as a **w**, and 4057
16: 1 *to* the ruler of the land from Sela to the **w**, 4057
16: 8 unto Jazer, they wandered *through* the **w**: 4057
23:13 founded it for **them that dwell in the w**: 6728
27:10 the habitation forsaken, and left like a **w**: 4057
32:15 the **w** be a fruitful field, and the fruitful 4057
32:16 judgment shall dwell in the **w**, and 4057
33: 9 Sharon is like a **w**; and Bashan and 6160
35: 1 The **w** and the solitary place shall be glad 4057
35: 6 for in the **w** shall waters break out, and 4057
40: 3 The voice of him that crieth in the **w**, 4057
41:18 I will make the **w** a pool of water, and 4057
41:19 I will plant in the **w** the cedar, the shittah 4057
42:11 Let the **w** and the cities thereof lift up *their* 4057
43:19 I will even make a way in the **w**, *and* 4057
43:20 because I give waters in the **w**, *and* rivers in 4057

Isa 50: 2 I dry up the sea, I make the rivers a **w**: 4057
51: 3 he will make her **w** like Eden, and 4057
63:13 as a horse in the **w**, *that* they should not 4057
64:10 Thy holy cities are a **w**, Zion is a 4057
64:10 Zion is a **w**, Jerusalem a desolation. 4057
Jer 2: 2 when thou wentest after me in the **w**, 4057
2: 6 that led us through the **w**, through a land of 4057
2:24 A wild ass used to the **w**, *that* snuffeth up 4057
2:31 Have I been a **w** unto Israel? a land of 4057
3: 2 thou sat for them, as the Arabian in the **w**; 4057
4:11 A dry wind of the high places in the **w** 4057
4:26 lo, the fruitful place *was* a **w**, and all 4057
9: 2 O that I had in the **w** a lodging place of 4057
9:10 for the habitations of the **w** a lamentation, 4057
9:12 the land perisheth *and* is burnt up like a **w**, 4057
9:26 in the utmost corners, that dwell in the **w**: 4057
12:10 made my pleasant portion a desolate **w**. 4057
12:12 come upon all high places through the **w**: 4057
13:24 that passeth away by the wind of the **w**. 4057
17: 6 shall inhabit the parched places in the **w**, 4057
22: 6 *yet* surely I will make thee a **w** *and* 4057
23:10 the pleasant places of the **w** are dried up, 4057
31: 2 were left of the sword found grace in the **w**; 4057
48: 6 your lives, and be like the heath in the **w**. 4057
50:12 the hindermost of the nations *shall be* a **w**, 4057
51:43 cities are a desolation, a dry land, and a **w**, 6160
La 4: 3 *is* become cruel, like the ostriches in the **w**. 4057
4:19 they laid wait for us in the **w**. 4057
5: 9 *of* our lives because of the sword of the **w**. 4057
Eze 6:14 more desolate than the **w** toward Diblath, 4057
19:13 now she *is* planted in the **w**, in a dry and 4057
20:10 land of Egypt, and brought them into the **w**. 4057
20:13 of Israel rebelled against me in the **w**: 4057
20:13 pour out my fury upon them in the **w**, 4057
20:15 also I lifted up my hand unto them in the **w**, 4057
20:17 neither did I make an end of them in the **w**. 4057
20:18 I said unto their children in the **w**, Walk ye 4057
20:21 my anger against them in the **w**. 4057
20:23 up mine hand unto them also in the **w**, 4057
20:35 I will bring you into the **w** of the people, 4057
20:36 Like as I pleaded with your fathers in the **w** 4057
23:42 sort *were* brought Sabeans from the **w**, 4057
29: 5 I will leave thee *thrown* into the **w**, thee 4057
34:25 they shall dwell safely in the **w**, and 4057
Hos 2: 3 make her as a **w**, and set her like a dry land, 4057
2:14 bring her *into* the **w**, and speak comfortably 4057
9:10 I found Israel like grapes in the **w**; I saw 4057
13: 5 I did know thee in the **w**, in the land of 4057
13:15 of the LORD *shall* come up from the **w**, 4057
Joel 1:19 the fire hath devoured the pastures of the **w**, 4057
1:20 the fire hath devoured the pastures of the **w**. 4057
2: 3 before them, and behind them a desolate **w**; 4057
2:22 for the pastures of the **w** do spring, for 4057
3:19 and Edom shall be a desolate **w**, 4057
Am 2:10 led you forty years through the **w**, 4057
5:25 and offerings in the **w** forty years, 4057
6:14 in of Hemath unto the river of the **w**. 6160
Zep 2:13 Nineveh a desolation, *and* dry like a **w**. 4057
Mal 1: 3 his heritage waste for the dragons of the **w**. 4057
Mt 3: 1 the Baptist, preaching in the **w** of Judea, *2048*
3: 3 saying, The voice of one crying in the **w**, *2048*
4: 1 Spirit into the **w** to be tempted of the devil. *2048*
11: 7 What went ye out into the **w** to see? *2048*
15:33 should we have so much bread in the **w**, *2047*
Mk 1: 3 The voice of one crying in the **w**, *2048*
1: 4 John did baptize in the **w**, and preach *2048*
1:12 the Spirit driveth him into the **w**. *2048*
1:13 And he was there in the **w** forty days, *2048*
8: 4 satisfy these *men* with bread here in the **w**? *2047*
Lk 3: 2 unto John the son of Zacharias in the **w**. *2048*
3: 4 saying, The voice of one crying in the **w**, *2048*
4: 1 and was led by the Spirit into the **w**, *2048*
5:16 And he withdrew himself into the **w**, and *2048*
7:24 What went ye out into the **w** for to see? *2048*
8:29 and was driven of the devil into the **w**.) *2048*
15: 4 doth not leave the ninety and nine in the **w**, *2048*
Jn 1:23 I *am* the voice of one crying in the **w**, *2048*
3:14 as Moses lifted up the serpent in the **w**, *2048*
6:49 Your fathers did eat manna in the **w**, and *2048*
11:54 went thence unto a country near to the **w**, *2048*
Ac 7:30 there appeared to him in the **w** of mount *2048*
7:36 and in the Red sea, and in the **w** forty years. *2048*
7:38 that was in the church in the **w** with *2048*
7:42 *by the space of* forty years in the **w**? *2048*
7:44 had the tabernacle of Witness in the **w**, *2048*
13:18 years suffered he their manners in the **w**. *2048*
21:38 leddest out into the **w** four thousand men *2048*
1Co 10: 5 for they were overthrown in the **w**. *2048*
2Co 11:26 *in* perils in the **w**, *in* perils in the sea, *2047*
Heb 3: 8 in the day of temptation in the **w**: *2048*
3:17 had sinned, whose carcases fell in the **w**? *2048*
Rev 12: 6 And the woman fled into the **w**, where she *2048*
12:14 that she might fly into the **w**, into her place, *2048*
17: 3 he carried me away in the spirit into the **w**: *2048*

WILES (2) [WILILY]

Nu 25:18 For they vex you with their **w**, 5231
Eph 6:11 that ye may be able to stand against the **w** *3180*

WILFULLY (1) [WILL]

Heb 10:26 For if we sin **w** after that *we* have received *1596*

W

WILILY (1) [WILES]

Jos 9: 4 They did work **w**, and went and 6195+871.1

WILL (3837) [FREEWILL, SELFWILL, SELFWILLED, WILFULLY, WILLETH, WILLING, WILLINGLY, WILT, WOULD]

Ge 2:18 be alone; I **w** make him a help meet for him. NIH
3:15 I **w** put enmity between thee and NIH
3:16 I **w** greatly multiply thy sorrow and NIH
6: 7 I **w** destroy man whom I have created from NIH
6:13 and behold, I **w** destroy them with the earth. NIH
6:18 with thee **w** I establish my covenant; and NIH
Ge 7: 4 I **w** cause it to rain upon the earth forty days NIH
7: 4 every living substance that I have made **w** I NIH
8:21 I **w** not again curse the ground any more for NIH
8:21 neither **w** I again smite any more every NIH
9: 5 surely your blood of your lives **w** I require; NIH
9: 5 at the hand of every beast **w** I require it, and NIH
9: 5 at the hand of every man's brother **w** I NIH
9:11 I **w** establish my covenant with you; NIH
9:15 I **w** remember my covenant, which *is* NIH
9:16 I **w** look upon it, that I may remember NIH
11: 6 and now nothing **w** be restrained from them, NIH
12: 1 unto a land that I **w** shew thee: NIH
12: 2 I **w** make of thee a great nation, and I will NIH
12: 2 I **w** bless thee, and make thy name great; NIH
12: 3 I **w** bless them that bless thee, and NIH
12: 7 and said, Unto thy seed **w** I give this land: NIH
12:12 they **w** kill me, but they will save thee alive. NIH
12:12 they will kill me, but they **w** save thee alive. NIH
13: 9 *take* the left hand, then I **w** go to the right; NIH
13: 9 *to* the right hand, then I **w** go to the left. NIH
13:15 to thee **w** I give it, and to thy seed for ever. NIH
13:16 I **w** make thy seed as the dust of the earth: NIH
13:17 in the breadth of it; for I **w** give it unto thee. NIH
14:23 That I **w** not *take* from a thread even to a NIH
14:23 that I **w** not take any thing that *is* thine, NIH
15:14 whom they shall serve, **w** I judge: NIH
16:10 I **w** multiply thy seed exceedingly, that it NIH
16:12 he **w** be a wild man; his hand *will be* against NIH
16:12 his hand *w be* against every man, and NIH
17: 2 I **w** make my covenant between me and NIH
17: 2 and thee, and **w** multiply thee exceedingly. NIH
17: 6 I **w** make thee exceeding fruitful, and I will NIH
17: 6 I **w** make nations of thee, and kings shall NIH
17: 7 I **w** establish my covenant between me and NIH
17: 8 I **w** give unto thee, and to thy seed after NIH
17: 8 and I **w** be their God. NIH
17:16 I **w** bless her, and give thee a son also of NIH
17:16 I **w** bless her, and she shall be *a mother* of NIH
17:19 I **w** establish my covenant with him for an NIH
17:20 **w** make him fruitful, and will multiply him NIH
17:20 and **w** multiply him exceedingly; NIH
17:20 he beget, and I **w** make him a great nation. NIH
17:21 my covenant **w** I establish with Isaac, NIH
18: 5 I **w** fetch a morsel of bread, and comfort ye NIH
18:10 I **w** certainly return unto thee according to NIH
18:14 At the time appointed I **w** return unto thee, NIH
18:19 that he **w** command his children and his NIH
18:21 I **w** go down now, and see whether they NIH
18:21 is come unto me; and if not, I **w** know. NIH
18:26 then I **w** spare all the place for their sakes. NIH
18:28 find there forty and five, I **w** not destroy *it*. NIH
18:29 And he said, I **w** not do *it* for forty's sake. NIH
18:30 Oh let not the Lord be angry, and I **w** speak: NIH
18:30 he said, I **w** not do *it*, if I find thirty there. NIH
18:31 he said, I **w** not destroy *it* for twenty's sake. NIH
18:32 be angry, and I **w** speak yet but *this* once: NIH
18:32 he said, I **w** not destroy *it* for ten's sake. NIH
19: 2 Nay; but we **w** abide in the street all night. NIH
19: 9 in to sojourn, and he **w** needs be a judge: NIH
19: 9 now **w** we deal worse with thee, than with NIH
19:13 For we **w** destroy this place, because the cry NIH
19:14 for the LORD **w** destroy this city. NIH
19:21 that I **w** not overthrow *this* city, for NIH
19:32 father drink wine, and we **w** lie with him, NIH
20:11 and they **w** slay me for my wife's sake. NIH
21: 6 *so that* all that hear **w** laugh with me. NIH
21:13 also of the son of the bondwoman **w** I make NIH
21:18 thine hand; for I **w** make him a great nation. NIH
21:24 And Abraham said, I **w** swear. NIH
22: 2 one of the mountains which I **w** tell thee of. NIH
22: 5 I and the lad **w** go yonder and worship, and NIH
22: 8 God **w** provide himself a lamb for a burnt NIH
22:17 That in blessing I **w** bless thee, and NIH
22:17 in multiplying I **w** multiply thy seed as NIH
23:13 I **w** give *thee* money for the field; take *it* of NIH
23:13 take *it* of me, and I **w** bury my dead there. NIH
24: 3 I **w** make thee swear by the LORD, NIH
24: 5 Peradventure the woman **w** not be willing to NIH
24: 7 Unto thy seed **w** I give this land; NIH
24: 8 if the woman **w** not be willing to follow NIH
24:14 Drink, and I **w** give thy camels drink also: NIH
24:19 she said, I **w** draw *water* for thy camels also, NIH
24:33 he said, I **w** not eat, until I have told mine NIH
24:39 Peradventure the woman **w** not follow me. NIH
24:40 **w** send his angel with thee, and prosper thy NIH
24:44 and I **w** also draw for thy camels: NIH
24:46 Drink, and I **w** give thy camels drink also: NIH
24:49 now if ye **w** deal kindly and truly with my 3426
24:57 We **w** call the damsel, and inquire at her NIH
24:58 go with this man? And she said, I **w** go. NIH
26: 3 I **w** be with thee, and will bless thee; NIH
26: 3 I will be with thee, and **w** bless thee; NIH
26: 3 I **w** give all these countries, and I will NIH
26: 3 I **w** perform the oath which I sware unto NIH
26: 4 I **w** make thy seed to multiply as the stars of NIH
26: 4 and **w** give unto thy seed all these countries; NIH
26:24 **w** bless thee, and multiply thy seed for my NIH
27: 9 I **w** make them savoury meat for thy father, NIH
27:12 My father peradventure **w** feel me, and NIH
27:25 near to me, and I **w** eat of my son's venison, NIH
27:41 are at hand; then **w** I slay my brother Jacob. NIH
27:45 I **w** send, and fetch thee from thence: why NIH
28:13 to thee **w** I give it, and to thy seed; NIH
28:15 **w** keep thee in all *places* whither thou goest, NIH
28:15 and **w** bring thee again into this land; NIH
28:15 for I **w** not leave thee, until I have done *that* NIH
28:20 If God **w** be with me, and will keep me in NIH
28:20 **w** keep me in this way that I go, and NIH
28:20 **w** give me bread to eat, and raiment to put NIH
28:22 of all that thou shalt give me I **w** surely give NIH
29:18 I **w** serve thee seven years for Rachel thy NIH
29:27 we **w** give thee this also for the service NIH
29:32 now therefore my husband **w** love me. NIH
29:34 Now *this* time **w** my husband be joined unto NIH
29:35 she said, Now **w** I praise the LORD: NIH
Ge 30:13 am I, for the daughters **w** call me blessed: NIH
30:20 now **w** my husband dwell with me, because NIH
30:28 Appoint me thy wages, and I **w** give *it*. NIH
30:31 for me, I **w** again feed *and* keep thy flock: NIH
30:32 I **w** pass through all thy flock to day, NIH
31: 3 and to thy kindred; and I **w** be with thee. NIH
31:52 that I **w** not pass over this heap to thee, and NIH
32: 9 to thy kindred, and I **w** deal well with thee: NIH
32:11 lest he **w** come and smite me, *and* NIH
32:12 I **w** surely do thee good, and make thy seed NIH
32:20 I **w** appease him with the present that goeth NIH
32:20 before me, and afterward I **w** see his face; NIH
32:20 his face; peradventure he **w** accept of me. NIH
32:26 he said, I **w** not let thee go, except thou NIH
33:12 and let us go, and I **w** go before thee. NIH
33:13 overdrive them one day, all the flock **w** die. NIH
33:14 I **w** lead on softly, according as the cattle NIH
34:11 and what ye shall say unto me I **w** give. NIH
34:12 I **w** give according as ye shall say unto me: NIH
34:15 in this **w** we consent unto you: If ye will be NIH
34:15 If ye **w** be as we *be*, that every male of you NIH
34:16 **w** we give our daughters unto you, and NIH
34:16 we **w** take your daughters to us, and we will NIH
34:16 we **w** dwell with you, and we will become NIH
34:16 we will dwell with you, and we **w** become one people. NIH
34:17 if ye **w** not hearken unto us, to be NIH
34:17 **w** we take our daughter, and we will be NIH
34:17 we take our daughter, and we **w** be gone. NIH
34:22 Only herein **w** the men consent unto us for NIH
34:23 unto them, and they **w** dwell with us. NIH
35: 3 I **w** make there an altar unto God, NIH
35:12 to thee I **w** give it, and to thy seed after thee NIH
35:12 and to thy seed after thee **w** I give the land. NIH
37:13 come, and I **w** send thee unto them. And he NIH
37:20 and cast him into some pit, and we **w** say, NIH
37:20 we shall see what **w** become of his dreams. NIH
37:35 For I **w** go down into the grave unto my son NIH
38:17 he said, I **w** send *thee* a kid from the flock. NIH
41:32 by God, and God **w** shortly bring it to pass. NIH
41:40 only *in* the throne **w** I be greater than thou. NIH
42:34 true *men*: *so* **w** I deliver you your brother, NIH
42:36 ye **w** take Benjamin *away*: all these things NIH
42:37 my hand, and I **w** bring him to thee again. NIH
43: 4 with us, we **w** go down and buy thee food: NIH
43: 5 if thou wilt not send *him*, we **w** not go NIH
43: 8 the lad with me, and we **w** arise and go; NIH
43: 9 I **w** be surety for him; of my hand shalt thou NIH
44: 9 and we also **w** be my lord's bondmen. NIH
44:26 brother be with us, then **w** we go down: NIH
44:31 that the lad *is* not *with us*, that he **w** die: NIH
45:11 there **w** I nourish thee; for yet *there are* five NIH
45:18 I **w** give you the good of the land of Egypt, NIH
45:28 *is* yet alive: I **w** go and see him before I die. NIH
46: 3 for I **w** there make of thee a great nation. NIH
46: 4 I **w** go down with thee into Egypt; and I will NIH
46: 4 I **w** also surely bring thee up *again*: and NIH
46:31 I **w** go up, and shew Pharaoh, and say unto NIH
47:16 I **w** give you for your cattle, if money fail. NIH
47:18 unto him, We **w** not hide *it* from my lord, NIH
47:19 and our land **w** be servants unto Pharaoh: NIH
47:25 of my lord, and we **w** be Pharaoh's servants. NIH
47:30 I **w** lie with my fathers, and thou shalt carry NIH
47:30 And he said, I **w** do as thou hast said. NIH
48: 4 I **w** make thee fruitful, and multiply thee, NIH
48: 4 and I **w** make of thee a multitude of people; NIH
48: 4 **w** give this land to thy seed after thee *for* an NIH
48: 9 I pray thee, unto me, and I **w** bless them. NIH
49: 7 I **w** divide them in Jacob, and scatter them NIH
50: 5 and bury my father, and I **w** come again. NIH
50:15 Joseph **w** peradventure hate us, and NIH
50:15 **w** certainly requite us all the evil which we NIH
50:21 I **w** nourish you and your little ones. And he NIH
50:24 God **w** surely visit you, and bring you out of NIH
50:25 God **w** surely visit you, and ye shall carry NIH
Ex 2: 9 nurse it for me, and I **w** give *thee* thy wages. NIH
3: 3 I **w** now turn aside, and see this great sight, NIH
3:10 and I **w** send thee unto Pharaoh, NIH
3:12 And he said, Certainly I **w** be with thee; and NIH
3:17 I **w** bring you up out of the affliction of NIH
3:19 I am sure that the king of Egypt **w** not let NIH
3:20 I **w** stretch out my hand, and smite Egypt NIH
3:20 smite Egypt with all my wonders which I **w** NIH
3:20 midst thereof: and after that he **w** let you go. NIH
3:21 I **w** give this people favour in the sight of NIH
4: 1 and said, But behold, they **w** not believe me, NIH
4: 1 for they **w** say, The LORD hath not NIH
4: 8 come to pass, if they **w** not believe thee, NIH
4: 8 that they **w** believe the voice of the latter NIH
4: 9 if they **w** not believe also these two signs, NIH
4:12 therefore go, and I **w** be with thy mouth, NIH
4:14 he seeth thee, he **w** be glad in his heart. NIH
4:15 I **w** be with thy mouth, and with his mouth, NIH
4:15 and **w** teach you what ye shall do. NIH
4:21 I **w** harden his heart, that he shall not let NIH
4:23 behold, I **w** slay thy son, *even* thy firstborn. NIH
5: 2 not the LORD, neither **w** I let Israel go. NIH
5:10 Thus saith Pharaoh, I **w** not give you straw. NIH
6: 1 Now shalt thou see what I **w** do to Pharaoh: NIH
6: 6 I **w** bring you out from under the burdens of NIH
6: 6 I **w** rid you out of their bondage, and I will NIH
6: 6 I **w** redeem you with a stretched out arm, NIH
6: 7 I **w** take you to me for a people, and I will NIH
6: 7 to me for a people, and I **w** be to you a God: NIH
6: 8 I **w** bring you in unto the land, NIH
6: 8 to Jacob; and I **w** give it you *for* an heritage: NIH
7: 3 I **w** harden Pharaoh's heart, and NIH
7:17 I **w** smite with the rod that *is* in mine hand NIH
8: 2 behold, I **w** smite all thy borders with frogs: NIH
8: 8 I **w** let the people go, that they may do NIH
8:21 I **w** send swarms *of flies* upon thee, and NIH
8:22 I **w** sever in that day the land of Goshen, NIH
8:23 I **w** put a division between my people and NIH
8:26 before their eyes, and **w** they not stone us? NIH
8:27 We **w** go three days' journey into NIH
8:28 Pharaoh said, I **w** let you go, that ye may NIH

Ex 8:29 I **w** intreat the LORD that the swarms *of* NIH
9:14 For I **w** at this time send all my plagues NIH
9:15 For now I **w** stretch out my hand, that I may NIH
9:18 to morrow about *this* time I **w** cause it to NIH
9:28 I **w** let you go, and ye shall stay no longer. NIH
9:29 I **w** spread abroad my hands unto NIH
9:30 I know that ye **w** not yet fear the LORD NIH
10:4 to morrow **w** I bring the locusts into thy NIH
10:9 We **w** go with our young and with our old, NIH
10:9 with our flocks and with our herds **w** we go; NIH
10:10 as I **w** let you go, and your little ones: NIH
10:29 spoken well, I **w** see thy face again no more. NIH
11:1 Yet **w** I bring one plague *more* upon NIH
11:1 afterwards he **w** let you go hence: NIH
11:4 About midnight **w** I go out into the midst of NIH
11:8 after that I **w** go out. And he went out from NIH
12:12 For I **w** pass through the land of Egypt this NIH
12:12 **w** smite all the firstborn in the land of NIH
12:12 against all the gods of Egypt I **w** execute NIH
12:13 I **w** pass over you, and the plague shall not NIH
12:23 For the LORD **w** pass through to smite NIH
12:23 the LORD **w** pass over the door, and NIH
12:23 **w** not suffer the destroyer to come in unto NIH
12:25 to the land which the LORD **w** give you, NIH
12:48 **w** keep the passover to the LORD, let all NIH
13:19 of Israel, saying, God **w** surely visit you; NIH
14:3 For Pharaoh **w** say of the children of Israel, NIH
14:4 I **w** harden Pharaoh's heart, that he shall NIH
14:4 I **w** be honoured upon Pharaoh, and upon all NIH
14:13 which he **w** shew to you to day: NIH
14:17 I **w** harden the hearts of the Egyptians, and NIH
14:17 I **w** get me honour upon Pharaoh, and NIH
15:1 spake, saying, I **w** sing unto the LORD, NIH
15:2 my God, and I **w** prepare him a habitation; NIH
15:2 my father's God, and I **w** exalt him. NIH
15:9 The enemy said, I **w** pursue, I will overtake, NIH
15:9 The enemy said, I will pursue, I **w** overtake, NIH
15:9 I will overtake, I **w** divide the spoil; NIH
15:9 I **w** draw my sword, my hand shall destroy NIH
15:26 I **w** put none of *these* diseases upon thee, NIH
16:4 Behold, I **w** rain bread from heaven for you; NIH
16:4 whether they **w** walk in my law, or no. NIH
16:23 bake *that* which you **w** bake *to day,* and NIH
16:23 bake *to day,* and seethe that ye **w** seethe; NIH
17:6 I **w** stand before thee there upon the rock in NIH
17:9 to morrow I **w** stand on the top of the hill NIH
17:14 for I **w** utterly put out the remembrance of NIH
17:16 ***w** have* war with Amalek from generation *to* NIH
18:19 I **w** give thee counsel, and God shall be with NIH
19:5 if ye **w** obey my voice indeed, and keep my NIH
19:8 All that the LORD hath spoken we **w** do. NIH
19:11 for the third day the LORD **w** come down NIH
20:7 for the LORD **w** not hold him guiltless that NIH
20:19 Speak thou with us, and we **w** hear: NIH
20:24 in all places where I record my name I **w** NIH
20:24 I will come unto thee, and I **w** bless thee. NIH
21:5 and my children; I **w** not go out free: NIH
21:13 I **w** appoint thee a place whither he shall NIH
21:22 according as the woman's husband **w** lay NIH
22:23 cry at all unto me, I **w** surely hear their cry; NIH
22:24 wax hot, and I **w** kill you with the sword; NIH
22:27 when he crieth unto me, that I **w** hear; NIH
23:7 slay thou not: for I **w** not justify the wicked. NIH
23:21 for he **w** not pardon your transgressions: NIH
23:22 I **w** be an enemy unto thine enemies, and NIH
23:23 and the Jebusites: and I **w** cut them off. NIH
23:25 I **w** take sickness away from the midst of NIH
23:26 thy land: the number of thy days I **w** fulfil. NIH
23:27 I **w** send my fear before thee, and NIH
23:27 **w** destroy all the people to whom thou shalt NIH
23:27 I **w** make all thine enemies turn their backs NIH
23:28 I **w** send hornets before thee, which shall NIH
23:29 I **w** not drive them out from before thee in NIH
23:30 little I **w** drive them out from before thee, NIH
23:31 I **w** set thy bounds from the Red sea even NIH
23:31 for I **w** deliver the inhabitants of the land NIH
23:33 their gods, it **w** surely be a snare unto thee. NIH
24:3 words which the LORD hath said **w** we do. NIH
24:7 All that the LORD hath said **w** we do, and NIH
24:12 and I **w** give thee tables of stone, and a law, NIH
25:22 there I **w** meet with thee, and I will NIH
25:22 I **w** commune with thee from above NIH
25:22 of all *things* which I **w** give thee in NIH
29:42 where I **w** meet you, to speak there unto NIH
29:43 there I **w** meet with the children of Israel, NIH
29:44 I **w** sanctify the tabernacle of NIH
29:44 I **w** sanctify also both Aaron and his sons, NIH
29:45 I **w** dwell amongst the children of Israel, NIH
29:45 the children of Israel, and **w** be their God. NIH
30:6 the Testimony, where I **w** meet with thee. NIH
30:36 the congregation, where I **w** meet with thee: NIH
32:10 and I **w** make of thee a great nation. NIH
32:13 I **w** multiply your seed as the stars of NIH
32:13 all this land that I have spoken of **w** I give NIH
32:30 now I **w** go up unto the LORD; NIH
32:33 against me, him **w** I blot out of my book. NIH
32:34 when I visit, I **w** visit their sin upon them. NIH
33:1 to Jacob, saying, Unto thy seed **w** I give it: NIH
33:2 I **w** send an angel before thee; and I will NIH
33:2 I **w** drive out the Canaanite, the Amorite, NIH
33:3 for I **w** not go up in the midst of thee; NIH
33:5 I **w** come up into the midst of thee in a NIH
33:14 shall go *with thee,* and I **w** give thee rest. NIH
33:17 I **w** do this thing also that thou hast spoken: NIH
33:19 I **w** make all my goodness pass before thee, NIH
33:19 I **w** proclaim the name of the LORD NIH
33:19 **w** be gracious to whom I will be gracious, NIH
33:19 will be gracious to whom I **w** be gracious, NIH
33:19 **w** shew mercy on whom I will shew mercy. NIH
33:19 will shew mercy on whom I **w** shew mercy. NIH
33:22 that I **w** put thee in a clift of the rock, and NIH
33:22 **w** cover thee with my hand while I pass by: NIH
33:23 I **w** take away mine hand, and thou shalt see NIH
34:1 I **w** write upon *these* tables the words that NIH
34:7 *that* **w** by no means clear *the guilty;* visiting NIH

Ex 34:10 before all thy people I **w** do marvels, NIH
34:10 for it *is* a terrible thing that I **w** do with thee. NIH
34:24 For I **w** cast out the nations before thee, and NIH
Lev 1:3 he shall offer it of his own **voluntary w** at 7522
2:1 when any **w** offer a meat offering unto NIH
9:4 for to day the LORD **w** appear unto you. NIH
10:3 I **w** be sanctified in them that come nigh NIH
10:3 and before all the people I **w** be glorified. NIH
16:2 for I **w** appear in the cloud upon the mercy NIH
17:10 I **w** even set my face against *that* soul that NIH
17:10 and **w** cut him off from among his people. NIH
19:5 the LORD, ye shall offer it at your own **w**. 7522
20:3 I **w** set my face against that man, and NIH
20:3 and **w** cut him off from among his people; NIH
20:5 I **w** set my face against that man, NIH
20:5 **w** cut him off, and all that go a whoring NIH
20:6 I **w** even set my face against that soul, and NIH
20:6 and **w** cut him off from among his people. NIH
20:24 and I **w** give it unto you to possess it, NIH
22:18 that **w** offer his oblation for all his vows, NIH
22:18 which they **w** offer unto the LORD for a NIH
22:19 *Ye shall offer* at your own **w** a male 7522
22:29 when ye **w** offer a sacrifice of thanksgiving NIH
22:29 unto the LORD, offer *it* at your own **w**. 7522
22:32 I **w** be hallowed among the children of NIH
23:30 the same soul **w** I destroy from among his NIH
25:21 I **w** command my blessing upon you in NIH
26:4 I **w** give you rain in due season, and NIH
26:6 I **w** give peace in the land, and ye shall lie NIH
26:6 I **w** rid evil beasts out of the land, NIH
26:9 For I **w** have respect unto you, and NIH
26:11 I **w** set my tabernacle amongst you: and NIH
26:12 I **w** walk among you, and will be your God, NIH
26:12 **w** be your God, and ye shall be my people. NIH
26:14 if ye **w** not hearken unto me, and will not do NIH
26:14 and **w** not do all these commandments; NIH
26:15 so that *ye* **w** not do all my commandments, NIH
26:16 I also **w** do this unto you; I will even NIH
26:16 I **w** even appoint over you terror, NIH
26:17 I **w** set my face against you, and ye shall be NIH
26:18 if ye **w** not yet for *all* this hearken unto me, NIH
26:18 I **w** punish you seven *times* more for your NIH
26:19 I **w** break the pride of your power; and NIH
26:19 I **w** make your heaven as iron, and your NIH
26:21 contrary unto me, and **w** not hearken unto me; 14
26:21 I **w** bring seven *times* moe plagues upon NIH
26:22 I **w** also send wild beasts among you, which NIH
26:23 if ye **w** not be reformed by me by these NIH
26:23 these *things,* but **w** walk contrary unto me; NIH
26:24 **w** I also walk contrary unto you, and NIH
26:24 **w** punish you yet seven *times* for your sins. NIH
26:25 I **w** bring a sword upon you, that shall NIH
26:25 I **w** send the pestilence among you; NIH
26:27 And if ye **w** not for *all* this hearken unto me, NIH
26:28 I **w** walk contrary unto you also in fury; NIH
26:28 **w** chastise you seven *times* for your sins. NIH
26:30 I **w** destroy your high places, and cut down NIH
26:31 I **w** make your cities waste, and bring your NIH
26:31 I **w** not smell the savour of your sweet NIH
26:32 I **w** bring the land into desolation: and NIH
26:33 And I **w** scatter you among the heathen, and NIH
26:33 and **w** draw out a sword after you: NIH
26:36 *upon* them that are left *alive* of you I **w** send NIH
26:42 **w** I remember my covenant with Jacob, NIH
26:42 also my covenant with Abraham **w** I NIH
26:42 I remember; and I **w** remember the land. NIH
26:44 I **w** not cast them away, neither will I abhor NIH
26:44 neither **w** I abhor them, to destroy them NIH
26:45 I **w** for their sakes remember the covenant NIH
27:13 if he **w** at all redeem it, then he shall add a NIH
27:15 if he that sanctified *it* **w** redeem his house, NIH
27:19 if he that sanctified the field **w** in any wise NIH
27:20 if he **w** not redeem the field, or if he have NIH
27:31 if a man **w** at all redeem *ought* of his tithes, NIH
Nu 6:27 the children of Israel; and I **w** bless them. NIH
9:8 I **w** hear what the LORD will command NIH
9:8 I will hear what the LORD **w** command NIH
9:14 and **w** keep the passover unto the LORD; NIH
10:29 of which the LORD said, I **w** give it you: NIH
10:29 come thou with us, and we **w** do thee good: NIH
10:30 he said unto him, I **w** not go; but I will NIH
10:30 I **w** depart to mine own land, and to my NIH
10:32 do unto us, the same **w** we do unto thee. NIH
11:17 I **w** come down and talk with thee there: NIH
11:17 and I **w** take of the spirit which *is* upon thee, NIH
11:17 which *is* upon thee, and **w** put *it* upon them; NIH
11:18 therefore the LORD **w** give you flesh, and NIH
11:21 thou hast said, I **w** give them flesh, that they NIH
12:6 *I* the LORD **w** make myself known unto NIH
12:6 a vision, *and* **w** speak unto him in a dream. NIH
12:8 With him **w** I speak mouth to mouth, NIH
14:8 he **w** bring us into this land, and give it us; NIH
14:11 How long **w** this people provoke me? NIH
14:11 how long **w** it be ere they believe me, for all NIH
14:12 I **w** smite them with the pestilence, and NIH
14:12 **w** make of thee a greater nation and NIH
14:14 they **w** tell *it* to the inhabitants of this land: NIH
14:15 which have heard the fame of thee **w** speak, NIH
14:24 him **w** I bring into the land whereinto he NIH
14:28 have spoken in mine ears, so **w** I do to you: NIH
14:31 them **w** I bring in, and they shall know NIH
14:35 I **w** surely do it unto all this evil NIH
14:40 **w** go up unto the place which the LORD NIH
14:43 therefore the LORD **w** not be with you. NIH
15:3 **w** make an offering by fire unto NIH
15:14 **w** offer an offering made by fire, of a sweet NIH
16:5 Even to morrow the LORD **w** shew who NIH
16:5 and **w** cause *him* to come near unto him: NIH
16:5 even *him* whom he hath chosen **w** he cause NIH
16:12 of Eliab: which said, We **w** not come up: NIH
16:14 the eyes of these men? we **w** not come up. NIH
17:4 the Testimony, where I **w** meet with you. NIH
17:5 I **w** make to cease from me the murmurings NIH
20:17 we **w** not pass through the fields, or NIH
20:17 neither **w** we drink *of* the water of the wells: NIH

Nu 20:17 we **w** go *by* the king's *high* way, we will not NIH
20:17 we **w** not turn *to* the right hand nor *to* NIH
20:19 said unto him, We **w** go by the high way: NIH
20:19 cattle drink *of* thy water, then I **w** pay for it: NIH
20:19 I **w** only, without *doing any* thing *else,* go NIH
21:2 then I **w** utterly destroy their cities. NIH
21:16 people together, and I **w** give them water. NIH
21:22 we **w** not turn into the fields, or into NIH
21:22 we **w** not drink *of* the waters of the well: NIH
21:22 *but* we **w** go along by the king's *high* way, NIH
22:8 *this* night, and I **w** bring you word again, NIH
22:17 For I **w** promote thee unto very great NIH
22:17 and I **w** do whatsoever thou sayest unto me: NIH
22:19 that I may know what the LORD **w** say NIH
22:34 if it displease thee, I **w** get me back again. NIH
23:3 Stand by thy burnt offering, and I **w** go: NIH
23:3 peradventure the LORD **w** come to meet NIH
23:3 and whatsoever he sheweth me I **w** tell thee. NIH
23:27 pray thee, I **w** bring thee unto another place; NIH
23:27 peradventure it **w** please God that thou NIH
24:13 *but* what the LORD saith, that **w** I speak? NIH
24:14 I **w** advertise thee what this people shall do NIH
32:15 he **w** yet again leave them in the wilderness; NIH
32:16 We **w** build sheepfolds here for our cattle, NIH
32:17 we ourselves **w** go ready armed before NIH
32:18 We **w** not return unto our houses, until NIH
32:19 For we **w** not inherit with them on *yonder* NIH
32:20 Moses said unto them, If ye **w** do this thing, NIH
32:20 if ye **w** go armed before the LORD to war, NIH
32:21 **w** go all of you armed over Jordan before NIH
32:23 if ye **w** not do so, behold, ye have sinned NIH
32:23 and be sure your sin **w** find you out. NIH
32:25 Thy servants **w** do as my lord commandeth. NIH
32:27 thy servants **w** pass over, every man armed NIH
32:29 the children of Reuben **w** pass with you NIH
32:30 But if they **w** not pass over with you armed, NIH
32:31 hath said unto thy servants, so **w** we do. NIH
32:32 We **w** pass over armed before the LORD NIH
33:55 if ye **w** not drive out the inhabitants of NIH
Dt 1:13 and I **w** make them rulers over you. NIH
1:17 for you, bring *it* unto me, and I **w** hear it. NIH
1:22 We **w** send men before us, and they shall NIH
1:36 to him **w** I give the land that he hath trodden NIH
1:39 unto them **w** I give it, and they shall possess NIH
1:41 against the LORD, we **w** go up and fight, NIH
2:5 for I **w** not give you of their land, no, not so NIH
2:9 for I **w** not give thee of their land *for* a NIH
2:19 for I **w** not give thee of the land of NIH
2:25 This day **w** I begin to put the dread of thee NIH
2:27 I **w** go along by the high way, I will neither NIH
2:27 I **w** neither turn *unto* the right hand nor *to* NIH
2:28 only I **w** pass through on my feet; NIH
3:2 for I **w** deliver him, and all his people, and NIH
4:10 and I **w** make them hear my words, NIH
4:31 he **w** not forsake thee, neither destroy thee, NIH
5:11 for the LORD **w** not hold *him* guiltless that NIH
5:25 for this great fire **w** consume us: if we hear NIH
5:27 unto thee; and we **w** hear *it,* and do *it.* NIH
5:31 I **w** speak unto thee all the commandments, NIH
7:4 For they **w** turn away thy son from NIH
7:4 **w** the anger of the LORD be kindled NIH
7:10 he **w** not be slack to him that hateth him, NIH
7:10 that hateth him, he **w** repay him to his face. NIH
7:13 he **w** love thee, and bless thee, and NIH
7:13 he **w** also bless the fruit of thy womb, and NIH
7:15 the LORD **w** take away from thee all NIH
7:15 **w** put none of the evil diseases of Egypt, NIH
7:15 but **w** lay them upon all *them* that hate thee. NIH
7:16 their gods; for that ***w** be* a snare unto thee. NIH
7:20 Moreover the LORD thy God **w** send NIH
7:22 the LORD thy God **w** put out those nations NIH
9:14 I **w** make of thee a nation mightier and NIH
10:2 I **w** write on the tables the words that were NIH
11:14 That I **w** give *you* the rain of your land in NIH
11:15 I **w** send grass in thy fields for thy cattle, NIH
11:23 **w** the LORD drive out all these nations NIH
11:28 if ye **w** not obey the commandments of NIH
12:20 I **w** eat flesh, because thy soul longeth to eat NIH
12:30 serve their gods? even so **w** I do likewise. NIH
15:16 he say unto thee, I **w** not go away from thee; NIH
17:12 And the man that **w** do presumptuously, and NIH
17:12 **w** not hearken unto the priest that standeth NIH
17:14 shalt say, I **w** set a king over me, NIH
18:15 The LORD thy God **w** raise up unto thee a NIH
18:18 I **w** raise them up a Prophet from among NIH
18:18 and **w** put my words in his mouth; NIH
18:19 *that* whosoever **w** not hearken unto my NIH
18:19 speak in my name, I **w** require *it* of him. NIH
20:12 if it **w** make no peace with thee, but NIH
20:12 **w** make war against thee, then thou shalt NIH
21:14 then thou shalt let her go whither she **w**; 5315
21:18 which **w** not obey the voice of his father, or NIH
21:18 chastened him, **w** not hearken unto them: NIH
21:20 and rebellious, he **w** not obey our voice; NIH
23:21 for the LORD thy God **w** surely require it NIH
25:7 he **w** not perform the duty of my husband's 14
25:9 So shall it be done unto *that* man that **w** not NIH
28:1 that the LORD thy God **w** set thee on high NIH
28:27 The LORD **w** smite thee with the botch of NIH
28:55 So that *he* **w** not give to any of them of NIH
28:59 the LORD **w** make thy plagues wonderful, NIH
28:60 Moreover he **w** bring upon thee all NIH
28:61 them **w** the LORD bring upon thee, NIH
28:63 the LORD **w** rejoice over you to destroy NIH
29:20 The LORD **w** not spare him, but then 14
30:3 the LORD thy God **w** turn thy captivity, NIH
30:3 **w** return and gather thee from all NIH
30:4 from thence **w** the LORD thy God gather NIH
30:4 and from thence **w** he fetch thee: NIH
30:5 the LORD thy God **w** bring thee into NIH
30:5 he **w** do thee good, and multiply thee above NIH
30:6 the LORD thy God **w** circumcise thine NIH
30:7 the LORD thy God **w** put all these curses NIH
30:9 the LORD thy God **w** make thee plenteous NIH
30:9 for the LORD **w** again rejoice over thee NIH

Dt 31: 3 he **w** go over before thee, *and* he will NIH
31: 3 he **w** destroy these nations from before thee, NIH
31: 6 he **w** not fail thee, nor forsake thee. NIH
31: 8 he **w** be with thee, he will not fail thee, NIH
31: 8 he will be with thee, he **w** not fail thee, NIH
31:16 this people **w** rise up, and go a whoring NIH
31:16 **w** forsake me, and break my covenant NIH
31:17 I **w** forsake them, and I will hide my face NIH
31:17 I **w** hide my face from them, and they shall NIH
31:17 so that they **w** say in that day, Are not these NIH
31:18 I **w** surely hide my face in that day for all NIH
31:20 **w** they turn unto other gods, and NIH
31:23 I sware unto them: and I **w** be with thee. NIH
31:29 For I know that after my death ye **w** utterly NIH
31:29 evil **w** befall you in the latter days; because NIH
31:29 ye **w** do evil in the sight of the LORD, NIH
32: 1 Give ear, O ye heavens, and I **w** speak; and NIH
32: 3 Because I **w** publish the name of NIH
32: 7 ask thy father, and he **w** shew thee; NIH
32: 7 shew thee; thy elders, and they **w** tell thee. NIH
32:20 he said, I **w** hide my face from them, I will NIH
32:20 I **w** see what their end *shall be:* for they *are* NIH
32:21 I **w** move them to jealousy with *those which* NIH
32:21 I **w** provoke them to anger with a foolish NIH
32:23 I **w** heap mischiefs upon them; I will spend NIH
32:23 I **w** spend mine arrows upon them. NIH
32:24 I **w** also send the teeth of beasts upon them, NIH
32:41 I **w** render vengeance to mine enemies, and NIH
32:41 and **w** reward them that hate me. NIH
32:42 I **w** make mine arrows drunk with blood, NIH
32:43 for he **w** avenge the blood of his servants, NIH
32:43 **w** render vengeance to his adversaries, and NIH
32:43 **w** be merciful *unto* his land, *and to* his NIH
33:16 *for* the **good w** of him that dwelt in 7522
34: 4 saying, I **w** give it unto thy seed: NIH
Jos 1: 5 as I was with Moses, *so* I **w** be with thee: NIH
1: 5 with thee: I **w** not fail thee, nor forsake thee. NIH
1:16 All that thou commandest us we **w** do, and NIH
1:16 whithersoever thou sendest us, we **w** go. NIH
1:17 in all *things,* so **w** we hearken unto thee: NIH
1:18 **w** not hearken unto thy words in all that NIH
2:12 that ye **w** also shew kindness unto my NIH
2:13 *that* ye **w** save alive my father, and NIH
2:14 that we **w** deal kindly and truly with thee. NIH
2:17 We *w be* blameless of this thine oath which NIH
2:19 *be* upon his head, and we *w be* guiltless: NIH
2:20 we **w** be quit of thine oath which thou hast NIH
3: 5 for to morrow the LORD **w** do wonders NIH
3: 7 This day **w** I begin to magnify thee in NIH
3: 7 as I was with Moses, *so* I **w** be with thee. NIH
3:10 *that* he **w** without fail drive out from before NIH
7:12 neither **w** I be with you any more, except ye NIH
8: 5 that *are* with me, **w** approach unto the city: NIH
8: 5 as at the first, that we **w** flee before them, NIH
8: 6 (For they **w** come out after us) till we have NIH
8: 6 for they **w** say, *They* flee before us, as at NIH
8: 6 at the first: therefore we **w** flee before them. NIH
8: 7 for the LORD your God **w** deliver it into NIH
8:18 toward Ai; for I **w** give it into thine hand. NIH
9:20 This we **w** do to them; we will even let NIH
9:20 we **w** even let them live, lest wrath be upon NIH
11: 6 for to morrow about this time **w** I deliver NIH
13: 6 them **w** I drive out from before the children NIH
14:12 if so be the LORD *w be* with me, then NIH
15:16 to him **w** I give Achsah my daughter to NIH
18: 4 I **w** send them, and they shall rise, and NIH
22:18 it **w** be, *seeing* ye rebel to day against NIH
22:18 that to morrow he **w** be wroth with NIH
23:13 **w** no more drive out *any of* these nations NIH
24:15 choose you *this* day whom you **w** serve; NIH
24:15 and my house, we **w** serve the LORD. NIH
24:18 *therefore* **w** we also serve the LORD; NIH
24:19 he **w** not forgive your transgressions nor NIH
24:20 he **w** turn and do you hurt, and NIH
24:21 Nay; but we **w** serve the LORD. NIH
24:24 The LORD our God **w** we serve, and his NIH
24:24 will we serve, and his voice **w** we obey. NIH
Jdg 1: 3 and I likewise **w** go with thee into thy lot. NIH
1:12 to him **w** I give Achsah my daughter to NIH
1:24 into the city, and we **w** shew thee mercy. NIH
2: 1 I **w** never break my covenant with you. NIH
2: 3 I **w** not drive them out from before you; NIH
2:21 I also **w** not henceforth drive out any from NIH
2:22 whether they **w** keep the way of the LORD NIH
4: 7 I **w** draw unto thee to the river Kishon NIH
4: 7 and I **w** deliver him into thine hand. NIH
4: 8 If thou wilt go with me, then I **w** go: NIH
4: 8 if thou wilt not go with me, *then* I **w** not go. NIH
4: 9 she said, I **w** surely go with thee: NIH
4:22 I **w** shew thee the man whom thou seekest. NIH
5: 3 I, *even* I, **w** sing unto the LORD; NIH
5: 3 I **w** sing *praise* to the LORD God of Israel. NIH
6:16 Surely I **w** be with thee, and thou shalt NIH
6:18 he said, I **w** tarry until thou come again. NIH
6:31 stood against him, **W** ye plead for Baal? NIH
6:31 **w** ye save him? he that will plead for him, NIH
6:31 he that **w** plead for him, let him be put to NIH
6:37 I **w** put a fleece of wool in the floor; NIH
6:39 hot against me, and I **w** speak but *this* once: NIH
7: 4 the water, and I **w** try them for thee there: NIH
7: 7 By the three hundred men that lapped **w** I NIH
8: 7 I **w** tear your flesh with the thorns of NIH
8: 9 again in peace, I **w** break down this tower. NIH
8:23 said unto them, I **w** not rule over you, NIH
8:25 We **w** willingly give *them.* And they spread NIH
10:13 wherefore I **w** deliver you no more. NIH
10:18 What man *is he* that **w** begin to fight against NIH
11:24 out from before us, them **w** we possess. NIH
11:31 and I **w** offer it up *for* a burnt offering. NIH
12: 1 we **w** burn thine house upon thee with fire. NIH
13:16 thou detain me, I **w** not eat of thy bread: NIH
14:12 I **w** now put forth a riddle unto you: NIH
14:12 I **w** give you thirty sheets and thirty change NIH
15: 1 I **w** go in to my wife into the chamber. NIH
15: 7 yet **w** I be avenged of you, and after *that* I NIH
Jdg 15: 7 be avenged of you, and after *that* I **w** cease. NIH
15:12 that ye **w** not fall upon me yourselves. NIH
15:13 we **w** bind thee fast, and deliver thee into NIH
15:13 surely we **w** not kill thee. And they bound NIH
16: 5 we **w** give thee every one *of us* eleven NIH
16:17 my strength **w** go from me, and I shall NIH
16:20 I **w** go out as at other times *before,* and NIH
17: 3 now therefore I **w** restore it unto thee. NIH
17:10 I **w** give thee ten *shekels* of silver by NIH
17:13 Now know I that the LORD **w** do me NIH
19:12 We **w** not turn aside hither into the city of a NIH
19:12 of Israel; we **w** pass over to Gibeah. NIH
19:24 them I **w** bring out now, and humble ye NIH
20: 8 We **w** not any *of us* go to his tent, NIH
20: 8 neither **w** we any *of us* turn into his house. NIH
20: 9 now this *shall be* the thing which we **w** do NIH
20: 9 do to Gibeah; *we w go up* by lot against it; NIH
20:10 we **w** take ten men of an hundred NIH
20:28 for to morrow I **w** deliver them into thine NIH
21: 7 we **w** not give them of our daughters to wives? NIH
21:22 that we **w** say unto them, Be favourable NIH
Ru 1:10 Surely we **w** return with thee unto thy NIH
1:11 why **w** you go with me? *are there* yet *any* NIH
1:16 for whither thou goest, I **w** go; and NIH
1:16 I will go; and where thou lodgest, I **w** lodge: NIH
1:17 **w** I die, and there will I be buried: NIH
1:17 will I die, and there **w** I be buried: NIH
3: 4 and he **w** tell thee what thou shalt do. NIH
3: 5 All that thou sayest unto me I **w** do. NIH
3:11 I **w** do to thee all that thou requirest: NIH
3:13 *that* if he **w** perform unto thee the part of a NIH
3:13 if he **w** not do the part of a kinsman to thee, 2654
3:13 **w** I do the part of a kinsman to thee, *as* NIH
3:18 until thou know how the matter **w** fall: NIH
3:18 for the man **w** not be in rest, until he have NIH
4: 4 I *am* after thee. And he said, I **w** redeem *it.* NIH
1Sa 1:11 I **w** give him unto the LORD all the days NIH
1:22 *I w not go up* until the child be weaned, and NIH
1:22 *then* I **w** bring him, that he may appear NIH
2: 9 He **w** keep the feet of his saints, and NIH
2:15 for he **w** not have sodden flesh of thee, but NIH
2:16 *it me* now: and if not, I **w** take *it* by force. NIH
2:30 for them that honour me I **w** honour, and NIH
2:31 that I **w** cut off thine arm, and the arm of NIH
2:35 I **w** raise me up a faithful priest, *that* shall NIH
2:35 I **w** build him a sure house; and he shall NIH
3:11 to Samuel, Behold, I **w** do a thing in Israel, NIH
3:12 In that day I **w** perform against Eli all *things* NIH
3:12 when I begin, I **w** also make an end. NIH
3:13 For I have told him that I **w** judge his house NIH
6: 5 peradventure he **w** lighten his hand from off NIH
7: 3 he **w** deliver you out of the hand of NIH
7: 5 and I **w** pray for you unto the LORD. NIH
7: 8 that he **w** save us out of the hand of NIH
8:11 This **w** be the manner of the king that shall NIH
8:11 He **w** take your sons, and appoint *them* for NIH
8:12 he **w** appoint him captains over thousands, NIH
8:12 *w set them* to ear his ground, and to reap his NIH
8:13 he **w** take your daughters to be NIH
8:14 he **w** take your fields, and your vineyards, NIH
8:15 he **w** take the tenth of your seed, and NIH
8:16 he **w** take your menservants, and your NIH
8:17 He **w** take the tenth of your sheep: and NIH
8:18 and the LORD **w** not hear you in that day. NIH
8:19 Nay, but we **w** have a king over us; NIH
9: 8 *that* **w** I give to the man of God, to tell us NIH
9:13 for the people **w** not eat until he come, NIH
9:16 To morrow about *this* time I **w** send thee a NIH
9:19 to morrow I **w** let thee go, and will tell thee NIH
9:19 and **w** tell thee all that *is* in thine heart. NIH
10: 2 they **w** say unto thee, The asses which thou NIH
10: 4 they **w** salute thee, and give thee two *loaves* NIH
10: 6 the spirit of the LORD **w** come upon thee, NIH
10: 8 behold, I **w** come down unto thee, to offer NIH
11: 1 a covenant with us, and we **w** serve thee. NIH
11: 2 On this *condition* **w** I make *a covenant* with NIH
11: 3 no man to save us, we **w** come out to thee. NIH
11:10 To morrow we **w** come out unto you, and NIH
12: 3 mine eyes therewith? and I **w** restore *it* you. NIH
12:10 hand of our enemies, and we **w** serve thee. NIH
12:14 If ye **w** fear the LORD, and serve him, and NIH
12:15 if ye **w** not obey the voice of the LORD, NIH
12:16 which the LORD **w** do before your eyes. NIH
12:17 I **w** call unto the LORD, and he shall send NIH
12:22 For the LORD **w** not forsake his people for NIH
12:23 I **w** teach you the good and the right way: NIH
13:12 The Philistines **w** come down now upon me NIH
14: 6 it may be that the LORD **w** work for us: NIH
14: 8 we **w** pass over unto *these* men, and we will NIH
14: 8 and we **w** discover ourselves unto them. NIH
14: 9 we **w** stand still in our place, and will not go NIH
14: 9 in our place, and **w** not go up unto them. NIH
14:10 Come up unto us; then we **w** go up: NIH
14:12 Come up to us, and we **w** shew you a thing. NIH
14:40 and Jonathan my son **w** be on the other side. NIH
15:16 I **w** tell thee what the LORD hath said to NIH
15:26 said unto Saul, I **w** not return with thee: NIH
15:29 also the Strength of Israel **w** not lie nor NIH
16: 1 go, I **w** send thee to Jesse the Beth-lehemite: NIH
16: 2 if Saul hear *it,* he **w** kill me. And NIH
16: 3 and I **w** shew thee what thou shalt do: NIH
16:11 for we **w** not sit down till he come hither. NIH
17: 9 and *to* kill me, then **w** we be your servants: NIH
17:25 the king **w** enrich him *with* great riches, and NIH
17:25 **w** give him his daughter, and make his NIH
17:32 thy servant **w** go and fight with this NIH
17:37 he **w** deliver me out of the hand of this NIH
17:44 I **w** give thy flesh unto the fowls of the air, NIH
17:46 This day **w** the LORD deliver thee into NIH
17:46 I **w** smite thee, and take thine head from NIH
17:46 I **w** give the carcases of the host of NIH
17:47 and he **w** give you into our hands. NIH
18:11 I **w** smite David even to the wall *with it.* NIH
18:17 daughter Merab, her **w** I give thee to wife: NIH
18:21 Saul said, I **w** give him her, that she may be NIH
1Sa 19: 3 I **w** go out and stand beside my father in NIH
19: 3 and I **w** commune with my father of thee; NIH
19: 3 of thee; and what I see, that I **w** tell thee. NIH
20: 2 my father **w** do nothing *either* great or NIH
20: 2 or small, but that he **w** shew it me: NIH
20: 4 thy soul desireth, I **w** even do *it* for thee. NIH
20:13 I **w** shew it thee, and send thee away, NIH
20:18 be missed, because thy seat **w** be empty. NIH
20:20 I **w** shoot three arrows on the side *thereof,* NIH
20:21 behold, I **w** send a lad, *saying,* Go, find out NIH
22: 3 with you, till I know what God **w** do for me. NIH
22: 7 **w** the son of Jesse give every one of you NIH
23: 4 for I **w** deliver the Philistines into thine NIH
23:11 **W** the men of Keilah deliver me up into his NIH
23:11 **W** Saul come down, as thy servant hath NIH
23:11 And the LORD said, He **w** come down. NIH
23:12 **W** the men of Keilah deliver me and my NIH
23:12 the LORD said, They **w** deliver *thee* up. NIH
23:23 me with the certainty, and I **w** go with you: NIH
23:23 that I **w** search him out throughout all NIH
24: 4 I **w** deliver thine enemy into thine hand, NIH
24:10 I **w** not put forth mine hand against my lord; NIH
24:19 find his enemy, **w** he let him go well away? NIH
25: 8 Ask thy young men, and they **w** shew thee. NIH
25:28 for the LORD **w** certainly make my lord a NIH
26: 6 Who **w** go down with me to Saul to NIH
26: 6 And Abishai said, I **w** go down with thee. NIH
26: 8 I **w** not *smite* him the second time. NIH
26:21 for I **w** no more do thee harm, because my NIH
27:11 *w be* his manner all the while he dwelleth in NIH
28: 2 Therefore **w** I make thee keeper of mine NIH
28:19 Moreover the LORD **w** also deliver Israel NIH
28:23 he refused, and said, I **w** not eat. But his NIH
30:15 and I **w** bring thee down to this company. NIH
30:22 we **w** not give them *ought* of the spoil that NIH
30:24 For who **w** hearken unto you in this matter? NIH
2Sa 2: 6 I also **w** requite you this kindness, because NIH
2:26 knowest thou not that it **w** be bitterness in NIH
3:13 he said, Well; I **w** make a league with thee: NIH
3:18 By the hand of my servant David I **w** save NIH
3:21 I **w** arise and go, and will gather all Israel NIH
3:21 **w** gather all Israel unto my lord the king, NIH
5:19 for I **w** doubtless deliver the Philistines into NIH
6:21 therefore **w** I play before the LORD. NIH
6:22 I **w** yet be more vile than thus, and will be NIH
6:22 than thus, and **w** be base in mine own sight: NIH
7:10 Moreover I **w** appoint a place for my people NIH
7:10 **w** plant them, that they may dwell in a place NIH
7:11 Also the LORD telleth thee that he **w** NIH
7:12 thy fathers, I **w** set up thy seed after thee, NIH
7:12 thy bowels, and I **w** establish his kingdom. NIH
7:13 I **w** stablish the throne of his kingdom for NIH
7:14 I **w** be his father, and he shall be my son. If NIH
7:14 I **w** chasten him with the rod of men, and NIH
7:27 thy servant, saying, I **w** build thee a house: NIH
9: 7 for I **w** surely shew thee kindness for NIH
9: 7 **w** restore thee all the land of Saul thy father; NIH
10: 2 I **w** shew kindness unto Hanun the son of NIH
10:11 for thee, then I **w** come and help thee. NIH
11:11 and *as* thy soul liveth, I **w** not do this thing. NIH
11:12 day also, and to morrow I **w** let thee depart. NIH
12:11 I **w** raise up evil against thee out of thine NIH
12:11 I **w** take thy wives before thine eyes, and NIH
12:12 I **w** do this thing before all Israel, and NIH
12:18 how **w** he then vex himself, if we tell him NIH
12:22 Who can tell *whether* GOD **w** be gracious NIH
13:13 for he **w** not withhold me from thee. NIH
14: 7 he slew; and we **w** destroy the heir also: NIH
14: 8 and I **w** give charge concerning thee. NIH
14:15 I **w** now speak unto the king; NIH
14:15 it may be that the king **w** perform NIH
14:16 For the king **w** hear, to deliver his handmaid NIH
14:17 the LORD thy God **w** be with thee. NIH
15: 8 *to* Jerusalem, then I **w** serve the LORD. NIH
15:21 *or* life, even there *also* **w** thy servant be. NIH
15:25 he **w** bring me again, and shew me *both* it, NIH
15:28 See, I **w** tarry in the plain of the wilderness, NIH
15:34 unto Absalom, I **w** be thy servant, O king; NIH
15:34 so *w* I now also *be* thy servant: NIH
16:12 It may be that the LORD **w** look on mine NIH
16:12 that the LORD **w** requite me good for his NIH
16:18 his **w** I be, and with him will I abide. NIH
16:18 his will I be, and with him **w** I abide. NIH
16:19 father's presence, so **w** I be in thy presence. NIH
17: 1 I **w** arise and pursue after David *this* night: NIH
17: 2 I **w** come upon him while he *is* weary and NIH
17: 2 and weak handed, and **w** make him afraid: NIH
17: 2 him shall flee; and I **w** smite the king only: NIH
17: 3 And I **w** bring back all the people unto thee: NIH
17: 8 of war, and **w** not lodge with the people. NIH
17: 9 it **w** come to pass, when *some* of them be NIH
17: 9 at the first, that whosoever heareth *it* **w** say, NIH
17:12 we *w light* upon him as the dew falleth on NIH
17:13 to that city, and we **w** draw it into the river, NIH
18: 2 I **w** surely go forth with you myself also. NIH
18: 3 for if we flee away, they **w** not care for us; NIH
18: 3 neither if half of us die, **w** they care for us: NIH
18: 4 unto them, What seemeth you best I **w** do. NIH
19: 7 there **w** not tarry one with thee *this* night: NIH
19: 7 that *w be* worse unto thee than all the evil NIH
19:26 for thy servant said, I **w** saddle me an ass, NIH
19:33 and I **w** feed thee with me in Jerusalem. NIH
19:36 Thy servant **w** go a little *way* over Jordan NIH
19:38 I **w** do to him *that* which shall seem good NIH
19:38 shalt require of me, *that* **w** I do for thee. NIH
20:21 him only, and I **w** depart from the city. NIH
21: 4 We **w** have no silver nor gold of Saul, NIH
21: 4 What you shall say, *that* **w** I do for you. NIH
21: 6 we **w** hang them up unto the LORD in NIH
21: 6 And the king said, I **w** give *them.* NIH
22: 3 The God of my rock; in him **w** I trust: *he is* NIH
22: 4 I **w** call on the LORD, who is *worthy* to be NIH
22:29 and the LORD **w** lighten my darkness. NIH
22:50 Therefore I **w** give thanks unto thee, NIH
22:50 and I **w** sing praises unto thy name. NIH

W

2Sa 24:24 Nay; but I **w** surely buy *it* of thee at a price: NIH
24:24 neither **w** I offer burnt offerings unto NIH
1Ki 1: 5 exalted himself, saying, I **w** be king: NIH
1:14 I also **w** come in after thee, and confirm thy NIH
1:30 my stead; even so **w** I certainly do this day. NIH
1:51 he **w** not slay his servant with the sword. NIH
1:52 If he **w** shew himself a worthy man, NIH
2: 8 I **w** not put thee to death with the sword. NIH
2:17 the king, (for he **w** not say thee nay,) NIH
2:18 Well; I **w** speak for thee unto the king. NIH
2:20 my mother: for I **w** not say thee nay. NIH
2:26 I **w** not at this time put thee to death, NIH
2:30 he said, Nay; but I **w** die here. And Benaiah NIH
2:38 lord the king hath said, so **w** thy servant do. NIH
3:14 David did walk, then I **w** lengthen thy days. NIH
5: 5 whom I **w** set upon thy throne in thy room, NIH
5: 6 unto thee **w** I give hire for thy servants NIH
5: 8 I **w** do all thy desire concerning timber of NIH
5: 9 I **w** convey them by sea *in* flotes unto NIH
5: 9 **w** cause them to be discharged there, and NIH
6:12 **w** I perform my word with thee, which I NIH
6:13 And I **w** dwell among the children of Israel, NIH
6:13 and **w** not forsake my people Israel. NIH
8:27 **w** God indeed dwell on the earth? behold, NIH
9: 5 I **w** establish the throne of thy kingdom NIH
9: 6 **w** not keep my commandments *and* NIH
9: 7 **w** I cut off Israel out of the land which I NIH
9: 7 for my name, **w** I cast out of my sight; NIH
11: 2 *for* surely they **w** turn away your heart after NIH
11:11 I **w** surely rend the kingdom from thee, and NIH
11:11 from thee, and **w** give it to thy servant. NIH
11:12 Notwithstanding in thy days I **w** not do it NIH
11:12 *but* I **w** rend it out of the hand of thy son. NIH
11:13 Howbeit I **w** not rend away all the kingdom; NIH
11:13 **w** give one tribe to thy son for David my NIH
11:31 I **w** rent the kingdom out of the hand of NIH
11:31 of Solomon, and **w** give ten tribes to thee: NIH
11:34 Howbeit I **w** not take the whole kingdom NIH
11:34 I **w** make him prince all the days of his life NIH
11:35 I **w** take the kingdom out of his son's hand, NIH
11:35 and **w** give it unto thee, *even* ten tribes. NIH
11:36 unto his son **w** I give one tribe, that David NIH
11:37 I **w** take thee, and thou shalt reign according NIH
11:38 that I **w** be with thee, and build thee a sure NIH
11:38 built for David, and **w** give Israel unto thee. NIH
11:39 I **w** for this afflict the seed of David, but NIH
12: 4 put upon us, lighter, and we **w** serve thee. NIH
12: 7 then they **w** be thy servants for ever. NIH
12:11 with a heavy yoke, I **w** add to your yoke: NIH
12:11 but I **w** chastise you with scorpions. NIH
12:14 your yoke heavy, and I **w** add to your yoke: NIH
12:14 but I **w** chastise you with scorpions. NIH
13: 7 refresh *thyself,* and I **w** give thee a reward. NIH
13: 8 me half thine house, I **w** not go in with thee, NIH
13: 8 neither **w** I eat bread nor drink water in this NIH
13:16 neither **w** I eat bread nor drink water with NIH
14:10 I **w** bring evil upon the house of Jeroboam, NIH
14:10 **w** cut off from Jeroboam *him that* pisseth NIH
14:10 **w** take away the remnant of the house of NIH
16: 3 I **w** take away the posterity of Baasha, and NIH
16: 3 **w** make thy house like the house of NIH
18: 1 and I **w** send rain upon the earth. NIH
18:15 I **w** surely shew myself unto him to day. NIH
18:23 fire *under:* and I **w** dress the other bullock, NIH
18:24 and I **w** call on the name of the LORD: NIH
19:20 and my mother, and *then* I **w** follow thee. NIH
20: 6 Yet I **w** send my servants unto thee to NIH
20: 9 send for to thy servant at the first I **w** do: NIH
20:13 I **w** deliver it into thine hand *this* day; NIH
20:22 the king of Syria **w** come up against thee. NIH
20:25 we **w** fight against them in the plain, *and* NIH
20:28 **w** I deliver all this great multitude into thine NIH
20:31 of Israel: peradventure he **w** save thy life. NIH
20:34 my father took from thy father, I **w** restore; NIH
20:34 *said Ahab,* I **w** send thee away with *this* NIH
21: 2 I **w** give thee for it a better vineyard than it; NIH
21: 2 I **w** give thee the worth of it *in* money. NIH
21: 4 I **w** not give thee the inheritance of my NIH
21: 6 I **w** give thee *another* vineyard for it: NIH
21: 6 he answered, I **w** not give thee my vineyard. NIH
21: 7 I **w** give thee the vineyard of Naboth NIH
21:21 I **w** bring evil upon thee, and will take away NIH
21:21 **w** take away thy posterity, and will cut off NIH
21:21 **w** cut off from Ahab *him that* pisseth NIH
21:22 **w** make thine house like the house of NIH
21:29 before me, I **w** not bring the evil in his days: NIH
21:29 in his son's days **w** I bring the evil upon his NIH
22:14 the LORD saith unto me, that **w** I speak. NIH
22:21 the LORD, and said, I **w** persuade him. NIH
22:22 I **w** go forth, and I will be a lying spirit in NIH
22:22 I **w** be a lying spirit in the mouth of all his NIH
22:30 I **w** disguise myself, and enter into NIH
2Ki 2: 2 and *as* thy soul liveth, I **w** not leave thee. NIH
2: 3 Knowest thou that the LORD **w** take away NIH
2: 4 and *as* thy soul liveth, I **w** not leave thee. NIH
2: 5 Knowest thou that the LORD **w** take away NIH
2: 6 and *as* thy soul liveth, I **w** not leave thee. NIH
3: 7 he said, I **w** go up: I *am* as thou *art,* my NIH
3:18 he **w** deliver the Moabites also into your NIH
4:30 and *as* thy soul liveth, I **w** not leave thee. NIH
5: 5 and I **w** send a letter unto the king of Israel. NIH
5:11 He **w** surely come out to me, and stand, and NIH
5:16 before whom I stand, I **w** receive none. NIH
5:17 for thy servant **w** henceforth offer neither NIH
5:20 I **w** run after him, and take somewhat of NIH
6: 3 with thy servants. And he answered, I **w** go. NIH
6:11 **W** ye not shew me which of us *is* for NIH
6:19 and I **w** bring you to the man whom ye seek. NIH
6:28 to day, and we **w** eat my son to morrow. NIH
7: 4 We **w** enter *into* the city, then the famine *is* NIH
7: 9 *some* mischief **w** come upon us: NIH
7:12 I **w** now shew you what the Syrians have NIH
9: 8 I **w** cut off from Ahab *him that* pisseth NIH
9: 9 I **w** make the house of Ahab like the house NIH
9:26 I **w** requite thee in this plat, saith NIH
2Ki 10: 5 and **w** do all that thou shalt bid us; NIH
10: 5 thou shalt bid us; we **w** not make any king: NIH
10: 6 *be* mine, and *if* ye **w** hearken unto my voice, NIH
18:14 *that* which thou puttest on me **w** I bear. NIH
18:21 it **w** go into his hand, and pierce it: NIH
18:23 and I **w** deliver thee two thousand horses, NIH
18:30 The LORD **w** surely deliver us, and NIH
18:32 saying, The LORD **w** deliver us. NIH
19: 4 It may be the LORD thy God **w** hear all NIH
19: 4 **w** reprove the words which the LORD thy NIH
19: 7 I **w** send a blast upon him, and he shall hear NIH
19: 7 I **w** cause him to fall by the sword in his NIH
19:23 **w** cut down the tall cedar trees thereof, *and* NIH
19:23 I **w** enter *into* the lodgings of his borders, NIH
19:28 therefore I **w** put my hook in thy nose, and NIH
19:28 I **w** turn thee back by the way by which NIH
19:34 For I **w** defend this city, to save it, for mine NIH
20: 5 behold, I **w** heal thee: on the third day thou NIH
20: 6 And I **w** add unto thy days fifteen years; and NIH
20: 6 I **w** deliver thee and this city out of the hand NIH
20: 6 I **w** defend this city for mine own sake, and NIH
20: 8 What *shall be* the sign that the LORD **w** NIH
20: 9 that the LORD **w** do the thing that he hath NIH
21: 4 In Jerusalem **w** I put my name. NIH
21: 7 tribes of Israel, **w** I put my name for ever: NIH
21: 8 Neither **w** I make the feet of Israel move NIH
21: 8 only if they **w** observe to do according to all NIH
21:13 I **w** stretch over Jerusalem the line of NIH
21:13 I **w** wipe Jerusalem as *a man* wipeth a dish, NIH
21:14 I **w** forsake the remnant of mine inheritance, NIH
22:16 I **w** bring evil upon this place, and upon NIH
22:20 I **w** gather thee unto thy fathers, and NIH
22:20 eyes shall not see all the evil which I **w** NIH
23:27 I **w** remove Judah also out of my sight, NIH
23:27 **w** cast off this city Jerusalem which I have NIH
1Ch 12:19 He **w** fall to his master Saul to *the jeopardy* NIH
14:10 Go up; for I **w** deliver them into thine hand. NIH
16:18 Unto thee **w** I give the land of Canaan, NIH
17: 9 Also I **w** ordain a place for my people NIH
17: 9 **w** plant them, and they shall dwell in their NIH
17:10 Moreover I **w** subdue all thine enemies. NIH
17:10 Furthermore I tell thee that the LORD **w** NIH
17:11 that I **w** raise up thy seed after thee, NIH
17:11 of thy sons; and I **w** stablish his kingdom. NIH
17:12 a house, and I **w** stablish his throne for ever. NIH
17:13 I **w** be his father, and he shall be my son: NIH
17:13 I **w** not take my mercy away from him, as I NIH
17:14 I **w** settle him in mine house and in my NIH
19: 2 I **w** shew kindness unto Hanun the son of NIH
19:12 be too strong for thee, then I **w** help thee. NIH
21: 3 doth my lord require this *thing?* why **w** he NIH
21:24 Nay; but I **w** verily buy *it* for the full price: NIH
21:24 for I **w** not take *that* which *is* thine for NIH
22: 5 I **w** *therefore* now make preparation for it. NIH
22: 9 I **w** give him rest from all his enemies round NIH
22: 9 I **w** give peace and quietness unto Israel in NIH
22:10 he shall be my son, and I *w be* his father; NIH
22:10 I **w** establish the throne of his kingdom over NIH
28: 6 him to be my son, and I **w** be his father. NIH
28: 7 Moreover I **w** establish his kingdom for NIH
28: 9 if thou seek him, he **w** be found of thee; but NIH
28: 9 forsake him, he **w** cast thee off for ever. NIH
28:20 LORD God, *even* my God, *w be* with thee; NIH
28:20 he **w** not fail thee, nor forsake thee, NIH
28:21 all the people *w be* wholly at thy NIH
2Ch 1:12 I **w** give thee riches, and wealth, and NIH
2:10 behold, I **w** give to thy servants, the hewers NIH
2:16 we **w** cut wood out of Lebanon, as much as NIH
2:16 we **w** bring it to thee *in* flotes by sea *to* NIH
6:18 **w** God in very deed dwell with men on NIH
7:14 **w** I hear from heaven, and will forgive their NIH
7:14 **w** forgive their sin, and will heal their land. NIH
7:14 will forgive their sin, and **w** heal their land. NIH
7:18 **w** I stablish the throne of thy kingdom, NIH
7:20 **w** I pluck them up by the roots out of my NIH
7:20 **w** I cast out of my sight, and will make it to NIH
7:20 **w** make it to be a proverb and a byword NIH
10: 4 that he put upon us, and we **w** serve thee. NIH
10: 7 to them, they **w** be thy servants for ever. NIH
10:11 yoke upon you, I **w** put more to your yoke: NIH
10:11 but I *w chastise you* with scorpions. NIH
10:14 made your yoke heavy, but I **w** add thereto: NIH
10:14 but I **w** *chastise you* with scorpions. NIH
12: 7 *therefore* I **w** not destroy them, but I will NIH
12: 7 but I **w** grant them some deliverance; NIH
15: 2 if ye seek him, he **w** be found of you; but NIH
15: 2 but if ye forsake him, he **w** forsake you. NIH
18: 3 and *we w be* with thee in the war. NIH
18: 5 for God **w** deliver *it* into the king's hand. NIH
18:13 even what my God saith, that **w** I speak. NIH
18:20 before the LORD, and said, I **w** entice him. NIH
18:21 I **w** go out, and be a lying spirit in NIH
18:29 I **w** disguise myself, and will go to NIH
18:29 will disguise myself, and **w** go to the battle; NIH
20:17 for the LORD *w be* with you. NIH
21:14 *with* a great plague **w** the LORD smite thy NIH
28:23 *therefore* **w** I sacrifice to them, that they NIH
30: 6 and he **w** return to the remnant of you, NIH
30: 9 and **w** not turn away *his* face from you, NIH
33: 7 tribes of Israel, **w** I put my name for ever: NIH
33: 8 Neither **w** I any more remove the foot of NIH
33: 8 that they **w** take heed to do all that I have NIH
34:24 I **w** bring evil upon this place, and upon NIH
34:28 I **w** gather thee to thy fathers, and thou shalt NIH
34:28 all the evil that I **w** bring upon this place, NIH
Ezr 4: 3 we ourselves together **w** build unto NIH
4:13 walls set up *again, then* they **w** not pay toll, NIH
7:18 and gold, *that* do after the **w** of your God. 7470
7:26 whosoever **w** not do the law of thy God, NIH
10: 4 we also *w be* with thee: be of good courage, NIH
Ne 1: 8 I **w** scatter you abroad among the nations: NIH
1: 9 *yet* **w** I gather them from thence, and NIH
1: 9 **w** bring them unto the place that I have NIH
2:19 that ye do? **w** ye rebel against the king? NIH
2:20 The God of heaven, he **w** prosper us; NIH
Ne 2:20 therefore we his servants **w** arise and build: NIH
4: 2 **w** they fortify themselves? will they NIH
4: 2 **w** they sacrifice? will they make an end in a NIH
4: 2 **w** they make an end in a day? will they NIH
4: 2 **w** they revive the stones out of the heaps of NIH
4:12 ye shall return unto us *they w be upon you.* NIH
5: 8 and **w** you even sell your brethren? NIH
5:12 We **w** restore *them,* and will require nothing NIH
5:12 and **w** require nothing of them; NIH
5:12 nothing of them; so **w** we do as thou sayest. NIH
6:10 for they **w** come to slay thee; yea, in NIH
6:10 yea, in the night **w** they come to slay thee. NIH
6:11 the temple to save his life? I **w** not go in. NIH
10:39 and we **w** not forsake the house of our God. NIH
13:21 if ye do *so* again, I **w** lay hands on you. NIH
Est 3: 9 I **w** pay ten thousand talents of silver to NIH
4:16 I also and my maidens **w** fast likewise; and NIH
4:16 so **w** I go in unto the king, which *is* not NIH
5: 8 and I **w** do to morrow as the king hath said. NIH
7: 8 **W** he force the queen also before me in NIH
Job 1:11 and he **w** curse thee to thy face. 518+3808
2: 4 all that a man hath **w** he give for his life. NIH
2: 5 and he **w** curse thee to thy face. 518+3808
5: 1 if there be *any* that **w** answer thee; NIH
6:24 Teach me, and I **w** hold my tongue: and NIH
7:11 Therefore I **w** not refrain my mouth; I will NIH
7:11 I **w** speak in the anguish of my spirit; NIH
7:11 I **w** complain in the bitterness of my soul. NIH
8:20 God **w** not cast away a perfect *man,* neither NIH
8:20 *man,* neither **w** he help the evil doers: NIH
9: 3 If he **w** contend with him, he cannot answer 2654
9:12 who **w** say unto him, What doest thou? NIH
9:13 *If* God **w** not withdraw his anger, the proud NIH
9:18 He **w** not suffer me to take my breath, but NIH
9:23 he **w** laugh at the trial of the innocent. NIH
9:27 If I say, I **w** forget my complaint, I will NIH
9:27 I **w** leave off my heaviness, and NIH
10: 1 I **w** leave my complaint upon myself; NIH
10: 1 I **w** speak in the bitterness of my soul. NIH
10: 2 I **w** say unto God, Do not condemn me; NIH
10:15 *if* I be righteous, *yet* **w** I not lift up my head. NIH
11:11 wickedness also; **w** he not then consider *it?* NIH
13: 7 **W** you speak wickedly for God? and NIH
13: 8 **W** ye accept his person? will ye contend for NIH
13: 8 accept his person? **w** ye contend for God? NIH
13:10 He **w** surely reprove you, if ye do secretly NIH
13:13 I may speak, and let come on me what **w**. NIH
13:15 Though he slay me, *yet* **w** I trust in him: but NIH
13:15 I **w** maintain mine own ways before him. NIH
13:19 Who *is* he *that* **w** plead with me? for now, NIH
13:20 then **w** I not hide myself from thee. NIH
13:22 call thou, and I **w** answer: or let me speak, NIH
14: 7 that it **w** sprout again, and that the tender NIH
14: 7 that the tender branch thereof **w** not cease. NIH
14: 9 *Yet* through the sent of water it **w** bud, and NIH
14:14 all the days of my appointed time **w** I wait, NIH
14:15 Thou shalt call, and I **w** answer thee: NIH
15:17 I **w** shew thee, hear me; and that which I NIH
15:17 and that which I have seen I **w** declare; NIH
17: 3 who *is* he *that* **w** strike hands with me? NIH
18: 2 How long *w it be ere* you make an end of NIH
18: 2 mark, and afterwards we **w** speak. NIH
19: 2 How long **w** ye vex my soul, and break me NIH
19: 5 If indeed ye **w** magnify *yourselves* against NIH
22: 4 **W** he reprove thee for fear of thee? will he NIH
22: 4 **w** he enter with thee into judgment? NIH
23: 6 **W** he plead against me with *his* great NIH
24:25 who **w** make me a liar, and make my speech NIH
27: 5 till I die I **w** not remove my integrity from NIH
27: 6 righteousness I hold fast, and **w** not let it go: NIH
27: 9 **W** God hear his cry when trouble cometh NIH
27:10 **W** he delight himself in the Almighty? NIH
27:10 the Almighty? **w** he always call upon God? NIH
27:11 I **w** teach you by the hand of God: NIH
27:11 *that* which *is* with the Almighty **w** I not NIH
30:24 Howbeit *he* **w** not stretch out *his* hand to NIH
32:10 Hearken to me; I also **w** shew mine opinion. NIH
32:14 neither **w** I answer him with your speeches. NIH
32:17 *I said,* I **w** answer also my part, I also will NIH
32:17 also my part, I also **w** shew mine opinion. NIH
32:20 I **w** speak, that I may be refreshed: I will NIH
32:20 be refreshed: I **w** open my lips and answer. NIH
33:12 I **w** answer thee, that God is greater than NIH
33:26 unto God, and he **w** be favourable unto him: NIH
33:26 for he **w** render unto man his righteousness. NIH
33:28 He **w** deliver his soul from going into NIH
33:31 unto me: hold thy peace, and I **w** speak. NIH
34:12 Yea, surely God **w** not do wickedly, NIH
34:12 neither **w** the Almighty pervert judgment. NIH
34:23 For he **w** not lay upon man more *than right;* NIH
34:31 I have borne *chastisement,* I **w** not offend NIH
34:32 if I have done iniquity, I **w** do no more. NIH
34:33 he **w** recompense it, whether thou refuse, or NIH
35: 3 What advantage **w** it be unto thee? NIH
35: 4 I **w** answer thee, and thy companions with NIH
35:13 Surely God **w** not hear vanity, neither will NIH
35:13 neither **w** the Almighty regard it. NIH
36: 2 I **w** shew thee that *I have* yet to speak on NIH
36: 3 I **w** fetch my knowledge from afar, and NIH
36: 3 and **w** ascribe righteousness to my Maker. NIH
36:19 **W** he esteem thy riches? *no,* not gold, NIH
37: 4 he **w** not stay them when his voice is heard. NIH
37:23 and *in* plenty of justice: he **w** not afflict. NIH
38: 3 for I **w** demand of thee, and answer thou NIH
39: 9 **W** the unicorn be willing to serve thee, or NIH
39:10 or **w** he harrow the valleys after thee? NIH
39:12 that he **w** bring home thy seed, and gather *it* NIH
40: 4 I **w** lay my hand upon my mouth. NIH
40: 5 Once have I spoken; but I **w** not answer: NIH
40: 5 yea, twice; but I **w** proceed no further. NIH
40: 7 I **w** demand of thee, and declare thou unto NIH
40:14 **w** I also confess unto thee that thine own NIH
41: 3 **W** he make many supplications unto thee? NIH
41: 3 unto thee? **w** he speak soft *words* unto thee? NIH
41: 4 **W** he make a covenant with thee? wilt thou NIH

Job 41:12 I **w** not conceal his parts, nor *his* power, NIH
42: 4 Hear, I beseech thee, and I **w** speak: I will NIH
42: 4 I **w** demand of thee, and declare thou unto NIH
42: 8 for him **w** I accept: lest *I* deal with you *after* NIH
Ps 2: 7 I **w** declare the decree: the LORD hath NIH
3: 6 I **w** not be afraid of ten thousands of people, NIH
4: 2 how long *w ye turn* my glory into shame? NIH
4: 2 *how long* **w** ye love vanity, *and* seek after NIH
4: 3 the LORD **w** hear when I call unto him. NIH
4: 6 many that say, Who **w** shew us *any* good? NIH
4: 8 I **w** both lay me down in peace, and sleep: NIH
5: 2 and my God: for unto thee **w** I pray. NIH
5: 3 *in* the morning **w** I direct *my prayer* unto NIH
5: 3 I direct *my prayer* unto thee, and **w** look up. NIH
5: 6 the LORD **w** abhor the bloody and NIH
5: 7 I **w** come *into* thy house in the multitude of NIH
5: 7 in thy fear **w** I worship toward thy holy NIH
6: 9 the LORD **w** receive my prayer. NIH
7:12 If he turn not, he **w** whet his sword; he hath NIH
7:17 I **w** praise the LORD according to his NIH
7:17 **w** sing *praise* to the name of the LORD NIH
9: 1 I **w** praise *thee,* O LORD, with my whole NIH
9: 1 I **w** shew forth all thy marvellous works. NIH
9: 2 I **w** be glad and rejoice in thee: I will sing NIH
9: 2 I **w** sing *praise* to thy name, O thou most NIH
9: 9 The LORD also **w** be a refuge for NIH
9:10 they that know thy name **w** put their trust in NIH
9:14 of Zion: I **w** rejoice in thy salvation. NIH
10: 4 **w** not seek *after God:* God *is* not *in* all his NIH
10:11 he hideth his face; he **w** never see *it.* NIH
12: 4 have said, With our tongue **w** we prevail; NIH
12: 5 the needy, now **w** I arise, saith the LORD; NIH
12: 5 I **w** set *him* in safety *from him that* puffeth NIH
13: 6 I **w** sing unto the LORD, because he hath NIH
16: 4 their drink offerings of blood **w** I not offer, NIH
16: 7 I **w** bless the LORD, who hath given me NIH
17:15 I **w** behold thy face in righteousness: NIH
18: 1 I **w** love thee, O LORD, my strength. NIH
18: 2 my God, my strength, in whom I **w** trust; NIH
18: 3 I **w** call upon the LORD, who is *worthy* to NIH
18:28 the LORD my God **w** enlighten my NIH
18:49 Therefore **w** I give thanks unto thee, NIH
20: 5 We **w** rejoice in thy salvation, and in NIH
20: 5 in the name of our God we **w** set up *our* NIH
20: 6 he **w** hear him from his holy heaven with NIH
20: 7 we **w** remember the name of the LORD NIH
21:13 *so* **w** we sing and praise thy power. NIH
22:22 I **w** declare thy name unto my brethren: NIH
22:22 in the midst of the congregation **w** I praise NIH
22:25 I **w** pay my vows before them that fear him. NIH
23: 4 of the shadow of death, I **w** fear no evil: NIH
23: 6 I **w** dwell in the house of the LORD for NIH
25: 8 **w** he teach sinners in the way. NIH
25: 9 The meek **w** he guide in judgment: and NIH
25: 9 and the meek **w** he teach his way. NIH
25:14 fear him; and he **w** shew them his covenant. NIH
26: 4 neither **w** I go in with dissemblers. NIH
26: 5 of evildoers; and **w** not sit with the wicked. NIH
26: 6 I **w** wash mine hands in innocency: so will I NIH
26: 6 so **w** I compass thine altar, O LORD: NIH
26:11 *as for* me, I **w** walk in mine integrity: NIH
26:12 in the congregations **w** I bless the LORD. NIH
27: 3 rise against me, in this **w** I *be* confident. NIH
27: 4 I desired of the LORD, that **w** I seek after; NIH
27: 6 **w** I offer in his tabernacle sacrifices of joy; NIH
27: 6 I **w** sing, yea, I will sing *praises* unto NIH
27: 6 yea, I **w** sing *praises* unto the LORD. NIH
27: 8 said unto thee, Thy face, LORD, **w** I seek. NIH
27:10 forsake me, then the LORD **w** take me up. NIH
27:12 Deliver me not over unto the **w** of mine 5315
28: 1 Unto thee **w** I cry, O LORD, my rock; NIH
28: 7 and with my song **w** I praise him. NIH
29:11 The LORD **w** give strength unto his NIH
29:11 the LORD **w** bless his people with peace. NIH
30: 1 I **w** extol thee, O LORD; for thou hast NIH
30:12 my God, I **w** give thanks unto thee for ever. NIH
31: 7 I **w** be glad and rejoice in thy mercy: NIH
32: 5 I **w** confess my transgressions unto NIH
32: 8 I **w** instruct thee and teach thee in the way NIH
32: 8 thou shalt go: I **w** guide thee with mine eye. NIH
34: 1 I **w** bless the LORD at all times: his praise NIH
34:11 I **w** teach you the fear of the LORD. NIH
35:18 I **w** give thee thanks in the great NIH
35:18 I **w** praise thee among much people. NIH
37:33 The LORD **w** not leave him in his hand, NIH
38:18 For I **w** declare mine iniquity; I will be NIH
38:18 mine iniquity; I **w** be sorry for my sin. NIH
39: 1 I said, I **w** take heed to my ways, that *I* sin NIH
39: 1 I **w** keep my mouth with a bridle, while NIH
40: 8 I delight to do thy **w**, O my God: yea, 7522
41: 1 the LORD **w** deliver him in time of NIH
41: 2 The LORD **w** preserve him, and keep him NIH
41: 2 thou wilt not deliver him unto the **w** of his 5315
41: 3 The LORD **w** strengthen him upon the bed NIH
42: 6 **w** I remember thee from the land of Jordan, NIH
42: 8 *Yet* the LORD **w** command his NIH
42: 9 I **w** say unto God my rock, Why hast thou NIH
43: 4 **w** I go unto the altar of God, unto God my NIH
43: 4 yea, upon the harp **w** I praise thee, O God NIH
44: 5 Through thee **w** we push down our enemies: NIH
44: 5 through thy name **w** we tread them under NIH
44: 6 For I **w** not trust in my bow, neither shall NIH
45:17 I **w** make thy name to be remembered in all NIH
46: 2 Therefore **w** not we fear, though the earth NIH
46:10 I **w** be exalted among the heathen, I will be NIH
46:10 the heathen, I **w** be exalted in the earth. NIH
48: 8 our God: God **w** establish it for ever. Selah. NIH
48:14 ever: he **w** be our guide *even* unto death. NIH
49: 4 I **w** incline mine ear to a parable: I will open NIH
49: 4 I **w** open my dark saying upon the harp. NIH
49:15 God **w** redeem my soul from the power of NIH
49:18 *men* **w** praise thee, when thou doest well to NIH
50: 7 Hear, O my people, and I **w** speak; O Israel, NIH
50: 7 O Israel, and I **w** testify against thee: NIH
50: 8 I **w** not reprove thee for thy sacrifices or NIH

Ps 50: 9 I **w** take no bullock out of thy house, *nor* he NIH
50:13 **W** I eat the flesh of bulls, or drink the blood NIH
50:15 I **w** deliver thee, and thou shalt glorify me. NIH
50:21 *but* I **w** reprove thee, and set *them* in order NIH
50:23 *aright* **w** I shew the salvation of God. NIH
51:13 *Then* **w** I teach transgressors thy ways; and NIH
52: 9 I **w** praise thee for ever, because thou hast NIH
52: 9 thou hast done *it:* and I **w** wait on thy name; NIH
54: 6 I **w** freely sacrifice unto thee: I will praise NIH
54: 6 I **w** praise thy name, O LORD; for *it is* NIH
55:16 *As for* me, I **w** call upon God; and NIH
55:17 and at noon, **w** I pray, and cry aloud: NIH
55:23 live out half their days; but I **w** trust in thee. NIH
56: 3 *What* time I am afraid, I **w** trust in thee. NIH
56: 4 In God I **w** praise his word, in God I have NIH
56: 4 I **w** not fear what flesh can do unto me. NIH
56:10 In God **w** I praise *his* word: in the LORD NIH
56:10 in the LORD **w** I praise *his* word. NIH
56:11 I **w** not be afraid what man can do unto me. NIH
56:12 O God: I **w** render praises unto thee. NIH
57: 1 in the shadow of thy wings **w** I make my NIH
57: 2 I **w** cry unto God most High; unto God that NIH
57: 7 my heart is fixed: I **w** sing and give praise. NIH
57: 8 and harp: I *myself* **w** awake early. NIH
57: 9 I **w** praise thee, O Lord, among the people: NIH
57: 9 I **w** sing unto thee among the nations. NIH
58: 5 Which **w** not hearken to the voice of NIH
59: 9 *Because of* his strength **w** I wait upon thee: NIH
59:16 I **w** sing of thy power; yea, I will sing aloud NIH
59:16 I **w** sing aloud of thy mercy in the morning: NIH
59:17 Unto thee, O my strength, **w** I sing: for God NIH
60: 6 I **w** rejoice, I will divide Shechem, and NIH
60: 6 I **w** divide Shechem, and mete out the valley NIH
60: 8 over Edom **w** I cast out my shoe: NIH
60: 9 Who **w** bring me *into* the strong city? NIH
60: 9 the strong city? who **w** lead me into Edom? NIH
61: 2 From the end of the earth **w** I cry unto thee, NIH
61: 4 I **w** abide in thy tabernacle for ever: I will NIH
61: 4 I **w** trust in the covert of thy wings. Selah. NIH
61: 8 So **w** I sing *praise* unto thy name for ever, NIH
62: 3 How long **w** ye imagine mischief against a NIH
63: 1 thou *art* my God; early **w** I seek thee: NIH
63: 4 Thus **w** I bless thee while I live: I will lift NIH
63: 4 I live: I **w** lift up my hands in thy name. NIH
63: 7 in the shadow of thy wings **w** I rejoice. NIH
66:13 I **w** go *into* thy house with burnt offerings: NIH
66:13 with burnt offerings: I **w** pay thee my vows, NIH
66:15 I **w** offer unto thee burnt sacrifices of NIH
66:15 of rams; I **w** offer bullocks with goats. NIH
66:16 I **w** declare what he hath done for my soul. NIH
66:18 in my heart, the Lord **w** not hear *me:* NIH
68:16 yea, the LORD **w** dwell *in it* for ever. NIH
68:22 Lord said, I **w** bring again from Bashan, NIH
68:22 I **w** bring *my people* again from the depths NIH
69:30 I **w** praise the name of God with a song; and NIH
69:30 and **w** magnify him with thanksgiving. NIH
69:35 For God **w** save Zion, and will build NIH
69:35 save Zion, and **w** build the cities of Judah: NIH
71:14 I **w** hope continually, and will yet praise NIH
71:14 and **w** yet praise thee more and more. NIH
71:16 I **w** go in the strength of the Lord GOD: NIH
71:16 I **w** make mention of thy righteousness, NIH
71:22 I **w** also praise thee with the psaltery, NIH
71:22 unto thee **w** I sing with the harp, O thou NIH
73:15 If I say, I **w** speak thus; behold, I should NIH
75: 2 When I shall receive the congregation I **w** NIH
75: 9 I **w** declare for ever; I will sing *praises* to NIH
75: 9 I **w** sing *praises* to the God of Jacob. NIH
75:10 All the horns of the wicked also **w** I cut off; NIH
77: 7 **W** the Lord cast off for ever? and will he be NIH
77: 7 for ever? and **w** he be favourable no more? NIH
77:10 *I* **w** *remember* the years of the right hand of NIH
77:11 I **w** remember the works of the LORD: NIH
77:11 surely I **w** remember thy wonders of old. NIH
77:12 I **w** meditate also of all thy work, and talk of NIH
78: 2 I **w** open my mouth in a parable: I will utter NIH
78: 2 in a parable: I **w** utter dark sayings of old: NIH
78: 4 We **w** not hide *them* from their children, NIH
79:13 sheep of thy pasture **w** give thee thanks for NIH
79:13 we **w** shew forth thy praise to all NIH
80:18 So **w** not we go *back* from thee: quicken us, NIH
80:18 quicken us, and we **w** call upon thy name. NIH
81: 8 O my people, and I **w** testify unto thee: NIH
81:10 open thy mouth wide, and I **w** fill it. NIH
82: 2 How long **w** ye judge unjustly, and NIH
82: 5 They know not, neither **w** they understand; NIH
84: 4 they **w** be still praising thee. Selah. NIH
84:11 the LORD **w** give grace and glory: NIH
84:11 no good *thing* **w** he withhold from them that NIH
85: 8 I **w** hear what God the LORD will speak: NIH
85: 8 I will hear what God the LORD **w** speak: NIH
85: 8 for he **w** speak peace unto his people, and NIH
86: 7 In the day of my trouble I **w** call upon thee: NIH
86:11 thy way, O LORD; I **w** walk in thy truth: NIH
86:12 I **w** praise thee, O Lord my God, with all NIH
86:12 and I **w** glorify thy name for evermore. NIH
87: 4 I **w** make mention of Rahab and Babylon to NIH
89: 1 I **w** sing of the mercies of the LORD for NIH
89: 1 with my mouth **w** I make known thy NIH
89: 4 Thy seed **w** I stablish for ever, and build up NIH
89:23 I **w** beat down his foes before his face, and NIH
89:25 I **w** set his hand also in the sea, and his right NIH
89:27 Also I **w** make him *my* firstborn, NIH
89:28 My mercy **w** I keep for him for evermore, NIH
89:29 His seed also **w** I make *to endure* for ever, NIH
89:32 **w** I visit their transgression with the rod, NIH
89:33 Nevertheless my lovingkindness **w** I not NIH
89:34 My covenant **w** I not break, nor alter NIH
89:35 Once have I sworn by my holiness that I **w** NIH
91: 2 I **w** say of the LORD, *He is* my refuge and NIH
91: 2 and my fortress: my God; in him **w** I trust. NIH
91:14 his love upon me, therefore **w** I deliver him: NIH
91:14 I **w** set him on high, because he hath known NIH
91:15 He shall call upon me, and I **w** answer him: NIH
91:15 I *w be* with him in trouble; I will deliver NIH

Ps 91:15 in trouble; I **w** deliver him, and honour him. NIH
91:16 *With* long life **w** I satisfy him, and NIH
92: 4 I **w** triumph in the works of thy hands. NIH
94: 8 and ye fools, when **w** ye be wise? NIH
94:14 For the LORD **w** not cast off his people, NIH
94:14 neither **w** he forsake his inheritance. NIH
94:16 Who **w** rise up for me against the evildoers? NIH
94:16 who **w** stand up for me against the workers NIH
95: 7 of his hand. To day if ye **w** hear his voice, NIH
101: 1 I **w** sing of mercy and judgment: unto thee, NIH
101: 1 judgment: unto thee, O LORD, **w** I sing. NIH
101: 2 I **w** behave myself wisely in a perfect way. NIH
101: 2 I **w** walk within my house with a perfect NIH
101: 3 I **w** set no wicked thing before mine eyes: NIH
101: 4 from me: I **w** not know a wicked *person.* NIH
101: 5 slandereth his neighbour, him **w** I cut off: NIH
101: 5 a high look and a proud heart **w** not I suffer. NIH
101: 8 I **w** early destroy all the wicked of the land; NIH
102:17 He **w** regard the prayer of the destitute, and NIH
103: 9 He **w** not always chide: neither will he keep NIH
103: 9 neither **w** he keep *his anger* for ever. NIH
104:33 I **w** sing unto the LORD as long as I live: NIH
104:33 I **w** sing *praise* to my God while I have my NIH
104:34 shall be sweet: I **w** be glad in the LORD. NIH
105:11 Unto thee **w** I give the land of Canaan, NIH
107:43 **w** observe these *things,* even they shall NIH
108: 1 I **w** sing and give praise, even *with* my NIH
108: 2 and harp: I *myself* **w** awake early. NIH
108: 3 I **w** praise thee, O LORD, among NIH
108: 3 I **w** sing *praises* unto thee among NIH
108: 7 I **w** rejoice, I will divide Shechem, and NIH
108: 7 I **w** divide Shechem, and mete out the valley NIH
108: 9 over Edom **w** I cast out my shoe; NIH
108: 9 cast out my shoe; over Philistia **w** I triumph. NIH
108:10 Who **w** bring me *into* the strong city? NIH
108:10 the strong city? who **w** lead me into Edom? NIH
109:30 I **w** greatly praise the LORD with my NIH
109:30 yea, I **w** praise him among the multitude. NIH
110: 4 The LORD hath sworn, and **w** not repent, NIH
111: 1 I **w** praise the LORD with *my* whole heart, NIH
111: 5 he **w** ever be mindful of his covenant. NIH
112: 5 he **w** guide his affairs with discretion. NIH
115:12 he **w** bless *us;* he will bless the house of NIH
115:12 he will bless *us;* he **w** bless the house of NIH
115:12 of Israel; he **w** bless the house of Aaron. NIH
115:13 He **w** bless them that fear the LORD, *both* NIH
115:18 we **w** bless the LORD from this time forth NIH
116: 2 therefore **w** I call upon *him* as long as I live. NIH
116: 9 I **w** walk before the LORD in the land of NIH
116:13 I **w** take the cup of salvation, and call upon NIH
116:14 I **w** pay my vows unto the LORD now in NIH
116:17 I **w** offer to thee the sacrifice of NIH
116:17 and **w** call upon the name of the LORD. NIH
116:18 I **w** pay my vows unto the LORD now in NIH
118: 6 The LORD *is* on my side; I **w** not fear: NIH
118:10 in the name of the LORD **w** I destroy NIH
118:11 in the name of the LORD I **w** destroy NIH
118:12 for in the name of the LORD I **w** destroy NIH
118:19 I **w** go into them, *and* I will praise NIH
118:19 go into them, *and* I **w** praise the LORD: NIH
118:21 I **w** praise thee: for thou hast heard me, and NIH
118:24 hath made; we **w** rejoice and be glad in it. NIH
118:28 Thou *art* my God, and I **w** praise thee: NIH
118:28 praise thee: *thou art* my God, I **w** exalt thee. NIH
119: 7 I **w** praise thee with uprightness of heart, NIH
119: 8 I **w** keep thy statutes: O forsake me not NIH
119:15 I **w** meditate in thy precepts, and NIH
119:16 I **w** delight myself in thy statutes: I will not NIH
119:16 in thy statutes: I **w** not forget thy word. NIH
119:32 I **w** run the way of thy commandments, NIH
119:45 I **w** walk at liberty: for I seek thy precepts. NIH
119:46 I **w** speak of thy testimonies also before NIH
119:46 also before kings, and **w** not be ashamed. NIH
119:47 I **w** delight myself in thy commandments, NIH
119:48 My hands also **w** I lift up unto thy NIH
119:48 have loved; and I **w** meditate in thy statutes. NIH
119:62 At midnight I **w** rise to give thanks unto NIH
119:69 I **w** keep thy precepts with *my* whole heart. NIH
119:74 They that fear thee **w** be glad when they see NIH
119:78 a cause: *but* I **w** meditate in thy precepts. NIH
119:93 I **w** never forget thy precepts: for with them NIH
119:95 *but* I **w** consider thy testimonies. NIH
119:106 I **w** perform *it,* that *I* will keep thy righteous NIH
119:106 I will perform *it,* that *I* **w** keep thy righteous NIH
119:115 for I **w** keep the commandments of my God. NIH
119:117 I **w** have respect unto thy statutes NIH
119:134 of man: so **w** I keep thy precepts. NIH
119:145 hear me, O LORD: I **w** keep thy statutes. NIH
121: 1 I **w** lift up mine eyes unto the hills, NIH
121: 3 He **w** not suffer thy foot to be moved: NIH
121: 3 he that keepeth thee **w** not slumber. NIH
122: 8 and companions' sakes, I **w** now say, NIH
122: 9 of the LORD our God I **w** seek thy good. NIH
132: 3 Surely I **w** not come into the tabernacle of NIH
132: 4 I **w** not give sleep to mine eyes, *or* NIH
132: 7 We **w** go into his tabernacles: we will NIH
132: 7 we **w** worship at his footstool. NIH
132:11 *in* truth unto David; he **w** not turn from it; NIH
132:11 Of the fruit of thy body **w** I set upon thy NIH
132:12 If thy children **w** keep my covenant and NIH
132:14 here **w** I dwell; for I have desired it. NIH
132:15 I **w** abundantly bless her provision: I will NIH
132:15 I **w** satisfy her poor *with* bread. NIH
132:16 I **w** also clothe her priests with salvation: NIH
132:17 There **w** I make the horn of David to bud: NIH
132:18 His enemies **w** I clothe with shame: but NIH
135:14 For the LORD **w** judge his people, and NIH
135:14 he **w** repent himself concerning his servants. NIH
138: 1 I **w** praise thee with my whole heart: NIH
138: 1 before the gods **w** I sing *praise* unto thee. NIH
138: 2 I **w** worship toward thy holy temple, and NIH
138: 8 The LORD **w** perfect that which NIH
139:14 I **w** praise thee; for I am fearfully and NIH
140:12 I know that the LORD **w** maintain NIH
143:10 Teach me to do thy **w**; for thou *art* my God: 7522

Ps 144: 9 I **w** sing a new song unto thee, O God: NIH
144: 9 an instrument of ten strings **w** I sing *praises* NIH
145: 1 I **w** extol thee, my God, O king; and I will NIH
145: 1 and I **w** bless thy name for ever and ever. NIH
145: 2 Every day **w** I bless thee; and I will praise NIH
145: 2 and I **w** praise thy name for ever and ever. NIH
145: 5 I **w** speak of the glorious honour of thy NIH
145: 6 terrible acts: and I **w** declare thy greatness. NIH
145:19 He **w** fulfil the desire of them that fear him: NIH
145:19 he also **w** hear their cry, and will save them. NIH
145:19 he also will hear their cry, and **w** save them. NIH
145:20 love him: but all the wicked **w** he destroy. NIH
146: 2 While I live **w** I praise the LORD: I will NIH
146: 2 I **w** sing *praises* unto my God while I have NIH
149: 4 he **w** beautify the meek with salvation. NIH
Pr 1: 5 A wise *man* **w** hear, and will increase NIH
1: 5 *man* will hear, and **w** increase learning; NIH
1:22 ye simple ones, **w** ye love simplicity? NIH
1:23 behold, I **w** pour out my spirit unto you, NIH
1:23 I **w** make known my words unto you. NIH
1:26 I also **w** laugh at your calamity; I will mock NIH
1:26 I **w** mock when your fear cometh; NIH
1:28 shall they call upon me, but I **w** not answer; NIH
3:28 and come again, and to morrow I **w** give; NIH
6:26 the adulteress **w** hunt for the precious life. NIH
6:34 he **w** not spare in the day of vengeance. NIH
6:35 He **w** not regard any ransom; neither will he NIH
6:35 neither **w** he rest content, though thou givest NIH
7:20 **w** come home at the day appointed. NIH
8: 6 Hear, for I **w** speak of excellent things; and NIH
8:21 and I **w** fill their treasures. NIH
9: 8 rebuke a wise *man*, and he **w** love thee. NIH
9: 9 to a wise *man*, and he **w** be yet wiser: NIH
9: 9 a just *man*, and he **w** increase in learning. NIH
10: 3 The LORD **w** not suffer the soul of NIH
10: 8 The wise in heart **w** receive NIH
12: 2 but a man of wicked devices **w** he condemn. NIH
14: 5 A faithful witness **w** not lie: but a false NIH
14: 5 will not lie: but a false witness **w** utter lies. NIH
15:12 neither **w** he go unto the wise. NIH
15:25 The LORD **w** destroy the house of NIH
15:25 but he **w** establish the border of the widow. NIH
16:14 of death: but a wise man **w** pacify it. NIH
18:14 The spirit of a man **w** sustain his infirmity; NIH
19: 6 Many **w** intreat the favour of the prince: and NIH
19:17 that which he hath given **w** he pay him NIH
19:24 **w** not so much as bring it to his mouth NIH
19:25 Smite a scorner, and the simple **w** beware: NIH
19:25 *and* he **w** understand knowledge. NIH
20: 3 from strife: but every fool **w** be meddling. NIH
20: 4 The sluggard **w** not plow by reason of NIH
20: 5 but a man of understanding **w** draw it out. NIH
20: 6 Most men **w** proclaim every one his own NIH
20:22 Say not thou, I **w** recompense evil; *but* NIH
21: 1 of water: he turneth it whithersoever he **w**. 2654
22: 6 and when he is old, he **w** not depart from it. NIH
22:23 For the LORD **w** plead their cause, and NIH
23: 9 for he **w** despise the wisdom of thy words. NIH
23:35 when shall I awake? I **w** seek it yet again. NIH
24:29 I **w** do so to him as he hath done to me: NIH
24:29 I **w** render to the man according to his work. NIH
26:27 he that rolleth a stone, it **w** return upon him. NIH
27:22 *yet* **w** not his foolishness depart from him. NIH
28: 8 he shall gather it for him that **w** pity NIH
28:21 for a piece of bread *that* man **w** NIH
29:19 A servant **w** not be corrected by words: NIH
29:19 for though he understand he **w** not answer. NIH
31:12 She **w** do him good and not evil all the days NIH
Ecc 2: 1 I **w** prove thee with mirth, therefore NIH
4:10 For if they fall, the one **w** lift up his fellow: NIH
4:13 who **w** no more be admonished. 3045
5:12 the abundance of the rich **w** not suffer him NIH
7: 2 all men; and the living **w** lay *it* to his heart. NIH
7:23 I said, I **w** be wise; but it *was* far from me. NIH
10:11 Surely the serpent **w** bite without NIH
10:12 but the lips of a fool **w** swallow up himself. NIH
11: 9 that for all these *things* God **w** bring thee NIH
SS 1: 4 Draw me, we **w** run after thee: the king hath NIH
1: 4 we **w** be glad and rejoice in thee, we will NIH
1: 4 we **w** remember thy love more than wine: NIH
1:11 We **w** make thee borders of gold with studs NIH
3: 2 I **w** rise now, and go about the city in NIH
3: 2 I **w** seek *him* whom my soul loveth: NIH
4: 6 I **w** get me to the mountain of myrrh, and NIH
6:13 What **w** ye see in the Shulamite? As it were NIH
7: 8 I said, I **w** go up to the palm tree, I will take NIH
7: 8 I **w** take hold of the boughs thereof: NIH
7:12 bud forth: there **w** I give thee my loves. NIH
8: 9 we **w** build upon her a palace of silver: NIH
8: 9 we **w** inclose her with boards of cedar. NIH
Isa 1: 5 ye **w** revolt more and more: the whole head NIH
1:15 your hands, I **w** hide mine eyes from you: NIH
1:15 when ye make many prayers, I **w** not hear: NIH
1:24 I **w** ease me of mine adversaries, and NIH
1:25 I **w** turn my hand upon thee, and purely NIH
1:26 I **w** restore thy judges as at the first, and NIH
2: 3 he **w** teach us of his ways, and we will walk NIH
2: 3 us of his ways, and we **w** walk in his paths: NIH
3: 4 I **w** give children *to be* their princes, and NIH
3: 7 shall he swear, saying, I **w** not be a healer; NIH
3:14 The LORD **w** enter into judgment with NIH
3:17 Therefore the Lord **w** smite with a scab NIH
3:17 the LORD **w** discover their secret parts. NIH
3:18 In that day the Lord **w** take away NIH
4: 1 We **w** eat our own bread, and wear our own NIH
4: 5 the LORD **w** create upon every dwelling NIH
5: 1 Now **w** I sing to my wellbeloved a song of NIH
5: 5 I **w** tell you what I *will* do to my vineyard: NIH
5: 5 I will tell you what I **w** do to my vineyard: NIH
5: 5 I **w** take away the hedge thereof, and it shall NIH
5: 6 I **w** lay it waste: it shall not be pruned, nor NIH
5: 6 I **w** also command the clouds that they rain NIH
5:26 he **w** lift up an ensign to the nations from NIH
5:26 **w** hiss unto them from the end of the earth: NIH
6: 8 Whom shall I send, and who **w** go for us? NIH

Isa 7: 9 If ye **w** not believe, surely ye shall not be NIH
7:12 Ahaz said, I **w** not ask, neither will I tempt NIH
7:12 I will not ask, neither **w** I tempt the LORD. NIH
7:13 weary men, but **w** ye weary my God also? NIH
8:17 I **w** wait upon the LORD, that hideth his NIH
8:17 the house of Jacob, and I **w** look for him. NIH
9: 7 The zeal of the LORD of hosts **w** perform NIH
9:10 but we **w** build *with* hewn stones: NIH
9:10 but we **w** change *them into* cedars. NIH
9:14 Therefore the LORD **w** cut off from Israel NIH
10: 3 what **w** ye do in the day of visitation, and NIH
10: 3 to whom **w** ye flee for help? and where will NIH
10: 3 for help? and where **w** ye leave your glory? NIH
10: 6 I **w** send him against a hypocritical nation, NIH
10: 6 against the people of my wrath **w** I give him NIH
10:12 I **w** punish the fruit of the stout heart of NIH
12: 1 thou shalt say, O LORD, I **w** praise thee: NIH
12: 2 *is* my salvation; I **w** trust, and not be afraid: NIH
13:11 I **w** punish the world for *their* evil, and NIH
13:11 I **w** cause the arrogancy of the proud to NIH
13:11 **w** lay low the haughtiness of the terrible. NIH
13:12 I **w** make a man more precious than fine NIH
13:13 Therefore I **w** shake the heavens, and NIH
13:17 Behold, I **w** stir up the Medes against them, NIH
14: 1 For the LORD **w** have mercy on Jacob, NIH
14: 1 **w** yet choose Israel, and set them in their NIH
14:13 said in thine heart, I **w** ascend *into* heaven, NIH
14:13 I **w** exalt my throne above the stars of God: NIH
14:13 I **w** sit also upon the mount of NIH
14:14 I **w** ascend above the heights of the clouds; NIH
14:14 of the clouds; I **w** be like the most High. NIH
14:22 For I **w** rise up against them, saith NIH
14:23 I **w** also make it a possession for the bittern, NIH
14:23 I **w** sweep it with the besom of destruction, NIH
14:25 That *I* **w** break the Assyrian in my land, and NIH
14:30 I **w** kill thy root with famine, and he shall NIH
15: 9 for I **w** bring more upon Dimon, lions upon NIH
16: 9 Therefore I **w** bewail with the weeping of NIH
16: 9 I **w** water thee *with* my tears, O Heshbon, NIH
18: 4 I **w** take my rest, and I will consider in my NIH
18: 4 I **w** consider in my dwelling place like a NIH
19: 2 I **w** set the Egyptians against the Egyptians: NIH
19: 3 and I **w** destroy the counsel thereof: NIH
19: 4 the Egyptians **w** I give over into the hand of NIH
21:12 if ye **w** inquire, inquire ye: return, come. NIH
22: 4 I **w** weep bitterly, labour not to comfort me, NIH
22:17 the LORD **w** carry thee away with a NIH
22:17 a mighty captivity, and **w** surely cover thee. NIH
22:18 He **w** surely violently turn and toss thee like NIH
22:19 I **w** drive thee from thy station, and NIH
22:20 that I **w** call my servant Eliakim the son of NIH
22:21 I **w** clothe him with thy robe, and NIH
22:21 I **w** commit thy government into his hand: NIH
22:22 the key of the house of David **w** I lay upon NIH
22:23 And I **w** fasten him *as* a nail in a sure place; NIH
23:17 *that* the LORD **w** visit Tyre, and she shall NIH
25: 1 I **w** exalt thee, I will praise thy name; NIH
25: 1 I will exalt thee, I **w** praise thy name; NIH
25: 7 he **w** destroy in this mountain the face of NIH
25: 8 He **w** swallow up death in victory; and NIH
25: 8 the Lord GOD **w** wipe away tears from off NIH
25: 9 we have waited for him, and he **w** save us: NIH
25: 9 we **w** be glad and rejoice in his salvation. NIH
26: 1 salvation **w** *God* appoint *for* walls and NIH
26: 9 *with* my spirit within me **w** I seek thee NIH
26: 9 the inhabitants of the world **w** learn NIH
26:10 *yet* **w** he not learn righteousness: NIH
26:10 in the land of uprightness **w** he deal NIH
26:10 **w** not behold the majesty of the LORD. NIH
26:11 *when* thy hand is lifted up, they **w** not see: NIH
26:13 by thee only **w** we make mention of thy NIH
27: 3 do keep it; I **w** water it every moment: NIH
27: 3 lest *any* hurt it, I **w** keep it night and day. NIH
27:11 he that made them **w** not have mercy on NIH
27:11 he that formed them **w** shew them no NIH
28:11 another tongue **w** he speak to this people. NIH
28:17 Judgment also **w** I lay to the line, and NIH
28:28 because he **w** not ever be threshing it, NIH
29: 2 Yet I **w** distress Ariel, and there shall be NIH
29: 3 And I **w** camp against thee round about, and NIH
29: 3 **w** lay siege against thee *with* a mount, and NIH
29: 3 a mount, and I **w** raise forts against thee. NIH
29:14 I **w** proceed to do a marvellous work NIH
30: 6 they **w** carry their riches upon the shoulders NIH
30: 9 children *that* **w** not hear the law of 14
30:16 ye said, No; for we **w** flee upon horses; NIH
30:16 and, We **w** ride upon the swift; therefore NIH
30:18 therefore **w** the LORD wait, that *he* may NIH
30:18 unto you, and therefore **w** he be exalted, NIH
30:19 he **w** be very gracious unto thee at the voice NIH
30:19 when *he* shall hear it, he **w** answer thee. NIH
30:32 and in battles of shaking **w** he fight with it. NIH
31: 2 **w** bring evil, and will not call back his NIH
31: 2 bring evil, and **w** not call back his words: NIH
31: 2 **w** arise against the house of the evildoers, NIH
31: 4 he **w** not be afraid of their voice, nor abase NIH
31: 5 so **w** the LORD of hosts defend Jerusalem; NIH
31: 5 defending also he **w** deliver *it; and* NIH
31: 5 and passing over he **w** preserve *it.* NIH
32: 6 For the vile person **w** speak villany, and NIH
32: 6 his heart **w** work iniquity, to practise NIH
32: 6 he **w** cause the drink of the thirsty to fail. NIH
33:10 Now **w** I rise, saith the LORD; now will I NIH
33:10 I rise, saith the LORD; now **w** I be exalted; NIH
33:10 will I be exalted, now **w** I lift up myself. NIH
33:21 there the glorious LORD **w** *be* unto us a NIH
33:22 the LORD *is* our king; he **w** save us. NIH
35: 4 behold, your God **w** come *with* vengeance, NIH
35: 4 a recompence; he **w** come and save you. NIH
36: 6 it **w** go into his hand, and pierce it: NIH
36: 8 and I **w** give thee two thousand horses, NIH
36:15 The LORD **w** surely deliver us: NIH
36:18 saying, The LORD **w** deliver us: NIH
37: 4 It may be the LORD thy God **w** hear NIH
37: 4 **w** reprove the words which the LORD thy NIH

Isa 37: 7 I **w** send a blast upon him, and he shall hear NIH
37: 7 I **w** cause him to fall by the sword in his NIH
37:24 and I **w** cut down the tall cedars thereof, *and* NIH
37:24 I **w** enter *into* the height of his border, *and* NIH
37:29 therefore **w** I put my hook in thy nose, and NIH
37:29 I **w** turn thee back by the way by which NIH
37:35 For I **w** defend this city to save it for mine NIH
38: 5 behold, I **w** add unto thy days fifteen years. NIH
38: 6 I **w** deliver thee and this city out of the hand NIH
38: 6 king of Assyria: and I **w** defend this city. NIH
38: 7 that the LORD **w** do this thing that he hath NIH
38: 8 I **w** bring again the shadow of the degrees, NIH
38:12 he **w** cut me off with pining sickness: NIH
38:13 *that,* as a lion, so **w** he break all my bones: NIH
38:20 we **w** sing my songs *to* the stringed NIH
40:10 the Lord GOD **w** come with strong *hand,* NIH
40:18 To whom then **w** ye liken God? or NIH
40:18 or what likeness **w** ye compare unto him? NIH
40:20 no oblation chooseth a tree *that* **w** not rot; NIH
40:25 To whom then **w** ye liken me, or shall I be NIH
41:10 I **w** strengthen thee; yea, I will help thee; NIH
41:10 yea, I **w** help thee; yea, I will uphold thee NIH
41:10 I **w** uphold thee with the right hand of my NIH
41:13 For I the LORD thy God **w** hold thy right NIH
41:13 saying unto thee, Fear not; I **w** help thee. NIH
41:14 I **w** help thee, saith the LORD, and NIH
41:15 I **w** make thee a new sharp threshing NIH
41:17 faileth for thirst, I the LORD **w** hear them, NIH
41:17 *I* the God of Israel **w** not forsake them. NIH
41:18 I **w** open rivers in high places, and NIH
41:18 I **w** make the wilderness a pool of water, NIH
41:19 I **w** plant in the wilderness the cedar, NIH
41:19 I **w** set in the desert the fir tree, *and* NIH
41:27 I **w** give to Jerusalem one that bringeth NIH
42: 6 **w** hold thine hand, and will keep thee, and NIH
42: 6 **w** keep thee, and give thee for a covenant of NIH
42: 8 my glory **w** I not give to another, neither my NIH
42:14 *now* **w** I cry like a travailing woman; I will NIH
42:14 I **w** destroy and devour at once. NIH
42:15 I **w** make waste mountains and hills, and NIH
42:15 I **w** make the rivers islands, and I will dry NIH
42:15 the rivers islands, and I **w** dry up the pools. NIH
42:16 I **w** bring the blind by a way *that* they knew NIH
42:16 I **w** lead them in paths *that* they have not NIH
42:16 I **w** make darkness light before them, and NIH
42:16 These things **w** I do unto them, and NIH
42:21 he **w** magnify the law, and make *it* NIH
42:23 Who among you **w** give ear to this? NIH
42:23 *who* **w** hearken and hear for the time to NIH
43: 2 passest through the waters, I **w** *be* with thee, NIH
43: 4 therefore **w** I give men for thee, and NIH
43: 5 I **w** bring thy seed from the east, and NIH
43: 6 I **w** say to the north, Give *up;* and to NIH
43:13 of my hand: I **w** work, and who shall let it? NIH
43:19 I **w** do a new *thing;* now it shall spring NIH
43:19 I **w** even make a way in the wilderness, *and* NIH
43:25 own sake, and **w** not remember thy sins. NIH
44: 2 thee from the womb, *which* **w** help thee; NIH
44: 3 For I **w** pour water upon *him that is* thirsty, NIH
44: 3 floods upon the dry *ground:* I **w** pour my NIH
44:15 for he **w** take thereof, and warm himself; NIH
44:26 and I **w** raise up the decayed places thereof: NIH
44:27 the deep, Be dry, and I **w** dry up thy rivers: NIH
45: 1 I **w** loose the loins of kings, to open before NIH
45: 2 I **w** go before thee, and make the crooked NIH
45: 2 I **w** break in pieces the gates of brass, and NIH
45: 3 And I **w** give thee the treasures of darkness, NIH
45:13 in righteousness, and I **w** direct all his ways: NIH
46: 4 *even* to hoar hairs **w** I carry *you:* I have NIH
46: 4 will I carry *you:* I have made, and I **w** bear; NIH
46: 4 even I **w** carry, and will deliver *you.* NIH
46: 4 even I will carry, and **w** deliver *you.* NIH
46: 5 To whom **w** ye liken me, and make *me* NIH
46:10 shall stand, and I **w** do all my pleasure: NIH
46:11 I have spoken *it,* I **w** also bring it to pass; NIH
46:11 it to pass; I have purposed *it,* I **w** also do it. NIH
46:13 I **w** place salvation in Zion for Israel my NIH
47: 3 I **w** take vengeance, and I will not meet *thee* NIH
47: 3 and I **w** not meet *thee as* a man. NIH
48: 6 **w** not ye declare *it?* I have shewed thee new NIH
48: 9 For my name's sake **w** I defer mine anger, NIH
48: 9 *for* my praise **w** I refrain for thee, that *I* cut NIH
48:11 **w** I do *it:* for how should *my name* be NIH
48:11 and I **w** not give my glory unto another. NIH
48:14 he **w** do his pleasure on Babylon, and NIH
49: 3 O Israel, in whom I **w** be glorified. NIH
49: 6 I **w** also give thee for a light to the Gentiles, NIH
49: 8 I **w** preserve thee, and give thee for a NIH
49:11 I **w** make all my mountains a way, and NIH
49:13 and **w** have mercy upon his afflicted. NIH
49:15 they may forget, yet **w** I not forget thee. NIH
49:22 I **w** lift up mine hand to the Gentiles, and NIH
49:25 for I **w** contend with him that contendeth NIH
49:25 with thee, and I **w** save thy children. NIH
49:26 I **w** feed them that oppress thee with their NIH
50: 7 For the Lord GOD **w** help me; therefore NIH
50: 8 that justifieth me; who **w** contend with me? NIH
50: 9 Behold, the Lord GOD **w** help me; who *is* NIH
51: 3 he **w** comfort all her waste places; and NIH
51: 3 he **w** make her wilderness like Eden, and NIH
51: 4 I **w** make my judgment to rest for a light of NIH
51:23 I **w** put it into the hand of them that afflict NIH
52:12 for the LORD **w** go before you; and NIH
52:12 and the God of Israel **w** *be* your rereward. NIH
53:12 Therefore **w** I divide him *a portion* with NIH
54: 7 but with great mercies **w** I gather thee. NIH
54: 8 with everlasting kindness **w** I have mercy NIH
54:11 I **w** lay thy stones with fair colours, and NIH
54:12 I **w** make thy windows *of* agates, and NIH
55: 3 I **w** make an everlasting covenant with you, NIH
55: 7 and he **w** have mercy upon him; NIH
55: 7 to our God, for he **w** abundantly pardon. NIH
56: 5 Even unto them **w** I give in mine house and NIH
56: 5 I **w** give them an everlasting name, NIH
56: 7 Even them **w** I bring to my holy mountain, NIH

Isa 56: 8 Yet **w** I gather *others* to him, besides those NIH
56:12 *say they,* I **w** fetch wine, and we will fill NIH
56:12 and we **w** fill ourselves with strong drink; NIH
57:12 I **w** declare thy righteousness, and thy NIH
57:16 For I **w** not contend for ever, neither will I NIH
57:16 for ever, neither **w** I be always wroth: NIH
57:18 I have seen his ways, and **w** heal him: I will NIH
57:18 I **w** lead him also, and restore comforts unto NIH
57:19 *is* near, saith the LORD; and I **w** heal him. NIH
58:14 I **w** cause thee to ride upon the high places NIH
59: 2 hid *his* face from you, that *he* **w** not hear. NIH
59:18 accordingly he **w** repay, fury to his NIH
59:18 to the islands he **w** repay recompence. NIH
60: 7 and I **w** glorify the house of my glory. NIH
60:12 kingdom that **w** not serve thee shall perish; NIH
60:13 and I **w** make the place of my feet glorious. NIH
60:15 that no man went through *thee,* I **w** make NIH
60:17 For brass I **w** bring gold, and for iron I will NIH
60:17 for iron I **w** bring silver, and for wood brass, NIH
60:17 I **w** also make thy officers peace, and NIH
60:22 I the LORD **w** hasten it in his time. NIH
61: 8 I **w** direct their work in truth, and I will NIH
61: 8 I **w** make an everlasting covenant with NIH
61:10 I **w** greatly rejoice in the LORD, my soul NIH
61:11 so the Lord GOD **w** cause righteousness NIH
62: 1 For Zion's sake **w** I not hold my peace, and NIH
62: 1 and for Jerusalem's sake I **w** not rest, NIH
62: 8 Surely I **w** no more give thy corn *to be* meat NIH
63: 3 for I **w** tread them in mine anger, and NIH
63: 3 my garments, and I **w** stain all my raiment. NIH
63: 6 I **w** tread down the people in mine anger, NIH
63: 6 I **w** bring down their strength to the earth. NIH
63: 7 I **w** mention the lovingkindnesses of NIH
63: 8 they *are* my people, children *that* **w** not lie: NIH
65: 6 I **w** not keep silence, but will recompense, NIH
65: 6 I will not keep silence, but **w** recompense, NIH
65: 7 **w** I measure their former work into their NIH
65: 8 so **w** I do for my servants' sakes, that *I* may NIH
65: 9 And I **w** bring forth a seed out of Jacob, and NIH
65:12 Therefore **w** I number you to the sword, and NIH
65:19 I **w** rejoice in Jerusalem, and joy in my NIH
65:24 to pass, that before they call, I **w** answer; NIH
65:24 and whiles they are yet speaking, I **w** hear. NIH
66: 2 to this *man* **w** I look, *even* to *him that is* NIH
66: 4 I also **w** choose their delusions, and NIH
66: 4 and **w** bring their fears upon them; NIH
66:12 I **w** extend peace to her like a river, and NIH
66:13 his mother comforteth, so **w** I comfort you; NIH
66:15 the LORD **w** come with fire, and with his NIH
66:16 by his sword **w** the LORD plead with all NIH
66:18 that *I* **w** gather all nations and tongues; NIH
66:19 I **w** set a sign among them, and I will send NIH
66:19 I **w** send those that escape of them unto NIH
66:21 I **w** also take of them for priests *and* NIH
66:22 and the new earth, which I **w** make, NIH
Jer 1:12 for I **w** hasten my word to perform it. NIH
1:15 I **w** call all the families of the kingdoms of NIH
1:16 I **w** utter my judgments against them NIH
2: 9 Wherefore I **w** yet plead with you, saith NIH
2: 9 and with your children's children **w** I plead. NIH
2:20 and thou saidst, I **w** not transgress; NIH
2:24 all they that seek her **w** not weary NIH
2:25 have loved strangers, and after them **w** I go. NIH
2:27 in the time of their trouble they **w** say, NIH
2:29 Wherefore **w** ye plead with me? ye all have NIH
2:31 are lords; we **w** come no more unto thee? NIH
2:35 Behold, I **w** plead with thee, because NIH
3: 5 **W** he reserve *his anger* for ever? will he NIH
3: 5 **w** he keep *it* to the end? Behold, thou hast NIH
3:12 I **w** not cause mine anger to fall upon you: NIH
3:12 *and* I **w** not keep *anger* for ever. NIH
3:14 I **w** take you one of a city, and two of a NIH
3:14 two of a family, and I **w** bring you *to* Zion: NIH
3:15 I **w** give you pastors according to mine NIH
3:22 *and* I **w** heal your backslidings. NIH
4: 6 for I **w** bring evil from the north, and a great NIH
4:12 now also **w** I give sentence against them. NIH
4:27 be desolate; yet **w** I not make a full end. NIH
4:28 *it,* I have purposed *it,* and **w** not repent, NIH
4:28 not repent, neither **w** I turn back from it. NIH
4:30 *thy* lovers **w** despise thee, they will seek thy NIH
4:30 will despise thee, they **w** seek thy life. NIH
5: 1 that seeketh the truth; and I **w** pardon it. NIH
5: 5 I **w** get me unto the great men, and NIH
5: 5 unto the great men, and **w** speak unto them; NIH
5:14 I **w** make my words in thy mouth fire, and NIH
5:15 Lo, I **w** bring a nation upon you from far, NIH
5:18 I **w** not make a full end with you. NIH
5:22 **w** ye not tremble at my presence, NIH
5:31 *it* so: and what **w** ye do in the end thereof? NIH
6:11 I **w** pour *it* out upon the children abroad, NIH
6:12 for I **w** stretch out my hand upon NIH
6:16 But they said, We **w** not walk *therein.* NIH
6:17 But they said, We **w** not hearken. NIH
6:19 behold, I **w** bring evil upon this people, NIH
6:21 I **w** lay stumblingblocks before this people, NIH
7: 3 and I **w** cause you to dwell in this place. NIH
7: 7 **w** I cause you to dwell in this place, in NIH
7: 9 **W** *ye* steal, murder, and commit adultery, NIH
7:14 Therefore **w** I do unto *this* house, which is NIH
7:15 I **w** cast you out of my sight, as I have cast NIH
7:16 intercession to me: for I **w** not hear thee. NIH
7:23 I **w** be your God, and ye shall be my people: NIH
7:27 unto them; but they **w** not hearken to thee: NIH
7:27 call unto them; but they **w** not answer thee. NIH
7:34 **w** I cause to cease from the cities of Judah, NIH
8:10 Therefore **w** I give their wives unto others, NIH
8:13 I **w** surely consume them, saith the LORD: NIH
8:17 For behold, I **w** send serpents, cockatrices, NIH
8:17 which **w** not *be* charmed, and they shall bite NIH
9: 4 for every brother **w** utterly supplant, NIH
9: 4 every neighbour **w** walk *with* slanders. NIH
9: 5 they **w** deceive every one his neighbour, NIH
9: 5 his neighbour, and **w** not speak the truth: NIH
9: 7 Behold, I **w** melt them, and try them; NIH

Jer 9:10 For the mountains **w** I take up a weeping NIH
9:11 I **w** make Jerusalem heaps, *and* a den of NIH
9:11 I **w** make the cities of Judah desolate, NIH
9:15 Behold, I **w** feed them, *even* this people, NIH
9:16 I **w** scatter them also among the heathen, NIH
9:16 I **w** send a sword after them, till I have NIH
9:25 that I **w** punish all *them which are* NIH
10:18 I **w** sling out the inhabitants of the land at NIH
10:18 **w** distress them, that they may find *it so.* NIH
11: 4 shall ye be my people, and I **w** be your God: NIH
11: 8 I **w** bring upon them all the words of this NIH
11:11 Behold, I **w** bring evil upon them, NIH
11:11 cry unto me, I **w** not hearken unto them. NIH
11:14 for I **w** not hear *them* in the time that they NIH
11:22 LORD of hosts, Behold, I **w** punish them: NIH
11:23 for I **w** bring evil upon the men of NIH
12:14 I **w** pluck them out of their land, and pluck NIH
12:15 I **w** return, and have compassion on them, NIH
12:15 **w** bring them again, every man to his NIH
12:16 if they **w** diligently learn the ways of my NIH
12:17 if they **w** not obey, I will utterly pluck up NIH
12:17 I **w** utterly pluck up and destroy that nation, NIH
13: 9 After this manner **w** I mar the pride of NIH
13:13 I **w** fill all the inhabitants of this land, NIH
13:14 I **w** dash them one against another, even NIH
13:14 I **w** not pity, nor spare, nor have mercy, but NIH
13:17 if ye **w** not hear it, my soul shall weep in NIH
13:24 Therefore **w** I scatter them as the stubble NIH
13:26 Therefore **w** I discover thy skirts upon thy NIH
14:10 he **w** now remember their iniquity, and NIH
14:12 When they fast, I **w** not hear their cry; and NIH
14:12 and an oblation, I **w** not accept them: NIH
14:12 I **w** consume them by the sword, and by NIH
14:13 but I **w** give you assured peace in this place. NIH
14:16 for I **w** pour their wickedness upon them. NIH
14:22 therefore we **w** wait upon thee: for thou NIH
15: 3 I **w** appoint over them four kinds, saith NIH
15: 4 I **w** cause them to be removed into all NIH
15: 6 **w** I stretch out my hand against thee, NIH
15: 7 I **w** fan them with a fan in the gates of NIH
15: 7 I **w** bereave *them* of children, I will destroy NIH
15: 7 *them* of children, I **w** destroy my people, NIH
15: 9 the residue of them **w** I deliver to the sword NIH
15:11 verily I **w** cause the enemy to entreat thee NIH
15:13 thy treasures **w** I give to the spoil without NIH
15:14 I **w** make *thee* to pass with thine enemies NIH
15:19 **w** I bring thee again, *and* thou shalt stand NIH
15:20 I **w** make thee unto this people a fenced NIH
15:21 I **w** deliver thee out of the hand of NIH
15:21 I **w** redeem thee out of the hand of NIH
16: 9 I **w** cause to cease out of this place in your NIH
16:13 Therefore **w** I cast you out of this land into NIH
16:13 and night; where I **w** not shew you favour. NIH
16:15 I **w** bring them again into their land that I NIH
16:16 Behold, I **w** send for many fishers, saith NIH
16:16 after **w** I send for many hunters, and NIH
16:18 first I **w** recompense their iniquity and NIH
16:21 I **w** this once cause them to know, NIH
16:21 I **w** cause them to know mine hand and my NIH
17: 3 I **w** give thy substance *and* all thy treasures NIH
17: 4 I **w** cause thee to serve thine enemies in NIH
17:27 if you **w** not hearken unto me to hallow NIH
17:27 **w** I kindle a fire in the gates thereof, and NIH
18: 2 and there I **w** cause thee to hear my words. NIH
18: 8 I **w** repent of the evil that I thought to do NIH
18:10 not my voice, then I **w** repent of the good, NIH
18:12 we **w** walk after our own devices, and NIH
18:12 we **w** every one do the imagination of his NIH
18:14 **W** *a man* leave the snow of Lebanon *which* NIH
18:17 I **w** scatter them as *with* an east wind before NIH
18:17 I **w** shew them the back, and not the face, NIH
19: 3 Behold, I **w** bring evil upon this place, NIH
19: 7 I **w** make void the counsel of Judah and NIH
19: 7 I **w** cause them to fall by the sword before NIH
19: 7 their carcases **w** I give to be meat for NIH
19: 8 I **w** make this city desolate, and a hissing; NIH
19: 9 I **w** cause them to eat the flesh of their sons NIH
19:11 Even so **w** I break this people and this city, NIH
19:12 Thus **w** I do unto this place, saith NIH
19:15 I **w** bring upon this city and upon all her NIH
20: 4 I **w** make thee a terror to thyself, and to all NIH
20: 4 I **w** give all Judah into the hand of the king NIH
20: 5 Moreover I **w** deliver all the strength of this NIH
20: 5 all the treasures of the kings of Judah **w** I NIH
20: 9 I said, I **w** not make mention of him, NIH
20:10 Report, *say they,* and we **w** report it. All my NIH
20:10 *saying,* Peradventure he **w** be enticed, and NIH
21: 2 be that the LORD **w** deal with us NIH
21: 4 I **w** turn back the weapons of war that *are* in NIH
21: 4 I **w** assemble them into the midst of this NIH
21: 5 I myself **w** fight against you with an NIH
21: 6 I **w** smite the inhabitants of this city, both NIH
21: 7 I **w** deliver Zedekiah king of Judah, and his NIH
21:14 I **w** punish you according to the fruit of your NIH
21:14 I **w** kindle a fire in the forest thereof, and NIH
22: 5 if ye **w** not hear these words, I swear by NIH
22: 6 *yet* surely I **w** make thee a wilderness *and* NIH
22: 7 I **w** prepare destroyers against thee, NIH
22:14 I **w** build me a wide house and NIH
22:21 thy prosperity; *but* thou saidst, I **w** not hear. NIH
22:25 I **w** give thee into the hand of them that seek NIH
22:26 I **w** cast thee out, and thy mother that bare NIH
23: 2 I **w** visit upon you the evil of your doings, NIH
23: 3 I **w** gather the remnant of my flock out of NIH
23: 3 and **w** bring them again to their folds; NIH
23: 4 I **w** set up shepherds over them which shall NIH
23: 5 that I **w** raise unto David a righteous NIH
23:12 for I **w** bring evil upon them, *even* the year NIH
23:15 I **w** feed them with wormwood, and NIH
23:33 I **w** even forsake you, saith the LORD. NIH
23:34 I **w** even punish that man and his house. NIH
23:39 **w** utterly forget you, and I will forsake you, NIH
23:39 I **w** forsake you, and the city that I gave you NIH
23:40 I **w** bring an everlasting reproach upon you, NIH
24: 5 **w** I acknowledge them that are carried away NIH

Jer 24: 6 For I **w** set mine eyes upon them for good, NIH
24: 6 and I **w** bring them again to this land: NIH
24: 6 I **w** build them, and not pull *them* down; NIH
24: 6 and I **w** plant them, and not pluck *them* up. NIH
24: 7 I **w** give them a heart to know me, that I *am* NIH
24: 7 shall be my people, and I **w** be their God: NIH
24: 8 So **w** I give Zedekiah the king of Judah, and NIH
24: 9 I **w** deliver them to be removed into all NIH
24:10 I **w** send the sword, the famine, and NIH
25: 6 of your hands; and I **w** do you no hurt. NIH
25: 9 I **w** send and take all the families of NIH
25: 9 **w** bring them against this land, and NIH
25: 9 **w** utterly destroy them, and make them an NIH
25:10 Moreover I **w** take from them the voice of NIH
25:12 *that* I **w** punish the king of Babylon, and NIH
25:12 and **w** make it perpetual desolations. NIH
25:13 I **w** bring upon that land all my words which NIH
25:14 I **w** recompense them according to their NIH
25:16 of the sword that I **w** send among them. NIH
25:27 of the sword which I **w** send among you. NIH
25:29 for I **w** call for a sword upon all NIH
25:31 with the nations, he **w** plead with all flesh; NIH
25:31 he **w** give them *that are* wicked to NIH
26: 3 If so be they **w** hearken, and turn every man NIH
26: 4 If ye **w** not hearken to me, to walk in my NIH
26: 6 **w** I make this house like Shiloh, and will NIH
26: 6 **w** make this city a curse to all the nations of NIH
26:13 the LORD **w** repent him of the evil that he NIH
27: 8 kingdom which **w** not serve the same NIH
27: 8 that **w** not put their neck under the yoke of NIH
27: 8 that nation **w** I punish, saith the LORD, NIH
27:11 those **w** I let remain still in their own land, NIH
27:13 Why **w** ye die, thou and thy people, by NIH
27:13 nation that **w** not serve the king of Babylon? NIH
27:22 **w** I bring them up, and restore them to this NIH
28: 3 Within two full years **w** I bring again into NIH
28: 4 I **w** bring again to this place Jeconiah NIH
28: 4 for I **w** break the yoke of the king of NIH
28:11 **w** I break the yoke of Nebuchadnezzar king NIH
28:16 I **w** cast thee from off the face of the earth: NIH
29:10 be accomplished at Babylon I **w** visit you, NIH
29:12 pray unto me, and I **w** hearken unto you. NIH
29:14 And I **w** be found of you, saith the LORD: NIH
29:14 I **w** turn away your captivity, and I will NIH
29:14 and I **w** gather you from all the nations, and NIH
29:14 I **w** bring you again into the place whence I NIH
29:17 Behold, I **w** send upon them the sword, NIH
29:17 and **w** make them like vile figs, NIH
29:18 I **w** persecute them with the sword, with NIH
29:18 **w** deliver them to be removed to all NIH
29:21 I **w** deliver them into the hand of NIH
29:32 I **w** punish Shemaiah the Nehelamite, and NIH
29:32 neither shall he behold the good that I **w** do NIH
30: 3 that I **w** bring again the captivity of my NIH
30: 3 I **w** cause them to return to the land that I NIH
30: 8 *that* I **w** break his yoke from off thy neck, NIH
30: 8 **w** burst thy bonds, and strangers shall no NIH
30: 9 their king, whom I **w** raise up unto them. NIH
30:10 I **w** save thee from afar, and thy seed from NIH
30:11 yet **w** I not make a full end of thee: NIH
30:11 I **w** correct thee in measure, and will not NIH
30:11 and **w** not leave thee altogether unpunished. NIH
30:16 all that prey upon thee **w** I give for a prey. NIH
30:17 For I **w** restore health unto thee, and I will NIH
30:17 I **w** heal thee of thy wounds, saith NIH
30:18 I **w** bring again the captivity of Jacob's NIH
30:19 I **w** multiply them, and they shall not be NIH
30:19 I **w** also glorify them, and they shall not be NIH
30:20 and I **w** punish all that oppress them. NIH
30:21 I **w** cause him to draw near, and he shall NIH
30:22 ye shall be my people, and I **w** be your God. NIH
31: 1 **w** I be the God of all the families of Israel, NIH
31: 4 Again I **w** build thee, and thou shalt be NIH
31: 8 I **w** bring them from the north country, and NIH
31: 9 and with supplications **w** I lead them: NIH
31: 9 I **w** cause them to walk by the rivers of NIH
31:10 He that scattered Israel **w** gather him, and NIH
31:13 for I **w** turn their mourning into joy, and NIH
31:13 **w** comfort them, and make them rejoice NIH
31:14 I **w** satiate the soul of the priests with NIH
31:20 I **w** surely have mercy upon him, saith NIH
31:27 that I **w** sow the house of Israel and NIH
31:28 so **w** I watch over them, to build, and NIH
31:31 that I **w** make a new covenant with NIH
31:33 this *shall be* the covenant that I **w** make NIH
31:33 I **w** put my law in their inward parts, and NIH
31:33 **w** be their God, and they shall be my NIH
31:34 for I **w** forgive their iniquity, and I will NIH
31:34 and I **w** remember their sin no more. NIH
31:37 I **w** also cast off all the seed of Israel for all NIH
32: 3 I **w** give this city into the hand of the king NIH
32:28 I **w** give this city into the hand of NIH
32:37 Behold, I **w** gather them out of all countries, NIH
32:37 I **w** bring them again unto this place, NIH
32:37 and I **w** cause them to dwell safely: NIH
32:38 shall be my people, and I **w** be their God: NIH
32:39 I **w** give them one heart, and one way, NIH
32:40 I **w** make an everlasting covenant with NIH
32:40 that I **w** not turn away from them, to do NIH
32:40 I **w** put my fear in their hearts, that *they* NIH
32:41 I **w** rejoice over them to do them good, NIH
32:41 I **w** plant them in this land assuredly with NIH
32:42 **w** I bring upon them all the good that I have NIH
32:44 for I **w** cause their captivity to return, NIH
33: 3 I **w** answer thee, and shew thee great and NIH
33: 6 I **w** bring it health and cure, and I will cure NIH
33: 6 I **w** cure them, and will reveal unto them NIH
33: 6 **w** reveal unto them the abundance of peace NIH
33: 7 I **w** cause the captivity of Judah and NIH
33: 7 to return, and **w** build them, as at the first. NIH
33: 8 I **w** cleanse them from all their iniquity, NIH
33: 8 I **w** pardon all their iniquities, whereby they NIH
33:11 For I **w** cause to return the captivity of NIH
33:14 that I **w** perform *that* good thing which I NIH
33:15 **w** I cause the Branch of righteousness to NIH

Jer 33:22 w I multiply the seed of David my servant, NIH
33:26 w I cast away the seed of Jacob, and NIH
33:26 that *I* w not take *any* of his seed *to be* rulers NIH
33:26 for I w cause their captivity to return, NIH
34: 2 I w give this city into the hand of the king NIH
34: 5 and they w lament thee, *saying,* Ah lord! NIH
34:17 I w make you to be removed into all NIH
34:18 I w give the men that have transgressed my NIH
34:20 I w even give them into the hand of their NIH
34:21 his princes w I give into the hand of their NIH
34:22 Behold, I w command, saith the LORD, NIH
34:22 I w make the cities of Judah a desolation NIH
35: 6 they said, We w drink no wine: for Jonadab NIH
35:13 W ye not receive instruction to hearken to NIH
35:17 I w bring upon Judah and upon all NIH
36: 3 It may be that the house of Judah w hear all NIH
36: 7 It may be they w present their supplication NIH
36: 7 and w return every one from his evil way: NIH
36:16 We w surely tell the king of all these words. NIH
36:31 I w punish him and his seed and his servants NIH
36:31 I w bring upon them, and upon NIH
38:14 said unto Jeremiah, I w ask thee a thing; NIH
38:16 made us this soul, I w not put thee to death, NIH
38:16 neither w I give thee into the hand of these NIH
38:25 not from us, and we w not put thee to death; NIH
39:16 I w bring my words upon this city for evil, NIH
39:17 I w deliver thee in that day, saith NIH
39:18 For I w surely deliver thee, and thou shalt NIH
40: 4 come; and I w look well unto thee: NIH
40:10 I w dwell at Mizpah to serve the Chaldeans, NIH
40:10 serve the Chaldeans, which w come unto us: NIH
40:15 I w slay Ishmael the son of Nethaniah, and NIH
42: 4 I w pray unto the LORD your God NIH
42: 4 shall answer you, I w declare *it* unto you; NIH
42: 4 unto you; I w keep nothing back from you. NIH
42: 6 we w obey the voice of the LORD our NIH
42:10 If ye w still abide in this land, then will I NIH
42:10 w I build you, and not pull *you* down, and NIH
42:10 and I w plant you, and not pluck *you* up: NIH
42:12 I w shew mercies unto you, that he may NIH
42:13 if ye say, We w not dwell in this land, NIH
42:14 we w go *into* the land of Egypt, where we NIH
42:14 hunger of bread; and there w we dwell: NIH
42:17 escape from the evil that I w bring upon NIH
42:20 so declare unto us, and we w do *it.* NIH
43:10 I w send and take Nebuchadrezzar the king NIH
43:10 w set his throne upon these stones that I NIH
43:12 I w kindle a fire in the houses of the gods of NIH
44:11 I w set my face against you for evil, and NIH
44:12 I w take the remnant of Judah, that have set NIH
44:13 For I w punish them that dwell in the land NIH
44:16 of the LORD, we w not hearken unto thee. NIH
44:17 we w certainly do whatsoever thing goeth NIH
44:25 We w surely perform our vows that we have NIH
44:25 ye w surely accomplish your vows, and NIH
44:27 I w watch over them for evil, and not for NIH
44:29 that I w punish you in this place, NIH
44:30 I w give Pharaoh-hophra king of Egypt into NIH
45: 4 *that* which I have built w I break down, and NIH
45: 4 *that* which I have planted I w pluck up, NIH
45: 5 for behold, I w bring evil upon all flesh, NIH
45: 5 thy life w I give unto thee for a prey in all NIH
46: 8 he saith, I w go up, *and* will cover the earth; NIH
46: 8 he saith, I will go up, *and* w cover the earth; NIH
46: 8 I w destroy the city and the inhabitants NIH
46:25 I w punish the multitude of No, and NIH
46:26 I w deliver them into the hand of those that NIH
46:27 I w save thee from afar off, and thy seed NIH
46:28 for I w make a full end of all the nations NIH
46:28 I w not make a full end of thee, but NIH
46:28 yet w I not leave thee wholly unpunished. NIH
47: 4 for the LORD w spoil the Philistines, NIH
47: 6 how long w *it be* ere thou be quiet? NIH
48:12 that I w send unto him wanderers, NIH
48:31 Therefore w I howl for Moab, and I will cry NIH
48:31 for Moab, and I w cry out for all Moab; NIH
48:32 I w weep for thee with the weeping of Jazer: NIH
48:35 Moreover I w cause to cease in Moab, NIH
48:44 for I w bring upon it, *even* upon Moab, NIH
48:47 Yet w I bring again the captivity of Moab in NIH
49: 2 that I w cause an alarm of war to be heard in NIH
49: 5 Behold, I w bring a fear upon thee, saith NIH
49: 6 afterward I w bring again the captivity of NIH
49: 8 for I w bring the calamity of Esau upon NIH
49: 8 Esau upon him, the time *that* I w visit him. NIH
49: 9 they w destroy till they have enough. NIH
49:11 fatherless children, I w preserve *them* alive; NIH
49:15 I w make thee small among the heathen, *and* NIH
49:16 I w bring thee down from thence, saith NIH
49:19 I w suddenly make him run away from her: NIH
49:19 who w appoint me the time? and who *is* that NIH
49:19 who *is* that shepherd that w stand before NIH
49:27 I w kindle a fire in the wall of Damascus, NIH
49:32 I w scatter into all winds them *that are* in NIH
49:32 I w bring their calamity from all sides NIH
49:35 Behold, I w break the bow of Elam, NIH
49:36 upon Elam w I bring the four winds from NIH
49:36 and w scatter them towards all those winds; NIH
49:37 For I w cause Elam to be dismayed before NIH
49:37 I w bring evil upon them, *even* my fierce NIH
49:37 I w send the sword after them, till I have NIH
49:38 I w set my throne in Elam, and will destroy NIH
49:38 w destroy from thence the king and NIH
49:39 *that* I w bring again the captivity of Elam, NIH
50: 9 I w raise and cause to come up against NIH
50:18 I w punish the king of Babylon and his land, NIH
50:19 I w bring Israel again to his habitation, and NIH
50:20 for I w pardon them whom I reserve. NIH
50:31 thy day is come, the time *that* I w visit thee. NIH
50:32 I w kindle a fire in his cities, and it shall NIH
50:42 they *are* cruel, and w not shew mercy: NIH
50:44 I w make them suddenly run away from her: NIH
50:44 who w appoint me the time? and who *is* that NIH
50:44 who *is* that shepherd that w stand before NIH
51: 1 I w raise up against Babylon, and NIH

Jer 51: 2 w send unto Babylon fanners, that shall fan NIH
51: 6 he w render unto her a recompence. NIH
51:14 *saying,* Surely I w fill thee *with* men, NIH
51:20 for with thee w I break in pieces the nations, NIH
51:20 and with thee w I destroy kingdoms: NIH
51:21 with thee w I break in pieces the horse and NIH
51:21 with thee w I break in pieces the chariot and NIH
51:22 With thee also w I break in pieces man and NIH
51:22 with thee w I break in pieces old and young; NIH
51:22 with thee w I break in pieces the young man NIH
51:23 I w also break in pieces with thee NIH
51:23 with thee w I break in pieces NIH
51:23 with thee w I break in pieces captains and NIH
51:24 I w render unto Babylon and to all NIH
51:25 I w stretch out mine hand upon thee, and NIH
51:25 and w make thee a burnt mountain. NIH
51:36 I w plead thy cause, and take vengeance for NIH
51:36 I w dry up her sea, and make her springs NIH
51:39 In their heat I w make their feasts, and I will NIH
51:39 I w make them drunken, that they may NIH
51:40 I w bring them down like lambs to NIH
51:44 I w punish Bel in Babylon, and I will bring NIH
51:44 I w bring forth out of his mouth that which NIH
51:47 that I w do judgment upon the graven NIH
51:52 that I w do judgment upon her graven NIH
51:57 I w make drunk her princes, and her wise NIH
51:64 shall not rise from the evil that I w bring NIH
La 3:24 saith my soul; therefore w I hope in him. NIH
3:31 For the Lord w not cast off for ever: NIH
3:32 yet w he have compassion according to NIH
4:16 divided them; he w no more regard them: NIH
4:22 he w no more carry thee away into NIH
4:22 he w visit thine iniquity, O daughter of NIH
4:22 daughter of Edom; he w discover thy sins. NIH
Eze 2: 1 upon thy feet, and I w speak unto thee. NIH
2: 5 whether they w hear, or whether they will NIH
2: 5 they will hear, or whether they w forbear, NIH
2: 7 whether they w hear, or whether they will NIH
2: 7 they will hear, or whether they w forbear: NIH
3: 7 the house of Israel w not hearken unto thee; 14
3: 7 unto thee; for they w not hearken unto me: 14
3:11 whether they w hear, or whether they will NIH
3:11 they will hear, or whether they w forbear. NIH
3:18 but his blood w I require at thine hand. NIH
3:20 but his blood w I require at thine hand. NIH
3:22 into the plain, and I w there talk with thee. NIH
3:26 I w make thy tongue cleave to the roof of NIH
3:27 I w open thy mouth, and thou shalt say unto NIH
4: 8 I w lay bands upon thee, and thou shalt not NIH
4:13 among the Gentiles, whither I w drive them NIH
4:16 I w break the staff of bread in Jerusalem: NIH
5: 2 and I w draw out a sword after them. NIH
5: 8 w execute judgments in the midst of thee in NIH
5: 9 I w do in thee that which I have not done, NIH
5: 9 and whereunto I w not do any more the like, NIH
5:10 I w execute judgments in thee, and NIH
5:10 the whole remnant of thee w I scatter into NIH
5:11 w I also diminish *thee;* neither shall mine NIH
5:11 mine eye spare, neither w I have any pity. NIH
5:12 I w scatter a third *part* into all the winds, NIH
5:12 and I w draw out a sword after them. NIH
5:13 I w cause my fury to rest upon them, and NIH
5:13 to rest upon them, and I w be comforted: NIH
5:14 Moreover I w make thee waste, and NIH
5:16 *and* which I w send to destroy you: NIH
5:16 I w increase the famine upon you, and NIH
5:16 upon you, and w break your staff of bread: NIH
5:17 So w I send upon you famine and NIH
5:17 and I w bring the sword upon thee. NIH
6: 3 w bring a sword upon you, and I will NIH
6: 3 upon you, and I w destroy your high places. NIH
6: 4 I w cast down your slain *men* before your NIH
6: 5 I w lay the dead carcases of the children of NIH
6: 5 I w scatter your bones round about your NIH
6: 8 Yet w I leave a remnant, that ye may have NIH
6:12 thus w I accomplish my fury upon them. NIH
6:14 So w I stretch out mine hand upon them, NIH
7: 3 I w send mine anger upon thee, and NIH
7: 3 and w judge thee according to thy ways, and NIH
7: 3 w recompense upon thee all thine NIH
7: 4 shall not spare thee, neither w I have pity: NIH
7: 4 but I w recompense thy ways upon thee, and NIH
7: 8 Now w I shortly pour out my fury upon NIH
7: 8 I w judge thee according to thy ways, and NIH
7: 8 w recompense thee for all thine NIH
7: 9 eye shall not spare, neither w I have pity: NIH
7: 9 I w recompense thee according to thy ways NIH
7:21 I w give it into the hands of the strangers for NIH
7:22 My face w I turn also from them, and NIH
7:24 Wherefore I w bring the worst of NIH
7:24 I w also make the pomp of the strong to NIH
7:27 I w do unto them after their way, and NIH
7:27 according to their deserts w I judge them; NIH
8:18 Therefore w I also deal in fury: mine eye NIH
8:18 eye shall not spare, neither w I have pity: NIH
8:18 *with* a loud voice, *yet* w I not hear them. NIH
9:10 neither w I have pity, *but* I will recompense NIH
9:10 I w recompense their way upon their head. NIH
11: 7 *I* w bring you forth out of the midst of it. NIH
11: 8 I w bring a sword upon you, saith the Lord NIH
11: 9 I w bring you out of the midst thereof, and NIH
11: 9 and w execute judgments among you. NIH
11:10 I w judge you in the border of Israel; and NIH
11:11 *but* I w judge you in the border of Israel: NIH
11:16 yet w I be to them as a little sanctuary in NIH
11:17 I w even gather you from the people, and NIH
11:17 and I w give you the land of Israel. NIH
11:19 I w give them one heart, and I will put a NIH
11:19 and I w put a new spirit within you; NIH
11:19 I w take the stony heart out of their flesh, NIH
11:19 their flesh, and w give them a heart of flesh: NIH
11:20 shall be my people, and I w be their God. NIH
11:21 I w recompense their way upon their own NIH
12: 3 it may be they w consider, though they *be* a NIH
12:13 My net also w I spread upon him, and NIH

Eze 12:13 I w bring him to Babylon *to* the land of NIH
12:14 I w scatter toward every wind all that *are* NIH
12:14 and I w draw out the sword after them. NIH
12:16 I w leave a few men of them from NIH
12:23 I w make this proverb to cease, and NIH
12:25 I w speak, and the word that I shall speak NIH
12:25 w I say the word, and will perform it, NIH
12:25 will I say the word, and w perform it, NIH
13:13 I w even rent *it with* a stormy wind in my NIH
13:14 So w I break down the wall that ye have NIH
13:15 Thus w I accomplish my wrath upon NIH
13:15 untempered *morter,* and w say unto you, NIH
13:18 W ye hunt the souls of my people, and NIH
13:18 w ye save the souls alive *that come* unto NIH
13:19 w ye pollute me among my people for NIH
13:20 I w tear them from your arms, and will let NIH
13:20 from your arms, and w let the souls go, NIH
13:21 Your kerchiefs also w I tear, and deliver my NIH
13:23 for I w deliver my people out of your hand: NIH
14: 4 I the LORD w answer him that cometh NIH
14: 7 I the LORD w answer him by myself: NIH
14: 8 I w set my face against that man, and NIH
14: 8 w make him a sign and a proverb, and I will NIH
14: 8 I w cut him off from the midst of my NIH
14: 9 I w stretch out my hand upon him, and NIH
14: 9 w destroy him from the midst of my people NIH
14:13 w I stretch out mine hand upon it, and NIH
14:13 w break the staff of the bread thereof, and NIH
14:13 w send famine upon it, and will cut off man NIH
14:13 and w cut off man and beast from it: NIH
15: 3 w *men* take a pin of it to hang any vessel NIH
15: 6 so w I give the inhabitants of Jerusalem. NIH
15: 7 I w set my face against them; they shall go NIH
15: 8 I w make the land desolate, because NIH
16:27 delivered thee unto the w of them that hate 5315
16:37 Behold therefore, I w gather all thy lovers, NIH
16:37 I w even gather them round about against NIH
16:37 w discover thy nakedness unto them, NIH
16:38 I w judge thee, as *women* that break NIH
16:38 I w give thee blood in fury and jealousy. NIH
16:39 I w also give thee into their hand, and NIH
16:41 I w cause thee to cease from playing NIH
16:42 So w I make my fury towards thee to rest, NIH
16:42 and I w be quiet, and will be no more angry. NIH
16:42 and I will be quiet, and w be no more angry. NIH
16:43 I also w recompense thy way upon *thine* NIH
16:53 *w I bring again* the captivity of thy captives NIH
16:59 I w even deal with thee as thou hast done, NIH
16:60 Nevertheless I w remember my covenant NIH
16:60 I w establish unto thee an everlasting NIH
16:61 I w give them unto thee for daughters, but NIH
16:62 I w establish my covenant with thee; and NIH
17:19 even it w I recompense upon his own head. NIH
17:20 I w spread my net upon him, and he shall be NIH
17:20 I w bring him to Babylon, and will plead NIH
17:20 w plead with him there *for* his trespass that NIH
17:22 I w also take of the highest branch of NIH
17:22 w set *it;* I will crop off from the top of his NIH
17:22 will set *it;* I w crop off from the top of his NIH
17:22 w plant *it* upon a high mountain and NIH
17:23 In the mountain of the height of Israel w I NIH
18:21 if the wicked w turn from all his sins that he NIH
18:30 Therefore I w judge you, O house of Israel, NIH
18:31 for why w ye die, O house of Israel? NIH
20: 3 Lord GOD, I w not be inquired of by you. NIH
20: 8 then I said, *I* w pour out my fury upon them, NIH
20:31 Lord GOD, I w not be inquired of by you. NIH
20:32 that ye say, We w be as the heathen, as NIH
20:33 and with fury poured out, w I rule over you: NIH
20:34 I w bring you out from the people, and NIH
20:34 w gather you out of the countries wherein NIH
20:35 I w bring you into the wilderness of NIH
20:35 and there w I plead with you face to face. NIH
20:36 so w I plead with you, saith the Lord NIH
20:37 I w cause you to pass under the rod, and NIH
20:37 I w bring you into the bond of the covenant: NIH
20:38 I w purge out from among you the rebels, NIH
20:38 I w bring them forth out of the country NIH
20:39 hereafter *also,* if ye w not hearken unto me: NIH
20:40 there w I accept them, and there will I NIH
20:40 there w I require your offerings, and NIH
20:41 I w accept you with *your* sweet savour, NIH
20:41 I w be sanctified in you before the heathen. NIH
20:47 I w kindle a fire in thee, and it shall devour NIH
21: 3 w draw forth my sword out of his sheath, NIH
21: 3 w cut off from thee the righteous and NIH
21: 4 that I w cut off from thee the righteous and NIH
21:17 I w also smite mine hands together, and NIH
21:17 and I w cause my fury to rest: NIH
21:23 he w call to remembrance the iniquity, NIH
21:27 I w[S] overturn, overturn, overturn it: and 7760
21:27 come whose right it is; and I w give it *him.* NIH
21:30 I w judge thee in the place where thou wast NIH
21:31 I w pour out mine indignation upon thee, NIH
21:31 I w blow against thee in the fire of my NIH
22:14 I the LORD have spoken *it,* and w do *it.* NIH
22:15 And I w scatter thee among the heathen, and NIH
22:15 and w consume thy filthiness out of thee. NIH
22:19 I w gather you into the midst of Jerusalem. NIH
22:20 melt *it;* so w I gather *you* in mine anger and NIH
22:20 and I w leave *you there,* and melt you. NIH
22:21 I w gather you, and blow upon you in NIH
23:22 Behold, I w raise up thy lovers against thee, NIH
23:22 I w bring them against thee on every side; NIH
23:24 I w set judgment before them, and they shall NIH
23:25 I w set my jealousy against thee, and NIH
23:27 Thus w I make thy lewdness to cease from NIH
23:28 I w deliver thee into the hand of *them* whom NIH
23:30 *I* w do these *things* unto thee, because NIH
23:31 therefore w I give her cup into thine hand. NIH
23:43 W they now commit whoredoms with her, NIH
23:46 *I* w bring up a company upon them, and NIH
23:46 and w give them to be removed and spoiled. NIH
23:48 Thus w I cause lewdness to cease out of NIH
24: 9 I w even make the pile for fire great. NIH

Eze 24:14 I **w** do *it;* I will not go back, neither will I NIH
24:14 I will do *it;* I **w** not go back, neither will I NIH
24:14 neither **w** I spare, neither will I repent; NIH
24:14 neither will I spare, neither **w** I repent; NIH
24:21 Behold, I **w** profane my sanctuary, NIH
25: 4 I **w** deliver thee to the men of the east for a NIH
25: 5 I **w** make Rabbah a stable for camels, and NIH
25: 7 I **w** stretch out mine hand upon thee, and NIH
25: 7 and **w** deliver thee for a spoil to the heathen; NIH
25: 7 I **w** cut thee off from the people, and I will NIH
25: 7 I **w** cause thee to perish out of the countries: NIH
25: 7 I **w** destroy thee; and thou shalt know that I NIH
25: 9 I **w** open the side of Moab from the cities, NIH
25:10 and **w** give them in possession, NIH
25:11 And I **w** execute judgments upon Moab; and NIH
25:13 I **w** also stretch out mine hand upon Edom, NIH
25:13 and **w** cut off man and beast from it; NIH
25:13 I **w** make it desolate from Teman; and NIH
25:14 I **w** lay my vengeance upon Edom by NIH
25:16 I **w** stretch out mine hand upon NIH
25:16 I **w** cut off the Cherethims, and destroy NIH
25:17 I **w** execute great vengeance upon them NIH
26: 3 **w** cause many nations to come up against NIH
26: 4 I **w** also scrape her dust from her, and NIH
26: 7 I **w** bring upon Tyrus Nebuchadrezzar king NIH
26:13 I **w** cause the noise of thy songs to cease; NIH
26:14 I **w** make thee like the top of a rock: NIH
26:21 I **w** make thee a terror, and thou *shalt be* no NIH
28: 7 I **w** bring strangers upon thee, NIH
28:16 I **w** cast thee as profane out of the mountain NIH
28:16 I **w** destroy thee, O covering cherub, NIH
28:17 I **w** cast thee to the ground, I will lay thee NIH
28:17 I **w** lay thee before kings, that *they* may NIH
28:18 **w** I bring forth a fire from the midst of thee, NIH
28:18 I **w** bring thee to ashes upon the earth in NIH
28:22 and I **w** be glorified in the midst of thee: NIH
28:23 For I **w** send into her pestilence, and NIH
29: 4 I **w** put hooks in thy jaws, and I will cause NIH
29: 4 I **w** cause the fish of thy rivers to stick unto NIH
29: 4 I **w** bring thee up out of the midst of thy NIH
29: 5 I **w** leave thee *thrown* into the wilderness, NIH
29: 8 I **w** bring a sword upon thee, and cut off NIH
29:10 I **w** make the land of Egypt utterly waste NIH
29:12 I **w** make the land of Egypt desolate in NIH
29:12 I **w** scatter the Egyptians among the nations, NIH
29:12 and **w** disperse them through the countries. NIH
29:13 At the end of forty years **w** I gather NIH
29:14 I **w** bring again the captivity of Egypt, and NIH
29:14 **w** cause them to return *into* the land of NIH
29:15 for I **w** diminish them, that *they* shall no NIH
29:19 I **w** give the land of Egypt unto NIH
29:21 In that day **w** I cause the horn of the house NIH
29:21 I **w** give thee the opening of the mouth in NIH
30:10 I **w** also make the multitude of Egypt to NIH
30:12 I **w** make the rivers dry, and sell the land NIH
30:12 I **w** make the land waste, and all that is NIH
30:13 I **w** also destroy the idols, and I will cause NIH
30:13 I **w** cause *their* images to cease out of Noph; NIH
30:13 and I **w** put a fear in the land of Egypt. NIH
30:14 I **w** make Pathros desolate, and will set fire NIH
30:14 **w** set fire in Zoan, and will execute NIH
30:14 in Zoan, and **w** execute judgments in No. NIH
30:15 I **w** pour my fury upon Sin, the strength of NIH
30:15 and I **w** cut off the multitude of No. NIH
30:16 I **w** set fire in Egypt: Sin shall have great NIH
30:19 Thus **w** I execute judgments in Egypt: and NIH
30:22 **w** break his arms, the strong, and that which NIH
30:22 I **w** cause the sword to fall out of his hand. NIH
30:23 I **w** scatter the Egyptians among the nations, NIH
30:23 and **w** disperse them through the countries. NIH
30:24 I **w** strengthen the arms of the king of NIH
30:24 I **w** break Pharaoh's arms, and he shall NIH
30:25 I **w** strengthen the arms of the king of NIH
30:26 I **w** scatter the Egyptians among the nations, NIH
32: 3 I **w** therefore spread out my net over thee NIH
32: 4 **w** I leave thee upon the land, I will cast thee NIH
32: 4 I **w** cast thee forth upon the open field, and NIH
32: 4 **w** cause all the fowls of the heaven to NIH
32: 4 I **w** fill the beasts of the whole earth with NIH
32: 5 I **w** lay thy flesh upon the mountains, and NIH
32: 6 I **w** also water with thy blood the land NIH
32: 7 I **w** cover the heaven, and make the stars NIH
32: 7 I **w** cover the sun with a cloud, and NIH
32: 8 All the bright lights of heaven **w** I make NIH
32: 9 I **w** also vex the hearts of many people, NIH
32:10 I **w** make many people amazed at thee, and NIH
32:12 By the swords of the mighty **w** I cause thy NIH
32:13 I **w** destroy also all the beasts thereof from NIH
32:14 **w** I make their waters deep, and cause their NIH
33: 6 his blood **w** I require at the watchman's NIH
33: 8 but his blood **w** I require at thine hand. NIH
33:11 for why **w** ye die, O house of Israel? NIH
33:20 I **w** judge you every one after his ways. NIH
33:27 him that *is* in the open field **w** I give to NIH
33:28 For I **w** lay the land most desolate, and NIH
33:31 hear thy words, but they **w** not do them: NIH
33:33 when this cometh to pass, (lo, it **w** come) NIH
34:10 I **w** require my flock at their hand, and NIH
34:10 for I **w** deliver my flock from their mouth, NIH
34:11 **w** both search my sheep, and seek them out. NIH
34:12 so **w** I seek out my sheep, and will deliver NIH
34:12 **w** deliver them out of all places where they NIH
34:13 I **w** bring them out from the people, and NIH
34:13 **w** bring them to their own land, and NIH
34:14 I **w** feed them in a good pasture, and NIH
34:15 I **w** feed my flock, and I will cause them to NIH
34:15 my flock, and I **w** cause them to lie down, NIH
34:16 I **w** seek that which was lost, and bring NIH
34:16 **w** bind up that which was broken, and NIH
34:16 and **w** strengthen that which was sick: NIH
34:16 I **w** destroy the fat and the strong; I will NIH
34:16 the strong; I **w** feed them with judgment. NIH
34:20 **w** judge between the fat cattle and NIH
34:22 Therefore **w** I save my flock, and they shall NIH
34:22 and I **w** judge between cattle and cattle. NIH

Eze 34:23 And I **w** set up one shepherd over them, and NIH
34:24 I the LORD **w** be their God, and NIH
34:25 I **w** make with them a covenant of peace, NIH
34:25 **w** cause the evil beasts to cease out of NIH
34:26 I **w** make them and the places round about NIH
34:26 I **w** cause the shower to come down in his NIH
34:29 I **w** raise up for them a plant of renown, NIH
35: 3 I **w** stretch out mine hand against thee, and NIH
35: 3 and I **w** make thee most desolate. NIH
35: 4 I **w** lay thy cities waste, and thou shalt be NIH
35: 6 I **w** prepare thee unto blood, and blood shall NIH
35: 7 Thus **w** I make mount Seir most desolate, NIH
35: 8 I **w** fill his mountains *with* his slain *men:* in NIH
35: 9 I **w** make thee perpetual desolations, and NIH
35:10 shall be mine, and we **w** possess it; NIH
35:11 I **w** even do according to thine anger, and NIH
35:11 and I **w** make myself known amongst them, NIH
35:14 earth rejoiceth, I **w** make thee desolate. NIH
35:15 because it was desolate, so **w** I do unto thee: NIH
36: 9 I **w** turn unto you, and ye shall be tilled and NIH
36:10 I **w** multiply men upon you, all the house of NIH
36:11 I **w** multiply upon you man and beast; and NIH
36:11 and I **w** settle you after your old estates, and NIH
36:11 **w** do better *unto you* than at your NIH
36:12 Yea, I **w** cause men to walk upon you, NIH
36:15 Neither **w** I cause *men* to hear in thee NIH
36:23 I **w** sanctify my great name, which was NIH
36:24 For I **w** take you from among the heathen, NIH
36:24 and **w** bring you into your own land. NIH
36:25 **w** I sprinkle clean water upon you, and NIH
36:25 and from all your idols, **w** I cleanse you. NIH
36:26 A new heart also **w** I give you, and a new NIH
36:26 and a new spirit **w** I put within you: NIH
36:26 I **w** take away the stony heart out of your NIH
36:26 your flesh, and I **w** give you a heart of flesh. NIH
36:27 I **w** put my spirit within you, and cause you NIH
36:28 ye shall be my people, and I **w** be your God. NIH
36:29 I **w** also save you from all your NIH
36:29 I **w** call for the corn, and will increase it, NIH
36:29 **w** increase it, and lay no famine upon you. NIH
36:30 I **w** multiply the fruit of the tree, and NIH
36:33 I **w** also cause *you* to dwell in the cities, and NIH
36:36 I the LORD have spoken *it,* and I **w** do *it.* NIH
36:37 I **w** yet *for* this be inquired of by the house NIH
36:37 I **w** increase them *with* men like a flock. NIH
37: 5 I **w** cause breath to enter into you, and NIH
37: 6 I **w** lay sinews upon you, and will bring up NIH
37: 6 **w** bring up flesh upon you, and cover you NIH
37:12 I **w** open your graves, and cause you to NIH
37:19 Behold, I **w** take the stick of Joseph, NIH
37:19 **w** put them with him, *even* with the stick of NIH
37:21 I **w** take the children of Israel from among NIH
37:21 **w** gather them on every side, and NIH
37:22 I **w** make them one nation in the land upon NIH
37:23 I **w** save them out of all their dwelling NIH
37:23 they have sinned, and **w** cleanse them: NIH
37:23 they be my people, and I **w** be their God. NIH
37:26 Moreover I **w** make a covenant of peace NIH
37:26 I **w** place them, and multiply them, and NIH
37:26 **w** set my sanctuary in the midst of them for NIH
37:27 I **w** be their God, and they shall be my NIH
38: 4 I **w** turn thee back, and put hooks into thy NIH
38: 4 I **w** bring thee forth, and all thine army, NIH
38:11 I **w** go up to the land of unwalled villages; NIH
38:11 I **w** go *to* them that are at rest, that dwell NIH
38:16 and I **w** bring thee against my land, NIH
38:21 I **w** call *for* a sword against him throughout NIH
38:22 I **w** plead against him with pestilence and NIH
38:22 I **w** rain upon him, and upon his bands, and NIH
38:23 Thus **w** I magnify myself, and NIH
38:23 I **w** be known in the eyes of many nations, NIH
39: 2 I **w** turn thee back, and leave but the sixth NIH
39: 2 **w** cause thee to come up from the north NIH
39: 2 **w** bring thee upon the mountains of Israel: NIH
39: 3 I **w** smite thy bow out of thy left hand, and NIH
39: 3 **w** cause thine arrows to fall out of thy right NIH
39: 4 I **w** give thee unto the ravenous birds of NIH
39: 6 I **w** send a fire on Magog, and among them NIH
39: 7 So **w** I make my holy name known in NIH
39: 7 I **w** not let *them* pollute my holy name any NIH
39:11 *that* I **w** give unto Gog a place there of NIH
39:21 I **w** set my glory among the heathen, and NIH
39:25 Now **w** I bring again the captivity of Jacob, NIH
39:25 and **w** be jealous for my holy name; NIH
39:29 Neither **w** I hide my face any more from NIH
43: 7 where I **w** dwell in the midst of the children NIH
43: 9 and I **w** dwell in the midst of them for ever. NIH
43:27 and I **w** accept you, saith the Lord GOD. NIH
44:14 I **w** make them keepers of the charge of NIH
Da 2: 4 and we **w** shew the interpretation. NIH
2: 5 if ye **w** not make known unto me the dream, NIH
2: 7 and we **w** shew the interpretation of it. NIH
2: 9 if ye **w** not make known unto me the dream, NIH
2:24 I **w** shew unto the king the interpretation. NIH
2:25 that **w** make known unto the king NIH
2:36 we **w** tell the interpretation thereof before NIH
3:17 he **w** deliver *us* out of thine hand, O king. NIH
3:18 O king, that we **w** not serve thy gods, 383
4:17 giveth it to whomsoever he **w**, and 6634
4:25 of men, and giveth it to whomsoever he **w**. 6634
4:32 of men, and giveth it to whomsoever he **w**. 6634
4:35 he doeth according to his **w** in the army of 6634
5:12 be called, and he **w** shew the interpretation. NIH
5:17 yet I **w** read the writing unto the king, and NIH
5:21 he appointeth over it whomsoever he **w**. 6634
6:16 thou servest continually, he **w** deliver thee. NIH
8: 4 he did according to his **w**, and 7522
8:19 I **w** make thee know what shall be in the last NIH
10:20 now **w** I return to fight with the prince of NIH
10:21 I **w** shew thee that which is noted in NIH
11: 2 now **w** I shew thee the truth. Behold, NIH
11: 3 great dominion, and do according to his **w**. 7522
11:16 him shall do according to his own **w**, 7522
11:36 the king shall do according to his **w**; and 7522
Hos 1: 4 I **w** avenge the blood of Jezreel upon NIH

Hos 1: 4 **w** cause to cease the kingdom of the house NIH
1: 5 that I **w** break the bow of Israel in the valley NIH
1: 6 for I **w** no more have mercy upon the house NIH
1: 6 of Israel; but I **w** utterly take them away. NIH
1: 7 I **w** have mercy upon the house of Judah, NIH
1: 7 **w** save them by the LORD their God, and NIH
1: 7 **w** not save them by bow, nor by sword, NIH
1: 9 not my people, and I **w** not be your *God.* NIH
2: 4 I **w** not have mercy upon her children; NIH
2: 5 for she said, I **w** go after my lovers, NIH
2: 6 I **w** hedge up thy way with thorns, and NIH
2: 7 I **w** go and return to my first husband; NIH
2: 9 Therefore **w** I return, and take *away* my NIH
2: 9 **w** recover my wool and my flax *given* to NIH
2:10 now **w** I discover her lewdness in the sight NIH
2:11 I **w** also cause all her mirth to cease, NIH
2:12 I **w** destroy her vines and her fig trees, NIH
2:12 I **w** make them a forest, and the beasts of NIH
2:13 I **w** visit upon her the days of Baalim, NIH
2:14 I **w** allure her, and bring her *into* NIH
2:15 And I **w** give her her vineyards from thence, NIH
2:17 For I **w** take away the names of Baalim out NIH
2:18 in that day **w** I make a covenant for them NIH
2:18 I **w** break the bow and the sword and NIH
2:18 and **w** make them to lie down safely. NIH
2:19 I **w** betroth thee unto me for ever; yea, I will NIH
2:19 I **w** betroth thee unto me in righteousness, NIH
2:20 I **w** even betroth thee unto me in NIH
2:21 I **w** hear, saith the LORD, I will hear NIH
2:21 I **w** hear the heavens, and they shall hear NIH
2:23 I **w** sow her unto me in the earth; and I will NIH
2:23 I **w** have mercy upon her that had not NIH
2:23 I **w** say to *them which were* not my people, NIH
3: 3 be for *another* man: so **w** I also *be* for thee. NIH
4: 5 *in* the night, and I **w** destroy thy mother. NIH
4: 6 rejected knowledge, I **w** also reject thee, NIH
4: 6 law of thy God, I **w** also forget thy children. NIH
4: 7 *therefore* **w** I change their glory into shame. NIH
4: 9 I **w** punish them for their ways, and NIH
4:14 I **w** not punish your daughters when they NIH
4:16 now the LORD **w** feed them as a lamb in a NIH
5: 4 They **w** not frame their doings to turn unto NIH
5:10 I **w** pour out my wrath upon them like NIH
5:12 Therefore **w** I *be* unto Ephraim as a moth, NIH
5:14 For I **w** *be* unto Ephraim as a lion, and as a NIH
5:14 I, *even* I, **w** tear and go away; I will take NIH
5:14 I **w** take away, and none shall rescue *him.* NIH
5:15 I **w** go *and* return to my place, till they NIH
5:15 in their affliction they **w** seek me early. NIH
6: 1 for he hath torn, and he **w** heal us; he hath NIH
6: 1 he hath smitten, and he **w** bind us up. NIH
6: 2 After two days **w** he revive us: in the third NIH
6: 2 in the third day he **w** raise us up, and NIH
7:12 they shall go, I **w** spread my net upon them; NIH
7:12 I **w** bring them down as the fowls of NIH
7:12 I **w** chastise them, as their congregation NIH
8: 5 how long **w** *it be* ere they attain to NIH
8:10 now **w** I gather them, and they shall sorrow NIH
8:13 now **w** he remember their iniquity, and NIH
8:14 I **w** send a fire upon his cities, and it shall NIH
9: 5 What **w** ye do in the solemn day, and in NIH
9: 9 *therefore* he **w** remember their iniquity, NIH
9: 9 their iniquity, he **w** visit their sins. NIH
9:12 up their children, yet **w** I bereave them, NIH
9:15 for the wickedness of their doings I **w** drive NIH
9:15 out of mine house, I **w** love them no more: NIH
9:16 yet **w** I slay *even* the beloved *fruit* of their NIH
9:17 My God **w** cast them away, because NIH
10:11 I **w** make Ephraim to ride; Judah shall plow, NIH
11: 9 I **w** not execute the fierceness of mine NIH
11: 9 I **w** not return to destroy Ephraim: NIH
11: 9 midst of thee: and I **w** not enter into the city. NIH
11:11 I **w** place them in their houses, saith NIH
12: 2 and **w** punish Jacob according to his ways; NIH
12: 2 according to his doings **w** he recompense NIH
12: 9 **w** yet make thee to dwell in tabernacles, NIH
13: 7 Therefore I **w** be unto them as a lion: as a NIH
13: 7 as a leopard by the way **w** I observe *them:* NIH
13: 8 I **w** meet them as a bear *that is* bereaved of NIH
13: 8 **w** rent the caul of their heart, and there will NIH
13: 8 and there **w** I devour them like a lion: NIH
13:10 I **w** be thy king: where *is any other* that may NIH
13:14 I **w** ransom them from the power of NIH
13:14 of the grave; I **w** redeem them from death: NIH
13:14 O death, I **w** be thy plagues; O grave, I will NIH
13:14 thy plagues; O grave, I **w** be thy destruction: NIH
14: 2 so **w** we render the calves of our lips. NIH
14: 3 we **w** not ride upon horses: neither will we NIH
14: 3 neither **w** we say any more to the work of NIH
14: 4 I **w** heal their backsliding, I will love them NIH
14: 4 heal their backsliding, I **w** love them freely: NIH
14: 5 I **w** be as the dew unto Israel: he shall grow NIH
Joel 1:19 O LORD, to thee **w** I cry: for the fire hath NIH
2:14 Who knoweth *if* he **w** return and repent, and NIH
2:18 **w** the LORD be jealous for his land, and NIH
2:19 the LORD **w** answer and say unto his NIH
2:19 I **w** send you corn, and wine, and oil, and NIH
2:19 I **w** no more make you a reproach among NIH
2:20 I **w** remove far off from you the northern NIH
2:20 **w** drive him into a land barren and desolate, NIH
2:21 rejoice: for the LORD **w** do great things. NIH
2:23 he **w** cause to come down for you the rain, NIH
2:25 I **w** restore to you the years that the locust NIH
2:28 that I **w** pour out my spirit upon all flesh; NIH
2:29 upon the handmaids in those days **w** I pour NIH
2:30 I **w** shew wonders in the heavens and in NIH
3: 2 I **w** also gather all nations, and will bring NIH
3: 2 **w** bring them down into the valley of NIH
3: 2 **w** plead with them there for my people and NIH
3: 4 **w** ye render me a recompence? and if ye NIH
3: 4 speedily **w** I return your recompence upon NIH
3: 7 I **w** raise them out of the place whither ye NIH
3: 7 **w** return your recompence upon your own NIH
3: 8 I **w** sell your sons and your daughters into NIH
3:12 for there **w** I sit to judge all the heathen NIH

Joel 3:16 but the LORD **w** *be* the hope of his people, NIH
3:21 For I **w** cleanse their blood *that* I have not NIH
Am 1: 2 The LORD **w** roar from Zion, and utter his NIH
1: 3 I **w** not turn away *the punishment* thereof; NIH
1: 4 But I **w** send a fire into the house of Hazael, NIH
1: 5 I **w** break also the bar of Damascus, and NIH
1: 6 I **w** not turn away *the punishment* thereof; NIH
1: 7 I **w** send a fire on the wall of Gaza, NIH
1: 8 And I **w** cut off the inhabitant from Ashdod, NIH
1: 8 and I **w** turn mine hand against Ekron: NIH
1: 9 I **w** not turn away *the punishment* thereof; NIH
1:10 I **w** send a fire on the wall of Tyrus, NIH
1:11 I **w** not turn away *the punishment* thereof; NIH
1:12 I **w** send a fire upon the Teman, which shall NIH
1:13 I **w** not turn away *the punishment* thereof; NIH
1:14 I **w** kindle a fire in the wall of Rabbah, and NIH
2: 1 I **w** not turn away *the punishment* thereof; NIH
2: 2 I **w** send a fire upon Moab, and it shall NIH
2: 3 I **w** cut off the judge from the midst thereof, NIH
2: 3 **w** slay all the princes thereof with him, NIH
2: 4 I **w** not turn away *the punishment* thereof; NIH
2: 5 I **w** send a fire upon Judah, and it shall NIH
2: 6 I **w** not turn away *the punishment* thereof; NIH
2: 7 and his father **w** go in unto the *same* maid, NIH
3: 2 I **w** punish you for all your iniquities. NIH
3: 4 **W** a lion roar in the forest, when he hath no NIH
3: 4 **w** a young lion cry out of his den, if he have NIH
3: 7 Surely the Lord GOD **w** do nothing, but he NIH
3: 8 The lion hath roared, who **w** not fear? NIH
3:14 upon him I **w** also visit the altars of Beth-el: NIH
3:15 I **w** smite the winter house with the summer NIH
4: 2 that he **w** take you away with hooks, and NIH
4:12 Therefore thus **w** I do unto thee, O Israel: NIH
4:12 *and* because I **w** do this unto thee, NIH
5:15 it may be that the LORD God of hosts **w** NIH
5:17 for I **w** pass through thee, saith the LORD. NIH
5:21 I **w** not smell in your solemn assemblies. NIH
5:22 I **w** not accept *them:* neither will I regard NIH
5:22 I will not accept *them:* neither **w** I regard NIH
5:23 for I **w** not hear the melody of thy viols. NIH
5:27 Therefore **w** I cause you to go into captivity NIH
6: 8 **w** I deliver up the city with all that is NIH
6:11 he **w** smite the great house *with* breaches, NIH
6:12 **w** *one* plow *there* with oxen? for ye have NIH
6:14 I **w** raise up against you a nation, NIH
7: 8 I **w** set a plumbline in the midst of my NIH
7: 8 I **w** not again pass by them any more: NIH
7: 9 I **w** rise against the house of Jeroboam with NIH
8: 2 I **w** not again pass by them any more. NIH
8: 5 Saying, When **w** the new moon be gone, NIH
8: 7 Surely I **w** never forget any of their works. NIH
8: 9 that I **w** cause the sun to go down at noon, NIH
8: 9 and I **w** darken the earth in the clear day: NIH
8:10 And I **w** turn your feasts into mourning, and NIH
8:10 I **w** bring up sackcloth upon all loins, and NIH
8:10 I **w** make it as the mourning of an only *son,* NIH
8:11 that I **w** send a famine in the land, NIH
9: 1 and I **w** slay the last of them with the sword: NIH
9: 2 up *to* heaven, thence **w** I bring them down: NIH
9: 3 I **w** search and take them out thence; NIH
9: 3 thence **w** I command the serpent, and NIH
9: 4 thence **w** I command the sword, and it shall NIH
9: 4 I **w** set mine eyes upon them for evil, and NIH
9: 8 I **w** destroy it from off the face of the earth; NIH
9: 8 saving that I **w** not utterly destroy the house NIH
9: 9 I **w** command, and I will sift the house of NIH
9: 9 I **w** sift the house of Israel among all NIH
9:11 In that day **w** I raise up the tabernacle of NIH
9:11 I **w** raise up his ruins, and I will build it as NIH
9:11 and I **w** build it as *in* the days of old: NIH
9:14 I **w** bring again the captivity of my people NIH
9:15 I **w** plant them upon their land, and NIH
Ob 1: 4 thence **w** I bring thee down, saith NIH
Jnh 1: 6 if so be that God **w** think upon us, that we NIH
2: 4 yet I **w** look again toward thy holy temple. NIH
2: 9 I **w** sacrifice unto thee with the voice of NIH
2: 9 I **w** pay *that* that I have vowed. NIH
3: 9 Who can tell *if* God **w** turn and repent, and NIH
Mic 1: 3 **w** come down and tread upon the high NIH
1: 6 Therefore I **w** make Samaria as a heap of NIH
1: 6 I **w** pour down the stones thereof into NIH
1: 6 and I **w** discover the foundations thereof. NIH
1: 7 and all the idols thereof **w** I lay desolate: NIH
1: 8 Therefore I **w** wail and howl, I will go stript NIH
1: 8 will wail and howl, I **w** go stript and naked: NIH
1: 8 I **w** make a wailing like the dragons, and NIH
1:15 Yet **w** I bring an heir unto thee, O inhabitant NIH
2:11 *saying,* I **w** prophesy unto thee of wine and NIH
2:12 I **w** surely assemble, O Jacob, all of thee; NIH
2:12 I **w** surely gather the remnant of Israel; NIH
2:12 I **w** put them together as the sheep of NIH
3: 4 unto the LORD, but he **w** not hear them: NIH
3: 4 he **w** even hide his face from them at that NIH
3:11 yet **w** they lean upon the LORD, and say, NIH
4: 2 he **w** teach us of his ways, and we will walk NIH
4: 2 us of his ways, and we **w** walk in his paths: NIH
4: 5 For all people **w** walk every one in the name NIH
4: 5 we **w** walk in the name of the LORD our NIH
4: 6 **w** I assemble her that halteth, and I will NIH
4: 6 I **w** gather her that is driven out, and *her* that NIH
4: 7 I **w** make her that halted a remnant, and NIH
4:13 for I **w** make thine horn iron, and I will NIH
4:13 horn iron, and I **w** make thy hoofs brass: NIH
4:13 I **w** consecrate their gain unto the LORD, NIH
5: 3 Therefore **w** he give them up, until the time NIH
5:10 that I **w** cut off thy horses out of the midst NIH
5:10 midst of thee, and I **w** destroy thy chariots: NIH
5:11 I **w** cut off the cities of thy land, and NIH
5:12 I **w** cut off witchcrafts out of thine hand; NIH
5:13 Thy graven images also **w** I cut off, and NIH
5:14 I **w** pluck up thy groves out of the midst of NIH
5:14 the midst of thee: so **w** I destroy thy cities. NIH
5:15 I **w** execute vengeance in anger and fury NIH
6: 2 with his people, and he **w** plead with Israel. NIH
6: 7 **W** the LORD be pleased with thousands of NIH

Mic 6:13 Therefore also **w** I make *thee* sick in NIH
6:14 *that* which thou deliverest **w** I give up to NIH
7: 7 Therefore I **w** look unto the LORD; I will NIH
7: 7 I **w** wait for the God of my salvation: NIH
7: 7 God of my salvation: my God **w** hear me. NIH
7: 9 I **w** bear the indignation of the LORD, NIH
7: 9 he **w** bring me forth to the light, *and* I shall NIH
7:15 **w** I shew unto him marvellous *things.* NIH
7:19 He **w** turn again, he will have compassion NIH
7:19 turn again, he **w** have compassion upon us; NIH
7:19 he **w** subdue our iniquities; and thou wilt NIH
Na 1: 2 the LORD **w** take vengeance on his NIH
1: 3 **w** not at all acquit *the wicked:* the LORD NIH
1: 8 with an overrunning flood he **w** make an NIH
1: 9 he **w** make an utter end: affliction shall not NIH
1:12 have afflicted thee, I **w** afflict thee no more. NIH
1:13 For now **w** I break his yoke from off thee, NIH
1:13 off thee, and **w** burst thy bonds in sunder. NIH
1:14 out of the house of thy gods **w** I cut off NIH
1:14 I **w** make thy grave; for thou art vile. NIH
2:13 I **w** burn her chariots in the smoke, and NIH
2:13 I **w** cut off thy prey from the earth, and NIH
3: 5 I **w** discover thy skirts upon thy face, and NIH
3: 5 and I **w** shew the nations thy nakedness, and NIH
3: 6 I **w** cast abominable filth upon thee, and NIH
3: 6 thee vile, and **w** set thee as a gazingstock. NIH
3: 7 who **w** bemoan her? whence shall I seek NIH
Hab 1: 5 for *I* **w** work a work in your days, *which* ye NIH
1: 5 *which* ye **w** not believe, though it be told NIH
2: 1 I **w** stand upon my watch, and set me upon NIH
2: 1 **w** watch to see what he will say unto me, NIH
2: 1 will watch to see what he **w** say unto me, NIH
2: 3 because it **w** surely come, it will not tarry. NIH
2: 3 because it will surely come, it **w** not tarry. NIH
3:16 he **w** invade them with his troops. NIH
3:18 Yet I **w** rejoice in the LORD, I will joy in NIH
3:18 I **w** joy in the God of my salvation. NIH
3:19 and he **w** make my feet like hinds' *feet,* and NIH
3:19 he **w** make me to walk upon mine high NIH
Zep 1: 2 I **w** utterly consume all *things* from off NIH
1: 3 I **w** consume man and beast; I will consume NIH
1: 3 I **w** consume the fowls of the heaven, and NIH
1: 3 I **w** cut off man from off the land, saith NIH
1: 4 I **w** also stretch out mine hand upon Judah, NIH
1: 4 I **w** cut off the remnant of Baal from this NIH
1: 8 that I **w** punish the princes, and the king's NIH
1: 9 In the same day also **w** I punish all those NIH
1:12 *that* I **w** search Jerusalem with candles, and NIH
1:12 in their heart, The LORD **w** not do good, NIH
1:12 will not do good, neither **w** he do evil. NIH
1:17 I **w** bring distress upon men, that they shall NIH
2: 5 of the Philistines, I **w** even destroy thee, NIH
2:11 The LORD **w** *be* terrible unto them: for he NIH
2:11 for he **w** famish all the gods of the earth; NIH
2:13 he **w** stretch out his hand against the north, NIH
2:13 **w** make Nineveh a desolation, *and* dry like a NIH
3: 5 *is* in the midst thereof; he **w** not do iniquity: NIH
3: 9 then **w** I turn to the people a pure language, NIH
3:11 I **w** take away out of the midst of thee them NIH
3:12 I **w** also leave in the midst of thee an NIH
3:17 he **w** save, he will rejoice over thee with NIH
3:17 will save, he **w** rejoice over thee with joy; NIH
3:17 he **w** rest in his love, he will joy over thee NIH
3:17 in his love, he **w** joy over thee with singing. NIH
3:18 I **w** gather *them that are* sorrowful for NIH
3:19 at that time I **w** undo all that afflict thee: NIH
3:19 I **w** save her that halteth, and gather her that NIH
3:19 I **w** get them praise and fame in every land NIH
3:20 At that time **w** I bring you *again,* even in NIH
3:20 for I **w** make you a name and a praise NIH
Hag 1: 8 I **w** take pleasure in it, and I will be NIH
1: 8 in it, and I **w** be glorified, saith the LORD. NIH
2: 6 I **w** shake the heavens, and the earth, and NIH
2: 7 I **w** shake all nations, and the desire of all NIH
2: 7 I **w** fill this house *with* glory, saith NIH
2: 9 in this place **w** I give peace, saith NIH
2:19 brought forth: from this day **w** I bless *you.* NIH
2:21 saying, I **w** shake the heavens and the earth; NIH
2:22 I **w** overthrow the throne of kingdoms, and NIH
2:22 I **w** destroy the strength of the kingdoms of NIH
2:22 I **w** overthrow the chariots, and those that NIH
2:23 **w** I take thee, O Zerubbabel, my servant, NIH
2:23 the LORD, and **w** make thee as a signet: NIH
Zec 1: 3 I **w** turn unto you, saith the LORD of NIH
1: 9 said unto me, I **w** shew thee what these *be.* NIH
2: 5 **w** be unto her a wall of fire round about, NIH
2: 5 and **w** be the glory in the midst of her. NIH
2: 9 I **w** shake mine hand upon them, and NIH
2:10 I come, and I **w** dwell in the midst of thee, NIH
2:11 I **w** dwell in the midst of thee, and NIH
3: 4 and *I* **w** clothe thee with change of raiment. NIH
3: 7 I **w** give thee places to walk among these NIH
3: 8 I **w** bring forth my servant the BRANCH. NIH
3: 9 behold, I **w** engrave the graving thereof, NIH
3: 9 I **w** remove the iniquity of that land in one NIH
5: 4 I **w** bring it forth, saith the LORD of hosts, NIH
6:15 if ye **w** diligently obey the voice of NIH
8: 3 and **w** dwell in the midst of Jerusalem: NIH
8: 7 I **w** save my people from the east country, NIH
8: 8 I **w** bring them, and they shall dwell in NIH
8: 8 I **w** be their God, in truth and NIH
8:11 now I **w** not *be* unto the residue of this NIH
8:12 I **w** cause the remnant of this people to NIH
8:13 so **w** I save you, and ye shall be a blessing: NIH
8:21 to seek the LORD of hosts: I **w** go also. NIH
8:23 that is a Jew, saying, We **w** go with you: NIH
9: 4 the Lord **w** cast her out, and he will smite NIH
9: 4 and he **w** smite her power in the sea; NIH
9: 6 and I **w** cut off the pride of the Philistines. NIH
9: 7 I **w** take away his blood out of his mouth, NIH
9: 8 I **w** encamp about mine house because NIH
9:10 I **w** cut off the chariot from Ephraim, and NIH
9:12 even to day do I declare *that* I **w** render NIH
10: 6 I **w** strengthen the house of Judah, and I will NIH
10: 6 I **w** save the house of Joseph, and I will NIH

Zec 10: 6 and I **w** bring them *again* to place them; NIH
10: 6 *am* the LORD their God, and **w** hear them. NIH
10: 8 I **w** hiss for them, and gather them; for I NIH
10: 9 I **w** sow them among the people: and they NIH
10:10 I **w** bring them again also out of the land of NIH
10:10 I **w** bring them into the land of Gilead and NIH
10:12 I **w** strengthen them in the LORD; and NIH
11: 6 For I **w** no more pity the inhabitants of NIH
11: 6 I **w** deliver the men every one into his NIH
11: 6 and out of their hand I **w** not deliver *them.* NIH
11: 7 I **w** feed the flock of slaughter, *even* you, NIH
11: 9 said I, I **w** not feed you: that that dieth, NIH
11:16 For lo, I **w** raise up a shepherd in the land, NIH
12: 2 I **w** make Jerusalem a cup of trembling unto NIH
12: 3 in that day **w** I make Jerusalem a 1961
12: 4 I **w** smite every horse with astonishment, NIH
12: 4 I **w** open mine eyes upon the house of NIH
12: 4 **w** smite every horse of the people with NIH
12: 6 In that day **w** I make the governors of Judah NIH
12: 9 *that* I **w** seek to destroy all the nations that NIH
12:10 I **w** pour upon the house of David, and NIH
13: 2 *that* I **w** cut off the names of the idols out of NIH
13: 2 also I **w** cause the prophets and the unclean NIH
13: 7 and I **w** turn mine hand upon the little ones. NIH
13: 9 And I **w** bring the third *part* through the fire, NIH
13: 9 **w** refine them as silver is refined, and NIH
13: 9 is refined, and **w** try them as gold is tried: NIH
13: 9 shall call on my name, and I **w** hear them: NIH
13: 9 I **w** say, It *is* my people: and they shall say, NIH
14: 2 For I **w** gather all nations against Jerusalem NIH
14:12 **w** smite all the people that have fought NIH
14:17 *that* whoso **w** not come up of *all* the families NIH
14:18 where*with* the LORD **w** smite the heathen NIH
Mal 1: 4 we **w** return and build the desolate places; NIH
1: 4 They shall build, but I **w** throw down; NIH
1: 5 The LORD **w** be magnified from NIH
1: 8 **w** he be pleased with thee, or accept thy NIH
1: 9 beseech God that he **w** be gracious unto us: NIH
1: 9 **w** he regard your persons? saith the LORD NIH
1:10 neither **w** I accept an offering at your hand. NIH
2: 2 If ye **w** not hear, and if ye will not lay *it* to NIH
2: 2 will not hear, and if ye **w** not lay *it* to heart, NIH
2: 2 I **w** even send a curse upon you, and NIH
2: 2 curse upon you, and **w** curse your blessings: NIH
2: 3 I **w** corrupt your seed, and spread dung NIH
2:12 The LORD **w** cut off the man that doth NIH
2:13 or receiveth *it with* **good w** at your hand. 7522
3: 1 I **w** send my messenger, and he shall NIH
3: 5 I **w** come near to you to judgment; and NIH
3: 5 I **w** be a swift witness against the sorcerers, NIH
3: 7 I **w** return unto you, saith the LORD of NIH
3: 8 **W** a man rob God? Yet ye *have* robbed me. NIH
3:10 if I **w** not open you the windows of heaven, NIH
3:11 And I **w** rebuke the devourer for your sakes, NIH
3:17 I **w** spare them, as a man spareth his own NIH
4: 5 I **w** send you Elijah the prophet before NIH
Mt 2:13 for Herod **w** seek the young child to *3195*
3:12 and he **w** throughly purge his floor, and NIG
3:12 **w** burn up the chaff with unquenchable fire. NIG
4: 9 unto him, All these *things* **w** I give thee, NIG
4:19 and I **w** make you fishers of men. NIG
5:40 And if any man **w** sue thee at the law, and *2309*
6:10 Thy **w** be done in earth, as *it is* in heaven. *2307*
6:14 your heavenly Father **w** also forgive you: NIG
6:15 neither **w** your Father forgive your NIG
6:21 your treasure is, there **w** your heart be also. NIG
6:24 for either he **w** hate the one, and love NIG
6:24 or else he **w** hold to the one, and despise NIG
7: 9 if his son ask bread, **w** he give him a stone? NIG
7:10 Or if he ask a fish, **w** he give him a serpent? NIG
7:21 he that doeth the **w** of my Father which is *2307*
7:22 Many **w** say to me in that day, Lord, Lord, NIG
7:23 And then **w** I profess unto them, I never NIG
7:24 doeth them, I **w** liken him unto a wise man, NIG
8: 3 *his* hand, and touched him, saying, I **w**; *2309*
8: 7 saith unto him, I **w** come and heal him. NIG
8:19 I **w** follow thee whithersoever thou goest. NIG
9:13 I **w** have mercy, and not sacrifice: NIG
9:15 but the days **w** come, when the bridegroom NIG
9:38 that he **w** send forth labourers into his NIG
10:17 for they **w** deliver you up to the councils, NIG
10:17 and they **w** scourge you in their synagogues; NIG
10:32 him **w** I confess also before my Father NIG
10:33 him **w** I also deny before my Father which NIG
11:14 And if ye **w** receive *it,* this is Elias, *2309*
11:27 *he* to whomsoever the Son **w** reveal *him.* *1014*
11:28 and are heavy laden, and I **w** give you rest. NIG
12: 7 I **w** have mercy, and not sacrifice, NIG
12:11 **w** he not lay hold on it, and lift *it* out? NIG
12:18 I **w** put my spirit upon him, and he shall NIG
12:29 strong *man?* and then he **w** spoil his house. NIG
12:44 I **w** return into my house from whence I NIG
12:50 For whosoever shall do the **w** of my Father *2307*
13:30 in the time of harvest I **w** say to the reapers, NIG
13:35 saying, I **w** open my mouth in parables; NIG
13:35 I **w** utter *things which have been* kept secret NIG
15:32 and I **w** not send them away fasting, *2309*
16: 2 it is evening, ye say, *It* **w** *be* fair weather: NIG
16: 3 in the morning, *It* **w** *be* foul weather to day: NIG
16:18 and upon this rock I **w** build my church; NIG
16:19 And I **w** give unto thee the keys of NIG
16:24 If any *man* **w** come after me, let him deny *2309*
16:25 For whosoever **w** save his life shall lose it: *2309*
16:25 whosoever **w** lose his life for my sake shall NIG
18:14 it is not the **w** of your Father which is in *2307*
18:16 But if he **w** not hear *thee, then* take with NIG
18:26 have patience with me, and I **w** pay thee all. NIG
18:29 Have patience with me, and I **w** pay thee all. NIG
20: 4 and whatsoever is right I **w** give you. NIG
20:14 I **w** give unto this last, even as unto thee. *2309*
20:15 Is it not lawful for me to do what I **w** with *2309*
20:26 but whosoever **w** be great among you, *2309*
20:27 And whosoever **w** be chief among you, *2309*
20:32 said, What **w** ye *that* I shall do unto you? *2309*
21: 3 of them; and straightway he **w** send them. NIG

W

Mt 21:24 said unto them, I also **w** ask you one thing, NIG
21:24 I in like wise **w** tell you by what authority I NIG
21:25 he **w** say unto us, Why did ye not then NIG
21:29 He answered and said, I **w** not: but *2309*
21:31 Whether of *them* twain did the **w** of *his* *2307*
21:37 his son, saying, They **w** reverence my son. NIG
21:40 what **w** he do unto those husbandmen? NIG
21:41 He **w** miserably destroy those wicked *men,* NIG
21:41 **w** let out *his* vineyard unto other NIG
21:44 it shall fall, it **w** grind him to powder. NIG
23: 4 they *themselves* **w** not move them with *2309*
24:28 there **w** the eagles be gathered together. NIG
25:21 hast been faithful over a few *things,* I **w** NIG
25:23 hast been faithful over a few *things,* I **w** NIG
26:15 And said *unto them,* What **w** ye give me, *2309*
26:15 ye give me, and I **w** deliver him unto you? NIG
26:18 I **w** keep the passover at thy house with my NIG
26:29 I **w** not drink henceforth of this fruit of NIG
26:31 I **w** smite the shepherd, and the sheep of NIG
26:32 But after I am risen *again,* I **w** go before you NIG
26:33 because of thee, *yet* **w** I never be offended. NIG
26:35 should die with thee, *yet* **w** I not deny thee. NIG
26:39 nevertheless not as I **w**, but as thou *wilt.* *2309*
26:42 from me, except I drink it, thy **w** be done. *2307*
27:17 Whom **w** ye *that* I release unto you? *2309*
27:21 Whether of the twain **w** ye *that* I release *2309*
27:42 down from the cross, and we **w** believe him. NIG
27:43 let him deliver him now, if he **w** have him: *2309*
27:49 let us see whether Elias **w** come to save NIG
27:63 yet alive, After three days I **w** rise *again.* NIG
28:14 we **w** persuade him, and secure you. NIG
Mk 1:17 and I **w** make you to become fishers of men. NIG
1:41 and touched him, and saith unto him, I **w**; *2309*
2:20 But the days **w** come, when the bridegroom NIG
2:22 wine is spilled, and the bottles **w** be marred: NIG
3:27 except he **w** first bind the strong *man;* and NIG
3:27 strong *man;* and then he **w** spoil his house. NIG
3:35 For whosoever shall do the **w** of God, *2307*
4:13 and how *then* **w** ye know all parables? NIG
6:22 whatsoever thou wilt, and I **w** give *it* thee. NIG
6:23 I **w** give *it* thee, unto the half of my NIG
6:25 I **w** that thou give me by and by in a *2309*
8: 3 their own houses, they **w** faint by the way: NIG
8:34 unto them, Whosoever **w** come after me, *2309*
8:35 For whosoever **w** save his life shall lose it; *2309*
9:50 his saltness, wherewith **w** you season it? NIG
10:43 but whosoever **w** be great among you, *2309*
10:44 And whosoever of you **w** be the chiefest, *2309*
11: 3 and straightway he **w** send him hither. NIG
11:26 neither **w** your Father which is in heaven NIG
11:29 I **w** also ask of you one question, and NIG
11:29 I **w** tell you by what authority I do these NIG
11:31 he **w** say, Why then did ye not believe him? NIG
12: 6 saying, They **w** reverence my son. NIG
12: 9 he **w** come and destroy the husbandmen, NIG
12: 9 and **w** give the vineyard unto others. NIG
14: 7 whensoever ye **w** ye may do them good: *2309*
14:15 And he **w** shew you a large upper room NIG
14:25 I **w** drink no more of the fruit of the vine, NIG
14:27 I **w** smite the shepherd, and the sheep shall NIG
14:28 I am risen, I **w** go before you into Galilee. NIG
14:29 Although all shall be offended, yet ***w*** not I. NIG
14:31 die with thee, I **w** not deny thee in any wise. NIG
14:36 nevertheless not that I **w**, but what thou *2309*
14:58 I **w** destroy this temple that is made with NIG
14:58 within three days I **w** build another made NIG
15: 9 **W** ye *that* I release unto you the King of *2309*
15:12 What **w** ye then *that* I shall do *unto him* *2309*
15:36 let us see whether Elias **w** come to take him NIG
Lk 2:14 and on earth peace, **good w** towards men. *2107*
3:17 and he **w** throughly purge his floor, and NIG
3:17 and **w** gather the wheat into his garner; NIG
3:17 the chaff he **w** burn with fire unquenchable. NIG
4: 6 All this power **w** I give thee, and the glory NIG
4: 6 unto me; and to whomsoever I **w** I give it. *2309*
4:23 Ye **w** surely say unto me this proverb, NIG
5: 5 nevertheless at thy word I **w** let down NIG
5:13 *his* hand, and touched him, saying, I **w**: *2309*
5:35 But the days **w** come, when the bridegroom NIG
5:37 else the new wine **w** burst the bottles, and NIG
6: 9 I **w** ask you one *thing;* Is it lawful on NIG
6:47 I **w** shew you to whom he is like: NIG
7:42 which of them **w** love him most? NIG
9: 5 And whosoever **w** not receive you, when ye NIG
9:23 If any *man* **w** come after me, let him deny *2309*
9:24 For whosoever **w** save his life shall lose it: *2309*
9:24 but whosoever **w** lose his life for my sake, NIG
9:57 I **w** follow thee whithersoever thou goest. NIG
9:61 another also said, Lord, I **w** follow thee; NIG
10:22 and *he* to whom the Son **w** reveal *him.* *1014*
10:35 when I come again, I **w** repay thee. NIG
11: 2 Thy **w** be done, as in heaven, so in earth. *2307*
11: 8 Though he **w** not rise and give him, because NIG
11: 8 because of his importunity he **w** rise and NIG
11:11 you that is a father, **w** he give him a stone? NIG
11:11 a fish, **w** he for a fish give him a serpent? NIG
11:12 shall ask an egg, **w** he offer him a scorpion? NIG
11:24 I **w** return unto my house whence I came NIG
11:49 I **w** send them prophets and apostles, and NIG
12: 5 But I **w** *fore*warn you whom you shall fear: NIG
12:18 And he said, This **w** I do: I will pull down NIG
12:18 I **w** pull down my barns, and build greater; NIG
12:18 and there **w** I bestow all my fruits and NIG
12:19 And I **w** say to my soul, Soul, thou hast NIG
12:28 how much more ***w*** *he clothe* you, O ye of NIG
12:34 your treasure is, there **w** your heart be also. NIG
12:36 when he **w** return from the wedding; NIG
12:37 to meat, and **w** come forth and serve them. NIG
12:44 that he **w** make him ruler over all that he NIG
12:46 The lord of that servant **w** come in a day NIG
12:46 and **w** cut him in sunder, and will appoint NIG
12:46 **w** appoint *him* his portion with NIG
12:47 which knew his lord's **w**, and prepared not *2307*
12:47 not *himself,* neither did according to his **w**, *2307*
12:48 of him they **w** ask the more. NIG
Lk 12:49 and what **w** I, if it be already kindled? *2309*
12:55 south wind blow, ye say, There **w** be heat; NIG
13:24 **w** seek to enter in, and shall not be able. NIG
13:31 and depart hence: for Herod **w** kill thee. *2309*
14: 5 **w** not straightway pull him out on NIG
15:18 I **w** arise and go to my father, and will say NIG
15:18 go to my father, and **w** say unto him, Father, NIG
16:11 who **w** commit to your trust the true *riches?* NIG
16:13 for either he **w** hate the one, and love NIG
16:13 or else he **w** hold to the one, and despise NIG
16:30 unto them from the dead, they **w** repent. NIG
16:31 the prophets, neither **w** they be persuaded, NIG
17: 1 It is impossible but that offences **w** come: NIG
17: 7 or feeding cattle, **w** say *unto him* by and by, NIG
17: 8 And **w** not *rather* say unto him, Make ready NIG
17:22 said unto the disciples, The days **w** come, NIG
17:37 Wheresoever the body *is,* thither **w** NIG
18: 5 this widow troubleth me, I **w** avenge her, NIG
18: 8 I tell you that he **w** avenge them speedily. *4160*
19:14 We **w** not have this *man* to reign over us. *2309*
19:22 Out of thine own mouth **w** I judge thee, NIG
20: 3 said unto them, I **w** also ask you one thing; NIG
20: 5 he **w** say, Why then believed ye him not? NIG
20: 6 if we say, Of men; all the people **w** stone us: NIG
20:13 I **w** send my beloved son: it may be they NIG
20:13 it may be they **w** reverence *him* when they NIG
20:18 it shall fall, it **w** grind him to powder. NIG
21: 6 *things* which ye behold, the days **w** come, NIG
21: 7 what sign ***w*** *there be* when these *things* NIG
21:15 For I **w** give you a mouth and wisdom, NIG
22:16 I say unto you, I **w** not any more eat thereof, NIG
22:18 I **w** not drink of the fruit of the vine, NIG
22:42 nevertheless not my **w**, but thine, be done. *2307*
22:67 unto them, If I tell you, you **w** not believe: NIG
22:68 And if I also ask *you,* you **w** not answer me, NIG
23:16 I **w** therefore chastise him, and release *him.* NIG
23:22 I **w** therefore chastise him, and let *him* go. NIG
23:25 but he delivered Jesus to their **w**. *2307*
Jn 1:13 not of blood, nor of the **w** of the flesh, *2307*
1:13 the flesh, nor of the **w** of man, but of God. *2307*
2:19 this temple, and in three days I **w** raise it up. NIG
4:25 when he is come, he **w** tell us all *things.* NIG
4:34 My meat is to do the **w** of him that sent me, *2307*
4:48 ye see signs and wonders, ye **w** not believe. NIG
5:20 he **w** shew him greater works than these, NIG
5:21 so the Son quickeneth whom he **w**. *2309*
5:30 is just; because I seek not mine own **w**, *2307*
5:30 but the **w** of the Father which hath sent me. *2307*
5:40 And ye **w** not come to me, that ye might *2309*
5:43 come in his own name, him ye **w** receive. NIG
5:45 Do not think that I **w** accuse you to NIG
6:37 him that cometh to me I **w** in no wise cast NIG
6:38 not to do mine own **w**, but the will of him *2307*
6:38 own will, but the **w** of him that sent me. *2307*
6:39 And this is the Father's **w** which hath sent *2307*
6:40 And this is the **w** of him that sent me, *2307*
6:40 and I **w** raise him up *at* the last day. NIG
6:44 and I **w** raise him up *at* the last day. NIG
6:51 and the bread that I **w** give is my flesh, NIG
6:51 which I **w** give for the life of the world. NIG
6:54 and I **w** raise him up *at* the last day. NIG
6:67 Jesus unto the twelve, **W** ye also go away? *2309*
7:17 If any *man* **w** do his will, he shall know of *2309*
7:17 If any *man* will do his **w**, he shall know of *2307*
7:31 **w** he do moe miracles than these which this NIG
7:35 Whither **w** he go, that we shall not find *3195*
7:35 **w** he go unto the dispersed among *3195*
8:22 Then said the Jews, **W** he kill himself? NIG
8:44 and the lusts of your father ye **w** do. *2309*
9:27 hear *it* again? **w** ye also be his disciples? *2309*
9:31 of God, and doeth his **w**, him he heareth. *2307*
10: 5 And a stranger **w** they not follow, but NIG
10: 5 will they not follow, but **w** flee from him: NIG
11:22 thou wilt ask of God, God **w** give *it* thee. NIG
11:48 him thus alone, all *men* **w** believe on him: NIG
11:56 think ye, that he **w** not come to the feast? NIG
12:26 *man* serve me, him **w** *my* Father honour. NIG
12:28 have both glorified *it,* and **w** glorify *it* again. NIG
12:32 up from the earth, **w** draw all *men* unto me. NIG
13:37 I **w** lay down my life for thy sake. NIG
14: 3 I **w** come again, and receive you unto NIG
14:13 ye shall ask in my name, that **w** I do, NIG
14:14 shall ask any *thing* in my name, I **w** do *it.* NIG
14:16 And I **w** pray the Father, and he shall give NIG
14:18 I **w** not leave you comfortless: I will come NIG
14:18 not leave you comfortless: I **w** come to you. NIG
14:21 and I **w** love him, and will manifest myself NIG
14:21 love him, and **w** manifest myself to him. NIG
14:23 If a man love me, he **w** keep my words: NIG
14:23 and my Father **w** love him, and we will NIG
14:23 and we **w** come unto him, and make *our* NIG
14:26 whom the Father **w** send in my name, NIG
14:30 Hereafter I **w** not talk much with you: NIG
15: 7 ye shall ask what ye **w**, and it shall be done *2309*
15:20 persecuted me, they **w** also persecute you; NIG
15:20 kept my saying, they **w** keep yours also. NIG
15:21 But all these *things* **w** they do unto you for NIG
15:26 whom I **w** send unto you from the Father, NIG
16: 2 that whosoever killeth you **w** think that he NIG
16: 3 And these *things* **w** they do unto you, NIG
16: 7 the Comforter **w** not come unto you; NIG
16: 7 but if I depart, I **w** send him unto you. NIG
16: 8 he **w** reprove the world of sin, and NIG
16:13 is come, he **w** guide you into all truth: NIG
16:13 and he **w** shew you *things* to come. NIG
16:22 but I **w** see you again, and your heart shall NIG
16:23 ask the Father in my name, he **w** give *it* you. NIG
16:26 unto you, that I **w** pray the Father for you: NIG
17:24 Father, I **w** that they also, whom thou hast *2309*
17:26 **w** declare *it:* that the love where*with* thou NIG
18:39 **w** ye therefore *that* I release unto you *1014*
20:15 thou hast laid him, and I **w** take him away. NIG
20:25 thrust my hand into his side, I **w** not believe. NIG
21:22 If I **w** that he tarry till I come, what *is that* *2309*
21:23 but, If I **w** that he tarry till I come, what *is* *2309*
Ac 2:17 I **w** pour out of my Spirit upon all flesh: NIG
2:18 on my handmaidens I **w** pour out in those NIG
2:19 And I **w** shew wonders in heaven above, NIG
3:23 every soul, which **w** not hear that prophet, NIG
5:38 this work be of men, it **w** come to nought: NIG
6: 4 But we **w** give ourselves continually to NIG
7: 7 to whom they shall be in bondage **w** I judge, NIG
7:34 And now come, I **w** send thee into Egypt. NIG
7:43 and I **w** carry you away beyond Babylon. NIG
7:49 what house **w** ye build me? saith the Lord: NIG
9:16 For I **w** shew him how great *things* he must NIG
13:22 mine own heart, which shall fulfil all my **w**. *2307*
13:34 I **w** give you the sure mercies of David. NIG
13:36 served his own generation by the **w** of God, *1012*
15:16 After this I **w** return, and will build again NIG
15:16 and **w** build again the tabernacle of David, NIG
15:16 and I **w** build again the ruins thereof, and NIG
15:16 again the ruins thereof, and I **w** set it up: NIG
17:18 And some said, What **w** this babbler say? *2309*
17:31 in the which he **w** judge the world in *3195*
17:32 We **w** hear thee again of this *matter.* NIG
18: 6 from henceforth I **w** go unto the Gentiles. NIG
18:15 look ye *to it;* for I **w** be no judge of such *1014*
18:21 but I **w** return again unto you, if God will. *2309*
18:21 but I will return again unto you, if God **w**. *2309*
21:14 saying, The **w** of the Lord be done. *2307*
21:22 for they **w** hear that thou art come. NIG
22:14 that *thou* shouldest know his **w**, and *2307*
22:18 for they **w** not receive thy testimony NIG
22:21 for I **w** send thee far hence unto NIG
23:14 that *we* **w** eat nothing until we have slain NIG
23:21 that *they* **w** neither eat nor drink till they NIG
23:35 I **w** hear thee, said he, when thine accusers NIG
24:22 I **w** know the uttermost of your matter. NIG
24:25 I have a convenient season, I **w** call for thee. NIG
26:16 *of those things* in the which I **w** appear unto NIG
27:10 I perceive that *this* voyage **w** be with hurt *3195*
28:28 unto the Gentiles, and *that* they **w** hear it. NIG
Ro 1:10 journey by the **w** of God to come unto you. *2307*
2: 6 Who **w** render to every *man* according to NIG
2:18 And knowest *his* **w**, and approvest *2307*
4: 8 Blessed *is* the man to whom the Lord **w** not NIG
5: 7 For scarcely for a righteous *man* **w** one die: NIG
7:18 dwelleth no good *thing:* for to **w** is present *2309*
8:27 for the saints according to *the* ***w*** *of* God. NIG
9: 9 At this time **w** I come, and Sara shall have a NIG
9:15 I **w** have mercy on whom I will have mercy, NIG
9:15 I will have mercy on whom I **w** have mercy, NIG
9:15 I **w** have compassion on whom I will have NIG
9:15 I will have compassion on whom I **w** have NIG
9:18 Therefore hath he mercy on whom he **w** *2309*
9:18 *have mercy,* and whom he **w** he hardeneth. *2309*
9:19 yet find fault? For who hath resisted his **w**? *1013*
9:25 saith also in Osee, I **w** call *them* my people, NIG
9:28 For he **w** finish the work, and cut *it* short in NIG
9:28 a short work **w** the Lord make upon NIG
10:19 I **w** provoke you to jealousy by *them that* NIG
10:19 *and* by a foolish nation I **w** anger you. NIG
12: 2 and acceptable, and perfect, **w** of God. *2307*
12:19 *is* mine; I **w** repay, saith the Lord. NIG
15: 9 For this cause I **w** confess to thee among NIG
15:18 For I **w** not dare to speak of any of *those* NIG
15:24 my journey into Spain, I **w** come to you: NIG
15:28 them this fruit, I **w** come by you into Spain. NIG
15:32 come unto you with joy by the **w** of God, *2307*
1Co 1: 1 of Jesus Christ through the **w** of God, *2307*
1:19 I **w** destroy the wisdom of the wise, and NIG
1:19 **w** bring to nothing the understanding of NIG
4: 5 who both **w** bring to light the hidden *things* NIG
4: 5 **w** make manifest the counsels of the hearts: NIG
4:19 But I **w** come to you shortly, if the Lord NIG
4:19 you shortly, if the Lord **w**, and will know, *2309*
4:19 to you shortly, if the Lord will, and **w** know, NIG
4:21 What **w** ye? shall I come unto you with a *2309*
6:12 I **w** not be brought under the power of any. NIG
6:14 and **w** *also* raise up us by his own power. NIG
7:36 and need so require, let him do what he **w**, *2309*
7:37 but hath power over his own **w**, and hath so *2307*
7:37 decreed in his heart that *he* **w** keep his NIG
7:39 is at liberty to be married to whom she **w**; *2309*
8:13 I **w** eat no flesh while the world standeth, NIG
9:17 but if **against** my **w**, a dispensation *of* *210*
10:13 who **w** not suffer you to be tempted above NIG
10:13 **w** with the temptation also make a way to NIG
11:34 And the rest **w** I set in order when I come. NIG
12:11 dividing to every man severally as he **w**. *1014*
14:15 I **w** pray with the spirit, and will pray with NIG
14:15 and **w** pray with the understanding also: NIG
14:15 I **w** sing with the spirit, and I will sing with NIG
14:15 and I **w** sing with the understanding also. NIG
14:21 and other lips **w** I speak unto this people; NIG
14:21 and yet for all that **w** they not hear me, NIG
14:23 unbelievers, **w** they not say that ye are mad? NIG
14:25 falling down on *his* face he **w** worship God, NIG
14:35 And if they **w** learn any *thing,* let them ask *2309*
15:35 But some *man* **w** say, How are the dead NIG
16: 3 them **w** I send to bring your liberality unto NIG
16: 5 Now I **w** come unto you, when I shall pass NIG
16: 6 And it may be that I **w** abide, yea, and NIG
16: 7 For I **w** not see you now by the way; but I *2309*
16: 8 But I **w** tarry at Ephesus until Pentecost. NIG
16:12 *his* **w** was not at all to come at this time; *2307*
16:12 he **w** come when he shall have convenient NIG
2Co 1: 1 an apostle of Jesus Christ by the **w** of God, *2307*
1:10 in whom we trust that he **w** yet deliver *us;* NIG
6:16 I **w** dwell in them, and walk in *them;* and NIG
6:16 and walk in *them;* and I **w** be their God, and NIG
6:17 not the unclean *thing;* and I **w** receive you, NIG
6:18 And **w** be a Father unto you, and ye shall be NIG
8: 5 to the Lord, and unto us by the **w** of God. *2307*
8:11 *of it;* that as *there was* a readiness to **w**, *2309*
10:11 such ***w*** *we be* also in deed when we are NIG
10:13 But we **w** not boast of *things* without *our* NIG
11: 9 to you, and *so* **w** I keep *myself.* NIG
11:12 But what I do, that I **w** do, that I may cut off NIG

W

2Co 11:18 many glory after the flesh, I **w** glory also. NIG
11:30 I **w** glory of the *things* which concern mine NIG
12: 1 I **w** come to visions and revelations of NIG
12: 5 Of such a one **w** I glory: yet of myself I will NIG
12: 5 yet of myself I **w** not glory, but in mine NIG
12: 6 I shall not be a fool; for I **w** say the truth: NIG
12: 9 therefore **w** I rather glory in my infirmities, NIG
12:14 to you; and I **w** not be burdensome to you: NIG
12:15 And I **w** very gladly spend and be spent for NIG
12:21 my God **w** humble *me* among you, and NIG
13: 2 all other, that, if I come again, I **w** not spare: NIG
Gal 1: 4 according to the **w** of God and our Father: *2307*
5:10 that you **w** be none otherwise minded: NIG
Eph 1: 1 an apostle of Jesus Christ by the **w** of God, *2307*
1: 5 according to the good pleasure of his **w**, *2307*
1: 9 made known unto us the mystery of his **w**, *2307*
1:11 all *things* after the counsel of his own **w**: *2307*
5:17 understanding what the **w** of the Lord *is.* *2307*
6: 6 doing the **w** of God from the heart; *2307*
6: 7 With **good w** doing service, as to the Lord, *2133*
Php 1: 6 **w** perform *it* until the day of Jesus Christ: NIG
1:15 and strife; and some also of **good w**: *2107*
1:18 and I therein do rejoice, yea, and **w** rejoice. NIG
2:13 it is God which worketh in you both to **w** *2309*
2:20 who **w** naturally care for your state. NIG
2:23 as I shall see **how it w go with** me. *3588+4012*
Col 1: 1 an apostle of Jesus Christ by the **w** of God, *2307*
1: 9 *with* the knowledge of his **w** in all wisdom *2307*
2:23 indeed a shew of wisdom in **w worship**, *1479*
4:12 and complete in all the **w** of God. *2307*
1Th 4: 3 For this is the **w** of God, *even* your *2307*
4:14 them also which sleep in Jesus **w** God bring NIG
5:18 for this *is* the **w** of God in Christ Jesus *2307*
5:24 *is* he that calleth you, who also **w** do *it.* NIG
2Th 2: 7 only he who now letteth **w** *let,* until he be NIG
3: 4 **w** do *the things* which we command you. NIG
1Ti 2: 4 Who **w have** all men to be saved, and *2309*
2: 8 I **w** therefore that men pray every where, *1014*
5:11 wax wanton against Christ, they **w** marry; *2309*
5:14 I **w** therefore that the younger *women* *1014*
6: 9 But they that **w** be rich fall into temptation *1014*
2Ti 1: 1 an apostle of Jesus Christ by the **w** of God, *2307*
2:12 *him:* if we deny *him,* he also **w** deny us: NIG
2:16 for they **w** increase unto more ungodliness. NIG
2:17 And their word **w** eat as *doth* a canker: NIG
2:25 if God peradventure **w** give them NIG
2:26 *who are* taken captive by him at his **w**. *2307*
3:12 all that **w** live godly in Christ Jesus shall *2309*
4: 3 For the time **w** come when they will not NIG
4: 3 For the time will come when they **w** not NIG
4:18 **w** preserve *me* unto his heavenly kingdom: NIG
Tit 3: 8 these *things* I **w** that thou affirm constantly, *1014*
Phm 1:19 I **w** repay *it:* albeit I do not say to thee how NIG
Heb 1: 5 I **w** be to him a Father, and he shall be to me NIG
2: 4 of the Holy Ghost, according to his own **w**? *2308*
2:12 I **w** declare thy name unto my brethren, NIG
2:12 in the midst of the church **w** I sing praise NIG
2:13 And again, I **w** put my trust in him. *1510*
3: 7 Ghost saith, To day if ye **w** hear his voice, NIG
3:15 it is said, To day if ye **w** hear his voice, NIG
4: 7 as it is said, To day if ye **w** hear his voice, NIG
6: 3 And this **w** we do, if God permit. NIG
6:14 Surely blessing I **w** bless thee, and NIG
6:14 and multiplying I **w** multiply thee. NIG
7:21 unto him, The Lord sware and **w** not repent, NIG
8: 8 when I **w** make a new covenant with NIG
8:10 For this *is* the covenant that I **w** make with NIG
8:10 I **w** put my laws into their mind, and NIG
8:10 and I **w** be to them a God, and they shall be NIG
8:12 For I **w** be merciful to their NIG
8:12 and their iniquities **w** I remember no more. NIG
10: 7 it is written of me,) to do thy **w**, O God. *2307*
10: 9 said he, Lo, I come to do thy **w**, O God. *2307*
10:10 By the which **w** we are sanctified through *2307*
10:16 This *is* the covenant that I **w** make with NIG
10:16 I **w** put my laws into their hearts, and NIG
10:16 and in their minds **w** I write them; NIG
10:17 and iniquities **w** I remember no more. NIG
10:30 unto me, I **w** recompense, saith the Lord. NIG
10:36 that, after ye have done the **w** of God, *2307*
10:37 *and* he that shall come **w** come, and NIG
10:37 that shall come will come, and **w** not tarry. NIG
13: 4 whoremongers and adulterers God **w** judge. NIG
13: 5 for he hath said, I **w** never leave thee, NIG
13: 6 and I **w** not fear what man shall do unto me. NIG
13:21 you perfect in every good work to do his **w**, *2307*
13:23 with whom, if he come shortly, I **w** see you. NIG
Jas 1:18 **Of** his **own w** begat he us with the word of *1014*
2:18 and I **w** shew thee my faith by my works. NIG
4: 4 **w** be a friend of the world is the enemy of *1014*
4: 7 Resist the devil, and he **w** flee from you. NIG
4: 8 nigh to God, and he **w** draw nigh to you. NIG
4:13 or to morrow we **w** go into such a city, NIG
4:15 If the Lord **w**, we shall live, and do this, or *2309*
1Pe 2:15 For so is the **w** of God, that with well doing *2307*
3:10 For he that **w** love life, and see good days, *2309*
3:13 And who *is* he that **w** harm you, if ye be NIG
3:17 For *it is* better, if the **w** of God be so, *2307*
4: 2 to the lusts of men, but to the **w** of God. *2307*
4: 3 us to have wrought the **w** of the Gentiles, *2307*
4:19 **w** of God commit the keeping of their souls *2307*
2Pe 1:12 Wherefore I **w** not be negligent to put you *3195*
1:15 Moreover I **w** endeavour that you may be NIG
1:21 came not in old time by the **w** of man: *2307*
3:10 But the day of the Lord **w** come as a thief in NIG
1Jn 2:17 he that doeth the **w** of God abideth for ever. *2307*
5:14 that, if we ask any *thing* according to his **w**, *2307*
3Jn 1:10 I **w** remember his deeds which he doeth, NIG
1:13 but I **w** not with ink and pen write unto *2309*
Jude 1: 5 I **w** therefore put you in remembrance, *1014*
Rev 2: 5 or else I **w** come unto thee quickly, and NIG
2: 5 **w** remove thy candlestick out of his place, NIG
2: 7 To him that overcometh **w** I give to eat of NIG
2:10 and I **w** give thee a crown of life. NIG
2:16 or else I **w** come unto thee quickly, and NIG
Rev 2:16 **w** fight against them with the sword of my NIG
2:17 To him that overcometh **w** I give to eat of NIG
2:17 and **w** give him a white stone, and in NIG
2:22 I **w** cast her into a bed, and them that NIG
2:23 And I **w** kill her children with death; and NIG
2:23 I **w** give unto every one of you according to NIG
2:24 I **w** put upon you none other burden. NIG
2:26 to him **w** I give power over the nations: NIG
2:28 And I **w** give him the morning star. NIG
3: 3 I **w** come on thee as a thief, and thou shalt NIG
3: 3 thou shalt not know what hour I **w** come NIG
3: 5 I **w** not blot out his name out of the book of NIG
3: 5 but I **w** confess his name before my Father, NIG
3: 9 I **w** make *them* of the synagogue of Satan, NIG
3: 9 I **w** make them to come and worship before NIG
3:10 I also **w** keep thee from the hour of NIG
3:12 Him that overcometh **w** I make a pillar in NIG
3:12 I **w** write upon him the name of my God, NIG
3:12 and *I* **w** *write upon him* my new name. NIG
3:16 nor hot, I **w** spue thee out of my mouth. *3195*
3:20 I **w** come in to him, and will sup with him, NIG
3:20 and **w** sup with him, and he with me. NIG
3:21 To him that overcometh **w** I grant to sit with NIG
4: 1 I **w** shew thee *things* which must be NIG
11: 3 And I **w** give *power* unto my two witnesses, NIG
11: 5 And if any *man* **w** hurt them, *2309*
11: 5 and if any *man* **w** hurt them, he must in this *2309*
11: 6 earth with all plagues, as often as they **w**. *2309*
17: 1 I **w** shew unto thee the judgment of NIG
17: 7 I **w** tell thee the mystery of the woman, and NIG
17:17 God hath put in their hearts to fulfil his **w**, *1106*
21: 3 and he **w** dwell with them, and they shall be NIG
21: 6 I **w** give unto him that is athirst of NIG
21: 7 shall inherit all *things;* and I **w** be his God, NIG
21: 9 *Come* hither, I **w** shew thee the bride, NIG
22:17 And whosoever **w**, let him take the water of *2309*

WILLETH (1) [WILL]

Ro 9:16 So then *it is* not of him that **w**, nor of him *2309*

WILLING (32) [WILL]

Ge 24: 5 Peradventure the woman will not be **w** to 14
24: 8 if the woman will not be **w** to follow thee, 14
Ex 35: 5 whosoever *is* of a **w** heart, let him bring it, 5081
35:21 and every one whom his spirit **made w**, *and* 5068
35:22 as many as were **w** hearted, *and* 5081
35:29 The children of Israel brought a **w offering** 5071
35:29 whose heart **made** them **w** to bring for all 5068
1Ch 28: 9 him with a perfect heart and with a **w** mind: 2655
28:21 **w** skilful *man,* for any *manner of* service. 5001
29: 5 is **w** to consecrate his service *this* day unto 5068
Job 39: 9 Will the unicorn be **w** to serve thee, or 14
Ps 110: 3 Thy people *shall be* **w** in the day of thy 5071
Isa 1:19 If ye be **w** and obedient, ye shall eat the good 14
Mt 1:19 and not **w** to make her a publick example, *2309*
26:41 the spirit indeed *is* **w**, but the flesh *is* weak. *4289*
Mk 15:15 And *so* Pilate, **w** to content the people, *1014*
Lk 10:29 But he, **w** to justify himself, said unto *2309*
22:42 Saying, Father, if thou be **w**, remove this *1014*
23:20 Pilate therefore, **w** to release Jesus, spake *2309*
Jn 5:35 ye were **w** for a season to rejoice in his *2309*
Ac 24:27 and Felix, **w** to shew the Jews a pleasure, *2309*
25: 9 But Festus, **w** to do the Jews a pleasure, *2309*
27:43 But the centurion, **w** to save Paul, *1014*
Ro 9:22 **w** to shew *his* wrath, and to make his power *2309*
2Co 5: 8 and **w** rather to be absent from the body, *2106*
8: 3 *their* power *they were* **w of themselves**; *830*
8:12 For if there be first a **w mind**, *it is* accepted *4288*
1Th 2: 8 we were **w** to have imparted unto you, *2106*
1Ti 6:18 ready to distribute, **w to communicate**; *2843*
Heb 6:17 **w** more abundantly to shew unto the heirs *1014*
13:18 in all *things* **w** to live honestly. *2309*
2Pe 3: 9 not **w** that any should perish, but that all *1014*

WILLINGLY (25) [WILL]

Ex 25: 2 of every man that **giveth** it **w** with his heart 5068
Jdg 5: 2 when the people **w offered** themselves. 5068
5: 9 that **offered** themselves **w** among 5068
8:25 We will **w give** *them.* And they 5414+5414
1Ch 29: 6 the rulers over the king's work, **offered w**, 5068
29: 9 for that they **offered w**, because 5068
29: 9 with perfect heart they **offered w** to 5068
29:14 that we should be able to **offer** so **w** after 5068
29:17 heart I have **w offered** all these *things:* 5068
29:17 are present here, to **offer w** unto thee. 5068
2Ch 17:16 who **w offered** himself unto the LORD; 5068
35: 8 his princes gave **w** unto the people, 5071+3807.1
Ezr 1: 6 beside all *that* was **w offered**. 5068
3: 5 of every one that **w offered** a freewill 5068
7:16 **offering w** for the house of their God 5069
Ne 11: 2 that **w offered** themselves to dwell at 5068
Pr 31:13 flax, and worketh **w** with her hands. 2656+871.1
La 3:33 For he doth not afflict **w** nor grieve 3820+4480
Hos 5:11 he **w** walked after the commandment. 2974
Jn 6:21 Then they **w** received him into the ship: *2309*
Ro 8:20 not **w**, but by reason of him who hath *1635*
1Co 9:17 For if I do this *thing* **w**, I have a reward: but *1635*
Phm 1:14 not be as *it were* of necessity, but **w**. *1595+2596*
1Pe 5: 2 oversight *thereof,* not by constraint, but **w**; *1596*
2Pe 3: 5 For this they **w** are ignorant of, that by *2309*

WILLOW (1) [WILLOWS]

Eze 17: 5 *it* by great waters, *and* set it *as* a **w tree**. 6851

WILLOWS (5) [WILLOW]

Lev 23:40 boughs of thick trees, and **w** of the brook; 6155
Job 40:22 the **w** of the brook compass him about. 6155
Ps 137: 2 We hanged our harps upon the **w** in 6155
Isa 15: 7 shall they carry away to the brook of the **w**. 6155
44: 4 among the grass, as **w** by the water courses. 6155

WILT (245) [WILL]

Ge 13: 9 if *thou* **w** *take* the left hand, then I will go to NIH
15: 2 Lord GOD, what **w** thou give me, NIH
Ge 16: 8 whither **w** thou go? And she said, I flee NIH
18:23 **W** thou also destroy the righteous with NIH
18:24 **w** thou also destroy and not spare the place NIH
18:28 **w** thou destroy all the city for *lack of* five? NIH
20: 4 Lord, **w** thou slay also a righteous nation? NIH
21:23 swear unto me here by God that thou **w** not NIH
23:13 saying, But if thou *w give it,* I pray thee, NIH
24:58 and said unto her, **W** thou go with this man? NIH
26:29 That thou **w** do us no hurt, as we have not NIH
30:31 if thou **w** do this thing for me, I will again NIH
38:16 she said, What **w** thou give me, that thou NIH
38:17 she said, **W** thou give *me* a pledge, till thou NIH
43: 4 If thou **w** send our brother with us, we will 3426
43: 5 if thou **w** not send *him,* we will not go NIH
Ex 4:13 by the hand *of him whom* thou **w** send. NIH
8:21 Else, if thou **w** not let my people go, behold, NIH
9: 2 refuse to let *them* go, and **w** hold them still, NIH
9:17 my people, that *thou* **w** not let them go? NIH
10: 3 How long **w** thou refuse to humble thyself NIH
13:13 if thou **w** not redeem *it,* then thou shalt NIH
15:26 If thou **w** diligently hearken to the voice of NIH
15:26 and **w** do that which is right in his sight, and NIH
15:26 **w** give ear to his commandments, and NIH
18:18 Thou **w** surely wear away, both thou, and NIH
20:25 if thou **w** make me an altar of stone, NIH
32:32 Yet now, if thou **w** forgive their sin; and NIH
33:12 thou hast not let me know whom thou **w** NIH
Nu 16:14 **w** thou put out the eyes of these men? NIH
16:22 **w** thou be wroth with all the congregation? NIH
21: 2 If thou **w** indeed deliver this people into my NIH
Dt 23:13 it shall be, when thou **w** ease thyself abroad, NIH
28:15 if thou **w** not hearken unto the voice of NIH
28:58 If thou **w** not observe to do all the words of NIH
30:17 so that thou **w** not hear, but shalt be drawn NIH
Jos 7: 9 and what **w** thou do unto thy great name? NIH
Jdg 1:14 and Caleb said unto her, What **w** thou? NIH
4: 8 If thou **w** go with me, then I will go: NIH
4: 8 if thou **w** not go with me, *then* I will not go. NIH
6:36 If thou **w** save Israel by mine hand, as thou 3426
6:37 shall I know that thou **w** save Israel by mine NIH
11:24 **W** not thou possess that which Chemosh thy NIH
13:16 if thou **w** offer a burnt offering, thou must NIH
Ru 4: 4 If thou **w** redeem *it,* redeem *it:* but if thou NIH
4: 4 but if thou **w** not redeem *it, then* tell me, NIH
1Sa 1:11 if thou **w** indeed look on the affliction of NIH
1:11 **w** give unto thine handmaid a man child, NIH
1:14 said unto her, How long **w** thou be drunken? NIH
14:37 **w** thou deliver them into the hand of Israel? NIH
16: 1 How long **w** thou mourn for Saul, NIH
19: 5 then **w** thou sin against innocent blood, NIH
21: 9 if thou **w** take that, take *it:* for *there is* no NIH
24:21 that thou **w** not cut off my seed after me, NIH
24:21 that thou **w** not destroy my name out of my NIH
25:17 know and consider what thou **w** do; NIH
30:15 unto me by God, that thou **w** neither kill me, NIH
2Sa 5:19 **w** thou deliver them into mine hand? NIH
13: 4 **w** thou not tell me? And Amnon said unto NIH
18:22 Joab said, Wherefore **w** thou run, my son, NIH
20:19 why **w** thou swallow up the inheritance of NIH
22:26 With the merciful thou **w** shew thyself NIH
22:26 with the upright man thou **w** shew thyself NIH
22:27 With the pure thou **w** shew thyself pure; and NIH
22:27 with the froward thou **w** shew thyself NIH
22:28 the afflicted people thou **w** save: but NIH
24:13 **w** thou flee three months before thine NIH
1Ki 3:14 if thou **w** walk in my ways, to keep my NIH
6:12 if thou **w** walk in my statutes, and execute NIH
9: 4 if thou **w** walk before me, as David thy NIH
9: 4 *and* **w** keep my statutes and my judgments: NIH
11:38 if thou **w** hearken unto all that I command NIH
11:38 **w** walk in my ways, and do that *is* right in NIH
12: 7 If thou **w** be a servant unto this people *this* NIH
12: 7 **w** serve them, and answer them, and NIH
13: 8 If thou **w** give me half thine house, I will NIH
22: 4 **W** thou go with me to battle *to* NIH
2Ki 3: 7 **w** thou go with me against Moab to battle? NIH
4:23 Wherefore **w** thou go to him to day? NIH
8:12 Because I know the evil that thou **w** do unto NIH
8:12 their strong holds **w** thou set on fire, and NIH
8:12 their young *men* **w** thou slay with NIH
8:12 **w** dash their children, and rip up their NIH
18:24 **w** thou turn away the face of one captain of NIH
1Ch 14:10 **w** thou deliver them into mine hand? NIH
17:25 hast told thy servant that *thou* **w** build him a NIH
2Ch 7:17 *as for* thee, if thou **w** walk before me, NIH
18: 3 **W** thou go with me *to* Ramoth-gilead? NIH
20: 9 in our affliction, then thou **w** hear and help. NIH
20:12 O our God, **w** thou not judge them? for we NIH
25: 8 if thou **w** go, do *it,* be strong for the battle: NIH
Ne 2: 6 when **w** thou return? So it pleased the king NIH
Est 5: 3 king unto her, What **w** thou, queen Esther? NIH
Job 4: 2 to commune with thee, **w** thou be grieved? NIH
5: 1 and to which of the saints **w** thou turn? NIH
7:19 How long **w** thou not depart from me, NIH
8: 2 How long **w** thou speak these *things?* and NIH
9:28 I know that thou **w** not hold me innocent. NIH
10: 9 and **w** thou bring me into dust again? NIH
10:14 thou **w** not acquit me from mine iniquity. NIH
13:25 **W** thou break a leaf driven to and fro? and NIH
13:25 and fro? and **w** thou pursue the dry stubble? NIH
14:15 thou **w** have a desire to the work of thine NIH
30:23 For I know *that* thou **w** bring me *to* death, NIH
34:17 and **w** thou condemn him that is most just? NIH
38:39 **W** thou hunt the prey for the lion? or fill NIH
39:11 **W** thou trust him, because his strength *is* NIH
39:11 *is* great? or **w** thou leave thy labour to him? NIH
39:12 **W** thou believe him, that he will bring home NIH
40: 8 **W** thou also disannul my judgment? NIH
40: 8 **w** thou condemn me, that thou mayest be NIH
41: 4 **w** thou take him for a servant for ever? NIH
41: 5 **W** thou play with him as *with* a bird? or NIH
41: 5 a bird? or **w** thou bind him for thy maidens? NIH
Ps 5:12 For thou, LORD, **w** bless the righteous; NIH
5:12 *with* favour **w** thou compass him as *with* a NIH
10:13 hath said in his heart, Thou **w** not require *it.* NIH

Ps 10:17 thou **w** prepare their heart, thou wilt cause NIH
10:17 their heart, thou **w** cause thine ear to hear: NIH
13: 1 How long **w** thou forget me, O LORD? NIH
13: 1 how long **w** thou hide thy face from me? NIH
16:10 For thou **w** not leave my soul in hell; NIH
16:10 neither **w** thou suffer thine Holy One to see NIH
16:11 Thou **w** shew me the path of life: in thy NIH
17: 6 upon thee, for thou **w** hear me, O God: NIH
18:25 With the merciful thou **w** shew thyself NIH
18:25 with an upright man thou **w** shew thyself NIH
18:26 With the pure thou **w** shew thyself pure; and NIH
18:26 with the froward thou **w** shew thyself NIH
18:27 For thou **w** save the afflicted people; but NIH
18:27 but **w** bring down high looks. NIH
18:28 For thou **w** light my candle: the LORD my NIH
35:17 Lord, how long **w** thou look on? rescue my NIH
38:15 do I hope: thou **w** hear, O Lord my God. NIH
41: 2 thou **w** not deliver him unto the will of his NIH
41: 3 thou **w** make all his bed in his sickness. NIH
51:17 a contrite heart, O God, thou **w** not despise. NIH
56:13 **w** not *thou deliver* my feet from falling, NIH
60:10 **W** not thou, O God, *which* hadst cast us NIH
61: 6 Thou **w** prolong the king's life: *and* NIH
65: 5 *By* terrible *things* in righteousness **w** thou NIH
79: 5 **w** thou be angry, for ever? shall thy jealousy NIH
80: 4 how long **w** thou be angry against NIH
81: 8 O Israel, if thou **w** hearken unto me; NIH
85: 5 **W** thou be angry with us for ever? wilt thou NIH
85: 5 **w** thou draw out thine anger to all NIH
85: 6 **W** thou not revive us again: that thy people NIH
86: 7 I will call upon thee: for thou **w** answer me. NIH
88:10 **W** thou shew wonders to the dead? shall NIH
89:46 **w** thou hide thyself, for ever? shall thy NIH
101: 2 O when **w** thou come unto me? I will walk NIH
108:11 **W** not *thou*, O God, *who* hast cast us off? NIH
108:11 **w** not thou, O God, go forth with our hosts? NIH
119:82 saying, When **w** thou comfort me? NIH
119:84 when **w** thou execute judgment on them that NIH
138: 7 in the midst of trouble, thou **w** revive me: NIH
139:19 Surely thou **w** slay the wicked, O God: NIH
Pr 2: 1 if thou **w** receive my words, and hide my NIH
5:20 why **w** thou, my son, be ravisht with a NIH
6: 9 How long **w** thou sleep, O sluggard? NIH
6: 9 when **w** thou arise out of thy sleep? NIH
23: 5 **W** thou set thine eyes upon that which is NIH
Isa 26: 3 Thou **w** keep *him in* perfect peace, *whose* NIH
26:12 LORD, thou **w** ordain peace for us: NIH
27: 8 it shooteth forth, thou **w** debate with it: NIH
36: 9 **w** thou turn away the face of one captain of NIH
38:12 from day *even* to night **w** thou make an end NIH
38:13 from day *even* to night **w** thou make an end NIH
38:16 so **w** thou recover me, and make me to live. NIH
58: 5 and ashes *under him*? **w** thou call this a fast, NIH
64:12 **W** thou refrain thyself for these *things*, O NIH
64:12 **w** thou hold thy peace, and afflict us very NIH
Jer 3: 4 **W** thou not from this time cry unto me, NIH
4: 1 If thou **w** return, O Israel, saith the LORD, NIH
4: 1 if thou **w** put away thine abominations out NIH
4:30 And when thou art spoiled, what **w** thou do? NIH
12: 5 how **w** thou do in the swelling of Jordan? NIH
13:21 What **w** thou say when he shall punish thee? NIH
13:27 **w** thou not be made clean? when *shall it* NIH
15:18 **w** thou be altogether unto me as a liar, *and* NIH
31:22 How long **w** thou go about, O thou NIH
38:15 **w** thou not surely put me to death? NIH
38:15 thee counsel, **w** thou not hearken unto me? NIH
38:17 If thou **w** assuredly go forth unto the king of NIH
38:18 if thou **w** not go forth to the king of NIH
47: 5 of their valley: how long **w** thou cut thyself? NIH
La 1:21 they are glad that thou hast done *it*: thou **w** NIH
Eze 9: 8 **w** thou destroy all the residue of Israel in NIH
11:13 **w** thou make a full end of the remnant of NIH
20: 4 **W** thou judge them, son of man, wilt thou NIH
20: 4 **w** thou judge *them*? cause them to know NIH
22: 2 Now, thou son of man, **w** thou judge, wilt NIH
22: 2 thou judge, **w** thou judge the bloody city? NIH
23:36 **w** thou judge Aholah and Aholibah? NIH
24:19 **W** thou not tell us what these *things are* to NIH
28: 9 **W** thou yet say before him that slayeth thee, NIH
37:18 **W** thou not shew us what thou meanest by NIH
Hos 9:14 what **w** thou give? give them a miscarrying NIH
Mic 7:19 thou **w** cast all their sins into the depths of NIH
7:20 Thou **w** perform the truth to Jacob, *and* NIH
Hab 1: 2 how long shall I cry, and thou **w** not hear? NIH
1: 2 unto thee *of* violence, and thou **w** not save? NIH
Zep 3: 7 I said, Surely thou **w** fear me, thou wilt NIH
3: 7 wilt fear me, thou **w** receive instruction; NIH
Zec 1:12 how long **w** thou not have mercy on NIH
3: 7 If thou **w** walk in my ways, and if thou wilt NIH
3: 7 if thou **w** keep my charge, then thou shalt NIH
Mt 4: 9 if thou **w** fall down and worship me. NIG
7: 4 Or how **w** thou say to thy brother, Let me NIG
8: 2 worshipped him, saying, Lord, if thou **w**, *2309*
13:28 **W** thou then *that* we go and gather them *2309*
15:28 be it unto thee *even* as thou **w**. And her *2309*
17: 4 if thou **w**, let us make here three *2309*
19:17 but if thou **w** enter into life, keep *2309*
19:21 If thou **w** be perfect, go *and* sell that thou *2309*
20:21 And he said unto her, What **w** thou? *2309*
26:17 Where **w** thou *that* we prepare for thee to *2309*
26:39 nevertheless not as I will, but as thou *w*. NIG
Mk 1:40 to him, and saying unto him, If thou **w**, *2309*
6:22 Ask of me whatsoever thou **w**, and I will *2309*
10:51 What **w** thou *that* I should do unto thee? *2309*
14:12 Where **w** thou *that* we go and prepare that *2309*
14:36 not that I will, but what thou *w*. NIG
Lk 4: 7 If thou therefore **w** worship me, all shall be NIG
5:12 and besought him, saying, Lord, if thou **w**, *2309*
9:54 **w** thou *that* we command fire to come *2309*
18:41 What **w** thou *that* I shall do unto thee? *2309*
22: 9 unto him, Where **w** thou *that* we prepare? *2309*
Jn 2:20 and **w** thou rear it up in three days? NIG
5: 6 he saith unto him, **W** thou be made whole? *2309*
11:22 even now, whatsoever thou **w** ask of God, NIG
13:38 **W** thou lay down thy life for my sake? NIG
Jn 14:22 how is it that thou **w** manifest thyself unto *3195*
Ac 1: 6 **w** thou at this time restore again NIG
2:27 Because thou **w** not leave my soul in hell, NIG
2:27 neither **w** thou suffer thine Holy One to see NIG
7:28 **W** thou kill me, as thou didst the Egyptian *2309*
9: 6 Lord, what **w** thou have me to do? NIG
13:10 **w** thou not cease to pervert the right ways of NIG
25: 9 **W** thou go up to Jerusalem, and there be *2309*
Ro 9:19 Thou **w** say then unto me, Why doth he yet NIG
11:19 Thou **w** say then, The branches were broken NIG
13: 3 **W** thou then not be afraid of the power? *2309*
Phm 1:21 knowing that thou **w** also do more than I NIG
Jas 2:20 But **w** thou know, O vain man, that faith *2309*

WILY See FROWARD

WIMPLES (1)

Isa 3:22 and the **w**, and the crisping pins, 4304

WIN (2) [WINNETH, WON]

2Ch 32: 1 and thought to **w** them for himself. 1234
Php 3: 8 count *them but* dung, that I may **w** Christ, *2770*

WIND (123) [WHIRLWIND, WHIRLWINDS, WINDING, WINDS, WINDY, WOUND]

Ge 8: 1 God made a **w** to pass over the earth, and 7307
41: 6 blasted with the **east w** sprang up after 6921
41:23 withered, thin, *and* blasted with the **east w**, 6921
41:27 the **east w** shall be seven years of famine. 6921
Ex 10:13 the LORD brought an east **w** upon 7307
10:13 the east **w** brought the locusts. 7307
10:19 the LORD turned a mighty strong west **w**, 7307
14:21 to go *back* by a strong east **w** all *that* night, 7307
15:10 Thou didst blow with thy **w**, the sea 7307
Nu 11:31 there went forth a **w** from the LORD, and 7307
2Sa 22:11 and he was seen upon the wings of the **w**. 7307
1Ki 18:45 the heaven was black *with* clouds and **w**, 7307
19:11 a great and strong **w** rent the mountains, 7307
19:11 *but* the LORD *was* not in the **w**: 7307
19:11 after the **w** an earthquake; *but* the LORD 7307
2Ki 3:17 Ye shall not see **w**, neither shall ye see rain; 7307
Job 1:19 there came a great **w** from the wilderness, 7307
6:26 of one that is desperate, *which are* as **w**? 7307
7: 7 O remember that my life *is* **w**: mine eye 7307
8: 2 the words of thy mouth *be like* a strong **w**? 7307
15: 2 and fill his belly *with* the **east w**? 6921
21:18 They are as stubble before the **w**, and 7307
27:21 The **east w** carrieth him away, and 6921
30:15 they pursue my soul as the **w**: and 7307
30:22 Thou liftest me up to the **w**; thou causest 7307
37:17 when he quieteth the earth by the south *w*? NIH
37:21 but the **w** passeth, and cleanseth them. 7307
38:24 *which* scattereth the **east w** upon the earth? 6921
Ps 1: 4 *are* like the chaff which the **w** driveth away. 7307
18:10 yea, he did fly upon the wings of the **w**. 7307
18:42 I beat them small as the dust before the **w**: 7307
35: 5 Let them be as chaff before the **w**: and 7307
48: 7 the ships of Tarshish with an east **w**. 7307
78:26 He caused an **east w** to blow in the heaven: 6921
78:26 by his power he brought in the **south w**. 8486
78:39 a **w** that passeth away, and cometh not 7307
83:13 like a wheel; as the stubble before the **w**. 7307
103:16 For the **w** passeth over it, and it is gone; 7307
104: 3 who walketh upon the wings of the **w**: 7307
107:25 he commandeth, and raiseth the stormy **w**, 7307
135: 7 he bringeth the **w** out of his treasuries. 7307
147:18 he causeth his **w** to blow, *and* the waters 7307
148: 8 and vapour; stormy **w** fulfilling his word: 7307
Pr 11:29 troubleth his own house shall inherit the **w**: 7307
25:14 false gift *is like* clouds and **w** without rain. 7307
25:23 The north **w** driveth away rain: so *doth* an 7307
27:16 hideth the **w**, and the ointment of his right 7307
30: 4 who hath gathered the **w** in his fists? 7307
Ecc 1: 6 The **w** goeth toward the south, and 7307
1: 6 the **w** returneth *again* according to his 7307
5:16 profit hath he that hath laboured for the **w**? 7307
11: 4 He that observeth the **w** shall not sow; and 7307
SS 4:16 Awake, O **north w**; and come thou south; 6828
Isa 7: 2 the trees of the wood are moved with the **w**. 7307
11:15 with his mighty **w** shall he shake his hand 7307
17:13 as the chaff of the mountains before the **w**, 7307
26:18 in pain, we have as it were brought forth **w**; 7307
27: 8 he stayeth his rough **w** in the day of the east 7307
27: 8 his rough wind in the day of the **east w**. 6921
32: 2 a man shall be as a hiding place from the **w**, 7307
41:16 the **w** shall carry them away, and 7307
41:29 their molten images *are* **w** and confusion. 7307
57:13 the **w** shall carry them all away; 7307
64: 6 our iniquities, like the **w**, have taken us 7307
Jer 2:24 *that* snuffeth up the **w** at her pleasure; 7307
4:11 A dry **w** of the high places in 7307
4:12 *Even* a full **w** from those *places* shall come 7307
5:13 the prophets shall become **w**, and the word 7307
10:13 bringeth forth the **w** out of his treasures. 7307
13:24 passeth away by the **w** of the wilderness. 7307
14: 6 they snuffed up the **w** like dragons; 7307
18:17 I will scatter them as *with* an east **w** before 7307
22:22 The **w** shall eat up all thy pastors, and 7307
51: 1 that rise up against me, a destroying **w**; 7307
51:16 bringeth forth the **w** out of his treasures. 7307
Eze 5: 2 a third *part* thou shalt scatter in the **w**; and 7307
12:14 I will scatter toward every **w** all that *are* 7307
13:11 shall fall; and a stormy **w** shall rent *it*. 7307
13:13 I will even rent *it with* a stormy **w** in my 7307
17:10 utterly wither, when the east **w** toucheth it? 7307
19:12 and the east **w** dried up her fruit: 7307
27:26 the east **w** hath broken thee in the midst of 7307
37: 9 Prophesy unto the **w**, prophesy, son of man, 7307
37: 9 prophesy, son of man, and say to the **w**, 7307
Da 2:35 the **w** carried them away, that no place was 7308
Hos 4:19 The **w** hath bound her up in her wings, and 7307
8: 7 For they have sown the **w**, and they shall 7307
12: 1 Ephraim feedeth on **w**, and followeth after 7307
12: 1 on wind, and followeth after the **east w**: 6921
Hos 13:15 among *his* brethren, an east **w** shall come, 7307
13:15 the **w** of the LORD *shall* come up from NIH
Am 4:13 createth the **w**, and declareth unto man 7307
Jnh 1: 4 the LORD sent out a great **w** into the sea, 7307
4: 8 that God prepared a vehement east **w**; 7307
Hab 1: 9 their faces shall sup up *as* the **east w**, and 6921
Zec 5: 9 two women, and the **w** *was* in their wings; 7307
Mt 11: 7 to see? A reed shaken with the **w**? *417*
14:24 tossed with waves: for the **w** was contrary. *417*
14:30 But when he saw the **w** boysterous, he was *417*
14:32 they were come into the ship, the **w** ceased. *417*
Mk 4:37 And there arose a great storm of **w**, and the *417*
4:39 and rebuked the **w**, and said unto the sea, *417*
4:39 And the **w** ceased, and there was a great *417*
4:41 is this, that even the **w** and the sea obey him? *417*
6:48 in rowing; for the **w** was contrary unto them: *417*
6:51 up unto them into the ship; and the **w** ceased: *417*
Lk 7:24 for to see? A reed shaken with the **w**? *417*
8:23 there came down a storm of **w** on the lake; *417*
8:24 and rebuked the **w** and the raging of *417*
12:55 And when *ye see* the **south w** blow, ye say, *3558*
Jn 3: 8 The **w** bloweth where it listeth, and *4151*
6:18 And the sea arose by reason of a great **w** that *417*
Ac 2: 2 from heaven as of a rushing mighty **w**, *4157*
27: 7 the **w** not suffering us, we sailed under *417*
27:13 And when the **south w** blew softly, *3558*
27:14 after there arose against it a tempestuous **w**, *417*
27:15 and could not bear up into the **w**, we let *her* *417*
27:40 and hoised up the mainsail to the **w**, and *4154*
28:13 and after one day the **south w** blew, and *3558*
Eph 4:14 and carried about with every **w** of doctrine, *417*
Jas 1: 6 is like a wave of the sea **driven with the w** *416*
Rev 6:13 when she is shaken of a mighty **w**. *417*
7: 1 that the **w** should not blow on the earth, *417*

WINDING (3) [WIND]

1Ki 6: 8 they went up with **w stairs** into the middle 3883
Eze 41: 7 a **w about** still upward to the side 5437
41: 7 for the **w about** of the house *went* still 5437

WINDOW (16) [WINDOWS]

Ge 6:16 A **w** shalt thou make to the ark, and in a 6672
8: 6 that Noah opened the **w** of the ark which he 2474
26: 8 king of the Philistims looked out at a **w**, 2474
Jos 2:15 she let them down by a cord through the **w**: 2474
2:18 in the **w** which thou didst let us down by: 2474
2:21 and she bound the scarlet line in the **w**. 2474
Jdg 5:28 The mother of Sisera looked out at a **w**, and 2474
1Sa 19:12 So Michal let David down through a **w**: and 2474
2Sa 6:16 Michal Saul's daughter looked through a **w**, 2474
2Ki 9:30 and tired her head, and looked out at a **w**. 2474
9:32 he lift up his face to the **w**, and said, Who *is* 2474
13:17 he said, Open the **w** eastward. And he 2474
1Ch 15:29 looking out at a **w** saw king David dancing 2474
Pr 7: 6 For at the **w** of my house I looked through 2474
Ac 20: 9 And there sat in a **w** a certain young man *2376*
2Co 11:33 And through a **w** in a basket was I let down *2376*

WINDOWS (30) [WINDOW]

Ge 7:11 and the **w** of heaven were opened. 699
8: 2 the deep and the **w** of heaven were stopped, 699
1Ki 6: 4 for the house he made **w** of narrow lights. 2474
7: 4 *there were* **w** *in* three rows, and light *was* 8261
7: 5 and posts *were* square, *with the* **w**: 8260
2Ki 7: 2 *if* the LORD would make **w** in heaven, 699
7:19 *if* the LORD should make **w** in heaven, 699
Ecc 12: 3 and those that look out of the **w** be darkened, 699
SS 2: 9 behind our wall, he looketh forth at the **w**, 2474
Isa 24:18 for the **w** from on high are open, and 699
54:12 I will make thy **w** *of* agates, and thy gates 8121
60: 8 fly as a cloud, and as the doves to their **w**? 699
Jer 9:21 For death is come up into our **w**, *and* 2474
22:14 and large chambers, and cutteth him out **w**; 2474
Eze 40:16 *there were* narrow **w** to the little chambers, 2474
40:16 **w** *were* round about inward: and upon *each* 2474
40:22 their **w**, and their arches, and their palm 2474
40:25 *there were* **w** in it and in the arches thereof 2474
40:25 arches thereof round about, like those **w**: 2474
40:29 *there were* **w** in it and in the arches thereof 2474
40:33 *there were* **w** therein and in the arches 2474
40:36 arches thereof, and the **w** to it round about: 2474
41:16 the narrow **w**, and the galleries round about 2474
41:16 *from* the ground up to the **w**, and 2474
41:16 to the windows, and the **w** *were* covered; 2474
41:26 *there were* narrow **w** and palm trees on 2474
Da 6:10 his **w** being open in his chamber toward 3551
Joel 2: 9 they shall enter in at the **w** like a thief. 2474
Zep 2:14 *their* voice shall sing in the **w**; 2474
Mal 3:10 if I will not open you the **w** of heaven, and 699

WINDS (23) [WINDY]

Job 28:25 To make the weight for the **w**; and 7307
Jer 49:32 I will scatter into all **w** them *that are* in 7307
49:36 upon Elam will I bring the four **w** from 7307
49:36 and will scatter them towards all those **w**; 7307
Eze 5:10 remnant of thee will I scatter into all the **w**. 7307
5:12 I will scatter a third *part* into all the **w**, and 7307
17:21 that remain shall be scattered towards all **w**: 7307
37: 9 Come from the four **w**, O breath, and 7307
Da 7: 2 the four **w** of the heaven strove upon 7308
8: 8 notable ones toward the four **w** of heaven. 7307
11: 4 shall be divided toward the four **w** of 7307
Zec 2: 6 for I have spread you abroad as the four **w** 7307
Mt 7:25 and the **w** blew, and beat upon that house; *417*
7:27 and the **w** blew, and beat upon that house; *417*
8:26 he arose, and rebuked the **w** and the sea; *417*
8:27 is this, that even the **w** and the sea obey him? *417*
24:31 gather together his elect from the four **w**, *417*
Mk 13:27 gather together his elect from the four **w**, *417*
Lk 8:25 for he commandeth even the **w** and water, *417*
Ac 27: 4 under Cyprus, because the **w** were contrary. *417*
Jas 3: 4 they be so great, and are driven of fierce **w**, *417*
Jude 1:12 *they are* without water, carried about of **w**; *417*
Rev 7: 1 holding the four **w** of the earth, that the wind *417*

W

WINDY (1) [WINDS]

Ps 55: 8 I would hasten my escape from the w storm 7307

WINE (232) [WINEBIBBER, WINEBIBBERS, WINEFAT, WINEPRESS, WINEPRESSES, WINES]

Ge 9:21 he drank of the w, and was drunken; and 3196
9:24 Noah awoke from his w, and knew what his 3196
14:18 king of Salem brought forth bread and w: 3196
19:32 let us make our father drink w, and we will 3196
19:33 they made their father drink w that night: 3196
19:34 let us make him drink w this night also; and 3196
19:35 they made their father drink w that night 3196
27:25 and he brought him w, and he drank. 3196
27:28 of the earth, and plenty of corn and w: 8492
27:37 and with corn and w have I sustained him: 8492
49:11 he washed his garments in w, and 3196
49:12 His eyes shall be red with w, and his teeth 3196
Ex 29:40 the fourth part of a hin of w for a drink 3196
Lev 10: 9 Do not drink w nor strong drink, thou, 3196
23:13 the drink offering thereof shall be of w, 3196
Nu 6: 3 He shall separate himself from w and 3196
6: 3 and shall drink no vinegar of w, or 3196
6:20 and after that the Nazarite may drink w. 3196
15: 5 the fourth part of a hin of w for a drink 3196
15: 7 thou shalt offer the third part of a hin of w, 3196
15:10 bring for a drink offering half a hin of w, 3196
18:12 and all the best of the w, and of the wheat, 8492
28: 7 strong w to be poured unto the LORD for 7941
28:14 their drink offerings shall be half a hin of w 3196
Dt 7:13 thy land, thy corn, and thy w, and thine oil, 8492
11:14 gather in thy corn, and thy w, and thine oil. 8492
12:17 or of thy w, or of thy oil, or the firstlings of 8492
14:23 of thy w, and of thine oil, and the firstlings 8492
14:26 or for w, or for strong drink, or 3196
16:13 thou hast gathered in thy corn and thy w: 3342
18: 4 of thy w, and of thy oil, and the first of 8492
28:39 dress them, but shalt neither drink of the w, 3196
28:51 w, or oil, or the increase of thy kine, or 8492
29: 6 neither have you drunk w or strong drink: 3196
32:33 Their w is the poison of dragons, and 3196
32:38 and drank the w of their drink offerings? 3196
33:28 Jacob shall be upon a land of corn and w; 8492
Jos 9: 4 and w bottles, old, and rent, and bound up; 3196
9:13 these bottles of w, which we filled, 3196
Jdg 9:13 Should I leave my w, which cheereth God 8492
13: 4 drink not w nor strong drink, and eat not 3196
13: 7 now drink no w nor strong drink, 3196
13:14 neither let her drink w or strong drink, 3196
19:19 there is bread and w also for me, and 3196
1Sa 1:14 be drunken? put away thy w from thee. 3196
1:15 I have drunk neither w nor strong drink, but 3196
1:24 a bottle of w, and brought him unto 3196
10: 3 and another carrying a bottle of w: 3196
16:20 a bottle of w, and a kid, and sent them by 3196
25:18 two bottles of w, and five sheep ready 3196
25:37 when the w was gone out of Nabal, and 3196
2Sa 6:19 a flagon of w. So all the people departed NIH
13:28 now when Amnon's heart is merry with w, 3196
16: 1 of summer fruits, and a bottle of w. 3196
16: 2 the w, that such as be faint in 3196
2Ki 18:32 a land of corn and w, a land of bread and 8492
1Ch 9:29 the w, and the oil, and the frankincense, 3196
12:40 w, and oil, and oxen, and sheep abundantly: 3196
16: 3 a good piece of flesh, and a flagon of w. NIH
27:27 over the increase of the vineyards for the w 3196
2Ch 2:10 twenty thousand baths of w, and 3196
2:15 and the barley, the oil, and the w, 3196
11:11 and store of victual, and of oil and w. 3196
31: 5 w, and oil, and honey, and of all 8492
32:28 also for the increase of corn, and w, and oil; 8492
Ezr 6: 9 the God of heaven, wheat, salt, w, and oil, 2562
7:22 to an hundred baths of w, and to an 2562
Ne 2: 1 Artaxerxes the king, that w was before him: 3196
2: 1 I took up the w, and gave it unto the king. 3196
5:11 of the corn, the w, and the oil, that ye exact 8492
5:15 had taken of them bread and w, beside forty 3196
5:18 and once in ten days store of all sorts of w: 3196
10:37 of trees, of w and of oil, unto the priests, 8492
10:39 of the new w, and the oil, unto 8492
13: 5 tithes of the corn, the new w, and the oil, 8492
13:12 the new w and the oil unto the treasuries. 8492
13:15 some treading w presses on the sabbath, 1660
13:15 as also w, grapes, and figs, and all manner 3196
Est 1: 7 royal w in abundance, according to 3196
1:10 the heart of the king was merry with w, 3196
5: 6 king said unto Esther at the banquet of w, 3196
7: 2 on the second day at the banquet of w, 3196
7: 7 the king arising from the banquet of w in 3196
7: 8 garden into the place of the banquet of w; 3196
Job 1:13 drinking w in their eldest brother's house: 3196
1:18 drinking w in their eldest brother's house: 3196
32:19 my belly is as w which hath no vent; 3196
Ps 4: 7 time that their corn and their w increased. 8492
60: 3 made us to drink the w of astonishment. 3196
75: 8 the LORD there is a cup, and the w is red; 3196
78:65 a mighty man that shouteth by reason of w. 3196
104:15 w that maketh glad the heart of man, 3196
Pr 3:10 and thy presses shall burst out with new w. 8492
4:17 of wickedness, and drink the w of violence. 3196
9: 2 killed her beasts; she hath mingled her w; 3196
9: 5 and drink of the w which I have mingled. 3196
20: 1 W is a mocker, strong drink is raging: and 3196
21:17 he that loveth w and oil shall not be rich. 3196
23:30 They that tarry long at the w; they that go 3196
23:30 at the wine; they that go to seek mixt w. 4469
23:31 Look not thou upon the w when it is red, 3196
31: 4 O Lemuel, it is not for kings to drink w; 3196
31: 6 and w unto those that be of heavy hearts. 3196
Ecc 2: 3 sought in mine heart to give myself unto w, 3196
9: 7 and drink thy w with a merry heart; 3196
10:19 is made for laughter, and w maketh merry: 3196
SS 1: 2 of his mouth: for thy love is better than w. 3196
1: 4 we will remember thy love more than w: 3196
4:10 how much better is thy love than w! and 3196
SS 5: 1 I have drunk my w with my milk: 3196
7: 9 the roof of thy mouth like the best w, 3196
8: 2 I would cause thee to drink of spiced w, 3196
Isa 1:22 is become dross, thy w mixt with water: 5435
5:11 continue until night, till w inflame them! 3196
5:12 and the viol, the tabret, and pipe, and w, 3196
5:22 Woe unto them that are mighty to drink w, 3196
16:10 the treaders shall tread out no w in their 3196
22:13 killing sheep, eating flesh, and drinking w: 3196
24: 7 The new w mourneth, the vine languisheth, 8492
24: 9 They shall not drink w with a song; 3196
24:11 There is a crying for w in the streets; all joy 3196
27: 2 day sing ye unto her, A vineyard of red w. 2561
28: 1 valleys of them that are overcome with w. 3196
28: 7 they also have erred through w, and 3196
28: 7 strong drink, they are swallowed up of w, 3196
29: 9 they are drunken, but not with w; 3196
36:17 a land of corn and w, a land of bread and 8492
49:26 with their own blood, as with sweet w: 6071
51:21 thou afflicted, and drunken, but not with w: 3196
55: 1 buy w and milk without money and without 3196
56:12 say they, I will fetch w, and we will fill 3196
62: 8 sons of the stranger shall not drink thy w, 8492
65: 8 As the new w is found in the cluster, and 8492
Jer 13:12 Every bottle shall be filled with w: 3196
13:12 that every bottle shall be filled with w? 3196
23: 9 like a man whom w hath overcome, 3196
25:15 Take the w cup of this fury at mine hand, 3196
31:12 for w, and for oil, and for the young of 8492
35: 2 of the chambers, and give them w to drink. 3196
35: 5 the house of the Rechabites pots full of w, 3196
35: 5 and cups, and I said unto them, Drink ye w. 3196
35: 6 they said, We will drink no w: for Jonadab 3196
35: 6 saying, Ye shall drink no w, neither ye, 3196
35: 8 to drink no w all our days, we, our wives, 3196
35:14 that he commanded his sons not to drink w, 3196
40:10 ye, gather ye w, and summer fruits, and oil, 3196
40:12 gathered w and summer fruits very much. 3196
48:33 I have caused w to fail from the wine 3196
48:33 caused wine to fail from the w presses: 3342
51: 7 the nations have drunken of her w; 3196
La 2:12 say to their mothers, Where is corn and w? 3196
Eze 27:18 in the w of Helbon, and white wool. 3196
44:21 Neither shall any priest drink w, when they 3196
Da 1: 5 king's meat, and of the w which he drank: 3196
1: 8 nor with the w which he drank: 3196
1:16 and the w that they should drink; 3196
5: 1 his lords, and drank w before the thousand. 2562
5: 2 Belshazzar, whiles he tasted the w, 2562
5: 4 They drank w, and praised the gods of 2562
5:23 and thy concubines, have drunk w in them; 2562
10: 3 neither came flesh nor w in my mouth, 3196
Hos 2: 8 w, and oil, and multiplied her silver and 8492
2: 9 my w in the season thereof, and 8492
2:22 shall hear the corn, and the w, and the oil; 8492
3: 1 look to other gods, and love flagons of w. 6025
4:11 Whoredom and w and new wine take away 3196
4:11 and wine and new w take away the heart. 8492
7: 5 have made him sick with bottles of w; 3196
7:14 they assemble themselves for corn and w, 8492
9: 2 feed them, and the new w shall fail in her. 8492
9: 4 They shall not offer w offerings to 3196
14: 7 the scent thereof shall be as the w of 3196
Joel 1: 5 howl, all ye drinkers of w, because of 3196
1: 5 ye drinkers of wine, because of the new w, 6071
1:10 the new w is dried up, the oil languisheth. 8492
2:19 w, and oil, and ye shall be satisfied 8492
2:24 and the fats shall overflow with w and oil. 8492
3: 3 and sold a girl for w, that they might drink. 3196
3:18 that the mountains shall drop down new w, 6071
Am 2: 8 they drink the w of the condemned in 3196
2:12 ye gave the Nazarites w to drink; 3196
5:11 but ye shall not drink w of them. 3196
6: 6 That drink w in bowls, and 3196
9:13 the mountains shall drop sweet w, and 6071
9:14 plant vineyards, and drink the w thereof; 3196
Mic 2:11 saying, I will prophesy unto thee of w and 3196
6:15 and sweet w, but shalt not drink wine. 8492
6:15 and sweet wine, but shalt not drink w. 3196
Hab 2: 5 Yea also, because he transgresseth by w, 3196
Zep 1:13 plant vineyards, but not drink the w thereof. 3196
Hag 1:11 upon the new w, and upon the oil, and 8492
2:12 or pottage, or w, or oil, or any meat, shall it 3196
Zec 9:15 shall drink, and make a noise as through w; 3196
9:17 young men cheerful, and new w the maids. 8492
10: 7 and their heart shall rejoice as through w: 3196
Mt 9:17 Neither do men put new w into old bottles: 3631
9:17 and the w runneth out, and the bottles 3631
9:17 but they put new w into new bottles, and 3631
Mk 2:22 And no man putteth new w into old bottles: 3631
2:22 else the new w doth burst the bottles, and 3631
2:22 and the w is spilled, and the bottles will be 3631
2:22 but new w must be put into new bottles. 3631
15:23 And they gave him to drink w mingled with 3631
Lk 1:15 and shall drink neither w nor strong drink; 3631
5:37 And no man putteth new w into old bottles; 3631
5:37 else the new w will burst the bottles, and 3631
5:38 But new w must be put into new bottles; 3631
5:39 No man also having drunk old w NIG
7:33 came neither eating bread nor drinking w; 3631
10:34 pouring in oil and w, and set him on his 3631
Jn 2: 3 And when they wanted w, the mother of 3631
2: 3 of Jesus saith unto him, They have no w. 3631
2: 9 feast had tasted the water that was made w, 3631
2:10 man at the beginning doth set forth good w; 3631
2:10 but thou hast kept the good w until now. 3631
4:46 of Galilee, where he made the water w. 3631
Ac 2:13 These men are full of new w. 1098
Ro 14:21 is good neither to eat flesh, nor to drink w, 3631
Eph 5:18 And be not drunk with w, wherein is 3631
1Ti 3: 3 Not given to w, no striker, not greedy of 3943
3: 8 not doubletongued, not given to much w, 3631
5:23 but use a little w for thy stomach's sake 3631
Tit 1: 7 not soon angry, not given to w, no striker, 3943
2: 3 not false accusers, not given to much w, 3631
1Pe 4: 3 lusts, excess of w, revellings, banquetings, 3632
Rev 6: 6 and see thou hurt not the oil and the w. 3631
14: 8 she made all nations drink of the w of 3631
14:10 The same shall drink of the w of the wrath 3631
16:19 to give unto her the cup of the w of 3631
17: 2 made drunk with the w of her fornication. 3631
18: 3 For all nations have drunk of the w of 3631
18:13 and w, and oil, and fine flour, and wheat, 3631

WINEBIBBER (2) [WINE]

Mt 11:19 and a w, a friend of publicans and sinners. 3630
Lk 7:34 and a w, a friend of publicans and sinners. 3630

WINEBIBBERS (1) [WINE]

Pr 23:20 Be not amongst w; amongst riotous eaters 3196

WINEFAT (2) [WINE]

Isa 63: 2 garments like him that treadeth in the w? 1660
Mk 12: 1 about it, and digged a place for the w, 5276

WINEPRESS (15) [PRESS, WINE]

Nu 18:27 and as the fulness of the w. 3342
18:30 and as the increase of the w. 3342
Dt 15:14 and out of thy floor, and out of thy w: 3342
Jdg 6:11 his son Gideon threshed wheat by the w, 1660
7:25 Zeeb they slew at the w of Zeeb, and 3342
2Ki 6:27 out of the barnfloor, or out of the w? 3342
Isa 5: 2 the midst of it, and also made a w therein: 3342
63: 3 I have trodden the w alone; and of 6333
La 1:15 the virgin, the daughter of Judah, as in a w. 1660
Hos 9: 2 The floor and the w shall not feed them, 3342
Mt 21:33 and digged a w in it, and built a tower, and 3025
Rev 14:19 cast it into the great w of the wrath of God. 3025
14:20 And the w was trodden without the city, 3025
14:20 and blood came out of the w, even unto 3025
19:15 and he treadeth the w of 3025+3631

WINEPRESSES (2) [PRESS, WINE]

Job 24:11 and tread their w, and suffer thirst. 3342
Zec 14:10 the tower of Hananeel unto the king's w. 3342

WINES (2) [WINE]

Isa 25: 6 a feast of w on the lees, of fat things full of 8105
25: 6 of marrow, of w on the lees well refined. 8105

WING (13) [LONGWINGED, WINGED, WINGS]

1Ki 6:24 five cubits was the one w of the cherub, 3671
6:24 and five cubits the other w of the cherub: 3671
6:24 from the uttermost part of the one w unto 3671
6:27 that the w of the one touched the one wall, 3671
6:27 the w of the other cherub touched the other 3671
2Ch 3:11 one w of the one cherub was five cubits, 3671
3:11 the other w was likewise five cubits, 3671
3:11 reaching to the w of the other cherub. 3671
3:12 one w of the other cherub was five cubits, 3671
3:12 the other w was five cubits also, joining to 3671
3:12 also, joining to the w of the other cherub. 3671
Isa 10:14 there was none that moved the w, or 3671
Eze 17:23 and under it shall dwell all fowl of every w; 3671

WINGED (2) [WING]

Ge 1:21 their kind, and every w fowl after his kind: 3671
Dt 4:17 the likeness of any w fowl that flieth in 3671

WINGS (76) [WING]

Ex 19: 4 how I bare you on eagles' w, and 3671
25:20 the cherubims shall stretch forth their w on 3671
25:20 covering the mercy seat with their w, 3671
37: 9 the cherubims spread out their w on high, 3671
37: 9 covered with their w over the mercy seat, 3671
Lev 1:17 he shall cleave it with the w thereof, but 3671
Dt 32:11 spreadeth abroad her w, taketh them, 3671
32:11 taketh them, beareth them on her w: 84
Ru 2:12 under whose w thou art come to trust. 3671
2Sa 22:11 and he was seen upon the w of the wind. 3671
1Ki 6:27 they stretched forth the w of the cherubims, 3671
6:27 their w touched one another in the midst of 3671
8: 6 to the most holy place, even under the w of 3671
8: 7 For the cherubims spread forth their two w 3671
1Ch 28:18 that spread out their w, and covered the ark NIH
2Ch 3:11 the w of the cherubims were twenty cubits 3671
3:13 The w of these cherubims spread 3671
5: 7 into the most holy place, even under the w 3671
5: 8 For the cherubims spread forth their w over 3671
Job 39:13 Gavest thou the goodly w unto 3671
39:13 or w and feathers unto the ostrich? 84
39:26 and stretch her w toward the south? 3671
Ps 17: 8 hide me under the shadow of thy w, 3671
18:10 yea, he did fly upon the w of the wind. 3671
36: 7 put their trust under the shadow of thy w. 3671
55: 6 O that I had w like a dove, for then would I 83
57: 1 in the shadow of thy w will I make my 3671
61: 4 I will trust in the covert of thy w. Selah. 3671
63: 7 in the shadow of thy w will I rejoice. 3671
68:13 yet shall ye be as the w of a dove covered 3671
91: 4 and under his w shalt thou trust: 3671
104: 3 who walketh upon the w of the wind: 3671
139: 9 If I take the w of the morning, and dwell in 3671
Pr 23: 5 for riches certainly make themselves w; 3671
Ecc 10:20 and that which hath w shall tell the matter. 3671
Isa 6: 2 each one had six w; with twain he covered 3671
8: 8 the stretching out of his w shall fill 3671
18: 1 Woe to the land shadowing with w, 3671
40:31 they shall mount up with w as eagles; 83
Jer 48: 9 Give w unto Moab, that it may flee and 6731
48:40 an eagle, and shall spread his w over Moab. 3671
49:22 as the eagle, and spread his w over Bozrah: 3671
Eze 1: 6 had four faces, and every one had four w. 3671
1: 8 they had the hands of a man under their w 3671
1: 8 and they four had their faces and their w. 3671
1: 9 Their w were joined one to another; they 3671
1:11 their w were stretched upward; two wings 3671
1:11 two w of every one were joined one to NIH
1:23 under the firmament were their w straight, 3671

Eze 1:24 they went, I heard the noise of their w, 3671
1:24 when they stood, they let down their w. 3671
1:25 when they stood, *and* had let down their w. 3671
3:13 *I heard* also the noise of the w of the living 3671
10: 5 the sound of the cherubims' w was heard 3671
10: 8 the form of a man's hand under their w. 3671
10:12 their hands, and their w, and the wheels, 3671
10:16 when the cherubims lift up their w to 3671
10:19 the cherubims lift up their w, and 3671
10:21 four faces apiece, and every one four w; 3671
10:21 of the hands of a man *was* under their w. 3671
11:22 did the cherubims lift up their w, and 3671
17: 3 A great eagle with great w, longwinged, 3671
17: 7 was also another great eagle with great w 3671
Da 7: 4 The first *was* like a lion, and had eagle's w: 1611
7: 4 I beheld till the w thereof were pluckt, and 1611
7: 6 which had upon the back of it four w of a 1611
Hos 4:19 The wind hath bound her up in her w, and 3671
Zec 5: 9 two women, and the wind *was* in their w; 3671
5: 9 for they had w like the wings of a stork: 3671
5: 9 for they had wings like the w of a stork: 3671
Mal 4: 2 of righteousness arise with healing in his w; 3671
Mt 23:37 a hen gathereth her chickens under *her* w, *4420*
Lk 13:34 as a hen *doth gather* her brood under *her* w, *4420*
Rev 4: 8 And the four beasts had each of them six w *4420*
9: 9 the sound of their w *was* as the sound of *4420*
12:14 And to the woman were given two w of a *4420*

WINK (2) [WINKED, WINKETH]
Job 15:12 thee away? and what do thine eyes w at, 7335
Ps 35:19 *neither* let them w *with* the eye that hate me 7169

WINKED (1) [WINK]
Ac 17:30 And the times of *this* ignorance God w at; *5237*

WINKETH (2) [WINK]
Pr 6:13 He w with his eyes, he speaketh with his 7169
10:10 He that w *with* the eye causeth sorrow: but 7169

WINNETH (1) [WIN]
Pr 11:30 *is* a tree of life; and he that w souls *is* wise. 3947

WINNOWED (1) [WINNOWETH]
Isa 30:24 which hath been w with the shovel and 2219

WINNOWETH (1) [WINNOWED]
Ru 3: 2 he w barley to night in the threshingfloor. 2219

WINTER (14) [WINTERED, WINTERHOUSE]
Ge 8:22 summer and w, and day and night shall not 2779
Ps 74:17 of the earth: thou hast made summer and w. 2779
SS 2:11 For lo, the w is past, the rain is over *and* 5638
Isa 18: 6 all the beasts of the earth shall w upon 2778
Am 3:15 I will smite the w house with the summer 2779
Zec 14: 8 hinder sea: in summer and in w shall it be. 2779
Mt 24:20 But pray ye that your flight be not in the w, *5494*
Mk 13:18 pray ye that your flight be not in the w. *5494*
Jn 10:22 *the feast of* the dedication, and it was w. *5494*
Ac 27:12 the haven was not commodious to w in, *3915*
27:12 might attain to Phenice, *and there* to w; *3914*
1Co 16: 6 be that I will abide, yea, and w with you, *3914*
2Ti 4:21 Do thy diligence to come before w. *5494*
Tit 3:12 for I have determined there to w. *3914*

WINTERED (1) [WINTER]
Ac 28:11 which had w in the isle, *whose* sign *was* *3914*

WINTERHOUSE (1) [HOUSE, WINTER]
Jer 36:22 Now the king sat *in* the w in 1004+2779

WIPE (8) [WIPED, WIPETH, WIPING]
2Ki 21:13 I will w Jerusalem as *a man* wipeth a dish, 4229
Ne 13:14 w not out my good deeds that I have done 4229
Isa 25: 8 the Lord GOD will w away tears from off 4229
Lk 7:38 and did w *them* with the hairs of her head, *1591*
10:11 cleaveth on us, we do w off against you: *631*
Jn 13: 5 to w *them* with the towel wherewith he was *1591*
Rev 7:17 God shall w away all tears from their eyes. *1813*
21: 4 And God shall w away all tears from their *1813*

WIPED (4) [WIPE]
Pr 6:33 and his reproach shall not be w away. 4229
Lk 7:44 and w *them* with the hairs of her head. *1591*
Jn 11: 2 and w his feet with her hair, whose brother *1591*
12: 3 feet of Jesus, and w his feet with her hair: *1591*

WIPETH (2) [WIPE]
2Ki 21:13 I will wipe Jerusalem as *a man* w a dish, 4229
Pr 30:20 she eateth, and w her mouth, and saith, 4229

WIPING (1) [WIPE]
2Ki 21:13 a dish, w *it,* and turning *it* upside down. 4229

WIRES (1)
Ex 39: 3 cut *it into* w, to work *it* in the blue, and 6616

WISDOM (234) [UNWISE]
Ex 28: 3 whom I have filled with the spirit of w, 2451
31: 3 in w, and in understanding, and 2451
31: 6 of all that are wise hearted I have put w, 2451
35:26 heart stirred them up in w spun goats' *hair.* 2451
35:31 in w, in understanding, and in knowledge, 2451
35:35 Them hath he filled *with* w of heart, 2451
36: 1 in whom the LORD put w and 2451
36: 2 in whose heart the LORD had put w, 2451
Dt 4: 6 and do *them;* for this *is* your w and 2451
34: 9 the son of Nun was full *of* the spirit of w; 2451
2Sa 14:20 according to the w of an angel of God, 2451
20:22 woman went unto all the people in her w. 2451
1Ki 2: 6 Do therefore according to thy w, and let not 2451
3:28 for they saw that the w of God *was* in him, 2451
4:29 God gave Solomon w and 2451
4:30 Solomon's w excelled the wisdom of all 2451
1Ki 4:30 Solomon's wisdom excelled the w of all 2451
4:30 of the east country, and all the w of Egypt. 2451
4:34 there came of all people to hear the w of 2451
4:34 of the earth, which had heard of his w. 2451
5:12 the LORD gave Solomon w, as he 2451
7:14 he was filled *with* w, and understanding, 2451
10: 4 queen of Sheba had seen all Solomon's w, 2451
10: 6 in mine own land of thy acts and of thy w. 2451
10: 7 thy w and prosperity exceedeth the fame 2451
10: 8 before thee, *and* that hear thy w. 2451
10:23 the kings of the earth for riches and for w. 2451
10:24 to hear his w, which God had put in his 2451
11:41 of Solomon, and all that he did, and his w, 2451
1Ch 22:12 Only the LORD give thee w and 7922
2Ch 1:10 Give me now w and knowledge, that I may 2451
1:11 hast asked w and knowledge for thyself, 2451
1:12 W and knowledge *is* granted unto thee; and 2451
9: 3 when the queen of Sheba had seen the w of 2451
9: 5 mine own land of thine acts, and of thy w: 2451
9: 6 *the one* half of the greatness of thy w was 2451
9: 7 continually before thee, and hear thy w. 2451
9:22 all the kings of the earth in riches and w. 2451
9:23 to hear his w, that God had put in his heart. 2451
Ezr 7:25 thou, Ezra, after the w of thy God, that *is* in 2452
Job 4:21 in them go away? they die, even without w. 2451
6:13 help in me? and is w driven *quite* from me? 8454
11: 6 that he would shew thee the secrets of w, 2451
12: 2 ye *are* the people, and w shall die with you. 2451
12:12 With the ancient *is* w; and *in* length of days 2451
12:13 With him *is* w and strength, he hath counsel 2451
12:16 With him *is* strength and w: the deceived 8454
13: 5 hold your peace, and it should be your w. 2451
15: 8 of God? and dost thou restrain w to thyself? 2451
26: 3 hast thou counselled *him that hath* no w? 2451
28:12 where shall w be found? and where *is* 2451
28:18 of pearls: for the price of w *is* above rubies. 2451
28:20 Whence then cometh w? and where *is* 2451
28:28 Behold, the fear of the Lord, that *is* w; 2451
32: 7 and multitude of years should teach w. 2451
32:13 Lest ye should say, We have found out w: 2451
33:33 hold thy peace, and I shall teach thee w. 2451
34:35 and his words *were* without w. 7919
36: 5 not *any: he is* mighty in strength *and* w. 3820
38:36 Who hath put w in the inward parts? or 2451
38:37 Who can number the clouds in w? or 2451
39:17 Because God hath deprived her of w, 2451
39:26 Doth the hawk fly by thy w, *and* stretch her 998
Ps 37:30 The mouth of the righteous speaketh w, and 2451
49: 3 My mouth shall speak of w; and 2454
51: 6 hidden *part* thou shalt make me to know w. 2451
90:12 that we may apply *our* hearts *unto* w. 2451
104:24 in w hast thou made them all: the earth is 2451
105:22 at his pleasure; and teach his senators w. 2449
111:10 fear of the LORD *is* the beginning of w: 2451
136: 5 To him that by w made the heavens: for his 8394
Pr 1: 2 To know w and instruction; to perceive 2451
1: 3 To receive the instruction of w, justice, and 7919
1: 7 *but* fools despise w and instruction. 2451
1:20 W crieth without; she uttereth her voice in 2454
2: 2 So that *thou* incline thine ear unto w, *and* 2451
2: 6 For the LORD giveth w: out of his mouth 2451
2: 7 He layeth up sound w for the righteous: 8454
2:10 When w entereth into thine heart, and 2451
3:13 Happy *is* the man *that* findeth w, and 2451
3:19 The LORD by w hath founded the earth; 2451
3:21 thine eyes: keep sound w and discretion: 8454
4: 5 Get w, get understanding: forget *it* not; 2451
4: 7 W *is* the principal thing; *therefore* 2451
4: 7 *is* the principal thing; *therefore* get w: 2451
4:11 I have taught thee in the way of w; I have 2451
5: 1 attend unto my w, *and* bow thine ear to my 2451
7: 4 Say unto w, Thou *art* my sister; and 2451
8: 1 Doth not w cry? and understanding put 2451
8: 5 O ye simple, understand w: and, ye fools, 6195
8:11 For w *is* better than rubies; and all 2451
8:12 I w dwell *with* prudence, and find out 2451
8:14 Counsel *is* mine, and sound w: I *am* 8454
9: 1 W hath builded her house, she hath hewn 2454
9:10 fear of the LORD *is* the beginning of w: 2451
10:13 In the lips of him that hath understanding w 2451
10:21 feed many: but fools die for want of w. 3820
10:23 but a man of understanding hath w. 2451
10:31 The mouth of the just bringeth forth w: but 2451
11: 2 cometh shame: but with the lowly *is* w. 2451
11:12 He that is void of w despiseth his 3820
12: 8 shall be commended according to his w: 7922
13:10 but with the well advised *is* w. 2451
14: 6 A scorner seeketh w, and *findeth it* not: but 2451
14: 8 The w of the prudent *is* to understand his 2451
14:33 W resteth in the heart of him that hath 2451
15:21 Folly *is* joy to *him that is* destitute of w: but 3820
15:33 fear of the LORD *is* the instruction of w; 2451
16:16 How much better *is it* to get w than gold! 2451
17:16 *there* a price in the hand of a fool to get w, 2451
17:24 W *is* before him that hath understanding; 2451
18: 1 seeketh *and* intermeddleth with all w. 8454
18: 4 *and* the wellspring of w *as* a flowing brook. 2451
19: 8 He that getteth w loveth his own soul: 3820
21:30 *There is* no w nor understanding nor 2451
23: 4 not to be rich: cease from thine own w. 998
23: 9 for he will despise the w of thy words. 7922
23:23 *also* w, and instruction, and understanding. 2451
24: 3 Through w is a house builded; and 2451
24: 7 W *is too* high for a fool: he openeth not his 2454
24:14 So shall the knowledge of w be unto thy 2451
29: 3 Whoso loveth w rejoiceth his father: but 2451
29:15 The rod and reproof give w: but a child left 2451
30: 3 I neither learned w, nor have 2451
31:26 She openeth her mouth with w; and in her 2451
Ecc 1:13 search out by w concerning all 2451+2050.2
1:16 have gotten more w than all *they* that have 2451
1:16 my heart had great experience of w and 2451
1:17 I gave my heart to know w, and to know 2451
1:18 For in much w *is* much grief: and he that 2451
2: 3 (yet acquainting mine heart with w) 2451
Ecc 2: 9 in Jerusalem: also my w remained with me. 2451
2:12 I turned myself to behold w, and madness, 2451
2:13 I saw that w excelleth folly, as far as light 2451
2:21 For there is a man whose labour *is* in w, 2451
2:26 giveth to a man that *is* good in his sight w, 2451
7:11 W *is* good with an inheritance: and *by it* 2451
7:12 For w *is* a defence, *and* money *is* a defence: 2451
7:12 the excellency of knowledge *is, that* w 2451
7:19 W strengtheneth the wise more than ten 2451
7:23 All this have I proved by w: I said, I will be 2451
7:25 to seek out w, and the reason *of things,* and 2451
8: 1 a man's w maketh his face to shine, and 2451
8:16 When I applied mine heart to know w, and 2451
9:10 nor knowledge, nor w, in the grave, 2451
9:13 This w have I seen also under the sun, and 2451
9:15 and he by his w delivered the city; 2451
9:16 said I, W *is* better than strength: 2451
9:16 nevertheless the poor *man's* w *is* despised, 2451
9:18 W *is* better than weapons of war: but 2451
10: 1 a little folly *him that is* in reputation for w 2451
10: 3 his w faileth *him,* and he saith to every one 3820
10:10 more strength: but w *is* profitable to direct. 2451
Isa 10:13 of my hand I have done *it,* and by my w; 2451
11: 2 the spirit of w and understanding, the spirit 2451
29:14 for the w of their wise *men* shall perish, 2451
33: 6 w and knowledge shall be the stability of 2451
47:10 Thy w and thy knowledge, it hath perverted 2451
Jer 8: 9 of the LORD; and what w *is* in them? 2451
9:23 Let not the wise *man* glory in his w, 2451
10:12 he hath established the world by his w, and 2451
49: 7 LORD of hosts; *Is* w no more in Teman? 2451
49: 7 from the prudent? is their w vanished? 2451
51:15 he hath established the world by his w, and 2451
Eze 28: 4 With thy w and with thine understanding 2451
28: 5 By thy great w *and* by thy traffick hast thou 2451
28: 7 their swords against the beauty of thy w, 2451
28:12 up the sum, full *of* w, and perfect in beauty. 2451
28:17 thou hast corrupted thy w by reason of thy 2451
Da 1: 4 skilful in all w, and cunning in knowledge, 2451
1:17 and skill in all learning and w: 2451
1:20 *in* all matters of w *and* understanding, 2451
2:14 w to Arioch the captain of the king's guard, 2942
2:20 for ever and ever: for w and might are his: 2452
2:21 he giveth w unto the wise, and 2452
2:23 who hast given me w and might, and 2452
2:30 this secret *is* not revealed to me for *any* w 2452
5:11 of thy father light and understanding and w, 2452
5:11 and wisdom, like the w of the gods, 2452
5:14 and excellent w is found in thee. 2452
Mic 6: 9 and *the man of* w shall see thy name: 8454
Mt 11:19 sinners. But w is justified of her children. *4678*
12:42 parts of the earth to hear the w of Solomon; *4678*
13:54 Whence hath this *man* this w, and *4678*
Mk 6: 2 and what w *is this* which is given unto him, *4678*
Lk 1:17 and the disobedient to the w of the just; *5428*
2:40 and waxed strong in spirit, filled with w: *4678*
2:52 And Jesus increased in w and stature, and *4678*
7:35 But w is justified of all her children. *4678*
11:31 parts of the earth to hear the w of Solomon; *4678*
11:49 Therefore also said the w of God, I will *4678*
21:15 For I will give you a mouth and w, *4678*
Ac 6: 3 full of the Holy Ghost and w, whom we *4678*
6:10 And they were not able to resist the w and *4678*
7:10 w in the sight of Pharaoh king of Egypt; *4678*
7:22 And Moses was learned in all the w of *4678*
Ro 11:33 O the depth of the riches both of the w and *4678*
1Co 1:17 not with w of words, lest the cross of Christ *4678*
1:19 I will destroy the w of the wise, and *4678*
1:20 hath not God made foolish the w of this *4678*
1:21 For after that in the w of God the world by *4678*
1:21 of God the world by w knew not God, *4678*
1:22 require a sign, and the Greeks seek after w: *4678*
1:24 Christ the power of God, and the w of God. *4678*
1:30 who of God is made unto us w, and *4678*
2: 1 not with excellency of speech or of w, *4678*
2: 4 *was* not with enticing words of man's w, *4678*
2: 5 That your faith should not stand in the w of *4678*
2: 6 Howbeit we speak w among *them that are* *4678*
2: 6 yet not the w of this world, nor of *4678*
2: 7 But we speak the w of God in a mystery, *4678*
2: 7 *even* the hidden w, which God ordained NIG
2:13 not in the words which man's w teacheth, *4678*
3:19 For the w of this world is foolishness with *4678*
12: 8 to one is given by the Spirit the word of w; *4678*
2Co 1:12 not with fleshly w, but by the grace of God, *4678*
Eph 1: 8 he hath abounded toward us in all w *4678*
1:17 may give unto you the spirit of w and *4678*
3:10 by the church the manifold w of God, *4678*
Col 1: 9 *with* the knowledge of his will in all w *4678*
1:28 and teaching every man in all w; *4678*
2: 3 In whom are hid all the treasures of w and *4678*
2:23 Which *things* have indeed a shew of w in *4678*
3:16 word of Christ dwell in you richly in all w; *4678*
4: 5 Walk in w toward them that are without, *4678*
Jas 1: 5 If any of you lack w, let him ask of God, *4678*
3:13 his works with meekness of w. *4678*
3:15 This w descendeth not from above, but *4678*
3:17 But the w that is from above is first pure, *4678*
2Pe 3:15 w given unto him hath written unto you; *4678*
Rev 5:12 and w, and strength, and honour, and glory, *4678*
7:12 and w, and thanksgiving, and honour, and *4678*
13:18 Here is w. Let him that hath understanding *4678*
17: 9 *And* here *is* the mind which hath w. *4678*

WISE (247) [WISELY, WISER]
Ge 3: 6 a tree to be desired to make *one* w, she 7919
41: 8 of Egypt, and all the w men thereof: 2450
41:33 let Pharaoh look out a man discreet and w, 2450
41:39 *there is* none so discreet and w as thou *art:* 2450
Ex 7:11 Pharaoh also called the w men and 2450
22:23 If thou afflict them in any w, 6031+6031
23: 8 for the gift blindeth the w, and 6493
28: 3 thou shalt speak unto all *that are* w hearted, 2450
31: 6 in the hearts of all that are w hearted I have 2450
35:10 every w hearted among you shall come, 2450

W

Ex 35:25 all the women that were w hearted did spin 2450
36: 1 and Aholiab, and every w hearted man, 2450
36: 2 and Aholiab, and every w hearted man, 2450
36: 4 all the w men, that wrought all the work of 2450
36: 8 every w hearted man among them that 2450
Lev 7:24 but ye shall in no w eat of it. 398+398+3808
19:17 thou shalt in any w rebuke thy 3198+3198
27:19 the field will in any w redeem it, 1350+1350
Nu 6:23 On this w ye shall bless the children of 3541
Dt 1:13 Take ye w men, and understanding, and 2450
1:15 w men, and known, and made them heads 2450
4: 6 Surely this great nation is a w and 2450
16:19 for a gift doth blind the eyes of the w, and 2450
17:15 Thou shalt in any w set him king 7760+7760
21:23 shalt in any w bury him that day; 6912+6912
22: 7 thou shalt in any w let the dam go, 7971+7971
32:29 O that they were w, that they understood 2449
Jos 6:18 in any w keep yourselves from 7535
23:12 Else if ye do in any w go back, 7725+7725
Jdg 5:29 Her w ladies answered her, yea, 2450
1Sa 6: 3 in any w return him a trespass 7725+7725
2Sa 14: 2 fetcht thence a w woman, and said unto 2450
14:20 my lord is w, according to the wisdom of 2450
20:16 cried a w woman out of the city, Hear, 2450
1Ki 2: 9 for thou art a w man, and knowest what 2450
3:12 I have given thee a w and an understanding 2450
3:26 the living child, and in no w slay it. 4191+4191
3:27 the living child, and in no w slay it: 4191+4191
5: 7 which hath given unto David a w son over 2450
11:22 howbeit let me go in any w. 7971+7971
1Ch 26:14 his son, a w counseller, they cast lots; 7922
27:32 was a counseller, a w man, and a scribe: 995
2Ch 2:12 who hath given to David the king a w son, 2450
Est 1:13 the king said to the w men, which knew 2450
6:13 said his w men and Zeresh his wife unto 2450
Job 5:13 He taketh the w in their own craftiness: and 2450
9: 4 He is w in heart, and mighty in strength: 2450
11:12 For vain man would be w, though man be 3823
15: 2 Should a w man utter vain knowledge, and 2450
15:18 Which w men have told from their fathers, 2450
17:10 for I cannot find one w man among you. 2450
22: 2 as he that is w may be profitable unto 7919
32: 9 Great men are not always w: neither do 2449
34: 2 O ye w men; and give ear unto me, 2450
34:34 tell me, and let a w man hearken unto me. 2450
37:24 he respecteth not any that are w of heart. 2450
Ps 2:10 Be w now therefore, O ye kings: 7919
19: 7 the LORD is sure, making w the simple. 2449
36: 3 he hath left off to be w, and to do good. 7919
37: 8 fret not thyself in any w to do evil. 389
49:10 For he seeth that w men die, likewise 2450
94: 8 and ye fools, when will ye be w? 7919
107:43 Whoso is w, and will observe these things, 2450
Pr 1: 5 A w man will hear, and will increase 2450
1: 5 understanding shall attain unto w counsels: 8458
1: 6 the words of the w, and their dark sayings. 2450
3: 7 Be not w in thine own eyes: fear 2450
3:35 The w shall inherit glory: but shame shall 2450
6: 6 consider her ways, and be w: 2449
8:33 and be w, and refuse it not. 2449
9: 8 rebuke a w man, and he will love thee. 2450
9: 9 Give instruction to a w man, and he will be 2450
9:12 If thou be w, thou shalt be wise for thyself: 2449
9:12 If thou be wise, thou shalt be w for thyself: 2449
10: 1 A w son maketh a glad father: but a foolish 2450
10: 5 He that gathereth in summer is a w son: but 7919
10: 8 The w in heart will receive 2450
10:14 W men lay up knowledge: but the mouth of 2450
10:19 not sin: but he that refraineth his lips is w. 7919
11:29 the fool shall be servant to the w of heart. 2450
11:30 tree of life; and he that winneth souls is w. 2450
12:15 but he that hearkeneth unto counsel is w. 2450
12:18 a sword: but the tongue of the w is health. 2450
13: 1 A w son heareth his father's instruction: but 2450
13:14 The law of the w is a fountain of life, 2450
13:20 He that walketh with w men shall be wise: 2450
13:20 He that walketh with wise men shall be w: 2449
14: 1 Every w woman buildeth her house: but 2450
14: 3 but the lips of the w shall preserve them. 2450
14:16 A w man feareth, and departeth from evil: 2450
14:24 The crown of the w is their riches: but 2450
14:35 The king's favour is toward a w servant: 7919
15: 2 The tongue of the w useth knowledge 2450
15: 7 The lips of the w disperse knowledge: but 2450
15:12 neither will he go unto the w. 2450
15:20 A w son maketh a glad father: but a foolish 2450
15:24 The way of life is above to the w, that he 7919
15:31 the reproof of life abideth among the w. 2450
16:14 of death: but a w man will pacify it. 2450
16:21 The w in heart shall be called prudent: and 2450
16:23 The heart of the w teacheth his mouth, and 2450
17: 2 A w servant shall have rule over a son that 7919
17:10 A reproof entereth more into a w man than 995
17:28 when he holdeth his peace, is counted w: 2450
18:15 and the ear of the w seeketh knowledge. 2450
19:20 that thou mayest be w in thy latter end. 2449
20: 1 whosoever is deceived thereby is not w. 2449
20:26 A w king scattereth the wicked, and 2450
21:11 scorner is punished, the simple is made w: 2449
21:11 when the w is instructed, he receiveth 2450
21:20 be desired and oil in the dwelling of the w; 2450
21:22 A w man scaleth the city of the mighty, and 2450
22:17 hear the words of the w, and apply thine 2450
23:15 My son, if thine heart be w, my heart shall 2449
23:19 and be w, and guide thine heart in the way. 2449
23:24 he that begetteth a w child shall have joy of 2450
24: 5 A w man is strong; yea, a man of 2450
24: 6 For by w counsel thou shalt make thy war: 8458
24:23 These things also belong to the w. It is not 2450
25:12 so is a w reprover upon an obedient ear. 2450
26: 5 to his folly, lest he be w in his own conceit. 2450
26:12 Seest thou a man w in his own conceit? 2450
27:11 My son, be w, and make my heart glad, 2449
28: 7 Whoso keepeth the law is a w son: but 995
28:11 The rich man is w in his own conceit; but 2450

Pr 29: 8 into a snare: but w men turn away wrath. 2450
29: 9 If a w man contendeth with a foolish man, 2450
29:11 but a w man keepeth it in till afterwards. 2450
30:24 the earth, but they are exceeding w: 2449+2450
Ecc 2:14 The w man's eyes are in his head; but 2450
2:15 even to me; and why was I then more w? 2449
2:16 For there is no remembrance of the w more 2450
2:16 And how dieth the w man? as the fool. 2450
2:19 who knoweth whether he shall be a w man 2450
2:19 wherein I have shewed myself w under 2449
4:13 and a w child than an old and foolish king, 2450
6: 8 For what hath the w more than the fool? 2450
7: 4 The heart of the w is in the house of 2450
7: 5 It is better to hear the rebuke of the w, 2450
7: 7 Surely oppression maketh a w man mad; 2450
7:16 over much; neither make thyself over w: 2449
7:19 Wisdom strengtheneth the w more than ten 2450
7:23 I said, I will be w; but it was far from me. 2449
8: 1 Who is as the w man? and who knoweth 2450
8: 5 a w man's heart discerneth both time and 2450
8:17 though a w man think to know it, yet shall 2450
9: 1 the righteous, and the w, and their works, 2450
9:11 to the strong, neither yet bread to the w, 2450
9:15 Now there was found in it a poor w man, 2450
9:17 The words of w men are heard in quiet, 2450
10: 2 A w man's heart is at his right hand; but 2450
10:12 The words of a w man's mouth are 2450
12: 9 because the Preacher was w, 2450
12:11 The words of the w are as goads, and 2450
Isa 5:21 Woe unto them that are w in their own 2450
19:11 the counsel of the w counsellers of Pharaoh 2450
19:11 I am the son of the w, the son of ancient 2450
19:12 where are thy w men? and let them tell thee 2450
29:14 for the wisdom of their w men shall perish, 2450
31: 2 Yet he also is w, and will bring evil, and 2450
44:25 that turneth w men backward, and 2450
Jer 4:22 they are w to do evil, but to do good they 2450
8: 8 We are w, and the law of the LORD is 2450
8: 9 The w men are ashamed, they are dismayed 2450
9:12 Who is the w man, that may understand 2450
9:23 Let not the w man glory in his wisdom, 2450
10: 7 forasmuch as among all the w men of 2450
18:18 nor counsel from the w, nor the word from 2450
50:35 and upon her princes, and upon her w men. 2450
51:57 her w men, her captains, and her rulers, and 2450
Eze 27: 8 thy w men, O Tyrus, that were in thee, 2450
27: 9 the w men thereof were in thee thy calkers: 2450
Da 2:12 commanded to destroy all the w men of 2445
2:13 the decree went forth that the w men should 2445
2:14 which was gone forth to slay the w men of 2445
2:18 with the rest of the w men of Babylon. 2445
2:21 he giveth wisdom unto the w, and 2445
2:24 ordained to destroy the w men of Babylon: 2445
2:24 Destroy not the w men of Babylon: 2445
2:27 cannot the w men, the astrologians, 2445
2:48 chief of the governors over all the w men of 2445
4: 6 in all the w men of Babylon before me, 2445
4:18 forasmuch as all the w men of my kingdom 2445
5: 7 and said to the w men of Babylon, 2445
5: 8 came in all the king's w men: but 2445
5:15 now the w men, the astrologers, have been 2445
12: 3 they that be w shall shine as the brightness 7919
12:10 but the w shall understand. 7919
Hos 14: 9 Who is w, and he shall understand these 2450
Ob 1: 8 even destroy the w men out of Edom, and 2450
Zec 9: 2 and Zidon, though it be very w. 2449
Mt 1:18 the birth of Jesus Christ was on this w: 3779
2: 1 there came w men from the east to 3097
2: 7 when he had privily called the w men, 3097
2:16 he saw that he was mocked of the w men, 3097
2:16 he had diligently inquired of the w men. 3097
5:18 one tittle shall in no w pass from the law, 3364
7:24 doeth them, I will liken him unto a w man, 5429
10:16 be ye therefore w as serpents, and 5429
10:42 unto you, he shall in no w lose his reward. 3364
11:25 thou hast hid these things from the w and 4680
21:24 I in like w will tell you by what authority I 2504
23:34 unto you prophets, and w men, and scribes: 4680
24:45 Who then is a faithful and w servant, 5429
25: 2 And five of them were w, and five were 5429
25: 4 But the w took oil in their vessels with their 5429
25: 8 And the foolish said unto the w, Give us of 5429
25: 9 But the w answered, saying, Not so; 5429
Mk 14:31 with thee, I will not deny thee in any w. 3364
Lk 10:21 that thou hast hid these things from the w 4680
12:42 Who then is that faithful and w steward, 5429
13:11 in no w lift up herself. 1519+3361+3588+3838
18:17 as a little child shall in no w enter therein. 3364
Jn 6:37 him that cometh to me I will in no w cast 3364
21: 1 and on this w shewed he himself. 3779
Ac 7: 6 And God spake on this w, That his seed 3779
13:34 to return to corruption, he said on this w, 3779
13:41 a work which you shall in no w believe, 3364
Ro 1:14 both to the w, and to the unwise. 4680
1:22 Professing themselves to be w, 4680
3: 9 are we better than they? No, in no w: 3843
10: 6 which is of faith speaketh on this w, 3779
11:25 lest ye should be w in your own conceits; 5429
12:16 low estate. Be not w in your own conceits. 5429
16:19 yet I would have you w unto that which is 4680
16:27 To God only w, be glory through Jesus 4680
1Co 1:19 I will destroy the wisdom of the w, and 4680
1:20 Where is the w? where is the scribe? 4680
1:26 how that not many w men after the flesh, 4680
1:27 things of the world to confound the w; 4680
3:10 as a w masterbuilder, I have laid 4680
3:18 If any man among you seemeth to be w in 4680
3:18 let him become a fool, that he may be w. 4680
3:19 He taketh the w in their own craftiness. 4680
3:20 The Lord knoweth the thoughts of the w, 4680
4:10 for Christ's sake, but ye are w in Christ; 5429
6: 5 that there is not a w man amongst you? 4680
10:15 I speak as to w men; judge ye what I say. 5429
2Co 10:12 themselves amongst themselves, are not w. 4920
11:19 fools gladly, seeing ye yourselves are w. 5429

Eph 5:15 walk circumspectly, not as fools, but as w, 4680
1Ti 1:17 immortal, invisible, the only w God, 4680
2Ti 3:15 which are able to make thee w unto 4679
Heb 4: 4 certain place of the seventh day on this w, 3779
Jas 3:13 Who is a w man and endued with 4680
Jude 1:25 To the only w God our Saviour, be glory 4680
Rev 21:27 And there shall in no w enter into it any 3364

WISELY (14) [WISE]

Ex 1:10 Come on, let us deal w with them; lest they 2449
1Sa 18: 5 Saul sent him, and behaved himself w: 7919
18:14 David behaved himself w in all his ways; 7919
18:15 Saul saw that he behaved himself very w, 7919
18:30 that David behaved himself more w than 7919
2Ch 11:23 he dealt w, and dispersed of all his children 995
Ps 58: 5 voice of charmers, charming never so w. 2449
64: 9 for they shall w consider of his doing. 7919
101: 2 I will behave myself w in a perfect way. 7919
Pr 16:20 He that handleth a matter w shall find 7919
21:12 The righteous man w considereth 7919
28:26 whoso walketh w, he shall be 2451+871.1
Ecc 7:10 dost not inquire w concerning this. 2451+4480
Lk 16: 8 the unjust steward, because he had done w: 5430

WISER (8) [WISE]

1Ki 4:31 For he was w than all men; than Ethan 2449
Job 35:11 and maketh us w than the fowls of heaven? 2449
Ps 119:98 hast made me w than mine enemies: 2449
Pr 9: 9 to a wise man, and he will be yet w: 2449
26:16 The sluggard is w in his own conceit than 2450
Eze 28: 3 Behold, thou art w than Daniel; there is no 2450
Lk 16: 8 generation w than the children of light. 5429
1Co 1:25 Because the foolishness of God is w than 4680

WISH (6) [WISHED, WISHING]

Job 33: 6 I am according to thy w in God's stead: 6310
Ps 40:14 and put to shame that w me evil. 2655
73: 7 they have more than heart could w. 4906
Ro 9: 3 For I could w that myself were accursed 2172
2Co 13: 9 and this also we w, even your perfection. 2172
3Jn 1: 2 I w above all things that thou mayest 2172

WISHED (2) [WISH]

Jnh 4: 8 and w in himself to die, and said, 7592
Ac 27:29 anchors out of the stern, and w for the day. 2172

WISHING (1) [WISH]

Job 31:30 my mouth to sin by w a curse to his soul.) 7592

WIST (13) [WIT]

Ex 16:15 for they w not what it was. And Moses said 3045
34:29 that Moses w not that the skin of his face 3045
Lev 5:17 though he w it not, yet is he guilty, and 3045
5:18 his ignorance wherein he erred and w it not, 3045
Jos 2: 4 unto me, but I w not whence they were: 3045
8:14 he w not that there were liers in ambush 3045
Jdg 16:20 he w not that the LORD was departed 3045
Mk 9: 6 For he w not what to say; for they were 1492
14:40 neither w they what to answer him. 1492
Lk 2:49 w ye not that I must be about my Father's 1492
Jn 5:13 And he that was healed w not who it was: 1492
Ac 12: 9 w not that it was true which was done by 1492
23: 5 Then said Paul, I w not, brethren, that he 1492

WIT (21) [UNWITTINGLY, WIST, WIT'S, WITTINGLY, WITTY, WOT, WOTTETH]

Ge 24:21 to w whether the LORD had made his 3045
Ex 2: 4 afar off, to w what would be done to him. 3045
Jos 17: 1 to w, for Machir the firstborn of Manasseh, NIH
1Ki 2:32 my father David not knowing thereof, to w, NIH
7:50 the doors of the house, to w, of the temple. NIH
13:23 to w, for the prophet whom he had brought NIH
2Ki 10:29 to w, the golden calves that were in Beth-el, NIH
1Ch 7: 2 heads of their fathers' house, to w, of Tola: NIH
27: 1 to w, the chief fathers and captains of NIH
2Ch 4:12 To w, the two pillars, and the pommels, and NIH
25: 7 to w, with all the children of Ephraim. NIH
25:10 Amaziah separated them, to w, the army 3807.1
31: 3 to w, for the morning and evening burnt NIH
Ne 11: 3 to w, Israel, the priests, and the Levites, and NIH
Est 2:12 to w, six months with oil of myrrh, and NIH
Jer 25:18 To w, Jerusalem, and the cities of Judah, NIH
34: 9 himself of them, to w, of a Jew his brother. NIH
Eze 13:16 To w, the prophets of Israel which prophesy NIH
Ro 8:23 to w, the redemption of our body. NIG
2Co 5:19 To w, that God was in Christ reconciling 5613
8: 1 we do you to w of the grace of God 1107

WIT'S (1) [WIT]

Ps 107:27 and are at their w end. 1104+2451+3605

WITCH (2) [WITCHCRAFT, WITCHCRAFTS]

Ex 22:18 Thou shalt not suffer a w to live. 3784
Dt 18:10 observer of times, or an enchanter, or a w, 3784

WITCHCRAFT (3) [CRAFT, WITCH]

1Sa 15:23 For rebellion is as the sin of w, and 7081
2Ch 33: 6 used w, and dealt with a familiar spirit, and 3784
Gal 5:20 Idolatry, w, hatred, variance, emulations, 5331

WITCHCRAFTS (4) [CRAFT, WITCH]

2Ki 9:22 thy mother Jezebel and her w are so many? 3785
Mic 5:12 I will cut off w out of thine hand; and 3785
Na 3: 4 the mistress of w, that selleth nations 3785
3: 4 and families through her w. 3785

WITH (6016) [HEREWITH, THEREWITH, WHEREWITH] See Index of Articles, Etc.

WITHAL (33) [WHEREWITHAL]

Ex 25:29 bowls thereof, to cover w: 834+871.1+2006.1
30: 4 for places for the staves to bear it w. 1992+871.1
30:18 to wash w: and thou shalt put it between NIH

Ex 36: 3 to make it w. And they brought yet unto NIH
37:16 and his covers to cover w, 871.1+2006.1
37:27 places for the staves to bear it w. 871.1+1992.1
38: 7 the sides of the altar, to bear it w; 871.1+1992.1
40:30 the altar, and put water there, to wash w. NIH
Lev 5: 3 it be that a man shall be defiled w, 871.1+1886.3
6:30 reconcile w in the holy place, shall be eaten: NIH
11:21 their feet, to leap w upon the earth; 871.1+2006.1
19:24 shall be holy to praise the LORD w. NIH
Nu 4: 7 and the bowls, and covers to cover w: 5262
Jdg 7:20 the trumpets in their right hands to blow w: NIH
1Sa 16:12 and w of a beautiful countenance, and 5973
1Ki 19: 1 w how he had slain all the prophets with 3605
2Ki 23:26 that Manasseh had provoked him w. NIH
1Ch 29: 4 to overlay the walls of the houses w: NIH
2Ch 24:14 to offer w, and spoons, and vessels of gold NIH
26:15 to shoot arrows and great stones w. 871.1
Est 6: 9 that they may array the man w whom NIH
Job 2: 8 a potsherd to scrape himself w; 871.1+2050.2
Ps 141:10 into their own nets, whilst that I w escape. 3162
Pr 22:18 they shall w be fitted in thy lips. 3162
Isa 30:14 the hearth, or to take water w out of the pit. NIH
30:23 thy seed, that thou shalt sow the ground w; NIH
Mk 10:39 with the baptism that I am baptized w shall NIG
Lk 6:38 For with the same measure that ye mete w it NIG
Ac 25:27 not w to signify the crimes laid against 3361
1Co 12: 7 the Spirit is given to every man to profit w. 4851
Col 4: 3 W praying also for us, that God would open 260
1Ti 5:13 And w they learn to be idle, wandering about 260
Phm 1:22 But w prepare me also a lodging: for I trust 260

WITHDRAW (11) [WITHDRAWEST, WITHDRAWETH, WITHDRAWN, WITHDREW]

1Sa 14:19 and Saul said unto the priest, W thine hand. 622
Job 9:13 If God will not w his anger, the proud 7725
13:21 W thine hand far from me: and let not thy 7368
33:17 That he may w man from his purpose, and 5493
Pr 25:17 W thy foot from thy neighbour's house; 3365
Ecc 7:18 yea, also from this w not thine hand: 3240
Isa 60:20 go down; neither shall thy moon w itself: 622
Joel 2:10 be dark, and the stars shall w their shining: 622
3:15 and the stars shall w their shining. 622
2Th 3: 6 that ye w yourselves from every brother 4724
1Ti 6: 5 that gain is godliness: from such w thyself. 868

WITHDRAWEST (1) [WITHDRAW]

Ps 74:11 Why w thou thy hand, even thy right hand? 7725

WITHDRAWETH (1) [WITHDRAW]

Job 36: 7 He w not his eyes from the righteous: but 1639

WITHDRAWN (6) [WITHDRAW]

Dt 13:13 have w the inhabitants of their city, saying, 5080
SS 5: 6 my beloved had w himself, and was gone: 2559
La 2: 8 he hath not w his hand from destroying: 7725
Eze 18: 8 that hath w his hand from iniquity, 7725
Hos 5: 6 they shall not find him; he hath w himself 2502
Lk 22:41 And he was w from them about a stone's 645

WITHDREW (6) [WITHDRAW]

Ne 9:29 w the shoulder, and hardened their 5414+5637
Eze 20:22 Nevertheless I w mine hand, and 7725
Mt 12:15 But when Jesus knew it, he w himself from 402
Mk 3: 7 But Jesus w himself with his disciples to 402
Lk 5:16 And he w himself into the wilderness, and 5298
Gal 2:12 were come, he w and separated himself, 5288

WITHER (11) [WITHERED, WITHERETH]

Ps 1: 3 his leaf also shall not w; and whatsoever he 5034
37: 2 like the grass, and w as the green herb. 5034
Isa 19: 6 and dried up: the reeds and flags shall w. 7060
19: 7 shall w, be driven away, and be no more. 3001
40:24 they shall w, and the whirlwind shall take 3001
Jer 12: 4 land mourn, and the herbs of every field w, 3001
Eze 17: 9 and cut off the fruit thereof, that it w? 3001
17: 9 it shall w in all the leaves of her spring, 3001
17:10 shall it not utterly w, when the east 3001+3001
17:10 it shall w in the furrows where it grew. 3001
Am 1: 2 shall mourn, and the top of Carmel shall w. 3001

WITHERED (25) [WITHER]

Ge 41:23 w, thin, and blasted with the east wind, 6798
Ps 102: 4 My heart is smitten, and w like grass; so 3001
102:11 that declineth; and I am w like grass. 3001
Isa 15: 6 for the hay is w away, the grass faileth, 3001
27:11 When the boughs thereof are w, they shall 3001
La 4: 8 their bones; it is w, it is become like a stick. 3001
Eze 19:12 her strong rods were broken and w; the fire 3001
Joel 1:12 even all the trees of the field, are w: 3001
1:12 joy is w away from the sons of men. 3001
1:17 barns are broken down; for the corn is w. 3001
Am 4: 7 and the piece whereupon it rained not w. 3001
Jnh 4: 7 next day, and it smote the gourd, that it w. 3001
Mt 12:10 there was a man which had his hand w. 3584
13: 6 because they had not root, they w away. 3583
21:19 for ever. And presently the fig tree w away. 3583
21:20 saying, How soon is the fig tree w away! 3583
Mk 3: 1 there was a man there which had a w hand. 3583
3: 3 And he saith unto the man which had the w 3583
4: 6 and because it had no root, it w away. 3583
11:21 the fig tree which thou cursedst is w away. 3583
Lk 6: 6 there was a man whose right hand was w. 3584
6: 8 and said to the man which had the w hand, 3584
8: 6 it w away, because it lacked moisture. 3583
Jn 5: 3 halt, w, waiting for the moving of 3584
15: 6 in me, he is cast forth as a branch, and is w; 3583

WITHERETH (8) [WITHER]

Job 8:12 not cut down, it w before any other herb. 3001
Ps 90: 6 in the evening it is cut down, and w. 3001
129: 6 the housetops, which w afore it groweth up: 3001
Isa 40: 7 The grass w, the flower fadeth: because 3001
40: 8 The grass w, the flower fadeth: but 3001
Jas 1:11 but it w the grass, and the flower thereof 3583
1Pe 1:24 The grass w, and the flower thereof falleth 3583
Jude 1:12 trees whose fruit w, without fruit, 5352

WITHHELD (6) [WITHHOLD]

Ge 20: 6 for I also w thee from sinning against me: 2820
22:12 seeing thou hast not w thy son, thine only 2820
22:16 hast not w thy son, thine only son: 2820
30: 2 who hath w from thee the fruit of 4513
Job 31:16 If I have w the poor from their desire, or 4513
Ecc 2:10 from them, I w not my heart from any joy; 4513

WITHHELDEST (1) [WITHHOLD]

Ne 9:20 w not thy manna from their mouth, and 4513

WITHHOLD (9) [WITHHELD, WITHHELDEST, WITHHOLDEN, WITHHOLDETH]

Ge 23: 6 none of us shall w from thee his sepulchre, 3607
2Sa 13:13 the king; for he will not w me from thee. 4513
Job 4: 2 but who can w himself from speaking? 6113
Ps 40:11 W not thou thy tender mercies from me, 3607
84:11 no good thing will he w from them that 4513
Pr 3:27 W not good from them to whom it is due, 4513
23:13 W not correction from the child: for if thou 4513
Ecc 11: 6 and in the evening w not thine hand: 3240
Jer 2:25 W thy foot from being unshod, and 4513

WITHHOLDEN (10) [WITHHOLD]

1Sa 25:26 seeing the LORD hath w thee from 4513
Job 22: 7 and thou hast w bread from the hungry. 4513
38:15 from the wicked their light is w, and 4513
42: 2 and that no thought can be w from thee. 1219
Ps 21: 2 and hast not w the request of his lips. 4513
Jer 3: 3 Therefore the showers have been w, and 4513
5:25 and your sins have w good things from you. 4513
Eze 18:16 hath not w the pledge, 2254+2258
Joel 1:13 the drink offering is w from the house of 4513
Am 4: 7 also I have w the rain from you, when there 4513

WITHHOLDETH (4) [WITHHOLD]

Job 12:15 Behold, he w the waters, and they dry up: 6113
Pr 11:24 there is that w more than is meet, but 2820
11:26 He that w corn, the people shall curse him: 4513
2Th 2: 6 And now ye know what w that he might be 2722

WITHIN (186) [IN]

Ge 6:14 pitch it w and without with pitch. 1004+4480
9:21 and he was uncovered w his tent. 8432+871.1
18:12 Therefore Sarah laughed w herself, 7130+871.1
18:24 there be fifty righteous w the city: 8432+871.1
18:26 If I find in Sodom fifty righteous w 8432+871.1
25:22 the children struggled together w 7130+871.1
39:11 was none of the men of the house there w. 871.1
40:13 Yet w three days shall Pharaoh lift up thine 871.1
40:19 Yet w three days shall Pharaoh lift 5750+871.1
Ex 20:10 nor thy stranger that is w thy gates: 871.1
25:11 shalt overlay it with pure gold, w 1004+4480
26:33 that thou mayest bring in thither w 1004+4480
37: 2 he overlaid it with pure gold w 1004+4480
Lev 10:18 the blood of it was not brought in w 413+6441
13:55 whether it be bare w or without. 7146
14:41 house to be scraped w round about, 1004+4480
16: 2 place w the vail before the mercy 1004+4480
16:12 beaten small, and bring it w the vail: 1004+4480
16:15 bring his blood w the vail, and 1004+4480
25:29 he may redeem it w a whole year after it is NIH
25:29 it is sold; w a full year may he redeem it. NIH
25:30 if it be not redeemed w the space of a full 5704
26:25 when ye are gathered together w your cities, 413
Nu 4:10 all the vessels thereof w a covering of 413
18: 7 of the altar, and w the vail; 1004+4480+3807.1
Dt 5:14 nor thy stranger that is w thy gates; 871.1
12:12 and the Levite that is w your gates; 871.1
12:17 Thou mayest not eat w thy gates the tithe 871.1
12:18 and the Levite that is w thy gates: 871.1
14:27 the Levite that is w thy gates; thou shalt 871.1
14:28 same year, and shalt lay it up w thy gates: 871.1
14:29 the widow, which are w thy gates, 871.1
15: 7 w any of thy gates in thy land which 871.1
15:22 Thou shalt eat it w thy gates: the unclean 871.1
16: 5 Thou mayest not sacrifice the passover w 871.1
16:11 the Levite that is w thy gates, and 871.1
16:14 and the widow, that are w thy gates. 871.1
17: 2 w any of thy gates which the LORD thy 871.1
17: 8 being matters of controversy w thy gates: 871.1
23:10 of the camp, he shall not come w the camp: 8432
24:14 of thy strangers that are in thy land w thy 871.1
26:12 they may eat w thy gates, and be filled; 871.1
28:43 The stranger that is w thee shall get 7130+871.1
31:12 and thy stranger that is w thy gates, 871.1
32:25 The sword without, and terror w, 2315+4480
Jos 1:11 for w three days ye shall pass over 5750+871.1
19: 1 their inheritance was w 8432+871.1
19: 9 w the inheritance of them. 8432+871.1
21:41 All the cities of the Levites w 8432+871.1
Jdg 7:16 and lamps w the pitchers. 8432+871.1
9:51 there was a strong tower w the city, 8432+871.1
11:18 but came not w the border of Moab: 871.1
11:26 did ye not recover them w that time? 871.1
14:12 if you can certainly declare it me w NIH
15: 1 it came to pass w a while after, 3117+4480
1Sa 13:11 thou camest not w the days appointed, 3807.1
14:14 w as it were a half acre of land, 871.1
25:36 Nabal's heart was merry w him, for he was 5921
25:37 that his heart died w him, and 7130+871.1
26: 7 Saul lay sleeping w the trench, and 871.1
2Sa 7: 2 the ark of God dwelleth w curtains. 8432+871.1
20: 4 Assemble me the men of Judah w three NIH
1Ki 6:15 w with boards of cedar, 1004+4480+1886.5
6:16 he even built them for it w, even for 1004+4480
6:18 the cedar of the house w was carved with 6441
6:19 oracle he prepared in the house w, 4480+6441
6:21 So Solomon overlaid the house w 4480+6441
6:23 w the oracle he made two cherubims of 871.1
6:27 he set the cherubims w the inner 8432+871.1
6:29 open flowers, w and without. 4480+6440+3807.1
6:30 the house he overlaid with gold, w 6441+3807.1
7: 8 dwelt had another court w the porch, 1004+4480
7: 9 sawed with saws, w and without, 1004+4480
7:31 the mouth of it w the chapiter and 1004+4480
2Ki 4:27 Let her alone; for her soul is vexed w her: 3807.1
6:30 he had sackcloth w upon his flesh. 1004+4480
7:11 and they told it to the king's house w. 6441
11: 8 he that cometh w the ranges, let him be 413
2Ch 3: 4 and he overlaid it w with pure gold. 4480+6441
Ezr 4:15 that they have moved sedition w the same 871.2
10: 8 that whosoever would not come w three 3807.1
10: 9 together unto Jerusalem w three days. 3807.1
Ne 4:22 with his servant lodge w Jerusalem, 8432+871.1
6:10 w the temple, and let us shut the doors 413+8432
Job 6: 4 For the arrows of the Almighty are w me, 5978
14:22 have pain, and his soul w him shall mourn. 5921
19:27 though my reins be consumed w me. 2436+871.1
20:13 it not; but keep it still w his mouth: 8432+871.1
20:14 is turned, it is the gall of asps w him. 7130+871.1
24:11 Which make oil w their walls, and tread their 996
32:18 of matter, the spirit w me constraineth me. 990
Ps 36: 1 of the wicked saith w my heart, 7130+871.1
39: 3 My heart was hot w me, while I was 7130+871.1
40: 8 My God: yea, thy law is w my heart. 8432+871.1
40:10 I have not hid thy righteousness w 8432+871.1
42: 6 O my God, my soul is cast down w me: 5921
42:11 why art thou disquieted w me? hope thou in 5921
43: 5 why art thou disquieted w me? hope in 5921
45:13 The king's daughter is all glorious w: 6441
51:10 and renew a right spirit w me. 7130+871.1
55: 4 My heart is sore pained w me: and 7130+871.1
94:19 In the multitude of my thoughts w 7130+871.1
101: 2 I will walk w my house with a 7130+871.1
101: 7 deceit shall not dwell w my house: 7130+871.1
103: 1 and all that is w me, bless his holy name. 7130
109:22 and my heart is wounded w me. 7130+871.1
122: 2 Our feet shall stand w thy gates, 871.1
122: 7 Peace be w thy walls, and 871.1
122: 7 thy walls, and prosperity w thy palaces. 871.1
122: 8 I will now say, Peace be w thee. 871.1
142: 3 When my spirit was overwhelmed w me, 5921
143: 4 Therefore is my spirit overwhelmed w me; 5921
143: 4 my heart w me is desolate. 8432+871.1
147:13 he hath blessed thy children w thee. 7130+871.1
Pr 22:18 thing if thou keep them w thee; 990+871.1
26:24 his lips, and layeth up deceit w him; 7130+871.1
Ecc 9:14 There was a little city, and few men w it; 871.1
SS 4: 1 thou hast doves' eyes w thy locks: 1157+4480
4: 3 piece of a pomegranate w thy locks. 1157+4480
6: 7 are thy temples w thy locks. 1157+4480
Isa 7: 8 w threescore and five years shall 5750+871.1
16:14 saying, W three years, as the years of a 871.1
21:16 W a year, according to the years of a 5750+871.1
26: 9 spirit w me will I seek thee early: 7130+871.1
56: 5 w my walls a place and a name better than 871.1
60:18 wasting nor destruction w thy borders; 871.1
63:11 is he that put his holy Spirit w him? 7130+871.1
Jer 4:14 thy vain thoughts lodge w thee? 7130+871.1
23: 9 Mine heart w me is broken because 7130+871.1
28: 3 W two full years will I bring again 5750+871.1
28:11 w the space of two full years. 5750+871.1
La 1:20 mine heart is turned w me; 7130+871.1
Eze 1:27 as the appearance of fire round about w it, 1004
2:10 and it was written w and without: 6440
3:24 Go, shut thyself w thine house. 8432+871.1
7:15 and the pestilence and the famine w: 1004+4480
11:19 and I will put a new spirit w you; 7130+871.1
12:24 divination w the house of Israel. 8432+871.1
36:26 and a new spirit will I put w you: 7130+871.1
36:27 I will put my spirit w you, and 7130+871.1
40: 7 of the gate w was one reed. 1004+4480+1886.1
40: 8 also the porch of the gate w, 1004+4480+1886.1
40:16 to their posts w the gate round 6441+3807.1
40:43 w were hooks, a hand 1004+871.1+1886.1
41: 9 side chambers that were w. 1004+1886.1+3807.1
41:17 all the wall round about w 6442+871.1+1886.1
44:17 the gates of the inner court, and w. 1004+1886.5
Da 6:12 a petition of any God or man w thirty days, 5705
11:20 w few days he shall be destroyed, 871.1
Hos 11: 8 mine heart is turned w me, my repentings 5921
Jnh 2: 7 When my soul fainted w me I remembered 5921
Mic 3: 3 the pot, and as flesh w the caldron. 8432+871.1
5: 6 and when he treadeth w our borders. 871.1
Zep 3: 3 Her princes w her are roaring lions; 7130+871.1
Zec 12: 1 and formeth the spirit of man w him. 7130+871.1
Mt 3: 9 And think not to say w yourselves, 1722
9: 3 certain of the scribes said w themselves, 1722
9:21 For she said w herself, If I may but 1722
23:25 but w they are full of extortion and excess. 2081
23:26 cleanse first that which is w the cup and 1787
23:27 but are w full of dead men's bones, and 2081
23:28 but w ye are full of hypocrisy and iniquity. 2081
Mk 2: 8 spirit that they so reasoned w themselves, 1722
7:21 For from w, out of the heart of men, 2081
7:23 All these evil things come from w, and 2081
14: 4 some that had indignation w themselves, 4314
14:58 w three days I will build another made 1223
Lk 3: 8 and begin not to say w yourselves, 1722
7:39 had bidden him saw it, he spake w himself, 1722
7:49 meat with him began to say w themselves, 1722
11: 7 And he from w shall answer and say, 2081
11:40 is without make that which is w also? 2081
12:17 And he thought w himself, saying, 1722
16: 3 Then the steward said w himself, 1722
17:21 for behold, the kingdom of God is w you. 1787
18: 4 but afterward he said w himself, Though I 1722
19:44 with the ground, and thy children w thee: 1722
24:32 one to another, Did not our heart burn w us, 1722
Jn 20:26 after eight days again his disciples were w, 2080
Ac 5:23 when we had opened, we found no man w. 2080
Ro 8:23 even we ourselves groan w ourselves, 1722
1Co 5:12 do not ye judge them that are w? 2080
2Co 7: 5 side; without were fightings, w were fears. 2081
Heb 6:19 and which entereth into that w the vail; 2082

W

Rev 4: 8 about *him;* and *they were* full of eyes **w**: *2081*
5: 1 him that sat on the throne a book written **w** *2081*

WITHOUT (426) [, OUT]

Ge 1: 2 the earth was **w form**, and void; and 8414
6:14 shalt pitch it within and **w** with pitch. 2351+4480
9:22 and told his two brethren **w**. 2351+871.1+1886.1
19:16 him forth, and set him **w** the city. 2351+4480
24:11 he made *his* camels to kneel down **w** 2351+4480
24:31 wherefore standest thou **w**? 2351+871.1+1886.1
37:33 Joseph is **w doubt rent in pieces**. 2963+2963
41:44 **w** thee shall no man lift up his hand or foot 1107
41:49 until he left numbering; for *it was* **w** number. 369
Ex 12: 5 Your lamb shall be **w blemish**, a male of 8549
21:11 unto her, then shall she go out free **w** money. 369
25:11 within and **w** shalt thou overlay it, 2351+4480
26:35 thou shalt set the table **w** the vail, 2351+4480
27:21 of the congregation **w** the vail, 2351+4480
29: 1 young bullock, and two rams **w blemish**, 8549
29:14 shalt thou burn with fire **w** the camp: 2351+4480
33: 7 pitched it **w** the camp, afar off from 2351+4480
33: 7 which *was* **w** the camp. 2351+4480
37: 2 it with pure gold within and **w**, 2351+4480
40:22 side of the tabernacle northward, **w** 2351+4480
Lev 1: 3 of the herd, let him offer a male **w blemish**: 8549
1:10 he shall bring it a male **w blemish**. 8549
3: 1 he shall offer it **w blemish** before 8549
3: 6 male or female, he shall offer it **w blemish**. 8549
4: 3 a young bullock **w blemish** unto 8549
4:12 forth **w** the camp unto a clean place, 2351+4480
4:21 he shall carry forth the bullock **w** 2351+4480
4:23 a kid of the goats, a male **w blemish**; 8549
4:28 a kid of the goats, a female **w blemish**, 8549
4:32 he shall bring it a female **w blemish**. 8549
5:15 LORD a ram **w blemish** out of the flocks, 8549
5:18 he shall bring a ram **w blemish** out of 8549
6: 6 a ram **w blemish** out of the flock, with thy 8549
6:11 carry forth the ashes **w** the camp 2351+4480
8:17 he burnt with fire **w** the camp; 2351+4480
9: 2 **w blemish**, and offer *them* before 8549
9: 3 first year, **w blemish**, for a burnt offering; 8549
9:11 hide he burnt with fire **w** the camp. 2351+4480
10:12 by fire, and eat it **w leaven** beside the altar: 4682
13:46 he shall dwell alone; **w** the camp 2351+4480
13:55 fret inward, *whether* it *be* bare within or **w**. 1372
14:10 day he shall take two he lambs **w blemish**, 8549
14:10 one ewe lamb of the first year **w blemish**, 8549
14:40 into an unclean place **w** the city: 2351+4480
14:41 off **w** the city into an unclean place: 2351+4480
16:27 shall *one* carry forth **w** the camp, 2351+4480
22:19 *offer* at your own will a male **w blemish**, 8549
23:12 **w blemish** of the first year for a burnt 8549
23:18 seven lambs **w blemish** of the first year, 8549
24: 3 **W** the vail of the Testimony, in 2351+4480
24:14 Bring forth him that hath cursed **w** 2351+4480
26:43 while she lieth desolate **w** them: 4480
Nu 5: 3 female shall ye put out, **w** the camp 2351+4480
5: 4 did so, and put them out **w** the camp: 2351+4480
6:14 one he lamb of the first year **w blemish** for 8549
6:14 one ewe lamb of the first year **w blemish** 8549
6:14 and one ram **w blemish** for peace offerings, 8549
15:24 **w** the **knowledge** of 4480+5869
15:35 stone him with stones **w** the camp. 2351+4480
15:36 all the congregation brought him **w** 2351+4480
19: 2 that they bring thee a red heifer **w spot**, 8549
19: 3 that he may bring her forth **w** 2351+4480
19: 9 *them* up **w** the camp in a clean place, 2351+4480
20:19 **w** *doing any* thing *else,* go through on my 369
28: 3 two lambs of the first year **w spot** day by 8549
28: 9 day two lambs of the first year **w spot**, 8549
28:11 seven lambs of the first year **w spot**; 8549
28:19 they shall be unto you **w blemish**: 8549
28:31 (they shall be unto you **w blemish**) 8549
29: 2 seven lambs of the first year **w blemish**: 8549
29: 8 they shall be unto you **w blemish**: 8549
29:13 of the first year; they shall be **w blemish**: 8549
29:17 fourteen lambs of the first year **w spot**: 8549
29:20 fourteen lambs of the first year **w blemish**; 8549
29:23 fourteen lambs of the first year **w blemish**: 8549
29:26 *and* fourteen lambs of the first year **w spot**: 8549
29:29 fourteen lambs of the first year **w blemish**: 8549
29:32 fourteen lambs of the first year **w blemish**: 8549
29:36 seven lambs of the first year **w blemish**: 8549
31:13 went forth to meet them **w** the camp. 2351+4480
31:19 do ye abide **w** the camp seven days: 2351+4480
35: 5 ye shall measure from **w** the city *on* the east 2351
35:22 if he thrust him suddenly **w** enmity, 3808+871.1
35:22 have cast upon him any thing **w** 3808+871.1
35:26 if the slayer shall at any time come *w* NIH
35:27 the revenger of blood find him **w** 2351+4480
Dt 8: 9 A land wherein thou shalt eat bread **w** 3808
23:12 Thou shalt have a place also **w** 2351+4480
25: 5 marry **w** unto a stranger: 2351+1886.1+1886.5
32: 4 a God of truth and **w** iniquity, just and 369
32:25 The sword **w**, and terror within, 2351+4480
Jos 3:10 *that* he will **w fail drive out** from 3423+3423
6:23 and left them **w** the camp of Israel. 2351+4480
Jdg 2:23 those nations, **w** driving them out hastily; 1115
6: 5 both they and their camels were **w** number: 369
7:12 their camels *were* **w** number, as the sand by 369
11:30 If thou shalt **w fail deliver** 5414+5414
Ru 4:14 which hath not **left** thee *this* day **w** a 7673
1Sa 19: 5 innocent blood, to slay David **w a cause**? 2600
30: 8 and **w fail recover** *all.* 5337+5337
2Sa 23: 4 the sun riseth, *even* a morning **w** clouds; 3808
1Ki 6: 6 for **w** *in the wall* of the house he 2351+1886.5
6:29 palm trees and open flowers, within and **w**. 2435
6:30 house he overlaid with gold, within and **w**. 2435
7: 9 sawed with saws, within and **w**, even 2351+4480
8: 8 and they were not seen **w**: 2351+1886.5
22: 1 they continued three years **w** war between 369
2Ki 10:24 fourscore men **w**, and said, 2351+871.1+1886.1
11:15 Have her forth **w** the ranges: 413+1004+4480
16:18 the house, and the king's entry **w**, 2435+1886.5
18:25 Am I now come up **w** the LORD 1107+4480
2Ki 23: 4 he burnt them **w** Jerusalem in 2351+4480
23: 6 from the house of the LORD, **w** 2351+4480
25:16 the brass of all these vessels was **w** weight. 3808
1Ch 2:30 and Appaim: but Seled died **w** children. 3808
2:32 and Jonathan: and Jether died **w** children. 3808
21:24 nor offer burnt offerings **w cost**. 2600
22: 3 and brass in abundance **w** weight; 369
22:14 of brass and iron **w** weight; for it is in 369
2Ch 5: 9 but they were not seen **w**. 2351+1886.5
12: 3 the people *were* **w** number that came with 369
15: 3 Israel *hath been* **w** the true God, 3808+3807.1
15: 3 **w** a teaching priest, and without 3808+3807.1
15: 3 a teaching priest, and **w** law. 3808+3807.1
21:20 and departed **w** being desired. 3808+871.1
24: 8 set it **w** at the gate of the house of 2351+1886.5
32: 3 the fountains which *were* **w** the city: 2351+4480
32: 5 another wall **w**, and repaired Millo 2351+1886.5
33:14 Now after this he built a wall **w** the city of 2435
Ezr 6: 9 let *it* be given them day by day **w** fail: 3809
7:22 *of* oil, and salt **w** prescribing *how much.* 3809
10:13 *we are* not able to stand **w**, 2351+871.1+1886.1
Ne 13:20 sellers of all *kind of* ware lodged **w** 2351+4480
Job 2: 3 me against him, to destroy him **w cause**. 2600
4:20 perish for ever **w** *any* regarding *it.* 1097+4480
4:21 go away? they die, even **w** wisdom. 3808+871.1
5: 9 marvellous *things* **w** number: 369+5704
6: 6 which is unsavoury be eaten **w** salt? 1097+4480
7: 6 and are spent **w** hope. 657+871.1
8:11 Can the rush grow up **w** mire? 3808+871.1
8:11 without mire? can the flag grow **w** water? 1097
9:10 yea, and wonders **w** number. 369+5704
9:17 and multiplieth my wounds **w cause**. 2600
10:22 **w any** order, and *where* the light is 3808+2050.1
11:15 For then shalt thou lift up thy face **w** spot; 4480
12:25 They grope *in* the dark **w** light, 3808+2050.1
24: 7 They cause the naked to lodge **w** 1097+4480
24:10 They cause *him* to go naked **w** clothing, 1097
26: 2 How hast thou helped *him that is* **w** power? 3808
30:28 I went mourning **w** the sun: I stood 3808+871.1
31:19 for want of clothing, or *any* poor **w** covering; 369
31:39 If I have eaten the fruits thereof **w** money, 1097
33: 9 I am clean **w** transgression, I *am* innocent; 1097
34: 6 my wound *is* incurable **w** transgression. 1097
34:20 and the mighty shall be taken away **w** hand. 3808
34:24 He shall break in pieces mighty *men* **w** 3808
34:35 Job hath spoken **w** knowledge, and 3808+871.1
34:35 and his words *were* **w** wisdom. 3808+871.1
35:16 he multiplieth words **w** knowledge. 1097+871.1
36:12 and they shall die **w** knowledge. 1097+3509.1
38: 2 darkeneth counsel by words **w** knowledge? 1097
39:16 *were* not hers: her labour *is* in vain **w** fear; 1097
41:33 is not his like, who is made **w** fear. 1097+3807.1
42: 3 Who *is* he that hideth counsel **w** 1097
Ps 7: 4 I have delivered him that **w cause** is mine 7387
25: 3 be ashamed which transgress **w cause**. 7387
31:11 did see me **w** fled from me. 2351+871.1+1886.1
35: 7 For **w cause** have they hid for me their net 2600
35: 7 *which* **w cause** they have digged for my 2600
35:19 wink *with* the eye that hate me **w a cause**. 2600
59: 4 and prepare themselves **w** *my* fault: 1097
69: 4 They that hate me **w a cause** are more than 2600
105:34 and caterpillars, and that **w** number, 369
109: 3 of hatred; and fought against me **w a cause**. 2600
119:78 they dealt perversely with me **w a cause**: 8267
119:161 Princes have persecuted me **w a cause**: but 2600
Pr 1:11 let us lurk privily for the innocent **w cause**: 2600
1:20 Wisdom crieth **w**; she 2351+871.1+1886.1
3:30 Strive not with a man **w cause**, if he have 2600
5:23 He shall die **w** instruction; and in 369+871.1
6:15 suddenly shall he be broken **w** remedy. 369
7:12 Now *is she* **w**, now in 2351+871.1+1886.1
11:22 *so is* a fair woman which is **w** discretion. 5493
15:22 **W** counsel purposes *are* disappointed: 369+871.1
16: 8 than great revenues **w** right. 3808+871.1
19: 2 Also, *that* the soul *be* **w** knowledge, 3808+871.1
22:13 *man* saith, *There is* a lion **w**, 2351+871.1+1886.1
23:29 who hath wounds **w cause**? who hath 2600
24:27 Prepare thy work **w**, and 2351+871.1+1886.1
24:28 a witness against thy neighbour **w cause**; 2600
25:14 of a false gift *is like* clouds and wind **w** rain. 369
25:28 *like* a city *that is* broken down, *and* **w** walls. 369
29: 1 suddenly be destroyed, and that **w** remedy. 369
Ecc 10:11 Surely the serpent will bite **w** 3808+871.1
SS 6: 8 fourscore concubines, and virgins **w** number. 369
8: 1 *when* I should find thee **w**, 2351+871.1+1886.1
Isa 5: 9 *even* great and fair, **w** inhabitant. 369+4480
5:14 opened her mouth **w** measure: 1097+3807.1
6:11 Until the cities be wasted **w** 369+4480
6:11 the houses **w** man, and the land be 369+4480
10: 4 **W** me they shall bow down under 1115
33: 7 their valiant ones shall cry **w**: 2351+1886.5
36:10 am I now come up **w** the LORD 1107+4480
45:17 nor confounded **world w end**. 5703+5704+5769
52: 3 and ye shall be redeemed **w** money. 3808+871.1
52: 4 Assyrian oppressed them **w cause**. 657+871.1
55: 1 buy wine and milk **w** money and 3808+871.1
55: 1 milk without money and **w** price. 3808+871.1
Jer 2:15 his cities are burnt **w** inhabitant. 1097+4480
2:32 yet my people have forgotten me days **w** 369
4: 7 thy cities shall be laid waste, **w** an 369+4480
4:23 the earth, and lo, *it was* **w form**, and void; 8414
5:21 O foolish people, and **w** understanding; 369
9:11 of Judah desolate, **w** an inhabitant. 1097+4480
9:21 to cut off the children from **w**, *and* 2351
15:13 will I give to the spoil **w** price, 3808+871.1
21: 4 which besiege you **w** the walls, and 2351+4480
22:13 *that* useth his neighbour's service **w wages**, 2600
26: 9 city shall be desolate **w** an inhabitant? 369+4480
32:43 ye say, *It is* desolate **w** man or beast; 369+4480
33:10 which ye say *shall be* desolate **w** man 369+4480
33:10 *be* desolate without man and **w** beast, 369+4480
33:10 that are desolate, **w** man, and without 369+4480
33:10 and **w** inhabitant, and without beast, 369+4480
33:10 and without inhabitant, and **w** beast, 369+4480
33:12 *which is* desolate **w** man and 369+4480
Jer 33:12 *which is* desolate without man and **w** beast, 5704
34:22 of Judah a desolation **w** an inhabitant. 369+4480
44:19 pour out drink offerings unto her, **w** 1107+4480
44:22 a curse, **w** an inhabitant, as *at* this day. 369+4480
46:19 be waste and desolate **w** an inhabitant. 369+4480
48: 9 the cities thereof shall be desolate, **w** 369+4480
49:31 that dwelleth **w care**, saith the LORD, 983
51:29 Babylon a desolation **w** an inhabitant. 369+4480
51:37 and a hissing, **w** an inhabitant. 369+4480
52:20 the brass of all these vessels was **w** weight. 3808
La 1: 6 they are gone **w** strength before 3808+871.1
3:49 and ceaseth not, **w any** intermission, 369+4480
3:52 chased me sore, like a bird, **w cause**. 2600
Eze 2:10 before me; and it *was* written within and **w**: 268
7:15 The sword *is* **w**, and 2351+871.1+1886.1
14:23 ye shall know that I have not done **w cause** 2600
17: 9 even **w** great power or many people 3808+871.1
33:15 of life, **w** committing iniquity; 1115+3807.1
38:11 all of them dwelling **w** walls, and 369+871.1
40:19 the forefront of the inner court **w**, 2351+4480
40:40 at the side **w**, as one goeth 2351+4480+1886.5
40:44 **w** the inner gate *were* 2351+4480+1886.5
41: 9 *was* for the side chamber **w**, 413+2351+1886.1
41:17 **w**, and by all the wall 2351+1886.1+3807.1
41:17 round about within and **w**, 2435+871.1+1886.1
41:25 upon the face of the porch **w**. 2351+4480+1886.1
42: 7 the wall that *was* **w** over 2351+1886.1+3807.1
43:21 the appointed place of the house, **w** 2351+4480
43:22 of the goats **w blemish** for a sin offering; 8549
43:23 shalt offer a young bullock **w blemish**, 8549
43:23 and a ram out of the flock **w blemish**. 8549
43:25 and a ram out of the flock, **w blemish**. 8549
45:18 thou shalt take a young bullock **w blemish**, 8549
45:23 seven rams **w blemish** daily the seven 8549
46: 2 the way of the porch of *that* gate **w**, 2351+4480
46: 4 sabbath day *shall be* six lambs **w blemish**, 8549
46: 4 without blemish, and a ram **w blemish**. 8549
46: 6 *it shall be* a young bullock **w blemish**, 8549
46: 6 and a ram: they shall be **w blemish**. 8549
46:13 *of* a lamb of the first year **w blemish**: 8549
47: 2 led me about the way **w** unto the utter gate 2351
Da 2:34 till that a stone was cut out **w** hands, 3809+871.2
2:45 cut out of the mountain **w** hands, 3809+871.2
8:25 but he shall be broken **w** hand. 657+871.1
11:18 **w** his own reproach he shall cause *it* to turn 1115
Hos 3: 4 of Israel shall abide many days **w** a king, 369
3: 4 **w** a prince, and without a sacrifice, and 369
3: 4 and **w** a sacrifice, and without an image, and 369
3: 4 **w** an image, and without an ephod, and 369
3: 4 and **w** an ephod, and *without* teraphim: 369
3: 4 and without an ephod, and *w* teraphim: NIH
7: 1 troop *of robbers* spoileth **w**. 2351+871.1+1886.1
7:11 Ephraim also is like a silly dove, **w** heart: 369
Joel 1: 6 strong, and **w** number, whose teeth *are* 369
Zec 2: 4 *as* **towns w walls** for the multitude of men 6519
Mt 5:22 **w a cause** shall be in danger of *1500*
10:29 one of them shall not fall on the ground **w** *427*
12:46 *his* mother and his brethren stood **w**, *1854*
12:47 thy mother and thy brethren stand **w**, *1854*
13:34 and **w** a parable spake he not unto them: *5565*
13:57 A prophet is not **w honour**, save in his own *820*
15:16 Are ye also yet **w understanding**? *801*
26:69 Now Peter sat **w** in the palace: and *1854*
Mk 1:45 into the city, but was **w** in desert places: *1854*
3:31 brethren and his mother, and, standing **w**, *1854*
3:32 and thy brethren **w** seek for thee. *1854*
4:11 but unto them that are **w**, all *these things* *1854*
4:34 But **w** a parable spake he not unto them: *5565*
6: 4 A prophet is not **w honour**, but in his own *820*
7:15 There is nothing **from w** a man, *1855*
7:18 Are ye so **w understanding** also? *801*
7:18 that whatsoever *thing* **from w** entereth into *1855*
11: 4 found the colt tied by the door **w** in a place *1854*
14:58 days I will build another **made w hands**. *886*
Lk 1:10 were praying **w** at the time of incense. *1854*
1:74 hand of our enemies might serve him **w fear**, *870*
6:49 is like a man that **w** a foundation built a *5565*
8:20 Thy mother and thy brethren stand **w**, *1854*
11:40 did not he that made that *which is* **w** make *1855*
13:25 and ye begin to stand **w**, and to knock at *1854*
20:28 having a wife, and he die **w children**, *815*
20:29 the first took a wife, and died **w children**. *815*
22:35 When I sent you **w** purse, and scrip, and *817*
Jn 1: 3 **w** him was not any *thing* made that was *5565*
8: 7 said unto them, He that is **w sin** among you, *361*
15: 5 much fruit: for **w** me ye can do nothing. *5565*
15:25 in their law, They hated me **w a cause**. *1432*
18:16 But Peter stood at the door **w**. Then went *1854*
19:23 now the coat was **w seam**, woven from *729*
20:11 But Mary stood **w** at the sepulchre *1854*
Ac 5:23 the keepers standing **w** before the doors: *1854*
5:26 and brought them **w** violence: *3326+3756*
9: 9 And he was three days **w** sight, and *3361*
10:29 Therefore came I *unto you* **w gainsaying**, *369*
12: 5 prayer was made **w ceasing** of the church *1618*
14:17 Nevertheless he left not himself **w witness**, *267*
25:17 when they were come hither, **w any** delay, *3367*
Ro 1: 9 that **w ceasing** I make mention of you, *89*
1:20 and Godhead; so that they are **w excuse**: *379*
1:31 **W understanding**, covenant-breakers, *801*
1:31 **w natural affection**, implacable, *794*
2:12 For as many as have sinned **w law** shall also *460*
2:12 sinned without law shall also perish **w law**: *460*
3: 3 unbelief **make** the faith of God **w effect**? *2673*
3:21 But now the righteousness of God **w** *5565*
3:28 is justified by faith **w** the deeds of the law. *5565*
4: 6 unto whom God imputeth righteousness **w** *5565*
5: 6 For when we were yet **w strength**, in due *772*
7: 8 For **w** the law sin *was* dead. *5565*
7: 9 For I was alive **w** the law once: but *5565*
10:14 and how shall they hear **w** a preacher? *5565*
11:29 and calling of God *are* **w repentance**. *278*
12: 9 *Let* love *be* **w dissimulation**. Abhor *that* *505*
1Co 4: 8 ye are rich, ye have reigned as kings **w** us: *5565*
5:12 have I to do to judge them also that are **w**? *1854*

1Co 5:13 But them that are **w** God judgeth. *1854*
6:18 Every sin that a man doeth is **w** the body; *1622*
7:32 But I would have you **w carefulness**. He *that* *275*
7:35 may attend upon the Lord **w distraction**. *563*
9:18 I may make the gospel of Christ **w charge**, *77*
9:21 To them *that are* **w law**, as without law, *459*
9:21 To them *that are* without law, as **w law**, *459*
9:21 (being not **w law** to God, but under the law *459*
9:21 that I might gain them *that are* **w law**. *459*
11:11 Nevertheless neither *is* the man **w** *5565*
11:11 neither the woman **w** the man, in the Lord. *5565*
14: 7 *And* even *things* **w life** giving sound, *895*
14:10 and none of them *is* **w signification**. *880*
16:10 see that he may be with you **w fear**: *870*
2Co 7: 5 *we were* troubled on every *side;* **w** *were* *1855*
10:13 we will not boast of *things* **w** *our* **measure**, *280*
10:15 Not boasting of *things* **w** *our* **measure**, *280*
11:28 Besides those *things* that are **w**, that which *3924*
Eph 1: 4 be holy and **w blame** before him in love: *299*
2:12 That at that time ye were **w** Christ, *5565*
2:12 having no hope, and **w God** in the world: *112*
3:21 all ages, **world w end**. *165+165+3588+3588*
5:27 but that it should be holy and **w blemish**. *299*
Php 1:10 and **w offence** till the day of Christ; *677*
1:14 much more bold to speak the word **w fear**. *870*
2:14 Do all *things* **w** murmurings and *5565*
2:15 and harmless, the sons of God **w rebuke**, *298*
Col 2:11 with the circumcision **made w hands**, *886*
4: 5 Walk in wisdom toward them that are **w**, *1854*
1Th 1: 3 Remembering **w ceasing** your work of faith, *89*
2:13 For this cause also thank we God **w ceasing**, *89*
4:12 may walk honestly toward them that are **w**, *1854*
5:17 Pray **w ceasing**. *89*
1Ti 2: 8 up holy hands, **w** wrath and doubting. *5565*
3: 7 have a good report of them which are **w**; *1855*
3:16 And **w controversy** great is the mystery of *3672*
5:21 that thou observe these *things* **w** preferring *5565*
6:14 That thou keep *this* commandment **w spot**, *784*
2Ti 1: 3 that **w ceasing** I have remembrance of thee in *88*
3: 3 **W natural affection**, trucebreakers, *794*
Phm 1:14 But **w** thy mind would I do nothing; *5565*
Heb 4:15 all *points* tempted like as *we are, yet* **w** sin. *5565*
7: 3 **W father**, without mother, without descent, *540*
7: 3 Without father, **w mother**, without descent, *282*
7: 3 Without father, without mother, **w descent**, *35*
7: 7 And **w** all contradiction the less is blessed *5565*
7:20 And inasmuch as not **w** an oath *he was* *5565*
7:21 (For those priests were made **w** an oath; but *5565*
9: 7 not **w** blood, which he offered for himself, *5565*
9:14 eternal Spirit offered himself **w spot** to God, *299*
9:18 the first *testament* was dedicated **w** blood. *5565*
9:22 and **w** shedding of blood is no remission. *5565*
9:28 the second time **w** sin unto salvation. *5565*
10:23 fast the profession of *our* hope **w wavering**; *186*
10:28 He that despised Moses' law died **w** mercy *5565*
11: 6 But **w** faith *it is* impossible to please *him:* *5565*
11:40 that they **w** us should not be made perfect. *5565*
12: 8 But if ye be **w** chastisement, whereof all are *5565*
12:14 **w** which no *man* shall see the Lord: *5565*
13: 5 *Let your* conversation *be* **w covetousness**; *866*
13:11 high priest for sin, are burnt **w** the camp. *1854*
13:12 with his own blood, suffered **w** the gate. *1854*
13:13 us go forth therefore unto him **w** the camp, *1854*
Jas 2:13 For he shall have judgment **w mercy**, *448*
2:18 shew me thy faith **w** thy works, and I will *5565*
2:20 O vain man, that faith **w** works is dead? *5565*
2:26 For as the body **w** the spirit is dead, so faith *5565*
2:26 spirit is dead, so faith **w** works is dead also. *5565*
3:17 **w partiality**, and without hypocrisy. *87*
3:17 without partiality, and **w hypocrisy**. *505*
1Pe 1:17 who **w respect of persons** judgeth according *678*
1:19 as of a lamb **w blemish** and without spot: *299*
1:19 as of a lamb without blemish and **w spot**: *784*
3: 1 they also may **w** the word be won by *427*
4: 9 Use hospitality one to another **w** grudging. *427*
2Pe 2:17 These are wells **w water**, clouds that are *504*
3:14 of him in peace, **w spot**, and blameless. *784*
Jude 1:12 feast with *you,* feeding themselves **w fear**: *870*
1:12 clouds *they are* **w water**, carried about of *504*
1:12 **w fruit**, twice dead, plucked up by the roots; *175*
Rev 11: 2 But the court which is **w** the temple leave *1855*
14: 5 for they are **w fault** before the throne of *299*
14:10 which is poured out **w mixture** into the cup *194*
14:20 And the winepress was trodden **w** the city, *1854*
22:15 For **w** *are* dogs, and sorcerers, and *1854*

WITHS (3)

Jdg 16: 7 If they bind me with seven green **w** that 3499
16: 8 seven green **w** which had not been dried, 3499
16: 9 he brake the **w**, as a thread of tow is broken 3499

WITHSTAND (10) [WITHSTOOD]

Nu 22:32 behold, I went out to **w** thee, because 7854
2Ch 13: 7 and could not **w** them. 2388+6440+3807.1
13: 8 now ye think to **w** the 2388+6440+3807.1
20: 6 so that none is **able to w** thee? 3320+5973
Est 9: 2 no man could **w** them; 5975+6440+3807.1
Ecc 4:12 prevail against him, two shall **w** him; 5048+5975
Da 11:15 the arms of the south shall not **w**, 5975
11:15 neither *shall there be any* strength to **w**. 5975
Ac 11:17 what was I, that I could **w** God? *2967*
Eph 6:13 that ye may be able to **w** in the evil day, and *436*

WITHSTOOD (6) [WITHSTAND]

2Ch 26:18 they **w** Uzziah the king, and 5921+5975
Da 10:13 kingdom of Persia **w** me one 5048+5975+3807.1
Ac 13: 8 **w** them, seeking to turn away the deputy *436*
Gal 2:11 I **w** him to the face, because he was *to be* *436*
2Ti 3: 8 Now as Jannes and Jambres **w** Moses, so *436*
4:15 ware also; for he hath greatly **w** our words. *436*

WITNESS (135) [EYEWITNESSES, WITNESSED, WITNESSES, WITNESSETH, WITNESSING]

Ge 21:30 that they may be a **w** unto me, that I have 5713
31:44 and let it be for a **w** between me and thee. 5707
31:48 This heap *is* a **w** between me and thee *this* 5707
31:50 with us; see, God *is* **w** betwixt me and thee. 5707
31:52 This heap *be* **w**, and *this* pillar *be* witness, 5707
31:52 This heap *be* witness, and *this* pillar *be* **w**, 5713
Ex 20:16 Thou shalt not bear false **w** against thy 5707
22:13 *then* let him bring it *for* **w**, *and* he shall not 5707
23: 1 with the wicked to be an unrighteous **w**. 5707
Lev 5: 1 *is* a **w**, whether he hath seen or known *of it;* 5707
Nu 5:13 be defiled, and *there be* no **w** against her, 5707
17: 7 before the LORD in the tabernacle of **W**. 5715
17: 8 Moses went into the tabernacle of **W**; 5715
18: 2 *shall minister* before the tabernacle of **W**. 5715
35:30 one **w** shall not testify against *any* person *to* 5707
Dt 4:26 I **call** heaven and earth **to w** against you 5749
5:20 Neither shalt thou bear false **w** against thy 5707
17: 6 at the mouth of one **w** he shall not be put to 5707
19:15 One **w** shall not rise up against a man for 5707
19:16 If a false **w** rise up against any man to 5707
19:18 *if* the **w** *be* a false witness, *and* 5707
19:18 *if* the witness *be* a false **w**, *and* 5707
31:19 that this song may be a **w** for me against 5707
31:21 this song shall testify against them as a **w**; 5707
31:26 that it may be there for a **w** against thee. 5707
Jos 22:27 But *that* it *may be* a **w** between us, and you, 5707
22:28 but it *is* a **w** between us and you. 5707
22:34 *be* a **w** between us that the LORD *is* God. 5707
24:27 Behold, this stone shall be a **w** unto us; 5713
24:27 it shall be therefore a **w** unto you, lest ye 5713
Jdg 11:10 The LORD be **w** between us, if we do not 8085
1Sa 12: 3 here I *am:* **w** against me before the LORD, 6030
12: 5 The LORD *is* **w** against you, and 5707
12: 5 against you, and his anointed *is* **w** this day, 5707
12: 5 in my hand. And they answered, *He is* **w**. 5707
1Ki 21:10 before him, to **bear w against** him, saying, 5749
2Ch 24: 6 of Israel, for the tabernacle of **W**? 5715
Job 16: 8 *which* is a **w** *against me:* and my leanness 5707
16: 8 my leanness rising up in me **beareth w** to 6030
16:19 behold my **w** *is* in heaven, and my record *is* 5707
29:11 and when the eye saw *me,* it **gave w to** me: 5749
Ps 89:37 as the moon, and *as* a faithful **w** in heaven. 5707
Pr 6:19 A false **w** *that* speaketh lies, and he that 5707
12:17 forth righteousness: but a false **w** deceit. 5707
14: 5 A faithful **w** will not lie: but a false witness 5707
14: 5 will not lie: but a false **w** will utter lies. 5707
14:25 A true **w** delivereth souls: but a deceitful 5707
14:25 but a deceitful *w* speaketh lies. NIH
19: 5 A false **w** shall not be unpunished, and 5707
19: 9 A false **w** shall not be unpunished, and 5707
19:28 An ungodly **w** scorneth judgment: and 5707
21:28 A false **w** shall perish: but the man that 5707
24:28 Be not a **w** against thy neighbour without 5707
25:18 A man that beareth false **w** against his 5707
Isa 3: 9 The shew of their countenance doth **w** 6030
19:20 for a **w** unto the LORD of hosts in 5707
55: 4 I have given him *for* a **w** to the people, 5707
Jer 29:23 even I know, and *am* a **w**, saith 5707
42: 5 be a true and faithful **w** between us, 5707
La 2:13 What *thing* shall I **take to w** for thee? 5749
Mic 1: 2 let the Lord GOD be **w** against you, 5707
Mal 2:14 Because the LORD hath been **w** between 5749
3: 5 I will be a swift **w** against the sorcerers, 5707
Mt 15:19 adulteries, fornications, thefts, **false w**, *5577*
19:18 shalt not steal, Thou shalt not **bear false w**, *5576*
24:14 in all the world for a **w** unto all nations; *3142*
26:59 the council, sought **false w** against Jesus, *5577*
26:62 what *is it which* these **w against** thee? *2649*
27:13 not how many *things* they **w against** thee? *2649*
Mk 10:19 not steal, Do not **bear false w**, Defraud not, *5576*
14:55 all the council sought for **w** against Jesus to *3141*
14:56 For many **bare false w** against him, but *5576*
14:56 but *their* **w** agreed not together. *3141*
14:57 and **bare false w** against him, saying, *5576*
14:59 But neither so did their **w** agree together. *3141*
14:60 what *is it which* these **w against** thee? *2649*
15: 4 behold how many *things* they **w against** *2649*
Lk 4:22 And all **bare** him **w**, and wondered at *3140*
11:48 Truly ye **bear w** that ye allow the deeds of *3140*
18:20 not kill, Do not steal, Do not **bear false w**, *5576*
22:71 they said, What need we any further **w**? *3141*
Jn 1: 7 The same came for a **w**, to bear witness of *3141*
1: 7 came for a witness, to **bear w** of the Light, *3140*
1: 8 but *was sent* to **bear w** of *that* Light. *3140*
1:15 John **bare w** of him, and cried, saying, *3140*
3:11 we have seen; and ye receive not our **w**. *3141*
3:26 to whom thou **barest w**, behold, the same *3140*
3:28 Ye yourselves **bear** me **w**, that I said, I am *3140*
5:31 If I **bear w** of myself, my witness is not *3140*
5:31 I bear witness of myself, my **w** is not true. *3141*
5:32 There is another that **beareth w** of me; and *3140*
5:32 I know that the **w** which he witnesseth of *3141*
5:33 unto John, and he **bare w** unto the truth. *3140*
5:36 But I have greater **w** than *that of* John: *3141*
5:36 the same works that I do, **bear w** of me, *3140*
5:37 which hath sent me, hath **borne w** of me. *3140*
8:18 I am *one* that **bear w** of myself, and *3140*
8:18 the Father that sent me **beareth w** of me. *3140*
10:25 in my Father's name, they **bear w** of me. *3140*
15:27 And ye also shall **bear w**, because ye have *3140*
18:23 If I have spoken evil, **bear w** of the evil: *3140*
18:37 that I should **bear w** unto the truth. *3140*
Ac 1:22 must one be ordained *to be* a **w** with us of *3144*
4:33 And with great power gave the apostles **w** *3142*
7:44 Our fathers had the tabernacle of **W** in *3142*
10:43 To him **give** all the prophets **w**, *3140*
14:17 Nevertheless he left not himself **without w**, *267*
15: 8 which knoweth the hearts, **bare** them **w**, *3140*
22: 5 As also the high priest doth **bear** me **w**, and *3140*
22:15 For thou shalt be his **w** unto all men of *3144*
23:11 so must thou **bear w** also at Rome. *3140*
26:16 a **w** both of *these things* which thou hast *3144*
Ro 1: 9 For God is my **w**, whom I serve with my *3144*
2:15 their conscience **also bearing w**, and *their* *4828*
8:16 The Spirit itself **beareth w with** our spirit, *4828*
9: 1 my conscience **also bearing** me **w** in *4828*
13: 9 shalt not steal, Thou shalt not **bear false w**, *5576*
1Th 2: 5 nor a cloke of covetousness; God *is* **w**: *3144*
Tit 1:13 This **w** is true. Wherefore rebuke them *3141*
Heb 2: 4 God **also bearing** *them* **w**, both with signs *4901*
10:15 *Whereof* the Holy Ghost also is a **w** to us: *3140*
11: 4 by which he **obtained w** that he was *3140*
Jas 5: 3 the rust of them shall be a **w** against you, *3142*
1Pe 5: 1 and a **w** of the sufferings of Christ, and *3144*
1Jn 1: 2 and we have seen *it,* and **bear w**, and *3140*
5: 6 And it is the Spirit that **beareth w**, because *3140*
5: 8 And there are three that **bear w** in earth, *3140*
5: 9 If we receive the **w** of men, the witness of *3141*
5: 9 the witness of men, the **w** of God is greater: *3141*
5: 9 for this is the **w** of God which he hath *3141*
5:10 on the Son of God hath the **w** in himself: *3141*
3Jn 1: 6 Which have **borne w** of thy charity before *3140*
Rev 1: 5 *who is* the faithful **w**, *and* the first begotten *3144*
3:14 saith the Amen, the faithful and true **w**, *3144*
20: 4 them that were beheaded for the **w** of Jesus, *3141*

WITNESSED (4) [WITNESS]

1Ki 21:13 the men of Belial **w against** him, 5749
Ro 3:21 being **w** by the law and the prophets; *3140*
1Ti 6:13 who before Pontius Pilate **w** a good *3140*
Heb 7: 8 there he *receiveth them,* of whom it is **w** *3140*

WITNESSES (49) [WITNESS]

Nu 35:30 shall be put to death by the mouth of **w**: 5707
Dt 17: 6 At the mouth of two **w**, or three witnesses, 5707
17: 6 At the mouth of two witnesses, or three **w**, 5707
17: 7 The hands of the **w** shall be first upon him 5707
19:15 at the mouth of two **w**, or at the mouth of 5707
19:15 or at the mouth of three **w**, shall the matter 5707
Jos 24:22 Ye *are* **w** against yourselves that ye have 5707
24:22 to serve him. And they said, *We are* **w**. 5707
Ru 4: 9 and *unto* all the people, Ye *are* **w** *this* day, 5707
4:10 the gate of his place: ye *are* **w** *this* day. 5707
4:11 in the gate, and the elders, said, *We are* **w**. 5707
Job 10:17 Thou renewest thy **w** against me, and 5707
Ps 27:12 for false **w** are risen up against me, and 5707
35:11 False **w** did rise up; they laid to my charge 5707
Isa 8: 2 I took unto me faithful **w** to record, Uriah 5707
43: 9 former *things?* let them bring forth their **w**, 5707
43:10 Ye *are* my **w**, saith the LORD, and 5707
43:12 therefore ye *are* my **w**, saith the LORD, 5707
44: 8 and have declared *it?* ye *are* even my **w**. 5707
44: 9 they *are* their own **w**; they see not, 5707
Jer 32:10 sealed *it,* and **took w**, and 5707+5749
32:12 in the presence of the **w** that subscribed 5707
32:25 thee the field for money, and **take w**; 5707+5749
32:44 and **take w** in the land of Benjamin, 5707+5749
Mt 18:16 or three **w** every word may be established. *3144*
23:31 Wherefore ye be **w** unto yourselves, that ye *3140*
26:60 yea, though many **false w** came, *yet* found *5575*
26:60 they none. At the last came two **false w**, *5575*
26:65 what further need have we of **w**? *3144*
Mk 14:63 and saith, What need we any further **w**? *3144*
Lk 24:48 And ye are **w** of these *things.* *3144*
Ac 1: 8 ye shall be **w** unto me both in Jerusalem, *3144*
2:32 hath God raised up, whereof we all are **w**. *3144*
3:15 raised from the dead; whereof we are **w**. *3144*
5:32 And we are his **w** of these things; and *so* *3144*
6:13 And set up false **w**, which said, This man *3144*
7:58 the **w** laid down their clothes at a young *3144*
10:39 And we are **w** of all *things* which he did *3144*
10:41 but unto **w** chosen before of God, *even* to *3144*
13:31 who are his **w** unto the people. *3144*
1Co 15:15 Yea, and we are found **false w** of God; *5575*
2Co 13: 1 or three **w** shall every word be established. *3144*
1Th 2:10 Ye *are* **w**, and God *also,* how holily and *3144*
1Ti 5:19 an accusation, but before two or three **w**. *3144*
6:12 a good profession before many **w**. *3144*
2Ti 2: 2 that thou hast heard of me among many **w**, *3144*
Heb 10:28 died without mercy under two or three **w**: *3144*
12: 1 about with so great a cloud of **w**, *3144*
Rev 11: 3 And I will give *power* unto my two **w**, and *3144*

WITNESSETH (2) [WITNESS]

Jn 5:32 I know that the witness which he **w** of me *3140*
Ac 20:23 Save that the Holy Ghost **w** in every city, *1263*

WITNESSING (1) [WITNESS]

Ac 26:22 unto this day, **w** both to small and great, *3140*

WITTINGLY (1) [WIT]

Ge 48:14 Manasseh's head, **guiding** his hands **w**; 7919

WITTY (1) [WIT]

Pr 8:12 and find out knowledge of **w inventions**. 4209

WIVES (132) [WIFE]

Ge 4:19 Lamech took unto him two **w**: the name of 802
4:23 Lamech said unto his **w**, Adah and Zillah, 802
4:23 ye **w** of Lamech, hearken unto my speech: 802
6: 2 they took them **w** of all which they chose. 802
6:18 and thy wife, and thy sons' **w** with thee. 802
7: 7 and his wife, and his sons' **w** with him, 802
7:13 the three **w** of his sons with them, into 802
8:16 and thy sons, and thy sons' **w** with thee. 802
8:18 and his wife, and his sons' **w** with him: 802
11:29 Abram and Nahor took them **w**: the name of 802
28: 9 took unto the **w** which he had Mahalath 802
30:26 Give *me* my **w** and my children, for whom I 802
31:17 and set his sons and his **w** upon camels; 802
31:50 if thou shalt take *other* **w** beside my 802
32:22 took his two **w**, and his two womenservants, 802
34:21 let us take their daughters to us for **w**, and let 802
34:29 their **w** took they captive, and spoiled even 802
36: 2 Esau took his **w** of the daughters of Canaan; 802
36: 6 Esau took his **w**, and his sons, and his 802
37: 2 and with the sons of Zilpah, his father's **w**: 802
45:19 for your **w**, and bring your father, and come. 802
46: 5 their father, and their little ones, and their **w**, 802
46:26 out of his loins, besides Jacob's sons' **w**, 802

Ex 19:15 against the third day: come not at *your* w. 802
22:24 your w shall be widows, and your children 802
32: 2 which *are* in the ears of your w, of your 802
Nu 14: 3 *that* our w and our children should be a 802
16:27 their w, and their sons, and their little 802
32:26 our w, our flocks, and all our cattle, 802
Dt 3:19 our w, and your little ones, and your cattle, 802
17:17 Neither shall he multiply w to himself, 802
21:15 If a man have two w, one beloved, and 802
29:11 your w, and thy stranger that *is* in thy camp, 802
Jos 1:14 Your w, your little ones, and your cattle, 802
Jdg 3: 6 they took their daughters to be their w, and 802
8:30 of his body begotten: for he had many w. 802
21: 7 How shall we do for w for them that remain, 802
21: 7 *we* will not give them of our daughters to w? 802
21:14 they gave them w which they had saved 802
21:16 How shall we do for w for them that remain, 802
21:18 Howbeit we may not give them w of our 802
21:23 and took *them* w, according to their number, 802
Ru 1: 4 they took them w of the women of Moab; 802
1Sa 1: 2 he had two w; the name of the one *was* 802
25:43 and they were also both of them his w. 802
27: 3 *even* David with his two w, Ahinoam 802
30: 3 their w, and their sons, and their daughters, 802
30: 5 David's two w were taken captives, 802
30:18 carried away: and David rescued his two w. 802
2Sa 2: 2 his two w also, Ahinoam the Jezreelitess, 802
5:13 *him* mo concubines and w out of Jerusalem, 802
12: 8 thy master's w into thy bosom, and 802
12:11 I will take thy w before thine eyes, and 802
12:11 he shall lie with thy w in the sight of this 802
19: 5 the lives of thy w, and the lives of thy 802
1Ki 11: 3 he had seven hundred w, princesses, and 802
11: 3 and his w turned away his heart. 802
11: 4 *that* his w turned away his heart after other 802
11: 8 likewise did he for all his strange w, 802
20: 3 thy w also and thy children, *even* 802
20: 5 and thy gold, and thy w, and thy children; 802
20: 7 for he sent unto me for my w, and for my 802
2Ki 4: 1 Now there cried a certain woman of the w of 802
24:15 the king's w, and his officers, and 802
1Ch 4: 5 Ashur the father of Tekoa had two w, Helah 802
7: 4 thirty thousand *men:* for they had many w. 802
8: 8 them away; Hushim and Baara *were* his w. 802
14: 3 David took moe w at Jerusalem: and 802
2Ch 11:21 the daughter of Absalom above all his w 802
11:21 (for he took eighteen w, and 802
11:23 in abundance. And he desired many w. 802
13:21 married fourteen w, and begat twenty and 802
20:13 their little ones, their w, and their children. 802
21:14 thy children, and thy w, and all thy goods: 802
21:17 king's house, and his sons also, and his w; 802
24: 3 Jehoiada took for him two w; and he begat 802
29: 9 and our w *are* in captivity for this. 802
31:18 their w, and their sons, and their daughters, 802
Ezr 10: 2 have taken strange w of the people of 802
10: 3 covenant with our God to put away all the w, 802
10:10 have transgressed, and have taken strange w, 802
10:11 people of the land, and from the strange w. 802
10:14 let all *them* which have taken strange w in 802
10:17 strange w by the first day of the first month. 802
10:18 there were found that had taken strange w: 802
10:19 hands that *they* would put away their w; 802
10:44 All these had taken strange w: and *some* of 802
10:44 *some* of them had w by *whom* they had 802
Ne 4:14 your daughters, your w, and your houses. 802
5: 1 of their w against their brethren the Jews. 802
10:28 their w, their sons, and their daughters, 802
12:43 the w also and the children rejoiced: so 802
13:23 saw I Jews *that* had married w of Ashdod, 802
13:27 against our God in marrying strange w? 802
Est 1:20 all the w shall give to their husbands honour, 802
Isa 13:16 houses shall be spoiled, and their w ravished. 802
Jer 6:12 unto others, *with their* fields and w together: 802
8:10 Therefore will I give their w unto others, *and* 802
14:16 them, their w, nor their sons, nor their 802
18:21 and let their w be bereaved of their children, 802
29: 6 Take ye w, and beget sons and daughters; 802
29: 6 take w for your sons, and give your 802
29:23 adultery with their neighbours' w, 802
35: 8 we, our w, our sons, nor our daughters; 802
38:23 So they *shall* bring out all thy w and thy 802
44: 9 the wickedness of their w, and your own 802
44: 9 and the wickedness of your w, 802
44:15 all the men which knew that their w had 802
44:25 your w have both spoken with your mouths, 802
Eze 44:22 Neither shall they take for their w a widow, 802
Da 5: 2 and his princes, his w, and his concubines, 7695
5: 3 and his princes, his w, and his concubines, 7695
5:23 and thy lords, thy w, and thy concubines, 7695
6:24 of lions, them, their children, and their w; 5389
Zec 12:12 the house of David apart, and their w apart; 802
12:12 the house of Nathan apart, and their w apart; 802
12:13 of the house of Levi apart, and their w apart; 802
12:13 the family of Shimei apart, and their w apart; 802
12:14 every family apart, and their w apart. 802
Mt 19: 8 hearts suffered you to put away your w: *1135*
Lk 17:27 they married *w*, they were given in NIG
Ac 21: 5 with w and children, till *we were* out of *1135*
1Co 7:29 that both they that have w be as though *1135*
Eph 5:22 W, submit yourselves unto your own *1135*
5:24 *let* the w *be* to their own husbands in every *1135*
5:25 Husbands, love your w, even as Christ also *1135*
5:28 So ought men to love their w as their own *1135*
Col 3:18 W, submit yourselves unto your own *1135*
3:19 love *your* w, and be not bitter against them. *1135*
1Ti 3:11 Even so *must their* w *be* grave, *1135*
1Pe 3: 1 Likewise, ye w, *be* in subjection to your *1135*
3: 1 word be won by the conversation of the w; *1135*

WIVES' (1) [WIFE]

1Ti 4: 7 But refuse profane and old w fables, and *1126*

WIZARD (2) [WIZARDS]

Lev 20:27 or that is a w, shall surely be put to death: 3049
Dt 18:11 familiar spirits, or a w, or a necromancer. 3049

WIZARDS (9) [WIZARD]

Lev 19:31 neither seek after w, to be defiled by them: 3049
20: 6 after w, to go a whoring after them, I will 3049
1Sa 28: 3 familiar spirits, and the w, out of the land. 3049
28: 9 familiar spirits, and the w, out of the land: 3049
2Ki 21: 6 and dealt with familiar spirits and w: 3049
23:24 the w, and the images, and the idols, and 3049
2Ch 33: 6 and dealt with a familiar spirit, and with w: 3049
Isa 8:19 and unto w that peep, and that mutter: 3049
19: 3 that have familiar spirits, and to the w. 3049

WOE (106) [WOEFUL, WOES]

Nu 21:29 W to thee, Moab! thou art undone, O people 188
1Sa 4: 7 they said, W unto us: for there hath not been 188
4: 8 W unto us: who shall deliver us out of 188
Job 10:15 If I be wicked, w unto me; and *if* I be 480
Ps 120: 5 W is me, that I sojourn *in* Mesech, *that* I 190
Pr 23:29 Who hath w? who hath sorrow? who hath 188
Ecc 4:10 w to him *that is* alone when he falleth; for *he* 337
10:16 W to thee, O land, when thy king *is* a child, 337
Isa 3: 9 W unto their soul! for they have rewarded 188
3:11 W unto the wicked! *it shall be* ill *with him:* 188
5: 8 W unto them that join house to house, 1945
5:11 W unto them that rise up early in 1945
5:18 W unto them that draw iniquity with cords 1945
5:20 W unto them that call evil good, and good 1945
5:21 W unto *them that are* wise in their own 1945
5:22 W unto *them that are* mighty to drink wine, 1945
6: 5 said I, W *is* me! for I am undone; because 188
10: 1 W unto them that decree unrighteous 1945
17:12 W to the multitude of many people, 1945
18: 1 W to the land shadowing with wings, 1945
24:16 My leanness, my leanness, w unto me! 188
28: 1 W to the crown of pride, to the drunkards 1945
29: 1 W to Ariel, to Ariel, the city *where* David 1945
29:15 W unto them that seek deep to hide *their* 1945
30: 1 W to the rebellious children, saith 1945
31: 1 W to them that go down *to* Egypt for help; 1945
33: 1 W to thee that spoilest, and thou *wast* not 1945
45: 9 W unto him that striveth with his maker! 1945
45:10 W unto him that saith unto *his* father, 1945
Jer 4:13 than eagles. W unto us! for we are spoiled. 188
4:31 spreadeth her hands, *saying,* W *is* me now! 188
6: 4 W unto us! for the day goeth away, for 188
10:19 W is me for my hurt! my wound *is* grievous: 188
13:27 W unto thee, O Jerusalem! wilt thou not be 188
15:10 W is me, my mother, that thou hast borne 188
22:13 W unto him that buildeth his house by 1945
23: 1 W be unto *the* pastors that destroy and 1945
45: 3 Thou didst say, W is me now! for 188
48: 1 of hosts, the God of Israel; W unto Nebo! 1945
48:46 W be unto thee, O Moab! the people of 188
50:27 w unto them! for their day is come, 1945
La 5:16 our head: w unto us, that we have sinned! 188
Eze 2:10 therein lamentations, and mourning, and w. 1958
13: 3 W unto the foolish prophets, that follow 1945
13:18 W to *the women* that sew pillows to all 1945
16:23 after all thy wickedness, (w, woe unto thee! 188
16:23 after all thy wickedness, (woe, w unto thee! 188
24: 6 W to the bloody city, to the pot whose scum 188
24: 9 saith the Lord GOD; W to the bloody city! 188
30: 2 Lord GOD; Howl ye, W worth the day! 1929
34: 2 W *be* to the shepherds of Israel that do feed 1945
Hos 7:13 W unto them! for they have fled from me: 188
9:12 w also to them when I depart from them! 188
Am 5:18 W unto *you* that desire the day of 1945
6: 1 W to them *that are* at ease in Zion, and trust 1945
Mic 2: 1 W to them that devise iniquity, and 1945
7: 1 W is me! for I am as when they have 480
Na 3: 1 W to the bloody city! it *is* all full *of* lies 1945
Hab 2: 6 W to him that increaseth *that which is* not 1945
2: 9 W to him that coveteth an evil 1945
2:12 W to him that buildeth a town with blood, 1945
2:15 W unto him that giveth his neighbour 1945
2:19 W unto him that saith to the wood, Awake, 1945
Zep 2: 5 W unto the inhabitants of the sea coast, 1945
3: 1 W to her that is filthy and polluted, to 1945
Zec 11:17 W to the idol shepherd that leaveth 1945
Mt 11:21 W unto thee, Chorazin, woe unto thee, *3759*
11:21 Chorazin, w unto thee, Bethsaida. *3759*
18: 7 W unto the world because of offences: *3759*
18: 7 w to that man by whom the offence *3759*
23:13 But w unto you, scribes and Pharisees, *3759*
23:14 W unto you, scribes and Pharisees, *3759*
23:15 W unto you, scribes and Pharisees, *3759*
23:16 W unto you, *ye* blind guides, which say, *3759*
23:23 W unto you, scribes and Pharisees, *3759*
23:25 W unto you, scribes and Pharisees, *3759*
23:27 W unto you, scribes and Pharisees, *3759*
23:29 W unto you, scribes and Pharisees, *3759*
24:19 And w unto them that are with child, *3759*
26:24 w unto that man by whom the Son of man *3759*
Mk 13:17 But w to them that are with child, and *3759*
14:21 w to that man by whom the Son of man is *3759*
Lk 6:24 But w unto you that are rich: for ye have *3759*
6:25 W unto you that are full: for ye shall *3759*
6:25 W unto you that laugh now: for ye shall *3759*
6:26 W unto you, when all men shall speak well *3759*
10:13 W unto thee, Chorazin, woe unto thee, *3759*
10:13 Chorazin, w unto thee, Bethsaida: *3759*
11:42 But w unto you, Pharisees! for ye tithe mint *3759*
11:43 W unto you, Pharisees! for ye love *3759*
11:44 W unto you, scribes and Pharisees, *3759*
11:46 And he said, W unto you also, *ye* lawyers! *3759*
11:47 W unto you! for ye build the sepulchres of *3759*
11:52 W unto you, lawyers! for ye have taken *3759*
17: 1 but w *unto him,* through whom they come. *3759*
21:23 But w unto them that are with child, and *3759*
22:22 w unto that man by whom he is betrayed. *3759*
1Co 9:16 yea, w is unto me, if I preach not *3759*
Jude 1:11 W unto them! for they have gone in *3759*
Rev 8:13 saying with a loud voice, W, woe, woe, *3759*
8:13 saying with a loud voice, Woe, w, woe, *3759*
8:13 saying with a loud voice, Woe, woe, w, *3759*
9:12 One w is past; *and* behold, there come two *3759*
11:14 The second w is past; *and* behold, the third *3759*
11:14 *and* behold, the third w cometh quickly. *3759*
12:12 W to the inhabiters of the earth and of *3759*

WOEFUL (1) [WOE]

Jer 17:16 neither have I desired the w day; 605

WOES (1) [WOE]

Rev 9:12 behold, there come two w more hereafter. *3759*

WOLF (6) [WOLVES]

Ge 49:27 Benjamin shall ravin *as* a w: in the morning 2061
Isa 11: 6 The w also shall dwell with the lamb, and 2061
65:25 The w and the lamb shall feed together, and 2061
Jer 5: 6 *and* a w of the evenings shall spoil them, 2061
Jn 10:12 seeth the w coming, and leaveth the sheep, *3074*
10:12 and the w catcheth them, and scattereth *3074*

WOLVES (7) [WOLF]

Eze 22:27 Her princes in the midst thereof *are* like w 2061
Hab 1: 8 and are more fierce than the evening w: 2061
Zep 3: 3 *are* roaring lions; her judges *are* evening w; 2061
Mt 7:15 but inwardly they are ravening w. *3074*
10:16 I send you forth as sheep in the midst of w: *3074*
Lk 10: 3 behold, I send you forth as lambs among w. *3074*
Ac 20:29 that after my departing shall grievous w *3074*

WOMAN (360) [BONDWOMAN, BONDWOMEN, FREEWOMAN, KINSWOMAN, KINSWOMEN, WOMAN'S, WOMANKIND, WOMEN, WOMEN'S, WOMENSERVANTS]

Ge 2:22 made he a w, and brought her unto the man. 802
2:23 she shall be called W, because she was taken 802
3: 1 And he said unto the w, Yea, hath God said, 802
3: 2 the w said unto the serpent, We may eat of 802
3: 4 the serpent said unto the w, Ye shall not 802
3: 6 when the w saw that the tree *was* good for 802
3:12 The w whom thou gavest *to be* with me, 802
3:13 the LORD God said unto the w, What *is* 802
3:13 the w said, The serpent beguiled me, and 802
3:15 I will put enmity between thee and the w, 802
3:16 Unto the w he said, I will greatly multiply 802
12:11 I know that thou *art* a fair w to look upon: 802
12:14 the Egyptians beheld the w that she *was* very 802
12:15 and the w was taken into Pharaoh's house. 802
20: 3 a dead man, for the w which thou hast taken; 802
24: 5 Peradventure the w will not be willing to 802
24: 8 if the w will not be willing to follow thee, 802
24:39 Peradventure the w will not follow me. 802
24:44 *let* the same *be* the w whom the LORD hath 802
46:10 and Shaul the son of a Canaanitish w. NIH
Ex 2: 2 the w conceived, and bare a son: and 802
2: 9 And the w took the child, and nursed it. 802
3:22 every w shall borrow of her neighbour, and 802
6:15 and Shaul the son of a **Canaanitish** w: 3669
11: 2 **every** w of her neighbour, jewels of silver, 802
21:22 hurt a w with child, so that her fruit depart 802
21:28 If an ox gore a man or a w, that they die: 802
21:29 him in, but that he hath killed a man or a w; 802
35:29 every man and w, whose heart made them 802
36: 6 Let neither man nor w make any more work 802
Lev 12: 2 If a w have conceived seed, and born a man 802
13:29 If a man or w hath a plague upon the head or 802
13:38 a w have in the skin of their flesh bright 802
15:18 The w also with whom man shall lie *with* 802
15:19 if a w have an issue, *and* her issue in her 802
15:25 if a w have an issue of her blood many days 802
15:33 of the w, and of him that lieth with her 5347
18:17 Thou shalt not uncover the nakedness of a w 802
18:19 Also thou shalt not approach unto a w to 802
18:23 neither shall any w stand before a beast to lie 802
19:20 whosoever lieth carnally with a w that *is* a 802
20:13 also lie with mankind, as he lieth with a w, 802
20:16 if a w approach unto any beast, and lie down 802
20:16 thou shalt kill the w and the beast: 802
20:18 if a man shall lie with a w having her 802
20:27 A man also or w that hath a familiar spirit, or 802
21: 7 neither shall they take a w put away from her 802
21:14 or a divorced *w*, or profane, *or* a harlot, NIH
24:10 the son of an Israelitish w, whose father *was* 802
24:10 *this* son of the Israelitish *w* and a man of NIH
Nu 5: 6 or w shall commit any sin that men commit, 802
5:18 the priest shall set the w before the LORD, 802
5:19 say unto the w, If no man have lain with 802
5:21 the priest shall charge the w with an oath of 802
5:21 the priest shall say unto the w, The LORD 802
5:22 to rot: And the w shall say, Amen, amen. 802
5:24 he shall cause the w to drink the bitter water 802
5:26 afterward shall cause the w to drink 802
5:27 and the w shall be a curse among her people. 802
5:28 if the w be not defiled, but *be* clean; then 802
5:30 shall set the w before the LORD, and 802
5:31 and this w shall bear her iniquity. 802
6: 2 w shall separate *themselves* to vow a vow of 802
12: 1 of the Ethiopian w whom he had married: 802
12: 1 for he had married an Ethiopian w. 802
25: 6 brought unto his brethren a Midianitish *w* in NIH
25: 8 man of Israel, and the w through her belly. 802
25:14 *even* that was slain with the **Midianitish** w, 4084
25:15 the name of the Midianitish w that was slain 802
30: 3 If a w also vow a vow unto the LORD, and 802
31:17 kill every w that hath known man by lying 802
Dt 15:12 a Hebrew man, or a **Hebrew** w, be sold 5680
17: 2 the LORD thy God giveth thee, man or w, 802
17: 5 shalt thou bring forth that man or that w, 802
17: 5 *even that* man or *that* w, and shalt stone 802
21:11 And seest among the captives a beautiful w, 802
22: 5 The w shall not wear that which pertaineth 802
22:14 say, I took this w, and when I came to her, 802
22:22 If a man be found lying with a w married to 802
22:22 *both* the man that lay with the w, and 802
22:22 the man that lay with the woman, and the w: 802

Dt 28:56 The tender and delicate *w* among you, NIH
29:18 be among you man, or **w**, or family, or tribe, 802
Jos 2: 4 the **w** took the two men, and hid them, and 802
6:21 both man and **w**, young and old, and ox, and 802
6:22 bring out thence the **w**, and all that she hath, 802
Jdg 4: 9 shall sell Sisera into the hand of a **w**. 802
9:53 a certain **w** cast a piece of a millstone upon 802
9:54 that *men* say not of me, A **w** slew him. 802
11: 2 for thou *art* the son of a strange **w**. 802
13: 3 angel of the LORD appeared unto the **w**, 802
13: 6 the **w** came and told her husband, saying, 802
13: 9 the angel of God came again unto the **w** as 802
13:10 the **w** made haste, and ran, and shewed her 802
13:11 *Art* thou the man that spakest unto the **w**? 802
13:13 Of all that I said unto the **w** let her beware. 802
13:24 the **w** bare a son, and called his name 802
14: 1 saw a **w** in Timnath of the daughters of 802
14: 2 I have seen a **w** in Timnath of the daughters 802
14: 3 *Is there* never a **w** among the daughters of 802
14: 7 he went down, and talked with the **w**; and 802
14:10 So his father went down unto the **w**: and 802
16: 4 that he loved a **w** in the valley of Sorek, 802
19:26 Then came the **w** in the dawning of the day, 802
19:27 the **w** his concubine *was* fallen down *at* 802
20: 4 the husband of the **w** that was slain, 802
21:11 and every **w** that hath lien by man. 802
Ru 1: 5 the **w** was left of her two sons and 802
3: 8 and behold, a **w** lay *at* his feet. 802
3:11 people doth know that thou *art* a virtuous **w**. 802
3:14 Let it not be known that a **w** came *into* 802
4:11 The LORD make the **w** that is come into 802
4:12 the LORD shall give thee of this **young w**. 5291
1Sa 1:15 No, my lord, I *am* a **w** of a sorrowful spirit: 802
1:18 So the **w** went her way, and did eat, and her 802
1:23 So the **w** abode, and gave her son suck until 802
1:26 my lord, I *am* the **w** that stood by thee here, 802
2:20 The LORD give thee seed of this **w** for 802
15: 3 slay both man and **w**, infant and suckling, 802
20:30 Thou son of the perverse rebellious *w*, do NIH
25: 3 and *she was* a **w** of good understanding, and 802
27: 9 left neither man nor **w** alive, and took away 802
27:11 David saved neither man nor **w** alive, 802
28: 7 Seek me a **w** that hath a familiar spirit, that I 802
28: 7 *there is* a **w** that hath a familiar spirit at 802
28: 8 with him, and they came to the **w** by night: 802
28: 9 the **w** said unto him, Behold, thou knowest 802
28:11 said the **w**, Whom shall I bring up unto thee? 802
28:12 when the **w** saw Samuel, she cried with a 802
28:12 the **w** spake to Saul, saying, Why hast thou 802
28:13 the **w** said unto Saul, I saw gods ascending 802
28:21 the **w** came unto Saul, and saw that he was 802
28:23 together with the **w**, compelled him; 802
28:24 the **w** had a fat calf in the house; and 802
2Sa 3: 8 me to day with a fault concerning *this* **w**? 802
11: 2 from the roof he saw a **w** washing *herself*; 802
11: 2 and the **w** *was* very beautiful to look upon. 802
11: 3 David sent and inquired after the **w**. And *one* 802
11: 5 the **w** conceived, and sent and told David, 802
11:21 did not a **w** cast a piece of a millstone upon 802
13:17 Put now this *w* out from me, and bolt NIH
14: 2 fetcht thence a wise **w**, and said unto her, 802
14: 2 be as a **w** *that had* a long time mourned for 802
14: 4 when the **w** of Tekoah spake to the king, 802
14: 5 I *am* indeed a widow **w**, and mine husband is 802
14: 8 the king said unto the **w**, Go to thine house, 802
14: 9 the **w** of Tekoah said unto the king, My lord, 802
14:12 the **w** said, Let thine handmaid, I pray thee, 802
14:13 the **w** said, Wherefore then hast thou thought 802
14:18 Then the king answered and said unto the **w**, 802
14:18 the **w** said, Let my lord the king now speak. 802
14:19 the **w** answered and said, *As* thy soul liveth, 802
14:27 she was a **w** of a fair countenance. 802
17:19 the **w** took and spread a covering over 802
17:20 when Absalom's servants came to the **w** to 802
17:20 the **w** said unto them, They be gone over 802
20:16 cried a wise **w** out of the city, Hear, hear; 802
20:17 near unto her, the **w** said, *Art* thou Joab? 802
20:21 the **w** said unto Joab, Behold, his head *shall* 802
20:22 the **w** went unto all the people in her 802
1Ki 3:17 the one **w** said, O my lord, I and this woman 802
3:17 O my lord, I and this **w** dwell in one house; 802
3:18 that this **w** was delivered also: 802
3:22 the other **w** said, Nay; but the living *is* my 802
3:26 spake the **w** whose the living child *was* unto 802
11:26 mother's name *was* Zeruah, a widow **w**, 802
14: 5 that she shall feign herself to be another *w*. NIH
17: 9 I have commanded a widow **w** there to 802
17:10 the widow **w** *was* there gathering of sticks: 802
17:17 *that* the son of the **w**, the mistress of 802
17:24 the **w** said to Elijah, Now *by* this I know that 802
2Ki 4: 1 Now there cried a certain **w** of the wives of 802
4: 8 passed to Shunem, where *was* a great **w**; 802
4:17 the **w** conceived, and bare a son at that 802
6:26 there cried a **w** unto him, saying, Help, 802
6:28 This **w** said unto me, Give thy son, 802
6:30 when the king heard the words of the **w**, 802
8: 1 spake Elisha unto the **w**, whose son he had 802
8: 2 the **w** arose, and did after the saying of 802
8: 3 that the **w** returned out of the land of 802
8: 5 that behold, the **w**, whose son he had 802
8: 5 O king, this *is* the **w**, and this *is* her son, 802
8: 6 when the king asked the **w**, she told him. 802
9:34 Go, see now this cursed *w*, and bury her: NIH
1Ch 16: 3 both man and **w**, to every one a loaf of 802
2Ch 2:14 The son of a **w** of the daughters of Dan, and 802
15:13 whether small or great, whether man or **w**. 802
24: 7 For the sons of Athaliah, *that* **wicked w**, 4849
Est 4:11 do know, that whosoever, *whether* man or **w**, 802
Job 14: 1 Man *that is* born of a **w** *is* of few days, and 802
15:14 *he which is* born of a **w**, that he should be 802
25: 4 or how can he be clean *that is* born of a **w**? 802
31: 9 If mine heart have been deceived by a **w**, or 802
Ps 48: 6 them there, *and* pain, as of a **w** in travail. NIH
58: 8 *like* the untimely birth of a **w**, *that* they may 802
113: 9 He maketh the barren *w* to keep house, NIH

Pr 2:16 To deliver thee from the strange **w**, 802
5: 3 For the lips of a strange *w* drop *as* a NIH
5:20 be ravisht with a strange *w*, and embrace NIH
6:24 To keep thee from the evil **w**, from 802
6:24 the flattery of the tongue of a strange *w*. NIH
6:26 For by means of a whorish **w** *a man is* 802
6:32 *But* whoso committeth adultery with a **w** 802
7: 5 That *they* may keep thee from the strange **w**, 802
7:10 there met him a **w** *with* the attire of a harlot, 802
9:13 A foolish **w** *is* clamorous: *she is* simple, and 802
11:16 A gracious **w** retaineth honour: and 802
11:22 *so is* a fair **w** which is without discretion. 802
12: 4 A virtuous **w** *is* a crown to her husband: but 802
14: 1 Every wise **w** buildeth her house: but 802
20:16 and take a pledge of him for a strange *w*. NIH
21: 9 than with a brawling **w** in a wide house. 802
21:19 than with a contentious and an angry **w**. 802
23:27 deep ditch; and a strange *w is* a narrow pit. NIH
25:24 than with a brawling **w** and in a wide house. 802
27:13 and take a pledge of him for a strange *w*. NIH
27:15 very rainy day and a contentious **w** are alike. 802
30:20 Such *is* the way of an adulterous **w**; 802
30:23 For an odious *w* when she is married; and NIH
31:10 Who can find a virtuous **w**? for her price *is* 802
31:30 *but* a **w** that feareth the LORD, she shall be 802
Ecc 7:26 I find more bitter than death the **w**, 802
7:28 but a **w** among all those have I not found. 802
Isa 13: 8 they shall be in pain as a **w** that travaileth: NIH
21: 3 upon me, as the pangs of a **w** that travaileth: NIH
26:17 Like as a **w** with child, *that* draweth near NIH
42:14 *now* will I cry like a **travailing w**; I will 3205
45:10 or to the **w**, What hast thou brought forth? 802
49:15 Can a **w** forget her sucking child, that *she* 802
54: 6 For the LORD hath called thee as a **w** 802
Jer 4:31 For I have heard a voice as of a **w** in travail, NIH
6: 2 of Zion *to* a comely and delicate *w*. NIH
6:24 hold of us, *and* pain, as of a **w** in travail. NIH
13:21 shall not sorrows take thee, as a **w** in travail? 802
22:23 upon thee, the pain as of a **w** in travail. NIH
30: 6 as a **w** in travail, and all faces are turned NIH
31: 8 the **w** with child and her that travaileth with NIH
31:22 in the earth, A **w** shall compass a man. 5347
44: 7 to cut off from you man and **w**, child and 802
48:41 day shall be as the heart of a **w** in her pangs. 802
49:22 of Edom be as the heart of a **w** in her pangs. 802
49:24 and sorrows have taken her as a **w** in travail. NIH
50:43 hold of him, *and* pangs as of a **w** in travail. NIH
51:22 thee also will I break in pieces man and **w**; 802
La 1:17 Jerusalem is as a menstruous *w* among NIH
Eze 16:30 *things*, the work of an imperious whorish **w**; 802
18: 6 neither hath come near to a menstruous **w**, 802
23:44 as *they* go in unto a **w** that playeth the harlot: 802
36:17 me as the uncleanness of a **removed w**. 5079
Hos 3: 1 Go yet, love a **w** beloved of *her* friend, 802
13:13 The sorrows of a travailing *w* shall come NIH
Mic 4: 9 for pangs have taken thee as a **w** in travail. NIH
4:10 O daughter of Zion, like a **w** in travail: NIH
Zec 5: 7 this *is* a **w** that sitteth in the midst of 802
Mt 5:28 That whosoever looketh on a **w** to lust after *1135*
9:20 (And behold, a **w**, which was diseased with *1135*
9:22 And the **w** was made whole from that *1135*
13:33 which a **w** took, and hid in three measures *1135*
15:22 a **w** of Canaan came out of the same coasts, *1135*
15:28 Jesus answered and said unto her, O **w**, *1135*
22:27 And last of all the **w** died also. *1135*
26: 7 There came unto him a **w** having an *1135*
26:10 he said unto them, Why trouble ye the **w**? *1135*
26:13 *there* shall also *this*, that this *w* hath done, NIG
Mk 5:25 And a certain **w**, which had an issue of *1135*
5:33 But the **w** fearing and trembling, *1135*
7:25 For a *certain* **w**, whose young daughter had *1135*
7:26 The **w** was a Greek, a Syrophenician by *1135*
10:12 And if a **w** shall put away her husband, and *1135*
12:22 and left no seed: last of all the **w** died also. *1135*
14: 3 there came a **w** having an alabaster box of *1135*
Lk 4:26 *a city* of Sidon, unto a **w** *that was* a widow. *1135*
7:37 And behold, a **w** in the city, which was a *1135*
7:39 what manner of **w** *this is* that toucheth him: *1135*
7:44 And he turned to the **w**, and said unto *1135*
7:44 and said unto Simon, Seest thou this **w**? *1135*
7:45 this *w* since the time I came in hath not NIG
7:46 this *w* hath anointed my feet with ointment. NIG
7:50 And he said to the **w**, Thy faith hath saved *1135*
8:43 And a **w** having an issue of blood twelve *1135*
8:47 And when the **w** saw that she was not hid, *1135*
10:38 a certain **w** named Martha received him *1135*
11:27 as he spake these *things*, a certain **w** of *1135*
13:11 there was a **w** which had a spirit of *1135*
13:12 he called *her to him*, and said unto her, **W**, *1135*
13:16 And ought not this *w*, being a daughter of NIG
13:21 which a **w** took and hid in three measures *1135*
15: 8 Either what **w** having ten pieces of silver, *1135*
20:32 Last of all the **w** died also. *1135*
22:57 he denied him, saying, **W**, I know him not. *1135*
Jn 2: 4 Jesus saith unto her, **W**, what have I to do *1135*
4: 7 There cometh a **w** of Samaria to draw *1135*
4: 9 Then saith the **w** of Samaria unto him, *1135*
4: 9 drink of me, which am a **w** of Samaria? *1135*
4:11 The **w** saith unto him, Sir, thou hast *1135*
4:15 The **w** saith unto him, Sir, give me this *1135*
4:17 The **w** answered and said, I have no *1135*
4:19 The **w** saith unto him, Sir, I perceive that *1135*
4:21 unto her, **W**, believe me, the hour cometh, *1135*
4:25 The **w** saith unto him, I know that Messias *1135*
4:27 and marvelled that he talked with *the* **w**: *1135*
4:28 The **w** then left her waterpot, and went her *1135*
4:39 believed on him for the saying of the **w**, *1135*
4:42 And said unto the **w**, *Now* we believe, not *1135*
8: 3 Pharisees brought unto him a **w** taken in *1135*
8: 4 Master, this **w** was taken in adultery, in *1135*
8: 9 left alone, and the **w** standing in the midst. *1135*
8:10 had lift up *himself*, and saw none but the **w**, *1135*
8:10 but the woman, he said unto her, **W**, *1135*
16:21 A **w** when she is in travail hath sorrow, *1135*
19:26 saith unto his mother, **W**, behold thy son. *1135*

Jn 20:13 they say unto her, **W**, why weepest thou? *1135*
20:15 Jesus saith unto her, **W**, why weepest thou? *1135*
Ac 9:36 this *w* was full of good works and NIG
16: 1 named Timotheus, the son of a certain **w**, *1135*
16:14 And a certain **w** named Lydia, a seller of *1135*
17:34 and a **w** named Damaris, and others with *1135*
Ro 1:27 the men, leaving the natural use of the **w**, *2338*
7: 2 For the **w** which hath a husband is bound *1135*
1Co 7: 1 *It is* good for a man not to touch a **w**. *1135*
7: 2 and let **every w** have her own husband. *1538*
7:13 And the **w** which hath a husband that *1135*
7:34 The unmarried *w* careth for the *things* of NIG
11: 3 and the head of the **w** *is* the man; and *1135*
11: 5 But every **w** that prayeth or *1135*
11: 6 For if the **w** be not covered, let her also be *1135*
11: 6 but *if it* be a shame for a **w** to be shorn or *1135*
11: 7 of God: but the **w** is the glory of the man. *1135*
11: 8 For the man is not of the **w**; but the woman *1135*
11: 8 is not of the woman; but the **w** of the man. *1135*
11: 9 Neither was the man created for the **w**; but *1135*
11: 9 for the woman; but the **w** for the man. *1135*
11:10 For this cause ought the **w** to have power *1135*
11:11 neither *is* the man without the **w**, *1135*
11:11 neither the **w** without the man, in the Lord. *1135*
11:12 For as the **w** *is* of the man, *even* so *is* *1135*
11:12 the man, *even* so *is* the man also by the **w**; *1135*
11:13 is it comely that a **w** pray unto God *1135*
11:15 But if a **w** have long hair, it is a glory to *1135*
Gal 4: 4 his Son, made of a **w**, made under the law, *1135*
1Th 5: 3 upon them, as travail upon a *w* with child; NIG
1Ti 2:11 Let the **w** learn in silence with all *1135*
2:12 But I suffer not a **w** to teach, nor to usurp *1135*
2:14 the **w** being deceived was in *1135*
5:16 any man or **w that believeth** have widows, *4103*
Rev 2:20 because thou sufferest *that* **w** Jezebel, *1135*
12: 1 a **w** clothed with the sun, and the moon *1135*
12: 4 the dragon stood before the **w** which was *1135*
12: 6 And the **w** fled into the wilderness, *1135*
12:13 he persecuted the **w** which brought forth *1135*
12:14 And to the **w** were given two wings of a *1135*
12:15 of his mouth water as a flood after the **w**, *1135*
12:16 And the earth helped the **w**, and the earth *1135*
12:17 And the dragon was wroth with the **w**, and *1135*
17: 3 I saw a **w** sit upon a scarlet coloured beast, *1135*
17: 4 And the **w** was arrayed in purple and *1135*
17: 6 And I saw the **w** drunken with the blood of *1135*
17: 7 I will tell thee the mystery of the **w**, and *1135*
17: 9 seven mountains, on which the **w** sitteth. *1135*
17:18 And the **w** which thou sawest is *that* great *1135*

WOMAN'S (7) [WOMAN]

Ge 38:20 to receive *his* pledge from the **w** hand: 802
Ex 21:22 according as the **w** husband will lay upon 802
Lev 24:11 the Israelitish **w** son blasphemed the name *of* 802
Nu 5:18 uncover the **w** head, and put the offering of 802
5:25 take the jealousy offering out of the **w** hand, 802
Dt 22: 5 neither shall a man put on a **w** garment: 802
1Ki 3:19 this **w** child died in the night; because 802

WOMANKIND (1) [WOMAN]

Lev 18:22 Thou shalt not lie with mankind, as with **w**: 802

WOMB (71) [WOMBS]

Ge 25:23 Two nations *are* in thy **w**, and two manner of 990
25:24 behold, *there were* twins in her **w**. 990
29:31 saw that Leah *was* hated, he opened her **w**: 7358
30: 2 hath withheld from thee the fruit of the **w**? 990
30:22 God hearkened to her, and opened her **w**. 7358
38:27 her travail, that, behold, twins *were* in her **w**. 990
49:25 blessings of the breasts, and of the **w**: 7356
Ex 13: 2 whatsoever openeth the **w** among 7358
Nu 8:16 instead of such as open every **w**, 7358
12:12 when he cometh out of his mother's **w**. 7358
Dt 7:13 he will also bless the fruit of thy **w**, and 990
Jdg 13: 5 shall be a Nazarite unto God from the **w**: 990
13: 7 to God from the **w** to the day of his death. 990
16:17 a Nazarite unto God from my mother's **w**: 990
Ru 1:11 *are there* yet *any moe* sons in my **w**, 4578
1Sa 1: 5 but the LORD had shut up her **w**. 7358
1: 6 because the LORD had shut up her **w**. 7358
Job 1:21 Naked came I out of my mother's **w**, and 990
3:10 it shut not up the doors of my *mother's* **w**, 990
3:11 Why died I not from the **w**? *why* did I *not* 7358
10:18 hast thou brought me forth out of the **w**? 7358
10:19 I should have been carried from the **w** to 990
24:20 The **w** shall forget him; the worm shall feed 7358
31:15 Did not he that made me in the **w** make him? 990
31:15 and did not one fashion us in the **w**? 7358
31:18 and I have guided her from my mother's **w**;) 990
38: 8 brake forth, *as if* it had issued out of the **w**? 7358
38:29 Out of whose **w** came the ice? and the hoary 990
Ps 22: 9 thou *art* he that took me out of the **w**: 990
22:10 I was cast upon thee from the **w**: thou *art* 7358
58: 3 The wicked are estranged from the **w**: 7358
71: 6 By thee have I been holden up from the **w**: 990
110: 3 in the beauties of holiness from the **w** of 7358
127: 3 *and* the fruit of the **w** *is his* reward. 990
139:13 thou hast covered me in my mother's **w**. 990
Pr 30:16 The grave; and the barren **w**; the earth *that* 7356
31: 2 what, the son of my **w**? and what, the son of 990
Ecc 5:15 As he came forth of his mother's **w**, 990
11: 5 *nor* how the bones *do grow* in the **w** of her 990
Isa 13:18 they shall have no pity on the fruit of the **w**; 990
44: 2 formed thee from the **w**, *which* will help 990
44:24 and he that formed thee from the **w**, 990
46: 3 the belly, which are carried from the **w**: 7356
48: 8 wast called a transgressor from the **w**. 990
49: 1 The LORD hath called me from the **w**; 990
49: 5 saith the LORD that formed me from the **w** 990
49:15 not have compassion on the son of her **w**? 990
66: 9 bring forth, and shut *the* **w**? saith thy God. NIH
Jer 1: 5 before thou camest forth out of the **w** I 7358
20:17 Because he slew me not from the **w**; or 7358
20:17 and her **w** *to be* always great *with me*. 7358

Jer 20:18 Wherefore came I forth out of the **w** to see 7358
Eze 20:26 pass through *the fire* all that openeth the **w**, 7356
Hos 9:11 and from the **w**, and from the conception. 990
9:14 give them a miscarrying **w** and dry breasts. 7358
9:16 will I slay *even* the beloved *fruit* of their **w**. 990
12: 3 He took his brother by the heel in the **w**, and 990
Mt 19:12 which were so born from *their* mother's **w**: *2836*
Lk 1:15 the Holy Ghost, even from his mother's **w**. *2836*
1:31 thou shalt conceive in *thy* **w**, and *1064*
1:41 of Mary, the babe leaped in her **w**; *2836*
1:42 and blessed *is* the fruit of thy **w**. *2836*
1:44 mine ears, the babe leaped in my **w** for joy. *2836*
2:21 the angel before he was conceived in the **w**. *2836*
2:23 Every male that openeth the **w** shall be *3388*
11:27 Blessed *is* the **w** that bare thee, and *2836*
Jn 3: 4 enter the second time into his mother's **w**, *2836*
Ac 3: 2 man lame from his mother's **w** was carried, *2836*
14: 8 being a cripple from his mother's **w**, *2836*
Ro 4:19 neither *yet* the deadness of Sara's **w**: *3388*
Gal 1:15 who separated me from my mother's **w**, *2836*

WOMBS (2) [WOMB]

Ge 20:18 For the LORD had fast closed up all the **w** 7358
Lk 23:29 and the **w** that never bare, and the paps *2836*

WOMEN (178) [WOMAN]

Ge 14:16 his goods, and the **w** also, and the people. 802
18:11 to be with Sarah after the manner of **w**. 802
24:11 *even* the time that **w** go out to draw *water*. NIH
31:35 before thee; for the custom of **w** *is* upon me. 802
33: 5 up his eyes, and saw the **w** and the children; 802
Ex 1:16 the office of a midwife to the **Hebrew w**, 5680
1:19 Because the **Hebrew w** *are* not as 5680
1:19 Hebrew women *are* not as the Egyptian **w**; 802
2: 7 and call to thee a nurse of the Hebrew **w**, 802
15:20 all the **w** went out after her with timbrels and 802
35:22 they came, both men and **w**, as many as were 802
35:25 all the **w** that were wise hearted did spin 802
35:26 all the **w** whose heart stirred them up in 802
38: 8 of the looking-glasses of *the* **w** assembling, NIH
Lev 26:26 ten **w** shall bake your bread in one oven, and 802
Nu 31: 9 the children of Israel took *all* the **w** of 802
31:15 unto them, Have ye saved all the **w** alive? 5347
31:18 all the **w** children, that have not known a 802
31:35 of **w** that had not known man by lying with 802
Dt 2:34 the **w**, and the little ones, of every city, 802
3: 6 the men, **w**, and children, of every city. 802
20:14 But the **w**, and the little ones, and the cattle, 802
31:12 **w**, and children, and thy stranger that *is* 802
Jos 8:25 both of men and **w**, *were* twelve thousand, 802
8:35 with the **w**, and the little ones, and 802
Jdg 5:24 Blessed above **w** shall Jael the wife of Heber 802
5:24 blessed shall she be above **w** in the tent. 802
9:49 died also, about a thousand men and **w**. 802
9:51 thither fled all the men and **w**, and all they of 802
16:27 Now the house was full *of* men and **w**; and 802
16:27 the roof about three thousand men and **w**, 802
21:10 of the sword, with the **w** and the children. 802
21:14 had saved alive of the **w** of Jabesh-gilead: 802
21:16 seeing the **w** are destroyed out of Benjamin? 802
Ru 1: 4 they took them wives of the **w of Moab**; 4125
4:14 the **w** said unto Naomi, Blessed *be* 802
4:17 the **w** *her* neighbours gave it a name, NIH
1Sa 2:22 how they lay with the **w** that assembled *at* 802
4:20 about the time of her death the **w** that stood NIH
15:33 As thy sword hath made **w** childless, so 802
15:33 so shall thy mother be childless among **w**. 802
18: 6 that the **w** came out of all cities of Israel, 802
18: 7 the **w** answered *one another* as they played, 802
21: 4 men have kept themselves at least from **w**. 802
21: 5 Of a truth **w** *have been* kept from us about 802
22:19 both men and **w**, children and sucklings, and 802
30: 2 had taken the **w** captives, that *were* therein: 802
2Sa 1:26 to me was wonderful, passing the love of **w**. 802
6:19 as well to the **w** as men, to every one a cake 802
15:16 the king left ten **w**, *which were* concubines, 802
19:35 singing *men* and singing **w**? wherefore then NIH
20: 3 the king took the ten **w** *his* concubines, 802
1Ki 3:16 came there two **w**, *that were* harlots, unto 802
11: 1 king Solomon loved many strange **w**, 802
11: 1 **w** *of the* Moabites, Ammonites, Edomites, NIH
2Ki 8:12 and rip up their **w with child**. 2030
15:16 all the **w** therein that were **with child** he 2030
23: 7 where the **w** wove hangings for the grove. 802
2Ch 28: 8 **w**, sons, and daughters, and took also away 802
35:25 the singing **w** spake of Josiah in their NIH
Ezr 2:65 two hundred singing *men* and singing **w**. NIH
10: 1 congregation *of* men and **w** and children: 802
Ne 7:67 and five singing *men* and singing **w**. NIH
8: 2 before the congregation both of men and **w**, 802
8: 3 before the men and the **w**, and those that 802
13:26 *nevertheless* even him did outlandish **w** 802
Est 1: 9 Also Vashti the queen made a feast for the **w** 802
1:17 of the queen shall come abroad unto all **w**, 802
2: 3 to the house of the **w**, unto the custody of 802
2: 3 the king's chamberlain, keeper of the **w**; 802
2: 8 to the custody of Hegai, keeper of the **w**. 802
2: 9 unto the best *place* of the house of the **w**. 802
2:12 according to the manner of the **w**, (for so 802
2:12 with *other* things for the purifying of the **w**;) 802
2:13 of the house of the **w** unto the king's house. 802
2:14 she returned into the second house of the **w**, 802
2:15 the keeper of the **w**, appointed. 802
2:17 the king loved Esther above all the **w**, and 802
3:13 both young and old, little children and **w**, 802
8:11 *both* little ones and **w**, and *to take* the spoil 802
Job 2:10 Thou speakest as one of the foolish **w** NIH
42:15 in all the land were no **w** found *so* fair as 802
Ps 45: 9 **w**: upon thy right hand did stand the queen NIH
Pr 22:14 The mouth of strange **w** *is* a deep pit: NIH
23:33 Thine eyes shall behold strange **w**, and NIH
31: 3 Give not thy strength unto **w**, nor thy ways 802
Ecc 2: 8 I gat me *men* singers and **w** singers, and NIH
SS 1: 8 If thou know not, O thou fairest among **w**, 802
5: 9 *another* beloved, O thou fairest among **w**? 802
SS 6: 1 thy beloved gone, O thou fairest among **w**? 802
Isa 3:12 *are* their oppressors, and **w** rule over them. 802
4: 1 in that day seven **w** shall take hold of one 802
19:16 In that day shall Egypt be like unto **w**: and 802
27:11 the **w** come, *and* set them on fire: for it *is* a 802
32: 9 Rise up, ye **w** that are at ease, hear my voice; 802
32:10 ye careless **w**: for the vintage shall fail, NIH
32:11 Tremble, ye **w** that are at ease; be troubled, NIH
Jer 7:18 kindle the fire, and the **w** knead *their* dough, 802
9:17 call for the mourning **w**, that they may NIH
9:17 send for cunning **w**, that they may come: NIH
9:20 O ye **w**, and let your ear receive the word of 802
38:22 all the **w** that are left in the king of Judah's 802
38:22 those **w** *shall* say, Thy friends have set thee NIH
40: 7 **w**, and children, and of the poor of the land, 802
41:16 and the **w**, and the children, and the eunuchs, 802
43: 6 **w**, and children, and the king's daughters, 802
44:15 and all the **w** that stood *by*, a great multitude, 802
44:20 to the **w**, and to all the people which had 802
44:24 to all the **w**, Hear the word of the LORD, 802
50:37 the midst of her; and they shall become as **w**: 802
51:30 their might hath failed; they became as **w**: 802
La 2:20 Shall the **w** eat their fruit, *and* children of a 802
4:10 The hands of the pitiful **w** have sodden their 802
5:11 They ravished the **w** in Zion, *and* the maids 802
Eze 8:14 behold, there sat **w** weeping for Tammuz. 802
9: 6 both maids, and little children, and **w**: 802
13:18 Woe to *the* **w** that sew pillows to all NIH
16:34 the contrary is in thee from *other* **w** in thy 802
16:38 as **w** that break wedlock and shed blood are NIH
16:41 judgments upon thee in the sight of many **w**: 802
23: 2 Son of man, there were two **w**, the daughters 802
23:10 she became famous among **w**; for they had 802
23:44 unto Aholah and unto Aholibah, the lewd **w**. 802
23:45 and after the manner of **w** that shed blood; NIH
23:48 that all **w** may be taught not to do after your 802
Da 11:17 he shall give him the daughter of **w**, 802
11:37 nor the desire of **w**, nor regard any god: 802
Hos 13:16 and their **w with child** shall be ript up. 2030
Am 1:13 they have ript up the **w with child** at 2030
Mic 2: 9 The **w** of my people have ye cast out from 802
Na 3:13 thy people in the midst of thee *are* **w**: 802
Zec 5: 9 there came out two **w**, and the wind *was* in 802
8: 4 and **old w** dwell in the streets of Jerusalem, 2205
14: 2 and the houses rifled, and the **w** ravished; 802
Mt 11:11 Among *them that are* born of **w** there hath *1135*
14:21 five thousand men, beside **w** and children. *1135*
15:38 four thousand men, beside **w** and children. *1135*
24:41 Two **w** *shall be* grinding at the mill; *the* one NIG
27:55 And many **w** were there beholding afar off, *1135*
28: 5 the angel answered and said unto the **w**, *1135*
Mk 15:40 There were also **w** looking on afar off: *1135*
15:41 many other **w** which came up with him unto NIG
Lk 1:28 *is* with thee: blessed *art* thou among **w**. *1135*
1:42 Blessed *art* thou among **w**, and blessed *is* *1135*
7:28 Among *those that are* born of **w** there is not *1135*
8: 2 And certain **w**, which had been healed of *1135*
17:35 Two **w** shall be grinding together; the one NIG
23:27 and of **w**, which also bewailed and *1135*
23:49 and the **w** that followed him from Galilee, *1135*
23:55 And the **w** also, which came with him from *1135*
24:10 of James, and other **w** *that were* with them, NIG
24:22 certain **w** *also* of our company made us *1135*
24:24 and found *it* even so as the **w** had said: *1135*
Ac 1:14 with the **w**, and Mary the mother of Jesus, *1135*
5:14 to the Lord, multitudes both of men and **w**.) *1135*
8: 3 and **w** committed *them* to prison. *1135*
8:12 they were baptized, both men and **w**. *1135*
9: 2 of *this* way, whether they were men or **w**, *1135*
13:50 stirred up the devout and honourable **w**, *1135*
16:13 spake unto the **w** which resorted *thither*. *1135*
17: 4 and of the chief **w** not a few. *1135*
17:12 also of honourable **w** which were Greeks, *1135*
22: 4 delivering into prisons both men and **w**. *1135*
Ro 1:26 for even their **w** did change the natural use *2338*
1Co 14:34 Let your **w** keep silence in the churches: *1135*
14:35 for it is a shame for **w** to speak in *1135*
Php 4: 3 help those **w** which laboured with me in NIG
1Ti 2: 9 that **w** adorn themselves in modest apparel, *1135*
2:10 But (which becometh **w** professing *1135*
5: 2 The elder **w** *as* mothers; the younger as NIG
5:14 I will therefore that the younger **w** marry, NIG
2Ti 3: 6 and lead captive **silly w** laden with sins, *1133*
Tit 2: 3 The **aged w** likewise, *that they be* in *4247*
2: 4 That they may teach the young **w** to be NIG
Heb 11:35 **W** received their dead raised to life again: *1135*
1Pe 3: 5 this manner in the old time the holy **w** also, *1135*
Rev 9: 8 And they had hair as the hair of **w**, and *1135*
14: 4 are they which were not defiled with **w**; *1135*

WOMEN'S (1) [WOMAN]

Est 2:11 every day before the court of the **w** house, 802

WOMENSERVANTS (3) [SERVE, WOMAN]

Ge 20:14 **w**, and gave *them* unto Abraham, and 8198
32: 5 and asses, flocks, and menservants, and **w**: 8198
32:22 his two **w**, and his eleven sons, and 8198

WON (3) [WIN]

1Ch 26:27 Out of the **spoils w** in battles did they 7998
Pr 18:19 A brother offended *is harder to be* **w** than a NIH
1Pe 3: 1 they also may without the word be **w** by *2770*

WONDER (15) [WONDERED, WONDERFUL, WONDERFULLY, WONDERING, WONDERS, WONDROUS, WONDROUSLY]

Dt 13: 1 of dreams, and giveth thee a sign or a **w**, 4159
13: 2 the sign or the **w** come to pass, whereof he 4159
28:46 shall be upon thee for a sign and for a **w**, 4159
2Ch 32:31 who sent unto him to inquire of the **w** that 4159
Ps 71: 7 I am as a **w** unto many; but thou *art* my 4159
Isa 20: 3 and **w** upon Egypt and upon Ethiopia; 4159
29: 9 Stay yourselves, and **w**; cry ye out, and cry: 8539
29:14 *even* a marvellous work and a **w**: 6382
Jer 4: 9 be astonished, and the prophets shall **w**. 8539
Hab 1: 5 and regard, and **w** marvellously: 8539
Ac 3:10 and they were filled with **w** and *2285*
13:41 Behold *ye* despisers, and **w**, and perish: *2296*
Rev 12: 1 And there appeared a great **w** in heaven; *4592*
12: 3 And there appeared another **w** in heaven; *4592*
17: 8 and they that dwell on the earth shall **w**, *2296*

WONDERED (15) [WONDER]

Isa 59:16 and **w** that *there was* no intercessor: 8074
63: 5 and I **w** that *there was* none to uphold: 8074
Zec 3: 8 for they *are* men **w at**: for behold, I *will* 4159
Mt 15:31 Insomuch that the multitude **w**, when they *2296*
Mk 6:51 in themselves beyond measure, and **w**. *2296*
Lk 2:18 And all they that heard *it* **w** at those *things* *2296*
4:22 **w** at the gracious words which proceeded *2296*
8:25 And they being afraid **w**, saying one to *2296*
9:43 But while they **w** every one at all *things* *2296*
11:14 the dumb spake; and the people **w**. *2296*
24:41 and **w**, he said unto them, Have ye here any *2296*
Ac 7:31 When Moses saw *it*, he **w** at the sight: and *2296*
8:13 and **w**, beholding *the* miracles and *1839*
Rev 13: 3 and all the world **w** after the beast. *2296*
17: 6 when I saw her, I **w** *with* great admiration. *2296*

WONDERFUL (21) [WONDER]

Dt 28:59 the LORD will **make** thy plagues **w**, and 6381
2Sa 1:26 thy love to me was **w**, passing the love of 6381
2Ch 2: 9 which I am about to build *shall be* **w** great. 6381
Job 42: 3 *things* too **w** for me, which I knew not. 6381
Ps 40: 5 *are* thy **w works** *which* thou hast done, and 6381
78: 4 and his **w works** that he hath done. 6381
107: 8 and *for* his **w works** to the children of men! 6381
107:15 and *for* his **w works** to the children of men! 6381
107:21 and *for* his **w works** to the children of men! 6381
107:31 and *for* his **w works** to the children of men! 6381
111: 4 He hath made his **w works** to be 6381
119:129 Thy testimonies *are* **w**: therefore doth my 6382
139: 6 *Such* knowledge *is* too **w** for me; it is high, 6383
Pr 30:18 There be three *things which* are too **w** for 6381
Isa 9: 6 and his name shall be called **W**, Counseller, 6382
25: 1 thy name; for thou hast done **w things**; 6382
28:29 which is **w** in counsel, *and* excellent in 6381
Jer 5:30 A **w** and horrible thing is committed in 8047
Mt 7:22 and in thy name done many **w works**? *1411*
21:15 and scribes saw the **w** *things* that he did, *2297*
Ac 2:11 speak in our tongues the **w works** of God. *3167*

WONDERFULLY (4) [WONDER]

1Sa 6: 6 when he had **wrought w** among them, did 5953
Ps 139:14 praise thee; for I am fearfully and **w made**: 6381
La 1: 9 her last end; therefore she came down **w**: 6382
Da 8:24 he shall destroy **w**, and shall prosper, and 6381

WONDERING (3) [WONDER]

Ge 24:21 the man **w** at her held his peace, to wit 7583
Lk 24:12 **w** in himself at that which was come to *2296*
Ac 3:11 porch that is called Solomon's, **greatly w**. *1569*

WONDERS (55) [WONDER]

Ex 3:20 smite Egypt with all my **w** which I will do 6381
4:21 see that thou do all *those* **w** before Pharaoh, 4159
7: 3 my signs and my **w** in the land of Egypt. 4159
11: 9 that my **w** may be multiplied in the land of 4159
11:10 and Aaron did all these **w** before Pharaoh: 4159
15:11 in holiness, fearful *in* praises, doing **w**? 6382
Dt 4:34 by **w**, and by war, and by a mighty hand, 4159
6:22 the LORD shewed signs and **w**, great and 4159
7:19 the **w**, and the mighty hand, and 4159
26: 8 and with signs, and with **w**: 4159
34:11 In all the signs and the **w**, which 4159
Jos 3: 5 for to morrow the LORD will do **w** among 6381
1Ch 16:12 his **w**, and the judgments of his mouth; 4159
Ne 9:10 shewedst signs and **w** upon Pharaoh, and 4159
9:17 neither were mindful of thy **w** that thou 6381
Job 9:10 finding out; yea, and **w** without number. 6381
Ps 77:11 surely I will remember thy **w** of old. 6382
77:14 Thou *art* the God that doest **w**: thou hast 6382
78:11 and his **w** that he had shewed them. 6381
78:43 in Egypt, and his **w** in the field of Zoan: 4159
88:10 Wilt thou shew **w** to the dead? shall 6382
88:12 Shall thy **w** be known in the dark? and 6382
89: 5 the heavens shall praise thy **w**, O LORD: 6382
96: 3 among the heathen, his **w** among all people. 6381
105: 5 his **w**, and the judgments of his mouth; 4159
105:27 among them, and **w** in the land of Ham. 4159
106: 7 Our fathers understood not thy **w** in Egypt; 6381
107:24 of the LORD, and his **w** in the deep. 6381
135: 9 sent tokens and **w** into the midst of thee, 4159
136: 4 To him who alone doeth great **w**: for his 6381
Isa 8:18 for **w** in Israel from the LORD of hosts, 4159
Jer 32:20 hast set signs and **w** in the land of Egypt, 4159
32:21 with **w**, and with a strong hand, and with a 4159
Da 4: 2 **w** that the high God hath wrought toward 8540
4: 3 how mighty *are* his **w**! his kingdom *is* an 8540
6:27 worketh signs and **w** in heaven and in earth, 8540
12: 6 How long *shall it be to* the end of *these* **w**? 6382
Joel 2:30 I will shew **w** in the heavens and in 4159
Mt 24:24 and shall shew great signs and **w**; *5059*
Mk 13:22 and shall shew signs and **w**, to seduce, if *it* *5059*
Jn 4:48 Except ye see signs and **w**, ye will not *5059*
Ac 2:19 And I will shew **w** in heaven above, and *5059*
2:22 among you by miracles and **w** and signs, *5059*
2:43 and many **w** and signs were done by *5059*
4:30 **w** may be done by the name of thy holy *5059*
5:12 and **w** wrought among the people; *5059*
6: 8 did great **w** and miracles among the people. *5059*
7:36 after that he had shewed **w** and signs in *5059*
14: 3 and **w** to be done by their hands. *5059*
15:12 **w** God had wrought among the Gentiles by *5059*
Ro 15:19 Through mighty signs and **w**, by the power *5059*
2Co 12:12 in signs, and **w**, and mighty deeds. *5059*
2Th 2: 9 Satan with all power and signs and lying **w**, *5059*
Heb 2: 4 both with signs and **w**, and with divers *5059*

Rev 13:13 And he doeth great **w**, so that he maketh *4592*

WONDROUS (15) [WONDER]
1Ch 16: 9 unto him, talk you of all his **w works**. 6381
Job 37:14 and consider the **w works** of God. 6381
37:16 the **w works** of *him which is* perfect in 4652
Ps 26: 7 and tell of all thy **w works**. 6381
71:17 and hitherto have I declared thy **w works**. 6381
72:18 God of Israel, who only doeth **w** *things*. 6381
75: 1 for *that* thy name *is* near thy **w works** 6381
78:32 and believed not for his **w works**. 6381
86:10 and doest **w** *things:* thou *art* God alone. 6381
105: 2 unto him: talk ye of all his **w works**. 6381
106:22 **W works** in the land of Ham, *and* 6381
119:18 that I may behold **w** *things* out of thy law. 6381
119:27 thy precepts: so shall I talk of thy **w works**. 6381
145: 5 honour of thy majesty, and of thy **w** works. 6381
Jer 21: 2 deal with us according to all his **w works**, 6381

WONDROUSLY (2) [WONDER]
Jdg 13:19 *the angel* did **w**; and Manoah and his wife 6381
Joel 2:26 that hath dealt **w** with you: 6381+3807.1

WONT (9)
Ex 21:29 if the ox *were* **w to push with his horn** in 5056
Nu 22:30 was I **ever w** to do so unto thee? 5532+5532
1Sa 30:31 and his men were **w to haunt**. 1980
2Sa 20:18 were **w to speak** in old time, saying, 1696+1696
Da 3:19 seven *times* more than *it was* **w** to be heat. 2370
Mt 27:15 Now at *that* feast the governor was **w** to *1486*
Mk 10: 1 and, as he was **w**, he taught them again. *1486*
Lk 22:39 and went, **as** he was **w**, *1485+2596+3588*
Ac 16:13 river side, where prayer was **w** to be made; *3543*

WOOD (140) [WOODS, WORMWOOD]
Ge 6:14 Make thee an ark of gopher **w**; rooms shalt 6086
22: 3 clave the **w** for the burnt offering, and 6086
22: 6 Abraham took the **w** of the burnt offering, 6086
22: 7 he said, Behold the fire and the **w**: but 6086
22: 9 laid the **w** in order, and bound Isaac his 6086
22: 9 and laid him on the altar upon the **w**. 6086
Ex 7:19 both in *vessels of* **w**, and in *vessels of* 6086
25: 5 and badgers' skins, and shittim **w**, 6086
25:10 they shall make an ark of shittim **w**: 6086
25:13 thou shalt make staves of shittim **w**, and 6086
25:23 Thou shalt also make a table *of* shittim **w**: 6086
25:28 thou shalt make the staves *of* shittim **w**, 6086
26:15 for the tabernacle *of* shittim **w** standing up. 6086
26:26 thou shalt make bars *of* shittim **w**; five for 6086
26:32 four pillars of shittim *w* overlaid with gold: NIH
26:37 for the hanging five pillars of shittim *w*, NIH
27: 1 thou shalt make an altar *of* shittim **w**, 6086
27: 6 staves of shittim **w**, and overlay them with 6086
30: 1 *of* shittim **w** shalt thou make it. 6086
30: 5 thou shalt make the staves *of* shittim **w**, 6086
35: 7 and badgers' skins, and shittim **w**, 6086
35:24 with whom was found shittim **w** for any 6086
35:33 of stones, to set *them*, and in carving of **w**, 6086
36:20 boards for the tabernacle *of* shittim **w**, 6086
36:31 he made bars of shittim **w**; five for 6086
36:36 he made thereunto four pillars of shittim *w*, NIH
37: 1 Bezaleel made the ark *of* shittim **w**: 6086
37: 4 he made staves of shittim **w**, and 6086
37:10 he made the table *of* shittim **w**: two cubits 6086
37:15 he made the staves *of* shittim **w**, and 6086
37:25 he made the incense altar *of* shittim **w**: 6086
37:28 he made the staves *of* shittim **w**, and 6086
38: 1 the altar of burnt offering *of* shittim **w**: 6086
38: 6 he made the staves *of* shittim **w**, and 6086
Lev 1: 7 and lay the **w** in order upon the fire: 6086
1: 8 in order upon the **w** that *is* on the fire which 6086
1:12 the priest shall lay them in order on the **w** 6086
1:17 the altar, upon the **w** that *is* upon the fire: 6086
3: 5 which *is* upon the **w** that *is* on the fire: 6086
4:12 and burn him on the **w** with fire: 6086
6:12 the priest shall burn **w** on it every morning, 6086
11:32 whether *it be* any vessel of **w**, or raiment, 6086
14: 4 clean, and cedar **w**, and scarlet, and hyssop: 6086
14: 6 the cedar **w**, and the scarlet, and the hyssop, 6086
14:49 and cedar **w**, and scarlet, and hyssop: 6086
14:51 he shall take the cedar **w**, and the hyssop, 6086
14:52 with the cedar **w**, and with the hyssop, and 6086
15:12 every vessel of **w** shall be rinsed in water. 6086
Nu 13:20 or lean, whether there be **w** therein, or not. 6086
19: 6 the priest shall take cedar **w**, and hyssop, 6086
31:20 of goats' *hair*, and all things made of **w**. 6086
35:18 *if* he smite him with a hand weapon of **w**, 6086
Dt 4:28 **w** and stone, which neither see, nor hear, 6086
10: 1 into the mount, and make thee an ark of **w**. 6086
10: 3 I made an ark of shittim **w**, and hewed two 6086
19: 5 As when *a man* goeth into the **w** with his 3293
19: 5 into the wood with his neighbour to hew **w**, 6086
28:36 shalt thou serve other gods, **w** and stone. 6086
28:64 thy fathers have known, *even* **w** and stone. 6086
29:11 from the hewer of thy **w** unto the drawer of 6086
29:17 their idols, **w** and stone, silver and gold, 6086
Jos 9:21 let them be hewers of **w** and drawers of 6086
9:23 hewers of **w** and drawers of water for 6086
9:27 Joshua made them that day hewers of **w** 6086
17:15 *then* get thee up to the **w** *country*, and 3293
17:18 for it *is* a **w**, and thou shalt cut it down: 3293
Jdg 6:26 offer a burnt sacrifice with the **w** of 6086
1Sa 6:14 they clave the **w** of the cart, and offered 6086
14:25 all *they of* the land came to a **w**; and 3293
14:26 when the people were come into the **w**, 3293
23:15 David *was* in the wilderness of Ziph in a **w**. 2793
23:16 went to David *into* the **w**, and 2793
23:18 David abode in the **w**, and Jonathan went to 2793
23:19 himself with us in strong holds in the **w**, 2793
2Sa 6: 5 on all *manner of instruments made of* fir **w**, 6086
18: 6 and the battle was in the **w** of Ephraim; 3293
18: 8 the **w** devoured more people that day than 3293
18:17 cast him into a great pit in the **w**, and laid a 3293
24:22 and *other* instruments of the oxen for **w**. 6086
1Ki 6:15 *and* he covered *them* on the inside with **w**, 6086
18:23 lay *it* on **w**, and put no fire *under:* and I will 6086
18:23 and lay *it* on **w**, and put no fire *under:* 6086
18:33 he put the **w** in order, and cut the bullock in 6086
18:33 in pieces, and laid *him* on the **w**, and said, 6086
18:33 pour *it* on the burnt sacrifice, and on the **w**. 6086
18:38 the **w**, and the stones, and the dust, and 6086
2Ki 2:24 there came forth two she bears out of the **w**, 3293
6: 4 they came to Jordan, they cut down **w**. 6086
19:18 but the work of men's hands, **w** and stone: 6086
1Ch 16:33 shall the trees of the **w** sing out at 3293
21:23 the threshing instruments for **w**, and 6086
22: 4 they of Tyre brought much cedar **w** to 6086
29: 2 *things of* iron, and **w** for *things of* wood; 6086
29: 2 *things of* iron, and wood for *things of* **w**; 6086
2Ch 2:16 we will cut **w** out of Lebanon, as much as 6086
Ne 8: 4 Ezra the scribe stood upon a pulpit of **w**, 6086
10:34 and the people, for the **w** offering, 6086
13:31 for the **w** offering, at times appointed, and 6086
Job 41:27 iron as straw, *and* brass as rotten **w**. 6086
Ps 80:13 The boar out of the **w** doth waste it, and 3293
83:14 As the fire burneth a **w**, and as the flame 3293
96:12 shall all the trees of the **w** rejoice 3293
132: 6 we found it in the fields of the **w**. 3293
141: 7 one cutteth and cleaveth *w* upon the earth. NIH
Pr 26:20 Where no **w** is, *there* the fire goeth out: so 6086
26:21 *As* coals *are* to burning coals, and **w** to fire; 6086
Ecc 2: 6 to water therewith the **w** that bringeth forth 3293
10: 9 he that cleaveth **w** shall be endangered 6086
SS 2: 3 As the apple tree among the trees of the **w**, 3293
3: 9 himself a chariot of the **w** of Lebanon. 6086
Isa 7: 2 as the trees of the **w** are moved with 3293
10:15 staff should lift up *itself, as if it were* no **w**. 6086
30:33 the pile thereof *is* fire and much **w**; 6086
37:19 but the work of men's hands, **w** and stone: 6086
45:20 they have no knowledge that set up the **w** 6086
60:17 and for **w** brass, and for stones iron: 6086
Jer 5:14 and this people **w**, and it shall devour them. 6086
7:18 The children gather **w**, and the fathers 6086
28:13 Thou hast broken the yokes of **w**; but 6086
46:22 come against her with axes, as hewers of **w**. 6086
La 5: 4 our water for money; our **w** is sold *unto us*. 6086
5:13 to grind, and the children fell under the **w**. 6086
Eze 15: 3 Shall **w** be taken thereof to do *any* work? or 6086
20:32 of the countries, to serve **w** and stone. 6086
24:10 Heap on **w**, kindle the fire, consume 6086
39:10 So that they shall take no **w** out of the field, 6086
41:16 cieled with **w** round about, and *from* 6086
41:22 The altar *of* **w** *was* three cubits high, and 6086
41:22 and the walls thereof, *were of* **w**: 6086
Da 5: 4 of silver, of brass, of iron, of **w**, and of stone. 636
5:23 gold, of brass, iron, **w**, and stone, which see 636
Mic 7:14 which dwell solitarily *in* the **w**, in the midst 3293
Hab 2:19 Woe unto him that saith to the **w**, Awake; 6086
Hag 1: 8 and bring **w**, and build the house; 6086
Zec 12: 6 of Judah like a hearth of fire among the **w**, 6086
1Co 3:12 silver, precious stones, **w**, hay, stubble; *3586*
2Ti 2:20 and of silver, but also **of w** and of earth; *3585*
Rev 9:20 and silver, and brass, and stone, and **of w**: *3585*
18:12 and all thyine **w**, and all *manner* vessels of *3586*
18:12 and all *manner* vessels of most precious **w**, *3586*

WOODCUTTER See HEWER

WOODS (1) [WOOD]
Eze 34:25 safely in the wilderness, and sleep in the **w**. 3293

WOOF (9)
Lev 13:48 Whether *it be* in the warp, or **w**; of linen, or 6154
13:49 or in the **w**, or in any thing of skin; 6154
13:51 or in the **w**, or in a skin, *or* in any work that 6154
13:52 whether warp or **w**, in woollen or in linen, 6154
13:53 or in the **w**, or in any thing of skin; 6154
13:56 the skin, or out of the warp, or out of the **w**: 6154
13:57 or in the **w**, or in any thing of skin; 6154
13:58 or **w**, or whatsoever thing of skin *it be*, 6154
13:59 *in* the warp, or **w**, or any thing of skins, 6154

WOOL (14) [WOOLLEN]
Jdg 6:37 Behold, I will put a fleece of **w** in the floor; 6785
2Ki 3: 4 and an hundred thousand rams, *with* the **w**. 6785
Ps 147:16 He giveth snow like **w**: he scattereth 6785
Pr 31:13 She seeketh **w**, and flax, and 6785
Isa 1:18 they be red like crimson, they shall be as **w**. 6785
51: 8 and the worm shall eat them like **w**: 6785
Eze 27:18 in the wine of Helbon, and white **w**. 6785
34: 3 eat the fat, and ye clothe you with the **w**, 6785
44:17 no **w** shall come upon them, whiles they 6785
Da 7: 9 and the hair of his head like the pure **w**: 6015
Hos 2: 5 my **w** and my flax, mine oil and my drink. 6785
2: 9 will recover my **w** and my flax *given* to 6785
Heb 9:19 and scarlet **w**, and hyssop, and *2053*
Rev 1:14 His head and *his* hairs *were* white like **w**, *2053*

WOOLLEN (6) [WOOL]
Lev 13:47 *whether it be* a **w** garment, or a linen 6785
13:48 *it be* in the warp, or woof; of linen, or of **w**; 6785
13:52 in **w** or in linen, or any thing of skin, 6785
13:59 of the plague of leprosy in a garment of **w** 6785
19:19 a garment **mingled of linen and w** 3610+8162
Dt 22:11 of divers sorts, *as* of **w** and linen together. 6785

WORD (698) [BYWORD, WORD'S, WORDS]
Ge 15: 1 After these things the **w** of the LORD 1697
15: 4 the **w** of the LORD *came* unto him, 1697
30:34 I would it might be according to thy **w**. 1697
37:14 well with the flocks; and bring me **w** again. 1697
41:40 according unto thy **w** shall all my people be 6310
44: 2 he did according to the **w** that Joseph had 1697
44:18 speak a **w** in my lord's ears, and let not 1697
Ex 8:10 he said, *Be it* according to thy **w**: that thou 1697
8:13 the LORD did according to the **w** of 1697
8:31 the LORD did according to the **w** of 1697
9:20 He that feared the **w** of the LORD 1697
9:21 he that regarded not the **w** of the LORD 1697
12:35 the children of Israel did according to the **w** 1697
14:12 *Is* not this the **w** that we did tell thee in 1697
32:28 the children of Levi did according to the **w** 1697
Lev 10: 7 And they did according to the **w** of Moses. 1697
Nu 3:16 Moses numbered them according to the **w** 6310
3:51 his sons, according to the **w** of the LORD, 6310
4:45 Aaron numbered according to the **w** of 6310
11:23 thou shalt see now whether my **w** shall 1697
13:26 brought back **w** unto them, and unto all 1697
14:20 I have pardoned according to thy **w**: 1697
15:31 Because he hath despised the **w** of 1697
20:24 ye rebelled against my **w** at the water of 6310
22: 8 *this* night, and I will bring you **w** again, 1697
22:18 I cannot go beyond the **w** of the LORD 6310
22:20 yet the **w** which I shall say unto thee, 1697
22:35 only the **w** that I shall speak unto thee, 1697
22:38 the **w** that God putteth in my mouth, that 1697
23: 5 the LORD put a **w** in Balaam's mouth, 1697
23:16 put a **w** in his mouth, and said, Go again 1697
27:21 at his **w** shall they go out, and at his word 6310
27:21 at his **w** they shall come in, *both* he, and 6310
30: 2 he shall not break his **w**, he shall do 1697
36: 5 of Israel according to the **w** of the LORD, 6310
Dt 1:22 bring us **w** again by what way we must go 1697
1:25 unto us, and brought us **w** again, and said, 1697
4: 2 Ye shall not add unto the **w** which I 1697
5: 5 to shew you the **w** of the LORD: 1697
8: 3 by every *w* that proceedeth out of the mouth NIH
9: 5 that he may perform the **w** which 1697
18:20 which shall presume to speak a **w** in my 1697
18:21 How shall we know the **w** which 1697
21: 5 by their **w** shall every controversy and 6310
30:14 the **w** *is* very nigh unto thee, in thy mouth, 1697
33: 9 for they have observed thy **w**, and kept thy 565
34: 5 according to the **w** of the LORD. 6310
Jos 1:13 Remember the **w** which Moses the servant 1697
6:10 neither shall *any* **w** proceed out of your 1697
8:27 according unto the **w** of the LORD which 1697
8:35 There was not a **w** of all that Moses 1697
14: 7 I brought him **w** again as *it was* in mine 1697
14:10 *even* since the LORD spake this **w** unto 1697
19:50 According to the **w** of the LORD they 6310
22: 9 according to the **w** of the LORD by 6310
22:32 of Israel, and brought them **w** again. 1697
1Sa 1:23 only the LORD establish his **w**. 1697
3: 1 the **w** of the LORD was precious in those 1697
3: 7 neither was the **w** of the LORD yet 1697
3:21 Samuel in Shiloh by the **w** of the LORD. 1697
4: 1 the **w** of Samuel came to all Israel. 1697
9:27 a while, that I may shew thee the **w** of God. 1697
15:10 came the **w** of the LORD unto Samuel, 1697
15:23 Because thou hast rejected the **w** of 1697
15:26 for thou hast rejected the **w** of the LORD, 1697
2Sa 3:11 he could not answer Abner a **w** again, 1697
7: 4 that the **w** of the LORD came unto 1697
7: 7 spake I a **w** with any of the tribes of Israel, 1697
7:25 the **w** that thou hast spoken concerning thy 1697
14:12 speak *one* **w** unto my lord the king. 1697
14:17 The **w** of my lord the king shall now be 1697
15:28 until there come **w** from you to certify me. 1697
19:10 why **speak** ye **not a w** of bringing the king 2790
19:14 so that they sent *this* **w** unto the king, NIH
22:31 way *is* perfect; the **w** of the LORD *is* tried: 565
23: 2 spake by me, and his **w** *was* in my tongue. 4405
24: 4 Notwithstanding the king's **w** prevailed 1697
24:11 the **w** of the LORD came unto the prophet 1697
1Ki 2: 4 That the LORD may continue his **w** which 1697
2:23 if Adonijah have not spoken this **w** against 1697
2:27 that *he* might fulfil the **w** of the LORD, 1697
2:30 Benaiah brought the king **w** again, saying, 1697
2:42 unto me, The **w** *that* I have heard *is* good. 1697
3:12 Behold, I have done according to thy **w**: lo, 1697
6:11 the **w** of the LORD came to Solomon, 1697
6:12 will I perform my **w** with thee, which I 1697
8:20 the LORD hath performed his **w** that he 1697
8:26 of Israel, let thy **w**, I pray thee, be verified, 1697
8:56 there hath not failed one **w** of all his good 1697
12:22 the **w** of God came unto Shemaiah the man 1697
12:24 therefore to the **w** of the LORD, 1697
12:24 according to the **w** of the LORD. 1697
13: 1 Judah by the **w** of the LORD unto Beth-el: 1697
13: 2 he cried against the altar in the **w** of 1697
13: 5 of God had given by the **w** of the LORD. 1697
13: 9 was it charged me by the **w** of the LORD, 1697
13:17 For it was said to me by the **w** of 1697
13:18 an angel spake unto me by the **w** of 1697
13:20 that the **w** of the LORD came unto 1697
13:26 who was disobedient unto the **w** of 6310
13:26 according to the **w** of the LORD, 1697
13:32 For the saying which he cried by the **w** of 1697
14:18 for him, according to the **w** of the LORD, 1697
16: 1 the **w** of the LORD came to Jehu the son 1697
16: 7 came the **w** of the LORD against Baasha, 1697
16:12 according to the **w** of the LORD, 1697
16:34 according to the **w** of the LORD, which he 1697
17: 1 nor rain these years, but according to my **w**. 1697
17: 2 the **w** of the LORD came unto him, 1697
17: 5 did according unto the **w** of the LORD: 1697
17: 8 the **w** of the LORD came unto him, 1697
17:16 according to the **w** of the LORD, which he 1697
17:24 *that* the **w** of the LORD in thy mouth *is* 1697
18: 1 that the **w** of the LORD came to Elijah in 1697
18:21 And the people answered him not a **w**. 1697
18:31 unto whom the **w** of the LORD came, 1697
18:36 *that* I have done all these things at thy **w**. 1697
19: 9 the **w** of the LORD *came* to him, and 1697
20: 9 and brought him **w** again. 1697
20:35 unto his neighbour in the **w** of the LORD, 1697
21: 4 of the **w** which Naboth the Jezreelite had 1697
21:17 the **w** of the LORD came to Elijah 1697
21:28 the **w** of the LORD came to Elijah 1697
22: 5 I pray thee, at the **w** of the LORD to day. 1697
22:13 let thy **w**, I pray thee, be like the word of 1697
22:13 be like the **w** of one of them, and speak *that* 1697

1Ki 22:19 Hear thou therefore the **w** of the LORD: 1697
22:38 according unto the **w** of the LORD which 1697
2Ki 1:16 *is* no God in Israel to inquire of his **w**? 1697
1:17 So he died according to the **w** of 1697
3:12 The **w** of the LORD is with him. 1697
4:44 left *thereof,* according to the **w** of 1697
6:18 with blindness according to the **w** of Elisha. 1697
7: 1 Elisha said, Hear ye the **w** of the LORD; 1697
7:16 a shekel, according to the **w** of the LORD. 1697
9:26 *ground,* according to the **w** of the LORD. 1697
9:36 he said, This *is* the **w** of the LORD, 1697
10:10 the earth nothing of the **w** of the LORD, 1697
14:25 according to the **w** of the LORD God of 1697
15:12 This *was* the **w** of the LORD which he 1697
18:28 spake, saying, Hear the **w** of the great king, 1697
18:36 held their peace, and answered him not a **w**: 1697
19:21 This *is* the **w** that the LORD hath spoken 1697
20: 4 that the **w** of the LORD came to him, 1697
20:16 unto Hezekiah, Hear the **w** of the LORD. 1697
20:19 Good *is* the **w** of the LORD which thou 1697
22: 9 and brought the king **w** again, and said, 1697
22:20 And they brought the king **w** again. 1697
23:16 according to the **w** of the LORD which 1697
24: 2 according to the **w** of the LORD, 1697
1Ch 10:13 *even* against the **w** of the LORD, which he 1697
11: 3 according to the **w** of the LORD by 1697
11:10 according to the **w** of the LORD 1697
12:23 to him, according to the **w** of the LORD. 6310
15:15 as Moses commanded according to the **w** of 1697
16:15 the **w** *which* he commanded to a thousand 1697
17: 3 that the **w** of God came to Nathan, saying, 1697
17: 6 spake I a **w** to any of the judges of Israel, 1697
21: 4 Nevertheless the king's **w** prevailed against 1697
21: 6 for the king's **w** was abominable to Joab. 1697
21:12 advise thyself what **w** I shall bring again to 1697
22: 8 the **w** of the LORD came to me, saying, 1697
2Ch 6:10 hath performed his **w** that he hath spoken: 1697
6:17 LORD God of Israel, let thy **w** be verified, 1697
10:15 that the LORD might perform his **w**, 1697
11: 2 the **w** of the LORD came to Shemaiah 1697
12: 7 the **w** of the LORD came to Shemaiah, 1697
18: 4 I pray thee, at the **w** of the LORD to day. 1697
18:12 let thy **w** therefore, I pray thee, be like one 1697
18:18 Therefore hear the **w** of the LORD; 1697
30:12 and of the princes, by the **w** of the LORD. 1697
34:16 brought the king **w** back again, saying, 1697
34:21 our fathers have not kept the **w** of 1697
34:28 the same. So they brought the king **w** again. 1697
35: 6 that *they* may do according to the **w** of 1697
36:21 To fulfil the **w** of the LORD by the mouth 1697
36:22 that the **w** of the LORD *spoken* by 1697
Ezr 1: 1 that the **w** of the LORD by the mouth of 1697
6:11 a decree, that whosoever shall alter this **w**, 6600
10: 5 that *they* should do according to this **w**. 1697
Ne 1: 8 the **w** that thou commandedst thy servant 1697
Est 1:21 the king did according to the **w** of 1697
7: 8 As the **w** went out of the king's mouth, 1697
Job 2:13 seven nights, and none spake a **w** unto him: 1697
Ps 17: 4 by the **w** of thy lips I have kept *me from* 1697
18:30 the **w** of the LORD is tried: he *is* a buckler 565
33: 4 For the **w** of the LORD *is* right; and all his 1697
33: 6 By the **w** of the LORD were the heavens 1697
56: 4 In God I will praise his **w**, in God I have 1697
56:10 In God will I praise *his* **w**: in the LORD 1697
56:10 *his* word: in the LORD will I praise *his* **w**. 1697
68:11 The Lord gave the **w**: great *was* 562
103:20 hearkening unto the voice of his **w**. 1697
105: 8 the **w** *which* he commanded to a thousand 1697
105:19 Until the time that his **w** came: the word of 1697
105:19 word came: the **w** of the LORD tried him. 565
105:28 it dark; and they rebelled not against his **w**. 1697
106:24 the pleasant land, they believed not his **w**: 1697
107:20 He sent his **w**, and healed them, and 1697
119: 9 by taking heed *thereto* according to thy **w**. 1697
119:11 Thy **w** have I hid in mine heart, that I might 565
119:16 in thy statutes: I will not forget thy **w**. 1697
119:17 thy servant, *that* I may live, and keep thy **w**. 1697
119:25 quicken thou me according to thy **w**. 1697
119:28 strengthen thou me according unto thy **w**. 1697
119:38 Stablish thy **w** unto thy servant, who *is* 565
119:41 *even* thy salvation, according to thy **w**. 565
119:42 that reproacheth me: for I trust in thy **w**. 1697
119:43 take not the **w** of truth utterly out of my 1697
119:49 Remember the **w** unto thy servant, 1697
119:50 my affliction: for thy **w** hath quickened me. 565
119:58 be merciful unto me according to thy **w**. 565
119:65 O LORD, according unto thy **w**. 1697
119:67 I went astray: but now have I kept thy **w**. 565
119:74 see me; because I have hoped in thy **w**. 1697
119:76 according to thy **w** unto thy servant. 565
119:81 for thy salvation: *but* I hope in thy **w**. 1697
119:82 Mine eyes fail for thy **w**, saying, When wilt 565
119:89 O LORD, thy **w** *is* settled in heaven. 1697
119:101 every evil way, that I might keep thy **w**. 1697
119:105 Thy **w** *is* a lamp unto my feet, and a light 1697
119:107 O LORD, according unto thy **w**. 1697
119:114 and my shield: I hope in thy **w**. 1697
119:116 Uphold me according unto thy **w**, that I may 565
119:123 and for the **w** of thy righteousness. 565
119:133 Order my steps in thy **w**: and let not any 565
119:140 Thy **w** *is* very pure: therefore thy servant 565
119:147 of the morning, and cried: I hoped in thy **w**. 1697
119:148 that *I* might meditate in thy **w**. 565
119:154 deliver me: quicken me according to thy **w**. 565
119:158 was grieved; because they kept not thy **w**. 565
119:160 Thy **w** *is* true *from* the beginning: and 1697
119:161 but my heart standeth in awe of thy **w**. 1697
119:162 I rejoice at thy **w**, as one that findeth great 565
119:169 give me understanding according to thy **w**. 1697
119:170 before thee: deliver me according to thy **w**. 565
119:172 My tongue shall speak of thy **w**: for all thy 565
130: 5 my soul doth wait, and in his **w** do I hope. 1697
138: 2 for thou hast magnified thy **w** above all thy 565
139: 4 For *there is* not a **w** in my tongue, *but* lo, 4405
147:15 *upon* earth: his **w** runneth very swiftly. 1697

Ps 147:18 He sendeth out his **w**, and melteth them: 1697
147:19 He sheweth his **w** unto Jacob, his statutes 1697
148: 8 and vapour; stormy wind fulfilling his **w**: 1697
Pr 12:25 it stoop: but a good **w** maketh it glad. 1697
13:13 Whoso despiseth the **w** shall be destroyed: 1697
14:15 The simple believeth every **w**: but 1697
15:23 a **w** *spoken* in due season, how good *is it!* 1697
25:11 A **w** fitly spoken *is like* apples of gold in 1697
30: 5 Every **w** of God *is* pure: he *is* a shield unto 565
Ecc 8: 4 Where the **w** of a king *is, there is* power: 1697
Isa 1:10 Hear the **w** of the LORD, ye rulers of 1697
2: 1 The **w** that Isaiah the son of Amoz saw 1697
2: 3 and the **w** of the LORD from Jerusalem. 1697
5:24 despised the **w** of the Holy One of Israel. 565
8:10 speak the **w**, and it shall not stand: 1697
8:20 if they speak not according to this **w**, *it is* 1697
9: 8 The Lord sent a **w** into Jacob, and it hath 1697
16:13 This *is* the **w** that the LORD hath spoken 1697
24: 3 for the LORD hath spoken this **w**. 1697
28:13 the **w** of the LORD was unto them precept 1697
28:14 Wherefore hear the **w** of the LORD, 1697
29:21 That make a man an offender for a **w**, and 1697
30:12 Because ye despise this **w**, and trust in 1697
30:21 thine ears shall hear a **w** behind thee, 1697
36:21 held their peace, and answered him not a **w**: 1697
37:22 This *is* the **w** which the LORD hath 1697
38: 4 came the **w** of the LORD to Isaiah, 1697
39: 5 Hear the **w** of the LORD of hosts: 1697
39: 8 Good *is* the **w** of the LORD which thou 1697
40: 8 but the **w** of our God shall stand for ever. 1697
41:28 when I asked of them, could answer a **w**. 1697
44:26 That confirmeth the **w** of his servant, and 1697
45:23 the **w** is gone out of my mouth *in* 1697
50: 4 that *I* should know how to speak a **w** in 1697
55:11 So shall my **w** be that goeth forth out of my 1697
66: 2 of a contrite spirit, and trembleth at my **w**. 1697
66: 5 Hear the **w** of the LORD, ye that tremble 1697
66: 5 of the LORD, ye that tremble at his **w**; 1697
Jer 1: 2 To whom the **w** of the LORD came in 1697
1: 4 the **w** of the LORD came unto me, saying, 1697
1:11 the **w** of the LORD came unto me, saying, 1697
1:12 for I will hasten my **w** to perform it. 1697
1:13 the **w** of the LORD came unto me 1697
2: 1 Moreover the **w** of the LORD came to me, 1697
2: 4 Hear ye the **w** of the LORD, O house of 1697
2:31 O generation, see ye the **w** of the LORD. 1697
5:13 become wind, and the **w** *is* not in them: 1699'
5:14 Because ye speak this **w**, behold, I will 1697
6:10 the **w** of the LORD is unto them a 1697
7: 1 The **w** that came to Jeremiah from 1697
7: 2 proclaim there this **w**, and say, Hear 1697
7: 2 say, Hear the **w** of the LORD, all *ye of* 1697
8: 9 lo, they have rejected the **w** of the LORD; 1697
9:20 Yet hear the **w** of the LORD, O ye 1697
9:20 let your ear receive the **w** of his mouth, and 1697
10: 1 Hear ye the **w** which the LORD speaketh 1697
11: 1 The **w** that came to Jeremiah from 1697
13: 2 according to the **w** of the LORD, and 1697
13: 3 the **w** of the LORD came unto me 1697
13: 8 the **w** of the LORD came unto me, saying, 1697
13:12 thou shalt speak unto them this **w**; 1697
14: 1 The **w** of the LORD that came to Jeremiah 1697
14:17 Therefore thou shalt say this **w** unto them; 1697
15:16 thy **w** was unto me the joy and rejoicing of 1697
16: 1 The **w** of the LORD came also unto me, 1697
17:15 unto me, Where *is* the **w** of the LORD? 1697
17:20 Hear ye the **w** of the LORD, ye kings of 1697
18: 1 The **w** which came to Jeremiah from 1697
18: 5 the **w** of the LORD came to me, saying, 1697
18:18 from the wise, nor the **w** from the prophet. 1697
19: 3 say, Hear ye the **w** of the LORD, O kings 1697
20: 8 the **w** of the LORD was made a reproach 1697
20: 9 *his* **w** was in mine heart as a burning fire NIH
21: 1 The **w** which came unto Jeremiah from 1697
21:11 *say,* Hear ye the **w** of the LORD. 1697
22: 1 the king of Judah, and speak there this **w**, 1697
22: 2 say, Hear the **w** of the LORD, O king of 1697
22:29 earth, earth, hear the **w** of the LORD. 1697
23:18 and hath perceived and heard his **w**? 1697
23:18 who hath marked his **w**, and heard *it?* 1697
23:28 he that hath my **w**, let him speak my word 1697
23:28 my word, let him speak my **w** faithfully. 1697
23:29 *Is* not my **w** like as a fire? saith 1697
23:36 for every man's **w** shall be his burden; 1697
23:38 Because you say this **w**, The burden of 1697
24: 4 Again the **w** of the LORD came unto me, 1697
25: 1 The **w** that came to Jeremiah concerning all 1697
25: 3 the **w** of the LORD hath come unto me, 1697
26: 1 of Judah came this **w** from the LORD, 1697
26: 2 thee to speak unto them; diminish not a **w**: 1697
27: 1 this **w** unto Jeremiah from the LORD, 1697
27:18 and if the **w** of the LORD be with them, 1697
28: 7 Nevertheless hear thou now this **w** that I 1697
28: 9 when the **w** of the prophet shall come to 1697
28:12 the **w** of the LORD came unto Jeremiah 1697
29:10 perform my good **w** towards you, in 1697
29:20 Hear ye therefore the **w** of the LORD, 1697
29:30 came the **w** of the LORD unto Jeremiah, 1697
30: 1 The **w** that came to Jeremiah from 1697
31:10 Hear the **w** of the LORD, O ye nations, 1697
32: 1 The **w** that came to Jeremiah from 1697
32: 6 The **w** of the LORD came unto me, 1697
32: 8 prison according to the **w** of the LORD, 1697
32: 8 I knew that this *was* the **w** of the LORD. 1697
32:26 came the **w** of the LORD unto Jeremiah, 1697
33: 1 Moreover the **w** of the LORD came unto 1697
33:19 the **w** of the LORD came unto Jeremiah, 1697
33:23 Moreover the **w** of the LORD came to 1697
34: 1 The **w** which came unto Jeremiah from 1697
34: 4 Yet hear the **w** of the LORD, O Zedekiah 1697
34: 5 for I have pronounced the **w**, saith 1697
34: 8 *This is* the **w** that came unto Jeremiah from 1697
34:12 Therefore the **w** of the LORD came to 1697
35: 1 The **w** which came unto Jeremiah from 1697
35:12 came the **w** of the LORD unto Jeremiah, 1697

Jer 36: 1 *that* this **w** came unto Jeremiah from 1697
36:27 the **w** of the LORD came to Jeremiah, 1697
37: 6 came the **w** of the LORD unto the prophet 1697
37:17 and said, Is there *any* **w** from the LORD? 1697
38:21 this *is* the **w** that the LORD hath shewed 1697
39:15 Now the **w** of the LORD came unto 1697
40: 1 The **w** which came to Jeremiah from 1697
42: 7 that the **w** of the LORD came unto 1697
42:15 therefore hear the **w** of the LORD, 1697
43: 8 came the **w** of the LORD unto Jeremiah in 1697
44: 1 The **w** that came to Jeremiah concerning all 1697
44:16 *As for* the **w** that thou hast spoken unto us 1697
44:24 all the women, Hear the **w** of the LORD, 1697
44:26 Therefore hear ye the **w** of the LORD, 1697
45: 1 The **w** that Jeremiah the prophet spake unto 1697
46: 1 The **w** of the LORD which came to 1697
46:13 The **w** that the LORD spake to Jeremiah 1697
47: 1 The **w** of the LORD that came to Jeremiah 1697
49:34 The **w** of the LORD that came to Jeremiah 1697
50: 1 The **w** that the LORD spake against 1697
51:59 The **w** which Jeremiah the prophet 1697
La 2:17 he hath fulfilled his **w** that he had 565
Eze 1: 3 The **w** of the LORD came expressly unto 1697
3:16 that the **w** of the LORD came unto me, 1697
3:17 therefore hear the **w** at my mouth, and 1697
6: 1 the **w** of the LORD came unto me, saying, 1697
6: 3 of Israel, hear the **w** of the Lord GOD; 1697
7: 1 Moreover the **w** of the LORD came unto 1697
11:14 Again the **w** of the LORD came unto me, 1697
12: 1 The **w** of the LORD also came unto me, 1697
12: 8 in the morning came the **w** of the LORD 1697
12:17 Moreover the **w** of the LORD came to me, 1697
12:21 the **w** of the LORD came unto me, saying, 1697
12:25 the **w** that I shall speak shall come to pass; 1697
12:25 will I say the **w**, and will perform it, 1697
12:26 Again the **w** of the LORD came to me, 1697
12:28 the **w** which I have spoken shall be done, 1697
13: 1 the **w** of the LORD came unto me, saying, 1697
13: 2 own hearts, Hear ye the **w** of the LORD; 1697
13: 6 to hope that *they* would confirm the **w**. 1697
14: 2 the **w** of the LORD came unto me, saying, 1697
14:12 The **w** of the LORD came again to me, 1697
15: 1 the **w** of the LORD came unto me, saying, 1697
16: 1 Again the **w** of the LORD came unto me, 1697
16:35 O harlot, hear the **w** of the LORD: 1697
17: 1 the **w** of the LORD came unto me, saying, 1697
17:11 Moreover the **w** of the LORD came unto 1697
18: 1 the **w** of the LORD came unto me again, 1697
20: 2 came the **w** of the LORD unto me, saying, 1697
20:45 Moreover the **w** of the LORD came unto 1697
20:46 drop *thy* **w** toward the south, and NIH
20:47 of the south, Hear the **w** of the LORD; 1697
21: 1 the **w** of the LORD came unto me, saying, 1697
21: 2 drop *thy* **w** toward the holy places, and NIH
21: 8 Again the **w** of the LORD came unto me, 1697
21:18 The **w** of the LORD came unto me again, 1697
22: 1 Moreover the **w** of the LORD came unto 1697
22:17 the **w** of the LORD came unto me, saying, 1697
22:23 the **w** of the LORD came unto me, saying, 1697
23: 1 The **w** of the LORD came again unto me, 1697
24: 1 the **w** of the LORD came unto me, saying, 1697
24:15 Also the **w** of the LORD came unto me, 1697
24:20 The **w** of the LORD came unto me, 1697
25: 1 The **w** of the LORD came again unto me, 1697
25: 3 Hear the **w** of the Lord GOD; 1697
26: 1 *that* the **w** of the LORD came unto me, 1697
27: 1 The **w** of the LORD came again unto me, 1697
28: 1 The **w** of the LORD came again unto me, 1697
28:11 Moreover the **w** of the LORD came unto 1697
28:20 Again the **w** of the LORD came unto me, 1697
29: 1 the **w** of the LORD came unto me, saying, 1697
29:17 the **w** of the LORD came unto me, saying, 1697
30: 1 The **w** of the LORD came again unto me, 1697
30:20 *that* the **w** of the LORD came unto me, 1697
31: 1 *that* the **w** of the LORD came unto me, 1697
32: 1 *that* the **w** of the LORD came unto me, 1697
32:17 *that* the **w** of the LORD came unto me, 1697
33: 1 Again the **w** of the LORD came unto me, 1697
33: 7 thou shalt hear the **w** at my mouth, 1697
33:23 the **w** of the LORD came unto me, saying, 1697
33:30 hear what *is* the **w** that cometh forth from 1697
34: 1 the **w** of the LORD came unto me, saying, 1697
34: 7 ye shepherds, hear the **w** of the LORD; 1697
34: 9 O ye shepherds, hear the **w** of the LORD; 1697
35: 1 Moreover the **w** of the LORD came unto 1697
36: 1 of Israel, hear the **w** of the LORD: 1697
36: 4 of Israel, hear the **w** of the Lord GOD; 1697
36:16 Moreover the **w** of the LORD came unto 1697
37: 4 O ye dry bones, hear the **w** of the LORD. 1697
37:15 The **w** of the LORD came again unto me, 1697
38: 1 the **w** of the LORD came unto me, saying, 1697
Da 3:28 have changed the king's **w**, and 4406
4:17 and the demand *by* the **w** of the holy ones: 3983
4:31 While the **w** *was* in the king's mouth, 4406
9: 2 where*of* the **w** of the LORD came to 1697
10:11 when he had spoken this **w** unto me, I stood 1697
Hos 1: 1 The **w** of the LORD that came unto 1697
1: 2 The beginning of the **w** of the LORD by 1699'
4: 1 Hear the **w** of the LORD, ye children of 1697
Joel 1: 1 The **w** of the LORD that came to Joel 1697
2:11 for *he is* strong that executeth his **w**: for 1697
Am 3: 1 Hear this **w** that the LORD hath spoken 1697
4: 1 Hear this **w**, ye kine of Bashan, that *are* in 1697
5: 1 Hear ye this **w** which I take up against you, 1697
7:16 therefore hear thou the **w** of the LORD: 1697
7:16 drop not *thy* **w** against the house of Isaac. NIH
8:12 run to and fro to seek the **w** of the LORD, 1697
Jnh 1: 1 Now the **w** of the LORD came unto Jonah 1697
3: 1 the **w** of the LORD came unto Jonah 1697
3: 3 according to the **w** of the LORD. 1697
3: 6 For **w** came unto the king of Nineveh, and 1697
Mic 1: 1 The **w** of the LORD that came to Micah 1697
4: 2 and the **w** of the LORD from Jerusalem. 1697
Hab 3: 9 *to* the oaths of the tribes, *even thy* **w**. 562
Zep 1: 1 The **w** of the LORD which came unto 1697

Zep 2: 5 the **w** of the LORD *is* against you; 1697
Hag 1: 1 came the **w** of the LORD by Haggai 1697
1: 3 came the **w** of the LORD by Haggai 1697
2: 1 came the **w** of the LORD by the prophet 1697
2: 5 *According to* the **w** that I covenanted with 1697
2:10 came the **w** of the LORD by Haggai 1697
2:20 again the **w** of the LORD came unto 1697
Zec 1: 1 came the **w** of the LORD unto Zechariah, 1697
1: 7 came the **w** of the LORD unto Zechariah, 1697
4: 6 This *is* the **w** of the LORD unto 1697
4: 8 Moreover the **w** of the LORD came unto 1697
6: 9 the **w** of the LORD came unto me, saying, 1697
7: 1 *that* the **w** of the LORD came unto 1697
7: 4 came the **w** of the LORD of hosts unto 1697
7: 8 the **w** of the LORD came unto Zechariah, 1697
8: 1 Again the **w** of the LORD of hosts came 1697
8:18 the **w** of the LORD of hosts came unto 1697
9: 1 The burden of the **w** of the LORD in 1697
11:11 me knew that it *was* the **w** of the LORD. 1697
12: 1 The burden of the **w** of the LORD for 1697
Mal 1: 1 The burden of the **w** of the LORD to 1697
Mt 2: 8 when ye have found *him*, **bring** me **w again**, *518*
2:13 and be thou there until I **bring** thee **w**: *3004*
4: 4 by every **w** that proceedeth out of *4487*
8: 8 but speak the **w** only, and my servant shall *3056*
8:16 and he cast out the spirits with *his* **w**, and *3056*
12:32 And whosoever speaketh a **w** against *3056*
12:36 That every idle **w** that men shall speak, *4487*
13:19 When any one heareth the **w** of *3056*
13:20 *places*, the same is he that heareth the **w**, *3056*
13:21 or persecution ariseth because of the **w**, *3056*
13:22 among the thorns is he that heareth the **w**; *3056*
13:22 choke the **w**, and he becometh unfruitful. *3056*
13:23 the good ground is he that heareth the **w**, *3056*
15:23 But he answered her not a **w**. And his *3056*
18:16 three witnesses every **w** may be *4487*
22:46 And no *man* was able to answer him a **w**, *3056*
26:75 And Peter remembered the **w** of Jesus, *4487*
27:14 And he answered him to never a **w**; *4487*
28: 8 and did run to **bring** his disciples **w**. *518*
Mk 2: 2 the door: and he preached the **w** unto them. *3056*
4:14 The sower soweth the **w**. *3056*
4:15 they by the way side, where the **w** is sown; *3056*
4:15 taketh away the **w** that was sown in their *3056*
4:16 who, when they have heard the **w**, *3056*
4:18 are sown among thorns; such as hear the **w**, *3056*
4:19 choke the **w**, and it becometh unfruitful. *3056*
4:20 such as hear the **w**, and receive *it*, and *3056*
4:33 such parables spake he the **w** unto them, *3056*
5:36 As soon as Jesus heard the **w** *that was* *3056*
7:13 Making the **w** of God of none effect *3056*
14:72 And Peter called to mind the **w** that Jesus *4487*
16:20 and confirming the **w** with signs following. *3056*
Lk 1: 2 were eyewitnesses, and ministers of the **w**; *3056*
1:38 the Lord; be it unto me according to thy **w**. *4487*
2:29 servant depart in peace, according to thy **w**: *4487*
3: 2 the **w** of God came unto John the son of *4487*
4: 4 live by bread alone, but by every **w** of God. *4487*
4:32 at his doctrine: for his **w** was with power. *3056*
4:36 saying, What a **w** *is* this! *3056*
5: 1 pressed upon him to hear the **w** of God, *3056*
5: 5 nevertheless at thy **w** I will let down *4487*
7: 7 but say in a **w**, and my servant shall be *3056*
8:11 parable is this: The seed is the **w** of God. *3056*
8:12 and taketh away the **w** out of their hearts, *3056*
8:13 when they hear, receive the **w** with joy; *3056*
8:15 having heard the **w**, keep *it*, and bring forth *3056*
8:21 my brethren are these which hear the **w** of *3056*
10:39 also sat at Jesus' feet, and heard his **w**. *3056*
11:28 blessed *are* they that hear the **w** of God, and *3056*
12:10 And whosoever shall speak a **w** against *3056*
22:61 And Peter remembered the **w** of the Lord, *3056*
24:19 and **w** before God and all the people: *3056*
Jn 1: 1 In the beginning was the **W**, and the Word *3056*
1: 1 and the **W** was with God, and the Word *3056*
1: 1 Word was with God, and the **W** was God. *3056*
1:14 And the **W** was made flesh, and *3056*
2:22 and the **w** which Jesus had said. *3056*
4:41 many moe believed because of his own **w**; *3056*
4:50 And the man believed the **w** that Jesus had *3056*
5:24 He that heareth my **w**, and believeth on him *3056*
5:38 And ye have not his **w** abiding in you: *3056*
8:31 If ye continue in my **w**, *then* are ye my *3056*
8:37 kill me, because my **w** hath no place in you. *3056*
8:43 *even* because ye cannot hear my **w**. *3056*
10:35 unto whom the **w** of God came, and *3056*
12:48 the **w** that I have spoken, the same shall *3056*
14:24 and the **w** which you hear is not mine, but *3056*
15: 3 Now ye are clean through the **w** which I *3056*
15:20 Remember the **w** that I said unto you, *3056*
15:25 But *this cometh to pass*, that the **w** might be *3056*
17: 6 gavest them me; and they have kept thy **w**. *3056*
17:14 I have given them thy **w**; and the world *3056*
17:17 them through thy truth: thy **w** is truth. *3056*
17:20 which shall believe on me through their **w**; *3056*
Ac 2:41 Then they that gladly received his **w** were *3056*
4: 4 Howbeit many of them which heard the **w** *3056*
4:29 with all boldness *they* may speak thy **w**, *3056*
4:31 and they spake the **w** of God with boldness. *3056*
6: 2 It is not reason that we should leave the **w** *3056*
6: 4 to prayer, and to the ministry of the **w**. *3056*
6: 7 And the **w** of God increased; and *3056*
8: 4 abroad went every where preaching the **w**. *3056*
8:14 that Samaria had received the **w** of God, *3056*
8:25 and preached the **w** of the Lord, *3056*
10:36 The **w** which *God* sent unto the children of *3056*
10:37 *That* **w**, *I say*, you know, which was *4487*
10:44 Ghost fell on all them which heard the **w**. *3056*
11: 1 Gentiles had also received the **w** of God. *3056*
11:16 Then remembered I the **w** of the Lord, *4487*
11:19 preaching the **w** to none but unto *the* Jews *3056*
12:24 But the **w** of God grew and multiplied. *3056*
13: 5 they preached the **w** of God in *3056*
13: 7 and Saul, and desired to hear the **w** of God. *3056*
13:15 if ye have *any* **w** of exhortation for *3056*

Ac 13:26 to you is the **w** of this salvation sent. *3056*
13:44 whole city together to hear the **w** of God. *3056*
13:46 It was necessary that the **w** of God should *3056*
13:48 were glad, and glorified the **w** of the Lord: *3056*
13:49 And the **w** of the Lord was published *3056*
14: 3 which gave testimony unto the **w** of his *3056*
14:25 And when they had preached the **w** in *3056*
15: 7 my mouth should hear the **w** of the gospel, *3056*
15:35 teaching and preaching the **w** of the Lord, *3056*
15:36 where we have preached the **w** of the Lord, *3056*
16: 6 of the Holy Ghost to preach the **w** in Asia, *3056*
16:32 And they spake unto him the **w** of the Lord, *3056*
17:11 in that they received the **w** with all *3056*
17:13 **w** of God was preached of Paul at Berea, *3056*
18:11 teaching the **w** of God among them. *3056*
19:10 in Asia heard the **w** of the Lord Jesus, *3056*
19:20 So mightily grew the **w** of God and *3056*
20:32 you to God, and to the **w** of his grace, *3056*
22:22 And they gave him audience unto this **w**, *3056*
28:25 after that Paul had spoken one **w**, *4487*
Ro 9: 6 Not as though the **w** of God hath taken *3056*
9: 9 For this *is* the **w** of promise, At this time *3056*
10: 8 The **w** is nigh thee, *even* in thy mouth, and *4487*
10: 8 that is, the **w** of faith, which we preach; *4487*
10:17 by hearing, and hearing by the **w** of God. *4487*
15:18 make the Gentiles obedient, by **w** and deed, *3056*
1Co 4:20 For the kingdom of God *is* not in **w**, but *3056*
12: 8 For to one is given by the Spirit the **w** of *3056*
12: 8 to another the **w** of knowledge by the same *3056*
14:36 came the **w** of God out from you? or *3056*
2Co 1:18 our **w** toward you was not yea and nay. *3056*
2:17 not as many, which corrupt the **w** of God: *3056*
4: 2 nor handling the **w** of God deceitfully; *3056*
5:19 hath committed unto us the **w** of *3056*
6: 7 By the **w** of truth, by the power of God, *3056*
10:11 such as we are in **w** by letters when we are *3056*
13: 1 three witnesses shall every **w** be *4487*
Gal 5:14 For all the law is fulfilled in one **w**, *even* in *3056*
6: 6 Let him that is taught in the **w** *3056*
Eph 1:13 *trusted*, after that ye heard the **w** of truth, *3056*
5:26 *it* with the washing of water by the **w**, *4487*
6:17 sword of the Spirit, which is the **w** of God: *4487*
Php 1:14 are much more bold to speak the **w** without *3056*
2:16 Holding forth the **w** of life; that I may *3056*
Col 1: 5 whereof ye heard before in the **w** of *3056*
1:25 given to me for you, to fulfil the **w** of God; *3056*
3:16 Let the **w** of Christ dwell in you richly in *3056*
3:17 And whatsoever ye do in **w** or deed, *do* all *3056*
1Th 1: 5 For our gospel came not unto you in **w** *3056*
1: 6 having received the **w** in much affliction, *3056*
1: 8 For from you sounded out the **w** of *3056*
2:13 when ye received the **w** of God which *ye* *3056*
2:13 ye received *it* not as the **w** of men, but as it *3056*
2:13 of men, but as it is in truth, the **w** of God, *3056*
4:15 For this we say unto you by the **w** of *3056*
2Th 2: 2 or be troubled, neither by spirit, nor by **w**, *3056*
2:15 whether by **w**, or by our epistle. *3056*
2:17 and stablish you in every good **w** and work. *3056*
3: 1 that the **w** of the Lord may have *free* *3056*
3:14 And if any *man* obey not our **w** by *this* *3056*
1Ti 4: 5 For it is sanctified by the **w** of God and *3056*
4:12 in **w**, in conversation, in charity, in spirit, *3056*
5:17 especially they who labour in the **w** and *3056*
2Ti 2: 9 unto bonds; but the **w** of God is not bound. *3056*
2:15 be ashamed, rightly dividing the **w** of truth. *3056*
2:17 And their **w** will eat as *doth* a canker: *3056*
4: 2 Preach the **w**; be instant in season, out of *3056*
Tit 1: 3 But hath in due times manifested his **w** *3056*
1: 9 Holding fast the faithful **w** as *he* hath been *3056*
2: 5 that the **w** of God be not blasphemed. *3056*
Heb 1: 3 upholding all *things* by the **w** of his power, *4487*
2: 2 For if the **w** spoken by angels was stedfast, *3056*
4: 2 but the **w** preached did not profit them, *3056*
4:12 For the **w** of God *is* quick, and powerful, *3056*
5:13 milk *is* unskilful in the **w** of righteousness: *3056*
6: 5 And have tasted the good **w** of God, and *4487*
7:28 but the **w** of the oath, which was since *3056*
11: 3 the worlds were framed by the **w** of God, *4487*
12:19 **w** should not be **spoken** to them any more: *3056*
12:27 And this **w**, Yet once *more*, signifieth NIG
13: 7 who have spoken unto you the **w** of God: *3056*
13:22 brethren, suffer the **w** of exhortation: *3056*
Jas 1:18 Of his own will begat he us with the **w** of *3056*
1:21 and receive with meekness the engrafted **w**, *3056*
1:22 But be ye doers of the **w**, and not hearers *3056*
1:23 For if any be a hearer of the **w**, and not a *3056*
3: 2 If any *man* offend not in **w**, the same *is* a *3056*
1Pe 1:23 by the **w** of God, which liveth and *3056*
1:25 But the **w** of the Lord endureth for ever. *4487*
1:25 And this is the **w** which by the gospel is *4487*
2: 2 desire the sincere milk of the **w**, *3050*
2: 8 *even to them* which stumble at the **w**, *3056*
3: 1 that, if any obey not the **w**, they also may *3056*
3: 1 they also may without the **w** be won by *3056*
2Pe 1:19 We have also a more sure **w** of prophecy; *3056*
3: 5 that by the **w** of God the heavens were of *3056*
3: 7 are now, by the same **w** are kept in store, *3056*
1Jn 1: 1 our hands have handled, of the **W** of life; *3056*
1:10 we make him a liar, and his **w** is not in us. *3056*
2: 5 But whoso keepeth his **w**, in him verily is *3056*
2: 7 The old commandment is the **w** which ye *3056*
2:14 and the **w** of God abideth in you, and *3056*
3:18 let us not love in **w**, neither in tongue; *3056*
5: 7 the Father, the **W**, and the Holy Ghost: *3056*
Rev 1: 2 Who bare record of the **w** of God, and *3056*
1: 9 for the **w** of God, and for the testimony of *3056*
3: 8 and hast kept my **w**, and hast not denied my *3056*
3:10 Because thou hast kept the **w** of my *3056*
6: 9 of them that were slain for the **w** of God, *3056*
12:11 the Lamb, and by the **w** of their testimony; *3056*
19:13 and his name is called The **W** of God. *3056*
20: 4 and for the **w** of God, and which had not *3056*

WORD'S (2) [WORD]

2Sa 7:21 For thy **w** sake, and according to thine own 1697
Mk 4:17 or persecution ariseth for the **w** sake, *3056*

WORDS (547) [WORD]

Ge 24:30 when he heard the **w** of Rebekah his sister, 1697
24:52 when Abraham's servant heard their **w**, 1697
27:34 when Esau heard the **w** of his father, he 1697
27:42 these **w** of Esau her elder son were told to 1697
31: 1 he heard the **w** of Laban's sons, saying, 1697
34:18 their **w** pleased Hamor, and Shechem 1697
37: 8 yet the more for his dreams, and for his **w**. 1697
39:17 she spake unto him according to these **w**, 1697
39:19 when his master heard the **w** of his wife, 1697
42:16 kept in prison, that your **w** may be proved, 1697
42:20 so shall your **w** be verified, and ye shall not 1697
43: 7 told him according to the tenor of these **w**: 1697
44: 6 and he spake unto them these *same* **w**. 1697
44: 7 Wherefore saith my lord these **w**? 1697
44:10 Now also *let* it *be* according unto your **w**: 1697
44:24 my father, we told him the **w** of my lord. 1697
45:27 they told him all the **w** of Joseph, which he 1697
49:21 *is* a hind let loose: he giveth goodly **w**. 561
Ex 4:15 speak unto him, and put **w** in his mouth: 1697
4:28 Moses told Aaron all the **w** of the LORD 1697
4:30 Aaron spake all the **w** which the LORD 1697
5: 9 and let them not regard vain **w**. 1697
19: 6 These *are* the **w** which thou shalt speak 1697
19: 7 laid before their faces all these **w** which 1697
19: 8 Moses returned the **w** of the people unto 1697
19: 9 Moses told the **w** of the people unto 1697
20: 1 And God spake all these **w**, saying, 1697
23: 8 and perverteth the **w** of the righteous. 1697
24: 3 told the people all the **w** of the LORD, 1697
24: 3 All the **w** which the LORD hath said will 1697
24: 4 Moses wrote all the **w** of the LORD, and 1697
24: 8 hath made with you concerning all these **w**. 1697
34: 1 I will write upon *these* tables the **w** that 1697
34:27 said unto Moses, Write thou these **w**: 1697
34:27 for after the tenor of these **w** I have made a 1697
34:28 he wrote upon the tables the **w** of 1697
35: 1 These *are* the **w** which the LORD hath 1697
Nu 11:24 told the people the **w** of the LORD, and 1697
12: 6 he said, Hear now my **w**: If there be a 1697
16:31 had made an end of speaking all these **w**, 1697
22: 7 and spake unto him the **w** of Balak. 1697
24: 4 He hath said, which heard the **w** of God, 561
24:16 which heard the **w** of God, and knew 561
Dt 1: 1 These *be* the **w** which Moses spake unto all 1697
1:34 the LORD heard the voice of your **w**, and 1697
2:26 Sihon king of Heshbon *with* **w** of peace, 1697
4:10 and I will make them hear my **w**, 1697
4:12 ye heard the voice of the **w**, but saw no 1697
4:36 thou heardest his **w** out of the midst of 1697
5:22 These **w** the LORD spake unto all your 1697
5:28 the LORD heard the voice of your **w**, 1697
5:28 I have heard the voice of the **w** of this 1697
6: 6 these **w**, which I command thee *this* day, 1697
9:10 on them *was written* according to all the **w**, 1697
10: 2 I will write on the tables the **w** that were in 1697
11:18 Therefore shall ye lay up these my **w** in 1697
12:28 and hear all these **w** which I command thee, 1697
13: 3 Thou shalt not hearken unto the **w** of that 1697
16:19 the wise, and pervert the **w** of the righteous. 1697
17:19 to keep all the **w** of this law and 1697
18:18 unto thee, and will put my **w** in his mouth; 1697
18:19 *that* whosoever will not hearken unto my **w** 1697
27: 3 thou shalt write upon them all the **w** of this 1697
27: 8 thou shalt write upon the stones all the **w** of 1697
27:26 Cursed *be* he that confirmeth not *all* the **w** 1697
28:14 thou shalt not go aside from any of the **w** 1697
28:58 If thou wilt not observe to do all the **w** of 1697
29: 1 These *are* the **w** of the covenant, which 1697
29: 9 Keep therefore the **w** of this covenant, 1697
29:19 when he heareth the **w** of this curse, 1697
29:29 that *we* may do all the **w** of this law. 1697
31: 1 and spake these **w** unto all Israel. 1697
31:12 and observe to do all the **w** of this law: 1697
31:24 end of writing the **w** of this law in a book, 1697
31:28 that I may speak these **w** in their ears, 1697
31:30 congregation of Israel the **w** of this song, 1697
32: 1 and hear, O earth, the **w** of my mouth. 561
32:44 spake all the **w** of this song in the ears of 1697
32:45 Moses made an end of speaking all these **w** 1697
32:46 Set your hearts unto all the **w** which I 1697
32:46 to observe to do, all the **w** of this law. 1697
33: 3 at thy feet; *every one* shall receive of thy **w**. 1703
Jos 1:18 will not hearken unto thy **w** in all that thou 1697
2:21 she said, According unto your **w**, so *be* it. 1697
3: 9 and hear the **w** of the LORD your God. 1697
8:34 afterward he read all the **w** of the law, 1697
22:30 heard the **w** that the children of Reuben and 1697
24:26 Joshua wrote these **w** in the book of the law 1697
24:27 for it hath heard all the **w** of the LORD 561
Jdg 2: 4 these **w** unto all the children of Israel, 1697
9: 3 ears of all the men of Shechem all these **w**: 1697
9:30 when Zebul the ruler of the city heard the **w** 1697
11:10 if we do not so according to thy **w**. 1697
11:11 Jephthah uttered all his **w** before 1697
11:28 unto the **w** of Jephthah which he sent him. 1697
13:12 Manoah said, Now let thy **w** come to pass. 1697
16:16 when she pressed him daily with her **w**, and 1697
1Sa 3:19 and did let none of his **w** fall to the ground. 1697
8:10 Samuel told all the **w** of the LORD unto 1697
8:21 Samuel heard all the **w** of the people, and 1697
15: 1 hearken thou unto the voice of the **w** of 1697
15:24 commandment of the LORD, and thy **w**: 1697
17:11 all Israel heard those **w** of the Philistine, 1697
17:23 and spake according to the same **w**: 1697
17:31 when the **w** were heard which David spake, 1697
18:23 Saul's servants spake those **w** in the ears of 1697
18:26 when his servants told David these **w**, 1697
21:12 David laid up these **w** in his heart, and 1697
24: 7 So David stayed his servants with *these* **w**, 1697
24: 9 Wherefore hearest thou men's **w**, saying, 1697
24:16 made an end of speaking these **w** unto Saul, 1697
25: 9 to all those **w** in the name of David, 1697

W

1Sa 25:24 and hear the **w** of thine handmaid. 1697
26:19 let my lord the king hear the **w** of his 1697
28:20 sore afraid, because of the **w** of Samuel: 1697
28:21 have hearkened unto thy **w** which thou 1697
2Sa 3: 8 was Abner very wroth for the **w** of 1697
7:17 According to all these **w**, and according to 1697
7:28 thy **w** be true, and thou hast promised this 1697
14: 3 unto him. So Joab put the **w** in her mouth. 1697
14:19 he put all these **w** in the mouth of thine 1697
19:43 the **w** of the men of Judah were fiercer than 1697
19:43 were fiercer than the **w** of the men of Israel. 1697
20:17 unto him, Hear the **w** of thine handmaid. 1697
22: 1 David spake unto the LORD the **w** of this 1697
23: 1 Now these *be* the last **w** of David. 1697
1Ki 1:14 will come in after thee, and confirm thy **w**. 1697
5: 7 when Hiram heard the **w** of Solomon, 1697
8:59 let these my **w**, wherewith I have made 1697
10: 7 Howbeit I believed not the **w**, until I came, 1697
12: 7 speak good **w** to them, then they will be thy 1697
13:11 the **w** which he had spoken unto the king, 1697
21:27 it came to pass, when Ahab heard those **w**, 1697
22:13 the **w** of the prophets *declare* good unto 1697
2Ki 1: 7 came up to meet you, and told you these **w**? 1697
6:12 telleth the king of Israel the **w** that thou 1697
6:30 when the king heard the **w** of the woman, 1697
18:20 Thou sayest, (but *they are but* vain **w**,) 1697
18:27 thy master, and to thee, to speak these **w**? 1697
18:37 and told him the **w** of Rab-shakeh. 1697
19: 4 thy God will hear all the **w** of Rab-shakeh, 1697
19: 4 will reprove the **w** which the LORD thy 1697
19: 6 Be not afraid of the **w** which thou hast 1697
19:16 hear the **w** of Sennacherib, which hath sent 1697
22:11 when the king had heard the **w** of the book 1697
22:13 concerning the **w** of this book that is found: 1697
22:13 our fathers have not hearkened unto the **w** 1697
22:16 *even* all the **w** of the book which the king 1697
22:18 *As touching* the **w** which thou hast heard; 1697
23: 2 he read in their ears all the **w** of the book of 1697
23: 3 to perform the **w** of this covenant that were 1697
23:16 God proclaimed, who proclaimed these **w**. 1697
23:24 that he might perform the **w** of the law 1697
1Ch 17:15 According to all these **w**, and according to 1697
23:27 For by the last **w** of David, the Levites 1697
25: 5 of Heman the king's seer in the **w** of God, 1697
2Ch 9: 6 Howbeit I believed not their **w**, until I 1697
10: 7 please them, and speak good **w** to them, 1697
11: 4 they obeyed the **w** of the LORD, and 1697
15: 8 when Asa heard these **w**, and the prophecy 1697
18:12 the **w** of the prophets *declare* good to 1697
29:15 by the **w** of the LORD, to cleanse 1697
29:30 unto the LORD with the **w** of David, 1697
32: 8 the people rested themselves upon the **w** of 1697
33:18 the **w** of the seers that spake to him in 1697
34:19 when the king had heard the **w** of the law, 1697
34:21 concerning the **w** of the book that is found: 1697
34:26 *concerning* the **w** which thou hast heard; 1697
34:27 when thou heardest his **w** against this place, 1697
34:30 he read in their ears all the **w** of the book of 1697
34:31 to perform the **w** of the covenant which are 1697
35:22 hearkened not unto the **w** of Necho from 1697
36:16 despised his **w**, and misused his prophets, 1697
Ezr 7:11 *even* a scribe of the **w** of 1697
9: 4 that trembled at the **w** of the God of Israel, 1697
Ne 1: 1 The **w** of Nehemiah the son of Hachaliah. 1697
1: 4 when I heard these **w**, *that* I sat down and 1697
2:18 as also the king's **w** that he had spoken 1697
5: 6 angry when I heard their cry and these **w**. 1697
6: 6 mayest be their king, according to these **w**. 1697
6: 7 reported to the king according to these **w**. 1697
6:19 deeds before me, and uttered my **w** to him. 1697
8: 9 when they heard the **w** of the law. 1697
8:12 they had understood the **w** that were 1697
8:13 even to understand the **w** of the law. 1697
9: 8 *say,* to his seed, and hast performed thy **w**; 1697
Est 4: 9 and told Esther the **w** of Mordecai. 1697
4:12 And they told to Mordecai Esther's **w**. 1697
9:26 Therefore for all the **w** of this letter, and 1697
9:30 of Ahasuerus, *with* **w** of peace and truth, 1697
Job 4: 4 Thy **w** have upholden him that was falling, 4405
6: 3 the sea: therefore my **w** are swallowed up. 1697
6:10 for I have not concealed the **w** of the Holy 561
6:25 How forcible are right **w**! but what doth your 561
6:26 Do ye imagine to reprove **w**, and 4405
8: 2 *how long shall* the **w** of thy mouth *be like* a 561
8:10 *and* tell thee, and utter **w** out of their heart? 4405
9:14 *and* choose out my **w** *to reason* with him? 1697
11: 2 Should not the multitude of **w** be 1697
12:11 Doth not the ear try **w**? and the mouth taste 4405
15:13 and lettest *such* **w** go out of thy mouth? 4405
16: 3 Shall vain **w** have an end? or 1697
16: 4 I could heap up **w** against you, and 4405
18: 2 long *will it be ere* you make an end of **w**? 4405
19: 2 my soul, and break me in pieces with **w**? 4405
19:23 O that my **w** were now written! O that they 4405
22:22 his mouth, and lay up his **w** in thine heart. 561
23: 5 I would know the **w** *which* he would 4405
23:12 I have esteemed the **w** of his mouth more 561
26: 4 To whom hast thou uttered **w**? and 4405
29:22 After my **w** they spake not again; and 1697
31:40 instead of barley. The **w** of Job are ended. 1697
32:11 Behold, I waited for your **w**; I gave ear to 1697
32:12 that convinced Job, *or* that answered his **w**: 561
32:14 Now he hath not directed *his* **w** against me: 4405
33: 1 hear my speeches, and hearken to all my **w**. 1697
33: 3 My **w** *shall be of* the uprightness of my 561
33: 5 set *thy* **w** in order before me, stand up. NIH
33: 8 I have heard the voice of *thy* **w**, 4405
34: 2 Hear my **w**, O ye wise *men;* and give ear 4405
34: 3 For the ear trieth **w**, as the mouth tasteth 4405
34:16 hear this: hearken to the voice of my **w**. 4405
34:35 and his **w** *were* without wisdom. 1697
34:37 and multiplieth his **w** against God. 561
35:16 he multiplieth **w** without knowledge. 4405
36: 4 For truly my **w** *shall* not *be* false: *he that is* 4405
38: 2 Who *is* this that darkeneth counsel by **w** 4405

Job 41: 3 unto thee? will he speak soft **w** unto thee? NIH
42: 7 that after the LORD had spoken these **w** 1697
Ps 5: 1 Give ear to my **w**, O LORD, consider my 561
7: T concerning the **w** of Cush the Benjamite. 1697
12: 6 The **w** of the LORD *are* pure words: 565
12: 6 The words of the LORD *are* pure **w**: 565
18: T who spake unto the LORD the **w** of this 1697
19: 4 and their **w** to the end of the world. 4405
19:14 Let the **w** of my mouth, and the meditation 561
22: 1 helping me, *and from* the **w** of my roaring? 1697
36: 3 The **w** of his mouth *are* iniquity and deceit: 1697
50:17 and castest my **w** behind thee. 1697
52: 4 Thou lovest all devouring **w**, O thou 1697
54: 2 O God; give ear to the **w** of my mouth. 561
55:21 *The* **w** *of* his mouth were smoother than NIH
55:21 his **w** were softer than oil, yet *were* they 1697
56: 5 Every day they wrest my **w**: all their 1697
59:12 the **w** of their lips let them even be taken in 1697
64: 3 *bows to shoot* their arrows, *even* bitter **w**: 1697
78: 1 incline your ears to the **w** of my mouth. 561
106:12 believed they his **w**; they sang his praise. 1697
107:11 Because they rebelled against the **w** of God, 561
109: 3 They compassed me about also *with* **w** of 1697
119:57 I have said that *I* would keep thy **w**. 1697
119:103 How sweet are thy **w** unto my taste! 565
119:130 The entrance of thy **w** giveth light; it giveth 1697
119:139 mine enemies have forgotten thy **w**. 1697
138: 4 when they hear the **w** of thy mouth. 561
141: 6 in stony places, they shall hear my **w**; 561
Pr 1: 2 to perceive the **w** of understanding; 561
1: 6 the **w** of the wise, and their dark sayings. 1697
1:21 in the city she uttereth her **w**, *saying,* 561
1:23 I will make known my **w** unto you. 1697
2: 1 if thou wilt receive my **w**, and hide my 561
2:16 the stranger *which* flattereth with her **w**; 561
4: 4 said unto me, Let thine heart retain my **w**: 1697
4: 5 neither decline from the **w** of my mouth. 561
4:20 My son, attend to my **w**; incline thine ear 1697
5: 7 and depart not from the **w** of my mouth. 561
6: 2 Thou art snared with the **w** of thy mouth, 561
6: 2 thou art taken with the **w** of thy mouth, 561
7: 1 keep my **w**, and lay up my commandments 561
7: 5 the stranger *which* flattereth with her **w**. 561
7:24 and attend to the **w** of my mouth. 561
8: 8 All the **w** of my mouth *are* in righteousness; 561
10:19 In the multitude of **w** there wanteth not sin: 1697
12: 6 The **w** of the wicked *are* to lie in wait *for* 1697
15: 1 away wrath: but grievous **w** stir up anger. 1697
15:26 but *the* **w** *of* the pure *are* pleasant words. NIH
15:26 but *the words of* the pure *are* pleasant **w**. 561
16:24 Pleasant **w** *are as* a honeycomb, sweet to 561
17:27 He that hath knowledge spareth his **w**: *and* 561
18: 4 The **w** of a man's mouth *are as* deep 1697
18: 8 The **w** of a talebearer *are* as wounds, and 1697
19: 7 he pursueth *them with* **w**, *yet* they *are* 561
19:27 *that causeth* to err from the **w** of knowledge. 561
22:12 he overthroweth the **w** of the transgressor. 1697
22:17 hear the **w** of the wise, and apply thine 1697
22:21 thee know the certainty of the **w** of truth; 561
22:21 that *thou* mightest answer the **w** *of* truth to 561
23: 8 shalt thou vomit up, and lose thy sweet **w**. 1697
23: 9 for he will despise the wisdom of thy **w**. 4405
23:12 and thine ears to the **w** of knowledge. 561
26:22 The **w** of a talebearer *are* as wounds, and 1697
29:19 A servant will not be corrected by **w**: 1697
29:20 Seest thou a man that is hasty in his **w**? 1697
30: 1 The **w** of Agur the son of Jakeh, *even* 1697
30: 6 Add thou not unto his **w**, lest he reprove 1697
31: 1 The **w** of king Lemuel, the prophecy that 1697
Ecc 1: 1 The **w** of the Preacher, the son of David, 1697
5: 2 thou upon earth: therefore let thy **w** be few. 1697
5: 3 a fool's voice *is known* by multitude of **w**. 1697
5: 7 and many **w** *there are* also *divers* vanities: 1697
7:21 Also take no heed unto all **w** that are 1697
9:16 *is* despised, and his **w** *are* not heard. 1697
9:17 The **w** of wise *men are* heard in quiet, 1697
10:12 The **w** of a wise *man's* mouth *are* gracious; 1697
10:13 The beginning of the **w** of his mouth *is* 1697
10:14 A fool also is full of **w**: a man cannot tell 1697
12:10 Preacher sought to find out acceptable **w**: 1697
12:10 *was* written *was* upright, *even* **w** of truth. 1697
12:11 The **w** of the wise *are* as goads, and as nails 1697
Isa 29:11 unto you as the **w** of a book that is sealed, 1697
29:18 in that day shall the deaf hear the **w** of 1697
31: 2 will bring evil, and will not call back his **w**: 1697
32: 7 devices to destroy the poor with lying **w**, 561
36: 5 I say, *sayest thou,* (but *they are but* vain **w**) 1697
36:12 to thy master and to thee to speak these **w**? 1697
36:13 said, Hear ye the **w** of the great king, 1697
36:22 and told him the **w** of Rabshakeh. 1697
37: 4 thy God will hear the **w** of Rabshakeh, 1697
37: 4 will reprove the **w** which the LORD thy 1697
37: 6 Be not afraid of the **w** that thou hast heard, 1697
37:17 hear all the **w** of Sennacherib, which hath 1697
41:26 yea, *there is* none that heareth your **w**. 561
51:16 I have put my **w** in thy mouth, and 1697
58:13 own pleasure, nor speaking *thine own* **w**: 1697
59:13 and uttering from the heart **w** of falsehood. 1697
59:21 and my **w** which I have put in thy mouth, 1697
Jer 1: 1 The **w** of Jeremiah the son of Hilkiah, 1697
1: 9 Behold, I have put my **w** in thy mouth. 1697
3:12 Go and proclaim these **w** toward the north, 1697
5:14 I will make my **w** in thy mouth fire, and 1697
6:19 they have not hearkened unto my **w**, 1697
7: 4 Trust ye not in lying **w**, saying, The temple 1697
7: 8 Behold, ye trust in lying **w**, *that* cannot 1697
7:27 Therefore thou shalt speak all these **w** unto 1697
11: 2 Hear ye the **w** of this covenant, and 1697
11: 3 Cursed *be* the man that obeyeth not the **w** 1697
11: 6 Proclaim all these **w** in the cities of Judah, 1697
11: 6 Hear ye the **w** of this covenant, and 1697
11: 8 I will bring upon them all the **w** of this 1697
11:10 which refused to hear my **w**; 1697
12: 6 though they speak fair **w** unto thee. NIH
13:10 evil people, which refuse to hear my **w**, 1697

Jer 15:16 Thy **w** were found, and I did eat them; and 1697
16:10 thou shalt shew this people all these **w**, 1697
18: 2 and there I will cause thee to hear my **w**. 1697
18:18 and let us not give heed to any of his **w**. 1697
19: 2 proclaim there the **w** that I shall tell thee, 1697
19:15 their necks, that *they* might not hear my **w**. 1697
22: 5 if ye will not hear these **w**, I swear by 1697
23: 9 and because of the **w** of his holiness. 1697
23:16 Hearken not unto the **w** of the prophets that 1697
23:22 had caused my people to hear my **w**, then 1697
23:30 that steal my **w** every one from his 1697
23:36 for ye have perverted the **w** of the living 1697
25: 8 of hosts; Because ye have not heard my **w**, 1697
25:13 I will bring upon that land all my **w** which I 1697
25:30 prophesy thou against them all these **w**, 1697
26: 2 all the **w** that I command thee to speak unto 1697
26: 5 To hearken to the **w** of my servants 1697
26: 7 these **w** in the house of the LORD. 1697
26:12 against this city all the **w** that ye have 1697
26:15 unto you to speak all these **w** in your ears. 1697
26:20 against this land according to all the **w** of 1697
26:21 and all the princes, heard his **w**, 1697
27:12 king of Judah according to all these **w**, 1697
27:14 Therefore hearken not unto the **w** of 1697
27:16 Hearken not to the **w** of your prophets that 1697
28: 6 the LORD perform thy **w** which thou hast 1697
29: 1 Now these *are* the **w** of the letter that 1697
29:19 Because they have not hearkened to my **w**, 1697
29:23 have spoken lying **w** in my name, which I 1697
30: 2 Write thee all the **w** that I have spoken unto 1697
30: 4 these *are* the **w** that the LORD spake 1697
34: 6 Jeremiah the prophet spake all these **w** unto 1697
34:18 which have not performed the **w** of 1697
35:13 not receive instruction to hearken to my **w**? 1697
35:14 The **w** of Jonadab the son of Rechab, 1697
36: 2 write therein all the **w** that I have spoken 1697
36: 4 mouth of Jeremiah all the **w** of the LORD, 1697
36: 6 the **w** of the LORD in the ears of 1697
36: 8 reading in the book the **w** of the LORD *in* 1697
36:10 read Baruch in the book the **w** of Jeremiah 1697
36:11 had heard out of the book all the **w** of 1697
36:13 Michaiah declared unto them all the **w** that 1697
36:16 to pass when they had heard all the **w**, 1697
36:16 We will surely tell the king of all these **w**. 1697
36:17 How didst thou write all these **w** at his 1697
36:18 He pronounced all these **w** unto me with 1697
36:20 and told all the **w** in the ears of the king. 1697
36:24 any of his servants that heard all these **w**. 1697
36:27 the **w** which Baruch wrote at the mouth of 1697
36:28 write in it all the former **w** that were in 1697
36:32 **w** of the book which Jehoiakim king of 1697
36:32 were added besides unto them many like **w**. 1697
37: 2 did hearken unto the **w** of the LORD, 1697
38: 1 heard the **w** that Jeremiah had spoken unto 1697
38: 4 the people, in speaking such **w** unto them: 1697
38:24 Let no man know of these **w**, and thou shalt 1697
38:27 he told them according to all these **w** that 1697
39:16 I *will* bring my **w** upon this city for evil, 1697
42: 4 the LORD your God according to your **w**; 1697
43: 1 people all the **w** of the LORD their God, 1697
43: 1 God had sent him to them, *even* all these **w**; 1697
44:28 shall know whose **w** shall stand, mine, or 1697
44:29 that ye may know that my **w** shall surely 1697
45: 1 when he had written these **w** in a book at 1697
51:60 *even* all these **w** that are written against 1697
51:61 and shalt see, and shalt read all these **w**; 1697
51:64 be weary. Thus far *are* the **w** of Jeremiah. 1697
Eze 2: 6 neither be afraid of their **w**, though briers 1697
2: 6 be not afraid of their **w**, nor be dismayed at 1697
2: 7 thou shalt speak my **w** unto them, 1697
3: 4 of Israel, and speak with my **w** unto them. 1697
3: 6 whose **w** thou canst not understand. 1697
3:10 all my **w** that I shall speak unto thee receive 1697
12:28 There shall none of my **w** be prolonged any 1697
33:31 they hear thy **w**, but they will not do them: 1697
33:32 for they hear thy **w**, but they do them not. 1697
35:13 and have multiplied your **w** against me: 1697
Da 2: 9 and corrupt **w** to speak before me, 4406
5:10 by reason of the **w** of the king and his lords, 4406
6:14 the king, when he heard *these* **w**, was sore 4406
7:11 of the voice of the great **w** which the horn 4406
7:25 he shall speak *great* **w** against the most 4406
9:12 he hath confirmed his **w**, which he spake 1697
10: 6 the voice of his **w** like the voice of a 1697
10: 9 Yet heard I the voice of his **w**: and when I 1697
10: 9 when I heard the voice of his **w**, then was I 1697
10:11 understand the **w** that I speak unto thee, and 1697
10:12 thy **w** were heard, and I am come for thy 1697
10:12 were heard, and I am come for thy **w**. 1697
10:15 when he had spoken such **w** unto me, I set 1697
12: 4 O Daniel, shut up the **w**, and seal the book, 1697
12: 9 for the **w** *are* closed up and sealed till 1697
Hos 6: 5 I have slain them by the **w** of my mouth: 561
10: 4 They have spoken **w**, swearing falsely in 1697
14: 2 Take with you **w**, and turn to the LORD: 1697
Am 1: 1 The **w** of Amos, who was among 1697
7:10 the land is not able to bear all his **w**. 1697
8:11 but of hearing the **w** of the LORD: 1697
Mic 2: 7 do not my **w** do good to him that walketh 1697
Hag 1:12 the **w** of Haggai the prophet, as the LORD 1697
Zec 1: 6 my **w** and my statutes, which I commanded 1697
1:13 the angel that talked with me *with* good **w** 1697
1:13 me *with* good words *and* comfortable **w**. 1697
7: 7 *Should ye* not *hear* the **w** which 1697
7:12 the **w** which the LORD of hosts hath sent 1697
8: 9 ye that hear in these days these **w** by 1697
Mal 2:17 Ye have wearied the LORD with your **w**. 1697
3:13 Your **w** have been stout against me, 1697
Mt 10:14 nor hear your **w**, when ye depart out of that *3056*
12:37 For by thy **w** thou shalt be justified, and *3056*
12:37 and by thy **w** thou shalt be condemned. *3056*
22:22 When they had heard *these* **w**, they NIG
24:35 pass away, but my **w** shall not pass away. *3056*
26:44 prayed the third time, saying the same **w**. *3056*
Mk 8:38 and of my **w** in this adulterous and *3056*

Mk 10:24 And the disciples were astonished at his **w**. 3056
12:13 and of the Herodians, to catch him in *his* **w**. 3056
13:31 pass away: but my **w** shall not pass away. 3056
14:39 and prayed, and spake the same **w**. 3056
Lk 1:20 because thou believest not my **w**, 3056
3: 4 As it is written in the book of the **w** of 3056
4:22 wondered at the gracious **w** which 3056
9:26 shall be ashamed of me and of my **w**, 3056
20:20 *men,* that they might take hold of his **w**, 3056
20:26 And they could not take hold of his **w** 4487
21:33 pass away: but my **w** shall not pass away. 3056
23: 9 Then he questioned *with* him in many **w**; 3056
24: 8 And they remembered his **w**, 4487
24:11 And their **w** seemed to them as idle tales, 4487
24:44 These *are* the **w** which I spake unto you, 3056
Jn 3:34 For he whom God hath sent speaketh the **w** 4487
5:47 his writings, how shall ye believe my **w**? 4487
6:63 the **w** that I speak unto you, *they* are spirit, 4487
6:68 shall we go? thou hast the **w** of eternal life. 4487
7: 9 When he had said these *w* unto them, NIG
8:20 These **w** spake Jesus in the treasury, as he 4487
8:30 As he spake these *w*, many believed on him. NIG
8:47 He that is of God heareth God's **w**: ye 4487
9:22 These *w* spake his parents, because NIG
9:40 which were with him heard these *w*, NIG
10:21 These are not the **w** of him that hath a 4487
12:47 And if any *man* hear my **w**, and believe not, 4487
12:48 that rejecteth me, and receiveth not my **w**, 4487
14:10 the **w** that I speak unto you, I speak not of 4487
14:23 If a man love me, he will keep my **w**: 3056
15: 7 If ye abide in me, and my **w** abide in you, 4487
17: 1 These *w* spake Jesus, and lift up his eyes to NIG
17: 8 For I have given unto them the **w** which 4487
18: 1 When Jesus had spoken these *w*, he went NIG
Ac 2:14 this known unto you, and hearken to my **w**: 4487
2:22 Ye men of Israel, hear these **w**; Jesus of 3056
2:40 And with many other **w** did he testify and 3056
5: 5 And Ananias hearing these **w** fell down, 3056
5:20 speak in the temple to the people all the **w** 4487
6:11 We have heard him speak blasphemous **w** 4487
6:13 blasphemous **w** against this holy place, 4487
7:22 and was mighty in **w** and in deeds. 3056
10:22 thee into his house, and to hear **w** of thee. 4487
10:44 While Peter yet spake these **w**, the Holy 4487
11:14 Who shall tell thee **w**, whereby thou and 4487
13:42 the Gentiles besought that these **w** might be 4487
15:15 And to this agree the **w** of the prophets; 3056
15:24 went out from us have troubled you with **w**, 3056
15:32 exhorted the brethren with many **w**, and 3056
16:38 And the sergeants told these **w** unto 4487
18:15 But if it be a question of **w** and names, and 3056
20:35 and to remember the **w** of the Lord Jesus, 3056
20:38 Sorrowing most *of all* for the **w** which he 3056
24: 4 wouldest hear us of thy clemency a **few w**. 4935
26:25 but speak forth *the* **w** of truth and 4487
28:29 And when he had said these *w*, the Jews NIG
Ro 10:18 and their **w** unto the ends of the world. 4487
16:18 and by **good w** and fair speeches deceive 5542
1Co 1:17 not with wisdom of **w**, lest the cross of 3056
2: 4 my preaching *was* not with enticing **w** of 3056
2:13 not in the **w** which man's wisdom teacheth, 3056
14: 9 except ye utter by the tongue **w** easy to be 3056
14:19 Yet in the church I had rather speak five **w** 3056
14:19 than ten thousand **w** in an *unknown* tongue. 3056
2Co 12: 4 and heard unspeakable **w**, which *it is* not 4487
Eph 3: 3 me the mystery; (as I wrote afore in few *w*, NIG
5: 6 Let no *man* deceive you with vain **w**: for 3056
Col 2: 4 *man* should beguile you with **enticing w**. 4086
1Th 2: 5 neither at any time used we flattering **w**, 3056
4:18 comfort one another with these **w**. 3056
1Ti 4: 6 nourished up in the **w** of faith and of good 3056
6: 3 and consent not to wholesome **w**, 3056
6: 3 *even* the *w* of our Lord Jesus Christ, and NIG
6: 4 but doting about questions and **strifes of w**, 3055
2Ti 1:13 Hold fast the form of sound **w**, which thou 3056
2:14 that *they* **strive** not **about w** to no profit, 3054
4:15 for he hath greatly withstood our **w**. 3056
Heb 12:19 the sound of a trumpet, and the voice of **w**; 4487
13:22 I have written a letter unto you in few *w*. NIG
2Pe 2: 3 with feigned **w** make merchandise of you: 3056
2:18 For when they speak great swelling *w* of NIG
3: 2 That *ye* may be mindful of the **w** which 4487
3Jn 1:10 prating against us with malicious **w**: 3056
Jude 1:16 their mouth speaketh great swelling *w*, NIG
1:17 remember ye the **w** which were spoken 4487
Rev 1: 3 and they that hear the **w** of *this* prophecy, 3056
17:17 until the **w** of God shall be fulfilled. 4487
21: 5 Write: for these **w** are true and faithful. 3056
22:18 heareth the **w** of the prophecy of this book, 3056
22:19 And if any *man* shall take away from the **w** 3056

WORK (419) [FELLOWWORKERS, HANDYWORK, NEEDLEWORK, NETWORK, NETWORKS, WORK'S, WORKER, WORKERS, WORKETH, WORKFELLOW, WORKING, WORKMAN, WORKMANSHIP, WORKMEN, WORKMEN'S, WORKS, WORKS']

Ge 2: 2 on the seventh day God ended his **w** which 4399
2: 2 he rested on the seventh day from all his **w** 4399
2: 3 that in it he had rested from all his **w** which 4399
5:29 *same* shall comfort us concerning our **w** 4639
Ex 5: 9 Let there more **w** be laid upon the men, 5656
5:11 not ought of your **w** *shall be* diminished. 5656
5:18 Go therefore now, *and* **w**; for there shall no 5647
12:16 no *manner of* **w** shall be done in them, 4399
14:31 Israel saw *that* great **w** which the LORD 3027
18:20 must walk, and the **w** that they must do. 4639
20: 9 days shalt thou labour, and do all thy **w**: 4399
20:10 *in it* thou shalt not do any **w**, thou, nor thy 4399
23:12 Six days thou shalt do thy **w**, and on 4639
24:10 as it were a paved **w** of a sapphire stone, 4639
25:18 *of* **beaten w** shalt thou make them, in 4749
25:31 *of* **beaten w** shall the candlestick be made: 4749
25:36 all it *shall be* one **beaten w** *of* pure gold. 4749

Ex 26: 1 *with* cherubims *of* cunning **w** shalt thou 4639
26:31 scarlet, and fine twined linen *of* cunning **w**: 4639
28: 6 fine twined linen, *with* cunning **w**. 4639
28: 8 be of the same, according to the **w** thereof; 4639
28:11 *With* the **w** of an engraver in stone, *like* 4639
28:14 *of* wreathen **w** shalt thou make them, and 4639
28:15 breastplate of judgment *with* cunning **w**; 4639
28:15 after the **w** of the ephod thou shalt make it; 4639
28:22 at the ends *of* wreathen **w** *of* pure gold. 4639
28:32 it shall have a binding of woven **w** round 4639
31: 4 to **w** in gold, and in silver, and in brass, 6213
31: 5 to **w** in all *manner of* workmanship. 6213
31:14 for whosoever doeth *any* **w** therein, that 4399
31:15 Six days may **w** be done; but in the seventh 4399
31:15 whosoever doeth *any* **w** in the sabbath day, 4399
32:16 the tables *were* the **w** of God, and 4639
34:10 thou *art* shall see the **w** of the LORD: 4639
34:21 Six days thou shalt **w**, but on the seventh 5647
35: 2 Six days shall **w** be done, but on 4399
35: 2 whosoever doeth **w** therein shall be put to 4399
35:21 the **w** of the tabernacle of the congregation, 4399
35:24 shittim wood for any **w** of the service, 4399
35:29 them willing to bring for all *manner of* **w**, 4399
35:32 to **w** in gold, and in silver, and in brass, 6213
35:33 to make any *manner of* cunning **w**. 4399
35:35 to **w** all *manner of* work, of the engraver, 6213
35:35 to work all *manner of* **w**, of the engraver, 4399
35:35 *even* of them that do any **w**, and of those 4399
35:35 and of **those that devise cunning w**. 2803+4284
36: 1 understanding to know how to **w** all 6213
36: 1 *of* **w** for the service of the sanctuary, 4399
36: 2 stirred him up to come unto the **w** to do it: 4399
36: 3 for the **w** of the service of the sanctuary, 4399
36: 4 all the wise *men*, that wrought all the **w** of 4399
36: 4 came every man from his **w** which they 4399
36: 5 more than enough for the service of the **w**, 4399
36: 6 more **w** for the offering of the sanctuary. 4399
36: 7 *had* was sufficient for all the **w** to make it, 4399
36: 8 **w** *of* the tabernacle made ten curtains *of* 4399
36: 8 *with* cherubims *of* cunning **w** made he 4639
36:35 *with* cherubims made he it *of* cunning **w**. 4639
37:17 *of* **beaten w** made he the candlestick; 4749
37:22 all of it *was* one **beaten w** *of* pure gold. 4749
37:29 *according to* the **w** of the apothecary. 4639
38:24 All the gold that was occupied for the **w** in 4399
38:24 **w** of the holy *place*, *even* the gold of 4399
39: 3 to **w** *it* in the blue, and in the purple, and 6213
39: 3 in the fine linen, *with* cunning **w**. 4639
39: 5 of the same, according to the **w** thereof; 4639
39: 8 he made the breastplate *of* cunning **w**, 4639
39: 8 *of* cunning work, like the **w** of the ephod; 4639
39:15 at the ends, *of* wreathen **w** *of* pure gold. 4639
39:22 he made the robe of the ephod *of* woven **w**, 4639
39:27 they made coats *of* fine linen *of* woven **w** 4639
39:32 Thus was all the **w** of the tabernacle of 5656
39:42 so the children of Israel made all the **w**. 5656
39:43 Moses did look upon all the **w**, and behold, 4399
40:33 of the court gate. So Moses finished the **w**. 4399
Lev 11:32 whatsoever vessel *it be*, wherein *any* **w** is 4399
13:51 in a skin, *or* in any **w** that is made of skin; 4399
16:29 do no **w** *at all, whether it be* one of your 4399
23: 3 Six days shall **w** be done: but the seventh 4399
23: 3 ye shall do no **w** *therein*: it *is* the sabbath of 4399
23: 7 ye shall do no servile **w** *therein*. 4399
23: 8 ye shall do no servile **w** *therein*. 4399
23:21 ye shall do no servile **w** *therein*: *it shall be* 4399
23:25 Ye shall do no servile **w** *therein*: but 4399
23:28 ye shall do no **w** in that same day: for it *is* a 4399
23:30 whatsoever soul *it be* that doeth any **w** in 4399
23:31 Ye shall do no *manner of* **w**: *it shall be* a 4399
23:35 ye shall do no servile **w** *therein*. 4399
23:36 *and* ye shall do no servile **w** *therein*. 4399
Nu 4: 3 to do the **w** in the tabernacle of 4399
4:23 to do the **w** in the tabernacle of 5656
4:30 to do the **w** of the tabernacle of 5656
4:35 for the **w** in the tabernacle of 5656
4:39 for the **w** in the tabernacle of 5656
4:43 for the **w** in the tabernacle of 5656
8: 4 this **w** of the candlestick *was of* beaten 4639
8: 4 unto the flowers thereof, *was* **beaten w**: 4749
28:18 ye shall do no *manner of* servile **w** *therein*: 4399
28:25 holy convocation; ye shall do no servile **w**. 4399
28:26 holy convocation; ye shall do no servile **w**: 4399
29: 1 holy convocation; ye shall do no servile **w**: 4399
29: 7 your souls: ye shall not do any **w** *therein*: 4399
29:12 ye shall do no servile **w**, and ye shall keep a 4399
29:35 ye shall do no servile **w** *therein*: 4399
31:20 all **w** of goats' *hair*, and all things made of 4639
Dt 4:28 the **w** of men's hands, wood and stone, 4639
5:13 days thou shalt labour, and do all thy **w**: 4399
5:14 *in it* thou shalt not do any **w**, thou, nor thy 4399
14:29 in all the **w** of thine hand which thou doest. 4639
15:19 thou shalt **do** no **w** with the firstling of thy 5647
16: 8 thy God: thou shalt do no **w** *therein*. 4399
24:19 may bless thee in all the **w** of thine hands. 4639
27:15 the **w** of the hands of the craftsman, and 4639
28:12 and to bless all the **w** of thine hand: 4639
30: 9 thee plenteous in every **w** of thine hand, 4639
31:29 to provoke him to anger through the **w** of 4639
32: 4 *He is* the Rock, his **w** *is* perfect: for all his 6467
33:11 and accept the **w** of his hands: 6467
Jos 9: 4 They did **w** wilily, and went and made as if 6213
Jdg 19:16 there came an old man from his **w** out of 4639
Ru 2:12 The LORD recompense thy **w**, and a full 6467
1Sa 8:16 and your asses, and put *them* to his **w**. 4399
14: 6 it may be that the LORD will **w** for us: 6213
1Ki 5:16 Solomon's officers which *were* over the **w**, 4399
5:16 ruled over the people that wrought in the **w**. 4399
6:35 *them* with gold fitted upon the **carved w**. 2707
7: 8 within the porch, *which* was of the like **w**. 4639
7:14 and cunning to **w** all works in brass. 6213
7:14 to king Solomon, and wrought all his **w**. 4399
7:17 *And* nets of checker **w**, *and* wreaths of 4639
7:17 of checker work, *and* wreaths of chain **w**, 4639
7:19 of the pillars *were* of lily **w** in the porch, 4639

1Ki 7:22 upon the top of the pillars *was* lily **w**: so 4639
7:22 so was the **w** of the pillars finished. 4399
7:28 the **w** of the bases *was on* this *manner*: they 4639
7:29 oxen *were certain* additions made of thin **w**. 4639
7:31 the mouth thereof *was* round *after* the **w** of 4639
7:33 the **w** of the wheels *was* like the work of a 4639
7:33 the work of the wheels *was* like the **w** of a 4639
7:40 So Hiram made an end of doing all the **w** 4399
7:51 So was ended all the **w** that king Solomon 4399
9:23 of the officers that *were* over Solomon's **w**, 4399
9:23 rule over the people that wrought in the **w**. 4399
16: 7 in provoking him to anger with the **w** of his 4639
21:20 thou hast sold thyself to **w** evil in the sight 6213
21:25 which did sell himself to **w** wickedness in 6213
2Ki 12:11 into the hands of *them* that did the **w**, 4399
19:18 but the **w** of men's hands, wood and stone: 4639
22: 5 it into the hand of the doers of the **w**, 4399
22: 5 let them give it to the doers of the **w** which 4399
22: 9 it into the hand of them that do the **w**, 4399
25:17 the **wreathen w**, and pomegranates upon 7639
25:17 had the second pillar with **wreathen w**. 7639
1Ch 4:23 there they dwelt with the king for his **w**. 4399
6:49 *were appointed* for all the **w** of the *place* 4399
9:13 very able men *for* the **w** of the service of 4399
9:19 *were* over the **w** of the service, 4399
9:33 for they were employed in *that* **w** day and 4399
16:37 ark continually, as every day's **w required**: 1697
22:15 *of* cunning *men* for every *manner of* **w**. 4399
23: 4 four thousand *were* to set forward the **w** of 4399
23:24 that did the **w** for the service of the house 4399
23:28 the **w** of the service of the house of God; 4639
27:26 over them that did the **w** of the field for 4399
28:13 for all the **w** of the service of the house of 4399
28:20 until *thou* hast finished all the **w** for 4399
29: 1 *is yet* young and tender, and the **w** *is* great: 4399
29: 5 for all *manner of* **w** *to be made* by 4399
29: 6 with the rulers over the king's **w**, 4399
2Ch 2: 7 therefore a man cunning to **w** in gold, 6213
2:14 skilful to **w** in gold, and in silver, in brass, 6213
2:18 six hundred overseers to **set** the people **a w**. 5647
3:10 house he made two cherubims of image **w**, 4639
4: 5 the brim of it like the **w** of the brim of a 4639
4:11 Huram finished the **w** that he was to make 4399
5: 1 Thus all the **w** that Solomon made for 4399
8: 9 did Solomon make no servants for his **w**; 4399
8:16 Now all the **w** of Solomon was prepared 4399
15: 7 be weak: for your **w** shall be rewarded. 6468
16: 5 off building of Ramah, and let his **w** cease. 4399
24:12 Jehoiada gave it to such as did the **w** of 4399
24:13 the **w** was perfected by them, and they set 4399
29:34 till the **w** was ended, and until the *other* 4399
31:21 in every **w** that he began in the service of 4639
32:19 *which were* the **w** of the hands of man. 4639
34:12 the men did the **w** faithfully: and 4399
34:13 *were* overseers of all that wrought the **w** in 4399
Ezr 2:69 ability unto the treasure of the **w** threescore 4399
3: 8 to set forward the **w** of the house of 4399
4:24 ceased the **w** of the house of the God which 5673
5: 8 this **w** goeth fast on, and prospereth in their 5673
6: 7 Let the **w** of this house of God alone; 5673
6:22 to strengthen their hands in the **w** of 4399
10:13 neither *is this* a **w** of one day or two: 4399
Ne 2:16 to the rulers, nor to the rest that did the **w**. 4399
2:18 strengthened their hands for *this* good *w*. NIH
3: 5 their nobles put not their necks to the **w** of 5656
4: 6 for the people had a mind to **w**. 6213
4:11 and slay them, and cause the **w** to cease. 4399
4:15 all of us to the wall, every one unto his **w**. 4399
4:16 the half of my servants wrought in the **w**, 4399
4:17 *one* with one of his hands wrought in the **w**, 4399
4:19 The **w** *is* great and large, and we *are* 4399
4:21 So we laboured in the **w**: and half of them 4399
5:16 Yea also I continued in the **w** of this wall, 4399
5:16 servants *were* gathered thither unto the **w**. 4399
6: 3 I *am* doing a great **w**, so that I cannot come 4399
6: 3 why should the **w** cease, whilst I leave it, 4399
6: 9 Their hands shall be weakened from the **w**, 4399
6:16 for they perceived that this **w** was wrought 4399
7:70 of the chief of the fathers gave unto the **w**. 4399
7:71 of the **w** twenty thousand drams *of* gold, 4399
10:33 and *for* all the **w** of the house of our God. 4399
11:12 their brethren that did the **w** of the house 4399
13:10 the Levites and the singers, that did the **w**, 4399
Job 1:10 thou hast blessed the **w** of his hands, and 4639
7: 2 a hireling looketh for the **reward of** his **w**: 6467
10: 3 that thou shouldest despise the **w** of thine 3018
14:15 thou wilt have a desire to the **w** of thine 4639
23: 9 where he doth **w**, but I cannot behold *him*: 6213
24: 5 asses in the desert, go they forth to their **w**; 6467
34:11 For the **w** of a man shall he render unto 6467
34:19 for they all *are* the **w** of his hands. 4639
36: 9 he sheweth them their **w**, and 6467
36:24 Remember that thou magnify his **w**, 6467
37: 7 every man; that all men may know his **w**. 4639
Ps 8: 3 the **w** of thy fingers, the moon and the stars, 4639
9:16 the wicked is snared in the **w** of his own 6467
28: 4 give them after the **w** of their hands; 4639
44: 1 *what* **w** thou didst in their days, in the times 6467
58: 2 Yea, in heart you **w** wickedness; you weigh 6466
62:12 renderest to *every* man according to his **w**. 4639
64: 9 shall fear, and shall declare the **w** of God; 6467
74: 6 now they break down the **carved w** thereof 6603
77:12 I will meditate also of all thy **w**, and talk of 6467
90:16 Let thy **w** appear unto thy servants, and 6467
90:17 establish thou the **w** of our hands upon us; 4639
90:17 yea, the **w** of our hands establish thou it. 4639
92: 4 LORD, hast made me glad through thy **w**: 6467
95: 9 tempted me, proved me, and saw my **w**. 6467
101: 3 I hate the **w** of them that turn aside; *it* shall 6213
102:25 and the heavens *are* the **w** of thy hands. 4639
104:23 Man goeth forth unto his **w** and to his 6467
111: 3 His **w** *is* honourable and glorious: and 6467
115: 4 *are* silver and gold, the **w** of men's hands. 4639
119:126 *It is* time for *thee*, LORD, to **w**: *for* they 6213
135:15 *are* silver and gold, the **w** of men's hands. 4639

Ps 141: 4 to practise wicked works with men that w 6466
143: 5 all thy works; I muse on the w of thy hands. 4639
Pr 11:18 The wicked worketh a deceitful w: but 6468
16:11 all the weights of the bag *are* his w. 4639
18: 9 He also that is slothful in his w *is* brother to 4399
20:11 whether his w *be* pure, and whether *it be* 6467
21: 8 strange: but *as for* the pure, his w *is* right. 6467
24:27 Prepare thy w without, and make it fit for 4399
24:29 I will render to the man according to his w. 6467
Ecc 2:17 the w that is wrought under the sun *is* 4639
3:11 that no man can find out the w that God 4639
3:17 there for every purpose and for every w. 4639
4: 3 who hath not seen the evil w that is done 4639
4: 4 I considered all travail, and every right w, 4639
5: 6 and destroy the w of thine hands? 4639
7:13 Consider the w of God: for who can make 4639
8: 9 applied my heart unto every w that is done 4639
8:11 Because sentence *against* an evil w is not 4639
8:14 according to the w of the wicked; 4639
8:14 according to the w of the righteous: 4639
8:17 I beheld all the w of God, that a man cannot 4639
8:17 that a man cannot find out the w that is 4639
9:10 for *there is* no w, nor device, 4639
12:14 For God shall bring every w into judgment, 4639
SS 7: 1 the w of the hands of a cunning workman. 4639
Isa 2: 8 they worship the w of their own hands, 4639
5:12 they regard not the w of the LORD, 6467
5:19 *and* hasten his w, that we may see *it:* and 4639
10:12 performed his whole w upon mount Zion 4639
17: 8 not look to the altars, the w of his hands, 4639
19: 9 Moreover they that w in fine flax, and 5647
19:14 they have caused Egypt to err in every w 4639
19:15 Neither shall there be *any* w for Egypt, 4639
19:25 Assyria the w of my hands, and Israel mine 4639
28:21 that *he* may do his w, his strange work; 4639
28:21 that *he* may do his work, his strange w; 4639
29:14 I will proceed to **do a marvellous w** 6381
29:14 *even* a **marvellous w** and a wonder: 6381
29:16 for shall the w say of him that made it, 4639
29:23 the w of mine hands, in the midst of him, 4639
31: 2 against the help of them that w iniquity. 6466
32: 6 his heart will w iniquity, to practise 6213
32:17 the w of righteousness shall be peace; and 4639
37:19 but the w of men's hands, wood and stone: 4639
40:10 reward *is* with him, and his w before him. 6468
41:24 ye *are* of nothing, and your w of nought: 6467
43:13 of my hand: I will w, and who shall let it? 6466
45: 9 makest thou? or thy w, He hath no hands? 6467
45:11 concerning the w of my hands command ye 6467
49: 4 with the LORD, and my w with my God. 6468
54:16 that bringeth forth an instrument for his w; 4639
60:21 the w of my hands, that *I* may be glorified. 4639
61: 8 I will direct their w in truth, and I will 6468
62:11 reward *is* with him, and his w before him. 6468
64: 8 and we all *are* the w of thine hand. 4639
65: 7 will I measure their former w into their 6468
65:22 mine elect shall long enjoy the w of their 4639
Jer 10: 3 the w of the hands of the workman, 4639
10: 9 the w of the workman, and of the hands of 4639
10: 9 they *are* all the w of cunning *men.* 4639
10:15 They *are* vanity, *and* the w of errors: in 4639
17:22 neither do ye any w, but hallow ye 4399
17:24 hallow the sabbath day, to do no w therein; 4399
18: 3 and behold, he wrought a w on the wheels. 4399
22:13 and giveth him not *for* his w; 6467
31:16 for thy w shall be rewarded, saith 6468
32:19 Great in counsel, and mighty in w: for thine 5950
32:30 me to anger with the w of their hands, 4639
48:10 Cursed *be* he that doeth the w of 4399
50:25 for this *is* the w of the Lord GOD of hosts 4399
50:29 recompense her according to her w; 6467
51:10 let us declare in Zion the w of the LORD 4639
51:18 They *are* vanity, the w of errors: in the time 4639
La 3:64 according to the w of their hands. 4639
4: 2 the w of the hands of the potter! 4639
Eze 1:16 their w *was* like unto the colour of a beryl: 4639
1:16 their w *was* as it were a wheel in the middle 4639
15: 3 Shall wood be taken thereof to do *any* w? 4399
15: 4 midst of it is burnt. Is it meet for *any* w? 4399
15: 5 when it was whole, it was meet for no w: 4399
15: 5 much less shall it be meet yet for *any* w, 4399
16:10 I clothed thee also with **broidered w**, and 7553
16:13 *of* fine linen, and silk, and **broidered w**; 7553
16:30 seeing thou doest all these *things,* the w of 4639
27: 7 Fine linen with **broidered w** from Egypt 7553
27:16 **broidered w**, and fine linen, and coral, and 7553
27:24 **broidered w**, and in chests of rich apparel, 7553
33:26 ye w abomination, and ye defile every one 6213
Da 11:23 after the league *made* with him he shall w 6213
Hos 6: 8 Gilead *is* a city of them that w iniquity, *and* 6466
13: 2 all of it the w of the craftsmen: 4639
14: 3 neither will we say any more to the w of 4639
Mic 2: 1 devise iniquity, and w evil upon their beds! 6466
5:13 thou shalt no more worship the w of thine 4639
Hab 1: 5 for *I will* w a work in your days, *which* ye 6466
1: 5 for *I will* work a w in your days, *which* ye 6467
2:18 that the maker of his w trusteth therein, 3336
3: 2 revive thy w in the midst of the years, 6467
Zep 2:14 for he shall uncover the **cedar w**. 731
Hag 1:14 did w in the house of the LORD of hosts, 4399
2: 4 of the land, saith the LORD, and w: 6213
2:14 so *is* every w of their hands; and *that* which 4639
Mal 3:15 yea, they that w wickedness are set up; yea, 6213
Mt 7:23 depart from me, ye that w iniquity. 2038
21:28 and said, Son, go w to day in my vineyard. 2038
26:10 for she hath wrought a good w upon me. 2041
Mk 6: 5 And he could there do no **mighty w**, 1411
13:34 and to every man his w, and 2041
14: 6 you her? she hath wrought a good w on me. 2041
Lk 13:14 are six days in which *men* ought to w: 2038
Jn 4:34 of him that sent me, and to finish his w. 2041
5:17 My Father worketh hitherto, and I w. 2038
6:28 we do, that we might w the works of God? 2038
6:29 and said unto them, This is the w of God, 2041
6:30 and believe thee? what dost thou w? 2038
Jn 7:21 I have done one w, and ye all marvel. 2041
9: 4 I must w the works of him that sent me, 2038
9: 4 the night cometh, when no *man* can w. 2038
10:33 saying, For a good w we stone thee not; 2041
17: 4 I have finished the w which thou gavest me 2041
Ac 5:38 for if this counsel or this w be of men, 2041
13: 2 Saul for the w whereunto I have called 2041
13:41 for I w a work in your days, a work which 2038
13:41 for I work a w in your days, a work which 2041
13:41 a w which you shall in no wise believe, 2041
14:26 grace of God for the w which they fulfilled. 2041
15:38 and went not with them to the w. 2041
27:16 **had much w** to come by the boat: 2480+3433
Ro 2:15 Which shew the w of the law written in 2041
7: 5 did w in our members to bring forth fruit 1754
8:28 And we know that all *things* **w together** for 4903
9:28 For he will finish the w, and cut *it* short in 3056
9:28 a short w will the Lord make upon 3056
11: 6 more grace: otherwise w is no more work. 2041
11: 6 more grace: otherwise work is no more w. 2041
14:20 For meat destroy not the w of God. 2041
1Co 3:13 Every man's w shall be made manifest: 2041
3:13 the fire shall try every man's w of what sort 2041
3:14 If any *man's* w abide which he hath built 2041
3:15 If any *man's* w shall be burnt, he shall 2041
9: 1 our Lord? are not you my w in the Lord? 2041
15:58 always abounding in the w of the Lord, 2041
16:10 for he worketh the w of the Lord, as I also 2041
2Co 9: 8 in all *things,* may abound to every good w: 2041
Gal 6: 4 But let every man prove his own w, and 2041
Eph 4:12 For the perfecting of the saints for the w of 2041
4:19 to w all uncleanness with greediness. 2039
Php 1: 6 w in you will perform *it* until the day of 2041
2:12 **w out** your own salvation with fear and 2716
2:30 Because for the w of Christ he was nigh 2041
Col 1:10 being fruitful in every good w, and 2041
1Th 1: 3 Remembering without ceasing your w of 2041
4:11 and to w with your own hands, 2038
2Th 1:11 and the w of faith with power: 2041
2: 7 For the mystery of iniquity doth already w: 1754
2:17 and stablish you in every good word and w. 2041
3:10 that if any would not w, neither should he 2038
3:12 that with quietness they w, and eat their 2038
1Ti 3: 1 the office of a bishop, he desireth a good w. 2041
5:10 she have diligently followed every good w. 2041
2Ti 2:21 *and* prepared unto every good w. 2041
4: 5 do the w of an evangelist, make full proof 2041
4:18 Lord shall deliver me from every evil w, 2041
Tit 1:16 and unto every good w reprobate 2041
3: 1 to be ready to every good w, 2041
Heb 6:10 For God *is* not unrighteous to forget your w 2041
13:21 Make you perfect in every good w to do his 2041
Jas 1: 4 But let patience have *her* perfect w, that ye 2041
1:25 but a doer of the w, this *man* shall be 2041
3:16 *is,* there *is* confusion and every evil w. 4229
1Pe 1:17 judgeth according to every man's w, 2041
Rev 22:12 to give every man according as his w shall 2041

WORK'S (1) [WORK]
1Th 5:13 them very highly in love for their w sake. 2041

WORKER (1) [WORK]
1Ki 7:14 his father *was* a man of Tyre, a w in brass: 2790

WORKERS (27) [WORK]
2Ki 23:24 Moreover the *w with* familiar spirits, and NIH
1Ch 22:15 hewers and w of stone and timber, and 2796
Job 31: 3 a strange punishment to the w of iniquity? 6466
34: 8 Which goeth in company with the w of 6466
34:22 where the w of iniquity may hide 6466
Ps 5: 5 in thy sight: thou hatest all w of iniquity. 6466
6: 8 Depart from me, all ye w of iniquity; 6466
14: 4 Have all the w of iniquity no knowledge? 6466
28: 3 with the wicked, and with the w of iniquity, 6466
36:12 There are the w of iniquity fallen: they are 6466
37: 1 neither be thou envious against the w of 6213
53: 4 Have the w of iniquity no knowledge? 6466
59: 2 Deliver me from the w of iniquity, and 6466
64: 2 from the insurrection of the w of iniquity: 6466
92: 7 and when all the w of iniquity do flourish; 6466
92: 9 all the w of iniquity shall be scattered. 6466
94: 4 *and* all the w of iniquity boast themselves? 6466
94:16 who will stand up for me against the w of 6466
125: 5 shall lead them forth with the w of iniquity: 6466
141: 9 for me, and the grins of the w of iniquity. 6466
Pr 10:29 but destruction *shall be* to the w of iniquity. 6466
21:15 but destruction *shall be* to the w of iniquity. 6466
Lk 13:27 depart from me, all *ye* w of iniquity. 2040
1Co 12:29 *are* all teachers? *are* all **w of miracles**? 1411
2Co 6: 1 as **w together** *with him,* beseech *you* also 4903
11:13 For such *are* false apostles, deceitful w, 2040
Php 3: 2 Beware of dogs, beware of evil w, 2040

WORKETH (37) [WORK]
Job 33:29 all these *things* w God oftentimes with 6466
Ps 15: 2 w righteousness, and speaketh the truth in 6466
101: 7 He that w deceit shall not dwell within my 6213
Pr 11:18 The wicked w a deceitful work: but *to* him 6213
26:28 by it; and a flattering mouth w ruin. 6213
31:13 and flax, and w willingly with her hands. 6213
Ecc 3: 9 What profit *hath* he that w in *that* where*in* 6213
Isa 44:12 The smith *with* the tongs both w in 6466
44:12 and w it with the strength of his arms: 6466
64: 5 him that rejoiceth and w righteousness, 6213
Da 6:27 he w signs and wonders in heaven and 5648
Jn 5:17 answered them, My Father w hitherto, 2038
Ac 10:35 and w righteousness, is accepted with him. 2038
Ro 2:10 and peace, to every *man* that w good, 2038
4: 4 Now to him that w is the reward not 2038
4: 5 But to him that w not, but believeth on him 2038
4:15 Because the law w wrath: for where no law 2716
5: 3 knowing that tribulation w patience; 2716
13:10 Love w no ill to *his* neighbour: therefore 2038
1Co 12: 6 but it is the same God which w all in all. 1754
1Co 12:11 But all these w *that* one and the selfsame 1754
16:10 for he w the work of the Lord, as I also *do.* 2038
2Co 4:12 So then death w in us, but life in you. 1754
4:17 w for us a far more exceeding *and* 2716
7:10 For godly sorrow w repentance to salvation 2716
7:10 but the sorrow of the world w death. 2716
Gal 3: 5 you the Spirit, and w miracles among you, 1754
5: 6 but faith which w by love. 1754
Eph 1:11 w all *things* after the counsel of his own 1754
2: 2 the spirit that now w in the children of 1754
3:20 think, according to the power that w in us, 1754
Php 2:13 For it is God which w in you both to will 1754
Col 1:29 to his working, which w in me mightily. 1754
1Th 2:13 which **effectually** w also in you that 1754
Jas 1: 3 that the trying of your faith w patience. 2716
1:20 For the wrath of man w not 2716
Rev 21:27 neither *whatsoever* w abomination, or 4160

WORKFELLOW (1) [FELLOW, WORK]
Ro 16:21 Timotheus my w, and Lucius, and Jason, 4904

WORKING (20) [WORK]
Ps 52: 2 like a sharp rasor, w deceitfully. 6213
74:12 of old, w salvation in the midst of the earth. 6466
Isa 28:29 is wonderful in counsel, *and* excellent in w. 8454
Eze 46: 1 *toward* the east shall be shut the six w days; 4639
Mk 16:20 the Lord **w with** *them,* and confirming 4903
Ro 1:27 men with men w that which is unseemly, 2716
7:13 w death in me by that which is good; 2716
1Co 4:12 And labour, w with our own hands: 2038
9: 6 Barnabas, have not we power to forbear w? 2038
12:10 To another the w of miracles; to another 1755
Eph 1:19 according to the w of his mighty power, 1753
3: 7 unto me by the **effectual** w of his power. 1753
4:16 according to the **effectual** w in the measure 1753
4:28 w with *his* hands the *thing which is* good, 2038
Php 3:21 according to the w whereby he is able even 1753
Col 1:29 I also labour, striving according to his w, 1753
2Th 2: 9 *Even him,* whose coming is after the w of 1753
3:11 w not at all, but are busybodies. 2038
Heb 13:21 w in you *that which is* well pleasing in his 4160
Rev 16:14 they are the spirits of devils, w miracles, 4160

WORKMAN (10) [MAN, WORK]
Ex 35:35 of the **cunning** w, and of the embroiderer, 2803
38:23 a **cunning** w, and an embroiderer in blue, 2803
SS 7: 1 the work of the hands of a **cunning** w. 542
Isa 40:19 The w melteth a graven image, and 2796
40:20 he seeketh unto him a cunning w to prepare 2796
Jer 10: 3 the work of the hands of the w, with 2796
10: 9 the work of the w, and of the hands of 2796
Hos 8: 6 the w made it; therefore it *is* not God: but 2796
Mt 10:10 yet staves: for the w is worthy of his meat. 2040
2Ti 2:15 a w that needeth not to be ashamed, 2040

WORKMANSHIP (7) [MAN, WORK]
Ex 31: 3 and in knowledge, and in all *manner of* w, 4399
31: 5 of timber, to work in all *manner of* w. 4399
35:31 and in knowledge, and in all *manner of* w; 4399
2Ki 16:10 pattern of it, according to all the w thereof. 4639
1Ch 28:21 *there shall be* with thee for all *manner of* w 4399
Eze 28:13 the w of thy tabrets and of thy pipes was 4399
Eph 2:10 For we are his w, created in Christ Jesus 4161

WORKMEN (11) [MAN, WORK]
2Ki 12:14 they gave that to the w, and 4399+6213
12:15 the money to be bestowed on w: 4399+6213
1Ch 22:15 Moreover *there are* w with thee in 4399+6213
25: 1 the number of the w according to their 376+4399
2Ch 24:13 So the w wrought, and 4399+6213+1886.1
34:10 w that had the oversight of 4399+6213+1886.1
34:10 they gave it *to* the w that 4399+6213+1886.1
34:17 and to the hand of the w. 4399+6213+1886.1
Ezr 3: 9 to set forward the w in the house of God: 6213
Isa 44:11 the w, they *are* of men: let them all be 2796
Ac 19:25 Whom he called together with the w of like 2040

WORKMEN'S (1) [MAN, WORK]
Jdg 5:26 and her right hand to the w hammer; 6001

WORKS (236) [WORK]
Ex 5: 4 and Aaron, let the people from their w? 4639
5:13 Fulfil your w, *your* daily tasks, as when 4639
23:24 nor serve them, nor do after their w: 4639
31: 4 To devise **cunning** w, to work in gold, and 4284
35:32 to devise **curious** w, to work in gold, and 4284
Nu 16:28 the LORD hath sent me to do all these w; 4639
Dt 2: 7 hath blessed thee in all the w of thy hand: 4639
3:24 that can do according to thy w, and 4639
15:10 thy God shall bless thee in all thy w, 4639
16:15 in all the w of thine hands, therefore 4639
Jos 24:31 which had known all the w of the LORD, 4639
Jdg 2: 7 who had seen all the great w of 4639
2:10 nor yet the w which he had done for Israel. 4639
1Sa 8: 8 According to all the w which they have 4639
19: 4 his w *have been* to thee-ward very good: 4639
1Ki 7:14 and cunning to work all w in brass. 4399
13:11 told him all the w that the man of God had 4639
2Ki 22:17 me to anger with all the w of their hands; 4639
1Ch 16: 9 unto him, talk you of all his **wondrous** w. 6381
16:12 Remember his **marvellous** w that he hath 6381
16:24 his **marvellous** w among all nations. 6381
28:19 upon me, *even* all the w of *this* pattern. 4399
2Ch 20:37 the LORD hath broken thy w. 4639
32:30 And Hezekiah prospered in all his w. 4639
34:25 me to anger with all the w of their hands; 4639
Ne 6:14 and Sanballat according to these their w, 4639
9:35 neither turned they from their wicked w. 4611
Job 34:25 Therefore he knoweth their w, and 4566
37:14 and consider the **wondrous** w of God. 6381
37:16 the **wondrous** w of *him which is* perfect in 4652
Ps 8: 6 to have dominion over the w of thy hands; 4639
9: 1 I will shew forth all thy **marvellous** w. 6381
14: 1 are corrupt, they have done abominable w, 5949

W

Ps 17: 4 Concerning the **w** of men, by the word of 6468
26: 7 and tell of all thy **wondrous w**. 6381
28: 5 Because they regard not the **w** of 6468
33: 4 *is* right; and all his **w** *are done* in truth. 4639
33:15 their hearts alike; he considereth all their **w**. 4639
40: 5 *are* thy **wonderful w** *which* thou hast done, 6381
46: 8 Come, behold the **w** of the LORD, 4659
66: 3 unto God, How terrible *art thou in* thy **w**! 4639
66: 5 Come and see the **w** of God: *he is* terrible 4659
71:17 hitherto have I declared thy **wondrous w**. 6381
73:28 Lord GOD, that *I* may declare all thy **w**. 4399
75: 1 for *that* thy name *is* near thy **wondrous w** 6381
77:11 I will remember the **w** of the LORD: 4611
78: 4 and his **wonderful w** that he hath done. 6381
78: 7 not forget the **w** of God, but keep his 4611
78:11 forgat his **w**, and his wonders that he had 5949
78:32 and believed not for his **wondrous w**. 6381
86: 8 neither *are there any* **w** like unto thy works. NIH
86: 8 neither *are there any works* like unto thy **w**. 4639
92: 4 I will triumph in the **w** of thy hands. 4639
92: 5 O LORD, how great are thy **w**! *and* 4639
103:22 all his **w** in all places of his dominion: 4639
104:13 the earth is satisfied with the fruit of thy **w**. 4639
104:24 O LORD, how manifold are thy **w**! 4639
104:31 for ever: the LORD shall rejoice in his **w**. 4639
105: 2 unto him: talk ye of all his **wondrous w**. 6381
105: 5 Remember his **marvellous w** that he hath 6381
106:13 They soon forgat his **w**; they waited not for 4639
106:22 **Wondrous w** in the land of Ham, *and* 6381
106:35 among the heathen, and learned their **w**. 4639
106:39 Thus were they defiled with their own **w**, 4639
107: 8 *for* his **wonderful w** to the children of 6381
107:15 *for* his **wonderful w** to the children of 6381
107:21 *for* his **wonderful w** to the children of 6381
107:22 and declare his **w** with rejoicing. 4639
107:24 These see the **w** of the LORD, and 4639
107:31 *for* his **wonderful w** to the children of 6381
111: 2 The **w** of the LORD *are* great, sought out 4639
111: 4 He hath made his **wonderful w** to be 6381
111: 6 hath shewed his people the power of his **w**, 4639
111: 7 The **w** of his hands *are* verity and 4639
118:17 but live, and declare the **w** of the LORD. 4639
119:27 so shall I talk of thy **wondrous w**. 6381
138: 8 forsake not the **w** of thine own hands. 4639
139:14 marvellous *are* thy **w**; and *that* my soul 4639
141: 4 to practise wicked **w** with men that work 5949
143: 5 the days of old; I meditate on all thy **w**; 6467
145: 4 One generation shall praise thy **w** to 4639
145: 5 of thy majesty, and of thy wondrous **w**. 1697
145: 9 and his tender mercies *are* over all his **w**. 4639
145:10 All thy **w** shall praise thee, O LORD; and 4639
145:17 in all his ways, and holy in all his **w**. 4639
Pr 7:16 *with* carved **w**, *with* fine linen of Egypt. NIH
8:22 beginning of his way, before his **w** of old. 4659
16: 3 Commit thy **w** unto the LORD, and 4639
24:12 he render to *every* man according to his **w**? 6467
31:31 and let her own **w** praise her in the gates. 4639
Ecc 1:14 I have seen all the **w** that are done under 4639
2: 4 I made me great **w**; I builded me houses; 4639
2:11 I looked on all the **w** that my hands had 4639
3:22 that a man should rejoice in his own **w**; 4639
9: 1 the righteous, and the wise, and their **w**, 5652
9: 7 merry heart; for God now accepteth thy **w**. 4639
11: 5 thou knowest not the **w** of God who maketh 4639
Isa 26:12 for thou also hast wrought all our **w** in us. 4639
29:15 their **w** are in the dark, and they say, 4639
41:29 they *are* all vanity; their **w** *are* nothing: 4639
57:12 I will declare thy righteousness, and thy **w**; 4639
59: 6 shall they cover themselves with their **w**: 4639
59: 6 their **w** *are* works of iniquity, and the act of 4639
59: 6 their works *are* **w** of iniquity, and the act of 4639
66:18 For I *know* their **w** and their thoughts: 4639
Jer 1:16 and worshipped the **w** of their own hands. 4639
7:13 because ye have done all these **w**, 4639
21: 2 with us according to all his **wondrous w**, 6381
25: 6 provoke me not to anger with the **w** of your 4639
25: 7 with the **w** of your hands to your own hurt. 4639
25:14 and according to the **w** of their own hands. 4639
44: 8 me unto wrath with the **w** of your hands, 4639
48: 7 For because thou hast trusted in thy **w** and 4639
Eze 6: 6 be cut down, and your **w** may be abolished. 4639
Da 4:37 all whose **w** *are* truth, and his ways 4567
9:14 *is* righteous in all his **w** which he doeth: 4639
Am 8: 7 Surely I will never forget any of their **w**. 4639
Jnh 3:10 God saw their **w**, that they turned from 4639
Mic 6:16 all the **w** of the house of Ahab, and ye walk 4639
Mt 5:16 that they may see your good **w**, and *2041*
7:22 and in thy name done many **wonderful w**? *1411*
11: 2 had heard in the prison the **w** of Christ, *2041*
11:20 wherein most of his **mighty w** were done, *1411*
11:21 for if the **mighty w** which were done in *1411*
11:23 for if the **mighty w**, which have been done *1411*
13:54 this *man* this wisdom, and *these* **mighty w**? *1411*
13:58 And he did not many **mighty w** there, *1411*
14: 2 **mighty w** do shew forth themselves in him. *1411*
16:27 shall reward every man according to his **w**. *4234*
23: 3 and do; but do not ye after their **w**: *2041*
23: 5 But all their **w** they do for to be seen of *2041*
Mk 6: 2 that even such **mighty w** are wrought by *1411*
6:14 **mighty w** do shew forth themselves in him. *1411*
Lk 10:13 for if the **mighty w** had been done in Tyre *1411*
19:37 for all the **mighty w** that they had seen; *1411*
Jn 5:20 and he will shew him greater **w** than these, *2041*
5:36 for the **w** which the Father hath given me to *2041*
5:36 the same **w** that I do, bear witness of me, *2041*
6:28 we do, that we might work the **w** of God? *2041*
7: 3 that thy disciples also may see the **w** that *2041*
7: 7 I testify of it, that the **w** thereof are evil. *2041*
8:39 ye would do the **w** of Abraham. *2041*
9: 3 that the **w** of God should be made manifest *2041*
9: 4 I must work the **w** of him that sent me, *2041*
10:25 the **w** that I do in my Father's name, *2041*
10:32 Many good **w** have I shewed you from my *2041*
10:32 for which of those **w** do ye stone me? *2041*
10:37 If I do not the **w** of my Father, believe me *2041*
Jn 10:38 though ye believe not me, believe the **w**: *2041*
14:10 Father that dwelleth in me, he doeth the **w**. *2041*
14:12 on me, the **w** that I do shall he do also; *2041*
14:12 and greater **w** than these shall he do; NIG
15:24 If I had not done among them the **w** which *2041*
Ac 2:11 in our tongues the **wonderful w** of God. *3167*
7:41 and rejoiced in the **w** of their own hands. *2041*
9:36 this *woman* was full of good **w** and *2041*
15:18 Known unto God are all his **w** from *2041*
26:20 turn to God, and do **w** meet for repentance. *2041*
Ro 3:27 of **w**? Nay: but by the law of faith. *2041*
4: 2 For if Abraham were justified by **w**, he hath *2041*
4: 6 God imputeth righteousness without **w**, *2041*
9:11 not of **w**, but of him that calleth;) *2041*
9:32 by faith, but as *it were* by the **w** of the law. *2041*
11: 6 And if by grace, *then is it* no more of **w**: *2041*
11: 6 But if *it be* of **w**, *then* is it no more grace: *2041*
13: 3 For rulers are not a terror to good **w**, but *2041*
13:12 let us therefore cast off the **w** of darkness, *2041*
2Co 11:15 whose end shall be according to their **w**. *2041*
Gal 2:16 a man is not justified by the **w** of the law, *2041*
2:16 faith of Christ, and not by the **w** of the law: *2041*
2:16 for by the **w** of the law shall no flesh be *2041*
3: 2 Received ye the Spirit by the **w** of the law, *2041*
3: 5 *doeth he it* by the **w** of the law, or by *2041*
3:10 For as many as are of the **w** of the law are *2041*
5:19 Now the **w** of the flesh are manifest, *2041*
Eph 2: 9 Not of **w**, lest any *man* should boast. *2041*
2:10 created in Christ Jesus unto good **w**, *2041*
5:11 with the unfruitful **w** of darkness, *2041*
Col 1:21 and enemies in *your* mind by wicked **w**, *2041*
1Ti 2:10 women professing godliness) with good **w**. *2041*
5:10 Well reported of for good **w**; if she have *2041*
5:25 Likewise also the good **w** *of some* are *2041*
6:18 that *they* be rich in good **w**, ready to *2041*
2Ti 1: 9 not according to our **w**, but according to his *2041*
3:17 throughly furnished unto all good **w**. *2041*
4:14 the Lord reward him according to his **w**: *2041*
Tit 1:16 but in **w** they deny *him*, being abominable, *2041*
2: 7 *things* shewing thyself a pattern of good **w**: *2041*
2:14 a peculiar people, zealous of good **w**. *2041*
3: 5 Not by **w** of righteousness which we have *2041*
3: 8 God might be careful to maintain good **w**. *2041*
3:14 And let ours also learn to maintain good **w** *2041*
Heb 1:10 and the heavens are the **w** of thine hands: *2041*
2: 7 and didst set him over the **w** of thy hands: *2041*
3: 9 proved me, and saw my **w** forty years. *2041*
4: 3 although the **w** were finished from *2041*
4: 4 God did rest the seventh day from all his **w**. *2041*
4:10 he also hath ceased from his own **w**, as God *2041*
6: 1 the foundation of repentance from dead **w**, *2041*
9:14 purge your conscience from dead **w** to *2041*
10:24 to provoke unto love and to good **w**: *2041*
Jas 2:14 a man say *he* hath faith, and have not **w**? *2041*
2:17 Even so faith, if it hath not **w**, is dead, *2041*
2:18 may say, Thou hast faith, and I have **w**: *2041*
2:18 shew me thy faith without thy **w**, and I will *2041*
2:18 and I will shew thee my faith by my **w**. *2041*
2:20 O vain man, that faith without **w** is dead? *2041*
2:21 Was not Abraham our father justified by **w**, *2041*
2:22 Seest thou how faith wrought with his **w**, *2041*
2:22 and by **w** was faith made perfect? *2041*
2:24 then how that by **w** a man is justified, *2041*
2:25 was not Rahab the harlot justified by **w**, *2041*
2:26 is dead, so faith without **w** is dead also. *2041*
3:13 his **w** with meekness of wisdom. *2041*
1Pe 2:12 they may by *your* good **w**, *which* they shall *2041*
2Pe 3:10 and the **w** that are therein shall be burnt up. *2041*
1Jn 3: 8 that he might destroy the **w** of the devil. *2041*
3:12 Because his own **w** were evil, and his *2041*
Rev 2: 2 I know thy **w**, and thy labour, and *2041*
2: 5 art fallen, and repent, and do the first **w**; *2041*
2: 9 I know thy **w**, *2041*
2:13 I know thy **w**, and where thou dwellest, *2041*
2:19 I know thy **w**, and charity, and service, *2041*
2:19 and faith, and thy patience, and thy **w**; *2041*
2:23 unto every one of you according to your **w**. *2041*
2:26 and keepeth my **w** unto the end, *2041*
3: 1 I know thy **w**, that thou hast a name that *2041*
3: 2 for I have not found thy **w** perfect before *2041*
3: 8 I know thy **w**: behold, I have set before *2041*
3:15 I know thy **w**, that thou art neither cold nor *2041*
9:20 *yet* repented not of the **w** of their hands, *2041*
14:13 their labours; and their **w** do follow them. *2041*
15: 3 saying, Great and marvellous *are* thy **w**, *2041*
18: 6 double unto her double according to her **w**: *2041*
20:12 written in the books, according to their **w**. *2041*
20:13 judged every man according to their **w**. *2041*

WORKS' (1) [WORK]

Jn 14:11 or else believe me for the very **w** sake. *2041*

WORLD (287) [WORLD'S, WORLDLY, WORLDS]

1Sa 2: 8 and he hath set the **w** upon them. 8398
2Sa 22:16 the foundations of the **w** were discovered, 8398
1Ch 16:30 the **w** also shall be stable, that it be not 8398
Job 18:18 into darkness, and chased out of the **w**. 8398
34:13 or who hath disposed the whole **w**? 8398
37:12 them upon the face of the **w** in the earth. 8398
Ps 9: 8 he shall judge the **w** in righteousness, 8398
17:14 thy hand, O LORD, from men of the **w**, 2465
18:15 the foundations of the **w** were discovered at 8398
19: 4 and their words to the end of the **w**. 8398
22:27 All the ends of the **w** shall remember and 776
24: 1 the **w**, and they that dwell therein. 8398
33: 8 let all the inhabitants of the **w** stand in awe 8398
49: 1 give ear, all ye inhabitants of the **w**: 2465
50:12 for the **w** *is* mine, and the fulness thereof. 8398
73:12 *are* the ungodly, who prosper in the **w**; 5769
77:18 the lightnings lightened the **w**: the earth 8398
89:11 *as for* the **w** and the fulness thereof, 8398
90: 2 ever thou hadst formed the earth and the **w**, 8398
93: 1 the **w** also is stablished, *that* it cannot be 8398
96:10 the **w** also shall be established *that* it shall 8398
96:13 he shall judge the **w** with righteousness, 8398
Ps 97: 4 His lightnings enlightened the **w**: the earth 8398
98: 7 the **w**, and they that dwell therein. 8398
98: 9 with righteousness shall he judge the **w**, 8398
Pr 8:26 nor the highest part of the dust of the **w**. 8398
Ecc 3:11 also he hath set the **w** in their heart, so that 5769
Isa 13:11 I will punish the **w** for *their* evil, and 8398
14:17 *That* made the **w** as a wilderness, and 8398
14:21 nor fill the face of the **w** *with* cities. 8398
18: 3 All ye inhabitants of the **w**, and dwellers on 8398
23:17 of the **w** upon the face of the earth. 776
24: 4 the **w** languisheth *and* fadeth away, 8398
26: 9 the inhabitants of the **w** will learn 8398
26:18 neither have the inhabitants of the **w** fallen. 8398
27: 6 bud, and fill the face of the **w** *with* fruit. 8398
34: 1 the **w**, and all things that come forth of it. 8398
38:11 man no more with the inhabitants of the **w**. 2309
45:17 confounded **w without end.** 5703+5704+5769
62:11 hath proclaimed unto the end of the **w**, 776
64: 4 For **since the beginning of the w** 4480+5769
Jer 10:12 he hath established the **w** by his wisdom, 8398
25:26 with another, and all the kingdoms of the **w**, 776
51:15 he hath established the **w** by his wisdom, 8398
La 4:12 the earth, and all the inhabitants of the **w**, 8398
Na 1: 5 yea, the **w**, and all that dwell therein. 8398
Mt 4: 8 and sheweth him all the kingdoms of the **w**, *2889*
5:14 Ye are the light of the **w**. A city that is set *2889*
12:32 it shall not be forgiven him, neither in this **w**, *165*
12:32 in this world, neither in the **w** to come. NIG
13:22 and the care of this **w**, and the deceitfulness *165*
13:35 kept secret from the foundation of the **w**. *2889*
13:38 The field is the **w**; the good seed are *2889*
13:39 the harvest is the end of the **w**; and *165*
13:40 in the fire; so shall it be in the end of this **w**. *165*
13:49 So shall it be at the end of the **w**: the angels *165*
16:26 if he shall gain the whole **w**, and lose his *2889*
18: 7 Woe unto the **w** because of offences: for it *2889*
24: 3 sign of thy coming, and of the end of the **w**? *165*
24:14 in all the **w** for a witness unto all nations; *3625*
24:21 as was not since the beginning of the **w** *2889*
25:34 for you from the foundation of the **w**: *2889*
26:13 gospel shall be preached in the whole **w**, *2889*
28:20 with you alway, *even* unto the end of the **w**. *165*
Mk 4:19 And the cares of this **w**, and *165*
8:36 if he shall gain the whole **w**, and lose his *2889*
10:30 and in the **w** to come eternal life. *165*
14: 9 shall be preached throughout the whole **w**, *2889*
16:15 Go ye into all the **w**, and preach the gospel *2889*
Lk 1:70 which have been since the **w** began:) *165*
2: 1 that all the **w** should be taxed. *3625*
4: 5 shewed unto him all the kingdoms of the **w** *3625*
9:25 if he gain the whole **w**, and lose himself, or *2889*
11:50 was shed from the foundation of the **w**, *2889*
12:30 For all these *things* do the nations of the **w** *2889*
16: 8 for the children of this **w** are in their *165*
18:30 and in the **w** to come life everlasting. *165*
20:34 The children of this **w** marry, and are given *165*
20:35 shall be accounted worthy to obtain that **w**, *165*
Jn 1: 9 lighteth every man *that* cometh into the **w**. *2889*
1:10 He was in the **w**, and the world was made *2889*
1:10 and the **w** was made by him, and the world *2889*
1:10 was made by him, and the **w** knew him not. *2889*
1:29 of God, which taketh away the sin of the **w**. *2889*
3:16 For God so loved the **w**, that he gave his *2889*
3:17 For God sent not his Son into the **w** to *2889*
3:17 his Son into the world to condemn the **w**; *2889*
3:17 but that the **w** through him might be saved. *2889*
3:19 that light is come into the **w**, and men loved *2889*
4:42 is indeed the Christ, the Saviour of the **w**. *2889*
6:14 *that* prophet that should come into the **w**. *2889*
6:33 from heaven, and giveth life unto the **w**. *2889*
6:51 which I will give for the life of the **w**. *2889*
7: 4 thou do these *things*, shew thyself to the **w**. *2889*
7: 7 The **w** cannot hate you; but me it hateth, *2889*
8:12 unto them, saying, I am the light of the **w**: *2889*
8:23 ye are of this **w**; I am not of this world. *2889*
8:23 ye are of this world; I am not of this **w**. *2889*
8:26 I speak to the **w** those *things* which I have *2889*
9: 5 As long as I am in the **w**, I am the light of *2889*
9: 5 I am in the world, I am the light of the **w**. *2889*
9:32 Since the **w** began was it not heard that any *165*
9:39 For judgment I am come into this **w**, *2889*
10:36 and sent into the **w**, Thou blasphemest; *2889*
11: 9 because he seeth the light of this **w**. *2889*
11:27 Son of God, which should come into the **w**. *2889*
12:19 behold, the **w** is gone after him. *2889*
12:25 he that hateth his life in this **w** shall keep it *2889*
12:31 Now is the judgment of this **w**: now shall *2889*
12:31 now shall the prince of this **w** be cast out. *2889*
12:46 I am come a light into the **w**, *2889*
12:47 for I came not to judge the **w**, but to save *2889*
12:47 not to judge the world, but to save the **w**. *2889*
13: 1 should depart out of this **w** unto the Father, *2889*
13: 1 having loved his own which were in the **w**, *2889*
14:17 whom the **w** cannot receive, because *2889*
14:19 a little while, and the **w** seeth me no more; *2889*
14:22 thyself unto us, and not unto the **w**? *2889*
14:27 not as the **w** giveth, give I unto you. Let not *2889*
14:30 for the prince of this **w** cometh, and *2889*
14:31 But that the **w** may know that I love *2889*
15:18 If the **w** hate you, ye know that it hated me *2889*
15:19 If ye were of the **w**, the world would love *2889*
15:19 of the world, the **w** would love his own: *2889*
15:19 but because ye are not of the **w**, but I have *2889*
15:19 but I have chosen you out of the **w**, *2889*
15:19 of the world, therefore the **w** hateth you. *2889*
16: 8 he will reprove the **w** of sin, and *2889*
16:11 because the prince of this **w** is judged. *2889*
16:20 and lament, but the **w** shall rejoice: *2889*
16:21 for joy that a man is born into the **w**. *2889*
16:28 from the Father, and am come into the **w**: *2889*
16:28 again, I leave the **w**, and go to the Father. *2889*
16:33 In the **w** ye shall have tribulation: but be of *2889*
16:33 be of good cheer; I have overcome the **w**. *2889*
17: 5 which I had with thee before the **w** was. *2889*
17: 6 the men which thou gavest me out of the **w**: *2889*

W

Jn 17: 9 I pray not for the **w**, but for *them* which 2889
17:11 And *now* I am no more in the **w**, but 2889
17:11 but these are in the **w**, and I come to thee. 2889
17:12 While I was with them in the **w**, I kept 2889
17:13 and these *things* I speak in the **w**, that they 2889
17:14 and the **w** hath hated them, because 2889
17:14 hated them, because they are not of the **w**, 2889
17:14 not of the world, even as I am not of the **w**. 2889
17:15 that thou shouldest take them out of the **w**, 2889
17:16 They are not of the **w**, even as I am not of 2889
17:16 not of the world, even as I am not of the **w**. 2889
17:18 As thou hast sent me into the **w**, even *so* 2889
17:18 even *so* have I also sent them into the **w**. 2889
17:21 that the **w** may believe that thou hast sent 2889
17:23 that the **w** may know that thou hast sent 2889
17:24 lovedst me before the foundation of the **w**. 2889
17:25 the **w** hath not known thee: 2889
18:20 answered him, I spake openly to the **w**; 2889
18:36 My kingdom is not of this **w**: 2889
18:36 this world: if my kingdom were of this **w**, 2889
18:37 I born, and for this cause came I into the **w**, 2889
21:25 I suppose that even the **w** itself could not 2889
Ac 3:21 of all his holy prophets since the **w** began. *165*
11:28 should be great dearth throughout all the **w**: *3625*
15:18 all his works from the beginning of the **w**. *165*
17: 6 These that have turned the **w** upside down *3625*
17:24 God that made the **w** and all *things* therein, 2889
17:31 in the which he will judge the **w** in *3625*
19:27 whom all Asia and the **w** worshippeth. *3625*
24: 5 among all the Jews throughout the **w**, *3625*
Ro 1: 8 faith is spoken of throughout the whole **w**. 2889
1:20 from the creation of the **w** are clearly seen, 2889
3: 6 for then how shall God judge the **w**? 2889
3:19 all the **w** may become guilty before God. 2889
4:13 that he should be the heir of the **w**, 2889
5:12 as by one man sin entered into the **w**, and 2889
5:13 For until the law sin was in the **w**: but sin is 2889
10:18 and their words unto the ends of the **w**. *3625*
11:12 if the fall of them *be* the riches of the **w**, 2889
11:15 away of them *be* the reconciling of the **w**, 2889
12: 2 And be not conformed to this **w**: but be ye *165*
16:25 was kept secret **since** the **w began**, *166+5550*
1Co 1:20 where *is* the disputer of this **w**? hath not God *165*
1:20 God made foolish the wisdom of this **w**? 2889
1:21 For after that in the wisdom of God the **w** 2889
1:27 *things* of the **w** to confound the wise; 2889
1:27 God hath chosen the weak *things* of the **w** 2889
1:28 And base *things* of the **w**, and *things* which 2889
2: 6 yet not the wisdom of this **w**, nor of *165*
2: 6 nor of the princes of this **w**, that come to *165*
2: 7 God ordained before the **w** unto our glory: *165*
2: 8 Which none of the princes of this **w** knew: *165*
2:12 not the spirit of the **w**, but the Spirit which 2889
3:18 among you seemeth to be wise in this **w**, *165*
3:19 For the wisdom of this **w** is foolishness 2889
3:22 or the **w**, or life, or death, or *things* present, 2889
4: 9 for we are made a spectacle unto the **w**, and 2889
4:13 we are made as the filth of the **w**, *and* 2889
5:10 altogether with the fornicators of this **w**, 2889
5:10 for then must ye needs go out of the **w**. 2889
6: 2 not know that the saints shall judge the **w**? 2889
6: 2 and if the **w** shall be judged by you, are ye 2889
7:31 And they that use this **w**, as not abusing *it*: 2889
7:31 as not abusing *it*: for the fashion of this **w** 2889
7:33 careth for the *things that are* of the **w**, 2889
7:34 is married careth for the *things* of the **w**, 2889
8: 4 we know that an idol *is* nothing in the **w**, 2889
8:13 I will eat no flesh while the **w** standeth, lest I *165*
10:11 upon whom the ends of the **w** are come. *165*
11:32 we should not be condemned with the **w**. 2889
14:10 so many kinds of voices in the **w**, and 2889
2Co 1:12 we have had our conversation in the **w**, and 2889
4: 4 In whom the god of this **w** hath blinded *165*
5:19 that God was in Christ reconciling the **w** 2889
7:10 but the sorrow of the **w** worketh death. 2889
Gal 1: 4 he might deliver us from *this* present evil **w**, *165*
4: 3 in bondage under the elements of the **w**: 2889
6:14 by whom the **w** is crucified unto me, and I 2889
6:14 is crucified unto me, and I unto the **w**. 2889
Eph 1: 4 us in him before the foundation of the **w**, 2889
1:21 not only in this **w**, but also in that which is to *165*
2: 2 walked according to the course of this **w**, *165*
2:12 having no hope, and without God in the **w**: 2889
3: 9 which from the **beginning of the w** hath *165*
3:21 all ages, **w without end**. *165+165+3588+3588*
6:12 against the rulers of the darkness of this **w**, *165*
Php 2:15 among whom ye shine as lights in the **w**; 2889
Col 1: 6 is come unto you, as *it is* in all the **w**; 2889
2: 8 after the rudiments of the **w**, and not after 2889
2:20 with Christ from the rudiments of the **w**, 2889
2:20 why, as though living in the **w**, are ye 2889
1Ti 1:15 that Christ Jesus came into the **w** to save 2889
3:16 believed on in the **w**, received up into 2889
6: 7 For we brought nothing into *this* **w**, *and* 2889
6:17 Charge *them that are* rich in this **w**, that *they* *165*
2Ti 1: 9 us in Christ Jesus before the **w began**, *166+5550*
4:10 having loved *this* present **w**, and is departed *165*
Tit 1: 2 promised before the **w began**; *166+5550*
2:12 and godly, in *this* present **w**; *165*
Heb 1: 6 he bringeth in the firstbegotten into the **w**, *3625*
2: 5 hath he not put in subjection the **w** to come, *3625*
4: 3 were finished from the foundation of the **w**. 2889
6: 5 of God, and the powers of the **w** to come, *165*
9:26 have suffered since the foundation of the **w**: 2889
9:26 now once in the end of the **w** hath he *165*
10: 5 Wherefore when he cometh into the **w**, 2889
11: 7 by the which he condemned the **w**, and 2889
11:38 (Of whom the **w** was not worthy:) 2889
Jas 1:27 *and* to keep himself unspotted from the **w**. 2889
2: 5 Hath not God chosen the poor of this **w** rich 2889
3: 6 And the tongue *is* a fire, a **w** of iniquity: so 2889
4: 4 know ye not that the friendship of the **w** is 2889
4: 4 will be a friend of the **w** is the enemy of 2889
1Pe 1:20 before the foundation of the **w**, 2889
5: 9 in your brethren that are in the **w**. 2889

2Pe 1: 4 the corruption that is in the **w** through lust: 2889
2: 5 And spared not the old **w**, but saved Noah 2889
2: 5 bringing in the flood upon the **w** of 2889
2:20 of the **w** through the knowledge of the Lord 2889
3: 6 Whereby the **w** that then was, 2889
1Jn 2: 2 but also for *the sins of* the whole **w**. 2889
2:15 Love not the **w**, neither the *things* that are 2889
2:15 neither the *things that are* in the **w**. 2889
2:15 If any *man* love the **w**, the love of 2889
2:16 For all that is in the **w**, the lust of the flesh, 2889
2:16 of life, is not of the Father, but is of the **w**. 2889
2:17 And the **w** passeth away, and the lust 2889
3: 1 therefore the **w** knoweth us not, because 2889
3:13 Marvel not, my brethren, if the **w** hate you. 2889
4: 1 false prophets are gone out into the **w**. 2889
4: 3 and *even* now already is it in the **w**. 2889
4: 4 is he that is in you, than he that is in the **w**. 2889
4: 5 They are of the **w**, therefore speak they of 2889
4: 5 therefore speak they of the **w**, and 2889
4: 5 they of the world, and the **w** heareth them. 2889
4: 9 God sent his only begotten Son into the **w**, 2889
4:14 sent the Son *to be* the Saviour of the **w**. 2889
4:17 because as he is, so are we in this **w**. 2889
5: 4 is born of God overcometh the **w**: 2889
5: 4 this is the victory that overcometh the **w**, 2889
5: 5 Who is he that overcometh the **w**, but he 2889
5:19 and the whole **w** lieth in wickedness. 2889
2Jn 1: 7 For many deceivers are entered into the **w**, 2889
Rev 3:10 which shall come upon all the **w**, to try *3625*
11:15 The kingdoms of *this* **w** are become 2889
12: 9 and Satan, which deceiveth the whole **w**: *3625*
13: 3 and all the **w** wondered after the beast. *1093*
13: 8 Lamb slain from the foundation of the **w**. 2889
16:14 the kings of the earth and of the whole **w**, *3625*
17: 8 book of life from the foundation of the **w**, 2889

WORLD'S (1) [WORLD]

1Jn 3:17 But whoso hath *this* **w** good, and seeth his 2889

WORLDLY (2) [WORLD]

Tit 2:12 and **w** lusts we should live soberly, 2886
Heb 9: 1 of divine service, and a **w** sanctuary. 2886

WORLDS (2) [WORLD]

Heb 1: 2 of all *things*, by whom also he made the **w**; *165*
11: 3 Through faith we understand that the **w** were *165*

WORM (14) [CANKERWORM, PALMERWORM, WORMS, WORMWOOD]

Ex 16:24 not stink, neither was there any **w** therein. 7415
Job 17:14 to the **w**, *Thou art* my mother, and 7415
24:20 the **w** shall feed sweetly on him; 7415
25: 6 How much less man, *that is* a **w**? and 7415
25: 6 a worm? and the son of man, *which is* a **w**? 8438
Ps 22: 6 I *am* a **w**, and no man; a reproach of men, 8438
Isa 14:11 the **w** is spread under thee, and the worms 7415
41:14 thou **w** Jacob, *and* ye men of Israel; 8438
51: 8 and the **w** shall eat them like wool: 5580
66:24 for their **w** shall not die, neither shall their 8438
Jnh 4: 7 God prepared a **w** when the morning rose 8438
Mk 9:44 Where their **w** dieth not, and the fire is not *4663*
9:46 Where their **w** dieth not, and the fire is not *4663*
9:48 Where their **w** dieth not, and the fire is not *4663*

WORMS (8) [WORM]

Ex 16:20 until the morning, and it bred **w**, and stank: 8438
Dt 28:39 nor gather *the grapes*; for the **w** shall eat 8438
Job 7: 5 My flesh is clothed with **w** and clods of 7415
19:26 *though* after my skin **w** destroy this *body*, NIH
21:26 in the dust, and the **w** shall cover them. 7415
Isa 14:11 is spread under thee, and the **w** cover thee. 8438
Mic 7:17 they shall move out of their holes like **w** of 2119
Ac 12:23 and he was **eaten of w**, and gave up *4662*

WORMWOOD (9) [WOOD, WORM]

Dt 29:18 among you a root that beareth gall and **w**; 3939
Pr 5: 4 her end is bitter as **w**, sharp as a twoedged 3939
Jer 9:15 with **w**, and give them water of gall to 3939
23:15 I will feed them with **w**, and make them 3939
La 3:15 he hath made me drunken *with* **w**. 3939
3:19 and my misery, the **w** and the gall. 3939
Am 5: 7 *Ye* who turn judgment to **w**, and leave off 3939
Rev 8:11 And the name of the star is called **W**: and *894*
8:11 and the third *part* of the waters became **w**; *894*

WORSE (26) [BAD]

Ge 19: 9 now will we **deal w** with thee, than with 7489
2Sa 19: 7 that *will be* **w** unto thee than all the evil 7489
1Ki 16:25 and did **w** than all that *were* before him. 7489
2Ki 14:12 Judah was **put to the w** before Israel; and 5062
1Ch 19:16 that they were **put to the w** before Israel, 5062
19:19 that they were **put to the w** before Israel, 5062
2Ch 6:24 if thy people Israel be **put to the w** before 5062
25:22 Judah was **put to the w** before Israel, and 5062
33: 9 to err, *and* to do **w** than the heathen, 7451
Jer 7:26 their neck: they **did w** than their fathers. 7489
16:12 ye have done **w** than your fathers; 7489
Da 1:10 for why should he see your faces **w liking** 2196
Mt 9:16 from the garment, and the rent is made **w**. *5501*
12:45 the last *state* of that man is **w than** the first. *5501*
27:64 so the last error shall be **w than** the first. *5501*
Mk 2:21 away *from* the old, and the rent is made **w**. *5501*
5:26 was nothing bettered, but rather grew **w**, *5501*
Lk 11:26 the last *state* of that man is **w than** the first. *5501*
Jn 2:10 *men* have well drunk, then that which is **w**: *1640*
5:14 sin no more, lest a **w** *thing* come unto thee. *5501*
1Co 8: 8 neither, if we eat not, are we the **w**. *5302*
11:17 together not for the better, but for the **w**. *2276*
1Ti 5: 8 denied the faith, and is **w than** an infidel. *5501*
2Ti 3:13 shall wax **w and worse**, *1909+3588+5501*
3:13 shall wax **worse and w**, *1909+3588+5501*
2Pe 2:20 the latter *end* is **w** with them **than** *5501*

WORSHIP (108) [WORSHIPPED, WORSHIPPER, WORSHIPPERS, WORSHIPPETH, WORSHIPPING]

Ge 22: 5 I and the lad will go yonder and **w**, and 7812
Ex 24: 1 of the elders of Israel; and **w** ye afar off. 7812
34:14 For thou shalt **w** no other god: for 7812
Dt 4:19 shouldest be driven to **w** them, and 7812
8:19 other gods, and serve them, and **w** them, 7812
11:16 and serve other gods, and **w** them; 7812
26:10 and **w** before the LORD thy God: 7812
30:17 and **w** other gods, and serve them; 7812
Jos 5:14 did **w**, and said unto him, What saith my 7812
1Sa 1: 3 this man went up out of his city yearly to **w** 7812
15:25 again with me, that I may **w** the LORD. 7812
15:30 with me, that I may **w** the LORD thy God. 7812
1Ki 9: 6 but go and serve other gods, and **w** them: 7812
12:30 for the people went *to* **w** before the one, NIH
2Ki 5:18 goeth *into* the house of Rimmon to **w** there, 7812
17:36 him shall ye **w**, and to him shall ye do 7812
18:22 Ye shall **w** before this altar in Jerusalem? 7812
1Ch 16:29 **w** the LORD in the beauty of holiness. 7812
2Ch 7:19 shall go and serve other gods, and **w** them; 7812
32:12 Ye shall **w** before one altar, and 7812
Ps 5: 7 in thy fear will I **w** toward thy holy temple. 7812
22:27 all the kindreds of the nations shall **w** 7812
22:29 *they that be* fat upon earth shall eat and **w**: 7812
29: 2 **w** the LORD in the beauty of holiness. 7812
45:11 for he *is* thy Lord; and **w** thou him. 7812
66: 4 All the earth shall **w** thee, and shall sing 7812
81: 9 neither shalt thou **w** *any* strange god. 7812
86: 9 hast made shall come and **w** before thee, 7812
95: 6 O come, let us **w** and bow down: let us 7812
96: 9 O **w** the LORD in the beauty of holiness: 7812
97: 7 themselves of idols: **w** him, all ye gods. 7812
99: 5 LORD our God, and **w** at his footstool; 7812
99: 9 the LORD our God, and **w** at his holy hill; 7812
132: 7 his tabernacles: we will **w** at his footstool. 7812
138: 2 I will **w** toward thy holy temple, and 7812
Isa 2: 8 they **w** the work of their own hands, 7812
2:20 which they made *each one* for himself to **w**, 7812
27:13 shall **w** the LORD in the holy mount at 7812
36: 7 to Jerusalem, Ye shall **w** before this altar? 7812
46: 6 it a god: they fall down, yea, they **w**. 7812
49: 7 shall see and arise, princes also shall **w**, 7812
66:23 shall all flesh come to **w** before me, 7812
Jer 7: 2 that enter in at these gates to **w** the LORD. 7812
13:10 other gods, to serve them, and to **w** them, 7812
25: 6 to **w** them, and provoke me not to anger 7812
26: 2 which come to **w** *in* the LORD'S house, 7812
44:19 did we make her cakes to **w** her, and 6087
Eze 46: 2 and he shall **w** at the threshold of the gate: 7812
46: 3 Likewise the people of the land shall **w** *at* 7812
46: 9 **w** shall go out *by* the way of the south gate; 7812
Da 3: 5 **w** the golden image that Nebuchadnezzar 5457
3:10 shall fall down and **w** the golden image: 5457
3:12 nor **w** the golden image which thou hast set 5457
3:14 nor **w** the golden image which I have set 5457
3:15 and **w** the image which I have made; 5457
3:15 *well*: but if ye **w** not, ye shall be cast 5457
3:18 nor **w** the golden image which thou hast set 5457
3:28 that they might not serve nor **w** any god, 5457
Mic 5:13 thou shalt no more **w** the work of thine 7812
Zep 1: 5 them that **w** the host of heaven upon 7812
1: 5 them that **w** *and* that swear by the LORD, 7812
2:11 *men* shall **w** him, every one from his place, 7812
Zec 14:16 even go up from year to year to **w** the King, 7812
14:17 of the earth unto Jerusalem to **w** the King, 7812
Mt 2: 2 his star in the east, and are come to **w** him. *4352*
2: 8 that I may come and **w** him also. *4352*
4: 9 give thee, if thou wilt fall down and **w** me. *4352*
4:10 Thou shalt **w** the Lord thy God, and *4352*
15: 9 But in vain they do **w** me, teaching for *4576*
Mk 7: 7 Howbeit in vain do they **w** me, teaching for *4576*
Lk 4: 7 If thou therefore wilt **w** me, all shall be *4352*
4: 8 Thou shalt **w** the Lord thy God, and *4352*
14:10 shalt thou have **w** in the presence of them *1391*
Jn 4:20 is the place where *men* ought to **w**. *4352*
4:21 nor *yet* at Jerusalem, **w** the Father. *4352*
4:22 Ye **w** ye know not what: we know what we *4352*
4:22 we know what we **w**: for salvation is of *4352*
4:23 when the true worshippers shall **w** *4352*
4:23 for the Father seeketh such to **w** him. *4352*
4:24 they that **w** him must worship *him* in spirit *4352*
4:24 they that worship him must **w** *him* in spirit *4352*
12:20 among them that came up to **w** at the feast: *4352*
Ac 7:42 and gave them up to **w** the host of heaven; *3000*
7:43 figures which ye made to **w** them: *4352*
8:27 and had come to Jerusalem for to **w**, *4352*
17:23 Whom therefore ye ignorantly **w**, *2151*
18:13 This *fellow* persuadeth men to **w** God *4576*
24:11 days since I went up to Jerusalem for to **w**. *4352*
24:14 call heresy, so **w** I the God of my fathers, *3000*
1Co 14:25 so falling down on *his* face he will **w** God, *4352*
Php 3: 3 which **w** God in the spirit, and rejoice in *3000*
Col 2:23 have indeed a shew of wisdom in **will w**, *1479*
Heb 1: 6 And let all the angels of God **w** him. *4352*
Rev 3: 9 make them to come and **w** before thy feet, *4352*
4:10 and **w** him that liveth for ever and ever, and *4352*
9:20 that they should not **w** devils, and idols of *4352*
11: 1 and the altar, and them that **w** therein. *4352*
13: 8 And all that dwell upon the earth shall **w** *4352*
13:12 them which dwell therein to **w** the first *4352*
13:15 cause that as many as would not **w** *4352*
14: 7 and **w** him that made heaven, and earth, *4352*
14: 9 If any *man* **w** the beast and his image, and *4352*
14:11 who **w** the beast and his image, and *4352*
15: 4 all nations shall come and **w** before thee; *4352*
19:10 And I fell at his feet to **w** him. And he said *4352*
19:10 **w** God: for the testimony of Jesus is *4352*
22: 8 I fell down to **w** before the feet of *4352*
22: 9 keep the sayings of this book: **w** God. *4352*

WORSHIPPED (70) [WORSHIP]

Ge 24:26 bowed down his head, and **w** the LORD. 7812
24:48 **w** the LORD, and blessed the LORD 7812

Ge 24:52 he **w** the LORD, *bowing himself* to 7812
Ex 4:31 then they bowed their heads and **w**. 7812
12:27 And the people bowed the head and **w**. 7812
32: 8 have **w** it, and have sacrificed thereunto, 7812
33:10 all the people rose up and **w**, every man *in* 7812
34: 8 bowed his head toward the earth, and **w**. 7812
Dt 17: 3 **w** them, either the sun, or moon, or any of 7812
29:26 and served other gods, and **w** them, 7812
Jdg 7:15 that he **w**, and returned into the host of 7812
1Sa 1:19 **w** before the LORD, and returned, and 7812
1:28 to the LORD. And he **w** the LORD there. 7812
15:31 again after Saul; and Saul **w** the LORD. 7812
2Sa 12:20 came *into* the house of the LORD, and **w**: 7812
15:32 to the top *of the mount,* where he **w** God, 7812
1Ki 9: 9 and have **w** them, and served them: 7812
11:33 have **w** Ashtoreth the goddess of 7812
16:31 and went and served Baal, and **w** him. 7812
22:53 **w** him, and provoked to anger the LORD 7812
2Ki 17:16 **w** all the host of heaven, and served Baal. 7812
21: 3 **w** all the host of heaven, and served them. 7812
21:21 the idols that his father served, and **w** them: 7812
1Ch 29:20 and **w** the LORD, and the king. 7812
2Ch 7: 3 **w**, and praised the LORD, *saying,* For *he* 7812
7:22 other gods, and **w** them, and served them: 7812
29:28 all the congregation **w**, and the singers 7812
29:29 present with him bowed themselves, and **w**. 7812
29:30 and they bowed their heads and **w**. 7812
33: 3 **w** all the host of heaven, and served them. 7812
Ne 8: 6 **w** the LORD *with their* faces to 7812
9: 3 and **w** the LORD their God. 7812
Job 1:20 and fell down upon the ground, and **w**, 7812
Ps 106:19 a calf in Horeb, and **w** the molten image. 7812
Jer 1:16 and **w** the works of their own hands. 7812
8: 2 they have sought, and whom they have **w**: 7812
16:11 have **w** them, and have forsaken me, and 7812
22: 9 and **w** other gods, and served them. 7812
Eze 8:16 and they **w** the sun towards the east. 7812
Da 2:46 **w** Daniel, and commanded that *they* should 5457
3: 7 **w** the golden image that Nebuchadnezzar 5457
Mt 2:11 his mother, and fell down, and **w** him: *4352*
8: 2 there came a leper and **w** him, saying, Lord, *4352*
9:18 came a *certain* ruler, and **w** him, saying, *4352*
14:33 they that were in the ship came and **w** him, *4352*
15:25 Then came she and **w** him, saying, Lord, *4352*
18:26 fell down, and **w** him, saying, Lord, *4352*
28: 9 and held him by the feet, and **w** him. *4352*
28:17 And when they saw him, they **w** him: but *4352*
Mk 5: 6 he saw Jesus afar off, he ran and **w** him, *4352*
15:19 upon him, and bowing *their* knees **w** him. *4352*
Lk 24:52 And they **w** him, and returned to Jerusalem *4352*
Jn 4:20 Our fathers **w** in this mountain; and ye say, *4352*
9:38 he said, Lord, I believe. And he **w** him. *4352*
Ac 10:25 and fell down at *his* feet, and **w** *him.* *4352*
16:14 of the city of Thyatira, which **w** God, *4576*
17:25 Neither is **w** with men's hands, as though *2323*
18: 7 named Justus, one that **w** God, *4576*
Ro 1:25 and **w** and served the creature more than *4573*
2Th 2: 4 above all that is called God, or that is **w**; *4574*
Heb 11:21 and **w**, *leaning* upon the top of his staff. *4352*
Rev 5:14 and **w** him that liveth for ever and ever. *4352*
7:11 the throne on their faces, and **w** God, *4352*
11:16 fell upon their faces, and **w** God, *4352*
13: 4 And they **w** the dragon which gave power *4352*
13: 4 and they **w** the beast, saying, Who *is* like *4352*
16: 2 and *upon* them which **w** his image. *4352*
19: 4 fell down and **w** God that sat on the throne, *4352*
19:20 of the beast, and them that **w** his image. *4352*
20: 4 and which had not **w** the beast, neither his *4352*

WORSHIPPER (2) [WORSHIP]

Jn 9:31 but if any *man* be a **w of God**, and *2318*
Ac 19:35 is a **w** of the great goddess Diana, *3511*

WORSHIPPERS (7) [WORSHIP]

2Ki 10:19 to the intent that *he* might destroy the **w** of 5647
10:21 all the **w** of Baal came, so that there was 5647
10:22 Bring forth vestments for all the **w** of Baal. 5647
10:23 said unto the **w** of Baal, Search, and 5647
10:23 of the LORD, but the **w** of Baal only. 5647
Jn 4:23 when the true **w** shall worship the Father in *4353*
Heb 10: 2 that the **w** once purged should have had no *3000*

WORSHIPPETH (6) [WORSHIP]

Ne 9: 6 them all; and the host of heaven **w** thee. 7812
Isa 44:15 **w** *it;* he maketh it a graven image, and 7812
44:17 **w** *it,* and prayeth unto it, and saith, 7812
Da 3: 6 **w** shall the same hour be cast into the midst 5457
3:11 whoso falleth not down and **w**, *that* he 5457
Ac 19:27 whom all Asia and the world **w**. *4576*

WORSHIPPING (5) [WORSHIP]

2Ki 19:37 as he was **w** *in* the house of Nisroch his 7812
2Ch 20:18 fell before the LORD, **w** the LORD. 7812
Isa 37:38 as he was **w** *in* the house of Nisroch his 7812
Mt 20:20 **w** *him,* and desiring a certain *thing* of him. *4352*
Col 2:18 in a voluntary humility and **w** of angels, *2356*

WORST (1) [BAD]

Eze 7:24 Wherefore I will bring the **w** of 7451

WORTH (9) [THANKWORTHY, UNWORTHILY, UNWORTHY, WORTHIES, WORTHILY, WORTHY]

Ge 23: 9 for as much money as it is **w** he shall give it 4392
23:15 the land *is* **w** four hundred shekels of silver; NIH
Lev 27:23 the priest shall reckon unto him the **w** of 4373
Dt 15:18 for he hath been **w** a double hired servant *to* 7939
2Sa 18: 3 now *thou art* **w** ten thousand of us: 3644
1Ki 21: 2 I will give thee the **w** of it *in* money. 4242
Job 24:25 a liar, and make my speech nothing **w**? 3807.1
Pr 10:20 the heart of the wicked *is* **little w**. 4592+3509.1
Eze 30: 2 Lord GOD; Howl ye, Woe **w** the day! 3807.1

WORTHIES (1) [WORTH]

Na 2: 5 He shall recount his **w**: they shall stumble in 117

WORTHILY (1) [WORTH]

Ru 4:11 do thou **w** in Ephratah, and be famous in 2428

WORTHLESS See NOUGHT; VANITIES; VANITY

WORTHY (68) [WORTH]

Ge 32:10 I am **not w** of the least of all the mercies, 6994
Dt 17: 6 shall he that is **w** of death be put to death; NIH
19: 6 whereas he *was* not **w** of death, 4941
21:22 if a man have committed a sin **w** of death, 4941
22:26 *there is* in the damsel no sin **w** of death: NIH
25: 2 if the wicked *man be* **w** to be beaten, 1121
1Sa 1: 5 unto Hannah he gave a **w** portion; for he 639
26:16 ye *are* **w to die**, because ye have not 1121+4194
2Sa 22: 4 call on the LORD, who is **w** to be praised: NIH
1Ki 1:52 If he will shew himself a **w** man, 2428
2:26 thine own fields; for thou *art* **w** of death: 376
Ps 18: 3 upon the LORD, who is **w** to be praised: NIH
Jer 26:11 all the people, saying, This man *is* **w** to die; 4941
26:16 to the prophets; This man *is* not **w** to die: 4941
Mt 3:11 than I, whose shoes I am not **w** to bear: *2425*
8: 8 I am not **w** that thou shouldest come under *2425*
10:10 yet staves: for the workman is **w** of his meat. *514*
10:11 or town ye shall enter, inquire who in it is **w**; *514*
10:13 And if the house be **w**, let your peace come *514*
10:13 but if it be not **w**, let your peace return to *514*
10:37 or mother more than me is not **w** of me: *514*
10:37 or daughter more than me is not **w** of me. *514*
10:38 and followeth after me, is not **w** of me. *514*
22: 8 but they which were bidden were not **w**. *514*
Mk 1: 7 the latchet of whose shoes I am not **w** to *2425*
Lk 3: 8 Bring forth therefore fruits **w** of repentance, *514*
3:16 the latchet of whose shoes I am not **w** to *2425*
7: 4 That he was **w** for whom he should do this: *514*
7: 6 for I am not **w** that thou shouldest enter *2425*
7: 7 Wherefore neither **thought** I myself **w** to *515*
10: 7 for the labourer is **w** of his hire. Go not from *514*
12:48 and did commit *things* **w** of stripes, *514*
15:19 And am no more **w** to be called thy son: *514*
15:21 and am no more **w** to be called thy son. *514*
20:35 But they which shall be **accounted w** to *2661*
21:36 that ye may be **accounted w** to escape all *2661*
23:15 and lo, nothing **w** of death is done unto him. *514*
Jn 1:27 whose shoe's latchet I am not **w** to unloose. *514*
Ac 5:41 rejoicing that they were **counted w** to *2661*
13:25 whose shoes of *his* feet I am not **w** to loose. *514*
23:29 to have nothing laid to his charge **w** of death *514*
24: 2 that **very w deeds** are done unto this nation *2735*
25:11 or have committed any *thing* **w** of death, *514*
25:25 that he had committed nothing **w** of death, *514*
26:31 This man doeth nothing **w** of death or *514*
Ro 1:32 that they which commit such *things* are **w** of *514*
8:18 **w** to be compared with the glory which shall *514*
Eph 4: 1 beseech you that *ye* walk **w** of the vocation *516*
Col 1:10 That ye might walk **w** of the Lord unto all *516*
1Th 2:12 That ye would walk **w** of God, who hath *516*
2Th 1: 5 that ye may be **counted w** of the kingdom *2661*
1:11 that our God would **count** you **w** of *this* *515*
1Ti 1:15 *is* a faithful saying, and **w** of all acceptation, *514*
4: 9 *is* a faithful saying and **w** of all acceptation. *514*
5:17 Let the elders that rule well be **counted w** of *515*
5:18 And, The labourer *is* **w** of his reward. *514*
6: 1 count their own masters **w** of all honour, *514*
Heb 3: 3 For this *man* was **counted w** of more glory *515*
10:29 suppose ye, shall he be **thought w**, *515*
11:38 (Of whom the world was not **w**:) *514*
Jas 2: 7 Do not they blaspheme *that* **w** name by *2570*
Rev 3: 4 shall walk with me in white: for they are **w**. *514*
4:11 Thou art **w**, O Lord, to receive glory and *514*
5: 2 Who is **w** to open the book, and to loose *514*
5: 4 because no *man* was found **w** to open and *514*
5: 9 Thou art **w** to take the book, and to open *514*
5:12 **W** is the Lamb that was slain to receive *514*
16: 6 given them blood to drink; for they are **w**. *514*

WOT (10) [WIT]

Ge 21:26 I **w** not who hath done this thing: 3045
44:15 **w** ye not that such a man as I can certainly 3045
Ex 32: 1 of Egypt, we **w** not what is become of him. 3045
32:23 of Egypt, we **w** not what is become of him. 3045
Nu 22: 6 for I **w** that *he* whom thou blessest *is* 3045
Jos 2: 5 whither the men went I **w** not: pursue after 3045
Ac 3:17 I **w** that through ignorance ye did *it,* as *did* *1492*
7:40 of Egypt, we **w** not what is become of him. *1492*
Ro 11: 2 **W** ye not what the scripture saith of Elias? *1492*
Php 1:22 my labour: yet what I shall choose I **w** not. *1107*

WOTTETH (1) [WIT]

Ge 39: 8 my master **w** not what *is* with me in 3045

WOULD (451) [WILL, WOULDEST]

Ge 2:19 brought *them* unto Adam to see what he **w** NIH
21: 7 she said, Who **w** have said unto Abraham, NIH
30:34 I **w** it might be according to thy word. 3863
42:21 when he besought us, and we **w** not hear; NIH
42:22 not sin against the child; and ye **w** not hear? NIH
43: 7 could we certainly know that he **w** say, NIH
44:22 he should leave his father, *his father* **w** die. NIH
Ex 2: 4 afar off, to wit what **w** be done to him. NIH
8:32 time also, neither **w** he let the people go. NIH
9:35 neither **w** he let the children of Israel go; NIH
10:20 so that he **w** not let the children of Israel go. NIH
10:27 Pharaoh's heart, and he **w** not let them go. 14
11:10 that he **w** not let the children of Israel go out NIH
13:15 to pass, when Pharaoh **w** hardly let us go, NIH
16: 3 **W to God** we had died by the hand 4310+5414
Nu 11:29 **w God that** all the LORD'S people 4310+5414
11:29 that the LORD **w** put his spirit upon them! NIH
14: 2 **W God that** we had died in the land of 3863
14: 2 or **w God** we had died in this wilderness! 3863
20: 3 **W God** that we had died when our brethren 3863
21:23 Sihon **w** not suffer Israel to pass through his NIH
22:18 If Balak **w** give me his house full *of* silver NIH
22:29 **I w** there were a sword in mine hand, 3863
22:29 a sword in mine hand, for now **w** I kill thee. NIH
24:13 If Balak **w** give me his house full *of* silver NIH
Dt 1:26 Notwithstanding ye **w** not go up, but 14
1:43 you **w** not hear, but rebelled against NIH
1:45 the LORD **w** not hearken to your voice, NIH
2:30 Sihon king of Heshbon **w** not let us pass by 14
3:26 with me for your sakes, and **w** not hear me: NIH
5:29 that they **w** fear me, and keep all my NIH
7: 8 he **w** keep the oath which he had sworn unto NIH
8:20 ye **w** not be obedient unto the voice of NIH
9:25 the LORD had said he **w** destroy you. NIH
10:10 time also, *and* the LORD **w** not destroy thee. 14
23: 5 Nevertheless the LORD thy God **w** not 14
23:21 require it of thee; and it **w** be sin in thee. NIH
28:56 which **w** not adventure to set the sole of her NIH
28:67 thou shalt say, **W God** it were even! 4310+5414
28:67 shalt say, **W God** it were morning! 4310+5414
32:26 I said, I **w** scatter them into corners, I would NIH
32:26 I **w** make the remembrance of them to cease NIH
32:29 *that* they **w** consider their latter end! NIH
Jos 5: 6 unto whom the LORD sware that *he* **w** not NIH
5: 6 sware unto their fathers that he **w** give us, NIH
7: 7 **w to God** we had been content, 3863+2050.1
17:12 but the Canaanites **w** dwell in that land. 2974
24:10 I **w** not hearken unto Balaam; therefore 14
Jdg 1:27 but the Canaanites **w** dwell in that land. 2974
1:34 for they **w** not suffer them to come down to NIH
1:35 the Amorites **w** dwell in mount Heres in 2974
2:17 yet they **w** not hearken unto their judges, NIH
3: 4 to know whether they **w** hearken unto NIH
8:19 if ye had saved them alive, I **w** not slay you. NIH
8:24 said unto them, I **w** desire a request of you, NIH
8:24 that you **w** give me every man the earrings NIH
9:29 **w to God** this people were under my 4310+5414
9:29 my hand; then **w** I remove Abimelech. NIH
11:17 the king of Edom **w** not hearken *thereto.* NIH
11:17 he **w** not consent: and Israel abode in NIH
13:23 he **w** not have received a burnt offering and NIH
13:23 neither **w** he have shewed us all these NIH
13:23 **w** as *at this* time have told us *such things* as NIH
14: 6 and he rent him as *he* **w** have rent a kid, and NIH
15: 1 But her father **w** not suffer him to go in. NIH
19:10 the man **w** not tarry *that* night, but he rose up 14
19:25 the men **w** not hearken to him: so the man 14
20:13 the children of Benjamin **w** not hearken to 14
Ru 1:13 **W** ye tarry for them till they were grown? NIH
1:13 **w** ye stay for them from having husbands? NIH
1Sa 2:16 he **w** answer him, *Nay;* but thou shalt give *it* NIH
2:25 because the LORD **w** slay them. 2654
13:13 for now **w** the LORD have established thy NIH
15: 9 *that was* good, and **w** not utterly destroy them: 14
18: 2 **w** let him go no more home *to* his father's NIH
20: 9 to come upon thee, then **w** not I tell it thee? NIH
22:17 the servants of the king **w** not put forth their 14
22:22 *was* there, that he **w** surely tell Saul: NIH
26:23 I **w** not stretch forth mine hand against 14
31: 4 his armourbearer **w** not; for he was sore 14
2Sa 2:21 Asahel **w** not turn aside from following of 14
4: 6 *as though* they **w** have fetched wheat; NIH
4:10 who *thought* that I **w** have given him a NIH
6:10 So David **w** not remove the ark of the LORD 14
11:20 knew ye not that they **w** shoot from NIH
12: 8 I **w** moreover have given unto thee such and NIH
12:17 he **w** not, neither did he eat bread with them. 14
12:18 and he **w** not hearken unto our voice: NIH
13:14 Howbeit he **w** not hearken unto her voice: but, 14
13:16 didst unto me. But he **w** not hearken unto her. 14
13:25 howbeit he **w** not go, but blessed him. 14
14:16 of the hand of the man *that* **w** destroy me NIH
14:29 him to the king; but he **w** not come to him: 14
14:29 he sent again the second time, he **w** not come. 14
15: 4 come unto me, and I **w** do him justice. NIH
18:11 I **w** have given thee ten *shekels of* silver, NIH
18:12 *yet* **w** I not put forth mine hand against NIH
18:33 **w** God I had died for thee, O Absalom, 4310
23:15 Oh that one **w** give me drink *of* the water of NIH
23:16 nevertheless he **w** not drink thereof, but 14
23:17 therefore he **w** not drink it. These *things* did 14
1Ki 8:12 The LORD said that *he* **w** dwell in NIH
13:33 whosoever **w**, he consecrated him, and 2655
18:32 as great as **w** contain two measures of seed. NIH
20:33 whether *any thing* **w** *come* from him, NIH
21: 4 turned away his face, and **w** eat no bread. NIH
22:18 Did I not tell thee that he **w** prophesy no NIH
22:49 servants in the ships. But Jehoshaphat **w** not. 14
2Ki 2: 1 when the LORD **w** take up Elijah *into* NIH
3:14 I **w** not look toward thee, nor see thee. NIH
5: 3 **W God** my lord *were* with the prophet that 305
5: 3 for he **w** recover him of his leprosy. NIH
7: 2 *if* the LORD **w** make windows in heaven, NIH
8:19 Yet the LORD **w** not destroy Judah for 14
13:23 Isaac, and Jacob, and **w** not destroy them, 14
14:11 Amaziah **w** not hear. Therefore Jehoash NIH
14:27 the LORD said not that *he* **w** blot out NIH
17:14 Notwithstanding they **w** not hear, but NIH
18:12 and **w** not hear *them,* nor do *them.* NIH
24: 4 which the LORD **w** not pardon. 14
1Ch 10: 4 his armourbearer **w** not; for he was sore 14
11:17 Oh that one **w** give me drink *of* the water of NIH
11:18 David **w** not drink *of* it, but poured it out to 14
11:19 Therefore he **w** not drink it. These *things* did 14
13: 4 all the congregation said that *they* **w** do so: NIH
19:19 neither **w** the Syrians help the children of 14
27:23 the LORD had said *he* **w** increase Israel NIH
2Ch 6: 1 The LORD hath said that *he* **w** dwell in NIH
10:16 when all Israel saw that the king **w** not NIH
12:12 that *he* **w** not destroy *him* altogether: NIH
15:13 That whosoever **w** not seek the LORD NIH
18:17 Did I not tell thee *that* he **w** not prophesy NIH
21: 7 Howbeit the LORD **w** not destroy the house 14

2Ch 24:19 against them: but they **w** not give ear. NIH
25:20 Amaziah **w** not hear; for it *came* of God, NIH
33:10 and to his people: but they **w** not hearken. NIH
35:22 Nevertheless Josiah **w** not turn his face from NIH
Ezr 10: 8 *that* whosoever **w** not come within three NIH
10:19 they gave their hands that *they* **w** put away NIH
Ne 6:11 *being* as I *am*, **w** go into the temple to save NIH
6:14 of the prophets, that **w** have put me in fear. NIH
9:24 that *they* might do with them as they **w**. 7522
9:29 and hardened their neck, and **w** not hear. NIH
9:30 yet **w** they not give ear: therefore NIH
10:30 that we **w** not give our daughters unto NIH
10:31 *that* we **w** not buy *it* of them on the sabbath, NIH
10:31 *that* we **w** leave the seventh year, and NIH
Est 3: 4 to see whether Mordecai's matters **w** stand: NIH
6: 6 To whom **w** the king delight to do honour NIH
8:11 the people and province that **w** assault them, NIH
9: 5 did what they **w** unto those that hated them. 7522
9:27 that they **w** keep these two days according 1961
Job 5: 8 I **w** seek unto God, and unto God would I 199
5: 8 and unto God **w** I commit my cause: NIH
6: 3 For now it **w** be heavier than the sand of NIH
6: 8 *that* God **w** grant *me* the thing that I long NIH
6: 9 Even *that* it **w** please God to destroy me: NIH
6: 9 *that* he **w** let loose his hand, and cut me off! NIH
6:10 yea, I **w** harden myself in sorrow; let him NIH
7:16 I loathe *it;* I **w** not live alway: let me alone; NIH
8: 6 surely now he **w** awake for thee, and NIH
9:15 *yet* **w** I not answer, *but* I would make NIH
9:15 *but* I **w** make supplication to my judge. NIH
9:16 *yet* **w** I not believe that he had hearkened NIH
9:21 I *were* perfect, *yet* **w** I not know my soul: NIH
9:21 I not know my soul: I **w** despise my life. NIH
9:35 *Then* **w** I speak, and not fear him; but *it is* NIH
11: 5 O that God **w** speak, and open his lips NIH
11: 6 that he **w** shew thee the secrets of wisdom, NIH
11:12 For vain man **w** be wise, though man be NIH
13: 3 Surely I **w** speak to the Almighty, and NIH
13: 5 O that you **w** altogether hold your peace, NIH
16: 5 *But* I **w** strengthen you with my mouth, and NIH
23: 4 I **w** order *my* cause before him, and fill my NIH
23: 5 I **w** know the words *which* he would answer NIH
23: 5 I would know the words *which* he **w** answer NIH
23: 5 and understand what he **w** say unto me. NIH
23: 6 No; but he **w** put *strength* in me. NIH
27:22 he **w fain flee** out of his hand. 1272+1272
30: 1 whose fathers I **w** have disdained to have NIH
31:12 and **w** root out all mine increase. NIH
31:35 O that one **w** hear me! behold, my desire *is,* NIH
31:35 my desire *is, that* the Almighty **w** answer NIH
31:36 Surely I **w** take it upon my shoulder, *and* NIH
31:37 I **w** declare unto him the number of my NIH
31:37 my steps; as a prince **w** I go near unto him. NIH
32:22 *so doing* my Maker **w** soon take me away. NIH
34:27 and **w** not consider any of his ways: NIH
36:16 **w** he have removed thee out of the strait NIH
41:32 after him; *one* **w** think the deep to be hoary. NIH
Ps 22: 8 He trusted on the LORD *that* he **w** deliver NIH
35:25 not say in their hearts, Ah, so **w** we have it: NIH
40: 5 *if* I **w** declare and speak *of them,* they are NIH
50:12 If I were hungry, I **w** not tell thee: for NIH
51:16 else **w** I give *it:* thou delightest not in burnt NIH
55: 6 a dove, *for then* **w** I fly away, and be at rest. NIH
55: 7 Lo, *then* **w** I wander far off, *and* remain in NIH
55: 8 I **w** hasten my escape from the windy storm NIH
55:12 then I **w** have hid myself from him: NIH
56: 1 for man **w** swallow me up; he fighting daily NIH
56: 2 Mine enemies **w** daily swallow *me* up: NIH
57: 3 save me *from* the reproach of him that **w** NIH
69: 4 they that **w** destroy me, *being* mine enemies NIH
81:11 my people **w** not hearken to my voice; and NIH
81:11 hearken to my voice; and Israel **w** none of me. 14
106:23 Therefore he said that *he* **w** destroy them, NIH
107: 8 Oh that *men* **w** praise the LORD *for* his NIH
107:15 Oh that *men* **w** praise the LORD *for* his NIH
107:21 Oh that *men* **w** praise the LORD *for* his NIH
107:31 Oh that *men* **w** praise the LORD *for* his NIH
119:57 I have said that *I* **w** keep thy words. NIH
142: 4 but *there was* no man that **w** know me: NIH
Pr 1:25 all my counsel, and **w** none of my reproof: 14
1:30 They **w** none of my counsel: they despised all 14
SS 3: 4 I held him, and **w** not let him go, until I had NIH
8: 1 I should find thee without, I **w** kiss thee; NIH
8: 2 I **w** lead thee, *and* bring thee into my NIH
8: 2 into my mother's house, *who* **w** instruct me: NIH
8: 2 I **w** cause thee to drink of spiced wine, NIH
8: 7 if a man **w** give all the substance of his NIH
8: 7 house for love, it **w** utterly be contemned. NIH
Isa 27: 4 who **w** set the briers *and* thorns against me NIH
27: 4 I **w** go through them, I would burn them NIH
27: 4 go through them, I **w** burn them together. NIH
28:12 and this *is* the refreshing: yet they **w** not hear. 14
30:15 shall be your strength: and ye **w** not. 14
42:24 for they **w** not walk in his ways, neither were 14
54: 9 have I sworn that *I* **w** not be wroth with NIH
Jer 8:18 *When* I **w** comfort myself against sorrow, NIH
10: 7 Who **w** not fear thee, O King of nations? NIH
13:11 and for a glory: but they **w** not hear. NIH
18:10 the good, wherewith I said *I* **w** benefit them. NIH
22:24 my right hand, yet **w** I pluck thee thence; NIH
29:19 and sending *them;* but ye **w** not hear, NIH
36:25 to the king that *he* **w** not burn the roll: NIH
36:25 not burn the roll: but he **w** not hear them. NIH
38:26 that *he* **w** not cause me to return *to* NIH
49: 9 **w** they not leave *some* gleaning grapes? NIH
51: 9 We **w** have healed Babylon, but she is not NIH
La 4:12 **w** not have believed that the adversary and NIH
Eze 3: 6 to them, they **w** have hearkened unto thee. NIH
6:10 *that* I have not said in vain that *I* **w** do this NIH
13: 6 they have made *others* to hope that *they* **w** NIH
20: 8 against me, and **w** not hearken unto me: 14
20:13 *I* **w** pour out my fury upon them in NIH
20:15 that *I* **w** not bring them into the land which I NIH
20:21 then I said, *I* **w** pour out my fury upon them, NIH
20:23 that *I* **w** scatter them among the heathen, NIH
Eze 38:17 that *I* **w** bring thee against them? NIH
Da 1: 8 Daniel purposed in his heart that he **w** not NIH
2: 8 I know of certainty that ye **w** gain the time, NIH
2:16 desired of the king that he **w** give him time, NIH
2:16 that *he* **w** shew the king the interpretation. NIH
2:18 That *they* **w** desire mercies of the God of NIH
5:19 whom he **w** he slew; and whom he would 6634
5:19 whom he **w** he kept alive; and whom he 6634
5:19 whom he **w** he set up; and whom he would 6634
5:19 he set up; and whom he **w** he put down. 6634
7:19 Then I **w** know the truth of the fourth beast, 6634
9: 2 that *he* **w** accomplish seventy years in NIH
Hos 7: 1 When I **w** *have* healed Israel, then NIH
11: 7 to the most High, none at all **w** exalt *him.* NIH
Ob 1: 5 **w** they not have stolen till they had enough? NIH
1: 5 came to thee, **w** they not leave *some* grapes? NIH
Jnh 3:10 that he had said that he **w** do unto them; NIH
4: 5 till he might see what **w** become of the city. NIH
Zec 7:13 *that* as he cried, and they **w** not hear; NIH
7:13 so they cried, and I **w** not hear, saith NIH
Mal 1:10 Who *is there* even among you that **w** shut NIH
Mt 2:18 and **w** not be comforted, because they are *2309*
5:42 from him that **w** borrow of thee turn not *2309*
7:12 Therefore all *things* whatsoever ye **w** that *2309*
8:34 they besought *him* that he **w** depart out of NIG
11:21 Sidon they **w have** repented long ago in *302*
11:23 in Sodom, it **w have** remained until this day. *302*
12: 7 ye **w** not **have** condemned the guiltless. *302*
12:38 saying, Master, we **w** see a sign from thee. *2309*
14: 5 And when he **w** have put him to death, *2309*
14: 7 an oath to give her whatsoever she **w** ask. NIG
16: 1 tempting desired him that *he* **w** shew them a NIG
18:23 which **w** take account of his servants. *2309*
18:30 And he **w** not: but went and cast him into *2309*
22: 3 to the wedding: and they **w** not come. *2309*
23:30 we **w** not **have** been partakers with them in *302*
23:37 how often **w** I have gathered thy children *2309*
23:37 chickens under *her* wings, and ye **w** not? *2309*
24:43 had known in what watch the thief **w** come, NIG
24:43 he **w have** watched, and would not have *302*
24:43 **w** not **have** suffered his house to be broken *302*
27:15 unto the people a prisoner, whom they **w**. *2309*
27:34 when he had tasted *thereof,* he **w** not drink. *2309*
Mk 3: 2 whether he **w** heal him on the sabbath day; NIG
3:13 and calleth unto *him* whom he **w**: *2309*
5:10 And he besought him much that he **w** not NIG
6:19 quarrel against him, and **w** have killed him; *2309*
6:26 for their sakes which sat with *him,* he **w** not *2309*
6:48 upon the sea, and **w** have passed by them. *2309*
7:24 and **w have** no *man* know *it:* but he could *2309*
7:26 she besought him that he **w** cast forth NIG
9:30 and he **w** not that any *man* should know *it.* *2309*
10:35 we **w** that thou shouldest do for us *2309*
10:36 What **w** ye that I should do for you? *2309*
11:16 And **w** not suffer that any *man* should carry NIG
Lk 1:62 to his father, how he **w** have him called. *302*
1:74 That he **w** grant unto us, that *we* being NIG
5: 3 prayed him that *he* **w** thrust out a little from NIG
6: 7 whether he **w** heal on the sabbath day; NIG
6:31 And as ye **w** that men should do to you, *2309*
7: 3 beseeching him that he **w** come and heal his NIG
7:36 desired him that he **w** eat with him. NIG
7:39 **w have** known who and what manner of *302*
8:31 And they besought him that he **w** not NIG
8:32 they besought him that he **w** suffer them to NIG
8:41 besought him that *he* **w** come into his NIG
9:53 his face was *as though he* **w** go to NIG
10: 1 and place, whither he himself **w** come. *3195*
10: 2 that he **w** send forth labourers into his NIG
12:39 had known what hour the thief **w** come, NIG
12:39 he **w have** watched, and not have suffered *302*
13:34 how often **w** I have gathered thy children *2309*
13:34 her brood under *her* wings, and ye **w** not? *2309*
15:16 And he **w fain** have filled his belly with *1937*
15:28 And he was angry, and **w** not go in: *2309*
16:26 that they which **w** pass from hence to you *2309*
16:26 they pass to us, that **w** *come* from thence. NIG
18: 4 And he **w** not for a while: but afterward he *2309*
18:13 **w** not lift up so much as *his* eyes unto *2309*
18:15 unto him also infants, that he **w** touch them: NIG
19:27 which **w** not that I should reign over them, *2309*
19:40 the stones **w** immediately cry out. NIG
22:49 which were about him saw what **w** follow, NIG
24:28 he made as though *he* **w** have gone further. NIG
Jn 1:43 The day following Jesus **w** go forth into *2309*
4:10 and he **w have** given thee living water. *302*
4:40 they besought him that *he* **w** tarry with NIG
4:47 and besought him that he **w** come down, NIG
5:46 ye believed Moses, ye **w have** believed me: *302*
6: 6 for he himself knew what he **w** do. *3195*
6:11 likewise of the fishes as much as they **w**. *2309*
6:15 therefore perceived that they **w** come and *3195*
7: 1 for he **w** not walk in Jewry, because *2309*
7:44 And some of them **w** have taken him; but *2309*
8:39 ye **w** do the works of Abraham. NIG
8:42 If God were your Father, ye **w** love me: *302*
9:27 wherefore **w** you hear *it* again? will ye also *2309*
12:21 desired him, saying, Sir, we **w** see Jesus. *2309*
14: 2 if *it were* not *so,* I **w have** told you. I go to *302*
14:28 If ye loved me, ye **w** rejoice, because I said, *302*
15:19 were of the world, the world **w** love his own: *302*
18:30 we **w** not **have** delivered him up unto thee. *302*
18:36 of this world, then **w** my servants fight, *302*
Ac 2:30 *he* **w** raise up Christ to sit on his throne; NIG
5:24 they doubted of them whereunto this **w** NIG
7: 5 yet he promised that *he* **w** give it to him for NIG
7:25 For he supposed his brethren **w** have NIG
7:25 how that God by his hand **w** deliver them: NIG
7:26 and **w** have set them at one *again,* saying, NIG
7:39 To whom our fathers **w** not obey, *2309*
8:31 And he desired Philip that *he* **w** come up NIG
9:38 desiring *him* that *he* **w** not delay to come to NIG
10:10 he became very hungry, and **w** have eaten: *2309*
11:23 that with purpose of heart *they* **w** cleave NIG
12: 6 And when Herod **w** have brought him *3195*
Ac 14:13 and **w** have done sacrifice with the people. *2309*
16: 3 Him **w** Paul have to go forth with him; and *2309*
16:27 out his sword, and **w have** killed himself, *3195*
17:20 we **w** know therefore what these *things* *1014*
18:14 reason **w** that I should bear with you: *302*
19:30 And when Paul **w** have entered in unto *1014*
19:31 desiring *him* that *he* **w** not adventure NIG
19:33 **w** have made *his* defence unto the people. *2309*
20:16 because he **w** not spend the time in Asia: NIG
21:14 And when he **w** not be persuaded, NIG
22:30 he **w** have known the certainty wherefore *1014*
23:12 saying that *they* **w** neither eat nor drink till NIG
23:15 as though ye **w** inquire something more *3195*
23:20 as though they **w** inquire somewhat of him *3195*
23:28 And when I **w** have known the cause *1014*
24: 6 and **w** have judged according to our law. *2309*
25: 3 that he **w** send for him to Jerusalem, NIG
25: 4 that he himself **w** depart shortly *thither.* *3195*
25:20 I asked *him* whether he **w** go to Jerusalem, *1014*
25:22 unto Festus, I **w** also hear the man myself. *1014*
26: 5 me from the beginning, if they **w** testify, *2309*
26:29 And Paul said, I **w** to God, that not *302+2172*
27:30 under colour as though they **w have** cast *3195*
28:18 **w have** let *me* go, because there was no *1014*
Ro 1:13 Now I **w** not have you ignorant, brethren, *2309*
5: 7 yet peradventure for a good *man* some **w** NIG
7:15 for what I **w**, that do I not; but what I hate, *2309*
7:16 If then I do that which I **w** not, I consent *2309*
7:19 For the good that I **w** I do not: but the evil *2309*
7:19 do not: but the evil which I **w** not, that I do. *2309*
7:20 Now if I do that I **w** not, it is no more I that *2309*
7:21 I find then a law, that, when I **w** do good, *2309*
11:25 For I **w** not, brethren, that ye should be *2309*
16:19 *yet* I **w** have you wise unto *that which is* *2309*
1Co 2: 8 for had they known *it,* they **w** not **have** *302*
4: 8 and I **w** *to God* ye did reign, that we also *3785*
4:18 puffed up, as though I **w** not come to you. NIG
7: 7 For I **w that** all men were even as I myself. *2309*
7:32 But I **w** have you without carefulness. *2309*
10: 1 brethren, I **w** not that ye should be ignorant, *2309*
10:20 I **w** not that ye should have fellowship with *2309*
11: 3 But I **w** have you know, that the head of *2309*
11:31 For if we **w** judge ourselves, we should not NIG
12: 1 *gifts,* brethren, I **w** not have you ignorant. *2309*
14: 5 I **w** that ye all spake with tongues, but *2309*
2Co 1: 8 For we **w** not, brethren, have you ignorant *2309*
2: 1 that *I* **w** not come again to you in heaviness. NIG
2: 8 Wherefore I beseech you that *you* **w** NIG
5: 4 not for that we **w** be unclothed, but *2309*
8: 4 Praying us with much intreaty that we **w** NIG
8: 6 he **w** also finish in you the same grace also. NIG
9: 5 that they **w** go before unto you, and NIG
10: 9 That I may not seem as if *I* **w** terrify you by NIG
11: 1 **W** *to God* you could bear with me a little in *3785*
12: 6 For though I **w** desire to glory, I shall not be NIG
12:20 I shall not find you such as I **w**, and *that* I *2309*
12:20 *that* I shall be found unto you such as ye **w** *2309*
Gal 1: 7 and **w** pervert the gospel of Christ. *2309*
2:10 Only *they* **w** that we should remember NIG
3: 2 This only **w** I learn of you, Received ye *2309*
3: 8 foreseeing that God **w** justify the heathen NIG
4:15 ye **w** have plucked out your own eyes, and NIG
4:17 yea, they **w** exclude you, that you might *2309*
5:12 I **w** they were even cut off which trouble *3785*
5:17 so that ye cannot do the *things* that ye **w**. *2309*
Eph 3:16 That he **w** grant you, according to the riches NIG
Php 1:12 But I **w** ye should understand, brethren, *1014*
Col 1:27 To whom God **w** make known what *is* *2309*
2: 1 For I **w** that ye knew what great conflict I *2309*
4: 3 that God **w** open unto us a door of NIG
1Th 2: 9 *we* **w** not be chargeable unto any of you, NIG
2:12 That ye **w** walk worthy of God, who hath NIG
2:18 Wherefore we **w** have come unto you, *2309*
4: 1 *so* ye **w** abound more *and more.* *2443*
4:13 But I **w** not have you to be ignorant, NIG
2Th 1:11 that our God **w** count you worthy of *this* NIG
3:10 that if any **w** not work, neither should he *2309*
Phm 1:13 Whom I **w** have retained with me, that in *1014*
1:14 But without thy mind **w** I do nothing; *2309*
Heb 4: 8 **w** he not afterward have spoken of another *302*
10: 2 then **w** they not **have** ceased to be offered? *302*
11:32 for the time **w** fail me to tell of Gedeon, and NIG
12:17 when he **w** have inherited the blessing, *2309*
1Jn 2:19 they **w** *no doubt* **have** continued with us: *302*
2Jn 1:12 unto you, I **w** not *write* with paper and ink: *1014*
3Jn 1:10 and forbiddeth them that **w**, and *1014*
Rev 3:15 cold nor hot: I **w** thou wert cold or hot. *3785*
13:15 cause that as many as **w** not worship *302*

WOULDEST (38) [WOULD]

Ge 30:15 **w** thou take away my son's mandrakes also? NIH
31:30 *though* thou **w** needs be gone, because NIH
31:31 Peradventure thou **w** take by force thy NIH
Ex 7:16 and behold, hitherto thou **w** not hear. NIH
23: 5 **w** forbear to help him, thou shalt surely help NIH
Dt 8: 2 whether thou **w** keep his commandments, or NIH
21:11 unto her, that thou **w** have *her* to thy wife; NIH
28:62 thou **w** not obey the voice of the LORD NIH
Jos 15:18 and Caleb said unto her, What **w** thou? 3807.1
2Sa 14:11 that thou **w** not suffer the revengers of NIH
18:13 thou thyself **w** have set thyself against *me.* NIH
1Ki 1:16 And the king said, What **w** thou? 3807.1
18: 9 that thou **w** deliver thy servant into the hand NIH
2Ki 4:13 **w** thou be spoken for to the king, or to 3426
5:13 **w** thou not have done *it?* how much rather NIH
6:22 Thou shalt not smite *them:* **w** thou smite NIH
1Ch 4:10 Oh that thou **w** bless me indeed, and NIH
4:10 that thou **w** keep *me* from evil, that it may NIH
2Ch 6:20 hast said that *thou* **w** put thy name there; NIH
20:10 whom thou **w** not let Israel invade, NIH
Ezr 9:14 **w** thou not be angry with us till *thou* hadst NIH
Ne 2: 5 that thou **w** send me unto Judah, unto NIH
Job 8: 5 If thou **w** seek unto God betimes, and NIH
14:13 O that thou **w** hide me in the grave, NIH
14:13 that thou **w** keep me secret, until thy wrath NIH

W

Job 14:13 that thou **w** appoint me a set time, and NIH
Isa 48: 8 for I knew *that* thou **w** deal very NIH
64: 1 O that thou **w** rend the heavens, that thou NIH
64: 1 rend the heavens, that thou **w** come down, NIH
Lk 16:27 that thou **w** send him to my father's house: NIG
Jn 4:10 thou **w have** asked of him, and he would *302*
11:40 Said I not unto thee, that, if thou **w** believe, NIG
21:18 and walkedst whither thou **w**: *2309*
21:18 and carry *thee* whither thou **w** not. *2309*
Ac 23:20 **w** bring down Paul to morrow into NIG
24: 4 I pray *thee* that thou **w** hear us of thy NIG
Heb 10: 5 Sacrifice and offering thou **w** not, but *2309*
10: 8 and *offering* for sin thou **w** not, *2309*

WOUND (25) [WIND, WOUNDED, WOUNDEDST, WOUNDETH, WOUNDING, WOUNDS]

Ex 21:25 for burning, **w** for wound, stripe for stripe. 6482
21:25 for burning, wound for **w**, stripe for stripe. 6482
Dt 32:39 I kill, and I make alive; I **w**, and I heal: 4272
1Ki 22:35 the blood ran out of the **w** into the midst of 4347
Job 34: 6 my **w** *is* incurable without transgression. 2671
Ps 68:21 God shall **w** the head of his enemies, *and* 4272
110: 6 he shall **w** the heads over many countries. 4272
Pr 6:33 A **w** and dishonour shall he get; and 5061
20:30 The blueness of a **w** cleanseth away evil: so 6482
Isa 30:26 and healeth the stroke of their **w**. 4347
Jer 10:19 my **w** *is* grievous: but I said, Truly this *is* a 4347
15:18 is my pain perpetual, and my **w** incurable, 4347
30:12 bruise *is* incurable, *and* thy **w** *is* grievous. 4347
30:14 for I have wounded thee *with* the **w** of an 4347
Hos 5:13 Judah *saw* his **w**, then went Ephraim to 4205
5:13 he not heal you nor cure you of your **w**. 4205
Ob 1: 7 *they that eat* thy bread have laid a **w** under 4204
Mic 1: 9 For her **w** *is* incurable; for it is come unto 4347
Na 3:19 no healing of thy bruise; thy **w** *is* grievous: 4347
Jn 19:40 and **w** it in linen clothes with the spices, *1210*
Ac 5: 6 **w** him **up**, and carried *him* out, and *4958*
1Co 8:12 the brethren, and **w** their weak conscience, *5180*
Rev 13: 3 to death; and his deadly **w** was healed: *4127*
13:12 the first beast, whose deadly **w** was healed. *4127*
13:14 which had the **w** by a sword, and did live. *4127*

WOUNDED (35) [WOUND]

Dt 23: 1 He that is **w** in the stones, or hath *his* privy 6481
Jdg 9:40 and many were overthrown *and* **w**, 2491
1Sa 17:52 the **w** of the Philistines fell down by 2491
31: 3 hit him; and he was sore **w** of the archers. 2342
2Sa 22:39 and **w** them, that they could not arise: 4272
1Ki 20:37 smote him, so that in smiting he **w** *him*. 6481
22:34 and carry me out of the host; for I am **w**. 2470
2Ki 8:28 in Ramoth-gilead; and the Syrians **w** Joram. 5221
1Ch 10: 3 hit him, and he was **w** of the archers. 2342
2Ch 18:33 mayest carry me out of the host; for I am **w**. 2470
35:23 Have me away; for I am sore **w**. 2470
Job 24:12 of the city, and the soul of the **w** crieth out: 2491
Ps 18:38 I have **w** them that they were not able to 4272
64: 7 *with* an arrow; suddenly shall they be **w**. 4347
69:26 talk to the grief of those whom thou hast **w**. 2491
109:22 and needy, and my heart is **w** within me. 2490
Pr 7:26 For she hath cast down many **w**: yea, 2491
18:14 his infirmity; but a **w** spirit who can bear? 5218
SS 5: 7 city found me, they smote me, they **w** me; 6481
Isa 51: 9 it that hath cut Rahab, *and* **w** the dragon? 2490
53: 5 he *was* **w** for our transgressions, *he was* 2490
Jer 30:14 for I have **w** thee *with* the wound of an 5221
37:10 there remained *but* **w** men among them, 1856
51:52 and through all her land the **w** shall groan. 2491
La 2:12 when they swooned as the **w** in the streets 2491
Eze 26:15 at the sound of thy fall, when the **w** cry, 2491
28:23 the **w** shall be judged in the midst of her by 2491
30:24 him *with* the groanings of a **deadly w** *man*. 2491
Joel 2: 8 fall upon the sword, they shall not be **w**. 1214
Zec 13: 6 *Those with* which I was **w** *in* the house of 5221
Mk 12: 4 and **w** *him* **in the head**, and sent *him* away *2775*
Lk 10:30 and **w** *him*, and departed, *2007+4127*
20:12 and they **w** him also, and cast *him* out. *5135*
Ac 19:16 *they* fled out of that house naked and **w**. *5135*
Rev 13: 3 And I saw one of his heads as *it were* **w** to *4969*

WOUNDEDST (1) [WOUND]

Hab 3:13 thou **w** the head out of the house of 4272

WOUNDETH (1) [WOUND]

Job 5:18 he **w**, and his hands make whole. 4272

WOUNDING (1) [WOUND]

Ge 4:23 for I have slain a man to my **w**, and 6482

WOUNDS (15) [WOUND]

2Ki 8:29 **w** which the Syrians had given him at 4347
9:15 of the **w** which the Syrians had given him, 4347
2Ch 22: 6 of the **w** which were given him at Ramah, 4347
Job 9:17 and multiplieth my **w** without cause. 6482
Ps 38: 5 My **w** stink *and* are corrupt because of my 2250
147: 3 the broken in heart, and bindeth up their **w**. 6094
Pr 18: 8 The words of a talebearer *are* as **w**, and 3859
23:29 who hath **w** without cause? who hath 6482
26:22 The words of a talebearer *are* as **w**, and 3859
27: 6 Faithful *are* the **w** of a friend; but the kisses 6482
Isa 1: 6 *but* **w**, and bruises, and putrifying sores: 6482
Jer 6: 7 in her; before me continually *is* grief and **w**. 4347
30:17 I will heal thee of thy **w**, saith the LORD; 4347
Zec 13: 6 unto him, What *are* these **w** in thine hands? 4347
Lk 10:34 And went to *him*, and bound up his **w**, *5134*

WOVE (1) [WEAVE]

2Ki 23: 7 where the women **w** hangings for the grove. 707

WOVEN (4) [WEAVE]

Ex 28:32 it shall have a binding of **w** work round 707
39:22 he made the robe of the ephod *of* **w** work, 707
39:27 they made coats *of* fine linen *of* **w** work for 707
Jn 19:23 without seam, **w** from the top throughout. *5307*

WRAP (2) [WRAPPED, WRAPT]

Isa 28:20 the covering narrower than that *he* can **w** 3664
Mic 7: 3 his mischievous desire: so they **w** it **up**. 5686

WRAPPED (9) [WRAP]

Ge 38:14 and **w** herself, and sat in an open place, 5968
1Ki 19:13 when Elijah heard *it*, that he **w** his face in 3874
Job 8:17 His roots are **w** about the heap, *and* 5440
Mt 27:59 the body, he **w** it in a clean linen cloth, *1794*
Mk 15:46 and **w** *him* **in** the linen, and laid him in a *1750*
Lk 2: 7 and **w** him **in swaddling clothes**, and *4683*
2:12 shall find *the* babe **w in swaddling clothes**, *4683*
23:53 and **w** it in linen, and laid it in a sepulchre *1794*
Jn 20: 7 but **w together** in a place by itself. *1794*

WRAPT (5) [WRAP]

1Sa 21: 9 it *is here* **w** in a cloth behind the ephod: 3874
2Ki 2: 8 **w** *it* **together**, and smote the waters, and 1563
Job 40:17 the sinews of his stones are **w together**. 8276
Eze 21:15 *is* made bright, *it is* **w up** for the slaughter. 4593
Jnh 2: 5 the weeds *were* **w about** my head. 2280

WRATH (198) [WRATHFUL, WRATHS, WROTH]

Ge 39:19 thy servant to me; that his **w** was kindled. 639
49: 7 *it was* fierce; and their **w**, for it was cruel: 5678
Ex 15: 7 thou sentest forth thy **w**, *which* consumed 2740
22:24 my **w** shall wax hot, and I will kill you with 639
32:10 that my **w** may wax hot against them, and 639
32:11 why doth thy **w** wax hot against thy people, 639
32:12 Turn from thy fierce **w**, and repent of *this* 639
Lev 10: 6 and lest **w** come upon all the people: 7107
Nu 1:53 that there be no **w** upon the congregation of 7110
11:33 the **w** of the LORD was kindled against 639
16:46 for there is **w** gone out from the LORD; 7110
18: 5 that there be no **w** any more upon 7110
25:11 hath turned my **w** away from the children 2534
Dt 9: 7 **provokedst** the LORD thy God **to w** in 7107
9: 8 in Horeb ye **provoked** the LORD **to w**, 7107
9:22 ye **provoked** the LORD **to w**. 7107
11:17 *then* the LORD'S **w** be kindled against you, 639
29:23 overthrew in his anger, and in his **w**: 2534
29:28 in **w**, and in great indignation, and 2534
32:27 Were it not that I feared the **w** of 3708
Jos 9:20 lest **w** be upon us, because of the oath 7110
22:20 and **w** fell on all the congregation of Israel? 7110
1Sa 28:18 nor executedst his fierce **w** upon Amalek, 639
2Sa 11:20 if so be that the king's **w** arise, and he say 2534
2Ki 22:13 for great *is* the **w** of the LORD that is 2534
22:17 my **w** shall be kindled against this place, 2534
23:26 turned not from the fierceness of his great **w**, 639
1Ch 27:24 because there fell **w** for it against Israel; 7110
2Ch 12: 7 my **w** shall not be poured out upon 2534
12:12 the **w** of the LORD turned from him, 639
19: 2 *is* **w** upon thee from before the LORD. 7110
19:10 *so* **w** come upon you, and upon your 7110
24:18 **w** came upon Judah and Jerusalem for this 7110
28:11 for the fierce **w** of the LORD *is* upon you. 639
28:13 is great, and *there is* fierce **w** against Israel. 639
29: 8 Wherefore the **w** of the LORD was upon 7110
29:10 that his fierce **w** may turn away from us. 639
30: 8 that the fierceness of his **w** may turn away 639
32:25 therefore there was **w** upon him, and 7110
32:26 that the **w** of the LORD came not upon 7110
34:21 for great *is* the **w** of the LORD that is 2534
34:25 my **w** shall be poured out upon this place, 2534
36:16 until the **w** of the LORD arose against his 2534
Ezr 5:12 had **provoked** the God of heaven **unto w**, 7265
7:23 for why should there be **w** against the realm 7109
8:22 his **w** *is* against all them that forsake him. 639
10:14 until the fierce **w** of our God for this matter 639
Ne 13:18 yet ye bring more **w** upon Israel by 2740
Est 1:18 *shall there arise* too much contempt and **w**. 7110
2: 1 when the **w** of king Ahasuerus was 2534
3: 5 him reverence, *then* was Haman full *of* **w**. 2534
7: 7 wine in his **w** *went* into the palace garden: 2534
7:10 Then was the king's **w** pacified. 2534
Job 5: 2 For **w** killeth the foolish man, and 3708
14:13 wouldest keep me secret, until thy **w** be past, 639
16: 9 He teareth *me in* his **w**, who hateth me: 639
19:11 He hath also kindled his **w** against me, and 639
19:29 for **w** *bringeth* the punishments of 2534
20:23 *God* shall cast the fury of his **w** upon him, 639
20:28 *goods shall* flow away in the day of his **w**. 639
21:20 and he shall drink of the **w** of the Almighty. 2534
21:30 they shall be brought forth to the day of **w**. 5678
32: 2 was kindled the **w** of Elihu the son of 639
32: 2 against Job was his **w** kindled, because 639
32: 3 Also against his three friends was his **w** 639
32: 5 of *these* three men, then his **w** was kindled. 639
36:13 the hypocrites in heart heap up **w**: they cry 639
36:18 Because *there is* **w**, *beware* lest he take thee 2534
40:11 Cast abroad the rage of thy **w**: and 639
42: 7 My **w** is kindled against thee, and against thy 639
Ps 2: 5 Then shall he speak unto them in his **w**, and 639
2:12 the way, when his **w** is kindled but a little: 639
21: 9 the LORD shall swallow them up in his **w**, 639
37: 8 Cease from anger, and forsake **w**: fret not 2534
38: 1 O LORD, rebuke me not in thy **w**: 7110
55: 3 iniquity upon me, and in **w** they hate me. 639
58: 9 with a whirlwind, both living, and in *his* **w**. 2740
59:13 Consume *them* in **w**, consume *them*, that 2534
76:10 Surely the **w** of man shall praise thee: 2534
76:10 the remainder of **w** shalt thou restrain. 2534
78:31 The **w** of God came upon them, and slew 639
78:38 anger away, and did not stir up all his **w**. 2534
78:49 **w**, and indignation, and trouble, 5678
79: 6 Pour out thy **w** upon the heathen that have 2534
85: 3 Thou hast taken away all thy **w**: thou hast 5678
88: 7 Thy **w** lieth hard upon me, and thou hast 2534
88:16 Thy **fierce w** goeth over me; thy terrors 2740
89:46 for ever? shall thy **w** burn like fire? 2534
90: 7 thine anger, and by thy **w** are we troubled. 2534
90: 9 For all our days are passed away in thy **w**: 5678
90:11 even according to thy fear, *so is* thy **w**. 5678
Ps 95:11 *Unto* whom I sware in my **w** that they should 639
102:10 Because of thine indignation and thy **w**: 7110
106:23 to turn away his **w**, lest *he* should destroy 2534
106:40 Therefore was the **w** of the LORD kindled 639
110: 5 shall strike through kings in the day of his **w**. 639
124: 3 when their **w** was kindled against us: 639
138: 7 thine hand against the **w** of mine enemies, 639
Pr 11: 4 Riches profit not in the day of **w**: but 5678
11:23 *but* the expectation of the wicked *is* **w**. 5678
12:16 A fool's **w** is presently known: but 3708
14:29 *He that is* slow to **w** *is* of great 639
14:35 but his **w** is *against* him that causeth shame. 5678
15: 1 A soft answer turneth away **w**: but 2534
16:14 The **w** of a king *is as* messengers of death: 2534
19:12 The king's **w** *is* as the roaring of a lion; but 2197
19:19 *A man* of great **w** *shall* suffer punishment: 2534
21:14 and a reward in the bosom strong **w**. 2534
21:24 *is* his name, who dealeth in proud **w**. 5678
24:18 and he turn away his **w** from him. 639
27: 3 but a fool's **w** *is* heavier than them both. 3708
27: 4 **W** *is* cruel, and anger *is* outrageous; but 2534
29: 8 city into a snare: but wise *men* turn away **w**. 639
30:33 so the forcing of **w** bringeth forth strife. 639
Ecc 5:17 *hath* much sorrow and **w** with his sickness. 7110
Isa 9:19 Through the **w** of the LORD of hosts is 5678
10: 6 against the people of my **w** will I give him 5678
13: 9 cruel both *with* **w** and fierce anger, to lay 5678
13:13 in the **w** of the LORD of hosts, and in 5678
14: 6 He who smote the people in **w** *with* a 5678
16: 6 of his haughtiness, and his pride, and his **w**: 5678
54: 8 In a little **w** I hid my face from thee for a 7110
60:10 for in my **w** I smote thee, but in my favour 7110
Jer 7:29 and forsaken the generation of his **w**. 5678
10:10 at his **w** the earth shall tremble, and 7110
18:20 *and* to turn away thy **w** from them. 2534
21: 5 even in anger, and in fury, and in great **w**. 7110
32:37 mine anger, and in my fury, and in great **w**; 7110
44: 8 In that *ye* **provoke** me **unto w** with 3707
48:30 I know his **w**, saith the LORD; but *it shall* 5678
50:13 Because of the **w** of the LORD it shall not 7110
La 2: 2 he hath thrown down in his **w** the strong 5678
3: 1 *that* hath seen affliction by the rod of his **w**. 5678
Eze 7:12 for my **w** *is* upon all the multitude thereof. 2740
7:14 for my **w** *is* upon all the multitude thereof. 2740
7:19 them in the day of the **w** of the LORD: 5678
13:15 Thus will I accomplish my **w** upon 2534
21:31 I will blow against thee in the fire of my **w**, 5678
22:21 blow upon you in the fire of my **w**, and 5678
22:31 have consumed them with the fire of my **w**: 5678
38:19 *and* in the fire of my **w** have I spoken, 5678
Hos 5:10 I will pour out my **w** upon them like water. 5678
13:11 in mine anger, and took *him away* in my **w**. 5678
Am 1:11 tear perpetually, and he kept his **w** for ever: 5678
Na 1: 2 and he reserveth ***w*** for his enemies. NIH
Hab 3: 2 years make known; in **w** remember mercy. 7267
3: 8 *was* thy **w** against the sea, that thou didst 5678
Zep 1:15 That day *is* a day of **w**, a day of trouble and 5678
1:18 deliver them in the day of the LORD'S **w**; 5678
Zec 7:12 came a great **w** from the LORD of hosts. 7110
8:14 when your fathers **provoked** me **to w**, 7107
Mt 3: 7 who hath warned you to flee from the **w** to *3709*
Lk 3: 7 who hath warned you to flee from the **w** to *3709*
4:28 they heard these *things*, were filled with **w**, *2372*
21:23 distress in the land, and **w** upon this people. *3709*
Jn 3:36 see life; but the **w** of God abideth on him. *3709*
Ac 19:28 heard *these sayings*, they were full of **w**, *2372*
Ro 1:18 For the **w** of God is revealed from heaven *3709*
2: 5 heart treasurest up unto thyself **w** *3709*
2: 5 up unto thyself wrath against the day of **w** *3709*
2: 8 obey unrighteousness, indignation and **w**, *3709*
4:15 Because the law worketh **w**: for where no *3709*
5: 9 we shall be saved from **w** through him. *3709*
9:22 willing to shew *his* **w**, and to make his *3709*
9:22 *the* vessels of **w** fitted to destruction: *3709*
12:19 but *rather* give place unto **w**: *3709*
13: 4 a revenger to *execute* **w** upon him that doeth *3709*
13: 5 not only for **w**, but also for conscience *3709*
Gal 5:20 emulations, **w**, strife, seditions, heresies, *2372*
Eph 2: 3 and were by nature the children of **w**, *3709*
4:26 let not the sun go down upon your **w**: *3950*
4:31 and **w**, and anger, and clamour, and *2372*
5: 6 of these *things* cometh the **w** of God upon *3709*
6: 4 ye fathers, **provoke** not your children **to w**: *3949*
Col 3: 6 For which *things'* sake the **w** of God *3709*
3: 8 **w**, malice, blasphemy, *2372*
1Th 1:10 which delivered us from the **w** to come. *3709*
2:16 for the **w** is come upon them to *3709*
5: 9 For God hath not appointed us to **w**, but *3709*
1Ti 2: 8 up holy hands, without **w** and doubting. *3709*
Heb 3:11 So I sware in my **w**, They shall not enter *3709*
4: 3 as *he* said, As I have sworn in my **w**, if they *3709*
11:27 not fearing the **w** of the king: *2372*
Jas 1:19 be swift to hear, slow to speak, slow to **w**: *3709*
1:20 For the **w** of man worketh not *3709*
Rev 6:16 on the throne, and from the **w** of the Lamb: *3709*
6:17 For the great day of his **w** is come; and *3709*
11:18 and thy **w** is come, and the time of *3709*
12:12 having great **w**, because he knoweth that he *2372*
14: 8 of the wine of the **w** of her fornication. *2372*
14:10 The same shall drink of the wine of the **w** *2372*
14:19 cast *it* into the great winepress of the **w** of *2372*
15: 1 for in them is filled up the **w** of God. *2372*
15: 7 seven golden vials full of the **w** of God, *2372*
16: 1 pour out the vials of the **w** of God upon *2372*
16:19 cup of the wine of the fierceness of his **w**. *3709*
18: 3 of the wine of the **w** of her fornication, *2372*
19:15 of the fierceness and **w** of Almighty God. *3709*

WRATHFUL (2) [WRATH]

Ps 69:24 and let thy **w** anger take hold of them. 2740
Pr 15:18 A **w** man stirreth up strife: but *he that is* 2534

WRATHS (1) [WRATH]

2Co 12:20 envyings, **w**, strifes, backbitings, *2372*

WREATH (1) [WREATHED, WREATHEN, WREATHS]
2Ch 4:13 two rows of pomegranates on each w, to 7639

WREATHED (1) [WREATH]
La 1:14 they are w, and come up upon my neck: 8276

WREATHEN (10) [WREATH]
Ex 28:14 of w work shalt thou make them, and 5688
28:14 and fasten the w chains to the ouches. 5688
28:22 chains at the ends of w work of pure gold. 5688
28:24 thou shalt put the two w chains of gold in 5688
28:25 the other two ends of the two w chains thou 5688
39:15 chains at the ends, of w work of pure gold. 5688
39:17 they put the two w chains of gold in 5688
39:18 the two ends of the two w chains they 5688
2Ki 25:17 the w work, and pomegranates upon 7639
25:17 these had the second pillar with w work. 7639

WREATHS (3) [WREATH]
1Ki 7:17 nets of checker work, and w of chain work, 1434
2Ch 4:12 the two w to cover the two pommels of 7639
4:13 four hundred pomegranates on the two w; 7639

WREST (5) [WRESTLE]
Ex 23: 2 cause to decline after many to w judgment: 5186
23: 6 Thou shalt not w the judgment of thy poor 5186
Dt 16:19 Thou shalt not w judgment; thou shalt not 5186
Ps 56: 5 Every day they w my words: all their 6087
2Pe 3:16 they that are unlearned and unstable w, 4761

WRESTLE (1) [WREST, WRESTLED, WRESTLINGS]
Eph 6:12 For we w not against flesh and 1510+3823

WRESTLED (3) [WRESTLE]
Ge 30: 8 With great wrestlings have I w with my 6617
32:24 there w a man with him until the breaking of 79
32:25 thigh was out of joint, as he w with him. 79

WRESTLINGS (1) [WRESTLE]
Ge 30: 8 With great w have I wrestled with my 5319

WRETCHED (2) [WRETCHEDNESS]
Ro 7:24 O w man that I am! who shall deliver me 5005
Rev 3:17 and knowest not that thou art w, and 5005

WRETCHEDNESS (1) [WRETCHED]
Nu 11:15 in thy sight; and let me not see my w. 7451

WRING (3) [WRINGED, WRINGING, WRUNG]
Lev 1:15 and w off his head, and burn it on the altar; 4454
5: 8 w off his head from his neck, but shall not 4454
Ps 75: 8 the wicked of the earth shall w them out, 4680

WRINGED (1) [WRING]
Jdg 6:38 w the dew out of the fleece, a bowl full of 4680

WRINGING (1) [WRING]
Pr 30:33 and the w of the nose bringeth forth blood: 4330

WRINKLE (1) [WRINKLES]
Eph 5:27 or w, or any such thing; but that it should 4512

WRINKLES (1) [WRINKLE]
Job 16: 8 thou hast filled me with w, which is a 7059

WRITE (91) [HANDWRITING, WRITER, WRITER'S, WRITEST, WRITETH, WRITING, WRITINGS, WRITTEN, WROTE]
Ex 17:14 W this for a memorial in a book, and 3789
34: 1 I will w upon these tables the words that 3789
34:27 said unto Moses, W thou these words: 3789
Nu 5:23 the priest shall w these curses in a book, 3789
17: 2 w thou every man's name upon his rod. 3789
17: 3 thou shalt w Aaron's name upon the rod of 3789
Dt 6: 9 thou shalt w them upon the posts of thy 3789
10: 2 I will w on the tables the words that were in 3789
11:20 thou shalt w them upon the door posts of 3789
17:18 that he shall w him a copy of this law in a 3789
24: 1 let him w her a bill of divorcement, and 3789
24: 3 w her a bill of divorcement, and giveth it in 3789
27: 3 thou shalt w upon them all the words of this 3789
27: 8 thou shalt w upon the stones all the words 3789
31:19 Now therefore w ye this song for you, 3789
2Ch 26:22 did Isaiah the prophet, the son of Amoz, w. 3789
Ezr 5:10 that we might w the names of the men that 3790
Ne 9:38 w it; and our princes, Levites, and priests, 3789
Est 8: 8 W ye also for the Jews, as it liketh you, 3789
Pr 3: 3 w them upon the table of thine heart: 3789
7: 3 w them upon the table of thine heart. 3789
Isa 8: 1 w in it with a man's pen concerning 3789
10: 1 that w grievousness which they have 3789
10:19 shall be few, that a child may w them. 3789
30: 8 w it before them in a table, and note it in a 3789
Jer 22:30 saith the LORD, W ye this man childless, 3789
30: 2 W thee all the words that I have spoken 3789
31:33 their inward parts, and w it in their hearts; 3789
36: 2 w therein all the words that I have spoken 3789
36:17 How didst thou w all these words at his 3789
36:28 w in it all the former words that were in 3789
Eze 24: 2 Son of man, w thee the name of the day, 3789
37:16 w upon it, For Judah, and for the children 3789
37:16 another stick, and w upon it, For Joseph, 3789
43:11 w it in their sight, that they may keep 3789
Hab 2: 2 W the vision, and make it plain upon 3789
Mk 10: 4 Moses suffered to w a bill of divorcement, 1125
Lk 1: 3 to w unto thee in order, most excellent 1125
16: 6 thy bill, and sit down quickly, and w fifty. 1125
16: 7 unto him, Take thy bill, and w fourscore. 1125
Jn 1:45 and the prophets, did w, Jesus of Nazareth, 1125
19:21 to Pilate, W not, The King of the Jews; 1125
Ac 15:20 But that we w unto them, that they abstain 1989
Ac 25:26 Of whom I have no certain thing to w unto 1125
25:26 I might have somewhat to w. 1125
1Co 4:14 I w not these things to shame you, but 1125
14:37 let him acknowledge that the things that I w 1125
2Co 1:13 For we w none other things unto you, 1125
2: 9 For to this end also did I w, that I might 1125
9: 1 it is superfluous for me to w to you: 1125
13: 2 being absent now I w to them which 1125
13:10 Therefore I w these things being absent, 1125
Gal 1:20 Now the things which I w unto you, 1125
Php 3: 1 To w the same things to you, to me indeed 1125
1Th 4: 9 love ye need not that I w unto you: 1125
5: 1 ye have no need that I w unto you. 1125
2Th 3:17 which is the token in every epistle: so I w. 1125
1Ti 3:14 These things w I unto thee, hoping to come 1125
Heb 8:10 into their mind, and w them in their hearts: 1924
10:16 and in their minds will I w them; 1924
2Pe 3: 1 second epistle, beloved, I now w unto you; 1125
1Jn 1: 4 And these things w we unto you, that your 1125
2: 1 these things w I unto you, that ye sin not. 1125
2: 7 I w no new commandment unto you, but 1125
2: 8 Again, a new commandment I w unto you, 1125
2:12 I w unto you, little children, because 1125
2:13 I w unto you, fathers, because ye have 1125
2:13 I w unto you, young men, because 1125
2:13 I w unto you, little children, because 1125
2Jn 1:12 Having many things to w unto you, I would 1125
1:12 unto you, I would not w with paper and ink: NIG
3Jn 1:13 I had many things to w, 1125
1:13 but I will not with ink and pen w unto thee: 1125
Jude 1: 3 when I gave all diligence to w unto you of 1125
1: 3 it was needful for me to w unto you, and 1125
Rev 1:11 w in a book, and send it unto the seven 1125
1:19 W the things which thou hast seen, and 1125
2: 1 Unto the angel of the church of Ephesus w; 1125
2: 8 unto the angel of the church in Smyrna w; 1125
2:12 to the angel of the church in Pergamos w; 1125
2:18 unto the angel of the church in Thyatira w; 1125
3: 1 unto the angel of the church in Sardis w; 1125
3: 7 the angel of the church in Philadelphia w; 1125
3:12 and I will w upon him the name of my God, 1125
3:12 and I will w upon him my new name. NIG
3:14 angel of the church of the Laodiceans w; 1125
10: 4 had uttered their voices, I was about to w: 1125
10: 4 the seven thunders uttered, and w them not. 1125
14:13 a voice from heaven saying unto me, W, 1125
19: 9 And he saith unto me, W, Blessed are they 1125
21: 5 And he said unto me, W: for these words 1125

WRITER (2) [WRITE]
Jdg 5:14 Zebulun they that handle the pen of the w. 5608
Ps 45: 1 the king: my tongue is the pen of a ready w. 5608

WRITER'S (2) [WRITE]
Eze 9: 2 with linen, with a w inkhorn by his side: 5608
9: 3 which had the w inkhorn by his side; 5608

WRITEST (2) [WRITE]
Job 13:26 For thou w bitter things against me, and 3789
Eze 37:20 the sticks whereon thou w shall be in thine 3789

WRITETH (1) [WRITE]
Ps 87: 6 shall count, when he w up the people, 3789

WRITING (38) [WRITE]
Ex 32:16 the w was the writing of God, graven upon 4385
32:16 the writing was the w of God, graven upon 4385
39:30 wrote upon it a w, like to the engravings of 4385
Dt 10: 4 according to the first w, the ten 4385
31:24 when Moses had made an end of w 3789
1Ch 28:19 me understand in w by his hand upon me, 3791
2Ch 2:11 Huram the king of Tyre answered in w, 3791
21:12 there came a w to him from Elijah 4385
35: 4 according to the w of David king of Israel, 3791
35: 4 and according to the w of Solomon his son. 4385
36:22 his kingdom, and put it also in w, saying, 4385
Ezr 1: 1 his kingdom, and put it also in w, saying, 4385
4: 7 the w of the letter was written in the Syrian 3791
Est 1:22 into every province according to the w 3791
3:12 every province according to the w thereof, 3791
3:14 The copy of the w for a commandment to 3791
4: 8 Also he gave him the copy of the w of 3791
8: 8 for the w which is written in the king's 3791
8: 9 unto every province according to the w 3791
8: 9 to the Jews according to their w, and 3791
8:13 The copy of the w for a commandment to 3791
9:27 keep these two days according to their w, 3791
Isa 38: 9 The w of Hezekiah, king of Judah, when he 4385
Eze 13: 9 neither shall they be written in the w of 3791
Da 5: 7 Whosoever shall read this w, and shew me 3792
5: 8 wise men: but they could not read the w, 3792
5:15 that they should read this w, and 3792
5:16 now if thou canst read the w, and 3792
5:17 yet I will read the w unto the king, and 3792
5:24 hand sent from him; and this w was written. 3792
5:25 this is the w that was written, MENE, 3792
6: 8 establish the decree, and sign the w, 3792
6: 9 Wherefore king Darius signed the w and 3792
6:10 Now when Daniel knew that the w was 3792
Mt 5:31 let him give her a w of divorcement: 647
19: 7 then command to give a w of divorcement, 975
Lk 1:63 And he asked for a w table, and wrote, 4093
Jn 19:19 And the w was, JESUS OF NAZARETH 1125

WRITINGS (1) [WRITE]
Jn 5:47 But if ye believe not his w, how shall ye 1121

WRITTEN (291) [WRITE]
Ex 24:12 a law, and commandments which I have w; 3789
31:18 tables of stone, w with the finger of God. 3789
32:15 the tables were w on both their sides; on 3789
32:15 the one side and on the other were they w. 3789
32:32 out of thy book which thou hast w. 3789
Nu 11:26 they were of them that were w, but 3789
Dt 9:10 tables of stone w with the finger of God; 3789
9:10 on them was w according to all the words, NIH
28:58 words of this law that are w in this book, 3789
28:61 which is not w in the book of this law, 3789
29:20 all the curses that are w in this book shall 3789
29:21 covenant that are w in this book of the law: 3789
29:27 to bring upon it all the curses that are w in 3789
30:10 his statutes which are w in this book of 3789
Jos 1: 8 to do according to all that is w therein: 3789
8:31 as it is w in the book of the law of Moses, 3789
8:34 according to all that is w in the book of 3789
10:13 Is not this w in the book of Jasher? So 3789
23: 6 to do all that is w in the book of the law of 3789
2Sa 1:18 behold, it is w in the book of Jasher.) 3789
1Ki 2: 3 as it is w in the law of Moses, 3789
11:41 are they not w in the book of the acts of 3789
14:19 behold they are w in the book of 3789
14:29 are they not w in the book of the chronicles 3789
15: 7 are they not w in the book of the chronicles 3789
15:23 are they not w in the book of the chronicles 3789
15:31 are they not w in the book of the chronicles 3789
16: 5 are they not w in the book of the chronicles 3789
16:14 are they not w in the book of the chronicles 3789
16:20 are they not w in the book of the chronicles 3789
16:27 are they not w in the book of the chronicles 3789
21:11 as it was w in the letters which she had sent 3789
22:39 are they not w in the book of the chronicles 3789
22:45 are they not w in the book of the chronicles 3789
2Ki 1:18 are they not w in the book of the chronicles 3789
8:23 are they not w in the book of the chronicles 3789
10:34 are they not w in the book of the chronicles 3789
12:19 are they not w in the book of the chronicles 3789
13: 8 are they not w in the book of the chronicles 3789
13:12 are they not w in the book of the chronicles 3789
14: 6 according unto that which is w in the book 3789
14:15 are they not w in the book of the chronicles 3789
14:18 are they not w in the book of the chronicles 3789
14:28 are they not w in the book of the chronicles 3789
15: 6 are they not w in the book of the chronicles 3789
15:11 they are w in the book of the chronicles of 3789
15:15 they are w in the book of the chronicles of 3789
15:21 are they not w in the book of the chronicles 3789
15:26 they are w in the book of the chronicles of 3789
15:31 they are w in the book of the chronicles of 3789
15:36 are they not w in the book of the chronicles 3789
16:19 are they not w in the book of the chronicles 3789
20:20 are they not w in the book of the chronicles 3789
21:17 are they not w in the book of the chronicles 3789
21:25 are they not w in the book of the chronicles 3789
22:13 to do according unto all that which is w 3789
23: 3 of this covenant that were w in this book. 3789
23:21 as it is w in the book of this covenant. 3789
23:24 w in the book that Hilkiah the priest found 3789
23:28 are they not w in the book of the chronicles 3789
24: 5 are they not w in the book of the chronicles 3789
1Ch 4:41 these w by name came in the days of 3789
9: 1 they were w in the book of the kings of 3789
16:40 to do according to all that is w in the law of 3789
29:29 they are w in the book of Samuel the seer, 3789
2Ch 9:29 are they not w in the book of Nathan 3789
12:15 are they not w in the book of Shemaiah 3789
13:22 are w in the story of the prophet Iddo. 3789
16:11 they are w in the book of the kings of Judah 3789
20:34 behold they are w in the book of Jehu 3789
23:18 as it is w in the law of Moses, 3789
24:27 behold they are w in the story of the book 3789
25: 4 did as it is w in the law in the book of 3789
25:26 are they not w in the book of the kings of 3789
27: 7 lo they are w in the book of the kings of 3789
28:26 they are w in the book of the kings of Judah 3789
30: 5 it of a long time in such sort as it was w. 3789
30:18 eat the passover otherwise than it was w. 3789
31: 3 as it is w in the law of the LORD. 3789
32:32 they are w in the vision of Isaiah 3789
33:18 they are w in the book of the kings of Israel. NIH
33:19 they are w among the sayings of the seers. 3789
34:21 to do after all that is w in this book. 3789
34:24 even all the curses that are w in the book 3789
34:31 of the covenant which are w in this book. 3789
35:12 as it is w in the book of Moses. 3789
35:25 and behold, they are w in the lamentations. 3789
35:26 according to that which was w in the law of 3789
35:27 they are w in the book of the kings of Israel 3789
36: 8 they are w in the book of the kings of Israel 3789
Ezr 3: 2 as it is w in the law of Moses the man of 3789
3: 4 as it is w, and offered the daily burnt 3789
4: 7 the writing of the letter was w in the Syrian 3789
5: 7 sent a letter unto him, wherein was w thus: 3790
6: 2 a roll, and therein was a record thus w: 3790
6:18 as it is w in the book of Moses. 3792
8:34 and all the weight was w at that time. 3789
Ne 6: 6 Wherein was w, It is reported among 3789
7: 5 came up at the first, and found w therein, 3789
8:14 they found w in the law which the LORD 3789
8:15 of thick trees, to make booths, as it is w. 3789
10:34 the LORD our God, as it is w in the law: 3789
10:36 as it is w in the law, and the firstlings of 3789
12:23 were w in the book of the chronicles, 3789
13: 1 therein was found w, that the Ammonite 3789
Est 1:19 let it be w among the laws of the Persians 3789
2:23 it was w in the book of the chronicles 3789
3: 9 let it be w that they may be destroyed: 3789
3:12 there was w according to all that Haman 3789
3:12 in the name of king Ahasuerus was it w, 3789
6: 2 it was found w, that Mordecai had told of 3789
8: 5 let it be w to reverse the letters devised by 3789
8: 8 for the writing which is w in the king's 3789
8: 9 it was w according to all that Mordecai 3789
9:23 and as Mordecai had w unto them; 3789
9:32 matters of Purim; and it was w in the book. 3789
10: 2 are they not w in the book of the chronicles 3789
Job 19:23 O that my words were now w! O that they 3789
31:35 and that mine adversary had w a book. 3789
Ps 40: 7 in the volume of the book it is w of me, 3789
69:28 the living, and not be w with the righteous. 3789

W

Ps 102:18 This shall be **w** for the generation to come: 3789
139:16 in thy book all *my members* were **w**, 3789
149: 9 To execute upon them the judgment **w**: 3789
Pr 22:20 Have not I **w** to thee excellent things in 3789
Ecc 12:10 *that which was* **w** *was* upright, *even* words 3789
Isa 4: 3 *even* every one that is **w** among the living 3789
65: 6 Behold, *it is* **w** before me: I will not keep 3789
Jer 17: 1 The sin of Judah *is* **w** with a pen of iron, 3789
17:13 they that depart from me shall be **w** in 3789
25:13 *even* all that is **w** in this book, which 3789
36: 6 the roll, which thou hast **w** from my mouth, 3789
36:29 Why hast thou **w** therein, saying, 3789
45: 1 when he had **w** these words in a book at 3789
51:60 *even* all these words that are **w** against 3789
Eze 2:10 and it *was* **w** within and without: 3789
2:10 *there was* **w** therein lamentations, and 3789
13: 9 neither shall they be **w** in the writing of 3789
Da 5:24 sent from him; and this writing *was* **w**. 7560
5:25 this *is* the writing that *was* **w**, MENE, 7560
9:11 the oath that *is* **w** in the law of Moses 3789
9:13 As *it is* **w** in the law of Moses, all this evil 3789
12: 1 every one that *shall* be found **w** in the book. 3789
Hos 8:12 I have **w** to him the great things of my law, 3789
Mal 3:16 a book of remembrance was **w** before him 3789
Mt 2: 5 of Judea: for thus it is **w** by the prophet, *1125*
4: 4 But he answered and said, It is **w**, Man *1125*
4: 6 for it is **w**, He shall give his angels charge *1125*
4: 7 Jesus said unto him, It is **w** again, *1125*
4:10 for it is **w**, Thou shalt worship the Lord thy *1125*
11:10 For this is *he*, of whom it is **w**, Behold, *1125*
21:13 And said unto them, It is **w**, My house shall *1125*
26:24 The Son of man goeth as it is **w** of him: but *1125*
26:31 for it is **w**, I will smite the shepherd, and *1125*
27:37 And set up over his head his accusation **w**, *1125*
Mk 1: 2 As it is **w** in the prophets, Behold, I send *1125*
7: 6 as it is **w**, This people honoureth me with *1125*
9:12 and how it is **w** of the Son of man, *1125*
9:13 whatsoever they listed, as it is **w** of him. *1125*
11:17 he taught, saying unto them, Is it not **w**, *1125*
14:21 Son of man indeed goeth, as it is **w** of him: *1125*
14:27 for it is **w**, I will smite the shepherd, and *1125*
15:26 of his accusation was **w over**, *1924*
Lk 2:23 (As it is **w** in the law of the Lord, Every *1125*
3: 4 As it is **w** in the book of the words of *1125*
4: 4 And Jesus answered him, saying, It is **w**, *1125*
4: 8 for it is **w**, Thou shalt worship the Lord thy *1125*
4:10 For it is **w**, He shall give his angels charge *1125*
4:17 he found the place where it was **w**, *1125*
7:27 This is *he*, of whom it is **w**, Behold, I send *1125*
10:20 because your names are **w** in heaven. *1125*
10:26 He said unto him, What is **w** in the law? *1125*
18:31 all *things* that are **w** by the prophets *1125*
19:46 Saying unto them, It is **w**, My house is *1125*
20:17 and said, What is this then that is **w**, *1125*
21:22 that all *things* which are **w** may be fulfilled. *1125*
22:37 that this that is **w** must yet be accomplished *1125*
23:38 And a superscription also was **w** over him *1125*
24:44 which were **w** in the law of Moses, and *1125*
24:46 Thus it is **w**, and thus it behoved Christ to *1125*
Jn 2:17 his disciples remembered that it was **w**, *1125*
6:31 as it is **w**, He gave them bread from heaven *1125*
6:45 It is **w** in the prophets, And they shall be all *1125*
8:17 It is also **w** in your law, that the testimony *1125*
10:34 Is it not **w** in your law, I said, Ye are gods? *1125*
12:14 found a young ass, sat thereon; as it is **w**, *1125*
12:16 remembered they that these *things* were **w** *1125*
15:25 might be fulfilled that is **w** in their law, *1125*
19:20 and it was **w** in Hebrew, *and* Greek, *and* *1125*
19:22 What I have **w** I have written. *1125*
19:22 What I have written I have **w**. *1125*
20:30 his disciples, which are not **w** in this book: *1125*
20:31 But these are **w**, that ye might believe that *1125*
21:25 the which, if they should be **w** every one, *1125*
21:25 not contain the books that should be **w**. *1125*
Ac 1:20 For it is **w** in the book of Psalms, Let his *1125*
7:42 as it is **w** in the book of the prophets, O *ye* *1125*
13:29 And when they had fulfilled all that was **w** *1125*
13:33 as it is also **w** in the second psalm, Thou art *1125*
15:15 agree the words of the prophets; as it is **w**, *1125*
21:25 we have **w** and concluded that they observe *1989*
23: 5 for it is **w**, Thou shalt not speak evil of *1125*
24:14 believing all *things* which are **w** in the law *1125*
Ro 1:17 as it is **w**, The just shall live by faith. *1125*
2:15 Which shew the work of the law **w** in their *1123*
2:24 among the Gentiles through you, as it is **w**. *1125*
3: 4 as it is **w**, That thou mightest be justified in *1125*
3:10 As it is **w**, There is none righteous, no, *1125*
4:17 (As it is **w**, I have made thee a father of *1125*
4:23 Now it was not **w** for his sake alone, that it *1125*
8:36 As it is **w**, For thy sake we are killed all *1125*
9:13 As it is **w**, Jacob have I loved, *1125*
9:33 As it is **w**, Behold, I lay in Sion a *1125*
10:15 as it is **w**, How beautiful *are* the feet of *1125*
11: 8 (According as it is **w**, God hath given them *1125*
11:26 as it is **w**, There shall come out of Sion *1125*
12:19 for it is **w**, Vengeance *is* mine; I will repay, *1125*
14:11 For it is **w**, *As* I live, saith the Lord, every *1125*
15: 3 but, as it is **w**, The reproaches of them that *1125*
15: 4 For whatsoever *things* were **w aforetime** *4270*
15: 4 written aforetime were **w** for our learning, *4270*
15: 9 as it is **w**, For this cause I will confess to *1125*
15:15 I have **w** the more boldly unto you in some *1125*
15:21 But as it is **w**, To whom he was not spoken *1125*
16: S **W** to the Romans from Corinthus, *and* *1125*
1Co 1:19 For it is **w**, I will destroy the wisdom of *1125*
1:31 That, according as it is **w**, He that glorieth, *1125*
2: 9 But as it is **w**, Eye hath not seen, nor ear *1125*
3:19 For it is **w**, He taketh the wise in their own *1125*
4: 6 not to think *of men* above that which is **w**, *1125*
5:11 But now I have **w** unto you not to keep *1125*
9: 9 For it is **w** in the law of Moses, Thou shalt *1125*
9:10 For our sakes, no doubt, *this* is **w**: that he *1125*
9:15 have I **w** these *things*, that it should be *1125*
10: 7 as it is **w**, The people sat down to eat and *1125*
10:11 and they are **w** for our admonition, *1125*

1Co 14:21 In the law it is **w**, With *men* of other *1125*
15:45 And so it is **w**, The first man Adam was *1125*
15:54 be brought to pass the saying that is **w**, *1125*
16: S The first *epistle* to the Corinthians was **w** *1125*
2Co 3: 2 Ye are our epistle **w** in our hearts, known *1449*
3: 3 **w** not with ink, but with the Spirit of *1449*
3: 7 **w** *and* engraven in stones, *1121+1722*
4:13 according as it is **w**, I believed, *and* *1125*
8:15 As it is **w**, He that *had gathered* much had *1125*
9: 9 (As it is **w**, He hath dispersed abroad; *1125*
13: S to the Corinthians was **w** from Philippi, *1125*
Gal 3:10 for it is **w**, Cursed *is* every one that *1125*
3:10 are **w** in the book of the law to do them. *1125*
3:13 for it is **w**, Cursed *is* every one that hangeth *1125*
4:22 For it is **w**, that Abraham had two sons, *1125*
4:27 For it is **w**, Rejoice, *thou* barren that bearest *1125*
6:11 Ye see how large a letter I have **w** unto you *1125*
6: S Unto the Galatians **w** from Rome. *1125*
Eph 6: S **W** from Rome unto the Ephesians by *1125*
Php 4: S It was **w** to the Philippians from Rome by *1125*
Col 4: S **W** from Rome to the Colossians by *1125*
1Th 5: S unto the Thessalonians was **w** from Athens. *1125*
2Th 3: S to the Thessalonians was **w** from Athens. *1125*
1Ti 6: S The first to Timothy was **w** from Laodicea, *1125*
2Ti 4: S was **w** from Rome, when Paul was brought *1125*
Tit 3: S It was **w** to Titus, ordained the first bishop *1125*
Phm 1:19 I Paul have **w** *it* with mine own hand, I will *1125*
1: S **W** from Rome to Philemon, by Onesimus a *1125*
Heb 10: 7 I come (in the volume of the book it is **w** of *1125*
12:23 which are **w** in heaven, and to God the Judge *583*
13:22 for I have **w a letter** unto you in few *1989*
13: S **W** to the Hebrews from Italy by Timothy. *1125*
1Pe 1:16 Because it is **w**, Be ye holy; for I am holy. *1125*
5:12 I have **w** briefly, exhorting, and *1125*
2Pe 3:15 wisdom given unto him hath **w** unto you; *1125*
1Jn 2:14 I have **w** unto you, fathers, because ye have *1125*
2:14 I have **w** unto you, young men, because *1125*
2:21 I have not **w** unto you because ye know not *1125*
2:26 These *things* have I **w** unto you concerning *1125*
5:13 These *things* have I **w** unto you that believe *1125*
Rev 1: 3 and keep those *things* which are **w** therein: *1125*
2:17 and in the stone a new name **w**, *1125*
5: 1 him that sat on the throne a book **w** within *1125*
13: 8 whose names are not **w** in the book of life *1125*
14: 1 having his Father's name **w** in their *1125*
17: 5 And upon her forehead *was* a name **w**, *1125*
17: 8 whose names were not **w** in the book of life *1125*
19:12 and he had a name **w**, that no *man* knew, *1125*
19:16 on *his* vesture and on his thigh a name **w**, *1125*
20:12 of those *things* which were **w** in the books, *1125*
20:15 And whosoever was not found **w** in *1125*
21:12 gates twelve angels, and names **w *there***on, *1924*
21:27 they which are **w** in the Lamb's book of *1125*
22:18 him the plagues that are **w** in this book: *1125*
22:19 *from* the *things* which are **w** in this book. *1125*

WRONG (26) [WRONGED, WRONGETH, WRONGFULLY]

Ge 16: 5 Sarai said unto Abram, My **w** *be* upon thee: 2555
Ex 2:13 he said to **him that did** the **w**, Wherefore 7563
Dt 19:16 man to testify against him *that which is* **w**; 5627
Jdg 11:27 but thou doest me **w** to war against me: 7451
1Ch 12:17 seeing *there is* no **w** in mine hands, the God 2555
16:21 He suffered no man to **do** them **w**: yea, 6231
Est 1:16 Vashti the queen hath not **done w** to 5753
Job 19: 7 Behold, I cry out *of* **w**, but I am not heard: 2555
Ps 105:14 He suffered no man to **do** them **w**: yea, 6231
Jer 22: 3 **do** no **w**, do no violence, to the stranger, 3238
22:13 his chambers by **w**; 3808+4941
La 3:59 O LORD, thou hast seen my **w**: 5792
Hab 1: 4 therefore **w** judgment proceedeth. 6127
Mt 20:13 one of them, and said, Friend, I do thee no **w**: *91*
Ac 7:24 And seeing one *of them* **suffer w**, *91*
7:26 ye are brethren; why do ye **w** one to another? *91*
7:27 But he that **did** his neighbour **w** thrust him *91*
18:14 If it were a matter of **w** or wicked lewdness, *92*
25:10 to the Jews have I **done** no **w**, as thou very *91*
1Co 6: 7 Why do ye not rather **take w**? why do ye not *91*
6: 8 you do **w**, and defraud, and that *your* brethren. *91*
2Co 7:12 *I did it* not for his cause that had **done** the **w**, *91*
7:12 nor for his cause that **suffered w**, but that our *91*
12:13 not burdensome to you? forgive me this **w**. *93*
Col 3:25 But he that **doeth w** shall receive *for* *91*
3:25 shall receive *for* the **w** which he hath **done**: *91*

WRONGED (2) [WRONG]

2Co 7: 2 we have **w** no *man*, we have corrupted no *91*
Phm 1:18 If he hath **w** thee, or oweth *thee* ought, *91*

WRONGETH (1) [WRONG]

Pr 8:36 he that sinneth *against* me **w** his own soul: 2554

WRONGFULLY (7) [WRONG]

Job 21:27 the devices *which* ye **w imagine** against 2554
Ps 35:19 Let not them that are mine enemies **w** 8267
38:19 and they that hate me **w** are multiplied. 8267
69: 4 *being* mine enemies **w**, are mighty: 8267
119:86 they persecute me **w**; help thou me. 8267
Eze 22:29 oppressed the stranger **w**. 3808+4941+871.1
1Pe 2:19 toward God endure grief, suffering **w**. *95*

WROTE (62) [WRITE]

Ex 24: 4 Moses **w** all the words of the LORD, and 3789
34:28 he **w** upon the tables the words of 3789
39:30 **w** upon it a writing, *like to* the engravings 3789
Nu 33: 2 Moses **w** their goings out according to their 3789
Dt 4:13 and he **w** them upon two tables of stone. 3789
5:22 he **w** them in two tables of stone, and 3789
10: 4 he **w** on the tables, according to the first 3789
31: 9 Moses **w** this law, and delivered it unto 3789
31:22 Moses therefore **w** this song the same day, 3789
Jos 8:32 he **w** there upon the stones a copy of 3789
8:32 which he **w** in the presence of the children 3789
24:26 Joshua **w** these words in the book of 3789

1Sa 10:25 **w** *it* in a book, and laid *it* up before 3789
2Sa 11:14 that David **w** a letter to Joab, and sent *it* by 3789
11:15 he **w** in the letter, saying, Set ye Uriah in 3789
1Ki 21: 8 So she **w** letters in Ahab's name, and 3789
21: 9 she **w** in the letters, saying, Proclaim a fast, 3789
2Ki 10: 1 Jehu **w** letters, and sent *to* Samaria, 3789
10: 6 he **w** a letter the second time to them, 3789
17:37 the commandment, which he **w** for you, 3789
1Ch 24: 6 **w** them before the king, and the princes, 3789
2Ch 30: 1 **w** letters also to Ephraim and Manasseh, 3789
32:17 He **w** also letters to rail on the LORD God 3789
Ezr 4: 6 **w** they *unto him* an accusation against 3789
4: 7 in the days of Artaxerxes **w** Bishlam, 3789
4: 8 Shimshai the scribe **w** a letter against 3790
4: 9 *w* Rehum the chancellor, and Shimshai NIH
Est 8: 5 which he **w** to destroy the Jews which *are* 3789
8:10 And he **w** in the king Ahasuerus' name, and 3789
9:20 Mordecai **w** these things, and sent letters 3789
9:29 and Mordecai the Jew, **w** with all authority, 3789
Jer 36: 4 Baruch **w** from the mouth of Jeremiah all 3789
36:18 and I **w** *them* with ink in the book. 3789
36:27 the words which Baruch **w** at the mouth of 3789
36:32 who **w** therein from the mouth of Jeremiah 3789
51:60 So Jeremiah **w** in a book all the evil that 3789
Da 5: 5 **w** over against the candlestick upon 3790
5: 5 the king saw the part of the hand that **w**. 3790
6:25 king Darius **w** unto all people, nations, 3790
7: 1 he **w** the dream, *and* told the sum of 3790
Mk 10: 5 For the hardness of your heart he **w** you *1125*
12:19 Master, Moses **w** unto us, If a man's *1125*
Lk 1:63 and **w**, saying, His name is John. *1125*
20:28 Saying, Master, Moses **w** unto us, If any *1125*
Jn 5:46 would have believed me: for he **w** of me. *1125*
8: 6 and with *his* finger **w** on the ground, *1125*
8: 8 he stooped down, and **w** on the ground. *1125*
19:19 And Pilate **w** a title, and put *it* on the cross. *1125*
21:24 and **w** these *things*: and we know that his *1125*
Ac 15:23 And they **w** *letters* by them after this *1125*
18:27 the brethren **w**, exhorting the disciples to *1125*
23:25 And he **w** a letter after this manner: *1125*
Ro 16:22 I Tertius, who **w** *this* epistle, salute you in *1125*
1Co 5: 9 I **w** unto you in an epistle not to company *1125*
7: 1 Now concerning *the things* whereof ye **w** *1125*
2Co 2: 3 And I **w** this same unto you, lest, when I *1125*
2: 4 anguish of heart I **w** unto you with many *1125*
7:12 Wherefore, though I **w** unto you, *I did it* not *1125*
Eph 3: 3 the mystery; (as I **w afore** in few *words*, *4270*
Phm 1:21 Having confidence in thy obedience I **w** *1125*
2Jn 1: 5 not as though I **w** a new commandment *1125*
3Jn 1: 9 I **w** unto the church: but Diotrephes, *1125*

WROTH (49) [WRATH]

Ge 4: 5 Cain was very **w**, and his countenance fell. 2734
4: 6 LORD said unto Cain, Why art thou **w**? 2734
31:36 Jacob was **w**, and chode with Laban: and 2734
34: 7 they were very **w**, because he had wrought 2734
40: 2 Pharaoh was **w** against two *of* his officers, 7107
41:10 Pharaoh was **w** with his servants, and 7107
Ex 16:20 and stank: and Moses was **w** with them. 7107
Nu 16:15 Moses was very **w**, and said unto 2734
16:22 wilt thou be **w** with all the congregation? 7107
31:14 Moses was **w** with the officers of the host, 7107
Dt 1:34 your words, and was **w**, and sware, saying, 7107
3:26 the LORD was **w** with me for your sakes, 5674
9:19 where*with* the LORD was **w** against you 7107
Jos 22:18 that to morrow he will be **w** with the whole 7107
1Sa 18: 8 Saul was very **w**, and the saying displeased 2734
20: 7 if he be **very w**, *then* be sure that evil 2734+2734
29: 4 the princes of the Philistines were **w** with 7107
2Sa 3: 8 was Abner very **w** for the words of 2734
13:21 heard of all these things, he was very **w**. 2734
22: 8 and shook, because he was **w**. 2734
2Ki 5:11 Naaman was **w**, and went away, and said, 7107
13:19 the man of God was **w** with him, and said, 7107
2Ch 16:10 Asa was **w** with the seer, and put him *in* a 3707
26:19 Uzziah was **w**, and *had* a censer in his hand 2196
26:19 while he was **w** with the priests, the leprosy 2196
28: 9 the LORD God of your fathers was **w** 2534
Ne 4: 1 he was **w**, and took great indignation, and 2734
4: 7 to be stopped, then they were very **w**, 2734
Est 1:12 therefore was the king very **w**, and 7107
2:21 were **w**, and sought to lay hand on the king 7107
Ps 18: 7 and were shaken, because he was **w**. 2734
78:21 the LORD heard *this*, and was **w**: 5674
78:59 When God heard *this*, he was **w**, and 5674
78:62 the sword; and was **w** with his inheritance. 5674
89:38 thou hast been **w** with thine anointed. 5674
Isa 28:21 he shall be **w** as *in* the valley of Gibeon, 7264
47: 6 I was **w** with my people, I have polluted 7107
54: 9 have I sworn that *I* would not be **w** with 7107
57:16 for ever, neither will I be always **w**: 7107
57:17 the iniquity of his covetousness was I **w**, 7107
57:17 was **w**, and he went on frowardly in 7107
64: 5 behold, thou art **w**; for we have sinned: 7107
64: 9 Be not **w** very sore, O LORD, 7107
Jer 37:15 Wherefore the princes were **w** with 7107
La 5:22 rejected us; thou art very **w** against us. 7107
Mt 2:16 was exceeding **w**, and sent forth, and *2373*
18:34 And his lord was **w**, and delivered him to *3710*
22: 7 But when the king heard *thereof*, he was **w**: *3710*
Rev 12:17 And the dragon was **w** with the woman, *3710*

WROUGHT (100) [WROUGHTEST]

Ge 34: 7 he had **w** folly in Israel in lying with 6213
Ex 10: 2 what things I have **w** in Egypt, and my 5953
26:36 twined linen, **w with needlework**. 4639+7551
27:16 fine twined linen, **w** with needlework: 4639
36: 1 **w** Bezaleel and Aholiab, and every wise 6213
36: 4 all the wise *men*, that **w** all the work of 6213
36: 8 every wise hearted *man* among them that **w** 6213
39: 6 they **w** onyx stones inclosed *in* ouches *of* 6213
Lev 20:12 they have **w** confusion; their blood *shall be* 6213
Nu 23:23 of Jacob and of Israel, What hath God **w**! 6466
31:51 took the gold of them, *even* all **w** jewels. 4639
Dt 13:14 *that* such abomination is **w** among you; 6213

W

Dt 17: 2 that hath **w** wickedness in the sight of 6213
17: 4 *that* such abomination is **w** in Israel: 6213
21: 3 which hath not been **w** with, *and* 5647
22:21 because she hath **w** folly in Israel, to play 6213
31:18 for all the evils which they shall have **w**, 6213
Jos 7:15 and because he hath **w** folly in Israel. 6213
Jdg 20:10 according to all the folly that they have **w** 6213
Ru 2:19 her mother in law with whom she had **w**, 6213
2:19 The man's name with whom I **w** to day *is* 6213
1Sa 6: 6 when he had **w wonderfully** among them, 5953
11:13 for to day the LORD hath **w** salvation in 6213
14:45 who hath **w** this great salvation in Israel? 6213
14:45 for he hath **w** with God this day. 6213
19: 5 the LORD **w** a great salvation for all 6213
2Sa 18:13 Otherwise I should have **w** falsehood 6213
23:10 the LORD **w** a great victory that day; 6213
23:12 and the LORD **w** a great victory. 6213
1Ki 5:16 which ruled over the people that **w** in 6213
7:14 came to king Solomon, and **w** all his work. 6213
7:26 the brim thereof was **w** like the brim of a 4639
9:23 which bare rule over the people that **w** in 6213
16:20 the acts of Zimri, and his treason that he **w**, 7194
16:25 Omri **w** evil in the eyes of the LORD, and 6213
2Ki 3: 2 he **w** evil in the sight of the LORD; but 6213
12:11 that **w** upon the house of the LORD, 6213
17:11 **w** wicked things to provoke the LORD to 6213
21: 6 he **w** much wickedness in the sight of 6213
1Ch 4:21 the families of the house of them that **w** 5656
22: 2 he set masons to hew **w** stones to build 1496
2Ch 3:14 and fine linen, and **w** cherubims thereon. 5927
21: 6 he **w** *that* which *was* evil in the eyes of 6213
24:12 also such as **w** iron and brass to mend 2796
24:13 So the workmen **w**, and the work was 6213
31:20 **w** *that* which *was* good and right and truth 6213
33: 6 he **w** much evil in the sight of the LORD, 6213
34:10 they gave it *to* the workmen that **w** in 6213
34:13 *were* overseers of all that **w** the work in any 6213
Ne 4:16 *that* the half of my servants **w** in the work, 6213
4:17 *every one* with one of his hands **w** in 6213
6:16 for they perceived that this work was **w** of 6213
9:18 out of Egypt, and had **w** great provocations; 6213
9:26 to thee, and they **w** great provocations. 6213
Job 12: 9 that the hand of the LORD hath **w** this? 6213
36:23 or who can say, Thou hast **w** iniquity? 6466
Ps 31:19 *which* thou hast **w** for them that trust in 6466
45:13 glorious within: her clothing *is* of **w** gold. 4865
68:28 O God, that which thou hast **w** for us. 6466
78:43 How he had **w** his signs in Egypt, and 7760
139:15 curiously **w** in the lowest parts of the earth. 7551
Ecc 2:11 on all the works that my hands had **w**, 6213
2:17 the work that is **w** under the sun *is* grievous 6213
Isa 26:12 for thou also hast **w** all our works in us. 6466
26:18 we have not **w** any deliverance *in* the earth; 6213
41: 4 Who hath **w** and done *it*, calling 6466
Jer 11:15 *seeing* she hath **w** lewdness *with* many, and 6213
18: 3 and behold, he **w** a work on the wheels. 6213
Eze 20: 9 I **w** for my name's sake, that *it* should not 6213
20:14 I **w** for my name's sake, that *it* should not 6213
20:22 mine hand, and **w** for my name's sake, 6213
20:44 when I have **w** with you for my name's 6213
29:20 because they **w** for me, saith the Lord 6213
Da 4: 2 wonders that the high God hath **w** toward 5648
Jnh 1:11 for the sea **w**, and was tempestuous. 1980
1:13 for the sea **w**, and was tempestuous against 1980
Zep 2: 3 of the earth, which have **w** his judgment; 6466
Mt 20:12 These last have **w** *but* one hour, and *4160*
26:10 for she hath **w** a good work upon me. *2038*
Mk 6: 2 that even such mighty works are **w** by his *1096*
14: 6 you her? she hath **w** a good work on me. *2038*
Jn 3:21 be made manifest, that they are **w** in God. *2038*
Ac 5:12 and wonders **w** among the people; *1096*
15:12 wonders God had **w** among the Gentiles by *4160*
18: 3 the same craft, he abode with them, and **w**: *2038*
19:11 And God **w** special miracles by the hands *4160*
21:19 had **w** among the Gentiles by his ministry. *4160*
Ro 7: 8 **w** in me all *manner of* concupiscence. *2716*
15:18 *things* which Christ hath not **w** by me, *2716*
2Co 5: 5 Now he that hath **w** us for the selfsame *2716*
7:11 what carefulness it **w** in you, yea, *2716*
12:12 Truly the signs of an apostle were **w** among *2716*
Gal 2: 8 (For he that **w effectually** in Peter to *1754*
Eph 1:20 Which he **w** in Christ, when he raised him *1754*
2Th 3: 8 but **w** with labour and travail night and day, *2038*
Heb 11:33 **w** righteousness, obtained promises, *2038*
Jas 2:22 Seest thou how faith **w with** his works, and *4903*
1Pe 4: 3 us to have **w** the will of the Gentiles, *2716*
2Jn 1: 8 we lose not *those things* which we have **w**, *2038*
Rev 19:20 with him the false prophet that **w** miracles *4160*

WROUGHTEST (1) [WROUGHT]

Ru 2:19 where **w** thou? blessed be he that did take 6213

WRUNG (4) [WRING]

Lev 1:15 the blood thereof shall be **w out** at the side 4680
5: 9 the rest of the blood shall be **w out** at 4680
Ps 73:10 and waters of a full *cup* are **w out** to them. 4680
Isa 51:17 of the cup of trembling, *and* **w** *them* **out**. 4680

X

XERXES See AHASUERUS

Y

YARN (4)

1Ki 10:28 horses brought out of Egypt, and **linen y**: 4723
10:28 the king's merchants received the **linen y** at 4723
2Ch 1:16 horses brought out of Egypt, and **linen y**: 4723
1:16 the king's merchants received the **linen y** at 4723

YE (3796) [YOU] See Index of Articles, Etc.

YEA (340)

Ge 3: 1 unto the woman, **Y**, hath God said, 637+3588
17:16 **y**, I will bless her, and she shall be *a* 2050.1
20: 6 God said unto him in a dream, **Y**, I know 1571
27:33 blessed him? **y**, *and* he shall be blessed. 1571
Lev 25:35 **y**, *though he be* a stranger, or a sojourner; NIH
Nu 10:32 shall be, if thou go with us, **y**, it shall be, 2050.1
Dt 33: 3 **Y**, he loved the people; all his saints *are* in 637
Jdg 5:29 Her wise ladies answered *her*, **y**, 637
1Sa 15:20 Saul said unto Samuel, **Y**, I have obeyed 834
21: 5 and *the bread is* in a manner common, **y**, 2050.1
24:11 see, **y** see the skirt of thy robe in my hand: 1571
2Sa 19:30 said unto the king, **Y**, let him take all, 1571
22:39 not arise: **y**, they are fallen under my feet. 2050.1
2Ki 2: 3 he said, **Y**, I know *it*; hold you your peace. 1571
2: 5 he answered, **Y**, I know *it*; hold you your 1571
16: 3 **y**, and made his son to pass through 1571
1Ch 16:21 **y**, he reproved kings for their sakes, 2050.1
2Ch 26:20 **y**, himself hasted also to go out, because 1571
Ezr 9: 2 **y**, the hand of the princes and rulers hath 2050.1
Ne 5:15 **y**, even their servants bare rule over NIH
5:16 **Y** also I continued in the work of this wall, 1571
6:10 **y**, in the night will they come to slay thee. 2050.1
9:18 **Y**, when they had made them a molten calf, 637
9:21 **Y**, forty years didst thou sustain them in 2050.1
Est 5:12 Haman said moreover, **Y**, Esther the queen 637
Job 1:15 **y**, they have slain the servants with 2050.1
1:17 **y**, and slain the servants with the edge of 2050.1
2: 4 the LORD, and said, Skin for skin, **y**, 2050.1
5:19 **y**, in seven there shall no evil touch thee. 2050.1
6:10 **y**, I would harden myself in sorrow; 2050.1
6:27 **Y**, ye overwhelm the fatherless, and you dig 637
6:29 **y**, return again, my righteousness *is* in it. 2050.1
9:10 **y**, and wonders without number. NIH
11:15 **y**, thou shalt be steadfast, and shalt not 2050.1
11:18 **y**, thou shalt dig *about thee, and* 2050.1
11:19 **y**, many shall make suit unto thee. 2050.1
12: 3 **y**, who knoweth not such *things* as these? 2050.1
14:10 **y**, man giveth up the ghost, and where *is* 2050.1
15: 4 **Y**, thou castest off fear, and 637
15: 6 **y**, thine own lips testify against thee. 2050.1
15:15 **y**, the heavens are not clean in his sight. 2050.1
18: 5 **Y**, the light of the wicked shall be put out, 1571
19:18 **Y**, young children despised me; I arose, and 1571
20: 8 **y**, he shall be chased away as a vision of 2050.1
20:25 **y**, the glistering sword cometh out of his 2050.1
21: 7 become old, **y**, are mighty *in* power? 1571
22:25 **Y**, the Almighty shall be thy defence, and 2050.1
25: 5 **y**, the stars are not pure in his sight. 2050.1
28:27 he prepared it, **y**, and searched it out. 2050.1
30: 2 **Y**, whereto *might* the strength of their 1571
30: 8 children of fools, **y**, children of base men: 1571
30: 9 am I their song, **y**, I am their byword. 2050.1
31: 8 **y**, let my offspring be rooted out. 2050.1
31:11 **y**, it *is* an iniquity *to be punished by* 2050.1
32:12 **Y**, I attended unto you, and behold, 2050.1
33:14 For God speaketh once, **y** twice, *yet man* 2050.1
33:22 **Y**, his soul draweth near unto the grave, 2050.1
34:12 **Y**, surely God will not do wickedly, 637
36: 7 **y**, he doth establish them for ever, and 2050.1
40: 5 **y**, twice; but I will proceed no further. 2050.1
41:24 **y**, as hard as a piece of the nether 2050.1
Ps 7: 4 (**y**, I have delivered him that without 2050.1
7: 5 enemy persecute my soul, and take *it*; **y**, 2050.1
8: 7 and oxen, **y**, and the beasts of the field; 2050.1
16: 6 lines are fallen unto me in pleasant *places*; **y**, 637
18:10 **y**, he did fly upon the wings of the wind. 2050.1
18:14 **Y**, he sent out his arrows, and 2050.1
18:48 **y**, thou liftest me up above those that rise up 637
19:10 *they* than gold, **y**, than much fine gold: 2050.1
23: 4 **Y**, though I walk through the valley of 1571
25: 3 **Y**, let none that wait on thee be ashamed: 1571
27: 6 I will sing, **y**, I will sing *praises* unto 2050.1
29: 5 **y**, the LORD breaketh the cedars of 2050.1
29:10 **y**, the LORD sitteth King for ever. 2050.1
31: 9 with grief, **y**, my soul and my belly. NIH
35:10 **y**, the poor and the needy from him that 2050.1
35:15 **y**, the abjects gathered themselves together NIH
35:21 **Y**, they opened their mouth wide against 2050.1
35:27 **y**, let them say continually, Let 2050.1
37:10 and the wicked *shall* not *be*: **y**, 2050.1
37:36 **y**, I sought him, but he could not be 2050.1
40: 8 O my God: **y**, thy law *is* within my heart. 2050.1
41: 9 **Y**, mine own familiar friend, in whom I 1571
43: 4 **y**, upon the harp will I praise thee, O God 2050.1
44:22 **Y**, for thy sake are we killed all the day 3588
57: 1 **y**, in the shadow of thy wings will I make 2050.1
58: 2 **Y**, in heart you work wickedness; you weigh 637
59:16 **y**, I will sing aloud of thy mercy in 2050.1
68: 3 **y**, let them exceedingly rejoice. 2050.1
68:16 **y**, the LORD will dwell *in it* for ever. 637
68:18 **y**, *for* the rebellious also, that the LORD 637
72:11 **Y**, all kings shall fall down before him: 2050.1
78:19 **Y**, they spake against God; they said, Can 2050.1
78:38 **y**, many a time turned he his anger away, 2050.1
78:41 **Y**, they turned *back* and tempted God, 2050.1
83:11 **y**, all their princes as Zebah, and 2050.1
83:17 **y**, let them be put to shame, and perish: 2050.1
84: 2 My soul longeth, **y**, even fainteth for 2050.1
84: 3 **Y**, the sparrow hath found a house, and 1571
85:12 **Y**, the LORD shall give *that which is* 1571
90:17 **y**, the work of our hands establish thou it. 2050.1
93: 4 **y**, *than* the mighty waves of the sea. NIH
94:23 **y**, the LORD our God shall cut them off. NIH
102:13 time to favour her, **y**, the set time, is come. 3588
102:26 **y**, all of them shall wax old like a 2050.1
105:12 **y**, *very* few, and strangers in it. 3509.1
105:14 **y**, he reproved kings for their sakes; 2050.1
106:24 **Y**, they despised the pleasant land, 2050.1
106:37 **Y**, they sacrificed their sons and their 2050.1
109:30 **y**, I will praise him among the multitude. 2050.1
116: 5 and righteous; **y**, our God *is* merciful. 2050.1
118:11 me about; **y**, they compassed me about: 1571
119:34 **y**, I shall observe it with *my* whole heart. 2050.1
119:103 **y**, *sweeter* than honey to my mouth! NIH
119:127 above gold; **y**, above fine gold. 2050.1
128: 6 **Y**, thou shalt see thy children's children, 2050.1
137: 1 of Babylon, there we sat down, **y**, we wept, 1571
138: 5 **Y**, they shall sing in the ways of 2050.1
139:12 **Y**, the darkness hideth not from thee; but 1571
144:15 **y**, happy *is that* people, whose God *is* NIH
Pr 2: 3 **Y**, if thou criest after knowledge, *and* 3588
2: 9 judgment, and equity; **y**, every good path. NIH
3:24 **y**, thou shalt lie down, and thy sleep shall 2050.1
6:16 **y**, seven *are* an abomination unto him: 2050.1
7:26 **y**, many strong *men have been* slain by 2050.1
8:18 **y**, durable riches and righteousness. NIH
8:19 fruit *is* better than gold, **y**, than fine gold; 2050.1
16: 4 **y**, even the wicked for the day of evil. 2050.1
22:10 go out; **y**, strife and reproach shall cease. 2050.1
23:16 **Y**, my reins shall rejoice, when thy lips 2050.1
23:34 **Y**, thou shalt be as he that lieth down in 2050.1
24: 5 **y**, a man of knowledge increaseth 2050.1
29:17 **y**, he shall give delight unto thy soul. 2050.1
30:15 **y**, four *things* say not, *It is* enough: NIH
30:18 for me, **y**, four which I know not: 2050.1
30:29 go well, **y**, four are comely in going: 2050.1
31:20 **y**, she reacheth forth her hands to 2050.1
Ecc 1:16 **y**, my heart had great experience of 2050.1
2:18 **Y**, I hated all my labour which I *had* 2050.1
2:23 **y**, his heart taketh not rest in the night. 1571
3:19 **y**, they have all one breath; so that a man 2050.1
4: 3 **Y**, better *is he* than both they, which hath 2050.1
4: 8 **y**, he hath neither child nor brother: 1571
4: 8 This *is* also vanity, **y**, it *is* a sore travail 2050.1
6: 6 **Y**, though he live a thousand years twice 2050.1
7:18 **y**, also from this withdraw not thine hand: 2050.1
8:17 *it* out, yet he shall not find *it*; **y** further, 2050.1
9: 3 **y**, also the heart of the sons of men is full 2050.1
10: 3 **Y** also, when he that is a fool walketh by 2050.1
12: 9 **y**, he gave good heed, and sought out, *and* 2050.1
SS 1:16 thou *art* fair, my beloved, **y**, pleasant: 637
5: 1 drink, **y**, drink abundantly, O beloved. 2050.1
5:16 **y**, he *is* altogether lovely. This *is* my 2050.1
6: 9 **y**, the queens and the concubines, and NIH
8: 1 kiss thee; **y**, I should not be despised. 1571
Isa 1:15 **y**, when ye make many prayers, I will not 1571
5:10 **Y**, ten acres of vineyard shall yield one 3588
5:29 **y**, they shall roar, and lay hold of 2050.1
14: 8 **Y**, the fir trees rejoice at thee, *and* 1571
19:21 **y**, they shall vow a vow unto the LORD, 2050.1
24:16 **y**, the treacherous dealers have dealt very 2050.1
26: 8 **Y**, *in* the way of thy judgments, O LORD, 637
26: 9 **y**, *with* my spirit within me will I seek thee 637
26:11 **y**, the fire of thine enemies shall devour 637
29: 5 **y**, it shall be at an instant suddenly. 2050.1
30:33 **y**, for the king it is prepared; he hath made 1571
32:13 **y**, upon all the houses of joy *in* the joyous 3588
40:24 **Y**, they shall not be planted; yea, they shall 637
40:24 not be planted; **y**, they shall not be sown: 637
40:24 **y**, their stock shall not take root in the earth: 637
41:10 **y**, I will help thee; yea, I will uphold thee 637
41:10 **y**, I will uphold thee with the right hand of 637
41:23 **y**, do good, or do evil, that we may be 637
41:26 **y**, *there is* none that sheweth, yea, *there is* 637
41:26 yea, *there is* none that sheweth, **y**, *there is* 637
41:26 yea, *there is* none that declareth, **y**, 637
42:13 he shall cry, **y**, roar; he shall prevail against 637
43: 7 I have formed him; **y**, I have made him. 637
43:13 **Y**, before the day *was* I *am* he; and *there is* 1571
44: 8 **y**, *there is* no God; I know not *any*. 2050.1
44:12 **y**, he is hungry, and his strength faileth: 1571
44:15 **y**, he kindleth *it*, and baketh bread; yea, 637
44:15 **y**, he maketh a god, and worshippeth *it*; he 637
44:16 **y**, he warmeth himself, and saith, Aha, I am 637
44:19 **y**, also I have baked bread upon the coals 637
45:21 *them* near; **y**, let them take counsel together: 637
46: 6 it a god: they fall down, **y**, they worship. 637
46: 7 **y**, *one* shall cry unto him, yet can he not 637
46:11 **y**, I have spoken *it*, I will also bring it to 637
47: 3 be uncovered, **y**, thy shame shall be seen: 1571
48: 8 **Y**, thou heardest not; yea, thou knewest 1571
48: 8 **y**, thou knewest not; yea, from that time 1571
48: 8 **y**, from that time *that* thine ear was not 1571
48:15 I, *even* I, have spoken; **y**, I have called him: 637
49:15 **y**, they may forget, yet will I not forget 1571
55: 1 **y**, come, buy wine and milk without 2050.1
56: 9 to devour, **y**, all ye beasts in the forest. NIH
56:11 **Y**, *they are* greedy dogs *which* can never 2050.1
59:15 **Y**, truth faileth; and he *that* departeth 2050.1
60:12 **y**, *those* nations shall be utterly wasted. 2050.1
66: 3 **Y**, they have chosen their own ways, and 1571
Jer 2:37 **Y**, thou shalt go forth from him, and 1571
5:28 **y**, they overpass the deeds of the wicked: 1571
8: 7 **Y**, the stork in the heaven knoweth her 1571
12: 2 hast planted them, **y**, they have taken root: 1571
12: 2 they grow, **y**, they bring forth fruit: thou *art* 1571
12: 6 **y**, they have called a multitude after thee: 1571
14: 5 **Y**, the hind also calved in the field, and 3583
14:18 **y**, both the prophet and the priest go about 3588
23:11 **y**, in my house have I found their 1571

Jer 23:26 y, *they are* prophets of the deceit of their 2050.1
27:21 Y, thus saith the LORD of hosts, the God 3588
31: 3 *saying*, Y, I have loved thee *with* an 2050.1
31:19 I was ashamed, y, even confounded, 1571
32:41 Y, I will rejoice over them to do them 2050.1
46:16 made many to fall, y, one fell upon another: 1571
51:44 not flow *together* any **more** unto him: y, 1571
La 1: 8 y, she sigheth, and turneth backward. 1571
Eze 6:14 upon them, and make the land desolate, y, 2050.1
16: 6 y, I said unto thee *when thou wast* in thy 2050.1
16: 8 y, I sware unto thee, and entered into a 2050.1
16: 9 y, I throughly washed away thy blood 2050.1
16:28 y, thou hast played the harlot with them, 2050.1
16:52 y, be thou confounded also, and bear thy 2050.1
17:10 Y behold, *being* planted, shall it prosper? 2050.1
22: 2 y, thou shalt shew her all her 2050.1
22:21 Y, I will gather you, and blow upon you 2050.1
22:29 y, they have oppressed the stranger 2050.1
23:36 y, declare unto them their abominations; 2050.1
26:18 y, the isles that *are* in the sea shall be 2050.1
28:26 y, they shall dwell with confidence, 2050.1
32:10 Y, I will make many people amazed at 2050.1
32:28 Y, thou shalt be broken in the midst of 2050.1
34: 6 y, my flock was scattered upon all 2050.1
36:12 Y, I will cause men to walk upon you, 2050.1
37:27 y, I will be their God, and they shall be 2050.1
39:13 Y, all the people of the land shall bury 2050.1
Da 8:11 Y, he magnified *himself even* to 2050.1
9:11 Y, all Israel have transgressed thy law, 2050.1
9:21 Y, whiles I *was* speaking in prayer, 2050.1
10:19 peace *be* unto thee, be strong, y, 2050.1
11:22 y also, the prince of the covenant. 2050.1
11:24 *y*, and he shall forecast his devices against NIH
11:26 Y, they that feed of the portion of his 2050.1
Hos 2:19 y, I will betroth thee unto me in 2050.1
4: 3 y, the fishes of the sea also shall be taken 2050.1
7: 9 y, gray hairs are here and there upon him, 1571
8:10 Y, though they have hired among 1571
9:12 *that there shall* not *be* a man *left*: y, 3588
9:16 y, though they bring forth, yet will I slay 1571
12: 4 Y, he had power over *the* angel, and 2050.1
12:11 y, their altars *are* as heaps in the furrows of 1571
Joel 1:16 *y*, joy and gladness from the house of our NIH
1:18 y, the flocks of sheep are made desolate. 1571
2: 3 them a desolate wilderness; y, 1571+2050.1
2:19 Y, the LORD will answer and say unto 2050.1
3: 4 Y, and what have ye to do with me, O Tyre, 1571
Am 8: 6 of shoes; *y*, and sell the refuse of the wheat? NIH
Ob 1:13 y, thou shouldest not have looked on their 1571
1:16 y, they shall drink, and they shall 2050.1
Jnh 3: 8 y, let them turn every one from his evil 2050.1
Mic 3: 7 y, they shall all cover their lips; for *there* 2050.1
Na 1: 5 y, the world, and all that dwell therein. 2050.1
Hab 2: 5 Y also, because he transgresseth *by* wine, 2050.1
Zep 2: 1 y, gather together, O nation not desired; 2050.1
Hag 2:19 y, as yet the vine, and the fig tree, and 2050.1
Zec 7:12 Y, they made their hearts *as* an adamant 2050.1
8:22 Y, many people and strong nations shall 2050.1
10: 7 y, their children shall see *it*, and be glad; 2050.1
14: 5 y, ye shall flee, like as ye fled from 2050.1
14:21 Y, every pot in Jerusalem and in Judah 2050.1
Mal 2: 2 y, I have cursed them already, 1571+2050.1
3:15 y, they that work wickedness are set up; 1571
3:15 y, *they that* tempt God are even delivered. 1571
4: 1 all the proud, y, and all that do wickedly, NIH
Mt 5:37 But let your communication be, Y, yea; *3483*
5:37 But let your communication be, Yea, y; *3483*
9:28 to do this? They said unto him, Y, Lord. *3483*
11: 9 y, I say unto you, and more than a prophet. *3483*
13:51 these *things*? They say unto him, Y, Lord. *3483*
21:16 And Jesus saith unto them, Y; have ye *3483*
26:60 y, though many false witnesses came, NIG
Lk 2:35 (Y, a sword shall pierce through thy own *1161*
7:26 Y, I say unto you, and much more than a *3483*
11:28 But he said, Y **rather**, blessed *are* they that *3304*
12: 5 cast into hell; y, I say unto you, Fear him. *3483*
12:57 *Y*, and why even of yourselves judge ye not NIG
14:26 and brethren, and sisters, y, *2089+5037*
24:22 Y, and certain women *also* of our company *235*
Jn 11:27 She saith unto him, Y, Lord: I believe that *3483*
16: 2 y, the time cometh, that whosoever killeth *235*
16:32 Behold, the hour cometh, y, is now come, *2532*
21:15 He saith unto him, Y, Lord; thou knowest *3483*
21:16 He saith unto him, Y, Lord; thou knowest *3483*
Ac 3:16 y, the faith which is by him hath given him *2532*
3:24 Y, and all the prophets from Samuel and *2532*
5: 8 so much? And she said, Y, for so much. *3483*
7:43 Y, ye took up the tabernacle of Moloch, *2532*
20:34 Y, ye yourselves know, that these hands *1161*
22:27 Tell me, art thou a Roman? He said, Y. *3483*
Ro 3: 4 y, let God be true, but every man a liar; as it NIG
3:31 God forbid: y, we establish the law. *235*
8:34 *It is* Christ that died, y rather, that is risen *1161*
14: 4 Y, he shall be holden up: for God is able to *1161*
15:20 Y, so have I strived to preach the gospel, *1161*
1Co 1:28 God chosen, *y*, and *things* which are not, NIG
2:10 for the Spirit searcheth all *things*, y, *2532*
4: 3 y, I judge not mine own self. *235*
9:16 y, woe is unto me, if I preach not *1161*
15:15 Y, and we are found false witnesses of *1161*
16: 6 be that I will abide, y, and winter with you, *2228*
2Co 1:17 that with me there should be y yea, and nay *3483*
1:17 that with me there should be yea y, and nay *3483*
1:18 our word toward you was not y and nay. *3483*
1:19 was not y and nay, but in him was yea. *3483*
1:19 was not yea and nay, but in him was y. *3483*
1:20 For all the promises of God in him *are* y, *3483*
5:16 y, though we have known Christ after *1161*
7:11 y, *what* clearing of yourselves, yea, *235*
7:11 y, *what* indignation, yea, *what* fear, yea, *235*
7:11 yea, *what* indignation, y, *what* fear, yea, *235*
7:11 yea, *what* indignation, yea, *what* fear, y, *235*
7:11 y, *what* zeal, yea, *what* revenge! *235*
7:11 yea, *what* zeal, y, *what* revenge! *235*
7:13 *y*, and exceedingly the more joyed we for NIG
2Co 8: 3 *y*, and beyond *their* power *they were* willing NIG
Gal 4:17 y, they would exclude you, that you might *235*
Php 1:18 and I therein do rejoice, y, and will rejoice. *235*
2:17 Y, and if I be offered upon the sacrifice and *235*
3: 8 Y doubtless, and I count all *things but* *235*
2Ti 3:12 Y, and all that will live godly in Christ *1161*
Phm 1:20 Y, brother, let me have joy of thee in *3483*
Heb 11:36 trial of *cruel* mockings and scourgings, y, NIG
Jas 2:18 Y, a man may say, Thou hast faith, and I *235*
5:12 but let your y be yea; and *your* nay, nay; *3483*
5:12 but let your yea be y; and *your* nay, nay; *3483*
1Pe 5: 5 Y, all *of you* be subject one to another, and NIG
2Pe 1:13 Y, I think it meet, as long as I am in this NIG
3Jn 1:12 y, and we also bear record; and ye know *1161*
Rev 14:13 Y, saith the Spirit, that they may rest from *3483*

YEAR (372) [YEAR'S, YEARLY, YEARS, YEARS']

Ge 7:11 In the six hundredth y of Noah's life, in 8141
8:13 to pass in the six hundredth and first y, 8141
14: 4 and *in* the thirteenth y they rebelled. 8141
14: 5 in the fourteenth y came Chedorlaomer, 8141
17:21 bear unto thee at this set time in the next y. 8141
26:12 received in the same y an hundredfold: 8141
47:17 with bread for all their cattle for that y. 8141
47:18 When that y was ended, they came unto 8141
47:18 they came unto him the second y, and 8141
Ex 12: 2 it *shall be* the first month of the y to you. 8141
12: 5 be without blemish, a male of the first y: 8141
13:10 keep this ordinance in his season from y to 3117
13:10 this ordinance in his season from year to y. 3117
23:11 the seventh *y* thou shalt let it rest and NIH
23:14 thou shalt keep a feast unto me in the y. 8141
23:16 of ingathering, *which is* in the end of the y, 8141
23:17 Three times in the y all thy males shall 8141
23:29 drive them out from before thee in one y; 8141
29:38 two lambs of the first y day by day 8141
30:10 y with the blood of the sin offering of 8141
30:10 once in the y shall he make atonement upon 8141
34:23 Thrice in the y shall all your men children 8141
34:24 before the LORD thy God thrice in the y. 8141
40:17 to pass in the first month in the second y, 8141
Lev 9: 3 a calf and a lamb, both of the first y, 8141
12: 6 she shall bring a lamb of the first y for a 8141
14:10 one ewe lamb of the first y without 8141
16:34 children of Israel for all their sins once a y. 8141
19:24 in the fourth y all the fruit thereof shall be 8141
19:25 in the fifth y shall ye eat of the fruit thereof, 8141
23:12 first y for a burnt offering unto the LORD. 8141
23:18 seven lambs without blemish of the first y, 8141
23:19 two lambs of the first y for a sacrifice of 8141
23:41 feast unto the LORD seven days in the y. 8141
25: 4 in the seventh y shall be a sabbath of rest 8141
25: 5 *for* it is a y of rest unto the land. 8141
25:10 ye shall hallow the fiftieth y, and 8141
25:11 A jubile shall that fiftieth y be unto you: 8141
25:13 In the y of this jubile ye shall return every 8141
25:20 shall say, What shall we eat the seventh y? 8141
25:21 my blessing upon you in the sixth y, 8141
25:22 ye shall sow the eighth y, and eat *yet* of old 8141
25:22 and eat *yet* of old fruit until the ninth y; 8141
25:28 him that hath bought it until the y of jubile: 8141
25:29 he may redeem it within a whole y after it 8141
25:29 it is sold; *within* a **full** y may he redeem it. 3117
25:30 not redeemed within the space of a full y, 8141
25:33 shall go out in the y *of* jubile: NIH
25:40 *and* shall serve thee unto the y of jubile: 8141
25:50 y that he was sold to him unto the year of 8141
25:50 that he was sold to him unto the y of jubile: 8141
25:52 but few years unto the y of jubile, 8141
25:54 then he shall go out in the y of jubile, 8141
27:17 If he sanctify his field from the y of jubile, 8141
27:18 *even* unto the y of the jubile, and it shall be 8141
27:23 *even* unto the y of the jubile: 8141
27:24 In the y of the jubile the field shall return 8141
Nu 1: 1 in the second y after they were come out of 8141
6:12 shall bring a lamb of the **first** y for a 1121+8141
6:14 one he lamb of the **first** y without 1121+8141
6:14 one ewe lamb of the **first** y without 1323+8141
7:15 one ram, one lamb of the **first** y, 1121+8141
7:17 he goats, five lambs of the **first** y: 1121+8141
7:21 one ram, one lamb of the **first** y, 1121+8141
7:23 he goats, five lambs of the **first** y: 1121+8141
7:27 one ram, one lamb of the **first** y, 1121+8141
7:29 he goats, five lambs of the **first** y: 1121+8141
7:33 one ram, one lamb of the **first** y, 1121+8141
7:35 he goats, five lambs of the **first** y: 1121+8141
7:39 one ram, one lamb of the **first** y, 1121+8141
7:41 he goats, five lambs of the **first** y: 1121+8141
7:45 one ram, one lamb of the **first** y, 1121+8141
7:47 he goats, five lambs of the **first** y: 1121+8141
7:51 one ram, one lamb of the **first** y, 1121+8141
7:53 he goats, five lambs of the **first** y: 1121+8141
7:57 one ram, one lamb of the **first** y, 1121+8141
7:59 he goats, five lambs of the **first** y: 1121+8141
7:63 one ram, one lamb of the **first** y, 1121+8141
7:65 he goats, five lambs of the **first** y: 1121+8141
7:69 one ram, one lamb of the **first** y, 1121+8141
7:71 he goats, five lambs of the **first** y: 1121+8141
7:75 one ram, one lamb of the **first** y, 1121+8141
7:77 he goats, five lambs of the **first** y: 1121+8141
7:81 one ram, one lamb of the **first** y, 1121+8141
7:83 he goats, five lambs of the **first** y: 1121+8141
7:87 the lambs of the **first** y twelve, 1121+8141
7:88 the lambs of the **first** y sixty. 1121+8141
9: 1 in the first month of the second y after they 8141
9:22 *it were* two days, or a month, or a y, 3117
10:11 *day* of the second month, in the second y, 8141
14:34 *even* forty days, each day for a y, shall ye 8141
15:27 he shall bring a she goat of the first y for a 8141
28: 3 two lambs of the **first** y without spot 1121+8141
28: 9 on the sabbath day two lambs of the first y 8141
28:11 lambs of the **first** y without spot; 1121+8141
28:14 month throughout the months of the y. 8141
28:19 and seven lambs of the **first** y: 1121+8141
28:27 one ram, seven lambs of the **first** y; 1121+8141
Nu 29: 2 lambs of the **first** y without blemish: 1121+8141
29: 8 *and* seven lambs of the **first** y; 1121+8141
29:13 *and* fourteen lambs of the **first** y; 1121+8141
29:17 lambs of the **first** y without spot: 1121+8141
29:20 fourteen lambs of the **first** y without 1121+8141
29:23 fourteen lambs of the **first** y without 1121+8141
29:26 lambs of the **first** y without spot: 1121+8141
29:29 fourteen lambs of the **first** y without 1121+8141
29:32 fourteen lambs of the **first** y without 1121+8141
29:36 lambs of the **first** y without blemish: 1121+8141
33:38 in the fortieth y after the children of Israel 8141
Dt 1: 3 it came to pass in the fortieth y, in 8141
11:12 from the beginning of the y even unto 8141
11:12 of the year even unto the end of the y. 8141
14:22 the field bringeth forth y **by year**. 8141+8141
14:22 the field bringeth forth **year by** y. 8141+8141
14:28 all the tithe of thine increase the same y, 8141
15: 9 saying, The seventh y, the year of release, 8141
15: 9 seventh year, the y of release, is at hand; 8141
15:12 in the seventh y thou shalt let him go free 8141
15:20 y **by year** in the place which 8141+8141+871.1
15:20 **year by** y in the place which 8141+8141+871.1
16:16 Three times in a y shall all thy males 8141
24: 5 *but* he shall be free at home one y, and 8141
26:12 all the tithes of thine increase the third y, 8141
26:12 *which is* the y of tithing, and hast given *it* 8141
31:10 in the solemnity of the y of release, in 8141
Jos 5:12 eat of the fruit of the land of Canaan that y. 8141
Jdg 10: 8 that y they vexed and oppressed 8141
11:40 of Jephthah the Gileadite four days in a y. 8141
17:10 will give thee ten *shekels* of silver by the y, 3117
1Sa 1: 7 *as* he did so y by year, when she went up to 8141
1: 7 *as* he did so year by y, when she went up to 8141
2:19 and brought *it* to him from y to year, 3117
2:19 and brought *it* to him from year to y, 3117
7:16 he went from y to year in circuit *to* Beth-el, 8141
7:16 he went from year to y in circuit *to* Beth-el, 8141
13: 1 Saul reigned one y; and when he had 8141
27: 7 in the country of the Philistines was a **full** y 3117
2Sa 11: 1 it came to pass, after the y was expired, 8141
21: 1 the days of David three years, y after year; 8141
21: 1 the days of David three years, year after y; 8141
1Ki 4: 7 each man *his* month in a y made provision. 8141
5:11 thus gave Solomon to Hiram y by year. 8141
5:11 thus gave Solomon to Hiram year by y. 8141
6: 1 eightieth y after the children of Israel were 8141
6: 1 in the fourth y of Solomon's reign over 8141
6:37 In the fourth y was the foundation of 8141
6:38 in the eleventh y, in the month Bul, 8141
9:25 three times in a y did Solomon offer burnt 8141
10:14 in one y was six hundred threescore 8141
10:25 spices, horses, and mules, a rate y by year. 8141
10:25 spices, horses, and mules, a rate year by y. 8141
14:25 it came to pass in the fifth y of king 8141
15: 1 Now in the eighteenth y of king Jeroboam 8141
15: 9 in the twentieth y of Jeroboam king of 8141
15:25 Israel in the second y of Asa king of Judah, 8141
15:28 Even in the third y of Asa king of Judah did 8141
15:33 In the third y of Asa king of Judah *began* 8141
16: 8 sixth y of Asa king of Judah *began* Elah 8141
16:10 and seventh y of Asa king of Judah, 8141
16:15 seventh y of Asa king of Judah did Zimri 8141
16:23 first y of Asa king of Judah *began* Omri to 8141
16:29 eighth y of Asa king of Judah *began* Ahab 8141
18: 1 of the LORD came to Elijah in the third y, 8141
20:22 for at the return of the y the king of Syria 8141
20:26 it came to pass at the return of the y, 8141
22: 2 it came to pass on the third y, that 8141
22:41 in the fourth y of Ahab king of Israel. 8141
22:51 y of Jehoshaphat king of Judah, 8141
2Ki 1:17 y of Jehoram the son of Jehoshaphat king 8141
3: 1 eighteenth y of Jehoshaphat king of Judah, 8141
8:16 in the fifth y of Joram the son of Ahab king 8141
8:25 In the twelfth y of Joram the son of Ahab 8141
8:26 to reign; and he reigned one y in Jerusalem. 8141
9:29 in the eleventh y of Joram the son of Ahab 8141
11: 4 the seventh y Jehoiada sent and fet 8141
12: 1 In the seventh y of Jehu Jehoash *began* to 8141
12: 6 twentieth y of king Jehoash the priests had 8141
13: 1 twentieth y of Joash the son of Ahaziah 8141
13:10 seventh y of Joash king of Judah *began* 8141
13:20 invaded the land *at* the coming in of the y. 8141
14: 1 In the second y of Joash son of Jehoahaz 8141
14:23 In the fifteenth y of Amaziah the son of 8141
15: 1 seventh y of Jeroboam king of Israel *began* 8141
15: 8 eighth y of Azariah king of Judah did 8141
15:13 thirtieth y of Uzziah king of Judah; 8141
15:17 thirtieth y of Azariah king of Judah *began* 8141
15:23 In the fiftieth y of Azariah king of Judah 8141
15:27 fiftieth y of Azariah king of Judah Pekah 8141
15:30 in the twentieth y of Jotham the son of 8141
15:32 In the second y of Pekah the son of 8141
16: 1 In the seventeenth y of Pekah the son of 8141
17: 1 In the twelfth y of Ahaz king of Judah 8141
17: 4 king of Assyria, as *he had done* y by year: 8141
17: 4 king of Assyria, as *he had done* year by y: 8141
17: 6 In the ninth y of Hoshea, the king of 8141
18: 1 Now it came to pass in the third y of 8141
18: 9 it came to pass in the fourth y of king 8141
18: 9 which *was* the seventh y of Hoshea son of 8141
18:10 *even* in the sixth y of Hezekiah, that *is* 8141
18:10 that *is* the ninth y of Hoshea king of Israel, 8141
18:13 Now in the fourteenth y of king Hezekiah 8141
19:29 Ye shall eat *this* y such things as grow of 8141
19:29 in the second y that which springeth of 8141
19:29 in the third y sow ye, and reap, and 8141
22: 3 it came to pass in the eighteenth y of king 8141
23:23 in the eighteenth y of king Josiah, 8141
23:36 and five y old when he *began* to reign; 8141
24:12 king of Babylon took him in the eighth y 8141
25: 1 it came to pass in the ninth y of his reign, 8141
25: 2 the city was besieged unto the eleventh y of 8141
25: 8 which *is* the nineteenth y of king 8141
25:27 thirtieth y of the captivity of Jehoiachin 8141
25:27 of Babylon, in the y that he *began* to reign, 8141

1Ch 20: 1 it came to pass, that after the y was expired, 8141
26:31 In the fortieth y of the reign of David they 8141
27: 1 month throughout all the months of the y, 8141
2Ch 3: 2 second month, in the fourth y of his reign. 8141
8:13 on the solemn feasts, three times in the y, 8141
9:13 came to Solomon in one y was six hundred 8141
9:24 spices, horses, and mules, a rate y by year. 8141
9:24 spices, horses, and mules, a rate year by y. 8141
12: 2 that in the fifth y of king Rehoboam 8141
13: 1 Now in the eighteenth y of king Jeroboam 8141
15:10 in the fifteenth y of the reign of Asa. 8141
15:19 the five and thirtieth y of the reign of Asa. 8141
16: 1 thirtieth y of the reign of Asa Baasha king 8141
16:12 ninth y of his reign was diseased in his feet, 8141
16:13 died in the one and fortieth y of his reign. 8141
17: 7 Also in the third y of his reign he sent to his 8141
22: 2 to reign, and he reigned one y in Jerusalem. 8141
23: 1 in the seventh y Jehoiada strengthened 8141
24: 5 the house of your God from y to year, 8141
24: 5 the house of your God from year to y, 8141
24:23 it came to pass at the end of the y, that 8141
27: 5 him the same y an hundred talents of silver, 8141
27: 5 unto him, both the second y, and the third. 8141
29: 3 He in the first y of his reign, in the first 8141
34: 3 For in the eighth y of his reign, while he 8141
34: 3 in the twelfth y he began to purge Judah 8141
34: 8 Now in the eighteenth y of his reign, 8141
35:19 In the eighteenth y of the reign of Josiah 8141
36:10 when the y was expired, king 8141
36:22 Now in the first y of Cyrus king of Persia, 8141
Ezr 1: 1 Now in the first y of Cyrus king of Persia, 8141
3: 8 Now in the second y of their coming unto 8141
4:24 So it ceased unto the second y of the reign 8140
5:13 in the first y of Cyrus the king of Babylon 8140
6: 3 In the first y of Cyrus the king *the same* 8140
6:15 which *was in* the sixth y of the reign of 8140
7: 7 in the seventh y of Artaxerxes the king. 8141
7: 8 which *was in* the seventh y of the king. 8141
Ne 1: 1 *in* the twentieth y, as I was in Shushan 8141
2: 1 *in* the twentieth y of Artaxerxes the king, 8141
5:14 from the twentieth y even unto the two 8141
5:14 and thirtieth y of Artaxerxes the king, 8141
10:31 *that* we would leave the seventh y, and 8141
10:34 of our fathers, at times appointed y by year, 8141
10:34 of our fathers, at times appointed year by y, 8141
10:35 y by year, unto the house of the LORD: 8141
10:35 year by y, unto the house of the LORD: 8141
13: 6 thirtieth y of Artaxerxes king of Babylon 8141
Est 1: 3 In the third y of his reign, he made a feast 8141
2:16 month Tebeth, in the seventh y of his reign. 8141
3: 7 in the twelfth y of king Ahasuerus, 8141
9:27 time **every y**; 3605+8141+8141+2050.1
Job 3: 6 let it not be joined unto the days of the y, 8141
Ps 65:11 Thou crownest the y with thy goodness; 8141
Isa 6: 1 In the y that king Uzziah died I saw also 8141
14:28 In the y that king Ahaz died was this 8141
20: 1 In the y that Tartan came unto Ashdod, 8141
21:16 Within a y, according to the years of a 8141
29: 1 add ye y to year; let them kill sacrifices. 8141
29: 1 add ye year to y; let them kill sacrifices. 8141
34: 8 the y of recompences for the controversy of 8141
36: 1 Now it came to pass in the fourteenth y of 8141
37:30 Ye shall eat *this* y such as groweth of itself; 8141
37:30 the second y that which springeth of 8141
37:30 in the third y sow ye, and reap, and 8141
61: 2 To proclaim the acceptable y of 8141
63: 4 and the y of my redeemed is come. 8141
Jer 1: 2 of Judah, in the thirteenth y of his reign. 8141
1: 3 unto the end of the eleventh y of Zedekiah 8141
11:23 of Anathoth, *even* the y of their visitation. 8141
17: 8 shall not be careful in the y of drought, 8141
23:12 *even* the y of their visitation, saith 8141
25: 1 y of Jehoiakim the son of Josiah king of 8141
25: 1 that *was* the first y of Nebuchadrezzar king 8141
25: 3 From the thirteenth y of Josiah the son of 8141
25: 3 this day, that *is* the three and twentieth y, 8141
28: 1 it came to pass the same y, in the beginning 8141
28: 1 in the fourth y, *and* in the fifth month, 8141
28:16 *this* y thou *shalt* die, because thou hast 8141
28:17 So Hananiah the prophet died the same y in 8141
32: 1 in the tenth y of Zedekiah king of Judah, 8141
32: 1 which *was* the eighteenth y of 8141
36: 1 it came to pass in the fourth y of Jehoiakim 8141
36: 9 it came to pass in the fifth y of Jehoiakim 8141
39: 1 In the ninth y of Zedekiah king of Judah, 8141
39: 2 *And* in the eleventh y of Zedekiah, in 8141
45: 1 in the fourth y of Jehoiakim the son of 8141
46: 2 y of Jehoiakim the son of Josiah king of 8141
48:44 *even* upon Moab, the y of their visitation, 8141
51:46 a rumour shall both come *one* y, and 8141
51:46 after that in *another* y *shall come* a rumour, 8141
51:59 *into* Babylon in the fourth y of his reign. 8141
52: 1 and twenty y old when he *began* to reign, 8141
52: 4 it came to pass in the ninth y of his reign, 8141
52: 5 the city was besieged unto the eleventh y 8141
52:12 which *was* the nineteenth y of 8141
52:28 in the seventh y three thousand Jews and 8141
52:29 In the eighteenth y of Nebuchadrezzar he 8141
52:30 twentieth y of Nebuchadrezzar 8141
52:31 thirtieth y of the captivity of Jehoiachin 8141
52:31 y of his reign lifted up the head of 8141
Eze 1: 1 Now it came to pass in the thirtieth y, in 8141
1: 2 which *was* the fifth y of king Jehoiachin's 8141
4: 6 I have appointed thee each day for a y 8141
8: 1 it came to pass in the sixth y, in the sixth 8141
20: 1 it came to pass in the seventh y, in the fifth 8141
24: 1 Again in the ninth y, in the tenth month, 8141
26: 1 it came to pass in the eleventh y, in the first 8141
29: 1 In the tenth y, in the tenth *month,* in 8141
29:17 came to pass in the seven and twentieth y, 8141
30:20 it came to pass in the eleventh y, in the first 8141
31: 1 it came to pass in the eleventh y, in 8141
32: 1 it came to pass in the twelfth y, in 8141
32:17 It came to pass also in the twelfth y, in 8141
33:21 it came to pass in the twelfth y of our 8141
Eze 40: 1 In the five and twentieth y of our captivity, 8141
40: 1 in the beginning of the y, in the tenth *day* of 8141
40: 1 in the fourteenth y after that the city was 8141
46:13 *of* a lamb of the first y without blemish: 8141
46:17 then it shall be his to the y of liberty; 8141
Da 1: 1 In the third y of the reign of Jehoiakim king 8141
1:21 Daniel continued *even* unto the first y of 8141
2: 1 in the second y of the reign of 8141
5:31 *being* about threescore and two y old. 8140
7: 1 In the first y of Belshazzar king of Babylon 8140
8: 1 In the third y of the reign of king 8141
9: 1 In the first y of Darius the son of 8141
9: 2 In the first y of his reign I Daniel 8141
10: 1 In the third y of Cyrus king of Persia a 8141
11: 1 Also I in the first y of Darius the Mede, 8141
Am 1: 1 king of Israel, **two y** before the earthquake. 8141
Mic 6: 6 with burnt offerings, with calves of a y old? 8141
Hag 1: 1 In the second y of Darius the king, in 8141
1:15 in the second y of Darius the king. 8141
2:10 the ninth *month,* in the second y of Darius, 8141
Zec 1: 1 the eighth month, in the second y of Darius, 8141
1: 7 the month Sebat, in the second y of Darius, 8141
7: 1 it came to pass in the fourth y of king 8141
14:16 go up from y to year to worship the King, 8141
14:16 go up from year to y to worship the King, 8141
Lk 2:41 Now his parents went to Jerusalem every y 2094
3: 1 Now in the fifteenth y of the reign of 2094
4:19 To preach the acceptable y of the Lord. 1763
13: 8 Lord, let it alone this y also, till I shall dig 2094
Jn 11:49 being the high priest that *same* y, said unto 1763
11:51 but being high priest that y, he prophesied 1763
18:13 which was the high priest that *same* y. 1763
Ac 11:26 that a whole y they assembled themselves 1763
18:11 And he continued *there* a y and six months, 1763
Ro 4:19 when he was about an **hundred y old,** 1541
2Co 8:10 to do, but also to be forward **a y ago.** 575+4070
9: 2 that Achaia was ready **a y ago;** 575+4070
Heb 9: 7 *went* the high priest alone once every y, 1763
9:25 the holy *place* every y with blood of others; 1763
10: 1 **y by year** continually make 1763+2596
10: 1 **year by y** continually make 1763+2596
10: 3 a remembrance *again made* of sins every y. 1763
Jas 4:13 and continue there a y, and buy and sell, 1763
Rev 9:15 and a day, and a month, and a y, for to slay 1763

YEAR'S (2) [YEAR]

Ex 34:22 and the feast of ingathering *at* the y end. 8141
2Sa 14:26 (for it was at **every y** end 3117+3117+3807.1

YEARLING See FATLING

YEARLY (9) [YEAR]

Lev 25:53 *And* as a y hired servant shall 8141+8141+871.1
Jdg 11:40 y to lament 3117+3117+4480+1886.5
21:19 y *in a place* which *is* 3117+3117+4480+1886.5
1Sa 1: 3 his city y to worship 3117+3117+4480+1886.5
1:21 went up to offer unto the LORD the y 3117
2:19 up with her husband to offer the y sacrifice. 3117
20: 6 for *there is* a y sacrifice there for all 3117
Ne 10:32 to charge ourselves y with the third *part* of 8141
Est 9:21 of the same, y, 3605+8141+8141+871.1+2050.1

YEARN, YEARNED See YERN, YERNED

YEARS (532) [YEAR]

Ge 1:14 and for seasons, and for days, and y: 8141
5: 3 Adam lived an hundred and thirty y, and 8141
5: 4 he had begotten Seth were eight hundred y: 8141
5: 5 Adam lived were nine hundred and thirty y: 8141
5: 6 Seth lived an hundred and five y, and 8141
5: 7 he begat Enos eight hundred and seven y, 8141
5: 8 of Seth were nine hundred and twelve y: 8141
5: 9 And Enos lived ninety y, and begat Cainan: 8141
5:10 begat Cainan eight hundred and fifteen y, 8141
5:11 days of Enos were nine hundred and five y: 8141
5:12 Cainan lived seventy y, and 8141
5:13 begat Mahalaleel eight hundred and forty y, 8141
5:14 of Cainan were nine hundred and ten y: 8141
5:15 Mahalaleel lived sixty and five y, and 8141
5:16 he begat Jared eight hundred and thirty y, 8141
5:17 were eight hundred ninety and five y: 8141
5:18 Jared lived an hundred sixty and two y, 8141
5:19 lived after he begat Enoch eight hundred y, 8141
5:20 of Jared were nine hundred sixty and two y: 8141
5:21 Enoch lived sixty and five y, and 8141
5:22 after he begat Methuselah three hundred y, 8141
5:23 Enoch were three hundred sixty and five y: 8141
5:25 lived an hundred eighty and seven y, 8141
5:26 Lamech seven hundred eighty and two y, 8141
5:27 were nine hundred sixty and nine y: 8141
5:28 Lamech lived an hundred eighty and two y, 8141
5:30 begat Noah five hundred ninety and five y, 8141
5:31 were seven hundred seventy and seven y: 8141
5:32 Noah was five hundred y old: and 8141
6: 3 his days shall be an hundred and twenty y. 8141
7: 6 Noah *was* six hundred y old when the flood 8141
9:28 after the flood three hundred and fifty y. 8141
9:29 of Noah were nine hundred and fifty y: 8141
11:10 Shem *was* an hundred y old, and 8141
11:10 and begat Arphaxad **two y** after the flood: 8141
11:11 after he begat Arphaxad five hundred y, 8141
11:12 Arphaxad lived five and thirty y, and 8141
11:13 he begat Salah four hundred and three y, 8141
11:14 And Salah lived thirty y, and begat Eber: 8141
11:15 he begat Eber four hundred and three y, 8141
11:16 Eber lived four and thirty y, and 8141
11:17 he begat Peleg four hundred and thirty y, 8141
11:18 And Peleg lived thirty y, and begat Reu: 8141
11:19 after he begat Reu two hundred and nine y, 8141
11:20 Reu lived two and thirty y, and 8141
11:21 he begat Serug two hundred and seven y, 8141
11:22 And Serug lived thirty y, and begat Nahor: 8141
11:23 lived after he begat Nahor two hundred y, 8141
11:24 Nahor lived nine and twenty y, and 8141
11:25 he begat Terah an hundred and nineteen y, 8141
Ge 11:26 Terah lived seventy y, and begat Abram, 8141
11:32 days of Terah were two hundred and five y: 8141
12: 4 five y old when he departed out of Haran. 8141
14: 4 Twelve y they served Chedorlaomer, and 8141
15: 9 Take me a heifer of **three y old,** and a she 8027
15: 9 a she goat of **three y old,** and a ram of 8027
15: 9 a ram of **three y old,** and a turtle-dove, and 8027
15:13 and they shall afflict them four hundred y; 8141
16: 3 after Abram had dwelt ten y in the land of 8141
16:16 Abram *was* fourscore and six y old, 8141
17: 1 when Abram was ninety y old and nine, 8141
17:17 be born unto him that is an hundred y old? 8141
17:17 and shall Sarah, that is ninety y old, bear? 8141
17:24 Abraham *was* ninety y old and nine, 8141
17:25 Ishmael his son *was* thirteen y old, when he 8141
21: 5 Abraham *was* an hundred y old, when his 8141
23: 1 an hundred and seven and twenty y **old:** 8141
23: 1 *these were* the y of the life of Sarah. 8141
25: 7 these *are* the days of the y of Abraham's 8141
25: 7 an hundred threescore and fifteen y. 8141
25: 8 full *of* y; and was gathered to his people. NIH
25:17 these *are* the y of the life of Ishmael, 8141
25:17 an hundred and thirty and seven y: 8141
25:20 Isaac was forty y old when he took 8141
25:26 Isaac *was* threescore y old when she bare 8141
26:34 Esau was forty y old when he took to wife 8141
29:18 I will serve thee seven y for Rachel thy 8141
29:20 Jacob served seven y for Rachel; and 8141
29:27 thou shalt serve with me yet seven other y. 8141
29:30 and served with him yet seven other y. 8141
31:38 This twenty y *have* I *been* with thee; 8141
31:41 Thus have I been twenty y in thy house; 8141
31:41 I served thee fourteen y for thy two 8141
31:41 thy two daughters, and six y for thy cattle: 8141
35:28 of Isaac were an hundred and fourscore y. 8141
37: 2 Joseph, *being* seventeen y old, was feeding 8141
41: 1 came to pass at the end of **two full y,** 3117+8141
41:26 The seven good kine *are* seven y; and 8141
41:26 and the seven good ears *are* seven y: 8141
41:27 kine that came up after them *are* seven y; 8141
41:27 the east wind shall be seven y of famine. 8141
41:29 there come seven y of great plenty 8141
41:30 there shall arise after them seven y of 8141
41:34 the land of Egypt in the seven plenteous y. 8141
41:35 let them gather all the food of those good y 8141
41:36 to the land against the seven y of famine, 8141
41:46 Joseph *was* thirty y old when he stood 8141
41:47 in the seven plenteous y the earth brought 8141
41:48 he gathered up all the food of the seven y, 8141
41:50 born two sons before the y of famine came, 8141
41:53 the seven y of plenteousness, that was in 8141
41:54 the seven y of dearth began to come, 8141
45: 6 For these **two y** *hath* the famine *been* in 8141
45: 6 yet *there are* five y, in the which *there shall* 8141
45:11 for yet *there are* five y of famine; lest thou, 8141
47: 9 The days of the y of my pilgrimage *are* an 8141
47: 9 my pilgrimage *are* an hundred and thirty y: 8141
47: 9 evil have the days of the y of my life been, 8141
47: 9 have not attained unto the days of the y of 8141
47:28 lived in the land of Egypt seventeen y: 8141
47:28 of Jacob was an hundred forty and seven y. 8141
50:22 and Joseph lived an hundred and ten y. 8141
50:26 *being* an hundred and ten y old: 8141
Ex 6:16 the y of the life of Levi *were* an hundred 8141
6:16 of Levi *were* an hundred thirty and seven y. 8141
6:18 the y of the life of Kohath *were* an hundred 8141
6:18 Kohath *were* an hundred thirty and three y. 8141
6:20 the y of the life of Amram *were* an hundred 8141
6:20 *were* an hundred and thirty and seven y. 8141
7: 7 Moses *was* fourscore y old, and 8141
7: 7 Aaron fourscore and three y old, when they 8141
12:40 in Egypt, *was* four hundred and thirty y. 8141
12:41 at the end of the four hundred and thirty y, 8141
16:35 the children of Israel did eat manna forty y, 8141
21: 2 buy a Hebrew servant, six y he shall serve: 8141
23:10 six y thou shalt sow thy land, and 8141
30:14 from twenty y old and above, shall give an 8141
38:26 from twenty y old and upward, for six 8141
Lev 19:23 three y shall it be as uncircumcised unto 8141
25: 3 Six y thou shalt sow thy field, and six years 8141
25: 3 and six y thou shalt prune thy vineyard, and 8141
25: 8 thou shalt number seven sabbaths of y unto 8141
25: 8 of years unto thee, seven times seven y; 8141
25: 8 the space of the seven sabbaths of y shall 8141
25: 8 of years shall be unto thee forty and nine y. 8141
25:15 According to the number of y after 8141
25:15 according unto the number of y of the fruits 8141
25:16 According to the multitude of y thou shalt 8141
25:16 according to the fewness of y thou shalt 8141
25:16 for *according to* the number *of the* y of NIH
25:21 it shall bring forth fruit for three y. 8141
25:27 Then let him count the y of the sale thereof, 8141
25:50 shall be according unto the number of y, 8141
25:51 If *there be* yet many y *behind,* according 8141
25:52 but few y unto the year of jubile, 8141
25:52 according unto his y shall he give *him* 8141
25:54 if he be not redeemed in these *y,* then NIH
27: 3 of the male from twenty y old even unto 8141
27: 3 twenty years old even unto sixty y old, 8141
27: 5 if *it be* from five y old even unto twenty 8141
27: 5 from five years old even unto twenty y old, 8141
27: 6 if *it be* from a month old even unto five y 8141
27: 7 if *it be* from sixty y old and above; if *it be* a 8141
27:18 the money according to the y that remain, 8141
Nu 1: 3 From twenty y old and upward, all that *are* 8141
1:18 from twenty y old and upward, by their 8141
1:20 every male from twenty y old and upward, 8141
1:22 every male from twenty y old and upward, 8141
1:24 from twenty y old and upward, all that *were* 8141
1:26 from twenty y old and upward, all that *were* 8141
1:28 from twenty y old and upward, all that *were* 8141
1:30 from twenty y old and upward, all that *were* 8141
1:32 from twenty y old and upward, all that *were* 8141
1:34 from twenty y old and upward, all that *were* 8141
1:36 from twenty y old and upward, all that *were* 8141

Nu 1:38 from twenty y old and upward, all that *were* 8141
1:40 from twenty y old and upward, all that *were* 8141
1:42 from twenty y old and upward, all that *were* 8141
1:45 from twenty y old and upward, 8141
4: 3 From thirty y old and upward even until 8141
4: 3 years old and upward even until fifty y old, 8141
4:23 From thirty y old and upward until fifty 8141
4:23 upward until fifty y old shalt thou number 8141
4:30 From thirty y old and upward even unto 8141
4:30 upward even unto fifty y old shalt thou 8141
4:35 From thirty y old and upward even unto 8141
4:35 years old and upward even unto fifty y old, 8141
4:39 From thirty y old and upward even unto 8141
4:39 years old and upward even unto fifty y old, 8141
4:43 From thirty y old and upward even unto 8141
4:43 years old and upward even unto fifty y old, 8141
4:47 From thirty y old and upward even unto 8141
4:47 years old and upward even unto fifty y old, 8141
8:24 from twenty and five y old and 8141
8:25 from the age of fifty y they shall cease 8141
13:22 *were.* (Now Hebron was built seven y 8141
14:29 from twenty y old and upward, 8141
14:33 shall wander in the wilderness forty y, 8141
14:34 *even* forty y, and ye shall know my breach 8141
26: 2 from twenty y old and upward, throughout 8141
26: 4 *Take the sum of the people,* from twenty y 8141
32:11 from twenty y old and upward, shall see 8141
32:13 them wander in the wilderness forty y, 8141
33:39 and three y old when he died in mount Hor. 8141
Dt 2: 7 these forty y the LORD thy God *hath been* 8141
2:14 the brook Zered, *was* thirty and eight y; 8141
8: 2 led thee these forty y in the wilderness, 8141
8: 4 neither did thy foot swell, these forty y. 8141
14:28 At the end of three y thou shalt bring forth 8141
15: 1 At the end of *every* seven y thou shalt make 8141
15:12 be sold unto thee, and serve thee six y; 8141
15:18 hired servant *to thee,* in serving thee six y: 8141
29: 5 I have led you forty y in the wilderness: 8141
31: 2 I *am* an hundred and twenty y old *this* day; 8141
31:10 saying, At the end of *every* seven y, 8141
32: 7 of old, consider the y of many generations: 8141
34: 7 an hundred and twenty y old when he died: 8141
Jos 5: 6 For the children of Israel walked forty y in 8141
13: 1 Now Joshua was old *and* stricken in y; and 3117
13: 1 Thou art old *and* stricken in y, and 3117
14: 7 Forty y old *was* I when Moses the servant 8141
14:10 me alive, as he said, these forty and five y, 8141
14:10 I *am this* day fourscore and five y old. 8141
24:29 died, *being* an hundred and ten y old. 8141
Jdg 2: 8 died, *being* an hundred and ten y old. 8141
3: 8 Israel served Chushan-rishathaim eight y. 8141
3:11 the land had rest forty y. And Othniel 8141
3:14 served Eglon the king of Moab eighteen y. 8141
3:30 of Israel. And the land had rest fourscore y. 8141
4: 3 twenty y he mightily oppressed the children 8141
5:31 in his might. And the land had rest forty y. 8141
6: 1 them into the hand of Midian seven y. 8141
6:25 even the second bullock of seven y old, and 8141
8:28 the country was in quietness forty y in 8141
9:22 When Abimelech had reigned three y over 8141
10: 2 he judged Israel twenty and three y, and 8141
10: 3 and judged Israel twenty and two y. 8141
10: 8 eighteen y, all the children of Israel that 8141
11:26 by the coasts of Arnon, three hundred y? 8141
12: 7 Jephthah judged Israel six y. Then died 8141
12: 9 for his sons. And he judged Israel seven y. 8141
12:11 judged Israel; and he judged Israel ten y. 8141
12:14 ten ass colts: and he judged Israel eight y. 8141
13: 1 into the hand of the Philistines forty y. 8141
15:20 in the days of the Philistines twenty y. 8141
16:31 his father. And he judged Israel twenty y. 8141
Ru 1: 4 and they dwelled there about ten y. 8141
1Sa 4:15 Now Eli *was* ninety and eight y old; and 8141
4:18 heavy. And he had judged Israel forty y. 8141
7: 2 for it was twenty y: and all the house of 8141
13: 1 and when he had reigned two y over Israel, 8141
29: 3 or these y, and I have found no *fault* in him 8141
2Sa 2:10 Ish-bosheth Saul's son *was* forty y old 8141
2:10 to reign over Israel, and reigned two y. 8141
2:11 over the house of Judah was seven y 8141
4: 4 was five y old when the tidings came of 8141
5: 4 David *was* thirty y old when he *began* to 8141
5: 4 he *began* to reign, *and* he reigned forty y. 8141
5: 5 In Hebron he reigned over Judah seven y 8141
5: 5 and three y over all Israel and Judah. 8141
13:23 it came to pass after two full y, 3117+8141
13:38 and went to Geshur, and was there three y. 8141
14:28 So Absalom dwelt two full y in 3117+8141
15: 7 it came to pass after forty y, that Absalom 8141
19:32 was a very aged man, *even* fourscore y old: 8141
19:35 I *am this* day fourscore y old: *and* can I 8141
21: 1 was a famine in the days of David three y, 8141
24:13 Shall seven y of famine come unto thee in 8141
1Ki 1: 1 Now king David was old *and* stricken in y; 3117
2:11 that David reigned over Israel *were* forty y: 8141
2:11 seven y reigned he in Hebron, and thirty 8141
2:11 thirty and three y reigned he in Jerusalem. 8141
2:39 it came to pass at the end of three y, 8141
6:38 of it. So was he seven y in building it. 8141
7: 1 was building his own house thirteen y, 8141
9:10 it came to pass at the end of twenty y, 8141
10:22 once in three y came the navy of Tharshish, 8141
11:42 in Jerusalem over all Israel *was* forty y. 8141
14:20 Jeroboam reigned *were* two and twenty y: 8141
14:21 and one y old when he *began* to reign, 8141
14:21 and he reigned seventeen y in Jerusalem, 8141
15: 2 Three y reigned he in Jerusalem. And his 8141
15:10 and one y reigned he in Jerusalem. 8141
15:25 of Judah, and reigned over Israel two y. 8141
15:33 over all Israel in Tirzah, twenty and four y. 8141
16: 8 to reign over Israel in Tirzah, two y. 8141
16:23 *began* Omri to reign over Israel, twelve y: 8141
16:23 twelve years: six y reigned he in Tirzah. 8141
16:29 over Israel in Samaria twenty and two y. 8141
17: 1 there shall not be dew nor rain these y, but 8141

1Ki 22: 1 they continued three y without war between 8141
22:42 and five y old when he *began* to reign; 8141
22:42 he reigned twenty and five y in Jerusalem. 8141
22:51 of Judah, and reigned two y over Israel. 8141
2Ki 3: 1 king of Judah, and reigned twelve y. 8141
8: 1 it shall also come upon the land seven y. 8141
8: 2 in the land of the Philistines seven y. 8141
8:17 two y old was he when he *began* to reign; 8141
8:17 and he reigned eight y in Jerusalem. 8141
8:26 twenty y old *was* Ahaziah when he *began* 8141
10:36 Israel in Samaria *was* twenty and eight y. 8141
11: 3 her hid *in* the house of the LORD six y. 8141
11:21 Seven y old *was* Jehoash when he *began* to 8141
12: 1 and forty y reigned he in Jerusalem. 8141
13: 1 Israel in Samaria, *and reigned* seventeen y. 8141
13:10 Israel in Samaria, *and reigned* sixteen y. 8141
14: 2 and five y old when he *began* to reign, 8141
14: 2 reigned twenty and nine y in Jerusalem. 8141
14:17 son of Jehoahaz king of Israel fifteen y. 8141
14:21 which *was* sixteen y old, and made him 8141
14:23 in Samaria, *and reigned* forty and one y. 8141
15: 2 Sixteen y old was he when he *began* to 8141
15: 2 and he reigned two and fifty y in Jerusalem. 8141
15:17 over Israel, *and reigned* ten y in Samaria. 8141
15:23 over Israel in Samaria, *and reigned* two y. 8141
15:27 Israel in Samaria, *and reigned* twenty y. 8141
15:33 twenty y old was he when he *began* to 8141
15:33 and he reigned sixteen y in Jerusalem. 8141
16: 2 Twenty y old *was* Ahaz when he *began* to 8141
16: 2 reigned sixteen y in Jerusalem, and did not 8141
17: 1 Elah to reign in Samaria over Israel nine y. 8141
17: 5 went up *to* Samaria, and besieged it three y. 8141
18: 2 five y old was he when he *began* to reign; 8141
18: 2 he reigned twenty and nine y in Jerusalem. 8141
18:10 at the end of three y they took it: *even* in 8141
20: 6 I will add unto thy days fifteen y; and I will 8141
21: 1 Manasseh *was* twelve y old when he *began* 8141
21: 1 and reigned fifty and five y in Jerusalem. 8141
21:19 and two y old when he *began* to reign, 8141
21:19 to reign, and he reigned two y in Jerusalem. 8141
22: 1 Josiah *was* eight y old when he *began* to 8141
22: 1 he reigned thirty and one y in Jerusalem. 8141
23:31 and three y old when he *began* to reign; 8141
23:36 and he reigned eleven y in Jerusalem. 8141
24: 1 and Jehoiakim became his servant three y: 8141
24: 8 Jehoiachin *was* eighteen y old when he 8141
24:18 and one y old when he *began* to reign, 8141
24:18 and he reigned eleven y in Jerusalem. 8141
1Ch 2:21 whom he married when he *was* threescore y 8141
3: 4 there he reigned seven y and six months: 8141
3: 4 in Jerusalem he reigned thirty and three y. 8141
23: 3 were numbered from the age of thirty y 8141
23:24 from the age of twenty y and upward. 8141
23:27 the Levites *were* numbered from twenty y 8141
27:23 not the number of them from twenty y old 8141
29:27 time that he reigned over Israel *was* forty y; 8141
29:27 seven y reigned he in Hebron, and thirty 8141
29:27 thirty and three y reigned he in Jerusalem. NIH
2Ch 8: 1 it came to pass at the end of twenty y, 8141
9:21 every three y once came the ships of 8141
9:30 reigned in Jerusalem over all Israel forty y. 8141
11:17 the son of Solomon strong, three y: 8141
11:17 for three y they walked in the way of David 8141
12:13 and forty y old when he *began* to reign, 8141
12:13 and he reigned seventeen y in Jerusalem, 8141
13: 2 He reigned three y in Jerusalem. 8141
14: 1 In his days the land was quiet ten y. 8141
14: 6 land had rest, and he had no war in those y; 8141
18: 2 after *certain* y he went down to Ahab to 8141
20:31 and five y old when he *began* to reign, 8141
20:31 he reigned twenty and five y in Jerusalem. 8141
21: 5 and two y old when he *began* to reign, 8141
21: 5 and he reigned eight y in Jerusalem. 8141
21:19 in process of time, after the end of two y, 3117
21:20 two y old was he when he *began* to reign, NIH
21:20 he reigned in Jerusalem eight y, and 8141
22: 2 two y old *was* Ahaziah when he *began* to 8141
22:12 with them hid in the house of God six y: 8141
24: 1 Joash *was* seven y old when he *began* to 8141
24: 1 and he reigned forty y in Jerusalem. 8141
24:15 and thirty y old *was he* when he died. 8141
25: 1 and five y old *when* he *began* to reign, 8141
25: 1 he reigned twenty and nine y in Jerusalem. 8141
25: 5 he numbered them from twenty y old and 8141
25:25 son of Jehoahaz king of Israel fifteen y. 8141
26: 1 who *was* sixteen y old, and made him king 8141
26: 3 Sixteen y old *was* Uzziah when he *began* to 8141
26: 3 and he reigned fifty and two y in Jerusalem. 8141
27: 1 and five y old when he *began* to reign, 8141
27: 1 and he reigned sixteen y in Jerusalem. 8141
27: 8 and twenty y old when he *began* to reign, 8141
27: 8 and reigned sixteen y in Jerusalem. 8141
28: 1 Ahaz *was* twenty y old when he *began* to 8141
28: 1 and he reigned sixteen y in Jerusalem: 8141
29: 1 to reign *when he was* five and twenty y old, 8141
29: 1 he reigned nine and twenty y in Jerusalem. 8141
31:16 of males, from three y old and upward, 8141
31:17 the Levites from twenty y old and upward, 8141
33: 1 Manasseh *was* twelve y old when he *began* 8141
33: 1 he reigned fifty and five y in Jerusalem: 8141
33:21 and twenty y old when he *began* to reign, 8141
33:21 to reign, and reigned two y in Jerusalem. 8141
34: 1 Josiah *was* eight y old when he *began* to 8141
34: 1 he reigned in Jerusalem one and thirty y. 8141
36: 2 and three y old when he *began* to reign, 8141
36: 5 and five y old when he *began* to reign, 8141
36: 5 and he reigned eleven y in Jerusalem: 8141
36: 9 Jehoiachin *was* eight y old when he *began* 8141
36:11 and twenty y old when he *began* to reign, 8141
36:11 to reign, and reigned eleven y in Jerusalem. 8141
36:21 kept sabbath, to fulfil threescore and ten y. 8141
Ezr 3: 8 appointed the Levites from twenty y old 8141
5:11 house that was builded these many y ago, 8140
Ne 5:14 *that is,* twelve y, I and my brethren have 8141
9:21 forty y didst thou sustain them in 8141

Ne 9:30 Yet many y didst thou forbear them, and 8141
Job 10: 5 the days of man? *are* thy y as man's days, 8141
15:20 the number of y is hidden to the oppressor. 8141
16:22 When a few y are come, then I shall go 8141
32: 7 and multitude of y should teach wisdom. 8141
36:11 days in prosperity, and their y in pleasures. 8141
36:26 neither can the number of his y be searched 8141
42:16 After this lived Job an hundred and forty y, 8141
Ps 31:10 is spent with grief, and my y with sighing: 8141
61: 6 king's life: *and* his y as many generations. 8141
77: 5 the days of old, the y of ancient times. 8141
77:10 *I will remember* the y of the right hand of 8141
78:33 consume in vanity, and their y in trouble. 8141
90: 4 For a thousand y in thy sight *are but* 8141
90: 9 we spend our y as a tale *that is told.* 8141
90:10 The days of our y *are* threescore years and 8141
90:10 The days of our years *are* threescore y and 8141
90:10 if by reason of strength *they be* fourscore y, 8141
90:15 *and* the y *wherein* we have seen evil. 8141
95:10 Forty y long was I grieved with *this* 8141
102:24 thy y *are* throughout all generations. 8141
102:27 *art* the same, and thy y shall have no end. 8141
Pr 4:10 and the y of thy life shall be many. 8141
5: 9 unto others, and thy y unto the cruel: 8141
9:11 and the y of thy life shall be increased. 8141
10:27 but the y of the wicked shall be shortened. 8141
Ecc 6: 3 beget an hundred *children,* and live many y, 8141
6: 3 so that the days of his y be many, and 8141
6: 6 though he live a thousand y twice *told,* yet 8141
11: 8 if a man live many y, *and* rejoice in them 8141
12: 1 nor the y draw nigh, when thou shalt say, 8141
Isa 7: 8 and five y shall Ephraim be broken, 8141
15: 5 *shall flee* unto Zoar, a heifer of three y old: 7992
16:14 saying, Within three y, as the years of a 8141
16:14 as the y of a hireling, and the glory of 8141
20: 3 barefoot three y *for* a sign and wonder upon 8141
21:16 according to the y of a hireling, and all 8141
23:15 that Tyre shall be forgotten seventy y, 8141
23:15 after the end of seventy y shall Tyre sing as 8141
23:17 come to pass after the end of seventy y, 8141
32:10 Many days and y shall ye be troubled, 8141
38: 5 behold, I will add unto thy days fifteen y. 8141
38:10 I am deprived of the residue of my y. 8141
38:15 softly all my y in the bitterness of my soul. 8141
65:20 for the child shall die an hundred y old; but 8141
65:20 the sinner *being* an hundred y old shall be 8141
Jer 25:11 shall serve the king of Babylon seventy y. 8141
25:12 to pass, when seventy y are accomplished, 8141
28: 3 Within two full y *will* I bring again 3117+8141
28:11 within the space of two full y. 3117+8141
29:10 That after seventy y be accomplished at 8141
34:14 At the end of seven y let ye go every man 8141
34:14 when he hath served thee six y, thou shalt 8141
48:34 unto Horonaim, *as* a heifer of three y old: 7992
52: 1 and he reigned eleven y in Jerusalem. 8141
Eze 4: 5 For I have laid upon thee the y of their 8141
22: 4 to draw near, and art come *even* unto thy y: 8141
29:11 neither shall it be inhabited forty y. 8141
29:12 *that are* laid waste shall be desolate forty y: 8141
29:13 At the end of forty y will I gather 8141
38: 8 in the latter y thou shalt come into the land 8141
38:17 which prophesied in those days *many* y, 8141
39: 9 and they shall burn them with fire seven y: 8141
Da 1: 5 so nourishing them three y, that at the end 8141
9: 2 understood by books the number of the y, 8141
9: 2 that *he* would accomplish seventy y in 8141
11: 6 in the end of y they shall join themselves 8141
11: 8 he shall continue *more* y than the king of 8141
11:13 shall certainly come after certain y with a 8141
Joel 2: 2 after it, *even* to the y of many generations. 8141
2:25 I will restore to you the y that the locust 8141
Am 2:10 led you forty y through the wilderness, 8141
4: 4 *and* your tithes after three y: 3117
5:25 and offerings in the wilderness forty y, 8141
Hab 3: 2 revive thy work in the midst of the y, 8141
3: 2 in the midst of the y make known; 8141
Zec 1:12 had indignation these threescore and ten y? 8141
7: 3 as I have done these so many y? 8141
7: 5 and seventh *month,* even those seventy y, 8141
Mal 3: 4 as *in* the days of old, and as *in* former y. 8141
Mt 2:16 coasts thereof, from two y old and under, *1332*
9:20 diseased with an issue of blood twelve y, *2094*
Mk 5:25 which had an issue of blood twelve y, *2094*
5:42 walked; for she was *of the age* of twelve y. *2094*
Lk 1: 7 and they both were *now* well stricken in y. *2250*
1:18 an old man, and my wife well stricken in y. *2250*
2:36 had lived with a husband seven y from her *2094*
2:37 *was* a widow of about fourscore and four y, *2094*
2:42 And when he was twelve y old, they went *2094*
3:23 himself began *to be* about thirty y of age, *2094*
4:25 when the heaven was shut up three y and *2094*
8:42 about twelve y of age, and she lay a dying. *2094*
8:43 a woman having an issue of blood twelve y, *2094*
12:19 thou hast much goods laid up for many y; *2094*
13: 7 *these* three y I come seeking fruit on this *2094*
13:11 which had a spirit of infirmity eighteen y, *2094*
13:16 Satan hath bound, lo *these* eighteen y, *2094*
15:29 *his* father, Lo, these many y do I serve thee, *2094*
Jn 2:20 Forty and six y was this temple in building, *2094*
5: 5 which had an infirmity thirty *and* eight y. *2094*
8:57 Thou art not yet fifty y old, and hast thou *2094*
Ac 4:22 For the man was above forty y old, *2094*
7: 6 and entreat *them* evil four hundred y. *2094*
7:23 And when he was full forty y old, it came *5063*
7:30 And when forty y were expired, *2094*
7:36 the Red sea, and in the wilderness forty y. *2094*
7:42 sacrifices *by the space of* forty y in *2094*
9:33 which had kept his bed eight y, and was *2094*
13:18 And about the time of forty y suffered he *5063*
13:20 about *the space of* four hundred and fifty y, *2094*
13:21 tribe of Benjamin, *by the space of* forty y. *2094*
19:10 And this continued by the space of two y; *2094*
20:31 that *by the space of* three y I ceased not to *5148*
24:10 been of many y a judge unto this nation, *2094*
24:17 Now after many y I came to bring alms to *2094*

Ac 24:27 But after **two y** Porcius Festus came into *1333*
28:30 And Paul dwelt **two** whole **y** in his own *1333*
Ro 15:23 having a great desire these many **y** to come *2094*
2Co 12: 2 I knew a man in Christ above fourteen **y** *2094*
Gal 1:18 Then after three **y** I went up to Jerusalem to *2094*
2: 1 Then fourteen **y** after I went up again to *2094*
3:17 which was four hundred and thirty **y** after, *2094*
4:10 and months, and times, and **y**. *1763*
1Ti 5: 9 into the number under threescore **y old**, *2094*
Heb 1:12 thou art the same, and thy **y** shall not fail. *2094*
3: 9 proved me, and saw my works forty **y**. *2094*
3:17 But with whom was he grieved forty **y**? *2094*
11:24 By faith Moses, when he was **come to y**, *3173*
Jas 5:17 not on the earth *by the space of* three **y** *1763*
2Pe 3: 8 one day *is* with the Lord as a thousand **y**, *2094*
3: 8 and a thousand **y** as one day. *2094*
Rev 20: 2 and Satan, and bound him a thousand **y**, *2094*
20: 3 till the thousand **y** should be fulfilled: *2094*
20: 4 and reigned with Christ a thousand **y**. *2094*
20: 5 again until the thousand **y** were finished. *2094*
20: 6 and shall reign with him a thousand **y**. *2094*
20: 7 And when the thousand **y** are expired, *2094*

YEARS' (2) [YEAR]
2Ki 8: 3 it came to pass at the seven **y** end, that 8141
1Ch 21:12 Either three **y** famine; or three months to be 8141

YELL (1) [YELLED]
Jer 51:38 like lions: they shall **y** as lions' whelps, 5286

YELLED (1) [YELL]
Jer 2:15 *and* **y**, and they made his land waste: 5414+6963

YELLOW (4)
Lev 13:30 *there be* in it a **y** thin hair; then the priest 6669
13:32 there be in it no **y** hair, and the scall *be* not 6669
13:36 the skin, the priest shall not seek for **y** hair: 6669
Ps 68:13 with silver, and her feathers with **y** gold. 3422

YERN (1) [YERNED]
Ge 43:30 for his bowels did **y** upon his brother: 3648

YERNED (1) [YERN]
1Ki 3:26 for her bowels **y** upon her son, and she said, 3648

YES (4)
Mt 17:25 He saith, **Y**. And when he was come into *3483*
Mk 7:28 she answered and said unto him, **Y**, Lord: *3483*
Ro 3:29 of the Gentiles? **Y**, of the Gentiles also: *3483*
10:18 **Y verily**, their sound went into all *3304*

YESTERDAY (9) [DAY]
Ex 5:14 fulfilled your task in making brick both **y** 8543
1Sa 20:27 son of Jesse to meat, neither **y**, nor to day? 8543
2Sa 15:20 *Whereas* thou camest *but* **y**, should I *this* 8543
2Ki 9:26 Surely I have seen **y** the blood of Naboth, 570
Job 8: 9 (For we *are but of* **y**, and know nothing, 8543
Ps 90: 4 thy sight *are but as* **y** when it is past, 865+3117
Jn 4:52 **Y** at the seventh hour the fever left him. *5504*
Ac 7:28 thou kill me, as thou didst the Egyptian **y**? *5504*
Heb 13: 8 Jesus Christ the same **y**, and to day, and *5504*

YESTERNIGHT (3) [NIGHT]
Ge 19:34 the younger, Behold, I lay **y** with my father: 570
31:29 but the God of your father spake unto me **y**, 570
31:42 the labour of my hands, and rebuked *thee* **y**. 570

YET (683)
Ge 6: 3 **y** his days shall be an hundred and 2050.1
7: 4 For **y** seven days, *and* I will cause 5750+3807.1
8:10 he stayed **y** other seven days; and again he 5750
8:12 he stayed **y** other seven days; and sent forth 5750
15:16 iniquity of the Amorites *is* not **y** full. 2008+5704
18:22 but Abraham stood **y** before the LORD. 5750
18:29 he spake unto him **y again**, and said, 3254+5750
18:32 be angry, and I will speak **y but** *this* once: 389
20:12 **y** indeed *she is* my sister; she *is* 1571
21:26 **neither y** heard I *of it*, but to 1571+3808+2050.1
25: 6 while he **y** lived, eastward, unto the east 5750
27:30 Jacob was **y** scarce gone out from 389
29: 7 he said, Lo, *it is* **y** high day, neither *is it* 5750
29: 9 **while** he **y** spake with them, Rachel came 5750
29:27 shalt serve with me **y** seven other years. 5750
29:30 and served with him **y** seven other years. 5750
31:14 *Is there* **y** any portion or inheritance for us 5750
31:30 *y* wherefore hast thou stolen my gods? NIH
37: 5 and they hated him **y the more**. 3254+5750
37: 8 they hated him **y the more** for his 3254+5750
37: 9 he dreamed **y** another dream, and told it his 5750
38: 5 she **y again** conceived, and bare a 3254+5750
40:13 **Y** within three days shall Pharaoh lift up 5750
40:19 **Y** within three days shall Pharaoh lift up thy NIH
40:23 **Y** did not the chief butler remember 2050.1
43: 6 *as* to tell the man whether ye had **y** a 5750
43: 7 our kindred, saying, *Is* your father **y** alive? 5750
43:27 old man of whom ye spake? *Is* he **y** alive? 5750
43:28 our father *is* in good health, he *is* **y** alive. 5750
44: 4 *and* not *y* far off, Joseph said unto his NIH
44:14 came to Joseph's house; for he *was* **y** there: 5750
45: 3 I *am* Joseph; doth my father **y** live? 5750
45: 6 **y** *there are* five years, *in* the which *there* 5750
45:11 for **y** *there are* five years of famine; 5750
45:26 Joseph *is* **y** alive, and he *is* governor over 5750
45:28 *It is* enough; Joseph my son *is* **y** alive: 5750
46:30 have seen thy face, because thou *art* **y** alive. 5750
48: 7 when **y** *there was* but a little way to come 5750
Ex 4:18 in Egypt, and see whether they be **y** alive. 5750
5:11 get you straw where you can find *it:* **y** not 3588
5:18 **y** shall ye deliver the tale of bricks. 2050.1
9:17 **As y** exaltest thou thyself against my 5750
9:30 I know that ye will **not y** fear the LORD 2962
9:34 he sinned **y** more, and hardened his heart, 2050.1
10: 7 knowest thou **not y** that Egypt is 2962
11: 1 **Y** will I bring one plague *more* upon 5750
21:22 *from her,* **and y** no mischief follow: 2050.1
32:32 **Y** now, if thou wilt forgive their sin; and 2050.1
33:12 **Y** thou hast said, I know thee by name, 2050.1
36: 3 to make it *withal.* And they brought **y** unto 5750
Lev 5:17 **y** is he guilty, and shall bear his iniquity. 2050.1
11: 7 **y** he cheweth not the cud; 2050.1
11:21 **Y** these may ye eat of every flying creeping 389
13:40 fallen off his head, he *is* bald: *y is* he clean. NIH
13:41 his face, he *is* forehead bald: *y is* he clean. NIH
25:22 and eat *y* of old fruit until the ninth year; NIH
25:51 If *there be* **y** many years *behind,* according 5750
26:18 if ye will not **y** for *all* this hearken unto me, 5704
26:24 will punish you **y** seven *times* for your sins. 1571
26:44 **y** for all that, when they be in the land of 637
Nu 9:10 **y** he shall keep the passover unto 2050.1
11:33 **while** the flesh *was* **y** between their teeth, 5750
19:13 be unclean; his uncleanness *is* **y** upon him. 5750
22:15 Balak sent **y** again princes, more, and 5750
22:20 **y** the word which I shall say unto thee, 389
30:16 *being* **y** in her youth *in* her father's house. NIH
32:14 to augment **y** the fierce anger of 5750
32:15 he will **y** again leave them in 5750
Dt 1:32 **Y** in this thing ye did not believe 2050.1
9:29 **Y** they *are* thy people and 2050.1
12: 9 For ye are not as **y** come to the rest 5704+6258
14: 8 divideth the hoof, **y** *cheweth* not the cud, 2050.1
20: 6 a vineyard, and hath not *y* eaten of it? NIH
22:17 *y* these *are the tokens of* my daughter's NIH
29: 4 **Y** the LORD hath not given you a heart 2050.1
31:27 while I am **y** alive with you *this* day, 5750
32:52 **Y** thou shalt see the land before *thee;* but 3588
Jos 3: 4 **Y** there shall be a space between you and it, 389
13: 1 there remaineth *y* very much land to be NIH
13: 2 This is the land that *y* remaineth: all NIH
14:11 **As y** I *am as* strong *this* day as *I was* in 5750
17:12 **Y** the children of Manasseh could not 2050.1
17:13 **Y** it came to pass, when the children of 2050.1
18: 2 which had not *y* received their inheritance. NIH
Jdg 1:35 **y** the hand of the house of Joseph 2050.1
2:10 nor **y** the works which he had done for 1571
2:17 **y** they would not hearken unto their judges, 1571
6:24 unto this day it *is* **y** in Ophrah of 5750
6:31 let him be put to death whilst *it is y* NIH
7: 4 unto Gideon, The people *are* **y** *too* many; 5750
8: 4 *were* with him, faint, **y** pursuing *them.* 2050.1
8:20 for he feared, because he *was* **y** a youth. 5750
9: 5 **notwithstanding y** Jotham the youngest 2050.1
10:13 **Y** ye have forsaken me, and served other 2050.1
15: 7 **y** will I be avenged of you, and 518+3588
17: 4 **Y** he restored the money unto his mother; 2050.1
19:19 **Y** there is both straw and provender for 2050.1
20:28 Shall I **y again** go out to battle 3254+5750
21:14 **and y** so they sufficed them not. 2050.1
Ru 1:11 *are there* **y** *any moe* sons in my womb, 5750
1Sa 3: 6 the LORD called **y** again, Samuel. 5750
3: 7 Now Samuel did **not y** know the LORD, 2962
3: 7 **neither** was the word of the LORD **y** 2962+2050.1
8: 9 **howbeit y** protest solemnly unto 389+3588
10:22 if the man should **y** come thither. 5750
12:20 **y** turn not aside from following the LORD, 389
13: 7 he *was* **y** in Gilgal, and all the people 5750
13:21 **Y** they had a file for the mattocks, and 2050.1
15:30 *y* honour me now, I pray thee, before NIH
16:11 There remaineth **y** the youngest, and 5750
18:29 Saul was **y** the more afraid of David; and 5750
20:14 thou shalt not only **while y** I live shew me 5750
23: 4 David inquired of the LORD **y** again. 5750
23:22 prepare **y**, and know and see his place 5750
24:11 **y** thou huntest my soul to take it. 2050.1
25:29 **Y** a man is risen to pursue thee, and 2050.1
2Sa 1: 9 upon me, because my life *is* **y** whole in me. 5750
3:35 cause David to eat meat while it was **y** day, 5750
5:13 there were **y** sons and daughters born to 5750
5:22 the Philistines came up **y** again, and 5750
6:22 I will **y** be more vile than thus, and will be 5750
7:19 this was **y** a small thing in thy sight, O Lord 5750
9: 1 Is there **y** *any* that is left of the house of 5750
9: 3 *Is there* not **y** any of the house of Saul, 5750
9: 3 Jonathan hath **y** a son, *which is* lame on *his* 5750
12:18 Behold, while the child was *y* alive, NIH
12:22 While the child *was* **y** alive, I fasted and 5750
14:14 **y** doth he devise means, that *his* banished 2050.1
18:12 *y* would I not put forth mine hand against NIH
18:14 **while** he *was* **y** alive in the midst of 5750
18:22 the son of Zadok **y again** to Joab, 3254+5750
19:28 **y** didst thou set thy servant among them 2050.1
19:28 have I **y** to cry any more unto the king? 5750
19:35 should thy servant be **y** a burden unto my 5750
21:15 Moreover the Philistines had **y** war **again** 5750
21:20 there was **y** a battle in Gath, where was a 5750
23: 5 **y** he hath made with me an everlasting 3588
1Ki 1:14 **while** thou **y** talkest there with the king, 5750
1:22 lo, **while** she **y** talked with the king, 5750
1:42 **while** he **y** spake, behold, Jonathan the son 5750
8:28 **Y** have thou respect unto the prayer of 2050.1
8:47 *Y* if they shall bethink themselves in NIH
11:17 go *into* Egypt; Hadad *being* **y** a little child. NIH
12: 2 the son of Nebat, who was **y** in Egypt, 5750
12: 5 Depart **y** *for* three days, then come again to 5750
12: 6 before Solomon his father while he *y* lived, NIH
14: 8 *y* thou hast not been as my servant David, NIH
19:18 **Y** I have left *me* seven thousand in Israel, 2050.1
20: 6 **Y** I will send my servants unto thee to 518+3588
20:32 he said, *Is* he **y** alive? he *is* my brother. 5750
22: 8 *There is* **y** one man, Micaiah the son of 5750
22:43 and burnt incense **y** in the high places. 5750
2Ki 3:17 **y** that valley shall be filled *with* water, 2050.1
4: 6 she said unto her son, Bring me **y** a vessel. 5750
6:33 **while** he **y** talked with them, behold, 5750
8:19 **Y** the LORD would not destroy Judah 2050.1
8:22 **Y** Edom revolted from under the hand of 2050.1
13:23 cast he them from his presence **as y**. 5704+6258
14: 3 of the LORD, **y** not like David his father: 7535
14: 4 as **y** the people did sacrifice and 5750
17:13 **Y** the LORD testified against Israel, and 2050.1
2Ki 19:30 of Judah shall *y* again take root downward, NIH
1Ch 12: 1 while he **y** kept himself close because NIH
14:13 the Philistines **y** again spread themselves 2050.1
17:17 *y* this was a small thing in thine eyes, NIH
20: 6 **And y** again there was war at Gath, 2050.1
26:10 **y** his father made him the chief;) 2050.1
29: 1 *is* *y* young and tender, and the work *is* great: NIH
2Ch 1:11 neither **y** hast asked long life; 1571
6:16 **y** so that thy children take heed to their way 7535
6:26 *y* if they pray towards this place, NIH
6:37 *Y* if they bethink themselves in the land NIH
10: 6 before Solomon his father while he *y* lived, NIH
13: 6 **Y** Jeroboam the son of Nebat, the servant 2050.1
14: 7 and bars, *while* the land *is* **y** before us; 5750
16: 8 **y**, because thou didst rely on the LORD, 2050.1
16:12 **y** in his disease he sought not *to* 1571+2050.1
18: 7 *There is* **y** one man, by whom *we* may 5750
20:33 for **as y** the people had not prepared their 5750
24:19 **Y** he sent prophets to them, to bring them 2050.1
27: 2 And the people did **y** corruptly. 5750
28:22 he trespass **y** more against the LORD: 2050.1
30:18 **y** did they eat the passover otherwise than it 3588
32:15 this *manner,* **neither y** believe him: 408+2050.1
32:16 his servants spake **y** *more* against 5750
33:17 *y* unto the LORD their God only. NIH
34: 3 year of his reign, while he was **y** young, 5750
Ezr 3: 6 of the temple of the LORD was not *y* laid. NIH
5:16 *it been* in building, and *y it is* not finished. NIH
9: 9 **y** our God hath not forsaken us in our 2050.1
9:15 for we remain *y* escaped, as *it is* this day: NIH
10: 2 **y** now there is hope in Israel concerning 2050.1
Ne 1: 9 *y* will I gather them from thence, and NIH
2:16 neither had I **as y** told *it* to the Jews, 3651+5704
5: 5 **Y** now our flesh *is* as the flesh of our 2050.1
5:18 **y** for *all* this required not I the bread of 2050.1
6: 4 **Y** they sent unto me four times after this 2050.1
9:19 **Y** thou in thy manifold mercies 2050.1
9:28 **y when** they returned, and cried unto 2050.1
9:29 **y** they dealt proudly, and hearkened not 2050.1
9:30 **Y** many years didst thou forbear them, 2050.1
9:30 **y** would they not give ear: therefore 2050.1
13:18 **y** ye bring more wrath upon Israel by 2050.1
13:26 **y** among many nations was there no king 2050.1
Est 2:20 Esther had not *y* shewed her kindred nor her NIH
5:13 **Y** all this availeth me nothing, so long as 2050.1
6:14 **while** they *were* **y** talking with him, came 5750
8: 3 Esther spake **y** again before the king, and 2050.1
Job 1:16 **While** he *was* **y** speaking, there came also 5750
1:17 **While** he *was* **y** speaking, there came also 5750
1:18 **While** he *was* **y** speaking, there came also 5704
3:26 I rest, neither was I quiet; **y** trouble came. 2050.1
5: 7 **Y** man is born unto trouble, as the sparks 3588
6:10 should I **y** have comfort; yea, I would 5750
8: 7 **y** thy latter end should greatly increase. 2050.1
8:12 **Whilst** it *is* **y** in his greenness, *and* not cut 5750
9:15 *y* would I not answer, *but* I would make NIH
9:16 *y* would I not believe that he had hearkened NIH
9:21 I *were* perfect, *y* would I not know my soul: NIH
9:31 **Y** shalt thou plunge me in the ditch, and 227
10: 8 round about; **y** thou dost destroy me. 2050.1
10:15 I be righteous, *y* will I not lift up my head. NIH
13:15 Though he slay me, *y* will I trust in him: but NIH
14: 9 *Y* through the sent of water it will bud, and NIH
19:26 this *body,* **y** in my flesh shall I see God: 2050.1
20: 7 *Y* he shall perish for ever like his own dung: NIH
20:14 *Y* his meat in his bowels is turned, *it is* NIH
21:32 **Y** shall he be brought to the grave, and 2050.1
22:18 **Y** he filled their houses *with* good *things:* 2050.1
24:12 **y** God layeth not folly *to them.* 2050.1
24:23 he resteth; **y** his eyes *are* upon their ways. 2050.1
29: 5 When the Almighty *was* **y** with me, 5750
32: 3 found no answer, and *y* had condemned Job. NIH
33:14 yea twice, *y* *man* perceiveth it not. NIH
35:14 shalt not see him, *y* judgment *is* before him; NIH
35:15 **y** he knoweth *it* not in great extremity: 2050.1
36: 2 I will shew thee that *I have* **y** to speak on 5750
Ps 2: 6 **Y** have I set my king upon my holy hill of 2050.1
37:10 For **y** a little while, and the wicked *shall* 5750
37:25 **y** have I not seen the righteous forsaken, 2050.1
37:36 **Y** he passed away, and lo, he *was* not: 2050.1
40:17 and needy; *y* the Lord thinketh upon me: NIH
42: 5 for I shall **y** praise him *for* the help of his 5750
42: 8 *Y* the LORD will command his NIH
42:11 for I shall **y** praise him, *who is* the health of 5750
43: 5 for I shall **y** praise him, *who is* the health of 5750
44:17 **y** have we not forgotten thee, neither have 2050.1
49:13 **y** their posterity approve their sayings. 2050.1
55:21 softer than oil, **y** *were* they drawn swords. 2050.1
68:13 *y shall ye be as* the wings of a dove covered NIH
71:14 **and** will **y** praise thee more and more. 2050.1
78:17 they sinned **y more** against him by 3254+5750
78:30 But **while** their meat *was* **y** in their mouths, 5750
78:56 **Y** they tempted and provoked the most 2050.1
90:10 **y** *is* their strength labour and sorrow; 2050.1
94: 7 **Y** they say, The LORD shall not see, 2050.1
107:41 **Y** setteth he the poor on high from 2050.1
119:51 *y* have I not declined from thy law. NIH
119:83 in the smoke; *y* do I not forget thy statutes. NIH
119:109 in my hand: **y** do I not forget thy law. 2050.1
119:110 for me: **y** I erred not from thy precepts. 2050.1
119:141 and despised: *y* do not I forget thy precepts. NIH
119:143 *y* thy commandments *are* my delights. NIH
119:157 *y* do I not decline from thy testimonies. NIH
129: 2 **y** they have not prevailed against me. 1571
138: 6 *be* high, **y** hath he respect unto the lowly: 2050.1
139:16 did see my **substance, y being unperfect**; 1564
139:16 when *as y there was* none of them. NIH
141: 5 for **y** my prayer also *shall be* in their 5750
Pr 6:10 *Y* a little sleep, a little slumber, a little NIH
8:26 **While as y** he had not made the earth, 5704
9: 9 to a wise *man,* and he will be **y** wiser: 5750
11:24 There is that scattereth, and **y** increaseth; 5750
13: 7 There is that **maketh** himself rich, **y** *hath* 2050.1
13: 7 maketh himself poor, **y** *hath* great riches. 2050.1
19: 7 *with* words, *y* they *are* wanting *to him.* NIH

Pr 19:19 for if thou deliver him, y thou must do it 2050.1
23:35 shall I awake? I will seek it y again. 3254+5750
24:33 Y a little sleep, a little slumber, a little NIH
27:22 y will not his foolishness depart from him. NIH
30:12 and y is not washed from their filthiness. NIH
30:25 y they prepare their meat in the summer; 2050.1
30:26 y make they their houses in the rocks; 2050.1
30:27 y go they forth all of them by bands; 2050.1
31:15 She riseth also while it is y night, and 5750
Ecc 1: 7 run into the sea; y the sea is not full; 2050.1
2: 3 (y acquainting mine heart with wisdom) 2050.1
2:19 y shall he have rule over all my labour 2050.1
2:21 y to a man that hath not laboured therein 2050.1
4: 2 dead more than the living which are y alive. 5728
4: 3 is he than both they, which hath not y been, 5728
4: 8 y is there no end of all his labour; 2050.1
6: 2 y God giveth him not power to eat 2050.1
6: 6 years twice told, y hath he seen no good: 2050.1
6: 7 his mouth, and y the appetite is not filled. 1571
7:28 Which y my soul seeketh, but I find not: 5750
8:12 y surely I know that it shall be well with 1571
8:17 it out, y he shall not find it; yea further, 2050.1
8:17 though a wise man think to know it, y shall NIH
9:11 to the strong, neither y bread to the wise, 1571
9:11 nor y riches to men of understanding, 1571
9:11 nor y favour to men of skill; 1571
9:15 y no man remembered that same poor 2050.1
11: 8 y let him remember the days of darkness; 2050.1
Isa 6:13 y in it shall be a tenth, and it shall return, 5750
10:22 of the sea, y a remnant of them shall return: NIH
10:25 For y a very little while, and 5750
10:32 As y shall he remain at Nob that day: 5750
14: 1 will y choose Israel, and set them in their 5750
14:15 Y thou shalt be brought down to hell, to 389
17: 6 Y gleaning grapes shall be left in it, as 2050.1
26:10 y will he not learn righteousness: NIH
27:10 Y the defenced city shall be desolate, and 3588
28: 4 while it is y in his hand he eateth it up. 5750
28:12 is the refreshing: y they would not hear. 2050.1
29: 2 Y I will distress Ariel, and there shall be 2050.1
29:17 Is it not y a very little while, and 5750
30:20 y shall not thy teachers be removed into a 2050.1
31: 2 Y he also is wise, and will bring evil, and 2050.1
42:25 him on fire round about, y he knew not; 2050.1
42:25 it burned him, y he laid it not to heart. 2050.1
44: 1 Y now hear, O Jacob my servant; and 2050.1
44:11 let them stand up; y they shall fear, and NIH
46: 7 shall cry unto him, y can he not answer, 2050.1
46:10 from ancient times the things that are not y NIH
49: 4 y surely my judgment is with the LORD, NIH
49: 5 y shall I be glorious in the eyes of 2050.1
49:15 they may forget, y will I not forget thee. 2050.1
53: 4 y we did esteem him stricken, smitten of 2050.1
53: 7 was afflicted, y he opened not his mouth: 2050.1
53:10 Y it pleased the LORD to bruise him; 2050.1
56: 8 Y will I gather others to him, besides those 5750
57:10 thy way; y saidst thou not, There is no hope: NIH
58: 2 Y they seek me daily, and delight to 2050.1
65:24 and whiles they are y speaking, I will hear. 5750
Jer 2: 9 Wherefore I will y plead with you, saith 5750
2:11 changed their gods, which are y no gods? 2050.1
2:21 Y I had planted thee a noble vine, 2050.1
2:22 y thine iniquity is marked before me, NIH
2:32 y my people have forgotten me days 2050.1
2:35 Y thou sayest, Because I am innocent, 2050.1
3: 1 y return again to me, saith the LORD. 2050.1
3: 8 y her treacherous sister Judah feared not, 2050.1
3:10 y for all this her treacherous sister Judah 1571
4:27 be desolate; y will I not make a full end. 2050.1
5:22 toss themselves, y can they not prevail; 2050.1
5:22 they roar, y can they not pass over it? 2050.1
5:28 the cause of the fatherless, y they prosper; 2050.1
7:26 Y they hearkened not unto me, 2050.1
9:20 Y hear the word of the LORD, O ye 3588
11: 8 Y they obeyed not, nor inclined their ear, 2050.1
12: 1 y let me talk with thee of thy judgments. 389
14: 9 y thou, O LORD, art in the midst of us, 2050.1
14:15 y they say, Sword and famine shall not be 2050.1
15: 1 y my mind could not be toward this people: NIH
15: 9 her sun is gone down while it was y day: 5750
15:10 y every one of them doth curse me. NIH
18:23 Y, LORD, thou knowest all their 2050.1
22: 6 y surely I will make thee a wilderness and NIH
22:24 my right hand, y would I pluck thee thence; 3588
23:21 I have not sent these prophets, y they ran: 2050.1
23:21 not spoken to them, y they prophesied. 2050.1
23:32 y I sent them not, nor commanded them: 2050.1
25: 7 Y ye have not hearkened unto me, 2050.1
27:15 y they prophesy a lie in my name; 2050.1
30:11 y will I not make a full end of thee: 389
31: 5 Thou shalt y plant vines upon 5750
31:23 As y they shall use this speech in the land 5750
31:39 the measuring line shall y go forth over 5750
32:33 teaching them, y they have not hearkened 2050.1
33: 1 while he was y shut up in the court of 5750
34: 4 Y hear the word of the LORD, O Zedekiah 389
36:24 Y they were not afraid, nor rent their 2050.1
37:10 y should they rise up every man in his tent, NIH
40: 5 Now while he was not y gone back, he said, 5750
44:28 Y a small number that escape the sword 2050.1
46:28 y will I not leave thee wholly unpunished. 2050.1
48:47 Y will I bring again the captivity of Moab 2050.1
51:33 y a little while, and the time of her harvest 5750
51:53 y from me shall spoilers come unto her, NIH
La 3:32 y will he have compassion according to 2050.1
4:17 our eyes as y failed for our vain help: 5750
Eze 2: 5 y shall know that there hath been a 2050.1
3:19 Y if thou warn the wicked, and he turn 2050.1
6: 8 Y will I leave a remnant, that ye may 2050.1
7:13 which is sold, although they were y alive: 5750
8: 6 turn thee y again, and thou shalt see greater 5750
8:13 Turn thee y again, and thou shalt see 5750
8:15 turn thee y again, and thou shalt see greater 5750
8:18 with a loud voice, y will I not hear them. NIH
11:16 y will I be to them as a little sanctuary in 2050.1

Eze 12:13 y shall he not see it, though he shall die 2050.1
14:22 Y behold, therein shall be left a remnant 2050.1
15: 5 how much less shall it be meet y for any 5750
16:28 with them, and y couldest not be satisfied. 1571
16:29 and y thou wast not satisfied herewith. 1571
16:47 Y hast thou not walked after their ways, 2050.1
18:19 Y say ye, Why? doth not the son bear 2050.1
18:25 Y ye say, The way of the Lord is not 2050.1
18:29 Y saith the house of Israel, The way of 2050.1
20:15 Y also I lifted up my hand unto them in 2050.1
20:27 Y in this your fathers have blasphemed me, 5750
23:19 Y she multiplied her whoredoms, 2050.1
23:44 Y they went in unto her, as they go in 2050.1
24:16 y neither shalt thou mourn nor 3808+2050.1
26:21 y shalt thou never be found again, 2050.1
28: 2 y thou art a man, and not God, 2050.1
28: 9 Wilt thou y say before him that slayeth 559+559
29:13 Y thus saith the Lord GOD; At the end of 3588
29:18 y had he no wages, nor his army, 2050.1
31:18 y shalt thou be brought down with 2050.1
32:24 y have they borne their shame with them 2050.1
32:25 y have they borne their shame with them 2050.1
33:17 Y the children of thy people say, The way 2050.1
33:20 Y ye say, The way of the Lord is not 2050.1
36:37 I will y for this be inquired of by the house 5750
44:11 Y they shall be ministers in my sanctuary, 2050.1
Da 4:23 y leave the stump of the roots thereof in 1297
5:17 y I will read the writing unto the king, and 1297
7:12 y their lives were prolonged for a season 2050.3
9:13 y made we not our prayer before 2050.1
10: 9 Y heard I the voice of his words: and 2050.1
10:14 for y the vision is for many days. 5750
11: 2 there shall stand up y three kings in Persia; 5750
11:27 for y the end shall be at the time appointed. 5750
11:33 y they shall fall by the sword, and 2050.1
11:35 because it is y for a time appointed. 5750
11:45 y he shall come to his end, and none shall 2050.1
Hos 1: 4 for y a little while, and I will avenge 5750
1:10 Y the number of the children of Israel 2050.1
3: 1 said the LORD unto me, Go y, love a 5750
3: 1 beloved of her friend, y an adulteress, 2050.1
4: 4 Y let no man strive, nor reprove another: 389
4:15 play the harlot, y let not Judah offend; NIH
5:13 y could he not heal you nor cure you of 2050.1
7: 9 and there upon him, y he knoweth not. 2050.1
7:13 y they have spoken lies against me. 2050.1
7:15 y do they imagine mischief against me. 2050.1
9:12 up their children, y will I bereave them, 2050.1
9:16 y will I slay even the beloved fruit of 2050.1
11:12 Judah y ruleth with God, and is faithful 5750
12: 8 Ephraim said, Y I am become rich, I have 389
12: 9 will y make thee to dwell in tabernacles, 5750
13: 4 Y I am the LORD thy God from 2050.1
Am 2: 9 Y destroyed I the Amorite before them, 2050.1
2: 9 y I destroyed his fruit from above, and 2050.1
4: 6 y have ye not returned unto me, saith 2050.1
4: 7 when there were y three months to 5750
4: 8 y have ye not returned unto me, saith 2050.1
4: 9 the palmerworm devoured them: y have 2050.1
4:10 y have ye not returned unto me, saith 2050.1
4:11 y have ye not returned unto me, saith 2050.1
6:10 sides of the house, Is there y any with thee? 5750
9: 9 y shall not the least grain fall upon 2050.1
Jnh 2: 4 y I will look again toward thy holy temple. 389
2: 6 y hast thou brought up my life from 2050.1
3: 4 Y forty days, and Nineveh shall be 5750
4: 2 my saying, when I was y in my country? 5704
Mic 1:15 Y will I bring an heir unto thee, 5750
3:11 y will they lean upon the LORD, and 2050.1
5: 2 y out of thee shall he come forth unto me NIH
6:10 Are there y the treasures of wickedness in 5750
Na 1:12 y thus shall they be cut down, 2050.1
2: 8 y they shall flee away. Stand, stand, 2050.1
3:10 Y was she carried away, she went into 1571
Hab 2: 3 For the vision is y for an appointed time, 5750
3:18 Y I will rejoice in the LORD, I will joy 2050.1
Hag 2: 4 Y now be strong, O Zerubbabel, saith 2050.1
2: 6 Y once, it is a little while, and I will shake 5750
2:17 y ye turned not to me, saith the LORD. 2050.1
2:19 Is the seed y in the barn? yea, as yet 5750
2:19 as y the vine, and the fig tree, and 5704
Zec 1:17 Cry y, saying, Thus saith the LORD of 5750
1:17 My cities through prosperity shall y be 5750
1:17 the LORD shall y comfort Zion, and 5750
1:17 and shall y choose Jerusalem. 5750
8: 4 There shall y old men and old women 5750
8:20 It shall y come to pass, that there shall 5750
11:15 Take unto thee y the instruments of a 5750
13: 3 that when any shall y prophesy, then 5750
Mal 1: 2 Y ye say, Wherein hast thou loved us? 2050.1
1: 2 saith the LORD: y I loved Jacob, 2050.1
2:14 Y ye say, Wherefore? Because 2050.1
2:14 y is she thy companion, and the wife of 2050.1
2:15 Y had he the residue of the spirit. And 2050.1
2:17 Y ye say, Wherein have we wearied him? 2050.1
3: 8 Y ye have robbed me. But ye say, Wherein 3588
3:13 Y ye say, What have we spoken so 2050.1
Mt 6:25 nor y for your body, what ye shall put on. 3366
6:26 y your heavenly Father feedeth them. 2532
6:29 And y I say unto you, That even Solomon 1161
10:10 two coats, neither shoes, nor y staves: 3366
12:46 While he y talked to the people, behold, 2089
13:21 Y hath he not root in himself, but dureth for 1161
15:16 Are ye also y without understanding? 188
15:17 Do not ye y understand, that whatsoever 3768
15:27 y the dogs eat of the crumbs which 1063+2532
16: 9 Do ye not y understand, neither remember 3768
17: 5 While he y spake, behold, a bright cloud 2089
19:20 I kept from my youth up: what lack I y? 2089
24: 6 must come to pass, but the end is not y. 3768
24:32 When his branch is y tender, and 2235
26:33 because of thee, y will I never be offended. NIG
26:35 should die with thee, y will I not deny thee. NIG
26:47 And while he y spake, lo, Judas, one of 2089
26:60 false witnesses came, y found they none. NIG

Mt 27:63 while he was y alive, After three days I 2089
Mk 5:35 While he y spake, there came from 2089
6:26 y for his oaths' sake, and for their sakes NIG
7:28 y the dogs under the table eat of 1063+2532
8:17 perceive ye not y, neither understand? 3768
8:17 have ye your heart y hardened? 2089
11:13 but leaves; for the time of figs was not y. NIG
12: 6 Having y therefore one son, 2089
13: 7 must needs be; but the end shall not be y. 3768
13:28 When her branch is y tender, and 2235
14:29 Although all shall be offended, y will not I. 235
14:43 while he y spake, cometh Judas, one of 2089
15: 5 But Jesus y answered nothing; so that Pilate 3765
Lk 3:20 Added y this above all, that he shut up John 2532
8:49 While he y spake, there cometh one from 2089
9:42 And as he was y a coming, the devil threw 2089
11: 8 y because of his importunity he will rise 1065
12:27 and y I say unto you, that Solomon in all 1161
14:22 thou hast commanded, and y there is room. 2089
14:32 Or else, while the other is y a great way off, 2089
14:35 fit for the land, nor y for the dunghill; 3777
15:20 But when he was y a great way off, 2089
15:29 and y thou never gavest me a kid, that I 2532
18: 5 Y because this widow troubleth me, I will 1065
18:22 Y lackest thou one thing: sell all that thou 2089
19:30 a colt tied, whereon y never man sat: 3762+4455
22:37 that this that is written must y be 2089
22:47 And while he y spake, behold a multitude, 2089
22:60 while he y spake, the cock crew. 2089
23:15 No, nor y Herod: for I sent you to him; 3761
24: 6 spake unto you when he was y in Galilee, 2089
24:41 And while they y believed not for joy, and 2089
24:44 while I was y with you, that all things must 2089
Jn 2: 4 I to do with thee? mine hour is not y come. 3768
3:24 For John was not y cast into prison. 3768
4:21 nor y at Jerusalem, worship the Father. NIG
4:27 y no man said, What seekest thou? or, 3305
4:35 There are y four months, and then cometh 2089
7: 6 said unto them, My time is not y come: 3768
7: 8 I go not up y unto this feast; for my time is 3768
7: 8 this feast; for my time is not y full come. 3768
7:19 the law, and y none of you keepeth the law? NIG
7:30 on him, because his hour was not y come. 3768
7:33 Y a little while am I with you, and then I go 2089
7:39 for the Holy Ghost was not y given; 3768
7:39 because that Jesus was not y glorified.) 3764
8:14 I bear record of myself, y my record is true: NIG
8:16 And y if I judge, my judgment is true: for I 2532
8:20 hands on him; for his hour was not y come. 3768
8:55 Y ye have not known him; but I know him: 2532
8:57 Thou art not y fifty years old, and hast thou 3768
9:30 he is, and y he hath opened mine eyes. NIG
11:25 in me, though he were dead, y shall he live: NIG
11:30 Now Jesus was not y come into the town, 3768
12:35 Y a little while is the light with you. 2089
12:37 before them, y they believed not on him: NIG
13:33 y a little while I am with you. 2089
14: 9 and y hast thou not known me, Philip? NIG
14:19 Y a little while, and the world seeth me no 2089
14:25 spoken unto you, being y present with you. NIG
16:12 I have y many things to say unto you, but 2089
16:32 and y I am not alone, because the Father is NIG
19:41 wherein was never man y laid. 3764
20: 1 when it was y dark, unto the sepulchre, and 2089
20: 5 the linen clothes lying; y went he not in. 3305
20: 9 For as y they knew not the scripture, 3764
20:17 for I am not y ascended to my Father: 3768
20:29 that have not seen, and y have believed. NIG
21:11 so many, y was not the net broken. NIG
21:23 y Jesus said not unto him, He shall not die; 2532
Ac 7: 5 y he promised that he would give it to him 2532
7: 5 seed after him, when as y he had no child. NIG
8:16 (For as y he was fallen upon none of them: 3768
9: 1 y breathing out threatenings and 2089
10:44 While Peter y spake these words, the Holy 2089
13:27 nor y the voices of the prophets which are NIG
13:28 y desired they Pilate that he should be slain. NIG
18:18 And Paul after this tarried there y a good 2089
19:37 nor y blasphemers of your goddess. 3777
22: 3 y brought up in this city at the feet of 1161
24:11 that there are y but twelve days since I NIG
25: 8 against the temple, nor y against Cesar, NIG
28: 4 the sea, y Vengeance suffereth not to live. NIG
28:17 y was I delivered prisoner from Jerusalem NIG
Ro 3: 7 why y am I also judged as a sinner? 2089
4:11 faith which he had y being uncircumcised: NIG
4:12 which he had being y uncircumcised. NIG
4:19 neither y the deadness of Sara's womb: NIG
5: 6 For when we were y without strength, 2089
5: 7 y peradventure for a good man some would 1063
5: 8 in that, while we were y sinners, 2089
8:24 what a man seeth, why doth he y hope for? 2532
9:11 (For the children being not y born, 3380
9:19 then unto me, Why doth he y find fault? 2089
11:30 y have now obtained mercy through their 1161
16:19 y I would have you wise unto that which is NIG
1Co 2: 6 y not the wisdom of this world, nor of 1161
2:15 But he that is spiritual judgeth all things, y 1161
3: 2 not able to bear it, neither y now are ye able. 235
3: 3 For ye are y carnal: for whereas there is 2089
3:15 he himself shall be saved; y so as by fire. 1161
4: 4 by myself; y am I not hereby justified: 235
4:15 in Christ, y have ye not many fathers: 235
5:10 Y not altogether with the fornicators of this 2532
7:10 married I command, y not I, but the Lord, NIG
7:25 y I give my judgment, as one that hath 1161
8: 2 he knoweth nothing y as he ought to know. 3764
9: 2 unto others, y doubtless I am to you: 235+1065
9:19 For though I be free from all men, y have I NIG
12:20 are they many members, y but one body. 1161
12:31 y shew I unto you a more excellent way. 2089
14:19 Y in the church I had rather speak five words 235
14:21 and y for all that will they not hear me, 3761
15:10 y not I, but the grace of God which was 1161
15:17 your faith is vain; ye are y in your sins. 2089

2Co 1:10 in whom we trust that he will y deliver *us;* 2089
1:23 that to spare you I came **not** as **y** unto 3765
4: 8 *We are* troubled on every *side,* **y** not 235
4:16 **y** the inward *man* is renewed day by day. 235
5:16 **y** now henceforth know we *him* no more. 235
6: 8 and good report: as deceivers, and **y** true; NIG
6: 9 As unknown, and **y** well known; as dying, NIG
6:10 As sorrowful, **y** alway rejoicing; as poor, 1161
6:10 as poor, **y** making many rich; as having 1161
6:10 having nothing, and **y** possessing all *things.* NIG
8: 9 was rich, **y** for your sakes he became poor, NIG
9: 3 **Y** have I sent the brethren, lest our boasting 1161
11: 6 *I be* rude in speech, **y** not in knowledge; 235
11:16 if otherwise, **y** as a fool receive me, that I 2579
12: 5 **y** of myself I will not glory, but in mine 1161
13: 4 **y** he liveth by the power of God. 235
Gal 1:10 for if I **y** pleased men, I should not be 2089
2:20 I live; **y** not I, but Christ liveth in me: NIG
3: 4 so many *things* in vain? if *it be* **y** in vain. 2532
3:15 but a man's covenant, **y** *if it be* confirmed, NIG
5:11 And I, brethren, if I **y** preach circumcision, 2089
5:11 why do I **y** suffer persecution? 2089
Eph 5:29 For no *man* **ever y** hated his own flesh; but 4218
Php 1: 9 that your love may abound **y** more and 2089
1:22 my labour: **y** what I shall choose I wot not. 2532
2:25 **Y** I supposed it necessary to send to you 1161
Col 1:21 wicked works, **y** now hath he reconciled 1161
2: 5 **y** am I with you in the spirit, joying and 235
1Th 2: 6 we glory, neither of you, nor **y** of others, NIG
2Th 2: 5 ye not, that, when I was **y** with you, 2089
3:15 **Y** count *him* not as an enemy, but 2532
2Ti 2: 5 **y** is he not crowned, except he strive NIG
2:13 If we believe not, **y** he abideth faithful: NIG
Phm 1: 9 **Y** for love's sake I rather beseech *thee,* NIG
Heb 2: 8 But now we see **not y** all *things* put under 3768
4:15 was in all *points* tempted like as *we are,* **y** NIG
5: 8 **y** learned he obedience by *the things* which NIG
7:10 For he was **y** in the loins of his father, 2089
7:15 And it is **y** far more evident: for that after 2089
9: 8 the holiest *of all* was **not y** made manifest, 3380
9: 8 **while as** the first tabernacle was **y** standing: 2089
9:25 **Nor y** that he should offer himself often, 3761
10:37 For **y** a little while, 2089
11: 4 and by it he being dead **y** speaketh. 2089
11: 7 warned of God of *things* **not** seen **as y,** 3369
12: 4 Ye have **not y** resisted unto blood, 3768
12:26 **Y** once *more* I shake not the earth only, but 2089
12:27 And this *word,* **Y** once *more,* signifieth 2089
Jas 2:10 and **y** offend in one *point,* he is guilty of all. NIG
2:11 if thou commit no adultery, **y** *if* thou kill, 1161
3: 4 **y** are they turned about with a very small NIG
4: 2 ye fight and war, **y** ye have not, because ye 1161
1Pe 1: 8 though now ye see *him* not, **y** believing, 1161
4:16 **Y** if *any man suffer* as a Christian, let him 1161
1Jn 3: 2 and it doth **not y** appear what we shall be: 3768
Jude 1: 9 **Y** Michael the archangel, when contending 1161
Rev 6:11 that they should rest **y** for a little season, 2089
8:13 of the three angels, which are **y** to sound. 3195
9:20 **y** repented not of the works of their hands, NIG
17: 8 the beast that was, and is not, **and y** is. 2539
17:10 and one is, *and* the other is **not y** come; 3768
17:12 which have received **no** kingdom **as y;** 3768

YIELD (30) [YIELDED, YIELDETH, YIELDING]

Ge 4:12 it shall not henceforth **y** unto thee her 5414
49:20 *shall be* fat, and he shall **y** royal dainties. 5414
Lev 19:25 that *it* may **y** unto you the increase thereof: 3254
25:19 the land shall **y** her fruit, and ye shall eat 5414
26: 4 the land shall **y** her increase, and the trees 5414
26: 4 and the trees of the field shall **y** their fruit. 5414
26:20 for your land shall not **y** her increase, 5414
26:20 neither shall the trees of the land **y** their 5414
Dt 11:17 be no rain, and *that* the land **y** not her fruit; 5414
2Ch 30: 8 *but* **y** yourselves unto the LORD, 3027+5414
Ps 67: 6 *Then* shall the earth **y** her increase; *and* 5414
85:12 *is* good; and our land shall **y** her increase. 5414
107:37 which may **y** fruits of increase. 6213
Pr 7:21 her much fair speech she **caused** him **to y,** 5186
Isa 5:10 ten acres of vineyard shall **y** one bath, and 6213
5:10 and the seed of a homer shall **y** an ephah. 6213
Eze 34:27 the tree of the field shall **y** her fruit, and 5414
34:27 the earth shall **y** her increase, and they shall 5414
36: 8 and **y** your fruit to my people of Israel; 5375
Hos 8: 7 the bud shall **y** no meal: if so be it yield, 6213
8: 7 if so be it **y,** *the* strangers shall swallow it 6213
Joel 2:22 the fig tree and the vine do **y** their strength. 5414
Hab 3:17 shall fail, and the fields shall **y** no meat; 6213
Mk 4: 8 and did **y** fruit that sprang up and 1325
Ac 23:21 But do not thou **y unto** them: for there lie 3982
Ro 6:13 Neither **y** ye your members *as* instruments 3936
6:13 but **y** yourselves unto God, as *those that are* 3936
6:16 that to whom ye **y** yourselves servants to 3936
6:19 now **y** your members servants to 3936
Jas 3:12 so *can* no fountain *both* **y** salt water and 4160

YIELDED (8) [YIELD]

Ge 49:33 **y up the ghost,** and was gathered unto his 1478
Nu 17: 8 and bloomed blossoms, and **y** almonds. 1580
Da 3:28 the king's word, and **y** their bodies, 3052
Mt 27:50 cried again with a loud voice, **y up** the ghost. 863
Mk 4: 7 grew up, and choked it, and it **y** no fruit. 1325
Ac 5:10 straightway at his feet, and **y up the ghost:** 1634
Ro 6:19 for as ye have **y** your members servants to 3936
Rev 22: 2 *of* fruits, *and* **y** her fruit every month: 591

YIELDETH (4) [YIELD]

Ne 9:37 it **y** much **increase** unto the kings whom 8393
Job 24: 5 the wilderness **y** food for them *and* for *their* NIH
Pr 12:12 but the root of the righteous **y** *fruit.* 5414
Heb 12:11 nevertheless afterward it **y** the peaceable 591

YIELDING (7) [YIELD]

Ge 1:11 the herb **y** seed, *and* the fruit tree yielding 2232
1:11 *and* the fruit tree **y** fruit after his kind, 6213
1:12 *and* herb **y** seed after his kind, and the tree 2232
1:12 the tree **y** fruit, whose seed *was* in itself, 6213
1:29 in the which *is* the fruit of a tree **y** seed; 2232
Ecc 10: 4 not thy place; for **y** pacifieth great offences. 4832
Jer 17: 8 of drought, neither shall cease from **y** fruit. 6213

YOKE (59) [YOKED, YOKEFELLOW, YOKES]

Ge 27:40 that thou shalt break his **y** from off thy 5923
Lev 26:13 I have broken the bands of your **y,** and 5923
Nu 19: 2 no blemish, *and* upon which never came **y:** 5923
Dt 21: 3 *and* which hath not drawn in the **y;** 5923
28:48 and he shall put a **y** of iron upon thy neck, 5923
1Sa 6: 7 on which there hath come no **y,** and tie 5923
11: 7 he took a **y** of oxen, and hewed them in 6776
14:14 of land, *which* a **y** *of oxen might plow.* 6776
1Ki 12: 4 Thy father made our **y** grievous: now 5923
12: 4 his heavy **y** which he put upon us, lighter, 5923
12: 9 Make the **y** which thy father did put upon 5923
12:10 Thy father made our **y** heavy, but 5923
12:11 my father did lade you with a heavy **y,** 5923
12:11 you with a heavy yoke, I will add to your **y:** 5923
12:14 My father made your **y** heavy, and I will 5923
12:14 your yoke heavy, and I will add to your **y:** 5923
19:19 who *was* plowing *with* twelve **y** *of oxen* 6776
19:21 took a **y** of oxen, and slew them, and boiled 6776
2Ch 10: 4 Thy father made our **y** grievous: now 5923
10: 4 his heavy **y** that he put upon us, and we will 5923
10: 9 Ease somewhat the **y** that thy father did put 5923
10:10 Thy father made our **y** heavy, but 5923
10:11 For whereas my father put a heavy **y** upon 5923
10:11 yoke upon you, I will put more to your **y:** 5923
10:14 My father made your **y** heavy, but I will 5923
Job 1: 3 five hundred **y** of oxen, and five hundred 6776
42:12 a thousand **y** of oxen, and a thousand she 6776
Isa 9: 4 For thou hast broken the **y** of his burden, 5923
10:27 his **y** from off thy neck, and the yoke shall 5923
10:27 the **y** shall be destroyed because of 5923
14:25 shall his **y** depart from off them, and 5923
47: 6 ancient hast thou very heavily laid thy **y.** 5923
58: 6 go free, and *that* ye break every **y?** 4133
58: 9 take away from the midst of thee the **y,** 4133
Jer 2:20 For of old time I have broken thy **y,** *and* 5923
5: 5 these have altogether broken the **y,** *and* 5923
27: 8 that will not put their neck under the **y** of 5923
27:11 the nations that bring their neck under the **y** 5923
27:12 Bring your necks under the **y** of the king of 5923
28: 2 I have broken the **y** of the king of Babylon. 5923
28: 4 for I will break the **y** of the king of 5923
28:10 Hananiah the prophet took the **y** from off 4133
28:11 will I break the **y** of Nebuchadnezzar king 5923
28:12 **y** from off the neck of the prophet 4133
28:14 I have put a **y** of iron upon the neck of all 5923
30: 8 *that* I will break his **y** from off thy neck, 5923
31:18 as a bullock unaccustomed *to the* **y,** turn NIH
51:23 pieces the husbandman and his **y of oxen;** 6776
La 1:14 The **y** of my transgressions is bound by his 5923
3:27 *It is* good for a man that he bear the **y** in his 5923
Eze 34:27 when I have broken the bands of their **y,** 5923
Hos 11: 4 I was to them as they that take off the **y** on 5923
Na 1:13 For now will I break his **y** from off thee, 4132
Mt 11:29 Take my **y** upon you, and learn of me; for I 2218
11:30 For my **y** *is* easy, and my burden is light. 2218
Lk 14:19 I have bought five **y** of oxen, and I go to 2201
Ac 15:10 to put a **y** upon the neck of the disciples, 2218
Gal 5: 1 be not entangled again with the **y** of 2218
1Ti 6: 1 Let as many servants as are under the **y** 2218

YOKED (1) [YOKE]

2Co 6:14 Be ye not **unequally y together** with 2086

YOKEFELLOW (1) [FELLOW, YOKE]

Php 4: 3 And I intreat thee also, true **y,** help those 4805

YOKES (4) [YOKE]

Jer 27: 2 Make thee bonds and **y,** and put them upon 4133
28:13 Thou hast broken the **y** of wood; but 4133
28:13 but thou shalt make for them **y** of iron. 4133
Eze 30:18 when I shall break there the **y** of Egypt: 4133

YONDER (7)

Ge 22: 5 I and the lad will go **y** and worship, 3541+5704
Nu 16:37 of the burning, and scatter thou the fire **y;** 1973
23:15 burnt offering, while I meet *the LORD* **y.** 3541
32:19 For we will not inherit with them on **y** side NIH
2Ki 4:25 his servant, Behold, **y** *is* that Shunammite: NIH
Mt 17:20 this mountain, Remove hence **to y place;** 1563
26:36 Sit ye here, while I go and pray **y.** 1563

YOU (2802) [YE, YOU-WARD, YOU-WARDS, YOUR, YOURS, YOURSELVES] See Index of Articles, Etc.

YOUNG (300) [YOUTH]

Ge 4:23 to my wounding, and a **y man** to my hurt. 3206
14:24 Save only that which the **y men** have eaten, 5288
15: 9 and a turtle-dove, and a **y pigeon.** 1469
18: 7 and good, and gave *it* unto a **y man;** 5288
19: 4 compassed the house round, both old and **y,** 5288
22: 3 took two of his **y men** with him, and Isaac 5288
22: 5 Abraham said unto his **y men,** Abide you 5288
22:19 So Abraham returned unto his **y men,** and 5288
31:38 and thy she goats have not **cast** their **y,** 7921
33:13 the flocks and herds with **y** *are* with me: 5763
34:19 And the **y man** deferred not to do the thing, 5288
41:12 *there was* there with us a **y man,** a Hebrew, 5288
Ex 10: 9 We will go with our **y** and with our old, 5288
23:26 There shall nothing **cast** their **y,** nor be 7921
24: 5 And he sent **y men** of the children of Israel, 5288
29: 1 Take one **y** bullock, and two rams without 1121
33:11 servant Joshua, the son of Nun, a **y man,** 5288
Lev 1:14 his offering of turtledoves, or of **y** pigeons. 1121
4: 3 a **y** bullock without blemish unto 1121
4:14 the congregation shall offer a **y** bullock for 1121
5: 7 two turtledoves, or two **y** pigeons, unto 1121
5:11 or two **y** pigeons, then he that sinned shall 1121
9: 2 Take thee a **y** calf for a sin offering, and 1121
12: 6 a **y** pigeon, or a turtledove, for a sin 1121
12: 8 shall bring two turtles, or two **y** pigeons; 1121
14:22 two turtledoves, or two **y** pigeons, such as 1121
14:30 or of the **y** pigeons, such as he can get; 1121
15:14 or two **y** pigeons, and come before 1121
15:29 or two **y** pigeons, and bring them unto 1121
16: 3 *place:* with a **y** bullock for a sin offering, 1121
22:28 shall not kill it and her **y** both in one day. 1121
23:18 first year, and one **y** bullock, and two rams: 1121
Nu 6:10 two turtles, or two **y** pigeons, to the priest, 1121
7:15 One **y** bullock, one ram, one lamb of 1121
7:21 One **y** bullock, one ram, one lamb of 1121
7:27 One **y** bullock, one ram, one lamb of 1121
7:33 One **y** bullock, one ram, one lamb of 1121
7:39 One **y** bullock, one ram, one lamb of 1121
7:45 One **y** bullock, one ram, one lamb of 1121
7:51 One **y** bullock, one ram, one lamb of 1121
7:57 One **y** bullock, one ram, one lamb of 1121
7:63 One **y** bullock, one ram, one lamb of 1121
7:69 One **y** bullock, one ram, one lamb of 1121
7:75 One **y** bullock, one ram, one lamb of 1121
7:81 One **y** bullock, one ram, one lamb of 1121
8: 8 let them take a **y** bullock with his meat 1121
8: 8 another **y** bullock shalt thou take for a sin 1121
11:27 there ran a **y man,** and told Moses, and 5288
11:28 *one* of his **y men,** answered and said, 979
15:24 that all the congregation shall offer one **y** 1121
23:24 a great lion, and lift up himself as a **y lion:** 738
28:11 two **y** bullocks, and one ram, seven lambs 1121
28:19 two **y** bullocks, and one ram, and 1121
28:27 two **y** bullocks, one ram, seven lambs of 1121
29: 2 one **y** bullock, one ram, *and* seven lambs of 1121
29: 8 one **y** bullock, one ram, *and* seven lambs of 1121
29:13 thirteen **y** bullocks, two rams, *and* 1121
29:17 on the second day *ye shall offer* twelve **y** 1121
Dt 22: 6 *whether they be* **y ones,** or eggs, and the dam 667
22: 6 the dam sitting upon the **y,** or upon the eggs, 667
22: 6 thou shalt not take the dam with the **y:** 1121
22: 7 wise let the dam go, and take the **y** to thee; 1121
28:50 person of the old, nor shew favour to the **y:** 5288
28:57 towards her **y one** that cometh out from 7988
32:11 fluttereth over her **y,** spreadeth abroad her 1469
32:25 shall destroy both the **y man** and the virgin, 970
Jos 6:21 **y** and old, and ox, and sheep, and ass, 5288
6:23 the **y men** that were spies went in, and 5288
Jdg 6:25 said unto him, Take thy father's **y** bullock, 6499
8:14 And caught a **y man** of the men of Succoth, 5288
9:54 he called hastily unto the **y man** his 5288
9:54 his **y man** thrust him through, and he died. 5288
14: 5 behold, a **y** lion roared against him. 3715
14:10 there a feast; for so used the **y men** to do. 970
17: 7 there was a **y man** out of Beth-lehem-judah 5288
17:11 the **y man** was unto him as one of his sons. 5288
17:12 the **y man** became his priest, and was in 5288
18: 3 they knew the voice of the **y man** 5288
18:15 came to the house of the **y man** the Levite, 5288
19:19 for the **y man** *which is* with thy servants: 5288
21:12 of Jabesh-gilead four hundred **y** virgins, 5291
Ru 2: 9 have I not charged the **y men** that *they* shall 5288
2: 9 drink of *that* which the **y men** have drawn. 5288
2:15 Boaz commanded his **y men,** saying, 5288
2:21 me also, Thou shalt keep fast by my **y men,** 5288
3:10 inasmuch as thou followedst not **y men,** 970
4:12 LORD shall give thee of this **y woman.** 5291
1Sa 1:24 the LORD *in* Shiloh: and the child *was* **y.** 5288
2:17 Wherefore the sin of the **y men** was very 5288
8:16 your goodliest **y men,** and your asses, and 970
9: 2 *was* Saul, a choice **y** *man,* and a goodly: NIH
9:11 they found **y maidens** going out to draw 5291
14: 1 said unto the **y man** that bare his armour, 5288
14: 6 Jonathan said to the **y man** that bare his 5288
17:58 to him, Whose son *art* thou, *thou* **y man?** 5288
20:22 if I say thus unto the **y man,** Behold, 5958
21: 4 if the **y men** have kept themselves at least 5288
21: 5 the vessels of the **y men** are holy, and 5288
25: 5 David sent out ten **y men,** and David said 5288
25: 5 David said unto the **y men,** Get you up to 5288
25: 8 Ask thy **y men,** and they will shew thee. 5288
25: 8 Wherefore let the **y men** find favour in 5288
25: 9 when David's **y men** came, they spake to 5288
25:12 So David's **y men** turned their way, and 5288
25:14 one of the **y men** told Abigail, 5288
25:25 I thine handmaid saw not the **y men** of my 5288
25:27 let it even be given unto the **y men** that 5288
26:22 let one of the **y men** come over and fetch it. 5288
30:13 he said, I *am* a **y man** of Egypt, servant to 5288
30:17 save four hundred **y men,** which rode 376+5288
2Sa 1: 5 David said unto the **y man** that told him, 5288
1: 6 the **y man** that told him said, As I 5288
1:13 David said unto the **y man** that told him, 5288
1:15 David called one of the **y men,** and said, 5288
2:14 Let the **y men** now arise, and play before 5288
2:21 lay thee hold on one of the **y men,** and 5288
4:12 David commanded *his* **y men,** and 5288
9:12 Mephibosheth had a **y** son, whose name 6996
13:32 have slain all the **y men** the king's sons; 5288
13:34 the **y man** that kept the watch lift up his 5288
14:21 bring the **y man** Absalom again. 5288
16: 2 and summer fruit for the **y men** to eat; 5288
18: 5 *Deal* gently for my sake with the **y man,** 5288
18:12 Beware that none *touch* the **y man** 5288
18:15 ten **y men** that bare Joab's armour 5288
18:29 the king said, *Is* the **y man** Absalom safe? 5288
18:32 unto Cushi, *Is* the **y man** Absalom safe? 5288
18:32 thee to do *thee* hurt, be as *that* **y man** *is.* 5288
1Ki 1: 2 Let there be sought for my lord the king a **y** 5291
11:28 Solomon seeing the **y man** that he was 5288
12: 8 consulted with the **y men** that were grown 3206
12:10 the **y men** that were grown up with him 3206
12:14 to them after the counsel of the **y men,** 3206
20:14 *Even* by the **y men** of the princes of 5288
20:15 he numbered the **y men** of the princes of 5288

1Ki 20:17 the y men of the princes of the provinces 5288
20:19 So these y men of the princes of 5288
2Ki 4:22 one of the y men, and one of the asses, 5288
5:22 two y men of the sons of the prophets: 5288
6:17 the LORD opened the eyes of the y man; 5288
8:12 their y men wilt thou slay with the sword, 970
9: 4 So the y man, even the young man 5288
9: 4 young man, even the y man the prophet, 5288
1Ch 12:28 a y man mighty of valour, and of his 5288
22: 5 Solomon my son is y and tender, and 5288
29: 1 is yet y and tender, and the work is great: 5288
2Ch 10: 8 took counsel with the y men that were 3206
10:10 the y men that were brought up with him 3206
10:14 them after the advice of the y men, 3206
13: 7 when Rehoboam was y and tender hearted, 5288
13: 9 to consecrate himself with a y bullock 1121
34: 3 eighth year of his reign, while he was yet y, 5288
36:17 who slew their y men with the sword in 970
36:17 had no compassion upon y man or maiden, 970
Ezr 6: 9 both y bullocks, and rams, and lambs, 1123
Est 2: 2 Let there be fair y virgins sought for 5291
2: 3 that they may gather together all the fair y 5291
3:13 all Jews, both y and old, little children and 5288
8:10 on mules, camels, and y dromedaries: 1121
Job 1:19 it fell upon the y men, and they are dead; 5288
4:10 and the teeth of the y lions, are broken. 3715
19:18 Yea, y children despised me; I arose, and 5759
29: 8 The y men saw me, and hid themselves: 5288
32: 6 I am y, and ye are very old; 3117+6810+3807.1
38:39 the lion? or fill the appetite of the y lions, 3715
38:41 when his y ones cry unto God, they wander 3206
39: 3 they bring forth their y ones, 3206
39: 4 Their y ones are in good liking, they grow 1121
39:16 She is hardened against her y ones, 1121
39:30 Her y ones also suck up blood: and where 667
Ps 17:12 as it were a y lion lurking in secret places. 3715
29: 6 a calf; Lebanon and Sirion like a y unicorn. 1121
34:10 The y lions do lack, and suffer hunger: but 3715
37:25 I have been y, and now am old; yet have I 5288
58: 6 break out the great teeth of the y lions, 3715
78:63 The fire consumed their y men; and 970
78:71 From following the ewes great with y he 5763
84: 3 where she may lay her y, even thine altars, 667
91:13 the y lion and the dragon shalt thou trample 3715
104:21 The y lions roar after their prey, and seek 3715
119: 9 Wherewithal shall a y man cleanse his 5288
147: 9 his food, and to the y ravens which cry. 1121
148:12 Both y men, and maidens; old men, and 970
Pr 1: 4 to the y man knowledge and discretion. 5288
7: 7 the youths, a y man void of understanding, 5288
20:29 The glory of y men is their strength: and 970
30:17 pick it out, and the y eagles shall eat it. 1121
Ecc 11: 9 Rejoice, O y man, in thy youth; and let thy 970
SS 2: 9 My beloved is like a roe or a y hart: behold, 6082
2:17 or a y hart upon the mountains of Bether. 6082
4: 5 Thy two breasts are like two y roes that are 6082
7: 3 Thy two breasts are like two y roes that are 6082
8:14 or to a y hart upon the mountains of spices. 6082
Isa 5:29 be like a lion, they shall roar like y lions: 3715
7:21 that a man shall nourish a y cow, 1241+5697
9:17 the Lord shall have no joy in their y men, 970
11: 6 the calf and the y lion and the fatling 3715
11: 7 their y ones shall lie down together: 3206
13:18 Their bows also shall dash the y men to 5288
20: 4 y and old, naked and barefoot, 5288
23: 4 neither do I nourish up y men, nor bring up 970
30: 6 from whence come the y[s] and old lion, 3833
30: 6 their riches upon the shoulders of y asses, 5895
30:24 the y asses that ear the ground shall eat 5895
31: 4 the lion and the y lion roaring on his prey, 3715
31: 8 and his y men shall be discomfited. 970
40:11 and shall gently lead those that are with y. 5763
40:30 be weary, and the y men shall utterly fall: 970
62: 5 For as a y man marrieth a virgin, so shall thy 970
Jer 2:15 The y lions roared upon him, and yelled, 3715
6:11 and upon the assembly of y men together: 970
9:21 and the y men from the streets. 970
11:22 the y men shall die by the sword; their sons 970
15: 8 mother of the y men a spoiler at noonday: 970
18:21 let their y men be slain by the sword in 970
31:12 and for the y of the flock and of the herd: 1121
31:13 in the dance, both y men and old together: 970
48:15 his chosen y men are gone down to 970
49:26 Therefore her y men shall fall in her streets, 970
50:30 Therefore shall her y men fall in the streets, 970
51: 3 spare ye not her y men; destroy ye utterly all 970
51:22 with thee will I break in pieces old and y; 5288
51:22 with thee will I break in pieces the y man 970
La 1:15 an assembly against me to crush my y men: 970
1:18 and my y men are gone into captivity. 970
2:19 toward him for the life of thy y children, 5768
2:21 The y and the old lie on the ground in 5288
2:21 and my y men are fallen by the sword; 970
4: 3 the breast, they give suck to their y ones: 1482
4: 4 the y children ask bread, and no man 5768
5:13 They took the y men to grind, and 970
5:14 from the gate, the y men from their musick. 970
Eze 9: 6 Slay utterly old and y, both maids, and 970
17: 4 He cropt off the top of his y twigs, and 3242
17:22 off from the top of his y twigs a tender one, 3127
19: 2 she nourished her whelps among y lions. 3715
19: 3 it became a y lion, and it learned to catch 3715
19: 5 of her whelps, and made him a y lion. 3715
19: 6 he became a y lion, and learned to catch 3715
23: 6 and rulers, all of them desirable y men, 970
23:12 upon horses, all of them desirable y men. 970
23:23 all of them desirable y men, captains and 970
30:17 The y men of Aven and of Phi-beseth shall 970
31: 6 the beasts of the field bring forth their y, 3205
32: 2 Thou art like a y lion of the nations, and 3715
38:13 with all the y lions thereof, shall say unto 3715
41:19 the face of a y lion toward the palm tree on 3715
43:19 Lord GOD, a y bullock for a sin offering. 1121
43:23 shalt offer a y bullock without blemish, 1121
43:25 they shall also prepare a y bullock, and 1121
Eze 45:18 thou shalt take a y bullock without blemish, 1121
46: 6 in the day of the new moon it shall be a y 1121
Hos 5:14 and as a y lion to the house of Judah: 3715
Joel 2:28 dream dreams, your y men shall see visions: 970
Am 2:11 and of your y men for Nazarites. 970
3: 4 will a y lion cry out of his den, if he have 3715
4:10 your y men have I slain with the sword, and 970
8:13 the fair virgins and y men faint for thirst. 970
Mic 5: 8 as a y lion among the flocks of sheep: 3715
Na 2:11 the feeding place of the y lions, where 3715
2:13 and the sword shall devour thy y lions: 3715
3:10 her y children also were dashed in pieces 5768
Zec 2: 4 unto him, Run, speak to this y man, saying, 5288
9:17 corn shall make the y men cheerful, and 970
11: 3 a voice of the roaring of y lions; for 3715
11:16 neither shall seek the y one, nor heal that 5289
Mt 2: 8 Go and search diligently for the y child; 3813
2: 9 and stood over where the y child was. 3813
2:11 they saw the y child with Mary his mother, 3813
2:13 and take the y child and his mother, and 3813
2:13 for Herod will seek the y child to destroy 3813
2:14 he took the y child and his mother by night, 3813
2:20 and take the y child and his mother, and 3813
2:20 they are dead which sought the y child's 3813
2:21 and took the y child and his mother, and 3813
19:20 The y man saith unto him, All these things 3495
19:22 But when the y man heard that saying, 3495
Mk 7:25 whose y daughter had an unclean spirit, 2365
10:13 And they brought y children to him, 3813
14:51 And there followed him a certain y man, 3495
14:51 and the y men laid hold on him: 3495
16: 5 they saw a y man sitting on the right side, 3495
Lk 2:24 A pair of turtledoves, or two y pigeons. 3502
7:14 And he said, Y man, I say unto thee, Arise. 3495
Jn 12:14 And Jesus, when he had found a y ass, 3678
21:18 verily, I say unto thee, When thou wast y, 3501
Ac 2:17 and your y men shall see visions, and 3495
5: 6 And the y men arose, wound him up, and 3501
5:10 and the y men came in, and found her dead, 3495
7:19 so that they cast out their y children, 1025
7:58 laid down their clothes at a y man's feet, 3494
20: 9 And there sat in a window a certain y man 3494
20:12 And they brought the y man alive, and 3816
23:17 Bring this y man unto the chief captain: 3494
23:18 prayed me to bring this y man unto thee, 3494
23:22 the chief captain then let the y man depart, 3494
Tit 2: 4 That they may teach the y women to be 3501
2: 6 Y men likewise exhort to be sober minded. 3501
1Jn 2:13 y men, because you have overcome 3495
2:14 y men, because ye are strong, and the word 3495

YOUNGER (31) [YOUTH]

Ge 9:24 knew what his y son had done unto him. 6996
19:31 the firstborn said unto the y, Our father is 6810
19:34 that the firstborn said unto the y, Behold, 6810
19:35 the y arose, and lay with him; and 6810
19:38 the y, she also bare a son, and called his 6810
25:23 and the elder shall serve the y. 6810
27:15 and put them upon Jacob her y son: 6996
27:42 she sent and called Jacob her y son, and 6996
29:16 and the name of the y was Rachel. 6996
29:18 thee seven years for Rachel thy y daughter. 6996
29:26 to give the y before the firstborn. 6810
43:29 and said, Is this your y brother, 6996
48:14 who was the y, and his left hand upon 6810
48:19 truly his y brother shall be greater than he, 6996
Jdg 1:13 the son of Kenaz, Caleb's y brother, took it: 6996
3: 9 the son of Kenaz, Caleb's y brother. 6996
15: 2 is not her y sister fairer than she? take her, 6996
1Sa 14:49 and the name of the y Michal: 6996
1Ch 24:31 fathers over against their y brethren. 6996
Job 30: 1 now they that are y than I have me in 3117+6810
Eze 16:46 thy y sister, that dwelleth at thy right hand, 6996
16:61 receive thy sisters, thine elder and thy y: 6996
Lk 15:12 And the y of them said to his father, Father, 3501
15:13 And not many days after the y son gathered 3501
22:26 is greatest among you, let him be as the y; 3501
Ro 9:12 said unto her, The elder shall serve the y. 1640
1Ti 5: 1 him as a father; and the y men as brethren; 3501
5: 2 as mothers; the y as sisters, with all purity. 3501
5:11 But the y widows refuse: for when they 3501
5:14 I will therefore that the y women marry, 3501
1Pe 5: 5 Likewise, ye y, submit yourselves unto 3501

YOUNGEST (18) [YOUTH]

Ge 42:13 the y is this day with our father, and one is 6996
42:15 except your y brother come hither. 6996
42:20 bring your y brother unto me; so shall your 6996
42:32 the y is this day with our father in the land 6996
42:34 bring your y brother unto me: then shall I 6996
43:33 and the y according to his youth: 6810
44: 2 in the sack's mouth of the y, and his corn 6996
44:12 and began at the eldest, and left at the y: 6996
44:23 Except your y brother come down with 6996
44:26 if our y brother be with us, then will we go 6996
44:26 man's face, except our y brother be with us. 6996
Jos 6:26 in his y son shall he set up the gates of it. 6810
Jdg 9: 5 notwithstanding yet Jotham the y son of 6996
1Sa 16:11 There remaineth yet the y, and behold, 6996
17:14 David was the y: and the three eldest 6996
1Ki 16:34 set up the gates thereof in his y son Segub, 6810
2Ch 21:17 left him, save Jehoahaz, the y of his sons. 6996
22: 1 made Ahaziah his y son king in his stead: 6996

YOUR (1776) [YOU]

Ge 3: 5 y eyes shall be opened, and ye shall be as 3641.1
9: 2 of the sea; into y hand are they delivered. 3641.1
9: 5 surely y blood of your lives will I require; 3641.1
9: 5 surely your blood of y lives will I require; 3641.1
9: 9 with you and with y seed after you; 3641.1
17:11 ye shall circumcise the flesh of y 3641.1
17:12 every man child in y generations, he that 3641.1
17:13 my covenant shall be in y flesh for an 3641.1
18: 4 wash y feet, and rest yourselves under 3641.1
Ge 18: 5 morsel of bread, and comfort ye y hearts; 3641.1
18: 5 for therefore are you come to y servant. 3641.1
19: 2 into y servant's house, and tarry all night, 3641.1
19: 2 wash y feet, and ye shall rise up early, 3641.1
19: 2 ye shall rise up early, and go on y ways. 3641.1
19: 8 and do ye to them as is good in y eyes: 3641.1
23: 8 If it be y mind that I should bury my dead 3641.1
31: 5 unto them, I see y father's countenance, 3654.1
31: 6 with all my power I have served y father. 3654.1
31: 7 y father hath deceived me, and 3654.1
31: 9 Thus God hath taken away the cattle of y 3641.1
31:29 the God of y father spake unto me 3641.1
34: 8 my son Shechem longeth for y daughter: 3641.1
34: 9 and give y daughters unto us, and take 3641.1
34:11 Let me find grace in y eyes, and what ye 3641.1
34:16 we will take y daughters to us, and 3641.1
35: 2 and be clean, and change y garments: 3641.1
37: 7 y sheaves stood round about, and 3641.1
42:15 except y youngest brother come hither. 3641.1
42:16 let him fetch y brother, and ye shall be 3641.1
42:16 in prison, that y words may be proved, 3641.1
42:19 If ye be true men, let one of y brethren be 3641.1
42:19 be bound in the house of y prison: 3641.1
42:19 carry corn for the famine of y houses: 3641.1
42:20 bring y youngest brother unto me; so 3641.1
42:20 so shall y words be verified, and ye shall 3641.1
42:33 leave one of y brethren here with me, 3641.1
42:33 take food for the famine of y households, 3641.1
42:34 bring y youngest brother unto me: then 3641.1
42:34 true men: so will I deliver you y brother, 3641.1
43: 3 my face, except y brother be with you. 3641.1
43: 5 my face, except y brother be with you. 3641.1
43: 7 our kindred, saying, Is y father yet alive? 3641.1
43: 7 that he would say, Bring y brother down? 3641.1
43:11 take of the best fruits in the land in y 3641.1
43:12 take double money in y hand; and 3641.1
43:12 brought again in the mouth of y sacks, 3641.1
43:12 of your sacks, carry it again in y hand; 3641.1
43:13 Take also y brother, and arise, go again 3641.1
43:14 that he may send away y other brother, 3641.1
43:23 y God, and the God of your father, 3641.1
43:23 your God, and the God of y father, 3641.1
43:23 hath given you treasure in y sacks: 3641.1
43:23 I had y money. And he brought Simeon 3641.1
43:27 said, Is y father well, the old man of 3641.1
43:29 and said, Is this y younger brother, 3641.1
44:10 also let it be according unto y words: 3641.1
44:17 for you, get you up in peace unto y father. 3641.1
44:23 Except y youngest brother come down 3641.1
45: 4 he said, I am Joseph y brother, whom ye 3641.1
45: 7 y lives by a great deliverance. 3641.1+3807.1
45:12 y eyes see, and the eyes of my brother 3641.1
45:17 lade y beasts, and go, get you unto 3641.1
45:18 take y father and your households, and 3641.1
45:18 take your father and y households, and 3641.1
45:19 out of the land of Egypt for y little ones, 3641.1
45:19 for y wives, and bring your father, and 3641.1
45:19 your wives, and bring y father, and come. 3641.1
45:20 Also regard not y stuff; for the good of all 3641.1
46:33 and shall say, What is y occupation? 3641.1
47: 3 unto his brethren, What is y occupation? 3641.1
47:16 Joseph said, Give y cattle; and I will give 3641.1
47:16 I will give you for y cattle, if money fail. 3641.1
47:23 you this day and y land for Pharaoh: 3641.1
47:24 four parts shall be y own, for seed of 3641.1
47:24 for y food, and for them of your 3641.1
47:24 for them of y households, and for food 3641.1
47:24 and for food for y little ones. 3641.1
48:21 bring you again unto the land of y fathers. 3641.1
49: 2 of Jacob; and hearken unto Israel y father. 3641.1
50: 4 now I have found grace in y eyes, speak, 3641.1
50:21 I will nourish you and y little ones. 3641.1
Ex 3:13 The God of y fathers hath sent me unto 3641.1
3:15 The LORD God of y fathers, the God of 3641.1
3:16 unto them, The LORD God of y fathers, 3641.1
3:22 ye shall put them upon y sons, and 3641.1
3:22 upon your sons, and upon y daughters; 3641.1
5: 4 from their works? get you unto y burdens. 3641.1
5:11 not ought of y work shall be diminished. 3641.1
5:13 Fulfil y works, your daily tasks, as when 3641.1
5:13 Fulfil your works, y daily tasks, as when NIH
5:14 Wherefore have ye not fulfilled y task in 3641.1
5:19 Ye shall not minish ought from y bricks 3641.1
5:19 ought from your bricks of y daily task. NIH
6: 7 shall know that I am the LORD y God, 3641.1
8:25 Go ye, sacrifice to y God in the land. 3641.1
8:28 that ye may sacrifice to the LORD y 3641.1
10: 8 unto them, Go, serve the LORD y God: 3641.1
10:10 as I will let you go, and y little ones: 3641.1
10:16 I have sinned against the LORD y God, 3641.1
10:17 this once, and intreat the LORD y God, 3641.1
10:24 let y flocks and your herds be stayed: 3641.1
10:24 let your flocks and y herds be stayed: 3641.1
10:24 let y little ones also go with you. 3641.1
12: 4 his eating shall make y count for the lamb. NIH
12: 5 Y lamb shall be without blemish, 3641.1+3807.1
12:11 with y loins girded, your shoes on your 3641.1
12:11 y shoes on your feet, and your staff in 3641.1
12:11 your shoes on y feet, and your staff in 3641.1
12:11 on your feet, and y staff in your hand; 3641.1
12:11 on your feet, and your staff in y hand; 3641.1
12:14 to the LORD throughout y generations; 3641.1
12:15 ye shall put away leaven out of y houses: 3641.1
12:17 for in this selfsame day have I brought y 3641.1
12:17 shall ye observe this day in y generations 3641.1
12:19 there be no leaven found in y houses: 3641.1
12:20 in all y habitations shall ye eat 3641.1
12:21 take you a lamb according to y families, 3641.1
12:23 to come in unto y houses to smite you. 3641.1
12:26 when y children shall say unto you, 3641.1
12:32 Also take y flocks and your herds, as ye 3641.1
12:32 Also take your flocks and y herds, as ye 3641.1
14:14 fight for you, and ye shall hold y peace. NIH
16: 7 for that he heareth y murmurings against 3641.1
16: 8 for that the LORD heareth y 3641.1

Y

Ex 16: 8 y murmurings are not against us, but 3641.1
16: 9 for he hath heard y murmurings. 3641.1
16:12 shall know that I am the LORD y God. 3641.1
16:16 according to the number of y persons; 3641.1
16:32 Fill an omer of it to be kept for y 3641.1
16:33 the LORD, to be kept for y generations. 3641.1
19:15 against the third day: come not at y wives. NIH
20:20 that his fear may be before y faces, 3641.1
22:24 y wives shall be widows, and 3641.1
22:24 be widows, and y children fatherless. 3641.1
23:21 for he will not pardon y transgressions: 3641.1
23:25 ye shall serve the LORD y God, and 3641.1
23:31 the inhabitants of the land into y hand; 3641.1
29:42 y generations at the door of the tabernacle 3641.1
30: 8 the LORD throughout y generations. 3641.1
30:10 upon it throughout y generations: 3641.1
30:15 to make an atonement for y souls. 3641.1
30:16 to make an atonement for y souls. 3641.1
30:31 oil unto me throughout y generations. 3641.1
31:13 and you throughout y generations; 3641.1
32: 2 which are in the ears of y wives, of your 3641.1
32: 2 of y sons, and of your daughters, and 3641.1
32: 2 of y daughters, and bring them unto me. 3641.1
32:13 I will multiply y seed as the stars of 3641.1
32:13 I have spoken of will I give unto y seed, 3641.1
32:30 I shall make an atonement for y sin. 3641.1
34:23 Thrice in the year shall all y men children 3509.2
35: 3 Ye shall kindle no fire throughout y 3641.1
Lev 1: 2 ye shall bring y offering of the cattle, 3641.1
3:17 It shall be a perpetual statute for y 3641.1
3:17 generations throughout all y dwellings, 3641.1
6:18 It shall be a statute for ever in y 3641.1
7:26 of fowl or of beast, in any of y dwellings. 3641.1
7:32 of the sacrifices of y peace offerings. 3641.1
8:33 until the days of y consecration be at an 3641.1
10: 4 carry y brethren from before 3641.1
10: 6 Ithamar his sons, Uncover not y heads, 3641.1
10: 6 not your heads, neither rend y clothes; 3641.1
10: 6 let y brethren, the whole house of Israel, 3641.1
10: 9 it shall be a statute for ever throughout y 3641.1
11:44 For I am the LORD y God: ye shall 3641.1
11:45 of the land of Egypt, to be y God: 3641.1+3807.1
14:34 in a house of the land of y possession; 3641.1
16:29 ye shall afflict y souls, and do no work at 3641.1
16:29 at all, whether it be one of y own country, 249
16:30 that ye may be clean from all y sins 3641.1
16:31 ye shall afflict y souls, by a statute for 3641.1
17:11 altar to make an atonement for y souls: 3641.1
17:15 beasts, whether it be one of y own country, 249
18: 2 say unto them, I am the LORD y God. 3641.1
18: 4 to walk therein: I am the LORD y God. 3641.1
18:26 neither any of y own nation, nor any 249
18:30 I am the LORD y God. 3641.1
19: 2 be holy: for I the LORD y God am holy. 3641.1
19: 3 my sabbaths: I am the LORD y God. 3641.1
19: 4 molten gods: I am the LORD y God. 3641.1
19: 5 ye shall offer it at y own will. 3641.1
19: 9 when ye reap the harvest of y land, 3641.1
19:10 and stranger: I am the LORD y God. 3641.1
19:25 increase thereof: I am the LORD y God. 3641.1
19:27 Ye shall not round the corners of y heads, 3641.1
19:28 Ye shall not make any cuttings in y flesh 3641.1
19:31 defiled by them: I am the LORD y God. 3641.1
19:33 if a stranger sojourn with thee in y land, 3641.1
19:34 land of Egypt: I am the LORD y God. 3641.1
19:36 I am the LORD y God, which brought 3641.1
20: 7 be ye holy: for I am the LORD y God. 3641.1
20:24 I am the LORD y God, which have 3641.1
20:25 ye shall not make y souls abominable by 3641.1
22: 3 Whosoever he be of all y seed among 3641.1
22: 3 be of all your seed among y generations, 3641.1
22:19 Ye shall offer at y own will a male 3641.1
22:24 you make any offering thereof in y land. 3641.1
22:25 offer the bread of y God of any of these; 3641.1
22:29 unto the LORD, offer it at y own will. 3641.1
22:33 of the land of Egypt, to be y God: 3641.1+3807.1
23: 3 sabbath of the LORD in all y dwellings. 3641.1
23:10 the firstfruits of y harvest unto the priest: 3641.1
23:14 ye have brought an offering unto y God: 3641.1
23:14 it shall be a statute for ever throughout y 3641.1
23:14 your generations in all y dwellings. 3641.1
23:17 Ye shall bring out of y habitations two 3641.1
23:21 y dwellings throughout your generations. 3641.1
23:21 your dwellings throughout y generations. 3641.1
23:22 when ye reap the harvest of y land, 3641.1
23:22 to the stranger: I am the LORD y God. 3641.1
23:27 ye shall afflict y souls, and offer an 3641.1
23:28 for you before the LORD y God. 3641.1
23:31 it shall be a statute for ever throughout y 3641.1
23:31 your generations in all y dwellings. 3641.1
23:32 of rest, and ye shall afflict y souls: 3641.1
23:32 unto even, shall ye celebrate y sabbath. 3641.1
23:38 beside y gifts, and beside all your vows, 3641.1
23:38 beside all y vows, and beside all your 3641.1
23:38 and beside all y freewill offerings, 3641.1
23:40 ye shall rejoice before the LORD y God 3641.1
23:41 It shall be a statute for ever in y 3641.1
23:43 That y generations may know that I made 3641.1
23:43 land of Egypt: I am the LORD y God. 3641.1
24: 3 it shall be a statute for ever in y 3641.1
24:22 the stranger, as for one of y own country: NIH
24:22 own country: for I am the LORD y God. 3641.1
25: 9 the trumpet sound throughout all y land. 3641.1
25:17 fear thy God: for I am the LORD y God. 3641.1
25:19 ye shall eat y fill, and dwell therein in NIH
25:24 in all the land of y possession ye shall 3641.1
25:38 I am the LORD y God, which brought 3641.1
25:38 land of Canaan, and to be y God. 3641.1+3807.1
25:45 are with you, which they begat in y land: 3641.1
25:45 and they shall be y possession. 3641.1+3807.1
25:46 ye shall take them as an inheritance for y 3641.1
25:46 they shall be y bondmen for ever: NIH
25:46 over y brethren the children of Israel, 3641.1
25:55 land of Egypt: I am the LORD y God. 3641.1
26: 1 ye set up any image of stone in y land, 3641.1

Lev 26: 1 down unto it: for I am the LORD y God. 3641.1
26: 5 y threshing shall reach unto 3641.1+3807.1
26: 5 ye shall eat y bread to the full, and 3641.1
26: 5 to the full, and dwell in y land safely. 3641.1
26: 6 neither shall the sword go through y land. 3641.1
26: 7 ye shall chase y enemies, and they shall 3641.1
26: 8 y enemies shall fall before you by 3641.1
26:12 will be y God, and ye shall be my 3641.1+3807.1
26:13 I am the LORD y God, which brought 3641.1
26:13 I have broken the bands of y yoke, and 3641.1
26:15 or if y soul abhor my judgments, so 3641.1
26:16 ye shall sow y seed in vain, for your 3641.1
26:16 seed in vain, for y enemies shall eat it. 3641.1
26:17 and ye shall be slain before y enemies; 3641.1
26:18 I will punish you seven times more for y 3641.1
26:19 I will break the pride of y power; and 3641.1
26:19 I will make y heaven as iron, and your 3641.1
26:19 your heaven as iron, and y earth as brass: 3641.1
26:20 y strength shall be spent in vain: for your 3641.1
26:20 for y land shall not yield her increase, 3641.1
26:21 plagues upon you according to y sins. 3641.1
26:22 which shall rob you of y children, and NIH
26:22 destroy y cattle, and make you few in 3641.1
26:22 y high ways shall be desolate. 3641.1
26:24 punish you yet seven times for y sins. 3641.1
26:25 when ye are gathered together within y 3641.1
26:26 have broken the staff of y bread, 3641.1+3807.1
26:26 ten women shall bake y bread in one 3641.1
26:26 they shall deliver you y bread again by 3641.1
26:28 will chastise you seven times for y sins. 3641.1
26:29 ye shall eat the flesh of y sons, and 3641.1
26:29 and the flesh of y daughters shall ye eat. 3641.1
26:30 I will destroy y high places, and cut down 3641.1
26:30 cut down y images, and cast your 3641.1
26:30 cast y carcases upon the carcases of your 3641.1
26:30 cast your carcases upon the carcases of y 3641.1
26:31 I will make y cities waste, and bring your 3641.1
26:31 bring y sanctuaries unto desolation, and 3641.1
26:31 I will not smell the savour of y sweet 3641.1
26:32 y enemies which dwell therein shall be 3641.1
26:33 y land shall be desolate, and your cities 3641.1
26:33 land shall be desolate, and y cities waste. 3641.1
26:34 and ye be in y enemies' land; 3641.1
26:35 because it did not rest in y sabbaths, 3641.1
26:37 ye shall have no power to stand before y 3641.1
26:38 the land of y enemies shall eat you up. 3641.1
26:39 in their iniquity in y enemies' lands; 3641.1
Nu 9:10 of y posterity shall be unclean by reason 3641.1
10: 8 for ever throughout y generations. 3641.1
10: 9 if ye go to war in y land against 3641.1
10: 9 remembered before the LORD y God, 3641.1
10: 9 and ye shall be saved from y enemies. 3641.1
10:10 Also in the day of y gladness, and in your 3641.1
10:10 in y solemn days, and in the beginnings 3641.1
10:10 and in the beginnings of y months, 3641.1
10:10 ye shall blow with the trumpets over y 3641.1
10:10 over the sacrifices of y peace offerings; 3641.1
10:10 be to you for a memorial before y God: 3641.1
10:10 your God: I am the LORD y God. 3641.1
11:20 until it come out at y nostrils, and it be 3641.1
14:29 Y carcases shall fall in this wilderness; 3641.1
14:29 according to y whole number, 3641.1
14:31 y little ones, which ye said should be a 3641.1
14:32 as for you, y carcases, they shall fall in 3641.1
14:33 y children shall wander in the wilderness 3641.1
14:33 bear y whoredoms, until your carcases be 3641.1
14:33 until y carcases be wasted in 3641.1
14:34 shall ye bear y iniquities, even forty 3641.1
14:42 that ye be not smitten before y enemies. 3641.1
15: 2 When ye be come into the land of y 3641.1
15: 3 a freewill offering, or in y solemn feasts, 3641.1
15:14 be among you in y generations, 3641.1
15:15 an ordinance for ever in y generations: 3641.1
15:20 Ye shall offer up a cake of the first of y 3641.1
15:21 Of the first of y dough ye shall give unto 3641.1
15:21 a heave offering in y generations. 3641.1
15:23 and henceforward among y generations; 3641.1
15:39 that ye seek not after y own heart and 3641.1
15:39 not after your own heart and y own eyes, 3641.1
15:40 and be holy unto y God. 3641.1
15:41 I am the LORD y God, which brought 3641.1
15:41 of the land of Egypt, to be y God: 3641.1+3807.1
15:41 to be your God: I am the LORD y God. 3641.1
18: 1 shall bear the iniquity of y priesthood. 3641.1
18: 6 I have taken y brethren the Levites from 3641.1
18: 7 thy sons with thee shall keep y priest's 3641.1
18: 7 I have given y priest's office unto you as 3641.1
18:23 it shall be a statute for ever throughout y 3641.1
18:26 given you from them for y inheritance, 3641.1
18:27 this y heave offering shall be reckoned 3641.1
18:28 offering unto the LORD of all y tithes, 3641.1
18:29 Out of all y gifts ye shall offer every 3641.1
18:31 eat it in every place, ye and y households: 3641.1
18:31 for it is y reward for your service 3641.1+3807.1
18:31 for it is your reward for y service in 3641.1
22:13 the princes of Balak, Get you into y land: 3641.1
28:11 in the beginnings of y months ye shall 3641.1
28:26 after y weeks be out, ye shall have a holy 3641.1
29: 7 and ye shall afflict y souls: 3641.1
29:39 shall do unto the LORD in y set feasts, 3641.1
29:39 besides y vows, and your freewill 3641.1
29:39 your vows, and y freewill offerings, 3641.1
29:39 for y burnt offerings, and for your meat 3641.1
29:39 for y meat offerings, and for your drink 3641.1
29:39 for y drink offerings, and for your peace 3641.1
29:39 drink offerings, and for y peace offerings. 3641.1
31:19 and y captives on the third day, 3641.1
31:20 purify all y raiment, and all that is made of NIH
31:24 ye shall wash y clothes on the seventh 3641.1
32: 6 Shall y brethren go to war, and shall ye 3641.1
32: 8 Thus did y fathers, when I sent them from 3641.1
32:14 ye are risen up in y fathers' stead, 3641.1
32:22 this land shall be y possession 3641.1+3807.1
32:23 and be sure y sin will find you out. 3641.1
32:24 Build ye cities for y little ones, and 3641.1

Nu 32:24 for your little ones, and folds for y sheep; 3641.1
32:24 do that which hath proceeded out of y 3641.1
33:54 lot for an inheritance among y families: 3641.1
33:54 according to the tribes of y fathers ye 3641.1
33:55 remain of them shall be pricks in y eyes, 3641.1
33:55 thorns in y sides, and shall vex you in 3641.1
34: 3 y south quarter shall be from 3641.1+3807.1
34: 3 y south border shall be 3641.1+3807.1
34: 4 y border shall turn from the south 3641.1+3807.1
34: 6 this shall be y west border. 3641.1+3807.1
34: 7 this shall be y north border: 3641.1+3807.1
34: 8 From mount Hor ye shall point out y border NIH
34: 9 this shall be y north border. 3641.1+3807.1
34:10 ye shall point out y east border 3641.1+3807.1
34:12 this shall be y land with 3641.1+3807.1
35:29 y generations in all your dwellings. 3641.1
35:29 your generations in all y dwellings. 3641.1
Dt 1: 7 take y journey, and go to the mount of 3641.1
1: 8 which the LORD sware unto y fathers, 3641.1
1:10 The LORD y God hath multiplied you, 3641.1
1:11 (The LORD God of y fathers make you 3641.1
1:12 How can I myself alone bear y 3641.1
1:12 and y burden, and your strife? 3641.1
1:12 and your burden, and y strife? 3641.1
1:13 known among y tribes, and I will make 3641.1
1:15 So I took the chief of y tribes, wise men, 3641.1
1:15 over tens, and officers among y tribes. 3641.1
1:16 I charged y judges at that time, saying, 3641.1
1:16 Hear the causes between y brethren, and 3641.1
1:26 the commandment of the LORD y God: 3641.1
1:27 ye murmured in y tents, and said, 3641.1
1:30 The LORD y God which goeth before 3641.1
1:30 he did for you in Egypt before y eyes; 3641.1
1:32 ye did not believe the LORD y God, 3641.1
1:33 to search you out a place to pitch y tents 3641.1
1:34 the LORD heard the voice of y words, 3641.1
1:35 which I sware to give unto y fathers, 3641.1
1:37 Also the LORD was angry with me for y 3641.1
1:39 Moreover y little ones, which ye said 3641.1
1:39 ye said should be a prey, and y children, 3641.1
1:40 take y journey into the wilderness by NIH
1:42 lest ye be smitten before y enemies. 3641.1
1:45 the LORD would not hearken to y voice, 3641.1
2: 4 Ye are to pass through the coast of y 3641.1
2:24 take y journey, and pass over the river NIH
3:18 The LORD y God hath given you this 3641.1
3:18 ye shall pass over armed before y 3641.1
3:19 y wives, and your little ones, and 3641.1
3:19 and y little ones, and your cattle, 3641.1
3:19 and your little ones, and y cattle, 3641.1
3:19 shall abide in y cities which I have given 3641.1
3:20 Until the LORD have given rest unto y 3641.1
3:20 y God hath given them beyond Jordan: 3641.1
3:21 y God hath done unto these two kings: 3641.1
3:22 for the LORD y God he shall fight for 3641.1
3:26 the LORD was wroth with me for y 3641.1
4: 1 the LORD God of y fathers giveth you. 3641.1
4: 2 LORD y God which I command you. 3641.1
4: 3 Y eyes have seen what the LORD did 3641.1
4: 4 ye that did cleave unto the LORD y God 3641.1
4: 6 and do them; for this is y wisdom and 3641.1
4: 6 y understanding in the sight of 3641.1
4:21 LORD was angry with me for y sakes, 3641.1
4:23 forget the covenant of the LORD y God, 3641.1
4:26 ye shall not prolong y days upon it, but NIH
4:34 according to all that the LORD y God 3641.1
4:34 God did for you in Egypt before y eyes? 3509.2
5: 1 which I speak in y ears this day, 3641.1
5:22 These words the LORD spake unto all y 3641.1
5:23 even all the heads of y tribes, and 3641.1
5:23 all the heads of your tribes, and y elders; 3641.1
5:28 the LORD heard the voice of y words, 3641.1
5:30 say to them, Get you into y tents again. 3641.1
5:32 as the LORD y God hath commanded 3641.1
5:33 the LORD y God hath commanded you, 3641.1
5:33 that ye may prolong y days in the land NIH
6: 1 which the LORD y God commanded to 3641.1
6:16 Ye shall not tempt the LORD y God, 3641.1
6:17 the commandments of the LORD y God, 3641.1
7: 8 oath which he had sworn unto y fathers, 3641.1
7:14 barren among you, or among y cattle. 3509.2
8: 1 which the LORD sware unto y fathers. 3641.1
8:20 the LORD destroyeth before y face, 3641.1
8:20 unto the voice of the LORD y God. 3641.1
9:16 ye had sinned against the LORD y God, 3641.1
9:17 two hands, and brake them before y eyes. 3641.1
9:18 because of all y sins which ye sinned, 3641.1
9:21 I took y sin, the calf which ye had made, 3641.1
9:23 the commandment of the LORD y God, 3641.1
10:16 therefore the foreskin of y heart, 3641.1
10:17 For the LORD y God is God of gods, 3641.1
11: 2 for I speak not with y children which 3641.1
11: 2 the chastisement of the LORD y God, 3641.1
11: 7 y eyes have seen all the great acts of 3641.1
11: 9 And that ye may prolong y days in the land, NIH
11: 9 which the LORD sware unto y fathers to 3641.1
11:13 to love the LORD y God, and to serve 3641.1
11:13 to serve him with all y heart and with all 3641.1
11:13 with all your heart and with all y soul, 3641.1
11:14 That I will give you the rain of y land in 3641.1
11:16 that y heart be not deceived, and ye turn 3641.1
11:18 shall ye lay up these my words in y heart 3641.1
11:18 my words in your heart and in y soul, 3641.1
11:18 and bind them for a sign upon y hand, 3641.1
11:18 that they may be as frontlets between y 3641.1
11:19 ye shall teach them y children, speaking 3641.1
11:21 That y days may be multiplied, and 3641.1
11:21 be multiplied, and the days of y children, 3641.1
11:21 sware unto y fathers to give them, 3641.1
11:22 to do them, to love the LORD y God, 3641.1
11:24 Every place whereon the soles of y feet 3641.1
11:24 even unto the uttermost sea shall y coast 3641.1
11:25 for the LORD y God shall lay the fear of 3641.1
11:27 the commandments of the LORD y God, 3641.1
11:28 the commandments of the LORD y God, 3641.1

Dt 11:31 land which the LORD **y** God giveth you, 3641.1
12: 4 shall not do so unto the LORD **y** God. 3641.1
12: 5 unto the place which the LORD **y** God 3641.1
12: 5 out of all **y** tribes to put his name there, 3641.1
12: 6 thither ye shall bring **y** burnt offerings, 3641.1
12: 6 **y** sacrifices, and your tithes, and heave 3641.1
12: 6 **y** tithes, and heave offerings of your 3641.1
12: 6 heave offerings of **y** hand, and 3641.1
12: 6 **y** vows, and your freewill offerings, and 3641.1
12: 6 **y** freewill offerings, and the firstlings of 3641.1
12: 6 the firstlings of **y** herds and of your 3641.1
12: 6 firstlings of your herds and of **y** flocks: 3641.1
12: 7 there ye shall eat before the LORD **y** 3641.1
12: 7 ye shall rejoice in all that you put **y** hand 3641.1
12: 7 ye and **y** households, where*in* the LORD 3641.1
12: 9 which the LORD **y** God giveth you. 3509.2
12:10 dwell in the land which the LORD **y** 3641.1
12:10 *when* he giveth you rest from all **y** 3641.1
12:11 there shall be a place which the LORD **y** 3641.1
12:11 **y** burnt offerings, and your sacrifices, 3641.1
12:11 **y** sacrifices, your tithes, and the heave 3641.1
12:11 **y** tithes, and the heave offering of your 3641.1
12:11 the heave offering of **y** hand, and all your 3641.1
12:11 all **y** choice vows which ye vow unto 3641.1
12:12 ye shall rejoice before the LORD **y** God, 3641.1
12:12 ye, and **y** sons, and your daughters, and 3641.1
12:12 **y** daughters, and your menservants, and 3641.1
12:12 **y** menservants, and your maidservants, 3641.1
12:12 **y** maidservants, and the Levite that *is* 3641.1
12:12 and the Levite that *is* within **y** gates; 3641.1
13: 3 for the LORD **y** God proveth you, 3641.1
13: 3 to know whether you love the LORD **y** 3641.1
13: 3 the LORD your God with all **y** heart 3641.1
13: 3 with all your heart and with all **y** soul. 3641.1
13: 4 Ye shall walk after the LORD **y** God, 3641.1
13: 5 turn *you* away from the LORD **y** God, 3641.1
14: 1 Ye *are* the children of the LORD **y** God: 3641.1
14: 1 nor make *any* baldness between **y** eyes 3641.1
20: 3 *this* day unto battle against **y** enemies: 3641.1
20: 3 let not **y** hearts faint, fear not, and do not 3641.1
20: 4 For the LORD **y** God *is* he that goeth 3641.1
20: 4 to fight for you against **y** enemies, to save 3641.1
20:18 should ye sin against the LORD **y** God. 3641.1
28:68 there ye shall be sold unto **y** enemies for 3509.2
29: 2 **y** eyes in the land of Egypt unto Pharaoh, 3641.1
29: 5 **y** clothes are not waxen old upon you, 3641.1
29: 6 might know that I *am* the LORD **y** God. 3641.1
29:10 day all of you before the LORD **y** God; 3641.1
29:10 **y** captains of your tribes, your elders, and 3641.1
29:10 your captains of **y** tribes, your elders, and 3641.1
29:10 **y** elders, and your officers, *with* all 3641.1
29:10 your elders, and **y** officers, *with* all 3641.1
29:11 **Y** little ones, your wives, and thy stranger 3641.1
29:11 **y** wives, and thy stranger that *is* in thy 3641.1
29:22 So that the generation to come of **y** 3641.1
30:18 *that* ye shall not prolong **y** days upon NIH
31: 5 the LORD shall give them up before **y** 3641.1
31:12 fear the LORD **y** God, and observe to do 3641.1
31:13 and learn to fear the LORD **y** God, 3641.1
31:26 ark of the covenant of the LORD **y** God, 3641.1
31:28 Gather unto me all the elders of **y** tribes, 3641.1
31:28 **y** officers, that I may speak these words 3641.1
31:29 to anger through the work of **y** hands. 3641.1
32:17 newly up, whom **y** fathers feared not. 3641.1
32:38 rise up and help you, *and* be **y** protection. 3641.1
32:46 Set **y** hearts unto all the words which I 3641.1
32:46 which ye shall command **y** children to 3641.1
32:47 a vain thing for you; because it *is* **y** life: 3641.1
32:47 through this thing ye shall prolong **y** days in NIH
Jos 1: 3 Every place that the sole of **y** foot shall 3641.1
1: 4 going down of the sun, shall be **y** coast. 3641.1
1:11 which the LORD **y** God giveth you to 3641.1
1:13 The LORD **y** God hath given you rest, 3641.1
1:14 **Y** wives, your little ones, and your cattle, 3641.1
1:14 Your wives, **y** little ones, and your cattle, 3641.1
1:14 Your wives, your little ones, and **y** cattle, 3641.1
1:14 ye shall pass before **y** brethren armed, 3641.1
1:15 Until the LORD have given **y** brethren 3641.1
1:15 which the LORD **y** God giveth them: 3641.1
1:15 ye shall return unto the land of **y** 3641.1
2: 9 that **y** terror is fallen upon us, and that all 3641.1
2:11 for the LORD **y** God, he *is* God in 3641.1
2:16 and afterward may ye go **y** way. 3641.1
2:21 According unto **y** words, so *be* it. 3641.1
3: 3 ark of the covenant of the LORD **y** God, 3641.1
3: 3 ye shall remove from **y** place, and 3641.1
3: 9 and hear the words of the LORD **y** God. 3641.1
4: 5 Pass over before the ark of the LORD **y** 3641.1
4: 6 *that* when **y** children ask *their fathers* in 3641.1
4:21 When **y** children shall ask their fathers in 3641.1
4:22 ye shall let **y** children know, saying, 3641.1
4:23 For the LORD **y** God dried up 3641.1
4:23 as the LORD **y** God did to the Red sea, 3641.1
4:24 that ye might fear the LORD **y** God for 3641.1
6:10 nor make any noise with **y** voice, 3641.1
6:10 neither shall *any* word proceed out of **y** 3641.1
7:14 ye shall be brought according to **y** tribes: 3641.1
8: 7 for the LORD **y** God will deliver it into 3641.1
8: 7 your God will deliver it into **y** hand. 3641.1
9:11 and say unto them, We *are* **y** servants: 3641.1
10:19 *but* pursue after **y** enemies, and smite 3641.1
10:19 for the LORD **y** God hath delivered 3641.1
10:19 God hath delivered them into **y** hand. 3641.1
10:24 put **y** feet upon the necks of these kings. 3641.1
10:25 for thus shall the LORD do to all **y** 3641.1
15: 4 this shall be **y** south coast. 3641.1+3807.1
18: 3 which the LORD God of **y** fathers hath 3641.1
20: 3 they shall be **y** refuge from 3641.1+3807.1
22: 3 Ye have not left **y** brethren these many 3641.1
22: 3 the commandment of the LORD **y** God. 3641.1
22: 4 now the LORD **y** God hath given rest 3641.1
22: 4 your God hath given rest unto **y** brethren, 3641.1
22: 4 get ye unto **y** tents, *and* unto the land of 3641.1
22: 4 *and* unto the land of **y** possession, 3641.1
22: 5 to love the LORD **y** God, and to walk in 3641.1
Jos 22: 5 to serve him with all **y** heart and with all 3641.1
22: 5 with all your heart and with all **y** soul. 3641.1
22: 8 Return with much riches unto **y** tents, and 3641.1
22: 8 divide the spoil of **y** enemies with your 3641.1
22: 8 divide the spoil of your enemies with **y** 3641.1
22:19 if the land of **y** possession *be* unclean, 3641.1
22:24 In time to come **y** children might speak 3641.1
22:25 shall **y** children make our children cease 3641.1
22:27 that **y** children may not say to our 3641.1
23: 3 ye have seen all that the LORD **y** God 3641.1
23: 3 for the LORD **y** God *is* he that hath 3641.1
23: 4 to be an inheritance for **y** tribes, 3641.1
23: 5 the LORD **y** God, he shall expel them 3641.1
23: 5 and drive them from out of **y** sight; 3641.1
23: 5 as the LORD **y** God hath promised unto 3641.1
23: 8 cleave unto the LORD **y** God, as ye 3641.1
23:10 for the LORD **y** God, he *it is* that 3641.1
23:11 that ye love the LORD **y** God. 3641.1
23:13 Know for a certainty that the LORD **y** 3641.1
23:13 scourges in **y** sides, and thorns in your 3641.1
23:13 in your sides, and thorns in **y** eyes, 3641.1
23:13 which the LORD **y** God hath given you. 3641.1
23:14 ye know in all **y** hearts and in all your 3641.1
23:14 know in all your hearts and in all **y** souls, 3641.1
23:14 the LORD **y** God spake concerning you; 3641.1
23:15 which the LORD **y** God promised you; 3641.1
23:15 which the LORD **y** God hath given you. 3641.1
23:16 the covenant of the LORD **y** God, 3641.1
24: 2 **Y** fathers dwelt on the *other* side of 3641.1
24: 3 I took **y** father Abraham from the *other* 3641.1
24: 6 I brought **y** fathers out of Egypt: and 3641.1
24: 6 the Egyptians pursued after **y** fathers with 3641.1
24: 7 **y** eyes have seen what I have done in 3641.1
24: 8 I gave them into **y** hand, that ye might 3641.1
24:11 and I delivered them into **y** hand. 3641.1
24:14 put away the gods which **y** fathers served 3641.1
24:15 whether the gods which **y** fathers served 3641.1
24:19 he will not forgive **y** transgressions nor 3641.1
24:19 nor forgive your transgressions nor **y** sins. 3641.1
24:23 incline **y** heart unto the LORD God of 3641.1
24:27 a witness unto you, lest ye deny **y** God. 3641.1
Jdg 2: 1 the land which I sware unto **y** fathers; 3641.1
2: 3 they shall be *as thorns* in **y** sides, and 3641.1
3:28 for the LORD hath delivered **y** enemies 3641.1
3:28 your enemies the Moabites into **y** hand. 3641.1
6:10 I said unto you, I *am* the LORD **y** God; 3641.1
7:15 for the LORD hath delivered into **y** hand 3641.1
8: 3 God hath delivered into **y** hands 3641.1
8: 7 I will tear **y** flesh with the thorns of 3641.1
9: 2 remember also that I *am* **y** bone and 3641.1
9: 2 also that I *am* your bone and **y** flesh. 3641.1
9:15 *then* come *and* put **y** trust in my shadow: NIH
9:18 of Shechem, because he *is* **y** brother;) 3641.1
10:14 let them deliver you in the time of **y** 3641.1
11: 9 before me, shall I be **y** head? 3641.1+3807.1
18: 6 the LORD *is* **y** way wherein ye go. 3641.1
18:10 for God hath given it into **y** hands; 3641.1
19: 5 a morsel of bread, and afterward go **y** way. NIH
19: 9 to morrow get you early on **y** way, that 3641.1
19:30 of it, take advice, and speak ***y** minds.* NIH
20: 7 give here **y** advice and counsel. 3641.1+3807.1
Ru 1:11 that they may be **y** husbands? 3641.1+3807.1
1:12 go ***y** way;* for I am too old to have a NIH
1:13 for it grieveth me much for **y** sakes that 3641.1
1Sa 2: 3 let *not* arrogancy come out of **y** mouth: 3641.1
2:23 for I hear of **y** evil dealings by all this 3641.1
6: 4 plague *was* on you all, and on **y** lords. 3641.1
6: 5 Wherefore ye shall make images of **y** 3641.1
6: 5 and images of **y** mice that mar the land; 3641.1
6: 5 from off **y** gods, and from off your land. 3641.1
6: 5 from off your gods, and from off **y** land. 3641.1
6: 6 Wherefore then do ye harden **y** hearts, 3641.1
7: 3 If ye do return unto the LORD with all **y** 3641.1
7: 3 prepare **y** hearts unto the LORD, and 3641.1
8:11 He will take **y** sons, and appoint *them* for 3641.1
8:13 He will take **y** daughters to be 3641.1
8:14 he will take **y** fields, and your vineyards, 3641.1
8:14 **y** vineyards, and your oliveyards, 3641.1
8:14 your vineyards, and **y** oliveyards, 3641.1
8:15 he will take the tenth of **y** seed, and 3641.1
8:15 of **y** vineyards, and give to his officers, 3641.1
8:16 he will take **y** menservants, and your 3641.1
8:16 **y** maidservants, and your goodliest young 3641.1
8:16 **y** goodliest young men, and your asses, 3641.1
8:16 and **y** asses, and put *them* to his work. 3641.1
8:17 He will take the tenth of **y** sheep: and 3641.1
8:18 of **y** king which ye shall have chosen you; 3641.1
10:19 ye have *this* day rejected **y** God, 3641.1
10:19 who himself saved you out of all **y** 3641.1
10:19 of all your adversities and **y** tribulations; 3641.1
10:19 yourselves before the LORD by **y** tribes, 3641.1
10:19 by your tribes, and by **y** thousands. 3641.1
11: 2 that *I* may thrust out all **y** right 3641.1+3807.1
12: 1 I have hearkened unto **y** voice in all that 3641.1
12: 6 that brought **y** fathers up out of the land 3641.1
12: 7 which he did to you and to **y** fathers. 3641.1
12: 8 **y** fathers cried unto the LORD, then 3641.1
12: 8 which brought forth **y** fathers out of 3641.1
12:11 delivered you out of the hand of **y** 3641.1
12:12 when the LORD **y** God *was* your king. 3641.1
12:12 when the LORD your God *was* **y** king. 3641.1
12:14 continue following the LORD **y** God: 3641.1
12:15 be against you, as *it was* against **y** fathers. 3641.1
12:16 which the LORD will do before **y** eyes. 3641.1
12:17 and see that **y** wickedness *is* great, 3641.1
12:20 but serve the LORD with all **y** heart; 3641.1
12:24 and serve him in truth with all **y** heart: 3641.1
12:25 ye shall be consumed, both ye and **y** king. 3641.1
17: 8 Why are ye come out to set ***y*** battle in NIH
17: 9 then will we be **y** servants: 3641.1+3807.1
26:16 to die, because ye have not kept **y** master, 3641.1
2Sa 1:24 who put on ornaments of gold upon **y** 3654.1
2: 5 that ye have shewed this kindness unto **y** 3641.1
2: 7 Therefore now let **y** hands be 3641.1
2: 7 for **y** master Saul is dead, and also 3641.1
2Sa 3:31 Rent **y** clothes, and gird you with 3641.1
4:11 now require his blood of **y** hand, 3641.1
10: 5 Tarry at Jericho until **y** beards be grown, 3641.1
15:27 **y** two sons with you, Ahimaaz thy son, 3509.2
1Ki 1:33 Take with you the servants of **y** lord, and 3641.1
8:61 Let **y** heart therefore be perfect with 3641.1
9: 6 you or **y** children, and will not keep my 3641.1
11: 2 *for* surely they will turn away **y** heart 3641.1
12:11 with a heavy yoke, I will add to **y** yoke: 3641.1
12:14 My father made **y** yoke heavy, and I will 3641.1
12:14 yoke heavy, and I will add to **y** yoke: 3641.1
12:16 to **y** tents, O Israel: now see to thine own 3509.2
12:24 nor fight against **y** brethren the children 3641.1
18:24 call ye on the name of **y** gods, and I will 3641.1
18:25 call on the name of **y** gods, but put no 3641.1
2Ki 2: 3 he said, Yea, I know *it;* hold you **y** peace. NIH
2: 5 Yea, I know *it;* hold you **y** peace. NIH
3:17 *both* ye, and **y** cattle, and your beasts. 3641.1
3:17 *both* ye, and your cattle, and **y** beasts. 3641.1
3:18 he will deliver the Moabites also into **y** 3641.1
9:15 If it be **y** minds, *then* let none go forth *nor* 3641.1
10: 2 seeing **y** master's sons *are* with you, and 3641.1
10: 3 the best and meetest of **y** master's sons, 3641.1
10: 3 and fight for **y** master's house. 3641.1
10: 6 take ye the heads of the men **y** master's 3641.1
10:24 I *have* brought into **y** hands escape, 3641.1
12: 7 no *more* money of **y** acquaintance, 3641.1
17:13 Turn ye from **y** evil ways, and keep my 3641.1
17:13 all the law which I commanded **y** fathers, 3641.1
17:39 the LORD **y** God ye shall fear; and 3641.1
17:39 you out of the hand of all **y** enemies. 3641.1
18:32 take you away to a land like **y own** land, 3641.1
19: 6 Thus shall ye say to **y** master, Thus saith 3641.1
23:21 the passover unto the LORD **y** God, 3641.1
1Ch 15:12 sanctify yourselves, *both* ye and **y** 3641.1
16:18 land of Canaan, the lot of **y** inheritance; 3641.1
19: 5 Tarry at Jericho until **y** beards be grown, 3641.1
22:18 *Is* not the LORD **y** God with you? and 3641.1
22:19 Now set **y** heart and your soul to seek 3641.1
22:19 and **y** soul to seek the LORD your God; 3641.1
22:19 and your soul to seek the LORD **y** God; 3641.1
28: 8 the commandments of the LORD **y** God: 3641.1
28: 8 leave *it* for an inheritance for **y** children 3641.1
29:20 Now bless the LORD **y** God. 3641.1
2Ch 10:11 yoke upon you, I will put more to **y** yoke: 3641.1
10:14 My father made **y** yoke heavy, but I will 3641.1
10:16 every man to **y** tents, O Israel: *and* now, 3509.2
11: 4 not go up, nor fight against **y** brethren: 3641.1
13:12 fight ye not against the LORD God of **y** 3641.1
15: 7 and let not **y** hands be weak: 3641.1
15: 7 be weak: for **y** work shall be rewarded. 3641.1
18:14 and they shall be delivered into **y** hand. 3641.1
19:10 what cause soever shall come to you of **y** 3641.1
19:10 come upon you, and upon **y** brethren: 3641.1
20:20 Believe in the LORD **y** God, so 3641.1
24: 5 the house of **y** God from year to year, 3641.1
28: 9 the LORD God of **y** fathers was wroth 3641.1
28: 9 he hath delivered them into **y** hand, and 3641.1
28:10 with you, sins against the LORD **y** God? 3641.1
28:11 ye have taken captive of **y** brethren: 3641.1
29: 5 house of the LORD God of **y** fathers, 3641.1
29: 8 and to hissing, as ye see with **y** eyes. 3641.1
30: 7 be not ye like **y** fathers, and like your 3641.1
30: 7 ye like your fathers, and like **y** brethren, 3641.1
30: 8 as **y** fathers *were, but* yield yourselves 3641.1
30: 8 serve the LORD **y** God, that 3641.1
30: 9 **y** brethren and your children *shall find* 3641.1
30: 9 **y** children *shall find* compassion before 3641.1
30: 9 for the LORD **y** God *is* gracious and 3641.1
32:14 that **y** God should be able to deliver you 3641.1
32:15 how much less shall **y** God deliver you 3641.1
33: 8 land which I have appointed for **y** fathers; 3641.1
35: 3 *be* a burden upon **y** shoulders: 3641.1+3807.1
35: 3 serve now the LORD **y** God, and his 3641.1
35: 4 prepare *yourselves* by the houses of **y** 3641.1
35: 4 after **y** courses, according to the writing 3641.1
35: 5 of the fathers of **y** brethren the people, 3641.1
35: 6 and prepare **y** brethren, 3641.1
Ezr 4: 2 for we seek **y** God, as ye *do;* and we do 3641.1
6: 6 and **y** companions the Apharsachites, 1952.1
7:17 the house of **y** God which *is* in Jerusalem. 3641.2
7:18 and gold, *that* do after the will of **y** God. 3641.2
8:28 unto the LORD God of **y** fathers. 3641.1
9:12 give not **y** daughters unto their sons, 3641.1
9:12 neither take their daughters unto **y** sons, 3641.1
9:12 leave *it* for an inheritance to **y** children 3641.1
10:11 unto the LORD God of **y** fathers, 3641.1
Ne 4:14 and terrible, and fight for **y** brethren, 3641.1
4:14 **y** sons, and your daughters, your wives, 3641.1
4:14 your sons, and **y** daughters, your wives, 3641.1
4:14 your daughters, **y** wives, and your houses. 3641.1
4:14 your daughters, your wives, and **y** houses. 3641.1
5: 8 and will you even sell **y** brethren? 3641.1
8: 9 *This* day *is* holy unto the LORD **y** God; 3641.1
8:10 Go ***y** way,* eat the fat, and drink the sweet, NIH
8:10 for the joy of the LORD *is* **y** strength. 3641.1
8:11 Hold **y** peace, for the day *is* holy; NIH
9: 5 *and* bless the LORD **y** God for ever and 3641.1
13:18 Did not **y** fathers thus, and *did not* our 3641.1
13:25 *saying,* Ye shall not give **y** daughters unto 3641.1
13:25 nor take their daughters unto **y** sons, or 3641.1
Job 6:22 or, Give a reward for me of **y** substance? 3641.1
6:25 but what doth **y** arguing reprove? 4480+3641.1
6:27 and you dig *a pit* for **y** friend. 3641.1
13: 5 O that you would altogether hold **y** peace, NIH
13: 5 it should be **y** wisdom. 3641.1+3807.1
13:12 **Y** remembrances *are* like unto ashes, 3641.1
13:12 unto ashes, **y** bodies to bodies of clay. 3641.1
13:13 Hold **y** peace, let me alone, that I may NIH
13:17 and my declaration with **y** ears. 3641.1
16: 4 I also could speak as ye *do:* if **y** soul were 3641.1
16: 5 the moving of my lips should asswage ***y*** NIH
18: 3 as beasts, *and* reputed vile in **y** sight? 3641.1
21: 2 my speech, and let this be **y** consolations. 3641.1
21: 5 and lay ***y*** hand upon *your* mouth. NIH

Job 21: 5 and lay *your* hand upon y mouth. NIH
21:27 I know y thoughts, and the devices *which* 3641.1
21:34 seeing *in* y answers there remaineth 3641.1
32:11 Behold, I waited for y words; I gave ear 3641.1
32:11 I gave ear to y reasons, whilst you 3641.1
32:14 will I answer him with y speeches. 3641.1
42: 8 lest *I* deal with you *after* y folly, in that ye NIH
Ps 4: 4 commune with y own heart upon your 3641.1
4: 4 commune with your own heart upon y 3641.1
4: 5 and put y trust in the LORD. NIH
11: 1 to my soul, Flee *as* a bird *to* y mountain? 3641.1
22:26 that seek him: y heart shall live for ever. 3641.1
24: 7 Lift up y heads, O ye gates; and be ye lift 3641.1
24: 9 Lift up y heads, O ye gates; even lift *them* 3641.1
31:24 and he shall strengthen y heart, 3641.1
47: 1 O clap y hands, all ye people; shout unto NIH
58: 2 you weigh the violence of y hands in 3641.1
58: 9 Before y pots can feel the thorns, he shall 3641.1
62: 8 ye people, pour out y heart before him: 3641.1
62:10 riches increase, set not y heart *upon them.* NIH
69:32 and y heart shall live that seek God. 3641.1
75: 5 Lift not up y horn on high: speak *not* with 3641.1
76:11 Vow, and pay unto the LORD y God: 3641.1
78: 1 incline y ears to the words of my mouth. 3641.1
95: 8 Harden not y heart, as *in* the provocation, 3641.1
95: 9 When y fathers tempted me, proved me, 3641.1
105:11 land of Canaan, the lot of y inheritance: 3641.1
115:14 you more and more, you and y children. 3641.1
134: 2 Lift up y hands *in* the sanctuary, and 3641.1
146: 3 Put not y trust in princes, *nor* in the son of NIH
Pr 1:26 I also will laugh at y calamity; I will 3641.1
1:26 I will mock when y fear cometh; 3641.1
1:27 When y fear cometh as desolation, and 3641.1
1:27 and y destruction cometh as a whirlwind; 3641.1
Isa 1: 7 Y country *is* desolate, your cities *are* 3641.1
1: 7 *is* desolate, y cities *are* burnt *with* fire: 3641.1
1: 7 y land, strangers devour it in your 3641.1
1: 7 strangers devour it in y presence, and *it is* 3641.1
1:11 To what purpose *is* the multitude of y 3641.1
1:12 who hath required this at y hand, to tread 3641.1
1:14 Y new moons and your appointed feasts 3641.1
1:14 and y appointed feasts my soul hateth: 3641.1
1:15 when ye spread forth y hands, I will hide 3641.1
1:15 I will not hear: y hands are full *of* blood. 3641.1
1:16 put away the evil of y doings from before 3641.1
1:18 though y sins be as scarlet, they shall be 3641.1
3:14 the spoil of the poor *is* in y houses. 3641.1
8:13 *let* him *be* y fear, and *let* him *be* your 3641.1
8:13 him *be* your fear, and *let* him *be* y dread. 3641.1
10: 3 and where will ye leave y glory? 3641.1
23: 7 *Is* this y joyous *city,* whose 3641.1+3807.1
23:14 of Tarshish: for y strength is laid waste. 3654.1
28:18 y covenant with death shall be 3641.1
28:18 and y agreement with hell shall not stand; 3641.1
28:22 not mockers, lest y bands be made strong: 3641.1
29:10 of deep sleep, and hath closed y eyes: 3641.1
29:10 the prophets and y rulers, the seers hath 3641.1
29:16 Surely y turning *of things* upside down 3641.1
30: 3 strength of Pharaoh be y shame, 3641.1+3807.1
30: 3 the trust in the shadow of Egypt *y* NIH
30:15 and in confidence shall be y strength: 3641.1
31: 7 which y own hands have made unto you 3641.1
32:11 ye bare, and gird *sackcloth* upon *y* loins. NIH
33: 4 y spoil shall be gathered *like* 3641.1
33:11 y breath, *as* fire, shall devour you. 3641.1
35: 4 behold, y God will come *with* vengeance, 3641.1
36:17 take you away to a land like y own land, 3641.1
37: 6 Thus shall ye say unto y master, 3641.1
40: 1 comfort ye my people, saith y God. 3641.1
40: 9 unto the cities of Judah, Behold y God. 3641.1
40:26 Lift up y eyes on high, and behold who 3641.1
41:21 Produce y cause, saith the LORD; 3641.1
41:21 bring forth y strong *reasons,* saith 3641.1
41:24 ye *are* of nothing, and y work of nought: 3641.1
41:26 yea, *there is* none that heareth y words. 3641.1
43:14 y redeemer, the Holy One of Israel; 3641.1
43:14 For y sake I have sent to Babylon, and 3641.1
43:15 I *am* the LORD, y Holy One, the creator 3641.1
43:15 Holy One, the creator of Israel, y King. 3641.1
46: 1 y carriages *were* heavy loaden; *they are* a 3641.1
46: 4 *even* to *y* old age I *am* he; and *even* to hoar NIH
50: 1 Where *is* the bill of y mother's 3641.1
50: 1 for y iniquities have you sold yourselves, 3641.1
50: 1 for y transgressions *is* your mother put 3641.1
50: 1 for your transgressions *is* y mother put 3641.1
50:11 walk in the light of y fire, and in 3641.1
51: 2 Look unto Abraham y father, and 3641.1
51: 6 Lift up y eyes to the heavens, and 3641.1
52:12 and the God of Israel *will be* y rereward. 3641.1
55: 2 y labour for *that which* satisfieth not? 3641.1
55: 2 and let y soul delight itself in fatness. 3641.1
55: 3 Incline y ear, and come unto me: hear, 3641.1
55: 3 hear, and y soul shall live; and I will 3641.1
55: 8 For my thoughts *are* not y thoughts, 3641.1
55: 8 neither *are* y ways my ways, saith 3641.1
55: 9 so are my ways higher than y ways, and 3641.1
55: 9 and my thoughts than y thoughts. 3641.1
58: 3 in the day of y fast you find pleasure, and 3641.1
58: 3 you find pleasure, and exact all y labours. 3641.1
58: 4 to make y voice to be heard on high. 3641.1
59: 2 y iniquities have separated between you 3641.1
59: 2 have separated between you and y God, 3641.1
59: 2 and y sins have hid *his* face from you, 3641.1
59: 3 For y hands are defiled with blood, and 3641.1
59: 3 with blood, and y fingers with iniquity; 3641.1
59: 3 y lips have spoken lies, your tongue hath 3641.1
59: 3 y tongue hath muttered perverseness. 3641.1
61: 5 strangers shall stand and feed y flocks, 3641.1
61: 5 the sons of the alien *shall be* y plowmen 3641.1
61: 5 *be* your plowmen and y vinedressers. 3641.1
61: 7 For y shame *you shall have* double; and 3641.1
65: 7 Y iniquities, and the iniquities of your 3641.1
65: 7 and the iniquities of y fathers together, 3641.1
65:15 ye shall leave y name for a curse unto my 3641.1
66: 5 Y brethren that hated you, that cast you 3641.1
Isa 66: 5 he *shall* appear to y joy, and they shall be 3641.1
66:14 when ye see *this,* y heart shall rejoice, 3641.1
66:14 and y bones shall flourish like an herb: 3641.1
66:20 they shall bring all y brethren *for* an 3641.1
66:22 so shall y seed and your name remain. 3641.1
66:22 so shall your seed and y name remain. 3641.1
Jer 2: 5 What iniquity have y fathers found in me, 3641.1
2: 9 with y children's children will I plead. 3641.1
2:30 In vain have I smitten y children; 3641.1
2:30 y own sword hath devoured your 3641.1
2:30 your own sword hath devoured y 3641.1
3:18 given for an inheritance unto y fathers. 3641.1
3:22 *and* I will heal y backslidings. 3641.1
4: 3 Break up y fallow ground, and 3641.1+3807.1
4: 4 take away the foreskins of y heart, 3641.1
4: 4 quench *it,* because of the evil of y doings. 3641.1
5:19 served strange gods in y land, so shall ye 3641.1
5:25 Y iniquities have turned away these 3641.1
5:25 y sins have withholden good *things* from 3641.1
6:16 and ye shall find rest for y souls. 3641.1
6:20 y burnt offerings *are* not acceptable, 3641.1
6:20 nor y sacrifices sweet unto me. 3641.1
7: 3 Amend y ways and your doings, and 3641.1
7: 3 Amend your ways and y doings, and 3641.1
7: 5 For if you throughly amend y ways and 3641.1
7: 5 throughly amend your ways and y doings; 3641.1
7: 6 walk after other gods to y hurt: 3641.1+3807.1
7: 7 in the land that I gave to y fathers, 3641.1
7:11 become a den of robbers in y eyes? 3641.1
7:14 which I gave to you and to y fathers, 3641.1
7:15 as I have cast out all y brethren, *even* 3641.1
7:21 Put y burnt offerings unto your sacrifices, 3641.1
7:21 Put your burnt offerings unto y sacrifices, 3641.1
7:22 For I spake not unto y fathers, 3641.1
7:23 I will be y God, and ye shall be 3641.1+3807.1
7:25 Since the day that y fathers came forth 3641.1
9:20 let y ear receive the word of his mouth, 3641.1
9:20 teach y daughters wailing, and every one 3641.1
11: 4 Which I commanded y fathers in the day 3641.1
11: 4 my people, and I will be y God: 3641.1+3807.1
11: 5 oath which I have sworn unto y fathers, 3641.1
11: 7 For I earnestly protested unto y fathers in 3641.1
12:13 they shall be ashamed of y revenues 3641.1
13:16 Give glory to the LORD y God, before 3641.1
13:16 before y feet stumble upon the dark 3641.1
13:17 my soul shall weep in secret places for *y* NIH
13:18 for y principalities shall come down, 3641.1
13:18 come down, *even* the crown of y glory 3641.1
13:20 Lift up y eyes, and behold them that 3641.1
16: 9 I will cause to cease out of this place in y 3641.1
16: 9 in y days, the voice of mirth, and 3641.1
16:11 Because y fathers have forsaken me, 3641.1
16:12 ye have done worse than y fathers; 3641.1
16:13 that ye know not, *neither* ye nor y fathers; 3641.1
17: 1 their heart, and upon the horns of y altars; 3641.1
17:22 Neither carry forth a burden out of y 3641.1
17:22 sabbath day, as I commanded y fathers. 3641.1
18:11 and make y ways and your doings good. 3641.1
18:11 and make your ways and y doings good. 3641.1
21: 4 the weapons of war that *are* in y hands, 3641.1
21:12 quench *it,* because of the evil of y doings. 3641.1
21:14 you according to the fruit of y doings, 3641.1
23: 2 I will visit upon you the evil of y doings, 3641.1
23:39 the city that I gave you and y fathers, *and* 3641.1
25: 4 not hearkened, nor inclined y ear to hear. 3641.1
25: 5 from the evil of y doings, and dwell in 3641.1
25: 5 and to y fathers for ever and ever: 3641.1
25: 6 not to anger with the works of y hands; 3641.1
25: 7 the works of y hands to your own hurt. 3641.1
25: 7 the works of your hands to y own hurt. 3641.1
25:34 for the days of y slaughter and of your 3641.1
25:34 and of y dispersions are accomplished. 3641.1
26:11 this city, as ye have heard with y ears. 3641.1
26:13 Therefore now amend y ways and 3641.1
26:13 now amend your ways and y doings, 3641.1
26:13 and obey the voice of the LORD y God; 3641.1
26:14 As for me, behold, I *am* in y hand: 3641.1
26:15 you to speak all these words in y ears. 3641.1
27: 4 Thus shall ye say unto y masters; 3641.1
27: 9 Therefore hearken not ye to y prophets, 3641.1
27: 9 nor to y diviners, nor to your dreamers, 3641.1
27: 9 nor to your diviners, nor to y dreamers, 3641.1
27: 9 nor to y enchanters, nor to your sorcerers, 3641.1
27: 9 nor to y sorcerers, which speak unto you, 3641.1
27:10 unto you, to remove you far from y land; 3641.1
27:12 Bring y necks under the yoke of the king 3641.1
27:16 Hearken not to the words of y prophets 3641.1
29: 6 take wives for y sons, and give your 3641.1
29: 6 give y daughters to husbands, that they 3641.1
29: 8 Let not y prophets and your diviners, 3641.1
29: 8 Let not your prophets and y diviners, 3641.1
29: 8 neither hearken to y dreams which ye 3641.1
29:13 ye shall search for me with all y heart. 3641.1
29:14 I will turn away y captivity, and I will 3641.1
29:16 *of* y brethren that are not gone forth with 3641.1
29:21 and he shall slay them before y eyes; 3641.1
30:22 my people, and I will be y God. 3641.1+3807.1
34:13 I made a covenant with y fathers in 3641.1
34:14 y fathers hearkened not unto me, 3641.1
35: 6 no wine, *neither* ye, nor y sons for ever: 3641.1
35: 7 but all y days ye shall dwell in tents; 3641.1
35:15 amend y doings, and go not after other 3641.1
35:15 I have given to you and to y fathers: 3641.1
35:15 ye have not inclined y ear, nor hearkened 3641.1
35:18 the commandment of Jonadab y father, 3641.1
37:19 Where *are* now y prophets which 3641.1
38: 5 the king said, Behold, he *is* in y hand: 3641.1
40:10 oil, and put *them* in y vessels, and 3641.1
40:10 and dwell in y cities that ye have taken. 3641.1
42: 4 I *will* pray unto the LORD y God 3641.1
42: 4 LORD your God according to y words; 3641.1
42: 9 unto whom ye sent me to present y 3641.1
42:12 and cause you to return to y own land. 3641.1
42:13 neither obey the voice of the LORD y 3641.1
42:15 If ye wholly set y faces to enter *into* 3641.1
Jer 42:20 For ye dissembled in y hearts, when ye 3641.1
42:20 when ye sent me unto the LORD y God, 3641.1
42:21 obeyed the voice of the LORD y God, 3641.1
44: 3 knew not, *neither* they, you, nor y fathers. 3641.1
44: 7 commit ye *this* great evil against y souls, 3641.1
44: 8 me unto wrath with the works of y hands, 3641.1
44: 9 Have ye forgotten the wickedness of y 3641.1
44: 9 y own wickedness, and the wickedness of 3641.1
44: 9 and the wickedness of y wives, 3641.1
44:10 that I set before you and before y fathers. 3641.1
44:21 ye, and y fathers, your kings, and 3641.1
44:21 y kings, and your princes, and the people 3641.1
44:21 and y princes, and the people of the land, 3641.1
44:22 because of the evil of y doings, *and* 3641.1
44:22 therefore is y land a desolation, and an 3641.1
44:25 y wives have both spoken with your 3641.1
44:25 your wives have both spoken with y 3641.1
44:25 and fulfilled with y hand, saying, 3641.1
44:25 ye will surely accomplish y vows, and 3641.1
44:25 your vows, and surely perform y vows. 3641.1
46: 4 and stand forth with *y* helmets; NIH
48: 6 save y lives, and be like the heath in 3641.1
50:12 Y mother shall be sore confounded; 3641.1
51:24 that they have done in Zion in y sight, 3641.1
51:46 lest y heart faint, and ye fear for 3641.1
51:50 and let Jerusalem come into y mind. 3641.1
Eze 5:16 and will break y staff of bread: 3641.1+3807.1
6: 3 and I will destroy y high places. 3641.1
6: 4 y altars shall be desolate, and 3641.1
6: 4 and y images shall be broken: 3641.1
6: 4 I will cast down y slain *men* before your 3641.1
6: 4 I will cast down your slain *men* before y 3641.1
6: 5 I will scatter y bones round about your 3641.1
6: 5 I will scatter your bones round about y 3641.1
6: 6 In all y dwelling places the cities shall be 3641.1
6: 6 that y altars may be laid waste and 3641.1
6: 6 y idols may be broken and cease, and 3641.1
6: 6 y images may be cut down, and 3641.1
6: 6 cut down, and y works may be abolished. 3641.1
9: 5 let not y eye spare, neither have ye pity: 3641.1
11: 5 for I know the things that come into y 3641.1
11: 6 Ye have multiplied y slain in this city, 3641.1
11: 7 Y slain whom ye have laid in the midst of 3641.1
11:11 This *city* shall not be y caldron, 3641.1+3807.1
12:11 Say, I *am* y sign: like as I have done, so 3641.1
12:25 for in y days, O rebellious house, will I 3641.1
13:19 y lying to my people that hear *your* lies? 3641.1
13:19 by your lying to my people that hear *y* lies? NIH
13:20 Behold, I *am* against y pillows, 3654.1
13:20 I will tear them from y arms, and will let 3641.1
13:21 Y kerchiefs also will I tear, and 3641.1
13:21 deliver my people out of y hand, and 3654.1
13:21 they shall be no more in y hand to be 3654.1
13:23 for I will deliver my people out of y 3654.1
14: 6 Repent, and turn *yourselves* from y idols; 3641.1
14: 6 turn away y faces from all your 3641.1
14: 6 turn away your faces from all y 3641.1
16:45 y mother *was* a Hittite, and your father an 3654.1
16:45 *was* a Hittite, and y father an Amorite. 3654.1
16:55 thy daughters shall return to y former 3654.1
18:25 my way equal? are not y ways unequal? 3641.1
18:29 my ways equal? are not y ways unequal? 3641.1
18:30 turn *yourselves* from all y transgressions; 3641.1
18:30 so iniquity shall not be y ruin. 3641.1+3807.1
18:31 Cast away from you all y transgressions, 3641.1
20: 5 saying, I *am* the LORD y God; 3641.1
20: 7 idols of Egypt: I *am* the LORD y God. 3641.1
20:18 Walk ye not in the statutes of y fathers, 3641.1
20:19 I *am* the LORD y God; walk in my 3641.1
20:20 that *ye* may know that I *am* the LORD y 3641.1
20:27 Yet *in* this y fathers have blasphemed me, 3641.1
20:30 Are ye polluted after the manner of y 3641.1
20:31 For when *ye* offer y gifts, when *ye* make 3641.1
20:31 when *ye* make y sons to pass through 3641.1
20:31 ye pollute yourselves with all y idols, 3641.1
20:32 that which cometh into y mind shall not 3641.1
20:36 Like as I pleaded with y fathers in 3641.1
20:39 pollute ye my holy name no more with y 3641.1
20:39 no more with your gifts, and with y idols. 3641.1
20:40 there will I require y offerings, and 3641.1
20:40 the firstfruits of y oblations, with all your 3641.1
20:40 of your oblations, with all y holy *things.* 3641.1
20:41 I will accept you with *y* sweet savour, NIH
20:42 lifted up mine hand to give it to y fathers. 3641.1
20:43 there shall ye remember y ways, and all 3641.1
20:43 all y doings, wherein ye have been 3641.1
20:43 ye shall lothe yourselves in y own sight 3641.1
20:43 for all y evils that ye have committed. 3641.1
20:44 not according to y wicked ways, 3641.1
20:44 nor according to y corrupt doings, O ye 3641.1
21:24 Because ye have made y iniquity to be 3641.1
21:24 in that y transgressions are discovered, so 3641.1
21:24 that in all y doings your sins do appear; 3641.1
21:24 that in all your doings y sins do appear; 3641.1
23:48 may be taught not to do after y lewdness. 3654.1
23:49 they shall recompense y lewdness upon 3654.1
23:49 and ye shall bear the sins of y idols: 3654.1
24:21 the excellency of y strength, the desire of 3641.1
24:21 the desire of y eyes, and that which your 3641.1
24:21 your eyes, and that which y soul pitieth; 3641.1
24:21 y sons and your daughters whom ye have 3641.1
24:21 y daughters whom ye have left shall fall 3641.1
24:22 ye shall not cover *y* lips, nor eat the bread of NIH
24:23 y tires *shall be* upon your heads, and 3641.1
24:23 your tires *shall be* upon y heads, and 3641.1
24:23 your heads, and y shoes upon your feet: 3641.1
24:23 your heads, and your shoes upon y feet: 3641.1
24:23 ye shall pine away for y iniquities, and 3641.1
33:11 turn ye, turn ye from y evil ways; for why 3641.1
33:25 lift up y eyes toward your idols, and 3641.1
33:25 lift up your eyes toward y idols, and 3641.1
33:26 Ye stand upon y sword, ye work 3641.1
34:18 ye must tread down with y feet 3641.1
34:18 ye must foul the residue of y pastures? 3641.1
34:18 but ye must foul the residue with y feet? 3641.1

Eze 34:19 that which ye have trodden with y feet; 3641.1
34:19 that which ye have fouled with y feet. 3641.1
34:21 and pushed all the diseased with y horns, 3641.1
34:31 *are* men, *and* I *am* y God, saith the Lord 3641.1
35:13 Thus with y mouth ye have boasted 3641.1
35:13 and have multiplied y words against me: 3641.1
36: 8 ye shall shoot forth y branches, and 3641.1
36: 8 and yield y fruit to my people of Israel; 3641.1
36:11 I will settle you after y old estates, and 3641.1
36:11 will do better *unto you* than at y 3641.1
36:22 I do not *this* for y sakes, O house of 3641.1
36:24 and will bring you into y own land. 3641.1
36:25 from all y filthiness, and from all your 3641.1
36:25 and from all y idols, will I cleanse you. 3641.1
36:26 I will take away the stony heart out of y 3641.1
36:28 ye shall dwell in the land that I gave to y 3641.1
36:28 my people, and I will be y God. 3641.1+3807.1
36:29 I will also save you from all y 3641.1
36:31 shall ye remember y own evil ways, and 3641.1
36:31 y doings that *were* not good, and 3641.1
36:31 shall lothe yourselves in y own sight for 3641.1
36:31 in your own sight for y iniquities 3641.1
36:31 your iniquities and for y abominations. 3641.1
36:32 Not for y sakes do I *this*, saith the Lord 3641.1
36:32 and confounded for y own ways, 3641.1
36:33 have cleansed you from all y iniquities, 3641.1
37:12 I *will* open y graves, and cause you to 3641.1
37:12 cause you to come up out of y graves, and 3641.1
37:13 when I have opened y graves, O my 3641.1
37:13 and brought you up out of y graves, 3641.1
37:14 and I shall place you in y own land: 3641.1
37:25 my servant, wherein y fathers have dwelt; 3641.1
43:27 the priests shall make y burnt offerings 3641.1
43:27 upon the altar, and y peace offerings; 3641.1
44: 6 let it suffice you of all y abominations, 3641.1
44: 7 because of all y abominations. 3641.1
44:30 of every *sort* of y oblations, shall be 3641.1
44:30 give unto the priest the first of y dough, 3641.1
45: 9 take away y exactions from my people, 3641.1
45:12 fifteen shekels, shall be y maneh. 3641.1+3807.1
47:14 up mine hand to give it unto y fathers: 3641.1
Da 1:10 hath appointed y meat and your drink: 3641.1
1:10 hath appointed your meat and y drink: 3641.1
1:10 for why should he see y faces worse 3641.1
1:10 than the children which *are* of y sort? 3641.1
2: 5 and y houses shall be made a dunghill. 3561.1
2:47 Of a truth *it is*, that y God *is* a God of 3561.1
10:21 me in these *things*, but Michael y prince. 3641.1
Hos 1: 9 and I will not be y *God*. 3641.1+3807.1
2: 1 Say ye unto y brethren, Ammi; and 3641.1
2: 1 Ammi; and to y sisters, Ruhamah. 3641.1
2: 2 Plead with y mother, plead: for she *is* not 3641.1
4:13 y daughters shall commit whoredom, 3641.1
4:13 and y spouses shall commit adultery. 3641.1
4:14 I will not punish y daughters when they 3641.1
4:14 y spouses when they commit adultery: 3641.1
5:13 he not heal you nor cure you of y wound. 3641.1
6: 4 for y goodness *is* as a morning cloud, and 3641.1
9:10 I saw y fathers as the firstripe in the fig 3641.1
10:12 break up y fallow ground: 3641.1+3807.1
10:15 unto you because of y great wickedness; 3641.1
Joel 1: 2 Hath this been in y days, or even in 3641.1
1: 2 or even in the days of y fathers? 3641.1
1: 3 Tell ye y children of it, and *let* your 3641.1
1: 3 *let* y children *tell* their children, and 3641.1
1: 5 new wine, for it is cut off from y mouth. 3641.1
1:13 is withholden from the house of y God. 3641.1
1:14 land *into* the house of the LORD y God, 3641.1
2:12 turn ye *even* to me with all y heart, and 3641.1
2:13 rent y heart, and not your garments, and 3641.1
2:13 not y garments, and turn unto the LORD 3641.1
2:13 and turn unto the LORD y God: 3641.1
2:14 a drink offering unto the LORD y God? 3641.1
2:23 and rejoice in the LORD y God: 3641.1
2:26 praise the name of the LORD y God, 3641.1
2:27 *that* I *am* the LORD y God, and 3641.1
2:28 y sons and your daughters shall prophesy, 3641.1
2:28 your sons and y daughters shall prophesy, 3641.1
2:28 y old men shall dream dreams, 3641.1
2:28 y young men shall see visions: 3641.1
3: 4 speedily will I return y recompence upon 3641.1
3: 4 your recompence upon y own head; 3641.1
3: 5 have carried into y temples my goodly 3641.1
3: 7 will return y recompence upon your own 3641.1
3: 7 will return your recompence upon y own 3641.1
3: 8 I will sell y sons and your daughters into 3641.1
3: 8 y daughters into the hand of the children 3641.1
3:10 Beat y plowshares into swords, and 3641.1
3:10 and y pruninghooks into spears: 3641.1
3:17 So shall ye know that I *am* the LORD y 3641.1
Am 2:11 I raised up of y sons for prophets, and 3641.1
2:11 and of y young men for Nazarites. 3641.1
3: 2 I will punish you for all y iniquities. 3641.1
4: 2 and y posterity with fishhooks. 3654.1
4: 4 bring y sacrifices *every* morning, *and* 3641.1
4: 4 *and* y tithes after three years: 3641.1
4: 6 you cleanness of teeth in all y cities, 3641.1
4: 6 and want of bread in all y places: 3641.1
4: 9 when y gardens and your vineyards and 3641.1
4: 9 and y vineyards and your fig trees and 3641.1
4: 9 and your vineyards and y fig trees and 3641.1
4: 9 your fig trees and y olive trees increased, 3641.1
4:10 y young men have I slain with the sword, 3641.1
4:10 the sword, and have taken away y horses; 3641.1
4:10 I have made the stink of y camps to come 3641.1
4:10 of your camps to come up unto y nostrils: 3641.1
5:11 as y treading *is* upon the poor, 3641.1
5:12 For I know y manifold transgressions and 3641.1
5:12 and y mighty sins: 3641.1
5:21 I despise y feast *days*, and I will not smell 3641.1
5:21 I will not smell in y solemn assemblies. 3641.1
5:22 me burnt offerings and y meat offerings, 3641.1
5:22 regard the peace offerings of y fat beasts. 3641.1
5:26 ye have borne the tabernacle of y Moloch 3641.1
5:26 of your Moloch and Chiun y images, 3641.1
Am 5:26 and Chiun your images, the star of y god, 3641.1
6: 2 or their border greater than y border? 3641.1
8:10 I will turn y feasts into mourning, and 3641.1
8:10 and all y songs into lamentation; 3641.1
Mic 2: 3 from which ye shall not remove y necks; 3641.1
2:10 Arise ye, and depart; for this *is* not y rest: NIH
3:12 Therefore shall Zion for y sake be plowed 3641.1
Hab 1: 5 for *I will* work a work in y days, 3641.1
Zep 3:20 when I turn back y captivity before your 3641.1
3:20 when I turn back your captivity before y 3641.1
Hag 1: 4 to dwell in y cieled houses, and this 3641.1
1: 5 the LORD of hosts; Consider y ways. 3641.1
1: 7 the LORD of hosts; Consider y ways. 3641.1
2: 3 *is it* not in y eyes in comparison of it as 3641.1
2:17 with hail *in* all the labours of y hands; 3641.1
Zec 1: 2 hath been sore displeased with y fathers. 3641.1
1: 4 Be ye not as y fathers, unto whom 3641.1
1: 4 Turn ye now from y evil ways, and 3641.1
1: 4 your evil ways, and *from* y evil doings: 3641.1
1: 5 Y fathers, where *are* they? and 3641.1
1: 6 did they not take hold of y fathers? 3641.1
6:15 obey the voice of the LORD y God. 3641.1
7:10 evil against his brother in y heart. 3641.1
8: 9 Let y hands be strong, ye that hear in 3641.1
8:13 fear not, *but* let y hands be strong. 3641.1
8:14 when y fathers provoked me to wrath, 3641.1
8:16 judgment of truth and peace in y gates: 3641.1
8:17 let none of you imagine evil in y hearts 3641.1
Mal 1: 5 y eyes shall see, and ye shall say, 3641.1
1: 9 this hath been by y means: will he regard 3641.1
1: 9 will he regard y persons? saith 3641.1
1:10 neither will I accept an offering at y hand. 3641.1
1:13 should I accept this of y hand? saith 3641.1
2: 2 upon you, and will curse y blessings: 3641.1
2: 3 I *will* corrupt y[S] seed, and spread dung 1886.1
2: 3 your seed, and spread dung upon y faces, 3641.1
2: 3 *even* the dung of y solemn feasts; 3641.1
2:13 or receiveth *it with* good will at y hand. 3641.1
2:15 Therefore take heed to y spirit, and 3641.1
2:16 therefore take heed to y spirit, that ye 3641.1
2:17 Ye have wearied the LORD with y 3641.1
3: 7 Even from the days of y fathers ye are 3641.1
3:11 I will rebuke the devourer for y sakes, 3641.1
3:11 he shall not destroy the fruits of y ground; 3641.1
3:11 neither shall y vine cast her fruit 3641.1+3807.1
3:13 Y words have been stout against me, 3641.1
4: 3 y feet in the day that I *shall* do *this*, saith 3641.1
Mt 5:12 for great *is* y reward in heaven: for so *4771*
5:16 Let y light so shine before men, that they *4771*
5:16 that they may see y good works, and *4771*
5:16 and glorify y Father which is in heaven. *4771*
5:20 That except y righteousness shall exceed *4771*
5:37 But let y communication be, Yea, yea; Nay, *4771*
5:44 But I say unto you, Love y enemies, *4771*
5:45 That ye may be the children of y Father *4771*
5:47 And if ye salute y brethren only, what do *4771*
5:48 even as y Father which is in heaven is *4771*
6: 1 Take heed that *ye* do not y alms before *4771*
6: 1 otherwise ye have no reward of y Father *4771*
6: 8 for y Father knoweth what *things* ye have *4771*
6:14 y heavenly Father will also forgive you: *4771*
6:15 neither will y Father forgive your *4771*
6:15 neither will your Father forgive y *4771*
6:21 For where y treasure is, there will your *4771*
6:21 your treasure is, there will y heart be also. *4771*
6:25 Take no thought for y life, what ye shall *4771*
6:25 nor yet for y body, what ye shall put on. *4771*
6:26 yet y heavenly Father feedeth them. *4771*
6:32 for y heavenly Father knoweth that ye *4771*
7: 6 neither cast ye y pearls before swine, *4771*
7:11 know how to give good gifts unto y *4771*
7:11 how much more shall y Father which is in *4771*
9: 4 Wherefore think ye evil in y hearts? *4771*
9:11 Why eateth y Master with publicans and *4771*
9:29 saying, According to y faith be it unto you. *4771*
10: 9 nor silver, nor brass in y purses; *4771*
10:10 Nor scrip for y journey, neither two coats, NIG
10:13 house be worthy, let y peace come upon it: *4771*
10:13 it be not worthy, let y peace return to you. *4771*
10:14 nor hear y words, when ye depart out of *4771*
10:14 or city, shake off the dust of y feet. *4771*
10:20 the Spirit of y Father which speaketh in *4771*
10:29 not fall on the ground without y Father. *4771*
10:30 But the very hairs of y head are all *4771*
11:29 in heart: and ye shall find rest unto y souls. *4771*
12:27 by whom do y children cast *them* out? *4771*
12:27 *them* out? therefore they shall be y judges. *4771*
13:16 But blessed *are* y eyes, for they see: and *4771*
13:16 for they see: and y ears, for they hear. *4771*
15: 3 the commandment of God by y tradition? *4771*
15: 6 of God of none effect by y tradition. *4771*
17:20 said unto them, Because of y unbelief: *4771*
17:24 and said, Doth not y master pay tribute? *4771*
18:14 it is not the will of y Father which is in *4771*
18:35 if ye from y hearts forgive not every one *4771*
19: 8 of the hardness of y hearts suffered you to *4771*
19: 8 hearts suffered you to put away y wives: *4771*
20:26 be great among you, let him be y minister; *4771*
20:27 be chief among you, let him be y servant: *4771*
23: 8 for one is y Master, *even* Christ; *4771*
23: 9 And call no *man* y father upon the earth: *4771*
23: 9 for one is y Father, which is in heaven. *4771*
23:10 for one is y Master, *even* Christ. *4771*
23:11 But he that is greatest among you shall be y *4771*
23:32 Fill ye up then the measure of y fathers. *4771*
23:34 *some* of them shall ye scourge in y *4771*
23:38 Behold, y house is left unto you desolate. *4771*
24:20 But pray ye that y flight be not in *4771*
24:42 for ye know not what hour y Lord doth *4771*
25: 8 foolish said unto the wise, Give us of y oil; *4771*
26:45 unto them, Sleep on now, and take y rest: NIG
27:65 go y way, make *it* as sure as you can. NIG
Mk 2: 8 Why reason ye these *things* in y hearts? *4771*
6:11 shake off the dust under y feet for a *4771*
7: 9 of God, that ye may keep y own tradition. *4771*
Mk 7:13 of God of none effect through y tradition, *4771*
8:17 have ye y heart yet hardened? *4771*
10: 5 For the hardness of y heart he wrote you *4771*
10:43 be great among you, shall be y minister: *4771*
11: 2 Go y way into the village over against you: NIG
11:25 that y Father also which is in heaven may *4771*
11:25 is in heaven may forgive you y trespasses. *4771*
11:26 neither will y Father which is in heaven *4771*
11:26 which is in heaven forgive y trespasses. *4771*
13:18 And pray ye that y flight be not in *4771*
14:41 unto them, Sleep on now, and take y rest: NIG
16: 7 But go y way, tell his disciples and Peter NIG
Lk 3:14 *any* falsely; and be content with y wages. *4771*
4:21 This day is this scripture fulfilled in y ears. *4771*
5: 4 the deep, and let down y nets for a draught. *4771*
5:22 said unto them, What reason ye in y hearts? *4771*
6:22 reproach *you*, and cast out y name as evil, *4771*
6:23 *joy:* for behold, y reward *is* great in heaven: *4771*
6:24 are rich: for ye have received y consolation. *4771*
6:27 I say unto you which hear, Love y enemies, *4771*
6:35 But love ye y enemies, and do good, and *4771*
6:35 and y reward shall be great, and ye shall be *4771*
6:36 merciful, as y Father also is merciful. *4771*
6:38 running over, shall *men* give into y bosom. *4771*
7:22 Go y *way*, and tell John what *things* ye have NIG
8:25 And he said unto them, Where is y faith? *4771*
9: 3 Take nothing for y journey, neither staves, NIG
9: 5 shake off the very dust from y feet for a *4771*
9:44 Let these sayings sink down into y ears: *4771*
10: 3 Go y ways: behold, I send you forth as NIG
10: 6 of peace be there, y peace shall rest upon it: *4771*
10:10 go y *ways* out into the streets of the same, NIG
10:11 Even the *very* dust of y city, which cleaveth *4771*
10:20 because y names are written in heaven. *4771*
11:13 know how to give good gifts unto y *4771*
11:13 how much more shall y heavenly Father NIG
11:19 by whom do y sons cast *them* out? *4771*
11:19 *them* out? therefore shall they be y judges. *4771*
11:39 but y inward part is full of ravening and *4771*
11:46 touch not the burdens with one of y fingers. *4771*
11:47 of the prophets, and y fathers killed them. *4771*
11:48 witness that ye allow the deeds of y fathers: *4771*
12: 7 But even the *very* hairs of y head are all *4771*
12:22 Take no thought for y life, what ye shall *4771*
12:30 y Father knoweth that ye have need of *4771*
12:32 for it is y Father's good pleasure to give *4771*
12:34 For where y treasure is, there will your *4771*
12:34 your treasure is, there will y heart be also. *4771*
12:35 Let y loins be girded about, and *your* lights *4771*
12:35 loins be girded about, and y lights burning; NIG
13:35 Behold, y house is left unto you desolate: *4771*
16:11 who will commit to y trust the true *riches?* *4771*
16:12 who shall give you that which is y own? *5212*
16:15 before men; but God knoweth y hearts: *4771*
19:30 which at y entering ye shall find a colt tied, NIG
21:14 Settle *it* therefore in y hearts, not to *4771*
21:15 which all y adversaries shall not be able to *4771*
21:18 But there shall not a hair of y head perish. *4771*
21:19 In y patience possess ye your souls. *4771*
21:19 In your patience possess ye y souls. *4771*
21:28 to pass, *then* look up, and lift up y heads; *4771*
21:28 your heads; for y redemption draweth nigh. *4771*
21:30 know of y own selves that summer is now *1438*
21:34 lest at any time y hearts be overcharged *4771*
22:53 but this is y hour, and the power of *4771*
23:28 but weep for yourselves, and for y children. *4771*
24:38 and why do thoughts arise in y hearts? *4771*
Jn 4:35 Lift up y eyes, and look on the fields; *4771*
6:49 Y fathers did eat manna in the wilderness, *4771*
6:58 not as y fathers did eat manna, and *4771*
7: 6 is not yet come: but y time is alway ready. *5212*
8:17 It is also written in y law, that *5212*
8:21 ye shall seek me, and shall die in y sins: *4771*
8:24 unto you, that ye shall die in y sins: *4771*
8:24 not that I am *he*, ye shall die in y sins. *4771*
8:38 ye do *that* which ye have seen with y *4771*
8:41 Ye do the deeds of y father. Then said they *4771*
8:42 If God were y Father, ye would love me: *4771*
8:44 Ye are of y father the devil, and the lusts of NIG
8:44 and the lusts of y father ye will do. *4771*
8:54 of whom ye say, that he is y God: *4771*
8:56 Y father Abraham rejoiced to see my day: *4771*
9:19 And they asked them, saying, Is this y son, *4771*
9:41 ye say, We see; therefore y sin remaineth. *4771*
10:34 Is it not written in y law, I said, Ye are *4771*
11:15 And I am glad for y sakes that I was not *4771*
12:30 came not because of me, but for y sakes. *4771*
13:14 If I then, y Lord and Master, have washed NIG
13:14 *your* Lord and Master, have washed y feet; *4771*
14: 1 Let not y heart be troubled: ye believe in *4771*
14:26 and bring all *things* to y remembrance, *4771*
14:27 Let not y heart be troubled, neither let it be *4771*
15:11 remain in you, and *that* y joy might be full. *4771*
15:16 forth fruit, and *that* y fruit should remain: *4771*
16: 6 *things* unto you, sorrow hath filled y heart. *4771*
16:20 but y sorrow shall be turned into joy. *4771*
16:22 and y heart shall rejoice, and your joy no *4771*
16:22 and y joy no *man* taketh from you. *4771*
16:24 and ye shall receive, that y joy may be full. *4771*
18:31 ye him, and judge him according to y law. *4771*
19:14 and he saith unto the Jews, Behold y King. *4771*
19:15 saith unto them, Shall I crucify y King? *4771*
20:17 I ascend unto my Father, and y Father; *4771*
20:17 your Father; and *to* my God, and y God. *4771*
Ac 2:17 and y sons and your daughters shall *4771*
2:17 your sons and y daughters shall prophesy, *4771*
2:17 and y young men shall see visions, and *4771*
2:17 and y old men shall dream dreams: *4771*
2:39 and to y children, and to all that are afar *4771*
3:17 ignorance ye did *it*, as *did* also y rulers. *4771*
3:19 that y sins may be blotted out, *4771*
3:22 A prophet shall the Lord y God raise up *4771*
3:22 your God raise up unto you of y brethren, *4771*
5:28 ye have filled Jerusalem with y doctrine, *4771*
7:37 A prophet shall the Lord y God raise up *4771*

Y

Ac 7:37 your God raise up unto you of **y** brethren, 4771
7:43 of Moloch, and the star of **y** god Remphan, 4771
7:51 the Holy Ghost: as **y** fathers *did,* so *do* ye. 4771
7:52 Which of the prophets have not **y** fathers 4771
13:41 for I work a work in **y** days, a work which 4771
15:24 subverting **y** souls, saying, *Ye must be* 4771
17:23 For as I passed by, and beheld **y** devotions, 4771
17:28 as certain also of **y own** poets have 2596+4771
18: 6 **Y** blood *be* upon your own heads; 4771
18: 6 Your blood *be* upon **y own** heads; 4771
18:15 of words and names, and *of* **y** law, 2596+4771
19:37 nor yet blasphemers of **y** goddess. 4771
20:30 Also of **y** own selves shall men arise, 4771
24:22 I will know the uttermost of **y** matter. 4771
27:34 for this is for **y** health: for there shall not a 5212
Ro 1: 8 that **y** faith is spoken of throughout 4771
6:12 Let not sin therefore reign in **y** mortal body, 4771
6:13 Neither yield ye **y** members *as* instruments 4771
6:13 **y** members *as* instruments of righteousness 4771
6:19 of men because of the infirmity of **y** flesh: 4771
6:19 for as ye have yielded **y** members servants 4771
6:19 now yield **y** members servants to 4771
6:22 ye have **y** fruit unto holiness, and the end 4771
8:11 **y** mortal bodies by his Spirit that dwelleth 4771
11:25 lest ye should be wise in **y own** conceits; 1438
11:28 the gospel, *they are* enemies for **y** sakes: 4771
11:31 that through **y** mercy they also may obtain 5212
12: 1 that *ye* present **y** bodies a living sacrifice, 4771
12: 1 unto God, *which is* **y** reasonable service. 4771
12: 2 be ye transformed by the renewing of **y** 4771
12:16 low estate. Be not wise in **y own** conceits. 1438
14:16 Let not then **y** good be evil spoken of: 4771
15:24 if first I be somewhat filled with **y** 4771
15:30 that *ye* strive together with me in *y* prayers NIG
16:19 For **y** obedience is come abroad unto all 4771
16:19 all *men.* I am glad therefore on **y** behalf: 4771
16:20 shall bruise Satan under **y** feet shortly. 4771
1Co 1: 4 I thank my God always on **y** behalf, for 4771
1:26 For ye see **y** calling, brethren, how that not 4771
2: 5 That **y** faith should not stand in the wisdom 4771
4: 6 to myself and *to* Apollos for **y** sakes; 4771
5: 6 **Y** glorying *is* not good. Know ye not that a 4771
6: 5 I speak to **y** shame. Is it so, that there is not 4771
6: 8 do wrong, and defraud, and that *y* brethren. NIG
6:15 Know ye not that **y** bodies are the members 4771
6:19 know ye not that **y** body is the temple of 4771
6:19 ye have of God, and ye are not **y own**? 1438
6:20 therefore glorify God in **y** body, and 4771
6:20 your body, and in **y** spirit, which are God's. 4771
7: 5 that Satan tempt you not for **y** 4771
7:14 else were **y** children unclean; but now are 4771
7:35 And this I speak for **y** own profit; not that I 4771
9:11 great *thing* if we shall reap **y** carnal *things?* 4771
14:34 Let **y** women keep silence in the churches: 4771
15:14 our preaching vain, and **y** faith *is* also vain. 4771
15:17 And if Christ be not raised, **y** faith *is* vain; 4771
15:17 your faith *is* vain; ye are yet in **y** sins. 4771
15:31 I protest by **y** rejoicing which I have in 5212
15:34 knowledge of God: I speak *this* to **y** shame. 4771
15:58 forasmuch as ye know that **y** labour is not 4771
16: 3 whomsoever ye shall approve by *y* letters, NIG
16: 3 them will I send to bring **y** liberality unto 4771
16:14 Let all **y** *things* be done with charity. 4771
16:17 for that which was lacking **on y part** they 4771
2Co 1: 6 *it is* for **y** consolation and salvation, 4771
1: 6 *it is* for **y** consolation and salvation. 4771
1:14 us in part, that we are **y** rejoicing, 4771
1:24 Not for that we have dominion over **y** faith, 4771
1:24 over your faith, but are helpers of **y** joy: 4771
2: 8 that *you* would confirm *y* love towards him. NIG
2:10 **y** sakes *forgave I it* in the person of Christ; 4771
4: 5 and ourselves **y** servants for Jesus' sake. 4771
4:15 For all *things are* for **y** sakes, that 4771
5:11 I trust also are made manifest in **y** 4771
5:13 or whether we be sober, *it is* for **y** cause. 4771
6:12 but ye are straitened in **y own** bowels. 4771
7: 7 when he told us **y** earnest desire, your 4771
7: 7 **y** mourning, your fervent mind toward me; 4771
7: 7 your mourning, **y** fervent mind toward me; 4771
7:13 Therefore we were comforted in **y** comfort: 4771
8: 7 *in* all diligence, and *in* **y** love to us, 1537+4771
8: 8 and to prove the sincerity of **y** love. 5212
8: 9 was rich, *yet* for **y** sakes he became poor, 4771
8:14 *that* now at *this* time **y** abundance *may be a* 4771
8:14 abundance also may be *a supply* for **y** want: 4771
8:19 and *declaration of* **y** ready mind: 4771
8:24 the proof of **y** love, and of our boasting on 4771
8:24 your love, and of our boasting on **y** behalf. 4771
9: 2 For I know the forwardness of **y** mind, 4771
9: 2 and **y** zeal hath provoked very many. 4771
9: 5 and make up beforehand **y** bounty, 4771
9:10 to the sower both minister bread for *y* food, NIG
9:10 and multiply **y** seed sown, and increase 4771
9:10 and increase the fruits of **y** righteousness;) 4771
9:13 **y** professed subjection unto the gospel of 4771
9:13 and *for y* liberal distribution unto them, and NIG
10: 6 when **y** obedience is fulfilled. 4771
10: 8 and not for **y** destruction, I should not be 4771
10:15 but having hope, when **y** faith is increased, 4771
11: 3 **y** minds should be corrupted from 4771
12:19 all *things,* dearly beloved, for **y** edifying. 4771
13: 5 ye be in the faith; prove **y own selves**. 1438
13: 5 Know ye not **y own selves**, how that Jesus 1438
13: 9 and this also we wish, *even* **y** perfection. 4771
Gal 4: 6 sent forth the Spirit of his Son into **y** hearts, 4771
4:15 ye would have plucked out **y own** eyes, and 4771
4:16 Am I therefore become **y** enemy, because 4771
6:13 that they may glory in **y** flesh. 5212
6:18 the grace of our Lord Jesus Christ *be* with **y** 4771
Eph 1:13 the word of truth, the gospel of **y** salvation: 4771
1:15 after I heard of **y** faith in the Lord Jesus, 4771
1:18 The eyes of **y** understanding being 4771
3:13 at my tribulations for you, which is **y** glory. 4771
3:17 That Christ may dwell in **y** hearts by faith; 4771
4: 4 even as ye are called in one hope of **y** 4771
Eph 4:23 And be renewed in the spirit of **y** mind; 4771
4:26 let not the sun go down upon **y** wrath: 4771
4:29 communication proceed out of **y** mouth, 4771
5:19 and making melody in **y** heart to the Lord; 4771
5:22 submit yourselves unto **y own** husbands, 2398
5:25 Husbands, love **y** wives, even as Christ also 1438
6: 1 Children, obey **y** parents in the Lord: 4771
6: 4 ye fathers, provoke not **y** children to wrath: 4771
6: 5 be obedient to *them that are y* masters NIG
6: 5 and trembling, in singleness of **y** heart, 4771
6: 9 knowing that **y** Master also is in heaven; 4771
6:14 having **y** loins girt about with truth, and 4771
6:15 And *y* feet shod with the preparation of NIG
6:22 and *that* he might comfort **y** hearts. 4771
Php 1: 5 For **y** fellowship in the gospel from the first 4771
1: 9 that **y** love may abound yet more and 4771
1:19 shall turn to my salvation through **y** prayer, 4771
1:25 continue with you all for **y** furtherance and 4771
1:26 That **y** rejoicing may be *more* abundant in 4771
1:27 Only let *y* conversation be as it becometh NIG
1:27 or *else* be absent, I may hear of **y** affairs, 4771
1:28 And in nothing terrified by *y* adversaries: NIG
2:12 work out **y own** salvation with fear and 1438
2:17 upon the sacrifice and service of **y** faith, 4771
2:19 be of good comfort, when I know **y** state. 4771
2:20 who will naturally care for **y** state. 4771
2:25 but **y** messenger, and he that ministered to 4771
2:30 to supply **y** lack of service toward me. 4771
4: 5 Let **y** moderation be known unto all men. 4771
4: 6 supplication with thanksgiving let **y** 4771
4: 7 shall keep **y** hearts and minds through 4771
4:10 that now at the last **y** care of me hath 3588
4:17 I desire fruit that *may* abound to **y** account. 4771
4:19 But my God shall supply all **y** need 4771
Col 1: 4 Since we heard of **y** faith in Christ Jesus, 4771
1: 8 Who also declared unto us **y** love in 4771
1:21 and enemies in *y* mind by wicked works, NIG
2: 5 joying and beholding **y** order, and 4771
2: 5 and the stedfastness of **y** faith in Christ. 4771
2:13 being dead in *y* sins and the uncircumcision NIG
2:13 *your* sins and the uncircumcision of **y** flesh, 4771
2:18 Let no *man* beguile you of **y** reward in a NIG
3: 2 Set **y** affection on *things* above, not on NIG
3: 3 and **y** life is hid with Christ in God. 4771
3: 5 **y** members which are upon the earth; 4771
3: 8 filthy communication out of **y** mouth. 4771
3:15 And let the peace of God rule in **y** hearts, 4771
3:16 singing with grace in **y** hearts to the Lord. 4771
3:18 submit yourselves unto **y own** husbands, 2398
3:19 love *y* wives, and be not bitter against them. NIG
3:20 obey *y* parents in all *things:* for this is well NIG
3:21 provoke not **y** children *to anger,* lest they 4771
3:22 obey in all *things y* masters according to NIG
4: 1 give unto *y* servants that which is just and NIG
4: 6 Let **y** speech *be* alway with grace, 4771
4: 8 that he might know **y** estate, and 4771
4: 8 know your estate, and comfort **y** hearts; 4771
1Th 1: 3 Remembering without ceasing **y** work of 4771
1: 4 brethren beloved, **y** election of God. 4771
1: 5 of *men* we were among you for **y** sake. 4771
1: 8 also in every place **y** faith to God-ward is 4771
2:14 suffered like *things* of **y own** countrymen, 2398
2:17 endeavoured the more abundantly to see **y** 4771
3: 2 and to comfort you concerning **y** faith: 4771
3: 5 no longer forbear, I sent to know **y** faith, 4771
3: 6 and brought us good tidings of **y** faith and 4771
3: 7 in all our affliction and distress, by **y** faith: 4771
3: 9 for all the joy wherewith we joy for **y** sakes 4771
3:10 exceedingly that *we* might see **y** face, 4771
3:10 might perfect that which is lacking in **y** 4771
3:13 To the end *he* may stablish **y** hearts 4771
4: 3 is the will of God, *even* **y** sanctification, 4771
4:11 and to do **y own** *business,* and to work with 2398
4:11 and to work with **y** own hands, 4771
5:23 and *I pray God* **y** whole spirit and soul and 4771
2Th 1: 3 because that **y** faith groweth exceedingly, 4771
1: 4 you in the churches of God for **y** patience 4771
1: 4 and faith in all **y** persecutions and 4771
2:17 Comfort **y** hearts, and stablish you in every 4771
3: 5 And the Lord direct **y** hearts into the love 4771
Phm 1:22 for I trust that through **y** prayers I shall be 4771
1:25 of our Lord Jesus Christ *be* with **y** spirit. 4771
Heb 3: 8 Harden not **y** hearts, as in the provocation, 4771
3: 9 When **y** fathers tempted me, proved me, 4771
3:15 harden not **y** hearts, as in the provocation. 4771
4: 7 ye will hear his voice, harden not **y** hearts. 4771
6:10 For God *is* not unrighteous to forget **y** work 4771
9:14 purge **y** conscience from dead works to 4771
10:34 and took joyfully the spoiling of **y** goods, 4771
10:35 Cast not away therefore **y** confidence, 4771
12: 3 lest ye be wearied and faint in **y** minds. 4771
12:13 And make straight paths for **y** feet, lest *that* 4771
13: 5 *Let y* conversation *be* without covetousness; NIG
13:17 for they watch for **y** souls, as they that must 4771
Jas 1: 3 Knowing *this,* that the trying of **y** faith 4771
1:21 which is able to save **y** souls. 4771
1:22 not hearers only, deceiving **y own selves**. 1438
2: 2 For if there come unto **y** assembly a man 4771
3:14 ye have bitter envying and strife in **y** hearts, 4771
4: 1 *even* of **y** lusts that war in your members? 4771
4: 1 *even* of your lusts that war in **y** members? 4771
4: 3 that ye may consume *it* upon **y** lusts. 4771
4: 8 Cleanse *y* hands, *ye* sinners, and purify *your* NIG
4: 8 and purify *y* hearts, *ye* double minded. NIG
4: 9 let **y** laughter be turned to mourning, and 4771
4: 9 turned to mourning, and *y* joy to heaviness. NIG
4:14 for what *is* **y** life? It is even a vapour, 4771
4:16 But now ye rejoice in **y** boastings: all such 4771
5: 1 howl for **y** miseries that shall come upon 4771
5: 2 **Y** riches are corrupted, and your garments 4771
5: 2 and **y** garments are motheaten. 4771
5: 3 **Y** gold and silver is cankered; and the rust 4771
5: 3 and shall eat **y** flesh as *it were* fire: 4771
5: 4 labourers which have reaped *down* **y** fields, 4771
5: 5 ye have nourished **y** hearts, as in a day of 4771
Jas 5: 8 Be ye also patient; stablish **y** hearts: for 4771
5:12 but let **y** yea be yea; and *your* nay, nay; 4771
5:12 but let your yea be yea; and *y* nay, nay; NIG
5:16 Confess *y* faults one to another, and NIG
1Pe 1: 7 That the trial of **y** faith, *being* much more 4771
1: 9 Receiving the end of **y** faith, *even* 4771
1: 9 of your faith, *even* the salvation of *y* souls. NIG
1:13 Wherefore gird up the loins of **y** mind, 4771
1:14 to the former lusts in **y** ignorance: 4771
1:17 pass the time of **y** sojourning *here* in fear: 4771
1:18 from **y** vain conversation received by 4771
1:18 received by tradition from *y* fathers; NIG
1:21 that **y** faith and hope might be in God. 4771
1:22 Seeing ye have purified **y** souls in obeying 4771
2:12 Having **y** conversation honest among 4771
2:12 they may by *y* good works, *which* they shall NIG
2:16 not using *y* liberty for a cloke of NIG
2:18 *be* subject to *y* masters with all fear; NIG
2:20 *is it,* if, when ye be buffeted for *y* faults, NIG
2:25 unto the Shepherd and Bishop of **y** souls. 4771
3: 1 *be* in subjection to **y own** husbands; 2398
3: 2 While they behold **y** chaste conversation 4771
3: 7 grace of life; that **y** prayers be not hindered. 4771
3:15 But sanctify the Lord God in **y** hearts: and 4771
3:16 they may be ashamed that falsely accuse **y** 4771
4:14 evil spoken of, but on **y** part he is glorified. 4771
5: 7 Casting all **y** care upon him; for he careth 4771
5: 8 because **y** adversary the devil, as a roaring 4771
5: 9 in **y** brethren that are in the world. 4771
2Pe 1: 5 giving all diligence, add to **y** faith virtue; 4771
1:10 give diligence to make **y** calling and 4771
1:19 day dawn, and the day star arise in **y** hearts: 4771
3: 1 in both which I stir up **y** pure minds by way 4771
3:17 of the wicked, fall from **y own** stedfastness. 2398
1Jn 1: 4 write we unto you, that **y** joy may be full. 4771
2:12 *y* sins are forgiven you for his name's sake. NIG
2Jn 1:10 this doctrine, receive him not into *y* house, NIG
Jude 1:12 These are spots in **y** feasts of charity when 4771
1:20 building up yourselves on **y** most holy 4771
Rev 1: 9 who also am **y** brother, and companion in 4771
2:23 every one of you according to **y** works. 4771
16: 1 Go *y* ways, and pour out the vials of NIG

YOURS (12) [YOU]

Ge 45:20 good of all the land of Egypt *is* **y**. 3641.1+3807.1
Dt 11:24 of your feet shall tread shall be **y**: 3641.1+3807.1
Jos 2:14 the men answered her, Our life for **y**, if 3641.1
2Ch 20:15 for the battle *is* not **y**, but God's. 3641.1+3807.1
Jer 5:19 strangers in a land *that is* not **y**. 3641.1+3807.1
Lk 6:20 *be ye* poor: for **y** is the kingdom of God. 5212
Jn 15:20 have kept my saying, they will keep **y** also. 5212
1Co 3:21 no *man* glory in men. For all *things* are **y**; 4771
3:22 *things* present, or *things* to come; all are **y**; 4771
8: 9 **y** become a stumblingblock to them that are 4771
16:18 For they have refreshed my spirit and **y**: 4771
2Co 12:14 burdensome to you: for I seek not **y**, 3588+4771

YOURSELVES (191) [SELF, YOU]

Ge 18: 4 wash your feet, and rest **y** under the tree: NIH
45: 5 be not grieved, nor angry with **y**, 3641.1
49: 1 unto his sons, and said, Gather **y** together, NIH
49: 2 Gather **y** together, and hear, ye sons of NIH
Ex 19:12 saying, Take heed to **y**, *that ye* go *not* up 3641.1
30:37 you shall not make to **y** according to 3641.1
32:29 Consecrate **y** to day to the LORD, 3641.1
Lev 11:43 Ye shall not make **y** abominable 5315+3641.1
11:43 neither shall ye make **y** unclean with them, NIH
11:44 ye shall therefore sanctify **y**, and ye shall be NIH
11:44 neither shall ye defile **y** with any 5315+3641.1
18:24 Defile not you **y** in any of these *things:* for NIH
18:30 before you, and that ye **defile** not **y** therein: 2930
19: 4 unto idols, nor make to **y** molten gods: 3641.1
20: 7 Sanctify **y** therefore, and be ye holy: for I NIH
Nu 11:18 Sanctify **y** against to morrow, and ye shall NIH
16: 3 lift you up **y** above the congregation of NIH
16:21 Separate **y** from among this congregation, NIH
31: 3 Arm some of **y** unto the war, and let them 3641.1
31:18 a man by lying with him, keep alive for **y**. 3641.1
31:19 purify *both* **y** and your captives on the third 859
Dt 2: 4 of you: take ye good heed unto **y** therefore: NIH
4:15 therefore good heed unto **y**; 5315+3641.1
4:16 Lest ye corrupt *y*, and make you a graven NIH
4:23 Take heed unto **y**, lest ye forget 3641.1
4:25 shall corrupt *y*, and make a graven image, NIH
11:16 Take heed to **y**, that your heart be not 3641.1
11:23 greater nations and mightier than **y**. 3641.1
14: 1 ye shall not cut **y**, nor make *any* baldness NIH
31:14 present **y** in the tabernacle of NIH
31:29 that after my death ye will utterly corrupt *y*, NIH
Jos 2:16 hide **y** there three days, until the pursuers be NIH
3: 5 Joshua said unto the people, Sanctify **y**: NIH
6:18 in any wise keep *y* from the accursed thing, NIH
6:18 lest ye make *y* accursed, when ye take of NIH
7:13 and say, Sanctify **y** against to morrow: NIH
8: 2 shall ye take for a prey unto **y**: 3641.1
23: 7 neither serve them, nor bow **y** unto them. NIH
23:11 Take good heed therefore unto **y**, 5315+3641.1
23:16 served other gods, and bowed **y** to them; NIH
24:22 Ye *are* witnesses against **y** that ye have 3641.1
Jdg 15:12 unto me, that ye will not fall upon me **y**. 859
1Sa 2:29 to make **y** fat with the chiefest of all 3641.1
4: 9 Be strong, and quit **y** like men, O ye NIH
4: 9 have been to you: quit **y** like men, and fight. NIH
10:19 present **y** before the LORD by your tribes, NIH
14:34 Disperse **y** among the people, and say unto NIH
16: 5 sanctify **y**, and come with me to NIH
1Ki 18:25 Choose you one bullock for **y**, and dress *it* NIH
20:12 Set **y** *in array.* And they set *themselves in* NIH
2Ki 17:35 nor bow **y** to them, nor serve them, NIH
1Ch 15:12 sanctify **y**, *both* ye and your brethren, 859
2Ch 20:17 shall not need to fight in this *battle:* set **y**, NIH
29: 5 sanctify now **y**, and sanctify the house of NIH
29:31 Now ye have consecrated **y** unto 3641.1
30: 8 fathers *were, but* yield **y** unto the LORD, NIH
32:11 you to give over **y** to die by famine 3641.1

2Ch 35: 4 And prepare y by the houses of your fathers, NIH
35: 6 and sanctify y, and prepare your brethren, NIH
Ezr 10:11 separate y from the people of the land, and NIH
Ne 13:25 their daughters unto your sons, or for y. 3641.1
Job 19: 3 you are not ashamed *that* you make y NIH
19: 5 If indeed ye will magnify y against me, and NIH
27:12 all ye y have seen *it;* why then are ye thus 859
42: 8 and offer up for y a burnt offering; 3641.1
Isa 8: 9 Associate y, O ye people, and ye shall be NIH
8: 9 gird y, and ye shall be broken in pieces; NIH
8: 9 gird y, and ye shall be broken in pieces. NIH
29: 9 Stay y, and wonder; cry ye out, and cry: NIH
45:20 Assemble y and come; draw near together, NIH
46: 8 Remember this, and **shew y men**: bring *it* 377
48:14 All ye, assemble y, and hear; which among NIH
49: 9 to *them* that *are* in darkness, Shew y. NIH
50: 1 for your iniquities have you sold y, and NIH
50:11 a fire, that compass y about with sparks: NIH
52: 3 the LORD, Ye have sold y for nought; NIH
57: 4 Against whom do ye sport y? against whom NIH
57: 5 Inflaming y with idols under every green NIH
61: 6 and in their glory shall you boast y. NIH
Jer 4: 4 Circumcise y to the LORD, and take away NIH
4: 5 Assemble y, and let us go into the defenced NIH
6: 1 gather y to flee out of the midst of NIH
8:14 assemble y, and let us enter into NIH
13:18 and to the queen, Humble y, sit down: NIH
17:21 Take heed to y, and bear no burden 5315+3641.1
25:34 wallow y *in the ashes,* ye principal of NIH
26:15 shall surely bring innocent blood upon y, 3641.1
37: 9 Deceive not y, saying, 5315+3641.1
44: 8 that ye might cut y off, and that *ye* might 3641.1
50:14 Put y in array against Babylon round about: NIH
Eze 14: 6 Repent, and turn y from your idols; and NIH
18:30 and turn y from all your transgressions; NIH
18:32 Lord GOD: wherefore turn y, and live ye. NIH
20: 7 and defile not y with the idols of Egypt: NIH
20:18 nor defile y with their idols: NIH
20:31 ye pollute y with all your idols, *even* unto NIH
20:43 ye shall lothe y in your own sight for all NIH
36:31 shall lothe y in your own sight for your NIH
39:17 beast of the field, Assemble y, and come; NIH
39:17 gather y on every side to my sacrifice that I NIH
44: 8 of my charge in my sanctuary for y. 3641.1
Hos 10:12 Sow to y in righteousness, reap in mercy; 3641.1
Joel 1:13 Gird y, and lament, ye priests: howl, NIH
3:11 Assemble y, and come, all ye heathen, and NIH
3:11 and gather y together round about: NIH
Am 3: 9 Assemble y upon the mountains of Samaria, NIH
5:26 the star of your god, which ye made to y. 3641.1
Zep 2: 1 Gather y together, yea, gather together, NIH
Zec 7: 6 did not ye eat *for* y, and drink *for* NIH
7: 6 not ye eat *for yourselves,* and drink *for* y? NIH
Mt 3: 9 And think not to say within y, We have *1438*
6:19 Lay not up for y treasures upon earth, *4771*
6:20 But lay up for y treasures in heaven, *4771*
16: 8 why reason ye among y, because ye have *1438*
23:13 for ye neither go in y, neither suffer ye *4771*
23:15 him twofold more *the* child of hell than y. *4771*
23:31 Wherefore ye be witnesses unto y, that ye *1438*
25: 9 go ye rather to them that sell, and buy for y. *1438*
Mk 6:31 Come ye y apart into a desert place, and *846*
9:33 What *was it that* ye disputed among y by *1438*
9:50 Have salt in y, and have peace one with *1438*
13: 9 But take heed to y: for they shall deliver *1438*
Lk 3: 8 and begin not to say within y, *1438*
11:46 ye y touch not the burdens with one of your *846*
11:52 ye entered not in y, and them that were *846*
12:33 provide y bags which wax not old, *1438*
12:36 And ye y like unto men that wait for their NIG
12:57 why even of y judge ye not what *is* right? *1438*
13:28 the kingdom of God, and you y thrust out. *4771*
16: 9 Make to y friends of the mammon of *1438*
16:15 Ye are they which justify y before men; *1438*
17: 3 Take heed to y: If thy brother trespass *1438*
17:14 said unto them, Go shew y unto the priests. *1438*
21:34 And take heed to y, lest at any time your *1438*
22:17 and said, Take this, and divide *it* among y: *1438*
23:28 but weep for y, and for your children. *1438*
Jn 3:28 Ye y bear me witness, that I said, I am not *846*
6:43 and said unto them, Murmur not among y. *240*
16:19 Do ye inquire among y of that I said, A little *240*
Ac 2:22 him in the midst of you, as ye y also know: *846*
2:40 Save y from this untoward generation. NIG
5:35 take heed to y what ye intend to do as *1438*
13:46 and judge y unworthy of everlasting life, *1438*
15:29 from which if ye keep y, ye shall do well. *1438*
20:10 and embracing *him* said, Trouble not y; NIG
20:28 Take heed therefore unto y, and to all *1438*
20:34 Yea, ye y know, that these hands have *846*
Ro 6:11 Likewise reckon ye also y to be dead *1438*
6:13 but yield y unto God, as *those that are* alive *1438*
6:16 that to whom ye yield y servants to obey, *1438*
12:19 avenge not y, but *rather* give place unto *1438*
1Co 5:13 Therefore put away from among y *that* *4771*
6: 7 why do ye not rather *suffer* y to be NIG
7: 5 that ye may give y to fasting and prayer, NIG
11:13 Judge in y: is it comely that a woman pray *4771*
16:16 That ye submit y unto such, and to every NIG
2Co 7:11 yea, *what* clearing of y, yea, NIG
7:11 In all *things* ye have approved y to be clear *1438*
11:19 ye suffer fools gladly, seeing ye y are wise. NIG
13: 5 Examine y, whether ye be in the faith; *1438*
Eph 2: 8 ye saved through faith; and that not of y: *4771*
5:19 Speaking to y in psalms and hymns and *1438*
5:21 Submitting y one to another in the fear of NIG
5:22 Wives, submit y unto your own husbands, NIG
Col 3:18 Wives, submit y unto your own husbands, NIG
1Th 2: 1 For y, brethren, know our entrance in unto *846*
3: 3 for y know that we are appointed thereunto. *846*
4: 9 for ye y are taught of God to love one *846*
5: 2 For y know perfectly that the day of the Lord *846*
5:11 Wherefore comfort **y together**, and *240*
5:13 work's sake. *And* be at peace among y. *1438*
5:15 *is* good, both among y, and to all *men.* *240*
2Th 3: 6 that ye withdraw y from every brother that NIG
3: 7 For y know how *ye* ought to follow us: *846*
Heb 10:34 knowing in y that *ye* have in heaven a *1438*
13: 3 suffer adversity, as being y also in the body. *846*
13:17 that have the rule over you, and submit y: NIG
Jas 2: 4 Are ye not then partial in y, and are become *1438*
4: 7 Submit y therefore to God. Resist the devil, NIG
4:10 Humble y in the sight of the Lord, and NIG
1Pe 1:14 not fashioning y according to the former NIG
2:13 Submit y to every ordinance of man for NIG
4: 1 arm y likewise with the same mind: *4771*
4: 8 all *things* have fervent charity among y: *1438*
5: 5 *ye* younger, submit y unto the elder. NIG
5: 6 Humble y therefore under the mighty hand NIG
1Jn 5:21 Little children, keep y from idols. Amen. *1438*
2Jn 1: 8 Look to y, that we lose not *those things* *1438*
Jude 1:20 building up y on your most holy faith, *1438*
1:21 Keep y in the love of God, looking for *1438*
Rev 19:17 gather y together unto the supper of NIG

YOUTH (70) [YOUNG, YOUNGER, YOUNGEST, YOUTHFUL, YOUTHS]

Ge 8:21 of man's heart *is* evil from his y; 5271
43:33 and the youngest according to his y: 6812
46:34 about cattle from our y even until now, 5271
Lev 22:13 as *in* her y, she shall eat of her father's 5271
Nu 30: 3 a bond, *being* in her father's house in her y; 5271
30:16 *being yet* in her y *in* her father's house. 5271
Jdg 8:20 the y drew not his sword: for he feared, 5288
8:20 for he feared, because he *was* yet a y. 5288
1Sa 17:33 for thou *art but* a y, and he a man of war 5288
17:33 a youth, and he a man of war from his y. 5271
17:42 for he was *but* a y, and ruddy, and of a fair 5288
17:55 of the host, Abner, whose son *is* this y? 5288
2Sa 19: 7 evil that befell thee from thy y until now. 5271
1Ki 18:12 *I* thy servant fear the LORD from my y. 5271
Job 13:26 me to possess the iniquities of my y. 5271
20:11 His bones are full *of the sin of* his y, 5934
29: 4 As I was in the days of my y, when 2779
30:12 Upon *my* right hand rise the y; they push 6526
31:18 (For from my y he was brought up *with* me, 5271
33:25 he shall return to the days of his y: 5934
36:14 They die in y, and their life *is* among 5290
Ps 25: 7 Remember not the sins of my y, nor my 5271
71: 5 Lord GOD: *thou art* my trust from my y. 5271
71:17 O God, thou hast taught me from my y: and 5271
88:15 ready to die from *my* y *up: while* I suffer 5290
89:45 The days of his y hast thou shortened: 5934
103: 5 *so that* thy y is renewed like the eagle's. 5271
110: 3 of the morning: thou hast the dew of thy y. 3208
127: 4 of a mighty *man;* so *are* children of the y. 5271
129: 1 a time have they afflicted me from my y, 5271
129: 2 a time have they afflicted me from my y: 5271
144:12 sons *may be* as plants grown up in their y; 5271
Pr 2:17 Which forsaketh the guide of her y, and 5271
5:18 and rejoice with the wife of thy y. 5271
Ecc 11: 9 Rejoice, O young man, in thy y; and let thy 3208
11: 9 let thy heart cheer thee in the days of thy y, 979
11:10 thy flesh: for childhood and y *are* vanity. 7839
12: 1 now thy Creator in the days of thy y, 979
Isa 47:12 wherein thou hast laboured from thy y; 5271
47:15 *even* thy merchants, from thy y: 5271
54: 4 for thou shalt forget the shame of thy y, and 5934
54: 6 and grieved in spirit, and a wife of y, 5271
Jer 2: 2 I remember thee, the kindness of thy y, 5271
3: 4 My father, thou *art* the guide of my y? 5271
3:24 the labour of our fathers from our y; 5271
3:25 from our y even unto this day, and have not 5271
22:21 This *hath been* thy manner from thy y, 5271
31:19 because I did bear the reproach of my y. 5271
32:30 have only done evil before me from their y: 5271
48:11 Moab hath been at ease from his y, and 5271
La 3:27 for a man that he bear the yoke in his y. 5271
Eze 4:14 for from my y up even till now have I not 5271
16:22 thou hast not remembered the days of thy y, 5271
16:43 thou hast not remembered the days of thy y, 5271
16:60 my covenant with thee in the days of thy y, 5271
23: 3 they committed whoredoms in their y: 5271
23: 8 for in her y they lay with her, and 5271
23:19 calling to remembrance the days of her y, 5271
23:21 to remembrance the lewdness of thy y, 5271
23:21 teats by the Egyptians for the paps of thy y. 5271
Hos 2:15 as *in* the days of her y, and as *in* the day 5271
Joel 1: 8 with sackcloth for the husband of her y. 5271
Zec 13: 5 man taught me *to keep cattle* from my y. 5271
Mal 2:14 witness between thee and the wife of thy y, 5271
2:15 deal treacherously against the wife of his y. 5271
Mt 19:20 All these *things* have I kept from my y up: *3503*
Mk 10:20 all these have I observed from my y. *3503*
Lk 18:21 he said, All these have I kept from my y up. *3503*
Ac 26: 4 My manner of life from *my* y, which was at *3503*
1Ti 4:12 Let no *man* despise thy y; but be thou an *3503*

YOUTHFUL (1) [YOUTH]

2Ti 2:22 Flee also y lusts: but follow righteousness, *3512*

YOUTHS (2) [YOUTH]

Pr 7: 7 the simple ones, I discerned among the y, 1121
Isa 40:30 Even the y shall faint and be weary, and 5288

YOU-WARD (2) [YOU]

2Co 13: 3 which to y is not weak, but is mighty in *4771*
Eph 3: 2 of the grace of God which is given me to y: *4771*

YOU-WARDS (1) [YOU]

2Co 1:12 in the world, and more abundantly to y. *4771*

Z

ZAANAIM (1)

Jdg 4:11 pitched his tent unto the plain of Z, 6815

ZAANAN (1)

Mic 1:11 the inhabitant of Z came not forth *in* 6630

ZAANANNIM (1)

Jos 19:33 from Allon to Z, and Adami, Nekeb, and 6815

ZAAVAN (1)

Ge 36:27 of Ezer *are* these; Bilhan, and Z, and Akan. 2190

ZABAD (8)

1Ch 2:36 Attai begat Nathan, and Nathan begat Z, 2066
2:37 Z begat Ephlal, and Ephlal begat Obed, 2066
7:21 Z his son, and Shuthelah his son, and Ezer, 2066
11:41 Uriah the Hittite, Z the son of Ahlai, 2066
2Ch 24:26 Z the son of Shimeath an Ammonitess, and 2066
Ezr 10:27 Mattaniah, and Jeremoth, and Z, and Aziza. 2066
10:33 Z, Eliphelet, Jeremai, Manasseh, *and* 2066
10:43 Z, Zebina, Jadau, and Joel, Benaiah. 2066

ZABBAI (2)

Ezr 10:28 Jehohanan, Hananiah, Z, *and* Athlai. 2079
Ne 3:20 After him Baruch the son of Z earnestly 2079

ZABBUD (1)

Ezr 8:14 Uthai, and Z, and with them seventy males. 2072

ZABDI (6)

Jos 7: 1 of Carmi, the son of Z, the son of Zerah, 2067
7:17 the Zarhites man by man; and Z was taken: 2067
7:18 of Carmi, the son of Z, the son of Zerah, 2067
1Ch 8:19 And Jakim, and Zichri, and Z, 2067
27:27 for the wine cellars *was* Z the Shiphmite: 2067
Ne 11:17 of Micha, the son of Z, the son of Asaph, 2067

ZABDIEL (2)

1Ch 27: 2 first month *was* Jashobeam the son of Z: 2068
Ne 11:14 their overseer *was* Z, the son of *one of* 2068

ZABUD (1)

1Ki 4: 5 Z the son of Nathan *was* principal officer, 2071

ZABULON (3) [ZEBULUN]

Mt 4:13 in the borders of Z and Nephthalim: *2194*
4:15 The land of Z, and the land of Nephthalim, *2194*
Rev 7: 8 Of the tribe of Z *were* sealed twelve *2194*

ZACCAI (2)

Ezr 2: 9 The children of Z, seven hundred and 2140
Ne 7:14 The children of Z, seven hundred and 2140

ZACCHEUS (3)

Lk 19: 2 And behold, *there was* a man named Z, *2195*
19: 5 unto him, Z, make haste, and come down; *2195*
19: 8 And Z stood, and said unto the Lord; *2195*

ZACCHUR (1)

1Ch 4:26 Hamuel his son, Z his son, Shimei his son. 2139

ZACCUR (8)

Nu 13: 4 the tribe of Reuben, Shammua the son of Z. 2139
1Ch 24:27 Beno, and Shoham, and Z, and Ibri. 2139
25: 2 Z, and Joseph, and Nethaniah, and 2139
25:10 The third *to* Z, *he,* his sons, and 2139
Ne 3: 2 And next to them builded Z the son of Imri. 2139
10:12 Z, Sherebiah, Shebaniah, 2139
12:35 the son of Z, the son of Asaph: 2139
13:13 next to them *was* Hanan the son of Z, 2139

ZACHARIAH (4) [ZACHARIAS, ZECHARIAH]

2Ki 14:29 of Israel; and Z his son reigned in his stead. 2148
15: 8 eighth year of Azariah king of Judah did Z 2148
15:11 the rest of the acts of Z, behold, they *are* 2148
18: 2 name also *was* Abi, the daughter of Z. 2148

ZACHARIAS (11) [ZACHARIAH]

Mt 23:35 Abel unto the blood of Z son of Barachias, *2197*
Lk 1: 5 the king of Judea, a certain priest named Z, *2197*
1:12 And when Z saw *him,* he was troubled, and *2197*
1:13 But the angel said unto him, Fear not, Z: *2197*
1:18 And Z said unto the angel, Whereby shall I *2197*
1:21 And the people waited for Z, and *2197*
1:40 And entered into the house of Z, and *2197*
1:59 and they called him Z, after the name of his *2197*
1:67 And his father Z was filled with the Holy *2197*
3: 2 unto John the son of Z in the wilderness. *2197*
11:51 the blood of Abel unto the blood of Z, *2197*

ZACHER (1)

1Ch 8:31 And Gedor, and Ahio, and Z. 2144

ZADOK (52) [ZADOK'S]

2Sa 8:17 Z the son of Ahitub, and Ahimelech the son 6659
15:24 lo Z also, and all the Levites *were* with 6659
15:25 the king said unto Z, Carry back the ark of 6659
15:27 The king said also unto Z the priest, *Art not* 6659
15:29 Z therefore and Abiathar carried the ark of 6659
15:35 *hast thou* not there with thee Z and 6659
15:35 thou shalt tell *it* to Z and Abiathar 6659
17:15 said Hushai unto Z and to Abiathar 6659

2Sa 18:19 said Ahimaaz the son of **Z**, Let me now 6659
18:22 said Ahimaaz the son of **Z** yet again to 6659
18:27 *is* like the running of Ahimaaz the son of **Z**. 6659
19:11 king David sent to **Z** and to Abiathar 6659
20:25 and **Z** and Abiathar *were* the priests: 6659
1Ki 1: 8 **Z** the priest, and Benaiah the son of 6659
1:26 **Z** the priest, and Benaiah the son of 6659
1:32 Call me **Z** the priest, and Nathan 6659
1:34 let **Z** the priest and Nathan the prophet 6659
1:38 So **Z** the priest, and Nathan the prophet, 6659
1:39 **Z** the priest took a horn of oil out of 6659
1:44 the king hath sent with him **Z** the priest, 6659
1:45 **Z** the priest and Nathan the prophet have 6659
2:35 **Z** the priest did the king put in the room of 6659
4: 2 he had; Azariah the son of **Z** the priest, 6659
4: 4 and **Z** and Abiathar *were* the priests: 6659
2Ki 15:33 name *was* Jerusha, the daughter of **Z**. 6659
1Ch 6: 8 Ahitub begat **Z**, and Zadok begat Ahimaaz, 6659
6: 8 Ahitub begat Zadok, and **Z** begat Ahimaaz, 6659
6:12 Ahitub begat **Z**, and Zadok begat Shallum, 6659
6:12 Ahitub begat Zadok, and **Z** begat Shallum, 6659
6:53 **Z** his son, Ahimaaz his son. 6659
9:11 the son of **Z**, the son of Meraioth, the son 6659
12:28 **Z**, a young man mighty of valour, and 6659
15:11 David called for **Z** and Abiathar the priests, 6659
16:39 **Z** the priest, and his brethren the priests, 6659
18:16 **Z** the son of Ahitub, and Abimelech the son 6659
24: 3 both **Z** of the sons of Eleazar, and 6659
24: 6 **Z** the priest, and Ahimelech the son of 6659
24:31 **Z**, and Ahimelech, and the chief of 6659
27:17 the son of Kemuel: of the Aaronites, **Z**: 6659
29:22 to be the chief governor, and **Z** to be priest. 6659
2Ch 27: 1 name also *was* Jerushah, the daughter of **Z**. 6659
31:10 Azariah the chief priest of the house of **Z** 6659
Ezr 7: 2 of Shallum, the son of **Z**, the son of Ahitub, 6659
Ne 3: 4 next unto them repaired **Z** the son of 6659
3:29 After them repaired **Z** the son of Immer 6659
10:21 Meshezabeel, **Z**, Jaddua, 6659
11:11 the son of **Z**, the son of Meraioth, the son 6659
13:13 **Z** the scribe, and of the Levites, Pedaiah: 6659
Eze 40:46 these *are* the sons of **Z** among the sons of 6659
43:19 priests the Levites that *be* of the seed of **Z**, 6659
44:15 the priests the Levites, the sons of **Z**, 6659
48:11 priests that are sanctified of the sons of **Z**; 6659

ZADOK'S (1) [ZADOK]
2Sa 15:36 Ahimaaz **Z** *son*, and 6659+3807.1

ZAHAM (1)
2Ch 11:19 him children; Jeush, and Shamariah, and **Z**. 2093

ZAIR (1)
2Ki 8:21 So Joram went over to **Z**, and all 6811

ZALAPH (1)
Ne 3:30 Hanun the sixth son of **Z**, another piece. 6764

ZALMON (2)
Jdg 9:48 Abimelech gat him up *to* mount **Z**, he and 6756
2Sa 23:28 **Z** the Ahohite, Maharai the Netophathite, 6756

ZALMONAH (2)
Nu 33:41 departed from mount Hor, and pitched in **Z**. 6758
33:42 they departed from **Z**, and pitched in 6758

ZALMUNNA (12)
Jdg 8: 5 I am pursuing after Zebah and **Z**, kings of 6759
8: 6 hands of Zebah and **Z** now in thine hand, 6759
8: 7 hath delivered Zebah and **Z** into mine hand, 6759
8:10 Now Zebah and **Z** *were* in Karkor, and 6759
8:12 when Zebah and **Z** fled, he pursued after 6759
8:12 and **Z**, and discomfited all the host. 6759
8:15 said, Behold Zebah and **Z**, with whom ye 6759
8:15 hands of Zebah and **Z** now in thine hand, 6759
8:18 said he unto Zebah and **Z**, What manner of 6759
8:21 Zebah and **Z** said, Rise thou, and fall upon 6759
8:21 slew Zebah and **Z**, and took away 6759
Ps 83:11 yea, all their princes as Zebah, and as **Z**. 6759

ZAMZUMMIMS (1)
Dt 2:20 old time; and the Ammonites call them **Z**; 2157

ZAMZUMMITES See ZAMZUMMIMS

ZANOAH (5)
Jos 15:34 **Z**, and En-gannim, Tappuah, and Enam, 2182
15:56 And Jezreel, and Jokdeam, and **Z**, 2182
1Ch 4:18 of Socho, and Jekuthiel the father of **Z**. 2182
Ne 3:13 repaired Hanun, and the inhabitants of **Z**; 2182
11:30 **Z**, Adullam, and *in* their villages, 2182

ZAPHENATH-PANEAH See ZAPHNATH-PAANEAH

ZAPHNATH-PAANEAH (1)
Ge 41:45 Pharaoh called Joseph's name **Z**; and 6847

ZAPHON (1)
Jos 13:27 and Beth-nimrah, and Succoth, and **Z**, 6829

ZARA (1) [ZARAH]
Mt 1: 3 And Judas begat Phares and **Z** of Thamar; *2196*

ZARAH (1) [ZARA]
Ge 38:30 upon his hand: and his name was called **Z**. 2226

ZAREAH (1)
Ne 11:29 at En-rimmon, and at **Z**, and at Jarmuth, 6881

ZAREATHITES (1)
1Ch 2:53 of them came the **Z**, and the Eshtaulites. 6882

ZARED (1)
Nu 21:12 and pitched in the valley of **Z**. 2218

ZAREPHATH (3) [SAREPTA]
1Ki 17: 9 Arise, get thee to **Z**, which *belongeth* to 6886
17:10 So he arose and went to **Z**. And when he 6886
Ob 1:20 *possess* that of the Canaanites, *even* unto **Z**; 6886

ZARETAN (1)
Jos 3:16 from the city Adam, that *is* beside **Z**: 6891

ZARETHAN See ZARETAN; ZARTANAH; ZARTHAN; ZEREDATHAH

ZARETH-SHAHAR (1)
Jos 13:19 Sibmah, and **Z** in the mount of the valley, 6890

ZARHITES (6)
Nu 26:13 Of Zerah, the family of the **Z**: of Shaul, 2227
26:20 the Pharzites: of Zerah, the family of the **Z**. 2227
Jos 7:17 of Judah; and he took the family of the **Z**: 2227
7:17 he brought the family of the **Z** man by man; 2227
1Ch 27:11 *was* Sibbecai the Hushathite, of the **Z**: 2227
27:13 *was* Maharai the Netophathite, of the **Z**: 2227

ZARTANAH (1)
1Ki 4:12 which *is* by **Z** beneath Jezreel, 6891

ZARTHAN (1)
1Ki 7:46 in the clay ground between Succoth and **Z**. 6891

ZATTHU (1)
Ne 10:14 Parosh, Pahath-moab, Elam, **Z**, Bani, 2240

ZATTU (3)
Ezr 2: 8 The children of **Z**, nine hundred forty and 2240
10:27 of the sons of **Z**; Elioenai, Eliashib, 2240
Ne 7:13 The children of **Z**, eight hundred forty and 2240

ZAVAN (1)
1Ch 1:42 The sons of Ezer; Bilhan, and **Z**, *and* Jakan. 2190

ZAZA (1)
1Ch 2:33 the sons of Jonathan; Peleth, and **Z**. 2117

ZEAL (16) [ZEALOUS, ZEALOUSLY]
2Sa 21: 2 Saul sought to slay them in his **z** to 7065
2Ki 10:16 with me, and see my **z** for the LORD. 7068
19:31 the **z** of the LORD *of hosts* shall do this. 7068
Ps 69: 9 For the **z** of thine house hath eaten me up; 7068
119:139 My **z** hath consumed me, because 7068
Isa 9: 7 The **z** of the LORD of hosts will perform 7068
37:32 the **z** of the LORD of hosts shall do this. 7068
59:17 *for* clothing, and was clad with **z** as a cloke. 7068
63:15 where *is* thy **z** and thy strength, 7068
Eze 5:13 that I the LORD have spoken *it* in my **z**, 7068
Jn 2:17 The **z** of thine house hath eaten me up. *2205*
Ro 10: 2 For I bear them record that they have a **z** of *2205*
2Co 7:11 yea, *what* **z**, yea, *what* revenge! *2205*
9: 2 and your **z** hath provoked very many. *2205*
Php 3: 6 Concerning **z**, persecuting the church; *2205*
Col 4:13 that he hath a great **z** for you, and them that *2205*

ZEALOT See ZELOTES

ZEALOUS (8) [ZEAL]
Nu 25:11 he was **z** for my sake among them, 7065+7068
25:13 because he was **z** for his God, and made an 7065
Ac 21:20 which believe; and they are all **z** of the law: *2207*
22: 3 and was **z** towards God, as ye all are this *2207*
1Co 14:12 forasmuch as ye are **z** of spiritual *gifts*, seek *2207*
Gal 1:14 being more exceedingly **z** of the traditions *2207*
Tit 2:14 himself a peculiar people, **z** of good works. *2207*
Rev 3:19 and chasten: be **z** therefore, and repent. *2206*

ZEALOUSLY (2) [ZEAL]
Gal 4:17 They **z affect** you, *but* not well; yea, *2206*
4:18 But *it is* good to be **z affected** always in a *2206*

ZEBADIAH (9)
1Ch 8:15 And **Z**, and Arad, and Ader, 2069
8:17 **Z**, and Meshullam, and Hezeki, and Heber, 2069
12: 7 Joelah, and **Z**, the sons of Jeroham of 2069
26: 2 Jediael the second, **Z** the third, Jathniel 2069
27: 7 brother of Joab, and **Z** his son after him: 2069
2Ch 17: 8 **Z**, and Asahel, and Shemiramoth, and 2069
19:11 **Z** the son of Ishmael, the ruler of the house 2069
Ezr 8: 8 **Z** the son of Michael, and with him 2069
10:20 And of the sons of Immer; Hanani, and **Z**. 2069

ZEBAH (12)
Jdg 8: 5 I am pursuing after **Z** and Zalmunna, 2078
8: 6 *Are* the hands of **Z** and Zalmunna now in 2078
8: 7 when the LORD hath delivered **Z** 2078
8:10 Now **Z** and Zalmunna *were* in Karkor, and 2078
8:12 when **Z** and Zalmunna fled, he pursued 2078
8:12 **Z** and Zalmunna, and discomfited all 2078
8:15 said, Behold **Z** and Zalmunna, with whom 2078
8:15 *Are* the hands of **Z** and Zalmunna now in 2078
8:18 said he unto **Z** and Zalmunna, 2078
8:21 **Z** and Zalmunna said, Rise thou, and 2078
8:21 slew **Z** and Zalmunna, and took away 2078
Ps 83:11 all their princes as **Z**, and as Zalmunna: 2078

ZEBAIM See POCHERETH OF ZEBAIM, POCHERETH ZEBAIM

ZEBEDEE (10) [ZEBEDEE'S]
Mt 4:21 James the *son* of **Z**, and John his brother, *2199*
4:21 his brother, in a ship with **Z** their father, *2199*
10: 2 the *son* of **Z**, and John his brother; *2199*
26:37 took with *him* Peter and the two sons of **Z**, *2199*
Mk 1:19 he saw James the *son* of **Z**, and John his *2199*
1:20 they left their father **Z** in the ship with *2199*
3:17 And James the *son* of **Z**, and John *2199*
10:35 And James and John, the sons of **Z**, *2199*
Lk 5:10 so *was* also James, and John, *the* sons of **Z**, *2199*
Jn 21: 2 and the *sons* of **Z**, and two other of his *2199*

ZEBEDEE'S (2) [ZEBEDEE]
Mt 20:20 Then came to him the mother of **Z** children *2199*
27:56 and Joses, and the mother of **Z** children. *2199*

ZEBIDAH See ZEBUDAH

ZEBINA (1)
Ezr 10:43 Zabad, **Z**, Jadau, and Joel, Benaiah. 2081

ZEBOIIM (2) [ZEBOIM]
Ge 14: 2 Shemeber king of **Z**, and the king of Bela, 6636
14: 8 the king of **Z**, and the king of Bela 6636

ZEBOIM (5) [ZEBOIIM]
Ge 10:19 Gomorrah, and Admah, and **Z**, even unto 6636
Dt 29:23 of Sodom, and Gomorrah, Admah, and **Z**, 6636
1Sa 13:18 to the valley of **Z** toward the wilderness. 6650
Ne 11:34 Hadid, **Z**, Neballat, 6650
Hos 11: 8 *how* shall I set thee as **Z**? mine heart is 6636

ZEBUDAH (1)
2Ki 23:36 his mother's name *was* **Z**, the daughter of 2080

ZEBUL (6)
Jdg 9:28 **Z** his officer? serve the men of Hamor 2083
9:30 when **Z** the ruler of the city heard 2083
9:36 Gaal saw the people, he said to **Z**, Behold, 2083
9:36 **Z** said unto him, Thou seest the shadow of 2083
9:38 said **Z** unto him, Where *is* now thy mouth, 2083
9:41 **Z** thrust out Gaal and his brethren, that *they* 2083

ZEBULONITE (2) [ZEBULUN]
Jdg 12:11 after him Elon, a **Z**, judged Israel; and 2075
12:12 Elon the **Z** died, and was buried in Aijalon 2075

ZEBULUN (45) [ZABULON, ZEBULONITE, ZEBULUNITES]
Ge 30:20 him six sons: and she called his name **Z**. 2074
35:23 and Levi, and Judah, and Issachar, and **Z**: 2074
46:14 the sons of **Z**; Sered, and Elon, and Jahleel. 2074
49:13 **Z** shall dwell at the haven of the sea; and 2074
Ex 1: 3 Issachar, **Z**, and Benjamin, 2074
Nu 1: 9 Of **Z**; Eliab the son of Helon. 2074
1:30 Of the children of **Z**, *by* their generations, 2074
1:31 *even* of the tribe of **Z**, *were* fifty and 2074
2: 7 *Then* the tribe of **Z**: and Eliab the son of 2074
2: 7 Helon *shall be* captain of the children of **Z**. 2074
7:24 prince of the children of **Z**, *did offer:* 2074
10:16 children of **Z** *was* Eliab the son of Helon. 2074
13:10 Of the tribe of **Z**, Gaddiel the son of Sodi. 2074
26:26 *Of* the sons of **Z** after their families: 2074
34:25 the prince of the tribe of the children of **Z**, 2074
Dt 27:13 Gad, and Asher, and **Z**, Dan, and Naphtali. 2074
33:18 of **Z** he said, Rejoice, Zebulun, in thy going 2074
33:18 he said, Rejoice, **Z**, in thy going out; 2074
Jos 19:10 the third lot came up for the children of **Z** 2074
19:16 This *is* the inheritance of the children of **Z** 2074
19:27 reacheth to **Z**, and to the valley of 2074
19:34 reacheth to **Z** on the south side, and 2074
21: 7 and out of the tribe of **Z**, twelve cities. 2074
21:34 the rest of the Levites, out of the tribe of **Z**, 2074
Jdg 1:30 Neither did **Z** drive out the inhabitants of 2074
4: 6 of Naphtali and of the children of **Z**? 2074
4:10 Barak called **Z** and Naphtali to Kedesh; 2074
5:14 out of **Z** they that handle the pen of 2074
5:18 **Z** and Naphtali *were* a people *that* 2074
6:35 unto Asher, and unto **Z**, and unto Naphtali; 2074
12:12 was buried in Aijalon in the country of **Z**. 2074
1Ch 2: 1 Simeon, Levi, and Judah, Issachar, and **Z**, 2074
6:63 and out of the tribe of **Z**, twelve cities. 2074
6:77 of Merari *were given* out of the tribe of **Z**, 2074
12:33 Of **Z**, such as went forth to battle, expert in 2074
12:40 *even* unto Issachar and **Z** and Naphtali, 2074
27:19 Of **Z**, Ishmaiah the son of Obadiah: 2074
2Ch 30:10 of Ephraim and Manasseh even unto **Z**: 2074
30:11 Manasseh and of **Z** humbled themselves, 2074
30:18 and Manasseh, Issachar, and **Z**, 2074
Ps 68:27 the princes of **Z**, *and* the princes of 2074
Isa 9: 1 at the first he lightly afflicted the land of **Z** 2074
Eze 48:26 east side unto the west side, **Z** a *portion*. 2074
48:27 by the border of **Z**, from the east side unto 2074
48:33 one gate of Issachar, one gate of **Z**. 2074

ZEBULUNITES (1) [ZEBULUN]
Nu 26:27 These *are* the families of the **Z** according to 2075

ZECHARIAH (39) [ZACHARIAH]
1Ch 5: 7 was reckoned, *were* the chief, Jeiel, and **Z**, 2148
9:21 *And* **Z** the son of Meshelemiah *was* porter 2148
9:37 And Gedor, and Ahio, and **Z**, and Mikloth. 2148
15:18 **Z**, Ben, and Jaaziel, and Shemiramoth, and 2148
15:20 **Z**, and Aziel, and Shemiramoth, and Jehiel, 2148
15:24 Amasai, and **Z**, and Benaiah, and Eliezer, 2148
16: 5 next to him **Z**, Jeiel, and Shemiramoth, and 2148
24:25 *was* Isshiah: of the sons of Isshiah; **Z**. 2148
26: 2 the sons of Meshelemiah *were*, **Z** 2148
26:11 the second, Tebaliah the third, **Z** the fourth: 2148
26:14 *for* **Z** his son, a wise counseller, they cast 2148
27:21 of Manasseh in Gilead, Iddo the son of **Z**: 2148
2Ch 17: 7 to **Z**, and to Nethaneel, and to Michaiah, 2148
20:14 upon Jahaziel the son of **Z**, the son of 2148
21: 2 **Z**, and Azariah, and Michael, and 2148
24:20 the spirit of God came upon **Z** the son of 2148
26: 5 he sought God in the days of **Z**, who had 2148
29: 1 name *was* Abijah, the daughter of **Z**. 2148
29:13 of the sons of Asaph; **Z**, and Mattaniah: 2148
34:12 **Z** and Meshullam, of the sons of 2148

Z

2Ch 35: 8 Hilkiah and Z and Jehiel, rulers of 2148
Ezr 5: 1 Haggai the prophet, and Z the son of Iddo, 2148
6:14 Haggai the prophet and Z the son of Iddo. 2148
8: 3 of Shechaniah, of the sons of Pharosh; Z: 2148
8:11 Z the son of Bebai, and with him twenty 2148
8:16 for Nathan, and for Z, and for Meshullam, 2148
10:26 Z, and Jehiel, and Abdi, and Jeremoth, and 2148
Ne 8: 4 and Hashbadana, Z, *and* Meshullam. 2148
11: 4 the son of Z, the son of Amariah, the son of 2148
11: 5 of Adaiah, the son of Joiarib, the son of Z, 2148
11:12 the son of Amzi, the son of Z, the son of 2148
12:16 Of Iddo, Z; of Ginnethon, Meshullam; 2148
12:35 *namely,* Z the son of Jonathan, the son of 2148
12:41 Michaiah, Elioenai, Z, *and* Hananiah, 2148
Isa 8: 2 the priest, and Z the son of Jeberechiah. 2148
Zec 1: 1 came the word of the LORD unto Z, 2148
1: 7 came the word of the LORD unto Z, 2148
7: 1 *that* the word of the LORD came unto Z 2148
7: 8 the word of the LORD came unto Z, 2148

ZEDAD (2)
Nu 34: 8 the goings forth of the border shall be to Z: 6657
Eze 47:15 the way of Hethlon, as *men* go to Z; 6657

ZEDEKIAH (61) [ZEDEKIAH'S]
1Ki 22:11 Z the son of Chenaanah made him horns of 6667
22:24 Z the son of Chenaanah went near, and 6667
2Ki 24:17 in his stead, and changed his name *to* Z. 6667
24:18 Z *was* twenty and one years old when he 6667
24:20 that Z rebelled against the king of Babylon. 6667
25: 2 besieged unto the eleventh year of king Z. 6667
25: 7 they slew the sons of Z before his eyes, 6667
25: 7 put out the eyes of Z, and bound him with 6667
1Ch 3:15 the third Z, the fourth Shallum. 6667
3:16 of Jehoiakim: Jeconiah his son, Z his son. 6667
2Ch 18:10 Z the son of Chenaanah had made him 6667
18:23 Z the son of Chenaanah came near, and 6667
36:10 and made Z his brother king over Judah and 6667
36:11 Z *was* one and twenty years old when he 6667
Jer 1: 3 unto the end of the eleventh year of Z 6667
21: 1 when king Z sent unto him Pashur the son 6667
21: 3 Jeremiah unto them, Thus shall ye say to Z: 6667
21: 7 I will deliver Z king of Judah, and his 6667
24: 8 So will I give Z the king of Judah, and his 6667
27: 3 come *to* Jerusalem unto Z king of Judah; 6667
27:12 I spake also to Z king of Judah according to 6667
28: 1 in the beginning of the reign of Z king of 6667
29: 3 whom Z king of Judah sent unto Babylon 6667
29:21 of Kolaiah, and of Z, the son of Maaseiah, 6667
29:22 The LORD make thee like Z and 6667
32: 1 in the tenth year of Z king of Judah, 6667
32: 3 For Z king of Judah had shut him up, 6667
32: 4 Z king of Judah shall not escape out of 6667
32: 5 he shall lead Z *to* Babylon, and there shall 6667
34: 2 Go and speak to Z king of Judah, and 6667
34: 4 word of the LORD, O Z king of Judah; 6667
34: 6 words unto Z king of Judah in Jerusalem, 6667
34: 8 after that the king Z had made a covenant 6667
34:21 Z king of Judah and his princes will I give 6667
36:12 Z the son of Hananiah, and all the princes. 6667
37: 1 king Z the son of Josiah reigned instead of 6667
37: 3 Z the king sent Jehucal the son of 6667
37:17 Z the king sent, and took him *out:* and 6667
37:18 Moreover Jeremiah said unto king Z, 6667
37:21 Z the king commanded that they should 6667
38: 5 Z the king said, Behold, he *is* in your hand: 6667
38:14 Z the king sent, and took Jeremiah 6667
38:15 Jeremiah said unto Z, If I declare *it* unto 6667
38:16 So Z the king sware secretly unto Jeremiah, 6667
38:17 said Jeremiah unto Z, Thus saith 6667
38:19 Z the king said unto Jeremiah, I am afraid 6667
38:24 said Z unto Jeremiah, Let no man know of 6667
39: 1 In the ninth year of Z king of Judah, in 6667
39: 2 *And* in the eleventh year of Z, in the fourth 6667
39: 4 *that* when Z the king of Judah saw them, 6667
39: 5 and overtook Z in the plains of Jericho: 6667
39: 6 the king of Babylon slew the sons of Z in 6667
44:30 as I gave Z king of Judah into the hand of 6667
49:34 beginning of the reign of Z king of Judah, 6667
51:59 when he went with Z the king of Judah *into* 6667
52: 1 Z *was* one and twenty year old when he 6667
52: 3 that Z rebelled against the king of Babylon. 6667
52: 5 besieged unto the eleventh year of king Z. 6667
52: 8 and overtook Z in the plains of Jericho; 6667
52:10 the king of Babylon slew the sons of Z 6667
52:11 he put out the eyes of Z; and the king of 6667

ZEDEKIAH'S (1) [ZEDEKIAH]
Jer 39: 7 Moreover he put out Z eyes, and 6667

ZEEB (6)
Jdg 7:25 two princes of the Midianites, Oreb and Z; 2062
7:25 Z they slew at the winepress of Zeeb, and 2062
7:25 Zeeb they slew at the winepress of Z, and 2062
7:25 and Z to Gideon on the *other* side Jordan. 2062
8: 3 hands the princes of Midian, Oreb and Z: 2062
Ps 83:11 Make their nobles like Oreb, and like Z: 2062

ZEKER See ZACHER

ZELAH (2)
Jos 18:28 Z, Eleph, and Jebusi, which *is* Jerusalem, 6762
2Sa 21:14 they in the country of Benjamin in Z, 6762

ZELEK (2)
2Sa 23:37 Z the Ammonite, Naharai the Beerothite, 6768
1Ch 11:39 Z the Ammonite, Naharai the Berothite, 6768

ZELOPHEHAD (11)
Nu 26:33 Z the son of Hepher had no sons, but 6765
26:33 the names of the daughters of Z *were* 6765
27: 1 came the daughters of Z, the son of 6765
27: 7 The daughters of Z speak right: thou shalt 6765
36: 2 of Z our brother unto his daughters. 6765
36: 6 command concerning the daughters of Z, 6765
36:10 so did the daughters of Z: 6765
36:11 and Milcah, and Noah, the daughters of Z, 6765
Jos 17: 3 Z, the son of Hepher, the son of Gilead, 6765
1Ch 7:15 and the name of the second *was* Z: 6765
7:15 *was* Zelophehad: and Z had daughters. 6765

ZELOTES (2)
Lk 6:15 the *son* of Alpheus, and Simon called Z, *2208*
Ac 1:13 and Simon Z, and Judas *the brother* of *2208*

ZELZAH (1)
1Sa 10: 2 sepulchre in the border of Benjamin at Z; 6766

ZEMARAIM (2)
Jos 18:22 And Beth-arabah, and Z, and Beth-el, 6787
2Ch 13: 4 Abijah stood up upon mount Z, which *is* in 6787

ZEMARITE (2)
Ge 10:18 the Arvadite, and the Z, and the Hamathite: 6786
1Ch 1:16 the Arvadite, and the Z, and the Hamathite. 6786

ZEMIRA (1)
1Ch 7: 8 Z, and Joash, and Eliezer, and Elioenai, and 2160

ZENAN (1)
Jos 15:37 Z, and Hadashah, and Migdal-gad, 6799

ZENAS (1)
Tit 3:13 Bring Z the lawyer and Apollos on their *2211*

ZEPHANIAH (10)
2Ki 25:18 Z the second priest, and the three keepers 6846
1Ch 6:36 of Joel, the son of Azariah, the son of Z, 6846
Jer 21: 1 Z the son of Maaseiah the priest, saying, 6846
29:25 and to Z the son of Maaseiah the priest, and 6846
29:29 Z the priest read this letter in the ears of 6846
37: 3 Z the son of Maaseiah the priest to 6846
52:24 Z the second priest, and the three keepers 6846
Zep 1: 1 which came unto Z the son of Cushi, 6846
Zec 6:10 go *into* the house of Josiah the son of Z; 6846
6:14 and to Jedaiah, and to Hen the son of Z, 6846

ZEPHATH (1)
Jdg 1:17 they slew the Canaanites that inhabited Z, 6857

ZEPHATHAH (1)
2Ch 14:10 they set the battle in array in the valley of Z 6859

ZEPHI (1) [ZEPHO]
1Ch 1:36 Omar, Z, and Gatam, Kenaz, and Timna, 6825

ZEPHO (2) [ZEPHI]
Ge 36:11 Omar, Z, and Gatam, and Kenaz. 6825
36:15 duke Omar, duke Z, duke Kenaz, 6825

ZEPHON (1) [BAAL-ZEPHON, ZEPHONITES]
Nu 26:15 of Z, the family of the Zephonites: 6827

ZEPHONITES (1) [ZEPHON]
Nu 26:15 of Zephon, the family of the Z: of Haggi, 6831

ZER (1)
Jos 19:35 Z, and Hammath, Rakkath, and Chinnereth, 6863

ZERAH (20)
Ge 36:13 Nahath, and Z, Shammah, and Mizzah: 2226
36:17 duke Nahath, duke Z, duke Shammah, 2226
36:33 Jobab the son of Z of Bozrah reigned in his 2226
46:12 and Onan, and Shelah, and Pharez, and Z: 2226
Nu 26:13 Of Z, the family of the Zarhites: of Shaul, 2226
26:20 of Z, the family of the Zarhites. 2226
Jos 7: 1 of Carmi, the son of Zabdi, the son of Z, 2226
7:18 of Carmi, the son of Zabdi, the son of Z, 2226
7:24 took Achan the son of Z, and the silver, and 2226
22:20 Did not Achan the son of Z commit a 2226
1Ch 1:37 Nahath, Z, Shammah, and Mizzah. 2226
1:44 Jobab the son of Z of Bozrah reigned in his 2226
2: 4 his daughter in law bare him Pharez and Z. 2226
2: 6 the sons of Z; Zimri, and Ethan, and 2226
4:24 and Jamin, Jarib, Z, *and* Shaul: 2226
6:21 Joah his son, Iddo his son, Z his son, 2226
6:41 The son of Ethni, the son of Z, the son of 2226
9: 6 of the sons of Z; Jeuel, and their brethren, 2226
2Ch 14: 9 there came out against them Z 2226
Ne 11:24 of the children of Z the son of Judah, 2226

ZERAHIAH (5)
1Ch 6: 6 Uzzi begat Z, and Zerahiah begat Meraioth, 2228
6: 6 Uzzi begat Zerahiah, and Z begat Meraioth, 2228
6:51 Bukki his son, Uzzi his son, Z his son, 2228
Ezr 7: 4 The son of Z, the son of Uzzi, the son of 2228
8: 4 Elihoenai the son of Z, and with him two 2228

ZERAHITE See ZARHITES

ZERED (3)
Dt 2:13 *said I,* and get you over the brook Z. 2218
2:13 And we went over the brook Z. 2218
2:14 until we were come over the brook Z, 2218

ZEREDA (1)
1Ki 11:26 an Ephrathite of Z, Solomon's servant, 6868

ZEREDATHAH (1)
2Ch 4:17 in the clay ground between Succoth and Z. 6868

ZERERATH (1)
Jdg 7:22 the host fled to Beth-shittah in Z, *and* to 6888

ZERESH (4)
Est 5:10 and called for his friends, and Z his wife. 2238
5:14 said Z his wife and all his friends unto him, 2238
6:13 Haman told Z his wife and all his friends 2238
6:13 said his wise *men* and Z his wife unto him, 2238

ZERETH (1)
1Ch 4: 7 the sons of Helah *were,* Z, and Jezoar, and 6889

ZERETH SHAHAR See ZARETHSHAHAR

ZERI (1)
1Ch 25: 3 Gedaliah, and Z, and Jeshaiah, Hashabiah, 6874

ZEROR (1)
1Sa 9: 1 the son of Abiel, the son of Z, the son of 6872

ZERUAH (1)
1Ki 11:26 whose mother's name *was* Z, a widow 6871

ZERUBBABEL (22) [ZOROBABEL]
1Ch 3:19 the sons of Pedajah *were,* Z, and Shimei: 2216
3:19 the son of Z; Meshullam, and Hananiah, 2216
Ezr 2: 2 Which came with Z: Jeshua, Nehemiah, 2216
3: 2 and Z the son of Shealtiel, and his brethren, 2216
3: 8 began Z the son of Shealtiel, and Jeshua 2216
4: 2 they came to Z, and to the chief of 2216
4: 3 Z, and Jeshua, and the rest of the chief of 2216
5: 2 rose up Z the son of Shealtiel, and 2217
Ne 7: 7 Who came with Z, Jeshua, Nehemiah, 2216
12: 1 the Levites that went up with Z the son of 2216
12:47 all Israel in the days of Z, and in the days 2216
Hag 1: 1 the prophet unto Z the son of Shealtiel, 2216
1:12 Z the son of Shealtiel, and Joshua the son 2216
1:14 the LORD stirred up the spirit of Z 2216
2: 2 Speak now to Z the son of Shealtiel, 2216
2: 4 Yet now be strong, O Z, saith the LORD; 2216
2:21 Speak to Z, governor of Judah, saying, 2216
2:23 will I take thee, O Z, my servant, the son of 2216
Zec 4: 6 This *is* the word of the LORD unto Z, 2216
4: 7 before Z *thou shalt* become a plain: and 2216
4: 9 The hands of Z have laid the foundation of 2216
4:10 shall see the plummet in the hand of Z *with* 2216

ZERUIAH (26)
1Sa 26: 6 to Abishai the son of Z, brother to Joab, 6870
2Sa 2:13 Joab the son of Z, and the servants of 6870
2:18 there were three sons of Z there, Joab, and 6870
3:39 these men the sons of Z *be* too hard for me: 6870
8:16 Joab the son of Z *was* over the host; and 6870
14: 1 Now Joab the son of Z perceived that 6870
16: 9 said Abishai the son of Z unto the king, 6870
16:10 What have I to do with you, ye sons of Z? 6870
17:25 of Nahash, sister to Z Joab's mother. 6870
18: 2 part under the hand of Abishai the son of Z, 6870
19:21 Abishai the son of Z answered and said, 6870
19:22 What have I to do with you, ye sons of Z, 6870
21:17 Abishai the son of Z succoured him, and 6870
23:18 the brother of Joab, the son of Z, 6870
23:37 armourbearer to Joab the son of Z, 6870
1Ki 1: 7 he conferred with Joab the son of Z, and 6870
2: 5 also what Joab the son of Z did to me, 6870
2:22 the priest, and for Joab the son of Z. 6870
1Ch 2:16 Whose sisters *were* Z, and Abigail. And 6870
2:16 the sons of Z; Abishai, and Joab, and 6870
11: 6 So Joab the son of Z went first up, and 6870
11:39 the armourbearer of Joab the son of Z, 6870
18:12 Moreover Abishai the son of Z slew of 6870
18:15 Joab the son of Z *was* over the host; and 6870
26:28 and Joab the son of Z, had dedicated; 6870
27:24 Joab the son of Z began to number, but 6870

ZETHAM (2)
1Ch 23: 8 the chief *was* Jehiel, and Z, and Joel, three. 2241
26:22 Z, and Joel his brother, *which were* over 2241

ZETHAN (1)
1Ch 7:10 and Z, and Tharshish, and Ahishahar. 2133

ZETHAR (1)
Est 1:10 Bigtha, and Abagtha, Z, and Carcas, 2242

ZEUS See JUPITER

ZIA (1)
1Ch 5:13 Jorai, and Jachan, and Z, and Heber, seven. 2127

ZIBA (16)
2Sa 9: 2 house of Saul a servant whose name *was* Z. 6717
9: 2 the king said unto him, *Art* thou Z? 6717
9: 3 Z said unto the king, Jonathan hath yet a 6717
9: 4 Z said unto the king, Behold, he *is* in 6717
9: 9 the king called to Z, Saul's servant, and 6717
9:10 Now Z had fifteen sons and 6717
9:11 said Z unto the king, According to all that 6717
9:12 all that dwelt in the house of Z *were* 6717
16: 1 Z the servant of Mephibosheth met him, 6717
16: 2 the king said unto Z, What meanest thou by 6717
16: 2 Z said, The asses *be* for the king's 6717
16: 3 Z said unto the king, Behold, he abideth at 6717
16: 4 said the king to Z, Behold, thine *are* all that 6717
16: 4 Z said, I humbly beseech thee *that* I may 6717
19:17 Z the servant of the house of Saul, and 6717
19:29 I have said, Thou and Z divide the land. 6717

ZIBEON (8)
Ge 36: 2 of Anah the daughter of Z the Hivite; 6649
36:14 of Anah, daughter of Z, Esau's wife: 6649
36:20 Lotan, and Shobal, and Z, and Anah, 6649
36:24 these *are* the children of Z; both Aiah, and 6649
36:24 as he fed the asses of Z his father. 6649
36:29 duke Shobal, duke Z, duke Anah, 6649
1Ch 1:38 Z, and Anah, and Dishon, and Ezer, and 6649
1:40 Onam. And the sons of Z; Aiah, and Anah. 6649

ZIBIA (1)
1Ch 8: 9 and Z, and Mesha, and Malcham, 6644

ZIBIAH (2)
2Ki 12: 1 his mother's name *was* Z of Beer-sheba. 6645
2Ch 24: 1 His mother's name also *was* Z of 6645

ZICHRI (12)
Ex 6:21 sons of Izhar; Korah, and Nepheg, and Z. 2147
1Ch 8:19 And Jakim, and Z, and Zabdi, 2147
8:23 And Abdon, and Z, and Hanan, 2147
8:27 Jaresiah, and Eliah, and Z, the sons of 2147
9:15 of Micah, the son of Z, the son of Asaph; 2147
26:25 and Z his son, and Shelomith his son. 2147
27:16 of the Reubenites *was* Eliezer the son of Z: 2147
2Ch 17:16 next him *was* Amasiah the son of Z, 2147
23: 1 Elishaphat the son of Z, into covenant with 2147
28: 7 Z, a mighty *man* of Ephraim, slew 2147
Ne 11: 9 Joel the son of Z *was* their overseer: 2147
12:17 Of Abijah, Z; of Miniamin, of Moadiah, 2147

ZICRI See ZICHRI

ZIDDIM (1)
Jos 19:35 the fenced cities *are* Z, Zer, and Hammath, 6661

ZIDKIJAH (1)
Ne 10: 1 the Tirshatha, the son of Hachaliah, and Z, 6667

ZIDON (21) [SIDON, ZIDONIANS]
Ge 49:13 of ships; and his border *shall be* unto Z. 6721
Jos 11: 8 chased them unto great Z, and 6721
19:28 Hammon, and Kanah, *even* unto great Z; 6721
Jdg 1:31 nor the inhabitants of Z, nor of Ahlab, 6721
10: 6 the gods of Z, and the gods of Moab, and 6721
18:28 because it *was* far from Z, and they had no 6721
2Sa 24: 6 and they came to Dan-jaan, and about to Z, 6721
1Ki 17: 9 which *belongeth* to Z, and dwell there: 6721
1Ch 1:13 Canaan begat Z his firstborn, and Heth, 6721
Ezr 3: 7 oil, unto them of Z, and to them of Tyre, 6722
Isa 23: 2 thou whom the merchants of Z, that pass 6721
23: 4 Be thou ashamed, O Z: for the sea hath 6721
23:12 O thou oppressed virgin, daughter of Z: 6721
Jer 25:22 all the kings of Z, and the kings of the isles 6721
27: 3 to the king of Tyrus, and to the king of Z, 6721
47: 4 and Z every helper that remaineth: 6721
Eze 27: 8 The inhabitants of Z and Arvad were thy 6721
28:21 set thy face against Z, and prophesy against 6721
28:22 Behold, I *am* against thee, O Z; and I will 6721
Joel 3: 4 and Z, and all the coasts of Palestine? 6721
Zec 9: 2 and Z, though it be very wise. 6721

ZIDONIANS (10) [ZIDON]
Jdg 10:12 The Z also, and the Amalekites, and 6722
18: 7 after the manner of the Z, quiet and secure; 6722
18: 7 they *were* far from the Z, and had no 6722
1Ki 11: 1 Ammonites, Edomites, Z, *and* Hittites; 6722
11: 5 went after Ashtoreth the goddess of the Z, 6722
11:33 worshipped Ashtoreth the goddess of the Z, 6722
16:31 the daughter of Ethbaal king of the Z, 6722
2Ki 23:13 for Ashtoreth the abomination of the Z, 6722
1Ch 22: 4 for the Z and they of Tyre brought much 6722
Eze 32:30 of the north, all of them, and all the Z, 6722

ZIF (2)
1Ki 6: 1 in the month Z, which *is* the second month, 2099
6:37 house of the LORD laid, in the month Z: 2099

ZIHA (3)
Ezr 2:43 the children of Z, the children of Hasupha, 6727
Ne 7:46 the children of Z, the children of Hashupha, 6727
11:21 and Z and Gispa *were* over the Nethinims. 6727

ZIKLAG (15)
Jos 15:31 And Z, and Madmannah, and Sansannah, 6860
19: 5 Z, and Beth-marcaboth, and Hazar-susah, 6860
1Sa 27: 6 Achish gave him Z that day: wherefore 6860
27: 6 wherefore Z pertaineth unto the kings of 6860
30: 1 his men were come *to* Z on the third day, 6860
30: 1 Z, and smitten Ziklag, and burnt it with 6860
30: 1 and smitten Z, and burnt it with fire; 6860
30:14 south of Caleb; and we burnt Z with fire. 6860
30:26 when David came to Z, he sent of the spoil 6860
2Sa 1: 1 and David had abode two days in Z; 6860
4:10 I took hold of him, and slew him in Z, 6860
1Ch 4:30 And at Bethuel, and at Hormah, and at Z, 6860
12: 1 these *are* they that came to David to Z, 6860
12:20 As he went to Z, there fell to him of 6860
Ne 11:28 at Z, and at Mekonah, and in the villages 6860

ZILLAH (3)
Ge 4:19 one *was* Adah, and the name of the other Z. 6741
4:22 Z, she also bare Tubal-cain, an instructor of 6741
4:23 his wives, Adah and Z, Hear my voice; 6741

ZILLETHAI See ZILTHAI

ZILPAH (7)
Ge 29:24 Laban gave unto his daughter Leah Z his 2153
30: 9 she took Z her maid, and gave her Jacob to 2153
30:10 And Z Leah's maid bare Jacob a son. 2153
30:12 Z Leah's maid bare Jacob a second son. 2153
35:26 the sons of Z, Leah's handmaid; Gad, and 2153
37: 2 and with the sons of Z, his father's wives: 2153
46:18 These *are* the sons of Z, whom Laban gave 2153

ZILTHAI (2)
1Ch 8:20 And Elienai, and Z, and Eliel, 6769
12:20 Michael, and Jozabad, and Elihu, and Z, 6769

ZIMMAH (3)
1Ch 6:20 Libni his son, Jahath his son, Z his son, 2155
6:42 The son of Ethan, the son of Z, the son of 2155
2Ch 29:12 Joah the son of Z, and Eden the son of 2155

ZIMRAN (2)
Ge 25: 2 she bare him Z, and Jokshan, and Medan, 2175
1Ch 1:32 she bare Z, and Jokshan, and Medan, and 2175

ZIMRI (15)
Nu 25:14 *was* Z, the son of Salu, a prince of a chief 2174
1Ki 16: 9 his servant Z, captain of half *his* chariots, 2174
16:10 Z went in and smote him, and killed him, 2174
16:12 Thus did Z destroy all the house of Baasha, 2174
16:15 seventh year of Asa king of Judah did Z 2174
16:16 Z hath conspired, and hath also slain 2174
16:18 to pass, when Z saw that the city was taken, 2174
16:20 Now the rest of the acts of Z, and 2174
2Ki 9:31 she said, *Had* Z peace, who slew his 2174
1Ch 2: 6 Z, and Ethan, and Heman, and Calcol, and 2174
8:36 begat Alemeth, and Azmaveth, and Z; 2174
8:36 and Zimri; and Z begat Moza, 2174
9:42 begat Alemeth, and Azmaveth, and Z; 2174
9:42 and Zimri; and Z begat Moza; 2174
Jer 25:25 all the kings of Z, and all the kings of 2174

ZIN (10)
Nu 13:21 searched the land from the wilderness of Z 6790
20: 1 *into* the desert of Z in the first month: 6790
27:14 my commandment in the desert of Z, 6790
27:14 Meribah in Kadesh *in* the wilderness of Z. 6790
33:36 pitched in the wilderness of Z, which *is* 6790
34: 3 of Z along by the coast of Edom, 6790
34: 4 the ascent of Akrabbim, and pass on to Z: 6790
Dt 32:51 of Meribah-Kadesh, *in* the wilderness of Z; 6790
Jos 15: 1 the wilderness of Z southward *was* 6790
15: 3 passed along to Z, and ascended up on 6790

ZINA (1) [ZIZAH]
1Ch 23:10 *were,* Jahath, Z, and Jeush, and Beriah. 2126

ZION (153) [SION, ZION'S]
2Sa 5: 7 David took the strong hold of Z: 6726
1Ki 8: 1 out of the city of David, which *is* Z. 6726
2Ki 19:21 The virgin the daughter of Z hath despised 6726
19:31 and they that escape out of mount Z: 6726
1Ch 11: 5 Nevertheless David took the castle of Z, 6726
2Ch 5: 2 out of the city of David, which *is* Z. 6726
Ps 2: 6 have I set my king upon my holy hill of Z. 6726
9:11 to the LORD, which dwelleth in Z: 6726
9:14 thy praise in the gates of the daughter of Z: 6726
14: 7 the salvation of Israel *were come* out of Z! 6726
20: 2 the sanctuary, and strengthen thee out of Z; 6726
48: 2 *is* mount Z, *on* the sides of the north, 6726
48:11 Let mount Z rejoice, let the daughters of 6726
48:12 Walk about Z, and go round about her: 6726
50: 2 Out of Z, the perfection of beauty, 6726
51:18 Do good in thy good pleasure unto Z: 6726
53: 6 the salvation of Israel *were come* out of Z! 6726
65: 1 Praise waiteth for thee, O God, in Z: and 6726
69:35 For God will save Z, and will build 6726
74: 2 this mount Z, wherein thou hast dwelt. 6726
76: 2 his tabernacle, and his dwelling place in Z. 6726
78:68 tribe of Judah, the mount Z which he loved. 6726
84: 7 *every one of them* in Z appeareth before 6726
87: 2 The LORD loveth the gates of Z more 6726
87: 5 of Z it shall be said, This and that man was 6726
97: 8 Z heard, and was glad, and the daughters of 6726
99: 2 The LORD *is* great in Z; and he *is* high 6726
102:13 Thou shalt arise, *and* have mercy upon Z: 6726
102:16 When the LORD shall build up Z, he shall 6726
102:21 To declare the name of the LORD in Z, 6726
110: 2 shall send the rod of thy strength out of Z: 6726
125: 1 trust in the LORD *shall be* as mount Z, 6726
126: 1 the LORD turned again the captivity of Z, 6726
128: 5 The LORD shall bless thee out of Z: and 6726
129: 5 be confounded and turned back that hate Z. 6726
132:13 For the LORD hath chosen Z; he hath 6726
133: 3 that descended upon the mountains of Z: 6726
134: 3 made heaven and earth bless thee out of Z. 6726
135:21 Blessed *be* the LORD out of Z, 6726
137: 1 yea, we wept, when we remembered Z. 6726
137: 3 *saying,* Sing us *one* of the songs of Z. 6726
146:10 *even* thy God, O Z, unto all generations. 6726
147:12 O Jerusalem; praise thy God, O Z. 6726
149: 2 let the children of Z be joyful in their King. 6726
SS 3:11 O ye daughters of Z, and behold king 6726
Isa 1: 8 the daughter of Z is left as a cottage in a 6726
1:27 Z shall be redeemed with judgment, and 6726
2: 3 for out of Z shall go forth the law, and 6726
3:16 Because the daughters of Z are haughty, 6726
3:17 crown of the head of the daughters of Z, 6726
4: 3 *that* he that is left in Z, and he that 6726
4: 4 away the filth of the daughters of Z, 6726
4: 5 upon every dwelling place of mount Z, 6726
8:18 of hosts, which dwelleth in mount Z. 6726
10:12 performed his whole work upon mount Z 6726
10:24 O my people that dwellest in Z, be not 6726
10:32 *against* the mount of the daughter of Z, 6726
12: 6 Cry out and shout, thou inhabitant of Z: 6726
14:32 That the LORD hath founded Z, and 6726
16: 1 unto the mount of the daughter of Z. 6726
18: 7 name of the LORD of hosts, the mount Z. 6726
24:23 the LORD of hosts shall reign in mount Z, 6726
28:16 Behold, I lay in Z for a foundation a stone, 6726
29: 8 the nations be, that fight against mount Z. 6726
30:19 For the people shall dwell in Z at 6726
31: 4 of hosts come down to fight for mount Z, 6726
31: 9 whose fire *is* in Z, and his furnace in 6726
33: 5 he hath filled Z *with* judgment and 6726
33:14 The sinners in Z are afraid; fearfulness hath 6726
33:20 Look upon Z, the city of our solemnities: 6726
34: 8 of recompences for the controversy of Z. 6726
35:10 come *to* Z with songs and everlasting joy 6726
37:22 The virgin, the daughter of Z, hath despised 6726
37:32 and they that escape out of mount Z: 6726
40: 9 O Z, that bringest good tidings, get thee up 6726
Isa 41:27 The first *shall say* to Z, Behold, 6726
46:13 I will place salvation in Z for Israel my 6726
49:14 Z said, The LORD hath forsaken me, and 6726
51: 3 For the LORD shall comfort Z: he will 6726
51:11 shall return, and come with singing *unto* Z; 6726
51:16 and say unto Z, Thou *art* my people. 6726
52: 1 Awake, awake; put on thy strength, O Z; 6726
52: 2 bands of thy neck, O captive daughter of Z. 6726
52: 7 that saith unto Z, Thy God reigneth! 6726
52: 8 when the LORD shall bring again Z. 6726
59:20 the redeemer shall come to Z, and 6726
60:14 The Z of the Holy One of Israel. 6726
61: 3 To appoint unto them that mourn in Z, 6726
62:11 Say ye to the daughter of Z, Behold, 6726
64:10 Z is a wilderness, Jerusalem a desolation. 6726
66: 8 for as soon as Z travailed, she brought forth 6726
Jer 3:14 two of a family, and I will bring you *to* Z: 6726
4: 6 Set up the standard toward Z: retire, 6726
4:31 the voice of the daughter of Z, 6726
6: 2 I have likened the daughter of Z *to* a 6726
6:23 men for war against thee, O daughter of Z. 6726
8:19 *Is* not the LORD in Z? *is* not her king in 6726
9:19 For a voice of wailing is heard out of Z, 6726
14:19 hath thy soul lothed Z? why hast thou 6726
26:18 Z shall be plowed *like* a field, and 6726
30:17 called thee an Outcast, *saying,* This *is* Z, 6726
31: 6 let us go up *to* Z unto the LORD our God. 6726
31:12 they shall come and sing in the height of Z, 6726
50: 5 They shall ask the way *to* Z with their faces 6726
50:28 to declare in Z the vengeance of 6726
51:10 let us declare in Z the work of the LORD 6726
51:24 evil that they have done in Z in your sight, 6726
51:35 shall the inhabitant of Z say; 6726
La 1: 4 The ways of Z do mourn, because 6726
1: 6 from the daughter of Z all her beauty is 6726
1:17 Z spreadeth forth her hands, *and there is* 6726
2: 1 the daughter of Z with a cloud in his anger, 6726
2: 4 in the tabernacle of the daughter of Z: 6726
2: 6 and sabbaths to be forgotten in Z, 6726
2: 8 to destroy the wall of the daughter of Z: 6726
2:10 The elders of the daughter of Z sit upon 6726
2:13 may comfort thee, O virgin daughter of Z? 6726
2:18 unto the Lord, O wall of the daughter of Z, 6726
4: 2 The precious sons of Z, comparable to fine 6726
4:11 hath kindled a fire in Z, and it hath 6726
4:22 iniquity is accomplished, O daughter of Z; 6726
5:11 They ravished the women in Z, *and* 6726
5:18 Because of the mountain of Z, which is 6726
Joel 2: 1 Blow ye the trumpet in Z, and sound an 6726
2:15 Blow the trumpet in Z, sanctify a fast, 6726
2:23 ye children of Z, and rejoice in the LORD 6726
2:32 for in mount Z and in Jerusalem shall be 6726
3:16 The LORD also shall roar out of Z, and 6726
3:17 I *am* the LORD your God dwelling in Z, 6726
3:21 not cleansed: for the LORD dwelleth in Z. 6726
Am 1: 2 The LORD will roar from Z, and utter his 6726
6: 1 Woe to them *that are* at ease in Z, and trust 6726
Ob 1:17 But upon mount Z shall be deliverance, and 6726
1:21 saviours shall come up on mount Z to 6726
Mic 1:13 beginning of the sin to the daughter of Z: 6726
3:10 They build up Z with blood, and 6726
3:12 Therefore shall Z for your sake be plowed 6726
4: 2 for the law shall go forth of Z, and 6726
4: 7 over them in mount Z from henceforth, 6726
4: 8 the strong hold of the daughter of Z, 6726
4:10 and labour to bring forth, O daughter of Z, 6726
4:11 her be defiled, and let our eye look upon Z. 6726
4:13 Arise and thresh, O daughter of Z: for I 6726
Zep 3:14 Sing, O daughter of Z; shout, O Israel; 6726
3:16 *and to* Z, Let not thine hands be slack. 6726
Zec 1:14 and for Z *with* a great jealousy. 6726
1:17 the LORD shall yet comfort Z, and 6726
2: 7 Deliver thyself, O Z, that dwellest *with* 6726
2:10 Sing and rejoice, O daughter of Z: for lo, 6726
8: 2 I was jealous for Z *with* great jealousy, and 6726
8: 3 I am returned unto Z, and will dwell in 6726
9: 9 Rejoice greatly, O daughter of Z; shout, 6726
9:13 O Z, against thy sons, O Greece, and 6726

ZION'S (1) [ZION]
Isa 62: 1 For Z sake will I not hold my peace, and 6726

ZIOR (1)
Jos 15:54 and Kirjath-arba, which *is* Hebron, and Z; 6730

ZIPH (10) [ZIPHIMS, ZIPHITES]
Jos 15:24 Z, and Telem, and Bealoth, 2128
15:55 Maon, Carmel, and Z, and Juttah, 2128
1Sa 23:14 in a mountain in the wilderness of Z. 2128
23:15 David *was* in the wilderness of Z in a 2128
23:24 they arose, and went to Z before Saul: but 2128
26: 2 and went down to the wilderness of Z, 2128
26: 2 to seek David in the wilderness of Z. 2128
1Ch 2:42 his firstborn, which *was* the father of Z; 2128
4:16 Z, and Ziphah, Tiria, and Asareel. 2128
2Ch 11: 8 And Gath, and Mareshah, and Z, 2128

ZIPHAH (1)
1Ch 4:16 Ziph, and Z, Tiria, and Asareel. 2129

ZIPHIMS (1) [ZIPH]
Ps 54: T when the Z came and said to Saul, 2130

ZIPHION (1)
Ge 46:16 Z, and Haggi, Shuni, and Ezbon, Eri, and 6837

ZIPHITES (2) [ZIPH]
1Sa 23:19 came up the Z to Saul to Gibeah, saying, 2130
26: 1 the Z came unto Saul to Gibeah, saying, 2130

ZIPHRON (1)
Nu 34: 9 the border shall go on to Z, and the goings 2202

ZIPPOR (7)
Nu 22: 2 Balak the son of **Z** saw all that Israel had 6834
22: 4 Balak the son of **Z** *was* king of 6834
22:10 Balak the son of **Z**, king of Moab, hath sent 6834
22:16 said to him, Thus saith Balak the son of **Z**, 6834
23:18 and hear; hearken unto me, thou son of **Z**: 6834
Jos 24: 9 Balak the son of **Z**, king of Moab, arose 6834
Jdg 11:25 any thing better than Balak the son of **Z**, 6834

ZIPPORAH (3)
Ex 2:21 and he gave Moses **Z** his daughter. 6855
4:25 **Z** took a sharp stone, and cut off 6855
18: 2 Moses' father in law, took **Z**, Moses' wife, 6855

ZITHRI (1)
Ex 6:22 of Uzziel; Mishael, and Elzaphan, and **Z**. 5644

ZIV See ZIF

ZIZ (1)
2Ch 20:16 behold, they come up by the cliff of **Z**; and 6732

ZIZA (2)
1Ch 4:37 **Z** the son of Shiphi, the son of Allon, 2124
2Ch 11:20 and Attai, and **Z**, and Shelomith. 2124

ZIZAH (1) [ZINA]
1Ch 23:11 Jahath was the chief, and **Z** the second: 2125

ZOAN (7)
Nu 13:22 was built seven years before **Z** in Egypt.) 6814
Ps 78:12 in the land of Egypt, *in* the field of **Z**. 6814
78:43 in Egypt, and his wonders in the field of **Z**: 6814
Isa 19:11 Surely the princes of **Z** *are* fools, 6814
19:13 The princes of **Z** are become fools, 6814
30: 4 For his princes were at **Z**, and 6814
Eze 30:14 will set fire in **Z**, and will execute 6814

ZOAR (10)
Ge 13:10 the land of Egypt, as thou comest unto **Z**. 6820
14: 2 and the king of Bela, which *is* **Z**. 6820
14: 8 and the king of Bela (the same *is* **Z**); 6820
19:22 the name of the city was called **Z**. 6820
19:23 upon the earth when Lot entered into **Z**. 6820
19:30 Lot went up out of **Z**, and dwelt in 6820
19:30 with him; for he feared to dwell in **Z**: 6820
Dt 34: 3 of Jericho, the city of palm trees, unto **Z**. 6820
Isa 15: 5 his fugitives *shall flee* unto **Z**, a heifer of 6820
Jer 48:34 from **Z** *even* unto Horonaim, *as* a heifer of 6820

ZOBA (2) [ZOBAH]
2Sa 10: 6 the Syrians of **Z**, twenty thousand footmen, 6678
10: 8 the Syrians of **Z**, and of Rehob, and 6678

ZOBAH (11) [ARAM-ZOBAH, HAMATH-ZOBAH, ZOBA]
1Sa 14:47 against the kings of **Z**, and against 6678
2Sa 8: 3 the son of Rehob, king of **Z**, 6678
8: 5 came to succour Hadadezer king of **Z**, 6678
8:12 of Hadadezer, son of Rehob, king of **Z**. 6678
23:36 Igal the son of Nathan of **Z**, Bani 6678
1Ki 11:23 fled from his lord Hadadezer king of **Z**: 6678
11:24 when David slew them *of* **Z**: and they went NIH
1Ch 18: 3 David smote Hadarezer king of **Z** unto 6678
18: 5 came to help Hadarezer king of **Z**, 6678
18: 9 smitten all the host of Hadarezer king of **Z**; 6678
19: 6 and out of Syria-maachah, and out of **Z**. 6678

ZOBEBAH (1)
1Ch 4: 8 **Z**, and the families of Aharhel the son of 6637

ZOHAR (4)
Ge 23: 8 and intreat for me to Ephron the son of **Z**, 6714
25: 9 in the field of Ephron the son of **Z** 6714
46:10 **Z**, and Shaul the son of a Canaanitish 6714
Ex 6:15 **Z**, and Shaul the son of a Canaanitish 6714

ZOHELETH (1)
1Ki 1: 9 and oxen and fat cattle by the stone of **Z**, 2120

ZOHETH (1)
1Ch 4:20 the sons of Ishi *were*, **Z**, and Ben-zoheth. 2105

ZOPHAH (2)
1Ch 7:35 **Z**, and Imna, and Shelesh, and Amal. 6690
7:36 The sons of **Z**; Suah, and Harnepher, and 6690

ZOPHAI (1)
1Ch 6:26 of Elkanah; **Z** his son, and Nahath his son, 6689

ZOPHAR (4)
Job 2:11 Bildad the Shuhite, and **Z** the Naamathite: 6691
11: 1 Then answered **Z** the Naamathite, and said, 6691
20: 1 Then answered **Z** the Naamathite, and said, 6691
42: 9 the Shuhite *and* **Z** the Naamathite went, 6691

ZOPHIM (1) [RAMATHAIM-ZOPHIM]
Nu 23:14 he brought him *into* the field of **Z**, to 6839

ZORAH (8)
Jos 19:41 the coast of their inheritance was **Z**, and 6881
Jdg 13: 2 there was a certain man of **Z**, of the family 6881
13:25 the camp of Dan, between **Z** and Eshtaol. 6881
16:31 buried him between **Z** and Eshtaol in 6881
18: 2 men of valour, from **Z** and from Eshtaol, 6881
18: 8 they came unto their brethren *to* **Z** and 6881
18:11 out of **Z** and out of Eshtaol, six hundred 6881
2Ch 11:10 **Z**, and Aijalon, and Hebron, which *are* in 6881

ZORATHITES (1)
1Ch 4: 2 and Lahad. These *are* the families of the **Z**. 6882

ZOREAH (1)
Jos 15:33 in the valley, Eshtaol, and **Z**, and Ashnah, 6881

ZORITES (1)
1Ch 2:54 and half of the Manahethites, the **Z**. 6882

ZOROBABEL (3) [ZERUBBABEL]
Mt 1:12 begat Salathiel; and Salathiel begat **Z**; *2216*
1:13 And **Z** begat Abiud; and Abiud begat *2216*
Lk 3:27 *the son* of Rhesa, which was *the son* of **Z**, *2216*

ZUAR (5)
Nu 1: 8 Of Issachar; Nethaneel the son of **Z**. 6686
2: 5 Nethaneel the son of **Z** *shall be* captain of 6686
7:18 On the second day Nethaneel the son of **Z**, 6686
7:23 *was* the offering of Nethaneel the son of **Z**. 6686
10:15 of Issachar *was* Nethaneel the son of **Z**. 6686

ZUPH (3)
1Sa 1: 1 son of Tohu, the son of **Z**, an Ephrathite: 6689
9: 5 *And* when they were come to the land of **Z**, 6689
1Ch 6:35 The son of **Z**, the son of Elkanah, the son 6689

ZUPHITE See RAMATHAIM-ZOPHIM

ZUR (5) [BETH-ZUR]
Nu 25:15 was slain *was* Cozbi, the daughter of **Z**; 6698
31: 8 and Rekem, and **Z**, and Hur, and Reba, 6698
Jos 13:21 Evi, and Rekem, and **Z**, and Hur, and Reba, 6698
1Ch 8:30 and **Z**, and Kish, and Baal, and Nadab, 6698
9:36 **Z**, and Kish, and Baal, and Ner, and Nadab, 6698

ZURIEL (1)
Nu 3:35 of Merari *was* **Z** the son of Abihail: 6700

ZURISHADDAI (5)
Nu 1: 6 Of Simeon; Shelumiel the son of **Z**. 6701
2:12 of Simeon *shall be* Shelumiel the son of **Z**. 6701
7:36 On the fifth day Shelumiel the son of **Z**, 6701
7:41 *was* the offering of Shelumiel the son of **Z**. 6701
10:19 of Simeon *was* Shelumiel the son of **Z**. 6701

ZUZIMS (1)
Ge 14: 5 the **Z** in Ham, and the Emims in Shaveh 2104

ZUZITES See ZUZIMS

INDEX OF ARTICLES, CONJUNCTIONS, PARTICLES, PREPOSITIONS AND PRONOUNS

AN (1267)

AND (51713)

Idx

ARE (2946)

AS (3520)

BE (7012)

BUT (3994)

BY (2633)

FOR (8985)

14, 24, 25; 13:9, 12; 14:2, 2, 5, 8, 9, 14, 17, 21, 22, 22, 22, 31, 33, 34, 35, 35; 15:3, 3, 9, 16, 21, 22, 25, 27, 29, 29, 32, 34, 41, 52, 53; 16:1, 5, 7, 9, 10, 11, 11, 17, 18

2Co 1:5, 6, 6, 8, 11, 11, 12, 13, 19, 20, 23, 24, 24; 2:2, 4, 9, 10, 10, 11, 15, 16, 17; 3:6, 7, 9, 10, 11, 14; 4:5, 5, 6, 11, 11, 15, 15, 16, 17, 17, 17, 18; 5:1, 2, 4, 4, 5, 7, 10, 12, 13, 13, 14, 14, 15, 15, 20, 21, 21; 6:2, 13, 14, 16; 7:3, 5, 8, 8, 8, 9, 10, 11, 12, 12, 12, 13, 14; 8:3, 9, 9, 10, 10, 10, 12, 13, 14, 14, 16, 17, 21; 9:1, 1, 2, 2, 7, 9, 10, 12, 13, 13, 14, 14, 15; 10:3, 4, 8, 8, 8, 10, 12, 14, 14, 18; 11:2, 2, 4, 5, 9, 13, 14, 19, 20, 31; 12:1, 4, 6, 6, 8, 9, 9, 10, 10, 11, 11, 13, 14, 14, 14, 14, 15, 19, 20; 13:4, 4, 8, 8, 9

Gal 1:4, 5, 10, 10, 12, 13; 2:5, 6, 8, 12, 16, 18, 19, 20, 21; 3:6, 10, 10, 11, 13, 13, 18, 21, 26, 27, 28; 4:12, 15, 20, 22, 24, 25, 27, 27, 30; 5:3, 5, 5, 6, 13, 14, 17; 6:3, 5, 7, 8, 9, 12, 13, 15, 17

Eph 1:16; 2:4, 8, 10, 14, 15, 18, 22; 3:1, 1, 13, 14; 4:12, 12, 12, 25, 32; 5:2, 2, 5, 6, 8, 9, 12, 13, 20, 23, 25, 29, 30, 31; 6:1, 12, 18, 19, 20, 22

Php 1:4, 5, 7, 8, 17, 19, 21, 23, 24, 25, 26, 27, 29, 29; 2:13, 18, 20, 20, 21, 26, 27, 30; 3:1, 3, 7, 8, 8, 12, 14, 17, 18, 20, 20; 4:1, 6, 11, 16, 20

Col 1:3, 5, 5, 7, 9, 9, 16, 16, 19, 24, 24, 25; 2:1, 1, 1, 1, 5, 9; 3:3, 6, 20, 24, 25; 4:3, 3, 8, 12, 13, 13

1Th 1:2, 5, 5, 8, 9, 10; 2:1, 3, 5, 9, 9, 13, 14, 14, 16, 17, 19, 20; 3:3, 4, 5, 8, 9, 9, 9, 9; 4:2, 3, 7, 9, 14, 15, 16; 5:2, 3, 7, 8, 9, 10, 13, 15, 18, 25

2Th 1:3, 4, 5, 11; 2:3, 7, 11, 13; 3:1, 2, 5, 7, 7, 8, 10, 11

1Ti 1:9, 9, 9, 9, 9, 9, 10, 10, 10, 10, 10, 12, 16, 16, 17; 2:1, 2, 2, 3, 5, 6, 13; 3:5, 13; 4:4, 5, 8, 10, 16; 5:4, 8, 8, 10, 11, 15, 18, 23; 6:7, 10, 19

2Ti 1:7, 12, 12, 16; 2:5, 10, 11, 16, 21; 3:2, 6, 9, 16, 16, 16, 16; 4:3, 6, 8, 10, 11, 11, 15, 18

Tit 1:5, 7, 10, 11; 2:11, 13, 14; 3:3, 9, 12, 14

Phm 1:7, 9, 10, 15, 15, 15, 22

Heb 1:3, 8, 14; 2:2, 3, 8, 9, 9, 10, 10, 11, 11, 16, 17, 18; 3:3, 4, 5, 14, 16; 4:2, 3, 4, 8, 10, 12, 15; 5:1, 1, 1, 2, 3, 3, 3, 6, 12, 12, 13, 13; 6:4, 4, 7, 7, 10, 13, 16, 16, 18, 18, 20, 20; 7:1, 10, 11, 12, 13, 14, 15, 17, 17, 18, 18, 19, 21, 21, 25, 26, 27, 27, 27, 28, 28; 8:3, 4, 5, 7, 7, 8, 10, 11, 12; 9:2, 7, 7, 9, 12, 13, 15, 15, 16, 17, 19, 24, 24, 26, 28; 10:1, 2, 4, 6, 8, 10, 12, 12, 14, 14, 15, 18, 20, 23, 26, 26, 27, 30, 34, 36, 37; 11:1, 2, 5, 6, 8, 10, 10, 14, 16, 16, 25, 26, 27, 32, 40; 12:2, 3, 6, 7, 10, 10, 10, 11, 13, 16, 17, 17, 18, 20, 25, 29; 13:2, 5, 8, 9, 11, 11, 14, 16, 17, 17, 17, 17, 18, 18, 21, 22

Jas 1:6, 7, 11, 12, 13, 20, 23, 24; 2:2, 10, 11, 13, 23, 26; 3:2, 7, 16; 4:14, 14, 15; 5:1, 3, 7, 7, 8, 10, 14, 16

1Pe 1:4, 6, 13, 16, 20, 23, 24, 25; 2:13, 14, 14, 15, 16, 19, 19, 20, 20, 20, 21, 21, 25; 3:5, 9, 9, 10, 12, 14, 17, 17, 17, 18, 18, 18; 4:1, 1, 3, 6, 6, 8, 11, 14, 14, 17; 5:2, 5, 7, 7, 11

2Pe 1:8, 10, 11, 16, 17, 21; 2:4, 8, 16, 17, 18, 19, 20, 21, 21; 3:4, 5, 12, 13, 14, 18

1Jn 1:2; 2:2, 2, 2, 12, 16, 17, 19; 3:2, 4, 8, 8, 9, 11, 16, 16, 20; 4:7, 8, 10, 20; 5:3, 4, 7, 9, 16, 16

2Jn 1:2, 2, 7, 11

3Jn 1:3, 7

Jude 1:3, 3, 4, 7, 11, 11, 13, 21

Rev 1:3, 6, 9, 9, 18; 2:3; 3:2, 4, 8; 4:9, 10, 11, 11; 5:9, 13, 14; 6:6, 6, 9, 9, 11, 17, 7:12, 17; 8:12; 9:15, 15, 19, 19; 10:6; 11:2, 15; 12:4, 10, 12, 14; 13:18; 14:4, 5, 7, 11, 15, 15, 15, 18; 15:1, 4, 4, 4, 7; 16:6, 6, 10, 14, 21; 17:14, 17; 18:3, 5, 7, 8, 9, 10, 10, 11, 15, 17, 19, 20, 23, 23; 19:2, 2, 3, 6, 7, 8, 10; 20:4, 5, 10, 11; 21:1, 2, 4, 5, 22, 23, 25; 22:2, 5, 5, 9, 10, 15, 18

FROM (3660)

Ge 1:4, 6, 7, 14, 18; 2:2, 3, 6, 10, 22; 3:8, 23, 23; 4:1, 10, 11, 11, 14, 14, 16; 6:7, 17; 7:4, 23; 8:2, 3, 7, 8, 8, 11, 13, 21; 9:10, 24; 10:19, 30; 11:2, 6, 8, 9, 31; 12:1, 1, 8; 13:3, 9, 11, 14, 14; 14:17, 23; 15:18; 16:2, 6, 8; 17:14, 22; 18:2, 3, 16, 17, 22, 25, 25; 19:4, 24, 26; 20:1, 6, 13; 22:12; 23:3, 6; 24:5, 7, 7, 7, 8, 41, 41, 46, 50, 62; 25:6, 18, 23, 29; 26:16, 22, 23, 26, 27, 31; 27:9, 30, 30, 39, 40, 45, 45; 28:2, 6, 10; 29:3, 8, 10; 30:2, 32; 31:13, 16, 27, 31, 40, 49; 32:11, 11; 33:18; 35:1, 7, 13, 16; 36:6; 37:25; 38:1, 14, 17, 19, 20; 39:5, 9; 40:19, 19; 41:42, 46; 42:2, 7, 24, 24; 43:34; 44:28, 29; 45:1; 46:5, 34; 47:10, 18, 21; 48:7, 12, 16, 17; 49:9, 10, 10, 24, 26, 32; 50:25

Ex 2:15; 3:5; 4:3; 5:4, 5, 19, 20; 6:6, 7, 26, 27; 7:5; 8:8, 8, 9, 11, 11, 11, 11, 12, 29, 29, 29, 29, 30, 31, 31, 31; 9:15, 33; 10:5, 6, 11, 17, 18, 23, 28; 11:5, 8; 12:5, 5, 15, 15, 19, 29, 31, 37, 41, 42; 13:3, 3, 10, 14, 14, 20, 22; 14:5, 19, 25; 15:22; 16:1, 4, 6, 32; 17:1, 14, 16; 18:4, 10, 13, 14; 19:2, 14; 20:22; 21:14, 22; 22:12; 23:7, 15, 25, 28, 29, 30, 31, 31; 25:15, 22, 22; 26:4, 28; 27:21; 28:1, 28, 42; 29:28, 28; 30:14, 33, 38; 31:14; 32:12, 12, 15, 27; 33:5, 7, 16; 34:18, 29, 29; 35:5, 20; 36:4, 6, 11, 22, 33; 38:26; 39:21; 40:36

Lev 2:9, 13; 4:8, 10, 13, 19, 31, 35; 5:2, 3, 4, 6, 8; 7:20, 21, 25, 27, 34, 34; 8:28; 9:22, 24; 10:2, 4, 7; 12:7; 13:12, 41, 58; 14:7, 19; 15:3, 16, 31, 32; 16:12, 19, 30; 17:4, 9, 10; 18:29; 19:8; 20:3, 4, 5, 6, 18, 24, 25, 26; 21:7; 22:2, 3, 4, 25, 27; 23:15, 15, 29, 30, 32; 24:3, 8; 25:41, 50; 26:36; 27:3, 5, 6, 7, 17, 18

Nu 1:3, 18, 20, 22, 24, 26, 28, 30, 32, 34, 36, 38, 40, 42, 45; 3:12, 15, 22, 28, 34, 39, 40, 43; 4:2, 3, 13, 18, 23, 30, 35, 39, 43, 47; 5:13, 19, 31; 6:3, 4; 7:89, 89; 8:6, 14, 16, 19, 24, 25; 9:13, 17, 21; 10:9, 11, 33; 11:31, 31, 35; 12:10, 14, 15, 16; 13:3, 21, 23, 24, 25; 14:9, 13, 19, 29, 43; 15:23, 30; 16:9, 15, 21, 24, 26, 27, 33, 35, 45, 46, 46; 17:5, 9, 10; 18:6, 9, 16, 26, 30, 32; 19:13, 20; 20:6, 9, 14, 21, 22, 28; 21:4, 7, 11, 12, 13, 16, 18, 19, 19, 20, 24, 28; 22:5, 16, 33, 33; 23:7, 9, 9, 13, 13, 27; 24:11, 24; 25:4, 7, 8, 11; 26:2, 4, 62; 27:4; 30:14; 31:14, 42; 32:7, 8, 11, 15, 21; 33:3, 5, 6, 7, 8, 9, 10, 11, 13, 14, 15, 16, 17, 18, 19, 20, 21, 22, 23, 24, 25, 26, 27, 28, 29, 30, 31, 32, 33, 34, 35, 36, 37, 41, 42, 43, 44, 45, 46, 47, 48, 49, 52, 55; 34:3, 4, 4, 5, 7, 8, 10, 11; 35:4, 5, 8, 8, 12; 36:3, 3, 4, 7, 9

Dt 1:2, 19; 2:8, 8, 8, 12, 14, 14, 15, 16, 22, 36, 36; 3:4, 8, 12, 16, 17; 4:2, 3, 9, 26, 29, 32, 34, 38, 48; 5:6; 6:12, 15, 19, 23; 7:4, 8, 15, 20, 24; 8:14; 9:4, 4, 5, 7, 12, 14, 15, 23, 24; 10:5, 6, 7, 7; 11:10, 12, 17, 23, 24, 24; 12:10, 21, 29, 30, 32; 13:5, 5, 7, 7, 10, 10, 13, 17; 14:24; 15:7, 12, 13, 16, 18; 16:9; 17:7, 11, 12, 15, 20; 18:3, 3, 6, 12, 15, 18; 19:5, 13, 19; 20:15; 21:9, 13, 21; 22:1, 4, 8, 21, 22, 24; 23:9, 13, 14, 15; 24:7; 25:9, 19, 19; 26:15, 15; 28:14, 21, 24, 31, 35, 49, 49, 57, 63, 64; 29:11, 18, 20, 22; 30:3, 4, 4, 11; 31:17, 17, 29; 32:20, 26, 42; 33:2, 2, 2, 2, 7, 16, 22, 27; 34:1

Jos 1:4, 7; 2:13, 23; 3:1, 3, 10, 13, 13, 14, 16, 16; 4:23, 23; 5:1, 9, 15; 6:18; 7:2, 5, 9, 12, 13, 19, 26; 8:4, 6, 7, 16, 29; 9:6, 8, 9, 22, 23, 24; 10:6, 7, 9, 11, 11, 29, 31, 34, 36, 41; 11:17, 21, 21, 21, 21, 21, 21, 23; 12:1, 2, 2, 2, 3, 3, 7; 13:3, 4, 5, 6, 6, 9, 16, 26, 26, 30; 14:7, 15; 15:2, 2, 4, 5, 7, 9, 10, 46; 16:1, 1, 2, 7, 8; 17:7; 18:4, 12, 13, 14, 15, 17; 19:12, 13, 29, 33, 33, 34; 20:3, 6; 22:9, 16, 17, 18, 23, 25, 29, 31, 32; 23:1, 4, 5, 5, 9, 13, 13, 15, 16; 24:3, 8, 12, 17, 18

Jdg 1:11, 14, 36, 36; 2:1, 3, 19, 19, 21; 3:3, 19, 19, 20, 21, 27; 4:11, 13, 14; 5:5, 5, 11, 20; 6:8, 9, 11, 13, 14; 7:3; 8:13, 22; 9:20, 20, 20, 35, 36, 48; 10:11, 11, 11, 11, 16; 11:3, 13, 16, 22, 22, 23, 24, 29, 31, 33; 12:9; 13:5, 7, 20; 15:13, 14; 16:12, 17, 17, 19, 20; 17:2, 3, 8; 18:2, 2, 2, 7, 11, 22, 28; 19:2, 16, 18, 18, 30; 20:1, 13, 31, 32; 21:6, 8, 19, 24

Ru 1:6, 13, 16; 2:4, 7, 8; 4:10, 10

1Sa 1:14; 2:8, 19, 30, 33; 3:17, 17, 18, 20; 4:4, 18, 21, 22; 5:1; 6:3, 5, 5, 5, 7, 20; 7:3, 14, 14, 16; 9:2, 25; 10:2, 3, 5, 9, 23; 12:2, 20; 13:3, 8, 11, 15; 14:17, 21, 31, 46; 15:2, 6, 6, 7, 11, 15, 23, 26, 28; 16:1, 13, 14, 14, 15, 16, 23, 23; 17:15, 24, 26, 30, 33, 46, 53, 57; 18:6, 9, 10, 12, 13; 19:8, 9; 20:1, 2, 9, 15, 15, 34; 21:4, 5, 6; 22:15; 23:13, 28, 29; 24:1, 13; 25:10, 26, 26, 33, 33, 34, 39, 39; 26:12, 12, 19; 28:15, 16, 23; 30:17, 25; 31:1, 12

2Sa 1:1, 2, 3, 4, 22, 22; 2:12, 19, 21, 22, 26, 27, 30; 3:10, 10, 15, 15, 22, 26, 26, 28, 29; 4:11; 5:9, 13, 25; 6:2, 2, 12; 7:1, 8, 8, 11, 15, 15, 23, 23; 8:4, 8, 8, 13; 9:5; 10:14; 11:2, 2, 4, 8, 10, 15, 20, 21, 24; 12:10, 17, 20, 30; 13:4, 9, 9, 13, 17, 32; 14:14, 18, 19, 25, 32; 15:12, 12, 14, 18, 28; 17:11; 18:13, 16; 19:7, 24, 31; 20:2, 2, 20, 21, 22; 21:5, 10, 12, 12, 13; 22:3, 4, 4, 17, 18, 18, 22, 23, 24, 44, 49, 49; 23:11, 17; 24:2, 4, 15, 15, 21, 25

1Ki 1:45, 53; 2:15, 27, 31, 31, 33, 40, 41; 3:20; 4:12, 21, 24, 25, 33, 34; 5:9; 6:24; 7:7, 9, 23; 8:35, 51, 53, 54, 54, 65; 9:6, 12, 28; 10:3, 11, 11; 11:9, 11, 23; 12:2, 15, 24, 25; 13:4, 5, 12, 14, 21, 26, 33, 34; 14:7, 8, 10; 15:5, 13, 19; 16:17; 18:12, 12, 26; 19:17, 21; 20:33, 34, 36, 36, 41; 21:21; 22:24, 33, 43

2Ki 1:4, 6, 10, 10, 12, 12, 14; 2:1, 3, 5, 9, 10, 13, 14, 21, 23, 25, 25; 3:27; 4:5, 27, 42; 5:19, 21, 22, 24, 26, 27; 6:32; 8:14, 20, 22; 9:2, 8; 10:21, 29, 29, 31, 33, 33; 11:2, 2, 11, 19; 12:18; 13:5, 6, 11, 17, 23; 14:13, 24, 25, 27; 15:9, 14, 16, 18, 24, 28; 16:3, 6, 11, 11, 12, 14, 14, 17, 17, 18; 17:7, 8, 9, 13, 21, 21, 22, 24, 24, 24, 24, 24, 27, 28, 33; 18:6, 8, 14, 16, 16, 17; 19:8; 20:14, 14, 14, 18; 21:16; 23:6, 8, 12, 17, 22, 26, 30; 24:7, 15, 20; 25:5

1Ch 2:23; 4:10; 5:9, 23; 9:25; 10:1; 11:8, 13; 13:5, 5; 14:14, 16; 16:20, 20, 23, 35; 17:5, 5, 7, 7, 8, 13, 13, 21; 18:4, 8, 8, 11, 11, 11, 11, 11, 11; 19:7; 20:2; 21:2, 22, 26; 22:9; 23:3, 24, 27; 27:23

2Ch 1:4, 13, 13; 4:2; 5:9; 6:21, 21, 23, 25, 26, 27, 30, 32, 33, 33, 35, 39, 39; 7:1, 8, 14, 14; 8:15; 9:2, 10, 26; 10:2; 11:4, 14; 12:12; 13:19; 15:8, 16; 16:3, 9; 18:23, 31, 32; 19:2, 4; 20:2, 10, 32; 21:8, 10, 10, 12; 22:11, 11; 23:10, 20; 24:5, 23, 25; 25:5, 12, 13, 14, 23, 27; 26:18, 19, 20, 21; 28:8, 12; 29:6, 10; 30:5, 6, 8, 9, 10; 31:16, 17; 32:22, 22, 23; 33:8; 34:3, 33; 35:11, 15, 18, 21, 22, 22; 36:12, 13, 20

Ezr 1:11; 2:59, 62; 3:6, 7, 8, 13; 4:12, 14, 21; 6:6, 11, 21; 7:6, 9; 8:1, 31, 31; 9:1, 5, 8, 11; 10:6, 8, 11, 11, 14

Ne 1:9; 3:15, 20, 21, 24, 25, 28; 4:5, 12, 16, 19, 21; 5:13, 13, 14, 14, 17; 6:9; 7:61, 64; 8:3, 18; 9:2, 13, 15, 19, 20, 27, 28, 35; 10:28; 11:30, 31; 12:28, 29, 38, 39; 13:3, 21, 28, 30

Est 1:1, 7, 19; 2:6; 3:7, 7, 8, 10; 4:4, 14; 7:7; 8:2, 9, 15; 9:16, 22, 22, 22, 28, 28

Job 1:7, 7, 12, 16, 19; 2:2, 2, 2, 7, 7, 11; 3:4, 10, 11, 17, 19; 4:2, 13, 20; 5:4, 15, 15, 15, 20, 20, 21; 6:13, 14, 23, 23; 7:19; 8:18; 9:34; 10:14, 19; 13:20, 21; 14:6, 11; 15:18; 17:4; 18:17, 18; 19:9, 13, 13; 20:24, 29; 21:9, 14, 16; 22:6, 7, 17, 18, 22, 23; 23:7, 12, 17; 24:1, 9, 10, 12; 26:4, 5; 27:5; 28:4, 4, 11, 21, 21, 28; 30:5, 10, 31:2, 2, 16, 18, 18, 22, 22, 23; 33:17, 17, 18, 18, 24, 28, 30; 34:10, 10, 27; 35:3; 36:3, 7, 10; 38:15; 39:22, 29; 42:2

Ps 2:3, 12; 3:T; 6:8; 7:1; 9:13; 12:1, 5, 7; 13:1; 14:2; 17:2, 4, 7, 9, 9, 13, 14, 14; 18:T, 3, 16, 17, 17, 21, 22, 23, 43, 48, 48; 19:6, 6, 12, 13, 13; 20:2, 6; 21:10, 10; 22:1, 1, 10, 10, 11, 19, 20, 20, 21, 21, 24; 24:5, 5; 27:9; 30:3; 31:11, 15, 15, 20, 20, 22; 32:7; 33:13, 14, 19; 34:4, 13, 13, 14, 16; 35:10, 10, 17, 17, 22; 37:8, 27, 40; 38:9, 10, 11, 21; 39:2, 8, 10; 40:10, 11; 41:13; 42:6, 6; 43:1; 44:7, 10, 18; 49:14, 15; 50:1, 4; 51:2, 2, 9, 11, 11, 14; 53:2; 55:1, 8, 11, 12, 18; 56:13, 13; 57:T, 3, 3; 58:3; 59:1, 1, 2, 2; 60:11; 61:2, 3; 62:1, 4, 5; 64:1, 2, 2; 66:20; 68:20, 22, 22, 26; 69:5, 14, 17; 71:5, 6, 12, 17, 20; 72:8, 8, 14; 73:27, 27; 75:6, 6, 6; 76:8; 78:4, 23, 30, 42, 50, 70, 71; 80:14, 18; 81:6, 6; 83:4; 84:7, 11; 85:3, 11; 86:13; 88:5, 8, 14, 15, 18; 89:33, 48; 90:2; 91:3, 3; 93:2; 94:13; 96:2; 101:4, 8; 102:2, 19, 19; 103:4, 12, 12, 17; 104:13, 21; 105:13, 13; 106:10, 10, 47, 48; 107:2, 3, 3, 3, 3, 20, 41; 108:12; 109:15, 17, 20, 31; 110:3; 113:2, 3; 114:1; 115:18; 116:8, 8, 8; 119:10, 19, 21, 22, 29, 37, 51, 101, 102, 110, 115, 118, 134, 150, 155, 157, 160; 120:2, 2; 121:1, 2, 7, 8; 125:2; 129:1, 2; 130:8; 131:3; 132:11; 135:7; 136:11, 24; 139:7, 7, 12, 15, 19; 140:1, 1, 4, 4; 141:9; 142:6; 143:7, 9; 144:7, 7, 10, 11; 148:1, 7

Pr 1:15, 33; 2:12, 12, 16, 16, 22; 3:7, 21, 26, 27; 4:5, 15, 21, 24, 24, 27; 5:7, 8; 6:5, 5, 24, 24; 7:5, 5; 8:23, 23; 10:2; 11:4; 13:14, 19; 14:7, 14, 16, 27; 15:24, 29; 16:1, 6, 17; 17:13; 19:4, 7, 14, 27; 20:3, 9; 21:23; 22:5, 6, 15, 27; 23:4, 13, 14; 24:18; 25:4, 5, 17, 25; 27:8, 8, 22; 28:9; 29:21, 26; 30:8, 12, 14, 14; 31:14

Ecc 1:7; 2:10, 10, 24; 3:5, 11, 14; 7:18, 23, 26; 8:10; 10:5; 11:10, 10; 12:11

SS 3:4; 4:1, 2, 8, 8, 8, 8, 8, 8, 15; 5:7; 6:5, 5, 6, 0.5

Isa 1:6, 15, 16; 2:3, 6, 22; 3:1, 1; 4:4, 6, 6, 6; 5:23, 26, 26; 6:6; 7:17, 17; 8:17, 18; 9:7, 14; 10:2, 2, 3, 27, 27; 11:11, 11, 11, 11, 11, 11, 11, 11, 12, 16; 13:5, 5, 6, 20; 14:3, 3, 3, 9, 9, 12, 22, 25, 25, 31; 16:1, 4; 17:1, 3, 3; 18:2, 7, 7; 19:5; 20:2, 2, 6; 21:1, 1, 15, 15, 15, 15; 22:3, 4, 14, 19, 19, 24; 23:1; 24:14, 16, 18, 18; 25:4, 4, 8, 8; 27:12; 28:9, 9, 19, 22, 29; 29:13, 15; 30:6, 11, 14, 27; 31:6, 8; 32:2, 2, 15; 33:15, 15, 15; 34:4, 4, 10, 17; 36:2; 37:8, 14, 20; 38:7, 12, 12, 13, 17; 39:3, 3, 3, 7; 40:21, 21, 27, 27; 41:2, 4, 9, 9, 25, 25, 26; 42:7, 10, 11; 43:5, 5, 6, 6; 44:2, 8, 24; 45:6, 6, 8, 21, 21; 46:3, 3, 7, 10, 10, 11, 11, 12; 47:11, 12, 13, 14, 15; 48:3, 5, 6, 7, 8, 8, 16, 16, 19, 20; 49:1, 1, 1, 5, 12, 12, 12, 12, 24; 50:6; 51:4, 8; 52:2, 2, 11; 53:3, 8, 8; 54:8, 10, 14, 14; 55:10; 56:2, 2, 3, 6, 11; 57:1; 58:7, 9, 13, 13; 59:2, 9, 11, 13, 13, 15, 19, 19, 20, 21; 60:4, 6, 9; 63:1, 1, 15, 15, 16, 17, 17; 64:7; 65:16; 66:6, 6, 23, 23

Jer 2:5, 25, 25, 35, 37; 3:1, 4, 19, 20, 23, 23, 24, 25; 4:6, 7, 7, 8, 12, 14, 15, 15, 16, 28; 5:15, 25; 6:8, 13, 13, 20, 20, 22, 22; 7:1, 28, 34, 34; 8:10, 10, 13, 16; 9:2, 3, 21, 21; 10:9, 9, 11, 11, 13; 11:1, 4, 15, 19; 12:2, 12, 14; 13:6, 7, 20, 25; 15:7, 19; 16:5, 15, 15, 16, 16, 16, 17, 17, 19; 17:4, 5, 8, 12, 13, 16, 26, 26, 26, 26, 26, 26, 26; 18:1, 8, 11, 14, 14, 15, 18, 18, 18, 20, 22, 23; 19:14; 20:13, 17; 21:1, 2, 7, 7, 7; 22:20, 21; 23:8, 14, 15, 22, 22, 30; 24:1, 10; 25:3, 5, 5, 10, 30, 30, 32, 32, 33; 26:1, 3, 10; 27:1, 10, 16, 20; 28:3, 6, 10, 11, 12, 16; 29:1, 1, 2, 4, 14, 14, 20; 30:1, 8, 10, 10, 21; 31:8, 8, 11, 13, 16, 16, 16, 34, 36, 36, 38; 32:1, 30, 31, 31, 40, 40; 33:5, 8; 34:1, 8, 12, 14, 21; 35:1, 15; 36:1, 2, 2, 3, 4, 6, 7, 9, 29, 32; 37:5, 9, 11, 17; 38:10, 14, 25; 40:1, 1, 4; 41:5, 5, 5, 6, 14, 15, 16, 16, 16; 42:1, 4, 8, 11, 17; 43:5, 12; 44:5, 7, 12; 46:16, 27, 27; 47:4; 48:2, 3, 10, 11, 11, 18, 33, 33, 33, 34, 34, 42, 44, 45; 49:5, 7, 14, 16, 19, 19, 32, 36, 38; 50:6, 9, 9, 16, 26, 39, 41, 41, 44, 44; 51:16, 25, 45, 48, 53, 54, 54, 64; 52:3, 8, 29

La 1:6, 13, 14, 16; 2:1, 3, 8, 9; 3:17, 18, 50, 66; 5:14, 14, 16, 19

Eze 1:19, 21, 25, 27, 27; 3:12, 17, 18, 19, 19, 20; 4:8, 10, 11, 14; 6:9; 7:20, 22, 26, 26; 8:2, 2, 6; 9:2, 3; 10:2, 4, 6, 6, 7, 16, 16, 18, 19; 11:15, 17, 18, 23, 24; 12:3, 16, 16, 16, 19; 13:20, 22; 14:5, 6, 6, 7, 8, 9, 11, 13, 17, 19, 21; 15:7; 16:9, 34, 41, 42; 17:22; 18:8, 17, 21, 23, 24, 26, 27, 28, 30, 31; 19:8; 20:17, 34, 38, 41, 47; 21:3, 4, 4; 22:5, 26; 23:8, 17, 18, 18, 22, 27, 27, 28, 40, 42; 24:13, 16, 25; 25:7, 9, 9, 13, 13; 26:4, 7, 16; 27:5, 7, 7, 29; 28:3, 15, 16, 18, 25; 29:10, 13; 30:6, 9; 31:12; 32:13; 33:6, 7, 8, 9, 9, 11, 11, 12, 14, 18, 19, 30; 34:10, 10, 13, 13; 35:7; 36:24, 25, 25, 29, 33; 37:9, 21; 38:8, 15; 39:2, 22, 23, 24, 27, 29; 40:13, 15, 19, 23, 27; 41:7, 16, 20; 42:6, 9, 9; 43:2, 9, 14, 14, 15; 44:10, 10, 15; 45:7, 7, 7, 9; 46:18; 47:1, 1, 1, 10, 15, 17, 18, 18, 18, 18, 18, 19, 20; 48:1, 2, 3, 4, 5, 6, 7, 8, 8, 22, 22, 23, 24, 25, 26, 27, 28, 35

Da 2:1, 5, 8, 15; 3:17; 4:3, 13, 14, 14, 16, 23, 25, 31, 31, 32, 33, 34; 5:20, 20, 21, 24; 6:18, 20, 27; 7:3, 3, 4, 7, 10, 19, 23, 24; 8:5; 9:5, 5, 13, 16, 25; 10:12; 11:22; 12:11

Hos 1:2; 2:2, 15; 4:12; 5:3, 6; 7:4, 13; 8:6; 9:1, 11, 11, 11, 12; 10:5, 9; 11:2, 7, 10; 12:9; 13:4, 14, 14, 14, 15; 14:4, 8

Joel 1:5, 9, 12, 13, 15, 16; 2:20; 3:6, 16, 20

Am 1:2, 2, 5, 5, 8, 8; 2:3, 9, 9, 10, 14; 3:1, 5, 11; 4:7; 5:11, 12, 19, 23; 6:2, 14; 8:12, 12; 9:3, 7, 7, 8

Ob 1:1;

Jnh 1:3, 3, 10, 15; 2:6; 3:5, 6, 6, 8, 8, 9, 10; 4:3, 6

Mic 1:2, 12, 16; 2:3, 4, 8, 8, 9, 9; 3:2, 2, 3, 4; 4:2, 7, 10; 5:2, 2, 6, 7; 6:5; 7:5, 12, 12, 12, 12, 12, 20

Na 1:13; 2:13; 3:7, 8

Hab 1:8, 12; 2:9; 3:3, 3, 17

Zep 1:2, 3, 4, 6, 10, 10, 10; 2:11; 3:10

Hag 1:10, 10; 2:15, 15, 18, 18, 18, 19

Zec 1:4, 4; 2:6; 3:4, 4; 6:1, 5, 10; 7:12; 8:7, 7; 9:5, 7, 10, 10, 10, 10; 13:5; 14:2, 5, 8, 10, 10, 10, 13, 16

Mal 1:5, 11; 2:6; 3:5, 7, 7

Mt 1:17, 17, 17, 21, 24; 2:1, 16; 3:7, 13, 17; 4:17, 21, 25, 25, 25, 25, 25; 5:18, 29, 30, 42; 6:13; 7:23; 8:1, 11, 30; 9:9, 15, 16, 22; 11:12, 25; 12:15, 38, 42, 44; 13:12, 27, 35, 49; 14:2; 15:8, 18, 27, 28, 29; 16:1, 21, 22; 17:9, 9, 18; 18:8, 9, 35; 19:1, 8, 12, 20; 20:8, 29; 21:8, 25, 25, 43; 22:46; 23:34, 35; 24:1, 29, 31, 31; 25:28, 29, 32, 32, 34, 41; 26:16, 39, 42, 47; 27:31, 40, 42, 45, 51, 55, 64; 28:2, 2, 7, 8

Mk 1:9, 11, 42, 45; 2:20, 21; 3:7, 7, 8, 8, 8, 22; 4:25; 5:35; 6:1, 2, 10, 14, 16; 7:1, 4, 6, 15, 17, 18, 21, 23, 24, 31, 33; 8:3, 4, 11; 9:9, 9, 10; 10:1, 6, 20; 11:12, 20, 30, 31; 12:2, 25, 34; 13:19, 27, 27; 14:35, 36, 43, 52; 15:20, 30, 32, 38; 16:3, 8

Lk 1:2, 3, 15, 26, 38, 45, 48, 50, 52, 71, 71, 78; 2:1, 4, 15, 36, 37; 3:7, 22; 4:1, 9, 13, 42; 5:3, 8, 10, 13, 35; 6:17, 22; 7:6; 8:18, 37, 49; 9:5, 7, 33, 37, 39, 45, 54; 10:7, 18, 21, 30, 42; 11:4, 7, 16, 22, 31, 50, 51; 12:36, 52, 58; 13:12, 15, 16, 27, 29, 29, 29, 29; 16:3, 18, 21, 26, 26, 30, 31; 17:7, 29; 18:21, 34; 19:8, 24, 26, 26, 39, 42; 20:4, 5, 35; 21:11; 22:41, 42, 43, 45; 23:5, 49, 55; 24:2, 9, 13, 46, 49, 51

Jn 1:6, 19, 32; 2:22; 3:2, 13, 27, 31, 31; 4:11; 5:24, 34, 41, 44; 6:23, 31, 32, 32, 33, 38, 41, 42, 50, 51, 58, 64, 66; 7:29; 8:23, 23, 25, 42, 44; 9:1, 29, 30; 10:5, 18, 32; 11:41, 53; 12:1, 9, 17, 27, 28, 32, 36; 13:3, 4; 14:7; 15:26, 26, 27; 16:22, 27, 28, 30; 17:8, 15; 18:3, 28, 36; 19:11, 12, 23, 27; 20:1, 9; 21:8, 14

Ac 1:4, 11, 12, 12, 22, 22, 25; 2:2, 40, 46; 3:2, 15, 19, 23, 24, 26; 4:2, 10; 5:38, 41; 7:3, 4, 33, 39; 8:10, 26, 33; 9:3, 8, 14, 18; 10:17, 21, 22, 23, 37, 41; 11:4, 5, 9, 11, 27; 12:7, 10, 11, 19, 25; 13:4, 8, 13, 13, 14, 29, 30, 31, 34, 39, 39, 46; 14:8, 15, 17, 19, 26; 15:1, 18, 19, 20, 20, 20, 20, 24, 29, 29, 29, 29, 29, 33, 38, 38, 39; 16:11, 12; 17:3, 27, 31, 33; 18:1, 2, 2, 5, 6, 16, 21; 19:9, 12, 12, 35; 20:6, 9, 17, 18, 20, 26; 21:1, 1, 7, 10, 25, 25, 25, 25, 22:5, 6, 22, 29, 30; 23:10, 21; 24:18; 25:1, 7; 26:4, 5, 10, 13, 17, 17, 18, 18, 23, 26; 27:4, 21, 34, 43; 28:13, 15, 17, 23

Ro 1:4, 7, 17, 18, 20; 4:24; 5:9, 14; 6:4, 7, 9, 13, 17, 18, 20, 22; 7:2, 3, 4, 6, 24; 8:2, 11, 11, 21, 35, 39; 9:3; 10:6, 7, 9; 11:15, 26; 15:19, 22, 31; 16:99

HE (10430)

HIS (8478)

I (8851)

IN (12674)

IS (6993)

IT (6132)

ME (4096)

MY (4370)

NOT (6596)

O (1086)

OF (34750)

Idx

OUR (1165)

OUT (2777)

SHALL (9838)

SHALT (1616)

SHE (981)

THAT (12914)

THE (64039)

Idx

THEE (3826)

THEIR (3931)

Idx

2Ch 1:17; 3:13, 13; 4:4, 7, 16, 20; 5:8, 12, 12, 13; 6:14, 16, 25, 26, 28, 28, 34, 35, 35, 35, 36, 37, 38, 38, 38, 38, 38, 39, 39, 39; 7:3, 6, 6, 10, 14, 14, 14, 22; 8:8, 14, 14, 14; 9:4, 4, 6; 10:16; 11:13, 14, 14, 16, 16; 13:10, 16, 18; 14:4; 15:4, 12, 12, 12, 15, 15; 17:14; 18:9; 19:4, 10; 20:13, 13, 13, 27, 33, 33; 21:3; 22:5; 24:18, 18, 24, 24; 25:4, 5, 10, 15, 20; 26:11, 13; 28:6, 8, 15; 29:6, 6, 15, 23, 24, 30, 34; 30:7, 16, 16, 22, 27, 27; 31:1, 2, 6, 15, 15, 16, 16, 16, 16, 17, 17, 17, 18, 18, 18, 18, 18, 19; 32:13, 17; 33:17; 34:5, 6, 25, 30, 32, 33, 33; 35:2, 10, 10, 11, 15, 15, 15, 25; 36:15, 17, 17
Ezr 1:6; 2:59, 59, 61, 62, 65, 65, 66, 66, 67, 67, 69, 70, 70; 3:8, 8, 9, 9, 10, 12; 4:5, 7, 9, 17, 23; 5:3, 5, 8, 10; 6:12, 13, 18, 18, 20, 22; 7:13, 16, 17, 17; 8:1, 19, 24, 26; 9:1, 2, 2, 11, 11, 12, 12, 12, 12; 10:16, 16, 19, 19, 19
Ne 2:18; 3:5, 5, 5, 18, 23; 4:3, 4, 4, 5, 5, 13, 13, 13, 13, 15; 5:1, 1, 5, 6, 8, 11, 11, 11, 11, 14, 15; 6:6, 9, 14, 16; 7:61, 61, 63, 64, 67, 67, 68, 68, 69, 73, 73; 8:6, 6, 6, 7, 12, 15, 16; 9:2, 2, 3, 3, 3, 4, 6, 9, 11, 15, 15, 16, 17, 17, 17, 20, 20, 21, 21, 23, 23, 24, 24, 26, 27, 27, 27, 28, 29, 35, 35, 37; 10:10, 28, 28, 28, 29, 29, 30; 11:3, 9, 12, 14, 14, 19, 25, 30, 31; 12:7, 9, 24, 27, 42, 45; 13:11, 13, 13, 24, 25, 25, 25
Est 1:17, 17, 20, 22; 2:3, 12; 3:8, 12; 8:9, 9, 9, 11, 13; 9:2, 2, 5, 10, 15, 16, 16, 16, 16, 22, 27, 27, 27, 28, 31, 31, 31
Job 1:4, 4, 5, 5, 13, 18; 2:12, 12, 12; 3:8, 15; 4:21; 5:5, 12, 12, 13, 15; 6:17, 18; 8:4, 8, 10; 11:3, 20; 12:18; 14:12; 15:18, 35; 16:10; 17:2, 4; 19:12, 15; 20:10; 21:8, 8, 8, 8, 9, 10, 10, 11, 11, 13, 16, 16, 17, 29; 22:6, 18; 24:5, 5, 11, 11, 18, 23; 27:23; 29:9, 9, 10, 10, 10, 23, 25; 30:2, 4, 9, 9, 12; 31:16, 39; 33:16; 34:24, 25; 36:9, 9, 10, 11, 11, 14, 15, 20; 37:8; 38:15, 40; 39:3, 3, 4; 40:12, 13, 22; 42:15, 15
Ps 2:3, 3, 12; 4:7, 7; 5:9, 9, 9, 10, 10, 11; 7:7; 9:5, 6, 10, 15; 10:17; 11:2, 2, 6; 16:4, 4, 4; 17:7, 10, 10, 11, 14, 14, 14; 18:45; 19:3, 4, 4; 21:10, 10, 12; 22:13; 26:10; 28:3, 3, 4, 4, 4, 4, 8; 33:15, 15, 19; 34:5, 15, 17; 35:6, 7, 16, 17, 21, 25; 36:7; 37:14, 15, 15, 15, 18, 39; 40:15; 44:1, 3, 3, 12; 49:6, 6, 8, 10, 11, 11, 11, 11, 11, 13, 13, 13, 13, 14, 14; 55:9, 15, 23; 56:5; 57:4; 58:4, 6, 6; 59:7, 7, 12, 12, 12; 62:4; 64:3, 3, 3, 8; 65:7; 68:27, 27; 69:22, 22, 23, 23, 25, 25, 27; 70:3; 72:14, 14; 73:4, 4, 7, 9, 9, 17, 20; 74:4, 8; 76:5, 5; 78:4, 5, 6, 7, 8, 8, 12, 18, 18, 28, 28, 29, 30, 30, 30, 33, 33, 35, 35, 36, 36, 37, 38, 44, 44, 46, 46, 47, 47, 48, 48, 50, 50, 51, 53, 55, 57, 58, 58, 63, 63, 64, 64; 79:3, 10, 12, 12; 81:12, 12, 14, 14, 15; 83:11, 11, 16; 85:2; 89:17, 32, 32; 90:10, 16; 91:12; 93:3, 3; 94:23, 23; 95:10; 98:8; 99:8; 102:17, 28; 104:11, 12, 17, 21, 21, 22, 27, 29, 29; 105:14, 24, 25, 29, 29, 30, 30, 31, 32, 33, 33, 33, 35, 35, 36, 36, 37; 106:11, 15, 15, 18, 20, 21, 25, 27, 29, 32, 35, 36, 37, 37, 38, 38, 39, 39, 42, 42, 43, 43, 44, 44; 107:5, 6, 6, 12, 13, 13, 14, 17, 17, 18, 19, 19, 20, 26, 27, 28, 28, 30, 38; 109:10, 10, 13, 25, 29; 115:2, 4, 7, 9, 9, 10, 10, 11, 11; 119:70, 118; 123:2; 124:3, 6; 125:3, 4, 5; 129:3; 132:12; 135:12, 17; 136:10, 21; 140:2, 3, 3, 9; 141:4, 5, 6, 10; 144:8, 11, 12; 145:15, 19; 147:3, 4; 149:2, 5, 6, 6, 8, 8
Pr 1:6, 15, 16, 18, 18, 22, 31, 31; 2:15; 4:16, 22; 8:21; 9:15; 10:15; 11:6, 20; 14:24; 17:6; 18:19; 20:29; 21:12; 22:23; 23:11, 11; 24:2, 2, 22; 25:27; 29:13, 16; 30:5, 11, 11, 12, 12, 13, 13, 14, 25, 26
Ecc 2:3; 3:11; 4:1, 9; 5:11, 13; 9:1, 3, 6, 6, 6
Isa 2:4, 4, 7, 7, 7, 7, 8, 8, 8; 3:4, 8, 8, 9, 9, 9, 10, 12, 16, 17, 18, 18, 18, 18; 5:12, 13, 13, 14, 14, 14, 17, 21, 21, 24, 24, 25, 27, 27, 28, 28, 28, 29; 6:10, 10, 10, 10, 10, 13; 8:12, 19, 21, 21; 9:17, 17; 10:2, 5, 13, 25, 29; 11:7, 14; 13:8, 10, 11, 11, 16, 16, 16, 16, 18, 18, 20, 21, 22, 22; 14:1, 2, 2, 9, 21, 25; 15:2, 3, 3, 3, 4; 16:10, 10; 18:2, 7; 20:4, 5, 5; 21:14; 24:14; 25:11, 11; 26:11, 14, 21; 28:25; 29:13, 13, 13, 13, 14, 14, 15, 15, 19; 30:6, 6, 7, 26; 31:3, 4; 33:2, 7, 9, 23, 24; 34:2, 3, 3, 3, 3, 4, 7, 7, 35:10; 36:12, 12, 20, 21, 22; 37:18, 19, 27; 40:24, 26, 31; 41:1, 17, 29, 29; 42:11, 15; 43:9, 14; 44:9, 9, 18, 18, 25; 45:12, 20; 46:1; 47:9; 49:9, 22, 22, 23, 23, 26, 26; 50:2, 3; 51:7, 11; 52:15; 53:11; 54:17; 55:12; 56:7, 7, 11; 57:2, 8; 58:1, 1, 2; 59:5, 6, 6, 6, 6, 7, 7, 7, 8, 18; 60:8, 9, 9, 10, 11; 61:6, 7, 7, 8, 9, 9; 62:6; 63:3, 6, 8, 9, 10; 65:2, 4, 6, 7, 7, 22, 23; 66:3, 3, 3, 4, 4, 18, 18, 24, 24
Jer 1:8, 16, 16, 17; 2:11, 11, 26, 26, 26, 26, 27, 27, 27; 3:17, 21, 21, 24, 24, 24, 24; 4:16; 5:3, 4, 5, 6, 6, 6, 16, 24, 27, 31; 6:3, 3, 10, 12, 12, 19, 23, 27; 7:18, 19, 24, 24, 26, 26, 26, 28, 28, 30, 31, 31; 8:1, 7, 10, 10, 12, 19; 9:3, 3, 5, 8, 14, 14, 16; 10:7, 9, 15, 21; 11:8, 8, 10, 10, 12, 14, 18, 22, 22, 23; 12:2, 2, 14; 13:10; 14:3, 3, 3, 3, 4, 6, 10, 10, 10, 11, 12, 14, 16, 16, 16, 16; 15:7, 8, 9; 16:3, 3, 4, 7, 7, 15, 15, 17, 17, 18, 18, 18; 17:1, 2, 2, 2, 23, 23, 25; 18:8, 15, 16, 17, 21, 21, 21, 21, 21, 21, 22, 23, 23, 23; 19:4, 5, 7, 7, 7, 9, 9, 9, 9, 15; 20:4, 5, 11; 21:7, 7; 22:9; 23:3, 8, 10, 10, 11, 12, 12, 16, 22, 22, 26, 27, 27, 31, 32, 32; 24:5, 7, 7, 9, 10; 25:12, 14, 14, 36, 38; 26:3; 27:4, 8, 11, 11; 29:23; 30:3, 9, 9, 10, 20, 20, 21, 21; 31:12, 13, 13, 17, 23, 32, 33, 33, 33, 34, 34; 32:18, 22, 30, 30, 32, 32, 32, 32, 34, 35, 35, 38, 39, 40, 44; 33:8, 8, 12, 20, 26; 34:14, 16, 20, 20, 20, 21, 21; 35:14, 16; 36:3, 3, 6, 7, 15, 24, 31; 37:7; 38:18, 19, 23; 40:7, 8, 9; 41:5, 5, 5, 8; 42:17; 43:1, 1; 44:3, 5, 5, 9, 12, 15; 46:5, 10, 21, 21, 25, 25, 26, 27; 47:3, 5; 48:12, 13, 33, 34, 44; 49:1, 3, 7, 20, 21, 29, 29, 29, 29, 32, 32, 32, 35, 37, 37; 50:4, 5, 6, 6, 7, 7, 9, 27, 27, 34, 34, 37, 37, 38, 42, 45; 51:5, 18, 24, 30, 30, 39, 39, 55, 56
La 1:11, 14, 19, 19, 22; 2:10, 10, 12, 12, 12, 15, 15, 16, 18, 20; 3:14, 46, 60, 60, 61, 61, 62, 63, 63, 63, 64; 4:3, 7, 8, 8, 8, 10, 10, 14, 20; 5:7, 8, 12, 14
Eze 1:5, 7, 7, 8, 8, 8, 9, 10, 11, 11, 11, 13, 16, 16, 16, 17, 18, 18, 20, 22, 23, 23, 24, 24, 25, 25, 26; 2:3, 6, 6, 6; 3:8, 8, 9; 4:4, 5, 12, 13, 17; 5:10, 16; 6:5, 9, 9, 9, 9, 13, 13, 13, 13, 14; 7:11, 18, 19, 19, 19, 19, 19, 19, 19, 20, 20, 24, 24, 27, 27; 8:16, 16, 17; 9:10, 10; 10:8, 10, 11, 12, 12, 12, 12, 16, 19, 21, 22, 22; 11:19, 20, 21, 21, 21, 21, 22; 12:3, 3, 4, 4, 5, 6, 7, 16, 19, 13:2, 3, 17; 14:3, 3, 3, 5, 5, 10, 11, 11, 14, 14, 20, 20, 22, 22, 23, 23; 16:39, 40, 45, 45, 47, 47, 53, 55, 55; 19:4, 7, 7, 8, 8; 20:4, 8, 16, 16, 18, 18, 18, 24, 24, 26, 28, 28, 28, 28, 30; 21:6, 14, 15, 15, 15, 23, 28, 29; 22:6, 10, 26, 31, 31; 23:3, 3, 3, 4, 7, 8, 15, 15, 15, 17, 20, 24, 30, 36, 37, 37, 37, 39, 39, 42, 42, 45, 47, 47, 47, 47; 24:25, 25, 25, 25, 25, 25; 25:4, 4; 26:10, 16, 16, 16, 17; 27:9, 11, 29, 30, 30, 32, 35, 35; 28:7, 25, 26; 29:7, 7, 14, 16; 30:11, 13; 31:6, 6, 14, 14, 14, 14; 32:2, 10, 14, 14, 24, 24, 25, 25, 26, 27, 27, 27, 27, 27, 29, 30, 30, 30; 33:2, 2, 17, 29, 31, 31, 31; 34:10, 10, 13, 14, 23, 24, 27, 27, 30; 35:5, 5; 36:5, 5, 7, 12, 17, 17, 17, 17, 18, 19, 19, 23; 37:10, 20, 21, 23, 23, 23, 23, 23, 25, 25, 25, 27; 38:16; 39:22, 23, 23, 24, 24, 26, 26, 26, 27, 28, 28; 40:16, 22, 22, 22, 41, 44; 41:16; 42:4, 11, 11, 11, 14; 43:7, 7, 7, 7, 8, 8, 8, 8, 9, 9, 10, 11; 44:10, 10, 12, 12, 13, 13, 18, 18, 19, 19, 20, 20, 20, 22, 28, 28; 45:4, 8; 46:16, 18; 47:10, 10, 12; 48:29, 34
Da 1:15, 16; 2:30; 3:21, 21, 21, 21, 27, 27, 28, 28, 29; 4:21; 6:24, 24, 24; 7:12, 12; 8:23; 9:7; 11:8, 8, 8, 32
Hos 1:7; 2:5, 17; 3:5, 5; 4:7, 8, 8, 9, 9, 12, 12, 12, 18, 19; 5:4, 4, 5, 6, 6, 7, 15, 15; 7:2, 2, 2, 3, 3, 6, 6, 7, 7, 10, 12, 14, 14, 15, 16, 16, 16; 8:4, 4, 13, 13; 9:4, 4, 4, 6, 6, 9, 9, 10, 11, 12, 15, 15, 15, 16, 16; 10:2, 2, 2, 8, 10; 11:3, 4, 6, 11; 12:11; 13:2, 2, 6, 6, 8, 16, 16; 14:4
Joel 1:3, 3, 17; 2:6, 7, 10, 17, 22; 3:6, 13, 15, 19, 21
Am 1:13, 15; 2:4, 4, 8; 3:10; 4:1; 5:12; 6:2, 4; 7:11; 8:7; 9:4, 15, 15
Ob 1:12, 13, 13, 13, 13, 13, 17
Jnh 1:2; 2:8; 3:8, 10, 10; 4:11, 11
Mic 2:1, 1, 9, 9, 12, 13; 3:2, 2, 2, 3, 3, 4, 5, 5, 7; 4:3, 3, 13, 13; 6:12, 12, 16; 7:4, 13, 16, 16, 16, 16, 17, 19
Na 2:2, 5, 7; 3:3, 3, 17
Hab 1:7, 7, 8, 8, 8, 9, 15, 15, 16, 16, 16, 16, 17; 2:15; 3:11, 14
Zep 1:9, 12, 12, 13, 13, 17, 17, 18, 18; 2:7, 7, 8, 10, 14; 3:6, 6, 6, 7, 7, 13
Hag 1:12, 12, 14; 2:14, 22
Zec 1:21; 2:9; 5:6, 9; 7:2, 11, 12; 8:8, 12; 9:16; 10:2, 5, 6, 7, 7, 7, 9; 11:3, 5, 6, 8, 16; 12:5, 5, 12, 12, 13, 13, 14; 14:12, 12, 12, 12, 12, 12
Mal 4:6;
Mt 1:21; 2:11, 12; 3:6; 4:6, 20, 21, 21, 22, 23; 6:2, 5, 7, 14, 15, 16, 16; 7:6, 16, 20; 8:22, 33, 34; 9:2, 4, 29, 30, 35; 10:17, 21; 11:1, 5, 16; 12:9, 25; 13:15, 15, 15, 15, 15, 43, 54, 58; 14:14; 15:2, 8, 8, 8, 27; 17:6, 8, 25; 18:10, 31, 35; 19:12; 20:4, 8, 31, 34, 34; 21:7, 8, 41; 22:5, 7, 16, 18, 22; 23:3, 4, 5, 5, 5; 25:1, 3, 4, 4, 7; 26:43, 67; 27:39
Mk 1:5, 18, 19, 20, 23, 39; 2:5, 6; 3:4, 5; 4:12, 15; 5:17; 6:6, 8, 8, 26, 52; 7:3, 6, 6; 8:3; 9:34, 44, 46, 48; 10:42; 11:4, 7, 8; 12:12, 15, 44; 13:12; 14:40, 46, 56, 59, 65; 15:19, 29; 16:14
Lk 1:16, 20, 51, 52, 66, 77; 2:8, 39, 44; 3:15; 4:11, 15, 29; 5:2, 6, 7, 11, 15, 20, 22, 30; 6:1, 8, 17, 22, 23, 26; 7:21; 8:3, 12; 9:47, 60; 11:17, 48; 12:36, 42; 13:1; 14:4; 16:4, 8; 17:13; 19:32, 35, 36, 40; 20:23, 26; 21:1, 4, 12; 22:66; 23:25, 48; 24:5, 11, 16, 31, 31, 45
Jn 3:19; 4:38; 8:9; 10:39; 11:19, 46; 12:40, 40, 40, 40; 13:12; 15:22, 25; 17:19, 20; 18:8; 19:3, 31; 20:10
Ac 1:9, 19, 26; 2:37, 45, 46; 4:5, 23, 24, 29; 5:18; 6:1, 6; 7:19, 34, 39, 41, 54, 57, 58, 60; 8:17, 36; 9:24; 10:9; 11:18; 12:17, 20, 20, 25; 13:3, 5, 18, 19, 22, 27, 33, 50, 51; 14:2, 3, 5, 11, 13, 14, 16; 15:3, 9, 13, 22, 26; 16:19, 22, 24, 33; 17:21, 26; 18:3; 19:18, 19; 21:21, 24; 22:22, 23, 30; 23:16, 28, 29; 25:19; 26:18; 27:13, 43; 28:6, 27, 27, 27, 27, 27
Ro 1:21, 21, 24, 24, 26, 27, 27, 28; 2:15, 15; 3:3, 13, 13, 13, 15, 16, 18; 10:3, 18, 18; 11:9, 10, 10, 11, 12, 24, 27, 30; 13:7; 15:27, 27, 27; 16:4, 5, 18
1Co 3:19; 8:7, 12; 14:35; 16:19
2Co 3:14, 15; 5:19; 6:16; 8:2, 2, 2, 3, 3, 5, 14, 14; 9:14; 11:15
Gal 2:13;
Eph 4:17, 18; 5:24, 28, 28
Php 2:21; 3:19, 19
Col 2:2;
1Th 2:15, 16; 5:13
2Th 3:12;
1Ti 3:11, 12, 12; 4:2; 5:4, 12; 6:1
2Ti 2:17; 3:2, 9; 4:3, 4, 16
Tit 1:12, 15; 2:4, 4, 5, 9; 3:13
Heb 2:10, 15; 3:10; 5:14; 7:5; 8:9, 10, 10, 12, 12, 12; 10:16, 16, 17; 11:16, 35; 12:10; 13:7
Jas 1:27; 3:3
1Pe 3:5, 12, 14; 4:14, 19
2Pe 2:2, 3, 8, 12, 13; 3:3, 16
3Jn 1:6;
Jude 1:6, 6, 13, 15, 15, 16, 16, 18
Rev 2:22; 3:4; 4:4, 10; 6:11, 11, 14; 7:3, 9, 11, 14, 17; 9:4, 5, 7, 7, 8, 9, 10, 10, 17, 18, 19, 19, 19, 19, 20, 21, 21, 21, 21; 10:3, 4; 11:5, 5, 6, 7, 8, 9, 9, 11, 12, 16, 16; 12:8, 11, 11; 13:16, 16; 14:1, 2, 5, 11, 13, 13; 15:6; 16:10, 11, 11, 11; 17:13, 17, 17; 18:11, 19; 19:19, 21; 20:4, 4, 12, 13; 21:3, 4, 8, 24; 22:4

THEM (6429)

Ge 1:14, 15, 17, 22, 26, 27, 28, 28; 2:1, 19, 19; 3:7, 21; 5:2, 2; 6:1, 2, 4, 7, 13, 13, 19, 20, 21; 7:13; 9:1, 19; 10:1; 11:3, 6, 8, 9, 29, 31; 12:3; 13:6; 14:8, 14, 15, 15, 15, 24; 15:5, 10, 11, 13, 13; 18:2, 2, 8, 8, 16, 16; 19:1, 1, 3, 3, 5, 5, 6, 8, 8, 9, 10, 12, 13, 17, 18; 20:14; 21:27, 27, 31; 22:6, 8; 23:8; 24:28, 53, 56, 60; 25:6, 26; 26:15, 15, 18, 18, 27, 30, 31; 27:9, 13, 14, 15; 28:11; 29:4, 5, 6, 7, 9, 9; 30:14, 35, 37, 40, 42; 31:5, 9, 32, 33, 34, 34, 34, 55; 32:2, 4, 16, 23, 23; 33:3, 13; 34:8, 14, 21, 21, 21, 23; 35:4, 5; 36:7; 37:6, 13, 17, 17, 18, 22; 38:26; 39:14; 40:3, 4, 4, 5, 6, 6, 8, 8, 11, 17, 22; 41:3, 6, 8, 8, 19, 21, 21, 23, 27, 30, 35, 35; 42:7, 7, 7, 7, 9, 9, 12, 14, 17, 18, 22, 23, 23, 24, 24, 24, 24, 25, 25, 27, 28, 29, 36; 43:2, 11, 16, 23, 24, 27, 32, 34; 44:4, 4, 6, 6, 15; 45:1, 15, 21, 21, 22, 24, 26, 27; 47:2, 6, 6, 6, 11, 17, 17, 20, 21, 22, 22, 24; 48:6, 9, 9, 10, 10, 10, 12, 13, 13, 16, 16, 20; 49:7, 7, 28, 28, 28, 29, 29; 50:12, 19, 21, 21
Ex 1:7, 10, 10, 11, 11, 12, 14, 16, 17, 18, 19, 21; 2:17, 17, 25; 3:8, 8, 9, 13, 13, 16, 22; 4:20; 5:4, 5, 7, 8, 9, 13, 14, 21; 6:1, 1, 3, 4, 4, 13; 7:5, 6, 13, 22; 8:2, 14, 15, 19; 9:2, 2, 12, 17, 19, 27; 10:2, 8, 10, 14, 14, 19, 27; 12:3, 16, 21, 33, 36, 38, 42; 13:17, 21, 21, 21; 14:3, 4, 7, 9, 9, 10, 13, 17, 19, 19, 20, 22, 23, 25, 25, 28, 28, 29; 15:5, 7, 7, 9, 9, 10, 12, 13, 15, 16, 17, 17, 19, 21, 25, 25; 16:3, 4, 4, 12, 15, 16, 20, 20, 23; 17:2; 18:8, 8, 11, 16, 20, 20, 21, 22, 25; 19:10, 10, 21, 22, 24, 25; 20:5, 5, 5, 6, 11; 21:1, 34; 22:11, 23; 23:23, 24, 24, 29, 30, 31, 32; 24:12, 14; 25:3, 8, 8, 12, 13, 14, 18, 28, 28, 29, 40; 26:1, 24, 37, 37; 27:6; 28:9, 11, 14, 25, 26, 27, 33, 40, 40, 41, 41, 41, 41, 42; 29:1, 1, 2, 3, 3, 4, 8, 9, 9, 13, 13, 17, 22, 24, 25, 25, 29, 30, 33, 35, 46, 46; 30:5, 12, 12, 12, 13, 14, 21, 29, 29, 30; 31:5; 32:2, 2, 3, 4, 8, 8, 10, 10, 12, 12, 12, 13, 18, 18, 18, 19, 21, 24, 24, 25, 27, 31, 34; 34:31, 31, 32, 33; 35:1, 1, 23, 26, 29, 33, 35, 35; 36:8, 8, 14, 29, 36, 36; 37:4, 7, 15, 28; 38:6, 25, 28; 39:7, 18, 19, 20, 43; 40:12, 14, 15
Lev 1:2, 12; 2:12; 3:4, 10, 15, 16; 4:2, 9, 10, 20, 20, 35; 5:8; 6:10, 17, 18; 7:4, 5, 7, 34, 35, 36, 36; 8:6, 10, 11, 13, 13, 13, 26, 27, 28, 28; 9:2, 7, 13, 14, 22; 10:1, 1, 2, 3, 4, 5, 11, 17; 11:1, 4, 4, 9, 22, 24, 25, 26, 28, 31, 32, 33, 42, 43; 13:58; 14:6, 12, 23, 24, 40, 42, 45, 51; 15:2, 14, 15, 29, 31; 16:4, 7, 16, 21, 23, 28; 17:2, 5, 5, 7, 8, 16; 18:2, 5, 29; 19:2, 10, 31, 31, 37; 20:6, 8, 11, 11, 12, 12, 13, 13, 16, 18, 22, 23, 27, 27; 21:1, 23; 22:3, 9, 16, 16, 18, 22, 25, 25, 31; 23:2, 10, 20, 22, 43; 24:6, 12; 25:2, 18, 31, 44, 45, 46, 46, 51; 26:3, 36, 36, 39, 41, 41, 43, 43, 44, 44, 44, 44; 27:2
Nu 1:3, 19, 21, 22, 23, 25, 27, 29, 31, 33, 35, 37, 39, 41, 43, 47, 49; 2:4, 13, 15, 19, 21, 23, 26, 28, 30; 3:6, 15, 16, 22, 22, 32, 34, 43, 47, 48, 49, 49, 51; 4:8, 12, 12, 12, 19, 19, 23, 26, 27, 29, 30, 36, 40, 44, 48; 5:3, 4, 12, 23; 6:2, 16, 19, 20, 23, 27; 7:1, 1, 2, 3, 5, 5, 6, 9, 13, 19, 25, 31, 37, 43, 49, 55, 61, 67, 73, 79; 8:6, 7, 7, 7, 7, 7, 8, 13, 15, 15, 16, 17, 20, 20, 21, 21, 21, 22; 9:8; 10:2, 2, 3, 33, 33, 34, 35; 11:1, 1, 3, 4, 12, 12, 16, 16, 17, 21, 22, 22, 22, 22, 24, 25, 26, 26, 28, 29, 31, 32; 12:9; 13:2, 3, 17, 17, 26, 26; 14:2, 6, 9, 9, 10, 11, 12, 12, 13, 14, 14, 16, 16, 23, 28, 31, 40, 45, 45; 15:2, 18, 25, 26, 29, 38, 38, 39; 16:3, 3, 3, 7, 9, 15, 15, 17, 18, 19, 21, 28, 30, 30, 31, 32, 33, 33, 34, 34, 38, 38, 38, 45, 46, 49; 17:2, 4; 18:8, 11, 12, 12, 18, 20, 24, 26, 26, 30; 19:9, 10, 21; 20:6, 8, 10, 12, 13, 25, 26, 28; 21:1, 3, 16, 30, 30, 33; 22:6, 6, 8, 11, 11, 11, 12, 20; 23:11, 13, 13, 13, 21, 22, 25, 25, 27; 24:8, 10; 25:4, 8, 11, 17; 26:3, 7, 10, 18, 22, 25, 27, 34, 37, 41, 43, 47, 50, 62, 62, 64, 65, 65; 27:3, 7, 7, 17, 17, 17, 17; 28:2, 3, 31; 30:12, 12, 12, 14, 14, 15, 15; 31:3, 6, 6, 8, 13, 15, 27, 27, 30, 36, 47, 51; 32:7, 8, 9, 13, 15, 17, 19, 20, 28, 29, 29, 33, 41; 33:4, 51, 55, 56; 34:2; 35:2, 3, 5, 6, 7, 8, 8, 10, 15; 36:6
Dt 1:3, 8, 8, 13, 15, 29, 39, 42; 2:5, 6, 6, 9, 11, 12, 12, 12, 12, 14, 15, 15, 19, 19, 20, 21, 21, 21, 22, 22, 23; 3:4, 6, 14, 20, 22, 28; 4:1, 3, 6, 7, 9, 10, 13, 14, 19, 19, 31, 37; 5:1, 1, 1, 9, 9, 9, 10, 22, 22, 29, 29, 30, 31, 31, 31; 6:1, 7, 7, 8, 9; 7:2, 2, 2, 2, 2, 3, 5, 9, 10, 10, 11, 12, 15, 15, 16, 17, 18, 20, 21, 22, 23, 23, 24, 25; 8:19, 19; 9:3, 3, 3, 3, 4, 4, 5, 10, 12, 12, 14, 17, 17, 28, 28, 28, 28, 28; 10:2, 4, 11, 15, 15; 11:4, 4, 6, 9, 16, 18, 19, 19, 20, 21, 22; 12:3, 18, 22, 22, 29, 29, 30; 13:2; 14:7, 7; 17:3, 5, 19; 18:2, 3, 12, 18, 18; 19:1, 9; 20:1, 3, 3, 17, 19, 19, 19, 19, 20; 21:5, 8, 10, 10, 18; 22:1, 1, 4, 4, 19, 22, 24, 24; 23:8; 24:8; 25:1, 5; 26:13, 13, 16; 27:2, 3, 4, 5, 26; 28:13, 14, 25, 26, 31, 32, 39, 39, 41, 55, 57, 61; 29:1, 2, 7, 9, 17, 25, 25, 26, 26, 28, 28; 30:1, 7, 17, 20; 31:2, 3, 4, 4, 5, 5, 6, 7, 7, 10, 16, 16, 17, 17, 17, 17, 20, 20, 21, 21, 21, 23, 28; 32:11, 11, 19, 20, 21, 21, 23, 23, 24, 26, 26, 28, 30, 30, 35, 38, 41, 46; 33:2, 2, 11, 11, 17, 27
Jos 1:2, 6, 14, 15; 2:4, 5, 5, 6, 6, 7, 7, 8, 15, 16, 21, 22, 22, 23; 4:3, 3, 3, 5, 7, 8, 8, 8, 12; 5:1, 5, 6, 7, 7; 6:6, 8, 13, 23, 26; 7:2, 5, 5, 5, 11, 21, 21, 23, 23, 23, 24, 25, 25; 8:3, 4, 5, 6, 6, 9, 11, 12, 15, 16, 20, 22, 22, 22, 24, 33, 33, 33, 35; 9:5, 8, 11, 11, 15, 15, 15, 15, 16, 16, 18, 18, 19, 19, 20, 20, 20, 21, 21, 21, 21, 22, 22, 26, 26, 26, 27; 10:1, 8, 8, 8, 9, 10, 10, 10, 10, 10, 11, 18, 19, 19, 19, 20, 20, 24, 25, 26, 26, 26, 27, 27, 28, 39, 41; 11:4, 6, 6, 7, 7, 8, 8, 8, 8, 8, 9, 11, 12, 12, 12, 13, 14, 17, 17, 20, 20, 21; 12:6; 13:6, 8, 8, 12, 14, 22, 22, 33; 14:1, 3, 12; 15:63; 17:4, 13, 15; 18:1, 4, 4, 7, 8, 10; 19:9, 9, 47, 49; 20:4, 4, 9; 21:2, 11, 21, 42, 44, 44; 22:2, 4, 6, 6, 7, 7, 8, 12, 15, 30, 32, 33; 23:2, 5, 5, 7, 7, 7, 7, 12, 12, 16; 24:5, 7, 7, 8, 8, 11, 12, 13, 25
Jdg 1:1, 4, 22, 25, 28, 29, 30, 32, 33, 34; 2:3, 10, 12, 12, 12, 14, 14, 14, 15, 15, 16, 16, 17, 18, 18, 18, 18, 18, 19, 19, 21, 22, 23, 23; 3:1, 2, 4, 8, 9, 15, 23, 25, 27, 28; 4:2; 5:14, 21, 30, 31; 6:1, 2, 3, 4, 8, 9, 20, 35; 7:1, 4, 4, 6, 17, 24; 8:2, 4, 8, 10, 11, 12, 16, 19, 20, 23, 24, 25, 34; 9:1, 7, 8, 9, 11, 13, 24, 25, 33, 38, 43, 43, 43, 44, 49, 49, 51, 51, 57; 10:7, 14, 16; 11:9, 11, 21, 24, 25, 26, 32, 32, 33, 35; 12:2, 3; 13:1; 14:9, 9, 12, 14, 18, 19, 19; 15:3, 3, 5, 7, 8, 11, 11, 12; 16:3, 3, 3, 8, 12, 23, 25, 26; 17:4; 18:1, 1, 2, 4, 6, 7, 8, 9, 18, 21, 27, 31; 19:6, 8, 14, 15, 23, 23, 24, 24, 24, 25; 20:13, 20, 25, 28, 32, 34, 40, 41, 42, 42, 42, 43, 43, 45, 45, 45; 21:6, 7, 7, 10, 12, 13, 14, 14, 15, 16, 17, 18, 22, 22, 22, 23, 23, 23
Ru 1:4, 5, 6, 9, 13, 13, 19, 20; 2:9, 16, 16
1Sa 2:8, 8, 8, 10, 16, 23, 25, 30, 34; 3:13; 5:6, 6, 6, 8; 6:6, 7, 10, 12, 15; 7:10, 11; 8:7, 8, 9, 9, 9, 11, 12, 14, 14, 16, 21, 22; 9:4, 4, 11, 12, 14, 20, 22, 22, 22, 26; 10:5, 6, 10, 18; 11:2, 7, 7, 8, 11, 12; 12:5, 8, 9, 9; 13:16, 19; 14:8, 9, 10, 11, 12, 21, 22, 32, 32, 34, 34, 34, 36, 36, 37, 47, 48, 48; 15:3, 4, 6, 9, 15, 18; 16:5, 20; 17:3, 8, 23, 23, 31, 36, 39, 39, 40; 18:16, 27; 19:8, 20; 20:11, 21, 40; 21:13; 22:2, 4, 11; 23:5, 26; 24:7, 22; 25:7, 7, 14, 15, 16, 18, 20, 29, 43; 26:12, 12, 13; 27:5; 30:2, 8, 8, 17, 17, 19, 19, 21, 22, 22, 27, 27, 27, 28, 28, 28, 29, 29, 29, 30, 30, 30, 31; 31:7, 12, 13
2Sa 1:10, 11, 18; 2:5, 7, 14; 3:22, 36; 4:7, 9, 12, 12; 5:3, 19, 20, 21, 23, 23; 6:22; 7:10, 10, 21; 8:1, 2, 2, 4, 7; 10:4, 5, 9, 10, 16, 19; 11:23; 12:11, 17, 31, 31; 13:9, 10, 11, 30; 14:6; 15:36, 36; 16:1; 17:9, 17, 18, 18, 20, 20, 22; 18:1, 4, 14, 31; 19:3, 28; 20:3, 3, 3, 8, 19; 21:2, 2, 2, 6, 6, 7, 9, 9, 10, 10, 12, 12, 13; 22:15, 15, 18, 23, 28, 31, 38, 38, 39, 39, 40, 41, 42, 43, 43, 43, 49; 23:6, 7, 18; 24:1, 12
1Ki 1:20, 33, 40; 2:7, 32; 5:3, 9, 9, 9, 9, 14, 18; 6:12, 15, 16, 32, 32, 35; 7:6, 6, 15, 25, 37, 46; 8:21, 34, 35, 36, 37, 44, 46, 46, 46, 47, 47, 48, 50, 50, 50, 50, 52, 53; 9:6, 7, 9, 9, 9, 13, 21; 10:17, 29; 11:2, 18, 24; 12:5, 7, 7, 7, 9, 10, 14, 16, 17, 28; 13:11, 12; 14:15, 23, 27, 28, 28; 15:18, 18, 22; 18:4, 4, 6, 13, 13, 23, 26, 27, 28, 40, 40, 40, 40, 40; 19:2, 21; 20:15, 18, 18, 19, 20, 23, 25, 27, 27; 21:8, 11, 11; 22:6, 10, 11, 13, 17

THEY (7376)

THOU (5474)

THY (4607)

TO (13641)

UNTO (9005)

UP (2381)

UPON (2763)

US (1449)

WAS (4531)

WE (1844)

WERE (2776)

WITH (6016)

YE (3796)

YOU (2802)

HEBREW-ARAMAIC DICTIONARY-INDEX TO THE OLD TESTAMENT

FEATURES OF THE HEBREW-ARAMAIC TO ENGLISH DICTIONARY-INDEX

STRONG NUMBER
Matches the number at the end of context lines; one- to four-digit numbers in non-italic type are Hebrew and Aramaic (see the introduction, pages xii–xiv).

LEXICAL FORM AND TRANSLITERATION
See the table below. Note that the lexical forms conform to modern resources and sometimes differ from Strong's original spelling.

PART OF SPEECH
The part of speech is abbreviated (see below and introduction, page xiv).

G/K NUMBER
Cross reference to the G/K numbering system, widely used in up-to-date word study reference resources (see the introduction, page xiv).

122 אָדֹם *'ādōm,* a. GK: 137 [→ 131; cf. 119].

RELATED WORDS LIST
Hebrew and Aramaic words related by cognate are listed by Strong number (see the introduction, pages xiv–xv).

red, ruddy (skin):–

DEFINITION AND ETYMOLOGY
Words are defined, often with expanded explanations, and if a proper name, the possible definition (etymology) is given in italics (see the introduction, pages xiv–xv).

red [7], ruddy [1]

KJV WORD AND (FREQUENCY COUNT)
Following the symbol :– KJV words are listed according to their exact textual spelling and are organized according to frequency (see the introduction, page xiv).

displeased (+7451+871.1) [1],

MULTIPLE WORDS / MULTIPLE NUMBERS
More than one KJV word and/or more than one Strong number indicate multiple-word translations (see the introduction, pages xiii–xiv).

same[S] [1]

SUPERSCRIPT "S"
Indicates "substitution" translation (see the introduction, pages xiii-xv).

HEBREW-ARAMAIC SIMPLIFIED TRANSLITERATION AND PRONUNCIATION TABLE

Heb

Consonants

א	'	[no sound]
בּ, ב	*b*	*b*oy
גּ, ג	*g*	*g*irl
דּ, ד	*d*	*d*og
ה	*h*	*h*ot
ו	*w*	*v*ote
ז	*z*	*z*ip
ח	*ḥ*	Ba*ch*
ט	*ṭ*	*t*ip
י	*y*	*y*es
כּ, כ, ך	*k*	*k*it
ל	*l*	*l*et
מ, ם	*m*	*m*other
נ, ן	*n*	*n*ot
ס	*s*	*s*ip
ע	'	[no sound]
פּ, פ, ף	*p*	*p*et
צ, ץ	*ṣ*	si*ts*
ק	*q*	tor*q*ue
ר	*r*	*r*ot
שׂ	*ś*	*s*ip
שׁ	*š*	*sh*ip
תּ, ת	*t*	*t*ip

Vowels

◌ָה	*â*	f*a*ther
◌ָ	*ā*	f*a*ther
◌ַ	*a*	f*a*ther
◌ֲ	*ᵃ*	b*a*ton
וּ	*û*	t*u*ne
◌ֻ	*u*	s*u*re
◌ֵי	*ê*	th*ey*
◌ֵ	*ē*	th*ey*
◌ֶ	*e*	g*e*t
◌ְ if (vocal)	*ᵉ*	s*e*lect
◌ֱ	*ᵉ*	s*e*lect
◌ִי	*î*	mach*i*ne
◌ִ	*i*	p*i*n
וֹ	*ô*	ph*o*ne
◌ֹ	*ō*	ph*o*ne
◌ָ	*o*	ph*o*ne
◌ֳ	*ᵒ*	m*o*tel

HEBREW-ARAMAIC DICTIONARY ABBREVIATIONS

&	and
+	plus: in combination with
?	uncertain
[]	uncertain part of speech
→	see these related words
√	see this organizing word
1	first person
2	second person
3	third person
a.	adjective
abst.	abstract
adv.	adverb
art.	article
c.	conjunction
col.	collective
com.	common gender
demo.	demonstrative
den.	denominative
du.	dual number
emph.	emphatic
excl.	exclamation
f.	feminine
fig.	figurative(ly)
g.	gentilic
indecl.	indeclinable
indef.	indefinite
inf.	infinitive
intens.	intensive
inter.	interrogative
interj.	interjection
l.	loanword
loc.	location
m.	masculine
n.	noun
neg.	negative
num.	numeral
ord.	ordinal
p.	pronoun
pl.	plural
poss.	possibly
pp.	preposition
pr.	proper [noun]
pref.	prefix
prob.	probably
pt.	particle
ptcp.	participle
rel.	relative
s.	singular
subst.	substantive
suf.	suffix
temp.	temporal
tt.	technical term in Psalm title
v.	verb
var.	variant
vbl.	verbal

Hebrew Verbal Stems

[H]	Hiphil
[Ho]	Hophal
[Hotpaal]	Hotpaal
[Hotpael]	Hotpael
[Hsh]	Histaphel
[Ht]	Hitpael
[Htpal]	Hitpalpel
[Htpalpal]	Hitpalpal
[Htpo]	Hitpoel
[Htpoal]	Hitpoal
[Htpol]	Hitpolel
[Htpolal]	Hitpolal
[N]	Niphal
[P]	Piel
[Pilal]	Pilal
[Pilel]	Pilel
[Pilpal]	Pilpal
[Pil]	Pilpel
[Po]	Poel
[Poal]	Poal
[Poalal]	Poalal
[Pol]	Polel
[Polal]	Polal
[Pu]	Pual
[Pualal]	Pualal
[Pul]	Pulal
[Pulpal]	Pulpal
[Q]	Qal
[Qp]	Qal passive

Aramaic Verbal Stems

[A]	Aphel
[H]	Haphel
[Ho]	Hophal
[Hp]	Haphel passive
[Hsh]	Hishtaphel
[Hth]	Hithaphal
[Htpa]	Hitpaal
[Htpe]	Hitpeel
[Htpol]	Hitpolel
[Htt]	Ettaphal
[Itpa]	Itpaal
[Itpe]	Itpeel
[Itpo]	Itpoal
[P]	Peal
[Pa]	Pael
[Pap]	Pael passive
[Peil]	Peil
[Po]	Poel
[Pol]	Polel
[Pp]	Peal passive (participle)

0.1 אָ- **-ā'**, p.suf.3.f.s. GK: 2 [cf. 1886.3]. she, her:– *not translated* [1]

0.2 אָ- **-ā'** (Aram.), art.suf. GK: 10002 [→ 1886.7]. the, a; indicates vocative: O; indicates emphatic state:– the [503], *usually untranslated* [258], O [24], a [13], that [5], continually (+8411+871.2) [2], the same [2], this [2], an [1], at what time (+1768+5732+871.2) [1], ever (+5705+5957) [1], ever (+5957) [1], for ever (+5957) [1], the same [1]

1 אָב **'āb**, n.m. GK: 3 [cf. 2 (also used with compound proper names)]. father, grandfather, forefather, ancestor; (pl.) ancestors (of both genders); by extension: originator, founder (of a city or profession); a title of respect referring to humans or god. The "house of a father" is a subdivision of a clan:– father [593], fathers [475], father's [118], fathers' [13], father's (+3807.1) [6], chief [2], families (+1004) [2], fatherless (+369) [1], forefathers (+7223) [1], patrimony [1], prince [1], principal [1]

2 אַב **'ab** (Aram.), n.m. GK: 10003 [cf. 1]. father, predecessor, ancestor (not necessarily male):– father [6], fathers [3]

3 אֵב **'ēb**, n.[m.]. GK: 4 [cf. 768; cf. 4]. new (plant) growth, shoot:– fruits [1], greenness [1]

4 אֵב **'ēb** (Aram.), n.m. GK: 10004 [cf. 3]. fruit:– fruit [3]

אֹב **'ōb**. See 178.

5 אֲבַגְתָא **'ᵃbagtā'**, n.pr.m. GK: 5. Abagtha:– Abagtha [1]

6 אָבַד **'ābad**, v. GK: 6 [→ 8, 9, 10, 11, 12, 13; cf. 7]. [Q] perish, [P, H] destroy, demolish, annihilate; "to destroy the heart" means "to lose courage":– perish [65], destroy [39], destroyed [17], perished [17], lost [9], perisheth [6], destroyeth [4], surely perish (+6) [4], cause to perish [3], ready to perish [3], utterly destroy (+6) [2], utterly perish (+6) [2], broken [1], destroyest [1], destruction [1], failed (+4480) [1], faileth [1], have no (+4480) [1], lose [1], made to perish [1], not (+4480) [1], spendeth [1], take [1], undone [1], void [1]

7 אֲבַד **'ᵃbad** (Aram.), v. GK: 10005 [cf. 6]. [P] to perish; [H] to execute; [Ho] to be destroyed:– destroy [4], perish [2], destroyed [1]

8 אֹבֵד **'ōbēd**, n.[m.]. GK: 7 [→ 6]. ruin:– perish [2]

9 אֲבֵדָה **'ᵃbēdâ**, n.f. GK: 8 [→ 6]. lost item:– lost [3], that which was lost [1]

10 אֲבַדֹּה **'ᵃbaddōh**, n.f. GK: 9 [→ 11; cf. 6]. destruction; this can refer to the nether world of the dead, with a focus that this is the place of decay:– destruction [1]

11 אֲבַדּוֹן **'ᵃbaddôn**, n.f. GK: 10 & 11 [→ 10; cf. 6]. destruction; some translate as a proper noun, the Place of Destruction (the realm of the dead):– destruction [5]

12 אַבְדָן **'abdān**, n.[m.]. GK: 12 [→ 6]. destruction:– destruction [1]

13 אָבְדַן **'obdān**, n.[m.]. GK: 13 [→ 6]. destruction:– destruction [1]

14 אָבָה **'ābâ**, v. GK: 14 [→ 17, 15?, 34?; cf. 2968, 8373?]. [Q] to be willing, consent, yield; with the negative, to be unwilling, refuse:– would [39], will [6], consent [4], willing [4], rest content [1]

15 אֲבִי **'ᵃbî**, interj. GK: 20 [→ 14?]. Oh, that!:– my desire [1]

16 אֵבֶה **'ēbeh**, n.[m.]. GK: 15. papyrus or reed (boat):– swift [1]

17 אֲבוֹי **'ᵃbôy**, interj. GK: 16 [→ 14]. sorrow (uneasiness); some parse as an interjection: woe!:– sorrow [1]

18 אֵבוּס **'ēbûs**, n.m. GK: 17 [→ 75]. manger:– crib [3]

19 אִבְחָה **'ibḥâ**, n.f. GK: 18 [cf. 2874]. slaughter:– point [1]

20 אֲבַטִּיחַ **'ᵃbaṭṭiaḥ**, n.[m.]. GK: 19 [→ 982]. melon:– melons [1]

21 אֲבִי **'ᵃbî**, n.pr.m. GK: 23 [→ 29]. Abijah, Abiezrite, "*[my] father is Yahweh, Abi [my] father*":– Abi [1]

22 אֲבִיאֵל **'ᵃbî'ēl**, n.pr.m. GK: 24 [→ 410+1]. Abiel, "*[my] father is God [El]*":– Abiel [3]

23 אֲבִיאָסָף **'ᵃbî'āsāp**, n.pr.m. GK: 25 [→ 43]. Abiasaph, "*[my] father has gathered*":– Abiasaph [1]

24 אָבִיב **'ābîb**, n.m. GK: 26 [cf. 8512]. (month of) Abib, the first month of the Canaanite calendar equal to Nisan (March-April); head (of grain), already ripe but still soft:– Abib [6], green ears of corn [1], in the ear [1]

25 אֲבִי גִבְעוֹן **'ᵃbî gib'ōn**, n.pr.m. GK: 3 + 1500 [→ 1+1391]. father of Gibeon (1 + 1391):–

26 אֲבִיגַיִל **'ᵃbîgayil**, n.pr.f. GK: 28 [→ 1+1523?]. Abigail, "*[my] father rejoices* or *father [cause] of joy*":– Abigail [17]

27 אֲבִידָן **'ᵃbîdān**, n.pr.m. GK: 29 [→ 1+1777]. Abidan, "*[my] father is judge*":– Abidan [5]

28 אֲבִידָע **'ᵃbîdā'**, n.pr.m. GK: 30 [→ 1+3045]. Abida, "*[my] father knows*":– Abidah [1], Abida [1]

29 אֲבִיָּה **'ᵃbiyyâ** or אֲבִיָּהוּ **'ᵃbiyyāhû**, n.pr.m. & f. GK: 31 & 32 [→ 21]. Abijah, "*[my] father is Yahweh*":– Abijah [20], Abiah [4], Abia [1]

30 אֲבִיהוּא **'ᵃbîhû'**, n.pr.m. GK: 33 [→ 1+1931]. Abihu, "*he is [my] father*":– Abihu [12]

31 אֲבִיהוּד **'ᵃbîhûd**, n.pr.m. GK: 34 [→ 1+1935]. Abihud, "*[my] father has majesty*":– Abihud [1]

32 אֲבִיהַיִל **'ᵃbîhayil** or אֲבִיחַיִל **'ᵃbîḥayil**, n.pr.m. GK: 35 & 38 [→ 1+2428]. Abihail, "*[my] father has strength/wealth* or *cause of strength/wealth*":– Abihail [6]

33 אֲבִי הָעֶזְרִי **'ᵃbî 'ezrî**, a.g. GK: 49 [→ 44]. Abiezrite, "*of Abiezer*":– Abi-ezrites [2], Abi-ezrite [1]

34 אֶבְיוֹן **'ebyôn**, a. GK: 36 [→ 14?]. poor, needy, often as a class of persons with physical needs, of low status and little political power, with an associative meaning of oppression and misery:– needy [35], poor [24], beggar [1], poor man [1]

35 אֲבִיּוֹנָה **'ᵃbiyyônâ**, n.f. GK: 37. caper berry (that stimulates desire):– desire [1]

אֲבִיחַיִל **'ᵃbîḥayil**. See 32.

36 אֲבִיטוּב **'ᵃbîṭûb**, n.pr.m. GK: 39 [→ 1+2896]. Abitub, "*[my] father is good*":– Abitub [1]

37 אֲבִיטַל **'ᵃbîṭāl**, n.pr.f. GK: 40 [→ 1+2919]. Abital, "*[my] father is [the] night dew*":– Abital [2]

38 אֲבִיָּם **'ᵃbiyyām**, n.pr.m. GK: 41 [→ 1+3220]. Abiyam, "*[my] father is Yam [the sea]*":– Abijam [5]

39 אֲבִימָאֵל **'ᵃbîmā'ēl**, n.pr.m. GK: 42 [→ 1+410]. Abimael, "*[my] father is God [El]*":– Abimael [2]

40 אֲבִימֶלֶךְ **'ᵃbîmelek**, n.pr.m. GK: 43 [→ 1+4428]. Abimelech, "*[my] father is king* or *[my] father is Molech*":– Abimelech [65], Abimelech's [2]

41 אֲבִינָדָב **'ᵃbînādāb**, n.pr.m. GK: 44 [→ 1+5068]. Abinadab, "*[my] father is generous* or *[my] father is Nadab*":– Abinadab [13]

42 אֲבִינֹעַם **'ᵃbînō'am**, n.pr.m. GK: 45 [→ 1+5278]. Abinoam, "*[my] father is graciousness*":– Abinoam [4]

אֲבִינֵר **'ᵃbînēr**. See 74.

43 אֶבְיָסָף **'ebyāsāp**, n.pr.m. GK: 47 [→ 23]. Ebiasaph, "*[my] father has gathered*":– Ebiasaph [3]

44 אֲבִיעֶזֶר **'ᵃbî'ezer**, n.pr.m. GK: 48 [→ 33]. Abiezer, "*[my] father is help*":– Abi-ezer [7]

45 אֲבִי־עַלְבוֹן **'ᵃbî-'albôn**, n.pr.m. GK: 50 [→ 1]. Abi-Albon, "*[my] father is Albon*":– Abialbon [1]

46 אָבִיר **'ābîr**, a. GK: 51 [→ 47, 82, 83, 84]. mighty, powerful; (as a divine title) the Mighty One:– mighty one [3], mighty [3]

47 אַבִּיר **'abbîr**, a. GK: 52 [→ 46]. mighty, powerful; this can refer to strong animals, social leaders, and angelic beings:– bulls [4], mighty [4], stouthearted (+3820) [2], strong [2], valiant [2], angels' [1], chiefest [1], strong ones [1]

48 אֲבִירָם **'ᵃbîrām**, n.pr.m. GK: 53 [→ 1+7311; cf. 87]. Abiram, "*[my] father is exalted*":– Abiram [11]

49 אֲבִישַׁג **'ᵃbîšag**, n.pr.f. GK: 54 [→ 1+7683]. Abishag, "*[my] father strays*":– Abishag [5]

50 אֲבִישׁוּעַ **'ᵃbîšûa'**, n.pr.m. GK: 55 [→ 1+7770]. Abishua, "*[my] father is salvation*":– Abishua [5]

51 אֲבִישׁוּר **'ᵃbîšûr**, n.pr.m. GK: 56 [→ 1+7794]. Abishur, "*[my] father is a wall*":– Abishur [2]

52 אֲבִישַׁי **'ᵃbîšay** or אַבְשַׁי **'abšay**, n.pr.m. GK: 57 & 93 [→ 1+7862]. Abishai, "*[my] father is Jesse* or *father exists*":– Abishai [25]

53 אֲבִישָׁלוֹם **'ᵃbîšālôm** or אַבְשָׁלוֹם **'abšālôm**, n.pr.m. GK: 58 & 94 [→ 1+7965]. Abishalom, "*[my] father is peace*":– Absalom [104], Absalom's [5], Abishalom [2]

54 אֶבְיָתָר **'ebyātār**, n.pr.m. GK: 59 [→ 1+3498]. Abiathar, "*[my] father gives abundance* or *the father is preeminent*":– Abiathar [29], Abiathar's (+3807.1) [1]

55 אָבַךְ **'ābak**, v. GK: 60 [cf. 2015]. [Ht] to roll upward, to be borne along:– mount up [1]

56 אָבַל **'ābal**, v. GK: 61 & 62 [→ 57, 60]. [Q] to dry up, lie parched; to mourn, lament, grieve; [H] cause to mourn; mourning can be the emotion or attitude of sorrow, as well as the active observation of mourning rites and ceremonies; [Ht] to mourn, lament, grieve:– mourn [15], mourned [10], mourneth [8], caused a mourning [1], feign to be a mourner [1], lamented [1], lament [1], made to lament [1], mourning [1]

57 אָבֵל **'ābēl**, a. GK: 63 [→ 56]. mourning, grieving, weeping:– mourn [3], mourners [2], mourning [2], mourneth [1]

58 אָבֵל **'ābēl**, n.m. GK: 64 [→ 59, 62, 63, 64, 65, 66, 67, 180; cf. 2986]. meadow:– plain [1]

59 אָבֵל **'ābēl**, n.pr.loc. GK: 64 [→ 58]. Abel, "*meadow*":– Abel [4], Abel-beth-maachah [2]

60 אֵבֶל **'ēbel**, n.m. GK: 65 [→ 56]. ceremony of mourning, period of mourning; a mourning ceremony was a ritual for burial of the dead, with distinctive clothing, music, behaviors, and a set time period for the ritual, generally a longer period for more important people:– mourning [24]

61 אֲבָל **'ᵃbāl**, adv. GK: 66 [→ 1077]. but; however, surely, indeed:– but [4], verily [3], indeed [2], nevertheless [2]

62 אָבֵל בֵּית מַעֲכָה **'ābēl bêt maᵃkâ**, n.pr.loc. GK: 68 [→ 58+1004+4601]. Abel Beth Maacah, "*meadow of the house of Maacah [oppression]*":–

63 אָבֵל הַשִּׁטִּים **'ābēl haššiṭṭîm**, n.pr.loc. GK: 69 [→ 58]. Abel Shittim, "*meadow of the acacia trees*":– Abel-shittim [1]

64 אָבֵל כְּרָמִים **'ābēl kᵉrāmîm**, n.pr.loc. GK: 70 [→ 58]. Abel Keramim, "*meadow of vineyards*":–

65 אָבֵל מְחוֹלָה **'ābēl mᵉḥôlâ**, n.pr.loc. GK: 71 [→ 58+4246; cf. 4259?]. Abel Meholah, "*meadow of the round dance*":– Abel-meholah [3]

66 אָבֵל מַיִם **'ābēl mayim**, n.pr.loc. GK: 72 [→ 58+4325]. Abel Maim, "*meadow of waters*":– Abel-maim [1]

67 אָבֵל מִצְרַיִם **'ābēl miṣrayim**, n.pr.loc. GK: 73 [→ 58+4714]. Abel Mizraim, "*meadow of Egypt* or *mourning of Egypt*":– Abel-mizraim [1]

68 אֶבֶן **'eben**, n.f. GK: 74 [→ 72, 70?; cf. 69]. stone, rock, natural or shaped, sometimes of specific size for use in a balance scale; a "precious stone" is a gem or jewel; by extension: hailstone. Rock is a title of God, with a focus of strength and stability, a place of refuge:– stones [142], stone [105], divers weights (+68+2050.1) [6], weight [4], great hailstones (+417) [3], weights [3], stony [2], carbuncles (+688) [1], chalkstones (+1615) [1], hailstones (+1259) [1], hailstones (+1259+1886.1) [1], headstone (+7222) [1], masons (+2796+7023) [1], plummet (+913) [1], slingstones (+7050) [1]

Heb

69 אֶבֶן **'eben** (Aram.), n.f. GK: 10006 [cf. 68]. rock, stone, including hewn or unhewn stones, stone slabs and bricks:– stone [6], stones [2]

70 אָבְנַיִם **'obnayim**, n.[m.]. GK: 78 [→ 68?]. potter's wheel; delivery stool:– stools [1], wheels [1]

71 אֲבָנָה **'ᵃbānâ**, n.pr.loc. GK: 76 [cf. 549]. Abana:– Abana [1]

72 אֶבֶן הָעֵזֶר **'eben hā'ēzer**, n.pr.loc. GK: 75 [→ 68+5828]. Ebenezer, "*stone of help*":– Eben-ezer [3]

73 אַבְנֵט **'abnēṭ**, n.[m.]. GK: 77. (linen) sash, wrapped around the waist:– girdle [6], girdles [3]

74 אַבְנֵר **'abnēr** or אֲבִינֵר **'ᵃbînēr**, n.pr.m. GK: 46 & 79 [→ 1+5216]. Abner, "*[my] father is Ner [a lamp]*":– Abner [62], Abner's [1]

75 אָבַס **'ābas**, v. GK: 80 [→ 18, 3965]. [Qp] to be fattened:– fatted [1], stalled [1]

76 אֲבַעְבֻּעֹת **'ᵃba'bu'ōt**, n.f.pl. GK: 81 [→ 5042]. festers, blisters:– blains [2]

77 אֶבֶץ **'ebeṣ**, n.pr.loc. GK: 82 [→ 78]. Ebez:– Abez [1]

78 אִבְצָן **'ibṣān**, n.pr.m. GK: 83 [→ 77]. Ibzan, "*swift*":– Ibzan [2]

79 אָבַק **'ābaq**, v.den. GK: 84 [cf. 3543?]. [N] to wrestle (with):– wrestled [2]

80 אָבָק **'ābāq**, n.m. GK: 85 [→ 81]. fine dust, powder:– dust [4], powder [1], small dust [1]

81 אֲבָקָה **'ᵃbāqâ**, n.f. GK: 86 [→ 80]. spice (scented powders):– powders [1]

82 אָבַר **'ābar**, v.den. GK: 87 [→ 83; cf. 46]. [H] to take flight, soar upward:– fly [1]

83 אֵבֶר **'ēber**, n.[m.]. GK: 88 [→ 82, 84; cf. 46]. feather, wing; other sources: the strong joint of the body to the wing, "pinion," with the associative meaning of strength that can bring freedom:– wings [2], longwinged (+750) [1]

84 אֶבְרָה **'ebrâ**, n.f. GK: 89 [→ 83; cf. 46]. feather, pinion, wing; in some contexts may have the associative meaning of protection:– feathers [2], wings [2]

85 אַבְרָהָם **'abrāhām**, n.pr.m. GK: 90 [cf. 87]. Abraham, "*father of many*":– Abraham [161], Abraham's [14]

86 אַבְרֵךְ **'abrēk**, l.excl. GK: 91. Make way!; others: Kneel down! or Watch out!:– bow the knee [1]

87 אַבְרָם **'abrām**, n.pr.m. GK: 92 [→ 1+7311; cf. 48, 85]. Abram, "*exalted father*":– Abram [54], Abram's [7]

אַבְשַׁי **'abšay**. See 52.

אַבְשָׁלוֹם **'abšālôm**. See 53.

88 אֹבֹת **'ōbōt**, n.pr.loc. GK: 95 [→ 2968?]. Oboth, "*fathers*":– Oboth [4]

89 אָגֵא **'āgē'**, n.pr.m. GK: 96. Agee, "[poss.] *fugitive*":– Agee [1]

90 אֲגַג **'ᵃgag**, n.pr.m. GK: 97 [→ 91?]. Agag, "[poss.] *violent*":– Agag [8]

91 אֲגָגִי **'ᵃgāgî**, a.g. GK: 98 [→ 90?]. Agagite, "*of Agag*":– Agagite [5]

92 אֲגֻדָּה **'ᵃguddâ**, n.f. GK: 99. bunch, bundle; group, band; cord, bands; foundation, structure:– troop [2], bunch [1], burdens [1]

93 אֱגוֹז **'ᵉgôz**, n.[m.]. GK: 100. nut tree:– nuts [1]

94 אָגוּר **'āgûr**, n.pr.m. GK: 101 [→ 103]. Agur, "*gatherer* [or poss.] *wage earner*":– Agur [1]

95 אֲגוֹרָה **'ᵃgôrâ**, n.f. GK: 102 [→ 107]. fee, payment, a piece of precious metal used as a medium of exchange (but not a minted coin):– piece [1]

96 אֵגֶל **'ēgel**, n.[m.]. GK: 103 [→ 97]. drop (of dew):– drops [1]

97 אֶגְלַיִם **'eglayim**, n.pr.loc. GK: 104 [→ 96]. Eglaim:– Eglaim [1]

98 אֲגַם **'ᵃgam**, n.[m.]. GK: 106 [→ 100]. swamp, pond, marsh (with reeds):– ponds [2], pools [2], pool [2], standing [2], reeds [1]

99 אָגֵם **'āgēm**, a. GK: 108 [cf. 5701]. sick, grieved:– ponds [1]

100 אַגְמוֹן **'agmôn**, n.[m.]. GK: 109 [→ 98]. reed; cord (made of reeds):– rush [2], bulrush [1], caldron [1], hook [1]

101 אַגָּן **'aggān**, n.[m.]. GK: 110. (large and deep) bowl, goblet:– basons [1], cups [1], goblet [1]

102 אֲגַף **'ᵃgap**, n.[m.]. GK: 111 [→ 1610]. troop, band:– bands [7]

103 אָגַר **'āgar**, v. GK: 112 [→ 94]. [Q] to gather (in):– gathereth [2], gather [1]

104 אִגְּרָה **'iggᵉrâ** (Aram.), n.f. GK: 10007 [cf. 107]. letter:– letter [3]

105 אֲגַרְטָל **'ᵃgarṭāl**, n.m. GK: 113. dish; in context made of precious metals:– chargers [2]

106 אֶגְרֹף **'egrōp**, n.[m.]. GK: 114 [→ 1640?]. fist (the hand clenched to strike):– fist [2]

107 אִגֶּרֶת **'iggeret**, n.f. GK: 115 [→ 95; cf. 104]. letter, document:– letters [6], letter [4]

108 אֵד **'ēd**, n.m. GK: 116. stream, fresh water that moves from a higher to lower place; in some contexts this may be an artesian spring:– mist [1], vapour [1]

109 אָדַב **'ādab**, v. GK: 117 [→ 110]. [H] to grieve:– grieve [1]

110 אַדְבְּאֵל **'adbᵉ'ēl**, n.pr.m. GK: 118 [→ 109+410]. Adbeel, "*[the] grief of God [El]*":– Adbeel [2]

111 אֲדַד **'ᵃdad**, n.pr.m. GK: 119 [→ 1908]. Hadad, "*sharp*":– Hadad [1]

112 אִדּוֹ **'iddô**, n.pr.m. GK: 120. Iddo, "[prob.] *Yahweh has adorned*":– Iddo [2]

אֱדוֹם **'ᵉdôm**. See 123.

אֱדוֹמִי **'ᵉdômî**. See 30.

113 אָדוֹן **'ādôn**, n.m. GK: 123 [→ 136, 137, 138, 138, 139, 140, 141]. lord, master, supervisor, one who has authority over another; husband; owner; the Lord, (with Yahweh [3068]) Sovereign. "Lord of lords" means the highest power or authority:– Lord/lord [216], master [77], master's [22], lord's [5], masters [5], lords [4], lord's (+3807.1) [3], masters' [1], owner [1], sir [1]

114 אַדּוֹן **'addôn**, n.pr.loc. GK: 124 [cf. 135]. Addon:– Addon [1]

115 אֲדוֹרַיִם **'ᵃdôrayim**, n.pr.m. GK: 126 [→ 1752?]. Adoraim, "[poss.] *pair of knolls*":– Adoraim [1]

116 אֱדַיִן **'ᵉdayin** (Aram.), adv. GK: 10008 [cf. 227]. then, thus, so then:– then (+871.2) [28], then [26], now (+1768) [1], that time [1], then (+4481+6925+871.2) [1]

117 אַדִּיר **'addîr**, a. GK: 129 [→ 142]. mighty, noble, majestic, splendid; (n.) any powerful or awesome person: noble, believer, elite soldier; (as a divine title) the Mighty One, with a focus on the power and splendor of God:– nobles [7], excellent [4], mighty [4], principal [3], famous [2], gallant [1], glorious [1], goodly [1], lordly [1], mightier [1], mighty one [1], worthies [1]

118 אֲדַלְיָא **'ᵃdalyā'**, n.pr.m. GK: 130. Adalia, "[poss.] *honorable*":– Adalia [1]

119 אָדֵם **'ādēm**, v. GK: 131 [→ 120, 121, 122, 123, 124, 125, 127, 130, 131, 132]. [Q] be ruddy; [Pu] be dyed red:– dyed red [5], red [3], made red [1], ruddy [1]

120 אָדָם **'ādām**, n.m. GK: 132 & 133 & 135 [→ 119]. man, human being; humankind, people, often in contrast to animals; "son of man" means a human being (Nu 23:9), but often assumes messianic significance (Ps 8):– man [388], men [106], Adam [20], man's [16], men's [10], persons (+5315) [3], persons [3], man (+1121) [2], man (+5315) [2], men (+1121) [2], person [2], another [1], husbandman (+376+5647) [1], hypocrite (+2611) [1], low (+1121) [1], men (+5315) [1], men of low degree (+1121) [1], sort [1]

121 אָדָם **'ādām**, n.pr.m. & loc. GK: 134 & 136 [→ 128; cf. 119]. Adam, "*[red] earth* or *[ruddy] skin color*":– Adam [2]

122 אָדֹם **'ādōm**, a. GK: 137 [→ 131; cf. 119]. red; ruddy (skin):– red [7], ruddy [1], same[S] [1]

123 אֱדוֹם **'ᵉdôm** or אֱדֹם **'ᵉdōm**, n.pr.m. GK: 121 & 139 [→ 130, 5654; cf. 119]. Edom, referring to a person and his ancestral territory S.E. of the Dead Sea, "*red*":– Edom [87], Edomites [9], Idumea [4]

124 אֹדֶם **'ōdem**, n.[f.]. GK: 138 [→ 119]. ruby:– sardius [3]

125 אֲדַמְדָּם **'ᵃdamdām**, a. GK: 140 [→ 119]. reddish, reddish-white:– reddish [4], somewhat reddish [2]

126 אַדְמָה **'admâ**, n.pr.loc. GK: 144. Admah, "*[red] earth*":– Admah [5]

127 אֲדָמָה **'ᵃdāmâ**, n.f. GK: 141 & 143 [→ 119]. earth, the entire surface of the place where humans dwell, as well as smaller regions: land; with a focus on the elements of the earth: ground, soil, dust. A "man of the soil" is a farmer; "fruit of the soil" are crops:– land [122], earth [52], ground [43], lands [3], country [1], dust [1], husbandman (+376+1886.1) [1], husbandry [1]

128 אֲדָמָה **'ᵃdāmâ**, n.pr.loc. GK: 142 [→ 121; cf. 119]. Adamah, "*[red] earth*":– Adamah [1]

אַדְמוֹנִי **'admônî**. See 132.

129 אֲדָמִי **'ᵃdāmî**, n.pr.loc. GK: 146 [→ 119]. Adami [with Nekeb 5346], "*ground [of piercing]*":– Adami [1]

130 אֲדוֹמִי **'ᵃdômî**, a.g. GK: 122 [→ 123; cf. 119; 726]. Edomite, "*of Edom*":– Edomite [7], Edomites [4]

131 אֲדֻמִּים **'ᵃdummîm**, n.pr.loc. GK: 147 [→ 122; cf. 119]. Adummim, "*red [streaks]*":– Adummim [2]

132 אַדְמוֹנִי **'admônî**, a. GK: 145 [→ 119]. red; ruddy (skin):– ruddy [2], red [1]

133 אַדְמָתָא **'admātā'**, n.pr.m. GK: 148. Admatha, "*unrestrained*":– Admatha [1]

134 אֶדֶן **'eden**, n.m. GK: 149. base, footing, pedestal:– sockets [54], foundations [1], socket [1]

אָדֹן **'ādōn**. See 113.

135 אַדָּן **'addān**, n.pr.loc. GK: 150 [cf. 114]. Addon:– Addan [1]

136 אֲדֹנָי **'ᵃdōnāy**, n.[pr.]m. GK: 151 [→ 113]. the Lord, a title of the one true God, with a focus on his majesty and authority:– Lord/lord [430], God [1], Lord's [1]

137 אֲדֹנִי־בֶזֶק **'ᵃdōnî bezeq**, n.pr.m. GK: 152 [→ 113+966]. Adoni-Bezek, "*lord of Bezek*":– Adoni-bezek [3]

138 אֲדוֹנִיָּה **'ᵃdôniyyâ** or אֲדֹנִיָּה **'ᵃdōniyyâ** or אֲדֹנִיָּהוּ **'ᵃdōniyyāhû**, n.pr.m. GK: 125 & 153 & 154 [→ 2899]. Adonijah, "*[my] lord is Yahweh*":– Adonijah [26]

139 אֲדֹנִי־צֶדֶק **'ᵃdōnî-ṣedeq**, n.pr.m. GK: 155 [→ 113+6664]. Adoni-Zedek, "*[my] lord is righteousness*":– Adoni-zedek [2]

140 אֲדֹנִיקָם **'ᵃdōnîqām**, n.pr.m. GK: 156 [→ 113+6965]. Adonikam, "*[my] lord arises*":– Adonikam [3]

141 אֲדֹנִירָם **'ᵃdōnîrām**, n.pr.m. GK: 157 [→ 151]. Adoniram, "*[my] lord is exalted*":– Adoniram [2]

142 אָדַר **'ādar**, v. GK: 158 [→ 117, 145, 143, 155]. [N] to prove oneself majestic, powerful; [H] to make glorious, make powerful:– become glorious [1], glorious [1], make honourable [1]

143 אֲדָר **'ᵃdār**, n.pr.[m.]. GK: 160 [→ 142; cf. 144]. Adar, "[poss.] *dark, clouded*":– Adar [8]

144 אֲדָר **'ᵃdār** (Aram.), n.pr.month. GK: 10009 [cf. 143]. Adar, "[poss.] *dark, clouded*":– Adar [1]

145 אֶדֶר **'eder**, n.[m.]. GK: 159 [→ 142]. splendor, handsomeness, of obvious quality:– goodly [1], robe [1]

146 אַדָּר **'addār**, n.pr.m. & loc. GK: 161 & 162 [→ 2692, 5853]. Addar, "*glorious*":– Adar [1], Addar [1]

147 אִדַּר **'iddar** (Aram.), n.m. GK: 10010. threshing floor:– threshingfloors [1]

148 אֲדַרְגָּזַר **'ᵃdargāzar** (Aram.), n.m. GK: 10011. adviser, counselor, likely the king's "minister of information":– judges [2]

149 אַדְרַזְדָּא **'adrazdā'** (Aram.), adv. GK: 10012. with diligence, zealously:– diligently [1]

150 אֲדַרְכֹנִים **'ᵃdarkōnîm**, n.[m.pl.?]. GK: 163 [→ 1871]. darics, Persian gold coins:– drams [2]

151 אֲדוֹרָם **'ᵃdôrām** or אֲדֹרָם **'ᵃdōrām**, n.pr.m. GK: 127 & 164 [→ 141]. Adoram:– Adoram [2]

152 אַדְרַמֶּלֶךְ **'adrammelek**, n.pr.m. GK: 165 & 166. Adrammelech (pagan god and king), "*nobility of Molech [king]*":– Adrammelech [3]

153 אֶדְרָע **'edrā'** (Aram.), n.[f.]. GK: 10013 [→ 1872; cf. 248, 2220]. arm; fig., power, force:– force [1]

154 אֶדְרֶעִי **'edre'î**, n.pr.loc. GK: 167. Edrei, "*strong*":– Edrei [8]

155 אַדֶּרֶת **'adderet**, n.f. GK: 168 [→ 142]. cloak, royal robe, (hairy) garment:– mantle [5], garment [4], glory [1], goodly [1], robe [1]

156 אָדַשׁ **'ādaš**, v. GK: 169 [cf. 1758]. to thresh; see definitions at 1758:– threshing (+156) [2]

157 אָהַב **'āhab**, v. GK: 170 [→ 159, 158, 160]. [Q] to love, like, be a friend; [N] to be loved; [P] be a lover, an ally; love can refer to friendship, familial love, romantic love, or covenant loyalty:– love [75], loved [48], loveth [38], lovers [17], friends [8], lovest [7], beloved [5], friend [4], lover [2], liketh [1], lovedst [1], lovely [1], loving [1]

158 אַהַב **'ahab**, n.[m.]. GK: 172 [→ 157]. lover (negative); loving, charming (positive):– lovers [1], loving [1]

159 אֹהַב **'ōhab**, n.[m.]. GK: 171 [→ 157]. love; something loved:– loves [1]

160 אַהֲבָה **'ahᵃbâ**, n.f. GK: 173 & 174 [→ 157]. love; friendship, familial love, romantic love, or covenant loyalty:– love [33], loved [7]

161 אֹהַד **'ōhad**, n.pr.m. GK: 176. Ohad:– Ohad [2]

162 אֲהָהּ **'ᵃhāh**, interj. GK: 177. Ah!, Oh!, Alas!; an exclamation of emphasis, surprise, or sorrow:– ah [8], alas [7]

163 אַהֲוָא **'ahᵃwā'**, n.pr.loc. GK: 178. Ahava:– Ahava [3]

164 אֵהוּד **'ēhûd**, n.pr.m. GK: 179 [cf. 261?]. Ehud, "*united*":– Ehud [9]

165 אֱהִי **'ᵉhî**, adv. GK: 180. Where?:– be [2], where (+645) [1]

166 אָהַל **'āhal**, v. GK: 183 [→ 1984]. [H] to be bright:– shineth [1]

167 אָהַל **'āhal**, v.den. GK: 182 [→ 168]. [Q, P] to pitch a tent:– pitch tent [1], pitched tent [1], removed tent [1]

168 אֹהֶל **'ōhel**, n.m. GK: 185 [→ 167, 169, 170 (also used with compound proper names)]. tent, tent-dwelling; by extension: home, dwelling place, a permanent dwelling; family group. "The Tent of Meeting" was the worship tent built before the Temple:– tabernacle [187], tent [91], tents [50], tabernacles [11], dwelling place [2], covering [1], dwelling [1], home [1], places [1]

169 אֹהֶל **'ōhel**, n.pr.m. GK: 186 [→ 168]. Ohel, "*tent*":– Ohel [1]

170 אָהֳלָה ***'oh°lâ***, n.pr.f. GK: 188 [→ 172, 173; cf. 168]. Oholah, "*she who has a tent*":– Aholah [5]

171 אָהֳלִיאָב ***'oh°lî'āb***, n.pr.m. GK: 190 [→ 168+1]. Oholiab, "*tent of [my] father*":– Aholiab [5]

172 אָהֳלִיבָה ***'oh°lîbâ***, n.pr.f. GK: 191 [→ 170+871.1+1886.3]. Oholibah, "*my tent is in her*":– Aholibah [6]

173 אָהֳלִיבָמָה ***'oh°lîbāmâ***, n.pr.m. & f. GK: 192 [→ 168+1116?]. Oholibamah, "*[my] tent is a high place*":– Aholibamah [8]

174 אֲהָלוֹת ***'ahālôt*** or אֲהָלִים ***'ahālîm***, n.[m.]. GK: 189 & 193. aloes; an aromatic wood from India:– aloes [3], trees of lign aloes [1]

175 אַהֲרֹן ***'ah'rôn***, n.pr.m. GK: 195. Aaron:– Aaron [315], Aaron's [26], Aaron's (+3807.1) [4], Aaronites [2]

176 אוֹ ***'ô***, c. GK: 196 [→ 194?]. or, or if, whether:– or [293], either [7], whether [7], and [2], nor [2], or if [2], also [1], at the least [1], if then (+227) [1], nor (+3808) [1], or else [1], otherwise [1], then [1]

177 אוּאֵל ***'û'ēl***, n.pr.m. GK: 198 [→ 183?+410]. Uel, "[poss.] *will of God [El]*":– Uel [1]

178 אוֹב ***'ôb***, n.m. GK: 199 & 200. wineskin, bag, a leather bag of goatskin turned inside out to hold fluids; medium, spiritist, one who communicates with and conjures ghosts or spirits:– familiar spirits [9], familiar spirit [7], bottles [1]

179 אוֹבִיל ***'ôbîl***, n.pr.m. GK: 201 [→ 2986]. Obil, "*camel driver*":– Obil [1]

180 אֻבָל ***'ubāl***, n.[m.]. GK: 67 [→ 58]. canal:– river [3]

181 אוּד ***'ûd***, n.m. GK: 202 [→ 343]. burning stick:– brand [1], firebrands [1], firebrand [1]

182 אֹדוֹת ***'ōdôt***, n.f. GK: 128. on account of, because of, for the reason that:– because of (+5921) [5], concerning (+5921) [2], causes [1], cause [1], sake [1]

183 אָוָה ***'āwâ***, v. GK: 203 [→ 185, 1942, 3970, 8378 (also used with compound proper names)]. [P, Ht] to crave, desire, yearn for, long for:– desireth [7], desired [5], desire [3], longed [2], coveteth greedily (+8378) [1], covet [1], desirous [1], fell a lusting (+8378) [1], greatly desire [1], longeth [1], lusted exceedingly (+8378) [1], lusted [1], lusteth after [1]

184 אָוָה ***'āwâ***, v. GK: 204 [→ 226?; cf. 8376, 8379, 8427]. [Ht] to run a line, measure:– point out [1]

185 אַוָּה ***'awwâ***, n.f. GK: 205 [→ 1942; cf. 183]. wanting, craving; earnestness:– desire [3], lusteth after [3], pleasure [1]

186 אוּזַי ***'ûzay***, n.pr.m. GK: 206. Uzai, "*Yahweh has given ear, listened*":– Uzai [1]

187 אוּזָל ***'ûzāl***, n.pr.loc. [& m.]. GK: 207. Uzal, a person and a place:– Uzal [2]

188 אוֹי ***'ôy***, interj. GK: 208 [→ 190]. Woe! Alas!:– woe [23], alas [1]

189 אֱוִי ***'ewî***, n.pr.m. GK: 209. Evi, "*desire*":– Evi [2]

אוֹיֵב ***'ôyēb***. See 341.

190 אוֹיָה ***'ôyâ***, interj. GK: 210 [→ 188]. Woe!, Alas!:– woe [1]

191 אֱוִיל ***'ewîl***, a. GK: 211 [→ 196, 200; cf. 2973]. foolish; (n.) a fool:– fool [11], fools [7], foolish [5], fool's [2], foolish man [1]

192 אֱוִיל מְרֹדַךְ ***'ewîl m'rōdak***, n.pr.m. GK: 213. Evil-Merodach, "*worshiper of Marduk[s]*; [corrupted to read] *fool of blessing*":– Evil-merodach [2]

193 אוּל ***'ûl***, n.[m.]. GK: 214 & 215 [→ 352; cf. 2974]. belly, sometimes referring to the whole body; leading man, noble; symbolic of strength:– strength [1]

194 אוּלַי ***'ûlay***, adv. GK: 218 [→ 176?+3808?]. what if, perhaps, maybe; this is in an expression of hope, pleading, or fear:– peradventure [23], if so be [8], it may be that [7], it may be [5], if so be that [1], unless [1]

195 אוּלַי ***'ûlay***, n.pr.loc. GK: 217. Ulai:– Ulai [2]

196 אֱוִלִי ***'ewilî***, a. GK: 216 [→ 191]. foolish, without understanding:– foolish [1]

197 אוּלָם ***'ûlām***, n.m. GK: 221 [→ 361]. portico; hall; colonnade:– porch [33], porches [1]

198 אוּלָם ***'ûlām***, n.pr.m. GK: 220. Ulam, "*first, leader*":– Ulam [4]

199 אוּלָם ***'ûlām***, adv. GK: 219. but, however, on the other hand, nevertheless:– but (+2050.1) [6], truly [4], but [2], in very deed [2], surely [2], howbeit [1], wherefore (+2050.1) [1], would [1]

200 אִוֶּלֶת ***'iwwelet***, n.f. GK: 222 [→ 191]. foolishness, folly; in some contexts this may refer to thoughtless speech:– folly [13], foolishness [10], foolishly [1], foolish [1]

201 אוֹמָר ***'ômār***, n.pr.m. GK: 223 [→ 559]. Omar, "*speaker*":– Omar [3]

202 אוֹן ***'ôn***, n.m. GK: 226 [→ 203, 207, 208, 209]. power, strength, vigor, manhood; wealth:– strength [7], might [2], force [1], goods [1], substance [1]

203 אוֹן ***'ôn***, n.pr.m. GK: 227 [→ 208; cf. 202]. On, "*Sun [god] city*":– On [1]

204 אוֹן ***'ôn***, n.pr.loc. GK: 228. On, "*Sun [god] city*":– On [3]

205 אָוֶן ***'āwen***, n.m. GK: 224 & 230 [→ 578, 1007, 1126, 8383?]. evil, wickedness, iniquity; evildoer; an unfavorable circumstance: calamity, trouble, injustice; this can also refer to idols, with a focus that they are morally evil; mourning:– iniquity [47], vanity [6], wicked [6], affliction [3], mischief [3], Aven [2], unrighteous [2], wickedness [2], evil [1], false [1], idol [1], mourners [1], mourning [1], nought [1], sorrow [1], unjust [1], vain [1]

206 אָוֶן ***'āwen***, n.pr.loc. GK: 225. Heliopolis; (Valley of) Aven, "*evil power, wickedness*":– Aven [1]

207 אוֹנוֹ ***'ônô***, n.pr.loc. GK: 229 [→ 202]. Ono, "*strong*":– Ono [5]

208 אוֹנָם ***'ônām***, n.pr.m. GK: 231 [→ 203; cf. 202]. Onam, "*intense, strong*":– Onam [4]

209 אוֹנָן ***'ônān***, n.pr.m. GK: 232 [→ 202]. Onan, "*powerful, intense*":– Onan [8]

210 אוּפָז ***'ûpāz***, n.pr.loc. GK: 233. Uphaz:– Uphaz [2]

211 אוֹפִיר ***'ôpîr***, n.pr.m. & loc. GK: 234 & 235 [cf. 665]. Ophir:– Ophir [13]

212 אוֹפָן ***'ôpan***, n.m. GK: 236 [cf. 655?]. wheel (of a vehicle):– wheels [24], wheel [11], fitly (+5921) [1]

אוֹפִר ***'ôpir***. See 211.

213 אוּץ ***'ûṣ***, v. GK: 237. [Q] to be in haste, be eager; to press (for an answer); to be small, narrow; [H] to urge, insist upon:– hasted [2], hastened [2], hasty [2], hasteth [1], labour [1], maketh haste [1], narrow [1]

214 אוֹצָר ***'ôṣār***, n.m. GK: 238 [→ 686]. treasury, storehouse, storeroom, storage vault:– treasures [50], treasure [11], treasuries [7], treasury [3], cellars [2], storehouses [2], armoury [1], garners [1], storehouse (+1004) [1], store [1]

215 אוֹר ***'ôr***, v. GK: 239 [→ 216, 217, 218, 219, 221, 224?, 3974, 3975? (also used with compound proper names)]. [Q] to shine, be bright; [H] to give light, make shine, brighten; [N] to be resplendent with light, shine on; the fig. extension "to make the face shine" is to establish favorable circumstance, peace and relief from trouble:– give light [8], cause to shine [5], enlightened [4], lighten [2], light [2], make to shine [2], maketh to shine [2], at break of day [1], enlightening [1], gave light [1], give light (+216) [1], giveth light [1], glorious [1], have light [1], kindle [1], lightened [1], lighteneth [1], make shine [1], set on fire [1], shew light [1], shewed light [1], shined [1], shineth [1], shine [1]

216 אוֹר ***'ôr***, n.m. GK: 240 [→ 219; cf. 215]. light, contrasted with darkness; by extension: brightness; lightning; daylight, sunshine; the fig. extension "light of the face" is a positive, happy attitude, resulting from relief from trouble:– light [111], day [2], lights [2], bright [1], clear [1], give light (+215) [1], herbs [1], lightning [1], morning [1], sun [1]

217 אוּר ***'ûr***, n.m. GK: 241 [cf. 215]. light; east [the region of light], the direction of the sunrise:– fire [4], fires [1], light [1]

218 אוּר ***'ûr***, n.pr.m. & loc. GK: 243 & 244 [→ 215]. Ur, "*flame, light*":– Ur [5]

219 אוֹרָה ***'ôrâ***, n.f. GK: 245 & 246 [→ 216; cf. 215]. light, morning light; happiness, serenity, cheerfulness; herb, mallow, a tasty, edible plant:– herbs [2], light [2]

220 אֻרָוָה ***'ʿwērâ***, n.f. GK: 774 [→ 723]. (animal) stall, pen, stable; cf. 723:– cotes [1]

221 אוּרִי ***'ûrî*** or אֻרִי ***'urî***, n.pr.m. GK: 247 & 788 [→ 215, 738]. Uri, "*Yahweh is [my] flame, light*":– Uri [8]

222 אוּרִיאֵל ***'ûrî'ēl***, n.pr.m. GK: 248 [→ 215+410]. Uriel, "*God [El] is [my] flame, light*":– Uriel [4]

223 אוּרִיָּה ***'ûriyyâ*** or אוּרִיָּהוּ ***'ûriyyāhû***, n.pr.m. GK: 249 & 250. Uriah, "*Yahweh is [my] flame, light*":– Uriah [26], Urijah [12], Uriah's [1]

224 אוּרִים ***'ûrîm***, n.m.[pl.]. GK: 242 & 251 [→ 215? *or* 717? *or* 779?]. Urim, devices used by the high priest to make God's will known, possibly related to radiating or reflecting light:– Urim [7]

אוֹרְנָה ***'ôrenâ***. See 728.

225 אוּת ***'ût***, v. GK: 252. [N] to consent, agree:– consent [3], consented [1]

226 אוֹת ***'ôt***, n.m. & f. GK: 253 [→ 184?; cf. 852]. sign, mark, symbol, a signal or event that communicates; a supernatural event or miracle as a sign from God:– sign [33], signs [27], token [10], tokens [4], miracles [2], ensigns [1], ensign [1], mark [1]

227 אָז ***'āz***, adv. GK: 255 [→ 233; cf. 116]. then, at that time, meanwhile:– then [114], since (+4480) [6], that time [3], the beginning [3], old [2], time [2], also [1], at which time [1], even from (+4480) [1], for [1], hitherto (+4480) [1], if then (+176) [1], now [1], than (+4480) [1], then (+3588) [1], when once (+4480) [1], yet [1]

228 אֲזָה ***'ªzâ*** (Aram.), v. GK: 10015. [P] to heat; [Pp] to be heated:– heat [2], hot [1]

229 אֶזְבָּי ***'ezbāy***, n.pr.m. GK: 256 [→ 231?]. Ezbai:– Ezbai [1]

230 אַזְדָּא ***'azdā'*** (Aram.), a. GK: 10014. firm, assured:– gone [2]

231 אֵזוֹב ***'ēzôb***, n.m. GK: 257 [→ 229?]. hyssop:– hyssop [10]

232 אֵזוֹר ***'ēzôr***, n.m. GK: 258 [→ 247]. garments that are wrapped: belt, sash, loincloth:– girdle [13], girdles [1]

233 אֲזַי ***'ªzay***, adv. GK: 259 [→ 227]. (if not ...) then:– then [3]

234 אַזְכָּרָה ***'azkārâ***, n.f. GK: 260 [→ 2142]. memorial offering, memorial portion; the portion of the meal burnt as a token of honor to the Lord:– memorial [7]

235 אָזַל ***'āzal***, v. GK: 261 [cf. 236]. [Q] to go about, go away; disappear:– fail [1], gaddest about [1], going to and fro (+4480) [1], gone way [1], gone [1], spent [1]

236 אֲזַל ***'ªzal*** (Aram.), v. GK: 10016 [cf. 235]. [P] to go, return:– went [5], go [1], went up [1]

237 אֶזֶל ***'ezel***, n.pr.loc. GK: 262. Ezel:– Ezel [1]

238 אָזַן ***'āzan***, v.den. GK: 263 [→ 241]. [H] to listen, pay attention, give ear:– give ear [29], hearken [5], gave ear [2], hear [2], giveth ear [1], hearkened [1], perceived by the ear [1]

239 אָזַן ***'āzan***, v. GK: 264. [P] to ponder, give serious thought, an extension of weighing and testing on scales:– gave good heed [1]

240 אָזֵן ***'āzēn***, n.[m.]. GK: 266 [cf. 241?]. equipment, tools, specifically a digging tool:– weapon [1]

241 אֹזֶן ***'ōzen***, n.f. GK: 265 [→ 238, 244, 245; cf. 240?]. ear: the organ for hearing; by extension: listening, and hence, responding, obeying. "To be in the ear" shows close proximity; "to reveal to the ear" means "to inform":– ears [100], ear [63], audience [7], hearing [5], shew (+1540) [4], advertise (+1540) [1], displeased (+7451+871.1) [1], hear (+8085) [1], revealed (+1540) [1], sheweth (+1540) [1], sheweth unto (+1540) [1], they[S] [1], told (+1540) [1]

242 אֻזֵּן שֶׁאֱרָה ***'uzzēn še'ʿrâ***, n.pr.loc. GK: 267 [cf. 7609]. Uzzen Sheerah, "[perhaps] *ear of Sheerah*":– Uzzen-sherah [1]

243 אַזְנוֹת תָּבוֹר ***'aznôt tābôr***, n.pr.loc. GK: 268 [cf. 8396]. Aznoth Tabor, "[poss.] *peaks of Tabor*":– Aznoth-tabor [1]

244 אָזְנִי ***'oznî***, n.pr.m. & a.g. GK: 269 & 270 [cf. 241]. Ozni, "*my ear, my hearing*"; Oznite, "*belonging to Ozni*":– Oznites [1], Ozni [1]

245 אֲזַנְיָה ***'ªzanyâ***, n.pr.m. GK: 271 [→ 241+3068]. Azaniah, "*Yahweh has listened*":– Azaniah [1]

246 אֲזִקִּים ***'ªziqqîm***, n.[m.]. GK: 272 [cf. 2131]. chains, which in context refer to manacles or wrist cuffs:– chains [2]

247 אָזַר ***'āzar***, v. GK: 273 [→ 232]. [Q] to gird up, belt on; [P] to gird someone; [N, Ht] to gird oneself; the action of wrapping a belt or sash around the waist; by extension "to take action" of various kinds: working, providing, going to battle:– girded [6], gird up [3], gird [2], girt [2], bindeth about [1], compass about [1], girdeth [1]

248 אֶזְרוֹעַ ***'ezrôa'***, n.f. GK: 274 [cf. 2220; cf. 153]. arm, with the associative meaning of power and potency:– arm [2]

Heb

249 אֶזְרָח ***'ezrāḥ***, n.m. GK: 275 [→ 2224]. native-born:– born [3], your own country [2], bay tree [1], born among [1], born in the country [1], born in the land [1], born of the country [1], homeborn [1], one born amongst [1], one of own country [1], that is born in land [1], that is born [1], that was born [1], your own nation [1]

250 אֶזְרָחִי ***'ezrāḥî***, a.g. GK: 276 [→ 2226; cf. 2224]. Ezrahite, "*of Ezrah*":– Ezrahite [3]

251 אָח ***'āḥ***, n.m. GK: 278 [→ 264, 269, 277; cf. 252 (also used with compound proper names)]. brother; by extension: family, kinsman, relative (of either gender); a term of endearment; anyone of the same race or large social group: countryman; associate. "Each to his brother" is usually translated "to each other" or "one to another.":– brethren [331], brother [244], brother's [24], another^S [24], brethren's [1], brother's (+3807.1) [1], brotherly [1], kindred [1], like [1], other^S [1]

252 אַח ***'aḥ*** (Aram.), n.m. GK: 10017 [cf. 251]. brother:– brethren [1]

253 אָח ***'āḥ***, interj. GK: 277. Alas!, Oh!:– ah [1], alas [1]

254 אַח ***'aḥ***, n.f. GK: 279. firepot:– hearth [3]

255 אֹחַ ***'ōaḥ***, n.[m.]. GK: 280. a howling animal: jackal, hyena, eagle owl:– doleful creatures [1]

256 אַחְאָב ***'aḥ'āb*** or אֶחָב ***'eḥāb***, n.pr.m. GK: 281 & 282 [→ 251+1]. Ahab, "*brother of father*":– Ahab [91], Ahab's [2]

257 אַחְבָּן ***'aḥbān***, n.pr.m. GK: 283. Ahban, "*brother of intelligent one*":– Ahban [1]

258 אָחַד ***'āḥad***, v. GK: 284 [→ 2300]. prob. same as 2300: [Ht] to slash; to go one way or another:– go one way or other [1]

259 אֶחָד ***'eḥād***, a.num. GK: 285 [→ 261; cf. 2297; 2300; cf. 2298]. one; a certain one; first:– one [681], a [60], first [37], another [35], other [31], any [15], once [11], certain [9], eleven (+6240) [9], each [8], every [7], some [7], an [5], together (+3509.1) [5], alone [4], eleventh (+6240) [4], every one [3], few [3], once (+6471) [3], somewhat [3], at once (+6471) [2], only [2], alike (+3509.1) [1], altogether (+871.1) [1], any (+3605) [1], apiece (+5982) [1], apiece [1], at once [1], daily (+3117+3807.1) [1], each man [1], each one [1], fro (+2008) [1], man [1], none (+369) [1], none (+3808) [1], once (+871.1) [1], one manner [1], one tenth deal (+6241) [1], one thing [1], the [1], threescore and one (+8346+2050.1) [1], to^S (+2008) [1]

260 אָחוּ ***'āḥû***, n.m.col. GK: 286. reeds:– meadow [2], flag [1]

261 אֵהוּד ***'ēḥûd***, n.pr.m. GK: 287 [→ 259; cf. 164?]. Ehud, "*united*":– Ehud [1]

262 אַחֲוָה ***'aḥ^{a}wâ***, n.f. GK: 289 [→ 2331]. what is said, declaration:– declaration [1]

263 אַחֲוָיָה ***'aḥ^{a}wāyâ*** (Aram.), n.f. GK: 10018 [→ 2324]. declaring:– shewing [1]

264 אַחֲוָה ***'aḥ^{a}wâ***, n.f. GK: 288 [→ 251]. brotherhood, community:– brotherhood [1]

265 אֲחוֹחַ ***$^{'a}$ḥôaḥ***, n.pr.m. GK: 291 [→ 266]. Ahoah, "*brotherly*":– Ahoah [1]

266 אֲחוֹחִי ***$^{'a}$ḥôḥî***, a.g. GK: 292 [→ 265]. Ahohite:– Ahohite [4], Ahohite (+1121) [1]

267 אֲחוּמַי ***$^{'a}$ḥûmay***, n.pr.m. GK: 293. Ahumai:– Ahumai [1]

268 אָחוֹר ***'āḥôr***, subst. GK: 294 [→ 322; cf. 309]. back (of the body), rear, hindquarters; backward, from behind; west, as a compass point, because east (the direction of the sunrise) is the direction of orientation:– back [15], backward [10], behind [3], hinder parts [3], behind (+4480) [2], afterwards [1], back parts [1], backside [1], backs [1], backward (+3807.1) [1], hereafter [1], time to come [1], without [1]

269 אָחוֹת ***'āḥôt***, n.f. GK: 295 [→ 251]. sister, by extension: half-sister, any female blood-relative; a term of endearment. "Each to her sister" is a marker of reciprocal reference: one to another:– sister [90], sisters [11], another^S [6], sister's [5], other^S [1], together (+413+802) [1]

270 אָחַז ***'āḥaz***, v. GK: 296 & 297 [→ 271, 272, 275, 276; (also used with compound proper names)]. [Q] grasp, seize, hold; to attach, cover, panel; [Qp] to be fastened; [N] to be caught, acquire; [Ho] be attached; [P] to cover:– take hold [7], hold [6], took [6], taken [5], take [4], caught [3], fastened [3], held [3], taken hold upon [3], took hold [3], lay hold [2], portion [2], affrighted (+8178) [1], bar [1], caught hold [1], come upon [1], get possessions [1], had possession [1], handle [1], have possessions [1], hold on [1], holden [1], holdest [1], holdeth back [1], lay hold on [1], possessed [1], rested [1], surprised [1], take possession [1], taketh hold on [1], taketh [1], took hold upon [1]

271 אָחָז ***'āḥāz***, n.pr.m. GK: 298 [→ 274; cf. 270]. Ahaz, "*he has grasped*":– Ahaz [41]

272 אֲחֻזָּה ***$^{'a}$ḥuzzâ***, n.f. GK: 299 [→ 270]. property, possession:– possession [64], possessions [2]

273 אַחְזַי ***'aḥzay***, n.pr.m. GK: 300 [→ 274]. Ahzai, "*Yahweh has grasped*":– Ahasai [1]

274 אֲחַזְיָה ***$^{'a}$ḥazyâ*** or אֲחַזְיָהוּ ***$^{'a}$ḥazyāhû***, n.pr.m. GK: 301 & 302 [→ 271, 273, 276]. Ahaziah, "*Yahweh has upheld*":– Ahaziah [37]

275 אֲחֻזָּם ***$^{'a}$ḥuzzām***, n.pr.m. GK: 303 [→ 270]. Ahuzzam, "*possessor*":– Ahuzam [1]

276 אֲחֻזַּת ***$^{'a}$ḥuzzat***, n.pr.m. GK: 304 [→ 274; cf. 270]. Ahuzzath, "*possession*":– Ahuzzath [1]

277 אֲחִי ***$^{'a}$ḥî***, n.pr.m. GK: 306 [→ 251]. Ahi, "*my brother,* [poss.] *Yahweh is [my] brother*":– Ahi [2]

278 אֵחִי ***'ēḥî***, n.pr.m. GK: 305 [→ 297]. Ehi, "*my brother [is exalted]*":– Ehi [1]

279 אֲחִיאָם ***$^{'a}$ḥî'ām***, n.pr.m. GK: 307 [→ 251+3963.1?]. Ahiam, "*brother of mother*":– Ahiam [2]

280 אֲחִידָה ***$^{'a}$ḥîdâ*** (Aram.), n.f. GK: 10019 [cf. 2420]. riddle:– hard sentences [1]

281 אֲחִיָּה ***$^{'a}$ḥiyyâ*** or אֲחִיָּהוּ ***$^{'a}$ḥiyyāhû***, n.pr.m. GK: 308 & 309 [→ 251+3068]. Ahijah, "*[my] brother is Yahweh*":– Ahijah [20], Ahiah [4]

282 אֲחִיהוּד ***$^{'a}$ḥîhûd***, n.pr.m. GK: 310 [→ 251+1935]. Ahihud, "*[my] brother has majesty*":– Ahihud [1]

283 אַחְיוֹ ***'aḥyô***, n.pr.m. GK: 311 [→ 251+3068]. Ahio, "*[my] brother is Yahweh*":– Ahio [6]

284 אֲחִיחֻד ***$^{'a}$ḥîḥud***, n.pr.m. GK: 312 [→ 251+1935]. Ahihud, "*[my] brother has majesty*":– Ahihud [1]

285 אֲחִיטוּב ***$^{'a}$ḥîṭûb***, n.pr.m. GK: 313 [→ 251+2896]. Ahitub, "*[my] brother is goodness*":– Ahitub [15]

286 אֲחִילוּד ***$^{'a}$ḥîlûd***, n.pr.m. GK: 314 [→ 251+3205?]. Ahilud, "*[my] brother is born*":– Ahilud [5]

287 אֲחִימוֹת ***$^{'a}$ḥîmôt***, n.pr.m. GK: 315 [→ 251+4191]. Ahimoth, "*[my] brother is my support* [or poss.] *[my] brother is Mot*":– Ahimoth [1]

288 אֲחִימֶלֶךְ ***$^{'a}$ḥîmelek***, n.pr.m. GK: 316 [→ 251+4428]. Ahimelech, "*[my] brother is king*":– Ahimelech [16], Ahimelech's [1]

289 אֲחִימַן ***$^{'a}$ḥîman***, n.pr.m. GK: 317 [→ 251+?]. Ahiman, "[poss.] *[my] brother is a gift*":– Ahiman [4]

290 אֲחִימַעַץ ***$^{'a}$ḥîma'aṣ***, n.pr.m. GK: 318 [→ 251+4619]. Ahimaaz, "*[my] brother is fury*":– Ahimaaz [15]

291 אַחְיָן ***'aḥyān***, n.pr.m. GK: 319 [→ 251+4993.1?]. Ahian, "*little brother*":– Ahian [1]

292 אֲחִינָדָב ***$^{'a}$ḥînādāb***, n.pr.m. GK: 320 [→ 251+5068]. Ahinadab, "*[my] brother is willing*":– Ahinadab [1]

293 אֲחִינֹעַם ***$^{'a}$ḥînō'am***, n.pr.f. GK: 321 [→ 251+5278]. Ahinoam, "*[my] brother is pleasant*":– Ahinoam [7]

294 אֲחִיסָמָךְ ***$^{'a}$ḥîsāmāk***, n.pr.m. GK: 322 [→ 251+5564]. Ahisamach, "*[my] brother is a support*":– Ahisamach [3]

295 אֲחִיעֶזֶר ***$^{'a}$ḥî'ezer***, n.pr.m. GK: 323 [→ 251+5828]. Ahiezer, "*[my] brother is a help*":– Ahiezer [6]

296 אֲחִיקָם ***$^{'a}$ḥîqām***, n.pr.m. GK: 324 [→ 251+6965]. Ahikam, "*[my] brother stands*":– Ahikam [20]

297 אֲחִירָם ***$^{'a}$ḥîrām***, n.pr.m. GK: 325 [→ 278, 298, 2361, 2438]. Ahiram, "*[my] brother is exalted*":– Ahiram [1]

298 אֲחִירָמִי ***$^{'a}$ḥîrāmî***, a.g. GK: 326 [→ 297]. Ahiramite, "*of Ahiram*":– Ahiramites [1]

299 אֲחִירַע ***$^{'a}$ḥîra'***, n.pr.m. GK: 327 [→ 251+7452 *or* 7453 *or* 7454]. Ahira, "*[my] brother is my friend* or *my brother is evil*":– Ahira [5]

300 אֲחִישַׁחַר ***$^{'a}$ḥîšaḥar***, n.pr.m. GK: 328 [→ 251+7835]. Ahishahar, "*[my] brother was born at early dawn*":– Ahishahar [1]

301 אֲחִישָׁר ***$^{'a}$ḥîšār***, n.pr.m. GK: 329. Ahishar, "*[my] brother is upright* or *[my] brother has sung*":– Ahishar [1]

302 אֲחִיתֹפֶל ***$^{'a}$ḥîtōpel***, n.pr.m. GK: 330 [→ 251+8603?]. Ahithophel, "[poss.] *[my] brother is in the desert* or *[my] brother is foolishness*":– Ahithophel [20]

303 אַחְלָב ***'aḥlāb***, n.pr.loc. GK: 331. Ahlab, "*fat, fruitful, healthy*":– Ahlab [1]

304 אַחְלַי ***'aḥlāy***, n.pr. GK: 333 [→ 251+410]. Ahlai, "*Alas! I wish that!*":– Ahlai [2]

305 אַחֲלַי ***'aḥ^{a}lay***, subst. GK: 332. Oh that!; If only!:– O that [1], would God [1]

306 אַחְלָמָה ***'aḥlāmâ***, n.f. GK: 334. amethyst (exact identification uncertain):– amethyst [2]

307 אַחְמְתָא ***'aḥm^{e}tā'*** (Aram.), n.pr.loc. GK: 10020. Ecbatana, "[perhaps] *place of gathering*":– Achmetha [1]

308 אֲחַסְבַּי ***$^{'a}$ḥasbay***, n.pr.m. GK: 335 [→ 2620+871.1?+3068?]. Ahasbai, "*I seek refuge in Yahweh*":– Ahasbai [1]

309 אָחַר ***'āḥar***, v. GK: 336 [→ 268, 310, 314, 319, 322, 4279, 4283; cf. 3186]. [Q] to remain, stay on; [P] to detain, delay, slow down; [H] to take longer (than a set time), come late:– tarry [3], defer [2], make tarrying [2], slack [2], continue [1], deferred [1], delay [1], hinder [1], late [1], stayed [1], tarried longer [1], tarry long [1]

310 אַחַר ***'aḥar***, subst. & adv. & pp. GK: 339 & 343 [cf. 309; cf. 311]. (temporal) after, afterward, later, some time later; (spatial) back, behind, following:– after [477], behind [35], following [26], afterward [22], followed (+1980) [16], followed [16], afterward (+3651) [15], from (+4480) [12], behind (+4480) [11], follow (+1980) [9], afterwards [5], follow [5], after (+4480) [4], afterwards (+3651) [4], posterity [4], after that (+3651) [2], at [2], behind (+413) [2], followed (+1961) [2], followeth (+935) [2], following (+1980) [2], forasmuch [2], pursuing [2], since [2], when [2], after (+413) [1], after that (+3651+2050.1) [1], afterward (+3651+4480) [1], again [1], away from (+4480) [1], backside [1], back [1], behind (+5921) [1], beside [1], by [1], follow (+1961) [1], follow (+935) [1], followed (+3318) [1], followedst (+1980) [1], followeth [1], following (+3651) [1], following after [1], forasmuch as [1], hereafter [1], hinder end [1], outlived (+748+3117) [1], overlived (+748+3117) [1], pursue (+1980) [1], remnant [1], seeing that (+834) [1], thenceforth (+3651) [1], when (+4970) [1], when (+834) [1], with [1]

311 אַחַר ***'aḥar*** (Aram.), pp. GK: 10021 [→ 320, 318; cf. 310]. after, in the future:– hereafter (+1836) [2], after [1]

312 אַחֵר ***'aḥēr***, a. GK: 337 [→ 313]. other, another, different; next, additional, more, extra:– other [96], another [55], others [9], next [2], another man's [1], following [1], other men [1], strange [1]

313 אַחֵר ***'aḥēr***, n.pr.m. GK: 338 [→ 312]. Aher, "*another, substitute*":– Aher [1]

314 אַחֲרוֹן ***'aḥ^{a}rôn***, a.f. GK: 340 [→ 309]. (temporal) next, later, last, end; (spatial) at the back, behind, west, as a compass point, because east (the direction of the sunrise) is the direction of orientation:– last [19], latter [6], come [4], to come [3], after [2], come after [2], latter end [2], utmost [2], after (+871.1+1886.1) [1], afterward (+871.1+1886.1) [1], afterwards [1], afterward [1], following [1], hindermost [1], hinder [1], hindmost [1], last (+871.1+1886.1) [1], rereward [1], uttermost [1]

315 אַחְרַח ***'aḥraḥ***, n.pr.m. GK: 341. Aharah, "*brother of Rah*":– Aharah [1]

316 אֲחַרְחֵל ***$^{'a}$ḥarḥēl***, n.pr.m. GK: 342. Aharhel, "*brother of Rachel*":– Aharhel [1]

317 אָחֳרִי ***'oḥ^{o}rî*** (Aram.), a.f. GK: 10023 [→ 321]. other, another:– another [5], other [1]

318 אָחֳרֵין ***'oḥ^{o}rên*** (Aram.), adv. GK: 10024 [→ 311]. finally, at last:– last [1]

319 אַחֲרִית ***'aḥ^{a}rît***, n.f. GK: 344 [→ 309; cf. 320]. (spatial) the far side, the other side; (temporal) at the last, at the end, (in days) to come:– end [21], latter [11], latter end [8], last [6], last end [4], posterity [3], reward [2], hindermost [1], latter time [1], length [1], remnant [1], residue [1], uttermost parts [1]

320 אַחֲרִי ***'aḥ^{a}rî*** (Aram.), n.f.constr. GK: 10022 [→ 311; cf. 319]. end (of days), (days) to come:– latter [1]

321 אָחֳרָן ***'oḥ^{o}rān*** (Aram.), a.m. GK: 10025 [→ 317]. other, another, someone else:– other [3], another [2]

אָחֳרֵן ***'oḥ^{o}rēn***. See 318.

322 אֲחֹרַנִּית ***$^{'a}$ḥōrannît***, adv. GK: 345 [→ 268; cf. 309]. backwardly, by turning around, in turning back:– backward [6], again [1]

Heb

323 אֲחַשְׁדַּרְפָּן ***'ᵃḥašdarpān***, n.m.pl. GK: 346 [cf. 324]. satraps, an administrative governor of a Persian province:– lieutenants [4]

324 אֲחַשְׁדַּרְפַּן ***'ᵃḥašdarpan*** (Aram.), n.m. GK: 10026 [cf. 323]. satrap, a viceroy or governor having considerable power:– princes [9]

325 אֲחַשְׁוֵרוֹשׁ ***'ᵃḥašwērôš*** or אֲחַשְׁרֹשׁ ***'ᵃḥašērôš***, n.pr.m. GK: 347 & 348. Ahaseurus, Xerxes:– Ahasuerus [30], Ahasuerus' [1]

326 אֲחַשְׁתָּרִי ***'ᵃḥaštārî*** or הָאֲחַשְׁתָּרִי ***hā'ᵃḥaštārî***, n.pr.m. *or* a.g. GK: 349 & 2028. Ahashtari; Haahashtari, "*the Ahashtarites*":– Haahashtari [1]

327 אֲחַשְׁתְּרָן ***'ᵃḥašt***ᵉ***rān***, a. GK: 350. royal, belonging to the king and used in the king's service:– camels [2]

328 אַט ***'aṭ***, subst. & n.m. GK: 351 & 356. spirits of the dead; (adv.) gently, meekly, slowly:– softly (+3807.1) [2], charmers [1], gently (+3807.1) [1], secret [1], softly [1]

329 אָטָד ***'āṭād*** or אָטָד ***'āṭād***, n.m. & n.pr.loc. GK: 353 & 354. thornbush; Atad, "*of the thorns [?]*":– bramble [3], Atad [2], thorns [1]

330 אֵטוּן ***'ēṭûn***, n.[m.]. GK: 355. linen, possibly red in color:– fine linen [1]

331 אָטַם ***'āṭam***, v. GK: 357. [Q] to stop up (one's ears); to hold (one's tongue); [Qp] to be narrow:– narrow [4], stoppeth [3], shutteth [1]

332 אָטַר ***'āṭar***, v. GK: 358 [→ 333, 334]. [Q] to close:– shut [1]

333 אָטֵר ***'āṭēr***, n.pr.m. GK: 359 [→ 332]. Ater, "[poss.] *crippled one, left-handed one*, or *Etir*":– Ater [5]

334 אִטֵּר ***'iṭṭēr***, a. GK: 360 [→ 332]. hindered on the right hand, (thus) left-handed; other sources: ambidextrous:– lefthanded (+3027+3225) [2]

335 אֵי ***'ê***, adv.inter. GK: 361 [→ 346, 349, 351, 370, 375, 645?]. where?, which way?:– where [11], where (+2088) [10], whence (+2088+4480) [5], from whence (+2088+4480) [2], which (+2088) [2], by what (+2088) [1], how [1], of what (+2088+4480) [1], what (+2088) [1], what [1], whether (+2088) [1], which way (+2088) [1]

336 אִי ***'î***, adv. GK: 364 [→ 348?, 350]. not: island [1]

337 אִי ***'î***, interj. GK: 365. Woe!:– woe [2]

338 אִי ***'î***, n.m. GK: 363 [cf. 339?]. hyena, jackals; some understand this to be a spirit or demon:– wild beasts of the islands [2], wild beasts of the island [1]

339 אִי ***'î***, n.m. & f. GK: 362 [cf. 338?]. island; coastland; distant shores:– isles [27], islands [5], isle [3], country [1]

340 אָיַב ***'āyab***, v. GK: 366 [→ 341, 342, 347]. [Q] to be an enemy, be hostile towards:– enemy [1]

341 אֹיֵב ***'ōyēb***, n.m. *or* v.ptcp. GK: 367 [→ 340]. enemy, foe:– enemies [199], enemy [77], enemies' [3], foes [2], enemy's [1]

342 אֵיבָה ***'êbâ***, n.f. GK: 368 [→ 340]. hostility, enmity:– enmity [3], hatred [2]

343 אֵיד ***'êd***, n.m. GK: 369 [→ 181]. disaster, calamity, destruction:– calamity [16], destruction [7], calamities [1]

344 אַיָּה ***'ayyâ***, n.f. GK: 370 [→ 345]. black kite; falcon; vulture:– kite [2], vulture's [1]

345 אַיָּה ***'ayyâ***, n.pr.m. GK: 371 [→ 344]. Aiah, "*black kite*":– Aiah [6]

346 אַיֵּה ***'ayyēh***, adv.inter. GK: 372 [→ 335]. Where?:– where [45]

347 אִיּוֹב ***'iyyôb***, n.pr.m. GK: 373 [→ 340]. Job, "*where is my father*, [or perhaps] *Where is my father, O God?*":– Job [57], Job's [1]

348 אִיזֶבֶל ***'îzebel***, n.pr.f. GK: 374 [→ 336?+2073?]. Jezebel, "[poss.] *unhusbanded, unexalted*":– Jezebel [21], Jezebel's [1]

349 אֵיךְ ***'êk*** or אֵיכָה ***'êkâ*** or אֵיכָכָה ***'êkākâ***, adv.inter. & excl. GK: 375 & 377 & 379 [→ 335; cf. 1963]. How? Why? How! Also!:– how [78], where [2], how can [1], what [1]

350 אִיכָבוֹד ***'îkābôd*** or אִי־כָבוֹד ***'î-kābôd***, n.pr.m. GK: 376 [→ 336+3519]. Ichabod, "*where is the glory?*":– Ichabod's [1], Ichabod [1]

351 אֵיכֹה ***'êkōh***, adv.inter. & excl. GK: 378 [→ 335]. Where?:– where [1]

אֵיכָה ***'êkâ***; אֵיכָכָה ***'êkākâ***. See 349.

352 אַיִל ***'ayil***, n.m. GK: 380 & 381 & 382 & 383 & 442 & 443 & 444 [→ 193, 354, 356, 358, 359?, 362, 424, 425, 427, 436, 437, 438, 439, 879]. ram, a male sheep generally more aggressive and protective of the flock; by extension: leading man, ruler; oaks; or any large, mighty tree without reference to a specific species; projecting wall; jamb:– ram [90], rams [61], posts [17], rams' [5], post [4], mighty [3], trees [2], lintel [1], mighty men [1], oaks [1]

353 אֱיָל ***'ᵉyāl***, n.m. GK: 384 [→ 360; cf. 352]. strength:– strength [1]

354 אַיָּל ***'ayyāl***, n.[m.] & f. GK: 385 [→ 355, 365, 357; cf. 352]. deer, young stag:– hart [9], harts [2]

355 אַיָּלָה ***'ayyālâ***, n.f. GK: 387 [→ 354]. deer, doe:– hinds [4], hinds' [3], hind [1]

356 אֵלוֹן ***'êlôn*** or אֵילֹן ***'êlôn***, n.pr.m. & loc. GK: 390 & 391 & 472 [→ 436, 440; cf. 352]. Elon, "*species of a mighty tree*":– Elon [6]

357 אַיָּלוֹן ***'ayyālôn***, n.pr.loc. GK: 389 [→ 354]. Aijalon, "*place of the deer*":– Aijalon [8], Ajalon [2]

358 אֵילוֹן בֵּית חָנָן ***'êlôn bêt ḥānān***, n.pr.loc. GK: 392 [→ 352+1004+2605]. Elon Bethhanan, "*tree of Bethhanan*":– Elon-beth-hanan [1]

359 אֵילוֹת ***'êlôt*** or אֵילַת ***'êlat***, n.pr.loc. GK: 393 & 397 [→ 352?]. Eloth, Elath, "*grove of large trees*":– Elath [5], Eloth [3]

360 אֱיָלוּת ***'ᵉyālût***, n.m. GK: 394 [→ 353; cf. 352]. Strength, Power, a title of the one true God, with a focus that he is potent to help:– strength [1]

361 אֵילָם ***'êlām***, n.m. GK: 395 [→ 197]. portico, porch, hall:– arches [15]

362 אֵילִם ***'êlim***, n.pr.loc. GK: 396 [→ 352; cf. 352]. Elim, "*big trees*":– Elim [6]

363 אִילָן ***'îlān*** (Aram.), n.m. GK: 10027 [cf. 436]. tree:– tree [6]

364 אֵיל פָּארָן ***'êl pā'rān***, n.pr.loc. GK: 386 [→ 352+6290]. El Paran, "*tree of Paran*":– El-paran [1]

אֵילֹן ***'êlōn***. See 356.

365 אַיֶּלֶת ***'ayyelet***, n.f. GK: 387 [→ 354]. deer, doe:– hind [2], Aijeleth [1]

אַיִם ***'ayim***. See 368.

366 אָיֹם ***'āyōm***, a. GK: 398 [→ 367]. fearful; majestic, with an implication that this majesty instills awe that borders on fear:– terrible [3]

367 אֵימָה ***'êmâ*** or אֵמָה ***'ēmâ***, n.f. GK: 399 & 568 [→ 366, 368; cf. 520; cf. 574]. terror, dread, fear:– fear [5], terror [4], terrors [3], terrible [2], dread [1], horror [1], idols [1]

368 אֵימִים ***'êmîm***, n.pr.m.pl. GK: 400 [→ 367]. Emites, "*frightening beings*":– Emims [3]

369 אַיִן ***'ayin***, subst.neg. GK: 401 [cf. 371]. there is no, not, none, without:– no [243], not [188], none [141], neither (+2050.1) [27], nothing [26], without [26], without (+4480) [18], no man [17], nor (+2050.1) [17], neither [13], nor any (+2050.1) [5], gone [4], never [4], nothing (+3972) [4], cannot [3], innumerable (+4557) [3], unsearchable (+2714) [3], without (+871.1) [3], neither any (+2050.1) [2], no (+3605) [2], no more [2], none (+376) [2], none (+4480) [2], nothing (+3605) [2], without (+5704) [2], abundance (+4557) [1], any [1], come to nought [1], else [1], except [1], faileth [1], fatherless (+1) [1], incurable (+4832) [1], infinite (+4557) [1], infinite (+7093) [1], infinite (+7097) [1], innumerable (+4557+5704) [1], more than (+3807.1) [1], neither (+637) [1], no (+1097) [1], no (+3605+3807.1) [1], no (+4480) [1], no where [1], none (+259) [1], none other [1], nor any thing (+2050.1) [1], nothing else (+1115) [1], past (+5704) [1], there be no [1], there is none [1], there is not [1], well nigh (+3509.1) [1], without any (+4480) [1]

370 אַיִן ***'ayin***, adv. GK: 402 [cf. 335]. where (from)?:– whence (+4480) [12], whence [4], where (+4480) [1]

371 אִין ***'în***, subst.neg. GK: 403 [cf. 369]. there is not:– not [1]

372 אִיעֶזֶר ***'î'ezer***, n.pr.m. GK: 404 [→ 373]. Iezer, "*my [father] is help*":– Jeezer [1]

373 אִיעֶזְרִי ***'î'ezrî***, a.g. GK: 405 [→ 372]. Iezerite, "*of Iezer*":– Jeezerites [1]

374 אֵיפָה ***'êpâ***, n.f. GK: 406. ephah (dry measure, about three-fifths of a bushel (22 liters); also a large basket of unspecified measure; "ephah and ephah" means "two differing measures," as a measure that is not standardized:– ephah [34], divers measures (+374+2050.1) [4], measure [2]

375 אֵיפֹה ***'êpōh***, adv. GK: 407 [→ 335+6311]. where?:– where [9], what manner [1]

376 אִישׁ ***'îš***, n.m. GK: 408 [→ 380, 792, 802 (also used with compound proper names)]. man, sometimes in contrast to woman, human, sometimes in contrast to animal (without gender distinction); by extension: husband, in contrast to wife; (p.) each, every, someone, a certain one, anyone, whoever. This word is often used in phrases meaning "one of a kind," so a "man of war" is a soldier; a "man of bow" is an archer, etc:– man [763], men [679], every man [163], every one [112], one [71], husband [66], man's [31], any [24], any man [17], certain [14], persons [10], every one (+376) [8], each man [7], another[S] [6], every man's [6], he[S] [6], none (+3808) [6], whatsoever man (+376) [6], each [5], whosoever (+834) [5], every man (+376) [4], footmen (+7273) [4], husbands [4], none (+408) [4], person [4], what man soever (+376) [4], whosoever [4], any man's [3], him[S] [3], some [3], Benjamite (+3227) [2], Israel (+3478) [2], any man (+376) [2], an [2], champion (+1143+1886.1) [2], each (+376) [2], either[S] [2], every man's (+376+2050.1) [2], husband's [2], male [2], men's [2], none (+1115) [2], none (+369) [2], none (+376+3808) [2], one man [2], people [2], stranger (+2214) [2], stranger (+5237) [2], they[S] [2], those[S] [2], whosoever (+376) [2], whoso [2], Amalekite (+6003) [1], Benjamite (+1121+3227) [1], Egyptian (+4713) [1], Egyptian (+4713+1886.1) [1], Ishi [1], Israelite (+3478) [1], adulteress (+802) [1], adversary (+6862) [1], adversary (+7379) [1], all (+3605) [1], also [1], archers (+3384+7198+871.1+1886.1) [1], a [1], bear[S] [1], bloodthirsty (+1818) [1], chapmen (+1886.1) [1], consent [1], counseller (+6098) [1], counsellers (+6098) [1], destroyer (+4889) [1], divers [1], each one [1], eloquent (+1697) [1], every man's (+3807.1) [1], every [1], evil speaker (+3956) [1], familiar friend (+7965) [1], famous (+8034) [1], fellows [1], fellow [1], friends (+7965) [1], goodman [1], had war with (+1961+4421) [1], had wars with (+1961+4421) [1], high (+1121) [1], hunter (+6718) [1], husbandman (+120+5647) [1], husbandman (+127+1886.1) [1], in the flower of age [1], lender (+3867) [1], liar (+3577) [1], man carnally (+2233+7902) [1], mankind (+1320) [1], master (+1167) [1], men (+1121) [1], men of high degree (+1121) [1], merchantmen (+5503) [1], merchantmen [1], none (+1097) [1], none (+3808+3807.1) [1], one man's [1], oppressor (+2555) [1], reprover [1], servants [1], shipmen (+591) [1], slothful (+6102) [1], steward (+834+5921) [1], stranger (+1616) [1], stranger (+2114) [1], strangers (+1616) [1], them[S] [1], this[S] [1], trade about cattle (+4735) [1], trade to feed cattle (+4735) [1], whatsoever [1], whosoever (+3605) [1], whosoever (+834+3605) [1], workmen (+4399) [1], worthy [1], young men (+5288) [1]

377 אָשַׁשׁ ***'āšaš*** or אִישׁ ***'îš***, v. GK: 899 [→ 809?; cf. 787]. [Htpol] to fix in one's mind:– shew yourselves men [1]

378 אִישׁ־בֹּשֶׁת ***'îš-bōšet***, n.pr.m. GK: 410 [→ 376+1322]. Ish-Bosheth, "*man of shame*":– Ish-bosheth [11]

379 אִישְׁהוֹד ***'îšhôd***, n.pr.m. GK: 412 [→ 376+1935]. Ishhod, "*man of grandeur*":– Ishod [1]

380 אִישׁוֹן ***'îšôn***, n.[m.]. GK: 413 & 854 [→ 376]. pupil, the black center of the eyeball, formally, "the little man (of the eye)," often translated as "the apple of the eye," an idiom of care and love:– apple [2], apple (+1323) [1], black [1], obscure [1]

אִישׁ חַי ***'îš-ḥay***. See 301.

381 אִישׁ־חַיִל ***'îš-ḥayil***, n.m. GK: 408 + 2657 [→ 376+2428]. valiant man (376 + 2428):–

382 אִישׁ־טוֹב ***'îš-ṭôb***, n.pr.m. GK: 411 [→ 376+2896]. Ish-Tob, "*man from Tob*":– Ish-tob [2]

אִישַׁי ***'îšay***. See 3448.

אִיתוֹן ***'îtôn***. See 2978.

383 אִיתַי ***'îtay*** (Aram.), pt. GK: 10029 [cf. 3426]. there is, there are; a marker of existence often called a "quasi-verb":– there is [5], be [3], have [2], art [1], have (+3807.2) [1], is [1], none (+1768+3809) [1], there are [1], will [1]

384 אִיתִיאֵל ***'îtî'ēl***, n.pr.m. GK: 417 [cf. 863]. Ithiel, "*God [El] is with me*": Ithiel [3]

385 אִיתָמָר ***'îtāmār***, n.pr.m. GK: 418. Ithamar, "[poss.] *[is]land of palms; [father] of Tamar*":– Ithamar [21]

386 אֵיתָן ***'êtān***, a. GK: 419 [→ 387, 388, 3496, 3497]. ever-flowing, of a stream that is always filled with water; by extension: never-failing, steady, established, eternal:– strong [5], mighty [4], strength [2], hard [1], rough [1]

387 אֵיתָן ***'êtān***, n.pr.m. GK: 420 [→ 386]. Ethan, "*long lived, ever-flowing [streams]*":– Ethan [8]

388 אֵתָנִים **'ētānîm**, n.pr.[m.]. GK: 923 [→ 386]. Ethanim, "*ever-flowing [streams]*":– Ethanim [1]

389 אַךְ **'ak**, adv. GK: 421 [→ 403]. but, surely, only, however:– only [35], surely [34], but [33], yet [12], nevertheless [11], notwithstanding [6], verily [6], also [4], howbeit [4], even [3], truly [3], at least [1], certainly [1], howbeit yet (+3588) [1], in any wise [1], indeed only (+7535) [1], notwithstanding (+2050.1) [1], of a surety [1], save [1], wherefore (+3588) [1], yet but [1]

390 אַכַּד **'akkad**, n.pr.loc. GK: 422. Akkad:– Accad [1]

391 אַכְזָב **'akzāb**, a. GK: 423 [→ 3576]. deceptive, deceitful, referring to a stream or a person:– liar [1], lie [1]

392 אַכְזִיב **'akzîb**, n.pr.loc. GK: 424 [→ 3576?]. Aczib, "*deceit*":– Achzib [4]

393 אַכְזָר **'akzār**, a. GK: 425 [→ 394, 395]. deadly, ruthless, fierce, heartless:– cruel [3], fierce [1]

394 אַכְזָרִי **'akzārî**, a. GK: 426 [→ 393]. cruel, merciless:– cruel [7], cruel one [1]

395 אַכְזְרִיּוּת **'akzᵉriyyût**, n.f. GK: 427 [→ 393]. cruelty:– cruel [1]

396 אֲכִילָה **'ᵃkîlâ**, n.f. GK: 428 [→ 398]. food:– meat [1]

397 אָכִישׁ **'ākîš**, n.pr.m. GK: 429. Achish, "*the king gives*":– Achish [21]

398 אָכַל **'ākal**, v. GK: 430 [→ 396, 400, 402, 3978, 3979, 3980, 4361; cf. 399]. [Q] to eat; [N] to be eaten; [Pu] be consumed, be destroyed; [H] to give to eat, feed; from the base meaning of eating food is the fig. extension of consuming and destroying something:– eat [471], eaten [74], devour [57], devoured [41], eateth [29], consumed [20], eat up [16], eating [13], consume [9], feed [8], devoureth [6], eaten at all (+398) [6], devouring [5], fed [5], meat [5], eaten up [4], eater [3], eatest [3], give to eat [3], ate [2], cause to eat [2], consumeth [2], consuming [2], eat in plenty (+398) [2], eaten freely (+398) [2], eateth up [2], freely eat (+398) [2], in no wise eat (+398+3808) [2], indeed eaten (+398) [2], quite devoured (+398) [2], burnt up [1], caused to eat [1], devourer [1], devourest up [1], dine [1], feedest [1], food [1], gave to eat [1], higher [1], moth-eaten (+6211) [1]

399 אֲכַל **'ᵃkal** (Aram.), v. GK: 10030 [cf. 398]. [P] to eat (food); to destroy, devastate, devour (an object):– accused (+7170) [2], devoured [2], devour [2], eat [1]

400 אֹכֶל **'ōkel**, n.m. GK: 431 [→ 398]. food; a general word for food as anything edible:– meat [18], food [16], eating [4], victuals [3], prey [2], mealtime (+6256+1886.1) [1]

401 אֻכָל **'ukāl**, n.pr.m. GK: 432 [→ 3615]. Ucal, "[poss.] *I am consumed* or *I cease*":– Ucal [1]

402 אָכְלָה **'oklâ**, n.f. GK: 433 [→ 398]. what is consumed, food, fuel:– meat [8], fuel [3], devour [2], eat [2], consume [1], devoured [1], food [1]

403 אָכֵן **'ākēn**, adv. GK: 434 & 435 [→ 389+2005]. Surely! Truly!, an exclamation to emphasize the unexpected:– surely [9], but [3], truly [2], verily [2], certainly [1], nevertheless [1]

404 אָכַף **'ākap**, v. GK: 436 [→ 405]. [Q] to drive, press hard:– craveth [1]

405 אֶכֶף **'ekep**, n.m. GK: 437 [→ 404]. hand, with a focus that this part of the body that can exert pressure or press hard:– hand [1]

406 אִכָּר **'ikkār**, n.m. GK: 438. farmer, people who work in fields and vineyards:– husbandmen [3], husbandman [2], plowmen [2]

407 אַכְשָׁף **'akšāp**, n.pr.loc. GK: 439 [→ 3784]. Acshaph, "*fascination*":– Achshaph [3]

408 אַל **'al**, adv.neg. GK: 440 [cf. 409]. no, not:– not [558], neither (+2050.1) [61], no [42], nor (+2050.1) [24], nay [8], neither [6], none (+376) [4], nothing (+1697) [3], nothing [3], never (+5769+3807.1) [2], cannot [1], neither (+1571) [1], neither (+1571+2050.1) [1], neither yet (+2050.1) [1], no (+3972) [1], none (+3605+871.1) [1], nothing (+3605) [1], than [1], whither [1]

409 אַל **'al** (Aram.), neg.adv. GK: 10031 [cf. 408]. not:– not [3], nor (+2050.3) [1]

410 אֵל **'ēl**, n.m. GK: 445 & 446 [→ 430, 433 (also used with compound proper names)]. God, the Mighty One, as a title of majesty and power, often used in combination with other titles; also any false god, gods; any person who is strong and capable: mighty one; strength:– God/god [229], mighty [3], power [3], God's [2], gods [2], goodly [1], great [1], idols [1], mighty (+1121) [1], mighty one [1], might [1], power (+3027) [1], strong [1]

411 אֵל **'ēl**, pr.pl.m. & f. GK: 447 [→ 428; cf. 412]. these:– these [7], those [2]

412 אֵל **'ēl** (Aram.), p.demo.pl. GK: 10032 [→ 1836; cf. 411]. these:– these [1]

413 אֶל **'el**, pp. GK: 448 [→ 454, 454]. to, toward; in, into; with regard to:– unto [2855], to [1183], into [308], upon [169], against [148], in [87], for [57], at [51], toward [49], on [44], with [44], by [27], of [26], over [23], concerning [17], towards [16], before (+6440) [15], before [8], after [7], among [6], over against (+6440) [4], under (+8478) [4], straight forward (+5676+6440) [3], whithersoever (+834+3605) [3], within [3], according to [2], among (+996) [2], because of [2], before (+4136+6440) [2], behind (+310) [2], beside [2], hands together (+3709+3709) [2], over against (+4136+6440) [2], regard (+6437) [2], therein (+1886.3) [2], through [2], touching [2], under [2], whereupon (+1992.1) [2]*

414 אֵלָא **'ēlā'**, n.pr.m. GK: 452 [cf. 425]. Ela:– Elah [1]

415 אֵל אֱלֹהֵי יִשְׂרָאֵל **'ēl 'ᵉlōhê yiśrā'ēl**, n.pr.loc. GK: 449 [→ 410+430+3478]. El Elohe Israel, "*God, the God of Israel*":– El-Elohe-Israel [1]

416 אֵל בֵּית־אֵל **'ēl bêt-'ēl**, n.pr.loc. GK: 450 [→ 410+1004+410]. El Bethel, "*God [El] of Bethel*":– El-beth-el [1]

417 אֶלְגָּבִישׁ **'elgābîš**, n.[m.]. GK: 453 [cf. 1378]. hail(stone) or clump of ice:– great hailstones (+68) [3]

418 אַלְגּוּמִּים **'algûmmîm**, n.[m.]pl. GK: 454 [cf. 484]. algum (wood); a transliteration of the Hebrew, the exact identification of which is uncertain:– algum [2], algum trees [1]

419 אֶלְדָּד **'eldād**, n.pr.m. GK: 455 [→ 410+1730]. Eldad, "*beloved of God [El];* [poss.] *Dadi is god*":– Eldad [2]

420 אֶלְדָּעָה **'eldā'â**, n.pr.m. GK: 456 [→ 410]. Eldaah, "*God [El] is [my] desire*":– Eldaah [2]

421 אָלָה **'ālâ**, v. GK: 458. [Q] to mourn, wail:– lament [1]

422 אָלָה **'ālâ**, v. GK: 457 [→ 423, 8381]. [Q] to utter a curse, swear an oath; [H] to bind under oath, take an oath:– swearing [2], adjured [1], cause to swear [1], cursedst [1], make swear [1]

423 אָלָה **'ālâ**, n.f. GK: 460 [→ 422]. curse, oath; sworn agreement; public charge:– oath [14], curse [9], curses [5], cursing [4], execration [2], swearing [2]

424 אֵלָה **'ēlâ**, n.f. GK: 461 [→ 425; cf. 352; cf. 363]. oak, terebinth, or any species of large tree:– oak [11], elms [1], teil tree [1]

425 אֵלָה **'ēlâ**, n.pr.m. & loc. GK: 462 & 463 [→ 352, 424; cf. 414]. Elah, "*a mighty tree*":– Elah [16]

426 אֱלָהּ **'ᵉlāh** (Aram.), n.m. GK: 10033 [cf. 433]. God, in the singular usually the true God, but see Da 4:8; 6:7 for a pagan god; gods, in the plural:– God/god [81], gods [14]

427 אַלָּה **'allâ**, n.f. GK: 464 [→ 352]. oak, or any species of large tree:– oak [1]

428 אֵלֶּה **'ēlleh**, pr.pl.m. & f. GK: 465 [→ 411; cf. 429]. these:– these [647], those [39], them [10], this [10], some [6], such [4], they [4], one [3], other [3], such (+3509.1) [3], the same [2], whom [2], another [1], others [1], so [1], these things [1], the [1], things [1], thus [1], which [1], who [1]

429 אֵלֶּה **'ēlleh** (Aram.), p.demo.pl. GK: 10034 [→ 1836; cf. 428]. these:– these [1]

אֱלֹהַּ **'ᵉlōah**. See 433.

430 אֱלֹהִים **'ᵉlōhîm**, n.pl.m. & f. GK: 466 [→ 433; cf. 410]. God (plural of majesty: plural in form but singular in meaning, with a focus on great power); gods (true grammatical plural); any person characterized by greatness or power: mighty one, great one, judge:– God/god [2363], gods [216], God's [6], judges [4], goddess [2], mighty [2], God's (+3807.1) [1], angels [1], exceeding (+3807.1) [1], godly [1], great [1], judge [1], to God-ward (+4136+1886.1) [1], very great [1]

431 אֲלוּ **'ᵃlû** (Aram.), interj. GK: 10035 [→ 718]. there!, behold!; a discourse marker of transition, emphasis, or attention:– behold [5]

432 אִלּוּ **'illû**, c. GK: 467 [→ 518+3863]. if:– if [1], though [1]

433 אֱלוֹהַּ **'ᵉlôah**, n.m. GK: 468 [→ 430; cf. 410; cf. 426]. God; god; idol:– God/god [56], God's [1]

434 אֱלוּל **'ᵉlûl**, n.m.?. GK: 470 [→ 457]. idols, images, gods:–

435 אֱלוּל **'ᵉlûl**, n.pr. GK: 469. Elul:– Elul [1]

436 אֵלוֹן **'ēlôn**, n.[f.]. GK: 471 [→ 356; cf. 352; cf. 363]. great tree, large tree of an unspecified species:– plain [7], plains [2]

437 אַלּוֹן **'allôn**, n.m. GK: 473 [→ 438; cf. 352]. oak tree, large tree of an unspecified species:– oaks [5], oak [3]

438 אַלּוֹן **'allôn**, n.pr.m. GK: 474 [→ 437; cf. 352]. Allon, "*oak*":– Allon [2]

439 אַלּוֹן בָּכוּת **'allôn bākût**, n.pr.loc. GK: 475 [→ 352+1058]. Allon Bacuth, "*oak of weeping*":– Allon-bachuth [1]

440 אֵלֹנִי **'ēlōnî**, a.g. GK: 533 [→ 356]. Elonite, "*of Elon*":– Elonites [1], Elon [1]

441 אַלּוּף **'allûp**, a. & n.m. GK: 476 & 477 [→ 502, 503]. close friend, partner, ally, companion; chief, leader:– duke [43], dukes [14], guide [4], governors [2], captains [1], chief friends [1], governor [1], oxen [1], ox [1], very friends [1]

442 אָלוּשׁ **'ālûš**, n.pr.loc. GK: 478. Alush:– Alush [2]

443 אֶלְזָבָד **'elzābād**, n.pr.m. GK: 479 [→ 410+2064]. Elzabad, "*God [El] has given*":– Elzabad [2]

444 אָלַח **'ālaḥ**, v. GK: 480. [N] to be, become (morally) corrupt, a fig. extension of milk turning sour, not found in the OT:– filthy [3]

445 אֶלְחָנָן **'elḥānān**, n.pr.m. GK: 481 [→ 410+2605]. Elhanan, "*God [El] is gracious*":– Elhanan [4]

אֵלִי **'ēlî**. See 1017.

446 אֱלִיאָב **'ᵉlî'āb**, n.pr.m. GK: 482 [→ 410+1]. Eliab, "*God [El] is [my] father*":– Eliab [20], Eliab's [1]

447 אֱלִיאֵל **'ᵉlî'ēl**, n.pr.m. GK: 483 [→ 410+2967.1+410]. Eliel, "*God [El] is [my] God*":– Eliel [10]

448 אֱלִיאָתָה **'ᵉlî'ātâ** or אֱלִיָּתָה **'ᵉliyyātâ**, n.pr.m. GK: 484 & 517 [→ 410+857]. Eliathah, "*God [El] comes*":– Eliathah [2]

449 אֱלִידָד **'ᵉlîdād**, n.pr.m. GK: 485 [→ 410+1730]. Elidad, "*God [El] is [my] beloved*":– Elidad [1]

450 אֶלְיָדָע **'elyādā'**, n.pr.m. GK: 486 [→ 410+3045]. Eliada, "*God [El] knows*":– Eliada [3], Eliadah [1]

451 אַלְיָה **'alyâ**, n.f. GK: 487. fat tail (of a sheep):– rump [5]

452 אֵלִיָּה **'ēliyyâ** or אֵלִיָּהוּ **'ēliyyāhû**, n.pr.m. GK: 488 & 489 [→ 410+3068]. Elijah, "*Yahweh is [my] God*":– Elijah [69], Eliah [2]

453 אֱלִיהוּ **'ᵉlîhû** or אֱלִיהוּא **'ᵉlîhû'**, n.pr.m. GK: 490 & 491 [→ 410+1931]. Elihu, "*Yahweh is [my] God*":– Elihu [11]

454 אֶלְיְהוֹעֵינַי **'elyᵉhô'ênay** or אֶלְיוֹעֵינַי **'elyô'ênay**, n.pr.m. GK: 492 & 493 [→ 413+3068+5869]. Eliehoenai, Elioenai, "*my eyes [look] to Yahweh*":– Elioenai [8], Elihoenai [1]

455 אֶלְיַחְבָּא **'elyaḥbā'**, n.pr.m. GK: 494 [→ 410+2244]. Eliahba, "*God [El] hides*":– Eliahba [2]

456 אֱלִיחֹרֶף **'ᵉlîḥōrep**, n.pr.m. GK: 495. Elihoreph:– Elihoreph [1]

457 אֱלִיל **'ᵉlîl**, n.m. GK: 496 [→ 434]. idols, images, gods:– idols [16], idol [1], images [1], of no value [1], thing of nought [1]

458 אֱלִימֶלֶךְ **'ᵉlîmelek**, n.pr.m. GK: 497 [→ 410+4428]. Elimelech, "*God [El] is [my] king*":– Elimelech [4], Elimelech's [2]

459 אִלֵּין **'illēn** (Aram.), p.demo.pl. GK: 10036 [→ 1836]. these:– these [4]

460 אֶלְיָסָף **'elyāsāp**, n.pr.m. GK: 498 [→ 410+3254]. Eliasaph, "*God [El] has added*":– Eliasaph [6]

461 אֱלִיעֶזֶר **'ᵉlî'ezer**, n.pr.m. GK: 499 [→ 410+5828]. Eliezer, "*God [El] is [my] help*":– Eliezer [14]

462 אֱלִיעֵנַי **'ᵉlî'ēnay**, n.pr.m. GK: 501 [→ 413+3068+5869]. Elienai, "*my eyes [look] to Yahweh*":– Elienai [1]

463 אֱלִיעָם **'ᵉlî'ām**, n.pr.m. GK: 500 [→ 410+5971]. Eliam, "*God [El] is [my] kinsman*":– Eliam [2]

464 אֱלִיפַז **'ᵉlîpaz**, n.pr.m. GK: 502 [→ 410+6337]. Eliphaz, "*God [El] is fine gold* or *God crushes*":– Eliphaz [15]

465 אֱלִיפַל **'ᵉlîpal**, n.pr.m. GK: 503 [→ 410+6419]. Eliphal, "*[my] God [El] sit in judgment*":– Eliphal [1]

466 אֱלִיפְלֵהוּ **'ᵉlîpᵉlēhû**, n.pr.m. GK: 504 [→ 410+6381?]. Eliphelehu, "*God [El] distinguish him!*":– Elipheleh [2]

467 אֱלִיפֶלֶט **'ᵉlîpeleṭ** or אֶלְפֶּלֶט **'elpeleṭ**, n.pr.m. GK: 505 & 550 [→ 410+6404]. Eliphelet, Elpelet, "*God [El] is [my] deliverance*":– Eliphelet [6], Eliphalet [2], Elpalet [1]

468 אֱלִיצוּר **ʾᵉlîṣûr**, n.pr.m. GK: 506 [→ 410+6697]. Elizur, "*God [El] is [my] Rock*":– Elizur [5]

469 אֱלִיצָפָן **ʾᵉlîṣāpān** or אֶלְצָפָן **ʾelṣāpān**, n.pr.m. GK: 507 & 553 [→ 410+6845]. Elizaphan, Elzaphan, "*God [El] is [my] hiding place*":– Elizaphan [4], Elzaphan [2]

470 אֱלִיקָא **ʾᵉlîqāʾ**, n.pr.m. GK: 508 [→ 410+6965?]. Elika:– Elika [1]

471 אֶלְיָקִים **ʾelyāqîm**, n.pr.m. GK: 509 [→ 410+6965]. Eliakim, "*God [El] establishes*":– Eliakim [12]

472 אֱלִישֶׁבַע **ʾᵉlîšebaʿ**, n.pr.f. GK: 510 [→ 410; cf. 7652]. Elisheba, "*God [El] is an oath; God [El] is my fill*":– Elisheba [1]

473 אֱלִישָׁה **ʾᵉlîšâ**, n.pr.loc. GK: 511. Elishah, "*God [El] saves*":– Elishah [3]

474 אֱלִישׁוּעַ **ʾᵉlîšûaʿ**, n.pr.m. GK: 512 [→ 410+7768]. Elishua, "*God [El] is my salvation*":– Elishua [2]

475 אֶלְיָשִׁיב **ʾelyāšîb**, n.pr.m. GK: 513 [→ 410+7725]. Eliashib, "*God [El] restores*":– Eliashib [17]

476 אֱלִישָׁמָע **ʾᵉlîšāmāʿ**, n.pr.m. GK: 514 [→ 410+8085]. Elishama, "*God [El] has heard*":– Elishama [17]

477 אֱלִישָׁע **ʾᵉlîšāʿ**, n.pr.m. GK: 515 [→ 410+3467?]. Elisha, "*God [El] is [my] salvation*":– Elisha [58]

478 אֱלִישָׁפָט **ʾᵉlîšāpāṭ**, n.pr.m. GK: 516 [→ 410+8199]. Elishaphat, "*God [El] is [my] judge*":– Elishaphat [1]

אֱלִיָּתָה **ʾᵉliātâ**. See 448.

479 אִלֵּךְ **ʾillēk** (Aram.), p.demo.pl. GK: 10037 [→ 1836]. these:– these [11], those [3]

480 אַלְלַי **ʾallay**, interj. GK: 518. Woe!, What misery!, Alas!:– woe [2]

481 אָלַם **ʾālam** or אָלַם **ʾālam**, v. GK: 519 & 520 [→ 483, 485, 492; cf. 481?]. [N] to be silenced, be speechless; [P] to bind:– dumb [6], became dumb [1], binding [1], put to silence [1]

482 אֵלֶם **ʾēlem**, n.[m.]. GK: 521 [cf. 481?]. silence [?]:– congregation [1]

אֵלָם **ʾēlām**. See 361.

אֻלָם **ʾālum**. See 485.

483 אִלֵּם **ʾillēm**, a. GK: 522 [→ 481]. mute, unable to speak:– dumb [6]

484 אַלְמֻגִּים **ʾalmuggîm**, n.[m.]pl. GK: 523 [cf. 418]. almugwood; a transliteration of the Hebrew, the exact identification of which is uncertain:– almug [3]

485 אֲלֻמָּה **ʾᵃlummâ**, n.f. GK: 524 [→ 481]. sheaf:– sheaves [3], sheaf [2]

486 אַלְמוֹדָד **ʾalmôdād**, n.pr. GK: 525. Almodad, "*God [El] is loved*":– Almodad [2]

487 אַלַּמֶּלֶךְ **ʾallammelek**, n.pr.loc. GK: 526 [→ 427?+4428]. Allammelech, "*oak of the king* or *oak of Molech*":– Alammelech [1]

488 אַלְמָן **ʾalmān**, a. & n.[f.]. GK: 527 & 528 [→ 490; cf. 759]. widowed (one forsaken); stronghold:– forsaken [1]

489 אַלְמֹן **ʾalmōn**, n.[m.]. GK: 529 [→ 490]. widowhood:– widowhood [1]

490 אַלְמָנָה **ʾalmānâ**, n.f. GK: 530 [→ 488, 489, 491]. widow:– widow [37], widows [12], widow's [3], desolate houses [1], desolate palaces [1], widow's (+802) [1]

491 אַלְמָנוּת **ʾalmānût**, n.f. GK: 531 [→ 490]. widowhood:– widowhood [3], widow's [1]

492 אַלְמֹנִי **ʾalmōnî**, a. GK: 532 [→ 481; cf. 6422, 6423]. a certain so-and-so, whoever, wherever, with a focus that this is not named or spoken out loud:– such a one (+6423) [1], such and such (+6423) [1], such [1]

אִלֵּן **ʾillēn**. See 459.

אֵלֹנִי **ʾēlōnî**. See 440.

493 אֶלְנַעַם **ʾelnāʿam**, n.pr.m. GK: 534 [→ 410+5278]. Elnaam, "*God [El] is pleasantness*":– Elnaam [1]

494 אֶלְנָתָן **ʾelnātān**, n.pr.m. GK: 535 [→ 410+5414]. Elnathan, "*God [El] is given*":– Elnathan [7]

495 אֶלָּסָר **ʾellāsār**, n.pr.loc. GK: 536. Ellasar:– Ellasar [2]

496 אֶלְעָד **ʾelʿād**, n.pr.m. GK: 537 [→ 410+5749]. Elead, "*God [El] has testified*":– Elead [1]

497 אֶלְעָדָה **ʾelʿādâ**, n.pr.m. GK: 538 [→ 410+5710]. Eleadah, "*God [El] has adorned*":– Eladah [1]

498 אֶלְעוּזַי **ʾelʿûzay**, n.pr.m. GK: 539 [→ 410+5797?]. Eluzai, "*God [El] is my strength*":– Eleuzai [1]

499 אֶלְעָזָר **ʾelʿāzār**, n.pr.m. GK: 540 [→ 410+5826]. Eleazar, "*God [El] is a help*":– Eleazar [72]

500 אֶלְעָלֵא **ʾelʿālēʾ** or אֶלְעָלֵה **ʾelʿālēh**, n.pr.loc. GK: 541 & 542 [→ 410+5927]. Elealeh, "*God [El] is high*":– Elealeh [5]

501 אֶלְעָשָׂה **ʾelʿāśâ**, n.pr.m. GK: 543 [→ 410+6213]. Eleasah, "*God [El] has fashioned*":– Eleasah [4], Elasah [2]

502 אָלַף **ʾālap**, v. GK: 544 [→ 441]. [Q] to learn, become familiar with; [P] to teach, instruct:– learn [1], teacheth [1], teach [1], uttereth [1]

503 אָלַף **ʾālap**, v.den. GK: 545 [→ 441, 505; cf. 504]. [H] to increase by thousands, produce in abundance:– bring forth thousands [1]

504 אֶלֶף **ʾelep**, n.m. GK: 546 [→ 441, 505; cf. 502]. cattle herd; oxen:– kine [4], oxen [3], family [1]

505 אֶלֶף **ʾelep**, n.m. GK: 547 & 548 [→ 503; cf. 506]. thousand; by extension from "thousand," this refers to any large unit or group: (family) clan, (military) unit:– thousand [418], thousands [46], two thousand [29], eleven hundred (+3967+2050.1) [3], forty two thousand (+702+7239) [2], eighteen thousand (+7239+8083+2050.1) [1], four [1], threescore and one thousand (+7239+8337+2050.1) [1], twelve hundred (+3967+2050.1) [1]

506 אֲלַף **ʾᵃlap** (Aram.), n.m. GK: 10038 [cf. 505]. thousand; the phrase "thousands upon thousands" is an indefinitely large number:– thousand [3], thousands [1]

507 אֶלֶף **ʾelep**, n.pr.loc. GK: 549. Eleph:– Eleph [1]

אַלֻּף **ʾallup**. See 441.

אֱלְפֶּלֶט **ʾelpeleṭ**. See 467.

508 אֶלְפַּעַל **ʾelpaʿal**, n.pr.m. GK: 551 [→ 410+6466]. Elpaal, "*God [El] creates*":– Elpaal [3]

509 אָלַץ **ʾālaṣ**, v. GK: 552. [P] to prod, urge, a fig. extension of pressing one object hard against another, not found in the OT:– urged [1]

אֶלְצָפָן **ʾelṣāpān**. See 469.

510 אַלְקוּם **ʾalqûm**, n.[m.]?. GK: 554. army:– no rising up [1]

511 אֶלְקָנָה **ʾelqānâ**, n.pr.m. GK: 555 [→ 410+7069]. Elkanah, "*God [El] has possessed*":– Elkanah [21]

512 אֶלְקֹשִׁי **ʾelqōšî**, a.g. GK: 556. Elkoshite, "*of Elkosh*":– Elkoshite [1]

513 אֶלְתּוֹלַד **ʾeltôlad**, n.pr.loc. GK: 557 [cf. 8434]. Eltolad, "*generation; kindred of God [El]; place where God [El] gives children*":– Eltolad [2]

514 אֶלְתְּקֵא **ʾeltᵉqēʾ** or אֶלְתְּקֵה **ʾeltᵉqēh**, n.pr.loc. GK: 558 & 559. Eltekeh, "*meeting place*":– Eltekeh [2]

515 אֶלְתְּקֹן **ʾeltᵉqôn**, n.pr.loc. GK: 560. Eltekon, "*God [El] has arranged*":– Eltekon [1]

516 אַל תַּשְׁחֵת **ʾal tašḥēt**, adv.neg.+v. GK: 440 + 8845 [→ 408+7843]. Al-taschith (408 + 7843), "Do not destroy":– Al-taschith [4]

517 אֵם **ʾēm**, n.f. GK: 562. mother, grandmother, ancestress; by extension: a term of endearment; caregiver; fork (in a road):– mother [143], mother's [67], dam [5], mothers [3], mothers' [1], parting [1]

518 אִם **ʾim**, c. & pt.inter. GK: 561 [→ 432]. if, whether, or; whenever, as often as:– if [587], but (+3588) [86], or [43], not [35], though [33], whether [28], surely (+3808) [23], when [20], save (+3588) [13], that [9], or (+2050.1) [8], nor (+2050.1) [7], except (+3588) [6], except (+3808) [5], no [5], surely not [4], surely [4], though (+3588) [4], neither [3], until (+5704) [3], until (+834+5704) [3], and (+3588) [2], either [2], for (+3588) [2], none [2], nor [2], sith [2], surely (+3588) [2], than (+3588) [2], verily (+3808) [2], will (+3808) [2], yet (+3588) [2]*

519 אָמָה **ʾāmâ**, n.f. GK: 563. slave woman; female servant, maidservant:– handmaid [22], maidservant [13], maid [5], bondwoman [4], maidservants [4], bondmaids [2], maids [2], handmaids [1], maidens [1], maidservant's [1], maidservants' [1]

אֵמָה **ʾēmâ**. See 367.

520 אַמָּה **ʾammâ**, n.f. GK: 564 & 567 [cf. 521]. cubit (measurement of length, from the elbow to end of fingers, about 18 to 22 inches [about half a meter]); an unspecified unit of time; pivot (of a door):– cubits [191], cubit [42], two cubits [9], measure [1], posts [1]

521 אַמָּה **ʾammâ** (Aram.), n.f. GK: 10039 [cf. 520]. cubit (measurement of distance from the elbow to the end of the fingers, about 18 to 22 inches):– cubits [4]

522 אַמָּה **ʾammâ**, n.pr.loc. GK: 565. Ammah, "*cubit*":– Ammah [1]

523 אֻמָּה **ʾummâ**, n.f. GK: 569 [cf. 524]. tribe, clan:– people [2], nations [1]

524 אֻמָּה **ʾummâ** (Aram.), n.f. GK: 10040 [cf. 523]. nation, people:– nations [7], nation [1]

525 אָמוֹן **ʾāmôn**, n.m. GK: 570 [→ 542]. one brought up:– one brought up [1]

526 אָמוֹן **ʾāmôn**, n.pr.m. GK: 571 [→ 532; cf. 527, 539]. Amon, "*trustworthy*":– Amon [17]

527 אָמוֹן **ʾāmôn**, n.pr.[m.]. GK: 572 [→ 528; cf. 526, 539]. multitude, crowd; see also 1995:– multitude [2], populous [1]

528 אָמוֹן **ʾāmôn**, n.pr.[m.]. GK: 572 [→ 527+4996; cf. 526, 539]. Amon (pagan god), "*trustworthy*":–

529 אֵמוּן **ʾēmûn**, n.[m.]. GK: 573 & 574 [→ 539]. faithful, trustworthy:– faithful [4], faith [1], truth [1]

530 אֱמוּנָה **ʾᵉmûnâ**, n.f. GK: 575 [→ 539]. faithfulness, steadiness, trustworthiness:– faithfulness [18], truth [13], faithfully (+871.1) [5], set office [5], faithful [3], faith [1], stability [1], steady [1], truly [1], verily [1]

531 אָמוֹץ **ʾāmôṣ**, n.pr.m. GK: 576 [→ 553]. Amoz, "*strong*":– Amoz [13]

532 אָמִי **ʾāmî**, n.pr.m. GK: 577 [→ 526; cf. 539]. Ami, "*trustworthy, reliable, faithful*":– Ami [1]

אֲמִינוֹן **ʾᵃmînôn**. See 550.

533 אַמִּיץ **ʾammîṣ**, a. GK: 579 [→ 553]. strong, mighty, brave:– strong [4], courageous (+3820) [1], mighty [1]

534 אָמִיר **ʾāmîr**, n.m. GK: 580 [→ 559]. branch:– branch [1], uppermost bough [1]

535 אָמַל **ʾāmal**, v. GK: 581 & 582 [→ 536, 537]. [Qp] to be weak-willed; to be hot, feverish; [Pul] to wither, languish, fade away:– languisheth [8], languish [5], languished [1], waxed feeble [1], weak [1]

536 אֻמְלַל **ʾumlal**, a. GK: 583 [→ 535]. faint, fading away:– weak [1]

537 אֲמֵלָל **ʾᵃmēlāl**, a. GK: 584 [→ 535]. feeble, fading:– feeble [1]

538 אֲמָם **ʾᵃmām**, n.pr.loc. GK: 585 [→ 4965]. Amam:– Amam [1]

539 אָמַן **ʾāman**, v. GK: 586 & 587 [→ 526, 527, 529, 530, 532, 543, 544, 545, 548, 546, 547, 550, 551, 1968?; cf. 540, cf. 3330]. [Q] to nurse, nurture, care for; be a trustee, be a guardian; [Qp, N] to be nurtured, cared for; to be faithful, be trustworthy, be established; [H] to believe, trust, have confidence:– believed [21], believe [19], faithful [19], sure [11], established [6], believeth [4], brought up [3], verified [3], long continuance [2], nurse [2], stedfast [2], trust [2], assurance [1], bringers up [1], fail (+3808) [1], nursed [1], nursing fathers [1], nursing father [1], put trust [1], putteth trust [1], stablished [1], stand fast [1], surely [1], trusted [1], trusty [1]

540 אֲמַן **ʾᵃman** (Aram.), v. GK: 10041 [cf. 539]. [H] to trust in; [Hp] be trustworthy:– believed [1], faithful [1], sure [1]

541 אָמַן **ʾāman**, v. GK: 3554 [→ 3225, 3231]. [H] to turn to the right; cf. 3231:– turn to the right hand [1]

542 אָמָּן **ʾommān**, n.m. GK: 588 [→ 525]. craftsman:– cunning workman [1]

543 אָמֵן **ʾāmēn**, adv. GK: 589 [→ 539]. amen, surely; truth:– amen [27], truth [2], so be it [1]

544 אֹמֶן **ʾōmen**, n.[m.]. GK: 590 [→ 551, 552; cf. 539]. faithfulness:– truth [1]

545 אָמְנָה **ʾomnâ**, n.f. GK: 594 [→ 539]. bringing up, caring, tending, fostering:– brought up [1]

546 אָמְנָה **ʾomnâ**, adv. GK: 593 [→ 539]. really, truly, indeed:– indeed [2]

547 אֹמְנָה **ʾōmᵉnâ**, subst. GK: 595 [→ 539?]. doorpost:– pillars [1]

548 אֲמָנָה **ʾᵃmānâ**, n.f. GK: 591 [→ 539]. binding agreement, trustworthy agreement:– certain portion [1], sure [1]

549 אֲמָנָה **ʾᵃmānâ**, n.pr.loc. GK: 592 [cf. 71]. Amana, "*constant*":– Amana [1]

אֱמֻנָה **ʾᵉmunâ**. See 530.

Heb

550 אֲמִינוֹן *'ᵃmînôn* or אַמְנוֹן *'amnôn*, n.pr.m. GK: 578 & 596 [cf. 539]. Amnon, "*trustworthy*":– Amnon [25], Amnon's [3]

551 אָמְנָם *'omnām*, adv. GK: 597 [→ 552; cf. 544, 539]. indeed, truly, assuredly:– of a truth [3], indeed [2], no doubt [1], surely [1], true [1], truly [1]

552 אֻמְנָם *'umnām*, adv. GK: 598 [→ 551; cf. 544, 539]. really, indeed; used in interrogative sentences:– indeed [3], in very deed [1], of a surety (+637) [1]

553 אָמֵץ *'āmēṣ*, v. GK: 599 [→ 531, 533, 554, 555, 556, 3981 (also used with compound proper names)]. [Q] to be strong, courageous; [P] to strengthen, support, establish; harden; [Ht] to persist, determine:– of good courage [9], strengthen [7], strengthened [3], courageous [2], made speed [2], madest strong [2], strengtheneth [2], stronger [2], strong [2], confirm [1], established [1], fortify [1], hardened [1], harden [1], increaseth [1], made obstinate [1], made strong [1], prevailed [1], stedfastly minded [1]

554 אָמֹץ *'āmōṣ*, a. GK: 600 [→ 553]. powerful, strong:– bay [2]

555 אֹמֶץ *'ōmeṣ*, n.[m.]. GK: 601 [→ 553]. strength:– stronger and stronger (+3254) [1]

אַמִּץ *'ammiṣ*. See 533.

556 אַמְצָה *'amṣâ*, n.f. GK: 602 [→ 553]. strength:– strength [1]

557 אַמְצִי *'amṣî*, n.pr.m. GK: 603 [→ 553; cf. 558?]. Amzi, "[poss.] *[Yahweh is] my strength*":– Amzi [2]

558 אֲמַצְיָה *'ᵃmaṣyâ* or אֲמַצְיָהוּ *'ᵃmaṣyāhû*, n.pr.m. GK: 604 & 605 [→ 557]. Amaziah, "*Yahweh is powerful*":– Amaziah [40]

559 אָמַר *'āmar*, v. GK: 606 & 607 [→ 201, 534, 561, 562, 565, 3982, 8560; cf. 560 (also used with compound proper names)]. [Q, H] to say, speak, think (say to oneself); [Qp, N] to be said; [Ht] to boast:– said [2776], saying [915], saith [581], say [560], spake [110], answered [91], speak [47], tell [29], commanded [25], saidst [19], sayest [18], spoken [15], told [14], answer [8], thought [8], speaketh [7], bade [6], bid [6], promised [5], called [4], call [3], commandeth [3], think [3], appointed [2], avouched [2], command [2], expressly say (+559) [2], intend [2], name [2], plainly say (+559) [2], purpose [2], reported [2], said indeed (+559) [2], say still (+559) [2], termed [2], verily thought (+559) [2], yet say (+559) [2], appoint [1], bidden [1], boast [1], certified [1], challengeth [1], charged [1], commandment [1], commune [1], consider [1], declared [1], demanded [1], desired [1], desireth [1], determined [1], gave a commandment [1], intendest [1], is [1], named [1], promisedst [1], published [1], requirest [1], spakest [1], suppose [1], talked [1], thinking [1], use[S] [1], uttereth [1]

560 אֲמַר *'ᵃmar* (Aram.), v. GK: 10042 [→ 3983; cf. 559]. [P] to say, tell; to command:– said [41], commanded [12], tell [5], told [4], saying [2], say [2], speak [2], declare [1], spake [1], spoken [1]

561 אֵמֶר *'ēmer*, n.m. GK: 609 & 610 & 611 [→ 559, 564; cf. 563]. word, saying; branched antlers; fawn, lamb:– words [43], sayings [2], speeches [2], answer [1], appointed unto [1]

562 אֹמֶר *'ōmer*, n.m. GK: 608 [→ 559]. saying, word:– speech [2], word [2], promise [1], thing [1]

563 אִמַּר *'immar* (Aram.), n.m. GK: 10043. male lamb:– lambs [3]

564 אִמֵּר *'immēr*, n.pr.m. & loc. GK: 612 & 613 [→ 561]. Immer, "*lamb*":– Immer [10]

565 אִמְרָה *'imrâ* or אֶמְרָה *'emrâ*, n.f. GK: 614 & 615 [→ 559]. word, saying, utterance:– word [26], speech [7], words [3], commandment [1]

566 אִמְרִי *'imrî*, n.pr.m. GK: 617 [→ 559+3068]. Imri, "*Yahweh spoke*":– Imri [2]

567 אֱמֹרִי *'ᵉmōrî*, a.g. GK: 616. Amorite, "[poss.] *hill dwellers; westerners*":– Amorites [73], Amorite [14]

568 אֲמַרְיָה *'ᵃmaryâ* or אֲמַרְיָהוּ *'ᵃmaryāhû*, n.pr.m. GK: 618 & 619. Amariah, "*Yahweh has said*":– Amariah [16]

569 אַמְרָפֶל *'amrāpel*, n.pr.m. GK: 620. Amraphel:– Amraphel [2]

570 אֶמֶשׁ *'emeš*, adv. GK: 621 [cf. 4871?]. last night; yesterday (evening):– yesternight [3], in former time [1], yesterday [1]

571 אֱמֶת *'ᵉmet*, n.f. GK: 622 [→ 573; cf. 539]. faithfulness, reliability, trustworthiness; truth, what conforms to reality in contrast to what is false; "the book of truth" is a reliable book, referring to heavenly scroll detailing future things:– truth [90], true [18], truly [4], right [3], truly (+871.1) [3], faithfully [2], assuredly (+871.1) [1], assured [1], establishment [1], faithful [1], sure [1], truth's [1], verity [1]

572 אַמְתַּחַת *'amtaḥat*, n.f. GK: 623 [→ 4969]. sack:– sacks [6], sack [5], sack's [3], sacks' [1]

573 אֲמִתַּי *'ᵃmittay*, n.pr.m. GK: 624 [→ 571; cf. 539]. Amittai, "*true*":– Amittai [2]

574 אֵימְתָן *'êmᵉtān* (Aram.), a. GK: 10028. frightening, terrible:– terrible [1]

575 אָן *'ān*, adv. GK: 625. how long?; where?:– whither (+1886.5) [16], how long (+5704+1886.5) [13], any whither (+575+1886.5+1886.5+2050.1) [4], where (+1886.5) [3], whither (+575+1886.5+1886.5+2050.1) [2], how long (+5704) [1], whithersoever (+1886.5) [1], whither [1]

אֹן *'ōn*. See 204.

576 אֲנָה *'ᵃnâ* (Aram.), p.1.com.s. GK: 10044 [cf. 589]. I:– I [14], me [2]

577 אָנָּא *'onnā'* or אָנָּה *'onnâ*, interj. GK: 626 & 629 [cf. 4994]. I ask you!, O! (preceding a request):– I beseech thee [5], beseech [2], oh [2], I pray thee [1], O [1], now [1], pray [1]

אֲנָה *'ᵃnâ*. See 576.

אָנָה *'ānâ*. See 575.

578 אָנָה *'ānâ*, v. GK: 627 [→ 205, 592, 3123, 8386; cf. 584, 596]. [Q] to mourn, lament, groan:– lament [1], mourn [1]

579 אָנָה *'ānâ*, v. GK: 628 [→ 8385]. [P] to make happen; [Pu] to befall, have happen to; [Ht] to pick a quarrel against:– befall (+413) [1], deliver [1], happen [1], seeketh a quarrel [1]

אָנָּה *'ānnâ*. See 577.

580 אֲנוּ *'ᵃnû*, p.com.pl. GK: 630 [→ 587]. we:– we [1]

אֹנוֹ *'ōnô*. See 207.

581 אִנּוּן *'innûn* (Aram.), p.3.m.pl. GK: 10045 [→ 1932]. they; those:– are [1], them [1], these [1], which [1]

582 אֱנוֹשׁ *'ᵉnôš*, n.m. GK: 632 [→ 583; cf. 605; cf. 606]. man, humankind, mortal, with an emphasis on frailty; "a man of peace" is a "friend":– man [29], men [7], man's [3], another[S] [1], familiars (+7965) [1], mortal man [1]

583 אֱנוֹשׁ *'ᵉnôš*, n.pr.m. GK: 633 [→ 582; cf. 605]. Enosh, "*[mortal] man*":– Enos [6], Enosh [1]

584 אָנַח *'ānaḥ*, v. GK: 634 [→ 585; cf. 578, 596, 5117]. [N] to groan, moan:– sigh [7], groan [1], mourn [1], sighed [1], sighest [1], sigheth [1]

585 אֲנָחָה *'ᵃnāḥâ*, n.f. GK: 635 [→ 584]. groaning, sighing:– sighing [5], groaning [4], mourning [1], sighs [1]

586 אֲנַחְנָא *'ᵃnaḥnā'* (Aram.), p.1.com.pl. GK: 10047 [cf. 587]. we:– we [4]

587 אֲנַחְנוּ *'ᵃnaḥnû*, p.com.pl. GK: 636 [→ 580, 589, 595, 5168; cf. 586]. we:– we [111], us [3], we ourselves [3]

588 אֲנָחֲרַת *'ᵃnāḥᵃrat*, n.pr.loc. GK: 637. Anaharath:– Anaharath [1]

589 אֲנִי *'ᵃnî*, p.com.s. GK: 638 [→ 587; cf. 576]. I:– I [839], me [24], myself [2], I myself [1], mine [1], my [1], we [1], who [1]

590 אֳנִי *'ᵒnî*, n.m. GK: 639 [→ 591]. ships, fleet of ships:– navy [6], galley [1]

591 אֳנִיָּה *'ᵒniyyâ*, n.f. GK: 641 [→ 590]. ship, trading ship; (pl.) fleet of ships:– ships [26], ship [4], shipmen (+376) [1]

592 אֲנִיָּה *'ᵃniyyâ*, n.f. GK: 640 [→ 578]. lamentation, mourning:– lamentation [1], sorrow [1]

אִנִּין *'innîn*. See 581.

593 אֲנִיעָם *'ᵃnî'ām*, n.pr.m. GK: 642. Aniam, "*I am kinsman*":– Aniam [1]

594 אֲנָךְ *'ᵃnāk*, n.[m.]. GK: 643. plummet, weight for a plumb line:– plumbline [4]

595 אָנֹכִי *'ānōkî*, p.com.s. GK: 644 [→ 587]. I:– I [354], me [4], my [1]

596 אָנַן *'ānan*, v. GK: 645 [cf. 578 *or* 584]. [Htpol] to complain:– complained [1], complain [1]

597 אָנַס *'ānas*, v. GK: 646 [cf. 598]. [Q] to compel; "there is no compelling" means "to allow":– compel [1]

598 אֲנַס *'ᵃnas* (Aram.), v. GK: 10048 [cf. 597]. [P] to oppress, make difficult:– troubleth [1]

599 אָנַף *'ānap*, v. GK: 647 [→ 639, 649, 2739; cf. 600]. [Q] to be, become angry; [Ht] to feel angry:– angry [13], displeased [1]

600 אֲנַף *'ᵃnap* (Aram.), n.m. GK: 10049 [cf. 599]. face; "to fall on the face" is to assume a position of honor or reverence:– face [1], visage [1]

601 אֲנָפָה *'ᵃnāpâ*, n.f. GK: 649. heron, an unclean bird:– heron [2]

602 אָנַק *'ānaq*, v. GK: 650 [→ 603; cf. 5008, 5009]. [Q, N] to groan, lament, sigh:– cry [3], groan [1]

603 אֲנָקָה *'ᵃnāqâ*, n.f. GK: 651 [→ 602]. groaning, sighing:– sighing [2], crying out [1], groaning [1]

604 אֲנָקָה *'ᵃnāqâ*, n.f. GK: 652. gecko:– ferret [1]

605 אָנַשׁ *'ānaš*, v. GK: 631 & 653 [→ 605, 582, 583; cf. 5136]. [N] be ill, sickly; incurable, beyond cure; despairing:– incurable [5], desperately wicked [1], desperate [1], very sick [1], woeful [1]

606 אֱנָשׁ *'ᵉnāš* (Aram.), n.m. GK: 10050 [cf. 582]. man, human being; humankind, people, often in contrast to animals; "son of man" often means a human being, but in Da 7:13 assumes messianic significance:– men [12], man [8], man's [3], whosoever (+1768+1768+3606) [1], whosoever (+3606) [1]

אַנְתְּ *'ant*. See 859.

607 אַנְתְּ *'ant* or אַנְתָּה *'antâ* (Aram.), p.2.m.s. GK: 10051 & 10052 [cf. 859]. you, your:– thou [14], thee [1]

608 אַנְתּוּן *'antûn* (Aram.), p.2.m.pl. GK: 10053 [cf. 859]. you (all):– ye [1]

609 אָסָא *'āsā'*, n.pr.m. GK: 654. Asa, "[poss.] *healer; myrtle*":– Asa [57], Asa's [1]

610 אָסוּךְ *'āsûk*, n.[m.]. GK: 655 [→ 5480]. small (oil) jar, flask:– pot [1]

611 אָסוֹן *'āsôn*, n.m. GK: 656. serious injury, harm:– mischief [5]

612 אֵסוּר *'ēsûr*, n.m. GK: 657 [→ 631; cf. 613]. bindings, chains, fetters, shackles:– bands [2], prison (+1004+1886.1) [1]

613 אֱסוּר *'ᵉsûr* (Aram.), n.[m.]. GK: 10054 [→ 633; cf. 612]. bond, fetter; (pl.) imprisonment:– band [2], imprisonment [1]

614 אָסִיף *'āsîp*, n.[m.]. GK: 658 [→ 622]. (Feast of) Ingathering; harvest (from a threshing floor and winepress before the rainy season):– ingathering [2]

615 אָסִיר *'āsîr*, n.m. GK: 659 [→ 631]. prisoner, captive:– prisoners [8], bound [2], prisoner [2]

616 אַסִּיר *'assîr*, n.m.[col.]. GK: 660 [→ 617; cf. 631]. captive, prisoner:– prisoners [3]

617 אַסִּיר *'assîr*, n.pr.m. GK: 661 [→ 616; cf. 631]. Assir, "*prisoner*":– Assir [5]

618 אָסָם *'āsām*, n.m. GK: 662. barn, storehouse:– barns [1], storehouses [1]

619 אַסְנָה *'asnâ*, n.pr.m. GK: 663. Asnah, "[poss.] *thornbush; he who belongs to Nah*":– Asnah [1]

620 אָסְנַפַּר *'āsᵉnappar* (Aram.), n.pr.m. GK: 10055. Ashurbanipal, "*Ashur creates a son*":– Asnappar [1]

621 אָסְנַת *'āsᵉnat*, n.pr.f. GK: 664. Asenath, "*[belonging to] Neith*":– Asenath [3]

622 אָסַף *'āsap*, v. GK: 665 [→ 614, 623, 624, 625, 626, 627, 628]. [Q] to store, gather, harvest; [Qp] to be a victim; [N] to be gathered, assembled; [P] to be a rear guard, to bring in, gather; [Pu] to be gathered, collected; [Ht] to assemble; [H] to bring together:– gathered [49], gathered together [43], gather [25], assemble [9], taken away [7], gather together [6], assembled [5], rereward [5], gathereth [4], recover [4], withdraw [4], gather in [3], bring [2], gather up [2], gathered in [2], gathered up [2], generally gathered (+622) [2], surely assemble (+622) [2], took [2], assembled together [1], brought in [1], brought together [1], brought [1], consumed [1], destroy [1], fet [1], gathered together (+626) [1], gat [1], gotten [1], lose [1], put all together [1], put up [1], received in [1], receiveth [1], surely consume (+5486) [1], take away [1], take up [1], taken [1], takest away [1], take [1], utterly [1]

623 אָסָף *'āsāp*, n.pr.m. GK: 666 [→ 622]. Asaph, "*gatherer*":– Asaph [45], Asaph's [1]

אסף *'āsip*. See 614.

624 אָסֹף *'āsōp*, n.[m.]. GK: 667 [→ 622]. storehouse, storeroom:– Asuppim [2], thresholds [1]

625 אֹסֶף *'ōsep*, n.m. GK: 668 [→ 622]. harvest (of fruit), gathering:– gathering [2], gathered [1]

626 אֲסֵפָה ***'ᵃsēpâ***, n.f.vbl. GK: 669 [→ 622]. gathering (prisoners); imprisonment:– gathered together (+622) [1]

627 אֲסֻפָּה ***'ᵃsuppâ***, n.f. GK: 670 [→ 622]. collection (of sayings):– assemblies [1]

628 אֲסַפְסֻף ***'ᵃsapsup***, n.[m.]. GK: 671 [→ 622]. rabble, collection (of grumblers):– mixt multitude [1]

629 אָסְפַּרְנָא ***'osparnā'*** (Aram.), adv. GK: 10056. with diligence, surely, fully:– speedily [4], fast [1], forthwith [1], with speed [1]

630 אַסְפָּתָא ***'aspātā'***, n.pr.m. GK: 672. Aspatha, "[poss.] *given from a sacred horse*":– Aspatha [1]

631 אָסַר ***'āsar***, v. GK: 673 [→ 612, 615, 616, 617, 632, 4147, 4149?, 4562?]. [Q] to bind, tie up; to obligate; [Qp] to be confined, be bound; [N] to be tied, be kept in prison; [Pu] to be captured, be taken prisoner:– bound [33], bind [11], bind fast (+631) [4], made ready [3], tied [3], prisoners [2], prison [2], bindeth [1], binding [1], girded [1], girdeth [1], harness [1], held [1], kept in prison [1], make ready [1], order [1], prepare [1], prison (+1004+1886.1) [1], put in bands [1], set in array [1], tie [1]

632 אִסָּר ***'issār***, n.m. GK: 674 [→ 631; cf. 633]. pledge, a binding obligation:– bond [7], bonds [3], binding [1]

633 אֱסָר ***'ᵉsār*** (Aram.), n.m. GK: 10057 [→ 613; cf. 632]. (enforced) decree, i.e., a legally binding edict, a fig. extension of a bond or fetter that inhibits or controls:– decree [7]

634 אֵסַר־חַדֹּן ***'ēsar-ḥaddōn***, n.pr.m. GK: 675. Esarhaddon, "*Ashur has given a brother [for a lost son]*":– Esar-haddon [3]

635 אֶסְתֵּר ***'estēr***, n.pr.f. GK: 676. Esther, "[Persian] *star* [poss.] *Ishtar*":– Esther [52], Esther's [3]

636 אָע ***'ā'*** (Aram.), n.m. GK: 10058 [cf. 6086]. wood, timber:– timber [3], wood [2]

637 אַף ***'ap***, c. GK: 677 [cf. 638]. how much (better, worse; more, less); really, truly; too, also, even more:– also [53], yea [36], even [7], how much more (+3588) [7], how much less (+3588) [5], and [3], how much more [2], also (+518) [1], although (+3588) [1], and (+2050.1) [1], and when [1], but [1], furthermore [1], how much less (+3588+3808) [1], how much less [1], how much more then (+3588) [1], how much rather [1], moreover [1], much less (+3588) [1], much less for (+3588) [1], much more (+3588) [1], neither (+369) [1], of a surety (+552) [1], so [1], though (+3588) [1], with [1], yea (+3588) [1], yet [1]

638 אַף ***'ap*** (Aram.), c. GK: 10059 [cf. 637]. even, also:– also [3], also (+2050.3) [1]

639 אַף ***'ap***, n.m. GK: 678 [→ 649; cf. 599; cf. 600]. nose (representing the face or some part of the face); "hot of nose" signifies anger; "long of nose" signifies patience; "high of nose" signifies arrogance:– anger [171], wrath [42], face [19], nostrils [13], nose [11], angry [4], longsuffering (+750) [4], faces [3], before (+3807.1) [1], before (+871.1) [1], countenance [1], forbearing [1], forehead [1], noses [1], provocation of anger [1], snout [1], worthy [1]

640 אָפַד ***'āpad***, v.den. GK: 679 [→ 642]. [Q] to fasten:– bound [1], gird [1]

אֵפֹד ***'ēpōd***. See 646.

641 אֵפֹד ***'ēpōd***, n.pr.m. GK: 681 [→ 646?; cf. 640]. Ephod, "*ephod*":– Ephod [1]

642 אֲפֻדָּה ***'ᵃpuddâ***, n.f. GK: 682 [→ 640]. skillfully woven covering:– ephod [2], ornament [1]

643 אַפֶּדֶן ***'appeden***, n.[m.]. GK: 683. palace tent, royal tent:– palace [1]

644 אָפָה ***'āpâ***, v. GK: 684 & 685 [→ 3989; cf. 8601?]. [Q] to bake; [N] to be baked:– baker [8], bake [7], baken [3], baked [2], bakers [2], bakemeats (+3978+4639) [1], bakers' [1], baketh [1]

אֵפָה ***'ēpâ***. See 374.

645 אֵפוֹא ***'ēpô'***, pt. GK: 686 [→ 335?+6311?]. then, so then:– now [10], where [3], here [1], where (+165) [1]

646 אֵפוֹד ***'ēpōd***, n.m. GK: 680 [→ 641?; cf. 640]. ephod, a garment of a priest used for adornment and as an aid in priestly service:– ephod [49]

647 אֲפִיחַ ***'ᵃpîaḥ***, n.pr.m. GK: 688. Aphiah:– Aphiah [1]

648 אָפִיל ***'āpîl***, a. GK: 689 [→ 652]. late-ripening, late in the season:– not grown up [1]

649 אַפַּיִם ***'appayim***, n.pr.m. GK: 691 [cf. 639, 599]. Appaim, "*[pair of] nostrils*":– Appaim [2]

650 אָפִיק ***'āpîq***, n.m. GK: 692 & 693 [→ 662]. stream, water channel; valley, ravine, the deepest part of a valley flowing with water; mighty, strong:– rivers [10], channels [3], brooks [1], mighty [1], scales (+4043) [1], streams [1], stream [1], strong pieces [1]

אֹפִיר ***'ōpîr***. See 211.

651 אָפֵל ***'āpēl***, a. GK: 695 [→ 652]. dark, gloomy:– very dark [1]

652 אֹפֶל ***'ōpel***, n.m. GK: 694 [→ 648, 651, 653, 3990?, 3991?]. darkness, the absence of light, often with the associative meaning of gloom, despair; shadows:– darkness [7], obscurity [1], privily (+1119) [1]

653 אֲפֵלָה ***'ᵃpēlâ***, n.f. GK: 696 [→ 652]. the dark, darkness, with the associative meaning of mental gloom and despair:– darkness [6], gloominess [2], dark [1], thick [1]

654 אֶפְלָל ***'eplāl***, n.pr.m. GK: 697 [→ 6419]. Ephlal, "*judgment, arbitration*":– Ephlal [2]

655 אֹפֶן ***'ōpen***, n.[m.]. GK: 698 [cf. 212?]. (right) time; aptly:–

אֹפָן ***'ōpān***. See 212.

656 אָפֵס ***'āpēs***, v. GK: 699 [→ 657, 658]. [Q] to come to an end, cease:– at an end [1], brought [1], clean gone [1], faileth [1], fail [1]

657 אֶפֶס ***'epes***, n.m. GK: 700 & 701 [→ 656; cf. 6446]. ends (of the earth); no, nothing; however, but, only, yet; an extremity of the body, which in context wades through shallow water: ankles, or possibly soles of the feet:– ends [13], none [4], no [4], nothing [3], none else [2], not [2], without (+871.1) [2], ankles [1], but [1], howbeit [1], nevertheless (+3588) [1], nor any (+2050.1) [1], not any [1], notwithstanding (+3588) [1], only [1], save [1], saving [1], thing of nought [1], uttermost parts [1], want [1], without cause (+871.1) [1]

658 אֶפֶס דַּמִּים ***'epes dammîm***, n.pr.loc. GK: 702 [→ 656]. Ephes Dammim, "*border of Dammim [blood]*":– Ephes-dammim [1]

659 אֶפַע ***'epa'***, n. *or* a. GK: 703. worthless:– nought [1]

660 אֶפְעֶה ***'ep'eh***, n.[m.]. GK: 704 [→ 6463?]. snake, variously identified as an adder or viper:– viper [2], viper's [1]

661 אָפַף ***'āpap***, v. GK: 705. [Q] to surround, entangle, engulf:– compassed [3], compassed about [2]

662 אָפַק ***'āpaq***, v. GK: 706 [→ 650]. [Ht] to control oneself, restrain oneself; to feel compelled:– refrained [3], refrain [2], forced [1], restrained [1]

663 אֲפֵק ***'ᵃpēq***, n.pr.loc. GK: 707 [→ 664]. Aphek, "*stronghold*":– Aphek [8], Aphik [1]

664 אֲפֵקָה ***'ᵃpēqâ***, n.pr.loc. GK: 708 [→ 663]. Aphekah, "*fortress*":– Aphekah [1]

665 אֵפֶר ***'ēper***, n.[m.]. GK: 709 [→ 211]. ashes, dust:– ashes [22]

666 אֲפֵר ***'ᵃpēr***, n.[m.]. GK: 710. headband:– ashes [2]

667 אֶפְרֹחַ ***'eprōaḥ***, n.m. GK: 711 [→ 6524]. young (of a bird), chick:– young ones [2], young [2]

668 אַפִּרְיוֹן ***'appiryôn***, n.[m.]. GK: 712. carriage; other sources: sedan chair, litter, or palanquin, a vehicle carried on poles by porters:– chariot [1]

669 אֶפְרַיִם ***'eprayim***, n.pr.m. GK: 713 [→ 6509?]. Ephraim, "*doubly fruitful*":– Ephraim [171], Ephraimites [5], Ephraim's [3], Ephraim's (+3807.1) [1]

670 אֲפָרְסָי ***'ᵃpārᵉsāy*** (Aram.), n.pr.pl.g. GK: 10060 [cf. 6539?]. Persian, from Persia:– Apharsites [1]

671 אֲפָרְסְכָי ***'ᵃparsᵉkāy*** (Aram.), n.m.pl.[pr.g.?]. GK: 10061 & 10062. officials; transliterated in the KJV and ASV as the proper name "Apharsachites":– Apharsachites [2], Apharsathchites [1]

672 אֶפְרָת ***'eprāt*** or אֶפְרָתָה ***'eprātâ***, n.pr.f. & loc. GK: 714 & 715 & 716 & 717 [→ 673, 3613]. Ephrath, Ephrathah, "*fruitful land*":– Ephratah [5], Ephrath [5]

673 אֶפְרָתִי ***'eprātî***, a.g. GK: 718 [→ 672]. Ephraimite, "*of Ephraim*":– Ephrathite [3], Ephraimite [1], Ephrathites [1]

674 אַפְּתֹם ***'appᵉtōm*** (Aram.), n.m. GK: 10063. revenue, treasury:– revenue [1]

675 אֶצְבּוֹן ***'eṣbōn***, n.pr.m. GK: 719. Ezbon:– Ezbon [2]

676 אֶצְבַּע ***'eṣba'***, n.f. GK: 720 [cf. 677]. digit appendage of hand or foot: finger, toe; "four fingers" is a measurement of width (Jer 52:21):– finger [19], fingers [10], fingers and toes [1], toes [1]

677 אֶצְבַּע ***'eṣba'*** (Aram.), n.f. GK: 10064 [cf. 676]. toe, finger:– toes [2], fingers [1]

678 אָצִיל ***'āṣîl***, n.[m.]. GK: 721 & 722 [→ 680, 682]. leader, with an implication of being noble and distinguished; far corner, the remote areas of the earth:– chief men [1], nobles [1]

679 אַצִּיל ***'aṣṣîl***, n.[f.]. GK: 723 [→ 680]. joint (of shoulder or wrist); "a cubit of the joint" (Eze 41:8) is an unknown length, translated as a "long cubit":– armholes (+3027) [2], great [1]

680 אָצַל ***'āṣal***, v.den. GK: 724 [→ 678, 679, 681, 683]. [Q] to turn aside; to take away; [N] to be smaller:– kept [1], reserved [1], straitened [1], take [1], took [1]

681 אֵצֶל ***'ēṣel***, subst.pp. GK: 725 [→ 680]. beside, near, at the side:– by [33], beside [11], with [3], at [2], from (+4480) [2], near [2], unto [2], besides [1], by (+4480) [1], hard by [1], near unto [1], toward [1], to [1]

682 אָצֵל ***'āṣēl***, n.pr.m. & loc. GK: 727 & 728 [→ 678]. Azel, "*noble*":– Azel [6], Azal [1]

683 אֲצַלְיָהוּ ***'ᵃṣalyāhû***, n.pr.m. GK: 729 [→ 680+3068]. Azaliah, "*Yahweh is keeping in reserve*":– Azaliah [2]

684 אֹצֶם ***'ōṣem***, n.pr.m. GK: 730. Ozem:– Ozem [2]

685 אֶצְעָדָה ***'eṣ'ādâ***, n.f. GK: 731 [→ 6805]. armlet, armband; an ornamental chain worn on the wrist or the ankle:– bracelet [1], chains [1]

686 אָצַר ***'āṣar***, v. GK: 732 [→ 214, 687?]. [Q] to store up; [N] be stored; [H] to be in charge of a storeroom:– laid up in store [2], made treasurers [1], store up [1], treasured [1]

687 אֵצֶר ***'ēṣer***, n.pr.m. GK: 733 [→ 686?]. Ezer, "*help*":– Ezer [5]

688 אֶקְדָּח ***'eqdāḥ***, n.[m.]. GK: 734 [→ 6919]. sparkling jewel; some sources: beryl stone:– carbuncles (+68) [1]

689 אַקּוֹ ***'aqqô***, n.m. GK: 735 [→ 3243]. wild goat:– wild goat [1]

690 אֲרָא ***'ᵃrā'***, n.pr.m. GK: 736. Ara:– Ara [1]

691 אֶרְאֵל ***'er'ēl***, n.[m.]. GK: 737 [→ 739?]. brave man, hero:– valiant ones [1]

692 אַרְאֵלִי ***'ar'ēli***, a.g. GK: 739 & 740 [→ 692; cf. 8634?]. Areli; Arelite, "*of Areli*":– Areli [2], Arelites [1]

693 אָרַב ***'ārab***, v. GK: 741 [→ 695, 696, 698?, 3993]. [Q] to lay in wait against, hide in ambush; [P] to ambush, waylay; [H] to set an ambush:– lie in wait [9], liers in wait [8], laid wait [5], ambush [4], lieth in wait [4], lay wait [3], lying in wait [2], ambushes [1], ambushments [1], lay in wait [1], lie in ambush [1], lie in wait against [1], liers in ambush [1]

694 אֲרָב ***'ᵃrāb***, n.pr.loc. GK: 742 [cf. 701?]. Arab, "*desert* or *steppe*":– Arab [1]

695 אֶרֶב ***'ereb***, n.[m.]. GK: 743 [→ 693]. cover, hiding place, lair; hiding place (for an ambush):– dens [1], lie in wait [1]

696 אֹרֶב ***'ōreb***, n.[m.]. GK: 744 [→ 693]. trap, intrigue:– wait [1]

אַרְבֵּאל ***'arbē'l***. See 1009.

697 אַרְבֶּה ***'arbeh***, n.m. GK: 746 [→ 7235?]. locust, mature locust:– locusts [11], locust [9], grasshoppers [3], grasshopper [1]

698 אָרְבָּה ***'orbâ***, n.f. GK: 747 [→ 693?]. cleverness, other sources: nimble movements (of the hands), perhaps some concrete survival skill, such as swimming:– spoils [1]

699 אֲרֻבָּה ***'ᵃrubbâ***, n.f. GK: 748. floodgate; window; nest (nesting hole):– windows [8], chimney [1]

700 אֲרֻבּוֹת ***'ᵃrubbôt***, n.pr.loc. GK: 749. Arubboth:– Aruboth [1]

701 אַרְבִּי ***'arbî***, a.g. GK: 750 [cf. 694?]. Arbite:– Arbite [1]

702 אַרְבַּע ***'arba'***, n.m. & f. GK: 752 [→ 704, 705, 706, 7153, 7243, 7251, 7253?, 7255, 7256; cf. 703]. four, (pl.) forty; fourth, fortieth:– four [264], fourteenth (+6240) [23], fourteen (+6240) [19], fourth [5], forty two thousand (+505+7239) [2], four apiece (+702) [2], threescore and fourteen (+7657+2050.1) [2], fourfold [1], thousand [1]

703 אַרְבַּע ***'arba'*** (Aram.), n.m. & f. GK: 10065 [→ 7244; cf. 702]. four:– four [8]

704 אַרְבַּע ***'arba'***, n.pr.m. GK: 753 [→ 702]. Arba:– Arbah [2], Arba [1]

אַרְבָּעָה ***'arbā'â***. See 702.

705 אַרְבָּעִים ***'arbā'îm***, n.pl.indecl. GK: 754 [→ 702]. forty (pl. of "four"):– forty [131], fortieth [4], forty's [1]

Heb

706 אַרְבַּעְתַּיִם ***'arba'tayim***, n.m. & f. GK: 752 [→ 702]. dual of 702: fourfold:–

707 אָרַג ***'ārag***, v. GK: 755 [→ 708]. [Q] to weave, spin (a web):– weaver's [4], woven [3], weaver [2], weave [2], weavest [1], wove [1]

708 אֶרֶג ***'ereg***, n.[m.]. GK: 756 [→ 707]. weaver's loom, weaver's shuttle:– beam [1], weaver's shuttle [1]

709 אַרְגֹּב ***'argōb***, n.pr.m. & loc. GK: 758 & 759 [cf. 7263]. Argob, "*mound*":– Argob [5]

710 אַרְגְּוָן ***'arg^{e}wān***, n.[m.]. GK: 760 [cf. 713]. purple (yarn):– purple [1]

711 אַרְגְּוָן ***'arg^{e}wān*** (Aram.), n.m. GK: 10066 [cf. 713]. purple (clothing), a sign of rulership:– scarlet [3]

712 אַרְגָּז ***'argaz***, n.m. GK: 761 [→ 7264]. chest (containing objects); other sources: saddlebag:– coffer [3]

713 אַרְגָּמָן ***'argāmān***, n.[m.]. GK: 763 [cf. 710; cf. 711]. purple (yarn):– purple [38]

714 אַרְדְּ ***'ard***, n.pr.m. GK: 764 [→ 715?, 716, 720?]. Ard, "*hunchbacked*":– Ard [2]

715 אַרְדּוֹן ***'ardôn***, n.pr.m. GK: 765 [→ 714?]. Ardon, "*hunchbacked*":– Ardon [1]

716 אַרְדִּי ***'ardî***, a.g. GK: 766 [→ 714]. Ardite, "*of Ard*":– Ardites [1]

717 אָרָה ***'ārâ***, v. GK: 768 [→ 224?]. [Q] to gather, pick (fruit):– gathered [1], pluck [1]

718 אֲרוּ ***'^{a}rû*** (Aram.), interj. GK: 10067 [→ 431]. there!, behold!, i.e., a discourse marker of introduction, transition, or emphasis:– behold [4], lo [1]

719 אַרְוָד ***'arwād***, n.pr.loc. GK: 770 [→ 721]. Arvad:– Arvad [2]

720 אֲרוֹד ***'^{a}rôd***, n.pr.m. GK: 769 [→ 714?]. Arod, see 722:– Arod [1]

721 אַרְוָדִי ***'arwādî***, a.g. GK: 773 [→ 719]. Arvadite, "*of Arvad*":– Arvadite [2]

722 אֲרוֹדִי ***'^{a}rôdî***, n.pr.m. & a.g. GK: 771 & 772. Arodi, "*hunchbacked*"; Arodite, "*of Arodi*":– Arodites [1], Arodi [1]

Heb

723 אֻרְוָה ***'urwâ*** or אֻרְיָה ***'uryâ***, n.f. GK: 774 & 795 [→ 220]. (animal) stall, pen, stable, manger, crib:– stalls [3]

724 אֲרוּכָה ***'^{a}rûkâ***, n.f. GK: 776 [→ 748]. healing, health; repair:– health [4], made up (+5927) [1], perfected (+5927) [1]

725 אֲרוּמָה ***'^{a}rûmâ***, n.pr.loc. GK: 777 [cf. 7316]. Arumah, "*lofty*":– Arumah [1]

726 אֲרוֹמִי ***'^{a}rômî***, a.g. GK: 122 [cf. 130]. var. of 130: Edomite, "*of Edom*":– Syrians [1]

727 אֲרוֹן ***'^{a}rôn***, n.m. & f. GK: 778. ark, chest, box; coffin:– ark [195], chest [6], coffin [1]

728 אֲרַוְנָה ***'^{a}rawnâ*** or אֲרַנְיָה ***'^{a}ranyâ***, n.pr.m. GK: 779 & 819. Araunah, Aranyah, "*strong*":– Araunah [9]

729 אָרוּז ***'ārûz***, a. GK: 775 [→ 730?]. tight, solid:– made of cedar [1]

730 אֶרֶז ***'erez***, n.m. GK: 780 [→ 729?, 731]. cedar; other sources: fir:– cedar [43], cedars [24], cedar trees [5], cedar tree [1]

731 אַרְזָה ***'arzâ***, n.f.col. GK: 781 [→ 730]. beam of cedar; other sources: paneling (made of fir):– cedar work [1]

732 אָרַח ***'āraḥ***, v. GK: 782 [→ 733?, 734, 736, 737?]. [Q] to go, travel; (ptcp.) traveler, wanderer; (ptcp.pl.) caravans:– wayfaring man [2], goeth [1], wayfaring men [1], wayfaring [1]

733 אָרַח ***'āraḥ***, n.pr.m. GK: 783 [→ 732?]. Arah, "*he wanders*":– Arah [4]

734 אֹרַח ***'ōraḥ***, n.m. GK: 784 [→ 732; cf. 735]. road, way, path, thoroughfare; by extension: way of life, manner of conduct; "the way of a woman" means "childbirth":– way [18], paths [16], path [9], ways [8], byways (+6128) [1], highways [1], manner [1], race [1], ranks [1], traveller [1], troops [1], wayfaring man (+5674) [1]

735 אֲרַח ***'^{a}raḥ*** (Aram.), n.[m.?]. GK: 10068 [cf. 734]. road, way; fig., conduct or way of life (only used fig. in the Aramaic portion of the Bible):– ways [2]

736 אֹרְחָה ***'ōrḥâ***, n.f. GK: 785 [→ 732]. caravan:– company [1], travelling companies [1]

737 אֲרֻחָה ***'^{a}ruḥâ***, n.f. GK: 786 [→ 732?]. allowance, provision; portion:– allowance [2], diet [2], dinner [1], victuals [1]

738 אֲרִי ***'^{a}rî***, n.m. GK: 787 & 793 [→ 221, 745; cf. 744]. (the African) lion, with the associative meanings of strength, fierceness, and sometimes nobility; sometimes fig. of people who are destructive:– lion [55], lions [17], lion's [4], lions' [2], young lion [1]

739 אֲרִאֵל ***'^{a}ri'ēl***, n.pr.m. GK: 738 [→ 691?]. best man, warrior, possibly "lionlike":– lion-like men [2]

740 אֲרִיאֵל ***'^{a}rî'ēl***, n.pr.m. & n.pr.f. GK: 790 & 791 [→ 741]. Ariel, "*lioness of God [El]*":– Ariel [6]

741 אֲרִיאֵל ***'^{a}rî'ēl***, n.m. GK: 789 [→ 739, 740; cf. 2025]. altar hearth:– altar [2]

742 אֲרִידַי ***'^{a}rîday***, n.pr.m. GK: 767. Aridai, "[perhaps] *delight of Hari*":– Aridai [1]

743 אֲרִידָתָא ***'^{a}rîdātā'***, n.pr.m. GK: 792. Aridatha, "[perhaps] *given by Hari*":– Aridatha [1]

אַרְיֵה ***'aryēh***. See 738.

744 אַרְיֵה ***'aryēh*** (Aram.), n.m. GK: 10069 [cf. 738]. lion, an animal with the associative meanings of being fierce and powerful, and so causing fear:– lions [8], lions' [1], lion [1]

745 אַרְיֵה ***'aryēh***, n.pr.m. GK: 794 [→ 738]. Arieh, "*lion*":– Arieh [1]

אֲרָיָה ***'^{a}rāyâ***. See 723.

746 אַרְיוֹךְ ***'aryôk***, n.pr.m. GK: 796 & 10070. Arioch; note this name is Hebrew twice in Genesis and Aramaic five times in Daniel:– Arioch [7]

747 אֲרִיסַי ***'^{a}rîsay***, n.pr.m. GK: 798. Arisai:– Arisai [1]

748 אָרַךְ ***'ārak***, v. GK: 799 [→ 724, 750, 752, 753; cf. 754]. [Q] to be, become long; [H] to lengthen, to have a long (life):– prolong [12], prolonged [5], long [3], drew out [2], lengthen [2], deferreth [1], defer [1], draw out [1], lengthened [1], made long [1], outlived (+310+3117) [1], overlived (+310+3117) [1], prolongeth [1], tarried long [1], tarried [1]

749 אֲרִיךְ ***'^{a}rîk*** (Aram.), a.vbl. GK: 10071. proper, fitting:– meet [1]

750 אָרֵךְ ***'ārēk***, a. GK: 800 [→ 748]. slow (to anger), patient, long-suffering:– slow [9], longsuffering (+639) [4], longwinged (+83) [1], patient [1]

751 אֶרֶךְ ***'erek***, n.pr.loc. GK: 804 [cf. 756]. Erech:– Erech [1]

752 אָרֹךְ ***'ārōk***, a. GK: 801 [→ 748]. length (spatial and temporal):– long [2], longer [1]

753 אֹרֶךְ ***'ōrek***, n.[m.]. GK: 802 [→ 748]. length (spatial and temporal):– length [70], long [21], ever (+3117) [2], high [1], so long [1]

754 אַרְכָה ***'arkâ*** (Aram.), n.f. GK: 10073 [cf. 752]. continuing, prolongation, lengthening of time:– lengthening [1], prolonged [1]

755 אַרְכֻבָּה ***'arkubbâ*** (Aram.), n.f. GK: 10072 [cf. 1288]. knee; "knocking of the knees" indicates fear:– knees [1]

אֲרֻכָה ***'^{a}rukâ***. See 724.

756 אַרְכְּוָי ***'ark^{e}wāy*** (Aram.), n.pr.g. GK: 10074 [cf. 751]. Erech:– Archevites [1]

757 אַרְכִּי ***'arkî***, a.g. GK: 805. Arkite:– Archite [5], Archi [1]

758 אֲרָם ***'^{a}rām***, n.pr.m. GK: 806 [→ 762, 761, 6307 (also used with compound proper names)]. Aram:– Syria [67], Syrians [56], Aram [7], Mesopotamia [1], Syria-damascus (+1834) [1], Syria-maachah [1]

759 אַרְמוֹן ***'armôn***, n.m. GK: 810 [→ 764; cf. 488, 7411]. fortress, citadel, palace, stronghold, a military defensive building usually small of base but many floors high:– palaces [27], palace [4], castle [1]

760 אֲרַם צוֹבָה ***'^{a}ram ṣôbâ***, n.pr.loc. GK: 809 [→ 758+6678]. Aram Zobah:– Aram-zobah [1]

761 אֲרַמִּי ***'^{a}rammî***, a.g. GK: 812 [→ 758]. Aramean:– Syrian [7], Syrians [3], Aramitess [1]

762 אֲרָמִית ***'^{a}rāmî***, adv. GK: 811 [→ 758]. in Aramaic:– in the Syrian language [2], in the Syrian tongue [2], in Syriack [1]

763 אֲרַם נַהֲרַיִם ***'^{a}ram nah^{a}rayim***, n.loc. GK: 808 [→ 758]. Aram Naharaim:– Mesopotamia [4], Aram-naharaim [1]

764 אַרְמֹנִי ***'armōnî***, n.pr.m. GK: 813 [→ 759]. Armoni, "*one born in the dwelling tower, the palace*":– Armoni [1]

765 אֲרָן ***'^{a}rān***, n.pr.m. GK: 814. Aran, "*wild goat*":– Aran [2]

766 אֹרֶן ***'ōren***, n.[m.]. GK: 815 [→ 767, 769?]. pine tree; other sources: laurel, sweet laurel, fir, cedar:– ash [1]

767 אֹרֶן ***'ōren***, n.pr.m. GK: 816 [→ 766]. Oren, "*fir* or *cedar; laurel*":– Oren [1]

אָרֹן ***'ārōn***. See 727.

768 אַרְנֶבֶת ***'arnebet***, n.f. GK: 817 [cf. 3]. rabbit; other sources: hare:– hare [2]

769 אַרְנוֹן ***'arnôn***, n.pr.loc. GK: 818 [→ 766?]. Arnon:– Arnon [25]

אַרְנִיָּה ***'arnîah***. See 728.

770 אַרְנָן ***'arnān***, n.pr.m. GK: 820. Arnan:– Arnan [1]

771 אָרְנָן ***'ornān***, n.pr.m. GK: 821. Araunah, "*strong*":– Ornan [12]

772 אֲרַע ***'^{a}ra'*** (Aram.), n.[f.]. GK: 10075 [→ 773, 778; cf. 776]. earth, world, the dwelling place of all peoples; land, ground, the dwelling place of a specific people:– earth [20], inferior [1]

773 אַרְעִי ***'ar'î*** (Aram.), n.f.den. GK: 10076 [→ 772]. floor, bottom:– bottom [1]

774 אַרְפָּד ***'arpād***, n.pr.loc. GK: 822. Arpad:– Arpad [4], Arphad [2]

775 אַרְפַּכְשַׁד ***'arpakšad***, n.pr.m. GK: 823. Arphaxad:– Arphaxad [9]

776 אֶרֶץ ***'ereṣ***, n.f. & m. GK: 824 [cf. 772, cf. 778]. world, earth, all inhabited lands; parts of the earth, land (in contrast to water), ground, soil; country, region, territory; "heaven and earth" means the totality of creation; "the ends of the earth" means "a very distant place":– land [1508], earth [712], ground [98], country [92], countries [48], lands [34], world [4], way [2], common [1], field [1], little way (+3530+1886.1) [1], nations [1], wilderness (+4057) [1]

777 אַרְצָא ***'arṣā'***, n.pr.m. GK: 825. Arza, "[perhaps] *gracious*":– Arza [1]

778 אֲרַק ***'^{a}raq*** (Aram.), n.[f.]. GK: 10077 [→ 772; cf. 776]. earth:– earth [1]

779 אָרַר ***'ārar***, v. GK: 826 [→ 224?, 3994]. [Q] to curse, place a curse; [Qp] to be cursed, be under a curse; [N] to be cursed; [P] to bring a curse; [Ho] to bring a curse upon one:– cursed [44], curse [9], causeth the curse [5], curseth [2], bitterly [1], causeth curse [1], cursest [1]

780 אֲרָרַט ***'^{a}rāraṭ***, n.pr.loc. GK: 827. Ararat:– Ararat [2], Armenia [2]

781 אָרַשׂ ***'āraś***, v. GK: 829. [P] to betroth, pledge to marriage; [Pu] to be betrothed, be pledged to be married:– betrothed [6], betroth [4], espoused [1]

782 אֲרֶשֶׁת ***'^{a}rešet***, n.f. GK: 830 [→ 4180]. request, desire:– request [1]

783 אַרְתַּחְשַׁסְתְּא ***'artaḥšast'*** or אַרְתַּחְשַׁשְׂתְּ ***'artaḥšaśt*** or אַרְתַּחְשַׁשְׂתָּא ***'artaḥšaśtā'***, n.pr.m. GK: 831 & 10078. Artaxerxes; note this name occurs nine times in Hebrew in Ezra and Nehemiah and six times in Aramaic in Ezra:– Artaxerxes [14], Artaxerxes' [1]

784 אֵשׁ ***'ēš***, n.f. & m. GK: 836 [→ 800, 801; cf. 785]. fire, flame; lightning; same as 800:– fire [372], fiery [2], burning [1], fire (+3956) [1], flaming [1], hot [1]

785 אֶשָּׁא ***'eššā'*** (Aram.), n.[f.]. GK: 10080 [cf. 784, 801]. fire:– flame [1]

786 אִשׁ ***'iš***, subst. GK: 838 [→ 3426]. there is:– are there [1], can [1]

787 אֹשׁ ***'ōš*** (Aram.), n.m. GK: 10079 [cf. 8357]. foundation:– foundations [2], foundation [1]

788 אַשְׁבֵּל ***'ašbēl***, n.pr.m. GK: 839 [→ 789; cf. 7640]. Ashbel, "[poss. a form of] *man of Baal; having a long upper lip*":– Ashbel [3]

789 אַשְׁבֵּלִי ***'ašbēlî***, a.g. GK: 840 [→ 788; cf. 7640]. Ashbelite, "*of Ashbel*":– Ashbelites [1]

790 אֶשְׁבָּן ***'ešbān***, n.pr.m. GK: 841. Eshban, "*man of understanding*":– Eshban [2]

791 אַשְׁבֵּעַ ***'ašbēa'***, n.pr.loc. GK: 842 [→ 1004+791]. Ashbea:– Ashbea [1]

792 אֶשְׁבַּעַל ***'ešba'al***, n.pr.m. GK: 843 [→ 376+1167]. Esh-Baal, "*man of Baal*":– Eshbaal [2]

793 אֶשֶׁד ***'ešed***, n.[m.]. GK: 845 [→ 794]. foundation, bottom, lower part (slope):– stream [1]

794 אֲשֵׁדָה ***'ašēd***, n.f. GK: 844 [→ 793, 799]. slopes, mountain slopes:– springs [3]

795 אַשְׁדּוֹד ***'ašdôd***, n.pr.loc. GK: 846 [→ 796, 797]. Ashdod, "[perhaps] *fortress*":– Ashdod [17]

796 אַשְׁדּוֹדִי ***'ašdôdî***, a.g. GK: 847 [→ 795]. from Ashdod:– Ashdodites [1], Ashdothites [1], of Ashdod [1], them of Ashdod [1], they of Ashdod [1]

797 אַשְׁדּוֹדִית ***'ašdôdît***, adv. GK: 848 [→ 795]. language of Ashdod:– in the speech of Ashdod [1]

798 אַשְׁדּוֹת הַפִּסְגָּה ***'ašdôt happisgâ***, n.pr.loc. GK: 849 [→ 794+1886.1+6449]. Ashdoth Pisgah:– Ashdoth-pisgah [3]

799 אֶשְׁדָּת ***'ešdāt***, n.f. GK: 850 [→ 794]. mountain slope:– *not translated* [1]

800 אֵשׁ ***'ēš***, n.f. & m. GK: 836 [→ 784]. fire, flame; lightning; same as 784:–

801 אִשֶּׁה ***'iššeh***, n.m. GK: 852 [→ 784; cf. 785]. offering made by fire:– offering made by fire [35], offerings made by fire [15], sacrifice made by fire [9], sacrifices made by fire [3], offering by fire [2], offering made by fire (+7133) [1]

802 אִשָּׁה ***'iššâ***, n.f. GK: 851 [→ 376; cf. 5389]. woman, in contrast to man; wife, in contrast to husband; "to take a woman" means "to marry":– wife [301], woman [211], wives [115], women [103], wife's [8], one [7], woman's [7], every one [3], each [2], female [2], married (+1961+3807.1) [2], marry (+1961+3807.1) [2], adulteress (+376) [1], every woman [1], every [1], married (+1167) [1], married (+3807.1) [1], none (+3808) [1], together (+269+413) [1], whore's (+2181) [1], widow's (+490) [1], wife (+3807.1) [1], womankind [1], women's [1]

803 אֲשׁוּיָה ***'ašûyâ*** or אָשְׁיָה ***'ošyâ***, n.f. GK: 853 & 859. tower:– foundations [1]

804 אַשּׁוּר ***'aššûr***, n.pr.g. & loc. GK: 855 [→ 839]. Asshur, Assyria:– Assyria [118], Assyrian [13], Asshur [8], Assyrians [6], Assyrians (+1121) [4], Assur [2]

805 אֲשׁוּרִי ***'ašûrî***, a.g. & n.pr.g.pl. GK: 856. Ashuri; Asshurite, "*of Asshur*":– Ashurites [1], Asshurim [1]

806 אַשְׁחוּר ***'ašḥûr***, n.pr.m. GK: 858. Ashhur:– Ashur [2]

807 אֲשִׁימָא ***'ašîmā'***, n.pr.[m.]. GK: 860. Ashima:– Ashima [1]

אֲשִׁירָה ***'ašêrâ***. See 842.

808 אָשִׁישׁ ***'āšîš***, n.m. GK: 861. man:– foundations [1]

809 אֲשִׁישָׁה ***'ašîšâ***, n.f. GK: 862 [→ 377?]. cake of raisins, made of dried, compressed grapes; used as food and as an offering:– flagons [2], flagon [2]

810 אֶשֶׁךְ ***'ešek***, n.[m.]. GK: 863. testicle:– stones [1]

811 אֶשְׁכּוֹל ***'eškôl***, n.m. GK: 864 [→ 812; cf. 7921]. cluster of grapes:– clusters [4], cluster [4], cluster of grapes [1]

812 אֶשְׁכּוֹל ***'eškôl***, n.pr.m. & loc. GK: 865 & 866 [→ 811]. Eshcol, "*[grape] cluster*":– Eshcol [6]

813 אַשְׁכְּנַז ***'aškenaz***, n.pr.m. GK: 867. Ashkenaz:– Ashchenaz [2], Ashkenaz [1]

814 אֶשְׁכָּר ***'eškār***, n.[m.]. GK: 868. gifts; payment:– gifts [1], present [1]

815 אֵשֶׁל ***'ēšel***, n.m. GK: 869. tamarisk tree:– tree [2], grove [1]

816 אָשַׁם ***'āšam***, v. GK: 870 [→ 817, 818, 819]. [Q] to be guilty; to be in a state of liable for a wrongdoing, with an implication of that one will suffer or be punished for the guilt; [N] to be suffering; [H] to declare guilty:– guilty [12], desolate [4], offend [4], certainly trespassed (+816) [2], greatly offended (+816) [2], made desolate [2], trespass [2], acknowledge offence [1], destroy [1], found faulty [1], found guilty [1], hath trespassed [1], hold guilty [1], offended [1]

817 אָשָׁם ***'āšām***, n.m. GK: 871 [→ 816]. guilt offering, atoning sacrifice; guilt, penalty:– trespass offering [35], trespass [6], sin [2], guiltiness [1], offering for sin [1], trespasses [1]

818 אָשֵׁם ***'āšēm***, a. GK: 872 [→ 816]. guilty, bearing guilt:– guilty [2], which is faulty [1]

819 אַשְׁמָה ***'ašmâ***, n.f. GK: 873 [→ 816]. guilt, guiltiness:– trespass [9], sins [2], sin [2], cause of trespass [1], offended [1], trespass offering [1], trespassed [1], trespasses [1], trespassing [1]

אַשְׁמוּרָה ***'ašmûrâ***. See 821.

820 אַשְׁמָן ***'ašmān***, n.[m.].pl. GK: 875 [→ 8081?]. strong one:– desolate places [1]

821 אַשְׁמוּרָה ***'ašmûrâ***, n.f. GK: 874 [→ 8104]. watch of the night (middle or last):– watch [4], watches [3]

822 אֶשְׁנָב ***'ešnāb***, n.[m.]. GK: 876 [→ 5380]. lattice, a barred or grated window:– casement [1], lattice [1]

823 אַשְׁנָה ***'ašnâ***, n.pr.loc. GK: 877. Ashnah:– Ashnah [2]

824 אֶשְׁעָן ***'eš'ān***, n.pr.loc. GK: 878. Eshan, "*support*":– Eshean [1]

825 אַשָּׁף ***'aššāp***, n.m. GK: 879 [cf. 826]. enchanter, conjurer, one of the profession of the secret arts, in communication with the dead:– astrologers [2]

826 אָשַׁף ***'āšap*** (Aram.), n.m. GK: 10081 [cf. 825]. enchanter, conjurer:– astrologers [4], astrologer [1], astrologians [1]

827 אַשְׁפָּה ***'ašpâ***, n.f. GK: 880. quiver (for arrows):– quiver [6]

828 אַשְׁפְּנַז ***'ašpenaz***, n.pr.m. GK: 881. Ashpenaz, "*guest*":– Ashpenaz [1]

829 אֶשְׁפָּר ***'ešpār***, n.m. GK: 882 [→ 7782]. cake of dates:– good piece [2]

830 אַשְׁפֹּת ***'ašpōt***, n.[m.]. GK: 883 [→ 8239]. ash heap; Dung (Gate):– dung [4], dunghill [2], dunghills [1]

831 אַשְׁקְלוֹן ***'ašqelôn***, n.pr.loc. GK: 884 [→ 832]. Ashkelon:– Ashkelon [9], Askelon [3]

832 אֶשְׁקְלוֹנִי ***'ešqelônî***, a.g. GK: 885 [→ 831]. Ashkelonite, "*of Ashkelon*":– Eshkalonites [1]

833 אָשַׁר ***'āšar***, v. GK: 886 & 887 [→ 835, 836, 837, 838, 843]. [Q] to walk (straight); [P] to lead, guide; reprove; to call blessed, pronounce happy, speak well of; [Pu] to be guided; to be blessed; in some contexts, to give a blessing is to act kindly and impart benefits to the one being blessed; to be blessed implies the happy state that results:– call blessed [4], blessed [3], go [2], call happy [1], guide [1], happy [1], leaders [1], lead [1], led [1], relieve [1]

834 אֲשֶׁר ***'ašer***, pt.rel. GK: 889. (rel.) who, which, what; (c.) that, in order that, so that:– which [1819], that [1671], as (+3509.1) [382], whom [262], who [94], what [75], whose [69], where (+8033) [54], when (+3509.1) [47], wherewith [41], whither (+8033+1886.5) [38], because [36], whatsoever (+3605) [33], when [32], how [28], where [28], for [27], until (+5704) [27], whither (+8033) [27], because (+5921) [26], wherein [25], as [23], because (+3282) [19], whereof [19], according as (+3509.1) [16], wherein (+871.1) [15], such as [14], wherein (+871.1+1886.3) [14], whereby [12], whithersoever (+3605+871.1) [12], because (+8478) [11], like as (+3509.1) [11], wherewith (+871.1) [11], whereon (+5921) [10], till (+5704) [9], wherewith (+5921) [8], whosoever (+3605) [8], such [7], where (+8033+1886.5) [7], where (+871.1) [7], wherein (+8033) [7], as soon as (+3509.1) [6], forasmuch as (+3282) [5], how that [5], whatsoever [5], whither [5], whosoever (+376) [5], as when (+3509.1) [4], because (+1697+5921) [4], if [4], that (+4616+3807.1) [4], that when (+3509.1) [4], what soever (+3605) [4], wherein (+871.1+2050.2) [4], wherein (+871.1+3963.1) [4]*

835 אֶשֶׁר ***'ešer***, n.[m.]. GK: 890 & 897 [→ 833, 837]. fortune, blessedness, happiness; (interj.) blessed!, happy!, a heightened state of happiness and joy, implying very favorable circumstances, often resulting from the kind acts of God:– blessed [27], happy [18]

836 אָשֵׁר ***'āšēr***, n.pr.m. GK: 888 [→ 843; cf. 833]. Asher, "*Happy One!*":– Asher [43]

837 אֹשֶׁר ***'ōšer***, n.[m.]. GK: 891 [→ 835; cf. 833]. fortune, blessedness, happiness:– happy [1]

838 אֲשֻׁר ***'ašur***, n.f. GK: 892 & 893 [→ 833]. steps, tracks:– steps [5], goings [2], going [1], step [1]

839 אַשֻּׁר ***'aššur***, n.pr.g. & loc. GK: 894 [→ 804]. Asshur, Asshurite; cf. 804:– Ashurites [1]

אַשֻּׁר ***'aššur***. See 804, 838.

840 אֲשַׂרְאֵל ***'aśar'ēl***, n.pr.m. GK: 832 [→ 841, 844, 845]. Asarel:– Asareel [1]

841 אֲשַׂרְאֵלָה ***'aśar'ēlâ***, n.pr.m. GK: 833 [→ 840; cf. 3480]. Asarelah:– Asarelah [1]

842 אֲשֵׁרָה ***'ašērâ***, n.pr.f. GK: 895 [cf. 6252?]. Asherah (pagan god), Asherah pole:– groves [24], grove [16]

843 אָשֵׁרִי ***'āšērî***, a.g. GK: 896 [→ 836; cf. 833]. people of Asher:– Asherites [1]

844 אַשְׂרִיאֵל ***'aśrî'ēl***, n.pr.m. GK: 835 [→ 840]. Asriel, "*God has filled with joy* or *[the object of] joy is God*":– Asriel [2], Ashriel [1]

845 אַשְׂרִאֵלִי ***'aśri'ēlî***, a.g. GK: 834 [→ 840]. Asrielite, "*of Asriel*":– Asrielites [1]

846 אֻשַּׁרְנָא ***'uššarnā'*** (Aram.), n.m. GK: 10082. structure, a building or part of a building (various sources translate more specifically: "beams, roofing, paneling, scaffolding," etc.):– walls [1], wall [1]

847 אֶשְׁתָּאוֹל ***'eštā'ôl***, n.pr.loc. GK: 900 [→ 848; cf. 7592]. Eshtaol, "*[place of oracles,] inquiry*":– Eshtaol [7]

848 אֶשְׁתָּאֻלִי ***'eštā'ulî***, a.g. GK: 901 [→ 847]. Eshtaolite, "*of Eshtaol*":– Eshtaulites [1]

849 אֶשְׁתַּדּוּר ***'eštaddûr*** (Aram.), n.m. GK: 10083 [→ 7712]. rebellion, sedition, revolt:– sedition [2]

850 אֶשְׁתּוֹן ***'eštôn***, n.pr.m. GK: 902. Eshton, "[poss.] *hen-pecked [husband]* or *effeminate*":– Eshton [2]

851 אֶשְׁתְּמֹה ***'eštemōh*** or אֶשְׁתְּמֹעַ ***'eštemōa'***, n.pr.m. & loc. GK: 903 & 904 [→ 8085]. Eshtemoa, Eshtemoh, "*[place where oracle is] heard*":– Eshtemoa [5], Eshtemoh [1]

אַתְּ ***'at***. See 859.

852 אָת ***'āt*** (Aram.), n.m. GK: 10084 [cf. 226]. miraculous sign:– signs [3]

853 אֵת ***'ēt***, pt. GK: 906 [cf. 3487]. usually not translated: marks the direct object:– *usually untranslated* [513], consecrated (+3027+4390) [5], consecrate (+3027+4390) [4], besought (+2470+6440) [3], aided (+2388+3027) [1]

854 אֵת ***'ēt***, pp. GK: 907 [→ 856]. with, to, upon, beside, among, against:– with [606], from (+4480) [81], of (+4480) [71], against [27], to [20], before (+6440) [16], unto [14], by (+4480) [10], by [9], among [7], in [7], upon [7], for [3], of [3], amongst [2], and (+2050.1) [2], before [2], from [2], hath [2], also [1], at the hand of (+4480) [1], beside (+2050.1) [1], beside [1], delivered to keep (+6485+6487) [1], doing (+4480) [1], for (+2050.1) [1], had [1], have [1], knoweth [1], lie with at all (+7901+7901) [1], lien with (+7901) [1], lieth carnally with (+2233+7901+7902) [1], on side [1], on the behalf of (+4480) [1], out of (+4480) [1], own [1], requite (+6213) [1], than (+4480) [1], therewith (+2050.2) [1], towards [1], undo (+6213) [1], with (+4480) [1]

855 אֵת ***'ēt***, n.[m.]. GK: 908. plowshare, mattock:– plowshares [3], coulters [1], coulter [1]

אַתָּה ***'attâ***. See 859.

אָתָא ***'ātā'***. See 857.

856 אֶתְבַּעַל ***'etba'al***, n.pr.m. GK: 909 [→ 854+1167]. Ethbaal, "*with [him is] Baal*":– Ethbaal [1]

857 אָתָה ***'ātâ***, v. GK: 910 [→ 2978, 448; cf. 858]. [Q] to come; [H] to bring:– come [9], came [4], cometh [3], to come [2], brought (+7125) [1], come upon [1], coming [1]

858 אֲתָה ***'atâ*** (Aram.), v. GK: 10085 [cf. 857]. [P] to come, go; [H] to bring; [Hp] to be brought:– brought [6], came [4], come [3], bring [2], brought out [1]

859 אַתָּה ***'attâ***, p.m.s.; אַתְּ ***'att*** or אַתִּי ***'attî***, p.f.s.; אַתֶּם ***'attem***, p.m.pl.; אַתֵּן ***'attēn***, p.f.pl. GK: 905 & 911 & 914 & 917 & 920 [cf. 607; cf. 608]. all forms of the second person pronoun: you, your, yourself; you (all), yours, yourselves:– thou [777], ye [251], you [29], thee [15], thyself [5], yourselves [4], thine [1], thy [1]

860 אָתוֹן ***'ātôn***, n.f. GK: 912. female donkey:– ass [16], asses [12], she asses [5], ass's [1]

861 אַתּוּן ***'attûn*** (Aram.), n.m. [& f.?]. GK: 10086. furnace:– furnace [10]

862 אַתּוּק ***'attûq*** or אַתִּיק ***'attîq***, n.m. GK: 913 & 916. gallery, porch; other sources: street, passage:– galleries [3], gallery [2]

אַתִּי ***'attî***. See 859.

863 אִתַּי ***'ittay*** or אִיתַי ***'îtay***, n.pr.m. GK: 416 & 915 [cf. 384]. Ithai, Ittai, "[poss.] *with me*":– Ittai [8], Ithai [1]

864 אֵתָם ***'ētām***, n.pr.loc. GK: 918. Etham, "[poss.] *fort*":– Etham [4]

אַתֶּם ***'attem***. See 859.

865 אֶתְמוֹל ***'etmôl***, subst.adv. GK: 919 [→ 8543]. yesterday; (adv.) before, formerly, lately, in the past:– before that time (+8032+3509.1) [1], beforetime (+4480+8032) [1], heretofore (+8032) [1], in time past (+1571+8032) [1], in times past (+8032) [1], late [1], old [1], yesterday (+3117) [1]

אַתֵּן ***'atten***. See 859.

866 אֶתְנָה *'etnâ*, n.f. GK: 921 [→ 869]. payment (of a prostitute):– rewards [1]

אַתְּנָה *'attenâ* or אַתְּנָה *'attēnnâ*. See 859.

867 אֶתְנִי *'etnî*, n.pr.m. GK: 922. Ethni, "*gift* or *hire*":– Ethni [1]

868 אֶתְנָן *'etnān*, n.pr.m. GK: 925 [→ 869]. Ethnan, "*hire [of a prostitute]*":– hire [7], reward [3], hires [1]

869 אֶתְנַן *'etnan*, n.m. GK: 924 [→ 866, 868, 8566; cf. 5414]. wages, payment (of a prostitute):– Ethnan [1]

870 אֲתַר *'ᵃtar* (Aram.), n.m. GK: 10087 & 10092 [→ 871.2; cf. 834]. site, place; after:– place [5], after [3]

871 אֲתָרִים *'ᵃtārîm*, n.pr.loc. GK: 926. Atharim, "[trad.] *way of the spies*":– spies [1]

871.1 -בְּ *bᵉ-*, pp.pref. GK: 928 [→ 1119, 1152, 1164, 1212; cf. 871.2]. in, on, among, over, through, against; when, whenever; a spatial, temporal, or logical marker to show relationship of objects, words, and phrases:– in [6850], with [1418], by [699], when [584], into [476], at [438], on [372], upon [340], against [335], among [299], of [274], for [248], through [152], to [151], among (+8432) [106], unto [104], therein (+1886.3) [86], over [71], throughout [64], after [51], according to [43], by (+3027) [42], among (+7130) [41], while [36], before (+2962) [35], therein (+2050.2) [35], within [35], as [34], under [31], obey (+8085) [26], within (+7130) [25], every morning (+1242+1242+871.1+1886.1+1886.1) [20], obeyed (+8085) [20], amongst [19], because of [19], in (+8432) [19], within (+8432) [18], without (+3808) [17], wherein (+834) [15], for sake (+5668) [14], wherein (+834+1886.3) [14], that [13], because [12], wherein (+4100) [12], whithersoever (+834+3605) [12], without (+2351+1886.1) [12], therewith (+1886.3) [11], wherewith (+834) [11], here (+2088) [10], that (+5668) [10], when (+3117) [10], wherein (+2050.2) [10], wherewith (+4100) [10], with (+3027) [10]*

871.2 -בְּ *bᵉ-* (Aram.), pp.pref. GK: 10089 [→ 870; cf. 871.1]. in, with, by:– in [103], then (+116) [28], at [18], with [15], by [6], into [4], over [4], aloud (+2429) [3], of [3], on [3], upon [3], concerning [2], continually (+0.2+8411) [2], without (+3809) [2], according to [1], at what time (+0.2+1768+5732) [1], for [1], more [1], then (+116+4481+6925) [1], therein (+1459+1886.9) [1], therein (+1886.9) [1], therein (+1952.1) [1], through [1], wherein (+1459) [1], wheresoever (+1768+3606) [1], whiles [1], within [1]

Heb

872 בִּאָה *bi'â*, n.f. GK: 929 [→ 935]. entrance:– entry [1]

873 בְּאִישׁ *bi'yš* (Aram.), a. GK: 10090 [→ 888]. wicked, evil, bad:– bad [1]

874 בָּאַר *bā'ar*, v. GK: 930. [P] to make plain, make clear, expound:– declare [1], make plain [1], plainly [1]

875 בְּאֵר *bᵉ'ēr*, n.f. GK: 931 [→ 876, 877, 879, 883, 884, 878, 880, 881, 882, 885, 953, 1269, 1269 (also used with compound proper names)]. well, a shaft in the ground for extraction of water; pit, a depression in the earth with no focus on water:– well [23], well's [6], pit [3], wells [3], full of slimepits (+875+2564) [2]

876 בְּאֵר *bᵉ'ēr*, n.pr.loc. GK: 932 [→ 875]. Beer, "*cistern, well*":– Beer [2]

877 בֹּאר *bō'r*, n.m. GK: 934 [→ 953; cf. 875]. pit, well, cistern; dungeon; a cistern is usually a shaft in the ground, hewn out of soft stone and plastered to hold water:–

878 בְּאֵרָא *bᵉ'ērā'*, n.pr.m. GK: 938 [→ 875]. Beera, "*cistern, well*":– Beera [1]

879 בְּאֵר אֵילִים *bᵉ'ēr 'êlîm*, n.pr.loc. GK: 935 [→ 875+352; cf. 352]. Beer Elim, "*cistern, well of Elim*":– Beer-elim [1]

880 בְּאֵרָה *bᵉ'ērâ*, n.pr.m. GK: 939 [→ 875]. Beerah, "*cistern, well*":– Beerah [1]

881 בְּאֵרוֹת *bᵉ'ērôt*, n.pr.loc. GK: 940 [→ 886; cf. 875]. Beeroth, "*cisterns, wells*":– Beeroth [6]

882 בְּאֵרִי *bᵉ'ērî*, n.pr.m. GK: 941 [→ 875]. Beeri, "*[my] cistern, well*":– Beeri [2]

883 בְּאֵר לַחַי רֹאִי *bᵉ'ēr laḥay rō'î*, n.pr.loc. GK: 936 [→ 875+3807.1+2421]. Beer Lahai Roi, "*well that belongs to the Living One seeing me*":– well Lahai-roi [2], Beer-lahai-roi [1]

884 בְּאֵר שֶׁבַע *bᵉ'ēr šeba'*, n.pr.loc. GK: 937 [→ 875+7651]. Beersheba, "*seventh well*":– Beer-sheba [34]

885 בְּאֵרֹת בְּנֵי־יַעֲקָן *bᵉ'ērōt bᵉnê-yaᵃqān*, n.pr.loc. GK: 942 [→ 875+1121+3292]. Beeroth Bene-Jaakan, "*wells of the sons of Jaakan*":–

886 בְּאֵרֹתִי *bᵉ'ērōtî*, a.g. GK: 943 [→ 881; cf. 1307]. Beerothite, "*of Beeroth*":– Beerothite [4], Beerothites [1]

887 בָּאַשׁ *bā'aš*, v. GK: 944 [→ 889, 891, 890; cf. 888]. [Q] to stink, smell; [N] to become a stench; [H] to make a stench, to cause a bad smell; [Ht] to make oneself a stench:– stank [3], stink [3], made utterly to abhor (+887) [2], abhorred [1], had in abomination [1], loathsome [1], made odious [1], made to be abhorred [1], make to stink [1], stinketh [1], stinking savour [1], stunk [1]

888 בְּאֵשׁ *bᵉ'ēš* (Aram.), v. GK: 10091 [→ 873; cf. 887]. [P] to be distressed:– displeased [1]

889 בְּאֹשׁ *bᵉ'ōš*, n.m. GK: 945 [→ 887]. stench, stink:– stink [3]

890 בָּאְשָׁה *bo'šâ*, n.f. GK: 947 [→ 887]. weeds, a plant of no value, variously identified:– cockle [1]

891 בְּאֻשִׁים *bᵉ'uš*, n.[m.]pl. GK: 946 [→ 887]. bad (putrid) fruit, rotten grapes:– wild grapes [2]

892 בָּבָה *bābâ*, n.f. GK: 949 [→ 893?]. apple (of the eye), eyeball, formally, "little child of the eye," a term of endearment:– apple [1]

893 בֵּבַי *bēbay*, n.pr.m. GK: 950 [→ 892?]. Bebai, "*child*":– Bebai [6]

894 בָּבֶל *bābel*, n.pr.loc. GK: 951 [cf. 3778; cf. 895]. Babel, Babylon, "*gate of god[s]*; [Ge 11:9] *confused*":– Babylon [249], Babylon's [8], Babylonians (+1121) [3], Babel [2]

895 בָּבֶל *bābel* (Aram.), n.pr.loc. GK: 10093 [→ 896; cf. 894]. Babylon, "*gate of god(s)*":– Babylon [25]

896 בָּבְלִי *bābᵉlî* (Aram.), a.g. GK: 10094 [→ 895]. Babylonian, from Babylon:– Babylonians [1]

897 בַּג *bag*, var. GK: 952 [cf. 957, 6598?]. plunder, loot, despoiling:–

898 בָּגַד *bāgad*, v. GK: 953 [→ 899, 900, 901]. [Q] to be unfaithful, be faithless; to betray, act treacherously:– dealt treacherously [10], transgressors [8], deal treacherously [6], treacherous [3], deal very treacherously (+898) [2], dealt deceitfully [2], dealt very treacherously (+898) [2], transgressor [2], treacherous dealers [2], deal very treacherously (+899) [1], dealest treacherously [1], dealeth treacherously [1], dealt unfaithfully [1], dealt very treacherously (+899) [1], offend [1], transgressed [1], transgresseth [1], transgress [1], treacherous dealer [1], treacherously [1], unfaithful [1]

899 בֶּגֶד *beged*, n.m. GK: 954 & 955 [→ 898]. clothing, garment, cloak, robe; treachery:– clothes [73], garments [70], garment [37], raiment [12], cloth [9], apparel [4], robes [4], wardrobe [2], clothing [1], deal very treacherously (+898) [1], dealt very treacherously (+898) [1], lap [1], rags [1], vestures [1]

900 בֹּגְדוֹת *bōgᵉdôt*, n.pl.abst. GK: 956 [→ 898]. treachery:– treacherous [1]

901 בָּגוֹד *bāgôd*, a. GK: 957 [→ 898]. unfaithful, pertaining to being adulterous, with the implication that the actions were deceptive and treacherous:– treacherous [2]

902 בִּגְוַי *bigway*, n.pr.m. GK: 958. Bigvai, "*fortunate*":– Bigvai [6]

903 בִּגְתָא *bigtā'*, n.pr.m. GK: 960 [→ 904]. Bigtha, "*gift of God*":– Bigtha [1]

904 בִּגְתָן *bigtān* or בִּגְתָנָא *bigtānā'*, n.pr.m. GK: 961 & 962 [→ 903]. Bigthana, "*gift of God*":– Bigthana [1], Bigthan [1]

905 בַּד *bad*, n.m. GK: 963 & 964 [→ 909]. part, member, limb; pole, bar; (adv.) alone, apart, only; in addition to:– alone (+3807.1) [39], only (+3807.1) [39], staves [37], beside (+4480+3807.1) [30], besides (+4480+3807.1) [13], apart (+3807.1) [11], by themselves (+3807.1) [6], by themselves (+3807.1+3963.1) [4], beside (+3807.1) [3], branches [3], by himself (+2050.2+3807.1) [3], each a like (+905+871.1) [2], strength [2], alone (+2050.2+3807.1) [1], bars [1], beside (+5921+3807.1) [1], besides (+3807.1) [1], by himself (+3807.1) [1], by themselves (+2006.1+3807.1) [1], by themselves (+3807.1+5089.1) [1], except (+3807.1) [1], myself (+2967.1) [1]

906 בַּד *bad*, n.[m.]. GK: 965 [→ 909]. formally, a "(cut) piece (of a garment)," likely linen of the flax plant:– linen [23]

907 בַּד *bad*, n.m. GK: 966 & 967 [→ 908]. boasting, idle talk; false prophet, with a focus on empty, idle talk:– lies [3], liars [2], parts [1]

908 בָּדָא *bādā'*, v. GK: 968 [→ 907]. [Q] to choose; to make up, devise:– devised [1], feignest [1]

909 בָּדַד *bādad*, v. GK: 969 [→ 905, 906, 910]. [Q] to be alone, isolated:– alone [3]

910 בָּדָד *bādād*, n.[m.]. GK: 970 [→ 909]. alone, by oneself, apart:– alone [6], alone (+3807.1) [1], desolate [1], only (+3807.1) [1], solitarily (+3807.1) [1], solitary [1]

911 בְּדַד *bᵉdad*, n.pr.m. GK: 971. Bedad, "*solitary*":– Bedad [2]

912 בֵּדְיָה *bēdᵉyâ*, n.pr.m. GK: 973. Bedeiah, "*servant of Yahweh*":– Bedeiah [1]

913 בְּדִיל *bᵉdîl*, n.[m.]. GK: 974 & 975 [→ 914]. tin, an inexpensive metal that could be used as a medium of exchange; impurities, slag, the dross of the smelting process, used as a figure of moral and ceremonial impurities:– tin [5], plummet (+68) [1]

914 בָּדַל *bādal*, v. GK: 976 [→ 913, 915, 3995]. [N] separate oneself, be expelled; [H] to separate, sever completely, distinguish between:– separated [17], separate [7], divide [4], put difference [3], divide asunder [2], divided [2], severed [2], utterly separated (+914) [2], make a difference [1], make a separation [1], sever out [1]

915 בָּדָל *bādāl*, n.[m.]. GK: 977 [→ 914]. piece (of an ear):– piece [1]

916 בְּדֹלַח *bᵉdōlaḥ*, n.[m.]. GK: 978. aromatic resin; some sources: bdellium-gum (an aromatic, yellowish gum):– bdellium [2]

917 בְּדָן *bᵉdān*, n.pr.m. GK: 979. Bedan, "*son of judgment*":– Bedan [2]

918 בָּדַק *bādaq*, v.den. GK: 980 [→ 919; cf. 1333]. [Q] to repair, mend:– repair [1]

919 בֶּדֶק *bedeq*, n.m. GK: 981 [→ 918]. breach (of a temple or a ship):– breaches [7], calkers (+2388) [2], breach [1]

920 בִּדְקַר *bidqar*, n.pr.m. GK: 982 [→ 1121?+1857?]. Bidkar, "*son of Deker [piercing]*":– Bidkar [1]

921 בְּדַר *bᵉdar* (Aram.), v. GK: 10095 [cf. 967, 6340]. [Pa] to scatter:– scatter [1]

922 בֹּהוּ *bōhû*, n.[m.]. GK: 983. emptiness, desolation, a void associated with chaos; "empty and void" is a state of total chaos:– void [2], emptiness [1]

923 בַּהַט *bahaṭ*, n.[m.]. GK: 985. porphyry (or some other precious stone):– red [1]

924 בְּהִילוּ *bᵉhîlû* (Aram.), n.f. GK: 10096 [→ 927; cf. 926]. hurry, haste; (as adv.) immediately:– haste [1]

925 בָּהִיר *bāhîr*, a. GK: 986 [→ 934]. bright, brilliant:– bright [1]

926 בָּהַל *bāhal*, v. GK: 987 [→ 928; cf. 1089; cf. 927, cf. 927]. [N] to be terrified, alarmed, dismayed, bewildered; [P] to make afraid, terrify; to make haste; [Pu] to be hastened, made to hurry; to cause terror; to cause to hurry:– troubled [13], vexed [3], afraid [2], amazed [2], hasty [2], troubleth [2], trouble [2], affrighted [1], dismayed [1], gotten hastily [1], hasted [1], hastened [1], hasteth [1], make afraid [1], make haste [1], rash [1], speedily [1], speedy [1], thrust out [1], vex [1]

927 בְּהַל *bᵉhal* (Aram.), v. GK: 10097 & 10218 [→ 924; cf. 926]. [Pa] to frighten, terrify; [Htpe] to hurry, be at once; [Htpa] to be frightened:– troubled [6], haste [3], trouble [2]

928 בֶּהָלָה *behālâ*, n.f. GK: 988 [→ 926; cf. 924]. sudden terror; misfortune:– trouble [2], terrors [1], terror [1]

929 בְּהֵמָה *bᵉhēmâ*, n.f. GK: 989 [→ 930?]. beast, animal, livestock, herds, cattle:– beast [84], cattle [53], beasts [51], beasts (+929+2050.1) [2]

930 בְּהֵמוֹת *bᵉhēmôt*, n.m. GK: 990 [→ 929?]. behemoth; sources variously identify as hippopotamus, crocodile, elephant; the plural form may indicate this is the ultimate creature, a composite description of the strongest attributes of the animal kingdom:– behemoth [1]

931 בֹּהֶן *bōhen*, n.[f.]. GK: 984 & 991 [→ 932?]. thumb, big toe:– great toe [6], thumb [6], thumbs (+3027) [2], great toes [1], thumbs [1]

932 בֹּהַן *bōhan*, n.pr.m. GK: 992 [→ 931?]. Bohan, "*thumb, big toe*":– Bohan [2]

933 בֹּהַק *bōhaq*, n.m. GK: 993. harmless rash:– freckled spot [1]

934 בַּהֶרֶת *baheret*, n.f. GK: 994 [→ 925]. spot, bright spot (on the skin):– bright spot [9], bright spots [3]

935 בּוֹא ***bô'***, v. GK: 995 [→ 872, 3996, 3997, 4126, 8393]. [Q] to come, go; [H] to bring, take; [Ho] to be brought:– come [627], came [621], brought [234], bring [222], go [88], cometh [83], enter [66], went [59], go in [58], went in [53], come in [39], entered [35], came in [31], brought in [25], bring in [23], comest [20], coming [14], goest [12], enter in [11], put [11], entering [10], carried [9], camest [8], come to pass [8], carry [7], entereth [7], get [7], goeth [7], gone [7], bringeth [6], certainly come (+935) [6], going down [6], bringing [5], cometh in [5], coming in [5], entering in [5], goeth in [5], stricken [5], attained [4], came to pass [4], down [4], go down [4], went down [4], go into [3], goeth down [3], apply [2], besieged (+4692+871.1+1886.1) [2], brought to pass [2], broughtest in [2], broughtest [2], come in (+935) [2], come upon [2], comest in [2], cometh surely to pass (+935) [2], doubtless come again (+935) [2], entered in [2], entrance [2], followeth (+310) [2], gat [2], gone in [2], indeed come (+935) [2], led [2], surely come (+935) [2], well stricken [2], abide (+871.1) [1], abideth (+871.1) [1], befell (+5921) [1], bring forth [1], bring to pass [1], bringest [1], bringing in [1], brought into [1], brought up [1], called for [1], came unto [1], came up [1], carried into [1], cause to come [1], cause to enter [1], cause to go down [1], caused to enter [1], cometh to pass [1], departed [1], eaten (+413+7130) [1], eaten up (+413+7130) [1], employ (+4480+6440) [1], enter into [1], entered into [1], entereth into [1], entereth in [1], fallen [1], fetch [1], follow (+310) [1], gave [1], get in [1], go in to [1], goest in [1], going [1], gone down [1], granted [1], had (+413) [1], have [1], invade (+871.1) [1], invaded (+871.1) [1], laid [1], lifted [1], mentioned [1], pulled in [1], pulled [1], resort [1], run down [1], runneth [1], send [1], set [1], taken [1], take [1], took in [1], way [1], went forward [1]

בּוּב ***bûb***. See 892, 5014.

936 בּוּז ***bûz***, v. GK: 996 [→ 937, 938?, 939, 940, 941]. [Q] to despise, scorn, deride:– despiseth [4], despise [4], despised [2], utterly contemned (+936) [2]

937 בּוּז ***bûz***, n.m. GK: 997 [→ 936]. contempt:– contempt [7], despised [2], contemptuously [1], shamed [1]

938 בּוּז ***bûz***, n.pr.m. GK: 998 [→ 936?]. Buz, "*contempt*":– Buz [3]

939 בּוּזָה ***bûzâ***, n.f. GK: 999 [→ 936]. contempt:– despised [1]

940 בּוּזִי ***bûzî***, a.g. GK: 1000 [→ 941; cf. 936]. Buzite, "*of Buz*":– Buzite [2]

941 בּוּזִי ***bûzî***, n.pr.m. GK: 1001 [→ 940; cf. 936]. Buzi, "*contempt*":– Buzi [1]

942 בַּוַּי ***bawway***, n.pr.m. GK: 1002 [cf. 1131]. Bavvai, cf. 1131:– Bavai [1]

943 בּוּךְ ***bûk***, v. GK: 1003 [→ 3998]. [N] to wander around, mill about; to be bewildered:– perplexed [2], entangled [1]

944 בּוּל ***bûl***, n.[m.]. GK: 1005 & 1006 [→ 8398?]. piece of wood, in context likely referring to a block of wood that has been crafted into an idol; produce, in context produce as a gift or tribute:– food [1], stock [1]

945 בּוּל ***bûl***, n.[m.]. GK: 1004. Bul (month), the eighth month of the Canaanite calendar (modern October-November):– Bul [1]

בּוּם ***bûm***. See 1116.

946 בּוּנָה ***bûnâ***, n.pr.m. GK: 1007. Bunah:– Bunah [1]

בּוּנִי ***bûnî***. See 1138.

947 בּוּס ***bûs***, v. GK: 1008 [→ 4001, 8395]. [Q, P] to trample down; loathe; [Htpol] to kick about; [Ho] to be trodden down:– tread down [4], polluted [2], loatheth [1], tread under foot [1], tread under [1], trodden down [1], trodden under feet [1], trodden under foot [1]

948 בּוּץ ***bûṣ***, n.[m.]. GK: 1009 [→ 949?, 1000]. fine linen; white linen:– fine linen [7], white linen [1]

949 בּוֹצֵץ ***bôṣēṣ***, n.pr.loc. GK: 1010 [→ 948? *or* 1206?]. Bozez, "*oozing place*":– Bozez [1]

950 בּוּקָה ***bûqâ***, n.f. GK: 1011 [→ 4003, 5802?]. pillage, that which is made desolate and emptied:– empty [1]

951 בּוֹקֵר ***bôqēr***, n.m.den. GK: 1012 [→ 1241; cf. 1239]. herdsman, usually a shepherd:– herdman [1]

952 בּוּר ***bûr***, v. GK: 1013. [Q] to conclude:– declare [1]

953 בּוֹר ***bôr***, n.m. GK: 1014 [→ 877; cf. 875, 3565, 6228]. pit, well, cistern; dungeon; a cistern is usually a shaft in the ground, hewn out of soft stone and plastered to hold water:– pit [41], dungeon [11], well [6], cistern [4], wells [3], cisterns [2], dungeon (+1004) [1], dungeon (+1004+1886.1) [1], fountain [1], pits [1]

954 בּוֹשׁ ***bôš***, v. GK: 1017 & 1018 [→ 955, 1317, 1322, 4016]. [Q] to be put to shame, be ashamed, be disgraced; [Polal] to be delayed, be long; [Htpolal] to feel ashamed; [H] to bring shame, to cause disgrace, act shamefully:– ashamed [74], confounded [29], at all ashamed (+954) [4], causeth shame [4], put to shame [3], shamed [2], bringeth to shame [1], delayed [1], done shamefully [1], greatly ashamed (+1322) [1], long [1], maketh ashamed [1], put to confusion [1], shame [1]

955 בּוּשָׁה ***bûšâ***, n.f. GK: 1019 [→ 954]. shame:– shame [4]

956 בִּית ***bît*** (Aram.), v.den. GK: 10102 [→ 1005]. [P] to spend the night:– passed the night [1]

957 בַּז ***baz***, n.[m.]. GK: 1020 [→ 4122; cf. 962]. plunder, loot, despoiling:– prey [15], spoil [4], spoiled [2], take a prey (+962) [2], booty [1], take prey (+962) [1]

958 בָּזָא ***bāzā'***, v. GK: 1021. [Q] to divide, likely referring to the washing out of rivers by force of the waters:– spoiled [2]

959 בָּזָה ***bāzâ***, v. GK: 1022 [→ 960, 963, 964, 5240]. [Q] to despise, scorn, ridicule, show contempt for; [Qp] to be despised; [N] to be despised, be contemptible; [H] to cause to despise:– despised [26], despise [6], despiseth [4], contemptible [3], contemned [1], disdained [1], scorn [1], vile person [1]

960 בָּזֹה ***bāzōh***, v.inf. GK: 1022 [→ 959]. inf. of 959: to despise, scorn, ridicule, show contempt for:– despiseth [1]

961 בִּזָּה ***bizzâ***, n.f. GK: 1023 [→ 962]. plunder, booty, spoils:– spoil [6], prey [4]

962 בָּזַז ***bāzaz***, v. GK: 1024 [→ 957, 961]. [Q] to plunder, loot, carry off spoils; [Qp, N, Pu] to be plundered:– spoiled [5], spoil [5], took for a prey [4], robbed [3], rob [3], take [3], prey [2], take a prey (+957) [2], take the spoil [2], utterly spoiled (+962) [2], caught [1], gathering [1], make a prey [1], prey upon [1], robbers [1], take away [1], take for a prey [1], take prey (+957) [1], taken spoil [1], took away [1], took spoil [1], took [1]

963 בִּזָּיוֹן ***bizzāyôn***, n.[m.]. GK: 1025 [→ 964; cf. 959]. disrespect, contempt:– contempt [1]

964 בִּזְיוֹתְיָה ***bizyôtᵉyâ***, n.pr.loc. GK: 1026 [→ 963+3068]. Biziothiah, "*contempt of Yahweh*":– Bizjothjah [1]

965 בָּזָק ***bāzāq***, n.[m.]. GK: 1027. flashes of lightning, lightning:– flash of lightning [1]

966 בֶּזֶק ***bezeq***, n.pr.loc. GK: 1028 [→ 137]. Bezek, "*scattering, sowing*":– Bezek [3]

967 בָּזַר ***bāzar***, v. GK: 1029 [cf. 6340; cf. 921]. [Q] to distribute; [P] to scatter:– scatter [2]

968 בִּזְּתָא ***bizzᵉtā'***, n.pr.m. GK: 1030. Biztha, "[perhaps] *eunuch* or *bound*":– Biztha [1]

969 בָּחוֹן ***bāḥôn***, n.[m.]. GK: 1031 [→ 974]. tester of metals, assayer:– tower [1]

970 בָּחוּר ***bāḥûr***, n.m. GK: 1033 & 1037 [→ 979]. young man, able (fighting) man; bridegroom:– young men [35], young man [5], young [2], choice [1], chosen [1]

בְּחוּרוֹת ***bᵉḥûrôt***. See 979.

בַּחֻרִים ***baḥûrîm***. See 980.

971 בַּחוּן ***baḥûn***, n.[m.]. GK: 1032 & 1039 [→ 975]. siege tower, a moveable military engine used to attack a walled city:– towers [1]

972 בָּחִיר ***bāḥîr***, n.m. GK: 1040 [→ 977]. chosen one, one preferred or selected by God with an implication of receiving special favor:– chosen [8], elect [4], choose [1]

973 בָּחַל ***bāḥal***, v. GK: 1041 & 1042. [Q] to detest, disdain, feel an attitude of loathing; [Pu] to be gotten by greed:– abhorred [1]

974 בָּחַן ***bāḥan***, v. GK: 1043 [→ 969, 976]. [Q] to test, try, probe, examine; [Qp, N, Pu] to be tested; to test and learn the genuineness of an object, fig. of assaying a metal to determine its purity or nature:– try [8], proved [6], tried [4], trieth [4], triest [3], examine [1], prove [1], tempt [1], trial [1]

975 בַּחַן ***baḥan***, n.[m.]. GK: 1044 [→ 971]. watchtower:– towers [1]

976 בֹּחַן ***bōḥan***, n.[m.]. GK: 1046 [→ 974]. tested (stone):– tried [1]

977 בָּחַר ***bāḥar***, v. GK: 1034 & 1047 & 1048 [→ 972, 2984, 4004, 4005, 4006]. [Q] to choose, select, desire, prefer; to enter into a covenant; [Qp, N] to be chosen, choice, the best, preferred; [Pu] to be joined:– chosen [78], choose [50], chose [22], choice [6], choose out [3], chooseth [3], choosest [2], chose out [2], acceptable [1], appoint [1], excellent [1], rather [1], require [1]

בָּחֻר ***bāḥur***. See 970.

978 בַּחֲרוּמִי ***baḥᵃrûmî***, a.g. GK: 1049. Baharumite:– Baharumite [1]

979 בְּחוּרוֹת ***bᵉḥûrôt*** or בְּחוּרִים ***bᵉḥûrîm***, n.f.&m.pl.abst. GK: 1035 & 1036 [→ 970]. youth, as a state of being:– youth [2], young men [1]

980 בַּחוּרִים ***baḥûrîm***, n.pr.loc. GK: 1038 [cf. 1273]. Bahurim, "*young men*":– Bahurim [5]

981 בָּטָא ***bāṭā'***, v. GK: 1051 [→ 4008]. [Q, P] to speak thoughtlessly, to speak rashly, recklessly:– pronounce [1], pronouncing [1], spake unadvisedly [1], speaketh [1]

982 בָּטַח ***bāṭaḥ*** or בָּטֵחַ ***bāṭaḥ***, v. GK: 1053 & 1054 [→ 20, 983, 985, 987, 986, 4009]. [Q] to trust, rely on, put confidence in; to stumble, fall to the ground; [Qp] to be confident; [H] to lead to believe, make trust:– trust [46], trusted [18], trusteth [14], put trust [9], trustest [6], put confidence [4], secure [4], careless [3], trustedst [3], confident [2], make trust [2], putteth trust [2], bold [1], caused to trust [1], hoped [1], make hope [1], makest to trust [1], sure [1], trusting [1]

983 בֶּטַח ***beṭaḥ***, n.[m.]. GK: 1055 [→ 982]. safety, security:– safely (+3807.1) [14], safety [8], carelessly (+3807.1) [3], safely [3], careless [2], safe [2], assurance [1], boldly [1], confidence [1], hope [1], in safety [1], securely (+3807.1) [1], securely [1], secure [1], surely [1], without care [1]

984 בֶּטַח ***beṭaḥ***, n.pr.loc. GK: 1056 [cf. 2880]. Betah, cf. 2875:– Betah [1]

985 בִּטְחָה ***biṭḥâ***, n.f. GK: 1057 [→ 982]. trust, confidence:– confidence [1]

986 בִּטָּחוֹן ***biṭṭāḥôn***, n.m. GK: 1059 [→ 982]. confidence, hope:– confidence [2], hope [1]

987 בַּטֻּחָה ***baṭṭuḥâ***, n.f.pl. GK: 1058 [→ 982]. security, safety:– secure [1]

988 בָּטַל ***bāṭal***, v. GK: 1060 [cf. 989]. [Q] to cease (activity):– cease [1]

989 בְּטֵל ***bᵉṭal*** (Aram.), v. GK: 10098 [cf. 988]. [P] to come to a standstill; [Pa] to stop (another):– cause to cease [2], ceased [2], hindered [1], made to cease [1]

990 בֶּטֶן ***beṭen***, n.f. GK: 1061. inmost part, viscera: abdomen, belly, stomach, womb; by extension: the inner person, the heart, the seat of emotion, thought, and desire:– womb [31], belly [30], body [8], as soon as born (+4480) [1], within (+871.1) [1], within [1]

991 בֶּטֶן ***beṭen***, n.pr.loc. GK: 1062 [cf. 992?]. Beten, "*womb, bowels*":– Beten [1]

992 בָּטְנָה ***boṭnâ***, n.[m.].[pl. GK: 1063 [cf. 991?, 993?]. pistachio nut:– nuts [1]

993 בְּטֹנִים ***bᵉṭōnîm***, n.pr.loc. GK: 1064 [cf. 992?]. Betonim, "*pistachio nuts*":– Betonim [1]

994 בִּי ***bî***, pt.entreaty. GK: 1065. O!, please!:– O [11], alas [1]

995 בִּין ***bîn***, v. GK: 1067 [→ 996, 998, 2985?, 8394]. [Q] to understand, discern, realize; be prudent; [N] to be discerning, be understanding; [Pol] to care for; to have skill, insight; to instruct, explain; [Htpolel/Htpolal] to look closely, consider with full attention, ponder:– understand [36], understanding [18], consider [17], understood [11], prudent [8], give understanding [5], hath understanding [5], understandeth [5], regard [4], make to understand [3], perceived [3], perceive [3], wise [3], caused to understand [2], consider diligently (+995) [2], considering [2], discern [2], discreet [2], giveth understanding [2], instructed [2], taught [2], understandest [2], attended [1], cause to understand [1], consider perfectly (+998) [1], considered (+413) [1], considereth [1], cunning [1], dealt wisely [1], diligently consider [1], directeth [1], discerned [1], eloquent [1], feel [1], had understanding [1], have understanding [1], having understanding [1], informed [1], instruct [1], intelligence [1], know [1], looketh well [1], make understand [1], mark [1], perceiveth [1], regardest [1], regardeth [1], skilful [1], skill [1], teacher [1], think [1], understand (+3045) [1], viewed [1]

996 בַּיִן ***bayin***, subst. & pp. GK: 1068 [→ 1143; cf. 995; cf. 997]. between; separate from; whether ... or:– between [194], among [28], betwixt [14], at even (+6153+1886.1) [6], at [6], from [4], in [4], whether [3], among (+413) [2], with [2], among (+4480) [1], among (+5921) [1], among (+871.1) [1], amongst [1], asunder [1], midst [1], once in [1], out of (+4480) [1], part (+5337) [1], spake unto [1], within [1]

997 בֵּין **bên** (Aram.), pp. GK: 10099 [cf. 996]. between, among:– among [1], between [1]

998 בִּינָה **bînâ**, n.f. GK: 1069 [→ 995; cf. 999]. understanding, insight, discernment, good sense, wisdom, usually referring to the wisdom that responds to the Lord and his instruction:– understanding [30], wisdom [2], come to understanding (+3045) [1], consider perfectly (+995) [1], had understanding (+3045) [1], knowledge [1], meaning [1], understand [1]

999 בִּינָה **bînâ** (Aram.), n.f. GK: 10100 [cf. 998]. discernment, insight:– understanding [1]

1000 בֵּיצָה **bêṣâ**, n.f. GK: 1070 [→ 948]. egg:– eggs [6]

1001 בִּירָה **bîrâ** (Aram.), n.f. GK: 10101 [cf. 1002]. citadel, fortress:– palace [1]

1002 בִּירָה **bîrâ**, n.f. GK: 1072 [cf. 1003; cf. 1001]. citadel, fort, palatial structure:– palace [16]

1003 בִּירָנִיָּה **bîrāniyyâ**, n.f. GK: 1073 [cf. 1002]. fortified place:– castles [2]

1004 בַּיִת **bayit**, n.m. GK: 1074 & 1428 [→ 1006, 1055; cf. 1005]. house, home; of royalty: palace; of deity: temple; a specific part of a house: room; place; by extension: household, family, clan, tribe; woven garment:– house [1766], houses [118], household [47], home [25], within (+4480) [14], temple [11], places [9], prison (+5470+1886.1) [8], households [7], place [7], inward (+1886.5) [5], prison (+3608+1886.1) [4], families (+1) [2], families [2], prison (+3608) [2], prison (+3628+1886.1) [2], within (+4480+1886.1) [2], contain [1], court [1], door [1], dungeon (+953) [1], dungeon (+953+1886.1) [1], family [1], hangings [1], homeborn (+3211) [1], inside [1], inward (+4480+1886.1) [1], inward [1], palace [1], prison (+612+1886.1) [1], prison (+631+1886.1) [1], prison (+6486+1886.1) [1], steward (+834+5921) [1], storehouse (+214) [1], tablets (+5315) [1], ward (+4931) [1], web [1], winterhouse (+2779) [1], within (+1886.1+3807.1) [1], within (+1886.5) [1], within (+4480+1886.5) [1], within (+4480+3807.1) [1], within (+871.1+1886.1) [1], within [1], without (+413+4480) [1]

1005 בַּיִת **bayit** (Aram.), n.m. GK: 10103 [→ 956; cf. 1004]. a place of residence: house, home; residence of royalty: palace; residence of God or a god: temple:– house [42], houses [2]

Heb

1006 בַּיִת **bayit**, n.m. GK: 1074 [→ 1004]. same as 1004: Bayit, "*house*":– Bajith [1]

1007 בֵּית אָוֶן **bêt 'āwen**, n.pr.loc. GK: 1077 [→ 1004+205]. Beth Aven, "*house of idolatry*":– Beth-aven [7]

1008 בֵּית־אֵל **bêt-'ēl**, n.pr.loc. GK: 1078 [→ 1004+410]. Bethel, "*temple [house] of God [El]*":– Beth-el [66]

1009 בֵּית אַרְבֵאל **bêt 'arbē'l**, n.pr.loc. GK: 1079 [→ 1004]. Beth Arbel, "*house of Arbel*":– Beth-arbel [1]

1010 בֵּית בַּעַל מְעוֹן **bêt ba'al mᵉ'ôn** or בֵּית מְעוֹן **bêt mᵉ'ôn**, n.pr.loc. GK: 1081 & 1110 [→ 1004+1186]. Beth Baal Meon, "*house of Baal Meon*"; Beth Meon, "*house of habitation*":– Beth-baal-meon [1], Beth-meon [1]

1011 בֵּית בִּרְאִי **bêt bir'î**, n.pr.loc. GK: 1082 [→ 1004]. Beth Biri, "*house of Biri* or *den of a lioness*":– Beth-birei [1]

1012 בֵּית בָּרָה **bêt bārâ**, n.pr.loc. GK: 1083 [→ 1004]. Beth Barah, "*house of Barah [the river ford]*":– Beth-barah [2]

1013 בֵּית־גָּדֵר **bêt-gādēr**, n.pr.loc. GK: 1084 [→ 1004+1445; cf. 1451]. Beth Gader, "*house of Gader* or *site of a stone hedge*":– Beth-gader [1]

1014 בֵּית גָּמוּל **bêt gāmûl**, n.pr.loc. GK: 1085 [→ 1004+1580]. Beth Gamul, "*house of recompense*":– Beth-gamul [1]

1015 בֵּית דִּבְלָתַיִם **bêt diblātayim**, n.pr.loc. GK: 1086 [→ 1004]. Beth Diblathaim, "*house of Diblathaim*":– Beth-diblathaim [1]

1016 בֵּית־דָּגוֹן **bêt-dāgôn**, n.pr.loc. GK: 1087 [→ 1004+1712]. Beth Dagon, "*temple [house] of Dagon*":– Beth-dagon [2]

1017 בֵּית הָאֱלִי **bêt hā'ᵉlî**, a.g. GK: 1088 [→ 1004+430; cf. 433]. the Bethelite, "*of Bethel*":– Bethelite [1]

1018 בֵּית הָאֵצֶל **bêt hā'ēṣel**, n.pr.loc. GK: 1089 [→ 1004+1886.1]. Beth Ezel, "*house of Ezel* or *site nearby*":– Beth-ezel [1]

1019 בֵּית הַגִּלְגָּל **bêt haggilgāl**, n.pr.loc. GK: 1090 [→ 1004+1886.1+1537]. Beth Gilgal:–

1020 בֵּית הַיְשִׁימוֹת **bêt hayᵉšîmôt**, n.pr.loc. GK: 1093 [→ 1004]. Beth Jeshimoth, "*house of Jeshimoth* or *site of desolation*":– Beth-jeshimoth [3], Beth-jesimoth [1]

1021 בֵּית־הַכֶּרֶם **bêt-hakkerem**, n.pr.loc. GK: 1094 [→ 1004]. Beth Hakkerem, "*house of Hakkerem* or *site of vineyard*":– Beth-haccerem [2]

1022 בֵּית־הַלַּחְמִי **bêt-hallaḥmî**, a.g. GK: 1095 [→ 1004]. the Bethlehemite, "*of Bethlehem*":– Beth-lehemite [4]

1023 בֵּית הַמֶּרְחָק **bêt hammerḥāq**, n.pr.loc. GK: 1092 [→ 1004+1886.1+7368]. Beth Hamerhaq:–

1024 בֵּית־הַמַּרְכָּבוֹת **bêt-hammarkābôt** or בֵּית מַרְכָּבוֹת **bêt markābôt**, n.pr.loc. GK: 1096 & 1112 [→ 1004]. Beth Marcaboth, "*site [house] of Marcaboth [chariots]*":– Beth-marcaboth [2]

1025 בֵּית הָעֵמֶק **bêt hā'ēmeq**, n.pr.loc. GK: 1097 [→ 1004+1886.1+6010]. Beth Emek, "*house of Emek* or *site of the valley*":– Beth-emek [1]

1026 בֵּית הָעֲרָבָה **bêt hā'ᵃrābâ**, n.pr.loc. GK: 1098 [→ 1004]. Beth Arabah, "*house of Arabah [desert, plain]*":– Beth-arabah [3]

1027 בֵּית הָרָם **bêt hārām**, n.pr.loc. GK: 1099 [→ 1004]. Beth Haram:– Beth-aram [1]

1028 בֵּית הָרָן **bêt hārān**, n.pr.loc. GK: 1100 [→ 1004+2039]. Beth Haran, "*house of the mountaineer*":– Beth-haran [1]

1029 בֵּית הַשִּׁטָּה **bêt haššiṭṭâ**, n.pr.loc. GK: 1101 [→ 1004]. Beth Shittah, "*house of Shittah [acacias]*":– Beth-shittah [1]

1030 בֵּית־שִׁמְשִׁי **bêt-šimšî**, a.g. GK: 1128 [→ 1004]. of Beth Shemesh:– Beth-shemite [2]

1031 בֵּית־חָגְלָה **bêt-ḥoglâ**, n.pr.loc. GK: 1102 [→ 1004+2295]. Beth Hoglah, "*house of Hoglah* or *site of the partridge*":– Beth-hoglah [2], Beth-hogla [1]

1032 בֵּית־חוֹרוֹן **bêt-ḥôrôn**, n.pr.loc. GK: 1103 [→ 1004]. Beth Horon, "*house of Horon* or *site of ravine*":– Beth-horon [14]

בֵּית חָנָן **bêt ḥānān**. See 358.

1033 בֵּית כָּר **bêt kār**, n.pr.loc. GK: 1105 [→ 1004]. Beth Car, "*site [house] of a lamb*":– Beth-car [1]

1034 בֵּית לְבָאוֹת **bêt lᵉbā'ôt**, n.pr.loc. GK: 1106 [→ 1004+3822]. Beth Lebaoth, "*house of Lebaoth* or *den of the lioness*":– Beth-lebaoth [1]

1035 בֵּית לֶחֶם **bêt leḥem**, n.pr.loc. GK: 1107 [→ 1004+3899]. Bethlehem, "*house of bread;* [poss.] *temple [house] of Lakhmu*":– Beth-lehem [31], Beth-lehem-judah (+3063) [10]

1036 בֵּית לְעַפְרָה **bêt lᵉ'aprâ**, n.pr.loc. GK: 1108 [→ 1004]. Beth Ophrah, "*house of Ophrah* or *house of dust*":– house of Aphrah [1]

1037 בֵּית מִלּוֹא **bêt millô'**, n.pr.loc. GK: 1109 [→ 1004+4390]. Beth Millo, "*house of Millo* or *site of earth fill*":–

1038 בֵּית מַעֲכָה **bêt ma'ᵃkâ**, n.pr.loc. GK: 1111 [→ 1004+4601]. Beth Maacah:– Beth-maachah [2]

1039 בֵּית נִמְרָה **bêt nimrâ**, n.pr.loc. GK: 1113 [→ 1004+5247]. Beth Nimrah, "*house of Nimrah [spotted leopard]; house of a basin of clear, limpid water*":– Beth-nimrah [2]

1040 בֵּית עֶדֶן **bêt 'eden**, n.pr.loc. GK: 1114 [→ 1004+5729]. Beth Eden, "*house of Eden; garden place*":–

1041 בֵּית־עַזְמָוֶת **bêt-'azmāwet**, n.pr.loc. GK: 1115 [→ 1004+5820]. Beth Azmaveth, "*strong of death; house of Azmaveth [camel fodder]*":– Beth-azmaveth [1]

1042 בֵּית־עֲנוֹת **bêt-'ᵃnôt**, n.pr.loc. GK: 1116 [→ 1004+6067]. Beth Anoth, "*house of Anath [plural]*":– Beth-anoth [1]

1043 בֵּית־עֲנָת **bêt-'ᵃnāt**, n.pr.loc. GK: 1117 [→ 1004+6067]. Beth Anath, "*house of Anath*":– Beth-anath [3]

1044 בֵּית־עֵקֶד **bêt-'ēqed**, n.pr.loc. GK: 1118 [→ 1004]. Beth Eked:– shearing [2]

1045 בֵּית עַשְׁתָּרוֹת **bêt 'aštārôt**, n.pr.loc.?. GK: 1119 [→ 1004+6252]. Beth Ashtaroth, "*temple of the Ashtoreths*":–

1046 בֵּית פֶּלֶט **bêt peleṭ**, n.pr.loc. GK: 1120 [→ 1004+6404]. Beth Pelet, "*house of Pelet [escape]*":– Beth-palet [1], Beth-phelet [1]

1047 בֵּית פְּעוֹר **bêt pᵉ'ôr**, n.pr.loc. GK: 1121 [→ 1004+6465]. Beth Peor, "*house of Peor*":– Beth-peor [4]

1048 בֵּית פַּצֵּץ **bêt paṣṣēṣ**, n.pr.loc. GK: 1122 [→ 1004]. Beth Pazzez:– Beth-pazzez [1]

1049 בֵּית־צוּר **bêt-ṣûr**, n.pr.loc. GK: 1123 [→ 1004+6697]. Beth Zur, "*cliff house*":– Beth-zur [4]

1050 בֵּית־רְחוֹב **bêt-rᵉḥôb**, n.pr.loc. GK: 1124 [→ 1004+7339]. Beth Rehob, "*house of Rehob [main street, market]*":– Beth-rehob [2]

1051 בֵּית רָפָא **bêt rāpā'**, n.pr.[loc.?]. GK: 1125 [→ 1004+7495]. Beth Rapha, "*house of Rapha [healing]*":– Beth-rapha [1]

1052 בֵּית־שְׁאָן **bêt-šᵉ'ān**, n.pr.loc. GK: 1126 [→ 1004]. Beth Shan, "*site [house] of Shan [repose]*":– Beth-shean [6], Beth-shan [3]

1053 בֵּית שֶׁמֶשׁ **bêt šemeš**, n.pr.loc. GK: 1127 [→ 1004+8121]. Beth Shemesh, "*temple [house] of Shemesh*":– Beth-shemesh [21]

1054 בֵּית־תַּפּוּחַ **bêt-tappûaḥ**, n.pr.loc. GK: 1130 [→ 1004+8598]. Beth Tappuah, "*house of Tappuah [apricot; apple]*":– Beth-tappuah [1]

1055 בִּיתָן **bîtān**, n.[m.]. GK: 1131 [→ 1004]. dwelling place, of royalty: palace, with a possible focus on the inner parts of the palace complex:– palace [3]

1056 בָּכָא **bākā'**, n.pr.loc. GK: 1133 [→ 1058]. Baca, "*balsam tree* or *weeping*":– Baca [1]

1057 בָּכָא **bākā'**, n.[m.]. GK: 1132 [→ 1058]. balsam tree; some sources: baka-shrub:– mulberry trees [4]

1058 בָּכָה **bākâ**, v. GK: 1134 [→ 1057, 1056, 1059, 1065, 1068; cf. 1066]. [Q] to weep, wail, cry, sob, mourn; [P] to weep for, mourn for; this can refer to ritual mourning as well as personal sorrow:– wept [51], weep [26], weeping [8], bewail [3], weepeth [3], wept sore (+1065+1419) [3], mourned [2], weep at all (+1058) [2], weep more (+1058) [2], weep sore (+1058) [2], weepeth sore (+1058) [2], wept sore (+1058) [2], bewail (+5921) [1], bewailed [1], complain [1], made lamentation [1], tears [1], weepest [1], wept sore (+1059) [1], wept sore (+1065) [1]

1059 בֶּכֶה **bekeh**, n.[m.]. GK: 1135 [→ 1058]. weeping:– wept sore (+1058) [1]

1060 בְּכֹר **bᵉkōr**, n.m. GK: 1147 [→ 1069]. firstborn, first male offspring (human or animal), the oldest son, with associative meanings of honor, status, prominence, and privileges of inheritance to the firstborn; by extension: one in a special relationship with God:– firstborn [102], firstling [9], eldest [3], eldest son [2], firstlings [1]

1061 בִּכּוּרִים **bikkûrîm**, n.m. GK: 1137 [→ 1069]. firstfruits, first ripened produce:– firstfruits [14], first ripe [2], firstripe figs [1], hasty fruit [1]

1062 בְּכֹרָה **bᵉkōrâ**, n.f. GK: 1148 [→ 1069]. birthright, rights of the firstborn:– birthright [9], firstlings [5], firstborn [1]

1063 בִּכּוּרָה **bikkûrâ**, n.f. GK: 1136 [→ 1069, 1073]. same as 1073: early ripened fruit, usually ripening in June (late fruit ripens in August):– firstripe fruit [1], firstripe [1]

1064 בְּכוֹרַת **bᵉkōrat**, n.pr.m. GK: 1138 [→ 1069]. Becorath, "*firstborn*":– Bechorath [1]

1065 בְּכִי **bᵉkî**, n.m. GK: 1140 [→ 1058]. weeping:– weeping [20], wept sore (+1058+1419) [3], continual weeping (+1065) [2], weep [2], overflowing [1], wept aloud (+5414+6963+871.1) [1], wept sore (+1058) [1]

1066 בֹּכִים **bōkîm**, n.pr.loc. GK: 1141 [cf. 1058]. Bokim, "*weepings*":– Bochim [2]

1067 בְּכִירָה **bᵉkîrâ**, n.f. GK: 1142 [→ 1069]. first born (daughter):– firstborn [6]

1068 בְּכִית **bᵉkît**, n.f. GK: 1143 [→ 1058]. mourning, weeping:– mourning [1]

1069 בָּכַר **bākar**, v. GK: 1144 [→ 1061, 1063, 1064, 1067, 1070, 1071, 1060, 1062, 1072, 1074, 1076, 1075]. [P] bear early fruit; give the rights of the firstborn; [Pu] be made a firstborn (dedication); [H] to bear one's first child:– bring forth new fruit [1], bringeth forth first child [1], firstling [1], make firstborn [1]

1070 בֵּכֶר **bēker**, n.f. GK: 1145 [→ 1071; cf. 1069]. young bull camel:– dromedaries [1]

1071 בֶּכֶר **beker**, n.pr.m. GK: 1146 [→ 1070, 1076, 1075; cf. 1069]. Beker, "*young male camel*":– Becher [5]

1072 בִּכְרָה **bikrâ**, n.f. GK: 1149 [→ 1069]. young cow-camel (having given birth to her first calf):– dromedary [1]

בְּכֹרָה **bᵉkōrâ**. See 1062.

1073 בִּכּוּרָה **bikkûrâ**, n.f. GK: 1136 [→ 1063]. same as 1063: early ripened fruit, usually ripening in June (late fruit ripens in August):– first ripe [1]

1074 בֹּכְרוּ **bōkᵉrû**, n.pr.m. GK: 1150 [→ 1069]. Bokeru, "*his first born*":– Bocheru [2]

1075 בִּכְרִי **bikrî**, n.pr.m. *or* a.g. GK: 1152 [→ 1071; cf. 1069]. Bicri, "*firstborn*":– Bichri [8]

1076 בַּכְרִי **bakrî**, a.g. GK: 1151 [→ 1071; cf. 1069]. Bekerite, "*of Beker*":– Bachrites [1]

1077 בַּל **bal**, adv. GK: 1153 [→ 61, 1107; cf. 1086]. no, not, cannot, never:– not [52], nor (+2050.1) [3], no [3], cannot [2], neither (+2050.1) [2], lest [1], never (+5331+3807.1) [1], never (+5769+3807.1) [1], none [1], nothing (+4100) [1], nothing [1]

1078 בֵּל **bēl**, n.pr.m. GK: 1155 [→ 1112, 1085, 1095, 1114]. Bel, "*Bel*":– Bel [3]

1079 בָּל **bāl** (Aram.), n.[m.]. GK: 10104. heart, mind:– heart [1]

1080 בְּלָה **bᵉlâ** (Aram.), v. GK: 10106 [cf. 1086]. [Pa] to oppress, wear down:– wear out [1]

1081 בַּלְאֲדָן **balʾᵃdān**, n.pr.m. GK: 1156 [→ 4757]. Baladan:– Baladan [2]

1082 בָּלַג **bālag**, v. GK: 1158 [→ 1083, 1084]. [H] to flash (with a focus on suddenness); by extension: to smile, rejoice, gleam, have a cheerful attitude:– comfort [1], recover strength [1], strengtheneth [1], take comfort [1]

1083 בִּלְגָּה **bilgâ**, n.pr.m. GK: 1159 [→ 1082]. Bilgah, "*gleam, smile*":– Bilgah [3]

1084 בִּלְגַּי **bilgay**, n.pr.m. GK: 1160 [→ 1082]. Bilgai, "*gleam, smile*":– Bilgai [1]

1085 בִּלְדַּד **bildad**, n.pr.m. GK: 1161 [→ 1078?+1730]. Bildad, "*Bel has loved*":– Bildad [5]

1086 בָּלָה **bālâ**, v. GK: 1162 [→ 61, 1077, 1087, 1094, 1097, 1107, 1115, 8399; cf. 1080]. [Q] to wear out, waste away; [P] to enjoy, use to the full; to decay; to grow old; to oppress:– waxed old [4], wax old [3], waxen old [2], become old [1], consumeth [1], consume [1], long enjoy [1], made old [1], waste [1]

1087 בָּלֶה **bāleh**, a. GK: 1165 [→ 1086]. old, worn-out:– old [5]

1088 בָּלָה **bālâ**, n.pr.loc. GK: 1163 [cf. 1090]. Balah, "*old, worn out*":– Balah [1]

1089 בָּלַה **bālah**, v. GK: 1164 [→ 1090?, 1091; cf. 926]. [P] to be troubled:–

1090 בִּלְהָה **bilhâ**, n.pr.f. & loc. GK: 1167 & 1168 [→ 1089?, 1172; cf. 1088]. Bilhah:– Bilhah [11]

1091 בַּלָּהָה **ballāhâ**, n.f. GK: 1166 [→ 1089]. sudden terror, horrible end; in some contexts a horrible end refers to death:– terrors [6], terror [3], trouble [1]

1092 בִּלְהָן **bilhān**, n.pr.m. GK: 1169. Bilhan, "*foolish*":– Bilhan [4]

1093 בְּלוֹ **bᵉlô** (Aram.), n.[m.]. GK: 10107. tribute, tax:– tribute [3]

1094 בְּלוֹי **bᵉlôy**, n.[m.]. GK: 1170 [→ 1086]. old, worn-out (things):– old [3]

1095 בֵּלְטְשַׁאצַּר **bēlṭᵉšaʾṣṣar**, n.pr.m. GK: 1171 [→ 1078; cf. 1096]. Belteshazzar, "*protect his life*":– Belteshazzar [2]

1096 בֵּלְטְשַׁאצַּר **bēlṭᵉšaʾṣṣar** (Aram.), n.pr.m. GK: 10108 [cf. 1113; cf. 1095]. Belteshazzar, "*protect his life*":– Belteshazzar [8]

1097 בְּלִי **bᵉlî**, subst. GK: 1172 [→ 1099, 1100; cf. 1086]. lacking, without; nothing:– not [10], without [9], no [5], without (+4480) [5], lack [3], none [3], none (+4480) [2], unwittingly (+1847+871.1) [2], without (+3807.1) [2], base men (+8034) [1], cannot [1], corruption [1], for want of (+4480) [1], ignorantly (+1847+871.1) [1], never (+5769+3807.1) [1], no (+369) [1], no (+4480) [1], no man [1], none (+376) [1], nothing (+3605) [1], nothing (+4100) [1], so long as endureth (+5704) [1], so that (+834+4480) [1], unawares (+1847+871.1) [1], want [1], without (+3509.1) [1], without (+871.1) [1]

1098 בְּלִיל **bᵉlîl**, n.m. GK: 1173. fodder, mash, fermented matter:– corn [1], fodder [1], provender [1]

1099 בְּלִימָה **bᵉlîmâ**, n.[m.]. GK: 1174 [→ 1097+4100]. nothing:–

1100 בְּלִיַּעַל **bᵉliyyaʿal**, n.[m.]. GK: 1175 [→ 1097+3276]. wicked one, vile one, evil one, worthless one, transliterated "Belial"; A "son of Belial" or "man of Belial" is a troublemaker and scoundrel:– Belial [16], wicked [5], ungodly men [2], ungodly [2], evil [1], naughty [1]

1101 בָּלַל **bālal**, v. GK: 1176 [→ 7642?, 8397, 8400; cf. 1104?]. [Q] to confuse; give fodder, feed; pour upon; [Qp] to mix (with); [Htpolal] to be thrown about, shaken back and forth:– mingled [37], confound [2], anointed [1], gave provender [1], mixed [1], tempered [1]

1102 בָּלַם **bālam**, v. GK: 1178. [Q] to be controlled, in check:– held in [1]

1103 בָּלַס **bālas**, v.den. GK: 1179. [Q] to nip (scratch open) unripe sycamore-fig fruit, so as to promote ripening and make more palatable:– gatherer [1]

1104 בָּלַע **bālaʿ**, v. GK: 1180 & 1181 & 1182 [→ 1105, 1106, 1108, 1109, 2991?; cf. 1101?]. [Q] to swallow up; [N] to be swallowed; be befuddled, confused; [P] to swallow up, gulp down, devour, consume; to communicate, spread abroad; confuse, turn away; [Pu] be swallowed up, be devoured; be communicated; to be led astray; [Ht] to be confused thoroughly:– swallowed up [17], swallow up [11], destroy [7], devoured [2], devoureth [2], swallow down [2], at wit's end (+2451+3605) [1], covered [1], destroyed [1], destroying [1], eateth up [1], spendeth up [1], swallowed down [1], swallowed [1]

1105 בֶּלַע **belaʿ**, n.[m.]. GK: 1183 & 1184 [→ 1104]. what is swallowed; harmful, with a likely focus on destruction, fig. of what is greedily swallowed up:– devouring [1], swallowed up [1]

1106 בֶּלַע **belaʿ**, n.pr.m. & loc. GK: 1185 & 1186 [→ 1104]. Bela, "*swallower, devourer*":– Bela [13], Belah [1]

1107 בִּלְעֲדֵי **balʿᵃdê**, adv. GK: 1187 [→ 1077+5704]. apart from, except for, besides:– beside (+4480) [3], save (+4480) [3], without (+4480) [3], besides (+4480) [2], not [2], besides [1], else beside (+4480+5750) [1], save [1], without [1]

1108 בַּלְעִי **balʿî**, a.g. GK: 1188 [→ 1104]. Belaite, "*of Bela*":– Belaites [1]

1109 בִּלְעָם **bilʿām** or בִּלְעָם **bilʿām**, n.pr.m. & loc. GK: 1189 & 1190 [→ 1104]. Balaam, "[poss.] *Baal [lord] of the people;* [poss.] *the clan brings forth; devourer, glutton*"; Bileam, "*[gift] brought to the people*":– Balaam [57], Balaam's [3], Bileam [1]

1110 בָּלַק **bālaq**, v. GK: 1191 [→ 1111]. [Q] to devastate; [Pu] to be stripped, devastated:– maketh waste [1], waste [1]

1111 בָּלָק **bālāq**, n.pr.m. GK: 1192 [→ 1110]. Balak, "*devastator*":– Balak [42], Balak's [1]

1112 בֵּלְאשַׁצַּר **bēlʾšaṣṣar**, n.pr.m. GK: 1157 [→ 1078; cf. 1113]. Belshazzar, "*Bel protect the king*":– Belshazzar [1]

1113 בֵּלְאשַׁצַּר **bēlʾšaṣṣar** (Aram.), n.pr.m. GK: 10105 & 10109 [cf. 1112]. Belshazzar, "*Bel protect the king*":– Belshazzar [7]

1114 בִּלְשָׁן **bilšān**, n.pr.m. GK: 1193 [→ 1078]. Bilshan, "*their Bel [lord]*":– Bilshan [2]

1115 בִּלְתִּי **biltî**, subst. & adv. & pp. GK: 1194 [→ 1086]. no, not, without; except for; besides:– not [56], none [10], no [6], beside [3], nothing [3], save [3], without [3], except [2], from (+3807.1) [2], lest (+3807.1) [2], none (+376) [2], nor (+2050.1+3807.1) [2], not (+3807.1) [2], but (+518) [1], but [1], cannot [1], continual (+5627) [1], except (+518) [1], lest that (+3807.1) [1], neither (+2050.1) [1], neither [1], no (+3605) [1], no (+3807.1) [1], no more [1], nothing else (+369) [1], that no more (+3807.1) [1], that not (+3807.1) [1], unsatiable (+7654) [1], without (+3807.1) [1]

1116 בָּמָה **bāmâ**, n.f. GK: 1195 [→ 173?, 1117, 1120]. high place, worship shrine (an elevated place, often artificial, for the worship of a god); heights:– high places [83], high place [18], heights [1], waves [1]

1117 בָּמָה **bāmâ**, n.pr.loc. GK: 1196 [→ 1116]. Bamah, "*high place*":– Bamah [1]

1118 בִּמְהָל **bimhāl**, n.pr.m. GK: 1197 [→ 1121+4107]. Bimhal, "*son of circumcision*":– Bimhal [1]

1119 בְּמוֹ **bᵉmô**, pp. GK: 1198 [→ 871.1]. by, with, in:– in [2], with [2], for [1], into [1], privily (+652) [1], through [1]

1120 בָּמוֹת **bāmôt** or בָּמוֹת בַּעַל **bāmôt baʿal**, n.pr.loc. GK: 1199 & 1200 [→ 1116+1167]. Bamoth, "*high places [for cultic worship]*", Bamoth Baal, "*high places for Baal [worship]*":– Bamoth [2], Bamoth-baal [1]

1121 בֵּן **bēn**, n.m. GK: 1201 [→ 1122, 1150; cf. 1129, 1248; cf. 1247 (also used with compound proper names)]. son, child (of either gender), descendant (in any generation), offspring (human or animal); by extension: a term of endearment; one of a class or kind or nation or family. A "son of man" is a "human being" (Nu 23:9), a term that often assumes messianic significance (Ps 8):– son [1906], children [1543], sons [1030], old [135], young [52], first year (+8141) [42], son's [21], sons' [21], men [17], Ammonites (+5983) [15], children's [15], child [10], first [9], strangers (+5236) [6], people (+5971) [5], sons' (+3807.1) [5], stranger (+5236) [5], Assyrians (+804) [4], valiant (+2428) [4], Babylonians (+894) [3], age [3], bullock (+1241) [3], Beno [2], calf (+1241) [2], calves [2], fruitful bough (+6509) [2], hostages (+8594) [2], in a night (+3915) [2], lambs (+6629) [2], man (+120) [2], man [2], men (+120) [2], nephews (+1121) [2], ones [2], surely die (+4194) [2], whelps [2], young ones [2], Ahohite (+266) [1], Benjamite (+376+3227) [1], Benjamite [1], Egyptians (+4714) [1], Gileadites (+1569) [1], Grecians (+3125) [1], Hachmonite (+2453) [1], Levites (+3878) [1], Muth-labben (+4192+1886.1+3807.1) [1], afflicted (+6040) [1], appointed to death (+8546) [1], appointed to destruction (+2475) [1], appointed to die (+8546) [1], arrow (+7198) [1], arrows[S] [1], born [1], branch [1], breed [1], calves (+1241) [1], children (+3807.1) [1], children's (+3807.1) [1], colts [1], colt [1], common [1], corn [1], father[S] [1], foal [1], high[S] (+376) [1], kids (+5795) [1], low[S] (+120) [1], meet for the war (+2428) [1], men (+376) [1], men of high degree (+376) [1], men of low degree (+120) [1], mighty (+410) [1], one born [1], one [1], people [1], rebels (+4805) [1], robbers (+6530) [1], soldiers [1], sparks (+7565) [1], steward (+4943) [1], stranger's (+5236) [1], strong (+2428) [1], them[S] [1], valiantest (+2428) [1], very fruitful (+8081) [1], worthy to die (+4194) [1], worthy [1], youths [1]

1122 בֵּן **bēn**, n.pr.m. GK: 1202 [→ 1121]. Ben:– Ben [1]

1123 בֵּן **bēn** (Aram.), n.m. GK: 10110. a direct descendant, human or animal, male or of either gender: son, child; a distant descendant: grandson, grandchild, descendant; fig., one of a class or kind:– children [6], sons [3], captives (+1547) [1], young [1]

1124 בְּנָה **bᵉnâ** (Aram.), v. GK: 10111 [→ 1147; cf. 1129]. [P] to build, construct, rebuild; [Pp] to be built; [Htpe] to be built, be constructed, be rebuilt:– builded [10], build [7], building [3], built [1], make [1]

1125 בֶּן־אֲבִינָדָב **ben-ʾᵃbînādab**, n.pr.m. GK: 1203 [→ 1121+1+5068]. Ben-Abinadab, "*son of Abinadab*":–

1126 בֶּן־אוֹנִי **ben-ʾônî**, n.pr.m. GK: 1204 [→ 1121+205]. Ben-Oni, "*son of my sorrow*":– Ben-oni [1]

1127 בֶּן־גֶּבֶר **ben-geber**, n.pr.m. GK: 1205 [→ 1121+1397]. Ben-Geber, "*son of strength*":–

1128 בֶּן־דֶּקֶר **ben-deqer**, n.pr.[loc.?]. GK: 1206 [→ 1121+1856]. Ben-Deker, "*son of Deker [pierces]*":–

1129 בָּנָה **bānâ**, v. GK: 1215 [→ 1131, 1137, 1138, 1140, 1146, 4011, 8403; cf. 1121, 1323; cf. 1124 (also used with compound proper names)]. [Q] to make, build, rebuild, establish; [Qp, N] to be built, established:– built [152], build [132], builded [35], building [13], builders [10], build up [7], buildeth [7], buildest [3], built up [3], made [3], in building [2], repaired [2], set up [2], surely built (+1129) [2], buildedst [1], have children [1], obtain children [1]

1130 בֶּן־הֲדַד **ben-hᵃdad**, n.pr.m. GK: 1207 [→ 1121+1908]. Ben-Hadad, "*son of Hadad*":– Ben-hadad [25]

1131 בִּנּוּי **binnûy**, n.pr.m. GK: 1218 [→ 1129; cf. 942]. Binnui, "*son*":– Binnui [7]

1132 בֶּן־זוֹחֵת **ben-zôḥēt**, n.pr.m. GK: 1209 [→ 1121+2105]. Ben-Zoheth, "*son of Zoheth*":– Ben-zoheth [1]

1133 בֶּן־חוּר **ben-ḥûr**, n.pr.m. GK: 1210 [→ 1121+2354]. Ben-Hur, "*son of Hur*":–

1134 בֶּן־חַיִל **ben-ḥayil**, n.pr.m. GK: 1211 [→ 1121+2428]. Ben-Hail, "*son of strength*":– Ben-hail [1]

1135 בֶּן־חָנָן **ben-ḥānān**, n.pr.m. GK: 1212 [→ 1121+2605]. Ben-Hanan, "*son of grace*":– Ben-hanan [1]

1136 בֶּן־חֶסֶד **ben-ḥesed**, n.pr.m. GK: 1213 [→ 1121+2617]. Ben-Hesed, "*son of Hesed [loyal love]*":–

1137 בָּנִי **bānî**, n.pr.m. GK: 1220 [→ 1129]. Bani, "*descendant*":– Bani [15]

1138 בֻּנִּי **bunnî**, n.pr.m. GK: 1221 [→ 1129]. Bunni:– Bunni [3]

1139 בְּנֵי־בְרַק **bᵉnê-bᵉraq**, n.pr.loc. GK: 1222 [→ 1121]. Bene Berak, "*sons of Barak [lightning]*":– Bene-berak [1]

1140 בִּנְיָה **binyâ**, n.f. GK: 1224 [→ 1129]. building, physical structure:– building [1]

1141 בְּנָיָה **bᵉnāyâ** or בְּנָיָהוּ **bᵉnāyāhû**, n.pr.m. GK: 1225 & 1226 [→ 1129+3068]. Benaiah, "*Yahweh has built*":– Benaiah [42]

1142 בְּנֵי יַעֲקָן **bᵉnê yaᵃqān**, n.pr.loc. GK: 1223. Bene Jaakan, "[poss.] *son of Jaakan*":– Bene-jaakan [2]

1143 בֵּנַיִם **bēnayim**, subst.[du.]. GK: 1227 [→ 996]. champion, single fighter:– champion (+376+1886.1) [2]

1144 בִּנְיָמִין **binyāmîn** or בֶּן־יָמִין **ben-yāmîn**, n.pr.m. GK: 1228 [→ 1145, 3227]. Benjamin, "*son of [the] right hand; southerner*":– Benjamin [158], Benjamin's [4], Benjamites [4]

1145 בֶּן־יְמִינִי **ben-yᵉmînî** or בֶּנְיְמִינִי **benyᵉmînî**, a.g. GK: 1229 [→ 1030]. Benjamite, of Benjamin, "*of Benjamin*":– Benjamite [5], Benjamites [3]

1146 בִּנְיָן **binyān**, n.m. GK: 1230 [→ 1129; cf. 1147]. building, structure; outer wall:– building [7]

1147 בִּנְיָן **binyān** (Aram.), n.[m.]. GK: 10112 [→ 1124; cf. 1146]. building:– building [1]

1148 בְּנִינוּ **bᵉnînû**, n.pr.m. GK: 1231 [→ 1121]. Beninu, "*our son*":– Beninu [1]

1149 בְּנַס **bᵉnas** (Aram.), v. GK: 10113. [P] to become angry:– angry [1]

1150 בִּנְעָא **bin'ā'**, n.pr.m. GK: 1232 [→ 1121]. Binea:– Binea [2]

1151 בֶּן־עַמִּי **ben-'ammî**, n.pr.m. GK: 1214 [→ 1121+5971+2967.1]. Ben-Ammi, "*son of my people*":– Ben-ammi [1]

1152 בְּסוֹדְיָה **bᵉsôdᵉyâ**, n.pr.m. GK: 1233 [→ 871.1+5475+3068; cf. 1153?]. Besodeiah, "*in secret council of Yahweh*":– Besodeiah [1]

1153 בֵּסַי **bēsay**, n.pr.m. GK: 1234 [cf. 1152?]. Besai, "*in secret council of Yahweh*":– Besai [2]

1154 בֶּסֶר **beser**, n.m. GK: 1235 [→ 1155]. unripe grapes, sour grapes:– unripe grape [1]

1155 בֹּסֶר **bōser**, n.m. GK: 1235 [→ 1154]. unripe grapes, sour grapes:– sour grape [3], sour grapes [1]

Heb

1156 בְּעָה **bᵉ'â** (Aram.), v. GK: 10114 [→ 1159; cf. 1158]. [P] to ask for, request; when petitioning deity: pray for, plead for:– sought [3], ask [2], desired [2], asked [1], desire [1], maketh petition (+1159) [1], praying [1], requested [1]

1157 בַּעַד **ba'ad**, subst.pp. GK: 1237. behind; through, over; around; from; on behalf of, for (benefit of):– for [61], upon [9], about [7], through [7], at [4], within (+4480) [3], by means of [1], by [1], concerneth [1], in [1], out at [1], over [1], sealeth up (+2856) [1], to [1]

1158 בָּעָה **bā'â** or בָּעָה **bā'â**, v. GK: 1239 & 1240 [cf. 1156]. [Q] to ask, inquire; to boil; [N] to be pillaged; other sources: searched out, with an implication that what is found would be taken and so ransacked; to bulge, be swollen:– inquire [2], causeth to boil [1], sought up [1], swelling out [1]

1159 בָּעוּ **bā'û** (Aram.), n.f. GK: 10115 [→ 1156]. prayer, petition, request:– maketh petition (+1156) [1], petition [1]

1160 בְּעוֹר **bᵉ'ôr**, n.pr.m. GK: 1242. Beor, "[perhaps] *a burning*":– Beor [10]

1161 בִּעוּת **bi'ût**, n.m.pl. GK: 1243 [→ 1204]. terror:– terrors [2]

1162 בֹּעַז **bō'az**, n.pr.m. GK: 1244 & 1245. Boaz, "[prob.] *in him is strength*":– Boaz [24]

1163 בָּעַט **bā'aṭ**, v. GK: 1246. [Q] to kick (in scorn):– kicked [1], kick [1]

1164 בְּעִי **bᵉ'î**, n.[m.]. GK: 1247 [→ 871.1+5856]. ?:–

1165 בְּעִיר **bᵉ'îr**, n.m. GK: 1248 [→ 1197, 1198]. animals, livestock, cattle:– beasts [3], cattle [2], beast [1]

1166 בָּעַל **bā'al**, v. GK: 1241 & 1249. [Q] to rule over; to marry, be a husband; [Qp, N] to be married, have a husband; (ptcp.) Beulah:– married [6], husband [3], Beulah [1], dominion [1], had dominion over [1], married wife [1], marrieth [1], marry [1], wife [1]

1167 בַּעַל **ba'al**, n.m. GK: 1251 [→ 1168, 1172, 1191, 4810; cf. 1166; cf. 1169 (also used with compound proper names)]. Baal (pagan god), "*master, owner, lord*"; husband, master, owner, citizen; used in many phrases to indicate mastery of an object: "lord of arrows" is a master archer; "lord of dreams" is an interpreter of dreams, etc.:– men [20], owner [10], husband [9], man [4], owners [4], having [2], him that hath [2], husbands [2], lords [2], master [2], adversary (+4941) [1], archers (+2671) [1], babbler (+3956+1886.1) [1], bird (+3671) [1], captain [1], chief man [1], confederate (+1285) [1], creditor (+3027+4874) [1], dreamer (+2472+1886.1) [1], furious (+2534) [1], had [1], him that is great [1], horsemen (+6571) [1], man's [1], married (+802) [1], master (+376) [1], master's [1], masters [1], person [1], sworn (+7621) [1], that which hath [1], them that have [1], them to whom is due [1], they[5] [1], those that are given to [1]

1168 בַּעַל **ba'al**, n.pr.m. GK: 1252 [→ 1167]. Baal, "*master, owner, lord*":– Baal [62], Baalim [18], Baal's [1]

1169 בְּעֵל **bᵉ'ēl** (Aram.), n.m. GK: 10116 [cf. 1167]. master, lord; with 2941: "lord of the decree" is "commanding officer":– chancellor (+2942) [3]

1170 בַּעַל בְּרִית **ba'al bᵉrît**, n.pr. GK: 1253 [→ 1167+1285]. Baal-Berith, "*Baal [lord] of the covenant*":– Baal-berith [2]

1171 בַּעַל גָּד **ba'al gād**, n.pr.loc. GK: 1254 [→ 1167+1410]. Baal Gad, "*lord [Baal] of good luck*":– Baal-gad [3]

1172 בַּעֲלָה **baᵃlâ**, n.f. GK: 1266 [→ 1090, 1173?, 1175; cf. 1167]. mistress (of sorceries); (female) owner:– hath [2], mistress [2]

1173 בַּעֲלָה **baᵃlâ**, n.pr.loc. GK: 1267 [→ 1172?]. Baalah, "[fem. of Baal] *lady*":– Baalah [5]

1174 בַּעַל הָמוֹן **ba'al hāmôn**, n.pr.loc. GK: 1255 [→ 1167+1995]. Baal Hamon, "*lord [Baal] of Hamon* or *possessor of abundance*":– Baal-hamon [1]

1175 בְּעָלוֹת **bᵉ'ālôt**, n.pr.loc. GK: 1268 [→ 1172]. Bealoth, "[fem. pl. of Baal] *lady*":– Aloth [1], Bealoth [1]

1176 בַּעַל זְבוּב **ba'al zᵉbûb**, n.pr. GK: 1256 [→ 1167+2070]. Baal-Zebub, "*Baal [lord] of the flies*":– Baal-zebub [4]

1177 בַּעַל חָנָן **ba'al ḥānān**, n.pr.m. GK: 1257 [→ 1167+2605]. Baal-Hanan, "*lord [Baal] is gracious*":– Baal-hanan [5]

1178 בַּעַל חָצוֹר **ba'al ḥāṣôr**, n.pr.loc. GK: 1258 [→ 1167+2691]. Baal Hazor, "*lord [Baal] of Hazor*":– Baal-hazor [1]

1179 בַּעַל חֶרְמוֹן **ba'al ḥermôn**, n.pr.loc. GK: 1259 [→ 1167+2768]. Baal Hermon, "*lord [Baal] of Hermon*":– Baal-hermon [2]

1180 בַּעְלִי **bᵉ'alî**, n.m. GK: 1251 + 3276 [→ 1167+2967.1]. my husband; my Baal (1167 + 2967.1); translated as a proper name in the KJV: Baali:– Baali [1]

1181 בַּעֲלֵי בָמוֹת **bᵃ'alê bāmôt**, n.pr.loc. GK: 1251 + 1195 [→ 1167+1116]. lords of the high places (1167 + 1116):–

1182 בְּעֶלְיָדָע **bᵉ'elyādā'**, n.pr.m. GK: 1269 [→ 1167+3045]. Beeliada, "*the lord [Baal] knows*":– Beeliada [1]

1183 בְּעַלְיָה **bᵉ'alyâ**, n.pr.m. GK: 1270 [→ 1167+3045+3068]. Bealiah, "*Yahweh is Lord*":– Bealiah [1]

1184 בַּעֲלֵי יְהוּדָה **bᵃ'alê yᵉhûdâ**, n.pr.m. GK: 1251 + 3373 [→ 1167+3063]. Baale of Judah (1167 + 3063):– Baale of Judah [1]

1185 בַּעֲלִיס **baᵃlîs**, n.pr.m. GK: 1271. Baalis, "[poss.] *son of delight* or *Baals*":– Baalis [1]

1186 בַּעַל מְעוֹן **ba'al mᵉ'ôn**, n.pr.loc. GK: 1260 [→ 1167+4583?]. Baal Meon:– Baal-meon [3]

1187 בַּעַל פְּעוֹר **ba'al pᵉ'ôr**, n.pr.m. GK: 1261 [→ 1167+6465]. Baal Peor, "*lord [Baal] of Peor*":– Baal-peor [6]

1188 בַּעַל־פְּרָצִים **ba'al-pᵉrāṣîm**, n.pr.loc. GK: 1262 [→ 1167+6556]. Baal Perazim, "*lord [Baal] of making a breech, breaking through*":– Baal-perazim [4]

1189 בַּעַל צְפֹן **ba'al ṣᵉpōn**, n.pr.loc. GK: 1263 [→ 1167+6828]. Baal Zephon, "*lord [Baal] of the north*":– Baal-zephon [3]

1190 בַּעַל שָׁלִשָׁה **ba'al šālišâ**, n.pr.loc. GK: 1264 [→ 1167+8031]. Baal Shalishah:– Baal-shalisha [1]

1191 בַּעֲלָת **baᵃlāt**, n.pr.loc. GK: 1272 [→ 1167]. Baalath, "*lady, goddess* [fem. of Baal]":– Baalath [3]

1192 בַּעֲלַת בְּאֵר **baᵃlat bᵉ'ēr**, n.pr.loc. GK: 1273 [→ 1167+875]. Baalath Beer, "*lord [Baal] of the well*":– Baalath-beer [1]

1193 בַּעַל תָּמָר **ba'al tāmār**, n.pr.loc. GK: 1265 [→ 1167+8558]. Baal Tamar, "*lord [Baal] of the palm tree*":– Baal-tamar [1]

1194 בְּעֹן **bᵉ'ōn**, n.pr.loc. GK: 1274. Beon:– Beon [1]

1195 בַּעֲנָא **baᵃnā'**, n.pr.m. GK: 1275 [→ 1196]. Baana, "*son of affliction*":– Baana [2], Baanah [1]

1196 בַּעֲנָה **baᵃnâ**, n.pr.m. GK: 1276 [→ 1195]. Baanah, "*son of affliction*":– Baanah [9]

1197 בָּעַר **bā'ar**, v. GK: 1277 & 1278 & 1279 [→ 1165, 1199, 1200, 8404]. [Q] to burn; to be senseless, to be brutal; [N] to be purged; to behave senselessly; [P] to light a fire, set a blaze; to purge, remove, get rid of; [Pu] to be burning; [Ht] to start a fire, consume with fire; [H] to graze:– burn [19], put away [13], kindled [9], brutish [7], burned [6], burning [6], burnt [6], burneth [4], kindle [4], take away [4], burnt up [2], eaten up [2], taken away [2], brought away [1], cause to be eaten [1], eaten [1], feed [1], heated [1], set on fire [1], set [1], taketh away [1], took out [1], wasted [1]

1198 בַּעַר **ba'ar**, n.m. GK: 1280 [→ 1165]. senselessness, stupidity, ignorance, comparable to an animal:– brutish [3], brutish person [1], foolish [1]

1199 בַּעֲרָא **baᵃrā'**, n.pr.f. GK: 1281 [→ 1200; cf. 1197]. Baara, "*passionate [burning] one*":– Baara [1]

1200 בְּעֵרָה **bᵉ'ērâ**, n.f. GK: 1282 [→ 1199; cf. 1197]. fire:– fire [1]

1201 בַּעְשָׁא **ba'šā'**, n.pr.m. GK: 1284. Baasha, "*boldness*":– Baasha [28]

1202 בַּעֲשֵׂיָה **baᵃśēyâ**, n.pr.m. GK: 1283. Baaseiah, "*the* LORD *is bold*":– Baaseiah [1]

1203 בְּעֶשְׁתְּרָה **bᵉ'eštᵉrâ**, n.pr.loc. GK: 1285 [cf. 6252?]. Be Eshtarah:– Beeshterah [1]

1204 בָּעַת **bā'at**, v. GK: 1286 [→ 1205, 1161]. [N] to be afraid, be terrified; [P] to torment, terrify, overwhelm:– make afraid [5], afraid [3], made afraid [2], terrify [2], affrighted [1], terrifiest [1], troubled [1], troubleth [1]

1205 בְּעָתָה **bᵉ'ātâ**, n.f. GK: 1287 [→ 1204]. terror:– trouble [2]

1206 בֹּץ **bōṣ**, n.[m.]. GK: 1288 [→ 949?, 1207, 8405?]. mud, silt:– mire [1]

1207 בִּצָּה **biṣṣâ**, n.f. GK: 1289 [→ 1206]. marsh, swamp, waterlogged ground:– fens [1], mire [1], miry places [1]

1208 בָּצוּר **bāṣûr**, a. GK: 1290 [→ 1219]. fortified:–

1209 בֵּצַי **bēṣay**, n.pr.m. GK: 1291. Bezai:– Bezai [3]

1210 בָּצִיר **bāṣîr**, n.m. GK: 1292 & 1293 [→ 1219]. grape harvest; grapes; vineyard; dense, inaccessible (forest):– vintage [8]

1211 בָּצָל **bāṣāl**, n.m. GK: 1294 [→ 1213?]. onion:– onions [1]

1212 בְּצַלְאֵל **bᵉṣal'ēl**, n.pr.m. GK: 1295 [→ 871.1+6738+410]. Bezalel, "*in the shadow of God [El]*":– Bezaleel [9]

1213 בַּצְלוּת **baṣlût** or בַּצְלִית **baṣlît**, n.pr.m. GK: 1296 & 1297 [→ 1211?]. Bazluth, Bazlith:– Bazlith [1], Bazluth [1]

1214 בָּצַע **bāṣa'**, v. GK: 1298 [→ 1215]. [Q] to cut off; to be greedy, make unjust gain; [P] to cut off; to finish; to make unjust gain:– cut off [2], greedy of gain (+1215) [2], coveteth [1], covetous [1], cut [1], finish [1], fulfilled [1], gained [1], get dishonest gain (+1215) [1], given to covetousness (+1215) [1], given [1], greedily gained [1], performed [1], wounded [1]

1215 בֶּצַע **beṣa'**, n.m. GK: 1299 [→ 1214]. ill-gotten gain, dishonest gain; cutting off:– covetousness [9], gain [5], profit [3], greedy of gain (+1214) [2], dishonest gain [1], get dishonest gain (+1214) [1], given to covetousness (+1214) [1], lucre [1]

1216 בָּצֵק **bāṣēq**, v. GK: 1301 [→ 1217, 1218]. [Q] to swell, become swollen:– swelled [1], swell [1]

1217 בָּצֵק **bāṣēq**, n.[m.]. GK: 1302 [→ 1216]. dough made of flour, not yet leavened:– dough [4], flour [1]

1218 בָּצְקַת **boṣqat**, n.pr.loc. GK: 1304 [→ 1216]. Bozkath, "*swollen* or *elevated spot*":– Boscath [1], Bozkath [1]

1219 בָּצַר **bāṣar**, v. GK: 1305 & 1306 & 1307 [→ 1208, 1210, 1221, 1223, 1224, 1225, 1226, 4013, 4014]. [Q] to harvest, gather grapes; to humble, break (the spirit); [N] to be impossible, be thwarted; [P] to strengthen, fortify:– fenced [16], defenced [5], fortify [2], gather [2], grapegatherers [2], cut off [1], gathered [1], gatherest grapes [1], grapegatherer [1], mighty [1], restrained [1], strong [1], walled up [1], walled [1], withholden [1]

1220 בֶּצֶר **beṣer**, n.[m.]. GK: 1309 [→ 1222]. same as 1222: gold ore:– defence [1], gold [1]

1221 בֶּצֶר **beṣer**, n.pr.m. & loc. GK: 1310 & 1311 [→ 1219]. Bezer, "*[metallic] ore* or *place of refuge*":– Bezer [5]

1222 בְּצַר ***bᵉṣar***, n.[m.]. GK: 1309 [→ 1220]. same as 1220: gold ore:– gold [1]

1223 בָּצְרָה ***boṣrâ***, n.f. GK: 1312 [→ 1219]. pen, sheep-fold:– Bozrah [1]

1224 בָּצְרָה ***boṣrâ***, n.pr.loc. GK: 1313 [→ 1219]. Bozrah, "*enclosure (for sheep), fortress*":– Bozrah [8]

1225 בִּצָּרוֹן ***biṣṣārôn***, n.[m.]. GK: 1315 [→ 1219]. fortress, stronghold:– strong hold [1]

1226 בַּצָּרָה ***baṣṣārâ*** or בַּצֹּרֶת ***baṣṣōret***, n.f. GK: 1314 & 1316 [→ 1219]. drought; trouble:– dearth [1], drought [1]

1227 בַּקְבּוּק ***baqbûq***, n.pr.m. GK: 1317 [→ 1228]. Bakbuk, "*gurgling (sound coming out of a bottle)*":– Bakbuk [2]

1228 בַּקְבֻּק ***baqbuq***, n.[m.]. GK: 1318 [→ 1227, 1229, 1231, 1232]. jar; in some contexts a flask:– bottle [2], cruse [1]

1229 בַּקְבֻּקְיָה ***baqbuqyâ***, n.pr.m. GK: 1319 [→ 1228+3068]. Bakbukiah, "*Yahweh pours out*":– Bakbukiah [3]

1230 בַּקְבַּקַּר ***baqbaqqar***, n.pr.m. GK: 1320. Bakbakkar, "*investigator*":– Bakbakkar [1]

1231 בֻּקִּי ***buqqî***, n.pr.m. GK: 1321 [→ 1228; cf. 1232]. Bukki, "*proved of Yahweh; mouth [gurgle sounds] of Yahweh*":– Bukki [5]

1232 בֻּקִּיָּהוּ ***buqqiyyāhû***, n.pr.m. GK: 1322 [→ 1228+3068?; cf. 1231]. Bukkiah, "*proved of Yahweh*":– Bukkiah [2]

1233 בְּקִיעַ ***bāqîa'***, n.[m.]. GK: 1323 [→ 1234]. breach (in a defense); bits, debris:– breaches [1], clefts [1]

1234 בָּקַע ***bāqa'***, v. GK: 1324 [→ 1233, 1235, 1237]. [Q] to divide, split, tear open; [N] to be split, burst open; [P] to split open, burst forth; [Pu] to be cracked open, broken through, ripped open; [H] to break through, divide; [Ho] to be broken through; [Ht] to split apart:– rent [7], broken up [5], clave [5], cleave [3], rip up [3], brake [2], cleaveth [2], divided [2], divide [2], hatch [2], brake into [1], break forth [1], break out [1], break through [1], breaketh out [1], broken in pieces [1], clave asunder [1], cleft [1], cutteth out [1], dividing [1], made a breach [1], make a breach [1], ready to burst [1], rent asunder [1], rip up [1], tare [1], tear [1], win [1]

1235 בֶּקַע ***beqa'***, n.[m.]. GK: 1325 [→ 1234]. beka (half-shekel, one fifth of an ounce [five or six grams]):– bekah [1], half a shekel [1]

1236 בִּקְעָה ***biq'â*** (Aram.), n.f. GK: 10117 [cf. 1237]. plain, (broad) valley:– plain [1]

1237 בִּקְעָה ***biq'â***, n.f. GK: 1326 [→ 1234; cf. 1236]. valley, plain:– valley [9], plain [7], valleys [4]

1238 בָּקַק ***bāqaq***, v. GK: 1327 & 1328 [cf. 2999?]. [Q] to lay waste, ruin, destroy; to grow abundantly, spread out; [N] to be laid waste; [P] to devastate:– empty [2], utterly emptied (+1238) [2], emptied out [1], emptiers [1], fail [1], make void [1], maketh empty [1]

1239 בָּקַר ***bāqar***, v. GK: 1329 [→ 1241, 1242, 1243, 1244; cf. 1240]. [P] to inspect, seek; look after; consider:– inquire [2], seek out [2], make inquiry [1], search [1], seek [1]

1240 בְּקַר ***bᵉqar*** (Aram.), v. GK: 10118 [cf. 1239]. [Pa] to make a search, inquire; [Htpa] to let a search be made:– search made [4], inquire [1]

1241 בָּקָר ***bāqār***, n.m. GK: 1330 [→ 951; cf. 1239]. animal, cow, bull; cattle, oxen, herd:– oxen [75], herds [30], bullock (+6499) [28], herd [14], beeves [7], bullocks (+6499) [5], bullocks [4], bullock (+1121) [3], ox [3], calf (+1121) [2], heifer (+5697) [2], kine [2], bullock [1], bulls [1], calf (+5695) [1], calves (+1121) [1], cattle [1], cow's [1], great cattle [1], young cow (+5697) [1]

1242 בֹּקֶר ***bōqer***, n.m. GK: 1332 [→ 1239]. morning:– morning [178], every morning (+1242+871.1+871.1+1886.1+1886.1) [20], morrow [4], day [3], every morning (+1242+1886.1+1886.1+3807.1+3807.1) [2], to morrow [2], days (+6153) [1], early (+1886.1+3807.1) [1], early (+871.1+1886.1) [1], early [1], to morrow (+871.1+1886.1) [1]

1243 בַּקָּרָה ***baqqārâ***, n.f.vbl. GK: 1333 [→ 1239]. looking after, caring for:– seeketh out [1]

1244 בִּקֹּרֶת ***biqqōret***, n.f. GK: 1334 [→ 1239]. due punishment (after investigation):– scourged [1]

1245 בָּקַשׁ ***bāqaš***, v. GK: 1335 [→ 1246]. [P] to seek, search, look for, inquire about; [Pu] be sought, be investigated:– seek [103], sought [48], seeketh [19], require [10], seek after [7], seekest [7], sought for [6], make request [3], required [3], seek out [3], besought [2], asked [1], ask [1], begging [1], desire [1], get [1], inquired of (+6440) [1], inquired [1], inquirest [1], inquisition was made [1], procureth [1], requested [1], requireth [1], sought after [1], sought out [1]

1246 בַּקָּשָׁה ***baqqāšâ***, n.m. GK: 1336 [→ 1245]. request:– request [8]

1247 בַּר ***bar*** (Aram.), n.m. GK: 10120 [cf. 1248, 1121]. a direct descendant, human or animal, male or of either gender: son, child; a distant descendant: grandson, grandchild, descendant; fig., one of a class or kind:– son [7], old [1]

1248 בַּר ***bar***, n.m. GK: 1337 [→ 1302; cf. 1121; cf. 1247]. son (exclusively male in the OT); the phrase translated "Kiss the Son" (Ps 2:12) is an act of homage to a king:– son [4]

1249 בַּר ***bar***, a. GK: 1338 [→ 1305]. pure; empty; favorite; radiant, bright:– clean [3], pure [2], choice [1], clear [1]

1250 בַּר ***bar***, n.m. GK: 1339 & 1340 [→ 1305; cf. 1257?; cf. 1251]. grain, wheat, that has been cleansed and threshed; wilds, in the open field:– corn [9], wheat [5]

1251 בַּר ***bar*** (Aram.), n.[m.]. GK: 10119 [cf. 1250]. open field, the wild, an area not populated by people, the place of undomesticated animals:– field [8]

1252 בֹּר ***bōr***, n.m. GK: 1341 [→ 1305]. cleanness:– cleanness [4], pureness [1]

1253 בֹּר ***bōr***, n.m. GK: 1342 [→ 1305]. soda, potash, lye, used in making soap:– make never so clean (+2141+871.1) [1], purely (+1886.1+3509.1) [1]

1254 בָּרָא ***bārā'***, v. GK: 1343 & 1344 & 1345 [→ 1256, 1274, 1277, 1278; cf. 4806]. [Q] to create, Creator; [N] to be created; can refers to creating from nothing as well as to reforming existing materials, as in "create in me a pure heart" (Ps 51:10); [P] to cut, cut down, clear (a forest); [H] to fatten:– created [33], create [8], creator [3], choose [2], cut down [2], createth [1], dispatch [1], done [1], made [1], make fat [1], make [1]

1255 בְּרֹאדַךְ־בַּלְאֲדָן ***bᵉrō'dak-bal'ᵃdān***, n.pr.m. GK: 1347 [→ 4757]. Berodach-Baladan; cf. 4757:– Berodach-baladan [1]

בִּרְאִי ***bir'î***. See 1011.

1256 בְּרָאיָה ***bᵉrā'yâ***, n.pr.m. GK: 1349 [→ 1254+3068]. Beraiah, "*Yahweh has created*":– Beraiah [1]

1257 בַּרְבֻּר ***barbur***, n.m.pl. GK: 1350 [cf. 1250?]. fowl, bird (of various species):– fowl [1]

1258 בָּרַד ***bārad***, v.den. GK: 1351 [→ 1259]. [Q] to shower hail:– hail [1]

1259 בָּרָד ***bārād***, n.m. GK: 1352 [→ 1258]. hail, hailstones:– hail [25], hailstones [2], hailstones (+68) [1], hailstones (+68+1886.1) [1]

1260 בֶּרֶד ***bered***, n.pr.m. & loc. GK: 1354 & 1355. Bered, "[poss.] *freezing rain*":– Bered [2]

1261 בָּרֹד ***bārōd***, a. GK: 1353. spotted, dappled:– grisled [4]

1262 בָּרָה ***bārâ***, v. GK: 1346 & 1356 & 1357 [→ 1267, 1279, 1285]. [Q] to eat; [H] to give to eat, urge to eat:– eat [3], cause to eat [1], choose [1], give [1], meat [1]

1263 בָּרוּךְ ***bārûk***, n.pr.m. GK: 1358 [→ 1288]. Baruch, "*be blessed*":– Baruch [26]

1264 בְּרֹמִים ***bᵉrōmîm***, n.[m.]. GK: 1394. multicolored, a fabric of two-color webbing:– rich apparel [1]

1265 בְּרוֹשׁ ***bᵉrôš***, n.m. GK: 1360 [cf. 1266]. pine tree; some sources: cypress or fir:– fir trees [8], fir [7], fir tree [5]

1266 בְּרוֹת ***bᵉrôt***, n.m. GK: 1361 [cf. 1265]. fir tree; some sources: juniper or cypress:– fir [1]

1267 בָּרוּת ***bārût***, n.f. GK: 1362 [→ 1262]. food:– meat [1]

1268 בֵּרוֹתָה ***bērôtâ*** or בֵּרֹתַי ***bērōtay***, n.pr.loc. GK: 1363 & 1408. Berothah, Berothai, "*well*":– Berothah [1], Berothai [1]

1269 בִּרְזָוִת ***birzāwit*** or בִּרְזַיִת ***birzāyit***, n.pr.f. GK: 1364 & 1365 [→ 875+2132]. Birzaith, Birzavith, "*well of olive oil*":– Birzavith [1]

1270 בַּרְזֶל ***barzel***, n.m. GK: 1366 [→ 1271; cf. 6523]. iron, iron (implements):– iron [73], axe head [1], head [1], smith (+2796) [1]

1271 בַּרְזִלַּי ***barzillay***, n.pr.m. GK: 1367 [→ 1270]. Barzillai, "*[made of] iron*":– Barzillai [12]

1272 בָּרַח ***bāraḥ***, v. GK: 1368 & 1369 & 1370 [→ 1280, 1281, 4015]. [Q] to flee, run away, escape; [H] to drive out, make flee; [H] to injure; to make impassable:– fled [39], flee [10], flee away [3], would fain flee (+1272) [2], chased [1], chaseth away [1], drove away [1], fleddest [1], fleeth [1], make flee [1], make haste [1], put to flight [1], ran away [1], reach [1], shoot [1]

בָּרִחַ ***bāriaḥ***. See 1281.

1273 בַּרְחֻמִי ***barḥumî***, a.g. GK: 1372 [cf. 980]. Barhumite:– Barhumite [1]

1274 בְּרִי ***bᵉrî***, a. GK: 1374 [→ 1254, 1277; cf. 4806]. fat, choice, healthy:– fat [1]

1275 בֵּרִי ***bērî***, n.pr.m. GK: 1373. Beri, "*wisdom*":– Beri [1]

1276 בֵּרִים ***bērîm***, a.g. GK: 1379. Berite:– Berites [1]

1277 בָּרִיא ***bārî'***, a. GK: 1374 [→ 1274]. fat, choice, healthy:– fat [5], fatfleshed (+1320) [2], rank [2], fatter [1], fed [1], firm [1], plenteous [1]

1278 בְּרִיאָה ***bᵉrî'â***, n.f. GK: 1375 [→ 1254]. created thing, with a possible implication that it is something new:– new thing [1]

1279 בִּרְיָה ***biryâ***, n.f. GK: 1376 [→ 1262]. food; in context it refers to food for sick people:– meat [3]

1280 בְּרִיחַ ***bᵉrîaḥ***, n.m. GK: 1378 [→ 1272]. bar, gate bar, crossbar:– bars [36], bar [4], fugitives [1]

1281 בָּרִחַ ***bāriaḥ***, a. GK: 1371 [→ 1272]. gliding; fugitive:– crooked [1], nobles [1], piercing [1]

1282 בָּרִיחַ ***bārîaḥ***, n.pr.m. GK: 1377. Bariah, "[poss.] *board, bar; fugitive; descendant*":– Bariah [1]

1283 בְּרִיעָה ***bᵉrî'â***, n.pr.m. GK: 1380 [→ 1284]. Beriah, "*prominent, excellent*":– Beriah [11]

1284 בְּרִיעִי ***bᵉrî'î***, a.g. GK: 1381 [→ 1283]. Beriite, "*of Beriah*":– Beriites [1]

1285 בְּרִית ***bᵉrît***, n.f. GK: 1382 [→ 1286, 1170, 1262]. covenant, treaty, compact, agreement, an association between two parties with various responsibilities, benefits, and penalties; "to cut a covenant" is "make a covenant," a figure of the act of ceremonially cutting an animal into two parts, with an implication of serious consequences for not fulfilling the covenant:– covenant [264], league [15], in league [2], confederacy [1], confederate (+1167) [1], confederate [1]

1286 בְּרִית ***bᵉrît***, n.pr.[loc.?]. GK: 451 [→ 410+1285]. Berith, "*covenant*":– Berith [1]

1287 בֹּרִית ***bōrît***, n.f. GK: 1383 [→ 1305]. soap, made from soap plants or potash:– sope [2]

1288 בָּרַךְ ***bārak***, v. GK: 1384 & 1385 [→ 1263, 1290, 1292, 1293, 3000; cf. 1289]. [Q] to kneel down; [P] to bless, pronounce blessings, give praise, give thanks, extol; [Qp, N, Pu] to be blessed, be praised; [Ht] to bless oneself, be blessed; this can mean to speak words invoking divine favor (bless), or speak of the excellence of someone (praise); [H] to make kneel:– blessed [173], bless [112], blesseth [8], salute [4], blessest [3], curse [3], abundantly bless (+1288) [2], altogether blessed (+1288) [2], blaspheme [2], bless at all (+1288) [2], bless indeed (+1288) [2], blessed altogether (+1288) [2], blessed still (+1288) [2], blessing [2], greatly bless (+1288) [2], congratulate [1], cursed [1], kneeled [1], kneel [1], made to kneel down [1], praised [1], praise [1], saluted [1], thanked [1]

1289 בְּרַךְ ***bᵉrak*** (Aram.), v. GK: 10121 & 10122 [→ 1291; cf. 1288]. [P] to kneel, an act of reverence to authority, often referring to God; [Pp] to be praised; [Pa] to praise; [Pap] to be praised, to give or receive words of excellence:– blessed [4], kneeled [1]

1290 בֶּרֶךְ ***berek***, n.f. GK: 1386 [→ 1288, 1296; cf. 755, cf. 1291]. knee, the "buckling of the knees" means to falter, implying great fear or despair; "to bow the knee" means to be reverent or submissive:– knees [24], knee [1]

1291 בְּרֵךְ ***bᵉrēk*** (Aram.), n.[f.]. GK: 10123 [→ 1289; cf. 1290]. knee; "to kneel down on the knees" is to assume a position of reverence or worship:– knees [1]

1292 בָּרַכְאֵל ***barak'ēl***, n.pr.m. GK: 1387 [→ 1288+410]. Barakel, "*God [El] blesses*":– Barachel [2]

1293 בְּרָכָה ***bᵉrākâ***, n.f. GK: 1388 [→ 1294; cf. 1288]. blessing; gift:– blessing [50], blessings [11], blessed [3], present [3], Berachah [2], liberal [1]

1294 בְּרָכָה ***bᵉrākâ***, n.pr.m. & loc. GK: 1389 & 1390 [→ 1293; cf. 1288]. Beracah, "*blessing*":– Berachah [1]

1295 בְּרֵכָה ***bᵉrēkâ***, n.f. GK: 1391. (man-made) pool, reservoir:– pool [15], pools [2], fishpools [1]

1296 בֶּרֶכְיָה ***berekyâ*** or בֶּרֶכְיָהוּ ***berekyāhû***, n.pr.m. GK: 1392 & 1393 [→ 1290+3068]. Berekiah, "*Yahweh blesses*":– Berechiah [10], Berachiah [1]

1297 בְּרַם **b^{e}ram** (Aram.), adv.advers. GK: 10124. but, however, nevertheless:– but [2], yet [2], nevertheless [1]

1298 בֶּרַע **bera'**, n.pr.m. GK: 1396. Bera, "*gift*":– Bera [1]

1299 בָּרַק **bāraq**, v. GK: 1397 [→ 1300, 1301, 1303]. [Q] to flash lightning:– cast forth lightning (+1300) [1]

1300 בָּרָק **bārāq**, n.m. GK: 1398 [→ 1301, 1303; cf. 1299]. lightning bolt, flash of lightning:– lightnings [9], glittering [4], lightning [4], bright [1], cast forth lightning (+1299) [1], glistering sword [1], glitter [1]

1301 בָּרָק **bārāq**, n.pr.m. GK: 1399 [→ 1300; cf. 1299]. Barak, "*lightning*":– Barak [13]

1302 בַּרְקוֹס **barqôs**, n.pr.m. GK: 1401 [→ 1248]. Barkos, "*son of Kos*":– Barkos [2]

1303 בַּרְקֹן **barqōn**, n.m.pl. GK: 1402 [→ 1300; cf. 1299]. brier, a thorny plant:– briers [2]

1304 בָּרֶקֶת **bāreqet** or בָּרְקַת **bār^{e}qat**, n.f. GK: 1403 & 1404. beryl (a green stone, exact identification uncertain):– carbuncle [3]

1305 בָּרַר **bārar**, v. GK: 1359 & 1405 & 1406 [→ 1249, 1250, 1252, 1253, 1287]. [Q] to purge; [Qp] to be chosen, be choice; to be sharpened, polished, [N] to keep clean, be pure; [P] purify; [H] to cleanse; to sharpen; [Ht] to show oneself pure:– pure [3], choice [2], chosen [2], shew pure [2], cleanse [1], clean [1], clearly [1], make bright [1], manifest [1], polished [1], purge out [1], purge [1], purified [1]

1306 בִּרְשַׁע **birša'**, n.pr.m. GK: 1407. Birsha, "*disagreeable in taste*":– Birsha [1]

1307 בֵּרֹתִי **bērōtî**, a.g. GK: 1409 [cf. 886]. Berothite, "*of Berothai [?]*":– Berothite [1]

1308 בְּשׂוֹר **b^{e}śôr**, n.pr.loc. GK: 1410. Besor:– Besor [3]

1309 בְּשֹׂרָה **b^{e}śōrâ**, n.f. GK: 1415 [→ 1319]. news, good news:– tidings [4], good tidings [1], reward for tidings [1]

1310 בָּשַׁל **bāšal**, v. GK: 1418 [→ 1311, 4018]. [Q] to ripen; boil; [P] to cook, boil, roast, bake; [Pu] to be cooked, be boiled; [H] ripen:– seethe [9], boil [4], sodden [4], boiled [2], baked [1], bake [1], brought forth ripe [1], ripe [1], roasted [1], roast [1], seething [1], sodden at all (+1311) [1], sod [1]

Heb

1311 בָּשֵׁל **bāšēl**, a. GK: 1419 [→ 1310]. cooked, boiled:– sodden at all (+1310) [1], sodden [1]

1312 בִּשְׁלָם **bišlām**, n.pr.m. GK: 1420. Bishlam, "*son of Shalom [peace]*":– Bishlam [1]

1313 בָּשָׂם **bāśām**, n.m. GK: 1411 [→ 1314, 1315, 3005]. same as 1314: spices, perfume, fragrance; this can refer to balsam oil or to perfume in general:– spice [1]

1314 בֹּשֶׂם **bōśem**, n.m. GK: 1411 [→ 1313]. same as 1313: spices, perfume, fragrance; this can refer to balsam oil or to perfume in general:– spices [22], spice [2], sweet odours [2], sweet [2], sweet smell [1]

1315 בָּשְׂמַת **bāś^{e}mat**, n.pr.f. GK: 1412 [→ 1313]. Basemath, "*fragrant*":– Bashemath [6], Basmath [1]

1316 בָּשָׁן **bāšān**, n.pr.loc. GK: 1421 & 1422. Bashan, "*fertile stoneless plain*":– Bashan [59], Bashan-havoth-jair (+2334) [1]

1317 בָּשְׁנָה **bošnâ**, n.f. GK: 1423 [→ 954]. disgrace, shame:– shame [1]

1318 בָּשַׁס **bāšas**, v. GK: 1424. [Po] to trample:– treading [1]

1319 בָּשַׂר **bāśar**, v. GK: 1413 [→ 1309]. [P] to bring (good) news, proclaim (good) news; [Ht] to hear news:– bringeth good tidings [4], bear tidings [3], shew forth [3], bringest good tidings [2], publish [2], bringest tidings [1], bringeth tidings [1], brought good tidings [1], brought tidings [1], carry tidings [1], messenger [1], preach good tidings unto [1], preached [1], published [1], tidings [1]

1320 בָּשָׂר **bāśār**, n.m. GK: 1414 [cf. 1321]. flesh, the soft tissue mass of any animal; the whole body; particular parts of the body: meat, skin, genitals, etc.; by extension: humankind, living things:– flesh [256], body [2], fatfleshed (+1277) [2], kin [2], leanfleshed (+1851) [2], leanfleshed (+7534) [1], mankind (+376) [1], myself (+2967.1) [1], nakedness (+6172) [1], skin [1], thereof[S] [1]

1321 בְּשַׂר **b^{e}śar** (Aram.), n.m. GK: 10125 [cf. 1320]. flesh (human or creatures):– flesh [3]

בְּשֹׂרָה **b^{e}sōrâ**. See 1309.

1322 בֹּשֶׁת **bōšet**, n.f. GK: 1425 [→ 378; cf. 954]. shame, disgrace, humiliation:– shame [20], confusion [7], ashamed [1], greatly ashamed (+954) [1], shameful thing [1]

1323 בַּת **bat**, n.f. GK: 1426 [→ 1337, 1339, 1340; cf. 1129]. daughter, female child of any generation (granddaughter, etc.); by extension: any female, girl, woman; a term of endearment; fig., outlying village or settlement (of a "mother" city):– daughter [280], daughters [245], towns [32], villages [12], owls (+3284) [6], daughter's [3], first [2], owl (+3284) [2], apple (+380) [1], apple [1], branches [1], company [1], first year (+8141) [1], old [1]

1324 בַּת **bat**, n.m. & f. GK: 1427 [cf. 1325]. bath (liquid measure, equal to an ephah, about six gallons [about 22 liters]; some sources: eight to nine gallons):– baths [7], bath [6]

1325 בַּת **bat** (Aram.), n.[m.]. GK: 10126 [cf. 1324]. bath (liquid measure):– baths [2]

1326 בָּתָה **bātâ**, n.f. GK: 1429 [→ 1327?]. wasteland:– waste [1]

1327 בַּתָּה **battâ**, n.f. GK: 1431 [→ 1326?]. steep ravine, face of a cliff:– desolate [1]

1328 בְּתוּאֵל **b^{e}tû'ēl**, n.pr.m. & loc. GK: 1432 & 1433 [→ 4962+410; cf. 1329?]. Bethuel, "*man of God [El]*":– Bethuel [10]

1329 בְּתוּל **b^{e}tûl**, n.pr.loc. GK: 1434 [cf. 1328?]. Bethul:– Bethul [1]

1330 בְּתוּלָה **b^{e}tûlâ**, n.f. GK: 1435 [→ 1331]. virgin, maiden; a marriageable woman who has never had sexual intercourse and still under the authority of her father; (unmarried) young woman:– virgin [24], virgins [14], maid [4], maidens [3], maids [3], maiden [2]

1331 בְּתוּלִים **b^{e}tûlîm**, n.f. GK: 1436 [→ 1330]. virginity; proof of virginity, referring to a cloth with blood from a virgin's first sexual encounter:– virginity [8], maid [2]

1332 בִּתְיָה **bityâ**, n.pr.f. GK: 1437. Bithiah, "[poss.] *worshiper of Yahweh* or *queen*":– Bithiah [1]

1333 בָּתַק **bātaq**, v. GK: 1438 [cf. 918]. [P] to hack to pieces, slaughter:– thrust through [1]

1334 בָּתַר **bātar**, v. GK: 1439 [→ 1335, 1336, 1338]. [Q, P] to cut in pieces:– divided [2]

1335 בֶּתֶר **beter**, n.m. GK: 1440 [→ 1334]. piece:– parts [2], Bether [1], piece [1]

1336 בֶּתֶר **beter**, n.m. GK: 1441 [→ 1334]. ruggedness, referring to mountains with rugged ravines:–

1337 בַּת־רַבִּים **bat-rabbîm**, n.pr.loc. GK: 1442 [→ 1323+7235]. Bath Rabbim, "*daughter of a multitude*":– Bath-rabbim [1]

1338 בִּתְרוֹן **bitrôn**, n.[pr.loc.?]. GK: 1443 [→ 1334]. Bithron, "*gully*":– Bithron [1]

1339 בַּת־שֶׁבַע **bat-šeba'**, n.pr.f. GK: 1444 [→ 1323; cf. 7652]. Bathsheba, "*seventh daughter* or *daughter of an oath*":– Bath-sheba [11]

1340 בַּת־שׁוּעַ **bat-šûa'**, n.pr.f. GK: 1445 [→ 1323+7651?]. Bath-Shua:– Bath-shua [1]

1341 גֵּא **gē'**, a. GK: 1447 [→ 1342]. proud, arrogant:– proud [1]

1342 גָּאָה **gā'â**, v. GK: 1448 [→ 1341, 1344, 1343, 1346, 1347, 1348, 1349, 1466]. [Q] to grow tall, be high, to rise up; by extension: to be exalted:– triumphed gloriously (+1342) [4], grow up [1], increaseth [1], risen [1]

1343 גֵּאֶה **gē'eh**, a. GK: 1450 [→ 1342]. proud, arrogant:– proud [8]

1344 גֵּאָה **gē'â**, n.f. GK: 1449 [→ 1342]. pride, arrogance:– pride [1]

1345 גְּאוּאֵל **g^{e}'û'ēl**, n.pr.m. GK: 1451 [→ 1341+410]. Geuel, "*splendor of God [El]*":– Geuel [1]

1346 גַּאֲוָה **ga^{a}wâ**, n.f. GK: 1452 [→ 1342]. surging; majesty, glory, triumph; pride, arrogance, conceit:– pride [10], excellency [3], haughtiness [2], highness [1], proudly (+871.1) [1], proud [1], swelling [1]

1347 גָּאוֹן **gā'ôn**, n.m. GK: 1454 [→ 1342]. surging (waves), lush (high) thickets; majesty, splendor, glory; pride, arrogance:– pride [19], excellency [10], majesty [7], pomp [5], arrogancy [3], swelling [3], excellent [1], proud [1]

1348 גֵּאוּת **gē'ût**, n.f. GK: 1455 [→ 1342]. surging (sea), rising (smoke); majesty, glory; pride, arrogance:– majesty [2], pride [2], excellent things [1], lifting up [1], proudly (+871.1) [1], raging [1]

1349 גַּאֲיוֹן **ga^{a}yôn**, a. GK: 1456 [→ 1342]. arrogant, proud:– proud [1]

1350 גָּאַל **gā'al**, v. GK: 1453 & 1457 [→ 1353, 3008]. [Q] to redeem, deliver; (n.) avenger; kinsman-redeemer; [Qp] to be redeemed; [N] to be redeemed, redeem oneself; often this redemption is in the context of saving from danger or hostility, as a figure of purchasing a slave or indentured person. A "kinsman-redeemer" purchases a relative from slavery (actual or potential); a "kinsman-avenger" provides justice on behalf of a relative; both concepts are in the image of God as Redeemer:– redeemed [24], redeem [22], redeemer [18], kinsman [7], avenger [6], revenger [6], at all redeem (+1350) [4], do the part of a kinsman [2], in any wise redeem (+1350) [2], near kinsman [2], ransomed [2], deliver [1], do the kinsman's part [1], kinsfolks [1], next kinsmen [1], perform the part of a kinsman [1], purchase [1], redeemeth [1], revengers [1], stain [1]

1351 גָּאַל **gā'al**, v. GK: 1458 [→ 1352; cf. 1602]. [N] to be stained, defiled; [P] to defile; [Pu] to be unclean, defiled; [H/Aphel] to stain; [Ht] to defile oneself:– polluted [7], defile [2], defiled [1], stain [1]

1352 גֹּאַל **gō'al**, n.[m.]. GK: 1459 [→ 1351]. defilement:– defiled [1]

1353 גְּאֻלָּה **g^{e}'ullâ**, n.f. GK: 1460 [→ 1350]. redemption (of a person or object); right of redemption; blood relatives:– redemption [3], price of redemption [2], redeem (+1961) [2], kindred [1], redeem (+4672) [1], redeemed (+1961) [1], redeemed [1], redeeming [1], redeem [1], right [1]

1354 גַּב **gab**, n.m. & f. GK: 1461 & 1462 [cf. 1355]. eyebrow; rim (of a wheel); mound, back; defense:– eminent place [3], bodies [2], rings [2], backs [1], back [1], bosses [1], eyebrows (+5869) [1], higher place [1], naves [1]

1355 גַּב **gab** (Aram.), n.[m.]. GK: 10128 [→ 1358?]. the back (body part):– back [1]

1356 גֵּב **gēb**, n.[m.]. GK: 1463 & 1464 [→ 1374; cf. 1358]. ditch; cistern; an architectural structure variously interpretated: beam, rafter, paneling:– full of ditches (+1356) [2], beams [1], pits [1]

1357 גֵּבָה **gēbâ**, n.[m.]. GK: 1466 [→ 1462]. swarm (of locust):– locusts [1]

1358 גֹּב **gōb** (Aram.), n.m. GK: 10129 [→ 1355?; cf. 1356]. den, pit (of lions), often an excavated hole:– den [10]

1359 גּוֹב **gôb**, n.pr.loc. GK: 1570 [→ 1461?]. Gob, "*cistern*":– Gob [2]

1360 גֶּבֶא **gebe'**, n.m. GK: 1465. cistern; marsh:– marishes [1], pit [1]

1361 גָּבַהּ **gābah**, v. GK: 1467 [→ 1362, 1364, 1363, 1365, 1405, 3011]. [Q] to be tall, tower high; to exalt; to be proud, haughty, arrogant; [H] to make high, grow tall; exalt; the attitude of pride or arrogance is a fig. extension the base meaning of being tall or high; something that is "too high" cannot be understood:– lifted up [6], exalted [5], haughty [5], higher [4], exalt [3], high [2], exalteth [1], height [1], lift up [1], make high [1], mount up [1], on high [1], proud [1], raised up a great height [1], upward [1]

1362 גָּבֵהַּ **gābēah**, a. GK: 1468 [→ 1361]. high, towered; proud, haughty; the attitude of pride or arrogance is a fig. extension the base meaning of being tall or high:– high [2], proud [2]

1363 גֹּבַהּ **gōbah**, n.m. GK: 1470 [→ 1361]. tallness, height; splendor, majesty; pride, haughtiness, conceit; the attitude of pride or arrogance is a fig. extension the base meaning of being tall or high:– height [9], high [3], pride [2], excellency [1], haughty [1], loftiness [1]

1364 גָּבֹהַּ **gābōah**, a. GK: 1469 [→ 1361]. high, tall; proud, haughty; the attitude of pride or arrogance is a fig. extension the base meaning of being tall or high:– high [24], higher [5], exceeding proudly (+1364) [2], lofty [2], haughty [1], height [1], highest [1], proud [1]

1365 גַּבְהוּת **gabhût**, n.f. GK: 1471 [→ 1361]. arrogance:– loftiness [1], lofty [1]

1366 גְּבוּל **g^{e}bûl**, n.m. GK: 1473 [→ 1367, 1379]. territory, boundary, border:– border [138], coast [46], coasts [23], borders [20], bound [4], landmark [4], space [2], bounds [1], limit [1], quarters [1]

1367 גְּבוּלָה **g^{e}bûlâ**, n.f. GK: 1474 [→ 1366]. boundary stone, border marker:– coasts [5], bounds [2], borders [1], landmarks [1], place [1]

1368 גִּבּוֹר **gibbôr**, a. GK: 1475 [→ 1396; cf. 1401]. mighty one, mighty warrior, special guard:– mighty [133], strong [5], valiant [5], men [4], mighty ones [3], mighties [2], champion [1], chief [1], excel [1], giant [1], man [1], mightiest [1], strongest [1]

1369 גְּבוּרָה ***gᵉbûrâ***, n.f. GK: 1476 [→ 1396; cf. 1370]. power, strength, might, achievement:– might [27], strength [17], power [8], mighty acts [4], force [1], mastery [1], mighty (+5973) [1], mighty power [1], mighty [1]

1370 גְּבוּרָה ***gᵉbûrâ*** (Aram.), n.f. GK: 10130 [→ 1400; cf. 1369]. power, might, strength:– might [2]

1371 גִּבֵּחַ ***gibbēaḥ***, a. GK: 1477 [→ 1372]. bald forehead:– forehead bald [1]

1372 גַּבַּחַת ***gabbaḥat***, n.f. GK: 1478 [→ 1371]. bald spot on the forehead; bare spot on cloth:– bald forehead [3], without [1]

1373 גַּבַּי ***gabbay***, n.pr.m. GK: 1480. Gabbai, "*collector*":– Gabbai [1]

1374 גֵּבִים ***gēbîm***, n.pr.loc. GK: 1481 [→ 1356]. Gebim, "*ditches*":– Gebim [1]

1375 גָּבִיעַ ***gābîa'***, n.m. GK: 1483 [→ 1392, 4021?]. cup, (drinking) bowl:– bowls [8], cup [5], pots [1]

1376 גְּבִיר ***gᵉbîr***, n.m. GK: 1484 [→ 1376; cf. 1396]. lord, master:– lord [2]

1377 גְּבִירָה ***gᵉbîrâ***, n.f. GK: 1485 [→ 1376; cf. 1396]. mistress (female lord); queen:– queen [6]

1378 גָּבִישׁ ***gābîš***, n.m. GK: 1486 [cf. 417]. jasper:– pearls [1]

1379 גָּבַל ***gābal***, v.den. GK: 1487 [→ 1366]. [Q] to set up a boundary; [H] to put limits around (a geographical area):– border [2], set bounds about [1], set bounds [1], set [1]

1380 גְּבַל ***gᵉbal***, n.pr.loc. GK: 1488 [→ 1382]. Gebal, "[poss.] *border; hill*":– Gebal [1]

1381 גְּבָל ***gᵉbāl***, n.pr.loc. GK: 1489. Gebal, "[poss.] *border; hill*":– Gebal [1]

גְּבֻלָה ***gᵉbulâ***. See 1367.

1382 גִּבְלִי ***giblî***, a.g. GK: 1490 [→ 1380]. Gebalite, "*of Gebal*":– Giblites [1], stonesquarers [1]

1383 גַּבְלֻת ***gablut***, n.f. GK: 1491 [→ 4020]. braided (gold chain):– at the ends [1], ends [1]

1384 גִּבֵּן ***gibbēn***, a. GK: 1492 [→ 1386; cf. 1385]. hunchbacked:– crookbackt [1]

1385 גְּבִינָה ***gᵉbînâ***, n.f. GK: 1482 [cf. 1384]. cheese:– cheese [1]

1386 גַּבְנֹן ***gabnôn***, n.[m.]. GK: 1493 [→ 1384]. ruggedness; a many-peaked mountain range with an appearance that suggests wonder and majesty:– high [2]

1387 גֶּבַע ***geba'***, n.pr.loc. GK: 1494 [→ 1389]. Geba, "*hill*":– Geba [13], Gibeah [4], Gaba [2]

1388 גִּבְעָא ***gib'ā'***, n.pr.m. GK: 1495 [→ 1389?]. Gibea, "*mound, hill*":– Gibea [1]

1389 גִּבְעָה ***gib'â***, n.f. GK: 1496 [→ 1387, 1388?, 1390, 1391, 1394, 1533]. hill, hill top, height:– hills [35], hill [30], little hills [4]

1390 גִּבְעָה ***gib'â***, n.pr.loc. GK: 1497 [→ 1395; cf. 1389]. Gibeah, "*mound, hill*":– Gibeah [44], Gibeath [1]

1391 גִּבְעוֹן ***gib'ōn***, n.pr.loc. GK: 1500 [→ 1393; cf. 1389]. Gibeon, "*mound, hill*":– Gibeon [37]

1392 גִּבְעֹל ***gib'ōl***, n.[m.]. GK: 1499 [→ 1375]. bloom:– bolled [1]

1393 גִּבְעֹנִי ***gib'ônî***, a.g. GK: 1498 [→ 1391; cf. 1389]. Gibeonite, of Gibeon, "*of Gibeon*":– Gibeonites [6], Gibeonite [2]

1394 גִּבְעַת ***gib'at***, n.pr.loc. GK: 1501 & 1502 [→ 1389]. same as 1390: Gibeath, "*mound, hill*":–

1395 גִּבְעָתִי ***gib'ātî***, a.g. GK: 1503 [→ 1390]. Gibeathite, "*of Gibeah*":– Gibeathite [1]

1396 גָּבַר ***gābar***, v. GK: 1504 [→ 1368, 1369, 1376, 1377, 1397, 1398, 1399, 1402, 1403, 1404]. [Q] to rise, flood; to be greater, stronger; to prevail, overwhelm; [P] to strengthen; [H] to cause to triumph, confirm (a covenant); [Ht] to show oneself as a victor:– prevailed [9], prevail [5], great [2], strengthen [2], confirm [1], exceeded [1], mighty [1], put to more [1], strengtheneth [1], stronger [1], valiant [1]

1397 גֶּבֶר ***geber***, n.m. GK: 1505 [→ 1127, 1398, 1399, 1403; cf. 1396; cf. 1400]. (strong, young) man; in some contexts an indefinite pronoun: certain ones:– man [53], men [6], man's [2], mighty [2], every one [1], man child [1]

1398 גֶּבֶר ***geber***, n.pr.m. GK: 1506 [→ 1397; cf. 1396]. Geber, "*[strong young] man*":– Geber [2]

1399 גְּבַר ***gᵉbar***, n.m. GK: 1505 [→ 1397]. (mighty) man; in some contexts an indefinite pronoun: certain ones:– man [1]

1400 גְּבַר ***gᵉbar*** (Aram.), n.m. GK: 10131 [→ 1370, 1401; cf. 1397]. (mighty) man; in some contexts an indefinite pronoun: certain ones:– men [16], certain [2], man [2], most mighty men (+1401+2429) [1]

1401 גִּבָּר ***gibbar*** (Aram.), n.m. GK: 10132 [→ 1400; cf. 1368]. strong man, mighty one:– most mighty men (+1400+2429) [1]

1402 גִּבָּר ***gibbār***, n.pr.m. GK: 1507 [→ 1396]. Gibbar, "*[young vigorous] man, hero*":– Gibbar [1]

גְּבֻרָה ***gᵉburâ***. See 1369.

1403 גַּבְרִיאֵל ***gabrî'ēl***, n.pr.m. GK: 1508 [→ 1397+410]. Gabriel, "*[strong] man of God [El]*":– Gabriel [2]

1404 גְּבֶרֶת ***gᵉberet***, n.f. GK: 1509 [→ 1396]. queen:– mistress [7], lady [2]

1405 גִּבְּתוֹן ***gibbᵉtôn***, n.pr.loc. GK: 1510 [→ 1361]. Gibbethon, "*mound, hill*":– Gibbethon [6]

1406 גָּג ***gāg***, n.m. GK: 1511. roof, top:– roof [9], housetops [6], top [4], housetop [3], top of house [3], roof of house [2], roofs [2], tops of houses [1]

1407 גַּד ***gad***, n.m. GK: 1512. coriander:– coriander [2]

1408 גַּד ***gad***, n.[m.]. GK: 1513 [→ 1409, 1410, 1426, 1427]. same as 1409: good fortune; (as a pagan god) Fortune:–

1409 גַּד ***gad***, n.[m.]. GK: 1513 [→ 1408]. same as 1408: good fortune; (as a pagan god) Fortune:– troop [2]

1410 גָּד ***gād***, n.pr.m. GK: 1514 [→ 1171, 1425, 1424; cf. 1408]. Gad, "*fortune*":– Gad [70]

1411 גְּדָבַר ***gᵉdābar*** (Aram.), n.m. GK: 10133 [cf. 1490; cf. 1489]. treasurer:– treasurers [2]

1412 גֻּדְגֹּדָה ***gudgōdâ***, n.pr.loc. GK: 1516. Gudgodah, "*cleft*":– Gudgodah [2]

1413 גָּדַד ***gādad***, v. GK: 1517 & 1518 [→ 1416, 1417, 1418, 1464?; cf. 1414]. [Q] to band together; [Htpolal] to band together against; to cut oneself, slash oneself:– cut [5], assembled by troops [1], gather in troops [1], gather together [1]

1414 גְּדַד ***gᵉdad*** (Aram.), v. GK: 10134 [cf. 1413]. [P] to cut down:– hew down [2]

גְּדֻדָה ***gᵉdudâ***. See 1417.

1415 גָּדָה ***gādâ***, n.f. GK: 1519 [→ 1428]. bank (of a river):– banks [4]

גַּדָּה ***gaddâ***. See 2693.

1416 גְּדוּד ***gᵉdûd***, n.m. GK: 1522 [→ 1413]. band of raiders; band of rebels; bandits; troops, divisions:– bands [9], troop [7], band [5], army [4], company [3], troops [3], armies [1], companies [1]

1417 גְּדוּד ***gᵉdûd***, n.m. & f. GK: 1521 [→ 1413]. ridge (of a furrow):– cuttings [1]

1418 גְּדוּדָה ***gᵉdûdâ***, n.m. & f. GK: 1523 [→ 1413]. slash, cut (of the skin):– furrows [1]

1419 גָּדוֹל ***gādôl***, a. GK: 1524 & 2045 [cf. 1431]. great, large; much, more; this can refer to physical size, quantity, degree, and social status (great king, high priest):– great [412], high [22], greater [20], loud [19], greatest [9], elder [7], mighty [7], eldest [6], more [4], wept sore (+1058+1065) [3], aloud (+6963+871.1) [1], displeased exceedingly (+3415+7451) [1], elder (+4480) [1], exceeding glad (+8055+8057) [1], exceedingly afraid (+3372+3374) [1], exceedingly [1], far [1], feared exceedingly (+3372+3374) [1], great men [1], great multitude [1], greatness [1], grew great [1], grieved exceedingly (+7451+7489) [1], hated exceedingly (+3966+8130+8135) [1], long [1], loud (+6963+871.1) [1], nobles [1], proud [1], very (+3966) [1], very [1]

1420 גְּדוּלָּה ***gᵉdûllâ***, n.f. GK: 1525 [→ 1431]. greatness, majesty, recognition, honor:– greatness [7], great things [3], dignity [1], majesty [1]

1421 גִּדּוּף ***giddûp*** or גִּדּוּפָה ***giddûpâ***, n.m. GK: 1526 & 1528 [→ 1442]. taunt, scorn, insult, reviling:– revilings [2], reproaches [1]

1422 גְּדוּפָה ***gᵉdûpâ***, n.f. GK: 1527 [→ 1442]. taunt, scorn, reviling:– taunt [1]

גְּדוֹר ***gᵉdôr***. See 1446.

1423 גְּדִי ***gᵉdî***, n.m. GK: 1531 [→ 1429, 5872]. (male) young goat:– kid (+5795) [7], kid [6], kids [3]

1424 גָּדִי ***gādî***, n.pr.m. GK: 1533 [→ 1410]. Gadi, "*my fortune*":– Gadi [2]

1425 גָּדִי ***gādî***, a.g. GK: 1532 [→ 1410]. Gadite, of Gad, "*of Gad*":– Gadites [14], Gadite [1], Gad [1]

1426 גַּדִּי ***gaddî***, n.pr.m. GK: 1534 [→ 1408]. Gaddi, "*my fortune*":– Gaddi [1]

1427 גַּדִּיאֵל ***gaddî'ēl***, n.pr.m. GK: 1535 [→ 1408+410]. Gaddiel, "*God [El] is my fortune; Gad is [my] God*":– Gaddiel [1]

1428 גִּדְיָה ***gidyâ***, n.f. GK: 1536 [→ 1415]. bank (of a river):–

1429 גְּדִיָּה ***gᵉdiyyâ***, n.f. GK: 1537 [→ 1423]. (female) young goat:– kids [1]

1430 גָּדִישׁ ***gādîš***, n.m. GK: 1538 & 1539. shock of grain, sheaf of grain; tomb:– shock of corn [1], shocks [1], stacks of corn [1], tomb [1]

1431 גָּדַל ***gādal***, v. GK: 1540 [→ 1419, 1420, 1432, 1433, 1435, 1434?, 1437, 4024, 4026 (also used with compound proper names)]. [Q] to grow up; be great, exalted; [P] to grow long, make great; to exalt, honor, glorify; [Pu] to be well-nurtured; [H] to make great, cause greatness; [Ht] to magnify oneself, show greatness:– magnified [17], great [16], magnify [15], grew [7], brought up [6], grown [5], grown up [4], greater [3]; make great [3], waxed great [3], great things [2], grew up [2], made great [2], make greater [2], much set by [2], waxen great [2], advanced [1], became great [1], boasted [1], bring up [1], come to great estate [1], exceeded (+4480) [1], exceeded [1], excellent [1], great giveth [1], great things done [1], grow [1], increased [1], lift up [1], madest grow [1], magnifical [1], nourish up [1], nourished [1], nourishing [1], nourish [1], passed (+4480) [1], promoted [1], promote [1], proudly [1]

1432 גָּדֵל ***gādēl***, a.vbl. *or* v.ptcp. GK: 1541 [→ 1431]. great, powerful:– great [2], grew [2]

1433 גֹּדֶל ***gōdel***, n.m. GK: 1542 [→ 1431]. greatness, majesty, strength; pride, arrogance:– greatness [11], stoutness [1], stout [1]

1434 גְּדִל ***gādil***, n.[m.]pl. GK: 1544 [→ 1431?]. tassel, festoon:– fringes [1], wreaths [1]

1435 גִּדֵּל ***giddēl***, n.pr.m. GK: 1543 [→ 1431]. Giddel, "*big*":– Giddel [4]

גָּדֹל ***gādōl***. See 1419.

גְּדֻלָּה ***gᵉdullâ***. See 1420.

1436 גְּדַלְיָה ***gᵉdalyâ*** or גְּדַלְיָהוּ ***gᵉdalyāhû***, n.pr.m. GK: 1545 & 1546 [→ 1431+3068]. Gedaliah, "*great is Yahweh*":– Gedaliah [32]

1437 גִּדַּלְתִּי ***giddaltî***, n.pr.m. GK: 1547 [→ 1431]. Giddalti, "*I pronounce [God as] Great; I reared up*":– Giddalti [2]

1438 גָּדַע ***gāda'***, v. GK: 1548 [→ 1439, 1440, 1441]. [Q] to cut short, cut off, break; [P] to cut down, cut to pieces; [Qp, N, Pu] to be cut off, be cut down:– cut down [9], cut off [7], cut asunder [3], cut in sunder [2], hew down [1], hewn down [1]

1439 גִּדְעוֹן ***gid'ôn***, n.pr.m. GK: 1549 [→ 1441; cf. 1438]. Gideon, "*one who cuts, hacks*":– Gideon [39]

1440 גִּדְעֹם ***gid'ōm***, n.pr.loc. GK: 1550 [→ 1438]. Gidom, "*cutting off, stop pursuit*":– Gidom [1]

1441 גִּדְעֹנִי ***gid'ōnî***, n.pr.m. GK: 1551 [→ 1439; cf. 1438]. Gideoni, "*one who cuts, hacks*":– Gideoni [5]

1442 גָּדַף ***gādap***, v. GK: 1552 [→ 1421, 1422]. [P] to blaspheme, revile:– blasphemed [5], blasphemeth [1], reproacheth [1]

גִּדֻּף ***giddup***, and גִּדֻּפָה ***giddupâ***. See 1421.

1443 גָּדַר ***gādar***, v. GK: 1553 [→ 1446, 1445, 1444, 1447, 1448, 1449, 1450, 1448, 1452, 1453]. [Q] to built a stone wall, heap up stones for a wall:– masons [2], close up [1], fenced up [1], hedged [1], inclosed [1], made up the hedge (+1447) [1], make a wall (+1447) [1], make up the hedge (+1447) [1], repairer [1]

1444 גֶּדֶר ***geder***, n.m. GK: 1555 [→ 1443, 1447]. same as 1447: wall, fence, a wall made of loose stones from the field without mortar:– wall [2]

1445 גֶּדֶר ***geder***, n.pr.loc. GK: 1554 [→ 1013; cf. 1013, 1443]. Geder, "*wall [of stones]*":– Geder [1]

1446 גְּדוֹר ***gᵉdôr***, n.pr.m. & loc. GK: 1529 & 1530 [→ 1443]. Gedor, "*wall; pock-marked*":– Gedor [7]

1447 גָּדֵר ***gādēr***, n.m. GK: 1555 [→ 1444]. same as 1444: wall, fence, a wall made of loose stones from the field without mortar:– wall [5], fence [1], hedges [1], hedge [1], made up the

Heb

hedge (+1443) [1], make a wall (+1443) [1], make up the hedge (+1443) [1], walls [1]

1448 גְּדֵרָה **gᵉdērâ** or גְּדֶרֶת **gᵉderet**, n.f. GK: 1556 & 1560 [→ 1443, 1449, 1450, 1452, 1453; cf. 1443]. wall, pen (for sheep) made of stone walls:– hedges [4], folds [3], sheepcotes (+6629) [1], sheepfolds (+6629) [1], wall [1]

1449 גְּדֵרָה **gᵉdērâ**, n.pr.loc. GK: 1557 [→ 1448; cf. 1443]. Gederah, "*stone pen, sheep corral*":– Gederah [1]

1450 גְּדֵרוֹת **gᵉdērôt**, n.pr.loc. GK: 1558 [→ 1448; cf. 1443]. Gederoth, "*stone pens, sheep corrals*":– Gederoth [2]

1451 גְּדֵרִי **gᵉdērî**, a.g. GK: 1559 [cf. 1013]. Gederite, "*of Geder*":– Gederite [1]

1452 גְּדֵרָתִי **gᵉdērātî**, a.g. GK: 1561 [→ 1448; cf. 1443]. Gederathite, "*of Geder[ath]*":– Gederathite [1]

1453 גְּדֵרֹתַיִם **gᵉdērōtayim**, n.pr.loc. GK: 1562 [→ 1448; cf. 1443]. Gederothaim, "*two stone pens, two sheep corrals*":– Gederothaim [1]

1454 גֵּה **gēh**, var. GK: 1563. var. of 2088: this:– this [1]

1455 גָּהָה **gāhâ**, v. GK: 1564 [→ 1456, 4010]. [Q] to heal:– cure [1]

1456 גֵּהָה **gēhâ**, n.f. GK: 1565 [→ 1455]. healing, cure; that which promotes healing: medicine:– medicine [1]

1457 גָּהַר **gāhar**, v. GK: 1566. [Q] to bow down; stretch out in prostration:– stretched [2], cast down [1]

1458 גַּו **gaw**, n.[m.]. GK: 1567 [→ 1460]. back (of the body); "to thrust behind the back" means "to reject":– back [2], backs [1]

1459 גַּו **gaw** (Aram.), n.m. GK: 10135 [cf. 1460]. middle, interior:– midst [10], the same (+1886.9) [1], therein (+871.2+1886.9) [1], wherein (+871.2) [1]

1460 גֵּו **gēw**, n.[m.]. GK: 1568 & 1569 [→ 1458, 1465, 1471?, 1472; cf. 1459]. back (of the body); "to walk upon the back" is a sign of conquest and subjugation; "to send sin behind the back" is "to forgive"; among; fellow people, community:– back [5], among [1], body [1]

1461 גּוּב **gûb**, v. GK: 1572 [→ 1359?]. [Q] to dig:–

1462 גּוֹב **gôb** or גֹּבַי **gōbay**, n.m.[col]. GK: 1571 & 1479 [→ 1357]. locust, locust swarm:– great grasshoppers (+1462) [2], grasshoppers [1]

1463 גּוֹג **gôg**, n.pr.m. GK: 1573 [→ 1996, 4031]. Gog, "*precious golden object*":– Gog [10]

1464 גּוּד **gûd**, v. GK: 1574 [→ 1413?]. [Q] to attack, invade:– overcome [2], invade with troops [1]

1465 גֵּוָה **gēwâ**, n.f. GK: 1576 [→ 1460]. back (of the body):– body [1]

1466 גֵּוָה **gēwâ**, n.f. GK: 1575 [→ 1342; cf. 1467]. pride, lifting up:– pride [2], lifting up [1]

1467 גֵּוָה **gēwâ** (Aram.), n.f. GK: 10136 [cf. 1466]. pride:– pride [1]

1468 גּוּז **gûz**, v. GK: 1577. [Q] to pass along, pass away:– brought [1], cut off [1]

1469 גּוֹזָל **gôzāl**, n.m. GK: 1578. young bird, hatchling:– young pigeon [1], young [1]

1470 גּוֹזָן **gôzān**, n.pr.loc. GK: 1579. Gozan:– Gozan [5]

1471 גּוֹי **gôy**, n.m. GK: 1580 & 1582. people, nation; regularly in the OT, any people in contrast to Israel: the Gentiles, pagan, heathen, uncultured:– nations [265], heathen [143], nation [107], Gentiles [30], people [11], every nation (+1471) [4], another [1]

1472 גְּוִיָּה **gᵉwiyyâ**, n.f. GK: 1581 [→ 1460]. dead body, corpse; carcass:– bodies [5], body [3], carcase [2], corpses [2], dead bodies [1]

1473 גּוֹלָה **gôlâ**, n.f. GK: 1583 [→ 1540; cf. 1547]. exile, captive, people deported to another place:– captivity [26], those carried away [3], carried away captives [2], carried away [2], removing [2], away [1], captives [1], captive [1], carried away captive [1], go into captivity [1], remove [1], them carried away [1]

1474 גּוֹלָן **gôlān**, n.pr.loc. GK: 1584. Golan:– Golan [4]

1475 גּוּמָּץ **gûmmāṣ**, n.m. GK: 1585. pit:– pit [1]

1476 גּוּנִי **gûnî**, n.pr.m. GK: 1586 [→ 1477]. Guni, "*spotted sand grouse*":– Guni [4]

1477 גּוּנִי **gûnî**, a.g. GK: 1587 [→ 1476]. Gunite, "*of Guni*":– Gunites [1]

1478 גָּוַע **gāwaʻ**, v. GK: 1588. [Q] to perish, die, breath one's last:– die [7], gave up the ghost [4], died [3], give up the ghost [2], dead [1], dying [1], given up the ghost [1], giveth up the ghost [1], perished [1], perish [1], ready to die [1], yielded up the ghost [1]

1479 גּוּף **gûp**, v. GK: 1589. [H] to shut (a door):– shut [1]

1480 גּוּפָה **gûpâ**, n.f. GK: 1590 [→ 1610]. dead body, corpse:– bodies [1], body [1]

1481 גּוּר **gûr**, v. GK: 1591 & 1592 & 1593 [→ 1483?, 1616, 1628, 4032, 4033, 4034, 4036; cf. 1624, 1482?, 3025]. [Q] to live as an alien, dwell as a stranger, implying less social rights than a native; to be terrified, be afraid, fear, revere; to attack, stir up; [Htpol] to stay, gather together:– sojourn [31], sojourneth [15], dwell [11], sojourned [11], afraid [6], strangers [6], abide [2], fear [2], gather together [2], surely gather together (+1481) [2], assemble [1], dwelleth [1], feared [1], gathered together [1], gathered [1], inhabitant [1], remain [1], sojourners [1], sojourning [1], stand in awe [1]

1482 גּוּר **gûr**, n.m. GK: 1594 [→ 1484; cf. 1481?]. cub (young of lions, jackals):– whelps [3], whelp [3], young ones [1]

1483 גּוּר **gûr**, n.pr.loc. GK: 1595 [→ 1481?]. Gur:– Gur [1]

1484 גֹּור **gôr**, n.[m.]. GK: 1596 [→ 1482]. cub (of lion):– whelps [2]

1485 גּוּר־בַּעַל **gûr-bāʻal**, n.pr.loc. GK: 1597 [cf. 3017]. Gur Baal, "*sojourn of Baal*":– Gur-baal [1]

1486 גּוֹרָל **gôrāl**, n.m. GK: 1598. lot, device by which a decision was made, often a pebble, stick, or pottery shard either thrown or blindly pulled from a container; by extension: what is decided by lot, allotment (of land):– lot [61], lots [16]

1487 גּוּשׁ **gûš**, n.[m.]. GK: 1599 & 1641. scab, something crusted:– clods [1]

1488 גֵּז **gēz**, n.[m.]. GK: 1600 [→ 1494]. fleece, sheared wool; grass mowed:– fleece [2], mowings [1], mown grass [1]

1489 גִּזְבָּר **gizbār**, n.m. GK: 1601 [cf. 1411, cf. 1490]. treasurer:– treasurer [1]

1490 גִּזְבַּר **gizbar** (Aram.), n.m. GK: 10139 [cf. 1411; cf. 1489]. treasurer:– treasurers [1]

1491 גָּזָה **gāzâ**, v. GK: 1602 [→ 1496]. [Q] to bring forth, cut off (the umbilical cord):– took [1]

1492 גִּזָּה **gizzâ**, n.f. GK: 1603 [→ 1494]. wool fleece:– fleece [7]

1493 גִּזוֹנִי **gizônî**, a.g. GK: 1604. Gizonite, "*of Gizon*":– Gizonite [1]

1494 גָּזַז **gāzaz**, v. GK: 1605 [→ 1488, 1492, 1495]. [Q] to shear sheep; to shave one's head (in mourning):– shear [4], shearers [3], sheepshearers [2], cut down [1], cut off [1], poll [1], shaved [1], shearing [1], sheepshearers (+6629) [1]

1495 גָּזֵז **gāzēz**, n.pr.m. GK: 1606 [→ 1494]. Gazez, "[poss.] *sheep shearer;* [poss.] *one born at the time of shearing*":– Gazez [2]

1496 גָּזִית **gāzît**, n.f. GK: 1607 [→ 1491]. dressed stone, stone hewn or cut for masonry:– hewed stones [3], hewn stone [3], hewed stone [1], hewed [1], hewn stones [1], hewn [1], wrought [1]

1497 גָּזַל **gāzal**, v. GK: 1608 [→ 1499, 1498, 1500]. [Q] to rob, seize, snatch, take way; [Qp, N] to be robbed, be forcibly taken from:– spoiled [7], violently taken away [3], rob [2], away [1], caught [1], consume [1], exercised robbery (+1498) [1], pluck off [1], plucked [1], pluckt [1], pluck [1], robbed [1], robbeth [1], spoileth [1], take away from [1], take by force [1], take by violence [1], taken away [1], took violently away (+1500) [1], torn [1], violently take away [1]

1498 גָּזֵל **gāzēl**, n.[m.]. GK: 1610 [→ 1500; cf. 1497]. stealing, robbery, implying violence:– robbery [2], exercised robbery (+1497) [1], thing taken away by violence [1]

1499 גֵּזֶל **gēzel**, n.[m.]. GK: 1609 [→ 1497]. denial of rights:– violence [1], violent perverting [1]

גֹּזָל **gōzāl**. See 1469.

1500 גְּזֵלָה **gᵉzēlâ**, n.f. GK: 1611 [→ 1498; cf. 1497]. plunder, spoil, stolen things:– violence [3], robbed [1], spoil [1], took violently away (+1497) [1]

1501 גָּזָם **gāzām**, n.m. GK: 1612 [→ 1502; cf. 3697]. locust swarm; some sources: caterpillar or a specific state in the development of a locust:– palmerworm [3]

1502 גַּזָּם **gazzām**, n.pr.m. GK: 1613 [→ 1501]. Gazzam, "*some kind of bird or insect*":– Gazzam [2]

1503 גֶּזַע **gezaʻ**, n.m. GK: 1614. stump, root stock:– stock [2], stem [1]

1504 גָּזַר **gāzar**, v. GK: 1615 & 1616 [→ 1506, 1507?, 1508, 1509, 1511, 4037; cf. 1629; cf. 1505, cf. 1510]. [Q] to cut in two, divide, cut down; decide on; to disappear; to devour, eat, with a possible focus on carving or chewing up food; [N] to be cut off, be excluded:– cut off [6], divide [2], cut down [1], decreed [1], decree [1], divided [1], snatch [1]

1505 גְּזַר **gᵉzar** (Aram.), v. GK: 10140 [→ 1510; cf. 1504]. [P] to determine; (as noun) diviner, astrologer; note that a diviner determines the future through interpretations of omens, such as the movement of the stars (astrologer), or through interpreting the fissures in bodily organs of animals, such as livers; [Htpe] to cut out; [Itpe] to cut out:– soothsayers [4], cut out [2]

1506 גֶּזֶר **gezer**, n.[m.]. GK: 1617 [→ 1504]. pieces (something divided and cut up):– parts [1], pieces [1]

1507 גֶּזֶר **gezer**, n.pr.loc. GK: 1618 [→ 1511; cf. 1504?]. Gezer, "[poss.] *pieces*":– Gezer [13], Gazer [2]

1508 גִּזְרָה **gizrâ**, n.f. GK: 1619 [→ 1504]. courtyard; appearance:– separate place [7], polishing [1]

1509 גְּזֵרָה **gᵉzērâ**, n.f. GK: 1620 [→ 1504; cf. 1510]. solitary place, unfertile land:– not inhabited [1]

1510 גְּזֵרָה **gᵉzērâ** (Aram.), n.f. GK: 10141 [→ 1505; cf. 1509]. decree, decision:– decree [2]

1511 גִּזְרִי **gizrî** or גִּרְזִי **girzî**, a.g. GK: 1621 & 1747 [→ 1507; cf. 1504]. Gizrite, Girzite:– Gezrites [1]

גִּחוֹן **giḥôn**. See 1521.

1512 גָּחוֹן **gāḥôn**, n.m. GK: 1623. belly (of reptile):– belly [2]

גֵּחֲזִי **gēḥᵃzî**. See 1522.

גָּחֹל **gāḥol**. See 1513.

1513 גַּחַל **gaḥal** or גַּחֶלֶת **gaḥelet**, n.f. GK: 1624 & 1625. burning coals, hot embers:– coals [11], burning coals [3], coal [2], coals of fire [1], hot coals [1]

1514 גַּחַם **gaḥam**, n.pr.m. GK: 1626. Gaham, "*burning brightly*":– Gaham [1]

1515 גַּחַר **gaḥar**, n.pr.m. GK: 1627. Gahar, "*[born in the] year of little rain*":– Gahar [2]

גֹּי **gōy**. See 1471.

1516 גַּיְא **gayʼ**, n.m. & f. GK: 1628 [→ 2798]. valley:– valley [52], valleys [8]

1517 גִּיד **gîd**, n.m. GK: 1630. sinew, tendon:– sinews [4], sinew [3]

1518 גִּיחַ **gîaḥ**, v. GK: 1622 & 1631 [→ 1520, 1521; cf. 1519]. [Q] to burst forth, surge, bring forth (a baby); [H] to charge; to thrash about:– brake forth [1], came forth [1], camest forth [1], draw up [1], labour to bring forth [1], took out [1]

1519 גּוּחַ **gûaḥ** (Aram.), v. GK: 10137 [cf. 1518]. [H] to churn up, stir up (the sea):– strove [1]

1520 גִּיחַ **gîaḥ**, n.pr.loc. GK: 1632 [→ 1518]. Giah, "*bubbling spring*":– Giah [1]

1521 גִּיחוֹן **giḥôn**, n.pr.loc. GK: 1633 [→ 1518]. Gihon, "*to gush forth*":– Gihon [6]

1522 גֵּיחֲזִי **gêḥᵃzî**, n.pr.m. GK: 1634. Gehazi, "[poss.] *valley of vision*":– Gehazi [12]

1523 גִּיל **gîl**, v. GK: 1635 [→ 26?, 1524, 1525]. [Q] to rejoice, be glad, be joyful, the attitude and action of favorable circumstance, often expressed in shouts and song:– rejoice [23], glad [10], joyful [4], joy [2], rejoiced [2], delight [1], greatly rejoice (+1524) [1], rejoiceth [1]

1524 גִּיל **gîl**, n.[m.]. GK: 1636 & 1637 [→ 1523]. gladness, delight, jubilance; age, stage in life:– joy [3], gladness [2], greatly rejoice (+1523) [1], rejoice exceedingly (+413+8056) [1], rejoice [1], rejoicing [1], sort [1]

1525 גִּילָה **gîlâ**, n.f. GK: 1638 [→ 1523]. rejoicing, delight:– joy [1], rejoicing [1]

גִּילֹה **gîlōh**. See 1542.

1526 גִּילֹנִי **gîlōnî**, a.g. GK: 1639 [→ 1542; cf. 1540]. Gilonite, "*of Gilon*":– Gilonite [2]

1527 גִּינַת **gînat**, n.pr.m. GK: 1640. Ginath, "*protector*":– Ginath [2]

1528 גִּיר **gîr** (Aram.), n.[m.]. GK: 10142 [cf. 1615]. plaster:– plaister [1]

גֵּיר **gêr**. See 1616.

1529 גֵּשָׁן **gêšān**, n.pr.m. GK: 1642. Geshan:– Geshan [1]

1530 גַּל **gal**, n.m. GK: 1643 & 1644 [→ 1554, 1556]. waves, breaker waves, surging waves; fountain; heap, pile (of rocks, rubble):– waves [14], heap [12], heaps [6], Gallim [1], billows [1], spring [1]

1531 גֹּל **gōl**, n.f.?. GK: 1646 [→ 1543]. same as 1543: bowl:– bowl [1]

גְּלָא **g^e lā'**. See 1541.

1532 גַּלָּב **gallāb**, n.[m.]. GK: 1647. barber:– barber's [1]

1533 גִּלְבֹּעַ **gilbōa'**, n.pr.loc. GK: 1648 [→ 1389]. Gilboa, "*bubbling*":– Gilboa [8]

1534 גַּלְגַּל **galgal**, n.m. GK: 1649 & 1650 [cf. 1556; cf. 1535]. wheel; whirlwind; tumbleweed (a wheel-shaped plant):– wheels [6], wheel [3], heaven [1], rolling thing [1]

1535 גַּלְגַּל **galgal** (Aram.), n.m. GK: 10143 [→ 1560; cf. 1534, 1536]. wheel:– wheels [1]

1536 גִּלְגָּל **gilgāl**, n.[m.]. GK: 1651 [→ 1556; cf. 1535]. wheel:– wheel [1]

1537 גִּלְגָּל **gilgāl**, n.pr.loc. GK: 1652 [→ 1019; cf. 1556]. Gilgal, "*circle of stones*":– Gilgal [41]

1538 גֻּלְגֹּלֶת **gulgōlet**, n.f. GK: 1653 [→ 1556]. skull; individual, person:– polls [6], skull [2], every man [1], head [1], man [1], poll [1]

1539 גֶּלֶד **geled**, n.m. GK: 1654. skin:– skin [1]

1540 גָּלָה **gālâ**, v. GK: 1655 [→ 1473, 1526, 1546, 1549, 1542; cf. 1541]. [Q] to tell, uncover, reveal; depart, leave, be exiled, banished; [Qp] to be opened, unseal; be made known; [N] to be revealed, be exposed; [P] to reveal, expose (nakedness) = sexual relations; [Pu] to be opened, exiled; [H] to deport, exile:– uncover [22], discovered [18], carried away [17], carried away captive [15], discover [10], revealed [10], uncovered [10], open [6], removed [4], shew (+241) [4], surely go into captivity (+1540) [4], departed [3], gone into captivity [3], opened [3], openeth [3], revealeth [3], carried captive [2], carry away [2], go captive [2], plainly appear (+1540) [2], published [2], remove [2], reveal [2], surely led away captive (+1540) [2], advertise (+241) [1], appeared [1], appeareth [1], bewray [1], brought [1], captives [1], captive [1], captivity [1], carry away captives [1], carry away into captivity [1], carry captive [1], carrying away captive [1], cause to go into captivity [1], caused to be carried away captives [1], caused to be carried away captive [1], caused to be carried away [1], caused to be led into captivity [1], depart [1], disclose [1], discovereth [1], exile [1], go into captivity [1], gone [1], led away captive [1], led captive [1], openly shewed [1], revealed (+241) [1], shamelessly uncovereth [1], shewed [1], sheweth (+241) [1], sheweth unto (+241) [1], shew [1], told (+241) [1], told in [1], uncovereth [1], went into captivity [1]

1541 גְּלָה **g^e lâ** (Aram.), v. GK: 10144 [cf. 1540]. [P] to reveal (mysteries); [Peil] to be revealed (i.e., mysteries); [H] to deport:– revealeth [3], revealed [2], brought over [1], carried away [1], revealer [1], reveal [1]

גֹּלָה **gōlâ**. See 1473.

1542 גִּלֹה **gilōh**, n.pr.loc. GK: 1656 [→ 1526; cf. 1540]. Giloh:– Giloh [2]

1543 גֻּלָּה **gullâ**, n.f. GK: 1657 & 1684 [→ 1531]. spring (of water); bowl-shaped capital (of a pillar):– springs [6], bowls [3], pommels [3], bowl [2]

1544 גִּלּוּלִים **gillûlîm**, n.m. GK: 1658 [→ 1556]. (pl.) idols:– idols [47], images [1]

1545 גְּלוֹם **g^e lôm**, n.[m.]. GK: 1659 [→ 1563?]. fabric:– clothes [1]

1546 גָּלוּת **gālût**, n.f. GK: 1661 [→ 1540; cf. 1547]. exile, captive:– captivity [10], captives [3], carried away captive [2]

1547 גָּלוּ **gālû** (Aram.), n.f. GK: 10145 [cf. 1546]. exile:– captivity [3], captives (+1123) [1]

1548 גָּלַח **gālaḥ**, v. GK: 1662. [P] to shave off, cut off; [Pu] be shaved off; [Ht] to have oneself shaven, shave oneself:– shave [7], shaven [5], shave off [4], polled [3], shaved [2], caused to shave off [1], shaved off [1]

1549 גִּלָּיוֹן **gillāyôn**, n.m. GK: 1663 [→ 1540]. scroll (some sources: wooden tablet with a wax cover); mirror:– glasses [1], roll [1]

1550 גָּלִיל **gālîl**, a. GK: 1664 [→ 1556]. turnable (door); rings; rods:– folding [2], rings [2]

1551 גָּלִיל **gālîl**, n.pr.loc. GK: 1665 [→ 1552, 1553; cf. 1556]. Galilee, "*ring, circle,* hence *region*":– Galilee [6]

1552 גְּלִילָה **g^e lîlâ**, n.f. GK: 1666 [→ 1553; cf. 1551]. region, district:– borders [3], coasts [1], country [1]

1553 גְּלִילוֹת **g^e lîlôt**, n.pr.loc. GK: 1667 [→ 1552]. Geliloth, "*region*":– Geliloth [1]

1554 גַּלִּים **gallîm**, n.pr.loc. GK: 1668 [→ 1530; cf. 1556]. Gallim, "*heaps*":– Gallim [1]

1555 גָּלְיָת **golyāt**, n.pr.m. GK: 1669. Goliath, "*exile*":– Goliath [6]

1556 גָּלַל **gālal**, v. GK: 1670 & 1671 [→ 1530, 1530, 1561, 1534, 1534, 1536, 1537, 1538, 1544, 1550, 1551, 1552, 1553, 1554, 1557, 1559, 4039; cf. 4038?; cf. 1560]. [Q] to roll down, roll away; to commit, turn over; [N] to be rolled; [P] to roll; [Polal] to be rolled; [Htpol] to roll about, wallow; "to commit, trust" is a figure of rolling care or responsibilty onto the Lord:– rolled [4], roll [3], commit [2], remove [1], roll down [1], rolled away [1], rolled together [1], rolleth [1], run down [1], seek occasion [1], trusted [1], wallowed [1]

1557 גָּלָל **gālāl**, n.[m.]. GK: 1672 [→ 1556]. dung, filth:– dung [1]

1558 גָּלָל **gālāl**, n.[m.]. GK: 1673. because of, on account of, for the sake of:– because of (+871.1) [4], sake [2], for (+871.1) [1], for sake (+871.1) [1], sakes [1], that for (+871.1) [1]

1559 גָּלָל **gālāl**, n.pr.m. GK: 1674 [→ 1562; cf. 1556]. Galal, "[poss.] *tortoise; roll away*":– Galal [3]

1560 גְּלָל **g^e lāl** (Aram.), n.[m.]. GK: 10146 [→ 1535, 4040; cf. 1556]. (col.) stone blocks, formally, "stones of rolling" i.e., stones too large to carry:– great [2]

1561 גֵּל **gēl**, n.m. GK: 1645 [→ 1556]. dung, excrement, used for fuel in some contexts:– dung [4]

1562 גִּלְלַי **gil^e lay**, n.pr.m. GK: 1675 [→ 1559]. Gilalai:– Gilalai [1]

1563 גָּלַם **gālam**, v. GK: 1676 [→ 1545?, 1564]. [Q] to roll up (clothing in a tight ball):– wrapt together [1]

1564 גֹּלֶם **gōlem**, n.[m.]. GK: 1677 [→ 1563]. unformed body, embryo:– substance yet being unperfect [1]

1565 גַּלְמוּד **galmûd**, a. GK: 1678. barren, haggard:– desolate [2], solitary [2]

1566 גָּלַע **gāla'**, v. GK: 1679. [Ht] to burst out (in quarrel); to defy:– intermeddleth [1], meddled with [1], meddling [1]

1567 גַּלְעֵד **gal'ēd**, n.pr.loc. GK: 1681. Galeed; "*heap of [stones that are a] witness*":– Galeed [2]

1568 גִּלְעָד **gil'ād**, n.pr.loc. [& m.?]. GK: 1680 [→ 1569, 3003, 7433]. Gilead, "[perhaps] *monument of stones*":– Gilead [100], Gileadites [2], Gilead's [1], Ramoth-gilead [1]

1569 גִּלְעָדִי **gil'ādî**, a.g. GK: 1682 [→ 1568]. Gileadite, of Gilead, "*of Gilead*":– Gileadite [9], Gileadites (+1121) [1], Gileadites [1]

1570 גָּלַשׁ **gālaš**, v. GK: 1683. [Q] to descend; some sources: to leap, frisk:– appear [2]

1571 גַּם **gam**, adv. GK: 1685 [cf. 4041]. also, surely, too; and, but, yet, even, moreover:– also [438], yea [55], even [49], and [45], both [30], yet [14], likewise [13], moreover [12], moreover (+2050.1) [10], nor [7], neither (+3808) [6], neither [6], also (+2050.1) [5], neither (+3808+2050.1) [5], likewise (+2050.1) [3], so [3], therefore [3], again [2], and (+2050.1) [2], and also [2], for [2], in like manner [2], in times past (+1571+8032+8543) [2], nay [2], nevertheless (+2050.1) [2], nor (+3808) [2], not [2], yea (+2050.1) [2], alike [1], and so much as [1], and yet [1], any [1], as soon as [1], as [1], both (+2050.1) [1], but (+2050.1) [1], but [1], either [1], except (+3588) [1], further [1], heretofore (+4480+4480+8032+8543) [1], howbeit (+2050.1) [1], in time past (+865+8032) [1], indeed [1], more yea [1], moreover as for [1], neither (+408) [1], neither (+408+2050.1) [1], neither yet (+3808+2050.1) [1], no not [1], nor (+3808+2050.1) [1], or [1], so much as [1], surely [1], then [1], therefore (+2050.1) [1], though [1], together with (+2050.1) [1], what [1], with [1], yet (+2050.1) [1]

1572 גָּמָא **gāmā'**, v. GK: 1686 [→ 1573?]. [P] to eat up, swallow up; [H] to give water (to sip):– drink [1], swalloweth [1]

1573 גֹּמֶא **gōme'**, n.m. GK: 1687 [→ 1572?]. papyrus:– bulrushes [2], rushes [1], rush [1]

1574 גֹּמֶד **gōmed**, n.m. GK: 1688 [→ 1575?]. unit of measure: short cubit (the length from the elbow to the knuckles, about 12 to 18 inches):– cubit [1]

1575 גַּמָּדִים **gammādîm**, n.pr.g. GK: 1689 [→ 1574?]. men of Gammad, "[prob.] *valiant men*":– Gammadims [1]

1576 גְּמוּל **g^e mûl**, n.m. GK: 1691 [→ 1580]. what is done; benefit; what is deserved, recompense:– recompence [10], reward [3], as[S] [1], benefits [1], benefit [1], desert [1], deserving [1], given [1]

1577 גָּמוּל **gāmûl**, n.pr.m. GK: 1690 [→ 1580]. Gamul, "*weaned*":– Gamul [1]

1578 גְּמוּלָה **g^e mûlâ**, n.f. GK: 1692 [→ 1580]. what is done; retribution, recompense:– deeds [1], recompences [1], reward [1]

1579 גִּמְזוֹ **gimzô**, n.pr.loc. GK: 1693. Gimzo, "*place of sycamore trees*":– Gimzo [1]

1580 גָּמַל **gāmal**, v. GK: 1694 [→ 1014, 1577, 1576, 1578, 1581?, 1582, 1583, 8408]. [Q] to do, produce, deal fully; to wean; to repay (what is deserved); [Qp, N] to be weaned:– weaned [9], rewarded [7], bestowed on [2], deal bountifully [2], dealt bountifully [2], did [2], recompense [2], weaned child [2], child weaned [1], doeth good [1], done [1], do [1], requite [1], reward [1], ripening [1], served [1], yielded [1]

1581 גָּמָל **gāmāl**, n.m. GK: 1695 [→ 1580?]. camel:– camels [45], camel [5], camels' [3], camel's [1]

1582 גְּמַלִּי **g^e mallî**, n.pr.m. GK: 1696 [→ 1580]. Gemalli, "*my reward*":– Gemalli [1]

1583 גַּמְלִיאֵל **gamlî'ēl**, n.pr.m. GK: 1697 [→ 1580+410]. Gamaliel, "*recompense of God [El]*":– Gamaliel [5]

1584 גָּמַר **gāmar**, v. GK: 1698 [→ 1586, 1587; cf. 1585]. [Q] to bring to an end, fail; fulfill:– ceaseth [1], come to an end [1], fail [1], perfect [1], performeth [1]

1585 גְּמַר **g^e mar** (Aram.), v. GK: 10147 [cf. 1584]. [Pp] to be finished; (as an introduction in a letter) Greetings:– perfect [1]

1586 גֹּמֶר **gōmer**, n.pr.m. & f. GK: 1699 & 1700 [→ 1584]. Gomer, "*complete*":– Gomer [6]

1587 גְּמַרְיָה **g^e maryâ** or גְּמַרְיָהוּ **g^e maryāhû**, n.pr.m. GK: 1701 & 1702 [→ 1584+3068]. Gemariah, "*Yahweh has accomplished*":– Gemariah [5]

1588 גַּן **gan**, n.m. GK: 1703 [→ 1593; cf. 1598]. garden: garden [39], gardens [3]

1589 גָּנַב **gānab**, v. GK: 1704 [→ 1590, 1591, 1592?]. [Q] to steal, be a thief, kidnap; to deceive; [Qp, N, Pu] to be stolen, forcibly carried off; [Ht] to steal oneself away, sneak in:– stolen [11], steal [9], indeed stolen away (+1589) [2], stealeth [2], stealing [2], stolen (+1589) [2], stole [2], carrieth away [1], secretly brought [1], stale away unawares (+3820) [1], stale [1], steal away from [1], steal away [1], stealeth away [1], stealth [1], stolen away unawares (+3824) [1], stolen away [1]

1590 גַּנָּב **gannāb**, n.m. GK: 1705 [→ 1589]. thief; kidnapper:– thief [13], thieves [4]

1591 גְּנֵבָה **g^e nēbâ**, n.f. GK: 1706 [→ 1589]. stolen possession:– theft [2]

1592 גְּנֻבַת **g^e nubat**, n.pr.m. GK: 1707 [→ 1589?]. Genubath, "*thief*":– Genubath [2]

1593 גַּנָּה **gannâ**, n.f. GK: 1708 [→ 1594, 1588; cf. 1598]. same as 1594: garden, grove:– gardens [9], garden [3]

1594 גִּנָּה **ginnâ**, n.f. GK: 1708 [→ 1593]. same as 1593: garden, grove:– garden [4]

1595 גֶּנֶז **genez**, n.[m.]. GK: 1709 & 1710 [→ 1597; cf. 1596]. (royal) treasury; rug, carpet:– treasuries [2], chests [1]

1596 גְּנַז **g^e naz** (Aram.), n.m. GK: 10148 [cf. 1595]. place of treasure and archived documents:– treasure [2], treasures [1]

1597 גַּנְזַךְ **ganzak**, n.[m.]. GK: 1711 [→ 1595]. (temple) storeroom, where treasures are kept:– treasuries [1]

1598 גָּנַן **gānan**, v. GK: 1713 [→ 1588, 1593, 1594, 4043]. [Q] to defend, shield, protect:– defend [7], defending [1]

1599 גִּנְּתוֹן **ginn^e tôn** or גִּנְּתוֹי **ginn^e tôy**, n.pr.m. GK: 1715 & 1714. Ginnethon, Ginnethoi:– Ginnethon [2], Ginnetho [1]

1600 גָּעָה **gā'â**, v. GK: 1716. [Q] to bellow, low (of cattle):– loweth [1], lowing [1]

1601 גֹּעָה **gō'â**, n.pr.loc. GK: 1717. Goah:– Goath [1]

1602 גָּעַל **gā'al**, v. GK: 1718 [→ 1604, 1603; cf. 1351]. [Q] to abhor, despise, loathe; [N] to be defiled; [H] to cause defiling = fail to impregnate:– abhor [4], lothed [2], abhorred [1], faileth [1], lotheth [1], vilely cast away [1]

1603 גַּעַל **ga'al**, n.pr.m. GK: 1720 [→ 1602]. Gaal, "*loathing*":– Gaal [9]

Heb

1604 גֹּעַל ***gōʿal***, n.m. GK: 1719 [→ 1602]. despising, loathing:– lothing [1]

1605 גָּעַר ***gāʿar***, v. GK: 1721 [→ 1606, 4045]. [Q] to rebuke, reprimand; prevent (insects):– rebuke [7], rebuked [4], corrupt [1], rebuketh [1], reproved [1]

1606 גְּעָרָה ***g^{e}ʿārâ***, n.f. GK: 1722 [→ 1605]. rebuke; threat:– rebuke [12], reproof [2], rebuking [1]

1607 גָּעַשׁ ***gāʿaš***, v. GK: 1723. [Q] to shake, tremble; [Pu] to be shaken; [Ht] to shake back and forth, stagger, surge, tremble back and forth:– moved [3], shook [3], shaken [1], toss [1], troubled [1]

1608 גַּעַשׁ ***gaʿaš***, n.pr.loc. GK: 1724. Gaash, "*rumble, quake*":– Gaash [4]

1609 גַּעְתָּם ***gaʿtām***, n.pr.m. GK: 1725. Gatam:– Gatam [3]

1610 גַּף ***gap***, n.m. GK: 1726 & 1727 [→ 102, 1480]. height, elevation; body; by oneself:– himself (+2050.2) [3], highest places (+4791) [1]

1611 גַּף ***gap*** (Aram.), n.f. GK: 10149. wing:– wings [3]

1612 גֶּפֶן ***gepen***, n.f. & m. GK: 1728. vine, grapevine:– vine [43], vines [9], plant of vine [1], tree [1], vine (+3196) [1]

1613 גֹּפֶר ***gōper***, n.[m.]. GK: 1729. cypress (wood); exact identity of the wood is uncertain; "gopher wood" is simply a transliteration of the Hebrew:– gopher [1]

1614 גָּפְרִית ***goprît***, n.f. GK: 1730. sulfur; older versions: brimstone:– brimstone [7]

1615 גִּר ***gir***, n.[m.]. GK: 1732 [cf. 1528]. chalk:– chalkstones (+68) [1]

1616 גֵּר ***gēr***, n.m. GK: 1731 [→ 1628; cf. 1481]. alien, stranger (in a foreign land):– stranger [69], strangers [18], alien [1], sojourner [1], stranger (+376) [1], stranger's [1], strangers (+376) [1]

גּוּר ***gur***. See 1482.

1617 גֵּרָא ***gērāʾ***, n.pr.m. GK: 1733. Gera, "[perhaps] *sojourner*":– Gera [9]

1618 גָּרָב ***gārāb***, n.[m.]. GK: 1734 [→ 1619]. festering sore:– scurvy [2], scab [1]

1619 גָּרֵב ***gārēb***, n.pr.m. & loc. GK: 1735 & 1736 [→ 1618]. Gareb, "*scabby*":– Gareb [3]

1620 גַּרְגַּר ***gargar***, n.m. GK: 1737. ripe olives:– berries [1]

1621 גַּרְגְּרוֹת ***garg^{e}rôt***, n.f.pl. GK: 1738. neck, throat:– neck [4]

1622 גִּרְגָּשִׁי ***girgāšî***, a.g. GK: 1739. Girgashite:– Girgashites [5], Girgashite [2]

1623 גָּרַד ***gārad***, v. GK: 1740. [Ht] to scrape oneself (with a broken piece of pottery):– scrape [1]

1624 גָּרָה ***gārâ***, v. GK: 1741 [→ 8409; cf. 1481]. [P] to stir up (a dispute); [Ht] to provoke (to war), engage (to battle):– meddle [4], contend [3], stirred up [3], stirreth up [3], striven [1]

1625 גֵּרָה ***gērâ***, n.f. GK: 1742 [→ 1641]. cud:– cud [11]

1626 גֵּרָה ***gērâ***, n.f. GK: 1743. gerah (measure, one-twentieth of a shekel, about half a gram):– gerahs [5]

גֹּרָה ***gōrâ***. See 1484.

1627 גָּרוֹן ***gārôn***, n.m. GK: 1744 [→ 1641]. throat, neck; by extension: mouth; an "outstretched neck" is a sign of arrogance and possibly of sexual misconduct:– throat [4], aloud (+871.1) [1], mouth [1], necks [1], neck [1]

1628 גֵּרוּת ***gērût***, n.f.[pr.loc.] GK: 1745 [→ 1616]. habitation; place name: Geruth:– habitation [1]

1629 גָּרַז ***gāraz***, v. GK: 1746 [→ 1631; cf. 1504]. [N] to be cut off, implying destruction:– cut off [1]

1630 גְּרִזִּים ***g^{e}rizîm***, n.pr.loc. GK: 1748. Gerizim:– Gerizim [3], Gerizzim [1]

1631 גַּרְזֶן ***garzen***, n.m. GK: 1749 [→ 1629]. ax, chisel:– axe [4]

1632 גָּרֹל ***gārōl***, a.var. GK: 1754. var. of 1419: large, great:–

גּוֹרָל ***gōrāl***. See 1486.

1633 גָּרַם ***gāram***, v.den. GK: 1750 & 1751 [→ 1634]. [Q] to leave, reserve; [P] to break, to break bones:– break [2], gnaw bones [1]

1634 גֶּרֶם ***gerem***, n.[m.]. GK: 1752 [→ 1633, 1636?; cf. 1635]. bone, rawboned, bony; bareness:– bones [2], bone [1], strong [1], top [1]

1635 גְּרַם ***g^{e}ram*** (Aram.), n.[m.]. GK: 10150 [cf. 1634]. bone:– bones [1]

1636 גַּרְמִי ***garmî***, a.g. GK: 1753 [→ 1634?]. Garmite:– Garmite [1]

1637 גֹּרֶן ***gōren***, n.m. GK: 1755. threshing floor:– threshingfloor [17], floor [10], void place [2], barnfloor [1], barn [1], cornfloor (+1715) [1], corn [1], floors [1], threshingfloors [1], threshingplace [1]

גָּרֹן ***gārōn***. See 1627.

1638 גָּרַס ***gāras***, v. GK: 1756. [Q] to be crushed; [H] to break, crush:– breaketh [1], broken [1]

1639 גָּרַע ***gāraʿ***, v. GK: 1757 & 1758 [→ 4052]. [Q] to take away, reduce, hinder; [Qp] to be cut off (of a beard); [N] to be reduced, be taken away, to disappear; [P] to draw up (drops of water):– diminish [6], taken [3], diminished [2], abated [1], clipt [1], done away [1], kept back [1], maketh small [1], minish [1], restrainest [1], restrain [1], taken away [1], withdraweth [1]

1640 גָּרַף ***gārap***, v. GK: 1759 [→ 106, 4053]. [Q] to sweep away (of a river):– swept away [1]

1641 גָּרַר ***gārar***, v. GK: 1760 [→ 1625, 1627, 4050; cf. 5064]. [Q] to chew; to drag away; [Polal] to be sawn; [Htpol] to drive, swirl:– catch [1], cheweth [1], continuing [1], destroy [1], sawed [1]

1642 גְּרָר ***g^{e}rār***, n.pr.loc. GK: 1761. Gerar, "*circle, region*":– Gerar [10]

1643 גֶּרֶשׂ ***gereś***, n.[m.]. GK: 1762. (coarse) crushed grain, grits, groats:– beaten corn [1], beaten out [1]

1644 גָּרַשׁ ***gāraš***, v. GK: 1763 & 1764 [→ 1645, 1646, 4054]. [Q] to cast up, toss up; to drive out; [Qp] to be divorced; [N] to be tossed, stirred up; to be banished; [P] to drive out, expel [Pu] to be banished:– drive out [11], cast out [8], thrust out [5], driven out [4], divorced [3], drave out [3], drove away [2], put away [2], surely thrust out (+1644) [2], cast up [1], driven forth [1], drive [1], driving out [1], drove out [1], expel [1], troubled [1]

1645 גֶּרֶשׁ ***gereš***, n.[m.]. GK: 1765 [→ 1644]. yield, produce:– put forth [1]

1646 גְּרֻשָׁה ***g^{e}rušâ***, n.f. GK: 1766 [→ 1644]. dispossession:– exactions [1]

1647 גֵּרְשֹׁם ***gēršōm***, n.pr.m. GK: 1768 [→ 1648]. Gershom, Gershon, "*temporary resident there*":– Gershom [14]

1648 גֵּרְשׁוֹן ***gēršôn***, n.pr.m. GK: 1767 [→ 1647, 1649]. Gershon, "*temporary resident there*":– Gershon [17]

1649 גֵּרְשֻׁנִּי ***gēršunnî***, a.g. GK: 1769 [→ 1648]. Gershonite, "*of Gershon*":– Gershonites [9], Gershonite [3], Gershon [1]

1650 גְּשׁוּר ***g^{e}šûr***, n.pr.m. GK: 1770 [→ 1651]. Geshur, "*bridge*":– Geshur [8], Geshurites [1]

1651 גְּשׁוּרִי ***g^{e}šûrî***, a.g. GK: 1771 [→ 1650]. Geshurite, people of Geshur, "*of Geshur*":– Geshurites [4], Geshuri [2]

1652 גָּשַׁם ***gāšam***, v.den. GK: 1772 [→ 1653, 1654, 1656]. [H] to bring rain:– cause rain [1]

1653 גֶּשֶׁם ***gešem***, n.m. GK: 1773 [→ 1654, 1656; cf. 1652]. rain, shower, downpour:– rain [29], shower [3], great rain [1], much rain [1], showers [1]

1654 גֶּשֶׁם ***gešem*** or גַּשְׁמוּ ***gašmû***, n.pr.m. GK: 1774 & 1776 [cf. 1652, 1653]. Geshem, Gashmu, "*rain shower*":– Geshem [3], Gashmu [1]

1655 גְּשֵׁם ***g^{e}šēm*** (Aram.), n.m. GK: 10151. body; the phrase "give up the body" is translated "to die":– body [3], bodies [2]

1656 גֹּשֶׁם ***gōšem***, n.[m.]. GK: 1775 [→ 1653; cf. 1652]. shower, rain:– rained upon [1]

גַּשְׁמוּ ***gašmû***. See 1654.

1657 גֹּשֶׁן ***gōšen***, n.pr.loc. GK: 1777. Goshen, "*mound of earth*":– Goshen [15]

1658 גִּשְׁפָּא ***gišpāʾ***, n.pr.m. GK: 1778. Gishpa, "*listener*":– Gispa [1]

1659 גָּשַׁשׁ ***gāšaš***, v. GK: 1779. [P] to grope along, feel one's way (as if blind):– grope [2]

1660 גַּת ***gat***, n.f. GK: 1780 [→ 1661, 1662, 1667, 1663, 1664, 1665]. winepress; also used as a hiding place:– winepress [2], press [1], wine presses [1], winefat [1]

1661 גַּת ***gat***, n.pr.loc. GK: 1781 [→ 1663, 1665; cf. 1660]. Gath, "*winepress*":– Gath [33], Gath-hepher [1], Gittah-hepher [1]

1662 גַּת הַחֵפֶר ***gat haḥēper*** or גַּת חֵפֶר ***gat ḥēper***, n.pr.loc. GK: 1783 [→ 1660+1886.1+2660]. Gath Hepher, "*winepress waterpit*":–

1663 גִּתִּי ***gittî***, a.g. GK: 1785 [→ 1661; cf. 1660]. Gittite, "*of Gath*":– Gittite [8], Gittites [2]

1664 גִּתַּיִם ***gittayim***, n.pr.loc. GK: 1786 [→ 1660]. Gittaim, "*two winepresses*":– Gittaim [2]

1665 גִּתִּית ***gittît***, tt. GK: 1787 [→ 1661; cf. 1660]. gittith: unknown musical term, possibly the name of the tune, or the name of the instrument that played it, or even related in some way to ceremonies associated with the winepress:– Gittith [3]

1666 גֶּתֶר ***geter***, n.pr.m. GK: 1788. Gether:– Gether [2]

1667 גַּת־רִמּוֹן ***gat-rimmôn***, n.pr.loc. GK: 1784 [→ 1660+7416]. Gath Rimmon, "*winepress of pomegranate*":– Gath-rimmon [4]

1668 דָּא ***dāʾ*** (Aram.), p.demo.f. GK: 10154 [cf. 2090, 2097, 2088]. this, this one:– another [2], one [2], this [2]

1669 דָּאַב ***dāʾab***, v. GK: 1790 [→ 1670, 1671]. [Q] to be dim (of eyes); to sorrow:– mourneth [1], sorrowful [1], sorrow [1]

1670 דְּאָבָה ***d^{e}ʾābâ***, n.f. GK: 1791 [→ 1669]. dismay, despair:– sorrow [1]

1671 דְּאָבוֹן ***d^{e}ʾābôn***, n.[m.]. GK: 1792 [→ 1669]. despair:– sorrow [1]

1672 דָּאַג ***dāʾag***, v. GK: 1793 [→ 1673, 1674]. [Q] to worry, dread, be troubled, be afraid:– afraid [3], careful [1], sorroweth [1], sorry [1], take thought [1]

1673 דֹּאֵג ***dōʾēg***, n.pr.m. GK: 1795 [→ 1672]. Doeg, "*anxious*":– Doeg [6]

1674 דְּאָגָה ***d^{e}ʾāgâ***, n.f. GK: 1796 [→ 1672]. fear, anxiety, restlessness:– carefulness [2], care [1], fear [1], heaviness [1], sorrow [1]

1675 דָּאָה ***dāʾâ***, v. GK: 1797 [→ 1676; cf. 1772]. [Q] to swoop down, pounce; to soar:– fly [3], flieth [1]

1676 דָּאָה ***dāʾâ***, n.f. GK: 1798 [→ 1675]. red kite (bird):– vulture [1]

1677 דֹּב ***dōb***, n.m. GK: 1800 [→ 1680; cf. 1678]. bear (animal):– bear [10], bears [2]

1678 דֹּב ***dōb*** (Aram.), n.[m.]. GK: 10155 [cf. 1677]. bear:– bear [1]

1679 דֹּבֶא ***dōbeʾ***, n.[m.]. GK: 1801. strength:– strength [1]

1680 דָּבַב ***dābab***, v. GK: 1803 [→ 1677, 1681?, 1686?]. [Q] to flow over gently:– causing to speak [1]

1681 דִּבָּה ***dibbâ***, n.f. GK: 1804 [→ 1680?]. bad report, slander, bad reputation, whisper:– slander [3], infamy [2], report [2], defaming [1], evil report [1]

1682 דְּבוֹרָה ***d^{e}bôrâ***, n.f. GK: 1805 [→ 1683; cf. 1696]. wild honey bee; (pl.) swarm of bees:– bees [3], bee [1]

1683 דְּבוֹרָה ***d^{e}bôrâ***, n.pr.f. GK: 1806 [→ 1682; cf. 1696]. Deborah, "*hornet, wasp, wild honey bee*":– Deborah [10]

1684 דְּבַח ***d^{e}baḥ*** (Aram.), v. GK: 10156 [→ 1685, 4056; cf. 2076]. [P] to present a sacrifice as an act of worship:– offered [1]

1685 דְּבַח ***d^{e}baḥ*** (Aram.), n.[m.]. GK: 10157 [→ 1684; cf. 2077]. sacrifice (i.e., animal):– sacrifices [1]

1686 דִּבְיֹנִים ***dibyōnîm***, n.[m.]. GK: 1807 [→ 1680?+3123]. seed pods or doves' dung:– dove's dung [1]

1687 דְּבִיר ***d^{e}bîr***, n.m. GK: 1808 [→ 1688; cf. 1696?]. inner sanctuary, referring to the Most Holy Place:– oracle [16]

1688 דְּבִיר ***d^{e}bîr***, n.pr.m. & loc. GK: 1809 [→ 1687; cf. 1696]. Debir, "*back room [of a shrine temple for oracle pronouncement]*":– Debir [14]

1689 דִּבְלָה ***diblâ***, n.pr.loc. GK: 1812. Diblah:– Diblath [1]

1690 דְּבֵלָה ***d^{e}bēlâ***, n.f. GK: 1811 [→ 1691?]. pressed fig cakes; poultice of figs:– cakes [2], lump [2], cake [1]

1691 דִּבְלַיִם ***diblayim***, n.pr.m. GK: 1813 [→ 1690?]. Diblaim, "*lump of [two dried fig] cakes*":– Diblaim [1]

דִּבְלָתַיִם ***diblātayim***. See 1015.

1692 דָּבַק ***dābaq***, v. GK: 1815 [→ 1695, 1694; cf. 1693]. [Q] to be united, hold fast, keep, cling to; [H] to overtake, cause to cleave, press hard upon; [Pu] to be joined fast, be stuck together; [Ho] be made to cleave, stick to; from the base joining or fastening objects together comes the figure of close association of people:– cleave [13], clave [6], cleaveth [6], cleaved [3], followed hard [3], overtook [3], keep [2], make cleave [2], abide fast [1], cause to stick [1], caused to cleave [1], cleave fast together [1], cleave to [1], follow close [1], followed hard after [1], followeth hard [1], joined together [1], joined [1], keep fast [1], kept fast [1], pursued hard [1], stick [1], stuck [1], take [1]

1693 דְּבַק ***dᵉbaq*** (Aram.), v. GK: 10158 [cf. 1692]. [P] to be united, having a very close association:– cleave [1]

1694 דֶּבֶק ***debeq***, n.m. GK: 1817 [→ 1692]. welding; sections (of armor):– joints [2], sodering [1]

1695 דָּבֵק ***dābēq***, a. GK: 1816 [→ 1692]. holding fast, sticking to:– cleave [1], joining [1], sticketh closer [1]

1696 דָּבַר ***dābar***, v. GK: 1818 & 1819 [→ 1682, 1683, 1687?, 1688, 1697, 1698, 1699, 1699', 1700, 1702, 1703, 1705, 4057]. [Q, P, Ht] to say, speak, tell, command, promise; [Qp, Pu] to be spoken (of); [N] to speak together; a general term for verbal communication, note the specific contextual translations in the KJV; [P] to depart; to destroy; [H] to subdue:– spake [318], speak [273], spoken [174], said [85], speaking [37], promised [29], talked [29], say [27], speaketh [22], told [15], communed [14], pronounced [13], speakest [11], talk [11], spakest [8], tell [7], saith [6], utter [5], commanded [4], commune [4], say on [4], gave [3], talking [3], bid [2], communing [2], promisedst [2], speak well (+1696) [2], talkest [2], taught [2], telleth [2], wont to speak (+1696) [2], answered [1], appointed [1], badest [1], bade [1], declared [1], declare [1], destroyed [1], give [1], named [1], pronounce [1], published [1], rehearsed [1], saidst [1], speak on [1], spokesman [1], subdueth [1], subdue [1], talketh [1], telling [1], thought [1], uttered [1], uttereth [1]

1697 דָּבָר ***dābār***, n.m. GK: 1821 [→ 1696]. what is said, word (or any unit of speech such as a clause, or the whole of communication); matter (any event); thing (any object):– word [434], words [372], thing [178], acts [51], things [49], matter [47], chronicles (+3117) [33], nothing (+3808) [20], saying [20], commandment [15], manner [15], matters [15], business [8], said [8], book [7], speech [7], answer [6], cause [6], promise [6], chronicles (+3117+1886.1) [5], commandments [5], sayings [5], because (+834+5921) [4], portion [4], tidings [4], because of (+5921) [3], concerning (+5921) [3], deed [3], errand [3], message [3], nothing (+408) [3], rate [3], sentence [3], advice [2], affairs [2], answered (+7725) [2], any thing [2], causes [2], certain rate [2], deeds [2], it[S] [2], of [2], ought [2], questions [2], report [2], request [2], spoken [2], talk [2], answer (+7725) [1], answered [1], any[S] [1], as the matter require [1], care [1], case [1], commune [1], communication [1], conferred (+1961) [1], counsel [1], dealings [1], decree [1], disease [1], due [1], duty required [1], duty [1], effect [1], eloquent (+376) [1], every thing [1], evil favouredness (+7451) [1], for (+5921) [1], for sake (+5921) [1], hurt [1], iniquities (+5771) [1], judgment (+4941) [1], language [1], lies (+3577) [1], lies (+8267) [1], lying (+8267) [1], no (+3808) [1], nothing (+3605+3808) [1], oracle [1], parts [1], provision [1], purpose [1], reason [1], sakes [1], sake [1], so (+2088+1886.1+1886.1+3509.1) [1], somewhat to say [1], some [1], song (+7892) [1], sort [1], spakest [1], such [1], tasks [1], task [1], that (+2088+1886.1+1886.1) [1], thing (+1886.1) [1], things concerning [1], thought [1], thus (+2088+1886.1+1886.1) [1], what (+4100+1886.1) [1], whatsoever (+4100) [1], what [1], wherewith [1], whit [1], word's [1], work required [1], works [1]

1698 דֶּבֶר ***deber***, n.m. GK: 1822 & 1823 [→ 1696]. plague, pestilence, disease, a pandemic occurrence of sickness and death; some sources identify specific diseases in specific contexts; thorn:– pestilence [47], murrain [1], plagues [1]

1699 דֹּבֶר ***dōber***, n.[m.]. GK: 1824 [→ 1696]. pasture, in a remote place:– fold [1], manner [1]

1699' דִּבֵּר ***dibbēr***, n.[m.]. GK: 1825 [→ 1696]. word (of God):– word [2]

דְּבִר ***dᵉbir***. See 1687, 1688.

1700 דִּבְרָה ***dibrâ***, n.f. GK: 1826 [→ 1696; cf. 1701]. cause; order; therefore, because: cause [1], end [1], estate [1], order [1], regard [1]

1701 דִּבְרָה ***dibrâ*** (Aram.), n.f. GK: 10159 [cf. 1700]. affair, matter:– intent [1], sakes [1]

דְּבֹרָה ***dᵉbōrâ*** or דְּבֹרָה ***dᵉbōrâ***. See 1682, 1683.

1702 דֹּבְרוֹת ***dōbᵉrôt***, n.f.pl. GK: 1827 [→ 1696]. raft, a collection of logs towed behind a ship:– flotes [1]

1703 דַּבֶּרֶת ***dabberet***, n.f. GK: 1830 [→ 1696]. instruction, word:– words [1]

1704 דִּבְרִי ***dibrî***, n.pr.m. GK: 1828. Dibri, "[poss.] *speak*":– Dibri [1]

1705 דָּבְרַת ***dābᵉrat***, n.pr.loc. GK: 1829 [→ 1696]. Daberath, "*pasture*":– Daberath [2], Dabareh [1]

1706 דְּבַשׁ ***dᵉbaš***, n.m. GK: 1831 [→ 3031]. honey:– honey [52], honeycomb (+3295+1886.1) [1], honeycomb (+6688) [1]

1707 דַּבֶּשֶׁת ***dabbešet***, n.f. GK: 1832 [→ 1708?]. hump (of a camel):– bunches [1]

1708 דַּבֶּשֶׁת ***dabbešet***, n.pr.loc. GK: 1833 [→ 1707?]. Dabbesheth, "*hump*":– Dabbasheth [1]

1709 דָּג ***dāg*** or דָּאג ***dā'g***, n.m. GK: 1834 & 1794 [→ 1711?, 1710, 1728, 1729, 1771; cf. 1770]. fish:– fish [11], fishes [8]

1710 דָּגָה ***dāgâ***, n.f. GK: 1836 [→ 1709]. fish:– fish [14], fish's [1]

1711 דָּגָה ***dāgâ***, v. GK: 1835 [→ 1709?]. [Q] to increase, multiply:– grow [1]

1712 דָּגוֹן ***dāgôn***, n.pr.m. GK: 1837 [→ 1016, 1715]. Dagon (pagan god), "*[god of] grain; fish*":– Dagon [12], Dagon's [1]

1713 דָּגַל ***dāgal***, v.den. GK: 1838 & 1839 [→ 1714]. [Q] to lift a banner; [Qp] to be outstanding, conspicuous; [N] be gathered around the banner(s), organized as troops:– banners [1], chiefest [1], set up banners [1], with banners [1]

1714 דֶּגֶל ***degel***, n.m. GK: 1840 [→ 1713]. standard, banner:– standard [10], standards [3], banner [1]

1715 דָּגָן ***dāgān***, n.m. GK: 1841 [→ 1712]. grain:– corn [37], wheat [2], cornfloor (+1637) [1]

1716 דָּגַר ***dāgar***, v. GK: 1842. [Q] to care for; hatch eggs:– gather [1], sitteth [1]

1717 דַּד ***dad***, n.m. GK: 1843. bosom, breast:– breasts [2], teats [2]

1718 דָּדָה ***dādâ***, v. GK: 1844. [Ht] to walk, lead:– go softly [1], went with [1]

1719 דְּדָן ***dᵉdān***, n.pr.loc. & g. GK: 1847 [→ 1720]. Dedan:– Dedan [11]

1720 דְּדָנִי ***dᵉdānî***, a.g. GK: 1848 [→ 1719]. Dedanite, "*of Dedan*":– Dedanim [1]

1721 דֹּדָנִים ***dōdānîm*** or רֹדָן ***rōdān***, n.pr.g.pl. GK: 1849 & 8102. Dodanim; Rhodes, Rodanim, "*people of Rhodes*":– Dodanim [2]

1722 דְּהַב ***dᵉhab*** (Aram.), n.m. GK: 10160 [cf. 2091]. gold:– gold [14], golden [9]

1723 דְּהוּא ***dᵉhû'*** (Aram.), pt. + pr. GK: 10161 & 10162 [→ 1768+1932]. that is (1768 + 1932):– Dehavites [1]

1724 דָּהַם ***dāham***, v. GK: 1850. [N] to be taken by surprise, be astounded:– astonied [1]

1725 דָּהַר ***dāhar***, v. GK: 1851 [→ 1726]. [Q] to gallop:– pransing [1]

1726 דַּהֲרָה ***dahᵃrâ***, n.f. GK: 1852 [→ 1725]. galloping:– pransings [2]

דּוֹאֵג ***dô'ēg***. See 1673.

1727 דּוּב ***dûb***, v. GK: 1853 [cf. 2100]. [H] to drain away, wear away; loss of life as a fig. extension of draining liquid out of a container:– cause sorrow [1]

דֹּב ***dōb***. See 1677.

1728 דַּוָּג ***dawwāg***, n.m. GK: 1854 [→ 1709]. fisherman:– fishers [1]

1729 דּוּגָה ***dûgâ***, n.f. GK: 1855 [→ 1709]. fishing (hooks):– fishhooks (+5518) [1]

1730 דּוֹד ***dôd***, n.m. GK: 1856 [→ 419, 449, 1085, 1732?, 1733, 1734?, 1737?]. uncle, cousin, relative; beloved one, lover; a term of endearment ranging from friendship and familial affection to romantic love:– beloved [32], uncle [10], love [7], uncle's [6], beloved's (+3807.1) [2], father's brothers' [1], father's brother [1], loves [1], well-beloved [1]

1731 דּוּד ***dûd***, n.m. GK: 1857. basket; kettle, caldron, pot:– basket [2], baskets [1], caldrons [1], kettle [1], pots [1], pot [1]

1732 דָּוִד ***dāwid***, n.pr.m. GK: 1858 [→ 1730?]. David, "*beloved one*":– David [1022], David's [50], David's (+3807.1) [3]

1733 דּוֹדָה ***dôdâ***, n.f. GK: 1860 [→ 1730]. aunt (father's sister):– aunt [1], father's sister [1], uncle's wife [1]

1734 דּוֹדוֹ ***dôdô*** or דֹּדִי ***dōdî***, n.pr.m. GK: 1861 & 1846 [→ 1730?]. Dodo, Dodai, "*beloved*":– Dodo [5]

1735 דֹּדָוָהוּ ***dōdāwāhû***, n.pr.m. GK: 1845. Dodavahu, "*beloved of Yahweh*":– Dodavah [1]

1736 דּוּדָאִים ***dûdā'îm*** or דּוּדַי ***dûday***, n.m. GK: 1859 & 1863. mandrake plant, thought to be a fertility aid or aphrodisiac:– mandrakes [6], baskets [1]

1737 דּוֹדַי ***dôday***, n.pr.m. GK: 1862 [→ 1730?]. Dodai, "*beloved*":– Dodai [1]

1738 דָּוָה ***dāwâ***, v. GK: 1864 [→ 1739, 1741, 1742, 1773?, 4064]. [Q] to have a monthly period, menstruate:– infirmity [1]

1739 דָּוֶה ***dāweh***, a. GK: 1865 [→ 1738]. pertaining to the menstrual cycle; fainting:– faint [2], having sickness [1], menstruous cloth [1], sick [1]

1740 דּוּחַ ***dûaḥ***, v. GK: 1866 [cf. 5080]. [H] to rinse, wash, cleanse:– washed [2], cast out [1], purged [1]

1741 דְּוַי ***dᵉway***, n.[m.]. GK: 1867 [→ 1738]. illness:– languishing [1], sorrowful [1]

1742 דַּוָּי ***dawwāy***, a. GK: 1868 [→ 1738]. faint; afflicted:– faint [3]

דָּוִיד ***dāwîd***. See 1732.

1743 דּוּךְ ***dûk***, v. GK: 1870 [→ 4085; cf. 1790, 1792, 1794, 1854]. [Q] to crush (in a mortar):– beat [1]

1744 דּוּכִיפַת ***dûkîpat***, n.f. GK: 1871. hoopoe:– lapwing [2]

1745 דּוּמָה ***dûmâ***, n.f. GK: 1872 [→ 1826]. silence:– silence [2]

1746 דּוּמָה ***dûmâ***, n.pr.loc. GK: 1873 & 1874. Dumah, "*silence*":– Dumah [4]

1747 דּוּמִיָּה ***dûmiyyâ***, n.f. GK: 1875 [→ 1826; cf. 1820]. silence, stillness; rest:– waiteth [2], silence [1], silent [1]

1748 דּוּמָם ***dûmām***, n.[m.]. GK: 1876 [cf. 1826]. in silence, quietly; lifeless:– dumb [1], quietly wait [1], silent [1]

דּוּמֶשֶׂק ***dûmešeq***. See 1833.

1749 דּוֹנַג ***dônag***, n.m. GK: 1880. wax:– wax [4]

1750 דּוּץ ***dûṣ***, v. GK: 1881. [Q] to leap:– turned into joy [1]

1751 דּוּק ***dûq***, v. GK: 1882 [→ 1785]. [Q] to review:–

1752 דּוּר ***dûr***, v. GK: 1883 & 1884 [→ 115, 1754, 1755, 4071; cf. 1756; cf. 1753]. [Q] to dwell; to pile logs (around, to burn):– burn [1], dwell [1]

1753 דּוּר ***dûr*** (Aram.), v. GK: 10163 [→ 1859, 4070, 8411; cf. 1752]. [P] to live, dwell:– dwell [3], dwelt [2], inhabitants [2]

1754 דּוּר ***dûr***, n.[m.]. GK: 1885 [→ 1752; cf. 8411]. all around, encircling; ball:– ball [1], round about (+1886.1+3509.1) [1]

1755 דּוֹר ***dôr***, n.m. GK: 1886 & 1887 [→ 1752; cf. 1859]. generation, generation to come; descendant; house, dwelling:– generation [57], generations [50], all generations (+1755+2050.1) [26], many generations (+1755+2050.1) [12], all generations (+1755) [4], age [2], all generations (+1755+3605+2050.1) [2], evermore (+1755+2050.1) [2], every generation (+1755+2050.1) [2], every generation (+1755+3605+2050.1) [2], generations (+1755+2050.1) [2], never (+1755+3808+2050.1) [2], throughout all generations (+1755) [2], another[S] [1], posterity [1]

1756 דּוֹר ***dôr*** or דֹּאר ***dō'r***, n.pr.loc. GK: 1888 & 1799 [→ 2576, 5874; cf. 1752]. Dor:– Dor [7]

1757 דּוּרָא ***dûrā'*** (Aram.), n.pr.loc. GK: 10164. Dura:– Dura [1]

1758 דּוּשׁ ***dûš***, v. GK: 1889 [→ 1786, 1788?, 4098; cf. 1759]. [Q] to tread, trample, thresh; [Qp, N, Ho] be trampled, be threshed:– thresh [3], threshed [2], threshing [2], trodden down [2], break [1], tear [1], tread out [1], treadeth out [1]

1759 דּוּשׁ ***dûš*** (Aram.), v. GK: 10165 [cf. 1758]. [P] to trample, tread down:– tread down [1]

1760 דָּחָה ***dāḥâ*** or דָּחַח ***dāḥaḥ***, v. GK: 1890 & 1891 [→ 1762, 4072; cf. 5080; cf. 1761]. [Q] to push, push away; trip up; [Qp] to totter; [N] to be brought down; to be pushed, pushed out; [Pu] to be thrown down:– outcasts [3], thrust sore (+1760) [2], cast down [1], chase [1], driven away [1], driven on [1], overthrow [1], tottering [1]

1761 דַּחֲוָה ***daḥᵃwâ*** (Aram.), n.f. GK: 10166. entertainment, variously interpreted as musical, dancing, sexual, culinary, etc:– instruments of musick [1]

1762 דְּחִי ***dᵉḥî***, n.[m.]. GK: 1892 [→ 1760]. stumbling:– falling [2]

1763 דְּחַל ***dᵉḥal*** (Aram.), v. GK: 10167 [cf. 2119]. [P] to fear, reverence; [Pp] to be terrified, be awesome; [Pa] to make afraid:– dreadful [2], feared [1], fear [1], made afraid [1], terrible [1]

Heb

1764 דֹּחַן ***dōḥan***, n.m. GK: 1893. (sorghum) millet:– millet [1]

1765 דָּחַף ***dāḥap***, v. GK: 1894 [→ 4073]. [Qp] to be spurred on, be in haste; [N] to be eager, be rushed, hurry:– hasted [2], hastened [1], pressed on [1]

1766 דָּחַק ***dāḥaq***, v. GK: 1895. [Q] to afflict, oppress:– thrust [1], vexed [1]

1767 דַּי ***day***, subst. GK: 1896 [→ 1838, 4078]. enough, sufficient:– enough [6], from (+4480) [5], since (+4480) [3], sufficient [3], when (+4480) [3], in (+871.1) [2], very [2], ability [1], able (+3027+4672) [1], able (+3027+5381+3509.1) [1], able to bring (+3027+4672) [1], able [1], according to (+3509.1) [1], after (+4480) [1], among (+871.1) [1], as oft as (+4480) [1], much [1], so much as is sufficient [1], sufffcient for [1], time [1]

1768 דִּי ***dî*** (Aram.), pt.rel. & c. GK: 10168 [cf. 2088, 2098]. who, that, of:– that [100], of [64], which [54], whom [13], forasmuch as (+3606+6903) [8], till (+5705) [8], for [5], because (+3606+6903) [4], when (+3509.4) [4], whereas [4], whomsoever (+4479) [4], whose [4], who [3], because [2], until (+5705) [2], whatsoever (+1768+3606) [2], what [2], whoso (+4479) [2], whosoever (+3606) [2], whosoever (+606+1768+3606) [2], as (+3509.4) [1], as (+3606+6903) [1], at what time (+0.2+5732+871.2) [1], because (+4481) [1], but [1], none (+383+3809) [1], now (+116) [1], seeing [1], than [1], that which [1], therefore (+3606+6903) [1], those [1], though (+3606+6903) [1], what (+3964+3807.2) [1], whatsoever (+3606) [1], whatsoever (+4101) [1], wheresoever (+3606+871.2) [1], where [1]

1769 דִּיבֹן ***dîbôn***, n.pr.loc. GK: 1897 [→ 1769+1410; cf. 1775, 1776]. Dibon:– Dibon [9], Dibon-gad [2]

1770 דִּיג ***dîg***, v.den. GK: 1899 [cf. 1709]. [Q] to catch fish:– fish [1]

1771 דַּיָּג ***dayyāg***, n.m. GK: 1900 [→ 1709]. fisherman:– fishers [2]

1772 דַּיָּה ***dayyâ***, n.f. GK: 1901 [cf. 1675]. falcon:– vultures [1], vulture [1]

1773 דְּיוֹ ***dᵉyô***, n.m. GK: 1902 [→ 1738?]. ink, a writing substance made of soot or metal shavings mixed with oil or resin:– ink [1]

1774 דִּי זָהָב ***dî zāhāb***, n.pr.loc. GK: 1903. Dizahab, "*that which has gold*":– Dizahab [1]

1775 דִּימוֹן ***dîmôn***, n.pr.loc. GK: 1904 [cf. 1769]. Dimon:– Dimon [2]

1776 דִּימוֹנָה ***dîmônâ***, n.pr.loc. GK: 1905 [cf. 1769]. Dimonah:– Dimonah [1]

1777 דִּין ***dîn***, v. GK: 1906 [→ 1779, 1781, 1783, 1835, 4066, 4068, 4079, 4082, 4090; cf. 1778 (also used with compound proper names)]. [Q] to judge, punish; to plead, defend, vindicate, contend for; [N] to argue:– judge [14], judged [2], at strife [1], contend [1], execute [1], judgeth [1], minister judgment [1], plead the cause [1], plead [1], strive [1]

1778 דִּין ***dîn*** (Aram.), v. GK: 10169 [→ 1780, 1782, 1784, 4083; cf. 1777]. [P] to administer justice, judge:– judge [1]

1779 דִּין ***dîn***, n.[m.]. GK: 1907 [→ 1777; cf. 1780]. cause, legal case; judgment, justice:– judgment [9], cause [8], plea [2], strife [1]

1780 דִּין ***dîn*** (Aram.), n.m. GK: 10170 [→ 1778; cf. 1779]. judgment, court (place of judgment):– judgment [5]

1781 דַּיָּן ***dayyān***, n.m. GK: 1908 [→ 1777; cf. 1782]. defender, judge:– judge [2]

1782 דַּיָּן ***dayyān*** (Aram.), n.m. GK: 10171 [→ 1778; cf. 1781]. judge:– judges [1]

1783 דִּינָה ***dînâ***, n.pr.f. GK: 1909 [→ 1777]. Dinah, "*female judge*":– Dinah [7], Dinah's [1]

1784 דִּינָיֵא ***dînāyēʾ*** (Aram.), n.pr.g. GK: 10172 [→ 1778]. judge:– Dinaites [1]

דִּיפַת ***dîpat***. See 7384.

1785 דָּיֵק ***dāyēq***, n.m. GK: 1911 [→ 1751]. siege works:– forts [3], fort [3]

1786 דַּיִשׁ ***dayiš***, n.m. GK: 1912 [→ 1758]. threshing (season):– threshing [1]

1787 דִּישׁוֹן ***dîšôn***, n.pr.m. GK: 1914 [→ 1788?]. Dishon, Dishan, "*ibex[?]*":– Dishon [6]

1788 דִּישׁוֹן ***dîšôn***, n.[m.]. GK: 1913 [→ 1787?, 1789?; cf. 1758?]. ibex:– pygarg [1]

1789 דִּישָׁן ***dîšān***, n.pr.m. GK: 1915 [→ 1788?]. Dishan, "*ibex[?]*":– Dishan [5], Dishon [1]

1790 דַּךְ ***dak***, a. GK: 1916 [→ 1795; cf. 1743, 1792, 1794, 1854]. oppressed:– oppressed [3], afflicted [1]

1791 דֵּךְ ***dēk*** (Aram.), p.demo.com. GK: 10173 [→ 1797]. this:– this [12], the same [1]

1792 דָּכָא ***dākāʾ***, v. GK: 1917 [→ 1793; cf. 1743, 1790, 1794, 1854]. [N] to be contrite; [P] to crush; [Pu] to be crushed, be dejected, be humbled; [Ht] to lie crushed:– break in pieces [3], broken [2], crushed [2], beat to pieces [1], broken in pieces [1], bruised [1], bruise [1], contrite ones [1], crush [1], destroyed [1], destroy [1], humbled [1], oppress [1], smitten down [1]

1793 דַּכָּא ***dakkāʾ***, a. & n.[m.]. GK: 1918 & 1919 [→ 1792]. crushed, contrite; dust:– contrite [2], destruction [1]

1794 דָּכָה ***dākâ***, v. GK: 1920 [→ 1796; cf. 1743, 1790, 1792, 1854]. [Q, P] to crush; [N] to be crushed, contrite:– broken [2], contrite [1], croucheth [1], sore broken [1]

1795 דַּכָּה ***dakkâ***, n.f. GK: 1921 [→ 1790]. crushing (of testicle):– stones [1]

1796 דֳּכִי ***dᵒkî***, n.[m.]. GK: 1922 [→ 1794]. pounding (waves):– waves [1]

1797 דִּכֵּן ***dikkēn*** (Aram.), p.demo.com. GK: 10174 [→ 1791]. that:– same [1], that [1], this [1]

1798 דְּכַר ***dᵉkar*** (Aram.), n.m. GK: 10175 [cf. 2145]. ram (male animal):– rams [3]

1799 דִּכְרוֹן ***dikrôn*** or דָּכְרָן ***dokrān*** (Aram.), n.[m.]. GK: 10176 & 10177 [cf. 2146]. memorandum, record:– records [2], record [1]

1800 דַּל ***dal***, a. GK: 1924 [→ 1803; cf. 1809]. poor, needy, humble; weak, haggard, scrawny:– poor [43], needy [2], lean [1], weaker [1]

1801 דָּלַג ***dālag***, v. GK: 1925. [Q, P] to scale, ascend, leap up over:– leaped over [2], leap [2], leaping [1]

1802 דָּלָה ***dālâ***, v. GK: 1926 & 1927 [→ 1805, 1806, 1808]. [Q, P] to draw up, draw water (from a well); [Q] to hang limp, dangle:– drew water enough (+1802) [2], draw out [1], drew water [1], lifted up [1]

1803 דַּלָּה ***dallâ***, n.f. GK: 1929 & 1930 [→ 1800, 1809]. poor, a class of people with little status, influence, and social value; threads remaining on the loom; flowing hair:– poor [5], hair [1], pining sickness [1], poorest sort [1]

1804 דָּלַח ***dālaḥ***, v. GK: 1931. [Q] to churn, stir up:– trouble [2], troubledst [1]

1805 דְּלִי ***dᵉlî***, n.[m.]. GK: 1932 [→ 1802]. (water) bucket, possibly made of leather:– buckets [1], bucket [1]

1806 דְּלָיָה ***dᵉlāyâ*** or דְּלָיָהוּ ***dᵉlāyāhû***, n.pr.m. GK: 1933 & 1934 [→ 1802+3068]. Delaiah, "*Yahweh draws up [like water in a bucket]*":– Delaiah [6], Dalaiah [1]

1807 דְּלִילָה ***dᵉlîlâ***, n.pr.f. GK: 1935 [→ 1809]. Delilah, "*tease*":– Delilah [6]

1808 דָּלִית ***dālît***, n.f. GK: 1936 [→ 1802]. branch, bough:– branches [8]

1809 דָּלַל ***dālal***, v. GK: 1937 & 1938 [→ 1800, 1803, 1807]. [Q] to be in need, be weak, fade; to dangle:– brought low [3], dried up [1], emptied [1], fail [1], impoverished [1], made thin [1], not equal [1]

1810 דִּלְעָן ***dilʿān***, n.pr.loc. GK: 1939. Dilean, "*cucumber; protrude*":– Dilean [1]

1811 דָּלַף ***dālap***, v. GK: 1940 & 1941 [→ 1812, 1813, 3044]. [Q] to leak; to pour out; to be weary, be sleepless:– droppeth through [1], melteth [1], poureth out [1]

1812 דֶּלֶף ***delep***, n.m. GK: 1942 [→ 1811]. leaky roof:– continual dropping (+2956) [1], dropping [1]

1813 דַּלְפוֹן ***dalpôn***, n.pr.m. GK: 1943 [→ 1811]. Dalphon, "*crafty; sleepless*":– Dalphon [1]

1814 דָּלַק ***dālaq***, v. GK: 1944 [→ 1816; cf. 1815]. [Q] to set on fire; to hunt, chase, pursue; [H] to inflame, kindle:– kindle [2], burning [1], chasing [1], hotly pursued [1], inflame [1], persecute [1], persecutors [1], pursued [1]

1815 דְּלַק ***dᵉlaq*** (Aram.), v. GK: 10178 [cf. 1814]. [P] to be ablaze, burn:– burning [1]

1816 דַּלֶּקֶת ***dalleqet***, n.f. GK: 1945 [→ 1814]. inflammation:– inflammation [1]

1817 דֶּלֶת ***delet***, n.f. [& m.?]. GK: 1923 & 1928 & 1946. door, gate; column, lid, leaf (of a door):– doors [48], door [21], gates [13], leaves [4], lid [1], two leaved gates [1]

1818 דָּם ***dām***, n.m. GK: 1947. blood, lifeblood; by extension: bloodshed, death; blood-colored fluids: grape juice, wine; "to pour out blood" is "to kill" since life is in the blood:– blood [342], bloody [15], bloodguiltiness [1], bloodthirsty (+376) [1], person[S] [1]

1819 דָּמָה ***dāmâ***, v. GK: 1948 [→ 1823, 1824, 1825; cf. 1821]. [Q] to be like, liken, resemble; [N] to be like; [P] to think, plan, intend; to liken; [Ht] to consider oneself equal to:– like [14], liken [4], thought [4], likened [2], compared [1], devised [1], meaneth [1], think [1], thoughtest [1], used similitudes [1]

1820 דָּמָה ***dāmâ***, v. GK: 1949 & 1950 [→ 1822?, 1824; cf. 1747, 1826]. [Q] to destroy; to cease; to be silent; [N] to perish, be ruined, be destroyed, be wiped out; to be silenced:– cut off [3], brought to silence [2], perish [2], utterly cut off (+1820) [2], ceaseth [1], cease [1], cut down [1], destroyed [1], destroy [1], undone [1]

1821 דְּמָה ***dᵉmâ*** (Aram.), v. GK: 10179 [cf. 1819]. [P] to look like, resemble:– like [2]

1822 דֻּמָה ***dumâ***, n.f. GK: 1951 [→ 1820?]. one silenced:– destroyed [1]

1823 דְּמוּת ***dᵉmût***, n.f. GK: 1952 [→ 1819]. likeness, figure, image, form:– likeness [19], similitude [2], fashion [1], like (+3509.1) [1], like as [1], manner [1]

1824 דְּמִי ***dᵉmî*** or דֳּמִי ***dᵒmî***, n.[m.]. GK: 1953 & 1954 [→ 1819, 1820]. silence, rest; prime (of life), a fig. extension of being at a midway point in a journey:– cutting off [1], keep silence [1], rest [1], silence [1]

1825 דִּמְיוֹן ***dimyôn***, n.[m.]. GK: 1955 [→ 1819]. likeness:– like [1]

1826 דָּמַם ***dāmam***, v. GK: 1957 & 1958 & 1959 [→ 1745, 1747, 1827; cf. 1748, 1820]. [Q] to perish; to be still, be silent, be quiet, rest; [N] to be laid waste, be silenced, be destroyed; [Po] to quiet; [H] to doom to perish:– silent [4], still [4], cut off [3], cut down [2], keep silence [2], kept silence [2], ceased [1], cease [1], forbear [1], held peace [1], keepeth silence [1], put to silence [1], quieted [1], rested [1], rest [1], stand still [1], stood still [1], tarry [1], wait [1]

1827 דְּמָמָה ***dᵉmāmâ***, n.f. GK: 1960 [→ 1826]. hush, whisper:– calm [1], silence [1], still [1]

1828 דֹּמֶן ***dōmen***, n.m. GK: 1961 [→ 4087]. refuse, dung:– dung [6]

1829 דִּמְנָה ***dimnâ***, n.pr.loc. GK: 1962. Dimnah, "*manure*":– Dimnah [1]

1830 דָּמַע ***dāmaʿ***, v. GK: 1963 [→ 1831, 1832]. [Q] to weep:– weep sore (+1830) [2]

1831 דֶּמַע ***demaʿ***, n.[m.]. GK: 1964 [→ 1830]. juice:– liquors [1]

1832 דִּמְעָה ***dimʿâ***, n.f. GK: 1965 [→ 1830]. tears, weeping:– tears [23]

1833 דְּמֶשֶׁק ***dᵉmešeq***, n.[m.?]. GK: 1967 [→ 1834?]. Damascus, damask [?]:– Damascus [1]

1834 דַּמֶּשֶׂק ***dammeśeq*** or דּוּמֶּשֶׂק ***dûmmeśeq*** or דַּרְמֶשֶׂק ***darmeśeq***, n.pr.loc. GK: 1877 & 1966 & 2008 [→ 1833?]. Damascus:– Damascus [44], Syria-damascus (+758) [1]

1835 דָּן ***dān***, n.pr.m. & loc. GK: 1968 [→ 1842, 1839; cf. 1777]. Dan, "*judge*":– Dan [71]

1836 דְּנָה ***dᵉnâ*** (Aram.), p.demo.com. GK: 10180 [→ 412, 429, 459, 479]. this, that:– this [38], therefore (+3606+6903) [3], these [3], hereafter (+311) [2], thus (+3509.4) [2], wherefore (+3606+6903) [2], aforetime (+4481+6928) [1], another [1], for this cause (+3606+6903) [1], one [1], such (+3509.4) [1], that (+3606+6903) [1], therefore (+5922) [1], which [1]

1837 דַּנָּה ***dannâ***, n.pr.loc. GK: 1972 [→ 4091]. Dannah, "*stronghold*":– Dannah [1]

1838 דִּנְהָבָה ***dinhābâ***, n.pr.loc. GK: 1973 [→ 1767+5107]. Dinhabah:– Dinhabah [2]

1839 דָּנִי ***dānî***, a.g. GK: 1974 [→ 1835]. Danite, men of Dan, "*of Dan*":– Danites [4], Dan [1]

1840 דָּנִאֵל ***dāniʾēl*** or דָּנִיֵּאל ***dāniyyēʾl***, n.pr.m. GK: 1971 & 1975 [→ 1777+410; cf. 1841]. Danel, Daniel; this can refer to four different persons, the most prominent being the sage and prophet of the captivity, "*God is [my] judge*":– Daniel [29]

1841 דָּנִיֵּאל ***dāniyyē'l*** (Aram.), n.pr.m. GK: 10181 [cf. 1840]. Daniel, "*God (El) is my judge*":– Daniel [52]

1842 דָּן יַעַן ***dān ya'an***, n.pr.loc. GK: 1970 [→ 1835]. Dan Jaan:– Dan-jaan [1]

1843 דֵּעַ ***dēa'***, n.[m.]. GK: 1976 [→ 1844; cf. 3045]. what is known, knowledge:– opinion [3], knowledge [2]

1844 דֵּעָה ***dē'â***, n.f. GK: 1978 [→ 1843; cf. 3045]. knowledge:– knowledge [6]

1845 דְּעוּאֵל ***d'û'ēl***, n.pr.m. GK: 1979 [→ 3045+410]. Deuel, "*known of God [El]*":– Deuel [4]

1846 דָּעַךְ ***dā'ak***, v. GK: 1980 [cf. 2193]. [Q] to snuff out, extinguish; [N] to vanish; [Pu] to die out:– put out [6], consumed [1], extinct [1], quenched [1]

1847 דַּעַת ***da'at***, n.f. & m. GK: 1981 & 1982 & 1983 [→ 3045]. knowledge; understanding, learning; claim:– knowledge [80], know [4], unwittingly (+1097+871.1) [2], cunning [1], hath knowledge (+3045) [1], have knowledge (+3045) [1], ignorantly (+1097+871.1) [1], knew [1], knowest (+5921) [1], unawares (+1097+871.1) [1]

1848 דֳּפִי ***d'pî***, n.[m.]. GK: 1984. blemish, stain; slander:– slanderest (+5414) [1]

1849 דָּפַק ***dāpaq***, v. GK: 1985 [→ 1850]. [Q] to drive hard; to knock hard (= worry); [Ht] to pound (on a door):– beat [1], knocketh [1], overdrive [1]

1850 דָּפְקָה ***dopqâ***, n.pr.loc. GK: 1986 [→ 1849]. Dophkah, "*drive [sheep]*":– Dophkah [2]

1851 דַּק ***daq***, a. GK: 1987 [→ 1854]. gaunt, thin, dwarfed; finely ground (incense), fine (dust):– thin [5], small [4], leanfleshed (+1320) [2], beaten small [1], dwarf [1], very little thing [1]

1852 דֹּק ***dōq***, n.[m.]. GK: 1988 [→ 1854]. canopy, thin veil:– curtain [1]

1853 דִּקְלָה ***diqlâ***, n.pr.m.[loc.]. GK: 1989. Diklah, "*[place of] date palms*":– Diklah [2]

1854 דָּקַק ***dāqaq***, v. GK: 1990 [→ 1851, 1852; cf. 1743, 1790, 1792, 1794; cf. 1855]. [Q] to finely crush or grind; [H] to grind to powder, break to pieces; [Ho] to be ground (to make bread):– powder [2], stampt small [2], beat in pieces [1], beat small [1], bruised [1], bruise [1], made dust [1], small [1], stamped [1], stamp [1], very small [1]

1855 דְּקַק ***d'qaq*** (Aram.), v. GK: 10182 [cf. 1854]. [P] to break to pieces; [H] to crush, smash, pulverize:– brake in pieces [5], break in pieces [3], breaketh in pieces [1], broken to pieces [1]

1856 דָּקַר ***dāqar***, v. GK: 1991 [→ 1128, 1857, 4094]. [Q] to drive through, pierce, stab; [Qp, N, Pu] to be pierced:– thrust through [8], pierced [1], stricken through [1], wounded [1]

1857 דֶּקֶר ***deqer***, n.pr.m. GK: 1992 [→ 1856]. Deker:– Dekar [1]

1858 דַּר ***dar***, n.[m.]. GK: 1993. mother-of-pearl:– white [1]

1859 דָּר ***dār*** (Aram.), n.[m.]. GK: 10183 [→ 1753; cf. 1755]. generation; the phrase "from generation to generation" indicates an unlimited span of time: "eternal, forever":– generation [4]

דֹּר ***dōr***. See 1755.

1860 דֵּרָאוֹן ***dērā'ôn***, n.m. GK: 1994. loathing, contempt, aversion:– abhorring [1], contempt [1]

1861 דָּרְבָן ***dorbān***, n.[m.]. GK: 1995 & 1996. (iron) goading stick:– goads [2]

1862 דַּרְדַּע ***darda'***, n.pr.m. GK: 1997 [cf. 1873]. Darda:– Darda [1]

1863 דַּרְדַּר ***dardar***, n.[m.]. GK: 1998. thistle:– thistles [1], thistle [1]

1864 דָּרוֹם ***dārôm***, n.m. GK: 1999. south; south wind:– south [17]

1865 דְּרוֹר ***d'rôr***, n.[m.]. GK: 2001 & 2002. freedom, liberty; an event required every fifty years to restore Israelite slaves to freedom and Israelite land to tribal allotments; oil of myrrh, stacte:– liberty [7], pure [1]

1866 דְּרוֹר ***d'rôr***, n.f. GK: 2000. a kind of bird, perhaps swallow or dove:– swallow [2]

1867 דָּרְיָוֶשׁ ***dār'yāweš***, n.pr.m. GK: 2003 [cf. 1868]. Darius, "*he who upholds the good*":– Darius [10]

1868 דָּרְיָוֶשׁ ***dār'yāweš*** (Aram.), n.pr.m. GK: 10184 [cf. 1867]. Darius, "*he who upholds the good*":– Darius [15]

1869 דָּרַךְ ***dārak***, v. GK: 2005 [→ 1870, 4096]. [Q] to go out, set out, march on, walk upon, trample; to bend (a bow); [Qp] to string (a bow), be bent (of a bow); [H] to shoot (a bow); to cause to tread, to enable to go; to lead, guide:– tread [12], bend [7], bent [7], trodden [6], treadeth [4], bendeth [2], lead [2], archers (+7198) [1], archer [1], come [1], drew [1], goeth [1], guide [1], leadeth [1], led forth [1], led [1], make go over [1], make to go [1], make to walk [1], shoot [1], thresh [1], tread out [1], tread upon [1], treaders [1], treader [1], treading [1], trodden down [1], trode down [1], trode [1], walk [1]

1870 דֶּרֶךְ ***derek***, n.m. GK: 2006 [→ 1869]. way, path, route, road, journey; by extension: conduct, way of life; a pagan god (Am 8:14):– way [460], ways [164], toward [29], journey [23], manner [8], conversation [2], towards [2], along by (+4480) [1], away (+871.1) [1], by [1], custom [1], eastward (+6921+1886.1) [1], high way [1], in the way go (+5921+6310) [1], journeyed (+6213) [1], pass by (+5674) [1], passengers (+5674) [1], pathway (+5410) [1], through [1], transgression (+6588) [1], way side [1], wayfaring men (+1980) [1], wayside (+3027) [1], whithersoever (+834+871.1+1886.1) [1]

1871 דַּרְכְּמוֹנִים ***dark'mônîm***, n.[m.]. GK: 2007 [→ 150]. (pl.) drachmas (Persian: a unit of weight used as a money, the value of which is uncertain):– drams [4]

1872 דְּרָע ***d'rā'*** (Aram.), n.[f.]. GK: 10185 [→ 153; cf. 2220]. arm:– arms [1]

1873 דָּרַע ***dāra'***, n.pr.m. GK: 2009 [cf. 1862]. Daraa:– Dara [1]

1874 דַּרְקוֹן ***darqôn***, n.pr.m. GK: 2010. Darkon, "[perhaps] *rough* or *stern*":– Darkon [2]

1875 דָּרַשׁ ***dāraš***, v. GK: 2011 [→ 4097]. [Q] to seek, inquire, consult; [Qp] to ponder, be sought after; [N] to let oneself be inquired of, to allow a search to be made:– seek [54], inquire [29], sought [19], require [10], inquired [5], seeketh [5], inquired of [4], inquire of [3], search [3], diligently sought (+1875) [2], inquired of at all (+1875) [2], required [2], searcheth [2], seeking [2], sought after [2], sought out [2], surely require (+1875) [2], ask [1], cared [1], careth for [1], examine [1], inquired for [1], make inquisition [1], maketh inquisition [1], necromancer (+413+1886.1) [1], questioned [1], regard [1], search for [1], searchest [1], seek after [1], seek out [1], seeketh after [1], sought for [1]

1876 דָּשָׁא ***dāšā'***, v. GK: 2012 [→ 1877]. [Q] to become green (of pastures); [H] to produce, cause to shoot forth:– bring forth [1], spring [1]

1877 דֶּשֶׁא ***deše'***, n.m. GK: 2013 [→ 1876; cf. 1883]. (new) green vegetation, (new) green grass:– grass [6], herb [4], tender grass [2], tender herb [2], green [1]

1878 דָּשֵׁן ***dāšēn***, v. GK: 2014 [→ 1879, 1880]. [Q] to thrive, grow fat; [P] to anoint, give health; to remove the (fat) ashes; [Pu] to prosper, be satisfied, be soaked (with fat); [Hotpaal] to be covered with fat:– made fat [5], accept [1], anointest [1], maketh fat [1], receive ashes [1], take away ashes [1], waxen fat [1]

1879 דָּשֵׁן ***dāšēn***, a. GK: 2015 [→ 1878]. rich (pertaining to food which is fresh and possibly juicy), fresh:– fat [3]

1880 דֶּשֶׁן ***dešen***, n.m. GK: 2016 [→ 1878]. fat; ashes (the burned wood of the altar fire soaked with fat); by extension: abundance, riches, choice food; in the ancient Near East fatness was a positive, enviable state, though extreme obesity could be denounced or ridiculed:– ashes [8], fatness [7]

1881 דָּת ***dāt***, n.f. GK: 2017 [cf. 1882]. command (either written or oral), prescription, custom, edict, law:– decree [9], law [6], laws [3], commandment [2], commissions [1], manner [1]

1882 דָּת ***dāt*** (Aram.), n.f. GK: 10186 [cf. 1881]. law, decree, usually a written, codified prescription by either human or deity; the "Law of God" can refer to the Torah, the first five books of the Hebrew Bible:– law [9], decree [3], laws [2]

1883 דֶּתֶא ***dete'*** (Aram.), n.[m.]. GK: 10187 [cf. 1877]. grass (of the open country):– tender grass [2]

1884 דְּתָבַר ***d'tābar*** (Aram.), n.m. GK: 10188 [cf. 1881]. judge:– counsellers [2]

1885 דָּתָן ***dātān***, n.pr.m. GK: 2018. Dathan, "*strong*":– Dathan [10]

1886 דֹּתָן ***dōtān***, n.pr.loc. GK: 2019. Dothan, "*two wells*":– Dothan [3]

1886.1 -הַ ***ha-***, art.pref. GK: 2021 [cf. 0.2 (also used with compound proper names)]. the, a, who, this, that; often not translated:– the [18118], that [957], a [767], which [269], an [87], who [55], O [53], to day (+3117) [50], every morning (+1242+1242+871.1+871.1+1886.1) [20], he [17], for ever (+3117+3605) [15], it [12], without (+2351+871.1) [12], daily (+3117+3605) [11], those [10]*

1886.2 -הֲ ***h'-***, inter.pt.pref. GK: 2022 [cf. 1886.6]. introduces a question; usually translated as a question mark:– *usually untranslated* [711], whether [23], if [5], as if [1], either [1], not [1], or [1]

1886.3 ־ָה ***-āh*** or ־הָ ***-hā*** or ־ָה ***-â*** or ־הָא ***-hā'***, p.f.s.suf. GK: 2023 [→ 1886.4, 1930.2, 1958.1, 1992.1, 1993.1, 2006.1, 2009.1, 2050.2, 3963.1, 4123.1, 4993.1, 5089.1, 5105.2]. she, her; it, its:– her [1518], it [649], thereof [343], therein (+871.1) [86], his [81], she [44], their [24], the[S] [18], them [15], wherein (+834+871.1) [14], that [13], whose [13], therewith (+871.1) [11], thereon (+5921) [10], whereof [10]*

1886.4 ־ה ***-ōh***, p.m.s.suf. GK: 2024 [→ 1886.3]. he, his, him:– his [11], it [3], one [3], them [3], they [3], he [1], same [1], thereof [1]

1886.5 ־ָה ***-â***, adv.suf. GK: 2025. to, toward; a suffixed adverb or remnant of an archaic case ending:– to [269], into [97], toward [58], thither (+8033) [50], unto [49], upward (+4605) [45], on [41], whither (+834+8033) [38], upon [32], there (+8033) [31], westward (+3220) [21], northward (+6828) [20], above (+4480+4605+3807.1) [18], whither (+575) [16], eastward (+4217) [15], west (+3220) [15], east (+6921) [14], at [13], how long (+575+5704) [13], southward (+5045) [13], in [12], upward (+4605+3807.1) [12], eastward (+6924) [9], north (+6828) [9], towards [9], abroad (+2351) [8], southward (+8486) [8], where (+834+8033) [7], above (+4605+3807.1) [6], without (+2351) [6], east (+6924) [5], inward (+1004) [5], on high (+4605+3807.1) [5], therein (+8033) [5], above (+4605) [4], any whither (+575+575+1886.5+2050.1) [4], eastward (+6921) [4], out (+2351) [3], where (+575) [3], yearly (+3117+3117+4480) [3], exceedingly (+4605+3807.1) [2], exceedingly (+4605+5704+3807.1) [2], forward (+4605) [2], south (+5045) [2], south (+8486+1886.5) [2], still (+4605+3807.1) [2], upward (+4480+4605+3807.1) [2], very high (+4605+4605+1886.5) [2], whither (+575+575+1886.5+2050.1) [2], whither (+8033) [2], without (+2351+4480) [2], abroad (+413+2351+1886.1) [1], by [1], east (+4217+6924) [1], exceeding (+4605) [1], exceeding (+4605+3807.1) [1], for [1], hither (+2008) [1], in north (+6828) [1], north side (+6828) [1], northwards (+6828) [1], on high (+4480+4605+3807.1) [1], outward (+2351) [1], over (+4480+4605+3807.1) [1], over (+4605+3807.1) [1], over and above (+4480+4605+3807.1) [1], overturned (+2015+4605+3807.1) [1], south (+8486) [1], south [1], thitherward (+8033) [1], through [1], unto (+8033) [1], up (+4605+3807.1) [1], very (+4605+3807.1) [1], westward (+4628) [1], whereinto (+834+8033) [1], whereunto (+834+8033) [1], whithersoever (+575) [1], within (+1004) [1], within (+1004+4480) [1], without (+2351+1886.1) [1], without (+2435) [1]

Heb

1886.6 -הֲ ***h'-*** (Aram.), inter.pt. GK: 10190 [cf. 1886.2]. introduces a question, translated as a question mark rather than as a word:– *not translated* [6]

1886.7 ־ָה ***-â*** (Aram.), art.suf. GK: 10191 [→ 0.2]. the, a:– the [32], The[S] [1], a [1], it [1], thereof [1], this [1]

1886.8 ־ֵהּ ***-ēh*** (Aram.), p.suf.3.m.s. GK: 10192 [→ 1958.2; cf. 1886.4]. he, him, his; it, its:– his [61], him [29], thereof [25], whose [11], it [4], the[S] [2], their [2], whom [2], he [1], his (+3807.2) [1], his own [1], same [1]

1886.9 ־ַהּ ***-ah*** (Aram.), p.suf.3.f.s. GK: 10193 [cf. 1886.3]. she, her; it, its:– it [21], his [5], same [3], whom [2], whose [2], the same (+1459) [1], therein (+1459+871.2) [1], therein (+871.2) [1], thereof [1]

1887 הֵא ***hē'***, interj. GK: 2026 [cf. 1888]. surely! see!, a discourse marker of emphasis:– behold [1], lo [1]

1888 הָא ***hā'*** or הֵא ***hē'*** (Aram.), demo.pt. GK: 10194 & 10195 [cf. 1887]. just as; look!, there!:– even [1], lo [1]

1889 הֶאָח ***he'āḥ***, interj. GK: 2027. Ah!, Aha!:– aha [10], ah [1], ha [1]

הָאֲרָרִי ***hā'rārî***. See 2043.

1890 הַבְהָב ***habhab***, n.m. GK: 2037. gift:– offerings [1]

1891 הָבַל ***hābal***, v.den. GK: 2038 [→ 1892]. [Q] to be worthless, meaningless; be proud, vain; [H] to fill with false hopes, cause to become vain:– vain [2], become vain [1], make vain [1]

1892 הֶבֶל ***hebel***, n.m. GK: 2039 [→ 1891; cf. 1893]. breath; by extension: something with no substance, meaninglessness, worthlessness, vanity, emptiness, futility; idol:– vanity [49], vanities [12], in vain [7], vain [4], altogether vain [1]

1893 הֶבֶל ***hebel***, n.pr.m. GK: 2040 [cf. 1892?]. Abel, "*morning mist*":– Abel [8]

1894 הָבְנִים ***hobnîm***, n.[m.]. GK: 2041. ebony:– ebeny [1]

1895 הָבַר ***hābar***, v. GK: 2042. [Q] (ptcp.) astrologer, one who divides (classifies) the night sky for the purpose of telling the future:– astrologers (+8064) [1]

1896 הֵגֶא ***hēgē'*** or הֵגַי ***hēgay***, n.pr.m. GK: 2043 & 2051. Hegai:– Hegai [3], Hege [1]

1897 הָגָה ***hāgâ***, v. GK: 2047 [→ 1899, 1900, 1902]. [Q] to utter a sound, moan, meditate; [H] to mutter; from the base meaning of uttering a sound of any kind comes figure of meditation, the act of thoughtful deliberation with the implication of speaking to oneself:– meditate [6], mourn [3], speak [3], imagine [2], mourn sore (+1897) [2], studieth [2], muttered [1], mutter [1], roaring [1], speaketh [1], talk [1], uttering [1], utter [1]

1898 הָגָה ***hāgâ***, v. GK: 2048 [cf. 3014]. [Q] to expel, remove:– take away [2], stayeth [1]

1899 הֶגֶה ***hegeh***, n.m. GK: 2049 [→ 1897]. moaning, mourning, rumbling:– mourning [1], sound [1], tale [1]

1900 הָגוּת ***hāgût***, n.f. GK: 2050 [→ 1897]. utterance, meditation, which can include thinking and planning:– meditation [1]

1901 הָגִיג ***hāgîg***, n.m. GK: 2052. sighing, meditation:– meditation [1], musing [1]

1902 הִגָּיוֹן ***higgāyôn***, n.m. GK: 2053 [→ 1897]. muttering (sounds spoken to no one in particular), meditation; Higgaion, melody:– Higgaion [1], device [1], meditation [1], solemn sound [1]

1903 הָגִין ***hāgîn***, a. GK: 2054. corresponding:– directly [1]

1904 הָגָר ***hāgār***, n.pr.f. GK: 2057 [→ 1905?]. Hagar, "*emigration, flight*":– Hagar [12]

1905 הַגְרִי ***hagrî***, a.g. [& n.pr.m.?]. GK: 2058 [→ 1904?]. Hagrites, of Hagri, "*wanderer*":– Hagarites [3], Hagarenes [1], Hagerite [1], Haggeri [1]

1906 הֵד ***hēd***, n.[m.]. GK: 2059 [→ 1959]. joyous shout:– sounding again [1]

1907 הַדָּבַר ***haddābar*** (Aram.), n.m. GK: 10196. royal adviser, official of the king:– counsellers [4]

1908 הֲדַד ***h^{a}dad***, n.pr.m. GK: 2060 [→ 111, 1130, 1909, 1910, 1913, 2582]. Hadad, "*thunderer*":– Hadad [12]

1909 הֲדַדְעֶזֶר ***h^{a}dad'ezer***, n.pr.m. GK: 2061 [→ 1908+5828]. Hadadezer, "*Hadad is a help*":– Hadadezer [9]

1910 הֲדַד־רִמּוֹן ***h^{a}dad-rimmôn***, n.pr.m.[loc.?]. GK: 2062 [→ 1908+7417]. Hadad Rimmon:– Hadadrimmon [1]

1911 הָדָה ***hādâ***, v. GK: 2063. [Q] to put, stretch out:– put [1]

1912 הֹדּוּ ***hōddû***, n.pr.loc. GK: 2064. India:– India [2]

1913 הֲדוֹרָם ***h^{a}dôrām***, n.pr.m. GK: 2066 & 2067 [→ 1908+7311]. Hadoram, "*Hadad is exalted*":– Hadoram [4]

1914 הִדַּי ***hidday***, n.pr.m. GK: 2068 [cf. 2355]. Hiddai:– Hiddai [1]

1915 הָדַךְ ***hādak***, v. GK: 2070. [Q] to crush by treading upon:– tread down [1]

1916 הֲדֹם ***h^{a}dōm***, n.m. GK: 2071. footstool:– footstool (+7272) [5], footstool (+7272+3807.1) [1]

1917 הַדָּם ***haddām*** (Aram.), n.[m.]. GK: 10197. pieces, members (of an execution by dismemberment):– pieces [2]

1918 הֲדַס ***h^{a}das***, n.m. GK: 2072 [→ 1919]. myrtle tree:– myrtle trees [3], myrtle [2], myrtle tree [1]

1919 הֲדַסָּה ***h^{a}dassâ***, n.pr.f. GK: 2073 [→ 1918]. Hadassah, "*myrtle;* [poss.] *bride* or *myrtle*":– Hadassah [1]

1920 הָדַף ***hādap***, v. GK: 2074. [Q] to shove, push, thrust, drive out:– thrust [3], cast out [2], drive [2], casteth away [1], driven [1], expel [1], thrust away [1]

1921 הָדַר ***hādar***, v. GK: 2075 & 2065 [→ 1926, 1925, 1927; cf. 1922]. [Q] to show favoritism; show respect; [Qp] to be in splendor; [N] to be shown respect; [Ht] to exalt oneself:– honour [2], countenance [1], crooked places [1], glorious [1], honoured [1], put forth [1]

1922 הֲדַר ***h^{a}dar*** (Aram.), v. GK: 10198 [→ 1923; cf. 1921]. [Pa] to glorify, honor, to speak words that elevate the status of another:– glorified [1], honoured [1], honour [1]

1923 הֲדַר ***h^{a}dar*** (Aram.), n.[m.]. GK: 10199 [→ 1922; cf. 1926, 1925]. splendor, honor, majesty:– honour [2], majesty [1]

1924 הֲדַר ***h^{a}dar***, n.pr.m. GK: 2076 [→ 1928]. Hadar; cf. 1908:– Hadar [1]

1925 הֶדֶר ***heder***, n.[m.]. GK: 2078 [→ 1921; cf. 1923]. splendor; "the royal splendor" may refer to the land of Israel, with the focus that this land is an valued ornament of the king:– glory [1]

1926 הָדָר ***hādār***, n.m. GK: 2077 [→ 1921; cf. 1923]. majesty, splendor, glory, nobility; often related to the appearance of an object that is beautiful and instills awe:– glory [7], majesty [6], honour [5], beauty [3], comeliness [3], excellency [2], beauties [1], full of majesty [1], glorious [1], goodly [1]

1927 הֲדָרָה ***h^{a}dārâ***, n.f. GK: 2079 [→ 1921]. splendor, glory:– beauty [4], honour [1]

הֲדֹרָם ***h^{a}dōrām***. See 1913.

1928 הֲדַרְעֶזֶר ***h^{a}dar'ezer***, n.pr.m. GK: 2080 [→ 1924+5828]. Hadarezer:– Hadarezer [12]

1929 הָהּ ***hāh***, interj. GK: 2081. Alas!:– woe [1]

1930 הוֹ ***hô***, interj. GK: 2082 [→ 1945]. ah! (doubled for emphasis), with a strong implication of mourning or sorrow:– alas [2]

1930.1 הוּ ***hû***, p.m.s. GK: 2083 [→ 1931]. he, she, it; that, which:– it [1]

1930.2 ־הוּ ***-hû***, p.m.s.suf. GK: 2084 [→ 1886.3]. he, his, him; it, its:– him [568], his [219], it [164], them [33], thereof [13], he [8], his own [4], that [3], their [3], they [3], which [3], whose [3], himself [2], the same [2], whom [2], her [1], himself (+4617) [1], man's^{S} [1], me [1], she [1], thereof (+4480) [1], there [1], whereof [1]

1931 הוּא ***hû'***, p.m.s. or הִיא ***hî'***, p.f.s. GK: 2085 & 2115 [→ 1930.1, 1992, 2007; cf. 1932 (also used with compound proper names)]. he, she, it; this, that:– he [623], that [432], it [245], she [103], this [63], which [63], the same [53], they [24], who [24], himself [16], same [14], him [13], the^{S} [6], her [2], such [2], their [2], the [2], those [2], his own [1], his [1], one [1], she herself [1], this same [1], thou [1], very [1], what (+834) [1], whom [1], whose [1]

1932 הוּא ***hû'***, p.3.m.s. or הִיא ***hî'*** (Aram.), p.3.f.s. GK: 10200 & 10205 [→ 581; cf. 1931]. he, she, it:– *usually untranslated* [10], he [6], it [3], this [2], that [1]

1933 הָוָה ***hāwâ***, v. GK: 2092 & 2093 [→ 1942, 1943, 1962; cf. 1961; cf. 1934]. [Q] to be, become; to get, have:– be [5], hath (+3807.1) [1]

1934 הֲוָה ***h^{a}wâ*** (Aram.), v. GK: 10201 [cf. 1961, 1933]. [P] to be, become, happen:– *usually untranslated* [34], be [21], was [5], come to pass [3], became [2], been [1], have [1], might [1], offer [1], shall [1], so (+2050.3) [1]

1935 הוֹד ***hôd***, n.m. GK: 2086 [→ 1936, 5989; cf. 3034 (also used with compound proper names)]. splendor, majesty, glory, strength:– glory [9], honour [6], majesty [4], beauty [1], comeliness [1], glorious [1], goodly [1], honourable [1]

1936 הוֹד ***hôd***, n.pr.m. GK: 2087 [→ 1935]. Hod, "*grandeur*":– Hod [1]

1937 הוֹדְוָה ***hôd^{e}wâ***, n.pr.m. GK: 2088 [→ 1938, 1939]. Hodaviah, "*give thanks to Yahweh*":– Hodevah [1]

1938 הוֹדַוְיָה ***hôdawyâ***, n.pr.m. GK: 2089 [→ 1939, 1937]. Hodaviah, "*give thanks to Yahweh*":– Hodaviah [3]

1939 הוֹדַוְיָהוּ ***hôdawyāhû***, n.pr.m. GK: 2069 & 2090 [→ 1937, 1938]. Hodaviah, "*give thanks to Yahweh*":– Hodaiah [1]

1940 הוֹדִיָּה ***hôdiyyâ***, n.pr.m. GK: 2091 [→ 1935+3068, 1941]. same as 1941: Hodiah, "*grandeur is Yahweh*":– Hodiah [1]

1941 הוֹדִיָּה ***hôdiyyâ***, n.pr.m. GK: 2091 [→ 1940]. same as 1940: Hodiah, Hodijah, "*grandeur is Yahweh*":– Hodijah [5]

הָוָה ***hāwâ***. See 1933.

הֲוָה ***h^{a}wâ***. See 1934.

1942 הַוָּה ***hawwâ***, n.f. GK: 2094 & 2095 [→ 185, 1962; cf. 183; 1933]. (evil) desire, craving; destruction, ruin, corruption:– calamity [3], wickedness [3], calamities [1], iniquity [1], mischiefs [1], mischievous things [1], mischievous [1], naughtiness [1], naughty [1], noisome [1], perverse things [1], substance [1]

1943 הֹוָה ***hōwâ***, n.f. GK: 2096 [→ 1933]. calamity, disaster:– mischief [3]

1944 הוֹהָם ***hôhām***, n.pr.m. GK: 2097. Hoham:– Hoham [1]

1945 הוֹי ***hôy***, interj. GK: 2098 [→ 1930]. woe!, ah!, oh!, alas!; (to invite) come!:– woe [36], ah [7], O [3], ho [3], alas [2]

1946 הוּךְ ***hûk*** (Aram.), v. GK: 10202 [→ 1981]. same as 1981: [P] to go, walk:– go [2], brought [1], came [1]

1947 הוֹלֵלוֹת ***hôlēlôt***, n.f. GK: 2099 [→ 1984]. madness, delusion, folly:– madness [4]

1948 הוֹלֵלוּת ***hôlēlût***, n.f. GK: 2100 [→ 1984]. madness, delusion, folly:– madness [1]

1949 הוּם ***hûm***, v. GK: 2101 [→ 4103; cf. 1993, 2000, 5098]. [Q] to throw into confusion; [N] to be stirred up, be shook; [H] to be distraught; to throng:– rang again [2], destroy [1], make a noise [1], make great noise [1], moved [1]

1950 הוֹמָם ***hômām***, n.pr.m. GK: 2102 [→ 1967]. Homam:– Homam [1]

1951 הוּן ***hûn***, v. GK: 2103 [→ 1952]. [H] to think it easy:– ready [1]

1952 הוֹן ***hôn***, n.m. GK: 2104 [→ 1951]. wealth, riches, possessions:– riches [10], substance [7], wealth [5], enough [2], nought (+3808) [1], rich [1]

1952.1 ־הוֹן ***-hôn*** (Aram.), p.suf.3.m.pl. GK: 10203 [cf. 1992.1]. they, them, their:– their [21], them [16], the^{S} [3], their own [1], therein (+871.2) [1], these [1], whom [1], whose [1], your [1]

1953 הוֹשָׁמָע ***hôšāmā'***, n.pr.m. GK: 2106 [→ 8085+3068]. Hoshama, "*Yahweh has heard*":– Hoshama [1]

1954 הוֹשֵׁעַ ***hôšēa'***, n.pr.m. GK: 2107 [→ 3467+410 *or* 3068]. Hoshea; Joshua, "*salvation*":– Hoshea [11], Hosea [3], Oshea [2]

1955 הוֹשַׁעְיָה ***hôša'yâ***, n.pr.m. GK: 2108 [→ 3467+3068]. Hoshaiah, "*Yahweh has saved*":– Hoshaiah [3]

1956 הוֹתִיר ***hôtîr***, n.pr.m. GK: 2110 [→ 3498]. Hothir, "*one who remains*":– Hothir [2]

1957 הָזָה ***hāzâ***, v. GK: 2111. [Q] to dream:– sleeping [1]

1958 הִי ***hî***, n.[m.]. GK: 2113. woe!, an exclamation of sorrow:– woe [1]

הִיא ***hî'***. See 1931, 1932.

1958.1 ־הִי ***-hî***, p.m.s.suf. GK: 2114 [→ 1886.3]. his, him:– his [1]

1958.2 ־הִי ***-hî*** (Aram.), p.suf.3.m.s. GK: 10204 [→ 1886.8; cf. 1958.1]. he, his, him; it, its:– his [37], him [20], it [3], thereof [3], which [2], whose [2], himself [1], the^{S} [1], thereon (+5922) [1], ye [1]

1959 הֵידָד ***hêdād***, n.m. GK: 2116 [→ 1906]. shout (of joy):– shouting [5], give a shout (+6030) [1], shout [1]

1960 הֻיְּדוֹת ***huyy^{e}dôt***, n.f.pl. GK: 2117 [→ 3034]. (pl.) songs of thanksgiving:– thanksgiving [1]

1961 הָיָה ***hāyâ***, v. GK: 2118 & 181 [cf. 1933; cf. 1934]. [Q] to be, become, happen; [N] to be done, happen; the common verb of being, referring to state of being, change of state, existence, and the occurring of events, or even possession:– be [1277], was [525], came to pass [389], were [228], came [146], come to pass [125], is [75], had (+3807.1) [72], have (+3807.1) [72], been [71], become [64], became [59], are [56], have [26], am [20], had [18], wast [15], come [10], done [8], shall [8], became (+3807.1) [7], hath (+3807.1) [6], become (+3807.1) [4], being [4], did [4], fell [4], hath (+871.1) [4], went [4], art [3], continued [3], endure [3], fell on [3], follow [3], should [3], abode [2], be (+3807.1) [2], be altogether (+1961) [2], becamest [2], been (+1961) [2], came expressly (+1961) [2], continue [2], escape (+6413) [2], followed (+310) [2], go [2], had at all (+1961+3807.1) [2], hadst (+3807.1) [2], hast (+3807.1) [2], having [2], made [2], married (+802+3807.1) [2], marry (+802+3807.1) [2], pertained [2], quit [2], received (+3807.1) [2], redeem (+1353) [2], seemed (+5869+871.1) [2], shew (+3807.1) [2], surely become (+1961) [2], surely come to pass (+1961) [2], was altogether (+1961) [2], accomplished [1], after that (+4480+7093) [1], be at all [1], brake [1], brought to pass [1], brought [1], came up [1], caused [1], cherish (+5532) [1], cherished (+5532) [1], come [1], cometh to pass [1], committed [1], conferred (+1697) [1], count (+3807.1) [1], coupled (+8535) [1], determined (+7760) [1], do [1], endured [1], enjoy (+3807.1) [1], escape (+6412) [1], fainted [1], follow (+310) [1], give (+413) [1], gone [1], had (+5973) [1], had before (+4480) [1], had wars with (+376+4421) [1], had with (+376+4421) [1], happened [1], hast [1], hath [1], have (+871.1) [1], having (+3807.1) [1], help

(+3444) [1], help (+8668) [1], keep (+4931) [1], keep [1], lasted [1], lay [1], let [1], lived (+2416) [1], liveth [1], make [1], marry [1], order (+4941) [1], pass [1], pertaineth [1], reach [1], redeemed (+1353) [1], rejoice (+8056) [1], remained [1], remain [1], required [1], seem (+5869+871.1) [1], shalt [1], since (+4480) [1], surely be [1], take (+3807.1) [1], trembled (+2730) [1], use (+3807.1) [1], waited on (+6440+3807.1) [1], wear (+5921) [1], will [1], would [1]

1962 הַיָּה **hayyâ**, n.f. GK: 2119 [→ 1942; cf. 1933]. destruction:–

1963 הֵיךְ **hêk**, adv. GK: 2120 [cf. 349]. how?:– how [2]

1964 הֵיכָל **hêkāl**, n.m. GK: 2121 [cf. 1965]. a building of some kind: temple, sanctuary, palace; main hall:– temple [68], palace [7], palaces [3], temples [2]

1965 הֵיכַל **hêkal** (Aram.), n.m. GK: 10206 [cf. 1964]. residence of a deity: temple; residence of royalty: palace:– temple [8], palace [5]

1966 הֵילֵל **hêlēl**, n.m.[pr.?]. GK: 2122 [→ 1984]. from the base meaning "shining one," this refers to an object in the night sky, often translated "morning star," and possibly referring the planet Venus; fig. used as a title of the king of Babylon (Isa 14:12). The Latin "lucifer" also means "shining one," and has become a title of Satan due to a traditional equation of the king of Babylon with the devil:– Lucifer [1]

1967 הֵימָם **hêmām**, n.pr.m. GK: 2123 [→ 1950]. Homam:– Hemam [1]

1968 הֵימָן **hêmān**, n.pr.m. GK: 2124 [→ 3225? *or* 539?]. Homam:– Heman [17]

1969 הִין **hîn**, n.m. GK: 2125. hin (liquid measure of volume, one-sixth of a bath, about one gallon [four liters]):– hin [22]

1970 הָכַר **hākar**, v. GK: 2128 & 2686. [Q] to attack (vigorously) or to make oneself strange:– make strange [1]

1971 הַכָּרָה **hakkārâ**, n.f. GK: 2129 [→ 5234]. look (on a face) as a non-verbal communication, which in context may refer to personal bias:– shew [1]

הַל **hal**. See 1973.

1972 הָלָא **hālā'**, v.den. GK: 2133. [N] to be driven away, be removed:– cast far off [1]

1973 הָלְאָה **hal'ā**, adv. GK: 2131 & 2134 [→ 1886.1+3807.1]. beyond; far (and wide), some distance away; out of the way!:– forward [5], beyond (+4480) [4], hitherto [2], back [1], beyond (+4480+2050.1) [1], henceforward [1], thenceforth [1], yonder [1]

1974 הִלּוּלִים **hillûlîm**, n.[m.]. GK: 2136 [→ 1984]. offering of praise; festival (related to a god):– merry [1], praise [1]

1975 הַלָּז **hallāz**, p.com.s. GK: 2137 [→ 1976]. this:– this [4], that [2], other [1]

1976 הַלָּזֶה **hallāzeh**, p.m. GK: 2138 [→ 1975, 1977; cf. 2098]. this:– this [2]

1977 הַלֵּזוּ **hallēzû**, p.f. GK: 2139 [→ 1976]. this:– this [1]

1978 הָלִיךְ **hālîk**, n.[m.]. GK: 2141 [→ 1980]. path, steps:– steps [1]

1979 הֲלִיכָה **h^{a}lîkâ**, n.f. GK: 2142 [→ 1980]. procession, way, walk; traveling merchants; affairs:– goings [2], ways [2], companies [1], walk [1]

1980 הָלַךְ **hālak**, v. GK: 2143 [→ 1978, 1979, 1982, 3212, 4108, 4109, 4447, 8418, 8437; cf. 1981]. [Q] to walk, go, travel; [N] to fade away; [P] to walk about, go about, [H] to drive back, get rid of; enable to walk; to lead; bring; [Ht] to move to and fro, wander, walk about; by extension: to walk as a lifestyle, a pattern of conduct:– go [417], went [348], walk [133], walked [97], come [78], departed [47], gone [35], walketh [34], goest [18], get [17], depart [16], followed (+310) [16], goeth [16], led [13], came [11], walking [11], going [10], follow (+310) [9], went away [9], brought [8], wentest [7], went on (+1980) [6], went on [5], bring [4], walkest [4], camest [3], carry [3], departed (+4480) [3], going on [3], march [3], passeth away [3], walk to and fro [3], went along [3], all along as went (+1980) [2], came apace (+1980) [2], came on (+1980) [2], carried [2], cause to go [2], cause to walk [2], come away [2], continually [2], conversant [2], departeth [2], flow [2], following (+310) [2], gat away [2], gat [2], go along [2], go away [2], go speedily (+1980) [2], go to [2], go up and down [2], goeth away [2], goeth forth (+1980) [2], leadeth away [2], lead [2], needs be gone (+1980) [2], quite gone (+1980) [2], ran [2], run [2], still went on (+1980) [2], surely depart (+1980) [2], surely go (+1980) [2], travelleth [2], walked to and fro [2], walking up and down [2], waxed greater (+1980) [2], weak [2], went forth on a time (+1980) [2], went on continually (+1980) [2], went out [2], went up and down [2], wrought [2], along [1], at the point [1], away [1], bear [1], behaved [1], carry away [1], cause to run [1], caused to go [1], cometh out [1], cometh [1], coming [1], continually (+7725+2050.1) [1], depart (+4480) [1], enter [1], exercise [1], flowed [1], follow (+7272+871.1) [1], followedst (+310) [1], followed [1], get away [1], go forward [1], go in [1], go up [1], goeth about [1], goeth on still [1], gone away [1], gone up [1], grow [1], lead forth [1], leadeth [1], let down [1], made go [1], may [1], moveth [1], on [1], pass away [1], passeth [1], prospered [1], pursue (+310) [1], ran along [1], return again (+7725) [1], run continually [1], running [1], sent [1], shineth more and more [1], sounded long [1], spread abroad [1], spread [1], take away [1], takest [1], take [1], talebearer (+7400) [1], travellers (+5410) [1], vanisheth away [1], walk on [1], walk up and down [1], walked up and down [1], wandered [1], wandering [1], waxed greater [1], waxed stronger [1], waxed weaker [1], waxed [1], wayfaring men (+1870) [1], went abroad [1], went forward [1], went way [1], whirleth about continually (+5437+5437) [1], wont to haunt [1]

1981 הֲלַךְ **h^{a}lak** (Aram.), v. GK: 10207 [→ 1983; cf. 1946; cf. 1980]. [P] to go; [Pa] to walk about; [H] to walk around:– walked [1], walking [1], walk [1]

1982 הֵלֶךְ **hēlek**, n.m. GK: 2144 [→ 1980]. oozing, flowing; visitor:– dropped [1], traveller [1]

1983 הֲלָךְ **h^{a}lāk** (Aram.), n.[m.]. GK: 10208 [→ 1981]. duty, toll, tax:– custom [3]

1984 הָלַל **hālal**, v. GK: 2145 & 2146 & 2147 & 2149 [→ 166, 1947, 1948, 1966, 1974, 1985, 4110, 8416 (also used with compound proper names)]. [Q] to be arrogant; [P] to praise; give thanks; cheer, extol; [Po] to make a fool of, to mock, rail against; [Pu] to be praised, be worthy of praise, be of renown; [Ht] to make one's boast in (the name of God); to act like a madman; act furiously; [H] to flash, radiate, shine; "Hallelujah" is a compound of the second person plural imperative and the personal name of God: hallelu-yah, praise Yah(weh):– praise [92], praised [19], glory [12], boast [5], mad [5], praising [4], boasteth [3], commended [2], foolish [2], maketh mad [2], rage [2], shined [2], boastest [1], celebrate [1], deal foolishly [1], feigned mad [1], fools [1], given to marriage [1], give [1], gloriest [1], glorieth [1], make boast [1], maketh fools [1], praises [1], praiseth [1], renowned [1], shine [1]

1985 הִלֵּל **hillēl**, n.pr.m. GK: 2148 [→ 1984]. Hillel, "*he has praises*": Hillel [2]

1986 הָלַם **hālam**, v. GK: 2150 [→ 1989, 4112]. [Q] to strike, smash, beat, trample:– smote [2], beaten [1], beating down [1], break down [1], broken down [1], broken [1], overcome [1], smite [1]

1987 הֵלֶם **hēlem**, n.pr.m. GK: 2152. Helem, "*health*":– Helem [1]

1988 הֲלֹם **h^{a}lōm**, adv. GK: 2151. to here:– hither [6], here [2], hitherto (+5704) [2], thither [1]

1989 הַלְמוּת **halmût**, n.f. GK: 2153 [→ 1986]. hammer:– hammer [1]

1990 הָם **hām**, n.pr.loc. GK: 2154. Ham:– Ham [1]

1991 הָם **hām**, n.[m.]. GK: 2155 [cf. 1998]. wealth:– *not translated* [1]

1992 הֵם **hēm** or הֵמָּה **hēmmâ**, p.m.pl. GK: 2156 & 2160 [→ 1931; cf. 1994]. they, them:– they [368], those [52], these [26], them [20], who [7], themselves [5], same [4], that [3], their [3], which [3], it [2], whom (+834) [2], whom [2], the things [1], this [1], whereby (+834) [1], withal (+871.1) [1], ye [1]

1992.1 הֶם- **-hem** or הֵם- **-hēm**, p.m.pl.suf. GK: 2157 [cf. 1886.3]. they, them, their:– them [1496], their [1187], they [90], their (+3807.1) [38], themselves [26], their own [23]*

1992.2 הֹם- **-hōm** (Aram.), p.suf.3.m.pl. GK: 10209 [→ 2006.2; cf. 1992.1]. they, them, their:– them [7], their [4]

1993 הָמָה **hāmâ**, v. GK: 2159 [→ 1995, 1997?, 1998, 1999?; cf. 1949, 2000, 5098]. [Q] to make a noise, be tumultuous:– roar [6], disquieted [4], make a noise [4], sound [3], troubled [2], clamorous [1], concourse [1], cry aloud [1], in an uproar [1], loud [1], make a tumult [1], maketh a noise [1], mourning [1], moved [1], noise [1], raged [1], raging [1], roared [1], roareth [1], tumultuous [1]

1993.1 הֵמָה- **-hēmâ**, p.m.pl.suf. GK: 2161 [→ 1886.3]. they, them:– their [1]

1994 הִמּוֹ **himmô** (Aram.), p.3.pl. GK: 10210 [cf. 1992]. they, them:– them [8], those [1]

1995 הָמוֹן **hāmôn**, n.m. GK: 2162 & 2171 [→ 1174, 1996, 1997; cf. 1993]. commotion, tumult, confusion; many, populace, hoards, army:– multitude [59], noise [4], tumult [4], abundance [3], many [3], multitudes [3], Hamon-gog [2], company [1], great store [1], multiplied [1], riches [1], rumbling [1], sounding [1], store [1]

הַמֹּלֶכֶת **ham-mōleket**. See 4447.

1996 הֲמוֹן גּוֹג **h^{a}môn gôg**, n.pr.loc. GK: 2163 [→ 1995+1463]. Hamon Gog, "*multitude of Gog*":–

1997 הֲמוֹנָה **h^{a}mônâ**, n.pr.loc. GK: 2164 [→ 1995?; cf. 1993]. Hamonah, "*multitude*":– Hamonah [1]

הֲמוּנֵךְ **h^{a}mûnēk**. See 2002.

1998 הֶמְיָה **hemyâ**, n.f. GK: 2166 [→ 1993; cf. 1991]. noise, sound, tone:– noise [1]

1999 הֲמֻלָּה **h^{a}mullâ**, n.f. GK: 2167 [→ 1993?]. tumult, sound, noise:– speech [1], tumult [1]

הַמֶּלֶךְ **ham-melek**. See 4429.

2000 הָמַם **hāmam**, v. GK: 2169 & 2170 [cf. 1949, 1993, 5098]. [Q] to throw into confusion; to rout; to drain:– discomfited [5], destroy [3], break [1], consume [1], crushed [1], troubled [1], vex [1]

הָמֹן **hāmōn**. See 1995.

2001 הָמָן **hāmān**, n.pr.m. GK: 2172. Haman:– Haman [50], Haman's [3], he^S [1]

2002 המונכ **hmwnk** or הַמְיָנֵךְ **hamyānak** (Aram.), n.[m.]. GK: 10211 & 10212. chain, necklace:– chain [3]

2003 הֲמָסִים **h^{a}māsîm**, n.[m.]. GK: 2173. twigs, brushwood:– melting [1]

2004 הֵן **hēn**, p.f.pl. GK: 2177 [→ 1886.3]. they, them, their:–

2005 הֵן **hēn**, adv.demo. *or* interj. GK: 2176 [→ 403, 2008, 2009, 5728; cf. 2006]. behold!, see!, surely!; if, yet, but, then:– behold [82], lo [11], if [5], though [1]

2006 הֵן **hēn** (Aram.), c. GK: 10213 [cf. 2005, cf. 518?]. if, then, whether:– if [12], or [2], whether [2]

2006.1 הֵן- **-hēn** or הֶן- **-hen**, p.f.pl.suf. GK: 2177 [→ 1886.3]. they, them, their:– their [90], them [52], they [6], therein (+871.1) [4], thereof [4], their (+3807.1) [2], their own [2], withal (+871.1) [2], by themselves (+905+3807.1) [1], it [1], thereby (+871.1) [1], these [1], those [1], wherein (+834+871.1) [1], wherein (+871.1) [1], withal (+834+871.1) [1]

2006.2 הֵן- **-hēn** (Aram.), p.suf.3.f.pl. GK: 10214 [→ 1992.2, 3861; cf. 1992.1]. they, them, their:– *usually untranslated* [6], the others [1], them [1]

2007 הֵנָּה **hēnnâ**, p.f.pl. GK: 2179 [→ 1931]. they, these, those:– they [13], these [7], them [4], those [3], such (+3509.1) [2], such things (+3509.1) [1], such [1], that [1], the [1], theirs [1], thence (+4480) [1], therein (+871.1+1886.1) [1], this [1], thither [1], wherein (+834+871.1) [1]

2008 הֵנָּה **hēnnâ**, adv. GK: 2178 [→ 5728; cf. 2005]. here, to here; on this side, on the opposite side:– hither [20], hitherto (+5704) [5], thither [3], here [2], hither (+5704) [2], thus far (+5704) [2], fro (+259) [1], hither (+1886.5) [1], hitherto (+5704+2050.1) [1], in hither [1], now [1], on this side [1], side [1], since (+5704) [1], that way [1], there [1], this side [1], this way [1], thitherward [1], to (+259) [1], yet (+5704) [1]

2009 הִנֵּה **hinnēh**, pt.demo. GK: 2180 [→ 2005]. look!, now!, here, there, a marker used to enliven a narrative, change a scene, emphasize an idea, or call attention to detail:– behold [928], lo [110], here [17], see [2], behold (+2088) [1], behold as soon as [1], behold here [1]

2009.1 הֵנָה- **-h^{e}nâ** or הֶנָה- **-henâ**, p.f.pl.suf. GK: 2181 [→ 1886.3]. they, them:– them [2], their [1]

2010 הֲנָחָה **h^{a}nāḥâ**, n.f. GK: 2182 [→ 3240]. holiday, an official day of rest and celebration:– release [1]

2011 הִנֹּם **hinnōm**, n.pr.m. & loc. GK: 2183. Hinnom:– Hinnom [13]

2012 הֵנַע **hēna'**, n.pr.loc. GK: 2184. Hena, "*Anath*":– Hena [3]

2013 הָסָה **hāsâ**, v.den. GK: 2187 & 2188. [H] to silence, cause to be still:– hold peace [2], keep silence [2], be silent [1], hold tongue [1], silence [1], stilled [1]

2014 הֲפֻגָה **h^{a}pugâ**, n.f. GK: 2198 [→ 6313]. relief, stopping:– intermission [1]

2015 הָפַךְ **hāpak**, v. GK: 2200 [→ 2016, 2017, 2018, 2019, 4114, 4115, 8419; cf. 55]. [Q] to overthrow, overturn, turn around, change; [Qp] to be turned over; [N] to be changed, transformed, turned into; [Ho] to be overwhelmed; [Ht] to tumble around, flash back and forth, swirl; from the base meaning of turning an object over comes the fig. extension of "changing one's mind":– turned [48], turn [7], overthrow [5], overthrew [4], overthrown [4], overturneth [3], turneth [3], changed [2], become [1], came [1], change [1], converted [1], gave [1], make [1], overturned (+4605+1886.5+3807.1) [1], overturn [1], perverse [1], perverted [1], retired [1], tumbled [1], turned aside [1], turned back [1], turned every way [1], turned into [1], turned up [1], turning [1]

2016 הֵפֶךְ **hēpek**, n.m. GK: 2201 [→ 2015, 2017]. opposite, turning of things upside down, perversion:– contrary [2]

2017 הֹפֶךְ **hōpek**, n.m. GK: 2201 [→ 2016]. opposite, turning of things upside down, perversion:– turning upside down [1]

2018 הֲפֵכָה **h^{a}pēkâ**, n.f. GK: 2202 [→ 2015]. catastrophe, demolition:– overthrow [1]

2019 הֲפַכְפַּךְ **h^{a}pakpak**, a. GK: 2203 [→ 2015]. devious, crooked:– froward [1]

2020 הַצָּלָה **haṣṣālâ**, n.f. GK: 2208 [→ 5337]. deliverance:– deliverance [1]

2021 הֹצֶן **hōṣen**, n.[m.]. GK: 2210. weapon (variously interpreted):– chariots [1]

2022 הַר **har**, n.m. GK: 2215 [→ 2023, 2042]. hill, mountain, range (of hills, mountains); referring to low hills as well as high mountains:– mount [224], mountains [156], mountain [105], hill [35], hills [23], hill country [1], hill's [1]

2023 הֹר **hōr**, n.pr.loc. GK: 2216 [→ 2022]. Hor, "[perhaps] *mountain*":– Hor [12]

2024 הָרָא **hārā'**, n.pr.loc. GK: 2217. Hara, "*hill, highland*":– Hara [1]

2025 הַרְאֵל **har'ēl**, n.[m.]. GK: 2219 [cf. 741]. altar hearth:– altar [1]

2026 הָרַג **hārag**, v. GK: 2222 [→ 2027, 2028]. [Q] to kill, put to death, murder, slaughter; [Qp, N, Pu] to be slain, be put to death, be slaughtered:– slew [57], slay [41], slain [31], kill [15], killed [3], slaying [3], kill out of hand (+2026) [2], killedst [2], slayeth [2], surely kill (+2026) [2], destroyed [1], killeth [1], killing [1], murderers [1], murderer [1], murder [1], put to death (+4194) [1], slaughter made (+2027) [1], slayer [1]

2027 הֶרֶג **hereg**, n.m. GK: 2223 [→ 2026]. slaughter, killing:– slaughter [3], slain [1], slaughter made (+2026) [1]

2028 הֲרֵגָה **h^{a}rēgâ**, n.f. GK: 2224 [→ 2026]. slaughter:– slaughter [5]

2029 הָרָה **hārâ**, v. GK: 2225 [→ 2030, 2032]. [Q] to conceive, become pregnant, be with child; [Gp; Pu] to be conceived, born:– conceived [34], conceive [4], with child [2], bare [1], conceiving [1], progenitors [1]

2030 הָרֶה **hāreh** or הָרִיָּה **hāriyyâ**, a.f. GK: 2226 & 2230 [→ 2029]. pregnant, expecting (child):– with child [7], women with child [4], conceive [3], child [1], great [1]

2031 הַרְהֹר **harhōr** (Aram.), n.[m.]. GK: 10217. mental image (in a dream-like state):– thoughts [1]

2032 הֵרוֹן **hērôn** or הֵרָיוֹן **hērāyôn**, n.[m.]. GK: 2228 & 2231 [→ 2029]. childbearing, pregnancy:– conception [3]

2033 הֲרוֹרִי **h^{a}rôrî**, a.g. GK: 2229. Harorite:– Harorite [1]

2034 הֲרִיסָה **h^{a}rîsâ**, n.f. GK: 2232 [→ 2040]. ruin:– ruins [1]

2035 הֲרִיסוּת **h^{a}rîsût**, n.f. GK: 2233 [→ 2040]. waste, ruin, destruction:– destruction [1]

2036 הֹרָם **hōrām**, n.pr.m. GK: 2235 [cf. 2037]. Horam, "*height*":– Horam [1]

2037 הָרוּם **hārûm**, n.pr.m. GK: 2227 [cf. 2036]. Harum, "*consecrated*":– Harum [1]

2038 הַרְמוֹן **harmôn**, n.pr.loc. GK: 2236. Harmon:– palace [1]

2039 הָרָן **hārān**, n.pr.m. GK: 2237 [→ 1028]. Haran, "*mountaineer* [perhaps *sanctuary*]":– Haran [7]

2040 הָרַס **hāras**, v. GK: 2238 [→ 2034, 2035]. [Q] to tear down, break down, destroy; [Qp] to be in ruins; [N] to be destroyed, in ruins; [P] to destroy:– thrown down [7], throw down [6], break down [4], broken down [4], destroyed [3], pull down [3], break through [2], overthrown [2], ruined [2], utterly overthrow (+2040) [2], beat down [1], breaketh down [1], break [1], destroyers [1], destroy [1], overthroweth [1], overthrow [1], plucketh down [1]

2041 הֶרֶס **heres**, n.[m.]. GK: 2239 [→ 5892+2041]. destruction (= Heliopolis):– destruction [1]

2042 הָרָר **hārār**, n.m. GK: 2215 [→ 2022]. hill, mountain, range (of hills, mountains); referring to low hills as well as high mountains:– mountains [8], hills [2], mountain [2], mount [1]

2043 הֲרָרִי **h^{a}rārî** or הָאֲרָרִי **hā'rārî**, a.g. GK: 2240 & 2034. Hararite:– Hararite [5]

2044 הָשֵׁם **hāšēm**, n.pr.m. GK: 2244. Hashem:– Hashem [1]

2045 הַשְׁמָעוּת **hašmā'ût**, n.f. GK: 2245 [→ 8085]. news, communication, information:– cause to hear [1]

2046 הִתּוּךְ **hittûk**, n.[m.]. GK: 2247 [→ 5413]. melting:– melted [1]

2047 הֲתָךְ **h^{a}tāk**, n.pr.m. GK: 2251. Hathach, "*good*":– Hatach [4]

2048 הָתַל **hātal**, v. GK: 2252 & 9438 [→ 2049, 4123]. [P] to taunt, mock:– mocked [4], deceived [2], deal deceitfully [1], deceive [1], mocketh [1], mock [1]

2049 הֲתֻלִים **h^{a}tulîm**, n.[m.]pl. GK: 2253 [→ 2048]. mockery:– mockers [1]

2050 הָתַת **hātat**, v. GK: 2109 & 2254. [Po] to overwhelm with reproaches:– imagine mischief [1]

2050.1 -וְ **w^{e}-**, c.pref. GK: 2256 [cf. 2050.3]. a marker showing the relationship between words, clauses, sentences, and sections; generally, coordinating: and, also; contrasting: but, yet, however; showing a logical relationship: because, so then; emphazing: even, indeed:– and [38504], but [1748], then [1316], that [991], so [597], also [592], therefore [524], neither (+3808) [415], and when [371], for [368], even [363], or [363], now [290], with [282], nor [254], nor (+3808) [242], yet [185], yea [151], when [142], moreover [120], so that [110], thus [81], wherefore [77], which [66], neither (+408) [61], both [58], again [36], nevertheless [33], though [31], seeing [28], neither (+369) [27], howbeit [26], as [24], nor (+408) [24], neither [23], but when [19], nor (+369) [17], as for [16], if [16], lest (+3808) [14], all generations (+1755+1755) [13], now when [13], likewise [11], notwithstanding [11], and as [10], moreover (+1571) [10], whereas [10], while [10]*

2050.2 -וֹ **-ô** or -ו **-w** or -וּ **-û**, p.m.s.suf. GK: 2257 [→ 1886.3]. he, him, his; it, its:– his [6106], him [2818], it [586], he [454], thereof [366], their [202], his own [152], them [138], his (+3807.1) [76], whose [72], himself [68], the^{S} [49], therein (+871.1) [35], thereon (+5921) [31], whom [27], her [23], the same [11], their own [11], wherein (+871.1) [10]*

2050.3 -וְ **w^{e}-** (Aram.), c.pref. GK: 10221 [cf. 2050.1]. (connecting) and; (contrasting) or, but, however; (furthering) then, now:– and [612], but [20], or [10], that [10], nor (+3809) [7], even [6], also [5], then [5], so [4], which [4], neither (+3809) [3], nor [3], now [3], for [2], therefore [2], to [2], with [2], also (+638) [1], and that [1], as concerning [1], both [1], moreover [1], nor (+409) [1], nor (+5922) [1], so (+1934) [1], so that [1], therefore (+4481) [1], thus [1], upharsin (+6537) [1], yet [1]

2051 וְדָן **w^{e}dān**, n.pr.loc.?. GK: 2258. Vedan; and Dan (2050.1 + 1835):–

2052 וָהֵב **wāhēb**, n.pr.loc.?. GK: 2259. Waheb:– what he did [1]

2053 וָו **wāw**, n.[m.]. GK: 2260. hook, peg:– hooks [13]

2054 וָזָר **wāzār**, a. GK: 2261. guilty:– strange [1]

2055 וַיְזָתָא **way^{e}zātā'**, n.pr.m. GK: 2262. Vaizatha, "[poss.] *given of the best one*":– Vajezatha [1]

2056 וָלָד **wālād**, n.m. GK: 2263 [→ 3205]. child:– child [2]

2057 וַנְיָה **wanyâ**, n.pr.m. GK: 2264. Vaniah, "[poss.] *worthy of love*":– Vaniah [1]

2058 וָפְסִי **wopsî**, n.pr.m. GK: 2265. Vophsi:– Vophsi [1]

2059 וַשְׁנִי **wašnî**, n.pr.m.?. GK: 2266. Vashni:– Vashni [1]

2060 וַשְׁתִּי **waštî**, n.pr.f. GK: 2267. Vashti, "*one beautiful, desired*":– Vashti [10]

2061 זְאֵב **z^{e}'ēb**, n.m. GK: 2269 [→ 2062]. wolf:– wolf [4], wolves [3]

2062 זְאֵב **z^{e}'ēb**, n.pr.m. GK: 2270 [→ 2061]. Zeeb, "*wolf*":– Zeeb [6]

2063 זֹאת **zō't**, p.demo. & adv. GK: 2271 [→ 2088]. this, these:– this [15], herewith (+871.1) [2], it [2], she [2], so [2], that [2], these [2], thus [2], hereby (+871.1) [1], herein (+871.1) [1], so much [1], such (+1886.1+3509.1) [1], such [1], the one [1], the other [1], the same [1], therefore (+871.1+2050.1) [1], thus (+871.1) [1]

2064 זָבַד **zābad**, v. GK: 2272 [→ 2065, 2066, 2067, 2071, 2072, 2080 (also used with compound proper names)]. [Q] to give (a gift), bestow:– endued [1]

2065 זֶבֶד **zēbed**, n.m. GK: 2273 [→ 2064]. gift:– dowry [1]

2066 זָבָד **zābād**, n.pr.m. GK: 2274 [→ 2064]. Zabad, "*he bestows*":– Zabad [8]

2067 זַבְדִּי **zabdî**, n.pr.m. GK: 2275 [→ 2064]. Zabdi, "*Yahweh bestows*":– Zabdi [6]

2068 זַבְדִּיאֵל **zabdî'ēl**, n.pr.m. GK: 2276 [→ 2064+410]. Zabdiel, "*God [El] bestows*":– Zabdiel [2]

2069 זְבַדְיָה **z^{e}badyâ** or זְבַדְיָהוּ **z^{e}badyāhû**, n.pr.m. GK: 2277 & 2278. Zebadiah, "*Yahweh bestows*":– Zebadiah [9]

2070 זְבוּב **z^{e}bûb**, n.m. GK: 2279 [→ 1176]. fly (insect):– flies [1], fly [1]

2071 זָבוּד **zābûd**, n.pr.m. GK: 2280 [→ 2064]. Zabud, "*[he has] bestowed upon*":– Zabud [1]

2072 זַבּוּד **zabbûd**, n.pr.f. GK: 2281 [→ 2064; cf. 2080]. Zabbud, "*[he has] bestowed upon*":– Zabbud [1]

2073 זְבֻל **z^{e}bul**, n.[m.]. GK: 2292 [→ 348?, 2074, 2082, 2083]. magnificent dwelling, princely mansion, lofty dwelling:– habitation [3], dwell in [1], dwelling [1]

2074 זְבוּלֻן **z^{e}bûlûn**, n.pr.m. GK: 2282 [→ 2075; cf. 2073]. Zebulun, "*honor Ge 30:20*":– Zebulun [45]

2075 זְבוּלֹנִי **z^{e}bûlōnî**, a.g. GK: 2283 [→ 2074; cf. 2073]. Zebulunite, "*of Zebulun*":– Zebulonite [2], Zebulunites [1]

2076 זָבַח **zābaḥ**, v. GK: 2284 [→ 2077, 2078, 4196; cf. 1684]. [Q, P] to offer a sacrifice; to slaughter, butcher:– sacrifice [44], sacrificed [29], offer [19], offered [17], sacrificeth [6], do sacrifice [3], kill [3], slew [3], killed [2], sacrificing [2], slain [2], offer a sacrifice (+2077) [1], offereth [1], offering [1], sacrificedst [1]

2077 זֶבַח **zebaḥ**, n.m. GK: 2285 [→ 2078; cf. 2076; cf. 1685]. sacrifice, offering:– sacrifice [101], sacrifices [53], offerings [6], offer a sacrifice (+2076) [1], offer [1]

2078 זֶבַח **zebaḥ**, n.pr.m. GK: 2286 [→ 2077; cf. 2076]. Zebah, "*sacrifice*":– Zebah [12]

2079 זַבַּי **zabbay**, n.pr.m. GK: 2287. Zabbai, "[perhaps] *God has given*":– Zabbai [2]

2080 זְבִידָה **z^{e}bîdâ**, n.pr.f. GK: 2288 [→ 2064; cf. 2072]. Zebidah, "*given*":– Zebudah [1]

2081 זְבִינָא **z^{e}bînā'**, n.pr.m. GK: 2289. Zebina, "*one bought, purchased*":– Zebina [1]

2082 זָבַל **zābal**, v. GK: 2290 [cf. 2073, 5445]. [Q] to honor, exalt; from the base meaning of lifting up or carrying an object, especially bringing presents, not found in the OT:– dwell with [1]

2083 זְבֻל **z^{e}bul**, n.pr.m. GK: 2291 [→ 2073]. Zebul, "*elevation, height, lofty [temple]*":– Zebul [6]

זְבֻלֻן **z^{e}bulūn**. See 2074.

2084 זְבַן **z^{e}ban** (Aram.), v. GK: 10223. [P] to try to gain (time), buy (time):– gain [1]

2085 זָג **zāg**, n.[m.]. GK: 2293 [cf. 2212]. skin, peel (of grape):– husk [1]

2086 זֵד **zēd**, a. GK: 2294 [→ 2087; cf. 2102]. arrogant, proud, haughty:– proud [12], presumptuous [1]

2087 זָדוֹן **zādôn**, n.m. GK: 2295 [→ 2086]. pride, arrogance, contempt, presumption:– pride [6], presumptuously (+871.1) [2], proud [2], most proud [1]

2088 זֶה **zeh**, p.demo. & adv. GK: 2296 [→ 2063, 2090, 2097, 2098; cf. 2098]. this, these, such:– this [1418], that [42], these [37], it [12], thus (+3509.1) [12], another [10], here (+871.1) [10], one [10], where (+335) [10], he [9], the [9], thus [9], hence (+4480) [7], the other [7], hence [6], such [5], whence (+335+4480) [5], one side [4], other side [4], same [4], such (+3509.1) [4], wherefore (+4100+3807.1) [4], hereby (+871.1) [3], that side [3]*

2089 זֶה **zeh**, n.m. & f. GK: 8445 [→ 7716]. lamb; var. for 7716:–

2090 זֹה **zōh**, p.demo. & adv. GK: 2297 [→ 2097; cf. 2088; cf. 1668]. this:– this [7], thus (+3509.1) [3], it [1], one [1], that [1]

2091 זָהָב ***zāhāb***, n.m. GK: 2298 [→ 4314; cf. 6668; cf. 1722]. gold, nugget of gold, gold piece or coin:– gold [348], golden [40], fair weather [1]

2092 זָהַם ***zāham***, v. GK: 2299 [→ 2093]. [P] to make repulsive, loathsome (to someone):– abhorreth [1]

2093 זַהַם ***zaham***, n.pr.m. GK: 2300 [→ 2092]. Zaham, "*putrid, loathsome*":– Zaham [1]

2094 זָהַר ***zāhar***, v. GK: 2302 [cf. 2114; cf. 2095]. [N] to be warned, take warning; [H] to give warning, dissuade; to shine:– warn [8], warned [4], admonished [2], taketh warning [2], give warning [1], given warning [1], givest warning [1], shine [1], teach [1], took warning [1]

2095 זְהִיר ***z^{e}hîr*** (Aram.), v. GK: 10224 [cf. 2094]. careful, cautious:– take heed [1]

2096 זֹהַר ***zōhar***, n.[m.]. GK: 2303. brightness, shining:– brightness [2]

2097 זוֹ ***zô***, p.demo. GK: 2305 [→ 2090; cf. 2088]. this:– this [1]

2098 זוּ ***zû***, p.demo. & rel. GK: 2306 [→ 2088; cf. 1976]. who, which, that:– this [4], that [3], wherein [2], which [2], that which [1], whom [1]

2099 זִו ***ziw***, n.pr. GK: 2304 [cf. 2122]. Ziv, "*bright [as colorful flowers]*":– Zif [2]

2100 זוּב ***zûb***, v. GK: 2307 [→ 2101; cf. 1727]. [Q] to flow, gush out; discharge (of body fluids); "flowing with milk and honey" is a figure of sweet abundance:– floweth [12], issue [11], flowing [9], gushed out [3], running issue [2], hath an issue [1], hath [1], have an issue (+2101) [1], pine away [1], run [1]

2101 זוֹב ***zôb***, n.m. GK: 2308 [→ 2100]. discharge (of body fluids):– issue [12], have an issue (+2100) [1]

2102 זִיד ***zîd***, v. GK: 2326 [→ 2121, 5138; cf. 2086; cf. 2103]. [Q] to treat arrogantly, defy; [H] to cook; to act arrogantly, be contemptuous:– dealt proudly [4], presumptuously [2], come presumptuously [1], presume [1], proud [1], sod [1]

2103 זוּד ***zûd*** (Aram.), v. GK: 10225 [cf. 2102]. [H] to act proudly, act haughtily:– pride [1]

2104 זוּזִים ***zûzîm***, n.pr.g. GK: 2309. Zuzite, "*strong nations; babblers*":– Zuzims [1]

2105 זוֹחֵת ***zôḥēt***, n.pr.m. GK: 2311 [→ 1132]. Zoheth, "*proud*":– Zoheth [1]

2106 זָוִית ***zāwît***, n.f. GK: 2312 [cf. 4200]. corner (of a palace, altar), pillar:– corner stones [1], corners [1]

2107 זוּל ***zûl***, v. GK: 2313 [→ 2108]. [Q] to pour out, weigh out:– despise [1], lavish [1]

2108 זוּלָה ***zûlâ***, n.[f.] pp.c. GK: 2314 [→ 2107]. but, only, except; apart from, besides:– save [6], besides [5], beside [2], but [2], only [1]

2109 זוּן ***zûn***, v. GK: 2315 & 3469 [→ 4202; cf. 2110, cf. 4203]. [Q] to feed; [Pu] to be fed; to be lusty, be in the rut:– fed [1]

2110 זוּן ***zûn*** (Aram.), v. GK: 10226 [→ 4203; cf. 2109]. [Htpe] to be fed, live on:– fed [1]

2111 זוּעַ ***zûa'***, v. GK: 2316 & 2398 [→ 2113; cf. 2189; cf. 2112]. [Q] to show fear, tremble; [Pil] to make tremble; terrify:– moved [1], tremble [1], vex [1]

2112 זוּעַ ***zûa'*** (Aram.), v. GK: 10227 [cf. 2111]. [P] to dread, fear, to have an attitude of terror or worship, a fig. extension of "to shake, tremble.":– trembled [1], tremble [1]

2113 זְוָעָה ***z^{e}wā'â***, n.f. GK: 2317 [→ 2111]. abhorrence, terror, object of dread:– vexation [1]

2114 זוּר ***zûr***, v. GK: 2319 & 2320 & 2424 [cf. 2094]. [Q, N, Ho] to go astray, turn aside, be estranged; [Q] to stink; by extension: to be offensive:– strangers [25], strange [20], stranger [18], estranged [4], another [2], another place [1], fanners [1], gone away [1], stranger (+376) [1], strangers' [1]

2115 זוּר ***zûr***, v. GK: 2318 [→ 2116]. [Q] to squeeze, press upon, crush; [Qp] to be crushed:– closed [1], crush [1], thrust together [1]

2116 זוּרֶה ***zûreh***, v.ptcp. GK: 2318 [→ 2115]. ptcp. of 2115: that which is crushed:– crushed [1]

2117 זָזָא ***zāzā'***, n.pr.m. GK: 2321. Zaza, "*form of a shortened nick name; term of endearment*":– Zaza [1]

2118 זָחַח ***zāḥaḥ***, v. GK: 2310 & 2322. [N] to come loose, get out of place; to swing out:– loosed [2]

2119 זָחַל ***zāḥal***, v. GK: 2323 & 2324 [→ 2120; cf. 1763]. [Q] to be afraid; to crawl, glide (of a snake):– afraid [1], serpents [1], worms [1]

2120 זֹחֶלֶת ***zōḥelet***, n.pr.loc. GK: 2325 [→ 2119]. Zoheleth, "*crawling thing* or *fearsome thing*":– Zoheleth [1]

2121 זֵידוֹן ***zêdôn***, a. GK: 2327 [→ 2102]. raging (water), implying it is out of control:– proud [1]

2122 זִיו ***zîw*** (Aram.), n.m. GK: 10228. radiant appearance: dazzling, splendor; terrified appearance: flushed, pale:– countenance [4], brightness [2]

2123 זִיז ***zîz***, n.m. GK: 2328 & 2329. creatures; nipple (of a lactating breast):– abundance [1], wild beasts [1], wild beast [1]

2124 זִיזָא ***zîzā'***, n.pr.m. GK: 2330 [→ 2125?]. Ziza, "*(childish abbreviation, like "mama," as a name of endearment)*":– Ziza [2]

2125 זִיזָה ***zîzâ***, n.pr.m. GK: 2331 [→ 2124?]. Ziza, "*(childish abbreviation, like "mama," as a term of endearment)*":– Zizah [1]

2126 זִינָא ***zînā'***, n.pr.m. GK: 2332 [cf. 2124]. Zina; cf. 2124:– Zina [1]

2127 זִיעַ ***zîa'***, n.pr.m. GK: 2333. Zia, "[poss.] *trembler*":– Zia [1]

2128 זִיף ***zîp***, n.pr.m. & loc. GK: 2334 & 2335 [→ 2130]. Ziph:– Ziph [10]

2129 זִיפָה ***zîpâ***, n.pr.m. GK: 2336. Ziphah:– Ziphah [1]

2130 זִיפִי ***zîpî***, a.g. GK: 2337 [→ 2128]. Ziphite, "*of Ziph*":– Ziphites [2], Ziphims [1]

2131 זִיקוֹת ***zîqôt*** or זֵק ***zēq***, n.[m.]. GK: 2338 & 2414 & 2415 [cf. 246]. flaming torch, firebrand; chains, fetters:– chains [3], sparks [2], fetters [1], firebrands [1]

2132 זַיִת ***zayit***, n.m. GK: 2339 [→ 1209, 1209, 2133, 2241?]. olive (tree, grove, oil, leaf):– olive [13], olive tree [8], olive trees [6], oliveyards [5], olives [4], Olivet [1], oliveyard [1]

2133 זֵיתָן ***zêtān***, n.pr.m. GK: 2340 [→ 2132]. Zethan, "*olive tree* or *one who deals in olives*":– Zethan [1]

2134 זַךְ ***zak***, a. GK: 2341 [→ 2141]. pure, clear; flawless, innocent, upright:– pure [9], clean [2]

2135 זָכָה ***zakâ***, v. GK: 2342 [cf. 2141; cf. 2136]. [Q] to be pure; be justified, be acquitted; [P] to keep pure; [Ht] to make oneself clean, pure; usually referring to moral purity as a superior quality:– clean [2], cleansed [1], cleanse [1], clear [1], count pure [1], made clean [1], make clean [1]

2136 זָכוּ ***zākû*** (Aram.), n.f. GK: 10229 [cf. 2135]. innocence:– innocency [1]

2137 זְכוֹכִית ***z^{e}kôkît***, n.[f.]. GK: 2343 [→ 2141]. crystal, referring to a transparent ornament):– crystal [1]

2138 זָכוּר ***zākûr***, n.m. GK: 2344 & 2345 [→ 2142]. male:– males [2], male [1], men children [1]

2139 זַכּוּר ***zakkûr***, n.pr.m. GK: 2346 [→ 2142]. Zaccur, "*remembering*":– Zaccur [8], Zacchur [1]

2140 זַכַּי ***zakkay***, n.pr.m. GK: 2347 [→ 2142+3068?] Zaccai, "*Yahweh has remembered,* [or perhaps] *Yahweh remember*":– Zaccai [2]

2141 זָכַךְ ***zākak***, v. GK: 2348 [→ 2134, 2137; cf. 2135]. [Q] to be pure, bright, clean:– clean [1], make never so clean (+1253+871.1) [1], purer [1], pure [1]

2142 זָכַר ***zākar***, v. GK: 2349 & 2350 & 4654 [→ 234, 2138, 2139, 2143, 2144, 2145, 2146 (also used with compound proper names)]. [Q] to remember, commemorate, consider; [Qp] to remember; [N] to be remembered, be mentioned; to be born male; [H] to bring to remembrance, remind, mention, record:– remember [117], remembered [46], make mention [12], recorder [9], mindful [6], call to remembrance [3], mentioned [3], remembereth [3], bring to remembrance [2], earnestly remember (+2142) [2], mention [2], record [2], still in remembrance (+2142) [2], think [2], well remember (+2142) [2], bringeth to remembrance [1], bringing to remembrance [1], burneth [1], calling to remembrance [1], come to remembrance [1], in remembrance [1], keep in remembrance [1], made mention of [1], made mention [1], made to be remembered [1], make to be remembered [1], maketh mention [1], male [1], mention made [1], put in remembrance [1], recount [1], rememberest [1], remembering [1], think on [1]

2143 זֵכֶר ***zēker*** or זֶכֶר ***zeker***, n.m. GK: 2352 & 2354 [→ 2142]. memory, memorial, remembrance (with an implication of honor, worship, and celebration); fame, renown:– remembrance [11], memorial [5], memory [5], remembered [1], sent [1]

2144 זֶכֶר ***zeker***, n.pr.m. GK: 2353 [→ 2142]. Zeker, "*memorial*":– Zacher [1]

2145 זָכָר ***zākār***, n.m. & a. GK: 2351 [→ 2142; cf. 1798]. male, man:– male [37], males [30], man [9], man child [2], mankind [2], him^{S} [1], men [1]

2146 זִכָּרוֹן ***zikkārôn***, n.m. GK: 2355 [→ 2142; cf. 1799]. memorial, remembrance (with an implication of honor, worship, and celebration), commemoration, reminder:– memorial [17], remembrance [5], records [1], remembrances [1]

2147 זִכְרִי ***zikrî***, n.pr.m. GK: 2356 [→ 2142?+3068?]. Zicri, "*Yahweh remembers*":– Zichri [12]

2148 זְכַרְיָה ***z^{e}karyâ*** or זְכַרְיָהוּ ***z^{e}karyāhû***, n.pr.m. GK: 2357 & 2358 & 10230. Zechariah, "*Yahweh remembers*": note this name is Aramaic twice in Ezra:– Zechariah [39], Zachariah [4]

2149 זֻלּוּת ***zullût***, n.f. GK: 2359 [→ 2151]. vileness:– vilest [1]

2150 זַלְזַל ***zalzal***, n.[m.]. GK: 2360 [→ 2151; cf. 5550]. shoots, sprigs, tendrils:– sprigs [1]

2151 זָלַל ***zālal***, v. GK: 2361 & 2362 [→ 2149, 2150]. [Q] to profligate, be a glutton, to gorge oneself; [N] to tremble (of mountains); [H] to despise, treat contemptibly:– glutton [2], vile [2], flow down [1], flowed down [1], riotous eaters [1], riotous [1]

2152 זַלְעָפָה ***zal'āpâ***, n.f. GK: 2363 [→ 2196]. raging (wind); indignation; fits of hunger:– horrible [1], horror [1], terrible [1]

2153 זִלְפָּה ***zilpâ***, n.pr.f. GK: 2364. Zilpah, "*short nosed person*":– Zilpah [7]

2154 זִמָּה ***zimmâ***, n.f. GK: 2365. lewdness, shamelessness, evil:– lewdness [14], wickedness [4], mischief [3], lewd [2], heinous crime [1], lewdly (+871.1) [1], purposes [1], thought [1], wicked devices [1], wicked mind [1]

2155 זִמָּה ***zimmâ***, n.pr.m. GK: 2366. Zimmah, "*consider, plan*":– Zimmah [3]

2156 זְמוֹרָה ***z^{e}môrâ***, n.[f.]. GK: 2367 [→ 2168; cf. 2231]. vine branch:– branch [3], slips [1], vine branches [1]

2157 זַמְזֻמִּים ***zamzummîm***, n.pr.g. GK: 2368 [→ 2161?]. Zamzummite, "*babblers*":– Zamzummims [1]

2158 זָמִיר ***zāmîr***, n.m. GK: 2369 [→ 2167]. song, music and song:– songs [3], psalmist [1], psalms [1], singing [1]

2159 זָמִיר ***zāmîr***, n.[m.]. GK: 2370 [→ 2168]. pruning (of vines); vintage:– branch [1]

2160 זְמִירָה ***z^{e}mîrâ***, n.pr.m. GK: 2371 [→ 2172?; cf. 2167]. Zemirah, "[poss.] *song [with instrumental accompaniment];* [poss.] *Yahweh has helped*":– Zemira [1]

2161 זָמַם ***zāmam***, v. GK: 2372 [→ 2157?, 2162, 4209]. [Q] to determine, plan, plot, intend, resolve:– thought [4], devised [3], purposed [2], considereth [1], imagined [1], plotteth [1], thought evil [1]

2162 זָמָם ***zāmām***, n.[m.]. GK: 2373 [→ 2161]. plan, plot:– wicked device [1]

2163 זָמַן ***zāman***, v. GK: 2374 [→ 2165; cf. 2164]. [Pu] to be set, be designated, appointed:– appointed [3]

2164 זְמַן ***z^{e}man*** (Aram.), v.den. GK: 10231 [→ 2166; cf. 2163]. [Htpe] to conspire, agree to; [H] to decide:– prepared [1]

2165 זְמָן ***z^{e}mān***, n.m. GK: 2375 [→ 2163; cf. 2166]. time, appointed time:– time [2], season [1], times [1]

2166 זְמַן ***z^{e}man*** (Aram.), n.m. GK: 10232 [→ 2166; cf. 2165]. time, event, occurrence; a unit of time: indefinite period of time, set time, season:– time [6], times [3], seasons [1], season [1]

2167 זָמַר ***zāmar***, v. GK: 2376 [→ 2158, 2160?, 2172, 2176, 4210; cf. 2170, cf. 2171]. [P] to sing, sing praises, to make music, to chant, sing, or play instruments to worship God and proclaim his excellence:– sing [38], give praise [2], sing psalms [2], praise [1], sing forth [1], sing praises [1]

2168 זָמַר ***zāmar***, v. GK: 2377 [→ 2156, 2159, 4211, 4212]. [Q] to prune (vines); [N] to be pruned:– prune [2], pruned [1]

2169 זֶמֶר ***zemer***, n.[m.]. GK: 2378 [cf. 2173?]. mountain sheep; some sources: gazelle:– chamois [1]

2170 זְמָר ***z^{e}mār*** (Aram.), n.[m.]. GK: 10233 [→ 2171; cf. 2167]. music in general, or string music in particular:– musick [4]

זָמִר ***zāmir***. See 2158.

Heb

זְמֹר **zᵉmōr**. See 2156.

2171 זַמָּר **zammār** (Aram.), n.m. GK: 10234 [→ 2170; cf. 2167]. singer:– singers [1]

2172 זִמְרָה **zimrâ**, n.f. GK: 2379 [→ 2160?; cf. 2167]. singing, song, (instrumental) music:– melody [2], psalm [2]

2173 זִמְרָה **zimrâ**, n.f. GK: 2380 [→ 2174; cf. 2169?]. best product, having a high value:– best fruits [1]

זְמִרָה **zᵉmirâ**. See 2158.

זְמֹרָה **zᵉmōrâ**. See 2156.

2174 זִמְרִי **zimrî**, n.pr.m. & loc. GK: 2381 & 2382 [→ 2173]. Zimri, "*wild goats, sheep;* [poss.] *awe of Yahweh*":– Zimri [15]

2175 זִמְרָן **zimrān**, n.pr.m. GK: 2383. Zimran, "*wild goats, sheep*":– Zimran [2]

2176 זִמְרָת **zimrāt**, n.f. GK: 2384 [→ 2167?]. song or strength:– song [3]

2177 זַן **zan**, n.[m.]. GK: 2385 [cf. 2178]. kind, sort:– all manner of store (+413+2177+4480) [2], divers kinds [1]

2178 זַן **zan** (Aram.), n.[m.]. GK: 10235 [cf. 2177]. kind, sort:– kinds [4]

2179 זָנַב **zānab**, v.den. GK: 2386 [→ 2180]. [P] to cut off from the rear position, attack from the rear, as a fig. extension of the base meaning "to cut off a tail":– smite the hindmost [1], smote the hindmost [1]

2180 זָנָב **zānāb**, n.m. GK: 2387 [→ 2179]. tail; stump:– tail [9], tails [2]

2181 זָנָה **zānâ**, v. GK: 2388 & 2389 [→ 2185, 2183, 2184, 8457]. [Q] to be, become a prostitute; to be sexually immoral, be promiscuous, commit adultery; to feel a dislike for; [Pu] to be solicited for prostitution; [H] to make a prostitute, to turn to prostitution:– harlot [18], go a whoring [8], played the harlot [8], commit whoredom [6], went a whoring [5], gone a whoring [4], whore [4], whorish [3], committed great whoredom (+2181) [2], committed whoredom continually (+2181) [2], committed whoredoms [2], harlot's [2], harlots [2], play the harlot [2], played the whore [2], playedst the harlot [2], playing the harlot [2], whores [2], cause to be a whore [1], caused to commit fornication [1], commit fornication [1], commit whoredom (+8457) [1], commit whoredoms [1], committed fornication [1], committest whoredom [1], fall to whoredom [1], harlots' [1], made to go a whoring [1], make go a whoring [1], play the whore [1], playeth the harlot [1], playing the whore [1], whore's (+802) [1], whoredoms [1], whoredom [1]

2182 זָנוֹחַ **zānôaḥ**, n.pr.m. & loc. GK: 2391 & 2392 [→ 2186]. Zanoah, "*rejected*":– Zanoah [5]

2183 זְנוּנִים **zᵉnûnîm**, n.[m.]. GK: 2393 [→ 2181]. wanton lust, prostitution, adultery; by extension: idolatry, as unfaithfulness to God:– whoredoms [11], whoredom [1]

2184 זְנוּת **zᵉnût**, n.f.abst. GK: 2394 [→ 2181]. prostitution, sexual immorality, unfaithfulness; by extension: idolatry, as unfaithfulness to God:– whoredom [7], whoredoms [2]

2185 זֹנָה **zōnâ**, n.f. *or* v. GK: 2390 [→ 2181]. prostitute, harlot; translated as "armor" in the KJV:– armour [1]

2186 זָנַח **zānaḥ**, v. GK: 2395 & 2396 [→ 2182]. [Q] to reject, cast out; [H] to declare rejected; to remove; to stink:– cast off [16], cast away [1], castest off [1], removed far off [1], turn far away [1]

2187 זָנַק **zānaq**, v. GK: 2397. [P] to spring out:– leap [1]

2188 זֵעָה **zēʿâ**, n.f. GK: 2399 [→ 3154]. sweat; the "sweat of the brow" refers to do heavy manual labor:– sweat [1]

2189 זַעֲוָה **zaʿᵃwâ**, n.f. GK: 2400 [→ 2190; cf. 2111]. thing of horror, terror:– removed [6], trouble [1]

2190 זַעֲוָן **zaʿᵃwān**, n.pr.m. GK: 2401 [→ 2189+4993.1?]. Zaavan, "[poss.] *trembling, terror*":– Zaavan [1], Zavan [1]

2191 זְעֵיר **zᵉʿêr**, n.[m.]. GK: 2402 [→ 4213; cf. 6819; cf. 2192]. little; a little longer:– little [5]

2192 זְעֵיר **zᵉʿêr** (Aram.), a. GK: 10236 [cf. 2191]. little, small; fig., insignificant, light in status:– little [1]

2193 זָעַךְ **zāʿak**, v. GK: 2403 [cf. 1846]. [N] to be extinguished:– extinct [1]

2194 זָעַם **zāʿam**, v. GK: 2404 [→ 2195]. [Q] to express wrath, show fury, denounce; [Qp] to be under wrath, be accursed; [N] to be scolded, be cursed:– indignation [4], angry [2], defy [2], abhorred [1], abhor [1], abominable [1], defied [1]

2195 זַעַם **zaʿam**, n.m. GK: 2405 [→ 2194]. wrath, anger, indignation, insolence:– indignation [20], anger [1], rage [1]

2196 זָעַף **zāʿap**, v. GK: 2406 & 2407 [→ 2152, 2197, 2198]. [Q] to rage against, become angry; to look dejected, look pitiful:– wroth [2], fretteth [1], sad [1], worse liking [1]

2197 זַעַף **zaʿap**, n.m. GK: 2408 [→ 2196]. rage, wrath:– indignation [2], rage [2], raging [1], wrath [1]

2198 זָעֵף **zāʿēp**, a. GK: 2409 [→ 2196]. angry, raging:– displeased [2]

2199 זָעַק **zāʿaq**, v. GK: 2410 [→ 2201; cf. 6817; cf. 2200]. [Q] to cry out, call to, weep aloud, howl; [N] to be called, be summoned; be assembled; [H] to summon, cause to gather together, issue a proclamation:– cried [26], cry [20], cried out [5], cry out [5], called [3], assemble [2], criest [2], gathered together [2], gathered [2], assembled [1], caused to be proclaimed [1], comest with a company [1], crieth out [1], crying [1], make to cry [1]

2200 זְעִק **zᵉʿiq** (Aram.), v. GK: 10237 [cf. 3815, cf. 6817]. [P] to call out, shout:– cried [1]

2201 זְעָקָה **zᵉʿāqâ**, n.f. GK: 2411 [→ 2199]. outcry, shout, lament, wail:– cry [17], crying [1]

2202 זִפְרֹן **ziprôn**, n.pr.loc. GK: 2412. Ziphron:– Ziphron [1]

2203 זֶפֶת **zepet**, n.f. GK: 2413. pitch (resin):– pitch [3]

זִק **ziq** or זֵק **zēq**. See 2131.

2204 זָקֵן **zāqēn**, v. GK: 2416 [→ 2206]. [Q] to be old; [H] to grow old; this can refer to maturity in contrast to youth or to advanced age:– old [22], waxed old [2], aged man [1], old man [1], wax old [1]

2205 זָקֵן **zāqēn**, a. GK: 2418 [→ 2206]. elder, old, aged, veteran; (n.) elder, leader, dignitary; "elder" can refer to a formal position as a community leader and arbiter:– elders [114], old [21], old men [11], ancients [9], old man [9], ancient [5], aged [3], ancient men [1], elder (+3117+3807.1) [1], eldest [1], old men's [1], old women [1], senators [1]

2206 זָקָן **zāqān**, n.m. GK: 2417 [→ 2204, 2205, 2207, 2209, 2208]. beard, whiskers (a sign of maturity or age); chin:– beard [15], beards [4]

2207 זֹקֶן **zōqen**, n.[m.]. GK: 2419 [→ 2206]. old age:– age [1]

2208 זְקֻנִים **zᵉqunîm**, n.pl.[m.]. GK: 2421 [→ 2206]. old age:– old age [4]

2209 זִקְנָה **ziqnâ**, n.f. GK: 2420 [→ 2206]. old age, growing old:– old age [3], old [3]

2210 זָקַף **zāqap**, v. GK: 2422 [cf. 2211]. [Q] to lift up:– raiseth up [1], raiseth [1]

2211 זְקַף **zᵉqap** (Aram.), v. GK: 10238 [cf. 2210]. [Pp] to be lifted up:– set up [1]

2212 זָקַק **zāqaq**, v. GK: 2423 [cf. 2085]. [Q] to refine, distill; [P] to refine; [Pu] to be refined, be purified:– refined [2], fine [1], pour down [1], purge [1], purified [1], well refined [1]

2213 זֵר **zēr**, n.m. GK: 2425 [→ 2237]. molding:– crown [10]

2214 זָרָא **zārāʾ**, n.[f.]. GK: 2426. loathsome thing:– stranger (+376) [2], loathsome [1], strangers [1]

2215 זָרַב **zārab**, v. GK: 2427. [Pu] to become dry:– wax warm [1]

2216 זְרֻבָּבֶל **zᵉrubbābel**, n.pr.m. GK: 2428 [→ 2232+894; cf. 2217]. Zerubbabel, "*offspring [seed] of Babylon; scion* i.e., *one grafted into the [plant of] Babylon*":– Zerubbabel [21]

2217 זְרֻבָּבֶל **zᵉrubbābel** (Aram.), n.pr.m. GK: 10239 [cf. 2216]. Zerubbabel, "*seed of Babylon* or *one grafted into Babylon*":– Zerubbabel [1]

2218 זֶרֶד **zered**, n.pr.loc. GK: 2429. Zered, "*[valley of some kind of] plant*":– Zered [3], Zared [1]

2219 זָרָה **zārâ**, v. GK: 2430 & 2431 [→ 2239, 4214, 4215]. [Q, P] to scatter, spread out; winnow; to measure off, discern; [N, Pu] to be scattered, spread out:– scatter [12], disperse [7], scattered [6], fan [4], scattereth [2], spread [2], cast away [1], compassest [1], dispersed [1], strawed [1], winnowed [1], winnoweth [1]

2220 זְרוֹעַ **zᵉrôaʿ**, n.f. GK: 2432 [cf. 248; cf. 153, cf. 1872]. arm, forearm, shoulder; power, strength, force:– arm [59], arms [24], power [3], shoulder [2], holpen [1], mighty [1], strength [1]

2221 זֵרוּעַ **zērûaʿ**, n.[m.]. GK: 2433 [→ 2232]. (plants from) seeds:– sowing [1], things that are sown [1]

2222 זַרְזִיף **zarzîp**, n.[m.]. GK: 2434 & 2449. dripping:– water [1]

זְרוֹעָה **zᵉrôʿâ**. See 2220.

2223 זַרְזִיר **zarzîr**, a. GK: 2435 [→ 2237?]. a strutting animal, variously interpreted: rooster, horse, greyhound:– greyhound (+4975) [1]

2224 זָרַח **zāraḥ**, v. GK: 2436 [→ 249, 250, 2225, 2226, 2227, 4217 (also used with compound proper names)]. [Q] to rise, dawn (of the sun); by extension: to appear bright red (as with a skin disorder):– ariseth [4], arise [3], risen [2], riseth [2], rose up [2], arose [1], rise [1], rose [1], shone [1], up [1]

2225 זֶרַח **zeraḥ**, n.[m.]. GK: 2437 [→ 2226, 2227; cf. 2224]. dawning (of light):– rising [1]

2226 זֶרַח **zeraḥ**, n.pr.m. GK: 2438 [→ 250; cf. 2224, 2225]. Zerah, "*dawning, shining* or *flashing [red or scarlet] light*":– Zerah [20], Zarah [1]

2227 זַרְחִי **zarḥî**, a.g. GK: 2439 [→ 2226; cf. 2224, 2225]. Zerahite, "*of Zerah*":– Zarhites [6]

2228 זְרַחְיָה **zᵉraḥyâ**, n.pr.m. GK: 2440 [→ 2224+3068]. Zerahiah, "*Yahweh shines brightly [red or scarlet]; Yahweh has risen [like the sun]*":– Zerahiah [5]

2229 זָרַם **zāram**, v. GK: 2441 & 2442 [→ 2230]. [Q] to sweep away, put an end to; [Po] to pour down:– carriest away as with a flood [1], poured out [1]

2230 זֶרֶם **zerem**, n.m. GK: 2443 [→ 2229]. rain, rainstorm, thunderstorm, torrent rains:– storm [3], tempest [3], flood [1], overflowing [1], showers [1]

2231 זִרְמָה **zirmâ**, n.f. GK: 2444 [cf. 2156]. male genitals or emission:– issue [2]

2232 זָרַע **zāraʿ**, v. GK: 2445 [→ 2221, 2233, 2235, 4218; cf. 2234 (also used with compound proper names)]. [Q] to sow seed, plant seed; [Qp] to be sown upon; [Pu] to be sown; [N] to be sown, be planted, to have children, have descendants; [H] to yield seed, to become pregnant; from the base meaning of scattering seed onto the ground comes the fig. extension "to have children":– sow [26], sown [14], yielding [3], sowed [2], sower [2], soweth [2], bearing [1], conceive seed (+2233) [1], conceived seed [1], set [1], sow seeds [1], sow with seed [1], sowedst [1]

2233 זֶרַע **zeraʿ**, n.m. GK: 2446 [→ 2232; cf. 2234]. seed, semen, that which propagates a species; by extension: that which is propagated, child, offspring, descendant, line, race:– seed [218], child [2], conceive seed (+2232) [1], fruitful [1], lie carnally (+5414+7903+3807.1) [1], lieth carnally with (+854+7901+7902) [1], man carnally (+376+7902) [1], seed (+7902) [1], seed's [1], seedtime [1], sowing time [1]

2234 זְרַע **zᵉraʿ** (Aram.), n.[m.]. GK: 10240 [cf. 2233]. seed, "seed" of a person is translated "descendant":– seed [1]

זְרֹעַ **zᵉrōaʿ**. See 2220.

2235 זֵרֹעִים **zērōʿîm** or זֵרְעֹנִים **zērʿōnîm**, n.[m.]. GK: 2447 & 2448 [cf. 2232]. vegetables:– pulse [2]

זְרֹעָה **zᵉrōʿâ**. See 2220.

2236 זָרַק **zāraq**, v. GK: 2450 & 2451 [→ 4219]. [Q] to sprinkle, to scatter, to toss (in the air); to creep in; [Pu] to be sprinkled:– sprinkled [16], sprinkle [14], scatter [2], here and there [1], sprinkleth [1], strowed [1]

2237 זָרַר **zārar**, v. GK: 2452 & 2453 [→ 2213, 2223?]. [Qp] to be pressed out; [Po] to sneeze:– neesed [1]

2238 זֶרֶשׁ **zereš**, n.pr.f. GK: 2454. Zeresh, "[poss.] *Kirsha; gold; mop-headed*":– Zeresh [4]

2239 זֶרֶת **zeret**, n.f. GK: 2455 [→ 2219]. handbreadth, span (of an open hand, a measure of about nine inches [23 cm]):– span [7]

2240 זַתּוּא **zattûʾ**, n.pr.m. GK: 2456. Zattu:– Zattu [3], Zatthu [1]

2241 זֵתָם **zētām**, n.pr.m. GK: 2457 [→ 2132?]. Zetham, "[poss.] *olive tree*":– Zetham [2]

2242 זֵתַר **zētar**, n.pr.m. GK: 2458. Zethar, "[poss.] *conqueror; slayer*":– Zethar [1]

2243 חֹב **ḥōb**, n.[m.]. GK: 2460 [→ 2245; cf. 2244]. heart:– bosom [1]

2244 חָבָא **ḥābāʾ**, v. GK: 2461 [→ 455, 4224; cf. 2243, 2246?, 2247, 3160?]. [N] to be hidden, to hide oneself; [Pu] to keep oneself in hiding; [H] to hide (another); [Ho] to be hidden away; [Ht] to keep oneself hidden:– hid [24], hide [7], held peace (+6963) [1], hideth [1], secretly [1]

2245 חָבַב ***ḥābab***, v. GK: 2462 [→ 2243, 2246?, 3160?]. [Q] to love:– loved [1]

2246 חֹבָב ***ḥōbāb***, n.pr.m. GK: 2463 [→ 2245?; cf. 2244?]. Hobab, "*beloved;* [poss.] *deceit*":– Hobab [2]

2247 חָבָה ***ḥābâ***, v. GK: 2464 [→ 2252, 2253; cf. 2244]. [Q] to hide; [N] to conceal oneself:– hide [4]

2248 חֲבוּלָה ***ḥ^{a}bûlâ*** (Aram.), n.f. GK: 10242 [→ 2255]. wrong, crime:– hurt [1]

2249 חָבוֹר ***ḥābôr***, n.pr.loc. GK: 2466. Habor:– Habor [3]

2250 חַבּוּרָה ***ḥabbûrâ***, n.f. GK: 2467 [→ 2266]. bruise, welt, wound, injury:– stripe [2], blueness [1], bruises [1], hurt [1], stripes [1], wounds [1]

2251 חָבַט ***ḥābaṭ***, v. GK: 2468. [Q] to thresh, beat out; [N] to be beaten:– beat off [1], beat out [1], beaten out [1], beatest [1], threshed [1]

2252 חֳבַיָּה ***ḥ^{o}bayyâ***, n.pr.m. GK: 2469 [→ 2247+3068]. Hobaiah, "*Yahweh has hidden*":– Habaiah [2]

2253 חֶבְיוֹן ***ḥebyôn***, n.[m.]. GK: 2470 [→ 2247]. hiding, covering:– hiding [1]

2254 חָבַל ***ḥābal***, v. GK: 2471 & 2472 & 2473 [→ 2256, 2258; cf. 2255]. [Q] to require a pledge, demand a security; to act wickedly, to offend; [P] to destroy, ruin, work havoc; to conceive, be pregnant, be in labor; [Pu] to be broken:– destroy [5], take a pledge [3], at all take to pledge (+2254) [2], bands [2], brought forth [2], dealt very corruptly (+2254) [2], destroyed [2], take to pledge [2], corrupt [1], laid to pledge [1], offend [1], spoil [1], take for a pledge [1], taken a pledge [1], taketh to pledge [1], travaileth [1], withholden the pledge (+2258) [1]

2255 חֲבַל ***ḥ^{a}bal*** (Aram.), v. GK: 10243 [→ 2248, 2257; cf. 2254]. [Pa] to destroy, hurt; [Htpa] to be destroyed:– destroyed [3], destroy [2], hurt [1]

2256 חֶבֶל ***ḥebel*** or חֵבֶל ***ḥēbel***, n.m. GK: 2474 & 2475 & 2476 & 2477 & 2482 [→ 2254, cf. 2259, 2260]. rope, cord, line, rigging; share, portion, region, district; procession, group, union; destruction, ruin; labor pains, anguish of birth pangs:– cords [12], sorrows [10], line [5], coast [4], cord [4], lot [3], region [3], ropes [3], company [2], lines [2], pangs [2], portions [2], portion [2], bands [1], country [1], destruction [1], pain [1], snare [1], tacklings [1]

2257 חֲבָל ***ḥ^{a}bāl*** (Aram.), n.m. GK: 10244 [→ 2255]. physical harm, wound, hurt; fig., damage resulting from the lowering of status:– hurt [2], damage [1]

2258 חֲבֹל ***ḥ^{a}bōl*** or חֲבֹלָה ***ḥ^{a}bōlâ***, n.[m.]. GK: 2478 & 2481 [→ 2254]. pledge for a loan:– pledge [3], withholden the pledge (+2254) [1]

2259 חֹבֵל ***ḥōbēl***, n.m. GK: 2480 [cf. 2256]. seaman, sailor:– pilots [4], shipmaster (+7227+1886.1) [1]

2260 חִבֵּל ***ḥibbēl***, n.[m.]. GK: 2479 [→ 2256]. (ship's) rigging, mast:– mast [1]

2261 חֲבַצֶּלֶת ***ḥ^{a}baṣṣelet***, n.f. GK: 2483. rose; crocus:– rose [2]

2262 חֲבַצִּנְיָה ***ḥ^{a}baṣṣinyâ***, n.pr.m. GK: 2484. Habazziniah, "[poss.] *exuberant in Yahweh*":– Habaziniah [1]

2263 חָבַק ***ḥābaq***, v. GK: 2485 [→ 2264]. [Q] to hold in one's arms, embrace; to fold one's hands; [P] to embrace, hug:– embrace [8], embraced [3], embracing [1], foldeth together [1]

2264 חִבֻּק ***ḥibbuq***, n.[m.]. GK: 2486 [→ 2263]. folding (of idle hands):– folding [2]

2265 חֲבַקּוּק ***ḥ^{a}baqqûq***, n.pr.m. GK: 2487. Habakkuk, "*garden plant*":– Habakkuk [2]

2266 חָבַר ***ḥābar***, v. GK: 2248 & 2488 & 2489 [→ 2250, 2267, 2268, 2270, 2271, 2272, 2274, 5683, 2275, 2276, 2277, 2278, 2279, 4226, 4225]. [Q] to join, unite, be attached, to be touching; to cast spells, to enchant; [Qp] to be joined; [P] to fasten, join; [Pu] to be fastened, be closely compacted; [Ht] to make an alliance, become allies; [H] to make fine speeches:– joined [6], coupled [5], couple together [3], coupled together [2], couple [2], joined together [2], charmer (+2267) [1], charming (+2267) [1], compact [1], fellowship [1], heap up [1], join together [1], joined to [1], join [1], league [1]

2267 חֶבֶר ***ḥeber***, n.[m.]. GK: 2490 [→ 2266]. sharing; band, group; magic spell:– enchantments [2], wide [2], charmer (+2266) [1], charming (+2266) [1], company [1]

2268 חֶבֶר ***ḥeber***, n.pr.m. GK: 2491 [→ 2277; cf. 2266]. Heber, "*associate*":– Heber [10], Heber's [1]

2269 חֲבַר ***ḥ^{a}bar*** (Aram.), n.m. GK: 10245 [→ 2273; cf. 2270]. friend, companion:– fellows [2], companions [1]

2270 חָבֵר ***ḥābēr***, a. & n.m. GK: 2492 [→ 2266; cf. 2269, cf. 2273]. companion, associate, partner, friend:– companions [5], fellows [3], companion [2], fellow [1], knit together [1]

2271 חַבָּר ***ḥabbār***, n.m. GK: 2493 [→ 2266]. (fellow) trader, one of a community of traders:– companions [1]

2272 חֲבַרְבֻּרוֹת ***ḥ^{a}barburôt***, n.f. GK: 2494 [→ 2266]. spots (of a leopard):– spots [1]

2273 חַבְרָה ***ḥabrâ*** (Aram.), n.f. GK: 10246 [→ 2269; cf. 2270]. companion (horn):– fellows [1]

2274 חֶבְרָה ***ḥebrâ***, n.f. GK: 2495 [→ 2266]. company, association:– company [1]

2275 חֶבְרוֹן ***ḥebrôn***, n.pr.m. & loc. GK: 2496 & 2497 [→ 2276; cf. 2266, 5683?]. Hebron, "*association*":– Hebron [71]

2276 חֶבְרוֹנִי ***ḥebrônî***, a.g. GK: 2498 [→ 2275; cf. 2266, 5683]. Hebronite, "*of Hebron*":– Hebronites [6]

2277 חֶבְרִי ***ḥebrî***, a.g. GK: 2499 [→ 2268; cf. 2266]. Heberite, "*of Heber*":– Heberites [1]

2278 חֲבֶרֶת ***ḥ^{a}beret***, n.f. GK: 2500 [→ 2266]. partner, (marriage) companion:– companion [1]

2279 חֹבֶרֶת ***ḥōberet***, n.f. GK: 2501 [→ 2266]. set (of curtains):– coupleth [2], coupling [2]

2280 חָבַשׁ ***ḥābaš***, v. GK: 2502 [cf. 2805]. [Q] to tie, bind, saddle; [Qp] to be saddled; to be twisted, wrapped around; [P] to bind up; [Pu] to be bound, bandaged:– saddled [10], bind up [3], bindeth up [3], bind [3], bound up [3], saddle [3], put [2], bindeth [1], bound [1], girded about [1], govern [1], healer [1], wrapt about [1]

2281 חֲבִתִּים ***ḥ^{a}bittîm***, n.[m.]pl. GK: 2503 [→ 4227]. offering bread (flat cakes, baked in a pan):– pans [1]

2282 חַג ***ḥag***, n.m. GK: 2504 [→ 2287]. religious feast, festival; festal procession:– feast [50], feasts [3], keep a feast (+2287) [2], sacrifice [2], solemn feasts [2], sacrifices [1], solemn feast [1], solemnity [1]

2283 חָגָּא ***ḥoggā'***, n.[f.]. GK: 2505. terror; some sources: confusion:– terror [1]

2284 חָגָב ***ḥāgāb***, n.m. GK: 2506 [→ 2285, 2286]. grasshopper, locust (in some cultures distinguished from a grasshopper and used as a food source):– grasshoppers [2], grasshopper [2], locusts [1]

2285 חָגָב ***ḥāgāb***, n.pr.m. GK: 2507 [→ 2286; cf. 2284]. Hagab, "*locust*":– Hagab [1]

2286 חֲגָבָא ***ḥ^{a}gābā'*** or חֲגָבָה ***ḥ^{a}gābâ***, n.pr.m. GK: 2508 & 2509 [→ 2285; cf. 2284]. Hagaba, Hagabah, "*locust*":– Hagabah [1], Hagaba [1]

2287 חָגַג ***ḥāgag***, v. GK: 2510 [→ 2282, 2291, 2292, 2293, 2294; cf. 2328]. [Q] to hold a festival, celebrate a festival; this can refer to a religious celebration or a revel:– keep [6], keep a feast (+2282) [2], celebrate [1], dancing [1], hold a feast [1], keep a feast [1], keep a solemn feast [1], keep feast [1], kept holyday [1], reel to and fro [1]

2288 חָגוּ ***ḥāgû***, n.m.pl. GK: 2511. clefts (of a rock) that can be used as a hiding place or retreat from danger:– clefts [3]

2289 חָגוֹר ***ḥāgôr***, a. GK: 2513 [→ 2296]. belted (around the waist):– girdle [2], girded with [1], girdles [1]

2290 חֲגוֹר ***ḥ^{a}gôr*** or חֲגוֹרָה ***ḥ^{a}gôrâ***, n.m. & f. GK: 2512 & 2514 [→ 2296]. covering; belt, sash:– girdle [3], aprons [1], gird [1], put on armour (+2296) [1]

2291 חַגִּי ***ḥaggî***, n.pr.m. & a.g. GK: 2515 [→ 2287]. Haggi, "*festal; born on the feast day*": Haggi [2], Haggites [1]

2292 חַגַּי ***ḥaggay***, n.pr.m. GK: 2516 & 10247 [→ 2287]. Haggai, "*festal; born on the feast day*": note this name is Aramaic twice in Ezra:– Haggai [11]

2293 חַגִּיָּה ***ḥaggiyyâ***, n.pr.m. GK: 2517 [→ 2287+3068]. Haggiah, "*feast of Yahweh*":– Haggiah [1]

2294 חַגִּית ***ḥaggît***, n.pr.f. GK: 2518 [→ 2287]. Haggith, "*festal, born on the feast day*": Haggith [5]

2295 חָגְלָה ***ḥoglâ***, n.pr.f. GK: 2519 [→ 1031; cf. 2728]. Hoglah, "*partridge*":– Hoglah [4]

2296 חָגַר ***ḥāgar***, v. GK: 2520 [→ 2289, 2290, 4228]. [Q] to tie, strap, fasten; to tuck (lower robe) into one's belt, gird; [Qp] to be tucked in, girded:– girded [13], gird with [7], gird [5], appointed [3], girded on [3], gird up [2], girded with [2], afraid [1], gird on [1], girdeth on [1], girdeth [1], girding with [1], on every side [1], put on armour (+2290) [1], restrain [1]

2297 חַד ***ḥad***, a. GK: 2522 [cf. 259]. one, each:– one [1]

2298 חַד ***ḥad*** (Aram.), a. & subst. GK: 10248 [cf. 259]. one, first, a; time, occurrence:– one [5], a [4], first [4], together (+3509.4) [1]

2299 חַד ***ḥad***, a. GK: 2521 [→ 2300]. sharp (sword):– sharp [4]

2300 חָדַד ***ḥādad*** or חָדָה ***ḥādâ***, v. GK: 2523 & 2527 [→ 258, 2299, 2303, 2307; cf. 2302]. [Q] to be fierce, sharp; to sharpen; [H] to sharpen; [Ho] to be sharpened; [Ht] to slash:– sharpened [3], sharpeneth [2], fierce [1]

2301 חֲדַד ***ḥ^{a}dad***, n.pr.m. GK: 2524. Hadad, "*sharp, fierce*":– Hadad [1]

2302 חָדָה ***ḥādâ***, v. GK: 2525 & 2526 [→ 2304, 3164, 3165; cf. 2300]. [Q] to be delighted; [N] to be seen; to be joined; [P] to make glad:– joined [1], made [1], rejoiced [1]

2303 חַדּוּד ***ḥaddûd***, a. GK: 2529 [→ 2300]. jagged, pointed:– sharp [1]

2304 חֶדְוָה ***ḥedwâ***, n.f. GK: 2530 [→ 2302; cf. 2305]. joy:– gladness [1], joy [1]

2305 חֶדְוָה ***ḥedwâ*** (Aram.), n.f. GK: 10250 [cf. 2304]. joy:– joy [1]

2306 חֲדֵה ***ḥ^{a}dēh*** (Aram.), n.m. GK: 10249 [cf. 2373]. chest, breast:– breast [1]

2307 חָדִיד ***ḥādîd***, n.pr.loc. GK: 2531 [→ 2300]. Hadid, "*sharp*":– Hadid [3]

2308 חָדַל ***ḥādal***, v. GK: 2532 & 2533 [→ 2310, 2311?]. [Q] to stop, cease, refrain, fail; to become fat, have success:– forbear [15], cease [12], ceased [6], left off [4], forbare [3], leave [3], left [2], alone (+4480) [1], alone [1], ceaseth [1], ceasing [1], endeth [1], failed [1], forbeareth [1], forborn [1], forsake [1], off [1], rest [1], unoccupied [1], wanteth [1]

2309 חֶדֶל ***ḥedel***, n.[m.]. GK: 2535. world (of the living); some sources: the Underworld, the realm of the dead:– world [1]

2310 חָדֵל ***ḥādēl***, a. GK: 2534 [→ 2308]. refused, rejected, fleeting:– forbeareth [1], frail [1], rejected [1]

2311 חַדְלָי ***ḥadlāy***, n.pr.m. GK: 2536 [→ 2220 *or* 2308]. Hadlai, "*resting; fat, stout*":– Hadlai [1]

2312 חֵדֶק ***ḥēdeq***, n.[m.]. GK: 2537. brier, thorn:– brier [1], thorns [1]

2313 חִדֶּקֶל ***ḥiddeqel***, n.pr.loc. GK: 2538. Hiddekel = Tigris, "*arrow*":– Hiddekel [2]

2314 חָדַר ***ḥādar***, v. GK: 2539 [→ 2315]. [Q] to close in on every side, surround:– entereth into privy chambers [1]

2315 חֶדֶר ***ḥeder***, n.m. GK: 2540 [→ 2314, 2316]. room, chamber, bedroom; shrine; "the chambers of the belly" means "the most inner parts"; "the chambers of death" means "Sheol":– chamber [10], inner chamber (+2315+871.1) [8], chambers [7], bedchamber (+4904) [4], bedchamber (+4296) [2], innermost parts [2], inward parts [2], parlours [1], south [1], within (+4480) [1]

2316 חֲדַר ***ḥ^{a}dar***, n.pr.m. GK: 2540 [→ 2315]. Hadar:– Hadar [1]

2317 חַדְרָךְ ***ḥadrāk***, n.pr.loc. GK: 2541. Hadrach:– Hadrach [1]

2318 חָדַשׁ ***ḥādaš***, v. GK: 2542 [→ 2319, 2320, 2321, 2322]. [Q] to renew, restore, repair, reaffirm; [Ht] to renew oneself:– renew [3], repair [3], renewed [2], renewest [2]

2319 חָדָשׁ ***ḥādāš***, a. GK: 2543 [→ 2318; cf. 2323]. new, recent, fresh:– new [52], fresh [1]

2320 חֹדֶשׁ ***ḥōdeš***, n.m. [& f.?]. GK: 2544 [→ 2321; cf. 2318]. month; new moon, new moon festival:– month [216], months [37], new moons [11], new moon [9], every month (+2320+871.1) [2], another[S] [1], monthly [1]

2321 חֹדֶשׁ ***ḥōdeš***, n.pr.f. GK: 2545 [→ 2320; cf. 2318]. Hodesh, "*new moon*":– Hodesh [1]

2322 חֲדָשָׁה ***ḥ^{a}dāšâ***, n.pr.loc. GK: 2546 [→ 2318]. Hadashah, "*new*":– Hadashah [1]

2323 חֲדַת ***ḥ^{a}dat*** (Aram.), a. GK: 10251 [cf. 2319]. new:– new [1]

2324 חֲוָה ***ḥ^{a}wâ*** (Aram.), v. GK: 10252 [→ 263; cf. 2331]. [Pa] to reveal, tell, show; [H, A] tell, explain, make known, interpret:– shew [14]

2325 חוּב ***ḥûb***, v. GK: 2549 [→ 2326]. [P] to forfeit (one's head):– make endanger [1]

2326 חוֹב ***ḥôb***, n.[m.]. GK: 2550 [→ 2325]. loan, debt:– debtor [1]

2327 חוֹבָה ***ḥôbâ***, n.pr.loc. GK: 2551. Hobah:– Hobah [1]

2328 חוּג ***ḥûg***, v. GK: 2552 [→ 2329, 4230; cf. 2287]. [Q] to encircle:– compassed with (+5921+6440) [1]

2329 חוּג ***ḥûg***, n.[m.]. GK: 2553 [→ 2328]. circle, horizon:– circle [1], circuit [1], compass [1]

2330 חוּד ***ḥûd***, v.den. GK: 2554 [→ 2420; cf. 258]. [Q] to tell a riddle, set forth an allegory:– put forth [3], put forth a riddle (+2420) [1]

2331 חָוָה ***ḥāwâ***, v. GK: 2555 [→ 262; cf. 263, cf. 2324]. [P] to tell, explain, show, display:– shew [5], sheweth [1]

2332 חַוָּה ***ḥawwâ***, n.pr.f. GK: 2558 [cf. 2421]. Eve, "*life*":– Eve [2]

2333 חַוָּה ***ḥawwâ***, n.f. GK: 2557. settlement, camp; an unwalled village, a tent camp of nomadic peoples, more or less permanent:– towns [3], small towns [1]

2334 חַוֹּת יָאִיר ***ḥawwōt yāʾîr***, n.pr.m. & n.f. GK: 2596 [cf. 2971]. Havvoth Jair, "*villages of Jair*":– Havoth-jair [2], Bashan-havoth-jair (+1316) [1]

2335 חוֹזָי ***ḥôzāy***, n.m. GK: 2559 [→ 2374; cf. 2372]. Hozai:–

2336 חוֹחַ ***ḥôaḥ***, n.m. GK: 2560 [cf. 2397]. thicket, thistle, thornbush, bramble, briers; hook:– thistle [4], thorns [3], thorn [2], brambles [1], thistles [1]

2337 חוֹחַ ***ḥôaḥ***, n.m. GK: 2561. hollows, cleft in rock; thicket:– thickets [1]

2338 חוּט ***ḥûṭ*** (Aram.), v. GK: 10253. [H] to repair:– joined [1]

2339 חוּט ***ḥûṭ***, n.m. GK: 2562 [cf. 2338]. line, cord, ribbon, thread:– thread [4], cord [1], fillet [1], line [1]

2340 חִוִּי ***ḥiwwî***, a.g. GK: 2563. Hivite:– Hivites [16], Hivite [9]

2341 חֲוִילָה ***ḥ*ᵃ*wîlâ***, n.pr.loc. GK: 2564 [→ 2344]. Havilah, "*stretch of sand*":– Havilah [7]

2342 חוּל ***ḥûl*** or חִיל ***ḥîl***, v. GK: 2565 & 2655 & 2656 [→ 2427, 2428, 2479, 4234, 4235, 4246, 4257?; cf. 2426]. [Q] to swirl, turn, fall, dance; to writhe, tremble, be in labor, give birth; to endure, prosper; [Pol] to wait; to dance (the round dance); to give birth; be in deep anguish, to twist; [Polal] to be brought forth, be given birth; [Htpalpal] be in distress; [Htpol] to be in torment; to wait patiently; to swirl down; in some contexts this refers to a whirlwind; [H] to shake; [Ho] to be born:– formed [5], in pain [4], brought forth [3], fear [2], grieved [2], grievous [2], have great pain (+2342) [2], shaketh [2], stayed [2], travailed [2], trembled [2], tremble [2], wounded [2], abide [1], afraid [1], bare [1], calve [1], danced [1], dance [1], driveth away [1], fall grievously [1], fall with pain [1], in anguish [1], look for [1], made to bring forth [1], made [1], maketh to calve [1], much pained [1], pained [1], rest [1], shapen [1], sore pained [1], sorely pained [1], sorrowful [1], sorrow [1], tarried [1], travail with child [1], travaileth with pain [1], travail [1], trust [1], wait patiently [1], waited carefully [1]

Heb

2343 חוּל ***ḥûl***, n.pr.m. GK: 2566. Hul:– Hul [2]

2344 חוֹל ***ḥôl***, n.m. GK: 2567 & 2568 [→ 2341]. sand, grains of sand, with the associative meanings that the sands are vast and innumerable; palm tree or phoenix bird:– sand [23]

2345 חוּם ***ḥûm***, a. GK: 2569 [→ 2552]. dark-colored; some shade of gray:– brown [4]

2346 חוֹמָה ***ḥômâ***, n.f. GK: 2570 [→ 3181]. wall, with various associative meanings: protection, safety, or impenetrability:– wall [92], walls [35], two walls [4], walled [2]

2347 חוּס ***ḥûs***, v. GK: 2571. [Q] to show pity, mercy, have compassion, spare:– spare [12], pity [5], spare (+5921) [2], spared [2], had pity [1], pitied [1], regard (+5869) [1]

2348 חוֹף ***ḥôp***, n.[m.]. GK: 2572 [→ 2653]. coast, seashore, haven (for ships):– haven [2], shore [2], coasts [1], coast [1], side [1]

2349 חוּפָם ***ḥûpām***, n.pr.m. GK: 2573 [→ 2350]. Hupham:– Hupham [1]

2350 חוּפָמִי ***ḥûpāmî***, a.g. GK: 2574 [→ 2349]. Huphamite, "*of Hupham*":– Huphamites [1]

2351 חוּץ ***ḥûṣ***, n.[m.]. GK: 2575 [→ 2435; cf. 2434]. out, outside; street, market area; countryside, fields, outdoors:– without (+4480) [43], streets [35], without (+871.1+1886.1) [12], out (+4480) [9], street [9], abroad (+1886.5) [8], abroad [6], out [6], without (+1886.5) [6], out (+1886.5) [3], without [3], abroad (+4480) [2], fields [2], forth [2], outside [2], without (+1886.1+3807.1) [2], without (+4480+1886.5) [2], abroad (+1886.1+3807.1) [1], abroad (+413+1886.1+1886.5) [1], abroad (+4480+1886.1) [1], abroad (+871.1+1886.1) [1], highways [1], more [1], outward (+1886.5) [1], utter [1], without (+1886.1+1886.5) [1], without (+413+1886.1) [1], without (+4480+1886.1) [1]

חוֹק ***ḥôq***. See 2436.

חוּקֹק ***ḥûqōq***. See 2712.

2352 חֻר ***ḥur***, n.[m.]. GK: 2987 [→ 2356]. hole, pit:– holes [1], hole [1]

2353 חוּר ***ḥûr***, n.[m.]. GK: 2580 [→ 2357]. white garments, white linen:– white [2]

2354 חוּר ***ḥûr***, n.pr.m. GK: 2581 [→ 1133, 5991?]. Hur, "[perhaps] *child*":– Hur [16]

2355 חוֹרָי ***ḥôrāy***, n.m. GK: 2583 [→ 2357]. fine linen:– networks [1]

2356 חֹר ***ḥōr***, n.[m.]. GK: 2986 [→ 2352, 2735]. hole (in various forms):– holes [3], hole [3], caves [1]

2357 חָוַר ***ḥāwar***, v. GK: 2578 [→ 2353, 2355, 2751; cf. 2358]. [Q] to grow pale:– wax pale [1]

2358 חִוָּר ***ḥiwwār*** (Aram.), a. GK: 10254. white, a color of purity and lack of defilement:– white [1]

חוֹרוֹן ***ḥôrôn***. See 1032.

חוֹרִי ***ḥôrî***. See 2753.

2359 חוּרִי ***ḥûrî***, n.pr.m. GK: 2585. Huri, "*linen weaver*":– Huri [1]

2360 חוּרַי ***ḥûray***, n.pr.m. GK: 2584. Hurai:– Hurai [1]

2361 חוּרָם ***ḥûrām***, n.pr.m. GK: 2586 & 2587 [→ 297?+1]. Huram, Hiram, "*[my] brother is elevated*":– Huram [12]

2362 חַוְרָן ***ḥawrān***, n.pr.loc. GK: 2588. Hauran, "*black*":– Hauran [2]

2363 חוּשׁ ***ḥûš***, v. GK: 2590 & 2591 [→ 2439, 2440, 4122]. same as 2439: [Q] to go quickly, hasten, rush upon; to be greatly disturbed; to find enjoyment; [Qp] to be ready; [H] to make hurry, hasten; to be dismayed:– make haste [9], hasten [4], hasted [2], haste [2], hasteth [1], made haste [1], ready [1]

2364 חוּשָׁה ***ḥûšâ***, n.pr.m. GK: 2592 [→ 2843]. Hushah, "[perhaps] *haste*":– Hushah [1]

2365 חוּשַׁי ***ḥûšay***, n.pr.m. GK: 2593 [cf. 7862?]. Hushai:– Hushai [14]

2366 חוּשִׁים ***ḥûšim*** or חֻשִׁים ***ḥušim*** or חֻשִׁם ***ḥušim***, n.pr.f. & m. GK: 2594 & 3123. Hushim, Hushite:– Hushim [4]

2367 חוּשָׁם ***ḥûšām***, n.pr.m. GK: 2595 [cf. 2828]. Husham:– Husham [4]

2368 חוֹתָם ***ḥôtām***, n.m. GK: 2597 [→ 2369; cf. 2856]. seal, signet ring:– signet [8], seal [5], signets [1]

2369 חוֹתָם ***ḥôtām***, n.pr.m. GK: 2598 [→ 2368; cf. 2856]. Hotham, "*signet ring, seal*":– Hotham [1], Hothan [1]

2370 חֲזָה ***ḥ*ᵃ*zâ*** (Aram.), v. GK: 10255 [→ 2376, 2379; cf. 2372]. [P] to see, look, watch, realize; [Pp] to be usual, be customary:– saw [9], sawest [7], beheld [6], see [4], seen [3], had[S] [1], wont [1]

2371 חֲזָאֵל ***ḥ*ᵃ*zāʾēl*** or חֲזָהאֵל ***ḥ*ᵃ*zāhʾēl***, n.pr.m. GK: 2599 & 2604 [→ 2372+410]. Hazael, "*God [El] sees*":– Hazael [23]

2372 חָזָה ***ḥāzâ***, v. GK: 2600 [→ 2335, 2374, 2377, 2380, 2378, 2384, 4236, 4237, 4238; cf. 2370 (also used with compound proper names)]. [Q] to see, to look, observe, gaze; by extension: to choose (one thing over another); to have visions, to prophesy:– see [15], seen [9], saw [8], behold [7], look [3], seeth [3], prophesy [2], seest [2], provide [1], sawest [1]

2373 חָזֶה ***ḥāzeh***, n.m. GK: 2601 [cf. 2306]. breast (portion of sacrifice):– breast [11], breasts [2]

2374 חֹזֶה ***ḥōzeh***, n.m. GK: 2602 & 2603 [→ 2335, 3626; cf. 2372]. seer, one who receives a communication from God, with a possible focus that the message has a visual component; agreement:– seer [11], seers [5], see [2], agreement [1], prophets [1], seeing [1], stargazers (+3556+871.1+1886.1) [1]

חֲזָהאֵל ***ḥ*ᵃ*zāhʾēl***. See 2371.

2375 חֲזוֹ ***ḥ*ᵃ*zô***, n.pr.m. GK: 2605. Hazo:– Hazo [1]

2376 חֵזוּ ***ḥ*ᵉ*zû*** (Aram.), n.m. GK: 10256 [→ 2370]. vision, appearance:– visions [9], vision [2], look [1]

2377 חָזוֹן ***ḥāzôn***, n.m. GK: 2606 [→ 2372]. vision, revelation, a message from God, with a possible focus on the visual aspects of the message:– vision [32], visions [3]

2378 חָזוּת ***ḥ*ᵃ*zôt***, n.[f.]. GK: 2608 [→ 2372]. visions:– visions [1]

2379 חֲזוֹת ***ḥ*ᵃ*zôt*** (Aram.), n.f. GK: 10257 [→ 2370]. visible sight:– sight [2]

2380 חָזוּת ***ḥāzût***, n.f. GK: 2607 [→ 2372]. vision; prominent appearance:– vision [2], agreement [1], notable ones [1], notable [1]

2381 חֲזִיאֵל ***ḥ*ᵃ*zîʾēl***, n.pr.m. GK: 2609 [→ 2372+410]. Haziel, "*vision of God [El]*":– Haziel [1]

2382 חֲזָיָה ***ḥ*ᵃ*zāyâ***, n.pr.m. GK: 2610 [→ 2372+3068]. Hazaiah, "*Yahweh sees*":– Hazaiah [1]

2383 חֶזְיוֹן ***ḥezyôn***, n.pr.m. GK: 2611. Hezion, "*vision; one with floppy ears*":– Hezion [1]

2384 חִזָּיוֹן ***ḥizzāyôn***, n.m. GK: 2612 [→ 2372]. vision, dream, revelation:– vision [6], visions [3]

2385 חֲזִיז ***ḥ*ᵃ*zîz***, n.[m.]. GK: 2613. storm cloud, dark and producing lightning and thunder:– lightning [2], bright clouds [1]

2386 חֲזִיר ***ḥ*ᵃ*zîr***, n.m. GK: 2614 [→ 2387, 3170]. pig, boar:– swine's [4], swine [2], boar [1]

2387 חֵזִיר ***ḥēzîr***, n.pr.m. GK: 2615 [→ 2386]. Hezir, "*boar*":– Hezir [2]

2388 חָזַק ***ḥāzaq***, v. GK: 2616 [→ 2389, 2390, 2391, 2392, 2393, 2394 (also used with compound proper names)]. [Q] to be strong, hard, harsh, severe; [P] to harden (one's heart); to give strength, repair, encourage; [H] to grasp, seize, hold; to make repairs; [Ht] to establish oneself firmly; to encourage, to rally strength; from the base meaning of physical hardness come by extension: physical and internal strength of character; (negative) hardness of the heart, failure to respond to a person or message:– repaired [39], strong [38], strengthened [28], strengthen [14], hardened [9], prevailed [8], repair [8], take hold [7], of good courage [6], caught [5], encouraged [5], held [5], hold [5], make strong [5], encourage [4], harden [4], laid hold [4], stronger [4], took hold [4], took [4], caught hold [3], hold fast [3], made strong [3], sore [3], taketh [3], calkers (+919) [2], confirm [2], courageous [2], fortified [2], lay hold [2], mend [2], prevail [2], taken hold [2], taken [2], withstand (+6440+3807.1) [2], aided (+853+3027) [1], became mighty [1], behave valiantly [1], clave [1], confirmed [1], constant [1], constrained [1], continued [1], courageously [1], established [1], fastened [1], fasten [1], force [1], fortify [1], give strength [1], good courage [1], held fast [1], help (+3027+871.1) [1], help [1], holden [1], holdeth fast [1], holdeth [1], lay hold on [1], layeth hold [1], leaneth [1], made harder [1], maintain [1], obtain [1], play the men [1], received [1], recovered [1], relieve [1], retained (+871.1) [1], retained [1], retaineth [1], retain [1], seized [1], shew strong [1], stout [1], stronger than [1], sure [1], take fast hold [1], taken hold on [1], taketh hold [1], took courage [1], urgent [1], waxed mighty [1], waxed sore [1], waxen strong [1]

2389 חָזָק ***ḥāzāq***, a. GK: 2617 [→ 2388]. mighty, powerful, strong, hard, severe; from the base meaning of physical hardness come by extension: physical and internal strength of character; (negative) hardness of the heart, failure to respond to a person or message:– strong [26], mighty [20], sore [3], stronger [2], harder [1], hottest [1], impudent (+4696) [1], loud [1], stiff [1]

2390 חָזֵק ***ḥāzēq***, a.vbl. GK: 2618 [→ 2388]. strong, loud:– stronger [1], waxed louder and louder (+3966) [1]

2391 חֵזֶק ***ḥēzeq***, n.[m.]. GK: 2619 [→ 2388]. strength:– strength [1]

2392 חֹזֶק ***ḥōzeq***, n.m. GK: 2620 [→ 2388]. might, strength, power:– strength [5]

2393 חֶזְקָה ***ḥezqâ***, n.f. GK: 2621 [→ 2388]. strength, power:– strong [2], mightily (+871.1) [1], strengthened [1], strength [1]

2394 חָזְקָה ***ḥozqâ***, n.f. GK: 2622 [→ 2388]. force, harshness, urgency:– force [2], mightily (+871.1) [1], repair [1], sharply (+871.1) [1]

2395 חִזְקִי ***ḥizqî***, n.pr.m. GK: 2623 [→ 2388+3068]. Hizki, "*Yahweh is [my] strength* or *my strength*":– Hezeki [1]

2396 חִזְקִיָּה ***ḥizqiyyâ*** or חִזְקִיָּהוּ ***ḥizqiyyāhû***, n.pr.m. GK: 2624 & 2625 [→ 2388+3068]. Hezekiah, "*Yahweh is [my] strength*":– Hezekiah [85], Hizkiah [1], Hizkijah [1]

2397 חָח ***ḥāḥ***, n.m. GK: 2626 [cf. 2336]. hook; brooch:– chains [2], hooks [2], hook [2], bracelets [1]

חָחִי ***ḥāḥî***. See 2397.

2398 חָטָא ***ḥāṭā'***, v. GK: 2627 [→ 2399, 2400, 2401, 2402, 2403]. [Q] to sin, do wrong, miss the way; [P] to purify, cleanse, to offer a sin offering; [H] to bring a sin upon, cause to commit a sin; [Ht] to purify oneself; "to sin," to willfully act contrary to the will and law of God, is a figure of missing or moving from a standard or mark:– sinned [101], sin [38], made to sin [20], sinneth [13], sinner [8], cleanse [7], purify [7], committed [5], cause to sin [4], made sin [4], offended [4], purified [3], bear the blame [2], done [2], make sin [2], sinning [2], bare loss [1], cleansing [1], fault [1], grievously sinned (+2399) [1], harm done [1], made reconciliation [1], make an offender [1], miss [1], offered for sin [1], offereth for sin [1], purge [1], purifieth [1], sin committed (+2403) [1], sinful [1], sinnest [1], trespass [1]

2399 חֵטְא ***ḥēṭ'***, n.m. GK: 2628 [→ 2398; cf. 2408]. sin, action contrary to the will and law of God, with a strong implication that guilt follows, error:– sin [21], sins [7], committed a sin [1], faults [1], grievously sinned (+2398) [1], offences [1], punishment of sins [1]

2400 חַטָּא ***ḥaṭṭā'***, a. & n.m. GK: 2629 [→ 2398]. sinful, guilty; (n.) sinner, wicked one:– sinners [16], offenders [1], sinful [1]

2401 חֲטָאָה ***ḥ***^a^***ṭā'â***, n.f. GK: 2630 & 2631 [→ 2398]. sin, guilt, condemnation; sin offering:– sin [7], sin offering [1]

2402 חַטָּאָה ***ḥaṭṭā'â***, n.f. GK: 2632 [→ 2398]. sin, wickedness, fault:–

2403 חַטָּאת ***ḥaṭṭā't***, n.f. GK: 2633 [→ 2398; cf. 2409]. sin, wrong, iniquity; sin offering, purification offering:– sin offering [115], sin [100], sins [70], punishment [2], purification for sin [2], punishment of sin [1], purifying [1], sin committed (+2398) [1], sin offerings [1], sinful [1], sinner [1], sins committed [1]

2404 חָטַב ***ḥāṭab***, v. GK: 2634. [Q] to cut, chop (wood); (n.) woodcutter, woodsman; [Pu] to carve:– hewers [5], cut down [1], hewer [1], hew [1], polished [1]

2405 חֲטֻבוֹת ***ḥ***^a^***ṭubôt***, n.f.pl. GK: 2635. colored, embroidered (fabric):– carved [1]

2406 חִטָּה ***ḥiṭṭâ***, n.f. GK: 2636 [→ 2590; cf. 2591]. wheat:– wheat [29], wheaten [1]

2407 חַטּוּשׁ ***ḥaṭṭûš***, n.pr.m. GK: 2637. Hattush:– Hattush [5]

2408 חֲטָי ***ḥ***^a^***ṭāy*** (Aram.), n.[m.]. GK: 10259 [→ 2409; cf. 2399]. sin:– sins [1]

2409 חַטָּיָא ***ḥaṭṭāyā'*** (Aram.), n.f. GK: 10260 [→ 2408; cf. 2403]. sin offering:– sin offering [1]

2410 חֲטִיטָא ***ḥ***^a^***ṭîṭā'***, n.pr.m. GK: 2638. Hatita:– Hatita [2]

2411 חַטִּיל ***ḥaṭṭîl***, n.pr.m. GK: 2639. Hattil, "*talkative*":– Hattil [2]

2412 חֲטִיפָא ***ḥ***^a^***ṭîpā'***, n.pr.m. GK: 2640 [→ 2414]. Hatipha, "*taken captive*":– Hatipha [2]

2413 חָטַם ***ḥāṭam***, v. GK: 2641 [→ 2748]. [Q] to hold back, restrain:– refrain [1]

2414 חָטַף ***ḥāṭap***, v. GK: 2642 [→ 2412]. [Q] to seize, carry off (by force):– catch [3]

2415 חֹטֶר ***ḥōṭer***, n.m. GK: 2643. rod, switch; shoot, twig:– rod [2]

2416 חַי ***ḥay***, n.m. & a. GK: 2644 & 2645 & 2646 & 2651 & 2652 & 2653 [→ 2421; cf. 2417; cf. 2423]. life, state of living (in contrast to death), lifetime; "as I live" is a formula for an oath, implying death should follow if what is sworn is not true; family, kin; band, army; animal, beast, livestock, living creature; living, alive, with an implication that life has movement and vigor; "living meat" is "raw meat"; "living water" is "fresh, running water":– life [143], living [80], liveth [67], live [46], beasts [41], beast [34], alive [30], living creatures [9], running [7], living creature [6], raw [5], lived [4], living thing [4], quick [3], congregation [2], lives [2], troop [2], alive (+871.1+1886.1) [1], appetite [1], company [1], life (+5315) [1], lifetime [1], lived (+1961) [1], lively [1], livest [1], maintenance [1], maketh merry (+8055) [1], multitude [1], old (+3117+8141) [1], quick raw (+4241) [1], springing [1], whole age (+3117+8141) [1], wild beasts [1]

2417 חַי ***ḥay*** (Aram.), a. GK: 10261 [→ 2418; cf. 2416]. living, alive:– living [4], life [1], lives [1], liveth [1]

2418 חְיָא ***ḥ***^e^***yâ*** (Aram.), v. GK: 10262 [→ 2417, 2423; cf. 2421]. [P] to live; [H] to spare, let live:– live [5], kept alive [1]

2419 חִיאֵל ***ḥî'ēl***, n.pr.m. GK: 2647 [→ 251+410]. Hiel, "*God [El] lives here*":– Hiel [1]

חִיֵּב ***ḥāyab***. See 2325.

2420 חִידָה ***ḥîdâ***, n.f. GK: 2648 [→ 2330; cf. 280]. riddle, hard question, allegory; hidden things, intrigue; scorn (the asking of a riddle as a game could imply scorn and ridicule toward the person asked):– riddle [8], dark sayings [2], hard questions [2], dark saying [1], dark sentences [1], dark speeches [1], proverb [1], put forth a riddle (+2330) [1]

2421 חָיָה ***ḥāyâ***, v. GK: 2649 [→ 2416, 2422, 2424, 2425, 4241; cf. 2332; cf. 2418 (also used with compound proper names)]. same as 2425: [Q] to live; recover, revive; [P] to keep alive, preserve life; [H] to keep alive, save a life, spare a life, restore a life:– live [113], lived [44], surely live (+2421) [18], quicken [12], save alive [10], God save [8], keep alive [8], revive [8], saved alive [8], recover [4], restored to life [4], revived [4], certainly recover (+2421) [2], kept alive [2], liveth [2], make alive [2], preserve alive [2], preserve [2], quickened [2], recovered [2], save life [2], surely recover (+2421) [2], given life [1], giveth life [1], left alive [1], make to live [1], maketh alive [1], nourished up [1], nourish [1], preservest [1], preserveth life [1], promising life [1], repaired [1], save lives [1], saved lives [1], save [1], saving [1], suffer to live [1], whole [1]

2422 חָיֶה ***ḥāyeh***, a. GK: 2650 [→ 2421]. vigorous:– lively [1]

2423 חֵיוָה ***ḥêwâ*** (Aram.), n.f. GK: 10263 [→ 2418; cf. 2416]. beast, animal; this can refer to physical creatures of earth as well as to fig. creatures of visions and parables:– beasts [13], beast [6], beast's [1]

2424 חַיּוּת ***ḥayyût***, n.f.abst. GK: 2654 [→ 2421]. lifetime:– living [1]

2425 חָיַי ***ḥāyay***, v. GK: 2649 [→ 2421]. same as 2421: [Q] to live; recover, revive; [P] to keep alive, preserve life; [H] to keep alive, save a life, spare a life, restore a life:–

2426 חֵיל ***ḥêl***, n.m. GK: 2658 [→ 2430; cf. 2342]. ramparts, outer fortification, defense walls:– host [2], rampart [2], army [1], bulwarks [1], trench [1], walls [1], wall [1]

חִיל ***ḥîl***. See 2342.

2427 חִיל ***ḥîl*** or חִילָה ***ḥîlâ***, n.m. GK: 2659 & 2660 [→ 2342]. pain, anguish, any kind of physical trauma, as a fig. extension of the labor pains of birth:– pain [3], pangs [2], sorrow [2]

2428 חַיִל ***ḥayil***, n.m. GK: 2657 [→ 32, 1134; cf. 2342; cf. 2429]. strength, capability, skill, valor, wealth; army, troop, warrior:– army [51], valour [37], host [28], valiant [16], forces [14], strength [12], riches [11], wealth [10], power [9], substance [8], might [6], valiantly [5], armies [4], strong [4], valiant (+1121) [4], able [3], virtuous [3], goods [2], activity [1], army (+6635) [1], band of men [1], band [1], company [1], hosts [1], meet for the war (+1121) [1], mighty [1], strong (+1121) [1], train [1], valiantest (+1121) [1], very able [1], virtuously [1], war [1], worthily [1], worthy [1]

2429 חַיִל ***ḥayil*** (Aram.), n.m. GK: 10264 [cf. 2428]. strength, power; an army:– aloud (+871.2) [3], army [2], most mighty men (+1400+1401) [1], power [1]

2430 חֵילָה ***ḥêlâ***, n.m. GK: 2658 [→ 2426]. ramparts, outer fortification, defense walls:– bulwarks [1]

2431 חֵילָם ***ḥêlām*** or חֵלָאם ***ḥēlā'm***, n.pr.loc. GK: 2663 & 2691. Helam, "*health*":– Helam [2]

2432 חִילֵן ***ḥîlēn***, n.pr.loc. GK: 2664. Hilen: Hilen [1]

2433 חִין ***ḥîn***, n.[m.]. GK: 2665 [→ 2603]. gracefulness:– comely [1]

2434 חַיִץ ***ḥayiṣ***, n.[m.]. GK: 2666 [cf. 2351]. flimsy wall, inner wall:– wall [1]

2435 חִיצוֹן ***ḥîṣôn***, a. GK: 2667 [→ 2351]. outer, outside, exterior:– utter [13], outward [7], without [3], without (+1886.5) [1], without (+871.1+1886.1) [1]

2436 חֵיק ***ḥêq*** or חוֹק ***ḥôq***, n.[m.]. GK: 2668 & 2576 [→ 2710]. lap, bosom, the area to which one holds and cradles a loved one; by extension: the inner person, heart, seat of affection; fold of a cloak, gutter:– bosom [32], bottom [3], lap [1], midst [1], within (+871.1) [1]

2437 חִירָה ***ḥîrâ***, n.pr.m. GK: 2669. Hirah:– Hirah [2]

2438 חִירוֹם ***ḥîrôm*** or חִירָם ***ḥîrām***, n.pr.m. GK: 2670 & 2671 [→ 297?]. Hiram, "*[my] brother is elevated*":– Hiram [22], Hiram's [1]

2439 חִישׁ ***ḥîš***, v. GK: 2590 [→ 2363]. same as 2363: [Q] to go quickly, hasten, rush upon; [Qp] to be ready; [H] to make hurry, hasten:–

2440 חִישׁ ***ḥîš***, adv. GK: 2673 [→ 2363]. quickly, in haste:– soon [1]

2441 חֵךְ ***ḥēk***, n.m. GK: 2674. (area of the) mouth: lips, tongue (taste), roof of the mouth:– mouth [9], roof of mouth [5], taste [4]

2442 חָכָה ***ḥākâ***, v. GK: 2675. [Q] to wait; [P] to lie in wait (ambush); hope for, long for:– wait [5], waiteth [3], tarry [2], waited [2], long for [1], wait for [1]

2443 חַכָּה ***ḥakkâ***, n.f. GK: 2676. fishhook:– angle [2], hook [1]

2444 חֲכִילָה ***ḥ***^a^***kîlâ***, n.pr.loc. GK: 2677 [→ 2447]. Hakilah:– Hachilah [3]

2445 חַכִּים ***ḥakkîm*** (Aram.), n.m. GK: 10265 [→ 2452; cf. 2450]. wise man (usually pertaining to a social class):– wise [14]

2446 חֲכַלְיָה ***ḥ***^a^***kalyâ***, n.pr.m. GK: 2678 [→ 2447+3068]. Hacaliah, "*dark*":– Hachaliah [2]

2447 חַכְלִילִי ***ḥaklîlî***, a. GK: 2679 [→ 2444, 2446, 2448]. darker; some sources: sparkling:– red [1]

2448 חַכְלִלוּת ***ḥaklilût***, n.f. GK: 2680 [→ 2447]. bloodshot (eyes); some sources: sparkling:– redness [1]

2449 חָכַם ***ḥākam***, v. GK: 2681 [→ 2450, 2451, 2454, 2453?; cf. 2445]. [Q] to be wise, be skillful, gain wisdom; [P] to make wiser, to teach wisdom; [Pu] to be skillful; [H] to make wise; [Ht] to deal shrewdly; to show oneself wise; to be wise implies understanding and acting in a manner that is effective and usually moral:– wise [15], wiser [2], deal wisely [1], exceeding wise (+2450) [1], made wiser [1], made wise [1], make wise [1], maketh wiser [1], making wise [1], shewed wise [1], teach wisdom [1], wisely [1]

2450 חָכָם ***ḥākām***, a. GK: 2682 [→ 2449; cf. 2445]. wise, skilled, shrewd, craftsman; (n.) wise person, sage, one who interprets divination or prophecy, one who has fear of the Lord and understanding that leads to effective (moral) action:– wise [120], cunning [10], unwise (+3808) [2], wise men [2], wiser [2], exceeding wise (+2449) [1], subtil [1]

2451 חָכְמָה ***ḥokmâ***, n.f. GK: 2683 [→ 2449; cf. 2452]. wisdom, skill, learning; this can refer to skill in life, trade, war, or spiritual things:– wisdom [144], at wit's end (+1104+3605) [1], skilful [1], wisdom (+2050.2) [1], wisely (+4480) [1], wisely (+871.1) [1]

2452 חָכְמָה ***ḥokmâ*** (Aram.), n.f. GK: 10266 [→ 2445; cf. 2451]. wisdom:– wisdom [8]

2453 חַכְמֹנִי ***ḥakmōnî***, n.pr.m.[g.?]. GK: 2685 [→ 2449?]. Hacmoni; Hacmonite, "*wise*":– Hachmonite (+1121) [1], Hachmoni [1]

2454 חָכְמוֹת ***ḥokmôt***, n.f.pl.abst. GK: 2684 [→ 2449]. wisdom; the plural form may imply in its essential or supreme condition:– wisdom [4]

חֵל ***ḥēl***. See 2426.

2455 חֹל ***ḥōl***, n.[m.]. GK: 2687 [→ 2490]. common use, not holy, ordinary:– profane [4], common [2], unholy [1]

2456 חָלָא ***ḥālā'***, v. GK: 2688 [→ 2457, 2458, 8463; cf. 2470]. [Q] to be ill:– diseased [1]

2457 חֶלְאָה ***ḥel'â***, n.f. GK: 2689 [→ 2458; cf. 2456]. deposit, encrustation, rust:– scum [5]

2458 חֶלְאָה ***ḥel'â***, n.pr.f. GK: 2690 [→ 2457; cf. 2456]. Helah, "*necklace; rust*":– Helah [2]

2459 חֵלֶב ***ḥēleb***, n.m. GK: 2693. fat, fat portions; by extension: finest, best part; callous (heart that is dull and unresponsive):– fat [79], best [5], fatness [4], finest [2], grease [1], marrow [1]

2460 חֵלֶב ***ḥēleb***, n.pr.m. GK: 2694 [cf. 2466]. Heleb, cf. 2466:– Heleb [1]

2461 חָלָב ***ḥālāb***, n.m. GK: 2692 [→ 2464]. milk:– milk [42], cheeses (+2757) [1], sucking [1]

2462 חֶלְבָּה ***ḥelbâ***, n.pr.loc. GK: 2695. Helbah, "*fertile region*":– Helbah [1]

2463 חֶלְבּוֹן ***ḥelbôn***, n.pr.loc. GK: 2696. Helbon, "*fertile*":– Helbon [1]

2464 חֶלְבְּנָה ***ḥelb***^e^***nâ***, n.f. GK: 2697 [→ 2461]. galbanum (aromatic gum resin used to make incense):– galbanum [1]

2465 חֶלֶד ***ḥeled***, n.[m.]. GK: 2698 [→ 2466, 2469]. life, duration of life; this world:– age [2], world [2], short time [1]

2466 חֵלֶד ***ḥēled***, n.pr.m. GK: 2699 [→ 2465]. Heled, "*mole*":– Heled [1]

2467 חֹלֶד ***ḥōled***, n.[m.]. GK: 2700 [→ 2468]. weasel; some sources: rat or mole:– weasel [1]

Heb

2468 חֻלְדָּה ***ḥuldâ***, n.pr.m. GK: 2701 [→ 2467]. Huldah, "*weasel*":– Huldah [2]

2469 חֶלְדַּי ***ḥelday***, n.pr.m. GK: 2702 [→ 2465]. Heldai, "*mole*":– Heldai [2]

2470 חָלָה ***ḥālâ***, v. GK: 2703 & 2704 [→ 2483, 4245, 4248?, 4249?, 4250?, 4251, 4257?; cf. 2456]. [Q] to be ill, be weak, be faint, become diseased, be wounded; [N] to be made sick, be incurable; [P] to afflict; to entreat, implore, seek favor, intercede; [Pu] to become weak; [H] to make ill, to cause to suffer; [Ho] to be wounded; [Ht] to pretend to be ill, to feel sick:– sick [24], fell sick [4], grievous [4], besought (+853+6440) [3], diseased [3], pray [3], weak [3], wounded [3], besought (+6440) [2], grieved [2], intreat [2], made sick [2], make sick [2], sore [2], become weak [1], beseech (+6440) [1], fallen sick [1], grief [1], in travail [1], infirmity [1], intreat favour (+6440) [1], intreated [1], laid [1], made prayer [1], made supplication [1], make suit [1], maketh sick [1], put to grief [1], put to pain [1], sorry [1]

2471 חַלָּה ***ḥallâ***, n.f. GK: 2705 [→ 2490]. (ring-shaped) bread cakes:– cakes [7], cake [7]

2472 חֲלוֹם ***ḥ***a***lôm***, n.m. GK: 2706 [→ 2492; cf. 2493]. dream, dreamer; this can refer to a supernatural revelation by God by words and images:– dream [44], dreams [19], dreamer (+1167+1886.1) [1], dreamers [1]

2473 חֹלוֹן ***ḥōlôn***, n.pr.loc. GK: 2708. Holon, "[perhaps] *sandy*":– Holon [3]

2474 חַלּוֹן ***ḥallôn***, n.m. & f. GK: 2707 & 2709 [→ 2490]. window, narrow openings, parapet openings:– windows [18], window [13]

2475 חֲלוֹף ***ḥ***a***lôp***, n.m. GK: 2710 [→ 2498]. destitute, vanishing:– appointed to destruction (+1121) [1]

2476 חֲלוּשָׁה ***ḥ***a***lûšâ***, n.f. GK: 2711 [→ 2522]. defeat:– overcome [1]

2477 חֲלַח ***ḥ***a***laḥ***, n.pr.loc. GK: 2712. Halah:– Halah [3]

2478 חַלְחוּל ***ḥalḥûl***, n.pr.loc. GK: 2713. Halhul:– Halhul [1]

2479 חַלְחָלָה ***ḥalḥālâ***, n.f. GK: 2714 [→ 2342]. anguish, pain, trembling:– great pain [2], much pain [1], pain [1]

2480 חָלַט ***ḥālaṭ***, v. GK: 2715. [Q] to accept a statement:– catch [1]

2481 חֲלִי ***ḥ***a***lî***, n.m. GK: 2717 [→ 2484]. ornament, jewel:– jewels [1], ornament [1]

2482 חֲלִי ***ḥ***a***lî***, n.pr.loc. GK: 2718. Hali, "*adornment*":– Hali [1]

2483 חֳלִי ***ḥ***o***lî***, n.m. GK: 2716 [→ 2470]. illness, sickness, affliction; wound, injury:– sickness [11], disease [7], grief [3], griefs [1], sicknesses [1], sick [1]

2484 חֶלְיָה ***ḥelyâ***, n.f. GK: 2719 [→ 2481]. jewelry, ornament:– jewels [1]

2485 חָלִיל ***ḥālîl***, n.m. GK: 2720 [→ 2490, 5155?]. flute:– pipes [3], pipe [3]

2486 חָלִילָה ***ḥālîl***, subst. GK: 2721 [→ 2490]. far be it!, never!:– God forbid [8], far be it [4], be it far [3], forbid [3], that be far [2], forbid it [1]

2487 חֲלִיפָה ***ḥ***a***lîpâ***, n.f. GK: 2722 [→ 2498]. set, sequence, shift; renewal, relief:– changes [7], change [4], courses [1]

2488 חֲלִיצָה ***ḥ***a***lîṣâ***, n.f. GK: 2723 [→ 2502]. belongings, equipment:– armour [1], spoil [1]

2489 חֵלְכָה ***ḥēlkâ***, a. GK: 2724. victim:– poor [3]

2490 חָלַל ***ḥālal***, v. GK: 2725 & 2726 & 2727 [→ 2455, 2471, 2474, 2485, 2486, 2491, 4247, 5155?, 8462]. [Q] to be wounded; to play the flute; [N] to defile oneself, be profaned, be desecrated; [P] to pierce, wound; to defile, profane, desecrate; to enjoy; to play the flute; [Pu] to be killed; to be defiled; [Pol] to pierce, wound; [Polal] to be wounded; [H] to begin, to proceed, launch; [Ho] to be begun:– began [33], profane [17], profaned [15], polluted [13], begin [12], pollute [8], begun [7], defiled [5], break [3], wounded [3], defile [2], polluting [2], profaning [2], beginnest [1], broken [1], cast as profane [1], defiledst [1], defileth [1], eat as common things [1], eaten [1], eat [1], first [1], gather the grapes [1], piped [1], players on instruments [1], profaneth [1], prostitute [1], slain [1], slayeth [1], sorrow [1], stain [1], take inheritance [1]

2491 חָלָל ***ḥālāl***, n.m. & a. GK: 2728 & 2729 [→ 2490]. dead, slain, casualty; defiled, profane (moral or ceremonial failure):– slain [73], wounded [9], slew [4], profane [3], kill [2], deadly wounded [1], that is slain [1], that were slain [1]

חָלִלָה ***ḥālilâ***. See 2486.

2492 חָלַם ***ḥālam***, v. GK: 2730 & 2731 [→ 2472]. [Q] to grow strong; to dream; [H] to restore to health; to encourage one to have dreams:– dreamed [19], dreamer [3], dreameth [2], dream [2], cause to be dreamed [1], in good liking [1], recover [1]

2493 חֵלֶם ***ḥēlem*** (Aram.), n.m. GK: 10267 [cf. 2472]. dream:– dream [21], dreams [1]

2494 חֵלֶם ***ḥēlem***, n.pr.m. GK: 2732 [cf. 2469]. Helem, cf. 2469:– Helem [1]

2495 חַלָּמוּת ***ḥallāmût***, n.f. GK: 2733. egg or mallow:– egg [1]

2496 חַלָּמִישׁ ***ḥallāmîš***, n.m. GK: 2734. flinty rock, hard rock:– flint [3], flinty [1], rock [1]

2497 חֵלֹן ***ḥēlōn***, n.pr.m. GK: 2735. Helon, "*strength, power*":– Helon [5]

2498 חָלַף ***ḥālap***, v. GK: 2736 [→ 2475, 2487, 2500, 4252?, 4253; cf. 2499]. [Q] to go by, pass on, sweep by; to be new; to pierce, cut through; [P] to change; [H] to change, exchange, replace, renew:– changed [6], change [4], groweth up [2], renew [2], abolish [1], alter [1], cut off [1], go on [1], over [1], pass through [1], passed away [1], passed [1], passeth on [1], pass [1], renewed [1], sprout [1], stricken through [1], strike through [1]

2499 חֲלַף ***ḥ***a***lap*** (Aram.), v. GK: 10268 [cf. 2498]. [P] to pass by, pass over:– pass [4]

2500 חֵלֶף ***ḥēlep***, n.[m.]. GK: 2739 [→ 2498]. in return for:– for [2]

2501 חֵלֶף ***ḥēlep***, n.pr.loc. GK: 2738. Heleph, "[poss.] *sharp, cutting*":– Heleph [1]

2502 חָלַץ ***ḥālaṣ***, v. GK: 2740 & 2741 [→ 2488, 2503, 4254]. [Q] to take off; [Qp] to be taken off; to be armed (for battle); [N] to be delivered, be rescued; to arm oneself; [P] to rescue, deliver; to tear out, rob; [H] to strengthen:– armed [11], delivered [9], deliver [5], delivereth [2], go armed [2], ready armed [2], armed soldiers [1], army [1], arm [1], draw out [1], loosed [1], loose [1], make fat [1], prepared [1], put off [1], ready prepared for [1], take away [1], taken away [1], withdrawn [1]

2503 חֶלֶץ ***ḥeleṣ***, n.pr.m. GK: 2742 [→ 2502]. Helez, "*vigor; he has saved*":– Helez [5]

2504 חֲלָצַיִם ***ḥ***a***lāṣayim***, n.[f.]. GK: 2743 [cf. 2783]. waist, stomach, the area between the lowest ribs and the hip-bones; by extension: body, flesh; the inner person, heart:– loins [9], reins [1]

2505 חָלַק ***ḥālaq***, v. GK: 2744 & 2745 & 2746 [→ 2506, 2509, 2510, 2511, 2512, 2513, 2514, 2515, 2517, 2518, 2519, 2520, 4256]. [Q] to be smooth, slippery; deceitful; to divide, apportion, assign; [N] to be divided, be dispersed, be distributed; [P] to divide, allot, apportion; to destroy; [Pu] to be divided; [Ht] to divide among themselves; [H] to speak deceit, flatter, be seductive; to get one's share:– divided [21], divide [18], flattereth [5], dealt [2], distributed [2], parted [2], part [2], distributeth [1], distribute [1], dividing [1], flatter [1], given [1], have part [1], imparted [1], partner [1], received [1], separate [1], smoother [1], smootheth [1], took away a portion [1]

2506 חֵלֶק ***ḥēleq***, n.m. GK: 2749 & 2750 [→ 2505, 2513, 2520; cf. 2505; cf. 2508 (also used with compound proper names)]. smoothness; share, portion, allotment, plot of ground:– portion [36], part [18], parts [4], portions [4], flattering [1], flattery (+3807.1) [1], inheritance [1], partaker [1]

2507 חֵלֶק ***ḥēleq***, n.pr.m. GK: 2751 [→ 2516; cf. 2518?]. Helek, "*portion, lot*":– Helek [2]

2508 חֲלָק ***ḥ***a***lāq*** (Aram.), n.[m.]. GK: 10269 [→ 4255; cf. 2506]. portion, lot in life:– portion [3]

2509 חָלָק ***ḥālāq***, a. GK: 2747 [→ 2505, 2511]. smooth, slippery, pleasant, flattering:– flattering [2], smoother [1], smooth [1]

2510 חָלָק ***ḥālāq***, n.pr.loc. GK: 2748 [→ 2505]. Halak:– Halak [2]

2511 חַלָּק ***ḥallāq***, a. GK: 2747 [→ 2509]. smooth, slippery, pleasant, flattering:– smooth [1]

2512 חַלֻּק ***ḥalluq***, a. GK: 2752 [→ 2505]. smooth (stones):– smooth [1]

2513 חֶלְקָה ***ḥelqâ***, n.f. GK: 2753 & 2754 [→ 2505, 2506]. smoothness; plot, field, tract:– portion [6], parcel [5], field [3], piece [3], flattering [2], piece of land [2], plat [2], smooth [2], flattery [1], ground [1], part [1], slippery [1]

2514 חֲלַקָּה ***ḥ***a***laqqâ***, n.f. GK: 2756 [→ 2505]. smoothness, flattery:– flatteries [1]

2515 חֲלֻקָּה ***ḥ***a***luqqâ***, n.f. GK: 2755 [→ 2505]. part, portion, division:– division [1]

2516 חֶלְקִי ***ḥelqî***, a.g. GK: 2757 [→ 2507]. Helekite, "*of Helek*":– Helekites [1]

2517 חֶלְקַי ***ḥelqāy***, n.pr.m. GK: 2758 [→ 2506+3068?]. Helkai, "*Yahweh is [my] portion*":– Helkai [1]

2518 חִלְקִיָּה ***ḥilqiyyâ*** or חִלְקִיָּהוּ ***ḥilqiyyāhû***, n.pr.m. GK: 2759 & 2760 [cf. 2507?]. Hilkiah, "*Yahweh is [my] portion*":– Hilkiah [33], Hilkiah's [1]

2519 חֲלַקְלַק ***ḥ***a***laqlaq***, n.f.abst. GK: 2761 [→ 2505]. slippery, slick and hard to walk on; by extension: slippery words, intrigue, insincere:– flatteries [2], slippery [2]

2520 חֶלְקַת ***ḥelqat***, n.pr.loc. GK: 2762 [→ 2521; cf. 2505, 2506]. Helkath, "*portion*":– Helkath [2]

2521 חֶלְקַת הַצֻּרִים ***ḥelqat haṣṣurîm***, n.pr.loc. GK: 2763 [→ 2520]. Helkath Hazzurim, "[poss.] *portion [field] of rock* or *swords; portion [field] of snare*":– Helkath-hazzurim [1]

2522 חָלַשׁ ***ḥālaš***, v. GK: 2764 & 2765 [→ 2476, 2523]. [Q] to be laid low; to overcome, defeat:– discomfited [1], wasteth away [1], weaken [1]

2523 חַלָּשׁ ***ḥallāš***, a. GK: 2766 [→ 2522]. weak, weakling:– weak [1]

2524 חָם ***ḥām***, n.m. GK: 2767 [→ 2537, 2545]. father-in-law:– father in law [4]

2525 חָם ***ḥām***, a. GK: 2768 [→ 2552]. hot, sweltering:– hot [1], warm [1]

2526 חָם ***ḥām***, n.pr.m. & loc. GK: 2769 [→ 2536, 2537]. Ham:– Ham [16]

2527 חֹם ***ḥōm***, n.m. GK: 2770 [→ 2552]. heat:– heat [9], hot [4], warm [1]

2528 חֱמָה ***ḥ***a***mâ*** (Aram.), n.f. GK: 10270 [cf. 2534]. fury, rage; "to be in fury and rage" refers to anger of highest degree:– fury [2]

חֵמָא ***ḥēmā'***. See 2534.

2529 חֶמְאָה ***ḥem'â***, n.f. GK: 2772 [cf. 4260]. curds, curdled milk; butter, cream:– butter [10]

2530 חָמַד ***ḥāmad***, v. GK: 2773 & 2776 [→ 2531, 2532, 2533, 4261, 4262]. [Q] to covet, lust, desire; delight in; [Qp] (n.) what is coveted: treasure, wealth; [N] to be pleasing, be desirable; [P] to delight; this can refer to proper delight and fondness, as well as to improper lust and desire:– desired [5], desire [4], covet [3], desireth [2], beauty [1], coveted [1], delectable [1], delight in [1], lust after [1], pleasant [1], with great delight [1]

2531 חֶמֶד ***ḥemed***, n.[m.]. GK: 2774 [→ 2530]. fruitfulness, lushness; pleasantness; handsomeness:– desirable [3], pleasant [2]

2532 חֶמְדָּה ***ḥemdâ***, n.f. GK: 2775 [→ 2530]. desirable, pleasant, fine, valuable (things):– pleasant [11], precious [4], desire [3], greatly beloved [3], goodly [2], desired [1], pleasant things [1]

2533 חֶמְדָּן ***ḥemdān***, n.pr.m. GK: 2777 [→ 2530; cf. 2566]. Hemdan, "*desirable*":– Hemdan [1]

2534 חֵמָה ***ḥēmâ*** or חֵמָא ***ḥēmā'***, n.f. GK: 2779 & 2771 [→ 3179; cf. 2528]. anger, wrath, fury, rage, from the base meaning of heat (as in "hot-headed"); by extension: venom (poison that causes a burning sensation):– fury [67], wrath [34], poison [6], furious [4], hot displeasure [3], rage [2], anger [1], bottles [1], furious (+1167) [1], furiously (+871.1) [1], heat [1], indignation [1], wrathful [1], wroth [1]

2535 חַמָּה ***ḥammâ***, n.f. GK: 2780 [→ 2552]. heat (of the sun):– sun [5], heat [1]

2536 חַמּוּאֵל ***ḥammû'ēl***, n.pr.m. GK: 2781 [→ 2526+410; cf. 2537]. Hammuel, "*God [El] of Ham*":– Hamuel [1]

2537 חֲמוּטַל ***ḥ***a***mûṭal*** or חֲמִיטַל ***ḥ***a***mîṭal***, n.pr.f. GK: 2782 & 2795 [→ 2524+2919; 2526]. Hamutal, Hamital, "*my husband's father is like dew*":– Hamutal [3]

2538 חָמוּל ***ḥāmûl***, n.pr.m. GK: 2783 [→ 2539; cf. 2550]. Hamul, "*pitied*":– Hamul [3]

2539 חָמוּלִי ***ḥāmûlî***, a.g. GK: 2784 [→ 2538; cf. 2550]. Hamulite, "*of Hamul*":– Hamulites [1]

2540 חַמּוֹן ***ḥammôn***, n.pr.loc. GK: 2785 [→ 2552]. Hammon, "*hot springs*":– Hammon [2]

2541 חָמוֹץ ***ḥāmôṣ***, n.[m.]. GK: 2787 [→ 2556]. oppressor; oppressed:– oppressed [1]

2542 חַמּוּק ***ḥammûq***, n.m. GK: 2788 [→ 2559]. gracefulness, curve:– joints [1]

2543 חֲמוֹר ***ḥ**a**môr***, n.m. GK: 2789 [→ 2544; cf. 2565, 2560]. donkey:– ass [55], asses [39], ass's [1], he asses [1]

2544 חֲמוֹר ***ḥ**a**môr***, n.pr.m. GK: 2791 [→ 2543; cf. 2560]. Hamor, "*male donkey*":– Hamor [12], Hamor's [1]

2545 חָמוֹת ***ḥāmôt***, n.f. GK: 2792 [→ 2524]. mother-in-law:– mother in law [11]

2546 חֹמֶט ***ḥōmeṭ***, n.[m.]. GK: 2793. skink (lizard):– snail [1]

2547 חֻמְטָה ***ḥumṭâ***, n.pr.loc. GK: 2794. Humtah, "*[unclean] reptile*":– Humtah [1]

2548 חָמִיץ ***ḥāmîṣ***, a. GK: 2796 [→ 2556]. sour mash, sorrel-fodder:– clean [1]

2549 חֲמִישִׁי ***ḥ**a**mîšî***, a.num.ord. GK: 2797 [→ 2568]. fifth:– fifth [45]

2550 חָמַל ***ḥāmal***, v. GK: 2798 & 2800 [→ 2538, 2539, 2551, 2602, 4263?]. [Q] to spare, take pity on, have mercy on:– spare [13], have pity [8], pitied [4], pity [4], spared [4], had compassion [3], had pity [2], have compassion [2], spareth [1]

2551 חֶמְלָה ***ḥemlâ***, n.f. GK: 2799 [→ 2550]. mercy:– merciful [1], pity [1]

2552 חָמַם ***ḥāmam***, v. GK: 2801 [→ 2345, 2525, 2527, 2535, 2540, 2553, 2575, 2578, 2577; cf. 3179]. [Q] to be hot, be warm; by extension: to be aroused; be in a rage; [N] to burn with lust; [P] to let warm; [Ht] to warm oneself:– warm [3], hot [2], warmeth [2], get heat [1], have heat [1], inflaming [1], warmed [1], waxed hot [1], waxed warm [1]

2553 חַמָּן ***ḥammān***, n.m. GK: 2802 [→ 2552]. incense altar:– images [7], idols [1]

2554 חָמַס ***ḥāmas***, v. GK: 2803 & 2804 [→ 2555, 8464?]. [Q] to do violence, harm, to lay waste; to be stripped off; to think up, devise; [N] to be mistreated:– do violence [1], done violence [1], made bare [1], shake off [1], violated [1], violently taken away [1], wrongeth [1], wrongfully imagine [1]

2555 חָמָס ***ḥāmās***, n.m. GK: 2805 [→ 2554]. violence, destruction, malice, ruthlessness, fierceness:– violence [39], violent [6], cruelty [4], wrong [3], false [2], cruel hatred (+8135) [1], damage [1], injustice [1], oppressor (+376) [1], unrighteous [1], violent dealing [1]

2556 חָמֵץ ***ḥāmeṣ***, v. GK: 2806 & 2807 & 2808 [→ 2541, 2548, 2557, 2558]. [Q] to have yeast added, be leavened; to be cruel, oppress; [Qp] to be stained crimson; [Ht] to be grieved, embittered:– leavened [4], cruel [1], dyed [1], grieved [1], that which is leavened [1]

2557 חָמֵץ ***ḥāmēṣ***, n.m. GK: 2809 [→ 2556]. something leavened, made with yeast:– leavened bread [5], leaven [5], leavened [1]

2558 חֹמֶץ ***ḥōmeṣ***, n.m. GK: 2810 [→ 2556]. vinegar, wine vinegar:– vinegar [6]

2559 חָמַק ***ḥāmaq***, v. GK: 2811 [→ 2542]. [Q] to leave, turn away; [Ht] to wander, turn here and there:– go about [1], withdrawn [1]

2560 חָמַר ***ḥāmar***, v. GK: 2812 & 2813 & 2814 [→ 2543, 2565, 2544, 2561, 2563, 2564, 3180]. [Q] to foam; to coat, cover, to apply pitch as a sealant; [Poalal] to be reddened, glow:– troubled [3], daubed [1], foul [1], red [1]

2561 חֶמֶר ***ḥemer***, n.[m.]. GK: 2815 [→ 2560; cf. 2562]. (foaming, fermenting) wine:– pure [1], red wine [1]

2562 חֲמַר ***ḥ**a**mar*** (Aram.), n.m. GK: 10271 [cf. 2561]. wine:– wine [6]

חֲמֹר ***ḥ**a**mōr***. See 2543.

2563 חֹמֶר ***ḥōmer***, n.[m.]. GK: 2816 & 2817 & 2818 [→ 2560]. churning, storming (sea waters); clay, mortar, mud; "defenses of clay" are weak arguments; homer (dry measure of volume, roughly the amount a donkey could carry, variously reckoned from six to eleven bushels [220 to 394 liters]):– clay [11], homer [10], morter [4], mire [2], upon heaps (+2563) [2], heap [1], homers [1]

2564 חֵמָר ***ḥēmār***, n.[m.]. GK: 2819 [→ 2560]. tar (used in waterproofing or mortar):– slime [2], full of slimepits (+875+875) [1]

2565 חֲמֹרָה ***ḥ**a**mōrâ***, n.f. GK: 2790 [→ 2560; cf. 2543]. heap:– heaps [2]

2566 חַמְרָן ***ḥamrān***, n.pr.m. GK: 2820 [cf. 2533]. Hamran, cf. 2533:– Amram [1]

2567 חָמַשׁ ***ḥāmaš***, v.den. GK: 2821 [→ 2571; cf. 2568]. [Qp] to be organized for war; [P] to take a fifth:– take up the fifth [1]

2568 חָמֵשׁ ***ḥāmēš***, n.m. & f. GK: 2822 [→ 2549, 2567, 2569, 2571, 2572]. five, (pl.) fifty:– five [299], fifteenth (+6240) [17], fifteen (+6240) [16], fifth [6], five apiece (+2568) [2], threescore and fifteen (+7657+2050.1) [2], fifteen (+6235+2050.1) [1], threescore and fifteen (+7657+2050.1+2050.1) [1]

2569 חֹמֶשׁ ***ḥōmeš***, n.[m.]. GK: 2823 [→ 2568]. fifth:– fifth [1]

2570 חֹמֶשׁ ***ḥōmeš***, n.m. GK: 2824. stomach, belly:– fifth [4]

2571 חָמֻשׁ ***ḥāmuš***, v.ptcp. GK: 2821 & 2826 [→ 2567; cf. 2568]. organized for war, armed:– armed [3], harnessed [1]

חֲמִשָּׁה ***ḥ**a**miššâ***. See 2568.

חֲמִשִּׁי ***ḥ**a**miššî***. See 2549.

2572 חֲמִשִּׁים ***ḥ**a**miššîm***, n.pl. GK: 2825 [→ 2568]. fifty (pl. of "five"):– fifty [149], fifties [6], fiftieth [4], by fifty (+2572) [2], fifty every where (+2572+871.1+1886.1) [2]

2573 חֵמֶת ***ḥēmet***, n.[m.]. GK: 2827. skin (for water or wine):– bottle [4]

2574 חֲמָת ***ḥ**a**māt***, n.pr.loc. GK: 2828 & 4217 [→ 2578, 2577]. Hamath, "*fortress*":– Hamath [34], Hemath [2], Hamath-zobah [1]

חֲמֹת ***ḥ**a**mōt***. See 2545.

2575 חַמַּת ***ḥammat***, n.pr.m. & loc. GK: 2830 & 2829 [→ 2576; cf. 2552]. Hammath, "*hot springs*":– Hammath [1], Hemath [1]

2576 חַמֹּת דֹּאר ***ḥammōt dō'r***, n.pr.loc. GK: 2831 [→ 2575+1756]. Hammoth Dor, "*hot spring of Dor*":– Hammoth-dor [1]

2577 חֲמָתִי ***ḥ**a**mātî***, a.g. GK: 2833 [→ 2574; cf. 2552]. Hamathite, "*of Hamath*":– Hamathite [2]

2578 חֲמַת צוֹבָה ***ḥ**a**māt ṣôbâ***, n.pr.loc. GK: 2832 [→ 2574+6678]. Hamath Zobah:–

2579 חֲמַת רַבָּה ***ḥ**a**māt rabbâ***, n.pr.loc. GK: 2828 + 8051 [→ 2574+7237]. Hamath Rabbah:–

2580 חֵן ***ḥēn***, n.m. GK: 2834 [→ 2582, 2584, 2600; cf. 2603 (also used with compound proper names)]. favor, grace; charm; grace is the moral quality of kindness, displaying a favorable disposition; "to find grace in someone's eyes" means to be in a state of favor:– grace [38], favour [26], gracious [2], pleasant [1], precious [1], wellfavoured (+2896) [1]

2581 חֵן ***ḥēn***, n.pr.m. GK: 2835 [→ 2603]. Hen, "*gracious*":– Hen [1]

2582 חֵנָדָד ***ḥēnādād***, n.pr.m. GK: 2836 [→ 2580+1908]. Henadad, "*favor of Hadad*":– Henadad [4]

2583 חָנָה ***ḥānâ***, v. GK: 2837 [→ 2588, 4264, 4266, 8466]. [Q] to set up camp, pitch camp, encamp:– pitched [67], encamped [33], encamp [10], pitch [9], abode in tents [3], camp [3], dwelt [2], encampeth [2], lie [2], pitch tents [2], pitched tent [2], rested in tents [2], abide [1], camped [1], encamp about [1], encamping [1], groweth to an end [1], pitched tents [1]

2584 חַנָּה ***ḥannâ***, n.pr.f. GK: 2839 [→ 2580; cf. 2603]. Hannah, "*favor*":– Hannah [13]

2585 חֲנוֹךְ ***ḥ**a**nôk***, n.pr.m. & loc. GK: 2840 & 2841 [→ 2599; cf. 2593, 2596]. Enoch; Hanoch, "*initiated; follower*":– Enoch [9], Hanoch [5], Henoch [2]

2586 חָנוּן ***ḥānûn***, n.pr.m. GK: 2842 [→ 2603]. Hanun, "*favored*":– Hanun [11]

2587 חַנּוּן ***ḥannûn***, a. GK: 2843 [→ 2603]. gracious, compassionate:– gracious [13]

2588 חָנוּת ***ḥānût***, n.f. GK: 2844 [→ 2583]. vaulted cell:– cabins [1]

2589 חַנּוֹת ***ḥannôt***, v. GK: 2838. verbal forms of 2603: gracious, intreated:– gracious [1], intreated [1]

2590 חָנַט ***ḥānaṭ***, v. GK: 2845 & 2846 & 2847 [→ 2406]. [Q] to embalm; to ripen:– embalmed [3], embalm [1], putteth forth [1]

2591 חִנְטָה ***ḥinṭâ*** (Aram.), n.f. GK: 10272 [cf. 2406]. wheat:– wheat [2]

2592 חַנִּיאֵל ***ḥannî'ēl***, n.pr.m. GK: 2848 [→ 2603+410]. Hanniel, "*favored of God [El]*":– Haniel [1], Hanniel [1]

2593 חָנִיךְ ***ḥānîk***, a. GK: 2849 [→ 2596; cf. 2585]. trained (and trusted person):– trained [1]

2594 חֲנִינָה ***ḥ**a**nînâ***, n.f. GK: 2850 [→ 2603]. favor, kindness:– favour [1]

2595 חֲנִית ***ḥ**a**nît***, n.f. GK: 2851. spear:– spear [34], javelin [6], spears [6], spear's [1]

2596 חָנַךְ ***ḥānak***, v. GK: 2852 [→ 2585, 2593, 2598, 2599]. [Q] to dedicate, to devote an object to deity; to train (morally and religiously):– dedicated [3], dedicate [1], train up [1]

2597 חֲנֻכָּה ***ḥ**a**nukkâ*** (Aram.), n.f. GK: 10273 [cf. 2598]. (ceremonial religious) dedication:– dedication [4]

2598 חֲנֻכָּה ***ḥ**a**nukkâ***, n.f. GK: 2853 [→ 2596; cf. 2597]. dedication, offering for dedication:– dedication [6], dedicating [2]

2599 חֲנֹכִי ***ḥ**a**nōkî***, a.g. GK: 2854 [→ 2585; cf. 2596]. Hanochite, "*of Hanoch*":– Hanochites [1]

2600 חִנָּם ***ḥinnām***, subst.adv. GK: 2855 [→ 2580; cf. 2603]. without cause, for no reason; for nothing:– without cause [10], for nought [6], without a cause [5], causeless [2], cost nothing [1], for nothing [1], freely [1], free [1], in vain [1], innocent [1], vain [1], without cost [1], without wages [1]

2601 חֲנַמְאֵל ***ḥ**a**nam'ēl***, n.pr.m. GK: 2856 [→ 2580+410]. Hanamel, "*God [El] is gracious*":– Hanameel [4]

2602 חֲנָמַל ***ḥ**a**nāmal***, n.[m.]. GK: 2857 [→ 2550]. sleet:– frost [1]

2603 חָנַן ***ḥānan***, v. GK: 2858 & 2859 [→ 2433, 2580, 2581, 2584, 2586, 2587, 2594, 2600, 2605, 8465?, 8467, 8468, 8469, 8470?; cf. 2604 (also used with compound proper names)]. [Q] to be gracious, to have mercy, to take pity, be kind; to be loathsome; [Pol] to move to pity, be kind, be charming; [Ho] to be shown compassion, mercy; [Ht] to plead for grace, beg for mercy; this word implies acts of kindness, not simply feelings of pity:– gracious [12], have mercy [12], merciful [12], make supplication [7], besought [3], favour [3], made supplication [3], hath mercy [2], have pity [2], shew favour [2], very gracious (+2603) [2], besought (+413) [1], dealt graciously [1], fair [1], favour shewed [1], favourable [1], favoured [1], findeth favour [1], graciously given [1], grant graciously [1], hath pity [1], intreated [1], pity [1], pray [1], shew mercy [1], sheweth favour [1], sheweth mercy [1]

2604 חֲנַן ***ḥ**a**nan*** (Aram.), v. GK: 10274 [cf. 2603]. [P] to be kind, show mercy; [Htpa] to ask, implore:– making supplication [1], shewing mercy [1]

2605 חָנָן ***ḥānān***, n.pr.m. GK: 2860 [→ 2603 (also used with compound proper names)]. Hanan, "*gracious*":– Hanan [12]

2606 חֲנַנְאֵל ***ḥ**a**nan'ēl***, n.pr.m. GK: 2861 [→ 2603+410]. Hananel, "*God [El] is gracious*":– Hananeel [4]

2607 חֲנָנִי ***ḥ**a**nānî***, n.pr.m. GK: 2862 [→ 2603+3068]. Hanani, "*gracious*":– Hanani [11]

2608 חֲנַנְיָה ***ḥ**a**nanyâ*** or חֲנַנְיָהוּ ***ḥ**a**nanyāhû***, n.pr.m. GK: 2863 & 2864 & 10275 [→ 2603+3068]. Hananiah, "*Yahweh is gracious*": note this name is Aramaic once in Daniel:– Hananiah [29]

2609 חָנֵס ***ḥānēs***, n.pr.loc. GK: 2865. Hanes:– Hanes [1]

2610 חָנֵף ***ḥānēp***, v. GK: 2866 [→ 2611, 2612, 2613]. [Q] to be desecrated, be defiled; [H] to corrupt, defile, pollute:– defiled [3], greatly polluted (+2610) [2], polluted [2], corrupt [1], defileth [1], pollute [1], profane [1]

2611 חָנֵף ***ḥānēp***, a. GK: 2867 & 2868 [→ 2610]. godless, ungodly; limping:– hypocrite [6], hypocrites [3], hypocritical [2], hypocrite (+120) [1], hypocrite's [1]

2612 חֹנֶף ***ḥōnep***, n.[m.]. GK: 2869 [→ 2610]. ungodliness, godlessness:– hypocrisy [1]

2613 חֲנֻפָּה ***ḥ**a**nuppâ***, n.f. GK: 2870 [→ 2610]. ungodliness, godlessness:– profaneness [1]

2614 חָנַק ***ḥānaq***, v. GK: 2871 [→ 4267]. [N] to hang oneself; [P] to strangle:– hanged [1], strangled [1]

2615 חַנָּתֹן ***ḥannātôn***, n.pr.loc. GK: 2872. Hannathon:– Hannathon [1]

2616 חָסַד ***ḥāsad***, v. GK: 2873 & 2874 [→ 1136, 2617, 2618, 2623, 2624]. [P] to put to shame, reproach, with the strong implication of an insult; [Ht] to conduct oneself as faithful:– shew merciful [2], put to shame [1]

2617 חֶסֶד ***ḥesed***, n.m. GK: 2875 & 2876 [→ 1136, cf. 2616, 2618, 2619?, 2623]. unfailing love, loyal love, devotion, kindness, often based on a prior relationship, especially a covenant relationship; disgrace:– mercy [137], kindness [38], lovingkindness [26], goodness [12], mercies [9], kindly [5], lovingkindnesses [4], favour [3], merciful [3], mercy's [3], merciful kindness [2], good deeds [1], goodliness [1], pity [1], reproach [1], wicked thing [1]

2618 חֶסֶד ***ḥesed***, n.pr.m. GK: 2877 [→ 2617; cf. 2616]. Hesed:– Hesed [1]

Heb

2619 חֲסַדְיָה **ḥ^{a}sadyâ**, n.pr.m. GK: 2878 [→ 2617+3068]. Hasadiah, "*Yahweh is faithful*":– Hasadiah [1]

2620 חָסָה **ḥāsâ**, v. GK: 2879 [→ 308, 2622, 4268 (also used with compound proper names)]. [Q] to take refuge in, to trust in:– trust [19], put trust [12], trusteth [2], hope [1], make refuge [1], putteth trust [1], trusted [1]

2621 חֹסָה **ḥōsâ**, n.pr.m. & loc. GK: 2880 & 2881. Hosah, "*refuge*":– Hosah [5]

2622 חָסוּת **ḥāsût**, n.f. GK: 2882 [→ 2620]. refuge:– trust [1]

2623 חָסִיד **ḥāsîd**, a.m. GK: 2883 [→ 2624; cf. 2616, 2617]. godly, saints, the people of God with a focus on their faithfulness; this can refer to a prominent individual, with messianic significance (Ps 16:10):– saints [19], godly [3], holy [3], merciful [3], holy one [2], good [1], ungodly (+3808) [1]

2624 חֲסִידָה **ḥ^{a}sîdâ**, n.f. GK: 2884 [→ 2623; cf. 2616]. stork; some sources: heron:– stork [5], ostrich [1]

2625 חָסִיל **ḥāsîl**, n.m. GK: 2885 [→ 2628]. grasshoppers, locusts at a particular stage of development:– caterpillar [5], caterpillars [1]

2626 חֲסִין **ḥ^{a}sîn**, a. GK: 2886 [→ 2634]. mighty, strong:– strong [1]

2627 חַסִּיר **ḥassîr** (Aram.), a. GK: 10276 [cf. 2638]. wanting, lacking in quality or quantity, deficient:– wanting [1]

2628 חָסַל **ḥāsal**, v. GK: 2887 [→ 2625]. [Q, H] to devour, consume:– consume [1]

2629 חָסַם **ḥāsam**, v. GK: 2888 [→ 4269]. [Q] to muzzle (an animal); to block (the way):– muzzle [1], stop [1]

2630 חָסַן **ḥāsan**, v.den. GK: 2889 [→ 2633; cf. 2631]. [N] to be stored up:– laid up [1]

2631 חֲסַן **ḥ^{a}san** (Aram.), v. GK: 10277 [→ 2632; cf. 2630]. [H] to take possession of, occupy:– possessed [1], possess [1]

2632 חֱסֵן **ḥ^{e}sēn** (Aram.), n.m. GK: 10278 [→ 2631; cf. 2633]. power, might, force:– power [2]

2633 חֹסֶן **ḥōsen**, n.m. GK: 2890 [→ 2630; cf. 2632]. stored treasure, riches, wealth:– strength [2], treasure [2], riches [1]

2634 חָסֹן **ḥāsōn**, a. GK: 2891 [→ 2626]. mighty, strong:– strong [2]

2635 חֲסַף **ḥ^{a}sap** (Aram.), n.[m.]. GK: 10279. (formed, molded) clay, baked clay:– clay [9]

2636 חַסְפַּס **ḥaspas**, v. GK: 2892. [Pualal] to flake; some sources: to be scale-like, pertaining to the shape of an object; to crisp, crackle, pertaining to the brittleness of an object:– round thing [1]

2637 חָסֵר **ḥāsēr**, v. GK: 2893 [→ 2638, 2639, 2640, 2642, 4270]. [Q] to lack; to have nothing; to go down, recede; [P] to make lower; to deprive; [H] to cause to lack, withhold:– want [4], lack [3], fail [2], lacked [2], wanteth [2], abated [1], bereave [1], cause to fail [1], decreased [1], had lack [1], have need [1], made lower [1], wanted [1]

2638 חָסֵר **ḥāsēr**, a. GK: 2894 [→ 2637]. lacking; wanting:– void [6], wanteth [4], lacketh [3], destitute [1], faileth [1], fail [1], lacked [1], need [1], want [1]

2639 חֶסֶר **ḥeser**, n.m. GK: 2895 [→ 2637]. poverty, lack:– poverty [1], want [1]

2640 חֹסֶר **ḥōser**, n.[m.]. GK: 2896 [→ 2637]. poverty, lack:– want [3]

2641 חַסְרָה **ḥasrâ**, n.pr.m. GK: 2897 [cf. 2745]. Hasrah:– Hasrah [1]

2642 חֶסְרוֹן **ḥesrôn**, n.m. GK: 2898 [→ 2637]. what is lacking:– that which is wanting [1]

2643 חַף **ḥap**, a. GK: 2899 [→ 2653]. clean, pure:– innocent [1]

2644 חָפָא **ḥāpā'**, v. GK: 2901. [P] to do secretly:– secretly [1]

2645 חָפָה **ḥāpâ**, v. GK: 2902 [→ 2646, 2647; cf. 2653]. [Q] to cover; [Qp] to be covered; [N] to be sheathed, be covered; [P] to panel, overlay, cover:– covered [7], overlaid [4], cieled [1]

2646 חֻפָּה **ḥuppâ**, n.f. GK: 2903 [→ 2647; cf. 2645]. canopy, shelter; chamber, pavilion (of marriage ceremony):– chamber [1], closet [1], defence [1]

2647 חֻפָּה **ḥuppâ**, n.pr.m. GK: 2904 [→ 2646; cf. 2645]. Huppah, "*canopy,* hence *protection*":– Huppah [1]

2648 חָפַז **ḥāpaz**, v. GK: 2905 [→ 2649]. [Q] to hurry away (in alarm or terror):– haste [3], hasted away [2], made haste [2], hasteth [1], tremble [1]

2649 חִפָּזוֹן **ḥippāzôn**, n.[m.]. GK: 2906 [→ 2648]. haste:– haste [3]

2650 חֻפִּים **ḥuppîm**, n.pr.m. & a.g. GK: 2907. Huppim; Huppite, "*coast people*":– Huppim [3]

2651 חֹפֶן **ḥōpen**, n.[m.]. GK: 2908. hollow of the hand, handful (sometimes as a measure of volume):– hands [2], both hands [1], fists [1], handfuls (+4393) [1], hand [1]

2652 חָפְנִי **ḥopnî**, n.pr.m. GK: 2909. Hophni, "*tadpole*":– Hophni [5]

2653 חָפַף **ḥāpap**, v. GK: 2910 [→ 2348, 2643; cf. 2645]. [Q] to shield, shelter:– cover [1]

2654 חָפֵץ **ḥāpēṣ**, v. GK: 2911 & 2912 [→ 2655, 2656, 2657]. [Q] to desire, delight in, be pleased with, have pleasure in; to sway; some sources: to hang:– delight [15], delighteth [12], delighted [10], pleased [7], desire [6], please [5], will [3], any pleasure at all (+2654) [2], desirest [2], like [2], pleasure [2], delight in [1], desired [1], favourest [1], favoureth [1], moveth [1], pleaseth [1], take delight in [1], well pleased [1], would [1]

2655 חָפֵץ **ḥāpēṣ**, a.vbl. GK: 2913 [→ 2654]. desire, delight, pleasure:– desire [2], pleasure [2], delight [1], desireth [1], favour [1], please [1], willing [1], wish [1], would [1]

2656 חֵפֶץ **ḥēpeṣ**, n.m. GK: 2914 [→ 2654]. desire, delight, pleasure:– pleasure [16], desire [9], delight [3], purpose [3], desired [2], acceptable [1], delightsome [1], desireth [1], matter [1], pleasant [1], willingly (+871.1) [1]

2657 חֶפְצִי־בָהּ **ḥepṣî-bāh**, n.pr.f. GK: 2915 [→ 2654+871.1+1886.3]. Hephzibah, "*my pleasure is in her*":– Hephzi-bah [2]

2658 חָפַר **ḥāpar**, v. GK: 2916 [→ 1662, 2660, 2663, 2661, 6512]. [Q] to dig, scoop, to paw, to make a hole of any depth in soil; by extension: to spy out, search for, look about, seek out:– digged [13], dig [3], search out [3], diggeth [1], paweth [1], seeketh [1]

2659 חָפֵר **ḥāpar**, v. GK: 2917. [Q] to feel dismay, be disgraced, be humiliated, be in confusion; [H] to bring disgrace, be ashamed, be humiliated:– confounded [6], ashamed [4], brought to confusion [2], bringeth reproach [1], brought unto shame [1], cometh to shame [1], put to shame [1], shame [1]

2660 חֵפֶר **ḥēper**, n.pr.m. & loc. GK: 2918 & 2919 [→ 1662, 2662; cf. 2658]. Hepher, "[perhaps] *help*":– Hepher [9]

2661 חֲפַרְפָּרָה **ḥ^{a}parpārâ**, n.f. GK: 2923 [→ 2658, 6512]. rodent (an object of worship):– moles (+6512) [1]

2662 חֶפְרִי **ḥeprî**, a.g. GK: 2920 [→ 2660]. Hepherite, "*of Hepher*":– Hepherites [1]

2663 חֲפָרַיִם **ḥ^{a}pārayim**, n.pr.loc. GK: 2921 [→ 2658]. Hapharaim, "*place of two trenches*":– Hapharaim [1]

חֲפַרְפֵּרָה **ḥ^{a}parpērâ**. See 2661.

2664 חָפַשׂ **ḥāpaś**, v. GK: 2924 [→ 2665]. [Q] to search for, examine, plot; [N] to be ransacked; [P] to search, look around, track down, hunt down; [Pu] to go into hiding, to devise; [Ht] to disguise oneself, become like:– disguised [5], search [5], disguise [2], search out [2], searched [2], changed [1], diligent [1], hidden [1], made diligent search [1], searched out [1], searchest for [1], searching [1]

2665 חֵפֶשׂ **ḥēpeś**, n.[m.]. GK: 2925 [→ 2664]. plan, plot:– search [1]

2666 חָפַשׁ **ḥāpaš**, v. GK: 2926 [→ 2670]. [Pu] to be freed:– free [1]

2667 חֹפֶשׁ **ḥōpeš**, n.[m.]. GK: 2927. material (for saddle blanket):– precious [1]

2668 חֻפְשָׁה **ḥupšâ**, n.f. GK: 2928 [→ 2670]. freedom:– freedom [1]

2669 חָפְשׁוּת **ḥopšût** or חָפְשִׁית **ḥopšît**, n.f. GK: 2929 & 2931 [→ 2670]. separation, exemption (from duties):– several [2]

2670 חָפְשִׁי **ḥopšî**, a. GK: 2930 [→ 2666, 2668, 2669]. free; set apart, exempt:– free [16], liberty [1]

2671 חֵץ **ḥēṣ**, n.m. GK: 2932 [→ 2678]. arrow; archer:– arrows [37], arrow [11], archers (+1167) [1], dart [1], shaft [1], wound [1]

חוּץ **ḥuṣ**. See 2351.

2672 חָצַב **ḥāṣēb**, v. GK: 2933 & 2934 & 2935 [→ 4274]. [Q] to dig; hew out, cut out; to strike (with lightning); [Qp, N, Pu] to be dug, be engraved, be cut out; [H] to cut in pieces:– hewers [4], digged [3], masons [3], hewed out [2], hew [2], cut [1], diggedst [1], dig [1], divideth [1], graven [1], hewed [1], heweth out [1], heweth [1], hewn out [1], hewn [1], made [1]

2673 חָצָה **ḥāṣâ**, v. GK: 2936 [→ 2676, 2677, 2677, 3183, 3185, 4275, 4276; cf. 2686, 2687]. [Q] to divide; set apart; to rise up to; [N] to be divided, be parceled out:– divided [8], divide [2], divide into two parts [1], live out half [1], midst [1], parted [1], part [1]

2674 חָצוֹר **ḥāṣôr**, n.pr.loc. GK: 2937 & 2938 [→ 2691, 5877]. Hazor, "*enclosure*":– Hazor [18]

2675 חָצוֹר חֲדַתָּה **ḥāṣôr ḥ^{a}dattâ**, n.pr.loc. GK: 2939 [→ 2691]. Hazor Hadattah, "*new Hazor*":– Hazor Hadattah [1]

2676 חֲצוֹת **ḥ^{a}ṣôt**, n.f. GK: 2940 [→ 2673]. middle (of the night), mid(night):– at midnight (+3915) [2], midnight (+3915+1886.1) [1]

2677 חֲצִי **ḥ^{a}ṣî**, n.m. GK: 2942 & 2944 [→ 2673, 2679, 2680]. half, halfway, middle, midst:– half [107], midst [8], midnight (+3915+1886.1) [4], part [3], middle [1], one half [1], two parts [1]

2678 חֵצִי **ḥēṣî**, n.m. GK: 2943 [→ 2671]. arrow:– arrow [4]

2679 חֲצִי הַמְּנֻחוֹת **ḥ^{a}ṣî hamm^{e}nuḥôt**, n.m.+a.g. GK: 2942 [→ 2677]. half of the Manahethites:– Manahethites [1]

2680 חֲצִי הַמְּנַחְתִּי **ḥ^{a}ṣî hamm^{e}naḥtî**, n.m.+a.g. GK: 2942 [→ 2677]. half of the Manahethites:– Manahethites [1]

2681 חָצִיר **ḥāṣîr**, n.[m.]. GK: 2948. home, abode, haunt:– court [1]

2682 חָצִיר **ḥāṣîr**, n.m. GK: 2945 & 2946 & 2947 [→ 2690, 2689, 2695, 2696]. (green) grass; hay; leeks; reed:– grass [17], hay [2], herb [1], leeks [1]

2683 חֵצֶן **ḥēṣen**, n.m. GK: 2949 [→ 2684, 2785?]. bosom (of a garment):– bosom [1]

2684 חֹצֶן **ḥōṣen**, n.m. GK: 2950 [→ 2683]. arms, folds of a robe:– arms [1], lap [1]

2685 חֲצַף **ḥ^{a}ṣap** (Aram.), v. GK: 10280. [H] to show harshness:– hasty [1], urgent [1]

2686 חָצַץ **ḥāṣaṣ**, v. GK: 2951 & 2952 [cf. 2673]. [Q] to be in order, in ranks; [P] to divide, share; to sing; some sources: to distribute water; [Pu] to come to an end:– archers [1], by bands [1], cut off in the midst [1]

2687 חָצָץ **ḥāṣāṣ**, n.[m.]. GK: 2953 [cf. 2673]. gravel:– arrows [1], gravel stones [1], gravel [1]

2688 חַצְצוֹן תָּמָר **ḥaṣ^{e}ṣôn tāmār**, n.pr.loc. GK: 2954 [cf. 8558]. Hazazon Tamar, "*Hazazon of the palm trees*":– Hazazon-tamar [1], Hazezon-tamar [1]

2689 חֲצֹצְרָה **ḥ^{a}ṣōṣ^{e}râ**, n.f. GK: 2956 [→ 2690; cf. 2682]. trumpet, a metal instrument used for signaling and music:– trumpets [26], trumpeters [2], trumpet [1]

2690 חַצְצַר **ḥaṣṣar** or חָצַר **ḥāṣar**, v.den. GK: 2955 & 2957 [→ 2689; cf. 2682]. [P] to sound a trumpet, play a trumpet:– sounded [2], blow [1], sounded trumpets [1], sounding [1], trumpeters [1]

2691 חָצֵר **ḥāṣēr**, n.m. GK: 2958 [→ 1178, 2674, 2675, 2691, 2692, 2693, 2694, 2701, 2702, 2703, 2704, 2705, 2699, 2700; cf. 2691]. courtyard, court of a house, enclosed areas; village, a permanent settlement but without walls:– court [116], villages [47], courts [24], Hazar-hatticon [1], towns [1]

2692 חֲצַר־אַדָּר **ḥ^{a}ṣar-'addār**, n.pr.loc. GK: 2960 [→ 146+2691]. Hazar Addar, "*settlement of Addar*":– Hazar-addar [1]

2693 חֲצַר גַּדָּה **ḥ^{a}ṣar gaddâ**, n.pr.loc. GK: 2961 [→ 2691]. Hazar Gaddah, "*settlement of Gad*":– Hazar-gaddah [1]

2694 חָצֵר הַתִּיכוֹן **ḥāṣēr hattîkôn**, n.pr.loc. GK: 2962 [→ 2691]. Hazer Hatticon, "*place of Hatticon*":–

2695 חֶצְרוֹ **ḥeṣrô** or חֶצְרַי **ḥeṣray**, n.pr.m. GK: 2968 & 2974 [→ 2682]. Hezro, Hezrai:– Hezrai [1], Hezro [1]

2696 חֶצְרוֹן **ḥeṣrôn**, n.pr.m. & loc. GK: 2969 & 2970 [→ 2697, 7152; cf. 2682]. Hezron, "*enclosure*":– Hezron [17], Hezron's [1]

2697 חֶצְרוֹנִי **ḥeṣrônî**, a.g. GK: 2971 [→ 2696; cf. 2682]. Hezronite, "*of Hezron*":– Hezronites [2]

2698 חֲצֵרוֹת **ḥ^{a}ṣērôt**, n.pr.loc. GK: 2972. Hazeroth, "*settlements*":– Hazeroth [6]

2699 חֲצֵרִים **ḥ^{a}ṣērîm**, n.pr.loc. GK: 2973 [→ 2691]. Hazerim:– Hazerim [1]

2700 חֲצַרְמָוֶת **ḥ^{a}ṣarmāwet**, n.pr.m. GK: 2975 [→ 2691+4194]. Hazarmaveth, "*village of Maveth*":– Hazarmaveth [2]

2701 חֲצַר סוּסָה **ḥᵃṣar sûsâ**, n.pr.loc. GK: 2963 [→ 2691+5484]. Hazar Susah, "*settlement of Susah [horse]*":– Hazar-susah [1]

2702 חֲצַר סוּסִים **ḥᵃṣar sûsîm**, n.pr.loc. GK: 2964 [→ 2691]. Hazar Susim, "*settlement of Susah [horse]*":– Hazar-susim [1]

2703 חֲצַר עֵינוֹן **ḥᵃṣar ʿênôn**, n.pr.loc. GK: 2965 [→ 2691]. Hazar Enan, "*settlement of Enan*":– Hazar-enan [1]

2704 חֲצַר עֵינָן **ḥᵃṣar ʿênān**, n.pr.loc. GK: 2966 [→ 2691+5881]. Hazar Enan, "*settlement of Enan*":– Hazar-enan [3]

2705 חֲצַר שׁוּעָל **ḥᵃṣar šûʿāl**, n.pr.loc. GK: 2967 [→ 2691+7776]. Hazar Shual, "*settlement of Shual [jackal]*":– Hazar-shual [4]

חֵק **ḥêq**. See 2436.

2706 חֹק **ḥōq**, n.m. GK: 2976 [→ 2708, 2711; cf. 2710]. decree, statute, prescription, a clear communication of what someone should do; allotment, share, portion, prescribed amount of something:– statutes [74], statute [13], decree [7], ordinance [6], due [4], law [4], ordinances [3], portion [3], bounds [2], custom [2], commandments [1], convenient [1], decreed [1], measure [1], necessary [1], ordinary [1], set time [1], task [1], thing that is appointed [1]

2707 חָקָה **ḥāqâ**, v. GK: 2977 [cf. 2710]. [Pu] to be carved, be portrayed; [Ht] mark for oneself; from the base meaning of carving or engraving is by extension of the act of writing; the communication itself, regulation:– pourtrayed [2], carved work [1], settest a print [1]

2708 חֻקָּה **ḥuqqâ**, n.f. GK: 2978 [→ 2706; cf. 2710]. decree, ordinance, regulation, statute:– statutes [57], statute [20], ordinance [12], ordinances [10], customs [2], appointed [1], manners [1], rites [1]

2709 חֲקוּפָא **ḥᵃqupa**, n.pr.m. GK: 2979. Hakupha, "*crooked*":– Hakupha [2]

2710 חָקַק **ḥāqaq**, v. GK: 2980 [→ 2436, 2706, 2708; cf. 2707]. [Q] to mark out, inscribe, chisel, engrave; [Qp] to be portrayed; [Po] to command, be a leader, ruler; staff (of a commander); [Pu] to be decreed; [Ho] to be written:– lawgiver [6], decree [2], governors [2], appointed [1], graven [1], graveth [1], law [1], note [1], pourtrayed [1], pourtray [1], printed [1], set [1]

2711 חֵקֶק **ḥēqeq**, n.m. GK: 2981 [→ 2706]. decree, statute, prescription:– decrees [1], thoughts [1]

2712 חֻקֹּק **ḥuqqōq** or חוּקֹק **ḥûqōq**, n.pr.loc. GK: 2982 & 2577. Hukkok, Hukok:– Hukkok [1], Hukok [1]

2713 חָקַר **ḥāqar**, v. GK: 2983 [→ 2714, 4278]. [Q] to explore, search out, probe; [N] to be determined, be searched; [P] to search out:– search [7], searched out [4], search out [3], searched [3], found out [2], searcheth out [2], make search [1], searcheth [1], seek [1], sought out [1], sounded [1], try [1]

2714 חֵקֶר **ḥēqer**, n.m. GK: 2984 [→ 2713]. searching, finding out, often negatively stated: what cannot be search thoroughly or found out:– search [3], unsearchable (+369) [3], searching [2], finding out [1], number [1], searched out [1], searchings [1]

2715 חֹר **ḥōr**, n.m. GK: 2985. noble, free person:– nobles [13]

חֻר **ḥur**. See 2352.

2716 חֲרָאִים **ḥᵃrāʾîm**, n.[m.]. GK: 2989 [→ 4280; cf. 2755]. filth, excrement:–

2717 חָרֵב **ḥārēb**, v. GK: 2990 & 2991 & 2993 [→ 2719, 2720, 2721, 2722?, 2723, 2724, 2725; cf. 2718]. [Q] to be dried up, be parched; be desolate, lay in ruins; to kill; [N] to be ruined, be desolate; to be slaughtered; [Pu] to be dried up; [H] to lay waste, devastate, cause to dry up; [Ho] to lie in ruins:– laid waste [8], dried up [6], desolate [3], dried [3], dry up [2], dry [2], made waste [2], surely slain (+2717) [2], utterly wasted (+2717) [2], wasted [2], decayeth [1], destroyed [1], destroyer [1], drieth up [1], lie waste [1], make waste [1], slay [1], waste [1]

2718 חֲרַב **ḥᵃrab** (Aram.), v. GK: 10281 [cf. 2717]. [Ho] to be destroyed, be devastated:– destroyed [1]

2719 חֶרֶב **ḥereb**, n.f. GK: 2995 [→ 2717]. sword; dagger; knife; cutting tool; by extension: battle, war; used fig. of God's judgment:– sword [385], swords [17], dagger [3], knives [3], knife [2], axes [1], mattocks [1], tool [1]

2720 חָרֵב **ḥārēb**, a. GK: 2992 [→ 2717]. dry, desolate, wasted, in ruins:– waste [6], desolate [2], dry [2]

2721 חֹרֶב **ḥōreb** or חֹרֶב **ḥōreb**, n.m. GK: 2996 & 2997 [→ 2717]. heat, dryness, drought, fever; waste, rubble, object of horror, desolation:– heat [6], drought [3], dry [3], waste [2], desolation [1], utterly waste (+2723) [1]

2722 חֹרֵב **ḥōrēb**, n.pr.loc. GK: 2998 [→ 2717?]. Horeb, "*dry, desolate*":– Horeb [17]

2723 חָרְבָּה **ḥorbâ**, n.f. GK: 2999 [→ 2717]. ruins, desolate place:– wastes [7], waste [7], desolation [5], desolate places [4], waste places [4], desolations [3], deserts [2], desolate [2], laid waste [2], decayed places [1], desert [1], destructions [1], places desolate [1], utterly waste (+2721) [1], wasted [1]

2724 חָרָבָה **ḥārābâ**, n.f. GK: 3000 [→ 2717]. dry land, dry ground:– dry [8]

2725 חֲרָבוֹן **ḥᵃrābôn**, n.m. GK: 3001 [→ 2717]. dry heat, implying a drought:– drought [1]

2726 חַרְבוֹנָא **ḥarbônāʾ** or חַרְבוֹנָה **ḥarbônâ**, n.pr.m. GK: 3002 & 3003. Harbona, "*donkey driver*":– Harbonah [1], Harbona [1]

2727 חָרַג **ḥārag**, v. GK: 3004. [Q] to come out trembling:– afraid [1]

2728 חַרְגֹּל **ḥargōl**, n.[m.]. GK: 3005 [cf. 2295]. cricket; some sources: locust, grasshopper:– beetle [1]

2729 חָרַד **ḥārad**, v. GK: 3006 [→ 2730, 2731, 2732?, 2733?]. [Q] to tremble, quake, shudder, be startled; [H] to make afraid, frighten, make tremble:– make afraid [10], afraid [8], tremble [6], trembled [4], fray away [2], made afraid [2], careful [1], discomfited [1], fray [1], quaked [1], trembled (+2731) [1], trembleth [1], trembling [1]

2730 חָרֵד **ḥārēd**, a.vbl. GK: 3007 [→ 2729]. trembling, fearful:– tremble [2], afraid [1], trembled (+1961) [1], trembled [1], trembleth [1]

2731 חֲרָדָה **ḥᵃrādâ**, n.f. GK: 3010 [→ 2729]. panic, fear, terror, horror:– trembling [4], fear [2], care [1], quaking [1], trembled (+2729) [1]

2732 חֲרָדָה **ḥᵃrādâ**, n.pr.loc. GK: 3011 [→ 2729?]. Haradah, "*place of fear*":– Haradah [2]

2733 חֲרֹדִי **ḥᵃrōdî**, a.loc. GK: 3012 & 3009 [→ 2729?]. Harodite:– Harodite [2]

2734 חָרָה **ḥārâ**, v. GK: 3013 [→ 2740, 2750, 8474; cf. 2787]. [Q] to be angry, be aroused; to burn with anger; [N] to rage; [H] to be jealous; [Tiphel] to compete, contend with; [Ht] to fret:– kindled [44], wroth [12], angry [8], hot [5], fret [4], wax hot [4], displeased [3], incensed [2], very wroth (+2734) [2], burn [1], displease (+5869+871.1) [1], earnestly [1], grieved [1], very angry [1], waxed hot [1]

2735 חֹר הַגִּדְגָּד **ḥōr haggidgād**, n.pr.loc. GK: 2988 [→ 2356]. Hor Haggidgad, "*cavern of the Gidgad*":– Hor-hagidgad [2]

2736 חַרְהֲיָה **ḥarhᵃyâ**, n.pr.m. GK: 3015 & 3029. Harhaiah:– Harhaiah [1]

2737 חֲרוּזִים **ḥᵃrûzîm**, n.[m.]pl. GK: 3016. string of jewels; some sources: string of beads or shells:– chains [1]

2738 חָרוּל **ḥārûl**, n.[m.]. GK: 3017. weeds, undergrowth, variously identified:– nettles [3]

חרון **ḥōrôn**. See 1032, 2772.

2739 חֲרוּמַף **ḥᵃrûmap**, n.pr.m. GK: 3018 [→ 2763+639]. Harumaph, "*disfigured nose*":– Harumaph [1]

2740 חָרוֹן **ḥārôn**, n.m. GK: 3019 [→ 2734]. fierce (anger), burning (anger), wrath:– fierce [23], fierceness [9], wrath [5], fierce wrath [1], fury [1], sore displeasure [1], wrathful [1]

2741 חֲרוּפִי **ḥᵃrûpî** or חֲרִיפִי **ḥᵃrîpî**, a.g. GK: 3020 & 3042 [→ 2756; cf. 2778]. Haruphite, Hariphite:– Haruphite [1]

2742 חָרוּץ **ḥārûṣ**, n.m. & a. GK: 3021 & 3022 & 3023 & 3025 & 3026 [→ 2782]. gold; trench, ditch, moat, a military defense; threshing sledge, sharp instrument for harvest; decision; diligent, industrious:– diligent [5], gold [4], decision [2], fine gold [2], threshing [2], sharp pointed [1], sharp [1], wall [1]

2743 חָרוּץ **ḥārûṣ**, n.pr.m. GK: 3027 [→ 2782?]. Haruz, "[perhaps] *gold* or *eager*":– Haruz [1]

2744 חַרְחוּר **ḥarḥûr**, n.pr.m. GK: 3028 [→ 2746; cf. 2787]. Harhur, "[poss.] *fever;* [poss.] *raven; one born during mother's fever*":– Harhur [2]

2745 חַרְחַס **ḥarḥas**, n.pr.m. GK: 3030 [cf. 2641]. Harhas:– Harhas [1]

2746 חַרְחֻר **ḥarḥur**, n.m. GK: 3031 [→ 2744; cf. 2787]. scorching heat; some souces: fever:– extreme burning [1]

2747 חֶרֶט **ḥereṭ**, n.[m.]. GK: 3032. pen; fashioning tool, stylus:– graving tool [1], pen [1]

חָרִט **ḥāriṭ**. See 2754.

2748 חַרְטֹם **ḥarṭōm**, n.m. GK: 3033 [→ 2413; cf. 2749]. magician:– magicians [11]

2749 חַרְטֹם **ḥarṭōm** (Aram.), n.m. GK: 10282 [cf. 2748]. magician:– magicians [4], magician [1]

2750 חֳרִי **ḥᵒrî**, n.m. GK: 3034 [→ 2734]. hot, burning, fierce (anger):– fierce [3], great [2], heat [1]

חֲרִי **ḥᵃrî**. See 2716.

2751 חֹרִי **ḥōrî**, n.[m.]. GK: 3035 [→ 2357]. (white) bread or cake:– white [1]

2752 חֹרִי **ḥōrî**, n.pr.m. GK: 3036. Hori, "*cave-dweller*":– Horites [3], Horims [2], Horite [1]

2753 חֹרִי **ḥōrî**, a.g. GK: 3037. Horite, "*of Hor[i]*":– Hori [4]

2754 חָרִיט **ḥārîṭ**, n.m. GK: 3038. bag, purse:– bags [1], crisping pins [1]

2755 חִרְייוֹנִים **ḥiryyônîm**, n.[m.]. GK: 3039 [cf. 2716+3123]. dove's dung [?], see 2716:–

2756 חָרִיף **ḥārîp**, n.pr.m. GK: 3040 [→ 2741; cf. 2778]. Hariph, "*one born at harvest time*":– Hariph [2]

2757 חָרִיץ **ḥārîṣ**, n.m. GK: 3043 & 3044 [→ 2782]. portion, slice; pick, hoe, an iron tool:– harrows [2], cheeses (+2461) [1]

2758 חָרִישׁ **ḥārîš**, n.m. GK: 3045 [→ 2790]. plowing, time of plowing:– earing time [1], earing [1], ground [1]

2759 חֲרִישִׁי **ḥᵃrîšî**, a. GK: 3046 [→ 2790?]. scorching:– vehement [1]

2760 חָרַךְ **ḥārak**, v. GK: 3047. [Q] to roast; some sources: to capture:– roasteth [1]

2761 חֲרַךְ **ḥᵃrak** (Aram.), v. GK: 10283. [Htpa] to be singed (i.e., hair burnt):– singed [1]

2762 חֲרַכִּים **ḥᵃrakkîm**, n.[m.]pl. GK: 3048. lattice, a window covered by crossed strips of wood:– lattice [1]

חָרֻל **ḥārul**. See 2738.

2763 חָרַם **ḥāram**, v. GK: 3049 & 3050 [→ 1179, 2739, 2764, 2766?, 2767, 2768, 2769]. [Qp] to be disfigured, mutilated, any split portion of the face, possibly a cleft palate; [H] to completely destroy, devote to destruction, exterminate, annihilate [Ho] to be destroyed, be devoted to destruction; this can refer to anything which is under the ban from common use, some things are set apart for use by priests, other things are destroyed utterly as devoted to the LORD:– utterly destroyed [19], utterly destroy [9], destroyed utterly [4], utterly destroy (+2763) [4], destroy utterly [3], destroying utterly [3], utterly destroying [2], consecrate [1], devoted [1], devote [1], flat nose [1], forfeited [1], make accursed [1], utterly make away [1], utterly to slay [1]

2764 חֵרֶם **ḥērem**, n.m. GK: 3051 & 3052 [→ 2763]. devoted, set apart for destruction; this can refer to anything which is under the ban from common use, some things are set apart for use by priests, other things are destroyed utterly as devoted to the LORD; net, fishnet, trap:– accursed thing [9], net [5], curse [4], nets [4], accursed [3], cursed thing [3], devoted [3], devoted thing [2], appointed to utter destruction [1], dedicate thing [1], thing accursed [1], things utterly destroyed [1], utter destruction [1]

2765 חֹרֵם **ḥᵒrēm**, n.pr.loc. GK: 3054. Horem, "*consecrated*":– Horem [1]

2766 חָרִם **ḥārim**, n.pr.m. GK: 3053 [→ 2763?]. Harim, "*consecrated [to Yahweh]*":– Harim [11]

2767 חָרְמָה **ḥormâ**, n.pr.loc. GK: 3055 [→ 2763]. Hormah, "*consecration*":– Hormah [9]

2768 חֶרְמוֹן **ḥermôn**, n.pr.loc. GK: 3056 [→ 1179, 2769; cf. 2763]. Hermon, "*consecrated place*":– Hermon [13]

2769 חֶרְמֹנִים **ḥermōnîm**, n.pr.loc. GK: 3057 [→ 2768; cf. 2763]. heights of Hermon:– Hermonites [1]

2770 חֶרְמֵשׁ **ḥermēš**, n.[m.]. GK: 3058. sickle (for harvest of grain):– sickle [2]

2771 חָרָן **ḥārān**, n.pr.m. & loc. GK: 3059 & 3060. Haran, "*mountaineer* perhaps *sanctuary*":– Haran [12]

חָרֹן **ḥārōn**. See 2740.

2772 חֹרֹנִי **ḥōrōnî**, a.g. GK: 3061. Horonite:– Horonite [3]

2773 חוֹרֹנַיִם **ḥôrōnayim**, n.pr.loc. GK: 2589. Horonaim, "*twin hollows, twin caves*":– Horonaim [4]

2774 חַרְנֶפֶר **ḥarneper**, n.pr.m. *or* loc. GK: 3062. Harnepher, "*Horus is merciful*":– Harnepher [1]

2775 חֶרֶס **ḥeres** or חַרְסָה **harᵉsâ**, n.m. GK: 3063 & 3064 & 3066 [→ 2776, 8556]. sun; itch, any eruptive skin rash:– sun [3], itch [1]

2776 חֶרֶס **ḥeres**, n.pr.loc. GK: 3065 [→ 2775, 8556]. Heres, "*sun*":– Heres [1]

2777 חַרְסוּת **ḥarsût** or חַרְסִית **ḥarsît**, n.f.col. GK: 3067 & 3068 [→ 2789]. potsherd:– east [1]

2778 חָרַף **ḥārap**, v. GK: 3069 & 3070 & 3071 & 3072 [→ 2756, 2741, 2779, 2780, 2781; cf. 2741?]. [Q] to treat with contempt, insult, reproach, taunt; to (spend the time of) winter; [N] to be promised to a man, engaged; [P] to defy, ridicule, taunt, mock, insult; to disillusion, confuse:– reproached [12], reproach [10], defied [5], reproacheth [5], defy [3], betrothed [1], blasphemed [1], jeoparded [1], rail [1], upbraid [1], winter [1]

2779 חֹרֶף **ḥōrep**, n.m. GK: 3074 [→ 2778]. winter (the early time of the harvest cycle); prime (the early time of one's youth):– winter [4], cold [1], winterhouse (+1004) [1], youth [1]

2780 חָרֵף **ḥārēp**, n.pr.m. GK: 3073 [→ 2778]. Hareph, "*autumn* or *sharp; scornful*":– Hareph [1]

2781 חֶרְפָּה **ḥerpâ**, n.f. GK: 3075 [→ 2778]. disgrace, contempt, scorn, insult:– reproach [65], shame [3], rebuke [2], reproaches [1], reproacheth [1], reproachfully (+871.1) [1]

2782 חָרַץ **ḥāraṣ**, v. GK: 3024 & 3076 & 3077 [→ 2742, 2743?, 2757]. [Q] to pronounce, determine; to pay attention, act quickly; [Qp, N] to be determined, be decreed; to be maimed, mutilated, pertaining to what has been cut:– determined [6], bestir [1], decided [1], decreed [1], maimed [1], moved [1], move [1]

2783 חֲרַץ **ḥᵃraṣ** (Aram.), n.[m.]. GK: 10284 [cf. 2504]. hips, hip joints:– loins [1]

חָרֻץ **ḥāruṣ**. See 2742.

2784 חַרְצֹב **ḥarṣōb**, n.[f.]. GK: 3078. struggle; chains:– bands [2]

חָרִץ **ḥāriṣ**. See 2757.

2785 חַרְצָן **ḥarṣān**, n.m.pl. GK: 3079 [→ 2683?]. seeds (of grapes); some sources: unripe fruit:– kernels [1]

2786 חָרַק **ḥāraq**, v. GK: 3080. [Q] to gnash, grind (teeth):– gnasheth [2], gnash [2], gnashed [1]

2787 חָרַר **ḥārar**, v. GK: 3081 & 3082 [→ 2744, 2746, 2788; cf. 2734]. [Q] to burn; (heated metal) glow; [N] be parched, burned, charred; to be hoarse; [Pil] to kindle, cause to burn, glow; by extension: to have a fever:– burnt [5], burned [2], angry [1], burn [1], dried [1], kindle [1]

2788 חֲרֵרִים **ḥᵃrērîm**, n.[m.]. GK: 3083 [→ 2787]. parched place, a hot, lifeless desert place:– parched places [1]

2789 חֶרֶשׂ **ḥereś**, n.[m.]. GK: 3084 [→ 2777, 7025]. clay pot, earthenware; potsherd, fragment of pottery:– earthen [8], potsherd [4], earth [1], potsherds [1], sheards [1], sheard [1], stones [1]

2790 חָרֵשׁ **ḥārēš**, v. GK: 3086 & 3087 [→ 2758, 2759?, 2791, 2792?, 2794, 2795, 2796, 2797?, 2798, 2799, 4281, 4282]. [Q] to plow; engrave; plan, plot; to be silent, be quiet; to become deaf; [Qp] to be inscribed; [N] to be plowed; [H] to be quiet, say nothing, be silent; [Ht] to make no moves, keep silent; [H] to plot against:– hold peace [11], held peace [8], plow [6], plowed [5], altogether hold peace (+2790) [4], devise [3], keep silence [3], altogether holdest peace (+2790) [2], deviseth [2], hold tongue [2], holdeth peace [2], kept silence [2], plowing [2], plowman [2], cease [1], conceal [1], deaf [1], ear [1], graven [1], held peace (+3509.1) [1], held tongue [1], holdest tongue [1], imagine [1], left off speaking [1], make hold peace [1], plowers [1], quiet [1], rest [1], secretly practised [1], silent [1], speak not a word [1], still [1], worker [1]

2791 חֶרֶשׁ **ḥereš**, n.[m.] (used as adv.). GK: 3089 [→ 2790]. secretly, silently:– artificer [1], craftsmen [1], secretly [1]

2792 חֶרֶשׁ **ḥereš**, n.pr.m. GK: 3090 [→ 2790?]. Heresh, "*deaf, silent*":– Heresh [1]

2793 חֹרֶשׁ **ḥōreš**, n.m.[loc.] GK: 3091 & 3092 [→ 2796?; cf. 2800]. wooded place, forest, thicket; as place name: Horesh, "*woodsman* or *craftsman*":– wood [4], bough [1], forests [1], shrowd [1]

2794 חָרָשׁ **ḥārāš**, v.ptcp. GK: 3086 [→ 2790]. ptcp. of 2790: one who plows; engraves; plans:– artificer [1]

2795 חֵרֵשׁ **ḥērēš**, a. GK: 3094 [→ 2790]. deaf (person):– deaf [9]

2796 חָרָשׁ **ḥārāš**, n.m. GK: 3088 & 3093 [→ 2790, 2793?]. skilled craftsman: blacksmith, carpenter, stonemason, gemcutter, idol-maker, etc.; the ironic phrase "craftsman of destruction" means people who are very good at destroying things (Eze 21:31); magic, sorcery:– carpenters [6], workman [5], craftsmen [4], carpenters (+6086) [3], engraver [3], artificers [2], smith [2], carpenter (+6086) [1], carpenter [1], craftsman [1], makers [1], masons (+68+7023) [1], masons (+7023) [1], skilful [1], smith (+1270) [1], workers [1], workmen [1], wrought [1]

2797 חַרְשָׁא **ḥaršā'**, n.pr.m. GK: 3095 [→ 8521; cf. 2790?]. Harsha, "*deaf*":– Harsha [2]

2798 חֲרָשִׁים **ḥᵃrāšîm**, n.pr.loc. GK: 3096 & 1629 [→ 1516; cf. 2790]. Harashim; Ge Harashim, "*valley of the craftsmen*":– Charashim [1]

2799 חֲרֹשֶׁת **ḥᵃrōšet**, n.f. GK: 3098 [→ 2790]. cutting (stone), working (wood):– carving [2], cutting [2]

2800 חֲרֹשֶׁת **ḥᵃrōšet**, n.pr.loc. GK: 3099 [→ 1471; cf. 2793]. Harosheth:– Harosheth [3]

2801 חָרַת **ḥarat**, v. GK: 3100. [Qp] to be engraved:– graven [1]

2802 חֶרֶת **ḥeret**, n.pr.loc. GK: 3101. Hereth:– Hareth [1]

2803 חָשַׁב **ḥāšab**, v. GK: 3108 & 3110 [→ 2807, 2808, 2809, 2810, 2811, 2815, 4284; cf. 2804]. [Q] to plan, plot, purpose, consider; to credit, account, impute; [N] to be thought, considered, regarded; be reckoned, accounted; [P] to determine, plan, plot; to compute, account; [Ht] to consider oneself:– counted [18], devise [12], cunning [9], thought [9], imagine [6], think [6], accounted [5], devised [5], deviseth [4], esteemed [4], purposed [4], reckoned [4], count [3], reckon [3], counteth [2], cunning workman [2], imagined [2], imputed [2], purpose [2], conceived [1], considered [1], esteemeth [1], esteem [1], find out [1], forecast against [1], forecast [1], holdest [1], imagineth [1], imputeth [1], impute [1], invent [1], like [1], makest account [1], meant [1], reckoning made [1], regardeth [1], regard [1], thinkest [1], thinketh [1], those that devise cunning work (+4284) [1], thought on [1]

2804 חֲשַׁב **ḥᵃšab** (Aram.), v. GK: 10285 [cf. 2803]. [Pp] to be regarded, be respected:– reputed [1]

2805 חֵשֶׁב **ḥēšeb**, n.m. GK: 3109 [cf. 2280]. waistband:– curious girdle [8]

2806 חַשַׁבְדָּנָה **ḥašbaddānâ**, n.pr.m. GK: 3111 [cf. 2811]. Hashbaddanah, "[prob.] *Yahweh has considered me*":– Hashbadana [1]

2807 חֲשֻׁבָה **ḥᵃšubâ**, n.pr.m. GK: 3112 [→ 2803]. Hashubah, "*consideration*":– Hashubah [1]

2808 חֶשְׁבּוֹן **ḥešbôn**, n.m. GK: 3113 [→ 2803]. scheme, plan:– account [1], device [1], reason [1]

2809 חֶשְׁבּוֹן **ḥešbôn**, n.pr.loc. GK: 3114 [→ 2803]. Heshbon, "*reckoning*":– Heshbon [38]

2810 חִשָּׁבוֹן **ḥiššābôn**, n.m. GK: 3115 [→ 2803]. catapult machine (for hurling against ramparts); scheme:– engines [1], inventions [1]

2811 חֲשַׁבְיָה **ḥᵃšabyâ** or חֲשַׁבְיָהוּ **ḥᵃšabyāhû**, n.pr.m. GK: 3116 & 3117 [→ 2803+3068; cf. 2806]. Hashabiah, "*Yahweh has reckoned*":– Hashabiah [15]

2812 חֲשַׁבְנָה **ḥᵃšabnâ**, n.pr.m. GK: 3118. Hashabnah, "[prob.] *Yahweh has considered me*":– Hashabnah [1]

2813 חֲשַׁבְנְיָה **ḥᵃšabnᵉyâ**, n.pr.m. GK: 3119. Hashabneiah, "[prob.] *Yahweh has considered me*":– Hashabniah [2]

2814 חָשָׁה **ḥāšâ**, v. GK: 3120. [Q] to be silent, be hushed; [H] to keep silent; to do nothing, hesitate:– hold peace [5], still [3], held peace [2], hold my peace [1], holden peace [1], keep silence [1], silence [1], silent [1], stilled [1]

2815 חַשּׁוּב **ḥaššûb**, n.pr.m. GK: 3121 [→ 2803]. Hasshub, "*considerate*":– Hashub [4], Hasshub [1]

2816 חֲשׁוֹךְ **ḥᵃšôk** (Aram.), n.[m.]. GK: 10286 [cf. 2822]. darkness:– darkness [1]

2817 חֲשׂוּפָא **ḥᵃśûpā'**, n.pr.m. GK: 3102. Hasupha:– Hashupha [1], Hasupha [1]

חָשׁוּק **ḥāšûq**. See 2838.

2818 חֲשַׁח **ḥᵃšaḥ**, v. or חַשְׁחָה **hašḥâ** (Aram.), n.f. GK: 10287 & 10288 [→ 2819]. [P] to be in need; (n.) need:– careful [1], have need of [1]

2819 חַשְׁחוּ **ḥašḥû** (Aram.), n.f.col. GK: 10289 [→ 2818]. what is needed:– needful [1]

חֲשֵׁכָה **ḥᵃšēkᵉh**. See 2825.

חֻשִׁים **ḥušîm**. See 2366.

2820 חָשַׂךְ **ḥāśak**, v. GK: 3104. [Q] to keep back, to withhold, halt, spare; [N] to be spared, be relieved:– spareth [3], spare [3], withheld [3], reserved [2], spared [2], asswaged [1], asswage [1], forbear [1], held back [1], hindereth [1], keep back [1], keepeth back [1], kept back [1], kept [1], punished [1], refrained [1], refraineth [1], refrain [1], withholdeth [1]

2821 חָשַׁךְ **ḥāšak**, v. GK: 3124 [→ 2822, 2823, 2824, 2825, 4285]. [Q] to grow dark, be dim, be black; [H] to darken, make dark; often darkness has the associative meanings of gloom, despair, terror, ignorance, or hard to understand:– darkened [7], dark [3], blacker [1], cause darkness [1], darkeneth [1], darken [1], dim [1], hideth [1], made dark [1], maketh dark [1]

2822 חֹשֶׁךְ **ḥōšek**, n.m. GK: 3125 [→ 2821; cf. 2816]. darkness, dark; blackness, gloom; often darkness has the associative meanings of gloom, despair, terror, ignorance, or hard to understand:– darkness [70], dark [7], obscurity [2], night [1]

2823 חָשֹׁךְ **ḥāšōk**, a. GK: 3126 [→ 2821]. obscure, dark, unknown:– mean [1]

2824 חֶשְׁכָה **ḥeškâ**, n.f. GK: 3128 [→ 2821, 2825]. same as 2825: darkness:– dark [1]

2825 חֲשֵׁכָה **ḥᵃšēkâ**, n.f. GK: 3128 [→ 2824]. same as 2824: darkness:– darkness [5]

2826 חָשַׁל **ḥāšal**, v. GK: 3129. [N] to lag (behind), be worn out:– feeble [1]

2827 חֲשַׁל **ḥᵃšal** (Aram.), v. GK: 10290. [P] to smash, pulverize:– subdueth [1]

2828 חָשֻׁם **ḥāšum**, n.pr.m. GK: 3130 [→ 2829, 2832; cf. 2367]. Hashum, "*broad-nosed*":– Hashum [5]

חֻשָׁם **ḥušām**. See 2367.

חֻשִׁם **ḥušim**. See 2366.

2829 חֶשְׁמוֹן **ḥešmôn**, n.pr.loc. GK: 3132 [→ 2828]. Heshmon:– Heshmon [1]

2830 חַשְׁמַל **ḥašmal**, n.[m.]. GK: 3133. glowing metal; some sources: electrum:– amber [3]

2831 חַשְׁמַן **ḥašman**, n.m. GK: 3134. envoy:– princes [1]

2832 חַשְׁמֹנָה **ḥašmōnâ**, n.pr.loc. GK: 3135 [→ 2828]. Hashmonah:– Hashmonah [2]

2833 חֹשֶׁן **ḥōšen**, n.m. GK: 3136. breastpiece:– breastplate [25]

2834 חָשַׂף **ḥāśap**, v. GK: 3103 & 3106 & 3107 [→ 2835, 4286]. [Q] to strip bare, lay bare; to scoop out, draw out; [Qp] to be bared; [P] to bring to premature birth:– made bare [2], uncovered [2], bare [1], discovereth [1], discover [1], draw out [1], made clean [1], make bare [1], take [1]

2835 חָשִׂף **ḥāśip**, n.m. GK: 3105 [→ 2834]. small flock:– little flocks [1]

2836 חָשַׁק **ḥāšaq**, v. GK: 3137 & 3138 [→ 2837, 2838, 2839]. [Q] to set one's affection, desire, love, be attached to; [P] to make bands, make joints for binding; [Pu] to have bands:– filleted [3], desired (+2837) [2], set love [2], had delight [1], hast a desire [1], in love [1], longeth [1]

2837 חֵשֶׁק **ḥēšeq**, n.m. GK: 3139 [→ 2836]. thing desired, thing longed for:– desired (+2836) [2], desire [1], pleasure [1]

2838 חָשׁוּק **ḥāšûq**, n.[m.]. GK: 3122 [→ 2836]. band, binding:– fillets [8]

2839 חִשֻּׁק **ḥiššuq**, n.[m.]. GK: 3140 [→ 2836]. spokes (of a wheel):– felloes [1]

2840 חִשֻּׁר **ḥiššur**, n.[m.]. GK: 3141 [→ 2841]. hub (of a wheel):– spokes [1]

2841 חַשְׁרָה **ḥašrâ**, n.f. GK: 3142 [→ 2840]. collection, mass:– dark [1]

חֲשֻׂפָא **ḥᵃśupā'**. See 2817.

2842 חֲשַׁשׁ **ḥᵃšaš**, n.m. GK: 3143. chaff, dry grass:– chaff [2]

2843 חֻשָׁתִי **ḥušātî**, a.g. GK: 3144 [→ 2364]. Hushathite:– Hushathite [5]

2844 חַת **ḥat**, n.m. & a. GK: 3145 & 3146 [→ 2865]. fear, dread, terror; terrified, broken:– broken [1], dismayed [1], dread [1], fear [1]

2845 חֵת **ḥēt**, n.pr.m. GK: 3147 [→ 2850]. Hittite, "*descendants of Heth*":– Heth [14]

Heb

2846 חָתָה **ḥātâ**, v. GK: 3149 [→ 4289]. [Q] to get, snatch, take away:– take [2], heap [1], take away [1]

2847 חִתָּה **ḥittâ**, n.f. GK: 3150 [→ 2865]. terror:– terror [1]

2848 חִתּוּל **ḥittûl**, n.[m.]. GK: 3151 [→ 2853]. splint, bandage:– roller [1]

2849 חַתְחַת **ḥatḥat**, n.[m.]. GK: 3152 [→ 2865]. horror, terror, danger:– fears [1]

2850 חִתִּי **ḥittî**, a.g. GK: 3153 [→ 2845]. Hittite, "*descendants of Heth*":– Hittite [26], Hittites [22]

2851 חִתִּית **ḥittît**, n.f. GK: 3154 [→ 2865]. terror:– terror [8]

2852 חָתַךְ **ḥātak**, v. GK: 3155. [N] to be decreed:– determined [1]

2853 חָתַל **ḥātal**, v. GK: 3156 [→ 2848, 2854]. [Pu, Ho] to be wrapped in strips of cloth: swaddled at all (+2853) [2]

2854 חֲתֻלָּה **ḥ*ᵃ*tullâ**, n.f. GK: 3157 [→ 2853]. band (of cloth) for wrapping:– swaddling band [1]

2855 חֶתְלֹן **ḥetlôn**, n.pr.loc. GK: 3158. Hethlon:– Hethlon [2]

2856 חָתַם **ḥātam**, v. GK: 3159 [→ 2368, 2369, 2858; cf. 2857]. [Q] to seal (with a signet ring); to seal up; by extension: to be a model; [Qp] to be sealed, be enclosed; [N] to be sealed; [P] to seal in; [H] to block, obstruct:– sealed [12], seal [5], sealed up [2], marked [1], seal up [1], sealest up [1], sealeth up (+1157) [1], sealeth up [1], sealeth [1], stopped [1]

2857 חֲתַם **ḥ*ᵃ*tam** (Aram.), v. GK: 10291 [cf. 2856]. [P] to seal (with a signet ring):– sealed [1]

חֹתָם **ḥōtām**. See 2368.

2858 חֹתֶמֶת **ḥōtemet**, n.f. GK: 3160 [→ 2856]. signet ring seal:– signet [1]

2859 חָתַן **ḥātan**, v.den. GK: 3161 & 3162 & 3165 [→ 2860]. [Q, Ht] to intermarry; to become or have a son-in-law:– father in law [21], son in law [5], make marriages [3], join in affinity [1], joined affinity [1], made affinity [1], mother in law [1]

2860 חָתָן **ḥātān**, n.m. GK: 3163 [→ 2859, 2861]. son-in-law; bridegroom:– bridegroom [8], son in law [8], husband [2], sons in law [2]

2861 חֲתֻנָּה **ḥ*ᵃ*tunnâ**, n.f. GK: 3164 [→ 2860]. wedding, marriage:– espousals [1]

2862 חָתַף **ḥātap**, v. GK: 3166 [→ 2863]. [Q] to snatch away:– taketh away [1]

2863 חֶתֶף **ḥetep**, n.[m.]. GK: 3167 [→ 2862]. bandit, robber:– prey [1]

2864 חָתַר **ḥātar**, v. GK: 3168 [→ 4290]. [Q] to dig, break into; row (in rough seas):– dig [5], digged [2], rowed hard [1]

2865 חָתַת **ḥātat**, v. GK: 3169 [→ 2844, 2847, 2849, 2851, 2866, 2867?, 4287?, 4288]. [Q] to be shattered, dismayed, terrified; [N] to be discouraged, terrified; [P] to frighten; break; [H] to shatter, terrify:– dismayed [26], afraid [5], broken in pieces [5], broken [3], broken down [2], abolished [1], affrighted [1], amazed [1], beaten down [1], broken to pieces [1], cause to be dismayed [1], chapt [1], confound [1], discouraged [1], go down [1], made afraid [1], scarest [1], terrify [1]

2866 חֲתַת **ḥ*ᵃ*tat**, n.[m.]. GK: 3170 [→ 2866; cf. 2865]. something dreadful, horrible:– casting down [1]

2867 חֲתַת **ḥ*ᵃ*tat**, n.pr.m. GK: 3171 [→ 2866?; cf. 2865?]. Hathath, "[poss.] *terror;* [poss.] *weakness*":– Hathath [1]

2868 טְאֵב **ṭ*ᵉ*'ēb** (Aram.), v. GK: 10293 [→ 2869; cf. 3191; cf. 2895, 3190]. [P] to be good = to have joy:– glad [1]

2869 טָב **ṭāb** (Aram.), a. GK: 10294 [→ 2868; cf. 2896]. good, pleasing, pure:– fine [1], good [1]

2870 טָבְאַל **ṭāb*ᵉ*'al** or טָבְאֵל **ṭāb*ᵉ*'ēl**, n.pr.m. GK: 3174 & 3175 [→ 2896+410]. Tabeal, Tabeel, "*God [El] is good*":– Tabeal [1], Tabeel [1]

2871 טְבוּלִים **ṭ*ᵉ*bûlîm**, n.m. GK: 3178. turban:– exceeding in dyed attire (+5628) [1]

2872 טַבּוּר **ṭabbûr**, n.[m.]. GK: 3179. center (of the land), as a fig. extension of the navel of the body, not found in the OT:– middle [1], midst [1]

2873 טָבַח **ṭābaḥ**, v. GK: 3180 [→ 2874, 2876, 2879, 2878, 4293]. [Q] to slaughter, butcher; [Qp] to be slaughtered:– killed [3], slaughter [3], slay [2], kill [1], slain [1], sore slaughter (+2874) [1]

2874 טֶבַח **ṭebaḥ**, n.m. GK: 3181 [→ 2875; cf. 19, 2873]. slaughtering:– slaughter [9], beasts [1], sore slaughter (+2873) [1]

2875 טֶבַח **ṭebaḥ**, n.pr.m. & loc. GK: 3182 & 3183 [→ 2874; cf. 2880]. Tebah, "[poss.] *one born at the time or place of the slaughtering*":– Tebah [1]

2876 טַבָּח **ṭabbāḥ**, n.m. GK: 3184 [→ 2879; cf. 2873; cf. 2877]. cook, butcher; by extension: executioner; guard, imperial guard:– guard [29], cook [2], guard's [1]

2877 טַבָּח **ṭabbāḥ** (Aram.), n.m. GK: 10295 [cf. 2876]. (royal) body-guard, executioner; an elite unit guarding a king, execution only one of its functions:– guard [1]

2878 טִבְחָה **ṭibḥâ**, n.f. GK: 3186 [→ 2873]. slaughtered meat, butchered meat:– slaughter [2], flesh [1]

2879 טַבָּחָה **ṭabbāḥâ**, n.f. GK: 3185 [→ 2876; cf. 2873]. (female) cook (of meat):– cooks [1]

2880 טִבְחַת **ṭibḥat**, n.pr.loc. GK: 3187 [cf. 984, 2875]. Tebah, "[poss.] *one born at the time or place of slaughtering*":– Tibhath [1]

2881 טָבַל **ṭābal**, v. GK: 3188. [Q] to dip, plunge; bathe, soak; [N] to be dipped:– dip [9], dipped [3], dipt [3], plunge [1]

2882 טְבַלְיָהוּ **ṭ*ᵉ*balyāhû**, n.pr.m. GK: 3189 [→ 2919+3807.1?+3068?]. Tabaliah, "*Yahweh has dipped*":– Tebaliah [1]

2883 טָבַע **ṭāba'**, v. GK: 3190 [→ 2884, 2885]. [Q] to sink down, to fall into; [Pu] to be drowned; [Ho] to be sunk, be settled into:– sunk [4], sink [2], drowned [1], fastened [1], settled [1], sunk down [1]

2884 טַבָּעוֹת **ṭabbā'ôt**, n.pr.m. GK: 3191 [→ 2885; cf. 2883]. Tabbaoth, "*[ornamental or signet] ring*":– Tabbaoth [2]

2885 טַבַּעַת **ṭabba'at**, n.f. GK: 3192 [→ 2884; cf. 2883]. ring; signet ring:– rings [40], ring [9]

2886 טַבְרִמֹּן **ṭabrimmōn**, n.pr.m. GK: 3193 [→ 2896+7417]. Tabrimmon, "*Rimmon is good*":– Tabrimmon [1]

2887 טֵבֵת **ṭēbēt**, n.pr. GK: 3194. Tebeth:– Tebeth [1]

2888 טַבָּת **ṭabbāt**, n.pr.loc. GK: 3195. Tabbath, "[poss.] *good*":– Tabbath [1]

2889 טָהוֹר **ṭāhôr**, a. GK: 3196 [→ 2891, 2890]. clean, pure, flawless, free from impurity; moral or ceremonial purity as a fig. extension of an object being free from defect or filth:– clean [51], pure [40], fair [2], pureness [1], purer [1]

2890 טְהוֹר **ṭ*ᵉ*hôr**, n.m. GK: 3196 [→ 2889]. same as 2889: cleanness, purity, flawlessness:–

2891 טָהֵר **ṭāhēr**, v. GK: 3197 [→ 2889, 2890, 2892, 2893]. [Q] to be (ceremonially) clean, purified; [P] to pronounce clean, cleanse, make ceremonially clean, to purify; [Ht] to cleanse oneself, purify oneself; this can mean moral or ceremonial purity:– clean [26], cleansed [23], cleanse [16], pronounce clean [10], purged [4], purified [3], purify [3], made clean [2], pure [2], cleanseth [1], make clean [1], maketh clean [1], purge [1], purifier [1]

2892 טֹהַר **ṭōhar**, n.[m.]. GK: 3198 & 3199 [→ 2891]. purity; cleanness; clearness, brightness, splendor:– purifying [2], clearness [1], glory [1]

2893 טָהֳרָה **ṭoh*ᵒ*râ**, n.f. GK: 3200 [→ 2891]. cleansing, purification; pronouncement of (ceremonial) cleansing:– cleansing [7], purifying [3], purification [2], cleansed [1]

2894 טֵאטֵא **ṭē'ṭē'**, v. GK: 3173 [→ 4292; cf. 2916]. [Pil] to sweep away:– sweep [1]

2895 טוֹב **ṭôb**, v. GK: 3201 [→ 2896, 2897, 2898; cf. 3190; cf. 2868, cf. 3191]. [Q] to be good, well, pleasing; [H] to do well, do good, prosper; this can refer to quality as well as to moral goodness:– well [8], good [5], please [4], do good [3], didst well [2], please (+5921) [2], better [1], cheer [1], do better [1], doest good [1], done well [1], do [1], goodly [1], made goodly [1]

2896 טוֹב **ṭôb**, a. & n.m. GK: 3202 & 3203 [→ 2895, 2897; cf. 2869 (also used with compound proper names)]. good, pleasing, desirable; goodness; this can refer to quality as well as to moral goodness:– good [361], better [72], well [20], goodness [16], goodly [8], merry [7], best [6], fair [6], prosperity [6], precious [4], wealth [3], any thing better (+2896) [2], fair (+4758) [2], fairer [2], fine [2], glad [2], goodliest [2], goods [2], kindly [2], pleasant [2], pleased (+5869+871.1) [2], pleaseth (+5869+871.1) [2], please [2], pleasure [2], beautiful (+4758) [1], beautiful [1], bountiful [1], cheerful [1], ease [1], favour (+5869+871.1) [1], fine (+6668) [1], good deeds [1], goodlier [1], goodly (+8389) [1], graciously [1], in favour [1], joyful [1], kindness [1], kind [1], liketh (+5869+871.1) [1], liketh best (+871.1+1886.1) [1], loving [1], most [1], pleaseth (+6440+3807.1) [1], pleasing [1], ready [1], sweet [1], think best (+5869+871.1) [1], welfare [1], wellfavoured (+2580) [1]

2897 טוֹב **ṭôb**, n.pr.loc. GK: 3204 [→ 2896; cf. 2895]. Tob, "*good*":– Tob [2]

2898 טוּב **ṭûb**, n.m. GK: 3206 [→ 2895]. good, best; goodness, prosperity; this can refer to quality as well as to moral goodness:– goodness [13], good [9], goods [3], fair [1], gladness [1], goeth well [1], good things [1], good thing [1], goodness' [1], joy [1]

2899 טוֹב אֲדוֹנִיָּה **ṭôb '*ᵃ*dôniyyâ**, n.pr.m. GK: 3207 [→ 2897+138]. Tob-Adonijah, "*good is [my] Lord Yahweh*":– Tob-adonijah [1]

2900 טוֹבִיָּה **ṭôbiyyâ** or טוֹבִיָּהוּ **ṭôbiyyāhû**, n.pr.m. GK: 3209 & 3210 [→ 2896+3068]. Tobiah; Tobijah, "*Yahweh is good*":– Tobiah [15], Tobijah [3]

2901 טָוָה **ṭāwâ**, v. GK: 3211 [→ 4299]. [Q] to spin (yarn):– spin [1], spun [1]

2902 טוּחַ **ṭûaḥ** or טָחַח **ṭāḥaḥ**, v. GK: 3212 & 3220 [→ 2915]. [Q] to cover with whitewash; overlay with plaster; [N] to be plastered, be coated:– daubed [6], plaistered [2], daub [1], overlay [1], plaister [1], shut [1]

2903 טוֹטָפֹת **ṭôṭāpōt**, n.f.pl. GK: 3213 [→ 5197]. symbol, sign (later, phylactery, a small box of Scripture verses worn as a sign of obedience to the covenant):– frontlets [3]

2904 טוּל **ṭûl**, v. GK: 3214 [→ 2925]. [P] to hurl; [H] to thrown, hurl; [Ho] to be overpowered, be fallen, be hurled:– cast forth [4], cast [4], cast out [2], carry away [1], cast down [1], sent out [1], utterly cast down [1]

2905 טוּר **ṭûr**, n.m. GK: 3215 [→ 2918]. row, course:– row [14], rows [12]

2906 טוּר **ṭûr** (Aram.), n.m. GK: 10296 [cf. 6697]. mountain:– mountain [2]

2907 טוּשׂ **ṭûś**, v. GK: 3216. [Q] to swoop down; some sources: to flutter:– hasteth [1]

2908 טְוָת **ṭ*ᵉ*wāt** (Aram.), adv. GK: 10297. without eating, in hunger, in fasting:– fasting [1]

2909 טָחָה **ṭāḥâ**, v. GK: 3217. [Pil] to shoot (an arrow the distance of a bowshot; the distance of a bowshot is still in sight, though it is out of hearing range): bowshot (+7198) [1]

2910 טֻחוֹת **ṭuḥôt**, n.f.pl. GK: 3219. inner parts; heart, with a possible focus that this is a mysterious and unknowable part of a person:– inward parts [2]

2911 טְחוֹן **ṭ*ᵉ*ḥôn**, n.[m.]. GK: 3218 [→ 2912]. hand-mill, grinding-mill:– grind [1]

2912 טָחַן **ṭāḥan**, v. GK: 3221 & 3223 [→ 2911, 2913]. [Q] to grind to flour, crush to powder:– grind [4], ground [2], grinders [1], ground very small [1]

2913 טַחֲנָה **ṭaḥ*ᵃ*nâ**, n.f. GK: 3222 [→ 2912]. grinding-mill:– grinding [1]

2914 טְחֹרִים **ṭ*ᵉ*ḥōrîm**, n.m. GK: 3224. tumor, hemorrhoids:– emerods [7]

2915 טִיחַ **ṭîaḥ**, n.[m.]. GK: 3225 [→ 2902]. coating (of whitewash); some sources: coating of clay:– daubing [1]

2916 טִיט **ṭîṭ**, n.m. GK: 3226 [→ 2894, 4292; cf. 2917]. mud, dirt, mire, clay:– mire [8], clay [3], dirt [2]

2917 טִין **ṭîn** (Aram.), n.[m.]. GK: 10298 [cf. 2916]. (wet) clay:– miry [2]

2918 טִירָה **ṭîrâ**, n.f. GK: 3227 [→ 2905; cf. 3195?]. camp (protected by stone walls); tower, battlement:– castles [2], goodly castles [1], habitation [1], palaces [1], palace [1], rows [1]

2919 טַל **ṭal**, n.m. GK: 3228 [→ 37, 2537, 2882; cf. 2920]. dew, night mist:– dew [31]

2920 טַל **ṭal** (Aram.), n.[m.]. GK: 10299 [cf. 2919]. dew:– dew [5]

2921 טָלָא **ṭālā'**, v. GK: 3229. [Qp] to be spotted; be variegated; [Pu] to be patched:– spotted [6], clouted [1], divers colours [1]

2922 טְלָא **ṭ*ᵉ*lā'**, n.m. GK: 3231 [→ 2923, 2924]. same as 2924: lamb:– lambs [1]

2923 טְלָאִים **ṭ*ᵉ*lā'îm**, n.pr.loc. GK: 3230 [→ 2922]. Telaim, "*lambs*":– Telaim [1]

2924 טָלֶה **ṭāleh**, n.m. GK: 3231 [→ 2922]. same as 2922: lamb:– lamb [2]

2925 טַלְטֵלָה **ṭalṭēlâ**, n.f. GK: 3232 [→ 2904]. hurling, throwing:– captivity [1]

2926 טָלַל **ṭālal**, v. GK: 3233 [cf. 6751]. [P] to cover with a roof:– covered [1]

2927 טְלַל **ṭᵉlal** (Aram.), v. GK: 10300 [cf. 6751]. [H] to find shelter:– shadow [1]

2928 טֶלֶם **ṭelem**, n.pr.m. & loc. GK: 3234 & 3235 [cf. 2929]. Telem, "*brightness*":– Telem [2]

2929 טַלְמוֹן **ṭalmôn**, n.pr.m. GK: 3236 [cf. 2928]. Talmon, "[perhaps] *brightness*":– Talmon [5]

2930 טָמֵא **ṭāmēʾ**, v. GK: 3237 & 3239 [→ 2931, 2932, 2933?]. [Q] to be unclean, defiled; [N] to be made unclean, become defiled, impure; [P] to make unclean, defile, desecrate; [Pu] to become defiled; [Ht] to make oneself unclean, defiled; [Hotpaal] to be defiled; this can mean to be ceremonially impure or to be immoral in action:– unclean [61], defiled [45], defile [24], polluted [12], pronounce unclean [10], pollute [2], pronounce utterly unclean (+2930) [2], defile yourselves [1], defileth [1], made unclean [1], make unclean [1], take uncleanness [1]

2931 טָמֵא **ṭāmēʾ**, a. GK: 3238 [→ 2930]. unclean, defiled, impure; this can mean to be ceremonial impurity or active immorality:– unclean [80], defiled [5], infamous (+8034+1886.1) [1], polluted [1], pollution [1]

2932 טֻמְאָה **ṭumʾâ**, n.f. GK: 3240 [→ 2930]. uncleanness, impurity, filthiness; this can mean ceremonial impurity or a physical impurity on the body or in an object:– uncleanness [25], filthiness [7], unclean [3], uncleannesses [1]

2933 טָמָה **ṭāmâ**, v. GK: 3241 [→ 2930?]. [N] to be considered stupid; some sources: to be regarded as unclean:– make unclean [1], reputed vile [1]

2934 טָמַן **ṭāman**, v. GK: 3243 [→ 4301]. [Q] to hide; bury; [Qp] to be hidden; [N] to hide oneself; [H] to keep hidden:– hid [17], hide [5], hideth [2], hidden [1], hiding [1], laid privily [1], laid [1], laying privily [1], privily laid [1], secret [1]

2935 טֶנֶא **ṭeneʾ**, n.m. GK: 3244. basket:– basket [4]

2936 טָנַף **ṭānap**, v. GK: 3245. [P] to soil, make dirty:– defile [1]

2937 טָעָה **ṭāʿâ**, v. GK: 3246 [cf. 8582]. [H] to lead astray:– seduced [1]

2938 טָעַם **ṭāʿam**, v. GK: 3247 [→ 2940, 4303; cf. 2939]. [Q] to taste; to see, discover by experience:– taste [5], did but taste (+2938) [2], tasted [2], perceiveth [1], tasteth [1]

2939 טְעֵם **ṭᵉʿēm** (Aram.), v. GK: 10301 [→ 2941; cf. 2938]. [Pa] to eat:– make to eat [2], fed [1]

2940 טַעַם **ṭaʿam**, n.m. GK: 3248 [→ 2938; cf. 2941]. taste; discretion; discernment; decree, judgment; "to turn from discernment" means "to pretend to be insane" (1Sa 21:13):– taste [5], behaviour [2], advice [1], decree [1], discretion [1], judgment [1], reason [1], understanding [1]

2941 טַעַם **ṭaʿam** (Aram.), n.m. GK: 10302 [→ 2939, 2942; cf. 2940]. same as 2942: order, decree, command:– commandment [2], commanded [1], matter [1]

2942 טְעֵם **ṭᵉʿēm** (Aram.), n.m. GK: 10302 [→ 2941]. same as 2941: order, decree, command; tact, good sense; report, advice; with 2562 "under the command of wine" means "to be intoxicated"; with 1169, "lord of the decree" is translated "commanding officer":– decree [13], chancellor (+1169) [3], commanded (+7761) [3], commandment [2], accounts [1], regarded (+7761) [1], tasted [1], wisdom [1]

2943 טָעַן **ṭāʿan**, v. GK: 3250. [Q] to load:– lade [1]

2944 טָעַן **ṭāʿan**, v. GK: 3249. [Pu] to be pierced:– thrust through [1]

2945 טַף **ṭap**, n.m. GK: 3251 & 3252 [→ 2952]. (little) children, women and children, those (as a class) not able or barely able to march; drops:– little ones [29], children [9], little children [3], families [1]

2946 טָפַח **ṭāpaḥ**, v.den. GK: 3253 & 3254 [→ 2947, 2948, 2949, 4304]. [P] to spread out; to care for; some sources: to bear healthy children:– spanned [1], swaddled [1]

2947 טֶפַח **ṭepaḥ** or טֹפַח **ṭōpaḥ**, n.[m.]. GK: 3255 & 3257 & 3258 [→ 2946, 2948]. span, handbreadth (the width of the hand at the base of the four fingers, about three inches (8 cm); a figure of a short unit of time, a few years; eaves:– handbreadth [3], coping [1]

2948 טֹפַח **ṭōpaḥ**, n.m. GK: 3256 [→ 2947; cf. 2946]. handbreadth, span of the hand:– hand breadth [2], handbreadth [2], hand broad [1]

2949 טִפֻּחִים **ṭippuḥîm**, n.[m.]pl.abst. GK: 3259 [→ 2946]. caring for (children):– span long [1]

2950 טָפַל **ṭāpal**, v. GK: 3260 [cf. 8602]. [Q] to smear, cover:– forged [1], forgers [1], sewest up [1]

2951 טִפְסָר **ṭipsār**, n.[m.]. GK: 3261. official, clerk:– captains [1], captain [1]

2952 טָפַף **ṭāpap**, v. GK: 3262 [→ 2945]. [Q] to take little steps, trip along:– mincing [1]

2953 טְפַר **ṭᵉpar** (Aram.), n.m. GK: 10303 [cf. 6856]. finger and toe nails (of a human); claws (of an animal):– nails [2]

2954 טָפַשׁ **ṭāpaš**, v. GK: 3263. [Q] to be unfeeling, insensible:– fat [1]

2955 טָפַת **ṭāpat**, n.pr.f. GK: 3264. Taphath, "[poss.] *little child*":– Taphath [1]

2956 טָרַד **ṭārad**, v. GK: 3265 [→ 4308; cf. 2957]. [Q] to constantly drip:– continual dropping (+1812) [1], continual [1]

2957 טְרַד **ṭᵉrad** (Aram.), v. GK: 10304 [cf. 2956]. [P] to drive away (as noun) one driven away; [Peil] to be driven away:– driven [2], drive [2]

2958 טְרוֹם **ṭᵉrôm**, adv.temp. GK: 3266 [→ 2961, 2962]. before:–

2959 טָרַח **ṭāraḥ**, v. GK: 3267 [→ 2960]. [H] to load down, burden with:– wearieth [1]

2960 טֹרַח **ṭōraḥ**, n.m. GK: 3268 [→ 2959]. burden, problem, load:– cumbrance [1], trouble [1]

2961 טָרִי **ṭārî**, a. GK: 3269 [→ 2958]. fresh (bone); open, moist (sore):– new [1], putrifying [1]

2962 טֶרֶם **ṭerem**, adv.temp. & c. GK: 3270 [→ 2958]. a marker of time: before; negative: not, not yet:– before (+871.1) [35], before [11], not yet [3], before (+3808+871.1) [2], ere [2], but ere (+871.1) [1], ere (+871.1) [1], neither yet (+2050.1) [1]

2963 טָרַף **ṭārap**, v. GK: 3271 [→ 2964, 2965, 2966]. [Q] to tear, mangle; [Qp, N, Pu] to be torn (to pieces); [H] to provide (to enjoy):– torn in pieces (+2963) [4], ravening [3], teareth [3], tear [3], catch [2], tear in pieces [2], without doubt rent in pieces (+2963) [2], feed [1], prey [1], ravin [1], teareth in pieces [1], torn in pieces [1], torn [1]

2964 טֶרֶף **ṭerep**, n.m. GK: 3272 [→ 2963]. prey (food for wild animals):– prey [18], meat [3], leaves [1], spoil [1]

2965 טָרָף **ṭārāp**, a. GK: 3273 [→ 2963]. fresh-picked (leaf or vegetation):– pluckt off [1]

2966 טְרֵפָה **ṭᵉrēpâ**, n.f. GK: 3274 [→ 2963]. animal torn by wild beasts:– torn [4], that which was torn [2], ravin [1], that which is torn [1], torn in pieces [1]

2967 טַרְפְּלָי **ṭarpᵉlāy** (Aram.), n.pr.g. GK: 10305. from Tripolis (Tarpel):– Tarpelites [1]

2967.1 ִי- **-î**, p.s.com.suf. GK: 3276 [→ 447, 5105.1, 5204.1]. I, me, my:– my [3551], me [1946], mine [494], I [241], my (+3807.1) [64], mine (+3807.1) [50], mine own [30], myself [21], our [7], us [7], me (+5315) [3], mine own (+3807.1) [3], the[S] [3], Ammi (+5971) [1], for my sake [1], me (+6440) [1], mine (+5978) [1], mine (+8478) [1], my (+871.1) [1], myself (+1320) [1]; myself (+3820) [1], myself (+5315) [1], myself (+905) [1], we [1]

2967.2 ִי- **-î** (Aram.), p.suf.1.com.s. GK: 10307 [→ 5204.2; cf. 2967.1]. I, me, my:– my [32], me [22], I [10], mine [5]

2968 יָאַב **yāʾab**, v. GK: 3277 [→ 88?, 3053?; cf. 14?, 8373?]. [Q] to long for:– longed [1]

2969 יָאָה **yāʾâ**, v. GK: 3278. [Q] to be fitting, be proper:– appertain [1]

יְאוֹר **yᵉʾôr**. See 2975.

2970 יַאֲזַנְיָה **yaʾᵃzanyâ** or יַאֲזַנְיָהוּ **yaʾᵃzanyāhû**, n.pr.m. GK: 3279 & 3280. Jaazaniah, "*Yahweh listens*":– Jaazaniah [4]

2971 יָאִיר **yāʾîr**, n.pr.m. GK: 3281 [→ 2334, 2972]. Jair, "*he gives light*":– Jair [9]

2972 יָאִרִי **yāʾirî**, a.g. GK: 3285 [→ 2971]. Jairite, "*of Jair*":– Jairite [1]

2973 יָאַל **yāʾal**, v. GK: 3282 [cf. 191]. [N] to become foolish, act foolish:– done foolishly [1], dote [1], foolish [1], fools [1]

2974 יָאַל **yāʾal**, v. GK: 3283 [cf. 193, 4136]. [H] to begin; to determine; be intent upon; to agree to; to be content, be pleased; to be bold:– content [7], please [3], would [3], taken upon [2], assayed [1], began [1], pleased [1], willingly [1]

2975 יְאֹר **yᵉʾōr**, n.m. GK: 3284. river, stream, the Nile river; likely the Tigris river in Daniel:– river [35], rivers [15], flood [6], brooks [5], river's [3], streams [1]

2976 יָאַשׁ **yāʾaš**, v. GK: 3286. [N] to be despairing of, be without hope, give up; [P] to let despair:– no hope [3], cause to despair [1], despair [1], desperate [1]

2977 יֹאשִׁיָּה **yōʾšiyyâ** or יֹאשִׁיָּהוּ **yōʾšiyyāhû**, n.pr.m. GK: 3287 & 3288 [cf. 3068]. Josiah, "*let* or *may Yahweh give*":– Josiah [53]

2978 יִאתוֹן **yiʾtôn** or אִיתוֹן **ʾîtôn**, n.m. GK: 3289 & 415 [→ 857]. entrance:– entrance [1]

2979 יְאָתְרַי **yᵉʾātᵉray**, n.pr.m. GK: 3290. Jeatherai:– Jeaterai [1]

2980 יָבַב **yābab**, v. GK: 3291 [→ 3103]. [P] to cry out, lament:– cried [1]

2981 יְבוּל **yᵉbûl**, n.m. GK: 3292 [→ 2986]. crops, produce, harvest:– increase [10], fruit [3]

2982 יְבוּס **yᵉbûs**, n.pr.loc. GK: 3293 [→ 2983]. Jebus:– Jebus [4]

2983 יְבוּסִי **yᵉbûsî**, a.g. GK: 3294 [→ 2982]. Jebusite, "*of Jebus*":– Jebusites [25], Jebusite [14], Jebusi [2]

2984 יִבְחָר **yibḥār**, n.pr.m. GK: 3295 [→ 977]. Ibhar, "*he chooses*":– Ibhar [3]

2985 יָבִין **yābîn**, n.pr.m. GK: 3296 [→ 995]. Jabin, "*perceptive*":– Jabin [7], Jabin's [1]

יָבִישׁ **yābêš**. See 3003.

2986 יָבַל **yābal**, v. GK: 3297 [→ 58, 179, 2981, 2988, 2989, 3105; cf. 2987]. [H] to bring, take (a gift); [Ho] to be brought, be led, be carried off:– brought [6], bring [5], carried [3], brought forth [1], carry [1], lead [1], led forth [1]

2987 יְבַל **yᵉbal** (Aram.), v. GK: 10308 [cf. 2986]. [H] to bring, take:– brought [2], carry [1]

יֹבֵל **yōbēl**. See 3104.

2988 יָבָל **yābāl**, n.[m.]. GK: 3298 [→ 2986]. stream, watercourse:– courses [1], streams [1]

2989 יָבָל **yābāl**, n.pr.m. GK: 3299 [→ 2986]. Jabal:– Jabal [1]

יֹבֵל **yōbēl**. See 3104.

2990 יַבֶּלֶת **yabbelet**, a. GK: 3301 [→ 3104]. wart; some sources: running sore:– having a wen [1]

2991 יִבְלְעָם **yiblᵉʿām**, n.pr.loc. GK: 3300 [→ 1104?]. Ibleam:– Ibleam [3]

2992 יָבַם **yābam**, v.den. GK: 3302 [→ 2993]. [P] to fulfill the procreational duty of the brother-in-law:– marry [1], perform the duty of a husband's brother [1], perform the duty of husband's brother [1]

2993 יָבָם **yābām**, n.m. GK: 3303 [→ 2992, 2994]. husband's brother:– husband's brother [2]

2994 יְבָמָה **yᵉbāmâ**, n.f. GK: 3304 [→ 2993]. brother's widow; sister-in-law, husband's brother's widow:– brother's wife [3], sister in law [2]

2995 יַבְנְאֵל **yabnᵉʾēl**, n.pr.loc. GK: 3305 [→ 1129+410; cf. 2996]. Jabneel, "*God [El] will build*":– Jabneel [2]

2996 יַבְנֵה **yabnēh**, n.pr.loc. GK: 3306 [cf. 2995]. Jabneh:– Jabneh [1]

2997 יִבְנְיָה **yibnᵉyâ**, n.pr.m. GK: 3307 [→ 1129+3068]. Ibneiah, "*Yahweh built*":– Ibneiah [1]

2998 יִבְנִיָּה **yibniyyâ**, n.pr.m. GK: 3308 [→ 1129+3068]. Ibnijah, "*Yahweh built*":– Ibnijah [1]

2999 יַבֹּק **yabbōq**, n.pr.loc. GK: 3309 [→ 1238? *or* 79?]. Jabbok, "*flowing* or *wrestling*":– Jabbok [7]

3000 יְבֶרֶכְיָהוּ **yᵉberekyāhû**, n.pr.m. GK: 3310 [→ 1288+3068]. Jeberekiah, "*Yahweh blesses*":– Jeberechiah [1]

3001 יָבֵשׁ **yābēš**, v. GK: 3312 [→ 3002, 3003, 3004, 3006]. [Q] to dry up, be dry, be withered, be shriveled up; [P] to make wither, dry up; [H] to make wither, dry up:– dried up [18], withered [9], wither [7], dry up [6], withereth [5], dry [3], clean dried up (+3001) [2], dried [2], utterly wither (+3001) [2], withered away [2], ashamed [1], confounded [1], driedst up [1], drieth up [1], drieth [1], make dry [1], maketh dry [1]

3002 יָבֵשׁ ***yābēš***, a.vbl. *or* v.ptcp. GK: 3313 [→ 3001]. dry, withered, by extension: a paralyzed person (whose limbs have a shriveled appearance):– dry [7], dried away [1], dried [1]

3003 יָבֵשׁ ***yābēš***, n.pr.m. & loc. GK: 3314 & 3315 & 3316 [→ 3001+1568]. Jabesh, "*dry*":– Jabesh-gilead [12], Jabesh [12]

3004 יַבָּשָׁה ***yabbāšâ***, n.f. GK: 3317 [→ 3001; cf. 3007]. dry ground, dry land (in contrast to bodies of water):– dry [13], land [1]

3005 יִבְשָׂם ***yibśām***, n.pr.m. GK: 3311 [→ 1313]. Ibsam, "*fragrance*":– Jibsam [1]

3006 יַבֶּשֶׁת ***yabbešet***, n.f. GK: 3318 [→ 3001]. dry ground, dry land:– dry [2]

3007 יַבְּשָׁה ***yabbᵉšâ*** (Aram.), n.f. GK: 10309 [cf. 3004]. earth; dry land (in contrast to the sea):– earth [1]

3008 יִגְאָל ***yig'āl***, n.pr.m. GK: 3319 [→ 1350]. Igal, "*he redeems*":– Igal [2], Igeal [1]

3009 יָגַב ***yāgab***, v. GK: 3320 [→ 3010]. [Q] to work a field, do farm work:– husbandmen [2]

3010 יָגֵב ***yāgēb***, n.m. GK: 3321 [→ 3009]. field:– fields [1]

3011 יָגְבְּהָה ***yogbᵉhâ***, n.pr.loc. GK: 3322 [→ 1361]. Jogbehah, "*height*":– Jogbehah [2]

3012 יִגְדַּלְיָהוּ ***yigdalyāhû***, n.pr.m. GK: 3323 [→ 1431+3068]. Igdaliah, "*Yahweh is great*":– Igdaliah [1]

3013 יָגָה ***yāgâ***, v. GK: 3324 [→ 3015, 8424; cf. 3014]. [N] to be grieved; [P] to bring grief; [H] to torment, bring grief:– afflicted [3], afflict [1], cause grief [1], grieve [1], sorrowful [1], vex [1]

3014 יָגָה ***yāgâ***, v. GK: 3325 [cf. 1898, 3013]. [H] to remove:– removed [1]

3015 יָגוֹן ***yāgôn***, n.[m.]. GK: 3326 [→ 3013]. sorrow, anguish, grief:– sorrow [12], grief [2]

3016 יָגוֹר ***yāgôr***, a.vbl. GK: 3328 [→ 3025]. fearing, filled with fear:– afraid [1], fearest [1]

3017 יָגוּר ***yāgûr***, n.pr.loc. GK: 3327 [cf. 1485]. Jagur:– Jagur [1]

3018 יְגִיעַ ***yᵉgîa'***, n.m. GK: 3330 [→ 3021]. labor, heavy work; the result of labor: produce, gain:– labour [12], labours [3], work [1]

3019 יָגִיעַ ***yāgîa'***, a. GK: 3329 [→ 3021]. weary, exhausted:– weary (+3581) [1]

3020 יָגְלִי ***yoglî***, n.pr.m. GK: 3332. Jogli, "[perhaps] *may God reveal*":– Jogli [1]

3021 יָגַע ***yāga'***, v. GK: 3333 [→ 3019, 3018, 3024, 3022, 3023]. [Q] to labor, toil, be weary; [P] to make weary; [H] to make weary:– labour [7], weary [7], wearied [5], laboured [4], fainted [1], make to labour [1], wearieth [1]

3022 יָגָע ***yāgā'***, n.[m.]. GK: 3334 [→ 3021]. what is toiled for, the produce of labor:– that which laboured for [1]

3023 יָגֵעַ ***yāgēa'***, a. GK: 3335 [→ 3021]. worn out, weary, wearisome:– weary [2], full of labour [1]

3024 יְגִיעָה ***yᵉgî'â***, n.f. GK: 3331 [→ 3021]. weariness:– weariness [1]

3025 יָגֹר ***yāgōr***, v. GK: 3336 [→ 3016; cf. 1481]. [Q] to fear, dread:– afraid [4], fear [1]

3026 יְגַר שָׂהֲדוּתָא ***yᵉgar śāhᵃdûtā'***, n.[m.] & n.m. GK: 3337. Jegar Sahadutha, the Aramaic name of a stone monument, "witness heap":– Jegar-sahadutha [1]

3027 יָד ***yād***, n.f. & m. GK: 3338 [cf. 3028]. hand, by extension: arm, finger; fig. of control, power, strength, direction, care:– hand [1087], hands [271], by (+871.1) [42], next unto (+5921) [13], power [11], with (+871.1) [10], place [8], tenons [6], coast [5], consecrate (+4390) [5], consecrated (+853+4390) [5], consecrate (+853+4390) [4], custody [4], means [4], next to (+5921) [4], parts [4], side [4], stays [4], beside (+5921) [3], large (+7342) [3], next (+5921) [3], able to get (+5381) [2], armholes (+679) [2], as able [2], axletrees [2], because of (+871.1) [2], by (+5921) [2], consecrated (+4390) [2], dominion [2], force [2], from (+4480) [2], ledges [2], lefthanded (+334+3225) [2], ministry [2], near (+5921) [2], of (+4480) [2], order [2], paw [2], service [2], state [2], thumbs (+931) [2], times [2], to (+871.1) [2], wide (+7342) [2], ability (+5381) [1], able (+1767+4672) [1], able (+1767+5381+3509.1) [1], able (+4979) [1], able (+5381) [1], able to bring (+1767+4672) [1], able to bring (+5381) [1], about (+3807.1) [1], aided (+853+2388) [1], as ordained by (+5921) [1], at (+3807.1) [1], beside (+3807.1) [1], borders [1], border [1], bounty [1], broad (+7342) [1], brokenhanded (+7667) [1], by side [1], by [1], can get (+5381) [1], charge [1], coasts [1], creditor (+1167+4874) [1], dominion (+4475) [1], drew with full strength (+4390+871.1) [1], exaction of debt (+4853) [1], fallen in decay (+4131) [1], fellowship (+8667) [1], for (+871.1) [1], get (+5381) [1], give (+5414+871.1) [1], hand is able to get (+5381) [1], handed [1], handstaves (+4731) [1], handywork (+4639) [1], he (+2050.2) [1], help (+2388+871.1) [1], in (+871.1) [1], labour [1], large enough (+7342) [1], near (+413) [1], occasion serve (+4672) [1], occupied (+5503) [1], of (+871.1) [1], ordained by (+5921) [1], ordinance [1], own [1], places [1], power (+410) [1], power (+871.1) [1], presumptuously (+7311+871.1) [1], sore [1], stroke [1], sware (+5375) [1], swear (+5375) [1], sworn (+3678+5921) [1], sworn [1], thee (+3509.2) [1], themselves [1], thou (+3509.2) [1], through (+871.1) [1], throwing [1], under (+871.1) [1], wait on [1], wax rich (+5381) [1], way side (+4570) [1], wayside (+1870) [1], where [1], work [1], yield (+5414) [1]

3028 יַד ***yad*** (Aram.), n.f. GK: 10311 [cf. 3027]. hand (of a human), paw (of an animal); fig., power, control, action:– hand [12], hands [4], power [1]

3029 יְדָה ***yᵉdâ*** (Aram.), v. GK: 10312 [cf. 3034]. [H] to give thanks, confess praise:– gave thanks [1], thank [1]

3030 יִדְאֲלָה ***yid'ᵃlâ***, n.pr.loc. GK: 3339. Idalah:– Idalah [1]

3031 יִדְבָּשׁ ***yidbāš***, n.pr.m. GK: 3340 [→ 1706]. Idbash, "*honey*":– Idbash [1]

3032 יָדַד ***yādad***, v. GK: 3341 [cf. 3034]. [Q] to cast (lots for decision making):– cast [3]

3033 יְדִדוּת ***yᵉdidût***, n.f. GK: 3342 [→ 3039]. loved one, beloved:– dearly beloved [1]

3034 יָדָה ***yādâ***, v. GK: 3343 & 3344 [→ 1935, 1937, 1938, 1939, 1960, 8426; cf. 3032; cf. 3029]. [Q] to shoot (a bow); [P] to throw (down); [H] to express praise, give thanks, extol, make a public confession, make an admission; to praise is to speak of the excellence of someone or something; to give thanks has a focus on the gratitude of the speaker:– praise [52], give thanks [31], confess [11], thank [4], confessed [3], thanksgiving [2], cast out [1], cast [1], confesseth [1], confessing [1], giving thanks [1], made confession [1], making confession [1], praised [1], shoot [1], thankful [1], thanking [1]

3035 יִדּוֹ ***yiddô*** or יַדַּי ***yadday***, n.pr.m. GK: 3345 & 3346 & 3350 [→ 3039?]. Iddo, Jaddai, "[prob.] *Yahweh has adorned*":– Iddo [1], Jadau [1]

3036 יָדוֹן ***yādôn***, n.pr.m. GK: 3347. Jadon, "*frail one* or *Yahweh rules*":– Jadon [1]

3037 יַדּוּעַ ***yaddûa'***, n.pr.m. GK: 3348 [→ 3045]. Jaddua, "*one known*":– Jaddua [3]

3038 יְדוּתוּן ***yᵉdûtûn*** or יְדִיתוּן ***yᵉdîtûn***, n.pr.m. GK: 3349 & 3357. Jeduthun:– Jeduthun [17]

3039 יְדִיד ***yādîd***, a. GK: 3351 & 3353 [→ 3033, 3035?, 3040, 3041]. lovely, beloved, love song (referring to a wedding song):– beloved [5], well-beloved [2], amiable [1], loves [1]

3040 יְדִידָה ***yᵉdîdâ***, n.pr.f. GK: 3352 [→ 3039]. Jedidah, "*beloved; lovely, beloved*":– Jedidah [1]

3041 יְדִידְיָה ***yᵉdîdᵉyāh***, n.pr.m. GK: 3354 [→ 3039+3068]. Jedidiah, "*beloved of Yahweh*":– Jedidiah [1]

3042 יְדָיָה ***yᵉdāyâ***, n.pr.m. GK: 3355. Jedaiah, "*Yahweh has favored* or *Yahweh knows*":– Jedaiah [2]

3043 יְדִיעֲאֵל ***yᵉdî'ᵃ'ēl***, n.pr.m. GK: 3356 [→ 3045+410]. Jediael, "*known of God [El]*":– Jediael [6]

3044 יִדְלָף ***yidlāp***, n.pr.m. GK: 3358 [→ 1811]. Jidlaph, "*he weeps*":– Jidlaph [1]

3045 יָדַע ***yāda'***, v. GK: 3359 [→ 1843, 1844, 1847, 3037, 3049, 4093, 4129, 4130; cf. 3046 (also used with compound proper names)]. [Q] to know, recognize, understand; to have sexual relations; [Qp] to be respected; [N] to be known, make oneself known; [P] to cause to know; [Pu] to be well known; [H] to show, teach, make known; [Ho] to be made aware; [Ht] to make oneself known; this can range in meaning from the mere acquisition and understaning of information to intimacy in relationship, including sexual relations:– know [404], knew [83], known [80], knowest [66], knoweth [58], make known [14], shew [12], perceived [11], knowledge [10], made known [8], tell [8], wist [7], acquaintance [6], certainly know (+3045) [6], perceive [6], wot [6], acknowledge [5], cause to know [5], knewest [5], make know [5], shewed [5], teach [5], consider [4], cunning [4], know certainly (+3045) [4], know for certain (+3045) [4], sure [4], understood [4], declared [3], declare [3], ignorant (+3808) [3], learned (+5612) [3], make to know [3], mark [3], skill [3], taught [3], understand [3], aware [2], certainly knoweth (+3045) [2], come to knowledge [2], considereth [2], could [2], diligent to know (+3045) [2], discern [2], endued [2], feel [2], knew certainly (+3045) [2], know assuredly (+3045) [2], know for a certain (+3045) [2], know for a certainty (+3045) [2], know of a surety (+3045) [2], knowing [2], skilful [2], takest knowledge [2], wit [2], acknowledged [1], acquainted with [1], advise [1], answer [1], appointed [1], can skill [1], cannot (+3808) [1], cause to discern [1], caused to know [1], come to understanding (+998) [1], comprehend [1], discerneth [1], discovered [1], familiar friends [1], famous [1], felt [1], given knowledge [1], had knowledge [1], had respect unto [1], had understanding (+998) [1], hast [1], hath knowledge (+1847) [1], hath [1], have knowledge (+1847) [1], have knowledge [1], have [1], having knowledge [1], instructed [1], kinsfolks [1], know well [1], madest known [1], make to be known [1], making known [1], perceivest [1], privy [1], prognosticators [1], regardeth [1], take knowledge [1], unawares (+3808) [1], understand (+995) [1], will [1], wotteth [1]

3046 יְדַע ***yᵉda'*** (Aram.), v. GK: 10313 [→ 4486; cf. 3045]. [P] to know, understand, acknowledge; [Pp] to be known; [H] to make known, tell, inform:– know [13], make known [12], known [5], made known [5], certify [3], knew [2], maketh known [2], certified [1], knewest [1], knoweth [1], made know [1], teach [1]

3047 יָדָע ***yādā'***, n.pr.m. GK: 3360. Jada, "*shrewd one; [God] has cared*":– Jada [2]

3048 יְדַעְיָה ***yᵉda'yâ***, n.pr.m. GK: 3361 [→ 3045+3068]. Jedaiah, "*Yahweh has favored* or *Yahweh knows*":– Jedaiah [11]

3049 יִדְּעֹנִי ***yiddᵉ'ōnî***, n.m. GK: 3362 [→ 3045]. spiritist, soothsayer:– wizards [9], wizard [2]

3050 יָהּ ***yāh***, n.pr.m. GK: 3363 [→ 3068]. LORD (Yahweh):– the LORD* [45], LORD* [3], Jah [1]

3051 יָהַב ***yāhab***, v. GK: 2035 & 3364 [cf. 3052]. [Q] to give; (interj.) come!, give!, put!, ascribe!:– give [24], go to [4], bring [2], ascribe [1], come on [1], set [1], take [1]

3052 יְהַב ***yᵉhab*** (Aram.), v. GK: 10314 [cf. 5415; cf. 3051]. [P] to give; [Pp] to be given; [Htpe] to be given as payment; be entrusted:– given [16], gave [4], give [2], delivered [1], giveth [1], laid [1], paid [1], were [1], yielded [1]

Heb

3053 יְהָב ***yᵉhāb***, n.[m.]. GK: 3365 [→ 2968?]. care, burden:– burden [1]

3054 יָהַד ***yāhad***, v.den. GK: 3366 [→ 3064; cf. 3063]. [Ht] to become a Jew, this can mean to join the Jewish faith or simply to act like a Jew:– became Jews [1]

3055 יְהֻד ***yᵉhûd***, n.pr.loc. GK: 3372. Jehud, "*declare*":– Jehud [1]

3056 יַהְדַּי ***yāhdāy***, n.pr.m. GK: 3367. Jahdai, "*Yahweh lead*":– Jahdai [1]

3057 יְהֻדִיָּה ***yᵉhudiyyâ***, a.g. GK: 3368 [→ 3063]. Jewish, Judean:– Jehudijah [1]

3058 יֵהוּא ***yēhû'***, n.pr.m. GK: 3369 [→ 3068+1931]. Jehu, "*Yahweh is he*":– Jehu [58]

3059 יְהוֹאָחָז ***yᵉhô'āḥāz***, n.pr.m. GK: 3370 [→ 3068+270]. Jehoahaz, "*Yahweh holds*":– Jehoahaz [20]

3060 יְהוֹאָשׁ ***yᵉhô'āš***, n.pr.m. GK: 3371 [→ 3068+376]. Joash; Jehoash, "*Yahweh bestows; man of Yahweh*":– Jehoash [17]

3061 יְהוּד ***yᵉhûd*** (Aram.), n.pr.loc. GK: 10315 [→ 3062; cf. 3063]. Judah, "*praised*":– Judah [5], Jewry [1], Judea [1]

3062 יְהוּדַי ***yᵉhûdāy*** (Aram.), n.g. GK: 10316 [→ 3061; cf. 3064]. Jew:– Jews [10]

3063 יְהוּדָה ***yᵉhûdâ***, n.pr.m. & loc. GK: 3373 [→ 3054, 3057, 3064, 3065, 3066, 3067; cf. 3061]. Judah, of Judah, Judean, "*praised*":– Judah [804], Beth-lehem-judah (+1035) [10], Judah's [4]

3064 יְהוּדִי ***yᵉhûdî***, a.g. GK: 3374 [→ 3054, 3065, 3067; cf. 3063; cf. 3062]. (person) of Judah, Judean, Jew, Jewish, "*of Judah*":– Jews [63], Jew [10], Jews' [2], Judah [1]

3065 יְהוּדִי ***yᵉhûdî***, n.pr.m. GK: 3375 [→ 3064; cf. 3063]. Jehudi, Yaudi, "*of Judah*":– Jehudi [4]

3066 יְהוּדִית ***yᵉhûdît***, a.g.f. (used as adv.). GK: 3376 [→ 3063]. in Hebrew (language), in the language of Judah:– in the Jews' language [5], in the Jews' speech [1]

3067 יְהוּדִית ***yᵉhûdît***, n.pr.f. GK: 3377 [→ 3064; cf. 3063]. Judith, "*Jewess* or *Judahite*":– Judith [1]

3068 יהוה ***yhwh*** or יְהוִה ***yehwih***, n.pr.m. GK: 3378 [→ 3050, 3069 (also used with compound proper names)]. LORD (Yahweh), the proper name of the one true God; knowledge and use of the name implies personal or covenant relationship; the name pictures God as the one who exists and/or causes existence:– the LORD* [6043], LORD* [365], GOD* [309], the LORD'S* [79], the LORD'S* (+3807.1) [28], Jehovah [4], LORD'S* [1], he[S] [1]

3069 יְהוִה ***yehwih***, n.pr.m. GK: 3378 [→ 3068]. same as 3068: LORD (Yahweh), with vowels points used in combination with 136:–

3070 יהוה יִרְאֶה ***yhwh yir'eh***, n.pr.loc. GK: 3378 + 8011 [→ 3068+7200]. Yahweh yireh, "The LORD (Yahweh) will see" (3068 + 7200):– Jehovah-jireh [1]

3071 יהוה נִסִּי ***yhwh nissî***, n.pr.loc. GK: 3378 + 5812 + 3276 [→ 3068+5251+2967.1]. "LORD (Yahweh) is my banner" (3068 + 5251 + 2967.1):– Jehovah-nissi [1]

3072 יהוה צִדְקֵנוּ ***yhwh ṣidqēnû***, n.pr.m. GK: 3378 + 7406 + 5646 [→ 3068+6664+5105.1]. "LORD (Yahweh) is our righteousness" (3068 + 6664 + 5105.1):–

3073 יהוה שָׁלוֹם ***yhwh šālôm***, n.pr.loc. GK: 3378 + 8934 [→ 3068+7965]. "LORD (Yahweh) is peace" (3068 + 7965):– Jehovah-shalom [1]

3074 יהוה שָׁמָּה ***yhwh šāmmâ***, n.pr.loc. GK: 3378 + 9004 + 2025 [→ 3068+8033+1886.5]. "LORD (Yahweh) is there" (3068 + 8033 + 1886.5):–

3075 יְהוֹזָבָד ***y^e^hôzābād***, n.pr.m. GK: 3379 [→ 3068+2064]. Jehozabad, "*Yahweh endows*":– Jehozabad [4]

3076 יְהוֹחָנָן ***y^e^hôḥānān***, n.pr.m. GK: 3380 [→ 3068+2603]. Jehohanan, "*Yahweh has been gracious*":– Jehohanan [6], Johanan [3]

3077 יְהוֹיָדָע ***y^e^hôyādā'***, n.pr.m. GK: 3381 [→ 3068+3045]. Jehoiada, "*Yahweh has known*":– Jehoiada [51]

3078 יְהוֹיָכִין ***y^e^hôyākîn***, n.pr.m. GK: 3382 [→ 3204, 3659]. Jehoiachin, "*Yahweh supports*":– Jehoiachin [10]

3079 יְהוֹיָקִים ***y^e^hôyāqîm***, n.pr.m. GK: 3383 [→ 3068+6965]. Jehoiakim, "*Yahweh lifts up, establishes*":– Jehoiakim [37]

3080 יְהוֹיָרִיב ***y^e^hôyārîb***, n.pr.m. GK: 3384 [→ 3068+7378]. Jehoiarib, "*Yahweh argues [for me]*":– Jehoiarib [2]

3081 יְהוּכַל ***y^e^hûkal***, n.pr.m. GK: 3385 [→ 3068+3201; cf. 3116]. Jehucal, "*Yahweh is capable*":– Jehucal [1]

3082 יְהוֹנָדָב ***y^e^hônādāb***, n.pr.m. GK: 3386 [→ 3068+5068]. Jonadab; Jehonadab, "*Yahweh is generous, noble*":– Jonadab [5], Jehonadab [3]

3083 יְהוֹנָתָן ***y^e^hônātān***, n.pr.m. GK: 3387 [→ 3068+5414]. Jonathan; Jehonathan, "*gift of Yahweh*":– Jonathan [76], Jehonathan [3], Jonathan's [3]

3084 יְהוֹסֵף ***y^e^hôsēp***, n.pr.m. GK: 3388 [cf. 3254]. Joseph, "*he will add*":– Joseph [1]

3085 יְהוֹעַדָּה ***y^e^hô'addâ***, n.pr.m. GK: 3389. Jehoaddah:– Jehoadah [2]

3086 יְהוֹעַדִּין ***y^e^hô'addîn*** or יְהוֹעַדָּן ***y^e^hô'addān***, n.pr.f. GK: 3390 & 3391. Jehoaddin, Jehoaddan, "[prob.] *Yahweh is delight*":– Jehoaddan [2]

3087 יְהוֹצָדָק ***y^e^hôṣādāq***, n.pr.m. GK: 3392 [→ 3068+6663; cf. 3136]. Jehozadak, "*Yahweh is just*":– Josedech [6], Jehozadak [2]

3088 יְהוֹרָם ***y^e^hôrām***, n.pr.m. GK: 3393 [→ 3068+7311]. Joram; Jehoram, "*Yahweh exalts*":– Jehoram [23], Joram [6]

3089 יְהוֹשֶׁבַע ***y^e^hôšeba'***, n.pr.f. GK: 3394 [→ 3068; cf. 7652]. Jehosheba, "*Yahweh is an oath; Yahweh gives plenty, satisfies*":– Jehosheba [1]

3090 יְהוֹשַׁבְעַת ***y^e^hôšab'at***, n.pr.f. GK: 3395 [→ 3068; cf. 7652]. Jehosheba, "*Yahweh is an oath; Yahweh gives plenty, satisfies*":– Jehoshabeath [2]

3091 יְהוֹשֻׁעַ ***y^e^hôšua'***, n.pr.m. GK: 3397 [→ 3068+7768]. Joshua, "*Yahweh saves*":– Joshua [216], Jehoshua [2]

3092 יְהוֹשָׁפָט ***y^e^hôšāpāṭ***, n.pr.m. & loc. GK: 3398 & 3399 [→ 3068+8199]. Jehoshaphat, "*Yahweh has judged*":– Jehoshaphat [84]

3093 יָהִיר ***yāhîr***, a. GK: 3400. arrogant, haughty:– haughty [1], proud [1]

3094 יְהַלֶּלְאֵל ***y^e^hallel'ēl***, n.pr.[m.]. GK: 3401 [→ 3094+410]. Jehallelel, "*he shall praise God [El]; God [El] shines forth*":– Jehaleleel [1], Jehalelel [1]

3095 יַהֲלֹם ***yāh^a^lōm***, n.[m.]. GK: 3402. emerald (precious stone, exact identification uncertain):– diamond [3]

3096 יַהַץ ***yahaṣ*** or יַהְצָה ***yahṣâ***, n.pr.loc. GK: 3403 & 3404. Jahaz, Jahzah, "[perhaps] *a trodden* or *open place*":– Jahaz [5], Jahazah [3], Jahzah [1]

3097 יוֹאָב ***yô'āb***, n.pr.m. GK: 3405 [→ 5854]. Joab, "*Yahweh is father*":– Joab [138], Joab's [8]

3098 יוֹאָח ***yô'āḥ***, n.pr.m. GK: 3406 [→ 3068+251]. Joah, "*Yahweh is brother*":– Joah [11]

3099 יוֹאָחָז ***yô'āḥāz***, n.pr.m. GK: 3407 [→ 3068+270]. Jehoahaz; Joahaz, "*Yahweh grips, holds*":– Jehoahaz [3], Joahaz [1]

3100 יוֹאֵל ***yô'ēl***, n.pr.m. GK: 3408 [→ 3068+410]. Joel, "*Yahweh is God [El]*":– Joel [19]

3101 יוֹאָשׁ ***yô'āš***, n.pr.m. GK: 3409 [→ 3068+376]. Joash; Jehoash:– Joash [47]

3102 יוֹב ***yôb***, n.pr.m. GK: 3410. Job:– Job [1]

3103 יוֹבָב ***yôbāb***, n.pr.m. GK: 3411 & 3412 [→ 2980]. Jobab, "*howl*":– Jobab [9]

3104 יוֹבֵל ***yôbēl***, n.m. GK: 3413 [→ 2990]. ram's horn; (blowing of ram's horn) jubilee, (Year of) Jubilee:– jubile [21], rams' horns [4], ram's [1], trumpet [1]

3105 יוּבַל ***yûbal***, n.[m.]. GK: 3414 [→ 2986]. stream, watercourse:– river [1]

3106 יוּבַל ***yûbal***, n.pr.m. GK: 3415. Jubal:– Jubal [1]

3107 יוֹזָבָד ***yôzābād***, n.pr.m. GK: 3416 [→ 3068+2064]. Jozabad, "*Yahweh bestowed*":– Jozabad [9], Josabad [1]

3108 יוֹזָכָר ***yôzākār***, n.pr.m. GK: 3417. Jozakar:– Jozachar [1]

3109 יוֹחָא ***yôḥā'***, n.pr.m. GK: 3418. Joha:– Joha [2]

3110 יוֹחָנָן ***yôḥānān***, n.pr.m. GK: 3419 [→ 3068+2603]. Johanan, "*Yahweh is gracious*":– Johanan [24]

יוּטָה ***yûṭâ***. See 3194.

3111 יוֹיָדָע ***yôyādā'***, n.pr.m. GK: 3421 [→ 3068+3045]. Joiada, "*Yahweh knows*":– Joiada [4], Jehoiada [1]

3112 יוֹיָכִין ***yôyākîn***, n.pr.m. GK: 3422 [→ 3068+3559]. Jehoiachin, "*Yahweh supports*":– Jehoiachin's [1]

3113 יוֹיָקִים ***yôyāqîm***, n.pr.m. GK: 3423 [→ 3068+6965]. Joiakim, "*Yahweh lifts up*":– Joiakim [4]

3114 יוֹיָרִיב ***yôyārîb***, n.pr.m. GK: 3424 [→ 3068+7378]. Joiarib, "*Yahweh contends, pleads [your case]*":– Joiarib [5]

3115 יוֹכֶבֶד ***yôkebed***, n.pr.f. GK: 3425 [→ 3068+3513]. Jochebed, "*Yahweh is glorious*":– Jochebed [2]

3116 יוּכַל ***yûkal***, n.pr.m. GK: 3426 [cf. 3081]. Jehucal, "*Yahweh is capable*":– Jucal [1]

3117 יוֹם ***yôm***, n.m. GK: 3427 & 3428 [→ 3119; cf. 3118]. day (24 hours), daytime (in contrast to night); by extension: an indefinite period of time, an era with a certain characteristic, such as "the day of the LORD" and the prophetic "on that day"; storm, wind; breath:– day [1217], days [666], time [54], to day (+1886.1) [50], chronicles (+1697) [33], for ever (+3605+1886.1) [15], days' [13], daily (+3117) [12], every day (+3117+871.1) [12], daily (+3605+1886.1) [11], daily (+3117+871.1) [10], when (+871.1) [10], continually (+3605+1886.1) [9], while [6], yearly (+3117+4480+1886.5) [6], year [6], age [5], as long as (+3605) [5], chronicles (+1697+1886.1) [5], daily (+1886.1+3807.1) [5], day's [5], two full years (+8141) [5], years [5], alway (+3605+1886.1) [4], two days [4], always (+3605+1886.1) [3], ever (+3605+1886.1) [3], life [3], season [3], space [3], times [3], whole [3], yearly [3], as long as (+834+3605+1886.1) [2], at all times (+3117+871.1) [2], at other times (+3117+871.1) [2], daily (+3117+2050.1) [2], daily [2], day by day (+1886.1+3807.1) [2], each day (+3117) [2], ever (+753) [2], every day (+3117+3605+2050.1) [2], every day's (+3117+871.1) [2], every sabbath (+3117+7676+7676+871.1+871.1+1886.1+1886.1) [2], every year's (+3117+3807.1) [2], for every day (+3117+871.1) [2], full month (+3391) [2], full year [2], in process of time (+3117+4480+3807.1) [2], live [2], now (+1886.1) [2], now [2], perpetually (+3605+1886.1) [2], prolong life (+3117+5921) [2], time (+4557) [2], upon day (+3117+871.1) [2], afternoon (+5186+1886.1) [1], ago [1], always (+3605) [1], any time [1], as long as (+3605+1886.1) [1], as long as (+871.1) [1], birthday (+3205) [1], continually (+3605) [1], continuance [1], daily (+259+3807.1) [1], daily (+3605+871.1) [1], day (+1886.1) [1], each[S] [1], elder (+2205+3807.1) [1], elder [1], everlasting (+5769) [1], evermore (+3605+1886.1) [1], for evermore (+3605+1886.1) [1], full weeks (+7620) [1], how long (+4100+8141+3509.1) [1], in process of time (+4480) [1], in process of time (+7235+1886.1) [1], in trouble (+7186) [1], livest[S] [1], midday (+4276+1886.1) [1], now a days (+1886.1) [1], old (+2416+8141) [1], old [1], outlived (+310+748) [1], overlived (+310+748) [1], presently (+1886.1+3509.1) [1], presently (+871.1+1886.1) [1], process of time (+7227+1886.1+1886.1) [1], remaineth [1], sabbath (+7676) [1], since (+4480) [1], since (+4480+1886.1+3807.1) [1], so long as (+3605+1886.1) [1], so long as (+4480) [1], then (+1886.1) [1], to morrow (+4279) [1], two[S] [1], weather [1], when [1], while (+1886.1+3509.1) [1], while (+4480) [1], whole age (+2416+8141) [1], whole weeks (+7620) [1], within a while after (+4480) [1], yesterday (+865) [1], young (+6810+3807.1) [1], younger (+6810) [1]

3118 יוֹם ***yôm*** (Aram.), n.m. GK: 10317 [cf. 3117]. a period of time which is indefinite in scope: it can range widely in meaning from "daytime" (in contrast to night); "day," a period of time approximately 24 hours; to longer periods (seasons or years). The title "Ancient of Days" is a title of God as old (eternal), emphasizing wisdom and power:– days [9], day [5], time [2]

3119 יוֹמָם ***yômām***, subst. & adv. GK: 3429 [→ 3117]. day; in the daytime, by day:– day [24], by day [17], in daytime [4], daytime [3], daily [2], by day time [1]

3120 יָוָן ***yāwān***, n.pr.g. GK: 3430 [→ 3125]. Javan; Greeks; Greece:– Javan [7], Grecia [3], Greece [1]

3121 יָוֵן ***yāwēn***, n.[m.]. GK: 3431. mire, mud, sediment:– mire [1], miry [1]

3122 יוֹנָדָב ***yônādāb***, n.pr.m. GK: 3432 [→ 3068+5068]. Jonadab, "*Yahweh is generous, noble*":– Jonadab [7]

3123 יוֹנָה ***yônâ***, n.f. GK: 3433 [→ 1686, 3124; cf. 578, 2755]. dove; pigeon:– dove [14], pigeons [9], doves [5], doves' [2], pigeon [1]

3124 יוֹנָה ***yônâ***, n.pr.m. GK: 3434 [→ 3123]. Jonah, "*dove*":– Jonah [19]

3125 יְוָנִי ***y^e^wānî***, a.g. GK: 3436 [→ 3120]. Javanite = Greek:– Grecians (+1121) [1]

3126 יוֹנֵק ***yônēq***, n.m. GK: 3437 [→ 3243]. infant, one nursing; tender shoot:– tender plant [1]

3127 יוֹנֶקֶת ***yôneqet***, n.f. GK: 3438 [→ 3243]. new shoot, young shoot (of a plant):– branches [3], branch [1], tender branch [1], young twigs [1]

3128 יוֹנַת אֵלֶם רְחֹקִים ***yônat 'ēlem r^e^ḥōqîm***, tt. GK: 3439 [→ 3123+352+7368]. Dove of the Distant Oaks:– Jonath-elem-rechokim [1]

3129 יוֹנָתָן ***yônātān***, n.pr.m. GK: 3440 [→ 3068+5414]. Jonathan, "*gift of Yahweh*":– Jonathan [42]

3130 יוֹסֵף ***yôsēp***, n.pr.m. GK: 3441 [→ 3254]. Joseph, "*he will add*":– Joseph [193], Joseph's [20]

3131 יוֹסִפְיָה ***yôsipyâ***, n.pr.m. GK: 3442 [→ 3254+3068]. Josiphiah, "*Yahweh will add*":– Josiphiah [1]

3132 יוֹעֵאלָה ***yô'ē'lâ***, n.pr.m. GK: 3443. Joelah, "*let him help*":– Joelah [1]

3133 יוֹעֵד ***yô'ēd***, n.pr.m. GK: 3444 [→ 3068+5707]. Joed, "*Yahweh is witness*":– Joed [1]

3134 יוֹעֶזֶר ***yô'ezer***, n.pr.m. GK: 3445 [→ 3068+5828]. Joezer, "*Yahweh is help*":– Joezer [1]

3135 יוֹעָשׁ ***yô'āš***, n.pr.m. GK: 3447 [→ 3068+5789]. Joash, "*Yahweh has bestowed*":– Joash [2]

3136 יוֹצָדָק ***yôṣādāq***, n.pr.m. GK: 3449 & 10318 [→ 3068+6663, 3087]. Jozadak, "*Yahweh is righteous*": note this name is Aramaic once in Ezra:– Jozadak [5]

3137 יוֹקִים ***yôqîm***, n.pr.m. GK: 3451 [→ 3068?+6965]. Jokim, "*Yahweh lifts up*":– Jokim [1]

3138 יוֹרֶה ***yôreh***, n.[m.]. GK: 3453 [→ 7301]. autumn (i.e., the time of the early rains, from the end of October to the beginning of December):– first rain [1], former [1]

3139 יוֹרָה ***yôrâ***, n.pr.m. GK: 3454. Jorah, "*one born during harvest*":– Jorah [1]

3140 יוֹרַי ***yôray***, n.pr.m. GK: 3455. Jorai, "[poss.] *Yahweh sees; whom Yahweh teaches*":– Jorai [1]

3141 יוֹרָם ***yôrām***, n.pr.m. GK: 3456 [→ 3068+7311]. Joram; Jehoram, "*Yahweh is exalted*":– Joram [20]

3142 יוֹשַׁב חֶסֶד ***yûšab ḥesed***, n.pr.m. GK: 3457. Jushab-Hesed, "*loyal love will be returned*":– Jushabhesed [1]

3143 יוֹשִׁבְיָה ***yôšibyâ***, n.pr.m. GK: 3458 [→ 3427+3068]. Joshibiah, "*Yahweh places*":– Josibiah [1]

3144 יוֹשָׁה ***yôšâ***, n.pr.m. GK: 3459. Joshah, "*gift of Yahweh*":– Joshah [1]

3145 יוֹשַׁוְיָה ***yôšawyâ***, n.pr.m. GK: 3460 [→ 3427+3068]. Joshaviah, "*Yahweh places*":– Joshaviah [1]

3146 יוֹשָׁפָט ***yôšāpāṭ***, n.pr.m. GK: 3461 [→ 3068+8199]. Joshaphat, "*Yahweh judges*":– Jehoshaphat [1], Joshaphat [1]

3147 יוֹתָם ***yôtām***, n.pr.m. GK: 3462 [→ 3068+8535]. Jotham, "*Yahweh will complete*":– Jotham [24]

3148 יוֹתֵר ***yôtēr***, n.m. *or* v.ptcp. GK: 3463 [→ 3498]. the rest; gain, advantage, profit; more than:– more [2], better [1], further [1], more than [1], moreover [1], over [1], profit [1]

3149 יְזוּאֵל ***y^{e}zûʾēl*** or יְזִיאֵל ***y^{e}zîʾēl***, n.pr.m. GK: 3464 & 3465 [cf. 3150?, 3151?]. Jeziel, Jezuel, "*may God sprinkle [in atonement]; God unites*":– Jeziel [1]

3150 יִזִּיָּה ***yizziyyâ***, n.pr.m. GK: 3466 [cf. 3149?]. Izziah, "*may Yahweh sprinkle [in atonement]; Yahweh unites*":– Jeziah [1]

3151 יָזִיז ***yāzîz***, n.pr.m. GK: 3467 [cf. 3149?]. Jaziz:– Jaziz [1]

3152 יִזְלִיאָה ***yizlîʾâ***, n.pr.m. GK: 3468. Izliah, "*long living, eternal; Yahweh delivers*":– Jezliah [1]

3153 יְזַנְיָה ***y^{e}zanyâ*** or יְזַנְיָהוּ ***y^{e}zanyāhû***, n.pr.m. GK: 3470 & 3471. Jezaniah, Jaazaniah, "*Yahweh listens*":– Jezaniah [2]

3154 יֶזַע ***yezaʿ***, n.[m.]. GK: 3472 [→ 2188]. perspiration, sweat:– sweat [1]

3155 יִזְרָח ***yizrāḥ***, a.g. GK: 3473. Izrahite:– Izrahite [1]

3156 יִזְרַחְיָה ***yizraḥyâ***, n.pr.m. GK: 3474 [→ 2224+3068]. Izrahiah; Jezrahiah, "*Yahweh shines* or *will arise*":– Izrahiah [2], Jezrahiah [1]

3157 יִזְרְעֶאל ***yizr^{e}ʿeʾl***, n.pr.m. & loc. GK: 3475 & 3476 [→ 3158, 3159]. Jezreel, "*God [El] will sow*":– Jezreel [36]

3158 יִזְרְעֵאלִי ***yizr^{e}ʿēʾlî***, a.g. GK: 3477 [→ 3157, 3159]. Jezreelite, of Jezreel, "*of Jezreel*":– Jezreelite [8]

3159 יִזְרְעֵאלִית ***yizr^{e}ʿēʾlît***, a.g. GK: 3477 [→ 3158]. f. of 3158: Jezreelite, of Jezreel, "*of Jezreel*":– Jezreelitess [5]

3160 יְחֻבָּה ***y^{e}ḥubbâ***, n.pr.m. GK: 3478 & 2465 [→ 2245?; cf. 2244?]. Jehubbah, "*God has hidden [someone from danger]*":– Jehubbah [1]

3161 יָחַד ***yāḥad***, v. GK: 3479 [→ 3162, 3173]. [Q] to join, be united; [P] to unite:– joined with [1], united [1], unite [1]

3162 יַחַד ***yaḥad***, n.[m.] or יַחְדָּו ***yaḥdāw***, adv. GK: 3480 & 3481 [→ 3161]. together, along with, in close proximity or concord either in space or time; by extension: close association in relationships, unity:– together [118], alike [5], altogether [5], at once [2], likewise [2], withal [2], at all [1], both [1], coupled together (+8535) [1], even as [1], knit (+3807.1) [1], only [1], together in unity [1]

3163 יַחְדוֹ ***yaḥdô***, n.pr.m. GK: 3482. Jahdo, "*[God] gives joy*":– Jahdo [1]

3164 יַחְדִּיאֵל ***yaḥdîʾēl***, n.pr.m. GK: 3484 [→ 2302+410]. Jahdiel, "*God [El] gives joy*":– Jahdiel [1]

3165 יֶחְדְּיָהוּ ***yeḥd^{e}yāhû***, n.pr.m. GK: 3485 [→ 2302+3068]. Jehdeiah, "*Yahweh rejoices [in his works]*":– Jehdeiah [2]

יְחַוְאֵל ***y^{e}ḥawʾēl***. See 3171.

3166 יַחֲזִיאֵל ***yaḥ^{a}zîʾēl***, n.pr.m. GK: 3487 [→ 2372+410]. Jahaziel, "*God [El] will see*":– Jahaziel [6]

3167 יַחְזְיָה ***yaḥz^{e}yâ***, n.pr.m. GK: 3488 [→ 2372+3068]. Jahzeiah, "*Yahweh sees*":– Jahaziah [1]

3168 יְחֶזְקֵאל ***y^{e}ḥezqēʾl***, n.pr.m. GK: 3489 [→ 2388+410]. Ezekiel; Jehezkel, "*God [El] gives strength*":– Ezekiel [2], Jehezekel [1]

3169 יְחִזְקִיָּה ***y^{e}ḥizqiyyâ*** or יְחִזְקִיָּהוּ ***y^{e}ḥizqiyyāhû***, n.pr.m. GK: 3490 & 3491 [→ 2388+3068]. Hezekiah, "*Yahweh is [my] strength*"; Jehizkiah, "*Yahweh gives strength*":– Hezekiah [43], Jehizkiah [1]

3170 יַחְזֵרָה ***yaḥzērâ***, n.pr.m. GK: 3492 [→ 2386]. Jahzerah, "*[poss.] prudent*":– Jahzerah [1]

3171 יְחוּאֵל ***y^{e}ḥûʾēl*** or יְחִיאֵל ***y^{e}ḥîʾēl***, n.pr.m. GK: 3486 & 3493 [→ 3172]. Jehuel, Jehiel, "*God [El] lives*":– Jehiel [14]

3172 יְחִיאֵלִי ***y^{e}ḥîʾēlî***, n.pr.m. GK: 3494 [→ 3171]. Jehieli, "*of Jehiel*":– Jehieli [2]

3173 יָחִיד ***yāḥîd***, a. & subst. GK: 3495 [→ 3161]. only son, only child (special and unique to the parents); precious life; alone, solitary:– only [7], darling [2], child [1], desolate [1], solitary [1]

3174 יְחִיָּה ***y^{e}ḥiyyâ***, n.pr.m. GK: 3496 [→ 2421+3068]. Jehiah, "*Yahweh lives*":– Jehiah [1]

3175 יָחִיל ***yāḥîl***, a.vbl. GK: 3497 [→ 3176]. waiting:– hope [1]

3176 יָחַל ***yāḥal***, v. GK: 3498 [→ 3175, 3177, 3178, 8431]. [N] to wait; [P] to wait for, put hope in, expect; [H] to wait, put hope in:– hope [17], waited [6], wait [5], hoped [3], tarry [2], trust [2], caused to hope [1], made to hope [1], stayed [1], tarried [1], waiteth [1]

3177 יַחְלְאֵל ***yaḥl^{e}ʾēl***, n.pr.m. GK: 3499 [→ 3178]. Jahleel, "*wait for God [El];* [poss.] *may God [El] show himself friendly*":– Jahleel [2]

3178 יַחְלְאֵלִי ***yaḥl^{e}ʾēlî***, a.g. GK: 3500 [→ 3177]. Jahleelite, "*of Jahleel*":– Jahleelites [1]

3179 יָחַם ***yāḥam***, v. GK: 3501 [→ 2534; cf. 2552]. [Q] to be in (breeding) heat, be in the rut; [P] to be in (breeding) heat, to mate, to conceive:– conceive [4], conceived [2], hot [2], gat heat [1], warm [1]

3180 יַחְמוּר ***yaḥmûr***, n.[m.]. GK: 3502 [→ 2560]. roebuck, the roe deer:– fallow deer [1], fallowdeer [1]

3181 יַחְמַי ***yaḥmay***, n.pr.m. GK: 3503 [→ 2346]. Jahmai, "*protect*":– Jahmai [1]

3182 יָחֵף ***yāḥēp***, a. GK: 3504. barefoot:– barefoot [4], unshod [1]

3183 יַחְצְאֵל ***yaḥṣ^{e}ʾēl***, n.pr.m. GK: 3505 [→ 3184]. Jahziel, Jahzeel, "*God [El] apportions*":– Jahzeel [2]

3184 יַחְצְאֵלִי ***yaḥṣ^{e}ʾēlî***, a.g. GK: 3506 [→ 3183]. Jahzeelite, "*of Jahzeel*":– Jahzeelites [1]

3185 יַחֲצִיאֵל ***yaḥ^{a}ṣîʾēl***, n.pr.m. GK: 3507 [→ 2673+410]. Jahziel:– Jahziel [1]

3186 יָחַר ***yāḥar***, v. GK: 3508 [cf. 309]. var. of 309: to wait, hesitate:–

3187 יָחַשׂ ***yāḥaś***, v. GK: 3509 [→ 3188]. [Ht] to enroll oneself in a genealogical record, be in a family register:– genealogy [5], reckoned by genealogies [5], reckoned by genealogy [5], genealogy reckoned [2], genealogies [1], number after genealogy [1], throughout genealogy [1]

3188 יַחַשׂ ***yaḥaś***, n.[m.]. GK: 3510 [→ 3187]. (book of) genealogy:– genealogy [1]

3189 יַחַת ***yaḥat***, n.pr.m. GK: 3511. Jahath, "*snatch up*":– Jahath [8]

3190 יָטַב ***yāṭab***, v. GK: 3512 [→ 3192, 3193, 4105, 4315; cf. 2895; cf. 2868, cf. 3191]. [Q] to be good, go well; to be glad, pleased; [H] to do good, right; to make successful, cause to prosper; "to be good in the eyes" indicates pleasure in and acceptance of a person or situation:– well [20], do good [14], pleased (+5869+871.1) [8], go well [4], merry [4], amend [3], do well [3], accepted [2], dealt well [2], diligently [2], doeth good [2], good [2], pleased well (+5869+871.1) [2], surely do good (+3190) [2], throughly amend (+3190) [2], benefit [1], best [1], better [1], comely [1], content (+5869+871.1) [1], deal well [1], diligent [1], doest well [1], done good [1], do [1], dresseth [1], earnestly (+3807.1) [1], entreated well [1], found favour [1], give [1], glad [1], made better [1], make better [1], make good [1], make sweet [1], maketh cheerful [1], making merry [1], please (+413) [1], pleased (+6440+3807.1) [1], pleased [1], pleaseth (+5869+871.1) [1], please [1], shewed more [1], skilfully [1], throughly [1], tired [1], trimmest [1], useth aright [1], very [1]

3191 יְטַב ***y^{e}ṭab*** (Aram.), v. GK: 10320 [cf. 2868; cf. 3190]. [P] to seem best, be pleasing:– seem good [1]

3192 יָטְבָה ***yoṭbâ***, n.pr.loc. GK: 3513 [→ 3190]. Jotbah, "*good, pleasant*":– Jotbah [1]

3193 יָטְבָתָה ***yoṭbātâ***, n.pr.loc. GK. 3514 [→ 3190]. Jotbathah, "*good, pleasant*":– Jotbathah [2], Jotbath [1]

3194 יוּטָּה ***yûṭṭâ***, n.pr.loc. GK: 3420. Juttah, "*extended, inclined*":– Juttah [2]

3195 יְטוּר ***y^{e}ṭûr***, n.pr.m. & g. GK: 3515 [cf. 2918?]. Jetur:– Jetur [3]

3196 יַיִן ***yayin***, n.m. GK: 3516. wine, an alcoholic beverage made of naturally fermented fruit juice (usually grapes), usually diluted with water for general consumption:– wine [137], banqueting [1], vine (+1612) [1], vine [1], winebibbers [1]

3197 יָךְ ***yak***, var. GK: 3517. var. of 3027: hand, side:–

יָכוֹל ***yākôl***. See 3201.

יְכוֹנְיָה ***y^{e}kôn^{e}yâ***. See 3204.

3198 יָכַח ***yākaḥ***, v. GK: 3519 [→ 8433]. [N] to reason together (in a legal case); to be vindicated; [H] to rebuke, discipline, punish; decide, argue, defend, judge; [Ho] to be chastened; [Ht] to lodge a charge against:– reprove [15], rebuke [7], reproved [4], plead [3], rebuketh [3], reproveth [3], correcteth [2], in any wise rebuke (+3198) [2], reason [2], surely reprove (+3198) [2], appointed out [1], appointed [1], arguing [1], chastened [1], chasten [1], convinced [1], correction [1], correct [1], daysman [1], dispute [1], judge [1], maintain [1], reason together [1], rebuked [1], reprover [1]

יְכִילְיָה ***y^{e}kîl^{e}yâ***. See 3203.

3199 יָכִין ***yākîn***, n.pr.m. GK: 3520 & 3521 [→ 3200, 3559]. Jakin, "*he establishes*":– Jachin [8]

3200 יָכִינִי ***yākînî***, a.g. GK: 3522 [→ 3199; cf. 3559]. Jakinite, "*of Jakin*":– Jachinites [1]

3201 יָכֹל ***yākôl***, v. GK: 3523 [→ 3203; cf. 3202 (also used with compound proper names)]. [Q] to be able, capable; overcome, prevail, have victory:– could [45], able [41], cannot (+3808) [35], prevail [12], may [11], can [10], prevailed [8], canst [5], mayest [5], any power at all (+3201) [2], any ways able (+3201) [2], endure [2], might [2], still prevail (+3201) [2], well able to overcome (+3201) [2], attain [1], can do [1], cannot away with (+3808) [1], canst do [1], could endure [1], couldest [1], prevailed against [1], suffer [1]

3202 יְכִל ***y^{e}kil*** (Aram.), v. GK: 10321 [cf. 3201]. [P] to be able:– able [4], canst [2], can [2], couldest [1], could [1], prevailed [1]

3203 יְכָלְיָה ***y^{e}kolyâ*** or יְכָלְיָהוּ ***y^{e}kolyāhû***, n.pr.f. GK: 3524 & 3525 [→ 3201+3068]. Jecoliah, "*Yahweh is able*":– Jecholiah [1], Jecoliah [1]

3204 יְכוֹנְיָה ***y^{e}kôn^{e}yâ*** or יְכָנְיָה ***y^{e}konyâ*** or יְכָנְיָהוּ ***y^{e}konyāhû***, n.pr.m. GK: 3518 & 3526 & 3527 [→ 3078]. Jeconiah, "*Yahweh supports*":– Jeconiah [7]

3205 יָלַד ***yālad***, v. GK: 3528 & 4256 [→ 2056, 3206, 3207, 3208, 3209, 3211, 4138, 4140, 8434?, 8435]. [Q] to give birth to, have a child, become the father of; [Qp, N, Pu, Ho] to be born, be a descendant; [P] to assist in childbirth, be a midwife; [H] to become the father of, cause to come to birth:– begat [179], bare [111], born [78], bear [17], bring forth [12], beget [10], brought forth [10], in travail [9], begotten [7], midwives [7], delivered [5], bearing [3], begetteth [3], borne [3], travailed [3], travaileth [3], beareth [2], begettest [2], birth [2], brought up [2], cause to bring forth [2], child [2], labour [2], midwife [2], bearest [1], birthday (+3117) [1], bring forth children [1], bring forth young [1], calved [1], children [1], come [1], declared pedigrees [1], delivered of a child [1], delivery [1], do the office of a midwife [1], gendered [1], hatcheth [1], maketh bring forth [1], son [1], travail with child [1], travaileth with child [1], travailing woman [1], travailing [1], travail [1]

3206 יֶלֶד ***yeled***, n.m. GK: 3529 [→ 3205]. male child, young boy; this can refer to a wide range of ages, from infant to young adult:– child [38], children [30], young men [6], sons [3], young ones [3], child's [2], men children [2], boys [1], boy [1], fruit [1], young man [1]

3207 יַלְדָּה ***yaldâ***, n.f. GK: 3530 [→ 3205]. female child, young girl; this can refer to a wide range of ages, from infant to young adult:– damsel [1], girls [1], girl [1]

3208 יַלְדוּת ***yaldût***, n.f. GK: 3531 [→ 3205]. youth, childhood:– youth [2], childhood [1]

3209 יִלּוֹד ***yillôd***, a. GK: 3533 [→ 3205]. born (children):– born [5]

3210 יָלוֹן ***yālôn***, n.pr.m. GK: 3534. Jalon:– Jalon [1]

3211 יָלִיד ***yālîd***, a. GK: 3535 [→ 3205]. born (child, slave child); (pl.) descendants, children:– children [4], born [2], sons [2], that is born [2], he that is born [1], homeborn (+1004) [1], that were born [1]

3212 יָלַךְ ***yālak***, v. GK: 2143 [→ 1980]. all forms of this assumed root are aligned with 1980:–

3213 יָלַל ***yālal***, v. GK: 3536 [→ 3214, 3215]. [H] to wail, howl:– howl [27], howled [1], howlings [1], make to howl [1]

3214 יְלֵל ***y^{e}lēl***, n.[m.]. GK: 3537 [→ 3213]. howling, wailing cry:– howling [1]

3215 יְלָלָה ***y^{e}lālâ***, n.f. GK: 3538 [→ 3213]. wailing, lamentation, howling:– howling [5]

3216 לָעַע ***lā'a'*** or יָלַע ***yāla'***, v. GK: 4363 [→ 3930; cf. 5966]. [Q] to sip, lap, slurp:– devoureth [1]

3217 יַלֶּפֶת ***yallepet***, n.f. GK: 3539. running sore; some sources: scab, ringworm:– scabbed [2]

3218 יֶלֶק ***yeleq***, n.m. GK: 3540. locust, grasshopper; young locust, possibly some stage in the development of the locust:– cankerworm [6], caterpillars [3]

3219 יַלְקוּט ***yalqûṭ***, n.[m.]. GK: 3541 [→ 3950]. pouch:– scrip [1]

3220 יָם ***yām***, n.m. GK: 3542 [cf. 39; cf. 3221]. sea; seashore; the west (the direction of the Mediterranean Sea relative to the Near East); by extension: a large container for holding water; the recurring image of the sea as a terrifying danger and opponent of the LORD has its source in the Sea (Yamm) as a hostile Canaanite god:– sea [297], west [33], seas [24], westward (+1886.5) [21], west (+1886.5) [15], west side [3], seafaring [1], south [1], western [1]

3221 יַם ***yam*** (Aram.), n.m. GK: 10322 [cf. 3220]. a body of water usually referring to ocean, sea, or lake; fig., the nether regions of mystery, chaos, and monsters:– sea [2]

3222 יֵמִם ***yēmim***, n.[m.]. GK: 3553 [→ 3224?]. hot springs; traditionally: mules; others: adders:– mules [1]

3223 יְמוּאֵל ***y^{e}mû'ēl***, n.pr.m. GK: 3543 [cf. 5241]. Jemuel:– Jemuel [2]

3224 יְמִימָה ***y^{e}mîmâ***, n.pr.f. GK: 3544 [→ 3222?]. Jemimah, "*dove*":– Jemima [1]

3225 יָמִין ***yāmîn***, n.f. GK: 3545 [→ 541, 1144, 1145, 1968?, 3226, 3228, 3233, 8486, 8488]. (direction) right; south, southward (south is right when facing east, the direction of orientation in the ancient Near East); the right is considered culturally to be stronger and of greater prestige than the left; to be seated on the right side of a ruler is a greater position than on the left side:– right hand [106], right [22], right side [6], south [3], lefthanded (+334+3027) [2]

3226 יָמִין ***yāmîn***, n.pr.m. GK: 3546 [→ 3228; cf. 3225]. Jamin, "[poss.] *right hand; south, an indication of [good] fortune*":– Jamin [6]

Heb

3227 יְמִינִי ***y^{e}mînî***, a.g. GK: 3549 [→ 1144]. Benjamite, "*of Benjamin*":– Benjamite (+376) [2], Benjamite (+376+1121) [1]

3228 יָמִינִי ***yāmînî***, a.g. GK: 3547 [→ 3226; cf. 3225]. Jaminite, "*of Jamin*":– Benjamites [1], Jaminites [1]

3229 יִמְלָא ***yimlā'*** or יִמְלָה ***yimlâ***, n.pr.m. GK: 3550 & 3551 [→ 4390]. Imla, Imlah, "*fullness*":– Imlah [2], Imla [2]

3230 יַמְלֵךְ ***yamlēk***, n.pr.m. GK: 3552 [→ 4427?]. Jamlech, "*he will reign*":– Jamlech [1]

3231 יָמַן ***yāman***, v.den. GK: 3554 [→ 541, 3225]. [H] to go the right; (ptcp.) right-handed:– go to the right [1], on the right hand [1], turn to the right hand [1], use the right hand [1]

3232 יִמְנָה ***yimnâ***, n.pr.m. GK: 3555 [→ 4487]. Imnah; Imnite, "*good fortune*":– Imnah [2], Jimnah [1], Jimna [1], Jimnites [1]

3233 יְמָנִי ***y^{e}mānî***, a. GK: 3556 & 3548 [→ 3225]. (direction) right:– right [32], right hand [1]

3234 יִמְנָע ***yimnā'***, n.pr.m. GK: 3557 [→ 4513]. Imna, "[poss.] *he is withheld; luck, fortune*":– Imna [1]

3235 יָמַר ***yāmar***, v. GK: 3558. [H] to change, exchange:– boast [1], changed [1]

3236 יִמְרָה ***yimrâ***, n.pr.m. GK: 3559 [→ 4784]. Imrah, "*he rebels*":– Imrah [1]

3237 יָמַשׁ ***yāmaš***, v. GK: 3560 [cf. 4184, 4959]. [H] to touch:–

3238 יָנָה ***yānâ***, v. GK: 3561 & 3435. [Q] to oppress, to crush; [H] to mistreat, take advantage of, oppress:– oppress [5], oppressed [3], oppressing [3], vexed [2], vex [2], destroy [1], do wrong [1], oppression [1], oppressor [1]

3239 יָנוֹחַ ***yānôaḥ*** or יָנוֹחָה ***yānôḥâ***, n.pr.loc. GK: 3562 & 3563 [→ 3240]. Janoah, Janohah, "*resting place*":– Janohah [2], Janoah [1]

יָנוּם ***yānum***. See 3241.

3240 יָנַח ***yānaḥ***, v. GK: 5663 [→ 2010, 3239, 4494, 4495, 4496, 4506, 5117, 5118, 5119?, 5183, 5184, 5207]. same as 5117: [Q] to settle, rest, wait; [H] to put, keep, settle, rest; to leave, allow; [Ho] to be placed, find rest:– leave [13], left [11], set [6], lay up [5], lay [5], put [5], let alone [4], laid up [3], laid [3], suffer [3], placed [2], set down [2], suffered [2], bestowed [1], cast down [1], laid down [1], leave off [1], pacifieth [1], place [1], remain still [1], withdraw [1], withhold [1]

3241 יָנוּם ***yānûm*** or יָנִים ***yānîm***, n.pr.loc. GK: 3564 & 3565 [→ 5123?]. Janum, Janim:– Janum [1]

3242 יְנִיקָה ***y^{e}nîqâ***, n.f. GK: 3566 [→ 3243]. shoot (of a plant):– young twigs [1]

3243 יָנַק ***yānaq***, v. GK: 3567 & 4787 [→ 689, 3126, 3127, 3242; cf. 5134]. [Q] to suck, be nursing; [H] to give nourishment, nurse:– nurse [7], suck [7], sucking child [3], sucklings [3], suckling [3], give suck [2], gave suck [1], given suck [1], made to suck [1], milch [1], nursing mothers [1], sucked [1], those that suck [1]

3244 יַנְשׁוּף ***yanšûp***, n.[m.]. GK: 3568 [→ 5398]. great owl (an unclean bird, variously identified):– great owl [2], owl [1]

3245 יָסַד ***yāsad***, v. GK: 3569 & 3570 [→ 3246, 3247, 3248, 4143, 4144, 4145, 4146, 4328, 4527; cf. 5475]. [Q] to lay a foundation, establish, ordain; [N] to be founded; to associate, conspire (together); [P] to lay a foundation, establish; [Pu, Ho] to be founded, have a foundation laid:– founded [8], foundation laid [7], laid foundation [5], established [2], foundation [2], laid foundations [2], lay foundations [2], lay foundation [2], appointed [1], instructed [1], laid [1], lay for a foundation [1], lay the foundation [1], layeth foundation [1], ordained [1], ordain [1], set [1], sure foundation (+4143) [1], take counsel [1], took counsel [1]

3246 יְסֻד ***y^{e}sud***, n.[m.]. GK: 3571 [→ 3245]. foundation, beginning:– began [1]

3247 יְסוֹד ***y^{e}sôd***, n.f. & m. GK: 3572 [→ 3245]. foundation; base (of an altar); foot (base of the body); by extension: what is firm or enduring:– bottom [9], foundation [7], foundations [3], repairing [1]

3248 יְסוּדָה ***y^{e}sûdâ***, n.f. GK: 3573 [→ 3245]. foundation:– foundation [1]

3249 יָסוּר ***yāsûr***, var. GK: 6073 [→ 5627, 5493; cf. 5494, 5495]. one who departs:–

3250 יִסּוֹר ***yissôr***, n.m. GK: 3574 [→ 3256]. corrector, fault-finder, reprover:– instruct [1]

3251 יָסַךְ ***yāsak***, v. GK: 3575 [cf. 5258, 5480]. same as 5480: [Q] to anoint, to use oils or perfumes or lotions:– poured [1]

3252 יִסְכָּה ***yiskâ***, n.pr.f. GK: 3576. Iscah:– Iscah [1]

3253 יִסְמַכְיָהוּ ***yismakyāhû***, n.pr.m. GK: 3577 [→ 5564+3068]. Ismakiah, "*Yahweh sustains*":– Ismachiah [1]

3254 יָסַף ***yāsap***, v. GK: 3578 [→ 23, 43, 460, 3130, 3131; cf. 3084, cf. 3255]. [Q] to add to, to do once more, to do again; [N] to be added to, to gain more, to be joined; [H] to increase, to cause to add to, to continue on, to add to, to happen again:– again [40], more [39], add [22], more (+5750) [10], any more [7], henceforth [6], again (+5750) [5], increaseth [5], yet again (+5750) [5], increased [4], increase [4], put [4], added [3], addeth [3], further [3], any more (+5750) [2], continued (+5375) [2], do more [2], exceed [2], make so many moe [2], more and more [2], yet the more (+5750) [2], added more [1], any more at all (+5750) [1], bring more [1], bring [1], came again [1], came more [1], can more (+5750) [1], caused again [1], cease [1], do again (+5750) [1], done [1], exceedest [1], exceedeth [1], gave [1], gotten more [1], increase (+5921) [1], increase more and more [1], increased more [1], join [1], longer [1], maketh [1], more (+5750+3807.1) [1], more also (+3541) [1], more also [1], more and more (+3605+5921) [1], moreover given [1], proceed further [1], proceeded [1], proceed [1], prolongeth [1], put more [1], set again [1], stronger and stronger (+555) [1], yet more (+5750) [1], yield [1]

3255 יְסַף ***y^{e}sap*** (Aram.), v. GK: 10323 [cf. 3254]. [Ho] to be added:– added [1]

3256 יָסַר ***yāsar***, v. GK: 3579 & 3580 & 3581 [→ 3250, 4148, 4561]. [Q] to correct, discipline; [N] to accept correction, be warned, be disciplined; [P] to punish, correct, discipline; to instruct, train; to strengthen; [H] to catch; [Nitpael] to let oneself take warning:– chastised [6], chastise [6], correct [6], instructed [5], chasten [3], instruct [3], chastened sore (+3256) [2], chasteneth [2], taught [2], bound [1], chastened [1], chastenest [1], chastiseth [1], corrected [1], punish [1], reformed [1], reproveth [1]

3257 יָע ***yā'***, n.[m.]. GK: 3582 [→ 3261]. shovel (for altar fires):– shovels [9]

3258 יַעְבֵּץ ***ya'bēṣ***, n.pr.m. & loc. GK: 3583 & 3584. Jabez, "*to grieve*":– Jabez [4]

3259 יָעַד ***yā'ad***, v. GK: 3585 [→ 4150, 4151, 4152, 5129; cf. 5712]. [Q] to select, appoint, set out; [N] to meet with, assemble, band together, join forces; [H] to summon, challenge; [Ho] to be set, be ordered:– meet [7], appointed [3], assembled [3], gathered together [3], appoint the time [2], betrothed [2], set [2], agreed [1], assemble [1], gather [1], made an appointment [1], meet together [1], met together [1], set a time [1]

יְעְדּוֹ ***y^e'dô***. See 3260.

3260 יְעְדּוֹ ***ye'dô*** or יֶעְדִּי ***ye'dî***, n.pr.m. GK: 3587 & 3588 [→ 5710 *or* 5716]. Iddo, Iddi, "[prob.] *Yahweh has adorned*":– Iddo [1]

3261 יָעָה ***yā'â***, v. GK: 3589 [→ 3257, 3262?, 3273?]. [Q] to sweep away:– sweep away [1]

3262 יְעוּאֵל ***y^e'û'ēl***, n.pr.m. GK: 3590 [→ 3273]. Jeuel, "*God [El] has preserved*":– Jeuel [1]

3263 יְעוּץ ***y^e'ûṣ***, n.pr.m. GK: 3591. Jeuz, "*he comes to help;* [poss.] *encouraged*":– Jeuz [1]

3264 יַעוֹר ***ya'ôr***, n.m. GK: 3623 [→ 3293, 3295]. same as 3293: forest, woods, thicket:–

3265 יָעוּר ***yā'ûr*** or יָעִיר ***yā'îr***, n.pr.m. GK: 3592 & 3600 [→ 5782]. Jaur, Jair, "*he gives light*":– Jair [1]

3266 יְעוּשׁ ***y^e'ûš***, n.pr.m. GK: 3593 [→ 5789; cf. 3274]. Jeush, "[perhaps] *may God aid*":– Jeush [8], Jehush [1]

3267 יָעַז ***yā'az***, v. GK: 3594 [cf. 5810]. [N] to be arrogant, be insolent:– fierce [1]

3268 יַעֲזִיאֵל ***ya^{a}zî'ēl***, n.pr.m. GK: 3595. Jaaziel, "*God [El] strengthens*":– Jaaziel [1]

3269 יַעֲזִיָּהוּ ***ya^{a}ziyyāhû***, n.pr.m. GK: 3596. Jaaziah, "*may Yahweh nourish*":– Jaaziah [2]

3270 יַעְזֵיר ***ya'zêr***, n.pr.loc. GK: 3597 [→ 5826]. Jazer, "*he helps*":– Jazer [11], Jaazer [2]

3271 יָעַט ***yā'aṭ***, v. GK: 3598 [cf. 5844]. [Q] to array, cover:– covered with [1]

3272 יְעַט ***y^e'aṭ*** (Aram.), v. GK: 10324 & 10325 [→ 5843; cf. 3289]. [Itpa] to take counsel together, implying mutual agreement and choices:– counsellers [2], consulted together [1]

3273 יְעִיאֵל ***y^e'î'ēl***, n.pr.m. GK: 3599 [→ 3262]. Jeiel, "*God [El] has preserved;* [poss.] *God [El] sweeps up*":– Jeiel [11], Jehiel [2]

יָעִיר ***yā'îr***. See 3265.

3274 יְעִישׁ ***y^e'îš***, n.pr.m. GK: 3601 [→ 5789; cf. 3266]. Jeish:–

3275 יַעְכָּן ***ya'kān***, n.pr.m. GK: 3602. Jacan:– Jachan [1]

3276 יָעַל ***yā'al***, v. GK: 3603 [→ 1100]. [H] to have value, have use, have value, have benefit:– profit [17], profit at all (+3276) [2], do good [1], profitable [1], profiteth [1], set forward [1]

3277 יָעֵל ***yā'ēl***, n.[m.]. GK: 3604 [→ 3278, 3279, 3280]. mountain goat, wild goat:– wild goats [3]

3278 יָעֵל ***yā'ēl***, n.pr.f. GK: 3605 [→ 3277]. Jael, "*mountain goat*":– Jael [6]

3279 יַעֲלָא ***ya^{a}lā'*** or יַעֲלָה ***ya^{a}lâ***, n.pr.m. GK: 3606 & 3608 [→ 3280; cf. 3277]. Jaala:– Jaalah [1], Jaala [1]

3280 יַעֲלָה ***ya^{a}lâ***, n.f. GK: 3607 [→ 3279; cf. 3277]. (female) mountain goat, ibex; deer:– roe [1]

3281 יַעְלָם ***ya'lām***, n.pr.m. GK: 3609 [→ 5934]. Jalam:– Jaalam [4]

3282 יַעַן ***ya'an***, subst.pp.c. GK: 3610 [→ 6031]. for, because, since:– because [56], because (+834) [19], forasmuch as (+834) [5], because (+3588) [3], because (+3282+871.1) [2], because (+871.1) [2], because of [2], because that [2], as [1], forasmuch as (+3588) [1], forsomuch as (+3588) [1], seeing then [1], that (+834) [1], therefore [1], whereas (+834) [1]

3283 יָעֵן ***yā'ēn***, n.[m.]. GK: 3612 [cf. 3284]. (male) ostrich:– ostriches [1]

3284 יַעֲנָה ***ya^{a}nâ***, n.f. GK: 3613 [cf. 3283]. owl; horned owl:– owls (+1323) [6], owl (+1323) [2]

3285 יַעְנַי ***ya'nay***, n.pr.m. GK: 3614 [→ 6030?]. Janai, "*he will answer*":– Jaanai [1]

3286 יָעֵף ***yā'ēp***, v. GK: 3615 [→ 3287, 3288; cf. 5774, 5889]. [Q] to grow tired, be faint, exhaust oneself:– weary [4], faint [3], caused to fly [1], fainteth [1]

3287 יָעֵף **yā'ēp**, a. GK: 3617 [→ 3286]. weary, exhausted, fatigued:– faint [2], weary [2]

3288 יְעָף **y^e'āp**, n.[m.]. GK: 3618 & 3616. flight; some source: tiredness, weariness:– swiftly (+871.1) [1]

3289 יָעַץ **yā'aṣ**, v. GK: 3619 & 3446 [→ 4156, 6098; cf. 5779; cf. 3272]. [Q] to give advise, give counsel; to purpose, plan, plot, determine; [Qp] to be determined; [N] to seek advise, consult; to confer, to plot (together); [Ht] to consult together, conspire against:– counsellers [12], counseller [10], consulted [7], purposed [5], took counsel [5], counselled [4], counsel [3], take counsel [3], taken counsel [3], counsel gave (+6098) [2], counsel given (+6098) [2], counsel give [2], determined [2], deviseth [2], give counsel (+6098) [2], give counsel [2], taken [2], took counsel with [2], advertise [1], advice give [1], advise [1], consulted with [1], consult [1], given counsel [1], guide [1], taken counsel (+6098) [1], took advice [1], well advised [1]

3290 יַעֲקֹב **ya^{a}qōb**, n.pr.m. & g. GK: 3620 [cf. 6119?, 6120?]. Jacob, "*follower, replacer, one who follows at the heel*":– Jacob [332], Jacob's [16], Jacob's (+3807.1) [1]

3291 יַעֲקֹבָה **ya^{a}qōbâ**, n.pr.m. GK: 3621. Jaakobah, "*may [deity] protect*":– Jaakobah [1]

3292 יַעֲקָן **ya^{a}qān**, n.pr.loc. GK: 3622 [→ 885; cf. 6130?]. Jaakan:– Jaakan [1], Jakan [1]

3293 יַעַר **ya'ar**, n.m. & pr. GK: 3623 & 3624 & 3625 [→ 3264, 3295]. forest, woods, thicket; (cultivated) tree groves; honeycomb; as n.pr. Jaar:– forest [37], wood [18], forests [1], honeycomb [1], woods [1]

3294 יַעְרָה **ya'râ** or יַעְדָּה **ya'dâ**, n.pr.m. GK: 3628 & 3586 [→ 5710?]. Jarah, Jadah, "*honeycomb*":– Jarah [2]

3295 יַעֲרָה **ya^{a}râ**, n.f. GK: 3626 & 3627 [→ 3264, 3293]. forest; honeycomb:– forests [1], honeycomb (+1706+1886.1) [1]

3296 יַעְרֵי אֹרְגִים **ya^{a}rê 'ōr^{e}gîm**, n.pr.m. GK: 3629. Jaare-Oregim:– Jaare-oregim [1]

3297 יְעָרִים **y^e'ārîm**, n.pr.loc. GK: 3630 [→ 7157]. Jearim, "*timberlands*":– Jearim [1]

3298 יַעֲרֶשְׁיָה **ya^{a}rešyâ**, n.pr.m. GK: 3631 [→ 3068]. Jaareshiah, "*Yahweh plants*":– Jaresiah [1]

3299 יַעֲשׂוּ **ya^{a}śû** or יַעֲשָׂי **ya^{a}śāy**, n.pr.m. GK: 3632 & 3633 [→ 6213]. Jaasu, Jaasai: Jaasau [1]

3300 יַעֲשִׂיאֵל **ya^{a}śî'ēl**, n.pr.m. GK: 3634 [→ 6213+410]. Jaasiel, "*God [El] does*":– Jaasiel [1], Jasiel [1]

3301 יִפְדְיָה **yipd^{e}yâ**, n.pr.m. GK: 3635. Iphdeiah, "*Yahweh redeems*":– Iphedeiah [1]

3302 יָפָה **yāpâ**, v. GK: 3636 [→ 3303, 3304, 3305?, 3308]. [Q] to be beautiful, delightful; [P] to adorn, make beautiful; [Ht] to adorn oneself:– fair [3], beautiful [2], deck [1], fairer [1], make fair [1]

3303 יָפֶה **yāpeh**, a. GK: 3637 [→ 3302]. beautiful, fair, lovely, handsome:– fair [20], beautiful [5], well [5], fairest [3], beautiful (+8389) [2], fair one [2], beauty [1], comely [1], fair (+8389) [1], goodly (+8389) [1], pleasant [1]

3304 יְפֵה־פִיָּה **y^{e}pêpiyyâ** or יְפֵה־פִיָּה **y^{e}pēh-piyyâ**, a.f. GK: 3645 & 3638 [→ 3302]. beautiful, pretty:– very fair [1]

3305 יָפוֹ **yāpô**, n.pr.loc. GK: 3639 [→ 3302?]. Joppa, "*beautiful*":– Joppa [3], Japho [1]

3306 יָפַח **yāpaḥ**, v. GK: 3640 [→ 3307; cf. 6315]. [Ht] to gasp for breath:– bewaileth [1]

3307 יָפֵחַ **yāpēaḥ**, a. GK: 3641 [→ 3306]. breathing out, with a strong implication that this breath results in an action or communication:– breathe out [1]

3308 יְפִי **y^{o}pî**, n.m. GK: 3642 [→ 3302]. beauty:– beauty [19]

3309 יָפִיעַ **yāpîa'**, n.pr.m. & loc. GK: 3644 [→ 3313]. Japhia, "[perhaps] *may the deity shine*":– Japhia [5]

3310 יַפְלֵט **yaplēṭ**, n.pr.m. GK: 3646 [→ 3311; cf. 6403]. Japhlet, "*he delivers;* [poss.] *he escapes*":– Japhlet [3]

3311 יַפְלֵטִי **yaplēṭî**, a.g. GK: 3647 [→ 3310; cf. 6403]. Japhletite, "*of Japhlet*":– Japhleti [1]

3312 יְפֻנֶּה **y^{e}punneh**, n.pr.m. GK: 3648 [→ 6437]. Jephunneh, "[perhaps] *may he [God] turn* or *turned*":– Jephunneh [16]

3313 יָפַע **yāpa'**, v. GK: 3649 [→ 3309, 3314]. [H] to shine forth, flash; smile:– shine [2], caused to shine [1], light [1], shew [1], shine forth [1], shined forth [1], shined [1]

3314 יִפְעָה **yip'â**, n.f. GK: 3650 [→ 3313]. shining splendor:– brightness [2]

3315 יֶפֶת **yepet**, n.pr.m. GK: 3651 [→ 6601]. Japheth, "*enlarge*":– Japheth [11]

3316 יִפְתָּח **yiptāḥ**, n.pr.m. & loc. GK: 3652 & 3653 [→ 6605]. Jephthah, Iphtah, "*Yahweh opens, frees*":– Jephthah [29], Jiphtah [1]

3317 יִפְתַּח־אֵל **yiptaḥ-'ēl**, n.pr.loc. GK: 3654 [→ 6605+410]. Iphtah El, "*God [El] opens*":– Jiphthah-el [2]

3318 יָצָא **yāṣā'**, v. GK: 3655 & 3448 [→ 3329, 4161, 4162, 4163, 6631, 6792, 8444]. [Q] to go out, come out; [H] to bring out, lead forth; produce; [Ho] to be brought out; emptied; by extension: to grow (of plants), to have offspring:– went out [162], go forth [92], go out [82], brought forth [70], came out [63], went forth [54], brought out [51], come out [48], bring forth [39], came forth [35], come forth [35], bring out [32], gone out [18], goeth out [13], bringeth forth [12], goeth forth [12], gone forth [12], cometh forth [10], departed [10], going out [10], carry forth [9], came [8], carry out [7], proceed [7], bringeth out [6], cometh out [6], proceedeth [6], goest out [5], broughtest out [4], camest forth [4], get out [4], goeth [4], issued out [4], broughtest forth [3], cometh [3], depart [3], going forth [3], go [3], lieth out [3], utter [3], assuredly go forth (+3318) [2], at any time come (+3318) [2], bring up [2], bring [2], brought up [2], brought [2], camest out [2], carried out [2], coming out [2], failed [2], go on [2], goest forth [2], got [2], have forth [2], issue [2], laid out [2], leddest out [2], proceeded [2], put away [2], scarce gone out (+3318) [2], surely come out (+3318) [2], surely go forth (+3318) [2], uttereth [2], wentest forth [2], appeared [1], bear out [1], begotten [1], be [1], break out [1], bringing forth [1], bringing out [1], bringing up [1], brought forth out of [1], brought forth out [1], brought of [1], camest [1], carried forth [1], carry forth out [1], carry [1], cause to go out [1], caused to go forth [1], come abroad [1], departing [1], departure [1], do^S [1], draw forth [1], drawn forth [1], drew forth [1], end [1], escaped [1], escape [1], exacted [1], fall out [1], falleth [1], fell out [1], fell [1], fet forth [1], fetch [1], followed (+310) [1], get away [1], get forth [1], get hence [1], go away [1], go way forth [1], goeth on [1], grow [1], have out [1], in departing [1], issue out [1], lead out [1], out [1], pluck out [1], plucked out [1], proceed out [1], pull out [1], risen [1], shooteth forth [1], spread [1], spring out [1], springeth out [1], stand out [1], take forth [1], took out [1], to [1], uttered [1], wentest out [1], went [1]

3319 שֵׁיצִיא **šēṣî'** or יְצָא **y^{e}ṣā'** (Aram.), v. GK: 10707. [Sh] to complete, finish:– finished [1]

3320 יָצַב **yāṣab**, v. GK: 3656 [cf. 5324; cf. 3321]. [Ht] to stand one's ground, confront; to stand before, present oneself, commit oneself:– stand [16], stood [7], present [5], set [5], presented [4], stand still [2], stand up [2], able to withstand (+5973) [1], remaining [1], resorted [1], setteth [1], stand fast [1], stand forth [1], standing [1]

3321 יְצַב **y^{e}ṣab** (Aram.), v. GK: 10326 [→ 3330; cf. 3320]. [Pa] to make certain, to know the truth:– know the truth [1]

3322 יָצַג **yāṣag**, v. GK: 3657 [cf. 3332]. [H] to set, place, present; touch; [Ho] to be left behind:– set [8], made [2], put [2], establish [1], leave [1], presented [1], stayed [1]

3323 יִצְהָר **yiṣhār**, n.[m.]. GK: 3658 [→ 3324, 3325; cf. 6671]. olive oil:– oil [22], anointed [1]

3324 יִצְהָר **yiṣhār**, n.pr.m. GK: 3659 [→ 3323; cf. 6671]. Izhar, "*the shining one*":– Izhar [8], Izehar [1]

3325 יִצְהָרִי **yiṣhārî**, a.g. GK: 3660 [→ 3323; cf. 6671]. Izharite, "*of Izhar*":– Izharites [3], Izeharites [1]

3326 יָצוּעַ **yāṣûa'** or יָצִיעַ **yāṣîa'**, n.m. GK: 3661 & 3662 & 3666 [→ 3331]. bed, couch; structure, room, often referring to an annex, wing, or level of a building:– bed [3], chambers [2], bed (+6210) [1], chamber [1], couch [1]

3327 יִצְחָק **yiṣḥāq**, n.pr.m. GK: 3663 [→ 6711; cf. 3446]. Isaac, "*he laugh, he will laugh* or *mock; [God] laughs*":– Isaac [104], Isaac's [4]

3328 יִצְחָר **yiṣḥār**, n.pr.m. GK: 3664 [cf. 6714]. Jizhar:– Jezoar [1]

3329 יָצִיא **yāṣî'**, a. GK: 3665 [→ 3318]. coming forth:– came forth [1]

3330 יַצִּיב **yaṣṣîb** (Aram.), a. GK: 10327 [→ 3321]. certain, true, reliable:– true [2], certainty [1], certain [1], truth [1]

יָצִיעַ **yāṣîa'**. See 3326.

3331 יָצַע **yāṣa'**, v. GK: 3667 [→ 3326, 4702]. [H] to spread out bedding; [Ho] to be spread out:– spread [2], lay [1], make bed [1]

3332 יָצַק **yāṣaq**, v. GK: 3668 [→ 3333, 4164, 4166, 4690?, 6694?; cf. 3322]. [Q] to pour out, cast out; [Qp] be cast out, be poured out, be smelted; [H] to pour out, spread out; [Ho] to be poured out, be washed away; be anointed:– cast [11], pour [11], poured [9], molten [6], poured out [4], firm [2], pour out [2], cleaveth fast [1], groweth [1], hard [1], laid out [1], overflown [1], ran out [1], set down [1], steadfast [1]

3333 יְצֻקָה **y^{e}ṣuqâ**, n.f. GK: 3669 [→ 3332]. casting (of metal), with a focus that this is one piece:– cast [1]

3334 יָצַר **yāṣar**, v. GK: 7674 [→ 4712, 6862, 6869, 6872, 6887; cf. 6696]. same as 6887: [Q] to bind up, wrap up, tie up; to hamper, oppress, be in distress; [Qp] be bound, be confined; [Pu] to be mended; [H] to bring trouble, distress, oppress:– distressed [4], straitened [2], in straits [1], narrow [1], vexed [1]

3335 יָצַר **yāṣar**, v. GK: 3670 & 3450 [→ 3336, 3337, 3338, 3339, 3340]. [Q] to form, fashion, shape, create; (of God) the Maker, the Creator; [N] to be formed; [Pu] to be formed; [Ho] to be forged, be formed; usually from existing material; God as Creator or Maker, has its focus his planning and forming the creation as a skilled craftsman:– formed [23], potter [8], potter's [7], maker [4], fashioneth [3], fashioned [2], former [2], formeth [2], made [2], earthen [1], form [1], framed [1], frameth [1], frame [1], make [1], potters' [1], potters [1], purposed [1]

3336 יֵצֶר **yēṣer**, n.m. GK: 3671 [→ 3337; cf. 3335]. something formed, creation; inclination, disposition, motivation:– imagination [4], frame [1], imaginations [1], mind [1], thing framed [1], work [1]

3337 יֵצֶר **yēṣer**, n.pr.m. GK: 3672 [→ 3339, 3340; cf. 3335, 3336]. Jezer, "*formed, fashioned*":– Jezer [3]

3338 יְצֻרִים **y^{e}ṣurîm**, n.m.pl. GK: 3674 [→ 3335]. frame, body, limbs, that which gives visible form to a person:– members [1]

3339 יִצְרִי **yiṣrî**, a.g. & n.pr.m. GK: 3673 [→ 3337; cf. 3335]. same as 3340: Izri; Jezerite, "*Yahweh designs*":– Izri [1]

3340 יִצְרִי **yiṣrî**, a.g. & n.pr.m. GK: 3673 [→ 3337]. same as 3339: Izri; Jezerite, "*Yahweh designs*":– Jezerites [1]

3341 יָצַת **yāṣat**, v. GK: 3675 [cf. 6702]. [Q] to set ablaze; [N] to burn, be burned; [H] to kindle, set on fire:– kindle [8], burnt [7], set [6], kindled [4], burnt up [2], desolate [1], set on [1]

3342 יֶקֶב **yeqeb**, n.m. GK: 3676 [cf. 5344]. winepress; (wine or oil) vat:– winepress [7], fats [2], presses [2], winepresses [2], pressfat [1], wine presses [1], wine [1]

3343 יְקַבְצְאֵל **y^{e}qabṣ^e'ēl**, n.pr.loc. GK: 3677 [→ 6908+410]. Jekabzeel, "*God [El] gathers*":– Jekabzeel [1]

3344 יָקַד **yāqad**, v. GK: 3678 & 3683 [→ 3350, 4168, 4169; cf. 3345, cf. 3346]. [Q] to burn; to kindle a fire; [Qp or n.m.] hearth (of a fireplace); [Ho] to be burning, be kindled:– burning [3], burn [3], burneth [1], hearth [1], kindle [1]

3345 יְקַד **y^{e}qad** (Aram.), v. GK: 10328 [→ 3346; cf. 3344]. [P] to burn:– burning [8]

3346 יְקֵדָה **y^{e}qēdâ** (Aram.), n.f. GK: 10329 [→ 3345]. blazing, burning:– burning [1]

3347 יָקְדְעָם **yoqd^e'ām**, n.pr.loc. GK: 3680. Jokdeam:– Jokdeam [1]

3348 יָקֶה **yāqeh**, n.pr.m. GK: 3681. Jakeh, "*prudent*":– Jakeh [1]

3349 יְקָהָה **y^{e}qāhâ**, n.f. GK: 3682. obedience:– gathering [1], obey [1]

3350 יְקוֹד **y^{e}qōd**, n.[m.]. GK: 3679 [→ 3344]. blazing, burning:– burning [2]

3351 יְקוּם **y^{e}qûm**, n.[m.]. GK: 3685 [→ 6965]. living thing, living creature:– living substance [2], substance [1]

3352 יָקוֹשׁ **yāqôš**, n.[m.]. GK: 3686 [→ 3369]. fowler, bait-layer:– fowler [1]

3353 יָקוּשׁ **yāqûš**, n.[m.]. GK: 3687 [→ 3369]. fowler, one who snares birds:– fowler [2], snares [1]

3354 יְקוּתִיאֵל **y^{e}qûtî'ēl**, n.pr.m. GK: 3688. Jekuthiel, "*God [El] will nourish*":– Jekuthiel [1]

3355 יָקְטָן **yoqṭān**, n.pr.m. GK: 3690 [→ 3364]. Joktan, "*smaller*":– Joktan [6]

3356 יָקִים **yāqîm**, n.pr.m. GK: 3691 [→ 6965]. Jakim, "*he will establish*":– Jakim [2]

3357 יַקִּיר **yaqqîr**, a. GK: 3692 [→ 3365; cf. 3358]. dear, precious:– dear [1]

3358 יַקִּיר **yaqqîr** (Aram.), a. GK: 10330 [→ 3367; cf. 3366]. honorable; difficult, with an implication that such difficulty makes something unlikely or improbable:– noble [1], rare [1]

3359 יְקַמְיָה ***y^{e}qamyâ***, n.pr.m. GK: 3693 [→ 6965+3068]. Jekamiah, "*Yahweh will establish*":– Jekamiah [2], Jecamiah [1]

3360 יְקַמְעָם ***y^{e}qam'ām***, n.pr.m. GK: 3694 [→ 6965+5971]. Jekameam, "*[my] kinsman establishes*":– Jekameam [2]

3361 יָקְמְעָם ***yoqm^e'ām***, n.pr.loc. GK: 3695 [→ 3362?]. Jokmeam, "*let the people arise*":– Jokmeam [1], Jokneam [1]

3362 יָקְנְעָם ***yoqn^e'ām***, n.pr.loc. GK: 3696 [→ 3361?]. Jokneam:– Jokneam [3]

3363 יָקַע ***yāqa'***, v. GK: 3697 [cf. 5361]. [Q] to turn (away), wrench; [H] to kill and expose; [Ho] to be killed and exposed:– alienated [2], hang up [2], hanged [2], depart [1], out of joint [1]

3364 יָקַץ ***yāqaṣ***, v. GK: 3699 [→ 3355; cf. 6972]. [Q] to wake up, awake:– awoke [6], awaked [4], awake [1]

יָקַף *yāqap*. See 5362.

3365 יָקַר ***yāqar***, v. GK: 3700 [→ 3357, 3368, 3366]. [Q] to be precious, be costly; become well known; [H] to make scarce:– precious [7], make precious [1], prised [1], set by [1], withdraw [1]

3366 יְקָר ***y^{e}qār***, n.m. GK: 3702 [→ 3365; cf. 3367]. honor, splendor, riches, valuable things:– honour [12], precious things [2], precious thing [1], precious [1], price [1]

3367 יְקָר ***y^{e}qār*** (Aram.), n.m. GK: 10331 [→ 3358; cf. 3366]. glory, honor, majesty:– glory [5], honour [2]

3368 יָקָר ***yāqār***, a. GK: 3701 [→ 3365]. precious, valuable, quality, pertaining to items that are rare, beloved, or splendid:– precious [25], costly [4], excellent [2], brightness [1], clear [1], fat [1], honourable [1], reputation [1]

3369 יָקֹשׁ ***yāqaš***, v. GK: 3704 [→ 3352, 3353, 3370, 4170; cf. 5367, 6983]. [Q] to lay a bird snare, set a trap; [N, Pu] to be ensnared, be trapped:– snared [5], fowlers [1], laid a snare [1], laid [1]

3370 יָקְשָׁן ***yoqšān***, n.pr.m. GK: 3705 [→ 3369]. Jokshan:– Jokshan [4]

3371 יָקְתְאֵל ***yoqt^e'ēl***, n.pr.loc. GK: 3706 [→ 410]. Joktheel:– Joktheel [2]

יָרָא *yārā'*. See 3384.

3372 יָרֵא ***yārē'***, v. GK: 3707 [→ 3373, 3374, 4172]. [Q] to be afraid, be frightened; to revere, respect; [N] to be awesome, be dreadful, be feared; [P] to frighten, terrify, intimidate; in some contexts fear relates to terror and fright, in other contexts fear relates to honor, respect and awe, as in "the fear of the LORD":– fear [146], afraid [75], feared [36], terrible [28], dreadful [5], feareth [2], fearful [2], made afraid [2], put in fear [2], reverence [2], affright [1], dread [1], durst not [1], exceedingly afraid (+1419+3374) [1], feared exceedingly (+1419+3374) [1], fearest [1], fearfully [1], fearing [1], had in reverence [1], reverend [1], terrible acts [1], terrible things [1], terribleness [1]

3373 יָרֵא ***yārē'***, a.vbl. GK: 3710 [→ 3372]. fear; worship:– fear [35], feareth [11], feared [9], afraid [3], fearful [2], one that feareth [2], fearest [1], one that feared [1]

3374 יִרְאָה ***yir'â***, n.f. GK: 3711 [→ 3372]. fear, reverence, piety:– fear [41], dreadful [1], exceedingly afraid (+1419+3372) [1], feared exceedingly (+1419+3372) [1], fearfulness [1]

3375 יִרְאוֹן ***yir'ôn***, n.pr.loc. GK: 3712. Iron:– Iron [1]

3376 יִרְאִיָּיה ***yir'iyyāyh***, n.pr.m. GK: 3713 [→ 7200+3068]. Irijah, "*Yahweh sees*":– Irijah [2]

3377 יָרֵב ***yārēb***, n.m. GK: 3714 [→ 7231]. great (king):– Jareb [2]

3378 יְרֻבַּעַל ***y^{e}rubba'al***, n.pr.m. GK: 3715 [→ 7231+1167]. Jerub-Baal, "*Baal contends*":– Jerubbaal [14]

3379 יָרָבְעָם ***yārob'ām***, n.pr.m. GK: 3716 [→ 7231+5971]. Jeroboam, "*the people increase*":– Jeroboam [102], Jeroboam's [2]

3380 יְרֻבֶּשֶׁת ***y^{e}rubbešet***, n.pr.m. GK: 3717 [→ 7231+954]. Jerub-Besheth, "*Shame [Baal] contends*":– Jerubbesheth [1]

3381 יָרַד ***yārad***, v. GK: 3718 [→ 3383, 4174]. [Q] to come down, go down, descend; [H] to bring down, lower; [Ho] to be brought down, be taken down:– go down [73], went down [63], come down [53], came down [41], bring down [26], brought down [17], gone down [14], descended [12], get down [9], descend [6], goeth down [5], let down [5], run down [5], took down [4], camest down [3], cast down [3], going down [3], take down [3], bringeth down [2], came indeed down (+3381) [2], carry down [2], cause to come down [2], coming down [2], down [2], fell [2], runneth down [2], abundantly [1], casteth down [1], caused to run down [1], cometh down [1], descending [1], goeth [1], hang down [1], let fall down [1], lighted down [1], lighted [1], put down [1], put off [1], ran down [1], sank [1], subdued [1], taken down [1], went [1]

3382 יֶרֶד ***yered***, n.pr.m. GK: 3719. Jared; Jered, "*rose; servant*":– Jared [5], Jered [2]

3383 יַרְדֵּן ***yardēn***, n.pr.loc. GK: 3720 [→ 3381]. Jordan, "*descending*":– Jordan [182]

3384 יָרָה ***yārâ***, v. GK: 3721 & 3722 & 3723 & 3452 [→ 3385, 3406, 3412, 4175, 4176, 8451, 8452]. [Q] to throw, cast; shoot; [N] to be shot through; [H] to shoot (an arrow), to hurl; to water upon, rain, shower; to teach, instruct, give guidance, in a formal or informal setting, with an implied authority for the teacher and the content of what is taught; [Ho] to be refreshed:– teach [33], shoot [11], shot [6], taught [5], cast [4], archers [3], teachers [3], teacheth [3], shot through (+3384) [2], archers (+376+7198+871.1+1886.1) [1], casteth [1], direct [1], former rain [1], inform [1], instructed [1], laid [1], rain [1], shewed [1], teacher [1], teaching [1], watered [1]

3385 יְרוּאֵל ***y^{e}rû'ēl***, n.pr.loc. GK: 3725 [→ 3384+410]. Jeruel, "*God [El] is a foundation*":– Jeruel [1]

3386 יָרוֹחַ ***yārôaḥ***, n.pr.m. GK: 3726 [→ 3391]. Jaroah, "*soft, delicate*":– Jaroah [1]

3387 יָרוֹק ***yārôq***, n.[m.]. GK: 3728 [→ 3418]. green plant:– green thing [1]

3388 יְרוּשָׁא ***y^{e}rûšā'*** or יְרוּשָׁה ***y^{e}rûšâ***, n.pr.f. GK: 3729 & 3730 [→ 3423]. Jerusha, "*possession*":– Jerushah [1], Jerusha [1]

3389 יְרוּשָׁלַםִ ***y^{e}rûšālaim***, n.pr.loc. GK: 3731 [cf. 3390]. Jerusalem, "*foundation of Shalem [peace]*":– Jerusalem [640], Jerusalem's [3]

3390 יְרוּשְׁלֶם ***y^{e}rûš^{e}lem*** (Aram.), n.pr.loc. GK: 10332 [cf. 3389]. Jerusalem, "*foundation of Shalem (peace)*":– Jerusalem [26]

3391 יֶרַח ***yeraḥ***, n.m. GK: 3732 [→ 3386, 3392, 3394, 3405; cf. 732; cf. 3393]. moon; (lunar) month:– months [5], month [4], full month (+3117) [2], moon [2]

3392 יֶרַח ***yeraḥ***, n.pr.m. GK: 3733 [→ 3391]. Jerah, "*moon [god?]*":– Jerah [2]

3393 יְרַח ***y^{e}raḥ*** (Aram.), n.m. GK: 10333 [cf. 3391]. month:– months [1], month [1]

3394 יָרֵחַ ***yārēaḥ***, n.m. GK: 3734 [→ 3391]. moon:– moon [26]

יְרֵחוֹ *y^{e}rēḥô*. See 3405.

3395 יְרֹחָם ***y^{e}rōḥām***, n.pr.m. GK: 3736 [→ 7355]. Jeroham, "*he will be compassionate*":– Jeroham [10]

3396 יְרַחְמְאֵל ***y^{e}raḥm^e'ēl***, n.pr.m. GK: 3737 [→ 7355+410]. Jerahmeel, "*God [El] will have compassion*":– Jerahmeel [8]

3397 יְרַחְמְאֵלִי ***y^{e}raḥm^e'ēlî***, a.g. GK: 3738 [→ 7355+410]. Jerahmeelite, "*of Jerahmeel*":– Jerahmeelites [2]

3398 יַרְחָע ***yarḥā'***, n.pr.m. GK: 3739. Jarha:– Jarha [2]

3399 יָרַט ***yāraṭ***, v. GK: 3740. [Q] to throw (into someone's custody); to be reckless, a fig. extension of going down a steep ravine:– perverse [1], turned over [1]

3400 יְרִיאֵל ***y^{e}rî'ēl***, n.pr.m. GK: 3741 [cf. 3404]. Jeriel, "*founded of God [El]; God [El] will see*":– Jeriel [1]

3401 יָרִיב ***yārîb***, n.[m.]. GK: 3742 [→ 7378]. contender, accuser, adversary, opponent:– contend with [1], contendeth with [1], strive with [1]

3402 יָרִיב ***yārîb***, n.pr.m. GK: 3743. Jarib, "*Yahweh contends*":– Jarib [3]

3403 יְרִיבַי ***y^{e}rîbay***, n.pr.m. GK: 3744 [→ 7380?]. Jeribai, "*Yahweh pleads*":– Jeribai [1]

3404 יְרִיָּה ***y^{e}riyyâ*** or יְרִיָּהוּ ***y^{e}riyyāhû***, n.pr.m. GK: 3745 & 3746 [cf. 3400]. Jeriah, "*Yahweh founds*":– Jeriah [2], Jerijah [1]

3405 יְרִיחוֹ ***y^{e}rîḥô*** or יְרִיחֹה ***y^{e}rîḥōh***, n.pr.loc. GK: 3735 & 3747 [→ 3391]. Jericho, "*moon city*":– Jericho [57]

3406 יְרִימוֹת ***y^{e}rîmôt*** or יְרָמוֹת ***y^{e}rāmôt*** or יְרֵמוֹת ***y^{e}rēmôt***, n.pr.m. GK: 3748 & 3755 & 3756 [→ 3384+4191?]. Jeramoth, Jeremoth; Jerimoth, "*swollen* or *obese*":– Jerimoth [8], Jeremoth [5]

3407 יְרִיעָה ***y^{e}rî'â***, n.f. GK: 3749 [→ 3415]. tent curtain; tent, shelter, dwelling:– curtains [31], curtain [23]

3408 יְרִיעוֹת ***y^{e}rî'ôt***, n.pr.m. GK: 3750 [→ 3415]. Jerioth, "*tents*":– Jerioth [1]

3409 יָרֵךְ ***yārēk***, n.f. GK: 3751 [→ 3411; cf. 3410]. the area and components of the torso: thigh, hip, breast, leg, side; by extension: side, base, of any object:– thigh [19], side [7], shaft [3], loins [2], thighs [2], body [1]

3410 יַרְכָה ***yarkā*** (Aram.), n.f. GK: 10334 [cf. 3409]. (upper) thigh; some sources translate as "loin" (the lower back, as the soft area between the lower ribs and the hip joints):– thighs [1]

3411 יְרֵכָה ***y^{e}rēkâ***, n.[f.]. GK: 3752 [→ 3409]. far end, ends (of the earth); remote area: heights, depths:– sides [15], two sides [4], coasts [3], parts [2], side [2], border [1], quarters [1]

3412 יַרְמוּת ***yarmût***, n.pr.loc. GK: 3754 [→ 3384+4191?]. Jarmuth, "*height*":– Jarmuth [7]

יְרֵמוֹת *y^{e}rēmôt*. See 3406.

3413 יְרֵמַי ***y^{e}rēmay***, n.pr.m. GK: 3757 [cf. 3414?]. Jeremai, "[poss.] *fat*":– Jeremai [1]

3414 יִרְמְיָה ***yirm^{e}yâ*** or יִרְמְיָהוּ ***yirm^{e}yāhû***, n.pr.m. GK: 3758 & 3759 [cf. 3413?]. Jeremiah, "*Yahweh loosens [the womb]; Yahweh lifts up;* [poss.] *Yahweh shoots, establishes*":– Jeremiah [146], Jeremiah's [1]

3415 יָרַע ***yāra'***, v. GK: 3760 [→ 3407, 3408]. [Q] to tremble, be faint-hearted:– displeased (+5869+871.1) [6], grieved [3], grievous [3], evil [2], displease (+7489+871.1) [1], displeased (+7489+871.1) [1], displeased exceedingly (+1419+7451) [1], do harm [1], go ill [1], ill [1], sad [1]

3416 יִרְפְּאֵל ***yirp^e'ēl***, n.pr.loc. GK: 3761 [→ 7495+410]. Irpeel, "*God [El] heals*":– Irpeel [1]

3417 יָרַק ***yāraq***, v. GK: 3762 [cf. 7556]. [Q] to spit (in the face as an act of contempt):– but spit (+3417) [2], spit [1]

3418 יֶרֶק ***yereq***, n.m. GK: 3764 [→ 3387, 3419, 3420, 3422]. green (of plants, foliage, shoots, grass):– green [3], green thing [2], grass [1]

3419 יָרָק ***yārāq***, n.[m.]. GK: 3763 [→ 3418]. vegetables, vegetable greens:– herbs [3], green [2]

יַרְקוֹן *yarqôn*. See 4313.

3420 יֵרָקוֹן ***yērāqôn***, n.m. GK: 3766 [→ 3418]. paleness (of face); mildew (of grain):– mildew [5], paleness [1]

3421 יָרְקְעָם ***yorq^o'ām***, n.pr.m. GK: 3767 [→ 7554]. Jorkeam:– Jorkoam [1]

3422 יְרַקְרַק ***y^{e}raqraq***, a. GK: 3768 [→ 3418]. yellowish-green, pale-green (mildew); shining-yellowish (gold):– greenish [2], yellow [1]

3423 יָרַשׁ ***yāraš***, v. GK: 3769 [→ 3388, 3424, 3425, 4180, 4181, 7558, 7568, 8492; cf. 7326]. [Q] to be an heir, gain an inheritance, have as a possession; [N] to become destitute, to be poor; [P] to take possession of; [H] to drive away, push out, destroy; to cause to inherit; many of these meanings have a common element of gaining (by right or violence) or losing possession (by force or circumstance):– possess [93], drive out [26], inherit [19], possessed [19], cast out [11], heir [9], utterly drive out (+3423) [4], come to poverty [3], succeeded [3], dispossessed [2], dispossess [2], drave out [2], driven out [2], enjoy [2], expelled [2], inherited [2], succeedest [2], take possession [2], without fail drive out (+3423) [2], consume [1], destroy [1], disinherit [1], drive [1], driving out [1], drove out [1], drove [1], given to inherit [1], giveth to possess [1], got in possession [1], have in possession [1], heirs [1], inheritor [1], leave an inheritance [1], magistrate (+6114) [1], makest to possess [1], maketh poor [1], poor [1], possessest [1], possesseth [1], seize upon [1], take in possession [1], take that have [1], taken possession [1]

3424 יְרֵשָׁה ***y^{e}rēšâ***, n.f. GK: 3771 [→ 3423]. possession conquered:– possession [2]

3425 יְרֻשָּׁה ***y^{e}ruššâ***, n.f. GK: 3772 [→ 3423]. possession, inheritance:– possession [11], inheritance [2], heritage [1]

3426 יֵשׁ ***yēš***, subst. GK: 3780 [→ 786, 3449?; cf. 8454; cf. 383]. there is, it exists:– there is [35], there be [16], is there [13], be [12], is [9], have (+3807.1) [8], there were [6], have [4], had (+3807.1) [3], are [2], hast [2], hath (+3807.1) [2], it is [2], it was [2], there [2], wilt [2], are there [1], do [1], had [1], hast (+3807.1) [1], hath (+871.1) [1], hath [1], have (+5973) [1], is able [1], it be [1], substance [1], there was [1], were [1], will [1], wouldest [1]

3427 יָשַׁב ***yāšab***, v. GK: 3782 [→ 4186, 7675, 7871?, 8453; cf. 3488 (also used with compound proper names)]. [Q] to live, inhabit, dwell, stay; [N] to be settled, be inhabited; [P] to set up; to cause to settle, make dwell, to cause to sit; by extension: to marry, with a focus that the spouses live together:– inhabitants [190], dwell [184], dwelt [182], sat [72], sit [54], abode [33], inhabitant [31], abide [29], inhabited [28], sitteth

[24], sat down [22], dwelleth [19], dwell in [16], dwelling [15], sitting [14], set [13], dwellest [12], tarry [12], remain [11], remained [10], inhabit [8], dwelled [6], sittest [6], tarried [6], placed [5], sit down [5], taken [5], abideth [4], dwelt in [4], continued [3], abiding [2], continue [2], dwellest in [2], endure [2], habitation [2], made to dwell [2], make to dwell [2], satest [2], sit still [2], situate [2], abide in [1], abodest [1], bring to place [1], cause to dwell in [1], cause to dwell [1], caused to dwell [1], downsitting [1], dwelleth in [1], dwelling in [1], dwelt amongst [1], dwelt at [1], dwelt with [1], ease [1], establish [1], haunt [1], inhabitest [1], inhabiteth [1], lurking [1], made dwell [1], made to abide [1], make to be inhabited [1], makest dwell [1], maketh to dwell [1], maketh to keep [1], married [1], marrying [1], not fail to sit [1], place [1], remainest [1], remaineth [1], setteth [1], settle [1], sit in [1], sit up [1], sitteth still [1], sitting down [1], still [1], tarrieth [1], tarry abroad [1]

3428 יֶשֶׁבְאָב ***yešeb'āb***, n.pr.m. GK: 3784 [→ 7725+1]. Jeshebeab, "*father lives*":– Jeshebeab [1]

3429 יֹשֵׁב בַּשֶּׁבֶת ***yōšēb baššebet***, n.pr.m. GK: 3783. Josheb-Basshebeth, "*one sitting in the seat*":–

3430 יִשְׁבּוֹ בְנֹב ***yišbô bᵉnōb*** or יִשְׁבִּי בְנֹב ***yišbî bᵉnōb***, n.pr.m. GK: 3785 & 3787. Ishbo-Benob, Ishbi-Benob:– Ishbi-benob [1]

3431 יִשְׁבָּח ***yišbāḥ***, n.pr.m. GK: 3786 [→ 7623]. Ishbah, "*he boasts, congratulates*":– Ishbah [1]

3432 יָשׁוּבִי ***yāšûbî***, a.g. GK: 3795 [→ 3437; cf. 7725]. Jashubite, "*of Jashub*":– Jashubites [1]

3433 יָשֻׁבִי לֶחֶם ***yāšubî leḥem***, n.pr.m. GK: 3788 [→ 3899]. Jashubi Lehem, "*[they] returned to Lehem*":– Jashubi-lehem [1]

3434 יָשָׁבְעָם ***yāšob'ām***, n.pr.m. GK: 3790. Jashobeam, "*the people return*":– Jashobeam [3]

3435 יִשְׁבָּק ***yišbāq***, n.pr.m. GK: 3791 [→ 7733]. Ishbak:– Ishbak [2]

3436 יָשְׁבְּקָשָׁה ***yošbᵉqāšâ***, n.pr.m. GK: 3792. Joshbekashah, "*one sitting in request [prayer?]*":– Joshbekashah [2]

3437 יָשׁוּב ***yāšûb*** or יָשִׁיב ***yāšîb***, n.pr.m. GK: 3793 & 3806 [→ 3432; cf. 7725]. Jashub, Jashib, "*he returns*":– Jashub [3]

3438 יִשְׁוָה ***yišwâ***, n.pr.m. GK: 3796 [→ 7737]. Ishvah, "*he will level*":– Ishuah [1], Isuai [1]

3439 יְשׁוֹחָיָה ***yᵉšôḥāyâ***, n.pr.m. GK: 3797 [→ 3068+7817?]. Jeshohaiah, "[poss.] *Yahweh humbles*":– Jeshohaiah [1]

3440 יִשְׁוִי ***yišwî***, n.pr.m. GK: 3798 [→ 7737]. Ishvi:– Ishui [2], Isuah [1], Jesui [1]

3441 יִשְׁוִי ***yišwî***, a.g. GK: 3799 [→ 7737]. Ishvite, "*of Ishvi*":– Jesuites [1]

3442 יֵשׁוּעַ ***yēšûa'***, n.pr.m. & loc. GK: 3800 & 3801 [cf. 3467; cf. 3443]. Jeshua, "*Yahweh saves*":– Jeshua [29]

3443 יֵשׁוּעַ ***yēšûa'*** (Aram.), n.pr.m. GK: 10336 [cf. 3442]. Jeshua, "*Yahweh saves*":– Jeshua [1]

3444 יְשׁוּעָה ***yᵉšû'â***, n.f. GK: 3802 [→ 3467]. salvation, deliverance, help, rescue from a dangerous circumstance or harmful state by a savior; divine salvation usually has its focus on rescue from earthly enemies, occasionally referring to salvation from guilt, sin, and punishment:– salvation [65], deliverance [2], health [2], help [2], deliverances [1], help (+1961) [1], helping [1], save [1], saving health [1], saving [1], welfare [1]

3445 יֶשַׁח ***yešaḥ***, n.[m.]. GK: 3803. emptiness; some sources: filth, dung:– casting down [1]

3446 יִשְׂחָק ***yiśḥāq***, n.pr.m. GK: 3773 [→ 7832; cf. 3327]. Isaac, "*he laughs, he will laugh* or *mock; [God] laughs*":– Isaac [4]

3447 יָשַׁט ***yāšaṭ***, v. GK: 3804. [H] to extend; hold out:– held out [2], hold out [1]

3448 יִשַׁי ***yišay***, n.pr.m. GK: 3805. Jesse:– Jesse [42]

יָשִׁיב ***yāšîb***. See 3437.

3449 יִשִּׁיָּה ***yiššiyyâ*** or יִשִּׁיָּהוּ ***yiššiyyāhû***, n.pr.m. GK: 3807 & 3808 [→ 3426?+3068]. Isshiah; Ishijah, "*Yahweh forgets*":– Isshiah [3], Jesiah [2], Ishiah [1], Ishijah [1]

3450 יְשִׂימִאֵל ***yᵉśîmi'ēl***, n.pr.m. GK: 3774 [→ 7760+410]. Jesimiel, "*God [El] will establish*":– Jesimiel [1]

3451 יְשִׁימָה ***yᵉšîmâ*** or יַשִּׁימָוֶת ***yaššîmāwet***, n.f. GK: 3809 & 3812 [→ 3456]. desolation, devastation:–

3452 יְשִׁימוֹן ***yᵉšîmôn***, n.m. GK: 3810 [→ 3456]. Jeshimon; wasteland:– Jeshimon [6], desert [4], wilderness [2], solitary [1]

יְשִׁימוֹת ***yᵉšîmôt***. See 1020, 3451.

3453 יָשִׁישׁ ***yāšîš***, a. GK: 3813 [→ 3454?; cf. 3486]. old, aged:– aged [1], ancient [1], very aged men [1], very old [1]

3454 יְשִׁישַׁי ***yᵉšîšay***, n.pr.m. GK: 3814 [→ 3453?]. Jeshishai, "*aged*":– Jeshishai [1]

3455 יָשַׂם ***yāśam***, v. GK: 3775 [cf. 7760]. prob. same as 7760: to place, set:– put [1]

3456 יָשַׁם ***yāšam***, v. GK: 3815 [→ 3451, 3452; cf. 8074]. [Q] to be desolate:– desolate [4]

3457 יִשְׁמָא ***yišmā'***, n.pr.m. GK: 3816 [→ 3458]. Ishma, "*desolate; God [El] he heard*":– Ishma [1]

3458 יִשְׁמָעֵאל ***yišmā'ē'l***, n.pr.m. GK: 3817 [→ 3457, 3459]. Ishmael, "*God [El] he heard*":– Ishmael [47], Ishmael's [1]

3459 יִשְׁמְעֵאלִי ***yišmᵉ'ē'lî***, a.g. GK: 3818 [→ 3458]. Ishmaelite, "*of Ishmael*":– Ishmeelites [4], Ishmaelites [2], Ishmaelite [1], Ishmeelite [1]

3460 יִשְׁמַעְיָה ***yišma'yâ*** or יִשְׁמַעְיָהוּ ***yišma'yāhû***, n.pr.m. GK: 3819 & 3820 [→ 3461?]. Ishmaiah, "*Yahweh heard*":– Ishmaiah [1], Ismaiah [1]

3461 יִשְׁמְרַי ***yišmᵉray***, n.pr.m. GK: 3821 [→ 3460?]. Ishmerai, "*Yahweh guards*":– Ishmerai [1]

3462 יָשֵׁן ***yāšēn***, v. GK: 3822 & 3823 [→ 3463, 3464?, 3465, 8142]. [Q] to sleep, fall asleep; [N] to live a long time, be old, chronic; [P] to put to sleep:– sleep [9], slept [5], made sleep [1], old store (+3465) [1], old [1], remained long [1], sleepest [1]

3463 יָשֵׁן ***yāšēn***, a. GK: 3825 [→ 3462]. sleeping, pertaining to sleep:– sleep [3], asleep [2], sleepeth [2], sleeping [1], slept [1]

3464 יָשֵׁן ***yāšēn***, n.pr.m. GK: 3826 [→ 3462?]. Jashen, "[poss.] *asleep*":– Jashen [1]

3465 יָשָׁן ***yāšān***, a. GK: 3824 [→ 3466?; cf. 3462]. old; pertaining to last year:– old [7], old store (+3462) [1]

3466 יְשָׁנָה ***yᵉšānâ***, n.pr.loc. GK: 3827 [→ 3465?]. Jeshanah, "*old*":– Jeshanah [1]

3467 יָשַׁע ***yāša'***, v. GK: 3828 & 3830 & 4635 [→ 3444, 3468, 4190, 4338, 4337, 8668 (also used with compound proper names)]. [N] to be rescued, be delivered, be saved; [H] to save, rescue, deliver; divine salvation has its focus on rescue from earthly enemies, occasionally referring to salvation from guilt, sin, and punishment:– save [103], saved [35], saviour [13], help [10], delivered [8], saveth [7], preserved [4], deliver [3], savest [3], avenging [2], brought salvation [2], deliverer [2], helped [2], save at all (+3467) [2], saviours [2], avenged [1], defend [1], gotten victory [1], having salvation [1], preservest [1], rescue [1], safe [1]

3468 יֶשַׁע ***yeša'***, n.m. GK: 3829 [→ 3442; cf. 3467 (also used with compound proper names)]. salvation, deliverance, protection, often implying a victory is at hand; (of God) Savior, a title of God that focuses on rescue from earthly enemies, occasionally referring to salvation from guilt, sin, and punishment:– salvation [32], safety [3], saving [1]

3469 יִשְׁעִי ***yiš'î***, n.pr.m. GK: 3831 [→ 3467?+3068?]. Ishi, "*God has saved*":– Ishi [5]

3470 יְשַׁעְיָה ***yᵉša'yâ*** or יְשַׁעְיָהוּ ***yᵉša'yāhû***, n.pr.m. GK: 3832 & 3833 [→ 3467+3068]. Jeshaiah, "*Yahweh will save*":– Isaiah [31], Jeshaiah [5], Jesaiah [2], Esai [1]

3471 יָשְׁפֵה ***yāšᵉpēh***, n.[m.]. GK: 3835. jasper (exact identification uncertain):– jasper [3]

3472 יִשְׁפָּה ***yišpâ***, n.pr.m. GK: 3834 [→ 8192]. Ishpah, "[poss.] *barren way, empty path*":– Ispah [1]

3473 יִשְׁפָּן ***yišpān***, n.pr.m. GK: 3836 [→ 8192?]. Ishpan, "[poss.] *may God judge*":– Ishpan [1]

3474 יָשַׁר ***yāšar***, v. GK: 3837 [→ 3475, 3476, 3477, 3483, 3484, 4334, 4339, 8289, 8290]. [Q] to do good, do right, be straight; [P] to make straight, make smooth; [Pu] to be evenly hammered; [H] to make straight, gaze straight; from the base meaning of straightening out a crooked object comes the fig. extension of doing an act that is not perverse, but right or just:– direct [3], make straight [3], pleased (+5869+871.1) [3], pleased well (+5869+871.1) [3], brought straight [1], directeth [1], esteem to be right [1], fitted [1], go right [1], good [1], look straight [1], meet [1], please (+5869+871.1) [1], pleaseth well (+5869) [1], right [1], took straight [1], uprightly [1], upright [1]

3475 יֵשֶׁר ***yēšer***, n.pr.m. GK: 3840 [→ 3474]. Jesher, "[perhaps] *the deity shows himself just*":– Jesher [1]

3476 יֹשֶׁר ***yōšer***, n.m. GK: 3841 [→ 3474]. uprightness, straightness, honesty, integrity:– uprightness [9], right [2], equity [1], meet [1], upright [1]

3477 יָשָׁר ***yāšār***, a. & n.pr.m. GK: 3838 & 3839 [→ 3474]. straight (not crooked or twisted); by extension, something morally straight: right, upright, innocent; (n.) upright person; as n.pr. Jashar:– right [53], upright [41], righteous [9], straight [3], Jasher [2], convenient for (+413+1886.1) [1], convenient [1], equity [1], just [1], meetest [1], meet [1], most upright [1], pleased well (+5869+871.1) [1], upright ones [1], uprightly [1], uprightness [1]

3478 יִשְׂרָאֵל ***yiśrā'ēl***, n.pr.m. & g. GK: 3776 [→ 415, 3481, 3482; cf. 8280; cf. 3479]. Israel, "*he struggles with God [El]*":– Israel [2476], Israelites [16], Israel's [10], Israel (+376) [2], Israelite (+376) [1]

3479 יִשְׂרָאֵל ***yiśrā'ēl*** (Aram.), n.pr.g. GK: 10335 [cf. 3478]. Israel, "*he struggles with God [El]*":– Israel [8]

3480 יְשַׂרְאֵלָה ***yᵉśar'ēlâ***, n.pr.m. GK: 3777 [cf. 841]. Jesarelah:– Jesharelah [1]

3481 יִשְׂרְאֵלִי ***yiśrᵉ'ēlî***, a.g. GK: 3778 [→ 3478, 3482]. Israelite, "*of Israel*":– Israelite [1], Israel [1]

3482 יִשְׂרְאֵלִית ***yiśrᵉ'ēlît***, a.g. GK: 3778 [→ 3481]. f. of 3481: Israelite, "*of Israel*":– Israelitish [3]

3483 יִשְׁרָה ***yišrâ***, n.f. GK: 3842 [→ 3474]. uprightness:– uprightness [1]

3484 יְשֻׁרוּן ***yᵉšurûn***, n.pr.m. GK: 3843 [→ 3474]. Jeshurun, "*upright*":– Jeshurun [4]

3485 יִשָּׂשכָר ***yiśśāśkār***, n.pr.m. GK: 3779 [→ 376+7939]. Issachar, "*there is reward* [Ge. 30:18]; *may [God] show mercy; hired hand*":– Issachar [43]

3486 יָשֵׁשׁ ***yāšēš***, a. GK: 3844 [→ 3453]. aged, decrepit:– him that stooped for age [1]

3487 יָת ***yāt*** (Aram.), pt. GK: 10337 [cf. 853]. not translated, indicates the direct object:–

3488 יְתִב ***yᵉtib*** (Aram.), v. GK: 10338 [cf. 3427]. [P] to live in, dwell; to sit, be seated; [H] to cause to settle, cause to dwell in:– set [2], sit [2], dwell [1]

3489 יָתֵד ***yātēd***, n.f. GK: 3845. tent peg, stake, pin (of a loom); tool for digging:– pins [10], nail [8], pin [3], stakes [2], paddle [1]

3490 יָתוֹם ***yātôm***, n.[m.]. GK: 3846. fatherless, orphan:– fatherless [38], fatherless children [2], fatherless child [1], orphans [1]

3491 יְתוּר ***yᵉtûr***, var. GK: 3847 [cf. 8446]. range, extent; poss. a form of 8446:– range [1]

3492 יַתִּיר ***yattîr***, n.pr.loc. GK: 3848 [→ 3498]. Jattir, "[poss.] *preeminence*":– Jattir [4]

3493 יַתִּיר ***yattîr*** (Aram.), a. GK: 10339 [cf. 3471]. exceptional, outstanding; (as adv.) so, very, exceedingly:– excellent [5], exceeding [2], exceedingly [1]

3494 יִתְלָה ***yitlâ***, n.pr.loc. GK: 3849 [→ 8518]. Ithlah, "*hanging, lofty place*":– Jethlah [1]

3495 יִתְמָה ***yitmâ***, n.pr.m. GK: 3850. Ithmah, "*fatherless; purity*":– Ithmah [1]

3496 יַתְנִיאֵל ***yatni'el***, n.pr.m. GK: 3853 [→ 386+410]. Jathniel, "*God [El] hires; God [El] is forever*":– Jathniel [1]

3497 יִתְנָן ***yitnān***, n.pr.loc. GK: 3854 [→ 386]. Ithnan:– Ithnan [1]

3498 יָתַר ***yātar***, v. GK: 3855 [→ 1956, 3148, 3492?, 3499, 3500, 3501, 3502, 3503, 3504, 3505, 3506, 3508, 4195, 4340; cf. 3493 (also used with compound proper names)]. [N] to remain, be left over, the rest; [H] to have left over, spare, preserve:– left [46], remain [12], rest [12], leave [6], remained [5], remainder [4], remaineth [4], remnant [3], residue [3], make plenteous [2], reserved [2], come to remain [1], excel [1], had reserved [1], leave a remnant [1], left behind [1], preserve [1], remaining [1], too much [1]

3499 יֶתֶר ***yeter***, n.m. GK: 3856 & 3857 [→ 3323, 4340; cf. 3498]. remainder, remnant, the rest, what is left over; thong, cord, bowstring:– rest [63], remnant [14], residue [8], excellency [3], left [3], withs [3], abundant [1], cord [1], exceeding [1], excellent [1], leave [1], plentifully [1], string [1]

3500 יֶתֶר ***yeter***, n.pr.m. GK: 3858 [→ 3505; cf. 3498, 3499]. Jether; Jethro:– Jether [8], Jethro [1]

3501 יִתְרָא ***yitrā'***, n.pr.m. GK: 3859 [→ 3498]. Jether, "*abundance*":– Ithra [1]

3502 יִתְרָה ***yitrâ***, n.f. GK: 3860 [→ 3498]. wealth, abundance:– abundance [1], riches [1]

Heb

3503 יִתְרוֹ ***yitrô***, n.pr.m. GK: 3861 [→ 3498]. Jethro, "*remainder*":– Jethro [9]

3504 יִתְרוֹן ***yitrôn***, n.[m.]. GK: 3862 [→ 3498]. profit, gain, increase:– profit [5], excelleth [2], better [1], excellency [1], profitable [1]

3505 יִתְרִי ***yitrî***, a.g. GK: 3863 [→ 3500; cf. 3498]. Ithrite:– Ithrite [4], Ithrites [1]

3506 יִתְרָן ***yitrān***, n.pr.m. GK: 3864 [→ 3498]. Ithran, "*what is over, profit; excellent*":– Ithran [3]

3507 יִתְרְעָם ***yitr^{e}ʿām***, n.pr.m. GK: 3865 [→ 3499+5971]. Ithream, "*remainder of the people*":– Ithream [2]

3508 יֹתֶרֶת ***yōteret***, n.f. GK: 3866 [→ 3498]. covering, lobe (of certain animal livers):– caul [11]

3509 יְתֵת ***y^{e}tēt***, n.pr.m. GK: 3867. Jetheth:– Jetheth [2]

3509.1 -כְּ ***k^{e}-***, subst.pref. GK: 3869 [→ 3644; cf. 3509.4]. marker of comparison: as, like; marker of similarity or correspondence: according to; marker of time: when, as soon as, about:– as [1044], as (+834) [382], according to [367], like [361], when [164], after [75], about [47], when (+834) [47], according unto [29], like unto [23], as it were [20], according as (+834) [16], as soon as [13], so [13], thus (+2088) [12], like as (+834) [11]*

3509.2 ךָ- ***-kā*** or ךְ- ***-ak*** or כָה- ***-kēh***, p.m.s.suf. GK: 3870 [→ 3509.3, 3641.1, 3654.1]. you, your:– thy [3403], thee [2501], thine [639], thou [282], thyself [46], thine own [45], you [34], thine (+3807.1) [29], thy (+3807.1) [24], your [8], ye [3], thine own (+3807.1) [2], his [1], of thy [1], the^{S} [1], thee (+3027) [1], thee (+3807.1) [1], thee-ward [1], thine own self [1], thou (+3027) [1], thyself (+3807.1) [1], whose [1]

3509.3 ךְ- ***-k*** or כִי- ***-kî***, p.f.s.suf. GK: 3871 [→ 3509.2]. you, your:– thy [619], thee [458], thine [101], thou [63], thine own [9], thy (+3807.1) [7], thine (+3807.1) [3], thyself [3], thyself (+5315) [1], whom [1]

3509.4 -כְּ ***k^{e}-*** (Aram.), pp.pref. GK: 10341 [cf. 3509.1]. as, like, according to:– like [10], as [9], according to [5], when (+1768) [4], after [2], how (+4101) [2], thus (+1836) [2], about [1], after sort [1], as (+1768) [1], for [1], such (+1836) [1], together (+2298) [1], when [1]

3509.5 ךְ- ***-k*** (Aram.), p.suf.2.m.s. GK: 10342 [cf. 3509.2]. you, your:– thee [44], thy [44], thine [7], thou [3], thyself [1]

3510 כָּאַב ***kāʾab***, v. GK: 3872 [→ 3511, 4341]. [Q] to feel pain, ache; [H] to bring pain:– sorrowful [2], grieving [1], have pain [1], made sad [1], maketh sore [1], mar [1], sore [1]

3511 כְּאֵב ***k^{e}ʾēb***, n.m. GK: 3873 [→ 3510]. pain, anguish, suffering:– sorrow [3], grief [2], pain [1]

3512 כָּאָה ***kāʾâ***, v. GK: 3874 [cf. 3543]. [N] to be brokenhearted, lose heart; [H] to dishearten, cause to lose heart:– broken [1], grieved [1], made sad [1]

3513 כָּבֵד ***kābēd***, v. GK: 3877 [→ 3514, 3515, 3516, 3517, 3519, 3520, 3520]. [Q] to be heavy; to be wealthy, honored, glorified; to be failing, dull; [N] to be glorified, honored, renowned; [P] to honor, glorify, reward; [Pu] to be honored; [H] to make heavy, make hard; [Ht] to make numerous; honor oneself. If the base meaning is "to be weighty or heavy," then by extension, negatively: hard, dull, stubborn, difficult in circumstance; positively: substantial, honored, glorious, wealthy:– honourable [15], honour [15], heavy [9], glorify [7], glorified [6], hardened [6], honoured [5], made heavy [5], glorious [4], honoureth [4], chargeable [2], heavier [2], make many [2], promote unto great honour (+3513) [2], promote unto honour (+3513) [2], went sore [2], abounding [1], boast [1], bring to honour [1], come to honour [1], dim [1], do honour [1], get honour [1], glorifieth [1], glory [1], gotten honour [1], grievous [1], had in honour [1], harden [1], heavily laid [1], honourest [1], ladeth with [1], made glorious [1], make glorious [1], make heavy [1], more grievously afflict [1], more laid [1], nobles [1], prevailed [1], promote to honour [1], rich [1], sore [1], stopped [1]

3514 כֹּבֶד ***kōbed***, n.[m.]. GK: 3880 [→ 3513]. heaviness; heavy mass (density, piles):– heavy [2], great number [1], grievousness [1]

3515 כָּבֵד ***kābēd***, a. GK: 3878 [→ 3513]. heavy, severe, difficult, an extended degree or amount, positive or negative:– heavy [9], great [8], grievous [8], sore [4], hard [2], much [2], slow [2], hardened [1], heavier [1], laden [1], thick [1]

3516 כָּבֵד ***kābēd***, n.m. GK: 3879 [→ 3513]. liver; heart:– liver [14]

כָּבֹד ***kābōd***. See 3519.

3517 כְּבֵדֻת ***k^{e}bēdut***, n.f. GK: 3881 [→ 3513]. difficulty, awkwardness:– heavily (+871.1) [1]

3518 כָּבָה ***kābâ***, v. GK: 3882. [Q] to be quenched, snuffed out; [P] to quench, put out, snuff out:– quenched [9], quench [8], put out [3], goeth out [2], go out [1], went out [1]

3519 כָּבוֹד ***kābôd***, n.m. GK: 3883 [→ 350; cf. 3513]. glory, honor, splendor, wealth; while related words can be positive or negative in context, this word is almost exclusively positive in the OT; "the Glory" a title for God focuses on his splendor and high status; "my glory" means "myself" (Ge 49:8):– glory [156], honour [32], glorious [10], gloriously [1], honourable [1]

3520 כְּבוּדָּה ***k^{e}bûddâ***, n.f. GK: 3884 & 3885 [→ 3513]. possession, valuable property; glorious, elegant:– carriage [1], glorious [1], stately [1]

3521 כָּבוּל ***kābûl***, n.pr.loc. GK: 3886 [→ 3525]. Cabul, "*good for nothing*":– Cabul [2]

3522 כַּבּוֹן ***kabbôn***, n.pr.loc. GK: 3887. Cabbon:– Cabbon [1]

3523 כָּבִיר ***kābîr***, n.[m.]. GK: 3889 [→ 3527]. something braided; in context referring to goat's hair:– pillow [2]

3524 כַּבִּיר ***kabbîr***, a. GK: 3888 [→ 3527]. great, mighty (of God and humans), with a focus on potency or ability:– mighty [5], much [2], feeble (+3808) [1], most [1], strong [1]

3525 כֶּבֶל ***kebel***, n.[m.]. GK: 3890 [→ 3521]. shackles, fetters:– fetters [2]

3526 כָּבַס ***kābas***, v. GK: 3891 [cf. 3533]. [Q] (ptcp.) washer, fuller; [P] to wash, launder; [Pu] to be washed; [Hotpael] to be washed off:– wash [39], washed [7], fuller's [3], fullers' [1], washing [1]

3527 כָּבַר ***kābar***, v. GK: 3892 [→ 3524, 3523, 3528, 3529, 3531, 3530, 4342, 4346]. [H] to multiply; provide in abundance:– multiplieth [1]

3528 כְּבָר ***k^{e}bār***, adv. GK: 3893 [→ 3527]. already, before:– already [5], now [4]

3529 כְּבָר ***k^{e}bār***, n.pr.loc. GK: 3894 [→ 3527]. Kebar:– Chebar [8]

3530 כִּבְרָה ***k^{e}bārâ***, n.f. GK: 3896 [→ 3527]. (a certain) distance; some sources: as far as a horse can run; as far as one can see; about seven miles:– little [2], little way (+776+1886.1) [1]

3531 כְּבָרָה ***k^{e}bārâ***, n.f. GK: 3895 [→ 3527]. sieve:– sieve [1]

3532 כֶּבֶשׂ ***kebeś***, n.m. GK: 3897 [→ 3535; cf. 3775]. ram-lamb, young ram sheep:– lambs [59], lamb [41], he lamb [3], sheep [2], he lambs [1], lamb (+7716) [1]

3533 כָּבַשׁ ***kābaš***, v. GK: 3899 [→ 3534, 3536; cf. 3526, 3728]. [Q] to subdue, overcome, enslave; [N] be subdued, be subject, be brought under control; [P] to subdue; [H] subdue, subjugate:– subdued [5], subdue [3], brought into subjection [2], bring into bondage [1], brought unto bondage [1], force [1], keep under [1]

3534 כֶּבֶשׁ ***kebeš***, n.[m.]. GK: 3900 [→ 3533]. footstool:– footstool [1]

3535 כִּבְשָׂה ***kibśâ***, n.f. GK: 3898 [→ 3532]. ewe-lamb, young female sheep:– ewe lambs [3], ewe lamb [3], lamb [2]

3536 כִּבְשָׁן ***kibšān***, n.m. GK: 3901 [→ 3533]. furnace, likely in context referring to a kiln or forge for making glass, pottery, smelting, etc:– furnace [4]

3537 כַּד ***kad***, n.f. GK: 3902. jar, pitcher (of the size that could by carried on the shoulder):– pitcher [10], pitchers [4], barrel [3], barrels [1]

3538 כְּדַב ***k^{e}dab*** (Aram.), a. GK: 10343 [cf. 3577]. misleading, false:– lying [1]

3539 כַּדְכֹּד ***kadkōd***, n.[m.]. GK: 3905. ruby (exact identification unknown):– agates [1], agate [1]

3540 כְּדָרְלָעֹמֶר ***k^{e}dorlāʿōmer*** or כְּדָר־לָעֹמֶר ***k^{e}dor-lāʿōmer***, n.pr.m. GK: 3906. Kedorlaomer, "*servant of [the deity] Lagamar*":– Chedorlaomer [5]

3541 כֹּה ***kōh***, adv.demo. GK: 3907 [→ 3602; cf. 3542]. this is what, thus:– thus [520], so [23], also [7], here [4], hitherto (+5704) [2], in the mean while (+3541+5704+5704+2050.1) [2], this [2], and (+2050.1) [1], and [1], more also (+3254) [1], much [1], on the other side [1], on this side [1], on this wise [1], such [1], that manner [1], that way [1], this manner [1], this way [1], yonder (+5704) [1], yonder [1]

3542 כָּה ***kâ*** (Aram.), adv. GK: 10345 [cf. 3541]. here, up to this point:– hitherto (+5705) [1]

3543 כָּהָה ***kāhâ***, v. GK: 3908 & 3909 [→ 3544, 3545; cf. 3512]. [Q] to grow dim, be weak; [P] to fade, become faint; to rebuke, set (someone) right, with an implication that future bad behavior is curtailed:– dim [3], utterly darkened (+3543) [2], fail [1], faint [1], restrained [1]

3544 כֵּהֶה ***kēheh***, a. GK: 3910 [→ 3543]. dull; weak; smoldering; despairing:– somewhat dark [5], darkish [1], dim [1], heaviness [1], smoking [1]

3545 כֵּהָה ***kēhâ***, n.f. GK: 3911 [→ 3543]. healing, relief:– healing [1]

3546 כְּהַל ***k^{e}hal*** (Aram.), v. GK: 10346 [cf. 3202]. [P] to be able:– able [2], could [2]

3547 כָּהַן ***kāhan***, v.den. GK: 3912 [→ 3548]. [P] to serve as a priest:– minister in the priest's office [15], executed the priest's office [2], ministered in the priest's office [2], decketh with [1], do the office of a priest [1], executing the priest's office [1], priest [1]

3548 כֹּהֵן ***kōhēn***, n.m. GK: 3913 [→ 3547, 3550; cf. 3549]. priest, who not only had religious duties, but also examined persons and things for medical diagnosis, policed the unruly, and taught the word of God:– priest [421], priests [298], priest's [14], priests' [8], his^{S} own (+1886.1) [2], priest's (+3807.1) [2], chief rulers [1], chief ruler [1], priests' (+3807.1) [1], princes [1], principal officer [1]

3549 כָּהֵן ***kāhēn*** (Aram.), n.m. GK: 10347 [cf. 3548]. priest:– priests [6], priest [2]

3550 כְּהֻנָּה ***k^{e}hunnâ***, n.f. GK: 3914 [→ 3548]. priesthood, priestly office:– priesthood [9], priest's office [4], priests' offices [1]

3551 כַּוָּה ***kawwâ*** (Aram.), n.f. GK: 10348. window:– windows [1]

3552 כּוּב ***kûb***, n.pr.g. GK: 3915. Kub:– Chub [1]

3553 כּוֹבַע ***kôbaʿ***, n.m. GK: 3916 [cf. 6959]. helmet:– helmet [4], helmets [2]

3554 כָּוָה ***kāwâ***, v. GK: 3917 [→ 3555, 3587, 4348]. [N] to be burned, be scorched:– burnt [2]

כּוֹחַ ***kôaḥ***. See 3581.

3555 כְּוִיָּה ***k^{e}wiyyâ***, n.f. GK: 3918 [→ 3458]. burn spot, scar (of a burn):– burning [2]

3556 כּוֹכָב ***kôkāb***, n.m. GK: 3919. star, planet, a luminary in the night sky; by extension: human power (such as a king), heavenly power (that serve God); stargazer, one who studies the movements of the stars to predict the future:– stars [34], star [2], stargazers (+2374+871.1+1886.1) [1]

3557 כּוּל ***kûl***, v. GK: 3920 [cf. 3634?]. [Q] to hold, seize; [Pil] to hold; to provide, supply, sustain; [H] to hold; to bear, endure:– sustain [4], contain [3], fed [3], feed [3], abide [2], contained [2], nourish [2], receive [2], able to abide [1], bear [1], comprehended [1], containeth [1], forbearing [1], guide [1], held [1], holding in [1], hold [1], made provision [1], nourished [1], nourisher [1], present [1], provided of sustenance [1], provided victuals [1], provided victual [1]

3558 כּוּמָז ***kûmāz***, n.[m.]. GK: 3921. ornament, necklace:– tablets [2]

3559 כּוּן ***kûn***, v. GK: 3922 & 5788 [→ 3078, 3112, 3199, 3562, 3651, 3663, 4349, 4350, 4368, 4369, 5225, 8498, 8499; cf. 3653]. [N] to be established, be steadfast, be firm, be prepared; [Pol] to establish, set in place, make secure; [Polal] to be made firm, be prepared; [H] to establish, make preparations, provide; [Ho] to be made ready, be established, be attached:– prepared [53], established [42], prepare [28], establish [12], ready [9], fixed [4], made ready [4], make ready [4], right [4], stablished [4], stablish [4], prepareth [3], set [3], certain [2], confirmed [2], fashioned [2], firm [2], order [2], provideth [2], provide [2], certainty [1], confirm [1], could frame [1], directed [1], directeth [1], direct [1], faithfulness [1], fashion [1], fastened [1], fitted [1], made provision [1], make preparation [1], meet [1], ordained [1], ordered [1], perfect [1], preparation [1], preparest [1], provided for [1], set aright [1], set forth [1], set in order [1], setteth fast [1], stable [1], stablisheth [1], standeth [1], stood [1], tarry [1], very deed [1]

3560 כּוּן ***kûn***, n.pr.loc. GK: 3923. Cun, "*chosen*":– Chun [1]

3561 כַּוָּן ***kawwān***, n.[m.]. GK: 3924. cake of bread (presented as an offering):– cakes [2]

3561.1 כוֹן- ***-kôn*** (Aram.), p.suf.2.m.pl. GK: 10349 [→ 3641.2; cf. 3641.1]. you, your:– you [6], ye [2], your [2]

3562 כּוֹנַנְיָהוּ ***kônanyāhû***, n.pr.m. GK: 3925 [→ 3559+3068]. Conaniah:– Cononiah [2], Conaniah [1]

3563 כּוֹס **kôs**, n.f. GK: 3926 & 3927. cup; little owl:– cup [30], little owl [2], cups [1], owl [1]

3564 כּוּר **kûr**, n.[m.]. GK: 3929 [cf. 3600]. (little) furnace (for smelting metals); by extension: the testing and purification process:– furnace [9]

כּוֹר **kôr**. See 3733.

3565 כּוֹר עָשָׁן **kôr 'āšān**, n.pr.loc. GK: 3930 [cf. 953]. Kor Ashan:– Chor-ashan [1]

3566 כּוֹרֶשׁ **kôreš**, n.pr.m. GK: 3931 [cf. 3567]. Cyrus:– Cyrus [15]

3567 כּוֹרֶשׁ **kôreš** (Aram.), n.pr.m. GK: 10350 [cf. 3566]. Cyrus:– Cyrus [8]

3568 כּוּשׁ **kûš**, n.pr.m. & loc. GK: 3932 & 3933 [→ 3569, 3570, 3571]. Cush:– Ethiopia [19], Cush [8], Ethiopians [3]

3569 כּוּשִׁי **kûšî**, a.g. GK: 3934 [→ 3568]. Cushite, "*of Cush*":– Cushi [10], Ethiopians [9], Ethiopian [8]

3570 כּוּשִׁי **kûšî**, n.pr.m. GK: 3935 [→ 3568]. Cushi:–

3571 כּוּשִׁית **kûšît**, a.g. GK: 3934 [→ 3569]. f. of 3569: Cushite, "*of Cush*":–

3572 כּוּשָׁן **kûšān**, n.pr.loc. GK: 3936. Cushan:– Cushan [1]

3573 כּוּשַׁן רִשְׁעָתַיִם **kûšan riš'ātayim**, n.pr.m. GK: 3937. Cushan-Rishathaim, "*man of Cush, doubly guilty*":– Chushan-rishathaim [4]

3574 כּוֹשָׁרָה **kôšārâ**, n.f. GK: 3938 [cf. 7891]. singing or prosperity, fortune:– chains [1]

3575 כּוּת **kût** or כּוּתָה **kûtâ**, n.pr.loc. GK: 3939 & 3940. Cuthah:– Cuthah [1], Cuth [1]

3576 כָּזַב **kāzab**, v. GK: 3941 [→ 391, 392?, 3577, 3578, 3580]. [Q] to lie; [N] to be proven a liar, be false; [P] to lie, deceive, prove false; to fail; [H] to prove someone a liar:– lie [8], lied [2], fail [1], found a liar [1], in vain [1], liars [1], lying [1], make a liar [1]

3577 כָּזָב **kāzāb**, n.m. GK: 3942 [→ 3576; cf. 3538]. lie, falsehood; by extension: delusion; false god (worshiped by a deluded person):– lies [21], leasing [2], lie [2], lying [2], deceitful [1], false [1], liar (+376) [1], lies (+1697) [1]

3578 כֹּזֵבָא **kōzēbā'**, n.pr.loc. GK: 3943 [→ 3576]. Cozeba, "*liar*":– Chozeba [1]

3579 כָּזְבִּי **kozbî**, n.pr.f. GK: 3944. Cozbi, "*deceitful; luxuriant*":– Cozbi [2]

3580 כְּזִיב **k^ezîb**, n.pr.loc. GK: 3945 [→ 3576]. Kezib, "*deceit*":– Chezib [1]

3581 כֹּחַ **kōaḥ**, n.m. GK: 3946 & 3947. strength, power, might, ability; often physical strength and the vigor of good health, sometimes simply ability to accomplish an action; monitor lizard; some sources: any kind of lizard:– strength [57], power [47], might [7], force [3], ability [2], able [2], able (+6113) [1], chameleon [1], fruits [1], in strength [1], powerful [1], substance [1], wealth [1], weary (+3019) [1]

3582 כָּחַד **kāḥad**, v. GK: 3948. [N] to be hidden; be destroyed, perish; [P] to hide, conceal, keep from; [H] to hide; to destroy, annihilate, get rid of:– cut off [10], hide [10], hid [6], concealed [2], conceal [2], cut down [1], desolate [1]

3583 כָּחַל **kāḥal**, v. GK: 3949. [Q] to paint (eyes):– paintedst [1]

3584 כָּחַשׁ **kāḥaš**, v. GK: 3950 [→ 3585, 3586]. [Q] to be thin; [N] to cringe, feign obedience; [P] to lie, deceive; fail; to cringe, feign obedience; [Ht] to cringe, feign obedience:– deny [3], submit [3], denied [2], fail [2], lying [2], belied [1], deal falsely [1], deceive [1], dissembled [1], faileth [1], found liars [1], lied [1], lieth [1], lie [1], submitted [1]

3585 כַּחַשׁ **kaḥaš**, n.m. GK: 3951 [→ 3584]. lie, deception; gauntness, thinness, leanness:– lies [4], leanness [1], lying [1]

3586 כֶּחָשׁ **keḥāš**, a. GK: 3952 [→ 3584]. deceitful, untruthful:– lying [1]

3587 כִּי **kî**, n.[m.]. GK: 3953 [→ 3554]. branding:– burning [1]

3588 כִּי **kî**, c. GK: 3954. a marker that shows the relationship between clauses, sentences, or sections; logical: for, that, because; contrast: but, except; introducing a statement, often untranslated:– for [2322], that [696], because [442], when [237], but [173], if [168], but (+518) [86], surely [44], though [37], save (+518) [13], seeing [12], how [11], yet [10], although [9], yea [9], therefore [8], how much more (+637) [7], even [6], except (+518) [6], how much less (+637) [5], how that [5], because (+5921) [4], for (+5921) [4], nevertheless [4], so that [4], though (+518) [4], until (+5704) [4], whereas [4], assuredly [3], because (+3282) [3], else [3], in that [3], so [3], while [3], and (+518) [2], as [2], because (+3651+5921) [2], because (+6118) [2], because that [2], for (+518) [2], for if [2], forasmuch as [2], if not [2], or (+2050.1) [2], surely (+518) [2], than (+518) [2], to be [2], truly [2], whether [2], yet (+518) [2], also [1], although (+637) [1], and when [1], and [1], because (+8478) [1], because of [1], but (+518+3808) [1], but for (+518) [1], but that (+518) [1], but that [1], certainly [1], doubtless [1], either [1], even so [1], except (+1571) [1], except (+3884) [1], except (+518+3808) [1], except [1], for (+2088) [1], for (+4480) [1], for (+5973) [1], for surely (+518) [1], for that (+8478) [1], for then [1], for though (+518) [1], forasmuch as (+3282) [1], forasmuch as (+3651+5921) [1], forasmuch [1], forsomuch as (+3282) [1], how much less (+637+3808) [1], how much more then (+637) [1], howbeit yet (+389) [1], howbeit [1], inasmuch as [1], moreover [1], most [1], much less (+637) [1], much less for (+637) [1], much more (+637) [1], neither (+3808) [1], nevertheless (+518) [1], nevertheless (+657) [1], notwithstanding (+657) [1], now (+6258) [1], now [1], of a truth (+518) [1], rightly [1], save only (+518) [1], saving (+518) [1], seeing that [1], shall (+518) [1], since [1], than that [1], that (+518) [1], that when [1], then (+227) [1], then [1], thereof [1], though (+5973) [1], though (+637) [1], thus [1], till (+5704) [1], too [1], to [1], unless (+3884) [1], unless (+518) [1], until (+518) [1], wherefore (+389) [1], which [1], whom [1], whose [1], yea (+637) [1]

3589 כִּיד **kîd**, n.[m.]. GK: 3957. destruction:– destruction [1]

3590 כִּידוֹד **kîdôd**, n.m. GK: 3958. spark:– sparks [1]

3591 כִּידוֹן **kîdôn**, n.[m.]. GK: 3959 [→ 3592?]. javelin, lance, spear:– spear [5], shield [2], lance [1], target [1]

3592 כִּידֹן **kîdōn**, n.pr.m. GK: 3961 [→ 3591?]. Kidon:– Chidon [1]

3593 כִּידוֹר **kîdôr**, n.[m.]. GK: 3960. attack, battle:– battle [1]

3594 כִּיּוּן **kiyyûn**, n.m. GK: 3962. pedestal:– Chiun [1]

3595 כִּיּוֹר **kiyyôr**, n.m. GK: 3963. basin, pan, firepot:– laver [15], lavers [5], hearth [1], pan [1], scaffold [1]

3596 כִּילַי **kîlay**, n.m. GK: 3964 [→ 5230?]. scoundrel:– churl [2]

3597 כֵּילַפּוֹת **kêlappôt**, n.[f.]. GK: 3965 [→ 3619?]. an iron-tipped tool: ax, crowbar, pickax, etc:– hammers [1]

3598 כִּימָה **kîmâ**, n.f. GK: 3966. Pleiades (a constellation):– Pleiades [2], seven stars [1]

3599 כִּיס **kîs**, n.m. GK: 3967. bag, purse:– bag [4], purse [1]

3600 כִּיר **kîr**, n.[m.]. GK: 3968 [cf. 3564]. cooking pot, stove, a small portable cooking hearth, the form of the word suggesting it is large enough for a pair of pots:– ranges for pots [1]

כִּיֹר **kîōr**. See 3595.

3601 כִּישׁוֹר **kîšôr**, n.[m.]. GK: 3969. distaff, spindle, whorl, the small disk at the bottom of a distaff to promote turning:– spindle [1]

3602 כָּכָה **kākâ**, adv. GK: 3970 [→ 3541]. this is what, this is how, thus:– thus [17], so [8], after this manner [3], even so [3], after that manner [1], even thus [1], in such a case [1], this [1]

3603 כִּכָּר **kikkār**, n.f. GK: 3971 [→ 3769; cf. 3604]. plain (geographical area); loaf of bread; cover (of lead); talent (unit of weight or value, about 75 pounds [34 kg]):– talents [35], plain [12], talent [10], two talents [3], loaf [2], loaves [2], piece [2], morsel [1], plain country [1]

3604 כַּכַּר **kakkar** (Aram.), n.[f.]. GK: 10352 [cf. 3603]. talent (unit of weight or value, probably about 75 lbs [34 k]):– talents [1]

3605 כֹּל **kōl**, n.m. GK: 3972 [→ 3626; cf. 3634; cf. 3606, cf. 3635]. all, everyone, everything, totality of a mass or collective; every, any, a particular of a totality:– all [4291], every [362], any [169], whole [130], every one [95], no (+3808) [43], whosoever [34], whatsoever (+834) [33], whatsoever [23], for ever (+3117+1886.1) [15], none (+3808) [13], whithersoever (+834+871.1) [12], daily (+3117+1886.1) [11], continually (+3117+1886.1) [9], wholly [9], whosoever (+834) [8], any thing [7], as long as (+3117) [5], altogether [4], alway (+3117+1886.1) [4], every man [4], every province (+4082+4082+2050.1) [4], every thing [4], nothing (+3808) [4], what soever (+834) [4], all things [3], always (+3117+1886.1) [3], always (+6256+871.1) [3], as many as [3], ever (+3117+1886.1) [3], nothing (+3808+1886.1) [3], what [3], whatsoever (+871.1) [3], whithersoever (+413+834) [3], whomsoever (+834) [3], as long as (+834+3117+1886.1) [2], every city (+5892+5892+2050.1) [2], no (+369) [2], nothing (+369) [2], perpetually (+3117+1886.1) [2], that [2], throughout (+871.1) [2], whatsoever (+3807.1) [2], whatsoever (+834+3509.1) [2], whoso [2], all (+376) [1], all generations (+1755+1755+2050.1) [1], all manner [1], all over [1], always (+3117) [1], always (+871.1) [1], any (+259) [1], any manner [1], any thing (+3972) [1], as (+834+3509.1) [1], as long as (+3117+1886.1) [1], as long as [1], as many as (+834) [1], as much as (+3509.1) [1], as much as (+834) [1], at wit's end (+1104+2451) [1], continually (+3117) [1], continually (+6256+871.1) [1], daily (+3117+871.1) [1], enough [1], everlasting (+5769) [1], evermore (+3117+1886.1) [1], every day (+3117+3117+2050.1) [1], every generation (+1755+1755+2050.1) [1], every man's [1], every where [1], every year (+8141+8141+2050.1) [1], for evermore (+3117+1886.1) [1], generally [1], howsoever (+834) [1], many [1], more and more (+3254+5921) [1], no (+1115) [1], no (+369+3807.1) [1], none (+408+871.1) [1], nor (+2050.1) [1], nothing (+1097) [1], nothing (+1697+3808) [1], nothing (+408) [1], open [1], ought else (+3972) [1], ought [1], so long as (+3117+1886.1) [1], so long as (+871.1) [1], soever [1], the^S [1], throughout all [1], utterly [1], whatsoever (+3509.1) [1], whatsoever (+3627+1886.1) [1], whensoever (+871.1) [1], wheresoever (+3807.1) [1], wheresoever (+413) [1], wheresoever (+834+871.1) [1], wheresoever any (+834+8033) [1], while (+5750) [1], whithersoever (+834+5921) [1], whithersoever (+834+8033) [1], whosoever (+2050.2) [1], whosoever (+376) [1], whosoever (+376+834) [1], withal [1], yearly (+8141+8141+871.1+2050.1) [1]

3606 כֹּל **kōl** (Aram.), n.m. GK: 10353 [→ 3635; cf. 3605]. all, totality, completion of an event; a part of a totality: any, every:– all [51], any [8], forasmuch as (+1768+6903) [8], whole [6], because (+1768+6903) [4], every [4], no (+3809) [3], therefore (+1836+6903) [3], wherefore (+1836+6903) [2], whosoever (+1768) [2], as (+1768+6903) [1], for this cause (+1836+6903) [1], manner [1], no^S [1], none (+3809) [1], that (+1836+6903) [1], therefore (+1768+6903) [1], though (+1768+6903) [1], whatsoever (+1768) [1], whatsoever (+1768+1768) [1], wheresoever (+1768+871.2) [1], whosoever (+606) [1], whosoever (+606+1768+1768) [1]

3607 כָּלָא **kālā'**, v. GK: 3973 & 3974 [→ 3608, 3628, 4356; cf. 3615, 3627]. [Q] to stop, withhold, contain; [Qp] to be confined; [N] to be restrained; [P] to finish:– shut up [4], stayed [3], refrained [2], restrained [2], withhold [2], finish [1], forbid [1], keep back [1], kept [1], retain [1]

3608 כֶּלֶא **kele'**, n.[m.]. GK: 3975 [→ 3607; cf. 3628]. prison, (house of) imprisonment:– prison (+1004+1886.1) [4], prison [4], prison (+1004) [2]

3609 כִּלְאָב **kil'āb**, n.pr.m. GK: 3976. Kileab:– Chileab [1]

3610 כִּלְאַיִם **kil'ayim**, n.[m.]. GK: 3977. (things of) two kinds:– diverse kind [1], divers [1], mingled of linen and woollen (+8162) [1], mingled [1]

3611 כֶּלֶב **keleb**, n.m. GK: 3978 [→ 3612; cf. 3619]. dog; by extension of a person of low status: a dead dog; an immoral person: male prostitute:– dogs [16], dog [14], dog's [2]

3612 כָּלֵב **kālēb**, n.pr.m. GK: 3979 [→ 3613, 3614, 3619, 3621; cf. 3611]. Caleb, "*dog; snappish, warding off*":– Caleb [31], Caleb's [4]

3613 כָּלֵב אֶפְרָתָה **kālēb 'eprātâ**, n.pr.loc. GK: 3980 [→ 3612+672]. Caleb Ephrathah:– Caleb-ephratah [1]

3614 כָּלִבִּי **kālibbî**, a.g. GK: 3981 & 3982 [→ 3612]. Calebite, "*of Caleb*":– of the house of Caleb [1]

3615 כָּלָה **kālâ**, v. GK: 3983 [→ 401, 3616, 3617, 3631, 3630, 4357, 8502, 8503; cf. 3607, 3627, 3634, 5239]. [Q] to finish, fulfill, complete; to fail, cease, perish; [P] to finish, complete, fulfill; to destroy, end, wipe out; [Pu] to be completed, be concluded:– made an end [41], consumed [36], consume [22], finished [19], fail [12], done [9], accomplished [7], ended [7], accomplish [5], determined [4], faileth [4], spend [4], spent [4], end [2], fainteth [2], fulfilled [2], left [2], make an end [2], bringeth to pass [1], caused to fail [1], ceaseth [1], cease [1], consumed away [1], destroy utterly [1], destroyeth [1], expired [1], failed [1], finish [1], fulfil [1], fully [1], left off [1], longed [1], make clean riddance [1], pluck [1], quite take away [1], utterly destroyed [1], wasted [1], waste [1], wholly reap (+3807.1) [1]

3616 כָּלֶה **kāleh**, a. GK: 3985 [→ 3615]. failing with desire, longing:– fail [1]

3617 כָּלָה **kālâ**, n.f. GK: 3986 [→ 3615]. destruction, complete destruction:– full end [8], altogether [3], consumption [2], utter end [2], consumed [1], consume [1], consummation [1], determined [1], end [1], riddance [1], utterly consume [1]

3618 כַּלָּה ***kallâ***, n.f. GK: 3987 [→ 3623]. (before marriage) bride; daughter-in-law:– daughter in law [14], bride [9], spouse [6], daughters in law [3], spouses [2]

כְּלוּא ***kᵉlûʾ***. See 3628.

3619 כְּלוּב ***kᵉlûb***, n.m. GK: 3990 [→ 3597?, 3611, 3612, 3619, 3620?]. (fruit) basket; (bird) cage:– basket [2], cage [1]

3620 כְּלוּב ***kᵉlûb***, n.pr.m. GK: 3991 [→ 3619?]. Kelub, "*basket*":– Chelub [2]

3621 כְּלוּבָי ***kᵉlûbāy***, n.pr.m. GK: 3992 [→ 3612]. Caleb, "*dog; snappish warding off*":– Chelubai [1]

3622 כְּלֻהַי ***kᵉluhî*** or כְּלוּהוּ ***kᵉlûhû***, n.pr.m. GK: 3988 & 3993. Keluhi:– Chelluh [1]

3623 כְּלוּלֹת ***kᵉlûlōt***, n.f. GK: 3994 [→ 3618]. time of betrothal, state of betrothal:– espousals [1]

3624 כֶּלַח ***kelaḥ***, n.m. GK: 3995. full vigor:– full age [1], old age [1]

3625 כֶּלַח ***kelaḥ***, n.pr.loc. GK: 3996. Calah, "*strength, vigor*":– Calah [2]

3626 כָּל־חֹזֶה ***kol-ḥōzeh***, n.pr.m. GK: 3997 [→ 3605+2374]. Col-Hozeh, "*every seer*":– Col-hozeh [2]

3627 כְּלִי ***kᵉlî***, n.m. GK: 3998 [cf. 3607?, 3615?]. article, utensil, thing; a general term that can be used of any object:– vessels [132], instruments [37], vessel [34], jewels [20], armourbearer (+5375) [18], weapons [17], stuff [14], thing [11], armour [10], furniture [7], weapon [4], bag [2], carriage [2], instrument [2], artillery [1], carriages [1], furnish (+6213) [1], jewel [1], one another[S] [1], pot [1], psaltery (+5035) [1], sacks [1], that is made [1], that which pertaineth [1], things made [1], tool [1], wares [1], whatsoever (+3605+1886.1) [1]

3628 כְּלוּא ***kᵉlûʾ*** or כְּלִיא ***kᵉlîʾ***, n.[m.]. GK: 3989 & 3999 [→ 3607; cf. 3608]. imprisonment:– prison (+1004+1886.1) [2]

3629 כִּלְיָה ***kilyâ***, n.f. GK: 4000. kidney; by extension: inmost being: heart, mind, spirit, the seat of thought and emotion of the inner person; kernel (of wheat):– kidneys [18], reins [13]

3630 כִּלְיוֹן ***kilyôn***, n.pr.m. GK: 4002 [→ 3615]. Kilion, "*annihilation*":– Chilion [2], Chilion's [1]

Heb

3631 כִּלָּיוֹן ***killāyôn***, n.m. GK: 4001 [→ 3615]. destruction, annihilation; weariness, failure (of the eyes):– consumption [1], failing [1]

3632 כָּלִיל ***kālîl***, a. & subst. GK: 4003 [→ 3634]. entire, whole, perfect; whole burnt offering:– wholly [4], perfect [3], all [2], whole [2], every whit [1], flame [1], perfection [1], utterly [1]

3633 כַּלְכֹּל ***kalkōl***, n.pr.m. GK: 4004 [→ 3634?]. Calcol:– Calcol [1], Chalcol [1]

3634 כָּלַל ***kālal***, v. GK: 4005 [→ 3605, 3626, 3632, 3633?, 3636, 4358, 4360, 4359; cf. 3557?, 3615; cf. 3606, cf. 3635]. [Q] to bring to perfection, make complete:– made perfect [1], perfected [1]

3635 כְּלַל ***kᵉlal*** (Aram.), v. GK: 10354 [→ 3606; cf. 3634]. [Sh] to finish, restore; [Hsh] to be finished:– set up [4], make up [2], finished [1]

3636 כְּלָל ***kᵉlāl***, n.pr.m. GK: 4006 [→ 3634]. Kelal, "*perfection, completeness*":– Chelal [1]

3637 כָּלַם ***kālam***, v. GK: 4007 [→ 3639, 3640]. [N] to be disgraced, be humiliated, be put to shame; [H] to disgrace, humble, bring to shame; [Ho] to be mistreated, be despairing:– ashamed [11], confounded [11], put to shame [5], blush [3], hurt [2], done shame [1], make ashamed [1], put to confusion [1], reproached [1], reproach [1], shameth [1]

3638 כִּלְמַד ***kilmad***, n.pr.loc. GK: 4008. Kilmad:– Chilmad [1]

3639 כְּלִמָּה ***kᵉlimmâ***, n.f. GK: 4009 [→ 3637]. disgrace, shame, scorn:– shame [20], confusion [6], dishonour [3], reproach [1]

3640 כְּלִמּוּת ***kᵉlimmût***, n.f. GK: 4010 [→ 3637]. shame, disgrace, insult:– shame [1]

3641 כַּלְנֵה ***kalnēh*** or כַּלְנוֹ ***kalnô***, n.pr.loc. GK: 4011 & 4012. Calneh, Calno, "*all of them*":– Calneh [2], Calno [1]

3641.1 כֶם- ***-kem***, p.m.pl.suf. GK: 4013 [→ 3509.2]. you, your:– you [1209], your [1175], ye [145], your (+3807.1) [44], your own [22], yourselves [22], yourselves (+5315) [6], yours (+3807.1) [4], thee [2], thou [1], thy [1], your (+4480) [1], yours [1]

3641.2 כֹם- ***-kōm*** (Aram.), p.suf.2.m.pl. GK: 10355 [→ 3641.2; cf. 3641.1]. you, your:– you [3], your [2]

3642 כָּמַהּ ***kāmah***, v. GK: 4014 [→ 3643]. [Q] to long for, yearn for:– longeth [1]

3643 כִּמְהָם ***kimhām*** or כִּמְוֹהָם ***kimwhām***, n.pr.m. GK: 4016 & 4018 [cf. 3642]. Kimham, Kimuham:– Chimham [4]

3644 כְּמוֹ ***kᵉmô***, adv. & c. GK: 4017 [→ 3509.1+4100]. like, as; for, with, when:– as [60], like [41], like unto [17], according to [2], as it were [2], as well as [2], like to [2], such as [2], and [1], both [1], even [1], in comparison of [1], like as [1], so [1], the like [1], thus [1], when [1], worth [1]

3645 כְּמוֹשׁ ***kᵉmôš*** or כְּמִישׁ ***kᵉmîš***, n.pr. GK: 4019 & 4020. Chemosh, Chemish (pagan god):– Chemosh [8]

3646 כַּמֹּן ***kammōn***, n.m. GK: 4021. cummin (a small, flavorful seed of the carrot family):– cummin [3]

3647 כָּמַס ***kāmas***, v. GK: 4022 [→ 4363]. [Qp] to be kept in reserve:– laid up in store [1]

3648 כָּמַר ***kāmar***, v. GK: 4023 [→ 3649]. [N] to become hot; become aroused, be excited (with compassion):– black [1], kindled [1], yerned [1], yern [1]

3649 כֹּמֶר ***kōmer***, n.m. GK: 4024 [→ 3648]. priest, in the OT always one who serves a foreign god, with a possible focus on manic rituals and altered states of awareness:– Chemarims [1], idolatrous priests [1], priests [1]

3650 כַּמְרִיר ***kamrîr***, n.m. GK: 4025. blackness, deep gloom:– blackness [1]

3651 כֵּן ***kēn***, a. & adv. GK: 4026 & 4027 [cf. 3559; cf. 3652]. honest; right, correct, orderly; (adv.) marker to show sequence of logic: so, thus, therefore; marker to show sequence of events: so, then:– so [283], therefore (+3807.1) [176], therefore (+5921) [125], wherefore (+5921) [22], thus [20], wherefore (+3807.1) [18], this [17], afterward (+310) [15], that [12], likewise [11], such [7], true [5], afterwards (+310) [4], right [4], as [3], because (+5921) [3], in like manner [3], like [3], well [3], after that (+310) [2], because (+3588+5921) [2], even so [2], surely (+3807.1) [2], according [1], after that (+310+2050.1) [1], afterward (+310+4480) [1], also [1], aright [1], as (+834+3509.1) [1], as yet (+5704) [1], certainly [1], even as (+834+3509.1) [1], following (+310) [1], for which cause (+3807.1) [1], for which cause (+5921) [1], forasmuch (+3807.1) [1], forasmuch as (+3588+5921) [1], howbeit (+2050.1) [1], if so (+518) [1], state [1], straightway [1], that (+5921) [1], the more [1], thenceforth (+310) [1], therefore [1], which thing [1]

3652 כֵּן ***kēn*** (Aram.), adv. GK: 10357 [cf. 3651]. this is what, thus:– thus [8]

3653 כֵּן ***kēn***, n.m. GK: 4029 & 4030 [→ 3662, 3663; cf. 3559]. position; place; stand (of a basin):– foot [8], estate [4], base [2], office [1], place [1], well [1]

3654 כֵּן ***kēn***, n.[m.]. GK: 4031 & 4038. gnats, flies:– lice [6], in manner [1]

3654.1 כֶן- ***-ken*** or כֶנָה- ***-kenâ***, p.f.pl.suf. GK: 4032 [→ 3509.2]. you, your:– your [16], you [2], ye [1]

3655 כָּנָה ***kānâ***, v. GK: 4033. [P] to bestow a title or name of honor; to flatter by giving a name of honor:– give flattering titles [2], surnamed [1], surname [1]

3656 כַּנֵּה ***kannēh***, n.pr.loc. GK: 4034. Canneh:– Canneh [1]

3657 כַּנָּה ***kannâ***, n.f. GK: 4035. root:– vineyard [1]

3658 כִּנּוֹר ***kinnôr***, n.m. GK: 4036. a stringed instrument: harp, lyre, lute, zither:– harp [25], harps [17]

3659 כָּנְיָהוּ ***konyāhû***, n.pr.m. GK: 4037 [→ 3078]. Jehoiachin:– Coniah [3]

3660 כְּנֵמָא ***kᵉnēmāʾ*** (Aram.), adv. GK: 10358. as follows, thus:– thus [2], after this manner [1], in this sort [1], so [1]

3661 כָּנַן ***kānan***, var. GK: *. to plant a vineyard:–

3662 כְּנָנִי ***kᵉnānî***, n.pr.m. GK: 4039 [→ 3663]. Kenani, "*Yahweh strengthens*":– Chenani [1]

3663 כְּנַנְיָה ***kᵉnanyâ*** or כְּנַנְיָהוּ ***kᵉnanyāhû*** or כָּנַנְיָהוּ ***kānanyāhû***, n.pr.m. GK: 4040 & 4041 & 4042 [→ 3068+3559, 3662]. Kenaniah, Conaniah, "*Yahweh strengthens*":– Chenaniah [3]

3664 כָּנַס ***kānas***, v. GK: 4043 [→ 4370; cf. 3673]. [Q, P] to assemble, gather, store up; [Ht] to wrap around:– gather together [3], gathered [2], gathereth together [2], gather [2], heap up [1], wrap [1]

3665 כָּנַע ***kānaʿ***, v. GK: 4044 [→ 3666]. [N] to be humbled, be subdued, be subjected; [H] to subdue, humble, subject:– humbled [13], subdued [9], bring down [2], humbleth [2], humble [2], bring low [1], brought down [1], brought into subjection [1], brought low [1], brought under [1], humbledst [1], subduedst [1], subdue [1]

3666 כִּנְעָה ***kinʿâ***, n.f. GK: 4045 [→ 3665]. bundle of belongings:– wares [1]

3667 כְּנַעַן ***kᵉnaʿan***, n.pr.m. & loc. GK: 4046 & 4047 [→ 3668?, 3669]. Canaan; Canaanite, "*land of purple, hence merchant, trader*"; merchant, trader:– Canaan [89], merchant [3], traffickers [1], traffick [1]

3668 כְּנַעֲנָה ***kᵉnaʿᵃnâ***, n.pr.m. GK: 4049 [→ 3667?]. Kenaanah, "*toward Canaan*":– Chenaanah [5]

3669 כְּנַעֲנִי ***kᵉnaʿᵃnî***, a.g. & n.m. GK: 4048 & 4050 & 4051 [→ 3667]. Canaanite, of Canaan, in Canaan, "*of Canaan*"; merchant, trader:– Canaanites [55], Canaanite [12], Canaanitess [1], Canaanitish woman [1], Canaanitish [1], Canaan [1], merchants [1], merchant [1]

3670 כָּנַף ***kānap***, v.den. GK: 4052 [→ 3671]. [N] to hide oneself, be hidden:– removed into a corner [1]

3671 כָּנָף ***kānāp***, n.f. GK: 4053 [→ 3670]. extreme part: wing (of creatures that fly); corner, hem (of garment); ends (of the earth):– wings [60], wing [13], skirt [12], borders [2], corners [2], ends [2], feathered [2], one another (+413+3671) [2], skirts [2], sort [2], winged [2], bird (+1167) [1], flying [1], other[S] [1], overspreading [1], quarters [1], two wings [1], uttermost part [1]

3672 כִּנְרוֹת ***kinrôt*** or כִּנֶּרֶת ***kinneret*** or כִּנֲרוֹת ***kinᵃrôt***, n.pr.loc. GK: 4054 & 4055. Kinnereth, Kinneroth, "*zithers, lyres*":– Chinnereth [3], Cinneroth [3], Cinnereth [1]

3673 כְּנַשׁ ***kᵉnaš*** (Aram.), v. GK: 10359 [cf. 3664]. [P] to assemble (persons); [Htpa] to be assembled:– gathered together [2], gather together [1]

3674 כְּנָת ***kᵉnāt***, n.f. GK: 4056 [cf. 3675]. associate, companion:– companions [1]

3675 כְּנָת ***kᵉnāt*** (Aram.), n.m. GK: 10360 [cf. 3674]. associate, colleague:– companions [7]

3676 כֵּס ***kᵉs***, var. GK: 4058 [→ 3678+3050; cf. 3764]. poss. short form of 3678: seat, throne:–

3677 כֶּסֶא ***keseʾ***, n.[m.]. GK: 4057 & 4060 [→ 3678]. full moon:– appointed [1], time appointed [1]

3678 כִּסֵּא ***kissēʾ*** or כִּסֵּה ***kissēh***, n.m. GK: 4058 & 4061 [→ 3676]. seat, chair; in a public or civic setting: place of authority, seat of honor; of royalty or deity: throne:– throne [123], seat [7], thrones [4], stool [1], sworn (+3027+5921) [1]

3679 כַּסְדָּי ***kasdāy*** (Aram.), n.pr.g. GK: 10361 [cf. 3779]. Chaldean:– Chaldean [1]

3680 כָּסָה ***kāsâ***, v. GK: 4059 [→ 3681, 3682, 4372, 4374]. [Qp] to be covered; [N] to be covered; [P] to cover, conceal; to decorate; to overwhelm; [Pu] to be covered, be shrouded; [Ht] to cover oneself, put on clothing:– covered [61], cover [50], covereth [21], concealeth [2], conceal [2], coveredst [2], covering [2], hide [2], hid [2], overwhelmed [2], clad [1], closed [1], clothed [1], coverest [1], flee to hide [1], hideth [1]

כֶּסֶה ***keseh***. See 3677.

כִּסֵּה ***kissēh***. See 3678.

3681 כָּסוּי ***kāsûy***, n.[m.]. GK: 4062 [→ 3680]. covering:– covering [2]

3682 כְּסוּת ***kᵉsût***, n.f. GK: 4064 [→ 3680]. covering, cloak, clothing:– covering [6], raiment [1], vesture [1]

3683 כָּסַח ***kāsaḥ***, v. GK: 4065. [Qp] to be cut down (of brush):– cut down [1], cut up [1]

3684 כְּסִיל ***kᵉsîl***, n.m. GK: 4067 [→ 3685; cf. 3688]. foolish, stupid, insolent; (n.) fool, insolent person:– fool [34], fools [22], foolish [9], fool's [4], fools' [1]

3685 כְּסִיל ***kᵉsîl***, n.m. GK: 4068 [→ 3684; cf. 3688]. Orion (and its adjoining constellations):– Orion [3], constellations [1]

3686 כְּסִיל ***kᵉsîl***, n.pr.loc. GK: 4069. Kesil:– Chesil [1]

3687 כְּסִילוּת ***kᵉsîlût***, n.f. GK: 4070 [→ 3688]. folly, stupidity, insolence, with a possible implication of rebellion:– foolish [1]

3688 כָּסַל ***kāsal***, v. GK: 4071 [→ 3694, 3684, 3685, 3687, 3689, 3690, 3693, 3692]. [Q] to be foolish, be stupid:– foolish [1]

3689 כֶּסֶל ***kesel***, n.m. GK: 4072 & 4073 [→ 3688, 3696?]. waist, back; (pl.) loins; trust, confidence; stupidity:– flanks [6], hope [3], folly [2], confidence [1], loins [1]

3690 כִּסְלָה ***kislâ***, n.f. GK: 4074 [→ 3688]. confidence; folly:– confidence [1], folly [1]

3691 כִּסְלֵו ***kislēw***, n.pr.[m.]. GK: 4075. Kislev:– Chisleu [2]

3692 כִּסְלוֹן ***kislôn***, n.pr.m. GK: 4077 [→ 3688]. Kislon, "*slow; strength*":– Chislon [1]

3693 כְּסָלוֹן ***kᵉsālôn***, n.pr.loc. GK: 4076 [→ 3688]. Kesalon:– Chesalon [1]

3694 כְּסֻלּוֹת ***kᵉsûlôt***, n.pr.loc. GK: 4063 [→ 3688]. Kesulloth, "*loins* or *flanks [of Mt. Tabor]*":– Chesulloth [1]

3695 כַּסְלֻחִים ***kasluḥîm***, n.pr.g. GK: 4078. Casluhite:– Casluhim [2]

3696 כִּסְלֹת תָּבוֹר ***kislōt tābôr***, n.pr.loc. GK: 4079 [→ 3689?+8396]. Kisloth Tabor:– Chislothtabor [1]

3697 כָּסַם ***kāsam***, v. GK: 4080 [→ 3698; cf. 1501, 3765]. [Q] to trip, clip (hair):– only poll (+3697) [2]

3698 כֻּסֶּמֶת ***kussemet***, n.f. GK: 4081 [→ 3697]. spelt, emmer wheat:– rye [2], fitches [1]

3699 כָּסַס ***kāsas***, v. GK: 4082 [→ 4371, 4373]. [Q] to determine, reckon, compute:– make count [1]

3700 כָּסַף ***kāsap***, v. GK: 4083 [→ 3701]. [Q] to long for; be hungry; [N] to long for, yearn for; to be ashamed:– sore longedst (+3700) [2], desired [1], greedy [1], have desire [1], longeth [1]

3701 כֶּסֶף ***kesep***, n.m. GK: 4084 [→ 3700; cf. 3702]. silver, silver piece = money:– silver [287], money [112], price [3], silverlings [1]

3702 כְּסַף ***kᵉsap*** (Aram.), n.m. GK: 10362 [cf. 3701]. silver:– silver [12], money [1]

3703 כָּסִפְיָא ***kāsipyā'***, n.pr.loc. GK: 4085. Casiphia:– Casiphia [2]

3704 כֶּסֶת ***keset***, n.f. GK: 4086. magic charm band:– pillows [2]

3705 כְּעַן ***kᵉ'an*** (Aram.), adv. GK: 10363 [→ 3706]. now, furthermore, to the present:– now [13]

3706 כְּעֶנֶת ***kᵉ'enet*** or כְּעֶת ***kᵉ'et*** (Aram.), adv. GK: 10364 & 10365 [→ 3705]. (and) now, a marker to connect what follows; the phrase "Peace and now" is a formal greeting in a letter:– at such a time [3], such a time [1]

3707 כָּעַס ***kā'as***, v. GK: 4087 [→ 3708; cf. 3708]. [Q] to be angry, be vexed, be incensed; [P] to anger, provoke; [H] to provoke to anger:– provoke to anger [24], provoked to anger [14], provoking to anger [3], angry [2], provoked [2], grieved [1], provoke unto wrath [1], provoked sore (+3708) [1], provoketh to anger [1], provoke [1], sorrow [1], took indignation [1], vex [1], wroth [1]

3708 כַּעַס ***ka'as*** or כַּעַשׂ ***ka'aś***, n.m. GK: 4088 & 4089 [→ 3707, 3708]. general uneasiness and anxiety, inwardly focused: anguish, grief; focused toward an object: anger, resentment:– grief [7], wrath [4], provocation [3], sorrow [3], anger [2], angry [1], indignation [1], provocations [1], provoked sore (+3707) [1], provoking [1], spite [1]

כְּעֶת ***kᵉ'et***. See 3706.

3709 כַּף ***kap***, n.f. GK: 4090 [→ 3721]. hand (of a person), palm of the hand, sole of the foot, paw (of an animal); by extension: power, strength; something hollowed: socket, (shallow) dish; a measure of quantity: handful:– hands [69], hand [55], sole [12], spoons [12], spoon [12], soles [7], hands together (+413+3709) [4], hollow [4], palms [3], handful (+4393) [2], palm of hand [2], apiece (+1886.1) [1], branches [1], clouds [1], foot (+7272) [1], handled (+8610+871.1+1886.1) [1], handles [1], middle [1], palms of hands [1], paws [1], power [1], took a handful (+4390) [1]

3710 כֵּף ***kēp***, n.[m.]. GK: 4091. rock:– rocks [2]

3711 כָּפָה ***kāpâ***, v. GK: 4092. [Q] to soothe, avert (anger):– pacifieth [1]

3712 כִּפָּה ***kippâ***, n.f. GK: 4093 [→ 3721]. palm branch, palm frond:– branch [3]

3713 כְּפוֹר ***kᵉpôr***, n.m. GK: 4094 & 4095 [→ 3722]. bowl, dish (made of gold or silver); frost:– basons [4], every bason (+3713+2050.1) [4], hoar frost [1], hoarfrost [1], hoary frost [1]

3714 כָּפִיס ***kāpîs***, n.m. GK: 4096. beam (of woodwork); some sources: rafter:– beam [1]

3715 כְּפִיר ***kᵉpîr***, n.m. GK: 4097 & 4099 [→ 3722, 3723]. young lion; village:– young lions [12], young lion [12], lion [4], lions [2], villages [1], young [1]

3716 כְּפִירָה ***kᵉpîrâ***, n.pr.loc. GK: 4098 [→ 3723]. Kephirah, "*village*":– Chephirah [4]

3717 כָּפַל ***kāpal***, v. GK: 4100 [→ 3718, 4375]. [Q] to fold double; [Qp] to be folded double; [N] to be doubled:– doubled [3], double [2]

3718 כֶּפֶל ***kepel***, n.[m.]. GK: 4101 [→ 3717]. double; two sides:– double [3]

3719 כָּפַן ***kāpan***, v. GK: 4102 [→ 3720]. [Q] to hunger, send out roots in hunger:– bend [1]

3720 כָּפָן ***kāpān***, n.[m.]. GK: 4103 [→ 3719]. hunger, famine:– famine [2]

3721 כָּפַף ***kāpap***, v. GK: 4104 [→ 3709, 3712]. [Q] to bow down in distress; [Qp] be bowed down; [N] bow down (before):– bowed down [3], bow down [1], bow [1]

3722 כָּפַר ***kāpar***, v. GK: 4105 & 4106 [→ 3713, 3715, 3724, 3725, 3727]. [Q] to coat, cover (with pitch); [Nitpael] to be atoned (for); [P] to make atonement; make amends, pardon, release, appease, forgive; [Pu] to be atoned for, be annulled; [Ht] to allow for atonement; atonement may be a figure of covering over and therefore forgetting (forgiving) sin:– make an atonement [58], make atonement [6], made an atonement [5], purged [5], make reconciliation [4], atonement made [2], merciful [2], purge away [2], purge [2], reconcile [2], appease (+6440) [1], cleansed [1], disannulled [1], forgave [1], forgiven [1], forgive [1], maketh an atonement [1], maketh atonement [1], pacified [1], pacify [1], pardon [1], pitch [1], put off [1], reconciling [1]

3723 כָּפָר ***kāpār***, n.m. GK: 4107 [→ 3716, 3715, 3724, 3726]. (unwalled) village:– villages [2]

3724 כֹּפֶר ***kōper***, n.m. GK: 4108 & 4109 & 4110 & 4111 [→ 3722, 3723]. pitch (used to cover and seal the ark of Noah); (unwalled) village; henna, henna blossom; ransom, compensation, payment; bribe:– ransom [8], bribe [2], camphire [2], satisfaction [2], pitch [1], sum of money [1], villages [1]

3725 כִּפֻּרִים ***kippurîm***, n.pl.abst. GK: 4113 [→ 3722]. atonement; atonement may be a figure of covering over and therefore forgetting (forgiving) sin; "day of Atonement" is an annual day of rest and with ceremonies accomplishing full atonement for the nation of Israel:– atonement [7], atonements [1]

3726 כְּפַר הָעַמֹּנִי ***kᵉpar hā'ammōnî***, n.pr.loc. GK: 4112 [→ 3723]. Kephar Ammoni, "*village of Ammonites*":– Chephar-haammonai [1]

3727 כַּפֹּרֶת ***kappōret***, n. GK: 4114 [→ 3722]. atonement cover (traditionally: mercy seat); the golden cover on the ark of the covenant, the place where atonement is made:– mercy seat [26], mercy seatward [1]

3728 כָּפַשׁ ***kāpaš***, v. GK: 4115 [cf. 3533]. [H] to trample down:– covered [1]

3729 כְּפַת ***kᵉpat*** (Aram.), v. GK: 10366. [Peil] to be bound; [Pa] to tie up; [Pap] to be tied:– bound [3], bind [1]

3730 כַּפְתּוֹר ***kaptôr***, n.m. GK: 4117. bud; top of a pillar or column:– knop [10], knops [6], lintel of the door [1], upper lintels [1]

3731 כַּפְתּוֹר ***kaptôr***, n.pr.loc. GK: 4116 [→ 3732]. Caphtor:– Caphtor [3]

3732 כַּפְתֹּרִי ***kaptōrî***, a.g. GK: 4118 [→ 3731]. Caphtorite, "*of Caphtor*":– Caphthorim [1], Caphtorims [1], Caphtorim [1]

3733 כַּר ***kar***, n.m. GK: 4119 & 4120 & 4121 [→ 3769]. (young) ram; battering ram; meadow, pastureland; saddle, saddle-bag:– lambs [9], pastures [2], rams [2], captains [1], furniture [1], lamb [1]

3734 כֹּר ***kōr***, n.[m.]. GK: 4123 & 10367. cor (measure of dry or liquid volume, about 60 gallons [220 liters]): note this word is Aramaic once in Ezra:– measures [8], cor [1]

3735 כְּרָה ***kᵉrâ*** (Aram.), v. GK: 10369. [Itpe] to be troubled, distressed:– grieved [1]

3736 כִּרְבֵּל ***kirbēl***, v.den. GK: 4124 [cf. 3737]. [Pu] to be clothed, be wrapped:– clothed [1]

3737 כַּרְבְּלָה ***karbᵉlâ*** (Aram.), n.f. GK: 10368. headdress of some kind: turban, cap; the etymology suggests something wrapped around the head:– hats [1]

3738 כָּרָה ***kārâ***, v. GK: 4125 & 4127 & 4128 [→ 3740, 3741, 4351, 4379]. [Q] to dig; to hew (stone); to hollow out; to prepare a feast; to tie together:– digged [8], dig [2], made [2], diggeth up [1], diggeth [1], opened [1], pierced [1]

3739 כָּרָה ***kārâ***, v. GK: 4126. [Q] to barter; purchase:– bought [1], buy [1], make a banquet [1], prepared [1]

3740 כֵּרָה ***kērâ***, n.f. GK: 4130 [→ 3738]. feast, banquet:– provision [1]

3741 כָּרָה ***kārâ***, n.f. GK: 4129 [→ 3738]. cistern, well:– cottages [1]

3742 כְּרוּב ***kᵉrûb***, n.m. GK: 4131. cherub, (pl.) cherubim, a class of supernatural beings that serve in the presence of God; used as ornamental figures on the atonement cover of the ark of the covenant and in the temple as well as on the walls and doors of the temple:– cherubims [63], cherub [27], cherubims' [1]

3743 כְּרוּב ***kᵉrûb***, n.pr.loc. GK: 4132. Kerub:– Cherub [2]

3744 כָּרוֹז ***kārôz*** (Aram.), n.m. GK: 10370 [→ 3745]. herald, proclaimer:– herald [1]

3745 כְּרַז ***kᵉraz*** (Aram.), v.den. GK: 10371 [→ 3744]. [H] to proclaim:– made a proclamation [1]

3746 כָּרִי ***kārî***, a.g. GK: 4133. Carite:– captains [2]

3747 כְּרִית ***kᵉrît***, n.pr.loc. GK: 4134 [→ 3772]. Kerith, "*cut off, perish*":– Cherith [2]

3748 כְּרִיתוּת ***kᵉrîtût***, n.f. GK: 4135 [→ 3772]. divorce:– divorcement [3], divorce [1]

3749 כַּרְכֹּב ***karkōb***, n.[m.]. GK: 4136. ledge, rim, edge:– compass [2]

3750 כַּרְכֹּם ***karkōm***, n.[m.]. GK: 4137. saffron (plant):– saffron [1]

3751 כַּרְכְּמִישׁ ***karkᵉmîš***, n.pr.loc. GK: 4138. Carchemish:– Carchemish [3]

3752 כַּרְכַּס ***karkas***, n.pr.m. GK: 4139. Carcas, "[perhaps] *vulture*":– Carcas [1]

3753 כִּרְכָּרָה ***kirkārâ***, n.f. GK: 4140 [→ 3769]. (fast running) female camel:– swift beasts [1]

3754 כֶּרֶם ***kerem***, n.m. GK: 4142 [→ 3755, 3756?, 3757?, 3759]. vineyard:– vineyards [45], vineyard [44], vines [3], vintage [1]

3755 כֹּרֵם ***kōrēm***, n.[m.] *or* v.ptcp. GK: 4144 [→ 3754]. worker in the vineyard, vine growers, vinedressers:– vinedressers [5]

3756 כַּרְמִי ***karmî***, n.pr.m. GK: 4145 [→ 3757; cf. 3754?]. Carmi, "[poss.] *[fruitful] vine, vineyard owner*":– Carmi [8]

3757 כַּרְמִי ***karmî***, a.g. GK: 4146 [→ 3756; cf. 3754?]. Carmite, "*of Carmi*":– Carmites [1]

3758 כַּרְמִיל ***karmîl***, n.[m.]. GK: 4147. crimson (yarn):– crimson [3]

3759 כַּרְמֶל ***karmel***, n.m. GK: 4149 & 4152 [→ 3760, 3761, 3762; cf. 3754]. fertile land, fruitful land; this can refer to an orchard or plantation; new grain, newly ripe grain:– fruitful field [6], plentiful field [2], corn of full ears [1], fruitful place [1], full ears of corn [1], green ears [1], plentiful [1]

3760 כַּרְמֶל ***karmel***, n.pr.loc. GK: 4150 & 4151 [→ 3759, 3761]. Carmel, "*orchard planted with vine and fruit trees*":– Carmel [26]

3761 כַּרְמְלִי ***karmᵉlî***, a.g. GK: 4153 [→ 3760, 3762; cf. 3759]. Carmelite, of Carmel, "*of Carmel*":– Carmelite [5], Carmelitess [2]

3762 כַּרְמְלִית ***karmᵉlît***, a.g. GK: 4153 [→ 3761]. f. of 3761: Carmelite, of Carmel, "*of Carmel*":–

3763 כְּרָן ***kᵉrān***, n.pr.m. GK: 4154. Keran:– Cheran [2]

3764 כָּרְסֵא ***korsē'*** (Aram.), n.m. GK: 10372 [cf. 3676]. seat, chair; of power and position: throne; "to come down from the throne" means to be deposed and so lose power:– throne [2], thrones [1]

3765 כִּרְסֵם ***kirsēm***, v. GK: 4155 [cf. 3697]. [P] to ravage, eat away:– waste [1]

3766 כָּרַע ***kāra'***, v. GK: 4156 [→ 3767]. [Q] to kneel down, crouch, often with the associative meaning of respect and honor or of readiness for action; [H] to make bow down, make kneel (an act of oppression), make miserable:– bowed [10], bow down [5], bow [4], boweth down [2], brought very low (+3766) [2], fell [2], subdued [2], bowed down [1], brought down [1], cast down [1], couched [1], feeble [1], kneeling [1], smote down [1], stooped down [1], sunk down [1]

3767 כְּרַע ***kera'***, n.[f.]. GK: 4157 [→ 3766]. leg bone (the shank bone, between the knee and ankle):– legs [9]

3768 כַּרְפַּס ***karpas***, n.m. GK: 4158. (fine) linen:– green [1]

3769 כָּרַר **kārar**, v. GK: 4159 [→ 3564?, 3603, 3733, 3753]. [Pil] to dance:– danced [1], dancing [1]

3770 כָּרֵשׂ **kārēś**, n.[m.]. GK: 4160. stomach, belly:– belly [1]

כֹּרֶשׁ **kōreš**. See 3567.

3771 כַּרְשְׁנָא **karšᵉnā'**, n.pr.m. GK: 4161. Carshena, "[poss.] *black*":– Carshena [1]

3772 כָּרַת **kārat**, v. GK: 4162 [→ 3747?, 3748, 3773]. [Q] to cut off, cut down; to make (a covenant, agreement); [Qp] to be cut off, broken off; [N] to be cut off, be destroyed; [Pu] to be cut down; [H] to cut off, get rid of, destroy, kill; [Ho] to be cut off; "to cut a covenant" is "make a covenant," a figure of the act of ceremonially cutting an animal into two parts, with an implication of serious consequences for not fulfilling the covenant:– cut off [146], made [52], make [30], cut down [21], cut [6], fail [5], want [3], covenanted [2], destroyed [2], destroy [2], hew [2], utterly cut off (+3772) [2], are [1], chewed [1], cut out [1], cutteth [1], fail (+3807.1) [1], feller [1], freed [1], hew down [1], heweth down [1], leese [1], madest [1], make a covenant [1], maketh [1], making [1], perish [1]

3773 כְּרֻתוֹת **kᵉrutôt**, n.[f.pl.]. GK: 4164 [→ 3772]. beams (trimmed and cut):– beams [3]

3774 כְּרֵתִי **kᵉrētî**, a.g. GK: 4165 [cf. 6432?]. Kerethite:– Cherethites [9], Cherethims [1]

3775 כֶּשֶׂב **keśeb**, n.[m.]. GK: 4166 [→ 3776; cf. 3532]. ram-lamb, young sheep:– sheep [8], lamb [3], lambs [1], sheep (+7716) [1]

3776 כִּשְׂבָּה **kiśbâ**, n.f. GK: 4167 [→ 3775]. ewe-lamb, young sheep:– lamb [1]

3777 כֶּשֶׂד **keśed**, n.pr.m. GK: 4168 [→ 3778]. Kesed, "*Chaldean, Babylonian*":– Chesed [1]

3778 כַּשְׂדִּים **kaśdîm**, n.pr.g. GK: 4169 [→ 3777; cf. 894; cf. 3679, cf. 3779]. Chaldean, Babylonian, astrologers:– Chaldeans [59], Chaldees [13], Chaldea [7], Chaldeans' [1], Chaldees' [1]

3779 כַּשְׂדָּי **kaśdāy** (Aram.), n.pr.g. GK: 10373 [cf. 3679; cf. 3778]. Chaldean; Babylonian; (as a common noun) astrologer:– Chaldeans [6], Chaldean [1]

3780 כָּשָׂה **kāśâ**, v. GK: 4170. [Q] to become sleek, heavy; stubborn, headstrong:– covered [1]

3781 כַּשִּׁיל **kaššîl**, n.[m.]. GK: 4172 [→ 3782]. axe:– axes [1]

3782 כָּשַׁל **kāšal**, v. GK: 4173 [→ 3781, 3783, 4383, 4384]. [Q] to stumble, falter, fail; [N] be caused to stumble, be brought down; [H] to cause to stumble, overthrow, bring to ruin; [Ho] to be overthrown:– fall [17], stumble [13], feeble [4], cast down [3], stumbled [3], cause to fall [2], caused to stumble [2], fallen [2], overthrown [2], utterly fall (+3782) [2], decayed [1], faileth [1], falling [1], fell down [1], fell [1], made to fall [1], make fall [1], make to fall [1], ruined [1], ruin [1], stumbleth [1], weak [1]

3783 כִּשָּׁלוֹן **kiššālôn**, n.[m.]. GK: 4174 [→ 3782]. falling down, stumbling:– fall [1]

3784 כָּשַׁף **kāšap**, v.den. GK: 4175 [→ 407, 3785, 3786]. [P] to engage in witchcraft, be a sorcerer:– sorcerers [3], witch [2], used witchcraft [1]

3785 כֶּשֶׁף **kešep**, n.m. GK: 4176 [→ 3784]. witchcraft, sorcery, often with the associative meanings of rebellion and seduction into false religion:– witchcrafts [4], sorceries [2]

3786 כַּשָּׁף **kaššāp**, n.m. GK: 4177 [→ 3784]. sorcerer:– sorcerers [1]

3787 כָּשֵׁר **kāšēr**, v. GK: 4178 [→ 3788]. [Q] to be right, successful; [H] to bring success:– direct [1], prosper [1], seem right [1]

3788 כִּשְׁרוֹן **kišrôn**, n.[m.]. GK: 4179 [→ 3787]. skill, achievement; benefit:– equity [1], good [1], right [1]

3789 כָּתַב **kātab**, v. GK: 4180 [→ 3791, 3793, 4385; cf. 3790]. [Q] to write, engrave (on stone tablets); [Qp] to be written, be inscribed; [N] to be written down, be listed, be recorded; [P] to issue a written statement; writing can refer to ink on leather or papyrus, stylus on wax or clay, or carving in stone:– written [137], write [35], wrote [34], describe [4], described [2], subscribed [2], subscribe [2], writest [2], prescribed [1], recorded [1], were written [1], writeth [1], writing [1]

3790 כְּתַב **kᵉtab** (Aram.), v. GK: 10374 [→ 3792; cf. 3789]. [P] to write; [Pp, Peil] to be written:– wrote [5], written [2], write [1]

3791 כְּתָב **kᵉtāb**, n.m. GK: 4181 [→ 3789; cf. 3792]. written communication in various forms: script, text, record, book (as a scroll or tablet):– writing [14], register [2], scripture [1]

3792 כְּתָב **kᵉtāb** (Aram.), n.m. GK: 10375 [→ 3790; cf. 3791]. writing, inscription, decree:– writing [10], prescribing [1], written [1]

3793 כְּתֹבֶת **kᵉtōbet**, n.f. GK: 4182 [→ 3789]. tattoo mark:– any [1]

3794 כִּתִּיִּים **kittiyyîm**, a. & n.g. GK: 4183. Kittim, Cyprus; western coastlands:– Chittim [6], Kittim [2]

3795 כָּתִית **kātît**, a. GK: 4184 [→ 3807]. beaten or pressed olives; in some contexts this refers to virgin olive oil:– beaten [4], pure [1]

3796 כֹּתֶל **kōtel**, n.[m.]. GK: 4185 [cf. 3797]. wall (of a house):– wall [1]

3797 כְּתַל **kᵉtal** (Aram.), n.[m.]. GK: 10376. wall:– walls [1], wall [1]

3798 כִּתְלִישׁ **kitlîš**, n.pr.loc. GK: 4186. Kitlish:– Kithlish [1]

3799 כָּתַם **kātam**, v. GK: 4187. [N] be stained, be defiled:– marked [1]

3800 כֶּתֶם **ketem**, n.m. GK: 4188 [cf. 4387?]. gold, pure gold:– fine gold [4], gold [3], golden wedge [1], most [1]

3801 כֻּתֹּנֶת **kuttōnet**, n.f. GK: 4189. garment, robe, tunic:– coat [16], coats [7], garments [3], garment [2], robe [1]

3802 כָּתֵף **kātēp**, n.f. GK: 4190. shoulder, the part an animal or human that carries a load; by extension: shoulder piece; slope (of a hill), side, wall (of a building):– side [30], shoulders [13], shoulder [9], shoulderpieces [4], sides [4], undersetters [4], corner [2], arm [1]

3803 כָּתַר **kātar**, v. GK: 4192 & 4193 & 4194 [→ 3804, 3805]. [P] to bear with, have patience with; to surround, encircle; [H] to gather about; hem in; to crown, wear as a headdress:– compass about [2], beset round [1], crowned [1], inclosed round about [1], suffer [1]

3804 כֶּתֶר **keter**, n.m. GK: 4195 [→ 3803]. crown (probably not jeweled), royal headdress, crest, high turban:– crown [3]

3805 כֹּתֶרֶת **kōteret**, n.f. GK: 4196 [→ 3803]. capital (of a pillar or column):– chapiters [12], chapiter [12]

3806 כָּתַשׁ **kātaš**, v. GK: 4197 [→ 4388]. [Q] to grind, pound (in a mortar):– bray [1]

3807 כָּתַת **kātat**, v. GK: 4198 [→ 3795, 3796]. [Q] to crush, beat; [Qp] to be crushed, be shattered; [P] to beat, crush, break to pieces; [Pu] to be crushed; [H] to beat down; [Ho] to be battered to pieces:– beat [3], destroyed [3], beat down [1], beaten down [1], beaten to pieces [1], beaten [1], brake in pieces [1], broken in pieces [1], crushed [1], discomfited [1], smite [1], smitten [1], stamped [1]

3807.1 -לְ **lᵉ-**, pp.pref. GK: 4200 [→ 1973, 2882?, 3815, 4192, 3926, 3927, 3942; cf. 3807.2]. to, toward; in, through; before, at, with; temporally: before, until, when; logically: so that, in order to; agency: by means of:– to [4509], unto [2352], for [2001], of [1133], before (+6440) [958], in [462], that [358], with [227], therefore (+3651) [176], that (+4616) [167], by [163], into [131], against [122], had [122], after [116], at [116], have [110], according to [102], why (+4100) [92], on [81], upon [81], his (+2050.2) [76], had (+1961) [72], have (+1961) [72], wherefore (+4100) [70], hath [64], my (+2967.1) [64], before [59], throughout [56], mine (+2967.1) [50], for sake (+4616) [45], your (+3641.1) [44], alone (+905) [39], only (+905) [39], their (+1992.1) [38], among [37], as [37], concerning [31], beside (+905+4480) [30], toward [30], thine (+3509.2) [29], the LORD'S* (+3068) [28], from [27], over [27], hast [26], thy (+3509.2) [24], to (+4616) [19], above (+4480+4605+1886.5) [18], before (+5048) [18], wherefore (+3651) [18], before (+4480+6440) [17], over against (+5980) [15], safely (+983) [14], and [13], besides (+905+4480) [13], our (+5105.1) [13], because of (+4616) [12], from (+4480) [12], upward (+4605+1886.5) [12], according to (+6310) [11], apart (+905) [11], when [10]*

3807.2 -לְ **lᵉ-** (Aram.), pp.pref. GK: 10378 [cf. 3807.1]. to, for, toward, into; belonging to, with regard to:– to [101], unto [54], for [21], into [16], of [10], had [6], at [5], against [4], that [4], before (+6903) [3], by [2], in [2], why (+4101) [2], according to (+6903) [1], according to [1], against (+6655) [1], hast [1], have (+383) [1], his (+1886.8) [1], never (+3809+5957) [1], on [1], over [1], upon [1], what (+1768+3964) [1]

3808 לֹא **lō'** or לֹה **lōh**, adv. GK: 4202 & 4257 [→ 194?, 3810, 3818, 3819; cf. 3809 (also used with compound proper names)]. no, not:– not [3448], no [490], neither (+2050.1) [415], nor (+2050.1) [242], none [71], neither [58], cannot [57], no (+3605) [43], cannot (+3201) [35], surely (+518) [23], nothing [21], nothing (+1697) [20], nay [18], never [17], without (+871.1) [17], lest (+2050.1) [14], nor [14], none (+3605) [13], never (+5769+3807.1) [9], without [9], neither (+1571) [6], none (+376) [6], except (+518) [5], neither (+1571+2050.1) [5], nothing (+3972) [5], ere [4], nothing (+3605) [4], ignorant (+3045) [3], neither any (+2050.1) [3], nothing (+3605+1886.1) [3], without (+3807.1) [3], before (+2962+871.1) [2], before (+871.1) [2], by no means [2], never (+5331+3807.1) [2], no more [2], nor (+1571) [2], nought [2], unequal (+8505) [2], unwise (+2450) [2], verily (+518) [2], will (+518) [2], afore [1], but (+518) [1], but (+518+3588) [1], but [1], cannot (+3045) [1], cannot (+518) [1], cannot away with (+3201) [1], else (+518) [1], except (+518+3588) [1], fail (+539) [1], feeble (+3524) [1], feeble (+6099) [1], forbidden [1], how much less (+637+3588) [1], in no wise eat (+398+398) [1], lest (+4616+3807.1) [1], lest (+834) [1], measured (+4058) [1], neither (+2050.2) [1], neither (+3588) [1], neither yet (+1571+2050.1) [1], never (+1755+1755+2050.1) [1], never (+4480+5769) [1], never (+5331+5704) [1], never (+5704+5769) [1], never (+8548) [1], never again (+5750) [1], nevertheless (+2050.1) [1], no (+1697) [1], no (+3972) [1], none (+2050.2) [1], none (+259) [1], none (+376+376) [1], none (+376+3807.1) [1], none (+4480) [1], none (+802) [1], none (+834) [1], nor (+1571+2050.1) [1], nor (+176) [1], not (+518) [1], not (+5704) [1], not even [1], nothing (+1697+3605) [1], notwithstanding (+2050.1) [1], nought (+1952) [1], nought (+3972) [1], of a truth (+518) [1], or ever (+834+5704) [1], or ever [1], otherwise than (+871.1+3509.1) [1], out of (+2050.1) [1], out of (+871.1) [1], unaccustomed (+3925) [1], unawares (+3045) [1], ungodly (+2623) [1], unless (+518) [1], unprofitable [1], unrighteousness (+6664) [1], want of [1], wanting [1], whether (+518) [1], without (+2050.1) [1], without any (+2050.1) [1], wrong (+4941) [1], wrongfully (+4941+871.1) [1], yet neither (+2050.1) [1]

3809 לָא **lā'** (Aram.), adv.neg. GK: 10379 & 10384 [cf. 3808]. no, not, never:– not [49], nor (+2050.3) [7], no [7], neither (+2050.3) [3], no (+3606) [3], nor [2], without (+871.2) [2], without [2], cannot [1], ever [1], never (+5957+3807.2) [1], none (+3606) [1], none (+383+1768) [1], none [1], nothing [1]

לֻא **lu'**. See 3863.

3810 לֹא דְבָר **lō' dābār** or לֹא דְבַר **lō' dᵉbār** or לוֹ דְבַר **lô dᵉbār**, n.pr.loc. GK: 4203 & 4274 [→ 3808+1696]. Lo Debar, "*no pasture*":– Lodebar [3]

3811 לָאָה **lā'â**, v. GK: 4206 [→ 8513; cf. 3856]. [Q] to be weary; [N] to wear oneself out, be weary; [H] to wear someone out, try one's patience, frustrate:– weary [9], wearied [5], faintest [1], grieved [1], grieveth [1], lothe [1], made weary [1]

3812 לֵאָה **lē'â**, n.pr.f. GK: 4207. Leah, "[poss.] *wild-cow; wild cow, gazelle; cow*":– Leah [29], Leah's [5]

לְאוֹם **lᵉ'owm**. See 3816.

3813 לָאַט **lā'aṭ**, v. GK: 4209 [cf. 3874]. [Q] to cover:– covered [1]

3814 לָאט **lā'ṭ**, n.[m.]. GK: 4319 [→ 3874, 3909]. same as 3909: quietly, privately, secretly, a fig. extension of the base meaning "no physical sound"; (pl.) secret arts, with a focus on mysterious and hidden elements of this magic:– softly (+871.1+1886.1) [1]

3815 לָאֵל **lā'ēl**, n.pr.m. GK: 4210 [→ 3807.1+410]. Lael, "*[belonging] to God [El]*":– Lael [1]

3816 לְאֹם **lᵉ'ōm**, n.m. GK: 4211. people, nation:– people [24], nations [9], folk [1], nation [1]

3817 לְאֻמִּים **lᵉ'ummîm**, n.pr.g. GK: 4212. Leummite:– Leummim [1]

3818 לֹא עַמִּי **lō' 'ammî**, n.pr.m. GK: 4204 [→ 3808]. Lo-Ammi, "*not my people*":– Lo-ammi [1]

3819 לֹא רֻחָמָה **lō' ruḥāmâ**, n.pr.f. GK: 4205 [→ 3808]. Lo-Ruhamah, "*no compassion*":– Lo-ruhamah [2]

3820 לֵב **lēb**, n.m. GK: 4213 [→ 3823, 3824, 3834; cf. 3821]. heart; by extension: the inner person, self, the seat of thought and emotion: conscience, courage, mind, understanding:– heart [483], hearts [20], midst [12], mind [12], understanding [10], hearted [9], wisdom [6], comfortably (+5921) [4], double heart (+3820+2050.1) [4], care (+7760) [2], considered (+7760) [2], friendly (+5921) [2], heart's [2], mark well (+7760) [2], regard (+7896) [2], stouthearted (+47) [2], well [2], bethink (+413+7725) [1], broken-hearted (+7665) [1], consent [1], consider (+7760) [1], considered (+7896) [1], courageous (+533) [1], hardhearted (+7186) [1], kindly (+5921) [1], kindly [1], merryhearted (+8056) [1], minded (+5973) [1], myself (+2967.1) [1], regard (+7760) [1], regarded (+7760) [1], stale away unawares (+1589) [1], take heed (+5414) [1], very heart (+7023) [1], willingly (+4480) [1]

3821 לֵב **lēb** (Aram.), n.[m.]. GK: 10380 [→ 3825; cf. 3820]. heart, mind:– heart [1]

3822 לְבָאוֹת **lᵉbā'ôt**, n.pr.loc. GK: 4219 [→ 1034; cf. 3833]. Lebaoth, "*lionesses*":– Lebaoth [1]

3823 לָבַב **lābab**, v.den. GK: 4220 & 4221 [→ 3826, 3834; cf. 3820]. [N] to be made wise, be made intelligent; [P] to steal one's heart (from a lover's glance); to make special bread or pastry (heart-shaped?):– ravished heart [2], made cakes [1], make cakes (+3834) [1], wise [1]

3824 לֵבָב **lēbāb**, n.m. & f. GK: 4222 [→ 3820; cf. 3825]. heart; by extension: the inner person, self, the seat of thought and emotion: conscience, courage, mind, understanding:– heart [208], hearts [23], consider (+7760) [5], mind [4], understanding [3], bethink (+413+7725) [1], breasts [1], comfortably (+5921) [1], courage [1], fainthearted (+7390+1886.1) [1], fainthearted (+7401) [1], hearted [1], midst [1], stolen away unawares (+1589) [1]

3825 לְבַב **lᵉbab** (Aram.), n.m. GK: 10381 [→ 3821; cf. 3824]. heart (a physical organ); fig., the inner person that thinks, feels, and chooses: mind, heart, will; "one's heart" can mean "oneself":– heart [7]

לְבִבָה **lᵉbibâ**. See 3834.

3826 לִבָּה **libbâ**, n.[f.]. GK: 4226 [→ 3823]. rage:– hearts [6], heart [2]

3827 לַבָּה **labbâ**, n.f. GK: 4225 [cf. 3852]. flame:– flame [1]

3828 לְבוֹנָה **lᵉbônâ** or לְבֹנָה **lᵉbōnâ**, n.f. GK: 4227 & 4247 [→ 3829, 3836]. frankincense:– frankincense [15], incense [6]

3829 לְבוֹנָה **lᵉbônâ**, n.pr.loc. GK: 4228 [→ 3828]. Lebonah, "*frankincense*":– Lebonah [1]

3830 לְבוּשׁ **lᵉbûš**, n.m. GK: 4229 & 4230 [→ 3847; cf. 3831]. clothing, garment, robe:– clothing [9], apparel [8], garment [7], garments [2], vesture [2], clothed [1], put on [1], raiment [1], vestments [1]

3831 לְבוּשׁ **lᵉbûš** (Aram.), n.m. GK: 10382 [→ 3848; cf. 3830]. clothing, garment:– garments [1], garment [1]

3832 לָבַט **lābaṭ**, v. GK: 4231. [N] to come to ruin, be trampled:– fall [3]

לֻבִּי **lubbî**. See 3864.

3833 לָבִיא **lābî'** or לְבִיָּא **lᵉbiyyā'** or לִבְאָה **lib'â** or לְבָא **lebe'**, n.m. & f. GK: 4216 & 4218 & 4233 & 4234 [→ 1034, 3822]. lion, lioness:– lion [4], great lion [3], old lion [2], lionesses [1], lioness [1], lions [1], stout lion's [1], young[S] [1]

3834 לְבִבָה **lᵉbibâ**, n.f. GK: 4223 [→ 3823; cf. 3820]. special bread (heart-shaped?):– cakes [2], make cakes (+3823) [1]

3835 לָבַן **lāban**, v. GK: 4235 & 4236 [→ 3828, 3829, 3836, 3837, 3838, 3839, 3840, 3841?, 3842, 3844]. [Q] to make bricks; [H] to make white, be whitened; [Ht] to show oneself spotless, purified:– made white [2], make brick (+3843) [2], make white [1], making brick [1], whiter [1], white [1]

3836 לָבָן **lābān**, a. GK: 4237 [→ 3828, 3837, 3842; cf. 3835]. white:– white [29]

3837 לָבָן **lābān**, n.pr.m. & loc. GK: 4238 & 4239 [→ 3836]. Laban, "*white*":– Laban [51], Laban's [4]

לַבֵּן **labbēn**. See 4192.

3838 לְבָנָה **lᵉbānâ** or לְבָנָא **lᵉbānāh'**, n.pr.loc. GK: 4245 & 4241 [→ 3842]. Lebanah; Lebana, "*white*":– Lebanah [1], Lebana [1]

3839 לִבְנֶה **libneh**, n.[m.]. GK: 4242 [→ 3835]. poplar tree; some sources: storax tree:– poplars [1], poplar [1]

3840 לִבְנָה **libnâ**, n.f. GK: 4246 [→ 3835, 3843, 4404]. same as 3843: brick; tablet:– paved [1]

3841 לִבְנָה **libnâ**, n.pr.loc. GK: 4243 [→ 3835?]. Libnah, "*white*":– Libnah [18]

3842 לְבָנָה **lᵉbānâ**, n.f. GK: 4244 [→ 3838; cf. 3836]. bright (full) moon:– moon [3]

3843 לְבֵנָה **lᵉbēnâ**, n.f. GK: 4246 [→ 3840]. same as 3840: brick; tablet:– bricks [4], brick [3], make brick (+3835) [2], altars of brick [1], tile [1]

לְבֹנָה **lᵉbōnâ**. See 3828.

3844 לְבָנוֹן **lᵉbānôn**, n.pr.loc. GK: 4248 [→ 3835]. Lebanon, "*white, snow*":– Lebanon [71]

3845 לִבְנִי **libnî**, n.pr.m. GK: 4249 [→ 3846]. Libni, "*[descendant of] Libni* or *white*":– Libni [5]

3846 לִבְנִי **libnî**, a.g. GK: 4250 [→ 3845]. Libnite, "*of Libni*":– Libnites [2]

3847 לָבַשׁ **lābaš**, v. GK: 4252 [→ 3830, 4403, 8516; cf. 3848]. [Q] to put on clothing, dress, clothe; [Qp] to be dressed; [Pu] to be dressed; [H] to dress another, clothe someone:– put on [30], clothed with [20], clothed [15], clothe with [8], put upon [8], clothed in [4], clothe [4], wear [4], armed [3], arrayed [3], came upon [3], array [2], put [2], apparelled [1], apparel [1], arrayed in [1], clothest with [1], put on clothing (+8516) [1]

3848 לְבַשׁ **lᵉbaš** (Aram.), v. GK: 10383 [→ 3831; cf. 3847]. [P] to be clothed; [H] to clothe (another):– clothed with [3]

לְבֻשׁ **lᵉbuš**. See 3830.

3849 לֹג **lōg**, n.m. GK: 4253. log (liquid measure, about a third of a quart or liter):– log [5]

3850 לֹד **lōd**, n.pr.loc. GK: 4254. Lod:– Lod [4]

לִדְבִר **lidbir**. See 3810.

3851 לַהַב **lahab**, n.m. GK: 4258 [→ 3852, 7957]. flame of fire; by extension: flash (of a blade), blade of a sword:– flame [6], blade [2], flames [2], bright [1], glittering [1]

3852 לֶהָבָה **lehābâ**, n.f. GK: 4259 [→ 3851; cf. 3827]. flame, blaze, flash; (iron) point (of a blade):– flame [12], flaming [5], flames [1], head [1]

3853 לְהָבִים **lᵉhābîm**, n.pr.g. GK: 4260. Lehabite:– Lehabim [2]

3854 לַהַג **lahag**, n.m. GK: 4261. study, devotion to books:– study [1]

3855 לַהַד **lāhad**, n.pr.m. GK: 4262. Lahad, "[perhaps] *slow, indolent*":– Lahad [1]

3856 לָהַהּ **lāhah**, v. GK: 3532 & 4263 & 4264 & 4271 [cf. 3811]. [Q] to languish, faint; [Ht] to behave like a madman:– fainted [1], mad [1]

3857 לָהַט **lāhaṭ**, v. GK: 4265 & 4266 [→ 3858; cf. 3938]. [Q] to burn, flame; to devour; (n.) ravenous beast; [P] to set afire, set ablaze, consume:– set on fire [3], burn up [1], burneth up [1], burneth [1], burnt up [1], burnt [1], flaming [1], kindleth [1], setteth on fire [1]

3858 לַהַט **lahaṭ**, n.[m.]. GK: 4267 & 4268 [→ 3857; cf. 3874]. flame; referring to the supernatural blade of a sword; secret arts, sorceries:– enchantments [1], flaming [1]

3859 לָהַם **lāham**, v. GK: 4269. [Ht] to let oneself swallow greedily; (ptcp.) choice morsels:– wounds [2]

3860 לָהֵן **lāhēn**, c. GK: 4270 [cf. 3861]. therefore:–

3861 לָהֵן **lāhēn** (Aram.), c. GK: 10385 & 10386 [→ 3809; cf. 3860]. so then, therefore; except, but, unless:– except [3], but [2], save [2], therefore [2], wherefore [1]

3862 לַהֲקָה **lahᵃqâ**, n.f. GK: 4272. group, community:– company [1]

לוֹא **lô'**. See 3808.

3863 לוּ **lû**, c. GK: 4273 [→ 432, 3884]. if! if only!; O that!:– if [6], O that [5], would God [2], I pray thee [1], I would [1], if haply [1], neither [1], oh that [1], peradventure [1], though (+2050.1) [1], would God that [1], would to God (+2050.1) [1], would [1]

3864 לוּב **lûb**, n.g.pl. GK: 4275. Libya, Libyan:– Lubims [2], Libyans [1], Lubim [1]

3865 לוּד **lûd**, n.pr.m. & g. GK: 4276 [→ 3866]. same as 3866: Lud, Ludite; Lydia, Lydians:– Lud [4], Ludim [2], Lydians [1], Lydia [1]

3866 לוּדִים **lûdîm**, n.pr.m. & g. GK: 4276 [→ 3865]. same as 3865: Lud, Ludite; Lydia, Lydians:–

3867 לָוָה **lāwâ**, v. GK: 4277 & 4278 [→ 3878, 3881, 3880, 3882; cf. 3924]. [Q] to accompany; to borrow; [N] to be joined, be attached, be bound to; [H] to lend:– joined [8], lend [4], lendeth [3], borrower [2], join [2], abide with [1], borrowed [1], borroweth [1], borrow [1], cleave [1], lender (+376) [1], lender [1]

3868 לוּז **lûz**, v. GK: 4279 [→ 3891]. [Q] to depart (from one's sight); [N] to be devious, be perverse, be deceitful; [H] to depart (from one's sight):– depart [2], froward [2], perverseness [1], perverse [1]

3869 לוּז **lûz**, n.[m.]. GK: 4280 [→ 3870]. almond tree (branch):– hazel [1]

3870 לוּז **lûz**, n.pr.loc. GK: 4281 [cf. 3869]. Luz, "*almond tree*":– Luz [8]

3871 לוּחַ **lûaḥ**, n.m. GK: 4283 [→ 3872; cf. 3892]. tablets (of stone); board, panel (of wood); plate (metal):– tables [34], boards [4], table [4], plates [1]

3872 לוּחִית **lûḥît** or לֻחוֹת **luḥôt**, n.pr.loc. GK: 4284 & 4304 [→ 3871; cf. 3892]. Luhith, Luhoth:– Luhith [2]

3873 לוֹחֵשׁ **lôḥēš** or הַלּוֹחֵשׁ **hallôḥēš**, n.pr.m. GK: 4285 & 2135 [→ 1886.1+3907]. Lohesh or Hallohesh, "*the whisperer*":– Hallohesh [2]

3874 לוּט **lûṭ**, v. GK: 4286 [→ 3875, 3814, 3909, 3910; cf. 3813, 3858]. [Q] to cover, enfold; [Qp] to be wrapped up; [H] to cover, wrap up:– cast [1], wrapped [1], wrapt [1]

3875 לוֹט **lôṭ**, n.m. GK: 4287 [→ 3874]. shroud, covering:– covering [1]

3876 לוֹט **lôṭ**, n.pr.m. GK: 4288 [→ 3877]. Lot:– Lot [32], Lot's [1]

3877 לוֹטָן **lôṭān**, n.pr.m. GK: 4289 [→ 3876]. Lotan, "*of Lot*":– Lotan [5], Lotan's [2]

3878 לֵוִי **lēwî**, n.pr.m. GK: 4290 [→ 3867; cf. 3879]. Levi; Levite, "*of Levi*":– Levi [64], Levites (+1121) [1]

3879 לֵוָי **lēwāy** (Aram.), n.g. GK: 10387 [cf. 3878, 3881]. Levite, "*of Levi*":– Levites [4]

3880 לִוְיָה **liwyâ**, n.f. GK: 4292 [→ 3867]. garland, wreath:– ornament [2]

3881 לֵוִי **lēwî**, a.g. GK: 4291 [→ 3867; cf. 3879]. Levite, of Levi, "*of Levi*":– Levites [259], Levite [26]

3882 לִוְיָתָן **liwyātān**, n.m. GK: 4293 [→ 3867]. Leviathan, sea-monster; this refers both to a serpent-like sea creature and to a mythological monster of chaos opposed to the true God:– leviathan [5], mourning [1]

3883 לוּל **lûl**, n.[m.]. GK: 4294. stairway; some sources: trap door:– winding stairs [1]

3884 לוּלֵא **lûlē'**, c. GK: 4295 [→ 3863]. if not, unless:– except [3], if not [3], unless [3], were it not that [2], except (+3588) [1], not [1], unless (+3588) [1]

3885 לוּן **lûn** or לִין **lîn**, v. GK: 4296 & 4328 [→ 4411, 4412, 8519; cf. 3915, 3917]. [Q] to spend the night, stay the night; [N] to grumble against, blame; [H] to grumble against, blame; to hold back overnight, leave overnight; [Htpolal] to stay for the night; by extension: to stay, dwell an indeterminate amount of time:– lodge [18], lodged [12], murmured [7], murmur [6], abideth [3], abide [3], remain [3], tarried all night [3], tarry all night [3], abide all night [2], lie all night [2], lodge in [2], remain all night [2], remaineth [2], tarry [2], all night [1], cause to lodge [1], continue [1], dwell [1], endure [1], grudge [1], lay all night [1], left [1], lodge all night [1], lodgest [1], lodging [1], made to murmur [1], tarry for a night [1], tarry night [1]

3886 לוּעַ **lûa'**, v. GK: 4362. [Q] to talk impetuously, to dedicate (something) rashly; a fig. extension of drinking in a hurried, careless manner:– swallow down [1], swallowed up [1]

3887 לוּץ **lûṣ** or לִיץ **lîṣ**, v. GK: 4329 & 4370 [→ 3944, 3945, 4426]. [Q] to mock, scorn, talk big; [H] to mock; [Htpolal] to show oneself a mocker:– scorner [11], scorners [3], interpreter [2], scorneth [2], ambassadors [1], had in derision [1], make a mock at [1], mockers [1], mocker [1], scornest [1], scornful [1], scorn [1], teachers [1]

3888 לוּשׁ **lûš**, v. GK: 4297. [Q] to knead (bread dough):– kneaded [3], knead [2]

3889 לָוִשׁ **lāwiš**, n.pr.m. GK: 4298 [→ 3918]. Lawish; var. of 3919:–

3890 לְוָת **lᵉwāt** (Aram.), pp. GK: 10388 [cf. 3807.2]. near, beside:– from (+4481) [1]

לֻחוֹת **luḥôt**. See 3872.

לָז **lāz** and לָזֶה **lāzeh**. See 1975 and 1976.

3891 לָזוּת **lāzût**, n.f. GK: 4299 [→ 3868]. crookedness, perversity, referring to a kind of speech:– perverse [1]

3892 לַח **laḥ**, a. GK: 4300 [→ 3871, 3872, 3893]. fresh, fresh-cut, still moist:– green [5], moist [1]

3893 לֵחַ **lēaḥ**, n.m. GK: 4301 [→ 3892]. strength:– natural force [1]

לֻחַ **luaḥ**. See 3871.

3894 לְחוּם **lᵉḥûm**, n.[m.]. GK: 4302 & 4303 [→ 3898]. entrails; blow, wound; act of eating:– eating [1], flesh [1]

3895 לְחִי **lᵉḥî**, n.m. GK: 4305 [→ 3896?, 7437?]. jaw, jawbone; by extension: cheek, jowl:– cheek [5], cheeks [4], jaws [4], jawbone [3], jaw [3], cheek bone [1], two cheeks [1]

3896 לְחִי **lᵉḥî**, n.pr.loc. GK: 4306 [→ 3895?]. Lehi, "*jawbone*":– Lehi [3]

3897 לָחַךְ **lāḥak**, v. GK: 4308. [Q] to lick up; [P] to lick up, subdue:– lick up [2], lick [2], licked up [1], licketh up [1]

3898 לָחַם **lāḥam**, v. GK: 4309 & 4310 [→ 3894, 3899, 3901, 4421]. [Q] to fight against, attack; to eat, dine; [Qp] to be consumed; [N] to fight against, attack:– fight [85], fought [57], warred [7], eat [5], made war [4], fighteth [3], ever fight (+3898) [2], fighting [2], make war [2], overcome [2], warring [2], devoured [1], fought against [1], maketh war [1], making war [1], prevail [1], war [1]

3899 לֶחֶם **leḥem**, n.m. & f. GK: 4312 [→ 1035, 3433, 3898; cf. 3900]. bread, bread loaf; any kind of food; time or act of eating, meal; "bread of the Presence" is a regular offering to the LORD presented on a designated table in the tabernacle and temple:– bread [238], food [21], meat [18], loaves [5], shewbread (+6440) [3], shewbread (+6440+1886.1) [3], shewbread (+4635+1886.1) [2], victuals [2], eat [1], feast [1], fruit [1], provision [1], shewbread (+4635) [1], shewbread [1]

3900 לְחֶם **lᵉḥem** (Aram.), n.m. GK: 10389 [cf. 3899]. bread; banquet meal:– feast [1]

3901 לָחֶם **lāḥem**, n.[m.]. GK: 4311 [→ 3898]. war; other sources vary:– war [1]

לָחֻם **lāḥum**. See 3894.

3902 לַחְמִי **laḥmî**, n.pr.m. GK: 4313. Lahmi:– Lahmi [1]

3903 לַחְמָס **laḥmās**, n.pr.loc. GK: 4314. Lahmas:– Lahmam [1]

3904 לְחֵנָה **lᵉḥēnâ** (Aram.), n.f. GK: 10390. concubine, a class of spouse generally of lower status than a wife (the exact marriage relationship of a concubine varied in different cultures), usually for status and pleasure of the husband, also translated "mistress, consort":– concubines [3]

3905 לָחַץ **lāḥaṣ**, v. GK: 4315 [→ 3906; cf. 5169]. [Q] to oppress, crush, confine; [N] to be pressed close:– oppressed [7], oppress [5], afflict [1], crusht [1], forced [1], hold fast [1], oppresseth [1], oppressors [1], thrust [1]

3906 לַחַץ **laḥaṣ**, n.m. GK: 4316 [→ 3905]. oppression, affliction; short ration (of bread or water):– oppression [7], affliction [5]

3907 לָחַשׁ **lāḥaš**, v. GK: 4317 [→ 3873, 3908; cf. 5172]. [P] to charm, enchant (i.e., whisper); [Ht] to whisper together:– charmers [1], whispered [1], whisper [1]

3908 לַחַשׁ **laḥaš**, n.[m.]. GK: 4318 [→ 3907]. charming, whispering; charm, enchanter:– charmed [1], earrings [1], enchantment [1], orator [1], prayer [1]

3909 לָט **lāṭ**, n.[m.]. GK: 4319 [→ 3814]. quietly, privately, secretly, a fig. extension of the base meaning "no physical sound"; (pl.) secret arts, with a focus on mysterious and hidden elements of this magic:– enchantments [3], privily (+871.1+1886.1) [1], secretly (+871.1+1886.1) [1], softly (+871.1+1886.1) [1]

3910 לֹט **lōṭ**, n.[m.]. GK: 4320 [→ 3874]. myrrh (a resinous, fragrant and slightly bitter to the taste); some sources: mastic bark (a resinous gum of the rockrose plant):– myrrh [2]

3911 לְטָאָה **lᵉṭāʾâ**, n.f. GK: 4321. wall lizard; some sources: gecko:– lizard [1]

3912 לְטוּשִׁם **lᵉṭûšim**, n.pr.g. GK: 4322 [→ 3913]. Letushite, "*sharpened*":– Letushim [1]

3913 לָטַשׁ **lāṭaš**, v. GK: 4323 [→ 3912]. [Q] to sharpen; to forge, hammer; to pierce (with the eyes); [Pu] to be sharpened:– instructor [1], sharpeneth [1], sharpen [1], sharp [1], whet [1]

3914 לֹיָה **lōyâ**, n.f. GK: 4324 [cf. 3924]. wreath, garland; some translate as a technical architectural term: border, rim:– additions [2], addition [1]

3915 לַיִל **layil** or לַיְלָה **laylâ**, n.m. GK: 4325 & 4326 [→ 3917; cf. 3885; cf. 3916]. night; sometimes with the implication that it is the time of illicit, illegal, or immoral activity:– night [199], nights [15], midnight (+2677+1886.1) [4], to night (+1886.1) [4], at midnight (+2676) [2], in a night (+1121) [2], night season [2], in night [1], midnight (+2676+1886.1) [1], midnight (+8432+1886.1) [1], night seasons [1], to night [1]

3916 לֵילֵי **lêlê** (Aram.), n.[m.]. GK: 10391 [cf. 3915]. night:– night [5]

3917 לִילִית **lîlît**, n.f. GK: 4327 [→ 3915; cf. 3885]. night creature; Lilith, a female demon of the night:– shrich owl [1]

3918 לַיִשׁ **layiš**, n.m. GK: 4330 [→ 3889, 3919]. lion:– old lion [2], lion [1]

3919 לַיִשׁ **layiš** or לַיְשָׁה **layᵉšâ**, n.pr.m. & loc. GK: 4331 & 4332 & 4333 [→ 3918; cf. 3959]. Laish, Laishah, "*lion*":– Laish [7]

3920 לָכַד **lākad**, v. GK: 4334 [→ 3921, 4434]. [Q] to capture, seize, take as a possession; [N] to be taken captive, be seized, be taken:– taken [44], took [43], take [19], taketh [5], caught [3], catch [2], taken at all (+3920) [2], frozen [1], holden [1], stick together [1]

3921 לֶכֶד **leked**, n.[m.]. GK: 4335 [→ 3920]. snaring, capturing:– taken [1]

3922 לֵכָה **lēkâ**, n.pr.loc. GK: 4336. Lecah, "*to you*":– Lecah [1]

3923 לָכִישׁ **lākîš**, n.pr.loc. GK: 4337. Lachish:– Lachish [24]

3924 לֻלָאֹת **lulāʾōt**, n.f. GK: 4339 [cf. 3867, 3914]. (pl.) loops:– loops [13]

3925 לָמַד **lāmad**, v. GK: 4340 [→ 3928, 4451, 8527]. [Q] to learn, train for; [Qp] to be trained; [P] to teach, instruct, cause to learn; [Pu] to be trained; with implication that the learning will be put to use:– teach [32], taught [17], learn [16], learned [5], teacheth [5], diligently learn (+3925) [2], instructed [2], expert [1], instruct [1], skilful [1], teachers [1], teachest [1], teaching [1], unaccustomed (+3808) [1]

לִמֻּד **limmud**. See 3928.

3926 לְמוֹ **lᵉmô**, pp. GK: 4344 [→ 3807.1]. for, in, over:– at [1], for [1], to [1], upon [1]

3927 לְמוּאֵל **lᵉmûʾēl**, n.pr.m. GK: 4345 [→ 3807.1+410]. Lemuel, "*[belonging] to God [El]*":– Lemuel [2]

3928 לִמֻּד **limmud**, a. GK: 4341 [→ 3925]. accustomed to; (n.) a disciple, one who is taught, a follower:– learned [2], accustomed to [1]; disciples [1], taught [1], used to [1]

3929 לֶמֶךְ **lemek**, n.pr.m. GK: 4347. Lamech:– Lamech [11]

3930 לֹעַ **lōaʿ**, n.[m.]. GK: 4350 [→ 3216]. throat:– throat [1]

3931 לָעַב **lāʿab**, v. GK: 4351. [H] to mock, make sport of (someone), make a game of (someone):– mocked [1]

3932 לָעַג **lāʿag**, v. GK: 4352 [→ 3933, 3934; cf. 5926]. [Q] to mock, scoff, ridicule; [N] to stammer, speak as a foreigner; [H] to mock, ridicule:– laughed to scorn [3], mocketh [3], laugh to scorn [2], laugh [2], mocked [2], mock [2], derision [1], have in derision [1], mockest [1], stammering [1]

3933 לַעַג **laʿag**, n.[m.]. GK: 4353 [→ 3932]. scorn, ridicule, derision:– derision [3], scorning [2], scorn [2]

3934 לָעֵג **lāʿēg**, a. GK: 4354 [→ 3932]. people of stammering lips or foreign language:– mockers [1], stammering [1]

3935 לַעְדָּה **laʿdâ**, n.pr.m. GK: 4355 [→ 3936]. Laadah, "[perhaps] *having a fat throat or neck*":– Laadah [1]

3936 לַעְדָּן **laʿdān**, n.pr.m. GK: 4356 [→ 3935]. Ladan:– Laadan [7]

3937 לָעַז **lāʿaz**, v. GK: 4357. [Q] to speak a foreign tongue, speak an unintelligible language:– strange language [1]

3938 לָעַט **lāʿaṭ**, v. GK: 4358 [cf. 3857]. [H] to let (someone) gulp down:– feed [1]

3939 לַעֲנָה **laʿănâ**, n.f. GK: 4360. gall (bitter to the taste, possibly poisonous); by extension: bitterness as a concept:– wormwood [7], hemlock [1]

3940 לַפִּיד **lappîd**, n.m. GK: 4365 [→ 3941?]. torch, firebrand; by extension: lightning:– lamps [4], lamp [3], brands [1], burning lamps [1], firebrands [1], firebrand [1], lightnings [1], torches [1], torch [1]

3941 לַפִּידוֹת **lappîdôt**, n.pr.m. GK: 4366 [→ 3940?]. Lappidoth, "*flames*":– Lapidoth [1]

3942 לִפְנֵי **lipnê**, pp.+n.m. GK: 4367 [→ 3807.1+6437]. before, in front of, in the presence of (3807.1 + 6440):–

3943 לָפַת **lāpat**, v. GK: 4369. [Q] to reach toward; [N] be turned aside; in some contexts there is an implication of touching or grasping the object reached toward:– took hold [1], turned aside [1], turned [1]

3944 לָצוֹן **lāṣôn**, n.[m.]. GK: 4371 [→ 3887]. mockery, scoffing, hostile speech of fools:– scornful [2], scorning [1]

3945 לָצַץ **lāṣaṣ**, n.[m.] *or* v.ptcp. GK: 4372 [→ 3887]. mocker, scoffer, with an implication that this class of person is foolish and rebellious:– scorners [1]

3946 לַקּוּם **laqqûm**, n.pr.loc. GK: 4373. Lakkum:– Lakum [1]

3947 לָקַח **lāqaḥ**, v. GK: 4374 [→ 3948, 3949, 4455, 4457, 4727, 4728]. [Q] to take, receive; [Qp] to be led away; [N] to be captured, taken away; [Pu] to be taken away, brought; [Ht] to flash back and forth; by extension: to gain possession, exercise authority; "to take a woman" means "to marry a wife":– took [347], take [343], taken [72], receive [35], received [22], fetch [19], bring [17], take away [16], took away [12], taketh [10], brought [9], taken away [9], fetched [5], fet [5], get [5], married [4], receiveth [4], carried away [3], buy [2], carry away [2], fetcht [2], have [2], accept [1], buyeth [1], drawn unto [1], getteth [1], infolding [1], mingled [1], placed [1], put [1], receiving [1], reserved [1], seize [1], sent for [1], take out [1], take up [1], taken up [1], takest [1], taketh away [1], taking [1], tookest [1], use [1], winneth [1]

3948 לֶקַח **leqaḥ**, n.m. GK: 4375 [→ 3947]. teaching, instruction, learning:– doctrine [4], learning [4], fair speech [1]

3949 לִקְחִי **liqḥî**, n.pr.m. GK: 4376 [→ 3947]. Likhi, "*take, marry*":– Likhi [1]

3950 לָקַט **lāqaṭ**, v. GK: 4377 [→ 3219, 3951]. [Q] to gather; [P] to gather, pick up, glean; [Pu] to be gathered up; [Ht] to gather oneself about; this act of gathering is general, and can refer to the second or final gleanings of the field or orchard:– gather [13], gathered [9], glean [7], gleaned [5], gathered up [2], gathereth [1]

3951 לֶקֶט **leqeṭ**, n.[m.]. GK: 4378 [→ 3950]. gleanings (of a harvest):– gleanings [1], gleaning [1]

3952 לָקַק **lāqaq**, v. GK: 4379. [Q, P] to lap up, lick up:– lapped [2], lappeth [2], licked up [1], licked [1], lick [1]

3953 לָקַשׁ **lāqaš**, v.den. GK: 4380 [→ 3954, 4456]. [P] to glean:– gather [1]

3954 לֶקֶשׁ **leqeš**, n.[m.]. GK: 4381 [→ 3953]. second crop, late grass at spring time:– latter growth [2]

3955 לָשָׁד **lāšād**, n.m. GK: 4382. moist (food), strength:– fresh [1], moisture [1]

3956 לָשׁוֹן **lāšôn**, n.m. GK: 4383 [→ 3960; cf. 3961]. tongue; by extension: language, speech, noise (of an animal); something tongue-shaped: wedge (of precious metal), bay, gulf, flame of fire:– tongue [89], language [9], tongues [9], bay [3], wedge [2], babbler (+1167+1886.1) [1], evil speaker (+376) [1], fire (+784) [1], languages [1], talkers [1]

3957 לִשְׁכָּה **liškâ**, n.f. GK: 4384 [cf. 5393]. room, chamber; hall; storeroom:– chambers [31], chamber [15], parlour [1]

3958 לֶשֶׁם **lešem**, n.[m.]. GK: 4385. jacinth (exact identification is uncertain):– ligure [2]

3959 לֶשֶׁם **lešem**, n.pr.loc. GK: 4386 [cf. 3919]. Leshem, "*lion*":– Leshem [2]

3960 לָשַׁן **lāšan**, v.den. GK: 4387 [→ 3956]. [Po] to slander; [H] to slander:– accuse [1], slandereth [1]

3961 לִשָּׁן **liššān** (Aram.), n.m. GK: 10392 [cf. 3956]. language, tongue:– languages [6], language [1]

3962 לֶשַׁע **lešaʿ**, n.pr.loc. GK: 4388. Lasha:– Lasha [1]

3963 לֶתֶךְ **lētek**, n.[m.]. GK: 4390. lethek (a dry measure, half a cor, about 6 bushels [220 liters]):– half homer [1]

מַ **ma-**, or מָ **mā-**. See 4100.

3963.1 ם◌ָ **-ām** or ם◌ **-m**, p.m.pl.suf. GK: 4392 [→ 279?, 1886.3]. they, them, their:– them [1859], their [1501], they [263], their own [46], it [16], whose [15], whom [14], these [11], those [11], themselves [10], thereof [9], the[S] [6], theirs [6], which [6], you [6], by themselves (+905+3807.1) [4], therein (+871.1) [4], wherein (+834+871.1) [4], themselves (+5315) [3], whom (+834) [3], his [2], thereby (+871.1) [2], ye [2], man's[S] [1], others [1], the[S] people [1], their the [1], they (+5315) [1], wherein (+871.1) [1], wherein [1], whereof (+834) [1], whereof [1], wherewith (+834+871.1) [1], wherewith (+871.1) [1]

3964 מָא **māʾ** (Aram.), p.inter. & indef. GK: 10394 [→ 4101; cf. 4100]. what?:– what (+1768+3807.2) [1]

3965 מַאֲבוּס **maʾăbûs**, n.[m.]. GK: 4393 [→ 75]. granary:– storehouses [1]

3966 מְאֹד **mᵉʾōd**, n.m. (used as adv.). GK: 4394. a marker of great degree or quanity: very, greatly, exceedingly, much:– very [129], greatly [47], sore [20], great [12], exceeding [10], exceeding (+3966+871.1) [8], much [7], very (+5704) [7],

Heb

exceeding (+3966) [6], exceedingly (+3966) [6], diligently [4], exceedingly (+3966+871.1) [4], exceedingly [4], good [3], far [2], greatly (+5704) [2], mightily [2], might [2], utterly (+5704) [2], very sore (+5704) [2], ask never so much (+7235) [1], diligent [1], especially [1], exceeding (+5704) [1], exceeding (+7235) [1], exceedingly (+7235) [1], far off [1], fast [1], hated exceedingly (+1419+8130+8135) [1], mighty [1], quickly [1], right well [1], so much [1], sore (+5704) [1], so [1], very (+1419) [1], very (+5704+3807.1) [1], very great [1], very much (+5704) [1], waxed louder and louder (+2390) [1], well [1]

3967 מֵאָה ***mēʾâ***, n.f. GK: 4395 [→ 3968?; cf. 3969]. hundred:– hundred [465], two hundred [76], hundreds [27], eleven hundred (+505+2050.1) [3], hundredth [3], one hundred [3], hundredfold (+6471) [1], hundredfold (+8180) [1], sixscore (+6242+2050.1) [1], twelve hundred (+505+2050.1) [1]

3968 מֵאָה ***mēʾâ***, n.pr.loc. GK: 4396 [→ 3967?; cf. 3969]. (the Tower of) the Hundred:– Meah [2]

3969 מְאָה ***mᵉʾâ*** (Aram.), n.f. GK: 10395 [cf. 3967, 3968]. hundred; (dual) two hundred:– hundred [7], two hundred [1]

3970 מַאֲוַיִּים ***maʾᵃwiyyîm***, n.[m.pl.]. GK: 4397 [→ 183]. desires:– desires [1]

מוֹאל ***môʾl***. See 4136.

3971 מְאוּם ***mᵉʾûm*** or מוּם ***mûm***, n.m. GK: 4398 & 4583 [→ 3972]. defect, blemish, flaw, injury; by extension: shame, defilement:– blemish [15], spot [3], blot [2], blemishes [1]

3972 מְאוּמָה ***mᵉʾûmâ***, p.indef. GK: 4399 [→ 3971]. something, anything; (with negation) nothing:– any thing [13], nothing (+3808) [5], nothing (+369) [4], ought [4], any thing (+3605) [1], no (+3808) [1], no (+408) [1], nought (+3808) [1], ought else (+3605) [1], somewhat [1]

3973 מָאוֹס ***māʾôs***, n.[m.]. GK: 4400 [→ 3988]. refuse, trash:– refuse [1]

3974 מָאוֹר ***māʾôr***, n.m. GK: 4401 [→ 215]. light source, luminary, light-bearer:– light [15], lights [3], bright [1]

3975 מְאוּרָה ***mᵉʾûrâ***, n.f. GK: 4402 [→ 215?]. nest hole (of a viper):– den [1]

3976 מֹאזְנַיִם ***mōʾznayim***, n.[m.]du. GK: 4404 [cf. 3977]. set of scales, (two) balance pans for weight measurement, with an emphasis on honesty and standardized measurements; by extension: righteous evaluation of motives and actions:– balances [8], balance [7]

3977 מֹאזְנֵא ***mōʾznēʾ*** (Aram.), n.m.emph. GK: 10396 [cf. 3976]. scale, balance, with a focus that the device is an objective implement for judging truth:– balances [1]

מֵאיָה ***mēʾyâ***. See 3967.

3978 מַאֲכָל ***maʾᵃkāl***, n.m. & f. GK: 4407 [→ 398]. food, supplies, something to eat:– meat [22], food [5], bakemeats (+644+4639) [1], fruit [1], victual [1]

3979 מַאֲכֶלֶת ***maʾᵃkelet***, n.f. GK: 4408 [→ 398]. (butcher) knife, sometimes with a ceremonial or sacrificial focus:– knife [3], knives [1]

3980 מַאֲכֹלֶת ***maʾᵃkōlet***, n.f. GK: 4409 [→ 398]. fuel (for a fire); a fig. extension of food that is consumed:– fuel [2]

3981 מַאֲמָץ ***maʾᵃmāṣ***, n.[m.]. GK: 4410 [→ 553]. effort, exertion:– forces [1]

3982 מַאֲמָר ***maʾᵃmār***, n.m. GK: 4411 [→ 559; cf. 3983]. command, decree, instruction:– commandment [2], decree [1]

3983 מֵאמַר ***mēʾmar*** (Aram.), n.[m.]. GK: 10397 [→ 560; cf. 3982]. declaration, request:– appointment [1], word [1]

3984 מָאן ***māʾn*** (Aram.), n.m. GK: 10398. article, container, goblet:– vessels [7]

3985 מָאֵן ***māʾan***, v. GK: 4412 [→ 3986, 3987]. [P] to refuse, reject:– refused [24], refuse [9], refuseth [5], utterly refuse (+3985) [2], refusedst [1]

3986 מָאֵן ***māʾēn***, a.v. GK: 4413 [→ 3985]. refusing:– refuse [4]

3987 מֵאֵן ***mēʾēn***, a. GK: 4414 [→ 3985]. refusing:– refuse [1]

3988 מָאַס ***māʾas***, v. GK: 4415 & 4416 [→ 3973, cf 4529, 4549]. [Q] to reject, despise, spurn, disdain; [N] to be rejected, become vile; to be festering, be dissolving; be vanishing:– rejected [16], despised [12], despise [9], cast away [7], refused [5], utterly rejected (+3988) [4], cast off [3], despiseth [3], refuse [3], abhorred [2], abhorreth [1], abhor [1], become loathsome [1], contemneth [1], contemn [1], disdained [1], loathe [1], melt away [1], refuseth [1], reject [1], reprobate [1], vile [1]

3989 מַאֲפֶה ***maʾᵃpeh***, n.[m.]. GK: 4418 [→ 644]. something baked:– baken [1]

3990 מַאֲפֵל ***maʾᵃpēl***, n.[m.]. GK: 4419 [→ 652?]. darkness:– darkness [1]

3991 מַאְפֵלְיָה ***maʾpēlyâ***, n.f. GK: 4420 [→ 652?]. great darkness:– darkness [1]

3992 מָאַר ***māʾar***, v. GK: 4421. [H] to be destructive; to be painful:– fretting [3], pricking [1]

מָאֹר ***māʾōr***. See 3974.

3993 מַאֲרָב ***maʾᵃrāb***, n.m. GK: 4422 [→ 693]. ambush; troops in an ambush:– ambushment [2], lie in ambush [1], lurking places [1], lying in wait [1]

3994 מְאֵרָה ***mᵉʾērâ***, n.f. GK: 4423 [→ 779]. curse:– curse [4], cursing [1]

מְאֹרָה ***mᵉʾōrâ***. See 3974.

3995 מִבְדָּלוֹת ***mibdālôt***, n.f. GK: 4426 [→ 914]. set aside, selected, singled out:– separate [1]

3996 מָבוֹא ***mābôʾ***, n.m. GK: 4427 [→ 3997, 4126; cf. 935]. entrance, entryway, gateway; "the place where the sun goes (sets)" is the direction west:– entry [5], going down [5], entrance [3], entering in [2], came [1], cometh [1], coming in [1], enter into [1], entering [1], goeth down [1], the west (+8121+1886.1) [1], westward (+8121+1886.1) [1]

3997 מְבוֹאָה ***mᵉbôʾâ***, n.m. GK: 4427 [→ 3996]. same as 3996: entrance, entryway, gateway:– entry [1]

3998 מְבוּכָה ***mᵉbûkâ***, n.f. GK: 4428 [→ 943]. confusion, confused terror:– perplexity [2]

3999 מַבּוּל ***mabbûl***, n.m. GK: 4429 [→ 5035]. flood (waters):– flood [13]

4000 מְבוֹנִים ***mᵉbônîm***, v.ptcp. GK: 4430. ptcp. of 995: knowing, taught:–

4001 מְבוּסָה ***mᵉbûsâ***, n.f. GK: 4431 [→ 947]. trampling down, implying subjugation:– treading down [1], trodden down [1], trodden under foot [1]

4002 מַבּוּעַ ***mabbûaʿ***, n.[m.]. GK: 4432 [→ 5042]. (a bubbling) spring (of water):– springs [2], fountain [1]

4003 מְבוּקָה ***mᵉbûqâ***, n.f. GK: 4433 [→ 950]. plundering, devastation, desertion:– void [1]

4004 מִבְחוֹר ***mibḥôr***, n.[m.]. GK: 4435 [→ 977]. choicest (trees); major (towns):– choice [2]

4005 מִבְחָר ***mibḥār***, n.[m.] & f. GK: 4436 [→ 4006; cf. 977]. choicest, best, elite, finest (persons or things):– choice [7], chosen [4], choicest [1]

4006 מִבְחָר ***mibḥār***, n.pr.m. GK: 4437 [→ 4005; cf. 977]. Mibhar, "*choice*":– Mibhar [1]

4007 מַבָּט ***mabbāṭ***, n.m. GK: 4438 [→ 5027]. hope, trust in, relying on:– expectation [3]

4008 מִבְטָא ***mibṭāʾ***, n.[m.]. GK: 4439 [→ 981]. rash promise, rashness:– that which uttered [1], uttered ought out [1]

4009 מִבְטָח ***mibṭāḥ***, n.[m.]. GK: 4440 [→ 982]. security, trust, confidence:– confidence [8], trust [4], confidences [1], hope [1], sure [1]

4010 מַבְלִיגִית ***mablîgît***, n.f. GK: 4443 [→ 1455]. comfort, smile, cheerfulness:– comfort [1]

4011 מִבְנֶה ***mibneh***, n.m. GK: 4445 [→ 1129]. building, structure:– frame [1]

4012 מְבֻנַּי ***mᵉbunnay***, n.pr.m. GK: 4446. Mebunnai, "*well built*":– Mebunnai [1]

4013 מִבְצָר ***mibṣār***, n.m. GK: 4448 & 4450 [→ 4014; cf. 1219]. fortress, fortification, stronghold; ore:– fenced [11], strong holds [10], defenced [4], fortress [4], fortresses [2], strong hold [2], strong [2], holds [1], most fenced [1]

4014 מִבְצָר ***mibṣār***, n.pr.m. GK: 4449 [→ 4013; cf. 1219]. Mibzar, "*bastion*":– Mibzar [2]

מִבְצָרָה ***mibṣārâ***. See 4013.

4015 מִבְרָח ***mibrāḥ***, n.m. GK: 4451 [→ 1272]. fleeing, refugee:– fugitives [1]

4016 מְבוּשִׁים ***mᵉbûšîm***, n.[m.]. GK: 4434 [→ 954]. private parts, (male) genitals, with a possible focus on shame if exposed:– secrets [1]

4017 מִבְשָׂם ***mibśām***, n.pr.m. GK: 4452. Mibsam, "*sweet odor*":– Mibsam [3]

4018 מְבַשְּׁלוֹת ***mᵉbaššᵉlôt***, n.f.pl. GK: 4453 [→ 1310]. places for fire, cooking-places:– boiling places [1]

מַג ***māg***. See 7248, 7249.

4019 מַגְבִּישׁ ***magbîš***, n.pr.m. GK: 4455. Magbish, "[perhaps] *thick*":– Magbish [1]

4020 מִגְבָּלוֹת ***migbālôt***, n.f.pl. GK: 4456 [→ 1383]. (braided) chains, (twisted) cords:– ends [1]

4021 מִגְבָּעָה ***migbāʿâ***, n.f.pl. GK: 4457 [→ 1375?]. headband:– bonnets [4]

4022 מֶגֶד ***meged***, n.m. GK: 4458 [→ 4023, 4025, 4030]. choice things, best gifts:– precious things [4], pleasant [3], precious [1]

4023 מְגִדּוֹ ***mᵉgiddô*** or מְגִדּוֹן ***mᵉgiddôn***, n.pr.loc. GK: 4459 & 4461 [cf. 4022]. Megiddo, "*place of troops*":– Megiddo [11], Megiddon [1]

4024 מִגְדּוֹל ***migdôl*** or מִגְדֹּל ***migdōl***, n.m. & n.pr.loc. GK: 4460 & 4465 [→ 1431, 4026]. Migdol, "*tower*"; great:– Migdol [4], tower [3]

4025 מַגְדִּיאֵל ***magdîʾēl***, n.pr.m. GK: 4462 [→ 4022+410]. Magdiel, "*choice gift of God [El]*":– Magdiel [2]

4026 מִגְדָּל ***migdāl***, n.m. GK: 4463 [→ 4024, 4027, 4028, 4029; cf. 1431]. tower, watchtower, usually a tall, narrow building used for defense; high platform (made of wood and used for public speaking to crowds); an elevated area such as a garden with mounds, terraces:– tower [34], towers [13], castles [1], flowers [1], pulpit [1]

מִגְדֹּל ***migdōl***. See 4024.

מִגְדָּלָה ***migdālâ***. See 4026.

4027 מִגְדַּל־אֵל ***migdal-ʾēl***, n.pr.loc. GK: 4466 [→ 4026+410; cf. 1431]. Migdal El, "*tower of God [El]*":– Migdal-el [1]

4028 מִגְדַּל־גָּד ***migdal-gad***, n.pr.loc. GK: 4467 [→ 4026+1410; cf. 1431]. Migdal Gad, "*tower of Gad*":– Migdal-gad [1]

4029 מִגְדַּל־עֵדֶר ***migdal-ʿēder***, n.pr.loc. GK: 4468 [→ 4026+5740]. Migdal Eder, "*tower of Eder [flock]*":–

4030 מִגְדָּנוֹת ***migdānôt***, n.f.[pl.]. GK: 4469 [→ 4022]. costly gifts, articles of value:– precious things [3], presents [1]

4031 מָגוֹג ***māgôg***, n.pr.loc. GK: 4470 [→ 1463]. Magog, "[perhaps] *land of Gog*":– Magog [4]

4032 מָגוֹר ***māgôr***, n.m. GK: 4471 [→ 4034; cf. 1481]. terror, horror:– fear [6], terrors [1], terror [1]

4033 מָגוֹר ***māgôr***, n.[m.]. GK: 4472 & 4473 [→ 1481, 4035, 4460]. to live as an alien, stay as a stranger; place to live, place to lodge; grain pit, storage chamber = heart, mind:– pilgrimage [4], stranger [3], dwellings [2], sojourn [1], strangers [1]

4034 מְגוֹרָה ***mᵉgôrâ***, n.f. GK: 4475 [→ 4032; cf. 1481]. dread, fear:– fear [1]

4035 מְגוּרָה ***mᵉgûrâ***, n.f. GK: 4476 [→ 4033]. barn, grain-pit, storage chamber:– fears [2], barn [1]

4036 מָגוֹר מִסָּבִיב ***māgôr missābîb***, n.pr.m. GK: 4474 [→ 1481]. Magor-Missabib, "*terror on every side*":– Magor-missabib [1]

4037 מַגְזֵרָה ***magzērâ***, n.f. GK: 4477 [→ 1504]. ax:– axes [1]

4038 מַגָּל ***maggāl***, n.[m.]. GK: 4478 [cf. 1556?]. sickle:– sickle [2]

4039 מְגִלָּה ***mᵉgillâ***, n.f. GK: 4479 [→ 1556; cf. 4040]. scroll (a rolled up document made of leather or papyrus):– roll [20], volume [1]

4040 מְגִלָּה ***mᵉgillâ*** (Aram.), n.f. GK: 10399 [→ 1560; cf. 4039]. scroll:– roll [1]

4041 מְגַמָּה ***mᵉgammâ***, n.f. GK: 4480 [cf. 1571]. horde:– sup up [1]

4042 מָגַן ***māgan***, v. GK: 4481 [→ 4043]. [P] to hand over, deliver to, present with:– deliver [2], delivered [1]

4043 מָגֵן ***māgēn***, n.m. GK: 4482 & 4483 & 4484 [→ 1598, 4042, 4044]. (small) shield used for defense, usually of oiled leather; by extension: ruler, a leader who protects; fig. of the impregnable scales of leviathan; insolent; gift, present (gifts made in return):– shield [33], shields [15], buckler [6], bucklers [3], armed [2], defence [2], rulers [1], scales (+650) [1]

4044 מְגִנָּה ***mᵉginnâ***, n.f. GK: 4485 [→ 4043]. veil, covering:– sorrow [1]

4045 מִגְעֶרֶת ***migʿeret***, n.f. GK: 4486 [→ 1605]. rebuke, reproach:– rebuke [1]

4046 מַגֵּפָה ***maggēpâ***, n.f. GK: 4487 [→ 5062]. plague; blow, strike, slaughter:– plague [20], slaughter [3], plagued [1], plagues [1], stroke [1]

4047 מַגְפִּיעָשׁ ***magpî'āš***, n.pr.m. GK: 4488. Magpiash, "*moth killer*":– Magpiash [1]

4048 מָגַר ***māgar***, v. GK: 4489 [cf. 4049]. [Qp] to be thrown; [P] to cast, throw down:– cast down [1], terrors [1]

4049 מְגַר ***m^{e}gar*** (Aram.), v. GK: 10400 [cf. 4048]. [Pa] to overthrow:– destroy [1]

4050 מְגֵרָה ***m^{e}gērâ***, n.f. GK: 4490 [→ 1641]. saw (stone-cutting tool):– saws [3], axes [1]

4051 מִגְרוֹן ***migrôn***, n.pr.loc. GK: 4491. Migron, "*precipice*":– Migron [2]

4052 מִגְרָעוֹת ***migrā'ôt***, n.f. GK: 4492 [→ 1639]. offset ledge, recess, rebatement (of a wall):– narrowed rests [1]

4053 מֶגְרָפָה ***megrāpâ***, n.f. GK: 4493 [→ 1640]. clods (of earth) or a digging instrument: hoe, spade, shovel:– clods [1]

4054 מִגְרָשׁ ***migrāš*** or מִגְרְשׁוֹת ***migr^{e}šôt***, n.m. GK: 4494 & 4495 [→ 1644]. pastureland, untilled open land (belonging to a town):– suburbs [114], cast out [1]

4055 מַד ***mad***, n.m. GK: 4496 [→ 4058; cf. 4063]. clothing, garment; measure, decree:– garment [3], armour [2], clothes [1], garments [1], judgment [1], measures [1], measure [1], raiment [1]

4056 מַדְבַּח ***madbaḥ*** (Aram.), n.[m.]. GK: 10401 [→ 1684; cf. 4196]. altar:– altar [1]

4057 מִדְבָּר ***midbār***, n.m. GK: 4497 & 4498 [→ 1696]. desert, wasteland, barren wilderness, desolate land that supports little life; open country, suitable for grazing; mouth, instrument of speech:– wilderness [255], desert [13], south [1], speech [1], wilderness (+776) [1]

4058 מָדַד ***mādad***, v. GK: 4499 [→ 4055, 4059, 4060, 4461]. [Q] to measure a distance; consider a plan; [N] to be measured; [P] to measure off; [Htpol] to stretch oneself out:– measured [39], measure [7], mete out [2], measured (+3808) [1], mete [1], stretched [1]

4059 מִדַּד ***middad***, v. GK: 4499 [→ 4058]. same as 4058: [P] to measure off:– gone [1]

Heb

4060 מִדָּה ***middâ***, n.f. GK: 4500 & 4501 [→ 4058; cf. 5414; cf. 4061]. measurement, size, length; section (of a wall), length of life; tax:– measure [15], measures [12], measuring [10], piece [7], size [3], stature [3], garments [1], great stature [1], meteyard [1], tribute [1], wide [1]

4061 מִדָּה ***middâ*** or מִנְדָּה ***mindâ*** (Aram.), n.f. GK: 10402 & 10429 [cf. 4060]. tax, revenue, tribute:– toll [3], tribute [1]

4062 מַדְהֵבָה ***madhēbâ***, n.f. GK: 4502 [cf. 7292]. fury; others: golden:– golden city [1]

4063 מַדּוּ ***mādû*** or מַדְוֶה ***madweh***, n.m. GK: 4503 [cf. 4055]. garment:– garments [2]

4064 מַדְוֶה ***madweh***, n.m. GK: 4504 [→ 1738]. disease, sickness:– diseases [2]

4065 מַדּוּחִים ***maddûḥîm***, n.[m.]. GK: 4505 [→ 5080]. misleading, able to deceive:– causes of banishment [1]

4066 מָדוֹן ***mādôn***, n.m. GK: 4506 [→ 4067; cf. 1777]. dissension, quarrel, strife, contention:– strife [7], contentions [4], contention [3], contentious [3], brawling [2], discord [2], strifes [1]

4067 מִדְיָן ***midyān*** or מָדוֹן ***mādôn***, n.m. GK: 4517 [→ 4066, 4079, 4080, 4084, 4090, 4092; cf. 1777]. quarrel, strife, contention:– stature [1]

4068 מָדוֹן ***mādôn***, n.pr.loc. GK: 4507 [→ 1777]. Madon, "*contention*":– Madon [2]

4069 מַדּוּעַ ***maddûa'***, adv. GK: 4508. Why?, What is the meaning?:– why [43], wherefore [28], how [1]

4070 מְדוֹר ***m^{e}dôr*** or מְדָר ***m^{e}dār*** (Aram.), n.[m.]. GK: 10403 & 10407 [→ 1753]. living, dwelling:– dwelling [4]

4071 מְדוּרָה ***m^{e}dûrâ***, n.f. GK: 4509 [→ 1752]. (circular) pile of wood, fire pit:– pile for fire [1], pile [1]

4072 מִדְחֶה ***midḥeh***, n.m. GK: 4510 [→ 1760]. ruin, downfall:– ruin [1]

4073 מַדְחֵפָה ***madḥēpâ***, n.f. GK: 4511 [→ 1765]. blow, thrust; (pl.) blow after blow:– overthrow [1]

4074 מָדַי ***māday***, n.pr.g. & loc. GK: 4512 [→ 4075; cf. 4076]. Madai; Media, Medes:– Medes [8], Media [6], Madai [2]

4075 מָדִי ***mādî***, a.g. GK: 4513 [→ 4074]. Mede:– Mede [1]

4076 מָדַי ***māday*** (Aram.), n.pr.g. GK: 10404 [cf. 4074, 4077]. same as 4077: Mede; Media:– Medes [5], Median [1]

4077 מָדַי ***māday*** (Aram.), n.pr.g. GK: 10404 [→ 4076]. same as 4076: Mede; Media:–

4078 מַדַּי ***madday***, n.[m.]. GK: 1896 [→ 1767]. prob. same as 1767: sufficiently:– sufficiently (+3807.1) [1]

4079 מִדְיָן ***midyān***, n.m. GK: 4506 [→ 4067; cf. 1777]. same as 4066: dissension, quarrel, strife, contention:–

4080 מִדְיָן ***midyān***, n.pr.m. & loc. GK: 4518 [→ 4084; cf. 1777, 4067]. Midian, Midianite:– Midian [39], Midianites [20]

4081 מִדִּין ***middîn***, n.pr.loc. GK: 4516. Middin:– Middin [1]

4082 מְדִינָה ***m^{e}dînâ***, n.f. GK: 4519 [→ 1777; cf. 4083]. province, district, region:– provinces [27], every province (+4082+2050.1) [10], every province (+3605+4082+2050.1) [8], province [8]

4083 מְדִינָה ***m^{e}dînâ*** (Aram.), n.f. GK: 10406 [→ 1778; cf. 4082]. province, district:– province [8], provinces [3]

4084 מִדְיָנִי ***midyānî***, a.g. GK: 4520 [→ 4080, 4092; cf. 1777, 4067]. Midianite, "*of Midian*":– Midianites [3], Midianitish [2], Medanites [1], Midianite [1], Midianitish woman [1]

4085 מְדֹכָה ***m^{e}dōkâ***, n.f. GK: 4521 [→ 1743]. mortar:– mortar [1]

4086 מַדְמֵן ***madmēn***, n.pr.loc. GK: 4522 [→ 4088, 4089]. Madmen, "*[sounds like] be silenced*":– Madmen [1]

4087 מַדְמֵנָה ***madmēnâ***, n.f. GK: 4523 [→ 1828]. manure-pile, dung-heap:– dunghill [1]

4088 מַדְמֵנָה ***madmēnâ***, n.pr.loc. GK: 4524 [→ 4086]. Madmenah, "*dunghill*":– Madmenah [1]

4089 מַדְמַנָּה ***madmannâ***, n.pr.m. & loc. GK: 4525 & 4526 [→ 4086]. Madmannah, "*dung place*":– Madmannah [2]

4090 מְדָן ***m^{e}dān***, n.m. GK: 4506 [→ 4067; cf. 1777]. same as 4066: dissension, quarrel, strife, contention:–

4091 מְדָן ***m^{e}dān***, n.pr.m. GK: 4527 [→ 1837]. Medan, "*dissension*":– Medan [2]

4092 מְדָנִי ***m^{e}dānî***, a.g. GK: 4520 [→ 4084]. same as 4084: Midianite, "*of Midian*":–

4093 מַדָּע ***maddā'***, n.m. GK: 4529 [→ 3045; cf. 4486]. knowledge:– knowledge [4], science [1], thought [1]

מֹדָע ***mōdā'***. See 4129.

מַדֻּעַ ***madua'***. See 4069.

4094 מַדְקֵרָה ***madqērâ***, n.f. GK: 4532 [→ 1856]. piercing (of a sword):– piercings [1]

מְדֹר ***m^{e}dōr***. See 4070.

4095 מַדְרֵגָה ***madrēgâ***, n.f. GK: 4533. cliff, (steep) mountainside (with footholds and hiding places):– stairs [1], steep places [1]

מְדֻרָה ***m^{e}durâ***. See 4071.

4096 מִדְרָךְ ***midrāk***, n.[m.]. GK: 4534 [→ 1869]. foot-width, footprint:– breadth [1]

4097 מִדְרָשׁ ***midrāš***, n.[m.]. GK: 4535 [→ 1875]. annotation, study, writing, exposition:– story [2]

4098 מְדֻשָׁה ***m^{e}dušâ***, n.f. GK: 4536 [→ 1758]. that which is crushed (by trampling on a threshing floor):– threshing [1]

4099 הַמְּדָתָא ***hamm^{e}dātā'*** or מְדָתָא ***m^{e}dātā'***, n.pr.m. GK: 2158. Hammedatha, "*given by the moon [god]*":– Hammedatha [5]

4100 מָה ***mâ***, p.inter. & indef. GK: 4537 [→ 1099, 3644, 4972; cf. 4478; cf. 3964, cf. 4101]. why?, what?, how?; O!, who, whoever, whatever:– what [404], why (+3807.1) [92], wherefore (+3807.1) [70], how [51], why [28], wherein (+871.1) [12], wherefore (+5921) [10], wherewith (+871.1) [10], that [6], wherefore [6], how long (+5704) [4], wherefore (+2088+3807.1) [4], why (+5921) [3], how great [2], how long (+3509.1) [2], how many (+3509.1) [2], how many (+5704+3509.1) [2], how much [2], how oft (+3509.1) [2], howsoever [2], what (+3509.1) [2], what (+3807.1) [2], wherein [2], which [2], because (+3807.1) [1], how (+3509.1) [1], how long (+3117+8141+3509.1) [1], nor (+2050.1) [1], nothing (+1077) [1], nothing (+1097) [1], not [1], so many (+3509.1) [1], thing [1], to what end (+3807.1) [1], until (+5704) [1], what (+1697+1886.1) [1], what (+2088) [1], what aileth (+3807.1) [1], what good (+3807.1) [1], what profit (+3807.1) [1], whatsoever (+1697) [1], whatsoever [1], whereby (+871.1) [1], wherefore (+8478) [1], wherein (+871.1+1886.1) [1], whereon (+5921) [1], whereto (+3807.1) [1], whereupon (+5921) [1], wherewithal (+871.1) [1], whether [1], why (+2088+3807.1) [1], why (+871.1) [1], why then (+2088+3807.1) [1]

4101 מָה ***mâ*** (Aram.), p.inter. & indef. GK: 10408 [→ 2987; cf. 4479; cf. 4100]. why?, what?; that which, what:– what [6], how (+3509.4) [2], why (+3807.2) [2], that which [1], whatsoever (+1768) [1], why (+5922) [1]

4102 מָהַהּ ***māhah***, v. GK: 4538. [Htpal] to wait, delay, linger, hesitate:– tarry [3], lingered [2], tarried [2], delayed [1], stay [1]

4103 מְהוּמָה ***m^{e}hûmâ***, n.f. GK: 4539 [→ 1949]. turmoil, confusion, panic, discomfiture:– destruction [3], trouble [3], discomfiture [1], tumults [1], tumult [1], vexations [1], vexation [1], vexed [1]

4104 מְהוּמָן ***m^{e}hûmān***, n.pr.m. GK: 4540. Mehuman:– Mehuman [1]

4105 מְהֵיטַבְאֵל ***m^{e}hêṭab'ēl***, n.pr.m. & f. GK: 4541 [→ 3190+410]. Mehetabel, "*God [El] does good*":– Mehetabel [2], Mehetabeel [1]

4106 מָהִיר ***māhîr***, a. GK: 4542 [→ 4116]. skilled, well versed, experienced; speedy, prompt:– ready [2], diligent [1], hasting [1]

4107 מָהַל ***māhal***, v. GK: 4543 [→ 1118; cf. 4135]. [Qp] to be diluted, changed to an adulterated state; referring to dilution by water:– mixt [1]

4108 מַהְלֵךְ ***mahlēk***, n.m. GK: 4544 [→ 1980, 4109]. same as 4109: passageway; journey:– places to walk [1]

4109 מַהֲלָךְ ***mah^{a}lāk***, n.m. GK: 4544 [→ 4108]. same as 4108: passageway; journey:– journey [3], walk [1]

4110 מַהֲלָל ***mah^{a}lāl***, n.[m.]. GK: 4545 [→ 4111; cf. 1984]. praise, good reputation:– praise [1]

4111 מַהֲלַלְאֵל ***mah^{a}lal'ēl***, n.pr.m. GK: 4546 [→ 4110+410]. Mahalalel, "*praise of God [El]*":– Mahalaleel [7]

4112 מַהֲלֻמוֹת ***mah^{a}lumôt***, n.f.pl. GK: 4547 [→ 1986]. (pl.) beating, thrashing, repeated blows to the body:– stripes [1], strokes [1]

4113 מַהֲמֹרוֹת ***mah^{a}mōrôt***, n.f.[pl.]. GK: 4549. miry pits, pits filled with rain water:– deep pits [1]

4114 מַהְפֵּכָה ***mahpēkâ***, n.f. GK: 4550 [→ 2015]. overthrow, destruction, demolishing:– overthrew [3], overthrow [2], overthrown [1]

4115 מַהְפֶּכֶת ***mahpeket***, n.f. GK: 4551 [→ 2015]. stocks (confining a prisoner, suggesting in a crooked posture or distortion):– prison [2], stocks [2]

4116 מָהַר ***māhar***, v. GK: 4554 [→ 4106, 4117, 4118, 4120, 4122]. [N] to be swept away; to be impetuous, rash, disturbed; [P] to be quick, hasten, hurry, do at once:– hasted [14], make haste [8], haste [5], made haste [5], soon [3], swift [3], hastened [2], hasten [2], hasteth [2], hastily [2], hasty [2], in haste [2], make speed [2], carried headlong [1], cause to make haste [1], fearful [1], fetch quickly [1], hasteneth [1], make ready quickly [1], quickly [1], rash [1], ready [1], shortly [1], speedily [1], straightway [1], suddenly [1]

4117 מָהַר ***māhar***, v.den. GK: 4555 & 4556 [→ 4116, 4119]. [Q] to pay the purchase price for a bride:– surely endow (+4117) [2]

4118 מַהֵר ***mahēr***, adv. GK: 4557 [→ 4116]. swiftly:– quickly [8], speedily [4], hastily [2], at once [1], hasteth [1], suddenly [1]

מָהִר ***mâhir***. See 4106.

4119 מֹהַר ***mōhar***, n.m. GK: 4558 [→ 4117, 4121]. bride-price, compensation to the father of the bride:– dowry [3]

4120 מְהֵרָה ***m^{e}hērâ***, n.f. GK: 4559 [→ 4116]. haste, quickness, speed; (adv.) quickly, swiftly, soon, at once:– quickly [8], speedily [4], hastily [1], make speed [1], pass quickly [1], quickly (+871.1) [1], shortly [1], soon [1], speed [1], very swiftly (+5704) [1]

4121 מַהֲרַי ***mah^{a}ray***, n.pr.m. GK: 4560 [→ 4119]. Maharai, "*impetuous*":– Maharai [3]

4122 מַהֵר שָׁלָל חָשׁ בַּז ***mahēr šālāl ḥāš baz***, n.pr.m. GK: 4561 [→ 4116+7998+2363+957]. Maher-Shalal-Hash-Baz, "*quick to the plunder, swift to the spoil*":– Maher-shalal-hash-baz [2]

4123 מַהֲתַלָּה ***mah^{a}tallâ***, n.f. GK: 4562 [→ 2048]. illusion, deception:– deceits [1]

4123.1 מוֹ- **-mô** or מוּ- **-mû**, p.suf. GK: 4564 [→ 1886.3]. he, him; they, them:– them [58], their [22], their (+3807.1) [6], themselves [6], they [5], he [2], him [2], his (+3807.1) [2], their own [2], whom [2], himself [1], his [1], that [1], thereto (+3807.1) [1], those [1], wherein (+5921) [1], which (+3807.1) [1]

4124 מוֹאָב **mô'āb**, n.pr.m. & loc. GK: 4565 & 4566 [→ 4125, 6355]. Moab, Moabite:– Moab [166], Moabites [15]

4125 מוֹאָבִי **mô'ābî**, a.g. GK: 4567 [→ 4124]. Moabite, from Moab, "*of Moab*":– Moabitess [6], Moabites [4], Moabite [3], Moabitish [1], of Moab [1], women of Moab [1]

מוֹאל **mô'l**. See 4136.

4126 מוֹבָא **môbā'**, n.[m.]. GK: 4569 [→ 3996; cf. 935]. coming in; entrance (way):– coming in [1], comings in [1]

4127 מוּג **mûg**, v. GK: 4570. [Q] to melt, waste away; [N] to melt away (in fear), be disheartened; to collapse; [Pol] to soften; to toss about; [Htpol] to melt away, flow from; from the base meaning the melting of a substance is the fig. extension of the inner person melting is fear:– dissolved [3], faint [3], melt [3], melted [2], consumed [1], dissolvest [1], fainthearted [1], makest soft [1], melt away [1], melted away [1]

4128 מוּד **môd**, v. GK: 4571. [Pol] to shake, convulse, set into motion:– measured [1]

4129 מֹדַע **mōdā'**, n.m. GK: 4530 [→ 4130; cf. 3045]. (distant) relative, kinsman:– kinsman [1], kinswoman [1]

4130 מֹדַעַת **mōda'at**, n.f. GK: 4531 [→ 4129; cf. 3045]. (distant) kinsman:– kindred [1]

4131 מוֹט **môṭ**, v. GK: 4572 [→ 4132, 4133]. [Q] to slip, fall, totter, stagger; [N] to be shaken, be caused to move, be toppled; [H] to bring down, to cause to fall; [Htpol] to be thoroughly shaken, be continually shaken:– moved [19], removed [5], moved exceedingly (+4131) [2], slippeth [2], carried [1], cast [1], fallen in decay (+3027) [1], falling down [1], fall [1], out of course [1], ready [1], shaketh [1], slide [1], slip [1]

4132 מוֹט **môṭ**, n.[m.]. GK: 4573 [→ 4131]. carrying frame; pole; yoke bar:– bar [2], moved [2], staff [1], yoke [1]

4133 מוֹטָה **môṭâ**, n.f. GK: 4574 [→ 4131]. yoke bar, pole, bar; by extension: oppression of subjected people:– yokes [4], yoke [4], bands [2], heavy [1], staves [1]

4134 מוּךְ **mûk**, v. GK: 4575 [cf. 4355]. [Q] to become poor:– waxen poor [3], poorer [1], wax poor [1]

4135 מוּל **mûl**, v. GK: 4576 & 4577 [→ 4139; cf. 4107, 5243]. [Q] to circumcise; [Qp] to be circumcised; [N] to be circumcised, undergo circumcision, circumcise oneself; "to circumcise the heart" means to commit to covenant obedience from within, not only formally; [H] to cut off, ward off:– circumcised [23], circumcise [5], destroy [3], must needs be circumcised (+4135) [2], circumcising [1], cut down [1], cut in pieces [1]

4136 מוּל **mûl** or מוֹאל **mô'l**, subst. & pp. GK: 4578 & 4568 [cf. 2974]. before, opposite, in front of:– over against [10], against [5], forefront (+6440) [3], over against (+4480) [3], before (+413+6440) [2], over against (+413+6440) [2], against (+413) [1], before (+413) [1], before [1], forepart (+6440) [1], from (+4480) [1], off (+4480) [1], over against (+413) [1], to God-ward (+430+1886.1) [1], towards (+413) [1], towards (+4480) [1], upon (+413) [1]

4137 מוֹלָדָה **môlādâ**, n.pr.loc. GK: 4579. Moladah, "*generation*":– Moladah [4]

4138 מוֹלֶדֶת **môledet**, n.f. GK: 4580 [→ 3205]. family, relatives, children; (land of) birth, native (land):– kindred [11], nativity [6], born [2], begotten [1], issue [1], native [1]

4139 מוּלָה **mûlâ**, n.f. GK: 4581 [→ 4135]. circumcision:– circumcision [1]

4140 מוֹלִיד **môlîd**, n.pr.m. GK: 4582 [→ 3205]. Molid, "*descendant*":– Molid [1]

מוּם **muwm**. See 3971.

מוּמְכָן **mômukān**. See 4462.

4141 מוּסָב **mûsāb**, v.ptcp. GK: 6015 [→ 4142, 4524, 5252, 5437, 5438, 5439]. ptcp. of 5437: turning, winding:–

4142 מוּסַבָּה **mûsabbâ**, v.ptcp. GK: 6015 [→ 4141]. ptcp. of 5437: turning, winding:–

4143 מוּסָד **mûsād**, n.m. GK: 4586 [→ 4145; cf. 3245]. foundation, laying the foundation stone:– foundation [1], sure foundation (+3245) [1]

4144 מוֹסָד **môsād**, n.m. GK: 4587 [→ 4146; cf. 3245]. foundation:– foundations [3]

4145 מוּסָדָה **mûsādâ**, n.f. GK: 4588 [→ 4143, 4328; cf. 3245]. foundation:– grounded [1]

4146 מוֹסָדָה **môsādâ**, n.m. GK: 4589 [→ 4144; cf. 3245]. foundation:– foundations [10]

4147 מוֹסֵר **môsēr** or מוֹסֵרָה **môsērâ**, n.m. GK: 4591 & 4593 [→ 4149; cf. 631]. bonds, shackles, straps, chains, fetters:– bands [6], bonds [5]

4148 מוּסָר **mûsār**, n.m. GK: 4592 [→ 4561; cf. 3256]. discipline, instruction, correction; wisdom and teaching that imply correcting errant behavior:– instruction [30], correction [8], chastening [3], chastisement [3], bond [1], chasteneth [1], check [1], discipline [1], doctrine [1], rebuker [1]

4149 מוֹסֵרָה **môsērâ** or מֹסֵרוֹת **mōsērôt**, n.pr.loc. GK: 4594 & 5035 [→ 631?]. Moserah, Moseroth, "*bond, prison [?]*":– Moseroth [2], Mosera [1]

4150 מוֹעֵד **mô'ēd**, n.m. GK: 4595 [→ 3259]. (Tent of) Meeting; appointed time, designated time, season:– congregation [149], time appointed [9], solemn feasts [8], feasts [6], set time [6], season [5], set feasts [5], appointed season [4], appointed [3], seasons [3], solemnities [3], time [3], solemn feast [2], solemn [2], appointed feasts [1], appointed sign [1], appointed times [1], appointed time [1], assemblies [1], assembly [1], congregations [1], due season [1], feast [1], places of assembly [1], solemn assembly [1], solemn days [1], solemnity [1], synagogues [1], times [1]

4151 מוֹעָד **mô'ād**, n.[m.]. GK: 4596 [→ 3259]. ranks, appointed place of a soldier:– appointed times [1]

4152 מוּעָדָה **mû'ādâ**, n.f. GK: 4597 [→ 3259]. designation, appointment:– appointed [1]

4153 מוֹעַדְיָה **mô'adyâ**, n.pr.m. GK: 4598 [→ 4154+3068; cf. 4572]. Moadiah, "[perhaps] *Yahweh assembles* or *Yahweh promises*":– Moadiah [1]

4154 מוּעֶדֶת **mû'edet**, v.ptcp. GK: 5048 [→ 4153, 4571, 4572, 4573, 5976]. ptcp. of 4571: dislocated:– out of joint [1]

4155 מוּעָף **mû'āp**, n.[m.]. GK: 4599 [→ 4588, 6079; cf. 5890]. gloom, darkness; fig. of the emotional state of sadness and despondency:– dimness [1], foundations [1]

4156 מוֹעֵצָה **mô'ēṣâ**, n.f. GK: 4600 [→ 3289]. plan, scheme, device, intrigue:– counsels [6], devices [1]

4157 מוּעָקָה **mû'āqâ**, n.f. GK: 4601 [→ 5781?]. burden, misery, hardship:– affliction [1]

4158 מוֹפַעַת **môpa'at** or מֵיפַעַת **mêpa'at**, n.pr.loc. GK: 4602 & 4789. Mophaath, Mephaath, "*splendor*":– Mephaath [4]

4159 מוֹפֵת **môpēt**, n.m. GK: 4603. wonder, sign, miracle, portent; symbol:– wonders [19], sign [8], wonder [6], miracles [1], miracle [1], wondered at [1]

4160 מֵץ **mēṣ** or מוּץ **mûṣ**, n.m. GK: 5160 [→ 4330]. oppressor:– extortioner [1]

4161 מוֹצָא **môṣā'**, n.m. GK: 4604 [→ 3318]. act of going out, springing out, exiting, moving on; by extension, (n.) what goes out: spring (of water), mine shaft, sunrise, east:– going forth [4], goings out [4], brought out [2], spring [2], watersprings (+4325) [2], bud [1], east [1], go forth [1], going out [1], outgoings [1], proceeded out [1], springs [1], that proceedeth out [1], that which came out of [1], that which is gone out [1], thing that is gone out [1], vein [1], watercourse (+4325) [1]

4162 מוֹצָא **môṣā'**, n.pr.m. GK: 4605 [→ 3318]. Moza, "*sunrise*":– Moza [5]

4163 מוֹצָאָה **môṣā'â**, n.f. GK: 4606 [→ 3318]. origin, coming out; latrine:– goings forth [1]

4164 מוּצָק **mûṣāq**, n.m. GK: 4607 [→ 4166; cf. 3332]. casting (of metal):– straitened [1], straitness [1], vexation [1]

4165 מוּצָק **mûṣāq**, n.[m.]. GK: 4608 [→ 6693]. restriction, constraint; distress, hardship:– casting [1], hardness [1]

4166 מוּצָקָה **mûṣāqâ**, n.f. GK: 4609 [→ 4164; cf. 3332]. casting (into one piece); channel, spout or lip (of a lamp):– cast [1], pipes [1]

4167 מוּק **mûq**, v. GK: 4610. [H] to scoff:– corrupt [1]

4168 מוֹקֵד **môqēd**, n.[m.]. GK: 4611 [→ 4169; cf. 3344]. hearth, (place of) glowing embers, burning embers:– burnings [1], hearth [1]

4169 מוֹקְדָה **môqᵉdâ**, n.f. GK: 4612 [→ 4168; cf. 3344]. hearth, place of burning:– burning [1]

4170 מוֹקֵשׁ **môqēš**, n.m. GK: 4613 [→ 3369]. snare, trap, that which captures prey; by extension: ensnarement, entrapment (of a person):– snare [14], snares [6], grins [2], ensnared [1], gin [1], snared [1], traps [1], trap [1]

4171 מוּר **mûr**, v. GK: 4614 & 4615 [→ 8545]. [N] to be changed; to shake, quake; [H] to exchange, substitute, change:– changed [4], change [3], at all change (+4171) [2], change at all (+4171) [2], changeth [1], exchange [1], removed [1]

4172 מוֹרָא **môrā'** or מוֹרָה **môrâ**, n.m. GK: 4616 & 4624 [→ 3372]. fear, terror, respect, reverence; awesome deed:– fear [6], terror [2], dread [1], feared [1], terribleness [1], terrors [1]

4173 מוֹרַג **môrag**, n.m. GK: 4617. threshing sledge:– threshing instruments [2], threshing instrument [1]

4174 מוֹרָד **môrād**, n.[m.]. GK: 4618 [→ 3381]. slope, road going down; something hammered down:– going down [3], made thin [1], steep place [1]

4175 מוֹרֶה **môreh**, n.[m.] *or* v.ptcp. GK: 4619 & 4620 & 4621 [→ 3384]. archer; autumn rains; teacher:– former rain [2], archers (+7198+871.1+1886.1) [1], rain [1], shooters [1]

4176 מוֹרֶה **môreh**, n.pr.[loc.?]. GK: 4622 [→ 3384]. Moreh:– Moreh [3]

4177 מוֹרָה **môrâ**, n.m. GK: 4623 [→ 6168]. razor:– rasor [3]

4178 מוֹרָט **môrāṭ**, v.ptcp. GK: 5307 [→ 4803; cf. 4804, cf. 4873]. ptcp. of 4803: polished, rubbed; skinned:– peeled [2]

4179 מֹרִיָּה **mōriyyâ**, n.pr.loc. GK: 5317. Moriah:– Moriah [2]

4180 מוֹרָשׁ **môrāš**, n.[m.]. GK: 4625 & 4626 [→ 782, 4181; cf. 3423]. possession, inheritance; desire:– possessions [1], possession [1], thoughts [1]

4181 מוֹרָשָׁה **môrāšâ**, n.f. GK: 4627 [→ 4180; cf. 3423]. possession:–possession [6], inheritance [2], heritage [1]

4182 מוֹרֶשֶׁת גַּת **môrešet gat**, n.pr.loc. GK: 4628 [→ 4183]. Moresheth Gath, "*possession of Gath*":– Moresheth-gath [1]

4183 מוֹרַשְׁתִּי **môraštî**, a.g. GK: 4629 [→ 4182]. of Moresheth:– Morasthite [2]

4184 מוּשׁ **mûš**, v. GK: 4630 [cf. 3237, 4959]. [Q] to touch, feel; [H] be able to feel, touch:– feel [2], handle [1]

4185 מוּשׁ **mûš**, v. GK: 4631. [Q] to depart, leave, move away, vanish; [H] to remove:– depart [8], remove [4], departed [2], removed [2], cease [1], departeth [1], gone back from [1], took away [1]

4186 מוֹשָׁב **môšāb**, n.m. GK: 4632 [→ 3427]. dwelling, settlement, place to live, place:– dwellings [8], habitations [8], seat [7], dwelling [4], habitation [4], dwelling places [3], dwelt [2], sitting [2], assembly [1], dwell in [1], dwelling place [1], inhabited places [1], situation [1], sojourning [1]

4187 מוּשִׁי **mûšî**, n.pr.m. GK: 4633 [→ 4188]. Mushi:– Mushi [8]

4188 מוּשִׁי **mûšî**, a.g. GK: 4634 [→ 4187]. Mushite, "*of Mushi*":– Mushites [2]

4189 מֹשְׁכוֹת **mōšᵉkôt**, n.f. GK: 5436 [→ 4900]. cords, chains, fetters:– bands [1]

4190 מוֹשָׁעָה **môšā'â**, n.f. GK: 4636 [→ 3467]. act of salvation, act of helping:– salvation [1]

4191 מוּת **mût**, v. GK: 4637 [→ 4194, 4463, 8546 (also used with compound proper names)]. [Q] to die, be killed, be dead; [Pol] to kill, slay, put to death; [H] to kill, make die, put to death, assassinate; [Ho] to be put to death, be murdered:– die [232], died [153], dead [134], surely put to death (+4191) [56], put to death [44], slew [40], surely die (+4191) [40], slay [38], kill [23], slain [18], dieth [16], death [10], killed [6], in wise slay (+4191) [4], die (+4191) [2], killeth [2], must needs die (+4191) [2], put at all to death (+4191) [2], surely be put to death (+4191) [2], surely kill (+4191) [2], cause to die [1], crying [1], dead man [1], destroyers [1], destroy [1], diest [1], slayeth [1], slaying [1]

4192 מוּת לַבֵּן **mût labbēn**, tt. GK: 4240 [→ 3807.1+1886.1+1121]. t.t. in Ps 9, poss. "death of the son" (4637 + 3807.1 + 1886.1 + 1121):– Muth-labben (+1121+1886.1+3807.1) [1]

4193 מוֹת **môt** (Aram.), n.[m.]. GK: 10409 [cf. 4194]. death:– death [1]

4194 מָוֶת **māwet**, n.m. GK: 4638 [→ 2700; cf. 4191; cf. 4193]. death, dying:– death [126], dead [8], died [8], die [6], dieth [5], surely die (+1121) [2], deadly [1], deaths [1], put to death (+2026) [1], slay [1], worthy to die (+1121) [1]

מוּת לַבֵּן **mût lab-bēn**. See 4192.

4195 מוֹתָר **môtār**, n.m. GK: 4639 [→ 3498]. profit, advantage:– hath preeminence [1], plenteousness [1], profit [1]

Heb

4196 מִזְבֵּחַ ***mizbēaḥ***, n.m. GK: 4640 [→ 2076; cf. 4056]. altar:– altar [349], altars [52]

4197 מֶזֶג ***mezeg***, n.m. GK: 4641. blended wine, mixed wine (likely spiced):– liquor [1]

4198 מָזֶה ***māzeh***, a. GK: 4642. empty (from hunger), implying an unhealthy loss of weight and breakdown in health:– burnt [1]

4199 מִזָּה ***mizzâ***, n.pr.m. GK: 4645. Mizzah, "*terror*":– Mizzah [3]

4200 מָזוּ ***māzû***, n.m. GK: 4646 [cf. 2106]. barn, granary:– garners [1]

4201 מְזוּזָה ***m^{e}zûzâ***, n.f. GK: 4647. doorframe, doorpost, doorjamb:– posts [10], side posts [4], post [3], door posts [1], door post [1]

4202 מָזוֹן ***māzôn***, n.m. GK: 4648 [→ 2109]. provisions, food:– meat [1], victual [1]

4203 מָזוֹן ***māzôn*** (Aram.), n.[m.]. GK: 10410 [→ 2110; cf. 2109]. food:– meat [2]

4204 מָזוֹר ***māzôr***, n.m. GK: 4650. trap, ambush:– wound [1]

4205 מָזוֹר ***māzôr***, n.[m.]. GK: 4649. sore, boil, ulcer:– wound [2], bound up [1]

מְזֻזָה ***m^{e}zuzâ***. See 4201.

4206 מֵזַח ***mēzaḥ*** or מָזִיחַ ***māzîaḥ***, n.m. GK: 4651 & 4652 & 4653 [→ 4231]. belt, leather girdle worn next to the skin; harbor; an area in which wind and wave are restricted as a fig. extension of a girdle or belt that restrains:– strength [2], girdle [1]

4207 מַזְלֵג ***mazlēg*** or מִזְלָגָה ***mizlāgâ***, n.m. & f. GK: 4656 & 4657 & 4658. (three-tined) meat fork:– fleshhooks [5], fleshhook [2]

4208 מַזָּל ***mazzāl***, n.[f.]pl. GK: 4655 [cf. 4216]. constellation (possibly of the zodiac signs):– planets [1]

4209 מְזִמָּה ***m^{e}zimmâ***, n.f. GK: 4659 [→ 2161]. discretion; scheme, plan, purpose, intent:– discretion [4], wicked devices [3], devices [2], thoughts [2], device [1], intents [1], lewdness [1], mischievous device [1], mischievous [1], thought [1], wickedly (+3807.1) [1], witty inventions [1]

4210 מִזְמוֹר ***mizmôr***, n.[m.]. GK: 4660 [→ 2167]. psalm, melody:– psalm [57]

4211 מַזְמֵרָה ***mazmērâ***, n.f. GK: 4661 [→ 2168]. pruning hook, pruning knife, vine-knife:– pruninghooks [3], pruning hooks [1]

4212 מְזַמֶּרֶת ***m^{e}zammeret***, n.f. GK: 4662 [→ 2168]. wick trimmer (scissors, possibly also used as a snuffer):– snuffers [5]

4213 מִזְעָר ***miz'ār***, n.[m.]. GK: 4663 [→ 2191]. small matter, few:– very little while (+4592) [2], few [1], small [1]

מָזֹר ***māzōr***. See 4205.

4214 מִזְרֶה ***mizreh***, n.[m.]. GK: 4665 [→ 2219]. winnowing fork, shovel:– fan [2]

4215 מְזָרִים ***m^{e}zārîm***, n.m. *or* v.ptcp. GK: 4668 [→ 2219]. driving (north) winds:– north [1]

4216 מַזָּרוֹת ***mazzārôt***, n.[f.]pl. GK: 4666 [cf. 4208]. constellations, variously specified:– Mazzaroth [1]

4217 מִזְרָח ***mizrāḥ***, n.[m.]. GK: 4667 [→ 2224]. direction of the sunrise, east, eastern; the east was the direction of orientation in the ancient Near East:– east [32], eastward (+1886.5) [15], rising [7], sunrising (+8121) [6], eastward [3], the sunrising (+8121+1886.1) [2], east (+6924+1886.5) [1], east side (+8121) [1], east side [1], eastward (+1886.1+3807.1) [1], eastward (+8121+1886.1) [1], rising of the sun [1], sunrising (+8121+1886.1) [1], sunrising [1], the east side (+8121+1886.1) [1]

4218 מִזְרָע ***mizrā'***, n.[m.]. GK: 4669 [→ 2232]. seeded field, land sown:– sown [1]

4219 מִזְרָק ***mizrāq***, n.m. GK: 4670 [→ 2236]. sacred bowl used for sprinkling (the altar):– bowl [13], basons [11], bowls [8]

4220 מֵחַ ***mēaḥ***, n.[m.]. GK: 4671 [→ 4221; cf. 4229]. fat sheep; (representing) the rich:– fat ones [1], fatlings [1]

4221 מֹחַ ***mōaḥ***, n.m. GK: 4672 [→ 4220; cf. 4229]. marrow (of the bones):– marrow [1]

4222 מָחָא ***māḥā'***, v. GK: 4673 [→ 4232; cf. 4229; cf. 4223]. [Q] to clap (hands in joy):– clap [2], clapped [1]

4223 מְחָא ***m^{e}ḥā'*** (Aram.), v. GK: 10411 [cf. 4272]. [P] to strike; [Pa] to hold back, prevent; [Htpe] to be impaled:– smote [2], hanged [1], stay [1]

4224 מַחֲבֵא ***maḥ^{a}bē'*** or מַחֲבֹא ***maḥ^{a}bō'***, n.[m.]. GK: 4675 & 4676 [→ 2244]. shelter, hiding place (from wind):– hiding place [1], lurking places [1]

4225 מַחְבֶּרֶת ***maḥberet***, n.f. GK: 4678 [→ 2266]. place of joining, seam, set (of curtains):– coupling [8]

4226 מְחַבְּרוֹת ***m^{e}ḥabb^{e}rôt***, n.f. GK: 4677 [→ 2266]. fittings, braces (of iron), joists, truss (of timber):– couplings [1], joinings [1]

4227 מַחֲבַת ***maḥ^{a}bat***, n.f. GK: 4679 [→ 2281]. (metal) griddle or baking pan:– pan [5]

4228 מַחֲגֹרֶת ***maḥ^{a}gōret***, n.f. GK: 4680 [→ 2296]. girding (of sackcloth wrapped around the body):– girding [1], king [1]

4229 מָחָה ***māḥâ***, v. GK: 4681 & 4682 & 4683 [→ 4239, 8547?; cf. 4220, 4221, 4222; cf. 4223]. [Q] to wash off, wipe out, blot out, destroy; to continue along, stretch along; [N] be blotted out, be wiped out, be exterminated; [Pu] (choice food-dishes) to be filled with marrow; [H] to cause to blot out:– blot out [9], blotted out [5], destroyed [3], destroy [2], put out [2], utterly put out (+4229) [2], wipeth [2], abolished [1], blotteth out [1], blot [1], destroyeth [1], full of marrow [1], reach [1], wipe away [1], wipe out [1], wiped away [1], wipe [1], wiping [1]

4230 מְחוּגָה ***m^{e}ḥûgâ***, n.f. GK: 4684 [→ 2328]. compass (for making circles):– compass [1]

4231 מָחוֹז ***māḥôz***, n.[m.]. GK: 4685 [→ 4206]. haven, harbor, which might include a population center like a repair yard and city:– haven [1]

4232 מְחוּיָאֵל ***m^{e}ḥûyā'ēl*** or מְחִיָּיאֵל ***m^{e}ḥiyyāy'ēl***, n.pr.m. GK: 4686 & 4696 [→ 4222+410]. Mehujael, Mehijael:– Mehujael [2]

4233 מַחֲוִים ***maḥ^{a}wîm***, a.g. GK: 4687. Mahavite:– Mahavite [1]

4234 מָחוֹל ***māḥôl***, n.m. GK: 4688 [→ 4235, 4246; cf. 2342]. circle-dancing, round-dancing:– dance [4], dances [1], dancing [1]

4235 מָחוֹל ***māḥôl***, n.pr.m. GK: 4689 [→ 4234; cf. 2342]. Mahol, "*place of round dancing*":– Mahol [1]

מְחוֹלָה ***m^{e}ḥôlâ***. See 65, 4246.

4236 מַחֲזֶה ***maḥ^{a}zeh***, n.[m.]. GK: 4690 [→ 2372]. vision:– vision [4]

4237 מֶחֱזָה ***meḥ^{e}zâ***, n.f. GK: 4691 [→ 2372]. light, place of seeing, in some contexts referring to a window:– light [4]

4238 מַחֲזִיאוֹת ***maḥ^{a}zî'ôt***, n.pr.m. GK: 4692 [→ 2372]. Mahazioth, "*visions*":– Mahazioth [2]

4239 מְחִי ***m^{e}ḥî***, n.[m.]. GK: 4693 [→ 4229]. blow (of a battering ram):– engines [1]

4240 מְחִידָא ***m^{e}ḥîdā'***, n.pr.m. GK: 4694. Mehida, "[poss.] *bought as slave*":– Mehida [2]

4241 מִחְיָה ***miḥyâ***, n.f. GK: 4695 [→ 2421]. saving of a life; raw flesh; food, sustenance; relief, recovering:– reviving [2], preserve life [1], quick raw (+2416) [1], quick [1], recover [1], sustenance [1], victuals [1]

מְחִיאֵל ***m^{e}ḥiyā'ēl***. See 4232.

4242 מְחִיר ***m^{e}ḥîr***, n.m. GK: 4697 [→ 4243]. price, cost, money:– price [11], gain [1], hire [1], sold (+871.1) [1], worth [1]

4243 מְחִיר ***m^{e}ḥîr***, n.pr.m. GK: 4698 [→ 4242]. Mehir, "*hired hand*":– Mehir [1]

4244 מַחְלָה ***maḥlâ***, n.pr.f. [& m.?]. GK: 4702. Mahlah, "[perhaps] *weak one*":– Mahlah [4], Mahalah [1]

4245 מַחֲלֶה ***maḥ^{a}leh*** or מַחֲלָה ***maḥ^{a}lâ***, n.m. & f. GK: 4700 & 4701 [cf. 2470]. sickness, disease:– sickness [3], diseases [1], disease [1], infirmity [1]

4246 מְחֹלָה ***m^{e}ḥōlâ***, n.f. GK: 4703 [→ 4234; cf. 65, 2342]. circle-dance, round-dance:– dances [5], dancing [2], company [1]

4247 מְחִלָּה ***m^{e}ḥillâ***, n.f. GK: 4704 [→ 2490]. hole:– caves [1]

4248 מַחְלוֹן ***maḥlôn***, n.pr.m. GK: 4705 [→ 2470?]. Mahlon:– Mahlon [3], Mahlon's [1]

4249 מַחְלִי ***maḥlî***, n.pr.m. GK: 4706 [→ 2470?]. Mahli, "[perhaps] *shrewd, cunning*":– Mahli [11], Mahali [1]

4250 מַחְלִי ***maḥlî***, a.g. GK: 4707 [→ 2470?]. Mahlite, "*of Mahli*":– Mahlites [2]

4251 מַחֲלֻיִים ***maḥ^{a}luyîm***, n.m. GK: 4708 [→ 2470]. sickness (caused by wounding):– diseases [1]

4252 מַחֲלָף ***maḥ^{a}lāp***, n.m. GK: 4709 [→ 2498?]. utensil, perhaps a pan:– knives [1]

4253 מַחְלָפָה ***maḥ^{a}lāpâ***, n.f. GK: 4710 [→ 2498]. braids (of hair):– locks [2]

4254 מַחֲלָצוֹת ***maḥ^{a}lāṣôt***, n.f.[pl.]. GK: 4711 [→ 2502]. fine robes, fine, white, festival garments:– change of raiment [1], changeable suits of apparel [1]

4255 מַחְלְקָה ***maḥl^{e}qâ*** (Aram.), n.f. GK: 10412 [→ 2508; cf. 4256]. group, division (of priests):– courses [1]

4256 מַחֲלֹקֶת ***maḥ^{a}lōqet***, n.f. GK: 4713 [→ 2505; cf. 4255]. portion, share (of land); division, group (of people):– course [18], courses [14], divisions [8], companies by course [1], portions [1]

4257 מָחֲלַת ***māḥ^{a}lat***, n.f. GK: 4714 [→ 2342? *or* 2470?]. mahalath (t.t. in the Psalms):– Mahalath [2]

4258 מָחֲלַת ***māḥ^{a}lat***, n.pr.f. GK: 4715. Mahalath, "*suffering of affliction NIV; sickness or suffering poem JB*":– Mahalath [2]

4259 מְחֹלָתִי ***m^{e}ḥōlātî***, a.g. GK: 4716 [cf. 65?]. Meholathite, of Meholah, "*of Meholah*":– Meholathite [2]

4260 מַחְמָאֹת ***maḥmā'ōt***, n.f.pl. GK: 4717 [cf. 2529]. butter; some sources: curds, yogurt:– butter [1]

4261 מַחְמָד ***maḥmād***, n.m. GK: 4718 [→ 2530]. thing of value, something of delight, treasure; "the delight of the eyes" is someone or something especially cherished:– pleasant things [4], desire [3], pleasant [3], beloved [1], goodly [1], lovely [1]

4262 מַחְמֹד ***maḥmōd***, n.[m.]. GK: 4719 [→ 2530]. treasure, something precious:– pleasant things [1]

4263 מַחְמָל ***maḥmāl***, n.[m.]. GK: 4720 [→ 2550?]. yearning:– pitieth [1]

4264 מַחֲנֶה ***maḥ^{a}neh***, n.m. & f. GK: 4722 [→ 4266; cf. 2583]. camp, group (military or civilian):– camp [129], host [57], camps [7], company [5], tents [5], hosts [4], armies [3], bands [2], battle [1], companies [1], drove [1], two armies [1]

4265 מַחֲנֵה־דָן ***maḥ^{a}nēh-dān***, n.pr.loc. GK: 4723. Mahaneh Dan, "*camp of Dan*":– Mahaneh-dan [1]

4266 מַחֲנַיִם ***maḥ^{a}nayim***, n.pr.loc. GK: 4724 [→ 4264; cf. 2583]. Mahanaim, "*double camp*":– Mahanaim [13]

4267 מַחֲנָק ***maḥ^{a}nāq***, n.[m.]. GK: 4725 [→ 2614]. strangling, suffocation:– strangling [1]

4268 מַחְסֶה ***maḥseh***, n.m. GK: 4726 [→ 4271; cf. 2620]. refuge, shelter:– refuge [13], hope [2], place of refuge [2], shelter [2], trust [1]

4269 מַחְסוֹם ***maḥsôm***, n.m. GK: 4727 [→ 2629]. muzzle, a covering for the mouth to keep silence:– bridle [1]

4270 מַחְסוֹר ***maḥsôr***, n.[m.]. GK: 4728 [→ 2637]. need, lack of, scarcity, hence poverty:– want [7], lack [1], need [1], penury [1], poor [1], poverty [1], wants [1]

4271 מַחְסֵיָה ***maḥsēyâ***, n.pr.m. GK: 4729 [→ 4268+3068]. Mahseiah:– Maaseiah [2]

4272 מָחַץ ***māḥaṣ***, v. GK: 4730 [→ 4273; cf. 4223]. [Q] to beat to pieces, crush, shatter:– wound [3], smite [2], wounded [2], dipped [1], pierce through [1], pierced [1], smiteth through [1], strike through [1], woundedst [1], woundeth [1]

4273 מַחַץ ***maḥaṣ***, n.[m.]. GK: 4731 [→ 4272]. wound (from a blow):– stroke [1]

4274 מַחְצֵב ***maḥṣēb***, n.[m.]. GK: 4732 [→ 2672]. dressed (stone), hewn (stone):– hewn [2], hewed [1]

4275 מֶחֱצָה ***meḥ^{e}ṣâ***, n.f. GK: 4733 [→ 2673]. half:– half [2]

4276 מַחֲצִית ***maḥ^{a}ṣît***, n.f. GK: 4734 [→ 2673]. half; noon, middle of the day:– half [14], half so much [1], midday (+3117+1886.1) [1]

4277 מָחַק ***māḥaq***, v. GK: 4735. [Q] to crush, smash, pierce:– smote off [1]

4278 מֶחְקָר ***meḥqār***, n.m. GK: 4736 [→ 2713]. (unexplored) depths (of the earth):– deep places [1]

4279 מָחָר ***māḥār***, n.m. (used as adv.). GK: 4737 [→ 4283; cf. 309]. tomorrow, the next day, in the future:– to morrow [43], in time to come [7], to come [1], to morrow (+3117) [1]

4280 מַחֲרָאָה ***maḥ^{a}rā'â***, n.f. GK: 4738 [→ 2716]. latrine:– draught house [1]

4281 מַחֲרֵשָׁה ***maḥ^{a}rēšâ***, n.f. GK: 4739 [→ 2790, 4282]. same as 4282: plowshare:– mattocks [1], mattock [1]

4282 מַחֲרֶשֶׁת ***maḥ^{a}rešet***, n.f. GK: 4739 [→ 4281]. same as 4281: plowshare:– share [1]

4283 מָחֳרָת **moḥ^o^rāt**, n.f. GK: 4740 [→ 4279; cf. 309]. the next day, the day after:– morrow [26], morrow after [3], next day [2], next [1]

4284 מַחֲשָׁבָה **maḥ^a^šābâ**, n.f. GK: 4742 [→ 2803]. thought, plan, scheme, plot, design:– thoughts [27], devices [8], device [4], imaginations [3], purposes [3], purpose [3], cunning works [1], cunning [1], curious works [1], devised [1], invented [1], means [1], those that devise cunning work (+2803) [1], thought [1]

4285 מַחְשָׁךְ **maḥšāk**, n.m. GK: 4743 [→ 2821]. place of darkness, hiding place:– darkness [4], dark places [2], dark [1]

4286 מַחְשֹׂף **maḥśōp**, n.m. GK: 4741 [→ 2834]. exposing, laying bare (of wood):– made appear [1]

4287 מַחַת **maḥat**, n.pr.m. GK: 4744 [→ 2865?]. Mahath, "[perhaps] *tough*":– Mahath [3]

4288 מְחִתָּה **m^e^ḥittâ**, n.f. GK: 4745 [→ 2865]. ruin, undoing; terror, horror:– destruction [7], terror [2], dismaying [1], ruin [1]

4289 מַחְתָּה **maḥtâ**, n.f. GK: 4746 [→ 2846]. censer, firepan, tray:– censers [8], censer [7], firepans [4], snuffdishes [3]

4290 מַחְתֶּרֶת **maḥteret**, n.m. GK: 4747 [→ 2864]. (the act of) breaking into (a house) and so trespassing:– breaking up [1], secret search [1]

4291 מְטָא **m^e^ṭā'** (Aram.), v. GK: 10413. [P] to reach out, extend towards:– came [4], reached [2], come [1], reacheth [1]

4292 מַטְאֲטֵא **maṭ'^a^ṭē'**, n.[m.]. GK: 4748 [→ 2894; cf. 2916]. broom:– besom [1]

4293 מַטְבֵּחַ **maṭbēaḥ**, n.[m.]. GK: 4749 [→ 2873]. place of slaughter, slaughter yard:– slaughter [1]

4294 מַטֶּה **maṭṭeh**, n.m. [& f.?]. GK: 4751 [→ 5186]. staff, rod, club, a stick used to assist in walking, discipline, and guidance, often highly individualized and used for identification; of royalty: scepter; by extension: tribe, as a major unit of national group or clan (fig. identified with or under authority of a leader's staff):– tribe [163], rod [42], tribes [20], staff [15], rods [8], staves [1]

4295 מַטָּה **maṭṭâ**, adv. GK: 4752 [→ 5186]. below, beneath, lower, bottom:– downward (+3807.1) [5], beneath (+4480+3807.1) [4], beneath [2], underneath (+4480+3807.1) [2], very low (+4295) [2], beneath (+3807.1) [1], down (+3807.1) [1], less [1], under [1]

4296 מִטָּה **miṭṭâ**, n.f. GK: 4753 [→ 5186]. bed, couch, a piece of furniture on which one reclines for rest or sleep; by extension: bier, to carry the dead; carriage or palanquin (a vehicle carried on poles by porters):– bed [23], bedchamber (+2315) [2], beds [2], bed's [1], bier [1]

4297 מֻטֶּה **muṭṭeh**, n.[m.]. GK: 4754 [→ 5186]. injustice, warping (of justice), crookedness (of law):– perverseness [1]

4298 מֻטָּה **muṭṭâ**, n.f. GK: 4755 [→ 5186]. outspreading (of wings):– stretching out [1]

4299 מַטְוֶה **maṭweh**, n.[m.]. GK: 4757 [→ 2901]. that which is spun, yarn:– spun [1]

4300 מְטִיל **m^e^ṭîl**, n.m. GK: 4758. (iron) rod:– bars [1]

4301 מַטְמוֹן **maṭmôn**, n.m. GK: 4759 [→ 2934]. (hidden) treasure, (hidden) riches:– hid treasures [2], hidden riches [1], treasures [1], treasure [1]

4302 מַטָּע **maṭṭā'**, n.m. GK: 4760 [→ 5193]. (the act or place of) planting:– planting [2], plantation [1], plantings [1], plants [1], plant [1]

4303 מַטְעָם **maṭ'ām**, n.m. GK: 4761 [→ 2938]. tasty food, delicacy:– savoury meat [6], dainties [1], dainty meats [1]

4304 מִטְפַּחַת **miṭpaḥat**, n.f. GK: 4762 [→ 2946]. cloak, shawl:– vail [1], wimples [1]

4305 מָטַר **māṭar**, v.den. GK: 4763 [→ 4306]. [N] to be rained upon; [H] to send rain down on; [Ho] to be rained upon; rain has a generally positive associations of growth and refreshment, though excessive or ill-timed rain is potentially destructive to crops and even life-threatening:– rained [5], rain [5], cause to rain [3], caused to rain [3], rained down [1]

4306 מָטָר **māṭār**, n.m. GK: 4764 [→ 4305, 4309]. rain, rain shower:– rain [35], great [1], showers [1], small [1]

4307 מַטָּרָה **maṭṭārâ**, n.f. GK: 4766 [→ 5201]. (the court of the) guard, i.e., place of confinement; (the Gate of the) Guard (a place); target:– prison [13], mark [3]

4308 מַטְרֵד **maṭrēd**, n.pr.f. GK: 4765 [→ 2956]. Matred, "[perhaps] *spear*":– Matred [2]

4309 מַטְרִי **maṭrî**, a.g. GK: 4767 [→ 4306]. Matri:– Matri [1]

4310 מִי **mî**, p.inter. GK: 4769 [→ 4316?, 4317, 4318, 4319, 4320, 4322, 4321, 4332]. who?, what?, which?; anyone, whoever:– who [284], whom [47], what [25], O that (+5414) [17], whose [11], whose (+3807.1) [7], which [6], oh that [3], whosoever [3], whoso [3], any [2], he [2], would God (+5414) [2], would to God (+5414) [2], him [1], none [1], that [1], what (+2088) [1], who else [1], whosoever (+834) [1], would God that (+5414) [1], would [1]

4311 מֵידְבָא **mêd^e^bā'**, n.pr.loc. GK: 4772. Medeba:– Medeba [5]

4312 מֵידָד **mêdād**, n.pr.m. GK: 4773. Medad, "*beloved*":– Medad [2]

4313 מֵי הַיַּרְקוֹן **mê hayyarqôn**, n.pr.loc. GK: 4770 [→ 4325]. Me Jarkon, "*waters of Jarkon [greenish?]*":– Me-jarkon [1]

4314 מֵי זָהָב **mê zāhāb**, n.pr.m. GK: 4771 [→ 4325+2091]. Me-Zahab, "*waters of gold*":– Mezahab [2]

4315 מֵיטָב **mêṭāb**, n.[m.]. GK: 4774 [→ 3190]. best (part of something):– best [6]

4316 מִיכָא **mîkā'**, n.pr.m. GK: 4775 [→ 4317?, 4318; cf. 4310?]. Mica, "*Who is like Yahweh?*":– Micha [4], Micah [1]

4317 מִיכָאֵל **mîkā'ēl**, n.pr.m. GK: 4776 [→ 4316?]. Michael, "*Who is like God [El]?*":– Michael [13]

4318 מִיכָה **mîkâ**, n.pr.m. GK: 4777 [→ 4316]. Micah; Mica; Micaiah, "*Who is like Yahweh?*":– Micah [24], Michah [4], Micah's [3], Micaiah [1]

4319 מִיכָהוּ **mîkāhû**, n.pr.m. GK: 4778 [→ 4310+3509.1+1930.2]. Micahu, cf. 4322:– @H = **4320** מִיכָיָה **mîkāyâ**, n.pr.m. GK: 4779 [→ 4322, 4321]. Micaiah, "*Who is like Yahweh?*":– Michaiah [3]

4321 מִיכָיְהוּ **mîkāy^e^hû**, n.pr.m. GK: 4781 [→ 4320]. Micaiah; Micah, "*Who is like Yahweh?*":– Micaiah [17], Micah [2], Michaiah [2]

4322 מִיכָיָהוּ **mîkāyāhû**, n.pr.m. & f. GK: 4780 [→ 4320]. Micaiah, "*Who is like Yahweh?*":– Michaiah [2]

4323 מִיכָל **mîkāl**, n.[m.]. GK: 4782 [→ 4324]. brook, stream; some sources: pool, reservoir:– brook [1]

4324 מִיכַל **mîkal**, n.pr.f. GK: 4783 [→ 4323]. Michal, "*Who is like God [El]?*":– Michal [18]

4325 מַיִם **mayim**, n.m. GK: 4784 [→ 66, 4313, 4314, 4956]. water; in nature: ocean, lake, flood, river; from the body: tears, urine:– water [306], waters [267], piss (+7272) [2], watersprings (+4161) [2], washing [1], watercourse (+4161) [1], waterflood (+7641) [1], watering [1]

4326 מִיָּמִין **miyyāmîn**, n.pr.m. GK: 4785 [→ 4509]. Mijamin, "*from the right hand*":– Miamin [2], Mijamin [2]

4327 מִין **mîn**, n.[m.]. GK: 4786 [→ 8544]. kind: genus or species:– kind [30], kinds [1]

4328 מְיֻסָּדָה **m^e^yussādâ**, v.ptcp. GK: 4588 [→ 4145]. ptcp. of 3245: foundation:– @H = **4329** מוּסָךְ **mûsāk** or מֵיסָךְ **mêsāk**, n.m. GK: 4590 & 4788 [→ 5526]. canopy:– covert [1]

מֵיפַעַת **mêpa'at**. See 4158.

4330 מִיץ **mîṣ**, n.m. GK: 4790 [→ 4160]. pressing, squeezing:– churning [1], forcing [1], wringing [1]

4331 מֵישָׁא **mêšā'**, n.pr.m. GK: 4791. Mesha:– Mesha [1]

4332 מִישָׁאֵל **mîšā'ēl**, n.pr.m. GK: 4792 [→ 4310+7945+410; cf. 4333]. Mishael, "*Who belongs to God [El]?*":– Mishael [7]

4333 מִישָׁאֵל **mîšā'ēl** (Aram.), n.pr.m. GK: 10414 [cf. 4332]. Mishael, "*who belongs to God (El)?*":– Mishael [1]

4334 מִישׁוֹר **mîšôr**, n.m. GK: 4793 [→ 3474]. (geographical) plateau, plain, level ground; (of ruling and right living) uprightness, justice, straightness:– plain [14], equity [2], even place [1], made straight [1], plains [1], righteously [1], right [1], straight [1], uprightness [1]

4335 מֵישַׁךְ **mêšak**, n.pr.m. GK: 4794 [cf. 4336]. Meshach, "[perhaps] *I have become weak*":– Meshach [1]

4336 מֵישַׁךְ **mêšak** (Aram.), n.pr.m. GK: 10415 [cf. 4335]. Meshach, "[perhaps] *I have become weak*":– Meshach [14]

4337 מֵישָׁע **mêšā'**, n.pr.m. GK: 4796 [→ 3467]. Mesha:– Mesha [1]

4338 מֵישַׁע **mêša'**, n.pr.m. GK: 4795 [→ 3467]. Mesha:– Mesha [1]

4339 מֵישָׁרִים **mêšārîm**, n.m. GK: 4797 [→ 3474]. uprightness, fairness, equity, justice; moral uprightness and justice are fig. extensions of an object that is straight rather than crooked:– equity [4], uprightly [3], uprightness [3], right things [2], agreement [1], aright (+871.1) [1], righteously (+871.1) [1], sweetly (+3807.1) [1], things that are equal [1], things that are right [1], upright [1]

4340 מֵיתָר **mêtār**, n.m. GK: 4798 [→ 3499]. rope, cord; bow-string:– cords [8], laid up [2], strings [1]

4341 מַכְאֹב **mak'ōb**, n.m. GK: 4799 [→ 3510]. pain, grief, sorrow, suffering:– sorrow [7], sorrows [5], grief [2], pain [2]

4342 מַכְבִּיר **makbîr**, v.ptcp. GK: 3892 [→ 3527]. ptcp. of 3527: abundance:– abundance [1]

4343 מַכְבֵּנָה **makbēnâ**, n.pr.loc. GK: 4800 [cf. 4344]. Macbenah, "*bond*":– Machbenah [1]

4344 מַכְבַּנַּי **makbannay**, n.pr.m. GK: 4801 [cf. 4343]. Macbannai, "*clad with a cloak*":– Machbanai [1]

4345 מִכְבָּר **mikbār**, n.m. GK: 4803 [→ 4346]. grating, lattice-work:– grate [6]

4346 מַכְבֵּר **makbēr**, n.[m.]. GK: 4802 [→ 4345]. thick cloth, with a focus that it is twisted, braided, or woven:– thick cloth [1]

4347 מַכָּה **makkâ**, n.f. GK: 4804 [→ 5221]. wound, injury, physical damage to the body; by extension: plague, affliction, calamity, disaster:– slaughter [13], plagues [9], wound [8], wounds [6], plague [2], stripes [2], stroke [2], beaten [1], blow [1], slaughter made (+5221) [1], smote [1], sores [1], wounded [1]

4348 מִכְוָה **mikwâ**, n.f. GK: 4805 [→ 3554]. burn (on the skin), scar; in context this is not an intentional mark or tattoo:– burning [4], burneth [1]

4349 מָכוֹן **mākôn**, n.m. GK: 4806 [→ 3559]. (established) place, site; foundation (of earth or throne):– place [11], dwelling place [2], habitation [2], foundations [1], settled place [1]

4350 מְכוֹנָה **m^e^kônâ**, n.f. GK: 4807 [→ 3559, 4369]. movable stand; (established) place, foundation:– bases [16], base [8], every (+1886.1) [1]

4351 מְכוּרָה **m^e^kûrâ**, n.f. GK: 4808 [→ 3738]. ancestry, origin, parentage:– birth [1], habitation [1], nativity [1]

4352 מָכִי **mākî**, n.pr.m. GK: 4809. Maki, "[perhaps] *reduced* or *bought*":– Machi [1]

4353 מָכִיר **mākîr**, n.pr.m. GK: 4810 [→ 4354]. Makir, Makirite, "*bought*":– Machir [22]

4354 מָכִירִי **mākîrî**, a.g. GK: 4811 [→ 4353]. Makirite, "*of Makir*":– Machirites [1]

4355 מָכַךְ **mākak**, v. GK: 4812 [cf. 4134]. [Q] to sink, go down, waste away; [N] to sag, be sunk down; [Ho] to be brought low:– brought low [2], decayeth [1]

4356 מִכְלָא **miklā'**, n.[m.]. GK: 4813 [→ 3607]. pen, fold (for sheep or goats):– folds [1], fold [1], sheepfolds (+6629) [1]

4357 מִכְלוֹת **miklôt**, n.[f.]. GK: 4816 [→ 3615]. solid (gold), purest (gold):– perfect [1]

4358 מִכְלוֹל **miklôl**, n.m. GK: 4814 [→ 3634]. fullness, completeness, perfection:– all sorts [1], most gorgeously [1]

4359 מִכְלָל **miklāl**, n.m. GK: 4817 [→ 3634]. perfection:– perfection [1]

4360 מַכְלוּל **maklûl**, n.m. GK: 4815 [→ 3634]. beautiful garment, finery, with a focus the excellence of the item:– all sorts of things [1]

4361 מַכֹּלֶת **makkōlet**, n.f. GK: 4818 [→ 398]. food:– food [1]

4362 מִכְמָן **mikmān**, n.[m.]. GK: 4819. (hidden) treasure:– treasures [1]

4363 מִכְמָס **mikmās** or מִכְמָשׂ **mikmāś**, n.pr.loc. GK: 4820 & 4825 [cf. 3647]. Micmas, Micmash, "[perhaps] *hidden place*":– Michmash [9], Michmas [2]

4364 מִכְמָר **mikmār** or מַכְמֹר **makmōr**, n.[m.]. GK: 4821 & 4822 [cf. 4365]. net, snare (for capture of game):– nets [1], net [1]

4365 מִכְמֶרֶת **mikmeret** or מִכְמֹרֶת **mikmōret**, n.f. GK: 4823 & 4824 [cf. 4364]. net, snare; fishing net, dragnet (for fish):– drag [2], nets [1]

מִכְמָשׂ **mikmāš**. See 4363.

4366 מִכְמְתָת **mikm^e^tāt**, n.pr.loc. GK: 4826. Micmethath:– Michmethah [2]

4367 מַכְנַדְבַי **maknadbay**, n.pr.m. GK: 4827. Macnadebai, "[poss.] *possession of Nebo*":– Machnadebai [1]

מְכֹנָה **m^e^kōnâ**. See 4350.

4368 מְכֹנָה **m^e^kōnâ**, n.pr.loc. GK: 4828 [→ 3559]. Meconah, "*foundation*":– Mekonah [1]

4369 מְכֻנָה ***mᵉkunâ***, n.f. GK: 4807 [→ 4350]. same as 4350: movable stand; (established) place, foundation:–

4370 מִכְנָס ***miknās***, n.m. GK: 4829 [→ 3664]. undergarment, some kind of shorts or trousers:– breeches [5]

4371 מֶכֶס ***mekes***, n.m. GK: 4830 [→ 3699]. tribute, cultic dues or taxes:– tribute [6]

4372 מִכְסֶה ***mikseh***, n.[m.]. GK: 4832 [→ 3680]. covering:– covering [16]

4373 מִכְסָה ***miksâ***, n.f. GK: 4831 [→ 3699]. number (of persons); amount, valuation (of a thing):– number [1], worth [1]

4374 מְכַסֶּה ***mᵉkasseh***, n.m. GK: 4833 [→ 3680]. covering (of a body or building); layer of fat (on the kidneys):– clothing [1], covered [1], covereth [1], cover [1]

4375 מַכְפֵּלָה ***makpēlâ***, n.pr.loc. GK: 4834 [→ 3717]. Machpelah, "*double [cave]*":– Machpelah [6]

4376 מָכַר ***mākar***, v. GK: 4835 [→ 4377, 4378?, 4465, 4466]. [Q] to sell; [N] to be sold; [Ht] to sell oneself:– sold [44], sell [22], selleth [5], seller [3], sell at all (+4376) [2], sell ought (+4465) [1], sellers [1], sellest [1], sold (+4466) [1]

4377 מֶכֶר ***meker***, n.m. GK: 4836 [→ 4376]. worth, value; merchandise:– pay (+5414) [1], price [1], ware [1]

4378 מַכָּר ***makkār***, n.m. GK: 4837 [→ 4376?]. treasurer:– acquaintance [2]

4379 מִכְרֶה ***mikreh***, n.m. GK: 4838 [→ 3738]. (salt) pit:– saltpits (+4417) [1]

4380 מְכֵרָה ***mᵉkērâ***, n.[f.]. GK: 4839. sword, weapon:– habitations [1]

מְכֹרָה ***mᵉkōrâ***. See 4351.

4381 מִכְרִי ***mikrî***, n.pr.m. GK: 4840. Micri:– Michri [1]

4382 מְכֵרָתִי ***mᵉkērātî***, a.g. GK: 4841. Mekerathite:– Mecherathite [1]

4383 מִכְשׁוֹל ***mikšôl***, n.m. GK: 4842 [→ 3782]. stumbling block, obstacle; (occasion of) stumbling, downfall:– stumblingblock [7], offence [2], caused to fall [1], offend [1], ruins [1], ruin [1], stumblingblocks [1]

Heb

4384 מַכְשֵׁלָה ***makšēlâ***, n.f. GK: 4843 [→ 3782]. heap of ruins, heap of rubble:– ruin [1], stumblingblocks [1]

4385 מִכְתָּב ***miktāb***, n.m. GK: 4844 [→ 3789]. writing, inscription, letter:– writing [9]

4386 מְכִתָּה ***mᵉkittâ***, n.f. GK: 4845 [→ 3807]. pieces, crushed fragments:– bursting [1]

4387 מִכְתָּם ***miktām***, n.[m.]. GK: 4846 [→ 3800?]. miktam (t.t. in the Psalms, of uncertain meaning):– Michtam [6]

4388 מַכְתֵּשׁ ***maktēš***, n.m. GK: 4847 [→ 3806, 4389]. hollow place; mortar; market district (at a hollow place in the city?):– hollow place [1], mortar [1]

4389 מַכְתֵּשׁ ***maktēš***, n.pr.m. GK: 4847 [→ 4388]. same as 4388 as n.pr.: Maktesh:– Maktesh [1]

מֻל ***mul***. See 4136.

4390 מָלֵא ***mālē'*** or מָלָה ***mālâ***, v. GK: 4848 & 4862 [→ 3229, 4392, 4393, 4394, 4395, 4396, 4402, 4407; cf. 4391 (also used with compound proper names)]. [Q] to fill up, be full; [Qp] to be ordained, fulfilled; [N] to be filled, become filled up; [P] to fill up, satisfy; ordain, consecrate; [Pu] to be set; [Ht] to unite together; "to fill the hand" means to ordain or consecrate for service to God:– filled [72], full [46], fill [32], fulfilled [20], fulfil [8], accomplished [6], wholly [6], consecrate (+3027) [5], consecrated (+853+3027) [5], replenished [5], set [5], consecrate (+853+3027) [4], expired [3], consecrated (+3027) [2], filleth [2], replenish [2], accomplish [1], at an end [1], become full [1], confirm [1], consecrate [1], drew with full strength (+3027+871.1) [1], durst presume [1], fenced [1], filledst [1], fillest [1], fully set [1], fully [1], fulness [1], furnish unto [1], gather together [1], gathered [1], gather [1], gave in full tale [1], overfloweth (+5921) [1], overflown (+5921) [1], satisfied [1], satisfy [1], space [1], took a handful (+3709) [1], went fully [1]

4391 מְלָא ***mᵉlā'*** (Aram.), v. GK: 10416 [cf. 4390]. [P] to fill; [Htpe] to be filled:– filled [1], full [1]

4392 מָלֵא ***mālē'***, a. GK: 4849 [→ 4390]. filled, full; "full of days" means "very old":– full [58], filled [2], all [1], fill [1], fully [1], multitude [1], with child [1], worth [1]

4393 מְלֹא ***mᵉlō'***, n.m. GK: 4850 [→ 4390]. what fills, what makes something full; fullness, everything:– full [12], fulness [8], all that is therein [6], fill [2], handful (+3709) [2], multitude [2], take handful (+7061+7062) [2], all along (+6967) [1], all that is in [1], all that therein is [1], handfuls (+2651) [1]

מִלֹּא ***millō'***. See 4407.

4394 מִלֻּאִים ***millu'îm***, n.m. GK: 4854 [→ 4390]. ordination, consecration (of a priest); mounting, setting (of gem stones):– consecration [6], consecrations [5], set [4]

4395 מְלֵאָה ***mᵉlē'â***, n.f. GK: 4852 [→ 4390]. full yield (of crops):– fruit [1], fulness [1], ripe fruits [1]

4396 מִלֻּאָה ***millu'â***, n.f. GK: 4853 [→ 4390]. mounting (of jewels), setting (of jewels):– inclosings [2], settings [1]

4397 מַלְאָךְ ***mal'āk***, n.m. GK: 4855 [→ 4399, 4400, 4401?; cf. 4398]. messenger, a human representative; angel, a supernatural representative of God, sometimes delivering messages, sometimes protecting God's people; the "angel of the LORD" sometimes shares divine characteristics and is sometimes thought to be an manifestation of God himself, or of the preincarnate Christ:– angel [101], messengers [74], messenger [24], angels [10], ambassadors [4]

4398 מַלְאַךְ ***mal'ak*** (Aram.), n.m. GK: 10417 [cf. 4397]. messenger; angel, a class of being that serves God, often to communicate with or rescue his faithful on earth:– angel [2]

4399 מְלָאכָה ***mᵉlā'kâ***, n.f. GK: 4856 [→ 4397]. work, deed, duty, craft, service; thing, something:– work [126], business [12], workmanship [5], workmen (+6213+1886.1) [4], workmen (+6213) [3], works [3], goods [2], cattle [1], industrious (+6213) [1], labour [1], made [1], occupation [1], occupied (+6213) [1], officers (+6213+1886.1) [1], stuff [1], thing [1], use [1], workmen (+376) [1]

4400 מַלְאֲכוּת ***mal'ăkût***, n.f. GK: 4857 [→ 4397]. message (from a commissioned messenger):– message [1]

4401 מַלְאָכִי ***mal'ākî***, n.pr.m. GK: 4858 [→ 4397?]. Malachi, "*my messenger* or *messenger of Yahweh*":– Malachi [1]

4402 מִלֵּאת ***millē't***, n.f. GK: 4859 [→ 4390]. setting, mounting, the solid base in which a gem is set:– fitly [1]

4403 מַלְבּוּשׁ ***malbûš***, n.m. GK: 4860 [→ 3847]. clothing, robe, attire, garment:– apparel [4], raiment [3], vestments [1]

4404 מַלְבֵּן ***malbēn***, n.[m.]. GK: 4861 [→ 3840]. brickwork, brick pavement; (the act of) brickmaking:– brickkiln [3]

4405 מִלָּה ***millâ***, n.f. GK: 4863 [→ 4448; cf. 4406]. word, what is said; the act of speaking, speech:– words [21], speech [4], speaking [2], speeches [2], word [2], answer (+7725) [1], any thing to say [1], byword [1], matter [1], speak [1], talking [1], what to say [1]

4406 מִלָּה ***millâ*** (Aram.), n.f. GK: 10418 [→ 4449; cf. 4405]. word, command; matter, thing, affair; a general term like the English "thing":– thing [9], words [5], matter [4], things [2], word [2], commandment [1], matters [1]

מְלוֹ ***mᵉlô*** or מְלוֹא ***mᵉlô'***. See 4393.

4407 מִלּוֹא ***millô'*** or מִלֹּא ***millō'***, n.pr.loc. GK: 4864 & 4851 [cf. 4390]. Millo, "supporting terrace":– Millo [10]

4408 מַלּוּחַ ***mallûaḥ***, n.[m.]. GK: 4865 [→ 4417]. salt herb (collected by the destitute and banished):– mallows [1]

4409 מַלּוּךְ ***mallûk*** or מַלּוּכִי ***mallûkî*** or מְלִיכוּ ***mᵉlîkû***, n.pr.m. GK: 4866 & 4868 & 4883 [→ 4428; cf. 4427]. Malluch, Melichu, "*counselor; king*":– Malluch [6], Melicu [1]

4410 מְלוּכָה ***mᵉlûkâ***, n.f. GK: 4867 [→ 4427]. kingship, rulership, royalty:– kingdom [18], royal [4], king's [2]

4411 מָלוֹן ***mālôn***, n.m. GK: 4869 [→ 3885]. place of overnight lodging, place where one spends the night:– inn [3], lodging place [2], lodgings [1], place where lodged [1], taken up lodging [1]

4412 מְלוּנָה ***mᵉlûnâ***, n.f. GK: 4870 [→ 3885]. hut, structure (of a watchman in the field):– cottage [1], lodge [1]

4413 מַלּוֹתִי ***mallôtî***, n.pr.m. GK: 4871 [→ 4448]. Mallothi, "*my expression*":– Mallothi [2]

4414 מָלַח ***mālaḥ***, v.den. GK: 4872 & 4873 [→ 4417, 4418]. [Q] to season with salt; [N] to vanish, be dispersed; [Pu] to be salted; [Ho] to be rubbed with salt:– salted at all (+4414) [2], season [1], tempered together [1], vanish away [1]

4415 מְלַח ***mᵉlaḥ*** (Aram.), v.den. GK: 10419 [→ 4416; cf. 4414]. [P] to eat salt (i.e., be under obligation to); "to eat the salt of the palace" is to be under the solemn obligation to the king's interests:– have maintenance (+4416) [1]

4416 מְלַח ***mᵉlaḥ*** (Aram.), n.m. GK: 10420 [→ 4415; cf. 4417]. salt, a condiment for food; also used in ceremonies:– salt [2], have maintenance (+4415) [1]

4417 מֶלַח ***melaḥ***, n.m. GK: 4875 [→ 4408, 4414, 4419, 4420, 5898, 8528; cf. 4415, cf. 4416]. salt, a staple of the ancient world; positively: for flavoring, as a nutrient, as a food preservative; as a medicine; for curing animal skins; negatively: used on fields to prevent or inhibit productive plant growth:– salt [28], saltpits (+4379) [1]

4418 מֶלַח ***melaḥ***, n.[m.]. GK: 4874 [→ 4414]. worn-out clothes, rags:– rotten rags [2]

4419 מַלָּח ***mallāḥ***, n.m. GK: 4876 [→ 4417]. sailor, mariner:– mariners [4]

4420 מְלֵחָה ***mᵉlēḥâ***, n.f. GK: 4877 [→ 4417]. salt flat, salt waste-lands, barren country:– barrenness [1], barren [1], salt [1]

4421 מִלְחָמָה ***milḥāmâ***, n.f. GK: 4878 [→ 3898]. fighting, battle (a particular engagement), war (as an ongoing event):– war [150], battle [144], wars [8], battles [6], fight [5], warriors (+6213) [2], battle (+6635) [1], fighting (+6213) [1], had wars with (+376+1961) [1], had with (+376+1961) [1]

4422 מָלַט ***mālaṭ***, v. GK: 4880 & 4881 [→ 4423?, 4424; cf. 6403]. [N] to deliver oneself, escape, flee; [P] to save, deliver, rescue; [H] to rescue; to deliver (a child); [Ht] to shoot out (of sparks); to escape; to be bald:– escaped [25], escape [21], delivered [16], deliver [16], save [4], escapeth [3], speedily escape (+4422) [2], surely deliver (+4422) [2], get away [1], lay [1], leap out [1], let alone [1], preserve [1], saved [1]

4423 מֶלֶט ***meleṭ***, n.[m.]. GK: 4879 [→ 4422?]. clay flooring:– clay [1]

4424 מְלַטְיָה ***mᵉlaṭyâ***, n.pr.m. GK: 4882 [→ 4422+3068]. Melatiah, "*Yahweh sets free*":– Melatiah [1]

4425 מְלִילָה ***mᵉlîlâ***, n.f. GK: 4884. (rubbed) kernels (of grain):– ears [1]

4426 מְלִיצָה ***mᵉlîṣâ***, n.[f.]. GK: 4886 [→ 3887]. allusive saying, parable; ridicule:– interpretation [1], taunting [1]

4427 מָלַךְ ***mālak***, v.den. GK: 4887 & 4888 [→ 3230?, 4410, 4428, 4467, 4468; cf. 4431]. [Q] to reign as king; [N] to ponder, consider carefully within oneself; [H] to make one a king, have a coronation; [Ho] be made a king:– reigned [159], reign [115], made king [30], reigneth [11], make king [10], king [4], made a king (+4428) [3], indeed reign (+4427) [2], surely be king (+4427) [2], consulted [1], made queen [1], made to reign [1], made [1], make a king (+4428) [1], queen [1], reigned over (+4428) [1], reigning [1], rule [1], set a king (+4428) [1], set up kings [1], set up to be king (+4428) [1]

4428 מֶלֶךְ ***melek***, n.m. GK: 4889 [→ 4409, 4429, 4432, 4436, 4435, 4438, 4445, 4446; cf. 4427; cf. 4430 (also used with compound proper names)]. king, royal ruler, human and divine; "the great king" is the more prominent of the leaders in a convenant agreement and is used of God (Ps 48:2); the "king of kings" is the supreme sovereign and is not used of God in the OT:– king [1966], kings [282], king's [254], king's (+871.1) [4], kings' [3], made a king (+4427) [3], king's (+3807.1) [2], royal [2], make a king (+4427) [1], reigned over (+4427) [1], set a king (+4427) [1], set up to be king (+4427) [1]

4429 מֶלֶךְ ***melek***, n.pr.m. GK: 4890 [→ 4428; cf. 4427]. Melech, "*king*":– Hammelech [2], Melech [2], Moloch [1]

4430 מֶלֶךְ ***melek*** (Aram.), n.m. GK: 10421 [→ 4433, 4437; cf. 4428]. king, royal ruler:– king [147], king's [17], kings [15], royal [1]

4431 מְלַךְ ***mᵉlak*** (Aram.), n.m. GK: 10422 [cf. 4427]. advice, counsel:– counsel [1]

4432 מֹלֶךְ ***mōlek***, n.pr.[m.]. GK: 4891 [→ 4428]. Molech (pagan god), "*(shameful) king*":– Molech [8]

4433 מַלְכָּה ***malkâ*** (Aram.), n.f. GK: 10423 [→ 4430; cf. 4436]. queen, the wife of a king, with very high status but not likely equal status to the king; queen mother, mother or grandmother of a king:– queen [2]

4434 מַלְכֹּדֶת ***malkōdet***, n.f. GK: 4892 [→ 3920]. trap, snare:– trap [1]

4435 מִלְכָּה ***milkâ***, n.pr.f. GK: 4894 [→ 4428; cf. 4427]. Milcah, "*queen*":– Milcah [11]

4436 מַלְכָּה ***malkâ***, n.f. GK: 4893 [→ 4428; cf. 4427; cf. 4433]. queen (outside Israel), a female ruler of a kingdom; wife of a king, royalty but without much actual governmental power:– queen [33], queens [2]

4437 מַלְכוּ ***malkû*** (Aram.), n.f. GK: 10424 [→ 4430; cf. 4438]. kingdom, dominion, reign:– kingdom [47], reign [4], realm [3], kingdoms [2], kingly [1]

4438 מַלְכוּת **malkût**, n.f. GK: 4895 [→ 4428; cf. 4427; cf. 4437]. kingdom, empire, realm; reign, royal power, position as a king:– kingdom [49], reign [21], royal [13], realm [4], kingdoms [2], empire [1], royal estate [1]

4439 מַלְכִּיאֵל **malkî'ēl**, n.pr.m. GK: 4896 [→ 4440]. Malkiel, "*God [El] is [my] king*":– Malchiel [3]

4440 מַלְכִּיאֵלִי **malkî'ēlî**, a.g. GK: 4897 [→ 4439]. Malkielite, "*of Malkiel*":– Malchielites [1]

4441 מַלְכִּיָּה **malkiyyâ** or מַלְכִּיָּהוּ **malkiyyāhû**, n.pr.m. GK: 4898 & 4899 [→ 4428+3068]. Malkijah, "*Yahweh is [my] king*":– Malchiah [9], Malchijah [6], Melchiah [1]

4442 מַלְכִּי־צֶדֶק **malkî-ṣedeq**, n.pr.m. GK: 4900 [→ 4428+6664]. Melchizedek, "*[my] king is Zedek [just]*":– Melchizedek [2]

4443 מַלְכִּירָם **malkîrām**, n.pr.m. GK: 4901 [→ 4428+7311]. Malkiram, "*[my] king is exalted*":– Malchiram [1]

4444 מַלְכִּי־שׁוּעַ **malkî-šûa'**, n.pr.m. GK: 4902 [→ 4428+7768]. Malki-Shua, "*[my] king saves*":– Malchishua [4], Melchishua [1]

4445 מַלְכָּם **malkām** or מִלְכֹּם **milkōm**, n.pr.m. GK: 4903 & 4904 [→ 4428+3963.1]. Malcam, Milcom, Molech, "*their king* or *[servant of] Malk*":– Milcom [3], Malcham [2]

4446 מְלֶכֶת **m^eleket**, n.f. GK: 4906 [→ 4428]. Queen (of Heaven):– queen [5]

4447 מֹלֶכֶת **mōleket** or הַמֹּלֶכֶת **hammōleket**, n.pr.f. GK: 4907 & 2168 [→ 1980]. Moleketh, Hammoleketh, "*the queen*":– Hammoleketh [1]

4448 מָלַל **mālal**, v. GK: 4910 & 4911 [→ 4405, 4413; cf. 4449]. [Q] to signal by rubbing or scraping; [P] to say, speak, proclaim:– utter [2], said [1], speaketh [1], speak [1]

4449 מְלַל **m^elal** (Aram.), v. GK: 10425 [→ 4406; cf. 4448]. [Pa] to speak:– spake [2], said [1], speaking [1], speak [1]

4450 מִלֲלַי **mil^alay**, n.pr.m. GK: 4912. Milalai:– Milalai [1]

4451 מַלְמָד **malmād**, n.[m.]. GK: 4913 [→ 3925]. oxgoad, cattle prod, a (metal-tipped) poker used to guide animals, which could also be used as a weapon:– goad [1]

4452 מָלַץ **mālaṣ**, v. GK: 4914. [N] to be smooth, pleasant, palatable, sweet:– sweet [1]

4453 מֶלְצַר **melṣar**, n.m. GK: 4915 [→ 5341]. guard, guardian, official:– Melzar [2]

4454 מָלַק **mālaq**, v. GK: 4916. [Q] to wring off, pinch off (the head of a bird):– wring off [2]

4455 מַלְקוֹחַ **malqôaḥ** or מַלְקוֹחַיִם **malqôḥayim**, n.m. GK: 4917 & 4918 [→ 3947]. spoils of war, plunder, war-booty; (du.) roof of the mouth, palate:– prey [6], booty [1], jaws [1]

4456 מַלְקוֹשׁ **malqôš**, n.m. GK: 4919 [→ 3953]. spring rains, latter rains of March-April:– latter rain [6], latter [2]

4457 מֶלְקָחַיִם **melqāḥayim**, n.[m.]du. GK: 4920 [→ 3947]. (pair of) wick trimmers; (pair of) tongs:– tongs [5], snuffers [1]

4458 מֶלְתָּחָה **meltāḥâ**, n.f. GK: 4921. wardrobe:– vestry [1]

4459 מַלְתָּעוֹת **maltā'ôt**, n.f.pl. GK: 4922 [→ 4973]. fangs, teeth; some sources: jawbone:– great teeth [1]

4460 מַמְּגֻרָה **mamm^egûrâ**, n.f.pl. GK: 4923 [→ 4033]. granary, grain-pit:– barns [1]

4461 מֵמַד **mēmād**, n.[m.]. GK: 4924 [→ 4058]. dimensions, measurement:– measures [1]

4462 מְמוּכָן **m^emûkān** or מוּמְכָן **m^ewmukān**, n.pr.m. GK: 4925 & 4584. Memucan, Mumecan:– Memucan [3]

4463 מָמוֹת **māmôt**, n.[m.]. GK: 4926 [→ 4191]. death:– deaths [2]

4464 מַמְזֵר **mamzēr**, n.m. GK: 4927. one born of a forbidden marriage; foreigner; this can have the associative meaning of being an unprivileged or despised class:– bastard [2]

4465 מִמְכָּר **mimkār**, n.m. GK: 4928 [→ 4376]. what is sold, goods, merchandise:– sale [2], sold [2], sell ought (+4376) [1], that was sold [1], that which cometh of sale [1], that which is sold [1], that which sold [1], ware [1]

4466 מִמְכֶּרֶת **mimkeret**, n.f. GK: 4929 [→ 4376]. selling, sale:– sold (+4376) [1]

4467 מַמְלָכָה **mamlākâ**, n.f. GK: 4930 [→ 4427]. kingdom, royal dominion, reign:– kingdom [62], kingdoms [48], royal [4], reign [2], king's [1]

4468 מַמְלָכוּת **mamlākût**, n.f. GK: 4931 [→ 4427]. kingdom, realm, royal dominion:– kingdom [8], reign [1]

4469 מִמְסָךְ **mimsāk**, n.m. GK: 4932 [→ 4537]. bowl of mixed wine, with a focus on the wine:– drink offering [1], mixt wine [1]

4470 מֶמֶר **memer**, n.[m.]. GK: 4933 [→ 4843]. bitterness, annoyance:– bitterness [1]

4471 מַמְרֵא **mamrē'**, n.pr.m. & loc. GK: 4934 & 4935 [→ 4806?]. Mamre, "*strength*":– Mamre [10]

4472 מַמְּרֹרִים **mamm^erōrîm**, n.m.[pl.]. GK: 4936 [→ 4843]. misery, bitterness:– bitterness [1]

4473 מִמְשַׁח **mimšaḥ**, n.[m.]. GK: 4937 [→ 4886]. anointing:– anointed [1]

4474 מִמְשָׁל **mimšāl**, n.[m.]. GK: 4938 [→ 4910]. leader, ruler; power, dominion, sovereign authority:– dominion [2], ruled [1]

4475 מֶמְשָׁלָה **memšālâ**, n.f. GK: 4939 [→ 4910]. dominion, power to govern, authority to rule:– dominion [10], rule [4], dominion (+3027) [1], government [1], power [1]

4476 מִמְשָׁק **mimšāq**, n.[m.]. GK: 4940 [→ 4943]. place, ground (overgrown with weeds):– breeding [1]

4477 מַמְתַקִּים **mamtaqqîm**, n.m.[pl.]. GK: 4941 [→ 4985]. sweetness, sweet things:– most sweet [1], sweet [1]

4478 מָן **mān**, n.m. GK: 4942 [cf. 4100]. manna, a food given by God to the generation of the Exodus: "the grain of heaven":– manna [14]

4479 מַן **man** (Aram.), p.inter. & indef. GK: 10426 [cf. 4101]. who? what?; anyone, whoever:– whomsoever (+1768) [4], who [3], whoso (+1768) [2], what [1]

4480 מִן **min** or מִנֵּי **minnî**, pp. GK: 4946 & 4974 [→ 4648; cf. 4481]. marker of a source or extension from a source: from, out of, of; temporary: since, after; logically: because of; of degree: more than:– from [2335], of [1397], out of [970], than [227], on [204], from (+5921) [152], at [116], for [103], from (+854) [81], more than [73], of (+854) [71], by [62], with [57], because of (+6440) [54], before (+6440) [50], from (+5973) [46], without (+2351) [43], above [38], in [38], thence (+8033) [34], because of [32], from (+6440) [31], too [31], beside (+905+3807.1) [30], by reason of [25], among [24], because [24], since [23], of (+6440) [20], round about (+5439) [20], above (+4605) [19], not [19], out of (+5921) [19], above (+4605+1886.5+3807.1) [18], afar off (+7350) [18], without (+369) [18], after [17], before (+6440+3807.1) [17], both [17], thereof (+5105.2) [16], on every side (+5439) [15], from among [14], within (+1004) [14], beneath (+8478) [13], besides (+905+3807.1) [13], of (+5973) [13], under (+8478) [13], above (+5921) [12], because (+6440) [12], for (+6440) [12], from (+310) [12], from (+3807.1) [12], through [12], whence (+370) [12], against [11], before [11], behind (+310) [11], that [11], upon (+5921) [11], by (+854) [10]*

4481 מִן **min** (Aram.), pp. GK: 10427 [cf. 4480]. from, to, out of, more than:– from [31], of [27], out of [11], part [6], before (+6925) [4], of (+6925) [3], with [3], according to [2], after [2], for [2], aforetime (+1836+6928) [1], ago (+6928) [1], because (+1768) [1], because [1], by [1], concerning (+6655) [1], from (+3890) [1], from (+6925) [1], more than [1], of a truth (+7187) [1], over (+5924) [1], partly (+7118) [1], partly [1], since [1], than [1], then (+116+6925+871.2) [1], therefore (+2050.3) [1], to [1], upon [1], when [1]

4482 מֵן **mēn**, n.[m.]. GK: 4944 & 4945 [→ 4487]. share, portion; (music of) stringed instruments:– in [1], stringed instruments [1], whereby [1]

4483 מְנָה **m^enâ** (Aram.), v. GK: 10431 [→ 4484, 4510; cf. 4487]. [P] to number; [Pa] to appoint, set (over):– set [3], numbered [1], ordained [1]

4484 מְנֵא **m^enē'** (Aram.), n.[m.]. GK: 10428 [→ 4483; cf. 4487]. mene (unit of weight, about 1.25 lbs. [0.6 kg]):– mene [3]

4485 מַנְגִּינָה **mangînâ**, n.f. GK: 4947 [→ 5059]. mocking song:– musick [1]

מִנְדָּה **mindâ**. See 4061.

4486 מַנְדַּע **manda'** (Aram.), n.[m.]. GK: 10430 [→ 3046; cf. 4093]. knowledge, understanding; in some contexts, sanity:– knowledge [2], reason [1], understanding [1]

מְנָה **m^enâ**. See 4483.

4487 מָנָה **mānâ**, v. GK: 4948 [→ 3232, 4482, 4488, 4490, 4489, 4507, 4521, 8553?, 8554, 8556?; cf. 4483]. [Q] to count, number, take a census; [N] to be counted, be numbered; [P] to assign, appoint, provide; [Pu] to be assigned, be appointed:– numbered [7], number [7], appointed [4], prepared [4], telleth [2], count [1], prepare [1], set [1], told [1]

4488 מָנֶה **māneh**, n.m. GK: 4949 [→ 4487; cf. 4484]. mina (unit of weight, about 1.25 pounds [0.6 kg]):– pound [4], maneh [1]

4489 מֹנֶה **mōneh**, n.[m.]. GK: 4951 [→ 4487]. time, occurrence:– times [2]

4490 מָנָה **mānâ**, n.f. GK: 4950 [→ 4487]. share, portion, piece:– portions [6], portion [4], part [3], such things as belonged [1]

4491 מִנְהָג **minhāg**, n.m. GK: 4952 [→ 5090]. driving (of a chariot):– driving [2]

4492 מִנְהָרָה **minhārâ**, n.f. GK: 4953. shelter, hole, cave (in mountain clefts):– dens [1]

4493 מָנוֹד **mānôd**, n.[m.]. GK: 4954 [→ 5110]. shaking of the head (in scorn or derision):– shaking [1]

4494 מָנוֹחַ **mānôaḥ**, n.m. GK: 4955 [→ 4495, 4496; cf. 3240]. resting place; the home of a person or the lair of an animal, with the focus that this is a place of rest, satisfaction, and contentment:– rest [6], place of rest [1]

4495 מָנוֹחַ **mānôaḥ**, n.pr.m. GK: 4956 [→ 4494; cf. 3240]. Manoah, "*rest*":– Manoah [18]

4496 מְנוּחָה **m^enûḥâ**, n.f. GK: 4957 [→ 4494; cf. 3240]. resting place:– rest [15], comfortable [1], quiet [1], resting places [1], resting place [1], still [1], with ease [1]

4497 מָנוֹן **mānôn**, n.m. GK: 4959. grief:– son [1]

4498 מָנוֹס **mānôs**, n.m. GK: 4960 [→ 4499; cf. 5127]. place to flee, place of escape, refuge:– refuge [4], escape [1], fled apace (+5127) [1], flight [1], way to flee [1]

4499 מְנוּסָה **m^enûsâ**, n.f. GK: 4961 [→ 4498; cf. 5127]. flight, fleeing:– fleeing [1], flight [1]

4500 מָנוֹר **mānôr**, n.m. GK: 4962. (weaver's) rod, beam (of weavers):– beam [4]

4501 מְנוֹרָה **m^enôrâ**, n.f. GK: 4963 [→ 5216]. lampstand (holding an oil lamp; not a candlestick, holding a wax candle):– candlestick [32], candlesticks [6], every candlestick (+4501+2050.1) [4]

4502 מִנְּזָר **minn^ezār**, n.[m.]pl. GK: 4964 [cf. 5144]. guard, watchman, with a possible implication of status and rank:– crowned [1]

4503 מִנְחָה **minḥâ**, n.f. GK: 4966 [cf. 4504]. grain offering; animal offering or sacrifice; gift, tribute, present:– meat offering [122], offering [29], present [22], meat offerings [10], gifts [6], presents [6], oblation [5], sacrifice [5], offerings [4], gift [1], oblations [1]

4504 מִנְחָה **minḥâ** (Aram.), n.f. GK: 10432 [cf. 4503]. offering, gift; grain offering:– meat offerings [1], oblation [1]

מְנֻחָה **m^enuḥâ**. See 4496.

מְנֻחוֹת **m^enuḥôt**. See 2679.

4505 מְנַחֵם **m^enaḥēm**, n.pr.m. GK: 4968 [→ 5162]. Menahem, "*comforter*":– Menahem [8]

4506 מָנַחַת **mānaḥat**, n.pr.m. & loc. GK: 4969 & 4970 [→ 3240]. Manahath, "*resting place*":– Manahath [3]

מְנַחְתִּי **m^enaḥtî**. See 2680.

4507 מְנִי **m^enî**, n.pr. GK: 4972 [→ 4487]. Destiny (pagan god):– number [1]

מִנִּי **minnî**. See 4480, 4482.

4508 מִנִּי **minnî**, n.pr.loc. GK: 4973. Minni:– Minni [1]

מְנָיוֹת **m^enāyôt**. See 4521.

4509 מִנְיָמִין **minyāmîn**, n.pr.m. GK: 4975 [→ 4326]. Miniamin, "*from the right, good, fortune*":– Miniamin [3]

4510 מִנְיָן **minyān** (Aram.), n.[m.]. GK: 10433 [→ 4483]. number:– number [1]

4511 מִנִּית **minnît**, n.pr.loc. GK: 4976. Minnith:– Minnith [2]

4512 מִנְלֶה **minleh**, n.[m.]. GK: 4978 [cf. 5186]. possession, acquisition:– perfection [1]

מְנֻסָּה **m^enusâ**. See 4499.

4513 מָנַע **māna'**, v. GK: 4979 [→ 3234]. [Q] to keep from, withhold, deny, refuse; [N] to be kept from, be withheld, be denied:– withholden [8], withhold [5], withheld [3], kept back [2], refrain [2], denied [1], deny [1], hinder [1], keep back [1], keep still [1], keepeth back [1], restrained [1], withheldest [1], withholdeth [1]

4514 מַנְעוּל ***man'ûl***, n.[m.]. GK: 4980 [→ 5274]. bolt, lock (of a door):– locks [5], lock [1]

4515 מִנְעָל ***min'āl***, n.m. GK: 4981 [→ 5274]. bolt (on a gate):– shoes [1]

4516 מַנְעַמִּים ***man'ammîm***, n.[m.]pl. GK: 4982 [→ 5276]. (edible) delicacies:– dainties [1]

4517 מְנַעַנְעִים ***m*ᵉ*na'an'îm***, n.[m.pl.]. GK: 4983 [→ 5128]. sistrum, rattle, percussion instrument not precisely identified:– cornets [1]

4518 מְנַקִּית ***m*ᵉ*naqqît***, n.f. GK: 4984 [→ 5352]. bowl (used for drink offering):– bowls [3], cups [1]

מְנֹרָה ***m*ᵉ*nōrâ***. See 4501.

4519 מְנַשֶּׁה ***m*ᵉ*naššeh***, n.pr.m. GK: 4985 [→ 4520; cf. 5382]. Manasseh, "*one that makes to forget*":– Manasseh [141], Manasseh's [3], Manasseh's (+3807.1) [1], Manassites [1]

4520 מְנַשִּׁי ***m*ᵉ*naššî***, a.g. GK: 4986 [→ 4519; cf. 5382]. Manassite, of Manasseh, "*of Manasseh*":– Manasseh [2], Manassites [2]

4521 מְנָת ***m*ᵉ*nāt***, n.f. GK: 4987 [→ 4487]. portion, lot, assigned share:– portion [4], portions [3]

4522 מַס ***mas***, n.m. GK: 4989. forced labor, slave labor:– tribute [12], levy [4], tributaries [4], discomfited [1], taskmasters (+8269) [1], tributary [1]

4523 מָס ***mās***, a. GK: 4988 [→ 4549]. despairing (man):– afflicted [1]

4524 מֵסַב ***mēsab*** or מְסִבָּה ***m*ᵉ*sibbâ***, n.[m.]. GK: 4990 & 4991 [cf. 4141]. surrounding; round table, circle of feasters; (adv.) around, round about:– round about [2], compass about [1], places round about [1], table [1]

מֻסַבָּה ***musabbâ***. See 4142.

4525 מַסְגֵּר ***masgēr***, n.[m.]. GK: 4993 & 4994 [cf. 5462]. prison, dungeon; artisan, craftsman; some sources: metalworker, locksmith:– smiths [4], prison [3]

4526 מִסְגֶּרֶת ***misgeret***, n.f. GK: 4995 [→ 5462]. side panels (of a building); rim (of a table and base); stronghold; den:– borders [8], border [6], close places [2], holes [1]

4527 מַסַּד ***massad***, n.[m.]. GK: 4996 [→ 3245]. foundation:– foundation [1]

מוֹסָדָה ***mōsādâ***. See 4146.

4528 מִסְדְּרוֹן ***misdᵉrôn***, n.[m.]. GK: 4997 [→ 5468?]. porch, vestibule:– porch [1]

4529 מָסָה ***māsâ***, v. GK: 4998 [cf. 3988, 4549]. [H] to melt, dissolve; to consume; to drench (with tears):– made melt [1], makest to consume away [1], melteth [1], water [1]

4530 מִסָּה ***missâ***, n.f. GK: 5002. proportion, measure:– tribute [1]

4531 מַסָּה ***massâ***, n.f. GK: 4999 & 5000 [→ 4532, 4549; cf. 5254]. trial, test, temptation; despair:– temptations [3], temptation [1], trial [1]

4532 מַסָּה ***massâ***, n.pr.loc. GK: 5001 [→ 4531?; cf. 5254?]. Massah, "*test, try*":– Massah [4]

4533 מַסְוֶה ***masweh***, n.[m.]. GK: 5003 [→ 5497]. veil, covering:– vail [3]

4534 מְסוּכָה ***m*ᵉ*sûkâ***, n.f. GK: 5004 [→ 4881]. thorn hedge:– thorn hedge [1]

4535 מַסָּח ***massāḥ***, n.m. *or* adv. GK: 5005 [cf. 5255?]. in turn, taking turns:– not broken down [1]

4536 מִסְחָר ***misḥār***, n.m. GK: 5006 [cf. 5503]. revenue:– traffick [1]

4537 מָסַךְ ***māsak***, v. GK: 5007 [→ 4469, 4538]. [Q] to mingle, mix (substances into drinks):– mingled [4], mingle [1]

4538 מֶסֶךְ ***mesek***, n.[m.]. GK: 5008 [→ 4537]. mixture (of spices):– mixture [1]

4539 מָסָךְ ***māsāk***, n.[m.]. GK: 5009 [→ 5526]. curtain, covering; by extension: shield, defense:– hanging [17], covering [7], curtain [1]

4540 מְסֻכָּה ***m*ᵉ*sukâ***, n.f. GK: 5010 [→ 5526]. (woven) covering:– covering [1]

4541 מַסֵּכָה ***massēkâ***, n.f. GK: 5011 & 5012 & 5013 [→ 5258, 5259]. image, idol (of cast metal); (woven) blanket, (interwoven) covering; alliance:– molten image [10], molten images [8], molten [7], covering [2], vail [1]

4542 מִסְכֵּן ***miskēn***, a. GK: 5014 [→ 4544; cf. 5533]. poor, needy (one):– poor [4]

4543 מִסְכְּנוֹת ***miskᵉnôt***, n.f.pl. GK: 5016 [→ 5532]. storage places, warehouses:– store [5], storehouses [1], treasure [1]

4544 מִסְכֵּנֻת ***miskēnut***, n.f. GK: 5017 [→ 4542; cf. 5533]. scarcity, poverty:– scarceness [1]

4545 מַסֶּכֶת ***masseket***, n.f. GK: 5018 [→ 5259]. warp-threads (the lengthwise threads of a loom):– web [2]

4546 מְסִלָּה ***m*ᵉ*sillâ***, n.f. GK: 5019 [→ 5549]. main road; (raised) highway, ramp, stairs; by extension: lifestyle, conduct in life:– highway [14], highways [5], causeway [2], courses [1], high way [1], paths [1], path [1], terraces [1], ways [1]

4547 מַסְלוּל ***maslûl***, n.m. GK: 5020 [→ 5549]. highway:– highway [1]

4548 מַסְמֵר ***masmēr***, n.m. GK: 5021 [→ 5568]. nail:– nails [4]

4549 מָסַס ***māsas***, v. GK: 5022 [→ 4523, 4531, 8557; cf. 3988, 4529, 4885]. [Q] to waste away, dissolve; [N] to be melted, dissolved; [H] to cause to melt:– melted [6], melt [4], melteth [2], utterly melt (+4549) [2], discouraged [1], fainteth [1], faint [1], loosed [1], melt away [1], molten [1], refuse [1]

4550 מַסַּע ***massa'***, n.[m.]. GK: 5023 [→ 5265]. journey, travels from place to place:– journeys [9], journeyings [1], journeying [1], journey [1]

4551 מַסָּע ***massā'***, n.[m.]. GK: 5024 & 5025 [→ 5265]. quarry; a weapon probably thrown like a spear or javelin; dart:– brought [1], dart [1]

4552 מִסְעָד ***mis'ād***, n.[m.]. GK: 5026 [→ 5582]. supports (for a building):– pillars [1]

4553 מִסְפֵּד ***mispēd***, n.m. GK: 5027 [→ 5594]. wailing, howling, weeping, mourning:– mourning [6], wailing [6], lamentation [3], mourneth [1]

4554 מִסְפּוֹא ***mispô'***, n.m. GK: 5028. fodder, animal feed:– provender [5]

4555 מִסְפָּחָה ***mispāḥâ***, n.f. GK: 5029 [→ 5596]. veil, (head) covering:– kerchiefs [2]

4556 מִסְפַּחַת ***mispaḥat***, n.f. GK: 5030 [→ 5597]. (uninfectious) breaking out of skin, rash or scab; referring to something relatively harmless:– scab [3]

4557 מִסְפָּר ***mispār***, n.m. GK: 5031 [→ 4558?, 4559?; cf. 5612]. number, quantity; listing, inventory, census:– number [109], few [5], all [3], innumerable (+369) [3], sum [2], time (+3117) [2], abundance (+369) [1], account [1], few (+4962) [1], infinite (+369) [1], innumerable (+369+5704) [1], numbered [1], numbers [1], tale [1], telling [1]

4558 מִסְפָּר ***mispār***, n.pr.m. GK: 5032 [→ 4559; cf. 4557?, 5612]. Mispar, "*number*":– Mizpar [1]

מוֹסֵרוֹת ***mōsᵉrôt***. See 4149.

4559 מִסְפֶּרֶת ***misperet***, n.pr.m. GK: 5033 [→ 4558; cf. 4557?]. Mispereth:– Mispereth [1]

4560 מָסַר ***māsar***, v. GK: 5034 [→ 4562?]. [Q] to supply, deliver; [N] to be supplied:– commit [1], delivered [1]

4561 מֹסָר ***mōsār***, n.m. GK: 5036 [→ 4148; cf. 3256]. same as 4148: instruction:– instruction [1]

4562 מָסֹרֶת ***māsōret***, n.f. GK: 5037 [→ 631? *or* 4560?]. bond, obligation, duty:– bond [1]

4563 מִסְתּוֹר ***mistôr***, n.[m.]. GK: 5039 [→ 5641]. hiding place, shelter (from the elements):– covert [1]

4564 מַסְתֵּר ***mastēr***, n.[m.]. GK: 5040 [→ 5641]. (the act of) hiding:– hid [1]

4565 מִסְתָּר ***mistār***, n.[m.]. GK: 5041 [→ 5641]. hiding place, covered place (from which to ambush):– secret places [7], secretly (+871.1+1886.1) [2], secret [1]

מְעָא ***m*ᵉ*'ā'***. See 4577.

4566 מַעְבָּד ***maᵃbād***, n.[m.]. GK: 5042 [→ 5647; cf. 4567]. deed, action:– works [1]

4567 מַעְבָּד ***maᵃbād*** (Aram.), n.[m.]. GK: 10434 [→ 5648; cf. 4566]. what one does, work:– works [1]

4568 מַעֲבֶה ***maᵃbeh***, n.[m.]. GK: 5043 [→ 5666]. mold, foundry:– clay [1]

4569 מַעֲבָר ***maᵃbār*** or מַעְבָּרָה ***ma'bārâ***, n.[m.]. GK: 5044 & 5045 [→ 5674]. stroke (of a rod); (geographical) pass; ford (of a river):– passages [4], fords [3], passage [2], ford [1], pass [1]

4570 מַעְגָּל ***ma'gāl***, n.m. GK: 5046 & 5047 [→ 5696]. (rutted) path (of a cart or wagon); (circled) camp, encampment:– paths [6], path [3], trench [3], goings [2], way side (+3027) [1], ways [1]

4571 מָעַד ***mā'ad***, v. GK: 5048 [→ 4154]. [Q] to slip, waver, wobble; [Pu] to become lame; [H] cause to wobble, to bend, wrench (one's back):– slip [3], slide [2], make to shake [1]

מוֹעֵד ***mō'ēd***. See 4150.

4572 מַעֲדַי ***maᵃday***, n.pr.m. GK: 5049 [→ 4573; cf. 4153]. Maadai, "*ornaments*":– Maadai [1]

4573 מַעַדְיָה ***ma'adyâ***, n.pr.m. GK: 5050 [→ 4572]. Moadiah, "[perhaps] *Yahweh assembles* or *Yahweh promises*":– Maadiah [1]

4574 מַעֲדַנִּים ***maᵃdannîm***, n.[m.pl.]. GK: 5052 [→ 5727]. delicacy; delight:– dainties [1], delicately (+3807.1) [1], delicately [1], delight [1]

4575 מַעֲדַנּוֹת ***maᵃdannôt***, n.[f.pl.]. GK: 5051 [→ 5727; cf. 6029]. beautiful; some sources: bands, cords used for binding; (adv.) confidently:– sweet influences [1]

4576 מַעְדֵּר ***ma'dēr***, n.[m.]. GK: 5053 [→ 5737]. hoe (to cultivate ground):– mattock [1]

4577 מְעֵה ***m*ᵉ*'ēh*** (Aram.), n.[m.]pl. GK: 10435 [cf. 4578]. belly:– belly [1]

4578 מֵעֶה ***mē'eh***, n.m. GK: 5055 [cf. 4577]. viscera: stomach, heart, bowels, womb; (body as a whole); by extension: of the inner person, the seat of emotions: anguish, tenderness:– bowels [27], belly [3], heart [1], womb [1]

4579 מָעָה ***mā'â***, n.f. GK: 5054. grain (of sand):– gravel [1]

4580 מָעוֹג ***mā'ôg***, n.[m.]. GK: 5056 [→ 5746]. provision, supply; some sources: flat bread:– cake [1], feasts [1]

4581 מָעוֹז ***mā'ôz***, n.m. GK: 5057 [cf. 5810]. refuge, stronghold, fortress, place of protection; (used with "head") helmet:– strength [24], fortress [3], strong [2], forces [1], fort [1], most strong [1], rock [1], strengthen [1], strong holds [1], strong hold [1]

4582 מָעוֹךְ ***mā'ôk***, n.pr.m. GK: 5059 [cf. 4601]. Maoch, "*poor one*":– Maoch [1]

4583 מָעוֹן ***mā'ôn***, n.[m.]. GK: 5060 & 5061 [→ 1010, 1186, 4584, 4585]. dwelling place; help:– habitation [9], dwelling place [3], dwelling [3], den [2], habitations [1], place [1]

4584 מָעוֹן ***mā'ôn***, n.pr.m. & g. & loc. GK: 5062 & 5063 [→ 4583]. Maon; Maonite, "*dwelling*":– Maon [7], Maonites [1]

4585 מְעוֹנָה ***m*ᵉ*'ônâ***, n.f. GK: 5104 [→ 4583]. hiding place, refuge; dwelling place, (animal) den:– dens [4], den [1], dwelling place [1], habitations [1], places [1], refuge [1]

4586 מְעוּנִים ***m*ᵉ*'ûnîm***, n.pr.g. GK: 5064. Meunim, Meunite, "*people of Maon*":– Mehunims [1], Mehunim [1], Meunim [1]

4587 מְעוֹנֹתַי ***m*ᵉ*'ônōtay***, n.pr.m. GK: 5065. Meonothai, "*my dwellings*":– Meonothai [1]

4588 מָעוּף ***mā'ûp***, n.[m.]. GK: 5066 [→ 4155]. gloom, darkness:– dimness [1]

4589 מָעוֹר ***mā'ôr***, n.[m.]. GK: 5067 [→ 5783]. exposed genitals, nakedness:– nakedness [1]

מָעֹז ***mā'ōz***. See 4581.

מָעֻז ***mā'uz***. See 4581.

4590 מַעַזְיָה ***ma'azyâ*** or מַעַזְיָהוּ ***ma'azyāhû***, n.pr.m. GK: 5068 & 5069. Maaziah, "*Yahweh is a refuge*":– Maaziah [2]

4591 מָעַט ***mā'aṭ***, v. GK: 5070 [→ 4592]. [Q] to dwindle, decrease, become few; [P] to become few; [H] to let reduce, make diminish, make collect little:– diminished [3], few [3], give less [3], diminish [2], little [2], bring to nothing [1], fewness [1], gathered least [1], gathered little [1], give few [1], less [1], make few in number [1], minished [1], suffereth to decrease [1]

4592 מְעַט ***m*ᵉ*'aṭ***, subst. GK: 5071 [→ 4591]. little (of size), few (of quantity), short (of time):– little [47], few [22], almost (+3509.1) [4], little while [4], small thing [4], by little and little (+4592) [2], small matter [2], small [2], soon (+3509.1) [2], very little while (+4213) [2], almost (+5750) [1], few (+4962) [1], fewer [1], fewest [1], lightly (+3509.1) [1], little worth (+3509.1) [1], some (+3509.1) [1], very little (+6985) [1], very small (+3509.1) [1], very [1]

4593 מָעֹט ***mā'ōṭ***, v.ptcp. GK: 6487 [→ 5844]. ptcp. of 5844: grasped, wrapped up:– wrapt up [1]

4594 מַעֲטֶה ***maᵃṭeh***, n.[m.]. GK: 5073 [→ 5844]. garment, mantle, wrap:– garment [1]

4595 מַעֲטֶפֶת ***maᵃṭepet***, n.f. GK: 5074 [→ 5848]. cape, outer garment:– mantles [1]

4596 מְעִי ***m^{e}'î***, n.[m.]. GK: 5075 [→ 5856]. heap (of ruins):– heap [1]

4597 מָעַי ***mā'ay***, n.pr.m. GK: 5076. Maai, "*to be compassionate*":– Maai [1]

4598 מְעִיל ***m^{e}'îl***, n.m. GK: 5077. robe, cloak:– robe [17], mantle [7], robes [2], cloke [1], coat [1]

מֵעִים ***mē'îm***. See 4578.

מְעִין ***m^{e}'în*** (Aram.). See 4577.

4599 מַעְיָן ***ma'yān***, n.m. GK: 5078 [→ 5869]. spring, fountain, well; by extension: source of life (satisfaction, blessing):– fountain [9], fountains [7], wells [3], springs [2], well [2]

מְעִינִי ***m^{e}'înî***. See 4586.

4600 מָעַךְ ***mā'ak***, v. GK: 5080. [Qp] be pressed (into the ground), be crushed, be bruised; [Pu] be fondled:– bruised [1], pressed [1], stuck [1]

4601 מַעֲכָה ***ma^{a}kâ*** or מַעֲכָת ***ma^{a}kāt***, n.pr.m. & f. & g. GK: 5081 & 5082 & 5083 [→ 4602; cf. 4582 (also used with compound proper names)]. Maacah, "[perhaps] *dull, stupid*":– Maachah [18], Maacah [3], Maachathites [1]

4602 מַעֲכָתִי ***ma^{a}kātî***, a.g. GK: 5084 [→ 4601]. Maacathite, of Maacah, "*of Maacah*":– Maachathite [4], Maachathites [3], Maachathi [1]

4603 מָעַל ***mā'al***, v. GK: 5085 [→ 4604]. [Q] to act unfaithfully, break faith, commit a violation:– trespassed [11], transgressed [5], commit a trespass (+4604) [4], committed a trespass (+4604) [3], transgress [2], committed trespass (+4604) [1], committed [1], do a trespass (+4604) [1], done trespass (+4604) [1], transgressed much (+4604) [1], transgressed sore (+4604) [1], transgresseth [1], transgression committed (+4604) [1], trespassing grievously (+4604) [1], trespass [1]

4604 מַעַל ***ma'al***, n.m. GK: 5086 [→ 4603]. unfaithfulness:– trespass [8], transgression [5], commit a trespass (+4603) [4], committed a trespass (+4603) [3], committed trespass (+4603) [1], do a trespass (+4603) [1], done trespass (+4603) [1], falsehood [1], transgressed much (+4603) [1], transgressed sore (+4603) [1], transgression committed (+4603) [1], trespasses [1], trespassing grievously (+4603) [1]

4605 מַעַל ***ma'al***, subst.adv. & pp. GK: 5087 [→ 5927]. above, beyond; this refer to spatial position, to degree, and to time (afterward):– upward (+1886.5) [45], above (+4480) [19], above (+4480+1886.5+3807.1) [18], upward (+1886.5+3807.1) [12], above (+1886.5+3807.1) [6], on high (+1886.5+3807.1) [5], above (+1886.5) [4], above [4], upon (+4480) [4], exceedingly (+1886.5+3807.1) [2], exceedingly (+5704+1886.5+3807.1) [2], forward (+1886.5) [2], still (+1886.5+3807.1) [2], upward (+4480+1886.5+3807.1) [2], very high (+4605+1886.5+1886.5) [2], above (+4480+3807.1) [1], exceeding (+1886.5) [1], exceeding (+1886.5+3807.1) [1], from above (+4480) [1], on high (+4480+1886.5+3807.1) [1], over (+1886.5+3807.1) [1], over (+4480+1886.5+3807.1) [1], over and above (+4480+1886.5 +3807.1) [1], overturned (+2015+1886.5+3807.1) [1], up (+1886.5+3807.1) [1], very (+1886.5+3807.1) [1]

מֵעַל ***mē'al***. See 5921.

4606 מֶעָל ***me'āl*** (Aram.), n.[m.]. GK: 10436 [→ 5954]. going in, (+ 8122) sunset:– going down [1]

4607 מֹעַל ***mō'al***, n.[m.]. GK: 5089 [→ 5927]. lifting (of hands):– lifting up [1]

4608 מַעֲלֶה ***ma^{a}leh***, n.m. GK: 5090 [→ 5927]. and ascent: hill, mount, (geographical) pass; stairs:– going up [9], ascent [2], chiefest [1], cliff [1], goeth up [1], hill [1], mounting up [1], stairs [1], up [1]

4609 מַעֲלָה ***ma^{a}lâ***, n.f. GK: 5091 & 5092 [→ 5927]. ascent: steps, stairway, paces; what goes through (or rises into) one's mind:– degrees [24], steps [11], stairs [5], dial [2], go up [1], high degree [1], stories [1], things that come into [1]

4610 מַעֲלֵה עַקְרַבִּים ***ma^{a}lēh 'aqrabbîm***, n.pr.loc. GK: 5091 + 6832 [→ 4609+6137]. Maaleh-akkrabim, the ascent of Akrabbim (of the Scorpions):– Maaleh-acrabbim [1]

4611 מַעֲלָל ***ma^{a}lāl***, n.m. GK: 5095 [→ 5953]. deeds, actions, practices, what is done:– doings [35], works [3], inventions [2], endeavours [1]

4612 מַעֲמָד ***ma^{a}mād***, n.[m.]. GK: 5096 [→ 5975]. attendance, serving; position of attendant:– attendance [2], office [1], place [1], state [1]

4613 מָעֳמָד ***mo^{o}mād***, n.[m.]. GK: 5097 [→ 5975]. foothold, firm ground:– standing [1]

4614 מַעֲמָסָה ***ma^{a}māsâ***, n.f. GK: 5098 [→ 6006]. heavy stone, hard-to-lift rock:– burdensome [1]

4615 מַעֲמַקִּים ***ma^{a}maqqîm***, n.m.pl. GK: 5099 [→ 6009]. depths (of waters or seas):– depths [3], deep [2]

4616 מַעַן ***ma'an***, subst.pp.c. GK: 5100 [→ 6031]. for the sake of, on account of, because; therefore, so that:– that (+3807.1) [167], for sake (+3807.1) [45], to (+3807.1) [19], because of (+3807.1) [12], for sakes (+3807.1) [5], for (+3807.1) [4], that (+834+3807.1) [4], to the end (+3807.1) [4], to the end that (+3807.1) [4], for that (+3807.1) [2], to the intent that (+3807.1) [2], lest (+3808+3807.1) [1], therefore (+3807.1) [1], to [1]

4617 מַעֲנֶה ***ma^{a}neh***, n.m. GK: 5101 & 5102 [→ 6030, 6031]. reply, answer, response; purpose:– answer [7], himself (+1930.2) [1]

4618 מַעֲנָה ***ma^{a}nâ***, n.f. GK: 5103 [cf. 6031]. furrow, plow path:– acre [1], furrows [1]

מְעֹנָה ***m^{e}'ōnâ***. See 4585.

4619 מַעַץ ***ma'aṣ***, n.pr.m. GK: 5106 [→ 290]. Maaz, "[perhaps] *angry* or *wrath*":– Maaz [1]

4620 מַעֲצֵבָה ***ma^{a}ṣēbâ***, n.f. GK: 5107 [→ 6087]. place of torment, place of pain:– sorrow [1]

4621 מַעֲצָד ***ma^{a}ṣād***, n.[m.]. GK: 5108. chiseling tool (for wood carving); some sources: ax, adze:– axe [1], tongs [1]

4622 מַעְצוֹר ***ma'ṣôr***, n.[m.]. GK: 5109 [→ 6113]. hindrance:– restraint [1]

4623 מַעְצָר ***ma'ṣār***, n.[m.]. GK: 5110 [→ 6113]. self-control:– rule [1]

4624 מַעֲקֶה ***ma^{a}qeh***, n.[m.]. GK: 5111. parapet, a short wall around the upper level of a house:– battlement [1]

4625 מַעֲקַשִּׁים ***ma^{a}qaššîm***, n.[m.]. GK: 5112 [→ 6140]. rough places, uneven terrain, rugged country:– crooked things [1]

4626 מַעַר ***ma'ar***, n.[m.]. GK: 5113 [→ 4629]. nakedness; available space:– nakedness [1], proportion [1]

4627 מַעֲרָב ***ma^{a}rāb***, n.m. GK: 5114 [→ 6148]. wares, goods (for trade, exchange, or barter):– merchandise [5], market [4]

4628 מַעֲרָב ***ma^{a}rāb***, n.[m.]. GK: 5115 [→ 6150]. west (the place of the sunset):– west [10], westward [2], westward (+1886.1+3807.1) [1], westward (+1886.5) [1]

4629 מַעֲרֶה ***ma^{a}reh***, n.[m.]. GK: 5116 [→ 4626]. approaches, vicinity:– meadows [1]

4630 מַעֲרָה ***ma^{a}râ***, n.f. GK: 5120 [→ 4634, 6186]. var. of 4634: things arranged in a row: battle line, row of army ranks:– @H = **4631** מְעָרָה ***m^{e}%ârâ***, n.f. GK: 5117. cave:– cave [32], caves [3], cave's [1], dens [1], den [1], holes [1]

4632 מְעָרָה ***m^{e}'ārâ***, n.f. GK: 5118 [→ 4638; cf. 6168]. wasteland, bare field:– Mearah [1]

4633 מַעֲרָךְ ***ma^{a}rāk***, n.[m.]. GK: 5119 [→ 6186]. plan, consideration, arrangement:– preparations [1]

4634 מַעֲרָכָה ***ma^{a}rākâ***, n.f. GK: 5120 [→ 4630]. things arranged in a row: battle line, row of army ranks; row, layer (of things); by extension: proper arrangement of something fitting and suitable:– army [8], armies [7], fight [1], ordered place [1], rank [1], rows [1], set in order [1]

4635 מַעֲרֶכֶת ***ma^{a}reket***, n.f. GK: 5121 [→ 6186]. (consecrated) bread set in rows:– shewbread [3], row [2], shewbread (+3899+1886.1) [2], in order [1], shewbread (+3899) [1]

4636 מַעֲרֹם ***ma^{a}rōm***, n.m. GK: 5122 [→ 6168]. nakedness, naked person:– naked [1]

4637 מַעֲרָצָה ***ma^{a}rāṣâ***, n.f. GK: 5124 [→ 6206]. terrifying power:– terror [1]

4638 מַעֲרָת ***ma^{a}rāt***, n.pr.loc. GK: 5125 [→ 4632?; cf. 6168]. Maarath, "*barren*":– Maarath [1]

4639 מַעֲשֶׂה ***ma^{a}śeh***, n.m. GK: 5126 [→ 4640, 4641; cf. 6213]. work, labor, deed, something made, something done:– work [116], works [73], acts [4], needlework (+7551) [4], art [3], doings [3], labours [3], wrought [3], deeds [2], network (+7568) [2], occupation [2], operation [2], wares of making [2], bakemeats (+644+3978) [1], business [1], deed [1], doing [1], do [1], handywork (+3027) [1], labour [1], possessions [1], purpose [1], things made [1], things offered [1], things that were made [1], well set hair (+4748) [1], working [1], workmanship [1], wrought with needlework (+7551) [1]

4640 מַעְשַׂי ***ma'śay***, n.pr.m. GK: 5127 [→ 4639+3068]. Maasai, "*work of Yahweh*":– Maasiai [1]

4641 מַעֲשֵׂיָה ***ma^{a}śēyâ*** or מַעֲשֵׂיָהוּ ***ma^{a}śēyāhû***, n.pr.m. GK: 5128 & 5129 [→ 4639+3068; cf. 6213]. Maaseiah, "*Yahweh is a refuge*":– Maaseiah [23]

4642 מַעֲשַׁקּוֹת ***ma^{a}šaqqôt***, n.f. GK: 5131 [→ 6229]. (col.pl) extortion:– oppressions [1], oppressor [1]

4643 מַעֲשֵׂר ***ma^{a}śēr***, n.m. GK: 5130 [→ 6237]. tithe, setting aside a tenth:– tithes [16], tithe [11], tenth part [2], tenth [2], tithing [1]

4644 מֹף ***mōp***, n.pr.loc. GK: 5132 [cf. 5297]. Moph = Memphis:– Memphis [1]

מְפִבֹשֶׁת ***m^{e}pibōšet***. See 4648.

4645 מִפְגָּע ***mipgā'***, n.[m.]. GK: 5133 [→ 6293]. target:– mark [1]

4646 מַפָּח ***mappāḥ***, n.[m.]. GK: 5134 [→ 5301]. (a dying) gasp, exhaling (of soul), with an implication of despair and affliction:– giving up of the ghost (+5315) [1]

4647 מַפֻּחַ ***mappuaḥ***, n.m. GK: 5135 [→ 5301]. bellows:– bellows [1]

4648 מְפִיבֹשֶׁת ***m^{e}pîbōšet*** or מְפִי־בֹשֶׁת ***m^{e}pî-bōšet***, n.pr.m. GK: 5136 [→ 4480+6310+1322]. Mephibosheth, "*from the mouth of Shame* [a derogatory name for Baal]":– Mephibosheth [15]

4649 מֻפִּים ***muppîm***, n.pr.m. GK: 5137. Muppim:– Muppim [1]

4650 מֵפִיץ ***mēpîṣ***, n.m. GK: 5138 [→ 6327]. war club:– maul [1]

4651 מַפָּל ***mappāl***, n.m. GK: 5139 [→ 4654; cf. 5307]. sweepings, waste, refuse (of wheat); (fleshy) folds (of the leviathan):– flakes [1], refuse [1]

4652 מִפְלָאוֹת ***miplā'ôt***, n.f.[pl.]. GK: 5140 [→ 6381]. wonders, marvelous works:– wondrous works [1]

4653 מִפְלַגָּה ***miplaggâ***, n.f. GK: 5141 [→ 6385]. division (of family groups), subgroup of a clan:– divisions [1]

4654 מַפָּלָה ***mappālâ*** or מַפֵּלָה ***mappēlâ***, n.f. GK: 5142 & 5143 [→ 4651; cf. 5307]. ruin, heap of rubble:– ruin [2], ruinous [1]

4655 מִפְלָט ***miplāṭ***, n.[m.]. GK: 5144 [→ 6403]. place of shelter, refuge, escape:– escape [1]

4656 מִפְלֶצֶת ***mipleṣet***, n.f. GK: 5145 [→ 6426]. repulsive image, disgraceful (idol):– idol [4]

4657 מִפְלָשׂ ***miplāś***, n.[m.]. GK: 5146. floating, hovering (clouds):– balancings [1]

4658 מַפֶּלֶת ***mappelet***, n.f. GK: 5147 [→ 5307]. downfall, collapse; (something downfallen) a shipwreck; carcass:– fall [5], ruin [2], carcase [1]

4659 מִפְעָל ***mip'āl*** or מִפְעָלָה ***mip'ālâ***, n.m. & f. GK: 5148 & 5149 [→ 6466]. deed, work:– works [3]

4660 מַפָּץ ***mappāṣ***, n.[m.]. GK: 5150 [→ 5310]. shattering, wrecking (weapon), implying death will follow its effective use:– slaughter [1]

4661 מַפֵּץ ***mappēṣ***, n.m. GK: 5151 [→ 5310]. war club:– battle axe [1]

4662 מִפְקָד ***mipqād***, n.m. & pr.loc. GK: 5152 [→ 4663, 6485]. appointment (by a king); number, counting (of the people); Inspection (Gate):– number [2], Miphkad [1], appointed place [1], commandment [1]

4663 מִפְקָד ***mipqād***, n.pr.loc. GK: 5152 [→ 4662]. same as 4662: Miphkad, "Inspection (Gate)":–

4664 מִפְרָץ ***miprāṣ***, n.[m.]. GK: 5153 [→ 6555]. cove, inlet, landing-place:– breaches [1]

4665 מַפְרֶקֶת ***mapreqet***, n.f. GK: 5154 [→ 6561]. neck:– neck [1]

4666 מִפְרָשׂ ***miprāś***, n.[m.]. GK: 5155 [→ 6566]. spreading (used of clouds and canvas sail):– spreadings [1], which spreadest forth [1]

4667 מִפְשָׂעָה ***mipśā'â***, n.f. GK: 5156 [cf. 6585]. buttocks, posterior area:– buttocks [1]

מֹפֵת ***mōpēt***. See 4159.

4668 מַפְתֵּחַ ***maptēaḥ***, n.m. GK: 5158 [→ 6605]. Key:– key [2], opening [1]

4669 מִפְתָּח ***miptāḥ***, n.[m.]. GK: 5157 [→ 6605]. opening (of lips):– opening [1]

4670 מִפְתָּן ***miptān***, n.[m.]. GK: 5159 [cf. 6596]. threshold:– threshold [8]

4671 מֹץ ***mōṣ***, n.m. GK: 5161. chaff:– chaff [8]

4672 מָצָא ***māṣā'***, v. GK: 5162. [Q] to find, find out, discover, uncover; [N] to be found out; be caught; [H] to hand over, present; to bring upon, cause to encounter; "to find favor in the eyes" means to "be please":– found [261], find [82], present [17], find out [16], findeth [12], come upon [5], found out [5], befallen [3], met [3], presented [3], certainly found (+4672) [2], findest [2], finding [2], get [2], gotten [2], here [2], hit [2], left [2], meet [2], suffice [2], able (+1767+3027) [1], able to bring (+1767+3027) [1], befall [1], befell [1], came to hand [1], came to [1], catch [1], cause to find [1], causeth to come [1], come on [1], come unto [1], cometh [1], delivered [1], deliver [1], enough [1], find occasion [1], foundest [1], gat hold upon [1], hath (+3807.1) [1], lighted on [1], lighteth upon [1], occasion serve (+3027) [1], ready [1], received [1], redeem (+1353) [1], sped [1], sufficed [1], taken hold on [1]

מֹצָא ***mōṣā'***. See 4161.

4673 מַצָּב ***maṣṣāb***, n.m. GK: 5163 [→ 4675; cf. 5324]. standing place; office; outpost, garrison:– garrison [7], stood [2], station [1]

4674 מֻצָּב ***muṣṣāb***, n.[m.]. GK: 5164 [→ 5324]. pillar, tower:– mount [1]

4675 מַצָּבָה ***maṣṣābâ*** or מִצָּבָה ***miṣṣābâ***, n.f. GK: 5165 & 5166 [→ 4673, 5324]. guard, watch, outpost, garrison of soldiers on the perimeter of a guarded area:– army [1], garrison [1]

4676 מַצֵּבָה ***maṣṣēbâ***, n.f. GK: 5167 [→ 4678; cf. 5324]. sacred (upright) stone, stone pillar:– images [13], pillar [9], image [4], pillars [2], garrisons [1], standing images [1], standing image [1]

4677 מְצֹבָיָה ***m^eṣōbāyâ***, a.g. GK: 5168. Mezobaite:– Mesobaite [1]

4678 מַצֶּבֶת ***maṣṣebet***, n.f. GK: 5169 & 5170 [→ 4676, 5324]. (tree) stump; sacred (upright) stone, stone pillar:– pillar [5], substance [2]

4679 מְצָד ***m^eṣād***, n.f. GK: 5171 [→ 6679; cf. 4686]. stronghold, fortress (with difficult access):– strong holds [5], hold [2], castle [1], forts [1], holds [1], munitions [1]

מְצֻדָה ***m^eṣudâ***. See 4686.

4680 מָצָה ***māṣâ***, v. GK: 5172 [cf. 4711]. [Q] to squeeze out; to drain dry; [N] to be drained out:– wrung out [4], suck out [1], wring out [1], wringed [1]

4681 מֹצָה ***mōṣâ***, n.pr.loc. GK: 5173. Mozah:– Mozah [1]

4682 מַצָּה ***maṣṣâ***, n.f. GK: 5174 [cf. 4711?]. unleavened bread, bread made without yeast; bread quickly made, without waiting for the dough to rise:– unleavened bread [34], unleavened [18], without leaven [1]

4683 מַצָּה ***maṣṣâ***, n.f. GK: 5175 [→ 5327]. quarrel, strife:– contention [1], debate [1], strife [1]

4684 מִצְהָלוֹת ***miṣhālôt***, n.f.[pl.]. GK: 5177 [→ 6670]. neighing:– neighings [1], neighing [1]

4685 מָצוֹד ***māṣôd*** or מְצוֹדָה ***m^eṣôdâ***, n.m. & f. GK: 5178 & 5179 & 5182 & 5183 [→ 6679]. fortress, prison (a place difficult to access); plunder; stronghold; (hunting) snare, net:– net [2], bulwarks [1], holds [1], munition [1], snares [1]

4686 מְצוּדָה ***m^eṣûdâ***, n.f. GK: 5180 & 5181 [→ 6679; cf. 4679]. stronghold, fortress, prison (a place difficult to access); (hunting) snare, net; prey:– fortress [6], hold [6], net [2], snare [2], castle [1], defence [1], fort [1], hunted [1], strong hold [1], strong place [1]

4687 מִצְוָה ***miṣwâ***, n.f. GK: 5184 [→ 6680]. command, order, prescription, instruction:– commandments [130], commandment [43], precepts [3], commanded [2], law [1], ordinances [1], precept [1]

4688 מְצוֹלָה ***m^eṣôlâ*** or מְצֻלָה ***m^eṣulâ***, n.f. GK: 5185 & 5198 [→ 4699, 6683]. depths, the deep:– deep [5], deeps [3], depths [2], bottom [1]

4689 מָצוֹק ***māṣôq***, n.[m.]. GK: 5186 [→ 4691; cf. 6693]. distress, suffering, stress, hardship:– straitness [4], anguish [1], distress [1]

4690 מָצוּק ***māṣûq***, n.m. GK: 5187 [→ 3332?]. foundation, pillar, support:– pillars [1], situate [1]

4691 מְצוּקָה ***m^eṣûqâ***, n.f. GK: 5188 [→ 4689; cf. 6693]. distress, anguish, stress, affliction:– distresses [5], anguish [1], distress [1]

4692 מָצוֹר ***māṣôr***, n.[m.]. GK: 5189 & 5190 [→ 4694; cf. 6696]. stronghold, fortification, defense; siege; siege works, ramparts:– siege [13], besieged (+871.1+1886.1) [2], besieged (+935+871.1+1886.1) [2], strong [2], bulwarks [1], defence [1], fenced [1], fortress [1], strong hold [1], tower [1]

4693 מָצוֹר ***māṣôr***, n.pr.loc. GK: 5191 [→ 4714]. Egypt:– besieged [2], defence [1], fortified [1], fortress [1]

4694 מְצוּרָה ***m^eṣûrâ*** or מְצֻרָה ***maṣṣārâ***, n.f. GK: 5193 & 5211 [→ 4692, 5341; cf. 6696]. fortification, defense, fortress; guard, watch:– fenced [5], forts [1], munition [1], strong holds [1]

4695 מַצּוּת ***maṣṣût***, n.f. GK: 5194 [→ 5327]. enemy, person of strife:– contended with [1]

4696 מֵצַח ***mēṣaḥ***, n.m. GK: 5195 [→ 4697; cf. 6705?]. forehead:– forehead [9], foreheads [2], brow [1], impudent (+2389) [1]

4697 מִצְחָה ***miṣḥâ***, n.f. GK: 5196 [→ 4696; cf. 6705?]. greaves (armor for the front or back of leg from ankle to knee):– greaves [1]

מְצֹלָה ***m^eṣōlâ***. See 4688.

מְצֻלָה ***m^eṣulâ***. See 4688.

4698 מְצִלָּה ***m^eṣillâ***, n.f. GK: 5197 [→ 6750]. (small) bell (on a horse):– bells [1]

4699 מְצֻלָּה ***m^eṣullâ***, n.f. GK: 5185 [→ 4688]. same as 4688: depths, the deep:– bottom [1]

4700 מְצִלְתַּיִם ***m^eṣiltayim***, n.f.du. GK: 5199 [→ 6750]. (pair of) cymbals:– cymbals [13]

4701 מִצְנֶפֶת ***miṣnepet***, n.f. GK: 5200 [→ 6801]. turban, headband:– mitre [11], diadem [1]

4702 מַצָּע ***maṣṣā'***, n.m. GK: 5201 [→ 3331]. bed, couch:– bed [1]

4703 מִצְעָד ***miṣ'ād***, n.[m.]. GK: 5202 [→ 6805]. step; (position of submission in a) train:– steps [2], goings [1]

4704 מִצְּעִירָה ***miṣṣ^e'îrâ***, a. GK: 5203 [→ 4705, 6819]. form of 4705: small, little, lowly:– little [1]

4705 מִצְעָר ***miṣ'ār***, n.m. GK: 5203 [→ 4704]. small quantity, few:– little one [2], small [2], little while [1]

4706 מִצְעָר ***miṣ'ār***, n.pr.loc. GK: 5204 [→ 6819]. Mizar, "*small*":– Mizar [1]

4707 מִצְפֶּה ***miṣpeh***, n.m. GK: 5205 [→ 4708, 4709; cf. 6822]. watchtower (used for military defense and surveillance), any place that overlooks:– watch tower [1], watchtower [1]

4708 מִצְפֶּה ***miṣpeh***, n.pr.loc. GK: 5206 [→ 4707; cf. 6822]. Mizpah, "*lookout point*":– Mizpeh [9], Mizpah [5]

4709 מִצְפָּה ***miṣpâ***, n.pr.loc. GK: 5207 [→ 4707; cf. 6822]. Mizpah, "*lookout point*":– Mizpah [18], Mizpeh [14]

4710 מַצְפֹּן ***maṣpôn***, n.[m.]. GK: 5208 [→ 6845]. hidden treasure, hiding place:– hid things [1]

4711 מָצַץ ***māṣaṣ***, v. GK: 5209 [cf. 4680?]. [Q] to drink deeply, quaff:– milk out [1]

מֻצָקָה ***muṣāqâ***. See 4166.

4712 מֵצַר ***mēṣar***, n.[m.]. GK: 5210 [→ 3334]. anguish, distress, hardship:– distress [1], pains [1], straits [1]

מָצֻק ***māṣuq***. See 4690.

מְצֻקָה ***m^eṣuqâ***. See 4691.

מְצֻרָה ***m^eṣurâ***. See 4694.

4713 מִצְרִי ***miṣrî***, a.g. GK: 5212 [→ 4714]. Egyptian:– Egyptian [16], Egyptians [5], Egyptian's [4], Egyptian (+376) [1], Egyptian (+376+1886.1) [1], Egypt [1], of Egypt [1]

4714 מִצְרַיִם ***miṣrayim***, n.pr.loc. & g. GK: 5213 [→ 67, 4693, 4713]. Mizraim; Egypt, Egyptian:– Egypt [585], Egyptians [90], Mizraim [4], Egyptian [2], Egyptians (+1121) [1]

4715 מַצְרֵף ***maṣrēp***, n.[m.]. GK: 5214 [→ 6884]. crucible, melting pot for metal:– fining pot [2]

4716 מַק ***maq***, n.m. GK: 5215 [→ 4743]. stench, smell of decay:– rottenness [1], stink [1]

4717 מַקֶּבֶת ***maqqebet***, n.f. GK: 5216 [→ 5344]. hammer:– hammers [2], hammer [2]

4718 מַקֶּבֶת ***maqqebet***, n.f. GK: 5217 [→ 5344]. quarry:– hole [1]

4719 מַקֵּדָה ***maqqēdâ***, n.pr.loc. GK: 5218 [→ 5348]. Makkedah, "*locality of shepherds*":– Makkedah [9]

4720 מִקְדָּשׁ ***miqdāš***, n.m. GK: 5219 [→ 6942]. holy place, sanctuary, shrine:– sanctuary [64], sanctuaries [5], holy places [2], chapel [1], hallowed [1], holy place [1]

4721 מַקְהֵל ***maqhēl***, n.[m.]. GK: 5220 [→ 6951]. assembly, congregation:– congregations [2]

4722 מַקְהֵלֹת ***maqhēlôt***, n.pr.loc. GK: 5221 [→ 6951]. Makheloth, "*assemblies*":– Makheloth [2]

4723 מִקְוֶה ***miqweh***, n.[m.]. GK: 5223 & 5224 [→ 6960]. hope; collection (of water), reservoir; other sources: linen yarn:– hope [4], linen yarn [4], abiding [1], gathering together [1], plenty [1], pools [1]

4724 מִקְוָה ***miqwâ***, n.f. GK: 5225 [→ 6960]. reservoir:– ditch [1]

4725 מָקוֹם ***māqôm***, n.m. GK: 5226 [→ 6965]. place, site:– place [370], places [20], home [3], room [3], whithersoever (+834) [2], country [1], open [1], space [1]

4726 מָקוֹר ***māqôr***, n.m. GK: 5227 [→ 6979]. fountain, spring, source (of a flow), often with an implication of abundance or freshness:– fountain [11], spring [2], wellspring [2], issue [1], springs [1], well [1]

4727 מִקָּח ***miqqāḥ***, n.[m.]. GK: 5228 [→ 3947]. taking, accepting (a bribe):– taking [1]

4728 מַקָּחוֹת ***maqqāḥôt***, n.f. GK: 5229 [→ 3947]. (pl.) merchandise, wares:– ware [1]

4729 מִקְטָר ***miqṭār***, n.m. GK: 5230 [→ 6999]. burning:– burn [1]

מְקַטְּרָה ***m^eqaṭṭ^erâ***. See 6999.

4730 מִקְטֶרֶת ***miqṭeret***, n.f. GK: 5233 [→ 6999]. censer, incense burner:– censer [2]

4731 מַקֵּל ***maqqēl***, n.m. & f. GK: 5234. branch, stick; staff, a stick used to assist in walking, discipline, and guidance; war club:– staff [7], rods [6], rod [2], staves [2], handstaves (+3027) [1]

4732 מִקְלוֹת ***miqlôt***, n.pr.m. GK: 5235. Mikloth, "*rods*":– Mikloth [4]

4733 מִקְלָט ***miqlāṭ***, n.[m.]. GK: 5236 [→ 7038]. refuge, place of protection:– refuge [20]

4734 מִקְלַעַת ***miqla'at***, n.f. GK: 5237 [→ 7049]. carving, engraving (on wood):– carved figures (+6603) [1], carved [1], carvings [1], gravings [1]

מָקֹם ***māqōm***. See 4725.

מְקֹמָה ***m^eqōmâ***. See 4725.

4735 מִקְנֶה ***miqneh***, n.m. GK: 5238 [→ 4737; cf. 7069]. livestock, (animals from) herds and flocks:– cattle [61], flocks [3], possession [3], possessions [2], substance [2], flocks (+6629) [1], herds [1], purchase [1], trade about cattle (+376) [1], trade to feed cattle (+376) [1]

4736 מִקְנָה ***miqnâ***, n.f. GK: 5239 [→ 7069]. something bought, purchased, acquisition:– bought [5], purchase [5], price [2], possession [1], that is bought [1], that were bought [1]

4737 מִקְנֵיָהוּ ***miqnēyāhû***, n.pr.m. GK: 5240 [→ 4735+3068; cf. 7069]. Mikneiah, "*Yahweh acquires*":– Mikneiah [2]

4738 מִקְסָם ***miqsām***, n.[m.]. GK: 5241 [→ 7080]. divination:– divination [2]

4739 מָקַץ ***māqaṣ***, n.pr.loc. GK: 5242. Makaz:– Makaz [1]

4740 מִקְצוֹעַ ***miqṣôa'***, n.m. GK: 5243 [→ 4742]. corner (of a base); angle of a wall:– corners [5], turning [5], every corner (+4740) [2]

4741 מַקְצֻעָה ***maqṣu'â***, n.[f.]. GK: 5244 [→ 7106]. (wood) chisel:– planes [1]

4742 מְקֻצְעָה ***m^equṣ'â***, v.ptcp. GK: 7910 [→ 4740, 7106]. ptcp. of 7106: made with corners:– corners [2]

4743 מָקַק ***māqaq***, v. GK: 5245 [→ 4716]. [N] to rot, waste away, fester; dissolve; [H] to cause to rot:– consume away [4], pine away [4], corrupt [1], dissolved [1]

מָקֹר ***māqōr***. See 4726.

4744 מִקְרָא ***miqrā'***, n.m. GK: 5246 [→ 7121]. assembly, calling the community together, usually for a religious ceremony:– convocation [16], convocations [3], assemblies [2], calling [1], reading [1]

4745 מִקְרֶה ***miqreh***, n.m. GK: 5247 [→ 7136]. happening by chance; fate, destiny:– befalleth [3], event [3], chance [1], happeneth [1], hap [1], something befallen [1]

4746 מְקָרֶה ***m^{e}qāreh***, n.[m.]. GK: 5248 [→ 6982]. rafters, roof beams:– building [1]

4747 מְקֵרָה ***m^{e}qērâ***, n.f. GK: 5249 [→ 6979]. coolness; cool room, summer home:– summer [2]

מֹקֵשׁ ***mōqēš***. See 4170.

4748 מִקְשֶׁה ***miqšeh***, n.[m.]. GK: 5250 [→ 4749]. well-dressed hair:– well set hair (+4639) [1]

4749 מִקְשָׁה ***miqšâ***, n.f. GK: 5251 [→ 4748]. hammered work; some sources: embossed metal work:– beaten work [6], beaten out of one piece [1], beaten [1], upright [1], whole piece [1]

4750 מִקְשָׁה ***miqšâ***, n.f. GK: 5252 [→ 7180]. melon field, cucumber field:– garden of cucumbers [1]

4751 מַר ***mar*** or מָרָה ***mārâ***, a. & subst. GK: 5253 & 5287 [cf. 4843]. bitter; bitterness, ranging from being merely disagreeable to the taste to being poisonous; by extension: anxiety, despair:– bitter [21], bitterness [9], bitterly [3], angry (+5315) [1], chafed [1], discontented (+5315) [1], great bitterness (+4843) [1], heavy [1]

4752 מַר ***mar***, n.[m.]. GK: 5254. drop (in a bucket):– drop [1]

4753 מֹר ***mōr***, n.m. GK: 5255 [→ 4843]. myrrh:– myrrh [12]

4754 מָרָא ***mārā'***, v. GK: 5256 & 5257 [cf. 4784]. [Q] to flap, spread the feathers as it runs; this can also refer to the feet kicking up dirt; [Ho] to be obstinate:– filthy [1], lifteth up [1]

4755 מָרָא ***mārā'***, n.pr.f. GK: 5259 [→ 4843]. Mara, "*bitter*":– Mara [1]

4756 מָרֵא ***mārē'*** (Aram.), n.m. GK: 10437. lord; (of God) the Lord; "Lord of kings" is one who is an authority over any and all other authorities:– Lord/lord [4]

מֹרָא ***mōrā'***. See 4172.

4757 מְרֹדַךְ־בַּלְאֲדָן ***m^{e}rōdak-bal^{a}dān***, n.pr.m. GK: 5282 [→ 4781+1081; cf. 1255]. Merodach-Baladan, "*Marduk has given a son*":– Merodach-baladan [1]

4758 מַרְאֶה ***mar'eh***, n.m. GK: 5260 [→ 7200]. what is seen with the eye, appearance; by extension: vision, supernatural revelation with a focus on visual communication, but can include verbal content:– appearance [33], vision [11], sight [10], countenance [9], favoured [8], in sight [8], look upon [4], appearances [2], countenances [2], fair (+2896) [2], apparently [1], appeareth [1], beautiful (+2896) [1], beauty [1], form [1], goodly [1], look on [1], look to [1], looketh (+5869) [1], pattern [1], saw [1], seem [1], see [1], visage [1]

4759 מַרְאָה ***mar'â***, n.f. GK: 5261 & 5262 [→ 7200]. vision; mirror:– vision [6], visions [5], looking-glasses [1]

4760 מֻרְאָה ***mur'â***, n.f. GK: 5263 [cf. 4784]. crop (of a bird):– crop [1]

מְרֹאוֹן ***m^{e}r'ôn***. See 8112.

4761 מְרַאֲשׁוֹת ***m^{e}ra^{a}šôt***, n.[f.]pl.den. GK: 5265 [→ 4762, 4763]. same as 4763: head rest, place near the head, headship:– principalities [1]

4762 מָרֵשָׁה ***mārēšâ***, n.pr.m. & loc. GK: 5358 & 5359 [→ 4761, 4763]. Mareshah, "[perhaps] *head place*":– Mareshah [8]

4763 מְרַאֲשׁוֹת ***m^{e}ra^{a}šôt***, n.[f.]pl.den. GK: 5265 [→ 4761]. same as 4761: head rest, place near the head:– bolster [6], pillows [2], head [1]

4764 מֵרַב ***mērab***, n.pr.f. GK: 5266 [→ 7231]. Merab, "*abundant*":– Merab [3]

4765 מַרְבַד ***marbad***, n.[m.]. GK: 5267 [→ 7234]. covering:– coverings of tapestry [2]

4766 מַרְבֶּה ***marbeh***, n.[m.]. GK: 5269 [→ 7235]. abundance, increase:– great [1], increase [1]

4767 מִרְבָּה ***mirbâ***, n.f. GK: 5268 [→ 7235]. so much:– much [1]

4768 מַרְבִּית ***marbît***, n.f. GK: 5270 [→ 7235]. great number; most, majority; profit:– increase [2], greatest part [1], greatness [1], multitude [1]

4769 מַרְבֵּץ ***marbēṣ***, n.[m.]. GK: 5271 [→ 7257]. lair, resting place, place to lie down:– couching place [1], place to lie down in [1]

4770 מַרְבֵּק ***marbēq***, n.[m.]. GK: 5272. fattening (of a calf):– stall [2], fatted [1], fat [1]

מֹרַג ***mōrag***. See 4173.

4771 מַרְגּוֹעַ ***margôa'***, n.[m.]. GK: 5273 [→ 7280]. resting place:– rest [1]

4772 מַרְגְּלוֹת ***marg^{e}lôt***, n.[f.]pl.den. GK: 5274 [→ 7272]. (place of) the feet:– feet [5]

4773 מַרְגֵּמָה ***margēmâ***, n.f. GK: 5275 [→ 7275]. sling:– sling [1]

4774 מַרְגֵּעָה ***margē'â***, n.f. GK: 5276 [→ 7280]. place of repose, resting-place:– refreshing [1]

4775 מָרַד ***mārad***, v. GK: 5277 [→ 4777, 4778?, 4780]. [Q] to rebel, revolt:– rebelled [12], rebel [8], rebellest [2], rebel against [1], rebellious [1], rebels [1]

4776 מְרַד ***m^{e}rad*** (Aram.), n.[m.]. GK: 10438 [→ 4779; cf. 4777]. rebellion:– rebellion [1]

4777 מֶרֶד ***mered***, n.[m.]. GK: 5278 [→ 4778; cf. 4775; cf. 4776]. rebellion:– rebellion [1]

4778 מֶרֶד ***mered***, n.pr.m. GK: 5279 [→ 4777?; cf. 4775]. Mered, "*rebel*":– Mered [2]

4779 מָרָד ***mārād*** (Aram.), a. GK: 10439 [→ 4776]. rebellious:– rebellious [2]

4780 מַרְדּוּת ***mardût***, n.f. GK: 5280 [→ 4775]. rebellion, revolt:– rebellious [1]

4781 מְרֹדָךְ ***m^{e}rōdāk***, n.pr. GK: 5281 [→ 4757, 4782]. Marduk, Merodak (pagan god):– Merodach [1]

4782 מָרְדֳּכַי ***mord^{o}kay***, n.pr.m. GK: 5283 [→ 4781]. Mordecai, "*Marduk*":– Mordecai [58], Mordecai's [2]

4783 מֻרְדָּף ***murdāp***, n.f. & m. GK: 5284 [→ 7291]. aggression:– persecuted [1]

4784 מָרָה ***mārâ***, v. GK: 5286 [→ 3236, 4805, 4812?, 4850; cf. 4754, 4760]. [Q] to rebel, defy, become disobedient; some: to be bitter; [H] to act as a rebel, defy by one's action:– rebelled [14], rebellious [9], provoked [4], rebel [4], disobedient [2], grievously rebelled (+4784) [2], provoke [2], bitter [1], changed [1], disobeyed [1], provocation [1], provoking [1], rebelled against [1], rebels [1]

4785 מָרָה ***mārâ***, n.pr.f. GK: 5288 [→ 4796; cf. 4843]. Marah, "*bitter*":– Marah [5]

מֹרֶה ***mōreh***. See 4175.

4786 מֹרָה ***mōrâ***, n.f. GK: 5289 [→ 4843]. bitterness, grief:– grief [1]

4787 מָרָּה ***morrâ***, n.f. GK: 5285 [→ 4843]. bitterness:– bitterness [1]

4788 מָרוּד ***mārûd***, n.[m.]. GK: 5291 [→ 7300]. wandering; wanderer; homeless, with a focus on poverty:– cast out [1], miseries [1], misery [1]

4789 מֵרוֹז ***mērôz***, n.pr.loc. GK: 5292. Meroz:– Meroz [1]

4790 מְרוֹחַ ***mārôaḥ***, n.[m.]. GK: 5293 [→ 4799]. damaged (by pounding or grinding):– broken [1]

4791 מָרוֹם ***mārôm***, n.m. GK: 5294 [→ 7311]. heights, (place) on high, being in an elevated position; by extension: pride, haughtiness, arrogance, an improperly high opinion of oneself; exaltation, high in honor and status:– high [16], on high [11], height [9], above [4], high places [4], dignity [1], far above [1], haughty [1], heights [1], high ones [1], highest places (+1610) [1], loftily (+4480) [1], on high (+871.1+1886.1) [1], upward [1], very high (+5704) [1]

4792 מֵרוֹם ***mērôm***, n.pr.loc. GK: 5295 [→ 7311]. Merom, "*high place*":– Merom [2]

4793 מֵרוֹץ ***mērôṣ***, n.[m.]. GK: 5296 [→ 7323]. foot race, running:– race [1]

4794 מְרוּצָה ***m^{e}rûṣâ***, n.f. GK: 5297 [→ 7323]. manner or mode of running; course of a race:– course [2], running [2]

4795 מְרוּקִים ***m^{e}rûqîm***, n.[m.]. GK: 5299 [→ 4838]. beauty treatments (including massage and ointments):– purifications [1]

מְרוֹר ***m^{e}rôr***. See 4844.

מְרוֹרָה ***m^{e}rôrâ***. See 4846.

4796 מָרוֹת ***mārôt***, n.pr.loc. GK: 5300 [→ 4785; cf. 4843]. Maroth, "*bitterness*":– Maroth [1]

4797 מִרְזֵחַ ***marzēaḥ***, n.m. GK: 5301 [→ 4798]. same as 4798: funeral meal; cultic feast:– banquet [1]

4798 מַרְזֵחַ ***marzēaḥ***, n.m. GK: 5301 [→ 4797]. same as 4797: funeral meal; cultic feast:– mourning [1]

4799 מָרַח ***māraḥ***, v. GK: 5302 [→ 4790]. [Q] to apply by spreading on or rubbing in:– lay for a plaister [1]

4800 מֶרְחָב ***merḥāb***, n.[m.]. GK: 5303 [→ 4800+3050; cf. 7337]. spaciousness, wideness, with the associative meaning that such a wide area is comfortable, and possibly safe and free:– large place [4], breadth [1], large room [1]

4801 מֶרְחָק ***merḥāq***, n.m. GK: 5305 [→ 7368]. distance, far away:– far [11], afar off (+4480) [2], afar [1], far countries [1], far off (+4480) [1], far off [1], very far off [1]

4802 מַרְחֶשֶׁת ***marḥešet***, n.f. GK: 5306 [→ 7370]. cooking pan (with a lid):– fryingpan [2]

4803 מָרַט ***māraṭ***, v. GK: 5307 [→ 4178]. [Q] to pull out (hair); [Qp] to be polished, rubbed; [N] to lose one's hair, become bald; [Pu] to be polished, burnished, smooth (skinned):– furbished [5], hair fallen off [2], bright [1], peeled [1], plucked off hair [1], pluckt off hair [1], pluckt off [1]

4804 מְרַט ***m^{e}raṭ*** (Aram.), v. GK: 10440 [cf. 4178]. [Peil] to be torn off, plucked out:– pluckt [1]

4805 מְרִי ***m^{e}rî***, n.m. GK: 5308 [→ 4784]. rebellion; some: bitter:– rebellious [17], rebellion [4], bitter [1], rebels (+1121) [1]

4806 מְרִיא ***m^{e}rî'***, n.[m.]. GK: 5309 [→ 1254, 1274, 1277, 4471?, 4813?]. fattened animal (choice for consumption):– fat cattle [3], fatlings [2], fat beasts [1], fatling [1], fed beasts [1]

4807 מְרִיב בַּעַל ***m^{e}rîb ba'al***, n.pr.m. GK: 5311 [→ 1167; cf. 4810]. Merib-Baal, "*Baal contends*":– Merib-baal [3]

4808 מְרִיבָה ***m^{e}rîbâ***, n.f. GK: 5312 [→ 4809; cf. 7378]. quarreling, strife; rebellion, with a focus on the feelings of enmity:– strife [5], provocation [1]

4809 מְרִיבָה ***m^{e}rîbâ***, n.pr.loc. GK: 5313 [→ 4808; cf. 7378]. Meribah:– Meribah [6], Meribah-Kadesh [1]

4810 מְרִי־בַעַל ***m^{e}rî-ba'al***, n.pr.m. GK: 5314 [→ 1167; cf. 4807]. Merib-Baal, "*Baal contends*":– Merib-baal [1]

4811 מְרָיָה ***m^{e}rāyâ***, n.pr.m. GK: 5316. Meraiah, "*loved by Yahweh*":– Meraiah [1]

מֹרִיָּה ***mōrîâ***. See 4179.

4812 מְרָיוֹת ***m^{e}rāyôt***, n.pr.m. GK: 5318 [→ 4784?]. Meraioth, "*rebellious*":– Meraioth [7]

4813 מִרְיָם ***miryām***, n.pr.f. & m. GK: 5319 [→ 4806?]. Miriam, "[variously] *bitterness; plump one; wished-for child; one who loves or is loved*":– Miriam [15]

4814 מְרִירוּת ***m^{e}rîrût***, n.f. GK: 5320 [→ 4843]. bitterness:– bitterness [1]

4815 מְרִירִי ***m^{e}rîrî***, a. GK: 5321 [→ 4843]. bitter, in context referring to something deadly:– bitter [1]

4816 מֹרֶךְ ***mōrek***, n.[m.]. GK: 5322 [→ 7401]. fearfulness, despondency:– faintness [1]

4817 מֶרְכָּב ***merkāb***, n.m. GK: 5323 [→ 7392]. seat, saddle, chariot:– chariots [1], covering [1], saddle [1]

4818 מֶרְכָּבָה ***merkābâ***, n.f. GK: 5324 [→ 7392]. chariot:– chariot [23], chariots [21]

4819 מַרְכֹּלֶת ***markōlet***, n.f. GK: 5326 [→ 7402]. marketplace, place of merchandising:– merchandise [1]

4820 מִרְמָה ***mirmâ***, n.f. GK: 5327 [→ 4821; cf. 7411]. deceit, deception, dishonesty, treachery:– deceit [19], deceitful [8], false [2], guile [2], craft [1], deceitfully (+3807.1) [1], deceitfully (+871.1) [1], deceitfully [1], deceits [1], feigned [1], subtilty [1], treachery [1]

4821 מִרְמָה ***mirmâ***, n.pr.m. GK: 5328 [→ 4820?; cf. 7411?]. Mirmah, "*deceit*":– Mirma [1]

4822 מְרֵמוֹת ***m^{e}rēmôt***, n.pr.m. GK: 5329. Meremoth, "*elevations*":– Meremoth [6]

4823 מִרְמָס ***mirmās***, n.[m.]. GK: 5330 [→ 7429]. trampling down, running over:– trodden down [3], that which trodden [1], tread down (+7760) [1], treading [1], trodden under foot [1]

4824 מֵרֹנֹתִי ***mērōnōtî***, a.g. GK: 5331. Meronothite, of Meronoth, "*of Meronoth*":– Meronothite [2]

4825 מֶרֶס ***meres***, n.pr.m. GK: 5332. Meres, "*worthy*":– Meres [1]

4826 מַרְסְנָא ***mars^{e}nā'***, n.pr.m. GK: 5333. Marsena:– Marsena [1]

4827 מֵרַע ***mēra'***, n.m. *or* v.ptcp. GK: 5334 [→ 7489]. evil, atrocity:– do mischief [1]

4828 מֵרֵעַ ***mērēa'***, n.[m.] *or* v.ptcp. GK: 5335 [→ 7462]. close friend, companion, personal adviser:– companion [3], friends [3], companions [1]

4829 מִרְעֶה ***mir'eh***, n.m. GK: 5337 [→ 7462]. pasture, grazing place:– pasture [11], feeding place [1], pastures [1]

4830 מַרְעִית ***mar'îṯ***, n.f. GK: 5338 [→ 7462]. pasture, place of grazing:– pasture [8], flocks [1], pastures [1]

4831 מַרְעֲלָה ***mar^{a}lâ***, n.pr.loc. GK: 5339 [→ 7477]. Maralah:– Maralah [1]

4832 מַרְפֵּא ***marpē'***, n.m. GK: 5340 & 5341 [→ 7503; cf. 7495]. healing, remedy; calmness, composure:– health [5], healing [3], remedy [3], cure [1], incurable (+369) [1], sound [1], wholesome [1], yielding [1]

4833 מִרְפָּשׂ ***mirpāś***, n.[m.]. GK: 5343 [→ 7511]. what is muddy, fouled (by trampling):– that which fouled [1]

4834 מָרַץ ***māraṣ***, v. GK: 5344. [N] to be painful, hurtful; [H] to provoke, irritate:– emboldeneth [1], forcible [1], grievous [1], sore [1]

4835 מְרוּצָה ***m^{e}rûṣâ***, n.f. GK: 5298 [→ 7533]. extortion:– violence [1]

4836 מַרְצֵעַ ***marṣēa'***, n.[m.]. GK: 5345 [→ 7527]. awl (piercing tool):– aul [2]

4837 מַרְצֶפֶת ***marṣepet***, n.f. GK: 5346 [→ 7528]. (stone) base, stone-layer:– pavement [1]

4838 מָרַק ***māraq***, v. GK: 5347 [→ 4795, 4839, 8562]. [Q] to polish; [Qp] to be polished; [Pu] to be thoroughly scoured; [H] to cleanse:– bright [1], furbish [1], scoured [1]

4839 מָרָק ***mārāq***, n.m. GK: 5348 [→ 4838]. broth (juice stewed out of meat):– broth [3]

4840 מֶרְקָח ***merqāḥ***, n.[m.]. GK: 5349 [→ 7543]. aromatic herb, scented spice, perfume:– sweet [1]

4841 מֶרְקָחָה ***merqāḥâ***, n.f. GK: 5350 [→ 7543]. ointment jar, spice-pot:– pot of ointment [1], well [1]

4842 מִרְקַחַת ***mirqaḥat***, n.f. GK: 5351 [→ 7543]. mixture of fragrant spices, blend of perfumes:– apothecaries' [1], compound [1], ointment [1]

4843 מָרַר ***mārar***, v. GK: 5352 [→ 4470, 4472, 4751, 4753, 4755, 4787, 4785, 4786, 4796, 4814, 4815, 4844, 4845, 4846, 8563]. [Q] to be bitter; suffer anguish; [P] to make bitter, weep bitterly; [H] to make bitter; to grieve bitterly; [Htpal] to enrage oneself, be furious; from the base meaning "to taste bitter" come extensions of bitter feelings: anger, fury, anguish, rebellion:– in bitterness [2], moved with choler [2], vexed [2], bitterly [1], bitterness [1], bitter [1], dealt bitterly [1], great bitterness (+4751) [1], grieved [1], grieveth [1], made bitter [1], provoke [1], sorely grieved [1]

4844 מָרֹר ***mārōr***, n.m. GK: 5353 [→ 4843]. bitter things:– bitter [2], bitterness [1]

4845 מְרֵרָה ***m^{e}rērâ***, n.f. GK: 5354 [→ 4843]. gall (bitter fluid from the gall bladder):– gall [1]

4846 מְרֹרָה ***m^{e}rōrâ***, n.f. GK: 5355 [→ 4843]. gall bladder; venom, poison (of snakes):– bitter [2], gall [2]

4847 מְרָרִי ***m^{e}rārî***, n.pr.m. GK: 5356 [→ 4848]. Merari; Merarite, "*bitter*":– Merari [39]

4848 מְרָרִי ***m^{e}rārî***, a.g. GK: 5357 [→ 4847]. Merarite, "*of Merari*":– Merarites [1]

מָרֵשָׁה ***mārēšâ***. See 4762.

4849 מִרְשַׁעַת ***mirša'at***, n.f. GK: 5360 [→ 7561]. wickedness, of a person (that) wicked woman:– wicked woman [1]

4850 מְרָתַיִם ***m^{e}rātayim***, n.pr.f. GK: 5361 [→ 4784]. Merathaim, "*double rebellion*":– Merethaim [1]

4851 מַשׁ ***maš***, n.pr.m. GK: 5390. prob. same as 4902: Mash, Meshech:– Mash [1]

4852 מֵשָׁא ***mēšā'***, n.pr.loc. GK: 5392 [→ 4854?]. Mesha:– Mesha [1]

4853 מַשָּׂא ***maśśā'***, n.m. GK: 5362 & 5363 [→ 4984]. burden, load, what is lifted and carried; by extension: oppression; singing (lifting the voice); oracle, prophetic utterance, pronouncement, with the focus on the content of the message:– burden [52], burdens [5], song [3], prophecy [2], carry away [1], exaction of debt (+3027) [1], set [1], tribute [1]

4854 מַשָּׂא ***maśśā'***, n.pr.g. & loc. GK: 5364 [→ 4852?]. Massa, "*burden, oracle*":– Massa [2]

4855 מַשָּׁא ***maššā'***, n.m. GK: 5391 [→ 5378]. debt; exacting of usury:– usury [2]

4856 מַשֹּׂא ***maśśō'***, n.m. GK: 5365 [→ 4984]. partiality:– respect [1]

4857 מַשְׁאָב ***maš'āb***, n.[m.]. GK: 5393 [→ 7579]. watering channel, place to draw water:– places of drawing [1]

מְשֹׁאָה ***m^{e}šō'â***. See 4875.

4858 מַשָּׂאָה ***maśśā'â***, n.f. GK: 5366 [→ 4984]. uplifted (clouds of smoke):– burden [1]

4859 מַשָּׁאָה ***maššā'â***, n.f. GK: 5394 [→ 5378]. (secured) loan:– debts [1], lend (+5383) [1]

מַשֻּׁאָה ***maššu'â***. See 4876.

4860 מַשָּׁאוֹן ***maššā'ôn***, n.[m.]. GK: 5396 [→ 5377]. deception:– deceit [1]

4861 מִשְׁאָל ***miš'āl***, n.pr.loc. GK: 5398 [cf. 4913]. Mishal:– Mishal [1], Misheal [1]

4862 מִשְׁאָלָה ***miš'ālâ***, n.f. GK: 5399 [→ 7592]. desire:– desires [1], petitions [1]

4863 מִשְׁאֶרֶת ***miš'eret***, n.f. GK: 5400 [→ 7603]. kneading trough:– kneadingtroughs [2], store [2]

4864 מַשְׂאֵת ***maś'ēt***, n.f. GK: 5368 [→ 4984]. what is lifted up: portion (of food), tax, tribute, gift, burden:– burdens [2], collection [2], flame [2], mess [2], burden [1], gifts [1], lifting up [1], messes [1], oblations [1], reward [1], sign of fire [1]

מֹשָׁב ***mōšāb***. See 4186.

מְשֻׁבָה ***m^{e}šubâ***. See 4878.

4865 מִשְׁבְּצוֹת ***mišb^{e}ṣôt***, n.f.pl. GK: 5401 [→ 7660]. filigree settings (ornamental work with fine gold wire usually for setting jewels):– ouches [8], wrought [1]

4866 מַשְׁבֵּר ***mašbēr***, n.[m.]. GK: 5402 [→ 7665]. opening of the womb, the point where birth first occurs:– birth [2], breaking forth [1]

4867 מִשְׁבָּר ***mišbār***, n.[m.]. GK: 5403 [→ 7665]. breakers, waves:– waves [4], billows [1]

4868 מִשְׁבָּת ***mišbāt***, n.[m.]. GK: 5404 [→ 7673]. destruction, cessation, finish:– sabbaths [1]

4869 מִשְׂגָּב ***miśgāb***, n.m. & loc. GK: 5369 [→ 7682]. fortress, refuge, stronghold; Misgab:– defence [6], refuge [5], high tower [3], Misgab [1], high fort [1], place of defence [1]

4870 מִשְׁגֶּה ***mišgeh***, n.m. GK: 5405 [→ 7686]. inadvertent mistake, oversight:– oversight [1]

4871 מָשָׁה ***māšâ***, v. GK: 5406 [→ 4872; cf. 570?]. [Q] to draw out; [H] to cause to draw out:– drew out [2], drew [1]

4872 מֹשֶׁה ***mōšeh***, n.pr.m. GK: 5407 [→ 4871]. Moses, "*drawn out* [Ex 2:10]; Egyptian for *child*":– Moses [750], Moses' [15], Moses' (+3807.1) [1]

4873 מֹשֶׁה ***mōšeh*** (Aram.), n.pr.m. GK: 10441 [cf. 4872]. Moses, "*drawn out* [Ex 2:10]; [Egyptian for] *child*":– Moses [1]

4874 מַשֶּׁה ***maššeh***, n.m. GK: 5408 [→ 5378]. credit, loan; "the lord of the loan" is a "creditor":– creditor (+1167+3027) [1]

4875 מְשׁוֹאָה ***m^{e}šô'â***, n.f. GK: 5409. wasteland, desolate land:– waste [2], desolation [1]

4876 מַשּׁוּאָה ***maššû'â*** or מַשֻּׁאוֹת ***maššu'ôt***, n.m. & f.[pl.]. GK: 5410 & 5397 [→ 5377]. ruin, rubble, desolation; deception:– desolations [1], destruction [1]

4877 מְשׁוֹבָב ***m^{e}šôbāb***, n.pr.m. GK: 5411 [→ 7725]. Meshobab:– Meshobab [1]

4878 מְשׁוּבָה ***m^{e}šûbâ***, n.f. GK: 5412 [→ 7725]. waywardness, backsliding, faithlessness, apostasy:– backsliding [7], backslidings [4], turning away [1]

4879 מְשׁוּגָה ***m^{e}šûgâ***, n.f. GK: 5413 [cf. 7683, 7686]. error:– error [1]

4880 מָשׁוֹט ***māšôṭ*** or מִשּׁוֹט ***miššôṭ***, n.[m.]. GK: 5414 & 5415 [→ 7751]. oar:– oars [1], oar [1]

4881 מְשׂוּכָּה ***m^{e}śûkkâ*** or מְשֻׂכָה ***m^{e}śukâ***, n.f. GK: 5372 & 5379 [→ 4534]. (thorn) hedge (which impedes movement):– hedge [2]

4882 מְשׁוּסָּה ***m^{e}šiwssâ***, var. GK: 5416 [cf. 4933]. plunder, loot, booty; cf. 4934:– @H = **4883** מַשּׂוֹר ***ma^{33}ôr***, n.m. GK: 5373. saw (cutting tool):– saw [1]

4884 מְשׂוּרָה ***m^{e}śûrâ***, n.f. GK: 5374. (liquid) measure of quantity, measure of capacity:– measure [4]

4885 מָשׂוֹשׂ ***māśôś***, n.m. GK: 5375 & 5376 [→ 7797; cf. 4549]. joy, delight, celebration; wasting away, rotting away:– joy [12], mirth [3], rejoiceth [1], rejoice [1]

4886 מָשַׁח ***māšaḥ***, v. GK: 5417 [→ 4473, 4888, 4899; cf. 4887]. [Q] to anoint; [Qp] to be spread, be anointed; [N] to be anointed; usually referring to pouring or smearing sacred oil on a person in a ceremony of dedication, possibly symbolizing divine empowering to accomplish the task or office:– anointed [42], anoint [25], anointedst [1], painted [1]

4887 מְשַׁח ***m^{e}šaḥ*** (Aram.), n.[m.]. GK: 10442 & 10443 [cf. 4888]. olive oil, used for food, lamp oil, and ceremonies; measure:– oil [2]

4888 מָשְׁחָה ***mošḥâ*** or מִשְׁחָה ***mišḥâ***, n.f. GK: 5418 & 5419 & 5420 & 5421 [→ 4886]. portion; anointing (oil), usually referring to pouring or smearing sacred oil on a person in a ceremony of dedication, possibly symbolizing divine empowering to accomplish the task or office:– anointing [24], anointed [1], ointment [1]

4889 מַשְׁחִית ***mašḥît***, n.[m.]. GK: 5422 [→ 7843]. destroyer, one who destroys; destruction, corruption; bird trap:– destroy [4], corruption [2], destruction [2], destroyer (+376) [1], destroying [1], trap [1], utterly (+3807.1) [1]

4890 מִשְׂחָק ***miśḥāq***, n.[m.]. GK: 5377 [→ 7832]. (scoffing) laughter:– scorn [1]

4891 מִשְׁחָר ***mišḥār***, n.[m.]. GK: 5423 [→ 7835]. dawn, early morning light:– morning [1]

4892 מַשְׁחֵת ***mašḥēt***, n.[m.]. GK: 5424 [→ 7843]. destruction, annihilation:– destroying [1]

4893 מִשְׁחַת ***mišḥat*** or מָשְׁחָת ***mošḥāt***, n.[m.]. GK: 5425 & 5426 [→ 7843]. deformity, defect, corruption, disfigurement, implying ugliness and repulsion:– corruption [1], marred [1]

4894 מִשְׁטוֹחַ ***mišṭôaḥ***, n.[m.]. GK: 5427 [→ 7849]. place for spreading out nets, drying yard for nets:– place to spread forth [1], spread upon [1], spreading [1]

4895 מַשְׂטֵמָה ***maśṭēmâ***, n.f. GK: 5378 [→ 7852]. hostility, animosity, enmity:– hatred [2]

4896 מִשְׁטָר ***mišṭār***, n.m. GK: 5428 [→ 7860]. dominion, rule; some sources: heavenly writing (the starry sky as God's communication):– dominion [1]

4897 מֶשִׁי ***mešî***, n.[m.]. GK: 5429. costly fabric for garments; possibly referring to silk:– silk [2]

מֻשִׁי ***mušî***. See 4187.

4898 מְשֵׁיזַבְאֵל ***m^{e}šêzab'ēl***, n.pr.m. GK: 5430 [cf. 7804]. Meshezabel, "*God [El] delivers*":– Meshezabeel [3]

4899 מָשִׁיחַ ***māšîaḥ***, n.m. GK: 5431 [→ 4886]. anointed (one), usually refers to pouring or smearing sacred oil on a person in a ceremony of dedication, possibly symbolizing divine empowering to accomplish the task or office; the Anointed One, the Messiah, God's ultimate chosen one, identified in the NT as Jesus:– anointed [37], Messiah [2]

4900 מָשַׁךְ ***māšak***, v. GK: 5432 [→ 4901, 4189]. [Q] to draw up, drag; to extend, spread out; [N] to be prolonged, delayed; [Pu] to be deferred; to be tall:– draw [7], drew [4], draw out [3], prolonged [3], draweth [2], drawn [2], scattered [2], continue [1], deferred [1], draw away [1], drew along [1], drew up [1], extend unto [1], forbear (+5921) [1], give [1], handle [1], make a long blast [1], soundeth long [1], soweth [1], stretched out [1]

4901 מֶשֶׁךְ ***mešek***, n.[m.]. GK: 5433 [→ 4900]. (leather) bag, pouch (= price):– precious [1], price [1]

4902 מֶשֶׁךְ ***mešek***, n.pr.g. GK: 5434. Meshech:– Meshech [8], Mesech [1]

4903 מִשְׁכַּב ***miškab*** (Aram.), n.[m.]. GK: 10444 [cf. 4904]. bed, formally "a place for lying," which can refer to simple mats and even outer cloaks, as well as to pieces of furniture:– bed [6]

4904 מִשְׁכָּב ***miškāb***, n.m. GK: 5435 [→ 7901; cf. 4903]. bed, couch, used as a place for sleep, meditation, convalescence, marital relations, and worship:– bed [28], beds [5], bedchamber (+2315) [4], lying with [4], couch [1], lay on a bed (+7901) [1], lien [1], lieth with [1]

מְשֻׂכָה ***m^{e}śukâ***. See 4881.

4905 מַשְׂכִּיל ***maśkîl***, n.m. GK: 5380 [→ 7919]. maskil (t.t. in the Psalms, perhaps "wisdom song"):– Maschil [13]

מַשְׁכִּים ***maškîm***. See 7925.

4906 מַשְׂכִּית ***maśkît***, n.f. GK: 5381. carved image, sculpture, figurine; what is imagined, imagination:– pictures [2], conceit [1], imagery [1], image [1], wish [1]

4907 מִשְׁכַּן ***miškan*** (Aram.), n.[m.]. GK: 10445 [→ 7932; cf. 4908]. dwelling, abode:– habitation [1]

4908 מִשְׁכָּן ***miškān***, n.m. GK: 5438 [→ 7931; cf. 4907]. dwelling place, habitat, tent, tabernacle, the tent used as the central place of worship before the temple:– tabernacle [114], dwellings [6], tabernacles [5], dwelling places [4], habitation [3], dwelling place [2], habitations [2], dwelling [1], tents [1], where dwelleth [1]

4909 מַשְׂכֹּרֶת ***maśkōret***, n.f. GK: 5382 [→ 7936]. wage:– wages [3], reward [1]

4910 מָשַׁל ***māšal***, v. GK: 5440 [→ 4474, 4475, 4915]. [Q] to rule, govern, control; [H] make one a ruler, (n.) dominion:– rule [15], ruler [14], ruleth [7], ruled [5], reign [4], rulers [4], governor [3], have dominion [3], reigned [3], have power [2], have rule [2], indeed have dominion (+4910) [2], rule over [2], rulest [2], ruling [2], bare rule [1], barest rule [1], bear rule [1], beareth rule [1], cause to rule over [1], dominion [1], governors [1], had dominion [1], madest to have dominion [1], reignest [1], ruler's [1]

4911 מָשַׁל ***māšal***, v. GK: 5439 [→ 4912, 4915, 4914]. [Q] to quote (a proverb or saying), to make up a proverb; [N] to liken, be like; [P] to tell a proverb; [H] to liken, compare to; [Ht] to show oneself like:– become like [3], like [2], use proverb (+4912) [2], compare [1], like unto [1], speak a parable (+4912) [1], speak in proverbs [1], speak [1], use as a proverb [1], use proverb [1], useth proverbs [1], utter [1]

4912 מָשָׁל ***māšāl***, n.m. GK: 5442 [→ 4911]. wisdom sayings of various types: proverb, a short, pithy saying, easy to remember; parable, a brief story with a symbolic meaning; oracle, a discourse type of prophecy; taunt, ridicule, a stylized form for mocking an enemy:– parable [16], proverb [12], proverbs [5], use proverb (+4911) [2], byword [1], like unto [1], parables [1], speak a parable (+4911) [1]

4913 מָשָׁל ***māšāl***, n.pr.loc. GK: 5443 [cf. 4861]. Mashal:– Mashal [1]

4914 מְשֹׁל ***m^e^šōl***, n.[m.]. GK: 5446 [→ 4911]. byword:– byword [1]

4915 מֹשֶׁל ***mōšel***, n.[m.]. GK: 5444 & 5445 [→ 4910, 4911]. likeness, similarity; power, dominion:– dominion [2], like [1]

מִשְׁלוֹשׁ ***mišlōš***. See 7969.

4916 מִשְׁלוֹחַ ***mišlôaḥ*** or מִשְׁלַח ***mišlaḥ***, n.[m.]. GK: 5447 & 5448 [→ 7971]. giving, sending (presents); laying on (hands): puttest unto [2], sending [2], settest unto [2], lay upon [1], put unto [1], sending forth [1], settest [1]

4917 מִשְׁלַחַת ***mišlaḥat***, n.f. GK: 5449 [→ 7971]. discharge (from military); band, company (of angels):– discharge [1], sending [1]

4918 מְשֻׁלָּם ***m^e^šullām***, n.pr.m. GK: 5450 [→ 4920; cf. 7999]. Meshullam, "*restitution*":– Meshullam [25]

4919 מְשִׁלֵּמוֹת ***m^e^šillēmôt***, n.pr.m. GK: 5451 [→ 4921; cf. 7999]. Meshillemoth, "*restitution*":– Meshillemoth [2]

4920 מְשֶׁלֶמְיָה ***m^e^šelemyâ*** or מְשֶׁלֶמְיָהוּ ***m^e^šelemyāhû***, n.pr.m. GK: 5452 & 5453 [→ 4918+3068]. Meshelemiah, "*Yahweh repays*":– Meshelemiah [4]

4921 מְשִׁלֵּמִית ***m^e^šillēmît***, n.pr.m. GK: 5454 [→ 4919; cf. 7999]. Meshillemith, "*restitution*":– Meshillemith [1]

4922 מְשֻׁלֶּמֶת ***m^e^šullemet***, n.pr.f. GK: 5455 [→ 7999]. Meshullemeth, "*restitution*":– Meshullemeth [1]

4923 מְשַׁמָּה ***m^e^šammâ***, n.f. GK: 5457 [→ 8074]. object of horror, desolate waste, dried up place:– desolate [3], most desolate (+8077+2050.1) [3], astonishment [1]

4924 מִשְׁמָן ***mišmān***, n.[m.]. GK: 5458 & 5460 [→ 8081]. fatness; by extension: sturdiness, stoutness; richness, fertility, abundance, prosperity; choice food, festive food, rich with oil or fat (rare and valued in the ancient Near East):– fatness [3], fat ones [1], fattest places [1], fattest [1], fat [1]

4925 מִשְׁמַנָּה ***mišmannâ***, n.pr.m. GK: 5459 [→ 8081]. Mishmannah, "*fatness*":– Mishmannah [1]

4926 מִשְׁמָע ***mišmā'***, n.[m.]. GK: 5461 [→ 4927; cf. 8085]. what one hears, rumor, hearsay:– hearing [1]

4927 מִשְׁמָע ***mišmā'***, n.pr.m. GK: 5462 [→ 4926, cf. 8085]. Mishma, "*rumor*":– Mishma [4]

4928 מִשְׁמַעַת ***mišma'at***, n.f. GK: 5463 [→ 8085]. bodyguard; subject, one obligated to allegiance:– guard [2], bidding [1], obey [1]

4929 מִשְׁמָר ***mišmār***, n.[m.]. GK: 5464 [→ 8104]. guard or guarding, custody, imprisonment:– ward [12], watch [4], guard [3], diligence [1], offices [1], prison [1]

4930 מַשְׂמְרָה ***maśmērâ***, n.m. GK: 5383 [cf. 5568]. nail (on the end of a goad):– nails [1]

4931 מִשְׁמֶרֶת ***mišmeret***, n.f. GK: 5466 [→ 8104]. responsibility, duty, service; requirement, obligation; guard, watch, what is cared for:– charge [45], kept [6], ward [5], watch [5], charges [4], ordinance [3], wards [3], watches [2], charge of [1], in safeguard [1], keep (+1961) [1], offices [1], ward (+1004) [1]

4932 מִשְׁנֶה ***mišneh***, n.[m.]. GK: 5467 [→ 8138]. second, next (in a series); twice, double:– second [9], double [8], next [6], college [2], copy [2], twice [2], fatlings [1], next to [1], second degree [1], second order [1], second sort [1], twice as much [1]

4933 מְשִׁסָּה ***m^e^šissâ***, n.f. GK: 5468 [→ 7601; cf. 4882]. plunder, loot, booty:– spoil [4], booties [1], booty [1]

4934 מִשְׁעוֹל ***miš'ôl***, n.m. GK: 5469 [→ 8168]. narrow path:– path [1]

4935 מִשְׁעִי ***miš'î***, n.f. GK: 5470. cleansing, implying cleansing by washing and rubbing:– supple [1]

4936 מִשְׁעָם ***miš'ām***, n.pr.m. GK: 5471. Misham:– Misham [1]

4937 מִשְׁעָן ***miš'ān*** or מַשְׁעֵן ***maš'ēn***, n.m. & f. GK: 5472 & 5473 [→ 8172]. support, supplies:– stay [5]

4938 מַשְׁעֵנָה ***maš'ēnâ*** or מִשְׁעֶנֶת ***miš'enet***, n.f. GK: 5474 & 5475 [→ 8172]. staff, stick; support, supply:– staff [11], staves [1]

4939 מִשְׂפָּח ***miśpāḥ***, n.[m.]. GK: 5384 [cf. 5596]. bloodshed, with a focus on violence:– oppression [1]

4940 מִשְׁפָּחָה ***mišpāḥâ***, n.f. GK: 5476 [→ 8198]. clan, family, people:– families [169], family [117], kindred [6], every family (+4940) [4], kindreds [3], every family (+4940+2050.1) [2], kinds [2]

4941 מִשְׁפָּט ***mišpāṭ***, n.m. GK: 5477 [→ 5880; cf. 8199]. justice, judgment; law, regulation, prescription, specification:– judgment [188], judgments [108], manner [34], right [18], cause [12], that which is lawful [7], ordinances [6], ordinance [5], worthy [4], after the manner [2], discretion [2], fashion [2], law [2], manners [2], measure [2], order [2], sentence [2], adversary (+1167) [1], as required [1], ceremonies [1], charge [1], crimes [1], custom [1], deserts [1], determination [1], disposing [1], due order [1], due [1], execute the judgment (+8199) [1], fashions [1], form [1], judged [1], judgment (+1697) [1], justice [1], justly [1], just [1], order (+1961) [1], order commanded [1], usest to do [1], wrong (+3808) [1], wrongfully (+3808+871.1) [1]

4942 מִשְׁפְּתַיִם ***mišp^e^tayim***, n.[m.]du. GK: 5478 [→ 8239]. (dual) campfires or two saddlebags:– sheepfolds [1], two burdens [1]

4943 מֶשֶׁק ***mešeq***, n.[m.]. GK: 5479 [→ 4476]. inheritance, possession:– steward (+1121) [1]

4944 מַשָּׁק ***maššāq***, n.[m.]. GK: 5480 [→ 8264]. onslaught, assault; formally "rushing," this is the sudden, aggressive movement of a swarm:– running to and fro [1]

4945 מַשְׁקֶה ***mašqeh***, n.m. GK: 5482 & 5483 [→ 8248]. cupbearer; drink (liquid); drinking vessel; irrigation:– drinking [2], drink [2], butlership [1], fat pastures [1], well watered [1]

4946 מִשְׁקוֹל ***mišqôl***, n.[m.]. GK: 5484 [→ 8254]. weight:– weight [1]

4947 מַשְׁקוֹף ***mašqôp***, n.[m.]. GK: 5485 [→ 8259]. top (upper crosspiece of a door), lintel:– lintel [2], upper door post [1]

4948 מִשְׁקָל ***mišqāl***, n.m. GK: 5486 [→ 8254]. weight:– weight [46], weigh [2], full weight [1]

4949 מִשְׁקֶלֶת ***mišqelet***, n.f. GK: 5487 [→ 8254?]. plumb line, leveling instrument:– plummet [2]

4950 מִשְׁקָע ***mišqā'***, n.[m.]. GK: 5488 [→ 8257]. clear (settled) water:– deep [1]

4951 מִשְׂרָה ***miśrâ***, n.f. GK: 5385 [→ 7786]. dominion, rule:– government [2]

4952 מִשְׁרָה ***mišrâ***, n.f. GK: 5489 [→ 8281]. (grape) juice:– liquor [1]

4953 מַשְׁרוֹקִי ***mašrôqî*** (Aram.), n.f. GK: 10446. flute, musical pipe, a cylinder-shaped instrument producing a high shrill sound, made of wood, reed, or bone:– flute [4]

4954 מִשְׁרָעִי ***mišrā'î***, a.g. GK: 5490. Mishraite:– Mishraites [1]

4955 מִשְׂרָפוֹת ***miśrāpôt***, n.[f.pl.]. GK: 5386 [→ 8313]. (complete) burning, funeral fire:– burnings [2]

4956 מִשְׂרְפוֹת מַיִם ***miśr^e^pôt mayim***, n.pr.loc. GK: 5387 [→ 8313+4325]. Misrephoth Maim, "*waters of Misrephoth [lime burning]*":– Misrephoth-maim [2]

4957 מַשְׂרֵקָה ***maśrēqâ***, n.pr.loc. GK: 5388 [→ 8320]. Masrekah, "[perhaps] *vineyard*":– Masrekah [2]

4958 מַשְׂרֵת ***maśrēt***, n.m. GK: 5389 [→ 7603]. cooking pan:– pan [1]

4959 מָשַׁשׁ ***māšaš***, v. GK: 5491 [cf. 3237, 4184]. [Q] to touch, feel; [P] to grope, search thoroughly; [H] to let one feel:– grope [3], felt [2], searched [2], feel [1], gropeth [1]

4960 מִשְׁתֶּה ***mišteh***, n.m. GK: 5492 [→ 8354; cf. 4961]. feast, banquet, dinner, with an focus on drinking:– feast [21], banquet [10], feasting [7], drink [3], drank [2], feasts [2], feasted (+6213) [1]

4961 מִשְׁתֵּא ***mištē'*** (Aram.), n.m. GK: 10447 [→ 8355; cf. 4960]. banquet (hall); feast (hall), a place of merriment and celebration, often associated with drinking bouts:– banquet [1]

4962 מַת ***mōt***, n.m. GK: 5493 [→ 1328, 4968]. men; few (people):– men [14], few [2], few (+4557) [1], few (+4592) [1], friends [1], number [1], persons [1], small [1]

4963 מַתְבֵּן ***matbēn***, n.[m.]. GK: 5495 [→ 8401]. heap of straw:– straw [1]

4964 מֶתֶג ***meteg***, n.m. GK: 5496 [→ 4965]. bridle or bit:– bridle [3], Metheg-ammah [1], bit [1]

4965 מֶתֶג הָאַמָּה ***meteg hā'ammâ***, n.pr.loc. GK: 5497 [→ 4964+1886.1+538]. Metheg Ammah:– @H = **4966** מָתוֹק ***mātôq***, a. GK: 5498 [→ 4985]. sweet, sweetness; by extension: pleasant, delightful:– sweet [8], sweeter [2], sweetness [2]

4967 מְתוּשָׁאֵל ***m^e^tûšā'ēl***, n.pr.m. GK: 5499 [→ 4191+7945+410]. Methushael, "[perhaps] *man of God*":– Methusael [2]

4968 מְתוּשֶׁלַח ***m^e^tûšelaḥ***, n.pr.m. GK: 5500 [→ 4962+7971?]. Methuselah, "*man of the javelin*":– Methuselah [6]

4969 מָתַח ***mātaḥ***, v. GK: 5501 [→ 572]. [Q] to spread out:– spreadeth out [1]

4970 מָתַי ***mātay***, adv.inter. GK: 5503. How long?; When?:– how long (+5704) [28], when [12], for how long (+5704) [1], when (+310) [1], when (+3807.1) [1]

מְתִים ***m^e^tîm***. See 4962.

4971 מַתְכֹּנֶת ***matkōnet***, n.f. GK: 5504 [→ 8505]. measure, formula:– composition [2], measure [1], state [1], tale [1]

4972 מַתְּלָאָה ***matt^e^lā'â***, p.indef.+n.f. GK: 5505 [→ 4100+8513]. what a burden! (4100 + 8513):– weariness [1]

4973 מְתַלְּעוֹת ***m^e^tall^e^'ôt***, n.f.pl. GK: 5506 [→ 4459]. jaw; teeth:– cheek teeth [1], jaw teeth [1], jaws [1]

4974 מְתֹם ***m^e^tōm***, n.[m.]. GK: 5507 [→ 8552]. health, soundness:– soundness [3], men [1]

מֶתֶן ***meten***. See 4981.

4975 מָתְנַיִם ***motnayim***, n.m.du. GK: 5516 [→ 4981?]. (dual) waist, lower back (lumbar region), loins; "girding the loins" involves tucking the skirt of a tunic or robe into the belt, thus preparing for action: running, working, fighting, etc:– loins [42], side [4], greyhound (+2223) [1]

4976 מַתָּן ***mattān***, n.m.col. GK: 5508 [→ 4977, 4982, 4983; cf. 5414; cf. 4978]. gift, present:– gift [4], giveth gifts [1]

4977 מַתָּן ***mattān***, n.pr.m. GK: 5509 [→ 4976; cf. 5414]. Mattan, "*gift*":– Mattan [3]

4978 מַתְּנָה ***matt^e^nâ*** (Aram.), n.f. GK: 10448 [→ 5415; cf. 4976]. gift:– gifts [3]

4979 מַתָּנָה ***mattānâ***, n.f. GK: 5510 [→ 4980; cf. 5414]. gift, something given, such as an offering to deity or a bribe:– gifts [11], gift [5], able (+3027) [1]

4980 מַתָּנָה ***mattānâ***, n.pr.loc. GK: 5511 [→ 4979; cf. 5414]. Mattanah, "*gift*":– Mattanah [2]

4981 מִתְנִי ***mitnî***, a.g. GK: 5512 [→ 4975?]. Mithnite:– Mithnite [1]

4982 מַתְּנַי ***matt^e^nay***, n.pr.m. GK: 5513 [→ 4976+3068]. Mattenai, "*gift*":– Mattenai [3]

4983 מַתַּנְיָה ***mattanyâ*** or מַתַּנְיָהוּ ***mattanyāhû***, n.pr.m. GK: 5514 & 5515 [→ 4976+3068]. Mattaniah, "*gift of Yahweh*":– Mattaniah [16]

מָתְנַיִם ***motnayim***. See 4975.

4984 מִתְנַשֵּׂא ***mitnaśśē'***, v.ptcp. GK: 5951 [→ 4853, 4853, 4856, 4858, 4864, 5375, 5379, 5385, 5387, 7613, 7721, 7863?, 7865?; cf. 5376]. ptcp. of 5375: lifted up, exalted:– @H = **4985** מָתַק ***mātaq***

Heb

, v. GK: 5517 [→ 4477, 4966, 4986, 4987, 4988, 4989?]. same as 4988: [Q] to be, become sweet; [H] to taste sweet, enjoy sweetness:– sweet [3], made sweet [1], took sweet [1]

4986 מֶתֶק ***mātēq***, n.m. GK: 5518 [→ 4985]. sweetness; by extension: pleasantness:– sweetness [2]

4987 מֹתֶק ***mōteq***, n.[m.]. GK: 5519 [→ 4985]. sweetness:– sweetness [1]

4988 מָתַק ***mātaq***, v. GK: 5517 [→ 4985]. same as 4985: [Q] to be, become sweet:– feed sweetly on [1]

4989 מִתְקָה ***mitqâ***, n.pr.loc. GK: 5520 [→ 4985?]. Mithcah, "*sweetness*":– Mithcah [2]

4990 מִתְרְדָת ***mitrᵉdāt***, n.pr.m. GK: 5521. Mithredath, "*gift to Mithra*":– Mithredath [2]

4991 מַתָּת ***mattat***, n.f. GK: 5522 [→ 4993; cf. 5414]. gift, something given:– gift [3], give [2], reward [1]

4992 מַתַּתָּה ***mattattâ***, n.pr.m. GK: 5523 [→ 5414]. Mattathah, "*gift*":– Mattathah [1]

4993 מַתִּתְיָה ***mattityâ*** or מַתִּתְיָהוּ ***mattityāhû***, n.pr.m. GK: 5524 & 5525 [→ 4991+3068]. Mattithiah, "*gift of Yahweh*":– Mattithiah [8]

4993.1 ־ָן ***-ān*** or ־ן ***-n***, p.f.pl.suf. GK: 5527 [→ 1886.3, 2190]. they, them, their:– their [14], them [11], they [8], thereof [1]

4994 נָא ***nā'***, pt. GK: 5528 [→ 577]. often not translated, marks entreaty or exhortation: please!, I beg you!, now!:– now [167], I pray thee [150], I pray you [34], I beseech thee [22], we pray thee [10], we beseech thee [6], oh [5], go to [3], I pray [2], let [2], O [1]

4995 נָא ***nā'***, a. GK: 5529. raw (meat):– raw [1]

4996 נֹא ***nō'***, n.pr.loc. GK: 5530 [→ 527+4996]. No = Thebes:– no [5]

4996.1 ־נָא ***-nā'*** (Aram.), p.suf.1.com.pl. GK: 10450 [cf. 5105.1]. we, our:– us [7], our [2], we [1]

4997 נֹאד ***nō'd***, n.m. GK: 5532. skin vessel (skinned in one piece, the appendages tied or sewn, the neck the funnel, used to hold liquid):– bottle [4], bottles [2]

נְאַדְּרִי ***ne'dārî***. See 142.

4998 נָאָה ***nā'â***, v. GK: 5533 [→ 5000; cf. 5115]. [Pilel] to be beautiful, adorn:– beautiful [1], becometh [1], comely [1]

4999 נָוָה ***nāwâ***, n.f. GK: 5661 [→ 5380]. pasture, pastureland; (generally) abode, dwelling, camp, place:– habitations [5], pastures [5], houses [1], pleasant places [1]

5000 נָאוֶה ***nā'weh***, a. GK: 5534 [→ 4998]. lovely, fitting, suited:– comely [6], seemly [2], becometh [1]

5001 נָאַם ***nā'am***, v.den. GK: 5535 [→ 5002]. [Q] to declare as a prophet:– say [1]

5002 נְאֻם ***nᵉ'um***, n.m. GK: 5536 [→ 5001]. declaration, oracle, utterance; often a marker introducing or punctuating prophetic discourse:– saith [366], said [9], spake [1]

5003 נָאַף ***nā'ap***, v. GK: 5537 [→ 5005, 5004; cf. 5130]. [Q, P] to commit adultery; [ptcp.] adulterer, adulteress; by extension: to be unfaithful to God (by having illicit relations with other gods):– commit adultery [6], committed adultery [6], adulterers [5], committeth adultery [4], adulterer [3], adulteresses [2], adulteress [2], adulterous [1], break wedlock [1], committing adultery [1]

5004 נִאֻפִים ***ni'upîm***, n.[m.]. GK: 5539 [→ 5003]. adultery:– adulteries [2]

5005 נַאֲפוּפִים ***na'ᵃpûpîm***, n.[m.pl.]. GK: 5538 [→ 5003]. (marks of) unfaithfulness, adultery; such marks might refer to jewelry or adornments which signal that a woman is available for illicit sex:– adulteries [1]

5006 נָאַץ ***nā'aṣ***, v. GK: 5540 [→ 5007]. [Q] to spurn, despise, reject; [P] to treat with contempt, revile, despise; [Htpo] be blasphemed, be reviled:– despised [6], abhorred [2], blasphemed [2], given great occasion to blaspheme (+5006) [2], provoked [2], provoke [2], abhorreth [1], abhor [1], blaspheme [1], contemned [1], contemn [1], despiseth [1], despise [1], provoked unto anger [1]

5007 נְאָצָה ***nᵉ'āṣâ*** or נֶאָצָה ***ne'āṣâ***, n.f. GK: 5541 & 5542 [→ 5006]. disgrace, shame; contemptible things, blasphemies:– blasphemy [2], provocations [2], blasphemies [1]

5008 נָאַק ***nā'aq***, v. GK: 5543 [→ 5009; cf. 602]. [Q] to groan:– groan [2]

5009 נְאָקָה ***nᵉ'āqâ***, n.f. GK: 5544 [→ 5008; cf. 602]. groaning:– groanings [2], groaning [2]

5010 נָאַר ***nā'ar***, v. GK: 5545. [P] to renounce, abandon:– abhorred [1], made void [1]

5011 נֹב ***nōb***, n.pr.loc. GK: 5546. Nob:– Nob [6]

5012 נָבָא ***nābā'***, v.den. GK: 5547 [→ 5030; cf. 5013]. [N, Ht] to prophesy, speak as a prophet; prophecy has its focus on encouraging or restoring covenant faithfulness, the telling of future events encourages obedience or warns against disobedience:– prophesy [68], prophesied [40], prophesieth [3], maketh a prophet [2], prophesying [2]

5013 נְבָא ***nᵉbā'*** (Aram.), v. GK: 10451 [→ 5017, 5029; cf. 5012]. [Htpa] to prophesy, act as a prophet:– prophesied [1]

5014 נָבַב ***nābab***, v. GK: 5554 & 5548. [Q] to hollow out; by extension: to be foolish:– hollow [3], vain [1]

5015 נְבוֹ ***nᵉbô***, n.pr.m. & loc. GK: 5549 & 5550 & 5551 [→ (used with compound proper names)]. Nebo (pagan god), Nebo (loc.), "*height* or *Mount of Nabu [Nebo]*":– Nebo [13]

5016 נְבוּאָה ***nᵉbû'â***, n.f. GK: 5553 [→ 5030; cf. 5017]. prophecy, the word of the prophet; prophecy has its focus on encouraging or restoring covenant faithfulness, the telling of future events encourages obedience or warns against disobedience:– prophecy [3]

5017 נְבוּאָה ***nᵉbû'â*** (Aram.), n.f. GK: 10452 [→ 5013; cf. 5016]. prophesying, preaching:– prophesying [1]

5018 נְבוּזַרְאֲדָן ***nᵉbûzar'ᵃdān*** or נְבוּזַר־אֲדָן ***nᵉbûzar-'ᵃdān***, n.pr.m. GK: 5555 [→ 5015+2232]. Nebuzaradan, "*Nebo [Nabu] has given seed [offspring]*":– Nebuzar-adan [15]

5019 נְבוּכַדְנֶאצַּר ***nᵉbûkadne'ṣṣar*** or נְבוּכַדְנֶצַּר ***nᵉbûkadneṣṣar*** or נְבוּכַדְנֶצּוֹר ***nᵉbûkadneṣṣôr*** or נְבוּכַדְרֶאצַּר ***nᵉbûkadre'ṣṣar*** or נְבוּכַדְרֶאצּוֹר ***nebûkadre'ṣṣôr***, n.pr.m. GK: 5556 & 5557 [→ 5015; cf. 5020]. Nebuchadnezzar, Nebuchadrezzar, "*Nebo protect my boundary stone; Nebo protect my son!*":– Nebuchadrezzar [31], Nebuchadnezzar [29]

5020 נְבוּכַדְנֶצַּר ***nᵉbûkadneṣṣar*** (Aram.), n.pr.m. GK: 10453 [cf. 5019]. Nebuchadnezzar, "*Nebo protect my boundary stone* or *Nebo protect my son!*":– Nebuchadnezzar [31]

5021 נְבוּשַׁזְבָּן ***nᵉbûšazbān*** or נְבוּשַׁז־בָּן ***nᵉbûšaz-bān***, n.pr.m. GK: 5558 [→ 5015]. Nebushazban, "*Nebo [Nabu] save me!*":– Nebushasban [1]

5022 נָבוֹת ***nābôt***, n.pr.m. GK: 5559. Naboth, "*sprout*":– Naboth [22]

5023 נְבִזְבָּה ***nᵉbizbâ*** (Aram.), n.f. GK: 10454. present, gift; this can be a gift given as a recompense for a proper service, a reward:– rewards [2]

5024 נָבַח ***nābaḥ***, v. GK: 5560 [→ 5025?]. [Q] to bark:– bark [1]

5025 נֹבַח ***nōbaḥ***, n.pr.m. & loc. GK: 5561 & 5562 [→ 5024?]. Nobah, "*barking*":– Nobah [3]

5026 נִבְחַז ***nibḥaz***, n.pr.[m.]. GK: 5563. Nibhaz (pagan god):– Nibhaz [1]

5027 נָבַט ***nābaṭ***, v. GK: 5564 [→ 4007, 5028]. [P] to look at; [H] to look at, gaze at, consider:– look [21], looked [11], behold [9], consider [5], regard [4], see [4], looketh [3], have respect [2], look down [2], beheld (+413) [1], beheld [1], beholdest [1], cause to behold [1], look upon [1], looked about [1], lookest [1], respect [1]

5028 נְבָט ***nᵉbāṭ***, n.pr.m. GK: 5565 [→ 5027]. Nebat, "*look to, regard [approvingly]*":– Nebat [25]

5029 נְבִיא ***nᵉbî'*** (Aram.), n.m. GK: 10455 [→ 5013; cf. 5030]. prophet, one who speaks for God in inspired utterance, often including the application of the message:– prophets [2], prophet [2]

5030 נָבִיא ***nābî'***, n.m. GK: 5566 [→ 5012, 5016, 5031; cf. 5029]. prophet (true or false):– prophet [165], prophets [147], prophecy [1], prophesy [1], prophet's [1]

5031 נְבִיאָה ***nᵉbî'â***, n.f. GK: 5567 [→ 5030]. prophetess (true or false):– prophetess [6]

5032 נְבָיוֹת ***nᵉbāyôt***, n.pr.g. GK: 5568. Nebaioth:– Nebajoth [5]

5033 נֵבֶךְ ***nēbek***, n.[m.]. GK: 5569. source springs (of the sea):– springs [1]

5034 נָבֵל ***nābēl***, v. GK: 5570 & 5571 [→ 5036, 5037, 5038, 5039, 5040?]. [Q] to wither, shrivel, fade, decay; to play the fool, act disdainfully; [P] to treat with contempt, dishonor, reject:– fadeth [3], fade [3], fade away [2], fadeth away [2], fading [2], surely wear away (+5034) [2], wither [2], cometh to nought [1], disgrace [1], dishonoureth [1], done foolishly [1], fall down [1], falleth off [1], falling [1], lightly esteemed [1], make vile [1]

5035 נֵבֶל ***nēbel***, n.m. GK: 5574 & 5575 [→ 3999]. (wine) skin; water jar, jug, pot (of clay); lyre, harp (stringed instrument):– psalteries [14], psaltery [8], bottle [5], bottles [3], viols [2], viol [2], flagons [1], pitchers [1], psaltery (+3627) [1], vessel [1]

5036 נָבָל ***nābāl***, a. GK: 5572 [→ 5037; cf. 5034]. foolish, lacking understanding, (n.) fool; often pertaining to insolence, pride, and disobedience to God:– foolish [7], fool [7], fools [2], vile person [2]

5037 נָבָל ***nābāl***, n.pr.m. GK: 5573 [→ 5036; cf. 5034]. Nabal, "*fool*":– Nabal [18], Nabal's [4]

5038 נְבֵלָה ***nᵉbēlâ***, n.f. GK: 5577 [→ 5034]. dead body, carcass:– carcase [28], carcases [7], dead body [3], dead bodies [2], dieth of itself [2], beast that dieth of itself [1], body [1], dead carcase [1], that is dead of itself [1], that which died of itself [1], that which dieth of itself [1]

5039 נְבָלָה ***nᵉbālâ***, n.f. GK: 5576 [→ 5034]. (very) wicked thing, disgraceful thing; vileness, something a fool would do:– folly [10], villany [2], vile [1]

5040 נַבְלוּת ***nablût***, n.f. GK: 5578 [→ 5034?]. (female) genitals:– lewdness [1]

5041 נְבַלָּט ***nᵉballāṭ***, n.pr.loc. GK: 5579. Neballat:– Neballat [1]

5042 נָבַע ***nāba'***, v. GK: 5580 [→ 76, 4002]. [H] to gush forth, bubble out, spew forth:– utter [3], poureth out [2], abundantly utter [1], belch out [1], cause to send forth [1], flowing [1], pour out [1], uttereth [1]

5043 נֶבְרְשָׁה ***nebrᵉšâ*** (Aram.), n.f.emph. GK: 10456. lampstand:– candlestick [1]

5044 נִבְשָׁן ***nibšān***, n.pr.loc. GK: 5581. Nibshan:– Nibshan [1]

5045 נֶגֶב ***negeb***, n.[pr.m.]. GK: 5582 [→ 7418]. south, the Negev:– south [88], southward (+1886.5) [13], south side [5], south (+1886.5) [2], south (+4480) [1], southward (+4480) [1], southward (+871.1+1886.1) [1], southward [1]

5046 נָגַד ***nāgad***, v. GK: 5583 [→ 5048, 5057; cf. 5047]. [H] to tell, report, inform; [Ho] to be told, have reported to:– told [150], tell [66], declare [45], shew [34], shewed [18], declared [13], sheweth [5], surely tell (+5046) [4], declareth [3], utter [3], certainly declare (+5046) [2], certainly told (+5046) [2], fully been shewed (+5046) [2], messenger [2], report [2], shew forth [2], telleth [2], told plainly (+5046) [2], uttered [2], another[S] [1], bewrayeth [1], certify [1], declaring [1], denounce [1], expounded [1], expound [1], profess [1], rehearsed [1], sheweth forth [1], speaketh [1]

5047 נְגַד ***nᵉgad*** (Aram.), v. GK: 10457 [→ 5049; cf. 5046]. [P] to flow:– issued [1]

5048 נֶגֶד ***neged***, subst. & adv. & pp. GK: 5584 [→ 5046; cf. 5049]. before, in front of, opposite of, beyond:– before [59], before (+3807.1) [18], over against [16], against [6], in (+3807.1) [4], in the presence [4], over against (+3807.1) [4], presence [4], before (+4480) [3], from (+4480) [3], over against (+4480) [3], against (+4480) [2], meet for (+3509.1) [2], straight before [2], view (+4480) [2], about [1], afar off (+4480) [1], against (+3807.1) [1], aloof from (+4480) [1], before (+6440) [1], far (+4480) [1], far off (+4480) [1], in presence [1], in the sight [1], in [1], of (+4480) [1], on the other side (+4480) [1], other side [1], over (+3807.1) [1], over [1], right against [1], sight [1], withstand (+5975) [1], withstood (+5975+3807.1) [1]

5049 נֶגֶד ***neged*** (Aram.), pp. GK: 10458 [→ 5047; cf. 5048]. toward, before, facing:– toward [1]

5050 נָגַהּ ***nāgah***, v. GK: 5585 [→ 5051, 5052, 5054]. [Q] to shine; [H] to cause to shine, give light:– shine [2], cause to shine [1], enlighten [1], lighten [1], shined [1]

5051 נֹגַהּ ***nōgah***, n.f. GK: 5586 [→ 5052; cf. 5050; cf. 5053]. brightness, radiance, splendor, brilliance:– brightness [11], shining [5], bright [1], clear shining [1], light [1]

5052 נֹגַהּ ***nōgah***, n.pr.m. GK: 5587 [→ 5051; cf. 5050]. Nogah, "*joy, splendor*":– Nogah [2]

5053 נְגַהּ ***nᵉgah*** (Aram.), n.[f.]. GK: 10459 [cf. 5051]. brightness (i.e., first light of dawn):– morning [1]

5054 נְגֹהָה ***nᵉgōhâ***, n.f. GK: 5588 [→ 5050]. brightness, luster:– brightness [1]

5055 נָגַח ***nāgaḥ***, v. GK: 5590 [→ 5056]. [Q] to gore (a bull into a person); [P] to gore, push back, butt; to engage in pushing back, butting, thrusting:– push [5], gored [2], gore [1], push down [1], pushing [1], pusht [1]

5056 נַגָּח **naggāḥ**, a. GK: 5591 [→ 5055]. (the act of) goring (a bull into a person):– used to push [1], wont to push with his horn [1]

5057 נָגִיד **nāgîd**, n.m. GK: 5592 [→ 5046]. leader, ruler, official, officer:– ruler [18], prince [8], captain [5], leader [3], captains [1], chief governor [1], chief ruler [1], chief [1], excellent things [1], governor [1], leaders [1], nobles [1], princes [1], rulers [1]

5058 נְגִינָה **n^{e}gînâ**, n.f. GK: 5593 [→ 5059]. stringed instrument; song that mocks, taunts:– Neginoth [6], song [4], Neginah [1], musick [1], songs [1], stringed instruments [1]

5059 נָגַן **nāgan**, v. GK: 5594 [→ 4485, 5058]. [Q] to play a stringed instrument, (n.) musician; [P] to play a stringed instrument:– played [4], play [3], minstrel [2], melody [1], play on an instrument [1], players on instruments [1], player [1], playing [1], sing the stringed instruments [1]

5060 נָגַע **nāga'**, v. GK: 5595 [→ 5061]. [Q] to touch; to strike; [Qp] to be plagued, be stricken; [N] to let oneself be driven back (in a battle); [P] to inflict, afflict; [Pu] to be plagued; [H] to extend, reach out, cause to touch; ranging in meaning from simple contact to violence:– toucheth [37], touch [31], touched [24], come [10], came [6], reacheth [4], reach [4], plagued [3], reaching [3], smote [3], bring [2], happeneth [2], beaten [1], bring down [1], bringeth [1], brought down [1], cast [1], come close [1], come nigh [1], cometh [1], draw near [1], draw nigh [1], draweth near [1], draweth nigh [1], drew near [1], getteth up [1], join [1], laid [1], near [1], reached [1], smitten [1], stricken [1], strike [1]

5061 נֶגַע **nega'**, n.m. GK: 5596 [→ 5060]. plague, blow (of various kinds): mildew, infection, sores, scourge, disaster:– plague [64], sore [5], stroke [4], stripes [2], plagues [1], stricken [1], wound [1]

5062 נָגַף **nāgap**, v. GK: 5597 [→ 4046, 5063]. [Q] to strike, afflict (with a plague); [N] to be defeated:– smitten [12], smite [9], smote [6], put to the worse [5], hurt [2], plagued [2], slain [2], smitten down (+5062) [2], smitten down [2], stumble [2], beaten [1], dash [1], plague [1], strake [1], struck [1]

5063 נֶגֶף **negep**, n.m. GK: 5598 [→ 5062]. plague; stumbling (caused by a stone):– plague [6], stumbling [1]

5064 נָגַר **nāgar**, v. GK: 5599 [cf. 1641]. [N] to be spilled, flow; [H] to pour out, hand over, deliver over; [Ho] to be poured down (a slope):– fall [1], flow away [1], pour down [1], pour out [1], poured [1], poureth out [1], ran [1], shed [1], spilt [1], trickleth down [1]

5065 נָגַשׂ **nāgaś**, v. GK: 5601 [cf. 5066]. [Q] to oppress, exploit, (n.) a slave driver; [N] to be oppressed, be hard pressed:– oppressor [5], taskmasters [5], exact [3], distressed [2], oppressed [2], oppressors [2], driver [1], exacted [1], exactors [1], taxes [1]

5066 נָגַשׁ **nāgaš**, v. GK: 5602 [cf. 5065]. [Q] to come near, approach; [N] to come near, approach; [H] to bring forth, present; [Ho] to be brought, be presented; [Ht] to draw near, assemble:– came near [17], come near [16], came [9], brought [8], come nigh [7], bring hither [6], come [6], drew near [6], draw near [5], approach [4], bring [4], offer [4], brought near [3], drew nigh [3], went near [3], bring forth [2], bring near [2], offered [2], overtake [2], approached nigh [1], brought forth [1], brought thither [1], came nigh [1], cause to come near [1], give place [1], go near [1], go [1], make to approach [1], near [1], offereth [1], presented [1], put [1], stand [1], went hard [1], went nigh [1]

5067 נֵד **nēd**, n.m. GK: 5603. heap, wall, barrier, dam:– heap [6]

5068 נָדַב **nādab**, v. GK: 5605 [→ 5070, 5071, 5081, 5082; cf. 5069 (also used with compound proper names)]. [Q] to be willing; to prompt, incite; [Ht] to willingly offer oneself, volunteer, give a freewill offering:– willingly offered [6], offered willingly [4], made willing [2], offer willingly [2], giveth willingly [1], offered freely [1], willing [1]

5069 נְדַב **n^{e}dab** (Aram.), v. GK: 10461 [cf. 5068]. [Htpa] to be willing, to give freely; (as noun) a freewill offering:– freely offered [1], freewill offering [1], minded of own freewill [1], offering willingly [1]

5070 נָדָב **nādāb**, n.pr.m. GK: 5606 [→ 5072; cf. 5068]. Nadab, "*volunteer, free will offering*":– Nadab [20]

5071 נְדָבָה **n^{e}dābâ**, n.f. GK: 5607 [→ 5068]. free, voluntary; freewill offering:– freewill offering [8], freewill offerings [7], free offerings [2], freely (+871.1) [1], freely [1], plentiful [1], voluntarily [1], voluntary offering [1], voluntary [1], willing offering [1], willingly (+3807.1) [1], willing [1]

5072 נְדַבְיָה **n^{e}dabyâ**, n.pr.m. GK: 5608 [→ 5070]. Nedabiah, "*Yahweh volunteers*":– Nedabiah [1]

5073 נִדְבָּךְ **nidbāk** (Aram.), n.m. GK: 10462. course (of timber or stone in building):– rows [1], row [1]

5074 נָדַד **nādad**, v. GK: 5610 [→ 5076; cf. 5077, 5110; cf. 5075]. [Q] to flee, be a fugitive; to wander, stray; [Pol] to flee away; [H] to banish, put to flight; [Ho] to be banished, be cast aside:– fled [8], wandereth [4], flee apace (+5074) [2], flee away [2], chased away [1], chased [1], could not [1], departed [1], flee [1], moved [1], removed [1], thrust away [1], wanderers [1], wandereth abroad [1], wandering [1], wander [1]

5075 נְדַד **n^{e}dad** (Aram.), v. GK: 10463 [cf. 5111; cf. 5074]. [P] to flee (i.e., sleep flees = insomnia):– went [1]

5076 נְדֻדִים **n^{e}dudîm**, n.[m.pl.]. GK: 5611 [→ 5074]. tossing and turning, restlessness (in bed in the night):– tossings to and fro [1]

5077 נָדָא **nādā'** or נָדָה **nādâ**, v. GK: 5604 & 5612 [→ 5079, 5206; cf. 5074, 5110]. [P] to exclude; to put off thoughts, suppose to be far off; [H] detach, remove from:– cast out [1], put far away [1]

5078 נֵדֶה **nēdeh**, n.m. GK: 5613. gift, reward; likely referring to a fee for service:– gifts [1]

5079 נִדָּה **niddâ**, n.[m.]. GK: 5614 [→ 5206; cf. 5077]. period of menstruation; (water used in) cleansing, "unclean" water; (act of) impurity, corruption, defilement:– separation [14], filthiness [2], flowers [2], menstruous [2], put apart [2], far [1], removed woman [1], removed [1], that was set apart [1], unclean thing [1], uncleanness [1], unclean [1]

5080 נָדַח **nādaḥ**, v. GK: 5615 & 5616 [→ 4065; cf. 1740, 1760]. [Q] to wield (an ax); (to have hand) be put (to the ax); [N] to be scattered, be exiled, be outcast; [Pu] be thrust into; [H] to cause to scatter, banish, drive out; to bring; [Ho] to be driven, be hunted:– driven [15], driven away [4], driven out [4], outcasts [4], cast out [3], drive [3], banished [2], drive out [2], bring [1], cast down [1], chased [1], compelled [1], drave [1], drawn away [1], expelled [1], fetcheth a stroke [1], forced [1], forcing [1], go astray [1], outcast [1], thrust away [1], thrust [1], withdrawn [1]

5081 נָדִיב **nādîb**, a. (used as noun). GK: 5618 [→ 5082; cf. 5068]. willing, generous; prince, noble, ruler, official:– princes [10], nobles [4], prince [4], willing [3], free [2], liberal [2], prince's [1]

5082 נְדִיבָה **n^{e}dîbâ**, n.f. GK: 5619 [→ 5081; cf. 5068]. something noble; dignity, nobility:– liberal [2], soul [1]

5083 נָדָן **nādān**, n.[m.]. GK: 5621 [cf. 5414]. gift, wages of illicit sexual favors:– gifts [1]

5084 נָדָן **nādān**, n.[m.]. GK: 5620 [cf. 5085]. sheath (of a sword):– sheath [1]

5085 נִדְנֶה **nidneh** (Aram.), n.[m.]. GK: 10464. sheath (of the spirit = the body):– body [1]

5086 נָדַף **nādap**, v. GK: 5622. [Q] to blow away, scatter; [N] to be windblown, be fleeting:– driven away [2], drive away [1], driven to and fro [1], driven [1], driveth away [1], shaken [1], thrusteth down [1], tossed to and fro [1]

5087 נָדַר **nādar**, v. GK: 5623 [→ 5088; cf. 5144, 5145]. [Q] to make a vow:– vowed [16], vow [10], vowest [2], made [1], vowedst [1], voweth [1]

5088 נֵדֶר **nēder**, n.m. GK: 5624 [→ 5087]. vow:– vows [30], vow [28], make a singular vow (+6381) [1], vowed [1]

5089 נֹהַּ **nōah**, n.[m.]. GK: 5625. value, distinction:– wailing [1]

5089.1 נָה- **-nâ**, p.f.s.suf. GK: 5626 [→ 1886.3]. her; it, its:– it [121], her [27], the same [11], them [9], she [5], thereof (+4480) [3], they [3], thence [2], therefrom (+4480) [2], thereof [2], by themselves (+905+3807.1) [1], their [1], therein [1], thereon [1], these things [1], this [1]

5090 נָהַג **nāhag**, v. GK: 5627 & 5628 [→ 4491, cf. 5101]. [Q] to drive, lead, guide; [Qp] to be led; [P] to drive, lead forth, guide; to moan, sob, lament:– lead [7], drave [4], carried away [3], brought [2], lead away [2], led forth [2], led [2], acquainting [1], brought away [1], brought in [1], drive away [1], driveth [1], drive [1], guided [1], guide [1], leadest [1]

5091 נָהָה **nāhâ**, v. GK: 5629 & 5630 [→ 5092, 5093, 5204]. [Q] to mourn, wail; [N] to be taunted (with a mournful song); to keep close, stay loyal:– lamented [1], lament [1], wail [1]

5092 נְהִי **n^{e}hî**, n.[m.]. GK: 5631 [→ 5204; cf. 5091]. wailing, mourning, often related to mournful songs: lamentation:– wailing [4], lamentation [2]

5093 נִהְיָה **nihyâ**, n.f. GK: 5632 [→ 5091]. wailing, lamentation, mourning:– doleful lamentation [1]

5094 נְהִיר **n^{e}hîr** or נַהִירוּ **nahîrû** (Aram.), n.m. GK: 10466 & 10467 [cf. 5105]. light; insight, illumination (of the mind):– light [3]

5095 נָהַל **nāhal**, v. GK: 5633 [→ 5096, 5097]. [P] guide, bring along, lead; [Ht] to move along:– guide [3], guided [2], carried [1], fed [1], gently lead [1], lead on [1], leadeth [1]

5096 נַהֲלָל **nah^{a}lāl** or נַהֲלֹל **nah^{a}lōl**, n.pr.loc. GK: 5634 & 5636 [→ 5095, 5097]. Nahalal, Nahalol, "*watering place*":– Nahalal [1], Nahallal [1], Nahalol [1]

5097 נַהֲלֹל **nah^{a}lōl**, n.m. GK: 5635 [→ 5096; cf. 5095]. watering hole:– bushes [1]

5098 נָהַם **nāham**, v. GK: 5637 [→ 5099, 5100; cf. 1949, 1993, 2000]. [Q] to growl, roar; to groan:– mourn [2], roar [2], roaring [1]

5099 נַהַם **naham**, n.[m.]. GK: 5638 [→ 5098]. roaring, growling:– roaring [2]

5100 נְהָמָה **n^{e}hāmâ**, n.f. GK: 5639 [→ 5098]. roaring, growling; anguish, groaning:– disquietness [1], roaring [1]

5101 נָהַק **nāhaq**, v. GK: 5640 [cf. 5090]. [Q] to bray (of a donkey):– brayed [1], bray [1]

5102 נָהַר **nāhar**, v. GK: 5641 & 5642 [→ 5104, 5105; cf. 5216]. [Q] to stream to (like a river flow); to be radiant (with joy), beam (with joy):– flow [5], lightened [1]

5103 נְהַר **n^{e}har** (Aram.), n.m. GK: 10468 [cf. 5104]. river, stream:– river [14], stream [1]

5104 נָהָר **nāhār**, n.m. GK: 5643 [→ 763, 5102; cf. 5103]. river, stream, canal; the River, which can refer to the Euphrates, Tigris, or Nile:– river [67], rivers [31], floods [10], flood [8], streams [2], river side [1]

5105 נְהָרָה **n^{e}hārâ**, n.f. GK: 5644 [→ 5102; cf. 5094]. (beaming) light:– light [1]

5105.1 נוּ- **-nû**, p.com.pl.suf. GK: 5646 [→ 2967.1]. us, our:– us [775], our [749], we [67], our (+3807.1) [13], our own [8], ours (+3807.1) [5], ourselves [4], it [1], ours [1], thereof (+4480) [1], us-ward (+413) [1], we (+5315) [1]

5105.2 נוּ- **-nû** or נוֹ- **-nô**, p.m.s.suf. GK: 5647 [→ 1886.3]. him, his; it, its:– him [217], it [120], them [36], he [34], thereof (+4480) [16], thereof [12], the same [4], they [4], his [2], themselves [2], thereat (+4480) [2], every one of them [1], him (+5315) [1], himself [1], the^{S} [1], their [1], thence [1], thereby [1], therefrom (+4480) [1], thereout (+4480) [1], therewith [1], which [1], whom (+834) [1], whom [1], whosoever (+834) [1]

5106 נוּא **nû'**, v. GK: 5648 [→ 8569]. [Q] to hinder; [H] to forbid, thwart, discourage:– disallowed [2], disallow [2], break [1], discouraged [1], discourage [1], maketh of none effect [1]

5107 נוּב **nûb**, v. GK: 5649 [→ 1838, 5108, 8570]. [Q] to bring forth, bear fruit, increase; [Pol] to make thrive:– bring forth fruit [1], bringeth forth [1], increase [1], make cheerful [1]

5108 נוֹב **nôb** or נִיב **nîb**, n.[m.]. GK: 5650 & 5762 [→ 5107]. fruit; "fruit of the lips" is praise:– fruit [2]

5109 נוֹבַי **nôbāy** or נֵיבָי **nêbāy**, n.pr.m. GK: 5651 & 5763. Nebai, Nobai, "*thrive*":– Nebai [1]

5110 נוּד **nûd**, v. GK: 5653 [→ 4493, 5112, 5113, 5205; cf. 5074, 5077; cf. 5111]. [Q] to sway, wander, be aimless, become homeless; to mourn, express sympathy (by shaking the head:– bemoan [5], remove [4], vagabond [2], bemoaned [1], bemoaning [1], flee [1], get [1], make move [1], mourn [1], removed [1], shaken [1], skippedst for joy [1], sorry [1], take pity [1], wag [1], wandering [1]

5111 נוּד **nûd** (Aram.), v. GK: 10469 [cf. 5075; cf. 5110]. [P] to flee:– get away [1]

5112 נוֹד **nôd**, n.[m.]. GK: 5654 [→ 5110]. lament; some sources: wandering, homelessness:– wanderings [1]

5113 נוֹד **nôd**, n.pr.loc. GK: 5655 [→ 5110]. Nod, "*wandering*":– Nod [1]

5114 נוֹדָב **nôdāb**, n.pr.g. GK: 5656. Nodab:– Nodab [1]

5115 נָוָה **nāwâ**, v. GK: 5657 & 5658 [→ 5116; cf. 4998]. [Q] to be at rest, reach one's aim; [H] to praise:– keepeth at home [1], prepare a habitation [1]

5116 נָוֶה **nāweh**, n.m. GK: 5659 & 5660 [→ 5115, 4999; cf. 4998]. dwelling, abiding; pasture, pastureland, with a possible focus that this is a place of rest and peace; (generally) abode, dwelling, house:– habitation [21], fold [3], dwelling [2], sheepcote [2], comely [1], dwelling place [1], dwellings [1], folds [1], habitations [1], pleasant place [1], stable [1], tarried [1]

5117 נוּחַ nûaḥ, v. GK: 5663 & 5664 [→ 3240; cf. 584]. [Q] to settle, rest, wait; to lament, wail; [H] to put, keep, settle, rest; to leave, allow; [Ho] to be placed, find rest:– rest [15], given rest [12], rested [7], cause to rest [4], give rest [4], at rest [3], caused to rest [3], gave rest [3], resteth [2], ceased [1], confederate [1], giveth rest [1], lay [1], let down [1], make to rest [1], quieted [1], quiet [1], remain [1], set down [1], set [1]

5118 נוֹחַ nôaḥ, n.f. GK: 5665 [→ 5119; cf. 3240]. resting place:– rested [2], resting place [1], rest [1]

5119 נוֹחָה nôḥâ, n.pr.m. GK: 5666 [→ 5118?; cf. 3240]. Nohah, "*rest*":– Nohah [1]

5120 נוּט nûṭ, v. GK: 5667. [Q] to shake, quake:– moved [1]

5121 נָוֹות nāwôt or **נָוִית nāwît**, n.pr.loc. GK: 5662 & 5668 & 5766. Navoth, Navith, Naioth, "*dwellings*":– Naioth [6]

5122 נְוָלוּ nᵉwālû (Aram.), n.f. GK: 10470. pile of rubble, garbage-heap:– dunghill [3]

5123 נוּם nûm, v. GK: 5670 [→ 3241?, 5124, 8572]. [Q] to sleep, slumber, implying detachment from activities and others; by extension: to be dead:– slumber [5], slept [1]

5124 נוּמָה nûmâ, n.f. GK: 5671 [→ 5123]. drowsiness:– drowsiness [1]

5125 נוּן nûn, v. GK: 5672 [cf. 5126?]. [N] to propagate, increase:– continued [1]

5126 נוּן nûn, n.pr.m. GK: 5673 [cf. 5125?]. Nun, "*fish* hence *fertile, productive*":– Nun [29], Non [1]

5127 נוּס nûs, v. GK: 5674 [→ 4498, 4499, 5211]. [Q] to flee away, escape; [Pol] to drive along; [H] to put to flight, get to safety:– fled [80], flee [52], flee away [8], fleeth [5], fled away [3], flee away (+5127) [2], abated [1], displayed [1], fled apace (+4498) [1], fleddest [1], fleeing [1], hide [1], lift up a standard [1], made flee [1], put to flight [1], ran away [1]

5128 נוּעַ nûa', v. GK: 5675 [→ 4517]. [Q] to shake, sway, swagger, wander; [N] to be shaken; [H] to make wander, to set trembling, shake, toss:– moved [5], promoted [3], shaken [3], wandered [3], continually vagabonds (+5128) [2], fugitive [2], reel to and fro (+5128) [2], shake [2], stagger [2], wag [2], wander [2], gone away [1], made wander [1], make [1], moveable [1], move [1], removed [1], scatter [1], set [1], shaked [1], sifted [1], sift [1], wander up and down [1]

5129 נוֹעַדְיָה nô'adyâ, n.pr.m. & f. GK: 5676 [→ 3259+3068]. Noadiah, "*meet with Yahweh*":– Noadiah [2]

5130 נוּף nûp, v. GK: 5677 & 5678 [→ 5299, 5317, 8573; cf. 5003]. [Q] to sprinkle with myrrh (a bed); [Pol] to wave (the fist) threateningly; [H] to wave, present (an offering) by waving; to shake, wield, sweep; to cause (rain) to fall; [Ho] to be waved:– wave [11], shake [5], waved [5], lift up [4], offer [3], offered [2], shaketh [2], move [1], perfumed [1], send [1], sift [1], strike [1]

5131 נוֹף nôp, n.[m.]. GK: 5679 [→ 5299, 5316]. loftiness, elevation, height:– situation [1]

5132 נוּץ nûṣ, v. GK: 5680. [Q] to leave, go away:– fled away [1]

5133 נֹצָה nōṣâ or **נוֹצָה nôṣâ**, n.f. GK: 5901 & 5902 & 5681. contents (of a bird's crop); plumage, feathers; falcon or other bird:– feathers [4]

5134 נוּק nûq, v. GK: 5682 [cf. 3243]. [H] to suckle, nurse:– nursed [1]

5135 נוּר nûr (Aram.), n.f. & m. GK: 10471 [cf. 5216]. fire; used for heat, purification, and as a form of execution:– fiery [10], fire [7]

5136 נוּשׁ nûš, v. GK: 5683 [cf. 605]. [Q] to be sick:– full of heaviness [1]

5137 נָזָה nāzâ, v. GK: 5684 & 5685. [Q] to spatter; [H] to sprinkle; to leap, spring:– sprinkle [17], sprinkled [6], sprinkleth [1]

5138 נָזִיד nāzîd, n.[m.]. GK: 5686 [→ 2102]. stew, thick boiled food:– pottage [6]

5139 נָזִיר nāzîr, n.m. GK: 5687 [→ 5144]. Nazirite, with the designated meaning of separation; a class of people dedicated to God; untended vine, dedicated to God in the sabbatical year of rest:– Nazarite [9], Nazarites [3], vine undressed [2], separate from [1], separated from [1]

5140 נָזַל nāzal, v. GK: 5688 & 5689. [Q] to flow down, pour down, stream down; [H] to make flow:– floods [3], streams [2], caused to flow [1], distil [1], drop [1], flow out [1], flowing [1], flow [1], gush out [1], melted [1], pour down [1], pour [1], running waters [1]

5141 נֶזֶם nezem, n.m. GK: 5690. ring (in the nose or ear of male or female):– earrings [9], earring [5], jewel [2], jewels [1]

5142 נְזַק nᵉzaq (Aram.), v. GK: 10472 [cf. 5143]. [P] to suffer loss; [H] to cause to suffer, be a detriment, be troublesome:– damage [1], endamage [1], hurtful [1], hurt [1]

5143 נֵזֶק nēzeq, n.[m.]. GK: 5691 [cf. 5142]. burden, trouble:– damage [1]

5144 נָזַר nāzar, v. GK: 5692 & 5693 [→ 5139, 5145; cf. 4502, 5087]. [N] to separate oneself, consecrate oneself; [H] to keep separate; to abstain, separate as a Nazirite:– separate [4], separateth [3], consecrate [1], separated [1], separating [1]

5145 נֵזֶר nēzer, n.m. GK: 5694 [→ 5144; cf. 5087]. separation, dedication (to God); diadem, crown (as a sign of consecration); Nazirite, a class of people dedicated to God:– crown [11], separation [11], consecration [2], hair [1]

5146 נֹחַ nōaḥ, n.pr.m. GK: 5695 [→ 5162]. Noah, "*rest, comfort*":– Noah [44], Noah's [2]

5147 נַחְבִּי naḥbî, n.pr.m. GK: 5696. Nahbi, "[perhaps] *hidden* or *timid*":– Nahbi [1]

5148 נָחָה nāḥâ, v. GK: 5697. [Q, H] to lead, guide:– lead [16], guide [4], led [4], bringeth [2], brought [2], guided [2], leddest [2], bestowed [1], govern [1], leadeth [1], led forth [1], led on [1], put [1], straiteneth [1]

5149 נְחוּם nᵉḥûm, n.pr.m. GK: 5700 [cf. 7348]. Nehum, "*comfort*":– Nehum [1]

5150 נִחֻמִים niḥumîm, n.m.[pl.]. GK: 5719 [→ 5162]. comfort, compassion:– comfortable [1], comforts [1], repentings [1]

5151 נַחוּם naḥûm, n.pr.m. GK: 5699 [→ 5162]. Nahum, "*comfort*":– Nahum [1]

5152 נָחוֹר nāḥôr, n.pr.m. GK: 5701. Nahor, "*the mound of Nahuru*":– Nahor [15], Nahor's [2], Nachor [1]

5153 נָחוּשׁ nāḥûš, a. GK: 5702 [→ 5178]. (made) of bronze:– brass [1]

5154 נְחוּשָׁה nᵉḥûšâ, n.f. GK: 5703 [→ 5178; cf. 5174]. copper, bronze:– brass [7], steel [3]

5155 נְחִילוֹת nᵉḥîlôt, n.f. GK: 5704 [→ 2485?; cf. 2490?]. flutes (a t.t. in Ps 5):– Nehiloth [1]

5156 נָחִיר nāḥîr, n.[m.]. GK: 5705 [→ 5170, 5170]. (dual) nostrils:– nostrils [1]

5157 נָחַל nāḥal, v.den. GK: 5706 [→ 5159]. [Q] to take as an appearance, take possession; [P] to assign an inheritance, allot; [H] to cause to inherit, give an inheritance; [Ho] to be allotted; [Ht] to obtain an inheritance for oneself; to distribute an inheritance:– inherit [16], cause to inherit [5], inherited [3], possess [3], giveth to inherit [2], have inheritance (+5159) [2], cause to possess [1], caused to inherit [1], distribute for inheritance [1], distributed for inheritance [1], divide an inheritance among [1], divide by inheritance [1], divide for an inheritance [1], divide inheritance unto [1], divided for an inheritance [1], divided inheritance [1], divide [1], dividing for inheritance [1], give inheritance [1], given for an inheritance [1], had [1], have inheritance [1], inheritance [1], inheriteth [1], leave for an inheritance [1], leaveth an inheritance [1], made to possess [1], make inherit [1], maketh to inherit [1], possession [1], take as inheritance [1], take for inheritance [1], taken as an heritage [1], took inheritance [1]

5158 נַחַל naḥal or **נַחְלָה naḥᵃlâ**, n.m. & loc. GK: 5707 & 5711 [→ 5160]. river, stream, brook, torrent; ravine, gorge, valley; wadi (of Egypt):– river [46], brook [37], valley [18], brooks [9], rivers [8], stream [7], valleys [5], streams [4], flood [3], floods [2]

5159 נַחֲלָה naḥᵃlâ, n.f. GK: 5709 [→ 5157]. inheritance, property:– inheritance [188], heritage [26], have inheritance (+5157) [2], inherit [2], river [2], have inheritance (+5307) [1], heritages [1], inheritances [1], possession [1]

5160 נַחֲלִיאֵל naḥᵃlî'ēl, n.pr.loc. GK: 5712 [→ 5158+410]. Nahaliel, "*wadi of God [El]*":– Nahaliel [2]

5161 נֶחֱלָמִי neḥᵉlāmî, a.g. GK: 5713. Nehelamite:– Nehelamite [3]

5162 נָחַם nāḥam, v. GK: 5714 [→ 4505, 5146, 5151, 5149, 5163, 5164, 5165, 5166, 5150, 5167, 8575, 8576]. [N] to relent, repent, change one's mind; be grieved; [P] to comfort, console, express sympathy; [Pu] to be comforted, be consoled; [Ht] to console oneself; to change one's mind; avenge oneself:– comfort [32], comforted [20], repent [19], repented [17], comforters [5], comforter [4], comforteth [3], repenteth [3], comfortedst [1], ease [1], receive comfort [1], repentest [1], repenting [1]

5163 נַחַם naḥam, n.pr.m. GK: 5715 [→ 5162]. Naham, "*repent, console*":– Naham [1]

5164 נֹחַם nōḥam, n.m. GK: 5716 [→ 5162]. compassion, pity:– repentance [1]

5165 נֶחָמָה neḥāmâ, n.f. GK: 5717 [→ 5162]. comfort, consolation:– comfort [2]

5166 נְחֶמְיָה nᵉḥemyâ, n.pr.m. GK: 5718 [→ 5162+3068]. Nehemiah, "*Yahweh has comforted*":– Nehemiah [8]

5167 נַחֲמָנִי naḥᵃmānî, n.pr.m. GK: 5720 [→ 5162]. Nahamani, "*Yahweh has consoled*":– Nahamani [1]

5168 נַחְנוּ naḥnû, p.com.pl. GK: 5721 [→ 587]. we:– we [6]

5169 נָחַץ nāḥaṣ, v. GK: 5722 [cf. 3905]. [Qp] to be urgent:– haste [1]

5170 נַחַר naḥar or **נַחֲרָה naḥᵃrâ**, n.m. & f. GK: 5724 & 5725 [→ 5156]. snorting (of a horse):– nostrils [1], snorting [1]

5171 נַחְרַי naḥray, n.pr.m. GK: 5726. Naharai:– Naharai [2]

5172 נָחַשׁ nāḥaš, v.den. GK: 5727 [→ 5173; cf. 3907]. [P] to practice divination, interpret omens and signs:– certainly divine (+5172) [2], indeed divineth (+5172) [2], used enchantments [2], diligently observe [1], enchanter [1], enchantments [1], learned by experience [1], use enchantment [1]

5173 נַחַשׁ naḥaš, n.[m.]. GK: 5728 [→ 5172]. sorcery, magic curse, spell:– enchantments [1], enchantment [1]

5174 נְחָשׁ nᵉḥāš (Aram.), n.m. GK: 10473 [cf. 5154, 5178]. bronze material; "brass" is a copper alloy dating from Roman times:– brass [9]

5175 נָחָשׁ nāḥāš, n.m. GK: 5729 [→ 5176, 5177]. snake, serpent; by extension: a mythological creature of chaos opposed to God:– serpent [25], serpents [4], serpent's [2]

5176 נָחָשׁ nāḥāš, n.pr.m. GK: 5731 [→ 5175]. Nahash, "*viper* or *copper*":– Nahash [9]

נְחֻשָׁה nᵉḥušâ. See 5154.

5177 נַחְשׁוֹן naḥšôn, n.pr.m. GK: 5732 [→ 5175]. Nahshon, "*small viper*":– Nahshon [9], Naashon [1]

5178 נְחֹשֶׁת nᵉḥōšet, n.m. GK: 5733 & 5734 [→ 5153, 5154; cf. 5180; cf. 5174]. copper, bronze; this can refer to bronze as a medium of exchange; menstruation:– brass [101], brasen [28], fetters [3], chains [2], fetters of brass [2], chain [1], copper [1], filthiness [1], steel [1]

5179 נְחֻשְׁתָּא nᵉḥuštā', n.pr.f. GK: 5735. Nehushta, "*[strong as or color of] bronze*":– Nehushta [1]

5180 נְחֻשְׁתָּן nᵉḥuštān, n.pr. GK: 5736 [cf. 5178]. Nehushtan, "*bronze viper*":– Nehushtan [1]

5181 נָחַת nāḥat, v. GK: 5737 [→ 5183, 5185; cf. 8478; cf. 5182]. [Q] to descend, go down; [N] to be pierced, penetrate; [P] to bend (a bow); to level off; [H] to bring down:– broken [2], cause to come down [1], come down [1], entereth [1], presseth sore (+5921) [1], settlest [1], stick fast [1]

5182 נְחַת nᵉḥat (Aram.), v. GK: 10474 [cf. 5181]. [P] to come down; [H, A] to deposit, store; [Ho] to be deposed:– came down [1], carry [1], coming down [1], deposed [1], laid up [1], place [1]

5183 נַחַת naḥat, n.f. & m. GK: 5738 & 5739 [→ 5181, 5184; cf. 3240]. coming down, descending; rest, peace, tranquillity:– rest [4], lighting down [1], quietness [1], quiet [1], that which be set on [1]

5184 נַחַת naḥat, n.pr.m. GK: 5740 [→ 5183; cf. 3240]. Nahath, "*descent;* [poss.] *rest*":– Nahath [5]

5185 נָחֵת nāḥēt, a. GK: 5741 [→ 5181]. going down, descending:– come down [1]

5186 נָטָה nāṭâ, v. GK: 5742 [→ 4294, 4295, 4296, 4297, 4298]. [Q] to spread out, stretch out; [Qp] to be outstretched, be spread out, be extended; [N] to be spread out, be stretched out; [H] to turn aside, pervert, lead astray; [Ho] to be outspread:– stretched out [37], stretch out [22], incline [15], inclined [13], stretched forth [9], turn aside [9], turned [9], pitched [8], turn [7], bowed [5], spread [5], stretch forth [5], bow down [4], stretcheth out [4], declined [3], decline [3], outstretched [3], turned aside [3], turned away [3], wrest [3], bow [2], carried aside [2], declineth [2], extended [2], pervert [2], stretcheth forth [2], afternoon (+3117+1886.1) [1], apply [1], bowing down [1], bowing [1], caused to yield [1], deliver [1], extend [1], go down [1], goeth down [1], gone [1], intended [1], laid [1], lay

Heb

down [1], let down [1], offer [1], overthrow [1], perverted [1], perverteth [1], prolong [1], put away [1], shewed [1], spread forth [1], spreadeth out [1], stretchedst out [1], stretched [1], stretchest out [1], stretch [1], took aside [1], turn away [1], turned in [1], turneth aside [1], turneth [1]

5187 נָטִיל ***nāṭîl***, a. GK: 5744 [→ 5190]. weighing (of precious metals); by extension, trading: buying, selling, and bartering:– bear [1]

5188 נְטִפָה ***n^{e}ṭipâ***, n.[f.]. GK: 5755 [→ 5197]. pendant, a drop-shaped ornament:– chains [1], collars [1]

5189 נְטִישׁוֹת ***n^{e}ṭîšôt***, n.f. GK: 5746 [→ 5203]. spreading branches, tendrils:– battlements [1], branches [1], plants [1]

5190 נָטַל ***nāṭal***, v. GK: 5747 [→ 5187, 5192; cf. 5191]. [Q] to lay upon; to weigh; [P] to lift:– bare [1], borne [1], offer [1], taketh up [1]

5191 נְטַל ***n^{e}ṭal*** (Aram.), v. GK: 10475 [cf. 5190]. [P] to raise up, lift up; [Peil] to be lifted up:– lift up [1], lifted up [1]

5192 נֵטֶל ***nēṭel***, n.[m.]. GK: 5748 [→ 5190]. burden, load:– weighty [1]

5193 נָטַע ***nāṭa'***, v. GK: 5749 [→ 4302, 5195, 5194, 5196]. [Q] to plant (seed or stock); by extension: to place, set, set up (any object on any surface):– plant [31], planted [21], plantedst [2], planteth [2], fastened [1], planters [1]

5194 נֶטַע ***neṭa'***, n.[m.]. GK: 5750 [→ 5193]. garden, plants; young plant:– plant [3], plants [1]

5195 נָטִיעַ ***nāṭîa'***, n.[m.]. GK: 5745 [→ 5193]. shoot (of a young plant):– plants [1]

5196 נְטָעִים ***n^{e}ṭā'îm***, n.pr.loc. GK: 5751 [→ 5193]. Netaim:– plants [1]

5197 נָטַף ***nāṭap***, v. GK: 5752 [→ 2903, 5188, 5198, 5199, 5200]. [Q] to pour down; gently fall, drip; [H] to (drip words) preach, prophesy:– drop [6], dropped [5], prophesy [4], drop down [1], dropping [1], prophet [1]

5198 נָטָף ***nāṭāp***, n.[m.]. GK: 5753 & 5754 [→ 5197]. gum resin, drops of stacte (the resin of a shrub); drop (of water):– drops [1], stacte [1]

5199 נְטֹפָה ***n^{e}ṭōpâ***, n.pr.loc. GK: 5756 [→ 5200; cf. 5197]. Netophah, "*trickle, drip*":– Netophah [2]

5200 נְטוֹפָתִי ***n^{e}ṭôpātî***, a.g. GK: 5743 [→ 5199; cf. 5197]. Netophathite, "*of Netophah*":– Netophathite [8], Netophathites [2], Netophathi [1]

5201 נָטַר ***nāṭar***, v. GK: 5757 [→ 4307; cf. 5341]. [Q] to care for, tend; to be angry, harbor a grudge:– keep [3], bear any grudge against [1], keepers [1], keeper [1], kept [1], reserveth [1], reserve [1]

5202 נְטַר ***n^{e}ṭar*** (Aram.), v. GK: 10476 [cf. 5341]. [P] to keep (in one's mind or heart):– kept [1]

5203 נָטַשׁ ***nāṭaš***, v. GK: 5759 [→ 5189]. [Q] to abandon, forsake, reject; [Qp] to be scattered; [N] to spread out; to be deserted; [Pu] to be abandoned:– forsake [7], left [7], forsaken [6], leave [5], spread [3], forsook [2], cast off [1], drawn [1], fall [1], joined [1], leave off [1], lie still [1], loosed [1], spread abroad [1], stretched out [1], suffered [1]

5204 נִי ***nî***, n.[m.]. GK: 5760 [→ 5092; cf. 5091]. wailing:– wailing [1]

5204.1 נִי- ***-nî***, p.com.s.suf. GK: 5761 [→ 2967.1]. I, me, my:– me [1072], I [217], my [7], us [3], myself [2], it [1], let me [1], mine (+4480) [1], mine [1], send me [1]

5204.2 נִי- ***-nî*** (Aram.), p.suf.1.com.s. GK: 10477 [→ 2967.2; cf. 5204.1]. I, me, my:– me [18]

5205 נִיד ***nîd***, n.m. GK: 5764 [→ 5110]. comfort:– moving [1]

5206 נִידָה ***nîdâ***, n.f. GK: 5765 [→ 5079; cf. 5077]. uncleanness, impurity:– removed [1]

5207 נִיחֹחַ ***nîḥōaḥ***, n.[m.]. GK: 5767 [→ 3240; cf. 5208]. pleasing, soothing, appeasing:– sweet [42], sweet odours [1]

5208 נִיחֹחַ ***niḥōaḥ*** (Aram.), n.[m.]. GK: 10478 [cf. 5207]. incense, pleasing scent:– sweet odours [1], sweet savours [1]

5209 נִין ***nîn***, n.[m.]. GK: 5769. offspring, children, posterity:– son [3]

5210 נִינְוֵה ***nîn^{e}wēh***, n.pr.loc. GK: 5770. Nineveh:– Nineveh [17]

5211 נִיס ***nîs***, n.m. *or* v. GK: 5771 [→ 5127]. flight, fleeing:– @H = **5212** נִיסָן ***nîsān***, n.pr. GK: 5772. Nisan:– Nisan [2]

5213 נִיצוֹץ ***nîṣôṣ***, n.[m.]. GK: 5773 [→ 5340]. spark:– spark [1]

5214 נִיר ***nîr***, v. GK: 5774 [→ 5215]. [Q] to break up, bring into cultivation:– break up [2]

5215 נִיר ***nîr***, n.[m.]. GK: 5776 [→ 5214]. unplowed ground, likely referring to ground not plowed for the current season:– fallow ground [2], plowing [1], tillage [1]

5216 נִיר ***nîr*** or נֵר ***nēr***, n.m. GK: 5775 & 5944 [→ 74, 4501, 5369, 5374; cf. 5102; cf. 5135]. lamp (fueled by olive oil); by extension: life (as a burning lamp); light (showing the way of truth):– lamps [26], lamp [9], candle [8], light [4], candles [1]

5217 נָכָא ***nākā'***, v. GK: 5777 [→ 5218, 5219?; cf. 5221]. [N] to be driven out (by whipping or scourging):– viler [1]

5218 נָכָא ***nākā'*** or נָכֵא ***nākē'***, a. GK: 5778 & 5779 [→ 5217]. crushed, beaten, broken; grieving (as one unmercifully beaten):– broken [2], stricken [1], wounded [1]

5219 נְכֹאת ***n^{e}kō't***, n.f. GK: 5780 [→ 5217?]. spices, resin:– spicery [1], spices [1]

5220 נֶכֶד ***neked***, n.[m.]. GK: 5781. descendant, progeny:– nephew [2], son's son [1]

5221 נָכָה ***nākâ***, v. GK: 5782 [→ 4347, 5223, 5222; cf. 5217]. [N] to be struck; [Pu] to be destroyed; [H] to kill, slaughter, destroy, defeat; [Ho] to be beat, be struck, be wounded, be killed:– smote [193], smite [95], slew [57], smitten [42], slain [21], killeth [11], smiteth [11], slay [8], slaughter [5], smiting [5], beaten [4], beat [4], kill [4], slay (+5315) [4], given [3], killed [3], stricken [3], wounded [3], indeed smitten (+5221) [2], killeth (+5315) [2], slaying [2], surely smite (+5221) [2], beatest [1], cast forth [1], clapt [1], murderers [1], punish [1], slaughter made (+4347) [1], slayer [1], slewest [1], smiters [1], smitest [1], smotest [1], strike [1], stripes give [1], stripes [1], strooke [1]

5222 נֵכֶה ***nēkeh***, a. GK: 5784 [→ 5221]. attacker:– abjects [1]

5223 נָכֶה ***nākeh***, a. GK: 5783 [→ 5221]. lame, crippled; contrite:– lame [2], contrite [1]

5224 נְכֹה ***n^{e}kōh*** or נְכוֹ ***n^{e}kô***, n.pr.m. GK: 5785 & 5786. Neco:– Necho [3]

5225 נָכוֹן ***nākôn***, n.pr.m. GK: 5789 [→ 3559]. Nacon, "*established*":– Nachon's [1]

5226 נֵכַח ***nēkaḥ***, subst. (used as pp. & adv.). GK: 5790 [→ 5227, 5228]. same as 5227: opposite, before, in front of:– before (+3807.1) [1], over against [1]

5227 נֹכַח ***nōkaḥ***, subst. (used as pp. & adv.). GK: 5790 [→ 5226]. same as 5226: opposite, before, in front of:– before [7], over against [7], against [4], before (+3807.1) [1], directly (+413) [1], for (+3807.1) [1], right before (+6440) [1], right on (+3807.1) [1]

5228 נָכֹחַ ***nākōaḥ***, a. & subst. GK: 5791 [→ 5226, 5229]. same as 5229: proper, right, honest, what is straight:– right [2], plain [1], uprightness [1]

5229 נְכֹחָה ***n^{e}kōḥâ***, a. & subst. GK: 5791 [→ 5228]. same as 5228: proper, right, honest, what is straight:– right [2], equity [1], uprightness [1]

5230 נָכַל ***nākal***, v. GK: 5792 [→ 3596?, 5231]. [Q, P] to cheat, treat cunningly; [Ht] to conspire, plot:– beguiled [1], conspired against [1], deal subtilly [1], deceiver [1]

5231 נֵכֶל ***nēkel***, n.[m.]. GK: 5793 [→ 5230]. deception, cunning:– wiles [1]

5232 נְכַס ***n^{e}kas*** (Aram.), n.[m.]. GK: 10479 [cf. 5233]. treasury; fine:– goods [2]

5233 נְכָסִים ***n^{e}kāsîm***, n.m.[pl.]. GK: 5794 [cf. 5232]. riches, wealth, possessions:– wealth [4], riches [1]

5234 נָכַר ***nākar***, v. GK: 5795 & 5796 [→ 1971, 5235, 5236, 5237]. [N] to disguise oneself, be not recognized; [P] to regard, consider; to favor; to misunderstand; to treat as foreign; [H] to recognize, acknowledge; [Ht] to pretend to be a stranger; to make known:– knew [8], know [8], acknowledge [6], discern [4], respect [4], discerned [2], known [2], take knowledge [2], acknowledged [1], behave strangely [1], could [1], delivered [1], dissembleth [1], estranged [1], feign to be another [1], feignest to be another [1], knoweth [1], made strange [1], perceived [1], regardeth [1], took notice [1]

5235 נֵכֶר ***nēker***, n.[m.]. GK: 5798 [→ 5234]. misfortune, disaster:– strange punishment [1], stranger [1]

5236 נֵכָר ***nēkār***, n.[m.]. GK: 5797 [→ 5234]. (one from a foreign land) foreigner, alien, stranger:– strange [17], strangers (+1121) [6], stranger (+1121) [5], strangers [3], stranger [3], alien [1], stranger's (+1121) [1]

5237 נָכְרִי ***nokrî***, a. GK: 5799 [→ 5234]. foreign, alien; (n.) foreigner:– strange [20], stranger [14], alien [3], stranger (+376) [2], strangers [2], aliens [1], foreigners [1], foreigner [1], outlandish [1]

5238 נְכֹת ***n^{e}kōt***, n.[f.]. GK: 5800. treasure, storage:– precious things [2]

5239 נָלָה ***nālâ***, v. GK: 5801 [cf. 3615]. [H] to stop:– make an end [1]

5240 נְמִבְזֶה ***n^{e}mibzeh***, v.ptcp. GK: 1022 [→ 959]. ptcp. of 959: despised, contemptible:– vile [1]

5241 נְמוּאֵל ***n^{e}mû'ēl***, n.pr.m. GK: 5803 [→ 5242; cf. 3223, 5272?]. Nemuel:– Nemuel [3]

5242 נְמוּאֵלִי ***n^{e}mû'ēlî***, a.g. GK: 5804 [→ 5241]. Nemuelite, "*of Nemuel*":– Nemuelites [1]

5243 נָמַל ***nāmal*** or מָלַל ***mālal***, v. GK: 4909 [cf. 4135]. [Q] to circumcise; to wither away; [N] to be cut off; [Pol] to wither; [Htpol] be blunted (of arrows):– cut down [2], cut off [2], circumcise [1]

5244 נְמָלָה ***n^{e}mālâ***, n.f. GK: 5805. ant:– ants [1], ant [1]

5245 נְמַר ***n^{e}mar*** (Aram.), n.[m.]. GK: 10480 [cf. 5246]. leopard, panther:– leopard [1]

5246 נָמֵר ***nāmēr***, n.m. GK: 5807 [cf. 5245]. leopard:– leopard [4], leopards [2]

נִמְרֹד ***nimrōd***. See 5248.

5247 נִמְרָה ***nimrâ***, n.pr.loc. GK: 5809 [→ 1039, 5249]. Nimrah, "*spotted leopard; basin of limpid [clear] water*":– Nimrah [1]

5248 נִמְרֹד ***nimrōd***, n.pr.m. GK: 5808. Nimrod, "[perhaps] *to rebel* or *the Arrow, the mighty hero*":– Nimrod [4]

5249 נִמְרִים ***nimrîm***, n.pr.loc. GK: 5810 [→ 5247]. Nimrim, "*limpid [clear] waters; wholesome waters;* [poss.] *waters of leopards*":– Nimrim [2]

5250 נִמְשִׁי ***nimšî***, n.pr.m. GK: 5811. Nimshi:– Nimshi [5]

5251 נֵס ***nēs***, n.[m.]. GK: 5812 [→ 5264; cf. 5263, 5264]. banner, standard, signal pole:– standard [7], ensign [6], banner [2], pole [2], sail [2], sign [1]

5252 נְסִבָּה ***n^{e}sibbâ***, n.f. GK: 5813 [→ 4141]. turn of events:– cause [1]

5253 נָסַג ***nāsag*** or סוּג ***sûg***, v. GK: 6047 [→ 5472, 7734; cf. 5473, 5509, 7873]. prob. same as 5472: [Q] to turn away, be faithless, be disloyal; [N] to be turned back, be disloyal, be faithless; [H] to move, displace; [Ho] to be driven back:– remove [4], departing away [1], removeth [1], take hold [1], take [1], turned away [1]

נְסָה ***n^{e}sâ***. See 5375.

5254 נָסָה ***nāsâ***, v. GK: 5814 [→ 4531, 4532?]. [P] to test (usually to prove character or faithfulness), to attempt; to test God implies a lack of confidence in his revealed character, thus is wicked:– prove [14], tempted [8], proved [5], tempt [4], adventure [1], assayed [1], assay [1], proveth [1], try [1]

5255 נָסַח ***nāsaḥ***, v. GK: 5815 [cf. 4535?; cf. 5256]. [Q] to tear down; [N] to be uprooted, be torn down:– destroy [1], plucked [1], pluck [1], rooted [1]

5256 נְסַח ***n^{e}saḥ*** (Aram.), v. GK: 10481 [cf. 5255]. [Htpe] to be pulled out:– pulled down [1]

5257 נָסִיךְ ***nāsîk***, n.m. GK: 5816 & 5817 [cf. 5258]. drink offering; metal image, idol; prince, leader:– princes [3], drink offerings [1], dukes [1], principal [1]

5258 נָסַךְ ***nāsak***, v. GK: 5818 & 5820 [→ 4541, 5257, 5262; cf. 3251, 5480; cf. 5260]. [Q] to pour out; to install, set; [N] to be poured out; to be appointed; [P] to pour out; [H] to pour out; [Ho] to be poured out; usually of pouring out a drink offering to deity:– poured out [7], pour out [5], cover [3], offer [2], poured [2], cause to be poured [1], melteth [1], molten [1], pour [1], set up [1], set [1]

5259 נָסַךְ ***nāsak***, v. GK: 5819 [→ 4541, 4545; cf. 5526, 7753]. [Qp] to be woven:– spread [1]

5260 נְסַךְ ***n^{e}sak*** (Aram.), v. GK: 10482 [→ 5261; cf. 5258]. [Pa] to present (an offering):– offer [1]

5261 נְסַךְ ***n^{e}sak*** (Aram.), n.[m.]. GK: 10483 [→ 5260; cf. 5262]. drink offering, libation:– drink offerings [1]

5262 נֶסֶךְ ***nesek***, n.m. GK: 5821 & 5822 [→ 5258; cf. 5261]. drink offering; metal image, idol:– drink offerings [30], drink offering [29], molten image [3], cover withal [1], molten images [1]

נִסְמָן ***nismān***. See 5567.

5263 נָסַס ***nāsas***, v. GK: 5823 [cf. 5251, 5264]. [Q] to falter:– standard-bearer [1]

5264 נָסַס ***nāsas***, v. GK: 5824 [→ 5251; cf. 5251, 5263]. [Htpol] to unfurl; to sparkle:– lifted up as an ensign [1]

5265 נָסַע ***nāsa'***, v. GK: 5825 [→ 4550, 4551]. [Q] to set out, move on, leave, travel on; [N] to be pulled up; [H] to lead, bring out; to pull out:– departed [30], journeyed [28], removed [26], set forward [13], went [8], took journey [7], take journey [5], go forward [3], brought [2], set forth [2], setteth forward [2], went away [2], brought out [1], caused to blow [1], get [1], go away [1], go forth [1], go [1], journeying [1], made to go forth [1], marched [1], on way [1], removeth [1], remove [1], set aside [1], still (+2050.1) [1], took [1], went forth [1], went onward [1], went out [1]

5266 נָסַק ***nāsaq*** or סָלַק ***sālaq***, v. GK: 5826. to go up:– ascend up [1]

5267 נְסַק ***n***^e^***saq*** or סְלַק ***s***^e^***laq*** (Aram.), v. GK: 10513 [→ 5559]. prob. same as 5559: [P] to come up, go up; [H] to lift up; [Ho] to be lifted up:– take up [1], taken up [1], took up [1]

5268 נִסְרֹךְ ***nisrōk***, n.pr.[m.]. GK: 5827. Nisroch (pagan god):– Nisroch [2]

5269 נֵעָה ***nē'â***, n.pr.loc. GK: 5828. Neah:– Neah [1]

5270 נֹעָה ***nō'â***, n.pr.f. GK: 5829. Noah, "*rest, comfort*":– Noah [4]

5271 נְעוּרִים ***n***^e^***'ûrîm*** or נְעוּרוֹת ***n***^e^***'ûrôt***, n.m. & f.pl. GK: 5830 & 5831 [→ 5286, 5288]. youth, childhood:– youth [46], childhood [1]

5272 נְעִיאֵל ***n***^e^***'î'ēl***, n.pr.loc. GK: 5832 [cf. 5241?]. Neiel:– Neiel [1]

5273 נָעִים ***nā'îm***, a. GK: 5833 & 5834 [→ 5276]. pleasant, charming; singing, sweetly sounding, musical:– pleasant [9], pleasures [2], sweet [2]

5274 נָעַל ***nā'al***, v. GK: 5835 & 5836 [→ 4514, 4515, 5275]. [Q] to lock up, bolt; to put on a sandal; [Qp] to be locked up, be sealed; [H] to provide with sandals:– locked [2], shod [2], bolted [1], bolt [1], inclosed [1], shut up [1]

5275 נַעַל ***na'al***, n.f. GK: 5837 [→ 5274]. sandal (normal footware); not to wear sandals could have the associative meaning of being in poverty, misery, or disgrace:– shoes [11], shoe [9], dryshod [1], shoelatchet (+8288) [1]

Heb

5276 נָעֵם ***nā'ēm***, v. GK: 5838 [→ 42, 293, 493, 4516, 5273, 5277, 5278, 5279, 5279, 5281, 5280, 5283, 5282]. [Q] to be pleasant, be dear, be favored:– pleasant [5], delight [1], in beauty [1], sweet [1]

5277 נַעַם ***na'am***, n.pr.m. GK: 5839 [→ 5276]. Naam, "*pleasant*":– Naam [1]

5278 נֹעַם ***nō'am***, n.m. GK: 5840 [→ 42, 293, 493; cf. 5276]. pleasantness, favor:– beauty [4], pleasant [2], pleasantness [1]

5279 נַעֲמָה ***na***^a^***mâ***, n.pr.f. & loc. GK: 5841 & 5842 [→ 5276]. Naamah, "*pleasant*":– Naamah [5]

5280 נַעֲמִי ***na***^a^***mî***, a.g. GK: 5844 [→ 5281; cf. 5276]. Naamite, "*of Naaman*":– Naamites [1]

5281 נָעֳמִי ***no***^o^***mî***, n.pr.f. GK: 5843 [→ 5276]. Naomi, "*my joy*":– Naomi [20], Naomi's [1]

5282 נַעֲמָנִים ***na***^a^***mānîm***, n.[m.]. GK: 5846 [→ 5276]. finest (of Adonis [?]):– pleasant [1]

5283 נַעֲמָן ***na***^a^***mān***, n.pr.m. GK: 5845 [→ 5280; cf. 5276]. Naaman, "*pleasantness*":– Naaman [15], Naaman's [1]

5284 נַעֲמָתִי ***na***^a^***mātî***, a.g. GK: 5847. Naamathite:– Naamathite [4]

5285 נַעֲצוּץ ***na***^a^***ṣûṣ***, n.[m.]. GK: 5848. thornbush:– thorns [1], thorn [1]

5286 נָעַר ***nā'ar***, v. GK: 5849 [→ 5271, 5289?, 5288?]. [Q] to growl:– yell [1]

5287 נָעַר ***nā'ar***, v. GK: 5850 [→ 5296]. [Q] to shake off; to refuse; [Qp] be shaken out; [N] to shake oneself free, be shaken off; [P] to shake off, sweep away; [Ht] to shake oneself free:– overthrew [2], shake [2], shake off [1], shake out [1], shaken out [1], shaken [1], shaketh [1], shook [1], tossed up and down [1]

5288 נַעַר ***na'ar***, n.m. GK: 5853 [→ 5271, 5290, 5291, 5292, 5294?; cf. 5286?]. young man, boy, child, ranging in age from infancy to young adulthood; by extension: servant, attendant, steward, with a possible focus on lower social status:– child [44], young men [39], young man [37], lad [32], servant [32], servants [22], young [14], children [7], youth [5], babe [1], boys [1], lads [1], men [1], young men (+376) [1], youths [1]

5289 נַעַר ***na'ar***, n.[m.]. GK: 5852 [→ 5286?]. scattering, shaking; (n.) scattered ones:– young one [1]

5290 נֹעַר ***nō'ar***, n.m. GK: 5854 [→ 5288]. youth:– youth [2], child's [1], child [1]

נָעוּר ***nā'ur***. See 5271.

5291 נַעֲרָה ***na***^a^***râ***, n.f. GK: 5855 [→ 5292; cf. 5288]. young woman, girl, ranging in age from infancy to young adulthood; by extension: servant, maid, with a possible focus on lower social status:– damsel [24], maidens [12], damsel's [8], maid [4], young [4], maiden [3], damsels [2], every maid's (+5291+2050.1) [2], maids [2], young maidens [1], young woman [1]

5292 נַעֲרָה ***na***^a^***râ***, n.pr.f. & loc. GK: 5856 & 5857 [→ 5291; cf. 5288, 5293?, 5295]. Naarah, "*[young] woman*":– Naarah [3], Naarath [1]

נְעֻרָה ***n***^e^***'urâ***. See 5271.

5293 נַעֲרַי ***na***^a^***ray***, n.pr.m. GK: 5858 [cf. 5292?]. Naarai, "*young man of Yahweh*":– Naarai [1]

5294 נְעַרְיָה ***n***^e^***'aryâ***, n.pr.m. GK: 5859 [→ 5288?+3068]. Neariah, "*[young] man of Yahweh*":– Neariah [3]

5295 נַעֲרָן ***na***^a^***rān***, n.pr.loc. GK: 5860 [cf. 5292]. Naaran:– Naaran [1]

5296 נְעֹרֶת ***n***^e^***'ōret***, n.f. GK: 5861 [→ 5287]. tinder (broken fibers shaken off flax):– tow [2]

נַעֲרָתָה ***na***^a^***rātâ***. See 5292.

5297 נֹף ***nōp***, n.pr.loc. GK: 5862 [cf. 4644]. Noph = Memphis:– Noph [7]

5298 נֶפֶג ***nepeg***, n.pr.m. GK: 5863. Nepheg, "*sprout, shoot*":– Nepheg [4]

5299 נָפָה ***nāpâ***, n.f. GK: 5864 & 5865 [→ 5130, 5131; cf. 5316]. height, yoke; sieve (winnowing device):– borders [1], coast [1], region [1], sieve [1]

5300 נְפוּשְׁסִים ***n***^e^***pûššîm*** or נְפוּסִים ***n***^e^***pûsîm*** or נְפִישְׁסִים ***n***^e^***pîs***^e^***sîm***, n.pr.g.?. GK: 5867 & 5866 & 5875 [→ 5304]. Nephushsim, Nephussim, Nephishsim:– Nephishesim [1], Nephusim [1]

5301 נָפַח ***nāpaḥ***, v. GK: 5870 [→ 4646, 4647, 8598; cf. 6315]. [Q] to blow upon, breathe upon; [Qp, Pu] to be blown upon; [H] to sniff out; to cause to breathe out:– blow [3], seething [2], bloweth [1], blown [1], breathed [1], breathe [1], caused to lose [1], given up the ghost (+5315) [1], snuffed [1]

5302 נֹפַח ***nōpaḥ***, n.pr.loc. GK: 5871. Nophah:– Nophah [1]

5303 נְפִילִים ***n***^e^***pîlîm***, n.m.pl. GK: 5872 [→ 5307]. Nephilim:– giants [3]

5304 נְפִיסִים ***n***^e^***pîsîm***, n.pr.g.?. GK: 5873 [→ 5300]. Nephissim:– @H = **5305** נָפִישׁ ***nāpîš***, n.pr.m. GK: 5874 [→ 5314]. Naphish, "*refreshed*":– Naphish [2], Nephish [1]

5306 נֹפֶךְ ***nōpek***, n.[m.]. GK: 5876. turquoise (green semi-precious stone):– emerald [3], emeralds [1]

5307 נָפַל ***nāpal***, v. GK: 5877 [→ 4651, 4654, 4658, 5303, 5309; cf. 5308]. [Q] to fall, fail; [Pilal?] to fall; [H] to cause to fall, to cast down, drop; (used of casting lots) to allocate; [Ht] to fall prostrate (to worship); to fall upon (to attack); by extension: to happen (of circumstance falling on a person):– fall [136], fell [98], fallen [52], fell down [20], cast [16], falleth [15], cast down [7], cause to fall [7], fall down [5], divide [4], failed [4], fallen down [3], falling [3], fell away [3], overthrown [3], present [3], rot [3], accepted [2], caused to fall [2], divided [2], fail [2], inferior [2], lay along [2], lighted [2], lost [2], overthrow [2], surely fall (+5307) [2], cast in [1], cast out [1], castedst down [1], casteth into [1], casting down [1], cause to lie down [1], ceased [1], died [1], fall away [1], fallest away [1], fell out [1], felled [1], fellest [1], felling [1], fugitives [1], have inheritance (+5159) [1], judged [1], keepeth [1], lay down [1], lay [1], liest [1], lighted down [1], lying [1], make fall [1], man^S^ [1], overwhelm (+5921) [1], perish [1], presented [1], presenting [1], slew [1], smite out [1], throw down [1]

5308 נְפַל ***n***^e^***pal*** (Aram.), v. GK: 10484 [cf. 5307]. [P] to fall:– fall down [3], fell [3], falleth down [2], fell down [2], have occasion [1]

5309 נֵפֶל ***nēpel***, n.m. GK: 5878 [→ 5307]. stillborn child, miscarriage:– untimely birth [3]

נְפִל ***n***^e^***pil***. See 5303.

5310 נָפַץ ***nāpaṣ***, v. GK: 5879 & 5880 [→ 4660, 4661, 5311; cf. 6327]. [Q] to shatter; to scatter; [P] to shatter; (of log raft) to separate; [Pu] to be crushed:– break in pieces [9], scattered [2], beaten in sunder [1], brake [1], break [1], broken [1], cause to be discharged [1], dash in pieces [1], dasheth [1], dash [1], dispersed [1], overspread [1], scatter [1]

5311 נֶפֶץ ***nepeṣ***, n.[m.]. GK: 5881 [→ 5310]. bursting, pelting (of rain):– scattering [1]

5312 נְפַק ***n***^e^***paq*** (Aram.), v. GK: 10485 [→ 5313]. [P] to go out, come out; [H] to take out, remove:– came forth [3], taken out [2], come forth [1], gone forth [1], take [1], took forth [1], took [1], went forth [1]

5313 נִפְקָה ***nipqâ*** (Aram.), n.f. GK: 10486 [→ 5312]. expense, cost:– expences [2]

5314 נָפַשׁ ***nāpaš***, v.den. GK: 5882 [→ 5305, 5315]. [N] to be refreshed, refresh oneself:– refreshed [3]

5315 נֶפֶשׁ ***nepeš***, n.f. GK: 5883 [→ 5314]. breath; by extension: life, life force, soul, an immaterial part of a person, the seat of emotion and desire; a creature or person as a whole: self, body, even corpse:– soul [416], life [100], souls [58], lives [18], persons [13], person [13], heart [12], mind [11], creature [9], himself (+2050.2) [8], yourselves (+3641.1) [6], dead [5], dead body [4], minds [4], slay (+5221) [4], will [4], desire [3], man [3], me (+2967.1) [3], persons (+120) [3], pleasure [3], themselves (+3963.1) [3], any [2], beast [2], body [2], hearts [2], herself (+1886.3) [2], him (+2050.2) [2], killeth (+5221) [2], lust [2], man (+120) [2], thing [2], angry (+4751) [1], appetite [1], breath [1], deadly (+871.1) [1], desire (+5375) [1], discontented (+4751) [1], fish [1], given to appetite [1], given up the ghost (+5301) [1], giving up of the ghost (+4646) [1], greedy (+5794) [1], have a desire (+5375) [1], he (+2050.2) [1], heart's [1], hearty [1], her (+1886.3) [1], he [1], him (+5105.2) [1], him^S^ [1], his own (+2050.2) [1], life (+2416) [1], men (+120) [1], mortally [1], moving creature [1], myself (+2967.1) [1], one [1], soul's [1], tablets (+1004) [1], they (+3963.1) [1], thyself (+3509.3) [1], we (+5105.1) [1]

5316 נֶפֶת ***nepet*** or נָפוֹת ***nāpôt***, n.f. or loc. GK: 5884 & 5868 [→ 5131; cf. 5299]. hill; or Nephet, Naphoth, "*heights*":– countries [1]

5317 נֹפֶת ***nōpet***, n.m. GK: 5885 [→ 5130]. honey of the honeycomb:– honeycomb [4], honeycomb (+6688) [1]

5318 נֶפְתּוֹחַ ***neptôaḥ***, n.pr.loc. GK: 5886. Nephtoah, "*opening*":– Nephtoah [2]

5319 נַפְתּוּלִים ***naptûlîm***, n.[m.pl.]. GK: 5887 [→ 6617]. struggles, wrestlings:– wrestlings [1]

5320 נַפְתֻּחִים ***naptuḥîm***, n.pr.loc. & a.g. GK: 5888. Naphtuhite:– Naphtuhim [2]

5321 נַפְתָּלִי ***naptālî***, n.pr.m. GK: 5889 [→ 6617?]. Naphtali, "*wrestling*":– Naphtali [50], Kedesh-naphtali (+6943) [1]

5322 נֵץ ***nēṣ***, n.m. GK: 5890 & 5891 [→ 5323, 5340]. blossom; hawk or falcon (bird of prey):– hawk [3], blossoms [1]

5323 נָצָא ***nāṣā'***, v. GK: 5892 [→ 5322]. [Q] to fly:– flee [1]

5324 נָצַב ***nāṣab***, v. GK: 5893 & 5894 [→ 4673, 4674, 4675, 4676, 4678, 5325, 5333, 5334; cf. 3320]. [N] to stand oneself before; (n.) officer, official; to be wretched, exhausted; [H] to station, set up, establish; [Ho] to be set up, be decreed:– stood [17], set [11], stand [8], set up [7], officers [6], standing [4], standeth [3], stood upright [2], Huzzab [1], appointed [1], at best state [1], deputy [1], erected [1], establish [1], laid [1], made to stand [1], pillar [1], present [1], reared up [1], settest [1], settled [1], sharpen [1], stablish [1], standeth still [1], stoodest [1]

נְצִב ***n***^e^***ṣib***. See 5333.

5325 נִצָּב ***niṣṣāb***, n.m. GK: 5896 [→ 5324]. handle, hilt (of sword, dagger or knife):– haft [1]

5326 נִצְבָּה ***niṣbâ*** (Aram.), n.f. GK: 10487. hardness, firmness, a quality of strength of a metal:– strength [1]

5327 נָצָה ***nāṣâ***, v. GK: 5897 & 5898 [→ 4683, 4695]. [Q] to lie in ruins; [N] to fight (quarreling that can come to blows and struggles); to be laid waste, be desolate; [H] to rebel, engage in a struggle:– strove together [3], strove [3], ruinous [2], strive [2], laid waste [1]

נֹצָה ***nōṣâ***. See 5133.

5328 נִצָּה ***niṣṣâ***, n.f. GK: 5900 [→ 5340]. blossom:– flower [2]

נְצוּרָה ***n***^e^***ṣûrâ***. See 5341.

5329 נָצַח ***nāṣaḥ***, v. GK: 5904 [→ 5331, 5335; cf. 5330]. [N] to be enduring, lasting; [P] to direct, supervise; (n.) director (of music, t.t. in the Psalms), supervisor:– chief Musician [55], set forward [4], overseers [2], chief singer [1], excel [1], oversee (+5921) [1], perpetual [1]

5330 נְצַח ***n***^e^***ṣaḥ*** (Aram.), v. GK: 10488 [cf. 5329]. [Htpa] to distinguish oneself:– preferred [1]

5331 נֵצַח ***nēṣaḥ***, n.m. GK: 5905 [→ 5329]. glory, majesty, splendor; forever, unending, everlasting, always; "the Glory of Israel" as a title of God probably emphasizes both glory and eternity:– ever [20], always (+3807.1) [2], end [2], ever (+3807.1) [2], for ever [2], never (+3808+3807.1) [2], perpetual [2], strength [2], victory [2], alway (+3807.1) [1], constantly (+3807.1) [1], for evermore [1], never (+1077+3807.1) [1], never (+3808+5704) [1], perpetual (+3807.1) [1], surely never (+518+3807.1) [1]

5332 נֵצַח ***nēṣaḥ***, n.m. GK: 5906. juice (= blood):– blood [1], strength [1]

5333 נְצִיב ***nᵉṣîb***, n.m. GK: 5907 [→ 5334; cf. 5324]. garrison, outpost; pillar:– garrisons [5], garrison [4], officer [1], pillar [1]

5334 נְצִיב ***nᵉṣîb***, n.pr.loc. GK: 5908 [→ 5333; cf. 5324]. Nezib, "*pillar, garrison*":– Nezib [1]

5335 נְצִיחַ ***nᵉṣîaḥ***, n.pr.m. GK: 5909 [→ 5329]. Neziah, "*director [of worship]*":– Neziah [2]

5336 נָצִיר ***nāṣîr***, a. GK: 5910 [→ 5341]. preserved:– @H =

5337 נָצַל ***nāṣal***, v. GK: 5911 [→ 2020; cf. 5338]. [N] to be saved, be delivered, be spared; [P] to plunder, take away, tear away; [H] to deliver, save, rescue; [Ho] to be snatched; [Ht] to strip off oneself:– deliver [112], delivered [56], delivereth [7], delivered at all (+5337) [4], surely deliver (+5337) [4], rid [3], pluckt [2], recovered [2], recover [2], without fail recover (+5337) [2], defended [1], deliverer [1], deliverest [1], escape (+5869) [1], escaped [1], part (+996) [1], preserved [1], rescued [1], rescue [1], saved [1], spoiled [1], spoil [1], stript off [1], stript [1], taken away [1], taken out [1], taken [1], taketh [1], take [1]

5338 נְצַל ***nᵉṣal*** (Aram.), v. GK: 10489 [cf. 5337]. [H] to save, rescue, deliver:– deliver [2], rescueth [1]

5339 נִצָּנִים ***niṣṣānîm***, n.[m.]. GK: 5912 [→ 5340]. blossoms:– flowers [1]

5340 נָצַץ ***nāṣaṣ***, v. GK: 5913 & 5914 [→ 5213, 5322, 5328, 5339]. [Q] to gleam, sparkle; [H] to bloom, blossom:– bud forth [1], budded [1], flourish [1], sparkled [1]

5341 נָצַר ***nāṣar***, v. GK: 5915 [→ 4453, 4694, 5336; cf. 5201; cf. 5202]. [Q] to guard, watch, protect, keep, preserve; [Qp] to be kept secret, be hidden:– keep [26], preserve [11], keepeth [7], kept [4], watchmen [3], besieged [2], hidden [1], keeper [1], keeping [1], monuments [1], observe [1], preserved [1], preserver [1], preserveth [1], subtil [1], watchers [1]

5342 נֵצֶר ***nēṣer***, n.m. GK: 5916. branch, shoot (of a plant):– branch [4]

5343 נְקֵא ***nᵉqē'*** (Aram.), a. GK: 10490 [cf. 5355]. pure, clean; this purity can be symbolized by the color white, as of lamb's wool:– pure [1]

5344 נָקַב ***nāqab***, v. GK: 5918 & 5919 [→ 4717, 4718, 5345, 5346, 5347; cf. 3342, 6895]. [Q] to bore (a hole), pierce; to designate, bestow; to blaspheme; [Qp] to have a hole; to be notable; [N] to be designated, be registered:– expressed [6], curse [4], blasphemeth [2], curse at all (+5344) [2], pierce [2], appoint [1], blasphemed [1], bore through [1], bored [1], cursed [1], holes [1], named [1], name [1], pierceth [1], strike through [1]

5345 נֶקֶב ***neqeb***, n.[m.]. GK: 5920 [→ 5344]. mounting (used in gold jewelry):– pipes [1]

5346 נֶקֶב ***neqeb***, n.pr.loc. GK: 5921 [→ 5344]. Nekeb:– Nekeb [1]

5347 נְקֵבָה ***nᵉqēbâ***, n.f. GK: 5922 [→ 5344]. female, woman:– female [18], woman [2], maid child [1], women [1]

5348 נָקֹד ***nāqōd***, a. GK: 5923 [→ 4719, 5351, 5350]. speckled, spotted:– speckled [9]

5349 נֹקֵד ***nōqēd***, n.m. GK: 5924. shepherd, one who raises sheep:– herdmen [1], sheepmaster [1]

5350 נִקֻּדִים ***niqqudîm***, n.[m.]. GK: 5926 [→ 5348]. (small) cakes; crumbling (food supplies):– mouldy [2], cracknels [1]

5351 נְקֻדָּה ***nᵉquddâ***, n.f. GK: 5925 [→ 5348]. point, drops (of silver on a gold earring):– studs [1]

5352 נָקָה ***nāqâ***, v. GK: 5927 [→ 4518, 5355, 5356]. [Q] to go unpunished; [N] be innocent, be released, go unpunished; [P] to leave unpunished, consider innocent, pardon:– unpunished [6], innocent [4], hold guiltless [3], altogether go unpunished (+5352) [2], at all acquit (+5352) [2], cleanse [2], clear (+5352) [2], clearing (+5352) [2], clear [2], cut off [2], free [2], guiltless [2], leave altogether unpunished (+5352) [2], leave wholly unpunished (+5352) [2], utterly unpunished (+5352) [2], acquit [1], blameless [1], cleansed [1], desolate [1], go unpunished [1], hold innocent [1], quit [1]

5353 נְקוֹדָא ***nᵉqôdā'***, n.pr.m. GK: 5928. Nekoda:– Nekoda [4]

5354 נָקַט ***nāqaṭ*** or קוּט ***qûṭ***, v. GK: 7752 [→ 6900, 6962, cf. 6973, 8262]. prob. same as 6962: [Q] to feel anger, loathing; [N] to feel loathing; [Htpolal] to loathe, abhor:– weary [1]

5355 נָקִי ***nāqî*** or נָקִיא ***nāqî'***, a. GK: 5929 & 5930 [→ 5352; cf. 5343]. innocent, free of blame, not guilty:– innocent [29], guiltless [4], blameless [2], innocents [2], quit [2], clean [1], clear [1], exempted [1], free [1]

5356 נִקָּיוֹן ***niqqāyôn***, n.[m.]. GK: 5931 [→ 5352]. cleanness, purity; by extension: moral or ceremonial innocence, purity, cleanness; "cleanness of teeth" is a sign of lack of food in famine:– innocency [4], cleanness [1]

5357 נָקִיק ***nāqîq***, n.m. GK: 5932. crevice, cleft, crack:– holes [2], hole [1]

5358 נָקַם ***nāqam***, v. GK: 5933 [→ 5359, 5360]. [Q] to seek vengeance, avenge; [N] to be avenged, avenge oneself; [P] to avenge; [Ho or Qp] to be avenged; [Ht] to take one's own vengeance:– avenged [8], avenge [7], avenger [2], revengeth [2], surely punished (+5358) [2], take vengeance [2], avenge (+5360) [1], avenge the quarrel (+5359) [1], avenged (+5359) [1], punished [1], revenged [1], revenge [1], take vengeance (+5359) [1], take vengeance (+5360) [1], taken vengeance (+5359) [1], taking vengeance (+5359) [1], tookest vengeance [1], vengeance taken [1]

5359 נָקָם ***nāqām***, n.m. GK: 5934 [→ 5360; cf. 5358]. vengeance, revenge:– vengeance [12], avenge the quarrel (+5358) [1], avenged (+5358) [1], take vengeance (+5358) [1], taken vengeance (+5358) [1], taking vengeance (+5358) [1]

5360 נְקָמָה ***nᵉqāmâ***, n.f. GK: 5935 [→ 5359; cf. 5358]. vengeance, revenge:– vengeance [18], avengeth (+5414) [2], revenge [2], avenge (+5358) [1], avenge (+5414) [1], avenged (+5414) [1], revenging [1], take vengeance (+5358) [1]

5361 נָקַע ***nāqa'***, v. GK: 5936 [cf. 3363]. [Q] to turn away in disgust:– alienated [3]

5362 נָקַף ***nāqap***, v. GK: 5937 & 5938 [→ 5363, 5364; cf. 8622]. [Q] to go through a yearly cycle; [P] to cut down; to be destroyed; [H] to surround, encircle, engulf:– compassed about [2], compassed [2], compassing [2], compass [2], go round about [2], compass about [1], cut down [1], destroy [1], going about [1], gone about [1], gone round about [1], inclosed [1], kill [1], round [1]

5363 נֹקֶף ***nōqep***, n.[m.]. GK: 5939 [→ 5362]. beating (fruit off olive tree in harvest):– shaking [2]

5364 נִקְפָּה ***niqpâ***, n.f. GK: 5940 [→ 5362]. rope (around waist):– rent [1]

5365 נָקַר ***nāqar***, v. GK: 5941 [→ 5366]. [Q] to gouge out, peck out (an eye); [P] to gouge out; to pierce; [Pu] to be hewn out (of quarry rock):– put out [2], digged [1], pick out [1], pierced [1], thrust out [1]

5366 נְקָרָה ***nᵉqārâ***, n.f. GK: 5942 [→ 5365]. cleft; cavern:– clifts [1], clift [1]

5367 נָקַשׁ ***nāqaš***, v. GK: 5943 [cf. 3369, 6983; cf. 5368]. [N] to be ensnared; [P] to lay out snares; [Ht] to lay out traps, set a trap:– snared [2], catch [1], lay snares [1], layest a snare [1]

5368 נְקַשׁ ***nᵉqaš*** (Aram.), v. GK: 10491 [cf. 5367]. [P] to knock (together):– smote [1]

נֵר ***nēr***, נִר ***nir***. See 5215, 5216.

5369 נֵר ***nēr***, n.pr.m. GK: 5945 [→ 5216]. Ner, "*lamp*":– Ner [16]

5370 נֵרְגַל ***nērᵉgal***, n.pr. GK: 5946 [→ 5371]. Nergal (pagan god):– Nergal [1]

5371 נֵרְגַל שַׂר־אֶצֶר ***nērgal śar-'eṣer***, n.pr.m. GK: 5947 [→ 5370+8272]. Nergal-Sharezer, "*Nergal protect the prince!*":– Nergal-sharezer [3]

5372 נִרְגָּן ***nirgān***, v.ptcp. GK: 8087 [→ 7279]. ptcp. of 7279: grumbling, gossiping:– talebearer [3], whisperer [1]

5373 נֵרְדְּ ***nērd***, n.m. GK: 5948. nard (aromatic ointment):– spikenard [3]

נֵרָה ***nērâ***. See 5216.

5374 נֵרִיָּה ***nēriyyâ*** or נֵרִיָּהוּ ***nēriyyāhû***, n.pr.m. GK: 5949 & 5950 [→ 4490]. Neriah, "*lamp of Yahweh*":– Neriah [10]

5375 נָשָׂא ***nāśā'***, v. GK: 5951 [→ 4984]. [Q] to bear, carry, lift up; forgive; [Qp] to be forgiven, honored, carried; [N] to be carried off, lifted up; [P] to elevate, carry along; [H] to cause to carry, to bring; [Ht] to exalt oneself, lift up oneself; from the base meaning of rise in elevation come fig. extensions "to exalt, honor," as the lifting up of a person in status, and "to forgive," as the removal of guilt and its penalties; "to lift up the eyes" means "to look up":– lift up [121], bear [96], lifted up [37], bare [33], take [30], took up [22], take up [20], armourbearer (+3627) [18], took [18], carry [14], borne [13], carried [13], brought [11], bearing [10], bring [8], forgive [8], take away [8], beareth [7], exalted [7], set up [7], accept [6], taken [5], took away [5], carry away [4], forgiven [4], honourable (+6440) [4], laid [4], obtained [4], suffer [4], bringing [3], carrying [3], pardon [3], receive [3], spare [3], stirred up [3], taken away [3], accept (+6440) [2], accepted (+6440) [2], advanced [2], bring forth [2], burnt [2], carried away [2], continued (+3254) [2], exalt [2], forgavest [2], forgiving [2], high [2], laden [2], lifteth up [2], must needs be borne (+5375) [2], regard [2], respect [2], set [2], taketh [2], utterly take away (+5375) [2], wear [2], able to bear [1], accepted [1], accepteth [1], arise [1], bare up [1], barest [1], bear up [1], been [1], brought forth [1], carrieth away [1], cast [1], contain [1], desire (+5315) [1], ease [1], exalted above [1], extolled [1], fetch [1], fet [1], furnished [1], furthered [1], gift [1], given [1], hadst [1], have a desire (+5315) [1], helped [1], help [1], hold up [1], laded [1], liftest up [1], lifting up [1], lofty [1], magnified [1], married (+3807.1) [1], offer [1], pardoneth [1], pluck up [1], raise up [1], raise [1], regard (+6440) [1], regard persons (+4480+6440) [1], regardeth [1], respected [1], setteth [1], suffer to bear [1], suffered [1], sware (+3027) [1], swear (+3027) [1], swear [1], taken up [1], takest [1], taketh up [1], wearing [1], went on journey (+7272) [1], yield [1]

5376 נְשָׂא ***nᵉśā'*** (Aram.), v. GK: 10492 [cf. 4984]. [P] to take away, carry away; [Htpa] to revolt, rise up:– carried away [1], made insurrection [1], take [1]

5377 נָשָׁא ***nāšā'***, v. GK: 5958 [→ 4860, 4876]. [N] to be deceived; [H] to deceive:– deceive [7], deceived [4], greatly deceived (+5377) [2], beguiled [1], seize [1], utterly forget (+5382) [1]

5378 נָשָׁא ***nāšā'***, v. GK: 5957 [→ 4855, 4859, 4874, 5383, 5386; cf. 5392]. [Q] to give a loan, be a creditor; [H] to make a loan; to subject one to tribute:– exact [2], debt [1], taker of usury [1]

נָשִׂא ***nāsi'***. See 5387.

נְשֻׂאָה ***nᵉsu'â***. See 5385.

5379 נִשֵּׂאת ***niśśē't***, v.ptcp. GK: 5951 [→ 4984]. ptcp. of 5375: something lifted up, taken; gift:–

5380 נָשַׁב ***nāšab***, v. GK: 5959 [→ 822; cf. 5395, 5398]. [Q] to blow; [H] to cause to blow; to drive away:– bloweth [1], causeth to blow [1], drove away [1]

5381 נָשַׂג ***nāśag***, v. GK: 5952. [H] to overtake, catch up, attain; to reach, to be able to afford:– overtake [13], overtook [7], take hold [3], able to get (+3027) [2], obtain [2], reach unto [2], surely overtake (+5381) [2], ability (+3027) [1], able (+1767+3027+3509.1) [1], able (+3027) [1], able to bring (+3027) [1], attain unto [1], attained unto [1], can get (+3027) [1], get (+3027) [1], get [1], hand is able to get (+3027) [1], layeth [1], overtaken [1], overtaketh [1], put [1], remove [1], take hold on [1], taken hold upon [1], take [1], wax rich (+3027) [1]

5382 נָשָׁה ***nāšâ***, v. GK: 5960 [→ 4519, 4520, 5388; cf. 7876]. [Q] to forget; [N] to be forgotten; [P] to make forget; [H] to make one forget; to allow one to forget:– deprived [1], exacteth [1], forgat [1], forgotten [1], made forget [1], utterly forget (+5377) [1]

5383 נָשָׁה ***nāšâ***, v. GK: 5957 [→ 5378]. same as 5378: [Q] to give a loan, be a creditor; [H] to make a loan; to subject one to tribute:– exact [2], lent on usury [2], creditors [1], creditor [1], extortioner [1], giver of usury [1], lend (+4859) [1], lendeth [1], lend [1], usurer [1]

5384 נָשֶׁה ***nāšeh***, n.[m.]. GK: 5962. tendon (attached to the hip), perhaps the sciatic nerve:– shrank [2]

5385 נְשׂוּאָה ***nᵉśû'â***, n.f. GK: 5953 [→ 4984]. burden, load (of images that are carried about):– carriages [1]

5386 נְשִׁי ***nᵉšî***, n.[m.]. GK: 5963 [→ 5378]. debt:– debt [1]

5387 נָשִׂיא ***nāśî'***, n.m. GK: 5954 & 5955 [→ 4984]. leader, ruler, chief, prince; cloud, rising mist, damp fog:– prince [55], princes [40], captain [12], chief [9], rulers [3], ruler [3], vapours [3], chief over [1], clouds [1], governor [1], prince's (+3807.1) [1], prince's [1]

5388 נְשִׁיָּה ***nᵉšiyyâ***, n.f. GK: 5964 [→ 5382]. oblivion, place forgotten (by the LORD):– forgetfulness [1]

נָשִׁים ***nāšîm***. See 802.

5389 נְשִׁין ***nᵉšîn*** (Aram.), n.f.pl. GK: 10493 [cf. 802]. wives, women:– wives [1]

5390 נְשִׁיקָה ***nᵉšîqâ***, n.f. GK: 5965 [→ 5401]. kiss:– kisses [2]

5391 נָשַׁךְ ***nāšak***, v. GK: 5966 & 5967 [→ 5392]. [Q] to bite; to earn interest; to claim interest against; [Qp] to be bitten; [P] to bite; [H] to charge interest:– bite [6], lend upon usury [3], biteth [2], bitten [2], bit [2], lent upon usury [1]

5392 נֶשֶׁךְ ***nešek***, n.[m.]. GK: 5968 [→ 5391; cf. 5378]. interest, usury:– usury [12]

5393 נִשְׁכָּה ***niškâ***, n.f. GK: 5969 [cf. 3957]. room (for various uses: living, storage, etc.):– chamber [2], chambers [1]

5394 נָשַׁל ***nāšal***, v. GK: 5970. [Q] to take off, come off; to drive out:– cast out [1], cast [1], drave [1], loose [1], put off [1], put out [1], slippeth [1]

5395 נָשַׁם ***nāšam***, v. GK: 5971 [→ 5397, 8580; cf. 5380, 5398]. [Q] to gasp, pant:– destroy [1]

5396 נִשְׁמָה ***nišmâ*** (Aram.), n.f. GK: 10494 [cf. 5397]. breath, air that enters and exhales the lungs; fig., that which is animate and conscious: life:– breath [1]

5397 נְשָׁמָה ***n***^e^***šāmâ***, n.f. GK: 5972 [→ 5395; cf. 5396]. breath, blast of breath; by extension: life, life force, spirit:– breath [11], blast [3], breathed [2], breathe [2], spirit [2], breath (+7307) [1], breatheth [1], inspiration [1], souls [1]

5398 נָשַׁף ***nāšap***, v. GK: 5973 [→ 3244, 5399; cf. 5380, 5395]. [Q] to blow:– blow [2]

5399 נֶשֶׁף ***nešep***, n.m. GK: 5974 [→ 5398]. dusk, dawn (of morning); twilight (of evening):– twilight [6], night [3], dark [1], dawning of the day [1], dawning of the morning [1]

5400 נָשַׂק ***nāśaq***, v. GK: 5956. [N] to be kindled; [H] to kindle a fire, burn:– burn [1], kindled [1], kindleth [1]

5401 נָשַׁק ***nāšaq***, v. GK: 5975 & 5976 [→ 5390, 5402]. [Q] to be equipped, arm oneself; to kiss; [P] to kiss (repeatedly or intensely); a kiss can show familial or romantic affection, as well as homage and submission; [H] to brush against, touch up against:– kissed [21], kiss [9], armed [3], ruled [1], touched [1]

5402 נֶשֶׁק ***nešeq***, n.[m.]. GK: 5977 [→ 5401]. weapon; armory:– armour [3], weapons [2], armed men [1], armoury [1], battle [1], harness [1], weapon [1]

5403 נְשַׁר ***n***^e^***šar*** (Aram.), n.m. GK: 10495 [cf. 5404]. eagle, vulture:– eagle's [1], eagles' [1]

5404 נֶשֶׁר ***nešer***, n.m. GK: 5979 [cf. 5403]. eagle; vulture:– eagle [19], eagles [5], eagle's [1], eagles' [1]

5405 נָשַׁת ***nāšat***, v. GK: 5980. [Q] to be dry, be parched; [N] to be dried up:– failed [1], faileth [1], fail [1]

נְתִבָה ***n***^e^***tibâ***. See 5410.

5406 נִשְׁתְּוָן ***ništ***^e^***wān***, n.[m.]. GK: 5981 [cf. 5407]. letter, writing:– letter [2]

5407 נִשְׁתְּוָן ***ništ***^e^***wān*** (Aram.), n.m. GK: 10496 [cf. 5406]. official letter, decree:– letter [3]

נָתוּן ***natûn***. See 5411.

5408 נָתַח ***nātaḥ***, v. GK: 5983 [→ 5409]. [P] to cut into pieces:– cut [4], cut in pieces [3], divided [1], hewed in pieces [1]

5409 נֵתַח ***nētaḥ***, n.m. GK: 5984 [→ 5408]. piece (of butchered things or persons):– pieces [9], piece [3], parts [1]

5410 נָתִיב ***nātîb*** or נְתִיבָה ***n***^e^***tîbâ***, n.m. & f. GK: 5985 & 5986. path, way, road; by extension: behavior, lifestyle:– paths [14], path [8], way [2], pathway (+1870) [1], travellers (+1980) [1]

5411 נָתִין ***nātîn***, n.m. GK: 5987 [cf. 5414; cf. 5412]. temple servant:– Nethinims [17]

5412 נְתִין ***n***^e^***tîn*** (Aram.), n.m.pl. GK: 10497 [→ 5415; cf. 5411]. temple servant:– Nethinims [1]

5413 נָתַךְ ***nātak***, v. GK: 5988 [→ 2046]. [Q] to pour out; [N] to be poured out, be melted; [H] to pour out (liquid or money); to melt; [Ho] to be melted:– poured out [7], poured forth [3], poured [3], melted [2], melt [2], dropped [1], gathered together [1], gathered [1], molten [1]

5414 נָתַן ***nātan***, v. GK: 5989 [→ 866, 869, 868, 4976, 4977, 4979, 4980, 4991, 4992, 5411, 5416; cf. 4060, 5083; cf. 5415 (also used with compound proper names)]. [Q] to give, put; [Qp] to be given, dedicated; [N] to be given; [Ho or Qp] to be given; note the many contextual translations in the KJV:– give [471], gave [252], given [246], put [185], set [99], delivered [94], giveth [77], deliver [72], make [66], made [41], lay [22], gavest [21], O that (+4310) [17], yield [13], grant [12], laid [11], suffer [11], bring [10], granted [9], recompense [9], appointed [7], caused [7], givest [7], suffered [7], give up [6], send [6], cast [5], cause [5], committed [5], giving [5], shew [5], uttered [5], let [4], sent [4], surely give (+5414) [4], traded [4], utter [4], wholly given (+5414) [4], appoint [3], brought [3], fasten [3], occupied [3], place [3], putteth [3], set up [3], uttereth [3], add [2], applied [2], ascribed [2], ascribe [2], assigned [2], avengeth (+5360) [2], bestowed [2], bestow [2], bringeth [2], deliver up [2], delivered up [2], doubtless deliver (+5414) [2], fastened [2], given forth [2], hang up [2], indeed deliver (+5414) [2], laid up [2], maketh [2], offer [2], ordained [2], pay [2], surely given (+5414) [2], willingly give (+5414) [2], without fail deliver (+5414) [2], would God (+4310) [2], would to God (+4310) [2], God [1], appoint out [1], are delivered [1], avenge (+5360) [1], avenged (+5360) [1], be [1], bring forth [1], bringeth forth [1], causeth [1], charged [1], charge [1], cometh [1], commit [1], considered [1], count [1], cried [1], crieth out (+6963+871.1) [1], cry (+6963) [1], deliver over [1], deliveredst [1], delivereth [1], direct [1], distribute [1], done [1], frame [1], gave up [1], gift [1], give (+3027+871.1) [1], give forth [1], give leave [1], give out [1], give over [1], given over [1], given up [1], gotten [1], hang [1], hath [1], having the oversight (+871.1) [1], layeth up [1], leave [1], left [1], lend [1], let (+3807.1) [1], let out [1], lie (+7903) [1], lie carnally (+2233+7903+3807.1) [1], lie with (+7903) [1], lift up [1], liftest up [1], made sit [1], paid [1], pay (+4377) [1], perform [1], placed [1], planted [1], plant [1], pour [1], presented [1], print [1], pulled [1], put forth [1], put in [1], put on [1], put out [1], puttest [1], putteth out [1], putting [1], recompensed [1], recompensing [1], render [1], requite [1], restored [1], send out [1], sendeth forth [1], sendeth [1], sent out [1], set forth [1], setting [1], shewedst [1], shewed [1], shoot forth [1], shoot up [1], shot up [1], sing (+6963) [1], slanderest (+1848) [1], strike [1], submitted [1], suffereth [1], surely delivered [1], take heed (+3820) [1], taken up [1], thrust [1], tied [1], took [1], turned [1], turn [1], wept aloud (+1065+6963+871.1) [1], withdrew (+5637) [1], would God that (+4310) [1], yelled (+6963) [1], yield (+3027) [1], yieldeth [1]

5415 נְתַן ***n***^e^***tan*** (Aram.), v. GK: 10498 [→ 4978, 5412; cf. 3052; cf. 5414]. [P] to give, provide, supply:– giveth [3], bestow [2], give [1], pay [1]

5416 נָתָן ***nātān***, n.pr.m. GK: 5990 [→ 5414]. Nathan, "*gift*":– Nathan [42]

5417 נְתַנְאֵל ***n***^e^***tan'ēl***, n.pr.m. GK: 5991 [→ 5321+410]. Nethanel, "*God [El] has given*":– Nethaneel [14]

5418 נְתַנְיָה ***n***^e^***tanyâ*** or נְתַנְיָהוּ ***n***^e^***tanyāhû***, n.pr.m. GK: 5992 & 5993 [→ 5414+3068]. Nethaniah, "*Yahweh has given*":– Nethaniah [20]

5419 נְתַן־מֶלֶךְ ***n***^e^***tan-melek***, n.pr.m. GK: 5994 [→ 5414+4428]. Nathan-Melech, "*gift of king* or *gift of Melek, Molech, Malk*":– Nathan-melech [1]

5420 נָתַס ***nātas***, v. GK: 5995 [cf. 5421, 5422, 5428]. [Q] to break up, tear up:– mar [1]

5421 נָתַע ***nāta'***, v. GK: 5996 [cf. 5420, 5422, 5428]. [N] to be broken down, be knocked out (of teeth):– broken [1]

5422 נָתַץ ***nātaṣ***, v. GK: 5997 [cf. 5420, 5421, 5428]. [Q] to break down, tear down, demolish; [Qp] to be broken down; [N] to be shattered, lay in ruins; [P] to tear down, break down, shatter, destroy; [Pu] to be demolished; [Ho] to be broken up:– brake down [12], break down [5], broken down [5], destroy [4], beat down [3], cast down [3], thrown down [3], pull down [2], break out [1], destroyed [1], overthrow [1], threw down [1], throw down [1]

5423 נָתַק ***nātaq***, v. GK: 5998 [→ 5424]. [Q] to draw away, pull off; [Qp] to be torn; [N] to be lured away, be shattered, be torn, be broken; [P] to break, tear; [H] to lure away, drag off; [Ho] to be drawn away:– broken [6], burst [3], brake [2], drawn away [2], brake in sunder [1], break asunder [1], break [1], broken off [1], burst in sunder [1], drawn [1], draw [1], lift up [1], pluck off [1], plucked away [1], pluck [1], pull out [1], pull up [1], rooted out [1]

5424 נֶתֶק ***neteq***, n.m. GK: 5999 [→ 5423]. diseased area of skin: itch; some sources: ringworm, eczema:– scall [13], dry scall [1]

5425 נָתַר ***nātar***, v. GK: 6000 & 6001 & 6002. [Q] to leap up; [P] to hop up; [H] to make leap up, jump up; to let loose, set free, release, untie; withdraw:– drove asunder [1], leap [1], loosed [1], looseth [1], loose [1], maketh [1], moved [1], undo [1]

5426 נְתַר ***n***^e^***tar*** (Aram.), v. GK: 10499. [H/A] to strip off, shake off:– shake off [1]

5427 נֶתֶר ***neter***, n.[m.]. GK: 6003. natron (a sodium carbonate for washing):– nitre [2]

5428 נָתַשׁ ***nātaš***, v. GK: 6004 [cf. 5420, 5421, 5422]. [Q] to uproot; [N] to be uprooted; [Ho] to be uprooted:– pluck up [6], plucked up [2], utterly pluck up (+5428) [2], destroyed [1], forsaken [1], pluck out [1], pluck up by the roots [1], plucked out [1], pluckt up [1], pluck [1], pulled up [1], root out [1], root up [1], rooted out [1]

5429 סְאָה ***s***^e^***'â***, n.f. GK: 6006. seah (dry measure, one-third of an ephah, about seven quarts or liters):– two measures [4], measure [3], measures [2]

5430 סְאוֹן ***s***^e^***'ôn***, n.[m.]. GK: 6007 [→ 5431]. boot:– battle [1]

5431 סָאַן ***sā'an***, v.den. GK: 6008 [→ 5430]. [Q] to tramp along in boots:– warrior [1]

5432 סַאסְּאָה ***sa'ss***^e^***'â***, n.f. GK: 6009. warfare, chasing away:– measure [1]

5433 סָבָא ***sābā'***, v. or סָבָא ***sābā'***, n.m. GK: 6010 [→ 5435]. [Q] to be a drunkard, drink too much; [Qp] to be drunk; others: bind-weed, shrub; others: Sabean, cf. 5434:– drunkard [2], drunken [1], fill [1]

5434 סְבָא ***s***^e^***bā'***, n.pr.m. GK: 6013 [→ 5436]. Seba:– Seba [4]

5435 סֹבֶא ***sōbe'***, n.m. GK: 6011 [→ 5433]. wine, drink, implying drunkenness:– drink [1], drunkards [1], wine [1]

5436 סְבָאִי ***s***^e^***bā'î***, n.pl.g. GK: 6014 [→ 5434]. Sabean:– Sabeans [2]

5437 סָבַב ***sābab***, v. GK: 6015 [→ 4141]. [Q] to go around, surround, encircle, engulf; [N] to change direction; to be surrounded; [P] to change; [Pol] to surround, shield, go about; [H] to turn about, circle around; [Ho] to be set, mounted, surrounded; to be changed:– turned [21], compassed [15], compassed about [10], turn [10], compass [9], compass about [7], turned about [6], went about [6], go about [5], carried about [3], compasseth [3], led about [3], beset round about [2], changed [2], compassed in [2], driven [2], fetch a compass [2], go round about [2], inclosed [2], remove [2], returned [2], turn away [2], turned away [2], whirleth about continually (+1980+5437) [2], winding about [2], about on every side [1], applied [1], avoided [1], beset about [1], besieged [1], bring about [1], bring again [1], brought about [1], came round about [1], cast about [1], caused about [1], circuit [1], closed round about [1], compass round about (+5439) [1], compass round about [1], compassed round [1], compasseth about [1], environ round [1], fetch about [1], fetched a compass [1], fetcht a compass [1], gone about [1], make about [1], occasioned [1], on every side [1], removed [1], round about compassing (+5439) [1], set [1], sit down [1], stood round about [1], turn aside [1], turn back [1], turned aside [1], turned back [1], turneth about [1], turneth [1], turning [1], walk about [1]

5438 סִבָּה ***sibbâ***, n.f. GK: 6016 [→ 4141]. turning, arrangement (of events):– cause [1]

5439 סָבִיב ***sābîb***, subst. (used as pp. & adv.). GK: 6017 [→ 4141]. all around, on all sides, surrounding, encircling:– round about [204], round about (+5439) [52], about [24], round about (+4480) [20], on every side (+4480) [15], on every side [7], every side [3], on every side (+5439) [2], about (+4480) [1], all about [1], circuits [1], compass round about (+5437) [1], compass [1], in compass [1], places round about [1], round about compassing (+5437) [1]

5440 סָבַךְ ***sābak***, v. GK: 6018 [→ 5442, 5441; cf. 7730]. [Qp, Pu] to be entangled, entwined:– folden together [1], wrapped [1]

5441 סְבֹךְ ***s***^e^***bōk***, n.[m.]. GK: 6020 [→ 5440]. thicket, underbrush (where animals can live or hide):– thicket [1]

5442 סְבַךְ ***s***^e^***bak***, n.[m.]. GK: 6019 [→ 5440]. thicket, underbrush:– thickets [2], thicket [1], thick [1]

5443 שַׂבְּכָא ***śabb***^e^***kā'*** or סַבְּכָא ***sabb***^e^***kā'*** (Aram.), n.[f.]. GK: 10676 & 10501 [cf. 7638]. lyre (triangular instrument with four strings):– sackbut [4]

5444 סִבְּכַי ***sibb***^e^***kay***, n.pr.m. GK: 6021. Sibbecai:– Sibbecai [2], Sibbechai [2]

5445 סָבַל ***sābal***, v. GK: 6022 [→ 5447, 5448, 5449, 5450; cf. 2082; cf. 5446]. [Q] to bear, carry, sustain; [Pu] to be (heavy) laden; [Ht] to drag oneself along:– carry [3], bear [2], borne [1], burden [1], carried [1], strong to labour [1]

5446 סְבַל ***s***^e^***bal*** (Aram.), v. GK: 10502 [cf. 5445]. [Po] to be laid:– strongly laid [1]

5447 סֵבֶל ***sēbel***, n.[m.]. GK: 6023 [→ 5445]. burden; forced labor:– burdens [1], burden [1], charge [1]

5448 סֹבֶל ***sōbel***, n.m. GK: 6024 [→ 5445]. burden:– burden [3]

5449 סַבָּל ***sabbāl***, n.[m.]. GK: 6025 [→ 5445]. carrier, burden-bearer:– bearers of burdens [3], burdens [2]

5450 סִבְלוֹת ***siblôt***, n.f. GK: 6026 [→ 5445]. forced labor, burden-bearer:– burdens [6]

5451 סִבֹּלֶת **sibbōlet**, n.f. GK: 6027 [cf. 7641]. Sibboleth, "*ear of grain* or *torrent of water*":– sibboleth [1]

5452 סְבַר **s^e^bar** (Aram.), v. GK: 10503 [cf. 7663]. [P] to try, strive, seek:– think [1]

5453 סִבְרַיִם **sibrayim**, n.pr.loc. GK: 6028. Sibraim:– Sibraim [1]

5454 סַבְתָּא **sabtā'** or סַבְתָּה **sabtâ**, n.pr.g. GK: 6029 & 6030. Sabta, Sabtah:– Sabtah [1], Sabta [1]

5455 סַבְתְּכָא **sabt^e^kā'**, n.pr.g. GK: 6031. Sabteca:– Sabtecha [2]

5456 סָגַד **sāgad**, v. GK: 6032 [cf. 5457]. [Q] to bow down (in worship):– fall down [2], falleth down [2]

5457 סְגִד **s^e^gid** (Aram.), v. GK: 10504 [cf. 5456]. [P] to worship, pay honor:– worship [8], worshipped [2], worshippeth [2]

5458 סְגוֹר **s^e^gôr**, n.[m.]. GK: 6033 [→ 5462]. enclosure, closing (of the heart):– caul [1], gold [1]

5459 סְגֻלָּה **s^e^gullâ**, n.f. GK: 6035. treasured possession, personal property:– peculiar treasure [3], peculiar [2], jewels [1], proper good [1], special [1]

5460 סְגַן **s^e^gan** (Aram.), n.m. GK: 10505 [cf. 5461]. prefect, governor:– governors [5]

5461 סֶגֶן **segen**, n.m. GK: 6036 [cf. 5532; cf. 5460]. official, officer, commander:– rulers [16], princes [1]

5462 סָגַר **sāgar**, v. GK: 6037 & 6034 [→ 4525, 4526, 5458, 5474; cf. 5534; cf. 5463]. [Q] to shut, close; [Qp] to be shut; [N] to be confined, to be shut up, be imprisoned; [P] to deliver; [Pu] to be shut up, be barred, be closed; [H] to surrender, give over, deliver up; to put in isolation:– shut [30], shut up [23], pure [8], deliver up [5], deliver [5], delivered up [3], delivered [3], gave over [2], straitly shut up (+5462+2050.1) [2], closed up [1], closed [1], gave up [1], given up [1], inclosed [1], repaired [1], shut in [1], shutteth up [1], shutting [1], stop [1]

5463 סְגַר **s^e^gar** (Aram.), v. GK: 10506 [cf. 5462]. [P] to shut, close up:– shut [1]

5464 סַגְרִיר **sagrîr**, n.[m.]. GK: 6039. heavy rain, downpour of rain:– very rainy [1]

5465 סַד **sad**, n.[m.]. GK: 6040 [cf. 7702]. shackles:– stocks [2]

5466 סָדִין **sādîn**, n.[m.]. GK: 6041. linen garment:– fine linen [2], sheets [2]

5467 סְדֹם **s^e^dōm**, n.pr.loc. GK: 6042. Sodom:– Sodom [39]

5468 סֵדֶר **sēder**, n.[m.]. GK: 6043 [→ 4528?; cf. 7713]. order, arrangement; "the land of disorder" refers to the Underworld, the region of darkness and chaos:– order [1]

5469 סַהַר **sahar**, n.[m.]. GK: 6044 [→ 5470]. roundness; referring to the shape of a bowl:– round [1]

5470 סֹהַר **sōhar**, n.[m.]. GK: 6045 [→ 5469]. prison:– prison (+1004+1886.1) [8]

5471 סוֹא **sô'**, n.pr.m. GK: 6046. So:– So [1]

5472 סוּג **sûg**, v. GK: 6047 [→ 5253]. [Q] to turn away, be faithless, be disloyal; [N] to be turned back, be disloyal, be faithless; [H] to move, displace; [Ho] to be driven back:– turned [6], turned away [3], backslider [1], driven [1], gone back [1], go [1], turned back [1]

5473 סוּג **sûg**, v. GK: 6048 [cf. 5253; 7735?]. [Qp] to be encircled, be bordered (by lilies):– set about [1]

סוּג **sûg**. See 5509.

5474 סוּגַר **sûgar**, n.[m.]. GK: 6050 [→ 5462]. cage; some sources: neck-stock (of iron or wood):– ward [1]

5475 סוֹד **sôd**, n.[m.]. GK: 6051 [→ 1152; cf. 3245]. confidential talk, conspiracy; council, confidant:– secret [7], assembly [5], counsel [5], secrets [2], inward [1], secret counsel [1]

5476 סוֹדִי **sôdî**, n.pr.m. GK: 6052. Sodi, "*Yahweh confides*":– Sodi [1]

5477 סוּחַ **sûaḥ**, n.pr.m. GK: 6053. Suah, "[poss.] *offal, dung, viscera*":– Suah [1]

5478 סוּחָה **suḥâ**, n.f. GK: 6054 [→ 5501]. refuse, garbage, offal:– torn [1]

סוּט **sûṭ**. See 7750.

5479 סוֹטַי **sôṭay**, n.pr.m. GK: 6055. Sotai:– Sotai [2]

5480 סוּךְ **sûk**, v. GK: 6057 [→ 610; cf. 3251, 5258]. [Q] to anoint, to use oils or perfumes or lotions; [H] to put on lotions; [Ho] to be poured on; this can refer to the application of oils, perfumes, lotions, or resins to the body:– anoint [4], anointed [3], anoint at all (+5480) [2]

סוֹלְלָה **sôl^e^lâ**. See 5550.

5481 סוּמְפֹּנְיָה **sûmpōn^e^yâ** or סוּפֹּנְיָא **sûppōn^e^yā'** or סִיפֹּנְיָא **sîppōn^e^yā'** (Aram.), n.f. GK: 10507 & 10510 & 10512. musical instrument; sources vary widely: a wind instrument: pipe, bagpipe, double flute; a stringed instrument: dulcimer; a percussion instrument: drum, cymbal:– dulcimer [3]

5482 סְוֵנֵה **s^e^wēnēh**, n.pr.loc. GK: 6059. Syene = Aswan:– Syene [2]

5483 סוּס **sûs**, n.m. GK: 6061 & 6062 [→ 5484, 5485]. (male) horse, stallion; swallow, swift:– horses [97], horse [35], crane [2], horseback [2], on horseback (+7392) [2], horsehoofs (+6119) [1], horses' [1]

5484 סוּסָה **sûsâ**, n.f. GK: 6063 [→ 2701; cf. 5483]. (female) horse, mare:– company of horses [1]

5485 סוּסִי **sûsî**, n.f. GK: 6064 [→ 5483]. Susi, "*[my] horse*":– Susi [1]

5486 סוּף **sûp**, v. GK: 6066 [→ 5490, 5492; cf. 5487]. [Q] to come to an end; demolish; die; [H] to sweep away:– consume [3], consumed [2], have an end [1], perish [1], surely consume (+622) [1]

5487 סוּף **sûp** (Aram.), v. GK: 10508 [→ 5491; cf. 5486]. [P] to be fulfilled; [H] to bring to an end:– consume [1], fulfilled [1]

5488 סוּף **sûp**, n.m. GK: 6068 [→ 5489, 5492]. reed; Reed Sea (traditionally, Red Sea):– Red [24], flags [3], weeds [1]

5489 סוּף **sûp**, n.pr.loc. GK: 6069 [→ 5488]. Suph, "*reeds, bushes*":– Red [1]

5490 סוֹף **sôp**, n.m. GK: 6067 [→ 5486; cf. 5491]. end, conclusion, destiny; rear guard:– end [3], conclusion [1], hinder part [1]

5491 סוֹף **sôp** (Aram.), n.[m.]. GK: 10509 [→ 5487; cf. 5490]. end (of space, time, or circumstance):– end [5]

5492 סוּפָה **sûpâ**, n.f. & loc. GK: 6070 & 6071 [→ 5486, 5488]. storm wind, whirlwind, tempest, gale; Suphah, "*reeds, bushes*"; poss. Red (Reed) Sea:– whirlwind [10], storm [3], Red sea [1], tempest [1], whirlwinds [1]

5493 סוּר **sûr** or שׂוּר **śûr**, v. GK: 6073 & 8462 [→ 3249, 7795?]. [Q] to turn away, depart, leave; to saw; [Qp] to be rejected; [Pol] to drag from, turn aside; [H] to remove, get rid of, take off; [Ho] to be removed, be abolished; by extension: to forsake, reject:– depart [41], take away [41], departed [31], removed [20], taken away [18], put away [14], remove [14], turn aside [14], turned aside [14], took away [10], turn in [7], took off [4], turn away [4], turned in [4], turned [4], departeth [3], taken [3], took [3], turn [3], depart away [2], departing [2], escheweth [2], go aside [2], put off [2], take off [2], taketh away [2], take [2], beheaded (+7218) [1], brought [1], call back [1], declined [1], decline [1], eschewed [1], get out [1], go away [1], goeth [1], gone aside [1], gone away [1], go [1], grievous [1], laid by [1], lay away [1], left undone [1], past [1], pluck away [1], put away (+4480) [1], put down [1], put [1], rebel [1], removeth away [1], removing to and fro [1], removing [1], revolted [1], sour [1], turned away [1], turned back [1], turneth away [1], went [1], withdraw [1], without [1]

5494 סוּר **sûr**, a.vbl. GK: 6074 [cf. 3249]. corrupt:– degenerate [1]

5495 סוּר **sûr**, n.pr.loc. GK: 6075 [cf. 3249]. Sur:– Sur [1]

5496 סוּת **sût**, v. GK: 6077. [H] to incite, entice, urge, mislead:– moved [4], persuade [3], stirred up [2], entice [1], movedst [1], persuaded [1], persuadeth [1], provoked [1], removed [1], set on [1], setteth on [1], take away [1]

5497 סוּת **sût**, n.[m.]. GK: 6078 [→ 4533]. robe, garment:– clothes [1]

5498 סָחַב **sāḥab**, v. GK: 6079 [→ 5499]. [Q] to drag down:– draw out [2], drawn [1], draw [1], tear [1]

5499 סְחָבָה **s^e^ḥābâ**, n.f. GK: 6080 [→ 5498]. rag:– cast clouts [2]

5500 סָחָה **sāḥâ**, v. GK: 6081 [cf. 5501]. [P] to scrape away:– scrape [1]

5501 סְחִי **s^e^ḥî**, n.[m.]. GK: 6082 [→ 5478; cf. 5500]. scum, refuse:– offscouring [1]

סָחִישׁ **sāḥîš**. See 7823.

5502 סָחַף **sāḥap**, v. GK: 6085. [Q] to wash away (of rain); [N] to be washed away, be laid low:– sweeping [1], swept away [1]

5503 סָחַר **sāḥar**, v. GK: 6086 [→ 5504, 5505, 5506; cf. 4536]. [Q] to be a trader, a merchant; [Pealal] to pound, throb (of the heart):– merchants [9], merchant [4], trade [2], go about [1], merchant's [1], merchantmen (+376) [1], occupied (+3027) [1], panteth [1], traffick [1]

5504 סַחַר **saḥar**, n.m. GK: 6087 [→ 5503]. same as 5505: merchandise, profit (from merchandising in the marketplace):– merchandise [4]

5505 סָחַר **sāḥar**, v. GK: 6087 [→ 5503]. same as 5504: merchandise, profit (from merchandising in the marketplace):– merchandise [2], mart [1]

5506 סְחֹרָה **s^e^ḥōrâ**, n.f. GK: 6088 [→ 5503]. customer:– merchandise [1]

5507 סֹחֵרָה **sōḥērâ**, n.f. GK: 6089. rampart, wall:– buckler [1]

5508 סֹחֶרֶת **sōḥeret**, n.f. GK: 6090. costly stone (not specifically defined):– black [1]

סֵט **sēṭ**. See 7750.

5509 סוּג **sûg** or סִיג **sîg**, n.[m.]. GK: 6049 & 6092 [cf. 5253, 7873]. dross (usually of silver):– dross [8]

5510 סִיוָן **sîwān**, n.pr. GK: 6094. Sivan:– Sivan [1]

5511 סִיחוֹן **sîḥôn**, n.pr.m. GK: 6095. Sihon:– Sihon [37]

5512 סִין **sîn**, n.pr.loc. GK: 6096 & 6097. Sin = Pelusium; Sin (a desert area between Sinai and Elim, having nothing to do with sinfulness), "*[desert] of clay* [or poss.] *[desert] of Sin*":– Sin [6]

5513 סִינִי **sînî**, a.g. GK: 6098. Sinite:– Sinite [2]

5514 סִינַי **sînay**, n.pr.loc. GK: 6099. Sinai, "*Sin; glare [from white chalk]*":– Sinai [35]

5515 סִינִים **sînîm**, a.g.pl. GK: 6100. Sinim, Chinese [?]:– Sinim [1]

5516 סִיסְרָא **sîs^e^rā'**, n.pr.m. GK: 6102. Sisera:– Sisera [21]

5517 סִיעָא **sî'ā'** or סִיעֲהָא **sî^a^hā'**, n.pr.m. GK: 6103 & 6104. Sia, Siaha, "*assembly*":– Siaha [1], Sia [1]

סִיפֹּנְיָא **sipon^e^ya'**. See 5481.

5518 סִיר **sîr** or סִירָה **sîrâ**, n.m. & f. GK: 6105 & 6106 [cf. 5626]. pot, pan, caldron, washbasin; thorn, thornbush; fishhook, barb:– pot [12], pots [9], thorns [4], caldron [3], caldrons [2], washpot (+7366) [2], fishhooks (+1729) [1], pans [1]

5519 סָךְ **sāk**, n.[m.]. GK: 6107 [→ 5526]. multitude, throng:– multitude [1]

5520 סֹךְ **sōk**, n.[m.]. GK: 6108 [→ 5521, 5523; cf. 7900]. covering, dwelling (of human or lion):– covert [1], den [1], pavilion [1], tabernacle [1]

5521 סֻכָּה **sukkâ**, n.f. GK: 6109 [→ 5523; cf. 5520]. tabernacle, shrine; booth, shelter, dwelling, tent:– booths [9], tabernacles [9], pavilions [3], tabernacle [3], booth [2], pavilion [2], cottage [1], covert [1], tents [1]

5522 סִכּוּת **sikkût**, n.pr.?. GK: 6110. Sikkut (pagan god?):– tabernacle [1]

5523 סֻכּוֹת **sukkôt**, n.pr.loc. GK: 6111 [→ 5521; cf. 5520]. Succoth, "*booths*":– Succoth [18]

5524 סֻכּוֹת בְּנוֹת **sukkôt b^e^nôt**, n.pr. GK: 6112. Succoth Benoth (pagan god):– Succoth-benoth [1]

5525 סֻכִּיִּים **sukkiyyîm**, n.pr.m.pl. GK: 6113. Sukkite:– Sukkiims [1]

5526 סָכַךְ **sākak**, v. GK: 6114 & 6115 [→ 4329, 4539, 4540, 5519, 5527; cf. 5259, 7753]. [Q] to cover, conceal, overshadow, shield; to knit together; [Pol] to knit together; [H] to cover, shield; to relieve oneself:– covered [8], cover [5], covereth [2], covering [2], defence [1], defendest (+5921) [1], hedged in [1], join together [1], set [1], shut up [1]

5527 סְכָכָה **s^e^kākâ**, n.pr.loc. GK: 6117 [→ 5526]. Secacah, "*thicket, cover*":– Secacah [1]

5528 סָכַל **sākal**, v. GK: 6118 [→ 5530, 5529, 5531]. [N] to do a foolish thing; [P] to turn into foolishness; [H] to act like a fool:– done foolishly [5], maketh foolish [1], played the fool [1], turn into foolishness [1]

5529 סֶכֶל **sekel**, n.m. GK: 6120 [→ 5528]. foolishness, fool:– folly [1]

5530 סָכָל **sākāl**, n.m. GK: 6119 [→ 5528]. foolish (one), senseless, stupid:– fool [4], foolish [2], sottish [1]

5531 סִכְלוּת **siklût** or שִׂכְלוּת **śiklût**, n.f. GK: 6121 & 8508 [→ 5528]. folly:– folly [5], foolishness [2]

Heb

5532 סָכַן ***sākan***, v. GK: 6122 & 6125 [→ 4543; cf. 5461]. [Q] to be of use, benefit, profit; [H] to be in the habit; be familiar with; to get along well with:– ever wont (+5532) [2], profitable [2], acquainted [1], acquaint [1], advantage [1], cherish (+1961) [1], cherished (+1961) [1], profiteth [1], treasurer [1]

5533 סָכַן ***sākan***, v. GK: 6123 & 6124 [cf. 4542, 4544]. [N] to be endangered; [Pu] to be poor:– endangered [1], so impoverished [1]

5534 סָכַר ***sākar***, v. GK: 6126 & 6127 [cf. 5462]. [N] to be closed; be silent; [P] to hand over, deliver:– stopped [2], give over [1]

5535 סָכַת ***sākat***, v. GK: 6129. [H] to be silent, be still:– take heed [1]

סֻכֹּת ***sukkōt***. See 5523.

5536 סַל ***sal***, n.m. GK: 6130. basket:– basket [13], baskets [2]

5537 סָלָא ***sālā'***, v. GK: 6131 [→ 5543, 5544?; cf. 5541]. [Pu] to be weighed (in correlation to gold):– comparable [1]

5538 סִלָּא ***sillā'***, n.pr.loc. GK: 6133. Silla, "*embankment*":– Silla [1]

5539 סָלַד ***sālad***, v. GK: 6134 [→ 5540?]. [P] to skip (for joy):– harden [1]

5540 סֶלֶד ***seled***, n.pr.m. GK: 6135 [→ 5539?]. Seled, "*jump for joy*":– Seled [2]

5541 סָלָה ***sālâ***, v. GK: 6136 & 6137 [cf. 5537]. [Q] to reject, toss aside; [P] to reject; [Pu] to be bought, be paid for:– valued [2], trodden down [1], trodden under foot [1]

5542 סֶלָה ***selâ***, n.[f.] GK: 6138 [cf. 5549?]. selah (t.t. in the Psalms):– Selah [74]

5543 סַלֻּא ***sallu'*** or סַלּוּ ***sallû*** or סָלוּא ***sālû'*** or סַלַּי ***sallay***, n.pr.m. GK: 6132 & 6139 & 6140 & 6144 [→ 5537]. Sallu, Salu, Sallai, "[poss.] *he restores*":– Sallu [3], Sallai [2], Salu [1]

5544 סִלּוֹן ***sillôn***, n.m. GK: 6141 [→ 5537?]. thorn, brier:– brier [1], thorns [1]

5545 סָלַח ***sālaḥ***, v. GK: 6142 [→ 5546, 5547]. [Q] to forgive, release, pardon; [N] to be forgiven:– forgive [18], forgiven [13], pardon [11], pardoned [2], forgiveth [1], spare [1]

5546 סַלָּח ***sallāḥ***, a. GK: 6143 [→ 5545]. forgiving:– ready to forgive [1]

סַלַּי ***sallay***. See 5543.

5547 סְלִיחָה ***s***e***lîḥâ***, n.f. GK: 6145 [→ 5545]. forgiveness, pardon:– forgivenesses [1], forgiveness [1], ready to pardon [1]

5548 סַלְכָה ***salkâ***, n.pr.loc. GK: 6146. Salecah:– Salcah [2], Salchah [2]

5549 סָלַל ***sālal***, v. GK: 6147 & 6148 [→ 4546, 4547, 5550, 5551, 5552; cf. 5542?]. [Q] to build up, heap up (a highway), extol; to pile up; [Pil] to esteem, cherish; [Htpol] to behave haughtily, insolently:– cast up [6], raise up [2], exaltest [1], exalt [1], extol [1], made plain [1]

5550 סֹלְלָה ***sōl***e***lâ***, n.f. GK: 6149 [→ 5549; cf. 2150]. siege ramp, siege mound:– mount [5], bank [3], mounts [3]

5551 סֻלָּם ***sullām***, n.m. GK: 6150 [→ 5549]. stairway; some sources: ladder:– ladder [1]

5552 סַלְסִלָּה ***salsillâ***, n.[f.]. GK: 6151 [→ 5549]. branch, shoot; some sources: basket:– baskets [1]

5553 סֶלַע ***sela'***, n.m. GK: 6152 [→ 5554, 5555, 5638?]. rock, stone; rock formation: cliff, crag; by extension: stronghold, fortress; God as a "Rock" focuses on stability, faithfulness, and protection:– rock [47], rocks [9], ragged rocks [1], stones [1], stony [1], strong hold [1]

5554 סֶלַע ***sela'***, n.pr.loc. GK: 6153 [→ 5553]. Sela, "*rock crags, cliffs*":– Selah [1], Sela [1]

5555 סֶלַע הַמַּחְלְקוֹת ***sela' hammaḥl***e***qôt***, n.pr.loc. GK: 6154 [→ 5553]. Sela Hammahlekoth:– Sela-hammahlekoth [1]

5556 סָלְעָם ***sol'ām***, n.m. GK: 6155 [→ 5553?]. edible locust or katydid:– bald locust [1]

5557 סָלַף ***sālap***, v. GK: 6156 [→ 5558]. [P] to twist; to overthrow; to frustrate:– overthroweth [4], perverteth [2], pervert [1]

5558 סֶלֶף ***selep***, n.m. GK: 6157 [→ 5557]. duplicity, perversity, deceit:– perverseness [2]

5559 סְלִק ***s***e***laq*** (Aram.), v. GK: 10513 [→ 5267]. [P] to come up, go up; [H] to lift up; [Ho] to be lifted up:– came up [4], came [1]

5560 סֹלֶת ***sōlet***, n.f. GK: 6159. fine flour (likely wheat flour):– fine flour [35], flour [17], fine [1]

5561 סַם ***sam***, n.m. GK: 6160. fragrant perfume:– sweet [13], sweet spices [3]

5562 סַמְגַּר־נְבוֹ ***samgar-n***e***bô***, n.pr.m. GK: 6162 [→ 5015]. Samgar-Nebo:– Samgar-nebo [1]

5563 סְמָדַר ***s***e***mādar***, n.m. GK: 6163. blossom (of a vine):– tender grape [2], tender grapes [1]

5564 סָמַךְ ***sāmak***, v. GK: 6164 [→ 294, 3253, 5565]. [Q] to sustain, uphold; to lay (one's hand upon); [Qp] to be braced, be steadfast; [N] to lean upon, rely upon, gain confidence; [P] to strengthen, refresh:– lay [12], laid [6], put [5], uphold [5], sustained [3], upholdeth [3], lean [2], stay [2], borne up [1], established [1], holden up [1], leaned [1], lieth hard [1], rested [1], set [1], stand fast [1], stayed [1], upheld [1]

5565 סְמַכְיָהוּ ***s***e***makyāhû***, n.pr.m. GK: 6165 [→ 5564]. Semakiah, "*Yahweh sustains, consecrates*":– Semachiah [1]

5566 סֶמֶל ***semel***, n.m. GK: 6166. image, idol:– idol [2], image [2], figure [1]

5567 סָמַן ***sāman***, v. GK: 6168. [N] to be appointed, apportioned:– appointed [1]

5568 סָמַר ***sāmar***, v. GK: 6169 [→ 4548, 5569; cf. 4930]. [Q] to tremble, shudder (i.e., to have goose bumps, gooseflesh); [P] to bristle, stand on end (of hair):– stood up [1], trembleth [1]

5569 סָמָר ***sāmār***, a. GK: 6170 [→ 5568]. bristling (locust):– rough [1]

5570 סְנָאָה ***s***e***nā'â*** or הַסְּנָאָה ***hass***e***nā'â***, n.pr.m. GK: 6171 & 2189 [→ 1886.1, 8130, cf. 5574]. Hassenaah, Senaah, "*the hated one*":– Senaah [2], Hassenaah [1]

סְנֻאָה ***s***e***nu'â***. See 5574.

5571 סַנְבַלַּט ***sanballaṭ***, n.pr.m. GK: 6172. Sanballat, "*Sin has given life*":– Sanballat [10]

5572 סְנֶה ***s***e***neh***, n.m. GK: 6174. bush, thorny shrub:– bush [6]

5573 סֶנֶּה ***senneh***, n.pr.loc. GK: 6175. Seneh, "*thorny;* [poss.] *[cliff shaped like] a tooth*":– Seneh [1]

סַנָּה ***sannâ***. See 7158.

5574 סְנוּאָה ***s***e***nû'â*** or הַסְּנֻאָה ***hass***e***nu'â***, n.pr.m. GK: 6176 & 2190 [→ 1886.1+8130; cf. 5570]. Senuah, Hassenuah, "*the hated one*":– Hasenuah [1], Senuah [1]

5575 סַנְוֵרִים ***sanwērîm***, n.[m.pl.]. GK: 6177. blindness:– blindness [3]

5576 סַנְחֵרִיב ***sanḥērîb***, n.pr.m. GK: 6178. Sennacherib, "*Sin has increased the brothers; Sin replace the [lost] brothers!*":– Sennacherib [13]

5577 סַנְסִנָּה ***sansinnâ***, n.[m.]pl. GK: 6180. fruit cluster (of date tree):– boughs [1]

5578 סַנְסַנָּה ***sansannâ***, n.pr.loc. GK: 6179. Sansannah, "*palm branch*":– Sansannah [1]

5579 סְנַפִּיר ***s***e***nappîr***, n.[m.]. GK: 6181. fin:– fins [5]

5580 סָס ***sās***, n.m. GK: 6182. (garment) moth; some sources: worm:– worm [1]

סֻס ***sus***. See 5483.

5581 סִסְמַי ***sismay***, n.pr.m. GK: 6183. Sismai, "[poss.] *belonging to Sisam*":– Sisamai [2]

5582 סָעַד ***sā'ad***, v. GK: 6184 [→ 4552; cf. 5583]. [Q] to sustain, support, refresh:– comfort [3], strengthen [2], held up [1], hold up [1], holden up [1], refresh [1], stablish [1], strengtheneth [1], upholden [1]

5583 סְעַד ***s***e***'ad*** (Aram.), v. GK: 10514 [cf. 5582]. [Pa] to help, support:– helping [1]

5584 סָעָה ***sā'â***, v. GK: 6185. [Q] to slander, defame, speak with malice:– storm [1]

5585 סָעִיף ***sā'îp***, n.[m.]. GK: 6186 & 6187 [→ 5586, 5587, 5588, 5589, 5634]. cleft, crag; bough, branch:– branches [2], top [2], clifts [1], tops [1]

5586 סָעַף ***sā'ap***, v.den. GK: 6188 [→ 5585]. [P] to lop off, trim down:– lop [1]

5587 סְעִפִּים ***s***e***'ippîm*** or שְׂעִפִּים ***ś***e***'ippîm***, n.f. GK: 6191 & 8546 [→ 5588, 8312; cf. 5585]. disquieted thoughts, troubled thoughts; division, divided opinion, a fig. extension of hobbling on crutches made of boughs:– thoughts [2], opinions [1]

5588 סֵעֵף ***sē'ēp***, a. GK: 6189 [→ 5587; cf. 5585]. double-minded, divided in heart:– thoughts [1]

5589 סְעַפָּה ***s***e***'appâ***, n.f. GK: 6190 [→ 5585]. bough:– boughs [2]

5590 סָעַר ***sā'ar***, v. GK: 6192 [→ 5591; cf. 8175]. [Q] to grow stormier, rougher; [N] to be enraged; [P] to scatter in a wind; [Po] to scatter, swirl; [Pu] to be lashed by storms:– tempestuous [2], came out as a whirlwind [1], driven with a whirlwind [1], scattered with a whirlwind [1], sore troubled [1], tossed with tempest [1]

5591 סַעַר ***sa'ar*** or סְעָרָה ***s***e***'ārâ***, n.m. GK: 6193 & 6194 [cf. 5590]. windstorm, tempest, gale:– whirlwind [11], tempest [6], stormy [4], storm [1], whirlwind (+7307) [1], whirlwinds [1]

5592 סַף ***sap***, n.m. GK: 6195 & 6196 & 6197 [→ 5605]. threshold, door frame, entrance, doorway; doorkeeper; basin, bowl; wool, hide, skin:– door [10], threshold [6], basons [2], bason [2], bowls [2], doors [2], gates [2], posts [2], thresholds [2], cup [1], door posts [1]

5593 סַף ***sap***, n.pr.m. GK: 6198 [cf. 5598]. Saph, "*basin, threshold*":– Saph [1]

5594 סָפַד ***sāpad***, v. GK: 6199 [→ 4553, 5636?]. [Q] to beat the breast, mourn, lament, weep; [N] to be mourned:– lament [9], mourn [9], mourned [6], lamented [4], mourners [1], wail [1]

5595 סָפָה ***sāpâ***, v. GK: 6200. [Q] to sweep away; take away; bring disaster; [N] to be swept away; be destroyed:– consumed [5], add [3], destroy [3], destroyed [2], perish [2], augment [1], consume [1], heap [1], joined [1], put [1]

5596 סָפַח ***sāpaḥ*** or שָׂפַח ***śāpaḥ***, v. GK: 6202 & 6203 & 8558 [→ 4555, 5599; cf. 4939, 8198]. [Q] to associate, attach to; [N] to be attached, be united; [P] to pour out; to bring sores, make scabby; [Pu] be joined together; [Ht] to feel oneself attached to:– abiding [1], cleave [1], gathered together [1], puttest [1], put [1], smite with a scab [1]

5597 סַפַּחַת ***sappaḥat***, n.f. GK: 6204 [→ 4556]. rash, skin eruption:– scab [2]

5598 סִפַּי ***sippay***, n.pr.m. GK: 6205 [cf. 5593]. Sippai:– Sippai [1]

5599 סָפִיחַ ***sāpîaḥ***, n.[m.]. GK: 6206 & 6207 [→ 5596]. what grows on its own, after-growth in a fallow year; torrent, downpour:– such as growth of itself [1], such things as grow of themselves [1], that which growth of it own accord [1], that which growth of itself [1], things which grow [1]

5600 סְפִינָה ***s***e***pînâ***, n.f. GK: 6208 [→ 5603]. ship (with a covering or deck):– ship [1]

5601 סַפִּיר ***sappîr***, n.[m.]. GK: 6209. sapphire; some sources: lapis lazuli:– sapphire [7], sapphires [3], sapphire stone [1]

5602 סֵפֶל ***sēpel***, n.[m.]. GK: 6210. bowl (for water or curdled milk):– bowl [1], dish [1]

5603 סָפַן ***sāpan***, v. GK: 6211 [→ 5600, 5604; cf. 8226]. [Q] to cover; [Qp] to be roofed, be paneled, be roofed:– covered [3], cieled [2], seated [1]

5604 סִפֻּן ***sippun***, n.[m.]. GK: 6212 [→ 5603]. ceiling:– cieling [1]

5605 סָפַף ***sāpap***, v.den. GK: 6214 [→ 5592]. [Htpol] to stand at the threshold:– doorkeeper [1]

5606 סָפַק ***sāpaq*** or שָׂפַק ***śāpaq***, v. GK: 6215 & 6216 & 8562 & 8563 [→ 5607]. [Q] to clap hands (in derision); beat one's breast; to punish, slap; to wallow, splash; to be enough; [H] to clasp hands:– clap [2], clappeth [1], please [1], smite [1], smote together [1], smote [1], striketh [1], suffice [1], wallow [1]

5607 סֵפֶק ***sepeq*** or שֵׂפֶק ***śēpeq***, n.[m.]. GK: 6217 & 8565 [→ 5606]. riches, abundance, plenty, sufficiency:– stroke [1], sufficiency [1]

5608 סָפַר ***sāpar***, v. GK: 6218 & 6221 [→ 5612; cf. 5613]. [Q] to count, number, take a census; [N] to be counted, be recorded; by extension: [P] to tell, proclaim, recount (an event or principle); [Pu] to be told:– scribe [42], told [26], declare [20], tell [12], numbered [11], number [10], scribes [6], shew forth [5], count [4], declared [4], counted [2], scribe's [2], speak [2], writer's [2], writer [2], accounted [1], commune [1], numberest [1], numbering [1], penknife (+8593+1886.1) [1], reckon [1], shewing [1], talk [1], tellest [1], telling [1], told out [1]

5609 סְפַר ***s***e***par*** (Aram.), n.m. GK: 10515 [→ 5613; cf. 5612]. record, archive, book (though not a book in the sense of a codex with bound pages); the phrase "book of Moses" means the first five books of the Bible:– book [3], books [1], rolls [1]

5610 סְפָר ***s***e***pār***, n.[m.]. GK: 6222 [→ 5612]. census:– numbering [1]

Heb

5611 סְפָר ***sᵉpār***, n.pr.loc. GK: 6223 [cf. 8234]. Sephar:– Sephar [1]

5612 סֵפֶר ***sēper*** or סִפְרָה ***siprâ***, n.m. GK: 6219 & 6225 [→ 4557, 4558?, 4559, 5608, 5610, 5615, 5618, 7158; cf. 5609]. book (as a scroll or tablet), scroll, letter, certificate, deed, dispatch:– book [136], letters [16], letter [13], evidence [6], bill [4], learned (+3045) [3], books [2], evidences [2], learning [2], register [1], scrole [1]

5613 סָפַר ***sāpar*** (Aram.), n.m. GK: 10516 [→ 5609; cf. 5608]. teacher of the Law; secretary (an official), scribe:– scribe [6]

5614 סְפָרַד ***sᵉpārad***, n.pr.loc. GK: 6224. Sepharad:– Sepharad [1]

סִפְרָה ***siprâ***. See 5612.

5615 סְפֹרוֹת ***sᵉpōrôt***, n.f. GK: 6228 [→ 5612]. measure, number; some sources: art of writing:– numbers [1]

5616 סְפַרְוִים ***sᵉparwîm***, a.g. GK: 6227 [→ 5617]. Sepharvite, "*of Sepharvaim*":– Sepharvites [1]

5617 סְפַרְוַיִם ***sᵉparwayim***, n.pr.loc. GK: 6226 [→ 5616]. Sepharvaim:– Sepharvaim [6]

5618 סֹפֶרֶת ***sōperet*** or סוֹפֶרֶת ***sôperet***, n.[pr.]m. GK: 6230 & 6072 [→ 5612]. (office of) scribes; as n.pr. Sophereth, "*scribe*":– Sophereth [2]

5619 סָקַל ***sāqal***, v. GK: 6232. [Q] to stone (as an execution); [N] to be stoned; [P] to throw stones (out or away), pelt with stones; [Pu] to be stoned:– stone [7], stoned [6], surely stoned (+5619) [4], cast [1], gathered out stones [1], gather [1], stoning [1], threw [1]

5620 סַר ***sar***, a. GK: 6234 [→ 5637]. sullen, dejected, discouraged:– heavy [2], so sad [1]

5621 סָרָב ***sārāb***, n.m. GK: 6235. briers:– briers [1]

5622 סַרְבָּל ***sarbāl*** (Aram.), n.[m.]. GK: 10517. robe, garment; variously translated as "hose, trousers, tunic, mantle, coat, cloak":– coats [2]

5623 סַרְגוֹן ***sargôn***, n.pr.m. GK: 6236. Sargon, "*firm, faithful king; the king is legitimate*":– Sargon [1]

5624 סֶרֶד ***sered***, n.pr.m. GK: 6237 [→ 5625]. Sered:– Sered [2]

5625 סַרְדִּי ***sardî***, a.g. GK: 6238 [→ 5624]. Seredite, "*of Sered*":– Sardites [1]

5626 סִרָה ***sirâ***, n.pr.[loc.]. GK: 6241 [→ 953+5626; cf. 5518]. Sirah:– Sirah [1]

5627 סָרָה ***sārâ***, n.f. GK: 6239 & 6240 [→ 3249, 5637]. ceasing, stopping; rebellion, revolt:– rebellion [2], revolt [2], continual (+1115) [1], revolted [1], turn away [1], wrong [1]

5628 סָרַח ***sāraḥ***, v. GK: 6243 & 6244 & 6242 [→ 5629; cf. 8294]. [Q] to hang down, overhang, spread over; [Qp] to be overhanged; [N] to be decayed, be spoiled, become stinking:– hang [2], exceeding in dyed attire (+2871) [1], spreading [1], stretched [1], stretch [1], vanished [1]

5629 סֶרַח ***seraḥ***, n.m. GK: 6245 [→ 5628]. overhang, what projects over:– remnant [1]

5630 סִרְיוֹן ***siryôn***, n.[m.]. GK: 6246 [cf. 8302, 8303]. (scale) armor, coat of mail:– brigandines [1], brigandine [1]

5631 סָרִיס ***sārîs***, n.m. GK: 6247 [→ 7249]. court official, palace officer, eunuch:– eunuchs [15], chamberlains [9], officers [7], officer [5], chamberlain [4], eunuch [2]

5632 סָרַךְ ***sārak*** (Aram.), n.m. GK: 10518. administrator:– presidents [5]

5633 סֶרֶן ***seren***, n.[m.]. GK: 6248 & 6249. axle; ruler, prince:– lords [21], plates [1]

5634 סַרְעַפָּה ***sar'appâ***, n.f. GK: 6250 [→ 5585]. bough:– boughs [1]

5635 סָרַף ***sārap***, v. GK: 6251 [cf. 8313]. [P] to burn:– burneth [1]

5636 סִרְפָּד ***sirpād***, n.[m.]. GK: 6252 [→ 5594?]. briers, stinging nettles:– brier [1]

5637 סָרַר ***sārar***, v. GK: 6253 [→ 5620, 5627]. [Q] to be stubborn, be obstinate, be rebellious:– rebellious [6], stubborn [4], revolters [2], away [1], backsliding [1], revolting [1], slideth back [1], withdrew (+5414) [1]

5638 סְתָו ***sᵉtāw***, n.m. GK: 6255. winter, rainy season:– winter [1]

5639 סְתוּר ***sᵉtûr***, n.pr.m. GK: 6256 [→ 5641]. Sethur, "*concealed [by deity]*":– Sethur [1]

5640 סָתַם ***sātam*** or שָׂתַם ***śātam***, v. GK: 6258 & 8608. [Q] to stop up, block off, seal; [Qp] to be closed up, (by extension) to be in a secret place; [N] to be closed; [P] to stop up:– stopped [5], shut up [2], stop [2], closed up [1], hidden [1], secret [1], shutteth out [1], stopt [1]

5641 סָתַר ***sātar***, v. GK: 6259 [→ 4563, 4564, 4565, 5639, 5643; cf. 5642]. [Q] to be hidden, be concealed, have a refuge; [P] to hide; [Pu] to be hidden; [H] to hide, conceal; [Ht] to hide oneself, keep oneself hidden:– hide [32], hid [29], hidest [5], hideth [5], secret [3], kept close [2], surely hide (+5641) [2], absent [1], conceal [1], keep secret [1]

5642 סְתַר ***sᵉtar*** (Aram.), v. GK: 10519 & 10520 [cf. 5641, cf. 8368]. [P] to destroy, demolish; [Pap] to be hidden; (as noun) hidden things:– destroyed [1], secret [1]

5643 סֵתֶר ***sēter*** or סִתְרָה ***sitrâ***, n.[m.]. GK: 6260 & 6261 [cf. 5641]. hiding place, secret place, shelter; covering, veil; (adv.) secretly, in secret:– secretly (+871.1+1886.1) [9], secret [9], covert [5], secret place [4], hiding place [3], backbiting [1], covering [1], disguiseth [1], privily [1], protection [1], secret places [1]

5644 סִתְרִי ***sitrî***, n.pr.m. GK: 6262. Sithri, "[poss.] *Yahweh is my hiding place*":– Zithri [1]

5645 עָב ***'āb***, n.m. GK: 6265 & 6266 [→ 5743]. clouds; thicket:– clouds [15], cloud [7], thick clouds [5], thick cloud [2], clay [1], thickets [1], thick [1]

5646 עָב ***'āb***, n.m. GK: 6264. overhang, overhanging roof:– thick beam [1], thick planks [1], thick [1]

5647 עָבַד ***'ābad***, v. GK: 6268 [→ 4566, 5650, 5652, 5653, 5656, 5657, 5659, 5744 (also used with compound proper names); cf. 5648]. [Q] to work, serve, labor, do; to worship, minister, work in ministry; [N] to be plowed, be cultivated; [Pu] to be worked; [H] to reduce to servitude, enslave, cause to serve; [Ho] to be caused to serve, worship (a god):– serve [153], served [61], do [14], worshippers [5], servants [4], till [4], do service [3], made to serve [3], serveth [3], work [3], caused to serve [2], dress [2], labour [2], serving [2], tilled [2], tilleth [2], been[S] [1], bondmen [1], bondservice [1], bring to pass [1], cause to serve [1], compel to serve (+5656) [1], do work [1], done [1], eared [1], ear [1], execute [1], husbandman (+120+376) [1], keep in bondage [1], keep [1], labouring [1], made serve [1], servant [1], servedst [1], set a work [1], tiller [1], tillest [1], useth service [1], wrought [1]

5648 עֲבַד ***ᵃbad*** (Aram.), v. GK: 10522 [→ 4567, 5649, 5673; cf. 5647]. [P] to do, make; [Htpe] to be done, be made, be turned into; a general word of activity and occurrence; the context determines the best translation, "do, make, obey, happen," etc:– made [7], do [5], done [4], cut [2], did [2], doest [1], doeth [1], executed [1], goeth on [1], kept [1], moved [1], worketh [1], wrought [1]

5649 עֲבֵד ***ᵃbēd*** (Aram.), n.m. GK: 10523 [→ 5648; cf. 5650]. servant:– servants [6], servant [1]

5650 עֶבֶד ***'ebed***, n.m. GK: 6269 [→ 5647, 5651, 5658, 5660, 5661; cf. 5649 (also used with compound proper names)]. servant, slave, attendant, indentured servants and owned slaves had varying levels of status and responsibilities; according to the OT Law, a Hebrew slave could be sold to a Hebrew master for only six years, but there was no time limit for Gentile slaves:– servants [370], servant [362], bondmen [15], manservant [12], bondage [10], menservants [9], servant's [8], bondman [6], servants' [4], bondservant [1], manservant's [1], manservants [1]

5651 עֶבֶד ***'ebed***, n.pr.m. GK: 6270 [→ 5650]. Ebed, "*servant*":– Ebed [6]

5652 עֲבָד ***ᵃbād***, n.m. GK: 6271 [→ 5647]. what is done, deed, act:– works [1]

5653 עַבְדָּא ***'abdā'***, n.pr.m. GK: 6272 [→ 5647]. Abda, "*servant of Yahweh*":– Abda [2]

5654 עֹבֵד־אֱדוֹם ***'ōbēd-'ᵉdôm***, n.pr.m. GK: 6273 [→ 5647+123]. Obed-Edom, "*servant [worshiper] of Edom*":– Obed-edom [20]

5655 עַבְדְּאֵל ***'abdᵉ'ēl***, n.pr.m. GK: 6274 [→ 5650+410; cf. 5661]. Abdeel, "*servant of God [El]*":– Abdeel [1]

5656 עֲבֹדָה ***ᵃbōdâ***, n.f. GK: 6275 [→ 5647; cf. 5673]. work, service, labor, task, duty, job; special work and service to God: service, ministry; forced labor: slavery:– service [94], servile [12], work [10], bondage [8], act [2], all manner of service (+5656+2050.1) [2], any manner of service (+5656+2050.1) [2], every kind of service (+5656+2050.1) [2], servitude [2], tillage [2], compel to serve (+5647) [1], effect [1], labour [1], ministering [1], ministry [1], office [1], serveth [1], use [1], wrought [1]

5657 עֲבֻדָּה ***ᵃbuddâ***, n.f. GK: 6276 [→ 5647]. servant, slave:– household [1], servants [1]

5658 עַבְדּוֹן ***'abdôn***, n.pr.m. & loc. GK: 6277 & 6278 [cf. 5650]. Abdon, "*servant*":– Abdon [8]

5659 עַבְדוּת ***'abdut***, n.f. GK: 6285 [→ 5647]. slavery, servitude:– bondage [3]

5660 עַבְדִּי ***'abdî***, n.pr.m. GK: 6279 [→ 5661?]. Abdi, "*servant of Yahweh* or *my servant*":– Abdi [3]

5661 עַבְדִּיאֵל ***'abdî'ēl***, n.pr.m. GK: 6280 [→ 5655, 5660?; cf. 5655]. Abdiel, "*servant of God [El]*":– Abdiel [1]

5662 עֹבַדְיָה ***'ōbadyâ*** or עֹבַדְיָהוּ ***'ōbadyāhû***, n.pr.m. GK: 6281 & 6282 [→ 5647+3068]. Obadiah, "*servant [worshiper] of Yahweh*":– Obadiah [20]

5663 עֶבֶד־מֶלֶךְ ***'ebed-melek***, n.pr.m. GK: 6283 [→ 5650+4428]. Ebed-Melech, "*servant of Melek [king]* or *Malk*":– Ebed-melech [6]

5664 עֲבֵד נְגוֹ ***ᵃbēd nᵉgô***, n.pr.m. GK: 6284 [→ 5650+5015; cf. 5665]. Abednego, "*servant of Nego* or *Nebo*":– Abed-nego [1]

5665 עֲבֵד נְגוֹ ***ᵃbēd nᵉgô*** (Aram.), n.pr.m. GK: 10524 [→ 5649; cf. 5664]. Abednego, "*servant of Nego* or *Nebo*":– Abed-nego [14]

5666 עָבָה ***'ābâ***, v. GK: 6286 [→ 4568, 5672]. [Q] to be thick:– thicker [2], grown thick [1]

5667 עֲבוֹט ***ᵃbôṭ***, n.[m.]. GK: 6287 [→ 5670, 5671]. pledge, (garment) security (for a loan):– pledge [4]

5668 עֲבוּר ***ᵃbûr***, pp. & c. GK: 6288. marker of cause or reason: for, because; marker of purpose or intent: on account of; in order to; a marker of result: then; benefit: for:– for sake (+871.1) [14], that (+871.1) [10], for (+871.1) [7], because of (+871.1) [5], to (+871.1) [3], because (+871.1) [2], for sakes (+871.1) [2], sake [2], and (+871.1) [1], for cause (+871.1) [1], for to (+871.1) [1], to (+871.1+3807.1) [1]

5669 עֲבוּר ***ᵃbûr***, n.[m.]. GK: 6289 [→ 5674]. produce, yield:– old corn [2]

5670 עָבַט ***'ābaṭ***, v.den. GK: 6292 & 6293 [→ 5667]. [Q] to borrow, i.e., take or receive a pledge; [P] to swerve, change (a course), implying a lack of purpose; [H] to lend on a pledge:– surely lend (+5670) [2], borrow [1], break [1], fetch [1], lend [1]

5671 עַבְטִיט ***'abṭîṭ***, n.[m.]intens. GK: 6294 [→ 5667]. heavy pledges, excessive mortgage for a debt; there may be an implication of undue force being used to keep the pledge:– thick clay [1]

5672 עֲבִי ***ᵃbî***, n.[m.]. GK: 6295 [→ 5666]. thickness, density, mold:– thickness [2], thick [2]

5673 עֲבִידָה ***ᵃbîdâ*** (Aram.), n.f. GK: 10525 [→ 5648; cf. 5656]. work, service, administration:– work [3], affairs [2], service [1]

5674 עָבַר ***'ābar***, v. GK: 6296 & 6297 [→ 4569, 5669, 5676, 5677, 5678, 5679, 5682]. [Q] to pass over, cross over, travel through; [N] to be crossed; [P] to extend; to breed; [H] to make pass through, let pass over, send over; by extensions: to forgive, as the passing over of guilt; [Ht] to be very angry, show oneself angry:– pass [46], passed over [43], pass over [40], passed [34], go over [29], passed by [17], went over [17], pass through [14], passeth [14], transgressed [12], went [11], gone over [10], passed on [10], come over [9], go [9], past [9], pass on [8], passed along [7], cause to pass [6], go through [6], gone [6], pass away [6], caused to pass [5], come [5], pass by [5], passeth by [5], wroth [5], goeth [4], passed through [4], passengers [4], passeth away [4], passing [4], put away [4], transgress [4], went on [4], caused to pass through [3], made pass [3], made to pass [3], make to pass [3], went through [3], at all brought over (+5674) [2], brought over [2], brought [2], carry over [2], cause to pass through [2], fail [2], go beyond [2], go by [2], go on [2], made a proclamation (+6963) [2], make go [2], overpast [2], passest over [2], passest [2], sent over [2], speedily pass over (+5674) [2], sweet smelling [2], take away [2], turn away [2], alienate [1], altered [1], beyond [1], bring over [1], brought through [1], came along [1], came by [1], came over [1], came [1], carried over [1], cause to sound [1], caused to be proclaimed (+6963) [1], charged (+5921) [1], cometh [1], coming on [1], conduct over [1], conducted [1], convey over [1], current [1], delivered [1], do away [1], enter [1], escape [1], gendereth [1], get over [1], go in [1], goeth forth [1], goeth over [1], going over [1], going [1], have away [1], have more than [1], laid [1], made a partition [1], made proclamation (+6963) [1], made to pass by [1], made to

Heb

pass through [1], make pass [1], make proclamation (+6963) [1], make sound [1], make to transgress [1], maketh to pass through [1], meddleth [1], overcome [1], overpass [1], overran [1], overrunning [1], over [1], pass away from [1], pass by (+1870) [1], passage [1], passed away [1], passed beyond [1], passedst over [1], passengers (+1870) [1], passest on [1], passeth along [1], passeth on along [1], passeth out [1], passeth over [1], passeth through [1], passing by [1], passing through [1], perishing [1], perish [1], proclaim (+6963) [1], provoketh to anger [1], rageth [1], raiser [1], removed [1], set apart [1], shave (+8593) [1], taken [1], took away [1], took [1], transgressest [1], transgressing [1], transgressors [1], translate [1], wayfaring man (+734) [1], went away [1], went forth [1], went throughout (+871.1) [1]

5675 עֲבַר **ʿăbar** (Aram.), n.m. GK: 10526 [cf. 5676]. the opposite bank (of a river); Trans(-Euphrates) or "beyond (the River)" is to the east of Israel:– beyond [7], side [7]

5676 עֵבֶר **ʿēber**, n.m. GK: 6298 [→ 5674; cf. 5675]. what is on the other side, what is beyond, across; i.e., east or west; Trans-Euphrates:– side [56], beyond (+871.1) [8], beyond [7], beyond (+4480) [6], sides [4], straight forward (+413+6440) [3], against (+6440) [1], by (+3807.1) [1], from (+4480) [1], over [1], passages [1], passage [1], quarter [1]

5677 עֵבֶר **ʿēber**, n.pr.m. GK: 6299 [→ 5674]. Eber, "*[regions] beyond [the river]*":– Eber [13], Heber [2]

5678 עֶבְרָה **ʿebrâ**, n.f. GK: 6301 [→ 5674]. wrath, anger, fury, rage; insolence:– wrath [31], rage [2], anger [1]

5679 עֲבָרָה **ʿăbārâ**, n.f. GK: 6302 [→ 5682; cf. 5674]. ford, crossing:– ferry boat [1]

5680 עִבְרִי **ʿibrî**, a. & n.g. GK: 6303 [→ 5681]. Hebrew:– Hebrews [17], Hebrew [11], Hebrew women [2], Hebrew man [1], Hebrew woman [1], Hebrewess [1], Hebrews' [1]

5681 עִבְרִי **ʿibrî**, n.pr.m. GK: 6304 [→ 5680]. Ibri, "*Hebrew*":– Ibri [1]

5682 עֲבָרִים **ʿăbārîm**, n.pr.loc. GK: 6305 [→ 5679; cf. 5674]. Abarim, "*geographical regions beyond*":– Abarim [4]

5683 עֶבְרֹן **ʿebrōn**, n.pr.loc. GK: 6306 [→ 2266; cf. 5658]. Ebron, Hebron, "*association*":– Hebron [1]

5684 עַבְרֹנָה **ʿabrōnâ**, n.pr.loc. GK: 6307. Abronah:– Ebronah [2]

5685 עָבַשׁ **ʿābaš**, v. GK: 6308. [Q] to shrivel, wither, dry up:– rotten [1]

5686 עָבַת **ʿābat**, v. GK: 6309 [→ 5687, 5688]. [P] to conspire, twist:– wrap up [1]

5687 עָבֹת **ʿābôt**, a. GK: 6290 [→ 5686]. leafy, dense, interwoven foliage:– thick [4]

5688 עֲבֹת **ʿăbōt**, n.m. GK: 6310 & 6291 [→ 5686]. rope, cord, chains, ties; fetters, harness; thick foliage:– wreathen [8], cords [5], bands [3], thick boughs [3], ropes [2], band [1], rope [1], thick branches [1]

5689 עָגַב **ʿāgab**, v. GK: 6311 [→ 5691, 5689; cf. 5748]. [Q] to lust, have sensual desire for:– doted [6], lovers [1]

5690 עֲגָבִים **ʿăgābîm**, n.[m.]. GK: 6313 [→ 5689]. devotion, love:– much love [1], very lovely [1]

5691 עֲגָבָה **ʿăgābâ**, n.f. GK: 6312 [→ 5689]. lust, sensual desire:– inordinate love [1]

5692 עֻגָה **ʿugâ**, n.f. GK: 6314 [→ 5746]. (round, flat) bread cakes:– cakes [4], cake [3]

עָגוֹל **ʿāgôl**. See 5696.

5693 עָגוּר **ʿāgûr**, n.[m.]. GK: 6315. (short footed) thrush (a bird):– swallow [2]

5694 עָגִיל **ʿāgîl**, n.[m.]. GK: 6316 [→ 5696]. earring:– earrings [2]

5695 עֵגֶל **ʿēgel**, n.m. GK: 6319 [→ 5696]. bull-calf; calf-shaped idol:– calf [20], calves [11], bullocks [1], bullock [1], calf (+1241) [1], calf's [1]

5696 עָגֹל **ʿāgōl**, a. GK: 6318 [→ 4570, 5694, 5696, 5695, 5697, 5698, 5699, 5700]. circular, round:– round [6]

5697 עֶגְלָה **ʿeglâ**, n.f. GK: 6320 [→ 5698; cf. 5696]. heifer-calf, young cow:– heifer [9], heifer (+1241) [2], calves [1], heifer's [1], young cow (+1241) [1]

5698 עֶגְלָה **ʿeglâ**, n.pr.f. GK: 6321 [→ 5697]. Eglah, "*heifer*":– Eglah [2]

5699 עֲגָלָה **ʿăgālâ**, n.f. GK: 6322 [→ 5696]. cart:– cart [15], wagons [8], chariot [1], wagon [1]

5700 עֶגְלוֹן **ʿeglôn**, n.pr.m. & loc. GK: 6323 & 6324 [→ 5696]. Eglon, "*circle; young bull*":– Eglon [13]

5701 עָגַם **ʿāgam**, v. GK: 6327 [cf. 99]. [Q] to grieve for, have pity on:– grieved [1]

5702 עָגַן **ʿāgan**, v. GK: 6328. [N] to keep withdrawn (from marital relations):– stay [1]

5703 עַד **ʿad**, n.m. GK: 6329. a unit of time, referring to the past: old, ancient; without limit: forever, eternal, for ever and ever; continual, always:– ever [39], everlasting [2], for ever [2], eternity [1], ever (+5769) [1], evermore [1], for ever (+5769+2050.1) [1], old [1], perpetually (+3807.1) [1], world without end (+5704+5769) [1]

5704 עַד **ʿad**, pp. GK: 6330 [→ 1107, 5728; cf. 5710?; cf. 5705]. until, up to, as far as:– unto [376], until [249], to [167], for [75], till [68], how long (+4970) [28], until (+834) [27], and [13], how long (+575+1886.5) [13], till (+834) [9], into [8], and (+2050.1) [7], both (+4480) [7], very (+3966) [7], by [5], even [5], hitherto (+2008) [5], or [5], how long (+4100) [4], toward [4], until (+3588) [4], until (+7945) [4], while [4]*

5705 עַד **ʿad** (Aram.), pp. & c. GK: 10527 [→ 5709?; cf. 5704]. up to, until:– till (+1768) [8], to [5], for [4], unto [4], till [3], until [3], until (+1768) [2], at [1], ever (+0.2+5957) [1], hitherto (+3542) [1], on [1], or [1], within [1]

5706 עַד **ʿad**, n.[m.]. GK: 6331 [→ 5710]. prey, plunder:– prey [3]

5707 עֵד **ʿēd**, n.m. GK: 6332 [→ 3133; cf. 5749]. witness, testimony; an object that serves as a memorial or a person giving of legal evidence:– witness [45], witnesses [21], take witnesses (+5749) [2], took witnesses (+5749) [1]

5708 עִדָּה **ʿiddâ**, n.f. GK: 6340. menstruation:– filthy [1]

עֹד **ʿōd**. See 5750.

5709 עֲדָה **ʿădâ** (Aram.), v. GK: 10528 [→ 5705?; cf. 5710]. [P] to be taken, be repealed; [H] to take away:– altereth [2], departed [1], pass away [1], passed [1], removeth [1], take away [1], taken away [1], took [1]

עֹדֵד **ʿōdēd**. See 5752.

5710 עָדָה **ʿādâ**, v. GK: 6334 & 6335 [→ 497, 3260?, 3294?, 5704?, 5711, 5706, 5716; cf. 5709]. [Q] to adorn oneself, put on jewelry; to prowl; [H] to take away, remove:– decked [3], adorned [1], adorneth with [1], deckedst with ornaments (+5716) [1], deckest with [1], deck [1], passed [1], taketh away [1]

5711 עָדָה **ʿādâ**, n.pr.f. GK: 6336 [→ 5716; cf. 5710]. Adah, "*adornment*":– Adah [8]

5712 עֵדָה **ʿēdâ**, n.f. GK: 6337 [cf. 3259]. community, assembly, with a possible focus on the unity of the congregation; this can refer to good or evil groups; human or animal groups:– congregation [124], company [13], assembly [8], assemblies [1], multitude [1], people [1], swarm [1]

5713 עֵדָה **ʿēdâ**, n.f. GK: 6338 [→ 5749]. witness:– testimonies [21], witness [4], testimony [1]

5714 עִדּוֹא **ʿiddō** or עִדּוֹ **ʿiddô**, n.pr.m. GK: 6333 & 6341 & 6342 & 10529. Iddo, "[prob.] *Yahweh has adorned*": note this name is Aramaic twice in Ezra:– Iddo [10]

5715 עֵדוּת **ʿēdût**, n.f. GK: 6343 [→ 5749]. testimony, statute, stipulation, regulation; this can also mean "the Testimony" as a formal written copy of the precepts and stipulations of a covenant:– testimony [40], testimonies [15], witness [4], Shoshannim-Eduth (+7799) [1]

5716 עֲדִי **ʿădî**, n.[m.]. GK: 6344 [→ 3260, 5711, 5717, 5718; cf. 5710 (also used with compound proper names)]. ornament, beautiful jewelry:– ornaments [7], excellent ornaments (+5716) [2], mouth [2], ornament [2], deckedst with ornaments (+5710) [1]

5717 עֲדִיאֵל **ʿădîʾēl**, n.pr.m. GK: 6346 [→ 5716+410]. Adiel, "*adornment of God [El]*":– Adiel [3]

5718 עֲדָיָה **ʿădāyâ** or עֲדָיָהוּ **ʿădāyāhû**, n.pr.m. GK: 6347 & 6348 [→ 5716+3068]. Adaiah, "*adornment of Yahweh*":– Adaiah [9]

5719 עָדִין **ʿādîn**, a. GK: 6349 [→ 5727]. voluptuous, wantonness:– given to pleasures [1]

5720 עָדִין **ʿādîn**, n.pr.m. GK: 6350 [→ 5727]. Adin, "*voluptuous, luxurious*":– Adin [4]

5721 עֲדִינָא **ʿădînāʾ**, n.pr.m. GK: 6351 [→ 5727]. Adina, "*adorned*":– Adina [1]

5722 עֲדִינוֹ **ʿădînô**, n.pr.m. GK: 6352. Adino:– Adino [1]

5723 עֲדִיתַיִם **ʿădîtayim**, n.pr.loc. GK: 6353. Adithaim, "*double [row] of adornments*":– Adithaim [1]

5724 עַדְלַי **ʿadlay**, n.pr.m. GK: 6354. Adlai, "*be just*":– Adlai [1]

5725 עֲדֻלָּם **ʿădullām**, n.pr.loc. GK: 6355 [→ 5726]. Adullam, "*retreat* or *refuge;* [poss.] *[they are] just*":– Adullam [8]

5726 עֲדֻלָּמִי **ʿădullāmî**, a.g. GK: 6356 [→ 5725]. Adullamite, of Adullam, "*of Adullam*":– Adullamite [3]

5727 עָדַן **ʿādan**, v.den. GK: 6357 [→ 4575, 4574, 5719, 5720, 5721, 5730; cf. 5734?]. [Ht] to revel in the good life, luxuriate:– delighted [1]

5728 עֲדֶן **ʿăden** or עֲדֶנָה **ʿădenâ**, adv. GK: 6362 & 6364 [→ 5704+2008]. yet, still:– yet [2]

5729 עֶדֶן **ʿeden**, n.pr.loc. GK: 6361 [→ 1040]. Eden, "*paradise, delight,* [poss.] *flat land*":– Eden [4]

5730 עֵדֶן **ʿēden** or עֶדְנָה **ʿednâ**, n.[m.]. GK: 6358 & 6366 [→ 5727, 5731, 5734; cf. 5733]. delight, delicacy; finery; (sexual) pleasure:– delicates [1], delights [1], pleasures [1], pleasure [1]

5731 עֵדֶן **ʿēden**, n.pr.m. & loc. GK: 6359 & 6360 [→ 5730]. Eden, "*paradise, delight,* [poss.] *flat land*":– Eden [16]

5732 עִדָּן **ʿiddān** (Aram.), n.m. GK: 10530. time (general or specific period); "time, times, and half a time" likely means three-and-one-half periods of time:– times [6], time [6], at what time (+0.2+1768+871.2) [1]

5733 עַדְנָא **ʿadnāʾ**, n.pr.m. GK: 6363 [cf. 5730, 5734]. Adna, "*delight*":– Adna [2]

5734 עַדְנָה **ʿadnâ**, n.pr.m. GK: 6365 & 6367 [→ 5730; cf. 5727?, 5733]. Adnah, "*delight*":– Adnah [2]

5735 עַדְעָדָה **ʿadʿādâ**, n.pr.loc. GK: 6368. Adadah:– Adadah [1]

5736 עָדַף **ʿādap**, v. GK: 6369. [Q] (ptcp.) what is left over, what is additional; [H] to have a surplus:– remaineth [3], had over [1], more [1], odd number [1], over and above (+5921) [1], overplus [1], remaineth over [1]

5737 עָדַר **ʿādar**, v. GK: 6370 & 6371 & 6372 [→ 4576, 5739; cf. 5826]. [Q] to help, serve; referring to a fighting unit that acts as a group; [N] to be cultivated, be weeded; to be missing; be lacking; [P] to let be lacking:– faileth [3], digged [2], lacked [2], fail [1], keep rank [1], keep [1], lacking [1]

5738 עֶדֶר **ʿeder**, n.pr.m. GK: 6376 [→ 5740]. Eder, "*flock*":– Ader [1]

5739 עֵדֶר **ʿēder**, n.m. GK: 6373 [→ 5737]. flock, herd:– flocks [16], flock [16], drove [2], every drove (+5739) [2], herds [2], droves [1]

5740 עֵדֶר **ʿēder**, n.pr.m. & loc. GK: 6374 & 6375 [→ 4029, 5738, 5741]. Eder, "*flock*":– Eder [3], Edar [1]

5741 עַדְרִיאֵל **ʿadrîʾēl**, n.pr.m. GK: 6377 [→ 5740+410]. Adriel, "*[my] help is God [El]*":– Adriel [2]

5742 עֲדָשִׁים **ʿădāšîm**, n.f. GK: 6378. lentils:– lentiles [4]

עַוָּא **ʿawwāʾ**. See 5755.

5743 עוּב **ʿûb**, v.den. GK: 6380 [→ 5645]. [H] to cover with a cloud:– covered with a cloud [1]

5744 עוֹבֵד **ʿôbēd**, n.pr.m. GK: 6381 [→ 5647]. Obed, "*servant [worshiper]*":– Obed [10]

5745 עוֹבָל **ʿôbāl**, n.pr.g. GK: 6382 [cf. 5858]. Obal:– Obal [1]

5746 עוּג **ʿûg**, v.den. GK: 6383 [→ 4580, 5692]. [Q] to bake a (round, flat) cake of bread:– bake [1]

5747 עוֹג **ʿôg**, n.pr.m. GK: 6384. Og:– Og [22]

5748 עוּגָב **ʿûgāb**, n.m. GK: 6385 [cf. 5689]. flute:– organ [3], organs [1]

5749 עוּד **ʿûd**, v.den. GK: 6386 & 6387 [→ 496, 5707, 5713, 5715, 5750, 5752, 8584]. [Q] to bear witness; [P] to surround (with ropes); [Pil] to sustain, relieve; [H] to admonish, warn, charge, declare; to testify, to call on a witness; [Ho] to be warned; [Htpol] to hold each other up; from the base meaning of binding (with ropes) come the fig. extensions of "to warn, charge, testify" (bind with words) and "to help, sustain" (bind oneself to another in aid and comfort):– testified [7], testify [6], call to record [2], earnestly protested (+5749) [2], protest solemnly (+5749) [2], protested [2], solemnly protest (+5749) [2], take witnesses (+5707) [2], testifiedst [2], admonished [1], bear witness against [1], call to witness [1], chargedst [1], charge [1], gave witness to [1], give warning [1], lifteth up [1], protesting [1], relieveth [1], robbed [1], stand upright [1], take to witness [1], took to record [1], took witnesses (+5707) [1], witnessed against [1], witness [1]

5750 עוֹד **'ôd**, subst. (used as adv.). GK: 6388 [→ 5749; cf. 5751]. longer, again, still, more:– yet [125], more [114], any more [72], again [44], still [21], while yet [12], else [10], more (+3254) [10], besides [6], again (+3254) [5], as yet [5], moreover [5], within (+871.1) [5], yet again (+3254) [5], moe [3], any longer [2], any more (+3254) [2], any more at all (+5750) [2], further [2], henceforth [2], longer [2], while have being (+871.1) [2], whiles [2], while [2], yet the more (+3254) [2], after [1], again (+2050.1) [1], all life long (+4480) [1], almost (+4592) [1], any more at all (+3254) [1], any [1], beside [1], but [1], can more (+3254) [1], do again (+3254) [1], else beside (+1107+4480) [1], ever since (+4480) [1], furthermore [1], good while [1], more (+3254+3807.1) [1], moreover (+2050.1) [1], mo [1], never again (+3808) [1], once [1], since [1], while (+3605) [1], while (+871.1) [1], whilst yet [1], within the space of (+871.1) [1], yet (+3807.1) [1], yet again [1], yet more (+3254) [1]

5751 עוֹד **'ôd** (Aram.), adv. GK: 10531 [cf. 5750]. still, yet:– while [1]

5752 עוֹדֵד **'ôdēd**, n.pr.m. GK: 6389 [→ 5749]. Oded, "*restorer*":– Oded [3]

5753 עָוָה **'āwâ**, v. GK: 6390 [→ 5754, 5771, 5773, 5856]. [Q] to do wrong; [N] to be perverse, be warped; [P] to ruin, make crooked; [H] to do wrong, pervert; from the base meaning of twisting an object comes the fig. extension of twisting morality: to be perverse, to do wrong:– commit iniquity [2], committed iniquity [2], perverse [2], perverted [2], bowed down [1], did perversely [1], done amiss [1], done perversely [1], done wickedly [1], done wrong [1], made crooked [1], troubled [1], turneth [1]

5754 עַוָּה **'awwâ**, n.f. GK: 6392 [→ 5857; cf. 5753]. ruin, wreckage, rubble:– overturn [3]

5755 עַוָּא **'awwā'** or עַוָּה **'awwâ** or עִוָּה **'iwwâ**, n.pr.loc. GK: 6379 & 6393 & 6394 [→ 5757, 5761]. Avva, Avvah, Ivvah:– Ivah [3], Ava [1]

עָוֹן **'āwôn**. See 5771.

5756 עוּז **'ûz**, v. GK: 6395 [→ 5797; cf. 5810]. [Q] to take refuge; [H] to bring to refuge, give shelter:– gather to flee [2], gather [1], retire [1]

5757 עַוִּים **'awwîm**, a.g. GK: 6398 [→ 5755]. Avvite:– @H =

5758 עֲוָיָה **‰ªwâyâ** (Aram.), n.f. GK: 10532. wickedness, iniquity:– iniquities [1]

5759 עֲוִיל **ªwîl**, n.m. GK: 6396 [→ 5763]. little boys:– little ones [1], young children [1]

5760 עֲוִיל **ªwîl**, n.m. GK: 6397 [→ 5765]. evil one, unjust one:– ungodly [1]

5761 עַוִּים **'awwîm**, n.pr.loc. GK: 6399 [→ 5755]. Avvim:– Avites [2], Avims [1], Avim [1]

5762 עֲוִית **ªwît** or עֲיוֹת **ªyôt**, n.pr.loc. GK: 6400 & 6511. Avith, Aioth:– Avith [2]

5763 עוּל **'ûl**, v. GK: 6402 [→ 5759, 5764, 5768]. [Q] to nurse, suckle:– milch [2], great with young [1], with young [1], young [1]

5764 עוּל **'ûl**, n.m. GK: 6403 [→ 5763]. nursing infant, baby:– infant [1], sucking child [1]

5765 עָוַל **'āwal**, v.den. GK: 6401 [→ 5760, 5766, 5767]. [P] to do evil, act wrong:– deal unjustly [1], unrighteous [1]

עוֹל **'ôl**. See 5923.

5766 עָוֶל **'āwel** or עַוְלָה **'awlâ** or עֹלָה **'ōlâ**, n.m. GK: 6404 & 6406 & 6593 [→ 5765]. wrong, evil, sin, injustice, what is morally perverted, warped, and twisted, an extension of the base meaning of a physically twisted, crooked object (not found in the OT):– iniquity [35], wickedness [7], unrighteousness [3], unjust [2], iniquities [1], perverseness [1], unjustly [1], unrighteously [1], wickedly [1], wicked [1]

5767 עַוָּל **'awwal**, n.m. GK: 6405 [→ 5765]. wicked one, evil one, unjust one:– wicked [3], unjust [1], unrighteous [1]

עוֹלָה **'ôlâ**. See 5930.

5768 עוֹלֵל **'olel** or עוֹלָל **'ôlāl**, n.m. GK: 6407 & 6408 [→ 5763]. child, little one:– children [10], young children [3], babes [2], infants [2], child [1], infant [1], little ones [1]

5769 עוֹלָם **'ôlām**, n.m. GK: 6409 [cf. 5865; cf. 5957]. everlasting, forever, eternity; from of old, ancient, lasting, for a duration:– ever [210], everlasting [59], for ever [47], perpetual [21], old [17], evermore [15], never (+3808+3807.1) [9], ever (+3807.1) [5], ancient [4], of old [4], everlasting (+3807.1) [3], alway (+3807.1) [2], always (+3807.1) [2], any more (+5704) [2], ever (+5704) [2], ever throughout [2], for ever (+3807.1) [2], long [2], never (+408+3807.1) [2], old time [2], world [2], always [1], ancient (+4480) [1], ancient times [1], any time [1], continuance [1], eternal [1], ever (+4480) [1], ever (+4480+1886.1) [1], ever (+5703) [1], ever of old (+4480) [1], everlasting (+3117) [1], everlasting (+3605) [1], for ever (+5703+2050.1) [1], lasting [1], long time [1], never (+1077+3807.1) [1], never (+1097+3807.1) [1], never (+3808+4480) [1], never (+3808+5704) [1], of old time (+3807.1) [1], of old time (+4480) [1], perpetual (+5704) [1], since the beginning of the world (+4480) [1], world without end (+5703+5704) [1]

5770 עָיַן **'āyan**, v.den. GK: 6523 [→ 5869]. [Q] to keep an eye on, look at (with suspicion or jealousy):– eyed [1]

5771 עָוֹן **'āwōn**, n.m. GK: 6411 [→ 5753; cf. 5758]. sin, wickedness, iniquity, often with a focus on the guilt or liability incurred, and the punishment to follow:– iniquity [167], iniquities [48], punishment of iniquity [5], punishment [4], fault [2], affliction [1], iniquities (+1697) [1], mischief [1], punishments [1], sin [1]

5772 עוֹנָה **'ōnâ**, n.f. GK: 6703 [→ 6031?]. marital rights (of intercourse):– duty of marriage [1], furrows [1]

5773 עִוְעִים **'iw'îm**, n.pl.abst. GK: 6413 [→ 5753]. (col. pl.) dizziness, staggering, frenzy:– perverse [1]

5774 עוּף **'ûp**, v. GK: 6414 & 6545 & 6758 [→ 5775, 5888, 5889; cf. 3286]. [Q] to fly; to be faint, be exhausted; [Pol] to dart about (of a flying bird or a snake); to brandish; [H] to let (eyes) glance; [Ht] to fly away:– fly [8], flying [6], fly away [5], faint [2], flieth [2], brandish [1], flew [1], flieth away [1], set [1], shine forth [1], waxed faint [1], weary [1]

5775 עוֹף **'ôp**, n.m. GK: 6416 [→ 5774; cf. 5776]. bird, winged creatures, flying creatures:– fowls [36], fowl [23], birds [6], bird [3], flying [2], flieth [1]

5776 עוֹף **'ôp** (Aram.), n.[m.]. GK: 10533 [cf. 5775]. bird; a "bird of heaven" is any wild bird:– fowls [1], fowl [1]

5777 עֹפֶרֶת **'ōperet**, n.m. GK: 6769. lead (a mineral):– lead [9]

5778 עֵיפַי **'êpay** or עוֹפַי **'ôpay**, n.pr.m. GK: 6550 & 6417. Ephai, Ophai, "*my bird*":– Ephai [1]

5779 עוּץ **'ûṣ**, v. GK: 6418 [cf. 3289]. [Q] to consider, devise, plan:– take advice [1], take counsel together (+6098) [1]

5780 עוּץ **'ûṣ**, n.pr.m. & loc. GK: 6419 & 6420. Uz:– Uz [7], Huz [1]

5781 עוּק **'ûq**, v. GK: 6421 [→ 4157?, 6125]. [Q] to crush, totter; [H] to crush, cause to totter:– pressed [2]

5782 עוּר **'ûr**, v. GK: 6424 [→ 3265, 5892, 5895, 6147, 6179, 6180]. [Q] to awake; [N] to be aroused, stirred up, wakened; [Pol] to awaken, arouse, raise up; [Pil] to raise, keep up; [H] to stir up, rouse, waken; [Htpol] to rouse oneself:– awake [24], stir up [12], raised up [9], stirred up [5], raise up [4], stirreth up [4], lift up [3], raised [3], raise [2], wakened [2], wakeneth [2], arise [1], awake up [1], awakest [1], dare stir up [1], lifting up [1], master [1], raising [1], wake up [1], waked [1], waketh [1]

5783 עוּר **'ûr**, v. GK: 6423 [→ 4589, 5785?; cf. 6168]. [N] to be uncovered, be laid bare:– made quite naked (+6181) [1]

5784 עוּר **'ûr** (Aram.), n.[m.]. GK: 10534. chaff, the husk particles of threshed grain, used fig. to indicate something worthless:– chaff [1]

5785 עוֹר **'ôr**, n.m. GK: 6425 [→ 5783?]. skin, hide, leather:– skin [73], skins [23], hide [2], leather [1]

5786 עָוַר **'āwar**, v. GK: 6422 [→ 5787, 5788]. [P] to make blind:– put out [3], blindeth [1], blind [1]

5787 עִוֵּר **'iwwēr**, a. GK: 6426 [→ 5786]. blind:– blind [26]

עֹרֵב **'ôrēb**. See 6159.

5788 עִוָּרוֹן **'iwwārôn** or עַוֶּרֶת **'awweret**, n.[m.]. GK: 6427 & 6428 [→ 5786]. blindness, blinding:– blindness [2], blind [1]

5789 עוּשׁ **'ûš**, v. GK: 6429 [→ 3135, 3266, 3274; cf. 5790]. [Q] to be quick or to help:– assemble [1]

5790 עוּת **'ût**, v. GK: 6431 [→ 5793; cf. 5789]. [Q] to sustain, help:– speak in season [1]

5791 עָוַת **'āwat**, v. GK: 6430 [→ 5792]. [P] to make crooked, pervert; [Pu] to be twisted, be made crooked; [Ht] to stoop down, bend over; from the base meaning of twisting an object comes the fig. extension of twisting morality: to pervert:– pervert [3], bow [1], crooked [1], dealt perversely with [1], falsifying [1], made crooked [1], overthrown [1], subvert [1], turneth upside down [1]

5792 עַוָּתָה **'awwātâ**, n.f. GK: 6432 [→ 5791]. wrong:– wrong [1]

5793 עוּתַי **'ûtay**, n.pr.m. GK: 6433 [→ 5790]. Uthai, "[poss.] *superiority of Yahweh;* [poss.] *[my] restoration*":– Uthai [2]

5794 עַז **'az**, a. GK: 6434 & 6435 [→ 5810, 5815?]. strong, mighty, powerful, fierce:– strong [12], fierce [4], mighty [3], greedy (+5315) [1], power [1], roughly [1], stronger [1]

5795 עֵז **'ēz**, n.m. GK: 6436 [→ 5810?; cf. 5796]. goat; goat hair:– goats [40], goats' [10], kid (+1423) [7], goat [5], she goats [3], he goat (+6842) [2], she goat [2], goat (+7716) [1], he goats (+6842) [1], kids (+1121) [1], kids [1], kid [1]

5796 עֵז **'ēz** (Aram.), n.[f.]. GK: 10535. goat (male and female):– he goats (+6841) [1]

5797 עֹז **'ōz**, n.m. GK: 6437 [→ 5813, 5818; cf. 5756, 5810]. strength, power, might; stronghold, fortification; strong-willed, stubborn;:– strength [60], strong [17], power [11], might [2], boldness [1], loud [1], mighty [1]

5798 עֻזָּא **'uzzā'** or עֻזָּה **'uzzâ**, n.pr.m. GK: 6438 & 6446 [→ 6560]. Uzza, Uzzah, "*strong, fierce one*":– Uzza [10], Uzzah [4]

5799 עֲזָאזֵל **ªzā'zēl**, n.[m. *or* pr.]. GK: 6439. scapegoat, a goat sent into the wilderness of the Day of Atonement, symbolically carrying away the sin of the community; some see this word as the name of the desert spirit (Azazel) to whom the goat is sent:– scapegoat [4]

5800 עָזַב **'āzab**, v. GK: 6440 & 6441 [→ 5801, 5805, 5806]. [Q] to leave, abandon, reject, desert; to restore, help; [Qp] be left, be abandoned, be freed; [N] be abandoned, be forsaken, be neglected; [Pu] be deserted, be abandoned:– forsaken [60], forsake [46], left [41], leave [20], forsook [16], forsaketh [3], faileth [2], forsookest [2], leave off [2], leaveth [2], left off [2], surely help (+5800) [2], committeth [1], fortified [1], fortify [1], help [1], left destitute [1], leftest [1], refuseth [1]

5801 עִזְבוֹנִים **'izbônîm**, n.[m.]. GK: 6442 [→ 5800]. merchandise, goods:– fairs [6], wares [1]

5802 עַזְבּוּק **'azbûq**, n.pr.m. GK: 6443 [→ 950?]. Azbuk:– Azbuk [1]

5803 עַזְגָּד **'azgād**, n.pr.m. GK: 6444. Azgad, "*strong is Gad*":– Azgad [4]

5804 עַזָּה **'azzâ**, n.pr.loc. GK: 6445 [→ 5841]. Gaza, "*strong*":– Gaza [18], Azzah [3]

5805 עֲזוּבָה **ªzûbâ**, n.f. GK: 6447 [→ 5800]. forsaking, desolation:– forsaking [1]

5806 עֲזוּבָה **ªzûbâ**, n.pr.f. GK: 6448 [→ 5800]. Azubah, "*adornment*":– Azubah [4]

5807 עֱזוּז **ªzûz**, n.[m.]. GK: 6449 [→ 5810]. power, strength:– strength [2], might [1]

5808 עִזּוּז **'izzûz**, a. GK: 6450 [→ 5810]. strong, powerful:– power [1], strong [1]

5809 עַזֻּר **'azzur**, n.pr.m. GK: 6473. Azzur, "*help*":– Azur [2], Azzur [1]

5810 עָזַז **'āzaz**, v. GK: 6451 [→ 4581, 5794, 5795?, 5807, 5808, 5811, 5812, 5815, 5819, 5821; cf. 3267, 5756, 5797]. [Q] to be strong, overpower; [H] to put on a bold face, be brazen:– strengthened [3], prevailed [2], strengthen [2], hardeneth [1], impudent [1], prevail [1], strengtheneth [1], strong [1]

5811 עָזָז **'āzāz**, n.pr.m. GK: 6452 [→ 5810]. Azaz, "*strong*":– Azaz [1]

5812 עֲזַזְיָהוּ **ªzazyāhû**, n.pr.m. GK: 6453 [→ 5810+3068]. Azaziah, "*Yahweh is strong*":– Azaziah [3]

5813 עֻזִּי **'uzzî**, n.pr.m. GK: 6454 [→ 5797]. Uzzi, "*Yahweh is [my] strength*":– Uzzi [11]

5814 עֻזִּיָּא **'uzziyyā'**, n.pr.m. GK: 6455 [cf. 5818]. Uzzia, "*[my] strength* or *Yahweh is [my] strength*":– Uzzia [1]

5815 עֲזִיאֵל **ªzî'ēl**, n.pr.m. GK: 6456 [→ 5794?+410?]. Aziel, "*God is my strength*":– Aziel [1]

5816 עֻזִּיאֵל **'uzzî'ēl**, n.pr.m. GK: 6457 [→ 5817]. Uzziel, "*God [El] is [my] strength*":– Uzziel [16]

5817 עֻזִּיאֵלִי **'ozzî'ēlî**, a.g. GK: 6458 [→ 5816]. Uzzielite, "*of Uzziel*":– Uzzielites [2]

5818 עֻזִּיָּה ***'uzziyyâ*** or עֻזִּיָּהוּ ***'uzziyyāhû***, n.pr.m. GK: 6459 & 6460 [→ 5797+3068; cf. 5814]. Uzziah, "*Yahweh is [my] strength*":– Uzziah [27]

5819 עֲזִיזָא ***ᵃzîzā'***, n.pr.m. GK: 6461 [→ 5810]. Aziza, "*powerful*":– Aziza [1]

5820 עַזְמָוֶת ***'azmāwet***, n.pr.m. & loc. GK: 6462 & 6463 [→ 1041]. Azmaveth, "*strong one of death; camel fodder, plant of the plumose family*":– Azmaveth [8]

5821 עַזָּן ***'azzān***, n.pr.m. GK: 6464 [→ 5810]. Azzan, "*strong*":– Azzan [1]

5822 עָזְנִיָּה ***'ozniyyâ***, n.f. GK: 6465. black vulture:– ospray [2]

5823 עָזַק ***'āzaq***, v. GK: 6466. [P] to dig:– fenced [1]

5824 עִזְקָה ***'izqâ*** (Aram.), n.f. GK: 10536. signet-ring, used to validate official business:– signet [2]

5825 עֲזֵקָה ***ᵃzēqâ***, n.pr.loc. GK: 6467. Azekah, "[poss.] *hoe [the ground]*":– Azekah [7]

5826 עָזַר ***'āzar***, v. GK: 6468 [→ 499, 3270, 5828, 5829, 5830, 5832, 5835, 5836, 5838; cf. 5737]. [Q] to help, support; [Qp] to be helped; [N] to be helped:– help [44], helped [17], helper [7], helpers [4], holpen [3], helpeth [2], succour [2], helped forward [1], succoured [1]

5827 עֵזֶר ***'ezer***, n.pr.m. GK: 6472 [→ 5828]. Ezer, "*help*":– Ezer [1]

5828 עֵזֶר ***'ēzer***, n.m. GK: 6469 [→ 5829, 5827, 5833, 5834; cf. 5826 (also used with compound proper names)]. help, helper:– help [21]

5829 עֵזֶר ***'ēzer***, n.pr.m. GK: 6470 [→ 5828; cf. 5826]. Ezer, "*help*":– Ezer [4]

עַזֻּר ***'azzur***. See 5809.

5830 עֶזְרָא ***'ezrā'***, n.pr.m. GK: 6474 [→ 5826; cf. 5831]. Ezra, "*help*":– Ezra [22]

5831 עֶזְרָא ***'ezrā'*** (Aram.), n.pr.m. GK: 10537 [cf. 5830]. Ezra, "*help*":– Ezra [3]

5832 עֲזַרְאֵל ***ᵃzar'ēl***, n.pr.m. GK: 6475 [→ 5826+410]. Azarel, "*God [El] has helped*":– Azareel [5], Azarael [1]

5833 עֶזְרָה ***'ezrâ***, n.f. GK: 6476 [→ 5834; cf. 5828]. help, aid, support; helper, ally:– help [24], helped [1], helpers [1]

5834 עֶזְרָה ***'ezrâ***, n.pr.m. GK: 6477 [→ 5833]. Ezrah:– Ezra [1]

5835 עֲזָרָה ***ᵃzārâ***, n.f. GK: 6478 [→ 5826]. court, enclosure; ledge, barrier:– settle [6], court [3]

5836 עֶזְרִי ***'ezrî***, n.pr.m. GK: 6479 [→ 5826+3068? *or* 2967.1?]. Ezri, "*my help*":– Ezri [1]

5837 עַזְרִיאֵל ***'azrî'ēl***, n.pr.m. GK: 6480 [→ 5828+410]. Azriel, "*God [El] is [my] help*":– Azriel [3]

5838 עֲזַרְיָה ***ᵃzaryâ*** or עֲזַרְיָהוּ ***ᵃzaryāhû***, n.pr.m. GK: 6481 & 6482 [→ 5826+3068; cf. 5839]. Azariah, "*Yahweh has helped*":– Azariah [48]

5839 עֲזַרְיָה ***ᵃzaryâ*** (Aram.), n.pr.m. GK: 10538 [cf. 5838]. Azariah, "*Yahweh has helped*":– Azariah [1]

5840 עַזְרִיקָם ***'azrîqām***, n.pr.m. GK: 6483 [→ 5828+6965]. Azrikam, "*[my] help arises*":– Azrikam [6]

5841 עַזָּתִי ***'azzātî***, a.g. GK: 6484 [→ 5804]. Gazite, "*of Gaza*":– Gazathites [1], Gazites [1]

5842 עֵט ***'ēṭ***, n.m. GK: 6485. (iron) engraving tool, stylus; (reed) pen:– pen [4]

5843 עֵטָא ***'ēṭâ*** (Aram.), n.f. GK: 10539 [→ 3272; cf. 6098]. counsel, wisdom:– counsel [1]

5844 עָטָה ***'āṭâ***, v. GK: 6486 & 6487 [→ 4593, 4594; cf. 3271]. [Q] to cover, wrap oneself; to grasp; [Pu] to be grasped; [H] cover, wrap another (thing):– cover [4], covered with [2], surely cover (+5844) [2], array with [1], clad with [1], covered [1], coverest [1], covereth [1], filleth [1], put a covering [1], putteth on [1], turneth aside [1]

5845 עֲטִין ***ᵃṭîn***, n.[m.]. GK: 6489. body, part of body; or pail, bucket:– breasts [1]

5846 עֲטִישָׁה ***ᵃṭîšâ***, n.f. GK: 6490. snorting, sneezing:– neesings [1]

5847 עֲטַלֵּף ***ᵃṭallēp***, n.[m.]. GK: 6491 [→ 5848+3807.1]. bat (animal):– bat [2], bats [1]

5848 עָטַף ***'āṭap***, v. GK: 6488 & 6493 & 6494 [→ 4595, 5847]. [Q] to clothe, mantle; to turn aside; to grow faint; [N] to be faint; [H] to be feeble; [Ht] to ebb away, grow faint:– overwhelmed [5], fainted [2], covered over [1], covereth [1], fail [1], faint [1], feebler [1], feeble [1], hideth [1], swooned [1], swoon [1]

5849 עָטַר ***'āṭar***, v. GK: 6496 & 6497 [→ 5850, 5851, 5852, 5853, 5854, 5855]. [Q] to surround, close in upon; [P] to crown, place a wreath (on the head); [H] to bestow a crown:– crowned [2], compassed round about [1], compass [1], crownest [1], crowneth [1], crowning [1]

5850 עֲטָרָה ***ᵃṭārâ***, n.f. GK: 6498 [→ 5849]. crown, wreath, placed on the head as a symbol of celebration or status; can be made of plants or precious metals:– crown [20], crowns [3]

5851 עֲטָרָה ***ᵃṭārâ***, n.pr.f. GK: 6499 [→ 5849]. Atarah, "*circlet, wreath*":– Atarah [1]

5852 עֲטָרוֹת ***ᵃṭārôt***, n.pr.loc. GK: 6500 [→ 5853, 5854; cf. 5849]. Ataroth, "*circlets, wreaths*":– Ataroth [5]

5853 עַטְרוֹת אַדָּר ***'aṭrôt 'addār***, n.pr.loc. GK: 6501 [→ 5852+146]. Ataroth Addar, "*wreaths of majesty*":– Ataroth-adar [1], Ataroth-addar [1]

5854 עַטְרוֹת בֵּית יוֹאָב ***'aṭrôt bêt yô'āb***, n.pr.loc. GK: 6502 [→ 5852+1004+3097]. Atroth Beth Joab, "*circlets, folds of the house of Joab*":– @H = **5855** עַטְרוֹת שׁוֹפָן ***‰a¬rôt šôpān***, n.pr.loc. GK: 6503 [→ 5849]. Atroth Shophan, "*circlets, folds of Shophan*":– Atroth Shophan [1]

5856 עִי ***'î***, n.[m.]. GK: 6505 [→ 1164, 4596, 5859, 5863, 5864; cf. 5753]. heap of rubble; (of a person) a broken man:– heaps [3], grave [1], heap [1]

5857 עַי ***'ay*** or עַיָּת ***'ayyat*** or עַיָּא ***'ayyâ***, n.pr.loc. GK: 6504 & 6509 & 6569 [cf. 5754]. Ai, Aiath, Ayyah; Aija, "*ruin, the heap*":– Ai [36], Hai [2], Aiath [1], Aija [1]

5858 עֵיבָל ***'êbāl***, n.pr.m. & g. & loc. GK: 6506 & 6507 & 6508 [cf. 5745]. Ebal:– Ebal [8]

עַיָּה ***'ayâ***. See 5857.

5859 עִיּוֹן ***'iyyôn***, n.pr.loc. GK: 6510 [→ 5856]. Ijon, "*place of heaps [of stone]*":– Ijon [3]

5860 עִיט ***'îṭ***, v. GK: 6512 & 6513 [→ 5861, 5862?]. [Q] to hurl insults; to pounce upon (with shrieks and screams):– flew [1], fly [1], railed [1]

5861 עַיִט ***'ayiṭ***, n.m. GK: 6514 [→ 5862?; cf. 5860]. (coll) birds of prey, carrion birds:– fowls [3], birds [1], bird [1], fowl [1], ravenous bird [1], ravenous [1]

5862 עֵיטָם ***'êṭām***, n.pr.loc. GK: 6515 [→ 5861?+3963.1?]. Etam, "[poss.] *place of birds of prey*":– Etam [5]

5863 עִיֵּי הָעֲבָרִים ***'iyyê hāᵃbārîm***, n.pr.loc. GK: 6516 [→ 5856]. Iye Abarim, "*heaps of Abarim [regions beyond]*":– Ije-abarim [2]

5864 עִיִּים ***'iyyîm***, n.pr.loc. GK: 6517 [→ 5856]. Iyim; Iim, "*heaps, ruins*":– Iim [2]

5865 עֵילוֹם ***'êlôm***, n.m. GK: 6518 [cf. 5769]. forever:– ever [1]

5866 עִילַי ***'îlay***, n.pr.m. GK: 6519. Ilai:– Ilai [1]

5867 עֵילָם ***'êlām***, n.pr.m. & g. & loc. GK: 6520 & 6521 [cf. 5962]. Elam, "*highland*":– Elam [28]

5868 עֲיָם ***ᵃyām***, n.[m.]. GK: 6522. scorching (of wind):– mighty [1]

5869 עַיִן ***'ayin***, n.f. & m. GK: 6524 [→ 4599, 5770, 5871, 5879, 5881; cf. 5870 (also used with compound proper names)]. eye; by extension: sight; spring, fountain; to be "evil of eye" is to be displeased; to be "good of eye" is to be pleased; to be "good in one's eyes" is to be pleasing "right in one's eyes" means acceptable by one's personal standards:– eyes [420], sight [216], eye [77], colour [12], face [10], well [10], seemeth unto (+871.1) [9], pleased (+3190+871.1) [8], presence [8], fountain [7], before (+3807.1) [6], displeased (+3415+871.1) [6], seem unto (+871.1) [6], seemeth (+871.1) [6], conceit [4], fountains [4], looks [3], look [3], pleased (+3474+871.1) [3], pleased well (+3474+871.1) [3], seemed to (+871.1) [3], thought (+871.1) [3], before (+871.1) [2], displease (+7489+871.1) [2], look well (+7760) [2], pleased (+2896+871.1) [2], pleased well (+3190+871.1) [2], pleaseth (+2896+871.1) [2], seemed (+1961+871.1) [2], seemeth to (+871.1) [2], thinkest (+871.1) [2], content (+3190+871.1) [1], countenance [1], displease (+2734+871.1) [1], displease (+6213+7451+871.1) [1], displeased (+7489+871.1) [1], escape (+5337) [1], eye sight [1], eye's [1], eyebrows (+1354) [1], eyed [1], eyesight [1], favour (+2896+871.1) [1], for (+871.1) [1], humble person (+7807) [1], liketh (+2896+871.1) [1], looketh (+4758) [1], open place (+6607) [1], openly (+871.1+1886.1) [1], outward appearance [1], please (+3474+871.1) [1], please not (+7451+871.1) [1], pleased not (+7451+871.1) [1], pleased well (+3477+871.1) [1], pleaseth (+3190+871.1) [1], pleaseth well (+3474) [1], regard (+2347) [1], resemblance [1], seem (+1961+871.1) [1], seem (+871.1) [1], seem to (+871.1) [1], seem unto (+3807.1) [1], seemed unto (+871.1) [1], think (+871.1) [1], think best (+2896+871.1) [1], thinking (+871.1) [1], wells [1], with (+871.1) [1], without knowledge (+4480) [1]

5870 עַיִן ***'ayin*** (Aram.), n.f. GK: 10540 [cf. 5869]. eye:– eyes [4], eye [1]

5871 עַיִן ***'ayin***, n.pr.loc. GK: 6526 [→ 5869]. Ain, "*eye[ball] or spring [of water]*":– Ain [5]

5872 עֵין גֶּדִי ***'ên gedî***, n.pr.loc. GK: 6527 [→ 5869+1423]. En Gedi, "*spring of young goat*":– En-gedi [6]

5873 עֵין גַּנִּים ***'ên gannîm***, n.pr.loc. GK: 6528 [→ 5869]. En Gannim, "*spring of gardens*":– En-gannim [3]

5874 עֵין־דֹּאר ***'ên-dō'r*** or עֵין־דּוֹר ***'ên-dôr***, n.pr.loc. GK: 6529 [→ 5869+1756]. Endor, "*spring of Dor*":– En-dor [3]

5875 עֵין הַקּוֹרֵא ***'ên haqqôrē'***, n.pr.loc. GK: 6530 [→ 5869]. En Hakkore, "*spring of the partridge* or *caller*":– En-hakkore [1]

עֵינוֹן ***'ênôn***. See 2703.

5876 עֵין חַדָּה ***'ên ḥaddâ***, n.pr.loc. GK: 6532 [→ 5869]. En Haddah, "*spring of gladness*":– En-haddah [1]

5877 עֵין חָצוֹר ***'ên ḥāṣôr***, n.pr.loc. GK: 6533 [→ 5869+2674]. En Hazor, "*spring of Hazor*":– En-hazor [1]

5878 עֵין חֲרֹד ***'ên ḥᵃrōd***, n.pr.loc. GK: 6534 [→ 5869]. En Harod, "*spring of Harod*":– Harod [1]

5879 עֵינַיִם ***'ênayim*** or עֵינָם ***'ênām***, n.pr.loc. GK: 6542 & 6543 [→ 5869+3963.1]. Enam, Enaim, "*two springs*":– Enam [1]

5880 עֵין מִשְׁפָּט ***'ên mišpāṭ***, n.pr.loc. GK: 6535 [→ 5869+4941]. En Mishpat, "*spring of judgment*":– En-mishpat [1]

5881 עֵינָן ***'ênān***, n.pr.m. GK: 6544 [→ 2704]. Enan, "*spring*":– Enan [5]

5882 עֵין עֶגְלַיִם ***'ên 'eglayim***, n.pr.loc. GK: 6536 [→ 5869]. En Eglaim, "*spring of two calves*":– En-eglaim [1]

5883 עֵין רֹגֵל ***'ên rōgēl***, n.pr.loc. GK: 6537 [→ 5869]. En Rogel, "*spring of the fuller* or *wanderer* or *spy*":– En-rogel [4]

5884 עֵין רִמּוֹן ***'ên rimmôn***, n.pr.loc. GK: 6538 [→ 5869+7417]. En Rimmon, "*spring of Rimmon*":– En-rimmon [1]

5885 עֵין שֶׁמֶשׁ ***'ên šemeš***, n.pr.loc. GK: 6539 [→ 5869+8121]. En Shemesh, "*spring of Shemesh*":– En-shemesh [2]

5886 עֵין תַּנִּים ***'ên tannîm***, n.pr.loc. GK: 6524 + 9478 [→ 5869+8565]. En Tannim, "Well of the Jackal" (5869 + 8565):–

5887 עֵין תַּפּוּחַ ***'ên tappûaḥ***, n.pr.loc. GK: 6540 [→ 5869+8599]. En Tappuah, "*spring of apple*":– En-tappuah [1]

5888 עִיף ***'îp***, v. GK: 6545 [→ 5774]. [Q] to be faint, be exhausted:– wearied [1]

5889 עָיֵף ***'āyēp***, a. GK: 6546 [→ 5774; cf. 3286]. weary, faint; famished, parched:– weary [8], faint [6], thirsty [3]

5890 עֵיפָה ***'êpâ***, n.f. GK: 6547 [→ 5891; cf. 4155]. darkness:– darkness [2]

5891 עֵיפָה ***'êpâ***, n.pr.m. & f. & g. GK: 6548 & 6549 [cf. 5890]. Ephah, "*darkness*":– Ephah [5]

5892 עִיר ***'îr***, n.f. GK: 6551 & 6552 [→ 5782, 6144? (also found with compound proper names)]. city, town, village, a general term for a population center; anguish, terror, wrath:– city [650], cities [421], several city (+5892+2050.1) [6], every city (+3605+5892+2050.1) [4], every city (+5892+2050.1) [4], town [4], towns [3], cities every one (+5892) [2]

5893 עִיר ***'îr***, n.pr.m. GK: 6553 [→ 5895]. Ir, "[poss.] *stallion donkey*":– Ir [1]

5894 עִיר ***'îr*** (Aram.), n.m. GK: 10541 [cf. 5782]. messenger (of God), watcher, one who is a sentinel to guard and protect:– watcher [2], watchers [1]

5895 עַיִר ***'ayir***, n.m. GK: 6554 & 6555 [→ 5782, 5893, 5896, 5901, 5902]. (male) donkey:– ass colts [2], colt [2], young asses [2], foals [1], foal [1]

5896 עִירָא ***'îrā'***, n.pr.m. GK: 6562 [→ 5895]. Ira, "[poss.] *stallion donkey*":– Ira [6]

5897 עִירָד *ʿîrād*, n.pr.m. GK: 6563 [→ 6171]. Irad:– Irad [2]

5898 עִיר הַמֶּלַח *ʿîr hammelaḥ*, n.pr.loc. GK: 6558 [→ 5892+1886.1+4417]. Ir Hammelak, "*the city of salt*":–

5899 עִיר הַתְּמָרִים *ʿîr hatt ͤmārîm*, n.pr.loc. GK: 6559 [→ 5892+1886.1+8558]. Ir Hattemarim, "*the city of palms*":–

5900 עִירוּ *ʿîrû*, n.pr.m. GK: 6564. Iru:– Iru [1]

5901 עִירִי *ʿîrî*, n.pr.m. GK: 6565 [→ 5895]. Iri, "[perhaps] *donkey's colt*":– Iri [1]

5902 עִירָם *ʿîrām*, n.pr.m. GK: 6566 [→ 5895+3963.1]. Iram:– Iram [2]

5903 עֵירֹם *ʿêrōm*, a. (used as noun). GK: 6567 [→ 6168]. naked; nakedness:– naked [9], nakedness [1]

5904 עִיר נָחָשׁ *ʿîr nāḥāš*, n.pr.loc. GK: 6560 [→ 5892]. Ir Nahash, "*city of Nahash*":– Irnahash [1]

5905 עִיר שֶׁמֶשׁ *ʿîr šemeš*, n.pr.loc. GK: 6561 [→ 5892+8121]. Ir Shemesh, "*city of Shemesh*":– Ir-shemesh [1]

5906 עַיִשׁ *ʿayiš* or עָשׁ *ʿāš*, n.f. GK: 6568 & 6933 [→ 6211]. constellation: the Bear or the Lion, or some other constellation:– Arcturus [2]

עַיָת *ʿayāt*. See 5857.

5907 עַכְבּוֹר *ʿakbôr*, n.pr.m. GK: 6570 [→ 5909]. Acbor, "*mouse* or *jerboa*":– Achbor [7]

5908 עַכָּבִישׁ *ʿakkābîš*, n.m. GK: 6571. spider:– spider's [2]

5909 עַכְבָּר *ʿakbār*, n.m. GK: 6572 [→ 5907]. (jumping) rat, jerboa:– mice [4], mouse [2]

5910 עַכּוֹ *ʿakkô*, n.pr.loc. GK: 6573. Acco:– Accho [1]

5911 עָכוֹר *ʿākôr*, n.pr.loc. GK: 6574 [→ 5916]. Achor, "*trouble*":– Achor [5]

5912 עָכָן *ʿākān*, n.pr.m. GK: 6575. Achan, "*troubler*":– Achan [6]

5913 עָכַס *ʿākas*, v.den. GK: 6576 [→ 5914, 5915]. [P] to jingle, rattle (of ankle ornaments):– making a tinkling [1]

5914 עֶכֶס *ʿekes*, n.[m.]. GK: 6577 [→ 5913]. bangle, ankle ornament:– stocks [1], tinkling ornaments [1]

5915 עַכְסָה *ʿaksâ*, n.pr.f. GK: 6578 [→ 5913]. Acsah, "*decorative anklet*":– Achsah [5]

5916 עָכַר *ʿākar*, v. GK: 6579 [→ 5911, 5917, 5918]. [Q] to bring trouble, make trouble; [N] to be troubled, be anguished:– troubled [4], troubleth [4], trouble [4], stirred [1], troubler [1]

5917 עָכָר *ʿākār*, n.pr.m. GK: 6580 [→ 5916]. Achar, "*trouble*":– Achar [1]

5918 עָכְרָן *ʿokrān*, n.pr.m. GK: 6581 [→ 5916]. Ocran, "*trouble*":– Ocran [5]

5919 עַכְשׁוּב *ʿakšûb*, n.m. GK: 6582. (horned) viper; other sources: asp:– adder's [1]

5920 עַל *ʿal*, subst. GK: 6583 [→ 5927; cf. 5921; cf. 5943]. (the) Most High:– above [2], most high [2], above (+4480) [1], on high [1]

5921 עַל *ʿal*, pp. & c. GK: 6584 [→ 4480+5921; cf. 5920; cf. 5922]. marker of relationship: spatial: on, upon, over, against, toward; logical: because of, according to; temporal: on, when, during:– upon [1572], against [538], over [413], in [318], for [305], on [292], by [215], to [167], from (+4480) [152], unto [150], therefore (+3651) [125], with [106], at [87], concerning [79], off [63], above [56], of [55], into [47], before (+6440) [43], according to [32], thereon (+2050.2) [31], because (+834) [26], because of [26], because [25], upon (+6440) [23], wherefore (+3651) [22], after [20], out of (+4480) [19], toward [15], next unto (+3027) [13], about [12], above (+4480) [12], beside [12], before [11], upon (+4480) [11], thereon (+1886.3) [10], wherefore (+4100) [10], whereon (+834) [10]*

5922 עַל *ʿal* (Aram.), pp. GK: 10542 [→ 5924, 5928, 5943, 5952, 5946; cf. 5921]. upon, over, against, toward, concerning:– upon [19], unto [16], over [13], in [10], against [7], to [7], concerning [6], for [6], of [5], about [3], above [1], from [1], more [1], nor (+2050.3) [1], on [1], therefore (+1836) [1], thereon (+1958.2) [1], why (+4101) [1], with [1]

5923 עֹל *ʿōl*, n.m. GK: 6585 [→ 5953]. yoke, placed on draft animals; by extension: a figure of oppression or of proper training:– yoke [40]

5924 עֵלָּא *ʿēllāʾ* (Aram.), adv. GK: 10543 [→ 5922; cf. 5921]. over, above:– over (+4481) [1]

5925 עֻלָּא *ʿullāʾ*, n.pr.m. GK: 6587 [→ 5927]. Ulla:– Ulla [1]

5926 עִלֵּג *ʿillēg*, a. GK: 6589 [cf. 3932]. speaking inarticulately; (pl.n.) stammerers:– stammerers [1]

5927 עָלָה *ʿālâ*, v. GK: 6590 [→ 500, 4605, 4607, 4608, 4609, 5920, 5925, 5929, 5930, 5933, 5935, 5941, 5940, 5942, 5933, 5944, 5945, 8585]. [Q] to go up, ascend, rise; [N] to be lifted up, withdraw, be exalted; [H] to take up, set up, offer a sacrifice; [Ho] to be offered up, be carried away, be recorded; [Ht] to raise oneself up; from the base meaning of rise in elevation comes the fig. extension "to exalt, honor," as the lifting up of a person in status:– went up [156], go up [123], come up [81], came up [77], brought up [58], offered [35], bring up [32], offer [29], gone up [21], get up [18], come [11], goeth up [10], taken up [9], offering [8], brought [7], gat up [7], ascended [6], came [6], cause to come up [6], cheweth [6], cometh up [6], offer up [5], rise up [5], ascended up [4], ascend [4], carry up [4], going up [4], go [4], mount up [4], take up [4], went [4], bringeth up [3], bring [3], carried up [3], causeth to ascend [3], chew [3], climb up [3], cometh [3], increased [3], made to come up [3], offereth [3], took up [3], arose [2], ascending [2], cast up [2], cause to burn [2], depart [2], exalted [2], fell [2], go up at once (+5927) [2], lifteth up [2], lighted [2], light [2], offered up [2], put [2], raised [2], setteth up [2], spring [2], surely bring up (+5927) [2], wentest up [2], arise up [1], ariseth [1], arise [1], ascend up [1], breaketh [1], breaking [1], broken up [1], broughtest up [1], broughtest [1], burnt [1], cause come up [1], caused to come up [1], causeth to come up [1], climbed up [1], climb [1], cometh in [1], cut off [1], dawning [1], departed [1], excellest [1], fetch up [1], fetched up [1], fetcht up [1], getteth up [1], goest up [1], goeth [1], gone away [1], grow up [1], groweth [1], grown over [1], grow [1], increaseth [1], laid [1], leaped [1], leap [1], lift up [1], lightest [1], lighteth [1], made to go up [1], made up (+724) [1], make rise up [1], make to pay [1], mentioned [1], offering up [1], perfected (+724) [1], prefer [1], put on [1], raised up [1], recovered [1], restore [1], riseth up [1], rising [1], rose up [1], rose [1], scaleth [1], set up [1], set [1], shooting up [1], shot forth [1], spring up [1], stir up [1], take away [1], upon levy [1], vapour [1], went away [1], wrought [1]

5928 עֲלָוָה *ʿᵃlāwâ* (Aram.), n.f. GK: 10545 [→ 5922; cf. 5930]. burnt offering:– burnt offerings [1]

5929 עָלֶה *ʿāleh*, n.m. GK: 6591 [→ 5927]. leaves, foliage:– leaf [11], branches [4], branch [1], leaves [1]

5930 עֹלָה *ʿōlâ*, n.f. GK: 6592 [→ 5927; cf. 5928]. burnt offering, wholly dedicated to God:– burnt offering [183], burnt offerings [82], burnt sacrifice [17], burnt sacrifices [4], ascent [1], go up [1]

5931 עִלָּה *ʿillâ* (Aram.), n.f. GK: 10544 [cf. 5953]. grounds, basis, pretext (for charges):– occasion [3]

5932 עַלְוָה *ʿalwâ*, n.f. GK: 6594. evil, wickedness:– iniquity [1]

5933 עַלְוָה *ʿalwâ* or עַלְיָה *ʿalyâ*, n.pr.m. GK: 6595 & 6607 [→ 5927]. Alvah, Aliah:– Aliah [1], Alvah [1]

5934 עֲלוּמִים *ʿᵃlûmîm*, n.pl.abst. GK: 6596 [→ 3281, 5958, 5959, 5961]. (abst.pl.) youthfulness, (the vigor of) youth:– youth [4]

5935 עַלְוָן *ʿalwān* or עַלְיָן *ʿalyān*, n.pr.m. GK: 6597 & 6615 [→ 5927]. Alvan, Alian, "[poss.] *ascending one* or *tall*":– Alian [1], Alvan [1]

5936 עֲלוּקָה *ʿᵃlûqâ*, n.f. GK: 6598. leech:– horseleach [1]

5937 עָלַז *ʿālaz*, v. GK: 6600 [→ 5938, 5947; cf. 5965]. [Q] to rejoice, be jubilant:– rejoice [8], joyful [2], rejoiced [2], triumph [2], greatly rejoiceth [1], rejoicest [1]

5938 עָלֵז *ʿālēz*, a. (used as n.). GK: 6601 [→ 5937]. reveling, exultant; (n.) reveler:– rejoiceth [1]

5939 עֲלָטָה *ʿᵃlāṭâ*, n.f. GK: 6602. darkness, dusk:– twilight [3], dark [1]

5940 עֱלִי *ʿᵉlî*, n.[m.]. GK: 6605 [→ 5927]. pestle (of a mortar):– pestle [1]

5941 עֵלִי *ʿēlî*, n.pr.m. GK: 6603 [→ 3068 *or* 410+5927]. Eli, "*Yahweh is exalted; God [El] is exalted*":– Eli [32], Eli's [1]

5942 עִלִּי *ʿillî*, a. GK: 6606 [→ 5927; cf. 5952]. upper:– upper [2]

5943 עִלַּי *ʿillāy* (Aram.), a. GK: 10546 [→ 5922]. highest, superior; the Most High, a title of God indicating his supreme status and power:– most high [9], high [1]

עַלְיָה *ʿalyâ*. See 5933.

5944 עֲלִיָּה *ʿᵃliyyâ*, n.f. GK: 6608 [→ 5927; cf. 5952]. upper room, upper parts:– chambers [4], chamber [4], parlour [4], going up [2], upper chambers [2], upper chamber [2], ascent [1], loft [1]

5945 עֶלְיוֹן *ʿelyôn*, a. GK: 6609 & 6610 [→ 5927; cf. 5943, cf. 5946]. upper, also used in place names; (the) Most High, a title of God with a focus on supremacy in status and power:– most high [27], high [9], upper [8], higher [4], highest [3], on high [1], uppermost [1]

5946 עֶלְיוֹן *ʿelyôn* (Aram.), a. GK: 10548 [→ 5922; cf. 5945]. highest, superior; (as a title) the Most High:– most high [4]

5947 עַלִּיז *ʿallîz*, a. GK: 6611 [→ 5937]. rejoicing, exulting; reveling, wild:– joyous [3], rejoice [3], rejoicing [1]

5948 עֲלִיל *ʿᵃlîl*, n.[m.]. GK: 6612 [→ 5953]. furnace:– furnace [1]

5949 עֲלִילָה *ʿᵃlîlâ*, n.f. GK: 6613 [→ 5953]. what is done, deed, action:– doings [13], works [3], deeds [2], occasions [2], actions [1], acts [1], doing [1], inventions [1]

5950 עֲלִילִיָּה *ʿᵃlîliyyâ*, n.f. GK: 6614. deed:– work [1]

עַלְיָן *ʿalyān*. See 5935.

5951 עֲלִיצֻת *ʿᵃlîṣut*, n.f. GK: 6617 [→ 5970; cf. 5965]. rejoicing, exaltation, including verbal expressions of joy and praise; from a negative perspective: haughtiness, presumption, gloating:– rejoicing [1]

5952 עִלִּי *ʿillî* (Aram.), n.f. GK: 10547 [→ 5922; cf. 5942]. upstairs room, a storage or guest room on the flat roof of a house:– chamber [1]

5953 עָלַל *ʿālal*, v. GK: 6618 & 6619 & 6620 & 6621 [→ 4611, 5923, 5948, 5949, 5955, 8586; cf. 5954]. [Po] to act or play the child; (n.) youths; to deal with; to glean, go over a second time; to thrust (in); [Poal] to be dealt with (in a way that causes suffering); [Ht] to deal harshly, abuse, mistreat; [Htpo] to take part in (wickedness):– done [3], abuse [2], glean [2], throughly glean (+5953) [2], abused [1], affecteth [1], children [1], defiled [1], do [1], gleaned [1], mocked [1], mock [1], practise [1], wrought wonderfully [1], wrought [1]

5954 עֲלַל *ʿᵃlal* (Aram.), v. GK: 10549 [→ 4606; cf. 5953]. [P] to go in; [H] to take in, bring before; [Ho] to be brought in, introduced before:– bring in [3], brought in [3], came in [3], went in [2], brought [1], came [1], went [1]

עֹלָל *ʿōlāl*. See 5768.

עֹלֵלָה *ʿōlēlâ*. See 5949.

5955 עֹלֵלוֹת *ʿōlēlôt*, n.f.pl.intens. GK: 6622 [→ 5953]. gleanings:– gleaning grapes [3], gleaning of grapes [1], grapegleanings [1], grapes [1]

5956 עָלַם *ʿālam*, v. GK: 6623 [→ 8587]. [Qp] to be in secret; [N] to be concealed, be hidden, be unaware; [H] to hide, shut off, conceal; [Ht] to hide oneself from, ignore:– hid [11], hide [7], any ways hide (+5956) [2], hideth [2], secret [2], blind [1], dissemblers [1], hidden [1], hidest [1]

5957 עָלַם *ʿālam* (Aram.), n.[m.]. GK: 10550 [cf. 5769]. forever, eternal, everlasting; ancient, a long time ago:– ever [10], everlasting [4], old [2], ever (+0.2) [1], ever (+0.2+5705) [1], for ever (+0.2) [1], never (+3809+3807.2) [1]

5958 עֶלֶם *ʿelem*, n.m. GK: 6624 [→ 5934]. boy, young man:– stripling [1], young man [1]

עֹלָם *ʿōlām*. See 5769.

5959 עַלְמָה *ʿalmâ*, n.f. GK: 6625 [→ 5934; cf. 5961]. girl, young woman, (in certain contexts) virgin:– maid [2], virgins [2], virgin [2], damsels [1]

5960 עַלְמוֹן *ʿalmôn*, n.pr.loc. GK: 6626 [→ 5963]. Almon:– Almon [1]

5961 עֲלָמוֹת *ʿᵃlāmôt*, n.f. GK: 6628 [→ 5934; cf. 5959]. alamoth (t.t. in the Psalms):– Alamoth [2]

עַלְמוּת *ʿalmût*. See 4192.

5962 עֵלְמָי *ʿēlmāy* (Aram.), n.g.pl. GK: 10551 [cf. 5867]. Elamite:– Elamites [1]

5963 עַלְמֹן דִּבְלָתָיְמָה *ʿalmôn diblātayim*, n.pr.loc. GK: 6627 [→ 5960]. Almon Diblathaim, "*way of the double fig cakes*":– Almon-diblathaim [2]

5964 עָלֶמֶת *ʿālemet*, n.pr.m. & loc. GK: 6630 & 6631. Alemeth, "*concealment*":– Alemeth [3], Alameth [1]

5965 עָלַס *ʿālas*, v. GK: 6632 [cf. 5937, 5951, 5970]. [Q] to enjoy; [N] to appear glad; [Ht] to enjoy one another:– peacocks [1], rejoice [1], solace [1]

5966 עָלַע *ʿālaʿ*, v. GK: 6633 [cf. 3216]. [Palpal] to drink, feast on:– suck up [1]

5967 עֲלַע *ʿᵃlaʿ* (Aram.), n.f. GK: 10552 [cf. 6763]. rib:– ribs [1]

5968 עָלַף *'ālap*, v. GK: 6634. [Pu] to faint; to be withered; be decorated, covered; [Ht] to disguise oneself; to grow faint:– fainted [2], faint [1], overlaid [1], wrapped [1]

5969 עֻלְפֶּה *'ulpeh*, var. GK: 6635. form of 5968: faint:– fainted [1]

5970 עָלַץ *'ālaṣ*, v. GK: 6636 [→ 5951; cf. 5965]. [Q] to rejoice, be jubilant:– rejoice [4], rejoiceth [2], joyful [1], triumph [1]

5971 עַם *'am*, n.[m.]. GK: 6638 & 6639 [cf. 5972 (also used with compound proper names)]. people, nation, countrymen; army, troop; father's relatives, one's people:– people [1829], nations [15], every people (+5971+2050.1) [8], people (+1121) [5], each people (+5971+2050.1) [2], folk [2], nation [2], people's [2], Ammi (+2967.1) [1], men [1]

5972 עַם *'am* (Aram.), n.m. GK: 10553 [cf. 5971]. people, nation:– people [15]

5973 עִם *'im*, pp. GK: 6640 [→ 6005; cf. 6004; cf. 5974]. marker of association or proximity: to, toward; with, among:– with [778], from (+4480) [46], against [36], unto [32], by [22], in [18], of (+4480) [13], among [11], to [11], and [7], for [5], of [5], before [4], by (+4480) [4], as [3], beside [3], at [2], towards [2], able to withstand (+3320) [1], accompanying [1], according to mind (+4480) [1], as long as [1], before (+4480) [1], besides [1], between [1], by reason of [1], for (+3588) [1], given of (+4480) [1], had (+1961) [1], had [1], have (+3426) [1], have [1], help [1], in the behalf of [1], lest (+2050.1) [1], lieth with (+7901) [1], like [1], mighty (+1369) [1], minded (+3820) [1], more than [1], near [1], on side [1], shew (+6213) [1], though (+3588) [1], to (+4480) [1], together with [1], toward [1], unto (+4480) [1], upon [1], withal [1]

5974 עִם *'im* (Aram.), pp. GK: 10554 [cf. 5973]. with, along with, to, for; a marker showing association in various meanings:– with [14], from [2], to [2], by [1], like [1], toward [1], unto [1]

5975 עָמַד *'āmad*, v. GK: 6641 [→ 4612, 4613, 5977, 5978, 5979, 5982]. [Q] to stand, stand up, stand still; [H] to cause to stand, present; to appoint, assign; [Ho] to be presented, be caused to stand:– stood [175], stand [123], set [31], standeth [13], stand up [12], set up [11], stood still [11], appointed [10], standing [10], stay [8], stayed [7], present [6], stand still [6], continue [4], endureth [4], remained [4], standest [4], stood up [4], waited [4], endure [3], establish [3], made [3], remain [3], abideth [2], abide [2], appoint [2], at a stay [2], confirmed [2], left [2], set forth [2], setteth [2], standing up [2], stayed up [2], stoodest [2], withstand [2], able to stand [1], abode [1], arise [1], arose [1], caused to stand [1], ceased [1], continued [1], continueth [1], dwell [1], employed [1], enduring [1], established [1], made to serve [1], made to stand [1], ordained [1], over (+5921) [1], placed [1], presented [1], raised up [1], raiseth [1], remaineth [1], repair [1], served (+6440+3807.1) [1], serve [1], settled [1], settle [1], stablished [1], stablisheth [1], stand by [1], standeth (+3807.1) [1], stood fast [1], tarried [1], tarry [1], waited on [1], withstand (+5048) [1], withstand (+6440+3807.1) [1], withstood (+5048+3807.1) [1], withstood (+5921) [1]

5976 עָמַד *'āmad* for מָעַד *mā'ad*, v. GK: 5048 [→ 4154]. var. of 4571: [H] cause to wobble, to bend:– madest to be at a stand [1]

5977 עֹמֶד *'ōmed*, n.[m.]. GK: 6642 [→ 5975]. standing-place (a position, station, or post):– place [6], upright (+5921) [2], stood [1], where stood [1]

5978 עִמָּד *'immād*, pp. GK: 6643 [→ 5975]. with:– with [25], unto [7], against [1], by [1], from (+4480) [1], in [1], mine (+2967.1) [1], of (+4480) [1], take [1], upon [1], within [1]

עַמֻּד *'ammud*. See 5982.

5979 עֶמְדָּה *'emdâ*, n.f. GK: 6644 [→ 5975]. place to stand, protection:– standing [1]

5980 עֻמָּה *'ummâ*, n.f. (used as pp.). GK: 6645 [→ 6004]. close by; alongside; adjoining:– over against (+3807.1) [15], against (+3807.1) [6], against [5], besides (+3807.1) [2], answerable (+3807.1) [1], at (+3807.1) [1], hard by (+3807.1) [1], points [1]

5981 עֻמָּה *'ummâ*, n.pr.loc. GK: 6646. Ummah:– Ummah [1]

5982 עַמּוּד *'ammûd*, n.m. GK: 6647 [→ 5975]. pillar, post, column; used fig. of the pillar-shaped cloud of God's presence:– pillars [80], pillar [29], apiece[S] (+259) [1], them[S] [1]

5983 עַמּוֹן *'ammôn*, n.pr.[loc.]. GK: 6648 [→ 5984; cf. 5971]. Ammonite; Ammon, "*my people [Ge 19:38]*":– Ammon [90], Ammonites (+1121) [15], Ammonites [1]

5984 עַמּוֹנִי *'ammônî*, a.g. GK: 6649 [→ 5983, 5985]. Ammonite, from Ammon, "*of Ammon*":– Ammonite [9], Ammonites [7], Ammonitess [4], of Ammon [1]

5985 עַמּוֹנִית *'ammônît*, a.g. GK: 6649 [→ 5984]. f. of 5984: Ammonite, from Ammon, "*of Ammon*":–

5986 עָמוֹס *'āmôs*, n.pr.m. GK: 6650 [→ 6006?]. Amos, "*burden bearer*":– Amos [7]

5987 עָמוֹק *'āmôq*, n.pr.m. GK: 6651 [→ 6009]. Amok, "*capable*":– Amok [2]

5988 עַמִּיאֵל *'ammî'ēl*, n.pr.m. GK: 6653 [→ 5971+410]. Ammiel, "*God [El] is my kinsman*":– Ammiel [6]

5989 עַמִּיהוּד *'ammîhûd*, n.pr.m. GK: 6654 [→ 5971+1935]. Ammihud, "*[my] people have majesty*":– Ammihud [10]

5990 עַמִּיזָבָד *'ammîzābād*, n.pr.m. GK: 6655 [→ 5971+2064]. Ammizabad, "*[my] people have given a gift*":– Ammizabad [1]

5991 עַמִּיחוּר *'ammîḥûr*, n.pr.m. GK: 6656 [→ 5971+2354?]. Ammihur, cf. 5989:– @H = **5992 עַמִּינָדָב *‰ammînâdâb***, n.pr.m. GK: 6657 [→ 5971+5068]. Amminadab, "*[my] people are generous*":– Amminadab [13]

5993 עַמִּי נָדִיב *'ammî Nādîb*, n.pr.m. GK: 6652 + 5618 [→ 5971+5081]. Amminadib, "*[my] people are generous*":– Ammi-nadib [1]

5994 עַמִּיק *'ammîq* (Aram.), a. GK: 10555 [cf. 6013]. deep; (as noun) the deep things, which are normally impenetrable and so secret and hidden, with the implication that such things are mysterious, profound, and valuable:– deep [1]

5995 עָמִיר *'āmîr*, n.[m.]. GK: 6658 [→ 6014]. (newly) cut grain:– sheaves [2], handful [1], sheaf [1]

5996 עַמִּישַׁדָּי *'ammîšaddāy*, n.pr.m. GK: 6659 [→ 5971+7706]. Ammishaddai, "*Shaddai is [my] kinsman*":– Ammishaddai [5]

5997 עָמִית *'āmît*, n.m. GK: 6660 [→ 6004]. neighbor, countryman, associate (one in close, united relation):– neighbour [7], another[S] [2], neighbour's [2], fellow [1]

5998 עָמַל *'āmal*, v. GK: 6661 [→ 5999, 6000, 6001]. [Q] to labor, toil, pour forth effort:– laboured [5], labour [2], taketh [2], laboureth [1], took [1]

5999 עָמָל *'āmāl*, n.m. & f. GK: 6662 [→ 5998]. trouble, work, labor, toil:– labour [25], mischief [9], misery [3], travail [3], trouble [3], sorrow [2], grievance [1], grievousness [1], iniquity [1], miserable [1], painful [1], pain [1], perverseness [1], toil [1], wearisome [1], wickedness [1]

6000 עָמָל *'āmāl*, n.pr.m. GK: 6663 [→ 5999; cf. 5998]. Amal, "*laborer, troubler*":– Amal [1]

6001 עָמֵל *'āmēl*, n.m. GK: 6664 & 6665 [→ 5998]. misery; workman, laborer:– laboureth [2], in misery [1], laboured [1], labour [1], taken [1], takest [1], wicked [1], workmen's [1]

6002 עֲמָלֵק *ªmālēq*, n.pr.m. GK: 6667 [→ 6003]. Amalek; Amalekite:– Amalek [24], Amalekites [15]

6003 עֲמָלֵקִי *ªmālēqî*, a.g. GK: 6668 [→ 6002]. Amalekite, "*of Amalek*":– Amalekites [9], Amalekite [2], Amalekite (+376) [1]

6004 עָמַם *'āmam*, v. GK: 6669 & 6670 [→ 5973, 5980, 5997]. [Q] to be rival to, be equal to; to grow dark; [Ho] to lose luster, grow dark:– hide [2], become dim [1]

6005 עִמָּנוּ אֵל *'immānû 'ēl*, n.pr.m. GK: 6672 [→ 5973+5105.1+410]. Immanuel, "*God with us*":– Immanuel [2]

6006 עָמַס *'āmas*, v. GK: 6673 [→ 4614, 5986?, 6007]. [Q] to load a burden, carry a burden; [Qp] to be burdensome, be upheld; [H] to lay a burden upon:– laded [2], borne [1], burden [1], heavy loaden [1], lade [1], lading (+5921) [1], loadeth [1], put [1]

6007 עֲמַסְיָה *ªmasyâ*, n.pr.m. GK: 6674 [→ 6006+3068]. Amasiah, "*Yahweh carries a load*":– Amasiah [1]

6008 עַמְעָד *'am'ād*, n.pr.loc. GK: 6675. Amad:– Amad [1]

6009 עָמַק *'āmaq*, v. GK: 6676 [→ 1025, 4615, 5987, 6010, 6013, 6011, 6012, 7104]. [Q] to be profound; [H] to make deep (in various senses):– deep [3], deeply [2], depth [1], made deep [1], profound to make [1], seek deep [1]

6010 עֵמֶק *'ēmeq*, n.m. GK: 6677 [→ 1025; cf. 6009]. valley; (low-lying) plain:– valley [54], valleys [9], vale [4], dale [2]

6011 עֹמֶק *'ōmeq*, n.[m.]. GK: 6679 [→ 6009]. depth:– depth [1]

6012 עָמֵק *'āmēq*, a. GK: 6680 [→ 6009]. obscure, unintelligible, by extension of what is physically deep (not found in the OT):– strange [2], deeper [1], depths [1]

6013 עָמֹק *'āmōq*, a. GK: 6678 [→ 6009; cf. 5994]. deep; profound:– deeper [8], deep [7], exceeding deep (+6013) [2]

6014 עָמַר *'āmar*, v.den. GK: 6682 & 6683 [→ 5995, 6016, 6017, 6019, 6020, 6192, 6191; cf. 6192]. [P] to bind sheaves (of newly cut grain); [Ht] to treat brutally, deal tyrannically with:– bindeth sheaves [1], make merchandise [1], maketh merchandise [1]

6015 עֲמַר *ªmar* (Aram.), n.m. GK: 10556 [cf. 6785]. wool:– wool [1]

6016 עֹמֶר *'ōmer*, n.m. GK: 6684 & 6685 [→ 6014]. sheaf of grain; omer (dry measure, one-tenth of an ephah, about two quarts or liters):– sheaf [6], omer [5], sheaves [2], omers [1]

6017 עֲמֹרָה *ªmōrâ*, n.pr.loc. GK: 6686 [→ 6014]. Gomorrah, "*to overwhelm with water*":– Gomorrah [19]

6018 עָמְרִי *'omrî*, n.pr.m. GK: 6687. Omri, "*thrive, live long*":– Omri [18]

6019 עַמְרָם *'amrām*, n.pr.m. GK: 6688 [→ 6020]. Amram, "*exalted people*":– Amram [13], Amram's [1]

6020 עַמְרָמִי *'amrāmî*, a.g. GK: 6689 [→ 6019]. Amramite, "*of Amram*":– Amramites [2]

עָמַשׂ *'āmaś*. See 6006.

6021 עֲמָשָׂא *ªmāśā'*, n.pr.m. GK: 6690 [→ 6022]. Amasa, "*[my] people are from Jesse*":– Amasa [16]

6022 עֲמָשַׂי *ªmāśay*, n.pr.m. GK: 6691 [→ 6021]. Amasai, "*[my] people are from Jesse*":– Amasai [5]

6023 עֲמַשְׁסַי *ªmaššay*, n.pr.m. GK: 6692. Amashai:– Amashai [1]

6024 עֲנָב *ªnāb*, n.pr.loc. GK: 6693 [→ 6025]. Anab, "*grape*":– Anab [2]

6025 עֵנָב *'ēnāb*, n.m. GK: 6694 [→ 6024]. cluster of grapes:– grapes [17], grape [1], wine [1]

6026 עָנַג *'ānag*, v. GK: 6695 [→ 6027, 6028, 8588]. [Pu] to be delicate; [Ht] to delight oneself, enjoy, to mock:– delight [5], delicateness [1], delicate [1], delighted [1], have delight [1], sport [1]

6027 עֹנֶג *'ōneg*, n.[m.]. GK: 6696 [→ 6026]. delight, luxury, enjoyment:– delight [1], pleasant [1]

6028 עָנֹג *'ānōg*, a. GK: 6697 [→ 6026]. sensitive, delicate:– delicate [3]

6029 עָנַד *'ānad*, v. GK: 6698 [cf. 4575]. [Q] to bind around, bind upon:– bind [1], tie [1]

6030 עָנָה *'ānâ*, v. GK: 6699 & 6702 & 4361 [→ 3285?, 4617, 6031?, 6043; cf. 6032]. [Q] to answer, reply, respond; to sing; [N] to be answered; usually verbal, the response can involve action; [P] to sing to or sing about; (inf.) leannoth (t.t. in Ps 88):– answered [175], answer [54], hear [29], heard [11], testify [8], answereth [5], sing [5], speak [5], spake [3], testified [3], answeredst [2], answerest [2], bear [2], cry [2], gave answer [2], witness [2], beareth witness [1], beareth [1], brought low [1], give a shout (+1959) [1], give an answer [1], given answer [1], giveth account [1], giveth answer [1], heardest [1], hearest [1], lift up [1], make answer [1], said [1], sang [1], scholar [1], shout [1], sung [1], testifieth [1], utter [1]

6031 עָנָה *'ānâ*, v. GK: 6700 & 6701 [→ 3282, 4616, 4617, 4618, 5772? 6030?, 6035, 6037, 6038, 6039, 6040, 6041, 6045, 6256, 6258, 6261, 6262, 8589]. [Q] to be afflicted; to stoop down; to be concerned about, be worried about; [N] to be afflicted, humbled, oppressed; [P] to afflict, oppress, subdue, humble, mistreat; [Pu] to be afflicted, deny oneself; [H] to afflict another, oppress; to keep occupied, keep oneself busy; [Ht] to humble oneself; humbling by force implies dishonor:– afflict [28], afflicted [21], humbled [7], forced [4], humble [4], afflict in any wise (+6031) [2], exercised [2], Leannoth [1], abase [1], afflictest [1], afflictions [1], answereth [1], chasten [1], dealt hardly with [1], defiled [1], force [1], gentleness [1], hurt [1], ravished [1], sing [1], submit [1], troubled [1], weakened [1]

6032 עֲנָה *ªnâ* (Aram.), v. GK: 10558 [cf. 6030]. [P] to answer, reply; usually a reaction to a direct question, but can be a more general response:– answered [16], spake [14]

6033 עֲנֵה *ªnēh* (Aram.), a. GK: 10559 [cf. 6041, 6035]. oppressed, needy, poor, implying that such persons are miserable in their life situation:– poor [1]

6034 עֲנָה *ªnâ*, n.pr.m. GK: 6704 [→ 6067]. Anah:– Anah [12]

Heb

6035 עָנָו **ʿānāw** or עָנָיו **ʿānāyw**, n.m. GK: 6705 & 6718 [cf. 6031; cf. 6033]. humble, afflicted, poor, oppressed:– meek [13], humble [5], lowly [2], poor [1]

6036 עָנוּב **ʿānûb**, n.pr.m. GK: 6707. Anub, "*fruitful*":– Anub [1]

6037 עַנְוָה **ʿanwâ**, n.f. GK: 6709 [→ 6031]. humility:– gentleness [1], meekness [1]

6038 עֲנָוָה **ʿᵃnāwâ**, n.f. GK: 6708 [→ 6031]. humility:– humility [3], meekness [1]

6039 עֱנוּת **ʿᵉnût**, n.f. GK: 6713 [→ 6031]. suffering, affliction:– affliction [1]

6040 עֳנִי **ʿᵒnî**, n.m. GK: 6715 [→ 6031]. affliction, suffering, misery:– affliction [32], trouble [3], afflicted (+1121) [1]

6041 עָנִי **ʿānî**, a. GK: 6714 [→ 6031; cf. 6033]. needy, poor, afflicted, oppressed, often referring to a class of persons of low status and lacking resources:– poor [59], afflicted [15], lowly [1]

6042 עֻנִּי **ʿunnî**, n.pr.m. GK: 6716. Unni, "*Yahweh has answered*":– Unni [3]

6043 עֲנָיָה **ʿᵃnāyâ**, n.pr.m. GK: 6717 [→ 6030+3068]. Anaiah, "*Yahweh responds*":– Anaiah [2]

עָנָיו **ʿānāyw** See 6035.

6044 עָנִים **ʿānîm**, n.pr.loc. GK: 6719. Anim, "*springs*":– Anim [1]

6045 עִנְיָן **ʿinyān**, n.m. GK: 6721 [→ 6031]. task, work, labor; misfortune, cares, troubles:– travail [6], business [2]

6046 עָנֵם **ʿānēm**, n.pr.loc. GK: 6722. Anem, "*springs*":– Anem [1]

6047 עֲנָמִים **ʿᵃnāmîm**, n.pr.g. GK: 6723. Anamite:– Anamim [2]

6048 עֲנַמֶּלֶךְ **ʿᵃnammelek**, n.pr.[m.]. GK: 6724 [→ 6067+4428]. Anammelech (pagan god), "*Anath is king*":– Anammelech [1]

6049 עָנַן **ʿānan**, v.den. GK: 6725 & 6726 [→ 6031, 6051, 6052, 6053, 6054, 6055]. [P] to bring clouds; [Po] to practice sorcery, practice divination, cast spells:– observed times [2], soothsayers [2], Meonenim [1], bring a cloud (+6051) [1], enchanters [1], observe times [1], observer of times [1], observers of times [1], sorceress [1]

6050 עֲנַן **ʿᵃnān** (Aram.), n.[m.]. GK: 10560 [cf. 6051]. cloud:– clouds [1]

6051 עָנָן **ʿānān**, n.m. GK: 6727 [→ 6053; cf. 6049; cf. 6050]. cloud, of moisture or smoke, natural or supernatural:– cloud [74], clouds [6], cloudy [6], bring a cloud (+6049) [1]

6052 עָנָן **ʿānān**, n.pr.m. GK: 6728 [→ 6051; cf. 6049]. Anan, "*cloud*":– Anan [1]

6053 עֲנָנָה **ʿᵃnānâ**, n.f. GK: 6729 [→ 6051; cf. 6049]. cloud, likely referring to a dense rain cloud:– cloud [1]

6054 עֲנָנִי **ʿᵃnānî**, n.pr.m. GK: 6730 [→ 6049+3068]. Anani, "*Yahweh is a covering*":– Anani [1]

6055 עֲנַנְיָה **ʿᵃnanᵉyâ**, n.pr.m. & loc. GK: 6731 & 6732 [→ 6049+3068]. Ananiah, "*Yahweh is a covering*":– Ananiah [2]

6056 עֲנַף **ʿᵃnap** (Aram.), n.[m.]. GK: 10561 [cf. 6057]. branch, bough:– branches [3], boughs [1]

6057 עָנָף **ʿānāp**, n.[m.]. GK: 6733 [→ 6058; cf. 6056]. branches:– boughs [3], branches [3], branch [1]

6058 עָנֵף **ʿānēp**, a. GK: 6734 [→ 6057]. full of branches:– full of branches [1]

6059 עָנַק **ʿānaq**, v.den. GK: 6735 [→ 6060]. [Q] to put on (as a necklace); [H] to supply, a fig. extension of putting an adornment around the neck:– furnish liberally (+6059) [2], compasseth about as a chain [1]

6060 עֲנָק **ʿᵃnāq**, n.m. GK: 6736 [→ 6059]. necklace chain:– chains [2], chain [1]

6061 עֲנוֹק **ʿᵃnôq**, n.pr.[m. *or* loc.]. GK: 6710 [→ 6062]. Anak, "*neck*":– Anak [9]

6062 עֲנָק **ʿᵃnāq**, n.[m.] & g. GK: 6737 [→ 6061]. Anak, "*neck*", Anakites:– Anakims [9]

6063 עָנֵר **ʿānēr**, n.pr.m. & loc. GK: 6738 & 6739. Aner:– Aner [3]

6064 עָנַשׁ **ʿānaš**, v.den. GK: 6740 & 6711 [→ 6066; cf. 6065]. [Q] to levy a fine (as a punishment or recompense); [N] to be fined, be punished:– punished [3], condemned [2], surely punished (+6064) [2], amerce [1], punish [1]

6065 עֲנָשׁ **ʿᵃnāš** (Aram.), n.[m.]. GK: 10562 [cf. 6066]. confiscation; some sources translate as "fine," a monetary penalty without the necessary confiscation of property:– confiscation [1]

6066 עֹנֶשׁ **ʿōneš**, n.[m.]. GK: 6741 [→ 6064]. levy, penalty, fine:– punishment [1], tribute [1]

עֶנֶת **ʿenet** See 3706.

6067 עֲנָת **ʿᵃnāt**, n.pr.m. GK: 6742 [→ 1042, 1043, 6034, 6048, 6068, 6069]. Anath, "*Semitic goddess*":– Anath [2]

6068 עֲנָתוֹת **ʿᵃnātôt**, n.pr.f. & loc. GK: 6743 & 6744 [→ 6067]. Anathoth, "*plural of Anath*":– Anathoth [15]

6069 עַנְּתֹתִי **ʿannᵉtōtî**, a.g. GK: 6745 [→ 6067]. Anathothite, from Anathoth, "*of Anathoth*":– Antothite [2], Anathoth [1], Anethothite [1], Anetothite [1]

6070 עַנְתֹתִיָּה **ʿantōtiyyâ**, n.pr.m. GK: 6746. Anthothijah:– Antothijah [1]

6071 עָסִיס **ʿāsîs**, n.m. GK: 6747 [→ 6072]. new wine (relatively sweet); nectar:– new wine [2], sweet wine [2], juice [1]

6072 עָסַס **ʿāsas**, v. GK: 6748 [→ 6071]. [Q] to trample down:– tread down [1]

6073 עֳפִי **ʿᵒpî**, n.[m.]. GK: 6751 [cf. 6074]. branch:– branches [1]

6074 עֳפִי **ʿᵒpî** (Aram.), n.m. GK: 10564 [cf. 6073]. leaves, foliage:– leaves [3]

6075 עָפַל **ʿāpal**, v. GK: 6752 & 6753 [→ 6076, 6077]. [Pu] to be puffed up, be swelled; [H] to have presumption, to have the audacity to:– lifted up [1], presumed [1]

6076 עֹפֶל **ʿōpel**, n.m. GK: 6754 [→ 6075]. tumor, hemorrhoid, abscess:– emerods [1], forts [1], tower [1]

6077 עֹפֶל **ʿōpel**, n.[m.]. GK: 6755 [→ 6076]. hill; (as a proper name) the hill of Ophel:– Ophel [5], strong hold [1]

6078 עָפְנִי **ʿopnî**, n.pr.loc. GK: 6756. Ophni:– Ophni [1]

6079 עַפְעַפַּיִם **ʿapʿappayim**, n.m. GK: 6757 [→ 4155]. flashing rays (of dawn); glances or flitting of eyes or eyelids:– eyelids [9], dawning [1]

6080 עָפַר **ʿāpar**, v.den. GK: 6759 [→ 6083]. [P] to shower (with dust or dirt):– cast [1]

6081 עֵפֶר **ʿēper**, n.pr.m. GK: 6761 [→ 6085]. Epher, "*[small] gazelle*":– Epher [4]

6082 עֹפֶר **ʿōper**, n.m. GK: 6762 [→ 6084; cf. 6083]. fawn (of a deer or gazelle):– young [5]

6083 עָפָר **ʿāpār**, n.m. GK: 6760 [→ 6080; cf. 6082]. dust, earth, soil in any form; used as a figure of something that cannot be counted:– dust [92], earth [8], powder [3], ashes [2], morter [2], rubbish [2], ground [1]

עָפְרָה **ʿaprâ**. See 1036.

6084 עָפְרָה **ʿoprâ**, n.pr.m. & loc. GK: 6763 & 6764 [cf. 6082]. Ophrah, "*young gazelle*":– Ophrah [8]

6085 עֶפְרוֹן **ʿeprôn**, n.pr.m. & loc. GK: 6766 & 6767 [cf. 6081]. Ephron, "*gazelle*":– Ephron [13], Ephrain [1]

עֹפֶרֶת **ʿōperet**. See 5777.

6086 עֵץ **ʿēṣ**, n.m. GK: 6770 [→ 6097; cf. 636]. tree; by extension, the product of the tree: wood, any wooden object:– wood [107], tree [84], trees [78], timber [23], stick [9], gallows [8], sticks [5], staff [4], carpenters (+2796) [3], stocks [2], stock [2], branches [1], carpenter (+2796) [1], helve [1], planks [1], stalks [1]

6087 עָצַב **ʿāṣab**, v. GK: 6771 & 6772 [→ 4620, 6089, 6090, 6091, 6092, 6093, 6094; cf. 6088]. [Q] to interfere with; [Qp] to be distressed; [N] to be grieved, be distressed; [P] to grieve; to shape; [H] to grieve; to make an image (of the Queen of Heaven); [Ht] to be filled with grief, be filled with pain:– grieved [8], grieve [2], displeased [1], hurt [1], made [1], sorry [1], vexed [1], worship [1], wrest [1]

6088 עֲצִיב **ʿᵃṣîb** (Aram.), v. GK: 10565. anguished, sorrowful:– lamentable [1]

6089 עֶצֶב **ʿeṣeb**, n.m. GK: 6775 & 6776 [→ 6087]. pot, vessel; pain, toil, hard work:– sorrow [2], grievous [1], idol [1], labours [1], labour [1], sorrows [1]

6090 עֹצֶב **ʿōṣeb**, n.m. GK: 6777 & 6778 [→ 6087]. idol; pain, toil:– sorrow [2], idol [1], wicked [1]

6091 עָצָב **ʿāṣāb**, n.[m.]. GK: 6773 [→ 6087]. idol, image, a crafted object believed to represent or even possess a spirit or god:– idols [16], images [1]

6092 עַצָּב **ʿaṣṣāb**, n.[m.]. GK: 6774 [→ 6087]. (hard) worker, toiler:– labours [1]

6093 עִצָּבוֹן **ʿiṣṣābôn**, n.[m.]. GK: 6779 [→ 6087]. pain, hardship, distress:– sorrow [2], toil [1]

6094 עַצֶּבֶת **ʿaṣṣebet**, n.f. GK: 6780 [→ 6087]. pain, sorrow, grief:– sorrows [2], sorrow [2], wounds [1]

6095 עָצָה **ʿāṣâ**, v. GK: 6781. [Q] to wink (the eye), as a non-verbal communication of what is evil, malicious, or lurid:– shutteth [1]

6096 עָצֶה **ʿāṣeh**, n.[m.]. GK: 6782. backbone, tailbone:– back bone [1]

6097 עֵצָה **ʿēṣâ**, n.f.col. GK: 6785 [→ 6086]. (coll.) wood; this can refer to wooden idols:– trees [1]

6098 עֵצָה **ʿēṣâ**, n.f. GK: 6783 [→ 3289; cf. 5843]. advice, counsel, plan, purpose, scheme:– counsel [72], counsel gave (+3289) [2], counsel given (+3289) [2], counsels [2], give counsel (+3289) [2], purpose [2], advice [1], advisement [1], counseller (+376) [1], counsellers (+376) [1], take counsel together (+5779) [1], taken counsel (+3289) [1]

6099 עָצוּם **ʿāṣûm**, a. GK: 6786 [→ 6110; cf. 6105]. strong, mighty, powerful:– strong [13], mighty [8], mightier [7], feeble (+3808) [1], great [1], much [1]

6100 עֶצְיוֹן גֶּבֶר **ʿeṣyôn geber**, n.pr.loc. GK: 6787. Ezion Geber, "*giant, the giant backbone*":– Ezion-geber [4], Ezion-gaber [3]

6101 עָצַל **ʿāṣal**, v. GK: 6788 [→ 6102, 6103, 6104]. [N] to hesitate, be sluggish, be slow:– slothful [1]

6102 עָצֵל **ʿāṣēl**, a. GK: 6789 [→ 6101]. sluggish, slow, lazy; (n.) sluggard, one with no discipline or motivation, a moral failure:– slothful [7], sluggard [6], slothful (+376) [1]

6103 עַצְלָה **ʿaṣlâ**, n.f. GK: 6790 & 6792 [→ 6101]. laziness, slowness, sluggishness:– much slothfulness [1], slothfulness [1]

6104 עַצְלוּת **ʿaṣlût**, n.f. GK: 6791 [→ 6101]. idleness, sluggishness, laziness:– idleness [1]

6105 עָצַם **ʿāṣam**, v. GK: 6793 & 6794 [→ 6099, 6106, 6107, 6108, 6108, 6109, 6111, 8592]. [Q] to close (the eyes); to be vast, powerful, numerous; [P] to tightly shut (the eyes); to crush bones; [H] to make numerous, make powerful, make vast:– increased [4], strong [4], mighty [2], moe [2], waxed mighty [2], broken bones [1], closed [1], great [1], made stronger [1], mightier [1], shutteth [1]

6106 עֶצֶם **ʿeṣem**, n.f. GK: 6795 [→ 6107; cf. 6105]. bone; by extension: the whole body, any part of the body, limb; strength of the body, vigor; (adv.) that very (day); "one's bone and flesh" is a close relative:– bones [89], bone [15], selfsame [11], same [5], body [2], very [2], life [1], strength [1]

6107 עֶצֶם **ʿeṣem**, n.pr.loc. GK: 6796 [→ 6106; cf. 6105]. Ezem, "*bone [strength]*":– Azem [2], Ezem [1]

6108 עֹצֶם **ʿōṣem**, n.[m.]. GK: 6797 & 6798 [→ 6105]. might, strength; framework (of bones of the human body):– might [1], strong [1], substance [1]

עָצֻם **ʿāṣum**. See 6099.

6109 עָצְמָה **ʿoṣmâ**, n.f. GK: 6800 [→ 6105]. power, potency, might:– strength [2], abundance [1]

6110 עֲצֻמוֹת **ʿᵃṣumôt**, n.f.[pl.]. GK: 6802 [→ 6099]. defensive arguments, strong words:– strong [1]

6111 עַצְמוֹן **ʿaṣmôn**, n.pr.loc. GK: 6801 [→ 6106; cf. 6105]. Azmon, "*strongly [built body]*":– Azmon [3]

6112 עֶצְנִי **ʿeṣnî**, n.pr. *or* a.g.?. GK: 6804. Eznite:– Eznite [1]

6113 עָצַר **ʿāṣar**, v. GK: 6806 [→ 4622, 4623, 6114, 6115, 6116]. [Q] to refrain, hold back, restrain; [Qp] to be enslaved, be constrained; [N] to be stopped, be detained:– shut up [15], stayed [7], detain [2], fast closed up (+6113) [2], retained [2], able (+3581) [1], able [1], be [1], detained [1], keep still [1], kept close [1], kept [1], prevail [1], recover [1], refrained [1], reign [1], restrained [1], retain [1], shut [1], slack [1], stop [1], withholdeth [1], withhold [1]

6114 עֶצֶר **ʿeṣer**, n.[m.]. GK: 6807 [→ 6113]. restraint, oppression:– magistrate (+3423) [1]

6115 עֹצֶר **ʿōṣer**, n.[m.]. GK: 6808 [→ 6113]. oppression; barrenness:– barren [1], oppression [1], prison [1]

6116 עֲצָרָה **ʿᵃṣārâ**, n.f. GK: 6809 [→ 6113]. assembly, usually on a festive day:– solemn assembly [8], assembly [1], solemn assemblies [1], solemn meeting [1]

6117 עָקַב **ʿāqab**, v. GK: 6810 [→ 6120; cf. 6119, 6120, 6906]. [Q] to deceive; to grasp at the heel; [P] to hold the heel, to hold back:– utterly supplant (+6117) [2], stay [1], supplanted [1], took by the heel [1]

6118 עֵקֶב **ʿēqeb**, n.[m.] (used as adv. & c.). GK: 6813 [→ 6119]. (c.) because; (n.) a reward; unto the end:– because [3], reward [3], because (+3588) [2], because (+834) [2], end [2], by [1], for [1], if [1]

6119 עָקֵב **ʿāqēb**, n.m. GK: 6811 [→ 6118, 6121; cf. 3290, 6117, 6120]. heel, hoof; footstep, footprint; by extension: rear guard of a military formation; a euphemism for private parts:– heel [4], footsteps [3], heels [2], horsehoofs (+5483) [1], last [1], liers in wait [1], steps [1]

6120 עָקֵב **ʿāqēb**, a.vbl. GK: 6812 [→ 6117, 6121, 6122; cf. 3290, 6117, 6119, 6906]. deceiver:– heels [1]

6121 עָקֹב **ʿāqōb**, a. [& n.] GK: 6814 & 6815 [→ 6119, 6120]. deceitful; rough, bumpy; footprint:– crooked [1], deceitful [1], polluted [1]

6122 עָקְבָה **ʿoqbâ**, n.f. GK: 6817 [→ 6120]. deceptiveness, cunning, craftiness:– subtilty [1]

6123 עָקַד **ʿāqad**, v. GK: 6818 [→ 6124]. [Q] to bind (feet):– bound [1]

עֵקֶד **ʿēqed**. See 1044.

6124 עָקֹד **ʿāqōd**, a. GK: 6819 [→ 6123]. streaked, striped:– ringstraked [7]

6125 עָקָה **ʿāqâ**, n.f. GK: 6821 [→ 5781]. pressure; oppressive look, stare, or actions:– oppression [1]

6126 עַקּוּב **ʿaqqûb**, n.pr.m. GK: 6822. Akkub, "*guard*":– Akkub [8]

6127 עָקַל **ʿāqal**, v. GK: 6823 [→ 6128, 6129]. [Pu] to be perverted, be distorted, be crooked:– wrong [1]

6128 עֲקַלְקַל **ᵃqalqāl**, a.intens. GK: 6824 [→ 6127]. crooked, winding:– byways (+734) [1], crooked ways [1]

6129 עֲקַלָּתוֹן **ᵃqallātôn**, a. GK: 6825 [→ 6127]. coiling (serpent):– crooked [1]

6130 עֲקָן **ᵃqān**, n.pr.m. GK: 6826 [→ 3292?]. Akan:– Akan [1]

Heb

6131 עָקַר **ʿāqar**, v.den. GK: 6827 & 6828 [→ 6135, 6133, 6134; cf. 6132, cf. 6136]. [Q] to root up; [N] to be uprooted; [P] to hamstring (to cut the tendon and render helpless or useless):– houghed [3], digged down [1], hough [1], pluck up [1], rooted up [1]

6132 עֲקַר **ᵃqar** (Aram.), v.den. GK: 10566 [→ 6136; cf. 6131]. [Itpe] to be uprooted, plucked out:– pluckt up by roots [1]

6133 עֵקֶר **ʿēqer**, n.m. GK: 6830 [→ 6131]. offspring, as the fig. extension of a plant that grows up from a root:– stock [1]

6134 עֵקֶר **ʿēqer**, n.pr.m. GK: 6831 [→ 6131?]. Eker, "[poss.] *offspring*":– Eker [1]

6135 עָקָר **ʿāqār**, a. GK: 6829 [→ 6131]. barren, sterile, without children:– barren [10], female barren [1], male[S] [1]

6136 עִקַּר **ʿiqqar** (Aram.), n.[m.]. GK: 10567 [→ 6132]. stump, root:– stump [3]

6137 עַקְרָב **ʿaqrāb**, n.m. GK: 6832 [→ 7128]. scorpion:– scorpions [6], Akrabbim [2]

6138 עֶקְרוֹן **ʿeqrôn**, n.pr.loc. GK: 6833 [→ 6139]. Ekron, "[perhaps] *barren place* or *fertile place*":– Ekron [22]

6139 עֶקְרוֹנִי **ʿeqrônî**, a.g. GK: 6834 [→ 6138]. Ekronite, of Ekron, "*of Ekron*":– Ekronites [2]

6140 עָקַשׁ **ʿāqaš**, v. GK: 6835 [→ 4625, 6141, 6142, 6143]. [N] to be perverse, be crooked; [P] to take crooked paths; to distort; [H] to pronounce guilty:– made crooked [1], perverse [1], perverteth [1], pervert [1], prove perverse [1]

6141 עִקֵּשׁ **ʿiqqēš**, a. GK: 6836 [→ 6142; cf. 6140]. perverse, crooked, warped:– froward [6], perverse [4], crooked [1]

6142 עִקֵּשׁ **ʿiqqēš**, n.pr.m. GK: 6837 [→ 6141; cf. 6140]. Ikkesh, "*crooked, perverted*":– Ikkesh [3]

6143 עִקְּשׁוּת **ʿiqqᵉšût**, n.f. GK: 6838 [→ 6140]. perversion, corruption, crookedness:– froward [2]

עָר **ʿār**. See 5892.

6144 עָר **ʿār**, n.pr.loc. GK: 6840 [→ 5892?]. Ar, "[poss.] *city*":– Ar [6]

6145 עָר **ʿār**, n.m. GK: 6839 [→ 6209?]. enemy, adversary:– enemies [1], enemy [1]

6146 עָר **ʿār** (Aram.), n.m. GK: 10568 [cf. 6862]. adversary, foe:– enemies [1]

6147 עֵר **ʿēr**, n.pr.m. GK: 6841 [→ 5782; cf. 5894]. Er, "*watchful, watcher*":– Er [10]

6148 עָרַב **ʿārab**, v. GK: 6842 & 6843 [→ 4627, 6154, 6157, 6161, 6162, 8594; cf. 6150; cf. 6151]. [Q] to put up a security, make a guarantee, give a pledge; [Ht] to make a bargain, make a wager; to mingle, join in with, share with:– surety [4], give pledges [2], meddle [2], mingled [2], surety for [2], became surety [1], becometh surety (+6161) [1], engaged [1], intermeddle [1], mortgaged [1], occupiers [1], occupy [1], put in a surety [1], sureties [1], undertake [1]

6149 עָרַב **ʿārab**, v. GK: 6844 [→ 6156]. [Q] to be pleasing, be pleasant, be acceptable:– sweet [5], pleasant [1], pleasing [1], taken pleasure [1]

6150 עָרַב **ʿārab**, v.den. GK: 6845 [→ 4628, 6153; cf. 6148]. [Q] to become evening; (opposite of joy) turn to gloom; [H] to do something in the evening:– evening [2], darkened [1]

6151 עֲרַב **ᵃrab** (Aram.), v. GK: 10569 [cf. 6148]. [Pap] to be mixed; [Htpa] (ptcp.) mixture:– mixed [2], mingle [1], mixt [1]

6152 עֲרַב **ᵃrab**, n.pr.loc. & g. GK: 6851 [→ 6160]. Arabia, Arab:– Arabia [5]

6153 עֶרֶב **ʿereb**, n.[m.]. GK: 6847 [→ 6150]. evening, twilight, dusk, the fading of the day; twilight can extend into the dark of the night:– even [67], evening [47], at even (+996+1886.1) [6], every evening (+6153+871.1+871.1+1886.1+1886.1) [4], night [4], mingled people [3], eveningtide (+6256) [2], Arabia [1], days (+1242) [1], eventide (+6256+1886.1) [1], eventide (+6437) [1], eventide [1], people [1]

6154 עֵרֶב **ʿēreb**, n.[m.]. GK: 6849 & 6850 [→ 6148]. foreign people; knitted or woven material:– woof [9], mixed multitude [1], mixed [1]

6155 עֲרָבָה **ᵃrābâ**, n.[f.]. GK: 6857 [→ 6164]. poplar tree:– willows [5]

6156 עָרֵב **ʿārēb**, a. GK: 6853 [→ 6149]. pleasant, sweet (voice):– sweet [2]

6157 עָרֹב **ʿārōb**, n.m. GK: 6856 [→ 6148]. swarms of flies:– swarms [5], divers sorts [2], swarm [2]

6158 עֹרֵב **ʿōrēb**, n.m. GK: 6854 [→ 6159]. raven:– raven [6], ravens [4]

6159 עֹרֵב **ʿōrēb**, n.pr.m. GK: 6855 [→ 6158]. Oreb, "*raven*":– Oreb [7]

6160 עֲרָבָה **ᵃrābâ**, n.f. GK: 6858 [→ 6152, 6163]. plains (a geographical region of desert, wilderness or wasteland); (pr.n.) Arabah:– plain [22], plains [20], desert [8], wilderness [5], Arabah [2], champaign [1], deserts [1], evenings [1], heavens [1]

6161 עֲרֻבָּה **ᵃrubbâ**, n.f. GK: 6859 [→ 6148]. security, pledge; assurance:– becometh surety (+6148) [1], pledge [1]

6162 עֵרָבוֹן **ʿērābôn**, n.[m.]. GK: 6860 [→ 6148]. pledge, security:– pledge [3]

6163 עַרְבִי **ʿarbî** or עֲרָבִי **ᵃrābî**, a.g. GK: 6861 & 6862 [→ 6160]. Arab, of Arabia; may also refer to bedouin in general:– Arabians [5], Arabian [4]

6164 עַרְבָתִי **ʿarbātî**, a.g. GK: 6863 [→ 6155]. Arbathite, "*of Arabah*":– Arbathite [2]

6165 עָרַג **ʿārag**, v. GK: 6864 [→ 6170?]. [Q] to pant for, long for (as a thirsty animal):– panteth [2], cry [1]

6166 עֲרָד **ᵃrād**, n.pr.m. & loc. GK: 6865 & 6866 [→ 6171]. Arad, "*wild donkey*":– Arad [5]

6167 עֲרָד **ᵃrād** (Aram.), n.m. GK: 10570 [cf. 6171]. wild donkey:– wild asses [1]

6168 עָרָה **ʿārâ**, v. GK: 6867 [→ 4177, 4632, 4636, 5903, 6172, 6174, 6181, 6196, 8593; cf. 6209, 5783]. [N] to be poured; [P] to lay bare, empty, expose, strip; [H] to make exposed; to cause to pour out; to dishonor; [Ht] to show oneself naked:– emptied [2], rase [2], discovered [1], discovering [1], discover [1], leave destitute [1], make naked [1], poured out [1], poured [1], spreading [1], uncovered [1], uncovereth [1], uncover [1]

6169 עָרָה **ʿārâ**, n.f. GK: 6868. plants, bulrushes:– paper reeds [1]

6170 עֲרוּגָה **ᵃrûgâ**, n.f. GK: 6870 [→ 6165?]. garden bed, garden plot:– furrows [2], beds [1], bed [1]

6171 עָרוֹד **ʿārôd**, n.[m.]. GK: 6871 [→ 5897, 6166; cf. 6167]. wild donkey:– wild ass [1]

6172 עֶרְוָה **ʿerwâ**, n.f. GK: 6872 [→ 6168; cf. 6173]. nakedness (indecent or shameful in certain situations); "to expose the nakedness" is to have sexual relations:– nakedness [50], nakedness (+1320) [1], shame [1], uncleanness [1], unclean [1]

6173 עַרְוָה **ʿarwâ** (Aram.), n.f. GK: 10571 [cf. 6172]. nakedness; fig., dishonor, lowering of one's status in a community resulting in disgrace or shame:– dishonour [1]

6174 עָרוֹם **ʿārôm**, a. GK: 6873 [→ 6174]. naked, stripped:– naked [16]

6175 עָרוּם **ʿārûm**, a. GK: 6874 [→ 6191]. wise and understanding; with a positive connotation: prudent, clever; with a negative connotation: crafty:– prudent [8], crafty [2], subtil [1]

6176 עֲרוֹעֵר **ᵃrôʿēr**, n.[m.]. GK: 6875 [→ 6177; cf. 6209]. (juniper) bush:– heath [1]

6177 עֲרוֹעֵר **ᵃrôʿēr** or עַרְעוֹר **ʿarʿôr**, n.pr.loc. GK: 6876 & 6898 [→ 6200; cf. 6176, 6209]. Aroer, "*juniper*":– Aroer [16]

6178 עָרוּץ **ʿārûṣ**, a. GK: 6877 [→ 6206]. dry or dreadful:– clifts [1]

6179 עֵרִי **ʿērî**, n.pr.m. GK: 6878 [→ 6180; cf. 5782]. Eri, "*watcher*":– Eri [2]

6180 עֵרִי **ʿērî**, a.g. GK: 6879 [→ 6179; cf. 5782]. Erite, "*of Eri*":– Erites [1]

6181 עֶרְיָה **ʿeryâ**, n.f. GK: 6880 [→ 6168]. bareness, nakedness, the state of being uncovered:– bare [4], made quite naked (+5783) [1], naked [1]

6182 עֲרִיסָה **ᵃrîsâ**, n.f. GK: 6881. ground meal (dough in the first phase of bread making):– dough [4]

6183 עֲרִיפִים **ᵃrîpîm**, n.[m.pl.]. GK: 6882 [→ 6201]. cloud:– heavens [1]

6184 עָרִיץ **ʿārîṣ**, a. GK: 6883 [→ 6206]. ruthless, cruel, fierce:– terrible [8], terrible ones [3], oppressors [2], great power [1], mighty [1], oppressor [1], strong [1], terrible one to nought [1], terrible one [1], violent [1]

6185 עֲרִירִי **ᵃrîrî**, a. GK: 6884 [→ 6209]. childless, very undesireable and even shameful in the ancient Near East:– childless [4]

6186 עָרַךְ **ʿārak**, v.[den.]. GK: 6885 [→ 6187, 4633, 4630, 4634, 4635]. [Q] to arrange in rows; put in order, take up (battle) positions; [Qp] to be arranged, be put in order, be put in formation; [H] to set a value:– put in array [14], set in array [12], order [6], set in order [5], lay in order [4], expert [3], value [3], equal [2], estimate [2], laid in order [2], ordained [2], ordered [2], prepared [2], prepare [2], compared [1], compare [1], directed [1], direct [1], esteem [1], furnished [1], furnish [1], handle [1], joined [1], preparest [1], put in order [1], reckoned up in order [1], set in order (+6187) [1], taxed [1]

6187 עֵרֶךְ **ʿērek**, n.m. GK: 6886 [→ 6186]. proper estimated value:– estimation [23], equal (+3509.1) [1], estimations [1], price [1], proportion [1], set at [1], set in order (+6186) [1], set in order [1], suit [1], taxation [1], valuest [1]

6188 עָרֵל **ʿāral**, v.den. GK: 6887 [→ 6190]. [Q] to regard as forbidden, leave unharvested:– count as uncircumcised (+6190) [1], foreskin uncovered [1]

6189 עָרֵל **ʿārēl**, a. GK: 6888 [→ 6190]. uncircumcised (i.e., having a foreskin of the penis):– uncircumcised [34], uncircumcised person [1]

6190 עָרְלָה **ʿorlâ**, n.f. GK: 6889 [→ 1394, 6188, 6189]. foreskin (of the penis):– foreskin [8], foreskins [5], uncircumcised [2], count as uncircumcised (+6188) [1]

6191 עָרַם **ʿāram**, v. GK: 6891 [→ 6175, 6193, 6195]. [Q] to be crafty, show prudence; [H] to initiate cunning plans:– dealeth very subtilly (+6191) [2], beware [1], prudent [1], taken crafty [1]

6192 עָרַם **ʿāram**, v. GK: 6890 [→ 6194; cf. 6014]. [N] to be piled up, be dammed up:– gathered together [1]

6193 עֹרֶם **ʿōrem**, n.[m.]. GK: 6892 [→ 6191]. craftiness:– craftiness [1]

עֵרֹם **ʿērōm**. See 5903.

עָרֹם **ʿārōm**. See 6174.

6194 עֲרֵמָה **ᵃrēmâ**, n.f. GK: 6894 [→ 6192]. heap, mound (of grain):– heaps [5], heap [3], by heaps (+6194) [2], sheaves [1]

6195 עָרְמָה **ʿormâ**, n.f. GK: 6893 [→ 6191]. prudence, cunning:– guile [1], prudence [1], subtilty [1], wilily (+871.1) [1], wisdom [1]

עֲרֵמָה **ʿarēmâ**. See 6194.

6196 עַרְמוֹן **'ermôn**, n.[m.]. GK: 6895 [→ 6168]. plane tree:– chesnut trees [1], chesnut tree [1]

6197 עֵרָן **'ērān**, n.pr.m. GK: 6896 [→ 6198]. Eran, "*watcher, watchful*":– Eran [1]

6198 עֵרָנִי **'ērānî**, a.g. GK: 6897 [→ 6197]. Eranite, "*of Eran*":– Eranites [1]

עַרְעוֹר **'ar'ôr**. See 6177.

6199 עַרְעָר **'ar'ār**, a. GK: 6899 [cf. 6209]. destitute, naked, stripped; (juniper) bush:– destitute [1], heath [1]

עֲרֹעֵר **'rō'ēr**. See 6177.

6200 עֲרֹעֵרִי **'rō'ērî**, a.g. GK: 6901 [→ 6177; cf. 6209]. Aroerite, "*of Aroer*":– Aroerite [1]

6201 עָרַף **'ārap**, v. GK: 6903 [→ 6183, 6205?; cf. 7491]. [Q] to trickle, drip:– drop down [1], drop [1]

6202 עָרַף **'ārap**, v.den. GK: 6904. [Q] to break; [Qp] be broken:– break neck [2], beheaded [1], break down [1], cut off neck [1], strike off neck [1]

6203 עֹרֶף **'ōrep**, n.m. GK: 6902 [→ 6204]. neck; to be "stiff of neck" is to be obstinate, stubborn, implying rebellion:– neck [11], necks [6], stiffnecked (+7186) [6], back [4], backs [3], stiffnecked (+7185) [1], stiffnecked [1], turn backs [1]

6204 עָרְפָּה **'orpâ**, n.pr.f. GK: 6905 [→ 6203]. Orpah, "*neck, the girl with the full mane[?]*":– Orpah [2]

6205 עֲרָפֶל **'rāpel**, n.m. GK: 6906 [→ 6201?]. dark or thick clouds; deep gloom:– thick darkness [8], darkness [3], dark [2], gross darkness [2]

6206 עָרַץ **'āraṣ**, v. GK: 6907 [→ 4637, 6178, 6184]. [Q] to shake, to shake in terror; [N] to be feared; [H] to dread, stand in awe:– afraid [3], dread [2], fear [2], shake terribly [2], affrighted [1], break [1], feared [1], oppress [1], prevail [1], terrified [1]

6207 עָרַק **'āraq**, v. GK: 6908. [Q] to gnaw:– flying [1], sinews [1]

6208 עַרְקִי **'arqî**, a.g. GK: 6909. Arkite:– Arkite [2]

6209 עָרַר **'ārar**, v. GK: 6910 [→ 6145?, 6176, 6177, 6185, 6199, 6200; cf. 6168]. [Q] to strip off; [Po] to strip; [Pil] to level, demolish; [Htpal] to be laid utterly bare:– utterly broken (+6209) [2], make bare [1], raised up [1]

6210 עֶרֶשׂ **'ereś**, n.f. GK: 6911. bed, couch:– bed [4], bedstead [2], couch [2], bed (+3326) [1], couches [1]

6211 עָשׁ **'āš**, n.m. GK: 6931 & 6933 [→ 5906, 6244]. moth, which consumes some natural fabrics; Bear or Lion (a constellation):– moth [6], moth-eaten (+398) [1]

6211' עֲשַׂב **'śab** (Aram.), n.[m.]. GK: 10572 [cf. 6212]. grass, (green) plants:– grass [5]

6212 עֵשֶׂב **'ēśeb**, n.m. GK: 6912 [cf. 6211']. green plant, vegetation, grass:– grass [16], herb [12], herbs [5]

6213 עָשָׂה **'āśâ**, v. GK: 6913 & 6914 [→ 501, 3299, 3300, 4639, 4640, 4641, 6214, 6221, 6222]. [Q] to do, make; [Qp] to be done; [N] to be done, be made; [P] to caress, squeeze; [Pu] to be made; a generic of action, seen in the many contextual translations of the KJV:– do [607], made [393], done [339], did [319], make [232], wrought [52], doeth [42], offer [41], keep [30], committed [27], execute [24], deal [23], maketh [23], prepare [22], work [22], shew [19], doest [18], kept [18], dealt [17], shewed [17], commit [16], executed [15], doing [14], maker [13], prepared [13], didst [12], perform [12], gotten [9], dealeth [7], dress [7], bring forth [6], maintain [6], offered [6], worketh [6], yield [6], dressed [5], executeth [5], performed [5], bear [4], brought forth [4], certainly make (+6213) [4], committeth [4], makest [4], workmen (+4399+1886.1) [4], bring to pass [3], doer [3], observe [3], ordained [3], practise [3], set [3], workmen (+4399) [3], yielding [3], accomplish [2], appointed [2], bruised [2], certainly do (+6213) [2], deal with [2], do great things (+6213) [2], do indeed (+6213) [2], doers [2], doth [2], fulfil [2], gat [2], get [2], holden [2], labour [2], made ready [2], meet [2], offering [2], procured [2], procure [2], sacrifice [2], sheweth [2], shewing [2], surely deal (+6213) [2], surely perform (+6213) [2], surely shew (+6213) [2], throughly execute (+6213) [2], used [2], warriors (+4421) [2], advanced [1], apt [1], at [1], become [1], bestow [1], bringeth to pass [1], bruising [1], busy [1], caused to be made [1], cause [1], charge [1], come to pass [1], committing [1], dealest [1], dealt with [1], deckedst [1], displease (+5869+7451+871.1) [1], effect [1], executedst [1], executest [1], executing [1], exercise [1], fashioned [1], feasted (+4960) [1], fighting (+4421) [1], fitteth [1], followed [1], fulfilled [1], fulfilling [1], furnish (+3627) [1], gathered [1], getteth [1], given [1], give [1], go about [1], govern [1], granted [1], held [1], hinder (+8442) [1], industrious (+4399) [1], journeyed (+1870) [1], laboured [1], madest [1], maintained [1], making [1], observed [1], occupied (+4399) [1], occupied [1], officers (+4399+1886.1) [1], pare [1], practised [1], preparest [1], preparing [1], provided [1], provide [1], put in execution [1], put [1], ready dressed [1], requite (+854) [1], sacrificed [1], served [1], shew (+5973) [1], shewest [1], sinneth through ignorance (+7684+871.1) [1], spendeth [1], surely [1], taken [1], take [1], trimmed [1], undo (+854) [1], used to do [1], vex (+7451) [1], workers [1], working [1], workmen [1], wroughtest [1]

6214 עֲשָׂהאֵל **'śāh'ēl** or עֲשָׂה־אֵל **'śāh-'ēl**, n.pr.m. GK: 6915 [→ 6213+410]. Asahel, "*God [El] has made*":– Asahel [18]

6215 עֵשָׂו **'ēśāw**, n.pr.m. GK: 6916. Esau, "*hairy*":– Esau [85], Esau's [12]

6216 עָשׁוֹק **'āšôq**, n.[m.]. GK: 6934 [→ 6231]. oppressor:– oppressor [1]

6217 עֲשׁוּקִים **'šûqîm**, n.pl.abst. GK: 6935 [→ 6231]. oppression:– oppressions [2], oppressed [1]

6218 עָשׂוֹר **'āśôr**, n.[m.]. GK: 6917 [→ 6237]. (group of) ten:– tenth [12], instrument of ten strings [3], ten [1]

6219 עָשׁוֹת **'āšôt**, a. GK: 6936 [→ 6245]. wrought, fashioned (iron):– bright [1]

6220 עַשְׁוָת **'ašwāt**, n.pr.m. GK: 6937. Ashvath, "[poss.] *wrought iron*":– Ashvath [1]

6221 עֲשִׂיאֵל **'śî'ēl**, n.pr.m. GK: 6918 [→ 6213+410]. Asiel, "*God [El] has made*":– Asiel [1]

6222 עֲשָׂיָה **'śāyâ**, n.pr.m. GK: 6919 [→ 6213+3068]. Asaiah, "*Yahweh has made*":– Asaiah [6], Asahiah [2]

6223 עָשִׁיר **'āšîr**, a. (used as n.). GK: 6938 [→ 6238]. rich, wealthy; (n.) the rich, rich person:– rich [23]

6224 עֲשִׂירִי **'śîrî**, a.num.ord. GK: 6920 [→ 6237]. tenth:– tenth [29]

6225 עָשַׁן **'āšan**, v.den. GK: 6939 [→ 6227, 6226]. [Q] to envelope in smoke, smolder:– smoke [5], angry [1]

6226 עָשֵׁן **'āšēn**, a. GK: 6942 [→ 6225]. smoking, smoldering:– smoking [2]

6227 עָשָׁן **'āšān**, n.m. GK: 6940 [→ 953+6228; cf. 6225]. smoke (billowing, ascending, blowing):– smoke [24], smoking [1]

6228 עָשָׁן **'āšān**, n.pr.loc. GK: 6941 [cf. 953]. Ashan, "*smoke*":– Ashan [4]

6229 עָשַׂק **'āśaq**, v. GK: 6921 [→ 4642]. [Ht] to dispute, quarrel:– strove [1]

6230 עֵשֶׂק **'ēśeq**, n.pr.loc. GK: 6922. Esek, "*dispute*":– Esek [1]

6231 עָשַׁק **'āšaq**, v. GK: 6943 [→ 6216, 6217, 6232, 6233, 6234]. [Q] to oppress, mistreat; to defraud, extort; [Qp] to be oppressed, be tormented; [Pu] to be crushed:– oppressed [10], oppress [9], oppresseth [3], defrauded [2], do wrong [2], oppressors [2], oppressor [2], cruelly oppressed (+6233) [1], deceitfully gotten (+6233) [1], deceived [1], defraud [1], doeth violence [1], drinketh up [1], used oppression (+6233) [1]

6232 עֵשֶׁק **'ēšeq**, n.pr.m. GK: 6944 [→ 6231]. Eshek, "*oppressor*":– Eshek [1]

6233 עֹשֶׁק **'ōšeq**, n.m. GK: 6945 [→ 6231]. oppression, tyranny; extortion:– oppression [11], cruelly oppressed (+6231) [1], deceitfully gotten (+6231) [1], extortion [1], used oppression (+6231) [1]

עָשֻׁק **'āšuq**. See 6217.

6234 עָשְׁקָה **'ošqâ**, n.f. GK: 6946 [→ 6233; cf. 6231]. trouble, oppression:– oppressed [1]

6235 עֶשֶׂר **'eśer** or עֲשָׂרָה **'śārâ**, n.m. & f. GK: 6924 & 6927 [→ 6237; cf. 6236]. ten:– ten [168], tens [3], fifteen (+2568+2050.1) [1], seventeen (+7651+2050.1) [1], ten's [1]

6236 עֲשַׂר **'śar** (Aram.), n.m. & f. GK: 10573 [→ 6243; cf. 6235]. ten:– ten [4], twelve (+8648) [2]

6237 עָשַׂר **'āśar**, v.den. GK: 6923 [→ 4643, 6218, 6224, 6235, 6240, 6241, 6242, 6240]. [Q] to take a tenth; [P] to give a tenth, set aside a tenth; [H] to give or receive a tenth:– surely give the tenth (+6237) [2], take the tenth [2], truly tithe (+6237) [2], take tithes [1], tithes [1], tithing [1]

6238 עָשַׁר **'āšar**, v. GK: 6947 [→ 6223, 6239]. [Q] to be, become rich; [H] to make rich, bring wealth:– rich [6], maketh rich [3], enrich [2], made rich [2], become rich [1], enrichest [1], richer (+6239) [1], waxen rich [1]

6239 עֹשֶׁר **'ōšer**, n.m. GK: 6948 [→ 6238]. wealth, riches:– riches [36], richer (+6238) [1]

6240 עָשָׂר **'āśār**, n. *or* a.num. GK: 6925 & 6926 & 6930 [→ 6237]. ten (always used in combined numbers):– twelve (+8147) [109], fourteenth (+702) [23], twelfth (+8147) [22], sixteen (+8337) [21], fourteen (+702) [19], eighteen (+8083) [18], fifteenth (+2568) [17], fifteen (+2568) [16], eleventh (+6249) [13], thirteen (+7969) [13], eighteenth (+8083) [11], thirteenth (+7969) [11], eleven (+259) [9], seventeen (+7651) [8], eleven (+6249) [6], seventeenth (+7651) [6], eleventh (+259) [4], nineteenth (+8672) [4], nineteen (+8672) [3], sixteenth (+8337) [3], sixscore (+8147) [1], ten [1]

עָשֹׂר **'āśōr**. See 6218.

6241 עִשָּׂרוֹן **'iśśārôn**, n.m. GK: 6928 [→ 6237]. tenth part:– tenth deals [18], several tenth deal (+6241) [10], tenth deal [3], one tenth deal (+259) [1], three tenth deals (+7969) [1]

6242 עֶשְׂרִים **'eśrîm**, n.pl.indecl. GK: 6929 [→ 6237; cf. 6243]. twenty (pl. of "ten"):– twenty [277], twentieth [36], sixscore (+3967+2050.1) [1], twenty's [1]

6243 עֶשְׂרִין **'eśrîn** (Aram.), n.pl.indecl. GK: 10574 [→ 6236; cf. 6242]. twenty; note that this is the grammatical plural of "ten":– twenty [1]

6244 עָשֵׁשׁ **'āšaš**, v. GK: 6949 [→ 6211]. [Q] to grow weak:– consumed [3]

6245 עָשַׁת **'āšat**, v. GK: 6950 & 6951 [→ 6219, 6247, 6248, 6250; cf. 6246]. [Q] to grow sleek (i.e., smooth or shiny); [Ht] to take notice:– shine [1], think [1]

6246 עֲשִׁת **'šit** (Aram.), v. GK: 10575 [cf. 6245]. [P] to plan, intend:– thought [1]

6247 עֶשֶׁת **'ešet**, n.[m.]. GK: 6952 [→ 6245]. polished piece, slab, plate:– bright [1]

6248 עַשְׁתּוּת **'aštût**, n.f. GK: 6953 [→ 6245]. thought:– thought [1]

6249 עַשְׁתֵּי **'aštê**, n. *or* a.num. GK: 6954. eleven, eleventh:– eleventh (+6240) [13], eleven (+6240) [6]

6250 עֶשְׁתֹּנֹת **'eštōnet**, n.f. GK: 6955 [→ 6245]. plan, thought:– thoughts [1]

6251 עַשְׁתָּרֶת **'ašteret**, n.f. GK: 6957. lamb or ewe:– flocks [4]

6252 עַשְׁתָּרֹת **'aštārōt**, n.pr.loc. GK: 6958 [→ 1045, 6253, 6255, 6254; cf. 842, 1203?]. Ashtaroth:– Ashtaroth [10], Astaroth [1]

6253 עַשְׁתֹּרֶת **'aštōret**, n.pr.f. GK: 6956 [→ 6252]. Ashtoreth (pagan god):– Ashtoreth [3], Ashtaroth [1]

6254 עַשְׁתְּרָתִי **'ašt^erātî**, a.g. GK: 6960 [→ 6252]. Ashterathite:– Ashterathite [1]

6255 עַשְׁתְּרֹת קַרְנַיִם **'ašt^erōt qarnayim**, n.pr.loc. GK: 6959 [→ 6252+7161]. Ashteroth Karnaim, "*Ashteroth of the pair of horns [twin peaks?]*":– Ashteroth Karnaim [1]

6256 עֵת **'ēt**, n.f. GK: 6961 [→ 6031]. time (in general); a unit of time (of various lengths), season:– time [233], times [24], season [8], due season [5], when (+871.1) [5], always (+3605+871.1) [3], eveningtide (+6153) [2], seasons [2], after (+3509.1) [1], after (+3807.1) [1], certain [1], continually (+3605+871.1) [1], due season (+2050.2) [1], eventide (+6153+1886.1) [1], long [1], mealtime (+400+1886.1) [1], noontide (+6672) [1], unto [1], when (+3807.1) [1], when [1]

6257 עָתַד **'ātad**, v. GK: 6963 [® 6259, 6260?, 6264]. [P] to make ready; [Ht] to be destined:– make fit [1], ready to become [1]

עַתֻּד **'attud**. See 6260.

6258 עַתָּה **'attâ**, adv. GK: 6964 [→ 6031]. now:– now [407], therefore [8], henceforth [6], this time forth [3], this time [2], I pray thee [1], as yet (+5704) [1], even now (+2088) [1], now (+3588) [1], straightway [1], whereas [1], yet (+5704) [1]

6259 עָתוּד **'ātûd**, a. GK: 6965 [→ 6257]. supply, treasure:– treasures [1]

6260 עַתּוּד **'attûd**, n.m. GK: 6966 [→ 6257?]. male goat; (of humans) a leader:– he goats [15], goats [11], rams [2], chief ones [1]

6261 עִתִּי **'ittî**, a. GK: 6967 [→ 6031]. available:– fit [1]

6262 עַתַּי **'attay**, n.pr.m. GK: 6968 [→ 6031]. Attai, "*timely,* [or perhaps] *an abbreviation of Athaiah*":– Attai [4]

6263 עֲתִיד **'tîd** (Aram.), a. GK: 10577 [cf. 6264]. ready:– ready [1]

6264 עָתִיד **'ātîd**, a. GK: 6969 [→ 6257; cf. 6263]. ready, prepared:– ready [4], things that shall come [1]

6265 עֲתָיָה **ʿᵃtāyâ**, n.pr.m. GK: 6970. Athaiah, "[poss.] *[the] superiority of Yahweh*":– Athaiah [1]

6266 עָתִיק **ʿātîq**, a. GK: 6971 [→ 6275]. fine, choice, select:– durable [1]

6267 עַתִּיק **ʿattîq**, a. GK: 6972 [→ 6275]. taken, removed (from place or time):– ancient [1], drawn [1]

6268 עַתִּיק **ʿattîq** (Aram.), a. GK: 10578. old, ancient; (as a title) the Ancient (of Days), a title of veneration and honor emphasizing wisdom and power:– ancient [3]

6269 עֲתָךְ **ʿᵃtāk**, n.pr.loc. GK: 6973. Athach:– Athach [1]

6270 עַתְלַי **ʿatlāy**, n.pr.m. & f. GK: 6974 [→ 6271]. Athlai, "[poss.] *Yahweh is exalted; oldest of Yahweh*":– Athlai [1]

6271 עֲתַלְיָה **ʿᵃtalyâ** or עֲתַלְיָהוּ **ʿᵃtalyāhû**, n.pr.m. & f. GK: 6975 & 6976 [→ 5830, 6270]. Athaliah, "[poss.] *Yahweh is exalted; oldest of Yahweh*":– Athaliah [17]

6272 עָתַם **ʿātam**, v. GK: 6977. [N] to be destroyed; in context, to be scorched:– darkened [1]

6273 עָתְנִי **ʿotnî**, n.pr.m. GK: 6978 [→ 6274]. Othni:– Othni [1]

6274 עָתְנִיאֵל **ʿotnîʾēl**, n.pr.m. GK: 6979 [→ 6273+410]. Othniel:– Othniel [7]

6275 עָתַק **ʿātaq**, v. GK: 6980 [→ 6266, 6267, 6277, 6276; cf. 6268]. [Q] to move; to grow old, grow weak; [H] to move on; to fail; to copy:– removed [4], become old [1], copied out [1], left off (+4480) [1], removeth [1], waxeth old [1]

6276 עָתֵק **ʿātēq**, a. GK: 6982 [→ 6275]. enduring (wealth):– durable [1]

6277 עָתָק **ʿātāq**, a. GK: 6981 [→ 6275]. arrogant, insolent, outstretched:– arrogancy [1], grievous things [1], hard [1], stiff [1]

6278 עֵת קָצִין **ʿēt qāṣîn**, n.pr.loc. GK: 6962 [cf. 7101]. Eth Kazin:– Ittah-kazin [1]

6279 עָתַר **ʿātar**, v. GK: 6983 [→ 6281?, 6282; cf. 6280?]. [Q] to pray; [N] to respond to prayer, be moved by an entreaty; [H] to pray, make entreaty:– intreated [12], intreat [6], make prayer [1], pray [1]

6280 עָתַר **ʿātar**, v. GK: 6984 [→ 6283; cf. 6279?]. [N] to be multiplied; [H] to multiply:– deceitful [1], multiplied [1]

6281 עֶתֶר **ʿeter**, n.pr.loc. GK: 6987 [→ 6279?]. Ether, "[perhaps] *perfume*":– Ether [2]

6282 עָתָר **ʿātār**, n.[m.]. GK: 6985 & 6986 [→ 6279]. worshiper; fragrance, perfume:– suppliants [1], thick [1]

6283 עֲתֶרֶת **ʿᵃteret**, n.f. GK: 6988 [→ 6280]. abundance:– abundance [1]

פֹּא **pōʾ**. See 6311.

6284 פָּאָה **pāʾâ**, v. GK: 6990 & 6991 [→ 6285]. [H] to split into pieces, scatter:– scatter into corners [1]

6285 פֵּאָה **pēʾâ**, n.f. GK: 6991 [→ 6284]. side, edge, boundary; forehead or crown of the head; piece, part:– side [63], corners [11], corner [5], quarter [3], end [1], part [1], quarter (+3807.1) [1], sides [1]

6286 פָּאַר **pāʾar**, v. GK: 6995 [→ 6287?, 8597]. [P] to honor, adorn, endow with splendor; to knock down olives a second time; [Ht] to glorify oneself, display one's splendor; (negatively) to boast:– glorified [6], beautify [3], boast [1], glorify [1], glory [1], go over the boughs [1], vaunt [1]

6287 פְּאֵר **pᵉʾēr**, n.m. GK: 6996 [→ 6286?]. turban, headdress:– bonnets [2], beauty [1], goodly [1], ornaments [1], tire of head [1], tires [1]

6288 פֹּארָה **pōʾrâ** or פֻּארָה **puʾrâ**, n.f. GK: 6997 & 6998. branch, leafy bough:– branches [4], boughs [1], bough [1], sprigs [1]

6289 פָּארוּר **pāʾrûr**, n.[m.]. GK: 6999 [→ 6517]. growing pale, turning pale; some sources: to burn, glow:– blackness [2]

6290 פָּארָן **pāʾrān**, n.pr.loc. GK: 7000 [→ 364; cf. 6501?]. Paran, "*plain*":– Paran [11]

6291 פַּג **pag**, n.f. GK: 7001. early fruit, in context, unripe fig buds:– green figs [1]

6292 פִּגּוּל **piggûl**, n.m. GK: 7002. (ceremonially) unclean meat, kept too long after a sacrifice:– abominable [3], abomination [1]

6293 פָּגַע **pāgaʿ**, n.m. GK: 7003 [→ 4645, 6294, 6295]. to strike, touch; intercede for, plead with; [H] to make intercession, intervene; strike; cause to encounter:– fall [6], meet [5], reacheth [5], fell [4], met [3], fall upon [2], intreat [2], made intercession [2], make intercession [2], meeteth [2], reached [2], came [1], cause to entreat [1], cometh betwixt [1], fell upon [1], intercessor [1], laid [1], lighted [1], meetest [1], met together [1], pray [1], run [1]

6294 פֶּגַע **pegaʿ**, n.m. GK: 7004 [→ 6293]. chance, occurrence:– chance [1], occurrent [1]

6295 פַּגְעִיאֵל **pagʿîʾēl**, n.pr.m. GK: 7005 [→ 6293+410]. Pagiel:– Pagiel [5]

6296 פָּגַר **pāgar**, v. GK: 7006 [→ 6297]. [P] to be exhausted:– faint [2]

6297 פֶּגֶר **peger**, n.m. GK: 7007 [→ 6296]. dead body, corpse; carcass; by extension: lifeless idol, with a focus that it is unclean and impotent:– carcases [12], dead bodies [6], corpses [2], carcase [1], dead carcases [1]

6298 פָּגַשׁ **pāgaš**, v. GK: 7008. [Q] to meet; to attack; [N] to have in common, to meet together; [P] to come upon, encounter:– met [6], meet [4], meet together [2], meeteth [1], met together [1]

6299 פָּדָה **pādâ**, v. GK: 7009 [→ 6302, 6303, 6304, 6306 (also used with compound proper names)]. [Q] to redeem, ransom, deliver, rescue, buy; [Qp] to be redeemed, be ransomed; [N] to be ransomed, be redeemed; [H] to let be ransomed; [Ho] to be brought to ransomed; this can mean to purchase a devoted animal from sacrifice or to purchase a person from slavery to freedom or new ownership; by extension: divine salvation from oppression, death, or sin:– redeemed [22], redeem [21], deliver [3], at all redeemed (+6299) [2], by any means redeem (+6299) [2], delivered [2], surely redeem (+6299) [2], ransomed [1], ransom [1], redeemedst [1], redeemeth [1], rescued [1]

6300 פְּדַהְאֵל **pᵉdahʾēl**, n.pr.m. GK: 7010 [→ 6299+410]. Pedahel, "*God [El] ransoms*":– Pedahel [1]

6301 פְּדָהצוּר **pᵉdāhṣûr** or פְּדָה־צוּר **pᵉdāh-ṣûr**, n.pr.m. GK: 7011 [→ 6299+6697]. Pedahzur, "*the Rock ransoms*":– Pedahzur [5]

6302 פְּדוּיִם **pᵉdûyim**, n.[m.]pl.abst. GK: 7012 [→ 6299]. redemption, ransom, paid to purchase firstborn Israelites from dedication to God:– redeemed [2], them that were redeemed [1], those that are redeemed [1]

6303 פָּדוֹן **pādôn**, n.pr.m. GK: 7013 [→ 6299]. Padon, "*ransom*":– Padon [2]

6304 פְּדוּת **pᵉdût** or פְּדֻת **pᵉdut**, n.f. GK: 7014 & 7151 [→ 6299, 6395]. redemption, ransom, always of divine action; distinction:– redemption [2], division [1], redeem [1]

6305 פְּדָיָה **pᵉdāyâ** or פְּדָיָהוּ **pᵉdāyāhû**, n.pr.m. GK: 7015 & 7016 [→ 6299+3068]. Pedaiah, "*Yahweh ransoms*":– Pedaiah [8]

6306 פִּדְיוֹם **pidyôm** or פִּדְיוֹן **pidyôn**, n.m. GK: 7017 & 7018 [→ 6299]. redemption, ransom; redemption money, ransom payment:– redemption [2], ransom [1]

6307 פַּדָּן **paddān** or פַּדַּן אֲרָם **paddan ʾᵃrām**, n.pr.loc. GK: 7019 & 7020 [→ 758]. Paddan, "*plain*"; Paddan Aram, "*plain of Aram*":– Padan-aram [10], Padan [1]

6308 פָּדַע **pādaʿ**, v. GK: 7021. [Q] to spare, deliver:– deliver [1]

6309 פֶּדֶר **peder**, n.[m.]. GK: 7022. suet (the hard fat about kidney's and loins of animals):– fat [3]

פְּדֻת **pᵉdut**. See 6304.

6310 פֶּה **peh**, n.m. GK: 7023 [→ 6366, 6374; cf. 6433]. mouth (human or animal); by extension: speech, command, testimony; any opening; edge (of a sword):– mouth [329], commandment [37], edge [35], word [15], mouths [12], according to (+3807.1) [11], according to (+3509.1) [6], hole [6], according to (+5921) [4], another[S] [3], according unto (+3509.1) [2], appointment [2], one end [2], portion [2], tenor [2], according as (+834+3509.1) [1], according to (+834+5921) [1], according unto (+3807.1) [1], accord [1], after (+3807.1) [1], collar [1], command [1], eat (+871.1) [1], edges [1], end [1], entry [1], file (+6477) [1], in (+3807.1) [1], in the way go (+1870+5921) [1], mind [1], out of (+4480) [1], parts [1], saith (+871.1) [1], sayings [1], skirts [1], so that (+3509.1) [1], sound [1], speech [1], spoken [1], talk [1], to (+3807.1) [1], told (+7760+871.1) [1], twoedged [1], when (+3807.1) [1], wish [1], with assent [1]

6311 פֹּה **pōh**, adv.loc. GK: 7024 [→ 375, 645?]. here:– here [44], that side [13], this side [12], one side [5], other side [5], hither [2], hitherto (+5704) [1]

פּוֹא **pôʾ**. See 375.

6312 פּוּאָה **pûʾâ** or פֻּוָּאָה **puwwāʾâ** or פֻּוָּה **puwwâ**, n.pr.m. GK: 7025 & 7026 & 7030 [→ 6324]. Puah, Puvah, "[perhaps] *girl*":– Puah [2], Phuvah [1], Pua [1]

6313 פּוּג **pûg**, v. GK: 7028 [→ 2014, 6314]. [Q] to grow numb, be feeble; [N] to be benumbed, be feeble:– ceased [1], fainted [1], feeble [1], slacked [1]

6314 פּוּגָה **pûgâ**, n.f. GK: 7029 [→ 6313]. relief, relaxation:– rest [1]

פֻּוָּה **puwwâ**. See 6312.

6315 פּוּחַ **pûaḥ**, v. GK: 7031 & 7032 [→ 6368; cf. 3306, 5301]. [Q] to blow, become dawn (of the day); to breathe out; [H] to blow (of wind); to breathe out, sneer, malign:– speaketh [5], blow [2], break [2], puffeth [2], bring into a snare [1], speak [1], utter [1]

6316 פּוּט **pûṭ**, n.pr.g. GK: 7033. Put:– Libya [2], Phut [2], Put [2], Libyans [1]

6317 פּוּטִיאֵל **pûṭîʾēl**, n.pr.m. GK: 7034 [→ 410]. Putiel, "*he whom God [El] gives*":– Putiel [1]

6318 פּוֹטִיפַר **pôṭîpar**, n.pr.m. GK: 7035 [cf. 6319]. Potiphar, "*he whom Ra gives*":– Potiphar [2]

6319 פּוֹטִי פֶרַע **pôṭî peraʿ**, n.pr.m. GK: 7036. Potiphera, "*he whom Ra gives*":– Poti-pherah [3]

6320 פּוּךְ **pûk**, n.[m.]. GK: 7037. turquoise (stone); (eye) paint, possibly derived from turquoise:– fair colours [1], glistering [1], painting [1]

6321 פּוֹל **pôl**, n.[m.]col. GK: 7038. beans:– beans [2]

6322 פּוּל **pûl**, n.pr.m. GK: 7040 [→ 6467; cf. 6466]. Pul:– Pul [4]

6323 פּוּן **pûn**, v. GK: 7041. [Q] to be in despair:– distracted [1]

6324 פּוּאִי **pûʾî** or פּוּנִי **pûnî**, a.g. GK: 7027 & 7043 [→ 6312]. Puite, Punite, "*of Puah*":– Punites [1]

6325 פּוּנֹן **pûnōn**, n.pr.loc. GK: 7044 [cf. 6373]. Punon:– Punon [2]

6326 פּוּעָה **pûʿâ**, n.pr.f. GK: 7045. Puah, "[perhaps] *girl*":– Puah [1]

6327 פּוּץ **pûṣ** or פָּצַץ **pāṣaṣ**, v. GK: 7046 & 7047 & 7207 [→ 1048, 4650, 6483, 8600; cf. 5310]. [Q] to be scattered; flow, overflow; [Qp] to be scattered; [N] to be scattered; [H] to cause to scatter; [Pol] to break to pieces, shatter; [Pil] to crush, smash; [Htpol] to be crumbled, be shattered:– scattered [31], scatter [16], scattered abroad [3], cast abroad [2], dispersed [2], scatter abroad [2], scattereth [2], spread abroad [2], breaketh in pieces [1], dasheth in pieces [1], disperse [1], drive [1], retired [1], scattereth abroad [1], shaken to pieces [1]

6328 פּוּק **pûq**, v. GK: 7048 [→ 6330; cf. 6329, 6375]. [Q] to stumble, totter; [H] to totter:– move [1], stumble [1]

6329 פּוּק **pûq**, v. GK: 7049 [cf. 6328]. [H] to bring out, furnish, promote:– obtaineth [2], affording [1], draw out [1], further [1], getteth [1], obtain [1]

6330 פּוּקָה **pûqâ**, n.f. GK: 7050 [→ 6328]. staggering, stumbling:– grief [1]

6331 פּוּר **pûr**, v. GK: 7051 [cf. 6565]. [H] to destroy:– bringeth to nought [1], broken [1], utterly take [1]

6332 פּוּר **pûr**, n.m. GK: 7052. pur (the lot), pebbles, sticks, or pottery shards that were thrown to make decisions; (pl.) Purim, a Jewish festival celebrating God's control over the casting of lots:– Purim [5], Pur [3]

6333 פּוּרָה **pûrâ**, n.f. GK: 7053. trough of the winepress; measure (equal to the filling of the winepress):– press [1], winepress [1]

פּוּרִים **pûrîm**. See 6332.

6334 פּוֹרָתָא **pôrātāʾ**, n.pr.m. GK: 7054. Poratha:– Poratha [1]

6335 פּוּשׁ **pûš**, v. GK: 7055 & 7056. [Q] to leap, frolic, gallop; this may refer to the playful pawing action of a young animal; [N] to be scattered:– grow up [1], grown fat [1], scattered [1], spread [1]

6336 פּוּתִי **pûtî**, a.g. GK: 7057. Puthite:– Puhites [1]

6337 פָּז **paz**, n.m. GK: 7058 [→ 464, 6338]. pure gold:– fine gold [8], pure gold [1]

6338 פָּזַז **pāzaz**, v. GK: 7059 [→ 6337]. [Ho] to be set with pure gold:– best [1]

6339 פָּזַז **pāzaz**, v. GK: 7060. [Q] to be limber; [P] to leap:– leaping [1], made strong [1]

6340 פָּזַר **pāzar**, v. GK: 7061 [cf. 967]. [Qp] to be scattered; [P] to scatter; [N] to be scattered; [Pu] to be dispersed:– scattered [6], scattereth [2], dispersed [1], scattered abroad [1]

6341 פַּח **paḥ**, n.m. GK: 7062 & 7063 [→ 6351]. thin sheets (of hammered metal); snare, bird trap:– snare [18], snares [5], gin [1], grin [1], plates [1], thin plates [1]

6342 פָּחַד **pāḥad**, v. GK: 7064 [→ 6343, 6345]. [Q] to tremble, be afraid; [P] to live in terror, fear; [H] to make shake, make tremble:– afraid [9], fear [8], feared [2], in great fear (+6343) [2], feareth [1], made to shake [1], standeth in awe [1]

6343 פַּחַד **paḥad**, n.m. GK: 7065 [→ 6342; cf. 6765]. fear, terror, dread:– fear [40], dread [3], in great fear (+6342) [2], terror [2], dreadful [1], greatly feared [1]

6344 פַּחַד **paḥad**, n.[m.]. GK: 7066. thigh:– stones [1]

6345 פַּחְדָּה **paḥdâ**, n.f. GK: 7067 [→ 6342]. awe, dread:– fear [1]

6346 פֶּחָה **peḥâ**, n.m. GK: 7068 [→ 6355?; cf. 6347]. governor, officer:– governor [10], captains [7], governors [7], captain [2], deputies [2]

6347 פֶּחָה **peḥâ** (Aram.), n.m. GK: 10580 [cf. 6346]. governor:– governor [6], captains [4]

6348 פָּחַז **pāḥaz**, v. GK: 7069 [→ 6349, 6350]. [Q] to be arrogant, be insolent:– light [2]

6349 פַּחַז **paḥaz**, n.[m.]. GK: 7070 [→ 6348]. turbulence, recklessness:– unstable [1]

6350 פַּחֲזוּת **paḥ^a^zût**, n.f. GK: 7071 [→ 6348]. insolence, arrogance, with an implication of recklessness:– lightness [1]

6351 פָּחַח **pāḥaḥ**, v.den. GK: 7072 [→ 6341]. [H] to trap; [Ho] to be entrapped:– snared [1]

6352 פֶּחָם **peḥām**, n.[m.]. GK: 7073. coal, charcoal:– coals [3]

6353 פֶּחָר **peḥār** (Aram.), n.m. GK: 10581. potter; sources translate "clay":– potter's [1]

6354 פַּחַת **paḥat**, n.m. GK: 7074 [→ 6356]. pit, cave:– pit [8], hole's [1], snare [1]

6355 פַּחַת מוֹאָב **paḥat mô'āb**, n.pr.m. GK: 7075 [→ 6346?+4124]. Pahath-Moab, "*supervisor of Moab*":– Pahath-moab [6]

6356 פְּחֶתֶת **p^e^ḥetet**, n.m. GK: 7076 [→ 6354]. mildew (that eats away at a garment):– fret [1]

6357 פִּטְדָה **piṭdâ**, n.f. [*or* m.?]. GK: 7077. topaz; some sources: chrysolite:– topaz [4]

6358 פָּטַר **pāṭar**, v.ptcp. GK: 7080 [→ 6359, 6362, 6363]. ptcp. of 6362: open:– open [4]

6359 פְּטִירִים **p^e^ṭîrîm**, var. GK: 7078 [→ 6358]. open, unoccupied:– @H = **6360** פַּטִּישׁ **pa¬¬îš**, n.m. GK: 7079. (sledge-)hammer:– hammer [3]

6361 פַּטִּישׁ **paṭṭîš** (Aram.), n.[m.]. GK: 10582. trousers, leggings; some sources identify as other parts of clothing: coat, tunic, shirt, trousers, hose, hat, etc:– hosen [1]

6362 פָּטַר **pāṭar**, v. GK: 7080 [→ 6358]. [Q] to elude, escape, release; [Qp] to be opened; [H] to open wide the mouth (as an insult):– dismissed [1], free [1], letteth out [1], shoot out [1], slipt away [1]

6363 פֶּטֶר **peṭer**, n.m. or פִּטְרָה **piṭrâ**, n.f. GK: 7081 & 7082 [cf. 6358]. first offspring, firstborn:– openeth [5], firstling [4], that openeth [2], open [1]

6364 פִּי־בֶסֶת **pî-beset**, n.pr.loc. GK: 7083. Bubastis (Piy-Beset), "*house of the cat goddess Basht*":– Phi-beseth [1]

6365 פִּיד **pîd**, n.[m.]. GK: 7085. misfortune, distress, calamity:– destruction [2], ruin [1]

6366 פִּיָה **pîyâ**, n.m. GK: 7023 [→ 6310]. f. of 6310: mouth; by extension: edge (of a sword):–

6367 פִּי הַחִירֹת **pî haḥîrôt**, n.pr.loc. GK: 7084. Pi Hahiroth, "*temple [house] of Hathor*":– Pi-hahiroth [4]

6368 פִּיחַ **pîaḥ**, n.[m.]. GK: 7086 [→ 6315]. soot (from a furnace):– ashes [2]

6369 פִּיכֹל **pîkōl**, n.pr.m. GK: 7087. Phicol:– Phichol [3]

6370 פִּלֶגֶשׁ **pilegeš**, n.f. GK: 7108. concubine, a female consort generally with lower status and fewer rights than a wife, with the function of giving social status or pleasure to the husband; once this refers to a woman's male consorts (Eze 23:20):– concubine [22], concubines [14], paramours [1]

6371 פִּימָה **pîmâ**, n.f. GK: 7089. fat, referring to an abundant life:– collops of fat [1]

6372 פִּינְחָס **pîn^e^ḥās**, n.pr.m. GK: 7090 [cf. 8471]. Phinehas, "*the black man*":– Phinehas [24], Phinehas' [1]

6373 פִּינֹן **pînōn**, n.pr.m. GK: 7091 [cf. 6325]. Pinon, "*darkness* [name related to famous copper mines]":– Pinon [2]

6374 פִּיפִיּוֹת **pîpiyyôt**, n.[f.pl.?]. GK: 7092 [→ 6310]. double-edged, with many teeth:– teeth [1], twoedged [1]

6375 פִּק **piq**, n.[m.]. GK: 7211 [cf. 6328]. giving way, shaking (of knees):– smite together [1]

6376 פִּישׁוֹן **pîšôn**, n.pr.loc. GK: 7093. Pishon:– Pison [1]

6377 פִּיתוֹן **pîtôn**, n.pr.m. GK: 7094. Pithon:– Pithon [2]

6378 פַּךְ **pak**, n.m. GK: 7095 [→ 6379]. flask, (small) jug:– box [2], vial [1]

6379 פָּכָה **pākâ**, v. GK: 7096 [→ 6378]. [P] to trickle:– ran out [1]

6380 פֹּכֶרֶת הַצְּבָיִים **pōkeret haṣṣ^e^bāyîm**, n.pr.m. GK: 7097. Pokereth-Hazzebaim, "*pitfall of gazelles, i.e., gazelle hunter*":– Pochereth Zebaim [1], Pochereth of Zebaim [1]

6381 פָּלָא **pālā'**, v.den. GK: 7098 [→ 466?, 4652, 6381, 6382, 6383, 6384, 6411, 6396; cf. 6395]. [N] to be wonderful, be marvelous, be amazing; to be hard, be amazing; [P] to fulfill; [H] to show a wonder, to cause to astound; [Ht] to show oneself marvelous:– wondrous works [10], wonders [9], marvellous [7], wonderful works [7], hard [5], wonderful [5], marvellous works [4], wondrous [4], marvellously [2], performing [2], accomplish [1], do a marvellous work [1], hidden [1], high [1], make a singular vow (+5088) [1], make wonderful [1], marvellous work [1], marvels [1], miracles [1], separate [1], shewed marvellous [1], shewest marvellous [1], wonderfully made [1], wonderfully [1], wondrously (+3807.1) [1], wondrously [1]

6382 פֶּלֶא **pele'**, n.m. GK: 7099 [→ 6381]. wonder, miracle, astounding thing:– wonders [7], wonderful [2], marvellous things [1], wonderful things [1], wonderfully [1], wonder [1]

6383 פִּלְאִי **pil'î**, a. GK: 7100 [→ 6381]. wonderful, beyond understanding:– secret [1], wonderful [1]

6384 פַּלֻּאִי **pallu'î**, a.g. GK: 7101 [→ 6396; cf. 6381]. Palluite, "*wonderful*":– Palluites [1]

פְּלָאיָה **p^e^lā'yâ**. See 6411.

פִּלְאֶסֶר **pil'eser**. See 8407.

6385 פָּלַג **pālag**, v. GK: 7103 [→ 4653, 6388, 6390, 6391; cf. 6418; cf. 6386, cf. 6387]. [N] to be divided; [P] to cut open, divide:– divided [3], divide [1]

6386 פְּלַג **p^e^lag** (Aram.), v. GK: 10583 [→ 6387, 6392; cf. 6385]. [Pp] to be divided:– divided [1]

6387 פְּלַג **p^e^lag** (Aram.), n.[m.]. GK: 10584 [→ 6386; cf. 6388]. half:– dividing [1]

6388 פֶּלֶג **peleg**, n.m. GK: 7104 [→ 6385]. stream, artificial irrigation canal:– rivers [8], river [1], streams [1]

6389 פֶּלֶג **peleg**, n.pr.m. GK: 7105. Peleg, "*water canal*":– Peleg [7]

6390 פְּלַגָּה **p^e^laggâ**, n.f. GK: 7106 [→ 6385]. district, division; stream:– divisions [2], rivers [1]

6391 פְּלֻגָּה **p^e^luggâ**, n.f. GK: 7107 [→ 6385; cf. 6392]. division (of a clan or family):– divisions [1]

6392 פְּלֻגָּה **p^e^luggâ** (Aram.), n.f. GK: 10585 [→ 6386; cf. 6391]. division (of priests):– divisions [1]

פִּלֶגֶשׁ **pilegeš**. See 6370.

6393 פְּלָדֹת **p^e^lādōt**, n.f. GK: 7110. (polished) metal:– torches [1]

6394 פִּלְדָּשׁ **pildāš**, n.pr.m. GK: 7109. Pildash, "*steely; spider*":– Pildash [1]

6395 פָּלָה **pālâ**, v. GK: 7111 [→ 6397, 6411, 6423, 6304; cf. 6381]. [N] to be distinguished; [H] to deal differently, make a distinction:– sever [2], marvellous [1], put a difference [1], separated [1], set apart [1], shew marvellous [1]

6396 פַּלּוּא **pallû'**, n.pr.m. GK: 7112 [→ 6384; cf. 6381]. Pallu, "*wonderful*":– Pallu [4], Phallu [1]

6397 פְּלוֹנִי **p^e^lônî**, a.g. GK: 7113 [→ 6395]. Pelonite:– Pelonite [3]

6398 פָּלַח **pālaḥ**, v. GK: 7114 [→ 6400, 6401; cf. 6399]. [Q] to plow; [P] to cut up, pierce; to bring forth (from the womb):– bring forth [1], cleaveth asunder [1], cutteth [1], shred [1], strike through [1]

6399 פְּלַח **p^e^laḥ** (Aram.), v. GK: 10586 [→ 6402; cf. 6398?]. [P] to serve, worship, work for (deity or deities):– serve [7], servest [2], ministers [1]

6400 פֶּלַח **pelaḥ**, n.f. GK: 7115 [→ 6398]. millstone; half (of a pomegranate); slice (of a cake):– piece [6]

6401 פִּלְחָא **pilḥā'**, n.pr.m. GK: 7116 [→ 6398]. Pilha, "*millstone; plowman; harelip*":– Pileha [1]

6402 פָּלְחָן **polḥān** (Aram.), n.[m.]. GK: 10587 [→ 6399]. worship, service, work (for deity):– service [1]

6403 פָּלַט **pālaṭ**, v. GK: 7117 [→ 3310, 3311, 4655, 6404, 6405, 6408, 6409, 6410, 6412, 6413; cf. 4422]. [Q] to escape; [P] to rescue, deliver; [H] to bring to safety:– deliver [11], deliverer [5], delivered [3], calveth [1], carry away safe [1], cause to escape [1], deliverest [1], delivereth [1], escape [1]

6404 פֶּלֶט **peleṭ**, n.pr.m. GK: 7118 [→ 6407; cf. 6403 (also used with compound proper names)]. Pelet, "*rescue*":– Pelet [2]

פָּלֵט **pālēṭ**. See 6412.

6405 פַּלֵּט **pallēṭ**, n.[m.]. GK: 7119 [→ 6403]. deliverance:– escape [3], deliverance [1], escaped [1]

פְּלֵטָה **p^e^lēṭâ**. See 6413.

6406 פַּלְטִי **palṭî**, n.pr.m. GK: 7120 [→ 6409]. Palti; Paltiel, "*God [El] is [my] deliverance*":– Palti [1], Phalti [1]

6407 פַּלְטִי **palṭî**, a.g. GK: 7121 [→ 6404]. Paltite:– Paltite [1]

6408 פִּלְטַי **pilṭāy**, n.pr.m. GK: 7122 [→ 6403]. Piltai, "*Yahweh rescues*":– Piltai [1]

6409 פַּלְטִיאֵל **palṭî'ēl**, n.pr.m. GK: 7123 [→ 6406]. Paltiel, "*God [El] is [my] deliverance*":– Paltiel [1], Phaltiel [1]

6410 פְּלַטְיָה **p^e^laṭyâ** or פְּלַטְיָהוּ **p^e^laṭyāhû**, n.pr.m. GK: 7124 & 7125 [→ 6403+3068]. Pelatiah, "*Yahweh rescues*":– Pelatiah [5]

פָּלִיא **pālî'**. See 6383.

6411 פְּלָאיָה **p^e^lā'yâ** or פְּלָיָה **p^e^lāyâ**, n.pr.m. GK: 7102 & 7126 [→ 6381+3068 *or* 6395+3068]. Pelaiah, "*Yahweh is spectacular*":– Pelaiah [3]

6412 פָּלִיט **pālîṭ** or פָּלֵיט **pālêṭ**, n.m. GK: 7127 & 7128 [→ 6403]. fugitive, one who escapes:– escape [9], escaped [6], escapeth [2], escape (+1961) [1], fugitives [1], one that escaped [1], that escaped [1]

6413 פְּלֵיטָה **p^e^lêṭâ**, n.f. GK: 7129 [→ 6403]. fugitive, one who escapes, survivors, remnant:– deliverance [5], escaped [4], escape [4], escape (+1961) [2], that is escaped [2], they that escape [2], escaping [1], him that escapeth [1], remnant to escape [1], remnant [1], such as are escaped [1], that are escaped [1], them that are escaped [1], them that be escaped [1], which is escaped [1]

6414 פָּלִיל **pālîl**, n.m. GK: 7130 [→ 6419]. judge:– judges [3]

6415 פְּלִילָה **p^e^lîlâ**, n.f. GK: 7131 [→ 6419]. decision:– judgment [1]

6416 פְּלִילִי **p^e^lîlî**, a. GK: 7132 [→ 6419]. for a judge, calling for judgment:– judge [1]

6417 פְּלִילִיָּה **p^e^lîliyyâ**, n.f. GK: 7133 [→ 6419]. rendering of a decision, the calling for a judgment:– judgment [1]

6418 פֶּלֶךְ **pelek**, n.[m.]. GK: 7134 & 7135 [cf. 6385]. spindle-whorl, which could be used as a crutch; district:– part [8], distaff [1], staff [1]

6419 פָּלַל **pālal**, v. GK: 7136 & 7137 [→ 654, 6414, 6415, 6416, 6417, 6420, 6421, 8605 (also used with compound proper names)]. [P] to mediate, intervene; to expect; to furnish justification; [Ht] to pray:– pray [35], prayed [30], praying [5], prayeth [4], executed judgment [1], intreat [1], judged [1], judge [1], made prayer [1], make supplication [1], make [1], prayer made [1], prayer make (+8605) [1], thought [1]

6420 פָּלָל **pālāl**, n.pr.m. GK: 7138 [→ 6419]. Palal, "*he has judged*":– Palal [1]

6421 פְּלַלְיָה **p^e^lalyâ**, n.pr.m. GK: 7139 [→ 6419+3068]. Pelaliah, "*Yahweh intercedes in arbitration*":– Pelaliah [1]

6422 פַּלְמֹנִי **palmōnî**, p. GK: 7140 [cf. 492, 6423]. certain one:– certain [1]

פִּלְנְאֶסֶר **piln^e^'eser**. See 8407.

6423 פְּלֹנִי **p^e^lōnî**, p. GK: 7141 [→ 6395; cf. 492, 6422]. certain one:– such a one (+492) [1], such and such (+492) [1], such [1]

פִּלְנֶסֶר **pilneser**. See 8407.

Heb

6424 פָּלַס ***pālas***, v.den. GK: 7142 & 7143 [→ 6425]. [P] to make level, make smooth, prepare; to examine, observe:– ponder [2], weigh [2], made [1], pondereth [1]

6425 פֶּלֶס ***peles***, n.[m.]. GK: 7144 [→ 6424]. balance, scale:– scales [1], weight [1]

פֶּלֶסֶר ***pᵉleser***. See 8407.

6426 פָּלַץ ***pālaṣ***, v. GK: 7145 [→ 4656, 6427, 8606]. [Ht] to tremble, shake:– tremble [1]

6427 פַּלָּצוּת ***pallāṣût***, n.f. GK: 7146 [→ 6426]. trembling, shuddering, shaking:– horror [2], fearfulness [1], trembling [1]

6428 פָּלַשׁ ***pālaš***, v. GK: 7147. [Ht] to roll oneself (in the dust or ash):– wallow [3], roll [1]

6429 פְּלֶשֶׁת ***pᵉlešet***, n.pr.loc. GK: 7148 [→ 6430]. Philistia; Philistine:– Palestina [3], Philistia [3], Palestine [1], Philistines [1]

6430 פְּלִשְׁתִּי ***pᵉlištî***, a.g. GK: 7149 [→ 6429]. Philistine:– Philistines [245], Philistine [33], Philistims [5], Philistines' [4], Philistim [1]

6431 פֶּלֶת ***pelet***, n.pr.m. GK: 7150. Peleth, "[perhaps] *swift* or *swiftness*":– Peleth [2]

6432 פְּלֵתִי ***pᵉlētî***, a.g. GK: 7152 [cf. 3774?]. Pelethite:– Pelethites [7]

6433 פֻּם ***pum*** (Aram.), n.m. GK: 10588. mouth:– mouth [5], mouths [1]

6434 פֵּן ***pēn***, n.m. GK: 7157 [→ 6437, 6438]. same as 6438: corner (of a structure), cornerstone (as a crucial element); stronghold; by extension: leader:– corner [2]

6435 פֶּן ***pen***, c. GK: 7153 [→ 6437?]. lest, not:– lest [114], not [7], lest peradventure [5], that not [4], none [1], peradventure [1], that [1]

6436 פַּנַּג ***pannag***, n.[m.]. GK: 7154. food, confection:– Pannag [1]

6437 פָּנָה ***pānâ***, v. GK: 7155 [→ 3312, 3942, 6435?, 6440, 6434, 6438, 6439, 6441, 6442]. [Q] to turn (in various senses); [P] to prepare; to turn away; [H] to turn; [Ho] to be caused to turn:– turned [33], turn [16], looked [14], looking [9], look [9], looketh [8], prepare [4], look back [3], respect [3], turneth [3], have respect [2], regard (+413) [2], beholdeth [1], cast out [1], cometh on [1], corner [1], dawning [1], empty [1], eventide (+6153) [1], goeth away [1], lieth [1], look toward [1], looked back [1], looked toward [1], mark (+413) [1], passed away [1], preparedst [1], prepared [1], regardeth (+413) [1], regard [1], respecteth (+413) [1], return [1], right [1], turn away [1], turn back [1], turned aside [1], turned back [1], turned faces [1], turnest [1], turneth away [1], when appeared (+3807.1) [1]

פָּנֶה ***pāneh***. See 6440.

6438 פִּנָּה ***pinnâ***, n.f. GK: 7157 [→ 6434]. same as 6434: corner (of a structure), cornerstone (as a crucial element); stronghold; by extension: leader:– corner [16], corners [6], chief [2], towers [2], bulwarks [1], stay [1]

6439 פְּנוּאֵל ***pᵉnû'ēl*** or פְּנִיאֵל ***pᵉnî'ēl***, n.pr.m. & loc. GK: 7158 & 7159 & 7160 & 7161 [→ 6437]. Penuel, Peniel, "*face of God [El]*":– Penuel [8], Peniel [1]

פָּנִי ***pānî***. See 6443.

6440 פָּנֶה ***pāneh***, n.m. & f. GK: 7156 [→ 6753, 6441; cf. 6437]. face; by extension: appearance, presence; (pp.) before, in front of, in the presence of; to "show one's face" is a sign of favor; to "turn" or "hide one's face" is a sign of rejection:– before (+3807.1) [958], face [328], presence [70], before [67], faces [63], because of (+4480) [54], before (+4480) [50], before (+5921) [43], sight [33], from (+4480) [31], countenance [30], upon (+5921) [23], of (+4480) [20], before (+4480+3807.1) [17], before (+854) [16], before (+413) [15], open [13], because (+4480) [12], for (+4480) [12], persons [10], person [10], by reason of (+4480) [9], fear [7], before (+871.1) [6], prospect [6], toward (+5921) [6], with (+3807.1) [6], against (+3807.1) [5], over against (+5921) [5], sight (+3807.1) [5], forefront [4], from (+4480+3807.1) [4], honourable (+5375) [4], in (+5921) [4], over against (+413) [4], presence (+3807.1) [4], according to (+5921) [3], anger [3], at (+4480) [3], because [3], beforetime (+3807.1) [3], besought (+853+2470) [3], favour [3], for (+3807.1) [3], forefront (+4136) [3], forepart [3], meet [3], of (+3807.1) [3], of (+4480+3807.1) [3], say nay (+7725) [3], shewbread (+3899) [3], shewbread (+3899+1886.1) [3], straight forward (+413+5676) [3], unto (+3807.1) [3], accept (+5375) [2], accepted (+5375) [2], afore (+3807.1) [2], aforetime (+3807.1) [2], before (+413+4136) [2], besought (+2470) [2], from (+3807.1) [2], from off (+4480+5921) [2], looketh [2], looks [2], of old (+3807.1) [2], over against (+413+4136) [2], seemeth unto (+3807.1) [2], to (+3807.1) [2], unto [2], withstand (+2388+3807.1) [2], against (+413) [1], against (+5676) [1], appease (+3722) [1], as (+5921) [1], as long as (+3807.1) [1], at (+3807.1) [1], attend upon [1], because (+834+4480) [1], because of (+4480+3807.1) [1], before (+5048) [1], before face [1], beforetime (+4480+3807.1) [1], beforetime [1], beseech (+2470) [1], by (+4480) [1], compassed with (+2328+5921) [1], deny (+7725) [1], disappoint (+6923) [1], edge [1], employ (+935+4480) [1], endure (+3807.1) [1], evident [1], first (+3807.1) [1], for (+4480+3807.1) [1], for fear of (+4480) [1], forefront (+3807.1) [1], forepart (+4136) [1], form [1], forward (+3807.1) [1], front [1], heaviness [1], himself (+2050.2) [1], impudent (+7186) [1], in former time (+3807.1) [1], in front (+5921) [1], in old time (+3807.1) [1], in presence (+7200) [1], in sight (+3807.1) [1], in the presence [1], in the sight (+3807.1) [1], in time past (+3807.1) [1], in times past (+3807.1) [1], inquired of (+1245) [1], intreat favour (+2470) [1], looked [1], look [1], me (+2967.1) [1], more than (+3807.1) [1], mouth [1], out of (+4480+5921) [1], over against [1], partial [1], pleased (+3190+3807.1) [1], pleaseth (+2896+3807.1) [1], purposed [1], regard (+5375) [1], regard persons (+4480+5375) [1], right before (+5227) [1], right forth (+3807.1) [1], send good speed (+7136+3807.1) [1], served (+5975+3807.1) [1], set [1], shewbread [1], state [1], themselves (+1992.1) [1], through (+4480) [1], throughout (+5921) [1], till (+3807.1) [1], towards (+3807.1) [1], towards (+4480) [1], toward [1], to [1], upside down (+5921) [1], upside down [1], waited on (+1961+3807.1) [1], whom (+834+4480) [1], with (+4480) [1], within (+4480+3807.1) [1], within [1], withstand (+5975+3807.1) [1]

6441 פְּנִימָה ***pᵉnîmâ***, adv. *or* pp. GK: 7163 [→ 6442; cf. 6440, 6437]. inner, inside, within:– within (+4480) [3], within [3], inward (+3807.1) [2], within (+3807.1) [2], inner part [1], in [1], within (+413) [1]

6442 פְּנִימִי ***pᵉnîmî***, a. GK: 7164 [→ 6441]. inner:– inner [30], inward (+413+1886.1) [1], within (+871.1+1886.1) [1]

6443 פְּנִינִים ***pᵉnînîm***, n.[f.]pl. GK: 7165 [→ 6444]. rubies or corals:– rubies [6]

6444 פְּנִנָּה ***pᵉninnâ***, n.pr.f. GK: 7166 [→ 6443]. Peninnah, "[poss.] *pearls, coral branches; woman with rich hair*":– Peninnah [3]

6445 פָּנַק ***pānaq***, v. GK: 7167. [P] to pamper:– delicately bringeth up [1]

6446 פַּס ***pas***, n.[m.]. GK: 7168 [→ 6450; cf. 657; cf. 6447]. ornamentation, many-colored or long-sleeved garment:– of many colours [3], divers colours [2]

6447 פַּס ***pas*** (Aram.), n.m. GK: 10589 [cf. 6446]. (palm of) hand; this may also refer to the entire hand:– part [2]

6448 פָּסַג ***pāsag***, v. GK: 7170. [P] to look over or to walk among:– consider [1]

6449 פִּסְגָּה ***pisgâ***, n.pr.loc. GK: 7171 [→ 798]. Pisgah:– Pisgah [5]

6450 פַּס דַּמִּים ***pas dammîm***, n.pr.loc. GK: 7169 [→ 6446]. Pas Dammim, "*place of blood*":– Pas-dammim [1]

6451 פִּסָּה ***pissâ***, n.f. GK: 7172. abundance, plenty:– handful [1]

6452 פָּסַח ***pāsaḥ***, v. GK: 7173 & 7174 [→ 6453, 6454, 6455, 8607]. [Q] to pass over; to be limp; [N] to become crippled; to worship in a limping dance:– pass over [2], became lame [1], halt [1], leapt [1], passed over [1], passing over [1]

6453 פֶּסַח ***pesaḥ***, n.m. GK: 7175 [→ 6452]. Passover; this can refer to the festival, the meal, or the lamb sacrificed at the festival:– passover [48], passovers [1]

6454 פָּסֵחַ ***pāsēaḥ***, n.pr.m. GK: 7176 [→ 6452]. Paseah, "*hobbling one*":– Paseah [3], Phaseah [1]

6455 פִּסֵּחַ ***pissēaḥ***, a. GK: 7177 [→ 6452]. lame, crippled:– lame [14]

6456 פָּסִיל ***pāsîl***, n.m. GK: 7178 [→ 6458]. idol, carved image:– graven images [18], carved images [3], quarries [2]

6457 פָּסַךְ ***pāsak***, n.pr.m. GK: 7179. Pasach, "*to divide*":– Pasach [1]

6458 פָּסַל ***pāsal***, v. GK: 7180 [→ 6456, 6459]. [Q] to chisel out, carve (stone or wood):– hew [3], hewed [2], graven [1]

6459 פֶּסֶל ***pesel***, n.m. GK: 7181 [→ 6458]. idol, usually an image carved of wood or stone:– graven image [26], carved image [2], graven images [2], graven [1]

6460 פְּסַנְתֵּרִין ***pᵉsantērîn*** (Aram.), n.[m.]. GK: 10590. harp (triangular stringed instrument):– psaltery [4]

6461 פָּסַס ***pāsas***, v. GK: 7182. [Q] to vanish:– fail [1]

6462 פִּסְפָּה ***pispâ***, n.pr.m. GK: 7183. Pispah:– Pispah [1]

6463 פָּעָה ***pā'â***, v. GK: 7184 [→ 660?]. [Q] to cry out, groan (in childbirth):– cry [1]

6464 פָּעוּ ***pā'û*** or פָּעִי ***pā'î***, n.pr.loc. GK: 7185 & 7187. Pau, Pai, "*groaning, bleating*":– Pai [1], Pau [1]

6465 פְּעוֹר ***pᵉ'ôr***, n.pr.loc. GK: 7186 [→ 1047, 1187; cf. 6473?]. Peor, "*opening*":– Peor [4], Peor's [1]

פָּעִי ***pā'î***. See 6464.

6466 פָּעַל ***pā'al***, v. GK: 7188 [→ 508, 4659, 6322, 6467, 6468, 6469]. [Q] to do, make:– workers [19], work [7], wrought [7], do [5], worketh [4], done [3], made [3], commit [1], didst [1], doers [1], doest [1], maker [1], maketh [1], ordaineth [1], working [1]

6467 פֹּעַל ***pō'al***, n.m. GK: 7189 [→ 6322; cf. 6466]. work, deed, labor:– work [27], deeds [2], done acts [2], works [2], act [1], do [1], getting [1], maker [1], reward of work [1]

6468 פְּעֻלָּה ***pᵉ'ullâ***, n.f. GK: 7190 [→ 6469; cf. 6466]. work, deed, recompense:– work [8], labour [2], works [2], reward [1], wages [1]

6469 פְּעֻלְּתַי ***pᵉ'ulᵉtay***, n.pr.m. GK: 7191 [→ 6468; cf. 6466]. Peullethai, "*worker, wage earner*":– Peulthai [1]

6470 פָּעַם ***pā'am***, v. GK: 7192 [→ 6471, 6472]. [Q] to push, impel; [N] to be troubled; [Ht] to be troubled:– troubled [4], move at times [1]

6471 פַּעַם ***pa'am***, n.f. GK: 7193 [→ 6472; cf. 6470]. step, foot; time, occurrence:– times [38], at other times (+6471+871.1) [12], time [12], once [8], feet [6], now [5], twice [5], steps [4], thrice (+7969) [4], corners [3], once (+259) [3], at once (+259) [2], now (+1886.1) [2], ranks [2], second time [2], anvil [1], footsteps [1], goings [1], hundredfold (+3967) [1], oftentimes (+7227) [1], oftentimes (+7969) [1], once (+871.1+1886.1) [1], order [1], two times [1], wheels [1]

6472 פַּעֲמוֹן ***paᵃmôn***, n.[m.]. GK: 7194 [→ 6471; cf. 6470]. bell (on a robe):– bell [4], bells [3]

6473 פָּעַר ***pā'ar***, v. GK: 7196 [cf. 6465?, 6474?]. [Q] to open wide (mouth):– opened [2], gaped [1], opened wide [1]

6474 פַּעֲרַי ***paᵃray***, n.pr.m. GK: 7197 [cf. 6473?]. Paarai, "*devotee of Peor*":– Paarai [1]

6475 פָּצָה ***pāṣâ***, v. GK: 7198. [Q] to open (mouth); to deliver, set free:– opened [7], open [3], rid [2], delivereth [1], gaped [1], uttered [1]

6476 פָּצַח ***pāṣaḥ***, v. GK: 7200. [Q] to break forth, burst forth; [P] to break (in pieces):– break forth [6], break [1], make a loud noise [1]

6477 פְּצִירָה ***pᵉṣîrâ***, n.f. GK: 7201. sharpening (of plowshare):– file (+6310) [1]

6478 פָּצַל ***pāṣal***, v. GK: 7202 [→ 6479]. [P] to peel (bark off boughs):– pilled [2]

6479 פְּצָלוֹת ***pᵉṣālôt***, n.f.pl. GK: 7203 [→ 6478]. stripes (made by peeling bark):– strakes [1]

6480 פָּצַם ***pāṣam***, v. GK: 7204. [Q] to tear open:– broken [1]

6481 פָּצַע ***pāṣa'***, v. GK: 7205 [→ 6482]. [Q] to bruise, wound; [Qp] to be emasculated (by crushing):– wounded [3]

6482 פֶּצַע ***peṣa'***, n.m. GK: 7206 [→ 6481]. wound, bruise:– wounds [4], wound [3], wounding [1]

פַּצֵּץ ***paṣṣēṣ***. See 1048.

6483 פִּצֵּץ ***piṣṣēṣ*** or הַפִּצֵּץ ***happiṣṣēṣ***, n.pr.m. GK: 7209 & 2204 [→ 1886.1+6327]. Pizzez, Happizzez, "*one who breaks*":– Aphses [1]

6484 פָּצַר ***pāṣar***, v. GK: 7210 [cf. 6555]. [Q] to insist on, bring pressure, persuade; [H] to be arrogant:– urged [4], pressed [2], stubbornness [1]

6485 פָּקַד ***pāqad***, v. GK: 7212 & 7217 [→ 4662, 6486, 6487, 6488, 6489, 6490, 6496]. [Q] to pay attention, care for; to count, number; to punish; [Qp] to be counted, listed; [N] to be missing, empty; [P] to muster; [Pu] to be robbed; to be recorded; [H] to appoint, give a charge; [Ho] to be appointed; [Ht] be mustered, counted; [Hotpaal] to be counted:– numbered [103], visit [31], punish [27], visited [17], number [14], appoint [10], set [6], surely visit (+6485) [6], made governor [5], appointed [4], committed [4], officers [4], punished [4], visiting [4], charged [3], counted [3], empty [3], missed [3], at all miss (+6485) [2], by any means missing (+6485) [2], commit [2], do judgment [2], lacking [2], laid up [2], made overseer [2], made ruler [2], numberest [2], overseers [2], oversight [2], surely visited

(+6485) [2], visitest [2], wanting [2], avenge [1], bestowed [1], calledst to remembrance [1], chargest [1], delivered to keep (+854+6487) [1], deprived [1], enjoined [1], given a charge [1], go see [1], had oversight [1], have oversight [1], hurt [1], lacked [1], lacketh [1], look [1], made rulers [1], make [1], missing [1], mustereth [1], reckon [1], remember [1], set over [1], sum [1], visiteth [1], want [1]

פִּקֻּד ***piqqud***. See 6490.

6486 פְּקֻדָּה ***p^{e}quddâ***, n.f. GK: 7213 [→ 6485]. positive: appointment, charge, visitation; negative: punishment:– visitation [13], office [3], officers [2], offices [2], oversight [2], account [1], charge [1], custody [1], numbers [1], orderings [1], prison (+1004+1886.1) [1], reckoning [1], that have charge over [1], that laid up [1]

6487 פִּקָּדוֹן ***piqqādôn***, n.m. GK: 7214 [→ 6485]. something entrusted, something in reserve:– delivered to keep (+854+6485) [1], store [1], that which was delivered to keep [1]

6488 פְּקִדֻת ***p^{e}qidut***, n.f. GK: 7215 [→ 6485]. (captain of the) guard:– ward [1]

6489 פְּקוֹד ***p^{e}qôd***, n.pr.loc. GK: 7216 [→ 6485]. Pekod, "*visitation*":– Pekod [2]

6490 פִּקּוּדִים ***piqqûdîm***, n.m.[pl.]. GK: 7218 [→ 6485]. precepts, directions, orders:– precepts [21], commandments [2], statutes [1]

6491 פָּקַח ***pāqaḥ***, v. GK: 7219 [→ 6492?, 6493, 6494, 6495]. [Q] to open; [Qp] to be opened; [N] to be opened:– open [10], opened [7], openeth [2], opening [1]

6492 פֶּקַח ***peqaḥ***, n.pr.m. GK: 7220 [→ 6491?]. Pekah, "*he has opened*":– Pekah [11]

6493 פִּקֵּחַ ***piqqēaḥ***, a. GK: 7221 [→ 6491]. (normal) sighted:– seeing [1], wise [1]

6494 פְּקַחְיָה ***p^{e}qaḥyâ***, n.pr.m. GK: 7222 [→ 6491+3068]. Pekahiah, "*Yahweh opens*":– Pekahiah [3]

6495 פְּקַח־קוֹחַ ***p^{e}qaḥ-qôaḥ***, n.[m.]. GK: 7223 [→ 6491]. opening (of eyesight); some sources: opening a prison house to release prisoners:– opening of the prison [1]

6496 פָּקִיד ***pāqîd***, n.m. GK: 7224 [→ 6485]. chief officer, supervisor, commissioner:– overseer [4], officers [3], officer [2], charge [1], governor [1], overseers [1], set [1]

6497 פְּקָעִים ***p^{e}qā'îm***, n.m.pl. GK: 7225 [→ 6498]. gourds:– knops [3]

6498 פַּקֻּעֹת ***paqqu'ōt***, n.[f.]pl. GK: 7226 [→ 6497]. gourds:– gourds [1]

6499 פַּר ***par***, n.m. GK: 7228 [→ 6510]. bull:– bullock [60], bullocks [31], bullock (+1241) [28], bullocks (+1241) [5], bullock's [3], bulls [2], oxen [2], calves [1], young [1]

6500 פָּרָא ***pārā'***, v. GK: 7229 [cf. 6509]. [H] to thrive in fruitfulness:– fruitful [1]

6501 פֶּרֶא ***pere'*** or פֶּרֶה ***pereh***, n.m. *or* f. GK: 7230 & 7241 [→ 6290?, 6502]. wild donkey; some sources: zebra, onager:– wild asses [4], wild ass [4], wild ass's [1], wild [1]

פֹּרָאה ***pōrā'h***. See 6288.

6502 פִּרְאָם ***pir'ām***, n.pr.m. GK: 7231 [→ 6501]. Piram, "[poss.] *wild donkey; indomitable;* [poss.] *zebra*":– Piram [1]

6503 פַּרְבָּר ***parbār*** or פַּרְוָר ***parwār***, n.[m.]. GK: 7232 & 7247. court (of the temple):– Parbar [2], suburbs [1]

6504 פָּרַד ***pārad***, v. GK: 7233 [→ 6505, 6506, 6507]. [Qp] to be spread out; [N] to be separated, be parted; [P] to consort with; [Pu] to be scattered; [H] to set apart, divide, separate; [Ht] to be scattered, be parted:– separated [8], divided [3], parted [2], separateth [2], separate [2], dispersed [1], out of joint [1], parteth [1], part [1], scattered abroad [1], scattered [1], severed [1], stretched [1], sundered [1]

6505 פֶּרֶד ***pered***, n.m. GK: 7234 [→ 6506; cf. 6504]. mule:– mules [8], mule [6], mules' [1]

6506 פִּרְדָּה ***pirdâ***, n.f. GK: 7235 [→ 6505]. (female) mule:– mule [3]

6507 פְּרֻדֹת ***p^{e}rudōt***, n.f. GK: 7237 [→ 6504]. grain (of seed); some sources: dried fig:– seed [1]

6508 פַּרְדֵּס ***pardēs***, n.[m.]. GK: 7236. park, forest, orchard:– forest [1], orchards [1], orchard [1]

6509 פָּרָה ***pārâ***, v. GK: 7238 [→ 669?, 6513, 6529; cf. 6500]. [Q] to be fruitful, flourish; [H] to make fruitful:– fruitful [13], make fruitful [5], increased [3], fruitful bough (+1121) [2], beareth [1], bring forth [1], bring fruit [1], caused to be fruitful [1], grew [1], grow [1]

6510 פָּרָה ***pārâ***, n.f. GK: 7239 [→ 6499]. cow, heifer:– kine [18], heifer [6], cow [2]

6511 פָּרָה ***pārâ***, n.pr.loc. GK: 7240. Parah, "*cow*":– Parah [1]

פֶּרֶה ***pereh***. See 6501.

6512 פֵּרוֹת ***pērôt*** or חֲפַרְפָּרָה ***ḥ^{a}parpārâ***, n.f. GK: 7249 & 2923 [→ 2658, 2661]. rodent (an object of worship):– moles (+2661) [1]

6513 פֻּרָה ***purâ***, n.pr.m. GK: 7242 [→ 6509]. Purah, "*branch; imposing*":– Phurah [2]

6514 פְּרוּדָא ***p^{e}rûdā'*** or פְּרִידָא ***p^{e}rîdā'***, n.pr.m. GK: 7243 & 7263. Peruda, Perida, "*single, unique*":– Perida [1], Peruda [1]

פְּרוֹזִי ***p^{e}rôzî***. See 6521.

6515 פָּרוּחַ ***pārûaḥ***, n.pr.m. GK: 7245 [→ 6524]. Paruah, "*blooming; cheerful*":– Paruah [1]

6516 פַּרְוַיִם ***parwayim***, n.pr.loc. GK: 7246. Parvaim:– Parvaim [1]

6517 פָּרוּר ***pārûr***, n.[m.]. GK: 7248 [→ 6289]. cooking pot:– pot [2], pans [1]

פַּרְוָר ***parwār***. See 6503.

6518 פָּרָז ***pārāz***, n.[m.]. GK: 7250. warrior:– villages [1]

6519 פְּרָזוֹת ***p^{e}rāzôt***, n.f.[pl.]. GK: 7252 [→ 6520, 6521, 6522]. rural, open country:– towns without walls [1], unwalled villages [1], unwalled [1]

6520 פְּרָזוֹן ***p^{e}rāzôn***, n.[m.]. GK: 7251 [→ 6519]. dwellers in the open country; warriors:– villages [2]

6521 פְּרָזִי ***p^{e}rāzî***, n.[m.]. GK: 7253 [cf. 6519]. rural, open country:– country [1], unwalled [1], villages [1]

6522 פְּרִזִּי ***p^{e}rizzî***, a.g. GK: 7254 [→ 6519]. Perizzite:– Perizzites [18], Perizzite [5]

6523 פַּרְזֶל ***parzel*** (Aram.), n.m. GK: 10591 [cf. 1270]. iron:– iron [20]

6524 פָּרַח ***pāraḥ***, v. GK: 7255 & 7256 & 7257 [→ 667, 6515, 6525, 6526?]. [Q] to sprout, blossom; break out, flourish; to fly; (n.) a bird; [H] to make flourish, bring to bud:– flourish [7], blossom [3], budded [3], blossom abundantly (+6524) [2], break out abroad (+6524) [2], breaking forth [2], broken out [2], bud [2], grow [2], make fly [2], break out [1], flourished [1], groweth [1], made to flourish [1], make to flourish [1], spreading [1], springeth up [1], spring [1], sprung up [1]

6525 פֶּרַח ***peraḥ***, n.m. GK: 7258 [→ 6524]. blossom, bud; floral work:– flowers [9], flower [5], blossom [1], buds [1], bud [1]

6526 פִּרְחַח ***pirḥaḥ***, n.m.col. GK: 7259 [→ 6524?]. offspring, brood, tribe, with a focus on energetic behavior:– youth [1]

6527 פָּרַט ***pāraṭ***, v. GK: 7260 [→ 6528?]. [Q] to strum, improvise (on a musical instrument):– chant [1]

6528 פֶּרֶט ***pereṭ***, n.[m.]col. GK: 7261 [→ 6527?]. fallen grapes:– grape [1]

6529 פְּרִי ***p^{e}rî***, n.m. GK: 7262 [→ 6509]. fruit, produce, crops; by extension: offspring of any creature; result of any action; "fruit of the lips" is speech, praise; "fruit of the hand" is something earned:– fruit [107], fruits [7], fruitful [2], boughs [1], firstfruits (+7225) [1], reward [1]

פְּרִידָא ***p^{e}rîdā'***. See 6514.

פֻּרִים ***purîm***. See 6332.

6530 פָּרִיץ ***pārîṣ***, n.m. GK: 7264 & 7265 [→ 6555]. ferocious (animal); robber; violent one:– robbers [2], destroyer [1], ravenous [1], robbers (+1121) [1], robber [1]

6531 פֶּרֶךְ ***perek***, n.[m.]. GK: 7266. ruthlessness, brutality, violence:– rigour [5], cruelty [1]

6532 פָּרֹכֶת ***pārōket***, n.f. GK: 7267. curtain:– vail [25]

6533 פָּרַם ***pāram***, v. GK: 7268. [Q] to tear; [Qp] to be torn:– rend [2], rent [1]

6534 פַּרְמַשְׁתָּא ***parmaš^{e}tā'***, n.pr.m. GK: 7269. Parmashta, "*very first*":– Parmashta [1]

6535 פַּרְנָךְ ***parnāk***, n.pr.m. GK: 7270. Parnach:– Parnach [1]

6536 פָּרַס ***pāras***, v. GK: 7271 [→ 6538?, 6541; cf. 6537]. [Q] to offer food, share food; [H] to have a divided hoof:– divideth [5], divide [4], parteth [2], deal [1], hoofs [1], tear [1]

6537 פְּרַס ***p^{e}ras***, v. and פְּרֵס ***p^{e}rēs*** (Aram.), n.[m.]. GK: 10592 [cf. 6536]. [Peil] to be divided; parsin, peres (unit of measure and weight):– divided [1], peres [1], upharsin (+2050.3) [1]

6538 פֶּרֶס ***peres***, n.[m.]. GK: 7272 [→ 6536?]. vulture:– ossifrage [2]

6539 פָּרַס ***pāras***, n.pr.loc. GK: 7273 [→ 6542; cf. 6540, cf. 6543]. Persia; Persian:– Persia [27], Persians [1]

6540 פָּרַס ***pāras*** (Aram.), n.pr.loc. & g. GK: 10594 [→ 6543; cf. 6539]. Persia, Persian:– Persians [4], Persia [2]

6541 פַּרְסָה ***parsâ***, n.f. GK: 7274 [→ 6536]. hoof:– hoof [12], hoofs [5], claws [2], clovenfooted (+8156+8157) [2]

6542 פַּרְסִי ***pār^{e}sî***, a.g. GK: 7275 [→ 6539; cf. 6543]. Persian:– Persian [1]

6543 פַּרְסָי ***parsāy*** (Aram.), a.g. GK: 10595 [→ 6540; cf. 6542]. Persian:– Persian [1]

6544 פָּרַע ***pāra'***, v.den. GK: 7276 & 7277 [→ 6546]. [Q] to take the lead; to be out of control, be unkempt; to ignore, avoid; [Qp] to be unkempt, be running wild; [N] be unrestrained; [H] to let neglect; to promote wickedness:– uncover [3], made naked [2], refuseth [2], avenging (+6546) [1], avoid [1], bare [1], go back [1], let [1], naked [1], perish [1], refuse [1], set at nought [1]

6545 פֶּרַע ***pera'***, n.[m.]. GK: 7279 [cf. 6546?]. long hair of head:– locks [2]

6546 פֶּרַע ***pera'***, n.[m.]. GK: 7278 [→ 6544; cf. 6545?]. leader, prince:– avenging (+6544) [1], revenges [1]

6547 פַּרְעֹה ***par'ōh***, n.m. GK: 7281 [→ 6548, 6549]. Pharaoh:– Pharaoh [222], Pharaoh's [43], Pharaoh's (+3807.1) [3]

6548 פַּרְעֹה חָפְרַע ***par'ōh ḥopra'***, n.pr.m. GK: 7281 + 2922 [→ 6547]. Pharaoh Hophra:– Pharaoh-hophra [1]

6549 פַּרְעֹה נְכֹה ***par'ōh n^{e}kōh***, n.pr.m. GK: 7281 + 5785 [→ 6547]. Pharaoh Neco:– Pharaoh-nechoh [4], Pharaoh-necho [1]

6550 פַּרְעֹשׁ ***par'ōš***, n.m. GK: 7282 [→ 6551]. flea:– flea [2]

6551 פַּרְעֹשׁ ***par'ōš***, n.pr.m. GK: 7283 [→ 6550]. Parosh, "*flea*":– Parosh [5], Pharosh [1]

6552 פִּרְעָתוֹן ***pir'ātôn***, n.pr.loc. GK: 7284 [→ 6553]. Pirathon:– Pirathon [1]

6553 פִּרְעָתוֹנִי ***pir'ātônî***, a.g. GK: 7285 [→ 6552]. Pirathonite, from Pirathon, "*of Pirathon*":– Pirathonite [5]

6554 פַּרְפַּר ***parpar***, n.pr.loc. GK: 7286. Pharpar:– Pharpar [1]

6555 פָּרַץ ***pāraṣ***, v. GK: 7287 [→ 1188, 4664, 6530, 6556, 6557, 6560, 6558, 6559; cf. 6484]. [Q] to break out, burst forth; [Qp] to be broken through; [N] to be spread abroad; [Pu] to be broken down; [Ht] to break oneself away:– broken down [5], increased [4], brake down [3], break down [3], break forth [3], breaketh [2], broken forth [2], broken up [2], broken [2], made a breach (+6556) [2], pressed [2], abroad every where [1], brake in [1], breaches [1], break away [1], break out [1], breaker [1], breaketh out [1], broken in upon [1], burst out [1], came abroad [1], compelled [1], dispersed [1], grew [1], increase [1], made a breach [1], open [1], scattered [1], spread abroad [1], urged [1]

6556 פֶּרֶץ ***pereṣ***, n.m. GK: 7288 [→ 1188, 7428; cf. 6555]. breech, break, gap caused by something breaking through; by extension: outburst of anger:– breach [9], breaches [3], breaking in [2], made a breach (+6555) [2], breaking forth [1], gaps [1], gap [1]

6557 פֶּרֶץ ***pereṣ***, n.pr.m. GK: 7289 [→ 6558; cf. 6555]. Perez, "*breaking out*":– Pharez [12], Perez [3]

6558 פַּרְצִי ***parṣî***, a.g. GK: 7291 [→ 6557; cf. 6555]. Perezite:– Pharzites [1]

6559 פְּרָצִים ***p^{e}rāṣîm***, n.pr.loc. GK: 7292 [→ 6556; cf. 6555]. Perazim, "*breaking out*":– Perazim [1]

6560 פֶּרֶץ עֻזָּא ***pereṣ 'uzzā'*** or פֶּרֶץ עֻזָּה ***pereṣ 'uzzâ***, n.pr.loc. GK: 7290 [→ 6556+5798]. Perez Uzzah, "*breaking out of Uzzah*":– Perez-uzzah [1], Perez-uzza [1]

6561 פָּרַק ***pāraq***, v. GK: 7293 [→ 4665, 6563, 6564; cf. 6562]. [Q] to rip to pieces; to free (by tearing away); [P] to take off, tear off; [Ht] to take off from oneself, tear off from oneself:– break off [2], brake off [1], break [1], broken [1], deliver [1], redeemed [1], rending in pieces [1], rent [1], tear in pieces [1]

6562 פְּרַק ***p^{e}raq*** (Aram.), v. GK: 10596 [cf. 6561]. [P] to break off, tear away; to loosen, abolish; to renounce:– break off [1]

6563 פֶּרֶק ***pereq***, n.[m.]. GK: 7294 [→ 6561]. crossroad; plunder:– crossway [1], robbery [1]

6564 פָּרָק ***pārāq***, n.[m.]. GK: 7295 [→ 6561]. fragment:– @H = **6565** פָּרַר ***pārar***, v. GK: 7296 & 7297 [cf. 6331]. [Q] to split asunder; [Pil] to shatter; [Pol] to split open; [Htpol] to split asunder; [H] to break, violate, nullify; [Ho] to be broken, revoked, thwarted:– break [13], broken [8], any ways make void (+6565) [2], brake [2], breaking [2], clean dissolved (+6565) [2], defeat [2], disannul [2], made void [2], utterly made void (+6565) [2], broken asunder [1], brought to nought [1], castest off [1], cause to cease [1], come to nought [1], disappointed [1], disappointeth [1], divide [1], fail [1], frustrateth [1], frustrate [1], make void [1], none effect [1]

6566 פָּרַשׂ ***pāraś***, v. GK: 7298 [→ 4666; cf. 6576]. [Q] to spread out, scatter; [Qp] to be spread out; [N] to be scattered; [P] to scatter, spread out:– spread [29], spread forth [10], spread out [6], spread abroad [4], spreadeth [3], scattered [2], spreadeth forth [2], stretch forth [2], breaketh [1], chop in pieces [1], layeth open [1], spreadeth abroad [1], stretch out [1], stretched forth [1], stretched out [1], stretcheth out [1], stretch [1]

6567 פָּרַשׁ ***pāraš***, v. GK: 7300 & 7301 [→ 6571, 6575; cf. 6569; cf. 6568]. [Q] to make clear; [N] to be given; [Pu] to be made clear; [H] to secrete poison:– declared [1], distinctly [1], scattered [1], shewed [1], stingeth [1]

6568 פְּרַשׁ ***p^e^raš*** (Aram.), v. GK: 10597 [cf. 6566]. [Pap] to be translated, be made clear, with an implication that each and every element of the letter be read and made clear:– plainly [1]

6569 פֶּרֶשׁ ***pereš***, n.[m.]. GK: 7302 [→ 6570; cf. 6567]. offal, dung or intestinal contents of a butchered animal:– dung [7]

6570 פֶּרֶשׁ ***pereš***, n.pr.m. GK: 7303 [→ 6569]. Peresh, "*offal eviscerated; dung; contents of stomach [not intestine]*":– Peresh [1]

6571 פָּרָשׁ ***pārāš***, n.m. GK: 7304 & 7305 [→ 6567]. horse; horseman:– horsemen [55], horseman [1], horsemen (+1167) [1]

6572 פַּרְשֶׁגֶן ***paršegen*** or פַּתְשֶׁגֶן ***patšegen***, n.m. GK: 7306 & 7358 [cf. 6573]. copy (of a text):– copy [4]

6573 פַּרְשֶׁגֶן ***paršegen*** (Aram.), n.m. GK: 10598 [cf. 6572]. copy (of a document):– copy [3]

6574 פַּרְשְׁדֹן ***parš^e^dōn***, n.[m.]. GK: 7307. back (of a person), back door [?]:– dirt [1]

6575 פָּרָשָׁה ***pārāšâ***, n.f. GK: 7308 [→ 6567]. exact amount, exact statement:– declaration [1], sum [1]

6576 פַּרְשֵׂז ***paršēz***, a.vbl. *or* v. GK: 7299 [cf. 6566]. spreading:– spreadeth [1]

6577 פַּרְשַׁנְדָּתָא ***paršandātā'***, n.pr.m. GK: 7309. Parshandatha:– Parshandatha [1]

6578 פְּרָת ***p^e^rāt***, n.pr.loc. GK: 7310. Euphrates (mighty river of Mesopotamia); Perath (small river or valley in the book of Jeremiah):– Euphrates [19]

פֹּרָת ***pōrāt***. See 6509.

6579 פַּרְתְּמִים ***part^e^mîm***, n.m.pl. GK: 7312. nobles, princes:– most noble [1], nobles [1], princes [1]

6580 פַּשׁ ***paš***, n.[m.]. GK: 7317. wickedness or weakness, foolishness:– extremity [1]

6581 פָּשָׂה ***pāśâ***, v. GK: 7313. [Q] to spread:– spread [13], spread much abroad (+6581) [6], spread much (+6581) [2], spreadeth [1]

6582 פָּשַׁח ***pāšaḥ***, v. GK: 7318. [P] to mangle:– pulled in pieces [1]

6583 פַּשְׁחוּר ***pašḥûr***, n.pr.m. GK: 7319. Pashhur, "[perhaps] *be quiet* and *round about*":– Pashur [14]

6584 פָּשַׁט ***pāšaṭ***, v. GK: 7320. [Q] to take off, strip; to make a sudden dash, raid; [P] to strip; [H] to take off, strip off; [Ht] to strip oneself:– put off [6], strip [6], invaded [4], flay [3], stripped [3], fell [2], spoileth [2], stript [2], flayed [1], made a road [1], made an invasion [1], pull [1], ran [1], rushed forward [1], rushed [1], set [1], spoil [1], spread abroad [1], spread [1], strip out of [1], stripped off [1], stript off [1], stript out of [1]

6585 פָּשַׂע ***pāśa'***, v. GK: 7314 [→ 6587; cf. 4667]. [Q] to march, step forth:– go [1]

6586 פָּשַׁע ***pāša'***, v. GK: 7321 [→ 6588]. [Q] to rebel, revolt (against human or divine authority):– transgressed [13], transgressors [8], rebelled [6], revolted [5], transgress [3], offended [1], revolt [1], transgressing [1], transgression [1], transgressor [1], trespassed [1]

6587 פֶּשַׂע ***peśa'***, n.[m.]. GK: 7315 [→ 6585]. step:– step [1]

6588 פֶּשַׁע ***peša'***, n.m. GK: 7322 [→ 6586]. rebellion, revolt, sin, transgression (against human or divine authority):– transgressions [46], transgression [37], trespass [5], sins [2], rebellion [1], sin [1], transgression (+1870) [1]

6589 פָּשַׂק ***pāśaq***, v. GK: 7316. [Q] to open wide (the lips in talking or smirking); [P] to spread the feet or legs (in immorality):– opened [1], openeth wide [1]

6590 פְּשַׁר ***p^e^šar*** (Aram.), v. GK: 10599 [→ 6591; cf. 6592, 6622]. [P] to give an interpretation; [Pa] to interpret; (as noun) an interpreter:– interpreting [1], make interpretations (+6591) [1]

6591 פְּשַׁר ***p^e^šar*** (Aram.), n.m. GK: 10600 [→ 6590; cf. 6592]. interpretation, explanation, what something means:– interpretation [30], make interpretations (+6590) [1]

6592 פֵּשֶׁר ***pēšer***, n.[m.]. GK: 7323 [cf. 6590, cf. 6591]. explanation, interpretation:– interpretation [1]

6593 פֵּשֶׁת ***pēšet***, n.[m.]. GK: 7324 [→ 6594]. flax, linen (made of flax):– linen [9], flax [7]

6594 פִּשְׁתָּה ***pištâ***, n.f. GK: 7325 [→ 6593]. flax, wick (made of flax):– flax [3], tow [1]

6595 פַּת ***pat*** or פְּתוֹת ***p^e^tôt***, n.f. GK: 7326 & 7336 [→ 6598, 6626]. little piece, morsel (of food):– morsel [8], pieces [2], piece [2], meat [1], morsels [1], part in pieces (+6626) [1]

6596 פֹּת ***pōt***, n.[f.]. GK: 7327 [cf. 4670]. scalp, forehead; socket (for doors):– hinges [1], secret parts [1]

פְּתָאִי ***p^e^tā'î***. See 6612.

6597 פִּתְאֹם ***pit'ōm***, subst. (used as adv.). GK: 7328 [→ 6621]. suddenly, unexpectedly, all at once, in an instant:– suddenly [20], sudden [2], straightway [1], suddenly (+871.1) [1], very suddenly (+6621+871.1) [1]

6598 פַּת־בַּג ***pat-bag***, n.[m.]. GK: 7329 [→ 6595+897?]. (fine) food, choice provisions:– portion of meat [5], meat [1]

6599 פִּתְגָם ***pitgām***, n.m. GK: 7330 [cf. 6600]. edict, decree; sentence (for a crime):– decree [1], sentence [1]

6600 פִּתְגָם ***pitgām*** (Aram.), n.m. GK: 10601 [cf. 6599]. word: report, reply, edict, decision, decree:– answer [2], matter [2], letter [1], word [1]

6601 פָּתָה ***pātâ***, v.den. GK: 7331 & 7332 [→ 3315, 6612, 6615; cf. 6613]. [Q] to be simple, easily deceived, enticed; [P] to seduce, entice, deceive, allure; [N] to be enticed, deceived; [Pu] to be deceived, enticed, persuaded; [H] to provide ample space, make spacious:– entice [7], deceived [6], persuade [3], deceive [2], enticed [2], allure [1], enlarge [1], enticeth [1], flattereth [1], flatter [1], persuaded [1], silly one [1], silly [1]

6602 פְּתוּאֵל ***p^e^tû'ēl***, n.pr.m. GK: 7333 [→ 6612+410]. Pethuel, "*God's opening*":– Pethuel [1]

6603 פִּתּוּחַ ***pittûaḥ***, n.m. GK: 7334 [→ 6605]. engraving, inscription:– engravings [5], graving [2], carved figures (+4734) [1], carved work [1], grave (+3807.1) [1], graven [1]

6604 פְּתוֹר ***p^e^tôr***, n.pr.loc. GK: 7335. Pethor:– Pethor [2]

6605 פָּתַח ***pātaḥ***, v. GK: 7337 & 7338 [→ 3316, 3317, 4669, 4668, 6603, 6607, 6608, 6609, 6610, 6611; cf. 6606]. [Q] to open; [Qp] to be opened; [N] to be opened; [P] to loosen, release, take off; to engrave, carve; [Pu] to be engraved; [Ht] to free oneself:– opened [51], open [47], loose [6], loosed [5], open wide (+6605) [4], openeth [4], grave [3], engrave [2], graved [2], openest [2], appear [1], break forth [1], drawn out [1], drawn [1], go free [1], graven [1], loose from [1], looseth [1], opening [1], put off [1], putteth off [1], set forth [1], set wide [1], spread out [1], ungirded [1], unstopped [1], vent [1]

6606 פְּתַח ***p^e^taḥ*** (Aram.), v. GK: 10602 [cf. 6605]. [Pp, Peil] to be opened:– opened [1], open [1]

6607 פֶּתַח ***petaḥ***, n.m. GK: 7339 [→ 6605]. entrance, opening; of a building or city: door, gate:– door [116], entering [17], doors [11], entry [7], gate [4], gates [3], entrance [2], entrances [1], entries [1], open place (+5869) [1], openings [1]

6608 פֵּתַח ***pētaḥ***, n.m. GK: 7340 [→ 6605]. revelation, disclosure, an extension opening a door or gate:– entrance [1]

פָּתֻחַ ***pātuaḥ***. See 6603.

6609 פְּתִיחָה ***p^e^tîḥâ***, n.[f.]. GK: 7347 [→ 6605]. drawn sword:– drawn swords [1]

6610 פִּתְחוֹן ***pittāḥôn***, n.[m.]. GK: 7341 [→ 6605]. opening (of mouth for communication):– opening [1], open [1]

6611 פְּתַחְיָה ***p^e^taḥyâ***, n.pr.m. GK: 7342 [→ 6605+3068]. Pethahiah, "*Yahweh opens*":– Pethahiah [4]

6612 פְּתִי ***petî***, n.f. & a. GK: 7343 & 7344 [→ 6601, 6602]. simple, naive, someone easily deceived or persuaded; simple ways, simplemindedness:– simple [15], simple ones [2], foolish [1], simplicity [1]

6613 פְּתָי ***p^e^tāy*** (Aram.), n.[m.]. GK: 10603. width, breadth:– breadth [2]

6614 פְּתִיגִיל ***p^e^tîgîl***, n.[m.]. GK: 7345. fine clothing:– stomacher [1]

6615 פְּתַיּוּת ***p^e^tayyût***, n.f. GK: 7346 [→ 6601]. undisciplined, deceptive:– simple [1]

6616 פָּתִיל ***pātîl***, n.m. GK: 7348 [→ 6617]. cord, strands, string:– lace [4], bracelets [2], bound [1], line [1], ribband [1], thread [1], wires [1]

6617 פָּתַל ***pātal***, v. GK: 7349 [→ 5319, 5321?, 6616, 6618]. [N] to have a struggle; to be wily, be crooked; [Ht] to show oneself shrewd:– froward [2], shew froward [1], shew unsavoury [1], wrestled [1]

6618 פְּתַלְתֹּל ***p^e^taltōl***, a. GK: 7350 [→ 6617]. crooked, perverse:– crooked [1]

6619 פִּתֹם ***pitōm***, n.pr.loc. GK: 7351. Pithom, "*temple [house] of Atum*":– Pithom [1]

6620 פֶּתֶן ***peten***, n.m. GK: 7352. cobra, serpent; some sources: viper:– asps [3], adder [2], asp [1]

6621 פֶּתַע ***peta'***, subst. (used as adv.). GK: 7353 [→ 6597]. instant; (adv.) suddenly, in an instant:– suddenly [3], instant [2], suddenly (+871.1) [1], very suddenly (+6597+871.1) [1]

6622 פָּתַר ***pātar***, v. GK: 7354 [→ 6623; cf. 6590, cf. 6591]. [Q] to interpret, give the meaning (of a dream):– interpret [4], interpreted [3], interpretation [1], interpreter [1]

6623 פִּתְרוֹן ***pittārôn***, n.m. GK: 7355 [→ 6622]. interpretation, meaning:– interpretation [4], interpretations [1]

6624 פַּתְרוֹס ***patrôs***, n.pr.loc. GK: 7356 [→ 6625]. Upper Egypt (Patros):– Pathros [5]

6625 פַּתְרֻסִים ***patrusîm***, a.g.pl. GK: 7357 [→ 6624]. Pathrusite:– Pathrusim [2]

פַּתְשֶׁגֶן ***patšegen***. See 6572.

6626 פָּתַת ***pātat***, v. GK: 7359 [→ 6595]. [Q] to crumble:– part in pieces (+6595) [1]

6627 צֵאָה ***ṣē'â***, n.f. GK: 7362. excrement, dung:– cometh from [1], cometh out [1]

צֹאָה ***ṣō'â***. See 6675.

צְאוֹן ***ṣ^e^'ôn***. See 6629.

6628 צֶאֱלִים ***ṣe'^e^lîm***, n.m.pl. GK: 7365. lotus plant:– shady trees [2]

6629 צֹאן ***ṣō'n***, n.col.f. *or* m. GK: 7366 [→ 6792; cf. 3318]. flock, sheep, goats (in contrast to larger mammals: cattle, donkeys, camels, etc.):– sheep [111], flock [84], flocks [53], cattle [14], lambs (+1121) [2], shepherds (+7462) [2], flocks (+4735) [1], lamb [1], sheepcotes (+1448) [1], sheepfolds (+1448) [1], sheepfolds (+4356) [1], sheepshearers (+1494) [1], shepherd (+7462) [1], small[S] [1]

6630 צַאֲנָן ***ṣa'^a^nān***, n.pr.loc. GK: 7367 [cf. 6799?]. Zaanan:– Zaanan [1]

6631 צֶאֱצָאִים ***ṣe'^e^ṣā'îm***, n.m.[pl.]. GK: 7368 [→ 3318]. offspring, descendant:– offspring [9], that come forth [1], that which cometh out [1]

6632 צָב ***ṣāb***, n.[m.]. GK: 7369 & 7370 [→ 6637, 6638?]. (covered) wagon; some sources: litter without wheels; lizard (of unspecified species):– covered [1], litters [1], tortoise [1]

6633 צָבָא ***ṣābā'***, v. GK: 7371 [→ 6635]. [Q] to fight, do battle; to serve in (temple) corps:– fight [3], assembled [2], mustered [2], warred [2], assembling [1], fought [1], perform service (+6635) [1], wait (+6635) [1]

6634 צְבָה ***ṣ^e^bâ*** (Aram.), v. GK: 10605 [→ 6640]. [P] to wish, desire, want, long for:– will [5], would [5]

6635 צָבָא ***ṣābā'***, n.m. & f. GK: 7372 [→ 6633]. army, host, divisions (of an army); as a title of God: of Hosts (the heavenly armies), the Almighty, with a focus on great power to conquer or rule, a fig. extension of the leader of an great army:– hosts [293], host [101], war [41], armies [22], army [7], battle [5], service [4], appointed time [2], warfare [2], army (+2428) [1], battle (+4421) [1], company [1], perform service (+6633) [1], soldiers [1], time appointed [1], wait (+6633) [1], waiting upon [1]

6636 צְבֹאִים ***ṣ^e^bō'îm*** or צְבִיִּים ***ṣ^e^bōyîm***, n.pr.loc. GK: 7375 & 7387 [cf. 6643]. Zeboiim, "*gazelles*":– Zeboim [3], Zeboiim [2]

6637 צֹבֵבָה ***ṣōbēbâ***, n.pr.m. GK: 7376 [→ 6632]. Zobebah:– Zobebah [1]

6638 צָבָה ***ṣābâ***, v. GK: 7377 [→ 6632?, 6639]. [Q] to swell; [H] to cause to swell:– fight [1], make to swell [1], swell [1]

6639 צָבֶה ***ṣābeh***, a. GK: 7379 [→ 6638]. swollen:– swell [1]

צֹבָה ***ṣōbâ***. See 6678.

6640 צְבוּ ***ṣᵉbû*** (Aram.), n.f. GK: 10606 [→ 6634]. situation, matter, affair, thing:– purpose [1]

6641 צָבוּעַ ***ṣābûaʿ***, a. GK: 7380 [→ 6641, 6648; 6649, 6650]. speckled, variegated, pertaining to the pattern on a winged creature:– speckled [1]

6642 צָבַט ***ṣābaṭ***, v. GK: 7381 [cf. 6653]. [Q] to offer (food to another person):– reached [1]

6643 צְבִי ***ṣᵉbî***, n.m. GK: 7373 & 7374 & 7382 & 7383 [→ 6644, 6645, 6646; cf. 6636, 6719; cf. 6634]. ornament, beautiful (thing), glory; gazelle:– glory [8], roe [6], glorious [5], roebuck [4], roes [3], beauty [2], beautiful [1], goodly [1], pleasant [1], roebucks [1]

6644 צִבְיָא ***ṣibyāʾ***, n.pr.m. GK: 7384 [→ 6643]. Zibia, "*gazelle*":– Zibia [1]

6645 צִבְיָה ***ṣibyâ***, n.pr.f. GK: 7385 [→ 6643]. Zibiah, "*gazelle*":– Zibiah [2]

6646 צְבִיָּה ***ṣᵉbiyyâ***, n.f. GK: 7386 [→ 6643]. (female) gazelle:– roes [2]

צְבִיִּם ***ṣᵉbiîm***. See 6636.

צְבָיִם ***ṣᵉbāyim***. See 6380.

6647 צְבַע ***ṣᵉbaʿ*** (Aram.), v. GK: 10607. [Pa] to drench, make wet; [Htpa] to be drenched, made wet:– wet [5]

6648 צֶבַע ***ṣebaʿ***, n.[m.]. GK: 7389 [→ 6641; cf. 6647]. colorful (dyed) garment:– divers colours [3]

6649 צִבְעוֹן ***ṣibʿôn***, n.pr.m. GK: 7390 [cf. 6641, 6650]. Zibeon, "*hyena*":– Zibeon [8]

6650 צְבֹעִים ***ṣᵉbōʿîm***, n.pr.loc. GK: 7391 [cf. 6641, 6649]. Zeboim, "*hyenas*":– Zeboim [2]

6651 צָבַר ***ṣabar***, v. GK: 7392 [→ 6652]. [Q] to store up, heap up, pile up:– gathered together [1], gathered [1], heap up [1], heaped up [1], heapeth up [1], heap [1], lay up [1]

6652 צִבֻּר ***ṣibbur***, n.m. GK: 7393 [→ 6651]. pile, heap:– heaps [1]

6653 צֶבֶת ***ṣebet***, n.[m.]pl. GK: 7395 [cf. 6642]. bundle (of grain with the stalk):– handfuls [1]

6654 צַד ***ṣad***, n.m. GK: 7396 [→ 6657; cf. 6655]. side (of something):– side [20], sides [9], beside (+4480) [3], another[5] [1]

6655 צַד ***ṣad*** (Aram.), n.[m.]. GK: 10608 [cf. 6654]. side:– against (+3807.2) [1], concerning (+4481) [1]

6656 צְדָא ***ṣᵉdāʾ*** (Aram.), n.[m.]. GK: 10609. purpose, (with 1886.6) is it true?:– true [1]

6657 צְדָד ***ṣādād***, n.pr.loc. GK: 7398 [→ 6654]. Zedad, "*side*":– Zedad [2]

6658 צָדָה ***ṣādâ***, v. GK: 7399 & 7400 [→ 6660]. [Q] to lie in wait, hunt down a person; [N] to be destroyed, be laid waste:– destroyed [1], huntest [1], lie in wait [1]

צֵדָה ***ṣēdâ***. See 6720.

6659 צָדוֹק ***ṣādôq***, n.pr.m. GK: 7401 [→ 6663]. Zadok, "*righteous one*":– Zadok [52], Zadok's (+3807.1) [1]

6660 צְדִיָּה ***ṣᵉdiyyâ***, n.f. GK: 7402 [→ 6658; cf. 6656]. ambush, lying-in-wait (with malicious intent):– laying of wait [2]

6661 צִדִּים ***ṣiddîm***, n.pr.loc. GK: 7403. Ziddim, "*place on the sides or flanks [of the hill]*":– Ziddim [1]

6662 צַדִּיק ***ṣaddîq***, a. GK: 7404 [→ 6663]. righteous, upright, just, innocent; in accordance with a proper (God's) standard, and so implying innocence:– righteous [163], just [42], lawful [1]

צִדֹנִי ***ṣidōnî***. See 6722.

6663 צָדַק ***ṣādaq***, v.den. GK: 7405 [→ 3087, 3136, 6659, 6662, 6664, 6666, 6667]. [Q] to be righteous, be innocent, be vindicated; in accordance with a proper (God's) standard, and so implying innocence:– justified [12], righteous [10], justify [7], just [3], justifieth [2], justifying [2], cleansed [1], clear [1], do justice [1], justice [1], turn to righteousness [1]

6664 צֶדֶק ***ṣedeq***, n.m. GK: 7406 [→ 139, 4442, 6667; cf. 6663]. righteousness, justice, rightness, acting according to a proper (God's) standard, doing what is right, being in the right:– righteousness [78], justice [10], just [10], righteous [8], righteously [3], right [3], altogether just (+6664) [2], even [1], righteous cause [1], righteousness' [1], unrighteousness (+3808) [1]

6665 צִדְקָה ***ṣidqâ*** (Aram.), n.f. GK: 10610 [cf. 6666]. what is right:– righteousness [1]

6666 צְדָקָה ***ṣᵉdāqâ***, n.f. GK: 7407 [→ 6663; cf. 6665]. righteousness, acting according to a proper (God's) standard, doing what is right, being in the right:– righteousness [124], justice [15], right [9], righteous acts [3], righteousnesses [3], moderately (+3807.1) [1], righteously [1], righteousness' [1]

6667 צִדְקִיָּה ***ṣidqiyyâ*** or צִדְקִיָּהוּ ***ṣidqiyyāhû***, n.pr.m. GK: 7408 & 7409 [→ 6664+3068]. Zedekiah, "*Yahweh is [my] righteousness*":– Zedekiah [61], Zedekiah's [1], Zidkijah [1]

6668 צָהַב ***ṣāhab***, v. GK: 7410 [→ 6669, 6678; cf. 2091]. [Ho] to be polished, gleaming copper color:– fine (+2896) [1]

6669 צָהֹב ***ṣāhōb***, a. GK: 7411 [→ 6668]. yellow, blond; some sources: gleaming red:– yellow [3]

6670 צָהַל ***ṣāhal***, v. GK: 7412 & 7413 [→ 4684, cf. 6671]. [Q] to shout out, celebrate; to neigh (of a horse); [H] to make shine:– cry aloud [2], bellow [1], cry out [1], lift up [1], make to shine [1], neighed [1], rejoiced [1], shout [1]

6671 צָהַר ***ṣāhar***, v.den. GK: 7414 [→ 3323, 3324, 3325, 6672; cf. 6670]. [H] to press olives; some sources: to spend the noontime:– make oil [1]

6672 צֹהַר ***ṣōhar***, n.f. and צָהֳרַיִם ***ṣohᵒrayim***, n.[m.]. GK: 7415 [→ 6671]. roof, covering (for the ark of Noah); noon, noonday, midday:– noon [11], noonday [8], midday [1], noon day [1], noondays [1], noontide (+6256) [1], window [1]

6673 צַו ***ṣaw***, n.[m.]. GK: 7417 [→ 7723? *or* 6680?]. worthless thing, an idol or utterance (perhaps a nonsense syllable, a mocking sound):– precept [8], commandment [1]

6674 צֹאִי ***ṣōʾî***, a. GK: 7364. filthy, befouled (with excrement):– filthy [2]

6675 צֹאָה ***ṣōʾâ***, n.f. GK: 7363. filth, excrement, dung; by extension: moral filth:– dung [2], filthiness [2], filth [1]

6676 צַוַּאר ***ṣawwaʾr*** (Aram.), n.m. GK: 10611 [cf. 6677]. neck:– neck [3]

6677 צַוָּאר ***ṣawwāʾr*** or צַוְּרֹנִים ***ṣawwᵉrōnîm***, n.m. GK: 7418 & 7454 [cf. 6676]. (back of) neck; necklace:– neck [32], necks [10]

6678 צוֹבָא ***ṣôbāʾ*** or צוֹבָה ***ṣôbâ***, n.pr.loc. GK: 7419 & 7420 [→ 760, 2578; cf. 6668]. Zobah:– Zobah [10], Zoba [2]

6679 צוּד ***ṣûd*** or צִיד ***ṣîd***, v. GK: 7421 & 7472 [→ 4679, 4685, 4686, 6718, 6719, 6720]. [Q] to hunt, stalk; [Pil] to ensnare; by extension to stalk people for capture or oppression; [Ht] to pack provisions for oneself:– hunt [10], chased sore (+6679) [2], hunt for [1], huntest [1], hunteth [1], taken [1], take [1], took provision [1]

6680 צָוָה ***ṣāwâ***, v. GK: 7422 [→ 4687, 6673?]. [P] to command, order, instruct, give direction; [Pu] to be commanded, be directed, be ordered:– commanded [333], command [84], charged [23], commandeth [6], appointed [4], commandedst [4], gave a charge [4], bade [3], gave charge [3], give a charge [3], give charge [3], charge [2], commandest [2], gave commandment [2], given a commandment [2], set in order [2], appoint [1], commander [1], commanding [1], forbad [1], forbidden [1], gave a commandment [1], gave in commandment [1], give in commandment [1], given a charge [1], given commandment [1], given in commandment [1], put in order [1], sent a messenger [1], sent with commandment [1]

6681 צָוַח ***ṣāwaḥ***, v. GK: 7423 [→ 6682]. [Q] to shout, cry aloud:– shout [1]

6682 צְוָחָה ***ṣᵉwāḥâ***, n.f. GK: 7424 [→ 6681]. cry of distress, wail:– cry [2], complaining [1], crying [1]

6683 צוּלָה ***ṣûlâ***, n.f. GK: 7425 [→ 4688, 4699; cf. 6749]. the watery deep, the ocean abyss:– deep [1]

6684 צוּם ***ṣûm***, v. GK: 7426 [→ 6685]. [Q] to fast, to voluntarily abstain from food as dedication to deity, as a sign of mourning, or possibly as a medical treatment:– fasted [11], fast [7], at all fast (+6684) [2], fasted (+6685) [1]

6685 צוֹם ***ṣôm***, n.m. GK: 7427 [→ 6684]. fast, time of fasting, act of fasting:– fast [16], fasting [8], fasted (+6684) [1], fastings [1]

6686 צוּעָר ***ṣûʿār***, n.pr.m. GK: 7428 [→ 6819]. Zuar, "*little one*":– Zuar [5]

6687 צוּף ***ṣûp***, v. GK: 7429 [→ 6688, 6689, 6824?]. [Q] to flow; [H] to make float; to overwhelm (with water):– flowed [1], made to overflow [1], swim [1]

6688 צוּף ***ṣûp***, n.m. GK: 7430 [→ 6687]. honeycomb (dripping with honey):– honeycomb (+1706) [1], honeycomb (+5317) [1]

6689 צוּף ***ṣûp*** or צוֹפַי ***ṣôpay*** or צוּפִי ***ṣûpî*** or צִיף ***ṣîp***, n.pr.m. & g. & loc. GK: 7431 & 7433 & 7434 & 7487 [→ 6687, 6688]. Zuph; Zuphite; Zophai; Ziph, "*[dripping, full] honeycomb*":– Zuph [3], Zophai [1]

6690 צוֹפַח ***ṣôpaḥ***, n.pr.m. GK: 7432 [→ 6838]. Zophah, "*bellied jug*":– Zophah [2]

צוֹפַי ***ṣôpay***. See 6689.

6691 צוֹפַר ***ṣôpar***, n.pr.m. GK: 7436 [→ 6833?]. Zophar, "[poss.] *peep, twitter [as a bird]*":– Zophar [4]

6692 צוּץ ***ṣûṣ***, v. GK: 7437 & 7438 [→ 6731, 6733, 6734]. [Q] to bud, blossom; [H] to put forth blossoms; to cause to flourish; to peer at, look at:– flourish [3], flourisheth [2], bloomed [1], blossomed [1], blossom [1], shewing [1]

6693 צוּק ***ṣûq***, v. GK: 7439 [→ 4165, 4689, 4691, 6695, 6695; cf. 6845]. [H] to oppress, compel, nag, inflict:– distress [5], oppressor [2], constraineth [1], lay sore upon [1], pressed [1], straiten [1]

6694 צוּק ***ṣûq***, v. GK: 7440 [→ 3332?]. [Q] to pour out:– poured out [2], molten [1]

6695 צוֹק ***ṣôq*** or צוּקָה ***ṣûqâ***, n.m. & f. GK: 7441 & 7442 [→ 6693]. trouble, distress, oppression:– anguish [3], troublous [1]

6696 צוּר ***ṣûr***, v. GK: 7443 & 7444 & 7445 [→ 4692, 4694, 6699, 6736?; cf. 6737, 3334]. [Q] to siege, besiege, enclose; to oppose, harass; to fashion, shape:– besieged [14], besiege [6], distress [2], lay siege [2], adversary [1], assault [1], beset [1], besiege (+5921) [1], bind up [1], bind [1], bound [1], cast [1], distressed [1], fashioned [1], fortify [1], inclose [1], laid siege [1], put up [1]

6697 צוּר ***ṣûr***, n.m. GK: 7446 & 7447 [→ 468, 1049, 6301, 6698, 6700, 6701, 6864; cf. 2906]. rock; pebble, flint; stone mass, rocky crag; a title of God, with a focus of stability, and possibly as a place of security and safety:– rock [57], rocks [7], strength [5], sharp [2], God [1], edge [1], mighty God [1], mighty one [1], stones [1], strong [1]

6698 צוּר ***ṣûr***, n.pr.m. GK: 7448 [→ 6697]. Zur, "*rock*":– Zur [5]

צוֹר ***ṣôr***. See 6865.

צַוָּר ***ṣawwār***. See 6677.

6699 צוּרָה ***ṣûrâ***, n.f. GK: 7451 [→ 6696]. design, form:– forms [2], form [2], beauty [1]

צַוְּרֹן ***ṣawwārōn***. See 6677.

6700 צוּרִיאֵל ***ṣûrîʾēl***, n.pr.m. GK: 7452 [→ 6697+410]. Zuriel, "*God [El] is [my] rock*":– Zuriel [1]

6701 צוּרִישַׁדַּי ***ṣûrîšadday*** or צוּרִי־שַׁדַּי ***ṣûrî-šadday***, n.pr.m. GK: 7453 [→ 6697+7706]. Zurishaddai, "*Shaddai is [my] rock*":– Zurishaddai [5]

6702 צוּת ***ṣût***, v. GK: 7455 [cf. 3341]. [H] to set on fire:– burn [1]

6703 צַח ***ṣaḥ***, a. GK: 7456 [→ 6705]. radiant, shimmering, scorching, clear:– clear [1], dry [1], plainly [1], white [1]

צִחָא ***ṣiḥaʾ***. See 6727.

6704 צִחֶה ***ṣiḥeh***, a. GK: 7457 [cf. 6705]. parched:– dried up [1]

6705 צָחַח ***ṣāḥaḥ***, v. GK: 7458 [→ 4696?, 4697?, 6703, 6706, 6707, 6710; cf. 6704, 6708]. [Q] to be white:– whiter [1]

6706 צָחִיחַ ***ṣāḥîaḥ***, n.[m.]. GK: 7460 [→ 6705; cf. 6708]. bare (rock or place in a wall):– top [4], higher places [1]

6707 צְחִיחָה ***ṣᵉḥîḥâ***, n.f. GK: 7461 [→ 6705]. bare, (sun-)scorched land:– dry [1]

6708 צְחִחִי ***ṣᵉḥiḥî***, n.[m.]. GK: 7459 [cf. 6705, 6706]. bare (rock or place in a wall):– @H = **6709** צַחֲנָה ***²a±ᵃnâ***, n.f. GK: 7462. putrid smell, stench:– ill savour [1]

6710 צַחְצָחוֹת ***ṣaḥṣāḥôt***, n.[f.pl.]. GK: 7463 [→ 6705]. bare, (sun-)scorched land:– drought [1]

6711 צָחַק ***ṣāḥaq***, v. GK: 7464 [→ 3327, 6712; cf. 7832]. [Q] to laugh; [P] to mock, make sport, caress; this can mean to laugh with delight or in scorn:– laughed [3], laugh [3], mock [2], made sport [1], mocked [1], mocking [1], play [1], sporting with [1]

6712 צְחֹק ***ṣᵉḥōq***, n.[m.]. GK: 7465 [→ 6711]. laughter, scorn:– laughed to scorn [1], laugh [1]

6713 צָהַר ***ṣāḥar***, n. & pr.m. GK: 7466 [→ 6715]. white; as n.pr. Zahar, "*yellowish red, tawny*":– white [1]

6714 צֹחַר ***ṣōḥar***, n.pr.m. GK: 7468 [→ 6715; cf. 3328]. Zohar, "*yellowish red, tawny*":– Zohar [4]

6715 צָחֹר ***ṣāḥōr***, a. GK: 7467 [→ 6713, 6714]. white, yellowish red, tawny:– white [1]

6716 צִי ***ṣî***, n.m. GK: 7469. ship:– ships [3], ship [1]

6717 צִיבָא ***ṣîbā'***, n.pr.m. GK: 7471. Ziba, "*gazelle*":– Ziba [16]

6718 צַיִד ***ṣayid***, n.m. GK: 7473 & 7474 [→ 6679]. food supply, provision; (hunting) game; hunter:– venison [8], hunter [2], provision [2], victuals [2], catcheth [1], food [1], hunter (+376) [1], hunting [1], took in hunting [1]

6719 צַיָּד ***ṣayyād***, n.m. GK: 7475 [→ 6679]. hunter:– hunters [1]

6720 צֵידָה ***ṣêdâ***, n.f. GK: 7476 [→ 6679]. food, provisions, supplies:– victuals [4], provision [2], victual [2], meat [1]

6721 צִידוֹן ***ṣîdôn***, n.pr.loc. GK: 7477 [→ 6722]. Sidon, "*fishery*":– Zidon [20], Sidon [2]

6722 צִידֹנִי ***ṣîdōnî***, a.g. GK: 7479 [→ 6721]. Sidonian, people of Sidon:– Zidonians [10], Sidonians [5], Zidon [1]

6723 צִיָּה ***ṣiyyâ***, n.f. GK: 7480 [→ 6728, 6724]. desert, parched land, dry land, waterless region:– dry [9], drought [2], wilderness [2], barren [1], dry land [1], solitary place [1]

6724 צָיוֹן ***ṣāyôn***, n.[m.]. GK: 7481 [→ 6723]. desert, waterless country:– dry place [2]

6725 צִיּוּן ***ṣiyyûn***, n.m. GK: 7483. sign, stone marker:– sign [1], title [1], waymarks [1]

6726 צִיּוֹן ***ṣiyyôn***, n.pr.loc. GK: 7482. Zion, "*citadel*":– Zion [153], Zion's [1]

6727 צִיחָא ***ṣîḥā'***, n.pr.m. GK: 7484. Ziha:– Ziha [3]

6728 צִי ***ṣî***, n.m. GK: 7470 [→ 6723]. desert creature, referring to known animals or presumed spirits or demons; tribe of the desert:– wild beasts of the desert [3], inhabiting the wilderness [1], that dwell in the wilderness [1], them that dwell in the wilderness [1]

6729 צִינֹק ***ṣînōq***, n.[m.]. GK: 7485. neck-iron, iron collar:– stocks [1]

6730 צִיעֹר ***ṣî'ōr***, n.pr.loc. GK: 7486 [→ 6819]. Zior, "*small, insignificant*":– Zior [1]

צִיף ***ṣîp***. See 6689.

6731 צִיץ ***ṣîṣ***, n.m. GK: 7488 & 7490 [→ 6692, 6733, 6734]. flower, blossom; (ornamental) plate; salt:– flower [6], flowers [4], plate [3], blossoms [1], wings [1]

6732 צִיץ ***ṣîṣ***, n.pr.loc. GK: 7489. Ziz, "[poss.] *ascent where the flowers grow*":– Ziz [1]

6733 צִיצָה ***ṣîṣâ***, n.f. GK: 7491 [→ 6731; cf. 6692]. flower:– flower [1]

6734 צִיצִת ***ṣîṣit***, n.f. GK: 7492 [→ 6731; cf. 6692]. tassel of threads; tuft of hair:– fringe [2], fringes [1], lock [1]

צִיקְלַג ***ṣîqᵉlag***. See 6860.

6735 צִיר ***ṣîr***, n.[m.]. GK: 7494 & 7495. hinge, (door-)pivot; pains, pangs, anguish; envoy, messenger:– ambassador [3], pangs [3], ambassadors [1], hinges [1], messengers [1], messenger [1], pains [1], sorrows [1]

6736 צִיר ***ṣîr***, n.m. GK: 7497 [→ 6696?]. idol:– idols [1]

6737 צִיר ***ṣîr***, v.den. GK: 7493 [cf. 6696]. [Ht] to act as a delegation:– made as if ambassadors [1]

6738 צֵל ***ṣēl***, n.m. GK: 7498 [→ 1212, 6741, 6752, 6757, 6765; cf. 6751]. shadow, shade, protection:– shadow [45], defence [3], shade [1]

6739 צְלָה ***ṣᵉlâ*** (Aram.), v. GK: 10612. [Pa] to pray:– prayed [1], pray [1]

6740 צָלָה ***ṣālâ***, v. GK: 7499 [→ 6748]. [Q] to roast (meat):– roasted [1], roasteth [1], roast [1]

6741 צִלָּה ***ṣillâ***, n.pr.f. GK: 7500 [→ 6738; cf. 4980]. Zillah, "*[God is my] shadow*, i.e., *protection*":– Zillah [3]

6742 צְלוּל ***ṣᵉlûl*** or צְלִיל ***ṣᵉlîl***, n.m. GK: 7501 & 7508. cake, round loaf:– cake [1]

6743 צָלַח ***ṣālaḥ***, v. GK: 7502 & 7503 [cf. 6744]. [Q] to be powerful, come forcefully; to rush; to prosper, prevail, succeed, avail; [H] to make a success, grant prosperity, make victorious:– prosper [33], prospered [6], came [5], made to prosper [3], came mightily [2], make prosperous [2], prosperous [2], break out [1], cause to prosper [1], come [1], good [1], made prosperous [1], meet [1], profitable [1], prospereth [1], prosperously effected [1], prosperously [1], send prosperity [1], went over [1]

6744 צְלַח ***ṣᵉlaḥ*** (Aram.), v. GK: 10613 [cf. 6743]. [H] to cause to prosper; to promote; to make progress:– prospered [2], promoted [1], prospereth [1]

6745 צַלַּחַת ***ṣallaḥat***, n.[f.]. GK: 7505 [→ 6746, 6747]. dish, pan:– pans [1]

6746 צְלֹחִית ***ṣᵉlōḥît***, n.f. GK: 7504 [→ 6745]. (shallow) bowl; some sources: pan, cruse, dish:– cruse [1]

6747 צֵלָחַת ***ṣēlaḥat***, n.[f.]. GK: 7506 [→ 6745]. pot for cooking:– bosom [2], dish [1]

6748 צָלִי ***ṣālî***, a. GK: 7507 [→ 6740]. roasted (meat):– roast [3]

6749 צָלַל ***ṣālal***, v. GK: 7510 [cf. 6683]. [Q] to sink down:– sank [1]

6750 צָלַל ***ṣālal***, v. GK: 7509 [→ 4698, 4700, 6767]. [Q] to tingle; to quiver:– tingle [3], quivered [1]

6751 צָלַל ***ṣālal***, v. GK: 7511 [→ 1212, 6738, 6741, 6752, 6753, 6757, 6765; cf. 2926; cf. 2927]. [Q] to grow dark; [H] to give shade:– dark [1], shadowing [1]

6752 צֵלֶל ***ṣēlel***, n.m. GK: 7498 [→ 6738]. same as 6738: shadow, shade, protection:– shadows [3], shadow [1]

6753 הַצְלֶלְפּוֹנִי ***haṣṣᵉlelpônî***, n.pr.f. GK: 2209 [→ 1886.1+6751+6440+2967.1]. Hazzelelponi:– Hazelelponi [1]

6754 צֶלֶם ***ṣelem***, n.m. GK: 7512 & 7513 [→ 6756?; cf. 6755]. image (usually referring to an object of worship), idol; phantom, fantasy, shadowy thing:– images [10], image [6], in a vain shew [1]

6755 צְלֵם ***ṣᵉlēm*** (Aram.), n.m. GK: 10614 [cf. 6754]. sculptured image, statue; this can refer to a statue, not necessarily worshiped, or to an idol, which is:– image [15], form [1], image's [1]

6756 צַלְמוֹן ***ṣalmôn***, n.pr.m. & loc. GK: 7514 & 7515 [→ 6754?]. Zalmon, "*in his image, copy*" or "*black hill*":– Zalmon [2], Salmon [1]

6757 צַלְמָוֶת ***ṣalmāwet***, n.[m.]. GK: 7516 [→ 6738+4191]. shadow, darkness, gloom, blackness:– shadow of death [18]

6758 צַלְמֹנָה ***ṣalmōnâ***, n.pr.loc. GK: 7517. Zalmonah, "*dark, gloomy, shaded place*":– Zalmonah [2]

6759 צַלְמֻנָּע ***ṣalmunnā'***, n.pr.m. GK: 7518. Zalmunna, "*protection refused*":– Zalmunna [12]

6760 צָלַע ***ṣāla'***, v. GK: 7519 [→ 6761]. [Q] to be lame, limp:– halted [2], halteth [2]

6761 צֶלַע ***ṣela'***, n.[m.]. GK: 7520 [→ 6760]. stumbling, falling, slipping:– adversity [1], halt [1]

6762 צֵלָע ***ṣēlā'***, n.pr.loc. GK: 7522 [→ 6763]. Zela, Zelah, "*side, slope*":– Zelah [2]

6763 צֵלָע ***ṣēlā'***, n.f. & m. GK: 7521 [→ 6762; cf. 5967]. side:– side [15], side chambers [7], sides [4], boards [2], corners [2], side chamber [2], another[S] [1], beams [1], chambers [1], chamber [1], halting [1], leaves [1], one[S] [1], planks [1], ribs [1], rib [1]

6764 צָלָף ***ṣālāp***, n.pr.m. GK: 7523. Zalaph, "*low, prickly shrub [caper plant]*":– Zalaph [1]

6765 צְלָפְחָד ***ṣᵉlopḥād***, n.pr.m. GK: 7524 [→ 6738+6343]. Zelophehad, "*shadow of dread, terror* i.e., *protection from terror or dread*":– Zelophehad [11]

6766 צֶלְצַח ***ṣelṣaḥ***, n.pr.loc. GK: 7525. Zelzah:– Zelzah [1]

6767 צְלָצַל ***ṣᵉlāṣal*** or צִלְצָל ***ṣilṣāl***, n.m. GK: 7526 & 7527 & 7528 & 7529 [→ 6750]. (swarm of) locust; some sources: cricket; whirring, buzzing; (fishing) spear; cymbals:– cymbals [3], locust [1], shadowing [1], spears [1]

6768 צֶלֶק ***ṣeleq***, n.pr.m. GK: 7530. Zelek, "*cry aloud*":– Zelek [2]

6769 צִלְּתַי ***ṣillᵉtay***, n.pr.m. GK: 7531. Zillethai, "*shadow of Yahweh*":– Zilthai [2]

צֹם ***ṣōm***. See 6685.

6770 צָמֵא ***ṣāmē'***, v. GK: 7532 [→ 6772, 6771, 6773, 6774]. [Q] to thirst, be thirsty:– athirst [2], thirsted [2], thirsteth [2], thirsty [2], suffer thirst [1], thirst [1]

6771 צָמֵא ***ṣāmē'***, a. GK: 7534 [→ 6770]. thirsty, used of humans and animals; used fig. of parched ground:– thirsty [7], thirsteth [1], thirst [1]

6772 צָמָא ***ṣāmā'***, n.[m.]. GK: 7533 [→ 6770]. thirst (of humans and animals); used fig. of parched ground:– thirst [16], thirsty [1]

6773 צִמְאָה ***ṣim'â***, n.f. GK: 7535 [→ 6770]. thirst:– thirst [1]

6774 צִמָּאוֹן ***ṣimmā'ôn***, n.[m.]. GK: 7536 [→ 6770]. thirsty ground:– drought [1], dry ground [1], thirsty land [1]

6775 צָמַד ***ṣāmad***, v. GK: 7537 [→ 6776, 6781]. [N] to be joined together; [Pu] to be strapped on; [H] to harness, attach to:– joined [2], fastened [1], frameth [1], joined unto [1]

6776 צֶמֶד ***ṣemed***, n.m. GK: 7538 [→ 6775]. yoke, team of two, pair; this can refer to a measurement of land, as the acreage a team of animals can plow:– yoke [6], couple [4], two [2], acres [1], together [1], yoke of oxen [1]

6777 צַמָּה ***ṣammâ***, n.f. GK: 7539. veil:– locks [4]

6778 צִמּוּקִים ***ṣimmûqîm***, n.m.[pl.]. GK: 7540 [→ 6784]. raisin cakes:– bunches of raisins [2], clusters of raisins [2]

6779 צָמַח ***ṣāmaḥ***, v. GK: 7541 [→ 6780]. [Q] to sprout up, spring up; [P] to grow; [H] to cause to grow, bring to fruition:– grown [3], spring forth [3], cause to spring forth [2], grew [2], grow [2], spring up [2], beareth [1], bring forth [1], bringeth forth [1], bud [1], cause to bud forth [1], cause to grow up [1], causeth to grow [1], causeth to spring forth [1], grow up [1], groweth [1], grown up [1], made to grow [1], make to bud [1], make to grow [1], maketh to grow [1], sprang up [1], spring out [1], spring [1], sprung up [1]

6780 צֶמַח ***ṣemaḥ***, n.m. GK: 7542 [→ 6779]. growth (which sprouts); (as a messianic title) the Branch:– branch [5], bud [3], grew [1], springing [1], spring [1], that which grew [1]

6781 צָמִיד ***ṣāmîd***, n.m. GK: 7543 & 7544 [→ 6775]. bracelet; lid, cover:– bracelets [6], covering [1]

6782 צַמִּים ***ṣammîm***, n.m. GK: 7545. snare:– robber [2]

6783 צְמִתֻת ***ṣᵉmitut***, n.f. GK: 7552 [→ 6789]. permanence, finality:– ever [2]

6784 צָמַק ***ṣāmaq***, v. GK: 7546 [→ 6778]. [Q] to be dry, shriveled (of breasts):– dry [1]

6785 צֶמֶר ***ṣemer***, n.m. GK: 7547 [→ 6787, 6788; cf. 6015]. wool:– wool [11], woollen [5]

6786 צְמָרִי ***ṣᵉmārî***, a.g. GK: 7548. Zemarite:– Zemarite [2]

6787 צְמָרַיִם ***ṣᵉmārayim***, n.pr.loc. GK: 7549 [→ 6785]. Zemaraim, "[poss.] *double peak*":– Zemaraim [2]

6788 צַמֶּרֶת ***ṣammeret***, n.f. GK: 7550 [→ 6785]. top (of a tree):– top [3], highest branch [2]

6789 צָמַת ***ṣāmat***, v. GK: 7551 [→ 6783]. [Q] to silence; [N] to be silenced; [Pil] to destroy; [P] to wear out; [H] to put to silence, destroy:– cut off [8], destroy [4], consumed [1], destroyed [1], vanish [1]

צְמִתֻת ***ṣᵉmitut***. See 6783.

6790 צִן ***ṣin***, n.pr.loc. GK: 7554. Zin:– Zin [10]

6791 צֵן ***ṣēn***, n.[m.]. GK: 7553 [→ 6793, 6796]. thorn; hook:– thorns [2]

6792 צֹנֶא ***ṣōnā'*** or צֹנֶה ***ṣōneh***, [n.m.]. GK: 7555 & 7556 [→ 6629; cf. 3318]. flocks (of sheep and goats):– sheep [2]

6793 צִנָּה ***ṣinnâ***, n.f. GK: 7557 & 7558 & 7559 [→ 6791]. coolness; (large) shield; hook:– shield [9], buckler [3], targets [3], bucklers [2], target [2], cold [1], hooks [1], shields [1]

6794 צִנּוֹר ***ṣinnôr***, n.m. GK: 7562 [→ 6804]. water shaft; waterfall:– gutter [1], waterspouts [1]

6795 צָנַח ***ṣānaḥ***, v. GK: 7563. [Q] to get down; to go down:– fastened [1], lighted off (+4480+5921) [1], lighted [1]

6796 צְנִינִים ***ṣᵉnînîm***, n.[m.pl.]. GK: 7564 [→ 6791]. thorns:– thorns [2]

6797 צָנוּף ***ṣānûp*** or צָנִיף ***ṣānîp*** or צְנִיפָה ***ṣᵉnîpâ***, n.m. GK: 7561 & 7565 & 7566 [→ 6801]. turban, an ornamental head wrap:– diadem [2], mitre [2], hoods [1]

6798 צָנַם ***ṣānam***, v. GK: 7567 & 7568. [Q] to dry up, harden, wither:– withered [1]

6799 צְנָן ***ṣᵉnān***, n.pr.loc. GK: 7569 [cf. 6630?]. Zenan, "*place of flocks*":– Zenan [1]

צָנִן ***ṣānin***. See 6796.

6800 צָנַע ***ṣāna'***, v. GK: 7570 & 7560 [→ 5204]. [H] to show a humble (walk with God), as an extension of acting in a cautious manner:– humbly [1], lowly [1]

Heb

6801 צָנַף **ṣānap**, v. GK: 7571 [→ 4701, 6797, 6802]. [Q] to wrap around, wind around:– surely violently turn and toss (+6801+6802) [2], attired [1]

6802 צְנֵפָה **ṣᵉnēpâ**, n.f. GK: 7572 [→ 6801]. winding, wrapping:– surely violently turn and toss (+6801+6801) [1]

6803 צִנְצֶנֶת **ṣinṣenet**, n.f. GK: 7573. vessel, receptacle, likely referring to a jar:– pot [1]

6804 צַנְתָּרוֹת **ṣantārôt**, n.m.pl. GK: 7574 [→ 6794]. pipes:– pipes [1]

6805 צָעַד **ṣā'ad**, v. GK: 7575 [→ 685, 4703, 6806, 6807]. [Q] to step, march; [H] to make march:– bring [1], gone paces (+6806) [1], go [1], march through [1], marchedst [1], march [1], run [1], went [1]

6806 צַעַד **ṣa'ad**, n.m. GK: 7576 [→ 6805]. step, stride:– steps [11], goings [1], gone paces (+6805) [1], go [1]

6807 צְעָדָה **ṣᵉ'ādâ**, n.f. GK: 7577 & 7578 [→ 6805]. marching; ankle chains:– going [2], ornaments of the legs [1]

6808 צָעָה **ṣā'â**, v. GK: 7579. [Q] to lay down, stoop, incline; [P] to tip, pour out:– captive exile [1], cause to wander [1], travelling [1], wanderers [1], wanderest [1]

צָעוֹר **ṣā'ôr**. See 6810.

6809 צָעִיף **ṣā'îp**, n.[m.]. GK: 7581. veil:– vail [3]

6810 צָעִיר **ṣā'îr**, a. GK: 7582 [→ 6819; cf. 6812]. younger, small, little, lowly:– younger [7], least [4], youngest [3], little ones [2], little [2], small one [1], small [1], young (+3117+3807.1) [1], younger (+3117) [1]

6811 צָעִיר **ṣā'îr**, n.pr.loc. GK: 7583. Zair, "*small, insignificant,* hence *narrow pass*":– Zair [1]

6812 צְעִירָה **ṣᵉ'îrâ**, n.f. GK: 7584 [cf. 6810]. youth, youngest (offspring):– youth [1]

6813 צָעַן **ṣā'an**, v. GK: 7585. [Q] to pack up, move (a tent):– taken down [1]

6814 צֹעַן **ṣō'an**, n.pr.loc. GK: 7586. Zoan:– Zoan [7]

6815 צַעֲנַנִּים **ṣa'ᵃnannîm**, n.pr.loc. GK: 7588. Zaanannim:– Zaanaim [1], Zaanannim [1]

6816 צַעֲצֻעִים **ṣa'ᵃṣu'îm**, n.[m.]pl. GK: 7589. sculptured work (by metal casting):– image [1]

6817 צָעַק **ṣā'aq**, v. GK: 7590 [→ 6818; cf. 2199; cf. 2200]. [Q] to cry; [N] to be called out, be summoned; [P] to keep crying; [H] to call together, summon:– cried [27], cry [13], gathered together [3], called together [2], cried out [2], crieth [2], cry at all (+6817) [2], criest [1], cry out [1], gathered themselves together [1], gathered [1]

6818 צְעָקָה **ṣᵉ'āqâ**, n.f. GK: 7591 [→ 6817]. cry of distress, outcry, wailing:– cry [19], crying [2]

6819 צָעַר **ṣā'ar**, v. GK: 7592 [→ 4704, 4705, 4706, 6686, 6730, 6810, 6820; cf. 2191]. [Q] to be trivial, insignificant, little:– brought low [1], little ones [1], small [1]

6820 צֹעַר **ṣō'ar**, n.pr.loc. GK: 7593 [→ 6819]. Zoar, "*small, insignificant*":– Zoar [10]

6821 צָפַד **ṣāpad**, v. GK: 7594. [Q] to shrivel:– cleaveth [1]

6822 צָפָה **ṣāpâ**, v. GK: 7595 [→ 4707, 4708, 4709, 6828, 6829, 6830, 6836, 6837?]. [Q] to keep watch, be a lookout; [Qp] to be spied out; [P] to watch, lookout:– watchman [14], watchmen [5], watch [4], beholding [1], behold [1], espy [1], kept watch [1], look up [1], looketh well [1], looketh [1], look [1], waited [1], watched [1], watcheth [1], watching [1], watchman's [1]

6823 צָפָה **ṣāpâ**, v. GK: 7596 [→ 6826, 6844, 6858, 6857?]. [Q] to arrange; [P] to overlay, cover, adorn; [Pu] to be overlaid, be coated:– overlaid [28], overlay [12], covered [5], garnished [1]

6824 צָפָה **ṣāpâ**, n.f. GK: 7597 [→ 6687?]. out-flow, discharge:– swimmest [1]

6825 צְפוֹ **ṣᵉpô** or צְפִי **ṣᵉpî**, n.pr.m. GK: 7598 & 7609. Zepho, Zephi, "[poss.] *gaze*":– Zepho [2], Zephi [1]

6826 צִפּוּי **ṣippûy**, n.[m.]. GK: 7599 [→ 6823]. overlaying, (metal) plating:– covering [3], overlaying [2]

6827 צְפוֹן **ṣᵉpôn**, n.pr.m. GK: 7602 [→ 6831; cf. 6837]. Zephon, "[poss.] *gaze;* [poss.] *look out [tower], watch*":– Zephon [1]

6828 צָפוֹן **ṣāpôn**, n.f. GK: 7600 [→ 1189, 6829, 6830; cf. 6822]. north, northern:– north [105], northward (+1886.5) [20], north side [10], north (+1886.5) [9], northward (+4480) [2], in north (+1886.5) [1], north side (+1886.5) [1], north side (+4480) [1], north wind [1], northern (+4480) [1], northwards (+1886.5) [1], northward [1]

6829 צָפוֹן **ṣāpôn**, n.pr.loc. GK: 7601 [→ 6828; cf. 6822]. Zaphon, "[poss.] *North* or *[proper name of a god], Zephon*":– Zaphon [1]

6830 צְפוֹנִי **ṣᵉpônî**, a. GK: 7603 [→ 6828; cf. 6822]. northern; (n.) northerner:– northern [1]

6831 צְפוֹנִי **ṣᵉpônî** or צִפְיוֹנִי **ṣipyônî**, a.g. GK: 7604 & 7612 [→ 6827, 6837]. Zephonite, "*of Zephon*":– Zephonites [1]

6832 צְפוּעַ **ṣāpûa'** or צָפִיעַ **ṣāpîa'**, n.[m.]. GK: 7605 & 7616. manure, dung:– dung [1]

6833 צִפּוֹר **ṣippôr**, n.f. & m. GK: 7606 [→ 6691?, 6834, 6855]. bird (individual and collective):– bird [21], birds [10], fowl [5], sparrow [2], bird's [1], fowls [1]

6834 צִפּוֹר **ṣippôr**, n.pr.m. GK: 7607 [→ 6833; cf. 6853]. Zippor, "*bird, swallow*":– Zippor [7]

6835 צַפַּחַת **ṣappaḥat**, n.f. GK: 7608 [→ 6838]. jug, jar (for liquid), a portable convex or spherical shape, with a lid or plug for transport:– cruse [7]

6836 צְפִיָּה **ṣippiyyâ**, n.f. GK: 7610 [→ 6822]. watchtower, lookout:– watching [1]

6837 צִפְיוֹן **ṣipyôn**, n.pr.m. GK: 7611 [→ 6831; cf. 6822?, 6827]. Ziphion, cf. 6829:– Ziphion [1]

6838 צַפִּיחִת **ṣappîḥit**, n.f. GK: 7613 [→ 6690, 6835]. wafer, flat-cake:– wafers [1]

6839 צֹפִים **ṣōpîm**, n.pr.[loc.?]. GK: 7614. Zophim:– Zophim [1]

6840 צָפִין **ṣāpîn**, n.[m.]. GK: 7615 [→ 6845]. hidden thing:– @H = **6841** צְפִיר **ᶻpîr** (Aram.), n.m. GK: 10615 [cf. 6842]. male goat:– he goats (+5796) [1]

6842 צָפִיר **ṣāpîr**, n.m. GK: 7618 [cf. 6841]. (male) goat:– goat [2], he goat (+5795) [2], he goats (+5795) [1], he goats [1]

6843 צְפִירָה **ṣᵉpîrâ**, n.f. GK: 7619. crown, wreath; doom:– morning [2], diadem [1]

6844 צָפִית **ṣāpît**, n.f. GK: 7620 [→ 6823]. rug, carpet:– watchtower [1]

6845 צָפַן **ṣāpan**, v. GK: 7621 & 7636 [→ 4710, 6840; cf. 6693 (also used with compound proper names)]. [Q] to hide, conceal, store up; [Qp] to be treasured, be cherished; [N] to be stored up, be concealed; [H] to hide:– hid [8], hide [5], laid up [3], hidden [2], hideth [2], lay up [2], layeth up [2], lurk privily [2], esteemed [1], hidden ones [1], keep secretly [1], privily set [1], secret places [1], secret [1]

צָפֹן **ṣāpōn**. See 6828.

6846 צְפַנְיָה **ṣᵉpanyâ** or צְפַנְיָהוּ **ṣᵉpanyāhû**, n.pr.m. GK: 7622 & 7623 [→ 6845+3068]. Zephaniah, "*Yahweh has hidden [to shelter]* or *Yahweh has hidden [as a treasure]*":– Zephaniah [10]

6847 צָפְנַת פַּעְנֵחַ **ṣāpᵉnat pa'nēaḥ**, n.pr.m. GK: 7624. Zaphenath-Paneah, "*the [pagan] god speaks and he [the newborn] lives*":– Zaphnath-paaneah [1]

6848 צֶפַע **ṣepa'** or צִפְעֹנִי **ṣip'ōnî**, n.m. GK: 7625 & 7626. viper, serpent:– cockatrice' [2], adder [1], cockatrices [1], cockatrice [1]

6849 צְפִיעָה **ṣᵉpî'â**, n.f. GK: 7617. offshoots, leaf:– issue [1]

צִפְעֹנִי **ṣip'ōnî**. See 6848.

6850 צָפַף **ṣāpap**, v. GK: 7627 [→ 6851]. [Pil] to chirp; to whisper:– chatter [1], peeped [1], peep [1], whisper [1]

6851 צַפְצָפָה **ṣapṣāpâ**, n.f. GK: 7628 [→ 6850]. willow:– willow tree [1]

6852 צָפַר **ṣāpar**, v. GK: 7629. [Q] to leave, depart:– depart early [1]

6853 צְפַר **ṣippar** (Aram.), n.f. GK: 10616 [cf. 6834]. bird:– fowls [3], birds' [1]

צִפֹּר **ṣippōr**. See 6833.

6854 צְפַרְדֵּעַ **ṣᵉpardea'**, n.f. GK: 7630. frogs:– frogs [13]

6855 צִפֹּרָה **ṣippōrâ**, n.pr.f. GK: 7631 [→ 6833]. Zipporah, "*bird, swallow*":– Zipporah [3]

6856 צִפֹּרֶן **ṣippōren**, n.[m.]. GK: 7632 [cf. 2953]. nail (of finger or toe); (flint or hard stone) point (of a stylus):– nails [1], point [1]

6857 צְפַת **ṣᵉpat**, n.pr.loc. GK: 7634 [→ 6823?]. Zephath, "*watcher*":– Zephath [1]

6858 צֶפֶת **ṣepet**, n.f. GK: 7633 [→ 6823]. capital (of a pillar):– chapiter [1]

6859 צְפָתָה **ṣᵉpatâ**, n.pr.loc. GK: 7635. Zephathah, "*watchtower*":– Zephathah [1]

צִץ **ṣiṣ**. See 6732.

6860 צִקְלַג **ṣiqlag**, n.pr.loc. GK: 7637. Ziklag:– Ziklag [15]

6861 צִקְלוֹן **ṣiqqālôn** or בִּצְקָלוֹן **biṣqālôn**, n.[m.]. GK: 7638 & 1303. head of grain; garment, bag:– husk [1]

6862 צַר **ṣar**, a. & n.m. GK: 7639 & 7640 & 7641 [→ 3334, 6864, 6887; cf. 6146]. (n.) trouble, distress, anguish; (a.) narrow; enemy, foe, adversary, opponent; flint, known for its hardness:– enemies [26], adversaries [21], trouble [17], enemy [10], adversary [5], distress [4], affliction [3], strait [3], enemy's [2], foes [2], narrow [2], adversary (+376) [1], adversity [1], afflicted [1], anguish [1], close [1], distresses [1], small [1], sorrow [1], tribulation [1]

6863 צֵר **ṣēr**, n.pr.loc. GK: 7643. Zer:– Zer [1]

6864 צֹר **ṣōr**, n.[m.]. GK: 7644 [→ 6697, 6862, 6865, 6872, 6876]. flint knife:– flint [2], sharp stone [1]

6865 צֹר **ṣōr** or צוֹר **ṣôr**, n.pr.loc. GK: 7645 & 7450 [→ 6876; cf. 6864]. Tyre, "*rocky place*":– Tyrus [22], Tyre [20]

צֻר **ṣur**. See 6697.

6866 צָרַב **ṣārab**, v. GK: 7646 [→ 6867]. [N] to be scorched:– burnt [1]

6867 צָרָב **ṣārāb** or צָרֶבֶת **ṣārebet**, a. & n.f. GK: 7647 & 7648 [→ 6866]. scorching; scar:– burning [2], inflammation [1]

6868 צְרֵדָה **ṣᵉrēdâ**, n.pr.loc. GK: 7649. Zeredah:– Zeredathah [1], Zereda [1]

6869 צָרָה **ṣārâ**, n.f. GK: 7650 & 7651 [→ 6862, 6887; cf. 3334]. trouble, distress, calamity, anguish; rival wife:– trouble [34], troubles [10], distress [8], affliction [7], anguish [5], adversity [4], tribulation [2], adversary [1], adversities [1], tribulations [1]

6870 צְרוּיָה **ṣᵉrûyâ**, n.pr.f. GK: 7653. Zeruiah, "*perfumed resin*":– Zeruiah [26]

6871 צְרוּעָה **ṣᵉrû'â**, n.pr.loc. GK: 7654 [→ 6879]. Zeruah, "*one with skin disease*":– Zeruah [1]

6872 צְרוֹר **ṣᵉrôr**, n.m. & pr. GK: 7655 & 7656 & 7657 [cf. 3334, 6864]. pouch, purse, sachet, bag; pebble; as n.pr. Zeror, "*money bag, pouch,* [or poss.] *pebbles*":– bag [3], bundle [3], Zeror [1], bindeth [1], bundles [1], least grain [1], small stone [1]

6873 צָרַח **ṣāraḥ**, v. GK: 7658. [Q] to shout, cry out; [H] to raise the battle cry:– cry [1], roar [1]

6874 צְרִי **ṣᵉrî**, n.pr.m. GK: 7662 [→ 6875]. Zeri, "*balsam*":– Zeri [1]

6875 צְרִי **ṣᵒrî**, n.[m.]. GK: 7661 [→ 6874]. balm, mastic (resin), usually obtained from processing from the bark of a tree:– balm [6]

6876 צֹרִי **ṣōrî**, a.g. GK: 7660 [→ 6865]. Tyrian, of Tyre:– Tyre [2], of Tyre [2], men of Tyre [1]

6877 צְרִיחַ **ṣᵉrîaḥ**, n.[m.]. GK: 7663. pit, (underground) stronghold, likely referring to a man-made pit:– hold [3], high places [1]

6878 צֹרֶךְ **ṣōrek**, n.[m.]. GK: 7664. need:– need [1]

6879 צָרַע **ṣāra'**, v.den. GK: 7665 [→ 6871, 6879?, 6883]. [Qp, Pu] to be leprous, afflicted with an infectious skin disease:– leper [13], leprous [6], lepers [1]

6880 צִרְעָה **ṣir'â**, n.f.col. GK: 7667 [→ 6879?]. hornets or discouragement:– hornet [2], hornets [1]

6881 צָרְעָה **ṣor'â**, n.pr.loc. GK: 7666 [→ 6882]. Zorah:– Zorah [8], Zareah [1], Zoreah [1]

6882 צָרְעִי **ṣor'î** or צָרְעָתִי **ṣārᵉ'ātî**, a.g. GK: 7668 & 7670 [→ 6881]. Zorite; Zorathite, "*of Zorah*":– Zareathites [1], Zorathites [1], Zorites [1]

6883 צָרַעַת **ṣāra'at**, n.f. GK: 7669 [→ 6879]. infectious skin disease; (of clothing) mildew:– leprosy [35]

6884 צָרַף **ṣārap**, v. GK: 7671 [→ 4715, 6885]. [Q] to smelt, refine (metals); (n.) (gold- or silver-)smith:– tried [8], founder [5], goldsmith [3], try [3], goldsmiths [2], pure [2], refined [2], casteth [1], finer [1], melteth [1], melt [1], purge away [1], refiner's [1], refiner [1], refine [1]

6885 צֹרְפִי **ṣōrᵉpî**, n.[m.]col. GK: 7672 [→ 6884]. (member of the) goldsmiths:– goldsmith's [1]

6886 צָרְפַת ***ṣārᵉpat***, n.pr.loc. GK: 7673. Zarephath, "[poss.] *smelting place; place of pigmenting, staining*":– Zarephath [3]

6887 צָרַר ***ṣārar***, v. GK: 7674 & 7675 & 7677 [→ 3334, 6862, 6869]. [Q] to be a rival-wife; to be an enemy, adversary; to bind up, wrap up, tie up; to hamper, oppress, be in distress; [Qp] be bound, be confined; [Pu] to be mended; [H] to bring trouble, distress, oppress:– enemies [9], enemy [5], vex [5], besiege [4], bound up [4], adversaries [3], distress [3], afflicted [2], afflict [2], bound [2], distressed [2], in a strait [2], in pangs [2], affliction [1], bind up [1], bindeth up [1], bring distress [1], in distress [1], in trouble [1], narrower [1], oppresseth [1], shut up [1], strait [1], trouble [1], vexed [1]

6888 צְרֵרָה ***ṣᵉrērâ***, n.p.loc. GK: 7678. Zererah:– Zererath [1]

6889 צֶרֶת ***ṣeret***, n.pr.m. GK: 7679 [→ 6890]. Zereth, "*splendor*":– Zereth [1]

6890 צֶרֶת הַשַּׁחַר ***ṣeret haššaḥar***, n.pr.loc. GK: 7680 [→ 6889]. Zereth Shahar, "*glory of dawn*":– Zareth-shahar [1]

6891 צָרְתָן ***ṣārᵉtān***, n.pr.loc. GK: 7681. Zarethan:– Zaretan [1], Zartanah [1], Zarthan [1]

6892 קֵא ***qē'*** or קִיא ***qî'***, n.m. GK: 7683 & 7795 [→ 6958]. vomit:– vomit [4]

6893 קָאַת ***qā'at***, n.[f.]. GK: 7684. desert owl:– pelican [3], cormorant [2]

6894 קַב ***qab***, n.[m.]. GK: 7685 [→ 6898]. cab (dry measure, one-eighteenth of an ephah, about one quart or liter):– kab [1]

6895 קָבַב ***qābab***, v. GK: 7686 [cf. 5344]. [Q] to curse:– curse [6], cursed [1]

6896 קֵבָה ***qēbâ***, n.f. GK: 7687 [→ 6897]. same as 6897: maw (4th stomach of cud-chewing animals); (of humans) belly, stomach area:– maw [1]

6897 קֹבָה ***qōbâ***, n.f. GK: 7687 [→ 6896]. same as 6896: maw (4th stomach of cud-chewing animals); (of humans) belly, stomach area:– belly [1]

6898 קֻבָּה ***qubbâ***, n.f. GK: 7688 [→ 6894]. woman's section (of a tent):– tent [1]

6899 קִבּוּץ ***qibbûṣ***, n.m. GK: 7689 [→ 6908]. collection (of idols):– companies [1]

6900 קְבוּרָה ***qᵉbûrâ***, n.f. GK: 7690 [→ 5354, 6912, 6962]. tomb, grave, burial:– sepulchre [5], burial [4], grave [4], buryingplace [1]

6901 קָבַל ***qābal***, v. GK: 7691 [→ 6904; cf. 6902]. [P] to receive, take; [H] to match, correspond:– received [3], receive [3], took [3], choose [1], held [1], take hold [1], undertook [1]

6902 קְבַל ***qᵉbal*** (Aram.), v.den. GK: 10618 [→ 6903; cf. 6901]. [Pa] to receive; to take over:– receive [1], take [1], took [1]

6903 קֳבֵל ***qᵒbēl*** (Aram.), subst. & pp. & c. GK: 10619 [→ 6902]. before, in front of; since, because of:– forasmuch as (+1768+3606) [8], because (+1768+3606) [4], before (+3807.2) [3], therefore (+1836+3606) [3], wherefore (+1836+3606) [2], according to (+3807.2) [1], against [1], as (+1768+3606) [1], for this cause (+1836+3606) [1], means [1], reason [1], that (+1836+3606) [1], therefore (+1768+3606) [1], though (+1768+3606) [1]

6904 קְבֹל ***qᵉbōl***, n.[m.]. GK: 7692 [→ 6901, 6905]. prob. same as 6905: (something) in front of, battering ram:– war [1]

6905 קְבֹל ***qᵉbōl***, n.[m.]. GK: 7692 [→ 6904]. prob. same as 6904: (something) in front of, battering ram:– before [1]

6906 קָבַע ***qāba'***, v. GK: 7693 [cf. 6117, 6120]. [Q] to rob, plunder:– robbed [3], rob [1], spoiled [1], spoil [1]

6907 קֻבַּעַת ***qubba'at***, n.f. GK: 7694. cup, goblet:– dregs [2]

6908 קָבַץ ***qābaṣ***, v. GK: 7695 [→ 6899, 6910, 6911 (also used with compound proper names)]. [Q] to collect, gather, assemble; [Qp] to be assembled; [N] to be gathered, be assembled, be joined; [P] to gather, assemble; [Pu] to be gathered; [Ht] to gather (themselves) together:– gather [43], gathered together [33], gathered [22], gather together [10], assemble [5], gathereth [4], gather up [2], surely gather (+6908) [2], assembled [1], brought together [1], gathered up [1], heapeth [1], resort [1], taketh up [1]

6909 קַבְצְאֵל ***qabṣᵉ'ēl***, n.pr.loc. GK: 7696 [→ 6908+410]. Kabzeel, "*God [El] collects*":– Kabzeel [3]

6910 קְבֻצָה ***qᵉbuṣâ***, n.f. GK: 7697 [→ 6908]. gathering:– gather [1]

6911 קִבְצַיִם ***qibṣayim***, n.pr.loc. GK: 7698 [→ 6908]. Kibzaim:– Kibzaim [1]

6912 קָבַר ***qābar***, v. GK: 7699 [→ 6900, 6913, 6914]. [Q] to store up, pile up, heap up:– buried [96], bury [32], burying [2], in any wise bury (+6912) [2], buriers [1]

6913 קֶבֶר ***qeber***, n.m. GK: 7700 [→ 6914]. burial site, tomb, grave:– grave [19], graves [16], sepulchre [14], sepulchres [12], buryingplace [6]

קְבֻרָה ***qᵉburâ***. See 6900.

6914 קִבְרוֹת הַתַּאֲוָה ***qibrôt hatta'ᵃwâ***, n.pr.loc. GK: 7701 [→ 6913]. Kibroth Hattaavah, "*graves of lust, greed*":– Kibroth-hattaavah [5]

6915 קָדַד ***qādad***, v. GK: 7702 [→ 6936?]. [Q] to bow low, bow down:– bowed down head [3], bowed heads [3], bowed down heads [2], bowed head [2], bowed [2], stooped [2], bowed the head [1]

6916 קִדָּה ***qiddâ***, n.f. GK: 7703. cassia (a spice):– cassia [2]

6917 קְדוּמִים ***qᵉdûmîm***, n.[m.pl.]. GK: 7704 [→ 6923]. age-old, ancient:– ancient [1]

6918 קָדוֹשׁ ***qādôš***, a. GK: 7705 [→ 6942; cf. 6922]. holy, sacred, consecrated, set apart as dedicated to God; by extension: pure, innocent, free from impurity; (n.) holy people of God, saints; as a title of God, "the Holy One" focuses on God as unique, wholly other:– holy [63], holy one [41], saints [9], saint [3]

6919 קָדַח ***qādaḥ***, v. GK: 7706 [→ 688, 6920]. [Q] to kindle, light (a fire):– kindled [3], burneth [1], kindle [1]

6920 קַדַּחַת ***qaddaḥat***, n.f. GK: 7707 [→ 6919]. fever, inflammation:– burning ague [1], fever [1]

6921 קָדִים ***qādîm***, n.m. GK: 7708 [→ 6923]. east, eastern, the direction of orientation in the ancient Near East (facing the sunrise); east is also the direction of the great desert, thus an east or desert wind is particularly hot:– east [36], east (+1886.5) [14], east wind [10], eastward (+1886.5) [4], eastward [3], east side [1], eastward (+1870+1886.1) [1]

6922 קַדִּישׁ ***qaddîš*** (Aram.), a. GK: 10620 [cf. 6918]. holy, ceremonial or moral purity; (as noun) holy one, saint, which can refer to human beings or angels:– saints [6], holy [4], holy one [2], holy ones [1]

6923 קָדַם ***qādam***, v.den. GK: 7709 [→ 6917, 6921, 6924, 6927, 6926, 6929, 6930, 6932, 6934, 6931, 6935; cf. 6925, cf. 6933]. [P] to be in front of, meet, confront:– prevented [8], prevent [6], come before [5], met [2], before [1], disappoint (+6440) [1], go before [1], preventest [1], went before [1]

6924 קֶדֶם ***qedem*** or קֵדְמָה ***qēdᵉmâ***, n.[m.]. GK: 7710 & 7711 & 7714 [→ 6923]. (as a direction) east, eastern; the direction of orientation in the ancient Near East (facing the sunrise); (used of time) ancient, eternal, long ago, possibly relating to east as the direction of origin (as the sunrise):– east [27], eastward (+1886.5) [9], old [9], of old [8], ancient [6], east (+1886.5) [5], east side [5], before [2], aforetime [1], ancient times [1], ancient time [1], before (+4480) [1], east (+4217+1886.5) [1], east country [1], east end [1], east parts [1], east part [1], eastward (+4480) [1], eastward [1], eternal [1], everlasting [1], forward [1], or ever was (+4480) [1], past [1]

6925 קֳדָם ***qᵒdām*** (Aram.), pp. GK: 10621 [→ 6928, 6933; cf. 6924]. before, in the presence of:– before [29], before (+4481) [4], of (+4481) [3], from (+4481) [1], in the presence [1], then (+116+4481+871.2) [1], thought [1]

קָדִם ***qādim***. See 6921.

6926 קִדְמָה ***qidmâ***, n.f. GK: 7713 [→ 6923]. east:– east [2], eastward [1], toward east [1]

6927 קַדְמָה ***qadmâ***, n.f. GK: 7712 [→ 6923; cf. 6928]. past, antiquity; ancient (city):– former estate [3], afore [1], antiquity [1], old estates [1]

6928 קַדְמָה ***qadmâ*** (Aram.), n.f. GK: 10622 [→ 6925; cf. 6927]. before times; (as adv.) formerly:– aforetime (+1836+4481) [1], ago (+4481) [1]

קֵדְמָה ***qēdmâ***. See 6924.

6929 קֵדְמָה ***qēdᵉmâ***, n.pr.m. GK: 7715 [→ 6923]. Kedemah, "*east*":– Kedemah [2]

6930 קַדְמוֹן ***qadmôn***, a. GK: 7716 [→ 6931, 6935; cf. 6923]. eastern:– east [1]

6931 קַדְמֹנִי ***qadmōnî***, a. GK: 7719 [→ 6930; cf. 6923]. (of a direction) eastern; (of time) old, former, past:– east [4], former [2], ancients [1], of old [1], old [1], they that went before [1]

6932 קְדֵמוֹת ***qᵉdēmôt***, n.pr.loc. GK: 7717 [→ 6923]. Kedemoth, "*east*":– Kedemoth [4]

6933 קַדְמָי ***qadmāy*** (Aram.), a. GK: 10623 [→ 6925; cf. 6924]. first; earlier, former:– first [3]

6934 קַדְמִיאֵל ***qadmî'ēl***, n.pr.m. GK: 7718 [→ 6923+410]. Kadmiel, "*[stand] before God [El]*":– Kadmiel [8]

קַדְמֹנִי ***qadmōnî***. See 6931.

6935 קַדְמֹנִי ***qadmōnî***, a.g. GK: 7720 [→ 6930; cf. 6923]. Kadmonite:– Kadmonites [1]

6936 קָדְקֹד ***qodqōd***, n.[m.]. GK: 7721 [→ 6915?]. top or crown of the head:– crown of the head [4], crown of head [2], crown [1], pate [1], scalp [1], top of head [1], top of the head [1]

6937 קָדַר ***qādar***, v. GK: 7722 [→ 6938, 6939, 6940, 6941]. [Q] to grow dark, be black; to mourn, wail, grieve; [H] to make dark, bring gloom; [Ht] to grow dark:– black [4], mourning [4], dark [2], make dark [2], blackish [1], caused to mourn [1], darkened [1], heavily [1], mourn [1]

6938 קֵדָר ***qēdār***, n.pr.g. GK: 7723 [→ 6937]. Kedar, "*mighty*":– Kedar [12]

6939 קִדְרוֹן ***qidrôn***, n.pr.loc. GK: 7724 [→ 6937]. Kidron:– Kidron [11]

6940 קַדְרוּת ***qadrût***, n.f. GK: 7725 [→ 6937]. darkness, blackness:– blackness [1]

6941 קְדֹרַנִּית ***qᵉdōrannît***, adv. GK: 7726 [→ 6937]. in mourner's attire, in an unkempt manner:– mournfully [1]

6942 קָדַשׁ ***qādaš***, v.den. GK: 7727 [→ 4720, 6918, 6943, 6944, 6945, 6946, 6947, 6948]. [Q] to be holy, sacred, consecrated; [N] to show oneself holy, be consecrated; [P] to consecrate, make holy; [Pu] to be dedicated, consecrated; [Ht] to consecrate oneself; [H] to set apart, consecrate, dedicate, regard as holy; to set apart as dedicated to God; by extension: pure, innocent, free from impurity:– sanctify [64], sanctified [45], hallow [15], hallowed [10], prepare [7], dedicated [5], holy [5], dedicate [4], consecrated [3], consecrate [2], wholly dedicated (+6942) [2], appointed [1], bid [1], defiled [1], holier [1], holy kept [1], holy places [1], keep holy [1], proclaim [1], purified [1], sanctified ones [1]

6943 קֶדֶשׁ ***qedeš***, n.pr.loc. GK: 7730 [→ 6942]. Kedesh, "*sacred place*":– Kedesh [11], Kedesh-naphtali (+5321) [1]

6944 קֹדֶשׁ ***qōdeš***, n.m. GK: 7731 [→ 6942]. holy or sacred thing, holy or sacred place, sanctuary; holiness, set apart as dedicated to God; the "holy of holies" is the most holy place, set apart exclusively for the Presence of God, with very limited high priestly access:– holy [256], most holy (+6944) [88], sanctuary [68], holiness [30], hallowed [9], dedicated [7], dedicate [5], consecrated [2], thing most holy (+6944) [2], holy dwelling [1], saints [1]

6945 קָדֵשׁ ***qādēš***, n.m. GK: 7728 [→ 6942, 6948]. (male or female) shrine prostitute:– sodomites [4], unclean [1], whore [1]

6946 קָדֵשׁ ***qādēš***, n.pr.loc. GK: 7729 [→ 4809+6946; cf. 6942]. Kadesh, "*sacred place*":– Kadesh [17]

קָדֹשׁ ***qādōš***. See 6918.

6947 קָדֵשׁ בַּרְנֵעַ ***qādēš barnēa'***, n.pr.loc. GK: 7732 [→ 6942]. Kadesh Barnea, "*sacred place of Barnea*":– Kadesh-barnea [10]

6948 קְדֵשָׁה ***qᵉdēšâ***, n.m. GK: 7728 [→ 6945]. f. of 6945: female shrine prostitute:– harlot [3], harlots [1], sodomite [1]

6949 קָהָה ***qāhâ***, v. GK: 7733. [Q] to be dull, blunt (of teeth); [P] to be dull:– set on edge [3], blunt [1]

6950 קָהַל ***qāhal***, v.den. GK: 7735 [→ 6951]. [N] to be gathered, be assembled; [H] to summon, call together, cause to assemble:– gathered together [15], assembled [8], gather together [7], gathered [5], assembled together [3], gather [1]

6951 קָהָל ***qāhāl***, n.m. GK: 7736 [→ 4721, 4722, 6950, 6951, 6952, 6953, 6954, 7035; cf. 6963]. assembly, community, often of Israel assembled for religious ceremony:– congregation [86], assembly [17], company [16], multitude [3], companies [1]

6952 קְהִלָּה ***qᵉhillâ***, n.f. GK: 7737 [→ 6951]. assembly, meeting:– assembly [1], congregation [1]

6953 קֹהֶלֶת ***qōhelet***, n.m. GK: 7738 [→ 6951]. (as a title or name) the Teacher, one who calls together and instructs the assembly:– preacher [7]

6954 קְהֵלָתָה ***qᵉhēlātâ***, n.pr.loc. GK: 7739 [→ 6951]. Kehelathah, "*assembly*":– Kehelathah [2]

6955 קְהָת ***qᵉhāt***, n.pr.m. GK: 7740 [→ 6956]. Kohath, Kohathite:– Kohath [32]

6956 קְהָתִי ***qᵉhātî***, a.g. GK: 7741 [→ 6955]. Kohathite, "*of Kohath*":– Kohathites [15]

6957 קָו ***qāw***, n.m. GK: 7742 & 7744 [→ 6960?, 6978; cf. 6961]. measuring line, ruler; qav (a mocking sound, like blah-blah):– line [20], rule [1]

6958 קִיא ***qîʾ***, v. GK: 7794 [→ 6892, 7006]. same as 7006: [Q] to vomit; [H] to vomit out, spit out:– spue out [2], vomit up [2], spued out [1], vomited out [1], vomiteth out [1], vomit [1]

6959 קוֹבַע ***qôbaʿ***, n.[m.]. GK: 7746 [cf. 3553]. helmet:– helmet [2]

6960 קָוָה ***qāwâ***, v. GK: 7747 & 7748 [→ 4723, 4724, 6957?, 8615, 8616]. [Q] to hope in; [N] to be gathered; [P] to hope for, wait for, look for:– wait [13], looked [8], waited [6], look [4], wait for [4], wait on [4], wait upon [2], waited patiently for (+6960) [2], gathered together [1], gathered [1], looked for [1], looketh [1], tarrieth [1], waited for [1]

6961 קָוֶה ***qāweh***, n.m. GK: 7749 [cf. 6957]. measuring line, ruler:– @HREF = קוֹה ***qôa±***. See 6495.

6962 קוּט ***qûṭ***, v. GK: 7752 & 7753 [→ 5354, 6900, 6990]. [Q] to feel anger, loathing; to be fragile; [N] to feel loathing; [Htpolal] to loathe, abhor:– grieved [3], lothe [3]

6963 קוֹל ***qôl*** or קֹל ***qōl***, n.m. GK: 7754 & 7825 & 7826 [→ 6964?, 7043; cf. 6951; cf. 7032]. sound, voice, noise; lightness, (i.e., frivolity or light-heartedness):– voice [381], noise [49], sound [39], thunder [7], thunders [3], made a proclamation (+5674) [2], thunderings [2], voices [2], aloud (+1419+871.1) [1], bleating [1], caused to be proclaimed (+5674) [1], crackling [1], crieth out (+5414+871.1) [1], cry (+5414) [1], cry [1], fame [1], held peace (+2244) [1], lightness [1], loud (+1419+871.1) [1], lowing [1], made proclamation (+5674) [1], make proclamation (+5674) [1], proclaim (+5674) [1], proclamation [1], shouted aloud (+7311+8643+871.1+3807.1) [1], sing (+5414) [1], speaketh [1], wept aloud (+1065+5414+871.1) [1], yelled (+5414) [1]

6964 קוֹלָיָה ***qôlāyâ***, n.pr.m. GK: 7755 [→ 6963?]. Kolaiah, "*Yahweh's voice*":– Kolaiah [2]

6965 קוּם ***qûm***, v. GK: 7756 [→ 3351, 3356, 4725, 6967, 6968, 7009, 7012, 7054, 8617, 8618; cf. 6966 (also used with compound proper names)]. [Q] to get up, arise, stand, establish; [P] to establish, confirm, restore; [Pol] to raise up; [H] to set up, establish, restore; [Ho] to be set up, be raised up; [Htpol] to raise up against:– arise [103], arose [101], rose up [62], rise up [45], rise [28], raise up [26], stand [25], set up [23], establish [17], stood up [15], perform [13], performed [11], risen up [11], up [10], raised up [9], reared up [9], rose [8], established [7], riseth up [6], risen [5], confirm [4], raise [4], set [4], stand up [4], arose up [3], confirmeth [3], continue [3], riseth [3], stablish [3], stirred up [3], ariseth [2], confirmed [2], lift up [2], made sure [2], newly set (+6965) [2], raiseth up [2], rear up [2], risest up [2], rose up against [2], stablished [2], surely accomplish (+6965) [2], surely lift up again (+6965) [2], surely stand (+6965) [2], abide [1], arise up [1], arising [1], assured [1], cleared [1], decreed [1], dim [1], endure [1], enemies [1], enjoined (+5921) [1], establisheth [1], get up [1], help up [1], hold [1], made to stand [1], make arise up [1], make good [1], maketh [1], ordained [1], performeth [1], pitch [1], raised [1], rear [1], remain [1], rise again [1], rise up again [1], rising up [1], rising [1], rouse up [1], stir up [1], strengthen [1], succeed [1], upholden [1], uprising [1]

6966 קוּם ***qûm*** (Aram.), v. GK: 10624 [→ 7010?, 7011; cf. 6965]. [P] to stand, rise up; [Pa] to issue (a decree); [H, A] to set up, establish; [Ho] to be set up, be established; from the base meaning of "standing up" (in contrast to sitting or lying) comes fig. extension of causing something to be or come into existence, implying a lively, active state:– set up [10], arise [4], stood [4], set [3], establish [2], rose up [2], setteth up [2], appointeth [1], arose [1], establisheth [1], made stand [1], made [1], raised up [1], rise [1], stand [1]

6967 קוֹמָה ***qômâ***, n.f. GK: 7757 [→ 6965]. height:– height [30], stature [7], high [5], tall [2], all along (+4393) [1]

6968 קוֹמְמִיּוּת ***qômᵉmiyyût***, n.f. GK: 7758 [→ 6965]. (adv.) with head held high:– upright [1]

6969 קִין ***qîn***, v.den. GK: 7801 [→ 7015]. [Pol] to chant a lament, sing a dirge:– lament [4], lamented [3], mourning [1]

6970 קוֹעַ ***qôaʿ***, n.pr.g. GK: 7760 [cf. 7772]. Koa:– Koa [1]

6971 קוֹף ***qôp***, n.[m.]. GK: 7761. ape:– apes [2]

6972 קִיץ ***qîṣ*** or קוּץ ***qûṣ***, v. GK: 7810 [→ 7019; cf. 3364]. [Q] to pass the summer; [H] to rouse, awaken:– summer [1]

6973 קוּץ ***qûṣ***, v. GK: 7762 [→ 6975?; cf. 5354, 8262]. [Q] to detest, be disgusted, loathe:– abhorred [2], weary [2], abhorrest [1], distressed [1], grieved [1], loatheth [1], vex [1]

6974 קוּץ ***qûṣ***, v. GK: 7763. [H] to rouse, awaken; to tear apart:– awake [10], awaked [4], awaketh [3], wake [2], arise [1], awakest [1], watcheth [1]

6975 קוֹץ ***qôṣ***, n.m. GK: 7764 & 7765 [→ 6976?; cf. 6973?, 7093]. thorns, thornbush; shreds of a wick:– thorns [10], thorn [2]

6976 הַקּוֹץ ***haqqôṣ*** or קוֹץ ***qôṣ***, n.pr.m. GK: 2212 & 7766 [→ 1886.1+6975?]. Hakkoz, Koz, "*the thorn*":– Koz [4], Coz [1], Hakkoz [1]

6977 קְוֻצּוֹת ***qᵉwuṣṣôt***, n.f.pl. GK: 7767. locks of hair:– locks [2]

6978 קַו־קָו ***qaw-qaw***, n.m. GK: 7743 & 7744 [→ 6957]. strange speech; qav-qav (a mocking sound, like blah-blah):– meted out (+6978) [4]

6979 קוּר ***qûr*** or קָרַר ***qārar***, v. GK: 7769 & 7981 & 7982 [→ 4726, 4747, 7119, 7120, 7135]. [Q] to dig (a well or water hole); [Pil] to tear down:– casteth out [2], digged [2], breaking down [1], destroy [1]

6980 קוּר ***qûr***, n.m. GK: 7770. thread (of a spider cobweb):– webs [1], web [1]

6981 קֹרֵא ***qōrēʾ***, n.pr.m. GK: 7927 [→ 7124; cf. 7121]. Kore, "*proclaimer*":– Kore [3]

6982 קוֹרָה ***qôrâ***, n.f. GK: 7771 [→ 4746]. beam, pole, roof beams, tree:– beams [2], beam [2], roof [1]

6983 קוּשׁ ***qûš***, v. GK: 7772 [cf. 3369, 5367]. [Q] to set a snare:– lay a snare [1]

6984 קוּשָׁיָהוּ ***qûšāyāhû***, n.pr.m. GK: 7773 [cf. 7029]. Kushaiah:– Kushaiah [1]

6985 קַט ***qaṭ***, pt. GK: 7775. little; soon:– very little (+4592) [1]

6986 קֶטֶב ***qeṭeb***, n.m. GK: 7776 [→ 6987]. same as 6987: plague, destruction:– destruction [2], destroying [1]

6987 קֹטֶב ***qōṭeb***, n.m. GK: 7776 [→ 6986]. same as 6986: plague, destruction:– destruction [1]

6988 קְטוֹרָה ***qᵉṭôrâ***, n.m. GK: 7777 [→ 6999]. smoke (of sacrifice):– incense [1]

6989 קְטוּרָה ***qᵉṭûrâ***, n.pr.f. GK: 7778 [→ 6999]. Keturah, "*incense, scented one*":– Keturah [4]

6990 קוּט ***qûṭ*** or קָטַט ***qāṭaṭ***, v. GK: 7752 & 7753 [→ 6962]. [Q] to be fragile; cut off; cf. 6962:– cut off [1]

6991 קָטַל ***qāṭal***, v. GK: 7779 [→ 6993; cf. 6992]. [Q] to slay, kill:– slay [2], killeth [1]

6992 קְטַל ***qᵉṭal*** (Aram.), v. GK: 10625 [cf. 6991]. [P] to put to death, kill; [Peil] to be slain; [Htpe] to be put to death; [Pa] to kill; [Htpa] to be put to death:– slain [4], slew [2], slay [1]

6993 קֶטֶל ***qeṭel***, n.[m.]. GK: 7780 [→ 6991]. slaughter:– slaughter [1]

6994 קָטֹן ***qāṭōn***, v. GK: 7781 [→ 6995, 6996, 6997]. [Q] to be unworthy, not enough, trifling; [H] to make a (measure) small:– small thing [2], making small [1], not worthy [1]

6995 קֹטֶן ***qōṭen***, n.m. GK: 7782 [→ 6994]. little finger; possibly a euphemism for penis:– little [2]

6996 קָטָן ***qāṭān*** or קָטֹן ***qāṭōn***, a. GK: 7783 & 7785 [→ 6994, 6997]. small (in size); few (in quantity); by extension, of status: lesser, insignificant; of age: young(est):– small [33], little [19], youngest [15], younger [14], least [10], less [3], lesser [2], little one [2], small quantity [1], smallest [1], young [1]

6997 קָטָן ***qāṭān*** or הַקָּטָן ***haqqāṭān***, n.pr.m. GK: 7784 & 2214 [→ 1886.1+6996; cf. 6994]. Katan, Hakkatan, "*the small one*":– Hakkatan [1]

6998 קָטַף ***qāṭap***, v. GK: 7786. [Q] to pick off (grain), break off (twigs); [N] to be picked off:– crop off [1], cropt off [1], cut down [1], cut up [1], pluck [1]

6999 קָטַר ***qāṭar***, v.den. GK: 7787 [→ 4729, 4730, 6988, 6989, 7002, 7003, 7004, 7008]. [P] to burn an offering (of incense smoke); [Pu] to be perfumed; [H] to make a burned smoking offering; [Ho] to be burned as an offering:– burn [34], burnt incense [25], burn incense [23], burnt [13], burned incense [3], burneth incense [2], not fail to burn (+6999) [2], offer [2], altars for incense [1], burn sacrifice [1], burned [1], burning incense [1], burnt incense (+7004) [1], incense [1], kindle [1], offer incense [1], offered incense [1], offered [1], offering incense [1], perfumed [1]

7000 קָטַר ***qāṭar***, v. GK: 7788. [Qp] to be enclosed:– joined [1]

7001 קְטַר ***qᵉṭar*** (Aram.), n.m. GK: 10626. joint (of the hip); difficult problem, "to solve a difficult problem" means to explain an enigma, as a fig. extension of untying a tight, hard-to-undo, knot:– doubts [2], joints [1]

7002 קִטֵּר ***qiṭṭēr***, n.f. GK: 7789 [→ 6999]. incense, often as or accompanying an offering to God:– incense [1]

7003 קִטְרוֹן ***qiṭrôn***, n.pr.loc. GK: 7790 [→ 6999]. Kitron, "*incense, [sacrificial] smoke*":– Kitron [1]

7004 קְטֹרֶת ***qᵉṭōret***, n.f. GK: 7792 [→ 6999]. incense, smoke offering, its pleasant fragrance symbolic of God's acceptance:– incense [56], perfume [3], burnt incense (+6999) [1]

7005 קַטָּת ***qaṭṭāt***, n.pr.loc. GK: 7793. Kattath:– Kattath [1]

7006 קִיא ***qîʾ*** or קָיָה ***qāyâ***, v. GK: 7794 & 7796 [→ 6958]. [Q] to vomit; [H] to vomit out, spit out:– spue [1]

7007 קַיִט ***qayiṭ*** (Aram.), n.[m.]. GK: 10627 [cf. 7019]. summer:– summer [1]

7008 קִיטוֹר ***qîṭôr***, n.m. GK: 7798 [→ 6999]. smoke:– smoke [3], vapour [1]

7009 קִים ***qîm***, n.m. GK: 7799 [→ 6965]. foe, adversary:– substance [1]

7010 קְיָם ***qᵉyām*** (Aram.), n.[m.]. GK: 10628 [→ 6966?]. edict, statute, decree:– statute [2]

7011 קַיָּם ***qayyām*** (Aram.), a. GK: 10629 [→ 6966]. enduring:– stedfast [1], sure [1]

7012 קִימָה ***qîmâ***, n.f. GK: 7800 [→ 6965]. standing up:– rising up [1]

קִימוֹשׁ ***qîmôš***. See 7057.

7013 קַיִן ***qayin***, n.[m.]. GK: 7802. spearhead, spear:– spear [1]

7014 קַיִן ***qayin***, n.pr.m. & g. & loc. GK: 7803 & 7804 & 7805 [→ 7017, 7018, 8423; cf. 7069]. Cain, "*metal worker; brought forth, acquired* [Ge 4:1]"; Kenite, "*metal workers*"; Kain, "*place of metal workers [?]*":– Cain [17], Kenites [1], Kenite [1]

7015 קִינָה ***qînâ***, n.f. GK: 7806 [→ 6969]. lament, mourning song, dirge:– lamentation [15], lamentations [3]

7016 קִינָה ***qînâ***, n.pr.loc. GK: 7807. Kinah, "*lament, dirge*":– Kinah [1]

7017 קֵינִי ***qênî***, a.g. GK: 7808 [→ 7014]. Kenite:– Kenites [7], Kenite [5]

7018 קֵינָן ***qênān***, n.pr.m. GK: 7809 [→ 7014]. Kenan:– Cainan [5], Kenan [1]

7019 קַיִץ ***qayiṣ***, n.m. GK: 7811 [→ 6972; cf. 7007]. summer; by extension, summer fruit, ripe fruit:– summer [11], summer fruits [6], summer fruit [3]

7020 קִיצוֹן ***qîṣôn***, a. GK: 7812 [→ 7093]. end, outermost:– uttermost [3], outmost [1]

7021 קִיקָיוֹן ***qîqāyôn***, n.m. GK: 7813. caster-oil vine; some sources: cucumber plant:– gourd [5]

7022 קִיקָלוֹן ***qîqālôn***, n.[m.]. GK: 7814 [→ 7043]. disgrace:– shameful spuing [1]

7023 קִיר ***qîr***, n.m. GK: 7815 [→ 7024; cf. 7176 (also used with compound proper names)]. wall (of a building or city); by extension, any surface of a construction: side, ceiling, surface; one who "urinates on a wall" is male:– wall [50], walls [16], sides [2], side [2], masons (+2796) [1], masons (+68+2796) [1], town [1], very heart (+3820) [1]

7024 קִיר ***qîr***, n.pr.loc. GK: 7816 & 7817 [→ 7023]. Kir, "*walled enclosure*":– Kir [5]

7025 קִיר־חֶרֶשׂ ***qîr-ḥereś*** or קִיר חֲרֶשֶׂת ***qîr ḥᵃreśet***, n.pr.loc. GK: 7818 & 7819 [→ 7023+2789]. Kir Heres, Kir Hareseth, "*walled [city] of pottery fragments*":– Kir-heres [2], Kir-haraseth [1], Kir-hareseth [1], Kir-haresh [1]

7026 קֵרֹס ***qêrōs***, n.pr.m. GK: 7820. Keros:– Keros [2]

7027 קִישׁ ***qîš***, n.pr.m. GK: 7821. Kish, "*bow, power*":– Kish [21]

7028 קִישׁוֹן ***qîšôn***, n.pr.loc. GK: 7822. Kishon, "*cunning*":– Kishon [5], Kison [1]

7029 קִישִׁי ***qîšî***, n.pr.m. GK: 7823 [cf. 6984]. Kishi, "[poss.] *gift; snarer*":– Kishi [1]

7030 קִיתְרֹס ***qîtᵉrōs*** or קַתְרוֹס ***qatrôs*** (Aram.), n.[m.]. GK: 10630 & 10644. a stringed instrument, translated variously as "zither, lute, lyre," etc.:– harp [4]

7031 קַל ***qal***, a. GK: 7824 [→ 7043]. fleet-footed, swift, speedy:– swift [9], swiftly [2], light [1], swifter [1]

7032 קָל ***qāl*** (Aram.), n.m. GK: 10631 [cf. 6963]. sound, voice:– sound [4], voice [3]

קֹל ***qōl***. See 6963.

7033 קָלָה ***qālâ***, v. GK: 7828 [→ 7039]. [Q] to burn; [Qp] to be roasted; [N] to have a burning sensation:– dried [1], loathsome [1], parched [1], roasted [1]

7034 קָלָה ***qālâ***, v. GK: 7829 [→ 7036; cf. 7043]. [N] to lightly esteemed, to be a nobody, be degraded; [H] to dishonor, treat with contempt:– base [1], contemned [1], despised [1], lightly esteemed [1], setteth light [1], vile [1]

7035 קָלַה ***qālah***, v.den. GK: 7827 [→ 6951]. var. of 6950: [N] to be gathered:– @H = **7036** קָלוֹן ***qālôn***, n.m. GK: 7830 [→ 7034]. shame, disgrace, dishonor:– shame [13], confusion [1], dishonour [1], ignominy [1], reproach [1]

7037 קַלַּחַת ***qallaḥat***, n.f. GK: 7831. caldron, (cooking) pot:– caldron [2]

7038 קָלַט ***qālaṭ***, v. GK: 7832 [→ 4733, 7042]. [Qp] to be stunted:– lacking in parts [1]

7039 קָלִי ***qālî***, n.m. GK: 7833 [→ 7033]. roasted grain, parched grain:– parched [6]

7040 קַלָּי ***qallāy***, n.pr.m. GK: 7834. Kallai, "*swift*":– Kallai [1]

7041 קֵלָיָה ***qēlāyâ***, n.pr.m. GK: 7835. Kelaiah, "[perhaps] *Yahweh has dishonored*":– Kelaiah [1]

7042 קְלִיטָא ***qᵉlîṭā'***, n.pr.m. GK: 7836 [→ 7038]. Kelita:– Kelita [3]

7043 קָלַל ***qālal***, v. GK: 7837 [→ 7022, 7031, 6963, 7044, 7045, 7052; cf. 7034]. [Q] to recede, grow smaller; to be vile, to disdain, despise; to be swift; [N] to be trivial, insignificant; to be swift; [P] to curse, blaspheme, revile; [Pu] to be accursed; [H] to lighten; to humble; to treat with contempt; [Htpal] to be shaken:– cursed [17], curse [17], curseth [6], swifter [5], light thing [4], make lighter [3], vile [3], abated [2], despised [2], ease somewhat [2], lighten [2], light [2], slightly (+5921) [2], accursed [1], bring into contempt [1], despise [1], easier (+4480) [1], easy [1], lightly afflicted [1], lightly esteemed [1], made bright [1], made vile [1], make somewhat lighter [1], moved lightly [1], revile [1], set light [1], swift [1], whet [1]

7044 קָלָל ***qālāl***, a. GK: 7838 [→ 7043]. burnished, polished:– burnished [1], polished [1]

7045 קְלָלָה ***qᵉlālâ***, n.f. GK: 7839 [→ 7043]. curse, condemnation:– curse [24], cursing [4], curses [3], accursed [1], cursings [1]

7046 קָלַס ***qālas***, v. GK: 7840 [→ 7047, 7048]. [P] to scorn; [Ht] to make fun of:– mocked [1], mock [1], scoff [1], scornest [1]

7047 קֶלֶס ***qeles***, n.[m.]. GK: 7841 [→ 7046]. derision, reproach:– derision [3]

7048 קַלָּסָה ***qallāsâ***, n.f. GK: 7842 [→ 7046]. laughingstock, object of derision:– mocking [1]

7049 קָלַע ***qāla'***, v. GK: 7843 & 7844 [→ 4734, 7050]. [Q] to hurl a stone (from a sling); to carve; [P] to hurl a stone (from a sling):– carved [3], sling out [2], slang [1], sling [1]

7050 קֶלַע ***qela'***, n.[m.]. GK: 7845 & 7846 [→ 7049, 7051]. sling (a weapon); curtains:– hangings [15], sling [4], leaves [1], slingstones (+68) [1], slings [1]

7051 קַלָּע ***qallā'***, n.m. GK: 7847 [→ 7050]. slinger (one who uses a sling):– slingers [1]

7052 קְלֹקֵל ***qᵉlōqēl***, a. GK: 7848 [→ 7043]. miserable (food), starvation (rations):– light [1]

7053 קִלְּשֹׁון ***qillᵉšôn***, n.[m.]. GK: 7849. (sharp pointed, three-pronged) fork:– forks (+7969) [1]

7054 קָמָה ***qāmâ***, n.f. GK: 7850 [→ 6965]. standing grain:– standing corn [5], corn [2], grown up [2], stalk [1]

7055 קְמוּאֵל ***qᵉmû'ēl***, n.pr.m. GK: 7851 [→ 6965+410]. Kemuel, "*God's [El's] mound*":– Kemuel [3]

7056 קָמוֹן ***qāmôn***, n.pr.loc. GK: 7852. Kamon:– Camon [1]

7057 קִמּוֹשׂ ***qimmôś***, n.m. GK: 7853 [→ 7063]. thorns, nettles, briers (weeds of all kinds):– nettles [2]

7058 קֶמַח ***qemaḥ***, n.[m.]. GK: 7854. flour:– meal [10], flour [4]

7059 קָמַט ***qāmaṭ***, v. GK: 7855. [Q] to seize; [Pu] to be seized:– cut down [1], filled with wrinkles [1]

7060 קָמַל ***qāmal***, v. GK: 7857. [Q] to wither:– hewn down [1], wither [1]

7061 קָמַץ ***qāmaṣ***, v. GK: 7858 [→ 7062]. [Q] to take a handful:– take handful (+4393+7062) [2], take a handful [1]

7062 קֹמֶץ ***qōmeṣ***, n.[m.]. GK: 7859 [→ 7061]. handful; (pl.) abundance:– take handful (+4393+7061) [2], handfuls [1], handful [1]

7063 קִמָּשׁוֹן ***qimmāšôn***, n.m. GK: 7853 [→ 7057]. same as 7057: thorns, nettles, briers (weeds of all kinds):– thorns [1]

7064 קֵן ***qēn***, n.m. GK: 7860 [→ 7077]. nest:– nest [12], rooms [1]

7065 קָנָא ***qānā'***, v.den. GK: 7861 [→ 7067, 7068, 7072]. [P] (of negative attitude) to be jealous, be envious; (of positive attitude) to be zealous:– jealous [8], envied [5], envious [4], very jealous (+7065) [4], envy [3], moved to jealousy [2], provoked to jealousy [2], enviest [1], move to jealousy [1], zealous (+7068) [1], zealous [1], zeal [1]

7066 קְנָה ***qᵉnâ*** (Aram.), v. GK: 10632 [cf. 7069]. [P] to buy:– buy [1]

7067 קַנָּא ***qannā'***, a. GK: 7862 [→ 7072; cf. 7065]. jealous; an adjective or title used exclusively of God, focusing on his desire for exclusive relationships:– jealous [6]

7068 קִנְאָה ***qin'â***, n.f. GK: 7863 [→ 7065]. jealousy, envy, zeal:– jealousy [24], zeal [9], envy [7], envied [1], jealousies [1], zealous (+7065) [1]

7069 קָנָה ***qānâ***, v. GK: 7864 & 7865 [→ 511, 4735, 4736, 4737, 7075; cf. 7014, cf. 7066]. [Q] to buy, acquire, get; to create, bring forth; (as a title of God) Creator; [N] to be bought:– bought [21], buy [21], get [9], purchased [5], buyer [3], getteth [3], got [3], possessed [3], buyest [2], possessor [2], surely buy (+7069) [2], verily buy (+7069) [2], attain [1], buy (+7075) [1], gotten [1], owner [1], possessors [1], provoketh to jealousy [1], recover [1], redeemed [1], taught [1]

7070 קָנֶה ***qāneh***, n.m. GK: 7866 [→ 7071]. branch, rod; (calamus) reed, stalk, shaft, cane; by extension: a measure of length, variously reckoned:– reed [22], branches [19]; reeds [6], branch [5], calamus [3], stalk [2], balance [1], bone [1], cane [1], spearmen [1], sweet cane [1]

7071 קָנָה ***qānâ***, n.pr.loc. GK: 7867 [→ 7070]. Kanah, "*reed*":– Kanah [3]

7072 קַנּוֹא ***qannô'***, a. GK: 7868 [→ 7067; cf. 7065]. jealous:– jealous [2]

7073 קְנַז ***qᵉnaz***, n.pr.m. GK: 7869 [→ 7074]. Kenaz, "*hunting*":– Kenaz [11]

7074 קְנִזִּי ***qᵉnizzî***, a.g. GK: 7870 [→ 7073]. Kenizzite:– Kenezite [3], Kenizzites [1]

7075 קִנְיָן ***qinyān***, n.[m.]. GK: 7871 [→ 7069]. goods, property, possessions:– substance [4], getting [2], goods [2], buy (+7069) [1], riches [1]

7076 קִנָּמוֹן ***qinnāmôn***, n.m. GK: 7872. cinnamon (a spice from the far east):– cinnamon [3]

7077 קָנַן ***qānan***, v.den. GK: 7873 [→ 7064]. [P] to make a nest; [Pu] to be nestled, nested:– made nests [1], make nests [1], make nest [1], makest nest [1], maketh nest [1]

7078 קֵנֶץ ***qeneṣ***, n.[m.]. GK: 7874 [cf. 7093]. end, an extension of a snare or net that captures or restrains (not found in the OT):– end [1]

7079 קְנָת ***qᵉnāt***, n.pr.loc. GK: 7875. Kenath, "*possession*":– Kenath [2]

7080 קָסַם ***qāsam***, v.den. GK: 7876 [→ 4738, 7081]. [Q] to practice divination, be a soothsayer, seek an omen:– diviners [7], divine [6], divination [1], divining [1], prudent [1], soothsayer [1], use divination (+7081) [1], used divination (+7081) [1], useth divination (+7081) [1]

7081 קֶסֶם ***qesem***, n.[m.]. GK: 7877 [→ 7080]. divination: pagan practice of determining the future by examining the position of stars, communication with the dead or with spirits, examining animal organs, or casting lots:– divination [4], divinations [1], divine sentence [1], rewards of divination [1], use divination (+7080) [1], used divination (+7080) [1], useth divination (+7080) [1], witchcraft [1]

7082 קָסַס ***qāsas***, v. GK: 7878 [cf. 7193]. [Pol] to strip off:– cut off [1]

7083 קֶסֶת ***qeset***, n.[f.]. GK: 7879. writing kit, writing-case:– inkhorn [3]

7084 קְעִילָה ***qᵉ'îlâ***, n.pr.loc. GK: 7881. Keilah:– Keilah [18]

7085 קַעֲקַע ***qa'ᵃqa'***, n.[m.]. GK: 7882. tattoo:– marks [1]

7086 קְעָרָה ***qᵉ'ārâ***, n.f. GK: 7883 [→ 8258]. plate, dish:– charger [13], dishes [3], chargers [1]

קֹף ***qōp***. See 6971.

7087 קָפָא ***qāpā'***, v. GK: 7884. [Q, N] to congeal, thicken; [H] to curdle:– congealed [1], cruddled [1], dark [1], settled [1]

7088 קָפַד ***qāpad***, v. GK: 7886 [→ 7090, 7089; cf. 7091]. [P] to roll up:– cut off [1]

7089 קְפָדָה ***qᵉpādâ***, n.[f.]. GK: 7888 [→ 7088]. terror, anguish:– destruction [1]

7090 קִפֹּד ***qippōd***, n.[m.]. GK: 7887 [→ 7088]. screech owl; some sources: hedgehog:– bittern [3]

7091 קִפּוֹז ***qippôz***, n.f. GK: 7889 [cf. 7088, 7092]. owl; some sources: tree snake:– great owl [1]

7092 קָפַץ ***qāpaṣ***, v. GK: 7890 [cf. 7091]. [Q] to draw together, shut; [N] to be gathered up; [P] to bound, leap:– shut [2], shut up [1], skipping [1], stoppeth [1], stop [1], taken out of the way [1]

7093 קֵץ ***qēṣ***, n.m. GK: 7891 [→ 7020; cf. 7078, 7112]. end, limit, boundary:– end [51], after (+4480) [6], after [2], after (+3807.1) [1], after that (+1961+4480) [1], borders [1], border [1], have an end [1], infinite (+369) [1], process [1], utmost border [1]

קֹץ ***qōṣ***. See 6975.

7094 קָצַב ***qāṣab***, v. GK: 7892 [→ 7095]. [Q] to cut off; [Qp] to be shorn, be cut off:– cut down [1], even shorn [1]

7095 קֶצֶב ***qeṣeb***, n.m. GK: 7893 [→ 7094]. shape, foundation:– size [2], bottoms [1]

7096 קָצָה ***qāṣâ***, v. GK: 7894 [→ 7097, 7098, 7099, 7117; cf. 7112]. [P] to cut off, reduce; [H] to scrape off:– cut short [1], cutteth off [1], cutting off [1], scrape off [1], scraped [1]

7097 קָצֶה ***qāṣeh*** or קֵצֶה ***qēṣeh***, n.[m.]. GK: 7895 & 7897 [→ 7096]. end, boundary, limit, outskirts, edge:– end [50], edge [6], ends [6], uttermost part [6], outside [3], border [2], other[S] [2], utmost part [2], after (+4480) [1], borders [1], brim [1], brink [1], coasts [1], every quarter [1], frontiers [1], infinite (+369) [1], other[S] (+8064) [1], outmost coast (+4480) [1], outmost parts [1], quarter [1], shore [1], side [1], some of (+4480) [1], utmost [1], uttermost (+4480) [1], uttermost part (+4480) [1], uttermost parts [1], uttermost [1]

7098 קָצָה ***qāṣâ***, n.f. & m.[pl.]. GK: 7896 [→ 7096]. end, fringe, edge:– ends [18], end [4], lowest [3], edges [2], selvedge [2], uttermost part [2], coasts [1], corners [1], parts [1], quarters [1]

7099 קָצוּ ***qāṣû***, n.[m.]. GK: 7898 [→ 7096]. ends, borders (of the earth):– ends [4], uttermost parts [1]

7100 קֶצַח ***qeṣaḥ***, n.m. GK: 7902. caraway, cummin:– fitches [3]

7101 קָצִין ***qāṣîn***, n.m. GK: 7903 [→ 6278]. commander, ruler, leader:– captain [2], princes [2], prince [2], rulers [2], ruler [2], captains [1], guide [1]

7102 קְצִיעָה ***qᵉṣî'â***, n.f. GK: 7904 [→ 7103; cf. 7106]. cassia:– cassia [1]

7103 קְצִיעָה ***qᵉṣî'â***, n.pr.f. GK: 7905 [→ 7102; cf. 7106]. Keziah, "*cassia [cinnamon]*":– Kezia [1]

7104 קְצִיץ ***qᵉṣîṣ***, n.pr.loc. GK: 7906 & 6681 [→ 6009; cf. 7093]. Keziz:– Keziz [1]

7105 קָצִיר ***qāṣîr***, n.m. GK: 7907 & 7908 [→ 7114]. harvest, time of reaping; branch, bough, twig, shoot:– harvest [46], boughs [3], branch [2], cuttest down harvest (+7114) [1], harvest time [1], harvestman [1]

7106 קָצַע ***qāṣa'***, v. GK: 7909 & 7910 [→ 4741, 4742, 7102, 7103]. [H] to scrape off; [Pu, Ho] to be made with corners:– cause to be scraped [1], corners [1]

7107 קָצַף ***qāṣap***, v. GK: 7911 [→ 7110; cf. 7108]. [Q] to be angry; [H] to provoke to anger; [Ht] to be enraged:– wroth [22], provoked to wrath [3], angry [2], sore displeased (+7110) [2], angered [1], displeased [1], fret [1], provokedst to wrath [1], wrath [1]

7108 קְצַף ***qᵉṣap*** (Aram.), v. GK: 10633 [→ 7109; cf. 7107]. [P] to become furious:– furious [1]

7109 קְצַף ***qᵉṣap*** (Aram.), n.[m.]. GK: 10634 [→ 7108; cf. 7110]. wrath, fury:– wrath [1]

7110 קֶצֶף **qeṣep**, n.m. GK: 7912 & 7913 [→ 7107, 7111; cf. 7109]. wrath, anger, fury; twig (snapped off):– wrath [23], indignation [3], sore displeased (+7107) [2], foam [1]

7111 קְצָפָה **qᵉṣāpâ**, n.f. GK: 7914 [→ 7110]. stump, splintering:– barked [1]

7112 קָצַץ **qāṣaṣ**, v. GK: 7915 & 7899 [cf. 7093, 7096]. [Q] to cut off; [P] to cut off, take away; [Pu] to be cut off, maimed:– cut off [6], in the utmost [3], cut in pieces [2], cut asunder [1], cutteth in sunder [1], cut [1]

7113 קְצַץ **qᵉṣaṣ** (Aram.), v. GK: 10635 [cf. 7112]. [Pa] to trim off, cut off:– cut off [1]

7114 קָצַר **qāṣar**, v. GK: 7917 & 7918 & 7900 [→ 7105, 7115, 7116]. [Q] to reap, harvest, gather; to be short; (by extension) to be impatient, angry; [P] to cut short; [H] to shorten, cut short:– reap [18], reapers [7], shortened [4], shortened at all (+7114) [2], shorter [2], cuttest down harvest (+7105) [1], discouraged [1], grieved [1], harvestman [1], lothed [1], mower [1], reaped [1], reaper [1], reapest [1], reapeth [1], reaping [1], straitened [1], troubled [1], vexed [1], waxed short [1]

7115 קֹצֶר **qōṣer**, n.[m.]. GK: 7919 [→ 7114]. discouragement, despondency, an extension of shortness or lack (of spirit):– anguish [1]

7116 קָצֵר **qāṣēr**, a. GK: 7920 [→ 7114]. shortened: quick-tempered, impatient:– small [2], few [1], hasty [1], soon [1]

7117 קְצָת **qᵉṣāt**, n.f. GK: 7921 [→ 7096; cf. 7118]. end, extremity:– end [3], part (+4480) [1], some (+4480) [1]

7118 קְצָת **qᵉṣāt** (Aram.), n.f. GK: 10636 [cf. 7117]. part; the end:– end [2], partly (+4481) [1]

7119 קַר **qar**, a. GK: 7922 [→ 6979]. cool, cold (water); cool-headed, even-tempered (of one's spirit):– cold [2]

קִר **qir**. See 7023.

7120 קֹר **qōr**, n.[m.]. GK: 7923 [→ 6979]. cold:– cold [1]

7121 קָרָא **qārā'**, v. GK: 7924 [→ 4744, 7124, 6981, 7148, 7150; cf. 7123]. [Q] to call, summon, announce, proclaim; [Qp] to be invited as a guest, be appointed; [N] to be called, be summoned; [Pu] to be called; "to call on the name of the LORD" means to proclaim or praise the excellence of Yahweh, to worship Yahweh, or to summon Yahweh by name for help:– called [366], call [115], cried [51], cry [35], read [35], proclaim [20], call upon [14], calleth [13], proclaimed [11], called upon [10], named [5], crieth [4], guests [4], called for [3], calledst [3], calling [3], cried unto [3], gave [3], invited [3], renowned [3], bidden [2], criest [2], cry unto [2], named (+8034) [2], preach [2], proclaiming [2], reading [2], bewrayeth [1], call for [1], call on [1], called forth [1], crying [1], famous (+8034) [1], famous [1], made proclamation [1], mentioned [1], proclaim (+871.1) [1], proclaimed (+871.1) [1], proclaimeth [1], pronounced [1], publish [1], readeth [1], said [1]

7122 קָרָא **qārā'**, v. GK: 7925 [→ 7125; cf. 7136]. [Q] to meet, encounter, happen; [N] to have met, have happened, [H] to cause to happen:– befall [4], met [2], befallen [1], came upon [1], caused to come upon [1], chance to be [1], come unto [1], come upon [1], falleth out [1], happened by chance [1], happened to be [1], happened unto [1]

7123 קְרָא **qᵉrā'** (Aram.), v. GK: 10637 [cf. 7121]. [P] to call, proclaim, read out loud; [Pp, Peil] to be read out loud; [Htpe] to be called, be summoned:– read [7], cried [3], called [1]

7124 קֹרֵא **qōrē'**, n.m. GK: 7926 [→ 6981; cf. 7121]. partridge:– partridge [2]

7125 קִרְאָה **qir'â**, v.inf. GK: 7925 [→ 7122]. inf. of 7122: meeting, encounter, happening:– meet [69], against [39], met [4], brought (+857) [1], come against [1], come [1], coming [1], help [1], in the way (+3807.1) [1], meet with [1], meeting [1], seek [1]

7126 קָרַב **qārab**, v. GK: 7928 [→ 6137, 7131, 7128, 7132, 7133, 7138; cf. 7127]. [Q] to come near, approach; [N] to present oneself, be brought near; [P] to bring near, approach; [H] to bring near, offer, present:– offer [79], bring [32], brought [24], come near [20], offered [16], came near [11], approach [9], offereth [9], came [6], come nigh [6], at hand [4], bring near [4], come [4], draw nigh [4], drew near [4], drew nigh [4], draw near [3], came nigh [2], cause to come near [2], cause to draw near [2], caused to come near [2], comest nigh [2], draweth near [2], go near [2], presented [2], went [2], approached [1], brought forth [1], brought near [1], came together [1], camest [1], cause to be brought [1], caused to draw near [1], causest to approach [1], draweth near the time [1], drewest near [1], goeth [1], go [1], joined [1], join [1], lay [1], made ready [1], near [1], offering [1], produce [1], stand [1], take [1], went near [1]

7127 קְרֵב **qᵉrēb** (Aram.), v. GK: 10638 [→ 7129; cf. 7126]. [P] to come near, approach; [Pa] to offer (a sacrifice); [H] to bring near, offer (a sacrifice):– came near [4], brought near [1], came [1], offered [1], offer [1], sacrifices [1]

7128 קְרָב **qᵉrāb**, n.[m.]. GK: 7930 [→ 6137; cf. 7126; cf. 7129]. war, battle:– battle [5], war [4]

7129 קְרָב **qᵉrāb** (Aram.), n.[m.]. GK: 10639 [→ 7127; cf. 7128]. war:– war [1]

7130 קֶרֶב **qereb**, n.[m.]. GK: 7931. inner parts; by extension: heart or mind as the seat of thought and emotion; interior, midst; (pp.) among, in the midst of:– midst [73], among (+871.1) [41], among [26], within (+871.1) [25], inwards [19], in (+871.1) [8], amongst (+871.1) [7], through (+871.1) [5], inward [3], out of (+4480) [3], amongst [2], into (+5921) [2], inward parts [2], before (+871.1) [1], bowels [1], charge [1], eaten (+413+935) [1], eaten up (+413+935) [1], heart [1], inwardly (+871.1) [1], purtenance [1], therein (+871.1) [1], therein (+871.1+1886.3) [1], within [1]

7131 קָרֵב **qārēb**, a.v. GK: 7929 [→ 7126]. approaching, coming near:– cometh nigh [4], come near [2], cometh near (+7131) [2], drew near [2], approach [1], came [1]

קָרֹב **qārōb**. See 7138.

7132 קִרְבָה **qirbâ**, n.f. GK: 7932 [→ 7126]. nearness, approach:– approaching to [1], draw near [1]

7133 קָרְבָּן **qorbān** or קֻרְבָּן **qurbān**, n.m. GK: 7933 & 7934 [→ 7126]. gift, offering, sacrifice; contribution, supply (of wood):– offering [65], oblation [11], oblations [1], offered [1], offering made by fire (+801) [1], offerings [1], sacrifice [1]

7134 קַרְדֹּם **qardōm**, n.[m.]. GK: 7935. ax; some sources: adze:– axes [3], axe [2]

7135 קָרָה **qārâ**, n.f. GK: 7938 [→ 6979]. cold:– cold [5]

7136 קָרָה **qārâ**, v. GK: 7936 [→ 4745, 7137, 7147; cf. 7122]. [Q] to happen, meet, encounter; [N] to meet with, have happen; [P] to make beams, build beams; [H] to give success, to select oneself:– met [4], happeneth [3], befall [2], happen [2], laid beams [2], appoint [1], befallen [1], befell [1], brought [1], come to pass [1], come [1], floor [1], happened [1], layeth beams [1], light on [1], make beams [1], meet [1], send good speed (+6440+3807.1) [1]

7137 קָרֶה **qāreh**, n.[m.]. GK: 7937 [→ 7136]. emission (at night):– chanceth [1]

קֹרָה **qōrâ**. See 6982.

7138 קָרוֹב **qārôb**, a. GK: 7940 [→ 7126]. near, close:– near [33], nigh [12], next [5], at hand [4], neighbours [3], approach [2], near of kin [2], neighbour [2], allied [1], come nigh [1], hand [1], kinsfolk [1], kinsmen [1], kin [1], near (+871.1) [1], near unto [1], nearer [1], newly (+4480) [1], nigh at hand [1], ready [1], short (+4480) [1], shortly (+4480) [1], short [1]

7139 קָרַח **qāraḥ**, v. GK: 7942 [→ 7142, 7143, 7141, 7144, 7145, 7146]. [Q] to shave, make bald; [N] to shave oneself, make oneself bald; [H] to shave another, make bald; [Ho] to be rubbed bare, be make bald:– make bald [2], make utterly bald (+7139) [2], made bald [1], make baldness (+7144) [1]

7140 קֶרַח **qeraḥ**, n.m. GK: 7943. ice, frost, hail:– frost [3], ice [3], crystal [1]

7141 קֹרַח **qōraḥ**, n.pr.m. GK: 7946 [→ 7145; cf. 7139]. Korah, "*shaven, bald*":– Korah [37]

7142 קֵרֵחַ **qērēaḥ**, a. GK: 7944 [→ 7139]. bald, bald-headed:– bald head [2], bald [1]

7143 קָרֵחַ **qārēaḥ**, n.pr.m. GK: 7945 [→ 7139]. Kareah, "*bald head*":– Kareah [13], Careah [1]

7144 קָרְחָה **qorḥâ**, n.f. GK: 7947 [→ 7139]. baldness, shaving the head:– baldness [8], bald [1], make baldness (+7139) [1]

7145 קָרְחִי **qorḥî**, a.g. GK: 7948 [→ 7141; cf. 7139]. Korahite, "*of Korah*":– Korhites [4], Korahites [2], Korahite [1], Kore [1]

7146 קָרַחַת **qāraḥat**, n.f. GK: 7949 [→ 7139]. bald spot (not the forehead area); bare spot (of articles):– bald head [3], bare within [1]

7147 קְרִי **qᵉrî**, n.[m.]. GK: 7950 [→ 7136]. hostile encounter, hostility:– contrary [7]

7148 קָרִיא **qārî'**, a. GK: 7951 [→ 7121]. summoned, called:– famous [2]

7149 קִרְיָא **qiryâ** (Aram.), n.f. GK: 10640 [cf. 7151]. city, town:– city [8], cities [1]

7150 קְרִיאָה **qᵉrî'â**, n.f. GK: 7952 [→ 7121]. message, appeal:– preaching [1]

7151 קִרְיָה **qiryâ** or קִרְיַת **qiryat**, n.f. [& pr.] GK: 7953 & 7956 [→ 7176; cf. 7149]. city, town; as n.pr. Kiriath:– city [32]

7152 קְרִיּוֹת **qᵉriyyôt**, n.pr.loc. GK: 7954 [→ 7176]. Kerioth, "*town*":– Kerioth [4]

7153 קִרְיַת אַרְבַּע **qiryat 'arba'** or קִרְיַת הָאַרְבַּע **qiryat hā'arba'**, n.pr.loc. GK: 7957 & 7959 [→ 7176+702]. Kiriath Arba, "*city of four*":– Kirjath-arba [6]

7154 קִרְיַת־בַּעַל **qiryat-ba'al**, n.pr.loc. GK: 7958 [→ 7176+1167]. Kiriath Baal:– Kirjath-baal [2]

7155 קִרְיַת חֻצוֹת **qiryat ḥuṣôt**, n.pr.loc. GK: 7960 [→ 7176]. Kiriath Huzoth, "*city of Huzoth [outside spaces]*":– Kirjath-huzoth [1]

7156 קִרְיָתַיִם **qiryātayim**, n.pr.loc. GK: 7964 [→ 7176]. Kiriathaim, "*two cities*":– Kiriathaim [3], Kirjathaim [3]

7157 קִרְיַת יְעָרִים **qiryat yᵉ'ārîm**, n.pr.loc. GK: 7961 [→ 7176+3297]. Kiriath Jearim, "*city of timberlands*":– Kirjath-jearim [18], Kirjath-arim [1], Kirjath [1]

7158 קִרְיַת־סַנָּה **qiryat-sannâ** or קִרְיַת־סֵפֶר **qiryat-sēper**, n.pr.loc. GK: 7962 & 7963 [→ 7176+5612]. Kiriath Sannah, "*city of Sannah*"; Kiriath Sepher, "*city of a scribe* or *book*":– Kirjath-sepher [4], Kirjath-sannah [1]

7159 קָרַם **qāram**, v. GK: 7965. [Q] to cover with, spread; [N] to be spread over:– cover with [1], covered [1]

7160 קָרַן **qāran**, v.den. GK: 7966 [→ 7161]. [Q] to be radiant; [H] to be with horns:– shone [3], horns [1]

7161 קֶרֶן **qeren**, n.f. or קַרְנַיִם **qarnayim**, n.pr.loc. GK: 7967 & 7969 [→ 6255, 7160, 7163; cf. 7162]. horn, (pair) of horns; something made of horns: wind instrument, container; horn often symbolizes strength and status, as in "horn of salvation"; as n.pr. Karnaim, "*horns*":– horns [43], horn [28], two horns [4], hill [1]

7162 קֶרֶן **qeren** (Aram.), n.f. GK: 10641 [cf. 7161]. horn (of an animal), also referring to a musical instrument:– horns [5], horn [5], cornet [4]

7163 קֶרֶן הַפּוּךְ **qeren happûk**, n.pr.f. GK: 7968 [→ 7161]. Keren-Happuch, "*horn of [cosmetic] eye shadow;* i.e., *cosmetic case*":– Keren-happuch [1]

7164 קָרַס **qāras**, v. GK: 7970 [→ 7165, 7166]. [Q] to stoop low, bend down:– stoopeth [1], stoop [1]

7165 קֶרֶס **qeres**, n.[m.]. GK: 7971 [→ 7164]. clasp, hook (of curtains):– taches [10]

קְרֹס **qērōs**. See 7026.

7166 קַרְסֹל **qarsōl**, n.[f.]. GK: 7972 [→ 7164]. (dual) ankles:– feet [2]

7167 קָרַע **qāra'**, v. GK: 7973 [→ 7168]. [Q] to tear, rend, rip; [Qp] to be torn; [N] to be torn to pieces, be split apart:– rent [46], rend [5], tear [3], surely rend (+7167) [2], cutteth out [1], cut [1], rend away [1], rent away [1], rent in pieces (+7168) [1], rentest [1], tare [1]

7168 קְרָעִים **qᵉrā'îm**, n.m.[pl.]. GK: 7974 [→ 7167]. torn pieces (of a garment), rags:– pieces [2], rags [1], rent in pieces (+7167) [1]

7169 קָרַץ **qāraṣ**, v. GK: 7975 [→ 7171; cf. 7170]. [Q] to maliciously wink, purse (the lips); [Pu] to be shaped:– winketh [2], formed [1], moving [1], wink [1]

7170 קְרַץ **qᵉraṣ** (Aram.), n.[m.]. GK: 10642. piece, "to eat pieces" is slander, denouncement:– accused (+399) [2]

7171 קֶרֶץ **qereṣ**, n.m. GK: 7976 [→ 7169]. gadfly; some sources: mosquito:– destruction [1]

7172 קַרְקַע **qarqa'**, n.[m.]. GK: 7977 [→ 7173, 7174]. floor:– floor [6], bottom [1], other[5] [1]

7173 קַרְקַע **qarqa'**, n.pr.loc. GK: 7978 [→ 7172]. Karka, "*floor, ground*":– Karkaa [1]

7174 קַרְקֹר **qarqōr**, n.pr.loc. GK: 7980 [→ 7172]. Karkor:– Karkor [1]

7175 קֶרֶשׁ **qereš**, n.m. GK: 7983. frame:– boards [33], board [17], benches [1]

7176 קֶרֶת **qeret**, n.f. GK: 7984 [→ 7151, 7152, 7156, 7177, 7178; cf. 7023 (also used with compound proper names)]. city, town:– city [5]

7177 קַרְתָּה **qartâ**, n.pr.loc. GK: 7985 [→ 7176]. Kartah, "*city*":– Kartah [1]

7178 קַרְתָּן ***qartān***, n.pr.loc. GK: 7986 [→ 7176]. Kartan:– Kartan [1]

7179 קַשׁ ***qaš***, n.m. GK: 7990 [→ 7197]. stubble, chaff, straw:– stubble [15], gather stubble (+7197) [1]

7180 קִשֻּׁאָה ***qiššuʾâ***, n.f. GK: 7991 [→ 4750]. cucumber:– cucumbers [1]

7181 קָשַׁב ***qāšab***, v. GK: 7992 [→ 7182, 7183]. [Q] to listen; [H] to pay attention, give heed, listen:– hearken [21], attend [7], hearkened [5], give heed [2], attend to [1], attend unto [1], attended [1], cause to be heard [1], cause to hear [1], giveth heed [1], hearkened diligently (+7182) [1], incline [1], mark well [1], marked [1], regarded [1]

7182 קֶשֶׁב ***qešeb***, n.m. GK: 7993 [→ 7181]. paying attention, responding:– hearing [1], hearkened diligently (+7181) [1], heed [1], regarded [1]

7183 קַשָּׁב ***qaššāb*** or קַשֻּׁב ***qaššub***, a. GK: 7994 & 7995 [→ 7181]. attentive:– attentive [3], attent [2]

7184 קַשְׂוָה ***qaśwâ***, n.f. GK: 7987. pitcher, jar:– covers [3], cups [1]

7185 קָשָׁה ***qāšâ***, v. GK: 7996 [→ 7186, 7190]. [Q] to be hard, harsh, cruel; [N] to be distressed; [P] to have great difficulty (in labor); [H] to make stiff, harden, be difficult:– hardened [8], hard [4], hardeneth [2], harden [2], made grievous [2], cruel [1], fiercer [1], hard thing [1], hardly bestead [1], hardly [1], made stiff [1], sore [1], stiffened [1], stiffnecked (+6203) [1]

7186 קָשֶׁה ***qāšeh***, a. GK: 7997 [→ 7185]. hard, harsh, difficult, fierce; stubborn, stiff(-necked), obstinate:– hard [6], stiffnecked (+6203) [6], roughly [5], cruel [3], grievous [3], sore [2], churlish [1], hardhearted (+3820) [1], heavy [1], impudent (+6440) [1], in trouble (+3117) [1], obstinate [1], prevailed [1], rough [1], sorrowful [1], stiff [1], stubborn [1]

7187 קְשֹׁט ***qᵉšōṭ*** (Aram.), n.[m.]. GK: 10643 [cf. 7189]. truth; (as adv.) surely, truly, rightly:– of a truth (+4481) [1], truth [1]

7188 קָשַׁח ***qāšaḥ***, v. GK: 7998. [H] to harden:– hardened against [1], hardened [1]

7189 קֹשְׁטְ ***qōšṭ*** or קֹשֶׁט ***qōšeṭ***, n.m. GK: 7999 & 8000 [cf. 7198; cf. 7187]. truth; bow (weapon):– certainty [1], truth [1]

קֹשֹׁט ***qōšōṭ***. See 7187.

7190 קְשִׁי ***qᵉšî***, n.[m.]. GK: 8001 [→ 7185]. stubbornness:– stubbornness [1]

7191 קִשְׁיוֹן ***qišyôn***, n.pr.loc. GK: 8002. Kishion:– Kishion [1], Kishon [1]

7192 קְשִׂיטָה ***qᵉśîṭâ***, n.f. GK: 7988. piece of silver (unknown unit of weight or value):– piece of money [1], pieces of money [1], pieces of silver [1]

7193 קַשְׂקֶשֶׂת ***qaśqeśet***, n.f. GK: 7989 [cf. 7082]. scales (as on skin of marine creatures); scale armor:– scales [7], mail [1]

7194 קָשַׁר ***qāšar***, v. GK: 8003 [→ 7195, 7196]. [Q] to tie, bind; to plot, conspire; [Qp] to be bound up; be strong; [N] to be joined with; [P] to bind; [Pu] to be strong; [Ht] to conspire together:– conspired [18], bind [11], made a conspiracy (+7195) [4], bound [3], stronger [2], bound up [1], conspiracy made (+7195) [1], conspirators [1], joined together [1], knit [1], wrought [1]

7195 קֶשֶׁר ***qešer***, n.m. GK: 8004 [→ 7194]. conspiracy, treason:– treason [5], conspiracy [4], made a conspiracy (+7194) [4], confederacy [2], conspiracy made (+7194) [1]

7196 קִשֻּׁרִים ***qiššurîm***, n.[m.]pl. GK: 8005 [→ 7194]. sashes, wedding ornaments:– attire [1], headbands [1]

7197 קָשַׁשׁ ***qāšaš***, v.den. GK: 8006 & 8007 [→ 7179]. [Q] to gather together; [Pol] to gather; [Htpol] to gather together:– gathering [3], gather together [2], gather stubble (+7179) [1], gathered [1], gather [1]

7198 קֶשֶׁת ***qešet***, n.f. [& m.?]. GK: 8008 [→ 7199; cf. 7189]. bow (weapon); by extension, something bow shaped: rainbow:– bow [55], bows [13], archers [2], archers (+1869) [1], archers (+376+3384+871.1+1886.1) [1], archers (+4175+871.1+1886.1) [1], arrow (+1121) [1], bowmen (+7411) [1], bowshot (+2909) [1]

7199 קַשָּׁת ***qaššāt***, n.m. GK: 8009 [→ 7198]. archer:– archer (+7235) [1]

7200 רָאָה ***rāʾâ***, v. GK: 8011 [→ 7204, 4758, 4759, 7201?, 7202, 7203, 7203, 7207, 7209, 7210, 7212 (also used with compound proper names)]. [Q] to see, look, view; to realize, know, consider; [Qp] to be selected; [N] to become visible, appear, show oneself; [Pu] to be seen; [H] to cause to see, show; [Ho] to be shown; [Ht] to look at each other, meet with; a general word for visual perception; note the many contextual translations in the KJV:– see [349], saw [305], seen [161], behold [57], looked [53], look [50], appeared [39], shewed [37], seest [27], seeth [27], shew [27], appear [24], beheld [23], consider [15], seeing [11], seer [10], sawest [6], spied [5], considered [4], looketh [4], perceived [4], appeareth [3], enjoy [3], lo [3], respect [3], sheweth [3], beholdeth [2], considereth [2], foreseeth [2], indeed look (+7200) [2], look out [2], looked on [2], looked upon [2], provided [2], provide [2], regarded [2], saw certainly (+7200) [2], see indeed (+7200) [2], surely seen (+7200) [2], take heed [2], advise [1], approveth [1], beholding [1], caused to see [1], considerest [1], discern [1], espied [1], gaze [1], had experience [1], hath respect [1], in presence (+6440) [1], joyfully [1], make enjoy [1], mark [1], meet [1], near [1], perceive [1], presented [1], regardeth [1], regard [1], respecteth [1], seemeth [1], seer's [1], shewedst [1], sight [1], spy [1], stare [1], thinketh [1], view [1], visions [1]

7201 רָאָה ***rāʾâ***, n.f. GK: 8012 [→ 7200?]. red kite:– glede [1]

7202 רָאֶה ***rāʾeh***, a. GK: 8013 [→ 7200]. seeing:– @H = **7203** רֹאֶה ***rōʾeh***, n.[m.]. GK: 8014 & 8015 [→ 7200]. seer; vision:– seers [1], vision [1]

7204 הָרֹאֶה ***hārōʾeh*** or רֹאֶה ***rōʾēh***, n.pr.m. GK: 2218 [→ 7200]. Haroeh, "*the seer*":– Haroeh [1]

7205 רְאוּבֵן ***rᵉʾûbēn***, n.pr.m. GK: 8017 [→ 7206]. Reuben, "*see, a son! [Ge 29:32]; substitute a son*":– Reuben [72]

7206 רְאוּבֵנִי ***rᵉʾûbēnî***, a.g. GK: 8018 [→ 7205]. Reubenite, of Reuben, "*of Reuben*":– Reubenites [16], Reubenite [1], Reuben [1]

7207 רַאֲוָה ***raʾᵃwâ***, n.f. GK: 8019 [→ 7200]. spectacle, sight:– beholding [1]

7208 רְאוּמָה ***rᵉʾûmâ***, n.pr.f. GK: 8020 [→ 7355? *or* 7214?]. Reumah:– Reumah [1]

7209 רְאִי ***rᵉʾî***, n.m. GK: 8023 [→ 7200]. mirror:– looking glass [1]

7210 רֳאִי ***rᵒʾî***, n.[m.]. GK: 8024 [→ 7200; cf. 7299]. appearance, spectacle:– seen [2], gazing-stock [1], look to [1], seest [1], seeth [1]

7211 רְאָיָה ***rᵉʾāyâ***, n.pr.m. GK: 8025 [→ 7200+3068]. Reaiah, "*Yahweh has seen*":– Reaiah [3], Reaia [1]

7212 רְאִית ***rᵉʾît***, n.f. GK: 8026 [→ 7200]. look, sight:– @H = **7213** רָאַם ***rāʾam***, v. GK: 8027 [→ 7216; cf. 7311]. [Q] to rise up high:– lifted up [1]

7214 רְאֵם ***rᵉʾēm***, n.m. GK: 8028 [→ 7208?]. wild oxen:– unicorn [6], unicorns [3]

7215 רָאמוֹת ***rāʾmôt***, n.[f.pl.]. GK: 8029. coral:– coral [2]

7216 רָאמוֹת ***rāʾmôt***, n.pr.loc. GK: 8030 [→ 7213; cf. 7311]. Ramoth, "*height*":– Ramoth [4]

7217 רֵאשׁ ***rēʾš*** (Aram.), n.m. GK: 10646 [cf. 7218]. head (for functions of sight and thought as a crucial part of the body); fig., leader; or the very first part of an event, the beginning:– head [11], chief [1], heads [1], sum [1]

7218 רֹאשׁ ***rōʾš***, n.m. GK: 8031 [→ 7220, 7221, 7222, 7223, 7224, 7225, 7226; cf. 7217]. head (of the body); by extension: top (of an object); high in status or authority: leader, chief; source or origin: first, beginning; "to lift up the head" can mean to take a census, to behead, or to restore to a position:– head [263], chief [95], heads [85], top [67], beginning [12], sum [9], tops [8], companies [7], captains [6], first [6], company [5], principal [5], captain [4], chapiters [4], high [3], bands [2], beginnings [2], ends [2], rulers [2], beheaded (+5493) [1], chief place [1], chief things [1], chiefest [1], every [1], excellent [1], forefront [1], height [1], highest part [1], lead [1], of [1]

7219 רֹאשׁ ***rōʾš***, n.m. GK: 8032. poison; gall; bitterness:– gall [9], hemlock [1], poison [1], venom [1]

7220 רֹאשׁ ***rōʾš***, n.pr.m. & g. & loc. GK: 8033 & 8396 [→ 7218]. Rosh, "*head, leader*":– Rosh [1]

רֵאשׁ ***rēʾš***. See 7389.

7221 רִאשָׁה ***riʾšâ***, n.f. GK: 8035 [→ 7218]. beginning, before:– beginnings [1]

7222 רֹאשָׁה ***rōʾšâ***, n.f. GK: 8036 [→ 7218]. uppermost, cap[stone]:– headstone (+68) [1]

7223 רִאשׁוֹן ***riʾšôn***, a. GK: 8037 [→ 7224; cf. 7218]. (of position) first, foremost; (of time) former, beginning, earlier:– first [128], former [32], beginning [4], chief [3], foremost [3], before (+871.1+1886.1) [2], old time [2], aforetime (+871.1+1886.1) [1], ancestors [1], beforetime (+871.1+1886.1) [1], before [1], eldest [1], first (+871.1+1886.1) [1], forefathers (+1) [1], past [1]

7224 רִאשֹׁנִי ***riʾšōnî***, a. GK: 8038 [→ 7223; cf. 7218]. first:– first [1]

7225 רֵאשִׁית ***rēʾšît***, n.f. GK: 8040 [→ 7218]. what is first; beginning:– beginning [18], firstfruits [10], first [10], chief [8], chiefest [1], first time [1], firstfruits (+6529) [1], firstfruit [1], principal thing [1]

7226 רַאֲשֹׁת ***raʾᵃšôt***, n.m. GK: 8031 [→ 7218]. pl. of 7218: place of the head:– @H = **7227** רַב ***rab***, a. & n. GK: 8041 & 8042 [→ 7237, 7248, 7249, 7262; cf. 7231; cf. 7229, cf. 7261]. many, much; great, abundant, numerous; commander, chief officer, high official:– many [191], great [117], much [33], captain [24], long [10], moe [8], enough [7], multitude [6], mighty [5], greater [4], more [4], greatly [3], manifold [3], plenteous [3], suffice [3], too much [3], abundantly [2], abundant [2], exceedingly [2], increased [2], long enough [2], many a time [2], princes [2], aboundeth [1], abound [1], common [1], elder [1], full [1], great men [1], great multitude [1], great one [1], great store [1], in abundance [1], in multitude [1], master [1], multiply [1], officers [1], oftentimes (+6471) [1], populous [1], process of time (+3117+1886.1+1886.1) [1], shipmaster (+2259+1886.1) [1], sufficient [1], too many [1]

7228 רַב ***rab***, n.m. GK: 8043 [→ 7232]. archer:– archers [2]

7229 רַב ***rab*** (Aram.), a. GK: 10647 [→ 7236, 7260; cf. 7227]. great, large, many, chief; this can refer to a large object (great, large), a large amount of objects (many, much), or high status (chief):– great [9], master [2], captain [1], chief [1], lord [1], very great [1]

רִב ***rib***. See 7378.

7230 רֹב ***rōb***, n.m. GK: 8044 [→ 7231]. greatness, abundance; multitude:– multitude [69], abundance [32], greatness [9], great [9], much [7], abundantly (+3807.1) [3], many [3], abundance (+3807.1) [2], long [2], plenty [2], abundantly [1], all [1], common [1], excellent [1], great number (+3807.1) [1], great things [1], greatly (+3807.1) [1], huge (+3807.1) [1], in abundance (+3807.1) [1], increased [1], most [1], much (+3807.1) [1], number [1], plentifully (+3807.1) [1], plenty (+3807.1) [1], very [1]

7231 רָבַב ***rābab***, v. GK: 8045 [→ 3377, 3378, 3379, 3380, 4764, 7227, 7230, 7233, 7237, 7239, 7241, 7245; cf. 7235]. [Q] to abound, increase, be great; [Pu] to increase by tens of thousands:– many [6], increased [3], multiplied [3], manifold [1], moe [1], more [1], multiply [1], ten thousands [1]

7232 רָבַב ***rābab***, v. GK: 8046 [→ 7228; cf. 7235]. [Q] to shoot (an arrow):– shot out [1], shot [1]

7233 רְבָבָה ***rᵉbābâ***, n.f. GK: 8047 [→ 7231]. ten thousand, myriad; (virtually) countless number:– ten thousands [8], ten thousand [5], many [1], millions [1], multiply [1]

7234 רָבַד ***rābad***, v. GK: 8048 [→ 4765, 7242]. [Q] to cover:– deckt [1]

7235 רָבָה ***rābâ***, v. GK: 8049 & 8050 & 2221 [→ 697?, 1337, 4767, 4766, 4768, 8635, 8636; cf. 7231, 7232; cf. 7236]. [Q] to increase in number, multiply, grow large; to shoot; (ptcp.) archer; [P] to rear (offspring); to gain; make numerous; [H] to cause to increase, make numerous, enlarge:– multiply [38], multiplied [29], much [24], increase [19], many [19], increased [15], great [6], increaseth [5], more [5], give more [3], long [3], made many [3], greatly multiply (+7235) [2], made great [2], make many [2], much more [2], multiplieth [2], multiply exceedingly (+7235) [2], over much [2], very [2], abundance [1], abundantly [1], any more [1], archer (+7199) [1], ask never so much (+3966) [1], brought in abundance [1], brought up [1], continued [1], enlarge [1], exceeding (+3966) [1], exceedingly (+3966) [1], excelled [1], full [1], gathered much [1], give many [1], givest many [1], great store [1], greater [1], grow up [1], had many [1], heap [1], in authority [1], in process of time (+3117+1886.1) [1], increasest [1], make to multiply [1], many a time [1], more and more [1], much greater [1], multipliedst [1], multiplying [1], nourished [1], number [1], plenteous [1], plenty [1], so much as (+4480) [1], sore [1], store [1], take much [1], throughly [1], use many [1]

7236 רְבָה ***rᵉbâ*** (Aram.), v. GK: 10648 [→ 7229, 7240?, 7238, 7260, 7261; cf. 7235]. [P] to become large, be great; [Pa] to place in a high position, make great:– grown [3], grew [2], made great [1]

7237 רַבָּה ***rabbâ***, n.pr.loc. GK: 8051 [→ 7227; cf. 7231]. Rabbah, "*chief, capital [city]*":– Rabbah [13], Rabbath [2]

7238 רְבוּ ***rᵉbû*** (Aram.), n.f. GK: 10650 [→ 7236]. greatness, high position:– majesty [3], greatness [2]

7239 רִבּוֹא **ribbô'**, n.f. GK: 8052 [→ 7231; cf. 7240]. ten thousand; myriad, (virtually) countless number:– thousand [3], forty two thousand (+505+702) [2], eighteen thousand (+505+8083+2050.1) [1], ten thousands [1], ten thousand [1], threescore and one thousand (+505+8337+2050.1) [1], twenty thousand [1]

7240 רִבּוֹ **ribbô** (Aram.), n.f. GK: 10649 [→ 7236?; cf. 7239]. ten thousand, myriad, (virtually) countless number:– ten thousand [2]

7241 רְבִיבִים **r**e**bîbîm**, n.m. GK: 8053 [→ 7231]. rain shower, abundant rain, gentle rain:– showers [6]

7242 רָבִיד **rābîd**, n.[m.]. GK: 8054 [→ 7234]. necklace, ornamental chain:– chain [2]

7243 רְבִיעִי **r**e**bî'î**, a.num.ord. GK: 8055 [→ 702; cf. 7244]. fourth:– fourth [55], foursquare [1]

7244 רְבִיעָי **r**e**bî'āy** (Aram.), a.num.ord. GK: 10651 [→ 703; cf. 7243]. fourth:– fourth [6]

7245 רַבִּית **rabbît**, n.pr.loc. GK: 8056 [→ 7231]. Rabbith, "*great*":– Rabbith [1]

7246 רָבַךְ **rābak**, v. GK: 8057. [Ho] to be kneaded, mixed (of dough):– fried [2], baken [1]

7247 רִבְלָה **riblâ**, n.pr.loc. GK: 8058. Riblah:– Riblah [11]

7248 רַב מָג **rab māg**, n.m. GK: 8059 [→ 7227]. high official:– Rab-mag [2]

7249 רַב־סָרִיס **rab-sārîs**, n.m. GK: 8060 [→ 7227+5631]. chief officer:– Rab-saris [3]

7250 רָבַע **rāba'**, v.den. GK: 8061 [→ 7252; cf. 7257]. [Q] to lie down with, have sexual relations with; [H] to mate, cross-breed:– lie down [2], gender with [1]

7251 רָבַע **rāba'**, v.den. GK: 8062 [→ 702]. [Qp, P] to be squared, have four corners:– foursquare [8], square [3], squared [1]

7252 רֶבַע **reba'**, v.inf. GK: 8061 [→ 7250]. inf. of 7250: to lie down:– lying down [1]

7253 רֶבַע **reba'**, n.m. GK: 8063 [→ 7254?; cf. 702?]. fourth-part, quarter; side (of a square thing):– sides [3], fourth part [2], squares [2]

7254 רֶבַע **reba'**, n.pr.m. GK: 8064 [→ 7253?; cf. 702?]. Reba:– Reba [2]

7255 רֹבַע **rōba'**, n.[m.]. GK: 8065 [→ 702]. fourth-part, quarter:– fourth part [2]

7256 רִבֵּעַ **ribbēa'**, a. GK: 8067 [→ 702]. fourth; (n.) the fourth generation:– fourth [4]

רְבִעִי **r**e**bi'î**. See 7243.

7257 רָבַץ **rābaṣ**, v. GK: 8069 [→ 4769, 7258; cf. 7250]. [Q] to lie down; [H] to make lie down; to cause to rest:– lie down [9], lieth [3], lie [3], lay down [2], lying [2], cause to lie down [1], causing to lie down [1], couched [1], coucheth [1], couching down [1], fell down [1], lay [1], make fold [1], makest to rest [1], maketh to lie down [1], sitting [1]

7258 רֵבֶץ **rēbeṣ**, n.[m.]. GK: 8070 [→ 7257]. resting place:– resting place [2], place to lie down in [1], where lay [1]

7259 רִבְקָה **ribqâ**, n.pr.f. GK: 8071. Rebekah, "[poss.] *choice calf*":– Rebekah [28], Rebekah's [2]

7260 רַבְרַב **rabrab** (Aram.), a. GK: 10647 [→ 7229]. same as 7229: great, large, many, chief; this can refer to a large object (great, large), a large amount of objects (many, much), or high status (chief):– great [7], stout [1]

7261 רַבְרְבָנִין **rabr**e**bānîn** (Aram.), n.m.pl. GK: 10652 [→ 7236]. nobles, lords:– lords [6], princes [2]

7262 רַב־שָׁקֵה **rab-šāqēh**, n.m. GK: 8072 [→ 7227+8248]. Assyrian officer: (field) commander, cupbearer:– Rab-shakeh [16]

7263 רֶגֶב **regeb**, n.m. GK: 8073 [→ 709]. clod of dirt:– clods [2]

7264 רָגַז **rāgaz**, v. GK: 8074 [→ 712, 7267, 7268, 7269; cf. 7265]. [Q] to quake, shake, tremble; to be angry, be in anguish; [H] to cause to shake, make tremble, cause a disturbance; [Ht] to enrage oneself (against):– tremble [8], rage [5], moved [4], trembled [3], troubled [3], disquieted [2], move [2], afraid [1], disquiet [1], fall out [1], fretted [1], made to tremble [1], much moved [1], provoke [1], quaked [1], quake [1], shaketh [1], shake [1], shook [1], stand in awe [1], wroth [1]

7265 רְגַז **r**e**gaz** (Aram.), v. GK: 10653 [→ 7266; cf. 7264]. [H] to anger, enrage:– provoked unto wrath [1]

7266 רְגַז **r**e**gaz** (Aram.), n.m. GK: 10654 [→ 7265; cf. 7267]. rage:– rage [1]

7267 רֹגֶז **rōgez**, n.m. GK: 8075 [→ 7264; cf. 7266]. turmoil, excitement, tumult:– trouble [2], fear [1], noise [1], rage [1], troubling [1], wrath [1]

7268 רַגָּז **raggāz**, a. GK: 8076 [→ 7264]. anxious, trembling:– trembling [1]

7269 רָגְזָה **rogzâ**, n.f. GK: 8077 [→ 7264]. shuddering, agitation:– trembling [1]

7270 רָגַל **rāgal**, v.den. GK: 8078 [→ 7272, 8637]. [Q] to slander; [P] to spy, explore:– spies [10], spy out [7], backbiteth [1], espy out [1], searched out [1], slandered [1], spied out [1], spy [1], taught to go [1], viewed [1], view [1]

7271 רְגַל **r**e**gal** (Aram.), n.[f.]. GK: 10655 [cf. 7272]. foot:– feet [7]

7272 רֶגֶל **regel**, n.f. GK: 8079 [→ 4772, 7270, 7273, 8637; cf. 7271]. foot; by extension, body parts associated with the foot: sole, legs, big toe, ankle; a euphemism for the genitals; footing or base of an object; footstep, as a measure of length:– feet [152], foot [63], footstool (+1916) [5], times [4], after (+871.1) [3], follow (+871.1) [3], great toes [2], piss (+4325) [2], able to endure (+3807.1) [1], after (+3807.1) [1], brokenfooted (+7667) [1], coming [1], follow (+1980+871.1) [1], followed (+871.1) [1], foot (+3709) [1], footstool (+1916+3807.1) [1], goeth [1], haunt [1], legs [1], possession [1], went on journey (+5375) [1]

7273 רַגְלִי **raglî**, a. GK: 8081 [→ 7272]. (persons) on foot (i.e., not riding):– footmen [7], footmen (+376) [4], on foot [1]

7274 רֹגְלִים **rōg**e**lîm**, n.pr.loc. GK: 8082. Rogelim, "*[place of] treaders, fullers [one who cleans clothes by kneading with no soap*":– Rogelim [2]

7275 רָגַם **rāgam**, v. GK: 8083 [→ 4773, 7277]. [Q] to execute by hurling stones:– stone [9], stoned [5], certainly stone (+7275) [2]

7276 רֶגֶם **regem**, n.pr.m. GK: 8084 [→ 7278; cf. 8638]. Regem, "*friend*":– Regem [1]

7277 רִגְמָה **rigmâ**, n.f. GK: 8086 [→ 7275]. great throng, crowd, a bustling, noisy group:– council [1]

7278 רֶגֶם מֶלֶךְ **regem melek**, n.pr.m. GK: 8085 [→ 7276+4428]. Regem-Melech, "*friend of the king;* [poss.] *chief of troops of the king*":– Regemmelech [1]

7279 רָגַן **rāgan**, v. GK: 8087 [→ 5372]. [Q] to complain; [N] to be grumbling, be gossiping:– murmured [3]

7280 רָגַע **rāga'**, v. GK: 8088 & 8089 & 8090 [→ 4771, 4774, 7281, 7282]. [Q] to stir up, churn up; to harden, crust over; [N] to cease; [H] to find repose, bring rest; to do something in an instant:– divideth [2], rest [2], suddenly [2], broken [1], cause to rest [1], divided [1], find ease [1], give rest [1], make to rest [1], moment [1]

7281 רֶגַע **rega'**, n.m. GK: 8092 [→ 7280]. moment, instant; peace, tranquillity:– moment [13], in a moment [3], instant [2], every moment (+3807.1) [1], in a moment (+3509.1) [1], space [1], suddenly [1]

7282 רָגֵעַ **rāgēa'**, a. GK: 8091 [→ 7280]. quiet, resting:– quiet [1]

7283 רָגַשׁ **rāgaš**, v. GK: 8093 [→ 7285; cf. 7284]. [Q] to be restless, be in tumult, likely referring to a rebellious conspiracy:– rage [1]

7284 רְגַשׁ **r**e**gaš** (Aram.), v. GK: 10656 [cf. 7283]. [H] to go in as a group (causing an uproar), implying that those in the group are bumping into one another:– assembled [3]

7285 רֶגֶשׁ **regeš** or רִגְשָׁה **rigšâ**, n.[m.]. GK: 8094 & 8095 [→ 7283]. crowd, throng:– company [1], insurrection [1]

7286 רָדַד **rādad**, v. GK: 8096 [→ 7289]. [Q] to subdue, beat down; [H] to hammer out flat:– spent [1], spread [1], subdueth [1], subdue [1]

7287 רָדָה **rādâ**, v. GK: 8097 & 8098 [→ 7288]. [Q] to rule over; to scoop out, scrape out; [H] to cause to dominate:– dominion [5], rule [5], ruled [3], bare rule [2], have dominion [2], made have dominion over [2], bear rule [1], made rule over [1], prevaileth [1], reign [1], rule over [1], ruler [1], taken [1], took [1]

7288 רַדַּי **radday**, n.pr.m. GK: 8099 [→ 7287]. Raddai, "[poss.] *beating down; Yahweh rules*":– Raddai [1]

7289 רְדִיד **r**e**dîd**, n.[m.]. GK: 8100 [→ 7286]. cloak, shawl, something wrapped around:– vails [1], vail [1]

7290 רָדַם **rādam**, v. GK: 8101 [→ 8639]. [N] to be in a heavy sleep:– fast asleep [2], in a deep sleep [2], cast into a dead sleep [1], sleeper [1], sleepeth [1]

7291 רָדַף **rādap**, v. GK: 8103 [→ 4783]. [Q] to pursue, chase, persecute; [N] to be pursued, be hounded; [P] to pursue, chase; [Pu] to be chased; [H] to chase:– pursued [35], pursue [28], persecute [15], chased [8], follow [8], persecutors [7], pursueth [7], chase [5], followeth after [5], persecuted [5], pursuers [5], pursuing [4], follow after [3], followed [2], followeth [1], hunt [1], past [1], persecution [1], pursuer [1], put to flight [1]

7292 רָהַב **rāhab**, v. GK: 8104 [→ 7293, 7294, 7296, 7295; cf. 4062]. [Q] to rise up against; press one's plea; [H] to overwhelm; make bold:– behave proudly [1], make sure [1], overcome [1], strengthenedst [1]

7293 רַהַב **rahab**, n.m. GK: 8105 [→ 7292]. same as 7294: pride, strength:– proud [2], strength [1]

7294 רַהַב **rahab**, n.pr. GK: 8105 [→ 7292]. same as 7293: Rahab, a sea monster of chaos that opposes God; used of the land of Egypt, with a focus on affliction or arrogance:– Rahab [3]

7295 רָהָב **rāhāb**, a. GK: 8107 [→ 7292]. proud, defiant:– proud [1]

7296 רֹהַב **rōhab**, n.[m.]. GK: 8106 [→ 7292]. pride or hurry:– strength [1]

7297 רָהָה **rāhâ** or יָרַהּ **yārah**, v. GK: 8109 & 3724. [Q] to fear:– afraid [1]

7298 רַהַט **rahaṭ**, n.[m.]. GK: 8110 & 8111 [→ 7351]. tress, rafter; watering trough:– gutters [2], galleries [1], troughs [1]

7299 רֵו **rēw** (Aram.), n.m. GK: 10657. appearance:– form [2]

רוּב **rûb**. See 7378.

7300 רוּד **rûd**, v. GK: 8113 [→ 4788]. [Q] to roam; [H] to grow restless, cause restlessness:– dominion [1], lords [1], mourn [1], ruleth [1]

7301 רָוָה **rāwâ**, v. GK: 8115 [→ 3138, 7302, 7310, 7377]. [Q] to drink to satisfaction, quench the thirst; [P] to drench, refresh, satisfy; [H] to lavish upon, cause to refresh; from the base meaning of quenching thirst come the fig. extensions of refreshment, satisfaction, and fulfillment:– watereth [2], abundantly satisfied [1], bathed [1], filled [1], made drunken [1], made drunk [1], satiated [1], satiate [1], satisfy [1], soaked [1], take fill [1], waterest abundantly [1], water [1]

7302 רָוֶה **rāweh**, a. GK: 8116 [→ 7301]. well-watered, drenched:– watered [2], drunkenness [1]

7303 רָהְגָה **rohgâ** or רוֹהֲגָה **rôh**a**gâ**, n.pr.m. GK: 8108 & 8117. Rohagah, Rohgah:– Rohgah [1]

7304 רָוַח **rāwaḥ**, v. GK: 8118 [→ 7305, 7307, 7309, 7306, 7381]. [Q] to feel relief; [Pu] to be spacious:– refreshed [2], large [1]

7305 רֶוַח **rewaḥ**, n.m. GK: 8119 [→ 7304]. relief; space:– enlargement [1], space [1]

7306 רִיחַ **rîaḥ** or רוּחַ **rûaḥ**, v. GK: 8193 [→ 7381; cf. 7304]. [H] to smell (an aroma or odor):– smell [5], smelled [2], accept [1], make of quick understanding [1], smelleth [1], toucheth [1]

7307 רוּחַ **rûaḥ**, n.f. GK: 8120 [→ 7304; cf. 7308]. breath, wind; by extension: spirit, mind, heart, as the immaterial part of a person that can respond to God, the seat of life; spirit being, especially the Spirit of God:– spirit [227], wind [81], breath [27], winds [11], mind [5], side [5], spirits [5], blast [4], vain [2], air [1], anger [1], breath (+5397) [1], cool [1], courage [1], quarters [1], sides [1], spiritual [1], tempest [1], whirlwind (+5591) [1], windy [1]

7308 רוּחַ **rûaḥ** (Aram.), n.f. GK: 10658 [cf. 7382; cf. 7307]. wind, breath, spirit; from the base meaning of "wind" (or "breath") come the meaning of "spirit" as an immaterial supernatural being, and as the immaterial part of the inner person, with a possible focus on the reasoning and thinking faculty: "mind" or "heart":– spirit [8], mind [1], winds [1], wind [1]

7309 רְוָחָה **r**e**wāḥâ**, n.f. GK: 8121 [→ 7304]. relief, respite:– breathing [1], respite [1]

7310 רְוָיָה **r**e**wāyâ**, n.f. GK: 8122 [→ 7301]. place of abundance, overflowing:– runneth over [1], wealthy [1]

7311 רוּם **rûm** or רָמַם **rāmam**, v. GK: 8123 & 8249 & 8225 [→ 4791, 4792, 7213, 7312, 7315, 7316, 7317, 7318, 7319, 7410, 7415, 7427, 8641, 8642; cf. 7413, 7426; cf. 7313 (also used with compound proper names)]. [Q] to be high, raise up; to be proud, haughty; to be full of maggots, be wormy; [Pol] to

Heb

exalt, lift high; [Polal] to be exalted, be lifted up; [H] to cause to lift up, present (an offering); to raise up against, rebel; [Ho] to be presented, be taken away; to exalt oneself; from the base meaning of being high in spatial position come the fig. extensions of being high in status: exalted, and high in attitude: proud, arrogant:– exalted [27], lift up [25], high [22], exalt [17], offer [11], lifted up [8], set up [6], take up [5], gave [4], exalteth [3], lifteth up [3], lofty [3], offer up [3], take off [3], take [3], tall [3], extol [2], heaved [2], held up [2], higher [2], liftest up [2], promotion [2], took up [2], bred [1], bring up [1], brought up [1], extolled [1], give [1], haughty [1], heaved up [1], heave [1], high ones [1], levy [1], lifted up on high [1], lifter up [1], lifteth [1], lifting up [1], loud [1], make on high [1], mount up [1], offered up [1], offered [1], presumptuously (+3027+871.1) [1], promote [1], proud [1], set up on high [1], setteth up [1], shouted aloud (+6963+8643+871.1+3807.1) [1], take away [1], taken away [1], taken off [1], taller [1], went up [1]

7312 רוּם ***rûm***, n.[m.]. GK: 8124 [→ 7311; cf. 7314]. height; haughtiness, pride:– haughtiness [3], high [2], height [1]

7313 רוּם ***rûm*** (Aram.), v. GK: 10659 [→ 7314; cf. 7311]. [P] to become arrogant; [Pol] to exalt, praise; [H] to promote, cause to rise (in rank); [Htpol] to rise up (against); all of these meanings are from the base meaning of "high":– lifted up [2], extol [1], set up [1]

7314 רוּם ***rûm*** (Aram.), n.m. GK: 10660 [→ 7313; cf. 7312?]. height; the top:– height [5]

7315 רוֹם ***rôm***, adv. GK: 8125 [→ 7311]. on high:– on high [1]

7316 רוּמָה ***rûmâ***, n.pr.loc. GK: 8126 [→ 7311; cf. 725]. Rumah, "*height*":– Rumah [1]

7317 רוֹמָה ***rômâ***, adv. GK: 8127 [→ 7311]. proudly, haughtily:– haughtily [1]

7318 רוֹמָם ***rômām***, n.[m.]. GK: 8128 [→ 7311]. praise, exaltation:– @H = **7319** רוֹמֵמֻת ***rômèmut***, n.f. GK: 8129 [→ 7311, 7427]. rising up, lifting up:– high [1]

7320 רֹמַמְתִּי עֶזֶר ***rōmamtî 'ezer***, n.pr.m. GK: 8251 [→ 7311+5828]. Romamti-Ezer, "*[he is my] highest help*":– Romamti-ezer [2]

7321 רוּעַ ***rûa'***, v. GK: 8131 [→ 7452, 8643]. [H] to raise a battle cry; sound a trumpet blast; shout in triumph or exaltation:– shouted [10], shout [10], make a joyful noise [7], triumph [3], cried [2], sound an alarm [2], blow an alarm [1], cry alarm [1], cry aloud [1], cry out aloud (+7452) [1], cry out [1], cry [1], gave a shout [1], shout for joy [1], shouted for joy [1], shouting [1], smart (+7451) [1]

7322 רָפַף ***rāpap*** or רוּף ***rûp***, v. GK: 8344. [Poal] to quake, shake:– tremble [1]

7323 רוּץ ***rûṣ***, v. GK: 8132 [→ 4793, 4794; cf. 7519?]. [Q] to run, hurry, be a messenger; [Pol] to dart about, run to and fro; [H] to chase; to bring quickly:– run [34], ran [28], guard [14], posts [6], running [6], runneth [4], make run [2], post [2], another[S] [1], brake down [1], brought hastily [1], divided speedily [1], footmen [1], runnest [1], stretch out [1]

7324 רִיק ***rîq*** or רוּק ***rûq***, v. GK: 8197 [→ 7385, 7386, 7387]. [H] to pour forth, empty out; to draw (a sword):– draw out [5], empty [4], draw [3], emptied [2], armed [1], cast out [1], make empty [1], pour out [1], poured forth [1]

7325 רִיר ***rîr*** or רוּר ***rûr***, v. GK: 8201 [→ 7388]. [Q] to flow:– run [1]

7326 רוּשׁ ***rûš***, v. GK: 8133 [→ 7389; cf. 3423]. [Q] to be poor, be in poverty, be oppressed; [Htpol] to pretend to be poor:– poor [21], lack [1], maketh poor [1], needy [1]

רוֹשׁ ***rôš***. See 7219.

7327 רוּת ***rût***, n.pr.f. GK: 8134 [→ 7462?]. Ruth, "*friendship; refreshed [as with water]*; [poss.] *comrade, companion*":– Ruth [12]

7328 רָז ***rāz*** (Aram.), n.m. GK: 10661. mystery, secret:– secret [6], secrets [3]

7329 רָזָה ***rāzâ***, v. GK: 8135 [→ 7330, 7332, 7334]. [Q] to destroy; [N] to waste away:– famish [1], wax lean [1]

7330 רָזֶה ***rāzeh***, a. GK: 8136 [→ 7329]. lean; barren:– lean [2]

7331 רְזוֹן ***r^ezôn***, n.pr.m. GK: 8139 [→ 7336]. Rezon, "*prince; high official*":– Rezon [1]

7332 רָזוֹן ***rāzôn***, n.[m.]. GK: 8137 [→ 7329]. wasting disease; short, scrimped (ephah):– leanness [2], scant [1]

7333 רָזוֹן ***rāzôn***, n.m. GK: 8138 [→ 7336]. prince, dignitary:– prince [1]

7334 רָזִי ***rāzî***, n.[m.]. GK: 8140 [→ 7329]. wasting away, leanness:– leanness [2]

7335 רָזַם ***rāzam***, v. GK: 8141. [Q] to wink, flash the eyes:– wink [1]

7336 רָזַן ***rāzan***, v. GK: 8142 [→ 7333, 7331]. [Q] to be a ruler; (ptcp.) a prince, ruler:– princes [5], rulers [1]

7337 רָחַב ***rāḥab***, v. GK: 8143 [→ 4800, 7338, 7341, 7342, 7343, 7339, 7345, 7346]. [Q] to be wide; to swell (with joy); to boast; [N] to be roomy, be broad; [H] to enlarge, broaden, make wide:– enlarged [8], enlarge [7], enlargeth [2], large [2], enlarging [1], made room [1], make wide [1], maketh room [1], open wide [1], opened wide [1]

7338 רַחַב ***raḥab***, n.[m.]. GK: 8144 [→ 7337]. spacious place, vast expanse:– breadth [1], broad place [1]

7339 רְחֹב ***r^eḥōb***, n.f. GK: 8148 [→ 1050, 7340, 7344; cf. 7337]. public square, open street:– street [21], streets [19], broad ways [2], broad places [1]

7340 רְחֹב ***r^eḥōb***, n.pr.m. & loc. GK: 8149 & 8150 [→ 7339]. Rehob, "*broad, wide [place, market]*":– Rehob [10]

7341 רֹחַב ***rōḥab***, n.[m.]. GK: 8145 [→ 7337]. breadth, width:– breadth [74], broad [22], thickness [2], largeness [1], thick [1], wideness [1]

7342 רָחָב ***rāḥāb***, a. GK: 8146 [→ 7343?; cf. 7337]. spacious, broad, roomy:– broad [4], large [4], large (+3027) [3], proud [3], wide (+3027) [2], broad (+3027) [1], broader [1], large enough (+3027) [1], liberty [1], wide [1]

7343 רָחָב ***rāḥāb***, n.pr.f. GK: 8147 [→ 7342?; cf. 7337]. Rahab, "*spacious, broad*":– Rahab [5]

7344 רְחֹבוֹת ***r^eḥōbôt***, n.pr.loc. GK: 8151 [→ 7339]. Rehoboth, "*broad, wide [places, markets]*":– Rehoboth [4]

7345 רְחַבְיָה ***r^eḥabyâ*** or רְחַבְיָהוּ ***r^eḥabyāhû***, n.pr.m. GK: 8152 & 8153 [→ 7337+3068]. Rehabiah, "*Yahweh has enlarged*":– Rehabiah [5]

7346 רְחַבְעָם ***r^eḥab'ām***, n.pr.m. GK: 8154 [→ 7337+5971]. Rehoboam, "*[my] people will enlarge, expand*":– Rehoboam [50]

רְחֹבֹת ***r^eḥōbōt***. See 7344.

7347 רֵחַיִם ***rēḥayim***, n.[m.]. GK: 8160. handmill; pair of mill stones:– millstones [2], mills [1], mill [1], nether [1]

רְחוֹב ***r^eḥôb***. See 7339, 7340.

7348 רְחוּם ***r^eḥûm***, n.pr.m. GK: 8156 & 10662 [→ 7355; cf. 5149, 7359]. Rehum, "*[he] is compassionate*": note this name is Aramaic four times in Ezra:– Rehum [8]

7349 רַחוּם ***raḥûm***, a. GK: 8157 [→ 7355]. compassionate, merciful:– merciful [8], full of compassion [5]

7350 רָחוֹק ***rāḥôq***, a. (used as noun). GK: 8158 [→ 7368; cf. 7352]. far, distant; (n.) distance, afar:– far [31], afar off (+4480) [18], far off [13], afar off [4], afar [3], great while to come (+4480) [2], long ago (+4480+3807.1) [2], old [2], afar off (+4480+5704+3807.1) [1], afar off (+5704) [1], afar off (+871.1) [1], even afar off (+4480) [1], far abroad (+4480+5704+3807.1) [1], far off (+4480) [1], long (+4480) [1], long ago (+4480) [1], space [1]

7351 רָהִיט ***rāhîṭ***, n.m.col. GK: 8112 [→ 7298]. rafters:– rafters [1]

7352 רַחִיק ***raḥîq*** (Aram.), a. GK: 10663 [cf. 7350]. far away:– far [1]

7353 רָחֵל ***rāḥēl***, n.f. GK: 8161 [→ 7354]. ewe-sheep:– ewes [2], sheep [2]

7354 רָחֵל ***rāḥēl***, n.pr.f. GK: 8162 [→ 7353]. Rachel, "*ewe*":– Rachel [41], Rachel's [5], Rahel [1]

7355 רָחַם ***rāḥam***, v.den. GK: 8163 [→ 3395, 3396, 3397, 7208?, 7348, 7349, 7362; cf. 7358]. [Q] to love; [P] to have compassion on, show mercy, take pity on; [Pu] to find compassion, be loved; feelings of compassion are usually accompanied by acts of compassion:– have mercy [22], have compassion [7], shew mercy [3], hath mercy [2], pitieth [2], surely have mercy (+7355) [2], Ruhamah [1], findeth mercy [1], had compassion [1], had mercy [1], have pity [1], love [1], merciful [1], mercy [1], obtained mercy [1]

7356 רַחֲמִים ***raḥ^amîm***, n.m.pl.abst. GK: 8171 [→ 7358; cf. 7359]. compassion, mercy, pity:– mercies [14], tender mercies [11], mercy [4], womb [4], bowels [2], compassions [2], compassion [2], damsel [1], mercies' [1], pitied [1], pity [1], tender love [1]

7357 רַחַם ***raḥam***, n.pr.m. GK: 8165 [→ 7360]. Raham, "*compassion*":– Raham [1]

7358 רֶחֶם ***reḥem***, n.m. GK: 8167 [→ 7361, 7356; cf. 7355]. womb; by extension: mother, any female, birth; an "open womb" is able to conceive; a "closed womb" cannot conceive:– womb [20], matrix [5], wombs [1]

7359 רַחֲמִין ***raḥ^amîn*** (Aram.), n.[m.]pl.intens. GK: 10664 [cf. 7348; cf. 7356]. mercy, compassion:– mercies [1]

7360 רָחָם ***rāḥām*** or רָחָמָה ***rāḥāmâ***, n.[m.]. GK: 8164 & 8168 [→ 7357]. carrion-vulture; some sources: osprey:– gier eagle [2]

7361 רַחֲמָה ***raḥ^amâ***, n.f. GK: 8169 [→ 7358]. womb; slang for woman:– two[S] [1]

7362 רַחֲמָנִי ***raḥ^amānî***, a. GK: 8172 [→ 7355]. compassionate:– pitiful [1]

7363 רָחַף ***rāḥap***, v. GK: 8173. [Q] to tremble, shake; [P] to hover:– fluttereth [1], moved [1], shake [1]

7364 רָחַץ ***rāḥaṣ***, v. GK: 8175 [→ 7366, 7367]. [Q] to wash, bathe; [Pu] to be cleansed; [Ht] to wash oneself:– wash [36], bathe [18], washed [16], washed away [1], washing [1]

7365 רְחַץ ***r^eḥaṣ*** (Aram.), v. GK: 10665. [Htpe] to put one's trust in, rely on:– trusted [1]

7366 רַחַץ ***raḥaṣ***, n.[m.]. GK: 8176 [→ 7364]. washing:– washpot (+5518) [2]

7367 רַחְצָה ***raḥṣâ***, n.f. GK: 8177 [→ 7364]. washing:– washing [2]

7368 רָחַק ***rāḥaq***, v. GK: 8178 [→ 1023, 3128, 4801, 7350, 7369]. [Q] to be far off; to avoid, stand aloof; [P] to send far away, extend; [H] to remove far away, drive far off, go very far:– far [19], far off [4], remove far [4], put away far [3], put far [3], far removed [2], go far [2], removed far [2], very far away (+7368) [2], afar off [1], cast far off [1], drive far [1], far away [1], flee far [1], go far off [1], gone away far [1], gone far [1], good way off [1], good way off [1], keep far [1], put far away [1], refrain [1], remove far off [1], removed far away [1], withdraw far [1]

7369 רָחֵק ***rāḥēq***, a.vbl. GK: 8179 [→ 7368]. one who is far away:– far from [1]

רָחֹק ***rāḥōq***. See 7350.

7370 רָחַשׁ ***rāḥaš***, v. GK: 8180 [→ 4802]. [Q] to be stirred up (one's heart):– inditing [1]

7371 רַחַת ***raḥat***, n.f. GK: 8181. winnowing fork, shovel:– shovel [1]

7372 רָטַב ***rāṭab***, v. GK: 8182 [→ 7373]. [Q] to be drenched, be wet:– wet [1]

7373 רָטֹב ***rāṭōb***, a. GK: 8183 [→ 7372]. well-watered (plant):– green [1]

7374 רֶטֶט ***reṭeṭ***, n.[m.]. GK: 8185 [cf. 7578]. panic:– fear [1]

7375 רֻטֲפַשׁ ***ruṭ^apaš***, v. GK: 8186. [Qp] to be renewed:– fresher [1]

7376 רָטַשׁ ***rāṭaš***, v. GK: 8187. [P] to dash to pieces; [Pu] to be dashed to pieces:– dashed in pieces [3], dash to pieces [1], dashed to pieces [1], dash [1]

7377 רִי ***rî***, n.[m.]. GK: 8188 [→ 7301]. moisture:– watering [1]

7378 רִיב ***rîb***, v. GK: 8189 [→ 3080, 3114, 3401, 4807, 4808, 4809, 7379]. [Q] to quarrel, contend, plead for:– plead [22], strive [7], contend [6], chide [4], contended [3], strove [3], chode [2], ever strive (+7378) [2], pleaded [2], throughly plead (+7378) [2], adversaries [1], complain [1], contend with [1], contendest [1], contendeth [1], debate with [1], debate [1], laid wait [1], plead for [1], pleadeth the cause [1], rebuked [1], strive together [1], striveth [1]

7379 רִיב ***rîb***, n.m. GK: 8190 & 8191 [→ 7378]. contention, grievance, strife, legal dispute:– cause [23], strife [14], controversy [12], contention [2], strivings [2], adversary (+376) [1], causes [1], chiding [1], contended [1], controversies [1], multitude [1], pleadings [1], strive with [1], suit [1]

7380 רִיבַי ***rîbay***, n.pr.m. GK: 8192 [→ 3403?]. Ribai, "*opponent*":– Ribai [2]

7381 רֵיחַ ***rêaḥ***, n.m. GK: 8194 [→ 7306; cf. 7304; cf. 7382]. aroma; pleasing and acceptable: fragrance; unpleasing and unacceptable: stench; both connotations are used of sacrifices as accepted or rejected by God:– savour [45], smell [11], sent [2]

7382 רֵיחַ ***rêaḥ*** (Aram.), n.f. GK: 10666 [cf. 7308; cf. 7381]. (singed, scorched) smell:– smell [1]

רֵים ***rêm***. See 7214.

Heb

רֵיעַ **rêa'**. See 7453.

7383 רִיפוֹת **rîpôt**, n.[f.]. GK: 8195. grain:– ground corn [1], wheat [1]

7384 רִיפַת **rîpat** or דִּיפַת **dîpat**, n.pr.g. GK: 8196 & 1910. Riphath, Diphath:– Riphath [2]

7385 רִיק **rîq**, n.[m.]. GK: 8198 [→ 7324]. emptiness, nothingness, vanity:– vain [8], vanity [2], empty [1], no purpose [1]

7386 רֵיק **rêq**, a. GK: 8199 [→ 7324]. empty; idle, worthless:– vain [7], empty [6], emptied [1]

7387 רֵיקָם **rêqām**, adv. GK: 8200 [→ 7324]. empty-handed, without cause or satisfaction:– empty [12], without cause [2], in vain [1], void [1]

7388 רִיר **rîr**, n.m. GK: 8202 [→ 7325]. saliva; white (of an egg); some sources: a kind of plant juice:– spittle [1], white [1]

7389 רֵישׁ **rêš**, n.m. GK: 8203 [→ 7326]. poverty:– poverty [7]

7390 רַךְ **rak**, a. GK: 8205 [→ 7401]. gentle, tender, weak, soft:– tender [10], soft [3], fainthearted (+3824+1886.1) [1], tender one [1], weak [1]

7391 רֹךְ **rōk**, n.[m.]. GK: 8204 [→ 7401]. gentleness, tenderness, softness:– tenderness [1]

7392 רָכַב **rākab**, v. GK: 8206 [→ 4817, 4818, 7393, 7395, 7394, 7396, 7398]. [Q] to ride or mount an riding animal:– rode [15], riding [10], ride [8], rider [7], rideth [7], riders [5], carried [3], caused to ride [3], put [3], cause to ride [2], made ride [2], on horseback (+5483) [2], ride on [2], set [2], bring [1], brought on horseback [1], causest to ride [1], gat up [1], made to ride [1], make to ride [1], ridden [1]

7393 רֶכֶב **rekeb**, n.m. GK: 8207 [→ 7392]. chariot; large upper mill stone:– chariots [86], chariot [29], millstone [2], upper millstone [1], wagons [1]

7394 רֵכָב **rēkāb**, n.pr.m. GK: 8209 & 8211 [cf. 7392]. Recab, "[prob.] *rider* or *horseman* [from to ride, mount]":– Rechab [13]

7395 רַכָּב **rakkāb**, n.m. GK: 8208 [→ 7392]. chariot driver, horseman:– chariot man [1], driver of chariot [1], horseman [1]

7396 רִכְבָּה **rikbâ**, n.f. GK: 8210 [→ 7392]. act of riding:– chariots [1]

7397 רֵכָה **rēkâ**, n.pr.loc. GK: 8212. Recah:– Rechabites [4], Rechah [1]

7398 רְכוּב **rᵉkûb**, n.[m.]. GK: 8213 [→ 7392]. chariot:– chariot [1]

7399 רְכוּשׁ **rᵉkûš**, n.m. GK: 8214 [→ 7408]. possessions, property, goods, equipment:– goods [12], substance [11], riches [5]

7400 רָכִיל **rākîl**, n.[m.]. GK: 8215 [→ 7402?]. slanderer, gossip:– slanders [2], talebearer [2], carry tales [1], talebearer (+1980) [1]

7401 רָכַךְ **rākak**, v. GK: 8216 [→ 4816, 7391, 7390]. [Q] to be soft, faint-hearted; [Pu] to be soothed; [H] to make faint:– faint [2], tender [2], fainthearted (+3824) [1], maketh soft [1], mollified [1], softer [1]

7402 רָכַל **rākal**, v. GK: 8217 [→ 4819, 7400?, 7403?, 7404]. [Q] to do trade, act as a merchant; (n.) trader, merchant:– merchants [14], merchant [3]

7403 רָכָל **rākāl**, n.pr.loc. GK: 8218 [→ 7402?]. Racal, "*trade*":– Rachal [1]

7404 רְכֻלָּה **rᵉkullâ**, n.f. GK: 8219 [→ 7402]. trading of merchandise:– merchandise [2], traffick [2]

7405 רָכַס **rākas**, v. GK: 8220 [→ 7406, 7407?; cf. 7409]. [Q] to tie, bind:– bind [2]

7406 רֶכֶס **rekes**, n.[m.]. GK: 8221 [→ 7405]. rugged place:– rough places [1]

7407 רֹכֶס **rōkes**, n.[m.]. GK: 8222 [→ 7405?]. intrigue, plot, conspiracy:– pride [1]

7408 רָכַשׁ **rākaš**, v. GK: 8223 [→ 7399]. [Q] to tie, bind:– gotten [3], gathered [1], got [1]

7409 רֶכֶשׁ **rekeš**, n.m.col. GK: 8224 [cf. 7405]. team of horses; fast horses (for couriers):– mules [2], dromedaries [1], swift beast [1]

רְכֻשׁ **rᵉkuš**. See 7399.

רֵם **rēm**. See 7214.

7410 רָם **rām**, n.pr.m. GK: 8226 [→ 7311]. Ram, "*high, exalted*":– Ram [7]

רֻם **rum**. See 7311.

7411 רָמָה **rāmâ**, v. GK: 8227 & 8228 [→ 759, 3414, 4820, 4821, 7419, 7423, 8649; cf. 7503?; cf. 7412]. [Q] to hurl (horse and rider); to shoot (arrows); [P] to deceive, betray:– deceived [4], beguiled [2], thrown [2], betray [1], bowmen (+7198) [1], carrying [1], deceiveth [1]

7412 רְמָה **rᵉmâ** (Aram.), v. GK: 10667 [cf. 7411]. [P] to throw; to impose; [Peil] to be thrown, be set in place; [Htpe] to be thrown:– cast [11], impose [1]

7413 רָמָה **rāmâ**, n.f. GK: 8229 [→ 7414, 7433, 7418, 7432, 7434, 7437, 7435; cf. 7311]. lofty shrine; height:– high place [3], high places [1]

7414 רָמָה **rāmâ** or רָמָתַיִם **rāmātayim**, n.pr.loc. GK: 8230 & 8259 [→ 7413]. Ramah; Ramoth, "*elevated spot, height*"; Ramathaim, "*two heights*":– Ramah [36], Ramath [1]

7415 רִמָּה **rimmâ**, n.f. GK: 8231 [→ 7311]. worm; maggot:– worm [5], worms [2]

7416 רִמּוֹן **rimmôn**, n.m. GK: 8232 [→ 1667, 7417, 7428]. pomegranate: the tree, its fruit, or decorative objects shaped like the fruit:– pomegranates [22], pomegranate [8], pomegranate tree [2]

7417 רִמּוֹן **rimmôn** or רִמּוֹנוֹ **rimmônô**, n.pr.m. & loc. GK: 8233 & 8234 & 8235 & 8237 [→ 1910, 2886, 5884]. Rimmon, "*pomegranate* or pagan god *Rimmon*"; for Remmon-methoar, see also 1886.1 and 8388:– Rimmon [14], Remmon-methoar (+8388+1886.1) [1], Remmon [1]

רָמוֹת **rāmôt**. See 7418, 7433.

7418 רָמוֹת־נֶגֶב **rāmôt-negeb**, n.pr.loc. GK: 8241 [→ 7418+5045]. Ramoth Negev, "*heights of Negev [the south]*":– Ramoth [1]

7419 רָמוּת **rāmût**, n.f. GK: 8239 [→ 7411]. remains, refuse, rubbish:– height [1]

7420 רֹמַח **rōmaḥ**, n.[m.]. GK: 8242. spear:– spears [9], spear [3], buckler [1], javelin [1], lancets [1]

7421 רַמִּי **rammî**, n.pr.m. GK: 8246. Ramite or Aramean:– Syrians [1]

7422 רַמְיָה **ramyâ**, n.pr.m. GK: 8243 [→ 7311?+3068?]. Ramiah, "*Yahweh is exalted*":– Ramiah [1]

7423 רְמִיָּה **rᵉmiyyâ**, n.f. GK: 8244 & 8245 [→ 7411]. laziness, laxness, slackness; deceit:– deceitful [4], deceitfully [3], deceit [2], slothful [2], false [1], guile [1], idle [1], slack [1]

7424 רַמָּכָה **rammākâ**, n.[f.]. GK: 8247. fast mare:– dromedaries [1]

7425 רְמַלְיָהוּ **rᵉmalyāhû**, n.pr.m. GK: 8248 [→ 3068]. Remaliah, "*Yahweh has adorned*":– Remaliah [11], Remaliah's [2]

7426 רָמַם **rāmam**, v. GK: 8250 [cf. 7311]. [Q] to be exalted; [N] to rise upward; to get away:– exalted [3], get up [1], lift up [1], lifted up [1], mounted up [1]

7427 רוֹמֵמֻת **rômēmut**, n.f. GK: 8129 [→ 7319]. same as 7319: rising up, lifting up:– lifting up [1]

רִמֹּן **rimmōn**. See 7416.

7428 רִמּוֹן פֶּרֶץ **rimmôn pereṣ**, n.pr.loc. GK: 8236 [→ 7416+6556]. Rimmon Perez, "*pomegranate pass [breach]*":– Rimmon-parez [2]

7429 רָמַס **rāmas**, v. GK: 8252 [→ 4823]. [Q] to trample, tread upon; [N] to be trampled:– tread down [4], tread [2], trode down [2], trode upon [2], oppressors [1], stamped upon [1], stamped [1], trample under feet [1], trample [1], treadeth down [1], treadeth [1], trodden [1], trode under foot [1]

7430 רָמַשׂ **rāmaś**, v. GK: 8253 [→ 7431]. [Q] to move along (ground or in the water):– creepeth [9], moveth [5], creep [2], moved [1]

7431 רֶמֶשׂ **remeś**, n.m. GK: 8254 [→ 7430]. creatures that move along (ground or sea):– creeping things [7], creeping thing [7], moving thing [1], thing that creepeth [1], things creeping [1]

7432 רֶמֶת **remet**, n.pr.loc. GK: 8255 [→ 7413]. Remeth, "*heights*":– Remeth [1]

7433 רָמוֹת גִּלְעָד **rāmôt gil'ād**, n.pr.loc. GK: 8240 [→ 7413+1568]. Ramoth Gilead, "*heights in Gilead*":– Ramoth-gilead [18], Ramoth [3]

7434 רָמַת הַמִּצְפֶּה **rāmat hammiṣpeh**, n.pr.loc. GK: 8256 [→ 7413]. Ramath Mizpah, "*height [hill] of Mizpah [watch tower]*":– Ramath-mizpeh [1]

7435 רָמָתִי **rāmātî**, a.g. GK: 8258 [→ 7413]. Ramathite, "*of Ramah*":– Ramathite [1]

7436 רָמָתַיִם צוֹפִים **rāmātayim ṣôpîm**, n.pr.loc. GK: 8259 + 7435 [→ 7413+6822]. Ramathaim Zophim:– Ramathaim-zophim [1]

7437 רָמַת לְחִי **rāmat lᵉḥî**, n.pr.loc. GK: 8257 [→ 7413+3895?]. Ramath Lehi, "*height [hill] of Lehi*":– Ramath-lehi [1]

רָן **rān**. See 1028.

7438 רֹן **rōn**, n.[m.]. GK: 8260 [→ 7442]. (joyful) song:– songs [1]

7439 רָנָה **rānâ**, v. GK: 8261 [→ 7440, 7441; cf. 7442]. [Q] to rattle:– rattleth [1]

7440 רִנָּה **rinnâ**, n.f. GK: 8262 [→ 7441; cf. 7439, 7442]. shout of joy, song of joy; cry of pleading:– cry [12], singing [9], joy [3], rejoicing [3], gladness [1], proclamation [1], shouting [1], sing [1], songs [1], triumph [1]

7441 רִנָּה **rinnâ**, n.pr.m. GK: 8263 [→ 7440; cf. 7439]. Rinnah, "*ringing cry [of joy] to Yahweh*":– Rinnah [1]

7442 רָנַן **rānan**, v. GK: 8264 [→ 7438, 7444, 7445, 7443; cf. 7439, 7440]. [Q] to shout for joy, sing for joy; to cry, plead; [P] to sing for joy; [Polal] to sing for joy; [H] to make sing, call for songs of joy:– sing [17], rejoice [9], shout for joy [4], sing aloud [4], crieth [2], caused to sing for joy [1], crieth out [1], cry out [1], greatly rejoice [1], into joy sing [1], joyful [1], makest to rejoice [1], sang [1], shout aloud for joy (+7444) [1], shouted [1], shouteth [1], shout [1], sing for joy [1], sing out [1], singing [1], triumph [1]

7443 רְנָנִים **rᵉnānîm**, n.[m.]pl. GK: 8266 [→ 7442]. female ostrich:– goodly [1]

7444 רַנֵּן **rannēn**, v.inf. GK: 8264 [→ 7442]. inf. of 7442: to shout for joy, sing for joy:– shout aloud for joy (+7442) [1], singing [1]

7445 רְנָנָה **rᵉnānâ**, n.f. GK: 8265 [→ 7442]. shout of joy, joyful song:– joyful voice [1], joyful [1], singing [1], triumphing [1]

7446 רִסָּה **rissâ**, n.pr.loc. GK: 8267 [→ 7450?]. Rissah, "*dew*":– Rissah [2]

7447 רָסִיס **rāsîs**, n.[m.]. GK: 8268 & 8269 [→ 7450]. broken piece (of rubble); drop (of moisture):– breaches [1], drops [1]

7448 רֶסֶן **resen**, n.m. GK: 8270. bridle:– bridle [4]

7449 רֶסֶן **resen**, n.pr.loc. GK: 8271. Resen:– Resen [1]

7450 רָסַס **rāsas**, v. GK: 8272 [→ 7446?, 7447]. [Q] to moisten, sprinkle:– temper [1]

7451 רַע **ra'**, a. & n. GK: 8273 & 8274 & 8288 [cf. 7489]. bad, disagreeable, inferior in quality; by extension: evil, wicked in ethical quality; what is disagreeable to God is ethically evil; God's actions of judgment are disagreeable to the wicked (Eze 14:21), but are not ethically evil:– evil [436], wickedness [58], wicked [25], hurt [20], mischief [19], bad [13], sore [9], trouble [9], evils [8], ill [6], affliction [5], harm [5], adversity [3], naught [3], grievous [2], ill favoured [2], mischiefs [2], noisome [2], sad [2], adversities [1], afflictions [1], calamities [1], displease (+5869+6213+871.1) [1], displeased (+241+871.1) [1], displeased exceedingly (+1419+3415) [1], displeasure [1], distress [1], doest evil [1], evil favouredness (+1697) [1], evil men [1], great wickedness (+7465) [1], grief [1], grieved exceedingly (+1419+7489) [1], heavy [1], hurtful [1], mischievous [1], misery [1], naughty [1], please not (+5869+871.1) [1], pleased not (+5869+871.1) [1], sadly [1], smart (+7321) [1], sorrow [1], troubles [1], vex (+6213) [1], wicked ones [1], wickedly (+871.1) [1], wickedly [1], worse [1], worst [1], wretchedness [1], wrong [1]

7452 רֵעַ **rēa'**, n.m.vbl. GK: 8275 [→ 7321]. shouting, roar:– cry out aloud (+7321) [1], noise [1], shouted [1]

7453 רֵעַ **rēa'**, n.m. GK: 8276 [→ 7462]. neighbor; friend, companion, associate:– neighbour [73], friend [28], neighbour's [26], another[S] [21], friends [14], fellow [8], companion [3], neighbours [2], other[S] [2], another's (+7794) [1], another's[S] [1], brother [1], companions' [1], companions [1], fellow's [1], fellows [1], husband [1], lovers [1], neighbour's (+3807.1) [1], neighbours' [1]

7454 רֵעַ **rēa'**, n.[m.]. GK: 8277. thought, intention:– thoughts [1], thought [1]

7455 רֹעַ **rōa'**, n.[m.]. GK: 8278 [→ 7489]. bad, disagreeable, inferior in quality; by extension: evil, wicked in ethical quality:– evil [11], wickedness [3], badness [1], bad [1], naughtiness [1], sadness [1], sorrow [1]

7456 רָעֵב ***rā'ēb***, v. GK: 8279 [→ 7458, 7457, 7459]. [Q] to be hungry, be famished, be starving:– hungry [3], hunger [2], suffer hunger [2], famished [1], suffer to famish [1], suffered to hunger [1]

7457 רָעֵב ***rā'ēb***, a. GK: 8281 [→ 7456]. hungry:– hungry [22], hunger-bitten [1]

7458 רָעָב ***rā'āb***, n.m. GK: 8280 [→ 7456]. hunger, famine, starvation:– famine [87], hunger [8], dearth [5], famished [1]

7459 רְעָבוֹן ***r^e'ābôn***, n.[m.]. GK: 8282 [→ 7456]. hunger, famine, starvation:– famine [3]

7460 רָעַד ***rā'ad***, v. GK: 8283 [→ 7461]. [Q, H] to tremble:– trembling [2], trembleth [1]

7461 רַעַד ***ra'ad*** or רְעָדָה ***r^e'ādâ***, n.m. & f. GK: 8284 & 8285 [→ 7460]. trembling:– trembling [4], fearfulness [1], fear [1]

7462 רָעָה ***rā'â***, v. GK: 8286 & 8287 & 8289 [→ 4828, 4829, 4830, 7327?, 7453, 7463, 7464, 7466, 7467, 7468, 7469, 7471, 7472, 7473, 7474]. [Q] to be a companion, be a friend; to be a shepherd, to care for flocks, graze; by extension: to rule, with a focus on care and concern; [P] to be an attendant of the groom (of a wedding):– feed [55], shepherds [31], shepherd [27], fed [11], herdmen [7], pastors [7], feedeth on [3], feeding [3], kept [3], companion [2], feedeth [2], shepherds (+6629) [2], broken [1], devour [1], eat up [1], eaten up [1], eat [1], evil entreateth [1], feedest [1], friend [1], keeper [1], keepeth company with [1], keepeth [1], keeping [1], make friendship [1], pastor [1], shepherd (+6629) [1], shepherd's [1], shepherds' [1], shew friendly [1], wander [1], waste [1]

7463 רֵעֶה ***rē'eh***, n.m. GK: 8291 [→ 7462]. friend, personal advisor:– friend [3]

7464 רֵעָה ***rē'â***, n.f. GK: 8292 [→ 7462]. companion, friend:– companions [2], fellows [1]

7465 רֹעָה ***rō'â***, v.ptcp. GK: 8318 [→ 7489; cf. 7492, 7533]. ptcp. of 7489: broken:– broken [1], great wickedness (+7451) [1]

7466 רְעוּ ***r^e'û***, n.pr.m. GK: 8293 [→ 7462; cf. 7472]. Reu, "*friend [of God]*":– Reu [4], Rehu [1]

7467 רְעוּאֵל ***r^e'û'ēl***, n.pr.m. GK: 8294 [→ 7462+410]. Reuel, "*friend of God [El]*":– Reuel [10], Raguel [1]

7468 רְעוּת ***r^e'ût***, n.f. GK: 8295 [→ 7462]. (female) neighbor; fellow (female):– another [2], mate [2], neighbour [2]

7469 רְעוּת ***r^e'ût***, n.f. GK: 8296 [cf. 7470]. chasing after:– vexation [7]

7470 רְעוּ ***r^e'û*** (Aram.), n.f. GK: 10668 [→ 7476; cf. 7469]. will, decision:– pleasure [1], will [1]

7471 רְעִי ***r^e'î***, n.[m.]. GK: 8297 [→ 7462]. pastured (cattle):– pastures [1]

7472 רֵעִי ***rē'î***, n.pr.m. GK: 8298 [→ 7462; cf. 7466]. Rei, "*friendly* or *[my] friend*":– Rei [1]

7473 רֹעִי ***rō'î***, v.ptcp. GK: 8286 [→ 7462]. ptcp. of 7462: shepherd:– shepherd's [1], shepherd [1]

7474 רַעְיָה ***ra'yâ***, n.f. GK: 8299 [→ 7462]. darling, beloved, formally, companion, a woman who is the object of a man's love and affection:– love [9]

7475 רַעְיוֹן ***ra'yôn***, n.[m.]. GK: 8301. chasing after, striving for:– vexation [3]

7476 רַעְיוֹן ***ra'yôn*** (Aram.), n.m. GK: 10669 [→ 7470; cf. 7475]. thought (in one's mind):– thoughts [5], cogitations [1]

7477 רָעַל ***rā'al***, v. GK: 8302 [→ 4831, 7478, 7479, 8653]. [Ho] to be made to quiver:– terribly shaken [1]

7478 רַעַל ***ra'al***, n.[m.]. GK: 8303 [→ 7477]. reeling:– trembling [1]

7479 רְעָלָה ***r^e'ālâ***, n.[f.]. GK: 8304 [→ 7477]. veil:– mufflers [1]

7480 רְעֵלָיָה ***r^e'ēlāyâ***, n.pr.m. GK: 8305 [cf. 7485]. Reelaiah:– Reelaiah [1]

7481 רָעַם ***rā'am***, v.den. GK: 8306 & 8307 [→ 7482, 7485]. [Q] to be confused, distorted; to storm, thunder; [H] to irritate, agitate; to make thunder, make storm:– roar [3], thundered [3], thundereth [3], thunder [2], make fret [1], troubled [1]

7482 רַעַם ***ra'am***, n.[m.]. GK: 8308 [→ 7481]. thunder; thunderous shout:– thunder [6]

7483 רַעְמָה ***ra'mâ***, n.f. GK: 8310. mane (of a horse):– thunder [1]

7484 רַעְמָה ***ra'mâ*** or רַעְמָא ***ra'mā'***, n.pr.m. & loc. GK: 8311 & 8309. Raamah:– Raamah [5]

7485 רַעַמְיָה ***ra'amyâ***, n.pr.m. GK: 8313 [→ 7481+3068; cf. 7480]. Raamiah, "*Yahweh has thundered*":– Raamiah [1]

7486 רַעְמְסֵס ***ra'm^esēs***, n.pr.loc. GK: 8314. Rameses, a town in Egypt and a region in the Nile Delta, "*Ra created him*":– Rameses [4], Raamses [1]

7487 רַעֲנַן ***ra^anan*** (Aram.), a. GK: 10670 [cf. 7488?]. prosperous, flourishing:– flourishing [1]

7488 רָעַן ***rā'an***, v. or רַעֲנָן ***ra^anān***, a. GK: 8316 [cf. 7487]. [Palel] to flourish; (n.) spreading (tree), verdant, luxuriant:– green [18], flourishing [1], fresh [1]

7489 רָעַע ***rā'a'***, v.den. GK: 8317 & 8318 [→ 4827, 7451, 7455, 7465]. [Q] to be distressed, be displeased; (by extension) to be bad, be evil; to break, shatter; [N] to suffer harm; [H] to do wickedness; bring trouble, mistreat; this refers to what is displeasing from a personal perspective; what is displeasing to God is ethically evil; [Htpol] to come to ruin:– evildoers [10], do evil [9], hurt [6], evil [4], wicked [4], afflicted [3], do harm [3], done evil [3], worse [3], afflict [2], break [2], displease (+5869+871.1) [2], done evil indeed (+7489) [2], done wickedly [2], evil entreated [2], still do wickedly (+7489) [2], utterly broken down (+7489) [2], associate [1], behaved ill [1], break in pieces [1], bring evil [1], broken [1], brought evil [1], deal worse [1], dealt ill [1], destroyed [1], did worse [1], displease (+3415+871.1) [1], displeased (+3415+871.1) [1], displeased (+5869+871.1) [1], do hurt [1], do wickedly [1], done mischief [1], evil doers [1], evildoer [1], grieved exceedingly (+1419+7451) [1], hurting [1], ill [1], punish [1], vexed [1], wicked doer [1], wickedly [1]

7490 רְעַע ***r^e'a'*** (Aram.), v. GK: 10671 [cf. 7533]. [P] to break, crush; [Pa] to break to pieces, shatter:– breaketh [1], bruise [1]

7491 רָעַף ***rā'ap***, v. GK: 8319 [cf. 6201]. [Q] to drop, fall, overflow; [H] to cause to rain:– drop down [2], drop [2], distil [1]

7492 רָעַץ ***rā'aṣ***, v. GK: 8320 [cf. 7465, 7533]. [Q] to shatter:– dashed in pieces [1], vexed [1]

7493 רָעַשׁ ***rā'aš***, v. GK: 8321 [→ 7494]. [Q] to shake, quake, tremble; [N] to be made to quake; [H] to cause to shake, make to tremble:– shake [13], trembled [5], tremble [3], moved [2], shook [2], made to shake [1], made to tremble [1], make afraid [1], quake [1], remove [1]

7494 רַעַשׁ ***ra'aš***, n.m. GK: 8323 [→ 7493]. commotion, rattling, earthquake; this can mean a quaking motion and the sounds from a quaking motion; by extension: any clamor, discord, or frenzy:– earthquake [6], rushing [3], shaking [3], commotion [1], confused noise [1], fierceness [1], quaking [1], rattling [1]

7495 רָפָא ***rāpā'***, v. GK: 8324 [→ 4832, 7498, 7500, 7505, 7499, 8644 (also used with compound proper names)]. [Q] to heal; [N] to be healed, be cured; [P] to heal, repair; [Ht] to recover:– healed [31], heal [21], healeth [4], physicians [4], cause to be thoroughly healed (+7495) [2], cure [1], made whole [1], make whole [1], physician [1], repaired [1]

7496 רְפָאִים ***r^epā'îm***, n.m. GK: 8327 [cf. 7503?]. dead, the spirits of the departed:– dead [7], deceased [1]

7497 רְפָאִים ***r^epā'îm***, n.pr.g. GK: 8328 & 8329 [cf. 7503?]. Rephaite, "*mighty*"; Rephaim, "*sunken, powerless ones [giants]*; [poss.] *shades, ghosts of the dead ones [giants]*":– giants [10], giant [7], Rephaim [6], Rephaims [2]

7498 רָפָא ***rāpā'*** or רָפָה ***rāpâ***, n.pr.m. GK: 8325 & 8334 [→ 7495; cf. 7501]. Rapha, Raphah, "[poss.] *one healed*":– Rapha [2]

7499 רְפוּאָה ***r^epû'â***, n.f. GK: 8337 [→ 7495]. healing:– medicines [2], healed [1]

7500 רִפְאוּת ***rip'ût***, n.f. GK: 8326 [→ 7495]. health, healing:– health [1]

7501 רְפָאֵל ***r^epā'ēl***, n.pr.m. GK: 8330 [→ 7495+410; cf. 7498]. Rephael, "*God [El] heals*":– Rephael [1]

7502 רָפַד ***rāpad***, v. GK: 8331 [→ 7507, 7508]. [Q] to spread (mud, so as to leave a trail); [P] to spread out; to refresh:– comfort [1], made [1], spreadeth [1]

7503 רָפָה ***rāpâ***, v. GK: 8332 [→ 4832, 7504, 7510; cf. 7411?, 7496?, 7497?]. [Q] to hang limp, sink down, be feeble; [N] to be lazy; [P] to lower; discourage; [H] to leave alone, abandon, withdraw; [Ht] to show oneself slack:– fail [4], let alone [4], feeble [3], idle [3], let go [3], slack [3], stay [3], faint [2], forsake [2], let down [2], waxed feeble [2], weakened [2], weakeneth [2], abated [1], cease [1], consumeth [1], draweth [1], give respite [1], go [1], leave [1], slothful [1], still [1], wax feeble [1], weak [1]

7504 רָפֶה ***rāpeh***, a. GK: 8333 [→ 7503]. weak, feeble:– weak [4]

רָפָה ***rāpâ, rāpâ***. See 7497, 7498.

רִפָּה ***ripâ***. See 7383.

7505 רָפוּא ***rāpû'***, n.pr.m. GK: 8336 [→ 7495]. Raphu, "*healed*":– Raphu [1]

7506 רֶפַח ***repaḥ***, n.pr.m. GK: 8338. Rephah, "[poss.] *rich; easy [life]*":– Rephah [1]

7507 רְפִידָה ***r^epîdâ***, n.f. GK: 8339 [→ 7502]. base (of a royal carriage); some sources: seat cover:– bottom [1]

7508 רְפִידִים ***r^epîdîm***, n.pr.loc. GK: 8340 [→ 7502]. Rephidim, "[poss.] *supports, rests; resting place*":– Rephidim [5]

7509 רְפָיָה ***r^epāyâ***, n.pr.m. GK: 8341 [cf. 7498?]. Rephaiah, "*Yahweh heals*":– Rephaiah [5]

7510 רִפְיוֹן ***rippāyôn***, n.[m.]. GK: 8342 [→ 7503]. hanging limp, possibly referring to despair:– feebleness [1]

7511 רָפַס ***rāpas*** or רָפַשׂ ***rāpaś***, v. GK: 8346 [→ 4833, 7515; cf. 7512]. same as 7515: [Q] to muddy (a stream by trampling through); [N] to be muddied; [Ht] to be humbled, humble oneself:– humble [1], submit [1]

7512 רְפַס ***r^epas*** (Aram.), v. GK: 10672 [cf. 7511]. [P] to trample down:– stamped [2]

7513 רַפְסֹדוֹת ***rapsōdôt***, n.[f.pl.]. GK: 8343. (log) rafts:– flotes [1]

7514 רָפַק ***rāpaq***, v. GK: 8345. [Ht] to lean oneself (upon):– leaning [1]

7515 רָפַשׂ ***rāpaś***, v. GK: 8346 [→ 7511]. same as 7511: [Q] to muddy (a stream by trampling through); [N] to be muddied; [Ht] to be humbled, humble oneself:– fouledst [1], foul [1], troubled [1]

7516 רֶפֶשׁ ***repeš***, n.[m.]. GK: 8347. mire (of the sea):– mire [1]

7517 רֶפֶת ***repet***, n.[m.]. GK: 8348. stall, enclosure for cattle:– stalls [1]

7518 רַץ ***raṣ***, n.[m.]. GK: 8349. bar (of silver):– pieces [1]

7519 רָצָא ***rāṣā'***, v. GK: 8351 & 8352 [→ 7521; cf. 7323?]. [Q] to take pleasure in, accept; to run forth:– ran [1]

7520 רָצַד ***rāṣad***, v. GK: 8353. [P] to gaze in hostility:– leap [1]

7521 רָצָה ***rāṣâ***, v. GK: 8354 & 8355 [→ 7519, 7522, 7525?, 7526?, 8656]. [Q] to be pleased, delight in, accept; to pay for (sin); [Qp] to be favored, be esteemed; [N] to be accepted; to be paid for; [P] to make amends; [H] to enjoy; [Ht] to regain favor:– accept [13], accepted [7], enjoy [3], favourable [3], please [3], taketh pleasure [3], accepteth [2], delighteth [2], pleased with [2], pleased [2], take pleasure [2], acceptable [1], accomplish [1], approve [1], consentedst [1], delight in [1], delightest in [1], delight [1], enjoyed [1], hadst a favour [1], hast pleasure [1], liked [1], pardoned [1], reconcile [1], set affection [1]

7522 רָצוֹן ***rāṣôn***, n.[m.]. GK: 8356 [→ 7521]. pleasure, acceptance, favor, will:– favour [15], will [9], acceptable [7], delight [5], accepted [4], pleasure [4], desire [3], good will [2], would [2], acceptable (+3807.1) [1], acceptance [1], good pleasure [1], selfwill [1], voluntary will [1]

7523 רָצַח ***rāṣaḥ***, v. GK: 8357 [→ 7524]. [Q] to murder, kill; [N] to be murdered, killed; [P] to murder, kill:– slayer [17], murderer [13], kill [4], murder [3], slain [3], manslayer [2], killed [1], killing [1], murderers [1], put to death [1], slayeth [1]

7524 רֶצַח ***reṣaḥ***, n.[m.]. GK: 8358 [→ 7523]. slaughter, murder, agony of death:– slaughter [1], sword [1]

7525 רִצְיָא ***riṣyā'***, n.pr.m. GK: 8359 [→ 7521?]. Rizia, "[poss.] *pleasant one*":– Rezia [1]

7526 רְצִין ***r^eṣîn***, n.pr.m. GK: 8360 [→ 7521?]. Rezin:– Rezin [11]

7527 רָצַע ***rāṣa'***, v. GK: 8361 [→ 4836]. [Q] to pierce (ear):– bore through [1]

7528 רָצַף ***rāṣap***, v. GK: 8362 [→ 4837, 7531]. [Qp] to be inlaid, be fitted:– paved [1]

7529 רֶצֶף ***reṣep***, n.f. GK: 8363 [→ 7530, 7531, 7532]. hot coals, live coals:– baken on the coals [1]

7530 רֶצֶף ***reṣep***, n.pr.loc. GK: 8364 [→ 7529]. Rezeph, "*heated stones, live coals*":– Rezeph [2]

7531 רִצְפָּה ***riṣpâ***, n.f. GK: 8365 & 8367 [→ 7528, 7529]. live coal, hot coal; (stone) pavement:– pavement [7], live coal [1]

7532 רִצְפָּה ***riṣpâ***, n.pr.f. GK: 8366 [→ 7529]. Rizpah, "*heated stones, live coals*":– Rizpah [4]

7533 רָצַץ ***rāṣaṣ***, v. GK: 8368 [→ 4835; cf. 7465, 7492; cf. 7490]. [Q] break, smash, oppress; [Qp] to be smashed, broken, splintered, oppressed; [N] to be broken, splintered; [P] to oppress, crush; [H] to crush to pieces; [Htpol] to jostle each other:– oppressed [6], broken [4], bruised [2], all to brake [1], brakest in pieces [1], break [1], crushed [1], crush [1], discouraged [1], struggled together [1]

7534 רַק ***raq***, a. GK: 8369 [→ 7535, 7541, 7542, 7550, 7557]. lean, thin, lank:– leanfleshed (+1320) [1], lean [1], thin [1]

7535 רַק ***raq***, adv. GK: 8370 [→ 7534]. only, but, however, except:– only [60], but [20], howbeit [5], nevertheless [5], surely [3], notwithstanding [2], save [2], yet [2], at the least [1], except [1], howsoever [1], in any wise [1], indeed only (+389) [1], nothing but [1], save only [1], save that [1], so that (+518) [1], so [1]

7536 רֹק ***rōq***, n.[m.]. GK: 8371 [→ 7556]. spit, saliva; "to swallow one's spit" means a very brief time:– spitting [1], spittle [1], spit [1]

7537 רָקַב ***rāqab***, v. GK: 8372 [→ 7538, 7539]. [Q] to rot, become worm-eaten:– rot [2]

7538 רָקָב ***rāqāb***, n.[m.]. GK: 8373 [→ 7537]. rottenness, decay:– rottenness [4], rotten thing [1]

7539 רִקָּבוֹן ***riqqābôn***, n.[m.]. GK: 8375 [→ 7537]. rottenness:– rotten [1]

7540 רָקַד ***rāqad***, v. GK: 8376. [Q] to skip, dance; [P] to leap about, dance; [H] to make skip:– dance [3], skipped [2], dancing [1], jumping [1], leap [1], maketh to skip [1]

7541 רַקָּה ***raqqâ***, n.f. GK: 8377 [→ 7534]. temple (of the head):– temples [5]

7542 רַקּוֹן ***raqqôn***, n.pr.loc. GK: 8378 [→ 7534]. Rakkon, "*narrow place*":– Rakkon [1]

7543 רָקַח ***rāqaḥ***, v. GK: 8379 [→ 4040, 4041, 4042, 7544, 7545, 7546, 7547, 7548]. [Q] to make perfume, mix spices; [Pu] to be blended (of perfume); [H] to mix spices:– apothecary [4], compoundeth [1], made [1], prepared [1], spice [1]

7544 רֶקַח ***reqaḥ***, n.[m.]. GK: 8380 [→ 7545; cf. 7543]. (powdered) spice:– spiced [1]

7545 רֹקַח ***rōqaḥ***, n.[m.]. GK: 8381 [→ 7544; cf. 7543]. fragrant blend, spice-blend:– confection [1], ointment [1]

7546 רַקָּח ***raqqāḥ***, n.m. GK: 8382 [→ 7543]. perfume-maker, ointment-mixer:– apothecaries [1]

7547 רִקֻּחַ ***riqquaḥ***, n.[m.]. GK: 8383 [→ 7543]. perfume, ointment:– perfumes [1]

7548 רַקָּחָה ***raqqāḥâ***, n.f. GK: 8384 [→ 7543]. perfume-maker, ointment-mixer:– confectionaries [1]

7549 רָקִיעַ ***rāqîa'***, n.m. GK: 8385 [→ 7554]. expanse (of the sky or heaven); the space above the earth that holds visible objects: clouds, planets, stars:– firmament [17]

7550 רָקִיק ***rāqîq***, n.m. GK: 8386 [→ 7534]. wafer, (thin, flat) cake:– wafers [4], wafer [3], cakes [1]

7551 רָקַם ***rāqam***, v. GK: 8387 [→ 7552?, 7553]. [Q] to embroider, weave colored thread; [Pu] to be woven together:– needlework (+4639) [4], embroiderer [2], curiously wrought [1], needlework [1], wrought with needlework (+4639) [1]

7552 רֶקֶם ***reqem*** or רָקֶם ***rāqem***, n.pr.m. & loc. GK: 8388 & 8389 & 8390 [→ 7551?]. Rakem, Rekem, "*friendship*":– Rekem [5], Rakem [1]

7553 רִקְמָה ***riqmâ***, n.f. GK: 8391 [→ 7551]. embroidered work; varied colored things:– broidered work [5], broidered [2], divers colours [2], needlework [2], raiment of needlework [1]

7554 רָקַע ***rāqa'***, v. GK: 8392 [→ 3421, 7549, 7555]. [Q] to spread out; stamp upon, trample; [P] to hammer out thin, overlay (with precious metal); [Pu] to be hammered, be beaten thin; [H] to cause to spread out, make into plated metal:– beat [1], made broad [1], spread abroad [1], spread forth [1], spread into plates [1], spread out [1], spreadeth abroad [1], spreadeth over [1], stamped [1], stamp [1], stretched out [1]

7555 רִקֻּעַ ***riqqua'***, n.[m.]. GK: 8393 [→ 7554]. sheet, something beaten thin:– broad [1]

7556 רָקַק ***rāqaq***, v. GK: 8394 [→ 7536; cf. 3417]. [Q] to spit saliva:– spit [1]

7557 רַקַּת ***raqqat***, n.pr.loc. GK: 8395 [→ 7534]. Rakkath, "*narrow place*":– Rakkath [1]

7558 רִשְׁיוֹן ***rišyôn***, n.[m.]. GK: 8397 [→ 3423]. authorization, permission:– grant [1]

7559 רָשַׁם ***rāšam***, v. GK: 8398 [cf. 7560]. [Qp] to be written, be inscribed:– noted [1]

7560 רְשַׁם ***rᵉšam*** (Aram.), v. GK: 10673 [cf. 7559]. [P] to put in writing, publish; [Peil] to be written, be published:– signed [4], written [2], sign [1]

7561 רָשַׁע ***rāša'***, v.den. GK: 8399 [→ 4849, 7562, 7563, 7564]. [Q] to do evil, act wickedly; to be guilty; [H] to declare guilty, condemn, inflict punishment; to do wrong:– condemn [11], do wickedly [4], done wickedly [4], wicked [4], condemneth [2], wickedly departed [2], committed wickedness [1], condemned [1], condemning [1], dealt wickedly [1], make trouble [1], very wickedly [1], vexed [1]

7562 רֶשַׁע ***reša'***, n.m. GK: 8400 [→ 7561]. evil, wickedness, wrongdoing:– wickedness [25], wicked [4], iniquity [1]

7563 רָשָׁע ***rāšā'***, a. GK: 8401 [→ 7561]. wicked, evil, guilty:– wicked [252], ungodly [8], condemned [1], guilty [1], him that did wrong [1]

7564 רִשְׁעָה ***riš'â***, n.f. GK: 8402 [→ 7561]. wickedness:– wickedness [13], fault [1], wickedly [1]

7565 רֶשֶׁף ***rešep***, n.m. GK: 8404 [→ 7566]. flame:– coals [2], arrows [1], burning coals [1], burning heat [1], hot thunderbolts [1], sparks (+1121) [1]

7566 רֶשֶׁף ***rešep***, n.pr.m. GK: 8405 [→ 7565]. Resheph, "*flame, flash of fire*":– Resheph [1]

7567 רָשַׁשׁ ***rāšaš***, v. GK: 8406 [→ 8658?, 8659?]. [Pol] to destroy, shatter; [Pu] to be crushed, shattered:– impoverished [1], impoverish [1]

7568 רֶשֶׁת ***rešet***, n.f. GK: 8407 [→ 3423]. net, snare, trap (for catching game); network (net-like metal grating):– net [20], network (+4639) [2]

7569 רַתּוֹק ***rattôq***, n.[m.]. GK: 8408 [→ 7576]. chain:– chain [1]

7570 רָתַח ***rātaḥ***, v. GK: 8409 [→ 7571]. [P] to bring to a boil; [Pu] to be caused to churn; [H] to make to churn:– boiled [1], make boil well (+7571) [1], maketh to boil [1]

7571 רֶתַח ***retaḥ***, n.[m.]. GK: 8410 [→ 7570]. boiling: make boil well (+7570) [1]

7572 רַתִּיקָה ***rattîqâ***, n.[m.]. GK: 8411 [→ 7576]. chain:– chains [1]

7573 רָתַם ***rātam***, v. GK: 8412 [→ 7574, 7575?]. [Q] to tie up, harness (horse team):– bind [1]

7574 רֹתֶם ***rōtem***, n.m. GK: 8413 [→ 7575; cf. 7573?]. broom tree:– juniper tree [2], juniper [2]

7575 רִתְמָה ***ritmâ***, n.pr.loc. GK: 8414 [→ 7574; cf. 7573?]. Rithmah, "*[place of] broom plants*":– Rithmah [2]

7576 רָתַק ***rātaq***, v. GK: 8415 [→ 7569, 7572, 7577]. [Pu] to be bound with chains:– bound [1], loosed [1]

7577 רְתֻקוֹת ***rᵉtuqôt***, n.[f.pl.]. GK: 8416 [→ 7576]. chains:– chains [1]

7578 רְתֵת ***rᵉtēt***, n.[m.]. GK: 8417 [cf. 7374]. trembling, fright:– trembling [1]

7578.1 -שֶׁ ***ša-***, pt rel.pref. GK: 8611 [→ 4332, 4967, 7706]. who, that, because; see under 7945:– @H = **7579** שָׁאַב ***šā„ab***, v. GK: 8612 [→ 4857]. [Q] to draw and carry water:– draw [9], drew [5], drawers [3], drawer [1], drawn [1]

7580 שָׁאַג ***šā'ag***, v. GK: 8613 [→ 7581]. [Q] to roar:– roar [10], roared [4], roaring [3], mightily roar (+7580) [2], roareth [1]

7581 שְׁאָגָה ***šᵉ'āgâ***, n.f. GK: 8614 [→ 7580]. roar, groan:– roaring [6], roarings [1]

7582 שָׁאָה ***šā'â***, v. GK: 8615 & 8616 [→ 7585, 7588, 7591, 7612, 7866?, 7898?, 8663]. [Q] to lie wasted; [N] to be ruined; to roar; [H] to turn into desolation:– lay waste [2], desolate [1], make a rushing [1], rush [1], wasted [1]

7583 שָׁאָה ***šā'â***, v. GK: 8617 [cf. 8159]. [Ht] to watch closely, gaze at:– wondering [1]

7584 שַׁאֲוָה ***ša'ᵃwâ***, n.f. GK: 8618. devastating storm: @H –
7585 שְׁאוֹל ***šᵉ„ôl***, n.f. & m. GK: 8619 [→ 7582; cf. 8040]. grave; by extension, realm of death, deepest depths, transliterated "Sheol":– hell [31], grave [30], pit [3], grave's [1]

7586 שָׁאוּל ***šā'ûl***, n.pr.m. GK: 8620 [→ 7587; cf. 7592]. Saul, Shaul, "*asked,* [poss.] *dedicated to God*":– Saul [368], Saul's [28], Shaul [7], Saul's (+3807.1) [3]

7587 שָׁאוּלִי ***šā'ûlî***, a.g. GK: 8621 [→ 7586]. Shaulite, "*of Shaul*":– Shaulites [1]

7588 שָׁאוֹן ***šā'ôn***, n.m. GK: 8623 [→ 7582]. roar, uproar, tumult, loud noise; waste, desolation:– noise [8], rushing [3], tumult [3], tumultuous [2], horrible [1], pomp [1]

7589 שְׁאָט ***šᵉ'āṭ***, n.[m.]. GK: 8624. malice:– despiteful [2], despite [1]

7590 שׂוּט ***šûṭ*** or שָׁאט ***šā'ṭ***, v. GK: 8764. [Q] to malign, act malicious:– despise [2], despised [1]

7591 שְׁאִיָּה ***šᵉ'iyyâ***, n.f. GK: 8625 [→ 7582]. desolation, ruin:– destruction [1]

7592 שָׁאַל ***šā'al***, v. GK: 8626 [→ 847, 848, 4862, 7586, 7587, 7956, 7957, 7961; cf. 7593 (also used with compound proper names)]. [Q] to ask, inquire, request; [Qp] to be given over; [N] to ask permission; [P] to ask intently, beg; [H] to give what is asked for:– asked [46], ask [38], inquired [15], inquire [7], asketh [4], borrow [4], desired [4], earnestly asked (+7592) [4], lent [4], required [4], asking [3], demand [3], requested [3], require [3], saluted (+7965+3807.1) [3], asked straitly (+7592) [2], beg [2], borrowed [2], desire [2], salute (+7965+3807.1) [2], surely ask (+7592) [2], ask on [1], ask petition (+7596) [1], askest [1], consulted [1], consulter [1], demanded [1], desire a request (+7596) [1], desiredst [1], desireth [1], greet (+7965+3807.1) [1], laid to charge [1], obtained [1], pray [1], wished [1], wishing [1]

7593 שְׁאֵל ***šᵉ'ēl*** (Aram.), v. GK: 10689 [→ 7595; cf. 7592]. [P] to ask, question:– asked [3], demanded [1], requireth [1], require [1]

7594 שְׁאָל ***šᵉ'āl***, n.pr.m. GK: 8627 [→ 7592]. Sheal, "*May God grant!, asking*":– Sheal [1]

שְׁאֹל ***šᵉ'ōl***. See 7585.

7595 שְׁאֵלָה ***šᵉ'ēlâ*** (Aram.), n.f. GK: 10690 [→ 7593; cf. 7596]. verdict, decision:– demand [1]

7596 שְׁאֵלָה ***šᵉ'ēlâ***, n.f. GK: 8629 [→ 7956; cf. 7592; cf. 7595]. petition, request:– petition [9], request [2], ask petition (+7592) [1], desire a request (+7592) [1], loan [1]

7597 שְׁאַלְתִּיאֵל ***šᵉ'altî'ēl*** or שַׁלְתִּיאֵל ***šaltî'ēl***, n.pr.m. GK: 8630 & 9003 [→ 7592+410]. Shealtiel, "*I have asked [him] of God [El];* [poss.] *God [El] is a shield, God [El] is a victor*":– Shealtiel [8], Salathiel [1]

7598 שְׁאַלְתִּיאֵל ***šᵉ'altî'ēl*** (Aram.), n.pr.m. GK: 10691 [cf. 7597]. Shealtiel:– Shealtiel [1]

Heb

7599 שָׁאַן ***šā'an***, v. GK: 8631 [→ 7600, 7946]. [Palpal] to be at ease, be at rest, be secure:– at ease [2], quiet [2], rest [1]

7600 שַׁאֲנָן ***ša'ᵃnān***, a. GK: 8633 [→ 7599]. at ease, complacent, secure; insolent, proud:– at ease [6], quiet [2], tumult [2]

7601 שָׁסַס ***šāsas*** or שָׁאַס ***šā'as***, v. GK: 9116 [→ 4933, 8155; cf. 8154]. same as 8155: [Q] to plunder, ransack; [N] to be looted, be ransacked:– spoil [1]

7602 שָׁאַף ***šā'ap***, v. GK: 8634 & 8635 [cf. 7779]. [Q] to pant after, long for, pursue; to trample, crush:– swallow up [4], desire [1], devour [1], earnestly desireth [1], hasteth [1], panted [1], pant [1], snuffed up [1], snuffeth up [1], swallowed up [1], swalloweth up [1]

7603 שְׂאֹר ***šᵉ'or***, n.m. GK: 8419 [→ 4958, 4863]. yeast, leaven:– leaven [4], leavened bread [1]

7604 שָׁאַר ***šā'ar***, v. GK: 8636 [→ 7605, 7610, 7609, 7611; cf. 7606]. [Q] to remain; [N] to be left, remain; [H] to leave, spare:– left [64], remained [23], remain [15], leave [12], remaineth [8], remnant [4], let [3], rest [2], left behind [1], reserve [1]

7605 שְׁאָר ***šᵉ'ār***, n.m. GK: 8637 [→ 7604; cf. 7606]. remainder, remnant, the rest:– remnant [11], rest [10], residue [4], other [1]

7606 שְׁאָר ***šᵉ'ār*** (Aram.), n.m. GK: 10692 [cf. 7605]. the rest, remainder:– rest [9], residue [2], more [1]

7607 שְׁאֵר ***šᵉ'ēr***, n.m. GK: 8638 [→ 7608]. flesh, meat; by extension: the body as a whole; blood relative, as one's "flesh and blood":– flesh [7], near kinswoman [2], body [1], food [1], kinsman [1], kin [1], near kin [1], near [1], that is nigh unto [1]

7608 שַׁאֲרָה ***ša'ᵃrâ***, var. GK: 8640 [→ 7607+1886.3]. blood relative, as one's "flesh and blood":– near kinswomen [1]

7609 שֶׁאֱרָה ***še'ᵉrâ***, n.pr.f. GK: 8641 [→ 7604; cf. 242]. Sheerah, "*blood relationship* or *female relative; remainder*":– Sherah [1]

7610 שְׁאָר יָשׁוּב ***šᵉ'ār yāšûb***, n.pr.m. GK: 8639 [→ 7604+3427]. Shear-Jashub, "*remnant will return*":– Shear-jashub [1]

7611 שְׁאֵרִית **še'ērît**, n.f. GK: 8642 [→ 7604]. remnant, remainder, the rest:– remnant [44], residue [13], rest [3], remainder [2], escaped [1], left [1], posterity [1], remain [1]

7612 שֵׁאת **šē't**, n.f. GK: 8643 [→ 7582]. ruin, desolation:– desolation [1]

7613 שְׂאֵת **śe'ēt**, n.f. GK: 8420 & 8421 [→ 4984, 7863?, 7865?; cf. 4984]. swelling; splendor, honor, loftiness, acceptance:– rising [7], dignity [2], excellency [2], accepted [1], highness [1], raiseth up [1]

7614 שְׁבָא **šebā'**, n.pr.m. & loc. GK: 8644 [→ 7615]. Sheba, "*seven or oath*":– Sheba [22], Sabeans [1]

7615 שְׁבָאִים **šebā'îm**, a.g. GK: 8645 [→ 7614]. Sabeans:– Sabeans [1]

7616 שְׁבָבִים **šebābîm**, n.[m.]pl. GK: 8646 [→ 7632]. broken pieces, splinters:– broken in pieces [1]

7617 שָׁבָה **šābâ**, v. GK: 8647 [→ 7619, 7622, 7628, 7633, 7870]. [Q] to take captive; [Qp, N] to be taken captive:– carried away captive [7], carried captives [5], carry away captives (+7617) [4], captives [3], carried away [3], taken captives [3], taken captive [3], carried captive [2], carry away captive [2], lead captive [2], took captives [2], brought away captive [1], carried away captives (+7633) [1], carry away captives [1], driven away [1], led away captive [1], led captive [1], take captives [1], taken captive (+7628) [1], took away [1], took captive [1], took prisoners (+7628) [1]

7618 שְׁבוֹ **šebô**, n.[f.]. GK: 8648. agate (exact identification is uncertain):– agate [2]

7619 שׁוּבָאֵל **šûbā'ēl** or שְׁבוּאֵל **šebû'ēl**, n.pr.m. GK: 8742 & 8649 [→ 7617?+410]. Shubael, Shebuel, "[poss.] *captive of God [El]* or *God [El] restores*":– Shebuel [3], Shubael [3]

7620 שָׁבוּעַ **šābûa'**, n.m. GK: 8651 [→ 7650]. week (a time period of seven); Feast of Weeks, a festival celebrating the first produce of the harvest; a unit of time used in the book of Daniel, possibly a "week" of seven years:– weeks [12], week [4], full weeks (+3117) [1], seven [1], two weeks [1], whole weeks (+3117) [1]

7621 שְׁבוּעָה **šebû'â**, n.f. GK: 8652 [→ 7650]. sworn oath:– oath [25], oaths [2], charge with an oath (+7650+871.1) [1], curse [1], sworn (+1167) [1]

Heb

7622 שְׁבוּת **šebût** or שְׁבִית **šebît**, n.f. GK: 8654 & 8669 [→ 7617]. captivity, exile; fortunes:– captivity [31], captives [1]

7623 שָׁבַח **šābaḥ**, v. GK: 8655 & 8656 [→ 3431; cf. 7624]. [P] to glorify, commend, extol; to keep still; [H] to cause stillness; [Ht] to glory in:– praise [4], commended [1], glory [1], keepeth [1], praised [1], stillest [1], stilleth [1], triumph [1]

7624 שְׁבַח **šebaḥ** (Aram.), v. GK: 10693 [cf. 7623]. [Pa] to praise, honor:– praised [3], praise [2]

7625 שְׁבַט **šebaṭ** (Aram.), n.m. GK: 10694 [cf. 7626]. tribe, a subgroup of a nation:– tribes [1]

7626 שֵׁבֶט **šēbeṭ**, n.m. GK: 8657 [→ 8275; cf. 7625]. rod, staff, a stick used to assist in walking, discipline, and guidance, often highly individualized and used for identification; of royalty: scepter; by extension: tribe, as a major unit of national group or clan (fig. identified with or under authority of a leader's staff), people, clan, family:– tribes [84], tribe [57], rod [34], sceptre [9], staff [2], correction [1], darts [1], pen [1], sceptres [1]

7627 שְׁבָט **šebāṭ**, n.pr.m. GK: 8658. Shebat, "*[month of] destroying [rain]*":– Sebat [1]

7628 שְׁבִי **šebî**, n.m. GK: 8660 [→ 7617]. captivity, exile; captive, prisoner:– captivity [35], captives [6], captive [3], prisoners [1], taken away [1], taken captive (+7617) [1], taken [1], took prisoners (+7617) [1]

7629 שֹׁבִי **šōbî**, n.pr.m. GK: 8661. Shobi, "[poss.] *captive* or *Yahweh returns*":– Shobi [1]

7630 שֹׁבַי **šōbay**, n.pr.m. GK: 8662. Shobai, "[poss.] *captive* or *Yahweh returns*":– Shobai [2]

7631 שְׁבִיב **šebîb** (Aram.), n.[m.]. GK: 10695 [cf. 7632]. flame:– flame [2]

7632 שָׁבִיב **šābîb**, n.m. GK: 8663 [→ 7616; cf. 7631]. flame; some sources: spark:– spark [1]

7633 שִׁבְיָה **šibyâ** or שְׁבִיָּה **šebiyyâ**, n.f. GK: 8664 & 8665 [→ 7617]. captive, prisoner; captivity:– captives [7], captivity [1], carried away captives (+7617) [1]

7634 שׁוֹבְיָה **šobyâ** or שָׂכְיָה **śākeyâ**, n.pr.m. GK: 8499 [→ 3068]. Shobia, "exile"; Sakia, "[poss.] *one who looks to Yahweh*":– Shachia [1]

7635 שְׁבִיל **šebîl**, n.[m.]. GK: 8666 [→ 7640]. way, path:– paths [1], path [1]

7636 שָׁבִיס **šābîs**, n.[m.]. GK: 8667. headband:– cauls [1]

7637 שְׁבִיעִי **šebî'î**, a.num.ord. GK: 8668 [→ 7651]. seventh:– seventh [98]

שְׁבִית **šebît**. See 7622.

7638 שָׂבָךְ **śābāk**, n.[m.]. GK: 8422 [→ 7639, 7730; cf. 5443]. same as 7639: network, lattice, interwoven mesh:–

שַׂבְּכָא **sabbekā'**. See 5443.

7639 שְׂבָכָה **śebākâ**, n.f. GK: 8422 [→ 7638]. same as 7638: network, lattice, interwoven mesh:– network [5], networks [2], wreathen work [2], wreaths [2], checker [1], lattice [1], nets [1], snare [1], wreath [1]

7640 שֹׁבֶל **šōbel**, n.[m.]. GK: 8670 [→ 788, 789, 7635, 7641]. skirt, hem of skirt:– leg [1]

7641 שִׁבֹּלֶת **šibbōlet**, n.f. GK: 8672 & 8673 [→ 7640; cf. 5451]. head of grain; flood, torrent, flow:– ears [11], ears of corn [3], branches [1], channel [1], floods [1], shibboleth [1], waterflood (+4325) [1]

7642 שַׁבְּלוּל **šabbelûl**, n.m. GK: 8671 [→ 1101?]. slug, snail; some sources: miscarriage:– snail [1]

שִׁבֹּלֶת **šibbōlet**. See 7641.

7643 שְׂבָם **śebām** or שִׂבְמָה **śibmâ**, n.pr.loc. GK: 8423 & 8424. Sebam, Sibmah, "*sweet smell*":– Sibmah [4], Shebam [1], Shibmah [1]

7644 שֶׁבְנָא **šebnā'** or שֶׁבְנָה **šebnâ**, n.pr.m. GK: 8674 & 8675 [→ 7645?]. Shebna, "*[Yahweh] return now*":– Shebna [9]

7645 שְׁבַנְיָה **šebanyâ** or שְׁבַנְיָהוּ **šebanyāhû**, n.pr.m. GK: 8676 & 8677 [→ 7644?]. Shebaniah:– Shebaniah [7]

7646 שָׂבַע **śāba'**, v. GK: 8425 [→ 7647, 7648, 7649, 7654, 7653]. [Q] to be satisfied, have enough, be satiated; the filling and even overfilling of appetites and desires:– satisfied [38], filled [21], full [14], satisfy [7], filleth [2], have enough [2], satisfieth [2], filled full [1], filledst [1], fill [1], had enough [1], had plenty [1], have plenty [1], satiate [1], satisfiest [1], sufficed [1], weary [1]

7647 שָׂבָע **śābā'**, n.m. GK: 8426 [→ 7646]. abundance, overflowing:– plenty [4], plenteous [2], abundance [1], plenteousness [1]

7648 שֹׂבַע **śōba'**, n.[m.]. GK: 8427 [→ 7646]. one's fill to contentment, all one wants:– full [3], fill [2], fulness [1], satisfying [1], sufficed [1]

7649 שָׂבֵעַ **śābēa'**, a. GK: 8428 [→ 7646]. full, abounding:– full [8], satisfied [2]

7650 שָׁבַע **šāba'**, v. GK: 8678 [→ 884, 7620, 7621, 7637, 7651, 7657, 7658, 7659]. [N] to swear an oath, make a sworn promise; [H] to make one swear an oath, give a charge:– sware [70], sworn [41], swear [32], sweareth [7], made swear [6], charge [5], swarest [5], took an oath [4], adjure [2], made to swear [2], straitly charged with an oath (+7650) [2], straitly sworn (+7650) [2], adjured [1], cause to swear [1], charge by an oath [1], charge with an oath (+7621+871.1) [1], charged with the oath [1], fed to the full [1], make swear [1], make to swear [1], swearers [1]

7651 שֶׁבַע **šeba'**, n.m. & f. GK: 8679 [→ 884, 1340?, 7637, 7658; cf. 7650; cf. 7655]. seven; (pl.) seventy:– seven [360], seventh [12], seventeen (+6240) [8], seventeenth (+6240) [6], by sevens (+7651) [4], sevenfold [1], seventeen (+6235+2050.1) [1], seventy [1], threescore and seventeen (+7657+2050.1) [1], threescore and ten [1]

7652 שֶׁבַע **šeba'**, n.pr.m. & loc. GK: 8680 & 8681 [cf. 472, 1339, 3089, 3090, 7656]. Sheba, "*seven* or *oath*":– Sheba [10]

שָׁבֻעַ **šābua'**. See 7620.

7653 שִׂבְעָה **śib'â**, n.f. GK: 8430 [→ 7646]. abundance, plenty:– fulness [1]

7654 שָׂבְעָה **śob'â**, n.f. GK: 8429 [→ 7646]. abundance, satisfaction, enough:– enough [2], full [1], satisfieth [1], sufficiently (+3807.1) [1], unsatiable (+1115) [1]

שִׁבְעָה **šib'â**. See 7651.

7655 שְׁבַע **šeba'** (Aram.), n.m. & f. GK: 10696 [cf. 7651]. seven; the phrase "seven times" (Da 3:19) likely means to be as hot as possible:– seven [6]

7656 שִׁבְעָה **šib'â**, n.pr.loc. GK: 8683 [cf. 7652]. Shibah:– Shebah [1]

שְׁבֻעָה **šebu'â**. See 7620.

שְׁבִיעִי **šebî'î**. See 7637.

7657 שִׁבְעִים **šib'îm**, n.pl. GK: 8684 [→ 7650]. seventy (pl. of "seven")]):– seventy [57], threescore and ten [21], threescore and fifteen (+2568+2050.1) [2], threescore and fourteen (+702+2050.1) [2], threescore and twelve (+8147+2050.1) [2], seven [1], threescore and fifteen (+2568+2050.1+2050.1) [1], threescore and seventeen (+7651+2050.1) [1], threescore and sixteen (+8337+2050.1) [1], threescore and thirteen (+7969+1886.1+2050.1) [1], threescore and thirteen (+7969+2050.1) [1]

7658 שִׁבְעָנָה **šib'ānâ**, n.m. GK: 8685 [→ 7651; cf. 7650]. seven:– seven [1]

7659 שִׁבְעָתַיִם **šib'ātayim**, n.f.du. GK: 8686 [→ 7650]. seven-fold, seven times:– sevenfold [5], seven times [1]

7660 שָׁבַץ **šābaṣ**, v. GK: 8687 [→ 4865, 7661, 8665]. [P] to weave; [Pu] to be woven (of fine metal), (n.) a filigree setting:– embroider [1], set [1]

7661 שָׁבָץ **šābāṣ**, n.m. GK: 8688 [→ 7660]. seizure, cramp, referring to death throes:– anguish [1]

7662 שְׁבַק **šebaq** (Aram.), v. GK: 10697. [P] to leave, have remain; [Htpe] to be left:– leave [3], alone [1], left [1]

7663 שָׂבַר **śābar**, v. GK: 8431 & 8432 [→ 7664; cf. 5452]. [Q] to examine; [P] to wait for, hope for:– hoped [2], viewed [2], wait [2], hope [1], tarry [1]

7664 שֵׂבֶר **śēber**, n.m. GK: 8433 [→ 7663]. hope:– hope [2]

7665 שָׁבַר **šābar**, v. GK: 8689 & 8653 [→ 4866, 4867, 7667, 7669, 7670, 7671; cf. 8406]. [Q] to break, destroy, crush; [Qp] to be broken; [N] to be destroyed, be smashed, be broken; [P] to break, smash, shatter; [H] to bring to break through (of birth); [Ho] to be crushed:– broken [63], break [30], brake [15], destroyed [7], breaketh [5], brake in pieces [4], brakest [4], hurt [3], destroy [2], quite break down (+7665) [2], torn [2], brake down [1], brake up [1], break down [1], break in pieces [1], breakest [1], bring to the birth [1], broken down [1], broken off [1], broken-hearted (+3820) [1], crush [1], quench [1]

7666 שָׁבַר **šābar**, v.den. GK: 8690 [→ 7668]. [Q] to buy grain or food; [H] to sell, allow to buy grain:– buy [14], sell [3], sold [2], bought [1], selleth [1]

7667 שֶׁבֶר **šeber** or שֵׁבֶר **šēber**, n.m. GK: 8691 & 8694 [→ 7671; cf. 7665]. destruction, brokenness, injury; "destruction of spirit" is discouragement, and so lacking motivation and being faint-hearted; interpretation (of a dream):– destruction [21], breach [6], hurt [4], affliction [2], breaking [2], bruise [2], breaches [1], breakings [1], brokenfooted (+7272) [1], brokenhanded (+3027) [1], crashing [1], interpretation [1], vexation [1]

7668 שֶׁבֶר **šeber**, n.[m.]. GK: 8692 [→ 7666]. grain:– corn [8], victuals [1]

7669 שֶׁבֶר **šeber**, n.pr.m. GK: 8693 [→ 7667 *or* 7668]. Sheber, "[poss.] *lion*; [poss.] *breaking* or *crushing* or *roughly broken grain*":– Sheber [1]

7670 שִׁבָּרוֹן **šibbārôn**, n.[m.]. GK: 8695 [→ 7665]. destruction, brokenness:– breaking [1], destruction [1]

7671 שְׁבָרִים **šebārîm**, n.m.[pl.]. GK: 8696 [→ 7667]. stone quarry:– Shebarim [1]

7672 שְׁבַשׁ **šebaš** (Aram.), v. GK: 10698. [Htpa] to be baffled, be perplexed:– astonied [1]

7673 שָׁבַת **šābat**, v. GK: 8697 [→ 4868, 7674, 7676, 7677, 7678]. [Q] to rest, observe the Sabbath; [N] to come to an end, disappear; [H] to put to an end, stop:– cause to cease [17], cease [9], ceased [6], rest [6], make to cease [5], ceaseth [4], rested [4], made to cease [3], caused to fail [1], causeth to cease [1], celebrate sabbath (+7676) [1], keep a sabbath (+7676) [1], kept sabbath [1], left without [1], make cease [1], make rest [1], make to fail [1], maketh to cease [1], put away [1], put down [1], puttest away [1], rid [1], still [1], suffer to be lacking [1], took away [1]

7674 שֶׁבֶת **šebet**, n.f. GK: 8700 [→ 7673]. cessation, doing-nothing:– cease [1], loss of time [1], sit still [1]

7675 שֶׁבֶת **šebet**, n.f. GK: 8699 [→ 3427]. place of sitting or settling, site, seat:– seat [3], habitation [1], place [1]

7676 שַׁבָּת **šabbāt**, n.f. & m. GK: 8701 [→ 7677, 7678; cf. 7673]. Sabbath, the seventh day of the week in the Hebrew calendar (modern Saturday) with a focus of this day as a day of rest and worship; by extension: sabbath, any day or year or period of rest:– sabbath [67], sabbaths [34], every sabbath (+3117+3117+7676+871.1+871.1+1886.1+1886.1) [2], every sabbath (+7676) [2], every sabbath (+7676+871.1) [2], another[S] [1], celebrate sabbath (+7673) [1], keep a sabbath (+7673) [1], sabbath (+3117) [1]

7677 שַׁבָּתוֹן ***šabbātôn***, n.m. GK: 8702 [→ 7676]. (day of) rest:– rest [8], sabbath [3]

7678 שַׁבְּתַי ***šabb^etay***, n.pr.m. GK: 8703 [→ 7676]. Shabbethai, "*one born at Sabbath*":– Shabbethai [3]

7679 שָׂגָא ***śāgā'***, v. GK: 8434 [→ 7689; cf. 7685; cf. 7680]. [H] to make great, extol:– increaseth [1], magnify [1]

7680 שְׂגָא ***ś^egā'*** (Aram.), v. GK: 10677 [→ 7690; cf. 7679, 7685]. [P] to grow great:– multiplied [2], grow [1]

7681 שָׁגֵה ***šāgēh***, n.pr.m. GK: 8707 [→ 7686?]. Shagee, "*wanderer, meanderer [like grazing sheep]*":– Shage [1]

7682 שָׂגַב ***śāgab***, v. GK: 8435 [→ 4869, 7687]. [Q] to be too strong for; [N] to be lofty, be exalted; [P] to lift high; to protect; [Pu] to be kept safe; [H] to act exalted:– exalted [5], high [3], defend [2], safe [2], exalteth [1], excellent [1], lofty [1], set on high [1], set up on high [1], set up [1], setteth on high [1], strong [1]

7683 שָׁגַג ***šāgag***, v. GK: 8704 [→ 49; cf. 4879, 7686]. [Q] to err unintentionally, go astray:– deceived [1], erred [1], sinneth ignorantly [1], went astray [1]

7684 שְׁגָגָה ***š^egāgâ***, n.f. GK: 8705 [cf. 7686]. unintentional wrong, accidental error:– ignorance [11], error [2], unawares (+871.1) [2], unawares [2], sinneth through ignorance (+6213+871.1) [1], unwittingly (+871.1) [1]

7685 שָׂגָה ***śāgâ***, v. GK: 8436 [cf. 7679]. [Q] to be prosperous, thrive, grow; [H] to increase (in wealth):– grow [2], increase [2]

7686 שָׁגָה ***šāgâ***, v. GK: 8706 [→ 4870; cf. 4879, 7683, 7684, 7681?, 7691]. [Q] to sin unintentionally, go astray, wander:– erred [6], err [4], ravisht [2], causeth to go astray [1], deceived [1], deceiver [1], erreth [1], go astray [1], maketh to wander [1], sin through ignorance [1], wandered [1], wander [1]

7687 שְׂגוּב ***ś^egûb*** or שְׂגִיב ***ś^egîb***, n.pr.m. GK: 8437 & 8439 [→ 7682]. Segub, Segib, "*exalted*":– Segub [3]

7688 שָׁגַח ***šāgaḥ***, v. GK: 8708. [H] to gaze, stare:– looketh [2], narrowly look [1]

7689 שַׂגִּיא ***śaggî'***, a. GK: 8438 [→ 7679; cf. 7690]. exalted:– excellent [1], great [1]

7690 שַׂגִּיא ***śaggî'*** (Aram.), a. GK: 10678 [→ 7680; cf. 7689]. great, large, abundant:– much [4], great [3], many [2], exceeding [1], greatly [1], sore [1], very [1]

7691 שְׂגִיאָה ***ś^egî'â***, n.f. GK: 8709 [cf. 7686]. error, mistake:– errors [1]

7692 שִׁגָּיוֹן ***šiggāyôn***, tt. *or* n.m. GK: 8710. shiggaion, shigionoth:– Shiggaion [1], Shigionoth [1]

7693 שָׁגַל ***šāgal***, v. GK: 8711 [→ 7694]. [Q] to ravish, sexually violate; [Qp, N, Pu] to be ravished, be raped:– lien [1]

7694 שֵׁגָל ***šēgal***, n.f. GK: 8712 [→ 7693; cf. 7695]. queen, royal bride:– queen [2]

7695 שֵׁגַל ***šēgal*** (Aram.), n.f. GK: 10699 [cf. 7694?]. wife, concubine:– wives [3]

7696 שָׁגַע ***šāga'***, v. GK: 8713 [→ 7697]. [Pu] to be mad, act like a maniac; [Ht] to carry on like a madman:– mad [5], mad men [1], play the mad man [1]

7697 שִׁגָּעוֹן ***šiggā'ôn***, n.m. GK: 8714 [→ 7696]. madness:– madness [2], furiously (+871.1) [1]

7698 שֶׁגֶר ***šeger***, n.f. GK: 8715. calf, offspring (of cattle):– increase [4], cometh [1]

7699 שַׁד ***šad*** or שֹׁד ***šōd***, n.m. GK: 8716 & 8718 [→ 7705]. (female) breast:– breasts [19], breast [3], paps [1], teats [1]

7700 שֵׁד ***šēd***, n.[m.]. GK: 8717. demon, evil spirit:– devils [2]

7701 שֹׁד ***šōd***, n.m. GK: 8719 [→ 7703]. destruction, ruin, violence:– destruction [7], spoil [4], spoiled [3], spoiling [3], desolation [2], robbery [2], wasting [2], oppression [1], spoiler [1]

7702 שָׂדַד ***śādad***, v. GK: 8440 [→ 7708; cf. 5465, 7713]. [P] to till, harrow, break up the ground:– break clods [1], break the clods [1], harrow [1]

7703 שָׁדַד ***šādad***, v. GK: 8720 [→ 7701, 7736]. [Q] to destroy, devastate; [Qp] to be destroyed; [H] to be ruined; [P, Pol] to ravage, destroy; [Pu] to be destroyed, be ruined; [Ho] to be ruined:– spoiled [19], spoiler [8], spoil [8], laid waste [5], spoilers [3], robbers [2], utterly spoiled (+7703) [2], wasted [2], dead [1], destroyed [1], destroyer [1], destroy [1], oppress [1], spoilest [1], spoileth [1], wasteth [1]

7704 שָׂדֶה ***śādeh*** or שָׂדַי ***śāday***, n.m. GK: 8441 & 8442. area of land, usually cultivated: field, open country, countryside:– field [245], fields [47], country [17], land [7], wild [7], ground [4], lands [4], soil [1], wild (+871.1+1886.1) [1]

7705 שִׁדָּה ***šiddâ***, n.f. GK: 8721 [→ 7699]. lady, concubine; (pl.) harem:– musical instruments of all sorts (+7705) [2]

7706 שַׁדַּי ***šadday***, n.[pr.m.]. GK: 8724 [→ 6701, 7707? (also used with compound proper names)]. Almighty:– Almighty [48]

7707 שְׁדֵיאוּר ***š^edê'ûr***, n.pr.m. GK: 8725 [→ 7706?+301]. Shedeur, "*Shaddai is light* or *Shaddai is fire*":– Shedeur [5]

7708 שִׂדִּים ***śiddîm***, n.pr.loc. GK: 8443 [→ 7702]. Siddim:– Siddim [3]

7709 שְׁדֵמָה ***š^edēmâ***, n.f. GK: 8727. (cultivated) field; terrace:– fields [5]

7710 שָׁדַף ***šādap***, v. GK: 8728 [→ 7711; cf. 7805]. [Qp] to be scorched:– blasted [3]

7711 שְׁדֵפָה ***š^edēpâ*** or שִׁדָּפוֹן ***šiddāpôn***, n.f. & m. GK: 8729 & 8730 [→ 7710]. scorching; blight:– blasting [5], blasted [2]

7712 שְׁדַר ***š^edar*** (Aram.), v. GK: 10700 [→ 849]. [Htpa] to make every effort, strive:– laboured [1]

7713 שְׂדֵרָה ***ś^edērâ***, n.f. GK: 8444 [cf. 5468, 7702]. ranks, rows; planks (architectural term):– ranges [3], boards [1]

7714 שַׁדְרַךְ ***šadrak***, n.pr.m. GK: 8731 [cf. 7715]. Shadrach, "*servant of Aku*":– Shadrach [1]

7715 שַׁדְרַךְ ***šadrak*** (Aram.), n.pr.m. GK: 10701 [cf. 7714]. Shadrach, "*servant of the (pagan moon god) Aku*":– Shadrach [14]

7716 שֶׂה ***śeh***, n.m. & f. GK: 8445 [→ 2089]. sheep, lamb:– sheep [17], lamb [16], cattle [8], ewe [1], goat (+5795) [1], lamb (+3532) [1], lesser cattle [1], sheep (+3775) [1], small cattle [1]

7717 שָׂהֵד ***śāhēd***, n.[m.]. GK: 8446. witness:– record [1]

7718 שֹׁהַם ***šōham***, n.m. GK: 8732 [→ 7719]. onyx (exact identification is uncertain):– onyx [11]

7719 שֹׁהַם ***šōham***, n.pr.m. GK: 8733 [→ 7718]. Shoham, "*carnelian [precious stone]*":– Shoham [1]

7720 שַׂהֲרֹנִים ***śah^arōnîm***, n.m. GK: 8448. ornamental crescent (or moon shaped) necklace:– ornaments [2], round tires like the moon [1]

שַׁו ***šaw***. See 7723.

7721 שׂוֹא ***śō'***, v.inf. GK: 5951 [→ 4984]. inf. of 5375: to lift up, arise:– @H = **7722** שׁוֹא ***šô„*** or שׁוֹאָה ***šô„â***, n.f. GK: 8738 & 8739. trouble, ruin, disaster, desolation; ravage:– desolation [5], desolate [2], destruction [2], destroy [1], destructions [1], storm [1], wasteness [1]

7723 שָׁוְא ***šāw'***, n.[m.]. GK: 8736 [→ 6673?]. worthlessness, vanity, falseness:– vanity [22], vain [17], false [5], in vain [3], in vain (+1886.1+3807.1) [2], lying [2], falsely [1], lies [1]

7724 שְׁוָא ***š^ewā'***, n.pr.m. GK: 8737 [→ 7737; cf. 7864]. Sheva, "*vanity, emptiness; one who will emulate*":– Sheva [2]

7725 שׁוּב ***šûb***, v. GK: 8740 [→ 3437, 3432, 4877, 4878, 7726, 7727, 7728, 7729, 8666; cf. 8421 (also used with compound proper names)]. [Q] to turn back, turn to, return; [Qp] to return; [Pol] to restore, bring back; [Polal] to be recovered; [H] to restore, recover, bring back; [Ho] to be returned, be brought back; from the base meaning of turning back comes the fig. extension of restoration of relationship, as when one returns in repentance to God:– return [223], returned [147], turn [71], bring again [54], turn away [36], turn again [32], turned [32], again [30], come again [30], brought again [25], restore [25], render [16], came again [15], restored [13], turned away [13], brought back [12], cause to return [12], turned back [12], answer [11], go again [11], turned again [10], turn back [9], turneth [9], bring back [6], bring [6], returneth [6], turneth away [6], recompensed [5], recovered [5], certainly return (+7725) [4], put again [4], went back [4], carry back [3], caused to return [3], cometh again [3], go back [3], recompense [3], relieve [3], rendered [3], repent [3], restored again [3], reverse [3], say nay (+6440) [3], answered (+1697) [2], answered [2], bring again indeed (+7725) [2], bringeth back [2], bringing back [2], brought [2], carried again [2], certainly requite (+7725) [2], deliver again [2], drew back [2], give again [2], gone back [2], hinder [2], in any case bring again (+7725) [2], in any case deliver again (+7725) [2], in any wise go back (+7725) [2], in any wise return (+7725) [2], may [2], must needs bring again (+7725) [2], restore again [2], restorer [2], return at all (+7725) [2], reward [2], surely bring back again (+7725) [2], turnest [2], went again [2], withdrawn [2], answer (+1697) [1], answer (+4405) [1], answereth [1], at all turn [1], averse [1], back again [1], bethink (+413+3820) [1], bethink (+413+3824) [1], bring home [1], bringeth [1], call [1], came back [1], camest back [1], carry again [1], cause to answer [1], cause to turn [1], causing to return [1], cease [1], considereth [1], consider [1], continually (+1980+2050.1) [1], converted [1], converting [1], converts [1], convert [1], deliver [1], deny (+6440) [1], drawn [1], fetch again [1], fro [1], gave [1], get again [1], get back again [1], giveth [1], give [1], go home [1], let [1], make return [1], makest to turn [1], more [1], out [1], past [1], pay [1], perverted [1], pull in again [1], put up again [1], put [1], recall [1], recover [1], refresheth [1], rendered again [1], reported [1], requited [1], requite [1], requiting [1], rescue [1], restoreth [1], retire [1], return again (+1980) [1], return again [1], returned back [1], rewardeth [1], sent back [1], set again [1], slidden back [1], still [1], take back [1], taken off [1], take [1], turn back again [1], turn from [1], turneth back [1], turning away [1], turning [1], withdrawest [1], withdraw [1], withdrew [1]

שׁוּבָאֵל ***šûbā'ēl***. See 7619.

7726 שׁוֹבָב ***šôbāb***, a. GK: 8743 [→ 7725]. faithless, rebellious, apostate:– backsliding [2], frowardly [1]

7727 שׁוֹבָב ***šôbāb***, n.pr.m. GK: 8744 [→ 7725]. Shobab, "*one who turns back, repents*":– Shobab [4]

7728 שׁוֹבֵב ***šôbēb***, a. GK: 8745 [→ 7725]. unfaithful, traitorous, apostate:– backsliding [2]

7729 שׁוּבָה ***šûbâ***, n.f. GK: 8746 [→ 7725]. returning, i.e., repentance:– returning [1]

7730 שׂוֹבֶךְ ***śôbek***, n.[m.]. GK: 8449 [→ 7638; cf. 5440]. tangle of branches:– thick boughs [1]

7731 שׁוֹבַךְ ***šôbak***, n.pr.m. GK: 8747 [cf. 7780]. Shobach:– Shobach [2]

7732 שׁוֹבָל ***šôbāl***, n.pr.m. GK: 8748. Shobal, "*basket*":– Shobal [9]

7733 שׁוֹבֵק ***šôbēq***, n.pr.m. GK: 8749 [→ 3435]. Shobek, "*victor*":– Shobek [1]

7734 סוּג ***sûg*** or שׂוּג ***śûg***, v. GK: 6047 [→ 5253]. same as 5472: [N] to be turned back, be disloyal:– turned [1]

7735 שׂוּג ***śûg***, v. GK: 8451 [cf. 5473?]. [Pil] to cause growth, raise:– make to grow [1]

7736 שׁוּד ***šûd*** or שָׁדַד ***šādad***, v. GK: 8720 [→ 7703]. same as 7703: [Q] to destroy, devastate:– wasteth [1]

שׁוֹד ***šōd***. See 7699, 7701.

7737 שָׁוָה ***šāwâ***, v. GK: 8750 & 8751 [→ 3438, 3440, 3441, 7724, 7740, 7741, 7862; cf. 7739]. [Q] to be like, be equal; to be appropriate, be deserved; [N] to be like; [P] to make smooth; to set, place, bestow; [H] to liken; to count as equal:– laid [3], compared [2], equal [2], maketh [2], alike [1], availeth [1], behaved [1], bringeth forth [1], countervail [1], like [1], made plain [1], make equal [1], profited [1], profit [1], reckoned [1], set [1]

7738 שָׁוָה ***šāwâ***, var. GK: *. to destroy:– @H = **7739** שְׁוָה ***š^ewâ*** (Aram.), v. GK: 10702 [cf. 7737]. [Peil] to be made like; [Pa] to make like; [Htpa] to be made into:– made [2]

7740 שָׁוֵה ***šāwēh***, n.pr.loc. GK: 8753 [cf. 7737]. Shaveh, "*level [valley]*":– Shaveh [1]

7741 שָׁוֵה קִרְיָתַיִם ***šāwēh qiryātayim***, n.pr.loc. GK: 8754 [→ 7737+7176]. Shaveh Kiriathaim:– Shaveh Kiriathaim [1]

7742 שׂוּחַ ***śûaḥ***, v. GK: 8452. [Q] to meditate:– meditate [1]

7743 שׁוּחַ ***šûaḥ***, v. GK: 8755 [→ 7745, 7746?, 7845; cf. 7812, 7817]. [Q] sink down:– bowed down [1], humbled [1], inclineth [1]

7744 שׁוּחַ ***šûaḥ***, n.pr.m. GK: 8756 [→ 7747]. Shuah, "*depression, lowland [an Aramean land on the Euphrates River]*":– Shuah [2]

7745 שׁוּחָה ***šûḥâ***, n.f. GK: 8757 [→ 7746?; cf. 7743, 7882]. pit, rift:– pit [3], ditch [1], pits [1]

7746 שׁוּחָה ***šûḥâ***, n.pr.[m.?]. GK: 8758 [→ 7745?; cf. 7743?]. Shuhah, "*pit, depression*":– Shuah [1]

7747 שׁוּחִי ***šûḥî***, a.g. GK: 8760 [→ 7744]. Shuhite:– Shuhite [5]

7748 שׁוּחָם ***šûḥām***, n.pr.m. GK: 8761 [→ 7749]. Shuham:– Shuham [1]

7749 שׁוּחָמִי ***šûḥāmî***, a.g. GK: 8762 [→ 7748]. Shuhamite, "*of Shuham*":– Shuhamites [2]

7750 שׂוּט ***śûṭ***, v. GK: 8454 [→ 7846?; cf. 7847]. [Q] to turn aside (to false gods):– turn aside [2]

7751 שׁוּט ***šûṭ***, v.den. GK: 8763 [→ 4880, 7752, 7850, 7885]. [Q] to roam, go about; to oar (a boat); [Pol] to wander, go here

Heb

and there; [Htpol] to rush here and there:– run to and fro [6], going to and fro [2], gone [1], go [1], mariners [1], rowers [1], went about [1]

7752 שׁוֹט שׁוט **šôṭ**, n.m. GK: 8765 & 8867 [→ 7850; cf. 7751]. whip, lash, scourge:– scourge [5], whips [4], whip [2]

7753 שׂוּךְ שׂוך **śûk**, v. GK: 8455 [→ 7754, 7755; cf. 5259, 5526]. [Q] to block with thorn hedges:– fenced [1], hedge up [1], made a hedge [1]

7754 שׂוֹךְ שׂוך **śôk** or שׂוֹכָה שׂוכה **śôkâ**, n.f. GK: 8456 & 8457 [→ 7753]. branch or brushwood:– bough [2]

7755 שׂוֹכֹה שׂוכה **śôkōh** or שׂוֹכוֹ שׂוכו **śôkô**, n.pr.loc. GK: 8458 & 8459 [→ 7753]. Soco, Socoh, "[poss.] *thorny place*":– Shochoh [2], Socoh [2], Shocho [1], Shoco [1], Sochoh [1], Socho [1]

7756 שׂוּכָתִי שׂוכתי **śûkātî**, a.g. GK: 8460. Sucathite:– Suchathites [1]

7757 שׁוּל שׁול **šûl**, n.m. GK: 8767 [cf. 7887]. hem (of a robe); skirt:– hem [5], skirts [4], hems [1], train [1]

7758 שׁוֹלָל שׁולל **šôlāl** or שֵׁילָל שׁילל **šêlāl**, a. GK: 8768 & 8871 [→ 7997]. barefoot, stripped:– spoiled [2], stript [1]

7759 שׁוּלַמִּית שׁולמית **šûlammît**, a.g.[f.]. GK: 8769. Shulammite:– Shulamite [2]

7760 שִׂים שׂים **śîm** or שׂוּם שׂום **śûm**, v. GK: 8492 [→ 3450, 8667; cf. 3455; cf. 7761]. [Q] to place, put, establish, appoint; [Qp] to be placed, set upon; [H] to cause to place, put; [Ho] to be set:– put [142], set [114], make [64], made [48], laid [35], lay [23], appoint [11], set up [10], appointed [8], maketh [8], consider (+3824) [5], give [5], putteth [5], brought [4], gave [4], layeth [4], makest [3], put in [3], care (+3820) [2], considered (+3820) [2], disposed [2], in any wise set (+7760) [2], lay up [2], look well (+5869) [2], mark well (+3820) [2], ordained [2], painted (+7760+871.1+1886.1) [2], placed [2], put on [2], put to [2], puttest [2], set on [2], take [2], turneth [2], wholly set (+7760) [2], bring [1], called [1], cast [1], caused to be set [1], change [1], charged [1], commit [1], consider (+3807.1) [1], consider (+3820) [1], consider [1], convey [1], determined (+1961) [1], doeth [1], done [1], gavest [1], get [1], given [1], had [1], heap up [1], holdeth [1], impute [1], laid up [1], laidst [1], lay down [1], layest [1], leave [1], made out [1], named (+8034) [1], ordain [1], ordereth [1], place [1], preserve [1], purposed [1], putting [1], regard (+3820) [1], regarded (+3820) [1], regarding [1], rehearse [1], rewarded [1], settest [1], setteth [1], shed [1], shewed [1], shew [1], stedfastly [1], told (+6310+871.1) [1], took [1], tread down (+4823) [1], turned [1], turn [1], will[S] [1], wrought [1]

Heb

7761 שִׂים שׂים **śîm** (Aram.), v. GK: 10682 [cf. 7760]. [P] to place (an order), issue (a decree); [Peil] to be placed, be issued; [Htpe] to be put, be laid (to rubble):– made [10], make [5], commanded (+2942) [3], laid [2], given [1], give [1], named (+8036) [1], regarded (+2942) [1], regardeth [1], set [1]

7762 שׁוּמִים שׁומים **šûmîm**, n.[m.]. GK: 8770. garlic:– garlick [1]

7763 שֹׁמֵר שׁמר **šōmēr**, n.pr.m. GK: 9071 [→ 8116]. Shomer, "*guardian, watchman*":– Shomer [2]

7764 שׁוּנִי שׁוני **šûnî**, n.pr.m. GK: 8771 [→ 7765]. Shuni:– Shuni [2]

7765 שׁוּנִי שׁוני **šûnî**, a.g. GK: 8772 [→ 7764]. Shunite, "*of Shuni*":– Shunites [1]

7766 שׁוּנֵם שׁונם **šûnēm**, n.pr.loc. GK: 8773 [→ 7767]. Shunem:– Shunem [3]

7767 שׁוּנַמִּי שׁונמי **šûnammî**, a.g. GK: 8774 [→ 7766]. Shunammite, "*of Shunem*":– Shunammite [8]

7768 שָׁוַע שׁוע **šāwa'**, v. GK: 8775 [→ 7769, 7771, 7773, 7775 (also used with compound proper names)]. [P] to cry for help, plead:– cried [10], cry [6], crieth out [1], crieth [1], cry aloud [1], cry out [1], shout [1]

7769 שׁוּעַ שׁוע **šûa'**, n.[m.]. GK: 8780 & 8782 [→ 7768, 7770; cf. 7771]. cry for help; wealth:– cry [1], riches [1]

7770 שׁוּעַ שׁוע **šûa'**, n.pr.m. GK: 8781 [→ 7769; cf. 7771]. Shua, "*prosperity*":– Shuah [2], Shua [1]

7771 שׁוֹעַ שׁוע **šôa'**, a. & n.m. GK: 8777 & 8779 [→ 50, 7768, 7770, 7769]. crying out; highly respected, noble; (n.) the rich:– bountiful [1], crying [1], rich [1]

7772 שׁוֹעַ שׁוע **šôa'**, n.pr.g. GK: 8778 [cf. 6970]. Shoa, "*rich*":– Shoa [1]

7773 שֶׁוַע שׁוע **šewa'**, n.[m.]. GK: 8776 [→ 7768]. cry for help:– cry [1]

7774 שׁוּעָא שׁועא **šû'ā'**, n.pr.f. GK: 8783. Shua, "*prosperity*":– Shua [1]

7775 שַׁוְעָה שׁועה **šaw'â**, n.f. GK: 8784 [→ 7768]. cry for help:– cry [11]

7776 שׁוּעָל שׁועל **šû'āl**, n.m. GK: 8785 [→ 2705, 7777]. fox; jackal:– foxes [6], fox [1]

7777 שׁוּעָל שׁועל **šû'āl**, n.pr.m. & loc. GK: 8786 & 8787 [→ 7776]. Shual, "*fox* or *jackal*":– Shual [2]

7778 שֹׁעֵר שׁוער **šō'ēr**, n.m. GK: 8788 [→ 8179; cf. 8652]. gatekeeper, doorkeeper:– porters [31], porter [4], doorkeepers [2]

7779 שׁוּף שׁוף **šûp**, v. GK: 8789 & 8790 [cf. 7602]. [Q] to strike; to crush; some sources: bruise, a wound that is not fatal:– bruise [2], breaketh [1], cover [1]

7780 שׁוֹפָךְ שׁופך **šôpak**, n.pr.m. GK: 8791 [cf. 7731]. Shophach:– Shophach [2]

7781 שׁוּפָמִי שׁופמי **šûpāmî**, a.g. GK: 8793 [→ 8197]. Shuphamite, "*of Shupham*":– Shuphamites [1]

שׁוֹפָן **šôpān**. See 5855.

7782 שׁוֹפָר שׁופר **šôpār**, n.m. GK: 8795 [→ 829; cf. 8231]. trumpet, ram's horn:– trumpet [48], trumpets [20], cornet [3], cornets [1]

7783 שׁוּק שׁוק **šûq**, v. GK: 8796 [→ 7785, 7784; cf. 8264?]. [H] to prove narrow, overflow; [Polel] to water abundantly:– overflow [2], waterest [1]

7784 שׁוּק שׁוק **šûq**, n.m. GK: 8798 [→ 7783]. street:– streets [3], street [1]

7785 שׁוֹק שׁוק **šôq**, n.[f.]. GK: 8797 [→ 7783; cf. 8243]. (lower) thigh; leg:– shoulder [13], legs [4], hip [1], thigh [1]

7786 שׂוּר שׂור **śûr**, v.den. GK: 8606 [→ 4951, 8269, 8323]. same as 8323: [Q] to rule, govern; [H] to choose a prince:– had power [1], made princes [1], reigned [1]

7787 שׂוּר שׂור **śûr**, v. GK: *. [Q] to saw:– cut [1]

7788 שׁוּר שׁור **šûr**, v. GK: 8801. [Q] to travel, descend:– sing [1], wentest [1]

7789 שׁוּר שׁור **šûr**, v. GK: 8800 [→ 7790, 7791, 7793?, 7791, 8284]. [Q] to see, look, view:– behold [5], see [4], lay wait [1], looketh [1], look [1], observed [1], observe [1], perceiveth [1], regard [1]

7790 שׁוּר שׁור **šûr**, n.[m.]. GK: 8803 [→ 7791, 7793; cf. 7789; cf. 7792]. enemy:– enemies [1]

7791 שׁוּר שׁור **šûr** or שׁוּרָה שׁורה **šûrâ**, n.m. & f. GK: 8803 & 8805 [→ 7790, 8284; cf. 7789]. wall, supporting wall (of a terrace):– wall [3], walls [1]

7792 שׁוּר שׁור **šûr** (Aram.), n.m. GK: 10703 [cf. 7790]. wall:– walls [3]

7793 שׁוּר שׁור **šûr**, n.pr.loc. GK: 8804 [→ 7790; cf. 7789?]. Shur, "*wall*":– Shur [6]

7794 שׁוֹר שׁור **šôr**, n.m. GK: 8802 [→ 51, 8670; cf. 8450]. bull, ox:– ox [54], bullock [11], oxen [8], cow [2], another's[S] (+7453) [1], bullocks [1], bull [1], wall [1]

7795 שׂוֹרָה שׂורה **śôrâ**, n.[f.]. GK: 8463 [→ 5493?; cf. 8184?]. place, row or a type of grain:– principal [1]

שׂוֹרֵק **sôrēq**. See 8321.

7796 שֹׂרֵק שׂרק **śōrēq**, n.pr.loc. GK: 8604 [→ 8320]. Sorek, "*blood red grapes*":– Sorek [1]

7797 שׂוּשׂ שׂושׂ **śûś**, v. GK: 8464 [→ 4885, 8342]. [Q] to rejoice, be pleased, be delighted:– rejoice [12], glad [4], rejoiced [3], rejoiceth [3], greatly rejoice (+7797) [2], exceedingly rejoice (+8057+871.1) [1], joy [1], make mirth [1]

7798 שַׁוְשָׁא שׁושׁא **šawšā'**, n.pr.m. GK: 8807. Shavsha:– Shavsha [1]

7799 שׁוּשַׁן שׁושׁן **šûšan**, n.m. GK: 8808. lily plant; some sources: lotus plant:– lilies [8], lily [5], Shoshannim [2], Shoshannim-Eduth (+5715) [1]

7800 שׁוּשַׁן שׁושׁן **šûšan**, n.pr.loc. GK: 8809 [cf. 7801]. Susa:– Shushan [21]

7801 שׁוּשַׁנְכָי שׁושׁנכי **šûšankāy** (Aram.), n.pr.g. & loc. GK: 10704 [cf. 7800]. of Susa:– Susanchites [1]

7802 שׁוּשַׁן עֵדוּת שׁושׁן עדות **šûšan 'ēdût**, t.t. GK: 8808 + 6343 [→ 7799+5715]. Shushan Eduth, "Lily of the covenant":– Shushan-eduth [1]

שׁוּשַׁק **šûšaq**. See 7895.

7803 שׁוּתֶלַח שׁותלח **šûtelaḥ**, n.pr.m. GK: 8811 [→ 8364]. Shuthelah:– Shuthelah [4]

7804 שֵׁיזִב שׁיזב **šēzib** (Aram.), v. GK: 10706. [Sh] to rescue, save:– deliver [6], delivered [2], delivereth [1]

7805 שָׁזַף שׁזף **šāzap**, v. GK: 8812 [cf. 7710]. [Q] to see; to be darkened:– looked [1], saw [1], seen [1]

7806 שָׁזַר שׁזר **šāzar**, v. GK: 8813. [Ho] to be finely twisted:– twined [21]

7807 שַׁח שׁח **šaḥ**, a. GK: 8814 [→ 7817]. downward, bent, low:– humble person (+5869) [1]

7808 שֵׂחַ שׂח **śēaḥ**, n.[m.]. GK: 8465 [→ 7878]. thoughts:– thought [1]

7809 שָׁחַד שׁחד **šāḥad**, v. GK: 8815 [→ 7810]. [Q] to give a gift; pay a bribe; pay a ransom:– give a reward [1], hirest [1]

7810 שֹׁחַד שׁחד **šōḥad**, n.m. GK: 8816 [→ 7809]. bribe, gift:– reward [7], gift [6], gifts [4], bribes [3], present [2], bribery [1]

7811 שָׂחָה שׂחה **śāḥâ**, v. GK: 8466 [→ 7813]. [Q] to swim; [H] to make swim, flood:– make to swim [1], swimmeth [1], swim [1]

7812 שָׁחָה שׁחה **šāḥâ**, v. GK: 8817 [cf. 7743, 7817]. [Q] to bow down; [H] to weigh down, cause to bow:– worship [54], worshipped [39], bowed [31], bow down [14], bowed down [4], made obeisance [4], bow [3], obeisance [3], reverence [3], worshippeth [3], worshipping [3], did obeisance [2], fall down [2], crouch [1], did reverence [1], fell down [1], fell flat [1], humbly beseech [1], maketh stoop [1], reverenced [1]

7813 שָׂחוּ שׂחו **śāḥû**, n.[m.]. GK: 8467 [→ 7811]. water deep enough to swim in:– swim [1]

7814 שְׂחוֹק שׂחוק **śᵉḥôq**, n.[m.]. GK: 8468 [→ 7832]. laughter, which can communicate joy or ridicule; object of ridicule: laughingstock:– laughter [6], derision [5], laughed to scorn [1], laughing [1], one mocked [1], sport [1]

7815 שְׁחוֹר שׁחור **šᵉḥôr**, n.[m.]. GK: 8818 [→ 7835]. soot:– coal [1]

שִׁחוֹר **šiḥôr**. See 7883.

שָׁחוֹר **šāḥôr**. See 7838.

7816 שְׁחוּת שׁחות **šᵉḥût**, n.f. GK: 8819 [→ 7825]. trap, pit:– pit [1]

7817 שָׁחַח שׁחח **šāḥaḥ** or שִׂיחַ שׂיח **śîaḥ**, v. GK: 8820 & 8863 [→ 7807; cf. 7743, 7812]. [Q] to bow down, bend low; [N] to be brought low; [H] to humble, bring low:– bowed down [4], cast down [4], bow [2], brought low [2], bending [1], boweth down [1], bring down [1], bringeth down [1], brought down [1], couch [1], humbleth [1], low [1], stoop [1]

7818 שָׂחַט שׂחט **śāḥaṭ**, v. GK: 8469. [Q] to squeeze out (juice from grapes):– pressed [1]

7819 שָׁחַט שׁחט **šāḥaṭ**, v. GK: 8821 & 8823 [→ 7821]. [Q] to slaughter, kill; [Qp, N] to be killed, be slaughtered:– kill [23], slew [21], killed [15], slay [9], slain [5], killeth [3], killing [1], offer [1], shot out [1], slaughter [1], slaying [1]

7820 שָׁחַט שׁחט **šāḥaṭ**, v. GK: 8822. [Qp] to be hammered, beaten; some sources: to be alloyed, blended, referring to the mixing of metals:– beaten [5]

7821 שְׁחִיטָה שׁחיטה **šᵉḥîṭâ**, n.f. GK: 8824 [→ 7819]. killing, slaughter:– killing [1]

7822 שְׁחִין שׁחין **šᵉḥîn**, n.m. GK: 8825. boils, skin sores:– boil [9], boils [2], botch [2]

7823 שָׁחִיס שׁחיס **šāḥîs** or סָחִישׁ סחישׁ **sāḥîš**, n.[m.]. GK: 8826 & 6084. growth, what springs up on its own (in the second year):– that which springeth of the same [2]

7824 שָׂחִיף שׂחיף **śāḥîp**, a. GK: 8470. covered, paneled:– cieled [1]

7825 שְׁחִית שׁחית **šᵉḥît**, n.f. GK: 8827 [→ 7816]. pit, trap, grave:– destructions [1], pits [1]

7826 שַׁחַל שׁחל **šaḥal**, n.m. GK: 8828 [→ 7827]. lion:– lion [4], fierce lion [3]

7827 שְׁחֵלֶת שׁחלת **šᵉḥēlet**, n.f. GK: 8829 [→ 7826]. onycha (a fragrant spice):– onycha [1]

7828 שַׁחַף שׁחף **šaḥap**, n.[m.]. GK: 8830. gull or possibly bat:– cuckow [2]

7829 שַׁחֶפֶת שׁחפת **šaḥepet**, n.f. GK: 8831. wasting disease, consumption:– consumption [2]

7830 שַׁחַץ שׁחץ **šaḥaṣ**, n.[m.]. GK: 8832 [→ 7831]. pride, dignity:– lion's [1], pride [1]

7831 שַׁחֲצוּמָה שׁחצומה **šaḥᵃṣûmâ** or שַׁחֲצִימָה שׁחצימה **šaḥᵃṣîmâ**, n.pr.loc. GK: 8833 & 8834 [→ 7830]. Shahazimah, Shahazumah, "*elevated place*":– Shahazimah [1]

7832 שָׂחַק שׂחק **śāḥaq**, v. GK: 8471 [→ 3446, 4890, 7814; cf. 6711]. [Q] to laugh, be amused; to laugh at, mock, scoff; [P] to celebrate, rejoice, frolic; [H] to scorn; this can communicate joy or ridicule:– laugh [8], play [5], played [3], make merry [2], playing [2], rejoicing [2], scorneth [2], deride [1], derision [1], in sport [1], laughed to scorn [1], laughed [1], laugheth [1], made sport [1], make sport [1], mockers [1], mocketh [1], mock [1], rejoice [1]

7833 שָׁחַק **šāḥaq**, v. GK: 8835 [→ 7834]. [Q] to grind, wear away:– beat small [2], beat [1], wear [1]

7834 שַׁחַק **šaḥaq**, n.m. GK: 8836 [→ 7833]. clouds, skies:– clouds [11], skies [5], heaven [2], sky [2], small dust [1]

שְׂחֹק **śᵉḥōq**. See 7814.

7835 שָׁחַר **šāḥar**, v. GK: 8837 [→ 300, 4891, 7815, 7838, 7225, 7839, 7840, 7842]. [Q] to become black:– black [1]

7836 שָׁחַר **šāḥar**, v.den. GK: 8838 [→ 7841; cf. 7837?]. [Q] to seek, look; [P] to earnestly seek, search for:– seek early [4], betimes [1], diligently seeketh [1], diligently seek [1], early seek [1], inquired early after [1], rising betimes [1], seek betimes [1], seek in the morning [1]

7837 שַׁחַר **šaḥar**, n.m. GK: 8840 [→ 7223, 7842; cf. 7836?]. dawn, daybreak:– morning [12], day [5], early [2], Shahar [1], day began [1], dayspring [1], light [1], riseth [1]

שִׁחֹר **šiḥōr**. See 7883.

7838 שָׁחֹר **šāḥōr**, a. GK: 8839 [→ 7835]. black, dark:– black [6]

7839 שַׁחֲרוּת **šaḥᵃrût**, n.f. GK: 8841 [→ 7835]. vigor, prime of youth, an extension of dark hair color (or perhaps of the dawn):– youth [1]

7840 שְׁחַרְחֹר **šᵉḥarḥōr**, a. GK: 8842 [→ 7835]. dark, swarthy (complexion):– black [1]

7841 שְׁחַרְיָה **šᵉḥaryâ**, n.pr.m. GK: 8843 [→ 7836]. Shehariah, "*he seeks Yahweh*":– Shehariah [1]

7842 שַׁחֲרַיִם **šaḥᵃrayim**, n.pr.m. GK: 8844 [→ 7837; cf. 7835]. Shaharaim, "*one born at early [reddish] dawn*":– Shaharaim [1]

7843 שָׁחַת **šāḥat**, v. GK: 8845 [→ 4889, 4892, 4893; cf. 7844]. [N] to be corrupt, be ruined, be marred; [P] to corrupt, destroy, ruin; [H] to destroy, corrupt, bring to ruin:– destroy [68], destroyed [22], corrupted [11], corrupt [10], destroying [5], mar [4], marred [3], corrupters [2], destroyer [2], destroyeth [2], spoilers [2], utterly corrupt (+7843) [2], waster [2], battered [1], cast off [1], corrupting [1], corruptly [1], destroyers [1], destroyest [1], destruction [1], lose [1], perish [1], spilled [1], wasted [1]

7844 שְׁחַת **šᵉḥat** (Aram.), v. GK: 10705 [cf. 7843]. [Pp] to be corrupt, wicked; (as noun) corruption:– fault [2], corrupt [1]

7845 שַׁחַת **šaḥat**, n.f. GK: 8846 [→ 7743]. pit, dungeon; corruption, decay:– pit [14], corruption [4], destruction [2], ditch [2], grave [1]

7846 שֵׂט **śēṭ**, n.[m.]. GK: 8473 [→ 7750?]. rebel:– revolters [1]

7847 שָׂטָה **śāṭâ**, v. GK: 8474 [cf. 7750]. [Q] to go astray:– gone aside [2], decline [1], go aside [1], goeth aside [1], turn [1]

7848 שִׁטָּה **šiṭṭâ**, n.f. GK: 8847 [→ 7851]. acacia wood:– shittim [27], shittah tree [1]

7849 שָׁטַח **šāṭaḥ**, v. GK: 8848 [→ 4894]. [Q] to spread out, enlarge, scatter; [P] to spread out:– spread all abroad (+7849) [2], spread [2], enlargeth [1], stretched out [1]

7850 שֹׁטֵט **šōṭēṭ**, n.[m.]. GK: 8849 [→ 7752; cf. 7751]. whip, scourge:– scourges [1]

7851 שִׁטִּים **šiṭṭîm**, n.pr.loc. GK: 8850 [→ 7848]. Shittim, "*acacia trees*":– Shittim [5]

7852 שָׂטַם **śāṭam**, v. GK: 8475 [→ 4895; cf. 7853]. [Q] to hold a grudge, hold hostility toward:– hated [2], hate [2], hateth [1], opposest [1]

7853 שָׂטַן **śāṭan**, v.den. GK: 8476 [→ 7854, 7855, 7856; cf. 7852]. [Q] to accuse, slander:– adversaries [5], resist [1]

7854 שָׂטָן **śāṭān**, n.m.[pr.]. GK: 8477 [→ 7853]. (human) adversary, accuser, one who opposes, slanderer; (as a proper name) Satan, the spirit being who is an opponent of God and slanderer of his creation:– Satan [19], adversary [6], adversaries [1], withstand [1]

7855 שִׂטְנָה **śiṭnâ**, n.f. GK: 8478 [→ 7856; cf. 7853]. accusation:– accusation [1]

7856 שִׂטְנָה **śiṭnâ**, n.pr.loc. GK: 8479 [→ 7855]. Sitnah, "*hostility*":– Sitnah [1]

7857 שָׁטַף **šāṭap**, v. GK: 8851 [→ 7858; cf. 8241]. [Q] to overflow, flood, wash away; [N] to be rinsed, be swept away; [Pu] to be rinsed:– overflow [10], overflowing [8], rinsed [3], drown [1], flowing [1], overflowed [1], overflown [1], overwhelmed [1], ran [1], rusheth [1], throughly washed away [1], washed [1], washest away [1]

7858 שֶׁטֶף **šeṭep**, n.m. GK: 8852 [→ 7857; cf. 8241]. flood, torrents (of rain):– flood [3], floods [1], outrageous [1], overflowing of waters [1]

7859 שְׁטַר **šᵉṭar** (Aram.), n.m. GK: 10680. side:– side [1]

7860 שֹׁטֵר **šāṭar**, n.m. GK: 8853 [→ 4896, 7861]. [Q] to keep a record; (n.) official, officer, foreman:– officers [23], overseer [1], ruler [1]

7861 שִׁטְרַי **šiṭray** or שִׁרְטַי **širṭay**, n.pr.m. GK: 8855 & 9231 [→ 7860]. Shitrai, Shirtai, "*scribe, officer*":– Shitrai [1]

7862 שַׁי **šay**, n.m. GK: 8856 [→ 52, 7737; cf. 2365?]. gift:– presents [2], present [1]

7863 שִׂיא **śî'**, n.m. GK: 8480 [→ 7865; cf. 4984; 7613?]. height:– excellency [1]

7864 שְׁיָא **šᵉyā'**, n.pr.m. GK: 8857 [cf. 7724]. Sheya, cf. 7724:– @H = **7865** שִׂיאֹן **ᵓî„ôn**, n.pr.loc. GK: 8481 [→ 7863; cf. 4984; 7613]. Siyon:– Sion [1]

7866 שִׁיאֹן **šî'ōn**, n.pr.loc. GK: 8858 [→ 7582?]. Shion:– Shion [1]

7867 שִׂיב **śîb**, v. GK: 8482 [→ 7869, 7872; cf. 7868]. [Q] to be gray(-haired); hence, old:– grayheaded [2]

7868 שִׂיב **śîb** (Aram.), v. GK: 10681 [cf. 7867]. [P] to be gray-haired, (ptcp.) elder, a community leader with considerable political, social, and judicial authority, as a fig. extension of being gray-haired, implying wisdom and honor:– elders [5]

7869 שֵׂב **śêb**, n.[m.]. GK: 8483 [→ 7867]. gray-headedness, old age:– age [1]

7870 שִׁיבָה **šîbâ**, n.f. GK: 8860 [→ 7617; cf. 7622]. captives:– captivity [1]

7871 שִׁיבָה **šîbâ**, n.f. GK: 8859 [→ 3427?]. stay:– lay [1]

7872 שֵׂיבָה **śêbâ**, n.f. GK: 8484 [→ 7867]. gray-haired (person), old age:– old age [6], gray hairs [5], hoar head [2], hoary head [2], gray head [1], grayheaded [1], hoar hairs [1], hoary [1]

7873 שִׂיג **śîg**, n.[m.]. GK: 8485 [cf. 5253, 5509]. busyness; perhaps: bowel movement:– pursuing [1]

7874 שִׂיד **śîd**, v.den. GK: 8486 [→ 7875]. [Q] to coat with (a whitewash) plaster:– plaister [2]

7875 שִׂיד **śîd**, n.[m.]. GK: 8487 [→ 7874]. lime, plaster (used as a whitewash):– lime [2], plaister [2]

7876 שָׁיָה **šāyâ**, v. GK: 8861 [cf. 5382]. [Q] to desert, forget:– unmindful [1]

7877 שִׁיזָא **šîzā'**, n.pr.m. GK: 8862. Shiza:– Shiza [1]

7878 שִׂיחַ **śîaḥ**, v.den. GK: 8488 [→ 7808, 7879, 7881]. [Q] to meditate, muse on, consider, think on:– meditate [5], talk [5], speak [4], commune [1], complained [1], complain [1], declare [1], muse [1], pray [1]

7879 שִׂיחַ **śîaḥ**, n.m. GK: 8490 [→ 7878]. complaint, lament:– complaint [9], babbling [1], communication [1], meditation [1], prayer [1], talking [1]

7880 שִׂיחַ **śîaḥ**, n.[m.]. GK: 8489. bush, shrub:– bushes [2], plant [1], shrubs [1]

7881 שִׂיחָה **śîḥâ**, n.f. GK: 8491 [→ 7878]. meditation:– meditation [2], prayer [1]

7882 שִׁיחָה **šîḥâ**, n.f. GK: 8864 [cf. 7745]. pit, pitfall:– pits [1], pit [1]

7883 שִׁיחוֹר **šîḥôr**, n.pr.loc. GK: 8865 [→ 7884]. Shihor, "[poss.] *black water*, [Egyptian] *Canal of Horus*":– Sihor [3], Shihor [1]

7884 שִׁיחוֹר לִבְנָת **šîḥôr libnāt**, n.pr.loc. GK: 8866 [→ 7883]. Shihor Libnath:– Shihor-libnath [1]

7885 שַׁיִט **šayiṭ**, n.[m.]. GK: 8868 [→ 7751]. oar:– oars [1]

7886 שִׁילֹה **šîlōh**, n.pr.loc.?. GK: 8869 [→ 7887]. Shiloh:– Shiloh [1]

7887 שִׁילוֹ **šîlô** or שִׁלוֹ **šilô** or שִׁלֹה **šilōh**, n.pr.loc. GK: 8870 & 8926 & 8931 [→ 7886, 7888; cf. 7757, 8387]. Shiloh:– Shiloh [32]

7888 שִׁילֹנִי **šîlōnî**, a.g. GK: 8872 [→ 7887, 8023]. Shilonite, of Shiloh, "*of Shiloh*":– Shilonite [5], Shilonites [1]

שֵׁילָל **šêlāl**. See 7758.

7889 שִׁימוֹן **šîmôn**, n.pr.m. GK: 8873. Shimon:– Shimon [1]

7890 שַׁיִן **šayin**, n.[m.]. GK: 8875 [→ 8366]. urine:– @H = **7891** שִׁיר **šîr**, v. GK: 8876 [→ 7892; cf. 3574]. [Q] to sing; [P ptcp.] singer, musician:– singers [36], sing [32], singing [9], sang [6], behold [1], singer [1], singeth [1], sung [1]

7892 שִׁיר **šîr**, n.m. & f. GK: 8877 & 8878 [→ 7891]. song, music:– song [62], songs [12], musick [7], singing [4], musical [2], singers [1], sing [1], song (+1697) [1]

שִׂישׂ **śîś**. See 7797.

7893 שַׁיִשׁ **šayiš**, n.[m.]. GK: 8880 [→ 8336]. alabaster:– marble [1]

7894 שִׁישָׁא **šîšā'**, n.pr.m. GK: 8881. Shisha:– Shisha [1]

7895 שׁוּשַׁק **šûšaq** or שִׁישַׁק **šîšaq**, n.pr.m. GK: 8810 & 8882. Shushak, Shishak:– Shishak [7]

7896 שִׁית **šît**, v. GK: 8883 [→ 7897, 8351, 8352; cf. 8371]. [Q] to place, put, set; [Ho] to be demanded:– set [21], make [12], put [11], laid [8], lay [5], made [5], appoint [2], regard (+3820) [2], alone (+4480) [1], apply [1], appointed [1], bring [1], considered (+3820) [1], lay up [1], layeth up [1], look [1], make turn [1], makest [1], mark [1], set in array [1], settest [1], shew [1], stayed [1], take [1]

7897 שִׁית **šît**, n.m. GK: 8884 [→ 7896]. garment:– attire [1], garment [1]

7898 שַׁיִת **šayit**, n.[m.]. GK: 8885 [→ 7582?]. thorns, thorn-bushes:– thorns [7]

7899 שֵׂךְ **śēk**, n.[m.]. GK: 8493. barb, splinter, thorn:– pricks [1]

7900 שֹׂךְ **śōk**, n.[m.]. GK: 8494 [cf. 5520]. dwelling place:– tabernacle [1]

7901 שָׁכַב **šākab**, v. GK: 8886 [→ 4904, 7902, 7903]. [Q] to lie down, rest; sleep with; (as a euphemism of sexual intercourse) to lie with, sleep with; [H] to make lie down; [Ho] to be laid down:– lie [41], slept [37], lay [32], lie down [15], lieth [15], lay down [11], sleep [10], laid down [9], laid [8], liest down [3], lieth down [3], lie with at all (+854+7901) [2], lien [2], lying [2], ravished [2], take rest [2], casting down [1], lain [1], lay down to sleep [1], lay on a bed (+4904) [1], lie together [1], lie with [1], lien with (+854) [1], liest [1], lieth carnally with (+854+2233+7902) [1], lieth with (+5973) [1], lodged [1], lying down [1], make to lie down [1], overlaid (+5921) [1], sleepest [1], stay [1], taketh rest [1]

7902 שִׁכְבָה **šikbâ**, n.f. GK: 8887 [→ 7901]. emission, discharge:– copulation [3], lay [2], lieth carnally with (+854+2233+7901) [1], man carnally (+376+2233) [1], seed (+2233) [1]

7903 שְׁכֹבֶת **šᵉkōbet**, n.f. GK: 8888 [→ 7901]. sexual relations, sexual intercourse:– lain [1], lie (+5414) [1], lie carnally (+2233+5414+3807.1) [1], lie with (+5414) [1]

7904 שָׂכָה **śākâ**, v. GK: 8889. [H] to be well-fed; lusting:– morning [1]

7905 שֻׂכָּה **śukkâ**, n.f. GK: 8496. harpoon:– barbed irons [1]

7906 שֵׂכוּ **śekû**, n.pr.loc. GK: 8497. Secu, "*lookout point*":– Sechu [1]

7907 שֶׂכְוִי **śekwî**, n.[m.]. GK: 8498. mind; some sources: mist:– heart [1]

7908 שְׁכוֹל **šᵉkôl**, n.[m.]. GK: 8890 [→ 7921]. forlornness, loss of children:– loss of children [2], spoiling [1]

7909 שַׁכּוּל **šakkûl** or שְׁכוּלָה **šᵉkûlâ**, a. GK: 8891 & 8892 [→ 7921]. bereaved (of children):– barren [2], bereaved of children [1], bereaved of whelps [1], robbed of whelps [1], robbed [1]

7910 שִׁכּוֹר **šikkôr**, a. GK: 8893 [→ 7937]. drunk, drunkenness; (n.) a drunkard:– drunken [6], drunkards [3], drunkard [2], drunk [2]

7911 שָׁכַח **šākaḥ**, v. GK: 8894 [→ 7913; cf. 7912]. [Q] to forget; [N] to be forgotten; [P] to make forget; [H] to make forget; [Ht] to be forgotten:– forget [46], forgotten [39], forgat [7], forgetteth [3], do at all forget (+7911) [2], forgettest [2], cause to forget [1], caused to be forgotten [1], forgot [1]

7912 שְׁכַח **šᵉkaḥ** (Aram.), v. GK: 10708 [cf. 7911]. [H] to find; [Htpe] to be found:– found [12], find [6]

7913 שָׁכֵחַ **šākēaḥ**, a. GK: 8895 [→ 7911]. forgetting:– forget [2]

7914 שְׂכִיָּה **śᵉkiyyâ**, n.f. GK: 8500. marine vessel, ship:– pictures [1]

7915 שַׂכִּין **śakkîn**, n.[m.]. GK: 8501. knife:– knife [1]

7916 שָׂכִיר **śākîr**, a. GK: 8502 [→ 7917, 7936]. hired worker, servant under contract:– hired servant [8], hireling [6], him that is hired [1], hired men [1], hired [1]

7917 שְׂכִירָה **śᵉkîrâ**, a. GK: 8502 [→ 7916]. f. of 7916: hired worker, servant under contract:– hired [1]

7918 שָׂכַךְ ***śākak***, v. GK: 8896. [Q] to recede, reside; [H] to get rid of:– appeased [1], asswaged [1], make to cease [1], pacified [1], setteth [1]

7919 שָׂכַל ***śākal***, v. GK: 8505 & 8506 [→ 4905, 7922; cf. 7920]. [Q] to have success; [P] to cross (the hands and arms in an extended motion); [H] to have insight, wisdom, understanding; to prosper, successful; the potent capacity to understand and so exercise skill in life, a state caused by proper training and teaching, enhanced by careful observation:– wise [11], understand [8], prosper [6], behaved wisely [4], understanding [4], instruct [2], prudent [2], understood [2], wisdom [2], behave wisely [1], considereth [1], consider [1], deal prudently [1], expert [1], give skill [1], guiding wittingly [1], handleth wisely [1], have good success [1], have understanding [1], instructed [1], made understand [1], make wise [1], prospered [1], prospereth [1], skilful [1], skill [1], taught knowledge (+7922) [1], teacheth [1], understandeth [1], wisely considereth [1], wisely consider [1]

7920 שְׂכַל ***śekal*** (Aram.), v. GK: 10683 [→ 7924; cf. 7919]. [Htpa] to think about, consider:– considered [1]

7921 שָׁכֹל ***šākal***, v. GK: 8897 [→ 811, 7908, 7909, 7923]. [Q] to be bereaved (of children); [P] to make childless, bring bereavement, suffer miscarriage; [H] to miscarry:– bereave [3], barren [2], bereaved of children [2], bereaved [2], cast young [2], bereave of children [1], bereave of men [1], bereaveth [1], cast fruit before the time [1], casteth her calf [1], childless [1], deprived [1], destroy [1], lost children [1], made childless [1], miscarrying [1], rob of children [1], spoil [1]

7922 שֶׂכֶל ***śekel***, n.m. GK: 8507 [→ 7919; cf. 7924]. understanding, wisdom, discretion:– understanding [7], wisdom [3], discretion [1], policy [1], prudence [1], sense [1], taught knowledge (+7919) [1], wise [1]

שִׂכֻּל ***śakkul***. See 7909.

שִׂכְלוּת ***siklût***. See 5531.

7923 שִׁכֻּלִים ***šikkulîm***, n.[m.]pl.abst. GK: 8898 [→ 7921]. (state of) bereavement (of children):– lost [1]

7924 שָׂכְלְתָנוּ ***śokletānû*** (Aram.), n.f. GK: 10684 [→ 7920]. intelligence, understanding, insight:– understanding [3]

7925 שָׁכַם ***šākam***, v.den. GK: 8899 [→ 7926]. [H] to do early in the morning; to do again and again:– rose up early [18], rose early [9], arose early [8], rising early [6], rising up early [6], rise up early [5], early [4], be up early [1], early rose up [1], gat up early [1], get early [1], get up early [1], morning [1], rise early [1], rising up betimes [1], rose up betimes [1]

7926 שְׁכֶם ***šekem***, n.m. GK: 8900 [→ 7925, 7927, 7928, 7929, 7930]. shoulder (upper part of the back); by extension: ridge of land:– shoulder [12], shoulders [5], back [2], consent [2], portion [1]

7927 שְׁכֶם ***šekem***, n.pr.m. & loc. GK: 8901 & 8902 [→ 7926]. Shechem, "*shoulders [and upper part of the back];* [poss.] *shoulder [saddle of a hill]*":– Shechem [49], Sichem [1]

7928 שֶׁכֶם ***šekem***, n.pr.m. GK: 8903 [→ 7930; cf. 7926]. Shechem, "*shoulders [and upper part of the back]*":– Shechem [13], Shechem's [2]

7929 שִׁכְמָה ***šikmâ***, n.m. GK: 8900 [→ 7926]. f. of 7926: shoulder (upper part of the back); by extension: ridge of land:– shoulder blade [1]

7930 שִׁכְמִי ***šikmî***, a.g. GK: 8904 [→ 7928]. Shechemite, "*of Shechem*":– Shechemites [1]

7931 שָׁכַן ***šākan***, v. GK: 8905 [→ 4908, 7933, 7934, 7935; cf. 7932]. [Q] to dwell, abide, live among, stay; [P] to make to dwell, make a home; [H] to cause to dwell, settle in, set up a dwelling:– dwell [61], dwelleth [8], dwelt [8], abode [6], place [5], cause to dwell [3], dwell in [3], dwellest [3], dwelt in [3], habitation [2], inhabit [2], placed [2], remain [2], set [2], abide [1], abiding [1], at rest [1], cause to remain [1], continue [1], dwellers [1], dwelleth in [1], dwelling [1], inhabitants [1], inhabited [1], inhabiteth [1], lay [1], made to dwell [1], make dwell [1], remaineth [1], remaining [1], rested [1], rest [1], set up [1]

7932 שְׁכַן ***šekan*** (Aram.), v. GK: 10709 [→ 4907; cf. 7931]. [P] to dwell; [Pa] to cause to dwell:– caused to dwell [1], habitation [1]

7933 שָׁכַן ***šākan***, v.inf. GK: 8905 [→ 7931]. inf. of 7931: to dwell, abide:– @H = **7934** שָׁכֵן ***šākēn***, a. GK: 8907 [→ 7931]. neighbor; inhabitant:– neighbours [11], neighbour [6], inhabitants [1], inhabitant [1], nigh [1]

7935 שְׁכַנְיָה ***šekanyâ*** or שְׁכַנְיָהוּ ***šekanyāhû***, n.pr.m. GK: 8908 & 8909 [→ 7931+3068]. Shecaniah, "*Yahweh has taken up his abode*":– Shechaniah [8], Shecaniah [2]

7936 שָׂכַר ***śākar*** or סָכַר ***sākar***, v. GK: 8509 & 6128 [→ 3485, 4909, 7916, 7917, 7938, 7939, 7940]. [Q] to hire; [Qp] to be hired; [N] to hire oneself; [Ht] to earn wages for oneself:– hired [12], earneth wages [2], hire [2], rewardeth [2], surely hired (+7936) [2], hired out [1]

7937 שָׁכַר ***šākar***, v. GK: 8910 & 8912 [→ 7910, 7941, 7943]. [Q] to become drunk, drink to one's fill; [P] to make drunk; [H] to make drunk; [Ht] to behave drunken:– drunken [8], make drunk [3], make drunken [2], drink abundantly [1], filled with drink [1], made drunken [1], made drunk [1], makest drunken [1], merry [1]

7938 שֶׂכֶר ***śeker***, n.[m.]. GK: 8512 [→ 7936]. wage, reward:– reward [1], sluces [1]

7939 שָׂכָר ***śākār***, n.m. GK: 8510 [→ 7940; cf. 7936 (also used with compound proper names)]. wage, reward:– hire [9], reward [7], wages [6], price [2], rewarded [2], fare [1], worth [1]

7940 שָׂכָר ***śākār***, n.pr.m. GK: 8511 [→ 7939; cf. 7936]. Sacar, "*reward [given by God],* [poss.] *hired hand*":– Sacar [2]

7941 שֵׁכָר ***šēkār***, n.[m.]. GK: 8911 [→ 7937]. fermented drink, beer:– strong drink [21], drunkards (+8354) [1], strong wine [1]

שִׁכֹּר ***šikkōr***. See 7910.

7942 שִׁכְּרוֹן ***šikkārôn***, n.pr.loc. GK: 8914. Shikkeron, "[poss.] *drunkenness; hog bean plant*":– Shicron [1]

7943 שִׁכָּרוֹן ***šikkārôn***, n.[m.]. GK: 8913 [→ 7937]. drunkenness:– drunkenness [2], drunken [1]

7944 שַׁל ***šal***, n.[m.]. GK: 8915. irreverent act:– error [1]

7945 שֶׁל ***šel***, pt. GK: 8611 [→ 4332, 4967, 7706]. what, which, usually as prefix 7578.1:– that [54], which [20], whom [7], who [6], when [5]; because [4], for [4], until (+5704) [4], wherein [3], whereof [3], till (+5704) [2], wherewith [2], as (+3509.1) [1], as [1], because (+871.1) [1], but (+5704) [1], by (+5921) [1], for cause (+871.1) [1], for sake (+871.1) [1], from whence [1], increase [1], it [1], of (+4480+3807.1) [1], when (+3509.1) [1], where [1], while (+5704) [1], whither (+8033) [1], whose (+2050.2) [1], whose [1]

7946 שַׁלְאֲנַן ***šalanan***, a. GK: 8916 [→ 7599]. secure:– at ease [1]

7947 שָׁלַב ***šālab***, v. GK: 8917 [→ 7948]. [Pu] to be joined, set parallel, dovetailed:– equally distant [1], set in order [1]

7948 שָׁלָב ***šālāb***, n.[m.]pl. GK: 8918 [→ 7947]. upright, crossbar:– ledges [3]

7949 שָׁלַג ***šālag***, v.den. GK: 8919 [→ 7950]. [H] to snow:– snow [1]

7950 שֶׁלֶג ***šeleg***, n.m. GK: 8920 & 8921 [→ 7949; cf. 8517]. snow; soap (processed from the soapwort plant):– snow [19], snowy [1]

7951 שָׁלָה ***šālâ***, v. GK: 8922 [→ 7961, 7959, 7962, 7968, 7987, 7988; cf. 7952]. [Q] to be at ease, have peace; [N] to give oneself to rest; [H] to raise hopes:– prosper [3], happy [1], in safety [1]

7952 שָׁלָה ***šālâ***, v. GK: 8923 [→ 7953, cf. 7951]. [Q] to take away, extract; to deceive:– deceive [1], negligent [1]

7953 שָׁלָה ***šālâ***, v. GK: 8923 [→ 7952]. prob. same as 7952: [Q] to take away, extract:– taketh away [1]

7954 שְׁלֵה ***šelēh*** (Aram.), a. GK: 10710 [→ 7960, 7963; cf. 7961]. contented, at ease:– rest [1]

שִׁלֹה ***šilōh***. See 7887.

7955 שָׁלָה ***šillâ*** (Aram.), n.f. GK: 10685 [cf. 5541]. insolence, rebellion:– @HREF = שֵׁלָה ***šēlâ***. See 7596.

7956 שֵׁלָה ***šēlâ***, n.f. & pr.m. GK: 8924 & 8925 [→ 8024; cf. 7592]. petition; n.pr. Shelah, "*missile [a weapon], sprout*":– Shelah [8]

7957 שַׁלְהֶבֶת ***šalhebet***, n.f. GK: 8927 [→ 3851]. flame:– flame [2], most vehement flame [1]

שָׁלַו ***šālaw***. See 7951.

7958 שְׂלָו ***śelāw***, n.f. GK: 8513. quail:– quails [4]

7959 שָׁלוּ ***šālû***, n.[m.]. GK: 8930 [→ 7951; cf. 7960]. secure feeling, ease:– prosperity [1]

שִׁלוֹ ***šilô***. See 7887.

7960 שָׁלוּ ***šālû*** (Aram.), n.f. GK: 10712 [→ 7954; cf. 7959]. negligence:– fail [2], any thing amiss [1], error [1]

7961 שָׁלֵו ***šālēw***, a. GK: 8929 [→ 7951; cf. 7954]. quiet, at ease, carefree:– at ease [2], peaceable [1], prosperity [1], prosper [1], quietness [1], quiet [1], wealthy [1]

7962 שַׁלְוָה ***šalwâ***, n.f. GK: 8932 [→ 7951; cf. 7963]. security, ease:– prosperity [3], abundance [1], peaceably (+871.1) [1], peaceably [1], peace [1], quietness [1]

7963 שְׁלֵוָה ***šelēwâ*** (Aram.), n.f. GK: 10713 [→ 7954; cf. 7962]. prosperity:– tranquillity [1]

7964 שִׁלּוּחִים ***šillûḥîm***, n.[m.]pl. GK: 8933 [→ 7971]. parting gifts; sending away:– presents [1], present [1], sent [1]

7965 שָׁלוֹם ***šālôm***, n.m. GK: 8934 [→ 53, 8010, 8015, 8019; cf. 7999; cf. 8001]. peace, safety, prosperity, well-being; intactness, wholeness; peace can have a focus of security, safety which can bring feelings of satisfaction, well-being, and contentment:– peace [174], well [13], peaceably [7], welfare [5], prosperity [4], safe [3], saluted (+7592+3807.1) [3], how did (+3807.1) [2], peaceable [2], perfect peace (+7965) [2], salute (+7592+3807.1) [2], all is well [1], did [1], familiar friend (+376) [1], familiars (+582) [1], fare [1], favour [1], friends (+376) [1], greet (+7592+3807.1) [1], how doest (+3807.1) [1], how prospered (+3807.1) [1], in good health [1], in health [1], peaceably (+3807.1) [1], peaceably (+871.1) [1], prosperous [1], rest [1], safely [1], salute [1], wholly [1]

7966 שִׁלּוּם ***šillûm***, n.[m.]. GK: 8936 [→ 7999]. retribution, reckoning; bribe, gift:– recompences [1], recompence [1], reward [1]

7967 שַׁלּוּם ***šallûm***, n.pr.m. GK: 8935 [→ 7999]. Shallum, "*peace, well-being, prosperity*":– Shallum [27]

שְׁלוֹמִית ***šelômît***. See 8019.

7968 שַׁלּוּן ***šallûn***, n.pr.m. GK: 8937 [→ 7951]. Shallun, "*recompense*":– Shallun [1]

7969 שָׁלֹשׁ ***šālōš***, n.m. & f. GK: 8993 [→ 7991, 7992, 8027, 8028, 8030, 8032, 8029, 7970; cf. 8531]. three; (pl.) thirty:– three [389], thirteen (+6240) [13], thirteenth (+6240) [11], third [9], thrice (+6471) [4], forks (+7053) [1], oftentimes (+6471) [1], three tenth deals (+6241) [1], threescore and thirteen (+7657+1886.1+2050.1) [1], threescore and thirteen (+7657+2050.1) [1]

7970 שְׁלֹשִׁים ***šelōšîm***, n.indecl. GK: 9001 [→ 7969]. thirty (pl. of "three"):– thirty [163], thirtieth [9], captains [1]

שָׁלוּת ***šālût***. See 7960.

7971 שָׁלַח ***šālaḥ***, v. GK: 8938 [→ 4916, 4917, 7964, 7973, 7975, 7974, 7976, 7977; cf. 7972]. [Q] to send, let out; [Qp] to be sent away; [N] to be sent; [P] to send away, let go, release; [Pu] to be sent away, thrust out; [H] to send out; "to let go" from a marriage relationship is to divorce:– sent [405], send [140], let go [69], sent away [36], put forth [24], send away [10], put [9], sent forth [9], sending [8], sent out [8], cast out [7], lay [7], stretch forth [7], cast [6], laid [6], put away [6], sendeth [5], set [5], put out [4], go [3], send forth [3], sentest [3], shot forth [3], soweth [3], stretch out [3], depart [2], earnestly send (+7971) [2], in any wise let go (+7971) [2], let depart [2], let down [2], let go in any wise (+7971) [2], let loose [2], put in [2], putteth forth [2], sendest away [2], sendest [2], sendeth out [2], stretched forth [2], stretched out [2], appoint [1], away [1], bring on way [1], brought [1], cast away [1], conduct [1], forsaken [1], gave up [1], givest [1], layeth [1], left [1], let go away [1], letting go [1], loose [1], push away [1], putting away [1], putting forth [1], reacheth forth [1], send out [1], sendest forth [1], sendest out [1], sendeth forth [1], sending away [1], sent for [1], sentest forth [1], shoot out [1], shooteth forth [1], shot [1], spreadeth out [1], suffer to grow long [1]

7972 שְׁלַח ***šelaḥ*** (Aram.), v. GK: 10714 [cf. 7971]. [P] to send out; [Pp, Peil] to be sent:– sent [12], put [1], send [1]

7973 שֶׁלַח ***šelaḥ*** or שְׁלָחִים ***šelāḥîm***, n.[m.]. GK: 8939 & 8945 [→ 7971]. weapon, sword, javelin; shoots, sprouts of a plant (in a closed, private garden):– sword [3], weapon [2], darts [1], plants [1], put off [1]

7974 שֶׁלַח ***šelaḥ***, n.pr.m. GK: 8941 [→ 7973?; cf. 7971]. Shelah, "*missile [a weapon], sprout*":– Salah [6], Shelah [3]

7975 שֶׁלַח ***šelaḥ*** or שִׁלֹחַ ***šilōaḥ***, n.pr.loc. GK: 8940 & 8942 [→ 7971]. Siloam, Shiloah, "*sent*":– Shiloah [1], Siloah [1]

שִׁלֻּחַ ***šilluaḥ***. See 7964.

7976 שְׁלֻחוֹת ***šeluḥôt***, n.f. GK: 8943 [→ 7971]. shoot (of a vine):– branches [1]

7977 שִׁלְחִי ***šilḥî***, n.pr.m. GK: 8944 [→ 7971]. Shilhi, "[poss.] *[my] javelin [thrower?]*":– Shilhi [2]

7978 שִׁלְחִים ***šilḥîm***, n.pr.loc. GK: 8946. Shilhim:– Shilhim [1]

7979 שֻׁלְחָן **šulḥān**, n.m. GK: 8947. table:– table [55], tables [14], every table (+7979+2050.1) [2]

7980 שָׁלַט **šālaṭ**, v. GK: 8948 [→ 7983, 7986, 7989; cf. 7981]. [Q] to control, lord over; [H] to let rule, enable:– bare rule [1], given power [1], giveth power [1], have dominion [1], have power [1], have rule [1], ruleth [1], rule [1]

7981 שְׁלֵט **š^e lēṭ** (Aram.), v. GK: 10715 [→ 7984, 7985, 7990; cf. 7980]. [P] to rule over, overpower; [H] to make rule over:– made ruler [2], ruler [2], bear rule [1], mastery [1], power [1]

7982 שֶׁלֶט **šeleṭ**, n.m. GK: 8949. small (round) shield:– shields [7]

7983 שִׁלְטוֹן **šilṭôn**, n.[m.]. GK: 8950 [→ 7980; cf. 7985]. supremacy:– power [2]

7984 שִׁלְטֹן **šilṭōn** (Aram.), n.m. GK: 10716 [→ 7981; cf. 7983]. high official:– rulers [2]

7985 שָׁלְטָן **šolṭān** (Aram.), n.m. GK: 10717 [→ 7981; cf. 7983?]. dominion, power, authority:– dominion [13], dominions [1]

7986 שַׁלֶּטֶת **šalleṭet**, a. GK: 8951 [→ 7980]. brazen, domineering:– imperious [1]

7987 שְׁלִי **š^e lî**, n.[m.]. GK: 8952 [→ 7951]. privateness, uninterruptedness:– quietly (+871.1+1886.1) [1]

7988 שִׁלְיָה **šilyâ**, n.f. GK: 8953 [→ 7951]. afterbirth:– young one [1]

שְׁלָיו **š^e lāyw**. See 7958.

שָׁלֵו **šalêw**. See 7961.

7989 שַׁלִּיט **šallîṭ**, a. GK: 8954 [→ 7980; cf. 7990]. ruler, governor:– governor [1], mighty [1], power [1], ruler [1]

7990 שַׁלִּיט **šallîṭ** (Aram.), a. GK: 10718 [→ 7981; cf. 7989]. mighty, powerful, sovereign, ruling:– ruleth [3], ruled [2], ruler [2], captain [1], lawful [1], rule [1]

7991 שָׁלִישׁ **šālîš** or שָׁלִשִׁי **šālišî**, n.[m.]. GK: 8955 & 8956 & 8998 [→ 7969]. [the] Three, a rank of officer; bowlful, basketful (a unit of measure, probably of one-third of something); (three-stringed?) lute:– captains [8], lord [3], captain [2], measure [2], excellent things [1], great lords [1], instruments of musick [1], princes [1]

7992 שְׁלִישִׁי **š^e lîšî**, a.num.ord. GK: 8958 [→ 7969; cf. 8523, cf. 8532]. third:– third [97], third part [3], third time [3], three years old [2], third rank [1], three [1]

7993 שָׁלַךְ **šālak**, v. GK: 8959 [→ 7994?, 7995]. [H] to throw, hurl, scatter; [Ho] to be thrown, be cast:– cast [77], cast out [13], cast away [11], cast down [11], cast forth [3], cast off [2], adventured [1], cast in [1], castest [1], casteth forth [1], hurl [1], pluckt [1], threwest [1], thrown [1]

7994 שָׁלָךְ **šālāk**, n.[m.]. GK: 8960 [→ 7993?]. cormorant:– cormorant [2]

7995 שַׁלֶּכֶת **šalleket**, n.f. GK: 8961 [→ 7993]. cutting down:– cast [1]

7996 שַׁלֶּכֶת **šalleket**, n.pr.loc. GK: 8962. Shalleketh, "[poss.] *[gate of] sending forth*":– Shallecheth [1]

7997 שָׁלַל **šālal**, v. GK: 8963 & 8964 [→ 7758, 7998]. [Q] to pull out; to plunder, loot; [Htpol] to be plundered:– spoiled [4], spoil [3], let fall of purpose (+7997) [2], take a spoil (+7998) [2], take [2], make a spoil [1], maketh prey [1], take spoil (+7998) [1]

7998 שָׁלָל **šālāl**, n.m. GK: 8965 [→ 4122; cf. 7997]. plunder, spoil, loot:– spoil [58], prey [10], take a spoil (+7997) [2], spoils won [1], spoils [1], take spoil (+7997) [1]

7999 שָׁלֵם **šālēm**, v. GK: 8966 [→ 4918, 4919, 4921, 4922, 7965, 7967, 7966, 8002, 8003, 8004, 8005, 8006, 8011, 8010, 8013, 8015, 8016, 8019, 8020, 8021 (also used with compound proper names)]. [Q] to be finished, be completed; be at peace; [Qp] to be at peace; [P] to repay, make restitution, fulfill (a vow); [Pu] be repaid, be fulfilled; [H] to make peace; cause to fulfill; [Ho] to be brought into peace:– pay [17], recompense [8], restore [8], render [7], made peace [6], make good [5], repay [5], perform [4], reward [4], at peace [3], finished [3], rewarded [3], rewardeth [3], ended [2], make an end [2], make full restitution (+7999) [2], make restitution [2], performeth [2], recompensed [2], requite [2], surely make good (+7999) [2], surely make restitution (+7999) [2], surely pay (+7999) [2], surely requite (+7999) [2], give again [1], make amends [1], make peace [1], make prosperous [1], maketh to be at peace [1], pay again [1], payed [1], payeth again [1], peaceable [1], perfect [1], performed [1], prospered [1], recompensest [1], renderest [1], rendereth [1], repayed [1], repayeth [1], requited [1]

8000 שְׁלִם **š^e lim** (Aram.), v. GK: 10719 [→ 8001; cf. 7999]. [P] to be finished; [H] to (deliver) completely, bring to an end:– finished [2], deliver [1]

8001 שְׁלָם **š^e lām** (Aram.), n.m. GK: 10720 [→ 8000; cf. 7965]. (as salutation) cordial greetings!; prosperity, well-being, good health:– peace [4]

8002 שֶׁלֶם **šelem**, n.[m.]. GK: 8968 [→ 7999]. fellowship (offering):– peace offerings [77], peace [6], peace offering [4]

8003 שָׁלֵם **šālēm**, a. GK: 8969 [→ 7999; cf. 8000]. safe, complete, whole:– perfect [16], whole [4], full [2], just [1], made ready [1], peaceable [1], perfected [1], quiet [1]

8004 שָׁלֵם **šālēm**, n.pr.loc. GK: 8970 [→ 7999]. Salem, "*peace*":– Salem [2], Shalem [1]

שָׁלֹם **šālōm**. See 7965.

8005 שִׁלֵּם **šillēm**, n.pr.loc. GK: 8972 [→ 7999]. recompense:– recompence [1]

8006 שִׁלֵּם **šillēm**, n.pr.m. GK: 8973 [→ 8016; cf. 7999]. Shillem, "*recompense;* [poss.] *whole, healthy, complete*":– Shillem [2]

שִׁלֻּם **šillum**. See 7966.

שַׁלֻּם **šallum**. See 7967.

8007 שַׂלְמָא **śalmā'**, n.pr.m. GK: 8514 [→ 8009, 8012]. Salma, "*little spark*":– Salma [4]

8008 שַׂלְמָה **śalmâ**, n.f. GK: 8515 [cf. 8071]. clothing, garment, cloak, robe:– raiment [5], garments [4], garment [4], clothes [3]

8009 שַׂלְמָה **śalmâ**, n.pr.m. GK: 8516 [→ 8007]. Salmah:– Salmon [1]

8010 שְׁלֹמֹה **š^e lōmōh**, n.pr.m. GK: 8976 [→ 7965; cf. 7999]. Solomon, "*peace, well-being*":– Solomon [271], Solomon's [18], Solomon's (+3807.1) [4]

8011 שִׁלֻּמָה **šillumâ**, n.f. GK: 8974 [→ 7999]. punishment, retribution:– reward [1]

8012 שַׂלְמוֹן **śalmôn**, n.pr.m. GK: 8517 [→ 8007] Salmon, "*little spark*":– Salmon [1]

8013 שְׁלֹמוֹת **š^e lōmôt**, n.pr.m. GK: 8977 [→ 7999]. Shelomoth, "*at peace*":– Shelomoth [2]

8014 שַׂלְמַי **śalmay**, n.pr.m. GK: 8518 [cf. 8073]. Salmai, cf. 8073:– Shalmai [1]

8015 שְׁלֹמִי **š^e lōmî**, n.pr.m. GK: 8979 [→ 8019; cf. 7965]. Shelomi, "*at peace*":– Shelomi [1]

8016 שִׁלֵּמִי **šillēmî**, a.g. GK: 8980 [→ 8006]. Shillemite, "*of Shillem*":– Shillemites [1]

8017 שְׁלֻמִיאֵל **š^e lumî'ēl**, n.pr.m. GK: 8981 [→ 7999+410]. Shelumiel, "*God [El] is [my] peace*":– Shelumiel [5]

8018 שֶׁלֶמְיָה **šelemyâ** or שֶׁלֶמְיָהוּ **šelemyāhû**, n.pr.m. GK: 8982 & 8983 [→ 7999+3068]. Shelemiah, "*Yahweh pays back* [poss.] *he restores peace offering of Yahweh*":– Shelemiah [10]

8019 שְׁלֹמִית **š^e lōmît**, n.pr.m. & f. GK: 8984 & 8985 [→ 8015; cf. 7999]. Shelomith, "*at peace*":– Shelomith [9]

8020 שַׁלְמַן **šalman**, n.pr.m. GK: 8986 [→ 7999]. Shalman, "[abbreviation of] *Shalmaneser*":– Shalman [1]

8021 שַׁלְמֹנִים **šalmōnîm**, n.[m.pl.]. GK: 8988 [→ 7999]. gifts:– rewards [1]

8022 שַׁלְמַנְאֶסֶר **šalman'eser**, n.pr.m. GK: 8987. Shalmaneser, "*Shulman is chief* or *Sulmanu is leader*":– Shalmaneser [2]

8023 שִׁלֹנִי **šilōnî**, a.g. GK: 8872 [→ 7888]. same as 7888: Shilonite, of Shiloh, "*of Shiloh*":– Shiloni [1]

8024 שֵׁלָנִי **šēlānî**, a.g. GK: 8989 [→ 7956]. Shelanite, of Shelah, "*of Shelah*":– Shelanites [1]

8025 שָׁלַף **šālap**, v. GK: 8990. [Q] to draw out (a sword); remove (a sandal); [Qp] to be drawn (sword):– drew [13], drawn [5], draw [4], drew off [1], groweth up [1], plucked off [1]

8026 שֶׁלֶף **šelep**, n.pr.m. GK: 8991. Sheleph, "*one plucked out, drawn out*":– Sheleph [2]

8027 שָׁלַשׁ **šālaš**, v.den. GK: 8992 [→ 7969]. [P] to do a third time, on the third day; [Pu] to be three years old, in three parts:– three years old [3], did the third time [1], divide into three parts [1], do the third time [1], stayed three days [1], threefold [1], three [1]

8028 שֶׁלֶשׁ **šeleš**, n.pr.m. GK: 8994 [→ 7969]. Shelesh, "*triplet;* [poss.] *obedient* or *gentle*":– Shelesh [1]

שָׁלֹשׁ **šālōš**. See 7969.

8029 שִׁלֵּשִׁים **šillēšîm**, a. GK: 9000 [→ 7969]. third (generation):– third [5]

8030 שִׁלְשָׁה **šilšâ**, n.pr.m. GK: 8996 [→ 7969]. Shilshah, "[poss.] *obedient* or *gentle; third [part, child?], triplet*":– Shilshah [1]

8031 שָׁלִשָׁה **šālišâ**, n.pr.loc. GK: 8995 [→ 1190]. Shalisha, "*third part*":– Shalisha [1]

שְׁלֹשָׁה **šālōšâ**. See 7969.

8032 שִׁלְשׁוֹם **šilšôm**, adv. GK: 8997 [→ 7969]. formally, three days ago; used with 8543: "yesterday and three days ago," as an adverb of time: formerly, previously:– heretofore (+8543) [4], in time past (+4480+8543) [4], before (+8543) [3], before that time (+865+3509.1) [1], beforetime (+4480+8543) [1], beforetime (+8543) [1], beforetime (+865+4480) [1], heretofore (+1571+4480+4480+8543) [1], heretofore (+4480+8543) [1], heretofore (+865) [1], in time past (+8543) [1], in time past (+865+1571) [1], in times past (+1571+1571+8543) [1], in times past (+4480+8543) [1], in times past (+865) [1], these three days (+8543) [1]

שְׁלֹשִׁים **š^e lōšîm**. See 7970.

שַׁלְתִּיאֵל **šaltî'ēl**. See 7597.

8033 שָׁם **šām**, adv. GK: 9004 [cf. 8536]. there, where:– there [424], thence [66], where (+834) [54], thither (+1886.5) [50], whither (+834+1886.5) [38], thence (+4480) [34], there (+1886.5) [31], whither (+834) [27], where [22], thither [20], where (+834+1886.5) [7], wherein (+834) [7], therein (+1886.5) [5], therein [5], thereof (+4480) [4], on [3], whence [3], here [2], whence (+834) [2], whence (+834+4480) [2], whereunto (+834) [2], whither (+1886.5) [2], whither [2], in it [1], place where [1], the same place [1], thereout (+4480) [1], thitherward (+1886.5) [1], unto (+1886.5) [1], where (+834+871.1) [1], whereinto (+834+1886.5) [1], wherein [1], wheresoever any (+834+3605) [1], whereunto (+834+1886.5) [1], which[S] [1], whither (+7945) [1], whithersoever (+834+3605) [1], whithersoever (+834+5921) [1], whom (+834) [1], whom[S] [1]

8034 שֵׁם **šēm**, n.m. GK: 9005 [→ 8035?, 8050, 8061, 8062; cf. 8036]. name, a proper designation of a person, place, or thing; by extension: renown, fame; "to call on the name of the LORD" means to proclaim or praise the excellence of Yahweh, to worship Yahweh, or to summon Yahweh by name for help:– name [738], names [81], name's [19], renown [7], fame [4], named [3], famous [2], named (+7121) [2], other names (+8034) [2], base men (+1097) [1], famous (+376) [1], famous (+7121) [1], infamous (+2931+1886.1) [1], named (+7760) [1], report [1]

8035 שֵׁם **šēm**, n.pr.m. GK: 9006 [→ 8034?]. Shem, "*name, fame*":– Shem [17]

8036 שֻׁם **šum** (Aram.), n.m. GK: 10721 [cf. 8034]. name, what someone is called:– name [8], names [3], named (+7761) [1]

8037 שַׁמָּא **šammā'**, n.pr.m. GK: 9007 [cf. 8048]. Shamma; Shammah, "*astonishment*":– Shamma [1]

8038 שֶׁמְאֵבֶר **šem'ēber**, n.pr.m. GK: 9008. Shemeber:– Shemeber [1]

8039 שִׁמְאָה **šim'â**, n.pr.m. GK: 9009 [cf. 8043]. Shimeah, "*he has heard* or *he is obedient*":– Shimeah [1]

8040 שְׂמֹאל **ś^e mō'l**, n.[m.]. GK: 8520 [→ 8041, 8042; cf. 7585]. left (opposite of right); north:– left [36], left hand [17], left side [1]

8041 שִׂמְאֵל **śim'ēl**, v.den. GK: 8521 [→ 8040]. [H] to go to the left; be left-handed:– left [2], go to the left [1], on the left [1], turn to the left [1]

8042 שְׂמָאלִי **ś^e mā'lî**, a. GK: 8522 [→ 8040]. on the left; northern:– left [9]

8043 שִׁמְאָם **šim'ām**, n.pr.m. GK: 9010 [cf. 8039]. Shimeam:– Shimeam [1]

8044 שַׁמְגַּר **šamgar**, n.pr.m. GK: 9011. Shamgar, "*Shimke gave [a son]*":– Shamgar [2]

8045 שָׁמַד **šāmad**, v. GK: 9012 [cf. 8046]. [N] to be destroyed; [H] to destroy, demolish, annihilate:– destroyed [42], destroy [39], destroyed (+8045) [2], utterly destroy (+8045) [2], bring to nought [1], destruction [1], overthrown [1], perished [1], quite pluck down [1]

8046 שְׁמַד **š^e mad** (Aram.), v. GK: 10722 [cf. 8045]. [H] to completely destroy, exterminate:– consume [1]

שָׁמֶה **šāmeh**. See 8064.

Heb

8047 שַׁמָּה ***šammâ***, n.f. GK: 9014 [→ 8074]. thing of horror; desolation, devastation, what is laid waste:– astonishment [13], desolation [11], desolate [10], waste [3], desolations [1], wonderful [1]

8048 שַׁמָּה ***šammâ***, n.pr.m. GK: 9015 [→ 8049, 8054, 8060?; cf. 8037, 8085? *or* 8121?]. Shammah, "*waste*":– Shammah [8]

8049 שַׁמְהוּת ***šamhût***, n.pr.m. GK: 9016 [→ 8054; cf. 8048]. Shamhuth, "[poss.] *one born at a time of a horrible event*":– Shamhuth [1]

8050 שְׁמוּאֵל ***šᵉmûʾēl***, n.pr.m. GK: 9017 [→ 8034+410]. Samuel; Shemuel, "*his name is God [El]; heard of God; the unnamed god is El*":– Samuel [137], Shemuel [3]

שְׁמֹנֶה ***šᵉmôneh***. See 8083.

שְׁמוֹנָה ***šᵉmônâ***. See 8083.

שְׁמוֹנִים ***šᵉmônîm***. See 8084.

8051 שַׁמּוּעַ ***šammûaʿ***, n.pr.m. GK: 9018 [→ 8085+3068?]. Shammua, "[poss.] *[Yahweh] hears; rumor*":– Shammua [5]

8052 שְׁמוּעָה ***šᵉmûʿâ***, n.f. GK: 9019 [→ 8085]. message, rumor, report:– rumour [9], tidings [8], report [4], fame [2], bruit [1], doctrine [1], mentioned [1], news [1]

8053 שָׁמוּר ***šāmûr***, n.pr.m. GK: 9020 [cf. 8069]. Shamur, cf. 8069:– @H = **8054** שַׁמּוֹת ***šammôt***, n.pr.m. GK: 9021 [→ 8049; cf. 8048]. Shammoth, "*desolation*":– Shammoth [1]

8055 שָׂמַח ***śāmaḥ***, v. GK: 8523 [→ 8056, 8057]. [Q] to rejoice, be glad, delight in:– rejoice [65], glad [33], rejoiced [19], make glad [4], maketh glad [4], rejoiceth [4], joy [3], made to rejoice [3], made glad [2], making very glad (+8055) [2], caused to rejoice [1], cheer up [1], cheereth [1], exceeding glad (+1419+8057) [1], hath joy [1], have joy [1], made joyful [1], made rejoice [1], make joyful [1], make rejoice [1], maketh merry (+2416) [1], merry [1], rejoicing [1]

8056 שָׂמֵחַ ***śāmēaḥ***, a.vbl. GK: 8524 [→ 8055]. rejoicing, gladness, delight:– glad [4], rejoiced [4], rejoice [4], joyful [3], merry [2], making merry [1], merrily [1], merryhearted (+3820) [1], rejoice (+1961) [1], rejoice exceedingly (+413+1524) [1], rejoicing [1]

8057 שִׂמְחָה ***śimḥâ***, n.f. GK: 8525 [→ 8055]. joy, gladness, pleasure, delight:– joy [43], gladness [32], mirth [8], rejoice [2], rejoicing [2], exceeding glad (+1419+8055) [1], exceedingly rejoice (+7797+871.1) [1], exceeding [1], glad [1], joyfulness [1], pleasure [1], rejoiced [1]

8058 שָׁמַט ***šāmaṭ***, v. GK: 9023 [→ 8059]. [Q] to drop down, stumble; to lie unplowed; [N] to be thrown down; [H] to cancel a debt:– release [2], discontinue [1], overthrown [1], rest [1], shook [1], stumbled [1], threw down [1], throw down [1]

8059 שְׁמִטָּה ***šᵉmiṭṭâ***, n.f. GK: 9024 [→ 8058]. canceling of debt:– release [5]

8060 שַׁמַּי ***šammay***, n.pr.m. GK: 9025 [→ 8085? *or* 8048?]. Shammai, "*Yahweh has heard*":– Shammai [6]

8061 שְׁמִידָע ***šᵉmîdāʿ***, n.pr.m. GK: 9026 [→ 8062]. Shemida, "[poss.] *the name knows;* [poss.] *Eshmun has known*":– Shemida [3]

8062 שְׁמִידָעִי ***šᵉmîdāʿî***, a.g. GK: 9027 [→ 8061; cf. 8034]. Shemidaite, "*of Shemida*":– Shemidaites [1]

8063 שְׂמִיכָה ***śᵉmîkâ***, n.f. GK: 8526. covering:– mantle [1]

8064 שָׁמַיִם ***šāmayim***, n.m. GK: 9028 [cf. 8065]. region above the earth: the heavens: place of the stars, sky, air; heaven: the invisible realm of God:– heaven [289], heavens [109], air [21], astrologers (+1895) [1], other (+7097) [1]

8065 שְׁמַיִן ***šᵉmayin*** (Aram.), n.m.pl. GK: 10723 [cf. 8064]. the heavens (of this world), sky, air; heaven (the realm of God); "heaven" is also a euphemism for "God"; the phrase "heaven and earth" combine into one meaning "the universe," the totality of all that exists:– heaven [35], heavens [3]

8066 שְׁמִינִי ***šᵉmînî***, a.num.ord. GK: 9029 [→ 8083]. eighth:– eighth [27], eight [1]

8067 שְׁמִינִית ***šᵉmînît***, tt. GK: 9030 [→ 8083]. sheminith:– Sheminith [3]

8068 שָׁמִיר ***šāmîr***, n.m. GK: 9031 & 9032 [→ 8104; cf. 8069?]. briers; hardest stone; (other contexts) flint or emery:– briers [8], adamant stone [1], adamant [1], diamond [1]

8069 שָׁמִיר ***šāmîr***, n.pr.m. & loc. GK: 9033 & 9034 [cf. 8053, 8068?]. Shamir, "[poss.] *thorny* or *emery [flint]*":– Shamir [4]

8070 שְׁמִירָמוֹת ***šᵉmîrāmôt*** or שְׁמָרִימוֹת ***šᵉmirîmôt***, n.pr.m. GK: 9035 & 9082. Shemirimoth, Shemiramoth, "*heights, heavens;* [poss. pr.n. of pagan goddess]":– Shemiramoth [4]

8071 שִׂמְלָה ***śimlâ***, n.f. GK: 8529 [→ 8072; cf. 8008]. clothing, garment, cloak:– raiment [11], clothes [6], garment [4], apparel [2], clothing [2], cloth [2], garments [2]

8072 שַׂמְלָה ***śamlâ***, n.pr.m. GK: 8528 [→ 8071, 8073]. Samlah:– Samlah [4]

8073 שַׂמְלַי ***śamlay*** or שַׁלְמַי ***šalmay*** or שַׁמְלַי ***šamlay***, n.pr.m. GK: 8530 & 8978 & 9036 [→ 8072; cf. 8014]. Samlai, Shalmai, Shamlai, "[perhaps] *Yahweh is well-being*":– Shalmai [1]

8074 שָׁמֵם ***šāmēm***, v. GK: 9037 [→ 4923, 8047, 8076, 8077, 8078; cf. 3456; cf. 8075]. [Q] to be desolate, be appalled; [N] to become desolate, be appalled; [Pol] to cause desolation, be appalled; [H] to bring to devastation, cause to be appalled; [Ho] to lie desolate; [Htpol] to destroy oneself, be appalled:– desolate [31], astonished [14], astonied [6], make desolate [5], desolations [4], made desolate [4], lieth desolate [3], destroy [2], laid desolate [2], laid waste [2], maketh desolate [2], wondered [2], astonishment [1], bring into desolation [1], bring unto desolation [1], desolate places [1], desolation [1], destitute [1], destroyed [1], lay desolate [1], lie waste [1], make amazed [1], make waste [1], make [1], making desolate [1], waste [1]

8075 שְׁמַם ***šᵉmam*** (Aram.), v. GK: 10724 [cf. 8074]. [Itpo] to be greatly perplexed, implying one is in a state of severe distress, a fig. extension of destroying an object:– astonied [1]

8076 שָׁמֵם ***šāmēm***, a. GK: 9038 [→ 8074]. desolate, deserted:– desolate [2]

8077 שְׁמָמָה ***šᵉmāmâ*** or שִׁמְמָה ***šimᵉmâ***, n.f. GK: 9039 & 9040 [→ 8074]. desolation, ruin, wasteland:– desolate [36], desolation [12], most desolate (+4923+2050.1) [3], desolations [2], most desolate (+8077+2050.1) [2], utterly [1], waste [1]

8078 שִׁמָּמוֹן ***šimmāmôn***, n.[m.]. GK: 9041 [→ 8074]. despair, which may border on feelings of horror and shuddering:– astonishment [2]

8079 שְׂמָמִית ***śᵉmāmît***, n.f. GK: 8532. lizard; some sources: gecko:– spider [1]

8080 שָׁמֵן ***šāmēn***, v. GK: 9042 [→ 8081]. [Q] to grow fat; [H] to show as well-fed; by extension: to be calloused, unresponsive of heart:– waxed fat [2], became fat [1], make fat [1], waxen fat [1]

8081 שֶׁמֶן ***šemen***, n.m. GK: 9043 [→ 820?, 4924, 4925, 4924, 8080, 8082]. olive, the tree and its products: olive berry, olive oil, olive wood; olive oil was a staple of diet in biblical times, and was also used as a medicine, lamp fuel, and in religious offerings and ritual:– oil [165], ointment [11], olive [4], ointments [3], fat things [2], fat [2], oiled [2], anointing [1], fatness [1], pine [1], very fruitful (+1121) [1]

8082 שָׁמֵן ***šāmēn***, a. GK: 9045 [→ 8081]. rich, fertile:– fat [8], lusty [1], plenteous [1]

8083 שְׁמֹנֶה ***šᵉmōneh***, n.m. & f. GK: 9046 [→ 8066, 8067, 8084]. eight; (pl.) eighty:– eight [74], eighteen (+6240) [18], eighteenth (+6240) [11], eighth [5], eighteen thousand (+505+7239+2050.1) [1]

8084 שְׁמֹנִים ***šᵉmōnîm***, n.pl.indecl. GK: 9047 [→ 8083]. eighty (pl. of "eight"):– fourscore [34], eighty [3], eightieth [1]

8085 שָׁמַע ***šāmaʿ***, v. GK: 9048 [→ 851, 2045, 3458, 3460, 3461, 4926, 4927, 4928, 8048, 8049, 8054, 8052, 8060, 8087, 8088, 8089, 8090, 8093, 8094, 8095, 8096, 8097, 8099, 8100, 8101; cf. 1002]. [Q] to hear, listen, obey; [N] to be heard; [P] to summon, call together; [H] to proclaim, summon, make hear; from the base meaning of hearing come the extensions of understanding and obedience:– heard [362], hear [350], hearken [112], hearkened [73], heareth [26], obey (+871.1) [26], obeyed (+871.1) [20], obeyed [14], publish [12], heardest [11], obey [11], obedient [8], hearest [6], hearing [6], understand [6], cause to be heard [5], cause to hear [4], diligently hearken (+8085) [4], hear diligently (+8085) [4], heareth (+8085) [4], hearken diligently (+8085) [4], publisheth [4], shewed [4], make to be heard [3], call together [2], carefully hearken (+8085) [2], certainly heard (+8085) [2], diligently obey (+8085) [2], discern [2], hear indeed (+8085) [2], hearkeneth [2], indeed obey (+8085) [2], made to hear [2], obey indeed (+8085+871.1) [2], obeyedst (+871.1) [2], obeyeth (+871.1) [2], reported [2], shew [2], surely hear (+8085) [2], surely heard (+8085) [2], tell [2], told [2], called together [1], caused to be heard [1], caused to hear [1], consented [1], considered [1], content [1], declared [1], declareth [1], declare [1], gathered together [1], gave ear [1], hear (+241) [1], hear attentively [1], hearken diligently [1], hearken unto [1], hearkenedst [1], hearkening [1], listen [1], made a sound [1], made proclamation [1], make a sound [1], make hear [1], make noise [1], make to hear [1], making a noise [1], obeyeth [1], obeying (+871.1) [1], obeying [1], perceived [1], perceive [1], proclaimed [1], published [1], regardeth [1], sang loud [1], shew forth [1], sounding [1], sound [1], understandest [1], understanding [1], understood [1], witness [1]

8086 שְׁמַע ***šᵉmaʿ*** (Aram.), v. GK: 10725 [cf. 8085]. [P] to hear; [Htpa] to obey:– heard [4], hear [4], obey [1]

8087 שֶׁמַע ***šemaʿ***, n.pr.m. GK: 9050. Shema, "*he hears*":– Shema [5]

8088 שֵׁמַע ***šēmaʿ***, n.[m.]. GK: 9051 [→ 8085]. what is heard, report, news, rumor:– fame [5], report [5], tidings [2], bruit [1], heard [1], hearing [1], hear [1], loud [1], speech [1]

8089 שֹׁמַע ***šōmaʿ***, n.m. GK: 9053 [→ 8085]. report; reputation:– fame [4]

8090 שְׁמַע ***šᵉmaʿ***, n.pr.loc. GK: 9054 [→ 8085]. Shema, "*he hears*":– Shema [1]

8091 שָׁמָע ***šāmāʿ***, n.pr.m. GK: 9052 [→ 8085+3068?]. Shama, "*one obedient [to Yahweh]*":– Shama [1]

8092 שִׁמְעָא ***šimʿāʾ***, n.pr.m. GK: 9055 [→ 8085+3068?]. Shimea; Shammua, "*he has heard* or *obedient one*":– Shimea [5], Shimma [1]

8093 שִׁמְעָה ***šimʿâ***, n.pr.m. GK: 9056 [→ 8101]. Shimeah, "*he has heard* or *he is obedient*":– Shimeah [2]

8094 שְׁמָעָה ***šᵉmāʿâ***, n.pr.m. GK: 9057 [→ 8085]. Shemaah, "[poss.] *Yahweh hears*":– Shemaah [1]

8095 שִׁמְעוֹן ***šimʿôn***, n.pr.m. GK: 9058 [→ 8099; cf. 8085]. Simeon, Simeonite, "*he has heard* or *obedient one*":– Simeon [43], Shimeon [1]

8096 שִׁמְעִי ***šimʿî***, n.pr.m. GK: 9059 [→ 8097]. Shimei, "*Yahweh has heard* or *famous*":– Shimei [41], Shimhi [1], Shimi [1]

8097 שִׁמְעִי ***šimʿî***, a.g. GK: 9060 [→ 8096]. Shimeites, of Shimei, "*of Shimei*":– Shimei [1], Shimites [1]

8098 שְׁמַעְיָה ***šᵉmaʿyâ*** or שְׁמַעְיָהוּ ***šᵉmaʿyāhû***, n.pr.m. GK: 9061 & 9062 [→ 8085+3068]. Shemaiah, "*Yahweh hears*":– Shemaiah [41]

8099 שִׁמְעֹנִי ***šimʿōnî***, a.g. GK: 9063 [→ 8095]. Simeonite, of Simeon, "*of Simeon*":– Simeonites [3], Simeon [1]

8100 שִׁמְעָת ***šimʿāt***, n.pr.f. GK: 9064 [→ 8085]. Shimeath, "*guardian, watcher*":– Shimeath [2]

8101 שִׁמְעָתִי ***šimʿātî***, a.g. GK: 9065 [→ 8093]. Shimeathite, "*of Shimeath*":– Shimeathites [1]

8102 שֶׁמֶץ ***šemeṣ***, n.[m.]. GK: 9066 [→ 8103?]. whisper:– little [2]

8103 שִׁמְצָה ***šimṣâ***, v. GK: 9067 [→ 8102?]. laughingstock, derision:– shame [1]

8104 שָׁמַר ***šāmar***, v. GK: 9068 [→ 821, 4929, 4931, 8068, 8105, 8106?, 8108, 8109, 8110, 8111, 8113, 8107, 8118, 8119 (also used with compound proper names)]. [Q] to keep, watch, observe, guard; [Qp] to be set aside, be secured; [N] to be careful, beware; [P] to cling to; [Ht] to keep oneself; to observe for oneself:– keep [183], kept [70], observe [41], take heed [31], keepeth [19], keepers [15], keeper [13], beware [9], preserve [9], keeping [7], preserved [6], preserveth [6], watch [5], diligently keep (+8104) [4], mark [4], watchman [4], watchmen [4], keepest [3], observed [3], regardeth [3], marked [2], regard [2], took heed [2], wait [2], circumspect [1], lay wait [1], lookest narrowly [1], markest [1], marketh [1], observest [1], observeth [1], reserveth [1], saved [1], save [1], spies [1], sure [1], takest heed [1], taking heed [1], wait on [1], waited [1], waiteth on [1], waiteth [1], waiting [1], watched [1], watcht [1]

8105 שֶׁמֶר ***šemer***, n.m. GK: 9069 [→ 8106?; cf. 8104]. dregs (of wine); aged wine:– lees [2], wines on the lees [2], dregs [1]

8106 שֶׁמֶר ***šemer***, n.pr.m. GK: 9070 [→ 8105?]. Shemer, "[poss.] *watch;* [poss.] *sediment of wine from which clear wine is made*":– Shamer [2], Shemer [2], Shamed [1]

8107 שִׁמֻּרִים ***šimmurîm***, n.[m.pl.]. GK: 9081 [→ 8104]. vigil, night-watch:– much observed [1], observed [1]

שֹׁמֵר ***šōmēr***. See 7763.

8108 שָׁמְרָה ***šomrâ***, n.f. GK: 9072 [→ 8104]. guard, watch:– watch [1]

8109 שְׁמֻרָה ***šᵉmurâ***, n.f. GK: 9073 [→ 8104]. eyelid (that covers and protects the eye):– waking [1]

8110 שִׁמְרוֹן ***šimrôn***, n.pr.m. & loc. GK: 9074 & 9075 [→ 8104, 8117]. Shimron, "*guardian, watchman*":– Shimron [5]

8111 שֹׁמְרוֹן **šōm^{e}rôn**, n.pr.m. GK: 9076 [→ 8118; cf. 8104; cf. 8115]. Samaria, the capital city of northern kingdom of Israel; by extension, the northern kingdom itself, "*belonging to the clan of Shemer [1Ki 16:24]*":– Samaria [109]

8112 שִׁמְרוֹן מְרֹאוֹן **šimrôn m^{e}r'ôn**, n.pr.loc. GK: 9077. Shimron Meron:– Shimron-meron [1]

8113 שִׁמְרִי **šimrî**, n.pr.m. GK: 9078 [→ 8104]. Shimri, "*Yahweh guards, preserves*":– Shimri [3], Simri [1]

8114 שְׁמַרְיָה **š^{e}maryâ** or שְׁמַרְיָהוּ **š^{e}maryāhû**, n.pr.m. GK: 9079 & 9080 [→ 8104+3068]. Shemariah, "*Yahweh guards, preserves*":– Shemariah [3], Shamariah [1]

שְׁמָרִימוֹת **š^{e}mārîmôt**. See 8070.

8115 שָׁמְרַיִן **šām^{e}rayin** (Aram.), n.pr.loc. GK: 10726 [cf. 8111]. Samaria, "*belonging to the clan of Shemer*":– Samaria [2]

8116 שִׁמְרִית **šimrît**, n.pr.f. GK: 9083 [→ 7763]. Shimrith, "*guardianess, watch woman*":– Shimrith [1]

8117 שִׁמְרֹנִי **šimrōnî**, a.g. GK: 9084 [→ 8110]. Shimronite, "*of Shimron*":– Shimronites [1]

8118 שֹׁמְרֹנִי **šōm^{e}rōnî**, a.g. GK: 9085 [→ 8111]. of Samaria, "*of Samaria*":– Samaritans [1]

8119 שִׁמְרָת **šimrāt**, n.pr.m. GK: 9086 [→ 8104]. Shimrath, "*guardian, watchman*":– Shimrath [1]

8120 שְׁמַשׁ **š^{e}maš** (Aram.), v. GK: 10727 [→ 8122?]. [Pa] to attend to, serve:– ministered [1]

8121 שֶׁמֶשׁ **šemeš**, n.f. & m. GK: 9087 [→ 1053, 1030, 5885, 5905, 8048, 8123; cf. 8122]. sun:– sun [119], sunrising (+4217) [6], the sunrising (+4217+1886.1) [2], east side (+4217) [1], eastward (+4217+1886.1) [1], sunrising (+4217+1886.1) [1], the east side (+4217+1886.1) [1], the west (+3996+1886.1) [1], westward (+3996+1886.1) [1], windows [1]

8122 שְׁמַשׁ **š^{e}maš** (Aram.), n.[m.]. GK: 10728 [→ 8120?, 8122; cf. 8121]. sun:– sun [1]

8123 שִׁמְשׁוֹן **šimšôn**, n.pr.m. GK: 9088 [→ 8121]. Samson, "*little one of Shemesh* or *strong*":– Samson [35], Samson's [3]

שִׁמְשִׁי **šimšî**. See 1030.

8124 שִׁמְשַׁי **šimšay** (Aram.), n.pr.m. GK: 10729 [→ 8122]. Shimshai, "*one given to (pagan sun god) Shemesh*":– Shimshai [4]

8125 שַׁמְשְׁרַי **šamš^{e}ray**, n.pr.m. GK: 9091. Shamsherai, "*may Shemesh guard*":– Shamsherai [1]

8126 שֻׁמָתִי **šumātî**, a.g. GK: 9092. Shumathite:– Shumathites [1]

8127 שֵׁן **šēn**, n.f. & m. GK: 9094 [→ 8143; cf. 8150; cf. 8128]. tooth (human or animal); by extension, anything tooth shaped: rocky crag; "cleanness of teeth" is a sign of lack of food in famine:– teeth [31], ivory [10], tooth [9], sharp [2], crag [1], forefront [1], tooth's [1]

8128 שֵׁן **šēn** (Aram.), n.[f.]. GK: 10730 [cf. 8127]. tooth; in the dual number it is a set of teeth, the upper and lower rows of teeth in a mouth:– teeth [3]

8129 שֵׁן **šēn**, n.pr.loc. GK: 9095 [→ 8150]. Shen, "*tooth, crag [of rock]*":– Shen [1]

8130 שָׂנֵא **śānē'**, v. GK: 8533 [→ 5570, 5574, 8135, 8146; cf. 8131]. [Q] to hate, be an enemy; [Qp] to be unloved; [N] to be hated, be shunned; [P] to be an adversary, be a foe; "hate" can be active, as an enemy or adversary; or passive, as someone unloved or shunned:– hate [68], hated [40], hateth [20], hatest [5], enemies [3], enemy [2], utterly hated (+8130) [2], foes [1], hated exceedingly (+1419+3966+8135) [1], hateful [1], haters [1], hating [1], odious [1]

8131 שְׂנֵא **ś^{e}nā'** (Aram.), v. GK: 10686 [cf. 8130]. [P] to hate; (as noun) an enemy:– hate [1]

8132 שָׁנָא **šānā'**, v. GK: 9096 [→ 8125?]. prob. same as 8138: [Q] to become dull; to change; [P] to change, alter; [Pu] to be changed:– changed [3]

8133 שְׁנָה **š^{e}nâ** (Aram.), v. GK: 10731 [→ 8140; cf. 8138]. [P] to be changed, be different; [Pa] to change; defy; [Pap] to be different; [H] to change, alter; [Itpa] to be changed, be turned into:– changed [12], diverse [5], alter [2], changeth [1], change [1]

שֵׁנָא **šēnā'**. See 8142.

8134 שִׁנְאָב **šin'āb**, n.pr.m. GK: 9098. Shinab, "*Sin is his father*":– Shinab [1]

8135 שִׂנְאָה **śin'â**, n.f. GK: 8534 [→ 8130]. hatred, malice:– hatred [12], hated [2], cruel hatred (+2555) [1], hated exceedingly (+1419+3966+8130) [1], hatefully (+871.1) [1]

8136 שִׁנְאָן **šin'ān**, n.[m.]. GK: 9099 [→ 8125?]. high in rank or number:– angels [1]

8137 שֶׁנְאַצַּר **šen'aṣṣar**, n.pr.m. GK: 9100. Shenazzar, "*may Sin protect*":– Shenazar [1]

8138 שָׁנָה **šānâ**, v. GK: 9101 [→ 4932, 8132?, 8136?, 8141, 8144?, 8145, 8147; cf. 8150; cf. 8133]. [Q] to repeat, do again; [N] to be repeated; [P] to change, alter; to pretend; [Pu] to be changed; [Ht] to disguise oneself:– changed [3], again [2], change [2], diverse [2], alter [1], changest [1], did the second time [1], disguise [1], do again [1], do the second time [1], doubled [1], given to change [1], pervert [1], preferred [1], repeateth [1], returneth [1], second time [1]

8139 שְׁנָה **š^{e}nâ** (Aram.), n.f. GK: 10733 [cf. 8142]. sleep:– sleep [1]

8140 שְׁנָה **š^{e}nâ** (Aram.), n.f. GK: 10732 [→ 8133; cf. 8141]. year:– year [6], years [1]

8141 שָׁנָה **šānâ**, n.f. GK: 9102 [→ 8138; cf. 8140]. year:– years [446], year [288], first year (+1121) [42], two years [6], two full years (+3117) [5], every year (+3605+8141+2050.1) [2], year by year (+8141) [2], year by year (+8141+871.1) [2], yearly (+3605+8141+871.1+2050.1) [2], yearly (+8141+871.1) [2], years old [2], years' [2], first year (+1323) [1], how long (+3117+4100+3509.1) [1], long [1], old (+2416+3117) [1], two year [1], whole age (+2416+3117) [1], year's [1], yearly [1]

8142 שֵׁנָא **šēnā'** or שֵׁנָה **šēnâ**, n.f. GK: 9097 & 9104 [→ 3462, 8153; cf. 8139]. sleep, with a focus of rest and inactivity, sometimes laziness; by extension: death:– sleep [23]

8143 שֶׁנְהַבִּים **šenhabbîm**, n.m.[pl.]. GK: 9105 [→ 8127]. ivory:– ivory [2]

8144 שָׁנִי **šānî**, n.[m.]. GK: 9106 [→ 8138?]. scarlet, crimson (thread):– scarlet (+8438) [31], scarlet [6], scarlet (+8438+1886.1) [2], scarlet thread [2], crimson [1]

8145 שֵׁנִי **šēnî**, a.num.ord. GK: 9108 [→ 8147; cf. 8138; cf. 8578, cf. 8579]. second:– second [84], other [37], second time [16], again [7], another [7], more [3], either [1], second rank [1]

8146 שָׂנִיא **śānî'**, a. GK: 8535 [→ 8130]. not loved, disdained:– hated [1]

8147 שְׁנַיִם **š^{e}nayim**, n.m. & f. GK: 9109 [→ 8145; cf. 8138; cf. 8648]. two:– two [528], twelve (+6240) [109], both [75], twelfth (+6240) [22], second [10], twain [6], double [5], twice [4], threescore and twelve (+7657+2050.1) [2], twenty [2], both twain [1], couple [1], sixscore (+6240) [1], twice (+871.1) [1]

8148 שְׁנִינָה **š^{e}nînâ**, n.f. GK: 9110 [→ 8150]. object of ridicule:– byword [3], taunt [1]

8149 שְׂנִיר **ś^{e}nîr**, n.pr.loc. GK: 8536. Senir:– Senir [2], Shenir [2]

8150 שָׁנַן **šānan**, v. GK: 9111 & 9112 [→ 8127, 8129, 8143, 8148; cf. 8138]. [Q] to sharpen; [Qp] be sharpened; [P] to impress, repeat; [Htpol] to be embittered:– sharp [4], whet [2], pricked [1], sharpened [1], teach diligently [1]

8151 שָׁנַס **šānas**, v. GK: 9113. [P] to tuck up the cloak (into the belt):– girded up [1]

8152 שִׁנְעָר **šin'ār**, n.pr.loc. GK: 9114. Shinar; Babylonia:– Shinar [7], Babylonish [1]

8153 שְׁנָת **š^{e}nāt**, n. GK: 9104 [→ 8142]. same as 8142: sleep:– sleep [1]

8154 שָׁסָה **šāsâ**, v. GK: 9115 [cf. 7601]. [Q] to raid, loot, plunder; [Qp] to be looted:– spoiled [3], spoil [3], spoilers [2], destroyers [1], robbed [1], rob [1]

8155 שָׁסַס **šāsas**, v. GK: 9116 [→ 7601]. same as 7601: [Q] to plunder, ransack; [N] to be looted, be ransacked:– spoiled [3], rifled [1], spoil [1]

8156 שָׁסַע **šāsa'**, v. GK: 9117 [→ 8157]. [Q] to divide; [Qp] be divided; [P] to tear apart:– clovenfooted (+6541+8157) [2], rent [2], cleaveth [1], cleave [1], clovenfooted (+8157) [1], cloven [1], stayed [1]

8157 שֶׁסַע **šesa'**, n.[m.]. GK: 9118 [→ 8156]. cleft (split hoof):– clovenfooted (+6541+8156) [2], cleft [1], clovenfooted (+8156) [1]

8158 שָׁסַף **šāsap**, v. GK: 9119. [P] to hack to pieces (for execution):– hewed in pieces [1]

8159 שָׁעָה **šā'â**, v. GK: 9120 [cf. 7583]. [Q] to look with favor, have regard for, pay attention to:– look [3], dismayed [2], respect [2], depart [1], dim [1], have respect [1], look away [1], looked [1], regard [1], spare [1], turn [1]

8160 שָׁעָה **šā'â** (Aram.), n.f. GK: 10734. moment, short time; (as adv.) immediately, suddenly, for a time:– hour [5]

שְׂעוֹר **ś^e'ôr**. See 8184.

שְׂעוֹרָה **ś^e'ôrâ**. See 8184.

8161 שְׁעָטָה **š^e'āṭâ**, n.f. GK: 9121. galloping, pounding (hooves):– stamping [1]

8162 שַׁעַטְנֵז **ša'aṭnēz**, n.m. GK: 9122. woven cloth; likely referring to a wide mesh:– garment of divers sorts [1], mingled of linen and woollen (+3610) [1]

8163 שָׂעִיר **śā'îr**, a. & n.m. GK: 8537 & 8538 & 8539 [→ 8166; cf. 8175]. hairy, shaggy; male goat; goat idol:– kid [26], goat [21], devils [2], goats [2], hairy [2], kids [2], he goats [1], rough [1], satyrs [1], satyr [1]

8164 שָׂעִיר **śā'îr**, n.[m.]. GK: 8540. rain shower:– small rain [1]

8165 שֵׂעִיר **śē'îr**, n.pr.m. & loc. GK: 8541 & 8542 & 8543 [→ 8167; cf. 8175]. Seir, "*hairy, shaggy, covered with trees;* [poss.] *the place of the goats* or *the place of Esau [Ge 25:25 BDB]; small forest, rich forest*":– Seir [39]

8166 שְׂעִירָה **ś^e'îrâ**, n.f. GK: 8544 [→ 8163]. female goat:– kid [2]

8167 שְׂעִירָה **ś^e'îrâ**, n.pr.loc. GK: 8545 [→ 8165]. Seirah, "*place of the goats;* [poss.] *woody hills; shaggy forest*":– Seirath [1]

8168 שֹׁעַל **šō'al**, n.[m.]. GK: 9123 [→ 4934, 8171?]. hollow of the hand; handful, a measure of volume:– handfuls [2], hollow of hand [1]

שֻׁעָל **šu'āl**. See 7776.

8169 שַׁעַלְבִים **ša'albîm** or שַׁעֲלַבִּין **ša^{a}labbîn**, n.pr.loc. GK: 9124 & 9125. Shaalbim, Shaalabbin, "*site of foxes*":– Shaalbim [2], Shaalabbin [1]

8170 שַׁעַלְבֹנִי **ša'albōnî**, a.g. GK: 9126. Shaalbonite:– Shaalbonite [2]

8171 שַׁעֲלִים **ša^{a}lîm**, n.pr.loc. GK: 9127 [→ 8168?]. Shaalim, "[poss.] *[land of] hollow depth*":– Shalim [1]

8172 שָׁעַן **šā'an**, v. GK: 9128 [→ 4937, 4938]. [N] to lean oneself upon, rely on:– stay [5], leaned [4], lean [4], relied [3], rest [2], leaneth [1], lieth [1], rely [1], resteth [1]

8173 שָׁעַע **šā'a'**, v. GK: 9129 & 9130 [→ 8191]. [Q] be blinded; [Pil] to take joy in, delight in; [Pulpal] to be dandled; [H] to make close the eyes; [Htpal] to blind oneself; a fig. extension of smearing over or pasting objects together; to delight oneself in:– delight [4], cry out [1], cry [1], dandled [1], play [1], shut [1]

שָׁעִף **sā'ip**. See 5587.

8174 שַׁעַף **ša'ap**, n.pr.m. GK: 9131. Shaaph:– Shaaph [2]

8175 שָׂעַר **śā'ar**, v.den. GK: 8547 & 8548 & 8549 [→ 8163, 8165, 8166, 8167, 8178, 8181, 8183, 8184, 8185; cf. 5590]. [Q] to shudder, bristle with horror; to sweep away (by the wind); to know about, be acquainted with; [N] to be in a storm; [P] to sweep away (by a wind); [Ht] to storm against:– afraid [1], as a storm hurleth [1], come like a whirlwind [1], feared [1], horribly afraid [1], sore afraid (+8178) [1], take away as with a whirlwind [1], tempestuous [1]

8176 שָׁעַר **šā'ar**, v. GK: 9132 [→ 8180]. [Q] to think, estimate, calculate:– thinketh [1]

8177 שְׂעַר **ś^e'ar** (Aram.), n.m. GK: 10687 [cf. 8181]. hair (of the head or body):– hair [2], hairs [1]

8178 שַׂעַר **śa'ar**, n.[m.]. GK: 8550 & 8551 [→ 8175]. horror, shudder, an extension of the bristling of hair (in excitement or fear); wind storm, gale:– affrighted (+270) [1], horribly [1], sore afraid (+8175) [1], storm [1]

8179 שַׁעַר **ša'ar**, n.m. GK: 9133 [→ 7778, 8182, 8189; cf. 8651]. gate, gateway; often referring to the entrance to a city, a key point of the city's defense and a place for public hearings and decisions:– gate [249], gates [112], every gate (+8179+2050.1) [6], cities [2], city [1], doors [1], door [1], porters [1], port [1]

8180 שַׁעַר **ša'ar**, n.[m.]. GK: 9134 [→ 8176]. measure (of grain):– hundredfold (+3967) [1]

שָׂעִר **sā'ir**. See 8163.

8181 שֵׂעָר ***śē'ār***, n.m. GK: 8552 [→ 8175; cf. 8177]. hair:– hair [23], hairy [3], hairs [1], rough [1]

שֹׁעֵר ***šō'ēr***. See 7778.

8182 שֹׁעָר ***šō'ār***, a. GK: 9135 [→ 8179]. burst open, i.e., poor quality (figs):– vile [1]

8183 שְׂעָרָה ***śᵉ'ārâ***, n.f. GK: 8554 [→ 8175]. storm, gale:– storm [1], tempest [1]

8184 שְׂעֹרָה ***śᵉ'ōrâ***, n.f. GK: 8555 [→ 8175; cf. 7795?]. barley:– barley [34]

8185 שַׂעֲרָה ***śaᵃrâ***, n.f. GK: 8553 [→ 8175]. hair:– hair [5], hairs [2]

8186 שַׁעֲרוּר ***šaᵃrûr*** or שַׁעֲרוּרִי ***šaᵃrûrî***, n.f. GK: 9136 & 9137. something horrible, shocking thing:– horrible thing [4]

8187 שְׁעַרְיָה ***šᵉ'aryâ***, n.pr.m. GK: 9138 [→ 3068]. Sheariah, "[poss.] *Yahweh breaks*":– Sheariah [2]

8188 שְׂעֹרִים ***śᵉ'ōrîm***, n.pr.m. GK: 8556. Seorim, "*one born at the time of the barley [harvest]*":– Seorim [1]

8189 שַׁעֲרַיִם ***šaᵃrayim***, n.pr.loc. GK: 9139 [→ 8179]. Shaaraim, "*double gates*":– Shaaraim [2], Sharaim [1]

שַׁעֲרוּרִיָּה ***šaᵃrîrîâ*** and שַׁעֲרֻרִת ***šaᵃrurit***. See 8186.

8190 שַׁעַשְׁגַז ***ša'ašgaz***, n.pr.m. GK: 9140. Shaashgaz:– Shaashgaz [1]

8191 שַׁעֲשׁוּעִים ***šaᵃšû'îm***, n.[m.]pl.intens. GK: 9141 [→ 8173]. delight:– delight [4], delights [3], pleasant [2]

8192 שָׁפָה ***šāpâ***, v. GK: 9142 [→ 3472, 3473?, 8194?, 8195?, 8205]. [N, Pu] to be swept bare:– high [1], stick out [1]

8193 שָׂפָה ***śāpâ***, n.f. & m. GK: 8557 [→ 8222]. lips (of the mouth); by extension: speech, language; edge of an object, rim, border; the "lip of the sea" is the seashore:– lips [110], bank [10], brim [8], edge [8], language [7], shore [6], speech [6], brink [5], border [3], side [3], lip [2], prating [2], vain [2], band [1], binding [1], full of talk [1], other [1]

8194 שְׁפוֹת ***šᵉpôt***, n.f. GK: 9147 [→ 8192?]. milk product: cream, curds, cheese, etc:– cheese [1]

8195 שְׁפוֹ ***šᵉpô*** or שְׁפִי ***šᵉpî***, n.pr.m. GK: 9143 & 9156 [→ 8192?, 8205?]. Shepho, Shephi, "[poss.] *barren way, empty path*":– Shephi [1], Shepho [1]

8196 שְׁפוֹט ***šᵉpôṭ***, n.m. GK: 9144 [→ 8199]. judgment, punishment:– judgment [2]

8197 שְׁפוּפָם ***šᵉpûpām*** or שְׁפוּפָן ***šᵉpûpān*** or שׁוּפָם ***šûpām***, n.pr.m. GK: 9145 & 9146 & 8792 [→ 7781, 8207?]. Shephupham, Shephuphan, Shupham; "[perhaps] *serpent*":– Shephuphan [1], Shupham [1]

8198 שִׁפְחָה ***šipḥâ***, n.f. GK: 9148 [→ 4940; cf. 5596]. maidservant, female slave:– handmaid [22], maid [12], handmaids [7], maidservants [5], bondwomen [3], maidservant [3], womenservants [3], handmaidens [2], maiden [2], bondmaid [1], maidens [1], servant [1], wench [1]

8199 שָׁפַט ***šāpaṭ***, v. GK: 9149 [→ 4941, 8195, 8196, 8201, 8202, 8204; cf. 8200 (also used with compound proper names)]. [Q] to judge, decide; lead, defend, vindicate; [N] to execute judgment, be brought to trial; to argue a matter; [Po] (ptcp.) judge:– judge [102], judges [37], judged [28], plead [7], judgeth [5], judging [4], avenged [2], judgest [2], needs be a judge (+8199) [2], plead with [2], condemn [1], contendeth [1], defend [1], deliver [1], execute the judgment (+4941) [1], execute [1], executing judgment [1], pleaded [1], pleadeth [1], reason [1], ruled [1]

8200 שְׁפַט ***šᵉpaṭ*** (Aram.), v. GK: 10735 [cf. 8199]. [P] to judge; (as noun) judge:– magistrates [1]

8201 שֶׁפֶט ***šepeṭ***, n.m. GK: 9150 [→ 8199]. judgment, punishment:– judgments [14], judgment [2]

8202 שָׁפָט ***šāpāṭ***, n.pr.m. GK: 9151 [→ 8199]. Shaphat, "*he judges*":– Shaphat [8]

8203 שְׁפַטְיָה ***šᵉpaṭyâ*** or שְׁפַטְיָהוּ ***šᵉpaṭyāhû***, n.pr.m. GK: 9152 & 9153 [→ 8199+3068]. Shephatiah, "*Yahweh has judged*":– Shephatiah [12], Shephathiah [1]

8204 שִׁפְטָן ***šipṭān***, n.pr.m. GK: 9154 [→ 8199]. Shiphtan, "*he has judged*":– Shiphtan [1]

8205 שְׁפִי ***šᵉpî***, n.m. GK: 9155 [→ 8195; cf. 8192]. barren height:– high places [8], high place [1]

8206 שֻׁפִּים ***šuppîm***, n.pr.m. & a.g. GK: 9157 & 9158 [→ 8221]. Shuppim; Shuppites:– Shuppim [3]

8207 שְׁפִיפֹן ***šᵉpîpōn***, n.[m.]. GK: 9159 [→ 8197?]. viper:– adder [1]

8208 שָׁפִיר ***šāpîr***, n.pr.loc. GK: 9160 [→ 8231]. Shaphir, "*lovely*":– Saphir [1]

8209 שַׁפִּיר ***šappîr*** (Aram.), a. GK: 10736 [→ 8232]. beautiful, fair, lovely:– fair [2]

8210 שָׁפַךְ ***šāpak***, v. GK: 9161 [→ 8211, 8212]. [Q] to pour out, shed, spill; [Qp, N, Pu] to be outpoured, be shed; [Ht] be scattered, ebb away; "to shed blood" means to kill:– shed [34], pour out [23], poured out [19], pour [10], cast [6], poured [6], poureth out [4], cast up [2], poureth [2], sheddeth [2], casting up [1], gushed out [1], pouredst out [1], pouring out [1], shed out [1], shedder [1], slipt [1]

8211 שֶׁפֶךְ ***šepek***, n.[m.]. GK: 9162 [→ 8210]. dump (for throwing out ash refuse):– poured out [2]

8212 שָׁפְכָה ***šopkâ***, n.f. GK: 9163 [→ 8210]. male organ (fluid duct):– privy member [1]

8213 שָׁפֵל ***šāpēl***, v. GK: 9164 [→ 8216, 8217, 8218, 8219, 8220; cf. 8214, cf. 8215]. [Q] to be humbled, be brought low; [H] to humble, bring low:– humbled [4], bring down [3], abase [2], brought down [2], humbleth [2], lay low [2], layeth low [2], made low [2], bring low [1], bringeth low [1], brought low [1], cast down [1], casteth down [1], debase [1], humble [1], low [1], put lower [1], putteth down [1]

8214 שְׁפַל ***šᵉpal*** (Aram.), v. GK: 10737 [→ 8215; cf. 8213]. [H] to humble, subdue, bring low:– abase [1], humbled [1], put down [1], subdue [1]

8215 שְׁפַל ***šᵉpal*** (Aram.), a. GK: 10738 [→ 8214; cf. 8217]. low; (as superlative) lowliest:– basest [1]

8216 שֵׁפֶל ***šēpel***, n.[m.]. GK: 9165 [→ 8213]. low estate, humble condition:– low estate [1], low place [1]

8217 שָׁפָל ***šāpāl***, a. GK: 9166 [→ 8213]. low, deep:– low [5], base [4], humble [4], lower [4], basest [1], lowly [1]

8218 שִׁפְלָה ***šiplâ***, n.f. GK: 9168 [→ 8213]. state of lowliness, condition of humiliation:– low place [1]

8219 שְׁפֵלָה ***šᵉpēlâ***, n.f. GK: 9169 [→ 8213]. (western) foothills, Shephelah, a major buffer area between the (Philistine) coastal plain and the highlands of Judah:– valley [6], vale [5], plain [3], low country [2], low plains [2], valleys [2]

8220 שִׁפְלוּת ***šiplût***, n.f. GK: 9170 [→ 8213]. idleness, inactivity, an extension of lowering the hands to a position of rest:– idleness [1]

8221 שְׁפָם ***šᵉpām***, n.pr.loc. GK: 9172 [→ 8225?]. Shepham, "*nakedness*":– Shepham [2]

8222 שָׂפָם ***śāpām***, n.[m.]. GK: 8559 [→ 8193]. (the area of the) mustache; lower part of the face:– lips [3], beard [1], upper lip [1]

8223 שָׁפָם ***šāpām***, n.pr.m. GK: 9171. Shapham:– Shapham [1]

8224 שִׂפְמוֹת ***śipmôt***, n.pr.loc. GK: 8560. Siphmoth:– Siphmoth [1]

8225 שִׁפְמִי ***šipmî***, a.g. GK: 9175 [→ 8221?]. Shiphmite:– Shiphmite [1]

8226 שָׂפַן ***śāpan***, v. GK: 8561 [cf. 5603]. [Qp] to be hidden:– treasures [1]

8227 שָׁפָן ***šāpān***, n.m. & n.pr.m. GK: 9176 & 9177. coney; n.pr. Shaphan, "*rock badger*":– Shaphan [30], conies [2], coney [1], cony [1]

8228 שֶׁפַע ***šepa'***, n.[m.]. GK: 9179. abundance:– abundance [1]

8229 שִׁפְעָה ***šip'â***, n.f. GK: 9180. (of water) flood; mass (of humans or animals):– abundance [3], company [2], multitude [1]

8230 שִׁפְעִי ***šip'î***, n.pr.m. GK: 9181. Shiphi, "*flowing abundance*":– Shiphi [1]

שָׂפַק ***sāpaq***. See 5606.

8231 שָׁפַר ***šāpar***, v. GK: 9182 [→ 8208, 8233, 8235, 8236, 8237; cf. 7782; cf. 8232]. [Q] to be delightful, pleasing:– goodly [1]

8232 שְׁפַר ***šᵉpar*** (Aram.), v. GK: 10739 [→ 8209, 8238?; cf. 8231]. [P] to be pleased, have pleasure:– acceptable [1], good [1], pleased [1]

8233 שֶׁפֶר ***šeper***, n.m. GK: 9183 [→ 8231]. beauty, loveliness:– goodly [1]

8234 שֶׁפֶר ***šeper***, n.pr.loc. GK: 9184 [cf. 5611]. Shepher:– Shapher [2]

שֹׁפָר ***šōpār***. See 7782.

8235 שִׁפְרָה ***šiprâ***, n.f. GK: 9185 [→ 8231]. fairness, clearness (of skies):– garnished [1]

8236 שִׁפְרָה ***šiprâ***, n.pr.f. GK: 9186 [→ 8231]. Shiphrah, "*beautiful, fair*":– Shiphrah [1]

8237 שַׁפְרוּר ***šaprûr*** or שַׁפְרִיר ***šaprîr***, n.[m.]. GK: 9187 & 9188 [→ 8231]. royal canopy, pavilion:– royal pavilion [1]

8238 שְׁפַרְפָּר ***šᵉparpār*** (Aram.), n.[m.]. GK: 10740 [→ 8232?]. dawn:– very early [1]

8239 שָׁפַת ***šāpat***, v.den. GK: 9189 [→ 830, 4942, 8240]. [Q] to place, put:– set on [3], brought [1], ordain [1]

8240 שְׁפַתַּיִם ***šᵉpattayim***, n.[m.]du. GK: 9190 & 9191 [→ 8239]. double-pronged hooks; area of inactivity: (place of the) fireplaces; some sources: saddlebags or sheepfolds:– hooks [1], pots [1]

8241 שֶׁצֶף ***šeṣep***, n.m. GK: 9192 [cf. 7857, 7858]. surging, flooding (of anger):– little [1]

8242 שַׂק ***śaq***, n.m. GK: 8566. sackcloth; sack:– sackcloth [41], sack [4], sacks [2], sackclothes [1]

8243 שָׁק ***šāq*** (Aram.), n.[m.]. GK: 10741 [cf. 7785]. lower leg, shank:– legs [1]

8244 שָׂקַד ***śāqad***, v. GK: 8567. [N] to be bound:– bound [1]

8245 שָׁקַד ***šāqad***, v. GK: 9193 [→ 8246, 8247]. [Q] to be awake, watch, stand guard:– watch [6], watched [2], hasten [1], remain [1], waketh [1], watching [1]

8246 מְשֻׁקָּד ***mᵉšuqqād***, n.m. GK: 5481 [cf. 8245]. shape of almond flowers:– made like almonds [3], made like unto almonds [2], made after the fashion of almonds [1]

8247 שָׁקֵד ***šāqēd***, n.[m.]. GK: 9196 [cf. 8245]. almond tree, almond nuts:– almond tree [2], almonds [2]

8248 שָׁקָה ***šāqâ***, v. GK: 9197 [→ 4945, 8249, 8250, 8268; cf. 8354]. [N] to be given a drink; [Pu] to be moistened; [H] to give a drink to:– water [9], butler [8], give drink [7], give to drink [6], watered [6], gave drink [5], made drink [5], cause to drink [4], make drink [4], made to drink [3], cupbearers [2], drink [2], gave to drink [2], given to drink [2], butlers [1], cupbearer [1], givest to drink [1], giveth drink [1], giving drink [1], moistened [1], wateredst [1], watereth [1]

8249 שִׁקֻּו ***šiqquw***, n.[m.]. GK: 9198 [→ 8248]. same as 8250: drink; nourishing drink:– drink [1]

8250 שִׁקּוּי ***šiqqûy***, n.[m.]. GK: 9198 [→ 8248]. same as 8249: drink; nourishing drink:– drink [1], marrow [1]

8251 שִׁקּוּץ ***šiqqûṣ***, n.m. GK: 9199 [→ 8262]. detestable thing, vileness, abomination:– abominations [13], abomination [7], detestable things [5], abominable filth [1], abominable idols [1], detestable [1]

8252 שָׁקַט ***šāqaṭ***, v. GK: 9200 [→ 8253; cf. 8367]. [Q] to be at rest, be at peace; [H] to keep silent, remain quiet, remain calm:– quiet [14], rest [5], had rest [4], at rest [2], in rest [2], quietness [2], still [2], appeaseth [1], give rest [1], giveth quietness [1], idleness [1], in quietness [1], in quiet [1], quieteth [1], rested [1], settled [1], take rest [1]

8253 שֶׁקֶט ***šeqeṭ***, n.[m.]. GK: 9201 [→ 8252]. quietness:– quietness [1]

8254 שָׁקַל ***šāqal***, v. GK: 9202 [→ 4946, 4948, 4949?, 8255; cf. 8625]. [Q] to weigh out, make payment; [N] to be weighed:– weighed [11], pay [4], throughly weighed (+8254) [2], weigh [2], receiver [1], receive [1], spend [1]

8255 שֶׁקֶל ***šeqel***, n.m. GK: 9203 [→ 8254; cf. 8625]. shekel (a unit of weight and value, about two-fifths of an ounce [11.5 grams]):– shekels [46], shekel [42]

8256 שִׁקְמָה ***šiqmâ***, n.f. GK: 9204. sycamore-fig tree:– sycomore trees [5], sycomore fruit [1], sycomores [1]

8257 שָׁקַע ***šāqa'***, v. GK: 9205 [→ 4950]. [Q] to sink down; [N] to sink; [H] to make sink down, make settle:– drowned [2], lettest down [1], make deep [1], quenched [1], sink [1]

8258 שְׁקַעֲרוּרָה ***šᵉqaᵃrûrâ***, n.f. GK: 9206 [→ 7086]. depression, hollow:– hollow strakes [1]

8259 שָׁקַף ***šāqap***, v. GK: 9207 [→ 4947, 8260?, 8261]. [N] to look down on, overlook; [H] to look down on:– looked [6], looked out [4], look down [3], looked down [3], looketh [3], appeareth [1], looketh forth [1], looking [1]

8260 שֶׁקֶף ***šeqep***, n.[m.]. GK: 9208 [→ 8259?]. frame work (of a door):– windows [1]

8261 שְׁקֻפִים ***šᵉqupîm***, n.m. GK: 9209 [→ 8259]. clerestory window (a high place window):– lights [1], windows [1]

8262 שָׁקַץ ***šāqaṣ***, v. GK: 9210 [→ 8251, 8263; cf. 5354, 6973]. [P] to detest, abhor, defile:– abomination [2], make abominable [2], utterly detest (+8262) [2], abhorred [1]

8263 שֶׁקֶץ ***šeqeṣ***, n.m. GK: 9211 [→ 8262]. detestable thing:– abomination [9], abominable [2]

שִׁקּוּץ ***šiqquṣ***. See 8251.

8264 שָׁקַק ***šāqaq***, v. GK: 9212 [→ 4944; cf. 7783?]. [Q] to rush forth, charge forth; [Htpal] to rush back and forth:– appetite [1], justle against [1], longing [1], ranging [1], run to and fro [1], run [1]

8265 שָׂקַר ***śāqar***, v. GK: 8568. [P] to flirt, ogle (with the eyes):– wanton [1]

8266 שָׁקַר ***šāqar***, v.den. GK: 9213 [→ 8267]. [Q] to deal falsely with; [P] to deceive, lie, betray:– lie [3], deal falsely [1], dealt falsely [1], suffer to fail [1]

8267 שֶׁקֶר ***šeqer***, n.m. GK: 9214 [→ 8266]. lie, falseness, deception; vanity:– lying [21], false [20], lies [18], falsehood [13], lie [10], falsely [7], falsely (+1886.1+3807.1) [4], wrongfully [4], vain [3], deceitful [2], deceit [1], falsely (+5921) [1], falsely (+871.1+1886.1) [1], feignedly (+871.1) [1], in vain (+1886.1+3807.1) [1], in vain [1], liar [1], lies (+1697) [1], lying (+1697) [1], vain thing [1], without a cause [1]

8268 שֹׁקֶת ***šōqet***, n.f. GK: 9216 [→ 8248]. watering-trough:– troughs [1], trough [1]

8269 שַׂר ***śar***, n.m. GK: 8569 [→ 5371, 8282, 8310; cf. 7786]. ruler of various spheres (military, religious, governmental): commander, official, prince, chief, leader; "Prince of Peace" is a title of the child who would rule on David's throne, referring to the Messiah:– princes [189], captains [80], captain [48], chief [33], rulers [23], prince [19], ruler [10], governor [4], chief captain [3], keeper [3], governors [2], principal [2], general [1], lords [1], master [1], stewards [1], taskmasters (+4522) [1]

8270 שֹׁר ***šōr***, n.[m.]. GK: 9219 [→ 8307, 8326]. navel; umbilical cord:– navel [2]

8271 שְׁרָא ***šᵉrā*** (Aram.), v. GK: 10742 [cf. 8281]. [P] to loosen, solve (a problem); [Pp] to be loosened; to dwell; [Pa] to begin; [Htpa] to be loose and shaking (of legs giving way):– began [1], dissolve [1], dissolving [1], dwelleth [1], loosed [1], loose [1]

8272 שַׂרְאֶצֶר ***śar'eṣer***, שַׂר־אֶצֶר ***śar-'eṣer***, n.pr.m. GK: 8570 [→ 5371]. Sharezer, "*[god] protect the king!*":– Sharezer [2], Sherezer [1]

8273 שָׁרָב ***šārāb***, n.m. GK: 9220 [→ 8274?]. parching heat; burning hot sand:– heat [1], parched ground [1]

8274 שֵׁרֵבְיָה ***šērēbyâ***, n.pr.m. GK: 9221 [→ 8273?+3068]. Sherebiah, "[poss.] *Yahweh has sent burning heat*":– Sherebiah [8]

8275 שַׁרְבִיט ***šarbîṭ***, n.m. GK: 9222 [→ 7626]. scepter, staff:– sceptre [4]

8276 שָׂרַג ***śārag***, v. GK: 8571 [→ 8299]. [Pu] to be close-knit, be intertwined; [Ht] to be woven together:– wrapt together [1], wreathed [1]

8277 שָׂרַד ***śārad***, v. GK: 8572 [→ 8300]. [Q] to run away, escape:– remained [1]

8278 שְׂרָד ***śᵉrād***, n.[m.]. GK: 8573 [→ 8279?]. woven material (with some kind of braiding woven in it):– service [4]

8279 שֶׂרֶד ***śered***, n.[m.]. GK: 8574 [→ 8278?]. marker (for wood chiseling):– line [1]

8280 שָׂרָה ***śārâ***, v. GK: 8575 [→ 415, 3478, 3481, 3482, 8304]. [Q] to struggle, contend:– as a prince hast power [1], had power [1]

8281 שָׁרָה ***šārâ***, v. GK: 9223 [→ 4952, 8302; cf. 8271]. [Q] to unleash; to deliver, set free:– remnant [1]

8282 שָׂרָה ***śārâ***, n.f. GK: 8576 [→ 8269, 8283; cf. 7786]. woman of nobility, lady of royal birth, queen:– ladies [2], princesses [1], princess [1], queens [1]

8283 שָׂרָה ***śārâ***, n.pr.f. GK: 8577 [→ 8282; cf. 8297]. Sarah, "*princess*":– Sarah [36], Sarah's [2]

8284 שָׁרָה ***šārâ***, n.[m.]. GK: 9224 [→ 7791; cf. 7789]. vineyard:– walls [1]

8285 שֵׁרָה ***šērâ*** or שֵׁר ***šēr***, n.[f.]. GK: 9225 & 9217. bracelet:– bracelets [1]

8286 שְׂרוּג ***śᵉrûg***, n.pr.m. GK: 8578. Serug, "*descendant* i.e., *younger branch*":– Serug [5]

8287 שָׁרוּחֶן ***šārûḥen***, n.pr.loc. GK: 9226. Sharuhen:– Sharuhen [1]

8288 שְׂרוֹךְ ***śᵉrôk***, n.[m.]. GK: 8579 [→ 8308]. thong (of a sandal):– latchet [1], shoelatchet (+5275) [1]

8289 שָׁרוֹן ***šārôn*** or לַשָּׁרוֹן ***laššārôn***, n.pr.loc. GK: 9227 & 4389 [→ 8290; cf. 3474]. Sharon, "*plain, level country*"; Lasharon, "*[belonging to] Sharon*":– Sharon [6], Lasharon [1]

8290 שָׁרוֹנִי ***šārônî***, a.g. GK: 9228 [→ 8289; cf. 3474]. Sharonite, "*of Sharon*":– Sharonite [1]

8291 שָׂרֹק ***śārōq***, n.[m.]. GK: 8602 [→ 8320]. choice vines:– principal plants [1]

8292 שְׁרוּקָה ***šᵉrûqâ*** or שְׁרִקָה ***šᵉriqâ***, n.[f.]. GK: 9229 & 9241 [→ 8319; cf. 8322]. whistling; scorn; some sources: flute playing:– bleatings [1], hissing [1]

8293 שֵׁרוּת ***šērût***, var. GK: 9230 [cf. 8281]. freedom:– @H = **8294** שֶׂרַח ***śeraḥ***, n.pr.f. GK: 8580 [cf. 5628]. Serah, "*one who explains, opens, extends; abundance*":– Serah [2], Sarah [1]

8295 שָׂרַט ***śāraṭ***, v. GK: 8581 [→ 8296]. [Q] to make a cut, incise the skin; [N] to make oneself incised, cut oneself:– cut in pieces (+8295) [2], make any cuttings (+8296) [1]

8296 שֶׂרֶט ***śereṭ*** or שָׂרֶטֶת ***śāreṭet***, n.[m.]. GK: 8582 & 8583 [→ 8295]. cut, incision; this may refer to a tattoo:– cuttings [1], make any cuttings (+8295) [1]

8297 שָׂרַי ***śāray***, n.pr.f. GK: 8584 [cf. 8283]. Sarai, "*princess*":– Sarai [16], Sarai's [1]

8298 שָׁרַי ***šāray***, n.pr.m. GK: 9232. Sharai:– Sharai [1]

8299 שָׂרִיג ***śārîg***, n.m. GK: 8585 [→ 8276]. branch, tendril (of grape vines and fig trees):– branches [3]

8300 שָׂרִיד ***śārîd***, n.m. GK: 8586 [→ 8277]. survivor; those left:– remaining [9], remain [8], left [3], remaineth [3], remnant [2], alive [1], remained [1], rest [1]

8301 שָׂרִיד ***śārîd***, n.pr.loc. GK: 8587. Sarid, "*survivor*":– Sarid [2]

8302 שִׁרְיָה ***širyâ*** or שִׁרְיוֹן ***širyôn***, n.f. GK: 9233 & 9234 [→ 8281; cf. 5630]. coat of scale armor; a weapon that is thrown: javelin, lance, light spear; some sources: arrowhead:– coat [3], habergeons [2], harness [2], breastplate [1], habergeon [1]

8303 שִׂרְיוֹן ***śiryôn***, n.pr.loc. GK: 8590 [cf. 5630]. Sirion, "*coat of mail*":– Sirion [2]

8304 שְׂרָיָה ***śᵉrāyâ*** or שְׂרָיָהוּ ***śᵉrāyāhû***, n.pr.m. GK: 8588 & 8589 [→ 8280+3068]. Seraiah, "*Yahweh persists; Yahweh is prince; Yahweh contends*":– Seraiah [20]

8305 שָׂרִיק ***śārîq***, a. GK: 8591. combed (flax, as a first step for making linen):– fine [1]

8306 שָׁרִיר ***šārîr***, n.[m.]. GK: 9235 [→ 8307]. muscle:– navel [1]

8307 שְׁרִירוּת ***šᵉrirût***, n.f. GK: 9244 [→ 8270, 8306, 8325, 8326]. stubbornness:– imagination [9], lust [1]

8308 שָׂרַךְ ***śārak***, v. GK: 8592 [→ 8288]. [P] to run here and there (aimlessly):– traversing [1]

8309 שְׁרֵמוֹת ***šᵉrēmôt***, var. GK: 9236. var. of 7709: field:– @H = **8310** שַׂר־סְכִים ***śar-sᵉkim***, n.pr.m. GK: 8593 [→ 8269]. Sarsekim:– Sarsechim [1]

8311 שָׂרַע ***śāra'***, v. GK: 8594. [Qp] to be deformed; [Ht] to stretch oneself:– hath any thing superfluous [1], stretch [1], superfluous [1]

8312 שַׂרְעַפִּים ***śar'appîm***, n.[m.]pl. GK: 8595 [→ 5587]. anxiety, anxious thoughts:– thoughts [2]

8313 שָׂרַף ***śārap***, v. GK: 8596 [→ 4955, 4956, 8314, 8315, 8316; cf. 5635]. [Q] to burn, set a fire; [Qp, N, Pu] to be burned up:– burnt [64], burn [38], burneth [4], burned [3], utterly burnt (+8313) [2], burn thoroughly (+8316+3807.1) [1], burn up [1], burnt up [1], cause to be burnt [1], kindled [1], made a burning (+8316) [1]

8314 שָׂרָף ***śārāp***, n.m. GK: 8597 [→ 8315; cf. 8313]. venomous snake; seraph (six-winged being):– fiery [3], fiery serpent [2], seraphims [2]

8315 שָׂרָף ***śārāp***, n.pr.m. GK: 8598 [→ 8314; cf. 8313]. Saraph, "*burning one, serpent*":– Saraph [1]

8316 שְׂרֵפָה ***śᵉrēpâ***, n.f. GK: 8599 [→ 8313]. burning:– burning [8], burnt [2], burn thoroughly (+8313+3807.1) [1], burnt up [1], made a burning (+8313) [1]

8317 שָׁרַץ ***šāraṣ***, v. GK: 9237 [→ 8318]. [Q] to teem, swarm, move about:– creepeth [4], bring forth abundantly [2], creep [2], breed abundantly [1], bring forth abundantly (+8318) [1], brought forth abundantly [1], brought forth in abundance [1], increased abundantly [1], moveth [1]

8318 שֶׁרֶץ ***šereṣ***, n.m. GK: 9238 [→ 8317]. creatures that teem, swarm, move about:– creeping thing [7], creeping things [4], creep [2], bring forth abundantly (+8317) [1], move [1]

8319 שָׁרַק ***šāraq***, v. GK: 9239 [→ 8322, 8292]. [Q] to whistle, hiss, scoff:– hiss [12]

8320 שָׂרֹק ***śārōq***, a. GK: 8601 [→ 4957, 7796, 8291, 8321]. brown, dark red (color of grapes):– speckled [1]

8321 שֹׂרֵק ***śōrēq*** or שְׂרֵקָה ***śᵉrēqâ***, n.m. & f. GK: 8603 & 8605 [→ 8320]. choice vines:– choicest vine [1], noble vine [1]

8322 שְׁרֵקָה ***šᵉrēqâ***, n.f. GK: 9240 [→ 8319; cf. 8292]. object of scorn, thing of derision, something held in contempt; an extension of the act of whistling or shrieking in derision:– hissing [7], choice vine [1]

8323 שָׂרַר ***śārar***, v.den. GK: 8606 [→ 7786]. [Q] to rule, govern; [H] to choose a prince; [Ht] to act out as a ruler:– make altogether a prince (+8323) [2], rule [2], bear rule [1]

8324 שׁוֹרֵר ***šôrēr***, n.m. GK: 8806. enemy, adversary:– enemies [5]

8325 שָׁרָר ***šārār***, n.pr.m. GK: 9243 [→ 8307]. Sharar, "*firm*":– Sharar [1]

8326 שֹׁרֶר ***šōrer***, n.m. GK: 9219 [→ 8270]. same as 8270: navel; umbilical cord:– navel [1]

8327 שָׁרַשׁ ***šāraš***, v.den. GK: 9245 [→ 8328]. [P] to uproot; [Poel/Poal] to take root; [Pu] to be uprooted; [H] to take root:– root out [2], cause to take deep root (+8328) [1], cause to take root [1], rooted out [1], take root [1], taken root [1], taking root [1]

8328 שֹׁרֶשׁ ***šōreš***, n.m. GK: 9247 [→ 8327, 8329; cf. 8330]. root of a plant; by extension: base or bottom of any object; source of a family line; "the Root of Jesse" is a messianic title, emphasizing Davidic origin:– root [16], roots [13], bottom [1], cause to take deep root (+8327) [1], heels [1], take root [1]

8329 שֶׁרֶשׁ ***šereš***, n.pr.m. GK: 9246 [→ 8328]. Sheresh, "*root, rootstock, sucker [of a plant]*":– Sheresh [1]

8330 שֹׁרֶשׁ ***šᵉrōš*** (Aram.), n.m. GK: 10743 [→ 8332; cf. 8328]. root:– roots [3]

8331 שַׁרְשָׁה ***šaršâ***, n.f. GK: 9248 [→ 8333]. chain:– chains [1]

8332 שְׁרֹשׁוּ ***šᵉrōšû*** or שְׁרֹשִׁי ***šᵉrōšî*** (Aram.), n.f. GK: 10744 & 10745 [→ 8330]. banishment, uprooting (from community):– banishment [1]

8333 שַׁרְשְׁרָה ***šaršᵉrâ***, n.f. GK: 9249 [→ 8331]. chain:– chains [6], chain [1]

8334 שָׁרַת ***šārat***, v. GK: 9250 [→ 8335]. [P] to minister, serve, attend:– minister [48], ministered [15], ministers [15], servant [4], served [4], serve [4], service [2], do service [1], ministering [1], servants [1], servitor [1], waited on [1]

8335 שָׁרֵת ***šārēt***, n.m. GK: 9251 [→ 8334]. cultic service:– minister [1], ministry [1]

8336 שֵׁשׁ ***šēš***, n.m. GK: 9253 & 9254 [→ 7893]. fine linen, byssus (processed from the flax plant); alabaster:– fine linen [37], marble [2], blue marble [1], silk [1]

8337 שֵׁשׁ ***šēš***, n.m. GK: 9252 [→ 8345, 8346; cf. 8353]. six; (pl.) sixty:– six [187], sixteen (+6240) [21], sixteenth (+6240) [3], sixth [2], threescore and one thousand (+505+7239+2050.1) [1], threescore and sixteen (+7657+2050.1) [1]

8338 שָׁשָׁא ***šāšā'***, v.intens. GK: 9255. [P] to lead along:– leave the sixth part [1]

8339 שֵׁשְׁבַּצַּר ***šēšbaṣṣar***, n.pr.m. GK: 9256 [cf. 8339]. Sheshbazzar, "*may Sin protect [the father]*":– Sheshbazzar [2]

8340 שֵׁשְׁבַּצַּר ***šēšbaṣṣar*** (Aram.), n.pr.m. GK: 10746 [cf. 8339]. Sheshbazzar, "*may (the pagan moon god) Sin protect (the father)*":– Sheshbazzar [2]

שָׂשָׂה ***śāśâ***. See 8154.

8341 שָׁשָׁה ***šāšâ***, v.den. GK: 9257. [P] to give a sixth part:– give the sixth part [1]

8342 שָׂשׂוֹן ***śāśôn***, n.m. GK: 8607 [→ 7797]. joy, gladness:– joy [15], gladness [3], mirth [3], rejoicing [1]

8343 שָׁשַׁי ***šāšay***, n.pr.m. GK: 9258. Shashai, "*noble*":– Shashai [1]

8344 שֵׁשַׁי ***šēšay***, n.pr.m. GK: 9259. Sheshai, "[poss.] *sixth [child]*":– Sheshai [3]

8345 שִׁשִּׁי ***šiššî***, a.num.ord. GK: 9261 [→ 8337]. sixth:– sixth [28]

8346 שִׁשִּׁים ***šiššîm***, n.indecl. GK: 9262 [→ 8337; cf. 8361]. sixty (pl. of "six"):– threescore [46], sixty [12], threescore and one (+259+2050.1) [1]

8347 שֵׁשַׁךְ ***šēšak***, n.pr.loc. GK: 9263. Sheshach, "[cryptogram for] *Babel*":– Sheshach [2]

8348 שֵׁשָׁן ***šēšān***, n.pr.m. GK: 9264. Sheshan:– Sheshan [5]

שׁשָׁן ***šōšān***. See 7799.

8349 שָׁשַׁק ***šāšaq***, n.pr.m. GK: 9265. Shashak:– Shashak [2]

8350 שָׁשַׁר ***šāšar***, n.[m.]. GK: 9266. red color (from lead, iron rust, or insects):– vermilion [2]

8351 שֵׁת ***šēt***, n.pr.m. GK: 9269 [→ 7896, 8352]. same as 8352: Seth, Sheth, "*determined, granted, Ge 4:25; restitution*":– @H = **8352** שֵׁת ***šèt***, n.pr.m. GK: 9269 [→ 8351]. same as 8353: Seth, Sheth, "*determined, granted, Ge 4:25; restitution*":– Seth [7], Sheth [2]

8353 שֵׁת ***šēt*** (Aram.), n.m. & f. GK: 10747 [→ 8361; cf. 8337]. six:– sixth [1], six [1]

8354 שָׁתָה ***šātâ***, v. GK: 9272 [→ 4960, 8358, 8360; cf. 8248; cf. 8355]. [Q] to drink; by extension: to be drunk; [N] to be drunken:– drink [160], drunk [17], drinking [12], drank [8], drinketh [6], drunken [3], assuredly drunken (+8354) [2], certainly drink (+8354) [2], drinketh up [2], surely drink (+8354) [2], banquet [1], drinkers [1], drunkards (+7941) [1]

8355 שְׁתָה ***šᵉtâ*** (Aram.), v. GK: 10748 [→ 4961; cf. 8354]. [P] to drink; this can refer to common consumption of liquid, or it can refer to drinking in worship to pagan gods and in insult to the true God (by drinking with his vessels):– drank [3], drink [1], drunk [1]

8356 שָׁתָה ***šātâ***, n.m. GK: 9271 [→ 8354?, 8359]. worker in weaving:– foundations [1], purposes [1]

8357 שֵׁת ***šēt***, n.[m.]. GK: 9268. foundation; buttocks:– buttocks [2]

8358 שְׁתִי ***šᵉtî***, n.[m.]. GK: 9275 [→ 8354]. drunkenness, drinking:– drunkenness [1]

8359 שְׁתִי ***šᵉtî***, n.m. GK: 9274 [→ 8356]. woven material, made on a loom; some sources: warp, the vertical threads on a loom:– warp [9]

Heb

8360 שְׁתִיָּה ***šᵉtiyyâ***, n.f. GK: 9276 [→ 8354]. (manner of) drinking:– drinking [1]

שְׁתַּיִם ***šᵉttayim***. See 8147.

8361 שִׁתִּין ***šittîn*** (Aram.), n.indecl. GK: 10749 [→ 8353; cf. 8346]. sixty:– threescore [4]

8362 שָׁתַל ***šātal***, v. GK: 9278 [→ 8363]. [Q] to plant; [Qp] to be planted:– planted [8], plant [2]

8363 שָׁתִיל ***šātîl***, n.[m.]. GK: 9277 [→ 8362]. slip, cutting (of a plant):– plants [1]

8364 שֻׁתַלְחִי ***šutalḥî***, a.g. GK: 9279 [→ 7803]. Shuthelahite, "*of Shuthelah*":– Shuthalhites [1]

שָׂתַם ***sātam***. See 5640.

8365 שָׁתַם ***šātam***, v. GK: 9280 & 9281. [Qp] to be opened:– open [2]

8366 שָׁתַן ***šātan*** or שִׁין ***šîn***, v. GK: 9282 & 8874 [→ 7890]. [H, Hiphtil] to urinate (against a wall), i.e., a male:– pisseth [6]

8367 שָׁתַק ***šātaq***, v. GK: 9284 [cf. 8252]. [Q] to become calm, die down:– calm [2], ceaseth [1], quiet [1]

8368 שָׂתַר ***śātar***, v. GK: 8609 [cf. 5642]. [N] to be broken out (with tumors):– secret parts [1]

8369 שֵׁתָר ***šētār***, n.pr.m. GK: 9285. Shethar:– Shethar [1]

8370 שְׁתַר בּוֹזְנַי ***šᵉtar bôzᵉnay*** (Aram.), n.pr.m. GK: 10750. Shethar-Bozenai:– Shethar-boznai [4]

8371 שָׁתַת ***šātat***, v. GK: 9286 [cf. 7896]. [Q] to be destined, appoint, lay claim:– laid [1], set [1]

8372 תָּא ***tā'***, n.m. GK: 9288. alcove for guards, guardroom:– little chambers [9], chamber [2], little chamber [2]

8373 תָּאַב ***tā'ab***, v. GK: 9289 [→ 8375; cf. 14? *or* 2968?]. [Q] to long for, desire:– longed [2]

8374 תָּאַב ***tā'ab***, v. GK: 9290 [cf. 8581]. [P] to abhor, loathe:– abhor [1]

8375 תַּאֲבָה ***ta'ᵃbâ***, n.f. GK: 9291 [→ 8373]. longing, desiring:– longing [1]

8376 תָּאָה ***tā'â***, v. GK: 9292 [cf. 184, 8427]. [P] to draw a line, mark out (territory):– point out [2]

8377 תְּאוֹ ***tᵉ'ô***, n.m. GK: 9293. antelope; some sources: wild ox or sheep:– wild bull [1], wild ox [1]

8378 תַּאֲוָה ***ta'ᵃwâ***, n.f. GK: 9294 [→ 183]. longing, desire, craving:– desire [14], coveteth greedily (+183) [1], dainty [1], fell a lusting (+183) [1], lusted exceedingly (+183) [1], lust [1], pleasant [1]

8379 תַּאֲוָה ***ta'ᵃwâ***, n.f. GK: 9295 [→ 8427]. boundary:– utmost bound [1]

8380 תּוֹאֲמִים ***tô'ᵃmîm*** or תְּאוֹמִים ***tᵉ'ômîm***, n.m. GK: 9339 & 9296 [→ 8382]. twins, (something) double:– twins [4]

8381 תַּאֲלָה ***ta'ᵃlâ***, n.f. GK: 9297 [→ 422]. curse:– curse [1]

8382 תָּאַם ***tā'am***, v.den. GK: 9298 [→ 8380]. [H] to have twins:– beareth twins [2], coupled together [1], coupled [1]

תָּאֹם ***tā'ōm***. See 8380.

8383 תְּאֻנִים ***tᵉ'unîm***, n.[m.]. GK: 9303 [→ 205?]. efforts, toil:– lies [1]

8384 תְּאֵנָה ***tᵉ'ēnâ***, n.f. GK: 9300. fig; fig tree:– fig tree [17], figs [15], fig trees [6], fig [1]

8385 תַּאֲנָה ***ta'ᵃnâ*** or תֹּאֲנָה ***tō'ᵃnâ***, n.f. GK: 9299 & 9301 [→ 579]. occasion, opportunity; (time of) heat, rut:– occasion [2]

8386 תַּאֲנִיָּה ***ta'ᵃniyyâ***, n.f. GK: 9302 [→ 578]. mourning:– heaviness [1], mourning [1]

8387 תַּאֲנַת שִׁלֹה ***ta'ᵃnat šilōh***, n.pr.loc. GK: 9304 [cf. 7887]. Taanath Shiloh, "[poss.] *approach to Shiloh*":– Taanath-shiloh [1]

8388 תָּאַר ***tā'ar***, v. GK: 9305 & 9306 [→ 8389; cf. 8446?]. [Q] to turn toward; [P] to mark out a form, make an outline; [Pu] to be turned toward:– drawn [5], marketh out [2], Remmon-methoar (+7417+1886.1) [1]

8389 תֹּאַר ***tō'ar***, n.m. GK: 9307 [→ 8388]. form, shape; beauty, fine-looking person:– form [3], beautiful (+3303) [2], favoured [2], comely [1], countenance [1], fair (+3303) [1], goodly (+2896) [1], goodly (+3303) [1], goodly [1], resembled (+3509.1) [1], visage [1]

8390 תַּאְרֵעַ ***ta'rēa'***, n.pr.m. GK: 9308 [cf. 8475]. Tarea:– Tarea [1]

8391 תְּאַשּׁוּר ***tᵉ'aššûr***, n.f. GK: 9309. cypress tree, cypress wood:– box tree [1], box [1]

8392 תֵּבָה ***tēbâ***, n.f. GK: 9310. box-shaped thing: chest, ark, basket:– ark [28]

8393 תְּבוּאָה ***tᵉbû'â***, n.f. GK: 9311 [→ 935]. harvest, crops, produce:– increase [22], fruit [7], fruits [6], revenues [3], revenue [2], gain [1], yieldeth increase [1]

8394 תְּבוּנָה ***tᵉbûnâ***, n.f. GK: 9312 [cf. 995]. understanding, insight; ability, skill, wisdom:– understanding [38], discretion [1], reasons [1], skilfulness [1], wisdom [1]

8395 תְּבוּסָה ***tᵉbûsâ***, n.f. GK: 9313 [→ 947]. downfall, ruin:– destruction [1]

8396 תָּבוֹר ***tābôr***, n.pr.loc. GK: 9314 [→ 3696; cf. 243]. Tabor:– Tabor [10]

8397 תֶּבֶל ***tebel***, n.[m.]. GK: 9316 [→ 1101]. perversion, abominable confusion:– confusion [2]

8398 תֵּבֵל ***tēbēl***, n.f. & m. GK: 9315 [→ 944?]. world, earth:– world [35], habitable part [1]

תֻּבַל ***tubal***. See 8422.

8399 תַּבְלִית ***tablît***, n.f. GK: 9318 [→ 1086]. destruction:– destruction [1]

8400 תְּבַלֻּל ***tᵉballul***, n.[m.]. GK: 9319 [→ 1101]. defect (obscuring vision); likely referring to a cataract:– blemish [1]

8401 תֶּבֶן ***teben***, n.m. GK: 9320 [→ 4963]. straw:– straw [15], chaff [1], stubble [1]

8402 תִּבְנִי ***tibnî***, n.pr.m. GK: 9321. Tibni:– Tibni [3]

8403 תַּבְנִית ***tabnît***, n.f. GK: 9322 [→ 1129]. image, form, shape:– pattern [9], likeness [5], form [3], similitude [2], figure [1]

8404 תַּבְעֵרָה ***tab'ērâ***, n.pr.loc. GK: 9323 [→ 1197]. Taberah, "*burning*":– Taberah [2]

8405 תֵּבֵץ ***tēbēṣ***, n.pr.loc. GK: 9324 [→ 1206?]. Thebez:– Thebez [3]

8406 תְּבַר ***tᵉbar*** (Aram.), v. GK: 10752 [cf. 7665]. [Pp] to be brittle, not to have flexibility, implying such an object is fragile and easy to break:– broken [1]

8407 תִּגְלַת פִּלְאֶסֶר ***tiglat pil'eser*** or תִּלְּגַת פִּלְנְאֶסֶר ***tillᵉgat pilnᵉ'eser*** or תִּלְּגַת פִּלְנֶסֶר ***tillᵉgat pilneser***, n.pr.m. GK: 9325 & 9433. Tiglath-Pileser, Tiglath-Pilneser, "*my trust is in the son of [the temple] Esharra*":– Tiglath-pileser [3], Tilgath-pilneser [3]

8408 תַּגְמוּל ***tagmûl***, n.m. GK: 9326 [→ 1580]. benefit, gracious act:– benefits [1]

8409 תִּגְרָה ***tigrâ***, n.f. GK: 9327 [→ 1624]. agitation, blow:– blow [1]

תֹּגַרְמָה ***tōgarmâ***. See 8425.

8410 תִּדְהָר ***tidhār***, n.[m.]. GK: 9329. fir tree; some sources: elm or ash tree:– pine tree [1], pine [1]

8411 תְּדִיר ***tᵉdîr*** (Aram.), n.f. GK: 10753 [→ 1753]. duration, encircling; (as adv.) continually:– continually (+0.2+871.2) [2]

8412 תַּדְמֹר ***tadmōr***, n.pr.loc. GK: 9330. Tadmor, "*palm tree*":– Tadmor [2]

8413 תִּדְעָל ***tid'āl***, n.pr.m. GK: 9331. Tidal:– Tidal [2]

8414 תֹּהוּ ***tōhû***, n.m. GK: 9332. formless, waste, empty; (of speech) useless, confused, vain:– vanity [4], confusion [3], in vain [2], vain [2], wilderness [2], without form [2], empty place [1], nothing [1], nought [1], thing of nought [1], waste [1]

8415 תְּהוֹם ***tᵉhôm***, n.f. & m. GK: 9333. the deep, depths, with the associative meanings of darkness and secrecy, controlled or inhabited by mysterious powers; "the depths of the earth" is the abode of the dead:– deep [19], depths [10], depth [5], deep places [1], deeps [1]

8416 תְּהִלָּה ***tᵉhillâ***, n.f. GK: 9335 [→ 1984]. praise, renown, glory; praise is proclaiming the excellence of a person or object:– praise [52], praises [5]

8417 תָּהֳלָה ***tohᵒlâ***, n.f. GK: 9334. error:– folly [1]

8418 תַּהֲלוּכָה ***tahᵃlûkâ***, n.f. GK: 9336 [→ 1980]. procession:– went [1]

תְּהֹם ***tᵉhōm***. See 8415.

8419 תַּהְפֻּכוֹת ***tahpukôt***, n.f. GK: 9337 [→ 2015]. perversity, confusing things:– frowardness [3], froward [3], froward things [2], perverse things [1], very froward [1]

8420 תָּו ***tāw***, n.m. GK: 9338 [→ 8427]. mark (on the forehead); signing (a document):– desire [1], mark [1], set a mark (+8427) [1]

8421 תּוּב ***tûb*** (Aram.), v. GK: 10754 [cf. 7725]. [P] to return, restore; [H] to give back, return, answer:– returned [4], answered [1], answer [1], restored [1], returned answer [1]

8422 תֻּבַל ***tubal***, n.pr.loc. GK: 9317. Tubal:– Tubal [8]

8423 תּוּבַל קַיִן ***tûbal qayin***, n.pr.m. GK: 9340 [→ 7014]. Tubal-Cain:– Tubal-cain [2]

תּוֹבֻנָה ***tôbunâ***. See 8394.

8424 תּוּגָה ***tûgâ***, n.f. GK: 9342 [→ 3013]. grief, sorrow:– heaviness [3], sorrow [1]

8425 תֹּגַרְמָה ***tōgarmâ***, n.pr.loc. GK: 9328. Togarmah:– Togarmah [4]

8426 תּוֹדָה ***tôdâ***, n.f. GK: 9343 [→ 3034]. thank offering; thanksgiving, confession of thankfulness; song of thanksgiving; thanks is the speaking of the excellence of a person or object, with a focus on the personal gratitude of the speaker:– thanksgiving [16], praise [4], thank offerings [3], thanks [3], confession [2], praises [1], sacrifice of praise [1], sacrifice of thanksgiving [1], thanksgivings [1]

8427 תָּוָה ***tāwâ***, v.den. GK: 9344 [→ 8379, 8420; cf. 184, 8376]. [P] to put a mark, place a sign:– scrabled [1], set a mark (+8420) [1]

8428 תָּוָה ***tāwâ***, v. GK: 9345. [H] to vex, bring pain:– limited [1]

8429 תְּוַהּ ***tᵉwah*** (Aram.), v. GK: 10755 [cf. 8539]. [P] to be amazed, be alarmed, an attitude or emotion that shows either fear or awe:– astonied [1]

8430 תּוֹחַ ***tôaḥ***, n.pr.m. GK: 9346 [cf. 8459]. Toah:– Toah [1]

8431 תּוֹחֶלֶת ***tôḥelet***, n.f. GK: 9347 [→ 3176]. hope, expectation:– hope [6]

תּוֹךְ ***tôk***. See 8496.

8432 תָּוֶךְ ***tāwek***, subst. GK: 9348 [→ 8484]. middle, midst, center, among, within:– midst [204], among (+871.1) [106], among [28], in (+871.1) [19], within (+871.1) [18], amongst (+871.1) [7], middle [6], midst (+871.1) [4], between (+871.1) [3], therein (+871.1+1886.3) [3], amongst [2], out of (+4480) [2], through (+871.1) [2], half [1], in (+413) [1], into

(+413) [1], into (+871.1) [1], midnight (+3915+1886.1) [1], of (+871.1) [1], to (+413) [1], unto (+413) [1], wherein (+834+871.1) [1], whereinto (+413) [1], with (+871.1) [1], within (+413) [1], within [1]

8433 תּוֹכֵחָה **tôkēḥâ** or תּוֹכַחַת **tôkaḥat**, n.f. GK: 9349 & 9350 [→ 3198]. rebuke, punishment, correction:– reproof [12], rebuke [4], rebukes [3], reproofs [2], reproved [2], arguments [1], chastened [1], correction [1], punishments [1], reasoning [1]

תּוּכִּי **tûkkî**. See 8500.

8434 תּוֹלָד **tôlād**, n.pr.loc. GK: 9351 [→ 3205?; cf. 513]. Tolad, "*birth, generation [?]*":– Tolad [1]

8435 תּוֹלֵדוֹת **tôlēdôt**, n.f.pl. GK: 9352 [→ 3205]. account, record, genealogy, family line:– generations [38], birth [1]

8436 תּוֹלוֹן **tôlôn** or תִּילוֹן **tîlôn**, n.pr.m. GK: 9353 & 9400. Tilon, Tolon:– Tilon [1]

8437 תּוֹלָל **tôlāl**, n.m. GK: 9354 [→ 1980]. tormentor, oppressor:– wasted [1]

8438 תּוֹלָע **tôlā'** or תּוֹלֵעָה **tôlē'â**, n.[m.]. GK: 9355 & 9357 [→ 8439, 8440, 8529]. (deep) red, purple; scarlet yarn, scarlet yarn; worm, maggot:– scarlet (+8144) [31], worm [5], worms [3], scarlet (+8144+1886.1) [2], crimson [1], scarlet [1]

8439 תּוֹלָע **tôlā'**, n.pr.m. GK: 9356 [→ 8440; cf. 8438]. Tola:– Tola [6]

8440 תּוֹלָעִי **tôlā'î**, a.g. GK: 9358 [→ 8439; cf. 8438]. Tolaite, "*of Tola*":– Tolaites [1]

8441 תּוֹעֵבָה **tô'ēbâ**, n.f. GK: 9359 [→ 8581?]. detestable thing, loathsome thing, abomination:– abominations [61], abomination [52], abominable [3], abominable things [1]

8442 תּוֹעָה **tô'â**, n.f. GK: 9360 [→ 8582]. trouble, error:– error [1], hinder (+6213) [1]

8443 תּוֹעָפוֹת **tô'āpôt**, n.f. GK: 9361. best, choice; strength; some sources: horns:– strength [3], plenty [1]

8444 תּוֹצָאוֹת **tôṣā'ôt**, n.f. GK: 9362 [→ 3318]. end, limit, starting point:– goings out [11], outgoings [7], issues [2], borders [1], going forth [1], goings forth [1]

8445 תָּוְקְהַת **towqᵉhat**, n.pr.m. GK: 9363. Tokehath, Tavkehath:– @H = **8446** תּוּר **tûr**, v. GK: 9365 [cf. 3491, 8388?]. [Q] to explore, investigate, search out; [H] to send out to spy:– search [6], searched [4], search out [3], spy out [2], espied [1], excellent [1], searching [1], seek [1], sent to descry [1], sought [1]

8447 תּוֹר **tôr**, n.m. GK: 9366 [→ 8448]. same as 8448: turning; earring:– turn [2], borders [1], rows [1]

8448 תּוֹר **tôr**, n.m. GK: 9366 [→ 8447]. same as 8447: turning; earring:– estate [1]

8449 תּוֹר **tôr**, n.f. & m. GK: 9367. dove:– turtle-doves [6], turtle-dove [3], turtles [3], turtle [2]

8450 תּוֹר **tôr** (Aram.), n.m. GK: 10756 [cf. 7794]. young bull or castrated bull, steer, ox, easier to handle for plowing, pulling, and threshing:– oxen [4], bullocks [3]

8451 תּוֹרָה **tôrâ**, n.f. GK: 9368 [→ 3384, 8452]. law, regulation, teaching, instruction; often referring to the five books of Moses in whole and in part:– law [206], laws [13]

8452 תּוֹרָה **tôrâ**, n.f. GK: 9368 [→ 8451]. same as 8451: manner, direction:– manner [1]

8453 תּוֹשָׁב **tôšāb**, n.m. GK: 9369 [→ 3427]. temporary resident, stranger, alien:– sojourner [7], sojourners [2], stranger [2], foreigner [1], inhabitants [1], strangers [1]

8454 תּוּשִׁיָּה **tûšiyyâ**, n.f. GK: 9370 [cf. 3426]. success, victory; sound judgment, wisdom:– wisdom [4], sound wisdom [3], enterprise [1], substance [1], that which is [1], thing as it is [1], working [1]

8455 תּוֹתָח **tôtāḥ**, n.m. GK: 9371. (stout) club:– Darts [1]

8456 תָּזַז **tāzaz**, v. GK: 9372. [H] to cut down:– cut down [1]

8457 תַּזְנוּת **taznût**, n.f.abst. GK: 9373 [→ 2181]. promiscuity, prostitution, act of lust:– whoredoms [14], whoredom [3], commit whoredoms (+2181) [1], fornications [1], fornication [1]

8458 תַּחְבֻּלוֹת **taḥbulôt**, n.f. GK: 9374. guidance, advice, giving direction:– counsels [2], counsel [1], good advice [1], wise counsels [1], wise counsel [1]

8459 תֹּחוּ **tōḥû**, n.pr.m. GK: 9375 [cf. 8430]. Tohu:– Tohu [1]

8460 תְּחוֹת **tᵉḥôt** (Aram.), pp. GK: 10757 [→ 8479, cf. 8478]. under:– under [4]

8461 תַּחְכְּמֹנִי **taḥkᵉmōnî**, a.g. GK: 9376. Tahkemonite:– Tachmonite [1]

8462 תְּחִלָּה **tᵉḥillâ**, n.f. GK: 9378 [→ 2490]. beginning, at first:– beginning [14], first [3], first (+871.1+1886.1) [2], first time [2], begin [1]

8463 תַּחֲלֻאִים **taḥᵃlu'îm**, n.pl.m. GK: 9377 [→ 2456]. diseases:– diseases [2], grievous [1], sicknesses [1], them that are sick [1]

8464 תַּחְמָס **taḥmās**, n.[m.]. GK: 9379 [→ 2554?]. screech owl:– night hawk [2]

8465 תַּחַן **taḥan**, n.pr.m. GK: 9380 [→ 8470; cf. 2603?]. Tahan, "[poss.] *grace, favor*":– Tahan [2]

8466 תַּחֲנָה **taḥᵃnâ**, n.f. GK: 9381 [→ 2583]. encampment:– camp [1]

8467 תְּחִנָּה **tᵉḥinnâ**, n.f. GK: 9382 [→ 8468; cf. 2603]. plea, petition, request, supplication:– supplication [21], favour [1], grace [1], supplication made [1], supplications [1]

8468 תְּחִנָּה **tᵉḥinnâ**, n.pr.m. GK: 9383 [→ 8467; cf. 2603]. Tehinnah, "*supplication for favor*":– Tehinnah [1]

8469 תַּחֲנוּן **taḥᵃnûn**, n.[m.]pl.abst. GK: 9384 [→ 2603]. plea for mercy, petition, supplication:– supplications [17], useth intreaties [1]

8470 תַּחֲנִי **taḥᵃnî**, a.g. GK: 9385 [→ 8465; cf. 2603?]. Tahanite, "*of Tahan*":– Tahanites [1]

8471 תַּחְפַּנְחֵס **taḥpanḥēs**, n.pr.loc. GK: 9387 [cf. 6372]. Tahpanhes, "*fortress of Penhase [the black man]*":– Tahpanhes [5], Tahapanes [1], Tehaphnehes [1]

8472 תַּחְפְּנֵיס **taḥpᵉnês**, n.pr.f. GK: 9388. Tahpenes, "*wife of the king*":– Tahpenes [3]

8473 תַּחְרָא **taḥrā'**, n.[m.]. GK: 9389. collar, edge around an opening in a garment:– habergeon [2]

8474 תַּחֲרָה **taḥᵃrâ**, v. GK: 3013 [→ 2734]. form of 2734: to be angry; to compete, contend with:– closest [1], contend [1]

8475 תַּחְרֵעַ **taḥrēa'**, n.pr.m. GK: 9390 [cf. 8390]. Tahrea, "[poss.] *clever one*":– Tahrea [1]

8476 תַּחַשׁ **taḥaš**, n.m. GK: 9391 [→ 8477]. (leather of) a sea cow:– badgers' [13], badgers' skins [1]

8477 תַּחַשׁ **taḥaš**, n.pr.m. GK: 9392 [→ 8476]. Tahash, "*species of dolphin*":– Thahash [1]

8478 תַּחַת **taḥat**, n.[m.] & adv. & pp. GK: 9393 [→ 8480, 8481, 8482; cf. 5181; cf. 8460]. under, in place of, succeeding (on a sequence):– under [220], in stead [89], for [59], instead of [32], beneath (+4480) [13], under (+4480) [13], because (+834) [11], in place [11], in room [5], in the room of [5], beneath [4], under (+413) [4], in [3], place [3], flat [2], for sake [2], in rooms [2], in the stead of [2], instead [2], as [1], because (+3588) [1], because [1], for that (+3588) [1], in a place [1], in places [1], in steads [1], in the place of [1], in the place where [1], in the place [1], in the same place [1], mine (+2967.1) [1], on behalf [1], room [1], underneath (+4480) [1], unto [1], where (+1886.3) [1], whereas (+834) [1], whereas [1], wherefore (+4100) [1], with [1]

8479 תְּחוֹת **tᵉḥôt** (Aram.), pp. GK: 10757 [→ 8460]. same as 8460: under:– under [1]

8480 תַּחַת **taḥat**, n.pr.m. & loc. GK: 9394 & 9395 [→ 8478]. Tahath, "*compensation*":– Tahath [6]

תְּחֹת **tᵉḥōt**. See 8460.

8481 תַּחְתּוֹן **taḥtôn**, a. GK: 9396 [→ 8478]. lower:– lower [5], nether [5], lowest [2], nethermost [1]

8482 תַּחְתִּי **taḥtî**, a. & subst. GK: 9397 [→ 8478]. lower; (n.) depths, below, sometimes referring to the underworld, the realm of the dead:– nether parts [5], lowest [3], nether [3], lower parts [2], lower [2], in low parts [1], lowest parts [1], low [1], nether part [1]

8483 תַּחְתִּים חָדְשִׁי **taḥtîm ḥodšî**, n.pr.loc. GK: 9398. Tahtim Hodshi:– Tahtim-hodshi [1]

8484 תִּיכוֹן **tîkôn**, a. GK: 9399 [→ 8432]. middle, center:– middle [8], middlemost [2], midst [1]

8485 תֵּימָא **têmā'**, n.pr.loc. [& m.?]. GK: 9401. Tema, "*on the right [not left] side, hence south country*":– Tema [5]

8486 תֵּימָן **têmān**, n.f. GK: 9402 [→ 8487; cf. 3225]. south, southward, south wind:– south [10], southward (+1886.5) [8], south side [2], south (+1886.5) [1], south (+1886.5+1886.5) [1], south wind [1]

8487 תֵּימָן **têmān**, n.pr.loc. GK: 9403 [→ 8489; cf. 3225, 8486]. Teman, "*on the right [not left] side, hence south country*":– Teman [11]

8488 תֵּימְנִי **têmᵉnî**, n.pr.m. GK: 9405 [→ 3225]. Temeni, "*one from the right [not left], hence southerner*":– Temeni [1]

8489 תֵּימָנִי **têmānî**, a.g. GK: 9404 [→ 8487]. Temanite, "*of Teman*":– Temanite [6], Temanites [1], Temani [1]

8490 תִּימָרָה **tîmārâ**, n.f. GK: 9406 [→ 8560?, 8564; cf. 8558]. column (of smoke):– pillars [2]

8491 תִּיצִי **tîṣî**, a.g. GK: 9407. Tizite:– Tizite [1]

8492 תִּירוֹשׁ **tîrôš**, n.m. GK: 9408 [→ 3423]. new wine:– wine [26], new wine [11], sweet wine [1]

8493 תִּירְיָא **tîrᵉyā'**, n.pr.m. GK: 9409. Tiria:– Tiria [1]

8494 תִּירָס **tîrās**, n.pr.loc. [& m.?]. GK: 9410. Tiras:– Tiras [2]

תִּירֹשׁ **tîrōš**. See 8492.

8495 תַּיִשׁ **tayiš**, n.m. GK: 9411. male goat:– he goats [3], he goat [1]

8496 תֹּךְ **tōk**, n.m. GK: 9412 [→ 8501]. oppression, threat:– deceit [2], fraud [1]

8497 תָּכָה **tākâ**, v. GK: 9413. [Pu] to bow down:– sat down [1]

8498 תְּכוּנָה **tᵉkûnâ**, n.f. GK: 9414 [→ 3559, 8499]. same as 8499: dwelling; arrangement, supply:– fashion [1], store [1]

8499 תְּכוּנָה **tᵉkûnâ**, n.f. GK: 9414 [→ 8498]. same as 8498: dwelling; arrangement, supply:– seat [1]

8500 תֻּכִּיִּים **tukkiyyîm**, n.m.[pl.]. GK: 9415. baboons; some sources: monkeys, peacocks, poultry:– peacocks [2]

8501 תְּכָכִים **tᵉkākîm**, n.m.pl. GK: 9412 [→ 8496]. pl. of 8496: oppression, threat:– deceitful [1]

8502 תִּכְלָה **tiklâ**, n.f. GK: 9416 [→ 3615]. perfection:– perfection [1]

8503 תַּכְלִית **taklît**, n.f. GK: 9417 [→ 3615]. end, limit, boundary:– perfection [2], come to an end [1], end [1], perfect [1]

8504 תְּכֵלֶת **tᵉkēlet**, n.f. GK: 9418. blue material:– blue [49]

8505 תָּכַן **tākan**, v. GK: 9419 [→ 4971, 8506, 8508; cf. 8626; cf. 8627]. [Q] to weigh, estimate; [N] to be just, be weighted; [P] to hold firm, mark off, understand; [Pu] to be determined:– equal [7], pondereth [2], unequal (+3808) [2], weigheth [2], bear up [1], directed [1], meted out [1], told [1], weighed [1]

8506 תֹּכֶן **tōken**, n.m. GK: 9420 [→ 8505]. full quota, fixed measure; size, measurement:– measure [1], tale [1]

8507 תֹּכֶן **tōken**, n.pr.loc. GK: 9421. Token, "*measure*":– Tochen [1]

8508 תָּכְנִית **toknît**, n.f. GK: 9422 [→ 8505]. (perfect) example, design:– pattern [1], sum [1]

8509 תַּכְרִיךְ **takrîk**, n.m. GK: 9423. robe, mantle:– garment [1]

8510 תֵּל **tēl**, n.[m.]. GK: 9424 [→ 8512, 8521, 8528, 8524, 8534?]. mound, heap, ruin:– heap [4], strength [1]

8511 תָּלָא **tālā'**, v. GK: 9428 [cf. 8518]. [Q] to hang; [Qp] to be suspended, be determined:– bent [1], hang in doubt [1], hanged [1]

8512 תֵּל אָבִיב **tēl 'ābîb**, n.pr.loc. GK: 9425 [→ 8510+24]. Tel Abib, "*mound of barley; mound of storm tide; mound of flood*":– Tel-abib [1]

8513 תְּלָאָה **tᵉlā'â**, n.f. GK: 9430 [→ 4972; cf. 3811]. hardship, burden:– travail [3], trouble [1]

8514 תַּלְאֻבוֹת **tal'ubôt**, n.f. GK: 9429. burning heat:– great drought [1]

8515 תְּלַאשָּׂר **tᵉla'śśār** or תְּלַשָּׂר **tᵉlaśśār**, n.pr.loc. GK: 9431 & 9445. Telassar, Tel Assar, "*ruined city, mound of Assar*":– Telassar [1], Thelasar [1]

8516 תִּלְבֹּשֶׁת **tilbōšet**, n.f. GK: 9432 [→ 3847]. clothing, what is worn:– put on clothing (+3847) [1]

8517 תְּלַג **tᵉlag** (Aram.), n.[m.]. GK: 10758 [cf. 7950]. snow:– snow [1]

תִּלְגַת **tilgat**. See 8407.

תֹּלְדָה **tōlᵉdâ**. See 8435.

8518 תָּלָה **tālâ**, v. GK: 9434 [→ 3494, 8522; cf. 8511]. [Q, P] to hang, suspend; [Qp, N] to be hung:– hanged [16], hang [7], hanged up [2], hangeth [1], hanging [1]

8519 תְּלֻנּוֹת ***tᵉlunnôt***, n.f. GK: 9442 [→ 3885]. grumbling, complaint:– murmurings [8]

8520 תֶּלַח ***telaḥ***, n.pr.m. GK: 9436. Telah, "*fissure, split, fracture*":– Telah [1]

8521 תֵּל חַרְשָׁא ***tēl ḥaršā'***, n.pr.loc. GK: 9426 [→ 8510+2793 *or* 2796]. Tel Harsha, "*mound of the forest* or *craftsman*":– Tel-haresha [1], Tel-harsa [1]

8522 תְּלִי ***tᵉlî***, n.[m.]. GK: 9437 [→ 8518]. quiver (case to hold arrows that hangs or dangles):– quiver [1]

8523 תְּלִיתָי ***tᵉlîtāy*** (Aram.), a. GK: 10759 [→ 8531; cf. 7992]. third:– third [2]

8524 תָּלוּל ***tālûl***, a. GK: 9435 [→ 8510]. lofty, towering:– eminent [1]

8525 תֶּלֶם ***telem***, n.m. GK: 9439 [→ 8526]. furrow, plowed line:– furrows [3], furrow [1], ridges [1]

8526 תַּלְמַי ***talmay***, n.pr.m. GK: 9440 [→ 8525]. Talmai, "[poss.] *[my] furrow maker*":– Talmai [6]

8527 תַּלְמִיד ***talmîd***, n.[m.]. GK: 9441 [→ 3925]. student, pupil:– scholar [1]

8528 תֵּל מֶלַח ***tēl melaḥ***, n.pr.loc. GK: 9427 [→ 8510+4417]. Tel Melah, "*mound of salt*":– Tel-melah [2]

תְּלֻנָּה ***tᵉlunnâ***. See 8519.

8529 תָּלַע ***tāla'***, v.den. GK: 9443 [→ 8438]. [Pu] to be clad in scarlet material:– in scarlet [1]

תֹּלַעַת ***tōla'at***. See 8438.

8530 תַּלְפִּיּוֹת ***talpiyyôt***, n.f.pl. GK: 9444. elegance or courses of stones:– armoury [1]

תְּלַשַּׂר ***tᵉlassar***. See 8515.

8531 תְּלָת ***tᵉlāt*** (Aram.), n.m. GK: 10760 [→ 8523, 8532, 8533; cf. 7969]. three:– third [2]

8532 תַּלְתָּא ***taltā'*** (Aram.), a.den. GK: 10761 [→ 8531; 7992]. third highest; this can refer to ruling over a third of the kingdom, or ruling as third in command, or ruling in a triumvirate; some sources translate less specifically as a high official of indeterminate rank:– three [10], third [1]

Heb

תַּלְתִּי ***taltiy***. See 8523.

8533 תְּלָתִין ***tᵉlātîn*** (Aram.), n.indecl. GK: 10762 [→ 8531; cf. 7970]. thirty:– thirty [2]

8534 תַּלְתַּל ***taltāl***, n.f.?. GK: 9446 [→ 8510?]. wavy:– bushy [1]

8535 תָּם ***tām***, a. GK: 9447 [→ 3147; cf. 8552]. blameless, flawless, perfect:– perfect [9], undefiled [2], coupled (+1961) [1], coupled together (+3162) [1], plain [1], upright [1]

8536 תַּמָּה ***tammâ*** (Aram.), adv. GK: 10764 [cf. 8033]. there:– there [2], thence [1], where [1]

8537 תֹּם ***tōm***, n.[m.]. GK: 9448 [→ 8550; cf. 8552]. blamelessness, integrity, innocence:– integrity [11], uprightness [2], upright [2], venture [2], full [1], perfection [1], perfect [1], simplicity [1], uprightly (+871.1) [1], uprightly [1]

תֵּמָא ***tēmā'***. See 8485.

8538 תֻּמָּה ***tummâ***, n.f. GK: 9450 [→ 8552]. integrity, blamelessness:– integrity [5]

8539 תָּמַהּ ***tāmah***, v. GK: 9449 [→ 8541; cf. 8429, cf. 8540]. [Q] to be astonished, be astounded, be stunned; [Htpal] to be stunned in oneself:– wonder [3], marvelled [2], amazed [1], astonished [1], marvellously [1], marvel [1]

8540 תְּמַהּ ***tᵉmah*** (Aram.), n.m. GK: 10763. wonder, miracle:– wonders [3]

8541 תִּמָּהוֹן ***timmāhôn***, n.[m.]. GK: 9451 [→ 8539]. confusion, panic:– astonishment [2]

8542 תַּמּוּז ***tammûz***, n.pr.[m.]. GK: 9452. Tammuz (pagan god):– Tammuz [1]

8543 תְּמוֹל ***tᵉmôl***, subst.adv. GK: 9453 [→ 865]. yesterday; (generally) before, in the past:– heretofore (+8032) [4], in time past (+4480+8032) [4], yesterday [4], before (+8032) [3], beforetime (+4480+8032) [1], beforetime (+8032) [1], heretofore (+1571+4480+4480+8032) [1], heretofore (+4480+8032) [1], in time past (+8032) [1], in times past (+1571+1571+8032) [1], in times past (+4480+8032) [1], these three days (+8032) [1]

8544 תְּמוּנָה ***tᵉmûnâ***, n.f. GK: 9454 [→ 4327]. form, image, likeness:– likeness [5], similitude [4], image [1]

8545 תְּמוּרָה ***tᵉmûrâ***, n.f. GK: 9455 [→ 4171]. substitution, transfer, exchange:– exchange [2], change [1], changing [1], recompence [1], restitution [1]

8546 תְּמוּתָה ***tᵉmûtâ***, n.f. GK: 9456 [→ 4191]. death:– appointed to death (+1121) [1], appointed to die (+1121) [1]

8547 תֶּמַח ***temaḥ***, n.pr.m. GK: 9457 [→ 4229?]. Temah:– Tamah [1], Thamah [1]

8548 תָּמִיד ***tāmîd***, n.m. (used as adv.). GK: 9458. (adv.) continually, constantly, regularly, daily:– continually [53], continual [26], daily [7], always [6], alway [4], ever [3], perpetual [2], continual employment [1], evermore [1], never (+3808) [1]

8549 תָּמִים ***tāmîm***, a. GK: 9459 [→ 8552]. without defect, blameless, perfect:– without blemish [44], perfect [18], upright [8], without spot [6], whole [4], uprightly [3], sincerely (+871.1) [2], complete [1], full [1], sincerity [1], sound [1], undefiled [1], uprightly (+871.1) [1]

8550 תֻּמִּים ***tummîm***, n.m.[pl.]. GK: 9460 [→ 8537; cf. 8552]. Thummim, formally "Perfections," devices used by the high priest to make God's will known, possibly related to the casting of lots:– Thummim [5]

8551 תָּמַךְ ***tāmak***, v. GK: 9461. [Q] to take hold of, grasp, hold secure; [N] to be seized:– uphold [3], holdeth [2], retaineth [2], retain [2], held up [1], hold up [1], holden [1], holding [1], hold [1], maintainest [1], stayed up [1], stay [1], take hold on [1], take hold [1], upholdest [1], upholdeth [1]

תְּמֹל ***tᵉmōl***. See 8543.

8552 תָּמַם ***tāmam***, v. GK: 9462 [→ 3147, 4974, 8535, 8537, 8538, 8549, 8550]. [Q] to complete, finish, perfect; [H] to end, stop, complete; [Ht] to show oneself blameless:– consumed [23], ended [5], finished [4], clean [3], spent [3], consume [2], done [2], end [2], failed [2], shew upright [2], wasted [2], accomplished [1], accomplish [1], all gone [1], all [1], cease [1], come to end [1], come to the full [1], make an end [1], makest perfect [1], perfect [1], sum [1], upright [1], utterly [1], whole [1]

תֵּמָן ***tēmān, tēmān***. See 8486, 8487.

8553 תִּמְנָה ***timnâ***, n.pr.loc. GK: 9463 [→ 8554; cf. 4487?]. Timnah, "*lot, portion*":– Timnath [8], Timnah [3], Thimnathah [1]

תְּמֻנָה ***tᵉmunâ***. See 8544.

8554 תִּמְנִי ***timnî***, a.g. GK: 9464 [→ 8553; cf. 4487?]. Timnite, "*of Timnah*":– Timnite [1]

8555 תִּמְנָע ***timna'***, n.pr.m. & f. GK: 9465. Timna, "*lot, portion*":– Timna [4], Timnah [2]

8556 תִּמְנַת־חֶרֶס ***timnat-ḥeres*** or תִּמְנַת־סֶרַח ***timnat-seraḥ***, n.pr.loc. GK: 9466 & 9467 [→ 4487?+2776]. Timnath Heres, Timnath Serah, "*place of the sun [worship]*":– Timnath-serah [2], Timnath-heres [1]

8557 תֶּמֶס ***temes***, n.m. GK: 9468 [→ 4549]. melting away:– melteth [1]

8558 תָּמָר ***tāmār***, n.m. GK: 9469 [→ 1193, 2688, 5899, 8559, 8560, 8561; cf. 8490]. palm tree:– palm trees [7], palm tree [4], palm [1]

8559 תָּמָר ***tāmār***, n.pr.f. & loc. GK: 9470 & 9471 [→ 8558]. Tamar, "*date palm*":– Tamar [24]

8560 תֹּמֶר ***tōmer***, n.m. & loc. GK: 9472 & 9473 [→ 559, 8490?, 8558]. the Palm (of Deborah), "*date palm*"; scarecrow:– palm tree [2]

8561 תִּמֹרָה ***timōrâ***, n.f. GK: 9474 [→ 8558]. palm tree:– palm trees [16], palm tree [3]

תַּמֹּר ***tammōr***. See 8412.

תִּמָרָה ***timārâ***. See 8490.

8562 תַּמְרוּק ***tamrûq***, n.[m.]. GK: 9475 [→ 4838]. beauty treatment (including massages and cleansing rituals), cosmetics:– things for purification [2], cleanseth away [1], things for the purifying [1]

8563 תַּמְרוּרִים ***tamrûrîm***, n.m. GK: 9476 [→ 4843]. bitterness:– bitter [2], most bitterly [1]

תַּמְרֻק ***tamruq*** and תַּמְרִיק ***tamrîq***. See 8562.

8564 תַּמְרוּרִים ***tamrûrîm***, n.m. GK: 9477 [→ 8490]. guidepost:– high heaps [1]

8565 תַּן ***tan***, n.[m. & f.]. GK: 9478 [→ 8568, 8577]. jackal:– @H = **8566** תָּנָה ***tānâ***, v. GK: 9479 [→ 869]. [Q, H] to sell oneself as a prostitute:– hired [2]

8567 תָּנָה ***tānâ***, v. GK: 9480. [P] to commemorate, recount:– lament [1], rehearse [1]

8568 תַּנָּה ***tannâ***, n.[m. & f.]. GK: 9478 [→ 8565]. same as 8565: jackal:– @H = **8569** תְּנוּאָה ***tᵉnû„â***, n.f. GK: 9481 [→ 5106]. fault, opposition, what one has against another:– breach of promise [1], occasions [1]

8570 תְּנוּבָה ***tᵉnûbâ***, n.f. GK: 9482 [→ 5107]. crop, produce:– fruit [2], increase [2], fruits [1]

8571 תְּנוּךְ ***tᵉnûk***, n.[m.]. GK: 9483. lobe (of the ear):– tip [8]

8572 תְּנוּמָה ***tᵉnûmâ***, n.f. GK: 9484 [→ 5123]. slumber, sleep:– slumber [4], slumberings [1]

8573 תְּנוּפָה ***tᵉnûpâ***, n.f. GK: 9485 [→ 5130]. wave offering, what it waved:– wave offering [13], offering [7], wave [6], shaking [2], wave offerings [1], waved [1]

8574 תַּנּוּר ***tannûr***, n.m. GK: 9486. oven, furnace, firepot (a portable oven for cooking bread):– oven [10], furnaces [2], furnace [2], ovens [1]

8575 תַּנְחוּמוֹת ***tanḥûmôt*** or תַּנְחוּמִים ***tanḥûmîm***, n.pl.m. & f. GK: 9487 & 9488 [→ 5162]. consolation, comfort:– consolations [3], comforts [1], consolation [1]

8576 תַּנְחֻמֶת ***tanḥumet***, n.pr.m. GK: 9489 [→ 5162]. Tanhumeth, "*comfort*":– Tanhumeth [2]

8577 תַּנִּין ***tannîn***, n.m. GK: 9490 [→ 8565]. serpent, snake; monster of the deep; (pr.n.) Jackal (Well); can refer to large sea creatures as well as to mythological monsters of chaos opposed to God:– dragons [16], dragon [6], serpent [2], whale [2], sea monsters [1], serpents [1], whales [1]

8578 תִּנְיָן ***tinyān*** (Aram.), a. GK: 10765 [→ 8648]. second:– second [1]

8579 תִּנְיָנוּת ***tinyānût*** (Aram.), adv. GK: 10766 [→ 8648]. once more, in the second time:– again [1]

8580 תִּנְשֶׁמֶת ***tinšemet***, n.f. GK: 9491 & 9492 [→ 5395]. white owl; chameleon:– swan [2], mole [1]

8581 תָּעַב ***tā'ab***, v.den. GK: 9493 [→ 8441?; cf. 8374]. [N] to be repulsive, be vile, be rejected; [P] to detest, abhor, loathe, despise; [H] to behave in a vile manner:– abhor [8], abominable [4], abhorred [2], abhorreth [2], done abominable [2], utterly abhor (+8581) [2], abominably [1], made to be abhorred [1]

תּוֹעֵבָה ***tō'ēbâ***. See 8441.

8582 תָּעָה ***tā'â***, v. GK: 9494 [→ 8442; cf. 2937]. [Q] to wander, go astray; [N] to deceive oneself; to stagger around (as a drunk); [H] to lead astray, make wander, mislead:– went astray [6], caused to err [4], cause to err [3], err [3], go astray [3], wandered [3], causeth to wander [2], erred [2], gone astray [2], made to err [2], out of the way [2], seduced [2], wander [2], caused to go astray [1], caused to wander [1], causing to err [1], deceived [1], dissembled [1], erreth [1], going astray [1], make err [1], maketh to stagger [1], panted [1], seduceth [1], staggereth [1], wandereth [1], wandering [1]

8583 תֹּעוּ ***tō'û*** or תֹּעִי ***tō'î***, n.pr.m. GK: 9495 & 9497. Toi, Tou:– Toi [3], Tou [2]

8584 תְּעוּדָה ***tᵉ'ûdâ***, n.f. GK: 9496 [→ 5749]. testimony; method of legalizing transactions (sandal transaction):– testimony [3]

8585 תְּעָלָה ***tᵉ'ālâ***, n.f. GK: 9498 & 9499 [→ 5927]. trench, channel, aqueduct; healing:– conduit [4], trench [3], cured [1], healing [1], little rivers [1], watercourse [1]

8586 תַּעֲלוּלִים ***ta'ᵃlûlîm***, n.m.pl.abst. GK: 9500 [→ 5953]. wantonness; harsh treatment, referring to impulsive people:– babes [1], delusions [1]

8587 תַּעֲלֻמָה ***ta'ᵃlumâ***, n.f. GK: 9502 [→ 5956]. secret; hidden thing:– secrets [2], thing that is hid [1]

8588 תַּעֲנוּג ***ta'ᵃnûg***, n.[m.]. GK: 9503 [→ 6026]. delight, pleasure; living in luxury:– delights [2], delicate [1], delight [1], pleasant [1]

8589 תַּעֲנִית ***ta'ᵃnît***, n.f. GK: 9504 [→ 6031]. self-abasement, mortification:– heaviness [1]

8590 תַּעְנָךְ ***ta'ᵃnak***, n.pr.loc. GK: 9505. Taanach:– Taanach [6], Tanach [1]

8591 תָּעַע ***tā'a'***, v. GK: 9506 [→ 8595]. [Pil] to mock; [Htpal] to scoff at:– deceiver [1], misused [1]

8592 תַּעֲצֻמוֹת ***ta'ᵃṣumôt***, n.f.[pl.]. GK: 9508 [→ 6105]. strength, might:– power [1]

8593 תַּעַר ***ta'ar***, n.m. GK: 9509 [→ 6168]. razor, knife, scabbard:– sheath [6], rasor [4], penknife (+5608+1886.1) [1], scabbard [1], shave (+5674) [1]

8594 תַּעֲרֻבוֹת ***taᵃrûbôt***, n.f.[pl.]. GK: 9510 [→ 6148]. hostage, formally "son of a pledge":– hostages (+1121) [2]

8595 תַּעְתֻּעִים ***ta'tu'îm***, n.[m.]pl.abst. GK: 9511 [→ 8591]. mockery:– errors [2]

8596 תֹּף ***tōp***, n.m. GK: 9512 & 9513 [→ 8608]. tambourine, timbrel; setting, jewelry; some sources uncertain in meaning:– tabrets [5], timbrel [5], timbrels [4], tabret [3]

8597 תִּפְאֶרֶת ***tip'eret***, n.f. GK: 9514 [→ 6286]. glory, splendor, honor:– glory [22], beauty [10], beautiful [6], honour [4], fair [3], glorious [3], bravery [1], comely (+3807.1) [1], excellent [1]

8598 תַּפּוּחַ ***tappûaḥ***, n.[m.]. GK: 9515 [→ 1054, 8599; cf. 5301]. apple, apple tree:– apple tree [3], apples [3]

8599 תַּפּוּחַ ***tappûaḥ***, n.pr.m. & loc. GK: 9516 & 9517 [→ 5887, 8598; cf. 5301]. Tappuah, "*apple*":– Tappuah [6]

8600 תְּפוֹצָה ***tᵉpûṣâ***, n.f.pl. GK: 9518 [→ 6327]. shattering, dispersing:– dispersions [1]

8601 תֻּפִינִים ***tupînîm***, n.[m.]pl. GK: 9519 [cf. 644?]. broken into pieces:– baken [1]

8602 תָּפֵל ***tāpēl***, n.[m.]. GK: 9521 & 9522 [→ 8604, cf. 2950]. tasteless (food); worthless (prophetic visions); whitewash:– untempered [5], foolish things [1], that which is unsavoury [1]

8603 תֹּפֶל ***tōpel***, n.pr.loc. GK: 9523 [→ 302?]. Tophel, "*cement*":– Tophel [1]

8604 תִּפְלָה ***tiplâ***, n.f. GK: 9524 [→ 8602]. repulsiveness, wrongdoing:– folly [2], foolishly [1]

8605 תְּפִלָּה ***tᵉpillâ***, n.f. GK: 9525 [→ 6419]. prayer, plea, petition:– prayer [74], prayers [2], prayer make (+6419) [1]

8606 תִּפְלֶצֶת ***tipleṣet***, n.f. GK: 9526 [→ 6426]. terror, horror, a state of great fear even to the point of shuddering:– terribleness [1]

8607 תִּפְסַח ***tipsaḥ***, n.pr.loc. GK: 9527 [→ 6452]. Tiphsah:– Tiphsah [2]

8608 תָּפַף ***tāpap***, v.den. GK: 9528 [→ 8596]. [Q] to tap (play) a tambourine; [Pol] to beat (the breast):– playing timbrels [1], tabring [1]

8609 תָּפַר ***tāpar***, v. GK: 9529. [Q] to sew, mend; [P] to sew (together):– sew [2], sewed together [1], sewed [1]

8610 תָּפַשׂ ***tāpaś***, v. GK: 9530. [Q] to take hold of, seize, capture; [Qp] to be covered; [N] to be seized, be caught, be captured; [P] to catch (a lizard):– took [17], taken [11], take [9], handle [5], caught [3], handleth [2], lay hold on [2], surely taken (+8610) [2], surprised [2], catch [1], handled (+3709+871.1+1886.1) [1], handling [1], holdest [1], hold [1], laid over [1], lay hold [1], stopped [1], take hold [1], taketh hold [1], taking [1], took hold [1]

8611 תֹּפֶת ***tōpet***, n.f. GK: 9531. spitting:– tabret [1]

8612 תֹּפֶת ***tōpet***, n.pr.loc. GK: 9532. Topheth:– Tophet [8], Topheth [1]

8613 תָּפְתֶּה ***topteh***, n.pr.loc. GK: 9533. Topheth:– Tophet [1]

8614 תִּפְתָּי ***tiptāy*** (Aram.), n.m.pl. GK: 10767. magistrate, a general or legal authority such as a chief of police:– sheriffs [2]

תֹּצָאָה ***tōṣā'â***. See 8444.

8615 תִּקְוָה ***tiqwâ***, n.f. GK: 9535 & 9536 [→ 6960, 8616]. hope, expectation; cord:– hope [23], expectation [7], line [2], expected [1], thing long for [1]

8616 תִּקְוָה ***tiqwâ***, n.pr.m. GK: 9537 [→ 8615; cf. 6960]. Tikvah, "*hope*":– Tikvah [2], Tikvath [1]

8617 תְּקוּמָה ***tᵉqûmâ***, n.f. GK: 9538 [→ 6965]. ability to stand:– power to stand [1]

8618 תְּקוֹמֵם ***tᵉqōmēm***, v.ptcp. GK: 9539 [→ 6965]. ptcp. of 6965: to rise up against:– rise up [1]

8619 תָּקוֹעַ ***tāqôa'***, n.[m.]. GK: 9540 [→ 8628]. trumpet, for battle signals:– trumpet [1]

8620 תְּקוֹעַ ***tᵉqôa'***, n.pr.loc. GK: 9541 [→ 8621; cf. 8628]. Tekoa:– Tekoa [6], Tekoah [1]

8621 תְּקוֹעִי ***tᵉqô'î***, a.g. GK: 9542 [→ 8620]. Tekoite, of Tekoa, "*of Tekoa*":– Tekoite [3], Tekoah [2], Tekoites [2]

8622 תְּקוּפָה ***tᵉqûpâ***, n.f. GK: 9543 [cf. 5362]. turning, course:– end [2], circuit [1], come about (+3807.1) [1]

8623 תַּקִּיף ***taqqîp***, a. GK: 9544 [→ 8630; cf. 8624]. strong, mighty:– mightier [1]

8624 תַּקִּיף ***taqqîp*** (Aram.), a. GK: 10768 [→ 8631; cf. 8623]. strong, powerful, mighty:– strong [3], mighty [2]

8625 תְּקַל ***tᵉqal***, v. or תְּקֵל ***tᵉqēl*** (Aram.), n.[m.]. GK: 10769 & 10770 [cf. 8254, cf. 8255]. [Peil] to be weighed; (n.) tekel, (i.e., shekel of weight):– tekel [2], weighed [1]

8626 תָּקַן ***tāqan***, v. GK: 9545 [cf. 8505; cf. 8627]. [Q] to be straight; [P] to straighten, set in order:– made straight [1], make straight [1], set in order [1]

8627 תְּקַן ***tᵉqan*** (Aram.), v. GK: 10771 [cf. 8626, 8505]. [Ho] to be restored, be reestablished:– established [1]

8628 תָּקַע ***tāqa'***, v. GK: 9546 & 9364 [→ 8619, 8620, 8621, 8629]. [Q] to sound (a trumpet); to pitch, camp; to strike, clap; [Qp] to be driven; [N] to be sounded (a trumpet); to put up a security:– blow [22], blew [18], fastened [4], blown [3], blowing [2], clap [2], pitched [2], sounded [2], strike [2], thrust [2], blow up [1], bloweth [1], cast [1], fasten [1], pitch [1], smote [1], stricken [1], striketh [1], suretiship [1]

8629 תֵּקַע ***tēqa'***, n.[m.]. GK: 9547 [→ 8628]. sounding, blast (of a trumpet):– sound [1]

תְּקֹעִי ***tᵉqō'î***. See 8621.

8630 תָּקַף ***tāqap***, v. GK: 9548 [→ 8623, 8633; cf. 8631]. [Q] to overpower, overwhelm:– prevail against [2], prevailest against [1]

8631 תְּקִף ***tᵉqip*** (Aram.), v. GK: 10772 [→ 8624, 8632; cf. 8630]. [P] to become strong, become hard; [Pa] to enforce, make hard:– strong [3], hardened [1], make firm [1]

8632 תְּקֹף ***tᵉqōp*** or תְּקָף ***tᵉqāp*** (Aram.), n.[m.]. GK: 10773 & 10774 [→ 8631; cf. 8633]. might, strength:– might [1], strength [1]

8633 תֹּקֶף ***tōqep***, n.m. GK: 9549 [→ 8630; cf. 8632]. power, strength, authority:– authority [1], power [1], strength [1]

תְּקֻפָה ***tᵉqupâ***. See 8622.

תֹּר ***tōr***. See 8447, 8449.

8634 תַּרְאֲלָה ***tar'ᵃlâ***, n.pr.loc. GK: 9550 [→ 692?]. Taralah:– Taralah [1]

8635 תַּרְבּוּת ***tarbût***, n.f. GK: 9551 [→ 7235]. a group of the same kind, brood:– increase [1]

8636 תַּרְבִּית ***tarbît***, n.f. GK: 9552 [→ 7235]. excessive interest, exorbitant interest:– increase [5], unjust gain [1]

8637 רָגַל ***rāgal*** or תִּרְגַּל ***tirgal***, v.den. GK: 8078 [→ 7270]. same as 7270: [Tiphil] to teach to walk:– @H = **8638** תִּרְגֵּם ***tirgēm***, v. GK: 9553 [→ 7276]. [Pu] to be interpreted, be translated:– interpreted [1]

תֹּרָה ***tōrâ***. See 8451.

8639 תַּרְדֵּמָה ***tardēmâ***, n.f. GK: 9554 [→ 7290]. deep (supernatural) sleep, often a state of divine revelation and activity:– deep sleep [7]

8640 תִּרְהָקָה ***tirhāqâ***, n.pr.m. GK: 9555. Tirhakah:– Tirhakah [2]

8641 תְּרוּמָה ***tᵉrûmâ***, n.f. GK: 9556 [→ 7311]. offering, special gift, contribution:– heave offering [21], offering [19], oblation [17], offerings [8], heave [4], heave offerings [3], oblations [2], gifts [1], offered [1]

8642 תְּרוּמִיָּה ***tᵉrûmiyyâ***, n.f.den. GK: 9557 [→ 7311]. special gift, tribute:– oblation [1]

8643 תְּרוּעָה ***tᵉrû'â***, n.f. GK: 9558 [→ 7321]. trumpet blast, battle cry:– shout [10], shouting [8], alarm [6], joy [2], blowing of trumpets [1], blowing trumpets [1], blow [1], high sounding [1], joyful sound [1], jubile [1], loud noise [1], rejoicing [1], shouted aloud (+6963+7311+871.1+3807.1) [1], sounding [1]

8644 תְּרוּפָה ***tᵉrûpâ***, n.f. GK: 9559 [→ 7495]. healing:– medicine [1]

8645 תִּרְזָה ***tirzâ***, n.f. GK: 9560. cypress tree:– cypress [1]

8646 תֶּרַח ***teraḥ*** or תָּרַח ***tāraḥ***, n.pr.m. & loc. GK: 9561 & 9562. Terah, Tarah:– Terah [11], Tarah [2]

8647 תִּרְחֲנָה ***tirḥᵃnâ***, n.pr.[f.?]. GK: 9563. Tirhanah:– Tirhanah [1]

8648 תְּרֵין ***tᵉrên*** or תַּרְתֵּין ***tartên*** (Aram.), n.m. & f. GK: 10775 & 10778 [→ 8578, 8579; cf. 8147]. two:– twelve (+6236) [2], second [1], two [1]

8649 תַּרְמוּת ***tarmût*** or תַּרְמִית ***tarmît***, n.f. GK: 9566 & 9567 [cf. 7411]. deceitfulness, delusion:– deceit [4], deceitful [1], privily (+871.1) [1]

תְּרֻמָה ***tᵉrumâ***. See 8641.

8650 תֹּרֶן ***tōren***, n.m. GK: 9568. (sailing) mast; flagstaff (on top of hill):– beacon [1], masts [1], mast [1]

8651 תְּרַע ***tᵉra'*** (Aram.), n.[m.]. GK: 10776 [→ 8652; cf. 8179]. gate, door; opening (of a furnace); (royal) court, the entourage of a king:– gate [1], mouth [1]

8652 תָּרָע ***tārā'*** (Aram.), n.m. GK: 10777 [→ 8651; cf. 7778]. gatekeeper, doorkeeper:– porters [1]

8653 תַּרְעֵלָה ***tar'ēlâ***, n.f. GK: 9570 [→ 7477]. staggering, reeling:– trembling [2], astonishment [1]

8654 תִּרְעָתִים ***tir'ātîm***, n.pr.m.pl. GK: 9571. Tirathite:– Tirathites [1]

8655 תְּרָפִים ***tᵉrāpîm***, n.m.pl. GK: 9572. household god, idol:– teraphim [6], images [5], image [2], idolatry [1], idols [1]

8656 תִּרְצָה ***tirṣâ***, n.pr.f. & loc. GK: 9573 & 9574 [→ 7521]. Tirzah, "*pleasant one* or *compensation*":– Tirzah [18]

8657 תֶּרֶשׁ ***tereš***, n.pr.m. GK: 9575. Teresh, "[perhaps] *desire*":– Teresh [2]

8658 תַּרְשִׁישׁ ***taršîš***, n.m. GK: 9577 [→ 7567?]. chrysolite:– beryl [7]

8659 תַּרְשִׁישׁ ***taršîš***, n.pr.m. & loc. GK: 9576 & 9578 [→ 7567?]. Tarshish, "[poss.] *yellow jasper;* [poss.] *greedy one; foundry, refinery*"; ships of Tarshish = trading ships:– Tarshish [24], Tharshish [4]

8660 תִּרְשָׁתָא ***tiršātā'***, n.m. GK: 9579. governor:– Tirshatha [5]

תַּרְתֵּין ***tartên***. See 8648.

8661 תַּרְתָּן ***tartān***, n.m. GK: 9580 [cf. 8648]. supreme commander, second in command:– Tartan [2]

8662 תַּרְתָּק ***tartāq***, n.pr.[m.]. GK: 9581. Tartak (pagan god):– Tartak [1]

8663 תְּשֻׁאָה ***tᵉšu'â***, n.f. GK: 9583 & 9589 [→ 7582]. shouting, commotion, thundering, storm:– crying [1], noise [1], shoutings [1], stirs [1]

תֹּשָׁב ***tōšāb***. See 8453.

8664 תִּשְׁבִּי ***tišbî***, a.g. or תִּשְׁבֵּי ***tišbê***, n.pr.loc. GK: 9585. Tishbe; Tishbite, "*of Tishbe*":– Tishbite [6]

8665 תַּשְׁבֵּץ ***tašbēṣ***, n.[m.]. GK: 9587 [→ 7660]. woven or checkered fabric:– broidered [1]

8666 תְּשׁוּבָה ***tᵉšûbâ***, n.f. GK: 9588 [→ 7725]. spring [time of year]; answer:– expired [3], return [3], answers [2]

8667 תְּשׂוּמֶת ***tᵉśûmâ***, n.f. GK: 9582 [→ 7760]. pledge, security:– fellowship (+3027) [1]

8668 תְּשׁוּעָה ***tᵉšû'â***, n.f. GK: 9591 [→ 3467]. deliverance, salvation, victory; divine salvation has its focus on rescue from earthly enemies, occasionally referring to salvation from guilt, sin, and punishment:– salvation [17], deliverance [5], help [4], safety [4], victory [3], help (+1961) [1]

8669 תְּשׁוּקָה ***tᵉšûqâ***, n.f. GK: 9592. desire, longing:– desire [3]

8670 תְּשׁוּרָה ***tᵉšûrâ***, n.f. GK: 9593 [→ 7794]. gift, present:– present [1]

תַּשְׁחֵת ***tašḥēt***. See 516.

תֻּשִׁיָּה ***tušîâ***. See 8454.

8671 תְּשִׁיעִי ***tᵉšî'î***, a.num.ord. GK: 9595 [→ 8672]. ninth:– ninth [18]

תְּשֻׁעָה ***tᵉšu'â***. See 8668.

8672 תֵּשַׁע ***tēša'***, n.m. & f. GK: 9596 [→ 8671, 8673]. nine, (pl.) ninety:– nine [45], ninth [6], nineteenth (+6240) [4], nineteen (+6240) [3]

8673 תִּשְׁעִים ***tiš'îm***, n.indecl. GK: 9597 [→ 8672]. ninety (pl. of "nine"):– ninety [20]

8674 תַּתְּנַי ***tattᵉnay*** (Aram.), n.pr.m. GK: 10779. Tattenai:– Tatnai [4]

GREEK DICTIONARY-INDEX TO THE NEW TESTAMENT

FEATURES OF THE GREEK TO ENGLISH DICTIONARY-INDEX

STRONG NUMBER
Matches the number at the end of context lines; Greek Strong numbers are in *italics* (see the introduction, pages xii, xiv).

LEXICAL FORM AND TRANSLITERATION
See the table below. Note that the lexical forms conform to modern resources and sometimes differ from Strong's original spelling.

PART OF SPEECH
The part of speech is abbreviated (see below and introduction, page xiv).

G/K NUMBER
Cross reference to the G/K numbering system, widely used in up-to-date word study reference resources (see the introduction, pages xiv).

223 **'Αλέξανδρος, *Alexandros*,** n.pr. GK: *235* [→ *221, 222*].

RELATED WORDS LIST
Greek words related by common elements are listed by Strong number (see the introduction, page xiv, xv).

Alexander, "*defender of men*":–

DEFINITION AND ETYMOLOGY
Words are defined, often with expanded explanations, and if a proper name, the possible definition (etymology) is given in italics (see the introduction, page xiv, xv).

Alexander [6],

KJV WORD AND (FREQUENCY COUNT)
Following the symbol :– KJV words are listed according to their exact textual spelling and are organized according to frequency (see the introduction, page xiv).

one another (+*1520*+*3588*) [2]

MULTIPLE WORDS / MULTIPLE NUMBERS
More than one KJV word and/or more than one Strong number indicate multiple-word translations (see the introduction, pages xii–xiv).

one another[S] [2]

SUPERSCRIPT "S"
Indicates "substitution" translation (see the introduction, pages xiii, xiv).

GREEK TRANSLITERATION AND PRONUNCIATION TABLE

Greek	Translit.	Sound	Greek	Translit.	Sound	Greek	Translit.	Sound	Greek	Translit.	Sound
Α, α	*A, a*	father	Κ, κ	*K, k*	kit	Τ, τ	*T, t*	tip	γγ	*ng*	thi*ng*
Β, β	*B, b*	boy	Λ, λ	*L, l*	let	Υ, υ	*Y, y*	put	γκ	*nk*	thi*nk*
Γ, γ	*G, g*	girl	Μ, μ	*M, m*	mother	Φ, φ	*Ph, ph*	phone	γξ	*nx*	thi*nks*
Δ, δ	*D, d*	dog	Ν, ν	*N, n*	not	Χ, χ	*Ch, ch*	Ba*ch*	γχ	*nch*	thi*nk*
Ε, ε	*E, e*	get	Ξ, ξ	*X, x*	fo*x*	Ψ, ψ	*Ps, ps*	li*ps*			
Ζ, ζ	*Z, z*	a*dz*e	Ο, ο	*O, o*	hot	Ω, ω	*Ō, ō*	phone	αυ	*au*	kr*au*t
Η, η	*Ē, ē*	they	Π, π	*P, p*	pot				ευ	*eu*	*you*
Θ, θ	*Th, th*	*th*ey	Ρ, ρ	*R, r*	rot	Ῥ, ῥ	*Rh, rh*	myr*rh*	ου	*ou*	thr*ou*gh
Ι, ι	*I, i*	pin, machine	Σ, σ, ς	*S, s, s*	sip	ʽ	*H, h*	*h*ot	υι	*ui*	*we*

GREEK DICTIONARY ABBREVIATIONS

&	and	comp.	comparative	inter.	interrogative	pl.	plural
?	uncertain	cond.	conditional	interj.	interjection	poss.	possessive
+	plus: in combination with	contr.	contraction	intr.	intransitive	pp.	preposition
[ ]	uncertain part of speech	demo.	demonstrative	l.	loanword	pp.*	improper preposition
→	see these related words	disj.	disjunctive	letter	letter of the alphabet	pr.	proper [noun]
√	see this organizing word	emph.	emphatic	mid.	middle	pt.	particle
a.	adjective	excl.	exclamation	n.	noun	recip.	reciprocal
act.	active	fig.	figurative(ly)	neg.	negative	reflex.	reflexive
adv.	adverb	g.	gentilic	neu.	neuter	rel.	relative
adver.	adversative	imper.	impersonal	num.	numeral	super.	superlative
aff.	affirmative	indef.	indefinite	p.	pronoun	temp.	temporal
art.	article	infer.	inferential	pass.	passive	trans.	transitional
c.	conjunction	inten.	intensive	pers.	personal	v.	verb

1 **α**, ***a***, letter. GK: *1 & 270* [→ *1*; ***1.1:*** *4, 22, 35, 36, 46, 50, 51, 52, 56, 57, 62, 77, 82, 83, 84, 87, 88, 89, 90, 91, 92, 93, 94, 95, 96, 97, 101, 102, 106, 110, 112, 113, 114, 115, 120, 121, 167, 168, 169, 170, 171, 172, 175, 176, 177, 178, 179, 180, 181, 182, 183, 185, 186, 192, 193, 194, 208, 209, 210, 215, 216, 225, 226, 227, 228, 230, 249, 253, 255, 261, 262, 263, 267, 269, 272, 273, 274, 275, 276, 277, 278, 279, 280, 282, 283, 298, 299, 335, 338, 358, 361, 368, 369, 370, 371, 379, 382, 410, 411, 412, 413, 415, 418, 419, 421, 422, 423, 428, 434, 448, 449, 453, 454, 458, 459, 460, 462, 504, 505, 506, 512, 517, 521, 531, 532, 540, 543, 544, 545, 551, 552, 562, 563, 564, 569, 570, 571, 639, 640, 676, 677, 678, 679, 691, 692, 729, 731, 732, 761, 762, 763, 764, 765, 766, 767, 769, 770, 771, 772, 776, 777, 781, 784, 786, 790, 793, 794, 795, 799, 800, 801, 802, 803, 804, 805, 806, 807, 808, 809, 810, 811, 812, 813, 814, 815, 818, 819, 820, 821, 823, 824, 852, 853, 854, 855, 857, 858, 861, 862, 865, 866, 870, 877, 878, 880, 884, 886, 888, 889, 890, 893, 895, 1280, 1820, 2673;* ***1.2:*** *12, 816;* ***1.3:*** *79, 271?, 1811, 1872, 2628, 3877, 4870, 5359, 5360, 5361, 5569*]. 1) letter of the Greek alphabet, Alpha, "*First* or *Beginning*"; 2) inseparable prefix: ***1.1*** alpha privative (as non- or un- in English), ***1.2*** prefix of intensity, ***1.3*** prefix of similarity, collectivity or association; also used as the numeral "1" in the superscriptions of some Greek manuscripts:– Alpha [4]

2 **Ἀαρών**, ***Aarōn***, n.pr. GK: *2.* Aaron (referring to both the person and his priesthood):– Aaron [4], Aaron's [1]

3 **Ἀβαδδών**, ***Abaddōn***, n.pr. GK: *3.* Abaddon, "*destruction*":– Abaddon [1]

4 **ἀβαρής**, ***abarēs***, a. GK: *4* [→ *1.1+922*]. not burdensome:– from being burdensome [1]

5 **ἀββά**, ***abba***, l.[n.]. GK: *5.* Aramaic for "father":– Abba [3]

6 **Ἅβελ**, ***Habel***, n.pr. GK: *6.* Abel, "*morning mist*":– Abel [4]

7 **Ἀβιά**, ***Abia***, n.pr. GK: *7.* Abijah, "*[my] father is Yahweh*":– Abia [3]

8 **Ἀβιαθάρ**, ***Abiathar***, n.pr. GK: *8.* Abiathar, "*[my] father gives abundance* or *the father is preeminent*":– Abiathar [1]

9 **Ἀβιληνή**, ***Abilēnē***, n.pr. GK: *9.* Abilene, a territory on the south end of the Ante-Lebanon mountain range, "[prob.] *meadow*":– Abilene [1]

10 **Ἀβιούδ**, ***Abioud***, n.pr. GK: *10.* Abiud, "*[my] father has majesty*":– Abiud [2]

11 **Ἀβραάμ**, ***Abraam***, n.pr. GK: *11.* Abraham, "*father of many*":– Abraham [68], Abraham's [5]

12 **ἄβυσσος**, ***abyssos***, n. GK: *12* [→ *1.2+1037*]. Abyss, the deep place, the underworld, the abode of the dead and demons, "*unfathomable depth*":– bottomless [7], deep [2]

13 **Ἅγαβος**, ***Hagabos***, n.pr. GK: *13.* Agabus:– Agabus [2]

14 **ἀγαθοεργέω**, ***agathoergeō***, v. GK: *14* [→ *18+2041*]. to do good:– do good [1]

15 **ἀγαθοποιέω**, ***agathopoieō***, v. GK: *16* [→ *18+4160*]. to do good, to do right:– do good [5], do well [2], well doing [2], did good [1], doeth good [1]

16 **ἀγαθοποιΐα**, ***agathopoiia***, n. GK: *17* [→ *18+4160*]. doing good:– well doing [1]

17 **ἀγαθοποιός**, ***agathopoios***, a. GK: *18* [→ *18+4160*]. one who does good, right:– do well [1]

18 **ἀγαθός**, ***agathos***, a. GK: *19* [→ *14, 15, 16, 17, 19, 865, 5358*]. good; good as a positive quality (vs. bad), good as a moral quality (vs. evil):– good [98], goods [2], benefit [1], well [1]

19 **ἀγαθωσύνη**, ***agathōsynē***, n. GK: *20* [→ *18*]. goodness:– goodness [4]

20 **ἀγαλλίασις**, ***agalliasis***, n. GK: *21* [→ *21*]. delight, great joy:– gladness [3], exceeding joy [1], joy [1]

21 **ἀγαλλιάω**, ***agalliaō***, v. GK: *22* [→ *20*]. to be filled with delight, with great joy:– rejoiced [4], rejoice [3], exceeding glad [1], exceeding joy [1], glad [1], greatly rejoice [1]

22 **ἄγαμος**, ***agamos***, n. GK: *23* [→ *1.1+1062*]. unmarried (man or woman):– unmarried [4]

23 **ἀγανακτέω**, ***aganakteō***, v. GK: *24* [→ *24*]. to be indignant:– had indignation [2], much displeased [2], indignation [1], moved with indignation [1], sore displeased [1]

24 **ἀγανάκτησις**, ***aganaktēsis***, n. GK: *25* [→ *23*]. indignation:– indignation [1]

25 **ἀγαπάω**, ***agapaō***, v. GK: *26* [→ *26, 27*]. to love; in the NT usually the active love of God for his Son and his people, and the active love his people are to have for God, each other, and even enemies:– love [73], loved [39], loveth [20], beloved [7], lovest [2], lovedst [1]

26 **ἀγάπη**, ***agapē***, n. GK: *27* [→ *25*]. love, in the NT usually the active love of God for his Son and his people, and the active love his people are to have for God, each other, and even enemies; love feast, the common meal shared by Christians in connection with church meetings:– love [85], charity [27], charitably (*+2596*) [1], dear [1], feasts of charity [1], love's [1]

27 **ἀγαπητός**, ***agapētos***, a. GK: *28* [→ *25*]. dearly loved one; the object of special affection and of special relationship, as with Jesus the beloved of the Father:– beloved [47], dearly beloved [9], dear [3], wellbeloved [3]

28 **Ἀγάρ**, ***Hagar***, n.pr. GK: *29.* Hagar:– Agar [2]

29 **ἀγγαρεύω**, ***angareuō***, v. GK: *30.* to force, compel, press into service in military or civil matters:– compel to go [1], compelled [1], compel [1]

30 **ἀγγεῖον**, ***angeion***, n. GK: *31.* jar, flask, a container for liquid, basket:– vessels [2]

31 **ἀγγελία**, ***angelia***, n. GK: *32* [→ *32*]. message:– message [1]

32 **ἄγγελος**, ***angelos***, n. GK: *34* [→ *31, 518, 312, 743, 1229, 1804, 1860, 1861, 1862, 2097, 2098, 2099, 2465, 2604, 2605, 3852, 3853, 4279, 4283, 4293; cf. 71*]. angel, messenger; this can refer to a human messenger, such as John the Baptist, or messengers sent by John the Baptist or Jesus, or to the supernatural class of being that serves God: the angel:– angel [96], angels [80], messenger [4], messengers [3], angel's [2]

33 **ἄγε**, ***agē***, v.imper. of *71.* GK: *72* [→ *71*]. look, pay attention, listen:–

34 **ἀγέλη**, ***agelē***, n. GK: *36* [→ *71*]. herd (of pigs):– herd [8]

35 **ἀγενεαλόγητος**, ***agenealogētos***, a. GK: *37* [→ *1.1+1096+3004*]. without genealogy:– without descent [1]

36 **ἀγενής**, ***agenēs***, a. GK: *38* [→ *1.1+1096*]. lowly, insignificant, implying low social standing:– base [1]

37 **ἁγιάζω**, ***hagiazō***, v. GK: *39* [→ *40*]. to sanctify, set apart, make holy; this can mean active dedication and service to God or the act of regarding or honoring as holy:– sanctified [16], sanctify [6], sanctifieth [4], hallowed [2], holy [1]

38 **ἁγιασμός**, ***hagiasmos***, n. GK: *40* [→ *40*]. holiness:– holiness [5], sanctification [5]

39 **ἅγιον**, ***hagion***, a.neut. of *40.* GK: *41* [→ *40*]. holy (moral quality), holy place = sanctuary:–

40 **ἅγιος**, ***hagios***, a. GK: *41* [→ *37, 38, 39, 41, 42; cf. 53*]. holy (moral quality), consecrated ([ceremonially] acceptable to God); holy person/people = saint(s), holy place = sanctuary:– holy [163], saints [60], holy one [4], sanctuary [4], holiest of all (*+40*) [2], holiest [2], holy thing [1], most holy [1], saints' [1], saint [1]

41 **ἁγιότης**, ***hagiotēs***, n. GK: *42* [→ *40*]. holiness, a characteristic of God, shared by his people, requiring a lifestyle acceptable to God:– holiness [1]

42 **ἁγιωσύνη**, ***hagiōsynē***, n. GK: *43* [→ *40*]. holiness, a characteristic of God, shared by his people, requiring a lifestyle acceptable to God:– holiness [3]

43 **ἀγκάλη**, ***ankalē***, n. GK: *44* [→ *1723*]. arm:– arms [1]

44 **ἄγκιστρον**, ***ankistron***, n. GK: *45* [→ *45*]. fish-hook, fish line with a hook on it:– hook [1]

45 **ἄγκυρα**, ***ankyra***, n. GK: *46* [→ *44*]. anchor; used fig. of security:– anchors [3], anchor [1]

46 **ἄγναφος**, ***agnaphos***, a. GK: *47* [→ *1.1+1102*]. unshrunk, new cloth that has not been laundered:– new [2]

47 **ἁγνεία**, ***hagneia***, n. GK: *48* [→ *53*]. purity, in the sense of moral purity and proper sexual conduct:– purity [2]

48 **ἁγνίζω**, ***hagnizō***, v. GK: *49* [→ *53*]. to purify, ceremonially cleanse:– purify [3], purified [2], purifieth [1], purifying [1]

49 **ἁγνισμός**, ***hagnismos***, n. GK: *50* [→ *53*]. purification:– purification [1]

50 **ἀγνοέω**, ***agnoeō***, v. GK: *51* [→ *1.1+1097*]. to be ignorant, not know, not understand:– ignorant [10], ignorantly [2], know not [2], understood not [2], unknown [2], have ignorant [1], knew not [1], not knowing [1], understand not [1]

51 **ἀγνόημα**, ***agnoēma***, n. GK: *52* [→ *1.1+1097*]. sin committed in ignorance:– errors [1]

52 **ἄγνοια**, ***agnoia***, n. GK: *53* [→ *1.1+1097*]. ignorance:– ignorance [4]

53 **ἁγνός**, ***hagnos***, a. GK: *54* [→ *47, 48, 49, 54, 55; cf. 40*]. pure (in some contexts morally pure), innocent:– pure [4], chaste [3], clear [1]

54 **ἁγνότης**, ***hagnotēs***, n. GK: *55* [→ *53*]. purity:– pureness [1]

55 **ἁγνῶς**, ***hagnōs***, adv. GK: *56* [→ *53*]. sincerely, purely:– sincerely [1]

56 **ἀγνωσία**, ***agnōsia***, n. GK: *57* [→ *1.1+1097*]. ignorance, with a focus on talk or action that opposes God:– ignorance [1], not knowledge [1]

57 **ἄγνωστος**, ***agnōstos***, a. GK: *58* [→ *1.1+1097*]. unknown:– unknown [1]

58 **ἀγορά**, ***agora***, n. GK: *59* [→ *59*]. marketplace (as a center of social and commercial life):– markets [4], marketplace [3], market [2], marketplaces [1], streets [1]

59 **ἀγοράζω**, ***agorazō***, v. GK: *60* [→ *58, 60, 238, 1215, 1805; cf. 71*]. to buy, purchase; this refers to buying and acquiring possessions, as in a market place, and to setting a slave free through purchase, often to God's purchase (redemption) of sinners:– bought [13], buy [13], redeemed [3], buyeth [2]

60 **ἀγοραῖος**, ***agoraios***, a. GK: *61* [→ *59*]. marketplace, place where the courts meet:– baser sort [1], law [1]

61 **ἄγρα**, ***agra***, n. GK: *62* [→ *64, 69, 70, 2221*]. catch (of fish), a net full:– draught [2]

62 **ἀγράμματος**, ***agrammatos***, a. GK: *63* [→ *1.1+1125*]. unschooled, probably in the sense of not having a formal rabbinic education:– unlearned [1]

63 **ἀγραυλέω**, ***agrauleō***, v. GK: *64* [→ *68+833*]. to live outdoors, spend a night in the elements:– in country abiding [1]

64 **ἀγρεύω**, ***agreuō***, v. GK: *65* [→ *61*]. to catch:– catch [1]

65 **ἀγριέλαιος**, ***agrielaios***, n. GK: *66* [→ *68+1636*]. wild olive tree:– olive tree which is wild [1], wild olive tree [1]

66 **ἄγριος**, ***agrios***, a. GK: *67* [→ *68*]. wild; undomesticated as well as uncontrolled:– wild [2], raging [1]

67 **Ἀγρίππας**, ***Agrippas***, n.pr. GK: *68* [→ *68+2462*]. Agrippa, "*wild horse*":– Agrippa [12]

68 **ἀγρός**, ***agros***, n. GK: *69* [→ *63, 65, 66, 67*]. field, countryside, both tilled and untilled ground:– field [21], country [8], lands [3], farm [1], fields [1], land [1], piece of ground [1]

69 **ἀγρυπνέω**, ***agrypneō***, v. GK: *70* [→ *61+5258*]. to keep awake, keep alert:– watch [3], watching [1]

70 **ἀγρυπνία**, ***agrypnia***, n. GK: *71* [→ *61+5258*]. sleeplessness, wakefulness:– watchings [2]

71 **ἄγω**, ***agō***, v. GK: *72* [→ *33, 34, 72, 321, 411, 520, 747, 1236, 1334, 1335, 1396, 1521, 1555, 1806, 1834, 1863, 1877, 1898, 1996, 2023, 2024, 2230, 2231, 2232, 2233, 3519, 2609, 2723, 3329, 3594, 3595, 3807, 3831, 3855, 3919, 3920, 3931, 4013, 4254, 4285, 4316, 4317, 4318, 4755, 4812, 4863, 4864, 4879, 5217, 5468, 5496, 5497, 5524; cf. 32, 59, 514, 2723*]. to bring, lead; as a command: look, pay attention, listen:– brought [32], bring [13], led [10], go [8], bring out [1], bringing [1], carried [1], going [1], is [1], kept [1], leadeth [1], lead [1], led away [1], open [1]

72 **ἀγωγή**, ***agōgē***, n. GK: *73* [→ *71*]. way of life, personal conduct:– manner of life [1]

73 **ἀγών**, ***agōn***, n. GK: *74* [→ *74, 75, 464, 1864, 2610, 4865*]. struggle, fight, often an athletic contest:– conflict [2], fight [2], contention [1], race [1]

74 **ἀγωνία**, ***agōnia***, n. GK: *75* [→ *73*]. anguish, anxiety:– agony [1]

75 **ἀγωνίζομαι**, ***agōnizomai***, v. GK: *76* [→ *73*]. to fight, struggle, often an athletic contest:– fight [2], fought [1], labouring fervently [1], striveth for the mastery [1], strive [1], striving [1]

76 **Ἀδάμ**, ***Adam***, n.pr. GK: *77.* Adam, "*[red] earth* or *[ruddy] skin color*":– Adam [8], Adam's [1]

77 **ἀδάπανος**, ***adapanos***, a. GK: *78* [→ *1.1+1160*]. free of charge, without payment:– without charge [1]

78 **Ἀδδί**, ***Addi***, n.pr. GK: *79.* Addi, "[poss.] *my witness* or *adorned*":– Addi [1]

79 **ἀδελφή**, ***adelphē***, n. GK: *80* [→ *80; cf. 1.3*]. sister, fellow countrywoman; by extension a female believer, a sister in the family of faith:– sister [15], sisters [8], sister's [1]

80 **ἀδελφός**, ***adelphos***, n. GK: *81* [→ *1.3, 79, 81, 5359, 5360, 5361, 5569*]. brother, fellow countryman, neighbor (often inclusive in gender); by extension a fellow believer in the family of faith; in the plural "brothers" regularly refers to men and women:– brethren [226], brother [113], brother's [7]

81 **ἀδελφότης**, ***adelphotēs***, n. GK: *82* [→ *80*]. brotherhood, fellowship of believers (men and women):– brethren [1], brotherhood [1]

82 **ἄδηλος**, ***adēlos***, a. GK: *83* [→ *1.1+1212*]. not clear:– appear not [1], uncertain [1]

83 **ἀδηλότης**, ***adēlotēs***, n. GK: *84* [→ *1.1+1212*]. uncertainty:– uncertain [1]

84 **ἀδήλως**, ***adēlōs***, adv. GK: *85* [→ *1.1+1212*]. aimlessly, uncertainly:– uncertainly [1]

85 **ἀδημονέω**, ***adēmoneō***, v. GK: *86 & 194.* to be troubled, distressed:– very heavy [2], full of heaviness [1]

86 **ᾅδης**, ***hadēs***, n. GK: *87.* Hades, the grave, the place of the dead, "*the underworld*":– hell [10], grave [1]

87 **ἀδιάκριτος**, ***adiakritos***, a. GK: *88* [→ *1.1+1223+2919*]. impartial, free from prejudice:– without partiality [1]

88 **ἀδιάλειπτος**, ***adialeiptos***, a. GK: *89* [→ *1.1+1223+3007*]. constant, unceasing:– continual [1], without ceasing [1]

89 **ἀδιαλείπτως**, ***adialeiptōs***, adv. GK: *90* [→ *1.1+1223+3007*]. constantly, unceasingly:– without ceasing [4]

90 **ἀδιαφθορία**, ***adiaphthoria***, n. GK: *91* [→ *1.1+1223+5351*]. sincerity, integrity:– uncorruptness [1]

91 **ἀδικέω**, ***adikeō***, v. GK: *92* [→ *1.1+1349*]. to do wrong, mistreat:– hurt [10], wrong [3], done wrong [2], unjust [2], wronged [2], did wrong [1], doeth wrong [1], injured [1], offender [1], suffer wrong [1], suffered wrong [1], take wrong [1], wrong done [1]

92 **ἀδίκημα**, ***adikēma***, n. GK: *93* [→ *1.1+1349*]. crime, unrighteous or unjust act:– evil doing [1], iniquities [1], wrong [1]

93 **ἀδικία**, ***adikia***, n. GK: *94* [→ *1.1+1349*]. wickedness, evil, wrongdoing:– unrighteousness [16], iniquity [6], unjust [2], wrong [1]

94 **ἄδικος**, ***adikos***, a. GK: *96* [→ *1.1+1349*]. unjust, unrighteous, used of things and persons; as a noun: unbeliever, wicked person:– unjust [8], unrighteous [4]

95 **ἀδίκως**, ***adikōs***, adv. GK: *97* [→ *1.1+1349*]. unjustly:– wrongfully [1]

96 **ἀδόκιμος**, ***adokimos***, a. GK: *99* [→ *1.1+1209*]. failing the test, rejected:– reprobates [3], reprobate [3], castaway [1], rejected [1]

97 **ἄδολος**, ***adolos***, a. GK: *100* [→ *1.1+1388*]. pure, uncontaminated or tainted:– sincere [1]

98 **Ἀδραμυττηνός**, ***Adramyttēnos***, a.pr.g. GK: *101.* of Adramyttium:– Adramyttium [1]

99 **Ἀδρίας**, ***Adrias***, n.pr. GK: *102.* Adriatic Sea:– Adria [1]

100 **ἁδρότης**, ***hadrotēs***, n. GK: *103.* liberal gift, liberality:– abundance [1]

101 **ἀδυνατέω**, ***adynateō***, v. GK: *104* [→ *1.1+1410*]. to be impossible:– unpossible [2]

102 **ἀδύνατος**, ***adynatos***, a. GK: *105* [→ *1.1+1410*]. impossible, powerless:– impossible [4], unpossible [2], could not do [1], impotent [1], not possible [1], weak [1]

103 **ᾄδω**, ***adō***, v. GK: *106* [→ *5603*]. to sing:– singing [2], sung [2], sing [1]

104 **ἀεί**, ***aei***, adv. GK: *107* [→ *126*]. always:– alway [4], always [3], ever [1]

105 **ἀετός**, ***aetos***, n. GK: *108.* eagle (a noble, powerful bird), vulture (a carrion bird):– eagles [2], eagle [2]

106 **ἄζυμος**, ***azymos***, a. GK: *109* [→ *1.1+2219*]. unleavened, (the Feast of) Unleavened Bread, made without yeast; fig. of purity:– unleavened bread [8], unleavened [1]

107 **Ἀζώρ**, ***Azōr***, n.pr. GK: *110.* Azor:– Azor [2]

108 **Ἄζωτος**, ***Azōtos***, n.pr. GK: *111.* Azotus, another name for Ashdod:– Azotus [1]

109 **ἀήρ**, ***aēr***, n. GK: *113* [→ *822; cf. 143, 833*]. air, sky:– air [7]

ἀθά, ***atha***. See ***3134***.

110 **ἀθανασία**, ***athanasia***, n. GK: *114* [→ *1.1+2348*]. immortality:– immortality [3]

111 **ἀθέμιτος**, ***athemitos***, a. GK: *116.* unlawful, detestable:– abominable [1], unlawful [1]

112 **ἄθεος**, ***atheos***, a. GK: *117* [→ *1.1+2316*]. without God, excluded from the heritage of Israel:– without God [1]

113 **ἄθεσμος**, ***athesmos***, a. GK: *118* [→ *1.1+5087*]. lawless, unprincipled:– wicked [2]

114 **ἀθετέω**, ***atheteō***, v. GK: *119* [→ *1.1+5087*]. to reject, set aside:– despiseth [6], reject [2], bring to nothing [1], cast off [1], despised [1], despise [1], disannulleth [1], frustrate [1], rejected [1], rejecteth [1]

115 **ἀθέτησις**, ***athetēsis***, n. GK: *120* [→ *1.1+5087*]. setting aside, doing away with:– disannulling [1], put away [1]

116 **Ἀθῆναι**, ***Athēnai***, n.pr. GK: *121* [→ *117*]. Athens:– Athens [6]

117 **Ἀθηναῖος**, ***Athēnaios***, a.pr.g. GK: *122* [→ *116*]. Athenian, resident of Athens:– Athenians [1], of Athens [1]

118 **ἀθλέω**, ***athleō***, v. GK: *123* [→ *119, 4866*]. to compete in a contest:– strive for masteries [1], strive [1]

119 **ἄθλησις**, ***athlēsis***, n. GK: *124* [→ *118*]. contest, struggle:– fight [1]

120 **ἀθυμέω**, ***athymeō***, v. GK: *126* [→ *1.1+2372*]. to be discouraged, lose heart:– discouraged [1]

121 **ἀθῷος**, ***athōos***, a. GK: *127* [→ *1.1+5087*]. innocent:– innocent [2]

122 **αἴγειος**, ***aigeios***, a. GK: *128.* of a goat:– goatskins (*+1192*) [1]

123 **αἰγιαλός**, ***aigialos***, n. GK: *129* [→ *217*]. shore, beach:– shore [6]

124 **Αἰγύπτιος**, ***Aigyptios***, a.pr.g. GK: *130* [→ *125*]. Egyptian, person of Egypt:– Egyptian [3], Egyptians [2]

125 **Αἴγυπτος**, ***Aigyptos***, n.pr. GK: *131* [→ *124*]. Egypt:– Egypt [24]

126 **ἀΐδιος**, ***aidios***, a. GK: *132* [→ *104*]. eternal (referring to God's power, chains of punishment):– eternal [1], everlasting [1]

127 **αἰδώς**, ***aidōs***, n. GK: *133 & 1290* [→ *335, 1167, 1168, 1169, 1171, 1175, 1174*]. decency, modesty:– reverence [1], shamefastness [1]

128 **Αἰθίοψ**, ***Aithiops***, n.pr.g. GK: *134.* Ethiopian, person of Ethiopia:– Ethiopians [1], Ethiopia [1]

129 **αἷμα**, ***haima***, n. GK: *135* [→ *130, 131*]. blood; extended meanings: killing, death, sacrifice:– blood [99]

130 **αἱματεκχυσία**, ***haimatekchysia***, n. GK: *136* [→ *129+1632*]. shedding, pouring out of blood:– shedding of blood [1]

131 **αἱμορροέω**, ***haimorroeō***, v. GK: *137* [→ *129+4482*]. to be subject to bleeding, to experience loss of blood:– diseased with an issue of blood [1]

132 **Αἰνέας**, ***Aineas***, n.pr. GK: *138* [→ *136*]. Aeneas, "[poss.] *praise*":– Aeneas [2]

133 **αἴνεσις**, ***ainesis***, n. GK: *139* [→ *136*]. praise, speaking of the excellence of someone or something:– praise [1]

134 **αἰνέω**, ***aineō***, v. GK: *140* [→ *136*]. to praise; in the NT, speaking of the excellence of God:– praising [6], praise [3]

135 **αἴνιγμα**, ***ainigma***, n. GK: *141.* poor reflection, indistinct image:– darkly (*+1722*) [1]

136 **αἶνος**, ***ainos***, n. GK: *142* [→ *132, 133, 134, 1866, 1867, 1868, 3867*]. praise:– praise [2]

137 **Αἰνών**, ***Ainōn***, n.pr. GK: *143.* Aenon, "*spring*":– Aenon [1]

138 **αἱρέομαι**, ***haireomai***, v. GK: *145* [→ *139, 140, 141, 336, 337, 830, 851, 1243, 1244, 1807, 2506, 2507, 4014, 4255*]. to choose:– choose [1], choosing [1], chosen [1]

139 **αἵρεσις**, ***hairesis***, n. GK: *146* [→ *138*]. sect (religious party), faction, heresy:– sect [5], heresies [3], heresy [1]

140 **αἱρετίζω**, ***hairetizō***, v. GK: *147* [→ *138*]. to choose (for the purpose of showing special favor):– chosen [1]

141 **αἱρετικός**, ***hairetikos***, a. GK: *148* [→ *138*]. divisive:– heretick [1]

142 **αἴρω**, ***airō***, v. GK: *149* [→ *522, 1808, 1869, 3332, 4868, 5097, 5098, 5229*]. to take up, take away:– take up [14], take [14], took up [13], taken away [9], take away [7], taketh away [6], away with [5], taketh [5], taken [4], taken up [3], took [3], bear up [2], bear [2], lifted up [2], removed [2], took away [2], borne [1], carry [1], lift up [1], lift [1], loosing [1], make to doubt (*+3588+5590*) [1], put away [1], takest up [1], taking up [1]

143 **αἰσθάνομαι**, ***aisthanomai***, v. GK: *150* [→ *144, 145; cf. 109*]. to grasp, understand, to have the capacity to perceive something clearly:– perceived [1]

144 **αἴσθησις**, ***aisthēsis***, n. GK: *151* [→ *143*]. insight:– judgment [1]

145 **αἰσθητήριον**, ***aisthētērion***, n. GK: *152* [→ *143*]. sense, faculty:– senses [1]

146 **αἰσχροκερδής**, ***aischrokerdēs***, a. GK: *153* [→ *150+2771*]. pursuing dishonest gain:– greedy of filthy lucre [2], given to filthy lucre [1]

147 **αἰσχροκερδῶς**, ***aischrokerdōs***, adv. GK: *154* [→ *150+2771*]. in greediness for money:– for filthy lucre [1]

148 **αἰσχρολογία**, ***aischrologia***, n. GK: *155* [→ *150+3004*]. filthy language, vulgar speech:– filthy communication [1]

149 **αἰσχρόν**, ***aischron***, a.neut. of *150.* GK: *156* [→ *150*]. disgraceful, shameful:– shame [3]

150 **αἰσχρός**, ***aischros***, a. GK: *156* [→ *146, 147, 148, 149, 151, 152, 153, 422, 1870, 2617*]. disgraceful, shameful:– filthy [1]

151 **αἰσχρότης**, ***aischrotēs***, n. GK: *157* [→ *150*]. obscenity:– filthiness [1]

152 **αἰσχύνη**, ***aischynē***, n. GK: *158* [→ *150*]. shamefulness:– shame [5], dishonesty [1]

153 **αἰσχύνομαι**, ***aischynomai***, v. GK: *159* [→ *150*]. to be ashamed:– ashamed [5]

154 **αἰτέω**, ***aiteō***, v. GK: *160* [→ *155, 523, 1809, 1871, 3868, 4319*]. to ask, ask for (of other humans or God), demand:– ask [38], desired [10], asketh [5], desire [5], asked [3], begged [2], desiring [2], asked for [1], askest [1], called for [1], craved [1], require [1], requiring [1]

155 **αἴτημα**, ***aitēma***, n. GK: *161* [→ *154*]. request:– petitions [1], requests [1], required [1]

156 **αἰτία**, ***aitia***, n. GK: *162* [→ *157, 158, 159, 338, 4256*]. (legal) charge; reason, cause:– cause [9], accusation [3], fault [3], wherefore (*+1223+3739*) [3], case [1], crimes [1]

157 **αἰτίαμα**, ***aitiama***, n. GK: *163 & 166* [→ *156*]. charge, complaint:– complaints [1]

158 **αἴτιον**, ***aition***, a.neut. of *159.* GK: *165* [→ *156*]. basis, reason or cause (for legal charges), source:– cause [2], fault [2]

159 **αἴτιος**, ***aitios***, a. GK: *165* [→ *156*]. basis, reason or cause (for legal charges), source:– author [1]

160 **αἰφνίδιος**, ***aiphnidios***, a. GK: *167* [→ *869?, 1810, 1819*]. sudden, unexpected:– sudden [1], unawares [1]

161 **αἰχμαλωσία**, ***aichmalōsia***, n. GK: *168* [→ *164*]. captivity:– captivity [3]

162 **αἰχμαλωτεύω**, ***aichmalōteuō***, v. GK: *169* [→ *164*]. to take captive:– lead captive [1], led captive [1]

163 **αἰχμαλωτίζω**, ***aichmalōtizō***, v. GK: *170* [→ *164*]. to take captive, take prisoner:– bringing into captivity [2], led away captive [1]

164 **αἰχμάλωτος**, ***aichmalōtos***, n. GK: *171* [→ *161, 162, 163, 4869; cf. 259*]. prisoner:– captives [1]

165 **αἰών**, ***aiōn***, n. GK: *172* [→ *166*]. eternity, age (time period); "this age" can mean the universe or even the current world system, the "god of this age" refers to the devil:– ever [68], world [35], never (*+1519+3361+3588+3756*) [5], ages [2], eternal [2], ever (*+1519+3588*) [2], evermore (*+165*) [2], evermore [2], world without end (*+165+3588+3588*) [2], worlds [2], beginning of the world [1], course [1], ever (*+1519+3588+3956*) [1], ever (*+2250*) [1], never (*+1487+1519+3588+3756*) [1], never (*+1519+3588+3756*) [1]

166 **αἰώνιος**, ***aiōnios***, a. GK: *173* [→ *165*]. eternal, long ago:– eternal [42], everlasting [25], world began (*+5550*) [2], for ever [1], since world began (*+5550*) [1]

167 **ἀκαθαρσία, *akatharsia***, n. GK: *174* [→ *1.1+2513*]. impurity, a state of moral filthiness, especially in relation to sexual sin:– uncleanness [10]

168 **ἀκαθάρτης, *akathartēs***, n. GK: *175* [→ *1.1+2513*]. uncleanness:– filthiness [1]

169 **ἀκάθαρτος, *akathartos***, a. GK: *176* [→ *1.1+2513*]. unclean, evil:– unclean [28], foul [2]

170 **ἀκαιρέομαι, *akaireomai***, v. GK: *177* [→ *1.1+2540*]. to have no opportunity, have no time:– lacked opportunity [1]

171 **ἀκαίρως, *akairōs***, adv. GK: *178* [→ *1.1+2540*]. out of season, lack of a favorable opportunity:– out of season [1]

172 **ἄκακος, *akakos***, a. GK: *179* [→ *1.1+2556*]. blameless, innocent, unsuspecting:– harmless [1], simple [1]

173 **ἄκανθα, *akantha***, n. GK: *180* [→ *206*]. thorn, thornbush:– thorns [14]

174 **ἀκάνθινος, *akanthinos***, a. GK: *181* [→ *206*]. of thorns, thorny:– of thorns [2]

175 **ἄκαρπος, *akarpos***, a. GK: *182* [→ *1.1+2590*]. unfruitful, unproductive, something generally useless:– unfruitful [6], without fruit [1]

176 **ἀκατάγνωστος, *akatagnōstos***, a. GK: *183* [→ *1.1+2596+1097*]. not condemned, what cannot be criticized:– cannot be condemned [1]

177 **ἀκατακάλυπτος, *akatakalyptos***, a. GK: *184* [→ *1.1+2596+2572*]. uncovered:– uncovered [2]

178 **ἀκατάκριτος, *akatakritos***, a. GK: *185* [→ *1.1+2596+2919*]. uncondemned, without a proper trial:– uncondemned [2]

179 **ἀκατάλυτος, *akatalytos***, a. GK: *186* [→ *1.1+2596+3089*]. indestructible, unstoppable:– endless [1]

180 **ἀκατάπαυστος, *akatapaustos***, a. GK: *187 & 188* [→ *1.1+2596+3973*]. never stopping:– cannot cease from [1]

181 **ἀκαταστασία, *akatastasia***, n. GK: *189* [→ *1.1+2596+2476*]. disorder, rebellion, riot:– confusion [2], tumults [2], commotions [1]

182 **ἀκατάστατος, *akatastatos***, a. GK: *190* [→ *1.1+2596+2476*]. unstable, restless:– unstable [1]

183 **ἀκατάσχετος, *akataschetos***, a. GK: *191* [→ *1.1+2596+2192*]. uncontrollable:– unruly [1]

184 **Ἀκελδαμάχ, *Hakeldamach***, n.pr. GK: *192*. Akeldama (traditionally located south of the valley of Hinnom), "*field of blood*":– Aceldama [1]

185 **ἀκέραιος, *akeraios***, a. GK: *193* [→ *1.1+2767*]. innocent, pure, not mixed with evil:– harmless [2], simple [1]

186 **ἀκλινής, *aklinēs***, a. GK: *195* [→ *1.1+2827*]. unswerving, without wavering:– without wavering [1]

187 **ἀκμάζω, *akmazō***, v. GK: *196* [→ *206*]. to be or become ripe:– fully ripe [1]

188 **ἀκμήν, *akmēn***, adv. GK: *197* [→ *206*]. still, even yet:– yet [1]

189 **ἀκοή, *akoē***, n. GK: *198* [→ *191*]. (act of) hearing, what is heard:– hearing [10], ears [4], fame [3], report [2], rumours [2], audience [1], heard [1], preached [1]

190 **ἀκολουθέω, *akoloutheō***, v. GK: *199* [→ *1.3, 1811, 1872, 2628, 3877, 4870*]. to follow; accompany; fig., to follow or be a disciple of a leader's teaching:– followed [53], follow [30], followeth [5], following [3], reached [1]

191 **ἀκούω, *akouō***, v. GK: *201* [→ *189, 1251, 1522, 1873, 3876, 3878, 4257, 5218, 5219, 5255*]. to hear, pay attention, understand, obey:– heard [239], hear [141], heareth [23], hearing [13], hearken [6], hearest [4], gave audience [2], hearers [2], came [1], come to ears (*+1909*) [1], give audience [1], in audience [1], noised [1], reported [1], understandeth [1]

192 **ἀκρασία, *akrasia***, n. GK: *202* [→ *1.1+2904*]. lack of self-control:– excess [1], incontinency [1]

193 **ἀκρατής, *akratēs***, a. GK: *203* [→ *1.1+2904*]. without self-control:– incontinent [1]

194 **ἄκρατος, *akratos***, a. GK: *204* [→ *1.1+2767*]. undiluted (of wine not watered down):– without mixture [1]

195 **ἀκρίβεια, *akribeia***, n. GK: *205* [→ *198*]. thoroughness, strictness:– perfect manner [1]

196 **ἀκριβέστατος, *akribestatos***, a.super. GK: *206* [→ *198*]. strictest:– most straitest [1]

197 **ἀκριβέστερον, *akribēstēron***, a.compar. GK: *206* [→ *198*]. more strict:– more perfectly [3], more perfect [1]

198 **ἀκριβόω, *akriboō***, v. GK: *208* [→ *195, 196, 197, 199*]. to find out exactly:– diligently inquired [1], inquired diligently [1]

199 **ἀκριβῶς, *akribōs***, adv. GK: *209* [→ *198*]. accurately, carefully, well:– diligently [2], circumspectly [1], perfectly [1], perfect [1]

200 **ἀκρίς, *akris***, n. GK: *210*. locust (in some cultures distinguished from a grasshopper and used as a food source):– locusts [4]

201 **ἀκροατήριον, *akroatērion***, n. GK: *211* [→ *202*]. audience room (of the procurator), in which hearings were held and justice was privately dispensed:– place of hearing [1]

202 **ἀκροατής, *akroatēs***, n. GK: *212* [→ *201, 1874*]. hearer:– hearers [2], hearer [2]

203 **ἀκροβυστία, *akrobystia***, n. GK: *213* [→ *206*]. uncircumcision, foreskin; fig., not of the Mosaic covenant, a Gentile:– uncircumcision [16], not circumcised [1], uncircumcised (*+1722*) [1], uncircumcised (*+2192*) [1], uncircumcised [1]

204 **ἀκρογωνιαῖος, *akrogōniaios***, a. GK: *214* [→ *206+1137*]. cornerstone, an essential stone in the construction of a building:– chief corner [2]

205 **ἀκροθίνιον, *akrothinion***, n. GK: *215* [→ *206*]. plunder, booty, fine spoils:– spoils [1]

206 **ἄκρον, *akron***, n. GK: *216* [→ *173, 174, 187, 188, 203, 204, 205, 891, 5230*]. end, top:– uttermost part [2], end [1], other[S] [1], tip [1], top [1]

207 **Ἀκύλας, *Akylas***, n.pr. GK: *217*. Aquila, "*eagle*":– Aquila [6]

208 **ἀκυρόω, *akyroō***, v. GK: *218* [→ *1.1+2964*]. to nullify, make void:– disannul [1], made of none effect [1], making of none effect [1]

209 **ἀκωλύτως, *akōlytōs***, adv. GK: *219* [→ *1.1+2967*]. without hinderance:– no forbidding [1]

210 **ἄκων, *akōn***, a. GK: *220* [→ *1.1+1635*]. not voluntary, unwilling:– against will [1]

211 **ἀλάβαστρος, *alabastros***, n. GK: *222 & 223*. alabaster jar; a long-necked flask, the top of which was broken off to empty its contents:– alabaster box [3], box [1]

212 **ἀλαζονεία, *alazoneia***, n. GK: *224* [→ *213, 214*]. boasting, pretension, arrogance:– boastings [1], pride [1]

213 **ἀλαζών, *alazōn***, n. GK: *225* [→ *212*]. boaster, braggart:– boasters [2]

214 **ἀλαλάζω, *alalazō***, v. GK: *226* [→ *212*]. to clang, wail:– tinkling [1], wailed [1]

215 **ἀλάλητος, *alalētos***, a. GK: *227* [→ *1.1+2980*]. inexpressible, unspeakable:– cannot be uttered [1]

216 **ἄλαλος, *alalos***, a. GK: *228* [→ *1.1+2980*]. mute, unable to speak:– dumb [3]

217 **ἅλας, *halas***, n. GK: *221 & 229* [→ *123, 231, 232, 233, 251, 252, 358, 1724, 3882; cf. 2281*]. salt; the impure salt of the ancient could become tasteless in adverse conditions, and its residue useless:– salt [8]

218 **ἀλείφω, *aleiphō***, v. GK: *230* [→ *1813*]. to pour on, anoint (usually with olive oil):– anointed [5], anoint [3], anointing [1]

219 **ἀλεκτοροφωνία, *alektorophōnia***, n. GK: *231* [→ *220+5456*]. crowing of a rooster; the third Roman watch of the night (about midnight to 3:00 a.m.):– cockcrowing [1]

220 **ἀλέκτωρ, *alektōr***, n. GK: *232* [→ *219*]. rooster:– cock [12]

221 **Ἀλεξανδρεύς, *Alexandreus***, n.pr.g. GK: *233* [→ *223*]. Alexandrian, person of Alexandria:– Alexandrians [1], at Alexandria [1]

222 **Ἀλεξανδρῖνος, *Alexandrinos***, a.pr.g. GK: *234* [→ *223*]. Alexandrian, of Alexandria:– Alexandria [2]

223 **Ἀλέξανδρος, *Alexandros***, n.pr. GK: *235* [→ *221, 222*]. Alexander, "*defender of men*":– Alexander [6]

224 **ἄλευρον, *aleuron***, n. GK: *236* [→ *229*]. flour:– meal [2]

225 **ἀλήθεια, *alētheia***, n. GK: *237* [→ *1.1+2990*]. truth, truthfulness; corresponding to reality:– truth [103], of a truth (*+1909*) [3], true [1], truly (*+1909*) [1], truth's [1], verity [1]

226 **ἀληθεύω, *alētheuō***, v. GK: *238* [→ *1.1+2990*]. to be truthful, tell the truth:– speaking the truth [1], tell the truth [1]

227 **ἀληθής, *alēthēs***, a. GK: *239* [→ *1.1+2990*]. true, genuine, reliable, trustworthy, valid:– true [23], truly [1], truth [1]

228 **ἀληθινός, *alēthinos***, a. GK: *240* [→ *1.1+2990*]. true, genuine:– true [27]

229 **ἀλήθω, *alēthō***, v. GK: *241* [→ *224*]. to grind grain (with a handmill operated by two women):– grinding [2]

230 **ἀληθῶς, *alēthōs***, adv. GK: *242* [→ *1.1+2990*]. truly, surely:– indeed [6], of a truth [6], surely [3], truly [2], in truth [1], of a surety [1], verily [1], very [1]

231 **ἁλιεύς, *halieus***, n. GK: *243* [→ *217*]. fisherman (by occupation):– fishers [4], fishermen [1]

232 **ἁλιεύω, *halieuō***, v. GK: *244* [→ *217*]. to catch fish, either by net or by line:– fishing [1]

233 **ἁλίζω, *halizō***, v. GK: *245* [→ *217*]. to salt, make salty:– salted [3]

234 **ἀλίσγημα, *alisgēma***, n. GK: *246*. pollution, ritually defiled:– pollutions [1]

235 **ἀλλά, *alla***, pt.adver. GK: *247* [→ *243*]. but, instead, yet, except:– but [573], yea [15], yet [11], nevertheless [10], howbeit [8], nay [4], therefore [3], and [2], save [2], also (*+2532*) [1], and (*+1065*) [1], howbeit (*+3303*) [1], moreover (*+2532*) [1], not so much as (*+3761*) [1], notwithstanding [1], no [1], than (*+2228*) [1], yet doubtless (*+1065*) [1]

236 **ἀλλάσσω, *allassō***, v. GK: *248* [→ *465, 525, 604, 1259, 2643, 2644, 3337, 3883; cf. 243*]. to change, exchange:– changed [4], change [2]

237 **ἀλλαχόθεν, *allachothen***, adv.pl. GK: *249* [→ *243*]. from another way:– some other way [1]

238 **ἀλληγορέω, *allēgoreō***, v. GK: *251* [→ *243+59*]. to take figuratively, speak allegorically, to employ an analogy or likeness in communication:– allegory [1]

239 **ἀλληλουϊά, *hallēlouia***, l.[v.+n.pr.]. GK: *252*. hallelujah; from Hebrew hallelu-yah, praise Yah(weh):– alleluia [4]

240 **ἀλλήλων, *allēlōn***, p.recip. GK: *253* [→ *243*]. one another, each other:– one another [74], themselves [12], yourselves [3], each other [2], one another's [2], one the other [2], mutual [1], one to the other [1], together (*+3326*) [1], together (*+4314*) [1], yourselves together [1]

241 **ἀλλογενής, *allogenēs***, a. GK: *254* [→ *243+1096*]. foreign:– stranger [1]

242 **ἅλλομαι, *hallomai***, v. GK: *256* [→ *1814, 2177; cf. 4531*]. to jump up, well up, quick movement of both humans and water:– leaped [1], leaping [1], springing up [1]

243 **ἄλλος, *allos***, a.&n. GK: *257* [→ *235, 237, 238, 240, 241, 244, 245, 246, 247, 526; cf. 236*]. another, other:– another [61], other [52], others [29], some [10], one [4], another (*+5100*) [1], moe [1], otherwise [1], some (*+3303*) [1]

244 **ἀλλοτριεπίσκοπος, *allotriepiskopos***, n. GK: *258* [→ *243+1909+4648*]. meddler, busybody; formally rendered "one who oversees what belongs to another" (in an unwarranted manner):– busybody in other men's matters [1]

245 **ἀλλότριος, *allotrios***, a. GK: *259* [→ *243*]. belonging to another:– another [4], strangers [3], other [2], strange [2], aliens [1], others [1], stranger [1]

246 **ἀλλόφυλος, *allophylos***, a. GK: *260* [→ *243+5443*]. Gentile, foreigner:– one of another nation [1]

247 **ἄλλως, *allōs***, adv. GK: *261* [→ *243*]. differently:– otherwise [1]

248 **ἀλοάω, *aloaō***, v. GK: *262* [→ *257, 3389, 3964*]. to tread, thresh, to separate grain kernels from the husks by beating or treading on:– treadeth out the corn [2], thresheth [1]

249 **ἄλογος, *alogos***, a. GK: *263* [→ *1.1+3004*]. unreasonable, without reason, brutish and living by instinct:– brute [2], unreasonable [1]

250 **ἀλόη, *aloe***, n. GK: *264*. aloes:– aloes [1]

251 **ἅλς, *hals***, n. GK: *265* [→ *217*]. salt:– salt [1]

252 **ἁλυκός, *halykos***, a. GK: *266* [→ *217*]. salt spring, salty:– salt [1]

253 **ἄλυπος, *alypos***, a. GK: *267* [→ *1.1+3077*]. free from anxiety; in the comparative, less anxiety:– less sorrowful [1]

254 **ἅλυσις, *halysis***, n. GK: *268*. chain (the state of imprisonment):– chains [7], chain [3], bonds [1]

255 ἀλυσιτελής, *alysitelēs*, a. GK: *269* [→ *1.1+3089+5056*]. unadvantageous, without special benefit:– unprofitable [1]

256 Ἁλφαῖος, *Halphaios*, n.pr. GK: *271*. Alphaeus:– Alpheus [5]

257 ἅλων, *halōn*, n. GK: *272* [→ *248*]. threshing floor:– floor [2]

258 ἀλώπηξ, *alōpēx*, n. GK: *273*. fox; this can refer to a wicked person with the probable implication of being cunning or treacherous:– foxes [2], fox [1]

259 ἅλωσις, *halōsis*, n. GK: *274* [→ *355, 2654, 4321; cf. 164*]. capture, catch:– taken [1]

260 ἅμα, *hama*, adv.&pp.*. GK: *275* [→ *537, 716; cf. 573*]. together, at the same time:– together [3], withal [3], also (+*2532*) [1], and [1], early in the morning (+*4404*) [1], with [1]

261 ἀμαθής, *amathēs*, a. GK: *276* [→ *1.1+3129*]. ignorant, without a formal education:– unlearned [1]

262 ἀμαράντινος, *amarantinos*, a. GK: *277* [→ *1.1+3133*]. unfading, without loss of pristine character:– fadeth not away [1]

263 ἀμάραντος, *amarantos*, a. GK: *278* [→ *1.1+3133*]. never fading:– fadeth not away [1]

264 ἁμαρτάνω, *hamartanō*, v. GK: *279* [→ *265, 266, 268, 361, 4258*]. to sin, do wrong; usually to do any act contrary to the will and law of God:– sin [16], sinned [15], sinneth [7], trespass [3], faults [1], offended [1]

265 ἁμάρτημα, *hamartēma*, n. GK: *280* [→ *264*]. sin, wrongdoing; usually any act contrary to the will and law of God:– sins [3], sin [1]

266 ἁμαρτία, *hamartia*, n. GK: *281* [→ *264*]. sin, wrongdoing; usually any act contrary to the will and law of God:– sin [94], sins [78], offence [1], sinful [1]

267 ἀμάρτυρος, *amartyros*, a. GK: *282* [→ *1.1+3144*]. without testimony, without witness:– without witness [1]

268 ἁμαρτωλός, *hamartōlos*, a. GK: *283* [→ *264*]. (a.) sinful, as an absolute moral failure; (n.) sinner, one who violates God's will or law; in some contexts, one who does not keep orthodox traditions and behaviors:– sinners [31], sinner [12], sinful [4]

269 ἄμαχος, *amachos*, a. GK: *285* [→ *1.1+3163*]. peaceable, not quarrelsome, without conflict:– no brawlers [1], not a brawler [1]

270 ἀμάω, *amaō*, v. GK: *286*. to mow, cut down:– reaped [1]

271 ἀμέθυστος, *amethystos*, n. GK: *287* [→ *1.3?+3184*]. amethyst, usually purple or violet in color:– amethyst [1]

272 ἀμελέω, *ameleō*, v. GK: *288* [→ *1.1+3199*]. to neglect, ignore:– neglect [2], made light of [1], negligent [1], regarded not [1]

273 ἄμεμπτος, *amemptos*, a. GK: *289* [→ *1.1+3201*]. blameless, faultless:– blameless [3], faultless [1], unblameable [1]

274 ἀμέμπτως, *amemptōs*, adv. GK: *290* [→ *1.1+3201*]. blamelessly:– blameless [1], unblameably [1]

275 ἀμέριμνος, *amerimnos*, a. GK: *291* [→ *1.1+3308*]. free from concern, free from care:– secure (+*4160*) [1], without carefulness [1]

276 ἀμετάθετος, *ametathetos*, a. GK: *292* [→ *1.1+3326+5087*]. unchangeable, unchanging:– immutability [1], immutable [1]

277 ἀμετακίνητος, *ametakinētos*, a. GK: *293* [→ *1.1+3326+2795*]. not moveable, immovable:– unmoveable [1]

278 ἀμεταμέλητος, *ametamelētos*, a. GK: *294* [→ *1.1+3326+3199*]. without regret, so, not revocable:– not repented of [1], without repentance [1]

279 ἀμετανόητος, *ametanoētos*, a. GK: *295* [→ *1.1+3326+3563*]. unrepentant:– impenitent [1]

280 ἄμετρος, *ametros*, a. GK: *296* [→ *1.1+3358*]. beyond limits, immeasurable:– without measure [2]

281 ἀμήν, *amēn*, l.[adv.]. GK: *297*. amen, the truth; a formula of solemn expression of certainty. In the Gospel of John it is doubled in the sayings of Jesus for emphasis:– verily [101], amen [51]

282 ἀμήτωρ, *amētōr*, a. GK: *298* [→ *1.1+3384*]. without a mother:– without mother [1]

283 ἀμίαντος, *amiantos*, a. GK: *299* [→ *1.1+3392*]. pure:– undefiled [4]

284 Ἀμιναδάβ, *Aminadab*, n.pr. GK: *300*. Amminadab, "*my people are generous*":– Aminadab [3]

285 ἄμμος, *ammos*, n. GK: *302*. sand, often used as a figure of things that cannot be counted:– sand [5]

286 ἀμνός, *amnos*, n. GK: *303*. lamb:– lamb [4]

287 ἀμοιβή, *amoibē*, n. GK: *304*. repayment, recompense:– requite (+*591*) [1]

288 ἄμπελος, *ampelos*, n. GK: *306* [→ *289, 290*]. vine, grapevine:– vine [9]

289 ἀμπελουργός, *ampelourgos*, n. GK: *307* [→ *288+2041*]. one who takes care of a vineyard:– dresser of vineyard [1]

290 ἀμπελών, *ampelōn*, n. GK: *308* [→ *288*]. vineyard:– vineyard [23]

291 Ἀμπλίας, *Amplias*, n.pr. GK: *309*. Amplias:– Amplias [1]

292 ἀμύνομαι, *amynomai*, v. GK: *310*. to defend, help, come to the aid of:– defended [1]

293 ἀμφίβληστρον, *amphiblēstron*, n. GK: *312* [→ *906*]. casting net, fishing net (not a dragnet):– net [2]

294 ἀμφιέννυμι, *amphiennymi*, v. GK: *313 & 314* [cf. *2439*]. to dress, clothe:– clothed [2], clothe [2]

295 Ἀμφίπολις, *Amphipolis*, n.pr. GK: *315* [→ *4172*]. Amphipolis, "*a city surrounded* or *a city conspicuous*":– Amphipolis [1]

296 ἄμφοδον, *amphodon*, n. GK: *316* [→ *3598*]. street, usually within a city:– place where two ways met [1]

297 ἀμφότερος, *amphoteros*, a. GK: *317*. both, all:– both [14]

298 ἀμώμητος, *amōmētos*, a. GK: *318* [→ *1.1+3201*]. blameless, unblemished:– blameless [1], without rebuke [1]

299 ἄμωμος, *amōmos*, a. GK: *320* [→ *1.1+3201*]. unblemished, blameless:– without blemish [2], faultless [1], unblameable [1], without blame [1], without fault [1], without spot [1]

300 Ἀμών, *Amōn*, n.pr. GK: *321*. Amon, "*trustworthy*":– Amon [2]

301 Ἀμώς, *Amōs*, n.pr. GK: *322*. Amos, "*burden bearer*":– Amos [1]

302 ἄν, *an*, pt. GK: *323* [→ *1437, 1875, 2579, 3752*]. not easily translated: indicates potential or condition:– whosoever (+*3739*) [32], till (+*2193*) [16], would have [15], would [8], should [7], whatsoever (+*3739*) [7], whatsoever (+*3745*) [6], until (+*2193*) [5], had [4], should have [4], whithersoever (+*3699*) [4], whomsoever (+*3739*) [4], as many as (+*3745*) [3], might [3], soever [3], that (+*3704*) [3], what (+*5101*) [3], whatsoever (+*3739+5100*) [3], whom (+*3739*) [3], whoso (+*3739*) [3], whosoever (+*3739+3956*) [3], whosoever (+*3748*) [3], as (+*5613*) [2], whatsoever (+*302+3739+5100*) [2], when (+*2259*) [2], wheresoever (+*3699*) [2], whosoever (+*3745*) [2], as (+*2530*) [1], as (+*3739+5100*) [1], as oft as (+*3740*) [1], as often as (+*3740*) [1], except (+*1509*) [1], he that (+*3739*) [1], how (+*1063+4459*) [1], howbeit whereinsoever (+*1161+1722+3739*) [1], if [1], may [1], might have [1], once (+*575+3739*) [1], so soon as (+*5613*) [1], soever (+*3739*) [1], that (+*3739*) [1], till (+*891+3739*) [1], whatsoever (+*3748*) [1], when (+*3704*) [1], when (+*5613*) [1], whereunto (+*5101*) [1], wherewith soever (+*3745*) [1], which (+*3748*) [1], which (+*5101*) [1], who (+*5101*) [1], would (+*2172*) [1], wouldest have [1]

303 ἀνά, *ana*, pp. GK: *324* [→ *306, 308, 309, 310, 311, 508, 312, 313, 314, 319, 320, 321, 322, 323, 324, 325, 326, 327, 328, 329, 330, 331, 333, 336, 337, 339, 340, 341, 342, 343, 344, 345, 346, 347, 348, 349, 350, 351, 352, 353, 354, 355, 356, 357, 359, 360, 362, 363, 364, 365, 366, 372, 373, 374, 376, 375, 377, 378, 380, 381, 383, 384, 385, 386, 387, 388, 389, 390, 391, 392, 394, 396, 397, 398, 399, 400, 401, 402, 403, 404, 414, 420, 424, 425, 429, 430, 433, 447, 450, 456, 461, 463, 466, 1815, 1817, 1877, 1878, 1879, 1880, 1881, 1882, 2654, 4320, 4321, 4322, 4323, 4872, 4873, 4874, 4875, cf. 395, 426, 455, 507*]. each, in turn, among:– by [3], apiece [2], every man [2], among (+*3319*) [1], between (+*3319*) [1], by course (+*3313*) [1], in [1], several (+*1520*) [1], through [1]

304 ἀναβαθμός, *anabathmos*, n. GK: *325* [→ *305*]. step; (pl.) a flight of steps:– stairs [2]

305 ἀναβαίνω, *anabainō*, v. GK: *326* [→ *304, 307, 531, 576, 898, 939, 949, 950, 951, 952, 953, 968, 1041, 1224, 1226, 1545, 1684, 1687, 1688, 1910, 1913, 2597, 2600, 2601, 3327, 3845, 3847, 3848, 4260, 4262, 4263, 4264, 4320, 4782, 4819, 4822, 4872, 5233*]. to go up, rise:– went up [23], go up [9], come up [7], ascended up [5], ascended [4], ascend [3], ascending [2], coming up [2], entered [2], going up [2], gone up [2], arise [1], arose [1], ascend up [1], ascendeth up [1], ascendeth [1], ascending up [1], came unto [1], came up [1], came [1], climbed up [1], climbeth up [1], cometh up [1], goeth up [1], grew up [1], groweth up [1], rise up [1], rose up [1], sprang up [1], sprung up [1], went upon [1]

306 ἀναβάλλω, *anaballō*, v. GK: *327* [→ *303+906*]. to adjourn a proceeding (a legal term):– deferred [1]

307 ἀναβιβάζω, *anabibazō*, v. GK: *328* [→ *305*]. to pull up, bring up:– drew [1]

308 ἀναβλέπω, *anablepō*, v. GK: *329* [→ *303+991*]. to look up, receive sight:– received sight [8], receive sight [7], looked up [5], looking up [3], look up [1], looked [1], see [1]

309 ἀνάβλεψις, *anablepsis*, n. GK: *330* [→ *303+991*]. recovery of sight:– recovering of sight [1]

310 ἀναβοάω, *anaboaō*, v. GK: *331* [→ *303+995*]. to cry out:– cried out [1], cried [1], crying aloud [1]

311 ἀναβολή, *anabolē*, n. GK: *332* [→ *303+906*]. delay, postponement:– delay (+*4160*) [1]

312 ἀναγγέλλω, *anangellō*, v. GK: *334* [→ *303+32*]. to tell, report, announce:– shew [4], told [4], declare [2], shewed [2], tell [2], declared [1], rehearsed [1], reported [1], spoken [1]

313 ἀναγεννάω, *anagennaō*, v. GK: *335* [→ *303+1096*]. to give new birth, cause to be born again; used in the sense of spiritual rebirth, similar to being born again/from above:– begotten again [1], born again [1]

314 ἀναγινώσκω, *anaginōskō*, v. GK: *336* [→ *303+1097*]. to read, read aloud:– read [28], readeth [3], readest [2]

315 ἀναγκάζω, *anankazō*, v. GK: *337* [→ *318*]. to compel, force:– compelled [3], constrained [3], compellest [1], compel [1], constrain [1]

316 ἀναγκαῖος, *anankaios*, a. GK: *338* [→ *318*]. necessary, indispensable:– necessary [5], more needful [1], near [1], necessity [1]

317 ἀναγκαστῶς, *anankastōs*, adv. GK: *339* [→ *318*]. a must, by compulsion:– by constraint [1]

318 ἀνάγκη, *anankē*, n. GK: *340* [→ *315, 316, 317, 1876*]. necessity; distress, hardship:– necessity [7], distress [3], must needs [2], necessities [2], necessary [1], needeth (+*2250*) [1], needful (+*2192*) [1], needs [1]

319 ἀναγνωρίζω, *anagnōrizō*, v. GK: *341* [→ *303+1097*]. to tell, make known again:– made known [1]

320 ἀνάγνωσις, *anagnōsis*, n. GK: *342* [→ *303+1097*]. reading, public reading:– reading [3]

321 ἀνάγω, *anagō*, v. GK: *343* [→ *303+71*]. to lead up, bring up; (mid.) to put out to sea:– brought [3], launched [3], departed [2], loosed [2], sailed [2], bring forth [1], bring up again [1], brought again [1], depart [1], launched forth [1], led up [1], led [1], loosing [1], offered [1], sail [1], set forth [1], taking up [1]

322 ἀναδείκνυμι, *anadeiknymi*, v. GK: *344* [→ *303+1166*]. to show, appoint:– appointed [1], shew [1]

323 ἀνάδειξις, *anadeixis*, n. GK: *345* [→ *303+1166*]. public appearance:– shewing [1]

324 ἀναδέχομαι, *anadechomai*, v. GK: *346* [→ *303+1209*]. to receive, welcome:– received [2]

325 ἀναδίδωμι, *anadidōmi*, v. GK: *347* [→ *303+1325*]. to deliver, hand over:– delivered [1]

326 ἀναζάω, *anazaō*, v. GK: *348* [→ *303+2198*]. to become alive again:– alive again [2], revived [2], lived again [1]

327 ἀναζητέω, *anazēteō*, v. GK: *349* [→ *303+2212*]. to look for, search for:– seek [1], sought [1]

328 ἀναζώννυμι, *anazōnnymi*, v. GK: *350* [→ *303+2224*]. to gird (the loins), bind (to prepare for action); used fig. of "girding the loins of the mind" (1Pe 1:13) to prepare mentally for action:– gird up [1]

329 ἀναζωπυρέω, *anazōpyreō*, v. GK: *351* [→ *303+2198+4442*]. to fan a flame, rekindle:– stir up [1]

330 ἀναθάλλω, *anathallō*, v. GK: *352* [→ *303+2337*]. to renew, cause to grow or bloom again:– flourished again [1]

331 **ἀνάθεμα, *anathema***, n. GK: *353* [→ *332, 334, 2652, 2653*]. curse, oath; one cursed:– accursed [4], anathema [1], bound under a great curse (*+332*) [1]

332 **ἀναθεματίζω, *anathematizō***, v. GK: *354* [→ *331*]. to bind with an oath:– bound under a curse [1], bound under a great curse (*+331*) [1], bound with an oath [1], curse [1]

333 **ἀναθεωρέω, *anatheōreō***, v. GK: *355* [→ *303+2334*]. to look carefully at:– beheld [1], considering [1]

334 **ἀνάθημα, *anathēma***, n. GK: *356* [→ *331*]. gifts dedicated to God, devoted exclusively to the service of deity:– gifts [1]

335 **ἀναίδεια, *anaideia***, n. GK: *357* [→ *1.1+127*]. boldness:– importunity [1]

336 **ἀναίρεσις, *anairesis***, n. GK: *358* [→ *303+138*]. death:– death [2]

337 **ἀναιρέω, *anaireō***, v. GK: *359* [→ *303+138*]. to kill, put to death; (mid.) take for oneself:– kill [6], killed [4], slain [3], slew [3], put to death [2], slay [2], didst [1], taketh away [1], took up [1]

338 **ἀναίτιος, *anaitios***, a. GK: *360* [→ *1.1+156*]. innocent:– blameless [1], guiltless [1]

339 **ἀνακαθίζω, *anakathizō***, v. GK: *361* [→ *303+2523*]. to sit up (from a reclining or lying position):– sat up [2]

340 **ἀνακαινίζω, *anakainizō***, v. GK: *362* [→ *303+2537*]. to bring back, restore:– renew [1]

341 **ἀνακαινόω, *anakainoō***, v. GK: *363* [→ *303+2537*]. to renew:– renewed [2]

342 **ἀνακαίνωσις, *anakainōsis***, n. GK: *364* [→ *303+2537*]. renewal:– renewing [2]

343 **ἀνακαλύπτω, *anakalyptō***, v. GK: *365* [→ *303+2572*]. to unveil, uncover:– open [1], untaken away (*+3361*) [1]

344 **ἀνακάμπτω, *anakamptō***, v. GK: *366* [→ *303+2578*]. to return, come back:– return [2], returned [1], turn again [1]

345 **ἀνάκειμαι, *anakeimai***, v. GK: *367* [→ *303+2749*]. to recline for a meal, dine (reclining was the normal posture at meals):– sat at meat [4], guests [2], sitteth at meat [2], leaning [1], lying [1], sat down [1], sat [1], set down [1], table [1]

346 **ἀνακεφαλαιόω, *anakephalaioō***, v. GK: *368* [→ *303+2776*]. to bring together under one head, summarize:– briefly comprehended [1], gather together in one [1]

347 **ἀνακλίνω, *anaklinō***, v. GK: *369* [→ *303+2827*]. to cause to lie down, recline (to eat):– sit down [3], laid [1], made sit down [1], make sit down to meat [1], make sit down [1], sat down to meat [1]

348 **ἀνακόπτω, *anakoptō***, v. GK: *370* [→ *303+2875*]. to hinder, restrain:– hinder [1]

349 **ἀνακράζω, *anakrazō***, v. GK: *371* [→ *303+2896*]. to cry out:– cried out [5]

350 **ἀνακρίνω, *anakrinō***, v. GK: *373* [→ *303+2919*]. to examine, judge (in both a general and a legal sense):– examined [4], judged [3], asking question [2], judgeth [2], discerned [1], examine [1], examining [1], judge [1], searched [1]

351 **ἀνάκρισις, *anakrisis***, n. GK: *374* [→ *303+2919*]. investigation:– examination [1]

352 **ἀνακύπτω, *anakyptō***, v. GK: *376* [→ *303+2955*]. to straighten up, stand erect:– lift up [3], look up [1]

353 **ἀναλαμβάνω, *analambanō***, v. GK: *377* [→ *303+2983*]. to take up, lift up, bring up:– received up [3], taken up [3], take in [1], take unto [1], take [1], taking [1], took in [1], took up [1], took [1]

354 **ἀνάλημψις, *analēmpsis***, n. GK: *378* [→ *303+2983*]. taking up, ascension:– received up [1]

355 **ἀναλίσκω, *analiskō***, v. GK: *379 & 384* [→ *303+259*]. to destroy, consume (with a possible implication of being used up):– consume [2], consumed [1]

356 **ἀναλογία, *analogia***, n. GK: *381* [→ *303+3004*]. proportion, right relationship:– proportion [1]

357 **ἀναλογίζομαι, *analogizomai***, v. GK: *382* [→ *303+3004*]. to consider, think carefully:– consider [1]

358 **ἄναλος, *analos***, a. GK: *383* [→ *1.1+217*]. not salty:– lost saltness [1]

359 **ἀνάλυσις, *analysis***, n. GK: *385* [→ *303+3089*]. departure (death):– departure [1]

360 **ἀναλύω, *analyō***, v. GK: *386* [→ *303+3089*]. to depart (die), return:– depart [1], return [1]

361 **ἀναμάρτητος, *anamartētos***, a. GK: *387* [→ *1.1+264*]. without sin:– without sin [1]

362 **ἀναμένω, *anamenō***, v. GK: *388* [→ *303+3306*]. to wait for, expect:– wait for [1]

363 **ἀναμιμνήσκω, *anamimnēskō***, v. GK: *389* [→ *303+3421*]. to remember, remind:– bring into remembrance [1], call to remembrance [1], called to mind [1], calling to remembrance [1], put in remembrance [1], remembereth [1]

364 **ἀνάμνησις, *anamnēsis***, n. GK: *390* [→ *303+3421*]. reminder, remembrance:– remembrance [4]

365 **ἀνανεόομαι, *ananeoomai***, v. GK: *391* [→ *303+3501*]. to be made new, renewed:– renewed [1]

366 **ἀνανήφω, *ananēphō***, v. GK: *392* [→ *303+3525*]. to come to one's senses:– recover [1]

367 **Ἁνανίας, *Hananias***, n.pr. GK: *393*. Ananias, "*Yahweh is gracious*":– Ananias [11]

368 **ἀναντίρρητος, *anantirrētos***, a. GK: *394* [→ *1.1+473+4487*]. undeniable, indisputable:– cannot be spoken against [1]

369 **ἀναντιρρήτως, *anantirrētōs***, adv. GK: *395* [→ *1.1+473+4487*]. without raising any objection, indisputable:– without gainsaying [1]

370 **ἀνάξιος, *anaxios***, a. GK: *396* [→ *1.1+514*]. not competent, unworthy:– unworthy [1]

371 **ἀναξίως, *anaxiōs***, adv. GK: *397* [→ *1.1+514*]. in an unworthy manner, possibly in a careless manner:– unworthily [2]

372 **ἀνάπαυσις, *anapausis***, n. GK: *398* [→ *303+3973*]. rest, resting place:– rest [4], rest (*+2192*) [1]

373 **ἀναπαύω, *anapauō***, v. GK: *399* [→ *303+3973*]. to rest, be refreshed; (act.) to give rest:– refreshed [3], rest [3], take rest [2], give rest [1], refresh [1], resteth [1], take ease [1]

374 **ἀναπείθω, *anapeithō***, v. GK: *400* [→ *303+3982*]. to persuade, with an implication of inciting resistance:– persuadeth [1]

375 **ἀναπέμπω, *anapempō***, v. GK: *402* [→ *303+3992*]. to send:– sent again [2], sent [2]

376 **ἀνάπειρος, *anapeiros***, a. GK: *401* [→ *303*]. crippled:– maimed [2]

377 **ἀναπίπτω, *anapiptō***, v. GK: *404* [→ *303+4098*]. recline, sit down, lie down (usually referring to the normal posture at meals):– sit down [4], sat down [3], leaned [1], sat down to meat [1], set down [1], sit down to meat [1]

378 **ἀναπληρόω, *anaplēroō***, v. GK: *405* [→ *303+4137*]. to fulfill, make complete:– fill up [1], fulfilled [1], fulfil [1], occupieth [1], supplied [1], supply [1]

379 **ἀναπολόγητος, *anapologētos***, a. GK: *406* [→ *1.1+575+3004*]. without excuse:– inexcusable [1], without excuse [1]

380 **ἀναπτύσσω, *anaptyssō***, v. GK: *408* [→ *303+4428*]. to unroll (a scroll):– opened [1]

381 **ἀνάπτω, *anaptō***, v. GK: *409* [→ *303+681*]. to set on fire:– kindled [2], kindleth [1]

382 **ἀναρίθμητος, *anarithmētos***, a. GK: *410* [→ *1.1+706*]. countless:– innumerable [1]

383 **ἀνασείω, *anaseiō***, v. GK: *411* [→ *303+4579*]. to stir up, incite:– moved [1], stirreth up [1]

384 **ἀνασκευάζω, *anaskeuazō***, v. GK: *412* [→ *303+4632*]. to trouble, upset:– subverting [1]

385 **ἀνασπάω, *anaspaō***, v. GK: *413* [→ *303+4685*]. to pull up, draw out:– drawn up [1], pull out [1]

386 **ἀνάστασις, *anastasis***, n. GK: *414* [→ *303+2476*]. resurrection, rising to life; from the base meaning of the act of rising from a prone or sitting position to a standing position. In the NT it means returning to life after death, usually referring to the raising to life of Jesus Christ:– resurrection [39], raised to life again (*+1537*) [1], rise [1], rising again [1]

387 **ἀναστατόω, *anastatoō***, v. GK: *415* [→ *303+2476*]. to cause trouble, start a revolt:– madest an uproar [1], trouble [1], turned upside down [1]

388 **ἀνασταυρόω, *anastauroō***, v. GK: *416* [→ *303+4716*]. to crucify again:– crucify afresh [1]

389 **ἀναστενάζω, *anastenazō***, v. GK: *417* [→ *303+4728*]. to sigh deeply:– sighed deeply [1]

390 **ἀναστρέφω, *anastrephō***, v. GK: *418* [→ *303+4762*]. to conduct oneself, live (in a certain way); to return:– had conversation [2], live [2], abode [1], behave [1], overthrew [1], pass [1], returned [1], return [1], used [1]

391 **ἀναστροφή, *anastrophē***, n. GK: *419* [→ *303+4762*]. way of life, behavior:– conversation [13]

392 **ἀνατάσσομαι, *anatassomai***, v. GK: *421* [→ *303+5021*]. to draw up (an account), compile:– set forth in order [1]

393 **ἀνατέλλω, *anatellō***, v. GK: *422* [→ *395*]. to rise, dawn:– up [2], arise [1], maketh to rise [1], rise out [1], risen [1], rising [1], sprang [1], sprung up [1]

394 **ἀνατίθημι, *anatithēmi***, v. GK: *423* [→ *303+5087*]. to set before, declare before:– communicated [1], declared [1]

395 **ἀνατολή, *anatolē***, n. GK: *424* [→ *393, 1816, cf. 303*]. east, rising of the sun; note that the east is the compass direction of orientation in the ancient Near East, just as the north is in the modern western world:– east [7], east (*+2246*) [2], dayspring [1]

396 **ἀνατρέπω, *anatrepō***, v. GK: *426* [→ *303+5157*]. to overturn, destroy:– overthrow [1], subvert [1]

397 **ἀνατρέφω, *anatrephō***, v. GK: *427* [→ *303+5142*]. to bring up, care for:– brought up [1], nourished up [1], nourished [1]

398 **ἀναφαίνω, *anaphainō***, v. GK: *428* [→ *303+5316*]. to appear:– appear [1], discovered [1]

399 **ἀναφέρω, *anapherō***, v. GK: *429* [→ *303+5342*]. to lead up, offer (a sacrifice), bear (sin):– offer up [2], bare [1], bear [1], bringeth up [1], carried up [1], leadeth up [1], offered up [1], offered [1], offer [1]

400 **ἀναφωνέω, *anaphōneō***, v. GK: *430* [→ *303+5456*]. to exclaim, cry out loudly:– spake out [1]

401 **ἀνάχυσις, *anachysis***, n. GK: *431* [→ *1632; cf. 303*]. flood, wide stream:– excess [1]

402 **ἀναχωρέω, *anachōreō***, v. GK: *432* [→ *303+5562*]. to withdraw, leave:– departed [8], withdrew [2], give place [1], gone aside [1], turned aside [1], went aside [1]

403 **ἀνάψυξις, *anapsyxis***, n. GK: *433* [→ *303+5594*]. refreshment, relaxation, relief:– refreshing [1]

404 **ἀναψύχω, *anapsychō***, v. GK: *434* [→ *303+5594*]. to refresh, revive:– refreshed [1]

405 **ἀνδραποδιστής, *andrapodistēs***, n. GK: *435* [→ *435+4228*]. slave trader, kidnapper:– menstealers [1]

406 **Ἀνδρέας, *Andreas***, n.pr. GK: *436* [→ *435*]. Andrew, "*manly*":– Andrew [13]

407 **ἀνδρίζομαι, *andrizomai***, v. GK: *437* [→ *435*]. to act courageously:– quit like men [1]

408 **Ἀνδρόνικος, *Andronikos***, n.pr. GK: *438* [→ *435+3529*]. Andronicus, "*victor over men*":– Andronicus [1]

409 **ἀνδροφόνος, *androphonos***, n. GK: *439* [→ *435+5408*]. murderer:– manslayers [1]

410 **ἀνέγκλητος, *anenklētos***, a. GK: *441* [→ *1.1+1722+2564*]. blameless, free from accusation:– blameless [4], unreproveable [1]

411 **ἀνεκδιήγητος, *anekdiēgētos***, a. GK: *442* [→ *1.1+1537+1223+71*]. indescribable, with the associative meanings of marvelous and wonderful:– unspeakable [1]

412 **ἀνεκλάλητος, *aneklalētos***, a. GK: *443* [→ *1.1+1537+2980*]. inexpressible:– unspeakable [1]

413 **ἀνέκλειπτος, *anekleiptos***, a. GK: *444* [→ *1.1+1537+3007*]. not exhaustible, unfailing:– faileth not [1]

414 **ἀνεκτός, *anektos***, a. GK: *445* [→ *303+2192*]. bearable, tolerable; used only in the comparative: more bearable:– more tolerable [6]

415 **ἀνελεήμων, *aneleēmōn***, a. GK: *446* [→ *1.1+1656*]. ruthless, merciless:– unmerciful [1]

416 **ἀνεμίζω, *anemizō***, v. GK: *448* [→ *417*]. to be moved by the wind:– driven with the wind [1]

417 **ἄνεμος, *anemos***, n. GK: *449* [→ *416*]. wind, gale:– wind [20], winds [11]

418 **ἀνένδεκτος, *anendektos***, a. GK: *450* [→ *1.1+1722+1209*]. impossible:– impossible [1]

419 ἀνεξεραύνητος, anexeraunētos, a. GK: *451* [→ *1.1+1537+2045*]. unsearchable, inscrutable:– unsearchable [1]

420 ἀνεξίκακος, anexikakos, a. GK: *452* [→ *303+2192+2556*]. not resentful, patient:– patient [1]

421 ἀνεξιχνίαστος, anexichniastos, a. GK: *453* [→ *1.1+1537+2487*]. unsearchable, incomprehensible:– past finding out [1], unsearchable [1]

422 ἀνεπαίσχυντος, anepaischyntos, a. GK: *454* [→ *1.1+1909+150*]. unashamed:– needeth not to be ashamed [1]

423 ἀνεπίλημπτος, anepilēmptos, a. GK: *455* [→ *1.1+1909+2983*]. above reproach, not open to blame:– blameless [2], unrebukeable [1]

424 ἀνέρχομαι, anerchomai, v. GK: *456* [→ *303+2064*]. to go up:– went up [3]

425 ἄνεσις, anesis, n. GK: *457* [→ *863; cf. 303*]. rest, relaxation, relief:– rest [3], eased [1], liberty [1]

426 ἀνετάζω, anetazō, v. GK: *458* [→ *1833; cf. 303*]. to question, examine, interrogate:– examined [2]

427 ἄνευ, aneu, pp.*. GK: *459*. without, apart from:– without [3]

428 ἀνεύθετος, aneuthetos, a. GK: *460* [→ *1.1+2095+5087*]. unsuitable, poor:– commodious [1]

429 ἀνευρίσκω, aneuriskō, v. GK: *461* [→ *303+2147*]. to find:– finding [1], found [1]

430 ἀνέχομαι, anechomai, v. GK: *462* [→ *303+2192*]. to put up with, endure:– suffer [7], bear with [4], endure [2], forbearing [2]

431 ἀνεψιός, anepsios, n. GK: *463*. cousin:– sister's son [1]

432 ἄνηθον, anēthon, n. GK: *464*. dill, a plant used for seasoning:– anise [1]

433 ἀνήκω, anēkō, v. GK: *465* [→ *303+2240*]. to be fitting, proper; to do one's duty:– convenient [2], fit [1]

434 ἀνήμερος, anēmeros, a. GK: *466* [→ *1.1*]. brutal, savage:– fierce [1]

435 ἀνήρ, anēr, n. GK: *467* [→ *405, 406, 407, 408, 409, 3527, 5220, 5362*]. man, male, husband; usually an adult male, but in some contexts the emphasis is on maturity rather than gender (1Co 13:11; Eph 4:13; Jas 3:2):– men [79], man [75], husband [38], husbands [12], sirs [6], fellows [1], man's [1], murderer (*+5406*) [1]

436 ἀνθίστημι, anthistēmi, v. GK: *468* [→ *473+2476*]. to resist, oppose, rebel, withstand:– resist [7], withstood [4], resisted [1], resisteth [1], withstand [1]

437 ἀνθομολογέομαι, anthomologeomai, v. GK: *469* [→ *473+3670*]. to give thanks, praise:– gave thanks unto [1]

438 ἄνθος, anthos, n. GK: *470*. flower, blossom:– flower [4]

439 ἀνθρακιά, anthrakia, n. GK: *471* [→ *440*]. charcoal fire:– fire of coals [2]

440 ἄνθραξ, anthrax, n. GK: *472* [→ *439*]. coal, charcoal:– coals [1]

441 ἀνθρωπάρεσκος, anthrōpareskos, a. GK: *473* [→ *444+700*]. one who wins favor, who pleases people:– menpleasers [2]

442 ἀνθρώπινος, anthrōpinos, a. GK: *474* [→ *444*]. human, common to mankind:– man's [3], after the manner of men [1], common to man [1], of mankind [1], of man [1]

443 ἀνθρωποκτόνος, anthrōpoktonos, n. GK: *475* [→ *444+615*]. murderer:– murderer [3]

444 ἄνθρωπος, anthrōpos, n. GK: *476* [→ *441, 442, 443, 5363, 5364*]. human being, person; humankind, people; man, husband; used of human beings in contrast to animals or deity; in some contexts it is used of male/husband in contrast to female/wife. "The Son of Man" is an OT phrase usually meaning "human being," that in the NT is used almost exclusively as a messianic title (see Da 7:13), emphasizing Jesus' humanity. "The outer person" is the corporeal body in contrast to "the inner (or hidden) person" of the spirit:– man [346], men [190], man's [10], men's [5], certain [2], Romans (*+4514*) [1], enemy (*+2190*) [1], householder (*+3617*) [1], men (*+3686*) [1], nobleman (*+2104*) [1]

445 ἀνθυπατεύω, anthypateuō, v. GK: *477* [→ *446*]. to be proconsul:– deputy [1]

446 ἀνθύπατος, anthypatos, n. GK: *478* [→ *445; cf. 473*]. proconsul:– deputy [3], deputies [1]

447 ἀνίημι, aniēmi, v. GK: *479* [→ *863; cf. 303*]. loosen, untie; leave, abandon:– loosed [2], forbearing [1], leave [1]

448 ἀνίλεως, anileōs, a. GK: *447 & 480* [→ *1.1+1656*]. merciless:– without mercy [1]

449 ἄνιπτος, aniptos, a. GK: *481* [→ *1.1+3538*]. unwashed:– unwashen [3]

450 ἀνίστημι, anistēmi, v. GK: *482* [→ *303+2476*]. to get up, stand up, come back to life:– arose [23], rise [14], arise [13], rose up [13], raise up [8], rise again [8], stood up [7], rose [5], raised up [4], risen again [4], rise up [2], risen [2], arise up [1], ariseth [1], lift up [1], raised up again [1], raised [1], rising up [1], rising [1], rose again [1], stand up [1], stand [1]

451 Ἅννα, Hanna, n.pr. GK: *483*. Anna, "*grace*":– Anna [1]

452 Ἅννας, Hannas, n.pr. GK: *484*. Annas, "*grace*":– Annas [4]

453 ἀνόητος, anoētos, a. GK: *485 & 493* [→ *1.1+3563*]. foolish, senseless:– foolish [4], fools [1], unwise [1]

454 ἄνοια, anoia, n. GK: *486* [→ *1.1+3563*]. folly, senselessness; fury:– folly [1], madness [1]

455 ἀνοίγω, anoigō, v. GK: *487 & 1986* [→ *457, 1272, 455; cf. 303*]. to open:– opened [53], open [21], openeth [3]

456 ἀνοικοδομέω, anoikodomeō, v. GK: *488* [→ *303+3624+1430*]. to rebuild:– build again [2]

457 ἄνοιξις, anoixis, n. GK: *489* [→ *455*]. (the act of) opening:– open [1]

458 ἀνομία, anomia, n. GK: *490* [→ *1.1+3551*]. wickedness, lawlessness, lawless deed:– iniquity [9], iniquities [3], transgresseth law (*+4160*) [1], transgression of law [1], unrighteousness [1]

459 ἄνομος, anomos, a. GK: *491* [→ *1.1+3551*]. without law, transgressing law (by not regarding it); as a noun this can mean a Gentile (without God's covenant law); Paul uses the definite article to speak of "the lawless one" (1Th. 2:8), often considered a title of the antichrist:– without law [4], transgressors [2], wicked [2], lawless [1], unlawful [1]

460 ἀνόμως, anomōs, adv. GK: *492* [→ *1.1+3551*]. apart from law, without law:– without law [2]

461 ἀνορθόω, anorthoō, v. GK: *494* [→ *303+3717*]. to restore, rebuild, strengthen:– lift up [1], made straight [1], set up [1]

462 ἀνόσιος, anosios, a. GK: *495* [→ *1.1+3741*]. unholy, wicked:– unholy [2]

463 ἀνοχή, anochē, n. GK: *496* [→ *303+2192*]. tolerance, forbearance, clemency:– forbearance [2]

464 ἀνταγωνίζομαι, antagōnizomai, v. GK: *497* [→ *473+73*]. to struggle against:– striving [1]

465 ἀντάλλαγμα, antallagma, n. GK: *498* [→ *473+236*]. something given in exchange:– in exchange for [2]

466 ἀνταναπληρόω, antanaplēroō, v. GK: *499* [→ *473+303+4137*]. to fill up, complete:– fill up [1]

467 ἀνταποδίδωμι, antapodidōmi, v. GK: *500* [→ *473+575+1325*]. to repay, return:– recompense [3], recompensed [2], render again [1], repay [1]

468 ἀνταπόδομα, antapodoma, n. GK: *501* [→ *473+575+1325*]. repayment, retribution:– recompence [2]

469 ἀνταπόδοσις, antapodosis, n. GK: *502* [→ *473+575+1325*]. reward, repayment:– reward [1]

470 ἀνταποκρίνομαι, antapokrinomai, v. GK: *503* [→ *473+575+2919*]. to talk back, answer (with implication of contradicting someone):– answer again [1], repliest against [1]

471 ἀντέπω, antepō, v. GK: *515* [→ *473+3004*]. to speak against, talk back, contradict:– gainsay [1], say against [1]

472 ἀντέχω, antechō, v. GK: *504* [→ *473+2192*]. to be devoted, hold firmly to; pay attention to:– hold to [2], holding fast [1], support [1]

473 ἀντί, anti, pp. GK: *505* [→ *368, 369, 436, 437, 464, 465, 466, 467, 468, 469, 470, 471, 472, 474, 475, 476, 477, 478, 479, 480, 481, 482, 483, 484, 485, 486, 487, 488, 489, 492, 493, 494, 495, 496, 497, 498, 499, 500, 503, 528, 529, 1725, 2658, 4876, 4877, 4878, 5221, 5222; cf. 446, 1725*]. in exchange for (often as a sign of benefaction), in place of (often as a sign of contrast), instead of (often as a sign of an exchange of a relationship), one after another (often as a sign of purpose or result). Note that this preposition used in absolute does not mean to be "against" or "in opposition to" something:– for [14], because (*+3739*) [4], for cause [1], for that (*+3588*) [1], in the room of [1], therefore (*+3739*) [1]

474 ἀντιβάλλω, antiballō, v. GK: *506* [→ *473+906*]. to discuss, exchange (words):– have [1]

475 ἀντιδιατίθημι, antidiatithēmi, v. GK: *507* [→ *473+1223+5087*]. to oppose:– oppose themselves [1]

476 ἀντίδικος, antidikos, n. GK: *508* [→ *473+1349*]. enemy, opponent (in battle or in court):– adversary [5]

477 ἀντίθεσις, antithesis, n. GK: *509* [→ *473+5087*]. opposition, objection:– oppositions [1]

478 ἀντικαθίστημι, antikathistēmi, v. GK: *510* [→ *473+2596+2476*]. to resist, oppose, contest against:– resisted [1]

479 ἀντικαλέω, antikaleō, v. GK: *511* [→ *473+2564*]. to invite in reciprocation:– bid again [1]

480 ἀντίκειμαι, antikeimai, v. GK: *512* [→ *473+2749*]. to be an opponent, in conflict:– adversaries [4], contrary [2], adversary [1], opposeth [1]

481 ἄντικρυς, antikrys, adv. GK: *513* [→ *473*]. opposite of, in proximity to:– over against [1]

482 ἀντιλαμβάνω, antilambanō, v. GK: *514* [→ *473+2983*]. to help, come to the aid of, benefit:– holpen [1], partakers [1], support [1]

483 ἀντιλέγω, antilegō, v. GK: *515* [→ *473+3004*]. to speak against, talk back, contradict:– spake against [2], spoken against [2], answering again [1], contradicting [1], deny [1], gainsayers [1], gainsaying [1], speaketh against [1]

484 ἀντίλημψις, antilēmpsis, n. GK: *516* [→ *473+2983*]. help, ability to aid:– helps [1]

485 ἀντιλογία, antilogia, n. GK: *517* [→ *473+3004*]. argument, opposition, rebellion:– contradiction [2], gainsaying [1], strife [1]

486 ἀντιλοιδορέω, antiloidoreō, v. GK: *518* [→ *473+3060*]. to retaliate:– reviled again [1]

487 ἀντίλυτρον, antilytron, n. GK: *519* [→ *473+3089*]. ransom; the purchase price to bring liberation from oppression; it is the means to redemption. This refers to Jesus (in person and work) as the price of salvation:– ransom [1]

488 ἀντιμετρέω, antimetreō, v. GK: *520* [→ *473+3358*]. to measure in return:– measured again [2]

489 ἀντιμισθία, antimisthia, n. GK: *521* [→ *473+3408*]. an exchange; penalty:– recompence [2]

490 Ἀντιόχεια, Antiocheia, n.pr. GK: *522* [→ *491*]. Antioch:– Antioch [18]

491 Ἀντιοχεύς, Antiocheus, n.pr.g. GK: *523* [→ *490*]. from Antioch:– Antioch [1]

492 ἀντιπαρέρχομαι, antiparerchomai, v. GK: *524* [→ *473+3844+2064*]. to pass by on the opposite side:– passed by on the other side [2]

493 Ἀντιπᾶς, Antipas, n.pr. GK: *525* [→ *473+3962*]. Antipas:– Antipas [1]

494 Ἀντιπατρίς, Antipatris, n.pr. GK: *526* [→ *473+3962*]. Antipatris:– Antipatris [1]

495 ἀντιπέρα, antipera, adv. GK: *527* [→ *473+4008*]. across from, opposite of:– over against [1]

496 ἀντιπίπτω, antipiptō, v. GK: *528* [→ *473+4098*]. to resist, oppose:– resist [1]

497 ἀντιστρατεύομαι, antistrateuomai, v. GK: *529* [→ *473+4756*]. to wage war against:– warring against [1]

498 ἀντιτάσσω, antitassō, v. GK: *530* [→ *473+5021*]. to oppose, rebel, resist:– resisteth [3], opposed [1], resist [1]

499 ἀντίτυπος, antitypos, a. GK: *531* [→ *473+5180*]. copy, representation:– figures [1], like figure [1]

500 ἀντίχριστος, antichristos, n. GK: *532* [→ *473+5547*]. antichrist:– antichrist [4], antichrists [1]

501 ἀντλέω, antleō, v. GK: *533* [→ *502*]. to draw (water):– draw [2], draw out [1], drew [1]

502 ἄντλημα, antlēma, n. GK: *534* [→ *501*]. container to draw water with:– draw with [1]

503 ἀντοφθαλμέω, antophthalmeō, v. GK: *535* [→ *473+3788*]. to head into, face (the wind):– bear up into [1]

504 ἄνυδρος, anydros, a. GK: *536* [→ *1.1+5204*]. arid, without water:– dry [2], without water [2]

505 **ἀνυπόκριτος**, ***anypokritos***, a. GK: *537* [→ *1.1+5259+2919*]. sincere, genuine, without hypocrisy; of good character, lacking pretense and prideful show:– unfeigned [4], without dissimulation [1], without hypocrisy [1]

506 **ἀνυπότακτος**, ***anypotaktos***, a. GK: *538* [→ *1.1+5259+5021*]. rebellious, disobedient; not made subject to, independent:– unruly [2], disobedient [1], not put under [1]

507 **ἄνω**, ***anō***, adv.pl. GK: *539* [→ *509, 510, 511, 1274, 1883, 5231; cf. 303*]. above, upward, heavenward, top:– above [5], up [2], high [1], the brim [1]

508 **ἀνάγαιον**, ***anagaion***, n. GK: *333* [→ *303+1093*]. upper room:– upper room [2]

509 **ἄνωθεν**, ***anōthen***, adv.pl. GK: *540* [→ *507*]. from above; from the beginning; again, anew:– from above [5], again [3], top [3], from beginning [1], from the very first [1]

510 **ἀνωτερικός**, ***anōterikos***, a. GK: *541* [→ *507*]. interior, upper (regions):– upper [1]

511 **ἀνώτερος**, ***anōteros***, a. GK: *542* [→ *507*]. higher, better in social standing; earlier, previously, first:– above [1], higher [1]

512 **ἀνωφελής**, ***anōphelēs***, a. GK: *543* [→ *1.1+5623*]. unprofitable, useless:– unprofitableness [1], unprofitable [1]

513 **ἀξίνη**, ***axinē***, n. GK: *544* [→ *2608*]. ax:– axe [2]

514 **ἄξιος**, ***axios***, a. GK: *545* [→ *370, 371, 515, 516, 2661; cf. 71*]. worthy, deserving, in keeping with, corresponding to:– worthy [35], meet for [2], meet [2], due reward [1], unworthy (*+3756*) [1]

515 **ἀξιόω**, ***axioō***, v. GK: *546* [→ *514*]. to consider worthy, consider wise or fitting:– counted worthy [2], thought worthy [2], count worthy [1], desire [1], thought good [1]

516 **ἀξίως**, ***axiōs***, adv. GK: *547* [→ *514*]. in a worthy manner, suitably:– worthy [3], becometh [2], after a sort [1]

517 **ἀόρατος**, ***aoratos***, a. GK: *548* [→ *1.1+3708*]. invisible, not seen:– invisible [5]

518 **ἀπαγγέλλω**, ***apangellō***, v. GK: *33 & 550* [→ *575+32*]. to tell, report, proclaim, announce, bring news, be a messenger:– told [19], shewed [6], tell [6], shew [4], declare [2], bring word again [1], bring word [1], declared [1], reported [1], report [1], shew again [1], told how [1]

519 **ἀπάγχω**, ***apanchō***, v. GK: *551*. to hang (oneself):– hanged [1]

520 **ἀπάγω**, ***apagō***, v. GK: *552* [→ *575+71*]. to lead away, bring before (an official):– led away [8], lead away [2], leadeth [2], bring [1], carried away [1], put to death [1], took away [1]

521 **ἀπαίδευτος**, ***apaideutos***, a. GK: *553* [→ *1.1+3816*]. stupid, uneducated:– unlearned [1]

522 **ἀπαίρω**, ***apairō***, v. GK: *554* [→ *575+142*]. to take away:– taken away [2], taken from [1]

523 **ἀπαιτέω**, ***apaiteō***, v. GK: *555* [→ *575+154*]. to demand back:– ask again [1], required [1]

524 **ἀπαλγέω**, ***apalgeō***, v. GK: *556*. to lose all sensitivity, become callous:– past feeling [1]

525 **ἀπαλλάσσω**, ***apallassō***, v. GK: *557* [→ *575+236*]. (act.) to set free, release; (pass.) to be reconciled, come to a settlement (in court); to be cured:– delivered [1], deliver [1], departed [1]

526 **ἀπαλλοτριόω**, ***apallotrioō***, v. GK: *558* [→ *575+243*]. to be excluded, separated, alienated:– alienated [2], aliens [1]

527 **ἁπαλός**, ***hapalos***, a. GK: *559*. tender (referring to sprouts):– tender [2]

528 **ἀπαντάω**, ***apantaō***, v. GK: *560* [→ *575+473*]. to meet, encounter:– met [5], meet [2]

529 **ἀπάντησις**, ***apantēsis***, n. GK: *561* [→ *575+473*]. (the act of) meeting, encountering:– meet [4]

530 **ἅπαξ**, ***hapax***, adv. GK: *562* [→ *2178*]. once, once more, once for all; the Greek idiom "once and yet twice" means to do something repeatedly, "again and again" (Php 4:16):– once [15]

531 **ἀπαράβατος**, ***aparabatos***, a. GK: *563* [→ *1.1+3844+305*]. permanent, unchangeable:– unchangeable [1]

532 **ἀπαρασκεύαστος**, ***aparaskeuastos***, a. GK: *564* [→ *1.1+3844+4632*]. unprepared, unready:– unprepared [1]

533 **ἀπαρνέομαι**, ***aparneomai***, v. GK: *565* [→ *575+720*]. to disown, deny, repudiate:– deny [11], denied [2]

534 **ἀπάρτι**, ***aparti***, adv. [pp.+adv.]. GK: *567* [→ *575+737*]. from now on, again:– henceforth [1]

535 **ἀπαρτισμός**, ***apartismos***, n. GK: *568* [→ *575+737*]. completion, finishing:– finish [1]

536 **ἀπαρχή**, ***aparchē***, n. GK: *569* [→ *575+757*]. firstfruits, the first of any crop or livestock offered to God before the rest could be used:– firstfruits [7], firstfruit [1]

537 **ἅπας**, ***hapas***, a. GK: *570* [→ *260+3956*]. all, every, whole:– all [39], whole [3], every one [1], every [1]

538 **ἀπατάω**, ***apataō***, v. GK: *572* [→ *539*]. to deceive, cheat, trick:– deceived [2], deceiveth [1], deceive [1]

539 **ἀπάτη**, ***apatē***, n. GK: *573* [→ *538, 1818, 5422, 5423*]. deception, deceitfulness:– deceitfulness [3], deceitful [1], deceit [1], deceivableness [1], deceivings [1]

540 **ἀπάτωρ**, ***apatōr***, a. GK: *574* [→ *1.1+3962*]. fatherless:– without father [1]

541 **ἀπαύγασμα**, ***apaugasma***, n. GK: *575* [→ *575+827*]. radiance, brilliance:– brightness [1]

542 **ἀπείδω**, ***apeidō***, v. GK: *927* [→ *575+3708*]. to fix one's eyes; look away:– see [1]

543 **ἀπείθεια**, ***apeitheia***, n. GK: *577* [→ *1.1+3982*]. disobedience:– unbelief [4], disobedience [3]

544 **ἀπειθέω**, ***apeitheō***, v. GK: *578* [→ *1.1+3982*]. to disobey, be disobedient:– believed not [4], disobedient [4], not believed [2], obey not [2], believeth not [1], not believe [1], not obey [1], unbelieving [1]

545 **ἀπειθής**, ***apeithēs***, a. GK: *579* [→ *1.1+3982*]. disobedient:– disobedient [6]

546 **ἀπειλέω**, ***apeileō***, v. GK: *580* [→ *547*]. to threaten, warn:– straitly threaten [1], threatened [1]

547 **ἀπειλή**, ***apeilē***, n. GK: *581* [→ *546, 4324*]. threat:– threatenings [2], threatening [1]

548 **ἄπειμι**[1], ***apeimi***[1], v. GK: *582* [→ *575+1510*]. to be absent:– absent [7]

549 **ἄπειμι**[2], ***apeimi***[2], v. GK: *583* [→ *575*]. to go away:– went [1]

550 **ἀπεῖπον**, ***apeipon***, v. GK: *584* [→ *575+3004*]. to renounce, disown:– renounced [1]

551 **ἀπείραστος**, ***apeirastos***, a. GK: *585* [→ *1.1+3984*]. incapable of being tempted, without temptation:– cannot be tempted (*+1510*) [1]

552 **ἄπειρος**, ***apeiros***, a. GK: *586* [→ *1.1+3984*]. not acquainted with:– unskilful [1]

553 **ἀπεκδέχομαι**, ***apekdechomai***, v. GK: *587* [→ *575+1537+1209*]. wait eagerly for:– look for [2], wait for [2], waiting for [2], waiteth for [1]

554 **ἀπεκδύομαι**, ***apekdyomai***, v. GK: *588* [→ *575+1537+1416*]. to take off, disarm:– put off [1], spoiled [1]

555 **ἀπέκδυσις**, ***apekdysis***, n. GK: *589* [→ *575+1537+1416*]. removal, putting off:– putting off [1]

556 **ἀπελαύνω**, ***apelaunō***, v. GK: *590* [→ *575+1643*]. to eject from (court), drive away:– drave [1]

557 **ἀπελεγμός**, ***apelegmos***, n. GK: *591* [→ *575+1651*]. disrepute, discredit:– nought [1]

558 **ἀπελεύθερος**, ***apeleutheros***, n. GK: *592* [→ *575+1658*]. freedman, one no longer a slave:– freeman [1]

559 **Ἀπελλῆς**, ***Apellēs***, n.pr. GK: *593*. Apelles:– Apelles [1]

560 **ἀπελπίζω**, ***apelpizō***, v. GK: *594* [→ *575+1680*]. to expect nothing in return:– hoping for again [1]

561 **ἀπέναντι**, ***apenanti***, pp.*. GK: *595* [→ *575+1725*]. opposite, in front of, against (opposition to):– before [2], over against [2], contrary [1], in the presence [1]

ἀπέπω, ***apepō***. See **550**.

562 **ἀπέραντος**, ***aperantos***, a. GK: *596* [→ *1.1+4008*]. endless, unlimited:– endless [1]

563 **ἀπερισπάστως**, ***aperispastōs***, adv. GK: *597* [→ *1.1+4012+4685*]. undivided, without distraction:– without distraction [1]

564 **ἀπερίτμητος**, ***aperitmētos***, a. GK: *598* [→ *1.1+4012+5114*]. uncircumcised (with a possible implication of being stubborn and obstinate):– uncircumcised [1]

565 **ἀπέρχομαι**, ***aperchomai***, v. GK: *599* [→ *575+2064*]. to go away, withdraw:– went [45], departed [23], go [17], went away [7], go away [4], come [3], depart [3], gone away [3], goest [2], past [2], came [1], depart out [1], go after [1], go aside [1], go out [1], goeth way [1], going [1], gone [1], passed away [1], went back (*+1519+3588+3694*) [1], went way [1]

566 **ἀπέχει**, ***apechei***, v.3.s. of *568*. GK: *600* [→ *575+2192*]. to receive (in full), have enough:–

567 **ἀπέχομαι**, ***apechomai***, v.mid. of *568*. GK: *600* [→ *575+2192*]. to abstain, avoid:–

568 **ἀπέχω**, ***apechō***, v. GK: *600* [→ *575+2192*]. to receive (in full); to be distant; (mid.) to abstain, avoid:– have [4], abstain from [3], abstain [3], from [3], enough [1], is from [1], off [1], received [1], receive [1]

569 **ἀπιστέω**, ***apisteō***, v. GK: *601* [→ *1.1+4103*]. to disbelieve, be faithless, unfaithful. In some contexts unbelief has no implication of faithlessness or hardheartedness (Lk 24:11); in other contexts unbelief is a moral failure, not acting like a true follower (2Ti 2:13):– believed not [4], believe not [1], believeth not [1], not believe [1]

570 **ἀπιστία**, ***apistia***, n. GK: *602* [→ *1.1+4103*]. unbelief, lack of faith (often with the implication of stubbornly refusing to believe or act in accord with God's will or law):– unbelief [12]

571 **ἄπιστος**, ***apistos***, a. GK: *603* [→ *1.1+4103*]. unbelieving, lacking in trust, doubting; as a noun: an unbeliever or outsider, one who does not believe the Gospel:– unbelieving [5], believe not [4], faithless [4], unbelievers [4], believeth not [3], infidel [2], incredible [1]

572 **ἁπλότης**, ***haplotēs***, n. GK: *605* [→ *573*]. Formally "the quality of singleness," translated "generosity," the state of giving things in a manner that shows liberality; "sincerity," the moral quality of honesty expressing singleness of purpose or motivation:– simplicity [3], singleness [2], bountifulness [1], liberality [1], liberal [1]

573 **ἁπλοῦς**, ***haplous***, a. GK: *606* [→ *572, 574; cf. 260*]. good in the sense of healthy, formally, "singleness." Some think "a good eye" means to be generous and liberal in giving.:– single [2]

574 **ἁπλῶς**, ***haplōs***, adv. GK: *607* [→ *573*]. generously, without reserve:– liberally [1]

575 **ἀπό**, ***apo***, pp. GK: *608* [→ *379, 467, 468, 469, 470, 518, 520, 522, 523, 525, 526, 528, 529, 533, 534, 535, 536, 541, 542, 548, 549, 550, 553, 554, 555, 556, 557, 558, 560, 561, 565, 566, 567, 568, 576, 577, 578, 579, 580, 581, 582, 583, 584, 585, 586, 587, 588, 589, 590, 591, 592, 593, 594, 595, 596, 597, 598, 599, 600, 601, 602, 603, 604, 605, 606, 607, 608, 609, 610, 611, 612, 613, 614, 616, 617, 618, 619, 620, 621, 622, 623, 626, 627, 628, 629, 630, 631, 632, 633, 634, 635, 636, 637, 638, 641, 642, 643, 644, 645, 646, 647, 648, 649, 650, 653, 654, 655, 656, 657, 658, 659, 660, 661, 662, 663, 664, 665, 666, 667, 668, 669, 670, 671, 672, 673, 674, 684, 851, 856, 864, 867, 868, 871, 872, 873, 874, 879, 3405, 3406, 4217, 4879, 4880, 4881; cf. 683, 863*]. from, away from; by means of; out of; against:– from [386], of [149], out of [25], for [10], at [9], by [9], off [6], afar off (*+3113*) [5], on [5], since [5], in [4], since (*+3739*) [4], with [4], from among [3], a year ago (*+4070*) [2], before [2], henceforth (*+737*) [2], hereafter (*+737*) [2], since began [2], a good while ago (*+744+2250*) [1], ago [1], away from [1], away [1], because of [1], forsake (*+646*) [1], from beginning [1], henceforth (*+3568+3588*) [1], hereafter (*+3568+3588*) [1], in that [1], now (*+737*) [1], once (*+302+3739*) [1], out [1], since the time (*+3739*) [1], somewhat (*+3313*) [1], some [1], space of [1], that (*+3739*) [1], upon [1]

576 **ἀποβαίνω**, ***apobainō***, v. GK: *609* [→ *575+305*]. to leave, get out; to result in, turn to, lead to:– come [1], gone out [1], turn to [1], turn [1]

577 **ἀποβάλλω**, ***apoballō***, v. GK: *610* [→ *575+906*]. to throw away:– cast away [1], casting away [1]

578 **ἀποβλέπω**, ***apoblepō***, v. GK: *611* [→ *575+991*]. to look ahead, pay attention:– respect [1]

579 **ἀπόβλητος**, ***apoblētos***, a. GK: *612* [→ *575+906*]. rejected (as unclean):– refused [1]

580 **ἀποβολή**, ***apobolē***, n. GK: *613* [→ *575+906*]. rejection; loss:– casting away [1], loss [1]

581 **ἀπογίνομαι**, ***apoginomai***, v. GK: *614* [→ *575+1096*]. to die:– dead [1]

582 **ἀπογραφή**, ***apographē***, n. GK: *615* [→ *575+1125*]. census, registration:– taxing [2]

583 **ἀπογράφω**, ***apographō***, v. GK: *616* [→ *575+1125*]. to take a census, register, record:– taxed [3], written [1]

584 **ἀποδείκνυμι, *apodeiknymi***, v. GK: *617* [→ *575+1166*]. to display, exhibit, proclaim; prove, accredit, attest:– approved [1], prove [1], set forth [1], shewing [1]

585 **ἀπόδειξις, *apodeixis***, n. GK: *618* [→ *575+1166*]. demonstration, proof:– demonstration [1]

586 **ἀποδεκατόω, *apodekatoō***, v. GK: *619 & 620* [→ *575+1176*]. to give a tenth, tithe; collect a tithe:– give tithes [1], pay tithe of [1], take tithes [1], tithe [1]

587 **ἀπόδεκτος, *apodektos***, a. GK: *621* [→ *575+1209*]. pleasing, pleasant:– acceptable [2]

588 **ἀποδέχομαι, *apodechomai***, v. GK: *622* [→ *575+1209*]. to welcome, accept, receive; acknowledge, acclaim:– received [3], accept [1], gladly received [1], receive [1]

589 **ἀποδημέω, *apodēmeō***, v. GK: *623* [→ *575+1218*]. to go away on a journey:– went into a far country [3], took journey [2], travelling into a far country [1]

590 **ἀπόδημος, *apodēmos***, a. GK: *624* [→ *575+1218*]. going away on a journey:– taking a far journey [1]

591 **ἀποδίδωμι, *apodidōmi***, v. GK: *625* [→ *575+1325*]. give, give away; pay, pay back:– give [8], render [8], pay [7], reward [6], sold [3], paid [2], delivered again [1], delivered [1], gave again [1], gave [1], payment made [1], perform [1], recompense [1], rendering [1], repay [1], requite (*+287*) [1], restore [1], rewarded [1], yielded [1], yieldeth [1]

592 **ἀποδιορίζω, *apodiorizō***, v. GK: *626* [→ *575+1223+3724*]. to divide, separate, cause a division:– separate [1]

593 **ἀποδοκιμάζω, *apodokimazō***, v. GK: *627* [→ *575+1209*]. to reject:– rejected [7], disallowed [2]

594 **ἀποδοχή, *apodochē***, n. GK: *628* [→ *575+1209*]. acceptance, approval:– acceptation [2]

595 **ἀπόθεσις, *apothesis***, n. GK: *629* [→ *575+5087*]. removal, putting aside, getting rid of; this can be a euphemism for death (2Pe 1:14):– put off [1], putting away [1]

596 **ἀποθήκη, *apothēkē***, n. GK: *630* [→ *575+2344*]. barn, storehouse:– barns [2], barn [2], garner [2]

597 **ἀποθησαυρίζω, *apothēsaurizō***, v. GK: *631* [→ *575+2344*]. to store up treasure:– laying up in store [1]

598 **ἀποθλίβω, *apothlibō***, v. GK: *632* [→ *575+2346*]. to press against, crowd up to:– press [1]

599 **ἀποθνήσκω, *apothnēskō***, v. GK: *633* [→ *575+2348*]. to die (in a literal or fig. sense); to be about to die, be mortal:– die [41], died [32], dead [29], dying [4], dieth [2], death [1], perished [1], slain (*+5408*) [1]

600 **ἀποκαθίστημι, *apokathistēmi***, v. GK: *634 & 635* [→ *575+2596+2476*]. to (completely) restore, reestablish, cure:– restored [5], restore again [1], restoreth [1], restore [1]

601 **ἀποκαλύπτω, *apokalyptō***, v. GK: *636* [→ *575+2572*]. to reveal, disclose:– revealed [22], reveal [4]

602 **ἀποκάλυψις, *apokalypsis***, n. GK: *637* [→ *575+2572*]. revelation, what is revealed, disclosure, to make information known with an implication that the information can be understood. This refers in the NT to God making information known, especially to his close associates:– revelation [10], revealed [2], revelations [2], appearing [1], coming [1], lighten [1], manifestation [1]

603 **ἀποκαραδοκία, *apokaradokia***, n. GK: *638 & 2839* [→ *575+2898+1380*]. eager expectation:– earnest expectation [2]

604 **ἀποκαταλλάσσω, *apokatallassō***, v. GK: *639* [→ *575+2596+236*]. to reconcile, reunite:– reconcile [2], reconciled [1]

605 **ἀποκατάστασις, *apokatastasis***, n. GK: *640* [→ *575+2596+2476*]. restoration:– restitution [1]

606 **ἀπόκειμαι, *apokeimai***, v. GK: *641* [→ *575+2749*]. to be stored up, destined:– laid up [3], appointed [1]

607 **ἀποκεφαλίζω, *apokephalizō***, v. GK: *642* [→ *575+2776*]. to behead:– beheaded [4]

608 **ἀποκλείω, *apokleiō***, v. GK: *643* [→ *575+2808*]. to close:– shut to [1]

609 **ἀποκόπτω, *apokoptō***, v. GK: *644* [→ *575+2875*]. to cut off; emasculate:– cut off [6]

610 **ἀπόκριμα, *apokrima***, n. GK: *645* [→ *575+2919*]. sentence, verdict:– sentence [1]

611 **ἀποκρίνομαι, *apokrinomai***, v. GK: *646* [→ *575+2919*]. to answer, reply; sometimes used in the NT in the Hebraic sense of continuing a discourse:– answered [201], answering [29], answer [12], answerest [4], answereth [4]

612 **ἀπόκρισις, *apokrisis***, n. GK: *647* [→ *575+2919*]. answer:– answer [3], answers [1]

613 **ἀποκρύπτω, *apokryptō***, v. GK: *648* [→ *575+2928*]. to hide, conceal:– hid [3], hid from [2], hidden [1]

614 **ἀπόκρυφος, *apokryphos***, a. GK: *649* [→ *575+2928*]. concealed, hidden, secret:– hid [2], kept secret [1]

615 **ἀποκτείνω, *apokteinō***, v. GK: *650 & 651* [→ *443*]. to kill (either natural life or spiritual life):– kill [28], killed [21], slain [7], put to death [6], slew [4], killeth [3], slay [3], killest [2], killing [1]

616 **ἀποκυέω, *apokyeō***, v. GK: *652* [→ *575+2949*]. to give birth to, bring into being:– begat [1], bringeth forth [1]

617 **ἀποκυλίω, *apokyliō***, v. GK: *375 & 653* [→ *575+2947*]. to roll away, roll back:– rolled away [2], roll away [1], rolled back [1]

618 **ἀπολαμβάνω, *apolambanō***, v. GK: *655* [→ *575+2983*]. to receive, be repaid:– receive [7], receive again [1], receivedst [1], received [1], receiving [1], took [1]

619 **ἀπόλαυσις, *apolausis***, n. GK: *656* [→ *575*]. enjoyment, pleasure:– enjoy [1], pleasures [1]

620 **ἀπολείπω, *apoleipō***, v. GK: *657* [→ *575+3007*]. to leave behind:– left [3], remaineth [3]

621 **ἀπολείχω, *apoleichō***, v. GK: *658 & 2143 & 3314 & 4336* [→ *575*]. lick, lick off:– licked [1]

622 **ἀπόλλυμι, *apollymi***, v. GK: *660* [→ *575+3639*]. to destroy (an inanimate object), to kill (by taking a life), cause to lose (especially a life); to die or perish. Violence and strife is often the associative meaning related to this word:– perish [25], destroy [19], lose [17], lost [13], destroyed [7], perished [5], perisheth [3], die [1], loseth [1], marred [1]

623 **Ἀπολλύων, *Apollyōn***, n.pr. GK: *661* [→ *575+3639*]. Apollyon, "*destroyer*":– Apollyon [1]

624 **Ἀπολλωνία, *Apollōnia***, n.pr. GK: *662* [→ *625*]. Apollonia:– Apollonia [1]

625 **Ἀπολλῶς, *Apollōs***, n.pr. GK: *663* [→ *624*]. Apollos:– Apollos [10]

626 **ἀπολογέομαι, *apologeomai***, v. GK: *664* [→ *575+3004*]. to defend oneself, speak in one's own behalf:– answer [3], answer for [1], answered for himself [1], answered for [1], excuse ourselves [1], excusing [1], made defence [1], spake for [1]

627 **ἀπολογία, *apologia***, n. GK: *665* [→ *575+3004*]. defense; answer or reply (of reason or accounting):– answer [3], defence [3], answer for [1], clearing [1]

628 **ἀπολούω, *apolouō***, v. GK: *666* [→ *575+3068*]. to wash away:– wash away [1], washed [1]

629 **ἀπολύτρωσις, *apolytrōsis***, n. GK: *667* [→ *575+3089*]. redemption, ransom, release:– redemption [9], deliverance [1]

630 **ἀπολύω, *apolyō***, v. GK: *668* [→ *575+3089*]. to release (forgive, grant clemency); divorce, send away:– let go [13], put away [13], release [13], sent away [7], send away [6], released [4], dismissed [2], loosed [2], set at liberty [2], departed [1], depart [1], divorced [1], forgiven [1], forgive [1], let depart [1], putteth away [1]

631 **ἀπομάσσω, *apomassō***, v. GK: *669* [→ *575+3146*]. to wipe off (this refers to an action of protest):– wipe off against [1]

632 **ἀπονέμω, *aponemō***, v. GK: *671* [→ *575+3551*]. to treat with, show, pay (respect):– giving [1]

633 **ἀπονίπτω, *aponiptō***, v. GK: *672* [→ *575+3538*]. to wash off:– washed [1]

634 **ἀποπίπτω, *apopiptō***, v. GK: *674* [→ *575+4098*]. to fall away, drop off:– fell [1]

635 **ἀποπλανάω, *apoplanaō***, v. GK: *675* [→ *575+4106*]. to deceive, mislead; (pass.) to wander:– erred [1], seduce [1]

636 **ἀποπλέω, *apopleō***, v. GK: *676* [→ *575+4126*]. to sail away from:– sailed [3], sail [1]

637 **ἀποπλύνω, *apoplynō***, v. GK: *677* [→ *575+4150*]. to wash off, wash out:– washing [1]

638 **ἀποπνίγω, *apopnigō***, v. GK: *678* [→ *575+4155*]. to choke, smother; (pass.) to be drowned, choked (with water):– choked [3]

639 **ἀπορέω, *aporeō***, v. GK: *679* [→ *1.1+4198*]. to be puzzled, at a loss, in wonder:– doubted [1], doubting [1], perplexed [1], stand in doubt [1]

640 **ἀπορία, *aporia***, n. GK: *680* [→ *1.1+4198*]. perplexity, consternation:– perplexity [1]

641 **ἀπορίπτω, *aporiptō***, v. GK: *681* [→ *575+4496*]. to jump into, throw oneself into:– cast [1]

642 **ἀπορφανίζω, *aporphanizō***, v. GK: *682* [→ *575+3737*]. to make an orphan of:– taken [1]

643 **ἀποσκευάζω, *aposkeuazō***, v. GK: *683 & 2171* [→ *575+4632*]. to pack up, get ready, make preparations:– took up carriages [1]

644 **ἀποσκίασμα, *aposkiasma***, n. GK: *684* [→ *575+4639*]. shadow:– shadow [1]

645 **ἀποσπάω, *apospaō***, v. GK: *685* [→ *575+4685*]. to draw out, draw away, attract; (pass.) to withdraw:– draw away [1], drew [1], gotten from [1], withdrawn [1]

646 **ἀποστασία, *apostasia***, n. GK: *686* [→ *575+2476*]. turning away, rebellion, abandonment, apostasy:– falling away [1], forsake (*+575*) [1]

647 **ἀποστάσιον, *apostasion***, n. GK: *687* [→ *575+2476*]. divorce:– divorcement [2], writing of divorcement [1]

648 **ἀποστεγάζω, *apostegazō***, v. GK: *689* [→ *575+4722*]. to make an opening in a roof, remove a roof:– uncovered [1]

649 **ἀποστέλλω, *apostellō***, v. GK: *690* [→ *651, 652, 1821, 4882, 5570*]. to send, send out, send away (especially used of the official sending out of the disciples):– sent [92], send [17], sent forth [8], send forth [5], sent away [3], sendeth forth [2], sent out [2], putteth in [1], send away [1], sendeth [1], set [1]

650 **ἀποστερέω, *apostereō***, v. GK: *691 & 935* [→ *575*]. to defraud, cheat, steal; deprive, deny, withhold, keep back:– defraud [3], defrauded [1], destitute [1], kept back by fraud [1]

651 **ἀποστολή, *apostolē***, n. GK: *692* [→ *649*]. apostleship, ministry / office of an apostle:– apostleship [4]

652 **ἀπόστολος, *apostolos***, n. GK: *693* [→ *649*]. apostle, representative, messenger, envoy; often used in a technical sense for the divinely appointed founders of the church:– apostles [54], apostle [19], apostles' [5], he that is sent [1], messengers [1], messenger [1]

653 **ἀποστοματίζω, *apostomatizō***, v. GK: *694* [→ *575+4750*]. to besiege with questions, interrogate closely:– provoke to speak [1]

654 **ἀποστρέφω, *apostrephō***, v. GK: *695* [→ *575+4762*]. to turn away from, rebel, mislead; to desert, reject; to return, put back:– turn away [3], brought again [1], perverteth [1], put up again [1], turn away from [1], turn from [1], turned away from [1], turning away [1]

655 **ἀποστυγέω, *apostygeō***, v. GK: *696* [→ *575+4767*]. to hate, abhor, loathe:– Abhor [1]

656 **ἀποσυνάγωγος, *aposynagōgos***, a. GK: *697* [→ *575+4864*]. put out of the synagogue, excommunicated:– put out of the synagogue [2], out of the synagogues [1]

657 **ἀποτάσσω, *apotassō***, v. GK: *698* [→ *575+5021*]. to say good-by, leave; give up, renounce, forsake:– bade farewell [1], bid farewell [1], forsaketh [1], sent away [1], taking leave of [1], took leave [1]

658 **ἀποτελέω, *apoteleō***, v. GK: *699* [→ *575+5056*]. to bring to completion; (pass.) to be full-grown, mature, completed:– finished [1]

659 **ἀποτίθημι, *apotithēmi***, v. GK: *700* [→ *575+5087*]. to put aside, get rid of:– put off [2], cast off [1], laid down [1], lay apart [1], lay aside [1], laying aside [1], putting away [1]

660 **ἀποτινάσσω, *apotinassō***, v. GK: *701* [→ *1614; cf. 575*]. to shake off, stomp off:– shake off [1], shook off [1]

661 **ἀποτίνω, *apotinō***, v. GK: *702* [→ *575+5099*]. to pay back, make restitution:– repay [1]

662 **ἀποτολμάω, *apotolmaō***, v. GK: *703* [→ *575+5111*]. to bring forth boldly:– very bold [1]

663 **ἀποτομία, *apotomia***, n. GK: *704* [→ *575+5114*]. sternness, severity:– severity [2]

664 **ἀποτόμως, *apotomōs***, adv. GK: *705* [→ *575+5114*]. harshly, sharply, severely, rigorously:– sharply [1], sharpness [1]

665 **ἀποτρέπω, *apotrepō***, v. GK: *706* [→ *575+5157*]. to have nothing to do with, turn away from completely, avoid:– from turn away [1]

666 **ἀπουσία**, ***apousia***, n. GK: *707* [→ *575+1510*]. absence:– absence [1]

667 **ἀποφέρω**, ***apopherō***, v. GK: *708* [→ *575+5342*]. to carry away, lead away:– carried away [3], bring [1], carried [1]

668 **ἀποφεύγω**, ***apopheugō***, v. GK: *709* [→ *575+5343*]. to escape (from):– escaped [2], escaped from [1]

669 **ἀποφθέγγομαι**, ***apophthengomai***, v. GK: *710* [→ *575+5350*]. to say, speak out, address, declare, in some contexts with the inference of urgency or boldness:– said [1], speak forth [1], utterance [1]

670 **ἀποφορτίζομαι**, ***apophortizomai***, v. GK: *711* [→ *575+5342*]. to unload:– unlade [1]

671 **ἀπόχρησις**, ***apochrēsis***, n. GK: *712* [→ *575+5530*]. using up, consumption:– using [1]

672 **ἀποχωρέω**, ***apochōreō***, v. GK: *713* [→ *575+5562*]. to go away from, leave:– departeth [1], departing [1], depart [1]

673 **ἀποχωρίζω**, ***apochōrizō***, v. GK: *714* [→ *575+5565*]. to part company, be separated; to recede, be split:– departed asunder [1], departed [1]

674 **ἀποψύχω**, ***apopsychō***, v. GK: *715* [→ *575+5594*]. to faint (some translate "to die"):– hearts failing [1]

675 **Ἄππιος**, ***Appios***, n.pr. GK: *716*. Appius:– Appii [1]

676 **ἀπρόσιτος**, ***aprositos***, a. GK: *717* [→ *1.1+4314*]. unapproachable:– which no can approach unto [1]

677 **ἀπρόσκοπος**, ***aproskopos***, a. GK: *718* [→ *1.1+4314+2875*]. blameless, clear; not causing one to stumble, not giving offense:– none offence [1], void of offence [1], without offence [1]

678 **ἀπροσωπολήμπτως**, ***aprosōpolēmptōs***, adv. GK: *719* [→ *1.1+4383+2983*]. impartially, without prejudice:– without respect of persons [1]

679 **ἄπταιστος**, ***aptaistos***, a. GK: *720* [→ *1.1+4417*]. without falling, without stumbling:– falling [1]

680 **ἅπτομαι**, ***haptomai***, v.mid. of *681*. GK: *721* [→ *381, 681, 860, 2510, 681*]. to touch, hold, handle; "to touch a woman" means "to get married":–

681 **ἅπτω**, ***haptō***, v. GK: *721 & 4312* [→ *680*]. to touch, hold, handle; (act.) to start a fire; "to touch a woman" means "to get married":– touched [21], touch [13], lighted [2], toucheth [2], kindled [1], light [1]

682 **Ἀπφία**, ***Apphia***, n.pr. GK: *722*. Apphia:– Apphia [1]

683 **ἀπωθέω**, ***apōtheō***, v. GK: *723* [→ *1856; cf. 575*]. to reject, repudiate, push aside:– cast away [2], put away [1], put from [1], thrust away [1], thrust from [1]

684 **ἀπώλεια**, ***apōleia***, n. GK: *724* [→ *575+3639*]. destruction, ruin, waste:– perdition [8], destruction [5], waste [2], damnable [1], damnation [1], die [1], perish (*+1510+1519*) [1], pernicious ways [1]

685 **ἀρά**, ***ara***, n. GK: *725* [→ *1944, 2671, 2672*]. curse:– cursing [1]

686 **ἄρα**, ***ara***, pt.infer. GK: *726*. then, so, therefore, consequently:– then [14], therefore (*+3767*) [7], so [4], therefore [4], so then [2], else (*+1893*) [1], haply (*+1065*) [1], haply [1], if so be that (*+1512*) [1], no doubt [1], now [1], perhaps [1], then (*+1065*) [1], truly [1], wherefore (*+1065*) [1], wherefore [1]

687 **ἆρα**, ***ara***, pt.inter. GK: *727*. difficult to translate directly: introduces direct questions, showing anxiety or impatience:– what (*+5101*) [2], therefore [1], what man (*+5101*) [1]

688 **Ἀραβία**, ***Arabia***, n.pr. GK: *728* [→ *690*]. Arabia, "*desert or steppe*":– Arabia [2]

ἄραγε, ***arage***. See **686** and **1065**.

689 **Ἀράμ**, ***Aram***, n.pr. GK: *730*. Aram, Ram, "*high, exalted*":– Aram [3]

690 **Ἄραψ**, ***Araps***, n.pr.g. GK: *732* [→ *688*]. Arab, "*desert dweller*":– Arabians [1]

691 **ἀργέω**, ***argeō***, v. GK: *733* [→ *1.1+2041*]. to be idle, grow weary:– lingereth [1]

692 **ἀργός**, ***argos***, a. GK: *734* [→ *1.1+2041*]. idle, lazy; useless, ineffective; careless:– idle [6], barren [1], slow [1]

693 **ἀργύρεος**, ***argyreos***, a. GK: *735* [→ *696*]. (made of) silver:– silver [2], of silver [1]

694 **ἀργύριον**, ***argyrion***, n. GK: *736* [→ *696*]. silver (always referring to money):– money [11], silver [9]

695 **ἀργυροκόπος**, ***argyrokopos***, n. GK: *737* [→ *696+2875*]. silversmith:– silversmith [1]

696 **ἄργυρος**, ***argyros***, n. GK: *738* [→ *693, 694, 695, 866, 5365, 5366*]. silver:– silver [5]

697 **Ἄρειος πάγος**, ***Areios pagos***, n.pr. GK: *740 & 4076* [→ *698*]. meeting of the Areopagus; Mars' Hill, "*hill of the Greek god Ares*":– Areopagus [1], Mars' hill [1]

698 **Ἀρεοπαγίτης**, ***Areopagitēs***, n.pr.g. GK: *741* [→ *697*]. member of the Areopagus:– Areopagite [1]

699 **ἀρεσκεία**, ***areskeia***, n. GK: *742* [→ *700*]. pleasing, striving to please:– pleasing [1]

700 **ἀρέσκω**, ***areskō***, v. GK: *743* [→ *441, 699, 701, 2100, 2101, 2102*]. to please, accommodate:– please [11], pleased [5], pleasing [1]

701 **ἀρεστός**, ***arestos***, a. GK: *744* [→ *700*]. pleasing, desirable, right:– pleased (*+1510*) [1], please [1], pleasing [1], reason [1]

702 **Ἀρέτας**, ***Haretas***, n.pr. GK: *745*. Aretas, "*virtuous*":– Aretas [1]

703 **ἀρετή**, ***aretē***, n. GK: *746*. (moral) goodness, excellence, virtue:– virtue [4], praises [1]

704 **ἀρήν**, ***arēn***, n. GK: *748* [→ *721*]. lamb:– lambs [1]

705 **ἀριθμέω**, ***arithmeō***, v. GK: *749* [→ *706*]. to count:– numbered [2], number [1]

706 **ἀριθμός**, ***arithmos***, n. GK: *750* [→ *382, 705, 2674*]. number:– number [18]

707 **Ἀριμαθαία**, ***Harimathaia***, n.pr. GK: *751*. Arimathea:– Arimathea [4]

708 **Ἀρίσταρχος**, ***Aristarchos***, n.pr. GK: *752* [→ *757*]. Aristarchus, "*best ruler*":– Aristarchus [5]

709 **ἀριστάω**, ***aristaō***, v. GK: *753* [→ *712*]. to eat (breakfast):– dine [2], dined [1]

710 **ἀριστερός**, ***aristeros***, a. GK: *754*. left side, left hand; the left is considered culturally to be weaker than the right; a weapon in the left hand is a defensive weapon; to be seated on the left side of a ruler is a lesser position than on the right side:– left [2], left hand [1]

711 **Ἀριστόβουλος**, ***Aristoboulos***, n.pr. GK: *755* [→ *1014*]. Aristobulus, "*best advisor*":– Aristobulus' [1]

712 **ἄριστον**, ***ariston***, n. GK: *756* [→ *709*]. meal, feast:– dinner [3]

713 **ἀρκετός**, ***arketos***, a. GK: *757* [→ *714*]. enough, sufficient:– enough [1], suffice [1], sufficient [1]

714 **ἀρκέω**, ***arkeō***, v. GK: *758* [→ *713, 841, 842, 1884*]. (mid./pass.) to be content, satisfied; (act.) to be sufficient:– content [4], sufficient [2], enough [1], sufficeth [1]

715 **ἄρκος**, ***arkos***, n. GK: *759 & 760*. bear:– bear [1]

716 **ἅρμα**, ***harma***, n. GK: *761* [→ *260*]. chariot, carriage (for traveling or military uses):– chariot [3], chariots [1]

717 **Ἁρμαγεδών**, ***Harmagedōn***, n.pr. GK: *762 & 3403*. Armageddon, "*Mount Megiddo*":– Armageddon [1]

718 **ἁρμόζω**, ***harmozō***, v. GK: *764* [→ *719, 4883*]. to promise for marriage, betroth:– espoused [1]

719 **ἁρμός**, ***harmos***, n. GK: *765* [→ *718*]. joint (where bones connect):– joints [1]

720 **ἀρνέομαι**, ***arneomai***, v. GK: *766* [→ *533*]. to deny, disown, renounce, repudiate:– denied [14], deny [7], denieth [4], denying [4], refused [2]

721 **ἀρνίον**, ***arnion***, n. GK: *768* [→ *704*]. lamb, sheep; the Lamb (a title of Christ):– lamb [27], lamb's [2], lambs [1]

722 **ἀροτριάω**, ***arotriaō***, v. GK: *769* [→ *723*]. to plow, furrow:– ploweth [1], plowing [1], plow [1]

723 **ἄροτρον**, ***arotron***, n. GK: *770* [→ *722*]. plow, furrow-maker:– plough [1]

724 **ἁρπαγή**, ***harpagē***, n. GK: *771* [→ *726*]. greediness, confiscation, robbery, plunder:– extortion [1], ravening [1], spoiling [1]

725 **ἁρπαγμός**, ***harpagmos***, n. GK: *772* [→ *726*]. something to hold onto:– robbery [1]

726 **ἁρπάζω**, ***harpazō***, v. GK: *773* [→ *724, 725, 727, 1283, 4884*]. to catch, steal, carry off:– caught up [4], take by force [3], pluck [2], catcheth away [1], catcheth [1], caught away [1], pulling [1]

727 **ἅρπαξ**, ***harpax***, a. GK: *774* [→ *726*]. swindling, robbing, implying violence in the process; (destructively) ferocious, ravenous; as a noun, a (violent) robber or swindler:– extortioners [3], extortioner [1], ravening [1]

728 **ἀρραβών**, ***arrabōn***, n. GK: *775*. deposit which guarantees, downpayment, pledge:– earnest [3]

729 **ἄραφος**, ***araphos***, a. GK: *731* [→ *1.1+4476*]. seamless:– without seam [1]

730 **ἄρρην**, ***arrēn***, n. GK: *776 & 781* [→ *733*]. male:– male [4], men [3], man [2]

731 **ἄρρητος**, ***arrētos***, a. GK: *777* [→ *1.1+4487*]. inexpressible, not to be spoken (in context, things or words too sacred to tell):– unspeakable [1]

732 **ἄρρωστος**, ***arrōstos***, a. GK: *778 & 779* [→ *1.1+4517*]. sick, ill:– sick [4], sickly [1]

733 **ἀρσενοκοίτης**, ***arsenokoitēs***, n. GK: *780* [→ *730+2749*]. one engaging in homosexual acts (likely referring to the active male partner), sexual deviant:– abusers with mankind [1], them that defile with mankind [1]

734 **Ἀρτεμᾶς**, ***Artemas***, n.pr. GK: *782* [→ *735+1325*]. Artemas, "*[given by] Artemis*":– Artemas [1]

735 **Ἄρτεμις**, ***Artemis***, n.pr. GK: *783* [→ *734*]. Artemis:– Diana [5]

736 **ἀρτέμων**, ***artemōn***, n. GK: *784*. foresail, sail:– mainsail [1]

737 **ἄρτι**, ***arti***, adv. GK: *785* [→ *534, 535, 738, 739, 1822, 2675, 2676, 2677, 4294*]. now, at once, immediately:– now [22], henceforth (*+575*) [2], hereafter (*+575*) [2], hitherto (*+2193*) [2], even now [1], henceforth [1], now (*+575*) [1], presently [1], present [1], this day [1], this hour [1], this present [1]

738 **ἀρτιγέννητος**, ***artigennētos***, a. GK: *786* [→ *737+1096*]. newborn:– newborn [1]

739 **ἄρτιος**, ***artios***, a. GK: *787* [→ *737*]. thorough, complete, capable, proficient, able to meet all demands:– perfect [1]

740 **ἄρτος**, ***artos***, n. GK: *788*. (loaf of) bread, food:– bread [72], loaves [22], shewbread (*+3588+4286*) [3], loaf [1], shewbread (*+4286*) [1]

741 **ἀρτύω**, ***artyō***, v. GK: *789*. to make salty, season:– seasoned [2], season [1]

742 **Ἀρφαξάδ**, ***Arphaxad***, n.pr. GK: *790*. Arphaxad:– Arphaxad [1]

743 **ἀρχάγγελος**, ***archangelos***, n. GK: *791* [→ *757+32*]. archangel:– archangel [2]

744 **ἀρχαῖος**, ***archaios***, a. GK: *792* [→ *757*]. ancient, of old:– old [8], of old time [3], a good while ago (*+575+2250*) [1]

745 **Ἀρχέλαος**, ***Archelaos***, n.pr. GK: *793* [→ *757+2992*]. Archelaus, "*ruler of people*":– Archelaus [1]

746 **ἀρχή**, ***archē***, n. GK: *794* [→ *757*]. beginning, origin, first; ruler, power, authority; position of authority, domain:– beginning [39], principalities [6], first [3], corners [2], principality [2], beginnings [1], first estate [1], magistrates [1], power [1], principles [1], rule [1]

747 **ἀρχηγός**, ***archēgos***, n. GK: *795* [→ *757+71*]. author, originator, founder; leader, ruler:– prince [2], author [1], captain [1]

748 **ἀρχιερατικός**, ***archieratikos***, a. GK: *796* [→ *757+2413*]. of the high priest:– high priest [1]

749 **ἀρχιερεύς**, ***archiereus***, n. GK: *797* [→ *757+2413*]. chief priest, high priest:– chief priests [63], high priest [51], high priest's [4], high priests [3], chief of the priests [1], priests [1]

750 **ἀρχιποίμην**, ***archipoimēn***, n. GK: *799* [→ *757+4166*]. chief shepherd:– chief shepherd [1]

751 **Ἄρχιππος**, ***Archippos***, n.pr. GK: *800* [→ *757+2462*]. Archippus, "*master of the horse*":– Archippus [2]

752 **ἀρχισυνάγωγος**, ***archisynagogos***, n. GK: *801* [→ *757+4864*]. leader of the synagogue, an official whose duty it was to care for the physical needs for the worship service:– ruler of the synagogue [5], ruler of the synagogue's [2], rulers of the synagogue [2]

753 **ἀρχιτέκτων**, ***architektōn***, n. GK: *802* [→ *757+5078*]. expert builder:– masterbuilder [1]

754 **ἀρχιτελώνης**, ***architelōnēs***, n. GK: *803* [→ *757+5057*]. chief tax collector:– chief among publicans [1]

755 ἀρχιτρίκλινος, architriklinos, n. GK: *804* [→ *757+5140+2827*]. master of the banquet, head waiter:– governor of the feast [2], ruler of the feast [1]

756 ἄρχομαι, archomai, v.mid. of *757.* GK: *806* [→ *757*]. to begin:– began [64], begin [11], beginning [7], begun [1], from the beginning [1]

757 ἄρχω, archō, v. GK: *806* [→ *536, 708, 743, 744, 745, 746, 747, 748, 749, 750, 751, 752, 753, 754, 755, 756, 758, 775, 1481, 1543, 1728, 1885, 3966, 3980, 4173, 4278, 4391, 4759, 5075, 5076, 5223, 5224, 5225, 5506*]. (act.) to rule; (mid.) to begin:– reign over [1], rule over [1]

758 ἄρχων, archōn, n. GK: *807* [→ *757*]. ruler, leader, official:– rulers [14], prince [8], ruler [8], princes [3], chief [2], magistrate [1], ruler's [1]

759 ἄρωμα, arōma, n. GK: *808.* spices, salves, scented oils, perfumes:– spices [4]

760 Ἀσά, Asa, n.pr. GK: *809 & 811.* Asa, "[poss.] *healer; myrtle*":– Asa [2]

761 ἀσάλευτος, asaleutos, a. GK: *810* [→ *1.1+4531*]. unshakable, immovable, fixed:– cannot be moved [1], unmoveable [1]

762 ἄσβεστος, asbestos, a. GK: *812* [→ *1.1+4570*]. unquenchable, inextinguishable:– never be quenched [2], unquenchable [2]

763 ἀσέβεια, asebeia, n. GK: *813* [→ *1.1+4576*]. ungodliness, godlessness, impiety (in thought and act):– ungodliness [4], ungodly [2]

764 ἀσεβέω, asebeō, v. GK: *814* [→ *1.1+4576*]. to do ungodly acts, act impiously:– those that live ungodly [1], ungodly committed [1]

765 ἀσεβής, asebēs, a. GK: *815* [→ *1.1+4576*]. ungodly, wicked, impious:– ungodly [9]

766 ἀσέλγεια, aselgeia, n. GK: *816* [→ *1.1*]. debauchery, sensuality, lewdness:– lasciviousness [6], wantonness [2], filthy [1]

767 ἄσημος, asēmos, a. GK: *817* [→ *1.1+4592*]. ordinary, obscure, insignificant:– mean [1]

768 Ἀσήρ, Asēr, n.pr. GK: *818.* Asher, "*happy one*":– Aser [2]

769 ἀσθένεια, astheneia, n. GK: *819* [→ *1.1+4599*]. weakness, illness, infirmity:– infirmities [10], infirmity [7], weakness [5], diseases [1], sickness [1]

770 ἀσθενέω, astheneō, v. GK: *820* [→ *1.1+4599*]. to be weak, ill:– sick [17], weak [16], impotent [2], diseased [1]

771 ἀσθένημα, asthenēma, n. GK: *821* [→ *1.1+4599*]. failing, weakness:– infirmities [1]

772 ἀσθενής, asthenēs, a. GK: *822* [→ *1.1+4599*]. weak, ill (of physical weakness or illness, also of moral or spiritual weakness):– weak [13], sick [6], weakness [2], impotent [1], more feeble [1], weaker [1], without strength [1]

773 Ἀσία, Asia, n.pr. GK: *823* [→ *774, 775*]. Asia:– Asia [19]

774 Ἀσιανός, Asianos, n.pr.g. GK: *824* [→ *773*]. one from the Roman province of Asia:– of Asia [1]

775 Ἀσιάρχης, Asiarchēs, n.pr. GK: *825* [→ *773+757*]. official of the province of Asia, Asiarch, a wealthy and influential man, probably connected with the Imperial cult:– chief of Asia [1]

776 ἀσιτία, asitia, n. GK: *826* [→ *1.1+4621*]. going without food:– abstinence [1]

777 ἄσιτος, asitos, a. GK: *827* [→ *1.1+4621*]. going without food:– fasting [1]

778 ἀσκέω, askeō, v. GK: *828.* to strive, do one's best:– exercise [1]

779 ἀσκός, askos, n. GK: *829.* wineskin, leather bag holding wine:– bottles [12]

780 ἀσμένως, asmenōs, adv. GK: *830* [→ *2237*]. warmly, gladly:– gladly [2]

781 ἄσοφος, asophos, a. GK: *831* [→ *1.1+4680*]. unwise, foolish:– fools [1]

782 ἀσπάζομαι, aspazomai, v. GK: *571 & 832* [→ *783*]. to give greetings (hello or good-bye):– salute [32], greet [14], saluted [5], saluteth [5], embraced [2], greeteth [1], taken leave [1]

783 ἀσπασμός, aspasmos, n. GK: *833* [→ *782*]. greeting:– salutation [6], greetings [3], salutations [1]

784 ἄσπιλος, aspilos, a. GK: *834* [→ *1.1+4696*]. without spot, defect or blemish:– without spot [3], unspotted [1]

785 ἀσπίς, aspis, n. GK: *835.* viper, asp, cobra:– asps [1]

786 ἄσπονδος, aspondos, a. GK: *836* [→ *1.1+4689*]. unforgiving, not reconcilable:– implacable [1], trucebreakers [1]

787 ἀσσάριον, assarion, n. GK: *837.* assarion (coin worth one-sixteenth of a day's wage):– farthings [1], farthing [1]

788 ἆσσον, asson, adv. GK: *839.* nearer:– close by [1]

789 *Ἄσσος, Assos, n.pr. GK: *840.* Assos:– Assos [2]

790 ἀστατέω, astateō, v. GK: *841* [→ *1.1+2476*]. to be homeless, a vagabond:– have no certain dwelling place [1]

791 ἀστεῖος, asteios, a. GK: *842.* not ordinary, beautiful, pleasing:– exceeding fair (*+2316+3588*) [1], proper [1]

792 ἀστήρ, astēr, n. GK: *843* [→ *798*]. star:– stars [13], star [11]

793 ἀστήρικτος, astēriktos, a. GK: *844* [→ *1.1+4741*]. unstable, weak:– unstable [2]

794 ἄστοργος, astorgos, a. GK: *845* [→ *1.1*]. without love, heartless:– without natural affection [2]

795 ἀστοχέω, astocheō, v. GK: *846* [→ *1.1*]. to wander away, miss the mark; to turn to, deviate from:– erred [2], swerved [1]

796 ἀστραπή, astrapē, n. GK: *847* [→ *797, 1823, 4015*]. lightning; light, ray of light:– lightnings [4], lightning [4], bright shining [1]

797 ἀστράπτω, astraptō, v. GK: *848* [→ *796*]. to flash, gleam like lightning:– lighteneth [1], shining [1]

798 ἄστρον, astron, n. GK: *849* [→ *792*]. star, constellation:– stars [3], star [1]

799 Ἀσύγκριτος, Asynkritos, n.pr. GK: *850* [→ *1.1+4862+2919*]. Asyncritus, "*incomparable*":– Asyncritus [1]

800 ἀσύμφωνος, asymphōnos, a. GK: *851* [→ *1.1+4862+5456*]. disagreeable, not harmonious:– agreed not (*+1510*) [1]

801 ἀσύνετος, asynetos, a. GK: *852* [→ *863*]. senseless, dull, without understanding, foolish:– without understanding [3], foolish [2]

802 ἀσύνθετος, asynthetos, a. GK: *853* [→ *1.1+4862+5087*]. faithless, untrustworthy:– covenantbreakers [1]

803 ἀσφάλεια, asphaleia, n. GK: *854* [→ *755; cf. 1.1*]. security, safety; certainty, truth:– safety [2], certainty [1]

804 ἀσφαλής, asphalēs, a. GK: *855* [→ *754, 757; cf. 1.1*]. safe, firm, certain; definite; the truth:– certainty [2], certain [1], safe [1], sure [1]

805 ἀσφαλίζω, asphalizō, v. GK: *856* [→ *755; cf. 1.1*]. to make secure; fasten:– made sure [2], made fast [1], make sure [1]

806 ἀσφαλῶς, asphalōs, adv. GK: *857* [→ *755; cf. 1.1*]. carefully, securely; under guard; assuredly, beyond a doubt:– safely [2], assuredly [1]

807 ἀσχημονέω, aschēmoneō, v. GK: *858* [→ *1.1+4976*]. to act improperly, dishonorably, indecently, rudely:– behave unseemly [1], behaveth uncomely [1]

808 ἀσχημοσύνη, aschēmosynē, n. GK: *859* [→ *1.1+4976*]. indecent act, shame:– shame [1], unseemly [1]

809 ἀσχήμων, aschēmōn, a. GK: *860* [→ *1.1+4976*]. unpresentable, shameful, indecent:– uncomely [1]

810 ἀσωτία, asōtia, n. GK: *861* [→ *1.1+4982*]. debauchery, dissipation, wildness:– riot [2], excess [1]

811 ἀσώτως, asōtōs, adv. GK: *862* [→ *1.1+4982*]. wildly, in debauchery, in dissipation:– riotous [1]

812 ἀτακτέω, atakteō, v. GK: *863* [→ *1.1+5021*]. to be idle, lazy:– behaved disorderly [1]

813 ἄτακτος, ataktos, a. GK: *864* [→ *1.1+5021*]. idle, lazy:– unruly [1]

814 ἀτάκτως, ataktōs, adv. GK: *865* [→ *1.1+5021*]. idly, irresponsibly:– disorderly [2]

815 ἄτεκνος, ateknos, a. GK: *866* [→ *1.1+5088*]. childless, without children:– without children [2], childless [1]

816 ἀτενίζω, atenizō, v. GK: *867* [→ *1614; cf. 1.2*]. to look intently, gaze, stare:– looked stedfastly [2], earnestly beholding [1], earnestly looked [1], fastened eyes [1], fastened [1], fastening eyes [1], look earnestly [1], looked [1], looking stedfastly [1], set eyes [1], stedfastly beholding [1], stedfastly behold [1], stedfastly look [1]

817 ἄτερ, ater, pp.*. GK: *868.* without, apart from:– in the absence of [1], without [1]

818 ἀτιμάζω, atimazō, v. GK: *869 & 870* [→ *1.1+5092*]. to dishonor, disgrace, treat shamefully, insult:– dishonour [2], despised [1], dishonourest [1], entreated shamefully [1], suffer shame [1]

819 ἀτιμία, atimia, n. GK: *871* [→ *1.1+5092*]. dishonor, disgrace, shame; common use:– dishonour [4], reproach [1], shame [1], vile [1]

820 ἄτιμος, atimos, a. GK: *872* [→ *1.1+5092*]. without honor, dishonored, despised:– without honour [2], despised [1], less honourable [1]

821 ἀτιμόω, atimoō, v. GK: *873* [→ *1.1+5092*]. to disgrace:– shamefully handled [1]

822 ἀτμίς, atmis, n. GK: *874* [→ *109*]. mist, vapor; billows (of smoke):– vapour [2]

823 ἄτομος, atomos, a. GK: *875* [→ *1.1+5114*]. in a flash, in a moment, an indivisible unit of time:– moment [1]

824 ἄτοπος, atopos, a. GK: *876* [→ *1.1+5117*]. wrong, wicked; unusual, surprising:– amiss [1], harm [1], unreasonable [1]

825 Ἀττάλεια, Attaleia, n.pr. GK: *877.* Attalia:– Attalia [1]

826 αὐγάζω, augazō, v. GK: *878 & 2964* [→ *827*]. to see; shine (forth):– shine [1]

827 αὐγή, augē, n. GK: *879* [→ *541, 826, 1306, 5081*]. daylight, dawn:– break of day [1]

828 Αὔγουστος, Augoustos, n.pr. GK: *880.* Augustus, "*reverant, holy*":– Augustus [1]

829 αὐθάδης, authadēs, a. GK: *881* [→ *846+2237*]. overbearing, arrogant, stubborn, self-willed:– selfwilled [2]

830 αὐθαίρετος, authairetos, a. GK: *882* [→ *846+138*]. on one's own initiative, of one's own accord:– of own accord [1], willing of themselves [1]

831 αὐθεντέω, authenteō, v. GK: *883* [→ *846*]. to have authority over:– usurp authority over [1]

832 αὐλέω, auleō, v. GK: *884* [→ *836*]. to play the flute:– piped [3]

833 αὐλή, aulē, n. GK: *885* [→ *63, 1886, 4259; cf. 109, 835*]. palace, house; courtyard, sheepfold:– palace [7], hall [2], court [1], fold [1], sheepfold (*+3588+4263*) [1]

834 αὐλητής, aulētēs, n. GK: *886* [→ *836*]. flute player:– minstrels [1], pipers [1]

835 αὐλίζομαι, aulizomai, v. GK: *887* [cf. *833*]. to spend the night, find lodging:– abode [1], lodged [1]

836 αὐλός, aulos, n. GK: *888* [→ *832, 834*]. flute:– pipe [1]

837 αὐξάνω, auxanō, v. GK: *889 & 891* [→ *838, 4885, 5232*]. to cause to grow; (intr.) to grow, increase:– grew [6], grow [5], increased [3], increase [2], gave increase [1], giveth increase [1], groweth [1], grown [1], increaseth [1], increasing [1]

838 αὔξησις, auxēsis, n. GK: *890* [→ *837*]. growth, increase:– increase [2]

839 αὔριον, aurion, adv. GK: *892* [→ *1887*]. tomorrow, the next day:– to morrow [9], morrow [4], next day [1], on morrow [1]

840 αὐστηρός, austēros, a. GK: *893* [→ *850*]. hard, severe, strict, exacting:– austere [2]

841 αὐτάρκεια, autarkeia, n. GK: *894* [→ *846+714*]. contentment, having all of one's needs, sufficiency:– contentment [1], sufficiency [1]

842 αὐτάρκης, autarkēs, a. GK: *895* [→ *846+714*]. content; (possibly) self-sufficient:– content [1]

843 αὐτοκατάκριτος, autokatakritos, a. GK: *896* [→ *846+2596+2919*]. self-condemned:– condemned of himself [1]

844 αὐτόματος, automatos, a. GK: *897* [→ *846*]. by itself, automatic:– of herself [1], of own accord [1]

845 αὐτόπτης, autoptēs, n. GK: *898* [→ *846+3708*]. eyewitness:– eyewitnesses [1]

846 αὐτός, *autos*, p.inten. GK: *899* [→ *829, 830, 831, 841, 842, 843, 844, 845, 847, 848, 849, 1438, 1683, 1763, 1824, 1888, 3910, 4572, 5024, 5367, 5615*]. he, she, it, they; also used as inten.p., himself, herself, itself, themselves; the same one; also an adv. of place: here, there, where:– him [1942], them [1145], his [1093], their [313], he [265], her [242], it [183], *usually untranslated* [166], they [134], same [77], himself [51], his own [30], thereof [29], therein (*+1722*) [16], their own [12], yourselves [12], myself [10], themselves [10], the same [9], she [8], itself [7], that [7], those [7], together (*+1909+3588*) [7], ourselves [6], this [5], therein (*+1519*) [4], there [4], very [4], ye [4], own [3], selfsame [3], theirs [3], thereof (*+1537*) [3], thereon (*+1722*) [3], thyself [3], whose [3], he himself [2], into one place (*+1909+3588*) [2], likeminded (*+3588+5426*) [2], thee [2], there (*+1722*) [2], thereby (*+1223*) [2], thereon (*+1883*) [2], thereon [2], therewith (*+1722*) [2], we [2], which [2], whom [2], who [2], I myself [1], I [1], Jesus[S] [1], and [1], even all one as if (*+1520+2532+3588*) [1], her own [1], here [1], herself [1], his own self [1], in one place (*+1909+3588*) [1], in the like manner (*+2596+3588*) [1], man's [1], myself (*+1473*) [1], nothing (*+1537+3361*) [1], one [1], own selves [1], so (*+2596+3588*) [1], the house[S] [1], the other[S] [1], the said [1], the same (*+3778*) [1], the very [1], their own company [1], thereat (*+1223*) [1], thereby (*+1722*) [1], thereinto (*+1519*) [1], therein [1], thereon (*+1909*) [1], thereunto (*+1519+3778*) [1], these [1], they themselves [1], the [1], things [1], together (*+2596+3588*) [1], we ourselves [1]

847 αὐτοῦ, *autou*, p.gen. of *846*. GK: *899* [→ *846*]. as an adv. of place: here, there, where:–

848 αὑτοῦ, *autou*, p.gen. of *846*. GK: *899* [→ *846*]. of him, her, it, them:–

849 αὐτόχειρ, *autocheir*, a. or n. GK: *901* [→ *846+5495*]. with one's own hand:– with own hands [1]

850 αὐχμηρός, *auchmēros*, a. GK: *903* [→ *840*]. dark:– dark [1]

851 ἀφαιρέω, *aphaireō*, v. GK: *904* [→ *575+138*]. to take away from, remove; to cut (off):– take away [5], cut off [2], smote off [1], taken away [1], taketh away [1]

852 ἀφανής, *aphanēs*, a. GK: *905* [→ *1.1+5316*]. hidden, invisible:– not manifest [1]

853 ἀφανίζω, *aphanizō*, v. GK: *906* [→ *1.1+5316*]. to destroy, disfigure; to perish, vanish, disappear:– corrupt [2], disfigure [1], perish [1], vanisheth away [1]

854 ἀφανισμός, *aphanismos*, n. GK: *907* [→ *1.1+5316*]. disappearance, destruction:– vanish away [1]

855 ἄφαντος, *aphantos*, a. GK: *908* [→ *1.1+5316*]. disappearing, invisible:– vanished out of sight (*+1096*) [1]

856 ἀφεδρών, *aphedrōn*, n. GK: *909* [→ *575+1476*]. latrine:– draught [2]

857 ἀφειδία, *apheidia*, n. GK: *910* [→ *1.1+5339*]. harsh treatment, unsparing:– neglecting [1]

858 ἀφελότης, *aphelotēs*, n. GK: *911* [→ *1.1*]. sincerity, simplicity:– singleness [1]

859 ἄφεσις, *aphesis*, n. GK: *912* [→ *863*]. forgiveness, pardon, release, cancellation of a debt:– remission [9], forgiveness [6], deliverance [1], liberty [1]

860 ἁφή, *haphē*, n. GK: *913* [→ *681*]. ligament, joint:– joints [1], joint [1]

861 ἀφθαρσία, *aphtharsia*, n. GK: *914* [→ *1.1+5351*]. imperishableness, immortality:– incorruption [4], immortality [2], sincerity [2]

862 ἄφθαρτος, *aphthartos*, a. GK: *915* [→ *1.1+5351*]. imperishable, immortal, lasting forever:– incorruptible [4], immortal [1], not corruptible [1], uncorruptible [1]

863 ἀφίημι, *aphiēmi*, v. GK: *918 & 1889* [→ *425, 447, 801, 859, 1455, 3929, 3935, 4907, 4908, 4920; cf. 575*]. to forgive, pardon, remit, cancel; to leave, abandon; to allow, permit, tolerate:– left [36], forgive [23], forgiven [21], leave [9], let [8], suffer [8], let alone [6], suffered [6], forsook [4], leaving [3], forgave [2], forsaken [2], leave undone [2], leaveth [2], put away [2], sent away [2], cried [1], forgiveth [1], laying aside [1], let be [1], let go [1], let have [1], omitted [1], remitted [1], remit [1], yielded up [1]

864 ἀφικνέομαι, *aphikneomai*, v. GK: *919* [→ *575+2425*]. to reach:– come abroad [1]

865 ἀφιλάγαθος, *aphilagathos*, a. GK: *920* [→ *1.1+5384+18*]. not loving good:– despisers of good [1]

866 ἀφιλάργυρος, *aphilargyros*, a. GK: *921* [→ *1.1+5384+696*]. not loving money, not greedy:– not covetous [1], without covetousness [1]

867 ἄφιξις, *aphixis*, n. GK: *922* [→ *575+2425*]. leaving, departure:– departing [1]

868 ἀφίστημι, *aphistēmi*, v. GK: *923* [→ *575+2476*]. to leave, withdraw, abandon; to revolt, mislead:– departed [6], depart [3], depart from [1], departing [1], drew away [1], fall away [1], refrain [1], withdraw [1]

869 ἄφνω, *aphnō*, adv. GK: *924* [→ *1607*]. suddenly:– suddenly [3]

870 ἀφόβως, *aphobōs*, adv. GK: *925* [→ *1.1+5401*]. fearlessly, without the slightest qualm, boldly:– without fear [4]

871 ἀφομοιόω, *aphomoioō*, v. GK: *926* [→ *575+3664*]. (pass.) to be like, similar:– made like unto [1]

872 ἀφοράω, *aphoraō*, v. GK: *927* [→ *575+3708*]. to fix one's eyes; look away:– looking [1]

873 ἀφορίζω, *aphorizō*, v. GK: *928* [→ *575+3724*]. to separate, set apart, exclude:– separated [4], separate [4], divideth [1], sever [1]

874 ἀφορμή, *aphormē*, n. GK: *929* [→ *575+3730*]. opportunity, opening, pretext:– occasion [7]

875 ἀφρίζω, *aphrizō*, v. GK: *930* [→ *876*]. to foam at the mouth:– foameth [1], foaming [1]

876 ἀφρός, *aphros*, n. GK: *931* [→ *875, 1890*]. foam, froth:– foameth (*+3326*) [1]

877 ἀφροσύνη, *aphrosynē*, n. GK: *932* [→ *1.1+5424*]. foolishness, lack of sense:– foolishly (*+1722*) [2], folly [1], foolishness [1]

878 ἄφρων, *aphrōn*, a. GK: *933* [→ *1.1+5424*]. foolish, ignorant:– fool [6], foolish [2], fools [2], unwise [1]

879 ἀφυπνόω, *aphypnoō*, v. GK: *934* [→ *575+5258*]. to fall asleep:– fell asleep [1]

880 ἄφωνος, *aphōnos*, a. GK: *936* [→ *1.1+5456*]. silent, mute, without speech; without meaning:– dumb [3], without signification [1]

881 Ἀχάζ, *Achaz*, n.pr. GK: *937 & 941*. Ahaz, "*he has grasped*":– Achaz [2]

882 Ἀχαΐα, *Achaia*, n.pr. GK: *938* [→ *883*]. Achaia:– Achaia [11]

883 Ἀχαϊκός, *Achaikos*, n.pr. GK: *939* [→ *882*]. Achaicus, "*belonging to Achaia*":– Achaicus [2]

884 ἀχάριστος, *acharistos*, a. GK: *940* [→ *1.1+5463*]. ungrateful:– unthankful [2]

885 Ἀχίμ, *Achim*, n.pr. GK: *943*. Akim, "*Yahweh is my brother*":– Achim [2]

886 ἀχειροποίητος, *acheiropoiētos*, a. GK: *942* [→ *1.1+5495+4160*]. not made by human hands, implying not of human origin:– made without hands [2], not made with hand [1]

887 ἀχλύς, *achlys*, n. GK: *944*. mistiness, dimness of sight:– mist [1]

888 ἀχρεῖος, *achreios*, a. GK: *945* [→ *1.1+5530*]. worthless, useless, unworthy:– unprofitable [2]

889 ἀχρειόω, *achreioō*, v. GK: *946* [→ *1.1+5530*]. (pass.) to become worthless, depraved:– unprofitable [1]

890 ἄχρηστος, *achrēstos*, a. GK: *947* [→ *1.1+5530*]. useless, worthless:– unprofitable [1]

891 ἄχρι, *achri*, pp.*&c. GK: *948* [→ *206*]. until, up to, as far as, as long as:– until [12], unto [12], till (*+3739*) [4], till [4], until (*+3739*) [4], as far as [2], for [2], while (*+3739*) [2], even to [1], even unto [1], hitherto (*+1204+3588*) [1], into [1], in [1], till (*+302+3739*) [1], to [1]

892 ἄχυρον, *achyron*, n. GK: *949*. chaff:– chaff [2]

893 ἀψευδής, *apseudēs*, a. GK: *950* [→ *1.1+5574*]. not a liar, free from deceit, trustworthy:– cannot lie [1]

894 ἄψινθος, *apsinthos*, n. GK: *951 & 952*. (m.) Wormwood, referring to a bitter herb (absinthe); (f.) bitterness:– wormwood [2]

895 ἄψυχος, *apsychos*, a. GK: *953* [→ *1.1+5594*]. lifeless, inanimate:– without life [1]

896 Βάαλ, *Baal*, n.pr. GK: *955*. Baal, "*master, owner, lord*":– Baal [1]

897 Βαβυλών, *Babylōn*, n.pr. GK: *956*. Babylon, "*gate of god[s]*":– Babylon [12]

898 βαθμός, *bathmos*, n. GK: *957* [→ *305*]. standing, rank:– degree [1]

899 βάθος, *bathos*, n. GK: *958* [→ *901*]. depth, deep thing; extreme:– depth [4], deep (*+2596*) [1], deep things [1], deepness [1], deep [1], depths [1]

900 βαθύνω, *bathynō*, v. GK: *959* [→ *901*]. to go down deep, dig deep:– deep [1]

901 βαθύς, *bathys*, a. GK: *960* [→ *899, 900*]. deep; (as a time of day) early:– deep [2], very early in the morning (*+3722*) [1]

902 βάϊον, *baion*, n. GK: *961*. (palm) branch:– branches [1]

903 Βαλαάμ, *Balaam*, n.pr. GK: *962*. Balaam, "[poss.] *Baal [lord] of the people* or *the clan brings forth*":– Balaam [3]

904 Βαλάκ, *Balak*, n.pr. GK: *963*. Balak, "*devastator*":– Balac [1]

905 βαλλάντιον, *ballantion*, n. GK: *964*. purse, money-bag:– purse [3], bags [1]

906 βάλλω, *ballō*, v. GK: *311 & 965* [→ *293, 306, 311, 474, 577, 579, 580, 956, 992, 1000, 1001, 1002, 1225, 1228, 1544, 1546, 1685, 1911, 1915, 2598, 2602, 3036, 3328, 3846, 3850, 3925, 4016, 4018, 4261, 4820, 5146, 5234, 5235, 5236, 5260*]. to throw, pour; to put, set:– cast [81], put [11], casting [6], laid [3], send [3], thrust [3], casteth [2], putteth [2], threw [2], thrust in [2], arose [1], cast in [1], dung (*+2874*) [1], lieth [1], lying [1], poured [1], poureth [1], put up [1], strike with the palms of hands (*+4475*) [1], thrown [1]

907 βαπτίζω, *baptizō*, v. GK: *966* [→ *911*]. to baptize, wash; the baptizer:– baptized [61], baptize [9], baptizing [4], baptizeth [2], Baptist [1], baptizest [1], washed [1], wash [1]

908 βάπτισμα, *baptisma*, n. GK: *967* [→ *911*]. baptism:– baptism [22]

909 βαπτισμός, *baptismos*, n. GK: *968* [→ *911*]. baptism, ceremonial washing:– washing [2], baptisms [1], washings [1]

910 βαπτιστής, *baptistēs*, n. GK: *969* [→ *911*]. Baptist, a surname of John:– Baptist [13], Baptist's [1]

911 βάπτω, *baptō*, v. GK: *970* [→ *907, 908, 909, 910, 1686*]. to dip (in):– dipped [1], dipt [1], dip [1]

912 Βαραββᾶς, *Barabbas*, n.pr. GK: *972*. Barabbas, "*son of a father* poss. *son of a rabbi*":– Barabbas [11]

913 Βαράκ, *Barak*, n.pr. GK: *973*. Barak, "*lightning*":– Barak [1]

914 Βαραχίας, *Barachias*, n.pr. GK: *974*. Berekiah, "*Yahweh blesses*":– Barachias [1]

915 βάρβαρος, *barbaros*, a. GK: *975*. non-Greek, foreign, "barbarian"; someone who speaks an unintelligible language:– barbarian [3], barbarians [2], barbarous people [1]

916 βαρέω, *bareō*, v. GK: *976* [→ *922*]. (pass.) to be burdened, under pressure:– heavy [3], burdened [1], charged [1], pressed [1]

917 βαρέως, *bareōs*, adv. GK: *977* [→ *922*]. with difficulty:– dull [2]

918 Βαρθολομαῖος, *Bartholomaios*, n.pr. GK: *978*. Bartholomew, "*son of Talmai*":– Bartholomew [4]

919 Βαριησοῦς, *Bariēsous*, n.pr. GK: *979*. Bar-Jesus, "*son of Jesus [Joshua]*":– Barjesus [1]

920 Βαριωνᾶς, *Bariōnas*, n.pr. GK: *980 & 981*. son of Jonah, Bar-Jona, "*son of Jonah* or *John*":– Barjona [1]

921 Βαρναβᾶς, *Barnabas*, n.pr. GK: *982*. Barnabas, "*son of comfort*":– Barnabas [29]

922 βάρος, *baros*, n. GK: *983* [→ *4, 916, 917, 925, 926, 927, 1912, 2599*]. burden, weight; this can refer either to difficulty or importance:– burden [3], burdensome (*+1722*) [1], burdens [1], weight [1]

923 Βαρσαββᾶς, *Barsabbas*, n.pr. GK: *984*. Barsabbas, "*son of the Sabbath* or *son of Saba*":– Barsabas [2]

924 Βαρτιμαῖος, *Bartimaios*, n.pr. GK: *985*. Bartimaeus, "*son of Timai* or *son of uncleanness*":– Bartimeus [1]

925 βαρύνω, *barynō*, v. GK: *986 & 2852* [→ *922*]. to burden, grieve:– overcharged [1]

926 βαρύς, *barys*, a. GK: *987* [→ *922*]. burdensome, heavy, important; savage, fierce:– grievous [3], heavy [1], weightier [1], weighty [1]

927 **βαρύτιμος**, ***barytimos***, a. GK: *988* [→ *922+5092*]. very expensive:– very precious [1]

928 **βασανίζω**, ***basanizō***, v. GK: *989* [→ *931*]. to torture, torment; (pass.) to be tortured, tormented, in pain:– tormented [5], torment [3], pained [1], toiling [1], tossed [1], vexed [1]

929 **βασανισμός**, ***basanismos***, n. GK: *990* [→ *931*]. torment, torture, agony:– torment [6]

930 **βασανιστής**, ***basanistēs***, n. GK: *991* [→ *931*]. torturer:– tormentors [1]

931 **βάσανος**, ***basanos***, n. GK: *992* [→ *928, 929, 930*]. torment, severe pain, torture:– torments [2], torment [1]

932 **βασιλεία**, ***basileia***, n. GK: *993* [→ *935*]. kingdom, kingship, royal rule:– kingdom [157], kingdoms [4], reigneth (*+2192*) [1]

933 **βασίλειον**, ***basileion***, a.neut. of *934*. GK: *994* [→ *935*]. as a noun, a residence of royalty: palace:– kings' courts [1]

934 **βασίλειος**, ***basileios***, a. GK: *994* [→ *935*]. royal, kingly; as a noun, a residence of royalty: palace:– royal [1]

935 **βασιλεύς**, ***basileus***, n. GK: *995* [→ *932, 933, 934, 936, 937, 938, 4821*]. king:– king [86], kings [29], king's [2], kings' [1]

936 **βασιλεύω**, ***basileuō***, v. GK: *996* [→ *935*]. to reign as a king, become king:– reign [13], reigned [5], kings [1], reigned as kings [1], reigneth [1]

937 **βασιλικός**, ***basilikos***, a. GK: *997 & 998* [→ *935*]. royal, noble, kingly; as a noun, royal official (possibly of the Herodian family):– nobleman [2], royal [2], king's [1]

938 **βασίλισσα**, ***basilissa***, n. GK: *999* [→ *935*]. queen:– queen [4]

939 **βάσις**, ***basis***, n. GK: *1000* [→ *305*]. foot:– feet [1]

940 **βασκαίνω**, ***baskainō***, v. GK: *1001*. to bewitch:– bewitched [1]

941 **βαστάζω**, ***bastazō***, v. GK: *1002* [→ *1419*]. to carry, bear up, carry off; to tolerate, help, support:– bear [11], bare [4], borne [4], bearing [3], bearest [1], carried [1], carrieth [1], carry [1], took up [1]

942 **βάτος**[1], ***batos***[1], n. GK: *1003*. bush, brier, thornbush:– bush [4], bramble bush [1]

943 **βάτος**[2], ***batos***[2], n. GK: *1004*. bath (a unit of liquid measure, between eight and nine gallons):– measures [1]

944 **βάτραχος**, ***batrachos***, n. GK: *1005*. frog:– frogs [1]

945 **βατταλογέω**, ***battalogeō***, v. GK: *1006* [→ *3004*]. to babble, prattle:– use vain repetitions [1]

946 **βδέλυγμα**, ***bdelygma***, n. GK: *1007* [→ *947, 948*]. abomination, something detestable:– abomination [4], abominations [2]

947 **βδελυκτός**, ***bdelyktos***, a. GK: *1008* [→ *946*]. detestable, abominable:– abominable [1]

948 **βδελύσσομαι**, ***bdelyssomai***, v. GK: *1009* [→ *946*]. (mid.) to abhor, detest; (pass.) to be vile, abhorrent:– abhorrest [1], abominable [1]

949 **βέβαιος**, ***bebaios***, a. GK: *1010* [→ *305*]. firm, sure, certain, binding:– stedfast [4], sure [2], firm [1], force [1], more sure [1]

950 **βεβαιόω**, ***bebaioō***, v. GK: *1011* [→ *305*]. to confirm; keep strong:– confirmed [2], confirm [2], confirming [1], established [1], stablished [1], stablisheth [1]

951 **βεβαίωσις**, ***bebaiōsis***, n. GK: *1012* [→ *305*]. confirmation:– confirmation [2]

952 **βέβηλος**, ***bebēlos***, a. GK: *1013* [→ *305*]. godless, irreligious, profane, worldly:– profane [5]

953 **βεβηλόω**, ***bebēloō***, v. GK: *1014* [→ *305*]. to desecrate, profane:– profane [2]

954 **Βεελζεβούλ**, ***Beelzeboul***, n.pr. GK: *1015*. Beelzebub, "*lord [baal] of the flies*":– Beelzebub [7]

955 **Βελίαλ**, ***Belial***, n.pr. GK: *1016*. Belial, "*wicked, without use*":– Belial [1]

956 **βέλος**, ***belos***, n. GK: *1018* [→ *906*]. arrow:– darts [1]

957 **βελτίων**, ***beltiōn***, a. GK: *1019*. having a detailed knowledge, translated "better, very well":– very well [1]

958 **Βενιαμίν**, ***Beniamin***, n.pr. GK: *1020 & 1021*. Benjamin, "*son of the right hand* or *Southerner*":– Benjamin [4]

959 **Βερνίκη**, ***Bernikē***, n.pr. GK: *1022* [→ *5342+3529*]. Bernice, "*victorious*":– Bernice [3]

960 **Βέροια**, ***Beroia***, n.pr. GK: *1023* [→ *961*]. Berea:– Berea [2]

961 **Βεροιαῖος**, ***Beroiaios***, a.pr.g. GK: *1024* [→ *960*]. Berean, person of Berea:– Berea [1]

962 **Βηθαβαρά**, ***Bēthabara***, n.pr. GK: *1028 & 1030*. Bethabara:– Bethabara [1]

963 **Βηθανία**, ***Bēthania***, n.pr. GK: *1029*. Bethany, "*House of Ananiah* [or *the poor* or *unripe figs*]":– Bethany [11]

964 **Βηθεσδά**, ***Bēthesda***, n.pr. GK: *1031 & 1032*. Bethesda, "*site [house] of mercy*":– Bethesda [1]

965 **Βηθλέεμ**, ***Bēthleem***, n.pr. GK: *1033*. Bethlehem, "*house of bread* poss. *temple of Lakhmu*":– Bethlehem [8]

966 **Βηθσαϊδά**, ***Bēthsaida***, n.pr. GK: *1034 & 1035*. Bethsaida, "*site [house] of fishing*":– Bethsaida [7]

967 **Βηθφαγή**, ***Bēthphagē***, n.pr. GK: *1036*. Bethphage, "*house of unripe figs*":– Bethphage [3]

968 **βῆμα**, ***bēma***, n. GK: *1037* [→ *305*]. judicial court, judge's seat; this can refer to human or divine judgment:– judgment seat [10], set on [1], throne [1]

969 **βήρυλλος**, ***bēryllos***, n. GK: *1039*. beryl, a semi-precious stone of sea-green color:– beryl [1]

970 **βία**, ***bia***, n. GK: *1040* [→ *971, 972, 973, 3849*]. force, violence, pounding (of surf):– violence [4]

971 **βιάζω**, ***biazō***, v. GK: *1041* [→ *970*]. (mid.) to force one's way:– presseth [1], suffereth violence [1]

972 **βίαιος**, ***biaios***, a. GK: *1042* [→ *970*]. violent, strong:– mighty [1]

973 **βιαστής**, ***biastēs***, n. GK: *1043* [→ *970*]. forceful one:– violent [1]

974 **βιβλαρίδιον**, ***biblaridion***, n. GK: *1044 & 1045* [→ *976*]. little scroll:– little book [4]

975 **βιβλίον**, ***biblion***, n. GK: *1046* [→ *976*]. scroll, book, certificate:– book [25], books [4], bill [1], scrole [1], writing [1]

976 **βίβλος**, ***biblos***, n. GK: *1047* [→ *974, 975*]. book, scroll:– book [12], books [1]

977 **βιβρώσκω**, ***bibrōskō***, v. GK: *1048* [→ *1033, 1034, 1035, 4598, 4662*]. to eat:– eaten [1]

978 **Βιθυνία**, ***Bithynia***, n.pr. GK: *1049*. Bithynia:– Bithynia [2]

979 **βίος**, ***bios***, n. GK: *1050* [→ *980, 981, 982, 3969*]. (everyday) life; what one lives on, property, possessions:– life [5], living [5], good [1]

980 **βιόω**, ***bioō***, v. GK: *1051* [→ *979*]. to live:– live [1]

981 **βίωσις**, ***biōsis***, n. GK: *1052* [→ *979*]. the way one lives:– manner of life [1]

982 **βιωτικός**, ***biōtikos***, a. GK: *1053* [→ *979*]. (lesser things) of this life:– of life [1], pertaining to life [1], that pertain to life [1]

983 **βλαβερός**, ***blaberos***, a. GK: *1054* [→ *984*]. harmful:– hurtful [1]

984 **βλάπτω**, ***blaptō***, v. GK: *1055* [→ *983*]. to hurt, injure:– hurt [2]

985 **βλαστάνω**, ***blastanō***, v. GK: *1056 & 1057* [→ *986*]. to sprout, bud:– brought forth [1], budded [1], spring [1], sprung up [1]

986 **Βλάστος**, ***Blastos***, n.pr. GK: *1058* [→ *985*]. Blastus, "*sprout [of a vine or branch]*":– Blastus [1]

987 **βλασφημέω**, ***blasphēmeō***, v. GK: *1059* [→ *988, 989; cf. 5346*]. to blaspheme, insult, slander, curse:– blasphemed [7], blaspheme [6], speak evil [5], evil spoken of [4], blasphemeth [2], blasphemers [1], blasphemest [1], blaspheming [1], blasphemously [1], defamed [1], railed on [1], railed [1], reviled [1], slanderously reported [1], speaking evil [1], spoken blasphemy [1]

988 **βλασφημία**, ***blasphēmia***, n. GK: *1060* [→ *987*]. blasphemy, slander, malicious talk:– blasphemy [11], blasphemies [5], evil speaking [1], railings [1], railing [1]

989 **βλάσφημος**, ***blasphēmos***, a. GK: *1061* [→ *987*]. blasphemous, slanderous, abusive, evil, hurtful (speech); as a noun, a reviler, blasphemer:– blasphemous [2], blasphemers [1], blasphemer [1], railing [1]

990 **βλέμμα**, ***blemma***, n. GK: *1062* [→ *991*]. act of seeing:– seeing [1]

991 **βλέπω**, ***blepō***, v. GK: *1063* [→ *308, 309, 578, 990, 1227, 1689, 1914, 4017, 4265*]. to see, look at; to watch out, beware, pay attention:– see [48], take heed [14], seeth [11], saw [9], seen [9], seeing [8], beware [7], seest [5], look [4], beholdest [3], behold [3], beheld [2], beholding [2], sight [2], lieth [1], look on [1], looked [1], looketh on [1], looking [1], perceive [1], regardest (*+1519*) [1], regardest [1]

992 **βλητέος**, ***blēteos***, a. GK: *1064* [→ *906*]. must be put:– must be put [1], put [1]

993 **Βοανηργές**, ***Boanērges***, l.[pr.n.]. GK: *1065*. Boanerges, "*sons of thunder*":– Boanerges [1]

994 **βοάω**, ***boaō***, v. GK: *1066* [→ *995*]. to call, cry out, shout:– crying [6], cried [3], cry [2]

995 **βοή**, ***boē***, n. GK: *1068* [→ *310, 994, 996, 997, 998, 1916*]. cry, shout:– cries [1]

996 **βοήθεια**, ***boētheia***, n. GK: *1069* [→ *995*]. help; support (to hold something together with ropes or cables):– helps [1], help [1]

997 **βοηθέω**, ***boētheō***, v. GK: *1070* [→ *995*]. to help, come to the aid of:– help [5], helped [1], succoured [1], succour [1]

998 **βοηθός**, ***boēthos***, a. GK: *1071* [→ *995*]. helpful (one):– helper [1]

999 **βόθυνος**, ***bothynos***, n. GK: *1072 & 1073*. pit, cistern:– ditch [2], pit [1]

1000 **βολή**, ***bolē***, n. GK: *1074* [→ *906*]. throwing:– cast [1]

1001 **βολίζω**, ***bolizō***, v. GK: *1075* [→ *906*]. to take a sounding (a nautical technical term):– sounded [2]

1002 **βολίς**, ***bolis***, n. GK: *1076* [→ *906*]. missile, arrow, javelin:– dart [1]

1003 **Βοόζ**, ***Booz***, n.pr. GK: *1067 & 1077 & 1078*. Boaz, "[perhaps] *in him is strength*":– Booz [3]

1004 **βόρβορος**, ***borboros***, n. GK: *1079*. mud, filth, slime:– mire [1]

1005 **βορρᾶς**, ***borras***, n. GK: *1080*. the north:– north [2]

1006 **βόσκω**, ***boskō***, v. GK: *1081* [→ *1008*]. to feed, tend; (pass.) to eat, graze:– feeding [3], feed [3], fed [2], kept [1]

1007 **Βοσόρ**, ***Bosor***, n.pr. GK: *1026 & 1027 & 1082*. Bosor:– Bosor [1]

1008 **βοτάνη**, ***botanē***, n. GK: *1083* [→ *1006*]. crop (from any kind of plant or vegetation):– herbs [1]

1009 **βότρυς**, ***botrys***, n. GK: *1084*. grape cluster, bunch of grapes:– clusters [1]

1010 **βουλευτής**, ***bouleutēs***, n. GK: *1085* [→ *1014*]. member of a council (an advisory or legislative body):– counseller [2]

1011 **βουλεύω**, ***bouleuō***, v. GK: *1086* [→ *1014*]. to make plans, consider, decide, plot:– minded [2], purpose [2], consulted [1], consulteth [1], determined [1], took counsel [1]

1012 **βουλή**, ***boulē***, n. GK: *1087* [→ *1014*]. plan, purpose, will, decision:– counsel [9], advised (*+5087*) [1], counsels [1], will [1]

1013 **βούλημα**, ***boulēma***, n. GK: *1088* [→ *1014*]. plan, will, choice:– purpose [1], will [1]

1014 **βούλομαι**, ***boulomai***, v. GK: *1089* [→ *711, 1010, 1011, 1012, 1013, 1917, 2103, 3851, 4823, 4824, 4825*]. to wish, will, desire; to choose, determine, plan:– will [11], would [10], willing [5], minded [2], disposed [1], intending [1], intend [1], listeth (*+2116*) [1], of own will [1], would have [1]

1015 **βουνός**, ***bounos***, n. GK: *1090*. hill:– hills [1], hill [1]

1016 **βοῦς**, ***bous***, n. GK: *1091*. ox, cattle:– oxen [4], ox [4]

1017 **βραβεῖον**, ***brabeion***, n. GK: *1092* [→ *1018*]. prize (from a contest or foot race):– prize [2]

1018 **βραβεύω**, ***brabeuō***, v. GK: *1093* [→ *1017, 2603*]. to rule:– rule [1]

1019 **βραδύνω**, ***bradynō***, v. GK: *1094* [→ *1021*]. to delay, hesitate:– slack [1], tarry long [1]

1020 **βραδυπλοέω**, ***bradyploeō***, v. GK: *1095* [→ *1021+4126*]. to sail slowly:– sailed slowly [1]

1021 **βραδύς**, ***bradys***, a. GK: *1096* [→ *1019, 1020, 1022*]. slow:– slow [3]

1022 βραδύτης, bradytēs, n. GK: *1097* [→ *1021*]. slowness:– slackness [1]

1023 βραχίων, brachiōn, n. GK: *1098* [→ *1024*]. arm; a figure of power and authority:– arm [3]

1024 βραχύς, brachys, a. GK: *1099* [→ *1023*]. little, short:– little [4], few [1], little space [1], little while [1]

1025 βρέφος, brephos, n. GK: *1100*. baby, infant:– babe [4], babes [1], child [1], infants [1], young children [1]

1026 βρέχω, brechō, v. GK: *1101* [→ *1028*]. to rain down (water or sulfur); to make wet:– rained [2], rain (+*5205*) [1], rain [1], sendeth rain [1], washed [1], wash [1]

1027 βροντή, brontē, n. GK: *1103*. thunder:– thunderings [4], thunders [4], thunder [3], thundered (+*1096*) [1]

1028 βροχή, brochē, n. GK: *1104* [→ *1026*]. rain:– rain [2]

1029 βρόχος, brochos, n. GK: *1105*. restriction, restraint (from the base meaning of a snare or noose, not found in the NT):– snare [1]

1030 βρυγμός, brygmos, n. GK: *1106* [→ *1031*]. gnashing, grinding:– gnashing [7]

1031 βρύχω, brychō, v. GK: *1107* [→ *1030*]. to gnash, grind:– gnashed [1]

1032 βρύω, bryō, v. GK: *1108*. to flow, pour forth:– send forth [1]

1033 βρῶμα, brōma, n. GK: *1109* [→ *977*]. food, what is eaten:– meat [10], meats [6], victuals [1]

1034 βρώσιμος, brōsimos, a. GK: *1110* [→ *977*]. eatable:– meat [1]

1035 βρῶσις, brōsis, n. GK: *1111* [→ *977*]. consumable, food, rust, corrosion:– meat [6], rust [2], eating [1], food [1], morsel of meat [1]

1036 βυθίζω, bythizō, v. GK: *1112* [→ *1037*]. (act.) to plunge; (pass.) to sink:– drown [1], sink [1]

1037 βυθός, bythos, n. GK: *1113* [→ *12, 1036*]. open sea, the deep:– deep [1]

1038 βυρσεύς, byrseus, n. GK: *1114*. tanner:– tanner [3]

1039 βύσσινος, byssinos, a. GK: *1115 & 3327* [→ *1040*]. made of fine linen, a product of the flax plant:– fine linen [4]

1040 βύσσος, byssos, n. GK: *1116* [→ *1039*]. fine linen:– fine linen [2]

1041 βωμός, bōmos, n. GK: *1117* [→ *305*]. altar:– altar [1]

1042 Γαββαθᾶ, Gabbatha, n.pr. GK: *1119*. Gabbatha, "[poss.] *height, ridge*":– Gabbatha [1]

1043 Γαβριήλ, Gabriēl, n.pr. GK: *1120*. Gabriel, "*[strong] man of God [El]*":– Gabriel [2]

1044 γάγγραινα, gangraina, n. GK: *1121*. gangrene:– canker [1]

1045 Γάδ, Gad, n.pr. GK: *1122*. Gad, "*fortune*":– Gad [1]

1046 Γαδαρηνός, Gadarēnos, a.pr.g. GK: *1123*. Gadarene, "*from Gadara*":– Gadarenes [3]

1047 γάζα[2], gaza[2], n. GK: *1125* [→ *1049*]. treasury:– treasure [1]

1048 Γάζα[1], Gaza[1], n.pr. GK: *1124*. Gaza, "*strong*":– Gaza [1]

1049 γαζοφυλάκιον, gazophylakion, n. GK: *1126* [→ *1047+5442*]. treasury, place where offerings are put:– treasury [5]

1050 Γάϊος, Gaios, n.pr. GK: *1127* [→ *1093*]. Gaius:– Gaius [5]

1051 γάλα, gala, n. GK: *1128*. milk:– milk [5]

1052 Γαλάτης, Galatēs, n.pr.g. GK: *1129* [→ *1053*]. Galatian, "*from Galatia*":– Galatians [2]

1053 Γαλατία, Galatia, n.pr. GK: *1130* [→ *1052, 1054*]. Galatia:– Galatia [4]

1054 Γαλατικός, Galatikos, a.pr.g. GK: *1131* [→ *1053*]. Galatian:– of Galatia [2]

1055 γαλήνη, galēnē, n. GK: *1132*. calm:– calm [3]

1056 Γαλιλαία, Galilaia, n.pr. GK: *1133* [→ *1057*]. Galilee, "*ring, circle*, hence *region*":– Galilee [63]

1057 Γαλιλαῖος, Galilaios, a.pr.g. GK: *1134* [→ *1056*]. Galilean, "*from Galilee*":– Galileans [5], Galilean [3], of Galilee [3]

1058 Γαλλίων, Galliōn, n.pr. GK: *1136*. Gallio:– Gallio [3]

1059 Γαμαλιήλ, Gamaliēl, n.pr. GK: *1137*. Gamaliel, "*recompense of God [El]*":– Gamaliel [2]

1060 γαμέω, gameō, v. GK: *1138* [→ *1062*]. to marry:– marry [16], married [9], marrieth [3], marrying [1]

1061 γαμίσκω, gamiskō, v. GK: *1139 & 1140* [→ *1062*]. to give in marriage, marry; (pass.) to be given in marriage:– given in marriage [1]

1062 γάμος, gamos, n. GK: *1141* [→ *22, 1060, 1061, 1547, 1548, 1918*]. wedding banquet (a festive time in the community):– marriage [9], wedding [7]

1063 γάρ, gar, c. GK: *1142* [→ *5105*]. shows inference or continuation: for, because, indeed, but:– for [1026], and [4], because [4], why [4], but [2], verily [2], yet (+*2532*) [2], as [1], even [1], how (+*302+4459*) [1], indeed [1], no doubt [1], seeing [1], that [1], then [1], therefore [1], when (+*5613*) [1], yet [1]

1064 γαστήρ, gastēr, n. GK: *1143*. belly, womb, gluttony:– with child (+*1722+2192*) [5], child [2], bellies [1], womb [1]

1065 γέ, ge, pt.emph. GK: *1145* [→ *2534, 2544, 3304, 3386*]. emphatic particle: indeed, surely:– yet [2], and (+*235*) [1], at least (+*2532*) [1], did [1], haply (+*686*) [1], then (+*686*) [1], wherefore (+*686*) [1], yet doubtless (+*235*) [1]

1066 Γεδεών, Gedeōn, n.pr. GK: *1146*. Gideon, "*one who cuts, hacks*":– Gedeon [1]

1067 γέεννα, geenna, n. GK: *1147*. Gehenna, hell, "*Valley of Hinnom*":– hell [12]

1068 Γεθσημανῆ, Gethsēmanē, n.pr. GK: *1148 & 1149*. Gethsemane, "*olive oil press*":– Gethsemane [2]

1069 γείτων, geitōn, n. GK: *1150*. neighbor:– neighbours [4]

1070 γελάω, gelaō, v. GK: *1151* [→ *1071, 2606*]. to laugh:– laugh [2]

1071 γέλως, gelōs, n. GK: *1152* [→ *1070*]. laughter:– laughter [1]

1072 γεμίζω, gemizō, v. GK: *1153* [→ *1073*]. to fill:– filled [7], fill [1], full [1]

1073 γέμω, gemō, v. GK: *1154* [→ *1072, 1117*]. to be full:– full [9], full of [2]

1074 γενεά, genea, n. GK: *1155* [→ *1096*]. generation, one's own kind or race, descendant; fig., age, period of time (as in "to all generations"):– generation [31], generations [6], ages [2], nation [1], times [1], time [1]

1075 γενεαλογέω, genealogeō, v. GK: *1156* [→ *1096+3004*]. to trace genealogical descent:– descent counted [1]

1076 γενεαλογία, genealogia, n. GK: *1157* [→ *1096+3004*]. genealogy, lineage:– genealogies [2]

1077 γενέσια, genesia, n. GK: *1158 & 1159 & 1160* [→ *1096*]. birthday (a day that was celebrated):– birthday [2]

1078 γένεσις, genesis, n. GK: *1161* [→ *1096*]. birth; genealogy, descent; (course of one's) life:– generation [1], natural [1], nature [1]

1079 γενετή, genetē, n. GK: *1162* [→ *1096*]. birth:– birth [1]

1080 γεννάω, gennaō, v. GK: *1164* [→ *1096*]. to become the father of; to bear, give birth to; (pass.) to be conceived, born:– begat [42], born [39], begotten [7], bare [1], bear [1], brought forth [1], conceived [1], delivered [1], gendereth [1], gender [1], made [1], sprang [1]

1081 γέννημα, gennēma, n. GK: *1163 & 1165* [→ *1096*]. fruit, product, yield, harvest; offspring, brood:– generation [4], fruit [3], fruits [2]

1082 Γεννησαρέτ, Gennēsaret, n.pr. GK: *1166*. Gennesaret:– Gennesaret [2], Genesaret [1]

1083 γέννησις, gennēsis, n. GK: *1167* [→ *1096*]. birth:– birth [2]

1084 γεννητός, gennētos, a. GK: *1168* [→ *1096*]. pertaining to birth; "those born among women" means "all humankind":– born [2]

1085 γένος, genos, n. GK: *1169* [→ *1096*]. family, offspring; nation, people, native (of a region); classification or kind:– kindred [3], kind [3], offspring [3], born [2], kinds [2], nation [2], stock [2], countrymen [1], diversities [1], generation [1], of the country of [1]

1086 Γεργεσηνός, Gergesēnos, a.pr.g. GK: *1170 & 1171*. Gergesene, "*from Gergesa*":– Gergesenes [1]

1087 γερουσία, gerousia, n. GK: *1172* [→ *1088*]. assembly of the elders:– senate [1]

1088 γέρων, gerōn, n. GK: *1173* [→ *1087; cf. 1094*]. old person:– old [1]

1089 γεύομαι, geuomai, v. GK: *1174*. to taste, eat, partake of (implying enjoyment of the experience):– taste [7], tasted [5], eaten [2], eat [1]

1090 γεωργέω, geōrgeō, v. GK: *1175* [→ *1093+2041*]. to farm, cultivate:– dressed [1]

1091 γεώργιον, geōrgion, n. GK: *1176* [→ *1093+2041*]. (farmer's) field:– husbandry [1]

1092 γεωργός, geōrgos, n. GK: *1177* [→ *1093+2041*]. farmer, tenant farmer, share cropper:– husbandmen [16], husbandman [3]

1093 γῆ, gē, n. GK: *1178* [→ *508, 1050, 1090, 1091, 1092, 1919*]. earth, world, country, region; land, ground, soil:– earth [188], land [42], ground [18], country [2], earthly (+*1537+3588*) [1], world [1]

1094 γῆρας, gēras, n. GK: *1179* [→ *1095; cf. 1088*]. old age:– old age [1]

1095 γηράσκω, gēraskō, v. GK: *1180* [→ *1094*]. to grow old, age:– old [1], waxeth old [1]

1096 γίνομαι, ginomai, v. GK: *1181* [→ *35, 36, 241, 313, 581, 738, 1074, 1075, 1076, 1077, 1078, 1079, 1080, 1081, 1083, 1084, 1085, 1103, 1104, 1118, 1230, 1549, 1920, 2104, 2225, 3439, 3824, 3854, 4266, 4269, 4772, 4773, 4836, 5041, 5042*]. to be, become, happen; to come into existence, be born. It is used in certain contexts to introduce a new section or paragraph in a narrative in Hebrew narrative style: and then, and it came to pass:– was [103], be [84], made [67], came to pass [65], done [63], come [27], were [26], become [21], came [21], is [20], became [17], God forbid (+*3361*) [15], come to pass [15], been [14], arose [11], are [5], have [5], become (+*1519*) [4], becometh [4], being [4], fulfilled [3], had [3], made (+*1519*) [3], married [3], ariseth [2], doing [2], grow [2], past [2], preferred before (+*1715*) [2], seemed [2], wrought [2], assembled [1], as [1], at even (+*3798*) [1], awaking out of sleep (+*1853*) [1], became (+*1519*) [1], befell [1], behaved [1], brought to pass [1], brought [1], came pass [1], camest [1], come by (+*4031*) [1], cometh to pass [1], cometh [1], continued [1], did [1], drawing [1], ended [1], falling headlong (+*4248*) [1], fell [1], finished [1], followed [1], found [1], give [1], happened [1], in [1], laid wait for (+*1917*) [1], obey (+*5255*) [1], ordained [1], partakest (+*4791*) [1], performed [1], preferred [1], published [1], purposed (+*1106*) [1], ran together (+*4890*) [1], require [1], shewed [1], sounded [1], spent [1], taken [1], there [1], thundered (+*1027*) [1], trembled (+*1719*) [1], trembled (+*1790*) [1], turned [1], used [1], vanished out of sight (+*855*) [1], was noised abroad (+*3588+5456*) [1], waxed (+*1519*) [1], waxed [1], wept (+*2805*) [1], were (+*1510*) [1]

1097 γινώσκω, ginōskō, v. GK: *1182* [→ *50, 51, 52, 56, 57, 176, 314, 319, 320, 1106, 1107, 1108, 1109, 1110, 1231, 1232, 1233, 1921, 1922, 2589, 2607, 4267, 4268, 4774*]. to know, come to know, recognize, understand; to have sexual relations:– know [94], known [45], knew [30], knoweth [16], perceived [7], knowest [5], knowing [5], understood [4], understand [3], perceive [2], sure [2], allow [1], canst speak [1], can [1], felt [1], knewest [1], knowledge [1], resolved [1], understandest [1], ware of [1], ware [1]

1098 γλεῦκος, gleukos, n. GK: *1183* [→ *1099*]. (sweet) wine:– new wine [1]

1099 γλυκύς, glykys, a. GK: *1184* [→ *1098*]. sweet, fresh (water):– sweet [3], fresh [1]

1100 γλῶσσα, glōssa, n. GK: *1185* [→ *1101, 2084*]. tongue; language; sometimes refers to the supernatural gift of tongues:– tongues [26], tongue [24]

1101 γλωσσόκομον, glōssokomon, n. GK: *1186* [→ *1100+2880*]. container for money:– bag [2]

1102 γναφεύς, gnapheus, n. GK: *1187* [→ *46; cf. 2833*]. bleacher, fuller, one who cleans and sizes woolen cloth:– fuller [1]

1103 γνήσιος, gnēsios, a. GK: *1188* [→ *1096*]. true, loyal, sincere, genuine:– own [2], sincerity [1], true [1]

1104 γνησίως, gnēsiōs, adv. GK: *1189* [→ *1096*]. genuinely, sincerely:– naturally [1]

1105 **γνόφος, *gnophos***, n. GK: *1190.* darkness:– blackness [1]

1106 **γνώμη, *gnōmē***, n. GK: *1191* [→ *1097*]. purpose, resolve; judgment; consent:– judgment [3], mind [2], advice [1], agree (+*1520+4160*) [1], purposed (+*1096*) [1], will [1]

1107 **γνωρίζω, *gnōrizō***, v. GK: *1192* [→ *1097*]. to make known, tell, reveal:– made known [9], make known [6], declare [3], certify [1], declared [1], give to understand [1], known [1], wit [1], wot [1]

1108 **γνῶσις, *gnōsis***, n. GK: *1194* [→ *1097*]. knowledge, understanding:– knowledge [28], science [1]

1109 **γνώστης, *gnōstēs***, n. GK: *1195* [→ *1097*]. one well acquainted with, expert in:– expert [1]

1110 **γνωστός, *gnōstos***, a. GK: *1196* [→ *1097*]. known:– known [11], acquaintance [2], know (+*1510*) [1], notable [1]

1111 **γογγύζω, *gongyzō***, v. GK: *1197* [→ *1112, 1113, 1234*]. to grumble, complain, mutter:– murmured [6], murmur [2]

1112 **γογγυσμός, *gongysmos***, n. GK: *1198* [→ *1111*]. complaint, grumbling; whispering, private talk:– murmuring [2], grudging [1], murmurings [1]

1113 **γογγυστής, *gongystēs***, n. GK: *1199* [→ *1111*]. grumbler, complainer:– murmurers [1]

1114 **γόης, *goēs***, n. GK: *1200.* imposter:– seducers [1]

1115 **Γολγοθᾶ, *Golgotha***, n.pr. GK: *1201.* Golgotha, "*skull*":– Golgotha [3]

1116 **Γόμορρα, *Gomorra***, n.pr. GK: *1202.* Gomorrah, "*to overwhelm with water*":– Gomorrha [5]

1117 **γόμος, *gomos***, n. GK: *1203* [→ *1073*]. cargo, freight:– merchandise [2], burden [1]

1118 **γονεύς, *goneus***, n. GK: *1204* [→ *1096*]. (pl.) parents:– parents [19]

1119 **γόνυ, *gony***, n. GK: *1205* [→ *1120*]. knee; "to bend the knee" means "to kneel (in submission or worship)":– kneeled down (+*3588+5087*) [5], knees [4], knee [3]

1120 **γονυπετέω, *gonypeteō***, v. GK: *1206* [→ *1119+4098*]. to kneel (before in submission or worship):– kneeling down [2], bowed the knee [1], kneeled [1]

1121 **γράμμα, *gramma***, n. GK: *1207* [→ *1125*]. letter (of the alphabet); document, Scriptures, written code; education:– letter [6], letters [3], bill [2], learning [1], scriptures [1], writings [1], written (+*1722*) [1]

1122 **γραμματεύς, *grammateus***, n. GK: *1208* [→ *1125*]. teacher or expert in the law, scholar, scribe, city clerk:– scribes [62], scribe [4], townclerk [1]

1123 **γραπτός, *graptos***, a. GK: *1209* [→ *1125*]. written:– written [1]

1124 **γραφή, *graphē***, n. GK: *1210* [→ *1125*]. (s.) a passage of Scripture; (pl.) the collective whole of the Scriptures; holy, authoritative collection of writings:– scripture [31], scriptures [20]

1125 **γράφω, *graphō***, v. GK: *1211 & 2863* [→ *62, 582, 583, 1121, 1122, 1123, 1124, 1449, 1923, 1924, 4270, 5261, 5498*]. to write:– written [135], write [50], wrote [21], describeth [1], writing [1]

1126 **γραώδης, *graōdēs***, a. GK: *1212* [→ *1491*]. old wives' tale:– old wives' [1]

1127 **γρηγορέω, *grēgoreō***, v. GK: *1213* [→ *1453*]. to keep watch, be on guard:– watch [16], watched [2], vigilant [1], wake [1], watcheth [1], watchful [1], watching [1]

1128 **γυμνάζω, *gymnazō***, v. GK: *1214* [→ *1131*]. to train, exercise:– exercised [3], exercise [1]

1129 **γυμνασία, *gymnasia***, n. GK: *1215* [→ *1131*]. training, exercise:– exercise [1]

1130 **γυμνητεύω, *gymnēteuō***, v. GK: *1216 & 1217* [→ *1131*]. to be in ragged clothing, poorly dressed:– naked [1]

1131 **γυμνός, *gymnos***, a. GK: *1218* [→ *1128, 1129, 1130, 1132*]. naked, without clothing; needing (more or better) clothing:– naked [14], bare [1]

1132 **γυμνότης, *gymnotēs***, n. GK: *1219* [→ *1131*]. nakedness, insufficiently clothed:– nakedness [3]

1133 **γυναικάριον, *gynaikarion***, n. GK: *1220* [→ *1135*]. weak-willed woman, "little woman":– silly women [1]

1134 **γυναικεῖος, *gynaikeios***, a. GK: *1221* [→ *1135*]. feminine, weaker:– wife [1]

1135 **γυνή, *gynē***, n. GK: *1222* [→ *1133, 1134*]. woman; wife:– woman [96], wife [80], women [33], wives [12]

1136 **Γώγ, *Gōg***, n.pr. GK: *1223.* Gog:– Gog [1]

1137 **γωνία, *gōnia***, n. GK: *1224* [→ *204, 5068*]. corner; cornerstone, capstone, keystone:– corner [6], corners [2], quarters [1]

1138 **Δαβίδ, *Dabid***, n.pr. GK: *1226 & 1253.* David, "*beloved one*":– David [58], David's [1]

1139 **δαιμονίζομαι, *daimonizomai***, v. GK: *1227* [→ *1140*]. to be demon-possessed:– possessed with devils [4], possessed with the devil [3], possessed of the devils [2], hath a devil [1], one possessed with a devil [1], possessed with a devil [1], vexed with a devil [1]

1140 **δαιμόνιον, *daimonion***, n. GK: *1228* [→ *1139, 1141, 1142, 1175, 1174*]. demon, (pagan) god:– devils [41], devil [18], gods [1]

1141 **δαιμονιώδης, *daimoniōdēs***, a. GK: *1229* [→ *1140+1491*]. of the devil, demonic:– devilish [1]

1142 **δαίμων, *daimōn***, n. GK: *1230* [→ *1140*]. demon, evil spirit:– devils [4], devil [1]

1143 **δάκνω, *daknō***, v. GK: *1231.* to bite:– bite [1]

1144 **δάκρυον, *dakryon***, n. GK: *1232* [→ *1145*]. teardrop:– tears [11]

1145 **δακρύω, *dakryō***, v. GK: *1233* [→ *1144*]. to weep, shed tears:– wept [1]

1146 **δακτύλιος, *daktylios***, n. GK: *1234* [→ *1147*]. (finger) ring:– ring [1]

1147 **δάκτυλος, *daktylos***, n. GK: *1235* [→ *1146, 5554; cf. 1166*]. finger:– finger [5], fingers [3]

1148 **Δαλμανουθά, *Dalmanoutha***, n.pr. GK: *1236.* Dalmanutha:– Dalmanutha [1]

1149 **Δαλματία, *Dalmatia***, n.pr. GK: *1237.* Dalmatia, "*deceitful*":– Dalmatia [1]

1150 **δαμάζω, *damazō***, v. GK: *1238* [→ *1151*]. to tame, subdue, control:– tamed [2], tame [2]

1151 **δάμαλις, *damalis***, n. GK: *1239* [→ *1150*]. heifer, young cow:– heifer [1]

1152 **Δάμαρις, *Damaris***, n.pr. GK: *1240.* Damaris:– Damaris [1]

1153 **Δαμασκηνός, *Damaskēnos***, a.pr.g. GK: *1241* [→ *1154*]. Damascene, "*from Damascus*":– Damascenes [1]

1154 **Δαμασκός, *Damaskos***, n.pr. GK: *1242* [→ *1153*]. Damascus:– Damascus [15]

1155 **δανείζω, *daneizō***, v. GK: *1244 & 1247* [→ *1156*]. to lend, (mid.) to borrow:– lend [3], borrow [1]

1156 **δάνειον, *daneion***, n. GK: *1245 & 1249* [→ *1155, 1157*]. debt, loan:– debt [1]

1157 **δανειστής, *daneistēs***, n. GK: *1246 & 1250* [→ *1156*]. moneylender, creditor:– creditor [1]

1158 **Δανιήλ, *Daniēl***, n.pr. GK: *1248.* Daniel, "*God [El] is my judge*":– Daniel [2]

1159 **δαπανάω, *dapanaō***, v. GK: *1251* [→ *1160*]. to spend; to pay expenses:– spent [2], charges [1], consume [1], spend [1]

1160 **δαπάνη, *dapanē***, n. GK: *1252* [→ *77, 1159, 1550, 4325*]. cost, expense:– cost [1]

1161 **δέ, *de***, pt.&c. GK: *1254* [→ *1847, 1848, 3365, 3366, 3367, 3368, 3369, 3760, 3761, 3762, 3763, 3764*]. but, and, then, rather:– and [1214], but [935], now [168], then [132], when [40], yet [20], for [19], so [15], howbeit [12], nevertheless [12], also [10], yea [10], moreover [9], notwithstanding [8], therefore [4], while [4], even [3], and yet [2], neither (+*3756*) [2], or [2], they (+*3588*) [2], though [2], wherefore [2], and forasmuch as [1], and part (+*3588*) [1], and partly (+*3778*) [1], and to [1], as for [1], as [1], but and [1], but though (+*1487+2532*) [1], but though [1], furthermore [1], howbeit whereinsoever (+*302+1722+3739*) [1], moreover (+*2089*) [1], moreover (+*3062+3739*) [1], neither any (+*3762*) [1], now about (+*2235*) [1], other (+*3588*) [1], so then [1], when (+*5613*) [1], who (+*3588*) [1]

1162 **δέησις, *deēsis***, n. GK: *1255* [→ *1189*]. prayer, request, petition:– prayer [7], prayers [5], supplication [4], supplications [2], request [1]

1163 **δεῖ, *dei***, v.imper. GK: *1256* [→ *1210*]. it is a must, it is necessary (one should, ought):– must [58], ought [25], must needs [5], ought to [3], meet [2], oughtest [2], should [2], behoved [1], must needs (+*3843*) [1], needful [1], need [1], ought to have [1], oughtest to have [1], should have [1], shouldest have [1]

1164 **δεῖγμα, *deigma***, n. GK: *1257* [→ *1165, 1730, 3856, 5262; cf. 1166*]. example:– example [1]

1165 **δειγματίζω, *deigmatizō***, v. GK: *1258* [→ *1164*]. to expose to public disgrace; to make a spectacle of:– made a shew [1]

1166 **δεικνύω, *deiknyō***, v. GK: *1259 & 1260* [→ *322, 323, 584, 585, 1731, 1732, 1925, 5263; cf. 1147, 1164*]. to show, point out, make known:– shew [20], shewed [8], sheweth [2], shewest [1]

1167 **δειλία, *deilia***, n. GK: *1261* [→ *127*]. timidity, cowardice:– fear [1]

1168 **δειλιάω, *deiliaō***, v. GK: *1262* [→ *127*]. to be afraid, cowardly, timid:– afraid [1]

1169 **δειλός, *deilos***, a. GK: *1264* [→ *127*]. afraid, cowardly, timid:– fearful [3]

1170 **δεῖνα, *deina***, n. GK: *1265.* a certain one, a person or thing one cannot or does not wish to name:– such a man [1]

1171 **δεινῶς, *deinōs***, adv. GK: *1267* [→ *127*]. terribly, fiercely:– grievously [1], vehemently [1]

1172 **δειπνέω, *deipneō***, v. GK: *1268* [→ *1173*]. to eat supper, dine:– sup [2], supped [1], supper [1]

1173 **δεῖπνον, *deipnon***, n. GK: *1270 & 1271* [→ *1172*]. banquet, supper, evening meal:– supper [13], feasts [3]

1174 **δεισιδαίμων, *deisidaimōn***, a. GK: *1273* [→ *127+1140*]. (compar.) very religious:– too superstitious [1]

1175 **δεισιδαιμονία, *deisidaimonia***, n. GK: *1272* [→ *127+1140*]. religion:– superstition [1]

1176 **δέκα, *deka***, n.num. GK: *1274* [→ *586, 586, 1177, 1178, 1179, 1180, 1181, 1182, 1183, 1427, 1428, 1429, 1733, 1734, 4003, 5065*]. ten:– ten [24], eighteen (+*2532+3638*) [3]

1177 **δεκαδύο, *dekadyo***, n.num. GK: *1275* [→ *1176+1417*]. twelve:– twelve [2]

1178 **δεκαπέντε, *dekapente***, n.num. GK: *1278* [→ *1176+4002*]. fifteen:– fifteen [3]

1179 **Δεκάπολις, *Dekapolis***, n.pr. GK: *1279* [→ *1176+4172*]. Decapolis, "*[league of] ten cities*":– Decapolis [3]

1180 **δεκατέσσαρες, *dekatessares***, n.num. GK: *1280* [→ *1176+5064*]. fourteen:– fourteen [5]

1181 **δεκάτη, *dekatē***, a.num.f. of *1182.* GK: *1281* [→ *1176*]. tenth in a series of things or events; as a noun, the tenth part, ten percent of something, tithe:– tenth [2], tithes [2]

1182 **δέκατος, *dekatos***, a.num. GK: *1281* [→ *1176*]. tenth in a series of things or events; as a noun, the tenth part, ten percent of something, tithe:– tenth [3]

1183 **δεκατόω, *dekatoō***, v. GK: *1282* [→ *1176*]. to collect a tenth; (pass.) to pay a tenth:– payed tithes [1], received tithes [1]

1184 **δεκτός, *dektos***, a. GK: *1283* [→ *1209*]. acceptable, favorable:– accepted [3], acceptable [2]

1185 **δελεάζω, *deleazō***, v. GK: *1284* [→ *1388*]. to entice, seduce, lure:– allure [1], beguiling [1], enticed [1]

1186 **δένδρον, *dendron***, n. GK: *1285.* tree:– tree [17], trees [9]

1187 **δεξιολάβος, *dexiolabos***, n. GK: *1286 & 1287* [→ *1188+2983*]. spearman; other sources: bowman, slinger, bodyguard:– spearmen [1]

1188 **δεξιός, *dexios***, a. GK: *1288* [→ *1187*]. the right hand or side in contrast to the left; the right is considered culturally to be stronger and of greater prestige than the left; to be seated on the right side of a ruler is a greater position than on the left side; to "give the right hand of fellowship" in Galatians is a sign of friendship, trust, and covenant:– right hand [38], right [12], right side [2], right hands [1]

1189 **δέομαι, *deomai***, v. GK: *1289* [→ *1162, 1729, 4326*]. to pray; ask, beg, plead:– pray [7], beseech [6], besought [3], prayed [2], praying [2], making request [1], prayed to [1]

δεόν, *deon*. See ***1163***.

1190* Δερβαῖος, *Derbaios, a.pr.g. GK: *1291* [→ *1191*]. from Derbe, "*from Derbe*":– of Derbe [1]

1191* Δέρβη, *Derbē, n.pr. GK: *1292* [→ *1190*]. Derbe:– Derbe [3]

1192* δέρμα, *derma, n. GK: *1293* [→ *1194*]. skin, leather:– goatskins (+*122*) [1]

1193* δερμάτινος, *dermatinos, a. GK: *1294* [→ *1194*]. made of leather:– leathern [1], skin [1]

1194* δέρω, *derō, v. GK: *1296* [→ *1192, 1193*]. to beat up, strike, flog, slap:– beaten [5], beat [5], beateth [1], beating [1], smitest [1], smite [1], smote [1]

1195* δεσμεύω, *desmeuō, v. GK: *1297* [→ *1210*]. to tie up, bind; to arrest:– binding [1], bind [1]

1196* δεσμέω, *desmeō, v. GK: *1298* [→ *1210*]. to tie, bind:– bound [1]

1197* δέσμη, *desmē, n. GK: *1299* [→ *1210*]. bundle:– bundles [1]

1198* δέσμιος, *desmios, n. GK: *1300* [→ *1210*]. prisoner, one under arrest:– prisoner [11], prisoners [3], bonds [1], in bonds [1]

1199* δεσμός, *desmos, n. GK: *1301* [→ *1210*]. chain, fetter, imprisonment:– bonds [14], bands [3], bond [1], chains [1], string [1]

1200* δεσμοφύλαξ, *desmophylax, n. GK: *1302* [→ *1210+5442*]. jailer, warden:– keeper of the prison [2], jailor [1]

1201* δεσμωτήριον, *desmōtērion, n. GK: *1303* [→ *1210*]. prison, jail:– prison [4]

1202* δεσμώτης, *desmōtēs, n. GK: *1304* [→ *1210*]. prisoner:– prisoners [2]

1203* δεσπότης, *despotēs, n. GK: *1305* [→ *3616, 3617; cf. 1210*]. master; Sovereign Lord:– Lord/lord [5], masters [4], master's [1]

1204* δεῦρο, *deuro, adv.pl. GK: *1306* [→ *1205*]. come, come here:– come [6], hither [2], hitherto (+*891+3588*) [1]

1205* δεῦτε, *deute, adv. GK: *1307* [→ *1204*]. come, come here (pl. of *1204*):– come [12], follow (+*3694*) [1]

1206* δευτεραῖος, *deuteraios, a. GK: *1308* [→ *1417*]. on the following day, on the second day:– next day [1]

1207* δευτερόπρωτος, *deuteroprōtos, a. GK: *1310* [→ *1417+4413*]. lit: "second-first":– second after the first [1]

1208* δεύτερος, *deuteros, a. GK: *1309 & 1311* [→ *1417*]. second; (adv.) for the second time, secondly:– second [36], second time (+*1537*) [4], again (+*1537*) [2], second time [2], afterward [1], again [1], secondarily [1]

1209* δέχομαι, *dechomai, v. GK: *1312* [→ *96, 324, 418, 553, 587, 588, 593, 594, 1184, 1237, 1240, 1381, 1382, 1383, 1384, 1403, 1523, 1551, 1561, 1735, 1926, 2144, 3580, 3829, 3830, 3858, 4327, 5264*]. to welcome, receive, accept:– receive [24], received [16], receiveth [11], take [3], accepted [2], took [2]

1210* δέω, *deō, v. GK: *1313* [→ *1163, 1195, 1196, 1197, 1198, 1199, 1200, 1201, 1202, 1338, 3611, 4019, 4886, 4887, 5265, 5266; cf. 1203*]. to tie, bind, imprison:– bound [28], bind [9], tied [4], in bonds [1], knit [1], wound [1]

1211* δή, *dē, pt.emph. GK: *1314* [→ *1221, 1222, 1894, 1895*]. indeed, therefore; can show urgency or certainty:– also [1], doubtless [1], now [1], therefore [1]

1212* δῆλος, *dēlos, a. GK: *1316* [→ *82, 83, 84, 1213, 1552, 2612, 4271*]. clear, plain, evident:– bewrayeth (+*4160*) [1], certain [1], evident [1], manifest [1]

1213* δηλόω, *dēloō, v. GK: *1317* [→ *1212*]. to make clear, bring to light, show, point:– declared [2], declare [1], shewed [1], signifieth [1], signifying [1], signify [1]

1214* Δημᾶς, *Dēmas, n.pr. GK: *1318* [→ *1218 or* 1216]. Demas, "*common folks*":– Demas [3]

1215* δημηγορέω, *dēmēgoreō, v. GK: *1319* [→ *1218+59*]. to deliver a public address:– made an oration [1]

1216* Δημήτριος, *Dēmētrios, n.pr. GK: *1320* [→ *1214?*]. Demetrius, "*of Demeter*":– Demetrius [3]

1217* δημιουργός, *dēmiourgos, n. GK: *1321* [→ *1218+2041*]. builder, craftsman, maker:– maker [1]

1218* δῆμος, *dēmos, n. GK: *1322* [→ *589, 590, 1214?, 1215, 1217, 1219, 1553, 1736, 1927, 3530, 3927, 4898*]. people, crowd:– people [4]

1219* δημόσιος, *dēmosios, a. GK: *1323* [→ *1218*]. public, publicly:– publickly [2], common [1], openly [1]

1220* δηνάριον, *dēnarion, n. GK: *1324*. denarius [about a day's wage]:– penny [9], pence [5], pennyworth [2]

1221* δήποτε, *dēpote, adv. GK: *1325* [→ *1211+4226*]. whatever:–

1222* δήπου, *dēpou, adv. GK: *1327* [→ *1211+4226*]. surely, of course:– verily [1]

1223* διά, *dia, pp. GK: *1328* [→ *87, 88, 89, 90, 411, 475, 592, 1224, 1225, 1226, 1227, 1228, 1229, 1230, 1231, 1232, 1233, 1234, 1235, 1236, 1237, 1238, 1239, 1240, 1241, 1242, 1243, 1244, 1245, 1246, 1251, 1252, 1253, 1254, 1255, 1256, 1257, 1258, 1259, 1260, 1261, 1262, 1263, 1264, 1265, 1266, 1267, 1268, 1269, 1270, 1271, 1272, 1273, 1274, 1275, 1276, 1277, 1278, 1279, 1280, 1281, 1282, 1283, 1284, 1285, 1286, 1287, 1288, 1289, 1290, 1291, 1292, 1293, 1294, 1295, 1296, 1297, 1298, 1299, 1300, 1301, 1302, 1303, 1304, 1305, 1306, 1307, 1308, 1309, 1310, 1311, 1312, 1313, 1314, 1315, 1316, 1326, 1327, 1328, 1329, 1330, 1331, 1334, 1335, 1336, 1338, 1339, 1340, 1352, 1353, 1355, 1357, 1358, 1360, 1368, 1555, 1928, 1930, 3859*]. (gen.) through, by means of; (acc.) because of, for the sake of, therefore:– by [247], through [86], for [58], therefore (+*3778*) [43], for sake [35], because of [24], because (+*3588*) [21], with [17], for this cause (+*3778*) [14], for sakes [12], because [9], in [8], wherefore (+*3778*) [7], after [3], always (+*3956*) [3], by reason of [3], of [3], throughout [3], whereby (+*3739*) [3], wherefore (+*156+3739*) [3], at [2], thereby (+*846*) [2], thereby [2], wherefore (+*3739*) [2], among [1], avoid [1], because by reason of [1], because that (+*3588*) [1], briefly (+*3641*) [1], by (+*3588*) [1], by (+*5495*) [1], by occasion [1], by reason hereof (+*3778*) [1], by reason of (+*3588*) [1], by the means of [1], continually (+*3956*) [1], for (+*3588*) [1], from [1], glorious (+*1391*) [1], out of [1], that (+*3588*) [1], thereat (+*846*) [1], therefore [1], though [1], throughout (+*3650*) [1], to [1], wherein (+*3739*) [1], within [1]

Δία, *Dia*. See ***2203***.

1224* διαβαίνω, *diabainō, v. GK: *1329* [→ *1223+305*]. to pass through, come over, cross:– come over [1], passed through [1], pass [1]

1225* διαβάλλω, *diaballō, v. GK: *1330* [→ *1223+906*]. (pass.) to have accusations brought upon someone:– accused [1]

1226* διαβεβαιόομαι, *diabebaioomai, v. GK: *1331* [→ *1223+305*]. to confidently affirm, stress, insist on:– affirm constantly [1], affirm [1]

1227* διαβλέπω, *diablepō, v. GK: *1332* [→ *1223+991*]. to see clearly; to open eyes wide:– see clearly [2]

1228* διάβολος, *diabolos, a. [used as n.]. GK: *1333* [→ *1223+906*]. devilish, malicious, slanderous; as a noun, the devil, Satan, or a wicked person who is like the devil:– devil [35], false accusers [2], slanderers [1]

1229* διαγγέλλω, *diangellō, v. GK: *1334* [→ *1223+32*]. to proclaim (throughout); to give notice:– declared [1], preach [1], signify [1]

1230* διαγίνομαι, *diaginomai, v. GK: *1335* [→ *1223+1096*]. to pass, elapse (of time):– after [1], past [1], spent [1]

1231* διαγινώσκω, *diaginōskō, v. GK: *1336* [→ *1223+1097*]. to determine, decide:– inquire [1], know the uttermost [1]

1232* διαγνωρίζω, *diagnōrizō, v. GK: *1337* [→ *1223+1097*]. to give an exact report:– made known abroad [1]

1233* διάγνωσις, *diagnōsis, n. GK: *1338* [→ *1223+1097*]. decision:– hearing [1]

1234* διαγογγύζω, *diagongyzō, v. GK: *1339* [→ *1223+1111*]. to mutter, grumble, complain:– murmured [2]

1235* διαγρηγορέω, *diagrēgoreō, v. GK: *1340* [→ *1223+1453*]. to become fully awake:– awake [1]

1236* διάγω, *diagō, v. GK: *1341* [→ *1223+71*]. to live, conduct one's life:– lead [1], living [1]

1237* διαδέχομαι, *diadechomai, v. GK: *1342* [→ *1223+1209*]. to receive (in turn):– came after [1]

1238* διάδημα, *diadēma, n. GK: *1343* [→ *1223+1210*]. crown, diadem:– crowns [3]

1239* διαδίδωμι, *diadidōmi, v. GK: *1344* [→ *1223+1325*]. to distribute, divide up:– distributed [1], distribute [1], distribution [1], divideth [1], give [1]

1240* διάδοχος, *diadochos, n. GK: *1345* [→ *1223+1209*]. successor:– came into room (+*2983*) [1]

1241* διαζώννυμι, *diazōnnymi, v. GK: *1346* [→ *1223+2224*]. to wrap around, tie around, put on:– girded [2], girt [1]

1242* διαθήκη, *diathēkē, n. GK: *1347* [→ *1223+5087*]. covenant, a solemn agreement between two parties; will, testament, a legal document by which property is transferred to heirs, usually upon death (Heb 9:16):– covenant [17], testament [13], covenants [3]

1243* διαίρεσις, *diairesis, n. GK: *1348* [→ *1223+138*]. difference, variety:– diversities [2], differences [1]

1244* διαιρέω, *diaireō, v. GK: *1349* [→ *1223+138*]. to divide, distribute, apportion:– divided [1], dividing [1]

1245* διακαθαρίζω, *diakatharizō, v. GK: *1350 & 1351* [→ *1223+2513*]. to clear out, clean out (with a possible implication that the cleaning is thorough):– throughly purge [2]

1246* διακατελέγχομαι, *diakatelenchomai, v. GK: *1352* [→ *1223+2596+1651*]. to refute (thoroughly):– convinced [1]

1247* διακονέω, *diakoneō, v. GK: *1354* [→ *1249*]. to serve, wait on, help, attend to; this often refers to spiritual and practical ministry in the Church. "To wait upon tables" (Ac 6:2) may mean to literally help in serving food, though some believe it refers (also) to the handling of finances:– ministered [14], minister [8], serve [7], administered [2], serveth [2], ministering [1], served [1], use the office of deacon [1], used the office of deacon [1]

1248* διακονία, *diakonia, n. GK: *1355* [→ *1249*]. ministry, service, this can refer to helps and service of various kinds which can range in meaning from "spiritual" biblical teaching (Ac 6:4) to the "practical" giving of provisions, supplies, support, and finances to those in need (2Co 9:12):– ministry [16], ministration [6], ministering [3], service [3], administrations [1], administration [1], minister [1], office [1], relief (+*1519*) [1], serving [1]

1249* διάκονος, *diakonos, n. GK: *1356* [→ *1247, 1248*]. servant, minister, a person who renders service and help to others, in some contexts with an implication of lower status; also transliterated as "deacon," a trusted officer of helps and service in the local church:– minister [14], ministers [6], servant [5], deacons [3], servants [3]

1250* διακόσιοι, *diakosioi, a.num. GK: *1357* [→ *1417*]. two hundred:– two hundred [8]

1251* διακούω, *diakouō, v. GK: *1358* [→ *1223+191*]. to give a (legal) hearing:– hear [1]

1252* διακρίνω, *diakrinō, v. GK: *1359* [→ *1223+2919*]. to make a distinction, judge a dispute; (mid./pass.) to doubt, hesitate, waver:– judge [3], doubting [2], doubt [2], contended [1], contending [1], discerning [1], discern [1], doubteth [1], maketh to differ [1], making a difference [1], partial [1], put difference [1], staggered [1], wavereth [1], wavering [1]

1253* διάκρισις, *diakrisis, n. GK: *1360* [→ *1223+2919*]. distinguishing, differentiation; passing judgment:– discerning [1], discern [1], disputations [1]

1254* διακωλύω, *diakōlyō, v. GK: *1361* [→ *1223+2967*]. to deter, prevent:– forbad [1]

1255* διαλαλέω, *dialaleō, v. GK: *1362* [→ *1223+2980*]. to talk about, discuss:– communed [1], noised abroad [1]

1256* διαλέγομαι, *dialegomai, v. GK: *1363* [→ *1223+3004*]. to reason, discuss, discourse; to argue, dispute:– reasoned [4], disputed [3], disputing [3], preached [1], preaching [1], speaketh [1]

1257* διαλείπω, *dialeipō, v. GK: *1364* [→ *1223+3007*]. to stop, cease:– ceased [1]

1258* διάλεκτος, *dialektos, n. GK: *1365* [→ *1223+3004*]. language, dialect, a communication code whether written or oral; in the NT this always refers to known languages commonly spoken in the ancient world:– tongue [5], language [1]

1259* διαλλάσσομαι, *diallassomai, v. GK: *1367* [→ *1223+236*]. to become reconciled:– reconciled [1]

1260* διαλογίζομαι, *dialogizomai, v. GK: *1368* [→ *1223+3004*]. to think, wonder about; to talk, discuss, argue:– reasoned [5], reason [5], cast in mind [1], consider [1], disputed [1], mused [1], reasoning [1], thought [1]

***1261* διαλογισμός, *dialogismos*,** n. GK: *1369* [→ *1223+3004*]. thought, doubt; argument, dispute:– thoughts [8], disputings [1], doubtful [1], doubting [1], imaginations [1], reasoning [1], thought [1]

***1262* διαλύω, *dialyō*,** v. GK: *1370* [→ *1223+3089*]. to disperse, break up:– scattered [1]

***1263* διαμαρτύρομαι, *diamartyromai*,** v. GK: *1371* [→ *1223+3144*]. to (solemnly) warn or charge; to (solemnly) testify about:– testified [6], testify [4], charge [2], charging [1], testifying [1], witnesseth [1]

***1264* διαμάχομαι, *diamachomai*,** v. GK: *1372* [→ *1223+3163*]. to argue vigorously, contend sharply:– strove [1]

***1265* διαμένω, *diamenō*,** v. GK: *1373* [→ *1223+3306*]. to remain (constantly):– continue [2], continued [1], remained [1], remainest [1]

***1266* διαμερίζω, *diamerizō*,** v. GK: *1374* [→ *1223+3313*]. to divide, distribute:– parted [5], divided [4], cloven [1], divide [1], parted among [1]

***1267* διαμερισμός, *diamerismos*,** n. GK: *1375* [→ *1223+3313*]. division:– division [1]

***1268* διανέμω, *dianemō*,** v. GK: *1376* [→ *1223+3551*]. (pass.) to be spread:– spread [1]

***1269* διανεύω, *dianeuō*,** v. GK: *1377* [→ *1223+3506*]. to make signs, nod, beckon:– beckoned [1]

***1270* διανόημα, *dianoēma*,** n. GK: *1378* [→ *1223+3563*]. thought:– thoughts [1]

***1271* διάνοια, *dianoia*,** n. GK: *1379* [→ *1223+3563*]. mind, thinking, understanding; this is a part of the inner person that thinks and processes information into understanding, including the making of choices, the seat of which is the heart:– mind [7], understanding [3], minds [2], imagination [1]

***1272* διανοίγω, *dianoigō*,** v. GK: *1380* [→ *455*; *cf. 1223*]. to open; (pass.) to be opened; to explain:– opened [6], openeth [1], opening [1]

***1273* διανυκτερεύω, *dianyktereuō*,** v. GK: *1381* [→ *1223+3571*]. to spend the (entire) night:– all night [1]

***1274* διανύω, *dianyō*,** v. GK: *1382* [→ *1223+507*]. to continue:– finished [1]

***1275* διαπαντός, *diapantos*,** adv. GK: *1383* [→ *1223+3956*]. always, continually, constantly:– always [3], alway [2], continually [1]

***1276* διαπεράω, *diaperaō*,** v. GK: *1385* [→ *1223+4008*]. to cross over:– passed over [3], gone over [1], pass [1], sailing over [1]

***1277* διαπλέω, *diapleō*,** v. GK: *1386* [→ *1223+4126*]. to sail across, sail through:– sailed over [1]

***1278* διαπονέομαι, *diaponeomai*,** v. GK: *1387* [→ *1223+4192*]. to be greatly disturbed, troubled, annoyed:– grieved [2]

***1279* διαπορεύομαι, *diaporeuomai*,** v. GK: *1388* [→ *1223+4198*]. to go through, travel through:– went through [2], in journey [1], pass by [1], went [1]

***1280* διαπορέω, *diaporeō*,** v. GK: *1389* [→ *1223+1.1+4198*]. to be perplexed, puzzled, in wonder:– doubted [2], perplexed [2], doubt [1]

***1281* διαπραγματεύομαι, *diapragmateuomai*,** v. GK: *1390* [→ *1223+4238*]. to gain, earn:– gained by trading [1]

***1282* διαπρίω, *diapriō*,** v. GK: *1391* [→ *1223+4249*]. (pass.) to be furious:– cut [2]

***1283* διαρπάζω, *diarpazō*,** v. GK: *1395* [→ *1223+726*]. to rob, carry off (many possessions):– spoil [4]

***1284* διαρήσσω, *diarēssō*,** v. GK: *1392 & 1393 & 1396* [→ *1223+4486*]. to tear (clothes), break (chains):– rent [3], brake [2]

***1285* διασαφέω, *diasapheō*,** v. GK: *1397* [→ *1223*]. to tell, explain (in detail):– told [1]

***1286* διασείω, *diaseiō*,** v. GK: *1398* [→ *1223+4579*]. to extort money, as a fig. extension of a violent shaking motion:– violence [1]

***1287* διασκορπίζω, *diaskorpizō*,** v. GK: *1399* [→ *1223+4650*]. to scatter:– scattered abroad [2], scattered [2], strawed [2], wasted [2], dispersed [1]

***1288* διασπάω, *diaspaō*,** v. GK: *1400* [→ *1223+4685*]. (pass.) to be torn to pieces:– plucked asunder [1], pulled in pieces [1]

***1289* διασπείρω, *diaspeirō*,** v. GK: *1401* [→ *1223+4687*]. (pass.) to be scattered:– scattered abroad [3]

***1290* διασπορά, *diaspora*,** n. GK: *1402* [→ *1223+4687*]. scattering, dispersion, Diaspora:– dispersed among [1], scattered abroad (*+1722+3588*) [1], scattered throughout [1]

***1291* διαστέλλω, *diastellō*,** v. GK: *1403* [→ *1223+4724*]. (mid.) to give orders, command, authorize; (pass.) what was commanded:– charged [6], commanded [1], gave commandment [1]

***1292* διάστημα, *diastēma*,** n. GK: *1404* [→ *1223+2476*]. later time, interval:– space after [1]

***1293* διαστολή, *diastolē*,** n. GK: *1405* [→ *1223+4724*]. difference, distinction:– difference [2], distinction [1]

***1294* διαστρέφω, *diastrephō*,** v. GK: *1406* [→ *1223+4762*]. (act.) to subvert, pervert, make turn away; (pass.) to be perverted, depraved, turned from the truth:– perverse [4], perverting [1], pervert [1], turn [1]

***1295* διασῴζω, *diasōzō*,** v. GK: *1407* [→ *1223+4982*]. save, spare, bring safely through a dangerous or distressing situation, with a focus that the rescue is complete or full; to heal, with a focus that the injured or sick person goes from the danger of ill health to the safety of a completely restored or healthy life:– escaped [2], bring safe [1], escaped safe [1], heal [1], made perfectly whole [1], saved [1], save [1]

***1296* διαταγή, *diatagē*,** n. GK: *1408* [→ *1223+5021*]. putting into effect, institution:– disposition [1], ordinance [1]

***1297* διάταγμα, *diatagma*,** n. GK: *1409* [→ *1223+5021*]. edict, command:– commandment [1]

***1298* διαταράσσω, *diatarassō*,** v. GK: *1410* [→ *1223+5015*]. (pass.) to be greatly troubled, perplexed, confused:– troubled [1]

***1299* διατάσσω, *diatassō*,** v. GK: *1411* [→ *1223+5021*]. (act./mid.) to command, order, direct; (pass.) to be required, ordered, put into effect:– commanded [6], appointed [4], ordained [2], commanding [1], given order [1], ordain [1], set in order [1]

***1300* διατελέω, *diateleō*,** v. GK: *1412* [→ *1223+5056*]. to continue, remain:– continued [1]

***1301* διατηρέω, *diatēreō*,** v. GK: *1413* [→ *1223+5083*]. to keep, treasure:– keep [1], kept [1]

***1302* διατί, *diati*,** pt.inter. GK: *1414* [→ *1223+5101*]. why?:– why [23], wherefore [4]

***1303* διατίθεμαι, *diatithemai*,** v. GK: *1415* [→ *1223+5087*]. to make a covenant or a will; to confer, assign; to decree, ordain:– make [2], testator [2], appointed [1], appoint [1], made [1]

***1304* διατρίβω, *diatribō*,** v. GK: *1417* [→ *1223+5147*]. to stay, remain, spend some time:– abode [4], continued [2], tarried [2], abiding [1], been [1]

***1305* διατροφή, *diatrophē*,** n. GK: *1418* [→ *1223+5142*]. food, sustenance:– food [1]

***1306* διαυγάζω, *diaugazō*,** v. GK: *1419* [→ *1223+827*]. to dawn, shine through:– dawn [1]

***1307* διαφανής, *diaphanēs*,** a. GK: *1420 & 1421* [→ *1223+5316*]. transparent:– transparent [1]

***1308* διαφέρω, *diapherō*,** v. GK: *1422* [→ *1223+5342*]. (tr.) to carry, spread out; (intr.) to differ; to be more valuable than:– better than [3], differeth from [2], more value than [2], carry [1], driven up and down [1], excellent [1], maketh matter [1], more excellent [1], published [1]

***1309* διαφεύγω, *diapheugō*,** v. GK: *1423* [→ *1223+5343*]. to escape, flee:– escape [1]

***1310* διαφημίζω, *diaphēmizō*,** v. GK: *1424 & 5775* [→ *1223+5346*]. to spread news about, circulate:– blaze abroad [1], commonly reported [1], spread abroad fame [1]

***1311* διαφθείρω, *diaphtheirō*,** v. GK: *1425* [→ *1223+5351*]. to destroy, corrupt:– destroy [2], corrupteth [1], corrupt [1], destroyed [1], perish [1]

***1312* διαφθορά, *diaphthora*,** n. GK: *1426* [→ *1223+5351*]. decay:– corruption [6]

***1313* διάφορος, *diaphoros*,** a. GK: *1427* [→ *1223+5342*]. different; superior, outstanding, excellent:– more excellent [2], differing [1], divers [1]

***1314* διαφυλάσσω, *diaphylassō*,** v. GK: *1428* [→ *1223+5442*]. to guard carefully:– keep [1]

***1315* διαχειρίζω, *diacheirizō*,** v. GK: *1429* [→ *1223+5495*]. (mid.) to kill, murder, formally, "to lay violent hands on":– kill [1], slew [1]

***1316* διαχωρίζω, *diachōrizō*,** v. GK: *1431* [→ *1223+5565*]. (pass.) to be separated:– departed [1]

***1317* διδακτικός, *didaktikos*,** a. GK: *1434* [→ *1321*]. able to teach, skillful at instructing:– apt to teach [2]

***1318* διδακτός, *didaktos*,** a. GK: *1435* [→ *1321*]. taught, instructed:– teacheth [2], taught [1]

***1319* διδασκαλία, *didaskalia*,** n. GK: *1436* [→ *1321*]. teaching, doctrine:– doctrine [15], doctrines [4], learning [1], teaching [1]

***1320* διδάσκαλος, *didaskalos*,** n. GK: *1437* [→ *1321*]. teacher, instructor, one who provides instruction, implying authority over the students or followers:– master [46], teachers [6], teacher [4], doctors [1], masters [1]

***1321* διδάσκω, *didaskō*,** v. GK: *1438* [→ *1317, 1318, 1319, 1320, 1322, 2085, 2312, 2567, 3547, 5572*]. to teach, instruct, to provide information in a manner intended to produce understanding, either in a formal or informal setting:– taught [40], teach [26], teaching [21], teachest [7], teacheth [3]

***1322* διδαχή, *didachē*,** n. GK: *1439* [→ *1321*]. (the activity or content of) teaching, instruction:– doctrine [28], doctrines [1], taught [1]

***1323* δίδραχμον, *didrachmon*,** n. GK: *1440* [→ *1417+1405*]. two-drachma (temple tax):– tribute money [1], tribute [1]

***1324* Δίδυμος, *Didymos*,** n.pr. GK: *1441* [→ *1417*]. Didymus, "*twin*":– Didymus [3]

***1325* δίδωμι, *didōmi*,** v. GK: *1442 & 1443* [→ *325, 467, 468, 469, 591, 734, 1239, 1390, 1394, 1395, 1431, 1432, 1433, 1434, 1554, 1560, 1929, 2130, 3330, 3405, 3406, 3860, 3862, 3970, 4272, 4273*; *cf. 1435*]. to give; that this can have many different specific meanings and referents depending on the context, as noted in the list of NIV translations:– give [141], given [123], gave [73], giveth [13], gavest [11], grant [7], put [5], giving [4], granted [3], shew [3], bestowed [2], delivered [2], had power [2], make [2], offer [2], suffer [2], adventure [1], brought forth [1], committed [1], deliver (*+4991*) [1], delivered up [1], gave forth [1], gave up [1], hinder (*+1464*) [1], minister [1], receive [1], set [1], shewed [1], smote with hands (*+4475*) [1], stroke with the palm of hand (*+4475*) [1], taking [1], utter [1], yielded [1], yield [1]

***1326* διεγείρω, *diegeirō*,** v. GK: *1444* [→ *1223+1453*]. to get up, arouse, stimulate:– arose [2], stir up [2], awake [1], awoke [1], raised [1]

***1327* διέξοδος, *diexodos*,** n. GK: *1447* [→ *1223+1537+3598*]. (street) corner:– highways (*+3588+3598*) [1]

***1328* διερμηνευτής, *diermēneutēs*,** n. GK: *1449 & 2256* [→ *1223+2059*]. interpreter, translator:– interpreter [1]

***1329* διερμηνεύω, *diermēneuō*,** v. GK: *1450* [→ *1223+2059*]. to interpret, translate, explain:– interpret [4], expounded [1], interpretation [1]

***1330* διέρχομαι, *dierchomai*,** v. GK: *1451* [→ *1223+2064*]. to go through, travel throughout:– passed through [5], go through [3], passed [3], pass [3], go [2], pass through [2], passing through [2], walketh through [2], went through [2], come [1], departed [1], go over [1], going [1], gone over [1], gone throughout [1], gone through [1], gone [1], pass over [1], passed by [1], passed into [1], passed throughout [1], past [1], pierce through [1], travelled [1], went about [1], went abroad [1], went every where [1], went over [1]

***1331* διερωτάω, *dierōtaō*,** v. GK: *1452* [→ *1223+2065*]. to find out, ask:– made inquiry [1]

***1332* διετής, *dietēs*,** a. GK: *1453* [→ *1417+2094*]. two years old:– two years old [1]

***1333* διετία, *dietia*,** n. GK: *1454* [→ *1417+2094*]. two years:– two years [2]

***1334* διηγέομαι, *diēgeomai*,** v. GK: *1455* [→ *1223+71*]. to tell, report, describe:– declared [2], tell [2], told [2], declare [1], shew [1]

***1335* διήγησις, *diēgēsis*,** n. GK: *1456* [→ *1223+71*]. account, narrative:– declaration [1]

1336 **διηνεκής, *diēnekēs***, a. GK: *1457* [→ *1223+5342*]. forever, endless, for all time:– continually (*+1519+3588*) [2], for ever (*+1519+3588*) [2]

1337 **διθάλασσος, *dithalassos***, a. GK: *1458* [→ *1417+2281*]. sandbar, sandbank (surrounded on both sides by sea):– where two seas met [1]

1338 **διϊκνέομαι, *diikneomai***, v. GK: *1459* [→ *1223+2425*]. to penetrate, pierce:– piercing [1]

1339 **διΐστημι, *diistēmi***, v. GK: *1460* [→ *1223+2476*]. to leave, pass:– gone further [1], parted [1], space after [1]

1340 **διϊσχυρίζομαι, *diischyrizomai***, v. GK: *1462* [→ *1223+2479*]. to assert, insist, maintain firmly:– confidently affirmed [1], constantly affirmed [1]

1341 **δικαιοκρισία, *dikaiokrisia***, n. GK: *1464* [→ *1349+2919*]. righteous judgment:– righteous judgment [1]

1342 **δίκαιος, *dikaios***, a. GK: *1465* [→ *1349*]. right, righteous, upright; in the NT this refers to God's proper standards and actions, expressed in the covenants; as a noun it refers to a person in accord with God's standards, in proper relationship with God: righteous [41], just [31], right [5], just one [2], meet [2]

1343 **δικαιοσύνη, *dikaiosynē***, n. GK: *1466* [→ *1349*]. righteousness, what is right, justice, the act of doing what is in agreement with God's standards, the state of being in proper relationship with God:– righteousness [90], righteousness' [2]

1344 **δικαιόω, *dikaioō***, v. GK: *1467* [→ *1349*]. to justify, vindicate, declare righteous, to put someone in a proper relationship with another, usually referring to God's relationship to humankind, implying a proper legal or moral relationship:– justified [31], justify [4], justifieth [2], freed [1], justifier [1], righteous [1]

1345 **δικαίωμα, *dikaiōma***, n. GK: *1468* [→ *1349*]. regulation, requirement, commandment; act of righteousness:– righteousness [4], ordinances [3], judgments [1], judgment [1], justification [1]

1346 **δικαίως, *dikaiōs***, adv. GK: *1469* [→ *1349*]. justly, uprightly, righteously:– justly [2], righteously [2], righteousness [1]

1347 **δικαίωσις, *dikaiōsis***, n. GK: *1470* [→ *1349*]. justification:– justification [2]

1348 **δικαστής, *dikastēs***, n. GK: *1471* [→ *1349*]. judge:– judge [3]

1349 **δίκη, *dikē***, n. GK: *1472 & 2869* [→ *91, 92, 93, 94, 95, 476, 1341, 1342, 1343, 1344, 1345, 1346, 1347, 1348, 1556, 1557, 1558, 1738, 2613, 2993, 2994, 5267*]. punishment, with a focus that the penalty is justly deserved and right; this can also refer to a pagan Greek goddess, "Justice" (Ac 28:4), who would seek out the guilty and punish the wrongdoer:– vengeance [2], judgment [1], punished (*+5099*) [1]

1350 **δίκτυον, *diktyon***, n. GK: *1473*. (fish) net:– nets [6], net [6]

1351 **δίλογος, *dilogos***, a. GK: *1474* [→ *1417+3004*]. insincere, double-tongued:– doubletongued [1]

1352 **διό, *dio***, c.infer. GK: *1475* [→ *1223+3739*]. therefore, that is why, for this reason:– wherefore [39], therefore [9], for which cause [2], therefore (*+2532*) [1], wherefore (*+2532*) [1], wherefore seeing that [1]

1353 **διοδεύω, *diodeuō***, v. GK: *1476* [→ *1223+3598*]. to go through, travel through:– passed through [1], went throughout [1]

1354 **Διονύσιος, *Dionysios***, n.pr. GK: *1477*. Dionysius, "*belonging to Dionysus*":– Dionysius [1]

1355 **διόπερ, *dioper***, c.infer. GK: *1478* [→ *1223+3739+4007*]. therefore, for this reason:– wherefore [3]

1356 **διοπετής, *diopetēs***, a. GK: *1479* [→ *2203+4098*]. (the image) fallen from heaven (given by the pagan god Zeus):– fell down from Jupiter [1]

1357 **διόρθωσις, *diorthōsis***, n. GK: *1481* [→ *1223+3717*]. a new order:– reformation [1]

1358 **διορύσσω, *diorysso***, v. GK: *1482* [→ *1223+3736*]. to break in:– break through [2], broken through [1], broken up [1]

Διός, *Dios*. See ***2203***.

1359 **Διόσκουροι, *Dioskouroi***, n.pr. GK: *1483* [→ *2203+2751*]. the twin gods Castor and Pollux, the Dioscuri, "*sons of Zeus*":– Castor and Pollux [1]

1360 **διότι, *dioti***, c. GK: *1484* [→ *1223+3739+5101*]. therefore, because:– because [11], for [8], because that [2], therefore [1]

1361 **Διοτρέφης, *Diotrephēs***, n.pr. GK: *1485* [→ *2203+5142*]. Diotrephes, "*nurtured by Zeus*":– Diotrephes [1]

1362 **διπλοῦς, *diplous***, a. GK: *1486 & 1487* [→ *1417*]. double, twice as much:– double [3], twofold more than [1]

1363 **διπλόω, *diploō***, v. GK: *1488* [→ *1417*]. to double, pay back double:– double [1]

1364 **δίς, *dis***, adv. GK: *1489* [→ *1417*]. twice, again:– twice [4], again [2]

Δίς, *Dis*. See ***2203***.

1365 **διστάζω, *distazō***, v. GK: *1491* [→ *1417*]. to doubt:– doubted [1], doubt [1]

1366 **δίστομος, *distomos***, a. GK: *1492* [→ *1417+4750*]. double-edged:– twoedged [2], with two edges [1]

1367 **δισχίλιοι, *dischilioi***, a.num. GK: *1493* [→ *1417+5507*]. two thousand:– two thousand [1]

1368 **διϋλίζω, *diylizō***, v. GK: *1494* [→ *1223+5208*]. to strain out, filter out:– strain out [1]

1369 **διχάζω, *dichazō***, v. GK: *1495* [→ *1417*]. to turn (one against another), cause a separation:– set at variance [1]

1370 **διχοστασία, *dichostasia***, n. GK: *1496* [→ *1417+2476*]. division, dissension:– divisions [2], seditions [1]

1371 **διχοτομέω, *dichotomeō***, v. GK: *1497* [→ *1417+5114*]. to cut to pieces, likely a figure for severe punishment rather than execution:– cut asunder [1], cut in sunder [1]

1372 **διψάω, *dipsaō***, v. GK: *1498* [→ *1373*]. to be thirsty:– thirst [10], athirst [3], thirsty [3]

1373 **δίψος, *dipsos***, n. GK: *1499* [→ *1372*]. thirst:– thirst [1]

1374 **δίψυχος, *dipsychos***, a. GK: *1500* [→ *1417+5594*]. double-minded:– double minded [2]

1375 **διωγμός, *diōgmos***, n. GK: *1501* [→ *1377*]. persecution:– persecutions [5], persecution [5]

1376 **διώκτης, *diōktēs***, n. GK: *1502* [→ *1377*]. persecutor:– persecutor [1]

1377 **διώκω, *diōkō***, v. GK: *1503* [→ *1375, 1376, 1559, 2614*]. to pursue, persecute, to systematically oppress and harass a person or group, as an extended meaning of pursuing a person on foot in a chase; also from the image of the chase comes the meaning of striving and pressing on to a goal with intensity: to press on:– persecuted [13], persecute [8], follow [7], persecutest [6], suffer persecution [3], followed [2], ensue [1], follow after [1], given to [1], persecuting [1], press [1]

1378 **δόγμα, *dogma***, n. GK: *1504* [→ *1380*]. decree, regulation:– decrees [2], ordinances [2], decree [1]

1379 **δογματίζω, *dogmatizō***, v. GK: *1505* [→ *1380*]. (pass.) to submit to a rule, regulation:– subject to ordinances [1]

1380 **δοκέω, *dokeō***, v. GK: *1506* [→ *603, 1378, 1379, 2106, 2107, 4328, 4329, 4909; cf. 1391*]. to think, consider, regard, an action of the mind and heart for processing information into understanding and choices, sometimes with a focus on appearances. Often in the impersonal form translated, "it seems" (Ac 17:18):– think [22], seemeth [5], seem [5], thought [5], thinkest [4], seemed good [3], seemed [3], suppose [3], accounted [2], pleased [2], supposed [2], supposing [2], thinketh [2], of reputation [1], pleasure [1], trow [1]

1381 **δοκιμάζω, *dokimazō***, v. GK: *1507* [→ *1209*]. to test, try, examine; interpret:– prove [6], proved [3], approve [2], try [2], allowed [1], alloweth [1], approvest [1], discern (*+1492*) [1], discern [1], examine [1], like [1], proving [1], tried [1], trieth [1]

1382 **δοκιμή, *dokimē***, n. GK: *1509* [→ *1209*]. character, test, proof:– proof [3], experience [2], experiment [1], trial [1]

1383 **δοκίμιον, *dokimion***, n. GK: *1510* [→ *1209*]. testing, proved genuineness:– trial [1], trying [1]

1384 **δόκιμος, *dokimos***, a. GK: *1511* [→ *1209*]. approved by testing, genuine:– approved [6], tried [1]

1385 **δοκός, *dokos***, n. GK: *1512*. plank, beam of wood:– beam [6]

δόκω, *dokō*. See ***1380***.

1386 **δόλιος, *dolios***, a. GK: *1513* [→ *1388*]. deceitful, dishonest, tricky:– deceitful [1]

1387 **δολιόω, *dolioō***, v. GK: *1514* [→ *1388*]. to practice deceit, deceive:– used deceit [1]

1388 **δόλος, *dolos***, n. GK: *1515* [→ *97, 1185, 1386, 1387, 1389*]. deceit, slyness, trickery, as a fig. extension of the base meaning (not used in the NT) of trapping an animal by baiting or by cunning:– guile [7], deceit [2], subtilty [2], craft [1]

1389 **δολόω, *doloō***, v. GK: *1516* [→ *1388*]. to distort, falsify:– handling deceitfully [1]

1390 **δόμα, *doma***, n. GK: *1517* [→ *1325*]. gift:– gifts [3], gift [1]

1391 **δόξα, *doxa***, n. GK: *1518* [→ *1392, 1740, 1741, 2754, 2755, 3861, 4888; cf. 1380*]. This word has a wide range of meanings in the NT, corresponding closely the Hebrew 3883: glory, splendor, brilliance, from the base meaning of the awesome light that radiates from God's presence and is associated with his acts of power; honor, praise, speaking of words of excellence and assigning highest status to God:– glory [145], glorious [6], honour [6], praise [4], glorious (*+1722*) [3], dignities [2], glorious (*+1223*) [1], worship [1]

1392 **δοξάζω, *doxazō***, v. GK: *1519* [→ *1391*]. to glorify, give praise, honor:– glorified [34], glorify [17], glorifying [3], full of glory [1], had glory [1], have glory [1], honoured [1], honoureth [1], honour [1], made glorious [1], magnify [1]

1393 **Δορκάς, *Dorkas***, n.pr. GK: *1520*. Dorcas, "*gazelle*":– Dorcas [2]

1394 **δόσις, *dosis***, n. GK: *1521* [→ *1325*]. gift, act of giving:– gift [1], giving [1]

1395 **δότης, *dotēs***, n. GK: *1522* [→ *1325*]. giver:– giver [1]

1396 **δουλαγωγέω, *doulagōgeō***, v. GK: *1524* [→ *1401+71*]. to enslave, bring to subjection:– bring into subjection [1]

1397 **δουλεία, *douleia***, n. GK: *1525* [→ *1401*]. slavery, bondage:– bondage [5]

1398 **δουλεύω, *douleuō***, v. GK: *1526* [→ *1401*]. to serve (as a slave):– serve [13], in bondage [4], serving [3], did service [1], do service [1], doing service [1], served [1], serveth [1]

1399 **δούλη, *doulē***, n. GK: *1527* [→ *1401*]. female servant, female slave:– handmaidens [1], handmaiden [1], handmaid [1]

1400 **δοῦλον, *doulon***, a.neut. of *1401*. GK: *1529* [→ *1401*]. slavish, servile, completely controlled, as a fig. extension of a slavery system in the ancient world, see *1401*:–

1401 **δοῦλος, *doulos***, n. GK: *1528* [→ *1396, 1397, 1398, 1399, 1400, 1402, 2615, 3787, 4889*]. servant, slave; in the NT a person owned as a possession for various lengths of times (Hebrew slaves no more than seven years, Gentile slaves without time limit), of lower social status than free persons or masters; slaves could earn or purchase their freedom:– servant [66], servants [53], bond [6], bondman [1], servant's [1]

1402 **δουλόω, *douloō***, v. GK: *1530* [→ *1401*]. to enslave, to cause one to become a slave; (pass.) to become enslaved; see also *1401*:– servants [2], bring into bondage [1], brought in bondage [1], given [1], in bondage [1], made servant [1], under bondage [1]

1403 **δοχή, *dochē***, n. GK: *1531* [→ *1209*]. banquet:– feast [2]

1404 **δράκων, *drakōn***, n. GK: *1532*. dragon:– dragon [13]

1405 **δράσσομαι, *drassomai***, v. GK: *1533* [→ *1323, 1406*]. to catch, seize:– taketh [1]

1406 **δραχμή, *drachmē***, n. GK: *1534* [→ *1405*]. silver coin, drachma:– piece [2], silver [1]

δρέμω, *dremō*. See ***5143***.

1407 **δρέπανον, *drepanon***, n. GK: *1535*. sickle:– sickle [8]

1408 **δρόμος, *dromos***, n. GK: *1536* [→ *5143*]. race, course; course (in life), career:– course [3]

1409 **Δρούσιλλα, *Drousilla***, n.pr. GK: *1537*. Drusilla:– Drusilla [1]

δῦμι, *dumi*. See ***1416***.

1410 **δύναμαι, *dynamai***, v. GK: *1538* [→ *101, 102, 1411, 1412, 1413, 1414, 1415, 1743, 2616*]. to be able, have ability, to have the power to accomplish an action; humans have variously limited abilities, God is unlimited:– can [63], cannot (*+3756*) [45], able [41], could [29], canst [9], may [8], mayest [4], might [3], cannot (*+3361*) [2], might have [2], been [1], can do [1], possible [1], power [1]

1411 **δύναμις, *dynamis***, n. GK: *1539* [→ *1410*]. power, ability; miracle; ruler, an extended meaning of a person or supernatural being who has administrative power:– power [71], mighty works [10], miracles [7], strength [7], powers [6], might [4], virtue [3], mighty [2], ability [1], abundance [1], meaning [1], mightily [1], mighty deeds [1], mighty work [1], miracle [1], violence [1], wonderful works [1], workers of miracles [1]

1412 **δυναμόω, *dynamoō***, v. GK: *1540* [→ *1410*]. (pass.) to be strengthened:– strengthened [1]

1413 **δυνάστης, *dynastēs***, n. GK: *1541* [→ *1410*]. ruler, sovereign, (court) official:– mighty [1], of great authority [1], potentate [1]

1414 **δυνατέω, *dynateō***, v. GK: *1542* [→ *1410*]. to be able, powerful, strong:– mighty [1]

1415 **δυνατός, *dynatos***, a. GK: *1543* [→ *1410*]. possible (based on power); powerful, able, the Mighty One:– possible [13], able [10], mighty [7], strong [3], could [1], power [1]

1416 **δύνω, *dynō***, v. GK: *1544* [→ *554, 555, 1424, 1562, 1737, 1742, 1744, 1745, 1746, 1902, 1903, 1931, 3921*]. to set (of the sun):– setting [1], set [1]

1417 **δύο, *dyo***, n.num. GK: *1545* [→ *1177, 1206, 1207, 1208, 1250, 1323, 1324, 1332, 1333, 1337, 1351, 1362, 1363, 1364, 1365, 1366, 1367, 1369, 1370, 1371, 1374, 1427, 1428, 1429*]. two:– two [123], twain [10], both [2], two hundred thousand thousand (*+3461*) [1]

1418 **δυσ-, *dus-***, inseparable prefix. GK: * [→ *1419, 1420, 1421, 1422, 1423, 1425, 1426*]. prefix conveying the idea of difficulty, opposition, injuriousness:–

1419 **δυσβάστακτος, *dysbastaktos***, a. GK: *1546* [→ *1418+941*]. hard to carry:– grievous to be borne [2]

1420 **δυσεντερία, *dysenteria***, n. GK: *1547 & 1548* [→ *1418; cf. 1722*]. dysentery:– bloody flixe [1]

1421 **δυσερμήνευτος, *dysermēneutos***, a. GK: *1549* [→ *1418+2059*]. hard to explain:– hard [1]

1422 **δύσκολος, *dyskolos***, a. GK: *1551* [→ *1418, 1423; cf. 2967*]. hard, difficult:– hard [1]

1423 **δυσκόλως, *dyskolōs***, adv. GK: *1552* [→ *1418, 1422*]. hard, with difficulty:– hardly [3]

1424 **δυσμή, *dysmē***, n. GK: *1553* [→ *1416*]. west (setting of the sun):– west [5]

1425 **δυσνόητος, *dysnoētos***, a. GK: *1554* [→ *1418+3563*]. hard to understand:– hard to be understood [1]

1426 **δυσφημία, *dysphēmia***, n. GK: *1556* [→ *1418+5346*]. bad report, slander:– evil report [1]

δύω, *duō*. See **1416**.

1427 **δώδεκα, *dōdeka***, n.num. GK: *1557* [→ *1417+1176*]. twelve:– twelve [72]

1428 **δωδέκατος, *dōdekatos***, a. GK: *1558* [→ *1417+1176*]. twelfth:– twelfth [1]

1429 **δωδεκάφυλον, *dōdekaphylon***, n. GK: *1559* [→ *1417+1176+5443*]. twelve tribes:– twelve tribes [1]

1430 **δῶμα, *dōma***, n. GK: *1560* [→ *456, 1739, 2026, 3618, 3619, 3620, 4925*]. roof, housetop:– housetop [4], housetops [2], house [1]

1431 **δωρεά, *dōrea***, n. GK: *1561* [→ *1325*]. gift:– gift [11]

1432 **δωρεάν, *dōrean***, adv. GK: *1562* [→ *1325*]. freely, free of charge, without payment:– freely [6], for nought [1], in vain [1], without a cause [1]

1433 **δωρέομαι, *dōreomai***, v. GK: *1563* [→ *1325*]. to give, confer, bestow:– given [2], gave [1]

1434 **δώρημα, *dōrēma***, n. GK: *1564* [→ *1325*]. gift:– gift [2]

1435 **δῶρον, *dōron***, n. GK: *1565* [→ *2333; cf. 1325*]. gift, offering:– gift [10], gifts [8], offerings [1]

1436 **ἔα, *ea***, pt.excl. GK: *1568*. ha!, aha!:– let alone [2]

1437 **ἐάν, *ean***, c. GK: *1569* [→ *1487+302*]. if (usually used in general conditions or conditions that imply some doubt):– if [214], whosoever (*+3739*) [19], whatsoever (*+3739*) [15], though [12], whomsoever (*+3739*) [4], if (*+4007*) [3], wheresoever (*+3699*) [3], that (*+3739*) [2], whatsoever (*+3745*) [2], when [2], whether (*+5037*) [2], whom (*+3739*) [2], according to that (*+2526*) [1], and whether (*+5037*) [1], as many as (*+3745*) [1], as often as (*+3740*) [1], but (*+3361*) [1], except (*+3361*) [1], in what place soever (*+3699*) [1], or (*+5037*) [1], though (*+2532*) [1], what (*+3739*) [1], whatsoever (*+3739+5100*) [1], whatsoever (*+3748+3956+5100*) [1], whensoever (*+5613*) [1], whithersoever (*+3699*) [1], whithersoever (*+3757*) [1], whomsoever (*+5100*) [1], whoso (*+3739*) [1]

ἐάν μή, *ean mē*. See **3361** and **3362**.

1438 **ἑαυτοῦ, *heautou***, p.reflex. GK: *1571* [→ *846*]. himself, herself, itself, themselves; (pl., in some contexts) reciprocal relationship, to one aother:– himself [111], themselves [57], yourselves [36], ourselves [20], his [19], their [15], itself [9], his own [8], their own [7], them [7], one another [6], herself [5], you [5], her [4], your own selves [4], your own [4], him [3], her own [2], they [2], alone (*+2596*) [1], he himself [1], he [1], our own [1], she [1], their own home [1], their own selves [1], thine own [1], thyself [1], ye [1], your [1]

1439 **ἐάω, *eaō***, v. GK: *1572* [→ *4330*]. to let, allow, permit:– suffered [5], suffer [2], committed [1], left [1], let alone [1], let [1], sufferest [1], suffereth [1]

1440 **ἑβδομήκοντα, *hebdomēkonta***, n.num. GK: *1573* [→ *2033*]. seventy:– seventy [2], threescore and fifteen (*+4002*) [1], threescore sixteen (*+1803*) [1], threescore ten [1]

1441 **ἑβδομηκοντάκις, *hebdomēkontakis***, adv. GK: *1574* [→ *2033*]. seventy times:– seventy times [1]

1442 **ἕβδομος, *hebdomos***, a. GK: *1575* [→ *2033*]. seventh:– seventh [9]

1443 **Ἔβερ, *Eber***, n.pr. GK: *1576*. Eber, "*[regions] beyond [the river]* or *source of the word "Hebrew"*":– Heber [1]

1444 **Ἑβραϊκός, *Hebraikos***, a.pr. GK: *1577* [→ *1445*]. Hebrew:– Hebrew [1]

1445 **Ἑβραῖος, *Hebraios***, n.pr.g. GK: *1578* [→ *1444, 1446, 1447*]. a Hebrew; a Hebraic Jew:– Hebrews [4], Hebrew [1]

1446 **Ἑβραΐς, *Hebrais***, n.pr. GK: *1579* [→ *1445*]. Aramaic, Hebrew dialect:– in Hebrew [3]

1447 **Ἑβραϊστί, *Hebraisti***, adv.pr. GK: *1580* [→ *1445*]. in Aramaic, in the Hebrew dialect:– in the Hebrew tongue [3], in the Hebrew [2], in Hebrew [1]

1448 **ἐγγίζω, *engizō***, v. GK: *1581* [→ *1451*]. come near, draw near:– at hand [9], come nigh [6], drew nigh [6], drew near [4], come near [3], draw nigh [3], draweth nigh [3], came near [2], came nigh [2], nigh [2], approacheth [1], approaching [1], draweth near [1]

1449 **ἐγγράφω, *engraphō***, v. GK: *1582* [→ *1722+1125*]. to write in, write on, record:– written [2]

1450 **ἔγγυος, *engyos***, a. GK: *1583*. (n.) guarantee, guarantor:– surety [1]

1451 **ἐγγύς, *engys***, adv. GK: *1584* [→ *1448, 1452, 4331*]. near, close:– nigh [12], at hand [6], nigh at hand [4], near [3], nigh to [2], from [1], near to [1], ready [1]

1452 **ἐγγύτερον, *engyteron***, adv.comp. GK: *1585* [→ *1451*]. nearer, closer:– nearer [1]

1453 **ἐγείρω, *egeirō***, v. GK: *1586* [→ *1127, 1235, 1326, 1454, 1825, 1892, 4891*]. to arise, to stand from a prone or sleeping position. From this base meaning are several fig. extended meanings: to wake from sleep; to restore from a dead or damaged state: to heal, raise to life; to cause something to exist: raise up (give birth to) a child:– raised [29], risen [20], raised up [16], rise [16], arise [13], arose [12], raise up [6], rise up [6], rose [4], awake [2], lift up [2], raise [2], risen up [2], ariseth [1], awoke [1], lift out [1], lifted up [1], raiseth up [1], raiseth [1], rear up [1], riseth [1], stand [1], took up [1]

1454 **ἔγερσις, *egersis***, n. GK: *1587* [→ *1453*]. resurrection:– resurrection [1]

1455 **ἐγκάθετος, *enkathetos***, a. GK: *1588* [→ *863*]. (n.) spy:– spies [1]

1456 **ἐγκαίνια, *enkainia***, n. GK: *1589* [→ *1722+2537*]. Feast of Dedication (Hanukkah):– dedication [1]

1457 **ἐγκαινίζω, *enkainizō***, v. GK: *1590* [→ *1722+2537*]. (pass.) to be put into effect, inaugurate; (act.) to open:– consecrated [1], dedicated [1]

1458 **ἐγκαλέω, *enkaleō***, v. GK: *1592* [→ *1722+2564*]. to bring charges, accuse; (pass.) to be charged with, have an accusation brought to:– accused [4], called in question [1], implead [1], lay to the charge [1]

1459 **ἐγκαταλείπω, *enkataleipō***, v. GK: *1593* [→ *1722+2596+3007*]. to forsake, leave, abandon:– forsaken [4], forsake [1], forsaking [1], forsook [1], leave [1], left [1]

1460 **ἐγκατοικέω, *enkatoikeō***, v. GK: *1594* [→ *1722+2596+3624*]. to live among:– dwelling [1]

1461 **ἐγκεντρίζω, *enkentrizō***, v. GK: *1596* [→ *1722+2759*]. to graft into:– graffed in [3], graff in [1], graffed into [1], graffed [1]

1462 **ἔγκλημα, *enklēma***, n. GK: *1598* [→ *1722+2564*]. charge, accusation:– crime laid [1], laid to charge [1]

1463 **ἐγκομβόομαι, *enkomboomai***, v. GK: *1599* [→ *1722*]. to clothe (oneself) with, put on:– clothed with [1]

1464 **ἐγκοπή, *enkopē***, n. GK: *1600 & 1715* [→ *1722+2875*]. hinderance, restraint:– hinder (*+1325*) [1]

1465 **ἐγκόπτω, *enkoptō***, v. GK: *1601* [→ *1722+2875*]. to hinder, stop, impede progress:– hindered from [1], hindered [1], tedious [1]

1466 **ἐγκράτεια, *enkrateia***, n. GK: *1602* [→ *1722+2904*]. self-control:– temperance [4]

1467 **ἐγκρατεύομαι, *enkrateuomai***, v. GK: *1603* [→ *1722+2904*]. to have control (of oneself):– contain [1], temperate [1]

1468 **ἐγκρατής, *enkratēs***, a. GK: *1604* [→ *1722+2904*]. disciplined, self-controlled:– temperate [1]

1469 **ἐγκρίνω, *enkrinō***, v. GK: *1605* [→ *1722+2919*]. to classify:– make of the number [1]

1470 **ἐγκρύπτω, *enkryptō***, v. GK: *1606* [→ *1722+2928*]. to mix, put into:– hid [2]

1471 **ἔγκυος, *enkyos***, a. GK: *1607* [→ *1722+2949*]. pregnant:– great with child [1]

1472 **ἐγχρίω, *enchriō***, v. GK: *1608* [→ *1722+5548*]. to put on, rub on, anoint:– anoint [1]

1473 **ἐγώ, *egō***, p.pers. GK: *1609* [→ *1683, 1691, 1698, 1699, 1700, 2248, 2249, 2251, 2254, 2257, 2504, 3165, 3365, 3427, 3450*]. I, me, my; we, us, our; often added for emphasis: myself, ourselves:– me [798], my [527], I [425], us [396], our [312], we [173], mine [24], mine own [4], ours [4], usward [2], myself (*+846*) [1], myself [1], ourselves [1], what have I to do (*+5101*) [1]

1474 **ἐδαφίζω, *edaphizō***, v. GK: *1610* [→ *1475*]. to dash to the ground, raze:– lay even with the ground [1]

1475 **ἔδαφος, *edaphos***, n. GK: *1611* [→ *1474*]. ground:– ground [1]

1476 **ἑδραῖος, *hedraios***, a. GK: *1612* [→ *856, 1477, 1747, 1748, 1749, 2145, 2516, 4332, 4892; cf. 2516*]. firm, steadfast:– stedfast [2], settled [1]

1477 **ἑδραίωμα, *hedraiōma***, n. GK: *1613* [→ *1476*]. foundation:– ground [1]

1478 **Ἑζεκίας, *Hezekias***, n.pr. GK: *1614*. Hezekiah, "*God [El] strengthens*":– Ezekias [2]

1479 **ἐθελοθρησκία, *ethelothrēskia***, n. GK: *1615* [→ *2309+2357*]. self-imposed religion:– will worship [1]

ἐθέλω, *ethelō*. See **2309**.

1480 **ἐθίζω, *ethizō***, v. GK: *1616* [→ *1485*]. (pass.) to be accustomed, required:– custom [1]

1481 **ἐθνάρχης, *ethnarchēs***, n. GK: *1617* [→ *1484+757*]. governor:– governor [1]

1482 **ἐθνικός, *ethnikos***, a. GK: *1618* [→ *1484*]. pagan, Gentile:– heathen [2]

1483 **ἐθνικῶς, *ethnikōs***, adv. GK: *1619* [→ *1484*]. like a Gentile, like a pagan:– after the manner of Gentiles [1]

1484 **ἔθνος, *ethnos***, n. GK: *1620* [→ *1481, 1482, 1483*]. Gentile, pagan; (foreign) nation, a people:– Gentiles [93], nations [37], nation [27], heathen [5], people [2]

1485 **ἔθος, *ethos***, n. GK: *1621* [→ *1480, 1486, 1486, 2239, 2550, 4914*]. custom, practice, habit:– customs [5], manner [4], custom [2], as wont (*+2596+3588*) [1]

1486 **ἔθω, *ethō***, v. GK: *1622 & 1665* [→ *1485*]. to be accustomed; to have a custom:– wont [2], custom [1], manner [1]

1487 **εἰ, *ei***, pt.cond. GK: *1623* [→ *1437, 3375, 1512, 1513, 1535, 2579, 5616, 5619*]. if, since:– if [270], whether [21], that [6], although (*+2532*) [1], but (*+1622+3361*) [1], but (*+3361*) [1], but though (*+1161+2532*) [1], except (*+1622+3361*) [1], forasmuch [1], had [1], if (*+3305*) [1], it may be (*+5177*) [1], it may chance (*+5177*) [1], never (*+165+1519+3588+3756*) [1], not [1], no [1], since [1], though (*+2532*) [1], unless (*+1622+3361*) [1], what if [1]

1488 **εἶ, *ei***, v.2.s of *1510*. GK: *1639* [→ *1510*]. you are, thou art; see *1510*:–

1489 **εἴγε, *eige*,** pt.emph. GK: *1623 + 1145* [→ *1487+1065*]. if indeed, seeing that, unless; (with neg.) otherwise:– if [4], if so be that [1]

1490 **εἰ δὲ μή (γε), *ei de mē (ge)*,** pt.emph. GK: *1623 + 1254 + 3590 (+ 1145)* [→ *1487+1161+3361+1065*]. but if not, or else, otherwise:– else [4], or else [4], if not [2], if otherwise [2], and if not [1], otherwise [1]

1491 **εἶδος, *eidos*,** n. GK: *1626* [→ *1126, 1141, 2396, 2397, 2400, 3708, 4075, 5237; cf. 1497*]. form, appearance, sight:– shape [2], appearance [1], fashion [1], sight [1]

1492 **εἴδω, *eidō*;** or **οἶδα, *oida*,** v. GK: *3857* [→ *4893?, 4894?; cf. 2467*]. to know, to possess information; recognize, realize, to come to know; to understand, to be able to use knowledge:– saw [188], know [176], see [78], knowing [38], seen [34], knew [28], knoweth [22], knowest [15], beheld [10], tell [9], seeing [8], sawest [7], known [6], looked [6], wist [6], behold [4], knewest [3], perceive [3], perceiving [3], sure [3], wot [3], can [2], know how [2], aware [1], consider [1], discern (*+1381*) [1], knowledge [1], looked on [1], understandeth [1], understand [1]

1493 **εἰδωλεῖον, *eidōleion*,** n. GK: *1627* [→ *1497*]. temple of an idol:– idol's temple [1]

1494 **εἰδωλόθυτος, *eidōlothytos*,** a. GK: *1628* [→ *1497+2380*]. (food) sacrificed to idols:– things offered to idols [2], things sacrificed unto idols [2], meats offered to idols [1], offered in sacrifice to idols [1], offered in sacrifice unto idols [1], thing offered unto an idol [1], things offered in sacrifice unto idols [1], things offered unto idols [1]

1495 **εἰδωλολατρία, *eidōlolatria*,** n. GK: *1630* [→ *1497+2999*]. idolatry, the reverence and worship of idols:– idolatry [3], idolatries [1]

1496 **εἰδωλολάτρης, *eidōlolatrēs*,** n. GK: *1629* [→ *1497+2999*]. idolater, one who worships idols and so practices idolatry:– idolaters [5], idolater [2]

1497 **εἴδωλον, *eidōlon*,** n. GK: *1631* [→ *1493, 1494, 1496, 1495, 2712; cf. 1491*]. idol, an object that is worshiped, formed by casting or carving (with the possible implication that a god or demon is intrinsic to the idol):– idols [7], idol [4]

1498 **εἴην, *eiēn*,** v.subj. or opt. of *1510*. GK: *1639* [→ *1510*]. it may (could, might, should, would) be; see *1510*:–

1499 **εἰ καί, *ei kai*,** conj. GK: *1623 + 2779* [→ *1487+2532*]. even if, although:– though [11], and if [1], if also [1], if that [1], though but [1]

1500 **εἰκῇ, *eikē*,** adv. GK: *1632*. in vain, for nothing, to no purpose:– in vain [5], vainly [1], without a cause [1]

1501 **εἴκοσι, *eikosi*,** n.num. GK: *1633*. twenty:– twenty [12]

1502 **εἴκω, *eikō*,** v. GK: *1634* [→ *5226*]. to give in, yield:– gave place [1]

1503 **ἔοικα, *eoika*,** v. GK: *2036* [→ *1504, 1932, 1933*]. to be like, resemble:– like [2]

1504 **εἰκών, *eikōn*,** n. GK: *1635* [→ *1503*]. image, likeness, portrait:– image [23]

1505 **εἰλικρίνεια, *eilikrineia*,** n. GK: *1636* [→ *1506*]. sincerity, the positive moral quality of purity (especially in motives), a fig. extension of an unadulterated or unmixed substance:– sincerity [3]

1506 **εἰλικρινής, *eilikrinēs*,** a. GK: *1637* [→ *1505*]. pure, wholesome:– pure [1], sincere [1]

1507 **εἱλίσσω, *heilissō*,** v. GK: *1813* [→ *1667*]. to roll up, roll together:– rolled together [1]

1508 **εἰ μή, *ei mē*,** conj. GK: *1623 + 3590* [→ *1487+3361*]. if not, except, but:– but [52], save [17], except [7], saving [2], more than [1], save only [1], till (*+3752*) [1]

1509 **εἰ μή τι, *ei mē ti*,** conj. GK: *1623 + 3590 + 5516* [→ *1508+5100*]. unless indeed, except, unless perhaps:– except [2], except (*+302*) [1]

1510 **εἰμί, *eimi*,** v. GK: *1639* [→ *548, 666, 1488, 1498, 1511, 1526, 1751, 1762, 1832, 1849, 1967, 2070, 2071, 2075, 2076, 2077, 2252, 2258, 2277, 2468, 3689, 3776, 3918, 3952, 4041, 4840, 4895, 5123, 5600, 5607; cf. 1849*]. to be, exist, be present; all forms of this verb are indexed under *1510*:– is [829], be [366], was [349], are [345], were [155], am [139], art [85], being [37], been [24], have [23], had [16], be (*+1519*) [9], wast [6], come to pass [4], come [3], shall [3], meaneth [2], meant [2], mean [2], agree together (*+2470*) [1], agreed not (*+800*) [1], agreed together (*+2470*) [1], agree [1], belonged [1], belongeth [1], belong [1], cannot (*+3756*) [1], cannot be tempted (*+551*) [1], cometh [1], consisteth [1], continued [1], did [1], down [1], dureth [1], endure [1], exceedingly fear (*+1630*) [1], followed (*+3326*) [1], follow [1], for [1], give [1], hast [1], have being [1], having [1], held [1], know (*+1110*) [1], let [1], live long (*+3118*) [1], love husbands (*+5362*) [1], make [1], may [1], meaneth (*+2309*) [1], must [1], oweth [1], pass the flower of age (*+5230*) [1], perish (*+684+1519*) [1], please well (*+2101*) [1], pleased (*+701*) [1], profiteth (*+5624*) [1], remaineth (*+3062+3588*) [1], should [1], sojourn (*+3941*) [1], so [1], stand [1], used to [1], were (*+1096*) [1], were (*+4218*) [1], wert [1], while (*+1722+3588*) [1], wholly given to idolatry (*+2712*) [1], will [1], wrestle (*+3823*) [1]

1511 **εἶναι, *einai*,** v.infin. of *1510*. GK: *1639* [→ *1510*]. to be, exist, be present; see *1510*:–

εἵνεκεν, *heineken*. See ***1752***.

1512 **εἴπερ, *eiper*,** pt.cond. GK: *1642* [→ *1487+4007*]. if indeed, if in fact, since:– if so that [2], if so be that (*+686*) [1], if so [1], seeing [1], though (*+2532*) [1]

1513 **εἴπως, *eipōs*,** pt. GK: *1643* [→ *1487+4226*]. if perhaps, if somehow:– if by any means [4]

1514 **εἰρηνεύω, *eirēneuō*,** v. GK: *1644* [→ *1515*]. to live in peace, be at peace:– have peace [1], live in peace [1], live peaceably [1], peace [1]

1515 **εἰρήνη, *eirēnē*,** n. GK: *1645* [→ *1514, 1516, 1517, 1518*]. peace, harmony, tranquility; safety, welfare, health; often with an emphasis on lack of strife or reconciliation in a relation, as when one has "peace with God." Often used as a verbal and written greeting. This word generally follows the meanings and usage of the Hebrew word 8934:– peace [89], quietness [1], rest [1], set at one (*+1519+4900*) [1]

1516 **εἰρηνικός, *eirēnikos*,** a. GK: *1646* [→ *1515*]. peace-loving, peaceable, peaceful, with a focus of having freedom from emotional worry and frustration:– peaceable [2]

1517 **εἰρηνοποιέω, *eirēnopoieō*,** v. GK: *1647* [→ *1515+4160*]. to make peace, to cause reconciliation between two parties, as in Christ causing the believer's peace with God:– made peace [1]

1518 **εἰρηνοποιός, *eirēnopoios*,** a. GK: *1648* [→ *1515+4160*]. peacemaker, one who restores peace and reconciliation between persons and even nations: peacemakers [1]

εἴρω, *eirō*. See ***1515, 4483, 5346***.

1519 **εἰς, *eis*,** pp. GK: *1650* [→ *1521, 1522, 1523, 1524, 1525, 1528, 1529, 1530, 1531, 1532, 1533, 1898, 2072, 2080, 2081, 2082, 3919, 3920, 3921, 3922, 3923, 4897*]. to, toward, into; for. Spatially: movement toward or into an area (extending to a goal); logically: a marker of purpose or result; of time: extending to or up to a certain time:– into [543], to [316], unto [206], for [141], in [140], on [59], against [27], that (*+3588*) [27], to (*+3588*) [24], upon [24], at [21], among [18], towards [15], toward [14], be (*+1510*) [9], that [6], whereunto (*+3739*) [6], concerning [5], never (*+165+3361+3588+3756*) [5], throughout [5], become (*+1096*) [4], of [4], therein (*+846*) [4], to the end (*+3588*) [4], back (*+3588+3694*) [3], made (*+1096*) [3], therefore (*+3778*) [3], wherein (*+3739*) [3], abroad (*+5318*) [2], before [2], by [2], continually (*+1336+3588*) [2], ever (*+165+3588*) [2], for ever (*+1336+3588*) [2], for purpose [2], for this cause (*+3778*) [2], so that (*+3588*) [2], thereunto (*+3778*) [2], to this end (*+3778*) [2], why (*+5101*) [2], abundantly (*+4050*) [1], afar off (*+3112*) [1], after that (*+3195+3588*) [1], again (*+3588+3694*) [1], as concerning (*+3056*) [1], backward (*+3588+3694*) [1], became (*+1096*) [1], before (*+4383*) [1], by continual (*+5056*) [1], despised (*+3049+3762*) [1], ever (*+165+3588+3956*) [1], far more exceeding (*+2596+5236+5236*) [1], for to (*+3588*) [1], forth (*+3319+3588*) [1], from [1], grew (*+2064*) [1], hereunto (*+3778*) [1], home (*+2398+3588*) [1], in among [1], in no wise (*+3361+3588+3838*) [1], insomuch that (*+3588*) [1], lest (*+3361+3588*) [1], made ready to hand (*+2092*) [1], make mad (*+3130+4062*) [1], make war against (*+4171+4820*) [1], never (*+165+1487+3588+3756*) [1], never (*+165+3588+3756*) [1], peculiar (*+4047*) [1], perish (*+684+1510*) [1], regardest (*+991*) [1], relief (*+1248*) [1], set at one (*+1515+4900*) [1], thereinto (*+846*) [1], thereunto (*+846+3778*) [1], throughout (*+3837*) [1], till [1], to end [1], to make [1], to the intent (*+3588*) [1], took shipping (*+1684+3588+4143*) [1], until [1], waxed (*+1096*) [1], went back (*+565+3588+3694*) [1], wherefore (*+3739*) [1], wherefore (*+5101*) [1], whereinto (*+3739*) [1], whereto (*+3739*) [1], wherewith [1], while standeth [1], whither (*+3739*) [1], with [1]

1520 **εἷς, *heis*,** n.num. GK: *1651* [→ *1733, 1734, 1775, 1847, 1848, 3367, 3391, 3762*]. one, single:– one [289], a [13], first [8], some [6], the other[S] [6], certain [5], any [2], an [2], man [2], one (*+5100*) [2], one another (*+1520+3588*) [2], agree (*+1106+4160*) [1], another [1], each (*+1538*) [1], even all one as if (*+846+2532+3588*) [1], every (*+1538+2596*) [1], every (*+1538*) [1], no not one (*+2193+3756*) [1], one by one (*+2596*) [1], only [1], other[S] [1], particularly (*+1538+2596*) [1], several (*+303*) [1], whether (*+3739*) [1]

1521 **εἰσάγω, *eisagō*,** v. GK: *1652* [→ *1519+71*]. to bring in, take in:– brought into [4], brought in [3], bring in [1], bringeth in [1], led into [1]

1522 **εἰσακούω, *eisakouō*,** v. GK: *1653* [→ *1519+191*]. (pass.) to be heard, listened to:– heard [4], hear [1]

1523 **εἰσδέχομαι, *eisdechomai*,** v. GK: *1654* [→ *1519+1209*]. to receive, welcome:– receive [1]

1524 **εἴσειμι, *eiseimi*,** v. GK: *1655* [→ *1519*]. to go in, enter:– entered [1], go [1], went in [1], went [1]

1525 **εἰσέρχομαι, *eiserchomai*,** v. GK: *1656* [→ *1519+2064*]. to go in, enter:– enter [55], entered [48], went into [14], went in [11], come in [8], came in [7], enter in [7], go in [7], come into [6], entered in [5], coming in [3], entereth [3], entering [3], came into [2], come [2], go into [2], arose [1], came to [1], camest in [1], come to [1], come unto [1], cometh into [1], enter in through [1], entereth in [1], entering in [1], goeth into [1], gone [1], go [1], in [1], wentest in [1], went [1]

1526 **εἰσί, *eisi*,** v.3.pl. of *1510*. GK: *1639* [→ *1510*]. they are; see *1510*.:–

1527 **εἷς καθ᾽ εἷς, *heis kath' heis*,** idiom. GK: *1651 + 2848* [→ *1520+2596+1520*]. one by one:– one by one [2], each [1]

1528 **εἰσκαλέομαι, *eiskaleomai*,** v. GK: *1657* [→ *1519+2564*]. to invite into:– called in [1]

1529 **εἴσοδος, *eisodos*,** n. GK: *1658* [→ *1519+3598*]. entering, entrance; reception, welcome:– coming [1], entering in [1], enter [1], entrance in [1], entrance [1]

1530 **εἰσπηδάω, *eispēdaō*,** v. GK: *1659* [→ *1519*]. to rush in:– ran in [1], sprang in [1]

1531 **εἰσπορεύομαι, *eisporeuomai*,** v. GK: *1660* [→ *1519+4198*]. to go in, enter:– entered [3], entereth [3], entereth in [2], entering [2], came in [1], come in [1], coming in [1], enter in [1], entering into [1], entering in [1], went into [1]

1532 **εἰστρέχω, *eistrechō*,** v. GK: *1661* [→ *1519+5143*]. to run in:– ran in [1]

1533 **εἰσφέρω, *eispherō*,** v. GK: *1662* [→ *1519+5342*]. to bring in, lead in:– bring in [2], brought [2], bringest [1], lead into [1], lead [1]

1534 **εἶτα, *eita*,** adv. GK: *1663* [→ *1899, 3347*]. then, after that, next:– then [11], after that [3], afterward [1], furthermore (*+3303+3588*) [1]

1535 **εἴτε, *eite*,** pt. GK: *1664* [→ *1487+5037*]. if, whether…or:– or [33], whether [28], or whether [3], if [1]

1536 **εἴ τις, *ei tis*,** pt.cond.+p. GK: *1623 + 5516* [→ *1487+5100*]. if any, whoever, whatever:– if any [45], if a man [6], that [2], whosoever [2], if ought [1], that which [1], whether any [1]

1537 **ἐκ, *ek*,** pp. GK: *1666* [→ *411, 412, 413, 419, 421, 553, 554, 555, 1327, 1544, 1545, 1546, 1547, 1548, 1549, 1550, 1551, 1552, 1553, 1554, 1555, 1556, 1557, 1558, 1559, 1560, 1561, 1562, 1567, 1568, 1569, 1570, 1571, 1572, 1573, 1574, 1575, 1576, 1577, 1578, 1579, 1580, 1581, 1582, 1583, 1584, 1585, 1586, 1587, 1588, 1589, 1590, 1591, 1592, 1593, 1594, 1597, 1598, 1599, 1600, 1601, 1602, 1603, 1604, 1605, 1606, 1607, 1608, 1609, 1610, 1611, 1612, 1613, 1615, 1620, 1622, 1624, 1625, 1626, 1627, 1628, 1629, 1630, 1631, 1633, 1634, 1804, 1805, 1806, 1807, 1808, 1809, 1810, 1811, 1813, 1814, 1815, 1816, 1817, 455, 1818, 1819, 1820, 1821, 1822, 1823, 1824, 1825, 1826, 1827, 1828, 1829, 1830, 1831, 1832, 1833, 1834, 1837, 1839, 1840, 1841, 1842, 1843, 1844, 1845, 1846, 1847, 1848, 1849, 1851, 1852, 1853, 1854, 1855, 1856, 1857, 2078, 2079, 3924, 4898, 4899, 5240; cf. 1614, 1632*]. of, out of; from, away from. Spatially: extension from a space to a goal outer in reference, separation; logically: the means or source of an activity, disassociation or separation:– of [441], from [185], out of [112], by [55], on [34], with [26], in [7], among [5], over [4], second time (*+1208*) [4], at [3], by reason of [3], from among [3], thereof (*+846*) [3], through [3], again (*+1208*) [2], because of [2], for [2], out [2], abundantly (*+4053*) [1], as much as lieth in [1], between [1], betwixt [1], beyond [1], by the means of [1], earthly (*+1093+3588*) [1], exceedingly (*+4053+5228*) [1], from thenceforth (*+3778*) [1], grudgingly (*+3077*) [1], heartily (*+5590*) [1], heavenly (*+3772*) [1], hereby (*+3778*) [1], highly (*+4053*) [1], nothing (*+846+3361*) [1], of company [1], off [1], over against (*+1727*) [1], raised to life again (*+386*) [1], since began [1], third time (*+5154*) [1], to [1], unto [1], vehemently (*+4053*) [1], whereof (*+3739*) [1], whereof [1], your (*+4771*) [1]

1538 **ἕκαστος, *hekastos***, a. GK: *1667* [→ *1539*]. each, every:– every man [34], every one [19], every [18], every man's [3], any man [1], both [1], daily (*+2250+2596*) [1], each (*+1520*) [1], each one [1], every (*+1520+2596*) [1], every (*+1520*) [1], every woman [1], particularly (*+1520+2596*) [1]

1539 **ἑκάστοτε, *hekastote***, adv. GK: *1668* [→ *1538+3739+5037*]. always, at any time:– always [1]

1540 **ἑκατόν, *hekaton***, n.num. GK: *1669* [→ *1541, 1542, 1543*]. hundred:– hundred [14], hundredfold [2], hundreds [1]

1541 **ἑκατονταετής, *hekatontaetēs***, a. GK: *1670* [→ *1540+2094*]. a hundred years old:– hundred year old [1]

1542 **ἑκατονταπλασίων, *hekatontaplasiōn***, a. GK: *1671* [→ *1540*]. a hundred times:– hundredfold [3]

1543 **ἑκατοντάρχης, *hekatontarchēs***, n. GK: *1672 & 1673* [→ *1540+757*]. centurion, officer:– centurion [17], centurions [3], centurion's [1]

1544 **ἐκβάλλω, *ekballō***, v. GK: *1675* [→ *1537+906*]. to take out, remove; to drive out, expel; bring out, send out:– cast out [46], bringeth forth [3], casteth out [3], casting out [3], cast [3], pull out [3], send forth [3], thrust out [3], put forth [2], cast forth [1], casteth [1], driveth [1], drove out [1], expelled [1], leave [1], pluck out [1], put out [1], putteth forth [1], put [1], sent away [1], sent out [1], took out [1]

1545 **ἔκβασις, *ekbasis***, n. GK: *1676* [→ *1537+305*]. way out; outcome, end, result:– end [1], way to escape [1]

1546 **ἐκβολή, *ekbolē***, n. GK: *1678* [→ *1537+906*]. throwing out (a ship's cargo), jettisoning:– lightened the ship (*+4160*) [1]

1547 **ἐκγαμίζω, *ekgamizō***, v. GK: *1679* [→ *1537+1062*]. to marry, give in marriage:– given in marriage [2], giveth in marriage [2], giving in marriage [1]

1548 **ἐκγαμίσκω, *ekgamiskō***, v. GK: *1680* [→ *1537+1062*]. to give in marriage:– given in marriage [2]

1549 **ἔκγονος, *ekgonos***, a. GK: *1681* [→ *1537+1096*]. (n.) grandchild:– nephews [1]

1550 **ἐκδαπανάω, *ekdapanaō***, v. GK: *1682* [→ *1537+1160*]. (pass.) to be completely expended, exhausted:– spent [1]

1551 **ἐκδέχομαι, *ekdechomai***, v. GK: *1683* [→ *1537+1209*]. to wait for, expect, look forward to:– expecting [1], look for [1], looked for [1], tarry for [1], waited for [1], waited [1], waiteth for [1], waiting for [1]

1552 **ἔκδηλος, *ekdēlos***, a. GK: *1684* [→ *1537+1212*]. clear, very evident, plain:– manifest [1]

1553 **ἐκδημέω, *ekdēmeō***, v. GK: *1685* [→ *1537+1218*]. to be away, absent:– absent [3]

1554 **ἐκδίδωμι, *ekdidōmi***, v. GK: *1686* [→ *1537+1325*]. (mid.) to rent, lease:– let out [3], let forth [1]

1555 **ἐκδιηγέομαι, *ekdiēgeomai***, v. GK: *1687* [→ *1537+1223+71*]. to tell:– declare [1], declaring [1]

1556 **ἐκδικέω, *ekdikeō***, v. GK: *1688* [→ *1537+1349*]. to avenge, take revenge; to grant justice, get justice:– avenge [4], avenged [1], revenge [1]

1557 **ἐκδίκησις, *ekdikēsis***, n. GK: *1689* [→ *1537+1349*]. justice; vengeance; punishment:– vengeance [4], avenge (*+3588+4160*) [1], avenged (*+4160*) [1], avenge [1], punishment [1], revenge [1]

1558 **ἔκδικος, *ekdikos***, a. GK: *1690* [→ *1537+1349*]. punishing, avenging:– avenger [1], revenger [1]

1559 **ἐκδιώκω, *ekdiōkō***, v. GK: *1691* [→ *1537+1377*]. to drive out, persecute (severely):– persecuted [1], persecute [1]

1560 **ἔκδοτος, *ekdotos***, a. GK: *1692* [→ *1537+1325*]. handed over, given up, delivered up:– delivered [1]

1561 **ἐκδοχή, *ekdochē***, n. GK: *1693* [→ *1537+1209*]. expectation:– looking for [1]

1562 **ἐκδύω, *ekdyō***, v. GK: *1694* [→ *1537+1416*]. to strip off clothing, unclothe:– stripped of raiment [1], stripped [1], took off from [1], took off [1], unclothed [1]

1563 **ἐκεῖ, *ekei***, adv. GK: *1695* [→ *1564, 1565, 1566, 1900, 2546, 2547, 2548, 5238*]. there, in a place where:– there [86], thither [7], thitherward [1], to yonder place [1], yonder [1]

1564 **ἐκεῖθεν, *ekeithen***, adv. GK: *1696* [→ *1563*]. from there, from that place:– thence [16], from thence [7], from that place [1], there [1]

1565 **ἐκεῖνος, *ekeinos***, p.demo. GK: *1697* [→ *1563*]. that, those; he, she, it:– that [105], he [40], those [40], they [15], the same [12], them [8], his [7], same [6], him [5], she [4], their [2], it [1], same (*+4012*) [1], selfsame [1], the other[S] [1], the same (*+2596*) [1], theirs [1], this [1]

1566 **ἐκεῖσε, *ekeise***, adv. GK: *1698* [→ *1563*]. there, a place where:– there [2]

1567 **ἐκζητέω, *ekzēteō***, v. GK: *1699* [→ *1537+2212*]. to seek out, seek earnestly; (pass.) to be held responsible:– required [2], after [1], diligently seek [1], inquired [1], seek after [1], sought carefully [1]

1568 **ἐκθαμβέω, *ekthambeō***, v. GK: *1701* [→ *1537+2285*]. (pass.) to be overwhelmed with wonder, distressed, alarmed:– affrighted [2], greatly amazed [1], sore amazed [1]

1569 **ἔκθαμβος, *ekthambos***, a. GK: *1702* [→ *1537+2285*]. (utterly) astonished:– greatly wondering [1]

1570 **ἔκθετος, *ekthetos***, a. GK: *1704* [→ *1537+5087*]. thrown out, exposed (to elements), abandoned:– cast out (*+4160*) [1]

1571 **ἐκκαθαίρω, *ekkathairō***, v. GK: *1705* [→ *1537+2513*]. to cleanse, clean out, get rid of:– purge out [1], purge [1]

1572 **ἐκκαίω, *ekkaiō***, v. GK: *1706* [→ *1537+2545*]. (pass.) to be inflamed, have a strong desire:– burned [1]

1573 **ἐκκακέω, *ekkakeō***, v. GK: *1591 & 1707* [→ *1537+2556*]. to give up, become discouraged, lose heart:– faint [4], weary [2]

1574 **ἐκκεντέω, *ekkenteō***, v. GK: *1708* [→ *1537+2759*]. to pierce:– pierced [2]

1575 **ἐκκλάω, *ekklaō***, v. GK: *1709* [→ *1537+2806*]. (pass.) to be broken off:– broken off [3]

1576 **ἐκκλείω, *ekkleiō***, v. GK: *1710* [→ *1537+2808*]. to alienate, shut out, exclude:– excluded [1], exclude [1]

1577 **ἐκκλησία, *ekklēsia***, n. GK: *1711* [→ *1537+2564*]. church, congregation, assembly; a group of people gathered together. It can refer to the OT assembly of believers (Ac 7:38), or a riotous mob (Ac 19:32), but usually to a Christian assembly, a church: as a totality (Eph 3:10), or in a specific locale (Col. 4:15). In the NT a church is never a building or meeting place:– church [78], churches [36], assembly [3], in every church (*+2596*) [1]

1578 **ἐκκλίνω, *ekklinō***, v. GK: *1712* [→ *1537+2827*]. to turn away, turn aside:– avoid [1], eschew [1], gone out of the way [1]

1579 **ἐκκολυμβάω, *ekkolymbaō***, v. GK: *1713* [→ *1537+2860*]. to swim away:– swim out [1]

1580 **ἐκκομίζω, *ekkomizō***, v. GK: *1714* [→ *1537+2889*]. to carry out:– carried out [1]

1581 **ἐκκόπτω, *ekkoptō***, v. GK: *1716* [→ *1537+2875*]. to cut off, cut down:– cut off [3], hewn down [3], cut down [2], cut off from [1], cut out [1], hindered [1]

1582 **ἐκκρεμάννυμι, *ekkremannymi***, v. GK: *1717* [→ *1537+2910*]. (mid.) to hang upon (words), to consider something seriously:– very attentive [1]

1583 **ἐκλαλέω, *eklaleō***, v. GK: *1718* [→ *1537+2980*]. to tell:– tell [1]

1584 **ἐκλάμπω, *eklampō***, v. GK: *1719* [→ *1537+2989*]. to shine:– shine forth [1]

1585 **ἐκλανθάνομαι, *eklanthanomai***, v. GK: *1720* [→ *1537+2990*]. to forget:– forgotten [1]

1586 **ἐκλέγομαι, *eklegomai***, v. GK: *1721* [→ *1537+3004*]. to chose, pick, select:– chosen [16], chose [3], chose out [1], made choice [1]

1587 **ἐκλείπω, *ekleipō***, v. GK: *1722* [→ *1537+3007*]. to fail, end, stop:– fail [3]

1588 **ἐκλεκτός, *eklektos***, a. GK: *1723* [→ *1537+3004*]. elect, chosen, the Chosen One:– elect [13], chosen [7], elect's [2], elects' [1]

1589 **ἐκλογή, *eklogē***, n. GK: *1724* [→ *1537+3004*]. election, choice, selection:– election [6], chosen [1]

1590 **ἐκλύω, *eklyō***, v. GK: *1725* [→ *1537+3089*]. (pass.) to lose heart; give up; collapse in weariness:– faint [5], fainted [1]

1591 **ἐκμάσσω, *ekmassō***, v. GK: *1726* [→ *1537+3146*]. to wipe off, dry off:– wiped [3], wipe [2]

1592 **ἐκμυκτηρίζω, *ekmyktērizō***, v. GK: *1727* [→ *1537+3456*]. to sneer at, ridicule:– derided [2]

1593 **ἐκνεύω, *ekneuō***, v. GK: *1728* [→ *1537+3506*]. to slip away, withdraw:– conveyed away [1]

1594 **ἐκνήφω, *eknēphō***, v. GK: *1729* [→ *1537+3525*]. to come to one's sense, become sober:– awake [1]

1595 **ἑκούσιος, *hekousios***, a. GK: *1730* [→ *1635*]. spontaneous, willing:– willingly (*+2596*) [1]

1596 **ἑκουσίως, *hekousiōs***, adv. GK: *1731* [→ *1635*]. willingly; deliberately, intentionally:– wilfully [1], willingly [1]

1597 **ἔκπαλαι, *ekpalai***, adv. GK: *1732* [→ *1537+3819*]. for a long time, long ago:– of a long time [1], of old [1]

1598 **ἐκπειράζω, *ekpeirazō***, v. GK: *1733* [→ *1537+3984*]. to test, put to a test, try, tempt:– tempt [3], tempted [1]

1599 **ἐκπέμπω, *ekpempō***, v. GK: *1734* [→ *1537+3992*]. to send away, send out:– sent away [1], sent forth [1]

ἐκπερισσοῦ, *ekperissou*. See **1537** and **4053**.

1600 **ἐκπετάννυμι, *ekpetannymi***, v. GK: *1736* [→ *1537+4072*]. to hold out, spread out:– stretched forth [1]

1601 **ἐκπίπτω, *ekpiptō***, v. GK: *1738* [→ *1537+4098*]. to fall off; to fail; to run aground, be dashed to pieces:– fallen [2], fall [2], cast [1], faileth [1], fall from [1], fall off [1], fallen from [1], falleth away [1], falleth [1], fell off [1], taken none effect [1]

1602 **ἐκπλέω, *ekpleō***, v. GK: *1739* [→ *1537+4126*]. to sail (from):– sailed away [1], sailed thence [1], sailed [1]

1603 **ἐκπληρόω, *ekplēroō***, v. GK: *1740* [→ *1537+4137*]. to (utterly) fulfill:– fulfilled [1]

1604 **ἐκπλήρωσις, *ekplērōsis***, n. GK: *1741* [→ *1537+4137*]. end, completion:– accomplishment [1]

1605 **ἐκπλήσσω, *ekplēssō***, v. GK: *1742* [→ *1537+4141*]. (pass.) to be amazed, astonished:– astonished [10], amazed [3]

1606 **ἐκπνέω, *ekpneō***, v. GK: *1743* [→ *1537+4154*]. to breathe one's last breath, die:– gave up the ghost [3]

1607 **ἐκπορεύομαι, *ekporeuomai***, v. GK: *1744* [→ *1537+4198*]. to go out, come out, leave:– went out [6], cometh out [2], depart [2], goeth out [2], proceeded [2], proceedeth [2], proceed [2], came forth [1], come forth [1], come out [1], come [1], departed [1], go forth [1], going out [1], gone forth [1], issued out [1], issued [1], out goeth [1], proceed out [1], proceeded out [1], proceedeth out [1], proceeding out [1], went [1]

1608 **ἐκπορνεύω, *ekporneuō***, v. GK: *1745* [→ *1537+4204*]. to engage in sexual immorality:– giving over to fornication [1]

1609 **ἐκπτύω, *ekptyō***, v. GK: *1746* [→ *1537+4429*]. to scorn, spit out:– rejected [1]

1610 **ἐκριζόω, *ekrizoō***, v. GK: *1748* [→ *1537+4491*]. to uproot:– plucked up by the roots [1], plucked up by the root [1], root up [1], rooted up [1]

1611 **ἔκστασις, *ekstasis***, n. GK: *1749* [→ *1537+2476*]. amazement, astonishment, bewilderment; a trance:– trance [3], amazed (*+2983*) [1], amazed [1], amazement [1], astonishment [1]

1612 **ἐκστρέφω, *ekstrephō***, v. GK: *1750* [→ *1537+4762*]. (pass.) to be warped, perverted:– subverted [1]

1613 **ἐκταράσσω, *ektarassō***, v. GK: *1752* [→ *1537+5015*]. to throw into an uproar, into confusion:– exceedingly trouble [1]

1614 **ἐκτείνω, *ekteinō***, v. GK: *1753* [→ *660, 816, 1616, 1617, 1618, 1619, 1621, 1901, 2159, 3905, 4385, 4401, 5239, 5500; cf. 1537*]. to stretch out, reach out; point, motion:– stretched forth [5], stretch forth [4], put forth [3], stretched out [2], cast [1], stretching forth [1]

1615 **ἐκτελέω, *ekteleō***, v. GK: *1754* [→ *1537+5056*]. to finish, bring to a conclusion:– finish [2]

1616 **ἐκτένεια, *ekteneia***, n. GK: *1755* [→ *1614*]. earnestness:– instantly (*+1722*) [1]

1617 **ἐκτενέστερον, *ektenesteron***, adv.compar. of *1618*. GK: *1757* [→ *1614*]. more deeply, more earnestly:– more earnestly [1]

1618 **ἐκτενής, *ektenēs***, a. GK: *1756* [→ *1614*]. deep, earnest:– fervent [1], without ceasing [1]

1619 **ἐκτενῶς, *ektenōs***, adv. GK: *1757* [→ *1614*]. deeply, earnestly:– fervently [1]

1620 **ἐκτίθημι, *ektithēmi***, v. GK: *1758* [→ *1537+5087*]. (mid.) to explain; (pass.) to be placed out in the elements, exposed, abandoned:– expounded [3], cast out [1]

1621 **ἐκτινάσσω, *ektinassō***, v. GK: *1759* [→ *1614*]. to shake off, shake out:– shake off [2], shook off [1], shook [1]

1622 **ἐκτός, *ektos***, adv. GK: *1760* [→ *1537*]. outside, beyond, except:– out of [2], but (*+1487+3361*) [1], except (*+1487+3361*) [1], excepted [1], other than [1], outside [1], unless (*+1487+3361*) [1], without [1]

1623 **ἕκτος, *hektos***, a. GK: *1761* [→ *1803*]. sixth, noon (the sixth hour):– sixth [14]

1624 **ἐκτρέπω, *ektrepō***, v. GK: *1762* [→ *1537+5157*]. to turn away, wander away from; be disabled:– turned aside [2], avoiding [1], turned out of the way [1], turned [1]

1625 **ἐκτρέφω, *ektrephō***, v. GK: *1763* [→ *1537+5142*]. to feed, nourish; to bring up, rear (children):– bring up [1], nourisheth [1]

1626 **ἔκτρωμα, *ektrōma***, n. GK: *1765* [→ *1537+5134*]. abnormal or untimely birth:– born out of due time [1]

1627 **ἐκφέρω, *ekpherō***, v. GK: *1766* [→ *1537+5342*]. to bring out, carry out; to produce:– carry out [2], beareth [1], bring forth [1], brought forth [1], carried out [1], carrying forth [1]

1628 **ἐκφεύγω, *ekpheugō***, v. GK: *1767* [→ *1537+5343*]. to escape:– escape [4], escaped [1], fled out [1], fled [1]

1629 **ἐκφοβέω, *ekphobeō***, v. GK: *1768* [→ *1537+5401*]. to frighten, terrify:– terrify [1]

1630 **ἔκφοβος, *ekphobos***, a. GK: *1769* [→ *1537+5401*]. frightened, terrified:– exceedingly fear (*+1510*) [1], sore afraid [1]

1631 **ἐκφύω, *ekphyō***, v. GK: *1770* [→ *1537+5453*]. to come out, put forth:– putteth forth [2]

1632 **ἐκχέω, *ekcheō***, v. GK: *1772 & 1773* [→ *130, 401, 2022, 2708, 4378, 4797, 4799, 5240, 5517, 5522; cf. 1537*]. to pour out, shed, scatter; (pass.) to be poured out, shed; to rush (for profit):– poured out [9], shed [9], pour out [3], spilled [2], gushed out [1], ran greedily after [1], runneth out [1], shed abroad [1], shed forth [1]

1633 **ἐκχωρέω, *ekchōreō***, v. GK: *1774* [→ *1537+5562*]. to go out, go away:– depart out [1]

1634 **ἐκψύχω, *ekpsychō***, v. GK: *1775* [→ *1537+5594*]. to die, expire:– gave up the ghost [2], yielded up the ghost [1]

1635 **ἑκών, *hekōn***, a. GK: *1776* [→ *210, 1595, 1596*]. voluntarily, by one's own choice:– willingly [2]

1636 **ἐλαία, *elaia***, n. GK: *1777* [→ *65, 1637, 1638, 2565*]. olive, olive tree; in the proper name "the Mount of Olives," a ridge on the east side of the Kidron Valley, overlooking Jerusalem and the Temple mount:– olives [11], olive tree [2], olive berries [1], olive trees [1]

1637 **ἔλαιον, *elaion***, n. GK: *1778* [→ *1636*]. olive oil:– oil [11]

1638 **ἐλαιών, *elaiōn***, n. GK: *1779* [→ *1636*]. Mount of Olives, olive grove:– Olivet [1]

1639 **Ἐλαμίτης, *Elamitēs***, n.pr.g. GK: *1780*. Elamite, "*highland*":– Elamites [1]

1640 **ἐλάσσων, *elassōn***, a. [also used as adv.]. GK: *1781 & 1784* [→ *1641, 1642, 1646, 1647*]. lesser, cheaper, younger:– less [1], under [1], worse [1], younger [1]

1641 **ἐλαττονέω, *elattoneō***, v. GK: *1782* [→ *1640*]. to have too little:– had lack [1]

1642 **ἐλαττόω, *elattoō***, v. GK: *1783* [→ *1640*]. to make lower than; (pass.) to be made lower than, become lesser, diminish:– decrease [1], made lower [1], madest lower [1]

1643 **ἐλαύνω, *elaunō***, v. GK: *1785* [→ *556, 4900*]. to row (with oars); (pass.) to be driven:– driven [2], carried [1], rowed [1], rowing [1]

1644 **ἐλαφρία, *elaphria***, n. GK: *1786* [→ *1645*]. lightness, levity:– lightness [1]

1645 **ἐλαφρός, *elaphros***, a. GK: *1787* [→ *1644*]. light, not burdensome:– light [2]

1646 **ἐλάχιστος, *elachistos***, a. GK: *1788* [→ *1640*]. least, very small, trivial:– least [9], very small [2], smallest matters [1], very little [1]

1647 **ἐλαχιστότερος, *elachistoteros***, a.compar. of *1646*. GK: *1788* [→ *1640*]. far less, smallest:– least [1]

1648 **Ἐλεάζαρ, *Eleazar***, n.pr. GK: *1789*. Eleazar, "*God [El] is a help*":– Eleazar [2]

1649 **ἔλεγξις, *elenxis***, n. GK: *1792* [→ *1651*]. rebuke, reproof:– rebuked [1]

1650 **ἔλεγχος, *elenchos***, n. GK: *1791 & 1793* [→ *1651*]. certainty, proof; rebuke, reproof:– evidence [1], reproof [1]

1651 **ἐλέγχω, *elenchō***, v. GK: *1794* [→ *557, 1246, 1649, 1650, 1827*]. to expose; to rebuke, refute, show fault; to convince, convict:– rebuke [4], reproved [3], reprove [3], convinced [2], convicted [1], convinceth [1], convince [1], rebuked [1], tell fault [1]

1652 **ἐλεεινός, *eleeinos***, a. GK: *1795* [→ *1656*]. pitiful:– miserable [1], most miserable [1]

1653 **ἐλεέω, *eleeō***, v. GK: *1790 & 1796* [→ *1656*]. to have mercy on, pity; to show mercy to, show pity to another who is in serious need, usually with a focus on an act of kindness that will help meet the need:– have mercy [14], obtained mercy [6], had compassion [2], obtain mercy [2], sheweth mercy [2], had mercy [1], had pity [1], hath mercy [1], have compassion [1], received mercy [1]

1654 **ἐλεημοσύνη, *eleēmosynē***, n. GK: *1797* [→ *1656*]. gift to the poor, alms, charitable gift; any act of generosity to someone in serious need, often referring to giving gifts of substance or money:– alms [13], almsdeeds [1]

1655 **ἐλεήμων, *eleēmōn***, a. GK: *1798* [→ *1656*]. merciful, including feelings of pity, with a focus of showing compassion to those in serious need:– merciful [2]

1656 **ἔλεος, *eleos***, n. GK: *1799* [→ *415, 448, 1652, 1653, 1654, 1655*]. mercy, pity; the moral quality of feeling compassion and especially of showing kindness toward someone in need. This can refer to a human kindness and to God's kindness to humankind:– mercy [27], tender mercy (*+4698*) [1]

1657 **ἐλευθερία, *eleutheria***, n. GK: *1800* [→ *1658*]. freedom, liberty, not enslaved:– liberty [11]

1658 **ἐλεύθερος, *eleutheros***, a. GK: *1801* [→ *558, 1657, 1659*]. free, released, liberated from various kinds of ownership, confinement, and distress: prison confinement, political domination and oppression, physical sickness, release from the marriage contract in death, and God's release of the sinner from sin. A free person is often contrasted to a slave:– free [19], freewoman [3], liberty [1]

1659 **ἐλευθερόω, *eleutheroō***, v. GK: *1802* [→ *1658*]. to set free, liberate, cause someone to receive liberty or freedom:– made free [4], make free [2], delivered [1]

ἐλεύθω, *eleuthō*. See **2064**.

1660 **ἔλευσις, *eleusis***, n. GK: *1803* [→ *2064*]. coming, advent:– coming [1]

1661 **ἐλεφάντινος, *elephantinos***, a. GK: *1804*. made of ivory (derivative of the Greek word for "elephant," not found in the NT):– ivory [1]

1662 **Ἐλιακείμ, *Eliakeim***, n.pr. GK: *1805 & 1806*. Eliakim, "*God [El] establishes*":– Eliakim [3]

1663 **Ἐλιέζερ, *Eliezer***, n.pr. GK: *1808*. Eliezer, "*God [El] is [my] help*":– Eliezer [1]

1664 **Ἐλιούδ, *Elioud***, n.pr. GK: *1809*. Eliud, "*God [El] is [my] grandeur*":– Eliud [2]

1665 **Ἐλισάβετ, *Elisabet***, n.pr. GK: *1810*. Elizabeth, "*God [El] is [my] oath*":– Elisabeth [8], Elisabeth's [1]

1666 **Ἐλισσαῖος, *Elissaios***, n.pr. GK: *1811 & 1812*. Elisha, "*God [El] is [my] salvation*":– Eliseus [1]

1667 **ἑλίσσω, *helissō***, v. GK: *1813* [→ *1507*]. to roll up:– fold up [1]

1668 **ἕλκος, *helkos***, n. GK: *1814* [→ *1669*]. sore, abscess:– sores [2], sore [1]

1669 **ἑλκόω, *helkoō***, v. GK: *1815* [→ *1668*]. (pass.) to be covered with sores:– full of sores [1]

1670 **ἑλκύω, *helkyō***, v. GK: *1816* [→ *1828*]. to drag, draw, pull in:– draw [4], drew [3], drew out [1]

1671 **Ἑλλάς, *Hellas***, n.pr. GK: *1817* [→ *1672*]. Greece:– Greece [1]

1672 **Ἕλλην, *Hellēn***, n.pr. GK: *1818* [→ *1671, 1673, 1674, 1675, 1676*]. Greek; Gentile, a class of person distinguished from the Jewish race and nation (not necessarily Greek):– Greeks [13], Greek [7], Gentiles [5], Gentile [2]

1673 **Ἑλληνικός, *Hellēnikos***, a.pr. GK: *1819* [→ *1672*]. Greek (language):– Greek [2]

1674 **Ἑλληνίς, *Hellēnis***, n.pr. GK: *1820* [→ *1672*]. Greek, Gentile, a class of person distinguished from the Jewish race and nation (not necessarily Greek):– Greeks [1], Greek [1]

1675 **Ἑλληνιστής, *Hellēnistēs***, n.pr.g. GK: *1821* [→ *1672*]. Grecian Jew, Hellenist:– Grecians [3]

1676 **Ἑλληνιστί, *Hellēnisti***, adv.pr. GK: *1822* [→ *1672*]. in Greek (language):– Greek [2]

1677 **ἐλλογέω, *ellogeō***, v. GK: *1823 & 1824* [→ *1722+3004*]. to charge (to one's account):– imputed [1], put on account [1]

ἔλλομαι, *hellomai*. See **138**.

1678 **Ἐλμωδάμ, *Elmōdam***, n.pr. GK: *1825 & 1826*. Elmodam:– Elmodam [1]

1679 **ἐλπίζω, *elpizō***, v. GK: *1827* [→ *1680*]. to hope, hope for, put hope in, expect, an attitude of confidently looking forward to what is good and beneficial:– trust [15], hope [5], hoped [3], hope for [2], trusted [2], hoped for [1], hopeth [1], hoping [1], trusteth [1]

1680 **ἐλπίς, *elpis***, n. GK: *1828* [→ *560, 1679, 4276*]. hope, expectation:– hope [53], hope's [1]

1681 **Ἐλύμας, *Elymas***, n.pr. GK: *1829*. Elymas, "[poss.] *wise one* hence *magician*":– Elymas [1]

1682 **ἐλωΐ, *elōi***, l.[n.+p.]. GK: *1830* [cf. *2241*]. Eloi [Aramaic: my God]:– eloi [2]

1683 **ἐμαυτοῦ, *emautou***, p.reflex. GK: *1831* [→ *1473+846*]. myself, my own, of my own accord:– myself [30], me [4], mine own self [2], mine own [1]

1684 **ἐμβαίνω, *embainō***, v. GK: *1832* [→ *1722+305*]. to get into, step into, embark:– entered [7], went [3], come [2], get [2], entering [1], stepped in [1], took shipping (*+1519+3588+4143*) [1], took [1]

1685 **ἐμβάλλω, *emballō***, v. GK: *1833* [→ *1722+906*]. to throw into:– cast [1]

1686 **ἐμβάπτω, *embaptō***, v. GK: *1834 & 1835* [→ *1722+911*]. to dip into:– dippeth [2], dipped [1]

1687 **ἐμβατεύω, *embateuō***, v. GK: *1836* [→ *1722+305*]. to go into great detail about:– intruding into [1]

1688 **ἐμβιβάζω, *embibazō***, v. GK: *1837* [→ *1722+305*]. to put on board (a vessel):– put [1]

1689 **ἐμβλέπω, *emblepō***, v. GK: *1838* [→ *1722+991*]. to look (closely, directly) at, gaze at:– beheld [3], looked upon [2], looking upon [2], beholding [1], behold [1], gazing up [1], saw [1], see [1]

1690 **ἐμβριμάομαι, *embrimaomai***, v. GK: *1839* [→ *1722*]. to warn sternly, rebuke harshly; to be deeply moved:– straitly charged [2], groaned [1], groaning [1], murmured against [1]

1691 **ἐμέ, *eme***, p.pers.acc. of *1473*. GK: *1609* [→ *1473*]. me; see *1473*:–

1692 **ἐμέω, *emeō***, v. GK: *1840*. to spit out:– spue [1]

1693 **ἐμμαίνομαι, *emmainomai***, v. GK: *1841* [→ *1722+3105*]. to be enraged:– mad against [1]

1694 **Ἐμμανουήλ, *Emmanouēl***, n.pr. GK: *1842*. Immanuel, "*God with us*":– Emmanuel [1]

1695 **Ἐμμαοῦς, *Emmaous***, n.pr. GK: *1843*. Emmaus, "*hot springs*":– Emmaus [1]

1696 **ἐμμένω, *emmenō***, v. GK: *1844* [→ *1722+3306*]. to remain in, stay in; remain faithful, continue in:– continue in [1], continued [1], continueth [1]

1697 **Ἐμμώρ, *Hemmōr***, n.pr. GK: *1846*. Hamor, "*male donkey*":– Emmor [1]

1698 **ἐμοί, *emoi***, p.pers.dat. of *1473*. GK: *1609* [→ *1473*]. in me; to me; my; see *1473*:–

1699 **ἐμός, *emos***, a.poss. GK: *1847* [→ *1473*]. my, mine:– my [49], mine [12], mine own [11], me [4], I have [1]

1700 **ἐμοῦ, *emou***, p.pers.gen. of *1473*. GK: *1609* [→ *1473*]. my, mine; see *1473*.:–

1701 **ἐμπαιγμός, *empaigmos***, n. GK: *1849* [→ *1722+3815*]. jeering, scoffing, mocking:– mockings [1]

1702 **ἐμπαίζω, *empaizō***, v. GK: *1850* [→ *1722+3815*]. to mock, ridicule:– mocked [8], mock [3], mocking [2]

1703 **ἐμπαίκτης**, ***empaiktēs***, n. GK: *1851* [→ *1722+3815*]. scoffer, mocker:– mockers [1], scoffers [1]

1704 **ἐμπεριπατέω**, ***emperipateō***, v. GK: *1853* [→ *1722+4012+3961*]. to walk among:– walk in [1]

1705 **ἐμπίπλημι**, ***empiplēmi***, v. GK: *1854 & 1855 & 1857 & 1858* [→ *1722+4130*]. (act.) to provide, fill, satisfy; (pass.) to be filled to satisfaction; to enjoy one's company:– filled [3], filling with [1], full [1]

1706 **ἐμπίπτω**, ***empiptō***, v. GK: *1860* [→ *1722+4098*]. to fall into:– fall [5], fallen [1], fell [1]

1707 **ἐμπλέκω**, ***emplekō***, v. GK: *1861* [→ *1722+4120*]. (mid./pass.) to be involved in, become entangled:– entangled [1], entangleth with [1]

ἐμπλήθω, ***emplēthō***. See ***1705***.

1708 **ἐμπλοκή**, ***emplokē***, n. GK: *1862 & 4451* [→ *1722+4120*]. braiding (possibly associated with high fashion):– plaiting [1]

1709 **ἐμπνέω**, ***empneō***, v. GK: *1863* [→ *1722+4154*]. to breath:– breathing out [1]

1710 **ἐμπορεύομαι**, ***emporeuomai***, v. GK: *1864* [→ *1722+4198*]. to carry on business; exploit:– buy and sell [1], make merchandise [1]

1711 **ἐμπορία**, ***emporia***, n. GK: *1865* [→ *1722+4198*]. business, trade:– merchandise [1]

1712 **ἐμπόριον**, ***emporion***, n. GK: *1866* [→ *1722+4198*]. market, marketplace:– merchandise [1]

1713 **ἔμπορος**, ***emporos***, n. GK: *1867* [→ *1722+4198*]. merchant:– merchants [4], merchant [1]

1714 **ἐμπρήθω**, ***emprēthō***, v. GK: *1856 & 1859 & 1868* [→ *1722+4092*]. to burn, set on fire:– burnt up [1]

1715 **ἔμπροσθεν**, ***emprosthen***, adv.&pp.*. GK: *1869* [→ *1722+4314*]. before, in front of, in the presence of:– before [38], in sight [2], preferred before (*+1096*) [2], against [1], at [1], in the presence [1], in the sight [1], of [1], went forth [1]

1716 **ἐμπτύω**, ***emptyō***, v. GK: *1870* [→ *1722+4429*]. to spit on, spit at:– spit upon [2], spit [2], spit on [1], spitted on [1]

1717 **ἐμφανής**, ***emphanēs***, a. GK: *1871* [→ *1722+5316*]. seen, revealed, visible:– manifest [1], openly [1]

1718 **ἐμφανίζω**, ***emphanizō***, v. GK: *1872* [→ *1722+5316*]. to show; report; to present (legal) charges; petition; (pass.) to appear:– informed [3], manifest [2], appeared [1], appear [1], declare plainly [1], shewed [1], signify [1]

1719 **ἔμφοβος**, ***emphobos***, a. GK: *1873* [→ *1722+5401*]. afraid, terrified:– afraid [3], affrighted [2], trembled (*+1096*) [1]

1720 **ἐμφυσάω**, ***emphysaō***, v. GK: *1874* [→ *1722+5453*]. to breathe on:– breathed on [1]

1721 **ἔμφυτος**, ***emphytos***, a. GK: *1875* [→ *1722+5453*]. implanted:– engrafted [1]

1722 **ἐν**, ***en***, pp. GK: *1877* [→ *410, 418, 1449, 1455, 1456, 1457, 1458, 1459, 1460, 1461, 1462, 1463, 1464, 1465, 1466, 1467, 1468, 1469, 1470, 1471, 1472, 1677, 1684, 1685, 1686, 1687, 1688, 1689, 1690, 1693, 1696, 1701, 1702, 1703, 1704, 1705, 1714, 1706, 1707, 1708, 1709, 1710, 1711, 1712, 1713, 1714, 1715, 1716, 1717, 1718, 1719, 1720, 1721, 1723, 1724, 1725, 1728, 1729, 1730, 1731, 1732, 1735, 1736, 1737, 1738, 1739, 1740, 1741, 1742, 1743, 1744, 1745, 1746, 1747, 1748, 1749, 1750, 1751, 1753, 1754, 1755, 1756, 1757, 1758, 1759, 1760, 1761, 1762, 1764, 1765, 1770, 1771, 1772, 1773, 1774, 1776, 1777, 1779, 1780, 1782, 1783, 1784, 1786, 1787, 1788, 1789, 1790, 1791, 1792, 1793, 1794, 1795, 1796, 1797, 1798, 1799, 1801, 1902, 1903, 2714, 3925, 3926, 4278, 5241; cf. 1420, 1785*]. Spatially: in, inside, at, among, with; logically: by means of, with, because of; of time: during, while:– in [1877], with [145], by [141], at [110], among [104], on [46], through [38], wherein (*+3739*) [23], to [18], therein (*+846*) [16], as (*+3588*) [15], of [15], within [13], into [12], when (*+3588*) [12], unto [9], amongst [8], hereby (*+3778*) [8], as [7], herein (*+3778*) [7], for [6], whereby (*+3739*) [6], among (*+3319*) [5], throughout [5], while (*+3588*) [5], with child (*+1064+2192*) [5], shortly (*+5034*) [4], upon [4], when [4], where (*+3739*) [4], glorious (*+1391*) [3], in (*+3588*) [3], openly (*+5318*) [3], thereon (*+846*) [3], towards [3], wherewith (*+5101*) [3], while (*+3739*) [3], almost (*+3641*) [2], always (*+2540+3956*) [2], because of [2], foolishly (*+877*) [2], quickly (*+5034*) [2], there (*+846*) [2], therein (*+3778*) [2], therewith (*+846*) [2], under [2], when (*+3739*) [2], whereas (*+3739*) [2], whereupon (*+3739*) [2], wherewith (*+3739*) [2], about [1], accused (*+2724*) [1], after (*+1836+3588*) [1], afterward (*+2517+3588*) [1], after [1], against [1], age (*+2250+4260*) [1], all (*+3650*) [1], altogether (*+4183*) [1], at (*+3588*) [1], because [1], before (*+3319+3588*) [1], before [1], being [1], between [1], boldly (*+3954*) [1], burdensome (*+922*) [1], by (*+3588*) [1], by way of [1], darkly (*+135*) [1], first (*+4413*) [1], for sake [1], gorgeously (*+1741*) [1], howbeit whereinsoever (*+302+1161+3739*) [1], in that (*+3588*) [1], in the mean time (*+3739*) [1], instantly (*+1616*) [1], inwardly (*+2927+3588*) [1], known openly (*+3954*) [1], namely (*+3588*) [1], openly (*+3954*) [1], outward (*+3588+5318*) [1], outwardly (*+3588+5318*) [1], over [1], plainly (*+3954*) [1], scattered abroad (*+1290+3588*) [1], speedily (*+5034*) [1], that (*+3588*) [1], that (*+3739*) [1], that [1], thereby (*+846*) [1], thereby [1], therein [1], throughly (*+3956*) [1], uncircumcised (*+203*) [1], wherein (*+3739+3778*) [1], wherein [1], while (*+1510+3588*) [1], whilst (*+3588*) [1], wholly to [1], written (*+1121*) [1]

1723 **ἐναγκαλίζομαι**, ***enankalizomai***, v. GK: *1878* [→ *1722+43*]. to take in one's arms:– taken in arms [1], took up in arms [1]

1724 **ἐνάλιος**, ***enalios***, a. GK: *1879* [→ *1722+217*]. creatures pertaining to the sea:– in the sea [1]

1725 **ἔναντι**, ***enanti***, adv. [used as pp.*]. GK: *1882* [→ *561, 1726, 1727, 2713, 5121, 5227*]. before (spatial); fig., in the eyes of:– before [1]

1726 **ἐναντίον**, ***enantion***, adv. [used as pp.*]. GK: *1883* [→ *1725*]. before (spatial); fig., in the sight of:– before [4], in the sight [1]

1727 **ἐναντίος**, ***enantios***, a. GK: *1885* [→ *1725*]. against, opposite, in hostility:– contrary [6], against [1], over against (*+1537*) [1]

1728 **ἐνάρχομαι**, ***enarchomai***, v. GK: *1887* [→ *1722+757*]. to begin:– begun [2]

1729 **ἐνδεής**, ***endeēs***, a. GK: *1890* [→ *1722+1189*]. needy, poor, impoverished:– lacked [1]

1730 **ἔνδειγμα**, ***endeigma***, n. GK: *1891* [→ *1722+1164*]. evidence, plain indication:– manifest token [1]

1731 **ἐνδείκνυμι**, ***endeiknymi***, v. GK: *1892* [→ *1722+1166*]. to show, display:– shew [6], shewing [2], did [1], shew forth [1], shewed [1]

1732 **ἔνδειξις**, ***endeixis***, n. GK: *1893* [→ *1722+1166*]. demonstration, proof, sign:– declare [2], evident token [1], proof [1]

1733 **ἕνδεκα**, ***hendeka***, n.num. GK: *1894* [→ *1520+1176*]. eleven:– eleven [6]

1734 **ἑνδέκατος**, ***hendekatos***, a. GK: *1895* [→ *1520+1176*]. eleventh:– eleventh [3]

1735 **ἐνδέχομαι**, ***endechomai***, v.imper. GK: *1896* [→ *1722+1209*]. it is possible:– cannot (*+3756*) [1]

1736 **ἐνδημέω**, ***endēmeō***, v. GK: *1897* [→ *1722+1218*]. to be at home:– present [2], at home [1]

1737 **ἐνδιδύσκω**, ***endidyskō***, v. GK: *1898* [→ *1722+1416*]. to put on, dress (another); (mid.) dress oneself:– clothed in [1], ware [1]

1738 **ἔνδικος**, ***endikos***, a. GK: *1899* [→ *1722+1349*]. just, deserved:– just recompence [1], just [1]

1739 **ἐνδόμησις**, ***endomēsis***, n. GK: *1900 & 1908* [→ *1722+1430*]. what something is made of, construction, material:– building [1]

1740 **ἐνδοξάζομαι**, ***endoxazomai***, v. GK: *1901* [→ *1722+1391*]. to be glorified, honored:– glorified [2]

1741 **ἔνδοξος**, ***endoxos***, a. GK: *1902* [→ *1722+1391*]. honored, having high status and so thought to be wonderful, a fig. extension of the feature of an object being radiant or expensive:– glorious [2], gorgeously (*+1722*) [1], honourable [1]

1742 **ἔνδυμα**, ***endyma***, n. GK: *1903* [→ *1722+1416*]. clothing, garment:– raiment [5], garment [2], clothing [1]

1743 **ἐνδυναμόω**, ***endynamoō***, v. GK: *1904* [→ *1722+1410*]. to give strength, strengthen; (mid./pass.) to be strong, strengthened:– strong [3], enabled [1], increased in strength [1], made strong [1], strengthened [1], strengtheneth [1]

1744 **ἐνδύνω**, ***endynō***, v. GK: *1905* [→ *1722+1416*]. to worm one's way, creep in:– creep [1]

1745 **ἔνδυσις**, ***endysis***, n. GK: *1906* [→ *1722+1416*]. putting on:– putting on [1]

1746 **ἐνδύω**, ***endyō***, v. GK: *1907* [→ *1722+1416*]. to clothe, dress; (mid.) clothe oneself:– put on [17], clothed in [2], clothed with [2], arrayed in [1], clothed with a garment [1], clothed [1], endued with [1], had on [1], having on [1], putting on [1]

ἐνέγκω, ***enegkō***. See ***5342***.

1747 **ἐνέδρα**, ***enedra***, n. GK: *1909* [→ *1722+1476*]. plot, ambush:– laying wait (*+4160*) [1], lying in wait [1]

1748 **ἐνεδρεύω**, ***enedreuō***, v. GK: *1910* [→ *1722+1476*]. to wait in ambush, lie in wait for:– laying wait for [1], lie in wait for [1]

1749 **ἔνεδρον**, ***enedron***, n. GK: *1911* [→ *1722+1476*]. plot, ambush:–

1750 **ἐνειλέω**, ***eneileō***, v. GK: *1912* [→ *1722*]. to wrap in:– wrapped in [1]

1751 **ἔνειμι**, ***eneimi***, v. GK: *1913* [→ *1722+1510*]. to be inside; contents:– have [1]

1752 **ἕνεκα**, ***heneka***; or **ἕνεκεν**, ***heneken***; or **εἵνεκεν**, ***heineken***, pp.*. GK: *1914 & 1915 & 1641*. for the sake of; for this reason, because:– for sake [14], for cause [2], for this cause (*+3778*) [2], because (*+3739*) [1], because that [1], by reason of [1], for causes [1], for [1], that [1], wherefore (*+5101*) [1]

1753 **ἐνέργεια**, ***energeia***, n. GK: *1918* [→ *1722+2041*]. working, power, energy:– working [4], effectual working [2], operation [1], strong [1]

1754 **ἐνεργέω**, ***energeō***, v. GK: *1919* [→ *1722+2041*]. to be at work in; to produce:– worketh [10], work [2], do [1], effectual fervent [1], effectually worketh [1], effectual [1], mighty in [1], shew forth in [1], shew forth [1], wrought effectually in [1], wrought [1]

1755 **ἐνέργημα**, ***energēma***, n. GK: *1920* [→ *1722+2041*]. working, activity:– operations [1], working [1]

1756 **ἐνεργής**, ***energēs***, a. GK: *1921* [→ *1722+2041*]. active, effective:– effectual [2], powerful [1]

1757 **ἐνευλογέω**, ***eneulogeō***, v. GK: *1922* [→ *1722+2095+3004*]. (pass.) to be blessed:– blessed [2]

1758 **ἐνέχω**, ***enechō***, v. GK: *1923* [→ *1722+2192*]. to oppose, be hostile toward, bear a grudge against; (pass.) to be burdened:– entangled [1], had a quarrel against [1], urge [1]

1759 **ἐνθάδε**, ***enthade***, adv. GK: *1924* [→ *1722*]. here, in this place, to this place:– hither [4], here [3], there [1]

1760 **ἐνθυμέομαι**, ***enthymeomai***, v. GK: *1445 & 1926* [→ *1722+2372*]. to consider, reflect on:– think [1], thought on [1], thought [1]

1761 **ἐνθύμησις**, ***enthymēsis***, n. GK: *1927* [→ *1722+2372*]. thought, reflection; design, idea:– thoughts [3], device [1]

1762 **ἔνι**, ***eni***, v. GK: *1928* [→ *1722+1510*]. there is:– is [5]

1763 **ἐνιαυτός**, ***eniautos***, n. GK: *1929* [→ *846*]. year:– year [11], years [2], year by year (*+2596*) [1]

1764 **ἐνίστημι**, ***enistēmi***, v. GK: *1931* [→ *1722+2476*]. to be present, (ptcp.) the present:– present [5], at hand [1], come [1]

1765 **ἐνισχύω**, ***enischyō***, v. GK: *1932* [→ *1722+2479*]. to strengthen (another); to regain (one's own) strength:– strengthened [1], strengthening [1]

1766 **ἔνατος**, ***enatos***, a. GK: *1888* [→ *1767*]. ninth (ninth hour = three p.m.):– ninth [10]

1767 **ἐννέα**, ***ennea***, n.num. GK: *1933* [→ *1766, 1768*]. nine:– nine [5]

1768 **ἐνενήκοντα**, ***enenēkonta***, n.num. GK: *1916* [→ *1767*]. ninety:– ninety [4]

1769 **ἐννεός**, ***enneos***, a. GK: *1917 & 1934*. speechless:– speechless [1]

1770 **ἐννεύω**, ***enneuō***, v. GK: *1935* [→ *1722+3506*]. to make a sign, nod:– made signs [1]

1771 **ἔννοια**, ***ennoia***, n. GK: *1936* [→ *1722+3563*]. attitude, thought:– intents [1], mind [1]

1772 **ἔννομος**, ***ennomos***, a. GK: *1937* [→ *1722+3551*]. under law, subject to the law; legal (assembly):– lawful [1], under law [1]

1773 **ἔννυχος**, ***ennychos***, a. [used as adv.]. GK: *1939* [→ *1722+3571*]. while it is still dark, at night:– before day [1]

1774 **ἐνοικέω**, ***enoikeō***, v. GK: *1940* [→ *1722+3624*]. to live in, live with:– dwelleth [2], dwell [2], dwelt [1]

1775 **ἑνότης**, ***henotēs***, n. GK: *1942* [→ *1520*]. unity:– unity [2]

1776 **ἐνοχλέω, *enochleō***, v. GK: *1943* [→ *1722+3793*]. (act.) to cause trouble; (pass.) to be troubled:– trouble [1]

1777 **ἔνοχος, *enochos***, a. GK: *1944* [→ *1722+2192*]. subject to; guilty, liable for:– guilty [4], in danger [4], danger [1], subject [1]

1778 **ἔνταλμα, *entalma***, n. GK: *1945* [→ *1785*]. rule, commandment, precept:– commandments [3]

1779 **ἐνταφιάζω, *entaphiazō***, v. GK: *1946* [→ *1722+5028*]. to prepare (a corpse) for burial, bury:– burial [1], bury [1]

1780 **ἐνταφιασμός, *entaphiasmos***, n. GK: *1947* [→ *1722+5028*]. preparation for burial, burial:– burying [2]

1781 **ἐντέλλω, *entellō***, v. GK: *1948* [→ *1785*]. (mid.) to command, give orders, give instructions:– commanded [6], command [4], gave commandment [2], give charge [2], charged [1], enjoined [1], given commandments [1]

1782 **ἐντεῦθεν, *enteuthen***, adv. GK: *1925 & 1949* [→ *1722*]. from here, from this place:– hence [6], from hence [3], of either side (*+1782+2532*) [2], on either side one (*+1782+2532*) [2]

1783 **ἔντευξις, *enteuxis***, n. GK: *1950* [→ *1722+5177*]. prayer, intercession:– intercessions [1], prayer [1]

1784 **ἔντιμος, *entimos***, a. GK: *1952* [→ *1722+5092*]. highly valued, honored, precious:– precious [2], dear [1], more honourable than [1], reputation [1]

1785 **ἐντολή, *entolē***, n. GK: *1953* [→ *1778, 1781; cf. 1722*]. command, commandment, regulation, an order that has authority:– commandment [42], commandments [27], precept [2]

1786 **ἐντόπιος, *entopios***, a. GK: *1954* [→ *1722+5117*]. resident, local:– place [1]

1787 **ἐντός, *entos***, adv. GK: *1955* [→ *1722*]. inside, within:– within [2]

1788 **ἐντρέπω, *entrepō***, v. GK: *1956* [→ *1722+5157*]. to cause shame; (pass.) to be ashamed; (mid.) to care about, respect:– reverence [3], ashamed [2], gave reverence [1], regarded [1], regard [1], shame [1]

1789 **ἐντρέφω, *entrephō***, v. GK: *1957* [→ *1722+5142*]. (pass.) to be brought up, reared, trained:– nourished up [1]

1790 **ἔντρομος, *entromos***, a. GK: *1958* [→ *1722+5141*]. trembling:– quake [1], trembled (*+1096*) [1], trembling [1]

1791 **ἐντροπή, *entropē***, n. GK: *1959* [→ *1722+5157*]. shame, humiliation:– shame [2]

1792 **ἐντρυφάω, *entryphaō***, v. GK: *1960* [→ *1722+5172*]. to revel, carouse:– sporting [1]

1793 **ἐντυγχάνω, *entynchanō***, v. GK: *1961* [→ *1722+5177*]. to intercede, appeal, petition:– maketh intercession [3], dealt with [1], make intercession [1]

1794 **ἐντυλίσσω, *entylissō***, v. GK: *1962* [→ *1722*]. to wrap up (a body); (pass.) to be folded:– wrapped [2], wrapped together [1]

1795 **ἐντυπόω, *entypoō***, v. GK: *1963* [→ *1722+5180*]. (pass.) to be engraved, carved:– engraven [1]

1796 **ἐνυβρίζω, *enybrizō***, v. GK: *1964* [→ *1722+5196*]. to insult:– done despite unto [1]

1797 **ἐνυπνιάζομαι, *enypniazomai***, v. GK: *1965* [→ *1722+5258*]. to (have supernatural) dreams or visions:– dreamers [1], dream [1]

1798 **ἐνύπνιον, *enypnion***, n. GK: *1966* [→ *1722+5258*]. dream:– dreams [1]

1799 **ἐνώπιον, *enōpion***, pp.*. GK: *1967* [→ *1722+3708*]. before, in the presence of; in behalf of, by authority of:– before [62], in the sight [16], in the presence [6], in sight [5], in presence [2], before face [1], here before [1], presence [1], to [1]

1800 **Ἐνώς, *Enōs***, n.pr. GK: *1968*. Enosh, "*[mortal] man*":– Enos [1]

1801 **ἐνωτίζομαι, *enōtizomai***, v. GK: *1969* [→ *1722+3775*]. to listen carefully, pay attention to:– hearken [1]

1802 **Ἐνώχ, *Henōch***, n.pr. GK: *1970*. Enoch, "*initiated; follower*":– Enoch [3]

ἐξ, *ex*. See ***1537***.

1803 **ἕξ, *hex***, n.num. GK: *1971* [→ *1623, 1812, 1835*]. six:– six [11], threescore sixteen (*+1440*) [1]

1804 **ἐξαγγέλλω, *exangellō***, v. GK: *1972* [→ *1537+32*]. to declare, proclaim:– shew forth [1]

1805 **ἐξαγοράζω, *exagorazō***, v. GK: *1973* [→ *1537+59*]. (act.) to redeem, as a fig. extension of the act of purchasing something in the marketplace; (mid.) to make the most (of the time):– redeeming [2], redeemed [1], redeem [1]

1806 **ἐξάγω, *exagō***, v. GK: *1974* [→ *1537+71*]. to lead out, bring out, escort:– brought out [5], led out [3], brought forth [1], fetch out [1], lead out [1], leadeth out [1], leddest out [1]

1807 **ἐξαιρέω, *exaireō***, v. GK: *1975* [→ *1537+138*]. (act.) to gouge, take out, tear out; (mid.) to rescue, set free:– delivered [2], deliver [2], pluck out [2], delivering [1], rescued [1]

1808 **ἐξαίρω, *exairō***, v. GK: *1976* [→ *1537+142*]. to expel, remove, drive away:– put away [1], taken away [1]

1809 **ἐξαιτέω, *exaiteō***, v. GK: *1977* [→ *1537+154*]. (mid.) to ask for:– desired [1]

1810 **ἐξαίφνης, *exaiphnēs***, adv. GK: *1978 & 2005* [→ *1537+160*]. suddenly, unexpectedly:– suddenly [5]

1811 **ἐξακολουθέω, *exakoloutheō***, v. GK: *1979* [→ *1537+190; cf. 1.3*]. to follow, obey:– followed [1], following [1], follow [1]

1812 **ἑξακόσιοι, *hexakosioi***, a.num. GK: *1980* [→ *1803*]. six hundred:– six hundred [1]

1813 **ἐξαλείφω, *exaleiphō***, v. GK: *1981* [→ *1537+218*]. to wipe away, blot out, cancel:– wipe away [2], blot out [1], blotted out [1], blotting out [1]

1814 **ἐξάλλομαι, *exallomai***, v. GK: *1982* [→ *1537+242*]. to jump up:– leaping up [1]

1815 **ἐξανάστασις, *exanastasis***, n. GK: *1983* [→ *1537+303+2476*]. resurrection:– resurrection [1]

1816 **ἐξανατέλλω, *exanatellō***, v. GK: *1984* [→ *395; cf. 1537*]. to spring up:– sprang up [1], sprung up [1]

1817 **ἐξανίστημι, *exanistēmi***, v. GK: *1985* [→ *1537+303+2476*]. to raise up (seed) = have children; (intr.) to stand up:– raise up [2], rose up [1]

1818 **ἐξαπατάω, *exapataō***, v. GK: *1987* [→ *1537+539*]. to deceive, cheat:– deceive [3], beguiled [1], deceived [1]

1819 **ἐξάπινα, *exapina***, adv. GK: *1988* [→ *1537+160*]. suddenly:– suddenly [1]

1820 **ἐξαπορέω, *exaporeō***, v. GK: *1989* [→ *1537+1.1+4198*]. (mid.) to despair; (pass.) to be in despair:– despaired [1], in despair [1]

1821 **ἐξαποστέλλω, *exapostellō***, v. GK: *1990* [→ *1537+649*]. to send out, send away:– sent away [4], sent forth [4], send [1], sent out [1], sent [1]

1822 **ἐξαρτίζω, *exartizō***, v. GK: *1992* [→ *1537+737*]. to finish, complete; (pass.) to be equipped, furnished:– accomplished [1], throughly furnished [1]

1823 **ἐξαστράπτω, *exastraptō***, v. GK: *1993* [→ *1537+796*]. to flash like lightning:– glistering [1]

1824 **ἐξαυτῆς, *exautēs***, adv. GK: *1994* [→ *1537+846*]. immediately, at once, right now:– immediately [2], by and by [1], immediately already [1], presently [1], straightway [1]

1825 **ἐξεγείρω, *exegeirō***, v. GK: *1995* [→ *1537+1453*]. to raise, awaken (from the dead):– raise up [1], raised up [1]

1826 **ἔξειμι, *exeimi***, v. GK: *1996* [→ *1537*]. to leave, go out, go away:– departed [1], depart [1], get [1], gone out [1]

1827 **ἐξελέγχω, *exelenchō***, v. GK: *1998* [→ *1537+1651*]. to convict:– convince [1]

1828 **ἐξέλκω, *exelkō***, v. GK: *1999* [→ *1537+1670*]. (pass.) to be dragged away:– drawn away [1]

1829 **ἐξέραμα, *exerama***, n. GK: *2000* [→ *1537*]. vomit, what is disgorged:– vomit [1]

1830 **ἐξεραυνάω, *exeraunaō***, v. GK: *2001* [→ *1537+2045*]. to search intently, inquire carefully:– searched diligently [1]

1831 **ἐξέρχομαι, *exerchomai***, v. GK: *2002* [→ *1537+2064*]. to go out, leave:– went out [59], came out [30], departed [22], went forth [19], come out [18], gone out [10], go out [9], depart [6], came forth [5], went [5], come forth [4], go forth [4], get out [3], came [2], come [2], go [2], out [2], spread abroad [2], went abroad [2], came out of [1], camest forth [1], cometh out [1], coming out [1], depart out [1], departing [1], escaped [1], go thence [1], gone [1], out come [1], proceeded forth [1], proceedeth [1], proceed [1], went away [1], went from [1]

1832 **ἔξεστι, *exesti***, v.imper. GK: *1997 & 2003* [→ *1537+1510*]. it is legal, it is proper, it is permitted:– lawful [28], lawful for [1], let [1], mayest [1], may [1]

1833 **ἐξετάζω, *exetazō***, v. GK: *2004* [→ *426; cf. 1537*]. to make a search; to ask, inquire, question:– ask [1], inquire [1], search [1]

1834 **ἐξηγέομαι, *exēgeomai***, v. GK: *2007* [→ *1537+71*]. to tell, make known, describe, report:– declared [4], declaring [1], told [1]

1835 **ἑξήκοντα, *hexēkonta***, n.num. GK: *2008* [→ *1803*]. sixty:– threescore [4], sixty [3], sixtyfold [1]

1836 **ἑξῆς, *hexēs***, adv. GK: *2009* [→ *2192*]. next, afterward:– next [2], after (*+1722+3588*) [1], following [1], on morrow [1]

1837 **ἐξηχέω, *exēcheō***, v. GK: *2010* [→ *1537+2279*]. (pass.) to ring out, be caused to sound out:– sounded out [1]

1838 **ἕξις, *hexis***, n. GK: *2011* [→ *2192*]. constant use, practice:– use [1]

1839 **ἐξίστημι, *existēmi***, v. GK: *2012 & 2013 & 2014* [→ *1537+2476*]. to amaze, astound; confuse; (intr.) to be amazed, out of one's senses:– amazed [6], astonished [5], bewitched [2], beside himself [1], besides ourselves [1], made astonished [1], wondered [1]

1840 **ἐξισχύω, *exischyō***, v. GK: *2015* [→ *1537+2479*]. to have power, be strong enough:– able [1]

1841 **ἔξοδος, *exodos***, n. GK: *2016* [→ *1537+3598*]. exodus, departure:– decease [2], departing [1]

1842 **ἐξολεθρεύω, *exolethreuō***, v. GK: *2017* [→ *1537+3639*]. (pass.) to be completely cut off from:– destroyed [1]

1843 **ἐξομολογέω, *exomologeō***, v. GK: *2018* [→ *1537+3670*]. (act.) to consent; (mid.) to openly confess, admit, praise:– confess [5], confessing [2], thank [2], confessed [1], promised [1]

ἐξόν, *exon*. See ***1832***.

1844 **ἐξορκίζω, *exorkizō***, v. GK: *2019* [→ *1537+3727*]. to charge under oath, adjure:– adjure [1]

1845 **ἐξορκιστής, *exorkistēs***, n. GK: *2020* [→ *1537+3727*]. one driving out evil spirits, exorcist:– exorcists [1]

1846 **ἐξορύσσω, *exoryssō***, v. GK: *2021* [→ *1537+3736*]. to dig through, tear out:– broken up [1], plucked out [1]

1847 **ἐξουδενόω, *exoudenoō***, v. GK: *2022 & 2023* [→ *1537+3756+1161+1520*]. (pass.) to be rejected, treated with contempt:– set at nought [1]

1848 **ἐξουθενέω, *exoutheneō***, v. GK: *2024 & 2025* [→ *1537+3756+1161+1520*]. to treat with contempt, look down on, ridicule; (pass.) to be rejected, despised:– despised [3], despise [3], set at nought [3], contemptible [1], least esteemed [1]

1849 **ἐξουσία, *exousia***, n. GK: *2026* [→ *1850, 2715*]. authority, power, the right to control or govern; dominion, the area or sphere of jurisdiction; a ruler, human or supernatural:– power [57], authority [28], powers [8], power over [4], right [2], authorities [1], jurisdiction [1], liberty [1], strength [1]

1850 **ἐξουσιάζω, *exousiazō***, v. GK: *2027* [→ *1849*]. to have power over; (pass.) to be mastered:– hath power [2], brought under power [1], exercise authority upon [1]

1851 **ἐξοχή, *exochē***, n. GK: *2029* [→ *1537+2192*]. leading, prominent:– principal [1]

1852 **ἐξυπνίζω, *exypnizō***, v. GK: *2030* [→ *1537+5258*]. to wake up, arouse:– awake out of sleep [1]

1853 **ἔξυπνος, *exypnos***, a. GK: *2031* [→ *1537+5258*]. awake, aroused:– awaking out of sleep (*+1096*) [1]

1854 **ἔξω, *exō***, adv. GK: *2032* [→ *1537*]. out, outside:– without [23], of [10], forth [6], out of [6], out [5], away [1], outward [1], strange [1]

1855 **ἔξωθεν, *exōthen***, adv. GK: *2033* [→ *1537*]. from the outside:– without [4], from without [2], outside [2], outward [2], outwardly [1]

1856 **ἐξωθέω, *exōtheō***, v. GK: *2034* [→ *683; cf. 1537*]. to drive out, expel; to run aground:– drave out [1], thrust in [1]

1857 **ἐξώτερος, *exōteros***, a. GK: *2035* [→ *1537*]. outside, farthest out (as a superlative):– outer [3]

1858 **ἑορτάζω, *heortazō***, v. GK: *2037* [→ *1859*]. to celebrate a festival:– keep the feast [1]

1859* ἑορτή, *heortē, n. GK: *2038* [→ *1858*]. feast, festival, in the NT this refers the joyous gathering of people for the celebrations of the Jewish calendar year, having a focus on ceremonial eating, such as Passover, Pentecost, and New Moon:– feast [26], holyday [1]

1860* ἐπαγγελία, *epangelia, n. GK: *2039* [→ *1909+32*]. promise:– promise [40], promises [12], message [1]

1861* ἐπαγγέλλομαι, *epangellomai, v. GK: *2040* [→ *1909+32*]. to promise; to profess, lay claim to:– promised [10], professing [2], made promise [1], promise made [1], promise [1]

1862* ἐπάγγελμα, *epangelma, n. GK: *2041* [→ *1909+32*]. promise:– promises [1], promise [1]

1863* ἐπάγω, *epagō, v. GK: *2042* [→ *1909+71*]. to bring upon; to make guilty:– bring upon [1], bringing in [1], bring [1]

1864* ἐπαγωνίζομαι, *epagōnizomai, v. GK: *2043* [→ *1909+73*]. to contend, fight:– earnestly contend for [1]

1865* ἐπαθροίζω, *epathroizō, v. GK: *2044* [→ *1909; cf. 4867*]. (pass.) to increase; to be collected:– gathered thick together [1]

1866* Ἐπαίνετος, *Epainetos, n.pr. GK: *2045* [→ *1909+136*]. Epenetus, "*praised*":– Epenetus [1]

1867* ἐπαινέω, *epaineō, v. GK: *2046* [→ *1909+136*]. to praise, commend:– praise [4], commended [1], laud [1]

1868* ἔπαινος, *epainos, n. GK: *2047* [→ *1909+136*]. praise, commendation:– praise [11]

1869* ἐπαίρω, *epairō, v. GK: *2048* [→ *1909+142*]. to lift up; "to lift up the eyes" means "to look up"; "to lift up the voice" means "to shout" or "talk loudly"; "to lift up the heel" means "to oppose someone" (implying hostility):– lift up [13], exalteth [1], exalt [1], hoised up [1], lifted up [1], lifting up [1], taken up [1]

1870* ἐπαισχύνομαι, *epaischynomai, v. GK: *2049* [→ *1909+150*]. to be ashamed of:– ashamed [11]

1871* ἐπαιτέω, *epaiteō, v. GK: *2050* [→ *1909+154*]. to beg:– beg [1]

1872* ἐπακολουθέω, *epakoloutheō, v. GK: *2051* [→ *1909+190; cf. 1.3*]. to follow after, accompany; be devoted to:– diligently followed [1], follow after [1], following [1], follow [1]

1873* ἐπακούω, *epakouō, v. GK: *2052* [→ *1909+191*]. to hear, listen to:– heard [1]

1874* ἐπακροάομαι, *epakroaomai, v. GK: *2053* [→ *1909+202*]. to listen to:– heard [1]

1875* ἐπάν, *epan, c.temp. GK: *2054* [→ *1909+302*]. when, as soon as:– when [3]

1876* ἐπάναγκες, *epanankes, adv. GK: *2055* [→ *1909+318*]. necessarily:– necessary [1]

1877* ἐπανάγω, *epanagō, v. GK: *2056* [→ *1909+303+71*]. to put out (to sea); to return:– launch out [1], returned [1], thrust out [1]

1878* ἐπαναμιμνήσκω, *epanamimnēskō, v. GK: *2057* [→ *1909+303+3421*]. to remind again:– putting in mind [1]

1879* ἐπαναπαύομαι, *epanapauomai, v. GK: *2058* [→ *1909+303+3973*]. to rest on, rely on:– restest [1], rest [1]

1880* ἐπανέρχομαι, *epanerchomai, v. GK: *2059* [→ *1909+303+2064*]. to return (home):– come again [1], returned [1]

1881* ἐπανίστημι, *epanistēmi, v. GK: *2060* [→ *1909+303+2476*]. to rebel against, rise up (in rebellion):– rise up against [1], rise up [1]

1882* ἐπανόρθωσις, *epanorthōsis, n. GK: *2061* [→ *1909+303+3717*]. correcting:– correction [1]

1883* ἐπάνω, *epanō, adv. GK: *2062* [→ *1909+507*]. above, on, upon; more than:– over [6], on [4], above [3], upon [3], thereon (+*846*) [2], more than [1], thereon [1]

1884* ἐπαρκέω, *eparkeō, v. GK: *2064* [→ *1909+714*]. to help, aid:– relieve [2], relieved [1]

1885* ἐπαρχεία, *eparcheia, n. GK: *2065 & 2066* [→ *1909+757*]. province:– province [2]

1886* ἔπαυλις, *epaulis, n. GK: *2068* [→ *1909+833*]. place to live, residence:– habitation [1]

1887* ἐπαύριον, *epaurion, adv. GK: *2069* [→ *839; cf. 1909*]. the next day, tomorrow:– next day [7], on morrow [7], day following [2], morrow [1]

1888* ἐπαυτοφώρῳ, *epautophōrō, a. GK: *2070* [→ *1909+846*]. pertaining to being caught in the act:– in the very act [1]

1889* Ἐπαφρᾶς, *Epaphras, n.pr. GK: *2071*. Epaphras, "*handsome*":– Epaphras [3]

1890* ἐπαφρίζω, *epaphrizō, v. GK: *576 & 2072* [→ *1909+876*]. to foam up:– foaming out [1]

1891* Ἐπαφρόδιτος, *Epaphroditos, n.pr. GK: *2073*. Epaphroditus, "*handsome*":– Epaphroditus [3]

1892* ἐπεγείρω, *epegeirō, v. GK: *2074* [→ *1909+1453*]. to stir up, arouse, excite:– raised [1], stirred up [1]

1893* ἐπεί, *epei, c. GK: *2075* [→ *1909*]. since, because, for otherwise:– because [7], otherwise [4], seeing [3], else [2], then [2], else (+*686*) [1], for that [1], for then [1], forasmuch as [1], forasmuch [1], for [1], seeing that [1], since [1], when [1]

1894* ἐπειδή, *epeidē, c. GK: *2076* [→ *1909+1211*]. when; since, because:– for [3], because [2], seeing [2], after that [1], forasmuch as [1], since [1]

1895* ἐπειδήπερ, *epeidēper, c. GK: *2077* [→ *1909+1211+4007*]. inasmuch as, since, whereas:– forasmuch as [1]

1896* ἐπεῖδον, *epeidon, v. GK: *2078 & 2393* [→ *1909+3708*]. to show favor, concern; to consider, look at:– behold [1], looked on [1]

1897* ἐπείπερ, *epeiper, c. GK: *2080* [→ *1909+4007*]. since, indeed:– seeing [1]

1898* ἐπεισαγωγή, *epeisagōgē, n. GK: *2081* [→ *1909+1519+71*]. introduction, bringing in:– bringing in [1]

1899* ἔπειτα, *epeita, adv. GK: *2083* [→ *1909+1534*]. then, later, afterward:– then [9], after that [4], afterward [2], afterwards [1]

1900* ἐπέκεινα, *epekeina, adv. GK: *2084* [→ *1909+1563*]. beyond, farther on:– beyond [1]

1901* ἐπεκτείνομαι, *epekteinomai, v. GK: *2085* [→ *1614; cf. 1909*]. to strain toward, stretch out:– reaching forth [1]

1902* ἐπενδύομαι, *ependyomai, v. GK: *2086* [→ *1909+1722+1416*]. to be clothed with:– clothed upon with [1], clothed upon [1]

1903* ἐπενδύτης, *ependytēs, n. GK: *2087* [→ *1909+1722+1416*]. outer garment, coat:– fisher's coat [1]

1904* ἐπέρχομαι, *eperchomai, v. GK: *2082 & 2088* [→ *1909+2064*]. to come, come upon, happen to, with a possible implication that it will happen suddenly and forcibly:– come upon [5], come [2], came thither [1], come on [1], coming on [1]

1905* ἐπερωτάω, *eperōtaō, v. GK: *2089* [→ *1909+2065*]. to ask, question:– asked [44], ask [8], demanded [2], asked after [1], askest [1], asking [1], desired [1], questioned [1]

1906* ἐπερώτημα, *eperōtēma, n. GK: *2090* [→ *1909+2065*]. pledge; some translate "request, appeal":– answer [1]

1907* ἐπέχω, *epechō, v. GK: *2091* [→ *1909+2192*]. (tr.) hold out, hold fast; (intr.) to give attention, watch, notice; to stay, stop:– heed [1], holding forth [1], marked [1], stayed [1], take heed [1]

1908* ἐπηρεάζω, *epēreazō, v. GK: *2092*. to mistreat, speak maliciously against:– despitefully use [2], falsely accuse [1]

1909* ἐπί, *epi, pp. GK: *2093* [→ *244, 422, 423, 1860, 1861, 1862, 1863, 1864, 1865, 1866, 1867, 1868, 1869, 1870, 1871, 1872, 1873, 1874, 1875, 1876, 1877, 1878, 1879, 1880, 1881, 1882, 1883, 1884, 1885, 1886, 1887, 1888, 1890, 1892, 1893, 1894, 1895, 1896, 1966, 1897, 1898, 1899, 1900, 1901, 1902, 1903, 1904, 1905, 1906, 1907, 1910, 1911, 1912, 1913, 1914, 1915, 1916, 1917, 1918, 1919, 1920, 1921, 1922, 1923, 1924, 1925, 1926, 1927, 1928, 1929, 1930, 1931, 1932, 1933, 1934, 1935, 1936, 1937, 1938, 1939, 1940, 1941, 1942, 1943, 1944, 1945, 1970, 1946, 1947, 1948, 1949, 1950, 1951, 1952, 1953, 1954, 1955, 1956, 1957, 1958, 1959, 1960, 1961, 1962, 1963, 1964, 1965, 1967, 1968, 1969, 1975, 1976, 1977, 1978, 1979, 1980, 1981, 1982, 1983, 1984, 1985, 1986, 1987, 1988, 1990, 1991, 1992, 1993, 1994, 1995, 1996, 1997, 1998, 1999, 2000, 2001, 2002, 2003, 2004, 2005, 2006, 2007, 2008, 2009, 2010, 2011, 2012, 2013, 2014, 2015, 2016, 2017, 2018, 2019, 2020, 2021, 2022, 2023, 2024, 2025, 2026, 2027, 2028, 2029, 2030, 2032, 2177, 2178, 2182, 2183, 2184, 2185, 2186, 2721, 3347, 3927, 4279, 4901, 4911; cf. 1971*]. (gen.) on, over, when; (dat.) on, at, in, while; (acc.) across, over, on, to, for, while:– on [182], upon [148], in [122], over [49], unto [45], at [43], against [38], to [36], for [30], before [17], into [16], of [16], with [9], by [8], together (+*846+3588*) [7], above [5], toward [5], about [4], after [4], among [4], whereon (+*3739*) [4], as long as (+*3745+5550*) [3], besides [3], further (+*4183*) [3], of a truth (+*225*) [3], under [3], wherein (+*3739*) [3], as long as (+*3745*) [2], bountifully (+*2129*) [2], inasmuch as (+*3745*) [2], into one place (+*846+3588*) [2], throughout [2], through [2], towards [2], a great while (+*4183*) [1], about the time [1], as touching [1], because of [1], being [1], by the space of [1], chamberlain (+*2846+3588*) [1], charge of [1], come to ears (+*191*) [1], for the space of [1], in one place (+*846+3588*) [1], in the days of [1], in the time of [1], inasmuch as (+*3303+3745+3767*) [1], kept (+*2621*) [1], long (+*4183*) [1], long while (+*2425*) [1], longer (+*4183*) [1], on behalf [1], the space of [1], thereon (+*846*) [1], thereon [1], therewith (+*3778*) [1], three times (+*5151*) [1], thrice (+*5151*) [1], touching [1], truly (+*225*) [1], wherefore (+*3739*) [1], worse and worse (+*3588+5501*) [1]

1910* ἐπιβαίνω, *epibainō, v. GK: *2094* [→ *1909+305*]. to go up, go upon, ride upon, board (a vessel):– came [1], come into [1], entering into [1], sitting [1], took [1], went aboard [1]

1911* ἐπιβάλλω, *epiballō, v. GK: *2095* [→ *1909+906*]. (tr.) to throw over; to place; lay hold of, seize, arrest; to sew on; (intr.) to break over:– laid [6], lay on [2], putteth [2], beat [1], cast on [1], cast [1], falleth to [1], laid on [1], put to [1], stretched forth [1], thought thereon [1]

1912* ἐπιβαρέω, *epibareō, v. GK: *2096* [→ *1909+922*]. to burden, weigh down excessively:– chargeable [2], overcharge [1]

1913* ἐπιβιβάζω, *epibibazō, v. GK: *2097* [→ *1909+305*]. to put (someone) on (a mount):– set on [2], set thereon [1]

1914* ἐπιβλέπω, *epiblepō, v. GK: *2098* [→ *1909+991*]. to look at, show special attention, consider, care about:– look upon [1], regarded [1], respect [1]

1915* ἐπίβλημα, *epiblēma, n. GK: *2099* [→ *1909+906*]. patch:– piece [4]

1916* ἐπιβοάω, *epiboaō, v. GK: *2100* [→ *1909+995*]. to cry out loudly:– crying [1]

1917* ἐπιβουλή, *epiboulē, n. GK: *2101* [→ *1909+1014*]. plan, plot:– laid wait for (+*1096*) [1], laid wait [1], laying await [1], lying in wait [1]

1918* ἐπιγαμβρεύω, *epigambreuō, v. GK: *2102* [→ *1909+1062*]. to marry (as next of kin):– marry [1]

1919* ἐπίγειος, *epigeios, a. GK: *2103* [→ *1909+1093*]. being on the earth, earthly, that which is inferior when in contrast to heavenly or divine things:– earthly [4], terrestrial [2], in earth [1]

1920* ἐπιγίνομαι, *epiginomai, v. GK: *2104* [→ *1909+1096*]. to come up, occur, happen:– blew [1]

1921* ἐπιγινώσκω, *epiginōskō, v. GK: *2105* [→ *1909+1097*]. to know (fully), recognize, realize, come to understand:– knew [14], know [8], acknowledge [4], known [3], perceived [3], knoweth [2], knowing [2], acknowledged [1], had knowledge [1], knowest [1], knowledge [1], took knowledge [1], well known [1]

1922* ἐπίγνωσις, *epignōsis, n. GK: *2106* [→ *1909+1097*]. knowledge, understanding, insight:– knowledge [16], acknowledging [3], acknowledgement [1]

1923* ἐπιγραφή, *epigraphē, n. GK: *2107* [→ *1909+1125*]. inscription, superscription, written notice:– superscription [5]

1924* ἐπιγράφω, *epigraphō, v. GK: *2108* [→ *1909+1125*]. (act.) to write; (pass.) to be written (upon), inscribed:– write [2], inscription [1], written over [1], written thereon [1]

1925* ἐπιδείκνυμι, *epideiknymi, v. GK: *2109* [→ *1909+1166*]. to show, call attention to; to prove, point out:– shew [6], shewing [2], shewed [1]

1926* ἐπιδέχομαι, *epidechomai, v. GK: *2110* [→ *1909+1209*]. to welcome, receive as a guest; to have to do with, accept, recognize:– receiveth [1], receive [1]

1927* ἐπιδημέω, *epidēmeō, v. GK: *2111* [→ *1909+1218*]. to live as a visitor, foreigner:– strangers [1], were there [1]

1928* ἐπιδιατάσσομαι, *epidiatassomai, v. GK: *2112* [→ *1909+1223+5021*]. to add to (a covenant):– added [1]

1929* ἐπιδίδωμι, *epididōmi, v. GK: *2113* [→ *1909+1325*]. to give, deliver, hand over to:– give [5], delivered [2], gave [2], let drive (+*5342*) [1], offer [1]

1930 ἐπιδιορθόω, ***epidiorthoō***, v. GK: *2114* [→ *1909+1223+3717*]. to straighten out, correct (in addition):– set in order [1]

1931 ἐπιδύω, ***epidyō***, v. GK: *2115* [→ *1909+1416*]. to go down, set (of the sun):– go down [1]

1932 ἐπιείκεια, ***epieikeia***, n. GK: *2116* [→ *1909+1503*]. gentleness, with an implication of tolerance and graciousness:– clemency [1], gentleness [1]

1933 ἐπιεικής, ***epieikēs***, a. GK: *2117* [→ *1909+1503*]. gentle, considerate:– gentle [3], moderation [1], patient [1]

1934 ἐπιζητέω, ***epizēteō***, v. GK: *2118* [→ *1909+2212*]. to look for, run after, seek earnestly:– seek [3], desire [2], seek after [2], seeketh after [2], after seek [1], desired [1], inquire [1], seeketh for [1], sought for [1]

1935 ἐπιθανάτιος, ***epithanatios***, a. GK: *2119* [→ *1909+2348*]. condemned to die:– appointed to death [1]

1936 ἐπίθεσις, ***epithesis***, n. GK: *2120* [→ *1909+5087*]. laying on:– laying on [3], putting on [1]

1937 ἐπιθυμέω, ***epithymeō***, v. GK: *2121* [→ *1909+2372*]. to long for, desire; covet, lust:– desire [4], covet [2], desired [2], coveted [1], desireth [1], desiring [1], lust after [1], lusted [1], lusteth [1], lust [1], would fain [1]

1938 ἐπιθυμητής, ***epithymētēs***, n. GK: *2122* [→ *1909+2372*]. one who desires, sets heart on (evil):– lust after [1]

1939 ἐπιθυμία, ***epithymia***, n. GK: *2123* [→ *1909+2372*]. desire, longing (in contexts where the desire is positive and proper); coveting, craving, lusting (in contexts where the desire is immoral and sinful):– lusts [22], lust [9], concupiscence [3], desire [3], lusted after [1]

1940 ἐπικαθίζω, ***epikathizō***, v. GK: *2125* [→ *1909+2523*]. to sit down (upon):– set [1]

1941 ἐπικαλέω, ***epikaleō***, v. GK: *2126* [→ *1909+2564*]. (act./pass.) to call (upon), name, be named; (mid.) appeal to, call upon for aid:– surname [6], call on [5], surnamed [5], call upon [3], called [3], appeal unto [2], appealed unto [2], appealed to [1], appealed [1], call for [1], called on [1], calling on [1], calling upon [1]

1942 ἐπικάλυμμα, ***epikalymma***, n. GK: *2127* [→ *1909+2572*]. cover-up, covering, veil:– cloke [1]

1943 ἐπικαλύπτω, ***epikalyptō***, v. GK: *2128* [→ *1909+2572*]. (pass.) to be covered:– covered [1]

1944 ἐπικατάρατος, ***epikataratos***, a. GK: *2063 & 2129* [→ *1909+2596+685*]. cursed:– cursed [3]

1945 ἐπίκειμαι, ***epikeimai***, v. GK: *2130* [→ *1909+2749*]. to lay upon; to press, crowd upon, demand insistently:– imposed [1], instant [1], laid thereon [1], laid upon [1], lay on [1], lay [1], pressed upon [1]

1946 Ἐπικούρειος, ***Epikoureios***, a.pr. or n.pr. GK: *2134* [→ *1909+2751*]. Epicurean, "*of Epicurus*":– Epicureans [1]

1947 ἐπικουρία, ***epikouria***, n. GK: *2135* [→ *1909+2751*]. help:– help [1]

1948 ἐπικρίνω, ***epikrinō***, v. GK: *2137* [→ *1909+2919*]. to decide, determine:– gave sentence [1]

1949 ἐπιλαμβάνομαι, ***epilambanomai***, v. GK: *2138* [→ *1909+2983*]. to take hold, catch, trap, seize:– took [10], caught [2], lay hold on [2], take hold [2], took on [2], laid hold upon [1]

1950 ἐπιλανθάνομαι, ***epilanthanomai***, v. GK: *2140* [→ *1909+2990*]. to forget:– forgotten [3], forget [2], forgetful [1], forgetteth [1], forgetting [1]

1951 ἐπιλέγω, ***epilegō***, v. GK: *2141* [→ *1909+3004*]. (pass.) to be called; (mid.) to choose:– called [1], chose [1]

1952 ἐπιλείπω, ***epileipō***, v. GK: *2142* [→ *1909+3007*]. to not have (time); to fail to have:– fail [1]

1953 ἐπιλησμονή, ***epilēsmonē***, n. GK: *2144* [→ *1909+2990*]. forgetfulness:– forgetful [1]

1954 ἐπίλοιπος, ***epiloipos***, a. GK: *2145* [→ *1909+3007*]. remaining, the rest:– rest [1]

1955 ἐπίλυσις, ***epilysis***, n. GK: *2146* [→ *1909+3089*]. interpretation, explanation:– interpretation [1]

1956 ἐπιλύω, ***epilyō***, v. GK: *2147* [→ *1909+3089*]. to explain; (pass.) to be settled, decided:– determined [1], expounded [1]

1957 ἐπιμαρτυρέω, ***epimartyreō***, v. GK: *2148* [→ *1909+3144*]. to testify that, bear witness about:– testifying [1]

1958 ἐπιμέλεια, ***epimeleia***, n. GK: *2149* [→ *1909+3199*]. needs, care, attention:– refresh (+*5177*) [1]

1959 ἐπιμελέομαι, ***epimeleomai***, v. GK: *2150* [→ *1909+3199*]. to take care of, look after:– take care of [2], took care of [1]

1960 ἐπιμελῶς, ***epimelōs***, adv. GK: *2151* [→ *1909+3199*]. carefully, diligently:– diligently [1]

1961 ἐπιμένω, ***epimenō***, v. GK: *2152* [→ *1909+3306*]. to stay, remain; to continue in, keep on, persevere:– continue in [4], tarry [4], tarried [3], abide [2], continued [2], abode [1], bide still in [1], continue [1]

1962 ἐπινεύω, ***epineuō***, v. GK: *2153* [→ *1909+3506*]. to accept, give consent:– consented [1]

1963 ἐπίνοια, ***epinoia***, n. GK: *2154* [→ *1909+3563*]. thought, intention:– thought [1]

1964 ἐπιορκέω, ***epiorkeō***, v. GK: *2155* [→ *1909+3727*]. to break an oath, swear falsely:– forswear [1]

1965 ἐπίορκος, ***epiorkos***, a. GK: *2156* [→ *1909+3727*]. perjured; as a noun, perjurer:– perjured [1]

1966 ἔπειμι, ***epeimi***, v. GK: *2079* [→ *1909*]. (ptcp.) the next day (from a verb that means "to follow, approach"):– next [3], following [2]

1967 ἐπιούσιος, ***epiousios***, a. GK: *2157* [→ *1909+1510*]. what recurs on a day to day basis, daily:– daily [2]

1968 ἐπιπίπτω, ***epipiptō***, v. GK: *2158* [→ *1909+4098*]. to fall upon, come eagerly, embrace; to come on:– fell on [5], fell [4], fallen upon [1], fell upon [1], lying [1], pressed upon [1]

1969 ἐπιπλήσσω, ***epiplēssō***, v. GK: *2159* [→ *1909+4141*]. to rebuke, strike at:– rebuke [1]

1970 ἐπιπνίγω, ***epipnigō***, v. GK: *4464* [→ *1909+4155*]. to overgrow, throttle, choke:–

1971 ἐπιποθέω, ***epipotheō***, v. GK: *2160* [→ *1972, 1973, 1974; cf. 1909*]. to long for, crave, desire:– long after [2], desire [1], desiring greatly [1], earnestly desiring [1], greatly desiring [1], longed after [1], long [1], lusteth [1]

1972 ἐπιπόθησις, ***epipothēsis***, n. GK: *2161* [→ *1971*]. longing (for):– earnest desire [1], vehement desire [1]

1973 ἐπιπόθητος, ***epipothētos***, a. GK: *2162* [→ *1971*]. longed for:– longed for [1]

1974 ἐπιποθία, ***epipothia***, n. GK: *2163* [→ *1971*]. longing, desire:– great desire [1]

1975 ἐπιπορεύομαι, ***epiporeuomai***, v. GK: *2164* [→ *1909+4198*]. to come to, go to:– come out of [1]

1976 ἐπιράπτω, ***epiraptō***, v. GK: *2165 & 2193* [→ *1909+4476*]. to sew on:– seweth [1]

1977 ἐπιρίπτω, ***epiriptō***, v. GK: *2166* [→ *1909+4496*]. to throw on:– cast upon [1], casting [1]

1978 ἐπισημος, ***episemos***, a. GK: *2168* [→ *1909+4592*]. notorious, prominent, outstanding:– notable [1], note [1]

1979 ἐπισιτισμός, ***episitismos***, n. GK: *2169* [→ *1909+4621*]. food, something to eat:– victuals [1]

1980 ἐπισκέπτομαι, ***episkeptomai***, v. GK: *2170* [→ *1909+4648*]. to visit, show concern, care for, come to help:– visited [5], visit [4], look out [1], visitest [1]

1981 ἐπισκηνόω, ***episkēnoō***, v. GK: *2172* [→ *1909+4633*]. to rest upon, take up residence:– rest [1]

1982 ἐπισκιάζω, ***episkiazō***, v. GK: *2173* [→ *1909+4639*]. to cast a shadow, overshadow; to envelope with a cloud:– overshadowed [3], overshadow [2]

1983 ἐπισκοπέω, ***episkopeō***, v. GK: *2174* [→ *1909+4648*]. to see to, care for; to serve as an overseer:– looking diligently [1], taking the oversight [1]

1984 ἐπισκοπή, ***episkopē***, n. GK: *2175* [→ *1909+4648*]. coming, visitation, the coming of divine power for recompense; an office of responsibility and place of leadership referring to an office of apostle in Acts, and the office of overseer or bishop in the local church:– visitation [2], bishoprick [1], office of bishop [1]

1985 ἐπίσκοπος, ***episkopos***, n. GK: *2176* [→ *1909+4648*]. overseer or bishop, a leader in a local church, an extension of one who guards, supervises, and helps:– bishop [5], bishops [1], overseers [1]

1986 ἐπισπάομαι, ***epispaomai***, v. GK: *2177* [→ *1909+4685*]. to (attempt to) conceal circumcision, formally "to pull over (the foreskin to conceal circumcision)":– become uncircumcised [1]

1987 ἐπίσταμαι, ***epistamai***, v. GK: *2179* [→ *1909+2476*]. to understand, know, be aware:– know [9], knowing [3], knoweth [1], understand [1]

1988 ἐπιστάτης, ***epistatēs***, n. GK: *2181* [→ *1909+2476*]. master:– master [7]

1989 ἐπιστέλλω, ***epistellō***, v. GK: *2182* [→ *1992*]. to write a letter:– write [1], written a letter [1], written [1]

1990 ἐπιστήμων, ***epistēmōn***, a. GK: *2184* [→ *1909+2476*]. understanding, expert, learned:– knowledge [1]

1991 ἐπιστηρίζω, ***epistērizō***, v. GK: *2185* [→ *1909+4741*]. to strengthen:– confirming [2], confirmed [1], strengthening [1]

1992 ἐπιστολή, ***epistolē***, n. GK: *2186* [→ *1989*]. letter, epistle:– epistle [13], letters [6], letter [3], epistles [2]

1993 ἐπιστομίζω, ***epistomizō***, v. GK: *2187* [→ *1909+4750*]. to silence, formally, "to stop the mouth":– mouths stopped [1]

1994 ἐπιστρέφω, ***epistrephō***, v. GK: *2188* [→ *1909+4762*]. to turn (around, back, from), return:– converted [6], return [4], turned [4], turn [4], turn to [3], turned about [3], returned [2], turned to [2], came again [1], converteth [1], convert [1], go again [1], turn again [1], turn back [1], turn unto [1], turned again [1], turned unto [1], turning about [1], turning [1]

1995 ἐπιστροφή, ***epistrophē***, n. GK: *2189* [→ *1909+4762*]. conversion, a fig. extension of *turning* an object, not found in the NT:– conversion [1]

1996 ἐπισυνάγω, ***episynagō***, v. GK: *2190* [→ *1909+4862+71*]. to gather together:– gathered together [4], gather together [2], gathereth [1]

1997 ἐπισυναγωγή, ***episynagōgē***, n. GK: *2191* [→ *1909+4864*]. gathering, meeting, assembling:– assembling together [1], gathering together [1]

1998 ἐπισυντρέχω, ***episyntrechō***, v. GK: *2192* [→ *1909+4862+5143*]. to run together to:– came running together [1]

1999 ἐπίστασις, ***epistasis***, n. GK: *2180 & 2194* [→ *1909+4862+2476*]. stirring up, disturbance, insurrection, rebellion; pressure:– cometh upon [1], raising up (+*4160*) [1]

2000 ἐπισφαλής, ***episphalēs***, a. GK: *2195* [→ *1909; cf. 755*]. dangerous, unsafe:– dangerous [1]

2001 ἐπισχύω, ***epischyō***, v. GK: *2196* [→ *1909+2479*]. to insist:– more fierce [1]

2002 ἐπισωρεύω, ***episōreuō***, v. GK: *2197* [→ *1909+4987*]. to gather a great number, accumulate:– heap [1]

2003 ἐπιταγή, ***epitagē***, n. GK: *2198* [→ *1909+5021*]. command, order; authority:– commandment [6], authority [1]

2004 ἐπιτάσσω, ***epitassō***, v. GK: *2199* [→ *1909+5021*]. to command, order:– commanded [4], commandeth [3], charge [1], command [1], enjoin [1]

2005 ἐπιτελέω, ***epiteleō***, v. GK: *2200* [→ *1909+5056*]. to finish, complete, end; to perfect, attain a goal; (mid.) to undergo:– perform [2], accomplished [1], accomplishing [1], do [1], finish [1], made perfect [1], make [1], perfecting [1], performance [1], performed [1]

2006 ἐπιτήδειος, ***epitēdeios***, a. GK: *2201* [→ *1909+3588*]. needful, necessary, suitable:– needful [1]

2007 ἐπιτίθημι, ***epitithēmi***, v. GK: *2202* [→ *1909+5087*]. to place, lay upon, put on:– laid on [7], put [4], laid [3], lay on [3], put upon [3], add [2], laid upon [2], lay [2], put on [2], putting on [2], laded with [1], lay upon [1], layeth [1], on laid [1], on lay [1], set on [1], set up [1], setteth on [1], set [1], surnamed (+*3686*) [1], surnamed [1], wounded (+*4127*) [1]

2008 ἐπιτιμάω, ***epitimaō***, v. GK: *2203* [→ *1909+5092*]. to rebuke, warn:– rebuked [17], rebuke [6], charged [4], rebuking [1], straitly charged [1]

2009 ἐπιτιμία, ***epitimia***, n. GK: *2204* [→ *1909+5092*]. punishment:– punishment [1]

2010 ἐπιτρέπω, ***epitrepō***, v. GK: *2205* [→ *1909+5157*]. to let, allow, permit, give permission:– suffer [6], suffered [4], gave leave [2], permitted [2], permit [2], gave liberty [1], given licence [1], let [1]

2011 **ἐπιτροπή, *epitropē***, n. GK: *2207* [→ *1909+5157*]. commission, permission:– commission [1]

2012 **ἐπίτροπος, *epitropos***, n. GK: *2208* [→ *1909+5157*]. foreman, manager, guardian; derived from a Greek verb, "to instruct," not found in the NT:– steward [2], tutors [1]

2013 **ἐπιτυγχάνω, *epitynchanō***, v. GK: *2209* [→ *1909+5177*]. to obtain, receive, gain:– obtained [4], obtain [1]

2014 **ἐπιφαίνω, *epiphainō***, v. GK: *2210* [→ *1909+5316*]. (act.) to appear, make an appearance, show oneself; (pass.) shine:– appeared [3], give light [1]

2015 **ἐπιφάνεια, *epiphaneia***, n. GK: *2211* [→ *1909+5316*]. appearing, appearance; usually referring to the return of Christ, cf. the English word "epiphany":– appearing [5], brightness [1]

2016 **ἐπιφανής, *epiphanēs***, a. GK: *2212* [→ *1909+5316*]. glorious, splendid:– notable [1]

2017 **ἐπιφαύσκω, *epiphauskō***, v. GK: *2213* [→ *1909+5316*]. to shine on:– give light [1]

2018 **ἐπιφέρω, *epipherō***, v. GK: *2214* [→ *1909+5342*]. to bring upon, inflict:– brought [2], add [1], bring against [1], taketh [1]

2019 **ἐπιφωνέω, *epiphōneō***, v. GK: *2215* [→ *1909+5456*]. to shout, cry out loudly:– cried against [1], cried [1], gave a shout [1]

2020 **ἐπιφώσκω, *epiphōskō***, v. GK: *2216* [→ *1909+5316*]. to dawn, begin, shine forth:– dawn [1], drew on [1]

2021 **ἐπιχειρέω, *epicheireō***, v. GK: *2217* [→ *1909+5495*]. to attempt, try to:– taken in hand [1], took upon [1], went about [1]

2022 **ἐπιχέω, *epicheō***, v. GK: *2219* [→ *1632; cf. 1909*]. to pour on, pour over:– pouring in [1]

2023 **ἐπιχορηγέω, *epichorēgeō***, v. GK: *2220* [→ *1909+5525+71*]. to support, supply; (pass.) to be supported, receive:– ministereth [2], add [1], ministered [1], nourishment ministered [1]

2024 **ἐπιχορηγία, *epichorēgia***, n. GK: *2221* [→ *1909+5525+71*]. support, help:– supplieth [1], supply [1]

2025 **ἐπιχρίω, *epichriō***, v. GK: *2222* [→ *1909+5548*]. to put on, anoint on, spread on:– anointed [2]

2026 **ἐποικοδομέω, *epoikodomeō***, v. GK: *2224* [→ *1909+3624+1430*]. to build up, build on:– build [2], buildeth thereon [1], buildeth thereupon [1], building up [1], built thereupon [1], built up [1], built [1]

2027 **ἐποκέλλω, *epokellō***, v. GK: *2131 & 2225* [→ *1909+2753*]. to run aground:– ran aground [1]

2028 **ἐπονομάζω, *eponomazō***, v. GK: *2226* [→ *1909+3686*]. (pass.) to be called, named:– called [1]

2029 **ἐποπτεύω, *epopteuō***, v. GK: *2227* [→ *1909+3708*]. to see, observe:– behold [2]

2030 **ἐπόπτης, *epoptēs***, n. GK: *2228* [→ *1909+3708*]. eyewitness:– eyewitnesses [1]

2031 **ἔπος, *epos***, n. GK: *2229*. word:– so[S] [1]

2032 **ἐπουράνιος, *epouranios***, a. GK: *2230* [→ *1909+3772*]. heavenly, celestial; heavenly realms:– heavenly [16], celestial [2], high [1], in heaven [1]

2033 **ἑπτά, *hepta***, n.num. GK: *2231* [→ *1440, 1441, 1442, 2034, 2035*]. seven:– seven [86], seventh [1]

2034 **ἑπτάκις, *heptakis***, adv. GK: *2232* [→ *2033*]. seven times:– seven times [4]

2035 **ἑπτακισχίλιοι, *heptakischilioi***, a.num. GK: *2233* [→ *2033+5507*]. seven thousand:– seven thousand [1]

2036 **ἔπω, *epō***, v. GK: *3306* [→ *3004*]. to speak, say:–

2037 **Ἔραστος, *Erastos***, n.pr. GK: *2235*. Erastus, "*beloved*":– Erastus [3]

ἐραυνάω, *eraunaō*. See ***2045***.

2038 **ἐργάζομαι, *ergazomai***, v. GK: *2237* [→ *2041*]. to work, be active, accomplish (something):– work [12], worketh [7], wrought [7], working [4], do [2], commit [1], doest [1], labouring [1], labour [1], minister [1], traded [1], trade [1]

2039 **ἐργασία, *ergasia***, n. GK: *2238* [→ *2041*]. trade, business, making money; indulgence:– gain [2], craft [1], diligence [1], gains [1], work [1]

2040 **ἐργάτης, *ergatēs***, n. GK: *2239* [→ *2041*]. worker, laborer, one who does (something):– labourers [8], workers [3], labourer [2], workman [2], workmen [1]

2041 **ἔργον, *ergon***, n. GK: *2240* [→ *14, 289, 691, 692, 1090, 1091, 1092, 1217, 1753, 1754, 1755, 1756, 2038, 2039, 2040, 2108, 2109, 2110, 2418, 2557, 2673, 2716, 3008, 3009, 3010, 3011, 3834, 3835, 4020, 4021, 4333, 4903, 4904, 4943; cf. 4468*]. work, deed, activity, task, job:– works [103], work [47], deeds [16], deed [6], doing [1], labour [1], work's [1], works' [1]

2042 **ἐρεθίζω, *erethizō***, v. GK: *2241*. to stir up, provoke, arouse; embitter, provoke, irritate:– provoked [1], provoke [1]

2043 **ἐρείδω, *ereidō***, v. GK: *2242*. to stick fast, make immovable, jam:– stuck fast [1]

2044 **ἐρεύγομαι, *ereugomai***, v. GK: *2243*. to utter, proclaim:– utter [1]

2045 **ἐραυνάω, *eraunaō***, v. GK: *2236* [→ *419, 1830; cf. 2065*]. to search, look into, try to find out:– searcheth [3], search [2], searching [1]

2046 **ἐρευνάω, *ereunaō***, v. GK: *3306* [→ *3004*]. to utter, speak say:–

2047 **ἐρημία, *erēmia***, n. GK: *2244* [→ *2048*]. remote place, desert, countryside, usually uninhabited areas:– wilderness [3], deserts [1]

2048 **ἔρημος, *erēmos***, a. GK: *2245* [→ *2047, 2049, 2050*]. deserted, remote, solitary; as a noun, desert, uninhabited wilderness, or grasslands, implying in some contexts to be a forsaken, desolate place:– wilderness [32], desert [12], desolate [4], deserts [1], solitary [1]

2049 **ἐρημόω, *erēmoō***, v. GK: *2246* [→ *2048*]. (pass.) to be brought to ruin, laid waste:– brought to desolation [2], come to nought [1], desolate [1], made desolate [1]

2050 **ἐρήμωσις, *erēmōsis***, n. GK: *2247* [→ *2048*]. desolation, devastation, destruction. "The Abomination of Desolation" is a phrase derived from Hebrew, formally, "the detestable thing of desolation." This abomination is a person, thing, or event that defiles a holy place and thus causes it to be abandoned, implying God detests this thing or action. Many refer this to desecration of the temple by Antiochus Epiphanes as analogous to a future event predicted by Jesus:– desolation [3]

2051 **ἐρίζω, *erizō***, v. GK: *2248* [→ *2054*]. to quarrel:– strive [1]

2052 **ἐριθεία, *eritheia***, n. GK: *2249* [→ *2054*]. selfish ambition, faction, strife:– strife [4], contention [1], contentious [1], strifes [1]

2053 **ἔριον, *erion***, n. GK: *2250*. wool:– wool [2]

2054 **ἔρις, *eris***, n. GK: *2251* [→ *2051, 2052*]. quarrel, strife, dissension, discord:– strife [4], contentions [2], debates [1], debate [1], variance [1]

2055 **ἐρίφιον, *eriphion***, n. GK: *2252* [→ *2056*]. goat:– goats [1]

2056 **ἔριφος, *eriphos***, n. GK: *2253* [→ *2055*]. (young) goat:– goats [1], kid [1]

2057 **Ἑρμᾶς, *Hermas***, n.pr. GK: *2254*. Hermas:– Hermas [1]

2058 **ἑρμηνεία, *hermēneia***, n. GK: *1448 & 2255* [→ *2059*]. interpretation, translation of meaning from one language to another, in the NT a gift of the Spirit necessary for understanding the gift of tongues in assembly:– interpretation [2]

2059 **ἑρμηνεύω, *hermēneuō***, v. GK: *2257* [→ *1328, 1329, 1421, 2058, 3177*]. to translate, give the meaning, interpret, explain:– by interpretation [3], interpreted [1]

2060 **Ἑρμῆς, *Hermēs***, n.pr. GK: *2258*. Hermes, "[poss.] *rock, cairn*":– Hermes [1], Mercurius [1]

2061 **Ἑρμογένης, *Hermogenēs***, n.pr. GK: *2259*. Hermogenes, "*born of Hermes*":– Hermogenes [1]

2062 **ἑρπετόν, *herpeton***, n. GK: *2260*. reptile:– creeping things [3], serpents [1]

2063 **ἐρυθρός, *erythros***, a. GK: *2261*. red:– Red [2]

2064 **ἔρχομαι, *erchomai***, v. GK: *2262* [→ *424, 492, 565, 1330, 1525, 1660, 1831, 1880, 1904, 2718, 3922, 3928, 4022, 4281, 4334, 4339, 4897, 4905*]. to come, go:– come [289], came [197], cometh [98], coming [27], went [11], comest [3], entered [2], go [2], resorted [2], accompanied (*+4862*) [1], appear [1], be [1], brought [1], camest [1], fallen out [1], for to come (*+3195*) [1], grew (*+1519*) [1], lighting [1], next [1], passing by [1], set [1]

2065 **ἐρωτάω, *erōtaō***, v. GK: *2263* [→ *1331, 1905, 1906; cf. 2045*]. to ask; beg, urge; pray:– ask [11], asked [10], pray [10], besought [9], beseech [4], desired [4], prayed [4], asketh [1], asking [1], beseeching [1], desireth [1], desire [1], intreat [1]

2066 **ἐσθής, *esthēs***, n. GK: *2264* [→ *2439*]. clothing, robe:– apparel [3], clothing [2], raiment [1], robe [1]

2067 **ἔσθησις, *esthēsis***, n. GK: *2265* [→ *2439*]. government:– garments [1]

2068 **ἐσθίω, *esthiō***, v. GK: *2266 & 2267* [→ *2068, 2719, 4906, 5315; cf. 3521, 5314*]. to eat, consume, devour:– eat [39], eateth [17], eating [6], devour [1], eaten [1], live [1]

2069 **Ἑσλί, *Hesli***, n.pr. GK: *2268*. Esli, "*Yahweh sets apart*":– Esli [1]

2070 **ἐσμέν, *esmen***, v.1.pl. of *1510*. GK: *1639* [→ *1510*]. we are; see *1510*:–

2071 **ἔσομαι, *esomai***, v.1.s.fut. of *1510*. GK: *1639* [→ *1510*]. will be; see *1510*:–

2072 **ἔσοπτρον, *esoptron***, n. GK: *2269* [→ *1519+3708*]. mirror:– glass [2]

2073 **ἑσπέρα, *hespera***, n. GK: *2270*. evening:– evening [2], eventide [1]

2074 **Ἑσρώμ, *Hesrōm***, n.pr. GK: *2272*. Hezron, "*enclosure*":– Esrom [3]

2075 **ἐστέ, *este***, v.2.pl. of *1510*. GK: *1639* [→ *1510*]. you are; see *1510*:–

2076 **ἐστί, *esti***, v.3.s. of *1510*. GK: *1639* [→ *1510*]. he, she, it is; see *1510*:–

2077 **ἔστω, *estō***, v.2.s.imper. of *1510*. GK: *1639* [→ *1510*]. be; see *1510*:–

2078 **ἔσχατος, *eschatos***, a. GK: *2274* [→ *1537*]. last (of a series), least, final:– last [48], lowest [2], ends [1], latter [1], uttermost part [1], uttermost [1]

2079 **ἐσχάτως, *eschatōs***, adv. GK: *2275* [→ *1537*]. finally; at the point of death:– lieth at the point of death (*+2192*) [1]

2080 **ἔσω, *esō***, adv. GK: *2276* [→ *1519*]. in, inner, inside, inwardly:– within [3], into [2], inner [1], inward [1]

2081 **ἔσωθεν, *esōthen***, adv. GK: *2277* [→ *1519*]. from within, from inside, inwardly:– within [7], from within [3], inward part [1], inwardly [1], inward [1], out [1]

2082 **ἐσώτερος, *esōteros***, a. GK: *2278* [→ *1519*]. inner:– inner [1], within [1]

2083 **ἑταῖρος, *hetairos***, n. GK: *2279*. friend, comrade, companion:– friend [3], fellows [1]

2084 **ἑτερόγλωσσος, *heteroglōssos***, a. GK: *2280* [→ *2087+1100*]. speaking in a foreign language:– other tongues [1]

2085 **ἑτεροδιδασκαλέω, *heterodidaskaleō***, v. GK: *2281* [→ *2087+1321*]. to teach false doctrine, teach heresy:– teach other doctrine [1], teach otherwise [1]

2086 **ἑτεροζυγέω, *heterozygeō***, v. GK: *2282* [→ *2087+2218*]. to yoke together in a mismatch:– unequally yoked together [1]

2087 **ἕτερος, *heteros***, a. GK: *2283* [→ *2084, 2085, 2086, 2088, 4220*]. other, different:– another [44], other [35], others [10], next [2], some [2], altered [1], another's [1], else [1], one [1], other's [1], strange [1]

2088 **ἑτέρως, *heterōs***, adv. GK: *2284* [→ *2087*]. differently, other, otherwise:– otherwise [1]

2089 **ἔτι, *eti***, adv. GK: *2285* [→ *3371, 3765*]. still, yet, again:– yet [42], more [16], while yet [7], any more [5], still [4], any further [3], further [3], longer [2], any longer [1], as yet [1], even [1], moreover (*+1161*) [1], moreover [1], no more (*+3367*) [1], now (*+3568*) [1], thenceforth [1], while as yet [1], yea (*+5037*) [1], yet a while [1]

2090 **ἑτοιμάζω, *hetoimazō***, v. GK: *2286* [→ *2092*]. to prepare, be ready:– prepared [18], prepare [11], make ready [6], made ready [4], provided [1]

2091 **ἑτοιμασία, *hetoimasia***, n. GK: *2288* [→ *2092*]. readiness, preparation:– preparation [1]

2092 **ἕτοιμος, *hetoimos***, a. GK: *2289* [→ *2090, 2091, 2093, 4282*]. ready, prepared:– ready [14], made ready to hand (*+1519*) [1], prepared [1], readiness [1]

2093 **ἑτοίμως, *hetoimōs***, adv. GK: *2290* [→ *2092*]. readily:– ready [3]

2094 **ἔτος, *etos***, n. GK: *2291* [→ *1332, 1333, 1541, 5063, 5148*]. year:– years [40], years old [4], year [3], years of age [2]

2095 **εὖ, *eu***, adv. GK: *2292* [→ *428, 1757, 2097, 2098, 2099, 2100, 2101, 2102, 2103, 2104, 2105, 2106, 2107, 2108, 2109, 2110, 2111, 2114, 2115, 2119, 2120, 2121, 2122, 2123, 2124, 2125, 2126, 2127, 2128, 2129, 2130, 2131, 2132, 2133, 2136, 2137, 2138, 2139, 2140, 2141, 2142, 2143, 2144, 2145, 2146, 2150, 2151, 2152, 2153, 2154, 2155, 2156, 2157, 2158, 2159, 2160, 2161, 2162, 2163, 2164, 2165, 2168, 2169, 2170, 2173, 2174, 2175, 2176, 4283, 4909, 4910*]. well; well done!:– well [5], good [1]

2096 **Εὕα, *Heua***, n.pr. GK: *2293*. Eve, "*life*":– Eve [2]

2097 **εὐαγγελίζω, *euangelizō***, v. GK: *2294* [→ *2095+32*]. to preach (bring) the good news (gospel), often with a focus on the content of the message which is brought. In the NT it always refers to the death, burial, resurrection, and witness about Jesus Christ, including its implications for humankind's relationship to God:– preached [12], preach the gospel [10], preached the gospel [6], preach [6], preaching [5], the gospel preached [3], gospel preached [2], preach gospel [2], bring glad tidings [1], bring good tidings [1], brought good tidings [1], declare glad tidings [1], declared [1], preacheth [1], preaching the gospel [1], shew glad tidings [1], shewing the glad tidings [1]

2098 **εὐαγγέλιον, *euangelion***, n. GK: *2295* [→ *2095+32*]. gospel, good news; see also *2097*:– gospel [74], gospel's [3]

2099 **εὐαγγελιστής, *euangelistēs***, n. GK: *2296* [→ *2095+32*]. evangelist, preacher of the gospel:– evangelist [2], evangelists [1]

2100 **εὐαρεστέω, *euaresteō***, v. GK: *2297* [→ *2095+700*]. to please:– pleased [1], please [1], well pleased [1]

2101 **εὐάρεστος, *euarestos***, a. GK: *2298* [→ *2095+700*]. pleasing, acceptable:– acceptable [4], well pleasing [3], accepted [1], please well (*+1510*) [1]

2102 **εὐαρέστως, *euarestōs***, adv. GK: *2299* [→ *2095+700*]. in an acceptable or pleasing manner:– acceptably [1]

2103 **Εὔβουλος, *Euboulos***, n.pr. GK: *2300* [→ *2095+1014*]. Eubulus, "*good counsel*":– Eubulus [1]

2104 **εὐγενής, *eugenēs***, a. GK: *2302* [→ *2095+1096*]. of noble birth, of noble character:– more noble than [1], nobleman (*+444*) [1], noble [1]

2105 **εὐδία, *eudia***, n. GK: *2304* [→ *2095+2203*]. fair weather:– fair weather [1]

2106 **εὐδοκέω, *eudokeō***, v. GK: *2305* [→ *2095+1380*]. to be well pleased, delight:– well pleased [7], pleased [5], pleasure [2], willing [2], good pleasure [1], had pleasure [1], have pleasure [1], take pleasure [1], thought good [1]

2107 **εὐδοκία, *eudokia***, n. GK: *2306* [→ *2095+1380*]. goodwill, good purpose, favor, pleasure, desire:– good pleasure [4], good will [2], good [2], desire [1]

2108 **εὐεργεσία, *euergesia***, n. GK: *2307* [→ *2095+2041*]. act of kindness, good deed:– benefit [1], good deed [1]

2109 **εὐεργετέω, *euergeteō***, v. GK: *2308* [→ *2095+2041*]. to do good to:– doing good [1]

2110 **εὐεργέτης, *euergetēs***, n. GK: *2309* [→ *2095+2041*]. benefactor; in context this is a title:– benefactors [1]

2111 **εὔθετος, *euthetos***, a. GK: *2310* [→ *2095+5087*]. fit, fit for service, useable, suitable:– fit [2], meet [1]

2112 **εὐθέως, *eutheōs***, adv. GK: *2311* [→ *2117*]. immediately, at once:– immediately [38], straightway [34], forthwith [8], by and by [3], anon [2], as soon as [2], shortly [1]

2113 **εὐθυδρομέω, *euthydromeō***, v. GK: *2312* [→ *2117+5143*]. to sail straight, run a straight course:– came with a straight course [1], straight course [1]

2114 **εὐθυμέω, *euthymeō***, v. GK: *2313* [→ *2095+2372*]. to keep up one's courage; to be happy, cheerful:– be of good cheer [2], merry [1]

2115 **εὔθυμος, *euthymos***, a. GK: *2314 & 2315* [→ *2095+2372*]. encouraged, cheerful, in good spirits:– more cheerfully [1], of good cheer [1]

2116 **εὐθύνω, *euthynō***, v. GK: *2316* [→ *2117*]. to make straight, straighten; to go straight:– listeth (*+1014*) [1], make straight [1]

2117 **εὐθύς, *euthys***, a. GK: *2317 & 2318* [→ *2112, 2113, 2116, 2118, 2720*]. straight, not crooked; by extension: right, upright, the moral quality of not being wrong or perverse to truth or purity:– straight [5], right [3]

2118 **εὐθύτης, *euthytēs***, n. GK: *2319* [→ *2117*]. righteousness, uprightness, a fig. extension of a straight (not crooked) object, not found in the NT:– righteousness [1]

2119 **εὐκαιρέω, *eukaireō***, v. GK: *2320* [→ *2095+2540*]. to have a chance to, have the opportunity to; to spend one's time:– had leisure [1], have convenient time [1], spent time [1]

2120 **εὐκαιρία, *eukairia***, n. GK: *2321* [→ *2095+2540*]. opportunity, the right moment:– opportunity [2]

2121 **εὔκαιρος, *eukairos***, a. GK: *2322* [→ *2095+2540*]. opportune, well timed, suitable; time of need:– convenient [1], time of need [1]

2122 **εὐκαίρως, *eukairōs***, adv. GK: *2323* [→ *2095+2540*]. opportunely, in season:– conveniently [1], in season [1]

2123 **εὔκοπος, *eukopos***, a. GK: *2324* [→ *2095+2875*]. easy; (compar.) easier:– easier [7]

2124 **εὐλάβεια, *eulabeia***, n. GK: *2325* [→ *2095+2983*]. reverence, reverent submission:– feared [1], godly fear [1]

2125 **εὐλαβέομαι, *eulabeomai***, v. GK: *2326* [→ *2095+2983*]. to have holy fear, reverence:– fearing [1], moved with fear [1]

2126 **εὐλαβής, *eulabēs***, a. GK: *2327* [→ *2095+2983*]. devout, godly, God-fearing:– devout [3]

2127 **εὐλογέω, *eulogeō***, v. GK: *2328* [→ *2095+3004*]. to praise, give thanks to, speak well of, extol; (pass.) to be blessed, receive blessing; in some contexts, to give a blessing is to act kindly and impart benefits to the one being blessed:– blessed [30], bless [10], blessing [3], praised [1]

2128 **εὐλογητός, *eulogētos***, a. GK: *2329* [→ *2095+3004*]. worthy of being praised, blessed, or commended:– blessed [8]

2129 **εὐλογία, *eulogia***, n. GK: *2330* [→ *2095+3004*]. blessing, praise, thanksgiving, the extolling of another; in some contexts, excessive praise is improper: flattery, by extention, generosity and (giving of) gifts:– blessing [10], bountifully (*+1909*) [2], bounty [2], blessings [1], fair speeches [1]

2130 **εὐμετάδοτος, *eumetadotos***, a. GK: *2331* [→ *2095+3326+1325*]. generous:– ready to distribute [1]

2131 **Εὐνίκη, *Eunikē***, n.pr. GK: *2332* [→ *2095+3529*]. Eunice, "*good victory*":– Eunice [1]

2132 **εὐνοέω, *eunoeō***, v. GK: *2333* [→ *2095+3563*]. to settle matters by coming to terms:– agree with [1]

2133 **εὔνοια, *eunoia***, n. GK: *2334* [→ *2095+3563*]. wholeheartedness, enthusiasm, eagerness:– benevolence [1], good will [1]

2134 **εὐνουχίζω, *eunouchizō***, v. GK: *2335* [→ *2135; cf. 2192*]. to emasculate, make (oneself) a eunuch; to be celibate, renounce marriage:– made eunuchs [2]

2135 **εὐνοῦχος, *eunouchos***, n. GK: *2336* [→ *2134*]. eunuch, court official:– eunuch [5], eunuchs [3]

2136 **Εὐοδία, *Euodia***, n.pr. GK: *2337* [→ *2095+3598*]. Euodia, "*good way* poss. *good fragrance*":– Euodias [1]

2137 **εὐοδόω, *euodoō***, v. GK: *2338* [→ *2095+3598*]. (pass.) to get along with; to have a way opened; to prosper, get along well:– have a prosperous journey [1], prospered [1], prospereth [1], prosper [1]

2138 **εὐπειθής, *eupeithēs***, a. GK: *2340* [→ *2095+3982*]. submissive, obedient, compliant:– easy to be intreated [1]

2139 **εὐπερίστατος, *euperistatos***, a. GK: *2341 & 2342* [→ *2095+4012+2476*]. easily entangling, constricting, obstructing:– easily beset [1]

2140 **εὐποιΐα, *eupoiia***, n. GK: *2343* [→ *2095+4160*]. doing good:– do good [1]

2141 **εὐπορέω, *euporeō***, v. GK: *2344* [→ *2095+4198*]. to have (financial) ability, have plenty, be well off:– ability [1]

2142 **εὐπορία, *euporia***, n. GK: *2345* [→ *2095+4198*]. prosperity, prosperous income:– wealth [1]

2143 **εὐπρέπεια, *euprepeia***, n. GK: *2346* [→ *2095+4241*]. beauty:– grace [1]

2144 **εὐπρόσδεκτος, *euprosdektos***, a. GK: *2347* [→ *2095+4314+1209*]. acceptable, favorable:– accepted [3], acceptable [2]

2145 **εὐπρόσεδρος, *euprosedros***, a. GK: *2348* [→ *2095+4314+1476*]. devoted, constant:– attend upon [1]

2146 **εὐπροσωπέω, *euprosōpeō***, v. GK: *2349* [→ *2095+4383*]. to make a good impression, make a good showing:– make a fair shew [1]

2147 **εὑρίσκω, *heuriskō***, v. GK: *2351* [→ *429, 2182*]. (act.) to find, discover, meet; (mid.) to obtain; (pass.) to be found:– found [112], find [46], findeth [12], finding [4], get [1], obtained [1], perceived [1]

2148 **εὐροκλύδων, *euroklydōn***, n. GK: *2352* [→ *2830*]. southeast wind, Euroclydon:– Euroclydon [1]

2149 **εὐρύχωρος, *eurychōros***, a. GK: *2353* [→ *5562*]. broad, spacious:– broad [1]

2150 **εὐσέβεια, *eusebeia***, n. GK: *2354* [→ *2095+4576*]. godliness, piety:– godliness [14], holiness [1]

2151 **εὐσεβέω, *eusebeō***, v. GK: *2355* [→ *2095+4576*]. to worship; to put religion into practice, show piety toward:– shew piety [1], worship [1]

2152 **εὐσεβής, *eusebēs***, a. GK: *2356* [→ *2095+4576*]. devout, godly, pious, reverent:– devout [3], godly [1]

2153 **εὐσεβῶς, *eusebōs***, adv. GK: *2357* [→ *2095+4576*]. in a godly manner:– godly [2]

2154 **εὔσημος, *eusēmos***, a. GK: *2358* [→ *2095+4592*]. intelligible, clear, distinct, easily recognizable:– easy to be understood [1]

2155 **εὔσπλαγχνος, *eusplanchnos***, a. GK: *2359* [→ *2095+4698*]. compassionate, tenderhearted:– pitiful [1], tenderhearted [1]

2156 **εὐσχημόνως, *euschēmonōs***, adv. GK: *2361* [→ *2095+4976*]. decently, fittingly, becomingly, properly:– honestly [2], decently [1]

2157 **εὐσχημοσύνη, *euschēmosynē***, n. GK: *2362* [→ *2095+4976*]. modesty, presentability:– comeliness [1]

2158 **εὐσχήμων, *euschēmōn***, a. GK: *2363* [→ *2095+4976*]. presentable, proper, right; prominent, of high standing:– honourable [3], comely [2]

2159 **εὐτόνως, *eutonōs***, adv. GK: *2364* [→ *1614; cf. 2095*]. vehemently, vigorously:– mightily [1], vehemently [1]

2160 **εὐτραπελία, *eutrapelia***, n. GK: *2365* [→ *2095+5157*]. coarse joking, vulgar jesting:– jesting [1]

2161 **Εὔτυχος, *Eutychos***, n.pr. GK: *2366* [→ *2095+5177*]. Eutychus, "*fortunate*":– Eutychus [1]

2162 **εὐφημία, *euphēmia***, n. GK: *2367* [→ *2095+5346*]. good report:– good report [1]

2163 **εὔφημος, *euphēmos***, a. GK: *2368* [→ *2095+5346*]. admirable, appealing, praiseworthy:– good report [1]

2164 **εὐφορέω, *euphoreō***, v. GK: *2369* [→ *2095+5342*]. to produce a good crop, be fruitful:– brought forth plentifully [1]

2165 **εὐφραίνω, *euphrainō***, v. GK: *2370* [→ *2166, 2167*]. (act.) to cause celebration, make glad; (mid./pass.) to celebrate, rejoice, be glad:– rejoice [5], make merry [3], merry [3], fared [1], maketh glad [1], rejoiced [1]

2166 **Εὐφράτης, *Euphratēs***, n.pr. GK: *2371* [→ *2165*]. Euphrates:– Euphrates [2]

2167 **εὐφροσύνη, *euphrosynē***, n. GK: *2372* [→ *2165*]. joy, gladness, cheerfulness:– gladness [1], joy [1]

2168 **εὐχαριστέω, *eucharisteō***, v. GK: *2373* [→ *2095+5463*]. to thank, give thanks, render gratitude; this can mean words that express gratitude or the emotion of gratitude:– thank [11], give thanks [8], gave thanks [6], given thanks [4], giving thanks [4], giveth thanks [2], givest thanks [1], thanked [1], thankful [1], thanks given [1]

2169 **εὐχαριστία, *eucharistia***, n. GK: *2374* [→ *2095+5463*]. expression of thanks, thanksgiving, gratitude:– thanksgiving [8], giving thanks [2], thanks [2], giving of thanks [1], thankfulness [1], thanksgivings [1]

2170 **εὐχάριστος, *eucharistos***, a. GK: *2375* [→ *2095+5463*]. thankful (in word and attitude):– thankful [1]

2171 **εὐχή, *euchē***, n. GK: *2376* [→ *2172*]. vow, oath; prayer:– vow [2], prayer [1]

2172 **εὔχομαι, *euchomai***, v. GK: *2377* [→ *2171, 4335, 4336*]. to pray for; wish for:– wish [3], pray [2], wished for [1], would (*+302*) [1]

2173 **εὔχρηστος, *euchrēstos***, a. GK: *2378* [→ *2095+5530*]. useful, helpful, serviceable:– profitable [2], meet for use [1]

2174 **εὐψυχέω, *eupsycheō***, v. GK: *2379* [→ *2095+5594*]. to be cheerful, glad:– of good comfort [1]

2175 **εὐωδία, *euōdia***, n. GK: *2380* [→ *2095+3605*]. aroma, fragrance:– sweet savour [1], sweet smell [1], sweetsmelling [1]

2176 **εὐώνυμος, *euōnymos***, a. GK: *2381* [→ *2095+3686*]. left (direction), south:– left [6], left hand [4]

2177 **ἐφάλλομαι, *ephallomai***, v. GK: *2383* [→ *1909+242*]. to jump on, leap upon:– leapt on [1]

2178 **ἐφάπαξ, *ephapax***, adv. GK: *2384* [→ *1909+530*]. once for all; at the same time:– once [3], at once [1], once for all [1]

2179 **Ἐφεσῖνος, *Ephesinos***, a.pr.g. GK: *2385* [→ *2181*]. Ephesian:– Ephesus [1]

2180 **Ἐφέσιος, *Ephesios***, a.pr.g. GK: *2386* [→ *2181*]. Ephesian, person of Ephesus:– Ephesians [5], Ephesian [1], of Ephesus [1]

2181 **Ἔφεσος, *Ephesos***, n.pr. GK: *2387* [→ *2179, 2180*]. Ephesus:– Ephesus [15]

2182 **ἐφευρετής, *epheuretēs***, n. GK: *2388* [→ *1909+2147*]. inventor, contriver:– inventors [1]

2183 **ἐφημερία, *ephēmeria***, n. GK: *2389* [→ *1909+2250*]. (priestly) division, group, class:– course [2]

2184 **ἐφήμερος, *ephēmeros***, a. GK: *2390* [→ *1909+2250*]. daily, for the day:– daily [1]

2185 **ἐφικνέομαι, *ephikneomai***, v. GK: *2391* [→ *1909+2425*]. to come (to), reach (to):– reached [1], reach [1]

2186 **ἐφίστημι, *ephistēmi***, v. GK: *2392* [→ *1909+2476*]. to approach, come near, stand beside, stop; to be imminent, at hand:– came upon [5], stood by [2], stood [2], assaulted [1], at hand [1], came to [1], came [1], come upon [1], cometh upon [1], come [1], coming in [1], instant [1], present [1], standing by [1], stood before [1]

2187 **Ἐφραίμ, *Ephraim***, n.pr. GK: *2394*. Ephraim, "*doubly fruitful*":– Ephraim [1]

2188 **ἐφφαθά, *ephphatha***, l.[v.]. GK: *2395*. ephphatha!, be opened!:– ephphatha [1]

2189 **ἔχθρα, *echthra***, n. GK: *2397* [→ *2190*]. hostility, hatred, antagonism:– enmity [5], hatred [1]

2190 **ἐχθρός, *echthros***, a. GK: *2398* [→ *2189*]. (n.) enemy:– enemies [19], enemy [10], foes [2], enemy (*+444*) [1]

2191 **ἔχιδνα, *echidna***, n. GK: *2399*. viper, snake:– vipers [4], viper [1]

2192 **ἔχω, *echō***, v. GK: *2400* [→ *183, 414, 420, 430, 463, 472, 566, 567, 568, 1758, 1777, 1836, 1838, 1851, 1907, 2517, 2558, 2697, 2722, 3348, 3352, 3353, 3562, 3794, 3930, 4023, 4042, 4122, 4123, 4124, 4284, 4337, 4465, 4778, 4830, 4910, 4912, 4928, 4975, 5242, 5247, 5254; cf. 2134, 4976*]. (tr.) to have, hold, keep; (intr.) to be:– have [262], hath [131], had [111], having [84], hast [27], need (*+5532*) [10], are [5], were [5], with child (*+1064+1722*) [5], sick (*+2560*) [4], next [3], thank (*+5485*) [3], was [3], am [2], counted [2], count [2], holding [2], hold [2], is [2], must [2], needeth (*+5532*) [2], accompany [1], art [1], been [1], began to amend (*+2866*) [1], being [1], be [1], cannot (*+3756*) [1], could [1], diseased (*+2560*) [1], do [1], eat (*+3542*) [1], enjoy [1], fear (*+5401*) [1], following [1], go to law (*+2917*) [1], held [1], hold fast [1], is of [1], kept [1], lacked (*+3361*) [1], lieth at the point of death (*+2079*) [1], needed (*+5532*) [1], needest (*+5532*) [1], needful (*+318*) [1], possessed with [1], possessed [1], recover (*+2573*) [1], reigneth (*+932*) [1], rest (*+372*) [1], retain [1], sabbath day's journey (*+3598+4521*) [1], sick people (*+2560*) [1], took [1], trembled (*+5156*) [1], uncircumcised (*+203*) [1], using [1], with [1]

2193 **ἕως, *heōs***, c.&pp.*. GK: *2401*. up to, until:– unto [31], until [23], till (*+302*) [16], to [16], till [14], till (*+3739*) [9], how long (*+4219*) [7], until (*+302*) [5], until (*+3739*) [5], while [5], as far as [3], hitherto (*+737*) [2], till (*+3748*) [2], until (*+3748*) [2], while (*+3739*) [2], even (*+2532*) [1], even [1], no not one (*+1520+3756*) [1], thus far (*+3778*) [1], up to [1], whiles (*+3748*) [1]

2194 **Ζαβουλών, *Zaboulōn***, n.pr. GK: *2404*. Zebulun, "*honor*":– Zabulon [3]

2195 **Ζακχαῖος, *Zakchaios***, n.pr. GK: *2405*. Zacchaeus, "*righteous one, pure one*":– Zaccheus [3]

2196 **Ζάρα, *Zara***, n.pr. GK: *2406*. Zerah, "*dawning, shining* or *flashing [red or scarlet] light*":– Zara [1]

2197 **Ζαχαρίας, *Zacharias***, n.pr. GK: *2408*. Zechariah, "*Yahweh remembers*":– Zacharias [11]

2198 **ζάω, *zaō***, v. GK: *2409* [→ *326, 329, 2221, 2222, 2225, 2226, 2227, 4800, 4806*]. to be alive, to live a life; in the NT this can also refer to the resurrection life, Jesus Christ is then "the Living One":– live [54], living [34], liveth [24], alive [15], lived [4], quick [4], lively [3], livest [2], lifetime [1], life [1]

2199 **Ζεβεδαῖος, *Zebedaios***, n.pr. GK: *2411*. Zebedee, "*Yahweh bestows*":– Zebedee [10], Zebedee's [2]

2200 **ζεστός, *zestos***, a. GK: *2412* [→ *2204*]. hot:– hot [3]

2201 **ζεῦγος, *zeugos***, n. GK: *2414* [→ *2218*]. yoke; by extension: a pair:– pair [1], yoke [1]

2202 **ζευκτηρία, *zeuktēria***, n. GK: *2415* [→ *2218*]. rope, band:– bands [1]

2203 **Ζεύς, *Zeus***, n.pr. GK: *2416* [→ *1356, 1359, 1361, 2105, 2211*]. Zeus, "*shine, bright*":– Jupiter [2]

2204 **ζέω, *zeō***, v. GK: *2417* [→ *2200; cf. 2205, 2219*]. to have great fervor, as a fig. extension something boiling or seething, not found in the NT:– fervent [2]

2205 **ζῆλος, *zēlos***, n. GK: *2419* [→ *2206, 2207, 2208, 3863; cf. 2204*]. zeal, ardent concern, enthusiasm, an attitude or emotion of deep, earnest concern; jealousy, envy, rage, morally corrupt zealous ill will:– zeal [6], envying [4], indignation [2], emulations [1], envyings [1], envy [1], fervent mind [1], jealousy [1]

2206 **ζηλόω, *zēloō***, v. GK: *2418 & 2420* [→ *2205*]. to desire, eagerly desire, show zeal, feel an attitude or emotion of deep concern; to be jealous, envious, to experience morally corrupt zealous ill will; covet, as a negative attitude of lust and desire for another's possessions:– desire [2], moved with envy [2], affect [1], covet earnestly [1], covet [1], envieth [1], jealous [1], zealously affected [1], zealously affect [1], zealous [1]

2207 **ζηλωτής, *zēlōtēs***, n. GK: *2421* [→ *2205*]. zealot, enthusiast, adherent, one who has the feelings or attitudes of deep commitment to a person or cause; in the NT this can technically refer to a person who belonged to a nationalist Jewish group that sought independence from Rome:– zealous [5]

2208 **Ζηλωτής, *Zēlōtēs***, n. GK: *2421* [→ *2205*]. same as *2207*; zealot, enthusiast, adherent, one who has the feelings or attitudes of deep commitment to a person or cause; in the NT this can technically refer to a person who belonged to a nationalist Jewish group that sought independence from Rome:– Zelotes [2]

2209 **ζημία, *zēmia***, n. GK: *2422* [→ *2210*]. loss, damage:– loss [3], damage [1]

2210 **ζημιόω, *zēmioō***, v. GK: *2423* [→ *2209*]. (pass.) to forfeit, suffer loss or damage:– lose [2], cast away [1], receive damage [1], suffer loss [1], suffered loss [1]

2211 **Ζηνᾶς, *Zēnas***, n.pr. GK: *2424* [→ *2203*]. Zenas, "*gift of Zeus*":– Zenas [1]

2212 **ζητέω, *zēteō***, v. GK: *2426* [→ *327, 1567, 1934, 2213, 2214, 4802, 4803, 4804*]. to look for, seek out; to try to obtain, desire to possess, strive for:– seek [44], sought [31], seeking [11], seeketh [9], seek for [3], sought for [3], desiring [2], inquire [2], required [2], seekest [2], about [1], desired [1], endeavoured [1], go about [1], goeth about [1], going about [1], seek after [1], seeking for [1], sought out [1], went about [1]

2213 **ζήτημα, *zētēma***, n. GK: *2427* [→ *2212*]. question for discussion, point of dispute, controversy:– questions [3], question [2]

2214 **ζήτησις, *zētēsis***, n. GK: *1700 & 2428* [→ *2212*]. argument, debate, controversy, discussion:– questions [5], question [1]

2215 **ζιζάνιον, *zizanion***, n. GK: *2429*. weed, darnel, or some other troublesome weed:– tares [8]

2216 **Ζοροβαβέλ, *Zorobabel***, n.pr. GK: *2431*. Zerubbabel, "*offspring of Babylon*":– Zorobabel [3]

2217 **ζόφος, *zophos***, n. GK: *2432*. blackness, darkness, gloom:– darkness [2], blackness [1], mist [1]

2218 **ζυγός, *zygos***, n. GK: *2433* [→ *2086, 2201, 2202, 4801, 4805, 5268*]. yoke, a frame and cross bar placed on draft animals to pull various objects; pair of scales, ancient balance-pan scales. "To be under a yoke" means to be in an oppressed condition such as slavery:– yoke [5], pair of balances [1]

2219 **ζύμη, *zymē***, n. GK: *2434* [→ *106, 2220; cf. 2204*]. yeast, leaven:– leaven [13]

2220 **ζυμόω, *zymoō***, v. GK: *2435* [→ *2219*]. to leaven, ferment, work as yeast:– leavened [2], leaveneth [2]

2221 **ζωγρέω, *zōgreō***, v. GK: *2436* [→ *2198+61*]. to capture (alive):– catch [1], taken captive [1]

2222 **ζωή, *zōē***, n. GK: *2437* [→ *2198*]. life, physical or spiritual; with *166*, "eternal life":– life [133], lifetime [1]

2223 **ζώνη, *zōnē***, n. GK: *2438* [→ *2224*]. belt, sash:– girdle [5], girdles [1], purses [1], purse [1]

2224 **ζώννυμι, *zōnnymi***, v. GK: *2439 & 2440* [→ *328, 1241, 2223, 4024, 5269*]. to dress, clothe oneself, put on a belt or sash:– girdedst [1], gird [1]

2225 **ζωογονέω, *zōogoneō***, v. GK: *2441* [→ *2198+1096*]. to give life, make alive; to preserve life, keep alive:– live [1], preserve [1]

2226 **ζῷον, *zōon***, n. GK: *2442* [→ *2198*]. living creature, animal:– beasts [16], beast [7]

2227 **ζωοποιέω, *zōopoieō***, v. GK: *2443* [→ *2198+4160*]. to make alive, give life to:– quickeneth [5], quickened [2], given life [1], giveth life [1], made alive [1], quickening [1], quicken [1]

2228 **ἤ, *ē***, pt.disj. or comp. GK: *2445* [→ *2260, 2273*]. or; (in a series) either…or; (in comparison) than:– or [260], than [36], either [8], before (*+4250*) [6], nor [5], or else [5], and [4], neither [3], what [3], but [2], rather than [2], but (*+3756+4183*) [1], except [1], rather [1], save [1], than (*+235*) [1], than (*+3123*) [1], yea [1]

2229 **ἦ, *ē***, adv. GK: *2446*. truly:– surely (*+3375*) [1]

ἡ, ***hē***. See ***3588***.

ἥ, ***hē***. See ***3739***.

ᾗ, ***ēi***. See ***5600***.

2230 **ἡγεμονεύω, *hēgemoneuō***, v. GK: *2448* [→ *71*]. to govern, lead, rule:– governor [2]

2231 **ἡγεμονία, *hēgemonia***, n. GK: *2449* [→ *71*]. reign, leadership, rulership:– reign [1]

2232 **ἡγεμών, *hēgemōn***, n. GK: *2450* [→ *71*]. ruler, prince, governor, prefect, procurator:– governor [16], governors [2], rulers [2], governor's [1], princes [1]

2233 **ἡγέομαι, *hēgeomai***, v. GK: *2451* [→ *71*]. to lead, rule, guide; to consider, think, regard:– count [7], chief [3], counted [3], have the rule over [3], esteem [2], governor [2], think [2], thought [2], account [1], esteeming [1], judged [1], supposed [1]

2234 **ἡδέως, *hēdeōs***, adv. GK: *2452* [→ *2237*]. gladly, with delight; in the superlative, most gladly, with utter delight:– gladly [3]

2235 **ἤδη, *ēdē***, adv. GK: *2453*. already, by this time, even now:– now [35], already [17], yet [2], by this time [1], far spent (*+2827*) [1], now about (*+1161*) [1], now already [1], now high time (*+5610*) [1], now ready [1]

2236 **ἥδιστα, *hēdista***, adv.super. of *2234*. GK: *2452* [→ *2237*]. most gladly, with utter delight:– most gladly [1], very gladly [1]

2237 **ἡδονή, *hēdonē***, n. GK: *2454* [→ *780, 829, 2234, 2236, 2238, 4913, 5369*]. pleasure, desire, enjoyment, usually with a negative sense:– lusts [2], pleasures [2], pleasure [1]

2238 **ἡδύοσμον, *hēdyosmon***, n. GK: *2455* [→ *2237+3605*]. mint:– mint [2]

2239 **ἦθος, *ēthos***, n. GK: *2456* [→ *1485*]. character, habit and custom:– manners [1]

2240 **ἥκω, *hēkō***, v. GK: *2457* [→ *433, 2520*]. to come, to have come, be present:– come [24], came [3]

2241 **ἠλί[1], *ēli*[1]**, l.[n.+p.]. GK: *2458* [cf. *1682*]. Eli [Hebrew: my God]:– eli [2]

2242 **Ἠλί[2], *Ēli*[2]**, n.pr. GK: *2459*. Heli, "*ascent [to God]*":– Heli [1]

2243 **Ἠλίας, *Ēlias***, n.pr. GK: *2460*. Elijah, "*Yahweh is [my] God*":– Elias [30]

2244 **ἡλικία, *hēlikia***, n. GK: *2461* [→ *2245*]. life, time in life, age; stature, height:– stature [5], age [2], age (*+2540*) [1]

2245 **ἡλίκος, *hēlikos***, a. GK: *2462* [→ *2244, 4080, 4915, 5082*]. how much, how great, how large:– how great [1], what great [1]

2246 **ἥλιος, *hēlios***, n. GK: *2463* [cf. *1506*]. sun:– sun [30], east (*+395*) [2]

2247 **ἧλος, *hēlos***, n. GK: *2464* [→ *4338*]. nail (used in crucifixion):– nails [2]

2248 **ἡμᾶς, *hēmas***, p.pers.acc.pl. of *1473* GK: *1609* [→ *1473*]. us, to us; see *1473*:–

2249 ἡμεῖς, ***hēmeis***, p.pers.nom.pl. of *1473* GK: *1609* [→ *1473*]. we, us, ourselves; see *1473*:–

2250 ἡμέρα, ***hēmera***, n. GK: *2465* [→ *2183, 2184, 2522, 3314, 3574, 3637, 4594*]. day, time of the day, time, indefinite period of time. "The children of the day" means "God's people," who walk in light. "The day of the Lord" and "the day of Christ" are periods of judgment and vindication, longer than twenty-four hours:– day [199], days [154], daily (*+2596*) [15], this day (*+4594*) [3], time [3], years [2], a good while ago (*+575+744*) [1], age (*+1722+4260*) [1], alway (*+3588+3956*) [1], another[S] [1], at midday (*+3319*) [1], daily (*+1538+2596*) [1], daily (*+2596+3956*) [1], daily (*+3956*) [1], day by day (*+2596*) [1], day time [1], day's [1], ever (*+165*) [1], good while (*+2425*) [1], judgment [1], needeth (*+318*) [1]

2251 ἡμέτερος, ***hēmeteros***, a. GK: *2466* [→ *1473*]. our, our own:– our [6], ours [2]

2252 ἤμην, ***ēmēn***, v.1.imperf. of *1510*. GK: *1639* [→ *1510*]. I was; see *1510*:–

2253 ἡμιθανής, ***hēmithanēs***, a. GK: *2467* [→ *2255+2348*]. half dead:– half dead [1]

2254 ἡμῖν, ***hēmin***, p.pers.dat.pl. of *1473*. GK: *1609* [→ *1473*]. for us, to us, our; see *1473*:–

2255 ἥμισυς, ***hēmisys***, a. GK: *2468* [→ *2253, 2256, 2256*]. half (temporal and spacial):– half [5]

2256 ἡμιώριον, ***hēmiōrion***, n. GK: *2469 & 2470* [→ *2255+5610*]. half an hour:– half an hour [1]

2257 ἡμῶν, ***hēmōn***, p.pers.gen.pl. of *1473*. GK: *1609* [→ *1473*]. our; see *1473*:–

2258 ἦν, ***ēn***, v.3.imperf. of *1510*. GK: *1639* [→ *1510*]. he, she, it was; see *1510*:–

2259 ἡνίκα, ***hēnika***, pt. GK: *2471*. when, whenever, at the time when:– when (*+302*) [2]

2260 ἤπερ, ***ēper***, pt.comp. GK: *2472* [→ *2228+4007*]. than:– than [1]

2261 ἤπιος, ***ēpios***, a. GK: *2473*. gentle, kind:– gentle [2]

2262 Ἤρ, ***Ēr***, n.pr. GK: *2474*. Er, "*watcher, watchful*": Er [1]

2263 ἤρεμος, ***ēremos***, a. GK: *2475*. peaceful, quiet, tranquil:– quiet [1]

2264 Ἡρῴδης, ***Hērōdēs***, n.pr. GK: *2476* [→ *2265, 2266, 2267*]. Herod:– Herod [40], Herod's [4]

2265 Ἡρῳδιανοί, ***Hērōdianoi***, n.pr.g. GK: *2477* [→ *2264*]. Herodians:– Herodians [3]

2266 Ἡρῳδιάς, ***Hērōdias***, n.pr. GK: *2478* [→ *2264*]. Herodias:– Herodias [4], Herodias' [2]

2267 Ἡρῳδίων, ***Hērōdiōn***, n.pr. GK: *2479* [→ *2264*]. Herodion:– Herodion [1]

2268 Ἡσαΐας, ***Ēsaias***, n.pr. GK: *2480*. Isaiah, "*Yahweh saves*":– Esaias [21]

2269 Ἠσαῦ, ***Ēsau***, n.pr. GK: *2481*. Esau, "*hairy*":– Esau [3]

2270 ἡσυχάζω, ***hēsychazō***, v. GK: *2483* [→ *2271, 2272*]. to be silent, have no objection; to rest; to lead a quiet life; to give up:– held peace [2], ceased [1], quiet [1], rested [1]

2271 ἡσυχία, ***hēsychia***, n. GK: *2484* [→ *2270*]. quietness, silence; settling down, lack of disturbance:– silence [3], quietness [1]

2272 ἡσύχιος, ***hēsychios***, a. GK: *2485* [→ *2270*]. quiet:– peaceable [1], quiet [1]

2273 ἤτοι, ***ētoi***, pt.disj. GK: *2486* [→ *2228+5104*]. (in a series) whether…or:– whether [1]

2274 ἡττάομαι, ***hēttaomai***, v. GK: *2273 & 2487* [→ *2276*]. to be inferior, lesser, worse off, with a focus on the manner in which someone is treated:– overcome [2], inferior [1]

2275 ἥττημα, ***hēttēma***, n. GK: *2488* [→ *2276*]. loss, defeat:– diminishing [1], fault [1]

2276 ἥττων, ***hetton***, a. GK: *2482 & 2489* [→ *2274, 2275*]. for the worse; (adv.) less:– less [1], worse [1]

2277 ἤτω, ***ētō***, v.3.s.imper. of *1510*. GK: *1639* [→ *1510*]. let it be:–

2278 ἠχέω, ***ēcheō***, v. GK: *2490* [→ *2279*]. to resound, ring out:– roaring [1], sounding [1]

2279 ἦχος[1], ***ēchos***[1], n. GK: *2491 & 2492 & 2493* [→ *1837, 2278, 2727*]. sound, tone, blast (of a trumpet); news, report:– sound [2], fame [1]

2280 Θαδδαῖος, ***Thaddaios***, n.pr. GK: *2497* [cf. *3002*]. Thaddaeus, "[poss.] *nipple*":– Thaddeus [2]

2281 θάλασσα, ***thalassa***, n. GK: *2498* [→ *1337, 3864; cf. 217*]. sea, lake, a general term for any natural body of water:– sea [92]

2282 θάλπω, ***thalpō***, v. GK: *2499*. to care for, cherish, comfort:– cherisheth [2]

2283 Θαμάρ, ***Thamar***, n.pr. GK: *2500*. Tamar, "*date palm*":– Thamar [1]

2284 θαμβέω, ***thambeō***, v. GK: *2501* [→ *2285*]. (pass.) to be amazed, astounded:– amazed [2], astonished [2]

2285 θάμβος, ***thambos***, n. GK: *2502* [→ *1568, 1569, 2284*]. amazement, astonishment, wonder:– amazed [1], astonished (*+4023*) [1], wonder [1]

2286 θανάσιμος, ***thanasimos***, a. GK: *2503* [→ *2348*]. deadly:– deadly [1]

2287 θανατηφόρος, ***thanatēphoros***, a. GK: *2504* [→ *2348+5342*]. deadly:– deadly [1]

2288 θάνατος, ***thanatos***, n. GK: *2505* [→ *2348*]. death:– death [116], deadly [2], deaths [1]

2289 θανατόω, ***thanatoō***, v. GK: *2506* [→ *2348*]. to put to death, kill:– put to death [7], killed [2], dead [1], mortify [1]

θάνω, ***thanō***. See **2348**.

2290 θάπτω, ***thaptō***, v. GK: *2507* [→ *4916; cf. 5028*]. to bury, entomb:– buried [7], bury [4]

2291 Θάρα, ***Thara***, n.pr. GK: *2508*. Terah:– Thara [1]

2292 θαρρέω, ***tharreō***, v. GK: *2509* [→ *2294*]. to have confidence, be bold:– bold [2], confident [2], boldly [1], have confidence [1]

2293 θαρσέω, ***tharseō***, v. GK: *2510* [→ *2294*]. take heart!, take courage!, cheer up!:– be of good cheer [5], be of good comfort [3]

2294 θάρσος, ***tharsos***, n. GK: *2511* [→ *2292, 2293*]. encouragement, courage:– courage [1]

2295 θαῦμα, ***thauma***, n. GK: *2512* [→ *2296*]. wonder, marvel, astonishment:– admiration [1]

2296 θαυμάζω, ***thaumazō***, v. GK: *1703 & 2513* [→ *2295, 2297, 2298; cf. 2300*]. to be amazed (at), in wonder, astonished, surprised:– marvelled [21], wondered [11], marvel [9], wonder [2], admired [1], having in admiration (*+4383*) [1], wondering [1]

2297 θαυμάσιος, ***thaumasios***, a. GK: *2514* [→ *2296*]. wonderful, remarkable:– wonderful [1]

2298 θαυμαστός, ***thaumastos***, a. GK: *2515* [→ *2296*]. wonderful, marvelous, remarkable:– marvellous [6], marvel [1]

2299 θεά, ***thea***, n. GK: *2516* [→ *2316*]. goddess:– goddess [3]

2300 θεάομαι, ***theaomai***, v. GK: *2517* [cf. *2296, 2302, 2334*]. to see, look at; visit:– saw [8], seen [8], see [4], beheld [2], look on [1], looked upon [1]

2301 θεατρίζω, ***theatrizō***, v. GK: *2518* [→ *2302*]. to publicly expose:– made a gazingstock [1]

2302 θέατρον, ***theatron***, n. GK: *2519* [→ *2301; cf. 2300*]. theatre, spectacle, theatrical play:– theatre [2], spectacle [1]

2303 θεῖον, ***theion***, n. GK: *2520* [→ *2306; cf. 2316 or* 2380]. sulfur:– brimstone [7]

2304 θεῖος, ***theios***, a. GK: *2521* [→ *2316*]. divine:– divine [2], Godhead [1]

2305 θειότης, ***theiotēs***, n. GK: *2522* [→ *2316*]. divine nature, divinity:– Godhead [1]

2306 θειώδης, ***theiōdēs***, a. GK: *2523* [→ *2303*]. (yellow) as sulfur:– brimstone [1]

θελέω, ***theleō***. See **2309**.

2307 θέλημα, ***thelēma***, n. GK: *2525* [→ *2309*]. will, decision, desire:– will [62], desires [1], pleasure [1]

2308 θέλησις, ***thelēsis***, n. GK: *2526* [→ *2309*]. will, decision:– will [1]

2309 θέλω, ***thelō***, v. GK: *2527* [→ *1479, 2307, 2308*]. to will, decide, want to; wish, desire:– would [69], will [68], wilt [21], desire [9], willing [8], have [5], wouldest [4], desirous [3], desiring [2], listed [2], willingly [2], desired [1], desireth [1], disposed [1], forward [1], had rather [1], intending [1], it hath pleased [1], listeth [1], love [1], meaneth (*+1510*) [1], mean [1], pleased [1], so[S] [1], voluntary [1], will have [1], willeth [1], would have [1], would that [1]

2310 θεμέλιος, ***themelios***, n. GK: *2528 & 2529* [→ *2311; cf. 5087*]. foundation:– foundation [12], foundations [4]

2311 θεμελιόω, ***themelioō***, v. GK: *2530* [→ *2310*]. to lay a foundation; to make steadfast:– founded [2], grounded [2], laid the foundation [1], settle [1]

2312 θεοδίδακτος, ***theodidaktos***, a. GK: *2531* [→ *2316+1321*]. taught by God:– taught of God [1]

2312' θεολόγος, ***theologos***, n. GK: *2532* [→ *2316+3004*]. one who speaks of God or divine things:–

2313 θεομαχέω, ***theomacheō***, v. GK: *2533* [→ *2316+3163*]. to fight against God:– fight against God [1]

2314 θεομάχος, ***theomachos***, a. GK: *2534* [→ *2316+3163*]. fighting against God:– fight against God [1]

2315 θεόπνευστος, ***theopneustos***, a. GK: *2535* [→ *2316+4154*]. God-breathed, inspired by God, referring to a communication from deity:– given by inspiration of God [1]

2316 θεός, ***theos***, n. GK: *2536* [→ *112, 2299, 2304, 2305, 2312, 2312', 2313, 2314, 2315, 2317, 2318, 2319, 2320, 2321, 2333, 5095, 5377; cf. 2303*]. God, usually refers to the one true God; in a very few contexts it refers to a (pagan) god or goddess. The "Son of God" as a title of Jesus emphasizes his unique relationship to the Father. "The god of this age" refers to the devil:– God/god [1309], God's [15], gods [8], godly [6], Godward [2], exceeding fair (*+791+3588*) [1], godly (*+2596*) [1]

2317 θεοσέβεια, ***theosebeia***, n. GK: *2537* [→ *2316+4576*]. worship of God, reverence for God:– godliness [1]

2318 θεοσεβής, ***theosebēs***, a. GK: *2538* [→ *2316+4576*]. godly, God-fearing, devout:– worshipper of God [1]

2319 θεοστυγής, ***theostygēs***, a. GK: *2539* [→ *2316+4767*]. God-hating:– haters of God [1]

2320 θεότης, ***theotēs***, n. GK: *2540* [→ *2316*]. Deity, Divinity:– Godhead [1]

2321 Θεόφιλος, ***Theophilus***, n.pr. GK: *2541* [→ *2316+5384*]. Theophilus, "*friend of God*":– Theophilus [2]

2322 θεραπεία, ***therapeia***, n. GK: *2542* [→ *2324*]. service, care; (hence) healing:– healing [2], household [2]

2323 θεραπεύω, ***therapeuō***, v. GK: *2543* [→ *2324*]. to serve, to give help, take care of another; by extension: to heal, cure; (pass.) to be healed:– healed [25], heal [10], cured [3], healing [3], cure [2], worshipped [1]

2324 θεράπων, ***therapōn***, n. GK: *2544* [→ *2322, 2323*]. servant, a person who renders service:– servant [1]

2325 θερίζω, ***therizō***, v. GK: *2545* [→ *2329*]. to reap, harvest:– reap [13], reapeth [3], reaped [2], reaping [2], reapest [1]

2326 θερισμός, ***therismos***, n. GK: *2546* [→ *2329*]. harvest:– harvest [13]

2327 θεριστής, ***theristēs***, n. GK: *2547* [→ *2329*]. harvester, reaper:– reapers [2]

2328 θερμαίνω, ***thermainō***, v. GK: *2548* [→ *2329*]. (mid.) to keep warm, warm (oneself):– warmed [5], warming [1]

2329 θέρμη, ***thermē***, n. GK: *2549* [→ *2325, 2326, 2327, 2328, 2330*]. heat:– heat [1]

2330 θέρος, ***theros***, n. GK: *2550* [→ *2329*]. summer:– summer [3]

2331 Θεσσαλονικεύς, ***Thessalonikeus***, n.pr.g. GK: *2552* [→ *2332*]. Thessalonian, "*from Thessalonica*":– Thessalonians [5], Thessalonica [1]

2332 Θεσσαλονίκη, ***Thessalonikē***, n.pr. GK: *2553* [→ *2331*]. Thessalonica:– Thessalonica [5]

2333 Θευδᾶς, ***Theudas***, n.pr. GK: *2554* [→ *2316+1435*]. Theudas, "*gift of God*":– Theudas [1]

θέω, ***theō***. See **5087**.

2334 θεωρέω, ***theoreo***, v. GK: *2555* [→ *333, 2335, 3865, cf. 2300*]. to see, look at, watch closely; perceive, experience:– see [17], seeth [10], saw [9], beheld [4], beholding [4], perceive [4], behold [3], seen [2], consider [1], looking on [1], seeing [1], seest [1]

2335 θεωρία, ***theōria***, n. GK: *2556* [→ *2334*]. sight, spectacle:– sight [1]

2336 θήκη, ***thēkē***, n. GK: *2557* [→ *5087*]. sheath, scabbard:– sheath [1]

2337 **θηλάζω, *thēlazō***, v. GK: *2558* [→ *330, 2338*]. to nurse a baby; (n.) nursing infant:– give suck [3], gave suck [1], sucked [1], sucklings [1]

2338 **θῆλυς, *thēlys***, a. GK: *2559* [→ *2337*]. female, pertaining to women:– female [3], woman [1], women [1]

2339 **θήρα, *thēra***, n. GK: *2560* [→ *2342*]. trap, net:– trap [1]

2340 **θηρεύω, *thēreuō***, v. GK: *2561* [→ *2342*]. to catch in a mistake, a fig. extension of catching hunted prey, not found in the NT:– catch [1]

2341 **θηριομαχέω, *thēriomacheō***, v. GK: *2562* [→ *2342+3163*]. to fight wild animals:– fought with beasts [1]

2342 **θηρίον, *thērion***, n. GK: *2563* [→ *2339, 2340, 2341*]. (wild) animal, (fiendish) beast, snake:– beast [40], beasts [3], wild beasts [3]

2343 **θησαυρίζω, *thēsaurizō***, v. GK: *2564* [→ *2344*]. to store up, gather, reserve:– lay up [3], heaped treasure together [1], in store [1], kept in store [1], layeth up treasure [1], treasurest up [1]

2344 **θησαυρός, *thēsauros***, n. GK: *2565* [→ *596, 597, 2343; cf. 5087*]. treasure, what is stored up; storeroom:– treasure [13], treasures [5]

2345 **θιγγάνω, *thinganō***, v. GK: *2566*. to touch:– touch [2], handle [1]

2346 **θλίβω, *thlibō***, v. GK: *2567* [→ *598, 2347, 4918*]. (act.) to press upon, crowd up to; cause trouble; (pass.) to be narrow; to be pressed, troubled, persecuted:– afflicted [3], troubled [3], narrow [1], suffer tribulation [1], throng [1], trouble [1]

2347 **θλῖψις, *thlipsis***, n. GK: *2568* [→ *2346*]. trouble, distress, oppression, tribulation:– tribulation [18], affliction [11], afflictions [6], tribulations [3], trouble [3], afflicted [1], anguish [1], burdened [1], persecution [1]

2348 **θνήσκω, *thnēskō***, v. GK: *2569* [→ *110, 599, 1935, 2253, 2286, 2287, 2288, 2289, 2349, 4880*]. (perf.) to have died, be dead:– dead [11], dead man [1], died [1]

2349 **θνητός, *thnētos***, a. GK: *2570* [→ *2348*]. mortal:– mortal [5], mortality [1]

2350 **θορυβέω, *thorybeō***, v. GK: *2572* [→ *2351*]. to start a riot, throw into disorder; (pass.) to be alarmed, in commotion, distressed:– make ado [1], making noise [1], set on an uproar [1], trouble [1]

2351 **θόρυβος, *thorybos***, n. GK: *2573* [→ *2350*]. uproar, riot, commotion, disturbance:– tumult [4], uproar [3]

2352 **θραύω, *thrauō***, v. GK: *2575*. (pass.) to be oppressed, downtrodden, a fig. extension of an object broken in pieces:– bruised [1]

2353 **θρέμμα, *thremma***, n. GK: *2576* [→ *5142*]. livestock, domestic animal (usually a sheep or goat):– cattle [1]

2354 **θρηνέω, *thrēneō***, v. GK: *2577* [→ *2355, 2360*]. to sing a funeral dirge, lament, mourn:– mourned [2], lamented [1], lament [1]

2355 **θρῆνος, *thrēnos***, n. GK: *2578* [→ *2354*]. dirge, funeral song:– lamentation [1]

2356 **θρησκεία, *thrēskeia***, n. GK: *2579* [→ *2357*]. religion, worship:– religion [3], worshipping [1]

2357 **θρῆσκος, *thrēskos***, a. GK: *2580* [→ *1479, 2356*]. religious:– religious [1]

2358 **θριαμβεύω, *thriambeuō***, v. GK: *2581*. to lead in a triumphal procession:– causeth to triumph [1], triumphing over [1]

2359 **θρίξ, *thrix***, n. GK: *2582* [→ *5155*]. hair, a hair:– hair [10], hairs [5]

2360 **θροέω, *throeō***, v. GK: *2583* [→ *2354*]. (pass.) to be alarmed, disturbed:– troubled [3]

2361 **θρόμβος, *thrombos***, n. GK: *2584*. drop:– drops [1]

2362 **θρόνος, *thronos***, n. GK: *2585*. throne:– throne [50], seats [4], thrones [4], seat [3]

2363 **Θυάτειρα, *Thyateira***, n.pr. GK: *2587*. Thyatira:– Thyatira [4]

2364 **θυγάτηρ, *thygatēr***, n. GK: *2588* [→ *2365*]. daughter, by extension a term of endearment toward (younger) woman:– daughter [24], daughters [5]

2365 **θυγάτριον, *thygatrion***, n. GK: *2589* [→ *2364*]. little daughter:– little daughter [1], young daughter [1]

2366 **θύελλα, *thyella***, n. GK: *2590* [→ *2372*]. storm:– tempest [1]

2367 **θύϊνος, *thyinos***, a. GK: *2591* [→ *2380*]. citron, from the citron tree (a scented wood):– thyine [1]

2368 **θυμίαμα, *thymiama***, n. GK: *2592* [→ *2380*]. incense; burning incense, offering of incense:– incense [4], odours [2]

2369 **θυμιατήριον, *thymiatērion***, n. GK: *2593* [→ *2380*]. incense altar:– censer [1]

2370 **θυμιάω, *thymiaō***, v. GK: *2594* [→ *2380*]. to burn incense, offer incense:– burn incense [1]

2371 **θυμομαχέω, *thymomacheō***, v. GK: *2595* [→ *2372+3163*]. to quarrel, be fighting mad:– highly displeased [1]

2372 **θυμός, *thymos***, n. GK: *2596* [→ *120, 1760, 1761, 1937, 1938, 1939, 2114, 2115, 2366, 2371, 2373, 3114, 3115, 3116, 3661, 4288, 4289, 4290*]. wrath, fury, anger, rage, a state of intense displeasure based in some real or perceived wrong. "The anger of God" is due to moral offense and has a focus on righteous punishment:– wrath [14], fierceness [2], indignation [1], wraths [1]

2373 **θυμόω, *thymoō***, v. GK: *2597* [→ *2372*]. (pass.) to become angry:– wroth [1]

2374 **θύρα, *thyra***, n. GK: *2598* [→ *2375, 2376, 2377*]. door, gate, entrance:– door [29], doors [9], gate [1]

2375 **θυρεός, *thyreos***, n. GK: *2599* [→ *2374*]. (long, oblong) shield:– shield [1]

2376 **θυρίς, *thyris***, n. GK: *2600* [→ *2374*]. window:– window [2]

2377 **θυρωρός, *thyrōros***, n. GK: *2601* [→ *2374*]. doorkeeper, watcher (at door or gate):– kept the door [2], porter [2]

2378 **θυσία, *thysia***, n. GK: *2602* [→ *2380*]. sacrifice, offering:– sacrifice [17], sacrifices [12]

2379 **θυσιαστήριον, *thysiastērion***, n. GK: *2603* [→ *2380*]. altar:– altar [22], altars [1]

2380 **θύω, *thyō***, v. GK: *2124 & 2604* [→ *1494, 2367, 2368, 2369, 2370, 2378, 2379; cf. 2303*]. to kill, butcher; to offer sacrifice:– killed [5], kill [3], sacrifice [3], done sacrifice [1], sacrificed [1], slay [1]

2381 **Θωμᾶς, *Thōmas***, n.pr. GK: *2605*. Thomas, "*twin*":– Thomas [12]

2382 **θώραξ, *thōrax***, n. GK: *2606*. breastplate:– breastplates [3], breastplate [2]

2383 **Ἰάϊρος, *Iairos***, n.pr. GK: *2608*. Jairus, "*he gives light*":– Jairus [2]

2384 **Ἰακώβ, *Iakōb***, n.pr. GK: *2609* [→ *2385*]. Jacob, "*follower, replacer, one who follows the heel*":– Jacob [26], Jacob's [1]

2385 **Ἰάκωβος, *Iakōbos***, n.pr. GK: *2610* [→ *2384*]. James, "*follower, replacer, one who follows the heel*":– James [42]

2386 **ἴαμα, *iama***, n. GK: *2611* [→ *2390*]. healing:– healing [2], healings [1]

2387 **Ἰαμβρῆς, *Iambrēs***, n.pr. GK: *2612*. Jambres:– Jambres [1]

2388 **Ἰανναί, *Iannai***, n.pr. GK: *2613*. Jannai:– Janna [1]

2389 **Ἰάννης, *Iannēs***, n.pr. GK: *2614*. Jannes:– Jannes [1]

2390 **ἰάομαι, *iaomai***, v. GK: *2615* [→ *2386, 2392, 2395*]. (mid.) to heal; (pass.) to be healed, freed:– healed [18], heal [7], healing [1], made whole [1], maketh whole [1]

2391 **Ἰάρετ, *Iaret***, n.pr. GK: *2616*. Jared, "*servant*":– Jared [1]

2392 **ἴασις, *iasis***, n. GK: *2617* [→ *2390*]. healing, cure:– cures [1], healing [1], heal [1]

2393 **ἴασπις, *iaspis***, n. GK: *2618*. jasper:– jasper [4]

2394 **Ἰάσων, *Iasōn***, n.pr. GK: *2619*. Jason, "*to heal*":– Jason [5]

2395 **ἰατρός, *iatros***, n. GK: *2620* [→ *2390*]. doctor, physician:– physician [5], physicians [2]

2396 **ἴδε, *ide***, pt. GK: *2623* [→ *1491*]. see!, look!; here, there:– behold [24], lo [3], look [1], see [1]

2397 **ἰδέα, *idea***, n. GK: *1624 & 2624* [→ *1491*]. appearance (usually implies a condition of reality):– countenance [1]

2398 **ἴδιος, *idios***, a. GK: *2625* [→ *2399*]. one's own, private:– his own [47], their own [14], privately (*+2596*) [8], apart (*+2596*) [7], own [6], your own [6], his [5], due [3], her own [2], our own [2], their [2], acquaintance [1], alone (*+2596*) [1], aside (*+2596*) [1], his proper [1], his several [1], home (*+1519+3588*) [1], private [1], proper [1], severally [1], thine own [1]

2399 **ἰδιώτης, *idiōtēs***, n. GK: *2626* [→ *2398*]. ordinary, untrained person, one who does not understand, an inquirer:– unlearned [3], ignorant [1], rude [1]

2400 **ἰδού, *idou***, pt. GK: *2627* [→ *1491*]. look!, suddenly, now; here, there; this particle is used to enliven a Hebrew narrative style, by marking the change of a scene, or emphasize some detail or idea, and is not always translated:– behold [181], lo [29], see [3]

2401 **Ἰδουμαία, *Idoumaia***, n.pr. GK: *2628*. Idumea, "*[land of] Edom*":– Idumea [1]

2402 **ἱδρώς, *hidrōs***, n. GK: *2629*. sweat, perspiration:– sweat [1]

2403 **Ἰεζάβελ, *Iezabel***, n.pr. GK: *2630*. Jezebel, "[poss.] *unexalted, without a husband*":– Jezebel [1]

2404 **Ἱεράπολις, *Hierapolis***, n.pr. GK: *2631* [→ *2413+4172*]. Hierapolis, "*[pagan] sacred city*":– Hierapolis [1]

2405 **ἱερατεία, *hierateia***, n. GK: *2632* [→ *2413*]. priestly office, priesthood:– office of priesthood [1], priest's office [1]

2406 **ἱεράτευμα, *hierateuma***, n. GK: *2633* [→ *2413*]. priesthood:– priesthood [2]

2407 **ἱερατεύω, *hierateuō***, v. GK: *2634* [→ *2413*]. to serve as a priest:– executed the priest's office [1]

2408 **Ἱερεμίας, *Ieremias***, n.pr. GK: *2635*. Jeremiah, "*Yahweh loosens [the womb]; Yahweh lifts up, establishes*":– Jeremie [2], Jeremias [1]

2409 **ἱερεύς, *hiereus***, n. GK: *2636* [→ *2413*]. priest:– priest [17], priests [15]

2410 **Ἱεριχώ, *Ierichō***, n.pr. GK: *2637*. Jericho, "*moon city*":– Jericho [7]

2411 **ἱερόν, *hieron***, n. GK: *2639* [→ *2413*]. temple, sanctuary; of the temple in Jerusalem, it can denote the entire temple complex:– temple [71]

2412 **ἱεροπρεπής, *hieroprepēs***, a. GK: *2640* [→ *2413+4241*]. reverent, pertaining to proper reverence, worthy of reverence:– as becometh holiness [1]

2413 **ἱερός, *hieros***, a. GK: *2641* [→ *748, 749, 2404, 2405, 2406, 2407, 2409, 2411, 2412, 2416, 2417, 2418, 2420*]. sacred, holy, set apart for God; (pl.) the holy things:– holy [2]

2414 **Ἱεροσόλυμα, *Hierosolyma***, n.pr. GK: *2642* [→ *2419*]. Jerusalem:– Jerusalem [59]

2415 **Ἱεροσολυμίτης, *Hierosolymitēs***, n.pr.g. GK: *2643* [→ *2419*]. inhabitant of Jerusalem:– Jerusalem [1], of Jerusalem [1]

2416 **ἱεροσυλέω, *hierosyleō***, v. GK: *2644* [→ *2413+4813*]. to rob temples:– commit sacrilege [1]

2417 **ἱερόσυλος, *hierosylos***, a. GK: *2645* [→ *2413+4813*]. temple robber:– robbers of churches [1]

2418 **ἱερουργέω, *hierourgeō***, v. GK: *2646* [→ *2413+2041*]. to perform priestly duty, serve as a priest:– ministering [1]

2419 **Ἱερουσαλήμ, *Ierousalēm***, n.pr. GK: *2647* [→ *2414, 2415*]. Jerusalem, "*foundation of Shalem [peace]*":– Jerusalem [83]

2420 **ἱερωσύνη, *hierōsynē***, n. GK: *2648* [→ *2413*]. priesthood:– priesthood [4]

2421 **Ἰεσσαί, *Iessai***, n.pr. GK: *2649*. Jesse:– Jesse [5]

2422 **Ἰεφθάε, *Iephthae***, n.pr. GK: *2650*. Jephthah, "*Yahweh opens, frees*":– Jephthae [1]

2423 **Ἰεχονίας, *Iechonias***, n.pr. GK: *2651*. Jeconiah, "*Yahweh supports*":– Jechonias [2]

2424 **Ἰησοῦς, *Iēsous***, n.pr. GK: *2652*. Jesus, Joshua, "*Yahweh saves*":– Jesus [964], Jesus' [10], him[S] [1]

2425 **ἱκανός, *hikanos***, a. GK: *2653* [→ *864, 867, 1338, 2185, 2426, 2427, 2428*]. sufficient, considerable, much; appropriate, competent, worthy, deserving:– many [11], much [6], long [5], worthy [5], sufficient [3], able [1], content (*+4160*) [1], enough [1], good while (*+2250*) [1], great number [1], great [1], large [1], long while (*+1909*) [1], meet [1], security [1], sore [1]

2426 **ἱκανότης, *hikanotēs***, n. GK: *2654* [→ *2425*]. competence, fitness, capability:– sufficiency [1]

2427 **ἱκανόω, *hikanoō***, v. GK: *2655* [→ *2425*]. to make competent, qualify one for, authorize:– made able [1], made meet [1]

2428 **ἱκετηρία, *hiketēria***, n. GK: *2656* [→ *2425*]. petition, supplication:– supplications [1]

2429 **ἰκμάς, *ikmas***, n. GK: *2657*. moisture:– moisture [1]

2430 **Ἰκόνιον, *Ikonion***, n.pr. GK: *2658*. Iconium:– Iconium [6]

2431 **ἱλαρός, *hilaros***, a. GK: *2659* [→ *2433*]. cheerful, without grudging, with an implication of a gracious attitude; note that the transliteration "hilarious" does not communicate the meaning of this attitude:– cheerful [1]

2432 **ἱλαρότης, *hilarotēs***, n. GK: *2660* [→ *2433*]. cheerfully, not grudgingly, with an implication of a gracious attitude:– cheerfulness [1]

2433 **ἱλάσκομαι, *hilaskomai***, v. GK: *2661* [→ *2431, 2432, 2434, 2435, 2436*]. (mid.) to make atonement for, with a focus on the means for accomplishing forgiveness, resulting in reconciliation; (pass.) to have mercy on, be merciful to:– make reconciliation [1], merciful [1]

2434 **ἱλασμός, *hilasmos***, n. GK: *2662* [→ *2433*]. atoning sacrifice, the means of forgiveness; traditionally propitiation:– propitiation [2]

2435 **ἱλαστήριον, *hilastērion***, n. GK: *2663* [→ *2433*]. atoning sacrifice; atonement cover, the place where sins are forgiven; traditionally propitiation or mercy seat:– mercy seat [1], propitiation [1]

2436 **ἵλεως, *hileōs***, a. GK: *2664* [→ *2433*]. forgiving, gracious; (may God be) gracious!, God forbid!:– be it far from [1], merciful [1]

2437 **Ἰλλυρικόν, *Illyrikon***, n.pr. GK: *2665*. Illyricum:– Illyricum [1]

2438 **ἱμάς, *himas***, n. GK: *2666*. (leather) thong, strap:– latchet [3], thongs [1]

2439 **ἱματίζω, *himatizō***, v. GK: *2667* [→ *2066, 2067, 2440, 2441; cf. 294*]. (pass.) to be dressed, clothed:– clothed [2]

2440 **ἱμάτιον, *himation***, n. GK: *2668* [→ *2439*]. clothing, cloak, robe:– garments [15], garment [15], clothes [12], raiment [12], cloke [2], robe [2], vesture [2], apparel [1]

2441 **ἱματισμός, *himatismos***, n. GK: *2669* [→ *2439*]. clothing:– vesture [2], apparelled [1], apparel [1], array [1], raiment [1]

2442 **ἱμείρομαι, *himeiromai***, v. GK: *2670*. to desire, long for:– affectionately desirous [1]

2443 **ἵνα, *hina***, c. GK: *2671* [→ *2444*]. a marker that shows purpose or result: in order that, in order to, so that, then; it can focus on the introduction of a discourse or on the content itself:– that [537], to [71], for to [5], after [1], albeit [1], because [1], must [1], so as [1], so that [1], to the intent that [1], to the intent [1], would [1]

ἵνα μή, *hina mē*. See ***3363***.

2444 **ἱνατί, *hinati***, pt.inter. GK: *2672* [→ *2443+5101*]. why?:– why [5], wherefore [1]

2445 **Ἰόππη, *Ioppē***, n.pr. GK: *2673*. Joppa, "*beautiful*":– Joppa [10]

2446 **Ἰορδάνης, *Iordanēs***, n.pr. GK: *2674*. Jordan, "*descending*":– Jordan [15]

2447 **ἰός, *ios***, n. GK: *2675* [→ *2728*]. poison, venom; corrosion, rust:– poison [2], rust [1]

2448 **Ἰουδά, *Iouda***, n.pr. GK: *2676* [→ *2455*]. Judah, "*praised*":– Juda [3]

2449 **Ἰουδαία, *Ioudaia***, n.pr. GK: *2677* [→ *2455*]. Judea, Judean, "*land of the Judahites*":– Judea [41], Jewry [2]

2450 **ἰουδαΐζω, *ioudaizō***, v. GK: *2678* [→ *2455*]. to follow Jewish customs, live as a Jew:– live as do the Jews [1]

2451 **Ἰουδαϊκός, *Ioudaikos***, a.pr. GK: *2679* [→ *2455*]. Jewish, "*Jewish*":– Jewish [1]

2452 **Ἰουδαϊκῶς, *Ioudaikōs***, adv.pr. GK: *2680* [→ *2455*]. like a Jew, in a Jewish manner, "*Jewish*":– as do the Jews [1]

2453 **Ἰουδαῖος, *Ioudaios***, a.pr.g. GK: *2681* [→ *2455*]. Jewish (people), "*Jewish*":– Jews [167], Jew [22], Jews' [4], Jewess [2], Judea [2]

2454 **Ἰουδαϊσμός, *Ioudaismos***, n.pr. GK: *2682* [→ *2455*]. Judaism, "*Judaism*":– Jews' religion [2]

2455 **Ἰούδας, *Ioudas***, n.pr. GK: *2683* [→ *2448, 2449, 2450, 2451, 2452, 2453, 2454*]. Judah, Judas, Jude, "*praised*":– Judas [33], Juda [8], Jude [1]

2456 **Ἰουλία, *Ioulia***, n.pr. GK: *2684* [→ *2457*]. Julia, "*of Julian [the family of Julius Caesar]*":– Julia [1]

2457 **Ἰούλιος, *Ioulios***, n.pr. GK: *2685* [→ *2456*]. Julius, "*of Julian [the family of Julius Caesar]*":– Julius [2]

2458 **Ἰουνιᾶς, *Iounias***, n.pr. GK: *2687*. Junias:– Junia [1]

2459 **Ἰοῦστος, *Ioustos***, n.pr. GK: *2688*. Justus, "*just*":– Justus [3]

2460 **ἱππεύς, *hippeus***, n. GK: *2689* [→ *2462*]. horseman, cavalryman:– horsemen [2]

2461 **ἱππικός, *hippikos***, a. GK: *2690* [→ *2462*]. mounted (troops), pertaining to a horseman:– horsemen [1]

2462 **ἵππος, *hippos***, n. GK: *2691* [→ *67, 751, 2460, 2461, 5374, 5375, 5376*]. horse:– horse [8], horses [7], horses' [1]

2463 **ἶρις, *iris***, n. GK: *2692*. rainbow; some translate as a brilliant halo or circle of light:– rainbow [2]

2464 **Ἰσαάκ, *Isaak***, n.pr. GK: *2693*. Isaac, "*he [God] laughs*":– Isaac [20]

2465 **ἰσάγγελος, *isangelos***, a. GK: *2694* [→ *2470+32*]. like an angel:– equal unto angels [1]

2466 **Ἰσαχάρ, *Isachar***, n.pr. GK: *2695 & 2704*. Issachar, "*there is a reward [Ge. 30:18]; may [God] show mercy; hired hand*":– Isachar [1]

2467 **ἴσημι, *isēmi***, v. GK: *3857* [cf. *1492*]. to know; presumed to be related to *1492*.:– know [2]

2468 **ἴσθι, *isthi***, v.2.s.imper. of *1510*. GK: *1639* [→ *1510*]. be; see *1510*:–

2469 **Ἰσκαριώτης, *Iskariōtēs***, n.pr.[g.?]. GK: *2696 & 2697*. Iscariot, "*man of Kerioth* or *of the assassins*":– Iscariot [11]

2470 **ἴσος, *isos***, a. GK: *2698* [→ *2465, 2471, 2472, 2473, 2481*]. equal, same; agreeable:– equal [4], agree together (*+1510*) [1], agreed together (*+1510*) [1], as much (*+3588*) [1], like [1]

2471 **ἰσότης, *isotēs***, n. GK: *2699* [→ *2470*]. equality, fairness:– equality [2], equal [1]

2472 **ἰσότιμος, *isotimos***, a. GK: *2700* [→ *2470+5092*]. as precious as, of equal value:– like precious [1]

2473 **ἰσόψυχος, *isopsychos***, a. GK: *2701* [→ *2470+5594*]. like, of like soul, heart or mind:– likeminded [1]

2474 **Ἰσραήλ, *Israēl***, n.pr. GK: *2702* [→ *2475*]. Israel, "*he struggles with God [El]*":– Israel [70]

2475 **Ἰσραηλίτης, *Israēlitēs***, n.pr.g. GK: *2703* [→ *2474*]. Israelite, (one) of Israel:– of Israel [5], Israelites [2], Israelite [2]

2476 **ἵστημι, *histēmi***, v. GK: *2705* [→ *181, 182, 386, 387, 436, 450, 478, 600, 605, 646, 647, 790, 868, 1292, 1339, 1370, 1611, 1764, 1815, 1817, 1839, 1881, 1987, 1988, 1990, 1999, 2139, 2186, 2525, 2688, 2721, 3179, 3936, 4026, 4291, 4368, 4414, 4712, 4713, 4714, 4715, 4739, 4911, 4921, 4955, 4956, 5287; cf. 4716, 4745*]. (intr.) to stand, to stand (firm), be present; to stop; (tr.) to make stand, place, put, establish:– stood [57], stand [34], standing [22], set [10], standeth [8], establish [3], stood still [3], appointed [2], established [2], standest [2], abode [1], brought [1], continue [1], covenanted [1], holden up [1], lay to charge [1], make stand [1], present [1], set up [1], setteth [1], stanched [1], stand still [1], standing up [1]

2477 **ἱστορέω, *historeō***, v. GK: *2707*. to get acquainted with, visit:– see [1]

2478 **ἰσχυρός, *ischyros***, a. GK: *2708* [→ *2479*]. powerful, strong, forceful:– strong [11], mighty [7], mightier than [3], stronger than [3], boysterous [1], powerful [1], valiant [1]

2479 **ἰσχύς, *ischys***, n. GK: *2709* [→ *1340, 1765, 1840, 2001, 2478, 2480, 2729*]. strength, power:– strength [4], power [3], might [2], ability [1], mightily [1]

2480 **ἰσχύω, *ischyō***, v. GK: *2710* [→ *2479*]. to be strong, powerful, able:– could [8], able [6], availeth [3], prevailed [3], whole [2], can do [1], cannot (*+3756*) [1], couldest [1], good [1], had much work (*+3433*) [1], might [1], strength [1]

2481 **ἴσως, *isōs***, adv. GK: *2711* [→ *2470*]. perhaps:– it may be [1]

2482 **Ἰταλία, *Italia***, n.pr. GK: *2712* [→ *2483*]. Italy:– Italy [5]

2483 **Ἰταλικός, *Italikos***, a.pr.g. GK: *2713* [→ *2482*]. Italian:– Italian [1]

2484 **Ἰτουραῖος, *Itouraios***, a.pr. GK: *2714*. Iturea, "*pertaining to Jetur*":– Iturea [1]

2485 **ἰχθύδιον, *ichthydion***, n. GK: *2715* [→ *2486*]. little fish:– little fishes [1], small fishes [1]

2486 **ἰχθύς, *ichthys***, n. GK: *2716* [→ *2485*]. fish:– fishes [15], fish [5]

2487 **ἴχνος, *ichnos***, n. GK: *2717* [→ *421*]. step, footstep; course of action:– steps [3]

2488 **Ἰωαθάμ, *Iōatham***, n.pr. GK: *2718*. Jotham, "*Yahweh will complete*":– Joatham [2]

2489 **Ἰωαννά, *Iōanna***, n.pr. GK: *2720* [cf. *2491*]. Joanna, "[prob.] *Yahweh is gracious*":– Joanna [2]

2490 **Ἰωαννᾶς, *Iōannas***, n.pr. GK: *2721* [cf. *2491*]. Joannas, "[prob.] *Yahweh is gracious*":– Joanna [1]

2491 **Ἰωάννης, *Iōannēs***, n.pr. GK: *2722* [cf. *2489, 2490*]. John, "*Yahweh is gracious*":– John [131], John's [2]

2492 **Ἰώβ, *Iōb***, n.pr. GK: *2724*. Job, "*where is my father* poss. *where is my father, O God?*":– Job [1]

2493 **Ἰωήλ, *Iōēl***, n.pr. GK: *2727*. Joel, "*Yahweh is God*":– Joel [1]

2494 **Ἰωνάμ, *Iōnam***; or **Ἰωνάν, *Iōnan***, n.pr. GK: *2729 & 2730*. Jonam, Jonan:– Jonan [1]

2495 **Ἰωνᾶς, *Iōnas***, n.pr. GK: *2731*. Jonah, "*dove*":– Jonas [12], Jona [1]

2496 **Ἰωράμ, *Iōram***, n.pr. GK: *2732*. Jehoram, "*Yahweh exalts*":– Joram [2]

2497 **Ἰωρίμ, *Iōrim***, n.pr. GK: *2733*. Jorim:– Jorim [1]

2498 **Ἰωσαφάτ, *Iōsaphat***, n.pr. GK: *2734*. Jehoshaphat, "*Yahweh has judged*":– Josaphat [2]

2499 **Ἰωσή, *Iōsē***, n.pr. GK: *2735* [cf. *2500*]. Jose, "*he will add*":– Jose [1]

2500 **Ἰωσῆς, *Iōsēs***, n.pr. GK: *2736* [cf. *2499*]. Joses, Joseph, "*he will add*":– Joses [6]

2501 **Ἰωσήφ, *Iōsēph***, n.pr. GK: *2737*. Joseph, "*he will add*":– Joseph [33], Joseph's [2]

2502 **Ἰωσίας, *Iōsias***, n.pr. GK: *2739*. Josiah, "*let* or *may Yahweh give*":– Josias [2]

2503 **ἰῶτα, *iōta***, n. GK: *2740*. smallest letter (of the Greek alphabet), which corresponds to the smallest letter of the Hebrew alphabet, *yodh*:– jot [1]

2504 **κἀγώ, *kagō***, contr. [c.+p.]. GK: *2743* [→ *2532+1473*]. and I, I also, but I:– and I [43], I also [19], I [5], even I [5], me also [3], so I [3], and me [2], I in like wise [1], also [1], both me [1], but me [1], even I also [1], that I [1], when I [1]

2505 **καθά, *katha***, c. or adv. GK: *2745* [→ *2596+3739*]. (just) as:– as [1]

2506 **καθαίρεσις, *kathairesis***, n. GK: *2746* [→ *2596+138*]. tearing down, demolishment, destruction:– destruction [2], pulling down [1]

2507 **καθαιρέω, *kathaireō***, v. GK: *2747* [→ *2596+138*]. to take down, demolish, overthrow; (pass.) to be robbed of, suffer the loss of:– took down [3], destroyed [2], casting down [1], pull down [1], put down [1], take down [1]

2508 **καθαίρω, *kathairō***, v. GK: *2748* [→ *2513*]. to prune, clear unproductive wood, cleanse:– purged [1], purgeth [1]

2509 **καθάπερ, *kathaper***, c. or adv. GK: *2749* [→ *2596+3739+4007*]. as, just as, like:– as [10], even as [2], as well [1]

2510 **καθάπτω, *kathaptō***, v. GK: *2750* [→ *2596+681*]. to fasten, attach, take hold of, seize:– fastened [1]

2511 **καθαρίζω, *katharizō***, v. GK: *2751 & 2760* [→ *2513*]. to make clean, cleanse, purify:– cleansed [9], cleanse [6], make clean [5], clean [3], cleanseth [1], purged [1], purge [1], purging [1], purified [1], purifying [1], purify [1]

2512 **καθαρισμός, *katharismos***, n. GK: *2752* [→ *2513*]. cleansing, purification, washing:– cleansing [2], purifying [2], purged (*+4160*) [1], purged [1], purification [1]

2513* καθαρός, *katharos, a. GK: *2754* [→ *167, 168, 169, 1245, 1571, 2508, 2511, 2512, 2514, 4027*]. clean, pure, clear of responsibility, innocent:– pure [17], clean [10], clear [1]

2514* καθαρότης, *katharotēs, n. GK: *2755* [→ *2513*]. cleanness, purity:– purifying [1]

2515* καθέδρα, *kathedra, n. GK: *2756* [→ *2516*]. seat, bench:– seats [2], seat [1]

2516* καθέζομαι, *kathezomai, v. GK: *2757* [→ *2515, 2521, 4410, 4775*]. to sit down, be seated:– sat [4], sitting [2]

2517* καθεξῆς, *kathexēs, adv. GK: *2759* [→ *2596+2192*]. in order, in a sequence:– in order [2], afterward (*+1722+3588*) [1], by order [1], follow after [1]

2518* καθεύδω, *katheudō, v. GK: *2761* [→ *2596*]. to sleep, fall asleep:– sleep [8], asleep [5], sleepeth [3], sleepest [2], sleeping [2], slept [2]

2519* καθηγητής, *kathēgētēs, n. GK: *2762* [→ *2596+71*]. teacher; derivative of a verb "to guide, to explain," not found in the NT:– master [2], masters [1]

2520* καθήκω, *kathēkō, v. GK: *2763* [→ *2596+2240*]. to be fitting; (pcpl.) things that ought to be, that are proper:– convenient [1], fit [1]

2521* κάθημαι, *kathēmai, v. GK: *2764* [→ *2516*]. to sit, seat, ride; to live, stay, reside:– sat [41], sitting [20], sit [12], sitteth [10], sat down [2], dwell [1], set down [1], sittest [1], sitting down [1]

2522* καθημερινός, *kathēmerinos, a. GK: *2766* [→ *2596+2250*]. daily:– daily [1]

2523* καθίζω, *kathizō, v. GK: *2767* [→ *339, 1940, 3869, 4776*]. (tr.) to place, seat (someone), appoint; (intr.) to sit down, come to rest upon; stay, live. "To sit on the right side" means to be in a position of high status, "to sit on the left" is a lesser position. "To sit on the seat of Moses" means to have the capacity to interpret the Law of Moses with authority:– sit [14], sat down [11], sat [10], set [3], set down [2], sitteth down [2], continued [1], set to judge [1], sit down [1], sitteth [1], sitting [1], tarry [1]

2524* καθίημι, *kathiēmi, v. GK: *2768* [→ *2596*]. to let down, lower:– let down [3], let down (*+5465*) [1]

2525* καθίστημι, *kathistēmi, v. GK: *2769 & 2770* [→ *2596+2476*]. to put in charge, appoint; to escort, bring, take; (pass.) to be made, become, be appointed:– made [6], make ruler [5], is [2], ordained [2], appoint [1], conducted [1], made ruler [1], maketh [1], make [1], ordain [1], set [1]

2526* καθό, *katho, adv. GK: *2771* [→ *2596+3739*]. insofar as, to the degree that:– according to that (*+1437*) [1], according to that [1], as we [1], inasmuch as [1]

2526'* καθολικός, *katholikos, a. GK: *2772* [→ *2596+3650*]. general, universal:–

2527* καθόλου, *katholou, adv. GK: *2773* [→ *2596+3650*]. at all, entirely, completely:– at all [1]

2528* καθοπλίζω, *kathoplizō, v. GK: *2774* [→ *2596+3696*]. (mid.) to fully arm or equip (oneself):– armed [1]

2529* καθοράω, *kathoraō, v. GK: *2775* [→ *2596+3708*]. (pass.) to be clearly seen, perceived:– clearly seen [1]

2530* καθότι, *kathoti, c. GK: *2776* [→ *2596+3739+5101*]. as, to the degree that; because:– according as [1], as (*+302*) [1], because that [1], because [1], forsomuch as [1]

2531* καθώς, *kathōs, adv. GK: *2777* [→ *2596+5613*]. as, just as, even as; in accordance with:– as [142], even as [27], according as [5], even [3], according to [1], as well as [1], how [1], seeing as [1], when [1]

2532* καί, *kai, c. GK: *2779* [→ *2504, 2534, 2539, 2543, 2544, 2546, 2547, 2548, 2579, 4003, 5065*]. (as a connective) and; (connecting and continuing) and then, then; (as a disjuntive) but, yet, however; (as an adv.) also, even, likewise:– and [8167], also [517], even [100], both [47], but [41], then [25], so [18], neither (*+3756*) [16], likewise [12], or [12], that [12], nor [11], yet [10], when [9], for [8], neither [8], with [6], yea [5], as [4], indeed [4], neither (*+3361*) [4], and also [3], eighteen (*+1176+3638*) [3], moreover [3], though [3], very [3], and yet [2], nor (*+3756*) [2], now [2], therefore [2], yet (*+1063*) [2], also (*+235*) [1], also (*+260*) [1], although (*+1487*) [1], and (*+5119*) [1], and again [1], and no so much as (*+3761*) [1], and when [1], as well [1], at least (*+1065*) [1], beside [1], but though (*+1161+1487*) [1], by [1], else [1], even (*+2193*) [1], even all one as if (*+846+1520+3588*) [1], if [1], insomuch [1], moreover (*+235*) [1], neither (*+3364*) [1], neither (*+3761*) [1], neither any (*+3762*) [1], neither at any time (*+3763*) [1], nevertheless (*+4133*) [1], of either side (*+1782+1782*) [1], on either side one (*+1782+1782*) [1], so in like manner (*+3779*) [1], so that (*+5620*) [1], so that [1], therefore (*+1352*) [1], though (*+1437*) [1], though (*+1487*) [1], though (*+1512*) [1], thus [1], verily [1], wherefore (*+1352*) [1], wherefore (*+5620*) [1], which [1]

2533* Καϊάφας, *Kaiaphas, n.pr. GK: *2780*. Caiaphas:– Caiaphas [9]

2534* καίγε, *kaige, pt. GK: *2781* [→ *2532+1065*]. even, even though:–

2535* Κάϊν, *Kain, n.pr. GK: *2782*. Cain, "*metal worker; brought forth, acquired [Ge. 4:1]*":– Cain [3]

2536* Καϊνάμ, *Kainam; or **Καϊνάν, *Kainan***, n.pr. GK: *2783 & 2784*. Cainam, Cainan, Kenan, "*worker in iron, metal worker*":– Cainan [2]

2537* καινός, *kainos, a. GK: *2785* [→ *340, 341, 342, 1456, 1457, 2538*]. new, latest, anew; in some contexts new is superior to old (Mt 9:17; Heb 8):– new [44]

2538* καινότης, *kainotēs, n. GK: *2786* [→ *2537*]. newness:– newness [2]

2539* καίπερ, *kaiper, c. GK: *2788* [→ *2532+4007*]. though, even though, although:– though [5], and yet [1]

2540* καιρός, *kairos, n. GK: *2789* [→ *170, 171, 2119, 2120, 2121, 2122, 4340*]. time (particular and general); right time, opportune time, proper time, appointed time:– time [53], times [11], season [8], seasons [4], always (*+1722+3956*) [2], due season [2], opportunity [2], age (*+2244*) [1], convenient season [1], due time [1], while [1]

2541* Καῖσαρ, *Kaisar, n.pr. GK: *2790* [→ *2542*]. Caesar:– Cesar [21], Cesar's [9]

2542* Καισάρεια, *Kaisareia, n.pr. GK: *2791* [→ *2541*]. Caesarea:– Cesarea [17]

2543* καίτοι, *kaitoi, pt. GK: *2792* [→ *2532+5104*]. and yet:– although [1]

2544* καίτοιγε, *kaitoige, pt. GK: *2793* [→ *2532+5104+1065*]. although, and yet:– though [2], nevertheless [1]

2545* καίω, *kaiō, v. GK: *2794* [→ *1572, 2575, 2618, 2738, 2739, 2740, 2741, 2742, 2743, 3646*]. to light (a wick), keep burning:– burning [6], burned [3], burneth [1], burn [1], light [1]

2546* κἀκεῖ, *kakei, contr. [c.+adv.]. GK: *2795* [→ *2532+1563*]. and there, and where:– and there [9], there also [1], thither also [1]

2547* κἀκεῖθεν, *kakeithen, contr. [c.+adv.]. GK: *2796* [→ *2532+1563*]. and from there:– and from thence [6], and thence [3], and afterward [1], thence also [1]

2548* κἀκεῖνος, *kakeinos, contr. [c.+p.demo.]. GK: *2797* [→ *2532+1563*]. and that one:– and he [4], and they [3], he also [3], and him [2], and the other [2], and them [2], they also [2], as them [1], even he [1], even they [1], him also [1], them also [1]

2549* κακία, *kakia, n. GK: *2798* [→ *2556*]. evil, wickedness, depravity, malice; in some contexts an "evil" situation means a difficult and hard circumstance rather than a morally corrupt circumstance (Mt 6:34):– malice [6], maliciousness [2], evil [1], naughtiness [1], wickedness [1]

2550* κακοήθεια, *kakoētheia, n. GK: *2799* [→ *2556+1485*]. malice:– malignity [1]

2551* κακολογέω, *kakologeō, v. GK: *2800* [→ *2556+3004*]. to curse, malign, speak evil of:– curseth [2], spake evil [1], speak evil [1]

2552* κακοπάθεια, *kakopatheia, n. GK: *2801* [→ *2556+3958*]. suffering:– suffering affliction [1]

2553* κακοπαθέω, *kakopatheō, v. GK: *2802* [→ *2556+3958*]. to suffer trouble, endure hardship:– afflicted [1], endure afflictions [1], endure hardness [1], suffer trouble [1]

2554* κακοποιέω, *kakopoieō, v. GK: *2803* [→ *2556+4160*]. to do evil, do what is wrong:– do evil [2], doeth evil [1], evil doing [1]

2555* κακοποιός, *kakopoios, a. GK: *2804* [→ *2556+4160*]. wrongdoing:– evildoers [3], evildoer [1], malefactor [1]

2556* κακός, *kakos, a. GK: *2805* [→ *172, 420, 1573, 2549, 2550, 2551, 2552, 2553, 2554, 2555, 2557, 2558, 2559, 2560, 2561, 4777, 4778*]. evil, wicked, wrong, bad, a perversion of what pertains to goodness; as a noun, an evil thing can refer to any crime, harm, or moral wrong:– evil [45], harm [2], bad [1], ill [1], noisome [1], wicked [1]

2557* κακοῦργος, *kakourgos, a. GK: *2806* [→ *2556+2041*]. criminal, evildoer:– malefactors [3], evil doer [1]

2558* κακουχέω, *kakoucheō, v. GK: *2807* [→ *2556+2192*]. (pass.) to be mistreated, maltreated, tormented:– suffer adversity [1], tormented [1]

2559* κακόω, *kakoō, v. GK: *2808* [→ *2556*]. to harm, mistreat, oppress, persecute; poison, embitter:– entreat evil [1], evil entreated [1], harm [1], hurt [1], made evil affected [1], vex [1]

2560* κακῶς, *kakōs, adv. GK: *2809* [→ *2556*]. badly, wrongly, terribly:– sick (*+2192*) [4], sick [3], evil [2], amiss [1], diseased (*+2192*) [1], diseased [1], grievously [1], miserably [1], sick people (*+2192*) [1], sore [1]

2561* κάκωσις, *kakōsis, n. GK: *2810* [→ *2556*]. oppression, mistreatment:– affliction [1]

2562* καλάμη, *kalamē, n. GK: *2811* [→ *2563*]. straw; note some translate "stubble":– stubble [1]

2563* κάλαμος, *kalamos, n. GK: *2812* [→ *2562*]. reed, staff, stick, measuring rod, pen:– reed [11], pen [1]

2564* καλέω, *kaleō, v. GK: *2813* [→ *410, 479, 1458, 1462, 1528, 1577, 1941, 2821, 2822, 3333, 3870, 3874, 3875, 4292, 4341, 4779, 4837*]. to call, invite, summon. The authority of the speaker dictates the nature of the calling (friends invite; kings summon). This is also translated "to name," the giving of attribution to someone or something:– called [103], call [16], bidden [10], calleth [6], bade [4], bid [2], calling [1], named [1], name [1], surname [1]

2565* καλλιέλαιος, *kallielaios, n. GK: *2814* [→ *2570+1636*]. cultivated olive tree:– good olive tree [1]

2566* καλλίον, *kalliōn, a.neut. of *2570*. GK: *2819* [→ *2570*]. good, right; beautiful, fine, excellent:–

2567* καλοδιδάσκαλος, *kalodidaskalos, a. GK: *2815* [→ *2570+1321*]. teaching what is good:– teachers of good things [1]

2568* Καλοὶ λιμένες, *Kaloi limenes, n.pr. GK: *2816* [→ *2570+3040*]. Fair Havens, "*fair havens*":– fair havens [1]

2569* καλοποιέω, *kalopoieō, v. GK: *2818* [→ *2570+4160*]. to do what is right or good:– well doing [1]

2570* καλός, *kalos, a. GK: *2819* [→ *2565, 2566, 2567, 2568, 2569, 2573*]. good, right; beautiful, fine, excellent:– good [82], better [6], honest [5], goodly [2], meet [2], better (*+3123*) [1], good thing [1], well [1], worthy [1]

2571* κάλυμμα, *kalymma, n. GK: *2820* [→ *2572*]. veil, covering:– vail [4]

2572* καλύπτω, *kalyptō, v. GK: *2821* [→ *177, 343, 601, 602, 1942, 1943, 2571, 2619, 3871, 4028, 4780*]. cover, veil, hide:– covered [2], cover [2], hid [2], covereth [1], hide [1]

2573* καλῶς, *kalōs, adv. GK: *2822* [→ *2570*]. rightly, well, sometimes with an implication of correctness:– well [30], good [3], full well [1], honestly [1], recover (*+2192*) [1], very well [1]

2574* κάμηλος, *kamēlos, n. GK: *2823*. camel:– camel [4], camel's [2]

2575* κάμινος, *kaminos, n. GK: *2825* [→ *2545*]. furnace, oven:– furnace [4]

2576* καμμύω, *kammyō, v. GK: *2826*. close, shut (the eyes):– closed [2]

2577* κάμνω, *kamnō, v. GK: *2827*. to grow weary; be sick:– fainted [1], sick [1], wearied [1]

2578* κάμπτω, *kamptō, v. GK: *2828* [→ *344, 4781*]. to bend, bow (on a knee):– bow [3], bowed [1]

2579* κἄν, *kan, contr. [c.+pt.]. GK: *2829* [→ *2532+1487+302*]. and if, even if:– and if [5], though [4], if but [2], also if [1], and though [1], at the least [1], yet [1]

2580* Κανά, *Kana, n.pr. GK: *2830* [→ *2581*]. Cana, "*reed*":– Cana [4]

2581* Κανανίτης, *Kananitēs, n.pr.g. GK: *2832* [→ *2580*]. Canaanite, from Cana:– Canaanite [2]

2582* Κανδάκη, *Kandakē, n.pr. GK: *2833*. Candace, "[title?] *queen*":– Candace [1]

2583* κανών, *kanōn, n. GK: *2834*. rule, standard; sphere of activity, limit:– rule [4], line [1]

2584* Καπερναούμ, *Kapernaoum, n.pr. GK: *2835 & 3019*. Capernaum, "*village of Nahum*":– Capernaum [16]

2585 καπηλεύω, ***kapēleuō***, v. GK: *2836*. to act as a peddler, trade in for profit:– corrupt [1]

2586 καπνός, ***kapnos***, n. GK: *2837*. smoke:– smoke [13]

2587 Καππαδοκία, ***Kappadokia***, n.pr. GK: *2838*. Cappadocia:– Cappadocia [2]

2588 καρδία, ***kardia***, n. GK: *2840* [→ *2589, 4641*]. heart, mind (seat of thought and emotion). The heart was thought to be the seat of the inner self (composed of life, soul, mind, and spirit). "Heart" is similar in meaning to "soul," but often the "heart" has a focus on thinking and understanding (Mk 2:8; Lk 1:51; 24:38):– heart [101], hearts [57], heart's [1]

2589 καρδιογνώστης, ***kardiognōstēs***, n. GK: *2841* [→ *2588+1097*]. knower of the heart:– knowest hearts [1], knoweth hearts [1]

2590 καρπός, ***karpos***, n. GK: *2843* [→ *175, 2591, 2592, 2593*]. fruit, crop, harvest, produce of vegetation; by extension: deed, activity, produce of a person:– fruit [54], fruits [12]

2591 Κάρπος, ***Karpos***, n.pr. GK: *2842* [→ *2590*]. Carpus, "*fruit(ful)*":– Carpus [1]

2592 καρποφορέω, ***karpophoreō***, v. GK: *2844* [→ *2590+5342*]. to produce a crop, bear fruit:– bring forth fruit [4], bringeth forth fruit [2], beareth fruit [1], fruitful [1]

2593 καρποφόρος, ***karpophoros***, a. GK: *2845* [→ *2590+5342*]. crop, fruitbearing:– fruitful [1]

2594 καρτερέω, ***kartereō***, v. GK: *2846* [→ *4342, 4343; cf. 2904*]. to persevere, endure:– endured [1]

2595 κάρφος, ***karphos***, n. GK: *2847*. speck, chip, particle:– mote [6]

2596 κατά, ***kata***, pp. GK: *2848* [→ *176, 177, 178, 179, 180, 181, 182, 183, 478, 600, 604, 605, 843, 1246, 1455, 1459, 1460, 1944, 2505, 2506, 2507, 2509, 2510, 2516, 2517, 2518, 2519, 2520, 2522, 2524, 2525, 2526, 2526', 2527, 2528, 2529, 2530, 2531, 2597, 2598, 2599, 2600, 2601, 2602, 2603, 2604, 2605, 2606, 2607, 2609, 2610, 2611, 2612, 2613, 2614, 2615, 2616, 2653, 2617, 2618, 2619, 2620, 2621, 2622, 2623, 2624, 2625, 2626, 2627, 2628, 2629, 2630, 2631, 2632, 2633, 2634, 2635, 2636, 2637, 2638, 2639, 2640, 2641, 2642, 2643, 2644, 2645, 2646, 2647, 2648, 2649, 2650, 2651, 2652, 2653, 2654, 2655, 2656, 2657, 2658, 2659, 2660, 2661, 2662, 2663, 2664, 2665, 2666, 2667, 2668, 2669, 2670, 2671, 2672, 2673, 2674, 2675, 2676, 2677, 2678, 2679, 2680, 2681, 2682, 2683, 2684, 2685, 2686, 2687, 2688, 2689, 2690, 2691, 2692, 2693, 2694, 2695, 2696, 2697, 2698, 2699, 2700, 2701, 2702, 2703, 2704, 2705, 2706, 2708, 2709, 2710, 2711, 2712, 2713, 2714, 2715, 2716, 2718, 2719, 2720, 2721, 2722, 2723, 2726, 2727, 2728, 2729, 2730, 2731, 2732, 2733, 2734, 2735, 2736, 2737, 3872, 4293, 4294, 4782, 4783, 4784, 4785, 5270; cf. 2608*]. (gen.) against, contrary to, opposed; down, throughout; (acc.) in, by, with, in accordance with, for:– according to [104], after [59], against [58], in [32], by [28], daily (*+2250*) [15], as [10], every [10], at [8], of [8], privately (*+2398*) [8], apart (*+2398*) [7], throughout [7], through [4], to [4], about [3], according [3], concerning [3], down [3], every (*+3956*) [3], in divers [3], toward [3], with [3], after the manner [2], among [2], as concerning [2], as touching [2], before [2], from house to house (*+3624*) [2], inasmuch as (*+3745*) [2], into [2], natural (*+5449*) [2], on part [2], on [2], over against [2], upon [2], according as [1], affairs (*+3588*) [1], after a manner [1], after a sort [1], after the manner of [1], alone (*+1438*) [1], alone (*+2398*) [1], alone (*+3441*) [1], as (*+3739+5158*) [1], as (*+3745*) [1], as much as [1], as pertaining to [1], as wont (*+1485+3588*) [1], aside (*+2398*) [1], beyond measure (*+5236*) [1], cause [1], charitably (*+26*) [1], covered [1], daily (*+1538+2250*) [1], daily (*+2250+3956*) [1], day by day (*+2250*) [1], deep (*+899*) [1], even as (*+3739+3779+5158*) [1], even thus (*+5024*) [1], every (*+1520+1538*) [1], every (*+3588*) [1], every house (*+3624*) [1], exceeding (*+5236*) [1], face to face (*+4383*) [1], far more exceeding (*+1519+5236+5236*) [1], for [1], godly (*+2316*) [1], in due [1], in every church (*+1577*) [1], in every house (*+3624*) [1], in every [1], in respect of [1], in the like manner (*+846+3588*) [1], in the presence (*+4383*) [1], like as (*+3665*) [1], matter (*+3588*) [1], mightily (*+2904*) [1], more excellent (*+5236*) [1], one by one (*+1520*) [1], out of measure (*+5236*) [1], particularly (*+1520+1538*) [1], particularly (*+3313*) [1], particular [1], pertaining to [1], reason (*+3056*) [1], so (*+846+3588*) [1], state [1], the same (*+1565*) [1], together (*+846+3588*) [1], touching [1], unto [1], whereby (*+5101*) [1], where [1], willingly (*+1595*) [1], year by year (*+1763*) [1], your (*+4771*) [1], your own (*+4771*) [1]

2597 καταβαίνω, ***katabainō***, v. GK: *2849* [→ *2596+305*]. to go down, descend:– come down [20], came down [16], went down [13], descended [7], descending [7], cometh down [4], descend [4], go down [2], coming down [1], falling down [1], fell [1], get down [1], goeth down [1], going down [1], steppeth down [1]

2598 καταβάλλω, ***kataballō***, v. GK: *2850* [→ *2596+906*]. (pass.) to be struck down; (mid.) to lay (a foundation):– cast down [2], laying [1]

2599 καταβαρέω, ***katabareō***, v. GK: *2851* [→ *2596+922*]. to burden, be a burden:– burden [1]

2600 κατάβασις, ***katabasis***, n. GK: *2853* [→ *2596+305*]. place that goes down, slope, down-grade:– descent [1]

2601 καταβιβάζω, ***katabibazō***, v. GK: *2854* [→ *2596+305*]. to bring down:– brought down [1], thrust down [1]

2602 καταβολή, ***katabolē***, n. GK: *2856* [→ *2596+906*]. creation (of the world), beginning, foundation:– foundation [10], conceive [1]

2603 καταβραβεύω, ***katabrabeuō***, v. GK: *2857* [→ *2596+1018*]. to disqualify for a prize, decide against:– beguile of reward [1]

2604 καταγγελεύς, ***katangeleus***, n. GK: *2858* [→ *2596+32*]. advocate, proclaimer:– setter forth [1]

2605 καταγγέλλω, ***katangellō***, v. GK: *2859* [→ *2596+32*]. to preach, proclaim, advocate, report:– preached [6], preach [4], shew [3], declare [1], declaring [1], spoken of [1], teach [1]

2606 καταγελάω, ***katagelaō***, v. GK: *2860* [→ *2596+1070*]. to laugh at, mock:– laughed to scorn [3]

2607 καταγινώσκω, ***kataginōskō***, v. GK: *2861* [→ *2596+1097*]. to condemn, convict; (pass.) to be in the wrong, condemned:– condemn [2], blamed [1]

2608 κατάγνυμι, ***katagnymi***, v. GK: *2862* [→ *513, 3489; cf. 2596*]. to break:– brake [2], break [1], broken [1]

2609 κατάγω, ***katagō***, v. GK: *2864* [→ *2596+71*]. to bring, bring down, land (on shore):– bring down [3], brought down [2], brought forth [1], brought [1], landed [1], landing [1], touched [1]

2610 καταγωνίζομαι, ***katagōnizomai***, v. GK: *2865* [→ *2596+73*]. (mid.) to conquer, defeat, overcome:– subdued [1]

2611 καταδέω, ***katadeō***, v. GK: *2866* [→ *2596+1210*]. to bandage, bind up:– bound up [1]

2612 κατάδηλος, ***katadēlos***, a. GK: *2867* [→ *2596+1212*]. clear, quite plain:– evident [1]

2613 καταδικάζω, ***katadikazō***, v. GK: *1463 & 2868* [→ *2596+1349*]. to judge, condemn:– condemned [4], condemn [1]

2614 καταδιώκω, ***katadiōkō***, v. GK: *2870* [→ *2596+1377*]. to look for, search for:– followed after [1]

2615 καταδουλόω, ***katadouloō***, v. GK: *2871* [→ *2596+1401*]. to make a slave, enslave:– bring into bondage [2]

2616 καταδυναστεύω, ***katadynasteuō***, v. GK: *2872* [→ *2596+1410*]. (act.) to exploit, oppress, dominate; (pass.) to be under the power of, oppressed by:– oppressed [1], oppress [1]

2617 καταισχύνω, ***kataischynō***, v. GK: *2875* [→ *2596+150*]. to dishonor, humiliate, shame, disappoint:– ashamed [6], confound [2], dishonoureth [2], confounded [1], maketh ashamed [1], shame [1]

2618 κατακαίω, ***katakaiō***, v. GK: *2876* [→ *2596+2545*]. to burn up, consume:– burnt up [3], burnt [3], burn [3], burn up [1], burned [1], utterly burnt [1]

2619 κατακαλύπτω, ***katakalyptō***, v. GK: *2877* [→ *2596+2572*]. (mid.) to cover (the head):– covered [2], cover [1]

2620 κατακαυχάομαι, ***katakauchaomai***, v. GK: *1595 & 2878* [→ *2596+2744*]. to boast about; to triumph over:– boast against [1], boast [1], glory [1], rejoiceth against [1]

2621 κατάκειμαι, ***katakeimai***, v. GK: *2879* [→ *2596+2749*]. to lie down (in bed); to recline (at dinner):– lay [5], sat at meat [2], kept (*+1909*) [1], lie [1], sat [1], sit at meat [1]

2622 κατακλάω, ***kataklaō***, v. GK: *2880* [→ *2596+2806*]. to break in pieces:– brake [2]

2623 κατακλείω, ***katakleiō***, v. GK: *1597 & 2881* [→ *2596+2808*]. to lock up:– shut up [2]

2624 κατακληροδοτέω, ***kataklērodoteō***, v. GK: *2882 & 2883* [→ *2596+2819+3551*]. to parcel out by lot:– divided by lot [1]

2625 κατακλίνω, ***kataklinō***, v. GK: *2884* [→ *2596+2827*]. (act.) to cause to sit; (pass.) to recline (at a table):– make sit down [1], sat at meat [1], sit down [1]

2626 κατακλύζω, ***kataklyzō***, v. GK: *2885* [→ *2596+2830*]. (pass.) to be deluged, flooded:– overflowed [1]

2627 κατακλυσμός, ***kataklysmos***, n. GK: *2886* [→ *2596+2830*]. flood, deluge:– flood [4]

2628 κατακολουθέω, ***katakoloutheō***, v. GK: *2887* [→ *2596+190; cf. 1.3*]. to follow:– followed after [1], followed [1]

2629 κατακόπτω, ***katakoptō***, v. GK: *2888* [→ *2596+2875*]. to cut:– cutting [1]

2630 κατακρημνίζω, ***katakrēmnizō***, v. GK: *2889* [→ *2596+2910*]. to throw down a cliff:– cast down headlong [1]

2631 κατάκριμα, ***katakrima***, n. GK: *2890* [→ *2596+2919*]. condemnation:– condemnation [3]

2632 κατακρίνω, ***katakrinō***, v. GK: *2891* [→ *2596+2919*]. to condemn:– condemned [8], condemn [7], damned [2], condemnest [1], condemneth [1]

2633 κατάκρισις, ***katakrisis***, n. GK: *2892* [→ *2596+2919*]. condemnation:– condemnation [1], condemn [1]

2634 κατακυριεύω, ***katakyrieuō***, v. GK: *2894* [→ *2596+2962*]. to lord it over, gain dominion over, subdue; in some contexts there is an implication that this exercise of authority is harsh:– exercise dominion over [1], exercise lordship over [1], lords over [1], overcame [1]

2635 καταλαλέω, ***katalaleō***, v. GK: *2895* [→ *2596+2980*]. to speak against, slander, accuse:– speak evil [2], speaketh evil [2], speak against [1]

2636 καταλαλιά, ***katalalia***, n. GK: *2896* [→ *2596+2980*]. slander, defamation, evil speech:– backbitings [1], evil speakings [1]

2637 κατάλαλος, ***katalalos***, a. GK: *2897* [→ *2596+2980*]. slanderous, defamatory:– backbiters [1]

2638 καταλαμβάνω, ***katalambanō***, v. GK: *2898* [→ *2596+2983*]. to obtain, attain, take hold of; seize, overtake; (mid.) to grasp, understand, realize, find out:– apprehended [2], taken [2], apprehend [1], attained [1], come upon [1], comprehended [1], comprehend [1], found [1], obtain [1], overtake [1], perceived [1], perceive [1], taketh [1]

2639 καταλέγω, ***katalegō***, v. GK: *2899* [→ *2596+3004*]. to put on a list, enroll, select:– taken into the number [1]

2640 κατάλειμμα, ***kataleimma***, n. GK: *2900 & 5698* [→ *2596+3007*]. remnant:– remnant [1]

2641 καταλείπω, ***kataleipō***, v. GK: *2901* [→ *2596+3007*]. to leave (behind), neglect; (pass.) remain (behind):– left [15], leave [6], forsaken [1], forsook [1], leaving [1], reserved [1]

2642 καταλιθάζω, ***katalithazō***, v. GK: *2902* [→ *2596+3037*]. to stone to death:– stone [1]

2643 καταλλαγή, ***katallagē***, n. GK: *2903* [→ *2596+236*]. reconciliation:– reconciliation [2], atonement [1], reconciling [1]

2644 καταλλάσσω, ***katallassō***, v. GK: *2904* [→ *2596+236*]. to reconcile (among human beings or between human beings and God):– reconciled [5], reconciling [1]

2645 κατάλοιπος, ***kataloipos***, a. GK: *2905* [→ *2596+3007*]. remaining, left over, (n.) remnant, the rest:– residue [1]

2646 κατάλυμα, ***katalyma***, n. GK: *2906* [→ *2596+3089*]. guest room; inn:– guestchamber [2], inn [1]

2647 καταλύω, ***katalyō***, v. GK: *2907* [→ *2596+3089*]. (tr.) throw down, abolish, destroy; (intr.) to be a guest, rest, find lodging:– destroy [6], thrown down [3], destroyest [2], come to nought [1], destroyed [1], dissolved [1], guest [1], lodge [1], overthrow [1]

2648 καταμανθάνω, ***katamanthanō***, v. GK: *2908* [→ *2596+3129*]. notice carefully, consider closely:– consider [1]

2649 καταμαρτυρέω, ***katamartyreō***, v. GK: *2909* [→ *2596+3144*]. to bring testimony against, bear testimony against:– witness against [4]

2650 καταμένω, ***katamenō***, v. GK: *2910* [→ *2596+3306*]. to stay, live:– abode [1]

2651 **καταμόνας**, ***katamonas***, a. GK: *2911* [→ *2596+3441*]. in private, alone:– alone [1]

2652 **κατανάθεμα**, ***katanathema***, n. GK: *2873 & 2912* [→ *2596+331*]. curse, that which is under the ban (devoted exclusively to God):– curse [1]

2653 **καταναθεματίζω**, ***katanathematizō***, v. GK: *2874 & 2913* [→ *2596+331*]. to (call down a) curse:– curse [1]

2654 **καταναλίσκω**, ***katanaliskō***, v. GK: *2914* [→ *2596+303+259*]. to consume:– consuming [1]

2655 **καταναρκάω**, ***katanarkaō***, v. GK: *2915* [→ *2596*]. to burden, be a burden:– burdensome [2], chargeable to [1]

2656 **κατανεύω**, ***kataneuō***, v. GK: *2916* [→ *2596+3506*]. to signal, nod:– beckoned [1]

2657 **κατανοέω**, ***katanoeō***, v. GK: *2917* [→ *2596+3563*]. to pay attention, notice, observe; consider, contemplate; this word has a strong implication that the attention paid is intense, and the contemplation is broad and thorough, resulting in complete understanding:– consider [4], behold [2], considered [2], beholdeth [1], beholding [1], considerest [1], discovered [1], perceived [1], perceivest [1]

2658 **καταντάω**, ***katantaō***, v. GK: *2918* [→ *2596+473*]. to come to, arrive at; attain, reach:– came [8], come [3], attain [2]

2659 **κατάνυξις**, ***katanyxis***, n. GK: *2919* [→ *2596+3572*]. stupor, bewilderment, unable to think:– slumber [1]

2660 **κατανύσσομαι**, ***katanyssomai***, v. GK: *2920* [→ *2596+3572*]. to be pierced, stabbed:– pricked [1]

2661 **καταξιόω**, ***kataxioō***, v. GK: *2921* [→ *2596+514*]. (pass.) to be counted worthy, considered worthy:– accounted worthy [2], counted worthy [2]

2662 **καταπατέω**, ***katapateō***, v. GK: *2922* [→ *2596+3961*]. to trample (an action that can show disdain):– trodden under foot [2], trample [1], trodden down [1], trode upon [1]

2663 **κατάπαυσις**, ***katapausis***, n. GK: *2923* [→ *2596+3973*]. rest:– rest [9]

2664 **καταπαύω**, ***katapauō***, v. GK: *2924* [→ *2596+3973*]. to keep from, restrain; to give rest; to rest, cease:– ceased [1], given rest [1], restrained [1], rest [1]

2665 **καταπέτασμα**, ***katapetasma***, n. GK: *2925* [→ *2596+4072*]. curtain:– vail [6]

2666 **καταπίνω**, ***katapinō***, v. GK: *2927* [→ *2596+4095*]. to swallow, devour; (pass.) to be swallowed up, overwhelmed, drowned:– swallowed up [4], devour [1], drowned [1], swallow [1]

2667 **καταπίπτω**, ***katapiptō***, v. GK: *2928* [→ *2596+4098*]. to fall down:– fallen down [1], fallen [1]

2668 **καταπλέω**, ***katapleō***, v. GK: *2929* [→ *2596+4126*]. to sail to:– arrived [1]

2669 **καταπονέω**, ***kataponeō***, v. GK: *2930* [→ *2596+4192*]. (pass.) to be oppressed, distressed:– oppressed [1], vexed [1]

2670 **καταποντίζω**, ***katapontizō***, v. GK: *2931* [→ *2596*]. (pass.) to be drowned; to sink:– drowned [1], sink [1]

2671 **κατάρα**, ***katara***, n. GK: *2932* [→ *2596+685*]. curse, imprecation:– curse [3], cursing [2], cursed [1]

2672 **καταράομαι**, ***kataraomai***, v. GK: *2933* [→ *2596+685*]. (mid.) to curse:– curse [4], cursedst [1], cursed [1]

2673 **καταργέω**, ***katargeō***, v. GK: *2934* [→ *2596+1.1+2041*]. to nullify, abolish, make ineffective; (pass.) cease, pass away:– done away [4], abolished [3], destroy [3], destroyed [2], become of no effect [1], bring to nought [1], ceased [1], come to nought [1], cumbereth [1], delivered [1], fail [1], loosed [1], made of none effect [1], make of none effect [1], make void [1], make without effect [1], put away [1], put down [1], vanish away [1]

2674 **καταριθμέω**, ***katarithmeō***, v. GK: *2935* [→ *2596+706*]. (pass.) to be numbered among, belong to:– numbered [1]

2675 **καταρτίζω**, ***katartizō***, v. GK: *2936* [→ *2596+737*]. to restore, put in order, mend; to make complete, equip, train; to prepare, ordain:– perfect [3], make perfect [2], mending [2], fitted [1], framed [1], perfected [1], perfectly joined together [1], prepared [1], restore [1]

2676 **κατάρτισις**, ***katartisis***, n. GK: *2937* [→ *2596+737*]. perfection, completion:– perfection [1]

2677 **καταρτισμός**, ***katartismos***, n. GK: *2938* [→ *2596+737*]. preparation, training, equipping:– perfecting [1]

2678 **κατασείω**, ***kataseiō***, v. GK: *2939* [→ *2596+4579*]. to motion, signal by waving or shaking:– beckoned [2], beckoning [2]

2679 **κατασκάπτω**, ***kataskaptō***, v. GK: *2940* [→ *2596+4626*]. (act.) to tear down; (pass.) to be ruined:– digged down [1], ruins [1]

2680 **κατασκευάζω**, ***kataskeuazō***, v. GK: *2941* [→ *2596+4632*]. to prepare, make ready; to build, construct; to set up, arrange, furnish; there is a strong implication that the preparation is thorough, and a possible implication that the act of building may be for a special purpose:– prepare [3], builded [2], prepared [2], built [1], made [1], ordained [1], preparing [1]

2681 **κατασκηνόω**, ***kataskēnoō***, v. GK: *2942* [→ *2596+4633*]. to perch, nest; to live, dwell:– lodge [2], lodged [1], rest [1]

2682 **κατασκήνωσις**, ***kataskēnōsis***, n. GK: *2943* [→ *2596+4633*]. nest:– nests [2]

2683 **κατασκιάζω**, ***kataskiazō***, v. GK: *2944* [→ *2596+4639*]. to overshadow:– shadowing [1]

2684 **κατασκοπέω**, ***kataskopeō***, v. GK: *2945* [→ *2596+4648*]. to spy on, lie in wait for:– spy out [1]

2685 **κατάσκοπος**, ***kataskopos***, n. GK: *2946* [→ *2596+4648*]. spy:– spies [1]

2686 **κατασοφίζομαι**, ***katasophizomai***, v. GK: *2947* [→ *2596+4680*]. to deal treacherously with:– dealt subtilly with [1]

2687 **καταστέλλω**, ***katastellō***, v. GK: *2948* [→ *2596+4724*]. (act.) to quiet, restrain:– appeased [1], quiet [1]

2688 **κατάστημα**, ***katastēma***, n. GK: *2949* [→ *2596+2476*]. the way one lives, behavior:– behaviour [1]

2689 **καταστολή**, ***katastolē***, n. GK: *2950* [→ *2596+4724*]. appearance, behavior:– apparel [1]

2690 **καταστρέφω**, ***katastrephō***, v. GK: *2951* [→ *2596+4762*]. to overturn, upset:– overthrew [2]

2691 **καταστρηνιάω**, ***katastrēniaō***, v. GK: *2952* [→ *2596+4764*]. to be filled with desires that conflict with dedication to someone:– wax wanton against [1]

2692 **καταστροφή**, ***katastrophē***, n. GK: *2953* [→ *2596+4762*]. ruin, destruction:– overthrow [1], subverting [1]

2693 **καταστρώννυμι**, ***katastrōnnymi***, v. GK: *2954* [→ *2596+4766*]. (pass.) to be scattered:– overthrown [1]

2694 **κατασύρω**, ***katasyrō***, v. GK: *2955* [→ *2596+4951*]. to drag away (by considerable force):– hale [1]

2695 **κατασφάττω**, ***katasphattō***, v. GK: *2956 & 2957* [→ *2596+4969*]. to kill, slaughter, strike down:– slay [1]

2696 **κατασφραγίζω**, ***katasphragizō***, v. GK: *2958* [→ *2596+4973*]. (pass.) to be sealed up:– sealed [1]

2697 **κατάσχεσις**, ***kataschesis***, n. GK: *2959* [→ *2596+2192*]. possession, taking into possession:– possession [2]

2698 **κατατίθημι**, ***katatithēmi***, v. GK: *2960* [→ *2596+5087*]. (mid.) to grant a favor, do a favor:– do [1], laid [1], shew [1]

2699 **κατατομή**, ***katatomē***, n. GK: *2961* [→ *2596+5114*]. mutilation, cutting away:– concision [1]

2700 **κατατοξεύω**, ***katatoxeuō***, v. GK: *2962* [→ *2596+5115*]. to shoot down:– thrust through [1]

2701 **κατατρέχω**, ***katatrechō***, v. GK: *2963* [→ *2596+5143*]. to run down:– ran down [1]

καταφάγω, ***kataphagō***. See ***2719***.

2702 **καταφέρω**, ***katapherō***, v. GK: *2965* [→ *2596+5342*]. to cast (a vote) against; to bring (charges); (pass.) to be overwhelmed (by sleep):– fallen into [1], gave [1], sunk down [1]

2703 **καταφεύγω**, ***katapheugō***, v. GK: *2966* [→ *2596+5343*]. to flee, take refuge:– fled for refuge [1], fled [1]

2704 **καταφθείρω**, ***kataphtheirō***, v. GK: *2967* [→ *2596+5351*]. (pass.) to be depraved, corrupt:– corrupt [1], utterly perish [1]

2705 **καταφιλέω**, ***kataphileō***, v. GK: *2968* [→ *2596+5384*]. to kiss:– kissed [5], kiss [1]

2706 **καταφρονέω**, ***kataphroneō***, v. GK: *2969* [→ *2707*]. to despise, look down on, scorn, show contempt:– despise [7], despisest [1], despising [1]

2707 **καταφρονητής**, ***kataphronētēs***, n. GK: *2970* [→ *2706*]. scoffer, despiser:– despisers [1]

2708 **καταχέω**, ***katacheō***, v. GK: *2972* [→ *1632; cf. 2596*]. to pour out, pour down:– poured [2]

2709 **καταχθόνιος**, ***katachthonios***, a. GK: *2973* [→ *2596*]. under the earth, subterranean; this may refer to the dead as a class of people, which generally are regarded as inhabiting the underworld. It is likely a more general term than the specific names for the abode of the dead: Hades, Gehenna, Tartaros, etc:– under the earth [1]

2710 **καταχράομαι**, ***katachraomai***, v. GK: *2974* [→ *2596+5530*]. to make full use of; to be engrossed in:– abuse [1], abusing [1]

2711 **καταψύχω**, ***katapsychō***, v. GK: *2976* [→ *2596+5594*]. to cool off, refresh with:– cool [1]

2712 **κατείδωλος**, ***kateidōlos***, a. GK: *2977* [→ *2596+1497*]. full of idols / images:– wholly given to idolatry (*+1510*) [1]

κατελεύθω, ***kateleuthō***. See ***2718***.

2713 **κατέναντι**, ***katenanti***, adv. GK: *2978* [→ *2596+1725*]. ahead, before, in the sight of; opposite of:– over against [4], before [1]

κατενέγκω, ***katenegkō***. See ***2702***.

2714 **κατενώπιον**, ***katenōpion***, adv.&pp.*. GK: *2979* [→ *2596+1722+3708*]. in the sight of, in the presence of; before:– before [2], before the presence [1], in the sight [1], sight [1]

2715 **κατεξουσιάζω**, ***katexousiazō***, v. GK: *2980* [→ *1849; cf. 2596*]. to exercise authority over:– exercise authority upon [2]

2716 **κατεργάζομαι**, ***katergazomai***, v. GK: *2981* [→ *2596+2041*]. to produce, accomplish, bring about, do:– worketh [7], wrought [6], do [3], done [2], working [2], causeth [1], doeth [1], perform [1], work out [1]

2717 , Not used in Strong's numbering system.

2718 **κατέρχομαι**, ***katerchomai***, v. GK: *2982* [→ *2596+2064*]. to go down, come down:– came down [4], came [2], went down [2], come down [1], come [1], departed [1], descendeth [1], landed [1]

2719 **κατεσθίω**, ***katesthiō***, v. GK: *2983 & 2984* [→ *2596+2068*]. to eat up, consume:– devour [6], devoured [3], devoured up [2], ate up [1], devoureth [1], eat up [1], eaten up [1]

2720 **κατευθύνω**, ***kateuthynō***, v. GK: *2985* [→ *2596+2117*]. to guide, direct, lead:– direct [2], guide [1]

2721 **κατεφίσταμαι**, ***katephistamai***, v. GK: *2987* [→ *2596+1909+2476*]. to make an attack upon, rise up against:– made insurrection against [1]

2722 **κατέχω**, ***katechō***, v. GK: *2988* [→ *2596+2192*]. to hold back, suppress, restrain; hold fast, possess; (pass.) to be bound:– hold fast [3], hold [2], keep [2], had [1], held [1], keep in memory [1], letteth [1], made [1], possessed [1], possessing [1], retained [1], seize [1], stayed [1], take [1], withholdeth [1]

2723 **κατηγορέω**, ***katēgoreō***, v. GK: *2989* [→ *2724, 2725*]. to accuse, bring charges against:– accuse [13], accused [6], accuseth [1], accusing [1], object [1]

2724 **κατηγορία**, ***katēgoria***, n. GK: *2990* [→ *2723*]. (legal) charge, accusation:– accusation [2], accusation against [1], accused (*+1722*) [1]

2725 **κατήγορος**, ***katēgoros***, n. GK: *2991 & 2992* [→ *2723*]. accuser:– accusers [6], accuser [1]

2726 **κατήφεια**, ***katēpheia***, n. GK: *2993* [→ *2596+5316*]. gloominess, a feeling of dejection:– heaviness [1]

2727 **κατηχέω**, ***katēcheō***, v. GK: *2994* [→ *2596+2279*]. (act.) to instruct; (pass.) to be instructed, informed:– informed [2], instructed [2], instructed in [1], taught [1], teacheth [1], teach [1]

2728 **κατιόω**, ***katioō***, v. GK: *2995* [→ *2596+2447*]. (pass.) to become corroded, tarnished:– cankered [1]

2729 **κατισχύω**, ***katischyō***, v. GK: *2996* [→ *2596+2479*]. to overcome, prevail; to be able:– prevail against [1], prevailed [1]

2730 **κατοικέω, *katoikeō***, v. GK: *2997 & 3001* [→ *2596+3624*]. to live in, reside in, settle:– dwell [19], dwelt [11], dwelleth [7], inhabiters [3], dwellers [2], dwelling [2], dwellest [1], dwelling at [1], dwelt in [1]

2731 **κατοίκησις, *katoikēsis***, n. GK: *2998* [→ *2596+3624*]. where one lives, residence:– dwelling [1]

2732 **κατοικητήριον, *katoikētērion***, n. GK: *2999* [→ *2596+3624*]. dwelling place, home:– habitation [2]

2733 **κατοικία, *katoikia***, n. GK: *3000* [→ *2596+3624*]. where one lives, dwelling place:– habitation [1]

2734 **κατοπτρίζω, *katoptrizō***, v. GK: *3002* [→ *2596+3708*]. (mid.) to reflect or to look at, contemplate:– beholding as in a glass [1]

2735 **κατόρθωμα, *katorthōma***, n. GK: *3003* [→ *2596+3717*]. success, prosperity, good order:– very worthy deeds [1]

2736 **κάτω, *katō***; or **κατωτέρω, *katōterō***, adv. GK: *3004 & 3006* [→ *2596*]. below; down, downward; bottom, under, lower:– down [5], beneath [3], bottom [2], under [1]

2737 **κατώτερος, *katōteros***, a. GK: *3005* [→ *2596*]. lower:– lower [1]

2738 **καῦμα, *kauma***, n. GK: *3008* [→ *2545*]. (scorching) heat:– heat [2]

2739 **καυματίζω, *kaumatizō***, v. GK: *3009 & 3010* [→ *2545*]. (act.) to scorch by heat, burn; (pass.) to be scorched, seared:– scorched [3], scorch [1]

2740 **καῦσις, *kausis***, n. GK: *3011* [→ *2545*]. burning:– burned [1]

2741 **καυσόω, *kausoō***, v. GK: *3012* [→ *2545*]. (pass.) to be consumed by fire, burned up:– fervent heat [2]

2742 **καύσων, *kausōn***, n. GK: *3014* [→ *2545*]. (scorching) heat, hot day:– heat [2], burning heat [1]

2743 **καυτηριάζω, *kautēriazō***, v. GK: *3013 & 3015* [→ *2545*]. (pass.) to be seared with a hot iron:– seared with a hot iron [1]

2744 **καυχάομαι, *kauchaomai***, v. GK: *3016* [→ *2620, 2745, 2746*]. to boast, brag about; to rejoice in, glory in; this can refer to proper or improper boasting, depending on the object of the boast:– glory [20], boast [6], rejoice [4], glorieth [2], makest boast [2], boasted [1], boasting [1], glorying [1], joy [1]

2745 **καύχημα, *kauchēma***, n. GK: *3017* [→ *2744*]. something to boast about, boasting; pride, joy:– rejoicing [4], glory [3], glorying [2], boasting [1], rejoice [1]

2746 **καύχησις, *kauchēsis***, n. GK: *3018* [→ *2744*]. boasting, pride; glorying in; this can refer to proper or improper boasting, depending on the object of the boast:– boasting [6], rejoicing [4], glorying [1], glory [1]

2747 **Κεγχρεαί, *Kenchreai***, n.pr. GK: *3020*. Cenchrea:– Cenchrea [3]

2748 **Κεδρών, *Kedrōn***, n.pr. GK: *3022*. Kidron:– Cedron [1]

2749 **κεῖμαι, *keimai***, v. GK: *3023* [→ *345, 480, 606, 733, 1945, 2621, 2837, 2838, 2845, 2846, 3873, 4029, 4295, 4873*]. to lay, lie, be laid, laid out; be destined, appointed:– laid [6], set [6], lying [4], lieth [2], appointed [1], is [1], laid up [1], lain [1], lay [1], lie [1], made [1], there [1]

2750 **κειρία, *keiria***, n. GK: *3024* [→ *2751*]. strip of linen, bandage, graveclothes:– graveclothes [1]

2751 **κείρω, *keirō***, v. GK: *3025* [→ *1359, 1946, 1947, 2750, 2772, 2773, 2877*]. (act.) to shear (another); (mid.) to have one's hair cut:– shorn [3], shearer [1]

2752 **κέλευσμα, *keleusma***, n. GK: *3026* [→ *2753*]. (loud) command, signal:– shout [1]

2753 **κελεύω, *keleuō***, v. GK: *3027* [→ *2027, 2752*]. to order, direct, command:– commanded [21], bid [1], commandest [1], commanding [1], commandment [1], command [1], gave commandment [1]

2754 **κενοδοξία, *kenodoxia***, n. GK: *3029* [→ *2756+1391*]. vain conceit, empty conceit, a state of pride that has no proper basis:– vainglory [1]

2755 **κενόδοξος, *kenodoxos***, a. GK: *3030* [→ *2756+1391*]. conceited, a state of pride that has no proper basis:– vain glory [1]

2756 **κενός, *kenos***, a. GK: *3031* [→ *2754, 2755, 2757, 2758, 2761*]. empty, empty-handed; by extension: vain, ineffective, useless, foolish:– vain [12], empty [4], in vain [2]

2757 **κενοφωνία, *kenophōnia***, n. GK: *3032* [→ *2756+5456*]. chatter, empty talk:– vain babblings [2]

2758 **κενόω, *kenoō***, v. GK: *3033* [→ *2756*]. to empty, deprive; (pass.) to be hollow, emptied, of no value:– in vain [1], made of no reputation [1], made of none effect [1], made void [1], make void [1]

2759 **κέντρον, *kentron***, n. GK: *3034* [→ *1461, 1574*]. sting, goad:– pricks [2], sting [2], stings [1]

2760 **κεντυρίων, *kentyriōn***, n. GK: *3035*. centurion, technically the commander of one hundred:– centurion [3]

2761 **κενῶς, *kenōs***, adv. GK: *3036* [→ *2756*]. without reason, in vain, to no purpose:– in vain [1]

2762 **κεραία, *keraia***, n. GK: *3037* [→ *2768*]. least stroke of a pen, projection [a portion of a letter of the alphabet], referring to the smallest detail of the Law:– tittle [2]

2763 **κεραμεύς, *kerameus***, n. GK: *3038* [→ *2766*]. potter:– potter's [2], potter [1]

2764 **κεραμικός, *keramikos***, a. GK: *3039* [→ *2766*]. pertaining to a potter:– potter [1]

2765 **κεράμιον, *keramion***, n. GK: *3040* [→ *2766*]. clay jar:– pitcher [2]

2766 **κέραμος, *keramos***, n. GK: *3041* [→ *2763, 2764, 2765*]. clay roof tile:– tiling [1]

2767 **κεράννυμι, *kerannymi***, v. GK: *3042* [→ *185, 194, 4786*]. to mix; (pass.) to be poured:– filled [1], fill [1], poured out [1]

2768 **κέρας, *keras***, n. GK: *3043* [→ *2762, 2769*]. horn, often a figure of power and position:– horns [10], horn [1]

2769 **κεράτιον, *keration***, n. GK: *3044* [→ *2768*]. carob pod:– husks [1]

κεράω, *keraō*. See **2767**.

2770 **κερδαίνω, *kerdainō***, v. GK: *2132 & 3045* [→ *2771*]. to gain; make money; win over; spare:– gain [8], gained [5], get gain [1], win [1], won [1]

2771 **κέρδος, *kerdos***, n. GK: *3046* [→ *146, 147, 2770*]. gain, profit:– gain [2], lucre's [1]

2772 **κέρμα, *kerma***, n. GK: *3047* [→ *2751*]. coin:– money [1]

2773 **κερματιστής, *kermatistēs***, n. GK: *3048* [→ *2751*]. money exchanger:– changers of money [1]

2774 **κεφάλαιον, *kephalaion***, n. GK: *3049* [→ *2776*]. the (main) point; price, sum of money:– sum [2]

2775 **κεφαλαιόω, *kephalaioō***, v. GK: *3050 & 3052* [→ *2776*]. to strike on the head:– wounded in the head [1]

2776 **κεφαλή, *kephalē***, n. GK: *3051* [→ *346, 607, 2774, 2775, 2777, 4030, 4344*]. head (of a body); top (stone in a building); by extension: someone or something in the primary place, the point of origin:– head [57], heads [19]

2777 **κεφαλίς, *kephalis***, n. GK: *3053* [→ *2776*]. section of a scroll:– volume [1]

2778 **κῆνσος, *kēnsos***, n. GK: *3056*. (poll) tax:– tribute [4]

2779 **κῆπος, *kēpos***, n. GK: *3057* [→ *2780*]. garden, grove:– garden [5]

2780 **κηπουρός, *kēpouros***, n. GK: *3058* [→ *2779*]. gardener:– gardener [1]

2781 **κηρίον, *kērion***, n. GK: *3059*. wax, honeycomb:–

2782 **κήρυγμα, *kērygma***, n. GK: *3060* [→ *2783*]. preaching, proclamation, message, with a focus on the content of what is preached:– preaching [8]

2783 **κῆρυξ, *kēryx***, n. GK: *3061* [→ *2782, 2784, 4296*]. herald, preacher, proclaimer:– preacher [3]

2784 **κηρύσσω, *kēryssō***, v. GK: *3062* [→ *2783*]. to preach, proclaim, tell, often urging acceptance of the message, with warnings of consequences for not doing so:– preach [22], preached [20], preaching [8], published [3], preacheth [2], publish [2], preacher [1], preachest [1], proclaimed [1], proclaiming [1]

2785 **κῆτος, *kētos***, n. GK: *3063*. huge fish:– whale's [1]

2786 **Κηφᾶς, *Kēphas***, n.pr. GK: *3064*. Cephas (Aramaic for Peter), "*rock*":– Cephas [6]

2787 **κιβωτός, *kibōtos***, n. GK: *3066*. ark, box, chest:– ark [6]

2788 **κιθάρα, *kithara***, n. GK: *3067* [→ *2789, 2790*]. harp, lyre:– harps [3], harp [1]

2789 **κιθαρίζω, *kitharizō***, v. GK: *3068* [→ *2788*]. to play the harp or lyre:– harped [1], harping [1]

2790 **κιθαρῳδός, *kitharōdos***, n. GK: *3069* [→ *2788+5603*]. harpist, lyre player:– harpers [2]

2791 **Κιλικία, *Kilikia***, n.pr. GK: *3070*. Cilicia:– Cilicia [8]

2792 **κινάμωμον, *kinamōmon***, n. GK: *3072 & 3077*. cinnamon:– cinnamon [1]

2793 **κινδυνεύω, *kindyneuō***, v. GK: *3073* [→ *2794*]. to be in danger:– in danger [2], in jeopardy [1], stand in jeopardy [1]

2794 **κίνδυνος, *kindynos***, n. GK: *3074* [→ *2793*]. danger, risk:– perils [8], peril [1]

2795 **κινέω, *kineō***, v. GK: *3075* [→ *277, 2796, 3334, 4787*]. to move, remove; to shake, stir up; (pass.) to be moved, removed; be aroused:– moved [2], move [2], wagging [2], mover [1], remove [1]

2796 **κίνησις, *kinēsis***, n. GK: *3076* [→ *2795*]. motion:– moving [1]

2797 **Κίς, *Kis***, n.pr. GK: *3078*. Kish, "*bow, power*":– Cis [1]

κίχρημι, *kichrēmi*. See **5531**.

2798 **κλάδος, *klados***, n. GK: *3080* [→ *2806*]. branch, twig:– branches [9], branch [2]

2799 **κλαίω, *klaiō***, v. GK: *3081* [→ *2805*]. to weep, cry, wail, mourn:– weep [16], wept [11], weeping [9], weepest [2], bewail [1], weep (*+4160*) [1]

2800 **κλάσις, *klasis***, n. GK: *3082* [→ *2806*]. breaking:– breaking [2]

2801 **κλάσμα, *klasma***, n. GK: *3083* [→ *2806*]. broken piece, fragment:– fragments [7], broken [2]

2802 **Κλαύδα, *Klauda***; or **Καῦδα, *Kauda***, n.pr. GK: *3007 & 3084 & 3085*. Clauda, Cauda:– Clauda [1]

2803 **Κλαυδία, *Klaudia***, n.pr. GK: *3086* [→ *2804*]. Claudia, "[poss.] *lame*":– Claudia [1]

2804 **Κλαύδιος, *Klaudios***, n.pr. GK: *3087* [→ *2803*]. Claudius:– Claudius [3]

2805 **κλαυθμός, *klauthmos***, n. GK: *3088* [→ *2799*]. weeping, crying:– weeping [6], wailing [2], wept (*+1096*) [1]

2806 **κλάω, *klaō***, v. GK: *3089* [→ *1575, 2622, 2798, 2800, 2801, 2814*]. to break:– brake [9], broken [3], break [2], breaking [1]

2807 **κλείς, *kleis***, n. GK: *3090* [→ *2808*]. key:– key [4], keys [2]

2808 **κλείω, *kleiō***, v. GK: *3091* [→ *608, 1576, 2623, 2807, 4788*]. to close, shut, lock:– shut [10], shut up [3], shutteth [2], shutteth up [1]

2809 **κλέμμα, *klemma***, n. GK: *3092* [→ *2813*]. theft, stealing:– thefts [1]

2810 **Κλεοπᾶς, *Kleopas***, n.pr. GK: *3093* [→ *2811+3962*]. Cleopas, "*renowned father*":– Cleopas [1]

2811 **κλέος, *kleos***, n. GK: *3094* [→ *2810*]. credit, honor:– glory [1]

2812 **κλέπτης, *kleptēs***, n. GK: *3095* [→ *2813*]. thief:– thief [12], thieves [4]

2813 **κλέπτω, *kleptō***, v. GK: *3096* [→ *2809, 2812, 2829*]. steal:– steal [11], stole [2]

2814 **κλῆμα, *klēma***, n. GK: *3097* [→ *2806*]. branch (in context, vine branches):– branch [3], branches [1]

2815 **Κλήμης, *Klēmēs***, n.pr. GK: *3098*. Clement, "*mild*":– Clement [1]

2816 **κληρονομέω, *klēronomeō***, v. GK: *3099* [→ *2819+3551*]. to inherit, acquire; see also *2817*.– inherit [14], heirs [1], heir [1], inheritance obtained [1], inherited [1]

2817 **κληρονομία, *klēronomia***, n. GK: *3100* [→ *2819+3551*]. inheritance, transfer of property and possessions from one generation to another, usually within a family or clan and usually upon the death of the owner. This word often has an implication of a legitimate, historic right to the objects inherited. In some contexts this refers to salvation, an inheritance shared with Jesus Christ, the true heir:– inheritance [14]

2818 **κληρονόμος, *klēronomos***, n. GK: *3101* [→ *2819+3551*]. heir, one who inherits:– heir [8], heirs [7]

2819 κλῆρος, *klēros*, n. GK: *3102* [→ *2624, 2816, 2817, 2818, 2820, 3490, 3647, 3648, 4345, 4789*]. (casting) lots; share, place, inheritance:– lots [6], inheritance [2], lot [2], part [2], heritage [1]

2820 κληρόω, *klēroō*, v. GK: *3103* [→ *2819*]. (pass.) to be chosen, appointed:– obtained an inheritance [1]

2821 κλῆσις, *klēsis*, n. GK: *3104* [→ *2564*]. call, calling; situation, station in life:– calling [10], vocation [1]

2822 κλητός, *klētos*, a. GK: *3105* [→ *2564*]. called, invited:– called [11]

2823 κλίβανος, *klibanos*, n. GK: *3106*. (fire of a) furnace, oven:– oven [2]

2824 κλίμα, *klima*, n. GK: *3107* [→ *2827*]. region:– regions [2], parts [1]

2825 κλίνη, *klinē*, n. GK: *3109* [→ *2827*]. bed, mat, stretcher:– bed [8], beds [1], tables [1]

2826 κλινίδιον, *klinidion*, n. GK: *3110* [→ *2827*]. bed, mat, stretcher (smaller and more temporary than a bed found in a home):– couch [2]

2827 κλίνω, *klinō*, v. GK: *3111* [→ *186, 347, 755, 1578, 2625, 2824, 2825, 2826, 2828, 4346, 4411*]. to bow down, lay down; to be over (late in the day):– lay [2], bowed down [1], bowed [1], far spent (*+2235*) [1], turned to flight [1], wear away [1]

2828 κλισία, *klisia*, n. GK: *3112* [→ *2827*]. group reclining for a meal:– company [1]

2829 κλοπή, *klopē*, n. GK: *3113* [→ *2813*]. theft, stealing:– thefts [2]

2830 κλύδων, *klydōn*, n. GK: *3114* [→ *2148, 2626, 2627, 2831*]. raging waters, waves:– raging [1], wave [1]

2831 κλυδωνίζομαι, *klydōnizomai*, v. GK: *3115* [→ *2830*]. to be tossed back and forth by waves:– tossed to and fro [1]

2832 Κλωπᾶς, *Klōpas*, n.pr. GK: *3116*. Clopas:– Cleophas [1]

2833 κνήθω, *knēthō*, v. GK: *3117* [cf. *1102*]. (pass.) to feel an itch:– itching [1]

2834 Κνίδος, *Knidos*, n.pr. GK: *3118*. Cnidus, "*age*":– Cnidus [1]

2835 κοδράντης, *kodrantēs*, n. GK: *3119*. penny, small Roman coin, about one-sixty-fourth of a denarius (a day's wage):– farthing [2]

2836 κοιλία, *koilia*, n. GK: *3120*. any and all internal organs, translated in context as: belly, stomach, womb, etc.; by extension: the source of feelings and emotions. "The fruit of the womb" means "a child.":– belly [11], womb [11], wombs [1]

2837 κοιμάω, *koimaō*, v. GK: *3121* [→ *2749*]. (pass.) to fall asleep, sleep; die:– sleep [4], slept [3], asleep [2], fallen asleep [2], fell asleep [2], sleeping [2], dead [1], fell on sleep [1], sleepeth [1]

2838 κοίμησις, *koimēsis*, n. GK: *3122* [→ *2749*]. (noun) sleep:– taking of rest [1]

2839 κοινός, *koinos*, a. GK: *3123* [→ *2840, 2841, 2842, 2843, 2844, 4790, 4791*]. common; (ceremonially) unclean, impure, unholy:– common [7], unclean [3], defiled [1], unholy [1]

2840 κοινόω, *koinoō*, v. GK: *3124* [→ *2839*]. to make (ceremonially) unclean, impure; to defile:– defile [6], defileth [5], call common [2], polluted [1], unclean [1]

2841 κοινωνέω, *koinōneō*, v. GK: *3125* [→ *2839*]. to share in, participate in:– partakers [2], partaker [2], communicated with [1], communicate [1], distributing [1], made partakers [1]

2842 κοινωνία, *koinōnia*, n. GK: *3126* [→ *2839*]. fellowship, the close association between persons, emphasizing what is common between them; by extension: participation, sharing, contribution, gift, the outcome of such close relationships:– fellowship [12], communion [4], communicate [1], communication [1], contribution [1], distribution [1]

2843 κοινωνικός, *koinōnikos*, a. GK: *3127* [→ *2839*]. willing to share, generous:– willing to communicate [1]

2844 κοινωνός, *koinōnos*, n. GK: *3128* [→ *2839*]. partner, participant, one who joins in with another in some enterprise or activity, in business or ministry:– partakers [4], partner [2], companions [1], fellowship [1], partaker [1], partners [1]

2845 κοίτη, *koitē*, n. GK: *3130* [→ *2749*]. (marriage) bed; conception; sexual immorality:– bed [2], chambering [1], conceived [1]

2846 κοιτών, *koitōn*, n. GK: *3131* [→ *2749*]. bedroom; trusted personal servant, chamberlain:– chamberlain (*+1909+3588*) [1]

2847 κόκκινος, *kokkinos*, a. GK: *3132* [→ *2848*]. scarlet, (bright) red; in some contexts, cloth that is scarlet or (bright) red (Rev 18:12,16):– scarlet [4], scarlet coloured [1], scarlet colour [1]

2848 κόκκος, *kokkos*, n. GK: *3133* [→ *2847*]. seed, kernel of grain:– grain of seed [5], corn [1], grain [1]

2849 κολάζω, *kolazō*, v. GK: *3134* [→ *2967*]. to punish:– punished [1], punish [1]

2850 κολακεία, *kolakeia*, n. GK: *3135*. flattery:– flattering [1]

2851 κόλασις, *kolasis*, n. GK: *3136* [→ *2967*]. punishment:– punishment [1], torment [1]

2852 κολαφίζω, *kolaphizō*, v. GK: *3139*. to strike with the fists, beat, torment; (pass.) receive a beating, be brutally treated:– buffeted [3], buffet [2]

2853 κολλάω, *kollaō*, v. GK: *3140* [→ *4347*]. (mid.) to join, associate with, cling to; (pass.) to be united, stuck to, piled up; to stay near, follow; to be hired out:– joined to [2], join [2], clave [1], cleaveth on [1], cleave [1], join to [1], joined [1], keep company [1]

2854 κολλούριον, *kollourion*, n. GK: *3141*. eye salve:– eyesalve [1]

2855 κολλυβιστής, *kollybistēs*, n. GK: *3142*. money exchanger:– moneychangers [2], changers' [1]

2856 κολοβόω, *koloboō*, v. GK: *3143* [→ *2967*]. to cut short, shorten:– shortened [4]

2857 Κολοσσαί, *Kolossai*, n.pr. GK: *3138 & 3145* [→ *2858*]. Colosse, "*punishment*":– Colosse [1]

2858 Κολοσσαεύς, *Kolossaeus*, n.pr.g. GK: *3137 & 3144* [→ *2857*]. Colossian:– Colossians [1]

2859 κόλπος, *kolpos*, n. GK: *3146*. lap area: side, bosom, chest; bay:– bosom [5], creek [1]

2860 κολυμβάω, *kolymbaō*, v. GK: *3147* [→ *1579, 2861*]. to swim:– swim [1]

2861 κολυμβήθρα, *kolymbēthra*, n. GK: *3148* [→ *2860*]. pool:– pool [5]

2862 κολωνία, *kolōnia*, n. GK: *3149*. Roman colony:– colony [1]

2863 κομάω, *komaō*, v. GK: *3150* [→ *2864*]. to have long hair:– have long hair [2]

2864 κόμη, *komē*, n. GK: *3151* [→ *2863*]. (long) hair:– hair [1]

2865 κομίζω, *komizō*, v. GK: *3152* [→ *2889*]. (act.) to bring; (mid.) to receive (what is due), reward, be repaid:– receive [6], received [3], brought [1], receiving [1]

2866 κομψότερον, *kompsoteron*, adv.comp. GK: *3153* [→ *2889*]. better:– began to amend (*+2192*) [1]

2867 κονιάω, *koniaō*, v. GK: *3154* [→ *2868*]. (pass.) to be whitewashed:– whited [2]

2868 κονιορτός, *koniortos*, n. GK: *3155* [→ *2867+3730*]. dust:– dust [5]

2869 κοπάζω, *kopazō*, v. GK: *3156* [→ *2875*]. to die down, abate:– ceased [3]

2870 κοπετός, *kopetos*, n. GK: *3157* [→ *2875*]. mourning, sorrowing, lamentation:– lamentation [1]

2871 κοπή, *kopē*, n. GK: *3158* [→ *2875*]. defeat, cutting down:– slaughter [1]

2872 κοπιάω, *kopiaō*, v. GK: *3159* [→ *2875*]. to work, labor, give effort; to become tired, grow weary:– labour [8], laboured [5], bestowed labour [3], laboureth [2], toil [2], labouring [1], toiled [1], wearied [1]

2873 κόπος, *kopos*, n. GK: *3160* [→ *2875*]. labor, work; bother, trouble, difficulty:– labour [8], labours [5], trouble (*+3930*) [4], troubleth (*+3930*) [1], weariness [1]

2874 κοπρία, *kopria*, n. GK: *3161 & 3162 & 3163*. manure pile, rubbish pile:– dung (*+906*) [1], dunghill [1]

2875 κόπτω, *koptō*, v. GK: *3164* [→ *348, 609, 677, 695, 1464, 1465, 1581, 2123, 2629, 2869, 2870, 2871, 2872, 2873, 2974, 4297, 4298, 4348, 4349, 4350*]. to cut; (mid.) to mourn, beat one's breast:– bewailed [2], cut down [2], lamented [1], lament [1], mourn [1], wail [1]

2876 κόραξ, *korax*, n. GK: *3165*. raven, crow:– ravens [1]

2877 κοράσιον, *korasion*, n. GK: *3166* [→ *2751*]. (little) girl:– damsel [6], maid [2]

2878 κορβᾶν, *korban*; or **κορβανᾶς, *korbanas***, n. GK: *3167 & 3168*. Corban, a gift dedicated to God, temple treasury:– Corban [1], treasury [1]

2879 Κόρε, *Kore*, n.pr. GK: *3169*. Korah, "*shaven, bald*":– Core [1]

2880 κορέννυμι, *korennymi*, v. GK: *3170*. (pass.) to be filled to the full, have enough:– eaten enough (*+5160*) [1], full [1]

2881 Κορίνθιος, *Korinthios*, n.pr.g. GK: *3171* [→ *2882*]. Corinthian:– Corinthians [4]

2882 Κόρινθος, *Korinthos*, n.pr. GK: *3172* [→ *2881*]. Corinth, "*decoration*":– Corinth [6], Corinthus [1]

2883 Κορνήλιος, *Kornēlios*, n.pr. GK: *3173*. Cornelius, "*of a horn*":– Cornelius [10]

2884 κόρος, *koros*, n. GK: *3174*. cor (dry measure between ten and twelve bushels):– measures [1]

2885 κοσμέω, *kosmeō*, v. GK: *3175* [→ *2889*]. to make beautiful, decorate, dress; trim (a lamp); (pass.) to put in order; be adorned, decorated, beautifully dressed:– adorned [3], garnished [3], adorn [2], garnish [1], trimmed [1]

2886 κοσμικός, *kosmikos*, a. GK: *3176* [→ *2889*]. earthly, worldly:– worldly [2]

2887 κόσμιος, *kosmios*, a. GK: *3177 & 3178* [→ *2889*]. respectable, honorable:– good behaviour [1], modest [1]

2888 κοσμοκράτωρ, *kosmokratōr*, n. GK: *3179* [→ *2889+2904*]. (pl.) powers of the world:– rulers [1]

2889 κόσμος, *kosmos*, n. GK: *3180* [→ *1101, 1580, 2865, 2866, 2885, 2886, 2887, 2888, 4792*]. world: earth, world system, whole universe; adornment. In some contexts, the world is simply the place where people live, in other contexts (especially in John), the world is a system opposed to God:– world [185], adorning [1], world's [1]

2890 Κούαρτος, *Kouartos*, n.pr. GK: *3181*. Quartus, "*fourth [born]*":– Quartus [1]

2891 κοῦμι, *koumi*, l.[v.]. GK: *3182 & 3183*. koumi (Aramaic: stand up!):– cumi [1]

2892 κουστωδία, *koustōdia*, n. GK: *3184*. guard:– watch [3]

2893 κουφίζω, *kouphizō*, v. GK: *3185*. to lighten, make lighter:– lightened [1]

2894 κόφινος, *kophinos*, n. GK: *3186*. basket of various sizes and considered typical of the Jews:– baskets [6]

2895 κράβαττος, *krabbatos*, n. GK: *3187 & 3188*. bed, (sleeping) mat:– bed [10], beds [1], couches [1]

2896 κράζω, *krazō*, v. GK: *3189* [→ *349, 2905, 2906*]. call out, cry out, shout, exclaim:– cried [30], cried out [13], crying [6], crieth [3], crying out [3], cry out [2], crieth out [1], cry [1], out [1]

2897 κραιπάλη, *kraipalē*, n. GK: *3190*. dissipation:– surfeiting [1]

2898 κρανίον, *kranion*, n. GK: *3191* [→ *603*]. skull:– skull [3], Calvary [1]

2899 κράσπεδον, *kraspedon*, n. GK: *3192*. edge, border, hem; tassel:– border [2], hem [2], borders [1]

2900 κραταιός, *krataios*, a. GK: *3193* [→ *2904*]. mighty, powerful:– mighty [1]

2901 κραταιόω, *krataioō*, v. GK: *3194* [→ *2904*]. (pass.) to be strong, become strong:– waxed strong [2], strengthened [1], strong [1]

2902 κρατέω, *krateō*, v. GK: *3195* [→ *2904*]. to arrest, seize into custody; to take, grab, hold onto, obtain; (pass.) to be kept from, held:– took [10], hold [5], hold fast [3], holding [3], laid hold on [3], lay hold on [3], take [3], held [2], holden [2], laid hold [2], fast [1], holdest fast [1], holdeth [1], kept [1], laid hands on [1], laid hold upon [1], lay hands on [1], lay hold upon [1], obtained [1], retained [1], retain [1]

2903 κράτιστος, *kratistos*, a. GK: *3196* [→ *2904*]. most excellent, "your Excellency":– most excellent [2], most noble [2]

2904 κράτος, *kratos*, n. GK: *3197* [→ *192, 193, 1466, 1467, 1468, 2888, 2900, 2901, 2902, 2903, 2908, 2909, 3841, 4031; cf. 2594*]. power, strength:– power [5], dominion [4], mightily (*+2596*) [1], mighty [1], strength [1]

2905 κραυγάζω, *kraugazō*, v. GK: *3198* [→ *2896*]. to shout, cry out:– cried out [3], cried [3], cry [1]

***2906* κραυγή, *kraugē*,** n. GK: *3199* [→ *2896*]. crying out, shouting, verbal brawling:– cry [3], crying [2], clamour [1]

***2907* κρέας, *kreas*,** n. GK: *3200*. meat:– flesh [2]

***2908* κρεῖσσον, *krēisson*,** a.neut. of a form of *2909*. GK: *3201* [→ *2904*]. better, superior, greater:– better [1]

***2909* κρείττων, *kreittōn*,** a. GK: *3202* [→ *2904*]. better, superior, greater:– better [17], best [1], better than [1]

***2910* κρεμάννυμι, *kremannymi*,** v. GK: *3203* [→ *1582, 2630, 2911*]. to hang on, hang upon:– hanged [4], hang [2], hangeth [1]

***2911* κρημνός, *krēmnos*,** n. GK: *3204* [→ *2910*]. steep bank, cliff:– steep place [3]

***2912* Κρής, *Krēs*,** n.pr.g. GK: *3205* [→ *2914*]. Cretan:– Cretians [2], Cretes [1]

***2913* Κρήσκης, *Krēskēs*,** n.pr. GK: *3206*. Crescens, "*increasing*":– Crescens [1]

***2914* Κρήτη, *Krētē*,** n.pr. GK: *3207* [→ *2912*]. Crete:– Crete [5]

***2915* κριθή, *krithē*,** n. GK: *3208* [→ *2916*]. barley; barley flour was used in the preparation of cheaper kinds of bread:– barley [1]

***2916* κρίθινος, *krithinos*,** a. GK: *3209* [→ *2915*]. made of barley (flour):– barley [2]

***2917* κρίμα, *krima*,** n. GK: *3210* [→ *2919*]. judgment, condemnation; sentence, punishment:– judgment [12], damnation [7], condemnation [5], avenged (*+2919*) [1], condemned [1], go to law (*+2192*) [1], judgments [1]

***2918* κρίνον, *krinon*,** n. GK: *3211*. lily:– lilies [2]

***2919* κρίνω, *krinō*,** v. GK: *3212* [→ *87, 178, 350, 351, 470, 505, 610, 611, 612, 799, 843, 1252, 1253, 1341, 1469, 1506, 1948, 2631, 2632, 2633, 2917, 2920, 2922, 2923, 2924, 4299, 4793, 4942, 5271, 5272, 5273; cf. 1506*]. to decide, consider, as preferring one thing over another or determining the correctness of a matter; by extension: to judge, pass judgment on, condemn in a legal sense:– judge [45], judged [26], judgeth [9], determined [7], judgest [6], called in question [2], condemned [2], esteemeth [2], judging [2], avenged (*+2917*) [1], concluded [1], condemneth [1], condemning [1], condemn [1], damned [1], decreed [1], go to law [1], goeth to law [1], ordained [1], sentence [1], sue at the law [1], thought [1]

***2920* κρίσις, *krisis*,** n. GK: *3213* [→ *2919*]. judgment (human or divine), justice, the concept of determining the correctness of a matter; negatively, punishment, condemnation:– judgment [39], condemnation [3], damnation [3], accusation [2], judgments [2]

***2921* Κρίσπος, *Krispos*,** n.pr. GK: *3214*. Crispus, "*curled*":– Crispus [2]

***2922* κριτήριον, *kritērion*,** n. GK: *3215* [→ *2919*]. court of law; legal dispute, lawsuit:– judge [1], judgment seats [1], judgments [1]

***2923* κριτής, *kritēs*,** n. GK: *3216* [→ *2919*]. judge:– judge [13], judges [4]

***2924* κριτικός, *kritikos*,** a. GK: *3217* [→ *2919*]. able to discern or judge:– discerner [1]

***2925* κρούω, *krouō*,** v. GK: *3218*. to knock (on a gate or door):– knock [4], knocketh [3], knocked [1], knocking [1]

***2926* κρύπτη, *kryptē*,** n. GK: *3219* [→ *2928*]. hidden place:– *untranslated* [1]

***2927* κρυπτός, *kryptos*,** a. GK: *3220 & 3224 & 3226* [→ *2928*]. hidden, unseen, secret:– secret [10], hidden [3], hid [3], secrets [2], inwardly (*+1722+3588*) [1], secret place [1]

***2928* κρύπτω, *kryptō*,** v. GK: *3221* [→ *613, 614, 1470, 2926, 2927, 2931, 4032*]. to hide:– hid [10], hide [2], hidden [1], hideth [1], kept secret [1], secretly [1]

***2929* κρυσταλλίζω, *krystallizo*,** v. GK: *3222* [→ *2930*]. to be clear as crystal:– clear as crystal [1]

***2930* κρύσταλλος, *krystallos*,** n. GK: *3223* [→ *2929*]. rock crystal; some translate "ice":– crystal [2]

***2931* κρυφῇ, *kryphē*,** adv. GK: *3225* [→ *2928*]. in secret:– secret [1]

***2932* κτάομαι, *ktaomai*,** v. GK: *3227* [→ *2933, 2934, 2935*]. to get, gain, buy; take along; to control:– possess [3], purchased [2], obtained [1], provide [1]

***2933* κτῆμα, *ktēma*,** n. GK: *3228* [→ *2932*]. wealth, possessions; piece of property, field:– possessions [3], possession [1]

***2934* κτῆνος, *ktēnos*,** n. GK: *3229* [→ *2932*]. (domestic) animal: donkey, horse, cattle:– beasts [3], beast [1]

***2935* κτήτωρ, *ktētōr*,** n. GK: *3230* [→ *2932*]. (land) owner:– possessors [1]

***2936* κτίζω, *ktizō*,** v. GK: *3231* [→ *2937, 2938, 2939*]. to create; (ptcp.) Creator:– created [12], creator [1], made [1], make [1]

***2937* κτίσις, *ktisis*,** n. GK: *3232* [→ *2936*]. creation, created thing, creature; governmental institution:– creature [11], creation [6], building [1], ordinance [1]

***2938* κτίσμα, *ktisma*,** n. GK: *3233* [→ *2936*]. creature, created thing:– creatures [2], creature [2]

***2939* κτίστης, *ktistēs*,** n. GK: *3234* [→ *2936*]. Creator:– creator [1]

***2940* κυβεία, *kybeia*,** n. GK: *3235*. cunning, craftiness, trickery:– sleight [1]

***2941* κυβέρνησις, *kybernēsis*,** n. GK: *3236* [→ *2942*]. administration; derived from a Greek verb meaning "to steer a ship, to guide," not found in the NT:– governments [1]

***2942* κυβερνήτης, *kybernētēs*,** n. GK: *3237* [→ *2941*]. sea captain, pilot:– master [1], shipmaster [1]

***2943* κυκλόθεν, *kyklothen*,** adv. GK: *3239* [→ *2945*]. (all) around; from all sides:– round about [3], about [1]

κυκλός, *kuklos*. See **2945**.

***2944* κυκλόω, *kykloō*,** v. GK: *3238 & 3240* [→ *2945*]. to surround: gather around, march around:– compassed about [2], came round about [1], compassed [1], stood round about [1]

***2945* κύκλῳ, *kyklō*,** adv. GK: *3241* [→ *2943, 2944, 4033*]. all around, in a circle, surrounding:– round about [7]

***2946* κύλισμα, *kylisma*,** n. GK: *3242 & 3243* [→ *2947*]. wallowing, rolling:– wallowing [1]

***2947* κυλίω, *kyliō*,** v. GK: *3244* [→ *617, 2946, 4351*]. (mid.) to roll around:– wallowed [1]

***2948* κυλλός, *kyllos*,** a. GK: *3245*. crippled, maimed:– maimed [4]

***2949* κῦμα, *kyma*,** n. GK: *3246* [→ *616, 1471*]. waves, surf:– waves [5]

***2950* κύμβαλον, *kymbalon*,** n. GK: *3247*. cymbal:– cymbal [1]

***2951* κύμινον, *kyminon*,** n. GK: *3248*. cummin:– cummin [1]

***2952* κυνάριον, *kynarion*,** n. GK: *3249* [→ *2965*]. (little or domesticated) dog:– dogs [4]

***2953* Κύπριος, *Kyprios*,** n.pr.g. GK: *3250* [→ *2954*]. from Cyprus:– Cyprus [3]

***2954* Κύπρος, *Kypros*,** n.pr. GK: *3251* [→ *2953*]. Cyprus, "*copper*":– Cyprus [5]

***2955* κύπτω, *kyptō*,** v. GK: *3252* [→ *352, 3870, 4794*]. to stoop down, bend down:– stooped [2], stoop down [1]

***2956* Κυρηναῖος, *Kyrēnaios*,** n.pr.g. GK: *3254* [→ *2957*]. from Cyrene:– Cyrenian [2], of Cyrene [2], Cyrene [1], Cyrenians [1]

***2957* Κυρήνη, *Kyrēnē*,** n.pr. GK: *3255* [→ *2956*]. Cyrene, "*wall*":– Cyrene [1]

***2958* Κυρήνιος, *Kyrēnios*,** n.pr. GK: *3256 & 3260*. Quirinius:– Cyrenius [1]

***2959* κυρία, *kyria*,** n. GK: *3257* [→ *2962*]. lady (female "lord"):– lady [2]

***2960* κυριακός, *kyriakos*,** a. GK: *3258* [→ *2962*]. pertaining to the Lord, the Lord's:– Lord's [2]

***2961* κυριεύω, *kyrieuō*,** v. GK: *3259* [→ *2962*]. to lord over, be master of, have authority over, one who rules or exercises authority; note in some contexts there is an implication that the authority exercised is harsh:– Lord/lord [1], dominion over [1], exercise lordship over [1], hath dominion over [1], have dominion over [1], lords [1], over [1]

***2962* κύριος, *kyrios*,** n. GK: *3261* [→ *2634, 2959, 2960, 2961, 2963; cf. 2964*]. lord, master. This can be a title of address to a person of higher status, "lord, sir"; a master of property or slaves; or a NT translation of the Hebrew 151 "Lord" or 3378 "LORD," that is "Yahweh," the proper name of God in the OT:– Lord/lord [703], Lord's/lord's [15], sir [11], masters [8], master [4], lords [3], God [1], masters' [1], owners [1], sirs [1]

***2963* κυριότης, *kyriotēs*,** n. GK: *3262* [→ *2962*]. authority, dominion, power, lordship:– dominion [2], dominions [1], government [1]

***2964* κυρόω, *kyroō*,** v. GK: *3263* [→ *208, 4300; cf. 2962*]. to reaffirm; to establish a covenant, ratify, validate:– confirmed [1], confirm [1]

***2965* κύων, *kyōn*,** n. GK: *3264* [→ *2952*]. dog:– dogs [4], dog [1]

***2966* κῶλον, *kōlon*,** n. GK: *3265*. dead body, corpse:– carcases [1]

***2967* κωλύω, *kōlyō*,** v. GK: *3266* [→ *209, 1254, 2849, 2851, 2856; cf. 1422*]. to hinder, stop, restrain, forbid; oppress; (pass.) to be prevented, kept from:– forbid [9], forbad [3], forbidding [3], forbidden [1], forbiddeth [1], hindered [1], hinder [1], kept from [1], let [1], not suffered [1], withstand [1]

***2968* κώμη, *kōmē*,** n. GK: *3267* [→ *2969, 2970*]. village, town:– village [10], town [8], villages [7], towns [3]

***2969* κωμόπολις, *kōmopolis*,** n. GK: *3268* [→ *2968+4172*]. village, market town:– towns [1]

***2970* κῶμος, *kōmos*,** n. GK: *3269* [→ *2968*]. orgy, revelry, carousing:– revellings [2], rioting [1]

***2971* κώνωψ, *kōnōps*,** n. GK: *3270*. gnat, mosquito:– gnat [1]

***2972* Κῶς, *Kōs*,** n.pr. GK: *3271*. Cos, "*summit*":– Cos [1]

***2973* Κωσάμ, *Kōsam*,** n.pr. GK: *3272*. Cosam, "*diviner*":– Cosam [1]

***2974* κωφός, *kōphos*,** a. GK: *3273* [→ *2875*]. unable to talk or speak, mute; deaf:– dumb [8], deaf [5], speechless [1]

***2975* λαγχάνω, *lanchanō*,** v. GK: *3275*. to choose by lot, decide by lot; receive (by lot or divine will):– obtained [2], cast lots [1], lot [1]

***2976* Λάζαρος, *Lazaros*,** n.pr. GK: *3276*. Lazarus, "*one whom God helps*":– Lazarus [15]

***2977* λάθρᾳ, *lathra*,** adv. GK: *3277* [→ *2990*]. secretly, quietly:– privily [3], secretly [1]

***2978* λαῖλαψ, *lailaps*,** n. GK: *3278*. storm, hurricane, whirlwind:– storm [2], tempest [1]

***2979* λακτίζω, *laktizō*,** v. GK: *3280*. to kick:– kick [2]

***2980* λαλέω, *laleō*,** v. GK: *3281* [→ *215, 216, 412, 1255, 1583, 2635, 2636, 2637, 2981, 3424, 4354, 4814*]. to speak, talk:– speak [103], spake [72], spoken [33], speaketh [23], speaking [11], told [10], talked [8], said [7], say [6], preached [4], speakest [4], uttered [3], saith [2], tell [2], preaching [1], preach [1], talkest [1], talketh [1], talking [1], talk [1], utter [1]

***2981* λαλιά, *lalia*,** n. GK: *3282* [→ *2980*]. speech, a way of speaking, language:– speech [3], saying [1]

***2982* λαμά, *lama*;** or **λεμά, *lema*,** l.[pp.+p.inter.]. GK: *3283 & 3316*. lama (Hebrew: why?):– lama [2]

***2983* λαμβάνω, *lambano*,** v. GK: *3284* [→ *353, 354, 423, 482, 484, 618, 678, 1187, 1949, 2124, 2125, 2126, 2638, 3028, 3335, 3336, 3880, 4301, 4355, 4356, 4380, 4381, 4382, 4815, 4838, 4843, 4878, 5274*]. to take, receive; (pass.) to be received, selected:– receive [61], received [57], took [55], take [32], receiveth [15], taken [12], taketh [4], taking [4], caught [3], had [2], obtain [2], took up [2], acceptest [1], accepteth [1], amazed (*+1611*) [1], attained [1], began [1], brought [1], call [1], came into room (*+1240*) [1], came [1], do [1], forgotten (*+3024*) [1], have [1], held [1], receiving [1]

***2984* Λάμεχ, *Lamech*,** n.pr. GK: *3285*. Lamech:– Lamech [1]

λαμμᾶ, *lamma*. See **2982**.

***2985* λαμπάς, *lampas*,** n. GK: *3286* [→ *2989*]. lamp, lantern, torch:– lamps [6], lamp [1], lights [1], torches [1]

***2986* λαμπρός, *lampros*,** a. GK: *3287* [→ *2989*]. bright, shining, splendorous, elegant:– bright [2], goodly [2], white [2], clear [1], gay [1], gorgeous [1]

***2987* λαμπρότης, *lamprotēs*,** n. GK: *3288* [→ *2989*]. brightness:– brightness [1]

***2988* λαμπρῶς, *lamprōs*,** adv. GK: *3289* [→ *2989*]. in luxury, splendidly:– sumptuously [1]

***2989* λάμπω, *lampō*,** v. GK: *3290* [→ *1584, 2985, 2986, 2987, 2988, 4034*]. to give light, shine:– shine [3], shined [2], giveth light [1], shineth [1]

2990 **λανθάνω, *lanthanō*,** v. GK: *3291* [→ *225, 226, 227, 228, 230, 1585, 1950, 1953, 2977, 3024*]. to keep secret, escape notice, be hidden:– hid [2], ignorant [2], hidden [1], unawares [1]

2991 **λαξευτός, *laxeutos*,** a. GK: *3292.* cut in rock:– hewn in stone [1]

2992 **λαός, *laos*,** n. GK: *3295* [→ *745, 2993, 2994, 3008, 3009, 3010, 3011, 3531, 3532*]. people, crowd; often denotes the people of God (either Israel or, by extension, the Christian church):– people [139], people's [2], peoples [2]

2993 **Λαοδίκεια, *Laodikeia*,** n.pr. GK: *3293* [→ *2992+1349*]. Laodicea:– Laodicea [6]

2994 **Λαοδικεύς, *Laodikeus*,** n.pr.g. GK: *3294* [→ *2992+1349*]. Laodicean:– Laodiceans [2]

2995 **λάρυγξ, *larynx*,** n. GK: *3296.* throat:– throat [1]

2996 **Λασαία, *Lasaia*,** n.pr. GK: *3297 & 3298.* Lasea:– Lasea [1]

2997 **λάσκω, *laskō*,** v. GK: *3279 & 3299.* to burst open:– burst asunder [1]

2998 **λατομέω, *latomeō*,** v. GK: *3300.* to cut, hew (rock):– hewn out [1], hewn [1]

2999 **λατρεία, *latreia*,** n. GK: *3301* [→ *1496, 1495, 3000*]. worship, ministry, service (to God):– service [4], divine service [1]

3000 **λατρεύω, *latreuō*,** v. GK: *3302* [→ *2999*]. to serve, minister (in religious duties):– serve [13], worship [3], served [2], service [1], serving [1], worshippers [1]

3001 **λάχανον, *lachanon*,** n. GK: *3303.* plant, herb, vegetable:– herbs [4]

3002 **Λεββαῖος, *Lebbaios*,** n.pr. GK: *3304* [cf. *2280*]. Lebbaeus, "*[one near to] my heart*":– Lebbeus [1]

3003 **λεγιών, *legiōn*,** n. GK: *3305.* legion, technically an army unit of 6,000 with 6,000 support troops. Twice in the NT it is the proper name of a collective of demons (Mk 5:9; Lk 8:30):– legion [3], legions [1]

3004 **λέγω, *legō*,** v. GK: *3306* [→ *35, 148, 249, 356, 357, 379, 471, 483, 485, 550, 626, 627, 945, 1075, 1076, 1256, 1258, 1260, 1261, 1351, 1586, 1588, 1589, 1677, 1757, 1951, 2036, 2046, 2127, 2128, 2129, 2312', 2551, 2639, 3048, 3049, 3050, 3051, 3052, 3053, 3054, 3055, 3056, 3150, 3151, 3473, 3670, 3881, 3884, 4086, 4180, 4277, 4280, 4302, 4691, 4758, 4816, 4817, 4883, 4899, 5378, 5542, 5573; cf. 3670*]. say, said, the most general term for speaking in the NT, translated contextually with more specific words such as say, tell; ask, answer:– said [995], saying [403], say [398], saith [298], tell [59], spake [50], spoken [45], called [39], speak [38], sayest [21], told [18], commanded [6], speaketh [6], calleth [4], call [4], bade [3], bid [3], callest [3], command [3], named [2], speakest [2], answer [1], asked [1], biddeth [1], boasting [1], bring word [1], describeth [1], giving out [1], grant [1], made [1], put forth [1], saidst [1], sayings [1], seen [1], shew [1], speaking [1], telleth [1], uttered [1]

3005 **λεῖμμα, *leimma*,** n. GK: *3307* [→ *3007*]. remnant:– remnant [1]

3006 **λεῖος, *leios*,** a. GK: *3308.* smooth, level:– smooth [1]

3007 **λείπω, *leipō*,** v. GK: *3309* [→ *88, 89, 413, 620, 1257, 1459, 1587, 1952, 1954, 2640, 2641, 2645, 3005, 3062, 3063, 3064, 4035, 5275, 5277*]. to lack, fall short:– wanting [3], destitute [1], lackest [1], lack [1]

3008 **λειτουργέω, *leitourgeō*,** v. GK: *3310* [→ *2992+2041*]. to perform religious duties; serve:– ministered [1], ministering [1], minister [1]

3009 **λειτουργία, *leitourgia*,** n. GK: *3311* [→ *2992+2041*]. religious service, ceremony; service, ministry, help:– service [3], ministry [2], ministration [1]

3010 **λειτουργικός, *leitourgikos*,** a. GK: *3312* [→ *2992+2041*]. ministering, engaged in holy service:– ministering [1]

3011 **λειτουργός, *leitourgos*,** n. GK: *3313* [→ *2992+2041*]. servant, minister, one who cares for (another), often with a focus on a specific task or duty, which can be practical or spiritual:– ministers [2], minister [2], ministered [1]

3012 **λέντιον, *lention*,** n. GK: *3317.* towel, likely made of linen:– towel [2]

3013 **λεπίς, *lepis*,** n. GK: *3318* [→ *3014, 3015, 3016*]. scale, flake:– scales [1]

3014 **λέπρα, *lepra*,** n. GK: *3319* [→ *3013*]. leprosy:– leprosy [4]

3015 **λεπρός, *lepros*,** a. GK: *3320* [→ *3013*]. leprous; (n.) leper:– lepers [5], leper [4]

3016 **λεπτός, *leptos*,** a. GK: *3321* [→ *3013*]. very small copper coin, worth about 1/128th of a denarius (a day's wage):– mites [2], mite [1]

3017 **Λευί, *Leui*,** n.pr. GK: *3322* [→ *3018, 3019, 3020*]. Levi, "[perhaps] *wild cow* or *person pledged for a debt or vow*":– Levi [5]

3018 **Λευίς, *Leuis*,** n.pr. GK: *3323* [→ *3017*]. Levi, "[perhaps] *wild cow* or *person pledged for a debt or vow*":– Levi [3]

3019 **Λευίτης, *Leuitēs*,** n.pr.g. GK: *3324* [→ *3017*]. Levite:– Levite [2], Levites [1]

3020 **Λευιτικός, *Leuitikos*,** a.pr.g. GK: *3325* [→ *3017*]. Levitical:– Levitical [1]

3021 **λευκαίνω, *leukainō*,** v. GK: *3326* [→ *3022*]. to bleach, whiten:– made white [1], white [1]

3022 **λευκός, *leukos*,** a. GK: *3328* [→ *3021*]. white; bright, gleaming:– white [25]

3023 **λέων, *leōn*,** n. GK: *3329.* lion:– lion [6], lions [3]

3024 **λήθη, *lēthē*,** n. GK: *3330* [→ *2990*]. forgetfulness:– forgotten (*+2983*) [1]

3025 **ληνός, *lēnos*,** n. GK: *3332* [→ *5276*]. winepress:– winepress [4], winepress (*+3631*) [1]

3026 **λῆρος, *lēros*,** n. GK: *3333.* nonsense, idle talk:– idle tales [1]

3027 **λῃστής, *lēstēs*,** n. GK: *3334.* robber, bandit; rebel, revolutionary; this word is derived from the Greek verb, "to practice robbery or piracy," not found in the NT:– thieves [8], thief [3], robbers [2], robber [2]

3028 **λῆμψις, *lēmpsis*,** n. GK: *3331 & 3335* [→ *2983*]. receiving:– receiving [1]

3029 **λίαν, *lian*,** adv. GK: *3336.* very much, greatly, completely:– exceeding [5], greatly [4], chiefest [2], great while [1], sore [1], very [1]

3030 **λίβανος, *libanos*,** n. GK: *3337* [→ *3031*]. frankincense, incense, an aromatic resinous gum:– frankincense [2]

3031 **λιβανωτός, *libanōtos*,** n. GK: *3338* [→ *3030*]. censer (bowl for burning incense):– censer [2]

3032 **Λιβερτῖνος, *Libertinos*,** n.pr. GK: *3339.* Freedman, "*Freedman*":– Libertines [1]

3033 **Λιβύη, *Libyē*,** n.pr. GK: *3340.* Libya:– Libya [1]

3034 **λιθάζω, *lithazō*,** v. GK: *3342* [→ *3037*]. to stone:– stoned [4], stone [4]

3035 **λίθινος, *lithinos*,** a. GK: *3343* [→ *3037*]. made of stone:– stone [2], of stone [1]

3036 **λιθοβολέω, *lithoboleō*,** v. GK: *3344* [→ *3037+906*]. to throw stones:– stoned [5], stonest [2], cast stones [1], stone [1]

3037 **λίθος, *lithos*,** n. GK: *3345* [→ *2642, 3034, 3035, 3036, 3038, 5555*]. stone, boulder; this can refer to stone as a material or substance, and to a stone as a piece of rock. A "precious stone" is a "gem.":– stone [37], stones [15], another[S] [4], stumblingstone (*+4348*) [2], millstone (*+3457*) [1], stone's [1]

3038 **λιθόστρωτος, *lithostrōtos*,** a. GK: *3346* [→ *3037+4766*]. (n.) stone pavement; translated in the NIV as a place name:– pavement [1]

3039 **λικμάω, *likmaō*,** v. GK: *3347.* to crush:– grind to powder [2]

3040 **λιμήν, *limēn*,** n. GK: *3348* [→ *2568, 3041*]. harbor:– haven [2]

3041 **λίμνη, *limnē*,** n. GK: *3349* [→ *3040*]. lake:– lake [10]

3042 **λιμός, *limos*,** n. GK: *3350.* hunger, famine, starvation:– famine [4], famines [3], hunger [3], dearth [2]

3043 **λίνον, *linon*,** n. GK: *3351.* linen (garment); wick of a lamp:– flax [1], linen [1]

3044 **Λίνος, *Linos*,** n.pr. GK: *3352.* Linus:– Linus [1]

3045 **λιπαρός, *liparos*,** a. GK: *3353.* costly, rich; (n.) riches:– dainty [1]

3046 **λίτρα, *litra*,** n. GK: *3354.* (Roman) pound (about 12 oz. or 327 gr.):– pound [2]

3047 **λίψ, *lips*,** n. GK: *3355.* southwest:– south west [1]

3048 **λογεία, *logeia*,** n. GK: *3356* [→ *3004*]. collection:– collection [1], gatherings [1]

3049 **λογίζομαι, *logizomai*,** v. GK: *3357* [→ *3004*]. to credit, count, reckon; regard, think, consider:– think [7], imputed [5], counted [4], reckoned [4], accounted [2], reckon [2], suppose [2], accounting [1], account [1], conclude [1], count [1], despised (*+1519+3762*) [1], esteemeth [1], imputeth [1], impute [1], imputing [1], laid to charge [1], numbered [1], reasoned [1], thinkest [1], thinketh [1], thought [1]

3050 **λογικός, *logikos*,** a. GK: *3358* [→ *3004*]. spiritual, logical:– reasonable [1], word [1]

3051 **λόγιον, *logion*,** n. GK: *3359* [→ *3004*]. (pl.) words, sayings, oracles:– oracles [4]

3052 **λόγιος, *logios*,** a. GK: *3360* [→ *3004*]. learned, eloquent:– eloquent [1]

3053 **λογισμός, *logismos*,** n. GK: *3361* [→ *3004*]. thought; argument, reasoning:– imaginations [1], thoughts [1]

3054 **λογομαχέω, *logomacheō*,** v. GK: *3362* [→ *3004+3163*]. to quarrel about words:– strive about words [1]

3055 **λογομαχία, *logomachia*,** n. GK: *3363* [→ *3004+3163*]. quarrel about words:– strifes of words [1]

3056 **λόγος, *logos*,** n. GK: *3364* [→ *3004*]. word, spoken or written, often with a focus on the content of a communication (note the many contextual translations in NIV); matter, thing. "The Word" is a title of Christ (Jn 1:1), emphasizing his own deity and communication of who God is and what he is like:– word [175], words [48], saying [34], sayings [16], account [8], speech [8], matter [4], utterance [4], communication [2], things [2], thing [2], work [2], as concerning (*+1519*) [1], cause [1], communications [1], doctrine [1], fame [1], given exhortation (*+3870*) [1], have to do [1], intent [1], mouth [1], none (*+3762*) [1], preaching [1], question [1], reason (*+2596*) [1], reason [1], reckoneth (*+4868*) [1], rumour [1], say [1], shew [1], speaker [1], talk [1], tidings [1], treatise [1], word spoken [1], word's [1]

3057 **λόγχη, *lonchē*,** n. GK: *3365.* spear, lance:– spear [1]

3058 **λοιδορέω, *loidoreō*,** v. GK: *3366* [→ *3060*]. to insult, curse:– reviled [3], revilest [1]

3059 **λοιδορία, *loidoria*,** n. GK: *3367* [→ *3060*]. insult, slander, verbal abuse:– railing [2], speak reproachfully [1]

3060 **λοίδορος, *loidoros*,** n. GK: *3368* [→ *486, 3058, 3059*]. slanderer, verbal abuser:– railer [1], revilers [1]

3061 **λοιμός, *loimos*,** n.&a. GK: *3369.* pestilence; troublemaker, public menace:– pestilences [2], pestilent [1]

3062 **λοιπός, *loipos*,** a. GK: *3370* [→ *3063*]. remaining, left over, the rest; in some contexts a marker for a conclusion, "finally," or an adverb of time, "from now on," or "henceforth":– other [17], rest [12], others [6], finally (*+3588*) [4], remnant [4], now (*+3588*) [2], besides [1], finally [1], from henceforth (*+3588*) [1], furthermore [1], henceforth (*+3588*) [1], henceforth [1], moreover (*+1161+3739*) [1], remaineth (*+1510+3588*) [1], remain [1], residue [1], then [1]

3063 **λοιπόν, *loipon*,** a.neut.s. of *3062.* GK: *3370* [→ *3007, 3062, 3064*]. remaining, left over, the rest; see *3062*:–

3064 **λοιποῦ, *loipou*,** a.gen.s. of *3062.* GK: *3370* [→ *3063*]. remaining, left over, the rest; see *3062*:–

3065 **Λουκᾶς, *Loukas*,** n.pr. GK: *3371* [→ *3066*]. Luke:– Lucas [2], Luke [2]

3066 **Λούκιος, *Loukios*,** n.pr. GK: *3372* [→ *3065*]. Lucius:– Lucius [2]

3067 **λουτρόν, *loutron*,** n. GK: *3373* [→ *3068*]. washing, bath:– washing [2]

3068 **λούω, *louō*,** v. GK: *3374* [→ *628, 3067*]. to wash, have a bath:– washed [6]

3069 **Λύδδα, *Lydda*,** n.pr. GK: *3375.* Lydda:– Lydda [3]

3070 **Λυδία, *Lydia*,** n.pr. GK: *3376.* Lydia:– Lydia [2]

3071 **Λυκαονία, *Lykaonia*,** n.pr. GK: *3377* [→ *3072*]. Lycaonia:– Lycaonia [1]

3072 **Λυκαονιστί, *Lykaonisti*,** adv.pr. GK: *3378* [→ *3071*]. in (the) Lycaonian (language):– in the speech of Lycaonia [1]

3073 **Λυκία, *Lykia*,** n.pr. GK: *3379.* Lycia:– Lycia [1]

3074 **λύκος**, ***lykos***, n. GK: *3380*. wolf:– wolves [4], wolf [2]

3075 **λυμαίνω**, ***lymainō***, v. GK: *3381*. to destroy, damage, ruin:– made havock [1]

3076 **λυπέω**, ***lypeō***, v. GK: *3382* [→ *3077*]. (act.) to cause sorrow, grief; (pass.) to be sorrowful, sad, distressed:– sorrowful [6], grieved [5], made sorry [5], sorry [3], sorrowed [2], caused grief [1], grieve [1], heaviness [1], make sorry [1], sorrow [1]

3077 **λύπη**, ***lypē***, n. GK: *3383* [→ *253, 3076, 4036, 4818*]. sorrow, grief, pain:– sorrow [11], heaviness [2], grief [1], grievous [1], grudgingly (*+1537*) [1]

3078 **Λυσανίας**, ***Lysanias***, n.pr. GK: *3384*. Lysanias:– Lysanias [1]

3079 **Λυσίας**, ***Lysias***, n.pr. GK: *3385*. Lysias:– Lysias [3]

3080 **λύσις**, ***lysis***, n. GK: *3386* [→ *3089*]. divorce:– loosed [1]

3081 **λυσιτελέω**, ***lysiteleō***, v. GK: *3387* [→ *3089+5056*]. to be advantageous, (imper. form) it is better:– better [1]

3082 **Λύστρα**, ***Lystra***, n.pr. GK: *3388*. Lystra:– Lystra [6]

3083 **λύτρον**, ***lytron***, n. GK: *3389* [→ *3089*]. ransom, the price of release, thus making redemption possible:– ransom [2]

3084 **λυτρόω**, ***lytroō***, v. GK: *3390* [→ *3089*]. to redeem, free a slave by paying a ransom; from the base meaning of slave redemption in the marketplace comes the figure of sinners redeemed by God from slavery to sin and death:– redeemed [2], redeem [1]

3085 **λύτρωσις**, ***lytrōsis***, n. GK: *3391* [→ *3089*]. redemption, ransoming, releasing:– redemption [2], redeemed (*+4160*) [1]

3086 **λυτρωτής**, ***lytrōtēs***, n. GK: *3392* [→ *3089*]. deliverer, redeemer:– deliverer [1]

3087 **λυχνία**, ***lychnia***, n. GK: *3393* [→ *3088*]. lampstand (not a candlestick):– candlesticks [6], candlestick [6]

3088 **λύχνος**, ***lychnos***, n. GK: *3394* [→ *3087*]. lamp, usually of clay or metal, with olive oil to fuel its wick (not a candle):– candle [8], light [5], lights [1]

3089 **λύω**, ***lyō***, v. GK: *3395* [→ *179, 255, 359, 360, 487, 629, 630, 1262, 1590, 1955, 1956, 2646, 2647, 3080, 3081, 3083, 3084, 3085, 3086, 3885, 3886*]. to loose, release, untie; to break, destroy:– loose [15], loosed [10], broken [4], unloose [3], destroy [2], dissolved [2], loosing [2], break [1], broken down [1], broken up [1], melt [1], put off from [1]

3090 **Λωΐς**, ***Lōis***, n.pr. GK: *3396*. Lois, "[perhaps] *more desirable, better*":– Lois [1]

3091 **Λώτ**, ***Lōt***, n.pr. GK: *3397*. Lot:– Lot [3], Lot's [1]

3092 **Μάαθ**, ***Maath***, n.pr. GK: *3399*. Maath, "*to be small*":– Maath [1]

3093 **Μαγδαλά**, ***Magdala***, n.pr. GK: *3400 & 3401* [cf. *3094*]. Magdala:– Magdala [1]

3094 **Μαγδαληνή**, ***Magdalēnē***, n.pr.g. GK: *3402* [cf. *3093*]. Magdalene, "*from Magdala*":– Magdalene [12]

3095 **μαγεία**, ***mageia***, n. GK: *3404 & 3406* [→ *3096*]. magic:– sorceries [1]

3096 **μαγεύω**, ***mageuō***, v. GK: *3405* [→ *3095, 3097*]. to practice sorcery, magic:– used sorcery [1]

3097 **μάγος**, ***magos***, n. GK: *3407* [→ *3096*]. sorcerer; (pl.) Magi:– wise men [4], sorcerer [2]

3098 **Μαγώγ**, ***Magōg***, n.pr. GK: *3408*. Magog, "[perhaps] *land of Gog*":– Magog [1]

3099 **Μαδιάμ**, ***Madiam***, n.pr. GK: *3409*. Midian:– Madian [1]

3100 **μαθητεύω**, ***mathēteuō***, v. GK: *3411* [→ *3129*]. (act./tr.) to teach; to make a disciple; (pass./intr.) to become a disciple:– disciple [1], instructed [1], taught [1], teach [1]

3101 **μαθητής**, ***mathētēs***, n. GK: *3412* [→ *3129*]. disciple, student, follower; a committed learner and follower, in the NT usually of Jesus Christ:– disciples [240], disciple [27], disciples' [1]

3102 **μαθήτρια**, ***mathētria***, n. GK: *3413* [→ *3129*]. (female) disciple, student, follower:– disciple [1]

3103 **Μαθουσαλά**, ***Mathousala***, n.pr. GK: *3417*. Methuselah, "*man of the javelin*":– Mathusala [1]

3104 **Μαϊνάν**, ***Mainan***, n.pr. GK: *3418*. Mainan:– Menan [1]

3105 **μαίνομαι**, ***mainomai***, v. GK: *3419* [→ *1693, 3130, 3132*]. to rave, be insane, out of one's mind, to think or reason in an irrational manner manifested by erratic actions or lack of reasonable speech:– mad [4], beside thyself [1]

3106 **μακαρίζω**, ***makarizō***, v. GK: *3420* [→ *3107, 3108*]. to call blessed; to consider blessed:– call blessed [1], count happy [1]

3107 **μακάριος**, ***makarios***, a. GK: *3421* [→ *3106*]. blessed (receiving God's favor), fortunate, good (in a position of favor), happy (feelings associated with receiving God's favor):– blessed [44], happy [5], happier [1]

3108 **μακαρισμός**, ***makarismos***, n. GK: *3422* [→ *3106*]. blessedness, joy:– blessedness [3]

3109 **Μακεδονία**, ***Makedonia***, n.pr. GK: *3423* [→ *3110*]. Macedonia:– Macedonia [24]

3110 **Μακεδών**, ***Makedōn***, n.pr.g. GK: *3424* [→ *3109*]. Macedonian, "*from Macedonia*":– Macedonia [3], Macedonian [1], of Macedonia [1]

3111 **μάκελλον**, ***makellon***, n. GK: *3425*. meat market, food market:– shambles [1]

3112 **μακράν**, ***makran***, adv.&pp.*. GK: *3426* [→ *3372*]. far away, distant, long way off:– far [4], afar off (*+1519*) [1], afar off [1], far hence [1], far off [1], good way off [1], great way [1]

3113 **μακρόθεν**, ***makrothen***, adv. GK: *3427* [→ *3372*]. from a distance, from far away:– afar off (*+575*) [5], afar [5], afar off [3], from far [1]

3114 **μακροθυμέω**, ***makrothymeō***, v. GK: *3428* [→ *3372+2372*]. to have patience; to be patient; to exhibit internal and external control in a difficult circumstance, which control could exhibit itself by delaying an action:– patient [3], have patience [2], bear long [1], hath long patience [1], longsuffering [1], patiently endured [1], suffereth long [1]

3115 **μακροθυμία**, ***makrothymia***, n. GK: *3429* [→ *3372+2372*]. patience, forbearance, internal and external control in a difficult circumstance, which control could exhibit itself by delaying an action:– longsuffering [12], patience [2]

3116 **μακροθύμως**, ***makrothymōs***, adv. GK: *3430* [→ *3372+2372*]. patiently:– patiently [1]

3117 **μακρός**, ***makros***, a. GK: *3431* [→ *3372*]. lengthy, long; distant, far away:– long [3], far [2]

3118 **μακροχρόνιος**, ***makrochronios***, a. GK: *3432* [→ *3372+5550*]. pertaining to having a long life:– live long (*+1510*) [1]

3119 **μαλακία**, ***malakia***, n. GK: *3433* [→ *3120*]. sickness, ailment:– disease [3]

3120 **μαλακός**, ***malakos***, a. GK: *3434* [→ *3119*]. fine, soft; (n.) male prostitute, a male homosexual who is the passive sex partner:– soft [3], effeminate [1]

3121 **Μαλελεήλ**, ***Maleleēl***, n.pr. GK: *3435*. Mahalalel, "*praise of God [El]*":– Maleleel [1]

3122 **μάλιστα**, ***malista***, adv.super. GK: *3436* [→ *3123*]. especially:– specially [5], especially [4], chiefly [2], most [1]

3123 **μᾶλλον**, ***mallon***, adv.comp. GK: *3437* [→ *3122*]. more, more than; rather, instead:– more [42], rather [34], better (*+2570*) [1], far (*+4183*) [1], more than [1], much more [1], much [1], than (*+2228*) [1]

3124 **Μάλχος**, ***Malchos***, n.pr. GK: *3438*. Malchus, "*king*":– Malchus [1]

3125 **μάμμη**, ***mammē***, n. GK: *3439*. grandmother:– grandmother [1]

3126 **μαμωνᾶς**, ***mamōnas***, n. GK: *3440*. wealth, assets:– mammon [4]

3127 **Μαναήν**, ***Manaēn***, n.pr. GK: *3441*. Manaen, "*comforter*":– Manaen [1]

3128 **Μανασσῆς**, ***Manassēs***, n.pr. GK: *3442*. Manasseh, "*one that makes to forget*":– Manasses [3]

3129 **μανθάνω**, ***manthanō***, v. GK: *3443* [→ *261, 2648, 3100, 3101, 3102, 4827*]. to learn, study, be instructed:– learn [13], learned [10], learning [1], understood [1]

3130 **μανία**, ***mania***, n. GK: *3444* [→ *3105*]. insanity, madness:– make mad (*+1519+4062*) [1]

3131 **μάννα**, ***manna***, n. GK: *3445*. manna, a food given by God to the generation of the Exodus: "the bread of heaven":– manna [5]

3132 **μαντεύομαι**, ***manteuomai***, v. GK: *3446* [→ *3105*]. to fortune-tell, divine:– soothsaying [1]

3133 **μαραίνω**, ***marainō***, v. GK: *3447* [→ *262, 263*]. (pass.) to fade away, disappear:– fade away [1]

3134 **μαράνα θά**, ***marana tha***, l.[n.+v.]. GK: *3448*. maranatha (Aramaic: "Come, Lord!"):– Maranatha [1]

3135 **μαργαρίτης**, ***margaritēs***, n. GK: *3449*. pearl:– pearls [7], pearl [2]

3136 **Μάρθα**, ***Martha***, n.pr. GK: *3450*. Martha, "*lady [female lord]*":– Martha [13]

3137 **Μαρία**, ***Maria***; or **Μαριάμ**, ***Mariam***, n.pr. GK: *3451 & 3452*. Mary, "[perhaps] *beloved* or *plump*":– Mary [54]

3138 **Μᾶρκος**, ***Markos***, n.pr. GK: *3453*. Mark, "*[Latin] large hammer*":– Mark [5], Marcus [3]

3139 **μάρμαρος**, ***marmaros***, n. GK: *3454*. marble:– marble [1]

μάρτυρ, ***martur***. See ***3144***.

3140 **μαρτυρέω**, ***martyreō***, v. GK: *3455* [→ *3144*]. to testify, give testimony; commend, speak well of, vouch for:– bear witness [15], testify [8], bear record [7], testified [6], bare record [5], bare witness [4], testifieth [4], beareth witness [3], witnessed [3], borne witness [2], gave testimony [2], obtained a good report [2], barest witness [1], bearest record [1], gave [1], give witness [1], good report [1], hath good report [1], having a good report [1], obtained witness [1], of honest report [1], testifying [1], testimony [1], well reported of [1], well reported [1], witnesses [1], witnesseth [1], witnessing [1], witness [1]

3141 **μαρτυρία**, ***martyria***, n. GK: *3456* [→ *3144*]. testimony, evidence; (good) reputation:– witness [15], testimony [14], record [7], report [1]

3142 **μαρτύριον**, ***martyrion***, n. GK: *3457* [→ *3144*]. testimony, proof:– testimony [15], witness [4], testified [1]

3143 **μαρτύρομαι**, ***martyromai***, v. GK: *3458* [→ *3144*]. to testify, declare; to insist on, urge:– testify [2], charged [1], take to record [1]

3144 **μάρτυς**, ***martys***, n. GK: *3459* [→ *267, 1263, 1957, 2649, 3140, 3141, 3142, 3143, 4303, 4828, 4901, 5576, 5577, 5575*]. witness, testimony; martyr (one who witnessed unto death):– witnesses [21], witness [8], martyr [2], record [2], martyrs [1]

3145 **μασσάομαι**, ***massaomai***, v. GK: *3460 & 3462* [→ *3146*]. to gnaw, bite:– gnawed [1]

3146 **μαστιγόω**, ***mastigoō***, v. GK: *3463* [→ *631, 1591, 3145, 3147, 3148*]. to flog, whip, scourge; to punish, chastise:– scourge [5], scourged [1], scourgeth [1]

3147 **μαστίζω**, ***mastizō***, v. GK: *3464* [→ *3146*]. to flog, scourge:– scourge [1]

3148 **μάστιξ**, ***mastix***, n. GK: *3465* [→ *3146*]. flogging device, whip; suffering; disease, sickness:– plagues [2], plague [2], scourgings [1], scourging [1]

3149 **μαστός**, ***mastos***, n. GK: *3410 & 3461 & 3466*. breast, chest:– paps [3]

3150 **ματαιολογία**, ***mataiologia***, n. GK: *3467* [→ *3152+3004*]. meaningless talk, empty talk:– vain jangling [1]

3151 **ματαιολόγος**, ***mataiologos***, a. GK: *3468* [→ *3152+3004*]. (n.) idle talker:– vain talkers [1]

3152 **μάταιος**, ***mataios***, a. GK: *3469* [→ *3150, 3151, 3153, 3154, 3155*]. worthless, futile, useless, empty:– vain [5], vanities [1]

3153 **ματαιότης**, ***mataiotēs***, n. GK: *3470* [→ *3152*]. emptiness, futility, frustration:– vanity [3]

3154 **ματαιόω**, ***mataioō***, v. GK: *3471* [→ *3152*]. (pass.) to become futile, given over to worthlessness:– vain [1]

3155 **μάτην**, ***matēn***, adv. GK: *3472* [→ *3152*]. in vain, to no end:– in vain [2]

3156 **Ματθαῖος**, ***Matthaios***; or **Μαθθαῖος**, ***Maththaios***, n.pr. GK: *3414 & 3473*. Matthew, "*gift of Yahweh*":– Matthew [5]

3157 **Ματθάν**, ***Matthan***, n.pr. GK: *3474*. Matthan, "*gift*":– Matthan [2]

3158 **Ματθάτ**, ***Matthat***; or **Μαθθάτ**, ***Maththat***, n.pr. GK: *3415 & 3475*. Mathat, "*gift*":– Matthat [2]

3159 **Ματθίας**, ***Matthias***, n.pr. GK: *3416 & 3476*. Matthias, "*gift of Yahweh*":– Matthias [2]

3160 **Ματταθά**, ***Mattatha***, n.pr. GK: *3477*. Mattatha, "*gift*":– Mattatha [1]

3161 **Ματταθίας**, ***Mattathias***, n.pr. GK: *3478*. Mattathias, "*gift of Yahweh*":– Mattathias [2]

3162 **μάχαιρα**, ***machaira***, n. GK: *3479* [→ *3163*]. (short) sword:– sword [23], swords [6]

3163 **μάχη**, ***machē***, n. GK: *3480* [→ *269, 1264, 2313, 2314, 2341, 2371, 3054, 3055, 3162, 3164*]. quarrel, conflict, fighting:– fightings [2], strifes [1], strivings [1]

3164 **μάχομαι**, ***machomai***, v. GK: *3481* [→ *3163*]. to fight, quarrel, argue:– strove [2], fight [1], strive [1]

3165 **μέ**, ***me***, p.pers.acc. of *1473*. GK: *1609* [→ *1473*]. me; see *1473*:–

3166 **μεγαλαυχέω**, ***megalaucheō***, v. GK: *3482* [→ *3173*]. to become proud, boast:– boasteth [1]

3167 **μεγαλεῖος**, ***megaleios***, a. GK: *3483* [→ *3173*]. (pl. n.) wonders, mighty deeds:– great things [1], wonderful works [1]

3168 **μεγαλειότης**, ***megaleiotēs***, n. GK: *3484* [→ *3173*]. majesty, greatness, grandeur:– magnificence [1], majesty [1], mighty power [1]

3169 **μεγαλοπρεπής**, ***megaloprepēs***, a. GK: *3485* [→ *3173+4241*]. majestic, magnificent:– excellent [1]

3170 **μεγαλύνω**, ***megalynō***, v. GK: *3486* [→ *3173*]. to glorify, regard highly, praise, exalt; to lengthen, expand:– magnified [3], magnify [2], enlarged [1], enlarge [1], shewed great [1]

3171 **μεγάλως**, ***megalōs***, adv. GK: *3487* [→ *3173*]. greatly:– greatly [1]

3172 **μεγαλωσύνη**, ***megalōsynē***, n. GK: *3488* [→ *3173*]. majesty:– majesty [3]

3173 **μέγας**, ***megas***, a. GK: *3489* [→ *3166, 3167, 3168, 3169, 3170, 3171, 3172, 3174, 3175, 3176, 3185, 3186, 3187*]. great; spatially: large; of quantity or degree: loud, intense, violent; of time: long (time); of position: great, important:– great [148], loud [33], greatest [2], high [2], large [2], come to years [1], exceedingly [1], great ones [1], great one [1], great things [1], mighty [1], sore [1], strong [1]

3174 **μέγεθος**, ***megethos***, n. GK: *3490* [→ *3173*]. greatness:– greatness [1]

3175 **μεγιστάν**, ***megistan***, n. GK: *3491* [→ *3173*]. great man, prince, high official:– great men [2], lords [1]

3176 **μέγιστος**, ***megistos***, a.super. GK: *3492* [→ *3173*]. very great:– exceeding great [1]

3177 **μεθερμηνεύω**, ***methermēneuō***, v. GK: *3493* [→ *3326+2059*]. to translate, give the meaning:– interpreted [6], by interpretation [1]

3178 **μέθη**, ***methē***, n. GK: *3494* [→ *3184*]. drunkenness:– drunkenness [3]

3179 **μεθίστημι**, ***methistēmi***; or **μεθιστάνω**, ***methistanō***, v. GK: *3495 & 3496* [→ *3326+2476*]. to move, remove; bring, lead astray; (pass.) to lose, be discharged:– put out [1], removed [1], remove [1], translated [1], turned away [1]

3180 **μεθοδεία**, ***methodeia***, n. GK: *3497* [→ *3326+3598*]. scheming, craftiness, strategy:– lie in wait [1], wiles [1]

3181 **μεθόριον**, ***methorion***, n. GK: *3498* [→ *3326+3724*]. boundary; (pl.) region:– borders [1]

3182 **μεθύσκω**, ***methyskō***, v. GK: *3499* [→ *3184*]. (pass.) to be or become drunk, intoxicated:– drunken [2], drunk [1], well drunk [1]

3183 **μέθυσος**, ***methysos***, n. GK: *3500* [→ *3184*]. drunkard:– drunkards [1], drunkard [1]

3184 **μεθύω**, ***methyō***, v. GK: *3501* [→ *271, 3178, 3182, 3183*]. to get drunk:– drunken [5], made drunk [1]

3185 **μεῖζον**, ***mēizon***, a.comp.n. of *3187*. GK: *3505* [→ *3173*]. greater, larger; older; louder; more:–

3186 **μειζότερος**, ***meizoteros***, a.comp. GK: *3504* [→ *3173*]. greater:– greater than [1]

3187 **μείζων**, ***meizōn***, a.comp. GK: *3505* [→ *3173*]. greater, larger; older; louder; more:– greater than [21], greater [13], greatest [9], more [2], elder [1]

3188 **μέλαν**, ***melan***, a.neut. of *3189*. GK: *3506* [→ *3189*]. the color black; ink, made of soot or other carbon source mixed with oil or resin:– ink [3]

3189 **μέλας**, ***melas***, a. GK: *3506* [→ *3188*]. the color black; ink, made of soot or other carbon source mixed with oil or resin:– black [3]

3190 **Μελεᾶς**, ***Meleas***, n.pr. GK: *3507*. Meleas:– Melea [1]

μέλει, ***melei***. See ***3199***.

3191 **μελετάω**, ***meletaō***, v. GK: *3509* [→ *3199*]. to plot, think about, meditate on; to give oneself wholly to, practice, cultivate:– imagine [1], meditate upon [1], premeditate [1]

3192 **μέλι**, ***meli***, n. GK: *3510* [→ *3193*]. honey:– honey [4]

3193 **μελίσσιος**, ***melissios***, a. GK: *3511 & 3512 & 3513* [→ *3192*]. pertaining to the bee, honeycomb:– honeycomb [1]

3194 **Μελίτη**, ***Melitē***, n.pr. GK: *3514 & 3515*. Melita:– Melita [1]

3195 **μέλλω**, ***mellō***, v. GK: *3516*. to be about to, on the point of; to be destined, must; to intend to; (what is) to come, the future:– should [21], shall [20], to come [14], will [7], would [7], about to [5], be [3], ready to [3], after [2], come [2], was to [2], would have [2], after that (*+1519+3588*) [1], afterwards [1], almost [1], at the point of [1], begin to [1], coming on [1], for to come (*+2064*) [1], hereafter [1], intending to [1], intend [1], meaning to [1], minding [1], ready [1], shall be [1], shalt [1], tarriest [1], time to come [1], to be [1], to [1], wilt [1], yet to [1]

3196 **μέλος**, ***melos***, n. GK: *3517*. part, member, limb:– members [29], member [5]

3197 **Μελχί**, ***Melchi***, n.pr. GK: *3518*. Melki, "*my king*":– Melchi [2]

3198 **Μελχισέδεκ**, ***Melchisedek***, n.pr. GK: *3519*. Melchizedek, "*[my] king is Zedek [just]*":– Melchisedec [9]

3199 **μέλω**, ***melō***, v. GK: *3508 & 3520* [→ *272, 278, 1958, 1959, 1960, 3191, 3338, 4304*]. to care, be concerned; (imper.) it is a care, it is a concern; (pers.) to trouble; to concern:– carest [3], careth [2], care for [1], cared for [1], cared [1], care [1], take care for [1]

3200 **μεμβράνα**, ***membrana***, n. GK: *3521*. parchment, a fine animal leather specially prepared for use in making scrolls:– parchments [1]

3201 **μέμφομαι**, ***memphomai***, v. GK: *3522* [→ *273, 274, 298, 299, 3202, 3437, 3469, 3470*]. to find fault with, blame:– find fault [1], finding fault with [1], found fault [1]

3202 **μεμψίμοιρος**, ***mempsimoiros***, a. GK: *3523* [→ *3201*]. fault-finding, complaining:– complainers [1]

3203 through ***3302*** are not used in Strong's numbering system.

3303 **μέν**, ***men***, pt.aff. GK: *3525* [→ *3304, 3305; cf. 3376*]. often untranslated; used with other particles to show contrast: on the one hand, one...or the other:– *usually untranslated* [121], indeed [22], verily [14], truly [12], some (*+3588*) [2], another (*+3739*) [1], as [1], even [1], for [1], furthermore (*+1534+3588*) [1], howbeit (*+235*) [1], inasmuch as (*+1909+3745+3767*) [1], one (*+3739*) [1], one [1], part (*+3588*) [1], partly (*+3778*) [1], some (*+243*) [1], some (*+3739*) [1], then [1]

3304 **μενοῦν**, ***menoun***; or **μενοῦνγε**, ***menounge***, pt. GK: *3528 & 3529* [→ *3303+3767+1065*]. rather, on the contrary, indeed:– doubtless [1], nay but [1], yea rather [1], yes verily [1]

3305 **μέντοι**, ***mentoi***, pt. GK: *3530* [→ *3303+5104*]. but, yet, nevertheless, really:– yet [2], but [1], howbeit [1], if (*+1487*) [1], likewise (*+3668*) [1], nevertheless (*+3676*) [1], nevertheless [1]

3306 **μένω**, ***menō***, v. GK: *3531* [→ *362, 1265, 1696, 1961, 2650, 3438, 3887, 4037, 4357, 4839, 5278, 5281*]. to stay, remain, live, dwell, abide; to be in a state that begins and continues, yet may or may not end or stop. "To abide in Christ" is to follow his example of a life obedient to the will of God:– abide [27], abideth [20], abode [12], dwelleth [10], remain [8], continue [7], tarry [7], remaineth [5], remained [3], abiding [2], continued [2], dwell [2], dwelt [2], endureth [2], tarried [2], continueth [1], continuing [1], dwellest [1], enduring [1], present [1], remaining [1], stand [1], tarried for [1]

3307 **μερίζω**, ***merizō***, v. GK: *3532* [→ *3313*]. to give, assign; (mid.) to divide, share; (pass.) to be divided:– divided [8], distributed [2], dealt [1], difference between [1], divide [1], gave [1]

3308 **μέριμνα**, ***merimna***, n. GK: *3533* [→ *275, 3309, 4305; cf. 3313*]. worry, concern, anxiety:– cares [3], care [3]

3309 **μεριμνάω**, ***merimnaō***, v. GK: *3534* [→ *3308*]. to worry, have anxiety, be concerned:– take thought [9], careth for [4], careful [2], taking thought [2], care for [1], have care [1]

3310 **μερίς**, ***meris***, n. GK: *3535* [→ *3313*]. district; part, share, what is common between:– part [4], partakers [1]

3311 **μερισμός**, ***merismos***, n. GK: *3536* [→ *3313*]. dividing, separation; distribution, apportionment:– dividing asunder [1], gifts [1]

3312 **μεριστής**, ***meristēs***, n. GK: *3537* [→ *3313*]. arbiter:– divider [1]

3313 **μέρος**, ***meros***, n. GK: *3538* [→ *1266, 1267, 3307, 3310, 3311, 3312, 4181, 4829; cf. 3308*]. part, share, portion; (pl.) district, region:– part [17], parts [7], coasts [3], portion [3], behalf [2], respect [2], by course (*+303*) [1], craft [1], particularly (*+2596*) [1], particular [1], partly (*+5100*) [1], piece [1], side [1], somewhat (*+575*) [1], sort [1]

3314 **μεσημβρία**, ***mesēmbria***, n. GK: *3540* [→ *3319+2250*]. (of time) noon, midday; (of place) south:– noon [1], south [1]

3315 **μεσιτεύω**, ***mesiteuō***, v. GK: *3541* [→ *3319*]. to confirm, guarantee:– confirmed [1]

3316 **μεσίτης**, ***mesitēs***, n. GK: *3542* [→ *3319*]. mediator:– mediator [6]

3317 **μεσονύκτιον**, ***mesonyktion***, n. GK: *3543* [→ *3319+3571*]. midnight:– midnight [3], at midnight [1]

3318 **Μεσοποταμία**, ***Mesopotamia***, n.pr. GK: *3544* [→ *3319+4215*]. Mesopotamia, "*[land] between rivers*":– Mesopotamia [2]

3319 **μέσος**, ***mesos***, a. GK: *3545* [→ *3314, 3315, 3316, 3317, 3318, 3320, 3321, 3322*]. middle, center, among; between; in front of, before:– midst [39], among [6], among (*+1722*) [5], in the midst [2], way [2], among (*+303*) [1], at midday (*+2250*) [1], at midnight (*+3571*) [1], before (*+1722+3588*) [1], between (*+303*) [1], forth (*+1519+3588*) [1], midnight (*+3571+3588*) [1]

3320 **μεσότοιχον**, ***mesotoichon***, n. GK: *3546* [→ *3319+5038*]. dividing wall:– middle wall [1]

3321 **μεσουράνημα**, ***mesouranēma***, n. GK: *3547* [→ *3319+3772*]. midair:– midst of heaven [3]

3322 **μεσόω**, ***mesoō***, v. GK: *3539 & 3548* [→ *3319*]. to be halfway through, at midpoint:– midst [1]

3323 **Μεσσίας**, ***Messias***, n.pr. GK: *3549*. Messiah, Anointed One; see also *5547*, "*anointed*":– Messias [2]

3324 **μεστός**, ***mestos***, a. GK: *3550* [→ *3325*]. full:– full [8]

3325 **μεστόω**, ***mestoō***, v. GK: *3551* [→ *3324*]. (pass.) to be filled:– full [1]

3326 **μετά**, ***meta***, pp. GK: *3552* [→ *276, 277, 278, 279, 2130, 3177, 3179, 3180, 3181, 3327, 3328, 3329, 3330, 3331, 3332, 3333, 3334, 3335, 3336, 3337, 3338, 3339, 3340, 3341, 3342, 3343, 3344, 3345, 3346, 3347, 3348, 3350, 3351, 3352, 3353, 3359, 4830*]. (gen.) with, among, a marker of association of various kinds and meanings; (acc.) after, later, a marker of time:– with [345], after [76], after (*+3588*) [12], among [5], afterward (*+3778*) [4], against [4], hereafter (*+3778*) [4], in [2], and [1], boldly (*+3954*) [1], foameth (*+876*) [1], followed (*+1510*) [1], freely (*+3954*) [1], hence (*+3778*) [1], joyfully (*+5479*) [1], of [1], on [1], setting [1], since [1], that should follow (*+3778*) [1], together (*+240*) [1], to [1], unto [1], upon [1], when (*+3588*) [1], when [1], without (*+3756*) [1]

3327 **μεταβαίνω**, ***metabainō***, v. GK: *3553* [→ *3326+305*]. to go on, leave, move from:– departed [4], depart [3], passed [2], remove [2], go [1]

3328 **μεταβάλλω**, ***metaballō***, v. GK: *3554* [→ *3326+906*]. (mid.) to change one's mind:– changed [1]

3329 **μετάγω**, ***metagō***, v. GK: *3555* [→ *3326+71*]. to turn, steer:– turn about [1], turned about [1]

3330 **μεταδίδωμι**, ***metadidōmi***, v. GK: *3556* [→ *3326+1325*]. to impart, share, contribute to needs:– impart [2], giveth [1], give [1], imparted [1]

3331 **μετάθεσις**, ***metathesis***, n. GK: *3557* [→ *3326+5087*]. removal, taking up; change, transformation:– change [1], removing [1], translation [1]

3332 **μεταίρω**, ***metairō***, v. GK: *3558* [→ *3326+142*]. to move on, leave:– departed [2]

3333 **μετακαλέω**, ***metakaleō***, v. GK: *3559* [→ *3326+2564*]. (mid.) to send for, summon, call to oneself:– called [2], call for [1], call hither [1]

3334 **μετακινέω**, ***metakineō***, v. GK: *3560* [→ *3326+2795*]. (pass.) to be moved, removed, shifted from:– moved away [1]

3335 **μεταλαμβάνω**, ***metalambanō***, v. GK: *3561* [→ *3326+2983*]. to share in, receive a share:– eat [1], have [1], partakers [1], partaker [1], receiveth [1], take [1]

3336 **μετάλημψις**, ***metalēmpsis***, n. GK: *3562* [→ *3326+2983*]. receiving, sharing with:– received [1]

3337 **μεταλλάσσω**, ***metallassō***, v. GK: *3563* [→ *3326+236*]. to exchange:– changed [1], change [1]

3338 **μεταμέλομαι**, ***metamelomai***, v. GK: *3564* [→ *3326+3199*]. (mid.) to regret, repent; (pass.) to be repentant, changed of mind, remorseful:– repented [3], repent [3]

3339 **μεταμορφόω**, ***metamorphoō***, v. GK: *3565* [→ *3326+3444*]. (pass.) to be transformed, transfigured, changed in form:– transfigured [2], changed [1], transformed [1]

3340 **μετανοέω**, ***metanoeō***, v. GK: *3566* [→ *3326+3563*]. to repent, to change any or all of the elements composing one's life: attitude, thoughts, and behaviors concerning the demands of God for right living:– repent [21], repented [11], repenteth [2]

3341 **μετάνοια**, ***metanoia***, n. GK: *3567* [→ *3326+3563*]. change of mind, repentance, the state of changing any or all of the elements composing one's life: attitude, thoughts, and behaviors concerning the demands of God for right living; note that this state can refer to the foundational salvation event in Christ, or to on-going repentance in the Christian life:– repentance [24]

3342 **μεταξύ**, ***metaxy***, adv. GK: *3568* [→ *3326+4862*]. (spacial) between; (temporal) meanwhile, next:– between [6], mean while [1], next [1]

3343 **μεταπέμπω**, ***metapempō***, v. GK: *3569* [→ *3326+3992*]. to summon, send for:– sent for [4], call for [2], send for [2]

3344 **μεταστρέφω**, ***metastrephō***, v. GK: *3570* [→ *3326+4762*]. to pervert; to turn into, change:– turned [2], pervert [1]

3345 **μετασχηματίζω**, ***metaschēmatizō***, v. GK: *3571* [→ *3326+4976*]. (act.) to transform, change (the form); (mid.) to masquerade, disguise (oneself):– transformed [2], change [1], in a figure transferred [1], transforming [1]

3346 **μετατίθημι**, ***metatithemi***, v. GK: *3572* [→ *3326+5087*]. to change (from one place or position to another); to bring back; to take away:– translated [2], carried over [1], changed [1], removed [1], turning [1]

3347 **μετέπειτα**, ***metepeita***, adv. GK: *3575* [→ *3326+1909+1534*]. afterward:– afterward [1]

3348 **μετέχω**, ***metechō***, v. GK: *3576* [→ *3326+2192*]. to share in, partake in, take part in:– partakers [3], partaker [2], pertaineth to [1], took part [1], useth [1]

3349 **μετεωρίζομαι**, ***meteōrizomai***, v. GK: *3577*. to worry about, be anxious:– doubtful mind [1]

3350 **μετοικεσία**, ***metoikesia***, n. GK: *3578* [→ *3326+3624*]. exile, deportation:– carrying away [2], brought [1], carried away [1]

3351 **μετοικίζω**, ***metoikizō***, v. GK: *3579* [→ *3326+3624*]. to send to another place, exile, deport:– carry away [1], removed [1]

3352 **μετοχή**, ***metochē***, n. GK: *3580* [→ *3326+2192*]. something in common, sharing, participation:– fellowship [1]

3353 **μέτοχος**, ***metochos***, a. GK: *3581* [→ *3326+2192*]. sharing in, partners with:– partakers [4], fellows [1], partners [1]

3354 **μετρέω**, ***metreō***, v. GK: *3582* [→ *3358*]. to measure:– measured [3], measure [3], mete [3], measuring [1]

3355 **μετρητής**, ***metrētēs***, n. GK: *3583* [→ *3358*]. measure (about nine or ten gallons):– firkins [1]

3356 **μετριοπαθέω**, ***metriopatheō***, v. GK: *3584* [→ *3358+3958*]. to deal gently:– have compassion [1]

3357 **μετρίως**, ***metriōs***, adv. GK: *3585* [→ *3358*]. not greatly, moderately:– little [1]

3358 **μέτρον**, ***metron***, n. GK: *3586* [→ *280, 488, 3354, 3355, 3356, 3357, 4620*]. measure, limit, what is apportioned:– measure [13]

3359 **μέτωπον**, ***metōpon***, n. GK: *3587* [→ *3326+3708*]. forehead:– foreheads [6], forehead [2]

3360 **μέχρι**, ***mechri***; or **μέχρις**, ***mechris***, c.&pp.*. GK: *3588 & 3589*. until, to the point of:– until [7], unto [7], at [1], till (+*3739*) [1], till [1], to [1]

3361 **μή**, ***mē***, pt.neg. GK: *3590* [→ *3365, 3366, 3367, 3368, 3369, 3371, 3379, 3380, 3381, 3383, 3385, 3387, 3386*]. no, not, absolutely not; a marker that negates a statement. At the beginning of a Greek question, it anticipates a negative response:– not [575], no [56], God forbid (+*1096*) [15], lest [14], never (+*165+1519+3588+3756*) [5], neither (+*2532*) [4], neither [3], none [3], but [2], cannot (+*1410*) [2], cannot [2], no (+*3956*) [2], none (+*5100*) [2], nor [2], not (+*3756*) [2], nothing (+*5100*) [2], any [1], but (+*1437*) [1], but (+*1487+1622*) [1], but (+*1487*) [1], but that [1], except (+*1437*) [1], except (+*1487+1622*) [1], forbear [1], in no wise (+*1519+3588+3838*) [1], lacked (+*2192*) [1], lacketh (+*3918*) [1], lest (+*1519+3588*) [1], never (+*3756+4218*) [1], never (+*3756+4455*) [1], never [1], no (+*5100*) [1], no more at all (+*3756+3765*) [1], not withal [1], nothing (+*5101*) [1], nothing (+*846+1537*) [1], nothing [1], unless (+*1487+1622*) [1], untaken away (+*343*) [1], without [1]

3362 **ἐὰν μή**, ***ean mē***, c.+pt.neg. GK: *1569 + 3590* [→ *1437+3361*]. if not, except, unless:– except [32], but [2], if not [1], not [1]

3363 **ἵνα μή**, ***hina mē***, c.+pt.neg. GK: *2671 + 3590* [→ *2443+3361*]. that not, lest:– lest [42]

3364 **οὐ μή**, ***ou mē***, pt.neg. GK: *4024 + 3590* [→ *3756+3361*]. intense negative: by no means, not at all, never:– not [58], no [7], in no wise [6], no at all [5], never [2], by any means [1], by no means [1], in no case [1], neither (+*2532*) [1], neither [1], nor ever [1], not at all [1], not in any wise [1], not one [1]

3365 **μηδαμῶς**, ***mēdamōs***, adv. GK: *3592 & 3598* [→ *3361+1161+1473*]. surely not, by no means, certainly not:– not so [1], so [1]

3366 **μηδέ**, ***mēde***, pt.neg.disj. GK: *3593* [→ *3361+1161*]. nor, or not, and not, but not:– neither [32], nor [17], not [4], nor yet [2], no not [1], not once [1], not so much as [1], or [1]

3367 **μηδείς**, ***mēdeis***, a. GK: *3594 & 3599* [→ *3361+1161+1520*]. no one, not anyone, nobody, nothing:– no [46], nothing [27], none [6], any [4], not any [2], no man [1], no more (+*2089*) [1], not a whit [1], not at all [1], not [1], without any [1]

3368 **μηδέποτε**, ***mēdepote***, adv. GK: *3595* [→ *3361+1161+4226*]. never:– never [1]

3369 **μηδέπω**, ***mēdepō***, adv. GK: *3596* [→ *3361+1161*]. not yet:– not as yet [1]

3370 **Μῆδος**, ***Mēdos***, n.pr.g. GK: *3597*. Mede:– Medes [1]

3371 **μηκέτι**, ***mēketi***, adv. GK: *3600* [→ *3361+2089*]. no longer, never again:– no more [8], no longer [4], henceforth not [2], any longer [1], henceforth [1], hereafter [1], no henceforward [1], not any more [1], not henceforth [1], no [1]

3372 **μῆκος**, ***mēkos***, n. GK: *3601* [→ *3112, 3113, 3114, 3115, 3116, 3117, 3118, 3373*]. length:– length [3]

3373 **μηκύνω**, ***mēkynō***, v. GK: *3602* [→ *3372*]. (pass.) to grow (long), become long:– grow up [1]

3374 **μηλωτή**, ***mēlōtē***, n. GK: *3603*. sheepskin:– sheepskins [1]

3375 **μήν**[1], ***mēn***[1], n. GK: *3604* [→ *3561, 5072, 5150*]. month:– surely (+*2229*) [1]

3376 **μήν**[2], ***mēn***[2], pt. GK: *3605* [cf. *3303*]. surely:– months [14], month [4]

3377 **μηνύω**, ***mēnyō***, v. GK: *3606*. to inform, report, tell:– shewed [2], shew [1], told [1]

3378 **μὴ οὐκ**, ***mē ouk***, pt.neg. GK: *3590 + 4024* [→ *3361+3756*]. intense negative: by no means, not at all, never:– not [4]

3379 **μήποτε**, ***mēpote***, pt.&c. GK: *3607* [→ *3361+4226*]. never, otherwise, that…not:– lest [12], lest at any time [7], lest haply [2], if peradventure [1], no at all [1], whether or not [1]

3380 **μήπω**, ***mēpō***, adv. GK: *3609* [→ *3361*]. not yet:– not yet [2]

3381 **μήπως**, ***mēpōs***, adv. GK: *3610* [→ *3361+4226*]. so that…somehow, lest:– lest [5], lest by any means [3], lest by some means [1], lest haply [1], lest perhaps [1], lest that by any means [1]

3382 **μηρός**, ***mēros***, n. GK: *3611*. thigh:– thigh [1]

3383 **μήτε**, ***mēte***, c.neg. GK: *3612* [→ *3361+5037*]. and not, neither, nor:– neither [20], nor [15], so much as [1]

3384 **μήτηρ**, ***mētēr***, n. GK: *3613* [→ *282, 3388, 3389, 3390*]. mother:– mother [76], mother's [7], mothers [2]

3385 **μήτι**, ***mēti***, pt.inter.neut. of *3387*. GK: *3614* [→ *3361+5100*]. often not translated; expects a no answer to a question: surely not, unless:– any [3], doth [1], is [1], not [1]

3386 **μήτιγε**, ***mētige***, pt.inter. GK: *3615* [→ *3361+5100+1065*]. how much more, not to speak of:– how much more [1]

3387 **μήτι**, ***mēti***, pt.inter. GK: *3614* [→ *3361+5100*]. often not translated; expects a no answer to a question: surely not, unless:–

3388 **μήτρα**, ***mētra***, n. GK: *3616* [→ *3384*]. womb:– womb [2]

3389 **μητραλῴας**, ***mētralōas***; or **μητρολῴας**, ***mētrolōas***, n. GK: *3617 & 3618* [→ *3384+248*]. one who kills a mother:– murderers of mothers [1]

3390 **μητρόπολις**, ***mētropolis***, n. GK: *3619* [→ *3384+4172*]. capital city:– chiefest city [1]

3391 **μία**, ***mia***, n.num.f. of *1520*. GK: *1651* [→ *1520*]. one, single; see *1520*:–

3392 **μιαίνω**, ***miainō***, v. GK: *3620* [→ *283, 3393, 3394*]. to pollute, stain, defile; (pass.) to be defiled, corrupted, become ceremonially unclean; this refers to both ceremonial and moral uncleanness:– defiled [4], defile [1]

3393 **μίασμα**, ***miasma***, n. GK: *3621* [→ *3392*]. corruption, defilement:– pollutions [1]

3394 **μιασμός**, ***miasmos***, n. GK: *3622* [→ *3392*]. corruption, pollution, defilement:– uncleanness [1]

3395 **μίγμα**, ***migma***, n. GK: *3623* [→ *3396*]. mixture, compound:– mixture [1]

3396 **μίγνυμι**, ***mignymi***, v. GK: *3502 & 3503 & 3624* [→ *3395, 4874*]. to mix, mingle:– mingled [4]

3397 **μικρόν**, ***mikrōn***, a.neut. of *3398*. GK: *3625* [→ *3398*]. little, small, short, lesser:–

3398 **μικρός**, ***mikros***, a. GK: *3625* [→ *3397*]. little, small, short, lesser:– little [16], little while [8], least [6], little ones [6], small [6], less than [1], less [1], little while (+*3745+3745*) [1], while [1]

3399 **Μίλητος**, ***Milētos***, n.pr. GK: *3626*. Miletus:– Miletus [2], Miletum [1]

3400 **μίλιον**, ***milion***, n. GK: *3627*. (Roman) mile (about 4,854 feet):– mile [1]

3401 **μιμέομαι**, ***mimeomai***, v. GK: *3628* [→ *3402, 4831*]. to imitate, follow an example, use as a model:– follow [4]

3402 **μιμητής**, ***mimētēs***, n. GK: *3629* [→ *3401*]. imitator, an example:– followers [7]

3403 **μιμνήσκομαι**, ***mimnēskomai***, v. GK: *3630* [→ *3421*]. to remember, recall, bring to remembrance, often with an implication that a response or action of some kind will occur:– mindful [1], remember [1]

3404 **μισέω**, ***miseō***, v. GK: *3631*. to hate; (pass.) to be hated, detestable:– hate [16], hated [12], hateth [10], hating [2], hateful [1], hatest [1]

3405 **μισθαποδοσία**, ***misthapodosia***, n. GK: *3632* [→ *3408+575+1325*]. reward; punishment:– recompence of reward [2], reward [1]

3406 **μισθαποδότης**, ***misthapodotēs***, n. GK: *3633* [→ *3408+575+1325*]. rewarder:– rewarder [1]

3407 **μίσθιος**, ***misthios***, n. GK: *3634* [→ *3408*]. hired worker:– hired [2]

3408 **μισθός**, ***misthos***, n. GK: *3635* [→ *489, 3405, 3406, 3407, 3409, 3410, 3411*]. wage; reward; what is paid back:– reward [24], hire [3], wages [2]

3409 **μισθόω**, ***misthoō***, v. GK: *3636* [→ *3408*]. to hire:– hired [1], hire [1]

3410 **μίσθωμα**, ***misthōma***, n. GK: *3637* [→ *3408*]. rented house, rented lodging:– hired house [1]

3411 **μισθωτός**, ***misthōtos***, n. GK: *3638* [→ *3408*]. hired worker:– hireling [3], hired servants [1]

3412 **Μιτυλήνη**, ***Mitylēnē***, n.pr. GK: *3639*. Mitylene:– Mitylene [1]

3413 **Μιχαήλ**, ***Michaēl***, n.pr. GK: *3640*. Michael, "*Who is like God [El]?*":– Michael [2]

3414 **μνᾶ**, ***mna***, n. GK: *3641*. mina (100 drachmas or denarii, about 100 days' wages):– pounds [5], pound [4]

3415 **μνάομαι, *mnaomai***, v. GK: *3642* [→ *3423*]. be engaged, betrothed:– remember [9], remembered [6], mindful [2], remembrance [2], came in remembrance [1], rememberest [1]

3416 **Μνάσων, *Mnasōn***, n.pr. GK: *3643*. Mnason:– Mnason [1]

3417 **μνεία, *mneia***, n. GK: *3644* [→ *3421*]. remembrance, mention:– mention [4], remembrance [3]

3418 **μνῆμα, *mnēma***, n. GK: *3645* [→ *3421*]. (burial) tomb:– sepulchre [4], tombs [2], graves [1]

3419 **μνημεῖον, *mnēmeion***, n. GK: *3646* [→ *3421*]. tomb, grave:– sepulchre [26], graves [4], grave [4], sepulchres [3], tombs [3], tomb [2]

3420 **μνήμη, *mnēmē***, n. GK: *3647* [→ *3421*]. remembrance, recalling, memory:– remembrance [1]

3421 **μνημονεύω, *mnēmoneuō***, v. GK: *3648* [→ *363, 364, 1878, 3403, 3417, 3418, 3419, 3420, 3422, 5279, 5280*]. to remember; to think of:– remember [16], made mention [1], mindful [1], remembered [1], remembereth [1], remembering [1]

3422 **μνημόσυνον, *mnēmosynon***, n. GK: *3649* [→ *3421*]. memory, remembrance; memorial offering:– memorial [3]

3423 **μνηστεύω, *mnēsteuō***, v. GK: *3650* [→ *3415*]. (pass.) to be pledged to marriage, betrothed, become engaged:– espoused [3]

3424 **μογιλάλος, *mogilalos***, a. GK: *3651 & 3652* [→ *3425+2980*]. hardly able to talk, speaking with difficulty; speaking in a hoarse or weak voice:– impediment in speech [1]

3425 **μόγις, *mogis***, adv. GK: *3653* [→ *3424, 3433, 3449*]. scarcely ever:– hardly [1]

3426 **μόδιος, *modios***, n. GK: *3654*. large bowl (holds about eight dry quarts):– bushel [3]

3427 **μοί, *mōi***, pers.p.dat. of *1473*. GK: *1609* [→ *1473*]. me, for me, to me; see *1473*:–

3428 **μοιχαλίς, *moichalis***, n. GK: *3655* [→ *3432*]. adulteress; (a.) adulterous:– adulterous [3], adulteress [2], adulteresses [1], adultery [1]

3429 **μοιχάω, *moichaō***, v. GK: *3656* [→ *3432*]. to commit adultery:– committeth adultery [4], commit adultery [2]

3430 **μοιχεία, *moicheia***, n. GK: *3657* [→ *3432*]. (the state or condition of) adultery:– adulteries [2], adultery [2]

3431 **μοιχεύω, *moicheuō***, v. GK: *3658* [→ *3432*]. (act.) to commit adultery; (pass.) to become an adulterer:– commit adultery [10], committeth adultery [2], adultery [1], committed adultery [1]

3432 **μοιχός, *moichos***, n. GK: *3659* [→ *3428, 3429, 3430, 3431*]. adulterer:– adulterers [4]

3433 **μόλις, *molis***, adv. GK: *3660* [→ *3425*]. with difficulty, hardly; very rarely:– scarcely [2], scarce [2], had much work (*+2480*) [1], hardly [1]

3434 **Μολόχ, *Moloch***, n.pr. GK: *3661*. Molech, " "*shameful" king*":– Moloch [1]

3435 **μολύνω, *molynō***, v. GK: *3662* [→ *3436*]. to defile, soil, stain, make impure:– defiled [3]

3436 **μολυσμός, *molysmos***, n. GK: *3663* [→ *3435*]. contamination, defilement:– filthiness [1]

3437 **μομφή, *momphē***, n. GK: *3664* [→ *3201*]. grievance, cause for complaint:– quarrel [1]

3438 **μονή, *monē***, n. GK: *3665* [→ *3306*]. room; dwelling place, abode:– abode [1], mansions [1]

3439 **μονογενής, *monogenēs***, a. GK: *3666* [→ *3441+1096*]. one and only, unique:– only begotten [6], one only [1], only child [1], only [1]

3440 **μόνον, *monon***, adv. GK: *3667* [→ *3441*]. only, alone; just, even, simply:– only [62], alone [3], but [1]

3441 **μόνος, *monos***, a. GK: *3668* [→ *2651, 3439, 3440, 3442, 3443*]. only, alone, by oneself:– only [24], alone [21], by themselves [2], alone (*+2596*) [1]

3442 **μονόφθαλμος, *monophthalmos***, a. GK: *3669* [→ *3441+3788*]. one-eyed:– one eye [2]

3443 **μονόω, *monoō***, v. GK: *3670* [→ *3441*]. (pass.) to be left alone:– desolate [1]

3444 **μορφή, *morphē***, n. GK: *3671* [→ *3339, 3445, 3446, 4832, 4833*]. form, outward appearance; nature, character:– form [3]

3445 **μορφόω, *morphoō***, v. GK: *3672* [→ *3444*]. (pass.) to be formed, take on a form:– formed [1]

3446 **μόρφωσις, *morphōsis***, n. GK: *3673* [→ *3444*]. embodiment, formulation; (outward) form, appearance:– form [2]

3447 **μοσχοποιέω, *moschopoieō***, v. GK: *3674* [→ *3448+4160*]. to make an idol in the shape of a calf:– made a calf [1]

3448 **μόσχος, *moschos***, n. GK: *3675* [→ *3447*]. calf, ox, young bull:– calf [4], calves [2]

3449 **μόχθος, *mochthos***, n. GK: *3677* [→ *3425*]. toil, hardship, exertion:– travail [2], painfulness [1]

3450 **μοῦ, *mōu***, pers.p.gen. of *1473*. GK: *1609* [→ *1473*]. my, mine; see *1473*:–

3451 **μουσικός, *mousikos***, a. GK: *3676*. (n.) musician:– musicians [1]

3452 **μυελός, *myelos***, n. GK: *3678*. marrow:– marrow [1]

3453 **μυέω, *myeō***, v. GK: *3679* [→ *3466*]. (pass.) to learn a secret:– instructed [1]

3454 **μῦθος, *mythos***, n. GK: *3680* [→ *3888, 3889, 3890*]. myth, story, tale:– fables [5]

3455 **μυκάομαι, *mykaomai***, v. GK: *3681*. to roar:– roareth [1]

3456 **μυκτηρίζω, *myktērizō***, v. GK: *3682* [→ *1592*]. (pass.) to be mocked, treated with contempt:– mocked [1]

3457 **μυλικός, *mylikos***, a. GK: *3683* [→ *3458*]. pertaining to a grinding mill:– millstone (*+3037*) [1]

3458 **μύλος, *mylos***, n. GK: *3685* [→ *3457, 3459*]. hand mill or millstone for grinding:– millstone (*+3684*) [2], millstone [2]

3459 **μυλών, *mylōn***, n. GK: *3686* [→ *3458*]. millhouse:– mill [1]

3460 **Μύρα, *Myra***, n.pr. GK: *3688 & 3694*. Myra:– Myra [1]

3461 **μυριάς, *myrias***, n. GK: *3689* [→ *3463*]. myriad, ten thousand; thousands upon thousands, a practically uncountable number:– ten thousand [2], fifty thousand (*+4002*) [1], innumerable company [1], innumerable multitude [1], ten thousands [1], thousands [1], two hundred thousand thousand (*+1417*) [1]

3462 **μυρίζω, *myrizō***, v. GK: *3690* [→ *3464*]. to pour perfume, anoint:– anoint [1]

3463 **μύριοι, *myrioi***, a.num. GK: *3691 & 3692* [→ *3461*]. ten thousand; a practically uncountable number:– ten thousand [3]

3464 **μύρον, *myron***, n. GK: *3693* [→ *3462*]. perfume, myrrh, ointment:– ointment [12], ointments [2]

3465 **Μυσία, *Mysia***, n.pr. GK: *3695*. Mysia:– Mysia [2]

3466 **μυστήριον, *mystērion***, n. GK: *3696* [→ *3453*]. mystery, secret; often refers to a misunderstood part of the OT that, with Christ's coming, is now unveiled:– mystery [22], mysteries [5]

3467 **μυωπάζω, *myōpazō***, v. GK: *3697*. to be nearsighted:– cannot see far off [1]

3468 **μώλωψ, *mōlōps***, n. GK: *3698*. wound, welt, bruise:– stripes [1]

3469 **μωμάομαι, *mōmaomai***, v. GK: *3699* [→ *3201*]. (mid.) to criticize, find fault, blame; (pass.) to be discredited, have fault found with:– blamed [1], blame [1]

3470 **μῶμος, *mōmos***, n. GK: *3700* [→ *3201*]. blemish:– blemishes [1]

3471 **μωραίνω, *mōrainō***, v. GK: *3701* [→ *3474*]. (act.) to make foolish, show one foolish; (pass.) to become a fool, be made a fool; (pass.) to become saltless, tasteless, inert:– lost savour [2], fools [1], made foolish [1]

3472 **μωρία, *mōria***, n. GK: *3702* [→ *3474*]. foolishness:– foolishness [5]

3473 **μωρολογία, *mōrologia***, n. GK: *3703* [→ *3474+3004*]. foolish talk:– foolish talking [1]

3474 **μωρός, *mōros***, a. GK: *3704* [→ *3471, 3472, 3473*]. foolish:– foolish [7], fools [3], fool [2], foolishness [1]

3475 **Μωσεύς, *Mōseus***; or **Μωσῆς, *Mōsēs***; or **Μωϋσῆς, *Mōysēs***, n.pr. GK: *3705 & 3706 & 3707*. Moses, "*drawn out* [Ex. 2:10]; [Egyptian] *son*":– Moses [77], Moses' [3]

3476 **Ναασσών, *Naassōn***, n.pr. GK: *3709*. Nahshon, "*small viper*":– Naasson [3]

3477 **Ναγγαί, *Nangai***, n.pr. GK: *3710*. Naggai:– Nagge [1]

3478 **Ναζαρέθ, *Nazareth***; or **Ναζαρέτ, *Nazaret***, n.pr. GK: *3711 & 3712 & 3713 & 3714 & 3715* [→ *3479, 3480*]. Nazareth, "[poss.] *sprout, branch* or *watchtower*":– Nazareth [12]

3479 **Ναζαρηνός, *Nazarēnos***, a.pr.g. GK: *3716* [→ *3478*]. of Nazareth; (n.) Nazarene (in no way connected to the OT Nazirite):– Nazareth [2], of Nazareth [2]

3480 **Ναζωραῖος, *Nazōraios***, n.pr.g. GK: *3717* [→ *3478*]. Nazarene, of Nazareth:– of Nazareth [13], Nazarenes [1], Nazarene [1]

3481 **Ναθάν, *Nathan***; or **Ναθάμ, *Natham***, n.pr. GK: *3718 & 3719*. Nathan, Natham, "*gift*":– Nathan [1]

3482 **Ναθαναήλ, *Nathanaēl***, n.pr. GK: *3720*. Nathanael, "*gift of God [El]*":– Nathanael [6]

3483 **ναί, *nai***, pt.aff. or emph. GK: *3721*. yes, indeed, a marker of strong agreement, affirmation, or emphasis:– yea [23], even so [5], yes [3], surely [1], truth [1], verily [1]

3484 **Ναΐν, *Nain***, n.pr. GK: *3723*. Nain, "*pleasant, delightful*":– Nain [1]

3485 **ναός, *naos***, n. GK: *3724* [→ *3511*]. temple; of the temple in Jerusalem, it generally denotes the temple building. Also used figuratively for the church as the dwelling place of the Holy Spirit:– temple [43], temples [2], shrines [1]

3486 **Ναούμ, *Naoum***, n.pr. GK: *3725*. Nahum, "*comfort*":– Naum [1]

3487 **νάρδος, *nardos***, n. GK: *3726*. nard, the oil of (spike)nard, extracted from the root:– spikenard (*+4101*) [2]

3488 **Νάρκισσος, *Narkissos***, n.pr. GK: *3727*. Narcissus:– Narcissus [1]

3489 **ναυαγέω, *nauageō***, v. GK: *3728* [→ *3491+2608*]. to be shipwrecked, have a shipwreck:– made shipwrack [1], suffered shipwrack [1]

3490 **ναύκληρος, *nauklēros***, n. GK: *3729* [→ *3491+2819*]. ship owner or captain:– owner of the ship [1]

3491 **ναῦς, *naus***, n. GK: *3730* [→ *3489, 3490, 3492*]. ship:– ship [1]

3492 **ναύτης, *nautēs***, n. GK: *3731* [→ *3491*]. sailor:– shipmen [2], sailers [1]

3493 **Ναχώρ, *Nachōr***, n.pr. GK: *3732*. Nahor:– Nachor [1]

3494 **νεανίας, *neanias***, n. GK: *3733* [→ *3501*]. young man:– young man [4], young man's [1]

3495 **νεανίσκος, *neaniskos***, n. GK: *3734* [→ *3501*]. young man:– young man [5], young men [5]

3496 **Νεάπολις, *Neapolis***, n.pr. GK: *3735 & 3736* [→ *3501+4172*]. Neapolis, "*new city*":– Neapolis [1]

3497 **Νεεμάν, *Neeman***; or **Ναιμάν, *Naiman***, n.pr. GK: *3722 & 3737*. Naaman, "*pleasantness*":– Naaman [1]

3498 **νεκρός, *nekros***, a. GK: *3738* [→ *3499, 3500*]. dead (can be used physically or fig., of both persons and things); (n.) dead person, corpse:– dead [131], one dead [1]

3499 **νεκρόω, *nekroō***, v. GK: *3739* [→ *3498*]. (act.) to put to death; (pass.) to be as good as dead:– as good as dead [1], dead [1], mortify [1]

3500 **νέκρωσις, *nekrōsis***, n. GK: *3740* [→ *3498*]. death, deadness:– deadness [1], dying [1]

3501 **νέος, *neos***, a. GK: *3742* [→ *365, 3494, 3495, 3496, 3502, 3503, 3504, 3512, 3555, 3556, 3561*]. new, fresh, young, younger:– new [12], younger [8], young [3], young men [1]

3502 **νεοσσός, *neossos***, n. GK: *3743 & 3801* [→ *3501*]. the young (of a bird):– young [1]

3503 **νεότης, *neotēs***, n. GK: *3744* [→ *3501*]. youth, childhood:– youth [5]

3504 **νεόφυτος, *neophytos***, a. GK: *3745* [→ *3501+5453*]. newly converted, a fig. extension of a new plant, not found in the NT:– novice [1]

3505 **Νέρων, *Nerōn***, n.pr. GK: *3746*. Nero, "*[family name]*":– Nero [1]

3506 **νεύω, *neuō***, v. GK: *3748* [→ *1269, 1593, 1770, 1962, 2656*]. to motion, nod (as a signal):– beckoned [2]

3507 **νεφέλη, *nephelē***, n. GK: *3749* [→ *3509*]. cloud:– cloud [18], clouds [8]

3508 Νεφθαλίμ, ***Nephthalim***, n.pr. GK: *3750*. Naphtali:– Nephthalim [3]

3509 νέφος, ***nephos***, n. GK: *3751* [→ *3507*]. cloud:– cloud [1]

3510 νεφρός, ***nephros***, n. GK: *3752*. mind, the part of the inner person that feels, desires, and gives intent; a fig. extension of the kidney (not found in the NT):– reins [1]

3511 νεωκόρος, ***neōkoros***, n. GK: *3753* [→ *3485*]. guardian of the temple:– worshipper [1]

3512 νεωτερικός, ***neōterikos***, a. GK: *3754* [→ *3501*]. pertaining to youth, youthful:– youthful [1]

νεώτερος, ***neōteros***. See ***3501***.

3513 νή, ***nē***, pt.aff. GK: *3755*. as surely as:– I protest [1]

3514 νήθω, ***nēthō***, v. GK: *3756*. to spin (yarn):– spin [2]

3515 νηπιάζω, ***nēpiazō***, v. GK: *3757* [→ *3516*]. to be (like) a child:– children [1]

3516 νήπιος, ***nēpios***, a. GK: *3758* [→ *3515*]. (n.) child, infant; (a.) childlike, childish, infantile, with a negative implication of immaturity or positive implication of innocence, depending on the context:– babes [5], child [5], children [2], babe [1], childish [1]

3517 Νηρεύς, ***Nēreus***, n.pr. GK: *3759*. Nereus:– Nereus [1]

3518 Νηρί, ***Nēri***, n.pr. GK: *3760*. Neri, "*lamp of Yahweh*":– Neri [1]

3519 νησίον, ***nēsion***, n. GK: *3761* [→ *3520*]. small island:– island [1]

3520 νῆσος, ***nēsos***, n. GK: *3762* [→ *3519*]. island:– island [6], isle [3]

3521 νηστεία, ***nēsteia***, n. GK: *3763* [→ *3522, 3523; cf. 2068*]. fasting, going without food:– fasting [4], fastings [3], fast [1]

3522 νηστεύω, ***nēsteuō***, v. GK: *3764* [→ *3521*]. to fast, go without food:– fast [16], fasted [3], fastest [1], fasting [1]

3523 νῆστις, ***nēstis***, n. GK: *3765* [→ *3521*]. hungry, without food:– fasting [2]

3524 νηφαλέος, ***nēphaleos***; or νηφάλιος, ***nēphalios***, a. GK: *3766 & 3767* [→ *3525*]. temperate (in the use of alcohol):– sober [2], vigilant [1]

3525 νήφω, ***nēphō***, v. GK: *3768* [→ *366, 1594, 3524*]. to be self-controlled, clear-headed:– sober [4], watch [2]

3526 Νίγερ, ***Niger***, n.pr. GK: *3769*. Niger, "*black*":– Niger [1]

3527 Νικάνωρ, ***Nikanōr***, n.pr. GK: *3770* [→ *3529+435*]. Nicanor, "*victor*":– Nicanor [1]

3528 νικάω, ***nikaō***, v. GK: *3771* [→ *3529*]. to overcome, overpower; to conquer, triumph:– overcometh [11], overcome [11], overcame [2], conquering [1], conquer [1], gotten the victory [1], prevailed [1]

3529 νίκη, ***nikē***, n. GK: *3772* [→ *408, 959, 2131, 3527, 3528, 3530, 3531, 3532, 3533, 3534, 5245*]. victory:– victory [1]

3530 Νικόδημος, ***Nikodēmos***, n.pr. GK: *3773* [→ *3529+1218*]. Nicodemus, "*victor over people*":– Nicodemus [5]

3531 Νικολαΐτης, ***Nikolaitēs***, n.pr.g. GK: *3774* [→ *3529+2992*]. Nicolaitan, "*follower of Nicolas*":– Nicolaitans [2]

3532 Νικόλαος, ***Nikolaos***, n.pr. GK: *3775* [→ *3529+2992*]. Nicolas, "*victor over people*":– Nicolas [1]

3533 Νικόπολις, ***Nikopolis***, n.pr. GK: *3776* [→ *3529+4172*]. Nicopolis, "*victory city*":– Nicopolis [2]

3534 νῖκος, ***nikos***, n. GK: *3777* [→ *3529*]. victory:– victory [4]

3535 Νινευί, ***Nineui***, n.pr. GK: *3778 & 3779* [→ *3536*]. Nineveh:– Nineveh [1]

3536 Νινευίτης, ***Nineuitēs***, n.pr.g. GK: *3780* [→ *3535*]. Ninevite:– Ninevites [1], of Nineveh [1]

3537 νιπτήρ, ***niptēr***, n. GK: *3781* [→ *3538*]. basin for washing:– bason [1]

3538 νίπτω, ***niptō***, v. GK: *3782* [→ *449, 633, 3537*]. to wash; bathe:– wash [11], washed [6]

3539 νοέω, ***noeō***, v. GK: *3783* [→ *3563*]. to understand, see with insight, reflect:– understand [8], perceive [2], consider [1], think [1], understanding [1], understood [1]

3540 νόημα, ***noēma***, n. GK: *3784* [→ *3563*]. thought, mind; scheme, design, plot:– minds [4], devices [1], thought [1]

3541 νόθος, ***nothos***, a. GK: *3785*. illegitimate, born out of wedlock:– bastards [1]

3542 νομή, ***nomē***, n. GK: *3786* [→ *3551*]. pasture:– eat (+*2192*) [1], pasture [1]

3543 νομίζω, ***nomizō***, v. GK: *3787* [→ *3551*]. to think, suppose, expect, consider:– supposed [4], supposing [4], think [4], suppose [1], thought [1], wont [1]

3544 νομικός, ***nomikos***, a. GK: *3788* [→ *3551*]. pertaining to the law; (n.) expert in the law, lawyer:– lawyers [5], lawyer [3], about law [1]

3545 νομίμως, ***nomimōs***, adv. GK: *3789* [→ *3551*]. properly, in accordance to the rules:– lawfully [2]

3546 νόμισμα, ***nomisma***, n. GK: *3790* [→ *3551*]. coin:– money [1]

3547 νομοδιδάσκαλος, ***nomodidaskalos***, n. GK: *3791* [→ *3551+1321*]. teacher of the law:– doctor of law [1], doctors of the law [1], teachers of the law [1]

3548 νομοθεσία, ***nomothesia***, n. GK: *3792* [→ *3551+5087*]. law, legislation:– giving of the law [1]

3549 νομοθετέω, ***nomotheteō***, v. GK: *3793* [→ *3551+5087*]. (pass.) to be given law; to be founded, enacted:– established [1], received law [1]

3550 νομοθέτης, ***nomothetēs***, n. GK: *3794* [→ *3551+5087*]. lawgiver:– lawgiver [1]

3551 νόμος, ***nomos***, n. GK: *3795* [→ *458, 459, 460, 632, 1268, 1772, 2624, 2816, 2817, 2818, 3542, 3543, 3544, 3545, 3546, 3547, 3548, 3549, 3550, 3621, 3622, 3623, 3891, 3892, 4789*]. law, regulation, principle; this has a broad range of meanings and referents, ranging from law as a principle revealed in nature or reason, to the OT Scriptures as a body, the first five books of the Scriptures, or any single command of the Scriptures:– law [195], laws [2]

3552 νοσέω, ***noseō***, v. GK: *3796* [→ *3554*]. to be unhealthy, ill:– doting [1]

3553 νόσημα, ***nosēma***, n. GK: *3797* [→ *3554*]. disease:– disease [1]

3554 νόσος, ***nosos***, n. GK: *3798* [→ *3552, 3553*]. disease, illness:– diseases [6], sickness [3], sicknesses [2], infirmities [1]

3555 νοσσιά, ***nossia***, n. GK: *3799* [→ *3501*]. chick, young (of a bird):– brood [1]

3556 νοσσίον, ***nossion***, n. GK: *3800* [→ *3501*]. young (of a bird):– chickens [1]

3557 νοσφίζω, ***nosphizō***, v. GK: *3802*. (mid.) to hold back for oneself, steal by misappropriating:– keep back [1], kept back [1], purloining [1]

3558 νότος, ***notos***, n. GK: *3803*. south, south wind:– south [4], south wind [3]

3559 νουθεσία, ***nouthesia***, n. GK: *3804* [→ *3563+5087*]. warning, admonition; instruction:– admonition [3]

3560 νουθετέω, ***noutheteō***, v. GK: *3805* [→ *3563+5087*]. to warn, admonish; instruct:– admonish [3], warn [3], admonishing [1], warning [1]

3561 νουμηνία, ***noumēnia***, n. GK: *3741 & 3806* [→ *3501+3375*]. New Moon Celebration:– new moon [1]

3562 νουνεχῶς, ***nounechōs***, adv. GK: *3807* [→ *3563+2192*]. wisely, thoughtfully:– discreetly [1]

3563 νοῦς, ***nous***, n. GK: *3808* [→ *279, 453, 454, 1270, 1271, 1425, 1771, 1963, 2132, 2133, 2657, 3340, 3341, 3539, 3540, 3559, 3560, 3562, 4306, 4307, 5282, 5283*]. mind, thinking; understanding, insight; "to open the mind" means "to understand something":– mind [15], understanding [7], minds [2]

3564 Νυμφᾶς, ***Nymphas***, n.pr. GK: *3809 & 3810* [→ *3565*]. Nymphas:– Nymphas [1]

3565 νύμφη, ***nymphē***, n. GK: *3811* [→ *3564, 3566, 3567*]. bride; daughter-in-law:– bride [5], daughter in law [3]

3566 νυμφίος, ***nymphios***, n. GK: *3812* [→ *3565*]. bridegroom:– bridegroom [15], bridegroom's [1]

3567 νυμφών, ***nymphōn***, n. GK: *3813* [→ *3565*]. bridegroom:– bridechamber [3]

3568 νῦν, ***nyn***, adv. GK: *3814* [→ *3570, 3569, 5106*]. now, as it is; (with the art.) the present (time):– now [119], present [4], henceforth (+*3588*) [3], this time (+*3588*) [2], at this time [1], henceforth (+*575+3588*) [1], henceforth [1], hereafter (+*575+3588*) [1], now (+*2089*) [1], now henceforth [1], of late [1], this (+*3588*) [1], this [1], time [1]

3569 ταννῦν, ***tanyn***, contr. [art.+adv.]. GK: *5422* [→ *3588+3568*]. concerning the present, now:– now [5]

3570 νυνί, ***nyni***, adv. GK: *3815* [→ *3568*]. now, as it is; indeed, in fact:– now [21]

3571 νύξ, ***nyx***, n. GK: *3816* [→ *1273, 1773, 3317, 3574*]. night, evening:– night [60], nights [3], at midnight (+*3319*) [1], midnight (+*3319+3588*) [1]

3572 νύσσω, ***nyssō***, v. GK: *3817* [→ *2659, 2660*]. to pierce, stab:– pierced [1]

3573 νυστάζω, ***nystazō***, v. GK: *3818*. to become drowsy; to sleep, be idle:– slumbered [1], slumbereth [1]

3574 νυχθήμερον, ***nychthēmeron***, n. GK: *3819* [→ *3571+2250*]. a night and a day, about 24 hours:– a night and a day [1]

3575 Νῶε, ***Nōe***, n.pr. GK: *3820*. Noah, "*rest, comfort*":– Noe [5], Noah [3]

3576 νωθρός, ***nōthros***, a. GK: *3821*. slow to learn; lazy, sluggish:– dull [1], slothful [1]

3577 νῶτος, ***nōtos***, n. GK: *3822*. back (of a human body); to have a "bent back" means to be "in trouble or oppression":– back [1]

3578 ξενία, ***xenia***, n. GK: *3825* [→ *3581*]. place to stay, guest room:– lodging [2]

3579 ξενίζω, ***xenizō***, v. GK: *3826* [→ *3581*]. to receive a guest, entertain; (pass.) to stay as a guest; to think of something as strange, be surprised, astonished:– lodged [4], think it strange [2], entertained [1], lodgeth [1], lodge [1], strange [1]

3580 ξενοδοχέω, ***xenodocheō***, v. GK: *3827* [→ *3581+1209*]. to show hospitality:– lodged strangers [1]

3581 ξένος, ***xenos***, a. GK: *3828* [→ *3578, 3579, 3580, 5381, 5382*]. strange, foreign, alien; (n.) foreigner, stranger, alien; host, one who shows hospitality:– strangers [6], stranger [4], strange [3], host [1]

3582 ξέστης, ***xestēs***, n. GK: *3829*. pitcher, jug:– pots [2]

3583 ξηραίνω, ***xērainō***, v. GK: *3830* [→ *3584*]. to wither, shrivel; become rigid:– withered away [6], dried up [3], withered [3], withereth [2], pineth away [1], ripe [1]

3584 ξηρός, ***xēros***, a. GK: *3831* [→ *3583*]. dried up, (n.) dry land; shriveled, by extension: withered, paralyzed, of an atrophied limb of the body:– withered [4], dry [2], land [1]

3585 ξύλινος, ***xylinos***, a. GK: *3832* [→ *3586, 3587*]. made of wood, wooden:– of wood [2]

3586 ξύλον, ***xylon***, n. GK: *3833* [→ *3585*]. wood; tree; wooden club, stocks:– tree [10], staves [5], wood [3], stocks [1]

3587 ξυράω, ***xyraō***, v. GK: *3834* [→ *3585*]. to have one's hair shaved:– shaven [2], shave [1]

3588 ὁ, ***ho***, art. GK: *3836* [→ *2006, 3592, 3634, 3569, 5024, 5107, 5108, 5120, 5121, 5122, 5602*]. (often not translated) the, this, that, who:– *usually untranslated* [9495], the [7887], he [450], which [392], that [353], them [267], they [259], a [179], him [134], who [93], those [41], that (+*1519*) [27], to (+*1519*) [24], because (+*1223*) [21], she [18], what [18], as (+*1722*) [15], after (+*3326*) [12], an [12], their [12], when (+*1722*) [12], his [11], some [10]*

ὅ, ***ho***. See ***3739***.

3589 ὀγδοήκοντα, ***ogdoēkonta***, n.num. GK: *3837* [→ *3638*]. eighty:– fourscore [2]

3590 ὄγδοος, ***ogdoos***, a. GK: *3838* [→ *3638*]. eighth:– eighth [5]

3591 ὄγκος, ***onkos***, n. GK: *3839* [→ *5246*]. hinderance, impediment:– weight [1]

3592 ὅδε, ***hode***, p.demo. GK: *3840* [→ *3588*]. this (one); thus:– these [7], after this manner [1], he [1], she [1], such [1], thus [1]

3593 ὁδεύω, ***hodeuō***, v. GK: *3841* [→ *3598*]. to travel:– journeyed [1]

3594 ὁδηγέω, ***hodēgeō***, v. GK: *3842* [→ *3598+71*]. to lead, guide; explain, instruct:– lead [3], guide [2]

3595 **ὁδηγός**, ***hodēgos***, n. GK: *3843* [→ *3598+71*]. guide, leader:– guides [2], guide [2], leaders [1]

3596 **ὁδοιπορέω**, ***hodoiporeō***, v. GK: *3844* [→ *3598+4198*]. to be on a journey, travel:– went on journey [1]

3597 **ὁδοιπορία**, ***hodoiporia***, n. GK: *3845* [→ *3598+4198*]. journey:– journeyings [1], journey [1]

3598 **ὁδός**, ***hodos***, n. GK: *3847* [→ *296, 1327, 1353, 1529, 1841, 2136, 2137, 3180, 3593, 3594, 3595, 3596, 3597, 3938, 4922, 4923*]. road, path, a general term for a thoroughfare to get from one place to another; by extension: way, manner of life; "the Way" is a term for the Christian lifestyle (Ac 9:2; 19:9):– way [75], ways [11], journey [5], way side [5], highways [2], as went (*+4160*) [1], highway side [1], highways (*+1327+3588*) [1], sabbath day's journey (*+2192+4521*) [1]

3599 **ὀδούς**, ***odous***, n. GK: *3848*. tooth:– teeth [10], tooth [2]

3600 **ὀδυνάω**, ***odynaō***, v. GK: *3849* [→ *3601*]. to grieve, be anxious, in agony:– sorrowing [2], tormented [2]

3601 **ὀδύνη**, ***odynē***, n. GK: *3850* [→ *3600*]. anguish, grief, pain:– sorrows [1], sorrow [1]

3602 **ὀδυρμός**, ***odyrmos***, n. GK: *3851*. deep sorrow, mourning, lamentation:– mourning [2]

3603 **ὅ ἐστι**, ***hō esti***; or **ὅ ἐστιν**, ***hō estin***, p.rel.+v. GK: *4005 + 1639* [→ *3739+1510*]. that is, which is; see *1510* and *3739*:–

3604 **Ὀζίας**, ***Ozias***, n.pr. GK: *3852*. Uzziah, "*Yahweh is [my] strength*":– Ozias [2]

3605 **ὄζω**, ***ozō***, v. GK: *3853* [→ *2175, 2238, 3744, 3750*]. to give off a bad odor, stink, smell:– stinketh [1]

3606 **ὅθεν**, ***hothen***, adv. GK: *3854* [→ *3739*]. from where, from there; therefore, this is why:– wherefore [4], whereupon [3], from whence [2], whence [2], where [2], from thence [1], whereby [1]

3607 **ὀθόνη**, ***othonē***, n. GK: *3855* [→ *3608*]. linen sheet:– sheet [2]

3608 **ὀθόνιον**, ***othonion***, n. GK: *3856* [→ *3607*]. (pl.) strips of linen, bandages:– linen clothes [5]

3609 **οἰκεῖος**, ***oikeios***, a. GK: *3858* [→ *3624*]. belonging to the household, of the immediate family:– household [1], house [1], of household [1]

3610 **οἰκέτης**, ***oiketēs***, n. GK: *3860* [→ *3624*]. house servant, domestic slave:– servant [3], household servants [1], servants [1]

3611 **οἰκέω**, ***oikeō***, v. GK: *3861* [→ *3624*]. to live, dwell:– dwelleth [4], dwell [4], dwelling [1]

3612 **οἴκημα**, ***oikēma***, n. GK: *3862* [→ *3624*]. cell, room in a prison:– prison [1]

3613 **οἰκητήριον**, ***oikētērion***, n. GK: *3863* [→ *3624*]. dwelling, home:– habitation [1], house [1]

3614 **οἰκία**, ***oikia***, n. GK: *3864* [→ *3624*]. house, home; family:– house [84], houses [8], from house to house (*+3588*) [1], home [1], household [1]

3615 **οἰκιακός**, ***oikiakos***, n. GK: *3865* [→ *3624*]. member of a household:– of household [2]

3616 **οἰκοδεσποτέω**, ***oikodespoteō***, v. GK: *3866* [→ *3624+1203*]. to manage one's home:– guide the house [1]

3617 **οἰκοδεσπότης**, ***oikodespotēs***, n. GK: *3867* [→ *3624+1203*]. head or owner of the house, landowner:– goodman of the house [4], householder [3], master of the house [3], goodman [1], householder (*+444*) [1]

3618 **οἰκοδομέω**, ***oikodomeō***, v. GK: *3868* [→ *3624+1430*]. to build, build up, rebuild, a physical edifice; by extension: to edify, strengthen, develop another person's life through acts and words of love and encouragement:– build [12], built [10], builders [5], edifieth [3], buildest [2], edified [2], edify [2], builded [1], building [1], emboldened [1]

3619 **οἰκοδομή**, ***oikodomē***, n. GK: *3869* [→ *3624+1430*]. building, construction, a physical edifice; by extension: building up, edification, strengthening, developing another person's life through acts and words of love and encouragement:– edifying [7], edification [4], buildings [3], building [3], edify [1]

3620 **οἰκοδομία**, ***oikodomia***, n. GK: *3870* [→ *3624+1430*]. edification:–

3621 **οἰκονομέω**, ***oikonomeō***, v. GK: *3872* [→ *3624+3551*]. to manage:– steward [1]

3622 **οἰκονομία**, ***oikonomia***, n. GK: *3873* [→ *3624+3551*]. management, administration, job of administration; what is put into effect, plan:– dispensation [4], stewardship [3], edifying [1]

3623 **οἰκονόμος**, ***oikonomos***, n. GK: *3874* [→ *3624+3551*]. manager, administrator, director, trustee:– steward [5], stewards [3], chamberlain [1], governors [1]

3624 **οἶκος**, ***oikos***, n. GK: *3875* [→ *456, 1460, 1774, 2026, 2730, 2731, 2732, 2733, 3350, 3351, 3609, 3610, 3611, 3612, 3613, 3614, 3615, 3616, 3617, 3618, 3619, 3620, 3621, 3622, 3623, 3625, 3626, 3832, 3939, 3940, 3941, 4039, 4040, 4924, 4925*]. house, home, a physical edifice; of royalty: palace; of deity: temple; by extension: family, lineage, people who live in or originated in a particular house:– house [96], home [5], houses [5], household [3], from house to house (*+2596*) [2], every house (*+2596*) [1], in every house (*+2596*) [1], temple [1]

3625 **οἰκουμένη**, ***oikoumenē***, n. GK: *3876* [→ *3624*]. the (inhabited) world, (Roman) world; humankind:– world [14], earth [1]

3626 **οἰκουρός**, ***oikouros***; or **οἰκουργός**, ***oikourgos***, a. GK: *3877 & 3878* [→ *3624*]. staying at home, domestic:– keepers at home [1]

3627 **οἰκτείρω**, ***oikteirō***, v. GK: *3879 & 3882* [→ *3628, 3629*]. to have compassion on:– have compassion [2]

3628 **οἰκτιρμός**, ***oiktirmos***, n. GK: *3880* [→ *3627*]. compassion, mercy, pity:– mercies [4], mercy [1]

3629 **οἰκτίρμων**, ***oiktirmōn***, a. GK: *3881* [→ *3627*]. merciful, compassionate:– merciful [2], tender mercy [1]

οἶμαι, ***oimai***. See **3633**.

3630 **οἰνοπότης**, ***oinopotēs***, n. GK: *3884* [→ *3631+4095*]. drunkard, wine-drinker:– winebibber [2]

3631 **οἶνος**, ***oinos***, n. GK: *3885* [→ *3630, 3632, 3943*]. wine:– wine [32], winepress (*+3025*) [1]

3632 **οἰνοφλυγία**, ***oinophlygia***, n. GK: *3886* [→ *3631+5397*]. drunkenness:– excess of wine [1]

3633 **οἴομαι**, ***oiomai***; or **οἶμαι**, ***oimai***, v. GK: *3883 & 3887*. to suppose, think, expect:– suppose [1], supposing [1], think [1]

3634 **οἷος**, ***hoios***, p.rel. GK: *3888* [→ *4169*]. what sort of, what kind of:– such as [5], as [4], what manner [2], which [2], so as [1], what [1]

οἴω, ***oiō***. See **5342**.

3635 **ὀκνέω**, ***okneō***, v. GK: *3890* [→ *3636*]. to delay, hesitate:– delay [1]

3636 **ὀκνηρός**, ***oknēros***, a. GK: *3891* [→ *3635*]. lazy, idle, not active; troublesome:– slothful [2], grievous [1]

3637 **ὀκταήμερος**, ***oktaēmeros***, a. GK: *3892* [→ *3638+2250*]. eighth day:– eighth day [1]

3638 **ὀκτώ**, ***oktō***, n.num. GK: *3893* [→ *3589, 3590, 3637*]. eight:– eight [6], eighteen (*+1176+2532*) [3]

3639 **ὄλεθρος**, ***olethros***, n. GK: *3897* [→ *622, 623, 684, 1842, 3644, 3645, 4881*]. destruction, ruin:– destruction [4]

3640 **ὀλιγόπιστος**, ***oligopistos***, a. GK: *3899* [→ *3641+4103*]. of little faith:– of little faith [5]

3641 **ὀλίγος**, ***oligos***, a. GK: *3900* [→ *3640, 3642, 3643*]. little, small, short; (pl.) few:– few [20], little [9], small [5], almost (*+1722*) [2], short [2], while [2], briefly (*+1223*) [1], long (*+3756*) [1], season [1]

3642 **ὀλιγόψυχος**, ***oligopsychos***, a. GK: *3901* [→ *3641+5594*]. timid, fainthearted, discouraged:– feebleminded [1]

3643 **ὀλιγωρέω**, ***oligōreō***, v. GK: *3902* [→ *3641*]. to make light of, despise:– despise [1]

3644 **ὀλοθρευτής**, ***olothreutēs***, n. GK: *3894 & 3904* [→ *3639*]. destroyer:– destroyer [1]

3645 **ὀλοθρεύω**, ***olothreuō***, v. GK: *3895 & 3905* [→ *3639*]. to destroy:– destroyed [1]

3646 **ὁλοκαύτωμα**, ***holokautōma***, n. GK: *3906* [→ *3650+2545*]. burnt offering, wholly consumed on the altar as dedicated to God:– burnt offerings [2], whole burnt offerings [1]

3647 **ὁλοκληρία**, ***holoklēria***, n. GK: *3907* [→ *3650+2819*]. completeness, wholeness (in healing):– perfect soundness [1]

3648 **ὁλόκληρος**, ***holoklēros***, a. GK: *3908* [→ *3650+2819*]. whole, complete:– entire [1], whole [1]

3649 **ὀλολύζω**, ***ololyzō***, v. GK: *3909*. to wail, cry out:– howl [1]

3650 **ὅλος**, ***holos***, a. GK: *3910* [→ *2526', 2527, 3646, 3647, 3648, 3651, 3654*]. all, whole, entire; throughout:– all [63], whole [43], every whit [2], all (*+1722*) [1], all long [1], altogether [1], throughout (*+1223*) [1]

3651 **ὁλοτελής**, ***holotelēs***, a. GK: *3911* [→ *3650+5056*]. through and through, wholly, completely:– wholly [1]

3652 **Ὀλυμπᾶς**, ***Olympas***, n.pr. GK: *3912*. Olympas:– Olympas [1]

3653 **ὄλυνθος**, ***olynthos***, n. GK: *3913*. late fig:– untimely figs [1]

3654 **ὅλως**, ***holōs***, adv. GK: *3914* [→ *3650*]. completely, (not) at all; actually:– at all [2], commonly [1], utterly [1]

3655 **ὄμβρος**, ***ombros***, n. GK: *3915*. rainstorm (that may include thunder and lightning):– shower [1]

3656 **ὁμιλέω**, ***homileō***, v. GK: *3917* [→ *3657, 3658, 4926; cf. 3664*]. to talk, converse:– communed [2], talked [2]

3657 **ὁμιλία**, ***homilia***, n. GK: *3918* [→ *3656*]. company, associations:– communications [1]

3658 **ὅμιλος**, ***homilos***, n. GK: *3919* [→ *3656*]. crowd, throng:– company [1]

3659 **ὄμμα**, ***omma***, n. GK: *3921* [→ *3708*]. eye:– eyes [1]

3660 **ὀμνύω**, ***omnyō***, v. GK: *3922 & 3923* [→ *3728, 4945*]. to declare an oath, swear an oath, promise with an oath:– swear [13], sware [7], sweareth [4], sworn [3]

3661 **ὁμοθυμαδόν**, ***homothymadon***, adv. GK: *3924* [→ *3664+2372*]. united, in togetherness, as one:– with one accord [11], one mind [1]

3662 **ὁμοιάζω**, ***homoiazō***, v. GK: *3925* [→ *3664*]. to be like, resemble:– agreeth [1]

3663 **ὁμοιοπαθής**, ***homoiopathēs***, a. GK: *3926* [→ *3664+3958*]. like, of the same quality or kind of desires:– of like passions with [1], subject to like passions [1]

3664 **ὅμοιος**, ***homoios***, a. GK: *3927* [→ *871, 3661, 3662, 3663, 3665, 3666, 3667, 3668, 3669, 3670, 3673, 3674, 3675, 3676, 3945, 3946, 4927; cf. 3656, 3670*]. like, similar, of a same or similar nature or quality:– like [41], like unto [4], unto [2]

3665 **ὁμοιότης**, ***homoiotēs***, n. GK: *3928* [→ *3664*]. similarity, likeness:– like as (*+2596*) [1], similitude [1]

3666 **ὁμοιόω**, ***homoioō***, v. GK: *3929* [→ *3664*]. to make like, compare; (pass.) to be like, become like:– liken [5], likened [4], like [2], made like [2], likeness [1], resemble [1]

3667 **ὁμοίωμα**, ***homoiōma***, n. GK: *3930* [→ *3664*]. likeness; looking like, image; form, appearance:– likeness [2], in likeness [1], like to [1], shapes [1], similitude [1]

3668 **ὁμοίως**, ***homoiōs***, adv. GK: *3931* [→ *3664*]. likewise, in the same way, similarly:– likewise [27], likewise (*+3305*) [1], moreover [1], so [1]

3669 **ὁμοίωσις**, ***homoiōsis***, n. GK: *3932* [→ *3664*]. likeness:– similitude [1]

3670 **ὁμολογέω**, ***homologeō***, v. GK: *3933* [→ *437, 1843, 3671, 3672*]. to confess, acknowledge, agree, admit, declare; this can be a profession of allegiance, an admission of bad behavior, or an emphatic declaration of a truth:– confess [12], confessed [3], confesseth [2], profess [2], confession made [1], giving thanks [1], professed [1], promised [1]

3671 **ὁμολογία**, ***homologia***, n. GK: *3934* [→ *3670*]. confession, profession, acknowledgment, to openly express commitment and allegiance:– profession [4], confession [1], professed [1]

3672 **ὁμολογουμένως**, ***homologoumenōs***, adv. GK: *3935* [→ *3670*]. beyond all question, most certainly:– without controversy [1]

3673 **ὁμότεχνος**, ***homotechnos***, a. GK: *3937* [→ *3664+5078*]. of the same trade:– same craft [1]

3674 **ὁμοῦ**, ***homou***, adv. GK: *3938* [→ *3664*]. together:– together [3]

3675 **ὁμόφρων**, ***homophrōn***, a. GK: *3939* [→ *3664+5424*]. living in harmony with, like-minded:– one mind [1]

ὁμόω, ***omoō***. See **3660**.

3676 **ὅμως**, ***homōs***, adv. GK: *3940* [→ *3664*]. just as; at the same time:– even [1], nevertheless (*+3305*) [1], though but [1]

3677* ὄναρ, *onar, n. GK: *3941.* dream:– dream [6]

3678* ὀνάριον, *onarion, n. GK: *3942* [→ *3688*]. young donkey:– young ass [1]

ὀνάω, *onaō*. See ***3685***.

3679* ὀνειδίζω, *oneidizō, v. GK: *3943* [→ *3681*]. to heap insults on, denounce, find fault, rebuke:– reproached [2], cast in teeth [1], reproach [1], reviled [1], revile [1], suffer reproach [1], upbraided [1], upbraideth [1], upbraid [1]

3680* ὀνειδισμός, *oneidismos, n. GK: *3944* [→ *3681*]. disgrace, insult:– reproach [3], reproaches [2]

3681* ὄνειδος, *oneidos, n. GK: *3945* [→ *3679, 3680*]. disgrace:– reproach [1]

3682* Ὀνήσιμος, *Onēsimos, n.pr. GK: *3946* [→ *3685*]. Onesimus, "*useful*":– Onesimus [4]

3683* Ὀνησίφορος, *Onēsiphoros, n.pr. GK: *3947* [→ *3685+5342*]. Onesiphorus, "*one bringing usefulness*":– Onesiphorus [2]

3684* ὀνικός, *onikos, a. GK: *3948* [→ *3688*]. pertaining to a donkey, millstone worked by a donkey:– millstone (*+3458*) [2]

3685* ὀνίνημι, *oninēmi, v. GK: *3949* [→ *3682, 3683*]. to have benefit or joy:– joy [1]

3686* ὄνομα, *onoma, n. GK: *3950* [→ *2028, 2176, 3687, 5122, 5581*]. name; title; reputation:– name [172], named [28], name's [11], names [11], called [4], men (*+444*) [1], surnamed (*+2007*) [1]

3687* ὀνομάζω, *onomazō, v. GK: *3951* [→ *3686*]. to give a name, designate a name; to confess; (mid.) to call oneself; (pass.) to be named; be known:– named [7], called [1], call [1], nameth [1]

3688* ὄνος, *onos, n. GK: *3952* [→ *3678, 3684*]. donkey (female or male):– ass [5], ass's [1]

3689* ὄντως, *ontōs, adv. GK: *3953* [→ *1510*]. really, certainly, surely:– indeed [6], certainly [1], clean [1], of a truth [1], verily [1]

3690* ὄξος, *oxos, n. GK: *3954* [→ *3691*]. wine vinegar:– vinegar [7]

3691* ὀξύς, *oxys, a. GK: *3955* [→ *3690, 3947, 3948*]. sharp; swift, quick:– sharp [7], swift [1]

3692* ὀπή, *opē, n. GK: *3956.* hole, opening:– caves [1], place [1]

3693* ὄπισθεν, *opisthen, adv. GK: *3957* [→ *3694*]. from behind; after:– behind [4], after [2], on the backside [1]

3694* ὀπίσω, *opisō, adv. GK: *3958* [→ *3693*]. behind, after, following:– after [22], behind [6], back (*+1519+3588*) [3], again (*+1519+3588*) [1], backward (*+1519+3588*) [1], back [1], follow (*+1205*) [1], went back (*+565+1519+3588*) [1]

3695* ὁπλίζω, *hoplizō, v. GK: *3959* [→ *3696*]. (mid.) to arm oneself with:– arm [1]

3696* ὅπλον, *hoplon, n. GK: *3960* [→ *2528, 3695, 3833*]. instrument, weapon, armor:– armour [2], instruments [2], weapons [2]

3697* ὁποῖος, *hopoios, a. GK: *3961* [→ *4226*]. what kind of, what sort of:– what manner of [2], of what sort [1], such as (*+5108*) [1], whatsoever [1]

3698* ὁπότε, *hopote, pt.temp. GK: *3962* [→ *4226*]. when:– when [1]

3699* ὅπου, *hopou, pt.pl. GK: *3963* [→ *4226*]. where, wherever; whenever:– where [58], whither [9], whithersoever (*+302*) [4], wheresoever (*+1437*) [3], whereas [2], wheresoever (*+302*) [2], in what place soever (*+1437*) [1], wheresoever [1], whithersoever (*+1437*) [1]

3700* ὀπτάνομαι, *optanomai, v. GK: *3964* [→ *3708*]. (mid.) to appear:– see [29], appeared [15], seen [8], appear [2], look [2], shewed [1]

3701* ὀπτασία, *optasia, n. GK: *3965* [→ *3708*]. (supernatural) vision:– vision [3], visions [1]

ὄπτομαι, *optomai*. See ***3700***.

3702* ὀπτός, *optos, a. GK: *3966.* broiled, roasted:– broiled [1]

3703* ὀπώρα, *opōra, n. GK: *3967* [→ *5352*]. fruit:– fruits [1]

3704* ὅπως, *hopōs, c.&adv. GK: *3968* [→ *4226*]. that, so that, (in order) to:– that [41], how [4], to [4], that (*+302*) [3], because [1], might [1], so that [1], when (*+302*) [1]

3705* ὅραμα, *horama, n. GK: *3969* [→ *3708*]. (supernatural) vision; sight (from God):– vision [11], sight [1]

3706* ὅρασις, *horasis, n. GK: *3970* [→ *3708*]. appearance; vision:– in sight [1], look [1], visions [1], vision [1]

3707* ὁρατός, *horatos, a. GK: *3971* [→ *3708*]. pertaining to things visible, things seen:– visible [1]

3708* ὁράω, *horaō, v. GK: *1625 & 3972* [→ *517, 542, 845, 872, 1799, 1896, 2029, 2030, 2072, 2529, 2714, 2734, 3359, 3659, 3700, 3701, 3705, 3706, 3707, 3799, 4275, 4308, 4383, 4659, 4893?, 4894?, 5299, 5432; cf. 3788, 4383*]. to see, notice; perceive; (pass.) to appear, be seen:– seen [33], see [12], saw [5], take heed [5], beholding [1], perceive [1], seeing [1], seeth [1]

3709* ὀργή, *orgē, n. GK: *3973* [→ *3710, 3711, 3949, 3950; cf. 3713*]. wrath, anger, the feeling and expression of strong displeasure and hostility; this can range from petty human anger to the righteous anger of God toward sinful disobedience:– wrath [31], anger [3], indignation [1], vengeance [1]

3710* ὀργίζω, *orgizō, v. GK: *3974* [→ *3709*]. (mid./pass.) to be angry, enraged, to feel and express strong displeasure and hostility; this can range from petty human anger to the righteous anger of God toward sinful disobedience:– angry [5], wroth [3]

3711* ὀργίλος, *orgilos, a. GK: *3975* [→ *3709*]. quick-tempered, inclined to anger:– soon angry [1]

3712* ὀργυιά, *orgyia, n. GK: *3976* [→ *3713*]. fathom (about six feet):– fathoms [2]

3713* ὀρέγω, *oregō, v. GK: *3977* [→ *3712, 3715; cf. 3709*]. (mid.) to set one's heart on, strive for, aspire to, desire:– desire [2], coveted after [1]

3714* ὀρεινός, *oreinos, a. GK: *3978* [→ *3735*]. hilly, (n.) hill country:– hill country [2]

3715* ὄρεξις, *orexis, n. GK: *3979* [→ *3713*]. lust, desire:– lust [1]

3716* ὀρθοποδέω, *orthopodeō, v. GK: *3980* [→ *3717+4228*]. to act in line with (the truth), act rightly:– walked uprightly [1]

3717* ὀρθός, *orthos, a. GK: *3981* [→ *461, 1357, 1882, 1930, 2735, 3716, 3718, 3723*]. straight, level:– straight [1], upright [1]

3718* ὀρθοτομέω, *orthotomeō, v. GK: *3982* [→ *3717+5114*]. to handle correctly, guide on a straight path:– rightly dividing [1]

3719* ὀρθρίζω, *orthrizō, v. GK: *3983* [→ *3722*]. to get up early in the morning:– came early in the morning [1]

3720* ὀρθρινός, *orthrinos, a. GK: *3984* [→ *3722*]. early in the morning:– morning [1]

3721* ὄρθριος, *orthrios, a. GK: *3985* [→ *3722*]. early in the morning:– early [1]

3722* ὄρθρος, *orthros, n. GK: *3986* [→ *3719, 3720, 3721*]. dawn, daybreak, early in the morning:– early in the morning (*+3588+5259*) [1], early in the morning [1], very early in the morning (*+901*) [1]

3723* ὀρθῶς, *orthōs, adv. GK: *3987* [→ *3717*]. correctly, rightly, plainly:– rightly [2], plain [1], right [1]

3724* ὁρίζω, *horizō, v. GK: *3988* [→ *592, 873, 3181, 3725, 3734, 4309, 4927*]. to determine, set, appoint, decree:– determined [3], ordained [2], declared [1], determinate [1], limiteth [1]

3725* ὅριον, *horion, n. GK: *3990* [→ *3724*]. region, area, vicinity:– coasts [10], borders [1]

3726* ὁρκίζω, *horkizō, v. GK: *1941 & 3991* [→ *3727*]. to command; implore, adjure:– adjure [2], charge [1]

3727* ὅρκος, *horkos, n. GK: *3992* [→ *1844, 1845, 1964, 1965, 3726, 3728*]. oath:– oath [7], oaths' [2], oaths [1]

3728* ὁρκωμοσία, *horkōmosia, n. GK: *3993* [→ *3727+3660*]. oath, taking of an oath:– oath [4]

3729* ὁρμάω, *hormaō, v. GK: *3994* [→ *3730*]. to rush (as in a stampede):– ran violently [3], ran [1], rushed [1]

3730* ὁρμή, *hormē, n. GK: *3995* [→ *874, 2868, 3729, 3731*]. plot, decision; impulse, desire:– assault [1], governor [1]

3731* ὅρμημα, *hormēma, n. GK: *3996* [→ *3730*]. sudden violence:– violence [1]

3732* ὄρνεον, *orneon, n. GK: *3997* [→ *3733*]. bird:– fowls [2], bird [1]

3733* ὄρνις, *ornis, n. GK: *3989 & 3998* [→ *3732*]. hen, bird:– hen [2]

3734* ὁροθεσία, *horothesia, n. GK: *3999* [→ *3724+5087*]. exact place, fixed boundary:– bounds [1]

3735* ὄρος, *oros, n. GK: *4001* [→ *3714*]. hill, hillside, mountain, mountainside; this can refer to any elevated place from mounds to high mountains:– mountain [28], mount [21], mountains [13], hill [3]

3736* ὀρύσσω, *oryssō, v. GK: *4002* [→ *1358, 1846*]. to dig up, dig out:– digged [3]

3737* ὀρφανός, *orphanos, a. GK: *4003* [→ *642*]. (n.) an orphan:– comfortless [1], fatherless [1]

3738* ὀρχέομαι, *orcheomai, v. GK: *4004.* to dance:– danced [4]

3739* ὅς, *hos, p.rel. GK: *4005* [→ *1352, 1355, 1360, 1539, 2505, 2509, 2526, 2530, 3606, 3634, 3746, 3748, 3755, 3752, 3753, 3754, 3757, 3842, 4212, 5119*]. who, which, what, that; anyone, someone, a certain one:– which [452], whom [267], that [144], who [85], whose [53], what [45], whosoever (*+302*) [32], wherein (*+1722*) [23], whosoever (*+1437*) [19], whatsoever (*+1437*) [15], whereof [15], some [14], he [10], one [9], till (*+2193*) [9], wherewith [9], another [8], whatsoever (*+302*) [7], whereby (*+1722*) [6], whereunto (*+1519*) [6], until (*+2193*) [5], whereunto [5], because (*+473*) [4], since (*+575*) [4], the [4], till (*+891*) [4], until (*+891*) [4], whatsoever [4], when [4], where (*+1722*) [4], whereon (*+1909*) [4], whomsoever (*+1437*) [4], whomsoever (*+302*) [4], as (*+5158*) [3], such [3], whatsoever (*+302+5100*) [3], whereby (*+1223*) [3], wherefore (*+156+1223*) [3], wherein (*+1519*) [3], wherein (*+1909*) [3], wherein [3], while (*+1722*) [3], whom (*+302*) [3], whoso (*+302*) [3], whosoever (*+302+3956*) [3], other [2], that (*+1437*) [2], when (*+1722*) [2], whereas (*+1722*) [2], wherefore (*+1223*) [2], whereof (*+4012*) [2], whereupon (*+1722*) [2], wherewith (*+1722*) [2], while (*+2193*) [2], while (*+891*) [2], whom (*+1437*) [2], another (*+3303*) [1], as (*+2596+5158*) [1], as (*+302+5100*) [1], as many as (*+3956*) [1], as [1], because (*+1752*) [1], called [1], even as (*+2596+3779+5158*) [1], even as (*+5158*) [1], he that (*+302*) [1], him [1], howbeit whereinsoever (*+302+1161+1722*) [1], in the mean time (*+1722*) [1], like [1], moreover (*+1161+3062*) [1], nothing (*+3756*) [1], once (*+302+575*) [1], one (*+3303*) [1], one man [1], others [1], since the time (*+575*) [1], soever (*+302*) [1], some (*+3303*) [1], that (*+1722*) [1], that (*+302*) [1], that (*+575*) [1], therefore (*+473*) [1], they [1], this [1], those [1], till (*+302+891*) [1], till (*+3360*) [1], what (*+1437*) [1], what (*+5101*) [1], whatsoever (*+1437+5100*) [1], whatsoever (*+302+302+5100*) [1], whatsoever (*+3956*) [1], whence [1], whereby (*+4012*) [1], whereby (*+4314*) [1], wherefore (*+1519*) [1], wherefore (*+1909*) [1], wherefore (*+5484*) [1], wherein (*+1223*) [1], wherein (*+1722+3778*) [1], wherein (*+4012*) [1], whereinto (*+1519*) [1], whereof (*+1537*) [1], whereon [1], whereto (*+1519*) [1], whereunto (*+3825*) [1], where [1], whether (*+1520*) [1], whither (*+1519*) [1], whomsoever (*+3956*) [1], whoso (*+1437*) [1], whosoever (*+3956*) [1]

3740* ὁσάκις, *hosakis, adv. GK: *4006* [→ *3745*]. as often as, whenever:– as oft as (*+302*) [1], as often as (*+1437*) [1], as often as (*+302*) [1]

3741* ὅσιος, *hosios, a. GK: *4008* [→ *462, 3742, 3743*]. holy, pious, devout; (n.) Holy One; divine decree (Ac 13:34):– holy [4], holy one [2], mercies [1]

3742* ὁσιότης, *hosiotēs, n. GK: *4009* [→ *3741*]. holiness:– holiness [2]

3743* ὁσίως, *hosiōs, adv. GK: *4010* [→ *3741*]. holy, in a devout manner:– holily [1]

3744* ὀσμή, *osmē, n. GK: *4011* [→ *3605*]. fragrance, odor:– savour [4], odour [2]

3745* ὅσος, *hosos, a. GK: *4012* [→ *3740, 4214*]. how great, how much, how far; as, just as:– as many as [25], whatsoever [17], that [9], whatsoever (*+302*) [6], how great [5], what [5], all that [4], as long as (*+1909+5550*) [3], as many as (*+302*) [3], as [3], how much [3], which [3], all [2], as long as (*+1909*) [2], inasmuch as (*+1909*) [2], inasmuch as (*+2596*) [2], little while (*+3398+3745*) [2], that ever [2], whatsoever (*+1437*) [2], whosoever (*+302*) [2], as (*+2590*) [1], as long as (*+5550*) [1], as many as (*+1437*) [1], as much as [1], ever [1], how many [1], inasmuch as (*+1909+3303+3767*) [1], more [1], so many as [1], what great [1], what soever [1], wherewith soever (*+302*) [1], who [1]

3746* ὅσπερ, *hosper, p.rel.&pt. GK: *4013* [→ *3739+4007*]. whosoever:– whomsoever [1]

3747* ὀστέον, *osteon; or **ὀστοῦν, *ostoun***, n. GK: *4014 & 4016.* bone:– bones [4], bone [1]

3748 **ὅστις, *hostis***, p.rel.&indef. GK: *4015* [→ *3739+5100*]. who, whoever, whatever; someone, anyone, everyone; a marker of time relationships: until, while:– which [82], who [30], whosoever [10], that [7], they [3], whosoever (*+302*) [3], till (*+2193*) [2], until (*+2193*) [2], whosoever (*+3956*) [2], as [1], a [1], he that [1], in that [1], such as [1], whatsoever (*+1437+3956+5100*) [1], whatsoever (*+302*) [1], what [1], whereas [1], which (*+302*) [1], whiles (*+2193*) [1]

3749 **ὀστράκινος, *ostrakinos***, a. GK: *4017*. made of clay:– earthen [1], of earth [1]

3750 **ὄσφρησις, *osphrēsis***, n. GK: *4018* [→ *3605*]. sense of smell:– smelling [1]

3751 **ὀσφῦς, *osphys***, n. GK: *4019*. waist, loins, body; belt:– loins [8]

3752 **ὅταν, *hotan***, pt.temp. GK: *4020* [→ *3739+5037+302*]. when, whenever; at once; as soon as:– when [115], as soon as [2], as long as [1], that [1], till (*+1508*) [1], whensoever [1], while [1]

3753 **ὅτε, *hote***, pt.temp. GK: *4021* [→ *3739+5037*]. when, while, after; as, as soon as:– when [99], after [3], as soon as [2], that [1], while [1], whilst [1]

3754 **ὅτι, *hoti***, c. GK: *4022* [→ *3739+5101*]. that; because, since; for:– that [622], for [265], *usually untranslated* [206], because [177], how that [20], how [11], because that [4], though [3], in that [1], seeing that [1], seeing [1], to [1], why [1]

3755 **ὅτου, *hotou***, p.rel.&indef.gen. of *3748*. GK: *4015* [→ *3739+5100*]. a marker of time relationships: until, while; see *3748*:–

3756 **οὐ, *ou***, adv.neg. GK: *4024* [→ *1847, 1848, 3760, 3761, 3762, 3763, 3764, 3765, 3766, 3768, 3777, 3780*]. no, not, not at all, in no way, absolutely not. At the beginning of a Greek question, it anticipates a positive response:– not [1209], no [140], cannot (*+1410*) [45], none [20], neither (*+2532*) [16], neither [12], nay [11], cannot [10], no (*+3956*) [7], never (*+165+1519+3361+3588*) [5], nothing [4], never [3], nothing (*+5101*) [3], neither (*+1161*) [2], nor (*+2532*) [2], nor [2], not (*+3361*) [2], but (*+2228+4183*) [1], cannot (*+1510*) [1], cannot (*+1735*) [1], cannot (*+2192*) [1], cannot (*+2480*) [1], long (*+3641*) [1], neither any (*+3762*) [1], never (*+165+1487+1519+3588*) [1], never (*+165+1519+3588*) [1], never (*+3361+4218*) [1], never (*+3361+4455*) [1], never before (*+3764*) [1], no more at all (*+3361+3765*) [1], no not one (*+1520+2193*) [1], none (*+3762*) [1], nothing (*+3739*) [1], nothing (*+3956+4487*) [1], nothing (*+5100*) [1], nothing at all (*+3762*) [1], special (*+3588+5177*) [1], unworthy (*+514*) [1], without (*+3326*) [1]

3757 **οὗ, *hou***, adv.pl. GK: *4023* [→ *3739*]. where; to which:– where [22], whither [2], whence [1], when [1], wherein [1], whithersoever (*+1437*) [1]

3758 **οὐά, *oua***, pt.interj. GK: *4025*. so!, aha!:– ah [1]

3759 **οὐαί, *ouai***, pt.interj. GK: *4026*. woe!, how dreadful!, alas!:– woe [40], alas [6], woes [1]

3760 **οὐδαμῶς, *oudamōs***, adv. GK: *4027* [→ *3756+1161*]. by no means:– not [1]

3761 **οὐδέ, *oude***, c.neg. GK: *4028* [→ *3756+1161*]. and not, nor, neither, not either, not even:– neither [68], nor [30], not [17], no [3], nor yet [2], not so much as [2], then not [2], also not [1], and no so much as (*+2532*) [1], and not [1], even not [1], neither (*+2532*) [1], never [1], no more [1], no not so much [1], not even [1], not so much as (*+235*) [1], nothing (*+5100*) [1], yet not [1]

3762 **οὐδείς, *oudeis***, a. GK: *4029 & 4032* [→ *3756+1161+1520*]. no one, not anyone, nothing:– no [116], nothing [68], none [26], any [7], man [2], not any [2], all [1], despised (*+1519+3049*) [1], neither any (*+1161*) [1], neither any (*+2532*) [1], neither any (*+3756*) [1], never (*+3768*) [1], none (*+3056*) [1], none (*+3756*) [1], not at all [1], nothing at all (*+3756*) [1], not [1], nought [1], ought [1], yet never (*+4455*) [1]

3763 **οὐδέποτε, *oudepote***, adv. GK: *4030* [→ *3756+1161+4226+5037*]. never:– never [14], neither at any time (*+2532*) [1], nothing at any time (*+3956*) [1]

3764 **οὐδέπω, *oudepō***, adv. GK: *4031* [→ *3756+1161*]. not yet, not ever:– as yet not [1], never before (*+3756*) [1], never yet [1], not yet [1], yet [1]

3765 **οὐκέτι, *ouketi***, adv. GK: *4033* [→ *3756+2089*]. no longer, not again, not any more, no further:– no more [29], any more [3], after that [2], not [2], now not [2], any moe [1], henceforth not [1], hereafter not [1], more [1], no longer [1], no more at all (*+3361+3756*) [1], not now [1], not yet [1], yet [1]

3766 **οὐκοῦν, *oukoun***, adv. GK: *4034* [→ *3756+3767*]. so, then (to introduce a question):– then [1]

3767 **οὖν, *oun***, pt.infer.&trans. GK: *4036* [→ *3304, 3766, 5105*]. therefore, then, so then:– therefore [257], then [195], so [16], and [9], now [9], wherefore [8], therefore (*+686*) [7], but [4], seeing then [3], then (*+5119*) [2], when [2], and so [1], forasmuch then as [1], forasmuch then [1], inasmuch as (*+1909+3303+3745*) [1], therefore seeing [1]

3768 **οὔπω, *oupō***, adv. GK: *4037* [→ *3756*]. not yet, still not; not ever:– not yet [20], hitherto not [1], never (*+3762*) [1], no as yet [1], yet [1]

3769 **οὐρά, *oura***, n. GK: *4038*. tail:– tails [4], tail [1]

3770 **οὐράνιος, *ouranios***, a. GK: *4039* [→ *3772*]. heavenly, in heaven, from heaven:– heavenly [6]

3771 **οὐρανόθεν, *ouranothen***, adv. GK: *4040* [→ *3772*]. from heaven:– from heaven [2]

3772 **οὐρανός, *ouranos***, n. GK: *4041* [→ *2032, 3321, 3770, 3771*]. sky, air, firmament, any area above the earth; heaven(s), the place of sun, moon, and stars; heaven, in which God dwells. "The third heaven" may be a Jewish technical term for God's dwelling place; "heaven" in some contexts is a euphemism for "God" (Lk 15:18):– heaven [248], heavens [19], air [10], sky [5], heaven's [1], heavenly (*+1537*) [1]

3773 **Οὐρβανός, *Ourbanos***, n.pr. GK: *4042*. Urbanus, "*refined, elegant*":– Urban [1]

3774 **Οὐρίας, *Ourias***, n.pr. GK: *4043*. Uriah, "*Yahweh is [my] flame, light*":– Urias [1]

3775 **οὖς, *ous***, n. GK: *4044* [→ *1801, 5621*]. ear; listening, responding:– ears [24], ear [13]

3776 **οὐσία, *ousia***, n. GK: *4045* [→ *1510*]. wealth; estate, property:– goods [1], substance [1]

3777 **οὔτε, *oute***, adv. [used as neg.]. GK: *4046* [→ *3756+5037*]. and not, neither, nor:– neither [45], nor [42], not [3], nor yet [2], none [1], nothing [1]

3778 **οὗτος, *houtos***, p.demo. GK: *4047* [→ *3779, 5023, 5025, 5026, 5082, 5108, 5118, 5123, 5124, 5125, 5126, 5127, 5128, 5129, 5130*]. this, this one, these; (as object) him, her, it, them:– this [666], these [358], that [58], therefore (*+1223*) [43], the same [36], he [33], him [30], thus [21], for this cause (*+1223*) [14], they [13], those [13], she [12], them [11], it [9], such [9], hereby (*+1722*) [8], herein (*+1722*) [7], wherefore (*+1223*) [7], same [6], so [6], the [6], afterward (*+3326*) [4], hereafter (*+3326*) [4], therefore (*+1519*) [3], for this cause (*+1519*) [2], for this cause (*+1752*) [2], therefore (*+3844*) [2], therein (*+1722*) [2], thereunto (*+1519*) [2], to this end (*+1519*) [2], and partly (*+1161*) [1], by reason hereof (*+1223*) [1], from thenceforth (*+1537*) [1], hence (*+3326*) [1], hereby (*+1537*) [1], hereof [1], hereunto (*+1519*) [1], her [1], one [1], partly (*+3303*) [1], that same [1], that should follow (*+3326*) [1], the same (*+846*) [1], their [1], themselves [1], thereabout (*+4012*) [1], therein [1], thereunto (*+846+1519*) [1], therewith (*+1909*) [1], therewith [1], thus far (*+2193*) [1], wherein (*+1722+3739*) [1], which [1], who [1]

3779 **οὕτως, *houtōs***, adv. GK: *4048* [→ *3778*]. in this manner, thus, in the same way, likewise:– so [171], thus [17], likewise [6], on this wise [6], after this manner [3], after that [1], as [1], can [1], even as (*+2596+3739+5158*) [1], for all that [1], in this manner [1], on this fashion [1], so in like manner (*+2532*) [1], what [1]

3780 **οὐχί, *ouchi***, adv.neg. GK: *4049* [→ *3756*]. not, no!:– not [51], nay [5]

3781 **ὀφειλέτης, *opheiletēs***, n. GK: *4050* [→ *3784*]. debtor, one who owes, is obligated, guilty:– debtors [3], debtor [2], ought [1], sinners [1]

3782 **ὀφειλή, *opheilē***, n. GK: *4051* [→ *3784*]. debt; marital duty; (pl.) taxes:– debt [1], dues [1]

3783 **ὀφείλημα, *opheilēma***, n. GK: *4052* [→ *3784*]. debt, obligation, what is owed:– debts [1], debt [1]

3784 **ὀφείλω, *opheilō***, v. GK: *4053* [→ *3781, 3782, 3783, 3785, 4359, 5533*]. to owe, be in debt; be bound by oath; be obligated, ought, must:– ought [17], owest [3], bound [2], due [2], duty [2], behoved [1], debtor [1], debt [1], guilty [1], indebted [1], must needs [1], need [1], oweth [1], owe [1], should [1]

3785 **ὄφελον, *ophelon***, pt. GK: *4054* [→ *3784*]. How I wish! How I hope!:– would [4]

3786 **ὄφελος, *ophelos***, n. GK: *4055* [→ *5623*]. good, gain, benefit:– profit [2], advantageth [1]

3787 **ὀφθαλμοδουλία, *ophthalmodoulia***, n. GK: *4056* [→ *3788+1401*]. eye-service, service performed to attract attention:– eyeservice [2]

3788 **ὀφθαλμός, *ophthalmos***, n. GK: *4057* [→ *503, 3442, 3787; cf. 3708*]. eye, the organ of sight; by extension: the faculty of mental perception and understanding:– eyes [71], eye [30], sight [1]

3789 **ὄφις, *ophis***, n. GK: *4058*. snake, serpent:– serpent [8], serpents [6]

3790 **ὀφρῦς, *ophrys***, n. GK: *4059*. eyebrow, brow (of a hill):– brow [1]

3791 **ὀχλέω, *ochleō***, v. GK: *4061* [→ *3793*]. (pass.) to be tormented, disturbed:– vexed [2]

3792 **ὀχλοποιέω, *ochlopoieō***, v. GK: *4062* [→ *3793+4160*]. to form a mob:– gathered a company [1]

3793 **ὄχλος, *ochlos***, n. GK: *4063* [→ *1776, 3791, 3792, 3926*]. crowd, people, multitude, mob, a gathering of any size, sometimes with the implication that these are common folk and not leaders or nobility:– people [83], multitude [59], multitudes [20], company [7], press [5], number [1]

3794 **ὀχύρωμα, *ochyrōma***, n. GK: *4065* [→ *2192*]. stronghold, fortress; some translate as "prison":– strong holds [1]

3795 **ὀψάριον, *opsarion***, n. GK: *4066* [→ *3800, 3953*]. (small) fish:– fish [3], fishes [1], small fishes [1]

3796 **ὀψέ, *opse***, adv. GK: *4067* [→ *3797, 3798*]. in the evening, late in the day; (pp.) after:– at even [1], even [1], in the end [1]

3797 **ὄψιμος, *opsimos***, a. GK: *4069* [→ *3796*]. late (in the season, April-May in the modern calendar), spring:– latter [1]

3798 **ὄψιος, *opsios***, a. GK: *4070* [→ *3796*]. late; (n.) evening:– even [8], evening [5], at even (*+1096*) [1], eventide (*+3588+5610*) [1]

3799 **ὄψις, *opsis***, n. GK: *4071* [→ *3708*]. face; appearance:– appearance [1], countenance [1], face [1]

3800 **ὀψώνιον, *opsōnion***, n. GK: *4072* [→ *3795+5608*]. pay, wage; support, compensation:– wages [3], charges [1]

3801 **ὁ ὢν καί ὁ ἦν καί ὁ ἐρχόμενος, *hō ōn kai hō én kai hō ērchōmēnōs***, rel.p.+v.+c. GK: *3836 + 1639 + 2779 + 2262* [→ *3588+1510+2064+2532*]. who is and who was and who is to come, a title of Christ:–

3802 **παγιδεύω, *pagideuō***, v. GK: *4074* [→ *4078*]. to trap, entrap:– entangle [1]

3803 **παγίς, *pagis***, n. GK: *4075* [→ *4078*]. trap, snare:– snare [5]

Πάγος, *Pagos*. See **697**.

3804 **πάθημα, *pathēma***, n. GK: *4077* [→ *3958*]. suffering, misfortune; passion:– sufferings [10], afflictions [3], affections [1], motions [1], suffering [1]

3805 **παθητός, *pathētos***, a. GK: *4078* [→ *3958*]. subject to suffering:– suffer [1]

3806 **πάθος, *pathos***, n. GK: *4079* [→ *3958*]. lust, sexual passion:– affections [1], inordinate affection [1], lust [1]

πάθω, *pathō*. See **3958**.

3807 **παιδαγωγός, *paidagōgos***, n. GK: *4080* [→ *3816+71*]. guardian, custodian, supervisor:– schoolmaster [2], instructors [1]

3808 **παιδάριον, *paidarion***, n. GK: *4081* [→ *3816*]. little boy, child:– children [1], lad [1]

3809 **παιδεία, *paideia***, n. GK: *4082* [→ *3816*]. discipline, training:– chastening [3], chastisement [1], instruction [1], nurture [1]

3810 **παιδευτής, *paideutēs***, n. GK: *4083* [→ *3816*]. instructor, teacher; discipliner, corrector:– corrected [1], instructor [1]

3811 **παιδεύω, *paideuō***, v. GK: *4084* [→ *3816*]. instruct, train, educate, as an on-going matter, in accord with rules and proper conduct; discipline, punish, for the purpose of better behavior:– chastened [3], chasteneth [2], chastise [2], chasten [1], instructing [1], learned [1], learn [1], taught [1], teaching [1]

3812 **παιδιόθεν, *paidiothen***, adv. GK: *4085 & 4088* [→ *3816*]. from childhood:– of a child [1]

3813 **παιδίον, *paidion***, n. GK: *4086* [→ *3816*]. child:– child [15], children [9], young child [8], little children [7], little child [5], damsel [4], children's [1], young child's [1], young children [1]

3814 **παιδίσκη, *paidiskē***, n. GK: *4087* [→ *3816*]. female servant, female slave, maidservant:– bondwoman [4], damsel [4], maid [2], bondmaid [1], maidens [1], maids [1]

3815 **παίζω, *paizō***, v. GK: *4089* [→ *1701, 1702, 1703; cf. 3816*]. to indulge in revelry, play, amuse oneself, dance, sometimes a euphemism for sexual immorality:– play [1]

3816 **παῖς, *pais***, n. GK: *4090* [→ *521, 3807, 3808, 3809, 3810, 3811, 3812, 3813, 3814; cf. 3815*]. boy, child, youth, usually below the age of puberty and not necessarily male; a personal servant, slave, attendant, with a possible implication of kind regard or close relationship; the word used in the Greek version of Isaiah, quoted in NT, for "servant" of the Lord:– servant [8], child [5], son [3], children [2], servants [2], maiden [1], maid [1], menservants [1], young man [1]

3817 **παίω, *paiō***, v. GK: *4091*. to strike, hit (and so wound):– smote [4], striketh [1]

3818 **Πακατιανός, *Pakatianos***, a.pr.g. GK: *4092*. Pacatian, "*in Pacatia*":– Pacatiana [1]

3819 **πάλαι, *palai***, adv. GK: *4093* [→ *1597, 3820, 3821, 3822*]. long ago, in the past, already:– any while [1], great while ago [1], long ago [1], of old [1], old [1], past [1]

3820 **παλαιός, *palaios***, a. GK: *4094* [→ *3819*]. old:– old [19]

3821 **παλαιότης, *palaiotēs***, n. GK: *4095* [→ *3819*]. the old way, obsoleteness, age:– oldness [1]

3822 **παλαιόω, *palaioō***, v. GK: *4096* [→ *3819*]. (act.) to make obsolete; (pass.) to wear out, become obsolete, become old:– wax old [2], decayeth [1], made old [1]

3823 **πάλη, *palē***, n. GK: *4097*. struggle:– wrestle (*+1510*) [1]

3824 **παλιγγενεσία, *palingenesia***, n. GK: *4098 & 4100* [→ *3825+1096*]. renewal; rebirth, regeneration:– regeneration [2]

3825 **πάλιν, *palin***, adv. GK: *4099* [→ *3824*]. again, once more; furthermore; on the other hand:– again [141], whereunto (*+3739*) [1]

3826 **παμπληθεί, *pamplēthei***, adv. GK: *4101 & 4113* [→ *3956+4130*]. with one voice, all together:– all at once [1]

3827 **πάμπολυς, *pampolys***, a. GK: *4102* [→ *3956+4183*]. very great:– very great [1]

3828 **Παμφυλία, *Pamphylia***, n.pr. GK: *4103* [→ *3956+5453*]. Pamphylia:– Pamphylia [5]

3829 **πανδοχεῖον, *pandocheion***, n. GK: *4104 & 4106* [→ *3956+1209*]. inn:– inn [1]

3830 **πανδοχεύς, *pandocheus***, n. GK: *4105 & 4107* [→ *3956+1209*]. innkeeper:– host [1]

3831 **πανήγυρις, *panēgyris***, n. GK: *4108* [→ *3956+71*]. joyful assembly, festal gathering:– general assembly [1]

3832 **πανοικεί, *panoikei***, adv. GK: *4109* [→ *3956+3624*]. with one's whole family:– all house [1]

3833 **πανοπλία, *panoplia***, n. GK: *4110* [→ *3956+3696*]. full armor, worn by a heavily armed soldier:– whole armour [2], all armour [1]

3834 **πανουργία, *panourgia***, n. GK: *4111* [→ *3956+2041*]. cunning, craftiness, deception, duplicity:– craftiness [3], cunning craftiness [1], subtilty [1]

3835 **πανοῦργος, *panourgos***, a. GK: *4112* [→ *3956+2041*]. crafty, clever, sly:– crafty [1]

3836 **πανταχόθεν, *pantachothen***, adv. GK: *4115* [→ *3956*]. from every direction:– from every quarter [1]

3837 **πανταχοῦ, *pantachou***, adv. GK: *4114 & 4116* [→ *3956*]. everywhere; in all directions:– every where [6], in all places [1], throughout (*+1519*) [1]

3838 **παντελής, *pantelēs***, a. GK: *4117* [→ *3956+5056*]. complete, perfect, absolute; at all:– in no wise (*+1519+3361+3588*) [1], uttermost [1]

3839 **πάντη, *pantē***, adv. GK: *4118* [→ *3956*]. in every way:– always [1]

3840 **πάντοθεν, *pantothen***, adv. GK: *4119* [→ *3956*]. from all directions; completely, entirely:– on every side [1], round about [1]

3841 **παντοκράτωρ, *pantokratōr***, n. GK: *4120* [→ *3956+2904*]. Almighty; this title for God translates the Hebrew 7372, [Lord] "of Hosts" (the heavenly armies), and Hebrew 8724, "Shaddai," (probably) God the Mountain, powerful and immovable:– Almighty [9], Omnipotent [1]

3842 **πάντοτε, *pantote***, adv. GK: *4121* [→ *3956+3739+5037*]. always, at all times, forever:– always [29], ever [6], alway [5], evermore [2]

3843 **πάντως, *pantōs***, adv. GK: *4122* [→ *3956*]. surely, certainly, by all possible means, quite:– altogether [2], by all means [2], at all [1], in no wise [1], must needs (*+1163*) [1], no doubt [1], surely [1]

3844 **παρά, *para***, pp. GK: *4123* [→ *492, 531, 532, 3845, 3846, 3847, 3848, 3849, 3850, 3851, 3852, 3853, 3854, 3855, 3856, 3858, 3859, 3860, 3861, 3862, 3863, 3864, 3865, 3866, 3867, 3868, 3869, 3870, 3871, 3872, 3873, 3874, 3875, 3876, 3877, 3878, 3879, 3880, 3881, 3882, 3883, 3884, 3885, 3886, 3887, 3888, 3889, 3890, 3891, 3892, 3893, 3894, 3895, 3896, 3897, 3898, 3899, 3900, 3901, 3902, 3903, 3904, 3905, 3906, 3907, 3908, 3909, 3910, 3911, 3912, 3914, 3915, 3916, 3918, 3919, 3920, 3921, 3922, 3923, 3924, 3925, 3926, 3927, 3928, 3929, 3930, 3931, 3935, 3936, 3938, 3939, 3940, 3941, 3943, 3944, 3945, 3946, 3947, 3948, 3949, 3950, 3951, 3952, 3953, 3970, 4836, 4837, 4838, 4839, 4840*]. (gen.) from; (dat.) with, before, among, in the sight of; (acc.) beside, along side, by, at:– of [53], with [42], from [24], by [14], at [12], by side [9], than [9], above [4], before [3], contrary to [3], against [2], among [2], any other than [2], in [2], more than [2], nigh unto [2], therefore (*+3778*) [2], amongst [1], friends (*+3588*) [1], had (*+3588*) [1], in the sight [1], past [1], save [1], such as give (*+3588*) [1]

3845 **παραβαίνω, *parabainō***, v. GK: *4124* [→ *3844+305*]. to break, transgress; to leave, turn aside:– transgress [2], by transgression fell [1], transgresseth [1]

3846 **παραβάλλω, *paraballō***, v. GK: *4125* [→ *3844+906*]. to come near (by ship); compare:– arrived [1], compare [1]

3847 **παράβασις, *parabasis***, n. GK: *4126* [→ *3844+305*]. transgression, breaking, violation:– transgression [4], transgressions [2], breaking [1]

3848 **παραβάτης, *parabatēs***, n. GK: *4127* [→ *3844+305*]. lawbreaker, transgressor:– transgressor [2], breaker [1], transgressors [1], transgress [1]

3849 **παραβιάζομαι, *parabiazomai***, v. GK: *4128* [→ *3844+970*]. to urge strongly, persuade:– constrained [2]

3850 **παραβολή, *parabolē***, n. GK: *4130* [→ *3844+906*]. parable, an illustration that teaches in a story or extended figure of speech; proverb, a short pithy saying:– parable [31], parables [15], figure [2], comparison [1], proverb [1]

3851 **παραβουλεύομαι, *parabouleuomai***; or **παραβολεύομαι, *paraboleuomai***, v. GK: *4131* [→ *3844+1014*]. to be careless, have no concern:– not regarding [1]

3852 **παραγγελία, *parangelia***, n. GK: *4132* [→ *3844+32*]. order, command; instruction:– charge [2], commandments [1], commandment [1], straitly command (*+3853*) [1]

3853 **παραγγέλλω, *parangellō***, v. GK: *4133* [→ *3844+32*]. to order, command, direct; to give instruction:– commanded [11], command [7], charged [3], charge [2], charging [1], commandeth [1], declare [1], gave commandment [1], give charge [1], give in charge [1], straitly command (*+3852*) [1]

3854 **παραγίνομαι, *paraginomai***, v. GK: *4134* [→ *3844+1096*]. to come, arrive, be present; to appear:– came [16], come [15], cometh [3], coming [1], present [1], went [1]

3855 **παράγω, *paragō***, v. GK: *4135* [→ *3844+71*]. to pass by, go on, walk beside; to pass away:– passed by [5], passeth away [2], departed [1], passed forth [1], past [1]

3856 **παραδειγματίζω, *paradeigmatizō***, v. GK: *4136* [→ *3844+1164*]. to subject to public disgrace, hold up to contempt:– make a publick example [1], put to open shame [1]

3857 **παράδεισος, *paradeisos***, n. GK: *4137*. paradise, a place of blessedness, from the base meaning of "garden":– paradise [3]

3858 **παραδέχομαι, *paradechomai***, v. GK: *4138* [→ *3844+1209*]. to accept, welcome, receive:– receive [4], receiveth [1]

3859 **παραδιατριβή, *paradiatribē***, n. GK: *4139* [→ *3844+1223+5147*]. useless occupation:– perverse disputings [1]

3860 **παραδίδωμι, *paradidōmi***, v. GK: *4140* [→ *3844+1325*]. to hand over, betray, deliver to prison; to entrust, commit:– delivered [39], betrayed [19], betray [17], deliver [9], deliver up [6], delivered up [4], gave up [4], betrayeth [3], committed [2], deliveredst [2], gave [2], recommended [2], betrayest [1], brought forth [1], cast into prison [1], delivered into [1], delivering up [1], delivering [1], gave over [1], given over [1], given [1], give [1], hazarded [1], put in prison [1]

3861 **παράδοξος, *paradoxos***, a. GK: *4141* [→ *3844+1391*]. remarkable, wonderful:– strange [1]

3862 **παράδοσις, *paradosis***, n. GK: *4142* [→ *3844+1325*]. tradition; teachings:– tradition [10], traditions [2], ordinances [1]

3863 **παραζηλόω, *parazēloō***, v. GK: *4143* [→ *3844+2205*]. to make envious, arouse jealousy:– provoke to jealousy [3], provoke to emulation [1]

3864 **παραθαλάσσιος, *parathalassios***, a. GK: *4144* [→ *3844+2281*]. by the lake, by the sea:– upon the sea coast [1]

3865 **παραθεωρέω, *paratheōreō***, v. GK: *4145* [→ *3844+2334*]. (pass.) to be overlooked, neglected:– neglected [1]

3866 **παραθήκη, *parathēkē***, n. GK: *4146* [→ *3844+5087*]. deposit, thing entrusted to:– committed unto [1]

3867 **παραινέω, *paraineō***, v. GK: *4147* [→ *3844+136*]. to warn, urge:– admonished [1], exhort [1]

3868 **παραιτέομαι, *paraiteomai***, v. GK: *4148* [→ *3844+154*]. to request, beg; to make excuses; to refuse, reject:– refuse [4], excused [2], avoid [1], intreated [1], make excuse [1], refused [1], reject [1]

3869 **παρακαθίζω, *parakathizō***, v. GK: *4149 & 4150* [→ *3844+2523*]. to sit down beside:– sat [1]

3870 **παρακαλέω, *parakaleō***, v. GK: *4151* [→ *3844+2564*]. to ask, beg, plead; to comfort, encourage, exhort, urge; to call, invite:– besought [21], beseech [20], exhort [14], comforted [13], comfort [8], desired [5], pray [4], exhorted [3], exhorting [3], beseeching [2], comforteth [2], desiring [2], intreat [2], prayed [2], called for [1], desiredst [1], exhortation [1], exhorteth [1], given exhortation (*+3056*) [1], intreated [1], of good comfort [1]

3871 **παρακαλύπτω, *parakalyptō***, v. GK: *4152* [→ *3844+2572*]. (pass.) to be hidden:– hid [1]

3872 **παρακαταθήκη, *parakatathēkē***, n. GK: *4153* [→ *3844+2596+5087*]. deposit:– committed to trust [1], committed unto [1]

3873 **παράκειμαι, *parakeimai***, v. GK: *4154* [→ *3844+2749*]. to be present, ready:– present [2]

3874 **παράκλησις, *paraklēsis***, n. GK: *4155* [→ *3844+2564*]. encouragement, comfort, consolation, appeal:– consolation [14], exhortation [8], comfort [6], intreaty [1]

3875 **παράκλητος, *paraklētos***, n. GK: *4156* [→ *3844+2564*]. counselor, intercessor, helper, one who encourages and comforts; in the NT it refers exclusively to the Holy Spirit and to Jesus Christ:– comforter [4], advocate [1]

3876 **παρακοή, *parakoē***, n. GK: *4157* [→ *3844+191*]. disobedience, unwillingness to hear:– disobedience [3]

3877 **παρακολουθέω, *parakoloutheō***, v. GK: *4158* [→ *3844+190; cf. 1.3*]. to follow, accompany; to know all about; to investigate:– attained [1], follow [1], fully known [1], understanding [1]

3878 **παρακούω, *parakouō***, v. GK: *4159* [→ *3844+191*]. to refuse to listen, ignore:– neglect to hear [2]

3879 **παρακύπτω, *parakyptō***, v. GK: *4160* [→ *3844+2955*]. to bend over; to look (intently):– looketh [1], look [1], stooped down and looked [1], stooping down and looking [1], stooping down [1]

3880 **παραλαμβάνω, *paralambanō***, v. GK: *4161* [→ *3844+2983*]. to take with; take charge of; to receive, accept:– took [14], received [13], taketh [6], taken [5], take [4], took unto [2], receive [1], receiving [1], take unto [1], taketh to [1], taketh with [1], took with [1]

3881 **παραλέγομαι, *paralegomai***, v. GK: *4162* [→ *3844+3004*]. to sail past, move along:– passing [1], sailed [1]

3882 **παράλιος, *paralios***, a. GK: *4163* [→ *3844+217*]. (located) by the sea; (n.) seacoast:– sea coast [1]

3883 **παραλλαγή, *parallagē***, n. GK: *4164* [→ *3844+236*]. change, variation:– variableness [1]

3884 **παραλογίζομαι, *paralogizomai***, v. GK: *4165* [→ *3844+3004*]. to deceive, delude:– beguile [1], deceiving [1]

3885 παραλυτικός, paralytikos, a. GK: *4166 & 4167* [→ *3844+3089*]. (n.) paralytic, lame person:– sick of the palsy [7], had the palsy [1], man sick of the palsy [1], one sick of the palsy [1]

3886 παραλύω, paralyō, v. GK: *4168* [→ *3844+3089*]. (pass.) to be paralyzed, disabled; (n.) paralytic:– sick of the palsy [2], feeble [1], taken with a palsy [1], taken with palsies [1]

3887 παραμένω, paramenō, v. GK: *4169* [→ *3844+3306*]. to continue; to remain with:– abide [1], continueth [1], continue [1]

3888 παραμυθέομαι, paramytheomai, v. GK: *4170* [→ *3844+3454*]. to comfort, encourage, console:– comforted [2], comfort [2]

3889 παραμυθία, paramythia, n. GK: *4171* [→ *3844+3454*]. comfort, consolation:– comfort [1]

3890 παραμύθιον, paramythion, n. GK: *4172* [→ *3844+3454*]. comfort, consolation, encouragement:– comfort [1]

3891 παρανομέω, paranomeō, v. GK: *4174* [→ *3844+3551*]. to violate the law, act contrary to the law:– contrary to law [1]

3892 παρανομία, paranomia, n. GK: *4175* [→ *3844+3551*]. wrongdoing, lawlessness:– iniquity [1]

3893 παραπικραίνω, parapikrainō, v. GK: *4176* [→ *3844+4089*]. to rebel, disobey:– provoke [1]

3894 παραπικρασμός, parapikrasmos, n. GK: *4177* [→ *3844+4089*]. rebellion, revolt:– provocation [2]

3895 παραπίπτω, parapiptō, v. GK: *4178* [→ *3844+4098*]. to fall away, commit apostasy:– fall away [1]

3896 παραπλέω, parapleō, v. GK: *4179* [→ *3844+4126*]. to sail past:– sail by [1]

3897 παραπλήσιος, paraplēsios, a. GK: *4180* [→ *3844+4139*]. (adv.) almost, nearly:– nigh unto [1]

3898 παραπλησίως, paraplēsiōs, adv. GK: *4181* [→ *3844+4139*]. in just the same way:– likewise [1]

3899 παραπορεύομαι, paraporeuomai, v. GK: *4182* [→ *3844+4198*]. to pass by, go through:– passed by [3], passed [1], went [1]

3900 παράπτωμα, paraptōma, n. GK: *4183* [→ *3844+4098*]. trespass, transgression, sin against, to sin as a moral failure to keep a command, fig., stepping out of the bounds of God's law:– trespasses [9], offence [5], sins [3], fall [2], offences [2], faults [1], fault [1]

3901 παραρρέω, pararreō, v. GK: *4184* [→ *3844+4482*]. to drift away, flow past, slip away:– slip [1]

3902 παράσημος, parasēmos, a. GK: *4185* [→ *3844+4592*]. distinguished, marked; (n.) figurehead, emblem (on a ship):– sign [1]

3903 παρασκευάζω, paraskeuazō, v. GK: *4186* [→ *3844+4632*]. (act.) to prepare; (mid.) to get ready; (mid./pass.) to be ready:– ready [2], made ready [1], prepare [1]

3904 παρασκευή, paraskeuē, n. GK: *4187* [→ *3844+4632*]. Preparation Day:– preparation [6]

3905 παρατείνω, parateinō, v. GK: *4189* [→ *1614; cf. 3844*]. to keep on, prolong, extend:– continued [1]

3906 παρατηρέω, paratēreō, v. GK: *4190* [→ *3844+5083*]. to watch closely, observe:– watched [5], observe [1]

3907 παρατήρησις, paratērēsis, n. GK: *4191* [→ *3844+5083*]. careful observation:– observation [1]

3908 παρατίθημι, paratithēmi, v. GK: *4192* [→ *3844+5087*]. (act.) to set before; (mid.) to entrust, commit:– set before [8], commend [2], commit [2], put forth [2], alleging [1], commended [1], commit the keeping [1], committed [1], set meat before (*+5132*) [1]

3909 παρατυγχάνω, paratynchanō, v. GK: *4193* [→ *3844+5177*]. to happen to be there:– met with [1]

3910 παραυτίκα, parautika, adv. GK: *4194* [→ *3844+846*]. (a.) momentary:– for a moment [1]

3911 παραφέρω, parapherō, v. GK: *4195* [→ *3844+5342*]. to take away, remove; (pass.) to be carried away:– remove [1], take away [1]

3912 παραφρονέω, paraphroneō, v. GK: *4196* [→ *3913*]. to be out of one's mind, insane:– fool [1]

3913 παραφρονία, paraphronia, n. GK: *4197* [→ *3912*]. madness, insanity:– madness [1]

3914 παραχειμάζω, paracheimazō, v. GK: *4199* [→ *3844+5510*]. to spend the winter:– winter [3], wintered [1]

3915 παραχειμασία, paracheimasia, n. GK: *4200* [→ *3844+5510*]. spending the winter:– winter in [1]

3916 παραχρῆμα, parachrēma, adv. GK: *4202* [→ *3844+5530*]. immediately, instantly, at once:– immediately [13], straightway [3], forthwith [1], presently [1], soon [1]

3917 πάρδαλις, pardalis, n. GK: *4203*. leopard:– leopard [1]

3918 πάρειμι, pareimi, v. GK: *4205* [→ *3844+1510*]. to be present, here; to have come:– present [12], come [6], came [1], have [1], here present [1], here [1], lacketh (*+3361*) [1]

3919 παρεισάγω, pareisagō, v. GK: *4206* [→ *3844+1519+71*]. to bring in secretly:– privily bring in [1]

3920 παρείσακτος, pareisaktos, a. GK: *4207* [→ *3844+1519+71*]. brought in secretly, infiltrated:– unawares brought in [1]

3921 παρεισδύω, pareisdyō, v. GK: *4208* [→ *3844+1519+1416*]. to slip in secretly:– crept in unawares [1]

3922 παρεισέρχομαι, pareiserchomai, v. GK: *4209* [→ *3844+1519+2064*]. to come in, sneak in; to add to:– came in privily [1], entered [1]

3923 παρεισφέρω, pareispherō, v. GK: *4210* [→ *3844+1519+5342*]. to do one's best:– giving [1]

3924 παρεκτός, parektos, adv.&pp.*. GK: *4211* [→ *3844+1537*]. (adv.) besides; (pp.) except for, apart from:– except [1], saving for [1], without [1]

3925 παρεμβολή, parembolē, n. GK: *4213* [→ *3844+1722+906*]. camp, barracks; army:– castle [6], camp [3], armies [1]

3926 παρενοχλέω, parenochleō, v. GK: *4214* [→ *3844+1722+3793*]. to make difficult, trouble:– trouble [1]

3927 παρεπίδημος, parepidēmos, a. GK: *4215* [→ *3844+1909+1218*]. (n.) stranger:– pilgrims [2], strangers [1]

3928 παρέρχομαι, parerchomai, v. GK: *4216* [→ *3844+2064*]. to go by, pass by; (pass.) to pass away, come to an end, disappear; be taken away:– pass away [10], pass [8], past [3], came [1], come forth [1], go [1], pass over [1], passed away [1], passed by [1], passeth by [1], passing by [1], past away [1], transgressed [1]

3929 πάρεσις, paresis, n. GK: *4217* [→ *863; cf. 3844*]. leaving unpunished, passing over:– remission [1]

3930 παρέχω, parechō, v. GK: *4218* [→ *3844+2192*]. to present, give; to show, give proof; to cause, bring about, promote; (mid.) to set (an example); to provide; to get for oneself:– trouble (*+2873*) [4], brought [2], do [1], give unto [1], given [1], giveth [1], kept [1], minister [1], offer [1], shewed [1], shewing [1], troubleth (*+2873*) [1]

3931 παρηγορία, parēgoria, n. GK: *4219* [→ *3844+71*]. comfort:– comfort [1]

3932 παρθενία, parthenia, n. GK: *4220* [→ *3933*]. virginity:– virginity [1]

3933 παρθένος, parthenos, n. GK: *4221* [→ *3932*]. virgin (male and female), one who has never engaged in sexual relations:– virgin [7], virgins [6], virgin's [1]

3934 Πάρθοι, Parthoi, n.pr.g. GK: *4222*. Parthian:– Parthians [1]

3935 παρίημι, pariēmi, v. GK: *4223* [→ *863; cf. 3844*]. to leave undone, neglect; (pass.) to be feeble, weakened, listless:– hang down [1]

3936 παρίστημι, paristēmi; or **παριστάνω, paristanō**, v. GK: *4225* [→ *3844+2476*]. to place beside, put at disposal; to present, make an offering; (intr.) to stand before, provide, come to aid:– stood by [11], present [7], yield [4], brought before [2], stand [2], assist [1], come [1], commendeth [1], give [1], presented before [1], presented [1], prove [1], provide [1], shewed [1], shew [1], stand before [1], standing by [1], stood up [1], stood with [1], stood [1], yielded [1]

3937 Παρμενᾶς, Parmenas, n.pr. GK: *4226*. Parmenas, "*steady, reliable*":– Parmenas [1]

3938 πάροδος, parodos, n. GK: *4227* [→ *3844+3598*]. passing by:– way [1]

3939 παροικέω, paroikeō, v. GK: *4228* [→ *3844+3624*]. to live as a stranger, visit; to migrate:– sojourned [1], stranger [1]

3940 παροικία, paroikia, n. GK: *4229* [→ *3844+3624*]. residence as a stranger:– dwelt as strangers [1], sojourning [1]

3941 πάροικος, paroikos, a. GK: *4230* [→ *3844+3624*]. strange; (n.) alien, foreigner, stranger:– foreigners [1], sojourn (*+1510*) [1], strangers [1], stranger [1]

3942 παροιμία, paroimia, n. GK: *4231*. figure of speech, proverb, maxim:– proverbs [2], proverb [2], parable [1]

3943 πάροινος, paroinos, a. GK: *4232* [→ *3844+3631*]. drunken, given to drunkenness:– given to wine [2]

3944 παροίχομαι, paroichomai, v. GK: *4233* [→ *3844*]. to pass by:– past [1]

3945 παρομοιάζω, paromoiazō, v. GK: *4234* [→ *3844+3664*]. to be like:– like [1]

3946 παρόμοιος, paromoios, a. GK: *4235* [→ *3844+3664*]. like, similar:– like [2]

3947 παροξύνω, paroxynō, v. GK: *4236* [→ *3844+3691*]. (intr.) to be greatly distressed; to be angered, irritated:– easily provoked [1], stirred [1]

3948 παροξυσμός, paroxysmos, n. GK: *4237* [→ *3844+3691*]. sharp disagreement; spurring on, encouraging:– contention sharp [1], provoke unto [1]

3949 παροργίζω, parorgizō, v. GK: *4239* [→ *3844+3709*]. to anger, exasperate:– anger [1], provoke to wrath [1]

3950 παροργισμός, parorgismos, n. GK: *4240* [→ *3844+3709*]. anger:– wrath [1]

3951 παροτρύνω, parotrynō, v. GK: *4241* [→ *3844*]. to incite, arouse:– stirred up [1]

3952 παρουσία, parousia, n. GK: *4242* [→ *3844+1510*]. presence; coming, advent; in the NT usually of the second coming of the Son of Man, arriving as a conquering king:– coming [22], presence [2]

3953 παροψίς, paropsis, n. GK: *4243* [→ *3844+3795*]. dish:– platter [2]

3954 παρρησία, parrēsia, n. GK: *4244* [→ *3956+4487*]. boldness, confidence, frankness; public, openness (of speech):– boldness [8], confidence [6], openly [4], plainly [3], boldly (*+1722*) [1], boldly (*+3326*) [1], boldly [1], boldness of speech [1], bold [1], freely (*+3326*) [1], known openly (*+1722*) [1], openly (*+1722*) [1], plainly (*+1722*) [1], plainness of speech [1]

3955 παρρησιάζομαι, parrēsiazomai, v. GK: *4245* [→ *3956+4487*]. to speak boldly, preach fearlessly:– speak boldly [2], boldly [1], bold [1], freely [1], preached boldly [1], spake boldly [1], speaking boldly [1], waxed bold [1]

3956 πᾶς, pas, a. GK: *4246* [→ *537, 1275, 3826, 3827, 3828, 3829, 3830, 3831, 3832, 3833, 3834, 3835, 3836, 3837, 3838, 3839, 3840, 3841, 3842, 3843, 3954, 3955*]. all, every (thing, one), whole; always:– all [976], every [133], whosoever [31], every one [28], whole [12], any [9], no (*+3756*) [7], whatsoever [7], always (*+1223*) [3], every (*+2596*) [3], whosoever (*+302+3739*) [3], always (*+1722+2540*) [2], no (*+3361*) [2], whosoever (*+3748*) [2], all manner [1], alway (*+2250+3588*) [1], any one [1], as many as (*+3739*) [1], as many as [1], continually (*+1223*) [1], daily (*+2250+2596*) [1], daily (*+2250*) [1], ever (*+165+1519+3588*) [1], every man [1], every one's [1], every thing [1], every where [1], nothing (*+3756+4487*) [1], nothing at any time (*+3763*) [1], throughly (*+1722*) [1], whatsoever (*+1437+3748+5100*) [1], whatsoever (*+3739*) [1], whomsoever (*+3739*) [1], whosoever (*+3739*) [1]

3957 πάσχα, pascha, n. GK: *4247*. Passover, Passover week; Passover meal; Passover lamb:– passover [28], Easter [1]

3958 πάσχω, paschō, v. GK: *4248* [→ *2552, 2553, 3356, 3663, 3804, 3805, 3806, 4310, 4777, 4834, 4835, 4841*]. to experience, suffer, endure (almost always in NT with reference to unpleasant experiences):– suffer [21], suffered [17], felt [1], passion [1], suffering [1], vexed [1]

3959 Πάταρα, Patara, n.pr. GK: *4249*. Patara:– Patara [1]

3960 πατάσσω, patassō, v. GK: *4250*. to hit, strike; kill:– smite [5], smote [4], stroke [1]

3961 πατέω, pateō, v. GK: *4251* [→ *1704, 2662, 4043*]. to trample on, tread on:– tread under foot [1], treadeth [1], tread [1], trodden down [1], trodden [1]

3962 πατήρ, patēr, n. GK: *4252* [→ *493, 494, 540, 2810, 3964, 3965, 3966, 3967, 3968, 3969, 3970, 3971, 4986, 4989*]. father, a male parent or ancestor; by extension: an honorific title, leader, archetype; (pl.) parents, ancestors (of both genders):– father [347], fathers [52], father's [17], fathers' [1], parents [1]

3963 Πάτμος, Patmos, n.pr. GK: *4253*. Patmos:– Patmos [1]

Grk

3964 **πατραλῴας**, ***patralōas***, n. GK: *4254 & 4260* [→ *3962+248*]. one who kills one's father:– murderers of fathers [1]

3965 **πατριά**, ***patria***, n. GK: *4255* [→ *3962*]. family, family line, clan; people, nation:– family [1], kindreds [1], lineage [1]

3966 **πατριάρχης**, ***patriarchēs***, n. GK: *4256* [→ *3962+757*]. patriarch, father of a nation:– patriarchs [2], patriarch [2]

3967 **πατρικός**, ***patrikos***, a. GK: *4257* [→ *3962*]. paternal, from one's ancestors:– fathers [1]

3968 **πατρίς**, ***patris***, n. GK: *4258* [→ *3962*]. hometown, homeland, land of one's ancestors:– country [8]

3969 **Πατροβᾶς**, ***Patrobas***, n.pr. GK: *4259* [→ *3962+979*]. Patrobas, "*father of existence*":– Patrobas [1]

3970 **πατροπαράδοτος**, ***patroparadotos***, a. GK: *4261* [→ *3962+3844+1325*]. handed down from forefathers:– received by tradition from fathers [1]

3971 **πατρῷος**, ***patrōos***, a. GK: *4262* [→ *3962*]. ancestral, from forefathers:– fathers [3]

3972 **Παῦλος**, ***Paulos***, n.pr. GK: *4263*. Paul, Paulus, "*little*":– Paul [157], Paul's [6], Paulus [1]

3973 **παύω**, ***pauō***, v. GK: *4264* [→ *180, 372, 373, 1879, 2663, 2664, 4875*]. (act.) to cause to stop; (mid.) to stop, cease, finish:– ceased [7], cease [4], left [2], ceaseth [1], refrain [1]

3974 **Πάφος**, ***Paphos***, n.pr. GK: *4265*. Paphos:– Paphos [2]

3975 **παχύνω**, ***pachynō***, v. GK: *4266*. to become calloused of heart, make fat, and so unable to understand:– waxed gross [2]

3976 **πέδη**, ***pedē***, n. GK: *4267* [→ *3978*]. foot shackle, fetter:– fetters [3]

3977 **πεδινός**, ***pedinos***, a. GK: *4268* [→ *3978*]. level, flat:– plain (*+5117*) [1]

3978 **πεζεύω**, ***pezeuō***, v. GK: *4269* [→ *3976, 3977, 3979, 4759, 4760, 5132, 5133*]. to go on foot, travel by walking:– go afoot [1]

3979 **πεζῇ**, ***pezē***, adv. GK: *4270 & 4271* [→ *3978*]. on foot:– afoot [1], on foot [1]

3980 **πειθαρχέω**, ***peitharcheō***, v. GK: *4272* [→ *3982+757*]. to obey; to take advice:– obey [2], hearkened [1], obey magistrates [1]

3981 **πειθός**, ***peithos***, a. GK: *4273* [→ *3982*]. persuasive:– enticing [1]

3982 **πείθω**, ***peithō***, v. GK: *4275* [→ *374, 543, 544, 545, 2138, 3980, 3981, 3988, 4006, 4086; cf. 4103*]. to convince, persuade; to trust in, have confidence in, be persuaded:– persuaded [16], trust [6], obey [5], believed [3], confidence [3], persuade [3], trusted [3], confident [2], having confidence [2], obeyed [2], persuading [2], agreed [1], assure [1], have confidence [1], made friend [1], persuadest [1], put trust [1], waxing confident [1], yield unto [1]

3983 **πεινάω**, ***peinaō***, v. GK: *4277* [→ *4361*]. to be hungry:– hungred [9], hunger [8], hungry [4], hungered [2]

3984 **πεῖρα**, ***peira***, n. GK: *4278* [→ *551, 552, 1598, 3985, 3986, 3987*]. to try to do, attempt; to face, experience:– assaying [1], trial [1]

3985 **πειράζω**, ***peirazō***, v. GK: *4279* [→ *3984*]. to test, tempt; to try to trap; to examine (oneself). The difference between a test and a temptation is found in the tester's motivations and expectations; the devil tempts that the believer might fail God's standards of faith and so sin; God tests that he might determine and sharpen true character, with no focus on making the believer fail:– tempted [15], tempting [7], tempt [6], tried [3], tempter [2], assayed [1], examine [1], gone about [1], prove [1], tempteth [1], try [1]

3986 **πειρασμός**, ***peirasmos***, n. GK: *4280* [→ *3984*]. test; trial; temptation:– temptation [15], temptations [5], try [1]

3987 **πειράω**, ***peiraō***, v. GK: *4281* [→ *3984*]. to try, attempt:– assayed [1], went about [1]

3988 **πεισμονή**, ***peismonē***, n. GK: *4282* [→ *3982*]. persuasion:– persuasion [1]

3989 **πέλαγος**, ***pelagos***, n. GK: *4283*. open sea; depths:– depth [1], sea [1]

3990 **πελεκίζω**, ***pelekizō***, v. GK: *4284*. to behead, a derivative of the Greek noun "ax," not found in the NT:– beheaded [1]

3991 **πέμπτος**, ***pemptos***, a. GK: *4286* [→ *4002*]. fifth:– fifth [4]

3992 **πέμπω**, ***pempō***, v. GK: *4287* [→ *375, 1599, 3343, 4311, 4842*]. to send:– sent [52], send [25], thrust in [2], sending [1], sent forth [1]

3993 **πένης**, ***penēs***, a. GK: *4288* [→ *3998; cf. 4192*]. poor:– poor [1]

3994 **πενθερά**, ***penthera***, n. GK: *4289* [→ *3995*]. mother-in-law:– mother in law [3], wife's mother [3]

3995 **πενθερός**, ***pentheros***, n. GK: *4290* [→ *3994*]. father-in-law:– father in law [1]

3996 **πενθέω**, ***pentheō***, v. GK: *4291* [→ *3997*]. to mourn, grieve (over):– mourn [5], mourned [2], wailing [2], bewail [1]

3997 **πένθος**, ***penthos***, n. GK: *4292* [→ *3996*]. mourning, grief, sadness:– sorrow [3], mourning [2]

3998 **πενιχρός**, ***penichros***, a. GK: *4293* [→ *3993*]. poor, needy:– poor [1]

3999 **πεντάκις**, ***pentakis***, adv. GK: *4294* [→ *4002*]. five times:– five times [1]

4000 **πεντακισχίλιοι**, ***pentakischilioi***, a.num. GK: *4295* [→ *4002+5507*]. five thousand:– five thousand [6]

4001 **πεντακόσιοι**, ***pentakosioi***, a.num. GK: *4296* [→ *4002*]. five hundred:– five hundred [2]

4002 **πέντε**, ***pente***, n.num. GK: *4297* [→ *1178, 3991, 3999, 4000, 4001, 4003, 4004, 4005*]. five:– five [36], fifty thousand (*+3461*) [1], threescore and fifteen (*+1440*) [1]

4003 **πεντεκαιδέκατος**, ***pentekaidekatos***, a. GK: *4298* [→ *4002+2532+1176*]. fifteenth:– fifteenth [1]

4004 **πεντήκοντα**, ***pentēkonta***, n.num. GK: *4299* [→ *4002*]. fifty:– fifty [5], fifties [2]

4005 **πεντηκοστή**, ***pentēkostē***, n. GK: *4300* [→ *4002*]. Pentecost, fiftieth (day after Passover):– Pentecost [3]

4006 **πεποίθησις**, ***pepoithēsis***, n. GK: *4301* [→ *3982*]. confidence, trust:– confidence [5], trust [1]

4007 **-περ**, ***-per***, pt.emph. GK: *4302* [→ *1355, 1512, 1895, 1897, 2260, 2509, 2539, 3746, 5618, 5619*]. an affix for various kinds of emphasis:– if (*+1437*) [3]

4008 **πέραν**, ***peran***, adv. GK: *4305* [→ *495, 562, 1276, 4009, 4070, 4097; cf. 4198*]. on the other side; (n.) opposite side, region across:– other side [10], beyond [7], over [3], on the other side [2], farther side [1]

4009 **πέρας**, ***peras***, n. GK: *4306* [→ *4008*]. end, limit:– ends [1], end [1], utmost parts [1], uttermost parts [1]

4010 **Πέργαμος**, ***Pergamos***, n.pr. GK: *4307*. Pergamum:– Pergamos [2]

4011 **Πέργη**, ***Pergē***, n.pr. GK: *4308*. Perga:– Perga [3]

4012 **περί**, ***peri***, pp. GK: *4309* [→ *563, 564, 1704, 2139, 4013, 4014, 681, 4015, 4016, 4017, 4018, 4019, 4020, 4021, 4022, 4023, 4024, 4025, 4026, 4027, 4028, 4029, 4030, 4031, 4032, 4033, 4034, 4035, 4036, 4037, 4038, 4039, 4040, 4041, 4042, 4043, 4044, 4045, 4046, 4047, 4048, 4049, 4059, 4060, 4061, 4062, 4063, 4064, 4065, 4066, 4067, 4843; cf. 4053*]. (gen.) about, concerning, in regard to; (acc.) around, about, nearby:– of [148], for [62], concerning [41], about [29], as touching [7], touching [4], at [3], against [2], as concerning [2], on [2], over [2], state (*+3588*) [2], whereof (*+3739*) [2], with [2], above [1], affairs (*+3588*) [1], affairs [1], among [1], company (*+3588*) [1], concern [1], estate [1], for sake [1], how it will go with (*+3588*) [1], in [1], of company [1], on behalf [1], pertaining [1], round about [1], same (*+1565*) [1], thereabout (*+3778*) [1], thereof [1], whereby (*+3739*) [1], wherein (*+3739*) [1], whereof (*+5101*) [1]

4013 **περιάγω**, ***periagō***, v. GK: *4310* [→ *4012+71*]. (tr.) to take (a wife); (intr.) to go about, travel about:– went about [3], compass [1], lead about [1], went [1]

4014 **περιαιρέω**, ***periaireō***, v. GK: *4311* [→ *4012+138*]. to take away; (pass.) to be taken away; to cut loose, set sail; to be given up, abandoned:– taken away [2], take away [1], taken up [1]

4015 **περιαστράπτω**, ***periastraptō***, v. GK: *4313* [→ *4012+796*]. to flash around, shine around:– shined round about [1], shone [1]

4016 **περιβάλλω**, ***periballō***, v. GK: *4314* [→ *4012+906*]. to dress, clothe, wrap around:– clothed [8], arrayed in [4], clothed in [3], clothed with [3], arrayed [2], cast about [2], cast [1], put on [1]

4017 **περιβλέπω**, ***periblepō***, v. GK: *4315* [→ *4012+991*]. to look around at:– looked round about [5], looked [1], looking round about [1]

4018 **περιβόλαιον**, ***peribolaion***, n. GK: *4316* [→ *4012+906*]. covering, robe:– covering [1], vesture [1]

4019 **περιδέω**, ***perideō***, v. GK: *4317* [→ *4012+1210*]. to wrap around:– bound about [1]

περιδρέμω, ***peridremō***. See ***4063***.

περιέλλω, ***periellō***. See ***4014***.

περιέλθω, ***perielthō***. See ***4022***.

4020 **περιεργάζομαι**, ***periergazomai***, v. GK: *4318* [→ *4012+2041*]. to be a busybody:– busybodies [1]

4021 **περίεργος**, ***periergos***, a. GK: *4319* [→ *4012+2041*]. meddlesome, curious; (n.) busybody; (pl.) sorcery, magical arts:– busybodies [1], curious arts [1]

4022 **περιέρχομαι**, ***perierchomai***, v. GK: *4320* [→ *4012+2064*]. to go around:– fet a compass [1], vagabond [1], wandered about [1], wandering about [1]

4023 **περιέχω**, ***periechō***, v. GK: *4321* [→ *4012+2192*]. to seize, encircle; to contain, to say:– after [1], astonished (*+2285*) [1], contained [1]

4024 **περιζώννυμι**, ***perizōnnymi***, v. GK: *4322 & 4323* [→ *4012+2224*]. to buckle a belt around, gird, dress for service:– gird [3], girded about [1], girded [1], girt about [1], girt [1]

4025 **περίθεσις**, ***perithesis***, n. GK: *4324* [→ *4012+5087*]. wearing, putting on:– wearing [1]

4026 **περιΐστημι**, ***periistēmi***, v. GK: *4325* [→ *4012+2476*]. to stand around; avoid, shun:– avoid [1], shun [1], stand by [1], stood round about [1]

4027 **περικάθαρμα**, ***perikatharma***, n. GK: *4326* [→ *4012+2513*]. scum, refuse:– filth [1]

4028 **περικαλύπτω**, ***perikalyptō***, v. GK: *4328* [→ *4012+2572*]. to blindfold, cover the face or eyes; to cover (with gold):– blindfolded [1], cover [1], overlaid [1]

4029 **περίκειμαι**, ***perikeimai***, v. GK: *4329* [→ *4012+2749*]. to surround, place or tie around; to be subject to:– bound with [1], compassed about [1], compassed with [1], hanged about [1], hanged [1]

4030 **περικεφαλαία**, ***perikephalaia***, n. GK: *4330* [→ *4012+2776*]. helmet:– helmet [2]

4031 **περικρατής**, ***perikratēs***, a. GK: *4331* [→ *4012+2904*]. secure, having power, being in command of, getting under control:– come by (*+1096*) [1]

4032 **περικρύπτω**, ***perikryptō***, v. GK: *4332* [→ *4012+2928*]. to seclude oneself, hide, conceal oneself:– hid [1]

4033 **περικυκλόω**, ***perikykloō***, v. GK: *4333* [→ *4012+2945*]. to encircle, surround:– compass round [1]

4034 **περιλάμπω**, ***perilampō***, v. GK: *4334* [→ *4012+2989*]. to shine around, blaze around:– shining round about [1], shone round about [1]

4035 **περιλείπομαι**, ***perileipomai***, v. GK: *4335* [→ *4012+3007*]. to be left, remain:– remain [2]

4036 **περίλυπος**, ***perilypos***, a. GK: *4337* [→ *4012+3077*]. overwhelmingly sorrowful; greatly distressing:– exceeding sorrowful [2], very sorrowful [2], exceeding sorry [1]

4037 **περιμένω**, ***perimenō***, v. GK: *4338* [→ *4012+3306*]. to wait for:– wait for [1]

4038 **πέριξ**, ***perix***, adv. GK: *4339* [→ *4012*]. around:– round about [1]

4039 **περιοικέω**, ***perioikeō***, v. GK: *4340* [→ *4012+3624*]. to live in a neighborhood; (n.) neighbor:– dwelt round about [1]

4040 **περίοικος**, ***perioikos***, a. GK: *4341* [→ *4012+3624*]. neighboring, (n.) neighbor:– neighbours [1]

4041 **περιούσιος**, ***periousios***, a. GK: *4342* [→ *4012+1510*]. one's very own, special:– peculiar [1]

4042 **περιοχή**, ***periochē***, n. GK: *4343* [→ *4012+2192*]. passage (of Scripture), portion:– place [1]

4043 **περιπατέω**, ***peripateō***, v. GK: *4344* [→ *4012+3961*]. to walk (around); to live, conduct one's life:– walk [56], walked [18], walking [12], walketh [4], walkest [2], go [1], occupied therein [1], walkedst [1], walketh about [1]

4044 **περιπείρω, *peripeirō***, v. GK: *4345* [→ *4012*]. to pierce:– pierced through [1]

4045 **περιπίπτω, *peripiptō***, v. GK: *4346* [→ *4012+4098*]. to fall into the hands of; to strike; to face, be involved in:– fall into [1], falling [1], fell among [1]

4046 **περιποιέω, *peripoieō***, v. GK: *4347* [→ *4012+4160*]. (mid.) to keep, save; to gain for oneself; to buy, acquire:– purchased [1], purchase [1]

4047 **περιποίησις, *peripoiēsis***, n. GK: *4348* [→ *4012+4160*]. possession, property; sharing in, gaining; saving:– obtaining [1], obtain [1], peculiar (*+1519*) [1], purchased possession [1], saving [1]

4048 **περιρήγνυμι, *perirēgnymi***, v. GK: *4351* [→ *4012+4486*]. to strip off, tear off:– rent off [1]

4049 **περισπάω, *perispaō***, v. GK: *4352* [→ *4012+4685*]. (pass.) to be distracted:– cumbered [1]

4050 **περισσεία, *perisseia***, n. GK: *4353* [→ *4053*]. abundance, prevalence:– abundance [2], abundantly (*+1519*) [1], superfluity [1]

4051 **περίσσευμα, *perisseuma***, n. GK: *4354* [→ *4053*]. overflow, plenty; what is left over, scraps:– abundance [4], left [1]

4052 **περισσεύω, *perisseuō***, v. GK: *4355* [→ *4053*]. to have abundance, more than enough, overflow, to have an excessive amount of something, ranging from moderate excess to a very great degree of excess:– abound [11], abounded [4], abundance [3], abounding [2], abundant [2], have abundance [2], remained [2], aboundeth [1], better [1], exceed (*+4183*) [1], exceed [1], excel [1], have enough and to spare [1], increased [1], increase [1], left [1], make abound [1], redound [1], remained over and above [1], remain [1]

4053 **περισσός, *perissos***, a. GK: *4356* [→ *4050, 4051, 4052, 4054, 4055, 4056, 4057, 5248, 5249; cf. 4012*]. exceeding, going beyond; full, abundant; (compar.) more than; (n.) advantage:– greater [2], more than [2], abundantly (*+1537*) [1], abundantly [1], advantage [1], exceedingly (*+1537+5228*) [1], highly (*+1537*) [1], measure [1], more [1], superfluous [1], vehemently (*+1537*) [1]

4054 **περισσότερον, *perissoteron***, adv. GK: *4357* [→ *4053*]. even more, so much more:– more [2], far more [1], great deal [1], greater [1], more abundantly than [1], more abundantly [1], much more than [1]

4055 **περισσότερος, *perissoteros***, a. GK: *4358* [→ *4053*]. more than, even more; greater than; with special honor:– more abundant [3], more (*+5100*) [1], overmuch [1]

4056 **περισσοτέρως, *perissoterōs***, adv. GK: *4359* [→ *4053*]. to a much greater degree; especially, frequently, extremely:– more abundantly [4], more abundant [2], more exceedingly [2], exceedingly [1], more earnest [1], more frequent [1], much more [1], rather [1]

4057 **περισσῶς, *perissōs***, adv. GK: *4360* [→ *4053*]. even more, all the more:– exceedingly [1], more [1], out of measure [1]

4058 **περιστερά, *peristera***, n. GK: *4361*. dove, pigeon:– doves [5], dove [4], pigeons [1]

4059 **περιτέμνω, *peritemnō***, v. GK: *4362* [→ *4012+5114*]. to circumcise:– circumcised [13], circumcise [4], circumcising [1]

4060 **περιτίθημι, *peritithēmi***, v. GK: *4363* [→ *4012+5087*]. to put on, set on; to treat with:– put on [3], bestow [1], put about [1], put upon [1], round about [1], set about [1]

4061 **περιτομή, *peritomē***, n. GK: *4364* [→ *4012+5114*]. circumcision; fig., the Jews (as a group of people who adhered to the ritual of circumcision):– circumcision [35], circumcised [1]

4062 **περιτρέπω, *peritrepō***, v. GK: *4365* [→ *4012+5157*]. to drive (to insanity):– make mad (*+1519+3130*) [1]

4063 **περιτρέχω, *peritrechō***, v. GK: *4366* [→ *4012+5143*]. to run throughout, run about:– ran through [1]

4064 **περιφέρω, *peripherō***, v. GK: *4367* [→ *4012+5342*]. to carry, carry around; (pass.) to be blown about, carried here and there:– carried about [3], bearing about [1], carry about [1]

4065 **περιφρονέω, *periphroneō***, v. GK: *4368* [→ *4012+5424*]. to despise, look down on:– despise [1]

4066 **περίχωρος, *perichōros***, a. GK: *4369* [→ *4012+5562*]. neighboring; (n.) surrounding country:– region round about [5], country round about [3], country about [1], region that lieth round about [1]

4067 **περίψημα, *peripsēma***, n. GK: *4370* [→ *4012+5597*]. refuse, garbage, that which is removed in the process of cleaning:– offscouring [1]

4068 **περπερεύομαι, *perpereuomai***, v. GK: *4371*. to boast, brag:– vaunteth [1]

4069 **Περσίς, *Persis***, n.pr. GK: *4372*. Persis, "*female Persian*":– Persis [1]

4070 **πέρυσι, *perysi***, adv. GK: *4373* [→ *4008*]. from last year, since last year:– a year ago (*+575*) [2]

πετάομαι, *petaomai*. See **4072**.

4071 **πετεινόν, *peteinon***, n. GK: *4374* [→ *4072*]. bird:– fowls [9], birds [5]

4072 **πέτομαι, *petomai***, v. GK: *4375* [→ *1600, 2665, 4071, 4419, 4420, 4421*]. to fly:– fly [3], flying [2]

4073 **πέτρα, *petra***, n. GK: *4376* [→ *4074, 4075*]. rock, bedrock, rocky crag, or other large rock formation, in contrast to individual stones (cf. *4074*), with a focus that this is a suitable, solid foundation:– rock [13], rocks [3]

4074 **Πέτρος, *Petros***, n.pr. GK: *4377* [→ *4073*]. Peter; this has the designative meaning "rock" or "individual stone", "*rock, stone*":– Peter [157], Peter's [4], stone [1]

4075 **πετρώδης, *petrōdēs***, a. GK: *4378* [→ *4073+1491*]. rocky, stony; (n.) rocky place, thin soil with larger rocks or bedrock underneath:– stony ground [2], stony [2]

4076 **πήγανον, *pēganon***, n. GK: *4379*. rue (a garden herb):– rue [1]

4077 **πηγή, *pēgē***, n. GK: *4380*. spring, well (of water); flow (of blood):– fountains [4], fountain [4], well [3], wells [1]

4078 **πήγνυμι, *pēgnymi***, v. GK: *4381* [→ *3802, 3803, 4362, 4634*]. to set up:– pitched [1]

4079 **πηδάλιον, *pēdalion***, n. GK: *4382*. rudder, steering paddle:– helm [1], rudder [1]

4080 **πηλίκος, *pēlikos***, a. GK: *4383* [→ *2245*]. how great, how large:– how great [1], how large [1]

4081 **πηλός, *pēlos***, n. GK: *4384*. mud, lump of clay:– clay [6]

4082 **πήρα, *pēra***, n. GK: *4385*. traveler's bag:– scrip [6]

4083 **πῆχυς, *pēchys***, n. GK: *4388*. measure of length: cubit, or time: hour:– cubits [2], cubit [2]

4084 **πιάζω, *piazō***, v. GK: *4389* [→ *4085*]. to seize, to grasp an object, usually with the hand; by extension: to arrest, capture, place in confinement:– take [4], caught [2], taken [2], apprehended [1], apprehend [1], laid hands on [1], took [1]

4085 **πιέζω, *piezō***, v. GK: *4390* [→ *4084*]. (pass.) to be pressed down:– pressed down [1]

4086 **πιθανολογία, *pithanologia***, n. GK: *4391* [→ *3982+3004*]. fine-sounding arguments, persuasive speech, a plausible yet false argument:– enticing words [1]

4087 **πικραίνω, *pikrainō***, v. GK: *4393* [→ *4089*]. to turn sour, make bitter; to become sour, embittered:– bitter [2], made bitter [1], make bitter [1]

4088 **πικρία, *pikria***, n. GK: *4394* [→ *4089*]. bitterness:– bitterness [4]

4089 **πικρός, *pikros***, a. GK: *4395* [→ *3893, 3894, 4087, 4088, 4090*]. bitter, salty:– bitter [2]

4090 **πικρῶς, *pikrōs***, adv. GK: *4396* [→ *4089*]. bitterly:– bitterly [2]

4091 **Πιλᾶτος, *Pilatos***, n.pr. GK: *4276 & 4397*. Pilate, "*[family name]*":– Pilate [55]

πίμπλημι, *pimplēmi*. See **4130**.

4092 **πίμπρημι, *pimprēmi***, v. GK: *4399* [→ *1714*]. to swell:– swollen [1]

4093 **πινακίδιον, *pinakidion***, n. GK: *4400 & 4401* [→ *4094*]. (small) writing tablet:– writing table [1]

4094 **πίναξ, *pinax***, n. GK: *4402* [→ *4093*]. platter, dish:– charger [4], platter [1]

4095 **πίνω, *pinō***, v. GK: *4403* [→ *2666, 3630, 4188, 4213, 4221, 4222, 4224, 4844, 4849, 5202; cf. 4215*]. to drink:– drink [52], drinketh [8], drinking [6], drank [5], drunk [3], drunken [1]

4096 **πιότης, *piotēs***, n. GK: *4404*. richness, nourishing sap:– fatness [1]

4097 **πιπράσκω, *pipraskō***, v. GK: *4405* [→ *4008*]. to sell:– sold [9]

4098 **πίπτω, *piptō***, v. GK: *4406* [→ *377, 496, 634, 1120, 1356, 1601, 1706, 1968, 2667, 3895, 3900, 4045, 4312, 4363, 4430, 4431*]. to fall, collapse; to bow down; to die:– fell [42], fall [20], fell down [14], fallen [5], falleth [3], fall down [2], fail [1], fallen down [1], falling down [1], light [1]

4099 **Πισιδία, *Pisidia***, n.pr. GK: *4407 & 4408*. Pisidia:– Pisidia [2]

4100 **πιστεύω, *pisteuō***, v. GK: *4409* [→ *4103*]. to believe, put one's faith in, trust, with an implication that actions based on that trust may follow; (pass.) entrust:– believe [115], believed [77], believeth [33], believest [8], believing [6], committed [3], believers [1], commit to trust [1], committed to trust [1], committed unto [1], commit [1], put in trust [1]

4101 **πιστικός, *pistikos***, a. GK: *4410* [→ *4103*]. pure:– spikenard (*+3487*) [2]

4102 **πίστις, *pistis***, n. GK: *4411* [→ *4103*]. faith, faithfulness, belief, trust, with an implication that actions based on that trust may follow; "the faith" often refers to the Christian system of belief and lifestyle:– faith [239], assurance [1], belief [1], believeth [1], believe [1], fidelity [1]

4103 **πιστός, *pistos***, a. GK: *4412* [→ *569, 570, 571, 3640, 4100, 4101, 4102, 4104; cf. 3982*]. faithful, trustworthy, reliable, believing:– faithful [53], believed [2], believe [2], believing [2], true [2], believers [1], believeth [1], faithfully [1], man[5] [1], sure [1], woman that believeth [1]

4104 **πιστόω, *pistoō***, v. GK: *4413* [→ *4103*]. (pass.) to be convinced of:– assured [1]

4105 **πλανάω, *planaō***, v. GK: *4414* [→ *4106*]. to lead astray, cause to wander, deceive; (mid./pass.) to be deceived, deluded:– deceived [10], deceive [10], err [6], deceiveth [3], gone astray [3], seduce [2], deceiving [1], going astray [1], out of the way [1], wandered [1], went astray [1]

4106 **πλάνη, *planē***, n. GK: *4415* [→ *635, 4105, 4107, 4108*]. error, delusion, deception:– error [7], deceit [1], deceive [1], delusion [1]

4107 **πλανήτης, *planētēs***, n. GK: *4417* [→ *4106*]. wanderer; (a.) wandering:– wandering [1]

4108 **πλάνος, *planos***, a. GK: *4418* [→ *4106*]. deceiving, leading astray; (n.) deceiver, imposter; fig. extensions of the base meaning "to wander off a path," not found in the NT:– deceivers [2], deceiver [2], seducing [1]

4109 **πλάξ, *plax***, n. GK: *4419*. stone tablet:– tables [3]

4110 **πλάσμα, *plasma***, n. GK: *4420* [→ *4111*]. what is formed, molded:– formed [1]

4111 **πλάσσω, *plassō***, v. GK: *4421* [→ *4110, 4112*]. to form, mold:– formed [2]

4112 **πλαστός, *plastos***, a. GK: *4422* [→ *4111*]. made up, fabricated, false:– feigned [1]

4113 **πλατεῖα, *plateia***, n. GK: *4423* [→ *4116*]. (main) street, wide road:– streets [6], street [3]

4114 **πλάτος, *platos***, n. GK: *4424* [→ *4116*]. width, breadth:– breadth [4]

4115 **πλατύνω, *platynō***, v. GK: *4425* [→ *4116*]. to open wide, make wide:– enlarged [2], make broad [1]

4116 **πλατύς, *platys***, a. GK: *4426* [→ *4113, 4114, 4115*]. wide, broad:– wide [1]

4117 **πλέγμα, *plegma***, n. GK: *4427* [→ *4120*]. something braided or woven:– broided hair [1]

πλεῖον, *pleion*. See **4119**.

4118 **πλεῖστος, *pleistos***, a.super. of *4183*. GK: *4498* [→ *4183*]. the most; very large:–

4119 **πλείων, *pleiōn***, a.compar. of *4183* GK: *4498* [→ *4183*]. more than, greater than:–

4120 **πλέκω, *plekō***, v. GK: *4428* [→ *1707, 1708, 4117*]. to twist together, weave, braid:– platted [3]

πλέον, *pleon*. See **4119**.

4121 **πλεονάζω, *pleonazō***, v. GK: *4429* [→ *4137*]. to make increase; (intr.) to grow, increase, have abundance:– abound [4], abounded [1], aboundeth [1], abundant [1], had over [1], make to increase [1]

4122 **πλεονεκτέω, *pleonekteō***, v. GK: *4430* [→ *4137+2192*]. to exploit, take advantage of, outwit:– make a gain [2], defrauded [1], defraud [1], get an advantage [1]

4123 πλεονέκτης, ***pleonektēs***, n. GK: *4431* [→ *4137+2192*]. greedy person:– covetous [3], covetous man [1]

4124 πλεονεξία, ***pleonexia***, n. GK: *4432* [→ *4137+2192*]. greediness, avarice:– covetousness [8], covetous practices [1], greediness [1]

4125 πλευρά, ***pleura***, n. GK: *4433*. side (of the body):– side [5]

4126 πλέω, ***pleō***, v. GK: *4434* [→ *636, 1020, 1277, 1602, 2668, 3896, 4142, 4143, 4144, 5284*]. to travel by ship, sail:– sailed [2], sail [2], sailing [1]

4127 πληγή, ***plēgē***, n. GK: *4435* [→ *4141*]. plague; punishment: beating, flogging, wounding:– plagues [10], stripes [5], wound [3], plague [2], wounded (*+2007*) [1]

4128 πλῆθος, ***plēthos***, n. GK: *4436* [→ *4130*]. large number, crowd, multitude, assembly:– multitude [29], bundle [1], company [1], multitudes [1]

4129 πληθύνω, ***plēthynō***, v. GK: *4437* [→ *4130*]. to increase, grow in numbers, abound:– multiplied [8], multiply [2], abound [1], multiplying [1]

4130 πίμπλημι, ***pimplēmi***, v. GK: *4398* [→ *1705, 3826, 4128, 4129, 4132, 4140*]. to fill; (pass.) to be filled, completed:– filled [18], accomplished [4], full came [1], furnished [1]

4131 πλήκτης, ***plēktēs***, n. GK: *4438* [→ *4141*]. violent man, bully:– striker [2]

4132 πλήμμυρα, ***plēmmyra***, n. GK: *4439* [→ *4130*]. flood, high water; in context likely a flash flood in a narrow valley (wadi):– flood [1]

4133 πλήν, ***plēn***, c.&pp.*. GK: *4440* [→ *4137*]. but, however, only, yet:– but [14], nevertheless [7], notwithstanding [4], but rather [2], except [1], nevertheless (*+2532*) [1], save [1], than [1]

4134 πλήρης, ***plērēs***, a. GK: *4441* [→ *4137*]. full:– full [17]

4135 πληροφορέω, ***plērophoreō***, v. GK: *4442* [→ *4137+5342*]. to fulfill (completely); (pass.) to be fully assured, convinced, persuaded:– fully persuaded [2], fully known [1], make full proof [1], most surely believed [1]

4136 πληροφορία, ***plērophoria***, n. GK: *4443* [→ *4137+5342*]. full assurance, certainty, conviction:– full assurance [3], assurance [1]

4137 πληρόω, ***plēroō***, v. GK: *4444* [→ *378, 466, 1603, 1604, 4121, 4122, 4123, 4124, 4133, 4134, 4135, 4136, 4138, 4322, 4845, 5250*]. to fulfill, make full; (pass.) to be filled, full, complete (often used with reference to the fulfillment of the OT Scriptures):– fulfilled [45], filled [15], full [7], fulfil [6], complete [2], ended [2], accomplish [1], after [1], expired [1], fill up [1], fill with [1], filled with [1], filleth [1], fill [1], full come [1], fully [1], make full [1], perfect [1], supply [1]

4138 πλήρωμα, ***plērōma***, n. GK: *4445* [→ *4137*]. fullness, fulfillment:– fulness [13], fulfilling [1], full [1], piece that filled up [1], put in to fill up [1]

4139 πλησίον, ***plēsion***, adv.&pp.*&n. GK: *4446* [→ *3897, 3898*]. near, close by; (n.) neighbor; (pp.) near:– neighbour [16], near [1]

4140 πλησμονή, ***plēsmonē***, n. GK: *4447* [→ *4130*]. indulgence, gratification:– satisfying [1]

4141 πλήσσω, ***plēssō***, v. GK: *4448* [→ *1605, 1969, 4127, 4131*]. (pass.) to be struck:– smitten [1]

4142 πλοιάριον, ***ploiarion***, n. GK: *4449* [→ *4126*]. (small) boat:– boat [2], boats [1], little ships [1], little ship [1], small ship [1]

4143 πλοῖον, ***ploion***, n. GK: *4450* [→ *4126*]. boat, ship:– ship [58], ships [8], took shipping (*+1519+1684+3588*) [1]

4144 πλόος, ***ploos***, n. GK: *4452 & 4453* [→ *4126*]. voyage, navigation:– course [1], sailing [1], voyage [1]

4145 πλούσιος, ***plousios***, a. GK: *4454* [→ *4149*]. rich, wealthy; (n.) rich person:– rich [28]

4146 πλουσίως, ***plousiōs***, adv. GK: *4455* [→ *4149*]. richly, generously, abundantly:– abundantly [2], richly [2]

4147 πλουτέω, ***plouteō***, v. GK: *4456* [→ *4149*]. to be rich; (pf.) to have acquired wealth:– rich [8], made rich [2], increased with goods [1], waxed rich [1]

4148 πλουτίζω, ***ploutizō***, v. GK: *4457* [→ *4149*]. to make rich; (pass.) to be enriched:– enriched [2], making rich [1]

4149 πλοῦτος, ***ploutos***, n. GK: *4458* [→ *4145, 4146, 4147, 4148*]. riches, wealth:– riches [22]

4150 πλύνω, ***plynō***, v. GK: *4459* [→ *637*]. to wash (things):– washed [1]

4151 πνεῦμα, ***pneuma***, n. GK: *4460* [→ *4154*]. wind, breath, things which are commonly perceived as having no material substance; by extension: spirit, heart, mind, the immaterial part of the inner person that can respond to God; spirit being: (evil) spirit, ghost, God the Holy Spirit:– spirit [257], ghost [92], spirits [32], life [1], spiritually [1], spiritual [1], wind [1]

4152 πνευματικός, ***pneumatikos***, a. GK: *4461* [→ *4154*]. spiritual, pertaining to the Spirit; (n.) spiritual person:– spiritual [26]

4153 πνευματικῶς, ***pneumatikōs***, adv. GK: *4462* [→ *4154*]. spiritually; figuratively:– spiritually [2]

4154 πνέω, ***pneō***, v. GK: *4463* [→ *1606, 1709, 2315, 4151, 4152, 4153, 4157, 5285*]. to blow (of wind):– blew [3], blow [2], bloweth [1], wind [1]

4155 πνίγω, ***pnigō***, v. GK: *4464* [→ *638, 1970, 4156, 4846*]. to choke or strangle; drown:– choked [1], took by the throat [1]

4156 πνικτός, ***pniktos***, a. GK: *4465* [→ *4155*]. strangled, choked; (n.) meat of strangled animals:– strangled [2], things strangled [1]

4157 πνοή, ***pnoē***, n. GK: *4466* [→ *4154*]. wind, breath:– breath [1], wind [1]

4158 ποδήρης, ***podērēs***, a. GK: *4468* [→ *4228*]. reaching to the feet; (n.) robe reaching to the feet:– down to the foot [1]

4159 πόθεν, ***pothen***, adv. GK: *4470*. from where, from which:– whence [20], from whence [8]

4160 ποιέω, ***poieō***, v. GK: *4472* [→ *15, 16, 17, 686, 1517, 1518, 2140, 2227, 2554, 2555, 2569, 3447, 3792, 4046, 4047, 4161, 4162, 4163, 4364, 4635, 4806, 5499*]. to do, make, practice, produce, a generic term of action or performance: note the many contextual translations in the NIV:– do [196], did [54], done [52], made [50], make [47], doeth [34], doest [13], doing [8], bringeth forth [7], maketh [6], making [6], bring forth [5], wrought [5], cause [4], committed [4], makest [4], shewed [4], causeth [3], committeth [3], bare [2], bear [2], caused [2], commit [2], continue [2], dealt [2], execute [2], fulfil [2], gave [2], keep [2], perform [2], put [2], working [2], able [1], abode [1], agree (*+1106+1520*) [1], appointed [1], as went (*+3598*) [1], avenge (*+1557+3588*) [1], avenged (*+1557*) [1], banded together (*+4963*) [1], been [1], bewrayeth (*+1212*) [1], bringing forth [1], bring [1], brought forth [1], cast out (*+1570*) [1], content (*+2425*) [1], delay (*+311*) [1], exerciseth [1], fulfilling [1], gained [1], held [1], journeying (*+4197*) [1], keepeth [1], kept [1], laying wait (*+1747*) [1], lightened the ship (*+1546*) [1], move [1], observe [1], ordained [1], provide [1], purged (*+2512*) [1], purposed [1], raising up (*+1999*) [1], redeemed (*+3085*) [1], secure (*+275*) [1], shewest [1], shooteth out [1], spent [1], tarried a space (*+5550*) [1], took [1], transgresseth law (*+458*) [1], weep (*+2799*) [1], will [1], worketh [1], yield [1]

4161 ποίημα, ***poiēma***, n. GK: *4473* [→ *4160*]. what is made, workmanship, creation:– things that are made [1], workmanship [1]

4162 ποίησις, ***poiēsis***, n. GK: *4474* [→ *4160*]. doing, working:– deed [1]

4163 ποιητής, ***poiētēs***, n. GK: *4475* [→ *4160*]. doer, keeper, obeyer; poet:– doer [3], doers [2], poets [1]

4164 ποικίλος, ***poikilos***, a. GK: *4476* [→ *4182*]. of various kinds, of all kinds:– divers [8], manifold [2]

4165 ποιμαίνω, ***poimainō***, v. GK: *4477* [→ *4166*]. to shepherd, take care of sheep; to rule, lead:– feed [4], rule [4], feedeth [1], feeding cattle [1], feeding [1]

4166 ποιμήν, ***poimēn***, n. GK: *4478* [→ *750, 4165, 4167, 4168*]. shepherd; pastor:– shepherd [13], shepherds [4], pastors [1]

4167 ποίμνη, ***poimnē***, n. GK: *4479* [→ *4166*]. flock:– flock [4], fold [1]

4168 ποίμνιον, ***poimnion***, n. GK: *4480* [→ *4166*]. flock:– flock [5]

4169 ποῖος, ***poios***, a. GK: *4481* [→ *3634*]. what?, which?, of what kind?:– what [29], which [4], what manner [1]

4170 πολεμέω, ***polemeō***, v. GK: *4482* [→ *4171*]. to fight, make war:– make war [3], fought [2], fight [1], war [1]

4171 πόλεμος, ***polemos***, n. GK: *4483* [→ *4170*]. war, battle, fight:– wars [6], battle [5], war [5], fight [1], make war against (*+1519+4820*) [1]

4172 πόλις, ***polis***, n. GK: *4484* [→ *295, 1179, 2404, 2969, 3390, 3496, 3533, 4173, 4174, 4175, 4176, 4177, 4847*]. city, town, village:– city [145], cities [19]

4173 πολιτάρχης, ***politarchēs***, n. GK: *4485* [→ *4172+757*]. city official, formally, "politarch":– rulers of the city [2]

4174 πολιτεία, ***politeia***, n. GK: *4486* [→ *4172*]. citizenship:– commonwealth [1], freedom [1]

4175 πολίτευμα, ***politeuma***, n. GK: *4487* [→ *4172*]. citizenship:– conversation [1]

4176 πολιτεύομαι, ***politeuomai***, v. GK: *4488* [→ *4172*]. to fulfill one's duty; to conduct oneself, lead one's life:– conversation [1], lived [1]

4177 πολίτης, ***politēs***, n. GK: *4489* [→ *4172*]. citizen, subjects of a kingdom; neighbor:– citizen [2], citizens [1]

4178 πολλάκις, ***pollakis***, adv. GK: *4490* [→ *4183*]. many times, again and again, often, constantly:– often [7], oft [5], oftentimes [3], ofttimes [3]

4179 πολλαπλασίων, ***pollaplasiōn***, a. GK: *4491* [→ *4183*]. many times as much:– manifold more [1]

4180 πολυλογία, ***polylogia***, n. GK: *4494* [→ *4183+3004*]. speaking many words, wordiness:– much speaking [1]

4181 πολυμερῶς, ***polymerōs***, adv. GK: *4495* [→ *4183+3313*]. at many times, in many ways:– times [1]

4182 πολυποίκιλος, ***polypoikilos***, a. GK: *4497* [→ *4183+4164*]. manifold, (very) many sided:– manifold [1]

4183 πολύς, ***polys***, a. GK: *4498* [→ *3827, 4118, 4119, 4178, 4179, 4180, 4181, 4182, 4184, 4185, 4186, 4187*]. many, great, large; (compar.) more than, greater than; (super.) the most; very large:– many [221], much [74], great [59], more [11], more than [7], greater than [4], greatly [4], long [4], moe [4], most [4], further (*+1909*) [3], more part [2], straitly [2], a great while (*+1909*) [1], above [1], abundant [1], altogether (*+1722*) [1], but (*+2228+3756*) [1], common [1], exceed (*+4052*) [1], far (*+3123*) [1], far passed [1], far [1], great deal [1], greater part [1], greater [1], long (*+1909*) [1], longer (*+1909*) [1], many moe [1], many things [1], moe than [1], more excellent [1], oftentimes (*+5550*) [1], oft [1], plenteous [1], sore [1], very great [1], very many [1]

4184 πολύσπλαγχνος, ***polysplanchnos***, a. GK: *4492 & 4499* [→ *4183+4698*]. full of compassion, full of mercy:– very pitiful [1]

4185 πολυτελής, ***polytelēs***, a. GK: *4500* [→ *4183+5056*]. expensive, of great worth, costly:– costly [1], great price [1], very precious [1]

4186 πολύτιμος, ***polytimos***, a. GK: *4501* [→ *4183+5092*]. expensive, of great worth, valuable:– great price [1], very costly [1]

4187 πολυτρόπως, ***polytropōs***, adv. GK: *4502* [→ *4183+5157*]. in various ways:– manners [1]

4188 πόμα, ***poma***, n. GK: *4503* [→ *4095*]. drink:– drinks [1], drink [1]

4189 πονηρία, ***ponēria***, n. GK: *4504* [→ *4190*]. evil, wickedness, malice, in the NT always a negative moral quality opposed to God and his goodness:– wickedness [6], iniquities [1]

4190 πονηρός, ***ponēros***, a. GK: *4505* [→ *4189, 4191; cf. 4192*]. bad, the negative quality of an object; evil, wicked, crime, the negative moral quality of a person or action opposed to God and his goodness; (n.) wicked deed, wicked thing; the Evil One, a title of Satan:– evil [52], wicked [11], wicked one [6], bad [1], evils [1], grievous [1], harm [1], lewd [1], malicious [1], wickedness [1]

4191 πονηρότερος, ***ponēroteros***, a.compar. of *4190* GK: *4505* [→ *4190*]. more evil, more wicked; see *4190*:– more wicked than [2]

4192 πόνος, ***ponos***, n. GK: *4506* [→ *1278, 2669; cf. 3993, 4190*]. pain, agony; hard work, toil:– pain [2], pains [1]

4193 Ποντικός, ***Pontikos***, a.pr.g. GK: *4507*. from Pontus:– Pontus [1]

4194 Πόντιος, ***Pontios***, n.pr. GK: *4508*. Pontius, "*[tribal name]*":– Pontius [4]

4195 Πόντος, ***Pontos***, n.pr. GK: *4510*. Pontus, "*sea*":– Pontus [2]

4196 **Πόπλιος, *Poplios***, n.pr. GK: *4511*. Publius, "*first*":– Publius [2]

4197 **πορεία, *poreia***, n. GK: *4512 & 4515* [→ *4198*]. journey, trip; going about one's business, way of life, conduct:– journeying (+*4160*) [1], ways [1]

4198 **πορεύομαι, *poreuomai***, v. GK: *4513* [→ *639, 640, 1279, 1280, 1531, 1607, 1710, 1711, 1712, 1713, 1820, 1975, 2141, 2142, 3596, 3597, 3899, 4197, 4200, 4313, 4365, 4848; cf. 4008*]. to come, go, travel:– go [74], went [44], goeth [7], departed [6], depart [5], walking [4], walk [4], gone [3], going [2], journeyed [2], made journey [1], take journey [1], walked [1]

4199 **πορθέω, *portheō***, v. GK: *4514*. to destroy, annihilate; to raise havoc, pillage:– destroyed [2], wasted [1]

4200 **πορισμός, *porismos***, n. GK: *4516* [→ *4198*]. means of gain:– gain [2]

4201 **Πόρκιος, *Porkios***, n.pr. GK: *4517*. Porcius, "*[tribal name]*":– Porcius [1]

4202 **πορνεία, *porneia***, n. GK: *4518* [→ *4204*]. sexual immorality, fornication, marital unfaithfulness, prostitution, adultery, a generic term for sexual sin of any kind:– fornication [24], fornications [2]

4203 **πορνεύω, *porneuō***, v. GK: *4519* [→ *4204*]. to commit sexual immorality of any kind, adultery:– commit fornication [3], committed fornication [3], committed [1], committeth fornication [1]

4204 **πόρνη, *pornē***, n. GK: *4520* [→ *1608, 4202, 4203, 4205*]. prostitute, a woman who practices sexual immorality for payment; this can refer to religious unfaithfulness:– harlots [4], harlot [4], whore [4]

4205 **πόρνος, *pornos***, n. GK: *4521* [→ *4204*]. one who is sexually immoral (male or female), in some contexts distinguished from an adulterer (1Co 6:9):– whoremongers [4], fornicators [3], fornicator [2], whoremonger [1]

4206 **πόρρω, *porrō***, adv. GK: *4522* [→ *4253*]. far, a long way off; (compar.) farther:– far [2], great way off [1]

4207 **πόρρωθεν, *porrōthen***, adv. GK: *4523* [→ *4253*]. from a distance, at a distance:– afar off [2]

4208 **πορρωτέρω, *porrōterō***, adv. GK: *4524* [→ *4253*]. farther:– further [1]

4209 **πορφύρα, *porphyra***, n. GK: *4525* [→ *4210, 4211*]. purple (cloth or robe):– purple [5]

4210 **πορφυροῦς, *porphyrous***, a. GK: *4526 & 4528* [→ *4209*]. purple, purple cloth, in some contexts implying royalty:– purple [3]

4211 **πορφυρόπωλις, *porphyropōlis***, n. GK: *4527* [→ *4209+4453*]. dealer in purple cloth:– seller of purple [1]

4212 **ποσάκις, *posakis***, adv. GK: *4529* [→ *3739*]. how many times?; how often!:– how often [2], how oft [1]

4213 **πόσις, *posis***, n. GK: *4530* [→ *4095*]. drinking; a drink:– drink [3]

4214 **πόσος, *posos***, a. GK: *4531* [→ *3745*]. how great?, how much?, how many?; how great!, how many!, how much!:– how much [13], how many [11], how great [1], how [1], what [1]

4215 **ποταμός, *potamos***, n. GK: *4532* [→ *3318, 4216; cf. 4095*]. river, stream, torrent:– river [6], rivers [3], floods [2], flood [2], stream [2], waters [1]

4216 **ποταμοφόρητος, *potamophorētos***, a. GK: *4533* [→ *4215+5342*]. swept away by a torrential flow of a river:– carried away of the flood [1]

4217 **ποταπός, *potapos***, a. GK: *4467 & 4534* [→ *575+4226*]. of what kind?; how great!:– what manner [4], what manner of man [1], what manner of [1], what [1]

4218 **ποτέ, *pote***, pt. GK: *4537* [→ *4226*]. once, at one time, formerly; now, now at last:– in time past [4], at any time [3], in times past [3], sometimes [3], sometime [3], in old time [2], once [2], aforetime [1], any time [1], at last [1], at length [1], ever yet [1], in time passed [1], never (+*3361+3756*) [1], were (+*1510*) [1], when [1]

4219 **πότε, *pote***, adv.inter. GK: *4536* [→ *4226*]. when? how long?:– when [12], how long (+*2193*) [7]

4220 **πότερον, *poteron***, a. or pt. GK: *4538* [→ *4226+2087*]. whether:– whether [1]

4221 **ποτήριον, *potērion***, n. GK: *4539* [→ *4095*]. cup:– cup [31], cups [2]

4222 **ποτίζω, *potizō***, v. GK: *4540* [→ *4095*]. to give or offer a drink; to water:– gave drink [3], gave to drink [2], give to drink [2], watereth [2], fed [1], give drink [1], made drink [1], made to drink [1], watered [1], watering [1]

4223 **Ποτίολοι, *Potioloi***, n.pr. GK: *4541*. Puteoli, "*rotten [sulphur] smell* or *well, spring*":– Puteoli [1]

4224 **πότος, *potos***, n. GK: *4542* [→ *4095*]. carousing, drinking party, orgy:– banquetings [1]

4225 **πού, *pou***, adv. GK: *4543* [→ *4226*]. somewhere, a place where; about, approximately:– a certain place [2], about [1]

4226 **ποῦ, *pou***, adv.inter.pl. GK: *4544* [→ *1221, 1222, 1513, 3368, 3379, 3381, 3697, 3698, 3699, 3704, 3763, 4217, 4219, 4218, 4220, 4225*]. where?, at what place?:– where [37], whither [10]

4227 **Πούδης, *Poudēs***, n.pr. GK: *4545*. Pudens, "*modest*":– Pudens [1]

4228 **πούς, *pous***, n. GK: *4546* [→ *405, 3716, 4158, 5074, 5286*]. foot; leg:– feet [76], foot [9]

4229 **πρᾶγμα, *pragma***, n. GK: *4547* [→ *4238*]. thing, matter, practice:– things [4], matter [3], thing [2], business [1], work [1]

4230 **πραγματεία, *pragmateia***, n. GK: *4548* [→ *4238*]. (pl.) affairs, concerns:– affairs [1]

4231 **πραγματεύομαι, *pragmateuomai***, v. GK: *4549* [→ *4238*]. to put capital to work, do business:– occupy [1]

4232 **πραιτώριον, *praitōrion***, n. GK: *4550*. Praetorium; palace (of the governor); palace guard:– judgment hall [4], Pretorium [1], common hall [1], hall of judgment [1], palace [1]

4233 **πράκτωρ, *praktōr***, n. GK: *4551* [→ *4238*]. officer, a bailiff or constable in charge of a debtor's prison:– officer [2]

4234 **πρᾶξις, *praxis***, n. GK: *4552* [→ *4238*]. deed, action, practice; function:– deeds [3], deed [1], office [1], works [1]

4235 **πρᾶος, *praos***, a. GK: *4553* [→ *4239*]. gentle, humble, considerate:– meek [1]

4236 **πραότης, *praotēs***, n. GK: *4554* [→ *4239*]. gentleness, humility, courtesy, considerateness:– meekness [9]

4237 **πρασιά, *prasia***, n. GK: *4555* [→ *5556*]. group; in context this word is doubled: group by group:– in ranks (+*4237*) [2]

4238 **πράσσω, *prassō***, v. GK: *4556* [→ *1281, 4229, 4230, 4231, 4233, 4234*]. to do, act, practice:– do [17], done [6], committed [3], doeth [3], commit [2], deeds [1], did [1], doest [1], exact [1], keep [1], required [1], used [1]

4239 **πραΰς, *praus***, a. GK: *4558* [→ *4235, 4236, 4240*]. gentle, meek, the positive moral quality of dealing with people in a kind manner, with humility and consideration:– meek [3]

4240 **πραΰτης, *prautēs***, n. GK: *4559* [→ *4239*]. gentleness, meekness, humility:– meekness [3]

4241 **πρέπω, *prepō***, v. GK: *4560* [→ *2143, 2412, 3169*]. to be proper, appropriate, fitting:– becometh [3], became [2], become [1], comely [1]

4242 **πρεσβεία, *presbeia***, n. GK: *4561* [→ *4245*]. delegation, ambassador:– ambassage [1], message [1]

4243 **πρεσβεύω, *presbeuō***, v. GK: *4563* [→ *4245*]. to be an ambassador:– ambassadors [1], ambassador [1]

4244 **πρεσβυτέριον, *presbyterion***, n. GK: *4564* [→ *4245*]. body or council of the elders, Sanhedrin:– elders [1], estate of the elders [1], presbytery [1]

4245 **πρεσβύτερος, *presbyteros***, a. GK: *4565* [→ *4242, 4243, 4244, 4246, 4247, 4850*]. older; ancestral; (n.) in the Gospels and Acts, "elder," usually as an official leader of the Jewish community, in the epistles, "older man" and "older woman," who may or may not be official leaders of the church, depending on the context:– elders [58], elder [7], eldest [1], old men [1]

4246 **πρεσβύτης, *presbytēs***, n. GK: *4562 & 4566* [→ *4245*]. older man, possibly an official of the church in some contexts:– aged men [1], aged [1], old man [1]

4247 **πρεσβῦτις, *presbytis***, n. GK: *4567* [→ *4245*]. older woman, possibly an official of the church in context:– aged women [1]

πρήθω, *prēthō*. See **4092**.

4248 **πρηνής, *prēnēs***, a. GK: *4568*. headlong, headfirst in prone position; some translate as "swollen, distended":– falling headlong (+*1096*) [1]

4249 **πρίζω, *prizō***, v. GK: *4569 & 4573* [→ *1282*]. (pass.) to be sawn in two:– sawn asunder [1]

4250 **πρίν, *prin***, adv. GK: *4570* [→ *4253*]. before:– before [7], before (+*2228*) [6], ere [1]

4251 **Πρίσκα, *Priska***, n.pr. GK: *4571* [→ *4252*]. Prisca, Priscilla:– Prisca [1]

4252 **Πρίσκιλλα, *Priskilla***, n.pr. GK: *4572* [→ *4251*]. Priscilla, Prisca:– Priscilla [5]

4253 **πρό, *pro***, pp. GK: *4574* [→ *4206, 4207, 4208, 4250, 4254, 4255, 4256, 4257, 4258, 4259, 4260, 4261, 4262, 4263, 4264, 4265, 4266, 4267, 4268, 4269, 4270, 4271, 4272, 4273, 4274, 4275, 4276, 4277, 4278, 4279, 4280, 4281, 4282, 4283, 4284, 4285, 4286, 4287, 4288, 4289, 4290, 4291, 4292, 4293, 4294, 4295, 4296, 4297, 4298, 4299, 4300, 4301, 4302, 4303, 4304, 4305, 4306, 4307, 4308, 4309, 4310, 4311, 4312, 4313, 4315, 4368, 4372, 4373, 4384, 4385, 4386, 4387, 4388, 4389, 4390, 4391, 4392, 4393, 4394, 4399, 4400, 4401, 4402, 4408, 5432; cf. 4404, 4413*]. (of place) before, at; (of time) before, some time ago:– before [37], before (+*3588*) [5], above [3], before (+*4383*) [1], before that (+*3588*) [1], ever (+*3588*) [1]

4254 **προάγω, *proagō***, v. GK: *4575* [→ *4253+71*]. to go on ahead, lead the way; to bring out, bring to trial:– went before [6], go before [5], brought forth [2], goeth before [2], going before [2], brought [1]

4255 **προαιρέω, *proaireō***, v. GK: *4576* [→ *4253+138*]. (mid.) to decide, determine:– purposeth [1]

4256 **προαιτιάομαι, *proaitiaomai***, v. GK: *4577* [→ *4253+156*]. to make a charge beforehand:– before proved [1]

4257 **προακούω, *proakouō***, v. GK: *4578* [→ *4253+191*]. to hear about beforehand:– heard before [1]

4258 **προαμαρτάνω, *proamartanō***, v. GK: *4579* [→ *4253+264*]. to sin earlier, to have sinned beforehand:– heretofore sinned [1], sinned already [1]

4259 **προαύλιον, *proaulion***, n. GK: *4580* [→ *4253+833*]. entryway, gateway:– porch [1]

4260 **προβαίνω, *probainō***, v. GK: *4581* [→ *4253+305*]. (spacial) to go on, go on farther; (temporal) to be well along (in years), advanced (in age):– well stricken [2], age (+*1722+2250*) [1], going on [1], gone further [1]

4261 **προβάλλω, *proballō***, v. GK: *4582* [→ *4253+906*]. to push to the front, cause to come to the front; to sprout, put forth:– putting forward [1], shoot forth [1]

4262 **προβατικός, *probatikos***, a. GK: *4583* [→ *4253+305*]. pertaining to sheep; (pr.n.) the Sheep (Gate):– sheep [1]

4263 **πρόβατον, *probaton***, n. GK: *4585* [→ *4253+305*]. sheep:– sheep [39], sheep's [1], sheepfold (+*833+3588*) [1]

4264 **προβιβάζω, *probibazō***, v. GK: *4586* [→ *4253+305*]. (pass.) to be prompted, caused to come forward:– before instructed [1], drew [1]

4265 **προβλέπω, *problepō***, v. GK: *4587* [→ *4253+991*]. (mid.) to plan, select, provide:– provided [1]

4266 **προγίνομαι, *proginomai***, v. GK: *4588* [→ *4253+1096*]. to commit beforehand, happen previously:– past [1]

4267 **προγινώσκω, *proginōskō***, v. GK: *4589* [→ *4253+1097*]. to know beforehand, foreknow; (mid.) to choose beforehand:– foreknew [1], foreknow [1], foreordained [1], knew [1], know before [1]

4268 **πρόγνωσις, *prognōsis***, n. GK: *4590* [→ *4253+1097*]. foreknowledge:– foreknowledge [2]

4269 **πρόγονος, *progonos***, a. GK: *4591* [→ *4253+1096*]. (pl.) parents, forefathers, ancestors:– forefathers [1], parents [1]

4270 **προγράφω, *prographō***, v. GK: *4592* [→ *4253+1125*]. to write beforehand; to show clearly, advertise, proclaim:– before ordained [1], evidently set forth [1], written aforetime [1], written [1], wrote afore [1]

4271 **πρόδηλος, *prodēlos***, a. GK: *4593* [→ *4253+1212*]. obvious, clear, evident:– evident [1], manifest beforehand [1], open beforehand [1]

4272 **προδίδωμι, *prodidōmi***, v. GK: *4594* [→ *4253+1325*]. to give beforehand:– first given [1]

4273 **προδότης, *prodotēs***, n. GK: *4595* [→ *4253+1325*]. traitor, betrayer, treacherous one:– betrayers [1], traitors [1], traitor [1]

προδρέμω, ***prodremō***. See **4390**.

4274 πρόδρομος, ***prodromos***, a. GK: *4596* [→ *4253+5143*]. going before, forerunner:– forerunner [1]

4275 προείδω, ***proeidō***, v. GK: *4632* [→ *4253+3708*]. to see previously; to see ahead, foresee:– foreseeing [1], seeing before [1]

προειρέω, ***proeireō***. See **4280**.

4276 προελπίζω, ***proelpizō***, v. GK: *4598* [→ *4253+1680*]. to be the first to hope, hope beforehand:– first trusted [1]

4277 προέπω, ***proepō***, v. GK: *4625* [→ *4253+3004*]. to tell beforehand; to speak in the past:–

4278 προενάρχομαι, ***proenarchomai***, v. GK: *4599* [→ *4253+1722+757*]. to begin beforehand, begin previously:– begun before [1], begun [1]

4279 προεπαγγέλλω, ***proepangellō***, v. GK: *4600* [→ *4253+1909+32*]. (mid.) to promise beforehand; (pass.) to be promised previously:– promised afore [1]

4280 προερέω, ***proereō***, v. GK: *4625* [→ *4253+3004*]. to tell beforehand; to speak in the past:–

4281 προέρχομαι, ***proerchomai***, v. GK: *4601* [→ *4253+2064*]. to go on ahead; to lead; to visit in advance:– went before [2], go before [1], going before [1], go [1], outwent [1], passed on [1], went forward [1], went further [1]

4282 προετοιμάζω, ***proetoimazō***, v. GK: *4602* [→ *4253+2092*]. to prepare in advance:– afore prepared [1], before ordained [1]

4283 προευαγγελίζομαι, ***proeuangelizomai***, v. GK: *4603* [→ *4253+2095+32*]. to announce the gospel in advance:– preached before the gospel [1]

4284 προέχω, ***proechō***, v. GK: *4604* [→ *4253+2192*]. (mid.) to be better off, have an advantage:– better [1]

4285 προηγέομαι, ***proēgeomai***, v. GK: *4605* [→ *4253+71*]. to put above, go before:– preferring [1]

4286 πρόθεσις, ***prothesis***, n. GK: *4606 & 4671* [→ *4253+5087*]. setting forth: plan, purpose, will; (a.) consecrated (bread):– purpose [8], shewbread (*+740+3588*) [3], shewbread (*+740*) [1]

4287 προθεσμία, ***prothesmia***, n. GK: *4607* [→ *4253+5087*]. set time, fixed or limited time:– time appointed [1]

4288 προθυμία, ***prothymia***, n. GK: *4608* [→ *4253+2372*]. eagerness, willingness, readiness:– forwardness of mind [1], readiness of mind [1], readiness [1], ready mind [1], willing mind [1]

4289 πρόθυμος, ***prothymos***, a. GK: *4609* [→ *4253+2372*]. willing, eager:– ready [2], willing [1]

4290 προθύμως, ***prothymōs***, adv. GK: *4610* [→ *4253+2372*]. eagerly, willingly:– of a ready mind [1]

4291 προΐστημι, ***proistēmi***, v. GK: *4613* [→ *4253+2476*]. (act/mid) to manage, direct, lead; (mid.) to devote oneself, busy oneself to:– maintain [2], ruleth [2], rule [2], over [1], ruling [1]

4292 προκαλέω, ***prokaleō***, v. GK: *4614* [→ *4253+2564*]. (mid.) to provoke, challenge:– provoking [1]

4293 προκαταγγέλλω, ***prokatangellō***, v. GK: *4615* [→ *4253+2596+32*]. to foretell, predict, announce beforehand:– before shewed [1], foretold [1], had notice before [1], shewed before [1]

4294 προκαταρτίζω, ***prokatartizō***, v. GK: *4616* [→ *4253+2596+737*]. to arrange for in advance, get ready beforehand:– make up beforehand [1]

4295 πρόκειμαι, ***prokeimai***, v. GK: *4618* [→ *4253+2749*]. (pass.) to be set before, present:– set before [3], first [1], set forth for [1]

4296 προκηρύσσω, ***prokēryssō***, v. GK: *4619* [→ *4253+2783*]. to preach beforehand:– before preached [1], first preached [1]

4297 προκοπή, ***prokopē***, n. GK: *4620* [→ *4253+2875*]. progress, advancement:– furtherance [2], profiting [1]

4298 προκόπτω, ***prokoptō***, v. GK: *4621* [→ *4253+2875*]. to go ahead, go forward, advance:– far spent [1], increased [1], increase [1], proceed [1], profited [1], wax [1]

4299 πρόκριμα, ***prokrima***, n. GK: *4622* [→ *4253+2919*]. partiality, discrimination, prejudice:– preferring [1]

4300 προκυρόω, ***prokyroō***, v. GK: *4623* [→ *4253+2964*]. to establish previously, ratify beforehand:– confirmed before [1]

4301 προλαμβάνω, ***prolambanō***, v. GK: *4624* [→ *4253+2983*]. to take beforehand; to go on ahead; (pass.) to be caught, detected:– come aforehand [1], overtaken [1], taketh before [1]

4302 προλέγω, ***prolegō***, v. GK: *4625* [→ *4253+3004*]. to tell beforehand; to speak in the past:– said before [4], told before [3], spoken before [2], foretell [1], foretold [1], forewarned [1], spake before [1], tell before [1], told in time past [1]

4303 προμαρτύρομαι, ***promartyromai***, v. GK: *4626* [→ *4253+3144*]. to predict, bear witness to beforehand:– testified beforehand [1]

4304 προμελετάω, ***promeletaō***, v. GK: *4627* [→ *4253+3199*]. to worry beforehand; some translate "to plan ahead":– meditate before [1]

4305 προμεριμνάω, ***promerimnaō***, v. GK: *4628* [→ *4253+3308*]. to worry or be anxious beforehand:– take thought beforehand [1]

4306 προνοέω, ***pronoeō***, v. GK: *4629* [→ *4253+3563*]. to provide for, care for; to consider, have regard for:– provide for [1], provide [1], providing [1]

4307 πρόνοια, ***pronoia***, n. GK: *4630* [→ *4253+3563*]. foresight, provision, care:– providence [1], provision for [1]

4308 προοράω, ***prooraō***, v. GK: *4632* [→ *4253+3708*]. to see previously; to see ahead, foresee; (mid.) to see in front of:– foresaw [1], seen before [1]

4309 προορίζω, ***proorizō***, v. GK: *4633* [→ *4253+3724*]. to predestine, decide beforehand:– predestinated [2], predestinate [2], determined before [1], ordained [1]

4310 προπάσχω, ***propaschō***, v. GK: *4634* [→ *4253+3958*]. to suffer previously:– suffered before [1]

4311 προπέμπω, ***propempō***, v. GK: *4636* [→ *4253+3992*]. to accompany, escort; to send on one's way, help on one's journey:– brought on way [3], bring on journey [2], accompanied [1], bring forward on journey [1], brought on [1], conduct forth [1]

4312 προπετής, ***propetēs***, a. GK: *4637* [→ *4253+4098*]. rash, reckless, thoughtless:– heady [1], rashly [1]

4313 προπορεύομαι, ***proporeuomai***, v. GK: *4638* [→ *4253+4198*]. to go before:– go before [1], go [1]

4314 πρός, ***pros***, pp. GK: *4639* [→ *676, 677, 1715, 2144, 2145, 4316, 4317, 4318, 4319, 4320, 4321, 4322, 4323, 4324, 4325, 4326, 4327, 4328, 4329, 4330, 4331, 4332, 4333, 4334, 4335, 4336, 4337, 4338, 4339, 4340, 4341, 4342, 4343, 4344, 4345, 4346, 4347, 4348, 4349, 4350, 4351, 4354, 4355, 4356, 4357, 4358, 4359, 4360, 4361, 4362, 4363, 4364, 4365, 4366, 4367, 4369, 4370, 4371, 4374, 4375, 4376, 4377, 4378, 4379, 4383; cf. 4352*]. (gen.) to, for; (dat.) on, at, near, by; (acc.) to, toward; with; in order to; against:– unto [344], to [200], with [43], for [26], against [24], among [18], at [15], toward [8], by [4], according to [3], in [3], of [3], that (*+3588*) [3], about [2], amongst [2], before [2], between [2], pertaining to [2], that [2], to (*+3588*) [2], towards [2], as [1], because (*+3588*) [1], because of [1], belong unto [1], compared with [1], for (*+3588*) [1], nigh unto [1], pertain to [1], to do [1], together (*+240*) [1], whereby (*+3739*) [1], whereby [1], within [1]

4315 προσάββατον, ***prosabbaton***, n. GK: *4640* [→ *4253+4521*]. day before the Sabbath (Friday):– day before the sabbath [1]

4316 προσαγορεύω, ***prosagoreuō***, v. GK: *4641* [→ *4314+71*]. to designate:– called [1]

4317 προσάγω, ***prosagō***, v. GK: *4642* [→ *4314+71*]. to bring to; to approach, come near:– bring [2], brought to [1], drew near [1]

4318 προσαγωγή, ***prosagōgē***, n. GK: *4643* [→ *4314+71*]. access; approach:– access [3]

4319 προσαιτέω, ***prosaiteō***, v. GK: *4644* [→ *4314+154*]. to beg:– begging [2], begged [1]

4320 προσαναβαίνω, ***prosanabainō***, v. GK: *4646* [→ *4314+303+305*]. to move up, go up:– go up [1]

4321 προσαναλίσκω, ***prosanaliskō***, v. GK: *4648 & 4649* [→ *4314+303+259*]. to spend lavishly or in addition:– spent [1]

4322 προσαναπληρόω, ***prosanaplēroō***, v. GK: *4650* [→ *4314+303+4137*]. to supply, fill up:– supplied [1], supplieth [1]

4323 προσανατίθημι, ***prosanatithēmi***, v. GK: *4651* [→ *4314+303+5087*]. to add; to consult, ask advice:– conferred [1], in conference added [1]

4324 προσαπειλέω, ***prosapeileō***, v. GK: *4653* [→ *4314+547*]. to threaten further:– further threatened [1]

4325 προσδαπανάω, ***prosdapanaō***, v. GK: *4655* [→ *4314+1160*]. to spend extra:– spendest more [1]

4326 προσδέομαι, ***prosdeomai***, v. GK: *4656* [→ *4314+1189*]. to need:– needed [1]

4327 προσδέχομαι, ***prosdechomai***, v. GK: *4657* [→ *4314+1209*]. to receive, welcome, accept; to wait for, anticipate:– looking for [3], receive [2], accepting [1], allow [1], looked for [1], receiveth [1], took [1], wait for [1], waited for [1], waited [1], waiting for [1]

4328 προσδοκάω, ***prosdokaō***, v. GK: *4659* [→ *4314+1380*]. to look forward to, expect, wait for:– look for [5], looked [2], waited for [2], expecting to [1], in expectation [1], looketh for [1], looketh [1], looking for [1], tarried [1], waiting for [1]

4329 προσδοκία, ***prosdokia***, n. GK: *4660* [→ *4314+1380*]. anticipation, expectation; apprehension:– expectation [1], looking after [1]

προσδρέμω, ***prosdremō***. See **4370**.

4330 προσεάω, ***proseaō***, v. GK: *4661* [→ *4314+1439*]. to allow to go farther:– suffering [1]

4331 προσεγγίζω, ***prosengizō***, v. GK: *4662* [→ *4314+1451*]. to approach, come near:– come nigh [1]

4332 προσεδρεύω, ***prosedreuō***, v. GK: *4663* [→ *4314+1476*]. to serve, wait upon:– wait at [1]

4333 προσεργάζομαι, ***prosergazomai***, v. GK: *4664* [→ *4314+2041*]. to earn more:– gained [1]

4334 προσέρχομαι, ***proserchomai***, v. GK: *4665* [→ *4314+2064*]. to come to, approach, draw near; to agree to:– came [35], came to [22], came unto [8], come unto [4], come [2], coming [2], went to [2], went unto [2], comers [1], cometh [1], coming to [1], consent to [1], draw near [1], drew near [1], go near [1], goeth [1], went [1]

4335 προσευχή, ***proseuchē***, n. GK: *4666* [→ *4314+2172*]. prayer; place of prayer:– prayer [21], prayers [15], prayed earnestly (*+4336*) [1]

4336 προσεύχομαι, ***proseuchomai***, v. GK: *4667* [→ *4314+2172*]. to pray:– pray [42], prayed [24], praying [12], prayeth [3], make prayers [2], prayest [2], make prayer [1], prayed earnestly (*+4335*) [1]

4337 προσέχω, ***prosechō***, v. GK: *4668* [→ *4314+2192*]. to watch out, be on guard, beware; to pay attention, devote, apply oneself:– beware [7], take heed [6], gave heed [2], giving heed [2], attended unto [1], gave attendance at [1], give attendance [1], give heed to [1], give heed [1], given to [1], had regard [1]

4338 προσηλόω, ***prosēloō***, v. GK: *4669* [→ *4314+2247*]. to nail to:– nailing [1]

4339 προσήλυτος, ***prosēlytos***, n. GK: *4670* [→ *4314+2064*]. Gentile convert (to Judaism), transliterated as "proselyte":– proselytes [2], proselyte [2]

4340 πρόσκαιρος, ***proskairos***, a. GK: *4672* [→ *4314+2540*]. lasting only for a short time, temporary:– for a time [1], for a while [1], season [1], temporal [1]

4341 προσκαλέω, ***proskaleō***, v. GK: *4673* [→ *4314+2564*]. (mid.) to call, summon, send for; gather together:– called unto [16], called [6], calleth unto [2], calling unto [2], call for [1], called for [1], called to [1], call [1]

4342 προσκαρτερέω, ***proskartereō***, v. GK: *4674* [→ *4314+2594*]. to join, adhere to; to be ready; to give attention, be faithful; to spend much time together:– continued [2], attending continually [1], continue in [1], continued stedfastly [1], continuing instant [1], continuing [1], give continually to [1], wait on [1], waited on continually [1]

4343 προσκαρτέρησις, ***proskarterēsis***, n. GK: *4675* [→ *4314+2594*]. perseverance, patience:– perseverance [1]

4344 προσκεφάλαιον, ***proskephalaion***, n. GK: *4676* [→ *4314+2776*]. cushion, pillow:– pillow [1]

4345 προσκληρόω, ***prosklēroō***, v. GK: *4677* [→ *4314+2819*]. (pass.) to be joined with, associated with:– consorted with [1]

4346 πρόσκλισις, ***prosklisis***, n. GK: *4680* [→ *4314+2827*]. favoritism, partiality:– partiality [1]

4347 προσκολλάω, ***proskollaō***, v. GK: *4681* [→ *4314+2853*]. (pass.) to be united to:– joined [2], cleave to [1], cleave [1]

4348 πρόσκομμα, proskomma, n. GK: *4682* [→ *4314+2875*]. stumbling block, something that causes one to stumble:– stumblingblock [2], stumblingstone (*+3037*) [2], offence [1], stumbling [1]

4349 προσκοπή, proskopē, n. GK: *4683* [→ *4314+2875*]. stumbling block, occasion for stumbling; fig. of sinning:– offence [1]

4350 προσκόπτω, proskoptō, v. GK: *4684* [→ *4314+2875*]. to strike, beat; (intr.) to stumble, fall:– stumbleth [3], dash [2], beat upon [1], stumbled [1], stumble [1]

4351 προσκυλίω, proskyliō, v. GK: *4685* [→ *4314+2947*]. to roll in front of, roll up to:– rolled [2]

4352 προσκυνέω, proskyneō, v. GK: *4686* [→ *4353; cf. 4314*]. to worship, pay homage, show reverence; to kneel down (before):– worship [35], worshipped [24], worshipping [1]

4353 προσκυνητής, proskynētēs, n. GK: *4687* [→ *4352*]. worshiper:– worshippers [1]

4354 προσλαλέω, proslaleō, v. GK: *4688* [→ *4314+2980*]. to talk with:– speak with [1], speaking to [1]

4355 προσλαμβάνω, proslambanō, v. GK: *4689* [→ *4314+2983*]. to take aside, take along; to partake; to welcome, accept:– receive [4], took [4], received [3], taken [1], take [1], took unto [1]

4356 πρόσληψις, proslēpsis, n. GK: *4691 & 4692* [→ *4314+2983*]. acceptance:– receiving [1]

4357 προσμένω, prosmenō, v. GK: *4693* [→ *4314+3306*]. to be with, continue in, remain, stay:– abide [1], been [1], cleave unto [1], continueth [1], continue [1], tarried [1]

4358 προσορμίζω, prosormizō, v. GK: *4694* [→ *4314*]. (pass.) to be anchored, come into harbor:– drew to shore [1]

4359 προσοφείλω, prosopheilō, v. GK: *4695* [→ *4314+3784*]. to owe (in addition):– owest besides [1]

4360 προσοχθίζω, prosochthizō, v. GK: *4696* [→ *4314*]. to be angry, provoked:– grieved [2]

4361 πρόσπεινος, prospeinos, a. GK: *4698* [→ *4314+3983*]. hungry:– hungry [1]

4362 προσπήγνυμι, prospēgnymi, v. GK: *4699* [→ *4314+4078*]. to nail to (the cross):– crucified [1]

4363 προσπίπτω, prospiptō, v. GK: *4700* [→ *4314+4098*]. to fall down before; to beat against, strike against:– fell down before [4], beat upon [1], falling down before [1], fell down at [1], fell [1]

4364 προσποιέω, prospoieō, v. GK: *4701* [→ *4314+4160*]. to act as if, pretend:– made as though [1]

4365 προσπορεύομαι, prosporeuomai, v. GK: *4702* [→ *4314+4198*]. to come to, approach:– come unto [1]

4366 προσρήγνυμι, prosrēgnymi, v. GK: *4703 & 4704* [→ *4314+4486*]. to strike upon:– against beat vehemently [1], beat vehemently upon [1]

4367 προστάσσω, prostassō, v. GK: *4705* [→ *4314+5021*]. (act./mid.) to command, order; (pass.) to be set, prescribed:– commanded [6], bidden [1]

4368 προστάτις, prostatis, n. GK: *4706* [→ *4253+2476*]. helper:– succourer [1]

4369 προστίθημι, prostithēmi, v. GK: *4707* [→ *4314+5087*]. to add to, increase ; (pass.) to be brought to, given:– added [7], add [2], again [2], added to [1], added unto [1], any more [1], increase [1], laid [1], more given [1], proceeded further [1]

4370 προστρέχω, prostrechō, v. GK: *4708* [→ *4314+5143*]. to run up to:– came running [1], ran to [1], running to [1]

4371 προσφάγιον, prosphagion, n. GK: *4709* [→ *4314+5314*]. (little) fish:– meat [1]

4372 πρόσφατος, prosphatos, a. GK: *4710* [→ *4253+5348 or* 5408]. new:– new [1]

4373 προσφάτως, prosphatōs, adv. GK: *4711* [→ *4253+5348 or* 5408]. recently:– lately [1]

4374 προσφέρω, prospherō, v. GK: *4712* [→ *4314+5342*]. to bring to, present, offer; to treat as, deal with:– brought [12], offered [12], offer [10], offered up [3], bring [2], brought unto [2], offering [2], brought to [1], dealeth [1], doeth [1], presented [1], put [1]

4375 προσφιλής, prosphilēs, a. GK: *4713* [→ *4314+5384*]. lovely, pleasing:– lovely [1]

4376 προσφορά, prosphora, n. GK: *4714* [→ *4314+5342*]. offering, presentation:– offering [7], offering up [1], offerings [1]

4377 προσφωνέω, prosphōneō, v. GK: *4715* [→ *4314+5456*]. to call out; speak to, address:– spake [2], called to [1], called unto [1], calling to [1], calling unto [1], spake unto [1]

4378 πρόσχυσις, proschysis, n. GK: *4717* [→ *1632; cf. 4314*]. sprinkling:– sprinkling [1]

4379 προσψαύω, prospsauō, v. GK: *4718* [→ *4314+5597*]. to touch:– touch [1]

4380 προσωποληπτέω, prosōpolēpteō, v. GK: *4719 & 4722* [→ *4383+2983*]. to show favoritism, partiality:– have respect to persons [1]

4381 προσωπολήπτης, prosōpolēptēs, n. GK: *4720 & 4723* [→ *4383+2983*]. one who shows favoritism, partiality:– respecter of persons [1]

4382 προσωποληψία, prosōpolēpsia, n. GK: *4721 & 4724* [→ *4383+2983*]. favoritism, partiality:– respect of persons [4]

4383 πρόσωπον, prosōpon, n. GK: *4725* [→ *678, 2146, 4380, 4381, 4382*]. face, a part of the body; by extension: in someone's presence, sight; (with various pp.) before, in front of, on the surface of:– face [49], faces [6], person [5], presence [5], countenance [3], appearance [1], before (*+1519*) [1], before (*+4253*) [1], face to face (*+2596*) [1], fashion [1], having in admiration (*+2296*) [1], in presence [1], in the presence (*+2596*) [1], outward appearance [1], persons [1]

4384 προτάσσω, protassō, v. GK: *4726* [→ *4253+5021*]. to determine beforehand, allot beforehand:– before appointed [1]

4385 προτείνω, proteinō, v. GK: *4727* [→ *1614; cf. 4253*]. to stretch out:– bound [1]

4386 πρότερον, protĕron, a.neut. of *4387*. GK: *4728* [→ *4253*]. before; (adv.) before, formerly, an earlier time:–

4387 πρότερος, proteros, a. GK: *4728* [→ *4253*]. before; (adv.) before, formerly, an earlier time:– before [5], former [3], first [2], at first [1]

4388 προτίθημι, protithēmi, v. GK: *4729* [→ *4253+5087*]. (mid.) to plan, purpose; to present, bring forth:– purposed [2], set forth [1]

4389 προτρέπω, protrepō, v. GK: *4730* [→ *4253+5157*]. to encourage, urge on:– exhorting [1]

4390 προτρέχω, protrechō, v. GK: *4731* [→ *4253+5143*]. to run ahead:– outrun (*+5030*) [1], ran before [1]

4391 προϋπάρχω, prouparchō, v. GK: *4732* [→ *4253+5259+757*]. to exist formerly:– beforetime [1], before [1]

4392 πρόφασις, prophasis, n. GK: *4733* [→ *4253+5316*]. excuse; pretense, show, cover:– pretence [3], cloke [2], shew [1], under colour [1]

4393 προφέρω, propherō, v. GK: *4734* [→ *4253+5342*]. to bring out:– bringeth forth [2]

4394 προφητεία, prophēteia, n. GK: *4735* [→ *4395, 4396, 4397, 4398, 5578*]. prophecy, an inspired message, sometimes encouraging obedience to God, sometimes proclaiming the future as a warning to preparedness and continued obedience:– prophecy [14], prophecies [2], prophesying [2], prophesyings [1]

4395 προφητεύω, prophēteuō, v. GK: *4736* [→ *4394*]. to prophesy, to speak an inspired message, sometimes encouraging obedience to God, sometimes proclaiming the future as a warning to preparedness and continued obedience:– prophesy [14], prophesied [9], prophesieth [4], prophesying [1]

4396 προφήτης, prophētēs, n. GK: *4737* [→ *4394*]. prophet, one who speaks inspired utterances; the writings of the OT prophets; see also *4394*:– prophets [81], prophet [67], prophet's [1]

4397 προφητικός, prophētikos, a. GK: *4738* [→ *4394*]. prophetic, prophesy; see also *4394*:– of prophecy [1], prophets [1]

4398 προφῆτις, prophētis, n. GK: *4739* [→ *4394*]. prophetess, a woman who speaks inspired utterances; see also *4394*:– prophetess [2]

4399 προφθάνω, prophthanō, v. GK: *4740* [→ *4253+5348*]. to anticipate, come before:– prevented [1]

4400 προχειρίζω, procheirizō, v. GK: *4741* [→ *4253+5495*]. (mid.) to choose, appoint:– chosen [1], make [1]

4401 προχειροτονέω, procheirotoneō, v. GK: *4742* [→ *1614*]. to choose beforehand, appoint beforehand:– chosen before [1]

4402 Πρόχορος, Prochoros, n.pr. GK: *4743* [→ *4253+5525*]. Procorus:– Prochorus [1]

4403 πρύμνα, prymna, n. GK: *4744*. stern (of a vessel):– hinder part of ship [1], hinder part [1], stern [1]

4404 πρωΐ, prōi, adv. GK: *4745* [→ *4405, 4406, 4407; cf. 4253*]. early in the morning:– in the morning [4], early [2], morning [2], early in the morning (*+260*) [1], early in the morning [1]

4405 πρωΐα, prōia, n. GK: *4746* [→ *4404*]. early morning:– morning [2], early [1], in the morning [1]

4406 πρώϊμος, prōimos, a. GK: *4611 & 4747* [→ *4404*]. early; (n.) autumn rains (in October of the modern calendar):– early [1]

4407 πρωϊνός, prōinos, a. GK: *4612 & 4748* [→ *4404*]. early, pertaining to the morning:– morning [1]

4408 πρῷρα, prōra, n. GK: *4749* [→ *4253*]. bow (of a vessel):– forepart [1], foreship [1]

4409 πρωτεύω, prōteuō, v. GK: *4750* [→ *4413*]. to be supreme, first, have first place:– preeminence [1]

4410 πρωτοκαθεδρία, prōtokathedria, n. GK: *4751* [→ *4413+2516*]. most important seat, seat of honor:– chief seats [2], highest seats [1], uppermost seats [1]

4411 πρωτοκλισία, prōtoklisia, n. GK: *4752* [→ *4413+2827*]. place of honor:– chief rooms [2], uppermost rooms [2], highest room [1]

4412 πρῶτον, prōton, adv. GK: *4754* [→ *4413*]. first; earlier; above all:– first [55], at first [2], at the beginning [1], before [1], chiefly [1], first of all [1]

4413 πρῶτος, prōtos, a. GK: *4755* [→ *1207, 4409, 4410, 4411, 4412, 4414, 4415, 4416, 5383; cf. 4253*]. first (chronologically or in order of importance):– first [86], chief [10], before [2], former [2], beginning [1], best [1], chiefest [1], first (*+1722*) [1]

4414 πρωτοστάτης, prōtostatēs, n. GK: *4756* [→ *4413+2476*]. ringleader, leader:– ringleader [1]

4415 πρωτοτόκια, prōtotokia, n. GK: *4757* [→ *4413+5088*]. inheritance rights (of the firstborn):– birthright [1]

4416 πρωτότοκος, prōtotokos, a. GK: *4758* [→ *4413+5088*]. firstborn (human or animal). In biblical culture, the firstborn had higher status and received a greater share of the inheritance. Jesus Christ, as the firstborn of God, is of supreme status and inherits all things:– firstborn [7], first begotten [1], firstbegotten [1]

4417 πταίω, ptaiō, v. GK: *4760* [→ *679*]. to stumble, fall, trip:– offend [3], fall [1], stumbled [1]

4418 πτέρνα, pterna, n. GK: *4761*. heel:– heel [1]

4419 πτερύγιον, pterygion, n. GK: *4762* [→ *4072*]. highest point:– pinnacle [2]

4420 πτέρυξ, pteryx, n. GK: *4763* [→ *4072*]. wing:– wings [5]

4421 πτηνός, ptēnos, a. GK: *4764* [→ *4072*]. what is winged or feathered; (n.) bird:– birds [1]

4422 πτοέω, ptoeō, v. GK: *4765* [→ *4423*]. (pass.) to be startled, frightened:– terrified [2]

4423 πτόησις, ptoēsis, n. GK: *4766* [→ *4422*]. something alarming:– amazement [1]

4424 Πτολεμαΐς, Ptolemais, n.pr. GK: *4767*. Ptolemais:– Ptolemais [1]

4425 πτύον, ptyon, n. GK: *4768* [→ *4429*]. winnowing fork or shovel:– fan [2]

4426 πτύρω, ptyrō, v. GK: *4769*. (pass.) to be frightened:– terrified [1]

4427 πτύσμα, ptysma, n. GK: *4770* [→ *4429*]. saliva, spit:– spittle [1]

4428 πτύσσω, ptyssō, v. GK: *4771* [→ *380*]. to roll up:– closed [1]

4429 πτύω, ptyō, v. GK: *4772* [→ *1609, 1716, 4425, 4427*]. to spit (saliva):– spit [2], spat [1]

4430 πτῶμα, ptōma, n. GK: *4773* [→ *4098*]. dead body, carcass, corpse:– dead bodies [3], carcase [1], corpse [1]

4431 **πτῶσις, *ptōsis***, n. GK: *4774* [→ *4098*]. falling, crash:– fall [2]

4432 **πτωχεία, *ptōcheia***, n. GK: *4775* [→ *4434*]. poverty:– poverty [3]

4433 **πτωχεύω, *ptōcheuō***, v. GK: *4776* [→ *4434*]. to be or become poor:– poor [1]

4434 **πτωχός, *ptōchos***, a. GK: *4777* [→ *4432, 4433*]. poor; (n.) poor, beggar, a person of few resources, culturally considered oppressed, despised, and miserable. "The poor in spirit" are not lacking in spirit, but have the positive moral quality of humility, realizing they have nothing to offer God but are in need of his free gifts:– poor [31], beggar [2], beggarly [1]

4435 **πυγμή, *pygmē***, n. GK: *4778* [→ *4437, 4438*]. fist; with a fist = NIV "ceremonial":– oft [1]

4436 **πύθων, *pythōn***, n. GK: *4780*. spirit of divination:– of divination [1]

4437 **πυκνός, *pyknos***, a. GK: *4781* [→ *4435*]. (a.) often, frequent, numerous; (adv.) often, as a comparative: quite often, as often as possible:– often [2], oftener [1]

4438 **πυκτεύω, *pykteuō***, v. GK: *4782* [→ *4435*]. to fight with the fist, box:– fight [1]

4439 **πύλη, *pylē***, n. GK: *4783* [→ *4440*]. (city) gate:– gate [8], gates [2]

4440 **πυλών, *pylōn***, n. GK: *4784* [→ *4439*]. gate, door, entryway:– gates [11], gate [6], porch [1]

4441 **πυνθάνομαι, *pynthanomai***, v. GK: *4785*. to ask, inquire, question:– asked [5], ask [2], demanded [2], inquired [1], inquire [1]; understood [1]

4442 **πῦρ, *pyr***, n. GK: *4786* [→ *329, 4443, 4445, 4446, 4447, 4448, 4449, 4450, 4451*]. fire, flames:– fire [73], fiery [1]

4443 **πυρά, *pyra***, n. GK: *4787* [→ *4442*]. fire:– fire [2]

4444 **πύργος, *pyrgos***, n. GK: *4788*. tower, watchtower:– tower [4]

4445 **πυρέσσω, *pyressō***, v. GK: *4789* [→ *4442*]. to burn with a fever:– sick of a fever [2]

4446 **πυρετός, *pyretos***, n. GK: *4790* [→ *4442*]. fever:– fever [6]

4447 **πύρινος, *pyrinos***, a. GK: *4791* [→ *4442*]. fiery red, the color of fire:– fire [1]

4448 **πυρόω, *pyroō***, v. GK: *4792* [→ *4442*]. to burn; to burn inwardly:– burn [2], burned [1], fiery [1], on fire [1], tried [1]

4449 **πυρράζω, *pyrrazō***, v. GK: *4793* [→ *4442*]. to be red, the color of fire:– red [2]

4450 **πυρρός, *pyrros***, a. GK: *4794* [→ *4442*]. fiery red, the color of fire:– red [2]

4451 **πύρωσις, *pyrōsis***, n. GK: *4796* [→ *4442*]. burning, painful:– burning [2], fiery trial [1]

4452 **-πω, *-pō***, pt. GK: * [→ *4458*]. an enclitic particle of indefiniteness; yet, even; used only in composition. See *3369, 3380, 3764, 3768, 4455*.:–

4453 **πωλέω, *pōleō***, v. GK: *4797* [→ *4211*]. to sell:– sold [14], sell [7], selleth [1]

4454 **πῶλος, *pōlos***, n. GK: *4798*. colt:– colt [12]

4455 **πώποτε, *pōpote***, adv. GK: *4799*. ever, at any time:– at any time [3], never (*+3361+3756*) [1], never [1], yet never (*+3762*) [1]

4456 **πωρόω, *pōroō***, v. GK: *4800* [→ *4457*]. to harden, deaden, make dull:– hardened [3], blinded [2]

4457 **πώρωσις, *pōrōsis***, n. GK: *4801* [→ *4456*]. hardening, stubbornness:– blindness [2], hardness [1]

4458 **πώς, *pōs***, pt. GK: *4803* [→ *4452*]. somehow, in some way:–

4459 **πῶς, *pōs***, pt.inter. GK: *4802*. how? in what way?; how!:– how [97], by what means [2], after what manner [1], how (*+302+1063*) [1], how can [1], that [1]

4460 **Ῥαάβ, *Rhaab***, n.pr. GK: *4805*. Rahab, "*spacious, broad*":– Rahab [2]

4461 **ῥαββί, *rhabbi***, l.[n.]. GK: *4806* [→ *4462*]. Rabbi, a title of a teacher:– master [9], Rabbi [8]

4462 **ῥαββονί, *rhabboni***; or **ῥαββουνί, *rhabbouni***, l.[n.]. GK: *4807 & 4808 & 4809* [→ *4461*]. Rabboni, a title of a teacher:– Lord [1], Rabboni [1]

4463 **ῥαβδίζω, *rhabdizō***, v. GK: *4810* [→ *4464*]. to beat with a rod:– beaten with rods [1], beat [1]

4464 **ῥάβδος, *rhabdos***, n. GK: *4811* [→ *4463, 4465, 4474, 4475*]. rod, staff, stick; measuring rod; scepter:– rod [6], sceptre [2], staff [2], staves [2]

4465 **ῥαβδοῦχος, *rhabdouchos***, n. GK: *4812* [→ *4464+2192*]. officer, the Roman *lictor*, a policeman:– sergeants [2]

4466 **Ῥαγαύ, *Rhagau***, n.pr. GK: *4814*. Reu, "*friend [of God]*":– Ragau [1]

4467 **ῥᾳδιούργημα, *rhadiourgēma***, n. GK: *4815* [→ *4468*]. crime, legal infraction:– lewdness [1]

4468 **ῥᾳδιουργία, *rhadiourgia***, n. GK: *4816* [→ *4467; cf. 2041*]. trickery:– mischief [1]

4469 **ῥακά, *rhaka***, l.[a.]. GK: *4819 & 4828*. Raca (a term of abuse, derived from Aramaic *rêqa'*, meaning "empty[-headed] one"), "*empty-headed [?]*":– Raca [1]

4470 **ῥάκος, *rhakos***, n. GK: *4820*. piece of cloth:– cloth [2]

4471 **Ῥαμά, *Rhama***, n.pr. GK: *4821*. Ramah, "*elevated spot*":– Rama [1]

4472 **ῥαντίζω, *rhantizō***, v. GK: *4822* [→ *4473*]. to sprinkle:– sprinkled [3], sprinkling [1]

4473 **ῥαντισμός, *rhantismos***, n. GK: *4823* [→ *4472*]. sprinkling:– sprinkling [2]

4474 **ῥαπίζω, *rhapizō***, v. GK: *4824* [→ *4464*]. to strike, slap:– smite [1], smote with the palms of hands [1]

4475 **ῥάπισμα, *rhapisma***, n. GK: *4825* [→ *4464*]. slap, strike:– smote with hands (*+1325*) [1], strike with the palms of hands (*+906*) [1], stroke with the palm of hand (*+1325*) [1]

4476 **ῥαφίς, *rhaphis***, n. GK: *4827* [→ *729, 1976*]. needle:– needle [2], needle's [1]

4477 **Ῥαχάβ, *Rhachab***, n.pr. GK: *4829*. Rahab, "*spacious, broad*":– Rachab [1]

4478 **Ῥαχήλ, *Rhachēl***, n.pr. GK: *4830*. Rachel, "*ewe*":– Rachel [1]

4479 **Ῥεβέκκα, *Rhebekka***, n.pr. GK: *4831*. Rebekah, "[poss.] *choice calf*":– Rebecca [1]

4480 **ῥέδη, *rhedē***, n. GK: *4832*. carriage:– chariots [1]

4481 **Ῥεμφάν, *Rhemphan***; or **Ῥαιφάν, *Rhaiphan***, n.pr. GK: *4818 & 4833 & 4834 & 4854* [→ *4481, 4481, 4481*]. Rephan, Remphan:– Remphan [1]

4482 **ῥέω, *rheō***, v. GK: *4835* [→ *131, 3901, 4511, 5493*]. to flow:– flow [1]

4483 **ῥέω, *rheō***; and **ἐρέω, *ereō***, v. GK: *3306* [→ *3004*]. to utter, speak, say:–

4484 **Ῥήγιον, *Rhēgion***, n.pr. GK: *4836*. Rhegium:– Rhegium [1]

4485 **ῥῆγμα, *rhegma***, n. GK: *4837* [→ *4486*]. destruction, ruin:– ruin [1]

4486 **ῥήγνυμι, *rhēgnymi***; or **ῥήσσω, *rhēssō***, v. GK. *4838* [→ *1284, 4048, 4366, 4405*]. to burst, break forth; to tear to pieces; to throw violently:– burst [2], break forth [1], break [1], rent [1], teareth [1], threw down [1]

4487 **ῥῆμα, *rhēma***, n. GK: *4839* [→ *368, 369, 731, 3954, 3955, 4489, 4490*]. word, saying; matter; thing:– words [31], word [25], saying [6], sayings [3], things [2], nothing (*+3756+3956*) [1], thing [1]

4488 **Ῥησά, *Rhēsa***, n.pr. GK: *4840*. Rhesa:– Rhesa [1]

4489 **ῥήτωρ, *rhētōr***, n. GK: *4842* [→ *4487*]. lawyer:– orator [1]

4490 **ῥητῶς, *rhētōs***, adv. GK: *4843* [→ *4487*]. clearly, exactly:– expressly [1]

4491 **ῥίζα, *rhiza***, n. GK: *4844* [→ *1610, 4492*]. root, rootstock:– root [16], roots [1]

4492 **ῥιζόω, *rhizoō***, v. GK: *4845* [→ *4491*]. (pass.) to be rooted, with the associative meaning that a rooted object is strong and healthy:– rooted [2]

4493 **ῥιπή, *rhipē***, n. GK: *4846 & 4856* [→ *4496*]. twinkling, rapid movement (of the eye); some translate as "the blink (of an eye)":– twinkling [1]

4494 **ῥιπίζω, *rhipizō***, v. GK: *4847* [→ *4496*]. (pass.) to be tossed about:– tossed [1]

4495 **ῥιπτέω, *rhipteō***, v. GK: *4848* [→ *4496*]. to throw off:– cast [1]

4496 **ῥίπτω, *rhiptō***, v. GK: *4849* [→ *641, 1977, 4493, 4494, 4495*]. to throw, drop; to lay; (pass.) to be helpless, laid out:– cast [4], cast down [1], scattered abroad [1], thrown [1]

4497 **Ῥοβοάμ, *Rhoboam***, n.pr. GK: *4850*. Rehoboam, "*[my] people will enlarge, expand*":– Roboam [2]

4498 **Ῥόδη, *Rhodē***, n.pr. GK: *4851*. Rhoda, "*rose*":– Rhoda [1]

4499 **Ῥόδος, *Rhodos***, n.pr. GK: *4852*. Rhodes, "*rose*":– Rhodes [1]

4500 **ῥοιζηδόν, *rhoizēdon***, adv. GK: *4853*. with a roar; a derivative of a Greek noun meaning, "the noise made by a passing arrow," not found in the NT:– great noise [1]

4501 **ῥομφαία, *rhomphaia***, n. GK: *4855*. (long) sword:– sword [7]

4502 **Ῥουβήν, *Rhoubēn***, n.pr. GK: *4857*. Reuben, "*See, a son! [Ge. 29:32]; substitute a son*":– Reuben [1]

4503 **Ῥούθ, *Rhouth***, n.pr. GK: *4858*. Ruth, "*friendship, poss. comrade, companion; refreshed*":– Ruth [1]

4504 **Ῥοῦφος, *Rhouphos***, n.pr. GK: *4859*. Rufus, "*red-haired*":– Rufus [2]

4505 **ῥύμη, *rhymē***, n. GK: *4860*. street, alley, lane:– street [2], lanes [1], streets [1]

4506 **ῥύομαι, *rhyomai***, v. GK: *4861*. to rescue, deliver:– delivered [9], deliver [8], deliverer [1]

4507 **ῥυπαρία, *rhyparia***, n. GK: *4864* [→ *4509*]. (moral) filth:– filthiness [1]

4508 **ῥυπαρός, *rhyparos***, a. GK: *4865* [→ *4509*]. shabby, dirty; moral vileness, filthiness:– vile [1]

4509 **ῥύπος, *rhypos***, n. GK: *4866* [→ *4507, 4508, 4510*]. dirt:– filth [1]

4510 **ῥυπόω, *rhypoō***, v. GK: *4867* [→ *4509*]. to defile, pollute:– filthy [2]

4511 **ῥύσις, *rhysis***, n. GK: *4868* [→ *4482*]. flow (of blood), bleeding:– issue [3]

4512 **ῥυτίς, *rhytis***, n. GK: *4869*. wrinkle:– wrinkle [1]

4513 **Ῥωμαϊκός, *Rhōmaikos***, a.pr. GK: *4870* [→ *4516*]. Roman, Latin:– Latin [1]

4514 **Ῥωμαῖος, *Rhōmaios***, a.pr.g. GK: *4871* [→ *4516*]. Roman, from Rome; (n.) Roman citizen:– Romans [6], Roman [5], Romans (*+444*) [1], of Rome [1]

4515 **Ῥωμαϊστί, *Rhōmaisti***, adv.pr. GK: *4872* [→ *4516*]. in Latin (language):– Latin [1]

4516 **Ῥώμη, *Rhōmē***, n.pr. GK: *4873* [→ *4513, 4514, 4515*]. Rome:– Rome [14]

4517 **ῥώννυμι, *rhōnnymi***, v. GK: *4874* [→ *732*]. to be strong; (pass.) farewell, goodbye, as the closing of a letter:– fare well [1], farewell [1]

4518 **σαβαχθάνι, *sabachthani***, l.[v.+p.]. GK: *2407 & 4876*. sabachthani (Aramaic: "you have forsaken me"):– sabachthani [2]

4519 **Σαβαώθ, *Sabaōth***, l.[pr.n.]. GK: *4877*. Almighty ["of Hosts"], a Greek transliteration of the Hebrew word 7372, "armies, hosts." This title has the associative meanings of power and potent authority, and pictures the Lord as a great, powerful, supreme general:– sabaoth [2]

4520 **σαββατισμός, *sabbatismos***, n. GK: *4878* [→ *4521*]. Sabbath-rest, Sabbath observance; "a sabbath's day journey" reckoned at 800 to 900 yards (2,000 cubits):– rest [1]

4521 **σάββατον, *sabbaton***, n. GK: *4879* [→ *4315, 4520*]. Sabbath:– sabbath [57], week [9], sabbath day's journey (*+2192+3598*) [1], sabbath days [1]

4522 **σαγήνη, *sagēnē***, n. GK: *4880*. (large) dragnet, a net with weights on the bottom and dragged through the water:– net [1]

4523 **Σαδδουκαῖος, *Saddoukaios***, n.pr. GK: *4881* [cf. *4524*]. Sadducee, "[poss.] *followers of Zadok; righteous*":– Sadducees [14]

4524 **Σαδώκ, *Sadōk***, n.pr. GK: *4882* [cf. *4523*]. Zadok, "*righteous one*":– Sadoc [2]

4525 **σαίνω, *sainō***, v. GK: *4883*. (pass.) to be unsettled, disturbed:– moved [1]

4526 σάκκος, ***sakkos***, n. GK: *4884*. sackcloth, a heavy coarse cloth used for making sacks, but worn by the penitent or mournful as a sign of contrition and sorrow:– sackcloth [4]

4527 Σαλά, ***Sala***, n.pr. GK: *4885*. Sala, "*missile [a weapon], sprout*":– Sala [1]

4528 Σαλαθιήλ, ***Salathiēl***, n.pr. GK: *4886*. Shealtiel, "*I have asked [him] of God [El]; poss. God [El] is a shield*":– Salathiel [3]

4529 Σαλαμίς, ***Salamis***, n.pr. GK: *4887*. Salamis, "*peace*":– Salamis [1]

4530 Σαλίμ, ***Salim***, n.pr. GK: *4890*. Salim:– Salim [1]

4531 σαλεύω, ***saleuō***, v. GK: *4888* [→ *761, 4535; cf. 242*]. to shake up; agitate; (pass.) to be shaken, swayed, unsettled:– shaken [11], moved [1], shake [1], shook [1], stirred up [1]

4532 Σαλήμ, ***Salēm***, n.pr. GK: *4889*. Salem, "*peace*":– Salem [2]

4533 Σαλμών, ***Salmōn***, n.pr. GK: *4891*. Salmon, "*little spark*":– Salmon [3]

4534 Σαλμώνη, ***Salmōnē***, n.pr. GK: *4892*. Salmone:– Salmone [1]

4535 σάλος, ***salos***, n. GK: *4893* [→ *4531*]. tossing motion, rolling motion (of the surging waves):– waves [1]

4536 σάλπιγξ, ***salpinx***, n. GK: *4894* [→ *4537*]. trumpet:– trumpet [7], trumpets [2], trump [2]

4537 σαλπίζω, ***salpizō***, v. GK: *4895* [→ *4536, 4538*]. to sound a trumpet, announce with a trumpet:– sounded [7], sound [3], sound a trumpet [1], trumpet sound [1]

4538 σαλπιστής, ***salpistēs***, n. GK: *4896* [→ *4537*]. trumpeter:– trumpeters [1]

4539 Σαλώμη, ***Salōmē***, n.pr. GK: *4897*. Salome, "*peaceful, prosperous one*":– Salome [2]

4540 Σαμάρεια, ***Samareia***, n.pr. GK: *4899 & 4900* [→ *4541, 4542*]. Samaria, "*belonging to the clan of Shemer [1Ki 16:24]*":– Samaria [11]

4541 Σαμαρίτης, ***Samaritēs***, n.pr.g. GK: *4901* [→ *4540*]. Samaritan:– Samaritans [6], Samaritan [3]

4542 Σαμαρῖτις, ***Samaritis***, n.pr.g.&a. GK: *4902* [→ *4540*]. Samaritan:– Samaria [2]

4543 Σαμοθρᾴκη, ***Samothrakē***, n.pr. GK: *4903*. Samothrace, "*Thracian Samos*":– Samothracia [1]

4544 Σάμος, ***Samos***, n.pr. GK: *4904*. Samos, "*heights, lofty place*":– Samos [1]

4545 Σαμουήλ, ***Samouēl***, n.pr. GK: *4905*. Samuel, "*his name is God [El]; heard of God [El]; the unnamed god is El*":– Samuel [3]

4546 Σαμψών, ***Sampsōn***, n.pr. GK: *4907*. Samson, "*little one of Shemesh [pagan sun god]* or *sunny*":– Samson [1]

4547 σανδάλιον, ***sandalion***, n. GK: *4908*. sandal:– sandals [2]

4548 σανίς, ***sanis***, n. GK: *4909*. plank, board:– boards [1]

4549 Σαούλ, ***Saoul***, n.pr. GK: *4910*. Saul, "*asked of God* or poss. *dedicated to God*":– Saul [9]

4550 σαπρός, ***sapros***, a. GK: *4911* [→ *4595*]. bad, rotten, decayed; unwholesome:– corrupt [7], bad [1]

4551 Σάπφιρα, ***Sapphira***, n.pr. GK: *4912* [→ *4552*]. Sapphira, "*beautiful*":– Sapphira [1]

4552 σάπφιρος, ***sapphiros***, n. GK: *4913* [→ *4551*]. sapphire stone:– sapphire [1]

4553 σαργάνη, ***sarganē***, n. GK: *4914*. (large flexible) basket, possibly made of ropes:– basket [1]

4554 Σάρδεις, ***Sardeis***, n.pr. GK: *4915*. Sardis:– Sardis [3]

4555 σάρδινος, ***sardinos***, n. GK: *4916* [→ *4556*]. carnelian, sard:– sardine [1]

4556 σάρδιον, ***sardion***, n. GK: *4917* [→ *4555, 4557*]. carnelian (a reddish precious stone):– sardius [1]

4557 σαρδόνυξ, ***sardonyx***, n. GK: *4918* [→ *4556*]. sardonyx (a variety of agate):– sardonyx [1]

4558 Σάρεπτα, ***Sarepta***, n.pr. GK: *4919*. Zarephath, "[poss.] *smelting place; place of pigmenting, staining*":– Sarepta [1]

[illegible]9 σαρκικός, ***sarkikos***, a. GK: *4920* [→ *4561*]. material; [illegible]lly, sinful; pertaining to the flesh; see also *4561*:– [illegible]al [9], fleshly [2]

4560 σάρκινος, ***sarkinos***, a. GK: *4921* [→ *4561*]. fleshly, made of flesh; human; worldly, unspiritual; see also *4561*:– fleshy [1]

4561 σάρξ, ***sarx***, n. GK: *4922* [→ *4559, 4560*]. flesh, body, the soft tissue of a creature, often in contrast to bone, ligament, or sinew; by extension human, humankind, with a focus on the fallen human nature, which is frail and corrupt in contrast to immaterial (spiritual) things, thus the NIV translation "sinful nature":– flesh [147], carnal [2], carnally [1], fleshly [1]

4562 Σαρούχ, ***Sarouch***; or Σερούχ, ***Serouch***, n.pr. GK: *4923 & 4951 & 4952*. Serug, "*descendant, i.e., younger branch*":– Saruch [1]

4563 σαρόω, ***saroō***, v. GK: *4924*. to sweep, sweep clean:– swept [2], sweep [1]

4564 Σάρρα, ***Sarra***, n.pr. GK: *4925*. Sarah, "*princess*":– Sara [3], Sara's [1]

4565 Σαρών, ***Sarōn***, n.pr. GK: *4926*. Sharon, "*plain, level country*":– Saron [1]

4566 Σατάν, ***Satan***, n.pr. GK: *4927* [→ *4567*]. Satan, "*hostile opponent*":– Satan [1]

4567 Σατανᾶς, ***Satanas***, n.pr. GK: *4928* [→ *4566*]. Satan, "*hostile opponent*":– Satan [35], Satan's [1]

4568 σάτον, ***saton***, n. GK: *4929*. seah (dry measure of about 12 quarts):– measures [2]

4569 Σαῦλος, ***Saulos***, n.pr. GK: *4930*. Saul, "*asked for* poss. *dedicated to God*":– Saul [17]

σαυτοῦ, ***sautou***. See **4572**.

4570 σβέννυμι, ***sbennymi***, v. GK: *4931* [→ *762*]. to extinguish, quench, snuff out:– quenched [4], quench [3], gone out [1]

4571 σέ, ***sē***, p.pers.a. of *4771*. GK: *5148* [→ *4771*]. you, thee; see *4771*:–

4572 σεαυτοῦ, ***seautou***, p.reflex. GK: *4932* [→ *4771+846*]. yourself:– thyself [38], thine own self [2], thee [1], thy [1]

4573 σεβάζομαι, ***sebazomai***, v. GK: *4933* [→ *4576*]. to worship:– worshipped [1]

4574 σέβασμα, ***sebasma***, n. GK: *4934* [→ *4576*]. object of worship; some translate as a place of worship: sanctuary:– devotions [1], worshipped [1]

4575 σεβαστός, ***sebastos***, a. GK: *4935* [→ *4576*]. (a.) revered, worthy of reverence, imperial (not found in the NT); (n.) Emperor, a title of reverence or veneration:– Augustus [2], Augustus' [1]

4576 σέβω, ***sebō***, v. GK: *4936* [→ *763, 764, 765, 2150, 2151, 2152, 2153, 2317, 2318, 4573, 4574, 4575, 4586, 4587*]. (mid.) to worship, be devout, God-fearing:– devout [3], worship [3], worshipped [2], religious [1], worshippeth [1]

4577 σειρά, ***seira***, n. GK: *4937*. chain:– chains [1]

4578 σεισμός, ***seismos***, n. GK: *4939* [→ *4579*]. earthquake; storm:– earthquake [10], earthquakes [3], tempest [1]

4579 σείω, ***seiō***, v. GK: *4940* [→ *383, 1286, 2678, 4578*]. to cause to shake; (pass.) to be shaken, stirred up:– shake [2], moved [1], quake [1], shaken [1]

4580 Σεκοῦνδος, ***Sekoundos***, n.pr. GK: *4941*. Secundus, "*second*":– Secundus [1]

4581 Σελεύκεια, ***Seleukeia***, n.pr. GK: *4942*. Seleucia:– Seleucia [1]

4582 σελήνη, ***selēnē***, n. GK: *4943* [→ *4583*]. moon:– moon [9]

4583 σεληνιάζομαι, ***selēniazomai***, v. GK: *4944* [→ *4582*]. (pass.) to have a seizure:– lunatick [2]

4584 Σεμεΐ, ***Semei***; or Σεμεΐν, ***Semein***, n.pr. GK: *4945 & 4946*. Semei, "*Yahweh has heard*":– Semei [1]

4585 σεμίδαλις, ***semidalis***, n. GK: *4947*. finely ground flour:– fine flour [1]

4586 σεμνός, ***semnos***, a. GK: *4948* [→ *4576*]. worthy of respect, noble:– grave [3], honest [1]

4587 σεμνότης, ***semnotēs***, n. GK: *4949* [→ *4576*]. holiness, seriousness, respect:– gravity [2], honesty [1]

4588 Σέργιος, ***Sergios***, n.pr. GK: *4950*. Sergius:– Sergius [1]

4589 Σήθ, ***Sēth***, n.pr. GK: *4953*. Seth, "*determined, granted [Ge 4:25]; restitution*":– Seth [1]

4590 Σήμ, ***Sēm***, n.pr. GK: *4954*. Shem, "*name, fame*":– Sem [1]

4591 σημαίνω, ***sēmainō***, v. GK: *4955* [→ *4592*]. to make known; to indicate (beforehand), predict, foretell:– signifying [3], signified [2], signify [1]

4592 σημεῖον, ***sēmeion***, n. GK: *4956* [→ *767, 1978, 2154, 3902, 4591, 4593, 4953*]. (miraculous) sign, signal, mark:– sign [29], signs [22], miracles [15], miracle [7], wonder [2], token [1], wonders [1]

4593 σημειόω, ***sēmeioō***, v. GK: *4957* [→ *4592*]. (mid.) to take special note of:– note [1]

4594 σήμερον, ***sēmeron***, adv. GK: *4958* [→ *2250*]. today, this day:– this day [19], to day [18], this day (*+2250*) [3], this day's [1]

4595 σήπω, ***sēpō***, v. GK: *4960* [→ *4550*]. to rot, decay:– corrupted [1]

4596 σηρικός, ***sērikos***; σιρικός, ***sirikos***, a. GK: *4961 & 4986*. silken; (n.) silk (cloth):– silk [1]

4597 σής, ***sēs***, n. GK: *4962* [→ *4598*]. moth:– moth [3]

4598 σητόβρωτος, ***sētobrōtos***, a. GK: *4963* [→ *4597+977*]. moth-eaten:– motheaten [1]

4599 σθενόω, ***sthenoō***, v. GK: *4964* [→ *769, 770, 771, 772*]. to strengthen, make strong:– strengthen [1]

4600 σιαγών, ***siagōn***, n. GK: *4965*. cheek:– cheek [2]

4601 σιγάω, ***sigaō***, v. GK: *4967* [→ *4602*]. to be or become silent; (pass.) to be hidden, concealed:– held peace [2], hold peace [2], keep silence [2], kept close [1], kept secret [1], kept silence [1]

4602 σιγή, ***sigē***, n. GK: *4968* [→ *4601*]. silence:– silence [2]

4603 σιδήρεος, ***sidēreos***, a. GK: *4969 & 4971* [→ *4604*]. made of iron:– of iron [4], iron [1]

4604 σίδηρος, ***sidēros***, n. GK: *4970* [→ *4603*]. iron:– iron [1]

4605 Σιδών, ***Sidōn***, n.pr. GK: *4972* [→ *4606*]. Sidon, "*fishery*":– Sidon [11]

4606 Σιδώνιος, ***Sidōnios***, a.pr.g. GK: *4973* [→ *4605*]. Sidonian, a person of Sidon:– Sidon [1]

4607 σικάριος, ***sikarios***, n. GK: *4974*. terrorist, assassin:– murderers [1]

4608 σίκερα, ***sikera***, l.[n.]. GK: *4975*. fermented drink, beer:– strong drink [1]

4609 Σίλας, ***Silas***, n.pr. GK: *4976* [→ *4610*]. Silas, "*asked for* poss. *dedicated to God*":– Silas [13]

4610 Σιλουανός, ***Silouanos***, n.pr. GK: *4977* [→ *4609*]. Silas, Silvanus, "*asked for* poss. *dedicated to God*":– Silvanus [4]

4611 Σιλωάμ, ***Silōam***, n.pr. GK: *4978*. Siloam, "*sent*":– Siloam [3]

4612 σιμικίνθιον, ***simikinthion***, n. GK: *4959 & 4980*. apron:– aprons [1]

4613 Σίμων, ***Simōn***, n.pr. GK: *4981* [→ *4826*]. Simon, "*he has heard* or *obedient one*":– Simon [68], Simon's [7]

4614 Σινά, ***Sina***, n.pr. GK: *4982*. Sinai, "*Sin [pagan moon god]; glare [from white chalk]*":– Sinai [2], Sina [2]

4615 σίναπι, ***sinapi***, n. GK: *4983*. mustard plant:– mustard [5]

4616 σινδών, ***sindōn***, n. GK: *4984*. linen (cloth or garment):– linen cloth [3], linen [2], fine linen [1]

4617 σινιάζω, ***siniazō***, v. GK: *4985*. to sift, shake in a sieve:– sift [1]

σῖτα, ***sita***. See **4621**.

4618 σιτευτός, ***siteutos***, a. GK: *4988* [→ *4621*]. fattened:– fatted [3]

4619 σιτιστός, ***sitistos***, a. GK: *4990* [→ *4621*]. fattened; (n.) fattened cattle:– fatlings [1]

4620 σιτομέτριον, ***sitometrion***, n. GK: *4991* [→ *4621+3358*]. measured allowance of food, ration of grain:– portion of meat [1]

4621 σῖτος, ***sitos***, n. GK: *4992* [→ *776, 777, 1979, 4618, 4619, 4620*]. wheat, grain:– wheat [12], corn [2]

4622 Σιών, ***Siōn***, n.pr. GK: *4994*. Zion, "*citadel*":– Sion [7]

4623 σιωπάω, ***siōpaō***, v. GK: *4995*. to be quiet, remain silent; to be calm, not agitated:– hold peace [5], held peace [4], dumb [1], peace [1]

4624 σκανδαλίζω, ***skandalizō***, v. GK: *4997* [→ *4625*]. to cause to sin, cause to fall (into sin), offend; to fall away (from the faith), go astray; to take offense:– offended [16], offend [12], make to offend [2]

4625 σκάνδαλον, ***skandalon***, n. GK: *4998* [→ *4624*]. stumbling block, obstacle, offense; something that causes sin:– offence [5], offences [4], stumblingblock [3], occasion of stumbling [1], occasion to fall [1], things that offend [1]

4626 σκάπτω, ***skaptō***, v. GK: *4999* [→ *2679, 4627*]. to dig:– dig [2], digged [1]

4627 σκάφη, ***skaphē***, n. GK: *5002* [→ *4626*]. lifeboat, (small) boat:– boat [3]

4628 σκέλος, ***skelos***, n. GK: *5003*. leg:– legs [3]

4629 σκέπασμα, ***skepasma***, n. GK: *5004*. clothing, covering; this can refer to shelter or personal covering:– raiment [1]

4630 Σκευᾶς, ***Skeuas***, n.pr. GK: *5005*. Sceva:– Sceva [1]

4631 σκευή, ***skeuē***, n. GK: *5006* [→ *4632*]. (ship's) tackle, gear:– tackling [1]

4632 σκεῦος, ***skeuos***, n. GK: *5007* [→ *384, 532, 643, 2680, 3903, 3904, 4631*]. possession, merchandise, object, thing; jar, vessel, dish; a general term that can refer to a human being:– vessel [11], vessels [8], goods [2], sail [1], stuff [1]

4633 σκηνή, ***skēnē***, n. GK: *5008* [→ *1981, 2681, 2682, 4634, 4635, 4636, 4637, 4638*]. tabernacle; tent, shelter, dwelling:– tabernacle [15], tabernacles [4], habitations [1]

4634 σκηνοπηγία, ***skēnopēgia***, n. GK: *5009* [→ *4633+4078*]. (Feast of) Tabernacles:– tabernacles [1]

4635 σκηνοποιός, ***skēnopoios***, n. GK: *5010* [→ *4633+4160*]. tentmaker; some translate more generally: leather worker:– tentmakers [1]

4636 σκῆνος, ***skēnos***, n. GK: *5011* [→ *4633*]. tent:– tabernacle [2]

4637 σκηνόω, ***skēnoō***, v. GK: *5012* [→ *4633*]. to live, dwell; to spread a tent:– dwell [4], dwelt [1]

4638 σκήνωμα, ***skēnōma***, n. GK: *5013* [→ *4633*]. tent, dwelling place, lodging place:– tabernacle [3]

4639 σκιά, ***skia***, n. GK: *5014* [→ *644, 1982, 2683*]. shadow, shade:– shadow [7]

4640 σκιρτάω, ***skirtaō***, v. GK: *5015*. to leap, with an implication that the one leaping is joyful:– leaped [2], leap [1]

4641 σκληροκαρδία, ***sklērokardia***, n. GK: *5016* [→ *4645+2588*]. hardness of heart, stubbornness, obstinacy:– hardness of heart [2], hardness of hearts [1]

4642 σκληρός, ***sklēros***, a. GK: *5017* [→ *4645*]. hard, harsh:– hard [5], fierce [1]

4643 σκληρότης, ***sklērotēs***, n. GK: *5018* [→ *4645*]. hardness, stubbornness:– hardness [1]

4644 σκληροτράχηλος, ***sklērotrachēlos***, a. GK: *5019* [→ *4645+5137*]. stiff-necked, stubborn:– stiffnecked [1]

4645 σκληρύνω, ***sklērynō***, v. GK: *5020* [→ *4641, 4642, 4643, 4644*]. to harden (the heart), make obstinate, make stubborn; (pass.) to be hardened, become obstinate:– harden [3], hardened [2], hardeneth [1]

4646 σκολιός, ***skolios***, a. GK: *5021*. crooked; corrupt:– crooked [2], froward [1], untoward [1]

4647 σκόλοψ, ***skolops***, n. GK: *5022*. thorn; some translate this as a "splinter":– thorn [1]

4648 σκοπέω, ***skopeō***, v. GK: *5023* [→ *244, 1980, 1983, 1984, 1985, 2684, 2685, 4649*]. to watch out for, take notice of, look to:– mark [2], considering [1], look at [1], look [1], take heed [1]

4649 σκοπός, ***skopos***, n. GK: *5024* [→ *4648*]. goal:– mark [1]

4650 σκορπίζω, ***skorpizō***, v. GK: *5025* [→ *1287, 4651*]. to scatter, disperse:– scattereth [2], dispersed abroad [1], scattered [1], scattereth abroad [1]

4651 σκορπίος, ***skorpios***, n. GK: *5026* [→ *4650*]. scorpion:– scorpions [3], scorpion [2]

4652 σκοτεινός, ***skoteinos***, a. GK: *5027* [→ *4655*]. dark:– full of darkness [2], dark [1]

4653 σκοτία, ***skotia***, n. GK: *5028* [→ *4655*]. darkness, the dark:– darkness [14], dark [2]

4654 σκοτίζομαι, ***skotizomai***, v. GK: *5029* [→ *4655*]. (pass.) to be or become dark, be darkened:– darkened [8]

4655 σκότος, ***skotos***, n. GK: *5030* [→ *4652, 4653, 4654, 4656*]. darkness, the dark:– darkness [32]

4656 σκοτόω, ***skotoō***, v. GK: *5031* [→ *4655*]. (pass.) to be or become darkened:– full of darkness [1]

4657 σκύβαλον, ***skybalon***, n. GK: *5032*. rubbish, refuse, dung; this can refer to any of a number of rotten, decaying things, all that is worth getting rid of:– dung [1]

4658 Σκύθης, ***Skythēs***, n.pr.g. GK: *5033*. Scythian:– Scythian [1]

4659 σκυθρωπός, ***skythrōpos***, a. GK: *5034* [→ *3708*]. to look somber, appear downcast, implying a sad or sullen attitude:– sad countenance [1], sad [1]

4660 σκύλλω, ***skyllō***, v. GK: *5035* [→ *4661*]. to bother, annoy; (pass.) to be harassed; (mid.) to trouble oneself:– trouble [2], troublest [1]

4661 σκῦλον, ***skylon***, n. GK: *5036* [→ *4660*]. (pl.) spoils, booty:– spoils [1]

4662 σκωληκόβρωτος, ***skōlēkobrōtos***, a. GK: *5037* [→ *4663+977*]. eaten by worms:– eaten of worms [1]

4663 σκώληξ, ***skōlēx***, n. GK: *5038* [→ *4662*]. worm:– worm [3]

4664 σμαράγδινος, ***smaragdinos***, a. GK: *5039* [→ *4665*]. (of) emerald:– emerald [1]

4665 σμάραγδος, ***smaragdos***, n. GK: *5040* [→ *4664*]. emerald:– emerald [1]

4666 σμύρνα[1], ***smyrna1***, n. GK: *5043* [→ *4667, 4668, 4669*]. myrrh, an aromatic resinous gum:– myrrh [2]

4667 Σμύρνα[2], ***Smyrna2***, n.pr. GK: *5044* [→ *4666*]. Smyrna:– Smyrna [1]

4668 Σμυρναῖος, ***Smyrnaios***, a.pr.g. GK: *5045* [→ *4666*]. Smyrnaean:– Smyrna [1]

4669 σμυρνίζω, ***smyrnizō***, v. GK: *5046* [→ *4666*]. to mix with myrrh, referring to wine mixed with myrrh as a drug to deaden the senses and mind:– mingled with myrrh [1]

4670 Σόδομα, ***Sodoma***, n.pr. GK: *5047*. Sodom:– Sodom [9], Sodoma [1]

4671 σοί, ***soi***, p.pers.dat. of *4771*. GK: *5148* [→ *4771*]. to you, for you, your; see *4771*:–

4672 Σολομών, ***Solomōn***, n.pr. GK: *4898 & 5048*. Solomon, "*peace, well being*":– Solomon [9], Solomon's [3]

4673 σορός, ***soros***, n. GK: *5049*. coffin, bier:– bier [1]

4674 σός, ***sos***, a.poss. GK: *5050* [→ *4771*]. (s.) your, yours:– thy [15], thine [9], thine own [3]

4675 σοῦ, ***sou***, p.pers.gen. of *4771*. GK: *5148* [→ *4771*]. of you, your; see *4771*:–

4676 σουδάριον, ***soudarion***, n. GK: *5051*. piece of cloth, burial cloth, handkerchief:– napkin [3], handkerchiefs [1]

4677 Σουσάννα, ***Sousanna***, n.pr. GK: *5052*. Susanna, "*lily*":– Susanna [1]

4678 σοφία, ***sophia***, n. GK: *5053* [→ *4680*]. wisdom (either secular or divine). Christ is called "the wisdom of God" in 1Co 1:24, 30. On the basis of the OT, wisdom can be personified:– wisdom [51]

4679 σοφίζω, ***sophizō***, v. GK: *5054* [→ *4680*]. to make wise; (pass.) to be cleverly invented:– cunningly devised [1], make wise [1]

4680 σοφός, ***sophos***, a. GK: *5055* [→ *781, 2686, 4678, 4679, 5385, 5386*]. wise; expert, skilled; (n.) a person who is skilled or expert, often as a class or kind, a wise man or woman:– wise [21], wiser than [1]

4681 Σπανία, ***Spania***, n.pr. GK: *5056*. Spain:– Spain [2]

4682 σπαράσσω, ***sparassō***, v. GK: *5057* [→ *4685*]. to convulse, shake violently:– rent [1], tare [1], teareth [1], torn [1]

4683 σπαργανόω, ***sparganoō***, v. GK: *5058*. to wrap (in cloth), to bind a newborn infant in strips of long cloth, a normal act of child care for warmth, security, etc:– wrapped in swaddling clothes [2]

4684 σπαταλάω, ***spatalaō***, v. GK: *5059*. to live in pleasure, in self-indulgence:– liveth in pleasure [1], wanton [1]

4685 σπάω, ***spaō***, v. GK: *5060* [→ *385, 563, 645, 1288, 1986, 4049, 4682, 4952*]. (mid.) to draw (a sword):– drew out [1], drew [1]

4686 σπεῖρα, ***speira***, n. GK: *5061*. company of soldiers, cohort; technically one tenth of a Roman legion: 600 fighting men:– band [7]

4687 σπείρω, ***speirō***, v. GK: *5062* [→ *1289, 1290, 4690, 4691, 4701, 4702, 4703*]. to sow seed, scatter seed:– sown [15], soweth [9], sowed [8], sow [8], sower [6], received seed [4], sowest [3]

4688 σπεκουλάτωρ, ***spekoulatōr***, n. GK: *5063*. executioner:– executioner [1]

4689 σπένδω, ***spendō***, v. GK: *5064* [→ *786*]. (pass.) to be poured out like a drink offering:– offered [2]

4690 σπέρμα, ***sperma***, n. GK: *5065* [→ *4687*]. seed, the part of a plant or animal that can propagate the species (cf. "sperm"); by extension: children, offspring, descendants:– seed [40], seeds [3], issue [1]

4691 σπερμολόγος, ***spermologos***, a. GK: *5066* [→ *4687+3004*]. babbler, chatterer, implying the person has low status, living by picking up scraps:– babbler [1]

4692 σπεύδω, ***speudō***, v. GK: *5067* [→ *4704, 4705, 4706, 4707, 4708, 4709, 4710*]. to hurry, hasten:– make haste [2], hasted [1], hasting [1], made haste [1], with haste [1]

4693 σπήλαιον, ***spēlaion***, n. GK: *5068*. den, cave, hideout:– den [3], dens [2], cave [1]

4694 σπιλάς, ***spilas***, n. GK: *5069* [→ *4696*]. blemish, spot:– spots [1]

4695 σπιλόω, ***spiloō***, v. GK: *5071* [→ *4696*]. to corrupt; (pass.) to be stained, defiled:– defileth [1], spotted [1]

4696 σπίλος, ***spilos***, n. GK: *5070* [→ *784, 4694, 4695*]. stain, blot:– spots [1], spot [1]

4697 σπλαγχνίζομαι, ***splanchnizomai***, v. GK: *5072* [→ *4698*]. to have compassion on, have pity on:– moved with compassion [5], had compassion [4], have compassion [3]

4698 σπλάγχνον, ***splanchnon***, n. GK: *5073* [→ *2155, 4184, 4697*]. inward parts of body: intestines; of emotion: *heart, affection, tenderness, compassion*:– bowels [9], inward affection [1], tender mercy (*+1656*) [1]

4699 σπόγγος, ***spongos***, n. GK: *5074*. sponge:– spunge [3]

4700 σποδός, ***spodos***, n. GK: *5075*. ashes:– ashes [3]

4701 σπορά, ***spora***, n. GK: *5076* [→ *4687*]. seed:– seed [1]

4702 σπόριμος, ***sporimos***, a. GK: *5077* [→ *4687*]. what is sown; (pl.n.) grainfield:– corn fields [2], corn [1]

4703 σπόρος, ***sporos***, n. GK: *5078* [→ *4687*]. seed:– seed [4], seed sown [1]

4704 σπουδάζω, ***spoudazō***, v. GK: *5079* [→ *4692*]. to be eager, make every effort, do one's best:– diligent [2], do diligence [2], endeavoured [1], endeavouring [1], endeavour [1], forward [1], give diligence [1], labour [1], study [1]

4705 σπουδαῖος, ***spoudaios***, a. GK: *5080* [→ *4692*]. zealous, eager, earnest; (compar.) more enthusiastic, very earnest:– diligent [1]

4706 σπουδαιότερον, ***spoudaioteron***, a.compar.neut. of *4705*. GK: *5080* [→ *4692*]. (compar.) more enthusiastic, very earnest:– very diligently [1]

4707 σπουδαιότερος, ***spoudaioteros***, a.compar. of *4705*. GK: *5080* [→ *4692*]. (compar.) more enthusiastic, very earnest:– diligent [1], more forward [1]

4708 σπουδαιοτέρως, ***spoudaioterōs***, adv.compar. of *4709*. GK: *5081* [→ *4692*]. (compar.) all the more eager, with special urgency:– more carefully [1]

4709 σπουδαίως, ***spoudaiōs***, adv. GK: *5081* [→ *4692*]. earnestly, zealously, with vigor; (compar.) all the more eager, with special urgency:– diligently [1], instantly [1]

4710 σπουδή, ***spoudē***, n. GK: *5082* [→ *4692*]. hurry, haste; earnestness, diligence, zeal, eagerness:– diligence [5], haste [2], business [1], carefulness [1], care [1], earnest care [1], forwardness [1]

4711 σπυρίς, ***spyris***, n. GK: *5083*. basket:– baskets [4], basket [1]

4712 στάδιον, ***stadion***, n. GK: *5084* [→ *2476*]. arena, stadium, race course; a unit of length: stade (about 200 yards):– furlongs [5], race [1]

4713 στάμνος, ***stamnos***, n. GK: *5085* [→ *2476*]. jar:– pot [1]

4714 **στάσις, *stasis***, n. GK: *5087* [→ *2476*]. continuance, state of existence; uprising, insurrection, riot; dispute, discord:– dissension [3], sedition [3], insurrection [1], standing [1], uproar [1]

4715 **στατήρ, *statēr***, n. GK: *5088* [→ *2476*]. four-drachma coin, stater (four days' wages):– piece of money [1]

4716 **σταυρός, *stauros***, n. GK: *5089* [→ *388, 4717, 4957; cf. 2476*]. cross:– cross [28]

4717 **σταυρόω, *stauroō***, v. GK: *5090* [→ *4716*]. to crucify:– crucified [31], crucify [15]

4718 **σταφυλή, *staphylē***, n. GK: *5091*. (bunch of) grapes:– grapes [3]

4719 **στάχυς[1], *stachys[1]***, n. GK: *5092* [→ *4720*]. head of grain:– ears of corn [3], ear [2]

4720 **Στάχυς[2], *Stachys[2]***, n.pr. GK: *5093* [→ *4719*]. Stachys, "*head of grain*":– Stachys [1]

4721 **στέγη, *stegē***, n. GK: *5094* [→ *4722*]. roof:– roof [3]

4722 **στέγω, *stegō***, v. GK: *5095* [→ *648, 4721, 5152*]. to put up with, stand, endure; to protect, cover:– forbear [2], beareth [1], suffer [1]

4723 **στεῖρα, *steira***, n. GK: *5096* [→ *4731*]. (state of) barrenness, infertility:– barren [4]

4724 **στέλλω, *stellō***, v. GK: *5097* [→ *649, 1291, 1293, 1992, 2687, 2689, 4749, 4958, 5288, 5289*]. (mid.) to avoid, keep away from:– avoiding [1], withdraw [1]

4725 **στέμμα, *stemma***, n. GK: *5098* [→ *4737*]. wreath, garland:– garlands [1]

4726 **στεναγμός, *stenagmos***, n. GK: *5099* [→ *4728*]. groan, sigh:– groanings [1], groaning [1]

4727 **στενάζω, *stenazō***, v. GK: *5100* [→ *4728*]. to groan, sigh; to grumble:– groan [3], grief [1], grudge [1], sighed [1]

4728 **στενός, *stenos***, a. GK: *5101* [→ *389, 4726, 4727, 4729, 4730, 4959*]. narrow:– strait [3]

4729 **στενοχωρέω, *stenochōreō***, v. GK: *5102* [→ *4728+5562*]. (pass.) to be crushed; to withhold, be restricted:– straitened [2], distressed [1]

4730 **στενοχωρία, *stenochōria***, n. GK: *5103* [→ *4728+5562*]. distress, hardship, difficulty:– distresses [2], anguish [1], distress [1]

4731 **στερεός, *stereos***, a. GK: *5104* [→ *4723, 4732, 4733*]. solid, strong; standing firm, steadfast:– strong [2], stedfast [1], sure [1]

4732 **στερεόω, *stereoō***, v. GK: *5105* [→ *4731*]. to make strong; (pass.) to become strong, be strengthened:– established [1], made strong [1], received strength [1]

4733 **στερέωμα, *stereōma***, n. GK: *5106* [→ *4731*]. firmness, steadfastness:– stedfastness [1]

4734 **Στεφανᾶς, *Stephanas***, n.pr. GK: *5107* [→ *4737*]. Stephanas, "*victor's wreath*":– Stephanas [4]

4735 **στέφανος[2], *stephanos[2]***, n. GK: *5109* [→ *4737*]. woven crown, wreath, victory garland; of various shapes and various materials, leaves, twigs, flowers, even metal, as a sign of victory, honor, and in some contexts, authority:– crown [15], crowns [3]

4736 **Στέφανος[1], *Stephanos[1]***, n.pr. GK: *5108* [→ *4737*]. Stephen, "*victor's wreath*":– Stephen [7]

4737 **στεφανόω, *stephanoō***, v. GK: *5110* [→ *4725, 4734, 4736, 4735*]. to crown, present a wreath:– crowned [2], crownedst [1]

4738 **στῆθος, *stēthos***, n. GK: *5111*. chest, breast:– breast [3], breasts [2]

4739 **στήκω, *stēkō***, v. GK: *5112* [→ *2476*]. to stand, stand firm, be steadfast:– stand fast [6], standeth [1], stand [1]

4740 **στηριγμός, *stērigmos***, n. GK: *5113* [→ *4741*]. security, firmness:– stedfastness [1]

4741 **στηρίζω, *stērizō***, v. GK: *5114* [→ *793, 1991, 4740*]. to strengthen, establish, stand firm; to be resolute:– stablish [6], strengthen [2], established [1], establish [1], fixed [1], stablished [1], stedfastly set [1]

4742 **στίγμα, *stigma***, n. GK: *5116* [→ *4743*]. mark, scar; in context Paul is likely referring to the scars he received in service to Jesus as marks of ownership by his master:– marks [1]

4743 **στιγμή, *stigmē***, n. GK: *5117* [→ *4742*]. instant, moment:– moment [1]

4744 **στίλβω, *stilbō***, v. GK: *5118*. to dazzle, be radiant:– shining [1]

4745 **στοά, *stoa***, n. GK: *5119* [→ *4770; cf. 2476*]. covered colonnade, portico:– porch [3], porches [1]

4746 **στοιβάς, *stoibas***; or **στιβάς, *stibas***, n. GK: *5115 & 5120*. leafy branch:– branches [1]

4747 **στοιχεῖον, *stoicheion***, n. GK: *5122* [→ *4748*]. principle, basic principle; element (of nature); elementary truths:– elements [4], rudiments [2], principles [1]

4748 **στοιχέω, *stoicheō***, v. GK: *5123* [→ *4747, 4960*]. to follow, walk in, adhere to:– walk [4], walkest orderly [1]

4749 **στολή, *stolē***, n. GK: *5124* [→ *4724*]. (flowing) robe:– robes [4], long clothing [1], long garment [1], long robes [1], robe [1]

4750 **στόμα, *stoma***, n. GK: *5125* [→ *653, 1366, 1993, 4751*]. mouth; by extension: edge (of a sword):– mouth [69], face [4], mouths [4], edge [2]

4751 **στόμαχος, *stomachos***, n. GK: *5126* [→ *4750*]. stomach:– stomach's [1]

4752 **στρατεία, *strateia***, n. GK: *5127* [→ *4756*]. warfare; fight:– warfare [2]

4753 **στράτευμα, *strateuma***, n. GK: *5128* [→ *4756*]. army, troops, soldiers:– armies [3], army [3], men of war [1], soldiers [1]

4754 **στρατεύομαι, *strateuomai***, v. GK: *5129* [→ *4756*]. (mid.) to serve as a soldier; to wage war, fight, battle:– war [4], goeth a warfare [1], soldiers [1], warreth [1]

4755 **στρατηγός, *stratēgos***, n. GK: *5130* [→ *4756+71*]. magistrate, praetor; captain, officer:– magistrates [5], captain [3], captains [2]

4756 **στρατιά, *stratia***, n. GK: *5131* [→ *497, 4752, 4753, 4754, 4755, 4757, 4758, 4759, 4760, 4961*]. host, army (of heaven), (celestial) bodies:– host [2]

4757 **στρατιώτης, *stratiōtēs***, n. GK: *5132* [→ *4756*]. soldier:– soldiers [21], soldier [4], soldiers' [1]

4758 **στρατολογέω, *stratologeō***, v. GK: *5133* [→ *4756+3004*]. to gather an army; (ptcp.) commanding officer, with a focus on enlisting soldiers:– chosen to be a soldier [1]

4759 **στρατοπεδάρχης, *stratopedarchēs***, n. GK: *5134 & 5135* [→ *4756+3978+757*]. military commander, commander of a camp:– captain of the guard [1]

4760 **στρατόπεδον, *stratopedon***, n. GK: *5136* [→ *4756+3978*]. army:– armies [1]

4761 **στρεβλόω, *strebloō***, v. GK: *5137* [→ *4762*]. to distort, twist:– wrest [1]

4762 **στρέφω, *strephō***, v. GK: *5138* [→ *390, 391, 654, 1294, 1612, 1994, 1995, 2690, 2692, 3344, 4761, 4962, 4963, 5290*]. to turn, turn away, return; to change, repent, turn one's life:– turned [12], turn [4], converted [1], turning [1]

4763 **στρηνιάω, *strēniaō***, v. GK: *5139* [→ *4764*]. to live in luxury, with an implication that this luxury contributes to improper sensuality and immorality:– lived deliciously [2]

4764 **στρῆνος, *strēnos***, n. GK: *5140* [→ *2691, 4763*]. luxury:– delicacies [1]

4765 **στρουθίον, *strouthion***, n. GK: *5141*. sparrow:– sparrows [4]

4766 **στρώννυμι, *strōnnymi***; or **στρωννύω, *strōnnyō***, v. GK: *5142 & 5143* [→ *2693, 3038, 5291*]. to spread out; (pass.) to be furnished:– furnished [2], spread [2], strawed [2], make bed [1]

4767 **στυγητός, *stygētos***, a. GK: *5144* [→ *655, 2319, 4768*]. hated:– hateful [1]

4768 **στυγνάζω, *stygnazō***, v. GK: *5145* [→ *4767*]. to be gloomy, sad, others translate "shocked, appalled"; (of weather) to be overcast, gloomy:– lowring [1], sad [1]

4769 **στῦλος, *stylos***, n. GK: *5146*. pillar, column; (fig.) leader:– pillars [2], pillar [2]

4770 **Στωϊκός, *Stōikos***, a.pr. GK: *5121 & 5147* [→ *4745*]. Stoic:– Stoicks [1]

4771 **σύ, *sy***, p.pers. GK: *5148* [→ *4571, 4671, 4572, 4674, 4675, 5209, 5210, 5212, 5213, 5216*]. you, your:– you [1194], thee [453], your [375], thy [363], ye [282], thou [213], thine [49], yourselves [9], thine own [8], your own [4], yours [4], youward [2], on your part [1], you (*+3588+5590*) [1], your (*+1537*) [1], your (*+2596*) [1], your own (*+2596*) [1], yours (*+3588*) [1], youwards [1]

4772 **συγγένεια, *syngeneia***, n. GK: *5149* [→ *4862+1096*]. family, relative, one's own people:– kindred [3]

4773 **συγγενής, *syngenēs***, a. GK: *5150 & 5151* [→ *4862+1096*]. family, relative, one's own race or people:– kinsmen [5], kinsman [2], cousins [1], cousin [1], kinsfolks [1], kinsfolk [1], kin [1]

4774 **συγγνώμη, *syngnōmē***, n. GK: *5152* [→ *4862+1097*]. concession:– permission [1]

4775 **συγκάθημαι, *synkathēmai***, v. GK: *5153* [→ *4862+2516*]. to sit with:– sat with [1], sat [1]

4776 **συγκαθίζω, *synkathizō***, v. GK: *5154* [→ *4862+2523*]. to sit down together; to be seated together:– made sit together [1], set down together [1]

4777 **συγκακοπαθέω, *synkakopatheō***, v. GK: *5155* [→ *4862+2556+3958*]. to suffer together with, endure hardship with:– partaker of afflictions [1]

4778 **συγκακουχέομαι, *synkakoucheomai***, v. GK: *5156* [→ *4862+2556+2192*]. (pass.) to be mistreated with:– suffer affliction with [1]

4779 **συγκαλέω, *synkaleō***, v. GK: *5157* [→ *4862+2564*]. (act.) to call together; (mid.) to call to one's side, summon:– called together [5], calleth together [2], call together [1]

4780 **συγκαλύπτω, *synkalyptō***, v. GK: *5158* [→ *4862+2572*]. to conceal:– covered [1]

4781 **συγκάμπτω, *synkamptō***, v. GK: *5159* [→ *4862+2578*]. (pass.) to be bent over:– bow down [1]

4782 **συγκαταβαίνω, *synkatabainō***, v. GK: *5160* [→ *4862+2596+305*]. to come, go down with:– go down with [1]

4783 **συγκατάθεσις, *synkatathesis***, n. GK: *5161* [→ *4862+2596+5087*]. agreement:– agreement [1]

4784 **συγκατατίθημι, *synkatatithēmi***, v. GK: *5163* [→ *4862+2596+5087*]. (mid.) to consent, agree with:– consented [1]

4785 **συγκαταψηφίζομαι, *synkatapsēphizomai***, v. GK: *5164* [→ *4862+2596+5586*]. (pass.) to be added, chosen together with:– numbered [1]

4786 **συγκεράννυμι, *synkerannymi***, v. GK: *5166* [→ *4862+2767*]. to combine, unite:– mixed [1], tempered together [1]

4787 **συγκινέω, *synkineō***, v. GK: *5167* [→ *4862+2795*]. to stir up, arouse:– stirred up [1]

4788 **συγκλείω, *synkleiō***, v. GK: *5168* [→ *4862+2808*]. to catch (fish hemmed up in a net); to confine, imprison, lock up:– concluded [2], inclosed [1], shut up [1]

4789 **συγκληρονόμος, *synklēronomos***, a. GK: *5169* [→ *4862+2819+3551*]. inheriting together; (n.) co-heir:– fellowheirs [1], heirs together [1], heirs with [1], jointheirs with [1]

4790 **συγκοινωνέω, *synkoinōneō***, v. GK: *5170* [→ *4862+2839*]. to share with, be connected with:– communicate with [1], have fellowship with [1], partakers [1]

4791 **συγκοινωνός, *synkoinōnos***, n. GK: *5171* [→ *4862+2839*]. sharer, companion, participant, partner:– companion [1], partaker with [1], partakers [1], partakest (*+1096*) [1]

4792 **συγκομίζω, *synkomizō***, v. GK: *5172* [→ *4862+2889*]. to bury, entomb:– carried [1]

4793 **συγκρίνω, *synkrinō***, v. GK: *5173* [→ *4862+2919*]. to express, explain; to compare:– compare with [1], comparing amongst [1], comparing [1]

4794 **συγκύπτω, *synkyptō***, v. GK: *5174* [→ *4862+2955*]. to bend over, be crippled:– bowed together [1]

4795 **συγκυρία, *synkyria***, n. GK: *5175* [→ *4862*]. event that just happens, coincidence:– chance [1]

4796 **συγχαίρω, *synchairō***, v. GK: *5176* [→ *4862+5463*]. to rejoice with:– rejoice with [5], rejoiced with [1], rejoiceth in [1]

4797 **συγχέω, *syncheō***; or **συγχύνω, *synchynō***, v. GK: *5177 & 5179* [→ *1632; cf. 4862*]. to baffle, confuse; to stir up, cause trouble; (pass.) to be bewildered, confused; to be in an uproar, stirred up:– confounded [2], confused [1], in an uproar [1], stirred up [1]

4798 συγχράομαι, ***synchraomai***, v. GK: *5178* [→ *4862+5530*]. to associate with, have (friendly) dealings with:– have dealings with [1]

4799 σύγχυσις, ***synchysis***, n. GK: *5180* [→ *1632; cf. 4862*]. uproar, confusion:– confusion [1]

4800 συζάω, ***syzaō***, v. GK: *5182* [→ *4862+2198*]. to live with:– live with [3]

4801 συζεύγνυμι, ***syzeugnymi***, v. GK: *5183* [→ *4862+2218*]. to join together:– joined together [2]

4802 συζητέω, ***syzēteō***, v. GK: *5184* [→ *4862+2212*]. to discuss; to debate, argue:– disputed [1], disputing [1], inquire [1], question with [1], questioned [1], questioning with [1], questioning [1], question [1], reasoned [1], reasoning together [1]

4803 συζήτησις, ***syzētēsis***, n. GK: *5185* [→ *4862+2212*]. dispute, discussion:– disputation [1], disputing [1], reasoning [1]

4804 συζητητής, ***syzētētēs***, n. GK: *5186* [→ *4862+2212*]. philosopher, debater:– disputer [1]

4805 σύζυγος, ***syzygos***, a. GK: *5187* [→ *4862+2218*]. yokefellow, comrade:– yokefellow [1]

4806 συζωοποιέω, ***syzōopoieō***, v. GK: *5188* [→ *4862+2198+4160*]. to make alive with (someone):– quickened together with [1], quickened together [1]

4807 συκάμινος, ***sykaminos***, n. GK: *5189*. mulberry tree:– sycamine tree [1]

4808 συκῆ, ***sykē***, n. GK: *5190* [→ *4810*]. fig tree:– fig tree [16]

4809 συκομορέα, ***sykomorea***, n. GK: *5191* [→ *4810*]. sycamore-fig tree:– sycomore tree [1]

4810 σῦκον, ***sykon***, n. GK: *5192* [→ *4808, 4809, 4811*]. fig:– figs [4]

4811 συκοφαντέω, ***sykophanteō***, v. GK: *5193* [→ *4810+5316*]. to accuse falsely, oppress; to cheat, extort:– accuse falsely [1], taken by false accusation [1]

4812 συλαγωγέω, ***sylagōgeō***, v. GK: *5194* [→ *4813+71*]. to take captive:– spoil [1]

4813 συλάω, ***sylaō***, v. GK: *5195* [→ *2416, 2417, 4812*]. to rob:– robbed [1]

4814 συλλαλέω, ***syllaleō***, v. GK: *5196* [→ *4862+2980*]. to talk with, discuss with, confer with:– communed with [1], conferred [1], spake [1], talked with [1], talking with [1], talking [1]

4815 συλλαμβάνω, ***syllambanō***, v. GK: *5197* [→ *4862+2983*]. to seize, arrest, capture; to become pregnant, conceive; to help, come to the aid of:– conceived [4], take [3], took [3], help [2], taken [2], caught [1], conceive [1]

4816 συλλέγω, ***syllegō***, v. GK: *5198* [→ *4862+3004*]. to pick, pull up, collect:– gather [3], gather up [2], gathered [2], gather together [1]

4817 συλλογίζομαι, ***syllogizomai***, v. GK: *5199* [→ *4862+3004*]. to discuss together:– reasoned [1]

4818 συλλυπέω, ***syllypeō***, v. GK: *5200* [→ *4862+3077*] (pass.) to be deeply distressed, grieved with:– grieved [1]

4819 συμβαίνω, ***symbainō***, v. GK: *5201* [→ *4862+305*]. to happen; to come about:– happened [5], befell [1], happen [1], so [1]

4820 συμβάλλω, ***symballō***, v. GK: *5202* [→ *4862+906*]. to dispute with; to confer with, meet with; to ponder; to engage in (war); (mid.) to help, assist:– conferred [1], encountered [1], helped [1], make war against (*+1519+4171*) [1], met with [1], pondered [1]

4821 συμβασιλεύω, ***symbasileuō***, v. GK: *5203* [→ *4862+935*]. to reign with, be king with:– reign with [2]

4822 συμβιβάζω, ***symbibazō***, v. GK: *5204* [→ *4862+305*]. (pass.) to be held together; to be united; (act.) to conclude; to prove; to instruct, teach, advise:– knit together [2], assuredly gathering [1], compacted [1], instruct [1], proving [1]

4823 συμβουλεύω, ***symbouleuō***, v. GK: *5205* [→ *4862+1014*]. to advise, counsel; (mid.) to plot, conspire, consult:– consulted [1], counsel [1], gave counsel [1], took counsel together [1], took counsel [1]

4824 συμβούλιον, ***symboulion***, n. GK: *5206* [→ *4862+1014*]. plan, plot; decision; council:– counsel [5], council [2], consultation [1]

4825 σύμβουλος, ***symboulos***, n. GK: *5207* [→ *4862+1014*]. counselor, advisor:– counseller [1]

4826 Συμεών, ***Symeōn***, n.pr. GK: *5208* [→ *4613*]. Simeon, Simon, "*he has heard* or *obedient one*":– Simeon [6], Simon [1]

4827 συμμαθητής, ***symmathētēs***, n. GK: *5209* [→ *4862+3129*]. fellow disciple:– fellowdisciples [1]

4828 συμμαρτυρέω, ***symmartyreō***, v. GK: *5210* [→ *4862+3144*]. to testify with; to confirm:– also bearing witness [2], beareth witness with [1], testify [1]

4829 συμμερίζομαι, ***symmerizomai***, v. GK: *5211* [→ *4862+3313*]. to share with:– partakers with [1]

4830 συμμέτοχος, ***symmetochos***, a. GK: *5212* [→ *4862+3326+2192*]. sharing with, being partner with, derived from the Greek verb "to share in the possession of something," not found in the NT:– partakers with [1], partakers [1]

4831 συμμιμητής, ***symmimētēs***, n. GK: *5213* [→ *4862+3401*]. fellow imitator:– followers together [1]

4832 σύμμορφος, ***symmorphos***, a. GK: *5215* [→ *4862+3444*]. conformed, being like:– conformed to [1], fashioned like unto [1]

4833 συμμορφόω, ***symmorphoō***, v. GK: *5214 & 5216* [→ *4862+3444*]. to give the same form:– made conformable [1]

4834 συμπαθέω, ***sympatheō***, v. GK: *5217* [→ *4862+3958*]. to sympathize with:– had compassion [1], touched with the feeling [1]

4835 συμπαθής, ***sympathēs***, a. GK: *5218* [→ *4862+3958*]. sympathetic:– compassion one of another [1]

4836 συμπαραγίνομαι, ***symparaginomai***, v. GK: *5219* [→ *4862+3844+1096*]. (mid.) to come together:– came together [1], stood with [1]

4837 συμπαρακαλέω, ***symparakaleō***, v. GK: *5220* [→ *4862+3844+2564*]. (pass.) to be mutually encouraged:– comforted together [1]

4838 συμπαραλαμβάνω, ***symparalambanō***, v. GK: *5221* [→ *4862+3844+2983*]. to take along with:– take with [2], took with [2]

4839 συμπαραμένω, ***symparamenō***, v. GK: *5222* [→ *4862+3844+3306*]. to stay with (someone) to help:– continue with [1]

4840 συμπάρειμι, ***sympareimi***, v. GK: *5223* [→ *4862+3844+1510*]. to be present with:– here present with [1]

4841 συμπάσχω, ***sympaschō***, v. GK: *5224* [→ *4862+3958*]. to suffer with, share in suffering:– suffer with [2]

4842 συμπέμπω, ***sympempō***, v. GK: *5225* [→ *4862+3992*]. to send with:– sent with [1], sent [1]

4843 συμπεριλαμβάνω, ***symperilambanō***, v. GK: *5227* [→ *4862+4012+2983*]. to put one's arms around, embrace:– embracing [1]

4844 συμπίνω, ***sympinō***, v. GK: *5228* [→ *4862+4095*]. to drink with:– drink with [1]

4845 συμπληρόω, ***symplēroō***, v. GK: *5230* [→ *4862+4137*]. (pass.) to be swamped, become full; to be fulfilled, come to an end:– come [1], filled [1], fully come [1]

4846 συμπνίγω, ***sympnigō***, v. GK: *5231* [→ *4862+4155*]. to choke; to crush:– choked [2], choke [2], thronged [1]

4847 συμπολίτης, ***sympolitēs***, n. GK: *5232* [→ *4862+4172*]. fellow citizen:– fellowcitizens with [1]

4848 συμπορεύομαι, ***symporeuomai***, v. GK: *5233* [→ *4862+4198*]. to go with, come together:– went with [3], resort [1]

4849 συμπόσιον, ***symposion***, n. GK: *5235* [→ *4862+4095*]. group:– by companies (*+4849*) [2]

4850 συμπρεσβύτερος, ***sympresbyteros***, n. GK: *5236* [→ *4862+4245*]. fellow elder:– also an elder [1]

συμφάγω, ***sumphagō***. See **4906**.

4851 συμφέρω, ***sympherō***, v. GK: *5237* [→ *4862+5342*]. to bring together; to be helpful, be gained; (n.) common good; (imper. verb) it is good, better, beneficial:– expedient [7], profitable [3], profit [3], better [1], brought together [1], good [1], profit withal [1]

4852 σύμφημι, ***symphēmi***, v. GK: *5238* [→ *4862+5346*]. to agree with:– consent [1]

4853 συμφυλέτης, ***symphyletēs***, n. GK: *5241* [→ *4862+5443*]. (pl.) one's own countrymen, people:– countrymen [1]

4854 σύμφυτος, ***symphytos***, a. GK: *5242* [→ *4862+5453*]. united, being one with:– planted together [1]

4855 συμφύω, ***symphyō***, v. GK: *5243* [→ *4862+5453*]. to grow up with:– sprang up with [1]

4856 συμφωνέω, ***symphōneō***, v. GK: *5244* [→ *4862+5456*]. to agree with; to match, fit in with:– agree [2], agree with [1], agreed together [1], agreed [1], agreeth [1]

4857 συμφώνησις, ***symphōnēsis***, n. GK: *5245* [→ *4862+5456*]. harmony, agreement:– concord [1]

4858 συμφωνία, ***symphōnia***, n. GK: *5246* [→ *4862+5456*]. music:– musick [1]

4859 σύμφωνος, ***symphonos***, a. GK: *5247* [→ *4862+5456*]. mutually consenting, agreeing; (n.) mutual agreement:– consent [1]

4860 συμψηφίζω, ***sympsēphizō***, v. GK: *5248* [→ *4862+5586*]. to calculate, compute:– counted [1]

4861 σύμψυχος, ***sympsychos***, a. GK: *5249* [→ *4862+5594*]. united in spirit, harmonious:– one accord [1]

4862 σύν, ***syn***, pp. GK: *5250* [→ *799, 800, 801, 802, 1996, 1998, 1999, 3342, 4772, 4773, 4774, 4775, 4776, 4777, 4778, 4779, 4780, 4781, 4782, 4783, 4784, 4785, 4786, 4787, 4788, 4789, 4790, 4791, 4792, 4793, 4794, 4795, 4796, 4797, 4798, 4799, 4800, 4801, 4802, 4803, 4804, 4805, 4806, 4814, 4815, 4816, 4817, 4818, 4819, 4820, 4821, 4822, 4823, 4824, 4825, 4827, 4828, 4829, 4830, 4831, 4832, 4833, 4834, 4835, 4836, 4837, 4838, 4839, 4840, 4841, 4842, 4843, 4844, 4845, 4846, 4847, 4848, 4849, 4850, 4851, 4852, 4853, 4854, 4855, 4856, 4857, 4858, 4859, 4860, 4861, 4863, 4864, 4865, 4866, 4867, 4868, 4869, 4870, 4872, 4873, 4874, 4875, 4876, 4877, 4878, 4879, 4880, 4881, 4882, 4883, 4884, 4885, 4886, 4887, 4888, 4889, 4890, 4891, 4892, 4893, 4894, 4895, 4896, 4897, 4898, 4899, 4900, 4901, 4902, 4903, 4904, 4905, 4906, 4907, 4908, 4909, 4910, 4911, 4912, 4913, 4914, 4915, 4916, 4917, 4918, 4919, 4920, 4921, 4922, 4923, 4924, 4925, 4926, 4927, 4928, 4929, 4930, 4931, 4932, 4933, 4934, 4935, 4936, 4937, 4938, 4939, 4940, 4941, 4942, 4943, 4944, 4945, 4952, 4953, 4954, 4955, 4956, 4957, 4958, 4959, 4960, 4961, 4962, 4963, 4964*]. with; as, besides, a marker which shows association with another thing or person:– with [121], accompanied (*+2064*) [1], and [1], beside [1], with also [1]

4863 συνάγω, ***synagō***, v. GK: *5251* [→ *4862+71*]. to gather together, assemble; invite, call together:– gathered together [20], gathered [8], gather [7], came together [6], assembled [4], gather together [3], gathereth [3], took in [3], assembled together [2], bestow [2], gather up [1], gathering [1], leadeth [1], resorted [1]

4864 συναγωγή, ***synagōgē***, n. GK: *5252* [→ *656, 752, 1997*]. synagogue, congregation, meeting, a gathering of worshipers, usually a Jewish congregation, though in some contexts it may refer to a Christian assembly; a synagogue building:– synagogue [33], synagogues [22], assembly [1], congregation [1]

4865 συναγωνίζομαι, ***synagōnizomai***, v. GK: *5253* [→ *4862+73*]. to join in a struggle, help, assist:– strive together with [1]

4866 συναθλέω, ***synathleō***, v. GK: *5254* [→ *4862+118*]. to contend at one's side, together:– laboured with [1], striving together [1]

4867 συναθροίζω, ***synathroizō***, v. GK: *5255* [→ *4862; cf. 1865*]. to bring together; (pass.) to be gathered:– gathered together [2], called together [1]

4868 συναίρω, ***synairō***, v. GK: *5256* [→ *4862+142*]. to settle (monetary accounts):– reckoneth (*+3056*) [1], reckon [1], take [1]

4869 συναιχμάλωτος, ***synaichmalōtos***, n. GK: *5257* [→ *4862+164*]. fellow prisoner:– fellowprisoner [2], fellowprisoners [1]

4870 συνακολουθέω, ***synakoloutheō***, v. GK: *5258* [→ *4862+190; cf. 1.3*]. to follow, accompany:– followed [1], follow [1]

4871 συναλίζω, ***synalizō***, v. GK: *5259*. to eat with:– assembled together with [1]

4872 συναναβαίνω, ***synanabainō***, v. GK: *5262* [→ *4862+303+305*]. to come with, travel with:– came up with [2]

4873 συνανάκειμαι, *synanakeimai*, v. GK: *5263* [→ *4862+303+2749*]. to eat with, have dinner with:– sat at meat with [2], sat with [2], sat also together with [1], sat at the table with [1], sat down with [1], sat with at meat [1], sit at meat with [1]

4874 συναναμείγνυμι, *synanameignymi*, v. GK: *5264* [→ *4862+303+3396*]. to associate with:– company with [1], have company with [1], keep company [1]

4875 συναναπαύομαι, *synanapauomai*, v. GK: *5265* [→ *4862+303+3973*]. to find rest together, be refreshed together:– with refreshed [1]

4876 συναντάω, *synantaō*, v. GK: *5267* [→ *4862+473*]. to meet; to happen to:– met [4], befall [1], meet [1]

4877 συνάντησις, *synantēsis*, n. GK: *5268* [→ *4862+473*]. meeting:– meet [1]

4878 συναντιλαμβάνομαι, *synantilambanomai*, v. GK: *5269* [→ *4862+473+2983*]. to help, come to the aid of:– helpeth [1], help [1]

4879 συναπάγω, *synapagō*, v. GK: *5270* [→ *4862+575+71*]. (pass.) to be led away, carried off; to associate with (the lowly):– carried away with [1], condescend to [1], led away with [1]

4880 συναποθνήσκω, *synapothnēskō*, v. GK: *5271* [→ *4862+575+2348*]. to die with:– dead with [1], die with [1], die [1]

4881 συναπόλλυμι, *synapollymi*, v. GK: *5272* [→ *4862+575+3639*]. (mid.) to die with, perish with:– perished with [1]

4882 συναποστέλλω, *synapostellō*, v. GK: *5273* [→ *4862+649*]. to send with:– sent [1]

4883 συναρμολογέω, *synarmologeō*, v. GK: *5274* [→ *4862+718+3004*]. (pass.) to be joined together, fit together:– fitly framed together [1], fitly joined together [1]

4884 συναρπάζω, *synarpazō*, v. GK: *5275* [→ *4862+726*]. to seize; (pass.) to be caught, seized:– caught [4]

4885 συναυξάνω, *synauxanō*, v. GK: *5277* [→ *4862+837*]. to grow together:– grow together [1]

4886 σύνδεσμος, *syndesmos*, n. GK: *5278* [→ *4862+1210*]. bond; sinew; captive:– bond [3], bands [1]

4887 συνδέω, *syndeō*, v. GK: *5279* [→ *4862+1210*]. (pass.) to be imprisoned with, bound with:– bound with [1]

4888 συνδοξάζω, *syndoxazō*, v. GK: *5280* [→ *4862+1391*]. (pass.) to be glorified with, share glory with:– glorified together [1]

4889 σύνδουλος, *syndoulos*, n. GK: *5281* [→ *4862+1401*]. fellow servant, fellow slave:– fellowservant [6], fellowservants [4]

συνδρέμω, *sundremō*. See **4936**.

4890 συνδρομή, *syndromē*, n. GK: *5282* [→ *4862+5143*]. running together:– ran together (*+1096*) [1]

4891 συνεγείρω, *synegeirō*, v. GK: *5283* [→ *4862+1453*]. to raise up with:– risen with [2], raised up together [1]

4892 συνέδριον, *synedrion*, n. GK: *5284* [→ *4862+1476*]. Sanhedrin; (local) council:– council [20], councils [2]

4893 συνείδησις, *syneidēsis*, n. GK: *5287* [→ *4862+1492 or* 3708]. conscience:– conscience [31], consciences [1]

4894 συνείδω, *syneidō*, v. GK: *5288* [→ *4862+1492 or* 3708]. to consider, know:– considered [1], know [1], privy [1], ware [1]

4895 σύνειμι[1], *syneimi*[1], v. GK: *5289* [→ *4862+1510*]. to be with; (n.) companion:– with [2]

4896 σύνειμι[2], *syneimi*[2], v. GK: *5290* [→ *4862*]. to gather together, come together:– gathered together [1]

4897 συνεισέρχομαι, *syneiserchomai*, v. GK: *5291* [→ *4862+1519+2064*]. to enter together with:– went in with [1], went with [1]

4898 συνέκδημος, *synekdēmos*, n. GK: *5292* [→ *4862+1537+1218*]. traveling companion:– companions in travel [1], travel with [1]

4899 συνεκλεκτός, *syneklektos*, a. GK: *5293* [→ *4862+1537+3004*]. chosen together with:– elected together with [1]

4900 συνελαύνω, *synelaunō*, v. GK: *5295* [→ *4862+1643*]. to drive, force, bring:– set at one (*+1515+1519*) [1]

4901 συνεπιμαρτυρέω, *synepimartyreō*, v. GK: *5296* [→ *4862+1909+3144*]. to testify at the same time:– also bearing witness [1]

4902 συνέπομαι, *synepomai*, v. GK: *5299* [→ *4862*]. to accompany:– accompanied [1]

4903 συνεργέω, *synergeō*, v. GK: *5300* [→ *4862+2041*]. to work together, work with; (n.) fellow worker:– helpeth with [1], work together [1], workers together [1], working with [1], wrought with [1]

4904 συνεργός, *synergos*, a. GK: *5301* [→ *4862+2041*]. fellow worker:– fellowlabourers [2], fellowlabourer [2], helpers [2], companion in labour [1], fellowhelpers [1], fellowhelper [1], fellowworkers [1], helper [1], labourers together with [1], workfellow [1]

4905 συνέρχομαι, *synerchomai*, v. GK: *5302* [→ *4862+2064*]. to come together, gather, assemble; to go along with, accompany:– come together [12], came together [4], came with [3], went with [3], come [2], accompanied [1], came [1], cometh together [1], companied with [1], go with [1], resorted [1], resort [1], with assembled [1]

4906 συνεσθίω, *synesthiō*, v. GK: *5303* [→ *4862+2068*]. to eat with:– eat [2], eat with [1], eateth with [1], with to eat [1]

4907 σύνεσις, *synesis*, n. GK: *5304* [→ *863; cf. 4862*]. understanding, insight; intelligence, the faculty of comprehension, often referring to wisdom and insight in spiritual matters:– understanding [6], knowledge [1]

4908 συνετός, *synetos*, a. GK: *5305* [→ *863; cf. 4862*]. intelligent, learned, with good sense:– prudent [4]

4909 συνευδοκέω, *syneudokeō*, v. GK: *5306* [→ *4862+2095+1380*]. to approve of, give approval; to be willing:– consenting [2], pleased [2], allow [1], pleasure [1]

4910 συνευωχέομαι, *syneuōcheomai*, v. GK: *5307* [→ *4862+2095+2192*]. to partake in a feast together:– feast with [2]

4911 συνεφίστημι, *synephistēmi*, v. GK: *5308* [→ *4862+1909+2476*]. to join in an attack:– rose up together [1]

4912 συνέχω, *synechō*, v. GK: *5309* [→ *4862+2192*]. to cover (ears); to crowd (against); to guard, hold in custody; to compel, urge on; (pass.) to suffer, be distressed; to be devoted to:– taken with [2], constraineth [1], held [1], in a strait [1], keep in [1], pressed [1], sick of [1], stopped [1], straitened [1], taken [1], throng [1]

4913 συνήδομαι, *synēdomai*, v. GK: *5310* [→ *4862+2237*]. to delight in agreement:– delight in [1]

4914 συνήθεια, *synētheia*, n. GK: *5311* [→ *4862+1485*]. custom, practice:– custom [2]

4915 συνηλικιώτης, *synēlikiōtēs*, n. GK: *5312* [→ *4862+2245*]. person of one's own age, contemporary:– equals [1]

4916 συνθάπτω, *synthaptō*, v. GK: *5313* [→ *4862+2290*]. (pass.) to be buried with:– buried with [2]

4917 συνθλάω, *synthlaō*, v. GK: *5314* [→ *4862*]. (pass.) to be broken to pieces:– broken [2]

4918 συνθλίβω, *synthlibō*, v. GK: *5315* [→ *4862+2346*]. to press around, crowd against:– thronged [1], thronging [1]

4919 συνθρύπτω, *synthryptō*, v. GK: *5316* [→ *4862*]. to break:– break [1]

4920 συνίημι, *syniēmi*, v. GK: *5317 & 5320* [→ *863; cf. 4862*]. to understand, realize:– understand [13], understood [7], understandeth [3], considered [1], understanding [1], wise [1]

4921 συνιστάω, *synistaō*; or **συνίστημι, *synistēmi***, v. GK: *5318 & 5319* [→ *4862+2476*]. to commend, recommend; to demonstrate, bring out, prove to be; (intr.) to stand with; to hold together; to be formed:– commend [5], commendeth [3], approved [1], approving [1], commended [1], commending [1], consist [1], make [1], standing [1], stood with [1]

4922 συνοδεύω, *synodeuō*, v. GK: *5321* [→ *4862+3598*]. to travel with:– journeyed with [1]

4923 συνοδία, *synodia*, n. GK: *5322* [→ *4862+3598*]. company of travelers, caravan:– company [1]

4924 συνοικέω, *synoikeō*, v. GK: *5324* [→ *4862+3624*]. to live with:– dwell with [1]

4925 συνοικοδομέω, *synoikodomeō*, v. GK: *5325* [→ *4862+3624+1430*]. (pass.) to be built up together:– builded together [1]

4926 συνομιλέω, *synomileō*, v. GK: *5326* [→ *4862+3656*]. to talk with, converse with:– talked with [1]

4927 συνομορέω, *synomoreō*, v. GK: *5327* [→ *4862+3664+3724*]. to be next door to:– joined hard to [1]

4928 συνοχή, *synochē*, n. GK: *5330* [→ *4862+2192*]. anguish, distress:– anguish [1], distress [1]

4929 συντάσσω, *syntassō*, v. GK: *5332* [→ *4862+5021*]. to command, direct, instruct:– appointed [2]

4930 συντέλεια, *synteleia*, n. GK: *5333* [→ *4862+5056*]. end, close, completion:– end [6]

4931 συντελέω, *synteleō*, v. GK: *5334* [→ *4862+5056*]. to finish, accomplish; (pass.) to be fulfilled, be over, accomplished:– ended [4], finish [1], fulfilled [1], make [1]

4932 συντέμνω, *syntemnō*, v. GK: *5335* [→ *4862+5114*]. to cut short, speed up:– cut short [1], short [1]

4933 συντηρέω, *syntēreō*, v. GK: *5337* [→ *4862+5083*]. to protect, defend; to treasure, preserve in memory; (pass.) to be preserved:– preserved [2], kept [1], observed [1]

4934 συντίθημι, *syntithēmi*, v. GK: *5338* [→ *4862+5087*]. (mid.) to agree, decide:– agreed [2], assented [1], covenanted [1]

4935 συντόμως, *syntomōs*, adv. GK: *5339* [→ *4862+5114*]. briefly:– few words [1]

4936 συντρέχω, *syntrechō*, v. GK: *5340* [→ *4862+5143*]. to run together, go together; by extension, to be closely associated in a particular behavior or undertaking:– ran together [1], ran [1], run with [1]

4937 συντρίβω, *syntribō*, v. GK: *5341* [→ *4862+5147*]. to break, destroy; (pass.) to be broken, bruised, dashed to pieces:– brake [1], broken in pieces [1], broken to shivers [1], brokenhearted [1], broken [1], bruised [1], bruise [1], bruising [1]

4938 σύντριμμα, *syntrimma*, n. GK: *5342* [→ *4862+5147*]. ruin, destruction:– destruction [1]

4939 σύντροφος, *syntrophos*, a. GK: *5343* [→ *4862+5142*]. brought up with (in a family); this can refer to a foster sibling or an intimate friend:– brought up with [1]

4940 συντυγχάνω, *syntynchanō*, v. GK: *5344* [→ *4862+5177*]. to come together with, meet:– come at [1]

4941 Συντύχη, *Syntychē*, n.pr. GK: *5345* [→ *4862+5177*]. Syntyche, "*coincidence, success*":– Syntyche [1]

4942 συνυποκρίνομαι, *synypokrinomai*, v. GK: *5347* [→ *4862+5259+2919*]. to join in one's hypocrisy:– dissembled with [1]

4943 συνυπουργέω, *synypourgeō*, v. GK: *5348* [→ *4862+5259+2041*]. to join to help:– helping together [1]

4944 συνωδίνω, *synōdinō*, v. GK: *5349* [→ *4862+5604*]. to join in the pains of childbirth, suffer agony together:– travaileth in pain together [1]

4945 συνωμοσία, *synōmosia*, n. GK: *5350* [→ *4862+3660*]. plot, conspiracy:– conspiracy [1]

4946 Συράκουσαι, *Syrakousai*, n.pr. GK: *5352*. Syracuse:– Syracuse [1]

4947 Συρία, *Syria*, n.pr. GK: *5353* [→ *4948*]. Syria:– Syria [8]

4948 Σύρος, *Syros*, n.pr.g. GK: *5354* [→ *4947, 4949*]. Syrian:– Syrian [1]

4949 Συροφοίνισσα, *Syrophoinissa*, n.pr.g. GK: *5356* [→ *4948+5404*]. Syrophoenician:– Syrophenician [1]

4950 Σύρτις, *Syrtis*, n.pr. GK: *5358* [→ *4951*]. Syrtis, feared for its shifting sandbars and unpredictable currents:– quicksands [1]

4951 σύρω, *syrō*, v. GK: *5359* [→ *2694, 4950*]. to drag, tow; to sweep:– drew [3], dragging [1], haling [1]

4952 συσπαράσσω, *sysparassō*, v. GK: *5360* [→ *4862+4685*]. to cause to convulse:– tare [1]

4953 σύσσημον, *syssēmon*, n. GK: *5361* [→ *4862+4592*]. signal:– token [1]

4954 σύσσωμος, *syssōmos*, a. GK: *5362* [→ *4862+4983*]. co-member of a body:– of same body [1]

4955 συστασιαστής, *systasiastēs*, n. GK: *5363* [→ *4862+2476*]. fellow insurrectionist:– made insurrection with [1]

4956 συστατικός, *systatikos*, a. GK: *5364* [→ *4862+2476*]. commendatory, recommended:– commendation [2]

4957 **συσταυρόω, *systauroō***, v. GK: *5365* [→ *4862+4716*]. (pass.) to be crucified with:– crucified with [5]

4958 **συστέλλω, *systellō***, v. GK: *5366* [→ *4862+4724*]. to wrap up, cover up; (pass.) to be shortened, limited:– short [1], wound up [1]

4959 **συστενάζω, *systenazō***, v. GK: *5367* [→ *4862+4728*]. to join in groaning, groan together:– groaneth [1]

4960 **συστοιχέω, *systoicheō***, v. GK: *5368* [→ *4862+4748*]. to correspond:– answereth to [1]

4961 **συστρατιώτης, *systratiōtēs***, n. GK: *5369* [→ *4862+4756*]. fellow soldier:– fellowsoldier [2]

4962 **συστρέφω, *systrephō***, v. GK: *5370* [→ *4862+4762*]. to gather up, bring together:– gathered [1]

4963 **συστροφή, *systrophē***, n. GK: *5371* [→ *4862+4762*]. commotion, disorderly gathering, mob; conspiracy, plot:– banded together (+*4160*) [1], concourse [1]

4964 **συσχηματίζω, *syschēmatizō***, v. GK: *5372* [→ *4862+4976*]. (mid.) to conform to a pattern or mold; (pass.) to be conformed to a pattern or mold:– conformed to [1], fashioning according to [1]

4965 **Συχάρ, *Sychar***, n.pr. GK: *4993 & 5373*. Sychar:– Sychar [1]

4966 **Συχέμ, *Sychem***, n.pr. GK: *5374*. Shechem, "[poss.] *shoulder [saddle of a hill]; shoulders [and upper back]*":– Sychem [2]

4967 **σφαγή, *sphagē***, n. GK: *5375* [→ *4969*]. slaughter:– slaughter [3]

4968 **σφάγιον, *sphagion***, n. GK: *5376* [→ *4969*]. offering for slaughter:– slain beasts [1]

4969 **σφάζω, *sphazō***, v. GK: *5377* [→ *2695, 4967, 4968*]. to kill, slay, murder:– slain [6], slew [2], kill [1], wounded [1]

4970 **σφόδρα, *sphodra***, adv. GK: *5379* [→ *4971*]. very, greatly, exceedingly:– exceeding [4], very [3], greatly [2], exceedingly [1], sore [1]

4971 **σφοδρῶς, *sphodrōs***, adv. GK: *5380* [→ *4970*]. violently:– exceedingly [1]

4972 **σφραγίζω, *sphragizō***, v. GK: *5381* [→ *4973*]. to seal, to put a mark on an object to show possession, authority, identity, or security:– sealed [20], seal [2], sealing [1], set a seal [1], set to seal [1]

4973 **σφραγίς, *sphragis***, n. GK: *5382* [→ *2696, 4972*]. seal:– seal [11], seals [5]

4974 **σφυρόν, *sphyron***, n. GK: *5383 & 5384*. ankle or heel:– ankle [1]

4975 **σχεδόν, *schedon***, adv. GK: *5385* [→ *2192*]. nearly, almost:– almost [3]

σχέω, *scheō*. See **2192**.

4976 **σχῆμα, *schēma***, n. GK: *5386* [→ *807, 808, 809, 2156, 2157, 2158, 3345, 4964; cf. 2192*]. form, outward appearance:– fashion [1], in fashion [1]

4977 **σχίζω, *schizō***, v. GK: *5387* [→ *4978*]. to tear, divide; (pass.) to be torn, divided, split (in opinion):– rent [5], divided [2], broken [1], maketh a rent [1], opened [1]

4978 **σχίσμα, *schisma***, n. GK: *5388* [→ *4977*]. tear, split, divide an object into parts, with an implication that the object is now damaged; by extension: division, dissension, implying discord and damage to the unity of the original group:– division [3], divisions [2], rent [2], schism [1]

4979 **σχοινίον, *schoinion***, n. GK: *5389*. (pl.) cords, ropes:– ropes [1], small cords [1]

4980 **σχολάζω, *scholazō***, v. GK: *5390* [→ *4981*]. to devote oneself to; to be unoccupied, stand empty:– empty [1], give [1]

4981 **σχολή, *scholē***, n. GK: *5391* [→ *4980*]. lecture hall, a building in which students meet for discussion and study, school:– school [1]

4982 **σῴζω, *sōzō***, v. GK: *5392* [→ *810, 811, 1295, 4986, 4989, 4990, 4991, 4992*]. to save, rescue, deliver; to heal; by extension: to be in right relationship with God, with the implication that the condition before salvation was one of grave danger or distress:– saved [53], save [41], made whole [9], healed [3], whole [2], do well [1], preserve [1]

4983 **σῶμα, *sōma***, n. GK: *5393* [→ *4954, 4984, 4985*]. body, the mass of anything, usually a corporeal tissue, human, animal, or plant, though it can also refer to a heavenly body; the church is said to be like a (human) body, emphasizing its essential unity with very important diversities of function within the unity:– body [132], bodies [11], bodily [1], body's [1], slaves [1]

4984 **σωματικός, *sōmatikos***, a. GK: *5394* [→ *4983*]. bodily, physical:– bodily [2]

4985 **σωματικῶς, *sōmatikōs***, adv. GK: *5395* [→ *4983*]. in bodily form, corporeally:– bodily [1]

4986 **Σώπατρος, *Sōpatros***, n.pr. GK: *5396* [→ *4982+3962*]. Sopater, "*saving one's father*":– Sopater [1]

4987 **σωρεύω, *sōreuō***, v. GK: *5397* [→ *2002*]. to heap up, pile up; (pass.) to be loaded down:– heap [1], laden [1]

4988 **Σωσθένης, *Sōsthenēs***, n.pr. GK: *5398*. Sosthenes:– Sosthenes [2]

4989 **Σωσίπατρος, *Sōsipatros***, n.pr. GK: *5399* [→ *4982+3962*]. Sosipater, "*saving one's father*":– Sosipater [1]

4990 **σωτήρ, *sōtēr***, n. GK: *5400* [→ *4982*]. Savior, one who delivers from grave danger; note that in the NT this always refers to God the Father and Jesus Christ as Savior of believers from righteous wrath to a proper relationship with God:– saviour [24]

4991 **σωτηρία, *sōtēria***, n. GK: *5401* [→ *4982*]. salvation, rescue, deliverance, the state of not being in grave danger and so being safe; this can refer to ordinary dangers and conditions on earth, but it usually refers to the state of believers being safe from righteous wrath in a proper relationship with God:– salvation [40], saved [2], deliver (+*1325*) [1], health [1], saving [1]

4992 **σωτήριον, *sōtērion***, n. GK: *5402* [→ *4982*]. salvation; this word can focus on the message or means of salvation:– salvation [5]

4993 **σωφρονέω, *sōphroneō***, v. GK: *5404* [→ *4994, 4995, 4996, 4997, 4998; cf. 5131*]. to be in a right state of mind, have sober judgment; to be self-controlled:– in right mind [2], sober [2], sober minded [1], soberly [1]

4994 **σωφρονίζω, *sōphronizō***, v. GK: *5405* [→ *4993*]. to train, encourage, advise, urge:– teach to be sober [1]

4995 **σωφρονισμός, *sōphronismos***, n. GK: *5406* [→ *4993*]. self-discipline, with an implication that this discipline demonstrates prudence and wisdom:– sound mind [1]

4996 **σωφρόνως, *sōphronōs***, adv. GK: *5407* [→ *4993*]. in self-control:– soberly [1]

4997 **σωφροσύνη, *sōphrosynē***, n. GK: *5408* [→ *4993*]. propriety, appropriateness; reasonableness, mental soundness:– sobriety [2], soberness [1]

4998 **σώφρων, *sōphrōn***, a. GK: *5409* [→ *4993*]. self-controlled, implied to be wise and prudent in nature:– sober [2], discreet [1], temperate [1]

τά, *ta*. See **3588**.

4999 **ταβέρναι, *tabernai***, n.pr. GK: *5411* [→ *5140+4999*]. tavern, shop, store:– taverns [1]

5000 **Ταβιθά, *Tabitha***, n.pr. GK: *5412*. Tabitha, "*gazelle*":– Tabitha [2]

5001 **τάγμα, *tagma***, n. GK: *5413* [→ *5021*]. turn, order, arrangement:– order [1]

5002 **τακτός, *taktos***, a. GK: *5414* [→ *5021*]. appointed, fixed:– set [1]

5003 **ταλαιπωρέω, *talaipōreō***, v. GK: *5415* [→ *5005*]. to grieve, lament:– afflicted [1]

5004 **ταλαιπωρία, *talaipōria***, n. GK: *5416* [→ *5005*]. misery, distress:– miseries [1], misery [1]

5005 **ταλαίπωρος, *talaipōros***, a. GK: *5417* [→ *5003, 5004*]. wretched, miserable:– wretched [2]

5006 **ταλαντιαῖος, *talantiaios***, a. GK: *5418* [→ *5007*]. weighing a talent (about 57 to 80 lbs.):– weight of a talent [1]

5007 **τάλαντον, *talanton***, n. GK: *5419* [→ *5006*]. talent (weight and monetary unit; about 57 to 80 lbs.); a talent of silver was about 6,000 days' wages (denarii) of a common laborer and a talent of gold was about 180,000 day's wages, often implying a vast, unattainable amount:– talents [12], talent [3]

5008 **ταλιθά, *talitha***, l.[n.]. GK: *5420*. talitha (Aramaic: "little girl"):– talitha [1]

5009 **ταμεῖον, *tameion***, n. GK: *5421* [→ *5114*]. room, inner room, storeroom:– closets [1], closet [1], secret chambers [1], storehouse [1]

ταννῦν, *tanun*. See **3568**.

5010 **τάξις, *taxis***, n. GK: *5423* [→ *5021*]. order, succession; kind, nature:– order [10]

5011 **ταπεινός, *tapeinos***, a. GK: *5424* [→ *5012, 5013, 5014*]. humble, lowly, downcast, timid:– humble [2], low degree [2], base [1], cast down [1], lowly [1], of low estate [1]

5012 **ταπεινοφροσύνη, *tapeinophrosynē***, n. GK: *5425* [→ *5011+5424*]. humility, humbleness, modesty:– humility [3], humbleness of mind [1], humility of mind [1], lowliness of mind [1], lowliness [1]

5013 **ταπεινόω, *tapeinoō***, v. GK: *5427* [→ *5011*]. (act.) to humble (oneself), lower (oneself); (pass.) to be humbled, brought low, in need:– humble [5], abased [4], humbleth [2], abasing [1], brought low [1], humbled [1]

5014 **ταπείνωσις, *tapeinōsis***, n. GK: *5428* [→ *5011*]. humbleness, lowliness, humiliation:– humiliation [1], low estate [1], made low [1], vile [1]

5015 **ταράσσω, *tarassō***, v. GK: *5429* [→ *1298, 1613, 5016, 5017*]. to trouble, disturb, throw into confusion; (pass.) to be disturbed, terrified, confused; to be stirred up:– troubled [15], troubleth [1], trouble [1]

5016 **ταραχή, *tarachē***, n. GK: *5430* [→ *5015*]. disturbance:– troubles [1], troubling [1]

5017 **τάραχος, *tarachos***, n. GK: *5431* [→ *5015*]. commotion; disturbance:– stir [2]

5018 **Ταρσεύς, *Tarseus***, n.pr.g. GK: *5432* [→ *5019*]. Tarsus:– Tarsus [2]

5019 **Ταρσός, *Tarsos***, n.pr. GK: *5433* [→ *5018*]. Tarsus:– Tarsus [3]

5020 **ταρταρόω, *tartaroō***, v. GK: *5434*. to send to hell, hold captive in Tartarus; a derivative of the Greek noun "Tartarus," a place of torture and torment lower than Hades in Greek and Jewish apocalyptic literature, not found in the NT:– cast down to hell [1]

5021 **τάσσω, *tassō***, v. GK: *5435* [→ *392, 498, 506, 657, 812, 813, 814, 1296, 1297, 1299, 1928, 2003, 2004, 4367, 4384, 4929, 5001, 5002, 5010, 5292, 5293*]. (act./mid.) to appoint, determine, arrange; devote; (pass.) to be established, appointed, assigned:– appointed [3], ordained [2], addicted [1], determined [1], set [1]

5022 **ταῦρος, *tauros***, n. GK: *5436*. bull, ox:– bulls [2], oxen [2]

5023 **ταῦτα, *tauta***, p.demo.neut.pl. of *3778*. GK: *4047* [→ *3778*]. these; see *3778*:–

5024 **ταὐτά, *tauta***, contr. [art.+p.]. GK: *5437* [→ *3588+846*]. the same things:– even thus (+*2596*) [1], like [1]

5025 **ταύταις, *tautais***, p.demo.fem.pl. of *3778*. GK: *4047* [→ *3778*]. to, for, by these; see *3778*:–

5026 **ταύτῃ, *tautē***, p.demo.fem.s. of *3778*. GK: *4047* [→ *3778*]. to, for, by this; see *3778*:–

5027 **ταφή, *taphē***, n. GK: *5438* [→ *5028*]. burial place:– bury [1]

5028 **τάφος, *taphos***, n. GK: *5439* [→ *1779, 1780, 5027; cf. 2290*]. tomb, grave:– sepulchre [5], sepulchres [1], tombs [1]

5029 **τάχα, *tacha***, adv. GK: *5440* [→ *5036*]. perhaps, possibly:– peradventure [1], perhaps [1]

5030 **ταχέως, *tacheōs***, adv. GK: *5441* [→ *5036*]. quickly, in haste; very soon:– shortly [6], quickly [3], soon [2], hastily [1], outrun (+*4390*) [1], sooner [1], suddenly [1], with all speed (+*5613*) [1]

5031 **ταχινός, *tachinos***, a. GK: *5442* [→ *5036*]. swift; soon, imminent:– shortly [1], swift [1]

5032 **τάχιον, *tachion***, adv.compar.neut. of *5030*. GK: *5441* [→ *5036*]. very quickly, in haste; very soon:–

5033 **τάχιστα, *tachista***, adv.super. of *5030*. GK: *5441* [→ *5036*]. most quickly, hastily; as soon as possible:–

5034 **τάχος, *tachos***, n. GK: *5443* [→ *5036*]. quickness, immediateness; (in pp. phrase) quickly, immediately, soon:– shortly (+*1722*) [4], quickly (+*1722*) [2], quickly [1], speedily (+*1722*) [1]

5035 **ταχύ, *tachu***, a.neut.s. of *5036*. GK: *5444* [→ *5036*]. (adv.) quickly, momentarily, soon:–

5036 **ταχύς, *tachys***, a. GK: *5444* [→ *5029, 5030, 5031, 5032, 5033, 5034, 5035*]. quick, swift; (adv.) quickly, momentarily, soon:– quickly [11], lightly [1], swift [1]

5037 τέ, *te*, pt. GK: *5445* [→ *1535, 1539, 3383, 3752, 3753, 3763, 3777, 3842, 5119, 5620*]. and, but (often not translated):– and [127], both [36], also [2], then [2], whether (*+1437*) [2], and whether (*+1437*) [1], between [1], even [1], inasmuch as both [1], or (*+1437*) [1], whether [1], yea (*+2089*) [1]

5038 τεῖχος, *teichos*, n. GK: *5446* [→ *3320, 5109*]. wall:– wall [8], walls [1]

5039 τεκμήριον, *tekmērion*, n. GK: *5447.* convincing proof:– infallible proofs [1]

5040 τεκνίον, *teknion*, n. GK: *5448* [→ *5088*]. dear children, little children:– little children [9]

5041 τεκνογονέω, *teknogoneō*, v. GK: *5449* [→ *5088+1096*]. to have children, bear a child:– bear children [1]

5042 τεκνογονία, *teknogonia*, n. GK: *5450* [→ *5088+1096*]. childbearing:– childbearing [1]

5043 τέκνον, *teknon*, n. GK: *5451* [→ *5088*]. child, son, daughter, offspring, descendant:– children [70], son [15], sons [6], child [5], children's [2], daughters [1]

5044 τεκνοτροφέω, *teknotropheō*, v. GK: *5452* [→ *5088+5142*]. to bring up children:– brought up children [1]

5045 τέκτων, *tektōn*, n. GK: *5454* [→ *5078*]. carpenter, woodworker; more generally: construction worker, including stonemason and metalworker:– carpenter's [1], carpenter [1]

5046 τέλειος, *teleios*, a. GK: *5455* [→ *5056*]. perfect, mature, finished:– perfect [16], full age [1], men [1], more perfect [1]

5047 τελειότης, *teleiotēs*, n. GK: *5456* [→ *5056*]. perfection, maturity, completeness:– perfection [1], perfectness [1]

5048 τελειόω, *teleioō*, v. GK: *5457* [→ *5056*]. to perfect, complete, finish; (pass.) to reach a goal, be fulfilled, completed, made perfect:– made perfect [9], perfected [4], finish [3], make perfect [3], fulfilled [2], consecrated [1], finished [1], perfect [1]

5049 τελείως, *teleiōs*, adv. GK: *5458* [→ *5056*]. fully, completely, perfectly:– end [1]

5050 τελείωσις, *teleiōsis*, n. GK: *5459* [→ *5056*]. perfection, accomplishment, fulfillment:– perfection [1], performance [1]

5051 τελειωτής, *teleiōtēs*, n. GK: *5460* [→ *5056*]. perfecter:– finisher [1]

5052 τελεσφορέω, *telesphoreō*, v. GK: *5461* [→ *5056+5342*]. to mature (to fruitfulness):– bring to perfection [1]

5053 τελευτάω, *teleutaō*, v. GK: *5462* [→ *5054; cf. 5056*]. to die:– dead [3], dieth [3], die [3], died [2], deceased [1]

5054 τελευτή, *teleutē*, n. GK: *5463* [→ *5053*]. death:– death [1]

5055 τελέω, *teleō*, v. GK: *5464* [→ *5056*]. to finish, complete, fulfill; (pass.) to be finished, be completed, fulfilled, perfected:– finished [8], accomplished [4], fulfilled [4], fulfil [3], pay [2], expired [1], filled up [1], gone over [1], made an end [1], performed [1]

5056 τέλος, *telos*, n. GK: *5465* [→ *255, 658, 1300, 1615, 2005, 3081, 3651, 3838, 4185, 4930, 4931, 5046, 5047, 5048, 5049, 5050, 5051, 5052, 5055; cf. 5053, 5057*]. end, result, outcome, finish, goal; revenue, tax, duty:– end [34], custom [3], by continual (*+1519*) [1], ending [1], ends [1], finally (*+3588*) [1], uttermost [1]

5057 τελώνης, *telōnēs*, n. GK: *5467* [→ *754, 5057, 5058*]. tax collector:– publicans [16], publican [6]

5058 τελώνιον, *telōnion*, n. GK: *5466 & 5468* [→ *5057*]. tax collector's booth:– receipt of custom [3]

5059 τέρας, *teras*, n. GK: *5469.* wonder, miracle, which is by implication a sign or portent:– wonders [16]

5060 Τέρτιος, *Tertios*, n.pr. GK: *5470.* Tertius, "*third*":– Tertius [1]

5061 Τέρτυλλος, *Tertyllos*, n.pr. GK: *5472.* Tertullus, "*third*":– Tertullus [2]

τέσσαρα, *tessara*. See **5064**.

5062 τεσσαράκοντα, *tessarakonta*, n.num. GK: *5473 & 5477* [→ *5064*]. forty:– forty [22]

5063 τεσσαρακονταετής, *tessarakontaetēs*, a.num. GK: *5474 & 5478* [→ *5064+2094*]. (of) forty years:– forty years [2]

5064 τέσσαρες, *tessares*, n.num. GK: *5475* [→ *1180, 5062, 5063, 5065, 5066, 5067, 5068, 5069, 5070, 5071, 5072, 5073, 5074, 5075, 5076, 5132, 5133*]. four:– four [42]

5065 τεσσαρεσκαιδέκατος, *tessareskaidekatos*, a.num. GK: *5476* [→ *5064+2532+1176*]. fourteenth:– fourteenth [2]

5066 τεταρταῖος, *tetartaios*, a. GK: *5479* [→ *5064*]. fourth (day):– four days [1]

5067 τέταρτος, *tetartos*, a. GK: *5480* [→ *5064*]. fourth in a series or collection; (n.) the fourth (fractional) part of something:– fourth [9], four [1]

5068 τετράγωνος, *tetragōnos*, a. GK: *5481* [→ *5064+1137*]. square, cubical:– foursquare [1]

5069 τετράδιον, *tetradion*, n. GK: *5482* [→ *5064*]. squad of four soldiers:– quaternions [1]

5070 τετρακισχίλιοι, *tetrakischilioi*, a.num. GK: *5483* [→ *5064+5507*]. four thousand:– four thousand [5]

5071 τετρακόσιοι, *tetrakosioi*, a.num. GK: *5484* [→ *5064*]. four hundred:– four hundred [4]

5072 τετράμηνος, *tetramēnos*, a. GK: *5485* [→ *5064+3375*]. (for) four months:– four months [1]

5073 τετραπλόος, *tetraploos*, a. [used as adv.]. GK: *5486 & 5487* [→ *5064*]. four times (as much):– fourfold [1]

5074 τετράπους, *tetrapous*, a. GK: *5488* [→ *5064+4228*]. four-footed; (n.) four-footed animal of any kind:– fourfooted beasts [3]

5075 τετραρχέω, *tetrarcheō*, v. GK: *5489* [→ *5064+757*]. to be a tetrarch:– tetrarch [3]

5076 τετράρχης, *tetrarchēs*, n. GK: *5490* [→ *5064+757*]. tetrarch, a ruler of less rank and authority than a king:– tetrarch [4]

τεύχω, *teuchō*. See **5177**.

5077 τεφρόω, *tephroō*, v. GK: *5491* [→ *5188*]. to reduce to ashes by fire:– turning into ashes [1]

5078 τέχνη, *technē*, n. GK: *5492* [→ *753, 3673, 5045, 5079; cf. 5088*]. skill, trade, craft:– art [1], craft [1], occupation [1]

5079 τεχνίτης, *technitēs*, n. GK: *5493* [→ *5078*]. craftsman, skilled worker, architect, designer, one who engages in a craft or trade, in some contexts with a focus or the design and planning of what is crafted:– craftsmen [2], builder [1], craftsman [1]

5080 τήκομαι, *tēkomai*, v. GK: *5494.* (pass.) to be melted:– melt [1]

5081 τηλαυγῶς, *tēlaugōs*, adv. GK: *5495* [→ *827*]. clearly, plainly:– clearly [1]

5082 τηλικοῦτος, *tēlikoutos*, p.demo. GK: *5496* [→ *2245+3778*]. so great, so large:– so great [2], great [1], mighty [1]

5083 τηρέω, *tēreō*, v. GK: *5498* [→ *1301, 3906, 3907, 4933, 5084*]. to keep, guard, obey, observe:– keep [32], kept [15], keepeth [10], reserved [7], observe [4], preserved [2], hold fast [1], keepers [1], reserve [1], watched [1], watching [1]

5084 τήρησις, *tērēsis*, n. GK: *5499* [→ *5083*]. jail, prison, custody; keeping, observance:– hold [1], keeping [1], prison [1]

τῇ, *tēi*, τήν, *tēn*, τῆς, *tēs*. See **3588**.

5085 Τιβεριάς, *Tiberias*, n.pr. GK: *5500* [→ *5086*]. Tiberias:– Tiberias [3]

5086 Τιβέριος, *Tiberios*, n.pr. GK: *5501* [→ *5085*]. Tiberius:– Tiberius [1]

5087 τίθημι, *tithēmi*, v. GK: *5502* [→ *113, 114, 115, 121, 276, 394, 428, 475, 477, 595, 659, 802, 1242, 1303, 1570, 1620, 1936, 2007, 2111, 2336, 2653, 2698, 3331, 3346, 3548, 3549, 3550, 3559, 3560, 3734, 3866, 3872, 3908, 4025, 4060, 4286, 4287, 4323, 4369, 4388, 4783, 4784, 4934, 5206, 5294; cf. 331, 2310, 2344, 2653*]. (act.) to place, put; (pass.) to be placed or put; (mid.) to set, appoint, decide, arrange:– laid [24], put [14], lay down [8], make [6], kneeled down (*+1119+3588*) [5], lay [5], appointed [4], set [4], made [3], appoint [2], laid down [2], ordained [2], putteth [2], advised (*+1012*) [1], bowing [1], committed [1], conceived [1], giveth [1], laid aside [1], laid up [1], layedst down [1], making [1], purposed [1], put in way [1], putting [1], set forth [1], settle [1], sink down [1]

5088 τίκτω, *tiktō*, v. GK: *5503* [→ *815, 4415, 4416, 5040, 5041, 5042, 5043, 5044, 5110, 5388; cf. 5078*]. to give birth to; bear, produce:– brought forth [4], delivered [4], born [3], bring forth [3], bringeth forth [2], bearest [1], delivered of a child [1], in travail [1]

5089 τίλλω, *tillō*, v. GK: *5504.* to pick (heads of grain):– pluck [2], plucked [1]

5090 Τιμαῖος, *Timaios*, n.pr. GK: *5505* [→ *5092*]. Timaeus, "*precious, valuable*":– Timeus [1]

5091 τιμάω, *timaō*, v. GK: *5506* [→ *5092*]. to honor, show respect, give recognition:– honour [14], honoureth [4], honoured [1], valued [1], value [1]

5092 τιμή, *timē*, n. GK: *5507* [→ *818, 819, 820, 821, 927, 1784, 2008, 2009, 2472, 4186, 5090, 5091, 5093, 5094, 5095, 5096, 5097, 5098, 5389*]. honor, value, respect; nobility, specialness; money, cost:– honour [32], price [7], honours [1], precious [1], prices [1], sum [1]

5093 τίμιος, *timios*, a. GK: *5508* [→ *5092*]. precious, valuable, honored; costly:– precious [8], most precious [2], dear [1], honourable [1], more precious [1], reputation [1]

5094 τιμιότης, *timiotēs*, n. GK: *5509* [→ *5092*]. wealth:– costliness [1]

5095 Τιμόθεος, *Timotheos*, n.pr. GK: *5510* [→ *5092+2316*]. Timothy, "*precious one of God*":– Timotheus [19], Timothy [9]

5096 Τίμων, *Timōn*, n.pr. GK: *5511* [→ *5092*]. Timon, "*precious, valuable*":– Timon [1]

5097 τιμωρέω, *timōreō*, v. GK: *5512* [→ *5092+142*]. to punish:– punished [2]

5098 τιμωρία, *timōria*, n. GK: *5513* [→ *5092+142*]. punishment:– punishment [1]

5099 τίνω, *tinō*, v. GK: *5514* [→ *661*]. to pay (a price or penalty), in context the penalty is suffering:– punished (*+1349*) [1]

5100 τὶς, *tis*, p.indef. GK: *5516* [→ *3385, 3387, 3386, 3748, 3755*]. one, anyone, anything; some, someone, something:– any [131], certain [114], some [79], one [36], man [25], a [14], ought [7], somewhat [6], something [5], whatsoever (*+302+3739*) [3], divers [2], he [2], none (*+3361*) [2], nothing (*+3361*) [2], one (*+1520*) [2], somebody [2], what [2], whose [2], another (*+243*) [1], as (*+302+3739*) [1], broken[S] pieces [1], every [1], kind [1], man's [1], matter [1], more (*+4055*) [1], no (*+3361*) [1], nothing (*+3756*) [1], nothing (*+3761*) [1], partly (*+3313*) [1], same [1], that [1], whatsoever (*+1437+3739*) [1], whatsoever (*+1437+3748+3956*) [1], whatsoever (*+302+302+3739*) [1], whatsoever [1], whomsoever (*+1437*) [1]

5101 τίς, *tis*, p.inter. GK: *5515* [→ *1302, 1360, 2444, 2530, 3754*]. who?, what?, which?, why?:– what [258], who [101], why [66], whom [25], which [16], how [10], whose [9], whether [8], whereunto [5], nothing (*+3756*) [3], what (*+302*) [3], wherefore [3], wherewith (*+1722*) [3], every [2], what (*+687*) [2], why (*+1519*) [2], any [1], how much [1], nothing (*+3361*) [1], one [1], that [1], what (*+3739*) [1], what have I to do (*+1473*) [1], what man (*+687*) [1], what mean [1], what purpose [1], whereby (*+2596*) [1], wherefore (*+1519*) [1], wherefore (*+1752*) [1], wherefore (*+5484*) [1], whereof (*+4012*) [1], whereunto (*+302*) [1], wherewithal [1], wherewith [1], where [1], which (*+302*) [1], who (*+302*) [1]

5102 τίτλος, *titlos*, n. GK: *5518.* sign, prepared notice, inscription:– title [2]

5103 Τίτος, *Titos*, n.pr. GK: *5519.* Titus:– Titus [15]

τίω, *tiō*. See **5099**.

τό, *to*. See **3588**.

5104 τοί, *toi*, pt. GK: *5520* [→ *2273, 2543, 2544, 3305, 5105, 5106*]. surely (emphasizing reliability):–

5105 τοιγαροῦν, *toigaroun*, pt. GK: *5521* [→ *5104+1063+3767*]. therefore, then:– therefore [1], wherefore seeing [1]

τοίγε, *toige*. See **2544**.

5106 τοίνυν, *toinyn*, pt.infer. GK: *5523* [→ *5104+3568*]. then, therefore:– therefore [3], then [1]

5107 τοιόσδε, *toiosde*, a. GK: *5524* [→ *3588*]. such as this, of this kind:– such [1]

5108 τοιοῦτος, *toioutos*, a. GK: *5525* [→ *3588+3778*]. such, such as this, of such a kind:– such [51], such a one [8], like occupation [1], such as (*+3697*) [1]

5109 τοῖχος, *toichos*, n. GK: *5526* [→ *5038*]. wall:– wall [1]

5110 τόκος, *tokos*, n. GK: *5527* [→ *5088*]. interest (on a monetary loan):– usury [2]

5111 **τολμάω, *tolmaō***, v. GK: *5528* [→ *662, 5112, 5113*]. to dare, be bold, courageous:– durst [7], bold [4], dare [4], boldly [1]

5112 **τολμηρότερον, *tolmēroteron***, adv.comp. GK: *5530* [→ *5111*]. rather boldly:– more boldly [1]

5113 **τολμητής, *tolmētēs***, n. GK: *5532* [→ *5111*]. bold man, daring man:– presumptuous [1]

5114 **τομός, *tomos***, a. GK: *5533* [→ *564, 663, 664, 823, 1371, 2699, 3718, 4059, 4061, 4932, 4935, 5009*]. cutting, sharp; (compar.) sharper:– sharper [1]

5115 **τόξον, *toxon***, n. GK: *5534* [→ *2700*]. bow (weapon):– bow [1]

5116 **τοπάζιον, *topazion***, n. GK: *5535*. topaz (a bright yellow precious stone):– topaz [1]

5117 **τόπος, *topos***, n. GK: *5536* [→ *824, 1786*]. place, location; passage (in a book); position; possibility, opportunity:– place [73], places [7], room [5], quarters [2], coasts [1], licence [1], plain (*+3977*) [1], rocks (*+5138*) [1], where [1]

5118 **τοσοῦτος, *tosoutos***, a. GK: *5537* [→ *3778*]. so great, so many, so large, so long:– so much [7], so great [5], so many [4], so long [2], all so many [1], large [1], these many [1]

5119 **τότε, *tote***, adv. GK: *5538* [→ *3739+5037*]. then, when, at that time:– then [147], that time [2], then (*+3767*) [2], after (*+5225*) [1], and (*+2532*) [1], that time forth [1], time [1], when [1]

5120 **τοῦ, *tou***, art.gen.s. of *3588*. GK: *3836* [→ *3588*]. (often not translated) his, her, its; see *3588*:–

5121 **τοὐναντίον, *tounantion***, contr. [art.+pp.*]. GK: *5539* [→ *3588+1725*]. but, on the contrary:– contrariwise [3]

5122 **τοὔνομα, *tounoma***, contr. [art.+n.]. GK: *5540* [→ *3588+3686*]. named, by name:– named [1]

5123 **τουτέστιν, *toutestin***, contr. [art.+v.]. GK: *5542* [→ *3778+1510*]. that is to say, by this we mean:–

5124 **τοῦτο, *touto***, p.demo.neut.s. of *3778*. GK: *4047* [→ *3778*]. this; see *3778*:–

5125 **τούτοις, *toutois***, p.demo.dat.pl. of *3778*. GK: *4047* [→ *3778*]. to, for, by these; see *3778*:–

5126 **τοῦτον, *touton***, p.demo.acc.s. of *3778*. GK: *4047* [→ *3778*]. this; see *3778*:–

5127 **τούτου, *toutou***, p.demo.gen.s. of *3778*. GK: *4047* [→ *3778*]. from, of this; see *3778*:–

5128 **τούτους, *toutous***, p.demo.acc.pl. of *3778*. GK: *4047* [→ *3778*]. these; see *3778*:–

5129 **τούτῳ, *toutō***, p.demo.dat.s. of *3778*. GK: *4047* [→ *3778*]. to, for, by this; see *3778*:–

5130 **τούτων, *toutōn***, p.demo.gen.pl. of *3778*. GK: *4047* [→ *3778*]. from, of these; see *3778*:–

5131 **τράγος, *tragos***, n. GK: *5543* [→ *5176*]. male goat:– goats [4]

5132 **τράπεζα, *trapeza***, n. GK: *5544* [→ *5064+3978*]. table:– table [9], tables [4], bank [1], set meat before (*+3908*) [1]

5133 **τραπεζίτης, *trapezitēs***, n. GK: *5545* [→ *5064+3978*]. banker:– exchangers [1]

5134 **τραῦμα, *trauma***, n. GK: *5546* [→ *1626, 5135*]. (pl.) wounds:– wounds [1]

5135 **τραυματίζω, *traumatizō***, v. GK: *5547* [→ *5134*]. to wound:– wounded [2]

5136 **τραχηλίζω, *trachēlizō***, v. GK: *5548* [→ *5137*]. (pass.) to be laid bare:– opened [1]

5137 **τράχηλος, *trachēlos***, n. GK: *5549* [→ *4644, 5136*]. neck, throat:– neck [6], necks [1]

5138 **τραχύς, *trachys***, a. GK: *5550* [→ *5139*]. rough, uneven:– rocks (*+5117*) [1], rough [1]

5139 **Τραχωνῖτις, *Trachonitis***, n.pr. GK: *5551* [→ *5138*]. Traconitis, "*rough, stony district*":– Trachonitis [1]

5140 **τρεῖς, *treis***, n.num. GK: *5552* [→ *755, 5144, 5145, 5146, 5148, 5150, 5151, 5152, 5153, 5154*]. three:– three [69]

5141 **τρέμω, *tremō***, v. GK: *5554* [→ *1790, 5156*]. to tremble, fear:– trembling [3], afraid [1]

5142 **τρέφω, *trephō***, v. GK: *5555* [→ *397, 1305, 1361, 1625, 1789, 2353, 4939, 5044, 5160, 5161, 5162*]. to care for, feed, nurse; (pass.) to be nurtured, cared for:– nourished [3], feedeth [2], brought up [1], fed [1], food [1]

5143 **τρέχω, *trechō***, v. GK: *5556* [→ *1408, 1532, 1998, 2113, 2701, 4063, 4274, 4370, 4390, 4890, 4936, 5163, 5164, 5295*]. to run; to strive, give effort:– run [10], ran [6], runneth [2], course [1], running [1]

5144 **τριάκοντα, *triakonta***, n.num. GK: *5558* [→ *5140*]. thirty:– thirty [9], thirtyfold [2]

5145 **τριακόσιοι, *triakosioi***, a.num. GK: *5559* [→ *5140*]. three hundred:– three hundred [2]

5146 **τρίβολος, *tribolos***, n. GK: *5560* [→ *5140+906*]. thistle:– briers [1], thistles [1]

5147 **τρίβος, *tribos***, n. GK: *5561* [→ *1304, 3859, 4937, 4938, 5551*]. path:– paths [3]

5148 **τριετία, *trietia***, n. GK: *5562* [→ *5140+2094*]. (for) three years:– three years [1]

5149 **τρίζω, *trizō***, v. GK: *5563*. to gnash, grind:– gnasheth [1]

5150 **τρίμηνος, *trimēnos***, a. GK: *5564* [→ *5140+3375*]. a period of three months:– three months [1]

5151 **τρίς, *tris***, adv. GK: *5565* [→ *5140*]. three times:– thrice [10], three times (*+1909*) [1], thrice (*+1909*) [1]

5152 **τρίστεγον, *tristegon***, n. GK: *5566* [→ *5140+4722*]. third story (of a building):– third loft [1]

5153 **τρισχίλιοι, *trischilioi***, a.num. GK: *5567* [→ *5140+5507*]. three thousand:– three thousand [1]

5154 **τρίτος, *tritos***, a. GK: *5568 & 5569* [→ *5140*]. third:– third [50], third time [5], third time (*+1537*) [1], thirdly [1]

τρίχες, *triches*. See **2359**.

5155 **τρίχινος, *trichinos***, a. GK: *5570* [→ *2359*]. made of hair, hairy:– of hair [1]

5156 **τρόμος, *tromos***, n. GK: *5571* [→ *5141*]. trembling, fear:– trembling [4], trembled (*+2192*) [1]

5157 **τροπή, *tropē***, n. GK: *5572* [→ *396, 665, 1624, 1788, 1791, 2010, 2011, 2012, 2160, 4062, 4187, 4389, 5158, 5159*]. shifting, turning, variation, change:– turning [1]

5158 **τρόπος, *tropos***, n. GK: *5573* [→ *5157*]. manner, way, kind; way of life:– as (*+3739*) [3], manner [2], means [2], way [2], as (*+2596+3739*) [1], conversation [1], even as (*+2596+3739+3779*) [1], even as (*+3739*) [1]

5159 **τροποφορέω, *tropophoreō***, v. GK: *5574* [→ *5157+5342*]. to endure, put up with:– suffered manners [1]

5160 **τροφή, *trophē***, n. GK: *5575* [→ *5142*]. food, nourishment:– meat [13], food [2], eaten enough (*+2880*) [1]

5161 **Τρόφιμος, *Trophimos***, n.pr. GK: *5576* [→ *5142*]. Trophimus, "*nourished [child]*":– Trophimus [3]

5162 **τροφός, *trophos***, n. GK: *5577* [→ *5142*]. mother, nurse:– nurse [1]

5163 **τροχιά, *trochia***, n. GK: *5579* [→ *5143*]. path, course:– paths [1]

5164 **τροχός, *trochos***, n. GK: *5580* [→ *5143*]. wheel; (fig.) whole course (of life):– course [1]

5165 **τρύβλιον, *tryblion***, n. GK: *5581*. bowl:– dish [2]

5166 **τρυγάω, *trygaō***, v. GK: *5582*. to gather or pick (grapes):– gather [2], gathered [1]

5167 **τρυγών, *trygōn***, n. GK: *5583*. (pl.) doves, turtledoves:– turtledoves [1]

5168 **τρυμαλιά, *trymalia***, n. GK: *5584* [→ *5169*]. eye (the tear-drop shaped hole of a needle through which thread is passed):– eye [2]

5169 **τρύπημα, *trypēma***, n. GK: *5585* [→ *5168*]. eye (of a needle):– eye [1]

5170 **Τρύφαινα, *Tryphaina***, n.pr. GK: *5586* [→ *5172*]. Tryphena, "*dainty*":– Tryphena [1]

5171 **τρυφάω, *tryphaō***, v. GK: *5587* [→ *5172*]. to live in luxury, lead a life of self-indulgence:– lived in pleasure [1]

5172 **τρυφή, *tryphē***, n. GK: *5588* [→ *1792, 5170, 5171, 5173*]. luxury, splendor; carousal, indulgence, reveling:– delicately [1], riot [1]

5173 **Τρυφῶσα, *Tryphōsa***, n.pr. GK: *5589* [→ *5172*]. Tryphosa, "*delicate*":– Tryphosa [1]

5174 **Τρῳάς, *Trōas***, n.pr. GK: *5590*. Troas:– Troas [6]

5175 **Τρωγύλλιον, *Trōgyllion***, n.pr. GK: *5591*. Trogyllium:– Trogyllium [1]

5176 **τρώγω, *trōgō***, v. GK: *5592* [→ *5131*]. to eat, feed on:– eateth [5], eating [1]

5177 **τυγχάνω, *tynchanō***, v. GK: *5593* [→ *1783, 1793, 2013, 2161, 3909, 4940, 4941, 5190, 5241*]. to take part in; to obtain, provide; (intr.) to happen a certain way, to be extraordinary; perhaps:– obtain [3], obtained [2], enjoy [1], it may be (*+1487*) [1], it may be [1], it may chance (*+1487*) [1], little [1], refresh (*+1958*) [1], special (*+3588+3756*) [1]

5178 **τυμπανίζω, *tympanizō***, v. GK: *5594* [→ *5180*]. (pass.) to be tortured, tormented:– tortured [1]

5179 **τύπος, *typos***, n. GK: *5596* [→ *5180*]. pattern, model, example, type, a visual form to be copied, such as in crafting an idol; by extension: a pattern of behavior to be emulated:– ensamples [3], ensample [2], pattern [2], print [2], examples [1], example [1], fashion [1], figures [1], figure [1], form [1], manner [1]

5180 **τύπτω, *typtō***, v. GK: *5597* [→ *499, 1795, 5178, 5179, 5296*]. to strike, beat, wound:– smote [4], smite [3], beat [2], beating [1], smiteth [1], smitten [1], stroke [1], wound [1]

5181 **Τύραννος[1], *Tyrannos[1]***, n.pr. GK: *5598*. Tyrannus, "*ruler*":– Tyrannus [1]

5182 **τυρβάζω, *tyrbazō***, v. GK: *5600*. (mid.) trouble oneself; (pass.) to be troubled:– troubled [1]

5183 **Τύριος, *Tyrios***, n.pr.g. GK: *5601* [→ *5184*]. Tyrian:– of Tyre [1]

5184 **Τύρος, *Tyros***, n.pr. GK: *5602* [→ *5183*]. Tyre, "*rocky place*":– Tyre [11]

5185 **τυφλός, *typhlos***, a. GK: *5603* [→ *5186*]. blind; (n.) blind person:– blind [43], blind man [7], blind men [3]

5186 **τυφλόω, *typhloō***, v. GK: *5604* [→ *5185*]. to cause blindness, deprive of sight:– blinded [3]

5187 **τυφόομαι, *typhoomai***, v. GK: *5605* [→ *5188*]. (pass.) to be or become conceited, implying foolishness:– highminded [1], lifted up with pride [1], proud [1]

5188 **τύφω, *typhō***, v. GK: *5606* [→ *5077, 5187*]. (pass.) to smolder, smoke:– smoking [1]

5189 **τυφωνικός, *typhōnikos***, a. GK: *5607*. of hurricane force:– tempestuous [1]

5190 **Τυχικός, *Tychikos***, n.pr. GK: *5608* [→ *5177*]. Tychicus, "*good fortune*":– Tychicus [7]

5191 **ὑακίνθινος, *hyakinthinos***, a. GK: *5610* [→ *5192*]. dark blue, *poss.* dark red:– jacinth [1]

5192 **ὑάκινθος, *hyakinthos***, n. GK: *5611* [→ *5191*]. jacinth:– jacinth [1]

5193 **ὑάλινος, *hyalinos***, a. GK: *5612* [→ *5194*]. of glass:– of glass [3]

5194 **ὕαλος, *hyalos***, n. GK: *5613* [→ *5193*]. glass, some translate "crystal":– glass [2]

5195 **ὑβρίζω, *hybrizō***, v. GK: *5614* [→ *5196*]. to insult, mistreat:– entreated spitefully [1], reproachest [1], shamefully entreated [1], spitefully entreated [1], use despitefully [1]

5196 **ὕβρις, *hybris***, n. GK: *5615* [→ *1796, 5195, 5197*]. insult, mistreatment; disaster, damage:– harm [1], hurt [1], reproaches [1]

5197 **ὑβριστής, *hybristēs***, n. GK: *5616* [→ *5196*]. insolent man, violent man:– despiteful [1], injurious [1]

5198 **ὑγιαίνω, *hygiainō***, v. GK: *5617* [→ *5199*]. to be healthy, sound:– sound [8], whole [2], health [1], wholesome [1]

5199 **ὑγιής, *hygiēs***, a. GK: *5618* [→ *5198*]. healthy, sound, well:– whole [13], sound [1]

5200 **ὑγρός, *hygros***, a. GK: *5619* [→ *5205*]. moist, green:– green [1]

5201 **ὑδρία, *hydria***, n. GK: *5620* [→ *5204*]. water jar:– waterpots [2], waterpot [1]

5202 **ὑδροποτέω, *hydropoteō***, v. GK: *5621* [→ *5204+4095*]. to drink water (exclusively):– drink water [1]

5203 **ὑδρωπικός, *hydrōpikos***, a. GK: *5622* [→ *5204*]. suffering from dropsy (edema, abnormal swelling from accumulated fluids):– had the dropsy [1]

5204 **ὕδωρ, *hydōr***, n. GK: *5623* [→ *504, 5201, 5202, 5203; cf. 5205*]. water:– water [64], waters [15]

5205 **ὑετός, *hyetos***, n. GK: *5624* [→ *5200; cf. 5204*]. rain:– rain [5], rain (*+1026*) [1]

5206* υἱοθεσία, *huiothesia, n. GK: *5625* [→ *5207+5087*]. adoption as sons, sonship; in NT culture a son received greater inheritance and honor, but in Christ men and women inherit equally:– adoption [3], adoption of children [1], adoption of sons [1]

5207* υἱός, *huios, n. GK: *5626* [→ *5206*]. son, child (of either gender), descendant (in any generation); by extension: a term of endearment; one of a class or kind, for example, a "son of the resurrection" is one who participates in the resurrection. "The Son of Man" is an OT phrase usually meaning "human being," that in the NT is used almost exclusively as a messianic title (see Da 7:13), emphasizing Jesus' humanity:– son [306], children [47], sons [24], child [3], foal [1]

5208* ὕλη, *hylē, n. GK: *5627* [→ *1368*]. forest, wood:– matter [1]

5209* ὑμᾶς, *humas, p.pers.acc.pl. of *4771*. GK: *5148* [→ *4771*]. you, your; see *4771*:–

5210* ὑμεῖς, *humeis, p.pers.nom.pl. of *4771*. GK: *5148* [→ *4771*]. you, your; see *4771*:–

5211* Ὑμέναιος, *Hymenaios, n.pr. GK: *5628*. Hymenaeus, "*of [pagan god] Hymen*":– Hymeneus [2]

5212* ὑμέτερος, *hymeteros, a. GK: *5629* [→ *4771*]. (pl.) your, your own:– your [7], yours [2], your own [1]

5213* ὑμῖν, *humin, p.pers.dat.pl. of *4771*. GK: *5148* [→ *4771*]. you, your; see *4771*:–

5214* ὑμνέω, *hymneō, v. GK: *5630* [→ *5215*]. to sing hymns, sing praises:– sung a hymn [2], sang praises [1], sing praise [1]

5215* ὕμνος, *hymnos, n. GK: *5631* [→ *5214*]. hymn, song of praise:– hymns [2]

5216* ὑμῶν, *humōn, p.pers.gen.pl. of *4771*. GK: *5148* [→ *4771*]. you, your; see *4771*:–

5217* ὑπάγω, *hypagō, v. GK: *5632* [→ *5259+71*]. to go (away):– go [53], goeth [9], goest [5], went [4], get [3], go away [2], departing [1], depart [1], get hence [1], going [1], went away [1]

5218* ὑπακοή, *hypakoē, n. GK: *5633* [→ *5259+191*]. obedience:– obedience [11], obedient [2], obeying [1], obey [1]

5219* ὑπακούω, *hypakouō, v. GK: *5634* [→ *5259+191*]. to obey, be obedient; to answer (the door):– obey [13], obeyed [5], obedient [2], hearken [1]

5220* ὕπανδρος, *hypandros, a. GK: *5635* [→ *5259+435*]. married, legally bound to a man in marriage:– husband [1]

5221* ὑπαντάω, *hypantaō, v. GK: *5636* [→ *5259+473*]. to go out to meet; to oppose:– met [4], went and met [1]

5222* ὑπάντησις, *hypantēsis, n. GK: *5637* [→ *5259+473*]. meeting:– meet [1]

5223* ὕπαρξις, *hyparxis, n. GK: *5638* [→ *5259+757*]. property, goods, possessions:– goods [1], substance [1]

5224* ὑπάρχοντα, *huparchonta, v.ptcp. of *5225*. GK: *5639* [→ *5259+757*]. possessions, property:–

5225* ὑπάρχω, *hyparchō, v. GK: *5639* [→ *5259+757*]. to have, possess; (n.) possessions; to be, exist:– being [13], was [8], be [7], goods [7], is [6], were [5], are [3], hath [2], have [2], after (*+5119*) [1], hast [1], live [1], possessed [1], possesseth [1], substance [1]

5226* ὑπείκω, *hypeikō, v. GK: *5640* [→ *5259+1502*]. to submit, yield:– submit [1]

5227* ὑπεναντίος, *hypenantios, a. GK: *5641* [→ *5259+1725*]. opposing, being against; (n.) enemy:– adversaries [1], contrary [1]

5228* ὑπέρ, *hyper, pp. GK: *5642* [→ *5229, 5230, 5231, 5232, 5233, 5234, 5235, 5236, 5237, 5238, 5239, 5240, 5241, 5242, 5243, 5244, 5245, 5246, 5247, 5248, 5249, 5250, 5251, 5252, 5253*]. (acc.) above, beyond, more than; (gen.) for, in behalf of, for the sake of; in place of:– for [104], above [12], of [12], for sake [7], more than [3], on behalf [3], very [3], than [2], beyond [1], by [1], concerning [1], exceedingly (*+1537+4053*) [1], exceeding [1], for sakes [1], in behalf of [1], in stead [1], more [1], on part [1], over [1], stead [1], toward [1], to [1]

5229* ὑπεραίρομαι, *hyperairomai, v. GK: *5643* [→ *5228+142*]. to become conceited, exalt oneself:– exalted above measure [2], exalteth [1]

5230* ὑπέρακμος, *hyperakmos, a. GK: *5644* [→ *5228+206*]. past one's prime, getting along in years:– pass the flower of age (*+1510*) [1]

5231* ὑπεράνω, *hyperanō, adv. GK: *5645* [→ *5228+507*]. far above, high above:– far above [2], over [1]

5232* ὑπεραυξάνω, *hyperauxanō, v. GK: *5647* [→ *5228+837*]. to grow more and more, increase abundantly:– groweth exceedingly [1]

5233* ὑπερβαίνω, *hyperbainō, v. GK: *5648* [→ *5228+305*]. to wrong, transgress against, sin against:– go beyond [1]

5234* ὑπερβαλλόντως, *hyperballontōs, adv. GK: *5649* [→ *5228+906*]. more severely, to a much greater degree:– above measure [1]

5235* ὑπερβάλλω, *hyperballō, v. GK: *5650* [→ *5228+906*]. to go beyond, surpass, be incomparable:– exceeding [3], excelleth [1], passeth [1]

5236* ὑπερβολή, *hyperbolē, n. GK: *5651* [→ *5228+906*]. all-surpassing, surpassingly great, most excellent, beyond measure:– far more exceeding (*+1519+2596+5236*) [2], abundance [1], beyond measure (*+2596*) [1], exceeding (*+2596*) [1], excellency [1], more excellent (*+2596*) [1], out of measure (*+2596*) [1]

5237* ὑπερείδω, *hypereidō, v. GK: *5653* [→ *5228+1491*]. to overlook, not punish:– winked at [1]

5238* ὑπερέκεινα, *hyperekeina, adv. GK: *5654* [→ *5228+1563*]. beyond; (n.) regions beyond:– beyond [1]

5239* ὑπερεκτείνω, *hyperekteinō, v. GK: *5657* [→ *1614; cf. 5228*]. to go too far, overextend, stretch out beyond:– stretch beyond [1]

5240* ὑπερεκχύννω, *hyperekchynnō, v. GK: *5658* [→ *1632*]. (pass.) to be running over, overflowing:– running over [1]

ὑπερεκπερισσοῦ, ***huperekperissou***. See ***5228*** and ***1537*** and ***4053***.

5241* ὑπερεντυγχάνω, *hyperentynchanō, v. GK: *5659* [→ *5228+1722+5177*]. to intercede:– maketh intercession [1]

5242* ὑπερέχω, *hyperechō, v. GK: *5660* [→ *5228+2192*]. to govern, have authority; to be better than, transcend; (n.) surpassing greatness:– better than [1], excellency [1], higher [1], passeth [1], supreme [1]

5243* ὑπερηφανία, *hyperēphania, n. GK: *5661* [→ *5228+5316*]. arrogance, pride:– pride [1]

5244* ὑπερήφανος, *hyperēphanos, a. GK: *5662* [→ *5228+5316*]. proud, arrogant:– proud [5]

ὑπερλίαν, ***huperlian***. See ***5228*** and ***3029***.

5245* ὑπερνικάω, *hypernikaō, v. GK: *5664* [→ *5228+3529*]. to thoroughly conquer, go beyond conquest:– more than conquerors [1]

5246* ὑπέρογκος, *hyperonkos, a. GK: *5665* [→ *5228+3591*]. boastful, bombastic:– great swelling [2]

5247* ὑπεροχή, *hyperochē, n. GK: *5667* [→ *5228+2192*]. authority, superiority:– authority [1], excellency [1]

5248* ὑπερπερισσεύω, *hyperperisseuō, v. GK: *5668* [→ *5228+4053*]. to increase all the more, exceed bounds, overflow:– exceeding [1], much more abound [1]

5249* ὑπερπερισσῶς, *hyperperissōs, adv. GK: *5669* [→ *5228+4053*]. beyond all measure, exceedingly:– beyond measure [1]

5250* ὑπερπλεονάζω, *hyperpleonazō, v. GK: *5670* [→ *5228+4137*]. to be (greatly) abundant:– exceeding abundant [1]

5251* ὑπερυψόω, *hyperypsoō, v. GK: *5671* [→ *5228+5311*]. to exalt to the highest place:– highly exalted [1]

5252* ὑπερφρονέω, *hyperphroneō, v. GK: *5672* [→ *5228+5424*]. to think too highly of oneself:– think highly [1]

5253* ὑπερῷον, *hyperōon, n. GK: *5673* [→ *5228*]. upstairs room, upper story:– upper chamber [3], upper room [1]

5254* ὑπέχω, *hypechō, v. GK: *5674* [→ *5259+2192*]. to experience:– suffering [1]

5255* ὑπήκοος, *hypēkoos, a. GK: *5675* [→ *5259+191*]. obedient:– obedient [2], obey (*+1096*) [1]

5256* ὑπηρετέω, *hypēreteō, v. GK: *5676* [→ *5257*]. to serve, care for needs:– ministered [1], minister [1], served [1]

5257* ὑπηρέτης, *hypēretēs, n. GK: *5677* [→ *5256; cf. 5259*]. servant, attendant, helper, one who serves or attends, not distinguished in status from other words for servant:– officers [10], servants [4], minister [3], ministers [2], officer [1]

5258* ὕπνος, *hypnos, n. GK: *5678* [→ *69, 70, 879, 1797, 1798, 1852, 1853*]. sleep, slumber:– sleep [6]

5259* ὑπό, *hypo, pp. GK: *5679* [→ *505, 506, 4391, 4942, 4943, 5217, 5218, 5219, 5220, 5221, 5222, 5223, 5224, 5225, 5226, 5227, 5254, 5255, 5260, 5261, 5262, 5263, 5264, 5265, 5266, 5267, 5268, 5269, 5270, 5271, 5272, 5273, 5274, 5275, 5276, 5277, 5278, 5279, 5280, 5281, 5282, 5283, 5284, 5285, 5286, 5287, 5288, 5289, 5290, 5291, 5292, 5293, 5294, 5295, 5296, 5297, 5298, 5299; cf. 5257*]. (gen.) by, by means of; (acc.) under (in space as well as in status or authority); at (a time of day):– of [117], under [48], by [42], with [14], from [2], among [1], early in the morning (*+3588+3722*) [1], into [1], unto [1], whereof [1]

5260* ὑποβάλλω, *hypoballō, v. GK: *5680* [→ *5259+906*]. to secretly persuade, instigate secretly:– suborned [1]

5261* ὑπογραμμός, *hypogrammos, n. GK: *5681* [→ *5259+1125*]. example, model:– example [1]

5262* ὑπόδειγμα, *hypodeigma, n. GK: *5682* [→ *5259+1164*]. example, model, pattern, copy:– example [4], ensample [1], patterns [1]

5263* ὑποδείκνυμι, *hypodeiknymi, v. GK: *5683 & 5684* [→ *5259+1166*]. to show; to warn:– shew [2], warned [2], forewarn [1], shewed [1]

5264* ὑποδέχομαι, *hypodechomai, v. GK: *5685* [→ *5259+1209*]. to welcome, receive as a guest:– received [4]

5265* ὑποδέω, *hypodeō, v. GK: *5686* [→ *5259+1210*]. (mid.) to put on (sandals):– shod [2], bind on [1]

5266* ὑπόδημα, *hypodēma, n. GK: *5687* [→ *5259+1210*]. sandal:– shoes [9], shoe's [1]

5267* ὑπόδικος, *hypodikos, a. GK: *5688* [→ *5259+1349*]. accountable, answerable:– guilty before [1]

5268* ὑποζύγιον, *hypozygion, n. GK: *5689* [→ *5259+2218*]. donkey:– ass [2]

5269* ὑποζώννυμι, *hypozōnnymi, v. GK: *5690* [→ *5259+2224*]. to undergird, brace:– undergirding [1]

5270* ὑποκάτω, *hypokatō, adv. GK: *5691* [→ *5259+2596*]. (pp.*) under:– under [9]

5271* ὑποκρίνομαι, *hypokrinomai, v. GK: *5693* [→ *5259+2919*]. to pretend, make believe; see also *5273*:– feign [1]

5272* ὑπόκρισις, *hypokrisis, n. GK: *5694* [→ *5259+2919*]. hypocrisy (an extension of an actor in a play, not found in the NT), implying arrogance and hardness of heart, utterly devoid of sincerity and genuineness:– hypocrisy [4], dissimulation [1], hypocrisies [1]

5273* ὑποκριτής, *hypokritēs, n. GK: *5695* [→ *5259+2919*]. hypocrite (an extension of an actor in a play, not found in the NT), implying arrogance and hardness of heart, utterly devoid of sincerity and genuineness:– hypocrites [17], hypocrite [3]

5274* ὑπολαμβάνω, *hypolambanō, v. GK: *5696* [→ *5259+2983*]. to take up; to show hospitality; to reply; to suppose, think, believe:– suppose [2], answering [1], received [1]

5275* ὑπολείπω, *hypoleipō, v. GK: *5699* [→ *5259+3007*]. (pass.) to be left, remaining:– left [1]

5276* ὑπολήνιον, *hypolēnion, n. GK: *5700* [→ *5259+3025*]. pit for a winepress:– winefat [1]

5277* ὑπολιμπάνω, *hypolimpanō, v. GK: *5701* [→ *5259+3007*]. to leave behind:– leaving [1]

5278* ὑπομένω, *hypomenō, v. GK: *5702* [→ *5259+3306*]. to stay behind; to stand firm, endure, persevere:– endure [5], endured [3], endureth [3], take it patiently [2], abode still [1], patient [1], suffer [1], tarried behind [1]

5279* ὑπομιμνήσκω, *hypomimnēskō, v. GK: *5703* [→ *5259+3421*]. to remind, call to mind; (pass.) to remember:– put in remembrance [3], bring to remembrance [1], put in mind [1], remembered [1], remember [1]

5280* ὑπόμνησις, *hypomnēsis, n. GK: *5704* [→ *5259+3421*]. reminder, memory, remembrance:– remembrance [2], putting in remembrance [1]

5281* ὑπομονή, *hypomonē, n. GK: *5705* [→ *5259+3306*]. perseverance, endurance, patience:– patience [29], enduring [1], patient continuance [1], patient waiting [1]

5282 **ὑπονοέω**, ***hyponoeō***, v. GK: *5706* [→ *5259+3563*]. to think, suppose; expect; to sense, suspect:– deemed [1], supposed [1], think [1]

5283 **ὑπόνοια**, ***hyponoia***, n. GK: *5707* [→ *5259+3563*]. suspicion:– surmisings [1]

5284 **ὑποπλέω**, ***hypopleō***, v. GK: *5709* [→ *5259+4126*]. to sail to the lee of, to move to the side that offers protection or shelter:– sailed under [2]

5285 **ὑποπνέω**, ***hypopneō***, v. GK: *5710* [→ *5259+4154*]. to blow gently (of wind):– blew softly [1]

5286 **ὑποπόδιον**, ***hypopodion***, n. GK: *5711* [→ *5259+4228*]. footstool:– footstool [9]

5287 **ὑπόστασις**, ***hypostasis***, n. GK: *5712* [→ *5259+2476*]. confidence, trust, being sure; being, essence:– confidence [2], confident [1], person [1], substance [1]

5288 **ὑποστέλλω**, ***hypostellō***, v. GK: *5713* [→ *5259+4724*]. (act.) to draw back, withdraw; (mid.) to hesitate, shrink back:– draw back [1], kept back [1], shunned [1], withdrew [1]

5289 **ὑποστολή**, ***hypostolē***, n. GK: *5714* [→ *5259+4724*]. shrinking back:– draw back [1]

5290 **ὑποστρέφω**, ***hypostrephō***, v. GK: *5715* [→ *5259+4762*]. to turn back toward, return; to turn one's back on, turn away:– returned [24], return [5], returning [3], come again [1], turned back again [1], turned back [1]

5291 **ὑποστρωννύω**, ***hypostrōnnyō***, v. GK: *5716* [→ *5259+4766*]. to spread out:– spread [1]

5292 **ὑποταγή**, ***hypotagē***, n. GK: *5717* [→ *5259+5021*]. obedience, submission:– subjection [4]

5293 **ὑποτάσσω**, ***hypotassō***, v. GK: *5718* [→ *5259+5021*]. to put in subjection, subject, subordinate; (pass.) to submit, be subject to:– subject [10], submit [6], put under [4], made subject [2], obedient [2], put in subjection [2], put [2], subject to [2], subjection [2], in subjection [1], put in subjection under [1], subdued [1], subdue [1], subjected [1], submitted [1], submitting [1], under obedience [1]

5294 **ὑποτίθημι**, ***hypotithēmi***, v. GK: *5719* [→ *5259+5087*]. (act.) to risk, lay down (a life); (mid.) to point out, teach:– laid down [1], put in remembrance [1]

5295 **ὑποτρέχω**, ***hypotrechō***, v. GK: *5720* [→ *5259+5143*]. to sail to the lee of, to move to the side that offers protection or shelter:– running under [1]

5296 **ὑποτύπωσις**, ***hypotypōsis***, n. GK: *5721* [→ *5259+5180*]. example, pattern:– form [1], pattern [1]

5297 **ὑποφέρω**, ***hypopherō***, v. GK: *5722* [→ *5259+5342*]. to endure, bear up under, stand up under:– bear [1], endured [1], endure [1]

5298 **ὑποχωρέω**, ***hypochōreō***, v. GK: *5723* [→ *5259+5562*]. to withdraw, retreat:– went aside [1], withdrew [1]

5299 **ὑπωπιάζω**, ***hypōpiazō***, v. GK: *5708 & 5724* [→ *5259+3708*]. to wear out, weaken, to beat up, treat roughly:– keep under [1], weary [1]

5300 **ὗς**, ***hys***, n. GK: *5725*. female pig, sow:– sow [1]

5301 **ὕσσωπος**, ***hyssōpos***, n. GK: *5727*. hyssop, highly aromatic leaves used in purification rites and at Passover:– hyssop [2]

5302 **ὑστερέω**, ***hystereō***, v. GK: *5728* [→ *5306*]. to lack, be in need, destitute; to be inferior; to fall short:– behind [2], come short [2], lacked [2], wanted [2], come behind [1], destitute [1], fail [1], in want [1], lackest [1], lack [1], suffer need [1], worse [1]

5303 **ὑστέρημα**, ***hysterēma***, n. GK: *5729* [→ *5306*]. what is lacking; poverty; what is needed:– lacking [3], want [3], behind [1], lack [1], penury [1]

5304 **ὑστέρησις**, ***hysterēsis***, n. GK: *5730* [→ *5306*]. need, poverty, lack:– want [2]

5305 **ὕστερον**, ***husteron***, a.neut. of *5306*. GK: *5731* [→ *5306*]. finally, last of all:–

5306 **ὕστερος**, ***hysteros***, a. GK: *5731* [→ *5302, 5303, 5304, 5305*]. (comp.) later, second; (neu.) finally, last of all:– afterward [7], last [3], afterwards [1], at the last [1], latter [1]

5307 **ὑφαντός**, ***hyphantos***, a. GK: *5733*. woven:– woven [1]

5308 **ὑψηλός**, ***hypsēlos***, a. GK: *5734* [→ *5311*]. high, mighty; proud, arrogant; highly valued; (compar.) more exalted:– high [9], higher than [1], highly esteemed [1]

5309 **ὑψηλοφρονέω**, ***hypsēlophroneō***, v. GK: *5735* [→ *5311+5424*]. to be arrogant, proud:– highminded [2]

5310 **ὕψιστος**, ***hypsistos***, a. GK: *5736* [→ *5311*]. highest, most exalted; (as a title of God) the Most High:– highest [8], most high [5]

5311 **ὕψος**, ***hypsos***, n. GK: *5737* [→ *5251, 5308, 5309, 5310, 5312, 5313*]. height, high position, heaven:– height [2], on high [2], exalted [1], high [1]

5312 **ὑψόω**, ***hypsoō***, v. GK: *5738* [→ *5311*]. to lift up, elevate, exalt:– exalted [10], lift up [3], lifted up [3], exalteth [2], exalt [2]

5313 **ὕψωμα**, ***hypsōma***, n. GK: *5739* [→ *5311*]. height; pretension:– height [1], high [1]

5314 **φάγος**, ***phagos***, n. GK: *5741* [→ *4371; cf. 2068*]. glutton:– gluttonous [2]

5315 **φάγω**, ***phagō***, v. GK: *2266* [→ *2068*]. to eat, consume, devour:– eat [88], eaten [5], meat [3], eating [1]

φαιλόνης, ***phailonēs***. Alternate spelling of ***5341***.

5316 **φαίνω**, ***phainō***, v. GK: *5743* [→ *398, 852, 853, 854, 855, 1307, 1717, 1718, 2014, 2015, 2016, 2017, 2020, 2726, 4392, 4811, 5243, 5244, 5318, 5319, 5320, 5321, 5322, 5324, 5325, 5326, 5334?, 5335?, 5402, 5457, 5458, 5459, 5460, 5461, 5462*]. (act.) to shine, give light; (mid./pass.) to appear, be visible;:– appear [9], appeared [5], shineth [5], appeareth [3], shine [3], seen [2], seemed [1], shining [1], shone [1], think [1]

5317 **Φάλεκ**, ***Phalek***, n.pr. GK: *5744*. Peleg, "*water canal*":– Phalec [1]

5318 **φανερός**, ***phaneros***, a. GK: *5745* [→ *5316*]. visible, clear, plain, known:– manifest [9], known [3], openly (*+1722*) [3], abroad (*+1519*) [2], appear [1], outward (*+1722+3588*) [1], outwardly (*+1722+3588*) [1], spread abroad [1]

5319 **φανερόω**, ***phaneroō***, v. GK: *5746* [→ *5316*]. (act.) to reveal, make known, show; (pass.) to appear, be disclosed, displayed, revealed:– made manifest [15], appear [9], manifested [9], shewed [4], appeared [3], make manifest [3], manifest [2], maketh manifest [1], manifested forth [1], manifestly declared [1], shew [1]

5320 **φανερῶς**, ***phanerōs***, adv. GK: *5747* [→ *5316*]. openly, publicly:– openly [2], evidently [1]

5321 **φανέρωσις**, ***phanerōsis***, n. GK: *5748* [→ *5316*]. manifestation, disclosure, revelation:– manifestation [2]

5322 **φανός**, ***phanos***, n. GK: *5749* [→ *5316*]. torch, lantern:– lanterns [1]

5323 **Φανουήλ**, ***Phanouēl***, n.pr. GK: *5750*. Phanuel, "*face of God [El]*":– Phanuel [1]

5324 **φαντάζω**, ***phantazō***, v. GK: *5751* [→ *5316*]. (pass.) to become visible; (n.) a sight:– sight [1]

5325 **φαντασία**, ***phantasia***, n. GK: *5752* [→ *5316*]. pomp, pageantry:– pomp [1]

5326 **φάντασμα**, ***phantasma***, n. GK: *5753* [→ *5316*]. ghost, apparition, transliterated as "phantasm":– spirit [2]

5327 **φάραγξ**, ***pharanx***, n. GK: *5754*. valley, ravine:– valley [1]

5328 **Φαραώ**, ***Pharaō***, n.pr. GK: *5755*. Pharaoh, "*the great house*":– Pharaoh [3], Pharaoh's [2]

5329 **Φαρές**, ***Phares***, n.pr. GK: *5756*. Perez, "*breaking out*":– Phares [3]

5330 **Φαρισαῖος**, ***Pharisaios***, n.pr. GK: *5757*. Pharisee, "*separate ones*":– Pharisees [86], Pharisee [11], Pharisee's [2], Pharisees' [1]

5331 **φαρμακεία**, ***pharmakeia***, n. GK: *5758* [→ *5332, 5333*]. witchcraft, magic, the use of spells and potions of magic, often involving drugs:– sorceries [2], witchcraft [1]

5332 **φαρμακεύς**, ***pharmakeus***, n. GK: *5759* [→ *5331*]. magician, sorcerer:– sorcerers [1]

5333 **φάρμακος**, ***pharmakos***, n. GK: *5761* [→ *5331*]. one who practices magical arts, magician:– sorcerers [1]

5334 **φάσις**, ***phasis***, n. GK: *5762* [→ *5346 or* 5316]. news, report:– tidings [1]

5335 **φάσκω**, ***phaskō***, v. GK: *5763* [→ *5346 or* 5316]. to claim, assert:– affirmed [1], professing [1], saying [1], say [1]

5336 **φάτνη**, ***phatnē***, n. GK: *5764*. manger, stall:– manger [3], stall [1]

5337 **φαῦλος**, ***phaulos***, a. GK: *5765*. evil, bad:– evil [4]

5338 **φέγγος**, ***phengos***, n. GK: *5766*. light, radiance:– light [3]

5339 **φείδομαι**, ***pheidomai***, v. GK: *5767* [→ *857, 5340*]. to spare, refrain from:– spared [4], spare [4], forbear [1], sparing [1]

5340 **φειδομένως**, ***pheidomenōs***, adv. GK: *5768* [→ *5339*]. sparingly:– sparingly [2]

5341 **φελόνης**, ***phelonēs***; or **φαιλόνης**, ***phailonēs***, n. GK: *5742 & 5769*. cloak:– cloke [1]

5342 **φέρω**, ***pherō***, v. GK: *5770* [→ *399, 667, 670, 959, 1308, 1313, 1336, 1533, 1627, 2018, 2164, 2287, 2592, 2593, 2702, 3683, 3911, 3923, 4064, 4135, 4136, 4216, 4374, 4376, 4393, 4851, 5052, 5159, 5297, 5409, 5411, 5412, 5413, 5414, 5459*]. to bring, bear, carry; lead:– brought [16], bring [14], bear [4], bringing [3], came [3], beareth [2], bring forth [2], bringeth forth [2], reach [2], bare [1], bearing [1], be [1], bring hither [1], brought forth [1], carry [1], driven [1], endured [1], endure [1], go on [1], laid [1], leadeth [1], let drive (*+1929*) [1], moved [1], rushing [1], upholding [1]

5343 **φεύγω**, ***pheugō***, v. GK: *5771* [→ *668, 1309, 1628, 2703, 5437*]. flee, escape, elude:– flee [15], fled [11], escaped [2], fleeth [2], escape [1]

5344 **Φῆλιξ**, ***Phēlix***, n.pr. GK: *5772*. Felix, "*fortunate, lucky*":– Felix [8], Felix' [1]

5345 **φήμη**, ***phēmē***, n. GK: *5773* [→ *5346*]. news, report:– fame [2]

5346 **φημί**, ***phēmi***, v. GK: *5774* [→ *1310, 2162, 2163, 4394, 4852, 5334?, 5335?, 5345; cf. 987, 1426, 4394*]. to say, declare, affirm:– said [47], saith [5], say [5], affirm [1]

5347 **Φῆστος**, ***Phēstos***, n.pr. GK: *5776*. Festus, "*festal, joyful*":– Festus [12], Festus' [1]

5348 **φθάνω**, ***phthanō***, v. GK: *5777* [→ *4372?, 4373?, 4399*]. to precede; to arrive, attain, come:– come [4], attained [2], prevent [1]

5349 **φθαρτός**, ***phthartos***, a. GK: *5778* [→ *5351*]. perishable, not lasting, mortal:– corruptible [6]

5350 **φθέγγομαι**, ***phthengomai***, v. GK: *5779* [→ *669, 5353*]. to speak, proclaim:– speak [2], speaking [1]

5351 **φθείρω**, ***phtheirō***, v. GK: *5780* [→ *90, 861, 862, 1311, 1312, 2704, 5349, 5352, 5356*]. to destroy, corrupt; (pass.) to be corrupted, destroyed, perish; to be led astray:– corrupt [4], corrupted [2], defile [1], destroy [1]

5352 **φθινοπωρινός**, ***phthinopōrinos***, a. GK: *5781* [→ *5351+3703*]. pertaining to the (late) autumn:– fruit withereth [1]

5353 **φθόγγος**, ***phthongos***, n. GK: *5782* [→ *5350*]. voice, sound; note, musical tone:– sounds [1], sound [1]

5354 **φθονέω**, ***phthoneō***, v. GK: *5783* [→ *5355*]. to envy, be jealous of:– envying [1]

5355 **φθόνος**, ***phthonos***, n. GK: *5784* [→ *5354*]. envy:– envy [7], envies [1], envyings [1]

5356 **φθορά**, ***phthora***, n. GK: *5785* [→ *5351*]. perishableness, destruction, corruption; depravity:– corruption [7], destroyed [1], perish [1]

5357 **φιάλη**, ***phialē***, n. GK: *5786*. bowl:– vial [7], vials [5]

5358 **φιλάγαθος**, ***philagathos***, a. GK: *5787* [→ *5384+18*]. loving what is good:– lover of good [1]

5359 **Φιλαδέλφεια**, ***Philadelpheia***, n.pr. GK: *5788* [→ *5384+80; cf. 1.3*]. Philadelphia, "*love of brother/sister*":– Philadelphia [2]

5360 **φιλαδελφία**, ***philadelphia***, n. GK: *5789* [→ *5384+80; cf. 1.3*]. brotherly love; brotherly kindness:– brotherly love [3], brotherly kindness [2], love of brethren [1]

5361 **φιλάδελφος**, ***philadelphos***, a. GK: *5790* [→ *5384+80; cf. 1.3*]. loving as brothers:– love as brethren [1]

5362 **φίλανδρος**, ***philandros***, a. GK: *5791* [→ *5384+435*]. loving one's husband:– love husbands (*+1510*) [1]

5363 **φιλανθρωπία**, ***philanthrōpia***, n. GK: *5792* [→ *5384+444*]. love, kindness:– kindness [1], love toward man [1]

5364 **φιλανθρώπως**, ***philanthrōpōs***, adv. GK: *5793* [→ *5384+444*]. in kindness, kindly:– courteously [1]

5365 **φιλαργυρία**, ***philargyria***, n. GK: *5794* [→ *5384+696*]. love of money, avarice, greed:– love of money [1]

5366 **φιλάργυρος, *philargyros***, a. GK: *5795* [→ *5384+696*]. money-loving, avaricious, greedy:– covetous [2]

5367 **φίλαυτος, *philautos***, a. GK: *5796* [→ *5384+846*]. loving oneself, selfish:– lovers of own selves [1]

5368 **φιλέω, *phileō***, v. GK: *5797* [→ *5384*]. to love, to have affection and regard of a very high order, not unlike *26,* and overlapping in meaning in some contexts:– love [10], loveth [6], kiss [3], loved [3], lovest [3]

5369 **φιλήδονος, *philēdonos***, a. GK: *5798* [→ *5384+2237*]. loving pleasure:– lovers of pleasures [1]

5370 **φίλημα, *philēma***, n. GK: *5799* [→ *5384*]. kiss:– kiss [7]

5371 **Φιλήμων, *Philēmōn***, n.pr. GK: *5800* [→ *5384*]. Philemon, "*beloved*":– Philemon [2]

5372 **Φίλητος, *Philētos***, n.pr. GK: *5801* [→ *5384*]. Philetus, "*beloved*":– Philetus [1]

5373 **φιλία, *philia***, n. GK: *5802* [→ *5384*]. friendship, love:– friendship [1]

5374 **Φιλιππήσιος, *Philippēsios***, n.pr.g. GK: *5803* [→ *5384+2462*]. Philippian:– Philippians [2]

5375 **Φίλιπποι, *Philippoi***, n.pr. GK: *5804* [→ *5384+2462*]. Philippi:– Philippi [6]

5376 **Φίλιππος, *Philippos***, n.pr. GK: *5805* [→ *5384+2462*]. Philip, "*horse lover*":– Philip [33], Philip's [3], Philippi [2]

5377 **φιλόθεος, *philotheos***, a. GK: *5806* [→ *5384+2316*]. loving God:– lovers of God [1]

5378 **Φιλόλογος, *Philologos***, n.pr. GK: *5807* [→ *5384+3004*]. Philologus, "*lover of words [education]*":– Philologus [1]

5379 **φιλονεικία, *philoneikia***, n. GK: *5808* [→ *5380; cf. 5384*]. dispute, strife:– strife [1]

5380 **φιλόνεικος, *philoneikos***, a. GK: *5809* [→ *5379*]. contentious, quarrelsome:– contentious [1]

5381 **φιλοξενία, *philoxenia***, n. GK: *5810* [→ *5384+3581*]. hospitality, entertainment of strangers:– entertain strangers [1], hospitality [1]

5382 **φιλόξενος, *philoxenos***, a. GK: *5811* [→ *5384+3581*]. hospitable:– given to hospitality [1], hospitality [1], lover of hospitality [1]

5383 **φιλοπρωτεύω, *philoprōteuō***, v. GK: *5812* [→ *5384+4413*]. to love to be first:– loveth to have preeminence among [1]

5384 **φίλος, *philos***, a. GK: *5813* [→ *865, 866, 2321, 2705, 4375, 5358, 5359, 5360, 5361, 5362, 5363, 5364, 5365, 5366, 5367, 5368, 5369, 5370, 5371, 5372, 5373, 5374, 5375, 5376, 5377, 5378, 5381, 5382, 5383, 5385, 5386, 5387, 5388, 5389, 5390, 5391; cf. 5379*]. (a.) friendly; (n.) friend (male or female):– friends [17], friend [12]

5385 **φιλοσοφία, *philosophia***, n. GK: *5814* [→ *5384+4680*]. philosophy, human wisdom:– philosophy [1]

5386 **φιλόσοφος, *philosophos***, n. GK: *5815* [→ *5384+4680*]. philosopher:– philosophers [1]

5387 **φιλόστοργος, *philostorgos***, a. GK: *5816* [→ *5384*]. devoted, loving dearly:– kindly affectioned [1]

5388 **φιλότεκνος, *philoteknos***, a. GK: *5817* [→ *5384+5088*]. loving one's children:– love children [1]

5389 **φιλοτιμέομαι, *philotimeomai***, v. GK: *5818* [→ *5384+5092*]. to have an ambition, aspire to a goal:– labour [1], strived [1], study [1]

5390 **φιλοφρόνως, *philophronōs***, adv. GK: *5819* [→ *5384+5424*]. hospitably, in a friendly manner:– courteously [1]

5391 **φιλόφρων, *philophrōn***, a. GK: *5820* [→ *5384+5424*]. well disposed, friendly, kind:– courteous [1]

5392 **φιμόω, *phimoō***, v. GK: *5821.* to muzzle; to silence; (pass.) to be quiet:– hold peace [2], muzzle [2], put to silence [2], speechless [1], still [1]

5393 **Φλέγων, *Phlegōn***, n.pr. GK: *5823* [→ *5395*]. Phlegon, "*burning*":– Phlegon [1]

5394 **φλογίζω, *phlogizō***, v. GK: *5824* [→ *5395*]. to set on fire:– set on fire [1], setteth on fire [1]

5395 **φλόξ, *phlox***, n. GK: *5825* [→ *5393, 5394*]. flame, blaze:– flame [6], flaming [1]

5396 **φλυαρέω, *phlyareō***, v. GK: *5826* [→ *5397*]. to gossip, talk nonsense:– prating against [1]

5397 **φλύαρος, *phlyaros***, a. GK: *5827* [→ *3632, 5396*]. gossipy:– tattlers [1]

5398 **φοβερός, *phoberos***, a. GK: *5829* [→ *5401*]. fearful, dreadful, terrible:– fearful [2], terrible [1]

5399 **φοβέω, *phobeō***, v. GK: *5828 & 5830* [→ *5401*]. to fear, be afraid, alarmed, in some contexts improper and an impediment to faith and love; to reverence, respect, worship, in other contexts a proper fear for God, a deep reverence and awe:– fear [35], afraid [28], feared [17], fearing [6], feareth [4], afraid (*+5401*) [1], feared (*+5401*) [1], reverence [1]

5400 **φόβητρον, *phobētron***, n. GK: *5831* [→ *5401*]. fearful event:– fearful sights [1]

5401 **φόβος, *phobos***, n. GK: *5832* [→ *870, 1629, 1630, 1719, 5398, 5399, 5400*]. fear, terror; respect, reverence:– fear [40], terror [3], afraid (*+5399*) [1], fear (*+2192*) [1], feared (*+5399*) [1], fears [1]

5402 **Φοίβη, *Phoibē***, n.pr. GK: *5833* [→ *5316*]. Phoebe, "*radiant*":– Phebe [2]

5403 **Φοινίκη, *Phoinikē***, n.pr. GK: *5834* [→ *5404*]. Phoenicia, "*land of purple [dye]*; poss. *land of date palms*":– Phenice [2], Phenicia [1]

5404 **φοῖνιξ[1], *phoinix*[1]**, n. GK: *5836* [→ *4949, 5403, 5405*]. palm tree, palm branch:– palm trees [1], palms [1]

5405 **Φοῖνιξ[2], *Phoinix*[2]**, n.pr. GK: *5837* [→ *5404*]. Phoenix:– Phenice [1]

5406 **φονεύς, *phoneus***, n. GK: *5838* [→ *5408*]. murderer:– murderers [4], murderer [2], murderer (*+435*) [1]

5407 **φονεύω, *phoneuō***, v. GK: *5839* [→ *5408*]. to commit murder, kill:– kill [8], killed [2], murder [1], slew [1]

5408 **φόνος, *phonos***, n. GK: *5840* [→ *409, 4372?, 4373?, 5406, 5407*]. murder, killing:– murders [4], murder [4], slain (*+599*) [1], slaughter [1]

5409 **φορέω, *phoreō***, v. GK: *5841* [→ *5342*]. to wear, bear:– beareth [1], bear [1], borne [1], weareth [1], wearing [1], wear [1]

5410 **φόρον, *phoron***, n. GK: *5842.* forum, used only as a compound proper name "Forum of Appius," a market town south of Rome:– forum [1]

5411 **φόρος, *phoros***, n. GK: *5843* [→ *5342*]. tax:– tribute [5]

5412 **φορτίζω, *phortizō***, v. GK: *5844* [→ *5342*]. to load down (with a burden); (pass.) to be burdened:– heavy laden [1], lade [1]

5413 **φορτίον, *phortion***, n. GK: *5845* [→ *5342*]. burden, load, cargo:– burdens [3], burden [2]

5414 **φόρτος, *phortos***, n. GK: *5846* [→ *5342*]. cargo:– lading [1]

5415 **Φορτουνᾶτος, *Phortounatos***, n.pr. GK: *5847.* Fortunatus, "*fortunate*":– Fortunatus [2]

5416 **φραγέλλιον, *phragellion***, n. GK: *5848* [→ *5417*]. whip:– scourge [1]

5417 **φραγελλόω, *phragelloō***, v. GK: *5849* [→ *5416*]. to flog:– scourged [2]

5418 **φραγμός, *phragmos***, n. GK: *5850* [→ *5420*]. barrier, wall, country lane:– hedged [1], hedges [1], hedge [1], partition [1]

5419 **φράζω, *phrazō***, v. GK: *5851.* to explain, interpret:– declare [2]

5420 **φράσσω, *phrassō***, v. GK: *5852* [→ *5418*]. to shut; (pass.) to be stopped, silenced:– stopped [2], stop [1]

5421 **φρέαρ, *phrear***, n. GK: *5853.* well, shaft, Abyss:– pit [5], well [2]

5422 **φρεναπατάω, *phrenapataō***, v. GK: *5854* [→ *5424+539*]. to deceive:– deceiveth [1]

5423 **φρεναπάτης, *phrenapatēs***, n. GK: *5855* [→ *5424+539*]. deceiver:– deceivers [1]

5424 **φρήν, *phrēn***, n. GK: *5856* [→ *877, 878, 3675, 4065, 5012, 5252, 5309, 5390, 5391, 5422, 5423, 5426, 5427, 5428, 5429, 5430, 5431; cf. 2165, 2706, 3912, 4993*]. (pl.) thinking, understanding:– understanding [2]

5425 **φρίσσω, *phrissō***, v. GK: *5857.* to shudder:– tremble [1]

5426 **φρονέω, *phroneō***, v. GK: *5858* [→ *5424*]. to think, regard, hold an opinion; to set one's mind on; to have a (certain) attitude:– mind [9], think [4], minded [3], regardeth [3], likeminded (*+846+3588*) [2], savourest [2], careful [1], care [1], regard [1], set affection on [1], thinkest [1], understood [1]

5427 **φρόνημα, *phronēma***, n. GK: *5859* [→ *5424*]. mind:– minded [2], mind [2]

5428 **φρόνησις, *phronēsis***, n. GK: *5860* [→ *5424*]. wisdom, understanding:– prudence [1], wisdom [1]

5429 **φρόνιμος, *phronimos***, a. GK: *5861* [→ *5424*]. wise, sensible, shrewd; conceited:– wise [13], wiser [1]

5430 **φρονίμως, *phronimōs***, adv. GK: *5862* [→ *5424*]. shrewdly, wisely:– wisely [1]

5431 **φροντίζω, *phrontizō***, v. GK: *5863* [→ *5424*]. to be careful, concerned:– careful [1]

5432 **φρουρέω, *phroureō***, v. GK: *5864* [→ *4253+3708*]. to guard; (pass.) to be held prisoner; to be shielded:– kept [3], keep [1]

5433 **φρυάσσω, *phryassō***, v. GK: *5865.* to rage, rave:– rage [1]

5434 **φρύγανον, *phryganon***, n. GK: *5866.* brushwood, firewood:– sticks [1]

5435 **Φρυγία, *Phrygia***, n.pr. GK: *5867.* Phrygia:– Phrygia [4]

5436 **Φύγελος, *Phygelos***, n.pr. GK: *5869.* Phygelus, "*fugitive*":– Phygellus [1]

5437 **φυγή, *phygē***, n. GK: *5870* [→ *5343*]. flight, fleeing:– flight [2]

5438 **φυλακή, *phylakē***, n. GK: *5871* [→ *5442*]. prison, jail, haunt; guard; watch (of the night):– prison [33], watch [5], prisons [3], cage [1], hold [1], imprisonments [1], imprisonment [1], keeping watch (*+5442*) [1], ward [1]

5439 **φυλακίζω, *phylakizō***, v. GK: *5872* [→ *5442*]. to imprison:– imprisoned [1]

5440 **φυλακτήριον, *phylaktērion***, n. GK: *5873* [→ *5442*]. phylactery, a small box containing Scripture verses, traditionally bound on the forehead and arm by the Jews during prayer:– phylacteries [1]

5441 **φύλαξ, *phylax***, n. GK: *5874* [→ *5442*]. guard, sentry:– keepers [3]

5442 **φυλάσσω, *phylassō***, v. GK: *5875* [→ *1049, 1200, 1314, 5438, 5439, 5440, 5441*]. to obey, keep; to guard, watch; to keep away from, abstain:– keep [11], kept [8], beware [2], keep from [2], be ware [1], keepest [1], keepeth [1], keeping watch (*+5438*) [1], observed [1], observe [1], saved [1]

5443 **φυλή, *phylē***, n. GK: *5876* [→ *246, 1429, 4853; cf. 5453*]. tribe; people, nation:– tribe [19], tribes [6], kindreds [4], kindred [2]

5444 **φύλλον, *phyllon***, n. GK: *5877.* leaf:– leaves [6]

5445 **φύραμα, *phyrama***, n. GK: *5878.* lump (of clay), batch (of dough); derived from a Greek verb, "to mix (wet or dry) substances," not found in the NT:– lump [5]

5446 **φυσικός, *physikos***, a. GK: *5879* [→ *5453*]. pertaining to things of nature: natural, instinctive; (n.) creatures of instinct:– natural [3]

5447 **φυσικῶς, *physikōs***, adv. GK: *5880* [→ *5453*]. by instinct, naturally:– naturally [1]

5448 **φυσιόω, *physioō***, v. GK: *5881* [→ *5453*]. to puff up, inflate; (pass.) to be proud, arrogant:– puffed up [5], puffeth up [1], puft up [1]

5449 **φύσις, *physis***, n. GK: *5882* [→ *5453*]. nature; natural state of being or characteristics:– nature [10], natural (*+2596*) [2], kind [1]

5450 **φυσίωσις, *physiōsis***, n. GK: *5883* [→ *5453*]. arrogance, pride:– swellings [1]

5451 **φυτεία, *phyteia***, n. GK: *5884* [→ *5453*]. plant:– plant [1]

5452 **φυτεύω, *phyteuō***, v. GK: *5885* [→ *5453*]. to plant:– planted [8], planteth [3]

5453 **φύω, *phyō***, v. GK: *5886* [→ *1631, 1720, 1721, 3504, 3828, 4854, 4855, 5446, 5447, 5448, 5449, 5450, 5451, 5452; cf. 5443*]. to grow up, come up, referring to plant growth:– sprang up [1], springing [1], sprung up [1]

5454 **φωλεός, *phōleos***, n. GK: *5887.* hole (in the ground), den:– holes [2]

5455 **φωνέω, *phōneō***, v. GK: *5888* [→ *5456*]. to call (out), summon:– called [16], crow [7], crew [5], cried [5], call [4], calleth [3], calleth for [1], calling [1]

5456 φωνή, ***phōnē***, n. GK: *5889* [→ *219, 400, 800, 880, 2019, 2757, 4377, 4856, 4857, 4858, 4859, 5455*]. voice, sound, tone, noise of any kind; by extension: speaking, language:– voice [116], voices [15], sound [8], noise [1], was noised abroad (*+1096+3588*) [1]

5457 φῶς, ***phōs***, n. GK: *5890* [→ *5316*]. light; daylight; firelight:– light [67], fire [2], lights [1]

5458 φωστήρ, ***phōstēr***, n. GK: *5891* [→ *5316*]. star; brilliance, splendor:– lights [1], light [1]

5459 φωσφόρος, ***phōsphoros***, a. GK: *5892* [→ *5316+5342*]. light-bearing; (n.) morning star, likely referring to the planet Venus:– day star [1]

5460 φωτεινός, ***phōteinos***, a. GK: *5893* [→ *5316*]. full of light; bright:– full of light [4], bright [1]

5461 φωτίζω, ***phōtizō***, v. GK: *5894* [→ *5316*]. to give light, shine; (pass.) to be enlightened, illuminated:– enlightened [2], bring to light [1], brought to light [1], give light [1], giveth light [1], illuminated [1], lightened [1], lighten [1], lighteth [1], make see [1]

5462 φωτισμός, ***phōtismos***, n. GK: *5895* [→ *5316*]. light, illumination:– light [2]

5463 χαίρω, ***chairō***, v. GK: *5897* [→ *884, 2168, 2169, 2170, 4796, 5479, 5483, 5484, 5485, 5486, 5487*]. to rejoice, be glad, delighted; (as a greeting) Hail!, Greetings!:– rejoice [26], glad [14], rejoiced [8], hail [6], rejoicing [5], greeting [3], joy [3], God speed [2], rejoiceth [2], farewell [1], joyed [1], joyfully [1], joying [1], rejoiceth greatly (*+5479*) [1]

5464 χάλαζα, ***chalaza***, n. GK: *5898*. hail, hailstorm, hailstone:– hail [4]

5465 χαλάω, ***chalao***, v. GK: *5899* [→ *5468, 5469*]. to lower, let down:– let down [5], let down (*+2524*) [1], strake [1]

5466 Χαλδαῖος, ***Chaldaios***, n.pr.g. GK: *5900*. Chaldean:– Chaldeans [1]

5467 χαλεπός, ***chalepos***, a. GK: *5901*. difficult, harsh; violent:– fierce [1], perilous [1]

5468 χαλιναγωγέω, ***chalinagōgeō***, v. GK: *5902* [→ *5465+71*]. to keep in check, keep a rein on one's mouth:– bridleth [1], bridle [1]

5469 χαλινός, ***chalinos***, n. GK: *5903* [→ *5465*]. bit, bridle:– bits [1], bridles [1]

5470 χάλκεος, ***chalkeos***, a. GK: *5905 & 5911* [→ *5475*]. made of bronze:– brass [1]

5471 χαλκεύς, ***chalkeus***, n. GK: *5906* [→ *5475*]. metalworker:– coppersmith [1]

5472 χαλκηδών, ***chalkēdōn***, n. GK: *5907* [→ *5475*]. chalcedony:– chalcedony [1]

5473 χαλκίον, ***chalkion***, n. GK: *5908* [→ *5475*]. (copper or bronze) kettle:– brasen vessels [1]

5474 χαλκολίβανον, ***chalkolibanon***, n. GK: *5909* [→ *5475*]. burnished bronze, fine bronze:– fine brass [2]

5475 χαλκός, ***chalkos***, n. GK: *5910* [→ *5470, 5471, 5472, 5473, 5474*]. copper, bronze; objects of copper:– brass [3], money [2]

5476 χαμαί, ***chamai***, adv. GK: *5912*. to the ground, on the ground:– on the ground [1], to the ground [1]

5477 Χανάαν, ***Chanaan***, n.pr. GK: *5913* [→ *5478*]. Canaan, "*land of purple* hence *merchant trader*":– Canaan [2]

5478 Χαναναῖος, ***Chananaios***, a.pr.g. GK: *5914* [→ *5477*]. Canaanite:– of Canaan [1]

5479 χαρά, ***chara***, n. GK: *5915* [→ *5463*]. joy, rejoicing, happiness, gladness:– joy [52], gladness [3], joyfully (*+3326*) [1], joyfulness [1], joyful [1], joyous [1], rejoiceth greatly (*+5463*) [1]

5480 χάραγμα, ***charagma***, n. GK: *5916* [→ *5481, 5482, 5489*]. mark, stamp; image, idol:– mark [8], graven [1]

5481 χαρακτήρ, ***charaktēr***, n. GK: *5917* [→ *5480*]. exact representation, reproduction:– express image [1]

5482 χάραξ, ***charax***, n. GK: *5918* [→ *5480*]. barricade, palisade (a defensive line or fence):– trench [1]

5483 χαρίζομαι, ***charizomai***, v. GK: *5919* [→ *5463*]. to give grace; to forgive, cancel (a debt); to grant; to hand over into custody:– forgave [4], given [4], forgive [3], deliver [2], forgiven [2], forgiving [2], gave [2], frankly forgave [1], freely given [1], freely give [1], granted [1]

5484 χάριν, ***charin***, c. or pp.*. GK: *5920* [→ *5463*]. therefore, because of this, for this reason:– for cause [3], because of [2], for sake [1], to [1], wherefore (*+3739*) [1], wherefore (*+5101*) [1]

5485 χάρις, ***charis***, n. GK: *5921* [→ *5463*]. grace, the state of kindness and favor toward someone, often with a focus on a benefit given to the object; by extension: gift, benefit; credit; words of kindness and benefit: thanks, blessing:– grace [130], favour [6], thanks [4], thank (*+2192*) [3], thank [3], pleasure [2], acceptable [1], benefit [1], gift [1], gracious [1], liberality [1], thanked [1], thankworthy [1]

5486 χάρισμα, ***charisma***, n. GK: *5922* [→ *5463*]. gracious gift; see also *5485*:– gift [8], gifts [7], free gift [2]

5487 χαριτόω, ***charitoō***, v. GK: *5923* [→ *5463*]. to give graciously, to show acts of kindness by freely giving; (n.) one highly favored; see also *5485*:– highly favoured [1], made accepted [1]

5488 Χαρράν, ***Charran***, n.pr. GK: *5924*. Haran, "[earlier] *mountaineer; perhaps sanctuary*":– Charran [2]

5489 χάρτης, ***chartēs***, n. GK: *5925* [→ *5480*]. (papyrus) paper:– paper [1]

5490 χάσμα, ***chasma***, n. GK: *5926*. chasm:– gulf [1]

5491 χεῖλος, ***cheilos***, n. GK: *5927*. lip; edge (of a shoreline):– lips [6], shore [1]

5492 χειμάζω, ***cheimazō***, v. GK: *5928* [→ *5494*]. (pass.) to be battered in a storm:– tossed with a tempest [1]

5493 χείμαρρος, ***cheimarros***, n. GK: *5929* [→ *5494+4482*]. valley, ravine, wadi:– brook [1]

5494 χειμών, ***cheimōn***, n. GK: *5930* [→ *5492, 5493*]. winter; stormy weather:– winter [4], foul weather [1], tempest [1]

5495 χείρ, ***cheir***, n. GK: *5931* [→ *849, 886, 1315, 2021, 4400, 5496, 5497, 5498, 5499; cf. 4401, 5500*]. hand, area or portion of the hand; power, control:– hands [90], hand [88], by (*+1223*) [1]

5496 χειραγωγέω, ***cheiragōgeō***, v. GK: *5932* [→ *5495+71*]. to lead by the hand:– led by the hand [2]

5497 χειραγωγός, ***cheiragōgos***, n. GK: *5933* [→ *5495+71*]. someone who leads by the hand, leader:– lead by the hand [1]

5498 χειρόγραφον, ***cheirographon***, n. GK: *5934* [→ *5495+1125*]. written code, record of debt:– handwriting [1]

5499 χειροποίητος, ***cheiropoiētos***, a. GK: *5935* [→ *5495+4160*]. hand-made, man-made:– made with hands [5], made by hands [1]

5500 χειροτονέω, ***cheirotoneō***, v. GK: *5936* [→ *1614; cf. 5495*]. to appoint, choose:– ordained [3], chosen [1]

5501 χείρων, ***cheirōn***, a. GK: *5937*. worse (than); more severe than:– worse than [5], worse [4], sorer [1], worse and worse (*+1909+3588*) [1]

5502 Χερούβ, ***Cheroub***, n.pr. GK: *5938*. (pl.) cherubim:– cherubims [1]

5503 χήρα, ***chēra***, n. GK: *5939*. widow:– widow [13], widows [11], widows' [3]

5504 χθές, ***chthes***, adv. GK: *5940*. yesterday:– yesterday [3]

5505 χιλιάς, ***chilias***, n. GK: *5942* [→ *5507*]. thousand:– thousand [21], thousands [2]

5506 χιλίαρχος, ***chiliarchos***, n. GK: *5941* [→ *5507+757*]. military officer, commander; technically an officer of 1,000 soldiers; in the ancient Roman military an officer of a cohort, one tenth of a legion, about 600 soldiers:– chief captain [17], chief captains [2], captains [1], captain [1], high captains [1]

5507 χίλιοι, ***chilioi***, a.num. GK: *5943* [→ *1367, 2035, 4000, 5070, 5153, 5506, 5505*]. thousand:– thousand [11]

5508 Χίος, ***Chios***, n.pr. GK: *5944*. Kios:– Chios [1]

5509 χιτών, ***chitōn***, n. GK: *5945*. tunic, robe, clothing, undergarment:– coats [5], coat [4], clothes [1], garment [1]

5510 χιών, ***chiōn***, n. GK: *5946* [→ *3914, 3915*]. snow:– snow [3]

5511 χλαμύς, ***chlamys***, n. GK: *5948*. robe, cloak, a heavy outer garment used by soldiers and travelers:– robe [2]

5512 χλευάζω, ***chleuazō***, v. GK: *5949*. to sneer, mock, scoff:– mocked [1], mocking [1]

5513 χλιαρός, ***chliaros***, a. GK: *5950*. lukewarm:– lukewarm [1]

5514 Χλόη, ***Chloē***, n.pr. GK: *5951* [→ *5515*]. Chloe, "*tender shoot*":– Chloe [1]

5515 χλωρός, ***chlōros***, a. GK: *5952* [→ *5514*]. light green; pale; (n.) green plant:– green [3], pale [1]

5516 χξϛ', ***chi xi stigma***, n.num. GK: *5953*. 666:– six hundred threescore six [1]

5517 χοϊκός, ***choikos***, a. GK: *5954* [→ *1632*]. made of dust, of the earth:– earthy [4]

5518 χοῖνιξ, ***choinix***, n. GK: *5955*. (almost one liter or) quart:– measures [1], measure [1]

5519 χοῖρος, ***choiros***, n. GK: *5956*. pig:– swine [14]

5520 χολάω, ***cholaō***, v. GK: *5957* [→ *5521*]. to be angry:– angry [1]

5521 χολή, ***cholē***, n. GK: *5958* [→ *5520*]. gall, bile:– gall [2]

5522 χόος, ***choos***, n. GK: *5959* [→ *1632*]. dust:– dust [2]

5523 Χοραζίν, ***Chorazin***, n.pr. GK: *5960 & 6002*. Korazin: Chorazin [2]

5524 χορηγέω, ***chorēgeō***, v. GK: *5961* [→ *5525+71*]. to supply, provide:– giveth [1], minister [1]

5525 χορός, ***choros***, n. GK: *5962* [→ *2023, 2024, 4402, 5524*]. dance; (pl.) dancing:– dancing [1]

5526 χορτάζω, ***chortazō***, v. GK: *5963* [→ *5528*]. to feed; (pass.) to be filled to satisfaction, eat one's fill:– filled [11], fed [1], fill [1], full [1], satisfy [1]

5527 χόρτασμα, ***chortasma***, n. GK: *5964* [→ *5528*]. food:– sustenance [1]

5528 χόρτος, ***chortos***, n. GK: *5965* [→ *5526, 5527*]. grass, plant, this can refer to plants in various forms and stages; hay, stalk, field, etc:– grass [12], blade [2], hay [1]

5529 Χουζᾶς, ***Chouzas***, n.pr. GK: *5966*. Cuza, "*little judge*":– Chuza [1]

5530 χράομαι, ***chraomai***, v. GK: *5968* [→ *671, 888, 889, 890, 2173, 2710, 3916, 4798, 5532, 5533, 5534, 5535, 5536, 5539, 5540, 5541, 5542, 5543, 5544; cf. 5531*]. to make use of, use; to do, act, proceed:– use [7], used [3], entreated [1]

5531 χράω, ***chraō***, v. GK: *5969* [→ *5537, 5538; cf. 5530*]. to lend:– lend [1]

5532 χρεία, ***chreia***, n. GK: *5970* [→ *5530*]. need, necessity:– need [25], need (*+2192*) [10], necessity [2], needeth (*+2192*) [2], business [1], lack [1], necessary [1], necessities [1], needed (*+2192*) [1], needest (*+2192*) [1], needful [1], uses [1], use [1], wants [1]

5533 χρεωφειλέτης, ***chreōpheiletēs***, n. GK: *5971 & 5972* [→ *5530+3784*]. debtor:– debtors [2]

5534 χρή, ***chrē***, pt. or v.imper. GK: *5973* [→ *5530*]. it should, it is necessary:– ought [1]

5535 χρῄζω, ***chrēzō***, v. GK: *5974* [→ *5530*]. to need, have need of:– have need [2], need [2], needeth [1]

5536 χρῆμα, ***chrēma***, n. GK: *5975* [→ *5530*]. money, wealth, possessions:– money [4], riches [3]

5537 χρηματίζω, ***chrēmatizō***, v. GK: *5976* [→ *5531*]. to warn; (pass.) to bear a name; to be warned, told about, revealed to:– warned of God [3], called [2], admonished of God [1], revealed [1], spake [1], warned from God [1]

5538 χρηματισμός, ***chrēmatismos***, n. GK: *5977* [→ *5531*]. proclamation or answer from God:– answer of God [1]

5539 χρήσιμος, ***chrēsimos***, n. GK: *5978* [→ *5530*]. pertaining to value, usefulness, advantage:– profit [1]

5540 χρῆσις, ***chrēsis***, n. GK: *5979* [→ *5530*]. relations, functions:– use [2]

5541 χρηστεύομαι, ***chrēsteuomai***, v. GK: *5980* [→ *5530*]. to be kind:– kind [1]

5542 χρηστολογία, ***chrēstologia***, n. GK: *5981* [→ *5530+3004*]. smooth talk, attractive speech:– good words [1]

5543 χρηστός, ***chrēstos***, a. GK: *5982* [→ *5530*]. easy, good; kind, loving, benevolent:– kind [2], better [1], easy [1], goodness [1], good [1], gracious [1]

5544 χρηστότης, ***chrēstotēs***, n. GK: *5983* [→ *5530*]. kindness, goodness:– goodness [4], kindness [4], gentleness [1], good [1]

***5545* χρῖσμα, chrisma**, n. GK: *5984* [→ *5548*]. anointing:– anointing [2], unction [1]

***5546* Χριστιανός, Christianos**, n.pr.g. GK: *5985* [→ *5547*]. Christian:– Christian [2], Christians [1]

***5547* Χριστός, Christos**, n.pr. GK: *5986* [→ *500, 5546, 5580; cf. 5548*]. Christ, Anointed One, Messiah, the Greek translation of the Hebrew 4899 (cf. Greek *3323*). The Messiah is the Son of David, an anointed leader expected to bring in an age of peace and liberty from all oppression. In the NT, the Messiah is Jesus, who came first to bring liberty from sin and peace with God and who will come again to bring all things under his control:– Christ [553], Christ's [16]

***5548* χρίω, chriō**, v. GK: *5987* [→ *1472, 2025, 5545; cf. 5547*]. to anoint (physically, with oil; spiritually, with the Holy Spirit), to assign a person to a special task, implying a giving of power by God to accomplish the task:– anointed [5]

***5549* χρονίζω, chronizō**, v. GK: *5988* [→ *5550*]. to take a long time, delay; to stay a long time:– delayeth [2], tarried long [1], tarried [1], tarry [1]

***5550* χρόνος, chronos**, n. GK: *5989* [→ *3118, 5549, 5551*]. time, period of time:– time [28], times [5], while [4], as long as (*+1909+3745*) [3], season [3], world began (*+166*) [2], as long as (*+3745*) [1], long ago [1], oftentimes (*+4183*) [1], old [1], seasons [1], since world began (*+166*) [1], space [1], tarried a space (*+4160*) [1]

***5551* χρονοτριβέω, chronotribeō**, v. GK: *5990* [→ *5550+5147*]. to spend time:– spend time [1]

***5552* χρύσεος, chryseos**, a. GK: *5991 & 5997* [→ *5557*]. made of gold:– golden [15], gold [2], of gold [1]

***5553* χρυσίον, chrysion**, n. GK: *5992* [→ *5557*]. gold; gold jewelry or coins:– gold [9]

***5554* χρυσοδακτύλιος, chrysodaktylios**, a. GK: *5993* [→ *5557+1147*]. having or wearing a gold ring:– with a gold ring [1]

***5555* χρυσόλιθος, chrysolithos**, n. GK: *5994* [→ *5557+3037*]. chrysolite:– chrysolite [1]

***5556* χρυσόπρασος, chrysoprasos**, n. GK: *5995* [→ *5557+4237*]. chrysoprase (an apple-green quartz):– chrysoprasus [1]

***5557* χρυσός, chrysos**, n. GK: *5996* [→ *5552, 5553, 5554, 5555, 5556, 5558*]. gold:– gold [12], decked with gold (*+5558*) [1]

***5558* χρυσόω, chrysoō**, v. GK: *5998* [→ *5557*]. (pass.) to be adorned with gold:– decked with gold (*+5557*) [1], decked [1]

***5559* χρώς, chrōs**, n. GK: *5999*. skin, surface of the body:– body [1]

***5560* χωλός, chōlos**, a. GK: *6000*. lame, crippled:– lame [10], halt [4], cripple [1]

***5561* χώρα, chōra**, n. GK: *6001* [→ *5562*]. country, land, region; countryside, field:– country [13], region [4], land [3], fields [2], coasts [1], countries [1], field [1], ground [1], regions [1]

***5562* χωρέω, chōreō**, v. GK: *6003* [→ *402, 672, 1633, 2149, 4066, 4729, 4730, 5298, 5561, 5564*]. to go, come; to accept; to make room, have room:– receive [4], come [1], containing [1], contain [1], goeth [1], hath place [1], room [1]

***5563* χωρίζω, chōrizō**, v. GK: *6004* [→ *5565*]. to divide, separate, leave; (pass.) to be separated from, set apart:– depart [6], separate [3], departed [2], put asunder [2]

***5564* χωρίον, chōrion**, n. GK: *6005* [→ *5562*]. place, parcel of land, field:– field [3], land [2], place [2], lands [1], parcel of ground [1], possessions [1]

***5565* χωρίς, chōris**, adv. GK: *6006* [→ *673, 1316, 5563*]. (adv.) by itself, separately; (pp.*) without, besides, apart from, independent from:– without [36], beside [2], besides [1], by itself [1]

***5566* χῶρος, chōros**, n. GK: *6008*. northwest:– north west [1]

***5567* ψάλλω, psallō**, v. GK: *6010* [→ *5568*]. to sing hymns, sing songs of praise:– sing [3], making melody [1], sing psalms [1]

***5568* ψαλμός, psalmos**, n. GK: *6011* [→ *5567*]. Psalms (book of or section of OT); psalm, hymn of praise:– psalms [5], psalm [2]

***5569* ψευδάδελφος, pseudadelphos**, n. GK: *6012* [→ *5574+80; cf. 1.3*]. false brother:– false brethren [2]

***5570* ψευδαπόστολος, pseudapostolos**, n. GK: *6013* [→ *5574+649*]. false apostle:– false apostles [1]

***5571* ψευδής, pseudēs**, a. GK: *6014* [→ *5574*]. false, lying; (n.) liar:– liars [2], false [1]

***5572* ψευδοδιδάσκαλος, pseudodidaskalos**, n. GK: *6015* [→ *5574+1321*]. false teacher:– false teachers [1]

***5573* ψευδολόγος, pseudologos**, a. GK: *6016* [→ *5574+3004*]. false of speech; (n.) liar:– speaking lies [1]

***5574* ψεύδομαι, pseudomai**, v. GK: *6017* [→ *893, 5569, 5570, 5571, 5572, 5573, 5576, 5577, 5575, 5578, 5579, 5580, 5581, 5582, 5583*]. to lie, speak untruths:– lie [10], falsely [1], lied [1]

***5575* ψευδόμαρτυς, pseudomartys**, n. GK: *6020* [→ *5574+3144*]. false witness, one who gives false testimony:– false witnesses [3]

***5576* ψευδομαρτυρέω, pseudomartyreō**, v. GK: *6018* [→ *5574+3144*]. to give false testimony:– bear false witness [4], bare false witness [2]

***5577* ψευδομαρτυρία, pseudomartyria**, n. GK: *6019* [→ *5574+3144*]. false testimony:– false witness [2]

***5578* ψευδοπροφήτης, pseudoprophētēs**, n. GK: *6021* [→ *5574+4394*]. false prophet:– false prophets [7], false prophet [4]

***5579* ψεῦδος, pseudos**, n. GK: *6022* [→ *5574*]. lie, falsehood, deception:– lie [7], lying [2]

***5580* ψευδόχριστος, pseudochristos**, n. GK: *6023* [→ *5574+5547*]. (pl.) false Christs:– false Christs [2]

***5581* ψευδώνυμος, pseudōnymos**, a. GK: *6024* [→ *5574+3686*]. falsely called or identified:– falsely called [1]

***5582* ψεῦσμα, pseusma**, n. GK: *6025* [→ *5574*]. falsehood, untruth:– lie [1]

***5583* ψεύστης, pseustēs**, n. GK: *6026* [→ *5574*]. liar:– liar [8], liars [2]

***5584* ψηλαφάω, psēlaphaō**, v. GK: *6027* [→ *5597*]. to touch, handle:– feel after [1], handled [1], handle [1], touched [1]

***5585* ψηφίζω, psēphizō**, v. GK: *6028* [→ *5586*]. to calculate; to estimate:– counteth [1], count [1]

***5586* ψῆφος, psēphos**, n. GK: *6029* [→ *4785, 4860, 5585; cf. 5597*]. stone, vote (cast by stones); in NT times a white stone usually meant a vote for innocence, a black stone a vote for guilt; the white stone of Rev 2:17 may picture the innocence of its owner:– stone [2], voice against [1]

***5587* ψιθυρισμός, psithyrismos**, n. GK: *6030* [→ *5588*]. whispering gossip:– whisperings [1]

***5588* ψιθυριστής, psithyristēs**, n. GK: *6031* [→ *5587*]. gossip, whisperer:– whisperers [1]

***5589* ψιχίον, psichion**, n. GK: *6033*. crumb, very small piece:– crumbs [3]

***5590* ψυχή, psychē**, n. GK: *6034* [→ *5594*]. life, soul; heart, mind; a person; the immaterial (and eternal) part of inner person, often meaning the animate self, which can be translated by pronouns: "my soul" = "I, myself":– soul [39], life [35], souls [19], lives [5], minds [2], heartily (*+1537*) [1], heart [1], make to doubt (*+142+3588*) [1], mind [1], you (*+3588+4771*) [1]

***5591* ψυχικός, psychikos**, a. GK: *6035* [→ *5594*]. pertaining to the natural state: physical, unspiritual, without the Spirit:– natural [4], sensual [2]

***5592* ψῦχος, psychos**, n. GK: *6036* [→ *5594*]. cold:– cold [3]

***5593* ψυχρός, psychros**, a. GK: *6037* [→ *5594*]. cold:– cold [4]

***5594* ψύχω, psychō**, v. GK: *6038* [→ *403, 404, 674, 895, 1374, 1634, 2174, 2473, 2711, 3642, 4861, 5590, 5591, 5592, 5593*]. (pass.) to grow cold:– wax cold [1]

***5595* ψωμίζω, psōmizō**, v. GK: *6039* [→ *5596*]. to feed; to give to the poor:– bestow to feed [1], feed [1]

***5596* ψωμίον, psōmion**, n. GK: *6040* [→ *5595; cf. 5597*]. piece of bread:– sop [4]

***5597* ψώχω, psōchō**, v. GK: *6041* [→ *4067, 4379, 5584; cf. 5586, 5596*]. to rub:– rubbing [1]

***5598* Ω[1], Ō[1]**, letter; n.pr. GK: *6042*. letter of the Greek alphabet; Omega:– Omega [4]

***5599* ὦ[2], ō[2]**, pt.interj. GK: *6043*. O!, Oh!:– O [16]

***5600* ὦ, ō**, v.subj. of *1510*. GK: *1639* [→ *1510*]. it may, might, could be; see *1510*:–

***5601* Ὠβήδ, Ōbēd**, n.pr. GK: *6044*. Obed, "*servant* or *worshiper*":– Obed [3]

***5602* ὧδε, hōde**, adv. GK: *6045* [→ *3588*]. here:– here [43], hither [13], here in a place [1], in this place [1], there [1], this place [1]

***5603* ᾠδή, ōdē**, n. GK: *6046* [→ *103, 2790*]. song:– song [5], songs [2]

***5604* ὠδίν, ōdin**, n. GK: *6047* [→ *4944, 5605*]. labor, birth pain; agony (of death):– sorrows [2], pains [1], travail [1]

***5605* ὠδίνω, ōdinō**, v. GK: *6048* [→ *5604*]. to suffer the pains of childbirth:– travail in birth [1], travailest [1], travailing in birth [1]

***5606* ὦμος, ōmos**, n. GK: *6049*. (pl.) shoulders:– shoulders [2]

***5607* ὤν, ōn**, v.ptcp. of *1510*. GK: *1639* [→ *1510*]. to be, exist, be present; all forms of this verb are indexed under *1510*:–

***5608* ὠνέομαι, ōneomai**, v. GK: *6050* [→ *3800; cf. 5057*]. to buy:– bought [1]

***5609* ᾠόν, ōon**, n. GK: *6051*. egg:– egg [1]

***5610* ὥρα, hōra**, n. GK: *6052* [→ *2256, 2256, 5611*]. hour, portion of time, while, moment:– hour [86], time [11], hours [3], season [3], day [1], eventide (*+3588+3798*) [1], instant [1], now high time (*+2235*) [1], short [1]

***5611* ὡραῖος, hōraios**, a. GK: *6053* [→ *5610*]. beautiful:– beautiful [4]

***5612* ὠρύομαι, ōryomai**, v. GK: *6054*. to roar:– roaring [1]

***5613* ὡς, hōs**, pt.&c. GK: *6055* [→ *2531, 5615, 5616, 5618, 5619, 5620*]. as, that, how, about, when; like, as:– as [352], when [39], how [18], as though [16], about [14], like [9], as soon as [7], that [6], while [4], according as [3], like unto [3], after [2], as (*+302*) [2], as it were [2], for [2], after that [1], and [1], are [1], as if [1], even as [1], how that [1], since [1], so soon as (*+302*) [1], so that [1], so [1], to wit [1], unto [1], when (*+1063*) [1], when (*+1161*) [1], when (*+302*) [1], whensoever (*+1437*) [1], with all speed (*+5030*) [1]

***5614* ὡσαννά, hōsanna**, l.[v.+pt.]. GK: *6057*. Hosanna! (exclamation of praise, originally "Save [us]!"):– hosanna [6]

***5615* ὡσαύτως, hōsautōs**, adv. GK: *6058* [→ *5613+846*]. in the same way, so also, likewise, similarly:– likewise [13], in like manner [2], after the same manner [1], even so [1]

***5616* ὡσεί, hōsei**, pt.comp. GK: *6059* [→ *5613+1487*]. like, as; about (an approximation):– about [18], as [8], like [5], as it had been [1], as it were [1], like as [1]

***5617* Ὡσηέ, Hōsēe**, n.pr. GK: *6060*. Hosea, "*salvation*":– Osee [1]

***5618* ὥσπερ, hōsper**, pt.comp. GK: *6061* [→ *5613+4007*]. as, just as; like:– as [39], even as [2], like as [1]

***5619* ὡσπερεί, hōsperei**, pt.comp. GK: *6062* [→ *5613+4007+1487*]. like, as though, as it were:– as [1]

***5620* ὥστε, hōste**, pt. GK: *6063* [→ *5613+5037*]. a marker for introducing clauses: for this reason, therefore, so; so that, resulting in; to, for the purpose of:– so that [24], wherefore [16], insomuch that [15], therefore [9], that [7], so then [5], to [3], as [1], because [1], insomuch as [1], so that (*+2532*) [1], wherefore (*+2532*) [1]

***5621* ὠτίον, ōtion**, n. GK: *6065* [→ *3775*]. ear:– ear [5]

***5622* ὠφέλεια, ōpheleia**, n. GK: *6066* [→ *5623*]. value, advantage:– advantage [1], profit [1]

***5623* ὠφελέω, ōpheleō**, v. GK: *6067* [→ *512, 3786, 5622, 5624*]. to be of good use; to have value; to help; to devote (as a gift) to God:– profited [4], profit [4], profiteth [3], prevail [2], advantaged [1], bettered [1]

***5624* ὠφέλιμος, ōphelimos**, a. GK: *6068* [→ *5623*]. valuable, useful, profitable:– profitable [3], profiteth (*+1510*) [1]

NAVE'S TOPICAL BIBLE REFERENCE SYSTEM

ABBREVIATIONS AND OTHER SYMBOLS

Books of the Bible

1Ch . . . . 1 Chronicles
1Co . . . . 1 Corinthians
1Jn . . . . 1 John
1Ki . . . . 1 Kings
1Pe . . . . 1 Peter
1Sa . . . . 1 Samuel
1Th . . . . 1 Thessalonians
1Ti . . . . 1 Timothy
2Ch . . . . 2 Chronicles
2Co . . . . 2 Corinthians
2Jn . . . . 2 John
2Ki . . . . 2 Kings
2Pe . . . . 2 Peter
2Sa . . . . 2 Samuel
2Th . . . . 2 Thessalonians
2Ti . . . . 2 Timothy
3Jn . . . . 3 John
Ac . . . . Acts
Am . . . . Amos
Col . . . . Colossians
Da . . . . Daniel
Dt . . . . Deuteronomy
Ecc . . . . Ecclesiastes
Eph . . . . Ephesians
Est . . . . Esther
Ex . . . . Exodus
Eze . . . . Ezekiel
Ezr . . . . Ezra
Gal . . . . Galatians
Ge . . . . Genesis
Hab . . . . Habakkuk
Hag . . . . Haggai
Heb . . . . Hebrews
Hos . . . . Hosea
Isa . . . . Isaiah
Jas . . . . James
Jdg . . . . Judges
Jer . . . . Jeremiah
Jn . . . . John
Jnh . . . . Jonah
Job . . . . Job
Joel . . . . Joel
Jos . . . . Joshua
Jude . . . . Jude
La . . . . Lamentations
Lev . . . . Leviticus
Lk . . . . Luke
Mal . . . . Malachi
Mic . . . . Micah
Mk . . . . Mark
Mt . . . . Matthew
Na . . . . Nahum
Ne . . . . Nehemiah
Nu . . . . Numbers
Ob . . . . Obadiah
Phm . . . . Philemon
Php . . . . Philippians
Pr . . . . Proverbs
Ps . . . . Psalms
Rev . . . . Revelation
Ro . . . . Romans
Ru . . . . Ruth
SS . . . . Song of Songs / Song of Solomon
Tit . . . . Titus
Zec . . . . Zechariah
Zep . . . . Zephaniah

Books of the Apocrypha

1Es . . . . 1 Esdras
1Mc . . . . 1 Maccabees
2Es . . . . 2 Esdras
2Mc . . . . 2 Maccabees
3Mc . . . . 3 Maccabees
4Mc . . . . 4 Maccabees
Bar . . . . Baruch
Bel . . . . Bel and the Dragon
Sir . . . . Sirach
Tob . . . . Tobit
Wis . . . . Wisdom

Other

& . . . . "and"; read this biblical text with the preceding
Antiq. . . . . Josephus, *Antiquities of the Jews.*
BDB . . . . Brown, Driver and Briggs *Hebrew and English Lexicon* (Oxford, 1907).
ISBE . . . . *International Standard Bible Encyclopedia* (Eerdmans, 1979-88).
KB . . . . Koehler and Baumgartner *Lexicon in Veteris Testamenti Libros* (Eerdmans, 1951-53).
JB . . . . Jerusalem Bible
KJV . . . . King James Version
NIV . . . . New International Version
NRSV . . . . New Revised Standard Version
w . . . . "with"; read this biblical text with the preceding
ZPBE . . . . *Zondervan Pictorial Bible Encyclopedia* (Zondervan, 1976).

A

AARON

Personal History:

Lineage of: a son of Amram of the Kohathites, and brother of Moses and Miriam (Ex 6:16-20; Nu 26:59-60; Jos 21:4, 10; 1Ch 6:2-3). His marriage to Elisheba, daughter of Amminadab (Ex 6:23). The children of: Nadab, Abihu, Eleazar and Ithamar (Ex 6:23, 25; 1Ch 6:3-4; 24:1-2). Descendants of (1Ch 6:3-15, 50-53; 24).

Character of (Ps 106:16).

As a Leader Ordained by God:

Meets Moses in the wilderness and is made spokesman for Moses (Ex 4:14-16, 27-31; 7:1-2, 6-7). Commissioned as a deliverer of Israel (Ex 6:13, 26-27; Jos 24:5; 1Sa 12:8; Ps 77:20; 105:26; Mic 6:4). Inspiration of (Ex 12:1; Lev 10:8; 11:1; 13:1; 15:1; Nu 2:1; 4:1, 17; 18:1; 19:1; 20:12). Summoned to Sinai with Nadab, Abihu, and seventy elders (Ex 19:24; 24:1, 9-10).

Events in the Life of:

Murmured against by the people (Ex 5:20-21; 16:2-12; Nu 14:2-5, 10; 16:3-11, 41; 20:2; Ps 106:16). Places pot of manna in the ark (Ex 16:34). With Hur supports the hands of Moses during battle (Ex 17:10-13). Judges Israel in the absence of Moses (Ex 24:13-14). Makes the golden calf (Ex 32; Dt 9:7-21; Ac 7:40-41).

His benedictions upon the people (Lev 9:22; Nu 6:23-26). Forbidden to mourn the death of his sons Nadab and Abihu (Lev 10:6, 19).

Gossips with Miriam about Moses because of jealousy (Nu 12:1). Intercedes for Miriam (Nu 12:11-12). Stops the plague started by Korah's rebellion, by priestly intercession (Nu 16:46-48).

Rod of buds (Nu 17; Heb 9:4), preserved in the ark of the covenant (Nu 17; Heb 9:4).

He and Moses dishonor God in the presence of the Israelites when the rock is struck (Nu 20:12, 23-29). Moses and Aaron are not allowed to enter the land of Canaan because of this lack of faith at the waters of Meribah Kadesh in the Desert of Zin (Dt 32:51-52).

Dies at 123 years of age on Mt. Hor (Nu 33:38-39). Death and burial of (Nu 20:27-28; Dt 10:6; 32:50).

As a Priest:

Priesthood of (Ex 28:1; 29:9; Nu 17; 18:1; Ps 99:6; Heb 5:4). Consecration of, to the priesthood (Ex 28; 29; Lev 8). Enters the priestly office (Lev 9).

Descendants of, ordained priests forever (Ex 28:40-43; 29:9; Nu 3:3; 18:1; 1Ch 23:13; 2Ch 26:18). *See Priest, High Priest.*

AARONITES Descendants of Aaron who were priests, numbering 3700 fighting men under Jehoiada who joined David at Hebron (1Ch 12:27). Their leader was Zadok (1Ch 27:17).

AB The Babylonian name of the fifth month in sacred sequence, month eleven in civil sequence. In the Bible it is referred to only as "the fifth month" (Nu 33:38; Ezr 7:8; Jer 1:3). The dry season (July-August); ripening season for grapes, figs, and olives. *See Month, 5.*

ABADDON (*destruction*). A Hebrew word for the underworld, meaning the place of destruction (Job 31:12, ftn), and in the OT is a synonym of death (Hell) and Sheol. The abode of the dead (Job 26:6, ftn; Pr 15:11, ftn; 27:20, ftn).

The name of the angel of the bottomless pit (Rev 9:11, ftn), whose Greek name is Apollyon which means destroyer.

ABAGTHA One of seven eunuchs that served King Xerxes (Est 1:10).

ABANA A river of Damascus mentioned by the leprous Naaman (2Ki 5:12).

ABARIM (*geographic regions beyond*). Either a region E of the Jordan and SE of the Dead Sea, or a mountain range NW of Moab (Nu 27:12; 33:47-48; Dt 32:49; Jer 22:20). *See Nebo, 2.*

ABBA An Aramaic word meaning *father,* which is a customary title of God in prayer. It is found in the Babylonian Talmud where it is used, of a child to his father, and also as a type of address to rabbis. It is equivalent to *papa.* This term conveys a sense of warm intimacy and also respect for the father. The Jews found it too presumptuous and nearly blasphemous; they would therefore never address God in this manner.

Jesus called God "Father" and gave that same right to his disciples (Mt 6:5-15). Paul sees this as symbolic of the Christian's adoption as a child of God and of possession of the Spirit (Mk 14:36; Ro 8:15; Gal 4:6).

ABDA (*servant of Yahweh*).

1. Father of Adoniram (1Ki 4:6).

2. A Levite of the family of Jeduthun, the son of Shammua (Ne 11:17).

ABDEEL (*servant of God [El]*). Father of Shelemiah, who was appointed by Jehoiakim, the king of Judah, "to arrest Baruch the scribe and Jeremiah the prophet" (Jer 36:26).

ABDI (*servant of Yahweh* or *my servant*).

1. A Levite in the reign of Hezekiah, the father of Kishi and grandfather of Ethan (1Ch 6:44; 2Ch 29:12).

2. A son of Elam (Ezr 10:26).

ABDIEL (*servant of God [El]*). A Gadite chief, the father of Ahi (1Ch 5:15).

ABDON (*servant*).

1. A Levitical city given to the tribe of Asher (Jos 19:28, ftn; 21:30; 1Ch 6:74).

2. A son of Hillel, from Pirathon in Ephraim, the hill country of the Amalekites; a judge of Israel for eight years (Jdg 12:13-15).

3. A son of Shashak (1Ch 8:23, 25, 28).

4. Firstborn son of Jeiel of Gibeon (1Ch 8:30; 9:35-36).

5. The son of Micah, an official of King Josiah (2Ch 34:20). Also called Acbor, son of Micaiah (2Ki 22:12).

ABEDNEGO (*servant of Nego* or *Nebo*). His Hebrew name was Azariah. He was taken as a captive to Babylon with Daniel, Hananiah, and Mishael, where each was given a Babylonian name (Da 1:6-20; 2:17, 49; 3:12-30). Azariah was given the Akkadian name Abednego, which was the Babylonian god of wisdom, connected with the planet Mercury.

Shadrach, Meshach, and Abednego were chosen to learn the language and the ways of the Chaldeans (Babylonians) so that they could enter the king's service (Da 1:3-5, 17-20). These three were eventually thrown into the king's furnace because they refused to bow down and worship Nebuchadnezzar's golden image (Da 3:1, 4-6, 8-30).

ABEL (proper name *morning mist;* place name *meadow* or *stream*).

1. The second son of Adam and Eve (Ge 4:1-2). The history of (Ge 4:1-15, 25). NT references to the death of (Mt 23:35; Lk 11:51; Heb 11:4; 12:24; 1Jn 3:12).

2. A city in Naphtali (2Sa 20:14, ftn; 20:18).

3. An element of certain place names. *See seven place names following.*

ABEL, GREAT STONE OF. KJV "the great *stone of* Abel" (1Sa 6:18) is "the large rock" in the NIV text; "Greater Abel" in the note.

ABEL BETH MAACAH (*meadow of the house of Maacah [oppression]*). Sheba son of Bicri fled there from King David (2Sa 20:14-22). A town in Naphtali (2Sa 20:15). Ben-Hadad later seized it (1Ki 15:20). Tiglath-Pileser, king of Assyria captured it (2Ki 15:29).

ABEL-CHERAMIM *See Abel Keramim.*

ABEL KERAMIM (*meadow of vineyards*). A place in Ammon, east of the Jordan, to which Jephthah pursued the Ammonites (Jdg 11:33).

ABEL MAIM (*meadow of waters*). A city conquered by Ben-Hadad (2Ch 16:4). Also known as Abel Beth Maacah (2Ch 16:4, ftn).

ABEL MEHOLAH (*meadow of the round dance*). A town probably in the Jordan Valley, named in conjunction with the retreat of the Midianites from Gideon (Jdg 7:22; 1Ki 4:12). Probably Elisha's birthplace (1Ki 19:16).

ABEL MIZRAIM (*meadow of Egypt,* or *mourning of Egypt*). The place was the threshing floor of Atad where the Israelites and all Pharaoh's officials mourned for Jacob (Ge 50:11).

ABEL SHITTIM (*meadow of the acacia trees*). A place where the Israelites made their final camp before crossing the Jordan into Canaan (Nu 33:49). *See Shittim.*

ABETTING *See Complicity.*

ABEZ *See Ebez.*

ABI *See Abijah, 7.*

ABIA, ABIAH *See Abijah, 1 & 3.*

ABI-ALBON (*[my] father is Albon*). Also called Abiel (1Ch 11:32). *See Abiel.* One of David's mighty men (2Sa 23:31).

ABIASAPH (*[my] father has gathered*). A Levite, and the last son of Korah (Ex 6:24). He is also identified as Ebiasaph (1Ch 6:23, 37; 9:19). *See Ebiasaph.*

ABIATHAR (*[my] father gives abundance* or *the father is preeminent*).

1. High priest under David.

He is the son of Ahimelech and, like his father, a high priest at Nob; he alone escaped from the massacre of his family and all the priests at Nob by Saul to join with David at Keilah, bringing an ephod with him (1Sa 22:6-23). Consults the ephod for David (1Sa 23:9; 30:7). David did not depose Zadok whom Saul had appointed to the priesthood; instead, the two constituted a double high priesthood (2Sa 15:35; 20:25; 1Ki 4:4; 1Ch 15:11). Abiathar was loyal to David when Absalom rebelled; leaves Jerusalem with the ark of the covenant, but is directed by David to return with the ark (2Sa 15:24-29). Helps David by sending his son Jonathan from Jerusalem to David with secret information concerning the counsel of Ahithophel (2Sa 15:35-36; 17:15-22; 1Ki 2:26).

Later he supports Adonijah's attempt to succeed David to the royal throne at David's death (1Ki 1:7). Because of this he is forced out of office by Solomon and is banished to Anathoth (1Ki 2:26-27). With this, the priestly line was confined to Zadok, an Aaronite, and the rule of Eli's house ended in fulfillment of prophecy (1Sa 2:31-35).

The reference to "Ahimelech son of Abiathar" as priest with Zadok is confusing because in other places "Abiathar son of Ahimelech" is known as the high priest. This problem is sometimes solved by saying that the names were transposed by a copyist error; many find this to be an improbable solution since the reference to Ahimelech, the son of Abiathar, as priest is too clear to make a mistake (2Sa 8:17; 1Ch 18:16; 24:3, 6, 31). One of the best explanations is that as the aged Abiathar came near to the end of David's reign, and his life, the responsibilities of office became heavy enough for him to shift many of those duties over to his oldest son Ahimelech; Ahimelech therefore became the functioning high priest.

When Jesus refers to "Abiathar as high priest" at Nob (instead of his father Ahimelech), it is perhaps best understood as Jesus referring to the "passage concerning Abiathar as high priest," by analogy with the way he refers to the burning bush (Mk 12:26).

2. *See Ahimelech, 3.*

ABIB (*heads or spikes of grain*). Hebrew name of the first month in sacred sequence, month seven in civil sequence (Ex 12:2). The name was changed to Nisan after the Exile (Ne 2:1; Est 3:7). The season of later rains (March-April); beginning of the barley and flax harvest.

The Passover and the Feast of Unleavened Bread were instituted, and the Israelites departed from Egypt in (Ex 13:4; 23:15; 34:18; Dt 16:1). It was to become a memorial month to the deliverance of the Israelites from Egypt (Ex 12, w 13:3-4; Dt 16:1-8, 16).

The order of events during the celebration month:

1. On the tenth day the Passover lamb was chosen.

2. On the fourteenth day the lamb was slain and eaten.

3. On the fifteenth day they began harvesting by gathering sheaves of the barley firstfruits.

4. On the sixteenth day they offered the sheaves.

The tabernacle, the Tent of Meeting, was set up in (Ex 40:2, 17). The Israelites arrived at the Desert of Zin, staying at Kadesh (Nu 20:1). Canaan entered in (Jos 4:19). Jordan's overflow in (1Ch 12:15).

See Month, 1; Nisan.

ABIDA (*[my] father knows*). Fourth of five sons of Midian, and the grandson of Abraham and Keturah (Ge 25:4; 1Ch 1:33).

ABIDAN (*[my] father is judge*). A son of Gideoni, and a prince of the tribe of Benjamin chosen to represent his tribe in the wilderness of Sinai (Nu 1:11; 2:22; 10:24). He was present at the dedication of the tabernacle (Nu 7:60, 65).

ABIEL (*[my] father is God [El]*).

1. The grandfather of Saul and Abner (1Sa 9:1; 14:51).

2. One of David's mighty men (1Ch 11:32), also called Abi-Albon (2Sa 23:31). Albon is a copyist's transference from the following verse; some mss of the LXX have Abiel here.

ABIEZER, ABIEZRITES (*[my] father is help*).

1. Founder of a clan of Manasseh (Jos 17:2; Jdg 6:34; 8:2). He was the second son of Hammoleketh, sister of Gilead and granddaughter of Manasseh (1Ch 7:17-18).

Also called Iezer, a shortened form, the progenitor of the Iezerites (Nu 26:30). *See Iezer, Iezerites.*

2. One of David's mighty men (2Sa 23:27; 1Ch 11:28; 27:12).

ABIGAIL (*[my] father rejoices* or *father [cause] of joy*).

1. The wife of Nabal of Carmel, a Calebite, and, after Nabal's death, of David (1Sa 25:3, 14-44; 27:3, 30:5; 2Sa 2:2), to whom she bore his second son, Kileab (2Sa 3:3), or Daniel (1Ch 3:1).

2. A sister of David, daughter of Nahash (Jesse), wife of Jether (Ithra, KJV) an Israelite (some Hebrew mss have Ishmaelite), and mother of Amasa, commander of David's army (2Sa 17:25; 1Ch 2:16-17).

ABIHAIL (*[my] father has strength/ wealth* or *cause of strength/wealth*).

1. A Levite, the father of Zuriel, leader of the Merarite clans (Nu 3:35).

2. The wife of Abishur (1Ch 2:29).

3. A Gadite who lived in Gilead of Bashan and on the pasturelands of Sharon (1Ch 5:14).

4. The wife of Rehoboam, king of Judah. A daughter of Eliab, David's oldest brother (2Ch 11:18).

5. The father of Queen Esther (Est 2:15; 9:29).

ABIHU (*he is [my] father*). Son of Aaron (Ex 6:23; Nu 3:2). Summoned by God to Sinai (Ex 24:1, 9). Called to the priesthood (Ex 28:1). Died because he and Nadab offered unauthorized fire to the Lord (Lev 10:1-2; Nu 26:61). Died childless (Nu 3:4).

ABIHUD (*[my] father has majesty*). A son of Bela, the oldest son of Benjamin (1Ch 8:3).

ABIJAH (*[my] father is Yahweh*).

1. The second son of Samuel; appointed, with his brother Joel, as judges but did not follow in Samuel's ways. They followed after dishonest gains, bribes, and perverted justice. Because of this the Israelites demanded a king to lead them (1Sa 8:1-5; 1Ch 6:28).

2. A son of Jeroboam I of Israel (1Ki 14:1-18). He died of illness when still a child, in fulfillment of a prediction by the prophet Ahijah.

3. The wife of Judah's grandson Hezron and mother of Ashhur the father of Tekoa (1Ch 2:24).

4. The seventh son of Beker, the son of Benjamin (1Ch 7:8).

5. The second king of Judah, the son and successor of Rehoboam, and the grandson of Solomon (1Ch 3:10). Name is spelled "Abijam" in 1 Kings 14 and 15 (See NIV ftn). He reigned three years (2Ch 12:16). Prosperity tempted him to follow the evil ways of his father (1Ki 15:3). He had fourteen wives by whom he had twenty-two sons and sixteen daughters (2Ch 13:21).

He made war on Jeroboam I, the king of Israel, in an effort to recover the ten tribes of Israel (2Ch 13). Before the battle, Abijah condemns the apostasy of the Northern kingdom and at the same time affirms a theocratic institution; he shows the folly of opposing Yahweh's kingdom and concludes by urging Israel not to fight against Yahweh. Jeroboam I, with a numerically stronger army, was routed by Yahweh; the two nations were not allied as they once were, but Jeroboam never made war with Abijah again (1Ki 15:1-8; 2Ch 11:22; 13). He was succeeded by Asa his son (1Ki 15:8; 2Ch 14:1).

6. A descendant of Aaron. The ancestral head of the eighth of the 24 groups into which David had divided the priests (1Ch 24:10).

7. The daughter of Zechariah, and mother of king Hezekiah (2Ch 29:1). Also called Abi (2Ki 18:2, ftn).
8. A priest of Nehemiah's time (Ne 10:7).
9. A chief of the priests who returned from Babylon with Zerubbabel (Ne 12:4, 17). Probably the same as 8.

ABIJAM (*[my] father is the sea* or *father of the West*). *See Abijah, 5.*

ABILENE (probably *meadow*). A territory surrounding the city of Abila NW of Damascus (Lk 3:1).

ABIMAEL (*[my] father is God [El]*). The ninth of the thirteen sons or descendants of Joktan, who was descended from Shem (Ge 10:28; 1Ch 1:22).

ABIMELECH (*[my] father is a king* or *[my] father is Molech*).
1. A Philistine king of Gerar, S of Gaza in the foothills of the Judean mountains (Ge 20:1-18).
2. A second king of Gerar, probably the son of the one mentioned in 1, at whose court Isaac tried to pass off his wife Rebekah as his sister (Ge 26:1-11).
3. The son of Gideon by a concubine (Jdg 8:31; 9:1-57, w 6:32 & 7:1).
4. A Philistine king mentioned in the title of Psalm 34, who very likely is the same as Achish, king of Gath (1Sa 21:10-22:1), with whom David sought refuge when he fled from Saul.
5. A priest in the days of David. A son of Abiathar (2Sa 8:17; 1Ch 18:16). Also called Ahimelech in the LXX and in the Chronicles (1Ch 24:6).
6. *See Achish; Ahimelech.*

ABINADAB (*[my] father is generous* or *[my] father is Nadab*).
1. A Levite, in whose house the ark of God rested twenty years (1Sa 7:1-2; 2Sa 6:3-4; 1Ch 13:7).
2. The second son of Jesse (1Sa 16:8; 17:13).
3. Son of Saul (1Sa 31:2), also called Ishvi (1Sa 14:49).
4. Father of one of Solomon's governors who supplied provisions for the king and the royal household. Also called Ben-Abinadab (1Ki 4:11).

ABINOAM (*[my] father is graciousness*). The father of Barak (Jdg 4:6, 12; 5:1, 12).

ABIRAM (*[my] father is exalted*).
1. One of the sons of Eliab, a Reubenite, who conspired with Dathan and with On against Moses and Aaron; the earth opened and swallowed them (Nu 16; 26:9-10; Dt 11:6; Ps 106:17).
2. The son of Hiel of Bethel; in rebuilding Jericho, Hiel's firstborn, Abiram, died, as well as his youngest son, Segub, in accordance with the word of the Lord spoken to Joshua (1Ki 16:34, w Jos 6:26).

ABISHAG (*[my] father strays*). The Shunammite who looked after David in his old age (1Ki 1:3-4, 15). After David died, Adonijah, his oldest son, wished to marry Abishag. He tried using Bathsheba as leverage to gain Abishag as his wife. Solomon saw this as an attempt to gain the throne by controlling and possessing the king's harem which was a royal right. Solomon had him killed (1Ki 2:13-25).

ABISHAI (*[my] father is Jesse* or *father exists*). The son of Zeruiah, David's sister (1Sa 26:6; 1Ch 2:16). Became the chief of the Three, David's chief men, because he killed 300 men with his spear (2Sa 23:18-19).

Goes into Saul's camp with David; they find Saul asleep with his spear planted in the ground near his head; Abishai tells David that he will pin Saul to the ground with one thrust of the spear, which David does not allow (1Sa 26:6-8). Abishai and his brother Joab pursue Abner all day until they reach the hill of Ammah near Giah; later they murder Joab (2Sa 2:24; 3:30). Defeats the Ammonites (2Sa 10:10, 14). Defeats 18,000 Edomites in the Valley of Salt (1Ch 18:12).

Seeks the life of Shimei son of Gera (2Sa 16:5-9; 19:18-23). Leads a division of David's army against Absalom (2Sa 18:2, 5). Overthrows Sheba (2Sa 20:1-22). Saves David from being killed by Ishbi-Benob, one of the descendants of Rapha, a Philistine (2Sa 21:16-17). Obtains water from the well of Bethlehem for David (1Ch 11:15-20).

ABISHALOM (*[my] father is peace*). A longer form of Absalom (1Ki 15:2, 10). *See Absalom.*

ABISHUA (*[my] father is salvation*).
1. The son of Phinehas the priest (1Ch 6:4-5, 50; Ezr 7:5).
2. A Benjamite of the family of Bela (1Ch 8:4).

ABISHUR (*[my] father is a wall*). A man of Judah, the son of Shammai (1Ch 2:28-29).

ABITAL (*[my] father is [the] night dew*). The fifth wife of David and mother of Shephatiah (2Sa 3:4; 1Ch 3:3).

ABITUB (*[my] father is good*). A Benjamite, son of Shaharaim and Hushim (1Ch 8:8-11).

ABIUD (*[my] father has majesty*). The son of Zerubbabel (Mt 1:13).

ABLUTION *See Washings.*

ABNER (*[my] father is Ner [lamp]*). Son of Ner. Cousin of Saul (1Sa 14:50-51). Commander of the army of Saul (1Sa 14:50; 17:55; 26:5, 14). Abner breaks with Ish-Bosheth and the house of Saul (2Sa 3:6-11) and transfers his loyalty to the house of David (2Sa 3:12-21). Murdered by Joab; David's sorrow for (2Sa 3:22-39). Dedicated spoils of war to the tabernacle (1Ch 26:27-28).

ABOMINATION Activities that are offensive in a moral, religious, or even a natural sense of repulsion.

God's Law Regarding:
Sexual relations: incest (Lev 18:6-18; Dt 27:20), lying with a woman in her monthly period (Lev 18:19; 20:18), adultery (Lev 18:20), homosexuality (Lev 18:22; 20:13), bestiality (Lev 18:23; 20:15-16). Idolatry (Dt 7:25-26; 27:15; 32:16-42), divination, sorcery, interpreting omens, witchcraft, casting spells, mediums or spiritists, those who consult the dead (Dt 18:9-15), offering children in sacrifice by fire to Molech (Dt 18:10, w Lev 18:21). Wearing clothes of opposite sex (Dt 22:5), the earnings of a female or a male prostitute to pay a vow (Dt 23:18), remarriage of defiled wife (Dt 24:1-4). Unjust weights and measures (Dt 25:13-16; Pr 11:1; 20:10, 23).
See Law.

Idols:
(Dt 7:25-26; 27:15; 29:17-18; Eze 7:20-21). Solomon, in his old age, followed other gods and was punished (1Ki 11:1-12), Ashtoreth of the Sidonians, Molech of the Ammonites, Chemosh of the Moabites (1Ki 11:5-8; 11:33; 2Ki 23:13).
There are no gods apart from God (Dt 6:4; 1Ch 17:20; Isa 43:10-13; 44:6-28). Conditions for blessing: Return to God and turn from worthless gods (Jer 4:1-2), or receive disaster (Eze 5:5ff).
Idols, the worship of, and related practices: (Eze 16:1-63; Hos 9:10).
See Idol; Idolatry.

Actions and Attitudes:
A false witness who pours out lies (Dt 19:15-21; Pr 6:19; 21:28), perverseness (Pr 3:32; 11:20), false pride (Pr 6:17; 16:5), murder (Pr 6:17), lying (Pr 6:17, 19; 12:22), one who devises wicked schemes (Pr 6:18), wicked imaginations, *i.e.,* the thoughts of the wicked (Pr 6:18; 15:26; 21:27), wickedness (Pr 8:7).
See Falsehood.

People, Types:
False witness (Pr 6:19; 17:15), trouble maker (Pr 6:19), mocker (Pr 24:9), dishonest (Pr 29:27).

Of Wicked:
Sacrifice (Pr 15:8; 21:27; Isa 1:13), ways (Pr 15:9), thoughts (Pr 15:26), prayer (Pr 28:9).
See Wicked.

ABOMINATION THAT CAUSES DESOLATION
An utterly abhorrent abomination (Da 9:27; 11:31; 12:11). Daniel's prophecies may refer to one or all of three events: to Antiochus' desecration of the temple in 167-169 B.C. (1Mc 1:21-61), to the destruction of Jerusalem in A.D. 70 (Mt 24:15; Mk 13:14), and to the setting up of the image of the beast (Rev 13:14-15). *See Antiochus, 4.*

ABORTION Induced termination of pregnancy by killing the fetus. Clinical abortions are not addressed in the Bible. But the value of the unborn is clearly seen in texts that speak of their value and of judgments on those who kill them.
The value of the unborn (Job 31:15; Ps 139:13-16; Ecc 11:5; Isa 44:2, 24; 49:1, 5; Jer 1:4; Lk 1:41-45).
Punishment for injury to a pregnant mother and her unborn child (Ex 21:22-25). Punishment for the atrocity of ripping open pregnant women (2Ki 8:12; 15:16; Hos 13:16; Am 1:13-15).
See Miscarry.

ABRAHAM, ABRAM (*father of many* or *exalted father*).

Events in the Life of:
Called Abram, son of Terah (Ge 11:26-27). Abram marries Sarai (Ge 11:29). Dwells in Ur of the Chaldeans, but moves. Terah, his father, took Abram and the rest of the family, intending to move to Canaan. On the way they stop and settle in Haran in NW Mesopotamia, where Terah dies (Ge 11:31; Ne 9:7; Ac 7:4). Eventually Abram, at seventy-five, sets out from Haran for the land of Canaan (Ge 12:1-6; Ac 7:4).
The divine call of (Ge 12:1-3; Jos 24:3; Ne 9:7-8; Isa 51:2; Ac 7:2-4; Heb 11:8). *See Call.*
Canaan given to (Ge 12:1, 6-7; 15:7-21; Eze 33:24). Dwells in the hills E of Bethel and W of Ai (Ge 12:8). Relocates to Egypt because of a famine in Canaan (Ge 12:10-20; 26:1). Upon leaving Egypt, they travel to the Negev and on to Bethel; since there is not enough land in one place to support their large herds of sheep, Abram gives Lot his choice of land; Lot chooses the plain of Jordan, leaving Abram to live at the great trees of Mamre the Amorite at Hebron (Ge 13; 14:13; 35:27). Dwells in Gerar and Beersheba (Ge 20; 21:22-34).
Defeats Kedorlaomer king of Elam (Ge 14:5-16; Heb 7:1). Is blessed by Melchizedek (Ge 14:18-20; Heb 7:1-10). *See Melchizedek.*
God's covenant with (Ge 15; 17:1-22; Mic 7:20; Lk 1:73; Ro 4:13; 15:8; Heb 6:13-15; Gal 3:6-29; 4:22-31). *See Covenants, Major in the Old Testament.*
Ishmael born to (Ge 16:3, 7-16). Renamed Abraham by the Lord (Ge 17:5; Ne 9:7). Circumcision of (Ge 17:10-14, 23-27). *See Circumcision.* Angels appear to (Ge 18:1-16; 22:11-12, 15; 24:7). His questions and intercession concerning the destruction of the righteous and wicked in Sodom (Ge 18:23-32). Witnesses the destruction of Sodom (Ge 19:27-29). Dwells in Gerar; deceives Abimelech concerning Sarah, his wife (Ge 20). Isaac born to Abraham when he is 100 years old according to the promise of Yahweh (Ge 21:1-5; Gal 4:22-30). Sends Hagar and Ishmael away (Ge 21:10-14; Gal 4:22-30).
Trial of his faith in the offering of Isaac (Ge 22:1-19; Heb 11:17-19; Jas 2:21). *See Faith, Instances of trial of.* Sarah, his wife, dies (Ge 23:1-2). He purchases a place for her burial and buries her in a cave (Ge 23:3-20). *See Burial; Burying Places.* Provides a wife for Isaac (Ge 24). Marries Keturah (Ge 25:1). Death (Ge 15:15; 25:8-10). In Paradise (Mt 8:11; Lk 13:28; 16:22-31).
Wealth of (Ge 13:2; 24:35). Children of (Ge 16:15; 21:2-3; 25:1-4; 1Ch 1:32-34). Inheritance of (Ge 25:5-6). *See Inheritance.* Age of at different periods (Ge 12:4; 16:16; 21:5; 25:7).

Character Qualities of:
Personal piety of and promises to (Ge 12:7-8; 13:4, 18; 18:18-33; 20:7; 21:33; 22:3-13; 26:5; Ne 9:7-8; 2Ch 20:7; Isa 41:8; Ro 4:16-18; Jas 2:23). *See Worship.* Unselfishness of (Ge 13:9; 21:25-30). Independence of, in character (Ge 14:23; 23:6-16). Faith of (Ge 15:6; Ro 4:1-22; Gal 3:6-9; Heb 11:8-19; Jas 2:21-24). *See Faith, Instances of.* A prophet (Ge 20:7). Friend of God (2Ch 20:7; Isa 41:8; Jas 2:23).
How regarded by his descendants (Mt 3:9; Lk 13:16, 28; 19:9; Jn 8:33-40, 52-59).

ABRAHAM'S SIDE In the Lukan account of the rich man and Lazarus, Lazarus is being comforted at Abraham's side [KJV "bosom"] while the rich man is being tormented in the fires of hell (Lk 16:22-23). *See Lazarus.*
In the Talmudic language, to sit in Abraham's side is to enter Paradise (compare 4Mc 13:17). It is the place where the righteous go at the moment of death and where judgment is enacted as preliminary and perhaps probationary, to the Final Judgment at the end of the age.
See Hades; Hell; Immortality; Paradise; Righteous, Promises to; Sheol; Spirit; Wicked, Punishment of.

ABRAM *See Abraham, Abram.*

ABRECH, ABREK Transliteration of a term, perhaps of Egyptian origin, translated "make way" or "bow down" in the NIV (Ge 41:43; see NRSV ftn).

ABRONAH A place where the Israelites camped (Nu 33:34-35).

ABSALOM (*father is peace*).
1. The third son of David by Maacah, daughter of Talmai, king of Geshur (2Sa 3:3; 1Ch 3:2), also known as Abishalom (1Ki 15:2, 10, w 1Ch 11:20-21).
Absalom hates Amnon, one of his stepbrothers and David's first son, because Amnon had raped his sister Tamar; after two years, Absalom avenges Tamar (2Sa 13:1-29). He flees to Geshur and stays there three years (2Sa 13:37-38). He is permitted by David to return to Jerusalem (2Sa 14:1-24). He is more handsome than anyone in all Israel (2Sa 14:25). Children of (2Sa 14:27; 1Ki 15:2, 10; 2Ch 11:20). He is not allowed to see David for two years after his return from exile in Geshur (2Sa 14:28), at which time he forces Joab to get him an audience with the king (2Sa 14:31-33).
His popularity (2Sa 15:2-6, 13). Conspiracy (2Sa 15-17). Death and burial (2Sa 18:9-17). Pillar of (2Sa 18:18). David's mourning for (2Sa 18:33; 19:1-8).
2. Rehoboam's father-in-law (2Ch 11:20-21).
3. In the Apocrypha, an ambassador of Judas Maccabaeus, the father of Mattathias and Jonathan (1Mc 11:70; 13:11; 2Mc 11:17).

ABSTEMIOUSNESS *See Abstinence; Temperance.*

ABSTINENCE

From Intoxicating Beverages:
Abuse of alcohol condemned (Pr 23:20, 31-35; Lk 21:34). Exemplified by Aaron and the Levitical priesthood, while on duty (Lev 10:8-11; Eze 44:21); Nazirites, while taking a special vow (Nu 6:2-4, 20); Manoah's wife, Samson's mother, during pregnancy (Jdg 13:2-5, 13-14); Kings and princes (Pr 31:4-5); John the Baptist (Lk 1:15).

Instances of:
Israelites in the wilderness (Dt 29:6). Samson (Jdg 16:17, w 13:3-5, 13-14 & Nu 6:3-4). Recabites, honoring an ancestral commitment (Jer 35:1-14). Daniel (Da 1:8, 12). John the Baptist (Mt 11:18; Lk 1:15; 7:33). *See Temperance.*

Other Things Abstained From:
Food, in fasting (Lev 16:29; 23:27; 1Sa 7:6; Ne 9:1; Joel 2:12; Mt 6:16-18). *See Fasting.* Sexual contact within marriage, temporarily (Ex 19:15; 1Co 7:1-5).

In Israel—
The use of blood or fat (Ge 9:4; Lev 3:17). The tendon of the hip (Ge 32:32). Meat not properly bled and prepared (Ex 22:31; Dt 14:21). Whole groups of animals (Lev 11). Contact with unclean person (Lev 15). *See Unclean.*

Christians—
From evil and immorality (Ac 15:20, 29; Eph 4:17-5:21; Col 3:1-11; 1Pe 2:11-12). For the sake of a weaker brother (Ro 14; 1Co 8). Wrongly used as a form of self-righteousness (Col 2:20-23; 1Ti 4:1-3). From an appearance of evil (1Th 5:22).

ABUNDANCE

General:
(Ecc 5:9-20; Isa 15:7; Mt 13:12; 25:29; Mk 12:42-44; Lk 21:1-4; 2Co 8:12-15). Steadfast love (Ex 34:6-7; Ps 69:13; 103; Jnh 4:2). Peace (Lev 26:3, 6; Ps 37:10-11; Jer 33:6-9). Pardon (Nu 14:17-19; 2Ch 30:18-20; Isa 1:18; 55:7; Joel 3:20-21; Mic 7:18-20). Prosperity (Dt 28:47). Anguish (1Sa 1:16). Wealth (2Ch 17:3-6; 18:1; 20:25-27; 24:8-14; Ps 37:16; 52:6-7; Jer 48:36-38; 51:12-13). Honor (2Ch 17:5; 18:1; 1Co 12:23-24). Glory of Zion (Isa 66:11). Overflow of the heart (Mt 12:34; Lk 6:45). Life (Jn 5:39-40; 10:10; 20:30-31), is not in the abundance of possessions (Lk 12:15). Grace (Ro 5; 2Co 4:15), of giving (2Co 8:1-15), through the knowledge of our God and Savior Jesus Christ (2Pe 1:2). Affection, brotherly (2Co 7:15). Plunder (2Ch 20:25). Immeasurably more than we ask (Eph 3:20). Holy Spirit (Tit 3:5-6).

From God:
Provisions, *i.e.* needs (Lev 26:3-5; Dt 30:9-10; Ps 132:13-15; Pr 3:9-10; Isa 30:23; Eze 36:29-30; Am 9:13; Zec 8:12; Php 4:19), grace (2Co 9:8), joys (Ps 36:8), life (Jn 10:10), power (Eph 3:20), participation in the divine nature and a rich welcome into the eternal kingdom (2Pe 1:3-11).

ABUSE

Substance Abuse: (1Co 6:12-13).
Of alcohol: Biblical condemnation of alcohol abuse may be generalized to apply to abuse of any mind- or behavior-altering

substance. Condemned (Pr 20:1; 21:17; 23:20, 30-35; Isa 5:22; Eph 5:18; 1Ti 3:8; Tit 2:3). Examples of (Ge 9:20-24; 19:30-36; Isa 28:7-8; 1Co 11:20-22). *See Abstinence; Temperance.*

Of food (Pr 23:1-3, 20-21; 25:16; 30:22; Isa 56:10-11; Am 6:4-7; 1Co 6:12-13; 1Co 11:20-22; Php 3:18-19).

Sexual Abuse:

Rape punished by death (Dt 22:25-27). Examples of: rape (Ge 34:1-7; Jdg 19:25-20:13; 2Sa 13:1-20; Zec 14:2), attempted homosexual rape (Ge 19:4-9; Jdg 19:22-24).

Abuse of Persons:

Physical injury: Punished in like kind (Ex 21:22-25; Lev 24:19-20).

Servants and slaves: Set free if physically abused (Ex 21:26-27).

Family: Under the law, an unfavored wife still had to be cared for (Ex 21:10-11; Dt 21:15-17). A child could be put to death for abuse of parents (Ex 21:15, 17; Dt 21:18-21). Corporal punishment, if done out of the motivation of love, is not abuse (Pr 3:11-12; 13:24; 29:15; Heb 12:7-11).

ABYSS (*unfathomable depth*). The abode of demons (Lk 8:31) and the place of the dead (Ro 10:7). The bottomless pit; a place of torment and of imprisoned demons (Rev 9:1-2, 11; 11:7; 17:8; 20:1-3).

ACACIA A tree (Isa 41:19). The ark of the covenant made of its wood (Ex 25:10), poles of the ark (Ex 25:13; 38:6), boards in the tabernacle (Ex 26:15-37), the altar of burnt offerings (Ex 38:1, 6).

ACBOR (*mouse* or *jerboa*).

1. The father of Baal-Hanan, a king of Edom (Ge 36:38-39; 1Ch 1:49).

2. The son of Micaiah, a messenger of King Josiah (2Ki 22:12-14). Also called Abdon the son of Micah (2Ch 34:20). *See Abdon, 5.*

3. The father of Elnathan (Jer 26:22; 36:12).

ACCAD *See Akkad.*

ACCEPTED BY GOD Lot's prayers (Ge 19:19-21), Job's prayers (Job 42:9), willing praise (Ps 119:108).

Israelites:

(Ex 28:38; Eze 20:40-41; 43:27). The OT prophets continually affirmed that offerings were only acceptable when the person was acceptable; the offerer never became acceptable to God by giving him gifts (Hos 8:13; Mal 1:6-14).

NT Believers:

People from every nation who fear God and do what is right (Ac 10:34-35). The believer's goal is to please God (2Co 5:9). Through Christ (Eph 1:4-6).

ACCEPTED TIME The time favorable for seeking God. When forgiven (Ps 32:5-6). When in trouble (Ps 69:13). Today, *i.e.,* now (Ps 95:7-8; Isa 49:8; 2Co 6:2).

ACCESS TO GOD Exemplified (Ex 24:2; 34:4-7). Typified (Lev 16:12-15, w Heb 10:19-22). In prayer (Dt 4:7; 2Ki 4:33; Mt 6:6; 1Pe 1:17). *See Prayer.* A privilege of believers (Dt 4:7; Ps 15; 23:6; 24:3-5). In his temple (Ps 15:1; 27:4-5; 43:3; 65:4). Blessedness of (Ps 16:11; 65:4; 73:28). Believers earnestly seek (Ps 27:4; 42:1-2; 43:3-4; 84:1-2). Is of God (Ps 65:4). Promises connected with (Ps 145:18-20; Isa 55:1-5; Mt 6:6; Jas 4:8). Urge others to seek (Isa 2:3; Jer 31:6). The wicked commanded to seek (Isa 55:6; Jas 4:8). Promised to repenting sinners (Hos 14:2; Joel 2:14). *See Repentance.* Is by Christ (Jn 10:7-10; 14:6-7; Ro 5:1-2; Eph 2:13; 3:12; Heb 7:18-19; 10:1-25; 1Pe 3:18). Obtained through faith (Ac 14:27; Ro 5:1-2; Eph 3:12; Heb 11:6). Is by the Holy Spirit (Eph 2:18). Believers have with confidence (Eph 3:12; Heb 4:16; 10:19-22). Follows upon reconciliation to God (Col 1:21-22). To obtain mercy and grace (Heb 4:16).

ACCESSORY *See Complicity.*

ACCO A town on the Mediterranean coast c. thirty miles south of Tyre, and ten from Mt. Carmel (Jdg 1:31, NIV). Also called Ptolemais by the ancient Greeks and Romans because Ptolemy, the Egyptian king, rebuilt the city in c. 100 B.C.; a town of Phoenicia (Ac 21:7, NIV, Ptolemais). *See Ptolemais.*

ACCOMPLICE *See Complicity.*

ACCOUNTABILITY *See Responsibility.*

ACCURSED People that are cursed (Dt 21:23; Jos 6:18; 7:1, 11, 13, 15; 1Ch 2:7; Isa 65:20; Ro 9:3; 1Co 12:3; Gal 1:8).

Things that are cursed (Jos 6:17-18; 7:12).

See Abomination; Anathema; Idolatry.

ACCUSATION, FALSE

Forbidden

(Ex 23:1, 7; Lev 19:16; Lk 3:14; Tit 2:3).

Consolation for falsely accused (Mt 5:11; Jn 15:19-21; 1Pe 4:14).

Instances of False Accusation:

Joseph by Potiphar's wife (Ge 39:7-20); Joseph's brothers by Joseph (Ge 42:6-14); Moses by Korah (Nu 16:1-3, 13), the prophet Ahimelech by Saul (1Sa 22:11-16); Abner by Joab (2Sa 3:24-27); Elijah by Ahab (1Ki 18:17-18); Naboth by Jezebel (1Ki 21:1-14); the Jews who returned under Ezra, accused by the men of Trans-Euphrates (Ezr 4:6-16; Ne 6:5-9); Job by Satan (Job 1:9-10; 2:4-5). David (Ps 41:5-9), by the princes of Ammon (2Sa 10:1-4; 1Ch 19:1-4), Jeremiah (Jer 26:8-15; 37:12-15; 43:1-4), Amos (Am 7:10-11), Mary (Mt 1:19), Jesus (Mt 9:34; 10:25; 12:2-14; 26:59-61; Mk 3:22; 14:53-65; Lk 23:2; Jn 18:30), Stephen (Ac 6:11-14), Paul (Ac 17:6-7; 21:27-29; 24:1-9, 12-13; 25:1-2, 7; Ro 3:8), Paul and Silas (Ac 16:19-21).

In last days, people will be slanderous (2Ti 3:3).

See Conspiracy; Evidence; False Witness; Persecution; Speaking, Evil; Talebearer.

ACELDAMA *See Akeldama.*

ACHAIA A region of Greece, on the S coast of the gulf of Corinth. Paul visits (Ac 18; 19:21; 1Co 16:15; 2Co 1:1). Generosity of the Christians in (Ro 15:26; 2Co 9:2; 11:10).

ACHAICUS (*belonging to Achaia*). A Corinthian Christian who helped Paul, visited him at Ephesus and was commended for his good will toward Paul (1Co 16:17-19).

ACHAN (a word play from Achar: *troubler*). The son of Carmi and a Judahite of Zerah's clan who participated in the assault upon Jericho; he also violated the sacrificial ban by stealing gold, silver, and a beautiful robe from the spoil taken. After Israel failed to take Ai, inquiry was made by lot, and Achan was found to be guilty. Sin and punishment of (Jos 7; 22:20; 1Ch 2:7).

ACHAR (*trouble*). A variant spelling of Achan (1Ch 2:7).

ACHAZ *See Ahaz.*

ACHBOR *See Acbor.*

ACHIM *See Akim.*

ACHISH (*the king gives*). King of the Philistines, also called Abimelech (Ps 34, title). David escapes to (1Sa 21:10-15; 27; 28:1-2; 29). Achish continues as king of Gath during the reign of Solomon (1Ki 2:39-40).

ACHMETHA *See Ecbatana.*

ACHOR (*trouble*). A valley near Jericho in which Achan was stoned (Jos 7:24-26; 15:7; Isa 65:10; Hos 2:15).

ACHSA, ACHSAH *See Acsah.*

ACHSHAPH *See Acshaph.*

ACHZIB *See Aczib.*

ACKNOWLEDGE

General (Isa 61:9; 63:16; 1Co 14:37-38).

Acknowledging, in an imperative sense, that the Lord is God and that there is no other (Dt 4:39; Pr 3:5-6), in an imprecatory sense (Ps 70:6-7; Jer 10:23-25).

We acknowledge our sins (Ps 32:5; 51:1-6; Isa 59:12-13), our rebellion, idolatry, and wickedness (Jer 3:13; 14:20).

Recognition (1Co 16:17-18).

ACRE The amount of land a pair of oxen could plow in a day (1Sa 14:14; Isa 5:10).

ACROPOLIS (*crest of city, high ground of city*). The upper or higher city, citadel, or castle of a Greek city. Especially the high rocky promontory in Athens where the treasury of the city and its finest temples were located.

ACROSTIC A literary device by which the first letter of each line of poetry forms either a word or the successive letters of the alphabet. An outstanding example is Psalm 119, in which each successive set of eight verses begins with a different letter of the Hebrew alphabet. The effect is not apparent in the English translation, but the Hebrew letters are given between the lines in order to show the construction. NIV notes identify other acrostic poems (Ps. 9-10; 24; 34; 37; 111; 112; 145; Pr 31:10-31; La 1; 2; 3; 4).

ACROSTIC POETRY *See Poetry.*

ACSAH (*decorative anklet*). Caleb's daughter (1Ch 2:49). Caleb offered her as a reward, to be married, to the man who would capture the city of Debir, which was formerly called Kiriath Sepher. Caleb's nephew, Othniel, took the city and won the prize (Jos 15:16-19; Jdg 1:9-15).

ACSHAPH (*fascination*). An important Canaanite city which Joshua captured with its king (Jos 11:1; 12:7, 20). It is named as being on the border of the lot assigned to Asher (Jos 19:24-25).

ACTIONS AT LAW Duty of defendant (Mt 5:40; 1Co 6:7). *See Adjudication at Law; Arbitration.*

ACTIVITY, EVIL Of sinners in general (Pr 1:10-16; 4:14-17; 6:18; Isa 59:7; Mic 2:1-2; 7:3; Ro 3:15-18). Of Pharisees (Mt 23:15). Of Paul in persecuting the church (Ac 9:2; 26:11; Gal 1:13; Php 3:6). Of busybodies in the church, stirring up strife (2Th 3:10-12; 1Ti 5:13; 1Pe 4:15). Of Satan (1Pe 5:8).

ACTS OF THE APOSTLES

Author: Anonymous; traditionally Luke, the companion of Paul

Date: Probably between A.D. 63 and 67

Outline:

I. Peter and the Beginnings of the Church in Israel (chs. 1-12).
  A. "Throughout Judea, Galilee and Samaria" (1:1-9:31; see 9:31).
    1. Introduction (1:1-2).
    2. Christ's post-resurrection ministry (1:3-11).
    3. The period of waiting for the Holy Spirit (1:12-26).
    4. The filling with the Spirit (ch. 2).
    5. The healing of the lame man and the resultant arrest of Peter and John (3:1-4:31).
    6. The community of goods (4:32-5:11).
    7. The arrest of the twelve apostles (5:12-42).
    8. The choice of the Seven (6:1-7).
    9. Stephen's arrest and martyrdom (6:8-7:60).
    10. The scattering of the Jerusalem believers (8:1-4).
    11. Philip's ministry (8:5-40).
      a. In Samaria (8:5-25).
      b. To the Ethiopian eunuch (8:26-40).
    12. Saul's conversion (9:1-31).
  B. "As far as Phoenicia, Cyprus and Antioch" (9:32-12:25; see 11:19).
    1. Peter's ministry on the Mediterranean coast (9:32-11:18).
      a. To Aeneas and Dorcas (9:32-43).
      b. To Cornelius (10:1-11:18).
    2. The new Gentile church in Antioch (11:19-30).
    3. Herod's persecution of the church and his subsequent death (ch. 12).
II. Paul and the Expansion of the Church From Antioch to Rome (chs. 13-28).
  A. "Throughout the region of Phrygia and Galatia" (13:1-15:35; see 16:6).
    1. Paul's first missionary journey (chs. 13-14).
    2. The Jerusalem conference (15:1-35).
  B. "Over to Macedonia" (15:36-21; see 16:9).
    1. Paul's second missionary journey (15:36-18:22).
    2. Paul's third missionary journey (18:23-21:16).
  C. "To Rome" (21:17-28:31; see 28:14).
    1. Paul's imprisonment in Jerusalem (21:17-23:35).
      a. Arrest (21:17-22:29).
      b. Trial before the Sanhedrin (22:30-23:11).
      c. Transfer to Caesarea (23:12-35).
    2. Paul's imprisonment in Caesarea (chs. 24-26).
      a. Trial before Felix (ch. 24).
      b. Trial before Festus (25:1-12).
      c. Hearing before Festus and Agrippa (25:13-26:32).
    3. Voyage to Rome (27:1-28:15).
    4. Two years under house arrest in Rome (28:16-31).

See Missionary Journeys of Paul.

ACZIB (*deceit*).

1. A city of Judah in the Shephelah (Jos 15:44; Mic 1:14) perhaps the same as modern Tell el-Beida, which is SW of Adullam. Taken by Sennacherib, c. 701 B.C. Also called Kezib (Ge 38:5) and Cozeba (1Ch 4:22).

2. A town in Asher on the coast N of Acco (Jos 19:29; Jdg 1:31).

ADADAH A city in Judah (Jos 15:22).

ADAH (*adornment*).

1. The wife of Lamech and mother of Jabal (Ge 4:19-20, 23).

2. The daughter of Elon the Hittite, and the first of three wives of Esau; she was the mother of Eliphaz (Ge 36:2, 4, 10, 12, 16).

ADAIAH (*adornment of Yahweh*).

1. A native of Bozkath, the father of Jedidah, the mother of Josiah, the king of Judah (2Ki 22:1).

2. A Levite of the family of Gershom; the son of Ethni and father of Zerah, in the ancestry of Asaph (1Ch 6:41-43).

3. The son of Shimei and one of the chief Benjamites in pre-exilic Jerusalem (1Ch 8:1, 21).

4. A priest and a Levite; the son of Jeroham (1Ch 9:10-12), also in the parallel list in Nehemiah, although the genealogies do not agree in all details (Ne 11:12).

5. The father of Maaseiah, an army officer who helped make Joash king in the overthrow of Athaliah (2Ch 23:1).

6. A man who married a foreign wife during the Exile and divorced her after the Captivity (Ezr 10:29).

7. Another man who did the same thing (Ezr 10:39).

8. A descendant of Judah whose posterity lived in Jerusalem after the captivity (Ne 11:5).

ADALIA (possibly *honorable*). The fifth son of Haman (Est 9:8).

ADAM (*[red] earth,* or *[ruddy] skin color*).

1. The first man. His creation (Ge 1:26-28; 2:7; 1Co 15:45; 1Ti 2:13). The history of, before he sinned (Ge 1:26-30; 2:16-25). His temptation and sin (Ge 3; Job 31:33, ftn; Isa 43:27; Hos 6:7; Ro 5:14-21; 1Ti 2:14). The subsequent history of (Ge 3:20-24; 4:1-2, 25; 5:1-5). His death (Ge 5:5). Progenitor of the human race (Dt 32:8; Mal 2:10). A type of Christ (Ro 5:14). Brought sin and death into the world (1Co 15:22, 45).

2. Christ: the last Adam (1Co 15:45).

3. A city in the Jordan Valley where the Israelites entered the promised land (Jos 3:16).

ADAMAH (*[red] earth*). A city of Naphtali (Jos 19:36). The location is disputed, yet it may be the modern city of Tell ed-Damiyeh.

ADAMANT NIV "hardest stone" (Eze 3:9; Zec 7:12). *See Diamond; Flint, 2; Hardest Stone; Minerals of the Bible, 1; Stones.*

ADAMI NEKEB (*the ground of piercing*). A place on the border of Naphtali (Jos 19:33).

ADAR (possibly *dark, clouded*).

Month twelve in sacred sequence, six in civil sequence (Ezr 6:15; Est 3:7; 8:12; 9:1, 15-21). The rainy season (February-March); the season for harvesting citrus fruit. *See Month, 12.*

ADAR SHENI (*Second Adar*). This intercalary month (not in Bible) was added about every three years so the lunar calendar would correspond to the solar year. *See Month, 13.*

ADBEEL (*[the] grief of God [El]*). The third son of Ishmael (Ge 25:13; 1Ch 1:29).

ADDAN *See Addon.*

ADDAR (*glorious*).

1. Also called Ard (Ge 46:21; Nu 26:40).

A son of Bela, and grandson of Benjamin (1Ch 8:3). Counted as a son of Benjamin and head of a family in the tribe.

2. A place on the S border of Judah (Jos 15:3).

See Hazar Addar; Ataroth Addar.

ADDER A poisonous snake (Job 20:16; Isa 30:6; 59:5). *See Cobra; Serpent.*

ADDI (*my witness,* or *adorned*). An ancestor of Joseph, the husband of Mary (Lk 3:28).

ADDICTION (1Co 6:12-13; 2Pe 2:19; Ro 6:16-21). *See Abuse.*

ADDON The inhabitants of Addon came up after the Babylonian captivity, but were unable to prove their lineage as descendants of Israel (Ezr 2:59; Ne 7:61).

ADER *See Eder.*

ADIEL (*adornment of God [El]*).

1. A descendant of Simeon who gained more pastoral land for himself in the region of Gedor in the time of Hezekiah (1Ch 4:36).

2. A priest, son of Jahzerah and the father of Maasai; Maasai returned after the Babylonian captivity and was very active in reconstructing the temple (1Ch 9:12).

3. Father of Azmaveth, who was supervisor of David's treasuries (1Ch 27:25).

ADIN (*voluptuous, luxurious*).

1. One whose family returned from exile with Zerubbabel (Ezr 2:15; Ne 7:20).

2. One whose posterity came back with Ezra (Ezr 8:6).

3. The name of a family sealing the covenant (Ne 10:16).

ADINA (*adorned*). The son of Shiza, a Reubenite; one of David's mighty men (1Ch 11:42).

ADINO (*his adorned one*). KJV "Adino the Eznite" is a variant reading in the NIV (2Sa 23:8, ftn). *See Josheb-Basshebeth.*

ADITHAIM (*double [row] of adornments*). A city of Judah in the Shephelah (Jos 15:36).

ADJUDICATION AT LAW To be avoided (Pr 17:14; 20:3; 25:8-10; Mt 5:25, 40; Lk 12:58). *See Actions at Law; Arbitration; Compromise; Court, of Law; Justice; Litigation.*

ADJURATION KJV "adjure" is in the NIV to "pronounce" or "bind under oath," to "make someone swear an oath." It is an act or appeal in which a person in authority imposes some obligation upon another with the strength and solemnity of an oath (Jos 6:26; 1Sa 14:24; 1Ki 22:16; 2Ch 18:15). In the NT the high priest calls upon Jesus to acknowledge that he was the Messiah (Mk 5:7). The oath was binding and required a reply. *See Oath.*

It is also used to exorcise demons (Ac 19:13).

ADLAI (*be just*). The father of Shaphat, who was David's chief herdsman (1Ch 27:29).

ADMAH (*[red] earth*). A city near Gomorrah and Zeboiim (Ge 10:19). The king was Shinab (Ge 14:2, 8). Admah was destroyed along with Sodom and Gomorrah (Dt 29:23, w Ge 19:24-28; Hos 11:8).

ADMATHA (*unrestrained*). The third named prince of Persia and Media (Est 1:14).

ADMINISTRATORS Officers who ruled in Darius's kingdom; satraps report to (Da 6:2-7).

ADMONITION *See Wicked, Warned.*

ADNA (*delight*).

1. A son of Pahath-Moab who had married a foreign wife during the Exile (Ezr 10:30).

2. A chief priest, and the head of his father's house in the days of Joiakim (Ne 12:12-15).

ADNAH (*delight*).

1. One of the captains of the tribe of Manasseh who joined David at Ziklag (1Ch 12:20).

2. A man of Judah who held high military rank under Jehoshaphat (2Ch 17:14).

ADONI-BEZEK (*lord of Bezek*). The king of Bezek, who had the thumbs and big toes of 70 kings cut off: when the Israelites routed the Canaanites and Perizzites and captured Adoni-Bezek, they had his thumbs and big toes cut off (Jdg 1:4-7). *See Bezek.*

ADONIJAH (*[my] lord is Yahweh*).

1. The fourth son of David by his wife Haggith (2Sa 3:4; 1Ki 1:5-6; 1Ch 3:2). Usurpation of, and downfall (1Ki 1). Executed by Solomon (1Ki 2:13, 25).

2. A Levite whom Jehoshaphat sent to assist in teaching the law to the people of Judah (2Ch 17:8).

3. A leader who with Nehemiah sealed the covenant (Ne 10:16). *See Adonikam.*

ADONIKAM (*[my] lord arises*). One of the Jews who returned with Ezra from Babylon with Zerubbabel (Ezr 2:13). Later three of his descendants came with Ezra (Ne 7:18). Probably the same as Adonijah, 3 (Ne 10:16).

ADONIRAM (*[my] Lord is exalted*). A man in charge of forced labor during the reigns of David (2Sa 20:24), and later under Solomon (1Ki 4:6; 5:14), and then Solomon's son, Rehoboam (1Ki 12:18; 2Ch 10:18). He was stoned to death by the people of Israel as their first act of rebellion and revolt, which was lead by Jeroboam, son of Nebat, during the division of the monarchy. Also spelled Adoram (1Ki 12:18; 2Sa 20:24) and Hadoram (2Ch 10:18, ftn).

ADONI-ZEDEK (*[my] lord is righteousness*). The Amorite king of Jerusalem who with four other kings was defeated in battle and slain by Joshua at Gibeon (Jos 10:1-27).

ADOPTION

Explained: (2Co 6:18).

Of Children:

Instances of: Of one born in Abram's house (Ge 15:3), of Joseph's sons (Ge 48:5, 14, 16, 22), of Moses (Ex 2:5-10; Ac 7:20-21; Heb 11:24), of Esther (Est 2:7).

Spiritual Adoption:

Of Israel (Ex 4:22-23; Nu 6:27; Dt 14:1-2; 26:18-19; 27:9; 28:9-10; 32:5-6; 2Ch 7:14; Isa 63:8, 16; Jer 3:19; 31:9, 20; Hos 1:9-10; 11:1; Ro 9:4); of Solomon (2Sa 7:14; 1Ch 22:10; 28:6).

Of the righteous (Pr 14:26; Isa 43:1-6; 63:8, 16; Mt 5:9, 44-45; 12:50; 13:43; Lk 6:35; Jn 11:52; Ro 9:8, 26; 2Co 6:17-18; Eph 2:19; Php 2:15; Heb 12:6-7, 9; 1Jn 3:1-2, 10; 4:4).

Of the Gentiles promised (Hos 2:23; Ro 9:24-26; Eph 3:6, 14-15; Heb 2:10-11, 13); testified to by the Holy Spirit (Ro 8:14-17, 19, 21, 29; Gal 4:5-7); through the gospel (Eph 3:6).

The Means of Adoption:

By God's grace (Eze 16:3-6; Ro 4:16-17; Eph 1:5-6, 11); by faith (Jn 1:12-13; Gal 3:7, 26, 29; Eph 1:5); through Christ (Jn 1:12-13; Gal 3:26; 4:4-5; Eph 1:5; Heb 2:10-11, 13); according to promise (Ro 9:8; Gal 3:29; Eph 3:6); through the gospel (Eph 3:6).

Role of the Holy Spirit:

Witnessed to by the Spirit (Ro 8:16); led by the Spirit as evidence of (Ro 8:14); the Spirit of sonship received (Ro 8:15; Gal 4:6).

Results:

A new name (Nu 6:27; Isa 62:2; Ac 15:17); disciplined by the Father (Dt 8:5; 2Sa 7:14; Pr 3:11-12; Heb 12:5-11); safety (Pr 14:26); God is Father-Redeemer (Isa 63:16); recipient of God's long-suffering mercy (Jer 31:1, 19-20); a new inheritance (Mt 13:43; Ro 8:17); the new birth (Jn 1:12-13); will become brothers and sisters of Christ (Jn 20:17; Heb 2:11-12).

A new lifestyle: A love of peace (Mt 5:9); desire for God's glory (Mt 5:16); likeness to God (Mt 5:44-45, 48); an avoiding of pretense (Mt 6:1-4); a forgiving spirit (Mt 6:14); confidence in God (Mt 6:25-34); a spirit of prayer (Mt 7:7-11); a merciful spirit (Lk 6:35-36); holiness (2Co 6:17-18; 7:1; Php 2:15); following God (Eph 5:1).

A new future: Gathered as one by Christ (Jn 11:52); final consummation (Ro 8:19, 23; 1Jn 3:2).

ADORAIM (possibly *pair of knolls*). A fortified city in SW Judah, five miles SW of Hebron, fortified by Rehoboam, son of Solomon (2Ch 11:9).

ADORAM *See Adoniram.*

ADORNING

Physical:

Bracelets (Ge 24:22; Nu 31:50; 2Sa 1:10). Earrings (Ge 35:4; Ex 32:2; 35:22; Nu 31:50; Jdg 8:24; Pr 25:12; Eze 16:12). Chains, used as ornaments (Ge 41:42; Pr 1:9; Eze 16:11; Da 5:29). Rings, for the fingers (Ge 41:42; Ex 35:22; Est 3:10; 8:8; Job 42:11; Isa 3:21; Hos 2:13; Lk 15:22). Ornaments, wearing of (Ex 33:4; Isa 3:18; Jer 2:32; 4:30; Eze 16:11; 23:40).

Jewels:

General references to (Ex 35:22; Nu 31:50). Discarded or refusal to wear (Ge 35:4; Ex 33:4; 1Pe 3:3). Brought as offerings to God (Ex 35:22; Nu 31:50; Mt 2:1-2, 9-11).

Spiritual:

Clothed in righteousness, salvation, strength (Job 29:14; Ps 132:16; Isa 52:1; 61:10; Zec 3:4; Mt 22:11). General references to (Ps 45:13; Pr 1:9; 4:9; SS 1:10; Isa 61:10; 1Pe 3:3-4; Rev 21:2). White clothing, the heavenly garment (Mt 17:2; Rev 3:5; 3:18; 4:4; 7:9; 19:8).

ADRAMMELECH (*nobility of Molech [king]*).

1. The name given to Adar, the god brought to Samaria from Assyria by the Sepharvites (2Ki 17:31).

2. One of the sons of Sennacherib, who along with his brother Sharezer, killed their father while he was worshiping in the temple of his god Nisroch (2Ki 19:37; Isa 37:38).

ADRAMYTTIUM (*the mansion of death*). A port city of Mysia, in the NW part of the Roman province of Asia (Ac 27:2).

ADRIATIC The Adriatic Sea, a body of water between Italy on the W and Dalmatia, Macedonia, and Achaia on the E (Ac 27:27).

ADRIEL (*[my] help is God [El]*). The son of Barzillai the Meholathite; Saul's son-in-law (1Sa 18:19; 2Sa 21:8-9).

ADULLAM, ADULLAMITE (*retreat* or *refuge;* possibly *[they are] just*).

1. A cave near the Dead Sea. David takes refuge in (1Sa 22:1; 2Sa 23:13; 1Ch 11:15). *See also the titles of Pss 57 and 142.*

2. An ancient city of Canaan (Ge 38:1; Jos 12:15; 15:35), fortified by Rehoboam (2Ch 11:5-7), inhabited after the Exile (Ne 11:25-30), referred to by Micah (Mic 1:15).

3. The people of Adullam, used of Hirah, Judah's friend (Ge 38:1, 12, 20).

ADULLAMITE *See Adullam, 3.*

ADULTERY

Defined:

(Mt 5:28, 32; 19:9; Mk 10:11-12; Lk 16:18; Ro 7:1-3). Laws concerning (Nu 5:11-31; Dt 22:13-29).

Repulsive to the righteous (Job 31:1-12; Eze 18:5-6, 9). Fatal consequences of (Pr 2:16-19; 5:3-4, 5-23; 6:23-35; 7:1-27; 9:13-18; 22:14; 23:26-28). Moral and spiritual corruption by (Jer 3:1-2; 5:7-8; Hos 4:1-2, 9-19). Source of: the heart (Mt 15:19; Mk 7:21-23), the sinful nature (Gal 5:19-21).

Figurative:

(Jer 3:1-2; 9:2; 23:10; Eze 16:15-16; Hos 1; 2:1-2; 3:1; 7:1-4; Ro 7:1-6).

Forbidden:

(Ex 20:14; Lev 18:20; 19:29; Dt 5:18; 23:17; Pr 31:3; Mt 5:27-28; 19:16-19; Mk 10:17-19; Lk 18:18-20; Ac 15:20, 29; Ro 13:9, 13; 1Co 5:9-11; 6:13-16-18; 10:7-8; Eph 4:17-19; 5:3; Col 3:5; 1Th 4:3-7; 1Ti 1:9-10; Jas 2:10-11).

Forgiveness of:

(Jdg 19:1-4; Jn 4:16-26, 39-42; 8:10-11).

Lack of Repentance in:

(Pr 30:20; Isa 57:3-4; Jer 7:9-15; Ro 1:28-32; 2Co 12:21; 1Pe 4:3-4; Rev 9:20-21).

Instances of:

The Sodomites (Ge 19:4-8; Jude 7). Lot and his two daughters (Ge 19:31-38). Shechem (Ge 34:1-2). Reuben (Ge 35:22). Judah (Ge 38:1-26). Potiphar's wife (Ge 39:6-12). Israelites (Ex 32:6; Jer 23:10-11; 29:23; Eze 22:9-11; 33:26; Hos 7:4). Gilead, the father of Jephthah (Jdg 11:1). Samson (Jdg 16:1). The Levite's concubine (Jdg 19:1-2). The men of Gibeah (Jdg 19:22-25). The sons of Eli (1Sa 2:22). David (2Sa 11:1-5). Amnon, David's oldest son by Ahinoam (2Sa 13:1-20). Absalom, David's third son by Maacah (2Sa 16:22). Herod (Mt 14:3-4; Mk 6:17-18; Lk 3:19). The Samaritan woman (Jn 4:17-18). The woman brought to Jesus in the temple (Jn 8:3-11). The Corinthians (1Co 5:1-5). Gentiles (Eph 4:17-20; 1Pe 4:3-4). Those living in the last days (2Ti 3:6).

Penalties for:

Curses (Nu 5:11-31; Dt 27:20-23; Job 24:15-18). Death (Ge 20:3, 7; 26:11; 38:24; Lev 20:10-12; 21:9; Dt 22:13-27; 2Sa 12:7-14; Eze 23:45-48; Jn 8:4-5). Fines (Ex 22:16-17; Dt 22:19, 28-29). Make a guilt offering (Lev 19:20-22). Divine judgments (2Sa 12:10-12; Jer 29:22-23; Eze 16:38-41; Mal 3:5; 1Co 10:8; Heb 13:4; 2Pe 2:9-10, 14; Rev 2:20-22; 18:9-10). Excommunication (1Co 5:1-13; Eph 5:11-12). Exclusion from the kingdom of God (1Co 6:9-10; Gal 5:19, 21; Eph 5:5-6; Jude 7; Rev 21:8; 22:14-15).

See Fornication; Idolatry; Lasciviousness; Prostitute; Rape; Sensuality; Homosexual; Prostitute.

ADUMMIM (*red [streaks]*). A pass on the road between Jerusalem and Jericho (Jos 15:7; 18:17), on the north border of Judah and the south border of Benjamin. Held to be the scene of Jesus' parable of the Good Samaritan (Lk 10:30-35).

ADVENT *See Jesus the Christ, Second Coming; Millennium.*

ADVERSARY In general, an enemy; personal, national, or supernatural (Ex 23:22; 1Sa 2:10; Na 1:2; Mt 5:25). Specifically, Satan is the enemy of all mankind (1Pe 5:8).

ADVERSITY *See Afflictions.*

ADVICE *See Counsel.*

ADVOCATE (*helper, Paraclete*). An advocate is one who pleads the case or the cause of another. The Holy Spirit or Counselor (Jn 14:16-17, 26; 15:26; 16:7), Jesus Christ himself (1Jn 2:1).

AENEAS (possibly *praise*). A paralytic, healed at Lydda by Peter (Ac 9:32-35).

AENON (*spring*). A place probably N of Jerusalem to the W of the Jordan Valley because the Johannine account indicates that there was "plenty of water." Some scholars identify ancient Salim with present-day Salim, which is about three to four miles E of Nablus (Shechem). A place near Salim, W of the Jordan, where John the Baptist baptized (Jn 3:22-23).

AEON (*a segment of time, eternity*). A Greek word indicating a period of time, usually translated ever or forever (Eph 3:21; Jn 6:51, 58), age or ages (Eph 1:21; Col 1:26), world (Ro 12:2; 2Ti 4:10).

AFFECTIONS

Of Believers:

Supremely set on God (Dt 6:5; Ps 42:1; 73:23-26; 119:9-20; Mk 12:30). Should be zealous for God (Ps 69:9; 119:139; Gal 4:18). Should not grow cold (Ps 106:12-13; Mt 24:12; Gal 4:14-16; Rev 2:4). Should be set upon the house and worship of God (1Ch 29:3; Ps 26:8; 27:4; 84:1-2), the people of God (Ps 16:3; Ro 12:10; 2Co 7:13-16; 1Th 2:8), the commandments and statutes of God (Ps 19:8-10; 119), heavenly things (Col 3:1-2).

Blessedness of making God the object of our affections (Ps 91:14). Christ claims the first place in (Mt 10:37; Lk 14:26). Stirred up by communion with Christ (Lk 24:32).

Of the Wicked:

Not sincerely set on God (Isa 58:1-2; Eze 33:31-32; Lk 8:13), are unnatural and perverted (Ro 1:18-32; 2Ti 3:1-9; 2Pe 2:10-22). Desires of the flesh, crucified in believers (Ro 6:5-7; Gal 5:24), should be put to death by the Spirit (Ro 8:12-13; 13:14; 1Co 9:27; Col 3:5-6; 1Th 4:3-7). False teachers seek to captivate (Gal 1:9-10; 4:17; 2Ti 3:6; 2Pe 2:3, 18; Rev 2:14, 20).

AFFLICTED

In General:

Sympathy with (Job 6:14; Mt 25:34-40). Help for (Job 22:29; Isa 58:6-7; Lk 10:30-37; 1Ti 5:9-10). Rewards of service to (Isa 53:10; Mt 25:34-45). Exhorted to pray (Jas 5:13). Prayer for healing (Jas 5:14-15).

Duty to:

Pity (Job 6:14), comfort (Job 16:5; 29:25; 2Co 1:3-5; 1Th 4:18), relieve (Job 31:19-20; Isa 58:9-12; Php 4:14; 1Ti 5:10), protect the poor (Ps 82:3; Pr 22:22; 31:5), pray (Ac 12:5; Php 1:19; Jas 5:14-16), sympathize (Ro 12:15; Gal 6:2), remember those in prison and those who are mistreated (Heb 13:3).

AFFLICTED BELIEVERS

God's Relation to:

God is a refuge and strength to (Ps 27:5-6; Isa 25:4; Jer 16:19; Na 1:7), delivers (Ps 34:4, 19; Pr 12:13; Jer 39:17-18), protects (Ps

34:20), is with (Ps 46:5, 7; Isa 43:2-3), comforts (Isa 49:13; Jer 31:13; Mt 5:4; 2Co 1:3-5; 7:6).

Christ comforts (Isa 61:2, w Lk 4:18-19; Mt 11:28-30; Lk 7:13; Jn 14:1; 16:33), preserves (Isa 63:9; Lk 21:18), is with (Jn 14:18), supports (2Ti 4:17; Heb 2:18), delivers (Rev 3:10).

Attitudes and Actions of:

Should be resigned (1Sa 3:18; 2Ki 20:19; Job 1:21; Ps 39:9), acknowledge the justice of their discipline (Ne 9:33; Job 2:10; Isa 64:5-7; La 3:39; Mic 7:9), not despise discipline (Job 5:17-18; Pr 3:11-12; Heb 12:5-6), trust in the goodness of God (Job 13:15; Ps 71:20; 2Co 1:9), avoid sin (Job 34:31-32; Jn 5:14; 1Pe 2:12), praise God (Ps 13:5-6; 56:8-11; 57:6-7; 71:20-23), take encouragement from former mercy (Ps 27:9; 2Co 1:10), call upon God in the day of trouble (Ps 50:15; 55:16-17). *See Affliction, Prayer under.* Turn and devote themselves to God (Ps 116:7-9; Jer 50:3-5; Hos 6:1), be patient (Lk 21:19; Ro 12:12; 2Th 1:4-7; Jas 1:4; 1Pe 2:20), imitate Christ (Heb 12:1-3; 1Pe 2:21-23), imitate the prophets (Jas 5:10).

Examples of:

Joseph (Ge 39:20-23; Ps 105:17-19), Eli (1Sa 3:11-18), David (2Sa 12:15-23), Nehemiah (Ne 1:3-4), Job (Job 1:20-22), Paul (Ac 20:22-24; 21:13), the apostles (1Co 4:13; 2Co 6:4-10), Moses (Heb 11:24-29).

AFFLICTION

Consolation Under:

God is the Author and Giver of (Ps 23:4; Ro 15:5; 2Co 1:3-4; 7:6-7; Col 1:11; 2Th 2:16-17). Christ is the Author and Giver of (Isa 61:1-3; Jn 14:18; 2Co 1:5). The Holy Spirit is the Author and Giver of (Jn 14:16-17; 15:26; 16:7; Ac 9:31).

In the prospect of death (Job 19:25-27; Ps 23:4; Jn 14:1-3; 2Co 5:1; 1Th 4:12-13; Heb 4:9-10; Rev 7:14-17; 14:13). Through the Holy Scriptures (Ps 119:50, 76; Ro 15:4). Pray for (Ps 119:81-83). By ministers of the gospel (Isa 40:1-2; 1Co 14:3; 2Co 1:4, 6). Promised (Ps 119:76; Isa 51:3, 12; 66:13; Eze 14:22-23; Hos 2:14; Zec 1:17). Believers should administer to each other (1Th 4:18; 5:11, 14). Under the infirmities of age (Ps 71:9, 18).

Is sought in vain from the world (Ps 69:20; Ecc 4:1; La 1:2), abundant (Ps 71:21; Isa 66:10-11), a cause of praise (Isa 12:1; 49:13), everlasting (2Th 2:16-17), firm and secure (Heb 6:17-20).

To the persecuted (Dt 33:27), the poor (Ps 10:14; 34:6, 9-10), those deserted by friends or family (Ps 27:10; 41:9-12; Jn 14:18; 15:18-19), the sick (Ps 41:3), the troubled in mind (Ps 42; 94:19; Jn 14:1, 27; 16:20-22), those who mourn for sin (Ps 51:17; Isa 1:18; 40:1-2; 61:1-3; Mic 7:18-19; Lk 4:18-19), the tempted (Ro 16:17-20; 1Co 10:13; 2Co 12:9; Jas 1:12; 4:7-10; 2Pe 2:9; Rev 2:10).

Prayer Under:

For the presence and support of God (Ps 10:1; 102:2). Exhortation to (Jas 5:13). That, God would consider our trouble (2Ki 19:16; Ne 9:32; Ps 9:13; La 5), we may be taught the uncertainty of life (Ps 39:4), the Holy Spirit may not be withdrawn (Ps 51:11), we may be turned to God (Ps 51:12-15; 80:7; 85:4-7; Jer 31:18).

For, protection and preservation from enemies (2Ki 19:19; 2Ch 20:12; Ps 17:8-9; 143:11-12), divine teaching and direction (Job 34:32; Ps 27:11; 143:10), divine comfort (Ps 4:6; 119:76-77), mercy (Ps 6:2; Hab 3:2), deliverance from troubles (Ps 25:17, 22; 39:10; Isa 64:9-12; Jer 17:14), pardon and deliverance from sin (Ps 39:8; 51:1-17; 79:8-9), relief from troubles (Ps 39:12-13), restoration of joy (Ps 51:8, 12; 69:29; 90:14-15), increase of faith (Mk 9:24).

AFFLICTIONS

In General:

God, determines the continuance of (Ge 15:13-14; Nu 14:33; Isa 10:25; Jer 29:10), appoints (2Ki 6:33; Job 5:6, 17; Ps 66:10-11; Am 3:6; Mic 6:9), dispenses as he will (Job 11:10; Isa 10:15-16; 45:7), regulates the measure of (Ps 80:5; Isa 9:1; Jer 46:28), does not willingly send (La 3:33).

Consequent upon the Fall (Ge 3:16-19). Frequently end in good (Ge 50:20; Ex 1:11-12, Dt 8:15-18; Jer 24:5-7; Eze 20:37). Sin visited with (2Sa 12:14; Ps 89:30-32; Isa 57:17, Ac 13:10-11). Sin produces (Job 4:8; 20:11; Pr 1:31).

Always less than we deserve (Ezr 9:13; Ps 103:10).Man is born to (Job 5:6-7; 14:1). Often severe (Job 16:7-16; Ps 42:7; 66:12; Rev 7:14). Tempered with mercy (Ps 78:38-39; 106:43-46; Isa 30:18-21; La 3:32; Mic 7:7-9; Na 1:12). Believers are to expect (Jn 16:33; Ac 14:22). Believers appointed to (1Th 3:3).

Of Believers:

Exhibit the love and faithfulness of God (Dt 8:5; Ps 119:75; Pr 3:11-12; 1Co 11:32; Heb 12:6-11; Rev 3:19-22). Believers have joy under (Job 5:17-18; Jas 5:11). Are but temporary (Ps 30:5; 103:9-10; Isa 54:7-8; Jn 16:20; 1Pe 1:6; 5:10). End in joy and blessedness (Ps 126:5-6; Isa 61:2-3; Mt 5:4; 1Pe 4:13-14). Often comes from the profession of the gospel (Mt 24:9; Jn 15:21; 2Ti 3:11-12). Are comparatively light (Ac 20:23-24; Ro 8:18; 2Co 4:17-18).

Benefits to Believers:

In, trying our faith and obedience (Ge 22:1-2, w Heb 11:17-18; Ex 15:23-25; Dt 8:2-3, 16; 1Pe 1:7; Rev 2:10), humbling us (Dt 8:3, 16; 2Ch 7:13-14; La 3:19-24; 2Co 12:7), leading us to confession of sin (Nu 21:7; Ps 32:4-5; 51:3-6), turning us to God (Dt 4:30-31; Ne 1:8-9; Ps 78:34-38; Isa 10:20-21; Hos 2:6-7), leading us to seek God in prayer (Jdg 4:3; Jer 31:18; La 2:17-19; Hos 5:14-15; Jnh 2:1), testing and exhibiting our sincerity (Job 23:10; Ps 66:10; Pr 17:3), keeping us from again departing from God (Job 34:31-32; Isa 10:20; Eze 14:10-11), convincing us of sin (Job 36:8-10; Ps 119:67; Lk 15:16, 18), exhibiting the power and faithfulness of God (Ps 34:19-20; 2Co 4:8-11), exercising our patience (Ps 40:1; Ro 5:3; Jas 1:3; 1Pe 2:20), teaching us the will of God (Ps 119:71; Isa 26:9), purifying us (Ecc 7:2-3; Isa 1:25-26; 48:10; Jer 9:6-7; Zec 13:9; Mal 3:2-3), promoting the glory of God (Jn 9:1-3; 11:3-4; 21:18-19), rendering us fruitful in good works (Jn 15:2; Heb 12:10-11), furthering the gospel (Ac 8:3-4; 11:19-21; Php 1:12-13; 2Ti 2:9-10; 4:16-18).

Examples of Benefits to Believers—

Joseph's brothers (Ge 42:21), Joseph (Ge 45:5-8), Israel (Dt 8:3-5), Josiah (2Ki 22:19), Hezekiah (2Ch 32:25-26), Manasseh (2Ch 33:12), Jonah (Jnh 2:7), Prodigal son (Lk 15:21).

Of the Wicked:

Are ineffective of themselves, for their conversion (Ex 9:30; Isa 9:13; Jer 2:30; Hag 2:17). God is glorified in (Ex 14:4; Eze 38:22-23). Their persecution of believers, a cause of (Dt 30:7; Ps 55:19; Zec 2:9; 2Th 1:6). Are multiplied (Dt 31:17; Job 20:12-18; Ps 32:10). Sometimes humble them (1Ki 21:27). Frequently harden (Ne 9:28-31; Jer 5:3). Are continual (Job 15:20; Ecc 2:23; Isa 32:10). Produce slavish fear (Job 15:24; Ps 73:19; Jer 49:3, 5). Are often judicially sent (Job 21:17; Ps 107:17; Jer 30:15). God holds in derision (Ps 37:13; Pr 1:26-27). Are for examples to others (Ps 64:7-9; Zep 3:6-7; 1Co 10:5-13; 2Pe 2:6). Are often sudden (Ps 73:19; Pr 6:15; Isa 30:12-13; Rev 18:10). Failure to repent is a cause of (Pr 1:30-31; Eze 24:13; Am 4:6-12; Zec 7:11-12; Rev 2:21-22). Believers should not be alarmed at (Pr 3:25-26).

Examples of Afflictions of the Wicked—

Pharaoh and the Egyptians (Ex 9:14-15; 14:24-25), Ahaziah (2Ki 1:1-4), Gehazi (2Ki 5:27), Jehoram (2Ch 21:12-16), Uzziah (2Ch 26:19-21), Ahaz (2Ch 28:5-8, 22).

AFTERWARD (Ps 73:24; Pr 20:17; Mt 25:11; Jn 13:36; 1Co 15:46; Gal 3:23; Heb 12:11, 17).

AGABUS A prophet living in Jerusalem who prophesied a world-wide famine which was fulfilled during the reign of Claudius (Ac 11:27-30). He also met Paul in Caesarea and warned him that he would be arrested in Jerusalem (Ac 21:10-11).

AGAG (possibly *violent*).

1. The king of Amalek, referred to by Balaam (Nu 24:2-3, 7).

2. Another king of Amalek. Saul spared Agag when he should have killed him. When Samuel came into the camp, he rebuked Saul and ordered that Agag be brought to him. Samuel killed Agag as Saul should have according to God's command (1Sa 15:8-33).

AGAGITE (possibly *violent*). A description of Haman (Est 3:1, 10; 8:3, 5; 9:24). The LXX understood the term to mean "enemy." Josephus explains it as a synonym of Amalek, a descendant of Agag (Ant. xi, 6, 5). *See Agag, 2.*

AGAPE (*love; volitional and self-sacrificial love*). A Greek word meaning "love" and "love feasts." *See Love; Love Feast.*

AGAR *See Hagar.*

AGATE A precious stone used in the high priest's breastpiece (Ex 28:19; 39:12). KJV "agates" is also translated "rubies" in the NIV (Isa 54:12; Eze 27:16). *See Minerals of the Bible, 1; Ruby; Stones.*

AGE *See Aeon.*

AGE (OLD), AGED *See Old Age.*

AGEE (possibly *fugitive*). A Hararite and the father of Shammah (2Sa 23:11).

AGENCY Duties entrusted to God's servants.

In salvation of people (Job 33:14-30; Ps 8:2; Mt 4:19; 5:13-16; Lk 1:17; 5:10; 10:17; 1Co 1:26-29; 1Th 2:4; 1Ti 1:11; 6:20; Jas 5:20).

In executing judgments (Ge 3:15; 1Sa 15:18; 2Sa 7:14; 2Ki 9:6-9; 19:25-26; 2Ch 22:7; Ps 17:13-14; Isa 10:5-6; 13:5; 41:15; Jer 27:8; 51:20-23).

AGONY Under judgment of God (Eze 30:16; Mic 4:10; Rev 9:5; 16:10). Of the rich man (Lk 16:24-25). Of Jesus (Ac 2:24).

AGORA (*marketplace*). In ancient cities the town meeting place was the market where the public met for the exchange of merchandise, information, and ideas (Mk 6:56; Ac 17:17).

AGRAPHA (*unwritten things*). Sayings ascribed to Jesus transmitted to us outside of the canonical Gospels. The number is not large, and most are obviously apocryphal or spurious. They are found in the NT outside of the Gospels (Ac 1:4ff; 11:16; 20:35; 1Co 7:10), ancient manuscripts of the NT, patristic literature, papyri, and apocryphal gospels.

AGRICULTURE The occupation of man before the Fall (Ge 2:15). Rendered laborious by the curse on the earth (Ge 3:17-19). Man condemned to labor in, after the Fall (Ge 3:23). Contributes to the support of all (Ecc 5:9). The providence of God to be acknowledged in the produce of (Jer 5:24; Hos 2:8).

Requires:

Hard work will be abundantly recompensed (Pr 12:11; 13:23; 28:19; Heb 6:7). Diligence (Pr 27:23-27; Ecc 11:6). Wisdom (Isa 28:26). Hard work (2Ti 2:6). Patience in waiting (Jas 5:7).

Persons Engaged in, Called:

Workers of the ground (Ge 4:2). Workers or hired men (Mt 9:37; 20:1).

In General:

Patriarchs engaged in (Ge 4:2; 9:20). The labor of, supposed to be lessened by Noah (Ge 5:29, w Ge 9:20). Soil of Canaan suited to (Ge 13:10; Dt 8:7-10). Climate of Canaan favorable to (Dt 11:10-12). The Israelites loved and followed (2Ch 26:10). Peace favorable to (Jer 31:24). War destructive to (Jer 5:16-17; 51:23).

Was Promoted Among the Israelites by:

The prohibition against usury (Ex 22:25). The right of redemption (Lev 25:23-28). The promises of God's blessing on (Lev 26:4; Dt 7:13; 11:14-15). Allotments to each family (Nu 36:7-9).

Enactments to Protect:

Against, the trespass of cattle (Ex 22:5), injuring the produce of (Ex 22:6). Not to, be engaged in during the Sabbatical year (Ex 23:10-11), covet the fields of another (Dt 5:21), move landmarks (Dt 19:14; Pr 22:28), cut down crops of another (Dt 23:25). Produce of, exported (1Ki 5:11; Eze 27:17). Often performed by hired help (1Ch 27:26; 2Ch 26:10; Mt 20:8; Lk 17:7). Produce of, often reduced in yield because of sin (Isa 5:10; 7:23; Jer 12:13; Joel 1:10-12). Grief resulted from the failure of the fruits of (Joel 1:11; Am 5:16-17).

Activities in:

Binding sheaves of grain or weeds into bundles (Ge 37:7; Mt 13:30). Stacking (Ex 22:6). Gleaning (Lev 19:9; Ru 2:3). Pruning (Lev 25:3; Isa 5:6; Jn 15:2). Watering (Dt 11:10; 1Co 3:6-8). Threshing (Dt 25:4; Jdg 6:11). Winnowing (Ru 3:2; Job 39:12; Mt 3:12). Plowing (Job 1:14). Harrowing (Job 39:10; Isa 28:24). Mowing (Ps 72:6; Am 7:1; Jas 5:4). Planting (Pr 31:16; Isa 44:14; Jer 31:5). Sowing (Ecc 11:4; Isa 32:20; Mt 13:3). Clearing out the stones (Isa 5:2). Hedging (Isa 5:2, 5; Hos 2:6). Digging (Lk 13:8; 16:3). Reaping (Isa 17:5). Fertilizing (Isa 25:10; Lk 14:34-35). Storing in barns (Mt 6:26; 13:30). Weeding (Mt 13:28). Grafting (Ro 11:17-19, 24).

Animals Used in:

The donkey (Dt 22:10), ox (Dt 22:10; 25:4), horse (Isa 28:28).

Tools of:

The sickle (Dt 16:9; 23:25), cart (1Sa 6:7; Isa 28:27-28), mattock (1Sa 13:20), ax (1Sa 13:20), plow (1Sa 13:20), fork (1Sa 13:21), iron pick (2Sa 12:31), hoe (Isa 7:25), pruning knives (Isa 18:5; Joel 3:10), rod (Isa 28:27), winnowing fork (Jer 15:7; Mt 3:12; Lk 3:17), shovel (Isa 30:24), threshing sledge (Isa 41:15), sieve (Am 9:9).

Illustrative of the:

Cultivating the heart (Jer 4:3; Hos 10:12). Cultivating the church (1Co 3:9).

AGRIPPA I Known in history as King Herod Agrippa I or Herod Agrippa, and in the NT as Herod, 10 B.C. to A.D. 44 He was the grandson of Herod the Great and ruled over the whole of Judea from A.D. 41 to 44. He killed James to please the Jews and intended to do the same to Peter (Ac 12:1-5). He died suddenly in Caesarea (Ac 12:19-23; Jos. Antiq. XIX.viii.2), A.D. 44.

AGRIPPA II Known in history as King Herod Agrippa II, Marcus Julius Agrippa, and in the NT as Agrippa, A.D. 28 to after A.D. 93, probably c. A.D. 100. He was the son of Agrippa I, and ruled over only a small part of his father's territory. Paul appeared before the tribunal of Agrippa and Festus (Ac 25:23-26). Died in c. A.D. 100.

AGUE NIV "fever"; a disease "that will destroy your sight and drain away your life" (Lev 26:16). *See Fever.*

AGUR (*gatherer,* possibly *wage earner*). The son of Jakeh; author or collector of the wise sayings of the Proverbs 30.

AHA A term of derision (Ps 35:21; 40:15; 70:3; Eze 25:3; 26:2).

AHAB (*brother of father*).

1. King of Israel for twenty-two years, reigning in Samaria (1Ki 16:29). Idolatry of (1Ki 16:30-33; 18:18-20; 21:25-26). Marries Jezebel (1Ki 16:31). Reproved by Elijah; assembles the prophets of Baal (1Ki 18:15-46). Defeats Ben-Hadad (1Ki 20). Illegally confiscates Naboth's vineyard (1Ki 21). Closing history and death of (1Ki 22:1-41; 2Ch 18). Succeeded by his son, Ahaziah (1Ki 22:40). Prophecies against (1Ki 20:42; 21:19-24; 22:19-28; 2Ki 9:8, 25-26). Other wickedness of (2Ki 3:2; 2Ch 21:6; 22:3-4; Mic 6:16). The seventy sons of, all his chief men, his close friends, and his priest were murdered (2Ki 10:1-11).

2. A false prophet (Jer 29:21-22).

AHARAH (*brother of Rah*). Also called Ashbel, Ahiram, and Aher, the third son of Benjamin (Ge 46:21; Nu 26:38; 1Ch 7:12; 8:1).

AHARHEL (*brother of Rachel*). A son of Harum, and the founder of a family enrolled in the tribe of Judah (1Ch 4:8).

AHASAI *See Ahzai.*

AHASBAI (*I seek refuge in Yahweh*). A Maacathite and the father of Eliphelet, one of David's heroes (2Sa 23:34). Possibly the same as Ur (1Ch 11:35). *See Ur.*

AHASUERUS Hebrew transliteration of the name of the Persian king Xerxes. *See Xerxes.*

AHAVA A Babylonian town on the Ahava Canal (Ezr 8:15, 21, 31).

AHAZ (*he has grasped*).

1. King of Judah, son and successor of Jotham (2Ki 15:38; 16:1; 2Ch 27:9; 28:1). Idolatrous abominations of (2Ki 16:3-4; 2Ch 28:2-4, 22-25). Kingdom of, invaded by the kings of Syria and Samaria (2Ki 16:5-6; 2Ch 28:5-8). Robs the temple to purchase aid from the king of Assyria (2Ki 16:7-9, 17-18; 2Ch 28:21). Visits Damascus, obtains a unique pattern of an altar, which he substitutes for the altar in the temple in Jerusalem and otherwise perverts the forms of worship (2Ki 16:10-16). Stairway of (2Ki 20:11; Isa 38:8). Prophets in the reign of (Isa 1:1; Hos 1:1; Mic 1:1). Prophecies concerning (Isa 7:13-25). Succeeded by Hezekiah (2Ki 16:20).

2. Son of Micah and great-grandson of Jonathan (1Ch 8:35; 9:41-42).

AHAZIAH (*Yahweh has upheld*).

1. King of Judah. Also called Azariah (2Ch 22:6, ftn) and Jehoahaz (2Ch 21:17, ftn). History of (2Ki 8:25-29; 9:16-29). Gifts of, to the temple (2Ki 12:18). Brothers of, slain (2Ki 10:13-14). Succeeded by Athaliah (2Ch 22:10-12).

2. King of Israel. History of (1Ki 22:40, 49, 51-53; 2Ch 20:35-37; 2Ki 1). Succeeded by Jehoram (2Ki 3:1).

AHBAN (*brother of intelligent one*). A Judahite, of the house of Jerahmeel (1Ch 2:29).

AHER (*another, a substitute*). A Benjamite (1Ch 7:12). *See Aharah.*

AHI (*my brother,* possibly *Yahweh is [my] brother*).
1. Chief of the Gadites in Gilead (1Ch 5:15).
2. A man of Asher, son of Shomer (1Ch 7:34).

AHIAH (*brother of Yahweh*).
1. A leader of Israel who agreed to the covenant of Nehemiah (Ne 10:26).
2. *See Ahijah.*

AHIAM (*brother of mother*). One of David's heroes (2Sa 23:33). The son of Sacar (1Ch 11:35).

AHIAN (*little brother*). Son of Shemida (1Ch 7:19).

AHIEZER (*[my] brother is a help*).
1. Captain of the tribe of Dan (Nu 1:12; 2:25-26). Contributes to the tabernacle (Nu 7:66-71).
2. One of David's valiant men (1Ch 12:3).

AHIHUD (*[my] brother has majesty*).
1. A prince of Asher, assists in allotting the land of Canaan among the tribes (Nu 34:27).
2. A son of Bela (1Ch 8:7).

AHIJAH (*[my] brother is Yahweh*).
1. Son of Bela (1Ch 8:7).
2. Son of Jerahmeel (1Ch 2:25).
3. A priest in Shiloh, probably identified with Ahimelech (1Sa 22:11). Was priest in Saul's reign (1Sa 14:3, 18). Killed (1Sa 22:11-19).
4. One of David's heroes (1Ch 11:36). Also called Eliam (2Sa 23:34).
5. A Levite who was treasurer in the tabernacle (1Ch 26:20).
6. Son of Shisha, secretary of Solomon (1Ki 4:3).
7. A prophet in Shiloh (1Ki 11:29-39; 12:15).
8. Father of Baasha (1Ki 15:27, 33; 2Ki 9:9).
See Ahiah.

AHIKAM (*[my] brother stands*). Son of Shaphan (2Ki 22:12-14; 25:22; 2Ch 34:20; Jer 26:24; 39:14; 40:5-16; 41:1-18; 43:6).

AHILUD (*[my] brother is born*). Father of: Baana (1Ki 4:12), Jehoshaphat (2Sa 8:16; 20:24; 1Ki 4:3; 1Ch 18:15).

AHIMAAZ (*[my] brother is fury*).
1. Father-in-law of king Saul (1Sa 14:50).
2. Son of Zadok, the high priest. Loyal to David (2Sa 15:36; 17:17-20; 18:19-33; 1Ch 6:8-9, 53).
3. One of Solomon's twelve district governors (1Ki 4:15). He married Basemath, the daughter of Solomon. Some suggest that he should be identified with the son of Zadok.

AHIMAN (possibly *[my] brother is a gift*).
1. One of the three giant sons of Anak seen in Mt. Hebron by the spies (Nu 13:22). Sheshai, Ahiman, and Talmai, were driven by Caleb from Hebron (Jos 15:14) and killed (Jdg 1:10).
2. A Levite gatekeeper (1Ch 9:17).

AHIMELECH (*[my] brother is king*).
1. Saul's high priest who helped David by giving him the bread of the Presence and Goliath's sword. Upon hearing this, Saul ordered the death of Ahimelech and the other priests with him (1Sa 21-22). Abiathar, son of Ahimelech, escaped.
2. A Hittite who, with Abishai, was asked to accompany David to Saul's camp (1Sa 26:6).
3. Son of Abiathar, and grandson of Ahimelech (2Sa 8:17; 1Ch 18:16; 24:6). *See Abiathar.*

AHIMOTH (*[my] brother is my support* possibly *my brother is Mot*). Son of Elkanah (1Ch 6:25), descendant of Kohath and a Levite.

AHINADAB (*[my] brother is willing*). Son of Iddo (1Ki 4:14).

AHINOAM (*[my] brother is pleasant*).
1. Wife of King Saul (1Sa 14:50).
2. One of David's wives, a Jezreelitess (1Sa 25:43), who lived with him at Gath (1Sa 27:3). Captured by the Amalekites at Ziklag (1Sa 30:5) but rescued by David (1Sa 30:18). Ahinoam bore Amnon, David's first son (2Sa 3:2).

AHIO (*[my] brother is Yahweh*).
1. A Levite, who drove the cart bearing the ark (2Sa 6:3-4; 1Ch 13:7).
2. A Benjamite (1Ch 8:14).
3. Son of Jeiel (1Ch 8:31; 9:37).

AHIRA (*[my] brother is my friend,* or *[my] brother is evil*). Prince captain of the tribe of Naphtali (Nu 1:15; 2:29; 7:78, 83; 10:27).

AHIRAM, AHIRAMITE (*[my] brother is exalted*). Son of Benjamin (Nu 26:38). *See Aharah.*

AHISAMACH (*[my] brother is a support*). A Danite, the father of Oholiab (Ex 31:6; 35:34; 38:23).

AHISHAHAR (*[my] brother was born at early dawn*). A descendant of Benjamin through Jediael and Bilhan (1Ch 7:10).

AHISHAR (*[my] brother is upright,* or *[my] brother has sung*). An official over Solomon's household (1Ki 4:6).

AHITHOPHEL (possibly *[my] brother is in the desert* or *[my] brother is foolishness*). One of David's counselors (2Sa 15:12; 1Ch 27:33). Joins Absalom (2Sa 15:31, 34; 16:15, 20-23; 17:1-23). Possibly referred to by David in Ps 55:12-14. Suicide of (2Sa 17:1-14, 23).

AHITUB (*[my] brother is goodness*).
1. High Priest, father of Ahiah (1Sa 14:3; 22:9, 11-12, 20).
2. Father of Zadok (2Sa 8:17; 1Ch 18:16).
3. Ruler of the house of God (1Ch 9:11; Ne 11:11).
4. The Ahitub mentioned (1Ch 6:8, 11-12) is probably identical with the last described above, or else he is confused with Azariah (2Ch 31:10).

AHLAB (*fat, fruitful, healthy*). A town of Asher from which the Israelites were not able to drive the inhabitants (Jdg 1:31).

AHLAI (*Alas! I wish that!*).
1. The father of Zabad, one of David's soldiers (1Ch 11:41).
2. A daughter of Sheshan who married her father's Egyptian slave Jarha. They had a son Attai (1Ch 2:31-35).

AHOAH (*brotherly*). A son of Bela (1Ch 8:4) and his descendants (2Sa 23:9, 28; 1Ch 11:12). *See Ahohite.* Also called Ahijah (1Ch 8:7) and Iri (1Ch 7:7).

AHOHITE A name given to the descendants of Ahoah, Dodo (2Sa 23:9), Zalmon (2Sa 23:28), Ilai (1Ch 11:29).

AHOLAH, AHOLA *See Oholah.*

AHOLIAB *See Oholiab.*

AHOLIBAH *See Oholah; Oholibah.*

AHOLIBAMAH *See Oholibamah.*

AHUMAI Son of Jahath (1Ch 4:2).

AHUZZAM (*possessor*). Son of Ashhur (1Ch 4:6).

AHUZZATH (*possession*). A "friend" of Abimelech, who made a peace treaty with Isaac at Beersheba after they saw that the Lord had blessed him (Ge 26:23-33).

AHZAI (*Yahweh has grasped*). A priest who lived in Jerusalem (Ne 11:13).

AI (*the ruin, the heap*).
1. A royal city of the Canaanites. Conquest and destruction of (Jos 7; 8). Population of (Jos 8:25). Rebuilt (Ezr 2:28).
Also called Aija (Ne 11:31) and Aiath (Isa 10:28).
2. A city of the Ammonites (Jer 49:3).

AIAH (*black kite [a type of hawk]*).
1. A Horite (Ge 36:24; 1Ch 1:40).
2. The father of Rizpah, Saul's concubine (2Sa 3:7; 21:8).

AIATH (possibly *ruin, heap*). Feminine form of the city Ai (Isa 10:28).

AIJA (*ruin, heap*). Another spelling of Ai (Ne 11:31). *See Ai, 1.*

AIJALON (*[the] place of the deer*).
1. A city of Dan (Jos 19:42). Assigned to the Levites (Jos 21:24; 1Sa 14:31; 1Ch 6:69). Amorites of, not exterminated (Jdg 1:35).
2. A city of Zebulun (Jdg 12:12).
3. A city of Judah (2Ch 28:18; 11:10).
4. A valley (Jos 10:12).

AIJELETH SHAHAR KJV title of Ps 22; NIV "The Doe of the Morning." A musical term which probably indicated the tune to which the psalm was sung. *See Music, Symbols Used in.*

AIN (*an eye[ball]* or *spring [of water]*).
1. A city of Simeon (Jos 19:7; 15:32; 21:16; 1Ch 4:32). Also called Ashan (1Ch 6:59). Possibly identical with En Rimmon (Ne 11:29).
2. A landmark on the northern boundary of Israel (Nu 34:11).

AIN FESHKA (*spring of Feshka*). Oasis on the W side of the Dead Sea, S of Khirbet Qumran. Used for farming by the community that produced the Dead Sea Scrolls.

AJAH *See Aiah.*

AJALON *See Aijalon.*

AKAN A Horite (Ge 36:27; 1Ch 1:42). Also spelled Jaakan (1Ch 1:42, ftn).

AKELDAMA (*field of blood*). The "Field of Blood" (Mt 27:8) purchased with money which Judas received for betraying Jesus (Ac 1:18-19).

AKHENATEN (*blessed spirit of [the god] Aten*). The name chosen by Amenhotep IV (1379-1362 B.C.), ruler in the Eighteenth Dynasty of Egypt, during the biblical era of the judges. He was a monotheist, demanding that all worship only the sun god under the name Aten. The Amarna Letters date from his era. *See Amarna, Tell El.*

AKIM (*Yahweh is my brother*). A descendant of Zerubbabel (Mt 1:14). Ancestor of Christ.

AKKAD An ancient center of Hamitic imperial power conquered by Nimrod (Ge 10:10). The city is evidently Agade which Sargon I brought into prominence as the capital of his Semitic empire, c. 2360-2180 B.C..

AKKUB (*guard*).
1. Son of Elioenai (1Ch 3:24).
2. A Levite who founded a family of temple gatekeepers (1Ch 9:17).
3. The head of a family of the temple servants (Ezr 2:45).
4. A Levite who helped expound the Law (Ne 8:7).

AKRABBIM (*scorpions*). *See Scorpion Pass.*

ALABASTER A white stone. Jars made of (Mt 26:7; Mk 14:3; Lk 7:37).

ALAMETH *See Alemeth.*

ALAMMELECH *See Allammelech.*

ALAMOTH A musical term (1Ch 15:20). In the title to Ps 46. *See Music, Symbols Used in.*

ALCOHOL *See Abstinence; Abuse, Substance Abuse; Beer; Drunkenness; Fermented Drink; Wine.*

ALEMETH (*concealment*).
1. A son of Beker and grandson of Benjamin (1Ch 7:8).
2. Son of Jehoaddah or Jadah (1Ch 8:36; 9:42).
3. A Levitical city (1Ch 6:60).
See Almon.

ALEXANDER (*man's defender*).
1. Son of Simon who carried the cross of Jesus (Mk 15:21).
2. A relative of the high priest, present at the defense of Peter and John (Ac 4:6).
3. A Jew of Ephesus (Ac 19:33).
4. A metalworker (1Ti 1:20; 2Ti 4:14).

ALEXANDER THE GREAT (*man's defender*). Son of Philip, King of Macedon. Lived from 356-323 B.C. He conquered the civilized world from Greece eastward to India. He is the "shaggy goat" of Da 8:5-8, 21. His hellenization of the world changed the trade language from Aramaic to Greek, the language of the NT. *See Testaments, Time Between.*

ALEXANDRA Wife of Aristobulus, King of the Jews (104-103 B.C.).

ALEXANDRIA A city of Egypt (Ac 6:9). Ships of (Ac 27:6; 28:11). Apollos born in (Ac 18:24).

ALGUM, ALGUMWOOD Probably a variant of almugwood (1Ki 10:11-12, ftn; 2Ch 2:8; 9:10-11). *See Almug, Almugwood.*

ALIAH *See Alvah.*

ALIAN *See Alvan.*

ALIENS (*sojourner, stranger, foreigner*). To be treated with justice (Ex 22:21; 23:9; Lev 19:33-34; Dt 1:16; 10:19 24:14, 17; 27:19; Jer 7:6; 22:3; Eze 22:29; Mal 3:5). Religious privileges of (Ex 12:48-49; Nu 9:14; 15:14-15). Kindness to Edomites, commanded (Dt 23:7).

Israelites Authorized:
To purchase, as slaves (Lev 25:44-45). To take usury from (Dt 15:3; 23:20). Not permitted to make kings of (Dt 17:15).
Forbidden to eat the passover (Ex 12:45). Partially exempt from the law (Dt 14:21). Numerous in times of David and Solomon (2Sa 22:45-46; 2Ch 2:17; 15:9). Oppressed (Eze 22:29). Rights of (Nu 35:15; Jos 20:9; Eze 47:22-23). David's kindness to (2Sa 15:19-20). Hospitality to, required by Jesus (Mt 25:35, 38, 43).
See Glean; Heathen; Hospitality; Inhospitableness; Proselyte; Strangers.

ALL THINGS The whole created order. God created and rules over (1Ch 29:12; Ps 119:91; Ecc 11:5; Isa 44:24; Jer 10:16; 51:19; Jn 1:3; Ro 8:28; 1Co 8:6; Rev 4:11). Under Jesus' authority (Mt 11:27; 28:20; Lk 10:22; Jn 13:3; Eph 1:10, 22; Col 1:16, 17, 20; Heb 1:2, 3). All things are possible with God (Mt 19:26; Mk 10:27).

ALLAMMELECH (*oak of the king* or *oak of [the god] Molech*). A town of Asher (Jos 19:26).

ALLEGORY

Explained:
Allegory is a literary genre that attempts to explain spiritual truths in pictorial forms. Some parables, for example, are a type of allegory. Allegory is also a method of interpretation that searches for a mysterious, hidden meaning beyond the literal understanding of the text.

In the OT:
Of the trees seeking a king (Jdg 9:8-15). Israel is a vine brought from Egypt (Ps 80). Wisdom is pictured as a noble woman (Pr 1:2-33); folly as a harlot (Pr 9:13-18). Messiah's kingdom represented by the wolf and the lamb dwelling together (Isa 11:6-8).

In the NT:
Jesus used allegory, as in the interpretation of his parable of the sower (Mt 13:18-23; Mk 4:14-20; Lk 8:11-15). Paul used allegory in using Hagar and Sarah to represent the differences between the Old and New Covenants (Gal 4:21-31). Many events and characters in the book of Revelation are used allegorically; most are clear or explained in context. For example, the Lamb and the Lion of Judah are both Jesus (Rev 5:5-14); the dragon is Satan (Rev 12:9).

Allegory in Interpretation:
Allegory is used as a literary device in the Bible. But, with the exception of Gal 4:21-31, allegory is not used in the NT to interpret the OT. However, allegory became increasingly important during the Apostolic period and into the Ante-Nicene period. The Alexandrian Jews of this period wished to reconcile Christianity with Greek thought. Origen taught a threefold sense of Scripture, corresponding to the body, soul, and the spirit.
In the Middle Ages four senses were found: historical, allegorical, moral, and anagogical (mystical). Jerusalem is *literally* a city in Israel, *allegorically* the church, *morally* the believing soul, *anagogically* the heavenly Jerusalem. The conquests of Joshua have been understood to be an allegory of the soul's victory over sin and self. Many Jewish scholars understand the Song of Songs to be

allegorical, depicting God's love for Israel. On the other hand, many Christian scholars understand this as Christ's love for his church.
See Fable; Parable; Symbols and Similitudes.

ALLELUIA *See Hallelujah.*

ALLIANCES

Forbidden:
(Ex 23:32; 34:12; Dt 7:2-3; 13:6, 8; Jos 23:6-7; Jdg 2:2; Ezr 9:12; Pr 1:10, 15; 2Co 6:14-17; Eph 5:11). Lead to idolatry (Ex 34:15-16; Nu 25:1-8; Dt 7:4; Jdg 3:5-7; Rev 2:20). Have led to murder and human sacrifice (Ps 106:37-38). Provoke the anger of God (Dt 7:4; 31:16-17; 2Ch 19:2; Ezr 9:13-14; Ps 106:29, 40; Isa 2:6). Provoke God to leave people to reap the fruits of them (Jos 23:12-13; Jdg 2:1-3).
Are ensnaring (Ex 23:33; Nu 25:18; Dt 12:30; 13:6; Ps 106:36). Are enslaving (2Pe 2:18-19). Are defiling (Ezr 9:1-2). Are degrading (Isa 1:23). Are ruinous to spiritual interests (Pr 29:24; Heb 12:14-15; 2Pe 3:17). Are ruinous to moral character (1Co 15:33). Are a proof of folly (Pr 12:11).
Children who enter into, bring shame upon their parents (Pr 28:7). Evil consequences of (Pr 28:19; Jer 51:7). The wicked are prone to (Ps 50:18; Jer 2:25). The wicked tempt believers to (Ne 6:2-4). Sin of, to be confessed, deeply repented of, and forsaken (Ezr 10).

Involve Believers:
In their guiltiness (2Jn 9-11; Rev 18:4). In their punishment (Nu 16:26; Jer 51:6; Rev 18:4). Unbecoming in those called believers (2Ch 19:2; 2Co 6:14, 16; Php 2:15). Exhortations to shun all inducements to (Pr 1:10-15; 4:14-15; 2Pe 3:17). Exhortations to hate and avoid (Pr 14:7; Ro 16:17; 1Co 5:9-11; Eph 5:6-7; 1Ti 6:5; 2Ti 3:5). A call to come out from (Nu 16:26; Ezr 10:11; Jer 51:6, 45; 2Co 6:17; 2Th 3:6; Rev 18:4). Means of preservation from (Pr 2:10-20; 19:27).
Blessedness of avoiding (Ps 1:1). Blessedness of forsaking (Ezr 9:12; Pr 9:6; 2Co 6:17-18). Believers grieve to meet with, in their dealings with the world (Ps 57:4; 120:5-6; 2Pe 2:7-8). Believers grieve to witness in their brothers (Ge 26:35; Ezr 9:3; 10:6). Believers hate and avoid (Ps 26:4-5; 31:6; 101:7; Rev 2:2). Believers deprecate (Ge 49:6; Ps 6:8; 15:4; 101:4, 7; 119:115; 139:19). Believers are separate from (Ex 33:16; Ezr 6:21). Believers should be careful when accidentally thrown into (Mt 10:16; Col 4:5; 1Pe 2:12). Pious parents prohibit, to their children (Ge 28:1). Persons in authority should denounce (Ezr 10:9-11; Ne 13:23-27). Punishment of (Nu 33:56; Dt 7:4; Jos 23:13; Jdg 2:3; 3:5-8; Ezr 9:7, 14; Ps 106:41-42; Rev 2:16, 22-23).

Exemplified:
Solomon (1Ki 11:1-8). Rehoboam (1Ki 12:8-9). Jehoshaphat (2Ch 18:3; 19:2; 20:35-38). Jehoram (2Ch 21:6). Ahaziah (2Ch 22:3-5). Israelites (Ezr 9:1-2). Israel (Eze 44:7). Judas Iscariot (Mt 26:14-16).

Examples of Avoiding—
Man of God (1Ki 13:7-10). Nehemiah (Ne 6:2-4; 10:29-31). David (Ps 101:4-7; 119:115). Jeremiah (Jer 15:17). Joseph of Arimathea (Lk 23:51). Church of Ephesus (Rev 2:6).

Examples of Forsaking—
Israelites (Nu 16:27; Ezr 6:21-22; 10:3-4, 16-17). Sons of the priests (Ezr 10:18-19).

Examples of God's Judgments Against—
Korah (Nu 16:32). Ahaziah (2Ch 22:7-8). Judas Iscariot (Ac 1:18).

ALLON (*oak*).
1. Son of Jedaiah (1Ch 4:37).
2. KJV Allon, a city of Naphtali (Jos 19:33), is "the large tree" in the NIV.

ALLON BACUTH (*oak of weeping*). Place where Rebekah was buried (Ge 35:8).

ALLOY *See Refining.*

ALMIGHTY (NIV rendering of *Shaddai* in the OT, *Pantokrator* in the NT). Used 56 times for: Identification (Ge 17:1). Invocation (Ge 28:3). Description (Eze 10:5). Praise (Rev 4:8). *See God, Names of.*

ALMODAD (*God [El] is loved*). First mentioned of Joktan's thirteen sons (Ge 10:26; 1Ch 1:20).

ALMON Levitical city of Benjamin (Jos 21:18). Called Alemeth (1Ch 6:60).

ALMON DIBLATHAIM (*way of the double fig cakes*). A stopping place in the wilderness journeys of the Israelites in Moab (Nu 33:46-47). Probably the same as Beth Diblathaim (Jer 48:22), and Diblah (Eze 6:14). *See Beth Diblathaim.*

ALMOND A tree (Ge 30:37). Fruit of (Ge 43:11). Aaron's rod of the (Nu 17:8). Bowls of lampstand in the tabernacle fashioned after the flowers of the (Ex 25:33-34; 37:19-20).

Figurative: Of old age (Ecc 12:5), of God's watching (Jer 1:11-12).

ALMS KJV "alms" is rendered "give (to the poor)" and "acts of righteousness" in the NIV.

To be Given:
Without public show (Mt 6:1-4; Ro 12:8). Freely (2Co 9:6-7). Commanded (Dt 15:7-11; Mt 5:42; 19:21; Lk 12:33; 2Co 9:5-7; Gal 2:10; 1Ti 6:18; Heb 13:16). Asked by the unfortunate (Jn 9:8; Ac 3:2). Withholding, not of love (1Jn 3:17).

Instances of Giving:
Zacchaeus (Lk 19:8). Dorcas (Ac 9:36). Cornelius (Ac 10:2). The early Christians (Ac 2:44-45; 4:34-37; 6:1-3; 11:29-30; 24:17; Ro 15:25-28; 1Co 16:1-4; 2Co 8:1-4; 9:1; Heb 6:10).
See Beneficence; Charitableness; Gifts From God; Giving; Liberality; Neighbor; Poor; Works, Good.

ALMUG, ALMUGWOOD Probably a variant of algum and algumwood (1Ki 10:11-12; 2Ch 2:8; 9:10-11, ftn). Trees of Ophir and Lebanon used in building the temple and musical instruments. *See Algum, Algumwood.*

ALOES Used as perfume (Ps 45:8; Pr 7:17; SS 4:14). In embalming the dead (Jn 19:39). Descriptive of the camping places of the Israelites (Nu 24:6).

ALOTH One of the districts in Israel during the reign of Solomon that shared the responsibility of supplying provisions for the king and the royal household for one month in the year (1Ki 4:16).

ALPHA AND OMEGA A title of Christ, meaning "First and Last" and "Beginning and End" (Rev 1:8, cf. 17; 21:6; 22:13; cf. Isa 41:4; 44:6; 48:12).

ALPHAEUS
1. Father of James (Mt 10:3; Mk 3:18).
2. Father of Levi (Mk 2:14).
3. Possibly Clopas, husband of the Mary at the cross (Jn 19:25; also Mk 15:40), as Clopas and Alphaeus are of Semitic derivation. Unlikely the Cleopas of the Emmaus road (Lk 24:18) since Clopas was a common Greek name.

ALTAR OF BURNT OFFERING Dimensions of (Ex 27:1; 38:1). Horns on the corners of (Ex 27:2; 38:2). Covered with bronze (Ex 27:2). All its vessels of bronze (Ex 27:3; 38:3). A network grating of bronze placed in (Ex 27:4-5; 38:4). Furnished with rings and poles (Ex 27:6-7; 38:5-7). Made after a divine pattern (Ex 27:8).

Called:
The bronze altar (Ex 39:39; 1Ki 8:64). The altar of God (Ps 43:4). The altar of the Lord (Mal 2:13). Placed in the court before the door of the tabernacle (Ex 40:6, 29). Sanctified by God (Ex 29:44). Anointed and sanctified with holy oil (Ex 40:10; Lev 8:10-11). Cleansed and purified with blood (Ex 29:36-37). Was most holy (Ex 40:10). Sanctified whatever touched it (Ex 29:37). All sacrifices to be offered on (Ex 29:38-42; Isa 56:7). All gifts to be presented at (Mt 5:23-24). Nothing polluted or defective to be offered on (Lev 22:22; Mal 1:7-8). Offering at the dedication of (Nu 7).

The Fire Upon:
Came from before the Lord (Lev 9:24). Was continually burning (Lev 6:13). Consumed the sacrifices (Lev 1:8-9). Sacrifices bound to the horns of (Ps 118:27, ftn). The blood of sacrifices put on the horns and poured at the foot of (Ex 29:12; Lev 4:7, 18, 25; 8:15).

The Priests:
Alone to serve (Nu 18:3, 7). Derived support from (1Co 9:13). Ahaz removed and profaned (2Ki 16:10-16). The Jews were condemned for swearing lightly by (Mt 23:18-19). A type of Christ (Heb 13:10).

ALTAR OF INCENSE Dimensions of (Ex 30:1-2; 37:25). Covered with gold (Ex 30:3; 37:26). Top of, surrounded with a crown of gold (Ex 30:3; 37:26). Had four rings of gold under the crown for the poles (Ex 30:4; 37:27). Poles of, covered with gold (Ex 30:5). Called the golden altar (Ex 39:38). Placed before the veil in the outer sanctuary (Ex 30:6; 40:5, 26). Said to be before the Lord (Lev 4:7; 1Ki 9:25). Anointed with holy oil (Ex 30:25-27). The priest burned incense on, every morning and evening (Ex 30:7-8). No strange incense nor any sacrifice to be offered on (Ex 30:9). Atonement made for, by the high priest once every year (Ex 30:10; Lev 16:18-19). The blood of all sin offerings put on the horns of (Lev 4:7, 18). Covered by the priests before removal from the sanctuary (Nu 4:11). A type of Christ (Rev 8:3; 9:3).
Punishment for: Offering unauthorized fire on (Lev 10:1-2). Unauthorized offering on (2Ch 26:16-19).

ALTARS
Designed for sacrifice (Ex 20:24). To be made of earth or uncut stone (Ex 20:24-25; Dt 27:5-6). Of brick, detestable to God (Isa 65:3). Natural rocks sometimes used as (Jdg 6:19-21; 13:19-20). Were not to have steps up to them (Ex 20:26). For idolatrous worship, often built on roofs of houses (2Ki 23:12; Jer 19:13; 32:29). Idolaters raised Asherah poles near (Jdg 6:30; 1Ki 16:32-33; 2Ki 21:3). The Israelites not to raise Asherah poles (Dt 16:21). For idolatrous worship, to be destroyed (Ex 34:13; Dt 7:5). Probable origin of inscriptions on (Dt 27:8).

Mentioned in Scripture:
Of Noah (Ge 8:20). Of Abraham (Ge 12:7-8; 13:18; 22:9). Of Isaac (Ge 26:25). Of Jacob (Ge 33:20; 35:1, 3, 7). Of Moses (Ex 17:15; 24:4). Of Balaam (Nu 23:1, 14, 29). Of Joshua (Jos 8:30-31). Of the temple of Solomon (2Ch 4:1, 19). Of the second temple (Ezr 3:2-3). Of Reubenites, E of Jordan (Jos 22:10). Of Gideon (Jdg 6:26-27). Of the people of Israel (Jdg 21:4). Of Samuel (1Sa 7:17). Of David (2Sa 24:21, 25). Of Jeroboam at Bethel (1Ki 12:33). Of Ahaz (2Ki 16:10-12). Of the Athenians (Ac 17:23). For burnt offering (Ex 27:1-8). For incense (Ex 30:1-6). Protection afforded by (1Ki 1:50-51). Afforded no protection to murderers (Ex 21:14; 1Ki 2:18-34).

AL-TASCHITH (*[do] not destroy*). In KJV titles of Pss 57-59; 75; NIV "Do Not Destroy." Probably the tune to which these psalms were sung. The phrase occurs in Isa 65:8, leading some to deduce it is the name of a vintage or wine-making song. *See Music, Symbols Used in.*

ALTRUISM (*concern and actions for the welfare of others*).

Jesus Commends:
By teaching (Mt 20:26-27; 23:11; Mk 9:35; 10:43-45; Lk 22:26-27; Jn 13:4-17; Ac 20:35). By example (Jn 13:4-17), came to serve (Mt 20:28; Php 2:7), went about doing good works (Ac 10:38), pleased not himself (Ro 15:3), became poor for others (2Co 8:9).

Paul Commends:
By teaching, to help the weak (Ac 20:33-35; Ro 15:1-2), to promote the welfare of others (1Co 10:24, 31-33; Gal 6:1-2, 10; Php 2:4-9). By example, became servant of all (1Co 9:18-22; 2Co 4:5), made many rich (2Co 6:10).

Motives Inspiring to:
Love of neighbor (Lk 10:25-37). To save people (1Co 9:22). For Jesus' sake (2Co 4:5). Example of Jesus (2Co 8:9; Php 2:3-8).
See Alms; Beneficence; Charitableness; Duty of People to People; Liberality; Love.

ALUSH Camping place of the Israelites (Nu 33:13).

ALVAH Chief of Edom, descended from Esau (Ge 36:40; 1Ch 1:51).

ALVAN (possibly *ascending one,* or *tall*). Son of Shobal, a descendant of Seir (Ge 36:23). Also spelled Alian (1Ch 1:40, ftn).

AMAD A town of Asher (Jos 19:26).

AMAL (*laborer, troubler*). Son of Helem (1Ch 7:35).

AMALEK Son of Eliphaz (Ge 36:12; 1Ch 1:36). Probably not the ancestor of the Amalekites mentioned in the time of Abraham (Ge 14:7).

AMALEKITE(S) Descent of (Ge 36:12, 16).

Character of:
Wicked (1Sa 15:18). Oppressive (Jdg 10:12). Warlike and cruel (1Sa 15:33). Governed by kings (1Sa 15:20, 32). A powerful and influential nation (Nu 24:7). Possessed cities (1Sa 15:5).

Country of:
In the south of Canaan (Nu 13:29; 1Sa 27:8). Extended from Havilah to Shur (1Sa 15:7). Was the scene of ancient warfare (Ge 14:7). Part of the Kenites dwelt among (1Sa 15:6).

Conflict With Israel:
Were the first to oppose Israel (Ex 17:8). Beaten at Rephidim, through the intercession of Moses (Ex 17:9-13). Doomed to utter destruction foretold (Nu 24:20). Presumption of Israel punished by (Nu 14:45). United with Eglon against Israel (Jdg 3:13). Part of their possessions taken by Ephraim (Jdg 5:14, w Jdg 12:15). With Midian, oppressed Israel (Jdg 6:3-5). Saul overcame, and delivered Israel (1Sa 14:48), commissioned to destroy (1Sa 15:1-3), massacred (1Sa 15:4-8), condemned for not utterly destroying (1Sa 15:9-26; 28:18). Agag, king of, slain by Samuel (1Sa 15:32-33). Invaded by David (1Sa 27:8-9). Pillaged and burned Ziklag (1Sa 30:1-2). Pursued and slain by David (1Sa 30:10-20). Spoil taken from, consecrated (2Sa 8:11-12). Confederated against Israel (Ps 83:5-7). Remnant of, completely destroyed during the reign of Hezekiah (1Ch 4:41-43).

AMAM A city of Judah (Jos 15:26). Probably within the district later assigned to Simeon (Jos 19:1-9).

AMANA (*constant*). A mountain near Lebanon (SS 4:8), from which flows the Abana River (2Ki 5:12). *See Abana.*

AMANUENSIS A secretary employed to write from dictation or to copy manuscripts.
Examples: Baruch (Jer 36:4; 45:1), Tertius (Ro 16:22), perhaps Silas (1Th 1:1; 2Th 1:1; 1Pe 5:12) and Timothy (2Co 1:1; Php 1:1; Col 1:1; 1Th 1:1; 2Th 1:1; Phm 1:1).

AMARANTHINE A type of straw flower that does not shrivel when picked. NIV "can never fade" (1Pe 1:4; 5:4).

AMARIAH (*Yahweh has said*).
1. Two Levites (1Ch 6:7, 52; 23:19; 24:23).
2. Chief priest in the reign of Jehoshaphat (2Ch 19:11).
3. A high priest, father of Ahitub (1Ch 6:11; Ezr 7:3).
4. A Levite, who assisted in distributing temple gifts (2Ch 31:15-19).
5. Son of Hezekiah (Zep 1:1).
6. Father of Zechariah (Ne 11:4).
7. A priest, returned from exile (Ne 10:3; 12:2). Probably also in Ne 12:13.
8. A returned exile. Divorces his idolatrous wife (Ezr 10:42).

AMARNA, TELL EL (*the hill Amarna*). The modern name for the ancient capital of Amenhotep IV (c. 1379-1362 B.C.), where in 1887 a large number of clay tablets containing the private correspondence between the ruling Egyptian pharaohs and the political leaders in Canaan were discovered. *See Akhenaten; Texts, Ancient Near Eastern Non-Biblical Texts Relating to the Old Testament..*

AMASA (*[my] people are from Jesse*).
1. Nephew of David (2Sa 17:25; 1Ch 2:17). Joins Absalom (2Sa 17:25). Returns to David and is made captain of the host (2Sa 19:13). Slain (2Sa 20:8-12; 1Ki 2:5, 32).
2. Son of Hadlai (2Ch 28:12).

AMASAI (*[my] people are from Jesse*).
1. A Levite and ancestor of Samuel (1Ch 6:25, 35).
2. Leader of a body of men unhappy with Saul, who joined David (1Ch 12:18).
3. A priest and trumpeter (1Ch 15:24).
4. A Levite of the Kohathites (2Ch 29:12).

AMASHSAI Priest in Nehemiah's time (Ne 11:13).

AMASIAH (*Yahweh carries a load*). A captain under Jehoshaphat (2Ch 17:16).

AMAZIAH (*Yahweh is powerful*).
1. A Levite (1Ch 6:45).
2. King of Judah. History of (2Ki 14; 2Ch 25).
3. An idolatrous priest at Bethel (Am 7:10-17).
4. Father of Joshah (1Ch 4:34).

A

AMBASSADORS

Sent by:
Moses to Edom (Nu 20:14), to the Amorites (Nu 21:21), by Gibeonites to the Israelites (Jos 9:4), Israelites to various nations (Jdg 11:12-28).
Hiram to David (2Sa 5:11), Solomon (1Ki 5:1).
Ben-Hadad to Ahab (1Ki 20:2-6), Amaziah to Jehoash (2Ki 14:8), Ahaz to Tiglath-Pileser (2Ki 16:7), Hoshea to So, king of Egypt (2Ki 17:4), Sennacherib through the field commander, to Hezekiah (2Ki 19:9), Merodach-Baladan to Hezekiah (2Ki 20:12; 2Ch 32:31), Zedekiah to Egypt (Eze 17:15).
Other references to (Pr 13:17; Isa 18:2; 30:4; 33:7; 36:11; 39:1-2; Lk 14:32).
Figurative (Job 33:23; Ob 1; 2Co 5:20; Eph 6:20).

AMBER NIV "glowing metal" (Eze 1:4, 27; 8:2). *See Glowing Metal; Minerals of the Bible, 1; Stones.*

AMBITION

Worthy: (1Ti 3:1).

Worldly: (Jas 4:1-2; 1Jn 2:16).
Cursed (Isa 5:8; Heb 2:9). Insatiable (Hab 2:5-6, 9). Perishable (Job 20:6-7; Ps 49:11-13). False accusation against Moses (Nu 16:13). Parable illustrating (2Ki 14:9). Rebuked by Jesus (Mt 16:26; 18:1-3; 20:20-28; 23:5-7, 12; Mk 9:33-37; 10:35-45; 12:38-39; Lk 9:25, 46-48; 11:43; 22:24-30; Jn 5:44). Temptation by Satan (Mt 4:8-10; Lk 4:5-8).

Instances of:
King of Babylon (Isa 14:12-15). Eve (Ge 3:5-6). Korah and his followers (Nu 16:3-35). Abimelech (Jdg 9:1-6). Absalom (2Sa 15:1-13; 18:18). Haman (Est 5:9-13). Disciples of Jesus (Mt 18:1-3; 20:20-24; Mk 9:33-37; 10:35-45; Lk 9:46-48; 22:24-30). Diotrephes (3Jn 9-10).

Disappointed: Ahithophel (2Sa 17:23), Adonijah (1Ki 1:5), Haman (Est 6:6-9).

AMBUSH

Instances of: At Ai (Jos 8:2-22), Shechem (Jdg 9:25, 34), Gibeah (Jdg 20:29-41), near Zemaraim (2Ch 13:13). By Jehoshaphat (2Ch 20:21-22).
See Armies.
Figurative (Jer 51:12).

AMEN (*so be it*). A word used to reinforce a statement (Nu 5:22; Dt 27:12-26; Ne 5:13; 2Co 1:20; Rev 5:14; 22:20).
Used in prayer (1Ki 1:36; 1Ch 16:36; Ne 8:6; Ps 41:13; 72:19; 89:52; 106:48; Jer 28:6; Mt 6:13; 1Co 14:16; Rev 5:14; 19:4).
A title of Christ (Rev 3:14).

AMETHYST A precious stone (Ex 28:19; 39:12; Rev 21:20). *See Minerals of the Bible, 1; Stones.*

AMI (*trustworthy, reliable, faithful*). A servant of Solomon (Ezr 2:57). Also called Amon (Ne 7:59). *See Amon.*

AMINADAB *See Amminadab.*

AMITTAI (*true*). Father of Jonah (2Ki 14:25; Jnh 1:1).

AMMAH (*cubit*). A hill around Gibeon where Joab and Abishai halted in their pursuit of Abner and his forces after they defeated him in the battle of Gibeon (2Sa 2:24-32).

AMMI (*my people*). Name given to Israel symbolizing acceptance (Hos 2:1, KJV); opposite of Lo-Ammi, "not my people" (Hos 1:9).

AMMIEL (*God [El] is my kinsman*).
1. The son of Gemalli and spy sent out by Moses (Nu 13:12).
2. The father of Makir of Lo Debar (2Sa 9:4-5; 17:27).
3. The father of Bathsheba, one of David's wives (1Ch 3:5). Called also Eliam (2Sa 11:3).
4. The sixth son of Obed-Edom who, with his family, was associated with the temple gatekeepers (1Ch 26:5).

AMMIHUD (*[my] people have majesty*).
1. The father of Elishama, chief of Ephraim (Nu 1:10; 2:18; 7:48, 53), and the son of Ladan (1Ch 7:26).
2. A man of Simeon and father of Shemuel (Nu 34:20).
3. A Naphtalite whose son, Pedahel, also assisted in the division of the land (Nu 34:28).
4. Father of Talmai and king of Geshur. Absalom fled to Talmai after he killed his brother Amnon (2Sa 13:37).
5. Son of Omri, father of Uthai (1Ch 9:4).

AMMIHUR *See Ammihud.*

AMMINADAB (*my people are generous*).
1. A Levite. Aaron's father-in-law (Ex 6:23).
2. A prince of Judah (Nu 1:7; 2:3; 7:12, 17; 10:14; Ru 4:19-20; 1Ch 2:10; Mt 1:4; Lk 3:33).
3. A son of Kohath, son of Levi (1Ch 6:22). Perhaps the same as 1.
4. A Kohathite who assisted in the return of the ark from the house of Obed-Edom (1Ch 15:10-11).

AMMINADIB KJV "chariots of Amminadib" are "royal chariots of my people" in the NIV (SS 6:12, see also ftn). *See Amminadab.*

AMMISHADDAI (*Shaddai is [my] kinsman*). Father of Abiezer, captain of the tribe of Dan in Moses' time (Nu 1:12; 2:25; 7:66, 71; 10:25).

AMMIZABAD (*[my] people have given a gift*). Son of Benaiah, third of David's captains (1Ch 27:6).

AMMON (*people*). Ammon or Ben-Ammi is the name of one of the sons of Lot born to him by his youngest daughter in Zoar (Ge 19:38). *See Ammonite(s).*

AMMONI *See Kephar Ammoni.*

AMMONITE(S)

History of:
Descendants of Ben-Ammi, one of the sons of Lot (Ge 19:38). Character of (Jdg 10:6; 2Ki 23:13; 2Ch 20:22-23; Jer 27:3, 9; Eze 25:1-7; Am 1:13; Zep 2:10). Territory of (Nu 21:24; Dt 2:19; Jos 12:2; 13:10, 25; Jdg 11:13).
Israelites forbidden to disturb (Dt 2:19, 37). Excluded from the congregation of Israel (Dt 23:3-6). Confederated with Moabites and Amalekites against Israel (Jdg 3:12-13). Defeated by the Israelites (Jdg 10:7-18; 11:32-33; 12:1-3; 1Sa 11; 2Sa 8:12; 10; 11:1; 12:26-31; 17:27; 1Ch 18:11; 20:1-3; 2Ch 20; 26:7-8; 27:5). Conspired against the Jews (Ne 4:7-8).
Solomon took wives from (1Ki 11:1; Ne 13:26). Rehoboam took wives from (2Ch 12:13). Jews intermarried with (Ezr 9:1, 10-12; 10:10-44; Ne 13:23).

Kings of: Baalis (Jer 40:14; 41:10).

Idols of: Molech (2Ki 23:13). *See Molech.*

Prophecies Concerning:
(Isa 11:14; Jer 9:25-26; 25:15-21; 27:1-11; 49:1-6; Eze 21:20, 28-32; 25:1-11; Da 11:41; Am 1:13-15; Zep 2:8-11).

AMNESTY For political offenses: Shimei (2Sa 19:16-23). Amasa (2Sa 19:13, w 17:25).

AMNON (*trustworthy*).
1. Son of David (2Sa 3:2; 1Ch 3:1). Incest of, and death (2Sa 13).
2. Son of Shimon (1Ch 4:20).

AMOK (*capable* KB). Priest who returned with Zerubbabel from exile (Ne 12:7, 20).

AMON (*trustworthy*).
1. Governor of the city of Samaria (1Ki 22:26; 2Ch 18:25).
2. King of Judah (2Ki 21:18-26; 2Ch 33:21-25; Zep 1:1; Mt 1:10).
3. Ancestor of one of the families of the temple servants (Ne 7:59). Called Ami (Ezr 2:57). *See Ami.*
4. A city thought by most scholars to be the same as the city of No (Hebrew) (Jer 46:25). It was the capital of Egypt. Thebes is the Greek name.

AMORITE(S) (possibly *hill dwellers* BDB; *westerners* KB). Descendants of Canaan (Ge 10:15-6; 1Ch 1:13-14). Were giants (Am 2:9). Conquered by Kedorlaomer and rescued by Abraham (Ge 14).
Territory of (Ge 14:7; Nu 13:29; 21:13; Dt 1:4, 7, 19; 3:8-9; Jos 5:1; 10:5; 12:2-3; Jdg 1:35-36; 11:22), given to descendants of Abraham (Ge 15:21; 48:22; Dt 1:20; 2:26-36; 7:1; Jos 3:10; Jdg 11:23; Am 2:10), allotted to Reuben, Gad, and Manasseh (Nu 32:33-42; Jos 13:15-21), conquest of (Nu 21:21-30; Jos 10:11; Jdg 1:34-36).
Chiefs of (Jos 13:21). Wickedness of (Ge 15:16; 2Ki 21:11; Ezr 9:1). Idolatry of (Jdg 6:10; 1Ki 21:26). Judgments denounced against (Ex 23:23-24; 33:2; 34:10-11; Dt 20:17-18). Hornets sent among (Jos 24:12). Not exterminated (Jdg 1:34-36; 3:1-3, 5-8; 1Sa 7:14; 2Sa 2:2; 1Ki 9:20-21; 2Ch 8:7). Intermarry with Jews (Ezr 9:1-2; 10:18-44). Kings of (Jos 10:3-26).

AMOS (*burden bearer*). A prophet (Am 1:1). Forbidden to prophesy in Israel (Am 7:10-17). Vision of (Am 8:2).

AMOS, BOOK OF

Author: Amos of Tekoa

Date: Probably between 760-750 B.C.

Outline:
I. Superscription (1:1).
II. Introduction to Amos's Message (1:2).
III. Judgments on the Nations (1:3-2:16).
 A. Judgment on Aram (1:3-5).
 B. Judgment on Philistia (1:6-8).
 C. Judgment on Phoenicia (1:9-10).
 D. Judgment on Edom (1:11-12).
 E. Judgment on Ammon (1:13-15).
 F. Judgment on Moab (2:1-3).
 G. Judgment on Judah (2:4-5).
 H. Judgment on Israel (2:6-16).
  1. Ruthless oppression of the poor (2:6-7a).
  2. Unbridled profanation of religion (2:7b-8).
  3. Contrasted position of the Israelites (2:9-12).
  4. The oppressive system will perish (2:13-16).
IV. Oracles Against Israel (3:1-5:17).
 A. Judgment on the Chosen People (ch. 3).
  1. God's punishment announced (3:1-2).
  2. The announcement vindicated (3:3-8).
  3. The punishment vindicated (3:9-15).
 B. Judgment on an Unrepentant People (ch. 4).
  1. Judgment on the socialites (4:1-3).
  2. Perversion of religious life (4:4-5).
  3. Past calamities brought no repentance (4:6-11).
  4. No hope for a hardened people (4:12-13).
 C. Judgment on an Unjust People (5:1-17).
  1. The death dirge (5:1-3).
  2. Exhortation to life (5:4-6).
  3. Indictment of injustices (5:7-13).
  4. Exhortation to life (5:14-15).
  5. Prosperity will turn to grief (5:16-17).
V. Announcements of Exile (5:18-6:14).
 A. A Message of Woe Against Israel's Perverted Religion (5:18-27).
 B. A Message of Woe Against Israel's Complacent Pride (6:1-7).
 C. A Sworn Judgment on the Proud and Unjust Nation (6:8-14).
VI. Visions of Divine Retribution (7:1-9:10).
 A. Judgment Relented (7:1-6).
  1. A swarm of locusts (7:1-3).
  2. A consuming fire (7:4-6).
 B. Judgment Unrelented (7:7-9:10).
  1. The plumb line (7:7-17).
   a. The vision (7:7-9).
   b. Challenged and vindicated (7:10-17).
  2. The basket of ripe fruit (ch. 8).
   a. The vision (8:1-3).
   b. The exposition (8:4-14).
  3. The Lord by the altar (9:1-10).
   a. The vision (9:1-4).
   b. The exposition (9:5-10).
VII. Restored Israel's Blessed Future (9:11-15).
 A. Revival of the House of David (9:11-12).
 B. Restoration of Israel to an Edenic Promised Land (9:13-15).
See Prophets, The Minor.

AMOZ (*strong*). Father of Isaiah (2Ki 19:2, 20; 20:1; Isa 1:1; 13:1).

AMPHIPOLIS (*a city surrounded* or *a city conspicuous*). City of Macedonia not far from Philippi. Paul passed through it (Ac 17:1).

AMPLIATUS A Christian to whom Paul sent a greeting (Ro 16:8).

AMRAM, AMRAMITES (*exalted people*).
1. Father of Moses (Ex 6:18, 20; Nu 26:58-59; 1Ch 6:3, 18; 23:12-13). Head of one of the branches of Levites (Nu 3:19, 27; 1Ch 26:23). Age of, at death (Ex 6:20).
2. Son of Bani (Ezr 10:34).
3. *See Hemdan.*

AMRAPHEL King of Shinar (Ge 14:1, 9).

AMULET *See Charmers and Charming.*

AMUN *See Amon.*

AMUSEMENTS AND WORLDLY PLEASURES

Belong to the works of the flesh (Gal 5:19, 21). Are transitory (Job 21:12-13; Heb 11:25), meaningless (Ecc 2:11), choke the Word of God in the heart (Lk 8:14), formed a part of idolatrous worship (Ex 32:4, 6, 19, w 1Co 10:7; Jdg 16:23-25).

Lead to:
Rejection of God (Job 21:12-15), poverty (Pr 21:17), disregard of the judgments and works of God (Isa 5:12; Am 6:1-6), sorrow (Pr 14:13), greater evil (Job 1:5; Mt 14:6-8), attempting to find fulfillment in (Ecc 2:1-8).

Indulgence in:
A proof of folly (Ecc 7:4), a characteristic of the wicked (Isa 47:8; Eph 4:17, 19; 2Ti 3:4; Tit 3:3; 1Pe 4:3), a proof of spiritual death (1Ti 5:6), an abuse of riches (Jas 5:1, 5), wisdom of abstaining from (Ecc 7:2-3), shunned by the early believers (1Pe 4:3).

Abstinence From:
Seems strange to the wicked (1Pe 4:4), denounced by God (Isa 5:11-12), exclude from the kingdom of God (Gal 5:21), punishment of (Ecc 11:9; 2Pe 2:13), renunciation of, exemplified by Moses (Heb 11:25).
See Dancing; Games; Pleasure, Worldly; Worldliness.

AMZI (possibly *Yahweh is my strength*).
1. A descendant of Merari and of Levi, and progenitor of Ethan, whom David set over the service of song (1Ch 6:44-46).
2. An ancestor of Adaiah, a priest in the second temple (Ne 11:12).

ANAB (*grape*). A city of the Anakites taken by Joshua (Jos 11:21). It fell to Judah (Jos 15:50). SE of Debir, SW of Hebron. It retains its ancient name.

ANAH

1. Daughter of Zibeon and mother of Oholibamah, Esau's wife (Ge 36:2, 14, 25).
2. Son of Seir, chief of Edom (Ge 36:20, 29; 1Ch 1:38).
3. Son Zibeon (Ge 36:24; 1Ch 1:40-41). Also called Beeri (Ge 26:34).

ANAHARATH City on the border of Issachar (Jos 19:19). Modern en-Naura.

ANAIAH (*Yahweh responds*).
1. A leader or priest who assisted in the reading of the law to the people (Ne 8:4).
2. A returned exile who, with Nehemiah, sealed the covenant (Ne 10:22). Possibly the same as 1.

ANAK (*[long] necked, tall*). Descendant of Arba (Jos 15:13), and the ancestor of the Anakites (Nu 13:22, 28, 33). *See Anakites.*

ANAKITES (*[long-] necked, tall*). Descent of (Nu 13:22; Jos 15:13). Called the descendants of Anak (Nu 13:33), Anakites (Dt 1:28; 9:2).
Divided into three tribes (Jos 15:14). Inhabited the mountains of Judah (Jos 11:21). Hebron, chief city of (Jos 14:15, w 21:11). Of gigantic strength and stature (Dt 2:10-11, 21). Israel terrified by (Nu 14:1, w 13:33). Hebron a possession of, given to Caleb for his faithfulness (Jos 14:6-14). Driven from Hebron by Caleb (Jos 15:13-14). Driven from Kiriath Sepher or Debir by Othniel (Jos 15:15-17; Jdg 1:12-13). Almost annihilated (Jos 11:21-22).

ANAMITES A tribe descended from Mizraim (Ge 10:13; 1Ch 1:11).

ANAMMELECH (*Anath is king*). An Assyrian idol (2Ki 17:31).

ANAN (*cloud*). A Jew, returned from Babylonian captivity (Ne 10:26).

ANANI (*Yahweh is a covering*). A descendant of David (1Ch 3:24).

ANANIAH (*Yahweh is a covering*).
1. Son of Maaseiah (Ne 3:23).
2. Town of Benjamin (Ne 11:32).

ANANIAS (*Yahweh is gracious*).
1. High priest, before whom Paul was tried (Ac 23:2-5; 24:1; 25:2).
2. A covetous member of church at Jerusalem. Falsehood and death of (Ac 5:1-11).
3. A Christian in Damascus (Ac 9:10-18; 22:12-16).

ANARCHY
In Israel: (Jdg 17:6; 18:1; 19:1; 21:25; Isa 3:5-8).

In the Early Church: Warned against (Gal 5:13-14). Insubordinate members hostile to authority (2Pe 2:10-19; Jude 8-13).

ANATH (*a Semitic goddess*).
1. Father of the judge Shamgar (Jdg 3:31; 5:6).
2. A Canaanite goddess of war and of love, sometimes identified with Astarte, Asherah, and Ashtoreth. She was the sister and consort of Baal. The name is reflected in the city Beth Anath (Jos 19:38; Jdg 1:33). *See Asherah; Ashtoreth; Beth Anath.*

ANATHEMA (*devoted to destruction*).
A thing devoted to God becomes his and is therefore irrevocably withdrawn from common use (Lev 27:28-29; Ro 9:3; 1Co 12:3; 16:22; Gal 1:9).

ANATHEMA MARANATHA These words from 1Co 16:22 were formerly interpreted as a double curse. *Anathema* does mean cursed (1Co 12:3). *Marana tha* is Aramaic for "Come, O Lord!" (cf. Rev 22:20).
See Blasphemy; Cursing; God, Name of; Oath.

ANATHOTH, ANATHOTHITE (*plural of Anath*).
1. A Levitical city in Benjamin (Jos 21:18; 1Ch 6:60). Abiathar confined in (1Ki 2:26).
Birthplace of Jeremiah (Jer 1:1; 32:7-12), of Abiezer (2Sa 23:27), of Jehu (1Ch 12:3). Prophecies against (Jer 11:21-23). Inhabitants of, after Babylonian captivity (Ezr 2:23; Ne 7:27).
2. Son of Beker (1Ch 7:8).
3. A Jew, who returned from Babylon (Ne 10:19).

ANCHOR Literal (Ac 27:17, 29, 30, 40). Figurative (Heb 6:19).

ANCIENT OF DAYS A title of Yahweh (Da 7:9, 13, 22).

ANCIENT TEXTS RELATING TO THE OLD TESTAMENT *See Texts, Ancient Near Eastern Non-Biblical Texts Relating to the Old Testament.*

ANCIENTS Those of the past (1Sa 24:13). *See Elders.*

ANDREW (*manly*). An apostle. A fisherman (Mt 4:18). Of Bethsaida (Jn 1:44). A disciple of John (Jn 1:40). Finds Peter, his brother, and brings him to Jesus (Jn 1:40-42). Call of (Mt 4:18; Mk 1:16). His name appears in the list of the apostles (Mt 10:2; Mk 3:18; Lk 6:14). Asks the Master privately about the destruction of the temple (Mk 13:3-4). Tells Jesus of the Greeks who wanted to see him (Jn 12:20-22). Reports the number of loaves at the feeding of the five thousand (Jn 6:8). Meets with the disciples after the Lord's ascension (Ac 1:13).

ANDRONICUS (*victor [over] man*). Relative of Paul; an apostle (Ro 16:7).

ANEM (*springs*). A Levitical city (1Ch 6:73).

ANER
1. A Canaanite chief and brother of Mamre (Ge 14:13, 24).
2. A Levitical city of Manasseh (1Ch 6:70).

ANGEL [OF THE LORD] (*messenger*). In addition to 54 occurrences of "the angel of the LORD" (Ex 3:2; Jdg 2:1), many uses of "angel" indicate a manifestation of God himself. These include: angel (Ac 7:30, 35 w Ex 3:2), my angel (Ex 23:20-23; 32:34), angel of God (Ex 14:19; Jdg 13:6; 2Sa 14:17, 20), angel of his Presence (Isa 63:9). *See Angels.*

ANGEL OF THE CHURCHES Heavenly messengers and guardians or earthly messengers and pastors (Rev 1:20; 2:1, 8, 18; 3:1, 7, 14).

ANGELS
Elect:
Created by God and Christ (Ne 9:6; Col 1:16). Worship God and Christ (Ne 9:6; Php 2:9-11; Heb 1:6). Are ministering spirits (1Ki 19:5; Ps 68:17; 104:4; Lk 16:22; Ac 12:7-11; 27:23; Heb 1:7, 14). Communicate the will of God and Christ (Da 8:16-17; 9:21-23; 10:11; 12:6-7; Mt 2:13, 20; Lk 1:19, 28; Ac 5:20; 8:26; 10:5; 27:23; Rev 1:1). Obey the will of God (Ps 103:20; Mt 6:10). Execute the purposes of God (Nu 22:22; Ps 103:21; Mt 13:39-42; 28:2; Jn 5:4; Rev 5:2). Execute the judgments of God (2Sa 24:16; 2Ki 19:35; Ps 35:5-6; Ac 12:23; Rev 16:1). Celebrate the praises of God (Job 38:7; Ps 148:2; Isa 6:3; Lk 2:13-14; Rev 5:11-12; 7:11-12). The law given by the mediation of (Ps 68:17; Ac 7:53; Heb 2:2).

Announced: The conception of Christ (Mt 1:20-21; Lk 1:31). The birth of Christ (Lk 2:10-12). The resurrection of Christ (Mt 28:5-7; Lk 24:23). The ascension and second coming of Christ (Ac 1:11). The conception of John the Baptist (Lk 1:13, 36).

Minister to Christ (Mt 4:11; Lk 22:43; Jn 1:51). Are subject to Christ (Eph 1:21; Col 1:16; 2:10; 1Pe 3:22). Shall execute the purposes of Christ (Mt 13:41; 24:31). Shall attend Christ at his second coming (Mt 16:27; 25:31; Mk 8:38; 2Th 1:7). Know and delight in the gospel of Christ (Eph 3:9-10; 1Ti 3:16; 1Pe 1:12). Mediation of, in response to prayer (Mt 26:53; Ac 12:5, 7). Rejoice over every repentant sinner (Lk 15:7, 10). Have charge over the children of God (Ps 34:7; 91:11-12; Da 6:22; Mt 18:10). Are of different orders (Isa 6:2; 1Th 4:16; 1Pe 3:22; Jude 9; Rev 12:7). Not to be worshiped (Col 2:18; Rev 19:10; 22:9). Are examples of meekness (2Pe 2:11; Jude 9). Are wise (2Sa 14:20). Are mighty (Ps 103:20). Are holy (Mt 25:31). Are elect (1Ti 5:21). Are innumerable (Job 25:3; Heb 12:22).

Fallen: (Job 4:18; Mt 25:41; 2Pe 2:4; Jude 6; Rev 2:9). *See Demons.*

ANGER
Forbidden (Ecc 7:9; Mt 5:22; Ro 12:19). A work of the flesh (Gal 5:20). A characteristic of fools (Pr 12:16; 14:29; 27:3; Ecc 7:9).

Connected With:
Pride (Pr 21:24). Cruelty (Ge 49:7; Pr 27:3-4). Clamor and evil-speaking (Eph 4:31). Malice and blasphemy (Col 3:8). Strife and contention (Pr 21:19; 29:22; 30:33). Brings its own punishment (Job 5:2; Pr 19:19; 25:28). Grievous words stir up (Jdg 12:4; 2Sa 19:43; Pr 15:1). Should not betray us into sin (Ps 37:8; Eph 4:26). In prayer be free from (1Ti 2:8). May be averted by wisdom (Pr 29:8). Meekness pacifies (Pr 15:1; Ecc 10:4). Children should not be provoked to (Eph 6:4; Col 3:21). Be slow to (Pr 15:18; 16:32; 19:11; Tit 1:7; Jas 1:19). Avoid those given to (Ge 49:6; Pr 22:24).

Justifiable, Exemplified:
Our Lord (Mk 3:5). Jacob (Ge 31:36). Moses (Ex 11:8; 32:19; Lev 10:16; Nu 16:15). Nehemiah (Ne 5:6; 13:17, 25).

Sinful, Exemplified:
Cain (Ge 4:5-6). Esau (Ge 27:45). Simeon and Levi (Ge 49:5-7). Moses (Nu 20:10-11). Balaam (Nu 22:27). Saul (1Sa 20:30). Ahab (1Ki 21:4). Naaman (2Ki 5:11). Asa (2Ch 16:10). Uzziah (2Ch 26:19). Haman (Est 3:5). Nebuchadnezzar (Da 3:13). Jonah (Jnh 4:4). Herod (Mt 2:16). Jews (Lk 4:28). High Priest (Ac 5:17; 7:54).

ANGER OF GOD
Turned away by Christ (Lk 2:11, 14; Ro 5:9; 2Co 5:18-19; Eph 2:14, 17; Col 1:20; 1Th 1:10). Is turned away from them that believe (Jn 3:14-18; Ro 3:25; 5:1). Is turned away upon confession of sin and repentance (Job 33:27-28; Ps 106:43-45; Jer 3:12-13; 18:7-8; 31:18-20; Joel 2:12-14; Lk 15:18-20). Is slow (Ps 103:8; Isa 48:9; Jnh 4:2; Na 1:3). Is righteous (Ps 58:10-11; La 1:18; Ro 2:6, 8; 3:5-6; Rev 16:6-7). The justice of, not to be questioned (Ro 9:18, 20, 22). Manifested in terrors (Ex 14:24; Ps 76:6-8; Jer 10:10; La 2:20-22). Manifested in judgments and afflictions (Job 21:17; Ps 78:49-51; 90:7; Isa 9:19; Jer 7:20; Eze 7:19; Heb 3:17). Cannot be resisted (Job 9:13; 14:13; Ps 76:7; Na 1:6). Aggravated by continual provocation (Nu 32:14). Specially reserved for the day of wrath (Zep 1:14-18; Mt 25:41; Ro 2:5, 8; 2Th 1:8; Rev 6:17; 11:18; 19:15).

Against:
The wicked (Ps 7:11; 21:8-9; Isa 3:8; 13:9; Na 1:2-3; Ro 1:18; 2:8; Eph 5:6; Col 3:6). Those who forsake him (Ezr 8:22; Isa 1:4). Unbelief (Ps 78:21-22; Jn 3:36; Heb 3:18-19). Impenitence (Ps 7:12; Pr 1:30-31; Isa 9:13-14; Ro 2:5). Apostasy (Heb 10:26-27). Idolatry (Dt 29:20, 27-28; 32:19-20, 22; Jos 23:16; 2Ki 22:17; Ps 78:58-59; Jer 44:3). Sin, in believers (Ps 89:30-32; 90:7-9; 99:8; 102:9-10; Isa 47:6). Extreme, against those who oppose the gospel (Ps 2:2-3, 5; 1Th 2:16). Folly of provoking (Jer 7:19; 1Co 10:22). To be dreaded (Ps 2:12; 76:7; 90:11; Mt 10:28). To be deprecated (Ex 32:11; Ps 6:1; 38:1; 74:1-2; Isa 64:9). Removal of, should be prayed for (Ps 39:10; 79:5; 80:4; Da 9:16; Hab 3:2). Tempered with mercy to believers (Ps 30:5; Isa 26:20; 54:8; 57:15-16; Jer 30:11; Mic 7:11). To be borne with submission (2Sa 24:17; La 3:39, 43; Mic 7:9). Should lead to repentance (Isa 42:24-25; Jer 4:8).

Exemplified Against:
The old world (Ge 7:21-23). Builders of Babel (Ge 11:8). Cities of the plain (Ge 19:24-25). Egyptians (Ex 7:20; 8:6, 16, 24; 9:3, 9, 23; 10:13, 22; 12:29; 14:27). Israelites (Ex 32:35; Nu 11:1, 33; 14:40-45; 21:6; 25:9; 2Sa 24:1, 15). Enemies of Israel (1Sa 5:6, 7:10). Nadab (Lev 10:2). The Spies (Nu 14:37). Korah (Nu 16:31, 35). Aaron and Miriam (Nu 12:9-10). Five Kings (Jos 10:25). Abimelech (Jdg 9:56). Men of Beth Shemesh (1Sa 6:19). Saul (1Sa 31:6). Uzzah (2Sa 6:7). Saul's family (2Sa 21:1). Sennacherib (2Ki 19:28, 35, 37).

ANIAM (*I am kinsman*). A son of Shemida, a Manassehite (1Ch 7:19).

ANIM (*springs*). A city of Judah (Jos 15:50).

ANIMALS
Creation of:
(Ge 1:24-25; 2:19; Jer 27:5). Food of (Ge 1:30). Named (Ge 2:20). Ordained as food for man (Ge 9:2-3; Lev 11:3, 9, 21-22; Dt 14:4-6, 9, 11, 20). God's care of (Ge 9:9-10; Dt 25:4; Job 38:41; Ps 36:6; 104:11, 21; 145:15-16; 147:9; Jn 4:11; Mt 6:26; 10:29; Lk 12:6, 24; 1Co 9:9). Under the curse (Ge 3:14; 6:7, 17). Suffer under divine judgments sent upon man (Jer 7:20; 14:4; 21:6; Eze 14:13, 17, 19-21; Joel 1:18-20). Two of every kind preserved in the ark (Ge 6:19-20; 7:2, 9, 14-15; 8:19). Seven clean of every kind preserved in the ark (Ge 7:2-3). Suffered the plagues of Egypt (Ex 8:17; 9:9-10, 19; 11:5). Perish at death (Ecc 3:21). Possessed by demons (Mt 8:31-32; Mk 5:13; Lk 8:33). Clean and unclean (Ge 7:2, 8; 8:20; Lev 7:21; 11; 20:25; Dt 14:3-20; Ac 10:11-15; 1Ti 4:3-5).

God's Control of:
(Ps 91:13; Lk 10:19). Instruments of God's will (Ex 8; 10:4-15, 19; Nu 21:6; 22:28; Jos 24:12; Joel 1:4). Belong to God (Ps 50:10-12). Sent in judgment (Lev 26:22; Nu 21:6-7; Dt 8:15; Eze 5:17; 14:15; Rev 6:8).

Nature of:
(Job 41; Ps 32:9; Jas 3:7). Habits of (Job 12:7-8; 37:8; 39; 40:20-21; Ps 104:20-25; Isa 13:21-22; 34:14). Breeding of (Ge 30:35-43; 31:8-9). Instincts of (Dt 32:11; Job 35:11; 39; 40:15-24; Ps 104:11-30; Pr 6:5-8; 30:25-28; Isa 1:3; Jer 2:24; 8:7; La 4:3; Mt 24:28). Abodes of (Job 24:5; 37:8; 39:5-10, 27-29; Ps 104:20, 22, 25; Isa 34:14-15; Jer 2:24; 50:39; Mk 1:13).

Cruelty to:
Of Balaam to his donkey (Nu 22:22-33). Hamstringing horses (2Sa 8:4; 1Ch 18:4).

Kindness to:
By the righteous (Pr 12:10). In not muzzling an ox while threshing (Dt 25:4; 1Ti 5:18). In relieving the overburdened (Ex 23:5; Dt 22:4). In rescuing from pits (Mt 12:11; Lk 13:15; 14:5). In feeding (Ge 24:32; 43:24; Jdg 19:21).

Instances of: Jacob in making shelters for his cattle (Ge 33:17). People of Gerar in providing tents for cattle (2Ch 14:15).

Laws Concerning:
Sabbath rest for (Ex 20:10; Dt 5:14).
Treatment of vicious (Ex 21:28-32, 35-36). Penalty for injury of (Ex 21:33-34). Hybridizing of, forbidden (Lev 19:19). Working of (Dt 22:10). Mother birds and their young (Dt 22:6-7).

Names of:
Antelopes (Dt 14:5; Isa 51:20). Apes (1Ki 10:22). Baboons (1Ki 10:22; 2Ch 9:21). Donkeys, beasts of burden (Ge 22:3; Nu 22:28; Dt 22:10; Jdg 5:10; 10:4 1Sa 9:3; Mt 21:2). Bears (1Sa 17:34; 2Sa 17:8; 2Ki 2:24; Pr 17:12; 28:15; Isa 11:7). Behemoth (Job 40:15-24). Boars (Ps 80:13). Bull, as offerings (Ex 29:10-11, 36; Lev 4:4; Nu 15:8; 1Ki 18:33; 2Ch 13:9; Ezr 6:17; Ps 66:15). Calves (Ge 18:7; 1Sa 28:24; Am 6:4; Lk 15:23). Camels (Ge 12:16; 30:43; Lev 11:4; Jdg 6:5; 1Sa 30:17; 1Ch 5:21; Job 1:3; Mt 19:24; 23:24). Cattle, livestock (Ge 1:25; 31:18; Ex 9:4; 20:10; Nu 32:1; Jos 14:4; Eze 39:18; Am 4:1). Coneys, rock badgers (Lev 11:5; Ps 104:18; Pr 30:26). Cows (Ge 32:15; Dt 7:13; 1Sa 6:7). Deer (Dt 14:5; 2Sa 2:18; 22:34; 1Ch 12:8; Ps 42:1; Pr 5:19; 6:5; Isa 35:6; Jer 14:5). Dogs (1Ki 14:11; 22:38; Ps 59:6; Pr 26:17; Ecc 9:4; Lk 16:21). Dragons (Rev 12:3-17). Elephants (Job 40:15, ftn). Foxes (Jdg 15:4; Ne 4:3; Ps 63:10; SS 2:15; Mt 8:20). Gecko (Lev 11:30). Goats, as offerings (Ge 15:9; Lev 4:24; 16:15; Jdg 13:19; 2Ch 29:23). Heifers, offered as sacrifices (Ge 15:9; Nu 19:2; Dt 21:3; Heb 9:13). Horses (Dt 17:16; 2Ki 23:11; Job 39:19; Ps 32:9; 33:17; Isa 31:1). Lambs, for offerings (Ex 29:38-39; Lev 3:7; 4:32; 5:6; Nu 6:12). Leopards (SS 4:8; Isa 11:6; Jer 5:6; 13:23; Hos 13:7; Hab 1:8). Lions, general references to (Jdg 14:5; 1Sa 17:34; 1Ki 13:24; Da 6:19), characteristics of (Dt 33:22; Jdg 14:18; 2Sa 17:10; Job 10:16; Ps 17:12; Pr 30:30; Isa 31:4; Na 2:12). Lizards (Lev 11:30). Mountain sheep (Dt 14:5). Mules (2Sa 13:29; 18:9; 1Ki 1:33; Ps 32:9; Zec 14:15). Oxen, laws concerning (Ex 21:28; 22:1; 23:4; Lev 17:3; Dt 5:14; 22:1; 25:4; Lk 13:15; 1Co 9:9; 1Ti 5:18). Pigs (Lev 11:7; Isa 65:4; 66:17; Mt 7:6; 8:30; Lk 15:15; 2Pe 2:22). Rabbit (Lev 11:6). Rams, used in sacrifices (Ge 15:9; 22:13; Ex 29:15; Lev 5:15; Nu 5:8). Rats (Lev 11:29; 1Sa 6:4; Isa 66:17). Rooster (Pr 30:31). Sheep (Ge 4:4; 30:32; Dt 18:4; 32:14; 2Ch 7:5; 15:11; Job 1:3; 42:12; Mt 12:11). Wild oxen (Nu 23:22; Dt 33:17; Job 39:9; Ps 29:6; Isa 34:7). Vipers, poisonous serpents (Job 20:16; Isa 30:6; 59:5). Weasel (Lev 11:29). Wolves, illustrative of the wicked (Mt 7:15; 10:16; Jn 10:12; Ac 20:29).
See Birds; Insects.

ANISE *See Dill.*

ANKLET An ornament worn by women on the ankles (Isa 3:16, 20). *See Jewel, Jewelry.*

ANNA (*grace*). A widow and prophetess who at the age of 84 recognized Jesus as the Messiah when He was brought into the Temple (Lk 2:36-38).

ANNAS (*grace*). Associate high priest with Caiaphas (Lk 3:2; Jn 18:13, 19, 24; Ac 4:6).

ANNIHILATION The belief that there is no existence after death or that there is no existence for the wicked after death.
Some texts seem to imply death as final (Job 14:12, 18-22; Ps 6:5; 88:10; Isa 26:14). The resurrection is the hope of all believers (Ps 16:9-11; Isa 53:11; Da 12:1-3). In the teaching of Jesus (Mt 22:23-32; Lk 14:14; Jn 11:24-26), of the apostles (Ac 4:1-4, 33; 23:6-8; 24:10-21; 1Co 15). *See Resurrection.*
Eternal punishment of the wicked is also clearly taught (Da 12:2; Mt 18:8-9; Jn 3:36; 2Th 1:9; Rev 14:11; 20:4-15). *See Wicked, Punishment of.*

ANNUAL FEASTS All but Purim and Dedication instituted by Moses.

Designated as:
Solemn feasts (Nu 15:3; 2Ch 8:13; La 2:6; Eze 46:9). Set feasts (Nu 29:39; Ezr 3:5). Appointed feasts (Isa 1:14). Holy convocations (Lev 23:4). First and last days were Sabbatic (Lev 23:39-40; Nu 28:18-25; 29:12, 35; Ne 8:1-18). Kept with rejoicing (Lev 23:40; Dt 16:11-14; 2Ch 30:21-26; Ezr 6:22; Ne 8:9-12, 17; Ps 122:4; Isa 30:29; Zec 8:19). Divine protection given during (Ex 34:24).
All males were required to attend (Ex 23:17; 34:23; Dt 16:16; Eze 36:38; Lk 2:41-42; Jn 4:45; 7). Aliens permitted to attend (Jn 12:20; Ac 2:1-11). Attended by women (1Sa 1:3, 9; Lk 2:41).

Observed:
By Jesus (Mt 26:17-20; Lk 2:41-42; 22:15; Jn 2:13, 23; 5:1; 7:10; 10:22). By Paul (Ac 20:6, 16; 24:11, 17).

New Moon:
(Nu 10:10; 28:11-15; 1Ch 23:31; 2Ch 31:3; Ezr 3:5). Buying and selling at time of, suspended (Am 8:5).

The Passover:
Institution of (Ex 12:3-49; 23:15-18; 34:18; Lev 23:4-8; Nu 9:2-5, 13-14; 28:16-25; Dt 16:1-8, 16; Ps 81:3, 5). Design of (Ex 12:21-28).
Special Passover, for those who were unclean, or on journey to be held in second month (Nu 9:6-12; 2Ch 30:2-4). Lamb killed by Levites, for those who were ceremonially unclean (2Ch 30:17; 35:3-11; Ezr 6:20). Strangers authorized to celebrate (Ex 12:48-49; Nu 9:14).
Observed at place designated by God (Dt 16:5-7). With unleavened bread (Ex 12:8, 15-20; 13:3, 6; 23:15; Lev 23:6; Nu

9:11; 28:17; Dt 16:3-4; Mk 14:12; Lk 22:7; Ac 12:3; 1Co 5:8). Penalty for neglecting to observe (Nu 9:13).

Reinstituted by Ezekiel (Eze 45:21-24).

Observation of—

Renewed, by the Israelites on entering Canaan (Jos 5:10-11). By Hezekiah (2Ch 30:1). By Josiah (2Ki 23:22-23; 2Ch 35:1, 18). After return from captivity (Ezr 6:19-20). Observed by Jesus (Mt 26:17-20; Lk 22:15; Jn 2:13, 23; 13). Jesus when twelve years old, in the temple at time of (Lk 2:41-50). Jesus crucified at time of (Mt 26:2; Mk 14:1-2; Jn 18:28). Lord's Supper ordained at (Mt 26:26-28; Mk 14:12-25; Lk 22:7-20). The lamb of, a type of Christ (1Co 5:7).

Prisoners released at, by the Romans (Mt 27:15; Mk 15:6; Lk 23:16-17; Jn 18:39). Peter imprisoned at time of (Ac 12:3).

Christ Called—

Our Passover lamb (1Co 5:7; see also Jn 1:36; Rev 5:6-14).

Pentecost:

Called Feast of Weeks (Ex 34:22; Dt 16:10). Feast of Harvest (Ex 23:16). Day of First Fruits (Nu 28:26). Day of Pentecost (Ac 2:1; 20:16; 1Co 16:8).

Institution of (Ex 23:16; 34:22; Lev 23:15-21; Nu 28:26-31; Dt 16:9-12, 16).

Holy Spirit given to the apostles on the day of (Ac 2).

Purim:

Instituted by Esther and Mordecai to commemorate the deliverance of the Jews from the plot of Haman (Est 9:20-32).

Tabernacles:

Also called Feast of Ingathering. Instituted (Ex 23:16; 34:22; Lev 23:34-43; Nu 29:12-40; Dt 16:13-16). Design of (Lev 23:42-43). The law read in connection with, every seventh year (Dt 31:10-12; Ne 8:18).

Observance of—

After the captivity (Ezr 3:4; Ne 8:14-18). By Jesus (Jn 7:2, 14). Observance of, omitted (Ne 8:17). Penalty for not observing (Zec 14:16-19).

Jeroboam institutes an idolatrous feast parallel to, in the eighth month (1Ki 12:32-33).

Trumpets:

When and how observed (Lev 23:24-25; Nu 29:1-6). Celebrated after the captivity with joy (Ne 8:2, 9-12).

Dedication or Hanukkah:

Instituted in the Intertestamental era, commemorating the dedication of the temple by Judas Maccabeus (1Mc 4:59). Observed by Jesus (Jn 10:22-39).

See Feasts; see also each feast by name.

ANOINTING

Of the body (Dt 28:40; Ru 3:3; Est 2:12; Ps 92:10; 104:15; 141:5; Pr 27:9, 16; Ecc 9:8; SS 1:3; 4:10; Isa 57:9; Am 6:6; Mic 6:15). Of guests (2Ch 28:15; Lk 7:46). The sick (Isa 1:6; Mk 6:13; Lk 10:34; Jas 5:14; Rev 3:18). The dead (Mt 26:12; Mk 14:8; 16:1; Lk 23:56). Of Jesus, as a token of love (Lk 7:37-38, 46; Jn 11:2; 12:3). Omitted in mourning (2Sa 12:20; 14:2; Isa 61:3; Da 10:3). God preserves those who receive (Ps 18:50; 20:6; 89:20-23). Believers receive (Isa 61:3; 1Jn 2:20).

In Consecration:

Of high priests (Ex 29:7, 29; 40:13; Lev 6:20; 8:12; 16:32; Nu 35:25; Ps 133:2).

Of priests (Ex 28:41; 30:30; 40:15; Lev 4:3; 8:30; Nu 3:3).

Of kings (Jdg 9:8, 15), Saul (1Sa 9:16; 10:1; 15:1), David (1Sa 16:3, 12-13; 2Sa 2:4; 5:3; 12:7; 9:21; 1Ch 11:3). Solomon (1Ki 1:39; 1Ch 29:22), Jehu (1Ki 19:16; 2Ki 9:1-3, 6, 12). Hazael (1Ki 19:15), Joash (2Ki 11:12; 2Ch 23:11), Jehoahaz (2Ki 23:30), Cyrus (Isa 45:1).

Of prophets (1Ki 19:16).

Of the tabernacle (Ex 30:26; 40:9; Lev 8:10; Nu 7:1), altars of (Ex 30:26-28; 40:10; Lev 8:11; Nu 7:1), vessels of (Ex 30:27-28; 40:9-10; Lev 8:10-11; Nu 7:1).

Jacob's pillar at Bethel (Ge 28:18; 31:13; 35:14).

See Dedication.

Figurative:

Of Christ's kingly and priestly office (Ps 45:7; 89:20; Isa 61:1; Da 9:24; Lk 4:18; Ac 4:27; 10:38; Heb 1:9). Of spiritual gifts (2Co 1:21; 1Jn 2:20, 27). Of God's choice and enabling of leaders (Ex 40:13-15; Lev 8:12; 1Sa 16:13; 1Ki 19:16).

Symbolic of Jesus' death (Mt 26:7-12; Jn 12:3-7).

ANOINTING OIL Formula of, given by Moses (Ex 30:22-25, 31-33). *See Oil; Ointment.*

ANOTH *See Beth Anoth.*

ANT Illustrate work ethic (Pr 6:6-8; 30:25).

ANTEDILUVIANS (*those who lived before the flood*). Worship God (Ge 4:3-4, 26). Occupations of (Ge 4:2-3, 20-22). Arts of (Ge 4:2-3, 20-22; 6:14-22). Enoch prophesies to (Jude 14-15). Noah preaches to (2Pe 2:5). Wickedness of (Ge 6:5-7). Destruction of (Ge 7:1, 21-23; Job 22:15-17; Mt 24:37-39; Lk 17:26-27; 2Pe 2:5). *See Flood.*

Longevity of. *See Longevity.*

Giants among. *See Giants.*

ANTELOPE (Dt 14:5; Isa 51:20). *See Deer.*

ANTHOTHIJAH Son of Shashak, a Benjamite (1Ch 8:24-25).

ANTHROPOMORPHISMS Figures of speech that attribute human anatomy, acts, and affections to God.

Anatomy:

Arm (Ps 89:13), body or form (Nu 11:25), ear (Ps 34:15), eye (2Ch 16:9; Isa 1:15), mouth (Ps 33:6), voice (Eze 1:24, 28), wings (Ps 36:7; 57:1).

See terms for body parts, e.g., Arm, Eye, Hand.

Intellectual Facilities:

Knowing (Ge 18:17-19), reason (Isa 1:18), remembering (Ge 9:16; 19:29; Ex 2:24; Isa 43:26; 63:11), understanding (Ps 147:5), will (Ro 9:19).

Actions:

Breathing (Ps 33:6), grasping, with hand (Ps 35:2), hearing (Ps 94:9), laughing (Ps 2:4; 37:13; 59:8; Pr 1:26), not tiring (Isa 40:28), resting (Ge 2:2-3, 19; Ex 20:11; 31:17; Dt 5:14; Heb 4:4, 10), seeing (Ge 18:21; Ex 14:24; Ps 94:9), sleeping (Ps 44:23; 78:65; 121:4), speaking (Ge 18:33; Nu 11:25; Ps 33:6), standing (Ps 35:2), walking (Ge 3:8; Lev 26:12; Dt 23:14; Job 22:14; Hab 3:15).

Affections and Emotions:

Amazement (Isa 59:16; 63:5; Mk 6:6), grief (Ge 6:6; Jdg 10:16; Ps 95:10; Heb 3:10, 17), jealousy (Ex 20:5; 34:13-14; Nu 25:11; Dt 29:20; 32:16, 21; 1Ki 14:22; Ps 78:58; 79:5; Isa 30:1-2; 31:1, 3; Eze 16:42; 23:25; 36:5-6; 38:19; Zep 1:18; 3:8; Zec 1:14; 8:2; 1Co 10:22), swearing an oath (Isa 62:8; Heb 6:16-17; 7:21, 28). *See Anger of God; Oath.*

ANTICHRIST(S) (*against* or *substitute Christ*). (Mt 24:5, 23-24, 26; Mk 13:6, 21-22; Lk 21:8; 2Th 2:3-12; 1Jn 2:18, 22; 4:3; 2Jn 7). To be destroyed (Rev 19:20; 20:10, 15).

ANTI-LEBANON *See Lebanon.*

ANTIOCH

1. A city of Syria. Disciples first called Christians in (Ac 11:19-30). Church in (Ac 13:1; 14:26-27). Barnabas and Paul make second visit to (Ac 14:26-28). Dissension in church of (Ac 15:22, w 15:1-35). Paul and Peter's controversy at (Gal 2:11-15).

2. A city of Pisidia. Persecutes Paul (Ac 13:14-52; Ac 14:19-22; 18:22; 2Ti 3:11).

ANTIOCHUS (*opposer*). A favorite name of the Seleucid kings of Syria, referred to as the kings of the North in Da 11.

1. Antiochus II Theos (286-246 B.C.) married Berenice, daughter of Ptolemy II, the "king of the South" (Da 11:6).

2. Antiochus III, the Great (242-187 B.C.) gained control of Israel in 198 B.C. (Da 11:10-19).

3. Antiochus IV (Epiphanes), son of III (215-163 B.C.); his attempt to hellenize the Jews led to the Maccabean revolt (Da 8:9-12, 23-25; 11:21-35; see also 1 and 2Mc). *See Abomination That Causes Desolation; Testaments, Time Between.*

ANTIPAS (possibly a contraction of *Antipater*).

1. A Christian martyr of Pergamum (Rev 2:13).

2. Herod Antipas, son of Herod the Great; ruled Galilee and Perea from 4 B.C. to A.D. 39. *See Herod.*

ANTIPATER *See Herod.*

ANTIPATRIS A city in Samaria (Ac 23:31).

ANTITYPE *See Types.*

ANTONIA, TOWER OF A fortress connected with the temple at Jerusalem, built by Herod the Great. It was garrisoned by Roman soldiers who watched the temple area (Ac 21:30ff).

ANTOTHIJAH *See Anthothijah.*

ANTOTHITE *See Anathoth, Anathothite.*

ANUB (*fruitful*). Son of Koz of the tribe of Judah (1Ch 4:8).

ANVIL (Isa 41:7).

ANXIETY Forbidden (Mt 6:25-34; Lk 12:11-12, 22-28; 1Co 7:32; Php 4:6; 1Pe 5:7).

Unavailing (Ps 39:6; Mt 6:27; Lk 12:25-26). Proceeds from unbelief (Mt 6:26, 28-30; Lk 12:24, 27-28). Martha rebuked for (Lk 10:40-41).

Remedy for (Ps 37:5; 55:22; Heb 13:5; 1Pe 5:6-7). *See Care, Worldly.*

APARTMENT (Jer 36:22). *See Winter Apartment, Winter House.*

APES In Solomon's zoological collections (1Ki 10:22; 2Ch 9:21).

APELLES A disciple in Rome (Ro 16:10).

APHARSACHITES, APHARSATHCHITES, APHARSITES Aramaic terms transliterated as proper names in the KJV are translated "officials" in the NIV (Ezr 5:6; 6:6).

APHEK (*stronghold*).

1. A city of the tribe of Asher (Jos 19:30). A city whose inhabitants were not driven out by Asher (Jdg 1:31).

2. A city of the tribe of Issachar. Philistines defeat Israelites at (1Sa 4:1-11). Saul slain at (1Sa 29:1, w 1Sa 31). Probably the same as the royal city of the Canaanites (Jos 12:18).

3. A city between Damascus and Israel. Ben-Hadad defeated at (1Ki 20:26-30).

APHEKAH (*the fortress*). A city in the mountains of Judah (Jos 15:53).

APHIAH Ancestor of Saul (1Sa 9:1).

APHIK *See Aphek.*

APHRAH *See Beth Ophrah; Ophrah.*

APHSES *See Happizzez.*

APOCALYPSE (*disclosure*). Greek title of the book of Revelation. *See Apocalyptic Literature; Revelation, Book of.*

APOCALYPTIC LITERATURE A type of prophetic literature that communicates the ultimate triumph of God over evil through dreams, visions, and symbols. Daniel and Revelation and parts of Ezekiel and Zechariah are canonical apocalypses. Many non-canonical apocalypses appeared between c. 200 B.C. and A.D. 200 in the style of Daniel, also claiming to have been written by a famous OT character. Major examples are 1 and 2 Enoch, Jubilees, Assumption of Moses, 2 Esdras, Apocalypse of Baruch, The Testaments of the Twelve Prophets, and the Psalms of Solomon.

APOCRYPHA (*hidden, obscure*). Books and chapters interspersed among the canonical books of the OT in the LXX and Vulgate, but not found in the Hebrew OT. The Jewish people, who produced them, and Protestants do not consider them canonical. The Roman Catholic Church received the following as deuterocanonical at the Council of Trent (1546): Tobit, Judith, Additions to Esther, Wisdom of Solomon, Ecclesiasticus, Baruch, Letter of Jeremiah, The Prayer of Azariah and the Song of the Three Young Men, Susanna, Bel and the Dragon, and 1 and 2 Maccabees. Other works are considered deuterocanonical by the Orthodox Church: 1 and 2 Esdras, The Prayer of Manasseh, Psalm 151, 3 and 4 Maccabees. *See Testaments, Time Between.*

APOLLONIA A city of Macedonia (Ac 17:1).

APOLLOS An eloquent Christian convert at Corinth (Ac 18:24-28; 19:1; 1Co 1:12; 3:4-7). Refuses to return to Rome (1Co 16:12). Paul writes Titus about (Tit 3:13). Born in Alexandria (Ac 18:24).

APOLLYON (*destroyer*). Angel of the bottomless pit (Rev 9:11).

APOSTASY (*abandoning God*).

Described:

(Dt 13:13, 32; 32:15; Isa 65:11-12; Mt 12:45; Lk 11:24-26; Ac 7:39-43; 1Ti 4:1-3; 2Ti 3:6-9; 4:3-4; Heb 3:12; 2Pe 2:15-22; Jude 8). Foretold (Mt 24:12; 2Th 2:3; 1Ti 4:1-3; 2Ti 3:1-9; 4:3-4; 2Pe 2:1).

Admonitions against (Mt 24:4-5; Mk 13:5-6; Heb 3:12; 2Pe 3:17; 2Jn 8; Jude 4-6). No remedy for (Heb 6:4-8; 10:26-29).

Punishment (1Ch 28:9; Isa 1:28; 65:12-15; Jer 17:5-6; Eze 3:20; 18:24, 26; 33:12-13, 18; Zep 1:4-6; Jn 15:6; 2Th 2:11-12; Heb 10:25-31, 38-39; 2Pe 2:17-22; Jude 6).

Caused by:

Persecution (Mt 13:20-21; 24:9-12; Mk 4:5-17; Lk 8:13). Worldliness (2Ti 4:10).

Instances of:

Israelites (Ex 32; Nu 14; Ac 7:39-43), Saul (1Sa 15:26-29; 18:12; 28:15, 18), Amaziah (2Ch 25:14, 27), disciples (Jn 6:66), Judas (Mt 26:14-16; 27:3-5; Mk 14:10-11; Lk 22:3-6, 47-48; Ac 1:16-18), Hymenaeus and Alexander (1Ti 1:19-20), Phygelus and Hermogenes (2Ti 1:15).

See Antichrist(s); Apostates; Backsliding, Instances of Israel's Backsliding; Backsliders; Reprobacy; Reprobates.

APOSTATES

Described:

(Dt 13:13; Heb 3:12). Persecution tends to make (Mt 24:9-10; Lk 8:13). A worldly spirit tends to make (2Ti 4:10). Never belonged to Christ (1Jn 2:19). Believers do not become (Ps 44:18-19; Heb 6:9; 10:39). It is impossible to restore (Heb 6:4-6). Guilt and punishment of (Zep 1:4-6; Heb 10:25-31, 39; 2Pe 2:17, 20-22). Cautions against becoming (Heb 3:12; 2Pe 3:17). Shall abound in the latter days (Mt 24:12; 2Th 2:3; 1Ti 4:1-3).

Examples of:

Amaziah (2Ch 25:14, 27). Professed disciples (Jn 6:66). Hymenaeus and Alexander (1Ti 1:19-20). *See Apostasy.*

APOSTLE (*to send off* or *out*). A title of Jesus (Heb 3:1). *See Apostles.*

APOSTLES (*to send off* or *out*).

The Twelve:

In the Gospels, a title distinguishing the twelve disciples, whom Jesus selected to be intimately associated with himself (Lk 6:13). Names of the twelve (Mt 10:2-4; Mk 3:16-19; Lk 6:13-16; Ac 1:13, 26).

Selection of (Mt 4:18, 22; 9:9-10; 10:2-4; Mk 3:13-19; Lk 6:13-16; Jn 1:43).

Commission of (Mt 10; 28:19-20; Mk 3:14-15; 6:7-11; 16:15; Lk 9:1-5; 22:28-30; Jn 20:23; 21:15-19; Ac 1; 2; 10:42). Uneducated (Mt 11:25; Ac 4:13). Miraculous power given to (Mt 10:1; Mk 3:15; 6:7; 16:17; Lk 9:1-2; 10:9, 17; Ac 2:4, 43; 5:12-16; 1Co 14:18; 2Co 12:12). Authority of (Mt 16:19; 18:18; 19:28).

Inspiration of (Mt 10:27; 16:17-19; Lk 24:45; Ac 1:2; 13:9). Duties of. *See above, Commission of.* For more information see Lk 24:48; Jn 15:27; Ac 1:8, 21-22; 2:32; 3:15; 4:33; 5:32; 10:39-41; 13:31; 2Pe 1:16, 18; 1Jn 1:1-3. *See Minister.*

Moral state of, before Pentecost (Mt 17:17; 18:3; 20:20-22; Lk 9:54-55). Slow to receive Jesus as Messiah (Mt 14:33). Forsake Jesus (Mk 14:50).

Fail to comprehend the nature and mission of Jesus, and the nature of the kingdom he came to establish (Mt 8:25-27; 15:23; 16:8-12, 21-22; 19:25; Mk 4:13; 6:51-52; 8:17-18; 9:9-10, 31-32; 10:13-14; Lk 9:44-45; 18:34; 24:19, 21; Jn 4:32-33; 10:6; 11:12-13; 12:16; 13:6-8; 14:5-9, 22; 16:6, 17-18, 32; 20:9; 21:12; Ac 1:6).

Other Than the Twelve:

Matthaias (Ac 1:26), Paul and Barnabas (Ac 14:1-4, 14), Paul (Ro 1:1), Andronicus and Junias (Ro 16:7). A spiritual gift (1Co 12:28-31; Eph 4:11-13).

See Andronicus; Barnabas; Junias; Matthias; Minister; Paul.

False: (2Co 11:13; Rev 2:2).

See Teachers, False.

APOTHECARY *See Perfume, Perfumer.*

APPAIM (*[a pair of] nostrils*). Son of Nadab (1Ch 2:30-31).

APPAREL *See Dress.*

APPEAL Paul makes, to Caesar (Ac 25:10-11, 21-27; 26:32; 28:19). *See Change of Venue; Court, of Law.*

APPEAL TO GOD To witness (Ge 31:50; Dt 30:19; Jdg 11:10; 1Sa 12:5; Job 16:19; Ro 1:9; 2Co 1:23; Php 1:8; 1Th 2:5).

APPEARANCES Of God to people (Ge 12:7; 17:1; 18:1; 26:2; 35:9; Ex 3:16; 1Ki 3:5; 9:2; 2Ch 3:1).

APPEARING *See Eschatology.*

APPELLATIO The judicial process of appealing to a higher magistrate (Ac 25:1-12).

APPETITE Kept in subjection (Pr 23:1-2; Da 1:8-16; 1Co 9:27). *See Temperance.*

APPHIA Christian at Colosse (Phm 2).

APPIAN WAY An ancient Roman road on which Paul traveled (Ac 28:13-16).

APPIUS, FORUM OF A market town forty-three miles from Rome, where Paul met a delegation of Roman Christians (Ac 28:15).

APPLE A fruit (Pr 25:11; SS 2:3, 5; 7:8; 8:5; Joel 1:12).

APPLE OF THE EYE The eyeball; symbolizing that which is precious and protected (Dt 32:10; Ps 17:8; Pr 7:2; Zec 2:8).

APRON *See Dress.*

AQABAH, GULF OF The eastern arm of the Red Sea, where Solomon's seaport was located (1Ki 9:26). *See Ezion Geber.*

AQUEDUCT (*water channel*). A channel made of stone to convey water to places where the water is to be used (2Ki 18:17; Isa 7:3; 36:1). Many fine Roman aqueducts survive.

AQUILA (*eagle*). A Jewish Christian, a tentmaker by trade, who with his wife Priscilla labored with Paul at Corinth and was of help to Apollos and many others (Ac 18:2, 18, 26; Ro 16:3-4; 1Co 16:19; 2Ti 4:19).

AR (possibly *city*). A city of Moab (Nu 21:15; Dt 2:9, 18, 24, 29). Destruction of (Nu 21:26-30; Isa 15:1).

ARA Son of Jether (1Ch 7:38).

ARAB (*desert* or *steppe*).
1. A city of Judah (Jos 15:52).
2. *See Arabia; Arabians.*

ARABAH (*desert*). A name applying to the rift running from Mt. Hermon to the Gulf of Aqabah. It is a narrow valley of varying breadth and productivity. The Israelites made stops there in their wilderness wanderings, and Solomon got iron and copper from its mines (Dt 1:1, 7; 11:30; Jos 3:16; 1Sa 23:24; Jer 39:4).

ARABIA (*desert* or *steppe*). Paid tribute to Solomon (2Ch 9:14) and Jehoshaphat (2Ch 17:11). Exports of (Eze 27:21). Prophecies against (Isa 21:13; Jer 25:24). Paul visits (Gal 1:17).

ARABIANS, ARABS (*desert plateau dwellers*). Paid tribute to Solomon (2Ch 9:14) and Jehoshaphat (2Ch 17:11). Invade and defeat Judah (2Ch 21:16-17; 22:1). Defeated by Uzziah (2Ch 26:7). Oppose Nehemiah's rebuilding the walls of Jerusalem (Ne 2:19; 4:7). Commerce of (Eze 27:21). Gospel preached to (Ac 2:11; Gal 1:17). Prophecies concerning (Isa 21:13-17; 42:11; 60:7; Jer 25:24).

ARAD (*wild donkey*).
1. A city on the S of Canaan (Nu 21:1; 33:40). Subdued by Joshua (Jos 12:14; Jdg 1:16).
2. Son of Beriah (1Ch 8:15).

ARAH (*he wanders*).
1. An Asherite (1Ch 7:39).
2. Father of a family that returned from exile (Ezr 2:5; Ne 7:10).
3. Jew whose granddaughter became the wife of Tobiah the Ammonite (Ne 6:18).
4. Town in NE Palestine belonging to Sidonians (Jos 13:4).

ARAM
1. Son of Shem (Ge 10:22-23).
2. Son of Kemuel, Abraham's nephew (Ge 22:21).
3. An Asherite (1Ch 7:34).
4. Ancestor of Jesus (Mt 1:3-4; Lk 3:33). *See Ram, 1.*
5. Place in Gilead (1Ch 2:23).
6. Region corresponding to modern Syria (Nu 23:7; 2Sa 8:5; 1Ki 20:20; Am 1:5). The Aramean people spread from Phoenicia to the Fertile Crescent and were closely related to Israel, with whom their history was intertwined. *See Syria.*

ARAM MAACAH Also called Maacah. A small kingdom in Northwest Mesopotamia (1Ch 19:6, ftn). The states of Aram Maacah, Aram Naharaim, and Zobah were N and NE of Israel and formed a solid block from the region of Lake Huleh through the Anti-Lebanons to beyond the Euphrates.
See Aram Naharaim; Aram Zobah; Zobah.

ARAM NAHARAIM A region in NW Mesopotamia (Ge 24:10; Dt 23:4; Jdg 3:8; 1Ch 19:6 and notes). *See Aram Maacah.*

ARAM ZOBAH Only in the Title of Ps 60 (Ps 60, ftn). *See Aram Maacah; Zobah.*

ARAMAIC A Semitic language closely related to Hebrew, which developed various dialects and spread to all of SW Asia. Aramaic portions in the OT are Da 2:4-7:28; Ezr 4:8-6:18; 7:12-26; Jer 10:11. Aramaic words occur in the NT (Mk 5:41; 15:34; Mt 27:46; Ro 8:15; Gal 4:6; 1Co 16:22). Aramaic was the colloquial language of Israel from the time of the return from the Exile.

ARAN (*wild goat*). Son of Dishan (Ge 36:28; 1Ch 1:42).

ARARAT Modern Armenia (2Ki 19:37; Isa 37:38, KJV) and to its mountain range (Ge 8:4), the resting place of Noah's ark. The region is now part of Turkey.

ARATUS A Cilician poet (315-240 B.C.). Paul quotes from his *Phaenomena* (Ac 17:28). *See Asceticism; Cleanthes; Stoicism; Stoics.*

ARAUNAH (*strong*). A Jebusite from whom David bought a site for an altar (2Sa 24:16-24). Also spelled Ornan (1Ch 21:15 ftn, 18-28).

ARBA (*four*). Giant ancestor of Anak (Jos 14:15; 15:13; 21:11).

ARBATHITE (*person from Arabah*). A native of Beth Arabah (2Sa 23:31; 1Ch 11:32).

ARBEL *See Beth Arbel.*

ARBITE Paarai, one of David's mighty men (2Sa 23:35).

ARBITRATION The two prostitutes before Solomon (1Ki 3:16-28). Urged by Paul as a mode of action for Christians (1Co 6:1-8). *See Court, of Law.*

ARCH *See Architecture.*

ARCHAEOLOGY (*study of ancient things*). Study of the material remains of the past by excavating ancient buried cities and examining their remains; deciphering inscriptions; and evaluating the language, literature, art, architecture, monuments, and other aspects of human life and achievement. Biblical archaeology is concerned with Israel and the countries with which the Hebrews and early Christians came into contact. Modern archaeology began with Napoleon's expedition to Egypt, on which many scholars accompanied him to study Egyptian monuments (1798), and with the work of Edward Robinson in Palestine (1838, 1852). Discoveries of great importance which throw much light upon the patriarchal period are the Mari Tablets, the Nuzi Tablets, the Tell-el Amarna Tablets, and the Ras Shamra Tablets. The discovery of the Dead Sea Scrolls and the excavation of Qumran are among the more recent archaeological finds of importance. Archaeology is of great help in better understanding the Bible, in dealing with critical questions regarding the Bible, and in gaining an appreciation of the ancient world.

ARCHANGEL (*ruling angel*). A high order of angels (1Th 4:16). Michael called a "prince" (Da 10:13, 21; 12:1; Jude 9; Rev 12:7). *See Angels.*

ARCHELAUS (*ruler of people*). The son of Herod the Great. He ruled over Judea, Samaria, and Idumea from 4 B.C. to A.D. 6 (Mt 2:22).

ARCHERS Hunters or warriors with bow and arrow, weapons universally used in ancient times (Ge 21:20; 1Sa 20:17-42; Isa 21:17). "Arrow" is often used figuratively (Job 6:4; Jer 9:8), as is also "bow" (Ps 7:12). *See Archery.*

ARCHERY Practiced by Ishmael (Ge 21:20), Esau (Ge 27:3), Jonathan (1Sa 20:20, 36-37), Sons of Ulam (1Ch 8:40), Philistines (1Sa 31:1-3; 1Ch 10:3), Persians (Isa 13:17-18), people of Kedar (Isa 21:17), Syrians (1Ki 22:31-34), Israelites (2Sa 1:18; 1Ch 5:18; 12:2; 2Ch 14:8; 26:14; Ne 4:13; Zec 9:13), Lydians (Jer 46:9).
In war (Ge 49:23; Jdg 5:11; 1Sa 31:3; Isa 22:3; Jer 4:29; Zec 10:4).
See Archers; Armies; Arrows; Bow; War.

ARCHEVITES *See Erech, 2.*

ARCHI, ARCHITES *See Arkite(s).*

ARCHIPPUS (*master of the horse*). An office bearer in the church at Colosse (Col 4:17; Phm 2).

ARCHITECTURE The materials of architecture in antiquity were wood, clay, brick (formed of clay, whether sun-baked or kiln-fired), and stone. The determining factor in the choice of material used was local availability. The homes of the poor had no artistic distinction. The wealthy and the nobility, however, adorned their palatial homes ornately with gold and ivory. Architectural remains—temples, city gates, arches, ziggurats, pyramids—survive intact in great abundance, and archaeology has uncovered the foundations of countless buildings. Each country had its own distinctive style of architecture. No architecture has surpassed that of Greece, although the temple of Solomon and the one rebuilt by Herod were universally admired.

ARCHIVES Storage place for royal documents (Ezr 4:15; 5:17; 6:1).

ARCTURUS Constellation: the Bear (Job 9:9; 38:32). *See Astronomy; Bear, Illustrative of.*

ARD, ARDITE (*hunchbacked*).
1. Son of Benjamin (Ge 46:21).
2. Son of Bela and his clan (Nu 26:40).

ARDON (*hunchbacked*). Son of Caleb (1Ch 2:18).

ARELI, ARELITE Son of Gad (Ge 46:16) and his clan (Nu 26:17).

AREOPAGITE A member of the Areopagus (Ac 17:34).

AREOPAGUS (*hill of the Greek god, Ares*).
1. The rocky hill of the Greek god of war Ares (Mars) on the Acropolis at Athens.
2. The name of a council which met on Mars Hill. In NT times it was primarily concerned with morals and education. Paul was brought before it (Ac 17:19-34).

ARETAS (*virtuous*). A Nabataean king, father-in-law of Herod Antipas (2Co 11:32).

ARGOB (*mound*).
1. A region in Bashan taken by the Israelites under Moses (Dt 3:4) and given to the half-tribe of Manasseh (Dt 3:13).
2. Could also be a place or a person (2Ki 15:25). The Hebrew text is uncertain.

ARIDAI (perhaps *delight of Hari*). Son of Haman killed by the Jews (Est 9:9).

ARIDATHA (perhaps *given by Hari*). A son of Haman killed by the Jews (Est 9:8).

ARIEH (*lion*). Either a person or a place. The text is uncertain (2Ki 15:25).

ARIEL (*lioness of God [El]*).
1. Leader under Ezra (Ezr 8:16-17).
2. Figurative name for Jerusalem (Isa 29:1-2, 7).
3. In 2Sa 23:20 and 1Ch 11:22 "best men" (KJV "lionlike men") translates a word similar to Ariel.

ARIMATHEA Home of Joseph who buried Jesus in his own tomb (Mt 27:57; Mk 15:43; Lk 23:51; Jn 19:38). Its location is in doubt, but it is conjectured to be Ramathaim-Zophim, c. twenty miles NW of Jerusalem.

ARIOCH
1. King of Ellasar (Ge 14:1, 9).
2. Captain of Nebuchadnezzar's guard (Da 2:14-15, 24-25).

ARISAI Son of Haman (Est 9:9).

ARISTARCHUS (*best ruler*). A Thessalonian traveling companion of Paul (Ac 19:29; 20:4; 27:2; Col 4:10; Phm 24).

ARISTOBULUS (*best adviser*). A Roman Christian greeted by Paul (Ro 16:10).

ARK (*box*).
1. A boat. Directions for building of (Ge 6:14-16). Noah and family preserved in (Ge 6:18; 7:8; Mt 24:38; Heb 11:7; 1Pe 3:20). Animals saved in (Ge 6:19-20; 7:1-16).
2. A box or chest. *See Ark of the Covenant.*

ARK OF THE COVENANT

Description of:
Dimensions of (Ex 25:10; 37:1). Entirely covered with gold (Ex 25:11; 37:2). Surrounded with a crown of gold (Ex 25:11). Furnished with rings and poles (Ex 25:12-15; 37:3-5). Tables of testimony alone placed in (Ex 25:16, 21; 1Ki 8:9, 21; 2Ch 5:10; Heb 9:4). Atonement cover laid upon (Ex 25:21; 26:34). Placed in the Most Holy Place (Ex 26:33; 40:21; Heb 9:3-4). The pot of manna and Aaron's rod laid up before (Heb 9:4, w Ex 16:33-34; Nu 17:10). A copy of the law laid in the side of (Dt 31:26). Anointed with sacred oil (Ex 30:26). Covered with the veil by the priests before removal (Nu 4:5-6).
A symbol of the presence and glory of God (Nu 14:43-44; Jos 7:6; 1Sa 14:18-19; Ps 132:8). Considered the glory of Israel (1Sa 4:21-22). Was holy (2Ch 35:3). Sanctified its resting place (2Ch 8:11). The Israelites inquired of the Lord before (Jos 7:6-9; Jdg 20:27; 1Ch 13:3). Profanation of, punished (Nu 4:5, 15; 1Sa 6:19; 1Ch 15:13). Protecting of, rewarded (1Ch 13:14).

Was Called the:
Ark of God (1Sa 3:3). Ark of God's might (2Ch 6:41; Ps 132:8). Ark of the covenant of the Lord (Nu 10:33). Ark of the testimony (Ex 30:6; Nu 7:89).

Was Carried:
By priests or Levites alone (Dt 10:8; Jos 3:14; 2Sa 15:24; 1Ch 15:2). Before the Israelites in their journeys (Nu 10:33; Jos 3:6). Sometimes to the camp in war (1Sa 4:4-5).

History and Miracles Connected With:
Jordan divided (Jos 4:7). Fall of the walls of Jericho (Jos 6:6-20). Captured by the Philistines (1Sa 4:11). Fall of Dagon (1Sa 5:1-4). Philistines plagued (1Sa 5:6-12). Manner of its restoration (1Sa 6:1-18). At Kiriath Jearim twenty years (1Sa 7:1-2). Removed from Kiriath Jearim to the house of Obed-Edom (2Sa 6:1-11). David made a tent for (2Sa 6:17; 1Ch 15:1). Brought into the city of David (2Sa 6:12-15; 1Ch 15:25-28). Brought by Solomon into the temple with great solemnity (1Ki 8:1-6; 2Ch 5:2-9). A type of Christ (Ps 40:8; Rev 11:19).

ARKITE(S) Descendants of Canaan (Ge 10:17; 1Ch 1:15). Member of a clan in Ephraim (Jos 16:2; 1Ch 27:33).

ARM Figurative of divine providence and salvation (Ex 6:6; 15:16; Dt 4:34; 5:15; 7:19; 9:29; 11:2; 26:8; 33:27; 1Ki 8:42; 2Ki 17:36; 2Ch 6:32; Ps 77:15; 89:10, 13, 21; 98:1; 136:12; SS 2:6; Isa 33:2; 40:10-11; 51:5, 9; 52:10; 53:1; 59:16; 62:8; 63:5, 12; Jer 21:5; 27:5; 32:17; Eze 20:33; Lk 1:51; Ac 13:17). *See Anthropomorphisms.*

ARMAGEDDON (*Mount of Megiddo*). Found only in Rev 16:16; the final battlefield between the forces of good and evil. Located on the S rim of Esdraelon, the scene of many decisive battles in the history of Israel (Jdg 5:19-20; 6:33; 1Sa 31; 2Ki 23:29-30). *See Megiddo.*

ARMENIA *See Ararat.*

ARMIES Those of the Israelites who were subject to service in (Nu 1:2-3; 26:2; 2Ch 25:5), who were exempt from service in (Nu 1:47-50; 2:33; Dt 20:5-9; Jdg 7:3). Numbering of Israel's military forces (Nu 1:2-3; 26:2; 1Sa 11:8; 2Sa 18:1-2; 24:1, 9; 1Ki 20:15; 2Ch 25:5). Levies for (Nu 31:4; Jdg 20:10). Compulsory service in (1Sa 14:52).
See Cowardice.

How Commanded:
Commander-in-chief (1Sa 14:50; 2Sa 2:8; 8:16; 17:25; 19:13; 20:23), Generals of corps and divisions (Nu 2:3-31; 1Ch 27:1-22; 2Ch 17:12-19), Captains of thousands (Nu 31:14, 48; 1Sa 17:18; 1Ch 28:1; 2Ch 25:5), of hundreds (Nu 31:14, 48; 2Ki 11:15; 1Ch 28:1; 2Ch 25:5), of fifties (2Ki 1:9; Isa 3:3). *See Cavalry; Chariot.*

Mustering of:
Methods employed in mustering: Sounding a trumpet (Nu 10:9; Jdg 3:27; 6:34; 1Sa 13:3-4), Cutting oxen in pieces, and sending the pieces throughout Israel (1Sa 11:7). Refusal to obey the summons, instance of (Jdg 21:5-11, w Jdg 20).

Tactics:
Camp and march (Nu 2). March in ranks (Joel 2:7). Move in attack in three divisions (Jdg 7:16; 9:43; 1Sa 11:11; 13:17, 18; 2Sa 18:2; Job 1:17). Flanks called wings (Isa 8:8). Orders delivered with trumpets (2Sa 2:28; 18:16; 20:1, 22; Ne 4:18, 20). *See Strategy.*

Strategies:
Ambushes at: Ai (Jos 8:2-22), Shechem (Jdg 9:25, 34), Gibeah (Jdg 20:29-43), Zemaraim (2Ch 13:4, 13). By Jehoshaphat (2Ch 20:20-22).

Reconnaissances:
Of Jericho (Jos 2:1-24), Ai (Jos 7:2-3), Bethel (Jdg 1:23-24), Laish (Jdg 18:2-10). Night attacks (Ge 14:15; Jdg 7:16-22). Decoy (Jos 8:4-22; Jdg 20:29-43; Ne 6). Delay (2Sa 17:7-14).

Speed of Action:
Abraham, in pursuit of Kedorlaomer (Ge 14:14-15). Joshua, against the Amorites (Jos 10:6, 9), the confederated kings (Jos 11:7). David's attack upon the Philistines (2Sa 5:23-25). Forced marches (Isa 5:26-27). Sieges (Jer 39:1), of Jericho (Jos 6), Samaria (2Ki 6:24-33:7), Jerusalem (2Ki 25:1-3).
Machines used (2Ch 26:15; Jer 6:6; Eze 26:9). Fortifications (Jdg 9:31; 2Sa 5:9; 2Ki 25:1; 2Ch 11:11; 26:9; Ne 3:8; 4:2; Isa 22:10; 25:12; 29:3; 32:14; Jer 6:6; 32:24; 33:4; 51:53; Eze 4:2; 17:17; 21:22; 26:8; 33:27; Da 11:15, 19; Na 2:1; 3:14).
Standards (Nu 2:2-3, 10, 17-18, 25, 31, 34; 10:14, 18, 22, 25). Uniforms of (Eze 23:6, 12; Na 2:3). Standing armies (1Sa 13:2; 1Ch 27; 2Ch 1:14; 17:12-19; 26:11-15).

Religious Ceremonies Attending:
Seeking counsel from God before battle (Nu 27:21; Jdg 1:1; 1Sa 14:19, 37-41; 23:2-12; 30:8; 2Sa 2:1; 5:19, 23; 1Ki 22:7-28; 2Ki 3:11-19; 1Ch 14:10, 14; Jer 37:7-10). Sacrifices (1Sa 13:11-12). Purifications (Nu 31:19-24). Prophets prophesy before (2Ch 20:14-17). Holiness required (Dt 23:9). Officers consecrate themselves to God (2Ch 17:16). Army choir and songs (2Ch 20:21-22). Ark taken to battle (Jos 6:6-7, 13; 1Sa 4:4-11).

Divine Assistance to:
When Aaron and Hur held up Moses' hands (Ex 17:11-12). In siege of Jericho (Jos 6). Sun stands still (Jos 10:11-14). Gideon's victory (Jdg 7). Samaria's deliverances (1Ki 20; 2Ki 7). Jehoshaphat's victories (2Ki 3; 2Ch 20). Angel of the Lord puts to death the Assyrians (2Ki 19:35).
Determine royal succession (2Sa 2:8-10; 1Ki 16:16; 2Ki 11:4-12).
Composed of insurgents (1Sa 22:1-2). Mercenaries (2Sa 10:6; 1Ch 19:6-7; 2Ch 25:5-6). Confederated (Jos 10:1-5; 11:1-5; Jdg 1:3; 2Sa 10:6, 15-16, 19; 1Ki 15:20; 22:1-4; 2Ki 16:9; 18:19-21; 1Ch 19:6-7; 2Ch 16:2-9; 18:1, 3; 20:1; 22:5; 28:16, 20; Ps 83:1-12; Isa 7:1-9; 8:9-12; 54:15). Exhorted before battle (Dt 20:1-9). Battle shouts (Jdg 7:18; 1Sa 17:20, 52).

Triumphs of, Celebrated:
With songs (Jdg 5; 1Sa 18:6-7), music (2Ch 20:28), dancing (1Sa 18:6-7).

Rewards for Meritorious Conduct:
The general offers his daughter in marriage (Jos 15:16-17). King offers his daughter (1Sa 17:25; 18:17-28). Promotion (2Sa 23:8-39; 1Ch 11:6, 10-47). Share the spoils (Nu 31:25-47).
Insubordination in, punished, Achan (Jos 7). Check roll call (1Sa 14:17; Nu 31:48-49).
Panics (Isa 30:17): Among the Midianites (Jdg 7:21), Philistines (1Sa 14:15-19), Syrians (2Ki 7:7-15). Soldiers destroy each other to escape captivity (1Sa 14:20; 31:4-6).
Champions fight instead of (1Sa 17:8-53; 2Sa 2:14-17; 21:15-22). Confidence in vain (Ps 33:16; 44:6). Escort duty performed by (2Ki 1:9; Ac 23:23-24, 31-33).

Roman Army:
Commanders of (Ac 22:24-29). Centurions (Mt 8:5, 8; 27:54; Lk 7:2; 23:47; Ac 10:1, 7, 22; 21:32; 22:26; 23:17, 23; 24:23; 27:1, 11, 43; 28:16). Divided into regiments (Ac 10:1; 27:1).
For other than armies of the Israelites and Romans: *See Amalekite(s); Assyria; Babylon; Egyptians; Midianite(s); Persia; Syria.*
For commissaries of: *See Commissary.*
For weapons used: *See Armor.*
See Ambush; Cavalry; Fort; Garrison; Herald; Hostage; Navy; Reconnaissance; Siege; Soldiers; Spies; Standard; Strategy; Truce; War.

Figurative: (Dt 33:2; 2Ki 6:17; Ps 34:7; 68:17; Rev 9:16).
See Army.

ARMLET, BRACELET An ornament usually for the upper arm, worn by both men and women (Ex 35:22; Nu 31:50; 2Sa 1:10; Isa 3:20). *See Bracelet.*

ARMONI (*[one] born in the dwelling tower, the palace*). A son of Saul by his concubine Rizpah, slain by the Gibeonites to satisfy justice (2Sa 21:8-11).

ARMOR The equipment of a soldier (1Sa 13:22; Jer 46:3-4; Eph 6:14-17).

Defensive:
Helmet (1Sa 17:5, 38; 2Ch 17:17; 26:14; Jer 46:4; Eze 23:24). Breastplate (Rev 9:9-17). Coat of armor (1Sa 17:5, 38; 1Ki 22:34; 2Ch 18:33). Greaves, protection for the leg (1Sa 17:6). Shield (2Sa 1:21; 8:7; 1Ki 10:16, 17; 14:27; 2Ch 9:16; 26:14; Ne 2:3).

Offensive:
Bows (Ge 21:16, 20). Made of bronze (2Sa 22:35; Job 20; Ps 18:34). Of wood (Eze 39:9). David instructed the Israelites in the use of, by writing war song (2Sa 1:18). Arrows (1Sa 31:3; 2Sa 22:15; 1Ki 22:34; 2Ki 19:32; 2Ch 17:17; Ps 7:13; Isa 22:3; Jer 51:3).
War club (Job 41:29; Jer 51:20). Spear (Nu 25:7; 1Sa 18:10; 2Sa 18:14). Javelin, a heavy lance (Eze 39:9). Used by Goliath (1Sa 17:6). By Saul (1Sa 18:11; 19:9-10).
Sling, used for throwing stones (Pr 26:8). David slays Goliath with (1Sa 17:40-50). Skilled use of (Jdg 20:16). Used in war (Jdg 20:16; 2Ki 3:25; 2Ch 26:14).
Sword, used by Gibeon (Jdg 7:20). By Peter (Mt 26:51; Jn 18:10). David's army equipped with (1Ch 21:5).

Figurative: (Ro 13:12; 2Co 6:7; 10:4; Eph 6:11-17; 1Th 5:8).

ARMOR-BEARER An attendant who carried a soldier's equipment.
Of Abimelech (Jdg 9:54), Jonathan (1Sa 14:6-7, 12, 14, 17), Saul (1Sa 16:21; 31:6), Goliath (1Sa 17:7), Joab (2Sa 18:15).

ARMORY A place for the storage of armor (Ne 3:19; SS 4:4; Isa 22:8; 39:2). In different parts of the kingdom (1Ki 10:17; 2Ch 11:12). *See Jerusalem.*
Figurative: (Jer 50:25).

ARMY
In Israel males (except Levites) were subject to military duty at the age of twenty (Nu 1:3, 17). Army divisions were subdivided into thousands and hundreds, with respective officers (Nu 31:14). Until Israel got its first king it had no standing army, but whenever there was need, God raised up men of special ability to save the country from its enemies. Down to the time of Solomon, Israel's armies were composed mostly of footmen (1Sa 4:10); later horsemen and chariots were added (2Sa 8:4; 1Ki 10:26, 28-29). The Roman army was composed of legions divided into cohorts, maniples, and centuries (Ac 10:1; 21:31).
See Armies.

ARNAN Name of a family descended from David (1Ch 3:21).

ARNON A river emptying into the Dead Sea from the east. Boundary between Moabites and Amorites (Nu 21:13-14, 26; 22:36; Dt 2:24, 36; 3:8, 16; Jos 12:1). Fords of (Isa 16:2). Miracles at (Nu 21:14).

ARODI, ARODITE (*hunchbacked*). The sixth son of Gad (Ge 46:16) and his clan (Nu 26:17).

AROER, AROERITE (*juniper*).
1. A city of the Amorites in the valley of the Arnon River (Dt 4:48). Conquered by Israelites (Dt 2:36; 3:12; Jdg 11:26). Taken by Hazael (2Ki 10:33).
2. A city built, or, probably more correctly, rebuilt, by the Gadites (Nu 32:34; Jos 13:25). Jephthah kills the Ammonites at (Jdg 11:33).
3. A city in Judah (1Sa 30:28). Birthplace of two of David's heroes (1Ch 11:44).

AROMATIC RESIN Fragrant gum or resin listed with precious stones (Ge 2:12; Nu 11:7). *See Minerals of the Bible, 1; Resin.*

ARPAD A fortified city of Syria, perhaps identical with Arvad (2Ki 18:34; 19:13). Idols of (Isa 36:19).

ARPHAXAD Son of Shem (Ge 10:22; 11:10-13; 1Ch 1:17-18, 24; Lk 3:36).

ARREST Of Jesus (Mt 26:57; Mk 14:46; Lk 22:54; Jn 18:12), apostles (Ac 5:17-18; 6:12), Paul and Silas (Ac 16:19), Paul (Ac 21:30). Paul authorized to arrest Christians (Ac 9:2).
See Extradition; Prison; Prisoners.

ARROGANCE (1Sa 2:3; Pr 8:13; Isa 13:11). *See Pride.*

ARROWS

Described:
Deadly and destructive weapons (Pr 26:18). Sharp (Ps 120:4; Isa 5:28). Bright and polished (Isa 49:2; Jer 51:11). Sometimes poisoned (Job 6:4). Carried in a quiver (Ge 27:3; Isa 49:2; Jer 5:16; La 3:13). Swiftness of, alluded to (Zec 9:14). The ancients divined by (Eze 21:21).

Discharged:
From a bow (Ps 11:2; Isa 7:24). From machines (2Ch 26:15). At a mark for amusement (1Sa 20:20-22). At the beasts of the earth (Ge 27:3). Against enemies (2Ki 19:32; Jer 50:14). With great force (Nu 24:8; 2Ki 9:24).

Figurative:
Of Christ (Isa 49:2). Of the word of Christ (Ps 45:5). Of God's judgment (Dt 32:23-42; Ps 7:13; 21:12; 64:7; Eze 5:16). Of severe afflictions (Job 6:4; Ps 38:2). Of bitter words (Ps 64:3). Of slanderous tongues (Jer 9:8). Of false witnesses (Pr 25:18). Of devices of the wicked (Ps 11:2). Of young children (Ps 127:4). Of lightning (Ps 77:17-18; Hab 3:11). Broken, of destruction of power (Ps 76:3). Falling from the hand, of the paralyzing power (Eze 39:3).

ARSON (Ps 74:7-8). Law concerning (Ex 22:6). Instances of: Samson (Jdg 15:4-5), Absalom (2Sa 14:30), Zimri (1Ki 16:18).

ART Seen in the gifting of Bezalel and Oholiab to build the tabernacle and its furnishings (Ex 31:1-12; 35:30-39:43); of Huram(-abi) and his work on the temple of Solomon (1Ki 7:13-45; 2Ch 2:13-4:16).
Israel was not to apply artistic talents to create idols (Ex 20:4, 23; 32:1-24; 34:17; Lev 26:1). *See Arts and Crafts; Bezalel; Huram; Tabernacle; Temple.*

ARTAXERXES (*kingdom of righteousness*). There are three kings with the name of Artaxerxes.
1. Artaxerxes I (465-425 B.C.), son of Xerxes I; known as Macrocheir or Longimanus. He overcame revolts in Egypt, where, with Athenian support, unrest started in 460 and lasted until 454, and in other parts of the Persian Empire. During that time some of the eastern possessions were lost. By the peace treaty of Callias (449), signed at Susa, the relations between Athens and Persia were stabilized on a *status quo ante bellum* basis. Artaxerxes was buried at Naqsi Rustam next to the tombs of his father and grandfather.
Artaxerxes I authorized Ezra's mission to Jerusalem in 458 (Ezr 7:8, 11-26). He temporarily halted the reconstruction of Jerusalem (4:7-23). Nehemiah's two missions were under his reign and with his permission, the first in 445 (Ne 2:1ff; 13:6).
2. Artaxerxes II (404-359 B.C.), son of Darius II and grandson of Artaxerxes I; known as Mnemon. He crushed the rebellion of his brother Cyrus (Battle of Cunaxa, 401), as related by Xenophon in his *Anabasis.* He lost Egypt probably in 402 or 401, repelled the meddling of Sparta in the affairs of Asia Minor (Peace of Antalcidas, 386), and suppressed other rebellious movements led by local satraps. Several of his inscriptions refer to his building activities. The palace he built at Susa is considered by some authorities to be identical with the palace described in Esther (Est 1:5-6).
3. Artaxerxes III (359-338 B.C.), son of Artaxerxes II; known as Ochus. By the use of skillful diplomacy and military force he succeeded in maintaining a superficially strong empire, until the time when he was murdered as the result of a conspiracy led by Bagoas (338).

ARTEMAS (*[given by] Artemis*). A companion of Paul (Tit 3:12).

ARTEMIS The Greek goddess of hunting, corresponding to the Roman Diana. Her largest and most famous temple was at Ephesus; it was regarded as one of the wonders of the ancient world (Ac 19:23-41).

ARTIFICER *See Arts and Crafts; Occupations and Professions.*

ARTILLERY *See Armory.*

ARTISANS *See Occupations.*

ARTS AND CRAFTS Armorer (1Sa 8:12). Baker (Ge 40:1; 1Sa 8:13). Brickmaker (Ge 11:3; Ex 5:7-8, 18). Blacksmith (Ge 4:22; 1Sa 13:19). Carver (Ex 31:5; 1Ki 6:18). Carpenter (2Sa 5:11; Mk 6:3). Caulker (Eze 27:9, 27). Dyer (Ex 25:5). Embroiderer (Ex 35:35; 38:23). Embalmer (Ge 50:2-3, 26). Engraver (Ex 28:11; Isa 49:16; 2Co 3:7). Gardener (Ge 4:2; 9:20; Jer 29:5; Jn 20:15). Goldsmith (Isa 40:19; Jer 10:9). Launderer (2Ki 18:17; Mk 9:3). Mariner (Eze 27:8-9). Mason (2Sa 5:11; 2Ch 24:12). Musician (1Sa 18:6; 1Ch 15:16). Perfumer (Ex 30:25, 35; 1Sa 8:13). Potter (Isa 64:8; Jer 18:3; La 4:2; Zec 11:13). Refiner of metals (1Ch 28:18; Mal 3:2-3). Rope-maker (Jdg 16:11). Silversmith (Jdg 17:4; Ac 19:24). Stonecutter (Ex 20:25; 1Ch 22:15). Shipbuilder (1Ki 9:26). Smelter of metals (Job 28:2). Spinner (Ex 35:25; Pr 31:19). Tailor (Ex 28:3). Tanner (Ac 9:43; 10:6). Tent maker (Ge 4:20; Ac 18:3). Tool maker (Ge 4:22; 2Ti 4:14). Weaver (Ex 35:35; Jn 19:23). Wine maker (Ne 13:15; Isa 63:3).

ARUBBOTH A district laid under tribute to Solomon's governor (1Ki 4:10).

ARUMAH (*lofty*). Place near Shechem where Abimelech lived (Jdg 9:41).

ARVAD, ARVADITES Island off the coast of Phoenicia (Eze 27:8, 11). Its people were descendants of Ham (Ge 10:18; 1Ch 1:16; Eze 27:8, 11).

ARZA (perhaps *gracious*). A steward of Elah (1Ki 16:9).

ASA (possibly *healer* BDB; *myrtle* KB).
1. King of Judah (1Ki 15:8-24; 1Ch 3:10; 2Ch 14; 15; 16; Mt 1:7).
2. A Levite (1Ch 9:16).

ASAHEL (*God [El] has made*).
1. Nephew of David and one of his captains (2Sa 2:18-24, 32; 3:27; 23:24; 1Ch 2:16; 11:26; 27:7).
2. A Levite commissioned by Jehoshaphat to teach the law to Judah (2Ch 17:8).
3. A Levite who had charge of tithes (2Ch 31:13).
4. Father of Jonathan (Ezr 10:15).

ASAIAH (*Yahweh has made*).
1. An officer of King Josiah (2Ki 22:12-20; 2Ch 34:20-28).
2. A Simeonite (1Ch 4:36).
3. Levite in the time of David (1Ch 6:30).
4. A Shilonite (1Ch 9:5).
5. Chief Levite in David's day who helped bring the ark to Jerusalem (1Ch 15:6, 11).

ASAPH (*gatherer*).
1. Father of Joah (2Ki 18:18; Isa 36:3, 22).
2. Son of Berekiah. One of the three leaders of music in David's organization of the tabernacle service (1Ch 15:16-19; 16:5-7; 25:1-9; 2Ch 5:12; 35:15; Ne 12:46). Appointed to sound the cymbals in the temple choir (1Ch 15:17, 19; 16:5, 7). A composer of sacred lyrics (2Ch 29:13-30). *See titles of Pss 50; 73-83.* Descendants of, in the temple choir (1Ch 25:1-9; 2Ch 20:14; 29:13; Ezr 2:41; 3:10; Ne 7:44; 11:22).

3. A Levite whose descendants lived in Jerusalem after the exile (1Ch 9:15).
4. A Kohath Levite (1Ch 26:1).
5. Keeper of forests (Ne 2:8).

ASAREL Son of Jehallelel (1Ch 4:16).

ASARELAH One of the temple choir (1Ch 25:2, 14), Probably identical with Azarel.

ASCENSION OF CHRIST Prophecies respecting (Ps 24:7; 68:18, w Eph 4:7-8). Foretold by himself (Jn 6:62; 7:33; 14:28; 16:5; 20:17). Forty days after his resurrection (Ac 1:3). Described (Ac 1:9). From Mount of Olives (Lk 24:50; w Mk 11:1; Ac 1:12). While blessing his disciples (Lk 24:50). When he had atoned for sin (Heb 9:12; 10:12). Was triumphant (Ps 68:18). Was to supreme power and dignity (Lk 24:26; Eph 1:20-21; 1Pe 3:22). As the Forerunner of His people (Heb 6:20). To intercede (Ro 8:34; Heb 9:24). To send the Holy Spirit (Jn 16:7; Ac 2:33). To receive gifts for people (Ps 68:18, w Eph 4:8-11). To prepare a place for his people (Jn 14:2). His second coming shall be in like manner as (Ac 1:10-11).
Typified (Lev 16:15, w Heb 6:20; 9:7, 9, 12).

ASCENTS, SONGS OF Title given Psalms 120 to 134. These psalms were, with 135 and 136, part of the liturgical collection "The Great Hallel." They were probably sung during the pilgrimage or "ascent" to Jerusalem required by the annual feasts.

ASCETICISM A philosophy that leads to severe self-discipline in subordinating the body to the control of the moral attributes of the mind. Extreme application of, rebuked by Jesus (Mt 11:19; Lk 7:34), by Paul (Col 2:20-23; 1Ti 4:1-4, 8). *See Stoicism; Stoics.*
Instances of the practice of: John the Baptist (Mt 11:18; Lk 7:33). Those who practiced celibacy for the kingdom of heaven (Mt 19:12).

ASENATH (*belonging to] the goddess Neith*). Wife of Joseph and mother of Manasseh and Ephraim (Ge 41:45, 50; 46:20).

ASER *See Asher.*

ASH *See Pine.*

ASHAN (*smoke*). A Levitical city of Judah, later of Simeon (Jos 15:42; 19:7; 1Ch 4:32; 6:59). *See Ain, 1.*

ASHBEA *See Beth Ashbea.*

ASHBEL, ASHBELITE (possibly a form of *man of Baal* BDB; *having a long upper lip* KB). Son of Benjamin (Ge 46:21; 1Ch 8:1) and his clan (Nu 26:38).

ASHCHENAZ *See Ashkenaz.*

ASHDOD (perhaps *fortress*). A city of the Philistines (Jos 13:3, 1Sa 6:17; Am 3:9). Anakites inhabit (Jos 11:22). Assigned to Judah (Jos 15:47). Dagon's temple in, in which was deposited the ark (1Sa 5).
Conquest of: by Uzziah (2Ch 26:6), by Assyrian supreme commander (Isa 20:1).
People of, conspire against the Jews (Ne 4:7-8). Jews intermarry with (Ne 13:23-24). Prophecies concerning (Jer 25:20; Am 1:8; 3; Zep 2:4; Zec 9:6). Called Azotus in NT times (Ac 8:40).

ASHDOTH-PISGAH (*slopes of Pisgah*). *See Pisgah.*

ASHER (*Happy One!*).
1. Son of Jacob, by Zilpah (Ge 30:13; 35:26; 49:20; Ex 1:4; 1Ch 2:2). Descendants of (Ge 46:17; Nu 26:44-47; Lk 2:36).
2. Tribe of.
Census of, by families (Nu 1:40-41; 26:44-47; 1Ch 7:40; 12:36). Station of, in camp (Nu 2:25, 27). Prophecies concerning by Moses (Dt 33:24-25), by John (Rev 7:6). Allotment to, of land in Canaan (Jos 19:24-31; Eze 48:2). Criticized by Deborah (Jdg 5:17). Summoned by Gideon (Jdg 6:35; 7:23). Join Hezekiah (2Ch 30:11).
3. A city of Shechem (Jos 17:7; 1Ki 4:16).

ASHERAH
1. Canaanite goddess, sometimes identified with Anath and Ashtoreth. *See Anath; Ashtoreth.*
2. Asherah poles: images of or trees planted to the goddess Asherah. Forbidden to be established (Ex 34:13; Dt 7:5; 16:21; Isa 1:29; 17:8; 27:9; Mic 5:14). Worshiped by Israelites (Jdg 3:7; 1Ki 14:15, 23; 15:13; 2Ki 13:6; 17:10, 16; 21:3-7; 2Ch 24:18; Jer 17:2). Destroyed by Gideon (Jdg 6:28), Hezekiah (2Ki 18:4), Josiah (2Ki 23:14; 2Ch 34:3-4), Asa (2Ch 14:3), Jehoshaphat (2Ch 17:6; 19:3). *See High Places; Idolatry.*

ASHES Uses of, in purification (Nu 19:9-10, 17; Heb 9:13). A symbol of mourning (2Sa 13:19; Est 4:1, 3). Sitting in (Job 2:8; Isa 58:5; Jer 6:26; Eze 27:30; Jnh 3:6; Lk 10:13). Repenting in (Job 42:6; Da 9:3; Jnh 3:6; Mt 11:21; Lk 10:13). Disguises of (1Ki 20:38, 41).

ASHHUR (possibly *darkness, dawn* BDB; *a Babylonian goddess* KB). Son of Hezron (1Ch 2:24; 4:5).

ASHIMA An idol (2Ki 17:30).

ASHKELON One of the five chief cities of the Philistines (Jos 13:3). Captured by the people of Judah (Jdg 1:18). Samson slays thirty men of (Jdg 14:19). Tumors of (1Sa 6:17). Prophecies concerning (Jer 25:20; 47:5, 7; Am 1:8; Zep 2:4, 7; Zec 9:5).

ASHKENAZ Son of Gomer (Ge 10:3; 1Ch 1:6). Descendants of (Jer 51:27).

ASHNAH A name of two towns in Judah (Jos 15:33, 43).

ASHPENAZ (*guest*). A prince in Nebuchadnezzar's court (Da 1:3).

ASHRIEL *See Asriel.*

ASHTAROTH
1. Plural form of Ashtoreth. *See Ashtoreth.*
2. The capital city of Bashan (Dt 1:4; Jos 9:10). Giants dwell at (Jos 12:4). Allotted to Manasseh (Jos 13:31; 1Ch 6:71). Possibly identical with Ashteroth Karnaim (Ge 14:5).

ASHTERATHITE A native of Ashtaroth (1Ch 11:44).

ASHTEROTH KARNAIM (*Ashteroth of the pair of horns, [two peaks?]*). An ancient city of Palestine taken by Kedorlaomer (Ge 14:5).

ASHTORETH An idol of the Philistines, Sidonians, and Phoenicians, sometimes identified with Anath and Asherah. *See Anath; Asherah.* Probably identical with queen of heaven (Jer 7:18). Worshiped by Israelites (Jdg 2:13; 10:6; 1Sa 7:3-4; 12:10; 1Ki 11:5, 33; 2Ki 23:13). Temple of (1Sa 31:10). High places of, at Jerusalem, destroyed (2Ki 23:13).

ASHUR *See Ashhur.*

ASHURBANIPAL (*Ashur creates a son*). King of Assyria who colonized the cities of Samaria after the Israelites were taken captive to Assyria (Ezr 4:10). Reigned from 688-626 B.C. He was a great lover of learning—his library (over 22,000 tablets) survives.

ASHURI A tribal region, possibly Asher (2Sa 2:9).

ASHURNASIRPAL II Ruthless king of Assyria, reigned early in ninth century B.C.

ASHVATH (possibly *wrought iron*). Son of Japhlet (1Ch 7:33).

ASIA Inhabitants of, in Jerusalem, at Pentecost (Ac 2:9; 21:27; 24:19). Paul and Silas forbidden by the Holy Spirit to preach in (Ac 16:6). Gospel preached in, by Paul (Ac 19; 20:4). Paul leaves (Ac 20:16). Churches of (1Co 16:19; Rev 1:4, 11). High officials of Asia were friends of Paul (Ac 19:31).

ASIARCHS High officials of Asia. *See Asia.*

ASIEL (*God [El] has made*). Grandfather of Jehu (1Ch 4:35).

ASKELON *See Ashkelon.*

ASNAH (possibly *thornbush* BDB; *he who belongs to [the god] Nah* IDB). Descendants of, return to Jerusalem (Ezr 2:50).

ASNAPPER *See Ashurbanipal; Samaria.*

ASP *See Cobra; Serpent; Viper.*

ASPATHA (possibly *given from a sacred horse*). Son of Haman (Est 9:7).

ASPHALTUM *See Caulkers; Pitch; Tar.*

ASRIEL (either *God has filled with joy,* or *[the object of] joy is God*).
1. Descendant of Manasseh (Nu 26:31; Jos 17:2).
2. Son of Manasseh, Asriel (1Ch 7:14).

ASS *See Donkey, Domestic; Donkey, Wild.*

ASSAR *See Tel Assar.*

ASSASSINATION David's abhorrence of (2Sa 4:9-12). Laws prohibiting (Dt 27:24).

Instances of:
Of Eglon, by Ehud (Jdg 3:15-22), Abner, by Joab (2Sa 3:27), Ish-Bosheth, by the sons of Rimmon (2Sa 4:5-7), Amnon, by Absalom (2Sa 13:28-29), Amasa, by Joab (2Sa 20:9-10), Joash, by his servants (2Ki 12:19-20), Sennacherib, by his sons (2Ki 19:37; Isa 37:38).

ASSAULT AND BATTERY

Laws Concerning:
(Ex 21:15, 18-19, 22-27; Dt 17:8-12; Mt 5:39; Lk 6:29). Damages and compensation for (Ex 21:18-19, 22).
See Abuse; Bruise(s); Flog, Flogging; Scourging; Stripes, 1-3; Stoning.

The Beating of Jesus:
Prophecies of (Isa 50:6; La 3:30). The attacks upon (Mt 26:67; 27:30; Mk 14:65; Lk 22:63; Jn 19:3).

ASSHUR Son of Shem, and ancestor of the Assyrians (Ge 10:11, 22; 1Ch 1:17; Eze 32:22). *See Assyria.*

ASSHURITES Descendants of Dedan (Ge 25:3).

ASSIR (*prisoner*).
1. Son of Korah (Ex 6:24; 1Ch 6:22).
2. Son of Ebiasaph (1Ch 6:23, 37).
3. Son of Jehoiachin (1Ch 3:17).

ASSOCIATION-SEPARATION

Evil associations:
Warnings concerning (Ex 23:2; 34:12; Ps 1:1; Pr 4:14; 24:1; 1Co 5:11; 2Co 6:14). Results of (Nu 33:55; 1Ki 11:2; 2Ch 19:2; Pr 28:7; Jn 18:18; 18:25; 1Co 15:33).
Contact with impurity (Lev 5:2; 15:11; Nu 19:13; Isa 52:11; 2Co 6:17; Col 2:21).
Separation from unclean (Lev 13:5, 21, 33, 46; Nu 5:3). Israel from nations (Lev 20:26; Nu 23:9; Dt 7:2; Jos 23:7; Jdg 2:2; Ezr 9:12; 10:11; Isa 52:11; Jer 15:19). Believers from evil associations (Jn 15:19; Ac 2:40; Eph 5:11; 2Th 3:6). Final separation of evil from good (Mt 13:30, 49; 25:32; Lk 16:26; 17:34).

Good associations:
Companionship (Ps 119:63; Pr 2:20; 13:20; 2Th 3:14). Personal contact with Jesus (Mt 9:20, 25; 14:34-36; Mk 3:10; 9:27; Lk 6:19), Peter (Ac 3:7; 9:41).

ASSOS A seaport in Mysia (Ac 20:13-14).

ASSURANCE
Produced by faith (Eph 3:12; 2Ti 1:12; Heb 10:22). Made full by hope (Heb 6:11, 19). Confirmed by love (1Jn 3:14, 19; 4:18). Is the effect of righteousness (Isa 32:17). Is abundant in the understanding of the gospel (Col 2:2; 1Th 1:5).

Believers Privileged to Have:
Their election (Ps 4:3; 1Th 1:4). Their redemption (Job 19:25). Their adoption (Ro 8:16; 1Jn 3:2). Their salvation (Isa 12:2). Eternal life (1Jn 5:13). The unalienable love of God (Ro 8:38-39). Union with God and Christ (1Co 6:15; 2Co 13:5; Eph 5:30; 1Jn 2:5; 4:13). Peace with God by Christ (Ro 5:1). Preservation (Ps 3:6, 8; 27:3-5; 46:3). Answers to prayer (1Jn 3:22; 5:14-15). Continuance in grace (Php 1:6). Comfort in affliction (Ps 73:26; Lk 4:18-19; 2Co 4:8-10, 16-18). Support in death (Ps 23:4). A glorious resurrection (Job 19:26; Ps 17:15; Php 3:21; 1Jn 3:2). A kingdom (Heb 12:28; Rev 5:10). A crown (2Ti 4:7-8; Jas 1:12). Give diligence to attain to (2Pe 1:10-11). Strive to maintain (Heb 3:14, 18). Confident hope in God restores (Ps 42:11).

Exemplified:
David (Ps 23:4; 73:24-26). Paul (2Ti 1:12; 4:18).

ASSYRIA Antiquity and origin of (Ge 10:8-11). Situated beyond the Euphrates (Isa 7:20). Watered by the Tigris River (Ge 2:14).

Called:
The land of Nimrod (Mic 5:6). Shinar (Ge 11:2; 14:1). Asshur (Nu 24:22, 24). Nineveh, chief city of (Ge 10:11; 2Ki 19:36). Governed by kings (2Ki 15:19, 29).

Celebrated for:
Fertility (2Ki 18:32; Isa 36:17). Extent of conquests (2Ki 18:33-35; 19:11-13; Isa 10:9-14). Extensive commerce (Eze 27:23-24). Idolatry, the religion of (2Ki 19:37).

Described:
Most formidable (Isa 28:2). Intolerant and oppressive (Na 3:19). Cruel and destructive (Isa 10:7). Selfish and reserved (Hos 8:9). Unfaithful (2Ch 28:20-21). Proud and haughty (2Ki 19:22-24; Isa 10:8). An instrument of God's vengeance (Isa 7:18-19; 10:5-6). Chief men of, described (Eze 23:6, 12, 23). Armies of, described (Isa 5:26-29).
Invaded Israel (2Ki 15:19). Bought off by Menahem (2Ki 15:19-20).

Tiglath-Pileser, King of:
Ravaged Israel (2Ki 15:29). Asked to aid Ahaz against Syria (2Ki 16:7-8). Took money from Ahaz, but did not strengthen him (2Ch 28:20-21). Conquered Syria (2Ki 16:9).

Shalmaneser, King of:
Reduced Israel to tribute (2Ki 17:3). Was conspired against by Hoshea (2Ki 17:4). Imprisoned Hoshea (2Ki 17:4). Carried Israel captive (2Ki 17:5-6). Repopulated Samaria from Assyria (2Ki 17:24).

Sennacherib, King of:
Invaded Judah (2Ki 18:13). Bought off by Hezekiah (2Ki 18:14-16). Insulted and threatened Judah (2Ki 18:17-32; 19:10-13). Blasphemed the Lord (2Ki 18:33-35). Prayed against by Hezekiah (2Ki 19:14-19). Reproved for pride and blasphemy (2Ki 19:20-34; Isa 37:21-29). His army destroyed by God (2Ki 19:35). Assassinated by his sons (2Ki 19:37). Condemned for oppressing God's people (Isa 52:4). Manasseh taken captive to (2Ch 33:11). The repopulating of Samaria from, completed by Ashurbanipal (Ezr 4:10). Idolatry of, brought into Samaria (2Ki 17:29). Judah condemned for trusting (Jer 2:18, 36). Israel condemned for trusting (Hos 5:13; 7:11; 8:9). The Jews condemned for following the idolatries of (Eze 16:28; 23:5, 7). The greatness, extent, duration, and fall of, illustrated (Eze 31:3-17).

Predictions Respecting:
Conquest of the Kenites by (Nu 24:22). Conquest of Syria by (Isa 8:4). Conquest and captivity of Israel by (Isa 8:4; Hos 9:3; 10:6; 11:5). Invasion of Judah by (Isa 5:26; 7:17-20; 8:8; 10:5-6, 12). Restoration of Israel from (Isa 27:12-13; Hos 11:11; Zec 10:10). Destruction of (Isa 10:12-19; 14:24-25; 30:31-33; 31:8-9; Zec 10:11). Participation in the blessings of the gospel (Isa 19:23-25; Mic 7:12).

ASTARTE *See Anath; Ashtaroth, 1; Ashtoreth.*

ASTONISHMENT Christ causes (Mt 13:54; 15:31; 22:22, 33; Mk 2:12; 4:41; 7:37; 10:24; Lk 2:48; 4:22, 26; 8:25).

ASTROLOGER, ASTROLOGY One who tries to find out the influence of the stars upon human affairs or to foretell events by their positions and aspects (Isa 47:13; Jer 10:1-2; Da 1:20; 2:27; 4:7; 5:7, 11; Isa 47:12-13). *See Astronomy; Sorcery.*

ASTRONOMY

Phenomena Concerning the Universe:
God the creator of (Job 9:6-9; 26:7, 13; 37:18; Ps 8:3; 136:5-9; Isa 40:22, 26). God the ruler of (Job 38:31-33; Ps 68:33; Eze 32:7-8; Am 5:8). Immeasurable (Jer 31:37; 33:22). Laws of, permanent (Ecc 1:5; Jer 31:35-36). Declares God's glory (Ps 19:1-6). Destruction of (Isa 34:4; Mt 24:35; 2Pe 3:10; Rev 6:12-14; 21:1).

Celestial Phenomena:
Fire from heaven, on the cities of the plain (Ge 19:24-25), on the two captains and their fifties (2Ki 1:10-14), on the flocks and servants of Job (Job 1:16).
Thunder and lightning on Mt. Sinai (Ex 19:16, 18; 20:18). Pillar of cloud and fire (Ex 13:21-22; 14:19, 24; 40:38; Nu 9:15-23; Ps 78:14). The sun and moon standing still (Jos 10:12-14). Hail on the Egyptians (Ex 9:22-34).

Darkness on the Egyptians (Ex 10:21-23), at the crucifixion of Christ (Mt 27:45; Lk 23:44-45).
Sun seemingly rotating (Ecc 1:5). Wandering stars (Jude 13).

Signs in the Sun, Moon and Stars:
(Joel 2:30-31; Isa 13:10). Foretold by Jesus as part of his second coming (Mt 24:29, 35; Mk 13:24-25; Lk 21:25; Ac 2:19-20). In the final judgments (Rev 8:10-12; 9:1-2; 10:1-2; 12:3-4; 13:13; 16:8-9; 19:11-14).

Constellations: Glory of (1Co 15:41). Darkened (Isa 13:10). The serpent (Job 26:13), Bear, Orion and Pleiades (Job 9:9; 38:31; Am 5:8).
See Constellations; Eclipse; Heaven; Meteorology; Moon; Stars; Sun.

ASUPPIM NIV "storehouses" at the S gate of the temple (1Ch 26:15, 17; Ne 12:25).

ASWAN Egyptian town on border of Egypt and Ethiopia (Isa 49:12; Eze 29:10; 30:6).

ASYNCRITUS (*incomparable*). A disciple at Rome (Ro 16:14).

ATAD (*thornbush*). The place where the sons of Jacob mourned for their father (Ge 50:10-11).

ATARAH (*circlet, wreath*). Wife of Jerahmeel (1Ch 2:26).

ATAROTH (*circlets, wreaths*). Also called Atroth.
1. A city E of Jordan (Nu 32:3, 34).
2. A city, or possibly two different cities, of Ephraim (Jos 16:2, 5, 7; 18:13).
3. A city of Judah (1Ch 2:54). Called Atroth Beth Joab. *See Atroth Beth Joab; Joab, 4.*
4. A city of Gad (Nu 32:35).

ATAROTH ADDAR (*wreaths of majesty*). *See Ataroth, 2.*

ATER (possibly *crippled one, left-handed one*, or *the proper name Etir*).
1. A descendant of Hezekiah who returned from Babylon (Ezr 2:16; Ne 7:21; 10:17).
2. A gatekeeper (Ezr 2:42; Ne 7:45).
3. An Israelite who agreed to Nehemiah's covenant (Ne 10:17).

ATHACH A city of Judah (1Sa 30:30).

ATHAIAH (possibly *[the] superiority of Yahweh*). Son of Uzziah (Ne 11:4).

ATHALIAH (possibly *Yahweh is exalted* BDB; *oldest of Yahweh* KB).
1. Wife of Jehoram, king of Judah (2Ki 8:18, 26; 11:1-3, 12-16, 20; 2Ch 22:10-12; 23:12-15, 21).
2. Son of Jehoram (1Ch 8:26).
3. Father of Jeshaiah (Ezr 8:7).

ATHARIM (traditionally *way of the spies*). The Israelites, under Moses, were attacked by the king of Arad, and some were taken captive (Nu 21:1ff).

ATHEISM Instances of (Ps 10:4; 14:1; 53:1). Arguments against (Job 12:7-25; Ro 1:19-20).
See God; Faith; Unbelief.

ATHENS, ATHENIANS A leading city of Greece and its inhabitants (Ac 17:15-34; 1Th 3:1).

ATHLAI (possibly *Yahweh is exalted* BDB; *oldest of Yahweh* KB). A son of Bebai (Ezr 10:28).

ATHLETE, ATHLETICS *See Games.*

ATOMS OF MATTER NIV "dust of the world" (Pr 8:26).

ATONEMENT
The divine act of grace in which God accepts an offering as a substitute for the punishment for sin. In the OT, the shed blood of sacrificial offerings effected atonement. The blood shed in the sacrifices was sacred. It epitomized the life of the sacrificial victim. Since life was sacred, blood (a symbol of life) had to be treated with respect (Ge 9:5-6). Eating blood was therefore strictly forbidden (Lev 7:26-27; Dt 12:16, 23-25; 15:23; 1Sa 14:32-34). Lev 17:14 stresses the intimate relationship between blood and life by twice declaring that "the life of every creature is its blood." Life is the precious and mysterious gift of God, and people are not to seek to preserve it or increase their life-force by eating "life" that is "in the blood" (Lev 17:11)—as many pagan peoples throughout history have thought they could do (Ge 9:4).
Practically every sacrifice included the sprinkling or smearing of blood on the altar or within the tabernacle (Lev 1:5; 3:2; 4:6, 25; 7:2; 17:6), thus teaching that atonement involves the substitution of life for life. The blood of the OT sacrifice pointed forward to the blood of the Lamb of God, who obtained for his people "eternal redemption" (Heb 9:12). "Without the shedding of blood there is no forgiveness" (Heb 9:22).
For tabernacle and furniture (Lev 16:15-20, 33). In consecration of the Levites (Nu 8:21). For those defiled by the dead (Nu 6:11). Made for houses (Lev 14:53). Sin. *See below, Sin.*

By:
Meat offerings (Lev 5:11-13), jewels (Nu 31:50), money (Ex 30:12-16; Lev 5:15-16; 2Ki 12:16), incense (Nu 16:46-50). By animals. *See below, Made by Animal Sacrifices.* By Jesus. *See below, Made by Jesus.*

Day of:
Time of (Ex 30:10; Lev 23:27; 25:9; Nu 29:7). How observed (Ex 30:10; Lev 16:2-34; 23:27-32; Nu 29:7-11; Heb 5:3; 9:7).

Made by Animal Sacrifices:
In the blood shed (Lev 17:11). In burnt offerings (Lev 1:4). For unintentional sin (Lev 4:13-21; Nu 15:22-28; 28:27-31; 29), for purification after childbirth (Lev 12:6-8).
In guilt offerings for sin (Lev 5:6-10; 6:7), for cleansing from a skin disease (Lev 14:12-32).
In sin offerings (Ex 29:36; Lev 4:20) for unintentional sins of a leader (Lev 4:22-35), of the descendants of Aaron (Lev 9:7; 10:17; 16:6-9). The scapegoat (Lev 16:10-34). On festival days (Nu 28:22; 29).
Forgiveness of sins through (Lev 5:10; 19:22).

Made by Jesus:
Through his blood shed (Lk 22:20; 1Co 1:23; Eph 2:13-15; Heb 9:12-15, 25-26; 12:24; 13:12, 20-21; 1Jn 5:6; Rev 1:5; 5:9; 7:14; 12:11), his death (Ro 3:24-26; 5:11-15; 1Th 1:10; Heb 13:12; 1Jn 2:2; 3:5; 4:10; Rev 5:6, 9; 13:8).
Typified in Passover lamb (Ex 12:5, 11, 14; 1Co 5:7), in sacrifices (Ex 24:8; Lev 16:30, 34; 17:11; 19:22; Heb 9:11-28). Compare Ge 4:4, w Heb 11:4; Ge 22:2, w Heb 11:17, 19; Ex 12:5, 11, 14, w 1Co 5:7; Ex 24:8, w Heb 9:10; Lev 16:30, 34, w Heb 9:7, 12, 28; Lev 17:11, w Heb 9:22.
Divinely inspired (Lk 2:30-31; Gal 4:4-5; Eph 1:3-12, 17-22; 2:4-10; Col 1:19-20; 1Pe 1:20; Rev 13:8). A mystery (1Co 2:7; 1Pe 1:8-12). Once for all (Heb 7:27; 9:24-28; 10:10, 12, 14; 1Pe 3:18). Made on our behalf (Isa 53:4-12; Mt 20:28; Jn 6:51; 11:49-51; Gal 3:13; Eph 5:2; 1Th 5:9-10; Heb 2:9; 1Pe 2:24).
For reconciliation (Da 9:24-27; Ro 5:1-21; 2Co 5:18-21; Eph 2:16-17; Col 1:20-22; Heb 2:17). For remission of sins (Zec 13:1; Mt 26:28; Lk 22:20; 24:46-47; Jn 1:29; Ro 4:25; 1Co 15:3; Gal 1:3-4; Eph 1:7; Col 1:14; Heb 1:3; 10:1-20; 1Jn 1:7; 3:5). For redemption (Mt 20:28; Ac 20:28; Gal 3:13; 1Ti 2:6; Heb 9:12; Rev 5:9).
See Blood; Jesus the Christ, Death of, Mission of, Sufferings of; Redemption; Salvation.

ATONEMENT COVER KJV "mercy seat." Description of (Ex 25:17-22). Placed on the ark of the testimony (Ex 26:34; 30:6; 31:7; 40:20; Heb 9:5). Materials of, to be a freewill offering (Ex 35:4-12). Made by Bezalel (Ex 37:1, 6-9).
Sprinkled with blood (Lev 16:14-15). There God met with his people (Ex 25:22; 30:6, 36; Lev 16:2; Nu 7:89; 17:4; 1Sa 4:4; 2Sa 6:2; 2Ki 19:15; 1Ch 13:6; Ps 80:1; Ps 99:1; Isa 37:16; Heb 4:16).
In Solomon's temple (1Ch 28:11).
See Tabernacle.

ATONEMENT, DAY OF *See Day of Atonement.*

ATONING SACRIFICE *See Propitiation.*

ATROPHY *See Disease; Shriveled Hand.*

ATROTH BETH JOAB (*circlets, folds of the house of Joab*). Descendants of Salma; the house of Joab, occurs in the genealogy of Judah (1Ch 2:54).

ATROTH SHOPHAN (*circlets, folds of Shophan*). Town built by Gadites E of Jordan (Nu 32:35).

ATTAI (*timely*, or perhaps *an abbreviation of Athaiah*).
1. A Gadite warrior (1Ch 12:11).
2. Son of Rehoboam (2Ch 11:20).
3. Grandson of Sheshan (1Ch 2:35-36).

ATTALIA A seaport of Pamphylia (Ac 14:25).

ATTORNEY *See Lawyer.*

ATTRIBUTES OF GOD *See God.*

AUGUSTUS (*reverent, holy*). A title of Roman emperors (Lk 2:1). "Emperor" and "Imperial" in Ac 25:21, 25; 27:1 are rendered Augustus in the KJV.

AUL *See Awl.*

AVA *See Avva.*

AVARICE Love of money: a root of evil (1Ti 6:10). Insatiable (Ecc 4:7-8; 5:10-11). Forbidden in overseer (1Ti 3:2-3; Tit 1:7).
Instances of: Descendants of Joseph (Jos 17:14-18). *See Covetousness; Greed; Rich, The; Riches.*

AVEN (*evil power, wickedness*).
1. Valley of Aven (Am 1:5, ftn).
2. Bethel (Am 5:5, ftn).
3. Beth Aven (Hos 10:8, ftn). *See Beth Aven.*
4. A possible spelling for On or Heliopolis (Eze 30:17, ftn).

AVENGER OF BLOOD

Premosaic:
Cain fears (Ge 4:14-15), Lamech fears (Ge 4:24). Edict of God (Ge 9:5-6).

Mosaic Law Concerning:
Cities of refuge from (Nu 35:6-34; Dt 19:1-13; Jos 20:1-9; 21:13, 21, 27, 32, 38; 1Ch 6:57, 67). Set aside by David (2Sa 14:4-11).

Figurative: (Ps 8:2; 44:16; Ro 13:4; 1Th 4:6).
See Homicide.

AVITH Capital city of the Edomites (Ge 36:35; 1Ch 1:46).

AVVA Also called Ivvah. A district near Babylon (2Ki 17:24; 18:34; 19:13; Isa 37:13).

AVVIM
1. A city of Benjamin (Jos 18:23).
2. A tribe in southern Palestine. *See Avvites.*

AVVITES
1. A people driven out of Canaan by the Philistines (Dt 2:23; Jos 13:3).
2. Colonists of Samaria (2Ki 17:31).

AWAKENINGS, REFORMS
General references (1Ki 18:39; 2Ch 30:11; Ezr 10:1; Lk 3:7-10; Jn 4:39; Ac 2:40-41; 8:6; 9:35; 11:21; 13:48; 18:8; 19:18).
Instances: Asa (1Ki 15:12). Jehu (1Ki 10:27). Jehoiada (2Ki 11:18). Josiah (2Ki 23:4). Jehoshaphat (2Ch 19:3). Hezekiah (2Ch 31:1). Manasseh (2Ch 33:15). Ezra (Ezr 10:3). Nehemiah (Ne 13:19).

AWL A sharp piercing tool (Ex 21:6; Dt 15:17).

AX, AXHEAD A tool for cutting wood (Dt 19:5; 20:19; 1Sa 13:20-21; 2Sa 12:31; Ps 74:5-6). A weapon of war (Jer 46:22). Elisha causes an axhead to float (2Ki 6:5-6).
Figurative of judgment (Jer 46:22; Mt 3:10).

AXLES Part of a wheeled vehicle, like the movable stands (1Ki 7:30-33).

AYYAH A city in Ephraim (1Ch 7:28).

AZAL *See Azel, 1.*

AZALIAH (*Yahweh is keeping in reserve*). Father of Shaphan (2Ki 22:3; 2Ch 34:8).

AZANIAH (*Yahweh has listened*). Father of Jeshua (Ne 10:9).

AZAREL (*God [El] has helped*).
1. Aaronite of the family of Korah (1Ch 12:6).
2. A musician in the temple (1Ch 25:18), also called Uzziel. *See Uzziel 4.*
3. A Danite prince (1Ch 27:22).
4. A son of Bani (Ezr 10:41).
5. A priest (Ne 11:13; 12:36).

AZARIAH (*Yahweh has helped*).
1. Man of Judah (1Ch 2:8).
2. King of Judah. *See Uzziah, 1.*
3. Son of Jehu (1Ch 2:38).
4. Son of Ahimaaz (1Ch 6:9).
5. Levite (1Ch 6:36).
6. Son of Zadok (1Ki 4:2).
7. High priest (1Ch 6:10).
8. Son of Nathan (1Ki 4:5).
9. Prophet (2Ch 15:1-8).
10. Son of King Jehoshaphat (2Ch 21:2).
11. Son of Jehoram (2Ch 22:6, ftn). *See Ahaziah.*
12. Son of Jehoram (2Ch 23:1).
13. Son of Johanan (2Ch 28:12).
14. Levite (2Ch 29:12).
15. High priest (2Ch 26:16-20).
16. Son of Hilkiah (1Ch 6:13-14).
17. Opponent of Jeremiah (Jer 43:2).
18. Jewish captive of Babylon (Da 1:7). *See Abednego.*
19. Son of Maaseiah (Ne 3:23).
20. Levite (Ne 8:7).
21. Priest (Ne 10:2).
22. Prince of Judah (Ne 12:32-33).

AZARIAHU A son of Jehoshaphat (2Ch 21:2).

AZAZ (*strong*). Father of Bela (1Ch 5:8).

AZAZEL NIV "scapegoat," one of the goats chosen for the service of the Day of Atonement (Lev 16:8, 10, 26). It has been interpreted both personally and impersonally as meaning: 1. remission of sin, 2. a place name, 3. an evil spirit, 4. the devil. *See Scapegoat.*

AZAZIAH (*Yahweh is strong*).
1. A harpist in the temple (1Ch 15:21).
2. Father of Hoshea (1Ch 27:20).
3. An overseer in the temple (2Ch 31:13).

AZBUK The father of Nehemiah (Ne 3:16).

AZEKAH (possibly *hoe [the ground]*). A town of Judah (Jos 10:10-11; 15:35; 1Sa 17:1; 2Ch 11:9; Ne 11:30; Jer 34:7).

AZEL (*noble*).
1. A place near Jerusalem (Zec 14:5).
2. A Benjamite (1Ch 8:37-38; 9:43-44).

AZEM *See Ezem.*

AZGAD (*strong is Gad*).
1. Ancestor of certain captives who returned from Babylon (Ezr 2:12; Ne 7:17).
2. A returned exile (Ezr 8:12).
3. A leader who signed Nehemiah's covenant (Ne 10:15).

AZIEL (*God is my strength*). A temple musician (1Ch 15:20).

AZIZA (*powerful*). Son of Zattu (Ezr 10:27).

AZMAVETH (*strong one of death* ISBE; *camel fodder, a plant of the plumose family* KB).
1. One of David's heroes (2Sa 23:31).
2. Benjamite (1Ch 12:3).
3. David's treasurer (1Ch 27:25).
4. Descendant of Jonathan (1Ch 8:36).
5. Place N of Anathoth (Ezr 2:24; Ne 12:29).

AZMON (*strongly [built body]*). A place on the S of Canaan (Nu 34:4, 5; Jos 15:4).

AZNOTH TABOR (possibly *peaks of Tabor*). A town in Naphtali (Jos 19:34).

AZOR (*help*). Ancestor of Jesus (Mt 1:13-14). Perhaps identical with Azrikam (1Ch 3:23).

AZOTUS The name of Ashdod in NT times (Ac 8:40). *See Ashdod.*

AZRIEL (*God [El] is [my] help*).
1. A chief of Manasseh (1Ch 5:24).
2. Father of Jerimoth (1Ch 27:19).
3. Father of Seraiah (Jer 36:26).

AZRIKAM (*[my] help arises*).
1. Son of Neariah (1Ch 3:23).
2. Son of Azel (1Ch 8:38; 9:44).
3. A Levite (1Ch 9:14; Ne 11:15).
4. Governor of the house of Ahaz (2Ch 28:7).

AZUBAH (*abandonment*).
1. Mother of Jehoshaphat (1Ki 22:42; 2Ch 20:31).
2. Wife of Caleb (1Ch 2:18-19).

AZUR *See Azzur.*

AZZAH *See Gaza, 1.*

AZZAN (*strong*). Father of Paltiel of the tribe of Issachar; chosen to help distribute the territory W of the Jordan among the various tribes who settled there (Nu 34:26).

AZZUR (*help*).
1. A leader who sealed Nehemiah's covenant (Ne 10:17).
2. A Gibeonite, the father of Hananiah, a false prophet in the days of King Zedekiah (Jer 28:1).
3. Father of Jaazaniah, an Israelite prince (Eze 11:1).

B

BAAL (*master, owner, lord*).
1. A god worshiped by the Canaanites and the Phoenicians; a god of storms and fertility. Often in the plural (Jdg 2:11; 3:7).
Wickedly worshiped by the Israelites in the time of the judges (Jdg 2:10-23; 1Sa 7:3-4), by the kingdom of Israel (2Ki 17:16; Jer 23:13; Hos 11:2; 13:1), under Ahab (1Ki 16:31-33; 18:18; 19:18), Jehoram (2Ki 3:2), by the Israelites (2Ki 21:3; 2Ch 22:2-4; 24:7; 28:2; 33:3). Jeremiah preaches against the worship of (Jer 2:8, 23; 7:9).
Altars of, destroyed by Gideon (Jdg 6:25-32), by Jehoiada (2Ki 11:18), by Josiah (2Ki 23:4-5).
Prophets of, slain by Elijah (2Ki 18:4). All worshipers of, destroyed by Jehu (2Ki 10:18-25).
2. A Benjamite (1Ch 8:30; 9:36).
3. A Reubenite (1Ch 5:5).
4. A city in the tribe of Simeon (1Ch 4:33). Called Baalath Beer (Jos 19:8).

BAAL-BERITH (*lord [Baal] of a covenant*). A god of the Shechemites (Jdg 9:4). Worshiped by Israelites (Jdg 8:33). Also called El-Berith (Jdg 9:46). *See El-Berith.*

BAAL GAD (*lord [Baal] of good luck*). A city of the Canaanites (Jos 11:17; 12:7; 13:5). Probably Baal Hermon (Jdg 3:3; 1Ch 5:23).

BAAL-GUR *See Gur Baal.*

BAAL HAMON (*lord [Baal] of Hamon,* or *possessor of abundance*). A place where Solomon had a vineyard (SS 8:11). Its location is unknown. Called Hammon (Jos 19:28).

BAAL-HANAN (*lord [Baal] is gracious*).
1. The son of Acbor and king of Edom (Ge 36:38; 1Ch 1:49).
2. An official under David (1Ch 27:28).

BAAL HAZOR (*lord [Baal] of Hazor*). Where Absalom had a sheep-range and where he brought about the death of Amnon in revenge for the rape of his sister (2Sa 13:23).

BAAL HERMON (*lord [Baal] of Hermon*).
1. A city near Mt. Hermon (1Ch 5:23). Probably identical with Baal Gad. *See Baal Gad.*
2. A mountain of Lebanon (Jdg 3:3).

BAAL MEON A city of the Reubenites (Nu 32:38; 1Ch 5:8; Eze 25:9). Also called: Beth Meon (Jer 48:23), Beth Baal Meon (Jos 13:17), Beon (Nu 32:3).

BAAL PEOR (*lord [Baal] of Peor*). An idol of Moab (Nu 25:3, 5; Dt 4:3; Ps 106:28; Hos 9:10).

BAAL PERAZIM (*lord [Baal] of making a breach, breaking through*). A place in the valley of Rephaim (2Sa 5:20; 1Ch 14:11). Called Mt. Perazim (Isa 28:21).

BAAL SHALISHAH (*lord [Baal] of Shalisha*). A place near Gilgal (1Sa 9:4; 2Ki 4:42).

BAAL TAMAR (*lord [Baal] of the palm tree*). A place near Gibeah (Jdg 20:33).

BAAL-ZEBUB (*lord [Baal] of the flies*). Name under which Baal was worshiped by the Philistines of Ekron (2Ki 1:2-3, 6). An intentional biblical corruption of the original name Baal-Zebul, "Baal the prince." *See Beelzebub.*

BAAL ZEPHON (*lord [Baal] of the North*). A place near which the Israelites encamped just before they crossed the Red Sea (Ex 14:2, 9; Nu 33:7). The site is unknown.

BAALAH (*[feminine of Baal] lady*).
1. A city in the S of Judah (Jos 15:29). Apparently identical with Balah (Jos 19:3) and Bilhah (1Ch 4:29).
2. A city in the N of Judah called also Kiriath Jearim. *See Kiriath Jearim.*
3. A mountain in Judah (Jos 15:11). Probably identical with Mt. Jearim.

BAALAH OF JUDAH (*lords [Baals] of Judah*). Town on N border of Judah; the same as Baalah and Kiriath Baal and Kiriath Jearim (2Sa 6:2; 1Ch 13:6).

BAALATH (feminine of Baal "lord" *lady*). A city of Dan (Jos 19:44; 1Ki 9:18; 2Ch 8:6).

BAALATH BEER (*lord [Baal] of the well*). A city in the tribe of Simeon (Jos 19:8). *See Baal, 4.*

BAALBEK (*city of Baal*). City of Coele-Syria, c. forty miles NW of Damascus, famous for its ruins.

BAALI (*my lord* or *my husband*). Name often given to Yahweh by Israel, no longer to be used when Baal worship is eradicated (Hos 2:16, ftn).

BAALIM Plural form of Baal in KJV (Jdg 2:11; 1Sa 7:4; Hos 2:13, 17; 11:2). *See Baal.*

BAALIS (possibly *son of delight,* or *Baals*). King of the Ammonites (Jer 40:14).

BAANA (*son of affliction*).
1. Son of Ahilud (1Ki 4:12).
2. Father of Zadok (Ne 3:4).
3. A son of Hushai (1Ki 4:16).

BAANAH (*son of affliction*).
1. A captain of Ish-Bosheth's army (2Sa 4:2, 5-6, 9).
2. Father of Heled (also Heleb) (2Sa 23:29, ftn; 1Ch 11:30).
3. Jewish leader of the Exile (Ezr 2:2; Ne 7:7; 10:27).
4. *See Baana, 3.*

BAARA (*passionate [burning] one*). Wife of Shaharaim (1Ch 8:8). Called Hodesh.

BAASEIAH (*the Lord is bold*). An ancestor of Asaph, the musician (1Ch 6:40).

BAASHA (*boldness*). King of Israel (1Ki 15:16-22, 27-34; 16:1-7; 21:22; 2Ki 9:9; 2Ch 16:1-6; Jer 41:9).

BABBLER A sarcastic title applied to Paul (Ac 17:18).

BABBLING Condemned (Mt 6:7; 1Ti 6:20; 2Ti 2:16).

BABEL (*gate of god[s]*; Ge 11:9 *confused*). A city in the plain of Shinar. Tower built and tongues confused at (Ge 11:1-9). *See Babylon.*

BABIES In the mouths of, praise is ordained (Mt 21:16).
Symbolize: Those without guile (Ps 8:2; Mt 11:25; Lk 10:21), the children of the kingdom of heaven (Mt 18:2-6; Mk 10:15; Lk 18:17), weak Christians (Ro 2:20; 1Co 3:1; Heb 5:13; 1Pe 2:2).
See Children; Parents.

BABOONS Imported by Solomon (1Ki 10:22; 2Ch 9:21).

BABYLON, BABYLONIA (*gate of god[s]*).

Described:
Origin of (Ge 10:8, 10). Origin of the name (Ge 11:8-9). Land of the Chaldeans (Eze 12:13). Land of Shinar in (Da 1:2; Zec 5:11, ftn). Land of Merathaim (Jer 50:21). Desert of the sea (Isa 21:1, 9) Sheshach, a cryptic term for Babylon (Jer 25:12, 26, ftn). Lady of kingdoms (Isa 47:5). Situated beyond the Euphrates (Ge 11:31, w Jos 24:2-3). Formerly a part of Mesopotamia (Ac 7:2). Conquered by the Assyrians and a part of their empire (2Ki 17:24, w Isa 23:13). Watered by the rivers Euphrates and Tigris (Ps 137:1; Jer 51:13). Composed of many nations (Da 3:4, 29). Governed by Kings (2Ki 20:12; Da 5:1). Languages spoken in (Da 1:4; 2:4). With Media and Persia divided by Darius into 120 provinces (Da 6:1). Administrators placed over (Da 2:48; 6:2). Babylon the chief province of (Da 3:1).

Babylon the Capital of:
Its antiquity (Ge 11:4, 9). Enlarged by Nebuchadnezzar (Da 4:30). Surrounded with a great wall and fortified (Jer 51:53, 58). Called the jewel of kingdoms and the glory of Babylonians' pride (Isa 13:19), the golden city (Isa 14:4, KJV), the city of merchants (Eze 17:4), Babylon the great (Da 4:30).

Remarkable for:
Antiquity (Jer 5:15). Naval power (Isa 43:14). Military power (Jer 5:16; 50:23). National greatness (Isa 13:19; Jer 51:41). Wealth (Jer 50:37; 51:13). Commerce (Eze 17:4). Manufacture of garments (Jos 7:21). Wisdom of officials (Isa 47:10; Jer 50:35).

Inhabitants of:
Idolatrous (Jer 50:38; Da 3:18). Addicted to magic (Isa 47:9, 12-13; Da 2:1-2). Profane and sacrilegious (Da 5:1-3). Wicked (Isa 47:10).

As a Power Was:
Arrogant (Isa 14:13-14; Jer 50:29, 31-32). Secure and self-confident (Isa 47:7-8). Grand and stately (Isa 47:1, 5). Covetous (Jer 51:13). Oppressive (Isa 14:4). Cruel and destructive (Isa 14:17; 47:6; Jer 51:25; Hab 1:6-7). An instrument of God's vengeance on other nations (Jer 51:7; Isa 47:6). Armies of, described (Hab 1:7-9).

Represented by:
A great eagle (Eze 17:3). A head of gold (Da 2:32, 37-38). A lion with eagle's wings (Da 7:4). Ambassadors of, sent to Hezekiah (2Ki 20:12). Figure of a woman (Rev 17).

Nebuchadnezzar, King of:
Made Jehoiakim vassal (2Ki 24:1). Besieged Jerusalem (2Ki 24:10-11). Took Jehoiachin captive to Babylon (2Ki 24:12, 14-16; 2Ch 36:10). Sacked the temple (2Ki 24:13). Made Zedekiah king (2Ki 24:17). Besieged and took Jerusalem (2Ki 24:20; 25:1-4). Burned Jerusalem (2Ki 25:9-10). Took Zedekiah captive to Babylon (2Ki 25:7, 11, 18-21; 2Ch 36:20). Sacked and burned the temple (2Ki 25:9, 13-17; 2Ch 36:18-19). Revolt of the Israelites from, and their punishment illustrated (Eze 17). The Israelites exhorted to be subject to, and settle in (Jer 27:17; 29:1-7). Treatment of the Israelites in (2Ki 25:27-30; Da 1:3-7). Grief of the Israelites in (Ps 137:1-6). Destroyed by the Medes (Da 5:30-31). Restoration of the Israelites from (2Ch 36:23; Ezr 1; 2:1-67). The gospel preached in (1Pe 5:13). A type of Antichrist (Rev 16:19; 17:5).

Predictions Respecting:
Conquests by (Jer 21:3-10; 27:2-6; 49:28-33; Eze 21:19-32; 29:18-20). Captivity of the Israelites by (Jer 20:4-6; 22:20-26; 25:9-11; Mic 4:10). Restoration of the Israelites from (Isa 14:1-4; 44:28; 48:20; Jer 29:10; 50:4, 8, 19). Destruction of (Isa 13; 14:4-22; 21:1-10; 47; Jer 25:12; 50; 51). Perpetual desolation of (Isa 13:19-22; 14:22-23; Jer 50:13, 39; 51:37). Acknowledgment of Yahweh (Ps 87:4).

BACA (*balsam tree,* or *weeping*). An unknown valley of Israel (Ps 84:6), figurative of an experience of sorrow turned into joy.

BACHRITES *See Beker, Bekerite.*

BACKBITING Evil of (Ps 15:1-3; Pr 25:23; Ro 1:29-30; 2Co 12:20).
See Accusation, False; Slander; Speaking, Evil.

BACKSLIDERS

Described as:
Blind (2Pe 1:9; Rev 3:17), godless (2Jn 9), idolaters (1Co 10:7), lukewarm (Rev 3:15-16), grumblers (Ex 17:7; 1Co 10:10), forsaking God (Jer 17:13), tempting Christ (1Co 10:9), forsaking God's covenant (Ps 78:10-11; Pr 2:17), turned aside to evil (Ps 125:5; 1Ti 5:15), unfit for God's kingdom (Lk 9:62).

God's Forbearance With:
(Dt 32:5-6, 26-27; Ezr 9:10, 14; Isa 42:3).
God's concern for (Dt 32:28-29; Ps 81:13-14; Isa 1:4-9, 21-22; 65:2-3; Jer 2:5, 11-13, 17, 31-32; 18:13-15; 50:6; Hos 6:4-11; 11:1-4; 11:7-9; Mt 23:37).
Called to repentance (Isa 30:9, 15; 31:6; Jer 3:4-7, 12-14, 21-22; 4:14; 6:16; Hos 14:1; Mal 3:7; Rev 2:4-5, 20-22; 3:2-3, 18-19).
Promises to penitent: Of finding the Lord (Dt 4:29-31; 2Ch 15:2 4). Of spiritual enlightenment (Isa 29:24; Jer 3:14-19; Hos 6:3). Of restoration (Dt 30:1-10; Pr 24:16; Isa 57:18-19; Hos 14:4; Zec 10:6). Of temporal prosperity (Lev 26:40-42; Dt 30:1-5, 7-10; Job 22:23-30). Return of (Jer 31:18-19; 50:4-5; Hos 3:5; Jnh 2:4).

Judgment of:
Warnings to (Dt 4:25-28; 28:58-59; 29:18; 31:16-18; 1Ki 9:6-9; 2Ch 7:19-22; Jer 7:13-34; 11:9-17; Mk 9:50).
Corrective judgments upon (Dt 32:16-25; 1Ki 8:33; 2Ch 7:19-22; Ne 9:26-30; Job 34:26-27; Isa 50:1; Jer 8:1-15; 16:22; Eze 22:18-22; Hos 8:14; 9:1-17).
Punishment of: By temporal loss (Dt 28:15-68; Ezr 8:22; Jer 13:24-25; Eze 15; Am 2:4-6). By being overthrown by enemies (Nu 14:43; Dt 4:27-28; Jdg 2:12-15; 2Ki 18:11-12; 2Ch 29:6-8; Ps 78:40-43, 56-64). By being forsaken of God (2Ch 24:20; Isa 2:6; Jer 6:30; 12:7; 14:7, 10; 15:1; Hos 4:6, 10). By bearing the fruits of their sin (Pr 14:14; Eze 11:21; 16:43; 23:35).

Instances of:
Saul (1Sa 15:11, 26-28). Solomon (1Ki 11:4-40; Ne 13:26). Amon (2Ki 21:22-23). Rehoboam (2Ch 12:1-2). Joash (2Ch 24:24). Amaziah (2Ch 25:27). Jonah (Jnh 1:3). Disciples of Jesus (Jn 6:66). Peter (Mt 26:69-75). Corinthian Christians (1Co 5:1-8). Galatians (Gal 1:6; 3:1; 4:9-11; 5:6-7). Hymenaeus and Alexander (1Ti 1:20). Phygelus and Hermogenes (2Ti 1:15). Demas (2Ti 4:10). Churches of Asia (2Ti 1:15; Rev 2:4; 3:2-3, 15-18).
See Apostasy; Backsliding; Church, The Body of Believers, Evil Conditions of; Reprobacy.

BACKSLIDING Turning from God (1Ki 11:9). Leaving the first love (Rev 2:4). Departing from the simplicity of the gospel (2Co 11:3; Gal 3:1-3; 5:4, 7).
God is displeased at (Ps 78:57, 59). Despised by believers (Ps 101:3). Warnings against (Ps 85:8; 1Co 10:12). Guilt and consequences of (Nu 14:43; Ps 125:5; Isa 59:2, 9-11; Jer 5:6; 8:5, 13; 15:6; Lk 9:62). Brings its own punishment (Pr 14:14; Jer 2:19). A haughty spirit leads to (Pr 16:18). Leaning to (Pr 24:16; Hos 11:7). Liable to continue and increase (Jer 8:5; 14:7). Exhortations to return from (2Ch 30:6; Isa 31:6; Jer 3:12, 14, 22; Hos 6:1). Pray to be restored from (Ps 80:3; 85:4; La 5:21). Punishment of tempting others to the sin of (Pr 28:10; Mt 18:6). Not hopeless (Ps 37:24; Pr 24:16).
Attempt to bring back those guilty of (Gal 6:1; Jas 5:10, 20). Sin of, to be confessed (Isa 59:12-14; Jer 3:13, 14; 14:7-9). Pardon of, promised (2Ch 7:14; Jer 3:12; 31:20; 36:3). Healing of, promised (Jer 3:22; Hos 14:4). Afflictions sent to heal (Hos 5:15). Blessedness of those who keep from (Pr 28:15; Isa 26:3-4; Col 1:21-23).

Instances of Israel's Backsliding:
At Meribah (Ex 17:1-7), when Aaron made the golden calf (Ex 32), after Joshua's death (Jdg 2), during Asa's reign (2Ch 15), Hezekiah's reign (2Ch 30:2-12).
See Apostasy; Backsliders.

BACUTH *See Allon Bacuth.*

BAD COMPANY *See Company, Evil.*

BADGER *See Sea Cow.*

B

BAG Sack or pouch made for holding anything. Many kinds are mentioned in Scripture (Dt 25:13; 2Ki 5:23; Mt 10:10).

BAGPIPE (RSV); NIV "pipes." A musical instrument (Da 3:5, 7, 10, 15). *See Music, Instruments of.*

BAHURIM, BAHARUMITE (*young men*). A village between Jericho and Jerusalem, on the eastern slope of the Mount of Olives; modern Ras et-Tmim (2Sa 3:16; 16:5; 17:18; 19:16; 1Ki 2:8).

BAIL *See Creditor; Debt; Debtor; Security, For Debt.*

BAJITH NIV "temple"; a place of idolatrous worship in Moab (Isa 15:2). *See Idolatry; Sanctuary, 4; Shrine.*

BAKBAKKAR (*investigator*). A Levite (1Ch 9:15).

BAKBUK (*gurgling [sound coming out of a bottle]*). The founder of a family of temple servants who returned from the Captivity with Zerubbabel (Ezr 2:51; Ne 7:53).

BAKBUKIAH (*Yahweh pours out*). A name occurring three times in Nehemiah (Ne 11:17; 12:9, 25), a Levite in high office in Jerusalem right after the Exile.

BAKER (1Sa 8:13; Jer 37:21; Hos 7:4, 6). Pharaoh's chief baker (Ge 40). *See Bread.*

BALAAM (possibly *Baal [lord] of the people* BDB; possibly *the clan brings forth* IDB; *devourer, glutton* KB). Son of Beor. From Mesopotamia (Dt 23:4). A soothsayer (Jos 13:22). A prophet (Nu 24:2-9; 2Pe 2:15-16). Balak sends for, to curse Israel (Nu 22:5-7; Jos 24:9; Ne 13:2; Mic 6:5). Anger of, rebuked by his donkey (Nu 22:22-35; 2Pe 2:16). Counsel of, an occasion of Israel's corruption with the Midianites (Nu 31:16; Rev 2:14-15). Greed of (2Pe 2:15; Jude 11). Death of (Nu 31:8; Jos 13:22).

BALAC *See Balak.*

BALADAN Father of Merodach-Baladan (2Ki 20:12; Isa 39:1).

BALAH (*old, worn out*). A city of Simeon (Jos 19:3). Called Bilhah (1Ch 4:29).

BALAK (*devastator*). King of Moab (Nu 22:4; Jos 24:9; Jdg 11:25; Mic 6:5). Tried to bribe Balaam to curse Israel (Nu 22:5-7, 15-17). *See Balaam.*

BALANCES Used for weighing (Job 31:6; Isa 40:12, 15; Eze 5:1). Money weighed with (Isa 46:6; Jer 32:10). Must be just (Lev 19:36; Pr 16:11; Eze 45:10).

False balance: Used (Hos 12:7; Am 8:5; Mic 6:11), an abomination (Pr 11:1; 20:23).

Figurative (Job 6:2; 31:6; Ps 62:9; Isa 40:12; Da 5:27; Rev 6:5).

BALD LOCUST *See Insects.*

BALDNESS (Lev 13:40, 41). A judgment (Isa 3:24; Jer 47:5; 48:37; Eze 7:18). Artificial, a sign of mourning (Isa 22:12; Jer 16:6; Eze 27:31; 29:18; Am 8:10; Mic 1:16). Artificial, as an idolatrous practice, forbidden (Lev 21:5; Dt 14:1).

Instance of: Elisha (2Ki 2:23).

BALL Playing at (Isa 22:18).

BALM A medicinal balsam (Ge 37:25; 43:11; Jer 8:22; 46:11; 51:8; Eze 27:17).

BALSAM TREES *See Tree.*

BAMAH (*high location [for cultic worship]*). A high place (Eze 20:29).

BAMOTH (*high locations [for cultic worship]*). A camping place of the Israelites (Nu 21:19-20).

BAMOTH BAAL (*high places for Baal [worship]*). A city assigned to Reuben as part of his inheritance (Jos 13:17).

BANI (*descendant*).

1. KJV a Gadite; NIV "son of" (2Sa 23:36).
2. Levite (1Ch 6:46).
3. Descendant of Judah (1Ch 9:4).
4. Levite (Ne 3:17).
5. Levite (Ne 9:4).
6. Levite (Ne 11:22).
7. Levite (Ne 10:13).
8. Man who signed covenant (Ne 10:14).
9. Ancestor of Jews who returned from the Captivity (Ezr 10:29).
10. KJV Bani; NIV "descendants of" (Ezr 10:38).

BANISHMENT (Ezr 7:26). Of Adam and Eve, from Eden (Ge 3:22-24). Of Cain, to be "a restless wanderer" (Ge 4:14). Of Jews, from Rome (Ac 18:2). Of John, to Patmos (Rev 1:9). *See Exile.*

BANK A primitive kind of banking was known in ancient times. Israelites could not charge each other interest (Ex 22:25) but could charge Gentiles (Dt 23:20). The concept of a bank as a savings institution was unknown. *See Borrowing; Interest; Lending.*

BANNER Banners, ensigns, or standards (not flags) were used in ancient times for military, national, and ecclesiastical purposes very much as they are today (Nu 2:2; Isa 5:26; 11:10; Jer 4:21).

BANQUET Social feasting was common among the Hebrews. There were feasts on birthdays (Ge 40:20), marriages (Ge 29:22), funerals (2Sa 3:35), grape-gatherings (Jdg 9:27), sheep-shearing (1Sa 25:2, 36), sacrifices (Ex 34:15), and on other occasions. Often a second invitation was sent on the day of the feast (Lk 7:45), and their feet were washed (Lk 7:44). Banquets were often invigorated with music, singing, and dancing (Lk 15:23-25).

BAPTISM (*dip*, or *immerse*).

As administered by John (Mt 3:5-12; Jn 3:23; Ac 13:24; 19:4). Sanctioned by Christ's submission to it (Mt 3:13-15; Lk 3:21). Adopted by Christ (Jn 3:22; 4:1-2). Appointed an ordinance of the Christian church (Mt 28:19-20; Mk 16:15-16). To be administered in the name of the Father, the Son, and the Holy Spirit (Mt 28:19). Water, the outward and visible sign in (Ac 8:36; 10:47). Regeneration, the inward and spiritual grace of (Jn 3:3, 5-6; Ro 6:3-4, 11). Remission of sins, signified by (Ac 2:38; 22:16). Unity of the church effected by (1Co 12:13; Gal 3:27-28). Confession of sin necessary to (Mt 3:6). Repentance necessary to (Ac 2:38). Faith necessary to (Ac 8:37; 18:8). There is but one (Eph 4:5).

Administered to: Individuals (Ac 8:38; 9:18). Households (Ac 16:15; 1Co 1:16). Emblematic of the influences of the Holy Spirit (Mt 3:11; Tit 3:5). Typified (1Co 10:2; 1Pe 3:20-21).

BAR An Aramaic word meaning "son"; in the NT used as a prefix (Mt 16:17, KJV). *See Barabbas; Barnabas; Barsabbas; Bartholomew; Bar-Jesus; Bar-Jona.*

BARABBAS (*son of a father*, possibly *son of a rabbi [teacher]*). A prisoner released by Pilate (Mt 27:16-26; Mk 15:7-15; Lk 23:18-25; Jn 18:40; Ac 3:14).

BARACHEL *See Barakel.*

BARACHIAH, BARAKIAH *See Berekiah, 5.*

BARAH *See Beth Barah.*

BARAK (*lightning*). Israelite who defeated Sisera at the command of Deborah the judge (Jdg 4-5; 1Sa 12:11; Heb 11:32).

BARAKEL (*God [El] blesses*). A Buzite, whose son Elihu was the last of Job's friends to reason with him (Job 32:2, 6).

BARBARIAN A foreigner (Ac 28:2-4; Ro 1:14; 1Co 14:11; Col 3:11). *See Strangers.*

BARBER A barber's razor (Eze 5:1).

BARHUMITE Azmaveth the Barhumite, one of the Thirty (2Sa 23:31).

BARIAH (possibly *board, bar; fugitive* ISBE; *descendant* KB). Son of Shecaniah (1Ch 3:22).

BAR-JESUS (*son of Joshua*). A false prophet (Ac 13:6).

BAR-JONA NIV "Simon son of Jonah," surname of Peter (Mt 16:17).

BARKOS (*son of [pagan god] Kos*). A Jew whose descendants returned from the Exile (Ezr 2:53; Ne 7:55).

BARLEY A product of: Egypt (Ex 9:31), Israel (Dt 8:8; 1Ch 11:13; Jer 41:8).

Fed to horses (1Ki 4:28). Used in offerings (Nu 5:15; Eze 45:15). Selling of (2Ch 2:10; Hos 3:2). Tribute in (2Ch 27:5). Priests estimated value of (Lev 27:16; 2Ki 7:1; Rev 6:6). Absalom burns Joab's field of (2Sa 14:30).

Loaves of (Jn 6:9, 13).

BARN A storehouse for crops (Dt 28:8; Ps 144:13; Pr 3:10; Hag 2:19; Mt 3:12; 6:26; 13:30; Lk 12:18, 24).

See Granary; Storehouse.

BARNABAS (*son of comfort*). Also called Joseph (Ac 4:36). A prophet (Ac 13:1). An apostle (Ac 14:14). A Levite who gave his possessions to be owned in common with other disciples (Ac 4:36-37). Goes to Tarsus to find Paul, brings him to Antioch (Ac 11:25-26). Accompanies Paul to Jerusalem (Ac 11:30). Returns with Paul to Antioch (Ac 12:25).

Goes With Paul to Seleucia (Ac 13), Iconium (Ac 14:1-7).

Called Jupiter (Ac 14:12-18). Goes to Derbe (Ac 14:20). Is sent as delegate to Jerusalem (Ac 15; Gal 2:1-9). Estranged from Paul (Ac 15:36-39). Is reconciled to Paul (1Co 9:6). Piety of (Ac 11:22-24). Devotion of, to Jesus (Ac 15:25-26).

BARNEA *See Kadesh Barnea.*

BARREL A clay jar (1Ki 17:12, 14, 16; 18:33). *See Jar(s); Pottery.*

BARRENNESS Inability of women to bear children. A reproach (Ge 30:22-23; 1Sa 1:6, 7; 2:1-11; Isa 4:1; Lk 1:25). Sent as a judgment (Ge 20:17-18). *See Childlessness.*

Barrenness miraculously removed: Sarai (Ge 17:15-21), Rebekah (Ge 25:21), Manoah's wife (Jdg 13), Hannah (1Sa 1:6-20), Elizabeth (Lk 1:5-25).

BARSABBAS (*son of the Sabbath* or *son of Saba*).

1. Surname of Joseph (Ac 1:23).
2. Judas (Ac 15:22).

BARTER (Job 6:27; 41:6; La 1:11). *See Commerce.*

BARTHOLOMEW (*son of Talmai*). One of the apostles (Mt 10:3; Mk 3:18; Lk 6:14; Ac 1:13).

BARTIMAEUS (*son of Timai*, or *son of uncleanness*). A blind man (Mt 20:29-34; Mk 10:46-52; Lk 18:35-43).

BARUCH (*be blessed*).

1. An amanuensis of Jeremiah (Jer 32:12-16; 36:4-32; 43:3-6; 45:1-2).
2. Son of Zabbai (Ne 3:20; 10:6).
3. A descendant of Perez (Ne 11:5).

BARUCH, BOOK OF Jewish pseudepigraphal book found in the Apocrypha; alleging to be a treatise by Jeremiah's scribe Baruch to Jewish exiles in Babylon.

BARZILLAI (*[made] of iron*).

1. A friend of David (2Sa 17:27-29; 19:31-39; 1Ki 2:7; Ezr 2:61; Ne 7:63).
2. Father of Adriel (2Sa 21:8).
3. A priest (Ezr 2:61; Ne 7:63).

BASE FELLOWS Derogatory term "sons of Belial"; NIV "evil" or "wicked men" (Dt 13:13; 1Sa 2:12; 10:27; 25:17; 30:22; 1Ki 21:10; 2Ch 13:7). *See Wicked.*

BASEMATH (*fragrant*).

1. Wife of Esau (Ge 26:34).
2. Ishmael's daughter (Ge 36:3-4, 13, 17). Also called Mahalath (Ge 28:9).
3. Solomon's daughter (1Ki 4:15).

BASHAN (*fertile stoneless plain*). A region E of the Jordan and N of Arnon (Ge 14:5); modern Golan Heights. Og, king of (Jos 13:12). Allotted to the two and one half tribes, which had their possession E of the Jordan (Nu 32:33; Dt 3:10-14; Jos 12:4-6; 13:29-31; 17:1). Invaded and taken by Hazael, king of Syria (2Ki 10:32-33). Retaken by Jehoash (2Ki 13:25). Fertility and productivity of (Isa 33:9; Jer 50:19; Na 1:4). Forests of famous (Isa 2:13; Eze 27:6; Zec 11:2). Distinguished for its fine cattle (Dt 32:14; Ps 22:12; Eze 39:18; Am 4:1; Mic 7:14).

See Argob; Ashtoreth; Edrei; Jair.

BASHAN-HAVOTH-JAIR *See Havvoth Jair.*

BASHEMATH, BASMATH *See Basemath.*

BASIC PRINCIPLES OF THIS WORLD Legalism and human traditions opposed to faith in Christ (Gal 4:3; Col 2:8, 20). *See Commandments and Statutes, of Men; Legalism.*

BASIN Made of gold (1Ki 7:50; 1Ch 28:17; 2Ch 4:8, 22; Ezr 1:10; 8:27), bronze (Ex 27:3; 38:3; 1Ki 7:45).

See Bronze Basin; Bronze Sea; Tabernacle.

BASKET (Ge 40:16-17; Ex 29:3, 23, 32; Lev 8:2; Nu 6:15; Dt 26:2; 28:5, 17; 2Ki 10:7). Received the fragments after the miracles of the loaves (Mt 14:20; 15:37; 16:9-10). Paul let down from the wall in (Ac 9:25; 2Co 11:33).

BASON *See Basin.*

BASTARD *See Illegitimate.*

BAT Unclean for food (Lev 11:19; Dt 14:18; Isa 2:20).

BATH

1. Bathing for physical cleanliness or refreshment is not often mentioned in the Bible, where most references to bathing are to partial washing. Bathing in the Bible stands primarily for ritual acts—purification of ceremonial defilement (Ex 30:19-21; Lev 16:4, 24; Mk 7:3-4).
2. A Hebrew measure for liquids, containing about six gallons or twenty-two liters (1Ki 7:26, 38; Ezr 7:22; Isa 5:10; Eze 45:10-11, 14). *See Measure.*

BATH RABBIM (*daughter of a multitude*). A gate in the city of Heshbon (SS 7:4).

BATHSHEBA (*seventh daughter* or *daughter of an oath*). Wife of Uriah and later wife of David. Also spelled Bathshua (1Ch 3:5, ftn). Adultery of (2Sa 11:2-5). Solomon's mother (1Ki 1:11-31; 2:13-21; 1Ch 3:5).

BATHSHUA (possibly *daughter of opulence* BDB).

1. The daughter of Shua (Ge 38:2; 1Ch 2:3).
2. *See Bathsheba.*

BATTERING RAM (2Sa 20:15; Eze 4:2; 21:22).

BATTERY *See Assault and Battery.*

BATTLE Shouting in (Jdg 7:20; 1Sa 17:20). Priests in (2Ch 13:12). Prayer before: by Asa (2Ch 14:11), Jehoshaphat (2Ch 20:3-12). *See Armies; War.*

BATTLE OF LIFE

Ancient Heroes:

Joshua (Jos 11:23). Gideon (Jdg 7:14). Jonathan (1Sa 14:6). David (1Sa 17:45). Elisha (2Ki 6:17). Jehoshaphat (2Ch 20:20).

The Spiritual Conflict:

An inward battle (Ro 7:23). Spiritual weapons (2Co 10:4). Invisible foes (Eph 6:12). Young soldiers enlisted (1Ti 1:18). A fight of faith (1Ti 6:12). Demands entire consecration (2Ti 2:4).

The Soul's Enemies:

(Ps 86:14; Jer 2:34; 18:20; Eze 13:18; 22:25; Lk 22:31; Eph 6:12; 1Pe 5:8).

Weapons and Armor:

(1Sa 17:45; 2Co 10:4; Eph 6:17; Heb 4:12; Rev 12:11).

Divine Protection:

Promised to believers (2Ch 16:9; Ps 34:7; 91:4; 125:2; Zec 2:5; Lk 21:18).

Examples of:

(Ge 35:5; Ex 14:20; 2Ki 6:17; Ezr 8:31; Da 6:22; Rev 7:3).

The Victory:

(Isa 53:12; Mt 12:20; Jn 16:33; 1Co 15:24; Rev 3:21; 6:2; 17:14).

BATTLE-AX *See Club.*

BATTLEMENTS Parapets on the tops of walls (Isa 54:11).

BAVAI *See Binnui, 1.*

BAY TREE NIV "tree" (Ps 37:35). *See Tree.*

BAZLUTH One of the temple servants (Ezr 2:52; Ne 7:54).

BDELLIUM *See Aromatic Resin; Minerals of the Bible.*

BE ESHTARAH A Levitical city (Jos 21:27). Called Ashtaroth (1Ch 6:71).

BEACON NIV "flagstaff" (Isa 30:17). *See Ensign; Standard.*

BEALIAH (*Yahweh is Lord*). A Benjamite soldier who joined David at Ziklag (1Ch 12:5).

BEALOTH (*feminine plural of Baal "lord" lady*). A town in Judah (Jos 15:24).

BEAM Large long piece of timber for use in houses (1Ki 6:9-10; 7:3). Used for impaling (Ezr 6:11). Used in figurative sense by Jesus; NIV "plank" (Mt 7:3; Lk 6:41).

BEANS Part of a simple diet (2Sa 17:28; Eze 4:9).

BEAR, THE

Described as:

Voracious (Da 7:5). Cunning (La 3:10). Cruel (Am 5:19). Often attacks men (2Ki 2:24; Am 5:19). Attacks the flock in the presence of the shepherd (1Sa 17:34). Particularly fierce when deprived of its young (2Sa 17:8; Pr 17:12). Growls when annoyed (Isa 59:11). Miraculously killed by David (1Sa 17:36-37).

Illustrative of:

God in his judgments (La 3:10; Hos 13:8). Peace in the Messianic era (Isa 11:7). Wicked rulers (Pr 28:15). The kingdom of the Medes (Da 7:5). The kingdom of Antichrist (Rev 13:2).

A constellation (Job 9:9; 38:32).

BEARD Worn long by Aaron (Ps 133:2), Samson (Jdg 16:17), David (1Sa 21:13; Eze 5:1).

Shaven by Egyptians (Ge 41:14). Untrimmed in mourning (2Sa 19:24). Plucked (Ezr 9:3). Cut (Isa 7:20; 15:2; Jer 41:5; 48:37). Lepers required to shave (Lev 13:29-33; 14:9). Idolatrous practice of marring forbidden (Lev 19:27; 21:5). Beards of David's ambassadors half shaven by the king of the Amorites (2Sa 10:4).

BEAST

1. A mammal, not man, distinguished from birds and fish (Ge 1:29-30).
2. A wild, as distinguished from a domesticated animal (Lev 26:22; Isa 13:21-22).
3. Any of the inferior animals, as distinguished from man (Ps 147:9; Ecc 3:19).
4. Apocalyptic symbol of brute force—sensual, lawless, and God opposing (Da 7; Rev 13:11-18).

BEATEN WORK Of metals (Ex 25:18; 37:17, 22; Nu 8:4).

BEATING As a punishment (Ex 5:14; Dt 25:3; Mk 13:9; Ac 5:40; 16:22, 37; 18:17; 21:32; 22:19).

See Assault and Battery; Punishment; Scourging.

BEATITUDES (*divine favor*). A word not found in the English Bible, but meaning either:

1. The joys of heaven.
2. A declaration of blessedness. Beatitudes occur frequently in the OT (Ps 32:1-2; 41:1). The Gospels contain isolated beatitudes by Christ (Mt 11:6; 13:16; Jn 20:29), but the word is most commonly used of those in Mt 5:3-11 and Lk 6:20-22, which set forth the qualities that should characterize his disciples. *See Graces; Sermon on the Mount.*

BEAUTY Vanity of (Ps 39:11; Pr 6:25; 31:30; Isa 3:24; Eze 16:14; 28:17). Consume away (Ps 39:11; 49:14).

Instances of:

Sarah (Ge 12:11). Rebekah (Ge 24:16). Rachel (Ge 29:17). Joseph (Ge 39:6). Moses (Ex 2:2; Heb 11:23). David (1Sa 16:12, 18). Bathsheba (2Sa 11:2). Tamar (2Sa 13:1). Absalom (2Sa 14:25) Abishag (1Ki 1:4). Vashti (Est 1:11). Esther (Est 2:7).

Spiritual:

(1Ch 16:29; Ps 27:4; 29:2; 45:11; 90:17; 110:3; Eze 16:14; Zec 9:17).

BEAUTY AND BANDS NIV "Favor" and "Union"; staffs representing God's favor and the union of Israel and Judah; broken (Zec 11:7-14).

BEBAI (*child*). The name of three Jews whose descendants came from exile (Ezr 2:11; 8:11; 10:28; Ne 7:16; 10:15).

BECHER *See Beker, Bekerite.*

BECORATH (*firstborn*). Son of Aphiah (1Sa 9:1).

BED Made of: iron (Dt 3:11), ivory (Am 6:4), gold and silver (Est 1:6). Used at meals (Am 6:4). Exempt from execution for debt (Pr 22:27). Perfumed (Pr 7:17).

Figurative (Ps 139:8).

BEDAD (*solitary*). Father of Hadad (Ge 36:35).

BEDAN (*son of judgment*).

1. In 1Sa 12:11 *See Barak.*
2. Son of Ulam (1Ch 7:17).

BEDEIAH (*servant of Yahweh*). A son of Bani who had taken a foreign wife (Ezr 10:35).

BEE In Israel (Dt 1:44; Jdg 14:8; Ps 118:12; Isa 7:18). Figurative of the Assyrians summoned for judgment (Isa 7:18). *See Honey.*

BEELIADA (*the lord [Baal] knows*). Son of David (1Ch 14:7). Called Eliada (2Sa 5:16; 1Ch 3:8)

BEELZEBUB (*lord of the flies*). The prince of demons (Mt 10:25; 12:24, 27; Mk 3:22; Lk 11:15, 18-19). *See Baal-Zebub.*

BEELZEBUL *See Baal-Zebub.*

BEER (as a place name *cistern, well*).

1. A stopping place of the Israelites (Nu 21:16-18).
2. A town in the tribe of Judah (Jdg 9:21).
3. A fermented, intoxicating beverage; its abuse condemned (1Sa 1:15; Pr 20:1; 31:4-6; Isa 28:7; 56:12; Mic 2:11). *See Abuse, Substance Abuse; Drunkenness; Fermented Drink; Wine.*

BEER ELIM (*cistern, well of Elim*).

A city of Moab (Isa 15:8).

BEER LAHAI ROI (*well that belongs to the Living One seeing me*).

A well, probably near Kadesh, where the Lord appeared to Hagar (Ge 16:7, 14) and where Isaac lived for some time (Ge 24:62; 25:11).

BEERA (*cistern, well*). Son of Zophah (1Ch 7:37).

BEERAH (*cistern, well*). A Reubenite (1Ch 5:6).

BEERI (*[my] cistern, well*).

1. A Hittite (Ge 26:34). *See Anah.*
2. Father of Hosea (Hos 1:1).

BEEROTH, BEEROTHITE (*cisterns, wells*).

1. NIV "wells" (Dt 10:6). *See Bene Jaakan.*
2. A city of the Hivites (Jos 9:17; 18:25; 2Sa 4:2; Ezr 2:25; Ne 7:29).
3. Inhabitants of Beeroth (2Sa 4:2, 5, 9; 23:37).

BEERSHEBA (*the seventh well*).

1. The most southern city of Israel (Jdg 20:1). Named by Abraham, who dwelt there (Ge 21:31-33; 22:19). The dwelling place of Isaac (Ge 26:23). Jacob went out from, toward Haran (Ge 28:10). Sacrifices offered at, by Jacob when traveling to Egypt (Ge 46:1). In the inheritance of Judah (Jos 15:20, 28; 2Sa 24:7). Afterward assigned to Simeon (Jos 19:2, 9; 1Ch 4:28). Two sons of Samuel were judges at (1Sa 8:2). Became a seat of idolatrous worship (Am 5:5; 8:14).
2. Well of, belonged to Abraham and Isaac (Ge 21:25-26).
3. Wilderness of, Hagar miraculously sees a well in (Ge 21:14-19). An angel fed Elijah in (1Ki 19:5, 7).

BEETLE NIV "cricket" (Lev 11:22). *See Insects.*

BEGGAR Set among princes (1Sa 2:8). Not the seed of the righteous (Ps 37:25). The children of the wicked (Ps 109:10; Pr 20:4; Lk 16:3).

Instances of: Bartimaeus (Mk 10:46), Lazarus (Lk 16:20-22), the blind man (Jn 9:8), the lame man (Ac 3:2-5).

See Poor.

BEHEADING Execution by: John the Baptist (Mt 14:10; Mk 6:27), James (Ac 12:2), martyrs (Rev 20:4). *See Punishment.*

BEHEMOTH The word is a Hebrew plural and means "beast par excellence," referring to a large land animal, possibly the hippopotamus or the elephant (Job 40:15, ftn). Much of the language used to describe it in vv. 16-24 is highly poetic and hyperbolic (Job 40:15-24).

BEKA A half shekel (Ex 38:26). *See Measure.*

BEKER, BEKERITE (*young male camel*).

1. Son of Benjamin (Ge 46:21; 1Ch 7:6, 8).
2. A family of Ephraim (Nu 26:35). Called Bered (1Ch 7:20).

BEL (Babylonian deity *Bel*). A Babylonian god (Isa 46:1; Jer 50:2; 51:44).

BELA, BELAITE (*swallower, devourer*)

1. A city called also Zoar (Ge 14:2, 8).
2. King of Edom (Ge 36:32-33; 1Ch 1:43-44).
3. Son of Benjamin (Ge 46:21; Nu 26:38, 40; 1Ch 7:6-7; 8:1, 3).
4. Son of Azaz (1Ch 5:8).

BELIAL (*wicked, without use*). A word meaning "worthlessness," "wickedness," "lawlessness" translated as a proper noun in the KJV (Dt 13:13; Jdg 19:22; 1Sa 25:25). Personified (2Co 6:15). *See Base Fellows; Wicked.*

BELIEVER *See Righteous.*

BELIEVING *See Faith.*

BELLOWS Used with the refiner's furnace (Jer 6:29).

BELLS Attached to the hem of the priest's robe (Ex 28:33-34; 39:25-26). On horses (Zec 14:20).

BELLY Used figuratively for the seat of the affections (Job 15:2, 35; 20:20; Ps 44:25; Pr 18:20; 20:27, 30; Hab 3:16; Jn 7:38; Tit 1:12).

BELOVED DISCIPLE Probably the apostle John (Jn 13:23; 19:26; 20:2; 21:7, 20).

BELSHAZZAR (*Bel protect the king*). King of Babylon (Da 5:1-30).

BELT Made of leather (2Ki 1:8; Mt 3:4), linen (Jer 13:1), gold (Da 10:5). Warrior's belt, used to bear arms (2Sa 18:11; 20:8), Jonathan gives his to David (1Sa 18:4).

Figurative (Isa 11:5; Eph 6:14).

Symbolic (Jer 13:1-11; Ac 21:11; Rev 15:6). *See Dress; Sash.*

BELTESHAZZAR (*protect his life*). His Hebrew name was Daniel. He was taken as a captive to Babylon with Hananiah, Mishael, and Azariah, where each one was given a Babylonian name (Da 1:6-20; 2:17, 49; 3:12-30). Daniel was given the name Belteshazzar. *See Daniel.*

B

BEMA *See Judgment Seat.*

BEN Hebrew word meaning "son" or "descendant"; possibly the name of a Levite (1Ch 15:18, ftn).

BEN-ABINADAB (*son of Abinadab*). *See Abinadab.*

BEN-AMMI (*son of my people*). Son of one of Lot's daughters; progenitor of Ammonites (Ge 19:38).

BEN-DEKER (*son of Deker [pierces]*). The father of one of Solomon's suppliers (1Ki 4:9).

BEN-GEBER (*son of strength*). *See Geber.*

BEN-HADAD (*son of Hadad*).

1. King of Syria (1Ki 15:18-20; 2Ch 16:2-4).
2. A king of Syria, who reigned in the time of Ahab, son of Ben-Hadad I (1Ki 20; 2Ki 5-7; 8:7-15).
3. Son of Hazael and king of Syria (2Ki 13:3, 24-25; Am 1:4).

BEN-HAIL (*son of strength*). A prince of Judah (2Ch 17:7).

BEN-HANAN (*son of grace*). A son of Shimon (1Ch 4:20).

BEN-HESED (*loyal love*). Father of one of Solomon's officers (1Ki 4:10).

BEN HINNOM (*valley of the son [or sons] of Hinnom*). A valley on the W and SW of Jerusalem which formed part of the border between Judah and Benjamin (Jos 15:8; 18:16; Ne 11:30-31). It later became the place of pagan sacrifice (2Ch 28:3; 33:6; Jer 32:35). Josiah defiled it by making it the city dump, where fires were kept constantly burning to consume the refuse (2Ki 23:10). Jewish apocalyptic writers called it the entrance to hell, and it became a figure of hell itself. Jesus used the term *gehenna* (NIV "hell") in this sense (Mt 5:22; 18:9; 23:15).

See Hades; Hell; Hinnom, Valley of; Topheth, Tophet.

BEN-HUR (*son of Hur*). *See Hur, 4.*

BEN-ONI (*son of my sorrow*). Name given Benjamin by Rachel (Ge 35:18). *See Benjamin.*

BEN-ZOHETH (*son of Zoheth*). Son of Ishi (1Ch 4:20).

BENAIAH (*Yahweh has built*).

1. Son of Jehoiada, commander of the Kerethites and Pelethites (2Sa 8:18; 1Ki 1:38). A distinguished warrior (2Sa 23:20-23; 1Ch 11:22-25; 27:5-6). Loyal to Solomon (1Ki 1:8, 10; 4:4).
2. An Ephraimite and distinguished warrior (2Sa 23:30; 1Ch 11:31; 27:14).
3. A Levitical musician (1Ch 15:18, 20; 16:5).
4. A priest (1Ch 15:24; 16:6).
5. Son of Jeiel (2Ch 20:14).
6. A Levite in time of Hezekiah (2Ch 31:13).
7. A chief of the Simeonites (1Ch 4:36).
8. Son of Parosh (Ezr 10:25).
9. Son of Pahath-Moab (Ezr 10:30).
10. Son of Bani (Ezr 10:35).
11. Son of Nebo (Ezr 10:43).
12. Father of Pelatiah (Eze 11:1, 13).

BENCHES Of those selling doves in the temple (Mt 21:12; Mk 11:15).

BENE BERAK (*sons of Barak [lightning]*). A city of Dan (Jos 19:45).

BENE JAAKAN (possibly *son of Jaakan*). A tribe that gave its name to certain wells in the wilderness (Nu 33:31-32; Dt 10:6). *See Jaakan, Jaakanites.*

BENEDICTIONS (*pronouncements of blessing*). Divinely appointed (Dt 10:8; 21:5; Nu 6:23-26).

By God:

Upon creatures he had made (Ge 1:22), mankind (Ge 1:28), Noah (Ge 9:1-2).

Instances of:

By Melchizedek upon Abraham (Ge 14:19-20; Heb 7:7). By Bethuel's household upon Rebekah (Ge 24:60). By Isaac upon Jacob (Ge 27:23-29, 37; 28:1-4), Esau (Ge 27:39-40). By Jacob upon Pharaoh (Ge 47:7-10), Joseph's sons (Ge 48), his own sons (Ge 49). By Moses upon the tribes of Israel (Dt 33). By Aaron (Lev 9:22-23), half the tribes who stood on Mt. Gerizim (Dt 11:29-30; 27:11-13; Jos 8:33). By Joshua upon Caleb (Jos 14:13), the Reubenites and Gadites, and the half tribe of Manasseh (Jos 22:6-7). By Naomi upon Ruth and Orpah (Ru 1:8-9). By the elders and people upon Ruth (Ru 4:11-12). By Eli upon Ruth (1Sa 1:17), upon Elkanah (1Sa 2:20). By David upon the people (2Sa 6:18), upon Barzillai (2Sa 19:39). By Araunah upon David (2Sa 24:23). By Solomon upon the people (1Ki 8:14, 55-58; 2Ch 6:3).

By Simeon upon Jesus (Lk 2:34). By Jesus (Lk 24:50).

Levitical: (Nu 6:23-26).

Apostolic: (Ro 1:7; 15:5, 13, 33; 16:20; 1Co 1:3; 16:23; 2Co 1:2; 13:14; Gal 1:3; 6:16, 18; Eph 1:2; 6:23-24; Php 1:2; 4:23; Col 1:2; 1Th 1:1; 5:23; 2Th 1:2; 3:16, 18; 1Ti 1:2; 6:21; 2Ti 1:2; 4:22; Tit 3:15; Phm 3, 25; Heb 13:20-21, 25; 1Pe 1:2; 5:10-11, 14; 2Pe 1:2-4; 2Jn 3; Jude 2; Rev 22:21).

BENEFACTOR A title of honor bestowed by ancient states upon those famous for notable deeds of benevolence (Lk 22:25).

B

BENEFICENCE (*goodness, kindness*).

Commanded:
(Lev 25:35-43; Dt 15:7-15, 18; Pr 3:27-28; 25:21-22; Mt 5:42; 19:21; 25:35-45; Mk 10:21; Lk 3:11; Ro 15:27; 1Co 13:3; 16:1-3; 2Co 8:7-15, 24; 9:1-15; Gal 2:10; 1Ti 5:8, 16; Heb 13:16; Jas 2:15-16; 1Jn 3:17).

Results:
Blessed (Ps 41:1; Pr 22:9). Rewarded (Ps 112:9; Pr 11:25; 28:27; Isa 58:6-11; Eze 18:5-9; Mt 19:21; Mk 9:41; 10:21; Heb 6:10).

Examples:
(Mt 25:35-45; Ac 11:29-30; Ro 15:25-27; 2Co 8:1-15; Php 4:10-18; 1Ti 6:18).
See Alms; Liberality; Poor, Duty to; Rich, The; Riches.

Instances of:
The old man of Gibeah (Jdg 19:16-21). Boaz (Ru 2). The Jews returned from Exile (Ne 5:8-12; 8:10-11). Job (Job 29:11-17; 31:16-23). The Temanites (Isa 21:14). The good Samaritan (Lk 10:33-35). Zacchaeus (Lk 19:8). The first Christians (Ac 2:44-46; 4:32-37). Cornelius (Ac 10:2, 4). Onesiphorus (2Ti 1:16-18).
See Alms; Poor, Duties to.

BENEVOLENCE *See Alms; Beneficence; Charitableness; Liberality; Love.*

BENINU (*our son*). A Levite (Ne 10:13).

BENJAMIN, BENJAMITE(S) (*son of [the] right hand* BDB; *southerner* KB).
1. Son of Jacob by Rachel (Ge 35:18, 24; 46:19). Taken into Egypt (Ge 42-45). Prophecy concerning (Ge 49:27). Descendants of (Ge 46:21; Nu 26:38-41).
2. Tribe of. Census of, at Sinai (Nu 1:37), in the plain of Moab (Nu 26:41). Clans of (Nu 26:38-40; 1Ch 7:6-12; 8). Position of, in camp and march (Nu 2:18, 22). Moses' benediction upon (Dt 33:12). Allotment in the land of Canaan (Jos 18:11-28). Reallotment (Eze 48:23). Did not exterminate the Jebusites (Jdg 1:21). Join Deborah in the war against Sisera (Jdg 5:14). Territory of, invaded by the Ammonites (Jdg 10:9). Did not avenge the crime of the Gibeonites against the Levite's concubine, the war that followed (Jdg 19-20). Saul, the first king of Israel, from (1Sa 9:1, 17; 10:20-21). Its rank in the time of Samuel (1Sa 9:21). Jerusalem within the territory of (Jer 6:1). A company of, joins David at Ziklag (1Ch 12:1-2, 16). Not enrolled by Joab when he took a census of the military forces of Israel (1Ch 21:6). Loyal to Ish-Bosheth, the son of Saul (2Sa 2:9, 15, 31; 1Ch 12:29). Subsequently joins David (2Sa 3:19; 19:16-17). Loyal to Rehoboam (1Ki 12:21; 2Ch 11:1). Military forces of, in the reign of Asa (2Ch 14:8), of Jehoshaphat (2Ch 17:17). Skill in archery and as slingers of stones (Jdg 3:15; 20:16; 1Ch 8:40; 12:2). Return to Israel from the Exile in Babylon (Ezr 1:5). Saints of, seen in John's vision (Rev 7:8). Paul, of the tribe of (Ro 11:1; Php 3:5).
See Israel.
3. Grandson of Benjamin (1Ch 7:10).
4. A son of Harim (Ezr 10:32). Probably identical with the man mentioned in Ne 3:23.
5. A Jew who assisted in purifying the wall of Jerusalem (Ne 12:34).
6. A gate of Jerusalem (Jer 20:2; 37:13; 38:7; Zec 14:10).

BENO (*his son*). A descendant of Merari (1Ch 24:26-27).

BENOTH *See Succoth Benoth.*

BEON A place E of Jordan, probably the same as Baal Meon (Nu 32:3, 38). *See Baal Meon.*

BEOR (perhaps *a burning*).
1. Father of Bela (Ge 36:32; 1Ch 1:43).
2. Father of Balaam (Nu 22:5; 24:3, 15; 31:8; Dt 23:4; Jos 13:22; 24:9; Mic 6:5; 2Pe 2:15).

BERA (*gift*). King of Sodom, defeated by Kedorlaomer in the days of Abraham (Ge 14:2, 8).

BERACAH (*blessing*).
1. An Israelite, who joined David at Ziklag (1Ch 12:3).
2. A valley in the S of Judah, where Jehoshaphat assembled the Israelites to offer praise to God for victory over the Ammonites and Moabites (2Ch 20:26). Between Bethlehem and Hebron.

BERACHIAH, BERECHIAH *See Berekiah.*

BERAIAH (*Yahweh creates*). Son of Shimei (1Ch 8:21).

BERAK *See Bene Berak.*

BEREA, BEREANS A city in the S of Macedonia (Ac 17:10, 13; 20:4). Its inhabitants are important as an example of comparing new teaching to the received Scriptures.

BEREAVEMENT From God (Hos 9:12). Mourning in, forbidden to Aaron, on account of his son's wickedness (Lev 10:6). To Ezekiel, for his wife (Eze 24:16-18).

Instances of:
Abraham, of Sarah (Ge 23:2). Jacob, of Joseph (Ge 37:34-35). Joseph, of his father (Ge 50:1, 4). The Egyptians, of their firstborn (Ex 12:29-33). Naomi, of her husband (Ru 1:3, 5, 20-21). David, of his child by Bathsheba (2Sa 12:15-23), of Absalom (2Sa 18:33; 19:4).

Resignation in:
Job (Job 1:18-21). David (2Sa 12:22, 30). Solomon (Ecc 7:2-4). Christians (1Th 4:13-18).
See Affliction, Consolation Under, Prayer Under; Resignation.

BERED (possibly *freezing rain*).
1. A town in the S of Israel (Ge 16:14).
2. A son of Shuthelah (1Ch 7:20). Probably the same as Beker (Nu 26:35).

BEREKIAH (*Yahweh blesses*).
1. Father of Asaph (1Ch 6:39; 15:17, 23).
2. A warrior of Ephraim (2Ch 28:12).
3. A brother of Zerubbabel (1Ch 3:20).
4. Son of Asa (1Ch 9:16).
5. Son of Iddo, father of Zechariah (Zec 1:1, 7; Mt 23:35).
6. Son of Meshullam (Ne 3:4, 30; 6:18).

BERI (*wisdom*). Son of Zophah (1Ch 7:36).

BERIAH, BERIITE (*prominent, excellent*).
1. Son of Asher (Ge 46:17; 1Ch 7:30) and his clan (Nu 26:44-45).
2. Son of Ephraim (1Ch 7:20-23).
3. A Benjamite (1Ch 8:13).
4. Son of Shimei (1Ch 23:10-11).

BERITES (*choice young men*). Followed Sheba in his rebellion against David (2Sa 20:14).

BERITH *See Baal-Berith.*

BERNICE (*victorious*). Daughter of Agrippa (Ac 25:13, 23; 26:30).

BERODACH-BALADAN *See Merodach-Baladan.*

BEROTHAH (*well*). Part of the northern boundary of Canaan (Eze 47:16).

BEROTHAI, BEROTHITE A city of Zobah (2Sa 8:8) and its inhabitants (1Ch 11:39).

BERYL (*yellow jasper*).
1. Set in the priestly breastplate (Ex 28:17; 39:10).
2. A precious stone (Eze 28:13).
3. John saw, in the foundation of the new Jerusalem (Rev 21:20).
See Minerals of the Bible, 1; Stones.

BESAI (*in secret council of Yahweh* KB). One of the temple servants (Ezr 2:49; Ne 7:52).

BESODEIAH (*in secret council of Yahweh*). Father of Meshullam (Ne 3:6).

BESOM *See Broom.*

BESOR A brook near Gaza (1Sa 30:9-10, 21).

BESTIALITY (*Sexual relations between a human and an animal*). (Ex 22:19; Lev 18:23; 20:16).

BETAH *See Tebah, 2.*

BETEN (*womb, bowels*). A city of Asher (Jos 19:25).

BETH The most common OT word for house, family or dynasty. Used in the more than fifty place names that follow.

BETH ANATH (*house of Anath*). A fortified city of Naphtali (Jos 19:38; Jdg 1:33).

BETH ANOTH (*house of Anath [plural]*). A city in Judah (Jos 15:59).

BETH ARABAH (*house of Arabah [desert plain]*). A city in the valley of the Dead Sea (Jos 15:6, 61; 18:22). Called Arabah (Jos 18:18).

BETH-ARAM *See Beth Haram.*

BETH ARBEL (*house of Arbel*). A city devastated by Shalman (Hos 10:14).

BETH ASHBEA (*house of Ashbea*). A descendant of Shelah (1Ch 4:21).

BETH AVEN (*house of idolatry*). A place on the mountains of Benjamin (Jos 7:2; 18:12; 1Sa 13:5; 14:23; Hos 4:15; 5:8; 10:5).

BETH AZMAVETH (*strong of death* ISBE; *house of Azmaveth [camel fodder, a plant of the plumose family]* KB). A town of Benjamin (Ne 7:28). Called Azmaveth (Ne 12:29; Ezr 2:24).

BETH BAAL MEON (*house of Baal Meon*). A place in the tribe of Reuben (Jos 13:17).
Called Baal Meon (Nu 32:38; Eze 25:9), Beon (Nu 32:3), Beth Meon (Jer 48:23).
Subdued by the Israelites (Nu 32:3-4). Assigned to the Reubenites (Jos 13:17).

BETH BARAH (*house of Barah [the river ford]*). A city E of the Jordan (Jdg 7:24).

BETH BIRI (*house of Biri* or *den of a lioness*). A town of Simeon S of Judah (1Ch 4:31). *See Beth Lebaoth.*

BETH CAR (*site [house] of a lamb*). A place W of Mizpah (1Sa 7:11).

BETH DAGON (*temple [house] of Dagon*).
1. A city of Judah (Jos 15:41).
2. A city of Asher (Jos 19:27).

BETH DIBLATHAIM (*house of Diblathaim*). A city of Moab (Jer 48:22). *See Almon Diblathaim.*

BETH EDEN (*house of Eden; garden place*). Probably another name for Damascus (Am 1:5). *See Damascus.*

BETH EKED Forty-two relatives of Ahaziah slaughtered there (2Ki 10:12-14).

BETH EMEK (*house of Emek* or *site of the valley*). A city of Asher (Jos 19:27).

BETH EZEL (*house of Ezel* or *site nearby*). A town of Judah (Mic 1:11).

BETH GADER (*house of Gader* or *site of a stone hedge*). A place in Judah (1Ch 2:51). Probably identical with Geder (Jos 12:13); and with Gedor (Jos 15:58).

BETH GAMUL (*house of recompense*). A city of Moab (Jer 48:23).

BETH GILGAL Perhaps an alternate name for Gilgal (Ne 12:29). *See Gilgal.*

BETH-HACCEREM *See Beth Hakkerem.*

BETH HAGGAN (*house of Haggan* or *site of the garden*). A garden house (2Ki 9:27). Probably identical with En Gannim (Jos 19:21).

BETH HAKKEREM (*house of Hakkerem* or *site of the vineyard*). A mountain in Judah (Ne 3:14; Jer 6:1).

BETH HARAM A fortified city of Gad, E of the Jordan (Jos 13:27).

BETH HARAN (*house of the mountaineer*). A fortified city E of Jordan (Nu 32:36).

BETH HOGLAH (*house of Hoglah* or *site of the partridge*). A place on the border of Judah (Jos 15:6; 18:19, 21).

BETH HORON (*house of Horon* or *site of a ravine*). Two ancient cities of Canaan, near which Joshua defeated the Amorites (Jos 10:10-11; 16:3, 5; 18:13-14; 1Sa 13:18; 1Ch 7:24). Solomon builds (1Ki 9:17; 2Ch 8:5). Taken from Judah by the ten tribes (2Ch 25:13).

BETH JESHIMOTH (*house of Jeshimoth* or *site of desolation*). A place in the plains of Moab, the S limit of Israel's encampment (Nu 33:49). It was assigned to the Reubenites (Jos 13:20), but was later in Moabite possession (Eze 25:9). Modern Tell el-Azeimeh, about twelve miles SE of Jericho (Jos 12:3).

BETH JOAB *See Atroth Beth Joab.*

BETH LEBAOTH (*house of Lebaoth* or *den of the lioness*). A town of Simeon in the S part of Judah (Jos 19:6). Called Lebaoth (Jos 15:32), and the same as Beth Biri (1Ch 4:31).

BETH-LEHEM-JUDAH *See Bethlehem; Judah.*

BETH-MAACHAH (*house of Maacah*). *See Abel Beth Maacah.*

BETH MARCABOTH (*site [house] of Marcaboth [chariots]*). A town of Simeon (Jos 19:5; 1Ch 4:31). Probably identical with Madmannah, which may have been its older name (Jos 15:31).

BETH MEON (*house of habitation*). A city of Moab (Jer 48:23); the same as Beth Baal Meon (Jos 13:17).

BETH MILLO (*house of Millo* or *site of earth fill*).
1. Beth Millo probably refers to the earthen fill used to erect a platform on which walls and other large structures were built (Jdg 9:6, 20). It may be identical to the "stronghold" of v. 46 (Jdg 9:46).
2. A name given to part of the citadel of Jerusalem, NIV "supporting terraces" (2Sa 5:9, ftn; 1Ch 11:8, ftn). King Solomon raised a levy to repair (1Ki 9:15, 24, ftn; 11:27, ftn). King Joash murdered at (2Ki 12:20). Repaired by King Hezekiah (2Ch 32:5, ftn).

BETH NIMRAH (*house of Nimrah [spotted leopard]* BDB; *house of a basin of clear, limpid water* KB). A fortified city E of Jordan (Nu 32:36; Jos 13:27).

BETH OPHRAH (*house of Ophrah* or *house of dust*). A city found in the Shephelah (Mic 1:10, ftn).

BETH-PALET *See Beth Pelet.*

BETH PAZZEZ A city in Issachar (Jos 19:21).

BETH PELET (*house of Pelet [escape]*). A city in Judah (Jos 15:27; Ne 11:26).

BETH PEOR (*house of Peor*). A place in the tribe of Reuben (Dt 3:29; 4:46; 34:6). Near the burial place of Moses (Jos 13:20).

BETH RAPHA (*house of Rapha [healing]*). Son of Eshton (1Ch 4:12).

BETH REHOB (*house of Rehob [main street, market]*). A place in Dan (Jdg 18:28; 2Sa 10:6). Called Rehob.

BETH SHAN (*site [house] of Shan [repose]*). A city of Manasseh (Jos 17:11; 1Ch 7:29). Not subdued (Jdg 1:27). Bodies of Saul and his sons exposed in (1Sa 31:10, 12). District of, under tribute to Solomon's governor (1Ki 4:12).

BETH-SHEAN *See Beth Shan.*

BETH SHEMESH (*temple [house] of Shemesh [pagan sun god]*).
1. A priestly city of Dan (Jos 21:16; 1Sa 6:15; 1Ch 6:59). On the northern border of Judah (Jos 15:10; 1Sa 6:9, 12). In later times transferred to Judah (2Ki 14:11). Mentioned in Solomon's governed districts (1Ki 4:9). Amaziah taken prisoner at (2Ki 14:11-13; 2Ch 25:21-23). Retaken by the Philistines (2Ch 28:18). Called Ir Shemesh (Jos 19:41).
2. A city near Jerusalem (Jos 19:22).

3. A fortified city of Naphtali (Jos 19:38; Jdg 1:33).
4. Literally "Beth Shemesh in Egypt," with the qualifying phrase being used to distinguish it from "Beth Shemesh in Judah" (2Ki 14:11). Called On (in Hebrew) in Egypt; also known as Heliopolis, about five miles NE of Cairo, where there was a temple of Ra (Jer 43:13, ftn).

BETH SHITTAH (*house of Shittah [acacias]*). A place near the Jordan (Jdg 7:22).

BETH TAPPUAH (*house of Tappuah [apricot;apple tree]*). A town of Judah (Jos 15:53).

BETH TOGARMAH A city in E Asia Minor (Eze 27:14; 38:6). *See Togarmah.*

BETH ZUR (*cliff house*). A town in Judah (Jos 15:58; 1Ch 2:45; 2Ch 11:7; Ne 3:16).

BETHANY (*house of Ananiah* or *poor ones* or *unripe figs*). A village on the eastern slope of the Mount of Olives (Jn 11:18). Mary, Martha, and Lazarus dwell at (Lk 10:38-41). Lazarus dies and is raised to life at (Jn 11). Jesus attends a feast in (Mt 26:6-13; Jn 12:1-9). The colt on which Jesus made his triumphal entry into Jerusalem obtained at (Mk 11:1-11). Jesus stays at (Mt 21:17; Mk 11:11-12, 19).

BETHEL (*temple [house] of God [El]*).
1. A city N of Jerusalem. The ancient city next to, and finally embraced in, was called Luz (Jos 18:13; Jdg 1:23-26). Abraham establishes an altar at (Ge 12:8; 13:3-4). The place where Jacob saw the vision of the stairway (Ge 28:10-22; 31:13; Hos 12:4), and builds an altar at (Ge 35:1-15). Deborah dies at (Ge 35:8). Conquered by Joshua (Jos 8:17, w 12:16), by the house of Joseph (Jdg 1:22-26). Allotted to Benjamin (Jos 18:13, 22). Court of justice held at, by Deborah (Jdg 4:5), by Samuel (1Sa 7:16).
Tabernacle at, and called House of God (Jdg 20:18, 31; 21:2). Jeroboam institutes idolatrous worship at (1Ki 12:25-33; 2Ki 10:29). Idolatry at (Jer 48:13; Am 4:4). Shalmaneser sends a priest to (2Ki 17:27-28). Prophecies against the idolatrous altars at (1Ki 13:1-6, 32; 2Ki 23:4, 15-20; Am 3:14). The company of prophets at (2Ki 2:3). Children of, mock Elisha (2Ki 2:23-24). People of, return from Babylon (Ezr 2:28; Ne 7:32). Prophecies against (Am 5:5).
2. A city in the S of Judah (1Sa 30:27).
3. A mountain (1Sa 13:2).

BETHER (perhaps *house [shrine] of the mountain*). Mountains of (SS 2:17, ftn, text "rugged hills").

BETHESDA (*site [house] of mercy*). A spring-fed pool in Jerusalem (Jn 5:1-16) into which the sick went for healing.

BETHHANAN *See Elon Bethhanan.*

BETHLEHEM (*house of bread;* possibly *temple [house] of Lakhmu [pagan deity]*).
1. A city SW of Jerusalem (Jdg 17:7; 19:18). Called Ephrathah and Ephrath (Ge 48:7; Ps 132:6; Mic 5:2), and Bethlehem in Judah (Jdg 17:7-9; 19:1, 18; Ru 1:1; 1Sa 17:12). Rachel dies and is buried at (Ge 35:16, 19; 48:7). The city of Boaz (Ru 1:1, 19; 2:4; 4). Taken and held by the Philistines (2Sa 23:14-16). Jeroboam converts it into a military stronghold (2Ch 11:6). The city of Joseph (Mt 2:5-6; Lk 2:4). Birthplace of Jesus (Mic 5:2; Mt 2; Lk 2:4, 15). Herod slays the children of (Mt 2:16-18).
2. A town of Zebulun, six miles W of Nazareth (Jos 19:15). Israel judged at (Jdg 12:10).

BETHPHAGE (*house of unripe figs*). A village on the Mount of Olives (Mt 21:1; Mk 11:1; Lk 19:29).

BETHSAIDA (*house of fishing*).
1. A city of Galilee. The city of Philip, Andrew, and Peter (Jn 1:44; 12:21). Jesus visits (Mk 6:45), cures a blind man in (Mk 8:22), prophesies against (Mt 11:21; Lk 10:13).
2. Secluded area E of the sea of Galilee; Jesus feeds five thousand people in (Mt 14:13; Mk 6:32, Lk 9:10).

BETHUEL (*man of God [El]*). Son of Nahor, father of Rebekah (Ge 22:22-23; 24:15, 24; 25:20; 28:2, 5).

BETHUL A city of Simeon (Jos 19:4). Called Kesil (Jos 15:30) and Bethuel (1Ch 4:30).

BETONIM (*pistachio nuts*). A town of Gad (Jos 13:26).

BETRAYAL Of Jesus (Mt 26:14-16, 45-50; Mk 14:10-11; Lk 22:3-6; 22:47-48; Jn 13:21). Of others, foretold (Mt 20:18; 24:10). Of David, by Doeg (1Sa 22:9-10, w 1Sa 21:1-10). Of cities (Jdg 1:24-25). *See Confidence, Betrayed.*

BETROTHAL Of Jacob (Ge 29:18-30). Exempts from military duty (Dt 20:7). A quasi-marriage (Mt 1:18; Lk 1:27).
Figurative (Isa 62:4; Hos 2:19-20; 2Co 11:2).
See Marriage.

BETTING By Samson (Jdg 14:12-19).

BEULAH (*married*). Poetic name for restored Israel (Isa 62:4).

BEZAI
1. Head of a Jewish family that returned from Babylon (Ezr 2:17; Ne 7:23).
2. A family that sealed the covenant with Nehemiah (Ne 10:18).

BEZALEL (*in the shadow of God [El]*).
1. A divinely inspired architect and master craftsman who built the tabernacle (Ex 31:2; 35:30-35; 36:1; 37:1; 38:1-7, 22).
2. Son of Pahath-Moab (Ezr 10:30).

BEZEK (*scattering, sowing*).
1. Residence of Adoni-Bezek (Jdg 1:5). *See Adoni-Bezek.*
2. A rendezvous of Israel under Saul (1Sa 11:8).

BEZER (*[metallic] ore*, or *place of refuge*).
1. A city of refuge, E of the Jordan (Dt 4:43; Jos 20:8; 21:36; 1Ch 6:78).
2. Son of Zophah (1Ch 7:37).

BIBLE, THE General references to (2Sa 22:31; Ps 12:6; 119:9, 50; 147:15; Mk 12:24; Lk 8:11; Eph 6:17). The Book of the ages (Ps 119:89; Mt 5:18; 24:35; 1Pe 1:25). Food for the soul (Dt 8:3; Job 23:12; Ps 119:103; Jer 15:16; 1Pe 2:2). Divinely inspired (Jer 36:2; Eze 1:3; Ac 1:16; 2Ti 3:16; 2Pe 1:21; Rev 14:13). Precepts written in the heart (Dt 6:6; 11:18; Ps 119:11; Lk 2:51; Ro 10:8; Col 3:16). Furnishes a light (Ps 19:8; 119:105, 130; Pr 6:23; 2Pe 1:19). Loved by the believers (Ps 119:47, 72, 82, 97, 140; Jer 15:16).
Mighty in its influence: a devouring flame (Jer 5:14), a crushing hammer (Jer 23:29), a life-giving force (Eze 37:7), a saving power (Ro 1:16), a penetrating sword (Eph 6:17; Heb 4:12).
Blessings to those who reverence it (Jos 1:8; Ps 19:11; Mt 7:24; Lk 11:28; Jn 5:24; 8:31; Rev 1:3). Purifies the life (Ps 119:9; Jn 15:3; 17:17; Eph 5:26; 1Pe 1:22). Written with a purpose (Jn 20:31; Ro 15:4; 1Co 10:11; 1Jn 5:13). The standard of faith (Pr 29:18; Isa 8:20; Jn 12:48; Gal 1:8; 1Th 2:13). Its words sacred (Dt 4:2; 12:32; Pr 30:6; Rev 22:19). The study of it commanded (Dt 17:19; Isa 34:16; Jn 5:39; Ac 17:11; Ro 15:4). Contains seed for the sower (Ps 126:6; Mk 4:14-15; 2Co 9:10). Absolutely trustworthy (1Ki 8:56; Ps 111:7; Eze 12:25; Mt 5:18; Lk 21:33). Profitable for instruction (Dt 4:10; 11:19; 2Ch 17:9; Ne 8:13; Isa 2:3). Ignorance of, dangerous (Mt 22:29; Jn 20:9; Ac 13:27; 2Co 3:15).
See Word of God.

BICRI (*first born*). Father of Sheba (2Sa 20:1).

BIDKAR (*son of Deker [piercing]*). Jehu's captain (2Ki 9:25).

BIER (2Sa 3:31; Lk 7:14).

BIGAMY *See Polygamy.*

BIGOTRY

Condemned:
Exhibited: In self-righteousness (Isa 65:5; Mk 2:16; Lk 15:2; 18:9-14). In intolerance (Lk 9:49-50; Ac 18:12-13).
Rebuked (Ac 10:28, 45). Paul's argument against (Ro 3:1-23; 4:1-25).

Instances of:
Joshua (Nu 11:27-29). The Jews with, the Samaritans (Jn 4:9, 27), Jesus (Lk 4:28; 7:39; 11:38-39; 15:22; 19:5-7; Jn 5:18), the blind man (Jn 9:29-34), Paul (Ac 21:28-29; 22:22). John (Mk 9:38-40; Lk 9:49-50). James and John (Lk 9:51-56). The early Christians (Ac 10:45; 11:2-3; 15:1-10, 24; Gal 2:3-5). Paul (Ac 9:1-2; 22:3-4; 26:9-11; Gal 1:13-14; Php 3:6).
See Intolerance, Religious; Persecution, Respect of Persons; Uncharitableness.

BIGTHA (*gift of God*). Eunuch and servant of Xerxes (Est 1:10).

BIGTHANA (*gift of God*). A conspiring Persian officer (Est 2:21-23: 6:2).

BIGVAI (*fortunate*).
1. Man who returned from the Captivity (Ezr 2:2; Ne 7:19).
2. Ancestor of family that returned from the Captivity (Ezr 2:14; Ne 7:19).
3. Probably the same as 2 above (Ezr 8:14).

BILDAD (*Bel has loved*). One of Job's friends (Job 2:11; 8:1; 18:1; 25:1).

BILEAM (*[a gift] brought to the people*). A town of Manasseh (1Ch 6:70). Called Ibleam (Jos 17:11) and Gath Rimmon (Jos 21:25).

BILGAH (*gleam, smile*).
1. One of the chiefs of the priestly courses in the temple (1Ch 24:14).
2. A priest (Ne 12:5, 18), perhaps identical with Bilgai (Ne 10:8).

BILGAI (*gleam, smile*). A priest (Ne 10:8).

BILHAH (perhaps *simplicity*, or *modesty*, or *to be without concern*).
1. Rachel's servant, bears children by Jacob (Ge 29:29; 30:3-4; 37:2). Mother of Dan and Naphtali (Ge 30:1-8; 35:25; 46:23, 25). Reuben's incest with (Ge 35:22; 49:4).
2. A place in the land of Simeon (1Ch 4:29). Called Balah (Jos 19:3) and Baalah (Jos 15:29).

BILHAN (*foolish*).
1. A Horite chief (Ge 36:27; 1Ch 1:42).
2. A Benjamite (1Ch 7:10).

BILL OF DIVORCE *See Divorce.*

BILSHAN (*their Bel [lord]*). A Jew of the Captivity (Ezr 2:2; Ne 7:7).

BIMHAL (*son of circumcision*). Son of Japhlet (1Ch 7:33).

BINDING AND LOOSING The carrying of a key or keys was a symbol of the delegated power of opening and closing (Mt 16:19; Rev 1:18). *See Key.*
The apostles were given power to bind and to loose (Mt 16:19; 18:18). Peter loosed the feet of the lame man at the temple gate (Ac 3:1-10), and Paul bound the sight of Elymas (Ac 13:8-11). Peter was present when the Holy Spirit was poured out on the Jews (Ac 2), Samaritans (Ac 8:14-17), and Gentiles (Ac 10:34-48).

BINEA A descendant of King Saul (1Ch 8:37; 9:43).

BINNUI (*a son*).
1. Man who helped rebuild walls of Jerusalem (Ne 3:18, ftn).
2. A Jew of the Captivity (Ne 7:15). Called Bani (Ezr 2:10).
3. A Levite of the Captivity (Ne 3:24; 12:8; 10:9).
4. Father of Noadiah (Ezr 8:33).
5. Descendant of Pahath-Moab who married a foreign wife (Ezr 10:30).
6. KJV; NIV "descendants of" (Ezr 10:38).

BIRDS Creation of, on the fifth creative day (Ge 1:20-30). Mankind's rule over (Ge 1:26, 28; 9:2-3; Ps 8:5-8; Jer 27:6; Da 2:38; Jas 3:7). Given for food (Ge 9:2-3; Dt 14:11-20). What species were unclean (Lev 11:13-20; Dt 14:12-19).
Used for sacrifice. *See Dove; Pigeon.* Divine care of (Job 38:41; Ps 147:9; Mt 10:29; Lk 12:6, 24). Songs of, at the break of day (Ps 104:12; Ecc 12:4; SS 2:12). Domesticated (Job 41:5; Jas 3:7). Solomon's proverbs of (1Ki 4:33). Nests of (Ps 104:17; Mt 8:20; 13:32). Instincts of (Pr 1:17). Habits of (Job 39:13-18, 26-30). Migrate (Jer 8:7).
Mosaic law protected the mother from being taken with the young (Dt 22:6-7). Cages of (Jer 5:27; Rev 18:2). *See Snare.*
Figurative (Isa 16:2; 46:11; Jer 12:9; Eze 39:4).
Symbolic (Da 7:6).
See Cormorant; Dove; Eagle; Falcon; Gull; Hawk; Hen, 2; Heron; Hoopoe; Kite; Osprey; Ostrich; Owl; Partridge; Pigeon; Quail; Raven; Red Kite; Screech Owl; Sparrow; Stork; Swallow; Swift; Thrush; Vulture; White Owl.

BIRSHA (*disagreeable in taste*). A king of Gomorrah (Ge 14:2-10).

BIRTH Pangs in giving (Ps 48:6; Isa 13:8; 21:3; Jer 4:31; 6:24; 30:6; 31:8). Giving, ordained to be in sorrow (Ge 3:16).
Famous births: Cain (Ge 4:1), Abel (Ge 4:2), Noah (Ge 5:28-29), Isaac (Ge 21:1-5), Esau and Jacob (Ge 25:24-26), the children of Jacob (Ge 29:31-30:24; 35:16-18), Moses (Ex 2:1-4), John the Baptist (Lk 1:5-25, 57), Jesus (Mt 1:18-25; Lk 1:26-38; 2:1-20).
See Abortion; Children.

BIRTHDAY Celebrated by feasts (Ge 40:20; Mt 14:6). Cursed (Job 3; Jer 20:14, 18).

BIRTHRIGHT

Described:
Belonged to the firstborn (Dt 21:15-16). Entitled the firstborn to a double portion of inheritance (Dt 21:15-17), a royal succession (2Ch 21:3). An honorable title (Ex 4:22; Ps 89:27; Jer 31:9; Ro 8:29; Col 1:15; Heb 1:6; 12:23; Rev 1:5).

Lost by Firstborn:
Sold by Esau (Ge 25:29-34; 27:36, w 25:33; Heb 12:16; Ro 9:12-13). Forfeited by Reuben (1Ch 5:1-2). Set aside: that of Manasseh (Ge 48:15-20), Adonijah (1Ki 2:15), Hosah's son (1Ch 26:10).
See Firstborn.

BIRZAITH (*well of olive oil*). A descendant of Asher (1Ch 7:31).

BISHLAM (*son of Shalom [peace]*). A Samaritan who obstructed the rebuilding of the temple at Jerusalem (Ezr 4:7-24).

BISHOP The same as elder or overseer (Ac 20:28; Php 1:1; 1Ti 3:1; Tit 1:7, ftns). *See Elders; Overseer.*

BIT Part of a bridle (Ps 32:9; Jas 3:3).

BITHIAH (possibly *worshiper of Yahweh* BDB; *[female pagan god] queen* KB). Daughter of Pharaoh; wife of Mered of Judah (1Ch 4:18).

BITHRON (*gully*). A district bordering on the Jordan (2Sa 2:29).

BITHYNIA A Roman province in Asia Minor (Ac 16:7; 1Pe 1:1).

BITTER HERBS Eaten symbolically with the Passover (Ex 12:8; Nu 9:11).

BITTER WATER At Marah (Ex 15:23). A ceremonial water used by the priest to determine marital faithfulness (Nu 5:18-27).

BITTERN *See Owl.*

BITTERNESS A poisonous and bitter plant (Hos 10:4; Am 6:12). *See Gall, 3.*
Of spirit (Dt 32:32; Jer 4:18; Ac 8:23; Ro 3:14; Eph 4:31; Heb 12:5; Jas 3:14).

BITUMEN *See Tar.*

BIZIOTHIAH (*contempt of Yahweh*). A town in Judah (Jos 15:28). Baalath Beer (Jos 19:8), and Balah (Jos 19:3).

BIZTHA (perhaps *eunuch*, or *bound*). A eunuch and servant of the Persian king Xerxes (Est 1:10).

BLACK VULTURE An unclean bird, not to be eaten under the law (Lev 11:13; Dt 14:13). *See Vulture.*

BLACKNESS Overcoming the day (Job 3:5). On the day of the LORD (Joel 2:6; Zep 1:15). God turning to dawn (Am 5:8).
See Colors, Figurative and Symbolic.

BLACKSMITH *See Smith.*

BLAIN *See Boil.*

BLASPHEMY (*speak against, revile*).

Described:
Reproaching God (2Ki 19:22; 2Ch 32:19; Ps 73:9, 11; 74:18; 139:20; Pr 30:9; Isa 5:19; 8:21-22; 37:23; 45:9; 52:5; Eze

35:12-13; Da 7:25; Mt 10:25). Defying God (Isa 29:15-16; 36:15-21; 37:10; Eze 8:12; 9:9; Mal 3:13-14). Denying God's word (Jer 17:15). Speaking lies against God (Hos 7:13). Attributing ignorance to God (Ps 10:11, 13; Isa 40:27). Exalting oneself above God (Da 11:36-37; 2Th 2:4). Calling Jesus accursed (1Co 12:3; Jas 2:7). Against the Holy Spirit (Mt 12:31-32; Mk 3:29-30; Lk 12:10). Occasioned by sins of believers (2Sa 12:14; Ro 2:24).

Foretold by Peter (2Pe 3:3-4). Foretold by John (Rev 13:1, 5-6; 16:9, 11, 21; 17:3).

Forbidden (Ex 20:7; 22:28; Lev 19:12; 22:32; Jas 3:10; 5:12).

Punishment for (Lev 24:10-16; Isa 65:7; Heb 10:29).

Instances of:

The depraved son of Shelomith, who, in a fight with an Israelite, cursed God (Lev 24:10-16). Of the Israelites, in grumbling against God (Nu 21:5-6). Infidels who used the adultery of David as an occasion to blaspheme (2Sa 12:14). Shimei, in his malice toward David (2Sa 16:5). One of Sennacherib's field commanders, in the siege of Jerusalem (2Ki 18:22; 19; Isa 36:15-20; 37:10-33). Job's wife, when she exhorted Job to curse God and die (Job 2:9). Israel (Eze 20:27-28). Peter, when accused of being a disciple of Jesus (Mt 26:74; Mk 14:71). The revilers of Jesus, when He was crucified (Mt 27:40-44, 63). The early Christians, persecuted by Saul of Tarsus compelled to blaspheme the name of Jesus (Ac 26:11; 1Ti 1:13). Two disciples, Hymenaeus and Alexander, who were delivered to Satan that they might learn not to blaspheme (1Ti 1:20). Man of sin (2Th 2:3-4). Backslidden Ephesians (Rev 2:9).

False Accusations of:

Against Naboth (1Ki 21:13). Against Jesus (Mt 9:3; 26:65; Mk 2:7; 14:58; Lk 5:21; 22:70-71; Jn 5:18; 10:33; 19:7). Against Stephen (Ac 6:11, 13).

BLAST

1. From God's nostrils, figurative of judgment (Ex 15:8; 2Sa 22:16; Job 4:9; Ps 18:15).

2. From a horn, a call to assemble (Ex 19:13, 16; Lev 23:24) or to battle (Jos 6:5, 16; Job 39:25).

BLASTUS (*sprout [of a vine, branch]*). One of Herod's officers (Ac 12:20).

BLEEDING, SUBJECT TO A woman who had been bleeding for twelve years could not be healed by physicians (Mt 9:20; Mk 5:25; Lk 8:43, ftn). The precise nature of the woman's problem is not known. Her existence was wretched because she was shunned by people generally, since anyone having contact with her was made ceremonially unclean (Lev 15:25-33). Jesus healed her (both physically, "be freed from your suffering," and spiritually, "go in peace"; Mk 5:34) as a result of her simple act of faith.

BLEMISH A physical deformity. Barred sons of Aaron from exercise of priestly offices (Lev 21:17-23). Animals with, forbidden to be used for sacrifice (Lev 22:19-25).

Figurative (Eph 5:27; 1Pe 1:19).

BLESSING For blessing before eating, *See Benedictions; Prayer, Thanksgiving, and Before Taking Food.*

BLESSINGS, SPIRITUAL

From God:

(Dt 33:25, 27; Ps 18:28-36; 29:11; 37:6, 17, 24, 39; 63:8; 66:8-9; 68:18, 28, 35; 84:5, 11; Isa 40:11, 29, 31; 41:10, 13, 16; Ac 3:19; 1Co 2:9; Php 4:13; Jas 1:17; Jude 24).

Guidance (Ex 33:16; Ps 23:2-3; 119:102; Isa 40:11; 58:11).

Sanctification (Ex 31:13; Lev 21:8; Isa 1:25; 4:3-4; 6:6-7; 1Jn 1:9; Jude 1).

The perfecting of salvation (2Co 1:21; Php 1:6; 2:13; 4:19; Col 1:11-12; 1Th 5:24; Heb 13:20-21; 1Pe 1:5; 2Pe 1:2-4).

The deposit of the Spirit, guaranteeing what is to come (2Co 1:22; 5:5).

Peace (Isa 26:12; 57:19; Mal 4:2; Php 4:7).

From Christ:

(Jn 1:16; Ro 1:7; 16:20; 1Co 1:3; 16:23; 2Co 1:2; 13:14; Gal 1:3; 6:16, 18; Eph 1:2; 6:23-24; Php 1:2; 4:23; 1Th 5:28; 2Th 1:2; 3:16, 18; 1Ti 1:2; 2Ti 1:2; Phm 3, 25; 2Pe 1:1; 2Jn 3).

Contingent Upon Obedience; Resulting in:

Divine favor (Ex 19:5; Jer 7:23), mercy (Ex 20:6; Dt 5:10, 16; 7:9; 1Ki 8:23; 2Ch 30:9), holiness (Dt 28:9; 30:1-3, 6; Col 1:22-23), eternal salvation (Mt 10:22; 24:13; Mk 13:13; Heb 3:6, 14; 10:36; Rev 2:10).

See Contingencies; Faithfulness; Regeneration; Salvation.

BLESSINGS, TEMPORAL

From God: (Ps 136:25).

Rain (Dt 11:14; 28:12; Job 37:6; 38:25-27; Ps 68:9; 135:7; 147:8; Jer 10:13; 14:22; 51:16; Joel 2:23; Am 4:7; Zec 10:1, 12; Mt 5:45; Ac 14:17).

Seedtime and harvest (Ge 8:22; Lev 25:20-22; 26:4-5; Ps 107:35-38; Isa 55:10; Jer 5:24; Eze 36:30; Mal 3:11; Ac 14:17).

Food and clothing (Ge 9:1-3; 28:20-21; Dt 8:3-4; 10:18; 29:5; Ru 1:6; 2Ch 31:10; Ps 65:9; 68:1-10; 81:16; 104:14-15, 27-28; 111:5; 132:15; 145:15-16; 146:7; Ecc 2:24; 3:13; Isa 33:15-16; Joel 2:26; Mt 6:26, 30-33; Lk 12:22-31; Jn 6:31).

Preservation of life (Dt 4:1, 40; 5:33; 7:15; Ps 21:4; 23:6; 91:16; 103:2-5; Da 6:20, 22).

Children (Ps 113:9; Ps 127:3-5).

Prosperity (Ge 24:56; 26:24; 49:24-25; Nu 10:29; Dt 8:7-10, 18; 1Sa 2:7-8; 1Ch 29:12, 14, 16; 2Ch 1:12; Ezr 8:22; Ps 147:13-14; Ecc 5:19; Isa 30:23; Hos 2:8).

National greatness (Ge 22:17; 26:3-4; Dt 1:10; 7:13-14; 15:4, 6; 26:18-19; 32:13-14; Job 12:23; Ps 69:35-36; Isa 51:2; Jer 30:19; Eze 36:36-38; Da 5:18), social peace (Lev 26:6; 1Ch 22:9), victory over enemies (Ex 23:22; Lev 26:6-9; Dt 28:7; Ps 44:3), worldly honors (2Sa 7:8-9; 1Ch 17:7-8).

Exemplified to:

Noah at the time of the Flood (Ge 7:1). Abraham (Ge 24:1). Isaac (Ge 26:12-24, 28). Jacob (Ge 35:9-15). Israelites in Egypt (Ex 11:3), in the wilderness, supplying water (Ex 17:1-7; Nu 20:10-11; Ps 78:15-20; 105:4), manna (Ex 16:14, 31; Nu 11:7-9; Ne 9:15; Ps 78:23-24), quail (Nu 11:31-33; Ps 78:23-30; 105:40). David (2Sa 5:10; 1Ch 14:17). Obed-Edom (2Sa 6:11). Solomon (1Ki 3:13; 1Ch 29:25; 2Ch 1:1). Elijah, fed by ravens (1Ki 17:2-7), by an angel (1Ki 19:5-8). The widow of Zarephath (1Ki 17:12-16). Hezekiah prospered (2Ki 18:6-7; 2Ch 32:29), restored to health (2Ki 20:1-7). Asa (2Ch 14:6-7). Jehoshaphat (2Ch 17:3-5; 20:30). Uzziah (2Ch 26:5-15). Jotham (2Ch 27:6). Job (Job 1:10; 42:10, 12). Daniel (Da 1:9).

Prayer for:

Rain (1Ki 8:36; 2Ch 6:27). Plentiful harvests (Ge 27:28; Dt 26:15; Dt 33:13-16). Daily bread (Mt 6:11; Lk 11:3), prosperity (Ge 28:3-4; 1Ch 4:10; Ne 1:11; 3Jn 2), providential guidance (Ge 24:12-14, 42-44; Ro 1:10; 1Th 3:11).

Instances of Prayer for:

Abraham (Ge 15:2-4). Abraham's servant (Ge 24:12). Laban (Ge 24:60). Isaac (Ge 25:21). Hannah (1Sa 1:11). Elijah (1Ki 17:20-21; 18:42, 44; Jas 5:17-18). Ezra (Ezr 8:21-23). Nehemiah (Ne 1:11; 2:4; 6:9).

Contingent Upon Obedience; Resulting in:

Longevity (Ex 20:12; Dt 4:40; 5:16; 1Ki 3:14; Pr 3:1-2). Deliverance from enemies (Ex 23:22; Lev 26:6-8; Dt 28:7; 30:1-4; Pr 16:7; Jer 15:19-21). Prosperity (Lev 26:3-5; Dt 7:12-14; 15:4-5; 28:2-12; 29:9; 30:1-5, 9-20; Jos 1:8; 1Ki 2:3-4; 9:3-9; 1Ch 22:13; 28:7-8; 2Ch 7:17-22; 26:5; 27:6; 31:10; Job 36:11; Isa 1:19; Jer 7:3-7; 11:1-5; 12:16; 17:24-27; 22:4-5, 15-16; Mal 3:10-12). Favors to children (Dt 4:1, 40; 5:29; 7:9; 12:25, 28). Preeminent honors (Dt 28:1, 13; Zec 3:7). Averted judgments (Ex 15:26; Dt 7:15).

See God, Goodness of, Providence of; Prosperity.

BLIGHT Destructive plant disease, sent as a judgment (Dt 28:22; 1Ki 8:37; Am 4:9; Hag 2:17).

BLIND Cruelty to, forbidden (Lev 19:14; Dt 27:18). Hated by David (2Sa 5:8). *See Blindness.*

BLINDNESS Disqualified for priestly office (Lev 21:18). Of animals, disqualified for a sacrifice (Lev 22:22; Dt 15:21; Mal 1:8). Miraculously inflicted upon the Sodomites (Ge 19:11), Syrians (2Ki 6:18-23), Saul of Tarsus (Ac 9:8-9), Elymas (Ac 13:11). Sent as a judgment (Dt 28:28).

Miraculous healing of (Mt 9:27-30; 11:5; 12:22; 21:14), Bartimaeus (Mt 20:30-34; Mk 10:46-52), a man of Bethsaida (Mk 8:22-25), a man born blind (Jn 9:1-7).

Instances of:

Isaac (Ge 27:1). Jacob (Ge 48:10). Eli (1Sa 4:14-15). Ahijah (1Ki 14:4).

Spiritual:

Instances of (Dt 29:4; Job 5:14; Isa 29:10-12; 56:10; 59:10; Jer 2:8; 5:21; 9:3; Eze 12:2; Ro 11:8). Foretold (Isa 60:2; Ro 2:4; 11:10).

Manifested:

In ignorance of God (Ex 5:2; Isa 1:3; Jer 4:22; Hos 4:1, 6; Jn 7:28; 15:21; 16:2-3; 17:25; Ac 17:23; 1Co 1:18-21; 2:8, 14-15; 15:34; Gal 4:8; Eph 4:17-19; 1Th 4:4-5; 1Jn 4:8; 3Jn 11), of Christ (Mt 16:3, 9; Lk 23:34; Jn 1:5, 10; 4:10-11, 15, 22; 8:15, 19, 27, 33, 42-43, 52-57; 9:29-39; Ac 3:14, 17; Ro 11:7-8, 25; 1Pe 1:14; 1Jn 3:1, 6), the Holy Spirit (Jn 14:17; Ac 19:2), of the Scriptures (Mt 22:29; Mk 12:24; Ac 13:27; 2Co 3:14-15; Heb 5:11-12; 2Pe 3:16).

In ignorance of moral truth (Dt 32:28; Pr 4:19; 28:5; Isa 5:13; Da 12:10; Mt 15:14, 16; 16:3, 9; 23:19, 24, 26; Mk 7:18; Lk 6:39; 12:48, 57; 2Ti 3:7; Jude 10), of the way of salvation (Lk 19:42; Jn 3:4; 6:52, 60; 2Pe 1:9; 1Jn 1:6, 8; 2:4, 9, 11; Rev 3:17), of God's ways (Ps 95:10; Jer 5:4; 8:7-9; Mic 4:12).

In unbelief (Ps 14:1, 4; Isa 15:1; Mk 16:14; Jn 12:35, 38; Ac 28:25, 27; 2Co 4:3-4, 6; 2Th 2:11-12). In insensibility (Dt 29:4; Jdg 16:20; Pr 7:7-23; 17:16; Isa 6:9-10; 42:18-20; 44:18-20; 48:8; Jer 16:10; Hos 7:11; Mt 6:23; 13:13-15; Mk 4:11-12; 6:52; 8:18; Lk 8:10; Jn 12:40; Ac 28:25-27). In presumption (Ps 10:5-6; 94:7-8; Isa 28:10-15; 40:21, 27-28; Jer 8:8-9; Am 9:10). In perversity (Job 21:14-15; Pr 1:7, 22, 29-30; 13:18; 19:2-3; Isa 5:20; 26:10-11; Jer 9:3, 6; Eze 12:2-3; Hos 5:4; Mt 21:32; Mk 3:5; Lk 11:52; Jn 3:19; Ro 1:19-23, 28-31). In hypocrisy (Tit 1:15-16).

Consequences of: (Pr 10:21; 14:12; Isa 27:11; Hos 4:6, 14; 2Th 1:8).

Remedy for: (Isa 9:2; 25:7; 35:5; 42:6-7; Lk 4:18; Jn 8:12; Ac 26:18; 2Co 4:6; Eph 5:8; Col 1:13; 1Pe 2:9).

See Affliction, Prayer Under; God, Providence of, Mysterious and Misinterpreted.

BLOOD Is the life (Ge 9:4; Lev 17:11, 14; 19:16; Dt 12:23; Mt 27:4, 24). Forbidden to be used as food (Ge 9:4; Lev 3:17; 7:26-27; 17:10-14; 19:26; Dt 12:16, 23; 15:23; Eze 33:25; Ac 15:20, 29; 21:25). Plague of (Ex 7:17-25; Ps 78:44; 105:29).

Sacrificial:

Sprinkled on altar and people (Ex 24:6-8; Eze 43:18, 20). Sprinkled on door posts (Ex 12:7-23; Heb 11:28). Without shedding of, no remission (Heb 9:22).

Of Sin Offering:

Sprinkled seven times before the veil (Lev 4;5-6, 17), on horns of the altar of sweet incense, and at the bottom of the altar of burnt offering (Ex 30:10; Lev 4:7, 18, 25, 30; 5:9; 9:9, 12). Of bull of sin offering, put on the horns of the altar (Ex 29:12; Lev 8:15), poured at the bottom of the altar (Ex 29:12; Lev 8:15). *See Offerings.*

Of Trespass Offering:

Sprinkled on the altar (Lev 7:2). *See Offerings.*

Of Burnt Offering:

Sprinkled round about, and upon the altar (Ex 29:16; Lev 1:5, 11, 15; 8:19; Dt 12:27). *See Offerings.* Used for cleansing of leprosy (Lev 14:6-7, 17, 28, 51-52). *See Offerings.*

Of Peace Offering:

Sprinkled about the altar (Lev 3:2, 8, 13; 9:19). Blood of the ram of consecration put on tip of right ear, thumb, and large toe of, and sprinkled upon, Aaron and his sons (Ex 29:20-21; Lev 8:23-24, 30). *See Offerings.*

Blood of the Covenant: (Ex 24:5-8; Zec 9:11; Mt 26:28; Heb 9:18-19, 22; 10:29; 13:20).

See Offerings.

Of Atonement:

Sprinkled on atonement cover (Lev 16:14-15, 18-19, 27; 17:11).

Figurative:

Of victories (Ps 58:10), oppression and cruelty (Hab 2:12), destruction (Eze 35:6), guilt (Lev 20:9; 2Sa 1:16; Eze 18:13), judgments (Eze 16:38; Rev 16:6).

Of Jesus:

Shed on the Cross (Jn 19:18, 34). Atoning (Mt 26:28; Mk 14:24; Lk 22:20; Ro 3:24-25; 5:9; Eph 2:13, 16; Heb 10:19-20; 12:24; 13:20; 1Jn 5:6, 8). Redeeming (Ac 20:28; Eph 1:7; Col 1:14, 20; Heb 9:12-14; 1Pe 1:18-19; Rev 1:5; 5:9; 7:14). Sanctifying (Heb 10:29; 13:12). Justification through (Ro 3:24-25; 5:9). Victory through (Rev 12:11). Eternal life by (Jn 6:53-56). Typified by the blood of sacrifices (Heb 9:6-28). Symbolized by the wine of the Lord's Supper (1Co 10:16; 11:25).

See Atonement; Jesus the Christ, Mission of, Sufferings of.

BLOOD, AVENGER One who took it upon himself to avenge the blood of a slain relative (Ge 9:6; Nu 35:6). *See Avenger of Blood.*

BLOOD, ISSUE OF *See Bleeding, Subject to; Disease.*

BLOOD MONEY Paid to Judas for betraying Jesus (Mt 27:6). *See Conscience Money.*

BLOODY SWEAT *See Disease; Sweat, Bloody.*

BLUE *See Colors, Figurative and Symbolic.*

BLUSHING With shame (Ezr 9:6; Jer 6:15; 8:12).

BOANERGES (*sons of thunder*). Surname of the sons of Zebedee (Mk 3:17).

BOARS, WILD (Ps 80:13). *See Pig.*

BOASTING Folly of (Ps 49:6-9; Pr 27:1; Isa 10:15; Jas 4:16). Deceitful (Pr 20:14; 25:14). Of the wicked (Ps 52:1; 94:4; Ro 1:30). Of the tongue (Jas 3:5). Forbidden (Jer 9:23).

Spiritual (Ps 52:1; 94:4; Ro 3:27; 11:17-21; 1Co 1:29; 4:6-7; 2Co 10:12-18; Eph 2:8-10).

Instances of:

Goliath (1Sa 17). Ben-Hadad (1Ki 20:10). Amaziah (2Ch 25:17-20). Sennacherib (2Ki 18:19, 28-35; 19:8-13; Isa 10:8-15). The disciples (Lk 10:17, 20).

See Ostentation.

BOAT *See Ship.*

BOAZ (perhaps *in him is strength*).

1. An ancestor of Jesus (Mt 1:5; Lk 3:32). History of, Ruth (Ru 2-4).

2. One of Solomon's bronze pillars erected at the temple. It stood on the left (north) side of the porch (1Ki 7:21; 2Ch 3:17).

BOAZ AND JAKIN *See Boaz, 2; Jakin, 2; Temple, Solomon's.*

BOCHERU *See Bokeru.*

BOCHIM *See Bokim.*

BODY

Called: house (2Co 5:1), house of clay (Job 4:19), golden bowl (Ecc 12:6), earthen vessel (2Co 4:7), tabernacle (2Pe 1:13), temple of God (1Co 3:16-17; 6:19), member of Christ (1Co 6:15).

Perishable (Job 17:14; 1Co 15:53-54). To be consecrated to God (Ro 12:1). To be kept unto holiness (1Co 6:13-20).

Resurrection of, to a spiritual body (1Co 15:19-54; 2Co 5:14; Php 3:21). *See Resurrection.*

BOHAN (*thumb, big toe*). A Reubenite (Jos 15:6; 18:17).

BOIL A tumor or running sore. Plague of Egyptians (Ex 9:9-10; Dt 28:27, 35), of the Philistines, (1Sa 5:6, 9; 1Sa 6:5). Of Hezekiah, healed (2Ki 20:7; Isa 38:21). Of Job (Job 2:7-8). Levitical ceremonies prescribed for (Lev 13:18-23).

BOILING POT Parable of (Eze 24:3-5).

BOKERU (*his first born*). Son of Azel (1Ch 8:38; 9:44).

BOKIM (*weepings*). A place W of Jordan, near Gilgal (Jdg 2:1, 5).

BOLDNESS OF THE RIGHTEOUS

Exemplified (Pr 28:1; Ac 18:26; 19:8; Heb 13:6). In prayer (Heb 4:16; 10:19; 1Jn 3:21-22; 5:14-15). Inspired by, fear of the Lord (Pr 14:26). Faith in Christ (Eph 3:12).

Instances of boldness in prayer: Abraham (Ge 18:23-32). Moses (Ex 33:12-18). In the day of judgment (1Jn 2:28; 4:17). Its effect on others (Ac 4:13).

See Courage.

BOLSTER *See Pillow.*

BOLT, FIERY (Hab 3:5).

BOND Of the covenant (Eze 20:37), of peace (Eph 4:3). Posting bond (Ac 17:9).

BONDAGE Of Israelites, in Egypt (Ex 1:14; 2:23; 6:6), in Persia (Ezr 9:9). *See Emancipation; Servant.*

BONDMAN *See Servant.*

BONES Vision of the dry (Eze 37:1-14). None of Christ's broken (Ps 34:20; Jn 19:36).

BONNET *See Dress; Turban.*

BOOK Genealogies kept in (Ge 5:1). Law of Moses written in (Nu 5:23; Dt 17:18; 31:9, 24, 26; 2Ki 22:8). Topography of Israel, recorded in (Jos 18:9).

Non-biblical books cited in the Bible:
Book of Jashar (Jos 10:13; 2Sa 1:18), records of Samuel, Nathan, and Gad (1Sa 10:25; 1Ch 29:29), Iddo (2Ch 12:15; 13:22), Isaiah (2Ch 26:22; 32:32; Isa 8:1).

Annals of the Kings of Judah and Israel:
Of David (1Ch 27:24), Solomon (1Ki 11:41), Jehu (2Ch 20:34), other kings (2Ch 24:27; 16:11; 25:26; 27:7; 28:26; 35:27; 36:8), the kings of Israel (1Ki 14:19; 2Ch 20:34; 33:18).
Other records kept in (Ezr 4:15; 6:1-2; Est 6:1; 9:32; Jer 32:12; Ac 19:19). Prophecies written in, by Jeremiah (Jer 25:13; 30:2; 45:1; 51:60, 63; Da 9:2). Other prophecies written in (2Ch 33:18-19). Lamentations written in (2Ch 35:25). Numerous (Ecc 12:12). Eating of (Jer 15:16; Eze 2:8-10; 3:1-3; Rev 10:2-10). Of magic (Ac 19:19). Paul's left at Troas (2Ti 4:13).
Made in a roll (Jer 36:4; Zec 5:1). Sealed (Isa 29:11; Da 12:4; Rev 5:1-5).
Kiriath Jearim was called Kiriath Sepher, which signifies a city of books (Jos 15:15-16; Jdg 1:11-12).

Figurative:
Of Life: righteous written in (Ex 32:32; Da 12:1; Lk 10:20; Php 4:3; Heb 12:23; Rev 3:5; 21:27), wicked blotted out of (Ex 32:33; Rev 22:18-19), wicked not written in (Rev 13:8; 17:8; 20:15).
Of remembrance (Ps 56:8; 139:16; Mal 3:16; Rev 20:12).

BOOTH Made for shelter (Jnh 4:5), for cattle (Ge 33:17), watchmen (Job 27:18; Isa 1:8; 24:20). Prescribed for the Israelites to dwell in during the Feast of Tabernacles to remember their wanderings in the wilderness (Lev 23:40-43; Ne 8:15-16).

BOOTY Spoils of war. Property and persons were sometimes preserved and sometimes completely destroyed (Jos 6:18-21; Dt 20:14, 16-18). Abraham gave a tenth (Ge 14:20), David ordered that booty be shared with baggage guards (1Sa 30:21-25).

BOOZ *See Boaz, 1.*

BOR ASHAN (*pit of smoke*). A town in Judah (1Sa 30:30). Perhaps identical with Ashan (Jos 15:42). *See Ain, 1; Ashan.*

BORING THE EAR *See Piercing the Ear.*

BORN AGAIN *See New Birth.*

BORROWING Dishonesty in (Ps 37:21). Obligations in (Ex 22:14-15). Distress from (Ne 5:1-5; Pr 22:7). Compassion toward debtors commanded (Ne 5:6-13). Christ's rule concerning (Mt 5:42).
See Lending; Interest.
Instances of: Israelites from the Egyptians (Ex 3:22; 11:2; 12:35), iron axhead (2Ki 6:5); returned exiles from each other (Ne 5:1-13).
Borrowing trouble. *See Security, For Debt.*

BOSCATH *See Bozkath.*

BOSOM Used in the sense of sexual intimacy (Pr 5:20; Eze 23:8, 21). KJV "bosom" is NIV "arms" (Ge 16:5; Nu 11:12; 2Sa 12:3), "side" (Jn 1:18), "next to" (Jn 13:23).

BOSOR *See Beor; Bozrah.*

BOSS *See Shield.*

BOTANICAL GARDENS Garden of Eden (Ge 2:8-3:24), of Uzza (2Ki 21:18, 25), king's garden (2Ki 25:4; Ne 3:15 w Ecc 2:5), of Susa (Est 1:5-6;7:7-8).

BOTANY Laws of nature in the vegetable kingdom uniform in action (Mt 7:16-18, 20; Lk 6:43-44; 1Co 15:36-38; Gal 6:7). Lily, beauty of (Mt 6:28-29). The size of the harvest is related to the amount of seed sown (2Co 9:6).
See Algum; Almond; Aloes; Apple; Balm; Barley; Bay Tree; Beans; Bramble; Broom Tree; Bush; Cane; Caraway; Cassia; Cedar; Cinnamon; Citron Wood; Coriander; Cucumbers; Cummin; Cypress Wood; Date; Ebony; Fig Tree; Fir Tree; Flax; Frankincense; Galbanum; Gall, 3; Garlic; Gourd; Grain; Grass; Gum Resin; Hemlock; Henna Blossoms; Husk; Hyssop; Leek; Lentil(s); Lily; Mandrake; Melon; Millet; Mint; Mulberry Tree; Mustard Seed; Myrrh; Myrtle; Nard; Nettles; Nut; Oak; Olive; Onion; Palm Tree; Perfume; Pine; Plants of the Bible; Pomegranate; Poplar; Reed; Rose; Rue; Salt Herbs; Shittim; Spelt; Sycamore-Fig; Terebinth; Thistle; Thorn; Tree; Vine; Weeds; Wheat; Willow; Wormwood.

BOTCH *See Boil.*

BOTTLE Perfume bottles (Isa 3:20). *See Wine; Wineskin.*

BOTTOMLESS PIT *See Abyss.*

BOUNDARY STONES Stones used, to mark the boundary of property (Jos 13:21), to remove them was forbidden (Dt 27:17).

BOW

A Weapon:
(Ge 21:16, 20). Made of, bronze (2Sa 22:35; Job 20:24; Ps 18:34), wood (Eze 39:9). Used in war (Isa 13:18; La 2:4; Eze 39:3) and in hunting (Ge 27:3). David's lament of the bow (2Sa 1:18-27). Used by the Elamites (Jer 49:35). *See Archery; Arrows.*

Figurative:
(Ge 49:24; Job 16:13; 29:20; Ps 78:57; La 3:12; Hos 1:5; Hab 3:9; Rev 6:2).

Rainbow:
A sign from God (Ge 9:8-16). A likeness of God's glory (Eze 1:28; Rev 4:3; 10:1).

BOWELS Diseased (2Ch 21:15-20). Judas's gushed out (Ac 1:18).
Figurative: Of the sensibilities (Ge 43:30; 1Ki 3:26; Job 30:27; Ps 22:14; SS 5:4; Jer 4:19; 31:20; La 1:20; Php 1:8; 2:1; Col 3:12; 1Jn 3:17).
See Heart.

BOWING In worship (2Ch 7:3). *See Obeisance; Worship, Attitudes in.*

BOWL Made of gold: for the tabernacle (Ex 25:29; 37:16), temple (1Ki 7:50; 1Ch 28:17; 2Ch 4:8). Of silver (Nu 4:7; 7:13, 19, 25, 31, 37, 43, 49, 55, 61, 67, 73, 79, 84). Stamped "HOLY TO THE LORD" (Zec 14:20-21). *See Basin.*
Figurative of fragile life (Ecc 12:6).
Symbolic: Of prayer (Rev 5:8). Seven bowls of judgment (Rev 15:7-16:17).

BOX Containing portions of Scripture (Mt 23:5, ftn). *See Jar(s).*

BOX TREE *See Cypress Wood.*

BOXING Figurative of personal discipline (1Co 9:26-27). *See Games.*

BOZEZ (*oozing place*). A rock near Gibeah (1Sa 14:4).

BOZKATH (*[swollen,] elevated spot*). A city of Judah (Jos 15:39; 2Ki 22:1).

BOZRAH (*enclosure [for sheep], fortress*).
1. A city of Edom (Ge 36:33). Prophecies concerning (Isa 34:6; 63:1; Jer 49:13, 22; Am 1:12).
2. A town of Moab (Jer 48:24).

BRACELET Present of (Ge 24:22). Worn by women (Ge 24:30; Isa 3:19); men, NIV "cord" (Ge 38:18, 25). Dedicated to the tabernacle (Ex 35:22; Nu 31:50). Taken as spoils (Nu 31:50; 2Sa 1:10).
Figurative of God's care for Israel (Eze 16:11).

BRAMBLE (Isa 34:13; Lk 6:44). Allegory of (Jdg 9:14-15).

BRANCH

Of Trees:
(Ge 30:37-43). Used in the Feast of Tabernacles (Lev 23:39-43; Ne 8:16-17). At the Triumphal Entry (Mt 21:6-9).

Figurative:
(Pr 11:28; Hos 14:6; Isa 60:21; Jn 15:2-5). Pruning of (Isa 18:5; Da 4:14; Jn 15:6; Ro 11:17, 21). Fruitless, cut off (Jn 15:2, 6). A title of Christ (Ps 80:15; Isa 4:2; 11:1; Jer 23:5; 33:15; Zec 3:8; 6:12). Symbolic name of Joshua (Zec 6:12).
See Graft.

BRASS *See Bronze.*

BRAVERY *See Boldness of the Righteous; Courage.*

BRAY The sound of a hungry donkey; a metaphor of humans crying out in need (Job 6:5; 30:7).

BRAZEN SEA *See Bronze Basin.*

BRAZEN SERPENT *See Bronze Snake.*

BRAZIER *See Coppersmith; Craftsman; Occupations and Professions.*

BREAD

Kinds of:
Bread of affliction (1Ki 22:27; Ps 127:2; Hos 9:4; Isa 30:20), leavened (Lev 7:13; 23:17; Hos 7:4; Am 4:5; Mt 13:33), unleavened (Ge 19:3; Ex 29:2; Jdg 6:19; 1Sa 28:24).
Made of wheat flour (Ex 29:2; 1Ki 4:22; 5:11; Ps 81:16), manna (Nu 11:8), meal (1Ki 17:12), barley (Jdg 7:13).

How Prepared:
Mixed with oil (Ex 29:2, 23), honey (Ex 16:31), with yeast. *See Yeast; see above, Kinds of.* Kneaded (Ge 18:6; Ex 8:3; 12:34; 1Sa 28:24; 2Sa 13:8; Jer 7:18; Hos 7:4).
Made into loaves (1Sa 10:3; 17:17; 25:18; 1Ki 14:3; Mk 8:14), cakes (2Sa 6:19; 1Ki 14:3; 17:12), wafers (Ex 16:21; 29:23.
Baked in ovens (Ex 8:3; Lev 2:4; 7:9; 11:35; 26:26; Hos 7:4), in pans (Lev 2:5, 7; 2Sa 13:6-9), on hearths (Ge 18:6), on coals (1Ki 19:6; Isa 44:19; Jn 21:9).
Made by men (Ge 40:2), women (Lev 26:26; 1Sa 8:13; Jer 7:18). Trade in (Jer 37:21; Mk 6:35-37).
Offered in sacrifice (Lev 21:6, 8, 17, 21-22; 22:25; 1Sa 2:36; 2Ki 23:9). By idolators (Jer 7:18; 44:19).
See Bread, Consecrated; Offerings.

Figurative:
(Isa 55:2; 1Co 10:17; 2Co 9:10). Christ: the bread of life (Jn 6:32-59).

Symbolic:
Of the body of Christ (Mt 26:26; Ac 20:7; 1Co 11:23-24).

BREAD, CONSECRATED (1Sa 21:4, 6; 1Ch 28:16; 2Ch 2:4; 29:18; Mt 12:4; Mk 2:26; Lk 6:4; Heb 9:2).
Required to be kept before the LORD continually (Ex 25:30; 2Ch 2:4). Placed on the table "in the Tent of Meeting" (Ex 40:22-23). *See Table of, below.* Ordinance concerning (Lev 24:5-9). Unlawfully eaten by David (1Sa 21:6; Mt 12:3-4; Mk 2:25-26; Lk 6:3-4). Prepared by the Levites (1Ch 9:32; 23:29). Provided by a yearly per capita tax (Ne 10:32-33).

Table of:
(Heb 9:2). Ordinances concerning (Ex 25:23-28; 37:10-15). Its situation in the tabernacle (Ex 26:35; 40:22). Furniture of (Ex 25:29-30; 37:16; Nu 4:7). Consecration of (Ex 30:26-27, 29). How removed (Nu 4:7, 15). For the temple (1Ki 7:48, 50; 2Ch 4:19, 22).

B

BREAST Breast in the Bible can simply refer to the chest area of the body (Lk 18:13). It can also refer to the female mammary glands (Ge 49:25; La 4:3; Lk 23:29), both in nurturing (Ps 22:9; Joel 2:16; Isa 60:16) and erotic contexts (SS 4:5; 7:7; Eze 23:3, 21). To beat one's breast with a fist was a sign of sorrow or repentence (Eze 21:12; Lk 18:13; 23:48). *See Bosom.*

BREASTPLATE
1. For high priest (Ex 25:7). Directions for the making of (Ex 28:15-30). Made by Bezalel (Ex 31:2-5; 39:8, 21). Freewill offering of materials for (Ex 35:9, 27). Worn by Aaron (Ex 29:5; Lev 8:8).
2. Armor for soldiers (Rev 9:9, 17).
Figurative (Isa 59:17; Eph 6:14; 1Th 5:8).

BREATH Of life (Ge 2:7; 7:22; Ac 17:25). Of God (2Sa 22:16; Job 4:9; 15:30; 33:4; 37:10; Ps 18:15; 33:6; Isa 30:33).
Figurative (Eze 37:9).

BREECHES *See Dress; Undergarments.*

BRETHREN *See Brother; Brothers of Our Lord.*

BRIBERY (Ps 26:9-10; Pr 15:27; Isa 33:15-16). Corrupts conscience (Ex 23:8; Dt 16:18-19; Ecc 7:7). Perverts justice (1Sa 8:1-3; 12:3; Pr 17:23; 28:21; Isa 1:23; 5:22-23; Eze 22:12; Am 5:12; Mic 7:3). Destroys national welfare (Pr 29:4). Profanes God (Eze 13:19). Condemnation of (Job 15:34; Eze 22:12-13). Punishment for (Dt 27:25; Am 2:6).

Instances of:
Delilah (Jdg 16:4-5). Samuel's sons (1Sa 8:1-3). The false prophet, Shemaiah (Ne 6:10-13). Ben-Hadad (1Ki 15:18-19). Haman bribes Xerxes to destroy the Jews (Est 3:8-9). Chief priests bribe Judas (Mt 26:15; 27:3-9; Mk 14:11; Lk 22:5). Soldiers bribed to declare that the disciples stole the body of Jesus (Mt 28:12-15). Felix seeks a bribe from Paul (Ac 24:26).

BRICK Used in building: Babel (Ge 11:3), cities in Egypt (Ex 1:11, 14), houses (Isa 9:10), altars (Isa 65:3). Made by Israelites (Ex 5:7-19), slave labor (2Sa 12:31), Ninevites (Na 3:14).

BRICKKILN *See Brick.*

BRIDE Presents to (Ge 24:53). Maids of (Ge 24:59, 61; 29:24, 29). Ornaments of (Isa 49:18; 61:10; Jer 2:32; Rev 21:2).
Figurative (Ps 45:10-17; Eze 16:8-14; Rev 19:7-8; 21:2, 9; 22:17).

BRIDECHAMBER *See Bridegroom; Wedding.*

BRIDEGROOM Ornaments of (Isa 61:10). Exempt from military duty (Dt 24:5). Companions of (Jdg 14:11). Joy with (Mt 9:15; Mk 2:19-20; Lk 5:34-35).
Parable of (Mt 25:1-13; SS 4:7-16).
Figurative (Eze 16:8-14).

BRIDGE "River crossings" (Jer 51:32) may have included bridges or ferries. The Israelites generally crossed streams at a ford (Ge 32:22; 2Sa 19:18).

BRIDLE To control an animal (Ps 32:9; Pr 26:3; Rev 14:20). *See Bit.*
Figurative (2Ki 19:28; Ps 39:1; Jas 1:26).

BRIER Figurative (Isa 5:6; 55:13; Eze 2:6; 28:24).

BRIGANDINE *See Armor.*

BRIMSTONE *See Sulfur.*

BRONZE An alloy of copper and tin. Smelted (Eze 22:20; Job 28:2). Found in Canaan (Dt 8:9; Jos 22:8), Syria (2Sa 8:8). Tyrians traded in (Eze 27:13). Abundance of, for the temple (1Ki 7:47; 1Ch 22:14).

Articles made of:
Altar, vessels, and other articles of the tabernacle and temple (Ex 38:28-31; 1Ki 7:14-47; Ezr 8:27), cymbals (1Ch 15:19), trumpets (1Co 13:1), armor (1Sa 17:5-6; 2Ch 12:10), bows *See Bow*, fetters (Jdg 16:21; 2Ki 25:7), gates (Ps 107:16; Isa 45:2), bars (1Ki 4:13), idols (Da 5:4; Rev 9:20), mirrors (Ex 38:8), household vessels (Mk 7:4).
Workers in: Tubal-Cain (Ge 4:22), Hiram (1Ki 7:13-14), Alexander (2Ti 4:14).
See Bronze Basin; Bronze Sea; Copper; Molding.

Figurative:
(Lev 26:19; Dt 33:25; Isa 48:4; Jer 1:18; Eze 1:7; Da 2:32, 39; 7:19; 10:6; Zec 6:1; Rev 1:15).

BRONZE BASIN Directions for making (Ex 30:18-20). Situation of, in the tabernacle, tent of the congregation, and the altar (Ex 40:7). Sanctified (Ex 30:28; 40:11; Lev 8:11). Used for washing (Ex 40:30-32).
Figurative (Rev 4:6; 15:2, w Ex 38:8).
See Bronze Sea; Tabernacle.

BRONZE SEA Made by Solomon for the temple (1Ki 7:23-26, 30, 38-39; 2Ch 4:2-14). Altered by Ahaz (2Ki 16:17). Broken and carried to Babylon by the Chaldeans (2Ki 25:13, 16; Jer 52:17, 20).
Figurative (Rev 4:6; 15:2, w 1Ki 7:23).
See Bronze Basin; Temple.

BRONZE SNAKE Made by Moses for the healing of the Israelites (Nu 21:8-9). Worshiped by Israelites (2Ki 18:4). A symbol of Christ's crucifixion (Jn 3:14-15).

BROOK *See River; River of Egypt.*

BROOM A metaphor of Babylon swept away in judgment (Isa 14:23).

BROOM TREE A desert shrub (1Ki 19:4-5; Job 30:4; Ps 120:4).

BROTH (Jdg 6:19-20; 2Ki 4:38; Isa 65:4). Symbolic (Eze 24:5).

BROTHEL *See Groves; High Places; Idolatry; Prostitute.*

BROTHER
Signifies a relative (Ge 14:16; 29:12), a neighbor (Dt 23:7; Jdg 21:6; Ne 5:7), any Israelite (Jer 34:9; Ob 10), an inclusive term for all mankind (Ge 9:5; Mt 18:35; 1Jn 3:15), a companion (2Sa 1:26; 1Ki 13:30; 20:33).
Love of (Pr 17:17; 18:24; SS 8:1). Unfaithful (Pr 27:10). Reuben's love for Joseph (Ge 37:21-22). Joseph's, for his brothers (Ge 43:30-34; 45:1-5; 50:19-25).
A fraternal title, especially among Christians. Instituted by Christ (Mt 12:50; 25:40; Heb 2:11-12). Used by disciples (Ac 9:17; 21:20; Ro 16:23; 1Co 7:12; 2Co 2:13), Peter (1Pe 1:22). Used among the Israelites (Lev 19:17; Dt 22:1-4).
Brother's widow, law concerning Levirate marriage of (Dt 25:5-10; Mt 22:24; Mk 12:19; Lk 20:28).
See Fraternity.

BROTHERLY KINDNESS *See Brother; Charitableness; Fellowship; Fraternity; Friendship; Love.*

BROTHERS OF OUR LORD James, Joseph, Simon, and Judas are called the Lord's brothers (Mt 13:55). He also had sisters (Mt 13:56). John records that his brothers did not believe in him (Jn 7:1-10). There are differences of opinion as to whether the "brothers" were full brothers, cousins, or children of Joseph by a former marriage.

BRUISE(S)
1. The so-called law of retaliation was meant to limit the punishment to fit the crime (Ex 21:25). By invoking the law of love, Jesus corrected the popular misunderstanding of the law of retaliation (Mt 5:38-42).
2. Castrated animals were not acceptable sacrifices (Lev 22:24).
3. Wounds inflicted, by shackles (Ps 105:18), because of drunkenness (physical and psychological effects) (Pr 29-35), by God upon Israel, because of the sins of the people, will be healed by the Lord (Isa 30:26). *See Bruised Reed, 1.*

BRUISED REED
1. Descriptive of someone who is weak; the "servant of the Lord" will mend broken lives (Isa 42:3; Mt 12:20).
2. NIV "splintered reed"; descriptive of depending on weak political alliances rather than relying on the Lord (2Ki 18:21; cf Isa 30:1-5; 31:1-3).
See Bruise(s).

BUBASTIS (*house of the cat goddess Basht*). One time capital of Lower Egypt; about forty miles NE of Cairo; modern Tel Basta. Prophesied against by Ezekiel (Eze 30:17, ftn). KJV Phi-Beseth.

BUCKET For water (Ex 7:19; Nu 24:7; Isa 40:15).

BUCKLER *See Shield.*

BUILDER Of the tabernacle. *See Bezalel; Master Craftsman.* Of the temple (2Ki 12:11; 22:6; Ezr 3:10). Of the wall of Jerusalem (Ne 4:18). Of the church (1Co 3:10). God (Heb 3:4; 11:10). Who rejected the capstone (Ps 118:22; Mt 21:42; Ac 4:11; 1Pe 2:7). *See Carpentry; Foundation.*

BUILDING The church as God's building (1Co 3:9; Eph 2:21). The eternal body compared to the earthly tent (2Co 5:1).

BUKKI (*proved of Yahweh* BDB; *mouth [gurgle sounds] of Yahweh* ISBE).
1. Son of Abishua (1Ch 6:5, 51; Ezr 7:4).
2. A prince of Dan (Nu 34:22).

BUKKIAH (*proved of Yahweh*). A Levite (1Ch 25:4, 13).

BUL Month eight in sacred sequence, month two in civil sequence. Also called Marcheshvan (not in Bible). The temple completed in (1Ki 6:38). Jeroboam institutes an idolatrous feast in, to correspond with the Feast of Tabernacles (1Ki 12:32-33). Time for planting wheat and barley (October-November). *See Month, 8.*

BULL
Uses of: For sacrifice (Ex 29:3, 10-14, 36; Lev 4:8, 16; Nu 7:87-88; 28:11-31; 29; Heb 9:13; 10:4), plowing (1Sa 14:14; 1Ki 19:19; Pr 14:4; Isa 32:20; Jer 31:18), treading out grain (Dt 25:4), with wagons (Nu 7:3-8; 2Sa 6:3-6).
Laws concerning: trespass by (Ex 21:28-36), theft of (Ex 22:1-10), rest for (Ex 23:12), not to be muzzled when treading grain (Dt 25:4; 1Co 9:9; 1Ti 5:18), not to be yoked with a donkey (Dt 22:10).
Twelve bronze, under the cast metal Sea in Solomon's temple (1Ki 7:25; 2Ch 4:4; Jer 52:20).
See Cattle; Offerings.
Symbolic (Eze 1:10; Rev 4:7).

BULRUSH *See Papyrus; Reed.*

BULWARK (Dt 20:20; 2Ch 26:15; Ecc 9:14). Figurative (Ps 48:13; Isa 26:1).

BUNAH Son of Jerahmeel (1Ch 2:25).

BUNNI
1. A Levite, a teacher with Ezra (Ne 9:4).
2. Ancestor of Shemaiah (Ne 11:15).
3. A family of Jews (Ne 10:15).

BURDEN Figurative: Of oppressions (Isa 58:6; Mt 23:4; Lk 11:46; Gal 6:2). Of the prophetic message (Isa 13:1; 15:1; 17:1; 19:1).

BURGLARY *See Theft.*

BURIAL Rites of (Jer 34:5). Soon after death (Dt 21:23; Jos 8:29; Jn 19:38-42; Ac 5:9-10). With spices (2Ch 16:14; Mk 16:1; Lk 23:56). Bier used at (2Sa 3:31; Lk 7:14).
Attended by relatives and friends: Of Jacob (Ge 50:5-9), Abner (2Sa 3:31), child of Jeroboam (1Ki 14:13), the son of the widow of Nain (Lk 7:12-13), Stephen (Ac 8:2).
Lack of, a disgrace (2Ki 9:10; Pr 30:17; Jer 16:4; 22:19; Eze 39:15). Directions given about, before death, by Jacob (Ge 49:29-30), Joseph (Ge 50:25). Burial of Gog (multitude) requiring 7 months (Eze 39:12-13).

BURNING As a punishment (Ge 19:28; Jos 6:24; 8:20; 11:13; Jdg 18:27; 1Sa 30:1; 1Ki 9:16; 2Ch 36:19; Job 1:16). *See Punishment.*

BURNING BUSH The LORD appears to Moses (Ex 3:2-5; Ac 7:30).

BURNT OFFERING *See Offerings, Burnt.*

BURYING PLACES Bought by Abraham (Ge 23; 25:9). Prepared by Jacob (Ge 50:5), Asa (2Ch 16:14), Joseph (Mt 27:60). On hills (2Ki 23:16; Jos 24:33). In valleys (Jer 7:32).
Family (Ge 47:30; 49:29; Ac 7:16). Of kings (1Ki 2:10; 2Ch 32:33), a place of honor (2Ch 24:16, 25; 21:20). For poor and strangers (Jer 26:23; Mt 27:7).
Tombs: In houses (1Sa 25:1; 1Ki 2:34), gardens (2Ki 21:18, 26; Jn 19:41), caves (Ge 23:9), under trees. Deborah's (Ge 35:8), King Saul's (1Sa 31:13).
Closed with stones (Mt 27:60, 66; Jn 11:38; 20:1). Sealed (Mt 27:66). Marked with pillars: Rachel's (Ge 35:20). Inscriptions (2Ki 23:17). Painted and decorated (Mt 23:27, 29).
Demon-possessed lived in (Mt 8:28). Any who touched were unclean (Nu 19:16, 18; Isa 65:4). Refused to the dead (Rev 11:9). Robbed (Jer 8:1).
See Cremation; Dead; Death, Physical; Elegy; Grave; Mourning.
Figurative (Isa 22:16; Ro 6:4; Col 2:12).

BUSH Desert shrubs (Ge 21:15; Jer 17:6). *See Burning Bush.*

BUSHELS (Lk 16:7). *See Measure.*

BUSINESS LIFE
Virtues Found in:
Diligence (Pr 10:4; 13:4; 22:29; 2Pe 3:14). Fidelity (Ge 39:6; 2Ch 34:11-12; Ne 13:13; Da 6:4; 1Co 4:2; Heb 3:5). Honesty (Lev 19:35-36; Dt 25:15; Pr 11:1; Ro 12:17; 13:8). Industry (Ge 2:15; Pr 6:6; 10:5; 12:11; 13:11; 20:13; Ro 12:11). Giving of just weights (Lev 19:36; Dt 25:13; Pr 11:1; 16:11; 20:10; Eze 45:10; Mic 6:11). Integrity (Ps 41:12; Pr 11:3; 19:1; 20:7).
Vices Found in:
Breach of trust (Lev 6:2; SS 1:6; Eze 16:17; Lk 16:12). Dishonesty (Dt 25:13; Pr 11:1; 20:14; 21:6; Hos 12:7). Extortion (Isa 10:2; Eze 22:12; Am 5:11; Mt 18:28; 23:25; Lk 3:13). Fraud (Lev 19:13; Mk 10:19; 1Co 6:8). Unjust gain (Pr 16:8; 21:6; 22:16; Jer 17:11; 22:13; Eze 22:13; Jas 5:4). Slothfulness (Pr 18:9; 24:30-31; Ecc 10:18; 2Th 3:11; Heb 6:12).

BUSYBODY Meddlers denounced (Pr 26:17; 1Ti 5:13; 2Th 3:11-12). Command against (Lev 19:16; 1Pe 4:15).
See Backbiting; Talebearer; Speaking, Evil.

BUTLER (1Ki 10:5; 2Ch 9:4; Ne 1:11; 2:1). Pharaoh's, imprisoned and released (Ge 40). *See Cupbearer.*

BUTTER (Ge 18:8; Dt 32:14; Jdg 5:25; 2Sa 17:29; Job 20:17; Isa 7:15, 22). Made by churning (Pr 30:33).

BUZ (*contempt*).
1. Son of Nahor (Ge 22:21).
2. Father of Jahdo (1Ch 5:14).

BUZI (*contempt*). The father of Ezekiel (Eze 1:3).

BYBLOS *See Gebal.*

BYWAYS NIV "winding paths," traveled to avoid danger (Jdg 5:6).

C

CAB A dry measure containing about two quarts (2Ki 6:25). *See Measure.*

CABBON A place in Judah (Jos 15:40).

CABINET Heads of departments in government. David's (2Sa 8:15-18; 15:12; 20:23-26; 1Ch 27:32-34), Solomon's (1Ki 4:1-7), Hezekiah's (Isa 36:3), Artaxerxes' (Ezr 7:14). *See Counselor.*

CABUL (*good for nothing*).
1. A city in the N of Israel (Jos 19:27).
2. Name given by Hiram to certain cities in Galilee (1Ki 9:13).

CAESAR
1. Augustus (Lk 2:1).
2. Tiberius (Lk 3:1; 20:22).
3. Claudius (Ac 11:28).
4. Nero (Php 4:22).

CAESAREA A seaport in Israel.
Home of Philip (Ac 8:40; 21:8), Cornelius, the centurion (Ac 10:1, 24), Herod (Ac 12:19-23), Felix (Ac 23:23-24).
Paul taken to, by the disciples to save him from his enemies (Ac 9:30), by Roman soldiers to be tried by Felix (Ac 23:23-35).

CAESAREA PHILIPPI A city in the N of Israel, visited by Jesus (Mt 16:13; Mk 8:27).

CAGE For birds (Jer 5:27; Rev 18:2).

CAIAPHAS High priest (Lk 3:2), son-in-law of Annas (Jn 18:13). Prophesies concerning Jesus (Jn 11:49-51; 18:14). Jesus tried before (Mt 26:2-3, 57, 63-65; Jn 18:24, 28). Peter and other disciples accused before (Ac 4:1-22).

CAIN (*metal worker* BDB KB; *brought forth, acquired* Ge. 4:1).
1. Son of Adam (Ge 4:1). Jealousy and crime of (Ge 4:3-15; Heb 11:4; 1Jn 3:12; Jude 11). Settles in the land of Nod (Ge 4:16). Children and descendants of (Ge 4:17-18).
2. *See Kain, 1.*

CAINAN (*worker in iron, metal worker*).
1. Also called Kenan. Son of Enos (Ge 5:9-15; 1Ch 1:2; Lk 3:37).
2. Son of Arphaxad (Lk 3:36).

CAKES Of unleavened bread (Ex 12:39), mixed with oil for offerings (Ex 29:2), offered to the Queen of Heaven (Jer 7:18); of raisins and figs (1Sa 25:18); of dates (2Sa 6:19); of barley (Eze 4:12).

CALAH (*strength, vigor*). An ancient city of Assyria (Ge 10:11-12).

CALAMUS A sweet cane (SS 4:14; Eze 27:19). An ingredient of the holy ointment (Isa 43:24). Imported (Jer 6:20; Eze 27:19).

CALCOL Son of Mahol (1Ki 4:31). Son of Zerah (1Ch 2:6).

CALDRON In the tabernacle (1Sa 2:14), the temple (2Ch 35:13; Jer 52:18-19). Figurative of judgment (Eze 11:3-11).

CALEB (*dog* BDB; *snappish, warding off* KB).
1. Son of Jephunneh. Also spelled Kelubai (1Ch 2:9, ftn). One of the two survivors of the Israelites permitted to enter the land of promise (Nu 14:30, 38; 26:63-65; 32:11-13; Dt 1:34-36; Jos 14:6-15). Sent to Canaan as a spy (Nu 13:6). Brings favorable report (Nu 13:26-30; 14:6-9). Assists in dividing Canaan (Nu 34:19). Life of, miraculously saved (Nu 14:10-12). Leader of the Israelites after Joshua's death (Jdg 1:11-12). Age of (Jos 14:7-10). Inheritance of (Jos 14:6-15; 15:13-16). Descendants of (1Ch 4:15).
2. Third son of Hezron (1Ch 2:9). Ancestor of Bezalel the craftsman who built the tabernacle (1Ch 2:18-20).
3. Brother of Jerahmeel (1Ch 2:42, 50), possibly the same as 1.

CALEB EPHRATHAH A place near Bethlehem (1Ch 2:24).

CALENDAR In the biblical era, time was reckoned solely on astronomical observations. Days, months, and years were determined by the sun and moon.
1. Days of the week were not named by the Israelites, but were designated by ordinal numbers. Jewish day began in the evening with the appearance of the first stars. Days were subdivided into hours and watches. Israelites divided nights into three watches (Ex 14:24; Jdg 7:19; La 2:19), the Romans four (Mt 14:25).
2. Egyptians had a week of ten days. The seven-day week is of Semitic origin (the Creation account), and ran consecutively irrespective of lunar or solar cycles. This was done for man's physical and spiritual welfare. The biblical records are silent regarding the observance of the Sabbath day from creation to the time of Moses. Sabbath observance was either revived or given special emphasis by Moses (Ex 16:23; 20:8).
3. The Hebrew month began with the new moon. Before the Exile months were designated by numbers. After the Exile names adopted from the Babylonians were used.
4. The Jewish calendar had two concurrent years, the sacred year, beginning in the spring with the month Nisan, and the civic year, beginning with Tishri (see chart below). The sacred year was instituted by Moses and consisted of lunar months of twenty-nine or thirty days each, with an intercalary month called Adar Sheni added about every three years. Every seventh year was a sabbatical year for the Israelites—a year of solemn rest for landlords, slaves, beasts of burden, and land, and freedom for Hebrew slaves. Every fiftieth year was a Jubilee year, observed by family reunions, canceled mortgages, and return of lands to original owners (Lev 25:8-17).

Synchronized Jewish Sacred Calendar

Sacred	Name	Modern Equivalent	Civic
1	Nisan	March-April	7
2	Iyyar	April-May	8
3	Sivan	May-June	9
4	Tammuz	June-July	10
5	Ab	July-August	11
6	Elul	August-September	12
7	Tishri	September-October	1
8	Bul	October-November	2
9	Kislev	November-December	3
10	Tebeth	December-January	4
11	Shebat	January-February	5
12	Adar	February-March	6

See Month; Time; also see each month under its respective topic heading.

CALF Offered in sacrifice (Mic 6:6). Golden idol, made by Aaron (Ex 32; Dt 9:16; Ne 9:18; Ps 106:19; Ac 7:41).

Images of, set up in Bethel and Dan by Jeroboam (1Ki 12:28-33; 2Ki 10:29). Worshiped by Jehu (2Ki 10:29). Prophecies against the golden calves at Bethel (1Ki 13:1-5, 32; Jer 48:13; Hos 8:5-6; 10:5-6, 15; 13:2; Am 3:14; 4:4; 8:14). Altars of, destroyed (2Ki 23:4, 15-20).

CALKERS *See Caulkers.*

CALL

Personal:

By Christ (Isa 55:5; Ro 1:6), his Spirit (Rev 22:17), his works (Ps 19:2-3; Ro 1:20), his ministers (Jer 35:15; 2Co 5:20), his gospel (2Th 2:14).

Is from darkness to light (1Pe 2:9). Addressed to all (Isa 45:22; Mt 20:16). Most reject (Pr 1:24; Mt 20:16). Effective to believers (Ps 110:3; Ac 13:48; 1Co 1:24). Not to many wise by human standards (1Co 1:26). To repentance (Isa 55:1).

To believers is of grace (Gal 1:6; 2Ti 1:9), according to the purpose of God (Ro 8:28; 9:11, 23-24), without repentance (Ro 11:29), high (Php 3:14), holy (2Ti 1:9), heavenly (Heb 3:1), to fellowship with Christ (1Co 1:9), to holiness (1Th 4:7), to a prize (Php 3:14), to liberty (Gal 5:13), to peace (1Co 7:15; Col 3:15), to glory and virtue (2Pe 1:3), to the eternal glory of Christ (2Th 2:14; 1Pe 5:10), to eternal life (1Ti 6:12).

Partakers of justified (Ro 8:30), walk worthy of (Eph 4:1; 2Th 1:11), blessedness of receiving (Rev 19:9), is to be made sure (2Pe 1:10), praise God for (1Pe 2:9), illustrated (Pr 8:3-4; Mt 23:3-9).

Rejected (Jer 6:16; Mt 22:3-7).

Rejection of leads to judicial blindness (Isa 6:9, w Ac 28:24-27; Ro 11:8-10), delusion (Isa 66:4; 2Th 2:10-11), withdrawal of the means of grace (Jer 26:4-6; Ac 13:46; 18:6; Rev 2:5), temporal judgments (Isa 28:12; Jer 6:16, 19; 35:17; Zec 7:12-14), rejection by God (Pr 1:24-32; Jer 6:19, 30), condemnation (Jn 12:48; Heb 2:1-3; 12:25), destruction (Pr 29:1; Mt 22:3-7).

To Special Religious Duty:

Abraham (Ge 12:1-3; Isa 51:2; Heb 11:8). Moses (Ex 3:2, 4, 10; 4:1-16; Ps 105:26; Ac 7:34-35). Aaron and his sons (Ex 4:14-16; 28:1; Ps 105:26; Heb 5:4). Joshua (Nu 27:18-19, 22-23; Dt 31:14, 23; Jos 1:1-9). Gideon (Jdg 6:11-16). Samuel (1Sa 3:4-10). Solomon (1Ch 28:6, 10). Jehu (2Ki 9:6-7; 2Ch 22:7). Cyrus (Isa 45:1-4). Amos (Am 7:14-15). Apostles (Mt 4:18-22; 9:9; Mk 1:16-17; 2:14; 3:13-19; Lk 5:27; 6:13-16; Jn 15:16). The rich young ruler (Mk 10:21-22). Paul (Ac 9:4-6, 15-16; 13:2-3; Ro 1:1; 1Co 1:1; 2Co 1:1; Gal 1:1, 15-16; Eph 1:1; Col 1:1; 1Ti 1:1; 2Ti 1:1).

To All Believers:

(Ro 8:30; 1Co 1:2, 9, 24; 1Th 2:11-12; 2Th 2:13-14; 2Ti 1:9; Heb 3:1-2, 3:7-8; 1Pe 5:10; 2Pe 1:3, 10; Jude 1; Rev 17:14).

See Minister, Call of; Backsliders; Seekers.

CALLING, THE CHRISTIAN (1Co 1:26; Eph 1:18; 4:1; Php 3:14; 1Th 2:12; 2Th 2:14; 2Ti 1:9; Heb 3:1; 1Pe 5:10; 2Pe 1:10). *See Call.*

CALNEH (*all of them*). Also called Canneh and Calno, a city of Assyria (Ge 10:10; Isa 10:9; Eze 27:23; Am 6:2).

CALNO (*all of them*). City which tried to resist the Assyrians (Isa 10:9).

CALVARY *See Golgotha.*

CAMEL Herds of (Ge 12:16; 24:35; 30:43; 1Sa 30:17; 1Ch 27:30; Job 1:3, 17; Isa 60:6). Docility of (Ge 24:11).

Uses of: For riding (Ge 24:10, 61, 64; 31:17), posts (Est 8:10, 14; Jer 2:23), drawing chariots (Isa 21:7), for carrying burdens (Ge 24:10; 37:25; 1Ki 10:2; 2Ki 8:9; 1Ch 12:40; Isa 30:6), for cavalry (1Sa 30:17), for milk (Ge 32:15). Forbidden as food (Lev 11:4). Hair of, made into cloth (Mt 3:4; Mk 1:6). Ornaments of (Jdg 8:21, 26). Stables for (Eze 25:5).

CAMEL'S HAIR John the Baptist wore a garment made of camel's hair (Mt 3:4; Mk 1:6). Such garments are still used in the Near East.

CAMON *See Kamon.*

CAMP Of the Israelites around the tabernacle (Nu 2; 3). *See Itinerary.*

CAMPHIRE *See Henna Blossoms.*

CANA (*reed*). Marriage at (Jn 2:1-11). Nobleman's son healed at (Jn 4:46-47). Nathanael's home at (Jn 21:2).

CANAAN (*land of purple* hence *merchant, trader*).

1. Son of Ham (Ge 9:18, 22, 25-27). Descendants of (Ge 10:6, 15; 1Ch 1:8, 13).

2. Land of (Ge 11:31; 17:8; 23:2). Called Israel (Ex 15:14), the land of Israel (1Sa 13:19), of the Hebrews (Ge 40:15), of the Jews (Ac 10:39), of promise (Heb 11:9), the Beautiful Land (Da 8:9), the holy land (Zec 2:12), the Lord's land (Hos 9:3), Immanuel's land (Isa 8:8), Beulah (Isa 62:4).

Promised to Abraham and his seed (Ge 12:1-7; 13:14-17; 15:18-21; 17:8; Dt 12:9-10; Ps 105:11) and the promise renewed to Isaac (Ge 26:3). Extent of: According to the promise (Ge 15:18; Ex 23:31; Dt 11:24; Jos 1:4; 15:1), after the Conquest by Joshua (Jos 12:1-8), in Solomon's time (1Ki 4:21, 24; 2Ch 7:8; 9:26). Prophecy concerning, after the restoration of Israel (Eze 47:13-20).

Fertility of (Dt 8:7-9; 11:10-13). Fruitfulness of (Nu 13:27; 14:7-8; Jer 2:7; 32:22). Products of: Fruits (Dt 8:8; Jer 40:10, 12), minerals (Dt 8:9). Exports of (Eze 27:17).

Famines in (Ge 12:10; 26:1; 47:13; Ru 1:1; 2Sa 21:1; 1Ki 17). *See Famine.*

Spies sent into, by Moses (Nu 13:17-29). Conquest of, by the Israelites (Nu 21:21-35; Dt 3:3-6; Jos 6-12; Ps 44:1-3). Divided by lot among the twelve tribes and families (Nu 26:55-56; 33:54; 34:13), by Joshua, Eleazar, and a prince from each tribe (Nu 34:16-29; 35:1-8; Jos 14-19). Divided into twelve provinces by Solomon (1Ki 4:7-19). Into two kingdoms, Judah and Israel (1Ki 11:29-36; 12:16-21). Roman provinces of (Lk 3:1; Jn 4:3-4). *See Canaanite(s).*

CANAANITE, SIMON THE *See Simon, 2; Zealot, Simon the.*

CANAANITE(S) (*land of purple* hence *merchant, trader*).

Eleven nations descended from Canaan (Ge 10:15-19; Dt 7:1; 1Ch 1:13-16). Territory of (Ge 10:19; 12:6; 15:18; Ex 23:31; Nu 13:29; 34:1-12; Jos 1:4; 5:1), given to the Israelites (Ge 12:6-7; 15:18; 17:8; Ex 23:23; Dt 7:1-3; 32:49; Ps 135:11-12).

Wickedness of (Ge 13:13; Lev 18:25, 27-28; 20:23). To be expelled from the land (Ex 33:2; 34:11). To be destroyed (Ex 23:23-24; Dt 19:1; 31:3-5). Not expelled (Jos 17:12-18; Jdg 1:1-33; 3:1-3). Defeat the Israelites (Nu 14:45; Jdg 4:1-3). Defeated by the Israelites (Nu 21:1-3; Jos 11:1-16; Jdg 4:4-24), by the Egyptians (1Ki 9:16). Chariots of (Jos 17:18).

Isaac forbidden by Abraham to take a wife from (Ge 28:1). Judah marries a woman of (Ge 38:2; 1Ch 2:3). The Jews intermarry with after the Exile (Ezr 9:2).

Prophecy concerning (Ge 9:25-27).

CANANAEAN *See Zealot, Simon the.*

CANDACE (roughly *queen*). Queen of Ethiopia (Ac 8:27).

CANDIDATE Instance of Absalom, campaigning for popular favor (2Sa 15:1-6).

CANDLE *See Lamp.*

CANDLESTICK *See Lampstand.*

CANE Probably the sweet calamus (Isa 43:24; Jer 6:20).

CANKER *See Gangrene.*

CANKERWORM *See Locust.*

CANNEH An alternate form of Calneh. A city of Assyria (Eze 27:23). *See Calneh.*

CANNIBALISM (Lev 26:29; Dt 28:53-57; 2Ki 6:28-29; Jer 19:9; La 2:20; 4:10; Eze 5:10).

CANONICITY By the canon is meant the list of the books of the Bible recognized by the Christian church as genuine and inspired. The Protestant canon includes thirty-nine books in the OT and twenty-seven in the New. The Roman Catholic canon has fourteen more books and additions to the OT; the Orthodox as many as eighteen. *See Apocrypha.* The Jewish canon is the same as the Protestant OT. The OT canon was formed before the time of Christ, as is evident from Josephus (*Against Apion* 1:8), who wrote c. A.D. 90. We know very little of the history of the acceptance of the OT books as canonical. There is much more documentary evidence regarding the formation of the NT canon. The Muratorian Canon (c. A.D. 170), which survives only as a fragment, lists most of the NT books. Some of the books were questioned for a time for various reasons, usually uncertainty of authorship, but by the end of the fourth century our present canon was almost universally accepted, and this was done not by arbitrary decree of bishops, but by the general consensus of the church.

CANTICLES *See Song of Solomon.*

CAPERNAUM (*village of Nahum*). A city on the shore of the Sea of Galilee. Jesus chose, as the place of his abode (Mt 4:13; Lk 4:31). Miracles of Jesus performed at (Mt 9:1-26; 17:24-27; Mk 1:21-45; 2; 3:1-6; Lk 7:1-10; Jn 4:46-53; 6:17-25, 59).

Jesus' prophecy against (Mt 11:23; Lk 10:15).

CAPHTOR Place from which the Philistines originally came (Am 9:7), probably from the island of Crete (Jer 47:4; Am 9:7).

CAPHTORITES People of Caphtor (Ge 10:14; Dt 2:23; 1Ch 1:12).

CAPITAL The uppermost member of a column or pilaster crowning the shaft and taking the weight of the entablature (Ex 36:38; 1Ki 7:16-42; 2Ki 25:17; 2Ch 4:12-13; Jer 52:22).

CAPITAL AND LABOR Strife between (Mt 21:33-41; Mk 12:1-9; Lk 20:9-10). *See Employee; Employer; Master; Rich, The; Servant.*

CAPITAL PUNISHMENT *See Punishment.*

CAPPADOCIA Easternmost Roman province of Asia Minor (Ac 2:9; 1Pe 1:1).

CAPSTONE The keystone of an arch or the last stone put in place to complete a building. Figurative of Jesus: first rejected; finally taking his rightful place of supremacy (Ps 118:22; Zec 4:7; Mt 21:42; Mk 12:10; Lk 20:17; Ac 4:11; 1Pe 2:7). *See Cornerstone.*

CAPTAIN Commander-in-chief of an army (Dt 20:9; Jdg 4:2; 1Sa 14:50; 1Ki 2:35; 16:16; 1Ch 27:34). Of the tribes (Nu 2). Of thousands (Nu 31:48; 1Sa 17:18; 1Ch 28:1). Of hundreds (2Ki 11:15). *See Centurion.* Of fifties (2Ki 1:9; Isa 3:3). Of the guard (Ge 37:36; 2Ki 25:8). Of the ward (Jer 37:13).

Signifying any commander (1Sa 9:16; 22:2; 2Ki 20:5), leader (1Ch 11:21; 12:34; 2Ch 17:14-19; Jn 18:12).

David's captains or chief heroes (2Sa 23; 1Ch 11; 12). King appoints (1Sa 18:13; 2Sa 17:25; 18:1).

Angel of the Lord called (Jos 5:14; 2Ch 13:12).

See Armies.

CAPTIVE Prisoner of war (Ge 14:12; 1Sa 30:1-2).

Cruelty to: Putting to death (Nu 31:9-20; Dt 20:13; 21:10; Jos 8:29; 10:15-40; 11:11; Jdg 7:25; 8:21; 21:11; 1Sa 15:32-33; 2Sa 8:2; 2Ki 8:12; Jer 39:6), 20,000 by Amaziah (2Ch 25:11-12), ripping open pregnant women (2Ki 8:12; 15:16; Am 1:13), enslaved or tortured with picks and axes (2Sa 12:31; 1Ch 20:3), blinded (Jdg 16:21; Jer 39:7), maimed (Jdg 1:6-7), ravished (La 5:11-13; Zec 14:2), enslaved (Dt 20:14; 2Ki 5:2; Ps 44:12; Joel 3:6), robbed (Eze 23:25-26), confined in pits (Isa 51:14). Other indignities to (Isa 20:4).

Kindness to (2Ki 25:27-30; Ps 106:46). Advanced to positions in state (Ge 41:39-45; Est 2:8; Da 1).

CAPTIVITY Of the, Israelites foretold (Lev 26:33; Dt 28:36), ten tribes (2Ki 17:6, 23-24; 18:9-12).

Of Judah in Babylon, prophecy of (Isa 39:6; Jer 13:19; 20:4; 25:2-11; 32:28), fulfilled (2Ki 24:11-16; 25; 2Ch 36; Jer 52:28-30). Israelites in, promises to (Ne 1:9). Jews return from (Ezr 2; 3; 8).

As a judgment (Ezr 5:12; 9:7; Isa 5:13; Jer 29:17-19; La 1:3-5; Eze 39:23-24).

Figurative:

(Isa 61:1; Ro 7:23; 1Co 9:27; 2Co 10:5; 2Ti 2:26; 3:6). "Take captive your captives" (Jdg 5:12), "led captives in your train" (Ps 68:18; Eph 4:8).

CAR *See Beth Car.*

CARAVAN Company of travelers united together for a common purpose or for mutual protection and generally equipped for a long journey, especially in desert country or through foreign and presumably hostile territory (Ge 32-33; 1Sa 30:1-20).

CARAWAY (Isa 28:25-27).

CARBUNCLE NIV "sparkling jewels," (Isa 54:12), "beryl," and "chrysolite." *See Beryl; Chrysolite, 1; Minerals of the Bible, 1; Stones.*

CARCAS (perhaps *vulture*). A eunuch and servant of the Persian king Xerxes (Est 1:10).

CARCASS The dead body of a human or animal. Israelites were ceremonially unclean if they touched a carcass (Lev 11:8-40; Nu 6:6-7; 9:10; Dt 14:8).

CARCHEMISH A Babylonian city on the Euphrates, against which the king of Egypt made war (2Ch 35:20; Isa 10:9; Jer 46:2).

CARE

Worldly (Ecc 4:8; Mt 6:25-34; 13:22; Mk 4:19; Lk 8:14; 12:27; 14:18-19; 21:34; 1Co 7:32-33; Php 4:6; 2Ti 2:4). In vain (Ps 39:6; 127:2; Mt 6:27; Lk 12:25-26). Proceeds from unbelief (Mt 6:26, 28-30; Lk 12:24, 27-28), Martha rebuked for (Lk 10:40-41).

Remedy for (Ps 37:5; 55:22; Pr 16:3; Jer 17:7-8; Mt 6:26-34; Lk 12:22-32; Php 4:6-7; Heb 13:5; 1Pe 5:6-7).

Instances of: Martha (Lk 10:40-41). Certain ones who desired to follow Jesus (Mt 8:19-22; Lk 9:57-62).

See Anxiety; Carnal Mindedness; Rich, The; Riches; Worldliness.

CAREAH *See Kareah.*

CARITES Mercenary soldiers from Caria in SW Asia Minor (2Ki 11:4, 19).

CARMEL (*orchard planted with vine and fruit trees*).

1. A fertile and lovely mountain in Israel (SS 7:5; Isa 33:9; 35:2; Jer 46:18; 50:19; Am 1:2). Forests of (2Ki 19:23). Caves of (Am 9:3). An idolatrous high place upon; Elijah builds an altar upon, and confronts the worshipers of Baal, putting to death 450 of its prophets (1Ki 18:17-46). Elisha's abode in (2Ki 2:25; 4:25).

2. A city of Judah (Jos 15:55). Saul erects a memorial at (1Sa 15:12). Nabal's possessions at (1Sa 25:2). King Uzziah, who delighted in agriculture, had vineyards at (2Ch 26:10).

CARMELITE Hezro, one of David's mighty men, a native of Judean Carmel (1Sa 27:3; 1Ch 11:37).

C

C

CARMI, CARMITE (possibly *[fruitful] vine, vineyard owner* IDB).
1. Son of Reuben (Ge 46:9; Ex 6:14).
2. Son of Hezron (1Ch 4:1).
3. Father of Achan (Jos 7:1, 18; 1Ch 2:7) and his clan (Nu 26:6).

CARNAL MINDEDNESS Is in conflict with, the inner being (Ro 7:14-22), the Holy Spirit (Gal 5:17). Is at enmity with God (Ro 8:6-8; Jas 4:4). In the children of wrath (Eph 2:3). To be crucified (Ro 8:13; Gal 5:24). Excludes from kingdom of God (Gal 5:19-21). Reaps corruption (Gal 6:8).
See Care, Worldly; Flesh; Riches; Sin, Fruits of; Worldliness.

CARNELIAN Seen in John's vision of the glory of God (Rev 4:3) and the foundation of the New Jerusalem (Rev 21:20).
See Minerals of the Bible, 1; Stones.

CARPENTRY Building the ark (Ge 6:14-16). Tabernacle and furniture of (Ex 31:2-9). *See Tabernacle.* David's palace (2Sa 5:11). Temple (2Ki 12:11; 22:6). *See Temple.* Making idols (Isa 41:7; 44:13). Carpenters (Jer 24:1; Zec 1:20), Joseph (Mt 13:55), Jesus (Mk 6:3).
See Carving; Master Craftsman.

CARPET *See Tapestry.*

CARPUS (*fruit[ful]*). A Christian at Troas (2Ti 4:13).

CARRIAGE A richly adorned royal means of transportation, a palanquin (SS 3:7, 9-10). In the description of fallen Babylon (Rev 18:13).

CARSHENA (possibly *black*). A Persian prince (Est 1:14).

CART(S) Vehicle(s) with wheels used for carrying goods as well as persons (Ge 45:19, 21; 46:5; 1Sa 6:7-14; 2Sa 6:3; Isa 28:27-28).

CARVING Woodwork of the temple was decorated with carvings of flowers, cherubim, and palm trees (1Ki 6:18, 29, 32, 35; Ps 74:6). Beds decorated with (Pr 7:16). Idols manufactured by (Dt 7:5; Isa 44:9-17; 45:20; Hab 2:18-19).
Persons skilled in: Bezalel (Ex 31:1-5), Huram (1Ki 7:13-51; 2Ch 2:13-14).

CASIPHIA A place in the Persian Empire (Ezr 8:17).

CASLUHITES A people whose progenitor was a son of Mizraim (Ge 10:14; 1Ch 1:12).

CASSIA An aromatic plant, probably cinnamon (Ps 45:8; Eze 27:19). An ingredient of the sacred oil (Ex 30:24).

CASTING *See Molding.*

CASTING LOTS To get a decision from God (Lev 16:8; Jos 18:6-10; 1Sa 14:42; 1Ch 24:31; 26:13-14; Jnh 1:7; Ac 1:26). To set a date (Est 3:7). To settle disputes (Pr 18:18). In divination (Eze 21:21). In gambling (Job 6:27; Ps 22:18; Mt 27:35). The decision is from the LORD (Pr 16:33). *See Lot, The.*

CASTLE *See Fort; Tower.* For the concept "My house is my castle" see Dt 24:10-11.

CASTOR AND POLLUX Twin sons of Zeus, Greek gods thought to have power over wind and wave (Ac 28:11).

CATACOMBS Subterranean burial places used by the early church. Most are in Rome, where they extend for 600 miles.

CATERPILLAR(S) *See Grasshopper; Locust.*

CATHOLIC EPISTLES *See General Letters.*

CATHOLICITY (liberality of religious sentiment, inclusiveness).

Taught:
In Christ's reproof of John (Mk 9:38-41; Lk 9:49-50). In Peter's vision of the sheet and visit to Cornelius (Ac 10:1-48). In Paul's commission (Ro 1:1-7, 14-16). In Paul's rebuke of Jewish exclusiveness (Ro 3:20-31; 4:1-25). In the judgment of apostolic church (Ac 15:1-31). In the unity of believers (Ro 5:1-2; Gal 3:27-28; Eph 2:14-17; Col 3:11-15). In the gifts of Holy Spirit to Gentiles as well as to Jews (Ac 10:44-48; 11:17-18).
See Heathen; Strangers.

Instances of:
Solomon, in his prayer (1Ki 8:41-43). Paul, in recognizing devout Gentiles (Ac 13:16, 26, 42-43). Peter (Ac 10:34-35). Rulers of the synagogue at Salamis, permitting the apostles to preach (Ac 13:5).

CATTLE Of the bovine species. Used for sacrifice (1Ki 8:63). *See Heifer; Offerings.* Sheltered (Ge 33:17). Pharaoh's dream of (Ge 41:2-7, 26-30). Stall-fed (Pr 15:17).
Gilead adapted to the raising of (Nu 32:1-4), and Bashan (Ps 22:12; Eze 39:18; Am 4:1).
See Animals; Bull; Cow; Heifer; Offerings.

CAUDA An island near Crete (Ac 27:16).

CAULKERS Those who drive some suitable substance into the seams of a ship's planking to render them watertight (Eze 27:9). *See Pitch; Tar.*

CAUL(S)
1. NIV "covering" of the liver. Burnt with sacrifice (Ex 29:13, 22; Lev 3:4, 10, 15; 4:9; 7:4; 8:16, 25; 9:10, 19).
2. NIV "headbands" (Isa 3:18). *See Headbands.*

CAUSE *See Actions at Law.*

CAUTION *See Expediency; Prudence.*

CAVALRY Mounted on, horses (Ex 14:23; 1Sa 13:5; 2Sa 8:4; 1Ki 4:26; 2Ch 8:6; 9:25; 12:3; Isa 30:16; 31:1; Jer 4:29; Zec 10:5; Rev 9:16-18), camels (1Sa 30:17).
See Armies.

CAVE Used as a dwelling: By Lot (Ge 19:30), Elijah (1Ki 19:9), Israelites (Eze 33:27), believers (Heb 11:38). Place of refuge (Jos 10:16-27; Jdg 6:2; 1Sa 13:6; 1Ki 18:4, 13; 19:9, 13). Burial place (Ge 23:9-20; 25:9; 49:29-32; 50:13; Jn 11:38).
Of Adullam (1Sa 22:1; 2Sa 23:13; 1Ch 11:15). En Gedi (1Sa 24:3-8).

CEDAR Valuable for building purposes (Isa 9:10). David's ample provision of, in Jerusalem, for the temple (2Ch 1:15; 22:4). Furnished by Hiram, king of Tyre, for Solomon's temple (1Ki 5:6-10; 9:11; 2Ch 2:16).
Used in rebuilding, the temple (Ezr 3:7), David's palace (2Sa 5:11; 1Ch 17:1), Solomon's palace (1Ki 7:2), masts of ships (Eze 27:5). Used in purifications (Lev 14:4, 6, 49-52; Nu 19:6).
Figurative (Ps 72:16; 92:12; Isa 2:13; 14:8; Jer 22:7; Eze 31:3; Zec 11:2).

CEDRON *See Kidron.*

CEILING A reference is to the walls of the temple (1Ki 6:15).

CELESTIAL PHENOMENA Fire from heaven, on the cities of the plain (Ge 19:24-25), on the two captains and their fifties (2Ki 1:10-14), on the flocks and servants of Job (Job 1:16). Hail, on the Egyptians (Ex 9:22-34).
Darkness, on the Egyptians (Ex 10:22-23), at the crucifixion of Jesus (Mt 27:45; Lk 23:44-45). Pillar of cloud and fire (Ex 13:21-22; 14:19, 24; 40:38; Nu 9:15-23; Ps 78:14). Thunder and lightning on Mt. Sinai (Ex 19:16, 18; 20:18). Sun stood still (Jos 10:12-13).
Prophecy of darkening of sun, moon, and stars (Joel 2:30, 32; Mt 24:29; Lk 21:25; Ac 2:19-20).
See Astronomy.

CELIBACY (*Abstaining from marriage and sexual activity*). Lamented by Jephthah's daughter (Jdg 11:38-39). Not obligatory (1Co 7:1-9, 25-26; 9:5; 1Ti 4:1-3). Practiced for kingdom of heaven's sake (Mt 19:10-12; 1Co 7:32-40). The 144,000 (Rev 14:1-4).

CELLAR *See Storehouse.*

CENCHREA A seaport near Corinth (Ac 18:18; Ro 16:1).

CENSER Used for offering incense (Lev 16:12; Nu 16:6-7, 16-18, 46; Rev 8:3). For the temple, made of gold (1Ki 7:50; 2Ch 4:22; Heb 9:4). Those which Korah used were converted into plates (Nu 16:37-39). Used in idolatrous rites (Eze 8:11).
Symbolic: (Rev 8:3, 5).

CENSORIOUSNESS *See Charitableness; Speaking, Evil; Uncharitableness.*

CENSUS Numbering of Israel by Moses (Ex 38:26; Nu 1; 3:14-43; 26), David (2Sa 24:1-9; 1Ch 21:1-8; 27:24).
A poll tax to be levied at each (Ex 30:12-16; 38:26).
Of the Roman Empire, by Caesar (Lk 2:1-3).

CENTURION (*ruler over 100*). A commander of 100 soldiers in the Roman army (Mk 15:44-45; Ac 21:32; 22:25-26; 23:17, 23; 24:23). Of Capernaum, comes to Jesus in behalf of his servant (Mt 8:5-13; Lk 7:1-10). In charge of the soldiers who crucified Jesus, testifies, "Truly this was the Son of God" (Mt 27:54; Mk 15:39; Lk 23:47).
See Cornelius; Julius.

CEPHAS (*rock*). *See Peter, Simon.*

CEREMONIAL WASHING The Mosaic Law, relative to cleansing, stresses that sin defiles. To keep this great truth constantly before the Israelites, specific ordinances concerning washings were given to Moses. The purpose was to teach, by this object lesson, that sin pollutes the soul, and that only those who were cleansed from their sins could be pure in the sight of the Lord (Heb 9:10; 10:22).
Of Garments (Ex 19:10, 14). Of priests (Ex 29:4; 30:18-21; 40:12, 31-32; Lev 8:6; 16:4, 24, 26, 28; Nu 19:7-10, 19; 2Ch 4:6). Of burnt offerings (Lev 1:9, 13; 9:14; 2Ch 4:6). Of the hands (Mt 15:2; Mk 7:2-5; Lk 11:38). Of the feet (1Ti 5:10).
For defilement (Lev 11:24-40). Of lepers (Lev 13:6; 14:9). Of those having bodily discharge (Lev 15:5-13). Of those having eaten or touched that which died (Lev 11:25, 40; 17:15-16).
Traditional forms of, not observed by Jesus (Lk 11:38-39).
See Defilement; Purification; Washings.

CERTIFICATE OF DIVORCE Given by the husband to his wife upon divorce (Dt 24:1-4; Mt 5:31; 19:7; Mk 10:4). Figurative of God's judgment on Israel (Isa 50:1; Jer 3:8). *See Divorce.*

CESAR *See Caesar.*

CESAREA *See Caesarea.*

CESAREA PHILIPPI *See Caesarea Philippi.*

CHAFF Winnowing of figurative of judgment (Job 21:18; Ps 1:4; 35:5; Isa 17:13; Da 2:35; Hos 13:3; Mt 3:12; Lk 3:17).

CHAINS Used as ornaments. Worn by princes (Ge 41:42; Da 5:7, 29), on ankles (Nu 31:50; Isa 3:19), on the breastplate of high priest (Ex 28:14; 39:15). As ornaments on camels (Jdg 8:26). A partition of, in the temple (1Ki 6:21; 7:17).
Used to confine prisoners (Ps 68:6; 149:8; Jer 40:4; Ac 12:6-7; 21:33; 28:20; 2Ti 1:16). *See Fetters.*
Figurative (Ps 73:6; Pr 1:9; La 3:7; Eze 7:23-27; Jude 6; 2Pe 2:4; Rev 20:1).

CHALCEDONY A precious stone (Rev 21:19). *See Minerals of the Bible, 1; Stones.*

CHALCOL *See Calcol.*

CHALDEA The southern portion of Babylonia. Often used interchangeably with Babylon as the name of the empire founded in the valley of the Euphrates. Abraham a native of (Ge 11:28, 31; 15:7). Founded by the Assyrians (Isa 23:13). Character of its people (Hab 1:6).
See Babylon; Chaldeans.

CHALDEAN ASTROLOGERS *See Wise Men.*

CHALDEANS
1. Virtually synonymous with the Babylonians (2Ki 25:4; 2Ch 36:17; Isa 13:19, ftns). *See Babylon; Chaldea.*
2. Learned and wise men of the east, NIV "astrologers" (Da 2:2, 4, 5, 10; 3:8; 4:7; 5:7).

CHALDEES *See Chaldeans; Ur.*

CHALK (Isa 27:9).

CHAMBERING *See Adultery; Fornication.*

CHAMBERLAIN *See Eunuch.*

CHAMBERS OF IMAGERY NIV "shrine of his own idol." Rooms in the temple where seventy elders of Israel worshiped idols (Eze 8:12).

CHAMELEON Forbidden as food (Lev 11:30).

CHAMOIS NIV "mountain sheep"; permitted as food (Dt 14:5). *See Animals.*

CHAMPAIGN Dt 11:30, KJV. *See Arabah.*

CHAMPIONSHIP Instances of battles decided by: Goliath and David (1Sa 17:8-53). Young men of David's and Abner's armies (2Sa 2:14-17). Representatives of the Philistines' and David's armies (2Sa 21:15-22).

CHANAAN *See Canaan.*

CHANCELLOR A state officer (Ezr 4:8-9, 17). *See Cabinet; Officer.*

CHANGE OF VENUE Granted Paul (Ac 23:17-35). Declined by Paul (Ac 25:9, 11).

CHANGERS OF MONEY *See Money Changers.*

CHAPITER *See Capital.*

CHAPMAN NIV "merchants" (2Ch 9:14). *See Merchant; Trade and Travel.*

CHARACTER

Of Believers:
Attentive to Christ's voice (Jn 10:3-4), blameless and harmless (Php 2:15), bold (Pr 28:1), contrite (Isa 57:15; 66:2), devout (Ac 8:2; 22:13), faithful (Rev 17:14), fearing God (Mal 3:16; Ac 10:2), following Christ (Jn 10:4, 27), godly (Ps 4:3; 2Pe 2:9), without falsehood (Jn 1:47), holy (Dt 7:6; 14:2; Col 3:12), humble (Ps 34:2; 1Pe 5:5), hungering for righteousness (Mt 5:6), just (Ge 6:9; Hab 2:4; Lk 2:25), led by the Spirit (Ro 8:14), generous (Isa 32:8; 2Co 9:13), loathing themselves (Eze 20:43), loving (Col 1:4; 1Th 4:9), lowly (Pr 16:19), meek (Isa 29:19; Mt 5:5), merciful (Ps 37:26; Mt 5:7), new creatures (2Co 5:17; Eph 2:10), obedient (Ro 16:19; 1Pe 1:14), poor in spirit (Mt 5:3), prudent (Pr 16:21), pure in heart (Mt 5:8; 1Jn 3:3), righteous (Isa 60:21; Lk 1:6), sincere (2Co 1:12; 2:17), steadfast (Ac 2:42; Col 2:5), taught of God (Isa 54:13; 1Jn 2:27), true (2Co 6:8), undefiled (Ps 119:1), upright (1Ki 3:6; Ps 15:2), watchful (Lk 12:37), zealous of good works (Tit 2:14). *See Righteous, Described.*

Of the Wicked:
Abominable (Rev 21:8), alienated from God (Eph 4:18; Col 1:21), blasphemous (Lk 22:65; Rev 16:9), blinded (2Co 4:4; Eph 4:18), boastful (Ps 10:3; 49:6), conspiring against believers (Ne 4:8; 6:2; Ps 38:12), corrupt (Mt 7:17; Eph 4:22), covetous (Mic 2:2; Ro 1:29), deceitful (Ps 5:6; Ro 3:13), delighting in the iniquity of others (Pr 2:14; Ro 1:32), despising believers (Ne 2:19; 4:2; 2Ti 3:3-4), destructive (Isa 59:7), disobedient (Ne 9:26; Tit 3:3; 1Pe 2:7), enticing to evil (Pr 1:10-14; 2Ti 3:6), envious (Ne 2:10; Tit 3:3), evildoers (Jer 13:23; Mic 7:3), fearful (Pr 28:1; Rev 21:8), fierce (Pr 16:29; 2Ti 3:3), foolish (Dt 32:6; Ps 5:5), forgetting God (Job 8:13), fraudulent (Pr 21:8; Isa 57:17), glorying in their shame (Php 3:19), hardhearted (Eze 3:7), hating the light (Job 24:13; Jn 3:20), heady and conceited (2Ti 3:4), hostile to God (Ro 8:7; Col 1:21), hypocritical (Isa 29:13; 2Ti 3:5), ignorant of God (Hos 4:1; 2Th 1:8), impudent (Eze 2:4), infidel (Ps 10:4; 14:1), loathsome (Pr 13:5), lovers of pleasure, not of God (2Ti 3:4), lying (Ps 58:3; 62:4; Isa 59:4), mischievous (Pr 24:8; Mic 7:3), murderous (Ps 10:8; 94:6; Ro 1:29), persecuting (Ps 69:26; 109:16), perverse (Dt 32:5), prayerless (Job 21:15; Ps 53:4), proud (Ps 59:12; Ob 3; 2Ti 3:2), rebellious (Isa 1:2; 30:9), rejoicing in the affliction of believers (Ps 35:15), reprobate (2Co 13:5; 2Ti 3:8; Tit 1:16), selfish (2Ti 3:2), sensual (Php 3:19; Jude 19), sold under sin (1Ki 21:20; 2Ki 17:17), stiff-hearted (Eze 2:4), stiff-necked (Ex 33:5; Ac 7:51), uncircumcised in heart (Jer 9:26), unclean (Isa 64:6; Eph 4:19), unjust (Pr 11:7; Isa 26:18), ungodly (Pr 16:27), unholy (2Ti 3:2), unmerciful (Ro 1:31), unprofitable (Mt 25:30; Ro 3:12), unruly (Tit 1:10), unthankful (Lk 6:35; 2Ti 3:2), unwise (Dt 32:6), without self-control (2Ti 3:3). *See Wicked, Described as.*

Good:
(Pr 22:1; Ecc 7:1). Defamation of, punished (Dt 22:13-19). Revealed in countenance (Isa 3:9).

Steadfastness of:
(Ps 57:7; 108:1; 112:7; Mk 4:20; 2Th 3:3). Exhortations to steadfastness (1Co 7:20; 15:58; 16:13; Eph 4:14-15; Php 1:27; 4:1; Col 1:23; 1Th 3:8; 2Th 2:15; Heb 3:6, 14; 10:23; 13:9; 1Pe 5:9; 2Pe 3:17; Rev 3:11). Reward of steadfastness (Mt 10:22; Jas 1:25). Continuing of (Rev 22:11).

Instances of Steadfastness:
Joseph (Ge 39:12). Moses (Heb 11:24-26). Joshua (Jos 24:15). Daniel (Da 1:8; 6:10). Three Hebrews (Da 3:16-18). Pilate (Jn 19:22). Peter and John (Ac 4:19-20). Paul (Ac 20:22-24; 21:13-14). *See Decision; Stability.*

Instability of:
(Pr 27:8; Jer 2:36; Hos 6:4; 7:8; 10:2; Mt 13:19-22; Mk 4:15-19; Lk 8:5-15; 2Pe 2:14; Rev 2:4). Warnings against (Pr 24:21-22; Lk 9:59-62; Eph 4:14; Heb 6:4-6; 13:9; Jas 1:6-8; 4:8; 2Pe 2:14).

Instances of Instability:
Reuben (Ge 49:3-4). Pharaoh (Ex 8:15, 32; 9:34; 14:5). Israelites (Ex 32:8; Jdg 2:17-19; 2Ch 11:17). Saul (1Sa 18:19). Solomon (1Ki 11:4-8). Rehoboam (2Ch 12:1). Pilate (Jn 18:37-40; 19:1-6). Demas (2Ti 4:10).

CHARASHIM *See Craftsman; Ge Harashim.*

CHARGE Delivered to ministers: *See Ministers.*

CHARGER *See Plate, Platter.*

CHARIOT For war (Ex 14:7, 9, 25; Jos 11:4; 1Sa 13:5; 1Ki 20:1, 25; 2Ki 6:14; 2Ch 12:2-3; Ps 20:7; Jer 46:9; 47:3; 51:21; Joel 2:5; Na 2:3-4; 3:2). Wheels of Pharaoh's, providentially taken off (Ex 14:25).
Commanded by captains (Ex 14:7; 1Ki 9:22; 22:31-33; 2Ki 8:21). Made of iron (Jos 17:18; Jdg 1:19). Introduced among Israelites by David (2Sa 8:4). Imported from Egypt by Solomon (1Ki 10:26-29). Cities for (1Ki 9:19; 2Ch 1:14; 8:6; 9:25). Royal (Ge 41:43; 46:29; 2Ki 5:9; 2Ch 35:24; Jer 17:25; Ac 8:29). Drawn by camels (Isa 21:7; Mic 1:13).
Kings ride in (2Ch 35:24; Jer 17:25; 22:4). Cherubim in Solomon's temple mounted on (1Ch 28:18).

Figurative:
Chariots of God (Ps 68:17; 104:3; 2Ki 6:17; Isa 66:15; Hab 3:8; Rev 9:9).

Symbolic: (Zec 6:1-8; 2Ki 2:11-12).

CHARISM, CHARISMA, CHARISMATA An inspired gift, bestowed on the apostles and early Christians without any claim of merit on the individual's part, for the good of the church (Mt 10:1, 8; Mk 16:17-18; Lk 10:1, 9, 17, 19; Ac 2:4; 10:44-46; 19:6; 1Co 12).
See Gifts From God; Miracles; Spiritual Gifts; Tongues, Gift of.

CHARITABLENESS Encouraged (Pr 10:12; 17:9). Commanded (Mt 5:23-24; 7:1-5; 18:21-22; Lk 6:36-42; 17:3-4; Jn 7:24; Ro 14:1-23; 15:1-2; 1Co 10:28-33; 16:14; 2Co 2:7; Gal 6:1; Eph 4:32; Col 3:13-14; 1Ti 1:5; 4:12; 2Ti 2:22; Jas 2:13; 4:11-12; 1Pe 3:9). Described (1Co 13:1-13). Covers sins (Pr 10:12; 17:9; 19:11; 1Pe 4:8). Pleases God (Mt 6:14-15; 18:23-35).
See Love; Uncharitableness.

CHARITY *See Alms; Beneficence; Liberality; Love.*

CHARMERS AND CHARMING Prohibited (Dt 18:11). Of serpents (Ps 58:4-5; Jer 8:17). Magic charms and amulets (Pr 17:8; Isa 3:20; Eze 13:18, 20). *See Sorcery.*

CHARRAN *See Haran, 4.*

CHASTISEMENT, FROM GOD A blessing (Job 5:17; Ps 94:12-13; Heb 12:11). Corrective (Dt 11:2-9; 2Sa 7:14-15; 2Ch 6:24-31; 7:13-14; Job 33:19; 34:31; Ps 73:14; 118:18; 119:67, 75; Isa 57:16-18; Jer 24:5-6; 46:28; 1Co 11:32).
Inflicted for sins (Lev 26:28; Ps 89:32; 107:10-12, 17; Isa 40:2; Jer 30:14; La 1:5; Hos 7:12; 10:10; Am 4:6). Administered in love (Dt 8:5; Pr 3:11-12; Heb 12:5-10; Rev 3:19).
Repentance under (Ps 106:43-44; 107:10-13, 17-19; Isa 26:16; Jer 31:18-19). Failure to repent under (Isa 42:25; Jer 2:30; Hag 2:17).
Prayer to be spared from (Ps 6:1; 38:1; 107:23-31). Vicariously borne by Jesus (Isa 53:4-5).
See Afflictions; Judgments; Punishment; Wicked, Punishment of.

CHASTITY

Commanded:
(Ex 20:14; Pr 2:10-11, 16-22; 5:3—21; 6:24-25; 7:1-5; 31:3; Mt 5:27-32; Ac 15:20; Ro 13:13; 1Co 6:13-19; 7:1-2, 7-9, 25-26, 36-37; Eph 5:3; Col 3:5; 1Th 4:3, 7).

Instances of:
Joseph (Ge 39:7-20). Boaz (Ru 3:6-13). Job (Job 31:1, 9-12). Paul (1Co 7). The 144,000 (Rev 14:1-5).
See Celibacy; Self-Control.

CHEATING *See Dishonesty.*

CHEBAR *See Kebar.*

CHEDORLAOMER *See Kedorlaomer.*

CHEERFULNESS *See Contentment.*

CHEESE (1Sa 17:18; 2Sa 17:29; Job 10:10).

CHELAL *See Kelal.*

CHELLUH *See Keluhi.*

CHELUB *See Kelub.*

CHELUBAI *See Caleb, 1.*

CHEMARIM NIV "pagan [priests]" (Zep 1:4). *See Groves; High Places; Idol; Idolatry; Priest, Corrupt.*

CHEMOSH An idol of the Moabites and Ammonites (1Ki 11:7, 33; 2Ki 23:13; Jer 48:7, 13, 46), and Amorites (Jdg 11:24).

CHENAANAH *See Kenaanah.*

CHENANI *See Kenani.*

CHENANIAH *See Kenaniah.*

CHEPHAR-HAAMMONAI *See Kephar Ammoni.*

CHEPHIRAH *See Kephirah.*

CHERAN *See Keran.*

CHERETHIMS, CHERETHITES *See Kerethite(s).*

CHERITH *See Kerith.*

CHERUB *See Kerub.*

CHERUBIM A classification or order of heavenly beings.
Eastward of the garden of Eden (Ge 3:24).
In the tabernacle (Ex 25:18-20; 37:7-9). Ark rested beneath the wings of (1Ki 8:6-7; 2Ch 5:7-8; Heb 9:5). Figures of, embroidered on walls of tabernacle (Ex 26:1; 36:8), and on the veil (Ex 26:31; 36:35).
In the temple (1Ki 6:23-29; 2Ch 3:10-13). Figures of, on the veil (2Ch 3:14), walls (1Ki 6:29-35; 2Ch 3:7), movable stands (1Ki 7:29, 36).
In Ezekiel's vision of the temple (Eze 41:18-20, 25).
Figurative (Eze 28:14, 16).
Symbolic (Eze 1; 10).

CHESALON *See Kesalon.*

CHESED *See Kesed.*

CHESIL *See Kesil.*

CHEST
1. The ark of the covenant (Ex 25:10-14; Dt 10:1-2).
2. For money (2Ki 12:9-10, 2Ch 24:8-11).
3. The torso (Job 41:24; Da 2:32; Rev 1:13).

CHESTNUT TREE *See Plane Tree.*

CHESULLOTH *See Kesulloth.*

CHEZIB *See Kezib.*

CHICKEN *See Hen, 2.*

CHIDING *See Rebuke.*

CHIDON *See Kidon.*

CHILDBEARING Pain of increased as part of the curse (Ge 3:16). Salvation through (1Ti 2:15), a verse of uncertain meaning.

CHILDLESSNESS A reproach (Ge 16:2; 29:32; 30:1-3, 13; 1Sa 1:6; Isa 4:1; Lk 1:25). *See Barrenness.*

CHILDREN

A Blessing:
[Ge 5:29; 30:1; Ps 127:3-5; Pr 17:6). The gift of God (Ge 4:1, 25; 17:16, 20; 22:17; 28:3; 29:32-35; 30:2, 5-6, 17-20, 22-24; 48:9, 16; Ru 4:13; Job 1:21; Ps 107:38, 41; 113:9; 127:3). Promised to the righteous (Dt 7:12, 14; Job 5:25; Ps 128:2-4, 6). Given in answer to prayer to, Abraham (Ge 15:2-5; 21:1-2), Isaac (Ge 25:21), Leah (Ge 30:17-22), Rachel (Ge 30:22-24), Hannah (1Sa 1:9-20), Zechariah (Lk 1:13).

In Infancy:
Circumcision of. *See Circumcision.* Dedicated to God, Samson (Jdg 13:5, 7), Samuel (1Sa 1:24-28), Jesus (Lk 2:22). Nurses for (Ex 2:7-9; Ru 4:16; 2Sa 4:4; 2Ki 11:2; Ac 7:20). Treatment of (Eze 16:4-6; Lk 2:7, 12). Weaning of (Ge 21:8; 1Sa 1:22; 1Ki 11:20; Ps 131:2; Isa 28:9).

In Early Childhood:
Amusements of (Job 21:11; Zec 8:5; Mt 11:16-17; Lk 7:31-32). Early piety of, Samuel (1Sa 2:18; 3), Jeremiah (Jer 1:5-7), John the Baptist (Lk 1:15, 80), Jesus (Lk 2:40, 46-47, 52). Taught to walk (Hos 11:3). Tutored (2Ki 10:1; Ac 22:3; Gal 3:24; 4:1-2). *See Tutor.*

God's Care Of:
(Ex 22:22-24; Dt 10:18; 14:29; Job 29:12; Ps 10:14, 17-18; 27:10; 68:5; 146:9; Jer 49:11; Hos 14:3; Mal 3:5). Blessed by Jesus (Mt 19:13-15; Mk 10:13-16; Lk 18:15-17). Intercessional sacrifices in behalf of (Job 1:5).

Commandments to—
To honor and obey parents (Ex 20:12; Lev 19:3, 32; Dt 5:16; Pr 1:8-9; 6:20-23; 23:22; Mt 15:4; Mk 10:19; Lk 18:20; Eph 6:1, 2-3; Col 3:20; 1Ti 3:4). To seek wisdom (Pr 4:1-11, 20-22; 5:1-2; 8:21-33; 27:11). To praise the Lord (Ps 148:12-13). To remember their Creator (Pr 23:26; Ecc 12:1). To obey (Ps 119:9; Pr 3:1-3; 6:20-25). To be pure (Ecc 11:9-10; La 3:27; 1Ti 4:12; 2Ti 2:22; Tit 2:6). *See Young Men.*

Miracles on behalf of—
Raised from the dead, by Elijah (1Ki 17:17-23), Elisha (2Ki 4:17-36), Jesus (Mt 9:18, 24-26; Mk 5:35-42; Lk 7:13-15; 8:49-56). Healing of (Mt 15:28; 17:18; Mk 7:29-30; 9:23-27; Lk 8:42-56; 9:38-42; Jn 4:46-54).

Prayer in behalf of—
For healing (2Sa 12:16). For divine favor (Ge 17:18). For spiritual wisdom (1Ch 22:12; 29:19). For sins (Job 1:5).

Promises and assurances to—
Promise of divine instruction (Isa 54:13). Long life to the obedient (Ex 20:12; Dt 5:16; Pr 3:1-10; Eph 6:2-3). Love and peace (Pr 8:17, 32; Isa 40:11; 54:13). Acceptance by Jesus (Mt 18:4-5, 10; 19:14-15; Mk 9:37; 10:16; Lk 9:48; 18:15-16). Joy to parents of wise children (Pr 23:15-16, 24-25; 29:3). Forgiven sins (1Jn 2:12-13).

The righteous, blessed by God—
In escaping judgments (Ge 6:18; 7:1; 19:12, 15-16; Lev 26:44-45; 1Ki 11:13; 2Ki 8:19; Pr 11:21; 12:7). In temporal prosperity (Ge 12:7; 13:15; 17:7-8; 21:13; 26:3-4, 24; Dt 4:37; 10:15; 12:28; 1Ki 15:4; Ps 37:26; 102:28; 112:2-3; Pr 13:22). In divine mercy (Ps 103:17-18; Pr 3:33; 20:7; Isa 44:3-5; 65:23; Jer 32:39; Ac 2:39; 1Co 7:14).

C

Parental Relationships:
Love of, for parents: Ruth (Ru 1:16-18), Jesus (Jn 19:26-27). Counsel of parents to (1Ki 2:1-4; 1Ch 22:6-13; 28:9-10, 20). Of ministers (1Ti 3:4; Tit 1:6).

Instruction of—
The law (Dt 6:6-9; 11:19-20; 31:12-13; Jos 8:35; Ps 78:1-8). The fear of the Lord (Ps 34:11). The providence of God (Ex 10:2; 12:26-27; 13:8-10, 14-16; Dt 4:9-10; Joel 1:3). Righteousness (Pr 1:1, 4; 22:6; Isa 28:9-10; 38:19). The Scriptures (Ac 22:3; Eph 6:4; 2Ti 3:15).
See Instruction; Tutor; Young Men.

Correction and punishment—
By discipline (Pr 19:18; 23:13; 29:15; Eph 6:4; Col 3:2). By the rod (Pr 13:24; 22:15; 23:13-14; 29:15). By death (Ex 21:15; 21:17; Lev 20:9; Dt 21:21; 27:16; Pr 20:20; 22:15; 30:17; Mt 15:4; Mk 7:10).

Differences and partiality—
Differences made between male and female (Lev 12). Partiality of parents, Rebekah for Jacob (Ge 27:6-17), Jacob for Joseph (Ge 37:3-4). Partiality among, forbidden (Dt 21:15-17).

Death and Mistreatment—
Death, as a judgment upon parents: Firstborn of Egypt (Ex 12:29; Nu 8:17; Ps 78:5), sons of Eli (1Sa 3:13-14), sons of Saul (1Sa 28:18-19), David's child by Uriah's wife (2Sa 12:14-19). Eaten. *See Cannibalism.* Edict to murder: Of Pharaoh (Ex 1:22), Jehu (2Ki 10:1-8), Herod (Mt 2:16-18). Caused to pass through fire (2Ki 16:3; 17:7; Jer 32:35; Eze 16:21). Sacrificed (2Ki 17:31; Eze 16:20-21). Sold for debt (2Ki 4:1; Ne 5:5; Job 24:9; Mt 18:25). Sold in marriage, law concerning (Ex 21:7-11). Instance of Leah and Rachel (Ge 29:15-30).

Religious Involvement:
Attend divine worship (Ex 34:23; Jos 8:35; 2Ch 20:13; 31:16; Ezr 8:21; Ne 8:2-3; 12:43; Mt 21:15; Lk 2:46). Entitled to enjoy religious privileges (Dt 12:12-13). Illegitimate excluded from privilege of congregation (Dt 23:2; Heb 12:8).

Covenant involvement—
Bound by covenants of parents (Ge 17:9-14). Share benefits of parents' covenant privileges (Ge 6:18; 12:7; 13:15; 17:7-8; 19:12; 21:23; 26:3-5, 24; Lev 26:44-45; Isa 65:23; 1Co 7:14). Involved in guilt of parents (Ex 20:5; 34:7; Lev 20:5; 26:39-42; Nu 14:18, 33; 1Ki 16:12; 21:29; Job 21:19; Ps 37:28; Isa 14:20-21; 65:6-7; Jer 32:18; Da 6:24). Not punished for parent's sake (2Ki 14:6; Jer 31:29-30; Eze 18:1-30).

Character of:
Known by conduct (Pr 20:11). Future state (Mt 18:10; 19:14). Status of minors (Gal 4:1-2). Alienated: Ishmael, to gratify Sarah (Ge 21:9-15). Adopted. *See Adoption; Parents.*

Good—
Have Lord's presence (1Sa 3:19). Blessed of God (Pr 3:1-4; Eph 6:2-3). Honor the aged (Job 32:6-7). Honor father (Mal 1:6). A joy to parents (Pr 10:1; 15:20; 23:24; 29:3; 29:17). Keep the law (Pr 28:7). Know the scriptures (2Ti 3:15). Love parents (Ge 46:29). Obey parents (Ge 28:7; 47:30; Pr 13:1), which pleases God (Col 3:20). Attend to parental teaching (Pr 13:1). Partake of God's promises (Ac 2:39). Extol the Savior (Mt 21:15-16; Ps 8:2). Take care of parents (Ge 45:9-11; 47:12; Mt 15:5). Wise (Ecc 4:13).
Illustrative of conversion (Mt 18:3), of a teachable spirit (Mt 18:4). Symbolic of regeneration (Mt 18:2-6, 10; 19:14-15; Mk 9:36-37; 10:13-15; Mk 10:16; Lk 9:46-48; 18:15, 17).

Good, Instances of—
Shem and Japheth (Ge 9:23). Isaac (Ge 22:6-12). Esau (Ge 28:6-9). Jacob (Ge 28:7). Judah (Ge 44:18-34). Joseph (Ge 45:9-13; 46:29; 47:11-12, 29-30; 48:12; 50:1-13). Moses (Ex 15:2; 18:7). Jephthah's daughter (Jdg 11:36-39). Ruth (Ru 1:15-17). Samuel (1Sa 2:26; 3:10). David (1Sa 22:3-4; Ps 71:5, 17). Solomon (1Ki 2:19-20; 3:3-13). Abijah (1Ki 14:13). Obadiah (1Ki 18:12). Jehoshaphat (1Ki 22:43; 2Ch 17:3). The captive maid (2Ki 5:2-4). Jewish children (2Ch 20:13; Ne 8:3; 12:43). Josiah (2Ch 34:1-3). Job (Job 29:4). Elihu (Job 32:4-7). Jeremiah (Jer 1:5-7). The Recabites (Jer 35:18-19). Daniel and the three Hebrews (Da 1:8-20). Children in the temple (Mt 21:15). John (Lk 1:80). Jesus (Lk 2:51-52). Timothy (2Ti 1:5; 3:15).

Wicked—
Disrespectful, to parents (Dt 27:16; Pr 15:20; 30:11; Eze 22:7; Mic 7:6; Job 19:18; 2Ki 2:23). Disobedient to parents (Dt 21:18-21; Pr 13:1; 15:5; 30:13; Ro 1:30; 2Ti 3:2). Defraud parents (Pr 28:7, 24; Mk 7:9-13). Disgrace parents (Pr 10:1; 17:2, 21, 25; 19:13, 26; 23:22). Betray parents (Mk 13:12).

Wicked, Instances of—
Canaan (Ge 4:25). Lot's daughters (Ge 19:14, 30-38). Ishmael (Ge 21:9). Eli's sons (1Sa 2:12, 22-25). Samuel's sons (1Sa 8:3). Absalom (2Sa 15). Adonijah (1Ki 1:5). Abijah (1Ki 15:3). Ahaziah (1Ki 22:52). Children at Bethel (2Ki 2:23-24). Samaritan's descendants (2Ki 17:41). Adrammelech and Sharezer (2Ki 19:37; 2Ch 32:31). Amon (2Ki 21:21).
See Babies; Young Men.

CHILDREN OF GOD *See Righteous.*

CHILEAB *See Kileab.*

CHILION *See Kilion.*

C

CHILMAD *See Kilmad.*

CHIMHAM *See Kimham.*

CHIMNEY NIV "window" (Hos 13:3). *See Window.*

CHINESE KJV "Sinim" is believed by some to be a reference to the Chinese; NIV has "Aswan" (Isa 49:12). *See Aswan.*

CHINNERETH, CHINNEROTH *See Kinnereth.*

CHIOS *See Kios.*

CHISLEU *See Kislev.*

CHISLON *See Kislon.*

CHISLOTH-TABOR *See Kisloth Tabor.*

CHITTIM *See Kittim.*

CHIUN NIV "pedestal"; perhaps the proper name "Kaiwan" (Am 5:26, ftn). *See Rephan.*

CHLOE (*tender shoot*). A Christian of Corinth (1Co 1:11).

CHOICE

Between life and death (Dt 30:19-20). God and false gods (Jos 24:15-18). Judgments by David (2Sa 24:12-14; 1Ch 21:11-13). Between God and Baal (1Ki 18:21, 39-40). Of Moses (Heb 11:24-25).

See Contingencies; Blessings, Spiritual Contingent Upon Obedience.

CHOIR Leaders of (1Ch 25:2-6; Ne 12:42). Presided over by chief musician (Ps 4; Hab 3:19). Instructed by teachers (1Ch 15:22, 27; 25:7-8).

In the tabernacle (1Ch 6:31-47). Composed of singers and instrumentalists (1Ch 15:16-21; 25:1-7; 2Ch 5:12-13; 23:13; Isa 38:20). Mixed choirs (2Ch 35:15, 25; Ezr 2:64-65). Sang every morning and evening (1Ch 9:33; 23:5, 30), during offering of sacrifices (1Ch 16:41-42; 2Ch 29:27-28), at restoration of the temple (Ezr 2:41; 3:10-11), at the dedication of the wall of Jerusalem (Ne 12:27-30). Appointed from the army to sing praises to God as a military strategy (2Ch 20:21).

See Music.

CHOOSING *See Choice.*

CHOR-ASHAN *See Bor Ashan.*

CHORAZIN *See Korazin.*

CHORUSES *See Music.*

CHOSEN Also referred to as elect (Mt 24:22, 24, 31). Few (Mt 20:16). Called (1Pe 2:9; Rev 17:14).

See Elect; Election; Foreknowledge of God; Predestination.

CHOZEBA *See Cozeba.*

CHRIST (*the Anointed One*). *See Jesus the Christ.*

CHRISTIAN (*follower of Christ*). Believers called (Ac 11:26; 26:28; 1Pe 4:16). *See Righteous.*

CHRISTIANITY The word does not occur in the Bible. It was first used by Ignatius, in the first half of the second century. It designates all that which Jesus Christ brings to people of faith, life, and salvation.

CHRISTMAS The anniversary of the birth of Christ and its observance. The date of the birth of Christ is not known. Celebrated by most Protestants and by Roman Catholics on December 25, by Eastern Orthodox churches on January 6, and by the Armenian church on January 19. The first mention of its observance on December 25 is in the time of Constantine, c. A.D. 325. The word *Christmas* is formed of *Christ* plus *Mass*, meaning a religious service in commemoration of the birth of Christ. It is not clear whether the early Christians thought of or observed Christmas, but once introduced, the observance spread throughout Christendom. Some Christian groups disapprove of the festival.

CHRONICLES, 1 and 2

Author: Anonymous; according to ancient Jewish tradition, Ezra

Date: Latter half of the fifth century B.C.

Outline:

I. Genealogies: Creation to Restoration (1Ch 1-9).
- A. The Patriarchs (ch. 1).
- B. The 12 Sons of Jacob/Israel (2:1-2).
- C. The Family of Judah (2:3-4:23).
- D. The Sons of Simeon (4:24-43).
- E. Reuben, Gad and the Half-Tribe of Manasseh (ch. 5).
- F. Levi and Families (ch. 6).
- G. Issachar, Benjamin, Naphtali, Manasseh, Ephraim and Asher (chs. 7-9).

II. The Reign of David (1Ch 10-29).
- A. Death of Saul (ch. 10).
- B. Capture of Jerusalem; David's Power Base (chs. 11-12).
- C. Return of the Ark; Establishment of David's Kingdom (chs. 13-16).
- D. Dynastic Promise (ch. 17).
- E. David's Conquest (chs. 18-20).
- F. The Census (ch. 21).
- G. Preparations for the Temple (ch. 22).
- H. Organization of the Temple Service (chs. 23-26).
- I. Administrative Structures of the Kingdom (ch. 27).
- J. David's Final Preparations for Succession and the Temple (28:1-29:20).

III. The Reign of Solomon (2Ch 1-9).
- A. The Gift of Wisdom (ch. 1).
- B. Building the Temple (2:1-5:1).
- C. Dedication of the Temple (5:2-7:22).
- D. Solomon's Other Activities (ch. 8).
- E. Solomon's Wisdom, Splendor and Death (ch. 9).

IV. The Schism, and the History of the Kings of Judah (2Ch 10-36).
- A. Rehoboam (chs. 10-12).
- B. Abijah (13:1-14:1).
- C. Asa (14:2-16:14).
- D. Jehoshaphat (17:1-21:3).
- E. Jehoram and Ahaziah (21:4-22:9).
- F. Joash (22:10-24:27).
- G. Amaziah (ch. 25).
- H. Uzziah (ch. 26).
- I. Jotham (ch. 27).
- J. Ahaz (ch. 28).
- K. Hezekiah (chs. 29-32).
- L. Manasseh (33:1-20).
- M. Amon (33:21-25).
- N. Josiah (34:1-36:1).
- O. Josiah's Successors (36:2-14).
- P. Exile and Restoration (36:15-23).

CHRONOLOGY, NEW TESTAMENT

In ancient times historians were not accustomed to recording history under exact dates, but were satisfied when some specific event was related to the reign of a noted ruler or a famous contemporary. Our method of dating events in reference to the birth of Christ was started by Dionysius Exiguus, a monk who lived in the sixth century, but who wrongly calculated Jesus' birth year. The birth of Christ must be dated in or before 5 B.C., as it is known that Herod the Great died in 4 B.C., and according to the Gospels Jesus was born some time before the death of the king. Luke gives the age of Jesus at his baptism as "about thirty years" (Lk 3:23). This would bring the baptism at c. A.D. 26 or 27. Since Herod began the reconstruction of the temple in 20 B.C., the "forty-six years" mentioned by the Jews during the first Passover of Jesus' public ministry (Jn 2:13-22), brings us to A.D. 27 for this first Passover. The ministry of John the Baptist began about the middle of A.D. 26. The time of the Crucifixion is determined by the length of the ministry of Jesus. Mark's Gospel seems to require at least two years. John's Gospel explicitly mentions three Passovers (Jn 2:23; 6:4; 11:55). If the feast (Jn 5:1) is also a Passover, as seems probable, then the length of the ministry of Jesus was a full three years and a little over. This places the Crucifixion at the Passover of A.D. 30.

As for the Apostolic Age the chronological data are very limited and uncertain. The death of Herod Agrippa I in A.D. 44 is one of the fixed dates of the NT. This was the year of Peter's arrest and miraculous escape from prison. The proconsulship of Gallio was between 51 and 53, and this would bring the beginning of Paul's ministry at Corinth to c. A.D. 50. The accession of Festus as governor, under whom Paul was sent to Rome, probably took place c. 59/60.

New Testament Chronology	
Birth of Jesus	7-5 B.C.
Baptism of Jesus	A.D. 26
Crucifixion of Jesus	30
Conversion of Saul	34/35
Death of Herod Agrippa I	44
James written	before 50 (?)
First Missionary Journey	46-48
Galatians written	48/49
Jerusalem Conference	49/50
Second Missionary Journey	50-52
Paul at Corinth	50-52
1 and 2 Thessalonians written	51
Arrival of Gallio as Proconsul	52
Third Missionary Journey	53-57
Paul at Ephesus	54-57
1 and 2 Corinthians written	55
Romans written	57
Paul's Arrest in Jerusalem	57
Imprisonment at Caesarea	57-59
On Island of Malta	59
Arrival at Rome	59
Roman Imprisonment	59-61/62
Colossians, Philemon, Ephesians	60
Philippians written	61
Paul's Release and Further Work	62-67
1 Timothy and Titus written	63-65
Synoptic Gospels and Acts written	before 67
1 and 2 Peter written	67/68
Peter's Death at Rome	67/68
Paul's Second Roman Imprisonment	67/68
2 Timothy written	67/68
Paul's Death at Rome	67/68
Jude written	c. 65-80
Writings of John	c. 90-100
Death of John	c. 100

CHRONOLOGY, OLD TESTAMENT

For the period from the Creation to the Flood the only Biblical data are the ages of the patriarchs in the genealogical tables of Genesis 5, 7, and 11. Extrabiblical sources for this period are almost completely lacking. For the period from the Flood to Abraham we are again dependent upon the genealogical data in the Bible. The numbers vary in the Masoretic text, the LXX, and the Samaritan Pentateuch. The construction of an absolute chronology from Adam to Abraham is not now possible on the basis of the available data.

The following chart is based on the early date of the Exodus. The later date (c. 1230 B.C.) only affects the dating of the patriarchs and judges.

Old Testament Chronology (From Abraham)	
Abram born	2166 B.C.
Abraham dies	1991
Jacob and family in Egypt	1876
Moses born	1526
The Exodus	1446
Moses dies; Israelites enter Canaan	1406
The Judges	1375-1050
Saul as king	10501010
David as king	1010-970
Solomon as king	970-930
Northern kingdom of Israel	930-722
Southern kingdom of Judah	930-586
Exile	586-538
First return under Zerubbabel	538
Temple rebuilt	536-516
Second return under Ezra	458
Wall of Jerusalem rebuilt	445
Third return under Nehemiah	432
Close of OT history and prophecy	c. 400

For the chronology of the kings, *See Kings.* For the approximate dates of OT books, see each by name.

CHRYSOLITE

1. One of the precious stones set in the priestly breastpiece (Ex 28:17; 39:10).

2. A precious stone used in poetic, prophetic, and apocalyptic literature (SS 5:14; Eze 1:16; 10:9; 28:13; Da 10:6; Rev 21:20).

See Minerals of the Bible, 1; Stones.

CHRYSOPRASE A precious stone (Rev 21:20).

See Minerals of the Bible, 1; Stones.

CHUB *See Libya.*

CHUN *See Cun.*

CHURCH, PLACE OF WORSHIP

Note: Nowhere in scripture does the word "church" identify a place of worship, but rather a group (or body) of believers, and only in the NT.

The Place Where God Was Worshiped:

Courts (Ps 65:4; 84:2, 10; 92:13; 96:8; 100:4; 116:19; Isa 1:12; 62:9; Zec 3:7). Holy Oracle (Ps 28:2). Holy place (Ex 28:29; 38:24;

Lev 6:16; 10:17; 14:13; 16:2-24; Jos 5:15; 1Ki 8:8; 1Ch 23:32; 2Ch 29:5; 30:27; 35:5; Ezr 9:8; Ps 24:3; 46:4; 68:17; Ecc 8:10; Isa 57:15; Eze 41:4; 42:13; 45:4; Mt 24:15; Ac 6:13; 21:28; Heb 9:12, 25). Holy temple (Ps 5:7; 11:4; 65:4; 79:1; 138:2; Jnh 2:4, 7; Mic 1:2; Hab 2:20; Eph 2:21; 3:17).

House of God (Ge 28:17, 22; Jos 9:23; Jdg 18:31; 20:18, 26; 21:2; 1Ch 9:11; 24:5; 2Ch 5:14; 22:12; 24:13; 33:7; 36:19; Ezr 5:8, 15; 7:20, 23; Ne 6:10; 11:11; 13:11; Ps 42:4; 52:8; 55:14; 84:10; Ecc 5:1; Isa 2:3; Hos 9:8; Joel 1:16; Mic 4:2; Zec 7:2; Mt 12:4; 1Ti 3:15; Heb 10:21; 1Pe 4:17). House of the Lord (Ex 23:19; 34:26; Dt 23:18; Jos 6:24; Jdg 19:18; 1Sa 1:7, 24; 2Sa 12:20; 1Ki 3:1; 6:37; 7:40; 8:10, 63; 10:5; 2Ki 11:3-4, 15, 18-19; 12:4, 9-10, 13, 16; 16:18; 20:8; 23:2, 7, 11; 25:9; 1Ch 6:31; 22:1, 11, 14; 23:4; 26:12; 2Ch 8:16; 26:21; 29:5, 15; 33:15; 34:15; 36:14; Ezr 7:27; Ps 23:6; 27:4; 92:13; 116:19; 118:26; 122:1, 9; 134:1; Isa 2:2; 37:14; Jer 17:26; 20:1-2; 26:2, 7; 28:1, 5; 29:26; 35:2; 36:5-6; 38:14; 41:5; 51:51; La 2:7; Eze 44:4; Hag 1:2; Zec 8:9). House of Prayer (Isa 56:7; Mt 21:13; Mk 11:17; Lk 19:46). My Father's House (Jn 2:16; 14:2).

Sanctuary (Ex 25:8; Lev 19:30; 21:12; Nu 3:28; 4:12; 7:9; 8:19; 10:21; 18:1, 5; 19:20; 1Ch 9:29; 22:19; 24:5; 28:10; 2Ch 20:8; 26:18; 29:21; 30:8, 19; Ne 10:39; Ps 20:2; 28:2; 63:2; 68:24; 73:17; 74:3, 7; 77:13; 78:69; 150:1; Isa 16:12; 63:18; La 2:7, 20; 4:1; Eze 5:11; 42:20; 44:5, 27; 45:3; 48:8, 21; Da 8:11, 13-14; 9:17, 26; 11:31; Heb 8:2; 9:1-2). Tabernacle (Ex 26:1; Lev 26:11; Jos 22:19; Ps 15:1; 61:4; 76:2; Heb 8:2, 5; 9:2, 11; Rev 13:6; 21:3). Temple (1Sa 1:9; 3:3; 2Ki 11:10, 13; Ezr 4:1; Ps 5:7; 11:4; 27:4; 29:9; 48:9; 68:29; Isa 6:1; Mal 3:1; Mt 4:5; 23:16; Lk 18:10; 24:53). Zion (Ps 9:11; 48:11; 74:2; 132:13; 137:1; Isa 35:10; Jer 31:6; 50:5; Joel 2:1, 15).

Buildings: *See Synagogue; Tabernacle; Temple.*

Nature:

Instituted by divine authority (Ex 25:8-9; Dt 12:11-14). Holy (Ex 30:26-29; 40:9; Lev 8:10-11; 16:33; 19:30; 21:12; 26:2; Nu 7:1; 8:19; 1Ki 9:3; 1Ch 29:3; 2Ch 3:8; Isa 64:11; Eze 23:39; 43:12). Should be shown reverence (Lev 19:30; 26:2). Figurative (1Co 3:17).

CHURCH, THE BODY OF BELIEVERS (*assembly*).

"Church" in this entry encompasses organized bodies of believers in both testaments. In the OT, the church was a group of "gathered together" Hebrew believers, a congregation. In the NT, the church (technically) was a group of "called out" Christian believers.

Called:

In the OT, the congregation, congregation of Israel, or community of Israel (Ex 12:3, 6, 19, 47; 16:1, 2, 9-10, 22; Lev 4:13, 15; 10:17; 24:14). Zion (2Ki 19:21, 31; Ps 9:11; 48:2, 11-12; 74:2; 132:13; 137:1; Isa 35:10; Isa 40:9; 49:14; 51:16; 52:1-2, 7-8; 60:14; 62:1, 11; Jer 31:6; 50:5; La 1:4; Joel 2:1, 15). Also (Ro 9:33; 11:26; 1Pe 2:16). Daughter of Zion (Isa 62:11; Zec 9:9). Also (Mt 21:5; Jn 12:15). In the NT, church (Mt 16:18; 18:17; Ac 2:47; 7:38; 20:28; 1Co 11:18; 14:19, 23, 28, 33-34; 15:9; Gal 1:13; Eph 1:22; 1Ti 3:15).

Described as:

Assembly of believers (Ps 89:7). The upright (Ps 111:1). Body of Christ (1Co 12:27; Eph 1:22-23; 4:12; Col 1:24). Branch of God's planting (Isa 60:21). Bride (Gal 6:16). Bride of Christ (Rev 21:9). Christ's body (Ro 12:5; 1Co 12:12, 27; Eph 1:22-23; 4:12; Col 1:24). Church of God (Ac 20:28). Church of the living God (1Ti 3:15). Church of the firstborn (Heb 12:23). Congregation of Believers (Ps 149:1). Congregation of the Lord's Poor (Ps 74:19). Dove (SS 2:14; 5:2). Family in heaven and earth (Eph 3:15). Flock of God (Eze 34:15; 1Pe 5:2). Fold of Christ (Jn 10:16). General Assembly of the Firstborn (Heb 12:23). The God of Jacob (Isa 2:3). Golden lampstand (Rev 1:20). God's building (1Co 3:9). God's field (1Co 3:9). God's heritage (Joel 3:2; 1Pe 5:3). Habitation of God (Eph 2:22). Heavenly Jerusalem (Gal 4:26; Heb 12:22). Holy City (Rev 21:2). Holy Mountain (Zec 8:3). Holy hill (Ps 2:6; 15:1). House (Heb 3:6). House of God (1Ti 3:15; Heb 10:21). House of Christ (Heb 3:6). Household of God (Eph 2:19). Inheritance (Ps 28:9; Isa 19:25). Israel of God (Gal 6:16). Joy of the whole earth (Ps 48:1-2, 11-13). Kingdom of God (Mt 6:33; 12:28; 19:24; 21:31). Kingdom of heaven (Mt 3:2; 4:17; 5:3, 10, 19-20; 10:7). His kingdom (Ps 103:19; 145:12; Mt 16:28; Lk 1:33). My kingdom (Jn 18:36). Your kingdom (Ps 45:6; 145:11, 13; Mt 6:10; Lk 23:42). Lamb's bride (Eph 5:22-32; Rev 22:17). Lamb's wife (Rev 19:7-9; 21:9). The Lord's portion (Dt 32:9). Lot of God's inheritance (Dt 32:9). Mount Zion (Heb 12:22). Mountain of the Lord's house (Isa 2:2). New Jerusalem (Rev 21:2). Pillar and ground of the truth (1Ti 3:15). Place of God's throne (Eze 43:7). Pleasant portion (Jer 12:10). River of gladness (Ps 46:4-5). Sanctuary of God (Ps 114:2). Sought out, a city not forsaken (Isa 62:12). Spiritual house (1Pe 2:5). Strength and Glory of God (Ps 78:61). Temple of God (1Co 3:16-17). Temple of the Living God (2Co 6:16). Vineyard (Jer 12:10; Mt 21:41).

Discipline:

In the Mosaic Institution—

(Ge 17:14; Ex 12:15; 30:33, 37-38; Lev 7:27; 17:8-9; 19:5-8; 20:18; 22:3; Nu 9:13; 15:31; 19:13, 20; Dt 13:12-18; 17:2—13; 19:16-21; 21:1-9, 18-21; 22:13-29; Ezr 10:7-8).

In the Christian Church—

Designed to save the sinner (Mt 18:15; 1Co 5:1-13; 2Th 3:14). Designed to warn others (1Ti 5:20). Designed to preserve sound doctrine (Ro 16:17; Gal 5:10, 1Ti 1:19-20; Tit 1:13). Exercised with kindness (2Co 2:6-11; Gal 6:1; Jude 22-23). Exercised with forbearance (Ro 15:1-3). Reasons for discipline: Heresy (1Ti 6:3-5; Tit 3:10-11; 2Jn 10-11). Reasons for discipline: Immorality (Mt 18:17-18; 1Co 5:1-7, 11-13; 2Th 3:6). For schism (Ro 16:17). Discipline by reproof (2Co 7:8; 10:1-11; 13:2, 10; 1Th 5:14; 2Th 3:15; 1Ti 5:1-2; 2Ti 4:2; Tit 2:15). Witnesses required in (Mt 18:16; 2Co 13:1; 1Ti 5:19).

Evil Conditions of:

Backslidden (Rev 2:1-5, 12-25; 3:1-4, 14-20). *See Backsliders; Backsliding.* Barren (Mt 21:19-20; Mk 11:13-14; Lk 13:6-9). Corrupt (Isa 5:1-7; Mt 21:33-46; Mk 12:1-12; Lk 20:9-19). Corruption in (Hos 4:9; Mic 3:1-4, 9, 11; Mt 21:33-41; 23:2-7, 13, 15-33; 26:14-16, 59-68; Mk 12:1-12; 14:10-11; Lk 22:3-6). Dissensions in (1Co 1:11-13; 3:3-4; 11:18-19; 2Co 12:20-21). Divisions in, to be shunned (Ro 16:17; 1Co 1:10; 3:3). Persecution of (Ac 8:1-3; 1Co 15:9; 1Th 2:14-15). *See Persecution.*

God's Care for:

Clothed in righteousness (Rev 19:8). Defended by God (Ps 89:18; Isa 4:5; 49:25; Mt 16:18). Edified by the Word (Ro 12:6; 1Co 14:4, 13; Eph 4:15-16; Col 3:16). Is glorious (Ps 45:13; Eph 5:27). Growth of continuous (Ac 2:47; 5:14; 11:24). Harmonious fellowship (Ps 133:1-3; Jn 13:34; Ac 4:32; Php 1:4; 2:1; 1Jn 3:4). Indwelt by God (Ps 132:14). Loved. *See below, Loved.* Not to be Despised (1Co 11:22). Privileges of (Ps 36:8; 87:5). Provides leaders (Jer 3:15; Eph 4:11-12). Punishment for defiling (1Co 3:17). Safe under God's care (Ps 46:1-2, 5). Triumphant (Gal 4:26; Heb 12:22-23; Rev 3:12; 21:3, 10).

Qualifications for Elders/Overseers and Deacons:		
Self-controlled	Elder	1Ti 3:2; Tit 1:8
Hospitable	Elder	1Ti 3:2; Tit 1:8
Able to teach	Elder	1Ti 3:2; 5:17; Tit 1:9
Not violent but gentle	Elder	1Ti 3:3; Tit 1:7
Not quarrelsome	Elder	1Ti 3:3
Not a lover of money	Elder	1Ti 3:3
Not a recent convert	Elder	1Ti 3:6
Good reputation with outsiders	Elder	1Ti 3:7
Not overbearing	Elder	Tit 1:7
Not quick-tempered	Elder	Tit 1:7
Loves what is good	Elder	Tit 1:8
Upright, holy	Elder	Tit 1:8
Disciplined	Elder	Tit 1:8
Above reproach (blameless)	Elder *Deacon*	1Ti 3:2; Tit 1:6 *1Ti 3:9*
Husband of one wife	Elder *Deacon*	1Ti 3:2; Tit 1:6 *1Ti 3:12*
Temperate	Elder *Deacon*	1Ti 3:2; Tit 1:7 *1Ti 3:8*
Respectable	Elder *Deacon*	1Ti 3:2 *1Ti 3:8*
Not given to drunkenness	Elder *Deacon*	1Ti 3:2; Tit 1:7 *1Ti 3:8*
Manages his own family well	Elder *Deacon*	1Ti 3:4 *1Ti 3:12*
Sees that his children obey him	Elder *Deacon*	1Ti 3:4-5; Tit 1:6 *1Ti 3:12*
Does not pursue dishonest gain	Elder *Deacon*	Tit 1:7 *1Ti 3:8*
Keeps hold of the deep truths	Elder *Deacon*	Tit 1:9 *1Ti 3:9*
Sincere	*Deacon*	*1Ti 3:8*
Tested	*Deacon*	*1Ti 3:10*

Government:

Of the Mosaic Institution: (Dt 17:8-13).

Of the Christian Church:

Authority of apostles (Mt 16:19; Jn 20:23; Ac 1:15, 23-26; 5:1-11; 1Co 7:17; 11:2, 33-34; Gal 2:9). Authority of apostolic council (Ac 15:1-31; 16:4-5). Authority of congregation (1Co 16:3, 16; Jude 22-23). Leadership by apostles. *See above, Authority of apostles.* Leadership by deacons (Ac 6:2-6; 1Ti 3:8-13). Leadership by elders (Ac 14:23; 20:17, 28, 1Ti 5:1, 17, 22; Tit 1:5; Jas 5:14-15; 1Pe 5:1-3). Leadership by overseers (1Ti 3:1-5). *See chart above: Qualifications for Elders/ Overseers and Deacons.* Leadership by prophets and teachers (Ac 13:1, 3, 5; 1Ti 4:14; 2Ti 1:6). Obedience to rulers (Heb 13:17, 24).

Responsibilities of Believers to Leaders—

To encourage (1Co 16:10-11). To esteem (Php 2:29; 1Th 5:12-13; 1Ti 5:17). To imitate the example of (1Co 11:1; Php 3:17; 2Th 3:7; Heb 13:7; 1Pe 5:3). To obey (Heb 13:17). To receive (Php 2:29). To reimburse (1Co 9:7-23; 2Co 12:13; Gal 6:6; Php 4:10-18; 2Th 3:7-9; 1Ti 5:17-18). To seek instruction from (Mal 2:7). Of leaders, to shepherd believers (Ac 20:28).

Loved:

By God (Isa 27:2-3; 43:1-7; 49:14-17; Jer 3:14-15; 13:11). By Christ (Jn 10:8, 11, 14; Eph 5:25-32; Rev 3:9). By believers (Ps 84:1-2; 87:7; 102:14; 137:5; 1Co 12:25; 1Th 4:9). Manifested, by prayer for (Ps 122:6; Isa 62:6). Manifested, by distress at misfortunes of (Ps 137:1-6; Isa 22:4; Jer 9:1; 14:17; 51:50-51; La 2:11; 3:48-51). Manifested, by joy at prosperity of (Isa 66:10, 13-14). Manifested, by zeal for (Isa 58:12; 62:1, 6-7).

New Testament Church:

List of NT Churches—

Antioch (Ac 13:1). Asia (1Co 16:19; Rev 1:4). Babylon (1Pe 5:13). Cenchrea (Ro 16:1). Caesarea (Ac 18:22). Cilicia (Ac 15:41). Corinth (1Co 1:2). Ephesus (Eph 1:22; Rev 2:1). Galatia (Gal 1:2). Galilee (Ac 9:31). Jerusalem (Ac 15:4). Joppa (Ac 9:42). Judea (Ac 9:31). Laodicea (Rev 3:14). Pergamum (Rev 2:12). Philadelphia (Rev 3:7). Samaria (Ac 9:31). Sardis (Rev 3:1). Smyrna (Rev 2:8). Syria (Ac 15:41). Thessalonica (1Th 1:1). Thyatira (Rev 2:18).

Described—

Beneficence of. *See Beneficence; Giving; Liberality.* Christ, the head of (Ps 118:22-23; Isa 28:16; 33:22; 55:4; Mt 12:6, 8; 21:42-43; 23:8, 10; Mk 2:28; 12:10; Lk 6:5; 20:17-18; Jn 13:13; 15:1-8; Ac 2:36; Ro 8:29; 9:5; 1Co 3:11; 11:3; 12:5; Eph 1:10, 22-23; 2:20-22; 4:15; 5:23-32; Col 1:13, 18; 2:10, 19; 3:11; Heb 3:3, 6; 1Pe 2:7; Rev 1:13; 2:1-28; 3:1, 7; 5:6; 21:22-23; 22:16). *See Jesus, Kingdom of.* Community in (Ac 4:32). Decrees of (Ac 15:28-29; 16:4). Design of (Ro 3:2; 9:4; Eph 2:20-22; 1Ti 3:15).

Discipline. *See above, Discipline.* Diversity of callings in (1Co 12:5, 28; Eph 4:11-12). Divinely established or instituted (Mt 16:15-18; Eph 2:20-22; 1Th 1:1; 2Th 1:1; 1Ti 3:15). Founded on the lordship of Christ (Mt 16:18). Duty. *See Responsibilities below.* Edification, by teachers (Eph 4:11-12). By public worship (Col 3:16; Heb 10:25). Government. *See above, Government.* Growth of, rapid (Ac 2:41, 47; 4:4; 5:14; 6:7; 9:35; 11:21, 24; 14:1; 19:17-20). Growth of, cut back (Isa 2:2; Eze 17:22-24; Da 4:35). Holiness of (2Co 11:2; Eph 5:27; 2Pe 3:14; Rev 19:8). Loved. *See above, Loved.* Membership in (Mt 12:50; 19:14; Mk 10:14; Lk 18:16; Jn 15:5-6; Ac 2:41, 47; 4:4; 5:14; 9:35, 42; 11:21; Ro 12:4-5; 1Co 3:11-15; 12:12-28; Eph 4:25; 5:30; Php 4:3; Rev 21:27). Militancy of (SS 6:10; Php 2:25; 2Ti 2:3; 4:7; Phm 2). Mission of. *See below, Mission.* Pastoral care of (Ac 20:28). Responsibilities. *See below, Responsibilities.* Unity of (Ps 133:1; Jn 10:16; 17:11, 21-23; Ro 12:4-5; 1Co 10:17; 12:5, 12-27; Gal 3:26-28; Eph 1:10; 2:14-21; 3:6, 15; 4:4-6, 12-16, 25; Col 3:11, 15). Union of, with Christ (Jn 15:1-7; Ro 11:17; 2Co 11:2; Eph 5:30, 32; Rev 19:7; 21:9). Worship, to be attended (Heb 10:25). To be conducted with order (Ecc 5:1, 3; 1Co 11:4-5, 33; 14:26, 33, 40; 1Ti 3:15).

Mission of—

To be entrusted with the oracles of God (Ro 3:2; 9:4). To bring peace (Ps 22:27-31; Isa 2:2-5; 11:6-9; 52:1, 2, 7-8; 61:1-3; 65:25). To bring spiritual enlightenment (Isa 2:3; 29:18-19; Joel 2:26-32; Hab 2:14; Ac 2:16-21). To bring moral transformation (Isa 4:2-6; 32:3-4, 15-17; 35:1-2, 5-7; 44:3-5; 55:10-13; Zep 3:9). To be the salt and light of the world (Mt 5:13).

Prophecies Concerning—

Its universality (Ge 12:3; Isa 2:2; 40:5; 42:3-4; 45:23; 52:10, 15; 54:1-5; 56:7-8; 59:19; 60:1-9; 66:12, 19, 23; Jer 3:17; 4:2; 16:19; 31:7-9, 34; 33:22; Da 2:35, 44; 7:13-14, 18, 22, 27; Am 9:11-12; Zep 2:11; Zec 9:1, 10; 14:6-9, 16; Mal 1:11; Mt 8:11; Jn 10:16; Rev 11:15; 15:4).

Its prosperity (Ps 72:7-11, 16, 19; 86:9; 102:15-16, 18; 132:15-18; Isa 4:2-6; 25:6-8; 33:20-21; 49:6-12, 13-18; 51:3-8; 52:1-8, 10, 15; 54:1-5, 11-14; 55:5, 10-13; 60:1-9, 19-20; 61:1-11; 62:2-3, 12; 65:18-19, 23-25; 66:12, 19, 23; Jer 31:34; Eze 17:22-24; 34:26, 29-31; 47:3-12; Joel 2:26-32; Am 9:11-12; Mic 4:3-4; 5:2, 4, 7; Hab 2:14; Zep 3:9; Hag 2:7-9; Zec 2:10-11; 6:15; 8:20-23).

Its lasting (Isa 9:7; 33:20; Da 7:14, 27; Mt 16:18; Eph 1:10; Heb 12:23-24, 27-28; Rev 5:10, 13-14; 11:15; 12:10; 15:4; 20:4-6; 21:9-27; 22:1-5). *See Jesus the Christ, Kingdom of.*

State: Relationship of Church and State:

Ecclesiastical Power Superior to Civil—

Appoints kings (1Sa 10:1). Directs administration (1Sa 15:1-4). Reproves rulers (1Sa 15:14-35), withdraws support and anoints a successor (1Sa 16:1-13; 2Ki 9:1-26; 11:4-12). Attempted usurpation of ecclesiastical functions by civil authorities reproved (1Sa 13:8-14; 2Ch 26:16-21).

State Superior to Church—

Evident, in David's appointments (1Ch 23-25; 2Ch 35:4). In Solomon's power (1Ki 2:26-27; 5-8). In Hezekiah reorganizing temple service (2Ch 31:2-19). In Jeroboam subverting the Jewish religion (1Ki 12:26-33). In Manasseh subverting and restoring the true religion (2Ch 33:2-9, 15-17). In Joash supervising the repairs of the temple (2Ki 12:14-18). In Ahaz transforming the altars (2Ki 16:10-16). In Josiah exercising the function of a priest (2Ch 34:29-33).

State Favorable to the Church—

Cyrus, in proclamation to restore the temple (2Ch 36:22-23; Ezr 1:1-11). Darius, in edict to further restoration of the temple (Ezr 6:1-14). Artaxerxes, in exempting religious institution from taxes (Ezr 7:24).

See Ecclesiasticism; Jesus the Christ, Kingdom of; Ministers; Usurpation, in Ecclesiastical Affairs.

CHURNING (Pr 30:33). *See Butter.*

CHUSHAN-RISHATHAIM *See Cushan-Rishathaim.*

CHUZA *See Cuza.*

CILICIA Maritime province of Asia Minor. Jews dwell in (Ac 6:9). Churches of (Ac 15:23, 41; Gal 1:21).

Sea of (Ac 27:5).

CINNAMON A spice (Pr 7:17; SS 4:14; Rev 18:13). An ingredient of the sacred oil (Ex 30:23).

CINNERETH, CINNEROTH *See Kinnereth; Galilee, Sea of.*

CIRCUMCISION
Institution of (Ge 17:10-14; Lev 12:3; Jn 7:22; Ac 7:8; Ro 4:11). A seal of righteousness (Ro 2:25-29; 4:11). Performed on all males on the eighth day (Ge 17:12-13; Lev 12:3; Php 3:5). Rite of, observed on the Sabbath (Jn 7:23). A prerequisite of the privileges of the Passover (Ex 12:48). Child named at the time of (Ge 21:3-4; Lk 1:59; 2:21). Neglected (Jos 5:7). Covenant promises of (Ge 17:4, 14; Ac 7:8; Ro 3:1; 4:11; 9:7-13; Gal 5:3). Necessity of, falsely taught by Judaizing Christians (Ac 15:1). Paul's argument against the continuance of (Ro 2:25, 28; Gal 6:13). Characterized by Paul as a yoke (Ac 15:10). Abrogated (Ac 15:5-29; Ro 3:30; 4:9-11; 1Co 7:18-19; Gal 2:3-4; 5:2-11; 6:12; Eph 2:11, 15; Col 2:11; 3:11).

Instances of:
Abraham (Ge 17:23-27; 21:3-4). Shechemites (Ge 34:24). Moses (Ex 4:25). Israelites at Gilgal (Jos 5:2-9). John the Baptist (Lk 1:59). Jesus (Lk 2:21). Paul (Php 3:5). Timothy (Ac 16:3).

Figurative:
(Ex 6:12, ftn; Dt 10:16; 30:6; Jer 4:4; 6:10, ftn; 9:26; Ro 2:28-29; 15:8, ftn; Php 3:3; Col 2:11; 3:11).
A designation of the Jews (Ac 10:45; 11:2; Ro 15:8, ftn; Eph 2:11; Col 4:11; Tit 1:10), of Christians (Php 3:3).

CIS *See Kish.*

CISTERN An artificial reservoir dug in the earth or rock for the collection and storage of water from rain or spring (Pr 5:15; Ecc 12:6; Isa 36:16; Jer 2:13). Cisterns were a necessity in Israel with its long, dry summers. Empty cisterns were sometimes used as prisons (Ge 37:22; Jer 38:6; Zec 9:11). *See Wells.*

Figurative: (2Ki 18:31; Pr 5:15; Ecc 12:6).

CITIES Ancient (Ge 4:17; 10:10-12). Fortified (Nu 32:36; Dt 9:1; Jos 10:20; 14:12; 2Ch 8:5; 11:10-12; 17:2, 19; 21:3; Isa 23:11). Gates of. *See Gates.*

Designated as:
Royal (Jos 10:2; 1Sa 27:5; 2Sa 12:26; 1Ch 11:7), treasure (Ge 41:48; Ex 1:11; 1Ki 9:19; 2Ch 8:4; 16:4; 17:12), chariot (2Ch 1:14; 8:6; 9:25), merchant (Isa 23:11; Eze 17:4; 27:3).
Town clerk of (Ac 19:35). Government of, by rulers (Ne 3:9, 12, 17-18; 7:2). *See Government.*
Suburbs of (Nu 35:3-5; Jos 14:4).
Watchmen of. *See Watchman.*

Figurative:
(Heb 11:10, 16; 12:22; 13:14).

CITIES OF REFUGE Six cities set apart by Moses and Joshua as places of asylum for those who had accidentally committed manslaughter: Bezer (Benjamin), Ramoth Gilead (Gad), Golan (Manasseh), Hebron (Judah), Shechem (Ephraim), Kedesh (Naphtali). There they remained until a fair trial could be held. If proved innocent of willful murder, they had to remain in the city of refuge until the death of the high priest (Nu 35; Dt 4:43; 9:1-13; Jos 20).

CITIES OF THE PLAIN Cities near the Dead Sea, including Sodom, Gomorrah, Admah, Zeboiim, and Zoar. Lot lived in Sodom (Ge 13:10-12). They were destroyed because of their wickedness (Ge 19). Josephus (Wars, 4.8.4) identified the area of the five cities at the "Lake Asphaltitus" (the Dead Sea) and said traces of the five cities were still visible. No archaeological evidence, however, backs up that siting and so the sites remain unidentified.

CITIZENS

Duties of:
Honors rulers (Ex 22:28; Nu 27:20; Job 34:18; Pr 16:14-15; 24:21; 25:6-7a, 15; Ecc 10:4, 20; Ac 23:5; 1Pe 2:17). Pray for rulers (Ezr 6:10; 1Ti 2:1-2). Promote peace (Jer 29:7). Obey the law (Ezr 7:26; 10:8; Ecc 4). Pay taxes (Mt 17:24-27; 22:17-21; Mk 12:14-17; Lk 20:22-25; Ro 13:5-7).

Rights of:
Public vindication when falsely accused (Ac 16:37). Protection from mob violence (Ac 19:36-41). Fair trial (Ac 22:25-29; 24:18-19; 25:5, 10-11, 16).

Loyal, Instances of:
Israelites (Jos 1:16-18; 2Sa 3:36-37; 15:23, 30; 18:3; 21:17; 1Ch 12:38). David (1Sa 24:6-11; 26:6-16; 2Sa 1:14). Hushai (2Sa 17:15-16). David's soldiers (2Sa 18:12-13; 23:15-16). Joab (2Sa 19:5-6). Barzillai (2Sa 19:32). Jehoiada (2Ki 11:4-12). Isaiah (Isa 22:4). Jeremiah (La 1-5). Mordecai (Est 2:21-23).

Wicked and Treacherous: (Pr 17:11; Pr 19:10, 12; 20:2; 2Ti 3:1-4; 2Pe 2:10; Jude 8).

Instances of—
Miriam and Aaron (Nu 12:1-11). Korah, Dathan, and Abiram (Nu 16:1-35; 26:9). Shechemites (Jdg 9:1-6, 22-25, 46-49). Ephraimites (Jdg 12:1-4). Israelites (1Sa 10:27; 1Ki 12:16-19). Absalom (2Sa 15:10-13). Ahithophel (2Sa 15:12; 17:1-4). Sheba (2Sa 20:1-2). Adonijah (1Ki 1:5-7). Jeroboam (1Ki 11:14-26; 12:20; 2Ch 13:5-9). Baasha (1Ki 15:27). Zimri (1Ki 16:9-10). Jozabad the son of Shimeath and Jehozabad son of Shomer (2Ki 12:19-21; 14:5). Shallum (2Ki 15:10). Menahem (2Ki 15:14). Pekah (2Ki 15:25). Hoshea (2Ki 15:30). Sons of Sennacherib (2Ki 19:37; 2Ch 32:21). Ishmael (Jer 40:14-16; 41). Bigthana and Teresh (Est 2:21). Jews (Eze 17:12-20). Barabbas (Mk 15:7). Theudas and 400 (Ac 5:36-37). An Egyptian (Ac 21:38).

Figurative:
Citizenship in heaven (Eph 2:12, 19; Php 3:20; 1Pe 2:11).

CITRON WOOD An aromatic wood; KJV "thyine" (Rev 18:12).

CITY CLERK An official in Greco-Roman cities of the first century, as at Ephesus (Ac 19:35-41).

CITY OF DAVID
1. Jebusite stronghold of Zion captured by David and made by him his royal residence (2Sa 5:6-9).
2. Bethlehem, the home of David (Lk 2:4).

CITY OF DESTRUCTION A city of Egypt; exact location unknown (Isa 19:18, ftn). Some mss of the Massoretic Text, Dead Sea Scrolls, and the Vulgate have "City of the Sun" (Heliopolis). *See Heliopolis.*

CIVIL DAMAGES *See Damages and Compensations.*

CIVIL ENGINEERING (Jos 18:9; Job 28:9-11).

CIVIL SERVICE School for (Da 1:3-21). Appointment in, on account of merit (Ge 39:1-6, 17-21; 41:38-44; 1Ki 11:28; Est 6:1-11; Da 1:7, 17-21; 6:1-3; Mt 25:14-15, 23-30; Lk 19:12-27). Corruption in (Ne 5:15; Da 6:4-17; Mk 15:15; Ac 24:26). Reform in (Ne 4:14-15). Influence in (1Ki 1:5-40; 2Ki 4:13; Mt 20:20-23; Mk 10:35).

CLAIRVOYANCE *See Sorcery.*

CLAP Clapping hands in joy (2Ki 11:12), in praise (Ps 47:1), in astonishment (Job 21:5), in scorn (Job 27:23; 34:37), in praise (Ps 98:8; Isa 55:12).

CLASP
1. Used to fasten the curtains on the tabernacle (Ex 26:6, 11, 33; 35:11, 13, 18, 33).
2. To shake hands in agreement and pledge for some obligation (Isa 2:6 w Pr 6:1).
3. Worshipers clasped Jesus' feet (Mt 28:9).

CLAUDA *See Cauda.*

CLAUDIA (possibly *lame*). A female disciple (2Ti 4:21).

CLAUDIUS The fourth Roman emperor (c. A.D. 41-54). The famine foretold by Agabus took place in his reign (Ac 11:28). He banished all Jews from Rome (Ac 18:2).

CLAUDIUS LYSIAS A Roman military officer (Ac 21:31-40; 22:23-30). Had Paul transferred from Jerusalem to Caesarea and wrote a letter to Governor Felix in order to protect him from an assassination plot (Ac 23:10-35; 24:7, ftn; 24:22).

CLAY Man formed from (Job 33:6). Seals made of (Job 38:14). Used by a potter (Isa 29:16; 41:25; 45:9). Blind man's eyes anointed with (Jn 9:6).
Figurative (Job 4:19; Ps 40:2; Isa 45:9; 64:8; Jer 18:6; Ro 9:21).
Symbolic (Da 2:33-41).

CLAY TABLETS Made of clay which, while still wet, had wedge-shaped letters imprinted on them with a stylus, and then were kiln-fired or sun-dried. They were made of various shapes, and were often placed in a clay envelope. Vast quantities have been excavated in the Near East. The earliest examples date to 3000 B.C.

CLEAN AND UNCLEAN ANIMALS *See Animals; Birds; Fish; Insects.*

CLEANLINESS Taught by frequent washings. *See Purification; Washing.* Regulation relating to, in camp (Dt 23:12-14).
Figurative (Ps 51:7, 10; 73:1; Pr 20:9; Isa 1:16; Eze 36:25; 1Jn 1:7, 9; Rev 1:5).
See Sanitation and Hygiene

CLEANSING *See Washing.*

CLEANTHES The son of Phanius of Assos and head of the Stoic school in Athens from 263-232 B.C. His poem, *Hymn to Zeus*, is quoted by Paul before the Areopagus Court (Ac 17:28). He made Stoicism more religious in its orientation by teaching that the universe was a living being, that God was its soul, and that the sun was its heart. He taught detachment from moral concerns. Doing good for gain was like feeding cattle for meat. He also maintained that evil thoughts were worse than evil deeds, just as a tumor which does not break open is more dangerous than one which does.
See Aratus; Asceticism; Stoicism; Stoics.

CLEMENCY Of David toward disloyal subjects: Shimei (2Sa 16:5-13; 19:16-23), Amasa (2Sa 19:13, w 2Sa 17:25).
Divine. *See God, Longsuffering of, and Mercy of; Kindness.*

CLEMENT (*mild*). A disciple at Philippi (Php 4:3).

CLEOPAS (*renowned father*). A disciple to whom Jesus appeared after his resurrection (Lk 24:18).

CLEOPHAS *See Clopas.*

CLERGYMAN *See Deacon; Elders; Minister; Pastor; Overseer.*

CLERK Town (Ac 19:35).

CLOAK Outer garment, not to be taken in pledge for a loan (Ex 22:26-27). Elijah's (1Ki 18:46; 19:13); used in calling Elisha (1Ki 19:19); parting the Jordan (2Ki 2:8; 2Ki 2:14); passes to Elisha (2Ki 2:13). Jesus' touched by the woman; her bleeding healed (Mt 9:20-21). Paul's left at Troas (2Ti 4:13).
Figurative of a curse (Ps 109:19).

CLOPAS Husband of Mary (Jn 19:25). *See Mary, 2.*

CLOSET *See Room.*

CLOTH Parable of old and new (Mt 9:16). Burial (Mt 27:59; Mk 15:46).

CLOTHING Of the Israelites, did not wear out (Dt 8:4; 29:5; Ne 9:21). *See Dress.*

CLOUD

Pillar of, With Fire:
Symbolic of the Lord's presence (Ex 13:21-22; 16:10; 19:9, 16; 24:16-18; 33:9-10; 34:5; Lev 16:2; Nu 11:25; 12:5, 10; 14:10; 16:19, 42; Dt 31:15; 1Ki 8:10-11; 2Ch 7:1-3; Isa 6:1, 4; Mt 17:5; Lk 9:34-35; 1Co 10:1). A guide to Israel (Ex 14:19, 24; 40:36-38; Nu 9:15-23; 10:11-12, 33-36; Dt 1:33; Ne 9:12, 19; Ps 78:14; 105:39; Isa 4:5). In Isaiah's prophecy (Isa 4:5). In Ezekiel's vision (Eze 10:3-4, 18-19; 11:22-23).
Figurative (Jer 4:13; Hos 6:4; 13:3).
Symbolic (Rev 14:14).
See Celestial Phenomena.

CLOUT *See Dress.*

CLUB War club or club used by shepherds (2Sa 23:21; Job 41:29; Pr 25:18; Jer 51:20; Eze 39:9).

CNIDUS (*age*). A city in Asia Minor (Ac 27:7).

CO-HEIRS As God's children, Christians share in Christ's glory (Ro 8:17). *See Inheritance.*

COAL The Bible never refers to true mineral coal, which has not been found in Israel proper. The references are always either to charcoal or to live embers of any kind. Hebrews usually used charcoal for warmth or cooking (Isa 47:14; Jn 18:18; 21:9).
Figurative (Pr 25:22).
Symbolic (Isa 6:6-7; 2Sa 14:7).

COAL OIL *See Oil.*

COAT OF ARMOR (1Sa 17:5, 38; 1Ki 22:34; 2Ch 18:33). *See Armor.*

COBRA A poisonous snake (Dt 32:33; Pr 23:32). Venom of, illustrates the speech of the wicked (Ps 58:4). Child playing with illustrates Messianic age (Isa 11:8-9).
See Serpent; Viper.

COCK *See Birds; Rooster.*

COCK CROWING *See Rooster.*

COCKATRICE *See Viper.*

COCKLE *See Weeds.*

COELE-SYRIA (*hollow Syria*). A name for that part of Syria that lay between the Lebanon and Anti-Lebanon Mountains.

COERCION Religious: Penalty for (Ex 22:20). Oath against (2Ch 15:12-15).
Instances of (Da 3:2-6, 29; 6:26-27).
See Bigotry; Intolerance.

COFFER *See Chest, 2; Treasury.*

COFFIN Joseph placed in for burial (Ge 50:26). *See Burial.*

COIN *See Money.*

COL-HOZEH (*every seer*). Father of Baruch (Ne 11:5).

COLLAR *See Dress.*

COLLECTION Of money for the poor.
See Alms; Beneficence; Giving; Liberality.

COLLEGE NIV "Second District" of the city of Jerusalem (2Ki 22:14; 2Ch 34:22). *See School.*

COLLOP NIV "bulges" of fat (Job 15:27).

COLLUSION In Sin (Lev 20:4-5). *See Complicity; Connivance.*

COLONIZATION Of conquered countries and people (2Ki 17:6, 24; Ezr 4:9-10).

COLORS, FIGURATIVE AND SYMBOLIC

Black:
Of affliction (Job 3:5; Ps 107:10-11; 143:3; Isa 9:19; 24:11). Of calamity (Isa 5:30; 8:22; 50:3; Joel 2:6, 10; 3:14-15; Na 2:10). Of the day of wrath (Zep 1:14-15). Of death (Job 10:20-22; Am 5:8). Of the abode of the lost (Mt 8:12; 22:13; 25:30; 2Pe 2:4; Jude 13; Rev 16:10).

Blue:
Of deity (Ex 25:3-4; 26:1; 28:28, 37; 38:18; 39:1-5, 21, 24, 29, 31; Nu 4:5-12; 15:38-40; 2Ch 2:7, 14; 3:14). Of royalty (Est 8:15; Eze 23:6). Predominant color in drapery and furnishings of the tabernacle, and in clothing of the priests (Ex 24:10; Jer 10:9; Eze 1:26; 10:1).

Crimson, Red, Purple, and Scarlet:
Of iniquity (Isa 1:18; Rev 17:3-4; 18:12, 16). Of prosperity (2Sa 1:24; Pr 31:21; La 4:5). Of conquest (Isa 63:2; Na 2:3; Rev 12:3). Of royalty (Jdg 8:26; Da 5:7, 16, 29; Mt 27:28). Types and shadows of the Atonement (Ex 25:3-5; 26:1, 14, 31, 36; 27:16; 28:4-6, 8, 15, 31, 33, 37; 35:5-7, 23-25, 35; 36:8, 19, 35, 37; 38:23; 39:1-43; Lev 14:4, 6, 49-52; Nu 4:7-8 13; 19:2, 5-6; Isa 63:1-3; Heb 9:19-23).

White:
Of Holiness (Lev 16:4, 32; Ps 51:7; Ecc 9:8; Isa 1:18; Da 7:9; 11:35; 12:10; Mt 17:1-2; 28:2-3; Mk 9:3; Rev 1:13-14; 2:17; 3:4-5, 18; 4:4; 6:2, 11; 7:9, 13-14; 15:6; 19:8, 11, 14; 20:11). Choir singers arrayed in white (2Ch 5:12).

COLOSSE (*punishment*). A city of Phrygia (Col 1:2, 7-8).

COLOSSIANS, BOOK OF

Author: The apostle Paul

Date: c. A.D. 60

Outline:

I. Introduction (1:1-14).
 A. Greetings (1:1-2).
 B. Thanksgiving (1:3-8).
 C. Prayer (1:9-14).
II. The Supremacy of Christ (1:15-23).
III. Paul's Labor for the Church (1:24-2:7).
 A. A Ministry for the Sake of the Church (1:24-29).
 B. A Concern for the Spiritual Welfare of His Readers (2:1-7).
IV. Freedom From Human Regulations Through Life With Christ (2:8-23).
 A. Warning to Guard Against the False Teachers (2:8-15).
 B. Pleas to Reject the False Teachers (2:16-19).
 C. An Analysis of the Heresy (2:20-23).
V. Rules for Holy Living (3:1-4:6).
 A. The Old Self and the New Self (3:1-17).
 B. Rules for Christian Households (3:18-4:1).
 C. Further Instructions (4:2-6).
VI. Final Greetings (4:7-18).

COLT Ridden by Jesus (Mt 21:2, 5, 7; Mk 11:2; Jn 12:15).

COMFORT *See Affliction, Consolation Under; Righteous, Promises to.*

COMFORTER *See God, Grace of; Holy Spirit.*

COMMANDMENT Used in the English Bible to translate a number of Hebrew and Greek words meaning law, ordinance, statute, word, judgment, precept, saying, charge, etc.

COMMANDMENTS AND STATUTES, OF GOD

Admonishing Against:

Backsliding (Dt 8:11-17; 28:18; Eze 33:12-13, 18; Lk 9:62; 1Co 10:12; Heb 3:12-13; 12:15; 2Pe 2:20-21). Conspiracy (Ex 23:1-2). Hypocrisy (Mt 6:1-5, 16; Lk 20:46-47; 1Pe 2:1). Lusts (Pr 31:3; Ro 13:13-14; Gal 5:16; 1Pe 2:11). Oppression of foreigners (Ex 22:21; 23:9; Dt 24:14; Zec 7:10). Popular corruption (Ex 23:2). Reviling rulers (Ex 22:28; Ac 23:5).

Concerning:

Children, commanding obedience to parents (Pr 6:20; Eph 6:1-3; Col 3:20). *See below, Commanding Reverence for Parents.* Debtors' protection (Dt 24:10, 12-13). Father's concern for children (Eph 6:4; Col 3:21). A husband's love for his wife (Eph 5:23; Col 3:19), honor for his wife (1Pe 3:7). Permanence of marriage (Ge 2:24; Mt 19:6; Mk 10:9; 1Co 7:1-16). Judges' justice in court (Dt 1:16). Lost property (Ex 23:4; Dt 22:1-3). Man's supremacy over animals (Ge 9:2). Masters', equity (Col 4:1), humane treatment of servants (Eph 6:9). Ministers (Ac 20:31; 1Ti 1:4; 3:2-13; 4:12-16; 5:20-22; 2Ti 2:1-3, 14-16, 22-24; Tit 1:5-9; 2:1-10, 15; 1Pe 5:2-3). Faithfulness (Col 4:17; 1Ti 6:11-12, 14; 2Ti 1:8, 13). Fortitude (2Ti 2:3). Foolish questions (2Ti 2:23). Sanctification (1Th 4:3). Strife (2Ti 2:24). Places of public worship (Dt 12:11). Restitution (Ex 21:30-36; 22:1-15; Lev 6:4-5; 24:18; Nu 5:7). Servants' obedience (Eph 6:5-8; Col 3:22-25; Tit 2:9-10; 1Pe 2:18-19). Vicious animals (Ex 21:28-32, 35-36). Wives' obedience (Eph 5:22; Col 3:18; 1Pe 3:1-4). Women (Eph 5:22, 24; Tit 2:3-5; 1Pe 3:1-3). Young men's parental obedience (Pr 6:20; 23:22).

The Decalogue: (Ex 20:3-17; Dt 5:6-21). *See Decalogue; Tablets of the Law.*

Commanding:

Hate, of the abominations of the wicked (Dt 7:25-26). Hatred of evil (Ro 12:9-21). Abiding in Christ (Jn 15:4, 9; 1Jn 2:28). Abstinence from evil (1Th 5:22). Accord with Christ, and concord with one another (Php 2:2-5). Admonition and encouragement (1Th 5:14). Altruistic service (Mt 20:26; Mk 9:35; 10:42-45; Lk 22:26; Jn 13:14; Ro 15:1-2; 1Co 10:24; Gal 6:10; Php 2:3-4). Assistance to the distressed (Ps 82:4; Pr 24:11).

Building a sanctuary (Ex 25:8). Casting anxiety upon the Lord (1Pe 5:7). Charitableness (Mt 18:10; Lk 6:37-38; Ro 14:1-3, 13, 19). Chastity (Pr 5:15-19; Mt 5:27-28). Cheerfulness (Ecc 9:7-9). Choice of wise men for rulers (Ex 18:21; Dt 1:13). Christian graces (2Co 13:11; Col 3:12-17; 2Ti 2:22). Christian tolerance toward the weak (Ro 15:1). Confession of sin (Nu 8:12; Jas 5:16). Contentment (Lk 3:14; Heb 13:5). Courage (Dt 31:6-7; Jos 1:6-7, 9; 1Ki 2:2-3; 1Ch 28:20; Ne 4:14; Jer 1:8; Eze 2:6). Cross bearing (Mt 16:24; Mk 8:34).

Destruction of idols (Ex 23:24; 34:13; Nu 33:52; Dt 7:25; 12:13). Diligence (Ecc 9:10; 11:6), in business (Pr 27:23). Discipleship (Mt 19:21; Mk 10:21; Lk 18:22). Discipline of, disorderly church members (2Th 3:6). Of Children (Mt 19:14; Mk 10:14; Lk 18:16-17). Discreet conduct (Ro 12:17; Eph 4:1-3; 5:15-16; Php 1:27, 5; 1Pe 2:11-12). Doing all to the glory of God (1Co 10:31; Col 3:17, 23).

Equity of servants (Col 4:1). Establishing and providing for the ordination of a holy ministry (Ex 28:1-3; 40:12-15; Lev 8:1-13). Esteem for pastors (1Th 5:12-13; 1Ti 5:17; Heb 13:7). Evangelism (Mt 28:19).

Faith (Ex 14:13; 2Ch 20:20; Ps 37:3, 5; 62:8; 115:9, 11; Pr 3:5; Isa 26:4; 50:10; Jer 49:11; Mk 1:15; 5:36; 11:22; Jn 6:29; 12:36; 14:1, 11; 20:27), in Christ (1Jn 3:23). Faithfulness to ministers (Col 4:17; 1Ti 6:11-12, 14; 2Ti 1:8, 13), to friends (Pr 27:10). Family support (1Ti 5:8). Fear of God (Lev 19:14, 32; 25:17; Dt 6:13; 10:12, 20; 13:4; Jos 24:14; 1Sa 12:24; 2Ki 17:39; Pr 3:7; 23:17; 24:21; Ecc 12:13; Isa 8:13; 1Pe 2:17). Fidelity in marriage (Ge 2:24; Mt 19:6; Mk 10:8; 1Co 7:10-11), to God (1Sa 12:20; Mt 22:21), to God and government (Mt 22:21; Mk 12:17; Lk 20:25), to vows (Nu 30:2; Dt 23:21-23; Ps 50:14; Ecc 5:4). Forbearance (Eph 4:2; Col 3:13). Forgiveness (Mt 18:22; Mk 11:25; Lk 17:3-4; Ro 12:14; Eph 4:32; Col 3:13). Fortitude under persecution (Mt 10:26-28; Mk 13:9, 11-13; 2Ti 2:3; Rev 2:10). Fraternal reproof (Mt 18:15-17; Lk 17:3-4). Fruits of righteousness (Lk 3:11, 14).

Gentleness (Tit 3:2). Godliness (Eph 5:1). Golden Rule, in conduct (Mt 7:12; Lk 6:31). Good works (1Pe 3:21). Growth in grace (Heb 6:1; 2Pe 1:5-8; 3:18; Jude 20-21).

Heed to instruction (Pr 4:10; 19:20; 22:17), to parental instruction (Pr 1:8; 23:22), to the truth (Mt 11:15; Mk 4:9; Rev 2:7). Helpfulness (1Co 10:24; Gal 6:1-2; Php 2:4; 1Th 5:11). Holiness (Ex 22:31; 30:29; Lev 11:44; 20:7, 25-26; 21:7; Nu 15:40; Dt 18:13; Jos 7:13; Isa 1:16-17; Jer 6:16; Am 5:14-15; 1Co 5:7; 2Co 7:1; Eph 4:22-32; Col 3:5, 8-9; 1Th 4:3-7; 2Ti 2:19, 22; Heb 12:14; Jas 1:21; 4:8; 1Pe 1:13-16; 2:11-12; 3:15; 3Jn 11). Holiness in ministers (Lev 21:6; Nu 8:14-15). Honesty (Lev 19:35-36; Dt 25:13-16; 1Th 4:12), in service (1Co 4:2; Eph 6:5-7; Col 3:22-23; Tit 2:9-10), in office (Lk 3:13). Honor, to civil rulers (1Pe 2:17), to wife (1Pe 3:7). Hospitality (Ro 12:13; Heb 13:2; 1Pe 4:9). Humane treatment of servants (Eph 6:9). Humility (Ro 12:16; Php 2:3; Jas 4:10; 1Pe 3:8; 5:6-7).

Imitation of Christ (Ro 13:14; Col 2:6-7). Industry (Pr 6:6; Eph 4:28; 1Th 4:11; 2Th 3:12). Influence for righteousness (Mt 5:16; Php 2:15). Joyfulness (Ro 12:12; Php 3:1; 4:4; 1Th 5:16). Justice (Lev 19:15; Isa 56:1; Zec 7:9-10; Jn 7:24), in courts (Dt 1:17; 25:1-2), to foreigners (Lev 19:33-34; 24:22).

Keeping the Sabbath holy (Ex 16:29; 20:8; 31:12-16; 35:2-3; Lev 19:3, 30; 26:2; Dt 5:12). Kindness (Pr 3:27-28; Eph 4:32; Col 3:12; 1Th 5:15). Kindness to animals (Dt 25:4). To enemies (Ex 23:4-5; Pr 25:21; Ro 12:20).

Labor (Ex 20:9; 35:2; Dt 5:13). Laying up treasure in heaven (Mt 6:20). Liberality (Pr 3:9; Ecc 11:1; Mt 5:42; Lk 6:30; 12:33; 2Co 8:7; Heb 13:16). Liberality in God's service (Mal 3:10), in support of religion (Dt 15:19; 16:17), toward the house of God (Ex 22:29; 30:12-16; 34:26; 35:4-9), to the poor (Lev 19:9-10; 23:22; Dt 15:7-15; 24:19-21; Ro 12:13; Heb 13:16; 1Jn 3:17). Love, for enemies (Mt 5:44; Lk 6:27-29; Ro 12:14-15), for foreigners (Lev 19:34; Dt 10:19). Love for God (Dt 6:5; 10:12; 11:1, 8, 13; 30:16; Jos 22:5; 23:11; Mt 22:37; Mk 12:30; Lk 10:27). Love for other people (Lev 19:18, 33-34; Mt 19:19; 22:39; Mk 12:31; Lk 10:27; Jn 13:34; 15:12, 17; Ro 12:9-10; 13:8-10; 1Co 16:14; Gal 5:14; Eph 5:2; Col 3:14; 1Th 3:12; 4:9; Heb 13:1; Jas 2:8; 1Pe 2:17; 3:8; 4:8; 1Jn 3:11, 18, 23; 1Jn 4:7, 21; 2Jn 5). Love for wife (Eph 5:23; Col 3:19). Loving truth and peace (Zec 8:19).

Maturity (1Co 16:13-14). Mature thinking (1Co 14:20; Tit 2:2). Meekness (Mt 5:39-40; Lk 6:29; Eph 4:2; Col 3:12; Tit 3:2). Mercy (Pr 3:3; Zec 7:9-10; Lk 6:36). Mercy to debtors (Dt 24:6).

Oaths in God's name (Dt 6:13; 10:20). Obedience (Pr 7:1-4; Lev 18:4-5, 26, 30; 19:19, 37; 20:8, 22; 22:31; 25:18; Nu 15:40; Dt 4:1, 6, 23, 30; 5:32-33; 6:17-18; 7:11; 8:1, 6; 10:12-13; 11:1, 8, 13, 32; 12:28, 32; 13:4; 27:1, 10; 29:9; 30:2, 8, 16; 1Sa 15:1; 1Ki 2:2-3; 2Ki 17:37-38; 1Ch 28:20; Pr 3:6; 4:20-21; 5:7; 7:5-14; Ecc 12:13; Jn 13:15). Obedience of children (Pr 6:20; Eph 6:1-3; Col 3:20), of servants (Eph 6:5-8; Col 3:22-25; Tit 2:9-10; 1Pe 2:18-19), of soldiers (Dt 20:3; Lk 3:14), of wives (Eph 5:22; Col 3:18; 1Pe 3:1-4), of young men (Pr 6:20; 23:22). Obedience to Christ as Lord (1Pe 3:15), to civil government (Ecc 8:2; Mk 12:17; Lk 20:25; Ro 13:1, 7; Tit 3:1; 1Pe 2:13), to God's law (Dt 11:8, 13, 32; 30:16; Jos 22:5; 2Ki 17:37-38; 1Ch 28:8), to parents (Pr 6:20; Eph 6:1-3; Col 3:20). Orderly conduct of divine worship (1Co 14:26-33).

Patience (Jas 1:4; 5:7-9). Patience under afflictions (Pr 3:11), under tribulations (Ro 12:12; Jas 1:2-4; 1Pe 4:1). Peaceableness (Ro 12:18; Col 3:15; 1Th 4:11; Heb 12:14). Perfection (Ge 17:1; Mt 5:48). Praise (Ps 146-150). *See Praise.* Prayer (Jer 33:3; Mt 7:7-11; Lk 11:9-13; Php 4:6; Col 4:2; 1Th 5:17-18; 1Ti 2:8), for more laborers in the Lord's vineyard (Mt 9:38), for rulers (1Ti 2:1-2). Prayerfulness (Lk 22:40; Ro 12:12; 1Th 5:17). Preparation for the Sabbath (Ex 16:23). Preparedness (Mt 24:44; 25:13, 1-12; 1Th 5:8). Propagation of children (Ge 9:1, 7). Propriety in worship (1Co 14:26-33, 40). Prudence (Col 4:5), in guests (Pr 23:1-2), in speech (Ecc 5:2, 6; 7:21; 10:20). Public instruction in the word of God (Dt 31:10-13). Worship (Ex 34:23; Dt 12:5-7, 11-14, 17-18, 26-27; 16:16). Pure conversation (Eph 4:29; 1Pe 3:10). Purity (2Co 7:1; Eph 5:1-4; 1Ti 5:22; Heb 13:4), in the family of a minister (Lev 21:9), of thought (Php 4:8). Quietness (1Th 4:11).

Rebuke of sin (Lev 19:17; Eph 5:11). Reconciliation between Christian brothers (Mt 5:23-25). Regard for consciences of others (1Co 10:28). Regulated enjoyments (Ecc 11:9-10). Religious instruction of children (Dt 4:9; 6:7-9; 11:19-20; 32:46; Eph 6:4). Remembrance, of God in youth (Ecc 12:1), of God's mercies (Dt 5:15; 8:2). Of the law (Dt 6:6-9; 11:18; 32:46; 1Ch 16:15). Renunciation of sources of temptation (Mt 5:29-30; 18:8-9; Mk 9:43-48). Repentance (Pr 1:23; Eze 33:11; Mal 3:7; Mt 3:2; 7:13-14; Mk 1:15; Ac 2:38; 17:30; Rev 3:19). Reproof of the erring (1Ti 5:20). Resistance of evil (Jas 4:7). Respect for religious instruction (1Th 5:20). Rest on the Sabbath (Ex 20:10; 23:12; 32:21; 35:2-3; Lev 23:3, 24; Dt 5:14). Restraint of temper (Ecc 7:9; Eph 4:26, 31; Jas 1:19). Returning good for evil (Mt 5:4; 1Co 6:7; 1Pe 3:9). Reverence, for God's house (Lev 19:30; 26:2; Ecc 5:1), for holy places (Ex 3:5; Jos 5:15; Ac 7:33), for parents (Ex 20:12; Lev 19:3; 20:9; Dt 5:16; Pr 23:22; Mt 15:4; 19:19; Lk 18:20; Eph 6:1-2), for the aged (Lev 19:32). Right conduct (Dt 6:18; Pr 4:26-27; Php 1:27; Jas 1:19). Righteousness (Ex 23:7; Eze 45:9; Hos 12:6; Lk 13:24; Ro 13:7-8). Rulers to study God's law (Dt 17:18-20).

Secrecy in giving alms (Mt 6:3). Seeking, the Lord (1Ch 16:11; Isa 55:6; Am 5:4, 6), the kingdom of God (Mt 16:24; Mk 8:34; 10:21; Lk 9:23; 18:22; Ro 15:2). Self-discipline (Mt 5:29-30; Mk 9:45-48). Self-examination (2Co 13:5). Service for God (Ex 23:25; Dt 6:13; 10:12, 20). Simplicity in worship (Mt 6:7). Six days of labor, and one day of rest (Ex 20:9-11; 35:2). Sobermindedness (Tit 2:6). Sobriety (1Th 5:8; 1Pe 1:13; 4:7; 5:8-9). Social peace (1Th 5:13). Spiritual diligence (Ro 12:11; 13:12; Heb 4:11; 2Pe 1:10; 3:14). Spirituality (Gal 5:16). Steadfastness (Dt 13:8, 10; Ro 12:21; 1Co 15:58; 16:13; Gal 5:1; Eph 6:11, 13-14, 18; Php 1:27; 4:1; 1Th 5:21; 2Th 2:15; 2Ti 1:13; 1Pe 1:13; Jude; Rev 3:11). Steadfastness in prayer (Ro 12:12; Eph 6:18; 1Th 5:17). Submission to God (2Ch 30:8; Pr 3:11; Jas 4:7), to fraternal counsel (Eph 5:21). Suffering, one for another (1Jn 3:16-17). Sympathy (Ro 12:15; Heb 13:3; 1Pe 3:8). Support of ministers (Dt 12:19; Gal 6:6; 1Ti 5:17-18).

Thankfulness (Dt 8:10; Col 2:6-7; 3:15). Thanksgiving (Eph 5:4, 20; Php 4:6; Col 3:17; 1Th 5:17-18; 1Ti 2:1; Heb 13:15). Tithing (Dt 12:6; 14:22). Truthfulness (Pr 3:3; Zec 8:16-17, 19; Eph 4:25).

Various Christian duties (Ro 12:6-8; Eph 6:10-20; Jas 4:8-11; 5:7-9, 12, 14; 1Pe 1:13-17; 2:11-25; 3:8-9, 15; 4:7-15; 5:5-8; 2Pe 1:5-7).

Watchfulness (Pr 4:23; Mt 24:42, 44; 25:13; Mk 13:35-37; Lk 12:35-40; 21:36; 1Co 16:13-14; Eph 5:15; Php 3:2; Col 4:2; 1Th 5:6; 1Pe 5:8-9; Rev 3:2). Watchfulness against backsliding (Dt 4:9; 8:11; 11:16, 28; 2Pe 3:17), against covetousness (Dt 15:9; Lk 12:15), against false Christs (Mt 24:23-26; Mk 13:21-23; Lk 17:23). Wholehearted service (Jos 22:5; 24:14; 1Sa 12:24; 1Ch 28:9; Ecc 9:10). Wisdom (Pr 3:21; 4:5, 13; 5:1; 8:5-6, 32-33; 23:12, 23), in speech (Pr 23:9; 26:4-5; Col 4:6). Wise self-restraint (Ecc 7:16-18, 21). Witnessing for Christ (Mk 5:19; 1Pe 3:15). Worship (Ge 35:1; Ex 20:24; Rev 19:10; 22:9; Eph 5:19; Col 3:16).

Zeal for righteousness (Jn 6:27; 1Co 15:58), for the faith (Jude 3), in one's calling (Ro 12:6-8).

Fixing Penalty for:

Adultery (Lev 20:10; 21:9; 1Co 6:9-10; Gal 5:19, 21). Arson (Ex 22:6).

Bestiality (Ex 22:19; Lev 20:13, 15-16). Blasphemy (Lev 24:16).

Carnality (Lev 19:20). Contempt of authority (Dt 17:12). Criminal neglect to safeguard life (Ex 21:28-36). Cursing parents (Ex 21:17; Lev 20:9).

Destruction of neighbor's property (Lev 24:18). Disobedience (Nu 15:30-31).

False Witness (Dt 19:18-19). Fornication (Ac 15:20; 1Co 6:18; 10:8).

Idolatry (Lev 20:2-5; Dt 17:2-5), enticement to idolatry (Dt 13:5, 9-10, 15). Impenitence (Lev 23:29). Incest (Lev 20:11-12, 14, 17, 19-21).

Kidnapping (Ex 21:16; Dt 24:7). Murder (Ex 21:12; Lev 24:17; Nu 35:31; Dt 19:11-13).

Laziness (2Th 3:10). Loss of borrowed property (Ex 22:14-15), of property held in trust (Ex 22:7, 13).

Personal injury (Ex 21:18-27; Lev 24:19-20).

Sabbath breaking (Ex 31:14; 35:2). Seduction (Ex 22:16).

Theft (Ex 22:1-4). Trespass (Ex 22:5).

Untimely cohabitation (Lev 20:18).

Witchcraft (Ex 22:18; Lev 20:27).

Forbidding:

Adultery (Ex 20:14; Lev 18:20; Dt 5:18; Mt 5:27; 19:18; Lk 18:20; Ro 13:9; 1Co 10:8). Anxiety (Mt 6:25-34; 10:19-23; Lk 12:11, 22-32; Jn 14:27; Php 4:6). Association with evil company (Pr 1:10-19), with harlots (Pr 2:16; 5:3-21; 6:20, 24-26; 7:1-27; 23:26-28).

Bestiality (Lev 18:23; 20:13, 15-16). Boasting (Dt 9:4). Bribe taking (Ex 23:8; Dt 16:19; 27:25).

Causeless strife (Pr 3:30). Change in God's law (Dt 4:2; 12:32). Class distinction (Ex 23:3; Lev 19:15; Nu 15:29; Dt 16:19), legislation (Lev 24:22). Company with drunkards (Pr 23:20). Conformity to the world (Lev 20:23). Contention (Ro 13:13; Php 2:14; 2Ti 2:14; Tit 3:2). Corrupt conversation (Eph 4:29; 5:4; Col 3:8). Covetousness (Ex 20:17; Dt 5:21; 7:25-26; Lk 12:15; Ro 13:9; Eph 5:3; Col 3:5; 1Ti 6:10-11; Heb 13:5).

Dishonesty in business (Lev 19:13, 35; 25:14; Dt 25:13-15; Mk 10:19). Divorce (1Co 7:10-11, w Mt 5:32; 19:9; Mk 10:11-12; Lk 16:18). Drunkenness (Ro 13:13; Eph 5:18).

Envy (Pr 3:31; 23:17; 24:1, 19; Ro 13:13; 1Pe 2:1). Evil speech (Ps 34:13; Pr 4:24; 30:10; Tit 3:2; 1Pe 3:10). Evil, to a neighbor (Ex 20:16; Lev 19:13, 16; Pr 3:29).

False, dealing (Lev 6:1-5; 19:11), swearing (Lev 19:12), witness (Ex 20:16; 23:1; Lev 19:16; Dt 5:20; Pr 24:28; Mt 19:18; Lk 18:20). Falsehood (Lev 19:11; Eph 4:25; Col 3:9). Fellowship with the wicked (Pr 1:10-15; 4:14-15; Ro 16:17; 1Co 5:9-11; 2Co 6:14, 17; Eph 5:11; 2Th 3:6; 2Ti 3:5). Foolish, unlearned questions (2Ti 2:23). Fraud (Lev 19:11, 13, 35; 1Th 4:6).

Giving cause for stumbling (1Co 8:9; 10:32). Grudges (Lev 19:18). Haste for riches (Pr 23:4), in litigation (Pr 25:8-9). Hatred (Lev 19:17; Eph 4:31; Col 3:8). Heed to false teachers (Dt 13:1-18).

Idolatry (Ex 20:3-5, 23; Lev 18:21; 20:2-5; 26:1; Dt 4:16-19, 23; 5:7-9; 6:14; 13:2-3; 16:21-22; Jos 24:14; 2Ki 17:35; Eze 20:18; 1Co 10:7; 1Jn 5:21). Impure marriages (Lev 21:7). Incest (Lev 18:6; 20:11-12, 13, 17, 19-21; Dt 22:30). Indulgence in wine (Pr 23:31; Eph 5:18; Tit 2:3). Injustice (Ex 23:2-3; Lev 19:15; 25:17; Dt 16:19), to foreigners (Ex 12:49; 22:21; Lev 19:33-34; Dt 1:16; 24:14, 17), to the poor (Ex 23:6). Intolerance (Mk 9:39; Lk 9:49-50). Improper respect of persons (Jas 2:1-9).

Labor on the Sabbath (Ex 20:10; 23:12; 34:21; 35:2-3; Lev 23:3; Dt 5:14). Lewdness (Pr 31:3; Ro 13:13; Eph 4:17-32; 5:3; 1Th 4:2-6; 2Ti 2:22). Lawlessness (Dt 12:8). Laziness (2Th 3:10). Love of the world (1Jn 2:15).

Malice (Lev 19:17-18; Eph 4:31; Col 3:8; 1Pe 2:1). Malicious mischief (Lev 19:14). Meddling (1Pe 4:15). Murder (Ex 20:13; Dt 5:17; Mt 5:21; 19:18; Ro 13:9; Jas 2:11; 1Pe 4:15). Murmuring (1Co 10:10; Php 2:14; Jas 5:9).

Offerings with blemish implying insincere or imperfect service of God (Lev 1:3, 10; 3:1, 6; 4:3, 23, 28, 32; 5:15, 18; 6:6; 9:2-3; 22:18-22; Dt 15:21; 17:1). Oppression (Lev 19:13; Pr 22:22), of the poor (Dt 24:14), of the widows and orphans (Ex 22:22-24; Jer 22:3; Zec 7:10). Ostentation in giving, in fasting, and in prayer (Mt 6:1, 5-6, 17-18).

Perjury (Lev 19:12). Perversion of justice (Dt 16:19-20; 24:17). Prejudice (Ex 23:3). Profane swearing (Mt 5:34-36; Jas 5:12). Profaning God's name (Ex 20:7; Lev 18:21; 19:12; 21:6; 22:32; Dt 5:11). Prostitution of a daughter (Lev 19:29). Putting a neighbor's life in peril by false witness (Lev 19:16).

Removal of landmarks (Dt 19:14; Pr 22:28; 23:10). Resistance (Mt 5:39). Retaliation (Lev 19:18; Pr 24:29; Mt 5:38-42; Ro 12:17; 1Th 5:15; 1Pe 3:9). Robbery (Lev 19:13; Pr 22:22).

Sabbath breaking (Ex 31:14; Jer 17:21-22). Self-confidence (Pr 3:5, 7). Self-pride (Ro 12:3). Self-praise (Pr 27:2). Selfishness (1Co 10:24; Php 2:4). Strife (2Ti 2:24). Homosexuality (Lev 18:22; 20:13).

Taking of interest (Ex 22:25; Lev 25:35, 37). Talebearing (Lev 19:16). Theft (Ex 20:15; Lev 19:11; Dt 5:19; Mt 19:18; Lk 18:20; Ro 13:9; Eph 4:28; 1Pe 4:15).

Uncharitable judgments (Mt 7:1-5; Lk 6:37, 42; Ro 14:1-3, 13). Uncharitableness (Pr 24:17; Mt 18:10). Unholy ambition (Php 2:3). Unrighteous anger (Mt 5:22). Unrighteous judgments (Lev 19:15). Use of alcohol by priests on duty (Lev 10:9).

Vain repetitions in prayer (Mt 6:7-8). Various vices (Ro 13:12-13; Gal 5:19-21; Eph 4:28-31; 5:3-6, 11, 18; Col 3:5, 8-9; 1Th 4:3-6; 5:15, 22; 1Ti 3:3, 8; 6:17; 2Ti 3:2-5; Tit 2:3, 10; Heb 13:5; Jas 1:21; 2:11; 4:11; 5:9, 12; 1Pe 2:11; 3:9; 4:3).

Witchcraft (Lev 19:26, 31; 20:6). Withholding a servant's wages (Lev 19:13). Worldliness (Mt 6:19; Ro 12:2; 1Jn 2:15). Worldliness of ministers (2Ti 2:4-5).

Implied:
Commanding an exact conscience (Mt 6:22-24). Against self-righteousness (Mt 7:3).

Precepts of Jesus:
Stated or implied (Mt 5:16, 22-24, 27-48; 6:1-4, 6-8, 16-25, 31-34; 7:1-29; 10:5-42; 16:24; 18:8-10, 15-17; 18:21-22; 19:16-19; 20:25-28; 22:21, 34-40; 24:42-51; 25:34-46; Mk 6:7-11; 8:34; 9:35-50; 10:9-12, 17, 22; 11:22; 12:17; 13:33-37; Lk 6:27-42; 10:28-37; 12:12-31; 13:24; Jn 7:24; 13:34-35; 14:11, 15, 23-24; 15:2-12, 17, 20-22).

Prescribing:
Law of evidence (Dt 17:6; 19:15). Number of stripes in punishment (Dt 25:3). Priestly benedictions (Nu 6:23-26). Stimulants for the perishing (Pr 31:6).

Warning: The rich (1Ti 6:17-19).

Warning against:
Covetousness (Lk 12:15). False teachers (Mt 7:15; Eph 5:6-7; Col 2:8). Love of money (Heb 13:5). Quenching the Spirit (1Th 5:19). Sensuality (Pr 6:24-25). Sinful indulgence (Lk 21:34). Sinning against the Holy Spirit (Eph 4:30; 1Th 5:19). Temptations (Pr 1:10-15; 19:27).

See Adultery; Children; Citizens; Homicide; Instruction; Ministers; Obedience, Commanded; Servant; Theft; Wife; Women.

COMMANDMENTS AND STATUTES, OF MEN
Traditions (Isa 29:13; Ro 14:1-6, 10-21; Gal 1:14; Col 2:8; 1Ti 4:1-3). Rejected by Jesus (Mt 15:2-20; Mk 7:2-23).

COMMERCE Laws concerning (Lev 19:36-37; 25:14, 17). Carried on by means of caravans (Ge 37:25, 27; Isa 60:6), ships (1Ki 9:27-28; 10:11; 22:48; Ps 107:23-30; Pr 31:14; Rev 18:19). Conducted in fairs (Eze 27:12, 19; Mt 11:16). Of the Arabs (Isa 60:6; Jer 6:20; Eze 27:21-24), Egyptians (Ge 42:2-34), Ethiopians (Isa 45:14), Ishmaelites (Ge 37:27-28), Israelites (1Ki 9:26-28; Ne 3:31-32; Eze 27:17), Ninevites (Na 3:16), Syrians (Eze 27:16, 18), Tyrians (2Sa 5:11; 1Ki 5:6; Isa 23:8; Eze 27; 28:5), Sidonians (Isa 23:2; Eze 27:8), Babylonians (Rev 18:3, 11-13), Israelites (Eze 27:17). From Tarshish (Jer 10:9; Eze 27:25).

Evil practices connected with (Pr 29:14; Eze 22:13; Hos 12:7).

Articles of:
Apes and baboons (1Ki 10:22), balm (Ge 37:25), blue cloth (Eze 27:24), bronze (Eze 27:13; Rev 18:12), cinnamon (Rev 18:13), cattle (Eze 27:21), chest of rich apparel (Eze 27:24), citron wood (Rev 18:12), clothes for chariots (Eze 27:20), embroidery (Eze 27:16, 24), frankincense (Jer 6:20; Rev 18:13), gold (1Ki 9:28; 10:22; 2Ch 8:18; Isa 60:6; Rev 18:12), honey (Eze 27:17), horses (1Ki 10:29; Eze 27:14; Rev 18:13), ivory (1Ki 10:22; 2Ch 9:21; Eze 27:15; Rev 18:12), iron (Eze 27:12, 19), land (Ge 23:13-16; Ru 4:3), lead (Eze 27:12), linen (Rev 18:12), oil (1Ki 5:11; Eze 27:17), pearls (Rev 18:12), perfumes (SS 3:6), precious stones (Eze 27:16, 22; 28:13, 16; Rev 18:12), purple (Eze 27:16; Rev 18:12), sheep (Rev 18:13), slaves (Ge 37:28, 36; Dt 24:7), silk (Rev 18:12), silver (1Ki 10:22; 2Ch 9:21; Rev 18:12), sweet cane (Jer 6:20), timber (1Ki 5:6, 8), tin (Eze 27:12), wheat (1Ki 5:11; Eze 27:17; Rev 18:13), white wool (Eze 27:18), wine (2Ch 2:15; Eze 27:18; Rev 18:13), human bodies and souls (Rev 18:13).

Transportation of passengers (Jnh 1:3; Ac 21:2; 27:2, 6, 37).

See Merchant; Tarshish, 2, 3; Trade and Travel; Traffic.

COMMISSARY For armies, cattle driven with (2Ki 3:9). *See Armies.* For royal households (2Ki 4:7-19, 27-28).

COMMITMENT Through the word of truth (Jn 17:17). To the Lord (Pr 16:3; 1Co 1:2; 2Co 7:1; 1Pe 1:15-16).

COMMONWEALTH *See Citizens.*

COMMUNION With God (Ps 16:7; Jn 14:23; 2Co 6:16; 1Jn 1:3). With Christ (Jn 14:23; 1Jn 1:3; Rev 3:20). With the Spirit (Jn 14:16-18; 2Co 13:14; Gal 4:6; Php 2:1-2). *See Fellowship.*

Instances of:
Enoch (Ge 5:22, 24). Noah (Ge 6:9, 13-22; 8:15-17). Abraham (Ge 12:1-3, 7; 17:1-2; 18:1-33; 22:1-2, 11-12, 16-18). Hagar (Ge 16:8-12). Isaac (Ge 26:2, 24), in dreams (Ge 28:13, 15; 31:3; 35:1, 7; 46:2-4). Moses (Ex 3; 4:1-17; 33:9, 11; 34:28-35; Nu 12:8). Joshua (Jos 6:11-24; 7:10-15). Gideon (Jdg 6:11-24). Solomon (1Ki 3:5-14; 2Ch 1:7-12).

Of Believers:
Unity (Ps 119:63; 133:1-3; Am 3:3; Jn 17:20-21; 1Co 10:16-17; 12:12-13). Commanded (Ro 12:15; 2Co 6:14-18; Eph 4:1-3; 5:11; Col 3:16; 1Th 4:18; 5:11, 14; Heb 3:13; 10:24-25; Jas 5:16). Exemplified (1Sa 23:16; Ps 55:14; Mal 3:16; Lk 22:32; 24:17, 32; Ac 2:42; 1Jn 1:3, 7). *See Eucharist; Fellowship.*

COMMUNITY Christian (Ac 2:44-45; 4:32-37; 5:1-10).

COMPANY

Evil:
Perils of (Ge 19:14-15; Nu 16:21-26; 33:55; Jdg 2:1-3; 2Ch 19:2; Ezr 9:14; Ps 50:18; 106:35-36; Pr 13:20; Hos 7:5, 8-9; Mic 6:16). Seductive (Pr 12:11, 26; 16:29; Ecc 9:18; Mt 24:12; 1Co 15:33; 2Pe 2:7-8, 18). Shunned by the righteous (Ps 6:8; 26:4-5, 9; 28:3; 31:6; 84:10; 101:4, 7; 119:115; 120:5-7; 139:19-22; 141:4; Pr 14:7; 17:12; Jer 9:2; 15:17; Hos 4:17; Rev 2:2).

Warnings against (Ge 49:6; 2Sa 23:6-7; Pr 2:11-12, 16, 19; 4:14-15; 5:8; 9:6; 20:19; 22:5, 10; 22:24-25; 23:6, 20; 24:1; 28:7, 19; 29:24; 1Ti 6:5). Forbidden (Ex 23:2, 32-33; 34:12-15; Lev 18:3; 20:23; Dt 7:2-4; 12:30; Jos 23:6-13; Pr 1:10-15; Isa 8:11-12; Jer 51:6, 45; Ro 16:17-18; 1Co 5:6, 9-11; 2Co 6:14-17; Gal 5:9; Eph 5:6-7, 11; 2Th 3:6; 1Ti 5:22; 2Ti 3:4-5; 2Jn 10-11; Rev 18:4).

See Example; Influence, Evil.

Good: (Ps 1:1; 15:1-5; Pr 13:20).

See Communion, Of Believers; Example; Fellowship; Influence, Good.

COMPASSES Carpenter's (Isa 44:13).

COMPASSION

Of God: *See God, Mercy of.*

Of Christ: *See Jesus the Christ, Compassion of.*

COMPEL By God (Ex 3:19; Ac 20:22; 1Co 9:16; 2Co 5:14). By people (Ezr 4:23; Gal 2:3; 6:12). By circumstances (1Sa 13:12; Ac 28:19).

COMPLACENCY Indifference to God is judged (Pr 1:32-33; Isa 32:9, 11; Am 6:1; Zep 1:12; Lk 11:23). *See Lukewarmness.*

COMPLAINT *See Murmuring.*

COMPLICITY

Warnings Against: (Ps 50:18; Pr 29:24; Ro 1:32; 2Jn 10-11).

Instances of:
Sarah, in deceiving Pharaoh (Ge 12:11-19), Abimelech (Ge 20:2-5, 11-14). Rebekah, in deceiving Isaac (Ge 27:5-17). The elders and nobles of Jezreel, in stoning Naboth (1Ki 21:7-14). Jews who opposed building the temple (Ne 6:10-19). Daughter of Herodias, in death of John the Baptist (Mt 14:8; Mk 6:25). Pilate, in the death of Christ (Mt 27:17-26; Mk 15:9-15; Lk 23:13-25; Jn 19:13-16). Paul, in death of Stephen (Ac 7:58).

See Collusion; Connivance; Conspiracy.

COMPROMISE Before litigation, commanded by Solomon (Pr 25:8-10), by Christ (Mt 5:25-26; Lk 12:58-59). *See Adjudication at Law; Arbitration; Court, Of Law; Justice.*

CONANIAH (*Yahweh sustains*).
1. A Levite (2Ch 31:12-13).
2. Another Levite (2Ch 35:9).

CONCEALMENT, EXPOSURE [*4059, 7621, *636, 649, 2821, 5158, 5745, 5746*].

Concealment of Sin:
(Ge 3:8; Jos 7:21; Pr 28:13; Isa 29:15; 30:1).

Secret Sins:
Warning against (2Ki 17:9; Job 24:16; Ps 19:12; 90:8; Eze 8:12; Eph 5:12). Called works of darkness (Job 24:14; Pr 7:8-9; Jn 3:20; Ro 13:12; Eph 5:11; 1Th 5:7).

Exposure of Sin:
Inevitable (Nu 32:23; Job 20:27; Pr 26:26; Ecc 12:14; Lk 12:2; 1Co 4:5). Rendered doubly certain (Job 10:14; 14:16; Jer 16:17; Eze 11:5; Hos 7:2; Am 5:12).

CONCEIT Of the foolish (Pr 12:15; 26:5, 12, 16; 28:26; Ro 1:22). Of the rich (Pr 28:11). Of the self-righteous (Ps 36:2; Lk 18:11-12). Warnings against (Pr 3:5, 7; 23:4; Isa 5:21; Jer 9:23; Ro 11:25; 12:16; 1Co 3:18; Gal 6:3).

See Hypocrisy; Pride; Self-Exaltation.

CONCEPTION Miraculous: By Sarah (Ge 21:1-2), Rebekah (Ge 25:21), Rachel (Ge 30:22), Manoah's wife (Jdg 13:3-24), Hannah (1Sa 1:19-20), Elizabeth (Lk 1:24-25, 36-37, 58), Mary (Mt 1:18, 20; Lk 1:31-35).

CONCISION *See Circumcision; Mutilators.*

CONCUBINAGE Laws concerning (Ex 21:7-11; Lev 19:20-22; Dt 21:10-14). Concubines might be dismissed (Ge 21:9-14). Called wives (Ge 37:2; Jdg 19:3-5). Children of, not heirs (Ge 15:4; 21:10).

Practiced by Abraham (Ge 16:3; 25:6; 1Ch 1:32). Nahor (Ge 22:23-24), Jacob (Ge 30:4), Eliphaz (Ge 36:12), Gideon (Jdg 8:31), a Levite (Jdg 19:1), Caleb (1Ch 2:46-48), Manasseh (1Ch 7:14), Saul (2Sa 3:7), David (2Sa 5:13; 15:16), Solomon (1Ki 11:3), Rehoboam (2Ch 11:21), Abijah (2Ch 13:21), Belshazzar (Da 5:2).

See Marriage; Polygamy.

CONCUPISCENCE Intense longing for what God would not have us to have (Ro 7:8; Col 3:5; 1Th 4:5). *See Covetousness.*

CONDEMNATION, SELF *See Self-Condemnation.*

CONDESCENSION

Of God:

In Reasoning With His Creatures—
Sets forth his reasons for sending the flood (Ge 6:11-13). Enters into covenant with Abraham (Ge 15:1-21; 18:1-22). Indulges Abraham's intercession for Sodom (Ge 18:23-33). Warns Abimelech in a dream (Ge 20:3-7). Reasons with Moses (Ex 4:2-17). Sends quail to the Israelites in response to their murmuring (Ex 16:12). Indulges Moses' prayer to see his glory (Ex 33:18-23). Indulges Gideon's tests (Jdg 6:36-40). Reasons with Job (Job 38; 39; 40; 41). Invites sinners, "Come now, let us reason together" (Isa 1:18-20). Expostulates with backsliding Israel (Isa 41:21-24; 43:1-19; 65:1-16; Jer 3:1-15; 4:1-31; 7:1-34; Eze 18:25-32; 33:10-20; Hos 2; Mic 6:1-9; Mal 3:7-15).

In His Care—
For mankind (Ps 8:4-6; 144:3). For the world (Ps 113:5-6). In redemption (Isa 45:11; Jn 3:16; Ro 5:8; Heb 2:11; 6:17-18; 1Jn 4:10, 19).

Of Christ: (Lk 22:27; Jn 13:5; 14; 2Co 8:9; Php 2:7-8; Heb 2:11).

CONDOLENCE Instances of: David, to Hanun (2Sa 10:2). King of Babylon, to Hezekiah (2Ki 20:12-13). The three friends of, to Job (Job 2:11). Jesus, to Mary and Martha (Jn 11:23-35).

See Affliction, Consolation Under; Sympathy.

CONDUCT, CHRISTIAN Believing God (Mk 11:22; Jn 14:11-12). Fearing God (Ecc 12:13; 1Pe 2:17). Loving God (Dt 6:5; Mt 22:37). Following God (Eph 5:1; 1Pe 1:15-16). Obeying God (Lk 1:6; 1Jn 5:3). Rejoicing in God (Ps 33:1; Hab 3:18). Believing in Christ (Jn 6:29; 1Jn 3:23). Loving Christ (Jn 21:15; 1Pe 1:7-8). Following the example of Christ (Jn 13:15; 1Pe 2:21-24). Obeying Christ (Jn 14:21; 15:14).

Living:
To Christ (Ro 14:8; 2Co 5:15). To righteousness (Mic 6:8; Ro 6:18; 1Pe 2:24). Soberly, righteously, and godly (Tit 2:12).

Walking:
Honestly (1Th 4:12). Worthy of God (1Th 2:12). Worthy of the Lord (Col 1:10). In the Spirit (Gal 5:25). After the Spirit (Ro 8:1). In newness of life (Ro 6:4). Worthy of our vocation (Eph 4:1). As children of light (Eph 5:8). Rejoicing in Christ (Php 3:1; 4:4). Loving one another (Jn 15:12; Ro 12:10; 1Co 13; Eph 5:2; Heb 13:1). Striving for the faith (Php 1:27; Jude 3). Putting away all sin (1Co 5:7; Heb 12:1). Abstaining from all appearance of evil (1Th 5:22). Perfecting holiness (Mt 5:48; 2Co 7:1; 2Ti 3:17). Hating defilement (Jude 23). Following after that which is good (Php 4:8; 1Th 5:15; 1Ti 6:11). Overcoming the world (1Jn 5:4-5). Adorning the gospel (Mt 5:16; Tit 2:10). Showing a good example (1Ti 4:12; Tit 2:7; 1Pe 2:12). Abounding in the work of the Lord (1Co 15:58; 2Co 8:7; 1Th 4:1). Shunning the wicked (Ps 1:1; 2Th 3:6). Controlling the body (1Co 9:27; Col 3:5). Subduing the temper (Eph 4:26; Jas 1:19). Submitting to injuries (Mt 5:39-41; 1Co 6:7). Forgiving injuries (Mt 6:14; Ro 12:20). Living peaceably with all (Ro 12:18; Heb 12:14). Visiting the afflicted (Mt 25:36; Jas 1:27). Doing as we would be done by (Mt 7:12; Lk 6:31). Sympathizing with others (Gal 6:2; 1Th 5:14). Honoring others (Ps 15:4; Ro 12:10). Fulfilling domestic duties (Eph 6:1-8; 1Pe 3:1-7). Submitting to authorities (Ro 13:1-7). Being liberal to others (Ac 20:35; Ro 12:13). Being contented (Php 4:11; Heb 13:4). Blessedness of maintaining (Ps 1:1-3; 19:9-11; 50:23; Mt 5:3-12; Jn 7:17; 15:10).

CONDUIT *See Aqueduct.*

CONEY Rock badger; unclean for food (Lev 11:5, ftn; Dt 14:7; Ps 104:18; Pr 30:26).

CONFECTION A blend of incense or perfume (Ex 30:35; 1Sa 8:12). Difficult term transliterated "Pannag" in KJV (Eze 27:17). *See Perfume.*

CONFECTIONARY A perfumer (1Sa 8:13). *See Perfume.*

CONFEDERACIES Of kings (Ge 14:1-2; Jos 10:1-5; 11:1-5; 1Ki 20:1). *See Alliances.*

CONFESSION To acknowledge one's faith in anything, as in the existence and authority of God, or the sins of which one has been guilty (Mt 10:32; Lev 5:5; Ps 32:5), to concede or allow (Jn 1:20; Ac 24:14; Heb 11:13), to praise God by thankfully acknowledging him (Ro 14:11; Heb 13:15).

Of Christ:
In baptism (Ac 19:4-5; Gal 3:27). To salvation (Mt 10:32; Lk 12:8; Ro 10:9-11). Inspired by the Holy Spirit (1Co 12:3; 1Jn 4:2-3). Fellowship with the Father through (1Jn 2:23; 4:15). Timid believers deterred from (Jn 12:42-43). Those refusing to make, rejected (Mt 10:33; Mk 8:38; Lk 12:9; 2Ti 2:12). Hypocritical (Mt 7:21-23; Lk 13:26; 1Jn 1:6; 2:4). Commanded (2Ti 1:8). Exemplified (Mt 3:11; 14:23; 16:16; Jn 1:15-18; 6:29; 9:22-38; 11:27; Ac 8:35-37; 9:20; 18:5; Ro 1:16).

Of Sin: *See Sin, Confession of.*

CONFIDENCE

In People:
Warned against (Jer 9:4; 12:6; Mic 7:5).

Betrayed—
Joshua, by the Gibeonites (Jos 9:3-15). Eglon, by Ehud (Jdg 3:15-23). Sisera, by Jael (Jdg 4:17-22). Samson, by Delilah (Jdg 16:17-20). Ahimelech, by David (1Sa 21:1-9). Abner, by Joab (2Sa 3:27). Amasa, by Joab (2Sa 20:9-10). Worshipers of Baal, by Jehu (2Ki 10:18-28). *See Betrayal.*

False: *See False Confidence.*

In God:
(Ps 118:8; Pr 3:26; 14:26; Ac 28:31; Eph 3:12; Heb 3:16; 10:35; 1Jn 2:28; 3:21; 5:14). *See Faith.*

CONFISCATION Of property: By David, that of Mephibosheth (2Sa 16:4). By Ahab, of Naboth's vineyard (1Ki 21:7-16). By Xerxes, of Haman's house (Est 8:1). As a penalty (Ezr 10:8).

CONFLAGRATIONS *See Burning.*

CONFORMITY
Conformity to the world, condemned (Ro 12:1-2; Eze 5:7; 11:12; 1Pe 1:14-16).

Conformity to Christ, commanded (Ro 8:29; Eph 5:1-2; 1Co 4:16; 1Th 1:6; 2:14; Heb 6:12; 13:7; 3Jn 11).

CONFUSION Of languages (Ge 11:1-9). Of Israel's enemies in battle (Ex 14:24; 23:27; Jos 10:10). Of Israel in judgment (Dt 28:20, 28; Jer 51:34). Of believers by false teachers (Gal 1:7; 5:10).

CONGESTION NIV "swelling" (Lev 13:28) or "inflamation" (Dt 28:22). *See Disease.*

CONGREGATION, OF ISRAEL Collective term for God's chosen in the OT, or an assembly of the people summoned for a definite purpose (1Ki 8:65), either the whole assembly, or a part (Nu 16:3; Ex 12:6; 35:1; Lev 4:13).

Often considered in a non-technical sense, as a gathering of believers or chosen, the church of the OT. For that purpose. *See Church, The Body of Believers.*

CONIAH (*Yahweh sustains*). A name given to Jehoiachin, king of Judah, who was carried captive by Nebuchadnezzar (Jer 22:24, ftn; 22:28; 37:1, ftn), c. 597 B.C. *See Jehoiachin.*

CONNIVANCE Judged (Lev 20:4; 1Sa 3:11-13). Result (Pr 10:10).

CONONIAH *See Conaniah.*

CONQUESTS Of the Gentiles by Israel (Jos 6:20; 8:24; 10:28-29; 11:8, 23; 12:7; Jdg 1:8; 3:30; 4:16; 8:28; 9:45; 11:33).

CONSCIENCE Guide (Ps 51:3; Pr 20:12; Mt 6:22-23; Lk 11:33-36; Ro 2:14-15; 7:18, 22; 2Co 5:11). Approves (Job 27:6; Pr 21:2; Ac 23:1; 24:16; Ro 9:1; 1Co 4:4; 2Co 1:12; 1Ti 1:5, 19; 3:9; 2Ti 1:3; Heb 13:18; 1Pe 2:19; 3:16, 21; 1Jn 3:20-21). Struggle with (Job 15:21, 24; Ps 51:3; Mt 6:22-23; Lk 11:33-36; Ro 7:15-23). Purged (Heb 9:14; 10:22). *See Honesty; Integrity.* Of another, to be respected (Ro 14:2-20; 1Co 8:7-13; 10:27-32; 2Co 4:2).

Instances of Faithful:

Pharaoh, when he took Sarah into his harem (Ge 12:18-19). Abimelech, when he took Sarah for a concubine (Ge 26:9-11). Jacob, in his care of Laban's property (Ge 31:39), in his greeting of Esau (Ge 33:1-12). Joseph, with Potiphar's wife (Ge 39:7-12). Nehemiah, with taxes (Ne 5:15). Daniel, with the king's meat (Da 1:8). Peter, in his preaching (Ac 4:19-20; 5:29).

Unfaithful Conscience:

Corrupt (Mt 6:23; Lk 11:34; Jn 16:2-3). Dead (Pr 16:25; 30:20; Jer 6:15; Am 6:1-6; Ro 1:21-25; Eph 4:17-29). Defiled (Tit 1:15). Seared (1Ti 4:2). Guilty (Job 15:21, 24; Ps 51:1-14; 73:21; Pr 28:1; Isa 59:9-14; Mt 14:1-2; 27:3-5; Mk 6:14, 16; Jn 8:9; Ac 2:37; 1Ti 4:2; Tit 1:15; Heb 9:14; 10:26-27). *See Blindness, Spiritual.*

Instances of Guilty—

Adam and Eve, after they sinned (Ge 3:7-8). Jacob, after defrauding Esau (Ge 33:1-12). Joseph's brothers (Ge 42:21; 44:16). Pharaoh, after the plagues (Ex 9:27). Micah, after stealing (Jdg 17:2). David, for his indignity to Saul (1Sa 24:5), for his adultery and for his murder of Uriah (Ps 32; 38; 40:11-12; 51), for numbering Israel (2Sa 24:10; 1Ch 21:1-8). The old prophet of Bethel (1Ki 13:18, 29-32). The lepers of Samaria (2Ki 7:8-10). Jonah (Jnh 1:12). Herod, for beheading John the Baptist (Mt 14:2; Lk 9:7). Peter, after denying the Lord (Mt 26:75; Mk 14:72; Lk 22:62). Judas (Mt 27:3-5). The accusers of the women taken in adultery (Jn 8:9).

CONSCIENCE MONEY *See Money.*

CONSCIENTIOUSNESS *See Integrity.*

CONSCRIPTION Of soldiers (1Sa 14:52). Of forced labor (1Ki 5:13-18; 19:15-23; 2Ki 25:19).

CONSECRATED THINGS Laws regarding (Lev 27; Nu 18:8-32). *See Firstborn; Firstfruits.*

CONSECRATION Of Aaron. *See Aaron.* Of Priests. *See Priest.* Of the altar. *See Altar.* Of the temple. *See Temple, Solomon's; Offerings.*

Commanded (Ex 32:29). Personal (Ps 51:17; Mt 13:44-46; Ro 6:13, 16, 19; 12:1; 2Co 8:5). Conditional (Ge 28:20-22; 2Sa 15:7-8).

Instances of: Cain and Abel (Ge 4:4-7). Abraham, of Isaac (Ge 22:9-12). Jephthah, of his daughter (Jdg 11:30-40). Hannah, of Samuel (1Sa 1:11, 24-28). David consecrates the water (2Sa 23:16; 1Ch 11:10). Zicri, of himself (2Ch 17:16).

See Dedication; Offerings.

CONSERVATION *See Ecology.*

CONSISTENCY Encouraged (Ne 5:9; Mt 6:24; Lk 16:13; Ro 14:22; 1Co 10:21).

See Deceit; Expediency; Hypocrisy; Inconsistency; Obduracy; Prudence.

CONSOLATION *See Affliction, Consolation Under; Holy Spirit.*

CONSPIRACY Law against (Ex 23:1-2).

Instances of:

Joseph's brothers, against Joseph (Ge 37:18-20). Miriam and Aaron, against Moses (Nu 12; 14:4; 16:1-35). Abimelech, against Gideon's sons (Jdg 9:1-6). Gaal, against Abimelech (Jdg 9:23-41). Delilah, against Samson (Jdg 16:4-21). Abner, against Ish-Bosheth (2Sa 3:7-21). Of Absalom (2Sa 15:10-13). Of Jeroboam (1Ki 14:2). Of Baasha (1Ki 15:27). Of Zimri (1Ki 16:9). Of Jezebel, against Naboth (1Ki 21:8-13). Of Jehu (2Ki 9:14-26). Of Jehoiada (2Ki 11:4-16). Of servants, against Joash (2Ki 12:20).

People in Jerusalem, against Amaziah (2Ki 14:19). Shallum, against Zechariah (2Ki 15:10). Pekahiah (2Ki 15:23-25). Pekah (2Ki 15:30). Amon (2Ki 21:23). Sennacherib (2Ki 19:37). Amaziah (2Ch 25:27). Xerxes (Est 2:21-23). Jeremiah (Jer 18:18). Daniel (Da 6:4-17). Shadrach, Meshach, and Abednego (Da 3:8-18).

Against Jeremiah (Jer 11:9, 19). Jesus (Mt 12:14; 21:38-41; 26:3-4; 27:1-2; Mk 3:6). Paul (Ac 18:12; 23:12-15).

Falsely accused of: Jonathan (1Sa 22:8).

CONSTANCY In obedience (Ps 119:31, 33). In friendship (Pr 27:10). Under suffering (Mt 5:12; Heb 12:5; 1Pe 4:12-16). In prayer (Lk 18:1; Ro 12:12; Eph 6:18; Col 4:2; 1Th 5:17). In beneficence (Gal 6:9). In profession (Heb 10:23).

Instances of: Ruth (Ru 1:14). Jonathan (1Sa 18:1; 20:16). Priscilla and Aquila (Ro 16:3-4).

See Character; Stability.

CONSTELLATIONS (2Ki 23:5; Job 9:9; 38:32; Isa 13:10). The serpent (Job 26:13). Orion (Job 9:9; Am 5:8).

See Astronomy.

CONSTITUTION Agreement between the ruler and the people. King commanded to study and obey the Mosaic Law (Dt 17:18-20). Made by David (2Sa 5:3; 1Ch 11:3). Made for Joash (2Ch 23:2-3, 11). Made by Zedekiah, proclaiming liberty (Jer 34:8-11). King of Medes and Persians bound by (Da 6:12-15). *See Covenant.*

CONSUMPTION NIV "wasting diseases" (Lev 26:16; Dt 28:22). *See Disease.*

CONTEMPT Sin of (Job 31:13-14; Pr 14:21). Folly of (Pr 11:12). A characteristic of the wicked (Pr 18:3; Isa 5:24; 2Ti 3:3).

Forbidden Toward:

Parents (Pr 23:22). Christ's little ones (Mt 18:10). Weak brothers (Ro 14:3). Young ministers (1Co 16:11). Believing masters (1Ti 6:2). The poor (Jas 2:1-3). Self-righteousness prompts to (Isa 65:5; Lk 18:9, 11). Pride and prosperity prompt to (Ps 123:4). Ministers should give no occasion for (1Ti 4:12). Of ministers, is a despising of God (Lk 10:16; 1Th 4:8).

Toward the Church:

Often turned into respect (Isa 60:14). Often punished (Eze 28:26). Causes believers to cry to God (Ne 4:4; Ps 123:3).

The Wicked Exhibit Toward:

Christ (Ps 22:6; Isa 53:3; Mt 27:29). Believers (Ps 119:141). Authorities (2Pe 2:10; Jude 8). Parents (Pr 15:5, 20). The afflicted (Job 19:18). The poor (Ps 14:6; Ecc 9:16). Believers sometimes guilty of (Jas 2:6).

Exemplified:

Hagar (Ge 16:4). Troublemakers (1Sa 10:27). Nabal (1Sa 25:10-11). Michal (2Sa 6:16). Sanballat (Ne 2:19; 4:2-3). False teachers (2Co 10:10).

CONTENTION *See Strife.*

CONTENTMENT Desirable (Pr 14:14; 15:13, 15, 30; 16:8; 17:1, 22; 30:8; Ecc 2:24; 4:6; 5:12; 6:9). Commanded (Ps 37:7; Ecc 9:7-9; Lk 3:14; 1Co 7:17, 20-24; Gal 5:26; 1Ti 6:6-8; Heb 13:5).

Instances of: Esau (Ge 33:9). Barzillai (2Sa 19:33-37). The Shunammite (2Ki 4:13). David (Ps 16:6). Paul (Php 4:11-12).

See Affliction, Consolation Under; Resignation.

CONTINENCE *See Chastity; Self-Control.*

CONTINENTS (Ge 1:9-10; Job 26:7, 10; 28:8-11; 38:4-18; Ps 95:5; 104:5-9; 136:6; Pr 8:29; 30:4). *See Geology.*

CONTINGENCIES

In Divine Government of Mankind:

Conditional Rewards (Ge 4:7; 18:19; Ex 19:5; Lev 26:3-4; Dt 7:12; 11:26-27; 30:15-16, 19; 1Ki 3:14; 1Ch 28:7; 2Ch 26:5; Job 36:11; Jer 11:4; 18:9-10; 22:4-5; Mt 19:17; 23:37; Jn 14:23; 15:7; Col 1:22-23; Heb 3:14; Rev 22:17). Conditional Punishment (Ge 2:16-17; 3:3; Lev 26:14-16; Dt 11:28; 30:15, 19; 1Ki 3:14; 20:42; Job 36:12; Jer 12:17; 18:8; Eze 33:14-16; Jnh 3:10; Mt 6:15; Jn 9:41; 15:6; 2Th 2:8-11; Rev 2:22; 3:3).

Instances of choice:

Joshua (Jos 24:15). David (2Sa 24:12-14). Jesus (Mt 26:39).

See Blessings, Spiritual, Contingent Upon Obedience; Predestination; Will.

CONTRACTS Binding force of (Jos 9:19; Pr 6:1-5; Mt 20:1-16; Gal 3:15). Penalty for breach of (Lev 6:1-7).

Dissolved:

By mutual consent (Ex 4:18), by blotting out (Col 2:14).

Ratified:

By giving presents (Ge 21:25-30; 1Sa 18:4), by consummating in the presence of the public at the gates of the city (Ge 23:17-18; Ru 4:1-11), by erecting a heap of stones (Ge 31:44-54), by oaths (Ge 26:3, 28, 31; Jos 9:15, 20; 1Ch 16:16; Heb 6:16-17), by joining hands (Pr 6:1; 17:18; 22:26), with salt (Nu 18:19), by taking off the sandal (Ru 4:6-8), by written instrument (Jer 32:10-15). By piercing the servant's ear (Ex 21:2-6).

Instances of:

Between Abraham and Abimelech, concerning wells of water (Ge 21:25-32), violated (Ge 26:15). Between Laban and Jacob, for Laban's daughter (Ge 29:15-20, 27-30), violated (Ge 29:23-27); regarding sharing flocks and herds (Ge 30:28-34), violated (Ge 30:27-43; 31:7). Between Joshua and Gibeonites (Jos 9:3-9, 15-19). Between Solomon and Hiram (1Ki 5:8-12; 9:11).

See Covenant; Land; Vows.

CONTRITION *See Repentance; Sin, Confession of.*

CONVENTION For counsel (Pr 15:22). *See Counsel.*

CONVERSATION Profane, forbidden (Mt 5:37; Jas 5:12). Corrupt, forbidden (Eph 4:29; Col 3:8). Edifying, commanded (Eph 4:29; Col 4:6). People judged by (Mt 12:36-37). *See Speaking.*

For KJV "conversation" *See Conduct, Christian.*

CONVERSION A turning, which may be literal or figurative, ethical or religious, either from God, or, more frequently, to God. It implies a turning from and a turning to something, and is therefore associated with repentance (Ac 3:19; 26:20), and faith (Ac 11:21). On its negative side it is turning from sin, and on its positive side it is faith in Christ (Ac 20:21). Although it is an act of man, it is done by the power of God (Ac 3:26). In the process of salvation, it is the first step in the transition from sin to God. *See Converts.*

CONVERTS Parable illustrating four levels of receiving the Word: "Along the path" (Mt 13:4, 19). "Rocky places" (Mt 13:5, 20-21). "Choked" (Mt 13:7, 22). "Good soil" (Mt 13:8, 23; Lk 8:4-15).

See Backsliders; Conversion; Proselyte; Revivals.

Instances of:

Ruth (Ru 1:16). Nebuchadnezzar (Da 4). The mariners with Jonah (Jnh 1:5-6, 14, 16). Ninevites (Jnh 3). Gerasenes (Lk 8:35-39). The Samaritans (Jn 4:28-42). The thief on the cross (Lk 23:39-43). At Pentecost, three thousand (Ac 2:41). Post-Pentecostal (Ac 4:4). The eunuch (Ac 8:35-38). Saul of Tarsus (Ac 9:3-18). Sergius Paulus (Ac 13:7, 12; 26:12-23). Cornelius (Ac 10). Jews and Greeks at Antioch (Ac 13:43). Lydia (Ac 16:14-15). Jailer (Ac 16:27-34). Greeks (Ac 17:4, 12).

Zealous:

Instances of: Nebuchadnezzar (Da 3:29; 4:1-37). Andrew (Jn 1:40-41). Philip (Jn 1:43-45). The woman of Samaria (Jn 4:28-29). The man possessed of demons (Lk 8:39). The blind men (Mt 9:31; Jn 9:8-38). The mute man (Mk 7:36).

CONVEYANCE Of land: *See Land.*

CONVICTION, OF SIN To convince or prove guilty. The first stage of repentance.

Produced:

By dreams (Job 33:14-17). By visions (Ac 9:3-9). By adversity (Job 33:18-30; La 1:20; Lk 15:17-21). By the gospel (Ac 2:37; 1Co 14:24-25). By conscience (Jn 8:9; Ro 2:15). By the Holy Spirit (Jn 16:7-11). By God (Dt 28:65-67; Ps 38:1-22; 51:1-4, 7-17).

Instances of:

Adam and Eve, after their disobedience (Ge 3:8-10). Cain, after he killed Abel (Ge 4:13). Joseph's brothers, because of their cruelty to him (Ge 42:21-22; 44:16; 45:3; 50:15-21). Pharaoh, after the plague of hail (Ex 9:27-28), of locusts (Ex 10:16-17), after the death of the firstborn (Ex 12:31).

The Israelites, after worshiping the golden calf and being rebuked (Ex 33:4), after the death of ten spies and their sentence (Nu 14:39-40), after murmuring against God and being bitten by the serpents (Nu 21:7). After being judged for disobedience (Dt 28:65-67; Eze 33:10). In the last days (Eze 7:16-18, 25-26).

Saul, after sparing Agag and the best of the spoils (1Sa 15:24). David, after the pestilence sent because he numbered the people (1Ch 21:8, 30). After his sin with Bathsheba (2Sa 9:12-13; Ps 51:1-17). In penitential Psalms (Ps 31:10; 38:1-22). *See Psalms.* Widow of Zarephath, when her son died (1Ki 17:18). Job, in his distress (Job 40:4-5).

Isaiah, after his vision of God's throne (Isa 6:5). Belshazzar, after the handwriting on the wall (Da 5:6). Darius, when Daniel was in the lions' den (Da 6:18). Mariners, after casting Jonah into the sea (Jnh 1:16). Ninevites, at the preaching of Jonah (Jnh 3; Mt 12:41; Lk 11:32). Jonah, in the fish's belly (Jnh 2).

Herod, when he heard of the fame of Jesus (Mt 14:2; Mk 6:14; Lk 9:7). Jews, who condemned the woman taken in adultery (Jn 8:9). Judas, after his betrayal of Jesus (Mt 27:3-5). Peter, after the large catch of fish (Lk 5:8). Paul, on the way to Damascus (Ac 9:4-18). Felix, under the preaching of Paul (Ac 24:25). Philippian jailer, after the earthquake (Ac 16:29-30).

See Penitent; Remorse; Repentance; Sin, Confession of; Wicked.

CONVOCATION NIV "assembly"; a religious festival during which no work could be done (Ex 12:16; Lev 23:2-37; Isa 1:13).

COOKING Of the Passover lamb (Ex 12:9). A young goat might not be cooked in the mother's milk (Ex 23:19; Dt 14:21). Spice used in (Eze 24:10). Ephraim, a cake unturned (Hos 7:8). In the temple (Eze 46:19-24).

See Bread; Oven.

COOS *See Cos.*

COPING NIV "eaves"; a parapet on the temple roof (1Ki 7:9).

COPPER A mineral resource of Israel (Dt 8:9; Job 28:2). Refining, figurative of judgment (Eze 22:20; 24:11). Used as money (Mt 10:9; Mk 12:42). Alloyed with tin to make bronze. *See Bronze; Money.*

COPPERSMITH NIV Alexander the "metalworker" (2Ti 4:14).

COPULATION Forbidden between persons near of kin (Lev 18:6-16). During menses (Lev 15:19; 18:19), with animals (Ex 22:19).

See Adultery; Bestiality; Homosexual; Lasciviousness.

COR A measure of dry capacity, equal to the homer, containing ten ephahs or baths (1Ki 4:22; 5:11; 2Ch 2:10; 27:5; Ezr 7:22; Eze 45:14). *See Measure.*

CORAL Ranked by Hebrews with precious stones (Job 28:18; Eze 27:16).

See Minerals of the Bible, 1; Stones.

CORBAN (*gift*). An offering dedicated to God (Lev 1:2-3; 2:1; 3:1; Nu 7:12-17; Mk 7:11).

CORD

Ancient Uses of:

In casting lots (Mic 2:5), fastening tents (Ex 35:18; 39:40; Isa 54:2), leading or binding animals (Ps 118:27, ftn; Hos 11:4), hitching to a cast or plow (Job 39:10), binding prisoners (Jdg 15:13), measuring ground (2Sa 8:2; Jos 17:14; Ps 78:55; Am 7:17; Zec 2:1), worn on the head as a sign of submission (1Ki 20:31).

Figurative:
Of spiritual blessings (Ps 16:6). Of sin (Pr 5:22). Of life (Ecc 12:6). Of friendship (Ecc 4:12; Hos 11:4).

Symbolic Uses of:
Tassels of thread on the corners of garments served as a reminder to obey God's commands (Nu 15:38; cf Dt 6:4-9). Signifying an inheritance (Jos 17:14). Token in mourning (1Ki 20:31-33; Job 36:8). Ribbon used in poetic imagery (SS 4:3).

C

CORIANDER A spice (Ex 16:31; Nu 11:7).

CORINTH (*decoration*). A city of Achaia.

Visited:
By Paul (Ac 18; 2Co 12:14; 13:1, w 1Co 16:5-7 & 2Co 1:16). Apollos (Ac 19:1), Titus (2Co 8:16-17; 12:18). Erastus, a Christian of (Ro 16:23; 2Ti 4:20).

Church of:
Schism in (1Co 1:12; 3:4). Immoralities in (1Co 5; 11). Writes to Paul (1Co 7:1). Alienation of, from Paul (2Co 10). Abuse of ordinances in (1Co 11:22; 14). Heresies in (1Co 15:12; 2Co 11). Lawsuits in (1Co 6). Liberality of (2Co 9). Paul's letters to (1Co 1:2; 16:21-24; 2Co 1:1, 13).

CORINTHIANS, 1 and 2

1 Corinthians:

Author: The apostle Paul

Date: c. Spring A.D. 55

Outline:
I. Introduction (1:1-9).
II. Divisions in the Church (1:10-4:21).
A. The Fact of the Divisions (1:10-17).
B. The Causes of the Divisions (1:18-4:13).
1. A wrong conception of the Christian message (1:18-3:4).
2. A wrong conception of Christian ministry and ministers (3:5-4:5).
3. A wrong conception of the Christian (4:6-13).
C. The Exhortation to End the Divisions (4:14-21).
III. Moral and Ethical Disorders in the Life of the Church (chs. 5-6).
A. Laxity in Church Discipline (ch. 5).
B. Lawsuits Before Non-Christian Judges (6:1-11).
C. Sexual Immorality (6:12-20).
IV. Instruction on Marriage (ch. 7).
A. The Prologue: General Principles (7:1-7).
B. The Problems of the Married (7:8-24).
C. The Problems of the Unmarried (7:25-40).
V. Instruction on the Questionable Practices (8:1-11:1).
A. The Principles Involved (ch. 8).
B. The Principles Illustrated (ch. 9).
C. A Warning From the History of Israel (10:1-22).
D. The Principles Applied (10:23-11:1).
VI. Instruction on Public Worship (11:2-14:40).
A. Propriety in Worship (11:2-16).
B. The Lord's Supper (11:17-34).
C. Spiritual Gifts (chs. 12-14).
1. The test of the gifts (12:1-3).
2. The unity of the gifts (12:4-11).
3. The diversity of the gifts (12:12-31a).
4. The necessity of exercising the gifts in love (12:31b-13:13).
5. The superiority of prophecy over tongues (14:1-25).
6. Rules governing public worship (14:26-40).
VII. Instruction on the Resurrection (ch. 15).
A. The Certainty of the Resurrection (15:1-34).
B. The Consideration of Certain Objections (15:35-37).
C. The Concluding Appeal (15:58).
VIII. Conclusion: Practical and Personal Matters (ch. 16).

2 Corinthians:

Author: The apostle Paul

Date: c. Fall A.D. 55

Outline:
I. Primarily Apologetic: Paul's Explanation of His Conduct and Apostolic Ministry (chs. 1-7).
A. Salutation (1:1-2).
B. Thanksgiving for Divine Comfort in Affliction (1:3-11).
C. The Integrity of Paul's Motives and Conduct (1:12-2:4).
D. Forgiving the Offender at Corinth (2:5-11).
E. God's Direction in the Ministry (2:12-17).
F. The Corinthian Believers—a Letter from Christ (3:1-11).
G. Seeing the Glory of God With Unveiled Faces (3:12-4:6).
H. Treasure in Clay Jars (4:7-16a).
I. The Prospect of Death and What It Means for the Christian (14:16b-5:10).
J. The Ministry of Reconciliation (5:11-6:10).
K. A Spiritual Father's Appeal to His Children (6:11-7:4).
L. The Meeting With Titus (7:5-16).
II. Hortatory: The Collection for the Christians at Jerusalem (chs. 8-9).
A. Generosity Encouraged (8:1-15).
B. Titus and His Companions Sent to Corinth (8:16-9:5).
C. Results of Generous Giving (9:6-15).
III. Polemical: Paul's Vindication of His Apostolic Authority (chs. 10-13).
A. Paul's Defense of His Apostolic Authority and the Area of His Mission (ch. 10).
B. Paul Forced Into Foolish Boasting (chs. 11-12).
C. Final Warnings (13:1-10).
D. Conclusion (13:11-14).

CORMORANT A bird forbidden as food (Lev 11:17; Dt 14:17). *See Birds.*

CORN *See Grain.*

CORNELIUS (*of a horn*). Roman centurion stationed at Caesarea, and the first Gentile convert (Ac 10:1).

CORNERSTONE Determined the design and structure of a building; the most important stone in the foundation (Isa 28:16). Figurative of Creation (Job 38:6). Of Christ (Isa 28:16; Zec 10:4; Eph 2:20; 1Pe 2:6).
See Capstone; Stones.

CORNET *See Music, Instruments of; Horn; Sistrums.*

CORPORAL PUNISHMENT *See Punishment.*

CORPULENCY Instances of: Eglon (Jdg 3:17), Eli (1Sa 4:18).

CORRECTION *See Afflictions, Of Believers; Chastisement, From God; Children, Correction of; Parents; Punishment; Reproof; Rod of Correction; Scourging.*

CORRUPTION

Physical Decomposition:
After death (Ge 3:19; Job 17:14; 21:26; 34:15; Ps 16:10; 49:9; 104:29; Ecc 3:20; 12:7; Jnh 2:6; Ac 2:27, 31; 13:34-37; 1Co 15:42, 50).

Figurative:
Of sin (Isa 38:17; Ro 8:21; Gal 6:8; 2Pe 1:4; 2:12, 19). Hill of (2Ki 23:13).

Judicial: *See Court, Of Law; Government; Judge.*

Ecclesiastical: *See Church, The Body of Believers, Corrupt; Ministers.*

Political: *See Bribery; Civil Service; Government; Politics.*

COS (*summit*). Island off the SW coast of Asia Minor (Ac 21:1).

COSAM (*diviner*). An ancestor of Christ (Lk 3:28).

COSMETICS Any of the various preparations used for beautifying the hair and skin (2Ki 9:30; Jer 4:30; Eze 23:40).

COTTON *See Linen.*

COUCH A piece of furniture for reclining, but sometimes only a rolled up mat (Am 6:4; Mt 9:6).

COULTER *See Plowshare.*

COUNCIL
1. Group of people gathered for deliberation (Ge 49:6; 2Ki 9:5).
2. The Jewish Sanhedrin (Mt 26:59; Ac 5:34) and lesser courts (Mt 10:17; Mk 13:9).

COUNSEL Wisdom in (Ex 18:14-23; Pr 1:5; 11:14; 15:22; 19:20; 20:18; 24:6). The wise profit by (Pr 1:5; 9:9; 12:15; 27:9). Rejected, by Rehoboam (1Ki 12:8-16), by rich young ruler (Mt 19:22). Consequences of rejecting divine (Pr 1:24-32).
See Prudence.

COUNSELOR A wise man, versed in law and diplomacy (1Ch 27:32-33). Ahithophel was, to David (2Sa 16:23; 1Ch 27:33), to Absalom (2Sa 16:23). A title of Christ (Isa 9:6). A title of the Holy Spirit (Jn 14:16, 26; 15:26; 16:7).

COUNTENANCE Angry (Pr 25:23). Cheerful (Job 29:24; Ps 4:6; 21:6; 44:3; Pr 15:13; 27:17). Fierce (Dt 28:50; Da 8:23). Guilty (Ge 4:5; Isa 3:9). Health indicated in (Ps 42:11; 43:5). Pride in (2Ki 5:1; Ps 10:4). Reading of (Ge 31:2, 5). Sad (1Sa 1:18; Ne 2:2-3; Ecc 7:3; Eze 27:35; Da 1:15; 5:6). Transfigured (Ex 34:29-35; Lk 9:29; 2Co 3:7, 13).
See Face.

COUNTRY Loved by Israelites in Exile (Ne 1; 2; 5; Ps 137:1-6). *See Church, The Body of Believers; Congregation, Of Israel; Patriotism.*

COURAGE Of the righteous (Pr 28:1; 2Ti 1:7). Exhortations to (Ps 31:24; Isa 51:7, 12-16; Eze 2:6; 3:9; Mt 10:28; Lk 12:4; 1Co 16:13; Php 1:27-28).

Commanded:
Upon Joshua (Dt 31:7-8, 22-23; Jos 1:1-9), the Israelites (Lev 26:6-8; Jos 23:6; 1Ch 19:13; 2Ch 32:7-8; Isa 41:10; 51:7, 12-16), Solomon (1Ch 22:13; 28:20), Asa (2Ch 15:1-7), the disciples (Mt 10:26, 28; Lk 12:4), Paul (Ac 18:9-10), other Christians (1Co 16:13; Php 1:27-28). By Jehoshaphat, upon judicial and executive officers (2Ch 19:11).

Instances of the Courage of Conviction:
Abraham, in leaving his fatherland (Ge 12:1-9), in offering Isaac (Ge 22:1-14). Gideon, in destroying the altar of Baal (Jdg 6:25-31). Ezra, in undertaking the perilous journey from Babylon to Israel without a guard (Ezr 8:22-23). The Jews, in returning answer to Tattenai (Ezr 5:11). The three Hebrews who refused to bow down to the image of Nebuchadnezzar (Da 3:16-18). Daniel, in persisting in prayer, regardless of the edict against praying (Da 6:10).
Peter and John, in refusing to obey men rather than God (Ac 4:19; 5:29).

Instances of Personal Bravery:
Joshua and Caleb, in advising that Israel go at once and possess the land (Nu 13:30; 14:6-12). Othniel, in killing Kiriath Sepher (Jos 15:16-17). Gideon, in attacking the confederate armies of the Midianites and Amalekites with 300 men (Jdg 7:7-23). Deborah, in leading Israel's armies (Jdg 4). Jael, in killing Sisera (Jdg 4:18-22). Agag, in the indifference with which he faced death (1Sa 15:32-33). David, in killing Goliath (1Sa 17:32-50), in entering the tent of Saul and carrying away Saul's spear (1Sa 26:7-12). David's captains (2Sa 23). Joab, in reproving King David (2Sa 19:5-7). Nehemiah, in refusing to take refuge in the temple (Ne 6:10-13). Esther, in going to the king to save her people (Est 4:8, 16; 5:7).
Joseph of Arimathea, in caring for the body of Jesus (Mk 15:43). Thomas, in being willing to die with Jesus (Jn 11:16). Peter and other disciples (Ac 3:12-26; 4:9-13, 19-20, 31). The apostles, under persecution (Ac 5:21, 29-32). Paul, in going to Jerusalem, despite his impressions that bonds and imprisonments awaited him (Ac 20:22-24; 24:14, 25).

See Boldness of the Righteous; Ministers; Reproof, Faithfulness in; Cowardice.

COURSE OF PRIESTS AND LEVITES David divided the priests and Levites into 24 groups, called courses (Lk 1:8), each with its own head (1Ch 24:1ff). Each course officiated a week at a time.

COURT, OF BUILDINGS

Of the Tabernacle:
(Ex 27:9, 12, 16-19; 35:17-18; 38:9, 15-20, 31; 39:40; 40:8, 33; Lev 6:16, 26; Nu 3:26, 37; 4:26).

Of the Temple:
(1Ch 28:12; 2Ch 4:9; 6:13; 23:5; 33:5). The inner court (1Ki 6:36; 7:12). The middle court (1Ki 8:64; 2Ch 7:7).

COURT, OF LAW

Ecclesiastical: (1Ch 26:29-32; 2Ch 19:8-11; Mt 18:15-18; Jn 20:23).
See Church, The Body of Believers, Discipline.

Civil:
Held, outside the camp (Lev 24:14), at the tabernacle (Nu 27:2), at the gates of the city (Dt 21:19; 22:15; 25:7; Jos 20:4; Ru 4:1; Zec 8:16), under a palm tree (Jdg 4:5). Circuit (1Sa 7:15-17).
Composition of, and mode of procedure (Ex 18:25-26; Dt 1:15-17; 17:9; Ru 4:2-5; 1Ch 26:29; 2Ch 19:8-11; Mt 26:54-71; Mk 14:53, 55-65; 15:1; Lk 22:50-71; Jn 18:13-28; Ac 5:17-21, 25-28, 34, 38-41). Accused spoke in his own defense (Jer 26:11-16; Mk 15:3-5; Ac 4:8-12, 18-20, 29-32). Stephen before the Sanhedrin (Ac 7:1-60). Paul before the Sanhedrin (Ac 23:1-7), before Agrippa (Ac 26:1-32). *See Appeal; Punishment; Witness.* Superior and inferior (Ex 18:21-26; 24:14; Dt 1:15-17; 17:8-13; 2Ch 19:5-10).
Justice required of (Ex 23:2-3, 6-8; Dt 1:15-17; 25:1; 27:19; 2Ch 19:5-10; Ac 25:16). Sentence of, final and obligatory (Dt 17:8-12). Contempt of (Dt 17:8-13; Mic 5:1; Ac 23:1-5). *See Judge; Justice.*
Corrupt (Pr 17:15; 29:26; Isa 1:23; 5:23; 10:1-2; Mic 3:11; 7:3; Zep 3:3; Mt 26:59-62; 27:18-26; Mk 14:53-65; 15:10; Ac 4:15-18; 6:11-14; 24:26-27). *See Bribery.*
See Judge; Justice; Priest.

COURTESY *See Manners.*

COURTSHIP Ancient customs of: Suitor visited the woman (Jdg 14:7), women proposed marriage (Ru 3:9-13). *See Marriage.*

COVENANT (*agreement, contract*).

Of God With People:
See Covenants, Major in the Old Testament. Salt is an emblem of (Lev 2:13; Nu 18:19; 2Ch 13:5). Confirmed with an oath (Ge 22:16; 26:3; 50:24; Ex 34:27-28; Nu 32:11; Ps 89:35; 105:9; Lk 1:73; Heb 6:13, 17-18). Binding (Lev 26; Jer 11:2-3; Gal 3:15). Everlasting (Ge 8:20-22; 9:1-17; Ps 105:8, 10; Isa 54:10; 61:8). God faithful to (Lev 26:44-45; Dt 4:31; 7:8-9; Jdg 2:1; 1Ki 8:23; Ps 105:8-11; 106:45; 111:5; Mic 7:20).

Instances of, With Individuals and Groups—
With Adam (Ge 2:16-17), Noah (Ge 6:18; 8:16; 9:8-17), Abraham (Ge 12:1-3; 15; 17:1-22; Ex 6:4-8; Ps 105:8-11; Ro 9:7-13; Gal 3). *See Circumcision.* Isaac (Ge 17:19), Jacob (Ge 28:13-15). Israel, to deliver them from Egypt (Ex 6:4-8), to destroy Amalek (Ex 17:14-16). Phinehas (Nu 25:12-13). Levites (Ne 13:29; Mal 2:4-5).

Instances of, with Israel at Sinai—
At Horeb (Ex 34:27; Dt 5:2-3), in Moab (Dt 29:1-15). Blood of (Ex 24:8). *See Blood, Blood of the Covenant.* Book of (Ex 24:7). The Sabbath (Ex 31:16). The Ten Commandments (Ex 34:28; Dt 5:2-3; 9:9).

Major Social Concerns in the Covenant—
1. Personhood. Everyone's person is to be secure (Ex 20:13; 21:16-21, 26-31; Lev 19:14; Dt 5:17; 24:7; 27:18).
2. False Accusation. Everyone is to be secure against slander and false accusation (Ex 20:16; 23:1-3; Lev 19:16; Dt 5:20; 19:15-21).
3. Woman. No woman is to be taken advantage of within her subordinate status in society (Ex 21:7-11, 20, 26-32; 22:16-17; Dt 21:10-14; 22:13-30; 24:1-5).
4. Punishment. Punishment for wrongdoing shall not be excessive so that the culprit is dehumanized (Dt 25:1-5).
5. Dignity. Every Israelite's dignity and right to be God's freedman and servant are to be honored and safeguarded (Ex 21:2, 5-6; Lev 25; Dt 15:12-18).
6. Inheritance. Every Israelite's inheritance in the promised land is to be secure (Lev 25; Nu 27:5-7; 36:1-9; Dt 25:5-10).
7. Property. Everyone's property is to be secure (Ex 20:15; 21:33-36; 22:1-15; 23:4-5; Lev 19:35-36; Dt 5:19; 22:1-4; 25:13-15).
8. Fruit of Labor. Everyone is to receive the fruit of his labors (Lev 19:13; Dt 24:14; 25:4).
9. Fruit of the Ground. Everyone is to share the fruit of the ground (Ex 23:10-11; Lev 19:9-10; 23:22; 25:3-55; Dt 14:28-29; 24:19-21).
10. Rest on Sabbath. Everyone, down to the humblest servant and the resident alien, is to share in the weekly rest of God's Sabbath (Ex 20:8-11; 23:12; Dt 5:12-15).
11. Marriage. The marriage relationship is to be kept inviolate (Ex 20:14; Dt 5:18; see also Lev 18:6-23; 20:10-21; Dt 22:13-30).
12. Exploitation. No one, however disabled, impoverished or powerless, is to be oppressed or exploited (Ex 22:21-27; Lev 19:14, 33-34; 25:35-36; Dt 23:19; 24:6, 12-15, 17; 27:18).
13. Fair Trial. Everyone is to have free access to the courts and is to be afforded a fair trial (Ex 23:6, 8; Lev 19:15; Dt 1:17; 10:17-18; 16:18-20; 17:8-13; 19:15-21).
14. Social Order. Every person's God-given place in the social order is to be honored (Ex 20:12; 21:15, 17; 22:28; Lev 19:3, 32; 20:9; Dt 5:16; 17:8-13; 21:15-21; 27:16).
15. Law. No one shall be above the law, not even the king (Dt 17:18-20).

16. Animals. Concern for the welfare of other creatures is to be extended to the animal world (Ex 23:5, 11; Lev 25:7; Dt 22:4, 6-7; 25:4).

Repudiated by God on account of Israelite's idolatry (Jer 44:26-27; Heb 8:9). Broken by the Israelites (Jer 22:9; Eze 16:59; Heb 8:9). Punishment for breaking (Lev 26:25-46).David (2Sa 7:12-16; 1Ch 17:11-14; 2Ch 6:16), David and his house (2Sa 23:5; Ps 89:20-37; Jer 33:21), God's people (Isa 55:3; 59:21).

Of People With God:

Jacob (Ge 28:20-22). Joshua (Jos 24:25). Absalom (2Sa 15:7-8). Jehoiada and Joash (2Ki 11:17). Josiah (2Ki 23:3). Asa (2Ch 15:12-15). Nehemiah (Ne 9:38; 10). Israelites (Ex 24:3, 7; 19:8; Dt 5:27; 26:17; Jer 50:5). *See Vows.*

Of People With People:

Sacred (Jos 9:18-21; Gal 3:15). Binding (Jos 9:18-20; Jer 34:8-21; Eze 17:14-18; Gal 3:15), on those represented as well (Dt 29:14-15). Breach of, punished (2Sa 21:1-6; Jer 34:8-22; Eze 17:13-19). National. *See Alliances.*

Ratified:

By giving the hand (Ezr 10:18; La 5:6; Eze 17:18), loosing the sandal (Ru 4:7-11), writing and sealing (Ne 9:38; Jer 32:10-12), giving presents (Ge 21:27-30; 1Sa 18:3-4), making a feast (Ge 26:30), erecting a monument (Ge 31:45-46, 49-53), offering a sacrifice (Ge 15:9-17; Jer 34:18-19), salting (Lev 2:13; Nu 18:19; 2Ch 13:5), taking an oath (Ge 21:23-24; 25:33; 26:28-31; 31:53; Jos 2:12-14; 14:9). *See Oath.*

See Contracts; Vows.

Instances of:

Abraham and Abimelech (Ge 21:22-32). Abimelech and Isaac (Ge 26:26-31). Jacob and Laban (Ge 31:44-54). Jonathan and David (1Sa 18:3-4; 20:16, 42; 2Sa 21:7). Jews with each other, to serve God (2Ch 15:12-15; Ne 10:28-32). King Zedekiah and his subjects (Jer 34:8). Ahab with Ben-Hadad (1Ki 20:34). Subjects with sovereign (2Ch 23:1-3, 16).

New Covenant:

Prophecy concerning (Jer 31:31-34; Isa 59:21; 61:8-9; Eze 16:59-63; 34:25-31; 37:24-28; Heb 8:4-13). Characterized by the Spirit rather than the letter (2Co 3:6-17). Purchased or ratified by the blood of Jesus (Mt 26:28; Mk 14:24; Lk 22:20; 1Co 11:25). Jesus the mediator (Heb 12:18-24). Everlasting (Heb 13:20).

See Covenants, Major in the Old Testament.

COVENANTS, MAJOR IN THE OLD TESTAMENT

Major Types:

***Royal Grant** (unconditional)—*

A king's grant (of land or some other benefit) to a loyal servant for faithful or exceptional service. The grant was normally perpetual and unconditional, but the servant's heirs benefited from it only as they continued their father's loyalty and service (1Sa 8:14; 22:7; 27:6; Est 8:1).

***Parity** (conditional)—*

A covenant between equals, binding them to mutual friendship or at least to mutual respect for each other's spheres and interests. Participants called each other "brothers" (Ge 21:27; 26:31; 31:44-54; 1Ki 5:12; 15:19; 20:32-34; Am 1:9).

***Suzerain-vassal** (unconditional)—*

A covenant regulating the relationship between a great king and one of his subject kings. The great king claimed absolute right of sovereignty, demanded total loyalty and service (the vassal must "love" his suzerain) and pledged protection of the subject's realm and dynasty, conditional on the vassal's faithfulness and loyalty to him. The vassal pledged absolute loyalty to his suzerain—whatever service his suzerain demanded—and exclusive reliance on the suzerain's protection. Participants called each other "lord" and "servant" or "father" and "son" (Jos 9:6, 8; Eze 17:13-18; Hos 12:1).

Major Instances:

1. Noahic—Ge 9:8-17.

Type: Royal Grant.

Participant: Made with "righteous" (Ge 6:9) Noah (and his descendants and every living thing on earth—all life that is subject to man's jurisdiction).

Description: An unconditional divine promise never to destroy all earthly life with some natural catastrophe; the covenant "sign" being the rainbow in the storm cloud.

2. Abrahamic A—Ge 15:9-21.

Type: Royal (land) Grant.

Participant: Made with "righteous" (his faith was "credited to him as righteousness," v. 6) Abram (and his descendants, v. 16).

Description: An unconditional divine promise to fulfill the grant of the land; a self-maledictory oath symbolically enacted it (v. 17).

3. Abrahamic B—Ge 17.

Type: Suzerain-vassal.

Participant: Made with Abraham as patriarchal head of his household.

Description: A conditional divine pledge to be Abraham's God and the God of his descendants (cf. "As for me," v. 4; "As for you," v. 9); the condition: total consecration to the Lord as symbolized by circumcision.

4. Sinaitic—Ex 19-24.

Type: Suzerain-vassal.

Participant: Made with Israel as the descendants of Abraham, Isaac and Jacob and as the people the Lord has redeemed from bondage to an earthly power.

Description: A conditional divine pledge to be Israel's God (as her Protector and the Guarantor of her blessed destiny); the condition: Israel's total consecration to the Lord as his people (his kingdom) who live by his rule and serve his purposes in history.

5. Phinehas—Nu 25:10-13.

Type: Royal Grant.

Participant: Made with the zealous priest Phinehas.

Description: An unconditionally divine promise to maintain the family of Phinehas in a "lasting priesthood" (implicitly a pledge to Israel to provide her forever with a faithful priesthood).

6. Davidic—2Sa 7:5-16.

Type: Royal Grant.

Participant: Made with faithful King David after his devotion to God as Israel's king and the Lord's vassal had come to special expression (v. 2).

Description: An unconditional divine promise to establish and maintain the Davidic dynasty on the throne of Israel (implicitly a pledge to Israel) to provide her forever with a godly king like David and through that dynasty to do for her what he had done through David—bring her into rest in the promised land (1Ki 4:20-21; 5:3-4).

7. New—Jer 31:31-34.

Type: Royal Grant.

Participant: Promised to rebellious Israel as she is about to be expelled from the promised land in actualization of the most severe covenant curse (Lev 26:27-39; Dt 28:36-37, 45-68).

Description: An unconditional divine promise to unfaithful Israel to forgive her sins and establish his relationship with her on a new basis by writing his law "on their hearts"—a covenant of pure grace.

See Covenant.

COVERING THE HEAD A symbol of sorrow and/or shame (2Sa 15:30; Est 6:12; Jer 14:3-4).

A symbol of authority (1Co 11:10). In Corinth men are commanded to pray and prophesy only with uncovered heads; women with heads covered with a veil or long hair (1Co 11:3-16).

COVETOUSNESS The Tenth Commandment against (Ex 20:17; Dt 5:21; Ro 13:9).

See Avarice; Bribery; Greed; Rich, The; Riches.

COW Used for pulling carts (1Sa 6:7-12; Hos 10:11). Milk of, used for food. *See Milk; Cattle.*

Figurative (Am 4:1).

COWARDICE Described (Jos 7:5). Disqualified for military service (Dt 20:8; Jdg 7:3). God inflicted on enemies (Jos 23:10). Inflicted as judgment (Lev 26:36-37; Dt 32:30). Rebuke for (Isa 51:12-13). Cause of adversity (Pr 29:25). Caused by adversity (Job 15:24; 18:11). Caused by wickedness (Pr 28:1).

Instances of:

Adam, in attempting to shift responsibility for his sin upon Eve (Ge 3:12). Abraham, in calling his wife his sister (Ge 26:7-9). Jacob, in flying from Laban (Ge 31:31). Aaron, in yielding to the Israelites when they demanded an idol (Ex 32:22-24). The ten spies (Nu 13:28, 31-33). Israelites, in fearing to attempt the conquest of Canaan (Nu 14:1-5; Dt 1:26-28), in the battle with the people of Ai (Jos 7:5), to meet Goliath (1Sa 17:24), to fight with the Philistines (1Sa 13:6-7). Twenty thousand of Gideon's army (Jdg 7:3). Ephraimites (Ps 78:9). Ephraimites and Manassites (Jos 17:14-18). Amorite kings (Jos 10:16). Canaanites (Jos 2:11; 5:1). Samuel, fearing to obey God's command to anoint a king in Saul's place (1Sa 16:2). David, in fleeing from Absalom (2Sa 15:13-17).

Nicodemus, in coming to Jesus by night (Jn 3:1-2). Joseph of Arimathea, secretly a disciple (Jn 19:38). Parents of the blind man, who was restored to sight (Jn 9:22). Early converts among the rulers (Jn 12:42-43). Disciples, in the storm at sea (Mt 8:26; Mk 4:38; Lk 8:25), when they saw Jesus walking on the water (Mt 14:25; Mk 6:50; Jn 6:19), when Jesus was apprehended (Mt 26:56). Peter, in denying the Lord (Mt 26:69-74; Mk 14:66-72; Lk 22:54-60; Jn 18:16-17, 25, 27). Pilate, in condemning Jesus, through fear of the people (Jn 19:12-16). Guards of the tomb of Jesus (Mt 28:4). The Philippian jailer (Ac 16:27). Peter and other Christians, at Antioch (Gal 2:11-14). False teachers (Gal 6:12). Companions of Paul (2Ti 4:16).

COZ *See Koz.*

COZBI (*deceitful* ISBE; *the luxuriant* KB). Daughter of Zur (Nu 25:15, 18).

COZEBA (*liar*). A city of Judah (1Ch 4:22). *See Kezib; Aczib.*

CRACKNEL *See Cakes.*

CRAFTINESS

Instances of: Satan, in the temptation of Eve (Ge 3:1-5). Jacob, in the purchase of Esau's birthright (Ge 25:31-33), obtaining Isaac's blessing (Ge 27:6-29), in management of Laban's flocks and herds (Ge 30:31-43). Gibeonites, in deceiving Joshua and the Israelites into a treaty (Jos 9:3-15). Sanballat, in trying to deceive Nehemiah into a conference (Ne 6). Jews, in seeking to entangle the Master (Mt 22:15-17, 24-28; Mk 12:13-14, 18-23; Lk 20:19-26), in seeking to slay Jesus (Mt 26:4; Mk 14:1).

CRAFTSMAN Valley of (1Ch 4:14, ftn; Ne 11:35).

See Art; Ge Harashim; Master Craftsman.

CRANE *See Swift.*

CREATION The Bible clearly teaches that the universe, "all things," came into existence through the will of the eternal God (Ge 1; 2; Jn 1:1-3; Heb 11:3; Rev 4:11). The Bible gives no information as to how long ago the original creation of matter occurred, or when the first day of creation began, or the sixth day ended. The two Creation accounts supplement each other (Ge 1; 2). Genesis 1 describes the creation of the universe as a whole, while Genesis 2 gives a more detailed account of the creation of man and says nothing about the creation of matter, light, heavenly bodies, plants, and animals, except to refer to the creation of animals as having taken place at an earlier time.

CREATOR Creator of the universe, God as (Ge 1:1; Ne 9:6; Job 26:7; Ps 102:25; Ac 14:15; Heb 11:3). The Word (Jesus) as (Jn 1:1-3). Holy Spirit as (Ge 1:2; Job 26:13; 33:4; Ps 104:30). Creator of mankind, God as (Ge 1;26; 2:7; 5:2; Dt 4:32; Job 33:4; Ps 8:5; 100:3; Isa 51:13; Mal 2:10; Ac 17:28).

CREATURE That which has been created (Ro 1:25; 8:39; Heb 4:13).

CREATURES, LIVING Heavenly beings with four faces and four or six wings (Eze 1:5-24; 3:13; 10:15-22; Rev 4:6-9; 5:6-14; 6:1-7; 7:11; 14:3; 15:7; 19:4). Identified as cherubim (Eze 10:15). *See Cherubim.*

CREDIT *See Borrowing; Creditor; Debt; Lending; Security, For Debt.*

CREDITOR

Mosaic laws concerning:

Release of debtor-servants (Ex 21:2-6). Must return cloak left as a pledge (Ex 22:25-27; Dt 24:10-13). Must not take, widows' cloak for pledge (Dt 24:17). Nor millstones (Dt 24:6). Must not extort interest of the poor (Lev 25:35-37; Dt 15:2-3; 23:19-20). Must not oppress neighbor (Lev 25:14-17).

Christ's injunctions to: (Mt 5:42; Lk 6:34).

Oppression by:

Seizing debtor's personal property (Job 22:6; 24:3, 10; Pr 22:26-27). Seizing debtor's houses (Job 20:18-20). Imprisoning debtor (Mt 5:25-26; 18:28-35; Lk 12:58-59). Enslaving debtor's children (2Ki 4:1; Ne 5:1-13; Job 24:9).

Merciful: (Ps 112:5; Mt 18:23-27; Lk 7:41-43).

See Debt; Debtor; Jubilee; Security, For Debt.

CREDULITY Willingness to trust too easily (Ge 3:6; Jos 9:14; Pr 14:15).

CREED A succinct statement of faith epitomizing the basic tenets of religious faith (Dt 4:4-6; 26:5-9). Various NT passages give the biblical foundation for the Christian creeds: the Apostles' Creed, the Nicene Creed, and the Athanasian Creed (Mt 16:16; 1Ti 3:16).

CREEK NIV "bay" (Ac 27:39). Identified as St. Paul's Bay, c. eight miles NW of the town of Zaletta on the island of Malta.

CREEPING THINGS NIV "creatures that move along the ground." A general term for animals (Ge 1:26; Lev 11:20-23, 29-31, 42; Ps 104:20, 25; Ro 1:23). Unclean (Lev 5:2; 11:20, 29-44; Dt 14:19). Clean (Lev 11:21-22). Used in idolatrous worship (Eze 8:10).

CREMATION (Jos 7:25; 1Sa 31:12; 2Ki 23:20; Am 2:1; 6:10).

See Burial.

CRESCENS (*increasing*). A disciple with Paul at Rome (2Ti 4:10).

CRETE, CRETAN An island in the Mediterranean, 165 miles long, 6 to 35 miles wide, forming a natural bridge between Europe and Asia Minor. It was the legendary birthplace of Zeus. Paul and Titus founded a church there (Tit 1:5-14). The Cretans in the OT are called Kerethites (1Sa 30:14; Eze 25:16). Cretans were in Jerusalem on the Day of Pentecost (Ac 2:11). According to Paul they were not of a high moral character (Tit 1:12).

CRIB *See Manger.*

CRICKET Permitted as food (Lev 11:22). *See Insects.*

CRIME Some lists (Eze 22:8-12, 27-30; Hos 4:1-2; Mt 15:19; Mk 7:21-22; Ro 1:24, 29-32; 3:14-18; 13:9; 1Co 5:11; Gal 5:19-21).

See various crimes or sins, such as Adultery, Arson, Homicide. See also, Punishment.

CRIMINALS Released at feasts (Mt 27:15, 21; Mk 15:6; Lk 23:17). Confined in prisons (Ge 39:20-23; Ezr 7:26; Ac 4:3; 12:4-5; 16:19-40), in dungeons (Ge 40:15; 41:14; Ex 12:29; Isa 24:22; Jer 37:16; 38:10; La 3:53, 55). Crucified with Jesus (Mt 27:38-44; Lk 23:32-39).

Cruelty to. *See Scourging; Stoning; Mocking.*

Punishment of. *See various crimes, such as Adultery, Arson, Homicide. See also, Punishments.*

CRIMINATION *See Self-Incrimination.*

CRIMSON Brilliant red dye obtained from an insect (2Ch 2:7, 14; Jer 4:30; Isa 1:18).

CRISPING PIN NIV "purses" (Isa 3:22). *See Purse.*

CRISPUS (*curled*). Former ruler of the Jewish synagogue at Corinth, converted by Paul (Ac 18:8; 1Co 1:14).

CRITICISM Unjust. *See Uncharitableness.*

CROCODILE *See Leviathan.*

CROCUS A flower (Isa 35:1). *See Plants of the Bible.*

CROP

1. Pouch-like enlargement in the gullet of many birds in which food is partially prepared for digestion (Lev 1:16).

2. Produce of the land (Ge 26:12; Ex 23:10). Cursed (Ge 4:12). In the New Jerusalem (Rev 22:2).

CROSS Jesus crucified on (Mt 27:32; Mk 15:21; Lk 23:26; Ac 2:23, 36; 4:10; 1Co 1:23; 2:2, 8; Eph 2:16; Php 2:8; Col 1:20; 2:14; Heb 12:2). Borne by Simon (Mt 27:32; Mk 15:21; Lk 23:26), by Jesus (Jn 19:17). Death on, a disgrace (Gal 3:13).

Figurative:

Of duty (Mt 10:38; 16:24; Mk 8:34; 10:21; Lk 9:23; 14:27). Of Christ's vicarious death (1Co 1:17-18; Gal 5:11; 6:14; Php 3:18).

See Crucifixion; Self-Denial.

CROSS-EXAMINED Skill in cross-examining (Pr 20:5). Instance of (Ac 12:19). *See Witness.*

CROW *See Birds; Rooster.*

CROWN Prescribed for priests (Ex 29:6; 39:30; Lev 8:9). Worn by kings (2Sa 1:10; 12:30; 2Ki 11:12; Est 6:8; SS 3:11; Rev 6:2), by queens (Est 1:11; 2:17; 8:15). Made of gold (Ps 21:3; Zec 6:11). An ornament (Eze 16:12; 23:42). Set with gems (2Sa 12:30; 1Ch 20:2; Zec 9:16; Isa 62:3). Given victor in games (1Co 9:25; 2Ti 2:5). Of thorns (Mt 27:29; Mk 15:17; Jn 19:5).

Figurative:
Of gracious visitation (Isa 28:5). Of heavenly reward (1Co 9:25; 2Ti 4:8; Jas 1:12; 1Pe 5:4; Rev 2:10; 3:11).

Symbolic: (Rev 4:4, 10; 6:2; 9:7; 12:1, 3; 13:1; 14:14; 19:12).

CRUCIBLE The crucible in which ore is melted to be purified and separated from dross (Pr 17:3; 27:21).

CRUCIFIXION The reproach of (Gal 3:13; 5:11). Of Jesus. *See Jesus the Christ, History of.* Of two criminals (Mt 27:38). Of disciples, foretold (Mt 23:34).

Figurative:
Of old nature (Ro 6:6; Gal 5:24). Of self-centered life (Gal 2:20; 6:14).
See Cross, Figurative.

CRUELTY
Instances of: Of Sarah to Hagar (Ge 16:6; 21:9-14). Egyptians to the Israelites (Ex 5:6-18). Peninnah to Hannah (1Sa 1:4-7; 2:3). Of Jews to Jesus (Mt 26:67; 27:28-31), soldiers to Jesus (Lk 22:64; Jn 19:3). In war (Isa 13:16, 18).
See Animals, Cruelty to; Kindness; Love; Malice; Prisoners, Of War.

CRUSE *See Jar(s).*

CRYING *See Mourning; Praise; Prayer; Weeping.*

CRYSTAL A precious stone (Job 28:17 Rev 4:6; 21:11; 22:1).
See Minerals of the Bible, 1; Stones.

CUB The young of a dog or a beast of prey; a cub (Ge 49:9; Dt 33:22; Jer 51:38; Na 2:11-12).

CUBIT A measure of distance, c. eighteen inches (Ge 6:16; Dt 3:11; Eze 40:5; 43:13; Rev 21:17). No one by worrying can add to his height (Mt 6:27; Lk 12:25 notes).

CUCKOO *See Gull.*

CUCUMBERS Vegetables enjoyed by Israel in Egypt (Nu 11:5).

CUD Chewing of, was one of the facts by which clean and unclean animals were distinguished (Lev 11:3-8; Dt 14:3-8).

CUMMIN A plant bearing a small aromatic seed (Isa 28:25, 27; Mt 23:23).

CUN (*chosen*). A Syrian city (1Ch 18:8). *See Tebah, 2; Berothai.*

CUNEIFORM A system of writing by symbolic wedge-shaped characters upon clay tablets used primarily in Mesopotamia in ancient times. More than half a million such clay tablets have been found.

CUP (Ge 40:11; 2Sa 12:3; 1Ki 7:26; Mt 23:25). Made of silver (Ge 44:2), gold (1Ch 28:17; Jer 52:19). Used in the institution of the Lord's Supper (Mt 26:27; Mk 14:23; Lk 22:20; 1Co 10:21). Of the table of demons (1Co 10:21).

Figurative:
Of sorrow (Ps 11:6; 73:10; 75:8; Isa 51:17, 22; Jer 25:15-28; Eze 23:31-34; Mt 20:22-23; 26:39; Mk 14:36; Lk 22:42; Jn 18:11; Rev 14:10). Of consolation (Jer 16:7). Of joy (Ps 23:5). Of salvation (Ps 116:13).

CUPBEARER A palace official who served wine at a king's table (Ge 40:11; 1Ki 10:5; 2Ch 9:4; Ne 1:11).

CUPIDITY *See Avarice; Covetousness; Lust.*

CURES Miraculous. *See Miracles; Disease; Physician.*

CURIOSITY Insatiable (Pr 27:20). Advised against (Ecc 7:21).

Instances of:
Of Eve (Ge 3:6). Of Abraham, to know whether God would destroy the righteous in Sodom (Ge 18:23-32). Of Jacob, to know the name of the angel (Ge 32:29). Of the Israelites, to see God (Ex 19:21, 24), to witness the offering in the Most Holy Place (Nu 4:19-20). Of Manoah, to know the name of an angel (Jdg 13:17-18). Of the people of Beth Shemesh, to see inside the ark (1Sa 6:19). Of the Babylonians, to see Hezekiah's treasures (2Ki 20:13). Of Daniel, to know a vision (Da 12:8-9).

Of Peter, to know what was being done with Jesus (Mt 26:58), to know what John would be appointed to do (Jn 21:21-22). A disciple, to know if there be few that be saved (Lk 13:23). Of Herod, to see Jesus (Lk 9:9; 23:8). Of the Jews, to see Lazarus, after he was raised from the dead (Jn 12:9), and to see Jesus (Jn 12:20-21). Of the disciples, to know whether Jesus would restore the kingdom of the Jews (Ac 1:6-7). Of the Athenians, to hear some new thing (Ac 17:19-21). Of angels, to look into the mysteries of salvation (1Pe 1:12).

CURSE Pronounced upon, the serpent (Ge 3:14-15), Adam and Eve (Ge 3:15-19), the ground (Ge 3:17-18), Cain (Ge 4:11-16), Canaan, Ham's son (Ge 9:24-27), the disobedient (Dt 28:15-68; Jer 11:3-17), Meroz (Jdg 5:23), Gehazi (2Ki 5:27). Barak commands Balaam to curse Israel (Nu 22:6; 23:11). Paternal (Ge 27:12-13; 49:5-7).

In the covenant with Abraham (Ge 12:3). Of the Mosaic law, enforcing the covenant (Dt 11:26-32; 27:12-26; 28:15-68; Jos 8:30-34).

Assumed for others (Mt 27:25). Rebekah for Jacob (Ge 27:13). Paul wishes he could assume for Israel (Ro 9:3). *See Blessings.* Christ assumed the curse of the Mosaic law for us (Gal 3:13). *See Jesus the Christ, Vicarious Death of.*

CURSING Of God (Lev 24:11-16; Isa 8:21). Of parents (Ex 21:17; Mt 15:4; Mk 7:10). Shimei curses David (2Sa 16:5-8). The precepts of Jesus concerning (Mt 5:44; Lk 6:28). Apostolic (Ro 12:14).
See Anathema Maranatha; Blasphemy; God, Name of; Oath.

CURTAINS

Of the tabernacle:
Ten curtains formed the inner lining of the tabernacle, of embroidered linen (Ex 26:1-6). Eleven curtains of goat hair formed the tent over it (Ex 26:7-13). A single linen curtain covered the entrance (Ex 26:36-37). The courtyard was fenced by curtains (Ex 27:9-18). Made by Bezalel and Oholiab (Ex 36:8-38).

A single linen curtain divided the Most Holy Place from the Holy Place (Ex 26:31-33; 35:12; 39:34; 40:21), also in the temple (2Ch 3:14); called the second curtain (Heb 9:3); used to cover the ark (Nu 4:5). A type of the humanity or body of Christ (Heb 10:20). Figurative of the believer's access to God (Heb 6:19).

Of the temple:
Divided the Most Holy Place from the Holy Place (2Ch 3:14). Torn at the time of the crucifixion of Christ (Mt 27:51; Mk 15:38; Lk 23:45).
See Tabernacle; Tapestry.

CUSH
1. Son of Ham (Ge 10:6-8; 1Ch 1:8-10).
2. A Benjamite, the title of the Psalm (Ps 7).
3. Land of (Ge 2:13; Ps 68:31; Isa 18:1). *See Cushite; Ethiopia.*

CUSHAN Poetic form of Cush (Hab 3:7). *See Ethiopia.*

CUSHAN-RISHATHAIM (*man of Cush, doubly guilty*). King of Aram Naharaim; that is, NW Mesopotamia (Jdg 3:8-10).

CUSHI
1. *See Cushite, 2.*
2. Father of Shelemiah (Jer 36:14).
3. Father of Zephaniah (Zep 1:1).

CUSHITE
1. Moses' wife (Nu 12:1).
2. A messenger who brought news to David (2Sa 18:21-32).
3. Tirhakah, king of Egypt. *See Tirhakah.*
4. Zerah, perhaps Pharaoh Oskoron I. *See Zerah, 7.*
5. Ebed-Melech, who pulled Jeremiah from the cistern (Jer 38:7-13). *See Ebed-Melech.*
6. A people, probably Ethiopians (2Ch 12:3; 14:12-13). *See Ethiopia.*

CUSTOM When not referring to a tax, usually means "manner," "way," or "statute" (Ge 31:35; Jdg 11:39; Jer 32:11). In the NT it means "manner," "usage" (Lk 1:9; Ac 6:14), and "religious practices."

CUSTOM, RECEIPT OF *See Tax.*

CUTHAH A district of Asia, from which colonists were transported to Samaria (2Ki 17:24-30; Ezr 4:10).

CUTTINGS A heathen practice, including tattooings, gashes, castrations, usually done in mourning for the dead and to propitiate deities. Forbidden to the Israelites (Lev 19:28; 21:5; Dt 14:1; Jer 16:6).

CUZA (*little judge*). Herod's steward (Lk 8:3).

CYLINDER SEALS *See Seal.*

CYMBAL A musical instrument. Of bronze (1Ch 15:19, 28; 1Co 13:1).

Used in the tabernacle service (2Sa 6:5; 1Ch 13:8; 15:16, 19, 28), in the temple service (2Ch 5:12-13; 1Ch 16:5, 42; 25:1, 6; Ps 150:5).

Used on special occasions: the Day of Atonement (2Ch 29:25), laying of the foundation of the second temple (Ezr 3:10-11), dedication of the wall (Ne 12:27, 36).

CYPRESS WOOD (Isa 44:14; SS 1:14; 4:13). Probably the wood from which Noah's ark was made; KJV "gopher wood" (Ge 6:14). Used in making idols (Isa 44:12-17).

CYPRUS (*copper*). An island (Ac 21:3; 27:4). Barnabas born in (Ac 4:36). Persecuted Jews preached the gospel at (Ac 11:19-20). Visited by Barnabas and Saul (Ac 13:4-12). Barnabas and Mark visit (Ac 15:39). Mnason, a disciple of (Ac 21:16).

CYRENE, CYRENIAN (*wall*). A city in N Africa, W of Egypt, c. ten miles from the coast. Originally a Greek city, it passed into the hands of the Romans. Simon, who helped Jesus carry his cross, came from there (Lk 23:26). People from Cyrene were in Jerusalem on the Day of Pentecost (Ac 2:10). Jews from the synagogue of the Cyrenians disputed with Stephen (Ac 6:9).

CYRENIUS *See Quirinius.*

CYRUS King of Persia. Issued a decree for the emancipation of the Jews and rebuilding the temple (2Ch 36:22-23; Ezr 1; 3:7; 4:3; 5:13-14; 6:3). Prophecies concerning (Isa 13:17-22; 21:2; 41:2; 44:28; 45:1-4, 13; 46:11; 48:14-15).

D

DABAREH *See Daberath.*

DABBESHETH (*hump*). A place on the boundary line of Zebulun (Jos 19:11).

DABERATH (*pasture*). A town of Issachar (Jos 19:12; 21:28). Assigned to the Levites (1Ch 6:72).

DAGGER A short sword (Jdg 3:16-22).

DAGON (*[god of] grain* IDB; *fish* ISBE). A pagan deity with the body of a fish, head and hands of a man. Probably the god of agriculture. Worshiped in Mesopotamia and Canaan, with temples in Ashdod (1Sa 5:1-7), Gaza (Jdg 16:21-30), and in Israel (1Ch 10:10). Samson destroyed the temple in Gaza (Jdg 16:30).

DAILY SACRIFICE Ordained in Mt. Sinai (Nu 28:6). A lamb as a burnt offering, morning and evening (Ex 29:38-39; Nu 28:3-4). Doubled on the Sabbath (Nu 28:9-10). Required to be with a meat and drink offering (Ex 29:40-41; Nu 28:5-8). Slowly and entirely consumed (Lev 6:9-12). Perpetually observed (Ex 29:42; Nu 28:3, 6). Pleasing (Nu 28:8; Ps 141:2). Secured God's presence and favor (Ex 29:43-44). Times of offering, were seasons of prayer (Ezr 9:5; Da 9:20-21, w Ac 3:1). Restored after the Captivity (Ezr 3:3). The abolition of, foretold (Da 9:26-27; 11:31).

Illustrative of:
Christ (Jn 1:29, 36; 1Pe 1:19). Acceptable prayer (Ps 141:2).
See Sacrifices.

DALAIAH *See Delaiah.*

DALE, THE KING'S *See Valley, Vale.*

DALMANUTHA South of the Plain of Gennesaret a cave has been found bearing the name "Talmanutha," perhaps the spot where Jesus landed. Matthew says Jesus went to the vicinity of Magadan (Mt 15:39). Dalmanutha and Magadan (of Magdala), located on the western shore of the Sea of Galilee, may be names for the same place or for two places located close to each other (Mk 8:10). *See Magadan.*

DALMATIA (*deceitful*). Province on the NE shore of the Adriatic Sea also called Illyricum (Ro 15:19; 2Ti 4:10).

DALPHON (*crafty* ISBE; *sleepless* KB). The son of Haman (Est 9:7).

DAMAGES AND COMPENSATIONS Listed (Nu 5:5-8). For assault (Ex 21:18-19, 22). For personal injury (Ex 21:28-34). For deception (Lev 6:1-5). For slander (Dt 22:13-19). For seduction (Dt 22:28-29). *See Fine.*

DAMARIS A female convert of Athens (Ac 17:34).

DAMASCUS, DAMASCENES An ancient city (Ge 14:15; 15:2). The capital of Syria (1Ki 20:34; Isa 7:8; Jer 49:23-29; Eze 47:16-17). Laid under tribute to David (2Sa 8:5-6). Besieged by Rezon (1Ki 11:23-24). Recovered by Jeroboam (2Ki 14:28). Taken by the king of Assyria (2Ki 16:9). Walled (Jer 49:27; 2Co 11:33). Garrisoned (2Co 11:32). Luxury in (Am 3:12). Paul's experiences in (Ac 9; 22:5-16; 26:12-20; 2Co 11:32; Gal 1:17). Prophecies concerning (Isa 8:4; 17:1-2; Jer 49:23-29; Am 1:3, 5; Zec 9:1).
Wilderness of (1Ki 19:15).
See Syria.

DAMMIM *See Ephes Dammim, Pas Dammim.*

DAMNATION When referring to the future it means primarily eternal separation from God with accompanying punishments (Mt 5:29; 10:28; 23:33; 24:51). The severity of the punishment is determined by the degree of sin (Lk 12:36-48), and is eternal (Isa 66:24; Mk 3:29; 2Th 1:9; Jude 6-7). *See Punishment; Wicked, Punishment of.*

DAN, DANITE(S) (*judge*).
1. The fifth son of Jacob and Bilhah (Ge 30:6; 35:25). Descendants of (Ge 46:23; Nu 26:42-43). *See below, Tribe of.* Blessed of Jacob (Ge 49:16-17).
2. Tribe of: Census of (Nu 1:39; 26:42-43). Inheritance of, according to the allotment of Joshua (Jos 19:40-47), of Ezekiel (Eze 48:1). Position of, in journey and camp, during the exodus out of Egypt (Nu 2:25, 31; 10:25). Blessed by Moses (Dt 33:22). Fail to conquer the Amorites (Jdg 1:34-35). Conquests by (Jos 19:47; Jdg 18:27-29). Deborah rebukes, for cowardice (Jdg 5:17). Idolatry of (Jdg 18). Commerce of (Jdg 5:17; Eze 27:19).
See Israel, Israelites.
3. A city of the tribe of Dan. Called Laish (Jdg 18:7, 13, 27, 29) and Leshem (Jos 19:47) and later known as Dan. *See Laish; Leshem.* Captured by the people of Dan (Jos 19:47). Idolatry established at (Jdg 18; 1Ki 12:28-29; Am 8:14). Captured by Ben-Hadad (1Ki 15:20; 2Ch 16:4).

DAN JAAN A place, probably in Dan, covered by David's census (2Sa 24:6).

DANCING Of children (Job 21:11). Of women (Ex 15:20; Jdg 11:34; 21:19-21; 1Sa 18:6; 21:11). Of David (2Sa 6:14-16; 1Ch 15:29). In the marketplace (Mt 11:16-17). At feasts (Jdg 21:19-21; Mt 14:6; Mk 6:22; Lk 15:23-25). As a religious ceremony (Ps 149:3; 150:4). Idolatrous (Ex 32:19; 32:25).
Figurative: Of joy (Ps 30:11; Ecc 3:4; Jer 31:4; 31:13; La 5:15).

DANIEL (*God [El] is my judge*).

1. An Israelite captive, also called Belteshazzar. *See Belteshazzar.* Educated at king's court (Da 1). Interprets visions (Da 2; 4; 5). Promotion and executive authority of (Da 2:48-49; 5:11, 29; 6:2). Conspiracy against, cast into the lions' den (Da 6).

Prophecies of (Da 4:8-9; 7-12; Mt 24:15).

Special diet of (Da 1:8-16). Wisdom of (Da 1:17; Eze 28:3). Devoutness of (Da 2:18; 6; 9; 10; 12; Eze 14:14). Courage and fidelity of (Da 4:27; 5:17-23; 6:10-23). Worshiped by Nebuchadnezzar (Da 2:6).

2. David's son. Also called Kileab (2Sa 3:3; 1Ch 3:1).

3. A descendant of Ithamar, and a companion of Ezra (Ezr 8:2; Ne 10:6).

DANIEL, BOOK OF

Author: Daniel

Date: c. 530 B.C.

Outline:

I. Prologue: The Setting (ch. 1; in Hebrew).
   A. Historical Introduction (1:1-2).
   B. Daniel and His Friends Are Taken Captive (1:3-7).
   C. The Young Men Are Faithful (1:8-16).
   D. The Young Men Are Elevated to High Positions (1:17-21).
II. The Destinies of the Nations of the World (chs. 2-7, in Aramaic, beginning at 2:4b).
   A. Nebuchadnezzar's Dream of a Large Statue (ch. 2).
   B. Nebuchadnezzar's Making of a Gold Image and His Decree That It Be Worshiped (ch. 3).
   C. Nebuchadnezzar's Dream of an Enormous Tree (ch. 4).
   D. Belshazzar's and Babylon's Downfall (ch. 5).
   E. Daniel's Deliverance (ch. 6).
   F. Daniel's Dream of Four Beasts (ch. 7).
III. The Destiny of the Nation of Israel (chs. 8-12; in Hebrew).
   A. Daniel's Vision of a Ram and a Goat (ch. 8).
   B. Daniel's Prayer and His Vision of the 70 "Sevens" (ch. 9).
   C. Daniel's Vision of Israel's Future (chs. 10-12).
      1. Revelation of things to come (10:1-3).
      2. Revelation from the angelic messenger (10:4-11:1).
      3. Prophecies concerning Persia and Greece (11:2-4).
      4. Prophecies concerning Egypt and Syria (11:5-35).
      5. Prophecies concerning the antichrist (11:36-45).
      6. Distress and deliverance (12:1).
      7. Two Resurrections (12:2-3).
      8. Instruction to Daniel (12:4).
      9. Conclusion (12:5-13).

DANNAH (*stronghold*). A city in the mountains of Judah (Jos 15:49).

DARA *See Darda.*

DARDA Also called Dara. A famous wise man (1Ki 4:31; 1Ch 2:6).

DARIC Persian gold coin used in Israel after the return from the Captivity; said to have been named from the first Darius (1Ch 29:7; Ezr 8:27). Although the NIV has "drachmas" for the following references, some believe that the coin intended was the daric (Ezr 2:69; Ne 7:70-72). *See Drachma.*

DARIUS (Old Persian *he who upholds the good*). A common name for Medo-Persian rulers.

1. Darius the Mede (Gubaru), the son of Xerxes (Da 5:31; 9:1), made governor of Babylon by Cyrus, but he seems to have ruled for only a brief time (Da 10:1; 11:1), prominent in the book of Daniel (Da 6:1, 6, 9, 25, 28; 11:1).

2. Darius I called the Great (spelled variously Hystaspos, Hystaspis, or Hystaspes), fourth and greatest of the Persian rulers (522-486 B.C.); reorganized the government into satraps and extended boundaries of the empire; a great builder; he was defeated by the Greeks at Marathon in 490 B.C.; renewed the edict of Cyrus and helped to rebuild the temple (Ezr 4:5, 24; 5:5-7; 6:1-12; Hag 1:1; 2:1, 10, 18; Zec 1:1, 7; 7:1). Died in 486 B.C. and was succeeded by Xerxes, the grandson of Cyrus the Great.

3. Darius, the Persian (spelled variously Codomanus or Codomannus), the last king of Persia (336-330 B.C.); defeated by Alexander the Great (330 B.C.) (Ne 12:22). Some scholars identify him with Darius II (Nothus), who ruled Persia and Babylon (423-404 B.C.).

DARKNESS Over the face of the earth (Ge 1:2; Job 38:9; Jer 4:23). Called "night" (Ge 1:5). God created (Isa 45:7). The NIV uses "[deep] darkness" to translate a word formerly translated "shadow of death," usually in a context of deep emotional despair or grief (Job 3:5; 10:21, 22; 12:22; 16:16; 24:17, 17; 28:3; 34:22; 38:17; Ps 23:4; 44:19; 107:10, 14; Isa 9:2; Jer 2:6; 13:16; Am 5:8).

Miraculous:

In Egypt (Ex 10:21-22; Ps 105:28), at Sinai (Ex 20:21; Heb 12:18), at the Crucifixion (Mt 27:45; Mk 15:33).

Figurative:

Of judgments (Pr 20:20; Isa 8:22, 13:10; Jer 4:28; 13:16; La 3:2; Eze 32:7-8; Joel 2:2, 10; Am 4:13; 5:18, 20; 8:9; Mic 7:8; Mt 24:29; Mk 13:24; Lk 23:45; Rev 8:12; 9:2). Of powers of evil (Lk 22:53; Eph 6:12; Col 1:13; 1Th 5:5; Rev 16:10).

Of the abode of the lost (Mt 8:12; 22:13; 25:30).

Of spiritual blindness (Isa 9:2; 42:16; 50:10; Mt 4:16; 6:22-23; Lk 1:79; 11:34; Jn 1:5; 3:19-21; 8:12; 11:9-10; Ac 26:18; Ro 1:21; 13:12-13; 1Co 4:5; 2Co 4:6; 6:14; Eph 5:8, 11; 1Th 5:4-5; 1Pe 2:9; 1Jn 1:5-7; 2:8-11). *See Blindness, Spiritual.*

Symbolic:

Of divine inscrutability (2Sa 22:10-12; Ps 18:11; 97:2). On Mt. Sinai (Ex 19:16; 20:21; Dt 4:11; 5:22; Heb 12:18). In the Sanctuary (1Ki 8:12; 2Ch 6:1).

See Tabernacle.

DARKON (perhaps *rough*, or *stern*). A descendant of Solomon's servant, Jaala, who returned with Zerubbabel from Exile (Ezr 2:56; Ne 7:58).

DART A weapon (Job 41:26). *See Armor; Arrows.*

DATE A fruit (2Ch 31:5).

DATHAN (*strong*). A conspirator against Moses (Nu 16:1-35; 26:9; Dt 11:6; Ps 106:17).

DAUGHTER Daughter can refer to both persons and things, often without regard to relationship or gender.

1. Daughter (Ge 11:29) or other female descendant (Ge 24:48).
2. Women in general (Ge 28:6; Nu 25:1).
3. Worshipers of the true God (Ps 45:10; Isa 62:11; Mt 21:5; Jn 12:15).
4. City (Isa 37:22).
5. Citizens (Zec 2:10).

DAUGHTER-IN-LAW

Filial: Instance of, Ruth (Ru 1:11-18; 4:15).

Unfilial: Prophecy of (Mic 7:6; Mt 10:35).

DAVID (*beloved one*).

1. King of Israel. Genealogy of (Ru 4:18-22; 1Sa 16:11; 17:12; 1Ch 2:3-15; Mt 1:1-6; Lk 3:31-38). A shepherd (1Sa 16:11). Kills a lion and a bear (1Sa 17:34-36). Anointed king, while a youth, by the prophet Samuel, and inspired (1Sa 16:1, 13; Ps 89:19-37). Chosen of God (Ps 78:70).

Described to Saul (1Sa 16:18). Detailed as armor-bearer and musician at Saul's court (1Sa 16:21-23). Slays Goliath (1Sa 17). Love of Jonathan for (1Sa 18:1-4). Popularity and discretion of (1Sa 18). Saul's jealousy of (1Sa 18:8-30). Is defrauded of Merab and given Michal for his wife (1Sa 18:17-27). Jonathan intercedes for (1Sa 19:1-7). Probably writes Ps 11 at this period of his life.

Conducts a campaign against, and defeats, the Philistines (1Sa 19:8). Saul attempts to slay him; he escapes to Ramah and dwells at Naioth, where Saul pursues him (1Sa 19:9-24). About this time he writes Ps 59. He returns, and Jonathan makes a covenant with him (1Sa 20). He escapes by way of Nob, where he obtains some consecrated bread and Goliath's sword from Abimelech (1Sa 21:1-6; Mt 12:3-4), to Gath (1Sa 21:10-15). At this time he probably writes Pss 34, 35, 52, 56, and 120. He recruits an army of insurgents, goes to Moab, returning to Hereth (1Sa 22). Probably writes Pss 17, 58, 64, 109, and 142. He saves Keilah (1Sa 23:1-13). He makes a second covenant with Jonathan (1Sa 23:16-18). He goes to the wilderness of Ziph, and is betrayed to Saul (1Sa 23:13-26). He writes Ps 54 about the betrayal and probably Pss 22, 31, and 140. Saul is diverted from pursuit of (1Sa 23:27-28). At this time he probably writes Ps 12. Goes to En Gedi (1Sa 23:29). Writes Ps 57. Covenants with Saul (1Sa 26). Marries Nabal's widow, Abigail, and Ahinoam (1Sa 25). Dwells in the wilderness of Ziph, has the opportunity to kill Saul but takes his spear only, Saul is contrite (1Sa 26). Flees to Achish and dwells in Ziklag (1Sa 27). List of men who join him (1Ch 12:1-22). Conducts an expedition against Amalekites, misinforms Achish (1Sa 27:8-12). At this time probably writes Ps 141. Is refused permission to accompany the Philistines to battle against the Israelites (1Sa 28:1-2; 29). Rescues the people of Ziklag, who had been captured by the Amalekites (1Sa 30). Probably writes Ps 13. Death and burial of Saul and his sons (1Sa 31; 2Sa 21:1-14). Slays the murderer of Saul (2Sa 1:1-16). Lamentation over Saul (2Sa 1:17-27).

After dwelling one year and four months at Ziklag (1Sa 27:7), goes to Hebron, and is anointed king by Judah (2Sa 2:1-4, 11; 5:5; 1Ki 2:11; 1Ch 3:4; 11:1-3). List of those who join him at Hebron (1Ch 12:23-40). Ish-Bosheth, the son of Saul, crowned (2Sa 2-4). David wages war against, and defeats, Ish-Bosheth (2Sa 2:13-32; 3:4). Demands the restoration of Michal, his wife (2Sa 3:14-16). Abner revolts from Ish-Bosheth, and joins David, but is slain by Joab (2Sa 3). David punishes Ish-Bosheth's murderers (2Sa 4).

Anointed king over all Israel, after reigning over Judah at Hebron seven years and six months, and reigns thirty-three years (2Sa 2:11; 5:5; 1Ch 3:4, 11:1-3; 12:23-40; 29:27). Makes a conquest of Jerusalem (2Sa 5:6; 1Ch 11:4-8; Isa 29:1). Builds a palace (2Sa 5:11; 2Ch 2:3). Friendship of, with Hiram, king of Tyre (2Sa 5:11; 1Ki 5:1). Prospered of God (2Sa 5:10, 12; 1Ch 11:9). Fame of (1Ch 14:17). Philistines make war against, and are defeated by him (2Sa 5:17, 25).

Assembles 30,000 men to escort the ark to Jerusalem with music and thanksgiving (2Sa 6:1-5). Uzzah is stricken when he attempts to steady the ark (2Sa 6:6-11). David is terrified and leaves the ark at the house of Obed-Edom (2Sa 6:9-11). After three months brings the ark to Jerusalem with dancing and great joy (2Sa 6:12-16; 1Ch 13). Organized the tabernacle service (1Ch 9:22; 15:16-24; 16:4-6, 37-43). Offers sacrifice, distributes gifts, and blesses the people (2Sa 6:17-19). Michal rebukes him for his religious enthusiasm (2Sa 6:20-23). Desires to build a temple, is forbidden, but receives promise that his seed should reign forever (2Sa 7:12-16; 23:5; 1Ch 17:11-14; 2Ch 6:16; Ps 89:3-4; 132:11-12; Ac 15:16; Ro 15:12). *See Covenants, Major in the Old Testament.* Interpretation and fulfillment of this prophecy (Ac 13:22-23). At this time, probably writes Pss 15, 16, 24, 101, and 138. Conquers the Philistines, Moabites, and Syria (2Sa 8).

Treats Mephibosheth, the lame son of Jonathan, with great kindness (2Sa 9:6; 19:24-30). Sends commissioners with a message of sympathy to Hanun, son of the king of Ammon; the message is misinterpreted and commissioners treated with indignity; David retaliates by invading his kingdom and defeating the combined armies of the Ammonites and Syrians (2Sa 10; 1Ch 19). Probably writes Pss 18, 20, and 21.

Commits adultery with Bathsheba (2Sa 11:2-5). Wickedly causes the death of Uriah (2Sa 11:6-25). Takes Bathsheba to be his wife (2Sa 11:26-27). Is rebuked by the prophet Nathan (2Sa 12:1-14). Repents of his crime and confesses his guilt (Pss 6; 32; 38; 39; 40; 51). Is disciplined on account of his crime (Ps 38; 41; 69). His infant son by Bathsheba dies (2Sa 12:15-23). Solomon is born (2Sa 12:24-25).

Ammonites defeated and tortured (2Sa 12:26-31). Amnon's crime, his murder by Absalom, and Absalom's flight (2Sa 13). Absalom's return (2Sa 14:1-24). Absalom's usurpation (2Sa 14-15). David's flight from Jerusalem (2Sa 15:13-37). He probably writes, at this time Pss 5, 7, 26, 61, 69, 70, 86, and 143. Shimei curses him (2Sa 16). Crosses the Jordan (2Sa 17:21-29). Absalom's defeat and death (2Sa 18). Laments the death of Absalom (2Sa 18:33; 19:1-4). Reprimanded by Joab (2Sa 19:5-7). David reprimands the priests for not showing loyalty amid the murmurings of the people against him (2Sa 19:9-15). Shimei sues for clemency (2Sa 19:16-23). Mephibosheth sues for the king's favor (2Sa 19:24-30). Barzillai rewarded (2Sa 19:31-40). Judah accused by the ten tribes of stealing him away (2Sa 19:41-43). Returns to Jerusalem (2Sa 20:1-3). At this time, probably composes Pss 27, 66, 122, and 144.

Sheba's conspiracy against David, and his death (2Sa 20). Makes Amasa general (2Sa 19:13). Amasa is slain (2Sa 20:4-10). Consigns seven sons of Saul to the Gibeonites to be slain to atone for Saul's persecution of the Gibeonites (2Sa 21:1-14). Buries the bones of Saul and his sons (2Sa 21:12-14).

Defeats the Philistines (2Sa 21:15-22; 1Ch 20:4-8). Takes the military strength of Israel without divine authority, and is reproved (2Sa 24; 1Ch 21; 27:24). Probably composes Pss 20, 131. Marries Abishag (1Ki 1:1-4). Probably composes Pss 19 and 111.

Reorganizes the tabernacle service (1Ch 22-26; 2Ch 7:6; 8:14; 23:18; 29:27-30; 35:15; Ezr 3:10; 8:20).

Adonijah usurps the scepter. Solomon is appointed to the throne (1Ki 1; 1Ch 23:1). Delivers his charge to Solomon (1Ki 2:1-11; 1Ch 22:6-19; 28: 29). Probably composes Pss 23 and 145.

Last words of (2Sa 23:1-7). Death probably (1Ki 2:10; 1Ch 29:28; Ac 2:29-30). Tomb of (Ac 2:29). Age of, at death (2Sa 5:4-5; 1Ch 29:28). Length of reign, forty years (1Ki 2:11; 1Ch 29:27-28).

Wives of (2Sa 3:2-5; 11:3, 27; 1Ch 3:5). Children born at Hebron (2Sa 3:2-5; 1Ch 3:4), at Jerusalem (2Sa 5:14-16; 1Ch 3:5-8; 14:4-7). Descendants of (1Ch 3).

Civil and military officers of (2Sa 8:16-18). *See Cabinet.*

List of his heroes and of their exploits (2Sa 23; 1Ch 11; 12:23-40).

Devoutness of (1Sa 13:14; 2Sa 6:5, 14-18; 7:18-29; 8:11; 24:25; 1Ki 3:14; 1Ch 17:16-27; 29:10; 2Ch 7:17; Zec 12:8; Ps 6; 7; 11; 13; 17; 22; 26; 27:7-14; 28; 31; 35; 37; 38; 39; 40:11-17; 42; 43; 51; 54; 55; 56; 57; 59; 60; 61; 62; 64:1-6; 66; 69; 70; 71; 86; 101; 108; 120:1-2; 140; 141; 142; 143; 144; Ac 13:22).

Justice in the administration of (2Sa 8:15; 1Ch 18:14). Discretion of (1Sa 18:14, 30). Meekness of (1Sa 24:7; 26:11; 2Sa 16:11; 19:22-23). Merciful (2Sa 19:23).

David as a musician (1Sa 16:21-23; 1Ch 15:16; 23:5; 2Ch 7:6; 29:26; Ne 12:36; Am 6:5), poet (2Sa 22). *See Psalms.* David as a prophet (2Sa 23:2-7; 1Ch 28:19; Mt 22:41-46; Ac 2:25-38; 4:25).

Type of Christ (Ps 2; 16; 18:43; 69:7-9, 20-21, 26, 29; 89:19-37). Jesus called son of (Mt 9:27; 12:23; 15:22; 20:30-31; 21:9; 22:42; Mk 10:47-48; Lk 18:37, 39).

Prophecies concerning him and his kingdom (Nu 24:17, 19; 2Sa 7:11-16; 1Ch 17:9-14; 22; 2Ch 6:5-17; 13:5; 21:7; Ps 89:19-37; Isa 9:7; 16:5; 22:20-25; Jer 23:5; 33:15-26; Lk 1:32-33).

Chronicles of, written by Samuel, Nathan, and Gad (1Ch 29:29-30).

2. A prophetic name for Christ (Jer 30:9; Eze 34:23-24; 37:24-25; Hos 3:5).

DAVID, CITY OF

1. Portion of Jerusalem occupied by David in c. 1003 B.C.; 2500 feet above sea level. Originally a Canaanite city (Eze 16:3), it dates back to the third millennium. Solomon enlarged the City of David for the temple and other buildings, and later kings enlarged the city still more (2Ch 32:4-5, 30; 2Ki 20:20; Isa 22:9-11).

2. Bethlehem (Lk 2:11).

DAY A creative period (Ge 1:5, 8, 13, 19, 23, 31; 2:2). Divided into twelve hours (Jn 11:9). Prophetic (Da 8:14, 26; 12:11-12; Rev 9:15; 11:3; 12:6). Six working days ordained (Ex 20:9; Eze 46:1). Sixth day of the week called preparation day (Mk 15:42; Jn 19:14, 31, 42). First day of the week called the Lord's Day (Rev 1:10). With the Lord as a thousand years (2Pe 3:8).

Day's journey, eighteen or twenty miles (Ex 3:18; 1Ki 19:4; Jnh 3:4). Sabbath day's journey, about two thousand paces (Ac 1:12). The seventh of the week ordained as a day of rest. *See Sabbath.*

DAY OF ATONEMENT An annual Hebrew feast when the high priest offered sacrifices for the sins of the nation (Lev 23:27; 25:9). It was the only fast period required by Mosaic law (Lev 16:29; 23:31). The day marked the only entry of the high priest into the Most Holy Place (Lev 16). It was observed on the tenth day of the seventh month; a day of great solemnity and strictest conformity to the law.

DAY OF CHRIST The period connected with reward and blessing at the coming of Christ for believers (1Co 1:8; Php 1:6, 10; 2:16). *See below, Day of the Lord.*

DAY OF THE LORD

1. A "day" of God's judgment on the nations (Isa 13:6-9; Eze 30:3; Joel 3:14; Ob 1:15), on Israel (Joel 1:15; 2:1, 11, 31; Am 5:18-20).

2. The period commencing with the second advent of Christ and terminating with the making of a new heaven and a new earth (Isa 65:17-19; 66:22; 2Th 2:2; 2Pe 2:13; Rev 21:1). Preceded and introduced by apocalyptic judgments (Rev 4:1-19:6).

DAY'S JOURNEY Eighteen or twenty miles (Ex 3:18; 1Ki 19:4; Jnh 3:4). Sabbath day's journey, about two thousand paces (Ac 1:12).

DAYSMAN NIV "someone to arbitrate" (Job 9:33). *See Mediation.*

DAYSPRING NIV "dawn" (Job 38:12) and "rising sun" (Lk 1:78).

DAYSTAR *See Morning Star.*

DEACON (*serve*). An officer charged with the temporal affairs of the church. The seven men chosen to help the apostles are often considered deacons (Ac 6:1-6). Qualifications of (1Ti 3:8-13). The Greek word translated deacon signifies servant, and is so translated (Mt 23:11; Jn 12:26). Also translated minister (Mk 10:43; 1Co 3:5; 1Th 3:2).

DEACONESS (*serve*). Phoebe is called a "servant of the church," which could be translated a "deaconess" (Ro 16:1, ftn). 1Ti 3:1-13 lists character qualities of deacons. V. 11 refers either to deacons' wives or to special qualities required of deaconesses (see ftn). *See Women, In Leadership.*

DEAD

Raised to life, instances of:

Son of the widow of Zarephath (1Ki 17:17-23), Shunammite's son (2Ki 4:32-37), young man laid in Elisha's tomb (2Ki 13:21), widow's son (Lk 7:12-15), Jairus' daughter (Lk 8:49-55), Lazarus (Jn 11:43-44), Dorcas (Ac 9:37-40), Eutychus (Ac 20:9-12, w Heb 11:35).

Prepared for burial by washing (Ac 9:37), anointing (Mt 26:12), wrapping in linen (Mt 27:59). Burned. *See Cremation.* Burnings of incense made for (2Ch 16:14; 21:19; Jer 34:5).

See Burial; Cremation; Embalming.

Pictured as:

Rest (Job 3:13-19). Sleep (Job 14:11-15, 21; Da 12:12). Hopelessness (Job 17:13-15; Ecc 9:5-6; Eze 32:27, 30). Separation from God (Ps 6:5; 30:9; 88:10-12; 115:17).

Life after (Job 14:12-15; Ps 49:15; Da 12:2; Lk 20:35-36; Jn 11:25). Understanding after (Eze 32:31; Lk 16:19-31).

Abode of:

The pit (Job 17:13-15). Abraham's side (Lk 16:22), hell (Lk 16:23). *See Hades; Hell; Grave; Sheol.* Paradise (Lk 23:43).

See Burial; Death, Physical; Mourning; Resurrection; Righteous, Promises to; Wicked, Punishment of.

DEAD SEA Lies SE of Jerusalem. Called the Salt Sea (Ge 14:3; Nu 34:12), Sea of the Plain (Dt 3:17; 4:49; Jos 3:16), eastern sea (Joel 2:20; Zec 14:8). Prophecy concerning (Eze 47:7-10, 18).

DEAD SEA SCROLLS Discovered in 1947 by a Bedouin in caves a mile or so W of the NW corner of the Dead Sea, at Qumran. So far mss have been found in 11 caves, and they are mostly dated as coming from the last two centuries B.C. and the first century A.D. At least 382 mss are represented by the fragments of Cave Four alone, c. 100 of which are biblical mss. These include fragments of every book of the Hebrew Bible except Esther. Some of the books are represented in many copies. Not all the mss are in fragments; some are complete or nearly complete. In addition to biblical books, fragments of apocryphal and apocalyptic books, commentaries, psalms, and sectarian literature have been found. Near the caves are the remains of a monastery of huge size, possibly the headquarters of a monastic sect of Jews called the Essenes. The discoveries at Qumran are important for biblical studies in general. They are of great importance for a study of the OT text, both Hebrew and the LXX. They are also of importance in relation to the NT, as they furnish the background to the preaching of John the Baptist and Jesus. There is no evidence that either John the Baptist or Jesus was a member of the group. *See Testaments, Time Between.*

DEAFNESS Law concerning (Lev 19:14). Inflicted by God (Ex 4:11). Miraculous cure of (Mt 11:5; Mk 7:32; 9:25).

Figurative of moral insensitivity (Isa 6:10; 29:18; 35:5; Eze 12:2; Mt 13:15; Jn 12:40; Ac 28:26-27).

See Blindness, Spiritual; Conscience, Dead; Impenitence; Obduracy.

DEATH, PHYSICAL Universal to mankind (Ecc 3:2, 19-21; Ro 5:12, 14; 1Pe 1:24). Time of, unknown (Ge 27:2; Ps 39:4, 13). Nearness to (Jos 23:14; 1Sa 20:3). Separates spirit and body (Ecc 12:5, 7).

Does not end conscious existence (Lk 20:34-38; 23:39-43; Rev 20:12-13). Exemplified in the appearance of Moses and Elijah at the transfiguration of Jesus (Mt 17:2-3; Mk 9:4-5; Lk 9:30-33).

Not to be feared by the righteous (Mt 10:28). Brings rest to the righteous (Job 3:13, 17-19). Dispossesses of earthly goods (Job 1:21; Ps 49:17; Lk 12:16-20; 1Ti 6:7).

A judgment (Ge 2:17; 3:19; 6:7, 11-13; 19:12-13, 24-25; Jos 5:4-6; 1Ch 10:13-14). God's power over (Dt 32:39; 1Sa 2:6; Ps 68:20; 2Ti 1:10). Christ's power over (Heb 2:14-15; Rev 1:18). To be destroyed (Isa 25:8; Hos 13:14; 1Co 15:21-22, 26, 55-57; Rev 20:14; 21:4).

Preparation for (2Ki 20:1; Lk 12:35-37). By Moses (Nu 27:12-23), by David (1Ki 2:1-10), by Ahithophel (2Sa 17:23). Apostrophe to (Hos 13:14; 1Co 15:55).

Described as:

Sleep (Dt 31:16; 1Ki 14:31; 15:8, 24; 16:6, 28; Job 7:21; 14:12; Ps 76:5-6; Jer 51:39; Da 12:2; Jn 11:11; Ac 7:60; 13:36; 1Co 15:6, 18, 51; 1Th 4:13-15). "Breathing one's last" or "giving up one's spirit" (Ge 25:8; 35:29; La 1:19; Ac 5:10). King of terrors (Job 18:14). A change (Job 14:14). Going to your fathers (Ge 15:15; 25:8; 35:29). Putting off this tabernacle (2Pe 1:14). Requiring the soul (Lk 12:20). Going the way from which there is no return (Job 16:22). Being gathered to our people (Ge 49:33). In silence (Ps 94:17; 115:17). Returning to dust (Ge 3:19). Being cut down (Job 14:2). Fleeing as a shadow (Job 14:2). Departing (Php 1:23).

Desired:

(Jer 8:3; Rev 9:6). By Moses (Nu 11:15). By Elijah (1Ki 19:4). By Job (Job 3; 6:8-11; Job 7:1-3, 15-16; 10:1). By Jonah (Jnh 4:8). By Simeon (Lk 2:29). By Paul (2Co 5:2, 8; Php 1:20-23).

Exemption from:

Enoch (Ge 5:24; Heb 11:5). Elijah (2Ki 2). Promised to saints, when Christ returns for believers (1Co 15:51; 1Th 4:15, 17). No death in heaven (Lk 20:36; Rev 21:4).

Inevitable:

(2Sa 14:14; Job 7:1, 8-10, 21; 10:21-22; 14:2, 5, 7-12, 14, 19-21; 16:22; 21:23, 25-26, 32-33; 30:23; 34:15, 19; Ps 49:7-10; 82:7; 89:48; 144:4; Ecc 2:14-18; 5:15; 8:8; 9:5, 10; Isa 51:12; Jer 9:21; Zec 1:5; Jn 9:4; Heb 9:27; 13:14; Jas 1:10-11).

Of the Righteous:

A transition (Lk 16:22; 23:43). Balaam extols (Nu 23:10). Peaceful (Ps 37:37). Precious in the sight of the Lord (Ps 116:15). A merciful providence in (Isa 57:1-2). Anticipated with confidence (Pr 14:32; Lk 2:29; Ac 7:59; Ro 14:7-8; 1Co 3:21-23; 2Co 5:1, 4, 8; 1Th 5:9-10; 2Ti 4:6-8; Heb 11:13). Hope in (Da 12:13; 1Co 15:51-57; 2Co 1:9-10; 1Th 4:13-14; 2Pe 1:11, 14; Rev 14:13).

Of the Wicked:

(Job 18:14, 18; 20:4-5, 8, 11; 21:13, 17-18, 23-26; 24:20, 24; 27:8, 19-23; Ps 37:1-2, 9-10, 35-36; 49:7, 9-10, 14, 17, 19-20; Pr 5:22-23; 11:7, 10; 21:16; Ecc 8:10; Isa 14:11, 15). Sudden (Nu 16:32; Pr 10:25, 27; Isa 17:14; Ac 5:3-10). A judgment (Nu 16:29-30; 1Sa 25:38; Job 36:12, 14, 18, 20; Ps 55:23; 58:9; 78:50; 92:7; Pr 2:22; 14:32; Isa 26:14; Jer 16:3-4; Eze 28:8, 10; Am 9:10; Lk 12:20).

Scenes of:

Jacob blessing his sons (Ge 49:1-33; Heb 11:21). Moses (Dt 34:1-7). Samson (Jdg 16:25-30). Eli (1Sa 4:12-18). The wife of Phinehas (1Sa 4:19-21). Zechariah (2Ch 24:22). Jesus (Mt 27:34-53; Mk 15:23-38; Lk 23:27-49; Jn 19:16-30). Stephen (Ac 7:59-60).

Death Penalty:

Shall not be remitted (Nu 35:31). In the Mosaic law the death penalty was inflicted for murder (Ge 9:5-6; Nu 35:16-21, 30-33; Dt 17:6), adultery (Lev 20:10; Dt 22:24), incest (Lev 20:11-12, 14), bestiality (Ex 22:19; Lev 20:15-16), sodomy (Lev 18:22; 20:13), rape of a betrothed virgin (Dt 22:25), perjury (Zec 5:4), kidnapping (Ex 21:16; Dt 24:7), upon a priest's daughter, who committed immorality (Lev 21:9), witchcraft (Ex 22:18), offering human sacrifice (Lev 20:2-5), striking or cursing father or mother (Ex 21:15, 17; Lev 20:9), disobedience to parents (Dt 21:18-21), theft (Zec 5:3-4), blasphemy (Lev 24:23), Sabbath desecration (Ex 35:2; Nu 15:32-36), prophesying falsely or propagating false doctrines (Dt 13:10), sacrificing to false gods (Ex 22:20), refusing to abide by the decision of the court (Dt 17:12), treason (1Ki 2:25; Est 2:23), sedition (Ac 5:36-37).

Not inflicted on the testimony of less than two witnesses (Nu 35:30; Dt 17:6; 19:15).

Modes of Execution of the Death Penalty—

Burning (Ge 38:24; Lev 20:14; 21:9; Jer 29:22; Eze 23:25; Da 3:19-23). Stoning (Lev 20:2, 27; Nu 14:10; 15:33-36; Dt 13:10; 17:5; 22:21, 24; Jos 7:25; 1Ki 21:10; Eze 16:40). Hanging (Ge 40:22; Dt 21:22-23; Jos 8:29; Est 7:10). Beheading (Mt 14:10; Mk 6:16, 27-28). Crucifixion (Mt 27:35, 38; Mk 15:24, 27; Lk 23:33). The sword (Ex 32:27-28; 1Ki 2:25, 34, 46; Ac 12:2).

Executed By—

The witnesses (Dt 13:9; 17:7; Ac 7:58). The congregation (Nu 15:35-36; Dt 13:9).

Figurative:

(Ro 6:2-11; 7:1-11; 8:10-11; Col 2:20; 2Ti 2:11).

Symbolized by the pale horse (Rev 6:8).

See Dead; Regeneration; Second Death; Spiritual Death.

DEBAR *See Lo Debar.*

DEBIR (*back room [of a shrine temple for oracle pronouncement]*).

1. King of Eglon (Jos 10:3-27).

2. A town in the mountains of Judah. Also called Kiriath Sepher which signifies a city of books (Jos 15:15-16). Anakites expelled from, by Joshua (Jos 11:21). Taken by Othniel (Jos 15:15-17, 49; Jdg 1:12-13). Allotted to the Aaronites (Jos 21:15).

3. A place near the Valley of Achor (Jos 15:7).

DEBORAH (*hornet, wasp, wild honey bee*).

1. A nurse to Rebekah (Ge 24:59). Buried beneath an oak under Bethel (Ge 35:8).

2. The prophetess, a judge of Israel (Jdg 4:4-5; 5:7). Inspires Barak to defeat Sisera (Jdg 4:6-16). Triumphant song of (Jdg 5).

DEBT Teaching against (Ro 13:8).

Security for: Warnings against becoming a guarantor for others (Pr 11:15; 22:26). Clothing taken as, must be returned by sundown (Ex 22:25-27; Dt 24:10-13; Job 22:6; Am 2:8). Houses and property (Ne 5:3-4). Children (Job 24:9). Millstones forbidden (Dt 24:6).

See Debtor; Creditor; Security, For Debt.

DEBTOR Laws concerning (Ex 21:2-6; 22:10-15; Lev 25:14-17, 25-41, 47-55; Dt 24:10-13; Ne 10:31; Mt 5:25-26, 40; 18:25). Sold for debt (2Ki 4:1-7; Ne 5:3-5; Mt 18:25). Imprisoned for debt (Mt 18:30). Oppressed (2Ki 4:1-7; Ne 5:3-5; Job 20:18-19; Mt 18:28-30). Mercy toward, commanded (Mt 18:23-27). Wicked (Lk 20:9-16).

See Creditor; Debt; Security, For Debt.

DECALOGUE (*ten words*). Written by God (Ex 24:12; 31:18; 32:16; Dt 5:22; 9:10; Hos 8:12). Divine authority of (Ex 20:1; 34:27-28; Dt 5:4-22). Called the Words of the Covenant (Ex 34:28; Dt 4:13). Tables of Testimony (Ex 31:18; 34:29; 40:20).

Listed (Ex 20:1-17; Dt 5:6-21). Confirmed, by Jesus (Mt 19:18-19; 22:34-40; Lk 10:25-28), by Paul (Ro 13:8-10).

See Commandments and Statutes, of God.

DECAPOLIS (*[league of] ten cities*). Ten cities situated in one district on the east of the Sea of Galilee (Mt 4:25; Mk 5:20; 7:31).

DECEIT Is falsehood (Ps 119:118). The tongue is an instrument of (Ro 3:13). Comes from the heart (Mk 7:22). Characteristic of the heart (Jer 17:9). God abhors (Ps 5:6). Forbidden (Pr 24:28; 1Pe 3:10). Christ was perfectly free from (Isa 53:9, w 1Pe 2:22).

Saints free from (Ps 24:4; Zep 3:13; Rev 14:5), purpose against (Job 27:4), avoid (Job 31:5), shun those addicted to (Ps 101:7), pray for deliverance from those who use (Ps 43:1; 120:2), delivered from those who use (Ps 72:14), should beware of those who teach (Eph 5:6; Col 2:8), should lay aside, in seeking truth (1Pe 2:1). Ministers should lay aside (2Co 4:2; 1Th 2:3).

The wicked are full of (Ro 1:29), devise (Ps 35:20; 38:12; Pr 12:5), utter (Ps 10:7; 36:3), work (Pr 11:18), increase in (2Ti 3:13), use, to themselves (Jer 37:9; Ob 7), delight in (Pr 20:17).

False teachers are workers of (2Co 11:13), preach (Jer 14:14; 23:26), impose on others by (Ro 16:18; Eph 4:14), sport themselves with (2Pe 2:13). Hypocrites practice (Hos 11:12). False witnesses use (Pr 12:17). A characteristic of Antichrist (2Jn 7). Characteristic of apostasy (2Th 2:10).

Evil of: Hinders knowledge of God (Jer 9:6). Keeps from turning to God (Jer 8:5). Leads to pride and oppression (Jer 5:27-28), to lying (Pr 14:25). Often accompanied by fraud and injustice (Ps 10:7; 43:1). Hatred often concealed by (Pr 26:24-26). The folly of fools is (Pr 14:8). The kisses of an enemy are (Pr 27:6). Punishment of (Ps 55:23; Jer 9:7-9).

Blessedness of being free from (Ps 24:4-5; 32:2).

See Confidence, False; Deception; Falsehood; Flattery; Hypocrisy.

DECEPTION

Instances of:

By Satan (Ge 3:4). Abraham, in saying that Sarah was his sister (Ge 12:13; 20:2). Isaac, in saying that his wife was his sister (Ge 26:7). Jacob and Rebekah, in imposing Jacob on his father, and Jacob's impersonating Esau (Ge 27:6-23). Jacob's sons, in entrapping the Shechemites (Ge 34:13-31), in representing to their father that Joseph had been destroyed by wild beasts (Ge 37:29-35). Joseph, in his ruse with his brothers (Ge 42-44). The Gibeonites, in misrepresenting their habitat (Jos 9:3-15). Ehud deceives Eglon, and slays him (Jdg 3:15-30). Delilah deceives Samson (Jdg 16:4-20). David feigns insanity (1Sa 21:10-15). Amnon deceives Tamar by feigning sickness (2Sa 13:6-14). Hushai deceives Absalom (2Sa 16:15-19). Sanballat tries to deceive Nehemiah (Ne 6). By Absalom, when he avenged his sister (2Sa 13:24-28), when he began his conspiracy (2Sa 15:7). The old prophet (1Ki 13:18). Gehazi (2Ki 5:20). Job's friends (Job 6:15). Doeg (Ps 52:2).

Herod (Mt 2:8). Pharisees (Mt 22:16). Chief priests (Mk 14:1). Lawyer (Lk 10:25). Ananias and Sapphira (Ac 5:1).

See Deceit; Hypocrisy; Falsehood; False Witness.

Self Deception: *See False Confidence; Flattery.*

DECISION

Teaching Concerning:

Choosing life (Dt 30:19). Committing to the Lord (Jos 24:15; 1Sa 12:20; 1Ki 18:21; Isa 50:7; Mt 6:24; 8:21-22; Lk 9:59-62; 1Co 15:58). Walking righteously (Jos 1:7; 2Ch 19:11; Pr 4:25-27; Mt 4:17; 2Th 3:13; 1Ti 6:11-14; Heb 12:1; 1Pe 1:13; 2Pe 1:10). Remaining in Christ (Jn 15:4-5, 7, 9; 1Jn 2:24, 28).

Endurance in:

Obedience (Jn 8:31; 1Co 15:58; Col 2:6-7; 2Th 2:15, 17; 2Pe 3:17-18; 2Jn 8), grace (Ac 13:43; 2Ti 2:1, 3), faith (Ac 14:22; 1Co 16:13; Php 1:27; Col 1:23; Heb 3:6-8, 14; 4:14; 10:23, 35; 1Pe 5:8-9; Jude 20-21), Christian liberty (Gal 5:1-26), the Lord (Php 4:1), holiness (1Th 3:8, 13), sound doctrine (Eph 4:14; 2Ti 1:13-14; Tit 1:7, 9; Heb 2:1; 13:9, 13).

Instances of:

Abel (Heb 11:4). Enoch (Heb 11:5-6). Noah (Heb 11:7). Abraham (Heb 11:8, 17-19). Jacob (Ge 28:20-22). Joseph (Ge 39:9). Moses (Nu 12:7; Heb 3:5; 11:24-26, 27). Israelites (Ex 19:7-8; 24:3, 7; Dt 4:4; 5:27; 26:17; Jos 22:34; 24:21-25; 1Ki 19:18; 2Ki 11:17; 2Ch 11:16; 13:10-11; 15:12, 15; 23:16; 29:10; Ezr 10:3-44; Ne 9:38; 10:28-31; Jer 34:15; 42:5-6; 50:5; Hos 11:12). Levites (Ex 32:26). Caleb (Nu 14:6-10, 24; Dt 1:36; Jos 14:14). Balaam (Nu 22:15-18; 24:13). Phinehas (Nu 25:7-13). Joshua (Jos 24:15). Gideon (Jdg 6:25-28). Ruth (Ru 1:16).

Saul (1Sa 11:4-7). David (1Sa 17:32-37; 2Sa 22:22-24). Psalmist (Ps 17:3; 26:6, 11; 27:3-8; 40:9-10; 56:12; 57:7-8; 71:17; 86:11; 101:2-3; 108:1; 116:9, 13-14, 16; 119:8, 30-31, 33-36, 57, 94, 106, 115, 125, 145-146). A prophet of Judah (1Ki 13:8-10). Elijah (1Ki 18:22). Jehoshaphat (1Ki 22:7-8; 2Ch 18:6-7). Micaiah (1Ki 22:13-14; 2Ch 18:6-7). Naaman (2Ki 5:13-17). Hezekiah (2Ki 18:6; 2Ch 15:17). Josiah (2Ki 22:2-3; 23:25; 2Ch 34:31). Nehemiah (Ne 2; 4:6; 6:11). Esther (Est 4:16). Job (Job 2:9-10). Daniel (Da 1:8). The three Hebrews (Da 3:11-12, 16-18).

Matthew (Mt 9:9). Joseph (Mk 15:43). Nathanael (Jn 1:49). Martha (Jn 11:27). Disciples (Lk 18:28; Jn 6:68-69; Ac 2:42). Paul (Ac 9:29; Ro 1:16; 8:38-39; Php 1:20-21; 2Ti 4:7-8). Church, of Ephesus (Rev 2:2-3). Of Sardis (Rev 3:4, 8, 10). Saints (Rev 14:4).

See Character.

DECISION, VALLEY OF *See Jehoshaphat, Valley of.*

DECREE An official ruling or law (Da 2:9; Est 1:20; Jnh 3:7; Ac 16:4; Rev 13:8).

DEDAN

1. A son of Raamah (Ge 10:7; 1Ch 1:9).

2. A son of Jokshan (Ge 25:3; 1Ch 1:32).

3. A country, probably bordering on Edom (Jer 49:8; Eze 25:13; 27:15, 20; 38:13).

DEDANITES Descendants of Dedan (Isa 21:13).

DEDICATION Law concerning dedicated things (Lev 27; Nu 18:14; 1Ch 26:26-27). Must be without blemish (Lev 22:18-23; Mal 1:14). Not redeemable (Lev 27:28-29). Offering must be voluntary (Lev 1:3; 22:19). *See Offerings; Vows.* Of the tabernacle (Nu 7). Solomon's temple (1Ki 8; 2Ch 7:5). Second temple (Ezr 6:16-17). Of the wall of Jerusalem (Ne 12:27-43). Of houses (Dt 20:5). Of Samuel by his mother (1Sa 1:11, 22).

Of Self. *See Consecration.*

For instances of liberality in dedicated things. *See Liberality.*

DEDICATION, FEAST OF Annual Jewish feast celebrating the restoration of the temple following its desecration

by Antiochus Epiphanes. Jesus delivered a discourse at this feast (Jn 10:22ff).
See Feasts; Hanukkah; Kislev; Maccabees; Month, 9.

DEED To the land (Jer 32:12, 14, 44). *See Land.* For works. *See Works, Good.*

DEEP The ocean (Ne 9:11), chaos (Ge 1:2), the deepest part of the sea (Ge 49:25), Abyss (Lk 8:31; Rev 9:1; 11:7).

DEER Also called doe, roe deer. Designated among the clean animals, to be eaten (Dt 12:15; 14:5). Provided for Solomon's household (1Ki 4:23). Swiftness of (2Sa 2:18; 1Ch 12:8; Pr 6:5; SS 8:14; Isa 35:6). Surefootedness of (2Sa 22:34). Gentleness of (Pr 5:19).

DEFENSE An argument made before a court. Of Jeremiah (Jer 26:12-16), Peter (Ac 4:8-13; 5:23-29), Stephen (Ac 7), Paul (Ac 22; 23:1-6; 24:10-21; 26:1-23). Military defenses. *See Fort; Armies.*

DEFILEMENT Laws relating to (Lev 7:18-21; 11:43; 22:2-7). Caused by, leprosy (Lev 13:3, 44-46; 14; 22:4-7), copulation (Lev 15:17), discharges (Lev 15:1-17), childbirth (Lev 12:2-8; Lk 2:22), menses (Lev 15:19-33; 2Sa 11:4), touching the dead (Nu 19:11-22; 31:19-20), touching carcass of any unclean animal (Lev 11:39-40; 17:15-16; 22:8), touching carcass of any unclean thing (Lev 5:2-13; 11:8, 24-28, 31-38; 14:46-57; 15:5-11; Dt 23:10-11), slaying in battle (Nu 31:19-20). Contact with sinners falsely supposed to cause (Jn 18:28). Of priests (Lev 16:26, 28; Nu 19:7-10; Eze 44:25-26).
Egyptian perspective (Ge 43:32).
See Purification; Unclean, Uncleanness; Washings.

DEFORMITY *See Blemish.*

DEGRADATION Of God's people (Ex 32:25; Eze 16:6; 20:31; 2Pe 2:22).

DEGREES NIV "steps" on the stairway of Ahaz (2Ki 20:9-11).

DEGREES, SONGS OF Title of Pss 120 to 134 in the KJV. *See Ascents, Songs of.*

DEHAVITES At the end of Ezra 4:9 the KJV lists three peoples: "the Susanchites, the Dehavites, *and* the Elamites," while the NIV reads "the Elamites of Susa." The KJV transliterated "the Dehavites" from a difficult Aramaic term, rightly rendered "of" in the NIV.

DEITY OF JESUS *See Jesus the Christ, Deity of.*

DEKAR *See Ben-Deker, Ben-Dekar.*

DELAIAH (*Yahweh draws up [like water in a bucket]*).
1. Descendant of David (1Ch 3:1-24).
2. Head of the twenty-third course of priests (1Ch 24:18).
3. Prince who tried to save Jeremiah's roll from destruction (Jer 36:12, 25).
4. An ancestor of the tribe that returned under Zerubbabel (Ezr 2:60; Ne 7:62).
5. The father of Shemaiah (Ne 6:10).

DELIGHTING IN GOD Commanded (Ps 37:4). Reconciliation leads to (Job 22:21, 26). Observing the Sabbath leads to (Isa 58:13-14).

Saints' Experience in:
Communion with God (SS 2:3). The law of God (Ps 1:2; 119:24, 35). The goodness of God (Ne 9:25). The comforts of God (Ps 94:19). Promises to (Ps 37:4). Blessedness of (Ps 112:1).

Hypocrites:
Pretend to (Isa 58:2). In heart despise (Job 27:10; Jer 6:10).

DELILAH (*tease*). Philistine woman who lured Samson to his ruin (Jdg 16:4-20).

DELIVERANCE *See Affliction; God, Providence of; Prayer, Answer to.*

DELIVERER A title of Jesus (Ro 11:26). *See Titles and Names.*

DELUGE *See Flood.*

DELUSION, SELF *See Self-Delusion.*

DEMAGOGISM Instances of: Absalom (2Sa 15:2-6). Pilate (Mt 27:17-26; Mk 15:15; Lk 23:13-24; Jn 18:38-40; 19:6-13). Felix (Ac 24:27). Herod (Ac 12:3).

DEMAS (*[common] folks*). Fellow laborer with Paul (Col 4:14; Phm 24), who later deserted him (2Ti 4:10).

DEMETRIUS (*of Demeter*).
1. A disciple praised by John (3Jn 12).
2. A silversmith at Ephesus who made trouble for Paul (Ac 19:23-27).

DEMONS

General:
Worship of (Lev 17:7; Dt 32:17; 2Ch 11:15; Ps 106:37; Mt 4:9; Lk 4:7; 1Co 10:20-21; 1Ti 4:1; Rev 13:4). Worship of, forbidden (Lev 17:7; Zec 13:2; Rev 9:20).
Testify to the deity of Jesus (Mt 8:29; Mk 1:23-24; 3:11; 5:7; Lk 8:28; Ac 19:15).
Adversaries of men (Mt 12:45). Sent to cause trouble between Abimelech and the Shechemites (Jdg 9:23). Messages given false prophets by (1Ki 22:21-23).
Believe and tremble (Jas 2:19). To be judged at the general judgment (Mt 8:29, w 2Pe 2:4; Jude 6).
Punishment of (Mt 8:29; 25:41; Lk 8:28; 2Pe 2:4; Jude 6; Rev 12:7-9).

Possession By:

instances of—
Saul (1Sa 16:14-23; 18:10-11; 19:9-10). Two men of the Gadarenes (Mt 8:28-34; Mk 5:2-20). The mute man (Mt 9:32-33). The blind and mute man (Mt 12:22; Lk 11:14). The daughter of the Syrian Phoenician (Mt 15:22-29; Mk 7:25-30). The child with seizures (Mt 17:14-18; Mk 9:17-27; Lk 9:37-42). The man in the synagogue (Mk 1:23-26; Lk 4:33-35). Mary Magdalene (Mk 16:9; Lk 8:2-3). The herd of pigs (Mt 8:30-32).
Jesus falsely accused of being possessed of (Mk 3:22-30; Jn 7:20; 8:48; 10:20).

Exorcised—
Cast out by Jesus (Mt 4:24; 8:16; Mk 3:22; Lk 4:41).
Power over, given the disciples (Mt 10:1; Mk 6:7; 16:17). Cast out by the disciples (Mk 9:38; Lk 10:17), by Peter (Ac 5:16), by Paul (Ac 16:16-18; 19:12), by Philip (Ac 8:7). The disciples could not expel (Mk 9:18, 28-29). Sceva's sons exorcise (Ac 19:13-16). The parable of the man repossessed (Mt 12:43-45).
See Devil; Satan.

DENARIUS *See Money.*

DENS Used as places of refuge (Jdg 6:2; Heb 11:38; Rev 6:15).

DENYING JESUS *See Jesus the Christ, Rejected.*

DEPRAVITY

In the Nature of Humanity: (Ge 6:5-8; 8:21; Job 4:17-19; 9:2-3, 20, 29-31; 11:12; 14:4; 15:14-16; 25:4-6; Ps 5:9; 51:5; 58:1-5; 94:11; 130:3; Pr 10:20; 20:6, 9; 21:8; Isa 1:5-6; 51:1; Jer 13:23; 16:12; 17:9; Hos 6:7; Mic 7:2-4; Mt 7:17; 12:34-35; 15:19; Mk 7:21-23; Jn 3:19; 8:23; 14:17; Ro 1:21-32; Ro 2:1; 6:6, 19-20; 7:5, 11-15, 18-25; 8:5-8, 13; 1Co 2:14; 3:3; 5:9-10; 2Co 5:14; Gal 5:17, 19-21; Eph 2:1-3, 12; 4:17-19, 22; Jas 4:5; 1Pe 1:18; 2:25; 1Jn 1:8, 10; 2:16).

Universal: (Ge 6:11-13; 2Ch 6:36; Ps 14:1-3; 53:1-3; 143:2; Ecc 7:20; Isa 53:6; 64:6; Mic 7:2-4; Ro 3:9-19, 23; 5:6, 12-14; 11:32; Gal 3:10-11, 22; Jas 3:2; 1Jn 5:19).
See Fall of Mankind, The; Sin.

DEPRESSION *See Despondency.*

DEPUTY An officer who administers the functions of a superior in his absence (1Ki 22:47; 2Ki 15:5; Ac 13:7-8; 18:12; 19:38).

DERBE A city of Lycaonia. Paul fled to (Ac 14:6, 20). Visited by Paul and Silas (Ac 16:1). Gaius born in (Ac 20:4).

DERISION The wicked held in, by God (Ps 2:4; Pr 1:26).
Instances of: Sarah, when the angels gave her the promise of a child (Ge 18:12). The evil children of Bethel deride Elisha (2Ki 2:23). The people of Israel scoff at Hezekiah (2Ch 30:1-10).
See Irony; Sarcasm; Scoffing.

DESERTS Vast barren plains (Ex 5:3; Jn 6:13). Uninhabited places (Mt 14:15; Mk 6:31).

Described as:
Uninhabited and lonesome (Jer 2:6). Uncultivated (Nu 20:5; Jer 2:2). Desolate (Eze 6:14). Dry and without water (Ex 17:1; Dt 8:15). Trackless (Isa 43:19). Great and terrible (Dt 1:19). Waste and howling (Dt 32:10). Infested with wild beasts (Isa 13:21; Mk 1:13). Infested with serpents (Dt 8:15). Infested with robbers (Jer 3:2; La 4:19). Danger of traveling in (Ex 14:3; 2Co 11:26). Guides required in (Nu 10:31; Dt 32:10).

Phenomena of, Alluded to:
Mirage or deceptive appearance of water (Jer 15:18). Scorching wind (Jer 4:11). Tornadoes or whirlwinds (Isa 21:1). Clouds of sand and dust (Dt 28:24; Jer 4:12-13).

Mentioned in Scripture:
Arabian or great desert (Ex 23:31). Beth Aven (Jos 18:12). Beersheba (Ge 21:14; 1Ki 19:3-4). Damascus (1Ki 19:15). Edom (2Ki 3:8). En Gedi (1Sa 24:1). Gibeon (2Sa 2:24). Judea (Mt 3:1). Jeruel (2Ch 20:16). Kedemoth (Dt 2:26). Kadesh (Ps 29:8). Maon (1Sa 23:24-25). Paran (Ge 21:21; Nu 10:12). Shur (Ge 16:7; Ex 15:22). Sin (Ex 16:1). Sinai (Ex 19:1-2; Nu 33:16). Ziph (1Sa 23:14-15). Zin (Nu 20:1; 27:14). Of the Red Sea (Ex 13:18). Near Gaza (Ac 8:26). Wastelands often found in (Jer 17:6). Parts of, afforded pasture (Ge 36:24; Ex 3:1). Inhabited by wandering tribes (Ge 21:20-21; Ps 72:9; Jer 25:24). The persecuted fled to (1Sa 23:14; Heb 11:38). The disaffected fled to (1Sa 22:2; Ac 21:38).

Illustrative of:
Barrenness (Ps 106:9; 107:33, 35). Those deprived of all blessings (Hos 2:3). The world (SS 3:6; 8:5). The Gentiles (Isa 35:1, 6; 41:19). What offers no support (Jer 2:31). Desolation by armies (Jer 12:10-13; 50:12).

DESIGN In nature, evidence of (Job 12:7-11; Pr 16:4).

DESIRED OF ALL NATIONS Some see as a title of Jesus (Hag 2:7). Others deny a messianic application and hold that it means the precious gifts of all nations (Hag 2:8 w Isa 60:5).

DESIRE, SPIRITUAL For divine piety (Ps 17:11; 51:1-4, 7-13; 119:82; Hab 3:2). For divine fellowship (Ps 62:1; 63:1, 8). For divine help (Ps 25:5, 15; 68:28; 119:77, 116-117).
Exhortations concerning (Ps 70:4; 105:4; Isa 55:1-2; 55:3, 6; Hos 10:12).
For God (Ps 24:6; 27:8; 33:20; 40:1; 42:1-11; 69:3; 73:26; 119:10, 12, 19-20, 25, 40, 81, 88, 123, 131-132, 135-136, 149, 156, 174; 123:1-2; 130:5-6; 143:6-12; Isa 8:17, 19; 26:8-9; Mt 13:17; Lk 10:42; Php 3:12-14; 1Pe 1:10). For his holy courts (Ps 84:2).
Reward of (Dt 4:29; Ps 34:10; 37:4, 9, 34; 107:9; 119:2; Pr 2:3-5; Isa 40:31; Jer 29:13; Mt 5:6; Lk 1:53; 6:21; Jn 6:35; Heb 11:6).
See Hunger, Figurative; Thirst.

Evil desire: *See Imagination; Lust.*

DESOLATION, ABOMINATION OF *See Abomination That Causes Desolation.*

DESPAIR *See Despondency.*

DESPISERS General references to (Pr 1:30; 9:8; Mt 7:6; Ac 13:41; Ro 2:4; 2Ti 3:3; Heb 10:28; 2Pe 2:10).

DESPONDENCY (Isa 35:3-4; Heb 12:12-13). Caused by corrective judgments (Nu 17:12-13; Dt 28:65-67; Isa 2:19; Hos 10:8; Mt 24:30; Lk 23:29-30; Rev 6:14-17; 9:5-6), deferred hope (Pr 13:12), adversity (Job 4:5; 9:16-35; 17:7-16).
Lament in (Job 3:1-26; 17:13-16; Ps 6:6; 22:1-2; 55:4-7; 77:7-9; 88:3-17; Ecc 2:20; Jer 8:20; La 3:1-20; 5:15-22; Mic 7:1-7).

Instances of:
Cain, when God pronounced judgment upon him (Ge 4:13-14). Hagar, when cast out of the household of Abraham (Ge 21:15-16). Moses, when sent on his mission to the Israelites (Ex 4:1, 10, 13; 6:12), at the Red Sea (Ex 14:15), when the people lusted for flesh (Nu 11:15). The Israelites, on account of the cruel oppressions of the Egyptians (Ex 6:9). Joshua, over the defeat at Ai (Jos 7:7-9). Elijah, when he fled from Jezebel to the wilderness and sat under the broom tree and wished to die (1Ki 19:4). Jonah, after he had preached to the Ninevites (Jnh 4:3, 8). The mariners with Paul (Ac 27:20).
See Affliction, Consolation Under; Righteous, Promises to.

DESPOTISM *See Government, Monarchical.*

DESTINY
1. Final determined end. Of all people (Ecc 7:2; 9:2-3; Heb 9:27). Of the wicked (Ps 73:17; Jer 15:2; 43:11). Of believers (1Co 2:7).
2. The pagan god of fate (Isa 65:11).

DETECTIVES *See Spies.*

DEUEL (*known of God [El]*). Also called Reuel (Nu 2:14, ftn). Captain of the tribe of Dan (Nu 1:14; 2:14; 7:42; 10:20).

DEUTERONOMY (*second [giving] of the law*).

Author: Moses, though the preamble (1:1-5) and report of Moses' death (ch. 34) were written by someone else.

Date: c. 1406 B.C.

Outline:
I. The Preamble (1:1-5).
II. The Historical Prologue (1:6-4:43).
III. The Stipulations of the Covenant (4:44-26:19).
A. The Great Commandment: The Demand for Absolute Allegiance (4:44-11:32).
B. Supplementary Requirements (chs. 12-26).
1. Ceremonial consecration (12:1-16:17).
2. Governmental leaders and a righteous nation (16:18-21:21).
3. Sanctity of God's kingdom (21:22-25:19).
4. Confession of God as Redeemer-King (ch. 26).
IV. Ratification; Curses and Blessings (chs. 27-30).
V. Covenant Leadership Succession (chs. 31-34).
A. Change of Leadership (31:1-29).
B. Song of Moses (31:30-32:47).
C. Moses' Testamental Blessing on the Tribes (32:48-33:29).
D. Death of Moses and Succession of Joshua (ch. 34).

Alternate Outline:
I. First Address (1:1-4:43).
II. Second Address (4:44-28:68).
III. Third Address (chs. 29-33).
IV. Moses' Death (ch. 34).

DEVIL (*slanderer* or *liar*). One of the principal titles of Satan, the archenemy of God and of mankind. It is not known how he originated, unless Isaiah and Ezekiel give us a clue (Isa 14:12-20; Eze 28:12-19), but it is certain that he was not created evil. He rebelled against God when in a state of holiness and apparently led other angels into rebellion with him (Jude 6; 2Pe 2:4). He is a being of superhuman power and wisdom but is not omnipotent or omniscient. He tries to frustrate God's plans and purposes for human beings. His principal method of attack is by temptation. His power is limited, and he can go only as far as God permits. On the Judgment Day he will be cast into hell to remain there forever.
See Satan.

DEVOTED THING That which is set apart to the Lord and therefore no longer belongs to the former owner (Lev 27:29, and ftn; Jos 7:1-15). *See Corban.*

DEVOTION

To God: *See Religion.*
For conspicuous instances of, study Enoch, Noah, Abraham, Moses, David, Solomon's early life, Josiah, Asa, Isaiah, Elijah, Jeremiah, Daniel, Shadrach, Meshach, and Abednego.

To Jesus: *See Peter, Simon; John; Paul; Mary.*
For elaborated topics covering the subject, *See Love, Of People for God; Consecration; Zeal.*

DEW A merciful providence (Dt 33:13). Forms imperceptibly (2Sa 17:12), in the night (Job 29:19). From the clouds (Pr 3:20). Called the dew of heaven (Da 4:15). Absence of (1Ki 17:1). Miraculous profusion and absence of (Jdg 6:36-40). *See Meteorology.*
Figurative (Ps 110:3; Isa 26:19; Hos 6:4; 13:3; 14:5).

DIADEM A golden plate worn on the turban of the high priest (Ex 29:6; 39:30; Lev 8:9). A royal crown (Isa 62:3). *See Crown.*

DIAL NIV "stairway" (2Ki 20:11; Isa 38:8). *See Stairs.*

D

DIAMOND *See Emerald; Flint; Minerals of the Bible, 1; Stones.*

DIANA Goddess of the Ephesians (Ac 19:24, 27-28, 35). *See Artemis.*

DIASPORA (*scattered [like] seed*). The name applied to the Jews living outside of Israel and maintaining their religious faith among the Gentiles (Jas 1:1; 1Pe 1:1). By the time of Christ the diaspora must have been several times the population of Israel. *See Dispersion; Testaments, Time Between.*

DIBLAH Probably an early copyist's error for Riblah, a town c. fifty miles S of Hamath (Eze 6:14).

DIBLAIM (*lump of [two dried fig] cakes*). Father of Hosea's wife (Hos 1:3).

DIBLATHAIM *See Almon Diblathaim; Beth Diblathaim.*

DIBON, DIBON GAD
1. Also called Dibon Gad and Dimon. A city on the northern banks of the Arnon (Nu 21:30). Israelites encamp at (Nu 33:45). Allotted to Gad and Reuben (Nu 32:3, 34; Jos 13:9, 17). Taken by Moab (Isa 15:2; Jer 48:18, 22).
2. A city in the tribe of Judah (Ne 11:25), probably identical with Dimonah (Jos 15:22).

DIBRI (possibly *speak*). The father of Shelomith (Lev 24:11).

DIDRACHMA (*two drachma*). The annual temple tax was two drachmas (Mt 17:24). *See Drachma; Money.*

DIDYMUS (*twin*). The surname of Thomas (Jn 11:16; 20:24; 21:2).

DIKLAH (*[place of] date palms*). The son of Joktan, and the name of a district inhabited by his descendants (Ge 10:27; 1Ch 1:21).

DILEAN (*cucumber* ISBE; *protrude* KB). A city of Judah (Jos 15:38).

DILIGENCE Jesus as an example of (Mk 1:35; Lk 2:49).

Required:
By God in seeking him (1Ch 22:19; Heb 11:6), obeying him (Dt 6:17; 11:13), listening to him (Isa 55:2), striving after perfection (Php 3:13-14), developing Christian qualities (2Pe 1:5), keeping the soul (Dt 4:9), keeping the heart (Pr 4:23), labors of love (Heb 6:10-12), following every good work (1Ti 3:10), guarding against defilement (Heb 12:15), seeking to be found spotless (2Pe 3:14), making our calling sure (2Pe 1:10), self-examination (Ps 77:6), lawful business (Pr 27:23; Ecc 9:10), teaching religion (2Ti 4:2; Jude 3), instructing children (Dt 6:7; 11:19), discharging official duties (Dt 19:18), saints should abound in (2Co 8:7).
Required in the service of God (Jn 9:4; Gal 6:9). Is not in vain (1Co 15:58). Preserves from evil (Ex 15:26). Leads to assured hope (Heb 6:11). God rewards (Dt 11:14; Heb 11:6).
In temporal matters leads to favor (Pr 11:27), prosperity (Pr 10:4; 13:4), honor (Pr 12:24; 22:29).

Figurative: (Pr 6:6-8).

Exemplified:
Ruth (Ru 2:17). Hezekiah (2Ch 31:21). Nehemiah and his helpers (Ne 4:6). Psalmist (Ps 119:60). Apostles (Ac 5:42). Apollos (Ac 18:25). Titus (2Co 8:22). Paul (1Th 2:9). Onesiphorus (2Ti 1:17).
See Industry; Zeal; Idleness; Slothfulness.

DILL A plant whose aromatic seeds are used in cooking (Mt 23:23).

DIMNAH (*manure*). A Levite town in Zebulun (Jos 21:35). May be the same as Rimmono (1Ch 6:77).

DIMON A town in Moab, generally called "Dibon," but it is called Dimon two times (Isa 15:9, ftn), c. four miles N of Aroer.

DIMONAH A town in the S of Judah (Jos 15:22), probably the same as the "Dibon" of Nehemiah (Ne 11:25).

DINAH (*female judge*). The daughter of Jacob and Leah (Ge 30:21). Rape of (Ge 34).

DINAITES NIV "judges" (Ezr 4:9).

DINHABAH A city of Edom (Ge 36:32; 1Ch 1:43).

DINNER Eaten at noon (Ge 43:16). *See Feasts.*

DIONYSIUS, THE AREOPAGITE (*belonging to Dionysus*). A member of the Areopagus, Athenian supreme court; converted by Paul (Ac 17:34).

DIOSCURI *See Castor and Pollux.*

DIOTREPHES (*nurtured by Zeus*). A domineering Christian leader condemned by John (3Jn 9-10).

DIPLOMACY

Ecclesiastical:
Paul, in winning souls to Christ (1Co 9:20-23), in circumcising Timothy (Ac 16:3), in performing certain temple services to placate the Jews (Ac 21:20-25, w Gal 6:12).

Corrupt practices in:
The officers of Nebuchadnezzar's court to secure the destruction of Daniel (Da 6:4-15).

Instances of:
Abimelech (Ge 21:22-23; 26:26-31). The Gibeonites, in securing a league with the Israelites through deception (Jos 9:3-16). Of Jephthah, with the king of Moab, unsuccessful (Jdg 11:12-28). Of Abigail (1Sa 25:23-31). Of Hiram, to secure the goodwill of David (2Sa 5:11). Of Tou, to promote the friendship of David (2Sa 8:10). David, in sending Hushai to Absalom's court (2Sa 15:32-37; 16:15-19; 17:1-14). The wise woman of Abel (2Sa 20:16-22). Absalom winning the people (2Sa 15:2-6). Solomon, in his alliance with Hiram (1Ki 5:1-12; 9:10-14, 26-27; 10:11), by intermarriage with other nations (1Ki 1:1-5). Ambassadors from Ben-Hadad to Ahab (1Ki 20:31-34). Jehoash purchases peace from Hazael (2Ki 12:18). Ahaz purchases aid from the king of Assyria (2Ki 16:7-9). The king of Assyria's field commander, in trying to entice Jerusalem to surrender by bombastic harangue (2Ki 18:17-37; 19:1-13; Isa 36:11-22). Sanballat, in an attempt to prevent the rebuilding of Jerusalem by Nehemiah (Ne 6).
The people of Tyre and Sidon, in securing the favor of Herod (Ac 12:20-22). Paul, in turning the Pharisees and Sadducees against each other at his trial (Ac 23:6-10).
See Prudence; Tact.

DISASTERS *See Burning.*

DISBELIEF *See Unbelief.*

DISCERNING OF SPIRITS The ability to discern between those who spoke by the Spirit of God and those who were moved by false spirits (1Co 12:10).

DISCHARGE, BODILY Caused ceremonial uncleanness. Of a male (Lev 15:2-15, 32). Of a female (Lev 15:25-33). Of a priest (Lev 22:3). *See Disease.*

DISCIPLE (*student*). A name given to the followers of any teacher. Of John the Baptist (Mt 9:14). Of the Pharisees (Lk 5:33). Of Jesus (Mt 10:1; 20:17; Ac 9:26; 14:20; 21:4). The seventy sent forth (Lk 10:1). First called Christians at Antioch (Ac 11:26).
See Apostles; Righteous.

DISCIPLESHIP Following Jesus.

Evangelism—Making Disciples: (Mt 28:18-20; Ac 6:7).

Personal Growth—Being a Disciple:
Characterized by putting Jesus first in all things (Mt 10:32-39; Mk 8:34-38; Lk 14:26-27, 33; Jn 21:15-19), by following Jesus' teaching (Jn 8:31-32), by fruitfulness (Jn 15:5-8), by love for other disciples (Jn 13:34-35).
See Commandments and Statutes, of God; Identification.

DISCIPLINE Of armies, for disobedience of orders (Jos 7:10-26; Jdg 21:5-12). *See Armies.*
Church Discipline: *See Church, The Body of Believers, Discipline.*
See Chastisement, From God; Graces; Self-Control; Self-Discipline.

DISCONTENTMENT *See Contentment; Murmuring.*

DISCOURAGEMENT *See Despondency.*

DISEASE Sent from God (Lev 14:34). As judgments (Ps 107:17; Isa 3:17).

Instances of:
Upon the Egyptians. *See Plague.* Upon Nabal (1Sa 25:38), David's child (2Sa 12:15), Gehazi (2Ki 5:27), Jeroboam (2Ch 13:20), Jehoram (2Ch 21:12-19), Uzziah (2Ch 26:17-20).
Threatened as judgments (Lev 26:16; Dt 7:15; 28:22, 27-28, 35; 29:22).
Healing of, from God (Ex 15:26; 23:25; Dt 7:15; 2Ch 16:12; Ps 103:3; 107:20).

In answer to prayer:
Of Hezekiah (2Ki 20:1-11; Isa 38:1-8), David (Ps 21:4; 116:3-8).
Miraculous healing *See Miracles.*
Physicians employed for (2Ch 16:12; Jer 8:22; Mt 9:12; Mk 5:26; Lk 4:23). Remedies used (Pr 17:22; 20:30; Isa 38:21; Jer 30:13; 46:11), medicinal compress (2Ki 20:7), ointments (Isa 1:6; Jer 8:22), wine and oil (Lk 10:34).
Of the sexual organs (Lev 15; 22:4; Nu 5:2; Dt 23:10). *See Bleeding, Subject to; Circumcision; Menstruation.* Treatment of fractures (Eze 30:21).
See Affliction.

Figurative: (Ps 38:7; Isa 1:6; Jer 30:12). Various kinds of: *See Bleeding, Subject to; Blindness; Boil; Congestion; Consumption; Deafness; Demons; Discharge, Bodily; Dropsy; Dysentery; Fever; Gout; Hemorrhage; Hemorrhoids; Indigestion; Inflammation; Insanity; Itch; Lameness; Leprosy; Paralysis; Pestilence; Seizures; Sore; Stammering; Sunstroke; Tumor; Worm.*
Of the bowels. *See Bowels.*

DISFELLOWSHIP

From God and People:
Of the uncircumcised (Ge 17:14). Of violators of the law, of unleavened bread (Ex 12:15), of sacrifices (Lev 17:9; 19:5-7), of purification (Nu 19:20). Of those defiled, by eating prohibited food (Lev 7:25, 27; 17:10; 19:8), by touching the dead (Nu 19:13), by committing abominations (Lev 18:29; 20:3-6).

Commanded:
For blasphemy (Nu 15:31). For schism (Ro 16:17). For heresy (1Ti 6:3-5; Tit 3:10-11; 2Jn 10-11). For immorality (Mt 18:17-18; 1Co 5:1-7, 11, 13; 2Th 3:6).
See Excommunication.

DISGUISES Examples of (Ge 38:14; 1Sa 28:8; 1Ki 14:2; 20:38; 22:30; 2Ch 35:22).

DISH Usually made either of baked clay or of metal. Orientals ate from a central platter or dish (Mt 26:23). Dishes used in the tabernacle and temple were made of gold (Ex 37:16; Nu 7:14ff; 2Ch 4:22, 24:14) or bronze (1Ki 7:38-40; 2Ki 25:14).

DISHAN (*ibex [?]*). The son of Seir (Ge 36:21, 30; 1Ch 1:38).

DISHON (*ibex [?]*).
1. The son of Seir (Ge 36:21, 30; 1Ch 1:38).
2. The grandson of Seir (Ge 36:25; 1Ch 1:41).

DISHONESTY In not paying debts (Ps 37:12, 21; Jas 5:4). In collusion with thieves (Ps 50:18). In wicked devices for gain (Job 24:2-11; Pr 1:10-14; 20:14; Isa 32:7; Jer 22:13; Eze 22:29; Hos 12:7; Am 3:10; 8:5; Mic 6:10-11).
Denounced (Jer 7:8-10; 9:4-6; 9:8; Hos 4:1-2; Na 3:1). Forbidden (Lev 19:13, 35-36; Dt 25:13-16; Ps 62:10; Pr 3:27-28; 11:1; 20:10, 23; 1Th 4:6). Penalties for (Lev 6:2-7; Pr 20:17; Zep 1:9; Zec 5:3-4). Parable concerning (Lk 16:1-8).

Instances of:
Abimelech's servants usurp a well of water (Ge 21:25; 26:15-22). Jacob obtains his brother's birthright by unjust advantage (Ge 25:29-33), steals his father's blessing (Ge 27:6-29), Laban's flocks by skillful manipulation (Ge 30:31-43). Rebekah's guile in Jacob's behalf (Ge 27:6-17). Laban's treatment of Jacob (Ge 29:21-30; 31:36-42). Rachel steals the household gods (Ge 31:19). Simeon and Levi deceive the Shechemites (Ge 34:15-31). Achan hides the wedge of gold and the Babylonian garment (Jos 7:11-26). Micah steals eleven hundred pieces of silver (Jdg 17:2). Micah's priest steals his images (Jdg 18:14-21). Joab's guile in securing Absalom's return (2Sa 14:2-20). Ahab usurps Naboth's vineyard (1Ki 21:2-16). Judas's hypocritical sympathy for the poor (Jn 12:6).
See Diplomacy; Hypocrisy; Injustice; Treason.

DISOBEDIENCE TO GOD Originated in Adam (Ro 5:19). Characteristic of all (Ro 1:32; Eph 2:2; 5:6; Col 3:6; Tit 1:16; 3:3; Heb 2:2; 1Pe 2:8). Temptation to (Ge 3:1-5). Denunciations against (Nu 14:11-12, 22-23; 32:8-13; Dt 18:19).

Punishment of:
Of the Israelites by covenant curses (Lev 26:14-46; Dt 28:15-68). *See Wicked.* Of the Egyptians by plagues. *See Plague; Sin, Punishment of.*

Instances of:
Of Adam and Eve, eating the forbidden fruit (Ge 3:6-11). Of Lot, in refusing to go to the mountain, as commanded by the angels (Ge 19:19-20). Of Lot's wife, in looking back upon Sodom (Ge 19:26). Of Moses, in making excuses when commissioned to deliver Israel (Ex 4:13-14), when he struck the rock (Nu 20:11, 23-24). Of Aaron, at the striking of the rock by Moses (Nu 20:23-24). Of Pharaoh, in refusing to let the Israelites go (Ex 5:2; 7:13, 22-23; 8:15, 19, 32; 9:12, 34; 10:20, 27; 11:10; 14:8). Of the Israelites, in gathering excessive quantities of manna (Ex 16:19-20), in refusing to enter the promised land (Dt 1:26, w Nu 14:1-10; Jos 5:6; Ps 106:24-25). Of Nadab and Abihu, in offering unauthorized fire (Lev 10:1-2). Of Balaam, in accompanying the messengers from Balak (Nu 22:22). Of Achan, in hiding the wedge of gold and the Babylonian garment (Jos 7:15-26).
Of Saul, in offering a sacrifice (1Sa 13:13), in sparing Agag and the spoils of the Amalekites (1Sa 15; 28:18). Of David, in his adultery, and in the killing of Uriah (2Sa 12:9). Of Solomon, in building places for idolatrous worship (1Ki 11:7-10). Of the prophet of Judah, in not keeping the commandment to deliver his message to Jeroboam without delay (1Ki 13). Of a man of Israel, who refused to smite the prophet (1Ki 20:35-36). Of Ahab, in suffering the king of Assyria to escape out of his hands (1Ki 20:42). Of priests, in not performing their functions after the due order (1Ch 15:13). Of the people of Judah (Jer 43:7), in going to dwell in Egypt contrary to divine command (Jer 44:12-14). Of Jonah, in refusing to deliver the message to the Ninevites (Jnh 1).
Of the blind men Jesus healed, and commanded not to tell of their healing (Mt 9:30-31). Of the leper whom Jesus healed, and commanded not to tell of the fact (Mk 1:45). Of Paul, in going to Jerusalem contrary to repeated admonitions (Ac 21:4, 10-14).
Of the righteous. *See Commandments and Statutes, of God.*
Of children. *See Children, Commandments to.*

DISPENSATION (*law or arrangement of a house*). The Greek word *oikonomia* means management or administration of a job or trust (Lk 16:2-4; 1Co 9:17; Eph 1:10; 3:2, 9; Col 1:25; 1Ti 1:4).

DISPENSATIONS An era of time during which mankind's obedience to God is tested according to the revelation of God available to him. From two dispensations (or covenants) to seven (innocence, conscience, human government, promise, law, grace, the kingdom) are held by various schools of interpretation.

DISPERSION Of the descendants of Noah (Ge 10). After building the tower of Babel (Ge 11:1-9; Dt 32:8). Of the Jews, foretold (Jer 16:15; 24:9; Jn 7:35). *See Diaspora.*

DISPLAY General references to (Est 1:4; 5:11; Isa 39:2; Lk 20:46; Ac 25:23).
In religious service (2Ki 10:16; Mt 6:2, 5, 16; 23:5).

DISPUTE About property. *See Property.*

DISSEMBLING *See Deception; Hypocrisy.*

DISSENSION In churches (1Co 1:10-13; 3:3-4; 11:18-19).

DISSIPATION Dangers of (Job 1:5). *See Drunkenness.*

DISTAFF Used in spinning thread (Pr 31:19).

DITCH *See Pit.*

DIVES (*rich*). In the Vulgate, the name given to the rich man in the parable of the rich man and Lazarus (Lk 16:19-31).

DIVIDING WALL The barrier between the Court of the Gentiles and the Court of the Jews in the temple in Jerusalem. For a Gentile to go beyond it meant death (Josephus, *Antiq.* 15.11.5). Figurative of Christ bringing Jews and Gentiles together as one in the church (Eph 2:14).

DIVINATION The practice of foreseeing or foretelling future events or discovering hidden knowledge; forbidden to Jews (Lev 19:26; Dt 18:10; Isa 19:3; Ac 16:16). Various means were used: reading omens, dreams, the use of the lot, astrology, necromancy, and others.

DIVINITY OF CHRIST *See Jesus the Christ, Deity of.*

DIVISIONS Forbidden in the church (1Co 1:10). Condemned in the church (1Co 1:11-13; 11:18). Improper in the church (1Co 12:24-25).

Are contrary to the: Unity of Christ (1Co 1:13; 12:13). Desire of Christ (Jn 17:21-23). Purpose of Christ (Jn 10:16). Spirit of the primitive church (1Co 11:16). Are a proof of a sinful spirit (1Co 3:3). Avoid those who cause (Ro 16:17). Evil of, illustrated (Mt 12:25).

DIVORCE Mosaic laws concerning (Ex 21:7-11; Dt 21:10-14; 24:1-4). Authorized for marital unfaithfulness (Mt 5:31-32; 19:3-11). Unjust reproved (Mal 2:14-16). From Gentile wives, required by Ezra (Ezr 10:1-16). Disobedience, a cause for, among the Persians (Est 1:10-22). Final, after remarriage of either party (Jer 3:1). Christ's injunctions concerning (Mk 10:2-12; Lk 16:18). Paul's injunctions concerning (1Co 7:10-17).

Figurative of God's judgment of Israel (Isa 50:1; 54:4-8; Jer 3:8). *See Certificate of Divorce; Marriage.*

DIZAHAB (*that which has gold*). A place in the region of Sinai where Moses gave a farewell address (Dt 1:1).

DOCTOR A physician (Mt 9:12; Mk 2:17; 5:26; Lk 5:31). Luke (Col 4:14).

See Physician; Disease.

DOCTRINES

Origin in God:

(Jn 7:16-17). Set forth by church councils (Ac 15:6-29).

False:

Jesus accuses scribes and Pharisees of false teaching (Mt 5:19-20; 15:9).

False teachers, to be avoided (Ro 16:17-18; 1Co 3:11, 21; 1Ti 1:3-7; 6:3-5, 20-21), accursed (Gal 1:6-8; Jude 4, 11), rejected (Tit 1:10-11, 14; 3:10-11; 2Jn 9-11). Admonitions against (Ro 16:17-18; Eph 4:14; Col 2:4, 8, 18-23; 1Ti 1:3-7; 4:7; 6:20-21; 2Ti 2:16; Tit 3:10-11; Heb 13:9).

False doctrine called: heresies (1Co 11:18-19; 2Pe 2:1-2), corruption (2Co 2:17; 11:3-4; Gal 1:6-8; 2Ti 2:14-18; 3:6-9; 2Pe 2:14-19).

Origin of false doctrine: people (Mt 15:9; Ro 16:17-18; 1Co 3:11, 21; 2Co 2:17; Eph 4:14; Col 2:4, 8, 18-23; 2Ti 3:6-9, 13; Tit 1:10-11, 14; 2Pe 2:1-3), Satan (2Co 11:3-4; 1Ti 4:1-3), Antichrist (1Jn 4:3; 2Jn 7, 9-11).

See Minister, False and Corrupt; Schism; Teachers, False.

DODAI (*beloved*). An officer in David's army (1Ch 27:4).

DODANIM *See Rodanim.*

DODAVAHU (*beloved of Yahweh*). Eliezer's father (2Ch 20:37).

DODO (*beloved*).

1. The grandfather of Tola (Jdg 10:1).
2. The son of Ahohite (2Sa 23:9).
3. The father of one of David's mighty men (2Sa 23:24).

DOEG (*anxious*). An Edomite, present when Ahimelech helped David (1Sa 21:7; 22:9, 22; Ps 52:T). Killed eighty-five priests (1Sa 22:18-19).

DOER OF THE WORD Example of belief (Mt 7:21; 12:50; Lk 11:28; Ro 2:13-15; 2Co 8:11; Jas 1:22-27; 4:11). *See Hearers.*

DOG Among the Israelites (Ex 11:7; 22:31). Shepherd dogs (Job 30:1).

Habits of:

Licking blood (1Ki 21:19; 22:38), licking sores (Lk 16:21), returns to his vomit (Pr 26:11; 2Pe 2:22), lapping of (Jdg 7:5). Mute and sleeping (Isa 56:10-11).

Title of contempt (1Sa 17:43; 24:14; 2Sa 3:8; 9:8; 16:9; 2Ki 8:13; Isa 56:10-11; Mt 15:26).

Figurative:

Of sinners (Php 3:2; Rev 22:15). Of male prostitutes (Dt 23:18).

DOGMATISM *See Commandments and Statutes, of Men.*

DOMICILE Rights of (Dt 24:10-11).

DOMINION, OF MANKIND *See Mankind, Design of.*

DONATIONS *See Liberality.*

DONKEY, DOMESTIC Unclean for food (Lev 11:2-3, 26; Ex 13:13).

Described as:

Knowing its master (Isa 1:3). Strong (Ge 49:14). Fond of ease (Ge 49:14-15). Formed a part of patriarchal wealth (Ge 12:16; 30:43; Job 1:3; 42:12).

Was Used:

In agriculture (Isa 30:6, 24). For bearing burdens (Ge 42:26; 1Sa 25:18). For riding (Ge 22:3; Nu 22:21-23). In harness (Isa 21:7). In war (2Ki 7:7, 10). Governed by a bridle (Pr 26:3). Urged on with a staff (Nu 22:23, 27). Women often rode on (Jos 15:18; 1Sa 25:20). Persons of rank rode on (Jdg 10:3-4; 2Sa 16:2). Judges of Israel rode on white (Jdg 5:10). Young, most valued for labor (Isa 30:6, 24). Trustworthy persons appointed to take care of (Ge 36:24; 1Sa 9:3; 1Ch 27:30). Often taken unlawfully by corrupt rulers (Nu 16:15; 1Sa 8:16; 12:3). Sometimes counted an ignoble creature (Jer 22:19).

Laws Respecting:

Not to be coveted (Ex 20:17). Fall under a burden, to be assisted (Ex 23:5). Astray, to be brought back to its owner (Ex 23:4; Dt 22:1). Astray, to be taken care of till its owner appeared (Dt 22:2-3). Not to be yoked with an ox (Dt 22:10). To enjoy the Sabbath rest (Dt 5:14). Firstborn of, if not redeemed, to have its neck broken (Ex 13:13; 34:20). Christ entered Jerusalem on (Zec 9:9; Jn 12:14).

Miracles Connected With:

Mouth of Balaam's opened to speak (Nu 22:28; 2Pe 2:16). A thousand men slain by Samson with a jawbone of (Jdg 15:15-17). Not torn by a lion (1Ki 13:28). Eaten during famine in Samaria (2Ki 6:25).

DONKEY, WILD

Inhabits wild and solitary places (Job 39:6; Isa 32:14; Da 5:21). Ranges the mountains for food (Job 39:8). Brays when hungry (Job 6:5). Suffers in time of scarcity (Jer 14:6).

Described as:

Fond of liberty (Job 39:5). Intractable (Job 11:12). Unsocial (Hos 8:9). Despises his pursuers (Job 39:5-7). Supported by God (Ps 104:10-11).

Illustrative of:

Intractableness of natural man (Job 11:12). The wicked in their pursuit of sin (Job 24:5). Israel in their love of idols (Jer 2:23-24). The Assyrian power (Hos 8:9). The Ishmaelites (Ge 16:12).

DOOR Posts of, sprinkled with the blood of the Passover lamb (Ex 12:22), the law to be written on (Dt 11:20). Hinges for (Pr 26:14), made of gold (1Ki 7:5). Doors of the temple made of two leaves, cherubim and flowers carved upon, covered with gold (1Ki 6:31-35).

Figurative:

Door of hope (Hos 2:15), of opportunity (1Co 16:9; Rev 3:8), closed (Mt 25:10; Lk 13:25; Rev 3:7).

DOORKEEPER Keeper of doors and gates in public buildings, temples, walled cities, etc., often called "gatekeepers" (2Ki 7:10; 1Ch 23:5; Ps 84:10; Ezr 7:24; Mk 13:34). *See Gatekeepers.*

DOPHKAH (*drive [sheep]*). The first stopping place of the Israelites after they left the wilderness of Sin. It is usually identified with the Egyptian mining center at Serabit el-Khadim in Sinai (Nu 33:12).

DOR A town and district of Israel (Jos 11:2). Conquered by Joshua (Jos 12:23; 1Ki 4:11). Allotted to Manasseh, although situated in the territory of Asher (Jos 17:11; Jdg 1:27).

DORCAS (*gazelle*). A Christian woman living at Joppa whom Peter raised from the dead (Ac 9:36-43).

DOTHAN (*two wells*). A place c. thirteen miles N of Shechem near where Joseph was sold (Ge 37:17) and where Elisha saw a vision of angels (2Ki 6:13-23).

DOUBLE-MINDED One who is a doubter, unstable (Ps 119:113; Jas 1:8).

DOUBTING In prayer (Mt 21:21; Jas 1:6-8). Admonishings against (Pr 24:10; Mt 8:26; 14:31; 17:17; Mk 4:40; 9:19; Lk 8:25; 9:40).

Instances of:

Job (Job 3; 4:3-6; 9:16-23; 30:20-21). Abraham (Ge 12:12-13; 15:8). Sarah (Ge 18:12-14). Lot (Ge 19:30). Moses (Ex 3:11; 4:1, 10, 13; 5:22-23; 6:12; Nu 11:21-22). Israelites (Ex 14:10-12, 15; 1Sa 17:11, 24; Isa 40:27-28; 49:14-15). Gideon (Jdg 6:13, 15). Samuel (1Sa 16:1-2). Psalmists (Ps 22:2; 31:22; 42:5-6; 49:5; 73:13-17; 77:3, 7-9). Obadiah (1Ki 18:7-14). Elijah (1Ki 19:13-18). Jeremiah (Jer 1:6; 8:18; 32:24-25; 45:3; La 3:8, 17-18; 5:20).

Christ's disciples (Mt 8:23-27; 14:29-31; 17:14-21; 28:17; Mk 4:38, 40; 9:14-29; 16:10-11; Lk 8:25; 9:40-41; Jn 14:8-11; 20:24-27). John the Baptist (Mt 11:2-3). Ananias (Ac 9:13-14). Peter (Mt 14:30-31). Thomas (Jn 20:25). Early believers (1Pe 1:6).

See Cowardice; Murmuring.

DOUGH First of, offered to God (Nu 15:19-21; Ne 10:37). Kneaded (Jer 7:18; Hos 7:4). Part of, for priest (Eze 44:30). *See Bread; Oven.*

DOVE Sent out from the ark by Noah (Ge 8:8-11). Mourning of (Isa 38:14; 59:11; Na 2:7). Domesticated (Isa 60:8). Nests of (Jer 48:28). Harmlessness of, typical of Christ's gentleness (Mt 10:16). Sacrificial uses of (Ge 15:9). Prescribed for purification, of women (Lev 12:6, 8; Lk 2:24), of Nazirites (Nu 6:10), of lepers (Lev 14:22). Burnt offering of (Lev 1:14-17). Trespass offering of, for the poor (Lev 5:7-10; 12:8). Sin offering, for those who touched any dead body (Nu 6:10). Market for, in the temple (Mt 21:12; Jn 2:14).

Symbolic of the Holy Spirit (Mt 3:16; Lk 3:22; Jn 1:32).

See Pigeon.

DOVE'S DUNG NIV "seed pods" (2Ki 6:25 and ftn). *See Plants of the Bible.*

DOWRY Sum paid to parents for a daughter taken as wife (Ex 22:16-17), by Shechem for Dinah (Ge 34:12), by Boaz for Ruth (Ru 4:3-9), by David to Saul for Michal (1Sa 18:25).

DOXOLOGY *See Praise.*

DRACHMA A Greek silver coin worth about a day's wages (Lk 15:8; Ac 19:19). The temple tax was two drachmas (Mt 17:24). In Ezr 2:69 and Ne 7:70-72 the term may refer to the Persian daric. *See Daric; Money.*

DRAGON Any terrible creature, as a venomous serpent (Dt 32:33; Ps 91:13), a sea monster (Ps 74:13; 148:7; Isa 27:1; Eze 29:3; 32:2). Figurative of forces opposed to God: Egypt (Isa 51:9), Satan (Rev 12; 13; 16:13; 20:2). *See Serpent.*

DRAM *See Daric.*

DRAMA *See Pantomime.*

DRAUGHT HOUSE *See Latrine.*

DRAWER OF WATER One who brought water from a well or a spring to a house (Dt 29:11; Jos 9:23-27).

DRAWING Of pictures on tile (Eze 4:1).

DREAM Transitory (Job 20:8). Vanity of (Ecc 5:3, 7).

Revelations by (Nu 12:6; Job 33:15-17; Jer 23:28; Joel 2:28; Ac 2:17). The dreams of the cupbearer and baker (Ge 40:8-23), of Pharaoh (Ge 41:1-36).

Interpreted by Joseph (Ge 40:12-13, 18-19; 41:25-32), by Daniel (Da 2:16-23, 28-30; 4). Delusive (Isa 29:7-8).

False prophets pretended to receive revelations through (Dt 13:1-5; Jer 23:25-32; 27:9; 29:8; Zec 10:2). *See Vision.*

Instances of:

Of Abimelech, concerning Sarah (Ge 20:3). Of Jacob, concerning the stairway (Ge 28:12), the speckled goats (Ge 31:10-13), concerning his going down into Egypt (Ge 46:2). Of Laban, concerning Jacob (Ge 31:24). Of Joseph, concerning the sheaves (Ge 37:5-10). Of the Midianite, concerning the cake of barley (Jdg 7:13). Of Solomon, concerning his choice of wisdom (1Ki 3:3-15). Of Eliphaz, of a spirit speaking to him (Job 4:12-21). Of Daniel, concerning the four beasts (Da 7). Of Joseph, concerning Mary's innocence (Mt 1:20-21), concerning the flight into Egypt (Mt 2:13), concerning the return into Israel (Mt 2:18-22). Of Pilate's wife, concerning Jesus (Mt 27:19). Cornelius's vision, concerning Peter (Ac 10:3-6). Peter's vision of the unclean beasts (Ac 10:10-16). Paul's vision of the man in Macedonia, crying, "Come over to Macedonia and help us" (Ac 16:9), relating to his going to Rome (Ac 23:11), concerning the shipwreck and the safety of all on board (Ac 27:23-24).

DRESS Of fig leaves (Ge 3:7). Of skins (Ge 3:21). Of other materials. *See Hair; Goats' Hair; Leather; Linen; Sackcloth; Silk; Wool.* Mixed materials in, forbidden (Dt 22:11). Men forbidden to wear women's, and women forbidden to wear men's (Dt 22:5). Rules with respect to women's (1Ti 2:9-10; 1Pe 3:3). Not to be held over night as a pledge for debt (Ex 22:26). Ceremonial purification of (Lev 11:32; 13:47-59; Nu 31:20). Tearing of. *See Mourning.*

Of the head:

Turbans prescribed by Moses, for the priests (Ex 28:40; 29:9; 39:28), by Ezekiel (Eze 44:18). Turbans and headdresses worn by men (Da 3:21) and by women (Isa 3:20; Eze 24:17, 23). Shawls (Isa 3:23). Veils (Eze 13:18, 21).

Various articles of:

Mantle, robe, or cloak (Ezr 9:3; 1Ki 19:13; 1Ch 15:27; Job 1:20), richly ornamented (2Sa 13:18), purple (Jn 19:2, 5). Robe (Ex 28:4; 1Sa 18:4). Capes (Isa 3:22). Embroidered coat (Ex 28:4, 40; 1Sa 2:19; Da 3:21). Sleeveless shirt, called coat (Mt 5:40; Lk 6:29; Jn 19:23; Ac 9:39). Cloak (2Ti 4:13; Jn 19:2, 5). Trousers (Da 3:21). Skirts (Eze 5:3). Sashes (Isa 3:20). *See Veil.*

Changes of clothing, the folly of excessive (Job 27:16). Uniform vestments kept in store for worshipers of Baal (2Ki 10:22-23; Zep 1:8), for wedding feast (Mt 22:11). Presents made of changes of clothing (Ge 45:22; 1Sa 18:4; 2Ki 5:5; Est 6:8; Da 5:7). Garments of priests. *See Priest.* Dress in mourning. *See Mourning.*

Symbolic:

Filthy, of unrighteousness and judgment (Isa 64:6; Zec 3:3-4). Clean, of acceptance (Zec 3:4-7).

See Colors, Figurative and Symbolic.

DRINK Beverages of the Israelites were water (Ge 24:11-18), wine (Ge 14:18; Jn 2:3), and milk (Jdg 4:19).

DRINK OFFERING *See Offerings, Drink; Libation.*

DRIVING Rapid, by Jehu (2Ki 9:20).

DROMEDARY *See Camel.*

DROPSY (Lk 14:2).

DROSS Refuse separated from molten ore or metal. Figurative of divine judgment (Ps 119:119; Pr 25:4; 26:23; Isa 1:22; Eze 22:18-19).

DROUGHT (Ge 31:40; 1Ki 17; 18; Jer 14:1-6). Sent by God as a judgment (Dt 28:23-24; 1Ki 8:35; 2Ch 6:26; 7:13; Hos 13:15).

See Famine; Meteorology; Rain.

Figurative: (Ps 32:4; Isa 44:3).

DRUG ABUSE Not mentioned in the Bible, but the principles derived from alcohol abuse would apply to drugs. *See Abuse, Substance Abuse; Drunkenness.*

DRUNKARD

Described:

(Pr 23:29-35). The psalmist mocked by (Ps 69:12). Fellowship with, forbidden (1Co 5:11).

End Result:

Poverty (Pr 23:21; Isa 28:1, 3), cut off (Joel 1:5), destroyed (Na 1:10), trodden under feet (Isa 28:1, 3), shame (Hab 2:16), death (Dt 21:20-21). Insatiable appetite of (Hab 2:5-6). Excluded from the kingdom (1Co 6:9-10). Punishment of (Dt 21:20-21).

See Drunkenness; Wine; Temperance; Abstinence.

DRUNKENNESS

Condemned:

Repugnancy of (Isa 28:7-8; 56:12; Hos 7:5, 14; Joel 1:5; 3:3; Am 2:8, 12; Mt 24:49; Lk 12:45). Mockery of (Ps 69:12; Pr 20:1).

Consequences of (Pr 21:17; 23:21, 29-35; Isa 19:14; 24:9-11; 28:7; Hos 4:11). Death penalty for (Dt 21:20-21; 29:19-20; Jer 25:27). Excludes from the kingdom of God (1Co 6:9-10; Gal 5:19-21).

D

Forbidden (1Sa 1:14; Pr 23:20, 31-32; 31:4-7; Lk 21:34; Ro 13:13; 1Co 11:21-30; Eph 5:18; 1Th 5:7-8; 1Pe 4:3). Woes denounced against (Isa 5:11-12, 22; 28:1, 3, 7-8; Am 6:1, 6; Na 1:10; Hab 2:15-16).

Figurative:
(Isa 28:8; 51:17, 21-23; 63:6; Jer 25:15-16, 27-28; 51:7-9; La 3:15; Eze 23:31-34; Hab 2:15-16).
See Abstinence; Drunkard; Sobriety; Wine.

Instances of:
Noah (Ge 9:21). Lot (Ge 19:33). Nabal (1Sa 25:36). Uriah (2Sa 11:13). Amnon (2Sa 13:28). Elah (1Ki 16:9). Ben-Hadad and his thirty-two confederate kings (1Ki 20:16). Xerxes (Est 1:10-11). Belshazzar (Da 5:1-6). Believers (1Co 11:21).

Falsely Accused of:
Hannah (1Sa 1:12-16). Jesus (Mt 11:19). The apostles (Ac 2:13-15).

E

DRUSILLA Daughter of Herod Agrippa I; married first to Azizus, king of Emesa; later to Felix, procurator of Judea (Ac 24:24-25).

DRY PLACES (Nu 20:2; 2Ki 3:9; Ps 68:6; Isa 1:30; Jer 14:3; 17:6).

DUKE NIV "chief." Of Edom (Ge 36:15-43; Ex 15:15; 1Ch 1:51-54). Of the Midianites (Jos 13:21).

DULCIMER NIV "pipes" (Da 3:5, 10, 15). *See Music, Instruments of.*

DUMAH (*silence, name of underworld*).
1. Son of Ishmael (Ge 25:14; 1Ch 1:30; Isa 21:11-12).
2. A city of Canaan assigned to Judah (Jos 15:52).

DUMB *See Mute.*

DUNG Laws were made regarding excrement of human beings and animals used in sacrifice (Dt 23:12-14; Ex 29:14; Lev 8:17). Dry dung was often used as fuel (Eze 4:12-15), also fertilizer (Isa 25:10; Lk 13:8).

DUNG GATE A gate in the Jerusalem wall that led out to the Valley of Hinnom where rubbish was dumped (Ne 3:14).

DUNGEON In prisons (Jer 38:6; La 3:53). *See Prison.*

DURA A plain of Babylon where Nebuchadnezzar set up his image (Da 3:1).

DUST Man made from (Ge 2:7; 3:19, 23; Ecc 3:20). Casting of, in anger (2Sa 16:13). Shaking from feet (Mt 10:14; Ac 13:51). Put on the head in mourning (Jos 7:6; 1Sa 4:12; 2Sa 1:2; 15:30; Job 2:12; 42:6).

DUTY
1. Tribute levied on foreign commerce by Solomon (1Ki 10:15).
2. Escape from, sought by Moses (Ex 3:11; 4:1, 10, 13; 6:12, 30), by Jonah (Jnh 1:1-15), by Ananias (Ac 9:13-14).

Of People to God:
To love (Dt 6:5; 11:1; 30:15-20; Jos 23:11; Ps 31:23; Mt 22:37; Lk 12:27). To obey (Dt 10:12-13; 30:15-20; Jos 22:5; Pr 23:26; Mt 12:50; 22:21; 23:23; Lk 17:10; Jn 14:15, 21; 15:14; Ac 4:19-20; 5:29).

Of People to People:
To love (Lev 19:18; Mt 19:19; 22:39; Mk 12:31; Jn 13:34; Ro 13:8-10; Gal 5:14; Jas 2:8). To help (Isa 58:6-7; Mt 25:34-46; Lk 10:23-36). To forgive (Mt 18:21-35; Lk 17:3-4; Eph 4:32; Col 3:13). To practice "the golden rule" toward (Mt 7:12). To respect a brother's conscience (Ro 14:1-23; 1Co 8:1-13). To restore a sinning brother (Gal 6:1-2).
See Commandments and Statutes, of God; Children; Husband; Minister, Duties of; Parents; Wife.

DWARFED Could not officiate at the altar (Lev 21:20).

DYEING Of fabric (Ex 25:5; 26:14; Isa 63:1; Eze 23:15).

DYING *See Death, Physical.*

DYSENTERY (Ac 28:8).

DYSPEPSIA *See Indigestion.*

E

EAGLE

General:
As food: Forbidden as food, classified as detestable (Lev 11:13; Dt 14:12). *See Birds.*
Species of: Osprey (Lev 11:18; Dt 14:17). Vulture (Job 15:23; Pr 30:17; Mic 1:16; Mt 24:28; Lk 17:37).
Flight of: The swift flight of, as an analogy of the swiftness of destruction to come (Dt 28:49; Jer 4:13; 48:40; 49:22; La 4:19). Its soaring capability (Job 39:27; Isa 40:31; Jer 49:22; Ob 4). Their graceful flight as a simile for various themes (Pr 23:5; Isa 40:31; Ob 4).
Care of young: Nest of (Dt 32:11; Job 39:27-30; Jer 49:16). Bears young on her wings (Dt 32:11). Life is renewed like an eagle's (Ps 103:5; Isa 40:31).

Figurative:
Of God's care (Ex 19:4; Dt 32:11). Of warriors (2Sa 1:23; Jer 4:13; 48:40; Hos 8:1). Of the swiftness of life (Job 9:26). Of renewed life (Isa 40:31).

Symbolic:
Of the glory of God (Eze 1:10; 10:14). An allegory, the "seed of the land" (Zedekiah) is planted by a "great eagle" (Nebuchadnezzar) and grows up to be a "spreading vine"; this spreading vine is then transplanted by another eagle (Hophra) (Eze 17:1-8). A lion with wings of an eagle representing the majesty and strength of Babylon (Da 7:4). Of redeemed man (Rev 4:7). Of the church (Rev 12:14).

EAR

Attentiveness:
To what God says, to what is right, to his voice, to his commands, and to keep all his decrees (Ex 15:26; 23:22; Dt 11:13; 15:5; 28:1; Jer 11:6; Mt 13:23; Lk 8:15; Ac 17:11). To a truth worthy of attention (Mt 11:15; 13:9, 43; Mk 4:23; Lk 14:35). To Jesus' words (Lk 19:48). A stringent demand for attention to the utterances of prophets who were inspired by the Spirit (Rev 2:7, 11, 29; 3:6, 13, 22; 13:9).

Blocked:
God will listen to the righteous, not to sinners (Ge 18:23-32; 1Sa 8; Ps 34:15-16; 145:18-19; Pr 15:29; Isa 59:1-2; Jn 9:31; 15:7; Jas 5:16-18; 1Jn 5:14-15). *See God, Access to; Righteous, Promises to; Wicked, Prayers of.*
The result of ignoring, the law (Nu 15:30-31; Dt 1:43-46; Pr 28:9; Isa 1:10-15; 24:4-13). Ignoring the Lord (1Sa 2:27-33; 8; Isa 65:12-15; 66:4; Zec 7:11-14; Lk 9:26; 2Ti 2:11-13; Heb 6:4-6; 2Pe 2:1). *See God, Rejected; Jesus the Christ, Rejected.* The result of ignoring the plight of the poor (Dt 15:7-11; Pr 21:13; 22:16, 22-23; 28:8; Isa 10:1-4; Eze 16:49-50; Zec 7:9-14; Jas 2:1-13). Hearing blocked by life's troubles (Mt 13:18-23, esp. 22). *See Sower.*
See Poor, Warning Against Neglect; Poor, Oppression of.
The inability of idols to hear (1Ki 18:22-39; Ps 115:4-8; 135:15-18; Isa 46:7; Jer 10:2-5; 1Co 8:4-6; 12:2). *See Idol; Idolatry, Folly of.*

Ceremonies:
Pierced as a sign of servitude (Ex 21:5-6; Dt 15:16-17). Blood put upon, in consecration of priests (Ex 29:20; Lev 8:23), in cleansing lepers (Lev 14:14, 25). *See Leprosy.* Anointed with oil in purifications (Lev 14:17, 28).

Deaf:
Hearing closed to prevent obedience and subsequent salvation (Jos 11:20; Isa 6:10; 63:17; Jn 12:37-41; Ro 9:10-18; 11:25). *See Deafness.* The Lord, in refusing to listen to a petition (Dt 1:45), is petitioned to hear and to not refuse to answer (1Ki 8:28-53, esp. vv. 28-30, 32, 34, 36, 39, 43, 45, 49, 52; 2Ki 19:16; Ne 1:6).

Fearful:
The nations, because of reports of what God had accomplished (Ex 15:13-16; Dt 2:24-25; Jos 2:8-9; 1Sa 4:6-9; Est 8:15-17; Ps 48:4-7), from the knowledge of God's majesty (Ps 99:1-3; 114:7-8; Eze 38:20). *See Fear of God.* Of hearing God speak (Ex 20:19; Dt 5:25; Heb 12:18-21). *See Voice, of God; Anthropomorphisms, Acts.* Israel, from reports of punishment (Dt 13:11; 17:12-13; 19:18-21; 1Ti 5:20). *See Punishment.*

Figurative:
Anthropomorphic uses of: (Ps 17:6; 39:12; 77:1; 80:1; 84:8).

Misguided:
The value of listening to instruction (Pr 1:8-9; 2:1-22; 3:1-2; 4; 5:1-6; 6:20-29; 7:1-5; 19:27; 22:17-19). *See Counsel; Instruction; Knowledge; Wisdom.*
Listening to the advice of fools (Pr 13:20; Ecc 7:5-6). *See Speaking, Speech, Foolish.*

Misunderstood:
Taking the words of others too seriously (Ecc 7:21-22). Those listening to Jesus' words from the cross (Mt 27:46-47; Mk 15:34-35). Those who heard the voice of God (Jn 12:29).

Quick to hear:
Listening carefully to what others say (Jas 1:19).

Rational:
Words are tested by hearing (Job 12:11; 34:3). Powerful presentation (Job 29:21-25; 32:11-12). God will teach men (Isa 54:13; Jer 31:33-34; Jn 6:45; 1Co 2:13; 1Th 4:9; 1Jn 2:26-27).

Refusal to listen:
A rebellious people (Eze 12:2; Zec 7:11-14). The Jews (Jn 8:43; 10:20; Ac 13:44-50). The Sanhedrin (Ac 7:57). Men will reject the truth and accept a lie (2Ti 4:2-4).

Unconcerned:
People are not concerned with the pleading of God by his Spirit or by his prophets (Ne 9:29-30; Zec 7:11-12). *See Holy Spirit, Sin Against; Holy Spirit, Withdrawn From Unrepentant Sinners.* Idols, are absolutely indifferent to the prayers of people (Ps 115:6).
Israel, with ears which are open yet unable to hear (Isa 6:9-10; 42:18-20; 43:8). Those not concerned to take Jesus' words seriously (Mt 7:26-27). The reason Jesus speaks in parables (Mt 13:13). Those who hear the word but do not do what it says (Jas 1:22-25).

Worthless:
The parable of the sower (Mt 13:20-22; Mk 4:16-19; Lk 8:13-14). John the Baptist and Herod (Mk 6:20). Paul, in Athens at the Areopagus (Ac 17:19, 32), before Felix (Ac 24:24-26), before Agrippa and Festus (Ac 26:1-29).

EAR OF GRAIN *See Grain.*

EARLY RAIN *See Rain.*

EARLY RISING

General references to:
To rise early (Ge 19:27; 26:31; Ex 8:20; 34:4; Jos 3:1; Jdg 6:38; 1Sa 5:4; 15:12; 17:20; 2Ch 20:20). Daybreak (Jos 6:15; 1Sa 9:26; Ps 46:5; 57:8; Da 6:19; Mk 16:2; Lk 24:22). Prior to daybreak (Ru 3:14; Pr 31:15). Morning (Ps 90:14; 101:8). *See Morning.*

To do evil: (Ex 32:6; Nu 14:40; Job 24:14; Isa 5:11).

EARNEST A pledge or token (Ps 86:17). The Spirit, as a guarantee of the future redemption of our bodies (Ro 8:23), of our inheritance (Ro 8:23; Eph 1:13-14), of the promise to come (2Co 1:22). *See Inheritance; Token, 1.*

EARNESTNESS An intense desire which results in repentance, produced by godly sorrow (2Co 7:11). Sincerity in your love (2Co 8:7-8). *See Sincerity; Zeal.*

EARRING

As an offering:
Offering of, for the golden calf (Ex 32:2-3). As a wave offering for the tabernacle (Ex 35:22). As an offering to the Lord to make atonement (Nu 31:50).

Types of:
Gold (Ex 32:2-3; Jdg 8:24; Pr 25:12). Gold studded with silver (SS 1:11).

Worn:
By the Israelites (Ex 32:2-3; Jdg 8:24). By Ishmaelites, as a cultural habit (Jdg 8:24). For idolatrous purposes (Ge 35:4; Isa 3:19).

EARTH

Creation of:
By God (Ge 1:1; Ex 20:11; 31:17; 2Ki 19:15; 2Ch 2:12; Ne 9:6; Job 38:4; Ps 90:2; 102:25; 104:5; 115:15; 124:8; 146:5-6; Pr 8:22-26; Isa 37:16; 45:18; 66:1-2; Jer 10:12; 27:5; 32:17; 51:15; Ac 14:15; Heb 11:3; 2Pe 3:5; Rev 10:6; 14:7). By Christ (Jn 1:3, 10; Heb 1:10). Primitive condition of (Ge 1:2, 6-7; Job 26:7; 38:4-7; Ps 104:5-9; Pr 3:19-20; Isa 40:22; Jer 4:23-26). *See Creation; God, Creator.* Created to be inhabited (Isa 45:18). By design (Isa 45:18).
Early divisions of (Ge 10-11; Dt 32:8; Ps 74:17).

Belongs to:
The Lord (Ex 9:29; 19:5; Dt 10:14; 1Sa 2:8; Ps 24:1; 50:12; Isa 66:1; 1Co 10:26). God controls (Job 9:6; Rev 7:1). God's footstool (Isa 66:1; La 2:1; Mt 5:35; Ac 7:49).

Cursed:
Cursed by God (Ge 3:17-19; 5:29; Ro 8:19-22).

Future of:
Perpetuity of (Ge 49:26; Dt 33:15; Ps 78:69; 104:5; Ecc 1:4; Hab 3:6). Will be judged (1Sa 2:10; Ps 96:13; 98:9). Destruction of, foretold (Ps 102:25-27; Isa 24:19-20; 51:6; Mt 5:17-18; 24:3, 6, 14, 29-31, 35-42; Mk 13:24-37; Lk 21:26-36; 2Pe 3:10-13; Rev 20:11; 21:1). A new earth (Isa 65:17; 66:22; 2Pe 3:13; Rev 21:1).

Residence of mankind: (Ps 115:16).

EARTHENWARE *See Pottery.*

EARTHQUAKES (*shaking, trembling*). (Job 9:6; Ps 18:7; 46:2-3; 104:32; Jer 4:24). *See Mountain.* As judgments (Ps 18:15; 60:2; Isa 13:13; 24:18-20; 29:6; Na 1:5; Rev 6:12-14; 11:13; 16:18, 20). *See Judgment.* Prophecies of (Eze 38:19-20; Zec 14:4; Mt 24:7; Mk 13:8; Lk 21:11; Rev 11:19).

Instances of:
At Sinai (Ex 19:18; Ps 68:8; 77:18; 114:4-7; Heb 12:26). When Korah, Dathan, and Abiram were swallowed up (Nu 16:31-34). When Jonathan and his armor-bearer attacked the garrison at Gibeah (1Sa 14:15). When the Lord revealed himself to Elijah in the still small voice (1Ki 19:11). In Canaan, in the days of Uzziah, king of Judah (Am 1:1; Zec 14:5). At the crucifixion of Jesus (Mt 27:51). At the resurrection of Jesus (Mt 28:2). When Paul and Silas were in prison at Philippi (Ac 16:26).

EAST

An Important Direction for God:
Glory of God from (Eze 43:2). Angel from (Rev 7:2).

An Important Direction for People:
The Garden of Eden (Ge 2:8; 3:24). *See Garden.* An east wind (Ge 41:6, 23, 27; Ex 10:13; 14:21; Job 15:2; 27:21; 38:24; Ps 48:7; 78:26; Isa 27:8; Jer 18:17; Eze 17:10; 19:12; 27:26; Hos 12:1; 13:15; Hab 1:9). *See Wind.* A significant direction for the Hebrews (Ex 38:13; Nu 3:38; 10:5; Eze 10:19; 11:23; 43:2, 4). God has removed our transgressions (Ps 103:12). Faces toward in worship (Eze 8:16).

People of:
Eastern people (Ge 29:1; Jdg 6:3, 33). Eastern people had a special reputation for wisdom (1Ki 4:30; Mt 2:1-12). "People of the east" denotes Arab groups who accompanied the Midianites and the Amalekites in attacking Israel (Job 1:3; Jer 49:28; Eze 25:4, 10). Kings of (Rev 16:12).

EAST WIND Hot, dry wind coming from the S and SE of Israel (Jer 4:11; Hos 13:15), destructive (Ge 41:6; Ps 48:7; Eze 17:10; 27:26), used as a means of salvation for Israel by God (Ex 14:21), used as a means of judgment by God (Isa 27:8; Jer 18:17; Jnh 4:8).

EASTER The day on which the church celebrates the resurrection of Jesus Christ. KJV "Easter" should be "Passover" as in NIV (Ac 12:4). *See Feasts; Passover.*

EASTERN SEA *See Dead Sea.*

EATING The host acting as waiter (Ge 18:8). Favored guests served an extra portion (Ge 43:34). *See Hospitality.* Sitting at table (Ex 32:6). *See Table.* Table used in (Jdg 1:7). Reclining on couches (Am 6:4, 7; Mt 26:7, 20; Mk 14:3, 18; Jn 12:2; 13:23). *See Couch.* Washing before (Mt 15:2).
See Feasts; Food; Gluttony.

EBAL
1. A Horite (Ge 36:23; 1Ch 1:40).

2. A mountain of Ephraim located N and directly opposite Mt. Gerizim. These two mountains form the two sides of an important E-W pass. Upon entering the land of Canaan, after the time of Moses, the Hebrews were to confirm their covenant with Yahweh. This required that half of the tribes were to be on Mt. Gerizim to proclaim the blessings, the other half of the tribes were to stand on Mt. Ebal to proclaim the curses of the covenant with the ark of the covenant between them (Dt 11:29; 27:12-13; Jos 8:33). Altar built on (Dt 27:4-6; Jos 8:30). They were to sacrifice a fellowship offering there, eating and rejoicing in the presence of the Lord (Dt 27:7). Traditionally these were called peace offerings (Dt 27:7, ftn). All the words of this covenant were to be written very clearly on the stones of the altar that they set up (Dt 27:8). *See Gerizim.*

3. Son of Joktan (1Ch 1:22). *See Obal.*

EBED (*servant*).

1. Father of Gaal, who led the rebellion against Abimelech at Shechem (Jdg 9:26-45).

2. The son of Jonathan, one of those who returned to Israel with Ezra (Ezr 8:6).

3. The title *Ebed* was adopted, apparently by David, from an Akkadian practice, which was also used in Edom and Ammon. It was a designation of the class of court officials as distinguished from the older institution of tribal elders. In Ebed-Melech it becomes a proper name.

EBED-MELECH (*servant of Melek [king]*). An Ethiopian eunuch in Zedekiah's court who interceded on Jeremiah's behalf before King Zedekiah to have Jeremiah pulled out of a mud filled cistern (Jer 38:1-13). The prophecy concerning Ebed-Melech promised that he would survive the destruction of the kingdom as a reward for his efforts (Jer 39:16-18).

EBENEZER (*stone of help*). A town of Ephraim near Aphek where the Israelites fought two battles with the Philistines and were defeated, losing the ark in the second battle (1Sa 4:1-11; 5:1). Later, after defeating the Philistines, the Israelites erected a memorial stone, naming it Ebenezer (1Sa 7:12).

EBER (*[regions] beyond [the river]*, or source of the word *Hebrew*).

1. The probable founder of the Hebrew race (Ge 10:21-25; 11:14-17; 1Ch 1:18-19, 25; Lk 3:35). Prophecy concerning (Nu 24:24). Perhaps Eber in this passage should be understood not as a proper name but as the word for "region beyond" (here, beyond the Euphrates), which is the same as the name Eber in Hebrew.

2. A Gadite (1Ch 5:13).

3. A Benjamite (1Ch 8:12).

4. Another family of the tribe of Benjamin (1Ch 8:22).

5. A postexilic priest (Ne 12:20).

6. Father of Peleg and Joktan (Lk 3:35).

EBEZ A town given by lot to Issachar (Jos 19:20).

EBIASAPH (*[my] father has gathered*). A son of Korah (1Ch 6:23, 37; 9:19; 26:1). *See Korah, 4.* Abiasaph is an alternate form (Ex 6:24). *See Abiasaph.* Called also Asaph (1Ch 26:1). *See Asaph.*

EBONY A highly prized core wood of a tree imported from S India, Ceylon, and perhaps Ethiopia. It was valued by the Egyptians, Phoenicians, Babylonians, Greeks, and Romans for its use, along with ivory, in fine furniture, vessels, and turned objects. It was also used in the Near East for idols. *See Image; Idol; Idolatry; Temple, Idolatrous.* Merchandise in (Eze 27:15).

EBRONAH *See Abronah.*

ECBATANA (perhaps *place of gathering*). A city located at the foot of the Alvand Mountain which is now Hamadan. The capital of Media, where during the reign of Darius I, a copy of Cyrus's decree was found which authorized the rebuilding of the temple in Jerusalem (Ezr 6:2, 3-12). *See Cyrus, Darius, Medes; Persia; Temple, The Second.*

ECCLESIASTES

Author and Date:

Several passages strongly suggest that King Solomon is the author (1:1, 12, 16; 2:4-9; 7:26-29; 12:9; cf. 1Ki 2:9; 3:12; 4:29-34; 5:12; 10:1-8). On the other hand, the writer's title ("Teacher," Hebrew *Qoheleth*), his unique style of Hebrew and his attitude toward rulers (suggesting that of a subject rather than a monarch—see, e.g., 4:1-2; 5:8-9; 8:2-4; 10:20) may point to another person and a later period.

Outline:

I. Author (1:1).
II. Theme: The Meaninglessness of Man's Efforts on Earth Apart From God (1:2).
III. Introduction: The Profitlessness of Working to Accumulate Things to Achieve Happiness (1:3-11).
IV. Discourse, Part 1: In Spite of Life's Apparent Enigmas and Meaninglessness, It is to be Enjoyed as a Gift From God (1:12-11:6).
V. Discourse, Part 2: Since Old Age and Death Will Soon Come, Man Should Enjoy Life in His Youth, Remembering That God Will Judge (11:7-12:7).
VI. Theme Repeated (12:8).
VII. Conclusion: Reverently Trust in and Obey God (12:9-14).

ECCLESIASTICISM Jewish, rebuked by Jesus (Mt 9:10-13; 23:2-35), to be overthrown (Mt 21:19-20, 28-44). Arrogance of (Mt 12:2-8; 23:4). Traditional rules of the Jewish (Mt 15:1-20; Mk 7:2-23). *See Church, The Body of Believers; Commandments and Statutes, of Men; Minister, False and Corrupt; Usurpation, in Ecclesiastical Affairs.*

ECLIPSE Of the sun and moon (Isa 13:10; 60:19; Eze 32:7-8; Joel 2:10, 31; 3:15; Am 8:9; Mic 3:6; Mt 24:29; Mk 13:24; Ac 2:20; Rev 6:12; 8:12). *See Sun; Moon.*

ECOLOGY Mankind created to care for the earth (Ge 1:28; 2:15; Ps 8:6-8; 115:16). The land was to enjoy rest every seven years (Lev 25:1-7); the land enjoyed its rest during Israel's exile (2Ch 36:20-21). Animals were to rest on the Sabbath (Ex 20:10). Fruit trees were not to be cut down in war time (Dt 20:19-20). A bird and its young were not to be caught together (Dt 22:6-7). Babylon judged for violence to the forests of Lebanon and its animals (Hab 2:17 w Isa 14:8).

ECONOMICS Political (Ge 41:33-57). Household (Pr 24:27; 31:10-31; Ecc 11:4-6; Jn 6:12-13). *See Family; Frugality; Industry.*

ECONOMY *See Economics; Government.*

ECUMENICISM (*the inhabited earth*). A movement among Christian religious groups—Protestant, Eastern Orthodox, Roman Catholic—to bring about a closer unity in work and organization. The word is not found in the NIV, but backing for the movement may be found in John 17 where Jesus prays for the unity of his church.

ED KJV transliterates the name of the altar erected by the tribes Reuben, Gad, and Manasseh at the fords of the Jordan (Jos 22:34); NIV "Witness."

EDAR *See Eder.*

EDEN (*paradise, delight*, possibly *flat land*).

1. The Garden of Eden (Ge 2:8-17; 3:23-24; 4:16; Isa 51:3; Eze 28:13; 31:9, 16, 18; 36:35; Joel 2:3).

2. Gods of (2Ki 19:12; Isa 37:12; Am 1:5).

3. A Gershonite (2Ch 29:12).

4. A Levite (2Ch 31:15).

5. A marketplace of costly merchandise (Eze 27:23-24).

EDER (*flock*).

1. A tower near Ephrath where Jacob encamped on the way back to Canaan (Ge 35:21).

2. A city of Judah (Jos 15:21).

3. A son of Beriah, grandson of Shaharaim, a Benjamite (1Ch 8:15).

4. A grandson of Merari (1Ch 23:23; 24:30).

EDICT A public proclamation, written and sealed with the king's signet and publicly read (Ezr 6:11-12; Est 2:8; 8:8-13; 9:1, 13). Penalties were severe for violating a Persian edict (Ezr 6:11). Moses' parents are listed as an example of those who were not afraid to transgress the royal edict (Heb 11:23).

EDIFICATION, EDIFY, EDIFYING (Latin *to build up*). The root of this Greek word is found in various words and compound words in the NT, i.e., build (Mt 23:29; 26:61), building (Jn 2:20), builder (1Co 3:10; Heb 3:3-4), builds up (1Co 8:1), strengthen (1Co 8:10), edified (1Co 14:5, 17), edification (Ro 14:19).

Paul uses the word group frequently but never in the literal sense of "building" a building. He uses it often in the metaphorical sense of "building" or "building up" the church, and of "building up" fellow believers. Paul refers to the church as a building (1Co 3:9; Eph 2:21), and of building the church upon the foundation that he and the apostles and the prophets laid (1Co 3:10, 12, 14; Eph 2:20).

Paul uses the words more frequently in the sense of "strengthening, unifying, making for peace." Christians are to build up each other in this sense (1Th 5:11). It is primarily love that "builds up" (1Co 8:1).

EDOM (*red*).

1. A name of Esau, possibly on account of his being covered with red hair (Ge 25:25, 30; 36:1, 8, 19).

2. A name of the land occupied by the descendants of Esau. It extended from the Gulf of Aqabah to the Red Sea, and was also called Idumea (Ge 32:3; 36:16-17, 21; Jer 40:11).

Prophecies concerning (Jer 25:21-23; 27:1-11; Da 11:41). Noted for its wise men (Ob 8). Sins of (Ob 10-14). Wilderness of (2Ki 3:8).

See Edomite(s).

Figurative of the foes of Zion (Isa 63:1).

EDOMITE(S) (*red*). Called also Edom. Land of (Ge 32:3; Dt 2:4-5, 12). Descendants of Esau (Ge 36). Rulers of (Ge 36:9-43; Ex 15:15; 1Ch 1:51-54). Kings of (Ge 36:31-39; Nu 20:14; 1Ch 1:43-50; Eze 32:29; Am 2:1).

Prophecies concerning (Ge 25:23; 27:29, 37-40; Nu 24:18; Isa 11:14; 21:11-12; 34; 63:1-6; Jer 9:25-26; 27:1-11; 49:7-22; La 4:21-22; Eze 25:12-14; 32:29-30; 36:5; Joel 3:19; Am 1:11-12; 9:12; Ob 1-21; Mal 1:2-5).

Protected by divine command from desolation by the Israelites (Dt 2:4-6), from being held in abhorrence by the Israelites (Dt 23:7). Children of the third generation might be received into the congregation of Israel (Dt 23:8). Refuse the Israelites passage through their country (Nu 20:18-21). Saul makes war against (1Sa 14:47). Garrisons of (2Sa 8:14). David conquers (1Ki 11:14-16; 1Ch 18:11-13), writes battle songs concerning his conquest of (Ps 60:8-9; 108:9-10). Ruled by a deputy king (1Ki 22:47). Become confederates of Jehoshaphat (2Ki 3:9, 26). Revolt in the days of Jehoram (2Ki 8:20-22; 2Ch 21:8-10). Amaziah, king of Judah, invades the territory of Edom, defeating ten thousand Edomites (2Ki 14:7, 10; 2Ch 25:11-12; 28:17). The Lord delivers the army of, into the hands of Jehoshaphat (2Ch 20:20, 23). A Jewish prophet in Babylon denounces (Ps 137:7; Eze 25:12-14; 35). Join Babylon in the war against the Israelites (Eze 35:5; Am 1:9-11; Ob 11-16).

EDREI (*strong*).

1. A chief city of Og, king of Bashan (Dt 1:4; Jos 12:4). Assigned to Manasseh (Jos 13:12, 31). Located c. ten miles NE of Ramoth-Gilead.

2. A city of Naphtali, the location is unknown (Jos 19:37).

EDUCATION *See Instruction; Teachers; School.*

EGG (*whiteness*). (Job 6:6; Lk 11:12). Appears also in the plural (Dt 22:6; Job 39:14; Isa 10:14).

EGLAH (*heifer*). The wife of David (2Sa 3:5; 1Ch 3:3).

EGLAIM A city on the border of Moab (Isa 15:8).

EGLATH SHELISHIYAH (possibly *the third Eglath*). A town near Zoar mentioned in prophetic oracles of judgment on Moab (Isa 15:5; Jer 48:34).

EGLON (*circle* ISBE; *young bull* KB).

1. A city of Canaan located between Gaza and Lachish (Jos 10:3, 5, 23), captured by Joshua (Jos 10:36-37; 12:12), assigned to Judah (Jos 15:39).

2. The king of Moab who captured Jericho (the City of Palms) from the Israelites as a judgment against them, controlling it for eighteen years (Jdg 3:12-14). Eglon was assassinated by Ehud, a judge, because the Israelites cried out to the Lord (Jdg 3:15-23).

E

EGOTISM *See Conceit.*

EGYPT

The Country of:

Fertility of (Ge 13:10). Imports of (Ge 37:25, 36). Productions of (Nu 11:5; Ps 78:47; Pr 7:16; Isa 19:5-10). Irrigation employed in (Dt 11:10). Called, Rahab which is the poetic name for Egypt (Ps 87:4; 89:10), the land of Ham (Ps 105:23; 106:21-22). Exports of (Pr 7:16; Eze 27:7), of horses (1Ki 10:28-29). Limits of (Eze 29:10).

Abraham dwells in (Ge 12:10-20; 13:1). The king acquires title to land of (Ge 47:18-26). Joseph's captivity in and subsequent rule over. *See Joseph, 1.* Israelites in bondage in. *See Israel, Israelites.* Plagues in. *See Plague.* Civil war in (Isa 19:2). Overflowed by the Nile (Am 8:8; 9:5). Joseph takes Jesus to (Mt 2:13-20).

Prophecies against (Ge 15:13-14; Isa 19; 20:2-6; 45:14; Jer 9:25-26; 43:8-13; 44:30; 46; Eze 29-32; Hos 8:13; Joel 3:19; Zec 10:11).

See Egyptians.

Famine in (Ge 41; Ac 7:11). *See Famine.* Magi of (Ge 41:8; Ex 7:11; 1Ki 4:30; Ac 7:22). *See Magi.* Priests of (Ge 41:45; 47:22). Army of destroyed in the Red Sea (Ex 14:5-31; Isa 43:17). *See Army.* Armies of (Ex 14:7; Isa 31:1). Idols of (Eze 20:7-8).

River, or Brook of:

Perhaps identical with Shihor. *See River of Egypt; Shihor.* A small stream flowing into the Mediterranean Sea, the western boundary of the land promised to the Israelites (Ge 15:18; Nu 34:5; Jos 13:3; 15:4, 47; 1Ki 8:65; 2Ki 24:7; Isa 27:12; Eze 47:19; 48:28).

Symbolic: (Rev 11:8).

EGYPTIANS Descendants of the Mizraim (Ge 10:6, 13-14, ftn). Hospitality of, to Abraham (Ge 12:10-20). Slaves bought by (Ge 37:36). The art of embalming the dead practiced by (Ge 50:2-3, 26). Oppressed the Israelites (Ex 1-2). Refuse to release the Israelites (Ex 5-10). Judged by plagues (Ex 7-12; Ps 78:43-51), firstborn of destroyed (Ex 12:29; Ps 78:51; 105:36; 136:10). Sent the Israelites away (Ex 12:31-42). Army pursued the Israelites, and was destroyed (Ex 14:5-31; Ps 106:7; Heb 11:29). Wisdom of (1Ki 4:30).

Refused to eat with the Hebrews (Ge 43:32). Abhorred shepherds (Ge 46:34). Eligible to membership in Israelite congregation in the third generation (Dt 23:7-8). Alliances with, without first consulting God, forbidden to the Israelites (Isa 30:1-5; 31:1-3; 36:6; Eze 17:15). Intermarry with the Israelites (1Ki 3:1).

Invasions of Israel: Under Shishak (1Ki 14:25-26; 2Ch 12:2-9), Pharaoh Neco (2Ki 23:29-35; 2Ch 35:20-24; 36:2-4). Aid the Israelites against the Chaldeans (Jer 37:5-11). An enthusiastic Egyptian instigated a rebellion against the Roman government (Ac 21:38).

Conversion of, foretold (Isa 19:18). Prophecies of dispersion and restoration of (Eze 29:12-16; 30:23-26).

See Egypt.

EHI (*my brother [is exalted]*). A son of Benjamin (Ge 46:21).

EHUD (*united*).

1. A Benjamite judge, the assassin of Eglon (Jdg 3:15-30; 1Ch 8:6). *See Eglon, 2.*

2. Son of Bilhan (1Ch 7:10).

EKED *See Beth Eked.*

EKER (possibly *offspring*). The son of Ram, part of the postexilic clan of Jerahmeel (1Ch 2:27).

EKRON, EKRONITES (perhaps *barren place* or *fertile place*). One of the five chief cities of the Philistines (Jos 13:3). Conquered and allotted to Judah (Jos 15:11, 45; Jdg 1:18). Allotted to Dan (Jos 19:43). The ark of God taken to (1Sa 5:10). Temple of Baal-Zebub, the god of Ekron, at (2Ki 1:2). Prophecies against (Jer 25:20; Am 1:8; Zep 2:4; Zec 9:5).

EL (*God; Mighty One*). A generic word for God in the Semitic languages. The chief Canaanite god was El. The God of Israel is usually referred to in the plural form, *Elohim*, or in compound names, as in the following articles. *See Elohim.*

EL-BERITH (*a god of a covenant*). An alternate name for the god worshiped at Shechem, in whose temple some of the people of Shechem took refuge when Abimelech destroyed the city (Jdg 9:46). *See Baal-Berith.*

EL BETHEL (*God [El] of Bethel*). A name given by Jacob to Luz because God there revealed Himself to him (Ge 35:7).

EL ELOHE ISRAEL (*God, the God of Israel*). Name of an altar erected by Jacob near Shechem (Ge 33:20).

EL PARAN (*tree of Paran*). A place in the wilderness of Paran (Ge 14:6).

EL SHADDAI (*God of mountains* or *God who is self-sufficient* KB or in older etymology *God of breasts*). Translated "God Almighty" in the NIV following the NT rendering of *Shaddai* by *pantokrator*. The name by which God appeared to Abraham, Isaac, and Jacob (Ex 6:3).
See God, Names of; Shaddai.

ELA The father of Shimei, one of Solomon's district governors (1Ki 4:18).

ELAH (*a species of a mighty tree*).
1. A chief of Edom (Ge 36:41).
2. The valley (valley of the terebinth), in which David killed Goliath (1Sa 17:2, 19; 21:9).
3. The king of Israel, son of Baasha; killed by Zimri (1Ki 16:8-10).
4. The father of Hoshea, the last king of Israel (2Ki 15:30; 17:1; 18:1, 9).
5. The son of Caleb (1Ch 4:15).
6. The Benjamite, son of Uzzi (1Ch 9:8).
7. *See Ela.*

ELAM (*highland*).
1. The son of Shem (Ge 10:22; 1Ch 1:17).
2. The son of Shashak (1Ch 8:24).
3. The son of Meshelemiah (1Ch 26:3).
4. The ancestor of a family which returned from the Exile (Ezr 2:7; Ne 7:12).
5. Another ancestor of a returned family (Ezr 2:31; Ne 7:34).
6. The father of two sons returned from the Exile (Ezr 8:7).
7. The ancestor of a man who married a foreign woman (Ezr 10:2, 26).
8. A chief who sealed a covenant with Nehemiah (Ne 10:14).
9. A priest who took part in the dedication of the wall (Ne 12:42).
10. A country situated on the E side of the Tigris opposite Babylonia; was one of the earliest civilizations; figures prominently in Babylonian and Assyrian history. Some of its people were brought to Samaria by the Assyrians (Ezr 4:9-10). Elamites at Jerusalem on the Day of Pentecost (Ac 2:9).

ELAMITES (*highland*). Descendants of Shem (Ge 10:22). They were present at Pentecost (Ac 2:9).

ELASAH (*God has fashioned*).
1. The son of Pashhur the priest, and one of those with foreign wives (Ezr 10:22).
2. The son of Shaphan and one of Zedekiah's emissaries to Nebuchadnezzar who took a letter to the exiles in Babylon for Jeremiah (Jer 29:3).

ELATH (*grove of large trees*). A city on the coast of Edom situated at the head of the Gulf of Arabah (Dt 2:8; 1Ki 9:26; 2Ch 8:17). The conquest of, by the Edomites (2Ki 16:6), by Uzziah (2Ch 26:1-2).

ELDAAH (*God [El] is [my] desire*). A descendant of Abraham (Ge 25:4; 1Ch 1:33).

ELDAD (*beloved of God [El]*; possibly *Dadi [pagan god] is god*). One of Moses' 70 elders (Nu 11:24-29).

ELDERS

In the Mosaic System: *See Elders, Council of; Government, Mosaic.*

In the NT Church:
Received gifts on behalf of church (Ac 11:29-30). Ordained (Ac 14:23; Tit 1:5-9). Overseers of the church (Ac 15:1-29; 16:4-5; 20:17, 28-32; 21:18; 1Ti 5:17-19; 1Pe 5:1-5). Performed ecclesiastical duties (1Ti 4:14; Jas 5:14-15).

John's Vision of the Twenty-four Elders:
(Rev 4:4, 10; 5:5-6, 8, 11, 14; 7:11, 13; 11:16; 14:3; 19:4).
See Bishop; Church, Government of the Christian Church; Deacon; Overseer.

ELDERS, COUNCIL OF

Described:
Chosen elders of the nation, vested with representative, judicial, and executive authority (Ex 4:29; 5:15, 19; 6:14-25; 12:21; Nu 11:16-30). Called the council (Nu 16:2; Mk 15:43); council of the elders (Ps 107:32; Lk 22:66); elders of Israel (Ex 3:16, 18), of Judah (1Sa 30:26), of the people (Ex 19:7), of the community (Lev 4:15), of the Jews (Ezr 5:5); Sanhedrin (Mt 5:22; 26:59; Ac 4:15; 5:21-41).
Closely associated with Moses and subsequent leaders (Ex 3:16-18; 4:29; 12:21; 17:5-6; 18:12; 19:7; 24:1, 14; Nu 16:25; Dt 5:23; 27:1; 29:10; 31:9, 28; Jos 7:6; 8:10, 33; 23:2; 24:1; Jdg 11:5-11; Ac 5:17-18, 21). Made confession of sin in behalf of the nation (Lev 4:15; 9:1).
A similar council existed among the Egyptians (Ge 50:7), the Midianites and Moabites (Nu 22:4, 7-8), the Gibeonites (Jos 9:11).

Events Relating to:
Demands a king (1Sa 8:4-10, 19-22). Saul pleads to be honored before (1Sa 15:30). Chooses David as king (2Sa 3:17-21; 5:3; 1Ch 11:3). Closely associated with David (2Sa 12:17; 1Ch 15:25; 21:16). Joins Absalom in his usurpation (2Sa 17:4). David rebukes (2Sa 19:11). Assists Solomon at the dedication of the temple (1Ki 8:1-3; 2Ch 5:2-4). Counsels King Rehoboam (1Ki 12:6-8, 13). Counsels King Ahab (1Ki 20:7-8). Josiah assembles, to hear the law of the Lord (2Ki 23:1; 2Ch 34:29, 31).
Legislates with Ezra in reforming certain marriages with the Gentiles (Ezr 10:8-14). Legislates in later times (Mt 15:2, 7-9; Mk 7:1-13). Sits as a court (Jer 26:10-24). Constitutes, with priests and scribes, a court for the trial of both civil and ecclesiastical causes (Mt 21:23; 26:3-5, 57-68; 27:1-2; Mk 8:31; 14:53-65; 15:1; Lk 22:52-71; Ac 4:1-21; 6:12-15). Seeks counsel from prophets (Eze 8:1; 14:1; 20:1, 3). Corrupt (1Ki 21:8-14; Eze 8:11-12; Mt 26:14-15; 27:3-4).

ELEAD (*God [El] has testified*). A descendant of Ephraim (1Ch 7:21).

ELEADAH (*God [El] has adorned*). The son of Ephraim (1Ch 7:20).

ELEALEH (*God [El] is high*). A city in Transjordan, rebuilt by the tribe of Reuben (Nu 32:3, 37). Repossessed by the Moabites (Isa 15:4; 16:9; Jer 48:34).

ELEASAH (*God [El] has fashioned*).
1. A person or family of the clan of Jerahmeel of the tribe of Judah (1Ch 2:39-40).
2. A member of the tribe of Benjamin, descended from Saul (1Ch 8:37; 9:43).

ELEAZAR (*God [El] is a help*).
1. The son of Aaron (Ex 6:23; 28:1). He married a daughter of Putiel, who bore him Phinehas (Ex 6:25). After the death of Nadab and Abihu he is made the chief of the tribe of Levi (Nu 3:32). The duties of (Nu 4:16).
He succeeds Aaron as the high priest (Nu 20:26, 28; Dt 10:6). Assists Moses in the census (Nu 26:63). With Joshua, divides Israel (Nu 34:17). Death and burial of (Jos 24:33). Descendants of (1Ch 24:1-19).
2. An inhabitant of Kiriath Jearim who attended the ark (1Sa 7:1-2).
3. Son of Dodai the Ahohite, and one of David's three mighty men (2Sa 23:9-10, 13; 1Ch 11:12).
4. A Merarite Levite (1Ch 23:21-22; 24:28).
5. The son of Phinehas (Ezr 8:33; Ne 12:42).
6. A returned Israelite exile (Ezr 10:25).
7. The great-grandfather of Joseph, the husband of Mary (Mt 1:15).

ELECT (*chosen*). Those chosen by God for some special purpose (Ps 106:23; Isa 43:10; 45:4). Among the elect mentioned in Scripture are Moses, the Israelites, Christ, the angels, Christ's disciples.

ELECTION By grace (Mt 22:14; Jn 15:16; 17:6; Ro 11:5; Eph 1:4; 2:10; 2Th 2:13; 1Pe 2:9).
Of Israel (Dt 7:6; Isa 45:4). Of rulers (Ne 11:1). Of Christ as Messiah (Isa 42:1; 1Pe 2:6). Of ministers (Lk 6:13; Ac 9:15). Of good angels (1Ti 5:21). Of churches (1Pe 5:13).
See Chosen; Elect; Predestination.

ELECTIONEERING By Absalom (2Sa 15:1-6). Adonijah (1Ki 1:7). *See Candidate.*

ELEGY A song of sorrow. By David, on Saul and Jonathan (2Sa 1:17, 19-27), on Abner (2Sa 3:33-34).
See Lamentations, Book of; Poetry.

ELEMENTS (*rows, series, alphabet, first principles of a science, physical elements, heavenly bodies, planets, personal cosmic powers*). Heathen deities and practices (Gal 4:3, 9), rudiments (Col 2:8, 20), first principles (Heb 5:12). *See Basic Principles of this World.*

ELEPH *See Haeleph.*

ELEPHANT The Hebrew *behemoth* may be the elephant or hippopotamus (Job 40:15, ftn). *See Ivory.*

ELEVEN, THE The eleven apostles who remained after the defection of Judas (Mk 16:14; Lk 24:9, 33; Ac 2:14).

ELHANAN (*God [El] is gracious*).
1. The son of Dodo, one of David's heroes (2Sa 23:24; 1Ch 11:26).
2. A distinguished warrior in the time of David who killed Lahmi the brother of Goliath the Gittite (1Ch 20:5), or the Bethlehemite who killed Goliath (2Sa 21:19). The two accounts may be harmonized if an early copyist of Samuel misread "Lahmi the brother of" as "the Bethlehemite."

ELI (*Yahweh is exalted* IDB; *[God [El]] is exalted* KB). Misjudges and rebukes Hannah (1Sa 1:13-14). His benediction upon Hannah (1Sa 1:17-18; 2:20). Officiates when Samuel is presented at the tabernacle (1Sa 1:24-28). High priest (1Sa 1:25; 2:11; 1Ki 2:27). Judge of Israel (1Sa 4:18, ftn). Indulgent of his corrupt sons (1Sa 2:22-25, 29; 3:11-14). His concern for the ark (1Sa 4:11-18). Death of (1Sa 4:18).
Prophecies of judgments upon his house (1Sa 2:27-36; 3:11-14, w 1Ki 2:27).

ELI, ELI, LAMA SABACHTHANI *See Eloi, Eloi, Lama Sabachthani.*

ELIAB (*God [El] is [my] father*).
1. Son of Helon (Nu 1:9; 2:7; 7:24, 29; 10:16).
2. A Reubenite, progenitor of Dathan and Abiram (Nu 16:1, 12; 26:8-9; Dt 11:6).
3. The son of Jesse, and eldest brother of David (1Sa 16:6; 17:13, 28; 1Ch 2:13). Elihu, an officer over the tribe of Judah (1Ch 27:18).
4. An ancestor of Samuel (1Ch 6:27). Called also Elihu in the parallel genealogies (1Sa 1:1), and Eliel (1Ch 6:34).
5. A hero of the tribe of Gad (1Ch 12:9).
6. A Levite, a gatekeeper and musician (1Ch 15:18, 20; 16:5).

ELIADA (*God [El] knows*).
1. The son of David (2Sa 5:16; 1Ch 3:8).
2. Father of Rezon (1Ki 11:23).
3. Benjamite general (2Ch 17:17).

ELIAHBA (*God [El] hides*). The Shaalbonite, one of David's heroes (2Sa 23:32; 1Ch 11:33).

ELIAKIM (*God [El] establishes*).
1. The master of Hezekiah's household; sent by the king to negotiate with invading Assyrians (2Ki 18:17-37; Isa 36:1-22), and then to seek help of Isaiah the prophet (2Ki 19:2; Isa 37:2).
2. The original name of King Jehoiakim (2Ki 23:34; 2Ch 36:4). *See Jehoiakim.*
3. Priest (Ne 12:41).
4. The ancestor of Jesus (Mt 1:13).
5. Another and earlier ancestor of Jesus (Lk 3:30).

ELIAM (*God [El] is [my] kinsman*).
1. The father of Bathsheba (2Sa 11:3). Called Ammiel (1Ch 3:5).
2. One of David's mighty men known as the "Thirty" (2Sa 23:34). Called Ahijah (1Ch 11:36).

ELIAS *See Elijah.*

ELIASAPH (*God [El] has added*).
1. The son of Deuel, a leader of the tribe of Gad (Nu 1:14; 2:14; 7:42, 47; 10:20).
2. The son of Lael, a leader of the families of the Gershonites (Nu 3:24).

ELIASHIB (*God [El] restores*).
1. A descendant of Zerubbabel and remotely related to David (1Ch 3:24).
2. A priest in the time of David (1Ch 24:12).
3. An ancestor of a man who helped Ezra (Ezr 10:6; Ne 12:10, 22-23).
4. A Levite who put away his foreign wife (Ezr 10:24).
5. A man who married a foreign woman (Ezr 10:27).
6. Another man who married a foreign woman (Ezr 10:36).
7. A high priest in the time of Nehemiah (Ne 3:1, 20-21; 13:4, 7, 28).

ELIATHAH (*God [El] comes*). A temple musician, the son of Heman (1Ch 25:4, 27).

ELIDAD (*God [El] is [my] beloved*). A Benjamite, the son of Kislon (Nu 34:21). Eleazar the priest and Joshua were appointed to assign the land west of the Jordan to the tribes who were to settle there. God also appointed one man from each of the tribes to help Eleazar and Joshua, Elidad being the leader from the tribe of Benjamin.

ELIEHOENAI (*my eyes [look] to Yahweh*).
1. A Korahite gatekeeper of the tabernacle (1Ch 26:3).
2. One of the family heads who returned with Ezra; the son of Zerahiah (Ezr 8:4). *See Elioenai.*

ELIEL (*God [El] is [my] God*).
1. The chief of Manasseh (1Ch 5:24).
2. The ancestor of Samuel (1Ch 6:34). Called Eliab (1Ch 6:27).
3. The son of Shimei (1Ch 8:20).
4. The son of Shashak (1Ch 8:22).
5. A Mahavite and a captain in David's army (1Ch 11:46).
6. One of David's heroes (1Ch 11:47).
7. A Gadite; perhaps the same as 5 or 6 (1Ch 12:11).
8. A chief Levite (1Ch 15:11).
9. A chief of Judah; perhaps the same as 5 (1Ch 15:9).
10. A Levite overseer (2Ch 31:13).

ELIENAI (*my eyes [look] to Yahweh*). A Benjamite citizen of Jerusalem (1Ch 8:20).

ELIEZER (*God [El] is [my] help*).
1. Steward of Abraham, who in place of a son, would have become Abraham's heir (Ge 15:2). Perhaps the same as the servant mentioned in (Ge 24).
2. The son of Moses and Zipporah (Ex 18:4; 1Ch 23:15, 17; 26:25).
3. The grandson of Benjamin (1Ch 7:8).
4. A priest (1Ch 15:24).
5. A Reubenite chief (1Ch 27:16).
6. A prophet who rebuked Jehoshaphat (2Ch 20:37).
7. A chieftain sent to induce the Israelites to return to Jerusalem (Ezr 8:16).
8. A priest who put away his foreign wife (Ezr 10:18).
9. A Levite who put away his foreign wife (Ezr 10:23).
10. A son of Harim who put away his foreign wife (Ezr 10:31).
11. An ancestor of Jesus (Lk 3:29).

ELIHOREPH A son of Shisha (1Ki 4:3).

ELIHU (*Yahweh is [my] God*).
1. A son of Tohu, an Ephraimite, an ancestor of Samuel (1Sa 1:1). Probably identical with Eliab (1Ch 6:27), and Eliel (1Ch 6:34).
2. A Manassite warrior, who joined David at Ziklag (1Ch 12:20).
3. A Korahite gatekeeper of the tabernacle (1Ch 26:7).
4. A chief of the tribe of Judah and one of David's brothers (1Ch 27:18). Possibly Eliab, the oldest brother of David (1Sa 16:6).
5. A son of Barakel the Buzite who speaks to Job when his three friends have failed to silence him (Job 32-37).

ELIJAH (*Yahweh is [my] God*).
1. The Tishbite, a Gileadite and prophet. Announces to Ahab the coming of a disastrous drought (1Ki 17:2-7). The severity of Ahab, which is noted in secular literature as well, i.e., Jos. *Antiq.* VIII.xiii.2, prompts Elijah to escape into the wilderness, where he is miraculously fed by ravens (1Ki 17:1-6). By divine direction, he goes to Zarephath of Sidon where he is sustained in the household of a widow (1Ki 17:8-16). The widow's son becomes fatally ill; Elijah prays over him with the result that his life is restored (1Ki 17:16-24). Paul has a similar experience with a young man named Eutychus (Ac 20:7-12). He returns and sends a message to Ahab through Obadiah, a devout believer in the Lord, who was in charge of Ahab's palace (1Ki 18:1-16). Meets Ahab and directs him to assemble the prophets of Baal (1Ki 18:17-20). Derisively challenges the priests of Baal to offer sacrifices (1Ki 18:25-29). Slays the prophets of Baal (1Ki 18:40). Escapes to the wilderness from the

fierceness of Jezebel (1Ki 19:1-18). Fasts forty days (1Ki 19:8). Despondency and murmuring of (1Ki 19:10, 14). Consolation given to (1Ki 19:11-18). Flees to the wilderness of Damascus; directed to anoint Hazael as king over Aram, Jehu son of Nimshi king over Israel, and Elisha to be a prophet in his own place (1Ki 19:9-21). Personal aspect of (2Ki 1:8).

Piety of (1Ki 19:10, 14; Lk 1:17; Ro 11:2; Jas 5:17). His translation to heaven in a whirlwind (2Ki 2:11). Antitype of John the Baptist (Mt 11:14; 17:10-13; Mk 9:11-13; Lk 1:17; Jn 1:21-25). Appears to Jesus at his transfiguration (Mt 17:1-4; Mk 9:2-5; Lk 9:28-33).

Miracles of:
Increases the oil of the widow of Zarephath (1Ki 17:14-16). Raises from the dead the son of the woman of Zarephath (1Ki 17:17-24). Causes fire to consume the sacrifice (1Ki 18:24, 36-38). Causes rain after a drought of three and a half years (1Ki 18:41-45; Jas 5:17-18). Calls fire down upon the soldiers of Ahaziah (2Ki 1:10-14; Lk 9:54, ftn).

Prophecies of:
Foretells, a drought (1Ki 17:1), the destruction of Ahab and his house (1Ki 21:17-29; 2Ki 9:25-37), the death of Ahaziah (2Ki 1:2-17), the plague sent as a judgment upon the people in the time of Jehoram, king of Israel (2Ch 21:12-15).

2. A Benjamite chief, the son of Jeroham (1Ch 8:27).
3. A postexilic Jew who divorced his foreign wife; a descendant of Harim (Ezr 10:21).
4. A postexilic Jew who divorced his foreign wife; a descendant of Elam (Ezr 10:26).

ELIKA A Harodite, one of David's mighty men known as the "Thirty" (2Sa 23:25).

ELIM (*big trees*). The fourth stopping place of the Israelites after they crossed the Red Sea; they found twelve springs and seventy palm trees (Ex 15:27; 16:1; Nu 33:9-10).

ELIMELECH (*God [El] is [my] king*). An Ephrathite from Bethlehem of Judah who, with his wife, Naomi and his two sons, immigrated from Judah to Moab in the days of the judges to escape a famine in the land (Ru 1:2, 3; 2:1, 3; 4:3, 9).

ELIOENAI (*my eyes [look] to Yahweh*).
1. The son of Neariah (1Ch 3:23-24).
2. A Simeonite leader (1Ch 4:36).
3. A Benjamite (1Ch 7:8).
4. A man who divorced his foreign wife (Ezr 10:22).
5. A man who divorced his foreign wife (Ezr 10:27).
6. A priest, perhaps the same as 4 (Ne 12:41).

ELIPHAL (*[my] God [El] sit in judgment*). Perhaps the same as Eliphelet (2Sa 23:34). One of David's mighty men known as the "Thirty" (1Ch 11:35).

ELIPHAZ (*God [El] is fine gold* or *God crushes*).
1. The oldest son of Esau by his Hittite wife Adah (Ge 36:4, 10-12, 15-16; 1Ch 1:35-36).
2. One of Job's three friends; wise, rich, and a ruler of men. He was probably the leader of this trio (Job 42:7), and also the oldest. He took for granted that Job must have committed some major sin as the only explanation for his tremendous suffering. He tries to make it as easy as possible for Job to repent because of the powerful impact of the dream he had had concerning man's sinful condition in the presence of God (Job 4:12-21). In his second address, Eliphaz's point of view is that Job's problems stem from his strong sense of personal righteousness; that Job believes that he has all the wisdom that he needs, therefore, he has no need of input from God or wise men (Job 15). In his third address, Eliphaz condemns Job of many sins, calling him back to right relationship and the resultant blessing of God (Job 22).

ELIPHELEHU (*God [El], distinguish him!*). A Levite musician (1Ch 15:18, 21).

ELIPHELET (*God [El] is [my] deliverance*).
1. A son of David, probably identical with #2 (2Sa 5:16; 1Ch 3:8; 14:7).
2. One of David's mighty men known as the "Thirty" (2Sa 23:34).
3. A son of David (1Ch 3:6; 14:7). Called Elpelet (1Ch 14:5).
4. A descendant of Saul (1Ch 8:39).
5. A companion of Ezra (Ezr 8:13).
6. A priest from among the Israelites who had married a foreign woman and had pledged to divorce his wife (Ezr 10:33).

ELISABETH *See Elizabeth.*

ELISHA (*God [El] is [my] salvation*). The successor to Elijah the prophet. Elijah is instructed to anoint (1Ki 19:16). Called by Elijah (1Ki 19:19). Ministers to Elijah (1Ki 19:21). Witnesses Elijah's translation, receives a double portion of his spirit (2Ki 2:1-15; 3:11). Mocked by the children of Bethel (2Ki 2:23-24). Causes the king to restore the property of the hospitable Shunammite (2Ki 8:1-6). Instructs that Jehu be anointed the king of Israel (2Ki 9:1-3). Life of, sought by Jehoram (2Ki 6:31-33). The death of (2Ki 13:14-20). Bones of, restore a dead man to life (2Ki 13:21).

Miracles of:
Divides the Jordan (2Ki 2:14). Purifies the waters of Jericho by casting salt into the fountain (2Ki 2:19-22). Increases the oil of the woman whose sons were to be sold for debt (2Ki 4:1-7). Raises from the dead the son of the Shunammite (2Ki 4:18-37). Neutralizes the poison of the stew (2Ki 4:38-41). Increases the bread to feed one hundred men (2Ki 4:42-44). Heals Naaman the leper (2Ki 5:1-19; Lk 4:27). Sends leprosy as a judgment upon Gehazi (2Ki 5:26-27). Recovers the axhead that had fallen into a stream by causing it to float (2Ki 6:6). Reveals the counsel of the king of Syria (2Ki 6:12). Opens the eyes of his servant to see the hosts of the Lord (2Ki 6:17). Brings blindness upon the army of Syria (2Ki 6:18).

Prophecies of:
Foretells a son to the Shunammite woman (2Ki 4:16); plenty to the starving in Samaria (2Ki 7:1); death of the unbelieving prince (2Ki 7:2); seven years' famine in the land of Canaan (2Ki 8:1-3); death of Ben-Hadad, king of Syria (2Ki 8:7-10); elevation of Hazael to the throne (2Ki 8:11-15); the victory of Jehoash over Syria (2Ki 13:14-19). Elisha is referred to once in the NT (Lk 4:27).

ELISHAH (*God [El] saves*). The son of Javan, whose name was given to an ancient land and its people, not identified (Ge 10:4; 1Ch 1:7; Eze 27:7).

ELISHAMA (*God [El] has heard*).
1. A leader of the tribe of Ephraim during the census in the wilderness. The grandfather of Joshua (Nu 1:10; 2:18; 7:48, 53; 10:22; 1Ch 7:26).
2. A son of David (2Sa 5:16; 1Ch 3:8; 14:7).
3. KJV Elishama, another son of David, is NIV Elishua (1Ch 3:6, ftn). *See Elishua.*
4. The grandfather of the Ishmael who killed Gedaliah the governor of Israel appointed by Nebuchadnezzar (2Ki 25:25; Jer 41:1).
5. Of the tribe of Judah, descended from Sheshan (1Ch 2:41).
6. A priest sent by Jehoshaphat to teach the law in Judah (2Ch 17:8).
7. A secretary to Jehoiakim (Jer 36:12, 20-21).

ELISHAPHAT (*God [El] is [my] judge*). One of five Judean commanders who helped Jehoiada the priest in the overthrow of Athaliah to make Joash king (2Ch 23:1).

ELISHEBA (*God [El] is an oath* BDB; *God [El] is [my] fill* KB). The daughter of Amminadab and wife of Aaron (Ex 6:23).

ELISHUA (*God [El] is [my] salvation*). A son of David (2Sa 5:15; 1Ch 14:5). Elishama (1Ch 3:6, ftn) is probably a scribal error in Hebrew mss.

ELIUD (*God [El] is [my] grandeur*). An ancestor of Jesus; in the fifth generation before Jesus, he was the son of Akim and the father of Eleazar (Mt 1:14-15).

ELIZABETH (God is [my] oath). The wife of Zechariah and mother of John the Baptist (Lk 1:5-60).

ELIZAPHAN (*God [El] is [my] hiding*).
1. A Levite (Ex 6:22; Lev 10:4). The son of Uzziel, the leader of the families of the Kohathite clans who had the responsibility to take care of the ark, the table, the lampstand, and the vessels of the sanctuary (Nu 3:30; 1Ch 15:8; 2Ch 29:13).
2. A leader of Zebulun (Nu 34:25).

ELIZUR (*God [El] is [my] rock*). A leader of Reuben, the son of Shedeur; one of the leaders who helped Moses take the census in the wilderness (Nu 1:5; 2:10; 7:30, 35; 10:18).

ELKANAH (*God [El] has possessed*).
1. The grandson of Korah (Ex 6:24; 1Ch 6:23).
2. The father of Samuel (1Sa 1:1, 4, 8, 19, 21, 23; 2:11, 20; 1Ch 6:27, 34).
3. A Levite (1Ch 6:25, 36).
4. Possibly identical with 3 (1Ch 6:26, 35).
5. A Levite (1Ch 9:16).
6. A Levite who joined David at Ziklag (1Ch 12:6).
7. A doorkeeper for the ark, perhaps identical with 6 (1Ch 15:23).
8. A prince of Ahaz (2Ch 28:7).

ELKOSH The birthplace of Nahum the prophet (Na 1:1).

ELLASAR A city-state in Babylonia in the time of Abraham (Ge 14:1, 9).

ELM *See Terebinth.*

ELMADAM An ancestor of Jesus (Lk 3:28).

ELNAAM (*God [El] is pleasantness*). The father of two of David's mighty men known as the "Thirty" (1Ch 11:46).

ELNATHAN (*God [El] has given*).
1. The grandfather of Jehoiachin (2Ki 24:8).
2. Levites who helped Ezra (Ezr 8:16).
3. The son of Acbor and a high official of King Jehoiakim (Jer 26:22; 36:12, 25).

ELOHE *See El Elohe Israel.*

ELOHIM (*a god, the God; Mighty One*).

Used of the God of Israel:
The most frequent Hebrew word for God, gods, angels, or magistrates. The plural *Elohim* when used for God in the OT is singular in meaning, and is often called "plural of majesty." *See God, Names of, Elohim; El.*

Used of Pagan Gods:
The Philistine god Dagon (Jdg 16:23-24), the Sidonian goddess Ashtoreth (1Ki 11:5, 33), the Moabite god Chemosh (1Ki 11:33), the Ammonite god Chemosh (1Ki 11:33), and Baal-Zebub of Ekron (2Ki 1:2, 3, 6) are also referred to in the plural.

Used of Other Groups:
Judges (Ex 21:6; 22:8-9), heavenly beings (Ps 8:5), those high among people (Ps 36:7).

ELOI, ELOI, LAMA SABACHTHANI (*My God, my God, why have you forsaken me?*). One of the seven cries of Jesus from the cross (Mt 27:46; Mk 15:34 w Ps 22:1).

ELON, ELONITE (*a species of a mighty tree*).
1. The father-in-law of Esau (Ge 26:34; 36:2).
2. A son of Zebulun (Ge 46:14) and his clan (Nu 26:26).
3. A town of Dan (Jos 19:43).
4. A Hebrew judge (Jdg 12:11-12).

ELON BETHHANAN (*tree of Bethhanan*). A town of Dan (1Ki 4:9). Perhaps identical with Elon (Jos 19:43).

ELOTH *See Elath.*

ELPAAL (*God [El] creates*). A Benjamite (1Ch 8:11-12, 18).

ELPELET (*God [El] is deliverance*). A son of David (1Ch 14:5). Called Eliphelet (1Ch 3:6).

ELTEKEH (*meeting place*). A city of Dan (Jos 19:44; 21:23).

ELTEKON (*God [El] has arranged*). A city of Judah (Jos 15:59).

ELTOLAD (*generation* IDB; *kindred of God [El]* ISBE; *God [El] + place where children could be obtained* KB). A city of Judah (Jos 15:30; 19:4). Called Tolad (1Ch 4:29).

E

ELUL The sixth month in sacred sequence, month twelve in civil sequence. The returned Jews finish the wall of Jerusalem in (Ne 6:15). Zerubbabel builds the temple in (Hag 1:14-15).

A transitional season from dry to rainy (August-September). The season for processing grapes, figs, and olives. *See Month, 6.*

ELUZAI (*God [El] is my strength*). A Benjamite warrior who joined David while he was in exile from Saul at the Philistine city of Ziklag (1Ch 12:5). He was able to use a bow or sling with either hand.

ELYMAS (possibly *wise one* hence *magician*). A Jewish magician and false prophet associated with Proconsul Sergius Paulus at Paphos on Cyprus. He was punished with blindness when he opposed Paul and Barnabas and tried to turn the proconsul from the faith (Ac 13:8-11).

ELZABAD (*God [El] has given*).
1. A Gadite warrior who joined David at Ziklag (1Ch 12:12).
2. A Korahite gatekeeper (1Ch 26:7).

ELZAPHAN *See Elizaphan.*

EMANCIPATION Of all Hebrew servants (Ex 21:2; Lev 25:8-17, 39-41; Dt 15:12).

Proclamation of. By Cyrus (2Ch 36:23; Ezr 1:1-4), by Zedekiah (Jer 34:8-11). *See Exodus; Jubilee.*

EMBALMING Of Jacob (Ge 50:2-3), of Joseph (Ge 50:26), of Asa (2Ch 16:14), of Jesus (Mk 15:46; 16:1; Jn 19:39-40).

EMBEZZLEMENT (Lk 16:1-7). *See Dishonesty.*

EMBLEMS OF THE HOLY SPIRIT *See Holy Spirit, Emblems of.*

EMBROIDERY In blue, purple, and scarlet, on the curtains of the tabernacle (Ex 26:1, 36; 27:16), on the ephod and coat of the high priest, mingled with gold (Ex 28:4-5, 39). Bezalel and Oholiab divinely inspired for in the work of the tabernacle (Ex 35:30-35; 38:22-23). On the garments of Sisera (Jdg 5:30). On the garments of women (Ps 45:14; Eze 16:10, 13, 18). On the garments of princes (Eze 26:16).

See Tapestry.

EMEK *See Beth Emek; Emek Keziz.*

EMEK KEZIZ (*valley of Keziz*). A valley and city of Benjamin (Jos 18:21).

EMERALD One of the jewels in the priestly breastplate (Ex 28:18; 39:11; Jer 17:1).

Figurative:
Ezekiel uses imagery of the Creation and the Fall to picture the career of the king of Tyre; unlike Adam, who was naked, the king is pictured as a fully clothed priest, ordained to guard God's holy place; the nine stones listed are among the twelve worn by the priest (Eze 28:13).

Since God dwells in "unapproachable light" and is one "whom no one has seen or can see" (1Ti 6:16), he is described in terms of the reflected brilliance of precious stones—an emerald rainbow around the throne (Rev 4:3).

Symbolic:
In the foundation of the holy city (Rev 21:19).
See Minerals of the Bible, 1; Stones.

EMERGENCY *See Decision.*

EMERODS *See Hemorrhoids.*

EMITES (*frightening beings*). Early inhabitants of the area around Kiriathaim which is E of the Dead Sea. They were defeated in the time of Abraham by the four invading kings (Ge 14:5). A race of giants who were "strong and numerous, and as tall as the Anakites" (Dt 2:10-11). *See Rephaites.*

EMMANUEL *See Immanuel.*

EMMAUS (*hot springs*). A village seven miles from Jerusalem (Lk 24:7-35).

EMPLOYEE

Rights of an Employee:
Prompt payment (Lev 19:13). Participation of produce (Lev 25:6). Just compensation (Mt 10:10; Lk 10:7; Ro 4:4; Col 4:1; 1Ti 5:18). Oppression of (Dt 24:14-15; Pr 22:16; Mal 3:5; Lk 15:15-17; Jas 5:4). Kindness to exemplified (Ru 2:4; Lk 15:17, 19).

Character of Unrighteous: (Job 7:1-3; 14:1, 6; Mt 20:1-16; 21:33-41; Jn 10:12-13).
See Employer; Master; Servant; Slave.

EMPLOYER Required: To grant a Sabbath rest (Ex 20:10; Dt 5:14). To make prompt payment (Lev 19:13; Dt 24:15; Jas 5:4-5). To be kind (Lev 25:39-43; Job 31:13-15; Eph 6:9; Phm 15-16). Not to oppress (Dt 24:14-15; Pr 22:16; Mal 3:5). To accord just compensation (Jer 22:13; Mt 10:10; 20:1-15; Lk 10:7; Ro 4:4; Col 4:1; 1Ti 5:18).

See Employee; Labor; Master; Servant.

EMULATION To create a desire for salvation (Ro 11:11, 14). To generosity in giving to aid others (2Co 8:1-8; 9:1-5). To love and good works (Heb 10:24).

Illustrated: In Esau's marriages (Ge 28:6-9). In Jacob's household (Ge 30:1-24).

EN EGLAIM (*spring of two calves*). Possibly modern Ain Feshka at the NW corner of the Dead Sea (Eze 47:10).

EN GANNIM (*spring of gardens*).

1. A city of Judah (Jos 15:34).
2. A city of Issachar (Jos 19:21; 21:29).

EN GEDI (*spring of young goat*). Called Hazazon Tamar. Built by the Amorites (Ge 14:7; 2Ch 20:2). A city allotted to Judah (Jos 15:62). Famous for its vineyards (SS 1:14).

Wilderness of, near the Dead Sea. David uses as a stronghold (1Sa 23:29; 24). Cave of (1Sa 24:3).

EN HADDAH (*spring of gladness*). A city of Issachar probably located c. six miles E of Mount Tabor (Jos 19:21).

EN HAKKORE (*spring of the partridge* or *spring of the caller*). A spring at Lehi from which Samson drank after slaughtering the Philistines (Jdg 15:19).

EN HAZOR (*spring of Hazor*). En Hazor was a fortified city assigned to Naphtali (Jos 19:37).

EN MISHPAT (*spring of judgment*). The ancient name of Kadesh (Ge 14:7). *See Kadesh.*

EN RIMMON (*spring of Rimmon*). A city of Judah in the Negev, later assigned to Simeon (Jos 19:7; 1Ch 4:32). Probably identical with Ain and Rimmon (Jos 15:32; 1Ch 4:32). Those returning from the Exile resettled at En Rimmon (Ne 11:29).

EN ROGEL (*spring of the fuller*, or *wanderer*, or *spy*). A spring near Jerusalem (Jos 15:7; 18:16; 2Sa 17:17), possibly the Jackal Well (Ne 2:13). A rebellious feast at (1Ki 1:9).

EN SHEMESH (*spring of Shemesh*, [sun or pagan god]). A place on the N boundary of Judah and the S boundary of Benjamin (Jos 15:7; 18:17). The last spring on the road between Jerusalem and the Jordan Valley was found there. En Shemesh has been called the "Spring of the Apostles" since the fifteenth century.

EN TAPPUAH (*spring of apple*). A spring of uncertain location at the S border of Manasseh (Jos 17:7); usually identified with modern Sheikh Abu Zarad c. eight miles S of Shechem. The town was a Canaanite stronghold that held out against the Israelites for a period of time during the conquest of the land by the Israelites.

ENAIM (*two springs*). It is most likely located in the high hill country SE of Jerusalem between Adullam and Timnah; KJV "open place" (Ge 38:14, 21).

ENAM A town in the western foothills of Judah (Jos 15:34).

ENAN (*spring*). The father of Ahira who was a military leader of the tribe of Naphtali and one who assisted in the Sinai census (Nu 1:15; 2:29; 7:78, 83; 10:27).

ENCAMPMENT Places where the Israelites encamped on the way from Egypt to Canaan (Nu 33). Also headquarters of armies (1Sa 13:16; 2Ch 32:1). *See Camp.*

ENCHANTMENT The use of any form of magic, including divination; forbidden to God's people (Dt 18:10; Ac 8:9, 11; 13:8, 10; 19:19). *See Divination; Magic; Sorcery.*

END OF THE WORLD Consummation of the age (Mt 13:39, 49; 24:3; 28:20; Heb 9:26). *See Eschatology.*

ENDOR (*spring of Dor*). A city of Issachar allotted to Manasseh (Jos 17:11). Deborah triumphs at, over Sisera (Jdg 4; Ps 83:10). The medium of, consulted by Saul (1Sa 28:7-25).

ENDURANCE *See Perseverance.*

ENEAS *See Aeneas.*

ENEMY

Kindness to:

Commanded (Ex 23:4-5; Pr 25:21-22; Mt 5:43-48; Lk 6:27-36; Ro 12:14, 20).

Forgiveness of:

Commanded (Mt 6:12-15; 18:21-35; Mk 11:25; Lk 17:3-4; Eph 4:31-32; Col 3:13; 1Pe 3:9).

Instances of Forgiveness—

Esau, of Jacob (Ge 33:4, 11). Joseph, of his brothers (Ge 45:5-15; 50:19-21). Moses, of Miriam and Aaron (Nu 12:1-13). David, of Saul (1Sa 24:10-12; 26:9, 23; 2Sa 1:14-17), of Shimei (2Sa 16:9-13; 19:23; 1Ki 2:8-9), of Absalom and his co-conspirators (2Sa 18:5, 12, 32-33; 19:6, 12-13). The prophet of Judah by Jeroboam (1Ki 13:3-6). Jesus, of his persecutors (Lk 23:34). Stephen, of his murderers (Ac 7:60).

Destruction of:

Requested by David (Ps 35:1-7). The wickedness of David's enemies (Ps 56:2, 5-6; 57:4, 6; 62:4; 69:4; 71:10; 102:8; 109:2-5; 129:1-3). *See Prayer, Imprecatory.*

Rejoicing at the destruction of, forbidden (Pr 24:17-18). Rejoicing at the destruction of, not practiced by Job (Job 31:29-30).

Figurative:

Of the devil (Mt 13:25, 28, 39).

ENGAGEMENT *See Betrothal.*

ENGINE NIV "machines" of war (2Ch 26:15) or "battering rams" (Eze 26:9). *See Armies; Fort.*

ENGRAFTING *See Graft.*

ENGRAVING On the stones set in the priest's breastplate (Ex 28:9-11, 21, 36; 39:8-14). In making idols (Ex 32:4), in the priest's ephod (Ex 39:6), in the priest's crown (Ex 39:30).

ENOCH (*initiated* ISBE; *follower* KB).

1. Cain's eldest son (Ge 4:17).
2. A city built by Cain (Ge 4:17).
3. The father of Methuselah (Ge 5:21-22). Walked with God and then was translated to heaven by God (Ge 5:24; Heb 11:5).

ENOCH, BOOKS OF Apocalyptic literature written by various authors and circulated under the name of Enoch; written c. 163 B.C. to A.D. 50. Possibly quoted in Jude 14-15.

ENON *See Aenon.*

ENOSH (*[mortal] man*). The son of Seth (Ge 4:26; 5:6-11; 1Ch 1:1; Lk 3:38).

ENQUIRING OF GOD *See Affliction, Prayer Under; Prayer.*

ENSIGN A standard or banner (Ps 74:4; Isa 5:26; 11:10, 12; 18:3; 30:17; 31:9; Zec 9:16). *See Banner; Standard.*

ENTERTAINMENTS Often great (Ge 21:8; Da 5:1; Lk 5:29). Preparations made for (Ge 18:6-7; Mt 22:4; Lk 15:23).

Given on Occasions of:

Weaning children (Ge 21:8). Ratifying covenants (Ge 26:30; 31:54). Offering voluntary sacrifice (Ge 31:54; Dt 12:6-7; 1Sa 1:4-5). After wine was trodden (Jdg 9:27). Harvest home (Ru 3:2-7; Isa 9:3). Festivals (1Sa 20:5, 24-26). Sheepshearing (1Sa 25:2, 36; 2Sa 13:23). Return of friends (2Sa 12:4; Lk 15:23). Coronation of kings (1Ki 1:9, 18-19; 1Ch 12:39-40; Hos 7:5). Taking leave of friends (1Ki 19:21). National deliverance (Est 8:17; 9:17-19). Marriage (Mt 22:2). Birth days (Mk 6:21).

Kinds of, Mentioned in Scripture:

Dinner (Ge 43:16; Mt 22:4; Lk 14:12). Banquet (Est 5:4-6). Served often by hired servants (Mt 22:3; Jn 2:5). Served often by members of the family (Lk 10:40; Jn 12:2). Supper (Lk 14:12; Jn 12:2). Under the direction of a master of the feast (Jn 2:8-9).

Invitations to:

Should be sent to the poor (Dt 14:29, w Lk 14:13). Often by the master in person (2Sa 13:24; Est 5:4; Zep 1:7; Lk 7:36). Often only to relatives and friends (1Ki 1:9; Lk 14:12). Often addressed to many (Lk 14:16). Repeated through servants when all things were ready (Lk 14:17).

Often Given in:

The house (Lk 5:29). Near landmarks (1Ki 1:9). The court of the house (Est 1:5-6; Lk 7:36-37). The upper room or guest chamber (Mk 14:14-15). The house (Lk 5:29).

Guests at:

Had their feet washed when they came a distance (Ge 18:4; 43:24; Lk 7:38, 44). Arranged according to rank (Ge 43:33; 1Sa 9:22; Lk 14:10). Often had separate dishes (Ge 43:34; 1Sa 1:4). A choice portion reserved for principal guests (Ge 43:34; 1Sa 1:5; 9:23-24). Began with thanksgiving (1Sa 9:13; Mk 8:6). Often scenes of great intemperance (1Sa 25:36; Da 5:3-4; Hos 7:5). Portions often sent to the absent (Ne 8:10; Est 9:19). None asked to eat more than he liked at (Est 1:8). Men and women did not usually meet at (Est 1:8-9; Mk 6:21, w Mt 14:11). Given by the guests in return (Job 1:4; Lk 14:12). Usually anointed (Ps 23:5; Lk 7:46). Music and dancing often introduced at (Am 6:5; Mk 6:22; Lk 15:25). Eager to take chief seats at, condemned (Mt 23:6; Lk 14:7-8). Often ate from the same dish (Mt 26:23). Concluded with a hymn (Mk 14:26). None admitted after the master had risen and shut the door (Lk 13:24-25). Offense given by refusing to go to (Lk 14:18, 24). Anxiety to have many guests at, alluded to (Lk 14:22-23). *See Feasts.*

ENTHUSIASM Instances of: Gideon (Jdg 6-7), Jehu (2Ki 9:1-14; 10:1-28).

See Zeal.

ENUMERATION *See Census.*

ENVY

Characteristic of:

Depravity (Ro 1:29; Tit 3:3). Worldliness (Ro 13:13; 1Co 3:3; 12:20; Gal 5:19-21; 1Ti 6:4; Jas 3:14, 16; 4:5).

Not characteristic of love (1Co 13:4).

Described as:

Destructive (Job 5:2). The cause of rotting bones (Pr 14:30). All consuming (Pr 27:4; SS 8:6). Drives people to achievement (Ecc 4:4). As unyielding as the grave (SS 8:6). Where envy and selfish ambition are found, disorder and every evil practice are found (Jas 3:16).

Forbidden: (Ps 37:1, 7; 49:16-20; Pr 3:31-32; 23:17-18; 24:1-2, 19-20; Ro 13:13; Gal 5:25-26; Jas 5:8-9; 1Pe 2:1-2).

Punishment for: (Eze 35:11).

Instances of:

Cain, of Abel (Ge 4:4-8). Sarah, of Hagar (Ge 16:5-6; 21:9-10). Philistines, of Isaac because of the large number of flocks and herds he owned (Ge 26:14). Rachel, of Leah (Ge 30:1). Leah, of Rachel (Ge 30:15). Laban's sons, of Jacob (Ge 31:1). Joseph's brothers, of Joseph (Ge 37:4-11, 18-20; Ac 7:9). Joshua, of Eldad and Medad (Nu 11:28-30). Miriam and Aaron, of Moses (Nu 12:1-10). Korah, Dathan, and Abiram, of Moses (Nu 16:3; Ps 106:16-18). Saul, of David (1Sa 18:8-9, 29; 1Sa 20:31). Haman, of Mordecai (Est 5:13). Asaph, at prosperity of wicked (Ps 73:2-3). The wicked, at the prosperity of the righteous (Ps 112:10; Isa 26:11). The princes of Babylon, of Daniel (Da 6:3-4).

Priests, of Jesus (Mt 27:18; Mk 15:10; Jn 11:47-48). Jews, of Paul and Barnabas (Ac 13:45; 17:5).

See Jealousy.

EPAENETUS *See Epenetus.*

EPAPHRAS (*handsome*). A co-worker with Paul (Col 1:7; 4:12; Phm 23).

EPAPHRODITUS (*handsome*). A messenger of Paul (Php 2:25; 4:18). Sick at Rome (Php 2:26-27, 30).

EPENETUS (*praised*). A convert to Christ in the province of Asia (Ro 16:5).

EPHAH (*darkness*).

1. A son of Midian (Ge 25:4; 1Ch 1:33; Isa 60:6).
2. Caleb's concubine (1Ch 2:46).
3. A son of Jahdai (1Ch 2:47).
4. A measure of about 3/5 bushel. *See Measure, Dry Capacity.*

EPHAI (*my bird*). A Netophathite (Jer 40:8). Sons warned Gedaliah (Jer 40:8-16; 41:3).

EPHER (*[small] gazelle*).

1. A son of Midian (Ge 25:4; 1Ch 1:33).
2. A son of Ezra (1Ch 4:17).
3. A chief of Manasseh (1Ch 5:24).

EPHES DAMMIM (*border of Dammim [blood]*). A place between Socoh and Azekah in Judah, where David killed Goliath (1Sa 17:1). Called Pas Dammim (1Ch 11:13).

EPHESIANS, EPISTLE TO THE

Author: The apostle Paul

Date: c. A.D. 60

Outline:

I. Greetings (1:1-2).
II. The Divine Purpose: The Glory and Headship of Christ (1:3-14).
III. Prayer That Christians May Realize God's Purpose and Power (1:15-23).
IV. Steps Toward the Fulfillment of God's Purpose (chs. 2-3).
- A. Salvation of Individuals by Grace (2:1-10).
- B. Reconciliation of Jew and Gentile Through the Cross (2:11-18).
- C. Uniting of Jew and Gentile in One Household (2:19-22).
- D. Revelation of God's Wisdom Through the Church (3:1-13).
- E. Prayer for Deeper Experience of God's Fullness (3:14-21).

V. Practical Ways to Fulfill God's Purpose in the Church (4:1-6:20).
- A. Unity (4:1-6).
- B. Maturity (4:7-16).
- C. Renewal of Personal Life (4:17-5:20).
- D. Deference in Personal Relationships (5:21-6:9).
  1. Principle (5:21).
  2. Husbands and wives (5:22-33).
  3. Children and parents (6:1-4).
  4. Slaves and masters (6:5-9).
- E. Strength in the Spiritual Conflict (6:10-20).

VI. Conclusion, Final Greetings and Benediction (6:21-24).

EPHESUS Paul visits and preaches in (Ac 18:19-21; 19; 20:16-38). Apollos visits and preaches in (Ac 18:18-28). Sceva's sons attempt to expel a demon in (Ac 19:13-16). Timothy directed by Paul to remain at (1Ti 1:3). Onesiphorus lives at (2Ti 1:18). Paul sends Tychicus to (2Ti 4:12). Church at (Rev 1:11). Apocalyptic message to (Rev 2:1-7).

See Ephesians, Epistle to the.

EPHLAL (*judgment, arbitration*). A descendant of Judah through Perez and the family of Jerahmeel (1Ch 2:37).

EPHOD

1. A sacred vestment worn by the high priest. Described (Ex 25:7; 28:6-14, 31-35). Breastplate attached to (Ex 28:22-30). Making of (Ex 39:2-26). Worn by Aaron (Ex 39:5).

An ephod made by his mother was worn by Samuel as a young boy ministering before the Lord (1Sa 2:18), by the common priests (1Sa 22:18), by David (2Sa 6:14). Used as an oracle (1Sa 23:9, 12; 30:7-8).

As an idol—

Gideon made an ephod out of gold, placing it in his hometown of Ophrah, the ephod subsequently becoming an idol to Israel (Jdg 8:27). Micah from the hill country of Ephraim made one of gold (Jdg 17:5; 18:14). Prophecy concerning the absence of an ephod from Israel (Hos 3:4).

2. A man of Manasseh (Nu 34:23).

EPHPHATHA (*to open*). An Aramaic passive imperative transliterated into the Greek (Mk 7:34).

EPHRAIM (*doubly fruitful*).

1. The second son of Joseph (Ge 41:52). Adopted by Jacob (Ge 48:5). Blessed before Manasseh; prophecies concerning (Ge 48:14-20). Descendants of (Nu 26:35-37; 1Ch 7:20-27). Mourns for his sons (1Ch 7:21-22).

2. A tribe of Israel. Prophecy concerning (Ge 49:25-26; Isa 7; 9:18-21; 11:13; 28:1-6; Jer 31; Hos 5:13-14; Zec 9:10-13; 10:7-12). Numbered at Sinai and in the plains of Moab (Nu 1:33; 26:37). Place in camp and march (Nu 2:18, 24; 10:22). Blessed by Moses (Dt 33:13-17).

Territory allotted to, after the conquest of Canaan (Jos 16:5-9; 17:9-10, 15-18; 1Ch 7:28-29). Fail to expel the Canaanites (Jos 16:10). Take Bethel in battle (Jdg 1:22-25). Join Gideon against the Midianites (Jdg 7:24-25). Rebuke Gideon for not summoning them to join the war against the Midianites (Jdg 8:1). Their jealousy of Jephthah (Jdg 12:1). Defeated by him (Jdg 12:4-6). Receive

Ish-Bosheth as king (2Sa 2:8-9). Revolt from the house of David (1Ki 12:25; 2Ch 10:16). Jeroboam set up a golden calf in Bethel (1Ki 12:29). Some of the tribe join Judah under Asa (2Ch 15:9). Chastise Ahaz and Judah (2Ch 28:7). Join Hezekiah in reinstituting the Passover (2Ch 30:18). Join in the destruction of idols in Jerusalem (2Ch 31:1). Submit to the scepter of Josiah (2Ch 34:1-6). Envied other tribes (Isa 11:13). Exalted by other tribes (Hos 13:1). Reallotment of territory to, by Ezekiel (Eze 48:5). Worshiped Baal (Hos 13:1). Sin of, remembered by God (Hos 13:12).

Name of, applied to the ten tribes (2Ch 17:2; 25:6-7; Isa 7:8-9; 11:12-13; 17:3; Jer 31:18, 20; Hos 4:17; 5:3, 5; 6:4, 10; 8:11; 12:14). Tribe of, called Joseph (Rev 7:8).

3. Mount of. A range of low mountains (Jos 17:15-18). Joshua has his inheritance in (Jdg 2:9). Residence of Micah (Jdg 17:8). A place of hiding for the Israelites (1Sa 14:22). Sheba resides in (2Sa 20:21). Prophecy concerning its conversion (Jer 31:6). Noted for rich pastures (Jer 50:19).

4. A wood E of the Jordan. Absalom killed in (2Sa 18:6-17).

5. A gate of Jerusalem (2Ki 14:13; 2Ch 25:23; Ne 8:16; 12:39).

6. A city in the territory of Ephraim to which Jesus escapes to evade the persecution of Caiaphas (Jn 11:54).

EPHRAIMITE (*doubly fruitful*). A member of the tribe of Ephraim (Jos 16:5-10; Jdg 12).

EPHRATH, EPHRATHAH (*fruitful land*).

1. A place near Bethel where Rachel died and was buried (Ge 35:16, 19; 48:7).
2. A name of Bethlehem (Ru 4:11; Mic 5:2).
3. The second wife of Caleb, mother of Hur (1Ch 2:19, 50; 4:4).
4. An area associated with Kiriath Jearim (Ps 132:6, ftn).

EPHRON (*gazelle*).

1. The son of Zohar; the Hittite from whom Abraham purchased the field containing the cave of Machpelah, to the E of Mamre (Ge 23:8-17; 25:9; 49:29-30; 50:13).
2. Mount Ephron, a district whose cities were on the border of Judah (Jos 15:9).
3. A city near Bethel from which Abijah took Jeroboam I (2Ch 13:19).
4. A strongly fortified city between Karnaim and Beth Shan (Scythopolis) in the Maccabean period. It tried to prevent the passage of Judas and the Israelites with him, but Judas took the city, plundered it, and killed all its male inhabitants (1Mc 5:46-52; 2Mc 12:27-29).

EPIC Heroic poetry. Miriam's song (Ex 15:1-19, 21). Deborah's song (Jdg 5). *See Poetry.*

EPICUREANS A style of life familiar to Solomon long before Epicurus (341-270 B.C.) defined the doctrine through his school of philosophy in Athens (Ecc 2:1-10). Paul confronts a group of Epicurean and Stoic philosophers at a meeting of the Court of the Areopagus (Mars Hill) which is NW of the Acropolis and connected to it (Ac 17:16-34). *See Aratus; Cleanthes; Stoicism; Stoics.* It is suspected that by the Christian era the responsibility of the Court of the Areopagus was to censor the religious life of the community, and because of Paul's teaching concerning Jesus and the Resurrection they were exercising that right of censor.

See Sensuality.

EPILEPSY *See Seizures.*

EPISTLE (*letter*). Formal letters containing Christian doctrine and exhortation, referring particularly to the twenty-one epistles of the NT, divided into Pauline and General epistles. Not all the letters of the apostles have survived (1Co 5:9; Col 4:16).

EPISTLES, GENERAL *See General Letters.*

EPISTLES, PASTORAL *See Pastoral Epistles.*

EQUALITY *See Mankind, Equality of All People.*

EQUITY *See Justice.*

ER (*watcher, watchful*).

1. The eldest son of Judah (Ge 38:3, 6-7; 46:12; Nu 26:19; 1Ch 2:3).
2. A son of Judah's son Shelah (1Ch 4:21).
3. An ancestor of Jesus (Lk 3:28).

ERAN, ERANITE (*watcher, watchful*). A grandson of Ephraim and his clan (Nu 26:36).

ERASTUS (*beloved*).

1. A convert of Paul sent with Timothy from Ephesus into Macedonia on an errand (Ac 19:22).
2. The "city treasurer" or the "city director of public works" of Corinth; a Christian (Ro 16:23).
3. A companion of Paul who remained in Corinth (2Ti 4:20). Possibly the same as 1 above.

ERECH

1. A Babylonian city founded by Nimrod (Ge 10:10), located forty miles NW of Ur toward Babylon.
2. The men of Erech along with the men of Tripolis, Persia, and Babylon were settled in the cities of Samaria and elsewhere in Trans-Euphrates by Ashurbanipal (Ezr 4:9-10).

ERI, ERITE (*watcher*). The fifth son of Gad, the grandson of Jacob (Ge 46:16) and his clan (Nu 26:16).

ERRORS In teachers and doctrines. *See Teachers, False.*

ESAIAS *See Isaiah.*

ESARHADDON (*Ashur has given a brother [for a lost son]*). The son and successor of Sennacherib after Sennacherib was murdered by his sons Adrammelech and Sharezer in 681 B.C.; ruled Assyria 681-669 B.C. (2Ki 19:37; 2Ch 32:21; Isa 37:38); restored the city of Babylon; conquered Egypt; brought deportees into Samaria (Ezr 4:2); took Manasseh captive (2Ch 33:11).

ESAU (*hairy*). The eldest of twin sons born to Isaac and Rebekah. Birth of (Ge 25:19-26; 1Ch 1:34). A hunter (Ge 25:27-28). Beloved by Isaac (Ge 25:27-28). Sold his birthright for a single meal of stew (Ge 25:29-34; 27:36; Heb 12:16). He was alternately called Edom because he had red coloring; Edom means red (Ge 25:25, 30). Married two Hittite women (Ge 26:34). Polygamy of (Ge 26:34; 28:9; 36:2-3). His marriages a grief to Isaac and Rebekah (Ge 26:35). Was defrauded of his father's blessing by Jacob (Ge 27; Heb 11:20). Met Jacob on the return of the latter from Haran (Ge 33:1). With Jacob, buried his father (Ge 35:29).

Descendants of (Ge 36; 1Ch 1:35-57). Called Edom (Ge 25:30; 36:1, 8). His name used to denote his descendants and their country (Dt 2:5; Jer 49:8, 10; Ob 6). Ancestor of Edomites (Jer 49:8). Enmity of descendants of, toward descendants of Jacob (Ob 10-14). Prophecies concerning (Ob 18).

ESCAPE

God Provides for the Righteous:

Noah and his family (Ge 7:7). The infant Jesus (Mt 2:13). By salvation (Ps 68:20). From temptation (Ecc 7:26; 1Co 10:13; 2Ti 2:26; 2Pe 1:4).

No Escape From the Judgment of God:

Adam and Eve (Ge 3:7-11). Cain (Ge 4:9-12). Mankind (Job 34:21-30; Ps 56:7; Isa 10:1-3; Mt 23:33; Ro 2:3; 1Th 5:2-3; Heb 2:2-3; 12:25-26; Rev 6:15-17).

See Sin, Fruits of; Punishment of; Judgment; Judgments.

ESCHATOLOGY (*study of last events*). Division of systematic theology dealing with the doctrine of last things such as death, resurrection, second coming of Christ, end of the age, divine judgment, and the future state. The OT teaches a future resurrection and judgment day (Job 19:25-27; Isa 25:6-9; 26:19-21; Da 12:2-3).

The NT interprets, enlarges, and completes the OT eschatology. It stresses the Resurrection (Ro 8:11; 1Co 15), the second coming of Christ (Mt 16:27; Lk 17:30; 1Co 1:7; 4:5; 1Th 2:19; 3:13; 4:13-18; 2Th 1:7-10; 2:1-6; 1Pe 1:7; 1Jn 2:28), the final judgment when the unsaved are cast into hell (Rev 20), and the righteous enter heaven (Mt 25:31-46). Christians differ on how the Millennium is to be interpreted, dividing themselves into amillennialists, postmillennialists, and premillennialists (Rev 20:1-6). *See Millennium.*

ESCHEAT *See Confiscation.*

ESDRAELON (*the valley of God's sowing* or *God will sow*). Mentioned as "Esdraelon" only in the Apocrypha. The Valley of Jezreel which lies between Galilee on the N and Samaria on the S (Jos 17:16; Jdg 6:33). Assigned to Issachar (Jos 15:56). Known as the "fertile valley."

ESDRAS, BOOKS OF *See Apocrypha.*

ESEK (*dispute*). A well dug by Isaac's servants in the valley near Gerar. A dispute arose between Isaac's herdsmen and the herdsmen of Gerar over rights to the water, so he named it Esek which means *dispute*. Isaac's men moved to another place and found the same problem, so he named it Sitnah which means *opposition*. Finally they dug a third well that no one quarreled over, so he named Rehoboth, which means *room* (Ge 26:19-22).

ESHAN (*support*). A city in Judah (Jos 15:52).

ESH-BAAL (*man of Baal*). Ish-Bosheth, the youngest son of Saul; he was made king over Israel by Abner to repudiate David's claim to the throne; he ruled two years and then was murdered by David's men (2Sa 2:8-10; 4:5-12). He was originally called Esh-baal (1Ch 8:33; 9:39).

ESHBAN (*man of understanding*). A son of Dishon, a Horite chief from the region of Mt. Seir (Ge 36:26; 1Ch 1:41).

ESHCOL (*[grape] cluster*).

1. An Amorite, and ally of Abraham (Ge 14:13, 24).
2. A valley or brook near Hebron (Nu 13:23-24; 32:9; Dt 1:24).

ESHEK (*oppressor*). A descendant of Jonathan (1Ch 8:38-40).

ESHTAOL, ESHTAOLITES (*[place of oracles] inquiry*). A town of Judah (Jos 15:33). Allotted to Dan (Jos 19:41; Jdg 18:2, 8, 11). Samson moved by the Spirit of the Lord near (Jdg 13:25). Samson buried near (Jdg 16:31).

ESHTEMOA, ESHTEMOH (*[place where oracle is] heard*).

1. A town of Canaan assigned to Judah (Jos 15:50). Allotted to the Aaronites (Jos 21:14; 1Ch 6:57). David shared the spoil with (1Sa 30:28).
2. A descendant of Ezra (1Ch 4:17, 19).

ESHTON (possibly *hen-pecked [husband]* or *effeminate*). A son of Mehir, the son of Kelub (1Ch 4:11-12).

ESLI (*Yahweh sets apart*). An ancestor of Jesus (Lk 3:25).

ESROM *See Hezron.*

ESSENES An important Jewish community which was flourishing in Israel during the lifetime of Jesus. They were not mentioned in the Bible, but described in Josephus and Philo, and are presumed to be the inhabitants of Qumran, where Dead Sea Scrolls were discovered. Most lived communal, celibate lives. They observed the law strictly; they practiced ceremonial baptisms; they were apocalyptic; they opposed the temple priesthood. *See Testaments, Time Between.*

ESTATE *See Land.*

ESTHER (Persian *star*, possibly *[Babylonian goddess] Ishtar*). Called also Hadassah (Est 2:7). The cousin of Mordecai (Est 2:7, 15). Chosen to be queen (Est 2:17). Tells the king of the plot against his life (Est 2:22). Fasts on account of the decree to destroy the Israelites; accuses Haman to the king; intercedes for her people (Est 4-9).

ESTHER, BOOK OF

Author: Anonymous

Date: Shortly after the events narrated, c. 460 B.C.

Outline:

I. The Feasts of Xerxes (1:1-2:18).
  A. Vashti Deposed (ch. 1).
  B. Esther Made Queen (2:1-18).
II. The Feasts of Esther (2:19-7:10).
  A. Mordecai Uncovers a Plot (2:19-23).
  B. Haman's Plot (ch. 3).
  C. Mordecai Persuades Esther to Help (ch. 4).
  D. Esther's Request to the King: First Banquet (5:1-8).
  E. A Sleepless Night (5:9-6:14).
  F. Haman Hanged: The Second Banquet (ch. 7).
III. The Feasts of Purim (chs. 8-10).
  A. The King's Edict in Behalf of the Jews (ch. 8).
  B. The Institution of Purim (ch. 9).
  C. The Promotion of Mordecai (ch. 10).

ETAM (possibly *place of birds of prey*).

1. A rock where Samson was bound and delivered to the Philistines (Jdg 15:8, 11-13).
2. A name in the list of Judah's descendants, but probably referring to 4 (1Ch 4:3).
3. A village of Simeon (1Ch 4:32).
4. A city in Judah (2Ch 11:6).

ETERNAL LIFE Participation in the life of Jesus Christ, the eternal Son of God (Jn 1:4; 10:10; 17:3; Ro 6:23), which reaches its fruition in the life to come (Mt 25:46; Jn 6:54; Ro 2:7; Tit 3:7). It is endless in its duration and divine in quality. *See Immortality; Life, Everlasting.*

ETERNAL PUNISHMENT *See Punishment, Eternal.*

ETERNITY God inhabits (Isa 57:15; Mic 5:2), rules (Jer 10:10).

God, adoration for (Ps 30:12; 41:13), steadfastness of (Ps 72:17; 90:2; Mt 6:13), righteousness of (Ps 119:142; 2Co 9:9). *See God, Eternity of.*

Priestly order of Melchizedek (Ps 110:4). *See Christ, Eternity of.*

Angels (Jude 6). *See Life, Everlasting; Punishment, Eternal.*

ETH KAZIN A landmark in the boundary line of Zebulun (Jos 19:13).

ETHAM (possibly *fort*). The second camping place of Israel (Ex 13:20; Nu 33:6-8).

ETHAN (*long lived, ever-flowing [streams]*).

1. An exceptionally wise man in Solomon's time; an Ezrahite (1Ki 4:31; Ps 89:T).
2. A son of Zerah (1Ch 2:6, 8).
3. A descendant of Gershon (1Ch 6:42-43).
4. A Levite singer (1Ch 6:44; 15:17, 19).

ETHANIM (*ever-flowing [streams]*). Seventh month in sacred sequence, First in civil sequence. The Feast of Trumpets in (Lev 23:23-25). The Day of Atonement, on the tenth day of (Lev 23:26-32). The Feast of Tabernacles, beginning on the fifteenth day of (Lev 23:33-43). The Jubilee proclaimed on the tenth day of the fiftieth year (Lev 25:9). The temple dedicated in and the ark restored (1Ki 8:2). The altar restored in, after the Captivity (Ezr 3:1, 6). Called Tishri in current Jewish calendar.

Beginning of the early rains (September-October), the time of plowing. *See Month, 7.*

ETHBAAL (*with [him is] Baal*). The king of Sidon; the father of Jezebel (1Ki 16:31).

ETHER (perhaps *perfume*). A city of Canaan. Assigned to Judah (Jos 15:42). Subsequently allotted to Simeon (Jos 19:7). Called Token in the parallel passage (1Ch 4:32).

ETHIOPIA A region in Africa, inhabited by the descendants of Ham, S of Egypt. Was called the land of Cush (Ge 10:6; 1Ch 1:9; Isa 11:11). Rivers of (Ge 10:6; Isa 18:1). Moses marries a Cushite woman (Nu 12:1). Tirhakah, the king of Ethiopia, attempted to stop Sennacherib's invasion of Israel in the time of Hezekiah (2Ki 19:9). Zerah was defeated by Asa in the Valley of Zephathah near Mareshah (2Ch 14:9-15; 16:8). Was ruled by Xerxes as a part of the Babylonian Empire (Est 1:1). Prophecies concerning the submission of (Ps 68:31; 87:4; Isa 45:14; Da 11:43). Desolation of (Isa 20:2-6; 43:3; Eze 30:4-9; Hab 3:7; Zep 2:12). Merchandise of (Isa 45:14). Ebed-Melech, an official in the royal palace, probably a eunuch and keeper of the royal harem, a native of; treats Jeremiah with kindness by interceding on his behalf before Zedekiah (Jer 38:7-13; 39:15-18). Warriors of (2Ch 12:3; 16:8; Jer 46:9; Eze 38:5). Bordered Egypt on the S (Eze 29:10). Candace, queen of (Ac 8:27). A eunuch from, becomes a disciple under the preaching of Philip (Ac 8:27-39).

ETHIOPIAN EUNUCH Treasurer of Candace, queen of the Ethiopians (Ac 8:26-39), became a Christian through Philip.

ETHNAN (*gift* or *hire*). One of the sons of Helah, of the tribe of Judah (1Ch 4:7); some identify him with Ithnan, a town in S Judah in the Negev (Jos 15:23).

ETHNI (*gift* or *hire*). An ancestor of Asaph, a musician (1Ch 6:41).

ETIQUETTE *See Manners.*

EUBULUS (*good counsel*). A Roman Christian who was a friend of Paul's during his second Roman imprisonment; he sent greetings with Paul's letter to Timothy (2Ti 4:21). His name is common in papyri and inscriptions.

EUCHARIST (*thanksgiving*). One name for the Lord's Supper, meaning "giving of thanks." *See Lord's Supper.*

Instituted (Mt 26:17-29; Mk 14:22-25; Lk 22:19-20; Jn 13:1-4). Celebrated by the early Church (Ac 2:42, 46; 20:7; 1Co 11:26). Bread and cup of, symbols of the body and blood of Christ (Mt 26:26-28; 1Co 10:16-17, 21-22; 11:23-25). Profanation of, forbidden (1Co 11:20-22, 33-34). Self-examination before taking, commanded (1Co 11:27-32).

EUNICE (*good victory*). The daughter of Lois, Timothy's mother, and the wife of a Gentile (Ac 16:1; 2Ti 1:5).

E

EUNUCH (*one emasculated*). Castrated males, used as custodians of royal harems and court officials (2Ki 20:18; Est 1:10-15; 2:21; Jer 41:16; Da 1:3; Ac 8:27). Not practiced by Israelites; eunuchs not allowed to enter the assembly of the Lord (Dt 23:1). *See Ethiopian Eunuch.*

Figurative of those who stay unmarried for the sake of the kingdom (Mt 19:10-12).

EUODIA (*good fragrance*). A Christian woman at Philippi (Php 4:2).

EUPHRATES (*to break forth*). A river in the Garden of Eden (Ge 2:14). The eastern limit of the kingdom of Israel (Ge 15:18; Ex 23:31; Dt 1:7; 11:24; Jos 1:4; 2Sa 8:3; 1Ki 4:21; 1Ch 5:9; 18:3). Pharaoh Neco, king of Egypt, made conquest to (2Ki 24:7; Jer 46:2-10). On the banks of, Jeremiah symbolically buries his belt (Jer 13:1-7; see v.4, ftn). Jeremiah instructs staff officer Seraiah son of Neriah to cast the roll containing prophecies against Babylon into the Euphrates (Jer 51:59-64).

Symbolic: Of the extension of the empire of Assyria (Isa 8:6-8). In the Apocalypse (Rev 9:14; 16:12).

EUROCLYDON, EURAQUILO *See Northeaster.*

EUTYCHUS (*fortunate*). A youth who fell asleep and fell out of the window to his death while Paul preached; was restored to life by Paul (Ac 20:9-10).

EVANGELISM *See Minister, Duties of; Zeal.*

EVANGELIST (*[a bringer of] good news*).

1. A Church leader (Eph 4:11). One who preached the good news of Jesus Christ from place to place (Ac 8:12, 26-39; 14:7; 1Co 1:17; 3:6). Philip is a typical example (Ac 21:8). Timothy was encouraged by Paul to do the work of an evangelist (2Ti 4:5).

2. In biblical studies: the author of a Gospel.

EVAPORATION (Ps 135:7; Jer 10:13; 51:16; Am 5:8; 9:6).

EVE (*life*). Creation of (Ge 1:26-28; 2:21-24; 1Ti 2:13). Named by Adam (Ge 2:23; 3:20). Deceived by Satan (Ge 3; 2Co 11:3; 1Ti 2:14). Clothed with fig leaves (Ge 3:7), with skins (Ge 3:21). Messiah promised to (Ge 3:15). Curse denounced against (Ge 3:16). Children of (Ge 4:1-2, 25; 5:3-4).

EVENING SACRIFICE One of two daily offerings prescribed in the Mosaic ritual (Ex 29:38-42; Nu 28:3-8).

EVENING, THE The day originally began with (Ge 1:5). Divided into two, commencing at 3 o'clock, and sunset (Ex 12:6; Nu 9:3).

Called the cool of the day (Ge 3:8). People cease from labor in (Ru 2:17; Ps 104:23). Wild beasts come forth in (Ps 59:6, 14). Where morning dawns and evening fades God calls forth songs of joy (Ps 65:8). The enemies of Jerusalem were so zealous to attack and defeat her that the soldiers encouraged each other to do battle at times of the day when attacks were rarely made, i.e., noon and evening (Jer 6:4-5).

A Time For:

Custom of sitting at the gates in (Ge 19:1). Meditation (Ge 24:63). Passover lamb killed in (Ex 12:6, 18). The golden lampstand lighted in (Ex 27:21, w Ex 30:8). Part of the daily sacrifice offered in (Ex 29:41; Ps 141:2; Da 9:21). All defiled persons unclean until (Lev 11:24-28; 15:5-7; 17:15; Nu 19:19). Humiliation often continued until (Jos 7:6; Jdg 20:23, 26; 21:2; Ezr 9:4-5). Exercise (2Sa 11:2). Prayer (Ps 55:17; Mt 14:15, 23). Taking food (Mk 14:17-18; Lk 24:29-30). The sky red in, a token of fair weather (Mt 16:2).

EVERLASTING ARMS (Dt 33:27).

EVERLASTING FIRE *See Fire, Figurative.*

EVERLASTING LIFE *See Life, Everlasting.*

EVERLASTING PUNISHMENT *See Punishment, Eternal.*

EVI (*desire*). One of five Midianite kings killed by the Israelites under Moses (Nu 31:8; Jos 13:21).

EVICTION Of tenants (Mt 21:41; Mk 12:9).

EVIDENCE False, forbidden (Ex 20:16; 23:1, 7; Pr 24:28; Mt 19:18). Concealment of, punished (Lev 5:1). The entire community involved in (Lev 24:14). Two or more witnesses required in to sustain an allegation (Nu 35:30; Dt 17:6-7; 19:15; Mt 18:16; Heb 10:28). Punishment for falsehood in (Dt 19:16-21). Self-incriminating, demanded (Jos 7:19-21).

See Witness; False Witness; Accusation, False; Self-Incrimination.

EVIL Tree of the knowledge of good and evil (Ge 2:9, 17). Knowledge of (Ge 3:5, 22). In the heart (Ge 6:5; 8:21; Lk 6:45).

To be forsaken (Ps 34:14; 37:27; Pr 3:7; 1Pe 3:11). To be abhorred (Ps 97:10; Am 5:15; Ro 12:9). You are not to repay evil for evil done to you (Ro 12:17; 1Th 5:15; 1Pe 3:9).

Appearance of to be avoided (Ro 14:1-23; 1Co 8:7-13; 10:28-33; 1Th 4:11-12; 5:22), exemplified by Paul, refusing to eat that which was offered to idols (1Co 8:13), in supporting himself (1Co 9:7-23).

See Company, Evil; Imagination, Of Mankind, Evil; Nonresistance.

EVIL-MERODACH (*worshiper of Marduk[s]* changed in textual transmission to read *fool of [blessing]*). Son and successor of Nebuchadnezzar. Released Jehoiachin from prison (2Ki 25:27-30; Jer 52:31-34).

EVIL FOR EVIL *See Retaliation.*

EVIL FOR GOOD (Ps 7:4-5; 35:12; 109:5; Pr 17:13).

Instances of:

Joseph accuses his brothers of rendering (Ge 44:4). Israelites, to Moses (Ex 5:21; 14:11; 15:24; 16:2-3; 17:3-4). Saul returns, to David (1Sa 19:1, 4-5, 10). Nabal returns, to David (1Sa 25:21), David, to Uriah (2Sa 11), to Joab (1Ki 2:4-6).

See Enemy; Good for Evil.

EVIL PUT AWAY (Dt 13:5; 17:7; 19:19; 21:21; 22:21; 24:7; Job 22:23; 1Co 5:13).

EVIL SPEAKING *See Speaking, Evil.*

EVIL SPIRITS *See Demons.*

EVILDOERS Warnings to (Ps 34:16; 37:9; 94:16; 119:115; Isa 9:17; 14:20; 31:2). Examples of (Jdg 2:11; 3:7; 4:1; 6:1; 10:6; 13:1; 1Ki 14:22; 15:26; 16:7; 2Ki 8:27; 13:2; 14:24; 15:9, 28; 17:2; 21:2; 23:32; 24:9; Ne 9:28; Isa 65:12; 2Ti 4:14).

EWE Female sheep.

EXALTATION

Of Christ *See Jesus the Christ, Exaltation of.*

Of Self *See Self-Exaltation.*

EXAMPLE

Bad:

Admonitions against (Lev 18:2-3; 20:23; Dt 18:9; 2Ch 30:7; Isa 8:11; Hos 4:9, 15; Zec 1:4; Mt 23:1-3; 1Co 8:9-13; 10:6; Eph 4:17; 3Jn 11). Corrupting (Pr 22:24-25; Jer 16:12; 17:1-2; Eze 20:18; Hos 4:9; 5:5).

Good:

Commanded (1Ti 4:12; Tit 2:7-8; 1Pe 5:3). Inspiring (Ne 5:8-19; 1Th 1:6-8; 1Pe 2:11-25). To be imitated (Heb 13:7; Jas 5:10-11). Illustrated (Ps 101:2; 1Pe 3:5-6).

God, our:

In holiness (Lev 11:44; 19:2). In perfection (Mt 5:48). In mercy (Lk 6:36). In not discriminating (Eph 6:9).

Christ, our:

In service (Mt 20:28; Mk 10:43-45; Lk 22:27; Jn 13:13-17, 34; Php 2:5-8). In meekness (2Co 10:1; 1Pe 2:20-25). In self-renunciation (Ro 15:2-7; 2Co 8:7; Eph 5:1-2; 1Jn 3:16). In enduring persecution (1Pe 3:17-18; 4:1). In forgiving (Col 3:13). In obedience (1Jn 2:6). In steadfastness (Heb 12:2-3). In perseverance (Rev 3:21). *See Jesus the Christ, Our Example.*

Paul, our:

Commanded (1Co 4:16; 11:1; Php 3:17; 4:9; 1Ti 1:16; 2Ti 1:13). In self-control (1Co 7:7-8). In self-maintenance (1Th 3:7-10). In beneficence (Ac 20:35).

See Influence.

EXCHANGERS *See Money Changers.*

EXCOMMUNICATION Disciplinary exclusion from church fellowship. Jews had temporary and permanent excommunication (Jn 9:22; 12:42; 16:2). Early church practiced it (1Co 5:5; 1Ti 1:20). *See Disfellowship.*

EXCUSES For disobedience (Ge 3:12-13; Ex 32:22-24; Dt 30:11-14). For rejecting salvation (Lk 14:18-20; Jn 15:22; Ac 24:25; Ro 1:20-21; 3:19). Inexcusable (Ro 2:1).

Examples:

For release from duty: By Moses, when commissioned to deliver Israel (Ex 3:11; 4:1, 10-14), by Gideon (Jdg 6:12-17), by Jesus' disciples (Mt 8:21; Lk 9:59-62).

When called to be a prophet: Elisha (1Ki 19:19-21), Isaiah (Isa 6:5-8), Jeremiah (Jer 1:5-10).

For physical healing: Naaman, the leper (2Ki 5:10-14).

EXECUTION *See Death, Death Penalty.*

EXECUTIONER (*punishment*). (Ge 37:36; Pr 16:14; Jer 39:9; Da 2:14; Mt 14:10). *See Punishment.*

EXHORTATIONS, SPECIAL To avoid various forms (Pr 4:15; Ro 16:17; 1Ti 6:20; 2Ti 2:16, 23; Tit 3:9). To choose between good and evil (Ex 32:26; Dt 30:19; Jos 24:15; 1Ki 18:21).

EXILE Usually refers to the period of time during which the Southern Kingdom (Judah) was forcibly detained in Babylon. Began in the reign of Jehoiakim (609-598 B.C.), culminating in the fall of Jerusalem (c. 586 B.C.). It ended with the decree of Cyrus permitting Jews to return to Israel c. 536 B.C. *See Diaspora; Outcasts.*

EXODUS (*a going out*). Departure of Israel from Egypt under Moses (Heb 11:22). *See Exodus, Book of.*

EXODUS, BOOK OF

Author: Moses

Date: c. 1445-1406 B.C.

Outline:

I. Divine Redemption (chs. 1-18).
  A. Fulfilled Multiplication (ch. 1).
    1. The promised increase (1:1-7).
    2. The first pogrom (1:8-14).
    3. The second pogrom (1:15-21).
    4. The third pogrom (1:22).
  B. Preparations for Deliverance (2:1-4:26).
    1. Preparing a leader (2:1-10).
    2. Extending the time of preparation (2:11-22).
    3. Preparing the people (2:23-25).
    4. Calling a deliverer (3:1-10).
    5. Answering inadequate objections (3:11-4:17).
    6. Preparing a leader's family (4:18-26).
  C. First Steps in Leadership (4:27-7:5).
    1. Reinforced by brothers (4:27-31).
    2. Rebuffed by the enemy (5:1-14).
    3. Rebuffed by the enslaved (5:15-21).
    4. Revisited by old objections (5:22-23).
    5. Reinforced by the name of God (6:1-8).
    6. Reminded of one's lowly origins (6:9-7:5).
  D. Judgment and Salvation Through the Plagues (7:6-11:10).
    1. Presenting the signs of divine authority (7:6-13).
    2. First plague: water turned to blood (7:14-24).
    3. Second plague: frogs (7:25-8:15).
    4. Third plague: gnats (8:16-19).
    5. Fourth plague: flies (8:20-32).
    6. Fifth plague: against livestock (9:1-7).
    7. Sixth plague: boils (9:8-12).
    8. Seventh plague: hail (9:13-35).
    9. Eighth plague: locusts (10:1-20).
    10. Ninth plague: darkness (10:21-29).
    11. Tenth plague announced: death of the firstborn (ch. 11).
  E. The Passover (12:1-28).
    1. Preparations for the Passover (12:1-13).
    2. Preparations for Unleavened Bread (12:14-20).
    3. Celebration of the Passover (12:21-28).
  F. The Exodus From Egypt (12:29-51).
    1. Death at midnight (12:29-32).
    2. Expulsion from Egypt (12:33-42).
    3. Regulations for the Passover (12:43-51).
  G. The Consecration of the Firstborn (13:1-16).
  H. Crossing the "Red Sea" (13:17-15:21).
    1. Into the wilderness (13:17-22).
    2. At the "Red Sea" (14:1-14).
    3. Across the "Red Sea" (14:15-31).
    4. Song at the sea (15:1-21).
  I. Journey to Sinai (15:22-18:27).
    1. The waters of Marah (15:22-27).
    2. The manna and the quail (ch. 16).
    3. The waters of Meribah (17:1-7).
    4. The war with Amalek (17:8-16).
    5. The wisdom of Jethro (ch. 18).

II. Covenant at Sinai (chs. 19-24).
  A. The Covenant Proposed (ch. 19).
  B. The Decalogue (20:1-17).
  C. The Reaction of the People to God's Fiery Presence (20:18-21).
  D. The Book of the Covenant (20:22-23:33).
    1. Prologue (20:22-26).
    2. Laws on slaves (21:1-11).
    3. Laws on homicide (21:12-17).
    4. Laws on bodily injuries (21:18-32).
    5. Laws on property damage (21:33-22:15).
    6. Laws on society (22:16-31).
    7. Laws on justice and neighborliness (23:1-9).
    8. Laws on sacred seasons (23:10-19).
    9. Epilogue (23:20-33).
  E. Ratification of the Covenant (ch. 24).

III. Divine Worship (chs. 25-40).
  A. Instructions Concerning the Tabernacle (chs. 25-31).
    1. Collection of the materials (25:1-9).
    2. Ark and atonement cover (25:10-22).
    3. Table of the bread of the Presence (25:23-30).
    4. Gold lampstand (25:31-40).
    5. Curtains and frames (ch. 26).
    6. Altar of burnt offering (27:1-8).
    7. Courtyard (27:9-19).
    8. Priesthood (27:20-28:5).
    9. Garments of the priests (28:6-43).
    10. Ordination of the priests (ch. 29).
    11. Altar of incense (30:1-10).
    12. Census tax (30:11-16).
    13. Bronze basin (30:17-21).
    14. Anointing oil and incense (30:22-38).
    15. Appointment of craftsmen (31:1-11).
    16. Sabbath rest (31:12-18).
  B. False Worship (chs. 32-34).
    1. The golden calf (32:1-29).
    2. Moses' mediation (32:30-35).
    3. Threatened separation and Moses' prayer (ch. 33).
    4. Renewal of the covenant (ch. 34).
  C. The Building of the Tabernacle (chs. 35-40).
    1. Summons to build (35:1-19).
    2. Voluntary gifts (35:20-29).
    3. Bezalel and his craftsmen (35:30-36:7).
    4. Progress of the work (36:8-39:31).
    5. Moses' blessing (39:32-43).
    6. Erection of the tabernacle (40:34-38).
    7. Dedication of the tabernacle (40:34-38).

EXORCISM (*to bind with an oath, to conjure*). The casting out of demons by means of magical formulas and ceremonies (Mt 12:27; Mk 9:38; Ac 19:13). *See Demons.*

EXPANSE The heavens above the earth (Ge 1:6-8, 14-17, 20).

EXPECTATION Of the righteous (Ps 62:5; Pr 24:14; Php 1:20). Of the wicked (Pr 10:28; 11:7, 23; Zec 9:5; Ac 12:11).

EXPEDIENCY To avoid offending others weaker (Ro 14:1-2, 14-22; 1Co 6:12; 8:8-13; 9:22-23; 10:23-29, 32-33). To save people (1Co 9:19-23). Rule governing (1Co 10:30-31). Exemplified by Paul, in circumcising Timothy (Ac 16:3), in purifying himself at the temple (Ac 21:23-27).

See Evil; Prudence.

EXPERIENCE Solomon's (Ecc 1:2). Religious, relating of. *See Testimony, Religious.*

EXPERIMENT In worldly pleasure, Solomon's (Ecc 1; 2).

EXPIATION The act or means of making amends or reparation for sin. *See Atonement.*

EXPORTS From Egypt: horses and chariots, and linen yarn (1Ki 10:28-29; 2Ch 1:16-17), grain (Ge 42; 43).

From Gilead: spices (Ge 37:25).

From Ophir: gold (1Ki 10:11; 22:48; 1Ch 29:4).

From Tarshish: gold (1Ki 10:22), ivory, apes, and baboons (1Ki 10:22), silver, iron, tin, lead, bronze, slaves (Eze 27:12-13).

From Arabia: sheep and goats (Eze 27:21).

From Israel: honey (Eze 27:17).

See Imports; Commerce.

EXPOSTULATION *See Reproof.*

EXTERMINATION *See War.*

EXTORTION Prayed upon the wicked by David (Ps 109:11). Warning against (Pr 22:16). Purged out of the land (Isa 16:4). Judged by God (Eze 22:12). Cruel (Mic 2:3).

Scribes and Pharisees accused of by Christ (Mt 23:25). Pharisee judges himself not guilty of (Lk 18:11).

Forbidden (Lk 3:13-14). Cause for disfellowship (1Co 5:10-11). Excludes from the kingdom of God (1Co 6:10).

Instances of:

Jacob, in demanding Esau's birthright for a bowl of stew (Ge 25:31). Pharaoh in exacting of the Egyptians lands and persons for grain (Ge 47:13-26). The Jews after the Captivity (Ne 5:1-13).

See Interest; Usury.

EXTRADITION Instances of: Elijah from hiding to Ahab by Obadiah (1Ki 18:7, 10). Uriah from Egypt to Jehoiakim by Elnathan and company (Jer 26:21-23). Early believers from Damascus chief priests, in Jerusalem by Paul (Ac 9:2, 14; 22:5).

EXTRAVAGANCE Not to be pursued (Pr 21:17, 20; Lk 16:19). *See Gluttony.*

EYE Anthropomorphisms, figurative of God's omniscience (Ps 11:4; Pr 15:3), justice (Am 9:8), holiness (Hab 1:13), care (Ps 33:18-19; 34:15; 121:3-5; Isa 1:15; 1Pe 3:12), glory (Isa 3:8). *See Anthropomorphisms.*

Figurative:

Of the moral state (Mt 7:3-5; 13:15-16; Mk 7:22). Of moral perception (Mt 6:22-23; Mk 8:18; Lk 10:23; Ac 26:18).

Of insatiable desire (Pr 27:20; Ecc 1:18; 2Pe 2:14; Hos 2:16). Of evil pleasure (Mt 5:29; 18:9; Mk 9:27).

EYE FOR EYE *See Retaliation.*

EYES, OPENED (Ge 21:19; Nu 22:31; 2Ki 6:17; Lk 24:31).

EYES, PAINTING OF *See Cosmetics.*

EYESALVE Used figuratively for restoration of spiritual vision (Rev 3:18).

EZBAI Father of Naarai (1Ch 11:37). Possibly identical with Paarai (2Sa 23:35).

EZBON

1. A son of Gad (Ge 46:16). Called Ozni (Nu 26:16).
2. A son of Bela (1Ch 7:7).

EZEKIAS *See Hezekiah.*

EZEKIEL (*God [El] strengthens*). A priest. The time of his prophecy (Eze 1:1-3). Persecution of (Eze 3:25). Visions of: Of God's glory (Eze 1; 8; 10; 11:22), of Israelites' abominations (Eze 8:5-6), of their punishment (Eze 9:10), of the valley of dry bones (Eze 37:1-14), of a man with a measuring line (Eze 40-48), of the river (Eze 47:1-5).

Teaches by pantomime: Feigns muteness (Eze 3:26; 24:27; 33:22), symbolizes the siege of Jerusalem by drawings on a tile (Eze 4), shaves himself (Eze 5:1-4), removes his belongings to illustrate the approaching Israelite captivity (Eze 12:3-7), sighs (Eze 21:6-7), employs a boiling pot to symbolize the destruction of Jerusalem (Eze 24:1-14), omits mourning at the death of his wife (Eze 24:16-27), prophesies by parable of an eagle (Eze 17:2-10). Other parables (Eze 15; 16; 19; 23).

Prophecies of concerning various nations (Eze 25 29). His popularity (Eze 33:31-32).

EZEKIEL, BOOK OF

Author: Ezekiel

Date: See chart below

Outline:

I. Oracles of Judgment Against Israel (chs. 1-24).
 A. Ezekiel's Inaugural Vision (chs. 1-3).
  1. The divine overwhelming (ch. 1).
  2. The equipping and commissioning (2:1-3:15).
  3. The watchman 3:16-21).
  4. Further stipulations (3:22-27).
 B. Symbolic Acts Portraying the Siege of Jerusalem (chs. 4-5).
  1. The city of Jerusalem on a clay tablet (4:1-3).
  2. Prophetic immobility (4:4-8).
  3. Diet for the siege and exile (4:9-17).
  4. The divine razor and its consequences (ch. 5).
 C. Oracles Explaining Divine Judgment (chs. 6-7).
  1. Doom for the mountains of Israel (ch. 6).
  2. The end (ch. 7).
 D. Vision of the Corrupted Temple (chs. 8-11).
  1. Four abominations (ch. 8).
  2. Destruction of the city (ch. 9).
  3. God's glory leaves Jerusalem (ch. 10).
  4. Conclusion of the vision (ch. 11).
 E. Symbolic Acts Portraying Jerusalem's Exile (ch. 12).
  1. An exile's baggage (12:1-16).
  2. Anxious eating (12:17-20).
  3. The nearness of judgment (12:21-28).
 F. Oracles Explaining Divine Judgment (chs. 13-24).
  1. False prophets and magic charms (ch. 13).
  2. The penalty for idolatry (14:1-11).
  3. Noah, Daniel and Job (14:12-23).
  4. Jerusalem as a burnt vine branch (ch. 15).
  5. Jerusalem as a wayward founding (16:1-43).
  6. Jerusalem compared to other cities (16:44-63).
  7. Jerusalem's kings allegorized (17:1-21).
  8. The new tree (17:22-24).
  9. The lesson of three generations (ch. 18).
  10. The twofold lament (ch. 19).
  11. Israel as a hardened repeater (ch. 20).
  12. The sword of the Lord (ch. 21).
  13. Jerusalem the city of blood (ch. 22).
  14. Oholah and Oholibah (ch. 23).
  15. The final fire: Jerusalem's end (24:1-14).
  16. The death of Ezekiel's wife and the destruction of the temple (24:15-27).
II. Oracles of Judgment Against the Nations (chs. 25-32).
 A. Against Ammon (25:1-7).
 B. Against Moab (25:8-11).
 C. Against Edom (25:12-14).
 D. Against Philistia (25:15-17).
 E. Against Tyre (26:1-28:19).
  1. The end of the city (ch. 26).
  2. A lament for Tyre (ch. 27).
  3. Against the king of Tyre (28:1-19).
 F. Against Sidon (28:20-24).
 G. A Note of Promise for Israel (28:25 26).
 H. Against Egypt (chs. 29-32).
  1. As a doomed monster (29:1-16).
  2. As a payment to Nebuchadnezzar (29:17-21).
  3. The approaching day (30:1-19).
  4. Pharaoh's arms are broken (30:20-26).
  5. As a felled cedar (ch. 31).
  6. A lament over Pharaoh (32:1-16).
  7. As consigned to the pit among the uncircumcised (32:17-32).
III. Oracles of Consolation for Israel (chs. 33 48).
 A. The Watchman (33:1-20).
 B. Jerusalem's Fall Reported and Explained (33:21-33).
 C. The Lord as the Good Shepherd (ch. 34).
 D. Oracles Against Edom (ch. 35).
 E. Consolations for the Mountains of Israel (36:1-15).
 F. Summary of Ezekiel's Theology (36:16-38).
 G. Vision of National Restoration (ch. 37).
  1. National resurrection (37:1-14).
  2. National reunification (37:15-28).
 H. The Final Battle (chs. 38-39).
 I. Vision of Renewed Worship (chs. 40-48).
  1. Wall around the temple (40:1-47).
  2. Temple exterior (40:48-41:26).
  3. Temple interior (ch. 42).
  4. The return of God's glory (ch. 43).
  5. The priesthood (ch. 44).
  6. Land allotment (ch. 45).
  7. The duties of the prince (ch. 46).
  8. Life-giving water (47:1-12).
  9. Land allotment (47:13-48:35).

EZEL *See Beth Ezel.*

EZEM (*bone [strength]*). A city in the S of Judah (Jos 15:29; 19:3; 1Ch 4:29).

EZER (*help*).

1. The sixth son of Seir; a clan chief of the native Horite inhabitants of Edom (Ge 36:21, 27, 30; 1Ch 1:38, 42).
2. A Judahite, father of Hushah (1Ch 4:4).
3. An Ephraimite slain by the men of Gath (1Ch 7:21).
4. A Gadite warrior who went over to David (1Ch 12:9).
5. A Levite, son of Jeshua, who repaired a section of the wall of Jerusalem under Nehemiah's direction (Ne 3:19).
6. A priest who participated in the dedication of the wall (Ne 12:42).

EZION GEBER (*giant, the giant backbone*). The last encampment of Israel before coming to the wilderness of Zin (Nu 33:35-36; Dt 2:8). Solomon, built a navy at (1Ki 9:26), visited (2Ch 8:17). Jehoshaphat's ships built at (2Ch 20:36), wrecked at (1Ki 22:48).

EZRA (*help*). A famous scribe and priest (Ezr 7:1-6, 10-12, 21; Ne 12:36). Appoints a fast (Ezr 8:21). Commissioned by Artaxerxes to rebuild the temple in Jerusalem which he directs (Ezr 7:8). Persecuted by Tattenai the governor (Ezr 6:3-17). Darius renews the decree of Cyrus for rebuilding the temple which he directs to completion (Ezr 6:1-15). His charge to the priests (Ezr 8:29). Exhorts people to put away heathen wives (Ezr 10:1-17). Reads the law (Ne 8). Reforms corruption (Ezr 10; Ne 13). Participates in the dedication of the wall of Jerusalem (Ne 12:27-43).

EZRA, BOOK OF

Author: According to Jewish tradition Ezra wrote Ezra and Nehemiah and also 1 and 2 Chronicles.

Date: c. 440 B.C.

Outline:

I. First Return From Exile and Rebuilding of the Temple (chs. 1-6).
 A. First Return of the Exiles (ch. 1).
  1. The edict of Cyrus (1:1-4).
  2. The return under Sheshbazzar (1:5-11).
 B. List of Returning Exiles (ch. 2).
 C. Revival of Temple Worship (ch. 3).
  1. The rebuilding of the altar (3:1-3).
  2. The Feast of Tabernacles (3:4-6).
  3. The beginning of temple reconstruction (3:7-13).
 D. Opposition to Rebuilding (4:1-23).
  1. Opposition during the reign of Cyrus (4:1-5).
  2. Opposition during the reign of Xerxes (4:6).
  3. Opposition during the reign of Artaxerxes (4:7-23).
 E. Completion of the Temple (4:24-6:22).
  1. Resumption of work under Darius (4:24).
  2. A new beginning inspired by Haggai and Zechariah (5:1-2).
  3. Intervention of Tattenai (5:3-5).
  4. Report to Darius (5:6-17).
  5. Search for the decree of Cyrus (6:1-5).
  6. Darius's order for the rebuilding of the temple (6:6-12).
  7. Completion of the temple (6:13-15).
  8. Dedication of the temple (6:16-18).
  9. Celebration of Passover (6:19-22).
II. Ezra's Return and Reforms (chs. 7-10).
 A. Ezra's Return to Jerusalem (chs. 7-8).
  1. Introduction (7:1-10).
  2. The authorization by Artaxerxes (7:11-26).
  3. Ezra's doxology (7:27-28).
  4. List of those returning with Ezra (8:1-14).
  5. The search for Levites (8:15-20).
  6. Prayer and fasting (8:21-23).
  7. The assignment of the sacred articles (8:24-30).
  8. The journey and arrival in Jerusalem (8:31-36).
 B. Ezra's Reforms (chs. 9-10).
  1. The offense of mixed marriages (9:1-5).
  2. Ezra's confession and prayer (9:6-15).
  3. The people's response (10:1-4).
  4. The public assembly (10:5-15).
  5. Investigation of the offenders (10:16-17).
  6. The list of offenders (10:18-43).
  7. Dissolution of mixed marriages (10:44).

EZRAH A Judahite (1Ch 4:17).

EZRAHITES The family or clan of Ethan and Heman, legendary wise men and poets (1Ki 4:31; Ps 88:T; 89:T). The word is probably a gentilic form of "Zerah," since 1Ch 2:6 designates Ethan and Heman as sons of Zerah.

EZRI (*my help*). Son of Kelub; the steward in charge of the agriculture of the crown lands in the time of David (1Ch 27:26).

F

FABLE (*talk, tale, legend, myth*). A type of literary genre in which animals and inanimate objects are used as persons or actors, speaking and using human behavior as if they actually were human beings. The fable is akin to the *allegory* and the *parable*. The fable is distinguished from the others in that there is a moral to the story; while the primary point of the allegory and the parable is to teach spiritual virtues.

There are two fables in the OT. In the first, the people of Shechem are warned by Jotham, the sole survivor of Abimelech's coup, that Abimelech is treacherous and will provide certain tyranny (Jdg 9:7-15). In the second, Jehoash, king of Israel, snubs Amaziah, king of Judah, with an insult, warning that he is courting disaster (2Ki 14:9).

In the NT, the debate among the parts of the body may be considered a fable (1Co 12:14-26). For KJV "fable" (1Ti 1:4; 4:7; 2Ti 4:4; Tit 1:14; 2Pe 1:16). *See Myths.*

See Allegory; Parable.

FACE

General References to:

Refers to the face of, the waters (Ge 1:2), the earth (Ge 1:29), a man (Ge 3:19; Jas 1:23), flocks (Ge 30:40), God (Nu 6:25), the moon (Job 26:9), the seraphs (Isa 6:2), and the sky (Mt 16:3), Christ (2Co 4:6), the living creatures around the throne (Rev 4:7). The man himself may be meant (Dt 7:10), as in the Oriental circumlocution for "I." Character revealed in (Isa 3:9). Disfiguring of, in fasting (Mt 6:16).

Reflects Feelings:

(Ge 4:5; Pr 15:13). Moses in the presence of God (Ex 3:6). Favors are granted when the face is lifted up (Nu 6:25). Ruth bowed with her face to the ground in humility (Ru 2:10). Mourning (2Sa 19:4). To turn away or to hide the face is rejection (Pr 13:1). To seek the face is a desire for an audience (Ps 105:4). To harden the face is to promise no appeal (Pr 21:29). To spit on the face is a serious insult (Mt 26:67). Determination was evident when Jesus set his face to go to Jerusalem (Lk 9:51).

Covered:
By a harlot (Ge 38:15). Moses, when talking to the people after he was in the presence of God (Ex 34:29-35; 2Co 3:13-18). David (2Sa 19:4). In the doom of Haman (Est 7:8).

Of God:
Applied to God, it denotes his presence. Jacob struggles with God until daybreak and lives; he names the place where he fought, Peniel, which means "face of God," because "I saw God face to face, and yet my life was spared" (Ge 32:30). God himself or his glory which could not be seen by Moses (or by any man) or he would die (Ex 33:20). God hides his face when angry (Job 13:24). God also hides his face from sin to show his displeasure (Pr 27:9) and to show that he has forgiven sin (Ps 51:9). John says that the Son of God alone has ever seen God face to face (Jn 1:18). The literal translation for the "bread of the Presence" would be the "bread of the face" (Ex 25:30).

Transfigured:
Moses (Ex 34:29-35), Jesus (Mt 17:2; Lk 9:29).
See Countenance.

FAIR Has the meaning of, just (Jdg 16:9; Pr 1:3; 2:9; 2Co 6:13; Col 4:1), clear skies (Job 26:13; Mt 16:2), persuasive (Pr 7:21), clean (Zec 3:5), beautiful (Hos 10:11; Ac 7:20).
It is not used to describe complexion.

FAIR HAVENS A small bay near Lasea on the S coast of Crete, about five miles E of Cape Matala. Paul stayed here for a short time on his way to Rome (Ac 27:8-12).

FAITH

General Explanation of:
Faith has both an active and a passive sense in the Bible. The former meaning relates to one's loyalty to a person or fidelity to a promise; the latter confidence in the word or assurance of another. Faith is not merely *what* a person believes, i.e., accurate doctrine or creed, but also and more importantly, that the object of his faith is valid. A man's life is governed by his thoughts; he will ultimately become that which he dwells most upon in his mind. This is the reason for Paul's instruction to the Romans, "Do not conform any longer to the pattern of this world, but be transformed by the renewing of your mind" (Ro 12:2). He wrote similar instruction to the Philippians, "Finally, brothers, whatever is true, whatever is noble, whatever is right, whatever is pure, whatever is lovely, whatever is admirable—if anything is excellent or praiseworthy—think about such things" (Php 4:8).

The Value of:
People are kept secure by (2Ch 20:20; Ro 11:20; 2Co 1:24; 1Jn 5:4), are established by (Isa 7:9), are saved by (Jn 3:15; Ac 16:31; Ro 9:30-32; Gal 2:16; Eph 2:8-9; Php 3:9), healed by (Ac 14:9; Jas 5:15), are sanctified by (Ac 26:18), receive the Holy Spirit by (Gal 3:5, 14), live by (2Co 5:7). Causes men to be a blessing to others (Jn 7:38). Disbelieving God is a great sin (Jn 16:9; Ro 14:23). Faith is necessary to please God (Heb 11:6).

The Gift of God:
The apostles ask Jesus to increase (Lk 17:5). God gives a certain measure of (Ro 12:3; 1Co 2:4-5). Given by the Spirit (1Co 12:8-9).

The Purpose of:
To gain understanding and to grow in the truth (Ps 119:97-105, 129-131; Jn 8:31-32; 2Ti 2:15; 1Jn 2:5, 14). To grow in the grace of God (Ac 2:42-47; Ro 4:4-5; 5:2; 1Co 15:10; Eph 4:15; Heb 4:16). To help us to rejoice through our faith (Ro 5:2-5, 11; 15:13; Php 1:18-19; 2:17-18). To strengthen the man of faith (Ro 6:12-14; 11:20; 1Co 9:27; Php 4:6-7; 2Th 3:3; 2Ti 4:7-8; 1Pe 1:3-5). To be transformed into the image of Christ (Ro 8:29; 1Co 15:49; 2Co 3:18; 4:3-6). To become strong people of faith (Eph 4:1-3, 11-13, 15-16).

The Effect of:
Faith not works (Gal 5:5-6). Produces good works (1Th 1:3; 2Th 1:11), internal changes (1Th 2:13), perseverance (Jas 1:3).

The Righteousness of:
The true righteousness of God comes from (Ro 1:17; 3:21-30; 4:3, 11; 9:31-33; 10:4-11; Gal 2:16; Php 3:9; Heb 11:7).

The Biblical Position Concerning:
Credited as righteousness (Ge 15:6; Ro 4:3; Gal 3:6; Jas 2:23). Inspired by God's goodness (Ps 36:7, 9). Inspired by the Holy Spirit (1Co 12:8-9). Explained (Ps 118:8-9; Lk 17:6; 18:8; 1Ti 4:12; Heb 11:1-3, 6). Worry, doubt, and the lack of faith (Mt 6:25-34; 14:31; Lk 9:40; 17:5). Prayer for increase of faith (Mk 9:24; Lk 17:5). The gift of God (Ro 12:3). The righteous live by (Hab 2:4; Ro 1:17; Gal 3:11; Heb 10:38). Miracles accomplished by (Mt 17:18-20; 21:21-22; Mk 9:23; 11:23-24). Secures salvation (Col 2:12; 2Th 2:13; Heb 4:1-11; 6:1, 12, 18).

The Old Testament Use:
In the OT, the word "faith" in the sense of belief occurs only five times (2Ch 20:20, 20; Isa 7:9; 26:2; Hab 2:4). Faith is also communicated by words such as "believe," "fear," "hope," "love," and "trust." Faith is seen in the examples of the servants of God who committed their lives to him in unwavering trust and obedience. OT faith is never mere assent to a set of doctrines or outward acceptance of the Law, but absolute confidence in the faithfulness of God and a loving obedience to his will.

The New Testament Use:
In the NT "faith" and "believe" occur almost 500 times. The NT makes the claim that the promised Messiah had come and that Jesus of Nazareth was this promised Messiah. To believe on him meant to become a Christian, and was pivotal in the experience of the individual. Jesus offered himself as the object of faith and made plain that faith in him was necessary for eternal life.
The first Christians called themselves believers (Ac 2:44) and endeavored to persuade others to believe in Jesus (Ac 6:7; 28:24). In the epistles of Paul, faith is contrasted with works as a means of salvation (Ro 3:20-22). Faith is trust in the person of Jesus, the truth of his teaching, and the redemptive work which he accomplished at Calvary.
Faith may also refer to the body of truth which constitutes the whole of the Christian message (Jude 3).

Examples in the NT: In God (Lk 1:38-55; Ac 27:25; Ro 4:24; Heb 6:1; 1Pe 1:21; 4:19; 1Jn 3:21).

Strengthened by Miracles:
Of Abraham (Ge 15:8-18), of Gideon (Jdg 6:17, 36-40), of Hezekiah (2Ki 20:8-11), of Zechariah (Lk 1:18-20, 64).

In Affliction:
Exemplified by Job (Job 13:15-16; 14:15; 16:19; 19:25-27).

In Adversity:
Exemplified by, Hagar (Ge 16:15), Moses (Nu 14:8-9), Asa (2Ch 14:11), Jehoshaphat (2Ch 20:12), Hezekiah (2Ch 32:7-8), Nehemiah (Ne 1:10; 2:20), the psalmist (Ps 3:3, 5-6; 4:3, 8; 6:8-9; Ps 7:1, 10; 9:3-4; 11:1; 13:5; 17:6; 20:5-7; 31:1, 3-6, 14-15; 32:7; 33:20-22; 35:10; 38:9, 15; 42:5-6, 8; 43:5; 44:5, 8; 46:1-3, 5, 7; 54:4; 55:16-17, 23; 56:3-4, 8-9; 57:1-3; 59:9, 17; 60:9-10, 12; 61:2, 4, 6-7; 62:1, 5-7; 63:6-7; 69:19, 35-36; 70:5; 71:1, 3, 5-7, 14, 16, 20-21; 73:23-24, 26, 28; 86:2, 7; 89:18, 26; 91:1-2, 9-10; 92:10, 15; 94:14-15, 17-18, 22; 102:13; 108:10-13; 118:6-7, 10, 14, 17; 119:42, 57, 74, 81, 114, 166; 121:2; 138:7-8; 140:6-7, 12; 142:3, 5; 143:8-9), Jeremiah (La 3:24), Daniel (Da 3:16-17), Jonah (Jnh 2:2), Micah (Mic 7:7-9, 20), Paul (Ac 27:25; 2Co 1:10; 4:8-9, 13, 16-18; Php 1:19-21; 1Ti 4:10; 2Ti 1:12-13; 4:7-8, 18), the author of the letter to the Hebrews (Heb 10:34).

Commanded:
(Ps 4:5; 115:9, 11; Ecc 11:1; Isa 26:4; Mt 6:25-34; Mk 1:15; 11:22; Lk 12:32; 1Ti 6:11-12, 17; Jas 1:6). In time of public danger (Ex 14:13; Nu 21:34; Dt 1:21, 29-30; 3:2, 22; 7:17-21; 20:1; 31:8, 23; Jos 10:25; Jdg 6:14-16; 2Ki 19:6-7; 2Ch 20:15, 17, 20; 32:7-8; Ne 4:14; Isa 37:6; Jer 42:11). In time of adversity (Ps 37:3, 5, 7; 55:22; 62:8; Isa 43:1-2, 5, 10; 44:2, 8).
Commanded upon public leaders (Jos 1:5-9; 2Ch 15:7). Upon the young (Pr 3:5-6, 24-26). Upon the discouraged (Isa 35:3-4; 41:10, 13-14; 50:10). Upon widows (Jer 49:11).

Exemplified:
By Asa (2Ch 14:11). By Jehoshaphat (2Ch 20:12). By Hezekiah (2Ch 32:8). By Job (Job 1:21-22; 2:10; 5:8-9; 19:25-27). By the psalmists, setting forth supreme confidence in God (Ps 4:3, 8; 11:1; 13:5-6; 16:1-2, 5, 8-11; 18:1-3, 30-50; 20:5-8; 23:1-6; 25:1-15; 27:1-14; 31:1-5, 22-23, 24; 40:1-11; 46:1-11; 56:10-13; 57:1-11; 60:6-12; 61:1-8; 62:5-12; 63:1-8). By the following Psalms in their entirety (Ps 91; 95; 105-108; 115-118; 121; 123-126; 130; 135-136; 138-140; 145-150). By Isaiah (Isa 8:10, 17; 12:2; 17:13-14; 25:9; 26:1, 8; 33:1, 22; 50:7-9; 63:16; 64:8). By Jeremiah (Jer 14:9, 22; 16:19; 17:17; 20:11).

Instances of:
Abel (Heb 11:4). Noah, in building the ark (Ge 6:14-22; Heb 11:7). Abraham, in forsaking the land of his birth at the command of God (Ge 12:1-4; Heb 11:8), in believing the promise of many descendants (Ge 12:7; 15:4-6; Ro 4:18-21; Heb 11:11-12), in the offering up of Isaac (Ge 22:1-10; Heb 11:17-19). Jacob, in blessing Joseph's sons (Ge 48:8-21; Heb 11:21). Joseph, concerning God's providence in his being sold into Egypt, and the final deliverance of Israel (Ge 50:20, 24; Heb 11:22). Job (Job 1:21-22; 2:10). Eliphaz, in the overruling providence of God, that afflictions are for the good of the righteous (Job 5:6-27).
Jochebed, in caring for Moses (Ex 2:2-3; Heb 11:23). Pharaoh's servants, who obeyed the Lord (Ex 9:20). Moses, in espousing the cause of his people (Heb 11:24-28), at the death of Korah (Nu 16:28-29). Israelites (Ps 22:4-5), when Aaron declared the mission of himself and Moses (Ex 4:31), for forty years wanderings (Dt 8:2), in the battle with the Canaanites (1Ch 5:20), and other conquests (2Ch 13:8-18), by the waters of Meribah (Ps 81:7). Caleb, in advising to take the land of promise (Nu 13:30; 14:6-9), when he asked for Hebron (Jos 14:12). Rahab, in hospitality to the spies (Jos 2:9, 11; Heb 11:31). The spies sent to look over Jericho (Jos 2:24). Conquest of Jericho (Jos 6; Heb 11:30). Manoah's wife (Jdg 13:23). Hannah (1Sa 1). Jonathan, in killing the Philistines (1Sa 14:6).
David, in killing Goliath, the hero of the Philistines (1Sa 17:37, 45-47), in choosing to fall into the hands of the Almighty in his punishment for numbering Israel (2Sa 24:14), in believing God's promise that his kingdom would be a perpetual kingdom (Ac 2:30). The widow of Zarephath, in feeding Elijah (1Ki 17:13-15). Elijah, in his controversy with the priests of Baal (1Ki 18:32-38). Hezekiah (2Ki 18:5, 19). Amaziah, in dismissing the Ephraimites in obedience to the command of God, and going alone to battle against the Edomites (2Ch 25:7-10).
The three Hebrews who refused to worship Nebuchadnezzar's idol (Da 3:13-27). Daniel, in the lions' den (Da 6). Nebuchadnezzar (Da 6:16). The Ninevites, in obeying Jonah (Jnh 3:5). Habakkuk (Hab 3:17-19). Ezra, in making the journey from Babylon to Jerusalem without a military escort (Ezr 8:22). Mordecai, in the deliverance of the Jews (Est 4:14). Esther, in going before the king (Est 4:9-5:4).
Joseph, in obeying the vision about Mary and to flee into Egypt (Mt 1:18-24; 2:13-14). Mary, in believing the angel of the Lord, and in submitting to the Lord's will (Lk 1:38). Simeon, when he saw Jesus in the temple (Lk 2:25-35). Paul (Ro 8:18, 28, 38-39; 1Co 9:24-27; 2Co 5:7; Gal 5:5). The great people of faith (Heb 11:32-34).

The Trial of:
To prove depth of faith (Dt 8:2; 1Ch 29:17; Ps 26:2). To test spirituality (Mt 13:9-22; Lk 8:13-14). By tribulations (Mt 24:21-25; 2Th 1:3-5). By deferred hope (Heb 6:13-15). By trials (Jas 1:3, 12). Is precious (1Pe 1:7).

Instances of—
Noah (Ge 6:14-22; Heb 11:7). Abraham, when commanded to leave his native land (Ge 12:1-4; Heb 11:8), when commanded to offer Isaac (Ge 22:1-19; Heb 11:17-19). Moses, when sent to Pharaoh (Ex 3:11-12; 4:10-17; Heb 11:25-29), at the Red Sea, by the murmurings of the people (Ex 14:15; Heb 11:29). Joshua and the Israelites, in the method of taking Jericho (Jos 6; Heb 11:30). Gideon, when commanded to deliver Israel (Jdg 6:36-40; Heb 11:32). Ezra, in leaving Babylon without a military escort (Ezr 8:22). Job, by affliction and adversity (Job 1; 2). The three Hebrews, when commanded to worship Nebuchadnezzar's image (Da 3:8-30; Heb 11:32-34). Daniel, when forbidden by decree to pray to Yahweh (Da 6:4-23; Heb 11:32-33).

The two blind men who appealed to Jesus for sight (Mt 9:28). The Syrian Phoenician woman (Mt 15:21-28; Mk 7:24-30). The disciples, by the question of Jesus, in the storm at sea (Mt 8:23-27; Mk 4:36-41; Lk 8:22-26), as to who he was (Mt 16:15-20; Lk 9:20-21), by their inability to cast out the evil spirit from the boy (Mt 17:14-21; Mk 9:14-29; Lk 9:37-42) Of Philip, when questioned by Jesus as to how the multitude would be fed (Jn 6:5-6). Of Peter, when asked whether he loved Jesus (Jn 21:15-17).
See Tribulation.

Rewards of:
Protection (2Sa 22:31; Ps 5:11; 9:9-10; 18:30; 33:18-20; Pr 29:25; 30:5; Jer 39:18; Na 1:7; Heb 13:5-6). Spiritual peace (Ps 2:12; 32:10; 40:4; 84:5, 12; Isa 26:3; Ro 15:13). Prosperity (Pr 28:25; Isa 57:13; Jer 17:7-8). Eternal life (2Ti 1:1, 8).
See Faith in Christ.

FAITH, TEACHINGS OF JESUS Beliefs held in common by apostles and early believers (Ac 6:7; 16:5; 1Co 16:13; Gal 1:23; 3:23, 25; 6:10; Php 1:27; 1Ti 3:9; 4:1; 5:8; 6:10, 21; 2Ti 3:8; 4:7; Tit 1:1, 4, 13; 3:15; Jude 3; Rev 2:13).

FAITH IN CHRIST

General References Concerning:
Commanded (Mt 17:7; Jn 6:20; 20:27, 29; 1Jn 3:23). All things possible by (Mt 21:22; Mk 9:23; Lk 17:6). Prayer for increase of (Mk 9:24).
Leads to salvation (Jn 1:12; 3:14-18, 36; 5:24; 6:40, 47; 7:38; 12:36, 46; 20:31; Ac 10:43; 13:48; 15:9, 11; 16:31; 20:21; 26:18; Ro 1:16-17; 3:22-28; 4:1-25; 5:1-2; 9:31-33; 10:4-10; 11:20; 1Co 1:21; 2:5; Gal 2:16; Gal 3:1-29; 5:5-6; Eph 1:12-14; 2:8; 3:12, 17; 1Ti 1:16; 2Ti 1:13; 3:15; 1Pe 1:9; 2:6-7; 2Pe 1:1; Rev 3:20). Will result in good works (Jn 14:12; Jas 2:1-26).
Christ, the focus of faith (Ps 2:12; Heb 12:2). The Christian triumphs by (Ro 8:35, 37; 2Co 1:24; Eph 4:13; 6:16; Php 3:9; Col 1:23; 2:7; Heb 10:22, 38-39; 13:7; 1Pe 1:5, 7-9; 1Jn 5:4-5, 10, 14).

Exemplified by:
The wise men of the East as they worship the infant King Jesus (Mt 2:1-2, 11). The disciples in response to the call of Jesus (Mt 4:18-22; Mk 1:16-20; Lk 5:4; Lk 5:5-11; Jn 1:35-49; 6:68-69; 16:27, 30, 33). Peter (Mt 4:18-22; 16:16; Mk 1:16-20; Lk 5:4-5; Jn 6:68-69). Andrew (Mt 4:18-22; Mk 1:16-20; Jn 1:41). James and John (Mt 4:21-22; Mk 1:19-20). Philip (Jn 1:43-46). Nathanael (Jn 1:46-49). The disciples, through the miracle at Cana of Galilee (Jn 2:11). Jews at Jerusalem (Jn 2:23; 8:30; 11:45; 12:11). The Samaritans, who believed through the preaching of Jesus (Jn 4:39-42), of Philip (Ac 8:9-12).
Those who were healed by Jesus: the leper (Mt 8:2; Mk 1:40; Lk 5:12-13). The centurion, for the healing of his servant (Mt 8:5-10, 13; Lk 7:3-9). Those who brought the paralytic to Jesus (Mt 9:1-2; Mk 2:1-5; Lk 5:18-20). Jairus, for the healing of his daughter (Mt 9:18, 23-25; Mk 5:22-43; Lk 8:41-56). The woman subject to bleeding (Mt 9:20-22; Mk 5:25-34; Lk 8:43-48). Two blind men (Mt 9:27-30). The disciples in the storm (Mt 14:33). The sick of Gennesaret (Mt 14:36; Mk 3:10; 6:54-56). The Syrian Phoenician woman (Mt 15:22-28; Mk 7:25-30). The people of Decapolis (Mt 15:30). The father of the demon-possessed child (Mt 17:14-15; Mk 9:24; Lk 9:38, 42). Blind Bartimaeus, and a fellow blind man (Mt 20:30-34; Mk 10:46-52; Lk 18:35-43). Those who brought the deaf and mute man to Jesus (Mk 7:32). The woman who was a sinner (Lk 7:38, 44-48, 50). Mary, the sister of Martha (Lk 10:38-42; Jn 11:32). The Samaritan leper (Lk 17:11-19).
The nobleman, for the healing of his son (Jn 4:46-47, 50). The people who saw the feeding of the five thousand (Jn 6:14). The blind man whom Jesus healed on the Sabbath (Jn 9:13-38). The people in Bethany beyond the Jordan (Jn 10:41-42). Zacchaeus (Lk 19:1-6). The thief, on the cross (Lk 23:42). John, the disciple, after the resurrection (Jn 20:8). Thomas, after the resurrection (Jn 20:28).
Those in the early church. By three thousand, at Pentecost (Ac 2:41). By five thousand (Ac 4:4). By multitudes (Ac 5:14). By Stephen (Ac 6:8; 7:55-56). By the Ethiopian eunuch (Ac 8:36, 38). By the cripple at Lystra (Ac 14:8-10). Paul (Ro 7:24-25; 2Co 12:9-10; Gal 2:20; Php 4:13; 2Ti 1:12; 4:18). Expressed as a response to the preaching of the gospel. Of Lydda and Sharon (Ac 9:35), of Joppa (Ac 9:42), of Antioch (Ac 11:21-24). Barnabas (Ac 11:24). Eunice, Lois, and Timothy (Ac 16:1; 2Ti 1:5). Lydia (Ac 16:14). Philippian jailer (Ac 16:31-34). Crispus (Ac 18:8). The Corinthians (Ac 18:8; 1Co 15:11). Jews at Rome (Ac 28:24). Ephesians (Eph 1:13, 15). Colossians (Col 1:2, 4). Thessalonians (1Th 1:6; 3:6-8; 2Th 1:3-4). Philemon (Phm 5). Church at Thyatira (Rev 2:19).

FAITHFUL SAYINGS These are trustworthy statements; words that you may depend upon as truthful and everlasting (1Ti 1:15; 3:1; 4:9; 2Ti 2:11; Tit 3:8).

FAITHFULNESS

Described:
Scarce (Ps 12:1; Pr 20:6). Tested (Lk 16:10-12). A fruit of the Spirit (Gal 5:22). Rewards of (Ps 31:23; Pr 28:20; Mt 10:22; 13:12; 25:29; Mk 13:13; Heb 10:34; Rev 2:10).

Required:
(Mt 24:45-51, w Lk 12:36-48; Mt 25:14-30, w Lk 19:12-27). Of those who are trusted (1Co 4:2). Of servants (Eph 6:5-9; Col 3:22).

Instances of:
Abraham's servant (Ge 24:33). Moses (Nu 12:7; Heb 3:3, 5). Ruth (Ru 1:15-18). Ittai the Gittite (2Sa 15:19-22). David (2Sa 22:22-25). Elijah (1Ki 19:10, 14). Workmen in temple repairs (2Ki 12:15; 2Ch 34:12). Josiah (2Ki 22:2). Abijah (2Ch 13:10-12). Jehoshaphat (2Ch 20:1-30). Hanani and Hananiah (Ne 7:2). Abraham (Ne 9:7-8; Gal 3:9). Nehemiah's treasurer (Ne 13:13). Job (Job 1:21-22; 2:9-10). The three Hebrew captives (Da 3:16-18). Daniel (Da 6:10). Jesus (Jn 4:34; Heb 3:2). Abraham (Gal 3:9). Paul (1Ti 1:12; 2Ti 4:7).
See Reward, A Motive, To Faithfulness.

See also, Jesus the Christ, Faithfulness of; God, Faithfulness of; Minister, Faithful.

FALCON A bird of prey (Job 28:7; Isa 34:15), unclean for food (Dt 14:13). *See Birds.*

FALL OF MANKIND, THE The fall of mankind as related in Genesis 3 is the historical choice by which Adam and Eve sinned voluntarily, and consequently involved all the human race in evil. Since the Fall, there is no person who continually does what is right and never sins (1Ki 8:46; Ps 130:3; 143:2; Pr 20:9; Ecc 7:20; Ro 3:8-10; 5:12; 1Co 15:22; 1Jn 1:8). By the Fall mankind was alienated from God. Mankind was created in God's own image, with a rational and moral nature like God's, with no inner impulse to sin, and with a will free to choose the will of God. Yielding to the outward temptation turned mankind from God and created an environment in which sin became a potent factor. Redemption from the Fall is accomplished through the second Adam, Jesus Christ (Ro 5:12-21; 1Co 15:21-22, 45-49).

Consequences of:

Knowledge of, nakedness (Ge 3:7). Guilt (Ge 3:8-10). Cursing of, the serpent (Ge 3:14-15). Cursing of the ground (Ge 3:17-18). Multiplying of sorrows (Ge 3:16-19). Death, physical (Ge 3:19; Ro 5:12, 14; 1Co 15:21-22). Spiritual (Ro 5:12, 14, 18-19, 21).

Means of:

By transgression of commandments (Ge 2:16-17; 3:1-3, 6, 11-12; Job 31:33; Isa 43:27; Hos 6:7). Through deception of Satan (Ge 3:4-5, 13; 2Co 11:3; 1Ti 2:14). Through evil desire (Ge 3:6; Ecc 7:29).

See Depravity.

FALLOW DEER *See Animals; Deer.*

FALLOW GROUND Land that is left idle for a growing season, after plowing and harrowing, so that weeds and insects are killed while the soil regains its fertility. *See Agriculture.*

Practical Application:

Israel is instructed to follow this practice every seventh year (Ex 23:11), but through much of its history, they failed to allow their land a sabbath rest (Lev 26:34-35).

Spiritual Application:

Israel is encouraged to seek God and to become spiritually active (Jer 4:3; Hos 10:12).

FALSE ACCUSATION *See Accusation, False.*

FALSE APOSTLES Paul speaks of false apostles in 2 Corinthians only. These people "masquerade as apostles of Christ" (2Co 11:13). Paul denounces them as servants of Satan (2Co 11:14), "masquerading as servants of righteousness," which is not surprising, since their master "masquerades as an angel of light" (2Co 11:14-15). Yet they claim to be servants of Christ (2Co 11:23). Apparently they boasted of their Jewish heritage, using this to help justify their self-proclaimed position as "apostle of Christ" (2Co 11:22).

FALSE CHRISTS These are people who make a false claim to be the Messiah. Jesus warned his disciples that imitators and pretenders would follow him who would try to deceive his followers (Mt 24:5-11, 23-25; Mk 13:6, 21, 23; Lk 21:8). False Christs are to be distinguished from the Antichrist. The false Christ is an impostor while the latter is one who opposes Christ. His opposition is mainly through the doctrines about Jesus' person and work which are contrary to the truth.

FALSE CONFIDENCE

Described:

In self (Dt 29:19; 1Ki 20:11; Pr 3:5, 7; 26:5, 12; 28:26; Isa 5:21; Ro 12:16; 2Co 1:9). In outward resources (Ps 20:7; 33:17; 44:6; 49:6; Pr 11:28; Isa 22:9-11; 31:1-3; Jer 48:7; Zec 4:6; Mk 10:24, ftn). In man (Ps 33:16; 62:9; 118:8; 146:3-4; Isa 2:22; Jer 17:5; Hos 5:13; 7:11).

Instances of:

At the tower of Babel (Ge 11:4). Sennacherib, in the siege of Jerusalem (2Ki 19:23). Asa, in relying on Syria rather than on God (2Ch 16:7-9). Hezekiah, in the defenses of Jerusalem (Isa 22:11). Peter, in asserting his devotion to Jesus (Mt 26:35; Lk 22:33-34; Jn 13:37-38).

See Confidence.

FALSE PROPHET Any person pretending to possess a message from God, but not possessing a divine commission (Jer 29:9). Test for (Dt 13:1-5; 18:20-22).

The False Prophet of the Apocalypse:

The false prophet is mentioned in the book of Revelation (Rev 19:20) and is usually identified with the two-horned beast of Revelation (Rev 13:11-18).

FALSE TEACHERS *See Teachers, False.*

FALSE WITNESS

Described:

Punishment for (Dt 19:16-20; Pr 19:5, 9; 21:28; Zec 5:3-4). Innocent suffer from (Ps 27:12; 35:11). Proverbs concerning (Pr 6:16-19; 12:17; 14:5, 8, 25; 19:5, 9; 21:28; 24:28; 25:18). God hates (Pr 6:16-19). Results from a corrupt heart (Mt 15:19).

See Evidence; Falsehood; Perjury; Witness.

Forbidden:

(Ex 20:16; 23:1-3; Lev 6:1-5; 19:11-12, 16; Dt 5:20; Pr 24:28; Mt 19:18; Lk 3:14; 18:20; 1Ti 1:9-10).

Instances of:

Witnesses against, Naboth (1Ki 21:13), Jesus (Mt 26:59-61; Mk 14:54-59), Stephen (Ac 6:11-13), Paul (Ac 16:20-21; 17:5-7; 24:5; 25:7-8).

FALSEHOOD

Described:

Atonement for (Lev 6:2-7). Punishment for (Ps 12:2-4; 52:4-5; 55:23; 63:11; Pr 10:10, 31; 12:19; 14:5, 25; 19:5, 9; Rev 21:8, 27; 22:15). Falsehood will be found out (Pr 10:9; 28:18). Destructive (Pr 11:9; 26:18-19, 24-26, 28; Isa 32:7).

See Accusation, False; Conspiracy; Deceit; Deception; False Witness; Flattery; Hypocrisy; Perjury; Teachers, False.

All guilty of (Job 13:4; Ps 116:11; Jer 9:3-5; Hos 7:13; Mic 6:12; Ro 3:4). Refrained from by the righteous (Job 27:4; 31:5-6, 33; 36:4; Pr 14:5, 25; Isa 63:8). Practiced by the wicked (Ps 10:7; 28:3; 36:3; 50:19-20; 52:2-4; 58:3; 62:4; 109:2; Pr 2:12-15; 12:17, 20; 21:6; Isa 28:15; 57:11; 59:3-4, 12-13; Jer 7:8, 28; 9:3, 5-6, 8; 12:6; Hos 4:1-2; Ob 7; Mic 6:12; Na 3:1; Jn 8:44-45; 1Ti 4:2; 1Pe 3:16). Wicked easily misled by (Pr 14:8; 17:4). An abomination to the Lord (Ps 5:6, 9; Pr 6:12-13, 16-19; 12:22). Abhorred by the righteous (Ps 31:18; 59:12; 101:5, 7; 119:29, 69, 163; 120:2-4; 144:8, 11; Pr 10:18; 13:5; 20:17).

Forbidden:

(Ex 20:16; 23:1; Lev 19:11-12, 16; Ps 34:13, w 1Pe 3:10; Pr 17:7; Ecc 5:6; Zep 3:13; Eph 4:25, 29; Col 3:9; 1Ti 1:9-10).

Instances of:

Satan, in deceiving Eve (Ge 3:4-5), in impugning Job's motives for being righteous (Job 1:9-10; 2:4-5), in his tempting of Jesus (Mt 4:8-9; Lk 4:6-7). Adam and Eve, in attempting to avoid responsibility (Ge 3:12-13). Cain, in denying knowledge of his brother (Ge 4:9). Abraham, in denying that Sarah was his wife (Ge 12:11-19; 20:2). Sarah, to the angels, denying her laugh of unbelief (Ge 18:15), in denying to the king of Gerar, that she was Abraham's wife (Ge 20:5, 16). Isaac, denying that Rebekah was his wife (Ge 26:7-10). Rebekah and Isaac, in the conspiracy against Esau (Ge 27:6-24, 46). Jacob's sons, in the scheme to destroy the Shechemites by first having them circumcised (Ge 34). Joseph's brothers in deceiving their father into a belief that Joseph was killed by wild beasts (Ge 37:29-35). Potiphar's wife, in falsely accusing Joseph (Ge 39:14-17). Joseph, in the deception he carried on with his brothers (Ge 42-44).

Pharaoh, in dealing deceitfully with the Israelites (Ex 7-12). Aaron, in attempting to shift responsibility for the making of the golden calf (Ex 32:1-24). Rahab, in denying that the spies were in her house (Jos 2:4-6). The Gibeonites' ambassadors, in the deception they perpetrated upon Joshua and the elders of Israel in leading them to believe that they came from a distant region, when in fact they dwelt in the immediate vicinity (Jos 9). Ehud, in pretending to bear secret messages to Eglon, king of Moab, while his object was to assassinate him (Jdg 3:16-22). Sisera, who instructed Jael to mislead his pursuers (Jdg 4:20).

Saul, in professing to Samuel to have obeyed the commandment to destroy all spoils of the Amalekites, when in fact he had not obeyed (1Sa 15:1-20), in accusing Ahimelech of conspiring with David against himself (1Sa 22:11-16), in deceiving the medium of Endor as to his identity (1Sa 28:7-12). Michal, in the false statement that David was sick, in order to save him from Saul's violence (1Sa 19:12-17).

David, who lied to Ahimelech, professing to have a mission from the king, in order that he might obtain provisions and armor (1Sa 21), in feigning madness (1Sa 21:13-15), and other deceits with the Philistines (1Sa 27:8-12), the falsehood he put in the mouth of Hushai, of friendship to Absalom (2Sa 15:34-37). The Amalekite who claimed to have slain Saul (2Sa 1:10-12). Hushai, in false professions to Absalom (2Sa 16:16-19), in his deceitful counsel to Absalom (2Sa 17:7-14). The wife of the Baharumite who saved the lives of Hushai's messengers, sent to inform David of the movements of Absalom's army (2Sa 17:15-22).

The old prophet of Bethel who misguided the prophet of Judah (1Ki 13:11-22), Jeroboam's wife, pretending to be another woman (1Ki 14:1-6). Jezebel, Ahab, and the conspirators against Naboth (1Ki 21:7-13). Gehazi, when he ran after Naaman and misrepresented that Elisha wanted a talent of silver and two changes of clothing (2Ki 5:20-24). Hazael, servant of the king of Syria, lied to the king in misrepresenting the prophet Elisha's message in regard to the king's recovery (2Ki 8:7-15). Jehu lied to the worshipers of Baal in order to gain advantage over them and destroy them (2Ki 10:18-28). Zedekiah, in violating his oath of allegiance to Nebuchadnezzar (2Ch 36:13; Eze 16:59; 17:13-20).

Samaritans, in their efforts to hinder the rebuilding of the temple at Jerusalem (Ezr 4). Sanballat, in trying to obstruct the rebuilding of Jerusalem (Ne 6). Haman, in his conspiracy against the Jews (Est 3:8). In the answers of Job's friends (Job 21:34). Jeremiah's adversaries in accusing him of joining the Chaldeans (Jer 37:13-15). Princes of Israel, when they went to Jeremiah for a vision from the Lord (Jer 42:20).

Herod, to the wise men, in professing to desire to worship Jesus (Mt 2:8). Jews, in falsely accusing Jesus of blasphemy, when he forgave sin (Mt 9:2-8; Mk 2:5-12; Lk 5:21-26), in falsely accusing Jesus of being a glutton and a drunkard (Mt 11:19), in refusing to bear truthful testimony concerning John the Baptist (Mt 21:24-27), when he announced that he was the Son of God (Mt 26:65; Mk 14:64; Jn 10:33-38). The disobedient son who promised to work in the vineyard but did not (Mt 21:30). Peter, in denying Jesus (Mt 26:69-75; Mk 14:66-72; Jn 18:16-18, 25-27). The Roman soldiers, who said the disciples stole the body of Jesus (Mt 28:13, 15).

Ananias and Sapphira falsely state that they had sold their land for a given sum (Ac 5:1-10). Stephen's accusers, who falsely accused him of blaspheming Moses and God (Ac 6:11-14). Paul's opponents, falsely accusing him of treason to Caesar (Ac 16:20-21; 17:5-7; 24:5; 25:7-8). The Cretans, who are always liars, evil brutes, lazy gluttons (Tit 1:12).

See Accusation, False; Conspiracy; False Witness; Hypocrisy; Perjury; Teachers, False.

FAME OF JESUS (Mt 4:24-25; 9:26, 31; 14:1; Mk 1:28, 45; Lk 4:14, 37; 5:15; 7:17).

FAMILIAR SPIRITS *See Spiritists.*

FAMILY The concept of the family in the Bible differs from the modern institution. The Hebrew family was larger than families today, including the father of the household, his parents, if living, his wife or wives and children, his daughters and sons-in-law, slaves, guests, and foreigners under his protection. Marriage was arranged by the father of the groom, and the family of the bride, for whom a dowry or purchase money was paid to her father (Ge 24). Polygamy and concubinage were practiced, though not favored by God. A husband could divorce his wife, but she could not divorce him.

The father of a family had the power of life and death over his children. To dishonor a parent was punishable by death (Ex 21:15, 17).

The NT concept followed that of the OT. Parents and children, husbands and wives, masters and slaves were commanded to live together in harmony and love (Eph 5:22-6:9; Col 3:18-4:1).

Good, Exemplified:

Abraham (Ge 18:19). Jacob (Ge 35:2). Joshua (Jos 24:15). David (2Sa 6:20). Job (Job 1:5). Lazarus of Bethany (Jn 11:1-5). Cornelius (Ac 10:2, 33). Lydia (Ac 16:15). The Philippian jailer (Ac 16:31-34). Crispus (Ac 18:8). Lois (2Ti 1:5).

Unhappiness in:

Caused, by indiscreetness (Pr 11:22; 12:4; 14:1; 30:21, 23). By hatred (Pr 15:17). By contention (Pr 18:19; 19:13; 21:9, 19; 25:24; 27:15-16).

Instances of —

Of Abraham, on account of Hagar (Ge 16:5; 21:10-11). Of Isaac, on account of disagreement between Jacob and Esau (Ge 27:4-46). Of Jacob, polygamous jealousy between Leah and Rachel (Ge 29:30-34; 30:1-25). Moses and Zipporah (Ex 4:25-26). Elkanah, on account of feuds (1Sa 1:4-7). David and Michal (2Sa 6:16, 20-23). Xerxes, on account of Vashti's refusing to appear before his drunken officials (Est 1:10-22).

Instituted:

(Ge 2:23-24). Government of (Ge 3:16; 18:19; Est 1:20, 22; 1Co 7:10; 11:3, 7-9; Eph 5:22-24; Col 3:18; 1Ti 3:2, 4-5, 12; 1Pe 3:1, 6). Husband should provide for (Ge 30:30; 1Ti 5:8). Duty to (Isa 58:7). Idolatrous (Jer 7:18).

Persian customs in (Est 1:10-22). *See Harem.*

See Children; Husband; Orphan; Widow; Wife.

Of Saints:

Live in unity (Ge 45:24; Ps 133:1). Live in mutual forbearance (Ge 50:17-21; Mt 18:21-22). Should be taught God's Word (Dt 4:9-10). Rejoice together before God (Dt 14:26). Warned against departing from God (Dt 29:18). Deceivers and liars should be removed from (Ps 101:7). Blessed (Ps 128:3, 6). Should be managed wisely (Pr 31:27; 1Ti 3:4-5, 12). Punishment of irreligious (Jer 10:25). Worship God together (1Co 16:19).

Religion in:

Purpose: To keep the way of the Lord (Ge 18:19), to keep children from sinning (Job 1:5), to be an example to the household (Ps 101:2).

Observed by: Abraham (Ge 12:7-8; 13:3-4; 18:19), Joshua (Jos 24:15), Job (Job 1:5), David (Ps 101:2).

Manifested in observance of religious rites (Ge 17:12-14; 35:2-4, 7; Lk 2:21; Ac 10:2, 47-48; 16:15; 16:25-34; 1Co 1:16), in religious instruction of children (Dt 4:9-10; 11:19-20), in household consecration (Dt 12:5-12; Jos 24:15; Ac 10:1-2; 18:8).

FAMINE

Described:

Pharaoh forewarned of, in dreams (Ge 41). Sent as a judgment (Lev 26:19-29; Dt 28:23-24, 38-42; 1Ki 17:1; 2Ki 8:1; 1Ch 21:12; Ps 105:16; 107:33-34; Isa 3:1-8; 14:30; Jer 14:15-22; 19:9; 29:17, 19; La 5:4-5, 10; Eze 4:16-17; 5:16-17; 14:13-14; Joel 1:15-16; Am 4:6-9; 5:16-17; Hag 1:10-11; Mt 24:7; Lk 21:11; Rev 6:5-8). Description of (Dt 28:53-57; Isa 5:13; 9:18-21; 17:11; Jer 5:17; 14:1-6; 48:33; La 1:11, 19; 2:11-22; 4:4-10; Joel 1:17-20). Righteous delivered from (Job 5:20; Ps 33:19; 37:19).

Cannibalism in (Dt 28:53; 2Ki 6:28).

Instances of:

In Canaan (Ge 12:10; 26:1; 2Sa 21:1; 1Ki 17; 18:1; 2Ki 6:25-29; 7:4). In Egypt (Ge 41:53-57). In Jerusalem, from siege (2Ki 25:3; Jer 52:6). Universal (Ac 11:28).

Figurative:

God will withdraw from those who will not listen to the words of his prophets in the same way that food and water is scarce during famine (Am 8:11).

FAN *See Winnow; Winnowing.*

FANATICISM Absolute and aggressive devotion to religion. The prophets of Baal (1Ki 18:28). The Jews against Christ (Jn 19:15). The Jews in stoning Stephen (Ac 7:57). Saul in persecuting the church (Ac 9:1). The Jews in their rage against Paul (Ac 21:36; 22:23).

FAREWELLS Allusions to (Ru 1:14; Lk 9:61; Ac 18:21; 20:38; 21:6; 2Co 13:11).

FARMER An agriculturalist (Isa 28:24; Jer 14:4; Mt 21:33-46; Mk 12:1-9; Jn 15:1; 1Co 3:9).

Parables of, describing the spread of the gospel (Mt 13:3-23); describing the unfaithful Jews, given over to corruption and hypocrisy (Mt 21:33-46; Mk 12:1-12; Lk 20:9-19).

Figurative:

Of God as the master gardener (Jn 15:1). Of the spread of the gospel (Mt 13:3-23); of Paul and Apollos 1Co 3:5-9). *See Agriculture; Farming.*

FARMING Was the chief occupation of the people of Israel after the conquest of Canaan. Each family received a piece of ground marked by boundaries that could not be removed (Dt 19:14). Plowing took place in the autumn when the ground was softened by the rain. Grain was sown during the month of February; harvest began in the spring and usually lasted from Passover to Pentecost. The grain was cut with a sickle, and gleanings were for the poor (Ru 2:2). The grain was threshed out on the threshing floor, a saucer-shaped area of beaten clay 25 or more feet in diameter, on which animals dragged a sledge over the sheaves to beat out the grain. The grain was winnowed by tossing it into the air to let the chaff blow away and was then sifted to remove impurities (Ps 1:4). Wheat and barley were the most important crops, but other grains and vegetables were cultivated as well. *See Agriculture; Fallow Ground.*

FARTHING NIV "penny." *See Money.*

FASTING

Described:

Accompanied by self-denial (Dt 9:18; Ne 9:1), confession of sin (1Sa 7:6; Ne 9:1-2), reading of the Scriptures (Jer 36:6), prayer (Da 9:3; Mt 17:21).

Commanded (Joel 1:14; 2:12-13). Precepts concerning (Mt 6:16-18).

Of the disobedient, unacceptable (Isa 58:3-7; Jer 14:12; Zec 7:5; Mt 6:16).

Observed:

In times of bereavement, of the people of Jabesh Gilead, for Saul and his sons (1Sa 31:13; 1Ch 10:12), of David, at the time of Saul's death (2Sa 1:12), of Abner's death (2Sa 3:35), of his child's sickness (2Sa 12:16, 21-23).

On occasions of, public calamities (2Sa 1:12; Ac 27:33), private afflictions (2Sa 12:16), approaching danger (Est 4:16; Ac 27:9, 33-34), afflictions (Ps 35:13; Da 6:18), religious observances (Zec 8:19), ordination of ministers (Ac 13:3; 14:23).

Habitual, of the Israelites (Zec 8:19), by John's disciples (Mt 9:14), by Pharisees (Mt 9:14; Mk 2:18; Lk 18:12), by Anna (Lk 2:37), by Cornelius (Ac 10:30), by Paul (2Co 6:5; 11:27).

Prolonged, forty days and nights, by Moses (Ex 24:18; 34:28; Dt 9:9, 18), forty days and nights, by Elijah (1Ki 19:8), three weeks, by Daniel (Da 10:2-3), forty days and nights, by Jesus (Mt 4:2; Mk 1:12-13; Lk 4:1-2).

See Humiliation and Self-Affliction; Humility.

Instances of:

Of the Israelites, in the conflict between the other tribes with the tribe of Benjamin, on account of the wrong suffered by a Levite's concubine (Jdg 20:26), when they went to Mizpah for the ark (1Sa 7:6).

Of David, at the death of Saul (2Sa 1:12), during the sickness of the child born to him by Bathsheba (2Sa 12:16-22), while interceding in prayer for his friends (Ps 35:13), in his zeal for Zion (Ps 69:10), in prayer for himself and his adversaries (Ps 109:4, 24). Of Ahab, when Elijah prophesied the destruction of himself and his house (1Ki 21:27, w 21:20-29). Of Jehoshaphat, at the time of the invasion of the confederated armies of the Canaanites and Syrians (2Ch 20:3).

Of the Jews, in Babylon, with prayer for divine deliverance and guidance (Ezr 8:21, 23), when Jeremiah prophesied against Judea and Jerusalem (Jer 36:9). Of Ezra, on account of the idolatrous marriages of the Jews (Ezr 10:6). Of Nehemiah, on account of the desolation of Jerusalem and the temple (Ne 1:4). Of Darius, when he put Daniel in the lions' den (Da 6:18). Of Daniel, on account of the captivity of the people, with prayer for their deliverance (Da 9:3), at the time of his vision (Da 10:1-3). Of the Ninevites, when Jonah preached to them (Jnh 3:5-10).

Of Paul, at the time of his conversion (Ac 9:9). Of the disciples, at the time of the consecration of Barnabas and Saul (Ac 13:2-3). Of the consecration of the elders (Ac 14:23).

FAT

Offered in Sacrifices:

The layer of fat around the kidneys and other viscera of sacrificial animals which was forbidden for food, but which was burned as an offering to Yahweh (Lev 4:31). Offered in sacrifice (Ex 23:18; 29:13, 22; Lev 1:8; 3:3-5, 9-11, 14-17; 4:8-10; 7:3-5; 8:16, 25-26; 10:15; 17:6; 1Sa 2:15-16; Isa 43:24). Belonged to the Lord (Lev 3:16). Forbidden as food (Lev 3:16-17; 7:23). Idolatrous sacrifices of (Dt 32:38).

Instances of Fat People:

Eglon king of Moab (Jdg 3:17, 22). Eli the priest (1Sa 4:18). *See Corpulency.*

FATHER

Described:

Has various meanings in the Bible:

1. The originator of a way of life (Ge 4:20).
2. A male ancestor, immediate or remote, the father of nations or peoples (Ge 17:4; Ro 9:5).
3. An immediate male progenitor (Ge 42:13).
4. An adviser (Jdg 17:10), or a source (Job 38:28).
5. A spiritual ancestor (Jn 8:44; Ro 4:11).

God is the Creator of the human race (Mal 2:10) and is called the Father of the universe (Jas 1:17).

FATHERHOOD, OF GOD *See God, Fatherhood of.*

FATHER-IN-LAW Unjust, Laban to Jacob (Ge 29:21-23; 31:7, 39-42). Hospitable to son-in-law, a man of Bethlehem in Judah (Jdg 19:3-9).

FATHERLESS *See Orphan.*

FATHERS' GOD (Ex 3:13; Dt 1:11; 4:1; Jos 18:3; 2Ch 28:9; 29:5). *See God.*

FATHOM *See Sounding.*

FATTENED CALF A clean animal fattened for offering to God (1Sa 28:24; 2Sa 6:13; Lk 15:23).

FAULT FINDING (Jude 16). *See Murmuring; Rebuke; Uncharitableness.*

FAVOR *See God, Grace of.*

FAVORITISM Instances of: Rebekah, for her son Jacob (Ge 27:6-17). Jacob, for Rachel (Ge 29:30, 34). Israel (Jacob), for Joseph (Ge 37:3-4). Joseph, for Benjamin (Ge 43:34). Forbidden in parents (Dt 21:15-17). Elkanah, for Hannah (1Sa 1:4-5).

See Partiality.

FEAR *See Cowardice; Fear of God.*

FEAR OF GOD

Described:

As, wisdom (Job 28:28; Pr 15:33), pure (Ps 19:9), the beginning of wisdom (Ps 111:10; Pr 9:10; 15:33), the beginning of knowledge (Pr 1:7), hating evil (Pr 8:13), adding length to life (Pr 10:27), a fountain of life (Pr 14:27), leading to life (Pr 19:23).

Commanded (Lev 19:14, 32; 25:36, 43; Dt 6:13; 10:20; 13:4; Jos 24:14; 1Sa 12:24; 2Ki 17:36; 1Ch 16:30; 2Ch 19:7, 9; Ne 5:9; Ps 2:11; 22:23; 34:9; 96:4; Pr 3:7; 23:17; 24:21; Ecc 5:7; 12:13; Isa 8:13; 29:23; Ro 11:20-21; Col 3:22; 1Pe 2:17; Rev 14:7). Cultivated by God (Ex 3:5; 19:12-13; Heb 12:18-24).

Deters from sin (Ex 20:18-20; Pr 16:6; Jer 32:39-40). Averts temporal calamity (Dt 28:47-49; 28:58-68; 2Ki 17:36-39). Secures divine blessing (Dt 5:29; Ps 25:12-14; 31:19-20; 33:18-19; 34:7, 9; 85:8-9; 103:11, 13, 17; 111:5; 112:1; 115:11, 13; 128:1-4; 145:18-19; Pr 22:4; Ecc 7:18; 8:12-13; Mal 4:2; Lk 1:50; Ac 10:34-35).

Universality of, foretold (Ps 76:11-12; 102:15). A bond of fellowship among righteous (Mal 3:16-18).

Instances of Guilty Fear:

Adam and Eve (Ge 3:8-13). The wicked (Job 15:20-25; 18:11; Pr 10:24). Those without moral direction (Pr 1:24-27). Those without God in general (Isa 2:19-21; 33:14). King Belshazzar (Da 5:6). The nations (Mic 7:17). Judas (Mt 27:3-5). The guards at Jesus' tomb (Mt 28:4). Christians no longer fear (Ro 8:15; 2Ti 1:7). Demons (Jas 2:19). The nations in the day of wrath (Rev 6:16).

Instances of Godly Fear:

Noah, in preparing the ark (Heb 11:7). Abraham, tested in the offering of his son Isaac (Ge 22:12). Jacob, in the vision of the stairway, and the covenant of God (Ge 28:16-17; 42:18). The midwives of Egypt, in refusing to take the lives of the Hebrew children (Ex 1:17, 21). The Egyptians, at the time of the plague of thunder and hail and fire (Ex 9:20).

Phinehas, in turning away the anger of God at the time of the plague (Nu 25:11, w 25:6-15). The nine-and-one-half tribes of Israel west of the Jordan (Jos 22:15-20). Obadiah, in his devotion to God, sheltered one hundred prophets against Jezebel because he feared God more than he feared the wrath of Jezebel (1Ki 18:3-4). Jehoshaphat, in proclaiming a fast when the land was about to be invaded by the armies of the Ammonites and Moabites (2Ch 20:3).

Nehemiah, in his reform of the public administration which had heavily taxed the people and lorded their rule over the people (Ne 5:15). Hanani, which qualified him to be ruler over Jerusalem (Ne 7:2). Job, according to the testimony of Satan (Job 1:8). David (Ps 119:38). Hezekiah, in his treatment of the prophet Micah, who prophesied evil against Jerusalem (Jer 26:19). The Israelites, in obeying the voice of the Lord (Hag 1:12).

The women at the tomb (Mt 28:8). Cornelius, who feared God with all his house (Ac 10:2).

Motivates God's:

Power (Jos 4:24; Ps 99:1; Jer 5:22; Mt 10:28; Lk 12:5), providence (1Sa 12:2-4), power and justice (Job 37:19-24), wrath (Ps 90:11), forgiveness (Ps 130:4), majesty (Jer 10:7).

See Conviction, of Sin; Faith.

Motivates People:

To respect others (Lev 19:14, 30; 25:17, 36, 43). To obedience (Nu 32:15; Dt 6:13-15; 7:1-4; 8:5-6; 10:12-13, 20; 13:4, 6-11; 17:11-13; 21:18-21; 28:14-68; 31:11-13; 1Sa 12:24-25; Job 13:21; 31:1-4, 13-23; Isa 1:20; Jer 4:4; 22:5; Mt 10:28; Lk 12:4-5; 2Co 5:10-11; 2Ti 4:1-2; 2Pe 3:10-12; Rev 14:9-10). To truthfulness (Dt 15:9; 19:16-20). To filial obedience (Dt 21:21).

Reverence:

Expressed in the Old Testament (Ge 35:5; Ex 18:21; 20:18-26; Lev 22:32; Dt 4:10; 5:29; 6:2; 10:12-13, 20-21; 14:23; 17:13; 28:58; Jos 24:14-15; 1Sa 12:14-15, 23-25; 2Sa 23:3-4; 1Ki 8:40; 2Ki 17:36-39; 1Ch 16:30; 2Ch 19:7, 9-10; Ezr 10:3; Job 28:28; 37:24; Ps 2:11; 15:4; 19:9; 22:23, 25; 31:19; 33:8, 18; 34:11; 37:7, 9, 11; 46:10; 52:6; 60:4; 64:9; 67:7; 72:5; 76:7, 11; 85:9; 86:11; 89:7; 90:11; 96:4, 9; 99:1; 102:15; 103:11, 13, 17; 111:5, 10; 112:1; 115:11, 13; 118:4; 119:63, 74, 79; 128:1, 4; 130:4; 135:20; 145:19; 147:11; Pr 1:7; 2:5; 3:7; 8:13; 9:10; 10:27; 14:2, 16, 26-27; 15:16, 33; 16:6; 19:23; 22:4; 23:17; 24:21; 28:14; 31:30; Ecc 3:14; 7:18; 8:12-13; 12:13; Isa 2:10, 19-21; 25:3; 33:6, 13; 50:10-11; 59:19; 60:5; Jer 5:22; 10:7; 32:39, 40; 33:9; Hos 3:5; Mic 7:16-20; Zep 3:7; Zec 2:13; Mal 3:16; 4:2).

Expressed in the New Testament (Mt 10:28; Lk 1:50; 12:5; 23:40; Ac 10:34-35; 13:26; Ro 11:20; 2Co 5:11; 7:1; Eph 5:21; 6:5; Php 2:12-13; Col 3:22; Heb 5:7; 12:28-29; Jas 2:19; 1Pe 1:17; 3:1-2; 1Jn 4:16-18; Rev 11:18; 14:7; 19:5).

See Punishment, Design of, to Secure Obedience; Reward, A Motive, To Faithfulness.

FEASTS

Described:

The host serves his guests (Ge 18:8). Men alone present at (Ge 40:20; 43:32, 34; 1Sa 9:22; Est 1:8; Mk 6:21; Lk 14:24), women alone (Est 1:9). Guests arranged according to age (Ge 43:33), rank (1Sa 9:22; Lk 14:8-10). Men and women attend (Ex 32:6, w 2-3; Da 5:1-4). Marriage feasts provided by the bridegroom (Jdg 14:10, 17). Given by kings (1Sa 20:5; 25:36; 2Sa 9:10; 1Ki 2:7; Est 1:3-8; Da 5:1-4). Drunkenness at (1Sa 25:36; Est 1:10; Da 5:1-4). Wine served at (Est 5:6; 7:7; Isa 5:12). Music at (Isa 5:12; Am 6:4-5; Lk 15:25). Reclined on couches (Am 6:4, 7; Jn 13:23, 25). Dancing at (Mt 14:6; Lk 15:25). Served in one dish (Mt 26:23). Were presided over by a master of the banquet (Jn 2:8-9). *See Entertainments.*

Covenants ratified by (Ge 26:28-31).

Annual Festivals:

Instituted by Moses: Divine protection given during (Ex 34:24). Designated as, sacred assemblies (Lev 23:4). First and last days were sabbatic (Lev 23:39-40; Nu 28:18-25; 29:12, 35; Ne 8:1-18). Kept with rejoicing (Lev 23:40; Dt 16:11-14; 2Ch 30:21-26; Ezr 6:22; Ne 8:9-12, 17; Ps 42:4; Isa 30:29; Zec 8:19). Solemn feasts (Nu 15:3; 2Ch 8:13; La 2:6; Eze 46:9), Appointed feasts (Nu 29:39; Ezr 3:5; Isa 1:14).

The three principal festivals were Passover, Pentecost, and Tabernacles. All males were required to attend (Ex 23:17; 34:23; Dt 16:16; Ps 42:4; 122:4; Eze 36:38; Lk 2:41; Jn 4:45; 7). Attended by women (1Sa 1:3, 9; Lk 2:41). Aliens permitted to attend (Jn 12:20; Ac 2:1-11).

Celebrations for:

Birthdays (Ge 40:20; Mk 6:21), coronations (1Ki 1:25; 1Ch 12:38-40), national deliverances (Est 8:17; 9:17-19).

Figurative:

(Mt 22:1-14; Lk 14:16-24; Rev 19:9, 17).

Observed:

By Jesus (Mt 26:17-20; Lk 2:41-42; 22:15; Jn 2:13, 23; 5:1; 7:10; 10:22-23), by Paul (Ac 20:6, 16; 24:11, 17).

See for full treatment of annual feasts: Dedication; Hanukkah; Kislev; Passover; Pentecost; Purim; Tabernacles, Feast of; Trumpets, Feast of.

FEET Sitting at (Lk 8:35; 10:39; Jas 2:3). Washing of, as an example, by Jesus (Jn 13:4-14). *See Washings.*

FELIX (*fortunate, lucky*). Governor of Judea. Paul tried before (Ac 23:24-35; 24). Trembles under Paul's preaching (Ac 24:25). Leaves Paul in bonds (Ac 24:26-27; 25:14).

FELLOES *See Rim.*

FELLOW A term of reproach (Ge 19:9; 1Sa 21:15; Mt 12:24; 26:61).

FELLOWSHIP Defined (Ecc 4:9, 12; Am 3:3).

Of the Righteous:

In brotherhood (Lev 18:19; 1Sa 23:16-18; Mt 23:8; Jn 13:34-35; 15:17; Ro 14:1-4, 10, 13-21; 1Co 1:10; 12:13; 16:19-20; Gal 6:10; Eph 2:14-21; 5:30; 1Th 4:9-10; Heb 13:1; 1Pe 1:22-23). In worship (Ps 55:13-14; 1Co 10:16-17; Eph 5:19; Col 3:16). In unity of purpose (Ps 119:63; 133:1-3; Am 3:3; Mal 3:16; Jn 17:11, 21-23; Ac 1:14; 2:1, 42, 44-47; Ro 15:6-7; 1Co 1:10; Php 1:3-6, 27-30; 2:1-4; Col 2:2; 1Pe 3:8-9). In ministry (Mt 20:25-28; Mk 10:42-45; Lk 22:32; Ac 20:34-35; Ro 1:12; 15:1-7; Gal 6:2, 10; 1Th 4:18; 5:11, 14; Heb 3:13; 10:24-25; 1Pe 2:17; 1Jn 3:14; 4:7-8, 11-13). Exemplified (Gal 2:9).

With God:

Signified in people walking with God (Ge 5:22, 24; 6:9). Signified in God dwelling with people (Ex 29:45; Ps 101:6; Isa 57:15; Zec 2:10; Jn 14:23; 2Co 6:16; 1Jn 3:24; 4:13; Rev 21:3-4). General (Ex 33:11, 14-17; Lev 26:12; Am 3:3; 2Co 13:11; 1Jn 1:3, 5-7). Possible only through Christ (Mk 9:37; Jn 17:21, 23). *See Communion, With God.*

With Christ:

Attained, by receiving Christ (Mk 9:37; Rev 3:20). By doing God's will (Mt 12:48-50; Lk 8:21). Through a gathering of believers (Mt 18:20; 28:20), commemorating Christ's death (1Co 10:16-17), by walking in the light (1Jn 1:3, 5-7). By abiding in Christ (1Jn 2:6, 24, 28; 3:6, 24). By keeping God's commandments (1Jn 3:6, 24). By continuing in his teaching (2Jn 9). General (Mt 18:20; Lk 24:32; 1Co 1:9; 10:16-17; 1Jn 1:3, 5-7; Rev 3:20). Signified in Christ dwelling with people (Jn 6:56; 14:23; Eph 3:17; Col 1:27; 1Jn 3:24; 4:13). Signified in our union with Christ (Jn 15:1-8; 17:21-23, 26; Ro 7:4; 8:1, 10, 17; 11:17; 12:5; 1Co 6:13-15, 17; 12:12, 27; 2Co 11:2; 13:5; Eph 5:30; Col 3:3; 1Th 5:9-10; Heb 2:11; 1Jn 5:12, 20). Through the Spirit (Jn 14:16; 1Jn 3:6, 24; 4:13). *See Communion, With the Spirit.*

With the Holy Spirit:

General (Jn 14:16-17; Ro 8:9; 1Co 3:16; 2Co 13:14; Gal 4:6; Php 2:1). *See Communion, With the Spirit.*

With the Wicked:

Abhorred by the righteous (Ge 49:6; Ex 33:15-16; Ezr 6:21-22; 9:14; Ps 6:8; 26:4-5). Implicating (Ps 50:18). Revelry (Ps 50:18; Pr 12:11; 29:24; 1Co 15:33; 2Pe 2:18-19). Impoverishing (Pr 28:19). Forbidden with those who provide the wrong type of influence (Ex 23:32-33; 34:12-16; Nu 16:26; Dt 7:2-3; 12:30; 13:6-11; Jos 23:6-8, 13; Ezr 9:12; 10:11; Ps 1:1; Pr 1:10-16; 4:14-17; 14:7; Mt 18:17; Ro 16:17; 1Co 5:9-13; 2Co 6:14-17; Eph 5:11; 2Th 3:6, 14-15; 1Ti 6:3-5; 2Ti 3:2-9; 2Pe 3:17-18; 2Jn 9-11; Rev 18:1-4). Punishment for fellowship with the wicked (Nu 25:1-8; 33:55-56; Dt 31:16-17; Jos 23:12-13; Jdg 3:5-8; Ezr 9:7, 14; Ps 106:34-35, 41-42; Rev 2:16, 22-23).

Instances of Evil Fellowship With the Wicked—

By Solomon (1Ki 11:1-8), Rehoboam (1Ki 12:8-9), Jehoshaphat (2Ch 18:3; 19:2; 20:35-37), Jehoram (2Ch 21:6), Ahaziah (2Ch 22:3-5), Israelites (Ezr 9:1-2), Israel (Eze 44:7), Judas Iscariot (Mt 26:14-16).

Instances of Avoiding Fellowship With the Wicked—

The man of God (1Ki 13:7-10). Nehemiah (Ne 6:2-4; 10:29-31). David (Ps 101:4-7; 119:115). Jeremiah (Jer 15:17). Joseph of Arimathea (Lk 23:51). Church of Ephesus (Rev 2:6).

See Company, Evil; Influence, Evil.

FELLOWSHIP OFFERINGS Traditionally "peace" offerings (Ex 20:24; 24:5; Lev 3:6; 7:11; 19:5). Offered by the leaders (Nu 7:17), by Joshua (Jos 8:31), by David (2Sa 6:17; 24:25). *See Offerings.*

FENCE Walls made of stone enclosing a field, town, etc. (Nu 22:24; Ps 62:3; Pr 24:30-31; Isa 5:2; Mic 7:11). Hedge (Job 1:10; Isa 5:5; Mic 7:4; Hos 2:6).

Figurative (Eze 22:30).

FENCED CITY *See Walled Cities.*

FERMENTED DRINK Intoxicating beverages, usually other than grape wine (Dt 14:26). Used in drink offerings (Nu 28:7).

Forbidden to priests on duty (Lev 10:9), to Nazirites while under a vow (Nu 6:3; cf. Jdg 13:4, 7, 14; Lk 1:15). *See Abstinence; Beer; Drunkenness; Wine.*

FERRET *See Gecko.*

FERTILE CRESCENT A modern description of the territory from the Persian Gulf to Egypt, which is watered by the Euphrates, Tigris, Orontes, Jordan, and Nile rivers. *See Canaan; Mesopotamia; Palestine.*

FESTIVALS *See Feasts.*

FESTUS, PORCIUS (*festal, joyful*). Was the Roman governor who succeeded Felix in the province of Judea (Ac 24:27). He presided at the hearing of the apostle Paul when he made his defense before Herod Agrippa II (Ac 24:27; 26:32). When Paul appealed to Caesar, Festus sent him to Rome. The date of Festus's accession is uncertain, probably A.D. 59/60. He died in office in A.D. 62.

FETTERS A translation of words which have the general meaning "anything that restricts or restrains" as well as those which bear the specific definition "shackle for the foot." Fetters were made from wood, bronze, or iron. The prisoner would have manacles on his wrists which were suspended from his neck by a rope. His feet would have been shackled and connected by a short piece of rope or chain so that the hobbled prisoner could take only short steps (2Sa 3:34; Job 36:13; Ps 2:3; 105:18; 149:8). Used for securing prisoners (2Ch 33:11; 36:6; Mk 5:4). *See Chains; Shackles.*

FEVER (Lev 26:16; Dt 28:22; Job 30:30; Mt 8:14; Ac 28:8).

FEW SAVED The number saved spoken of as few (Mt 7:14; 22:14; Lk 13:24; 1Pe 3:20; Rev 3:4).

FICKLENESS *See Instability.*

FIELD The biblical field was generally not enclosed, but was marked off from its neighbors by boundary markers (Dt 19:14; 27:17; Job 24:2; Pr 22:28; 23:10; Hos 5:10). A cultivated area where crops are grown (Ru 2:2; Ps 107:37), a place where herds could graze (Ge 34:5; Ex 9:21; Nu 22:24).

FIG Aprons made of fig leaves, by Adam and Eve (Ge 3:7). Common to Palestine (Nu 13:23; Dt 8:8), to Egypt (Ps 105:33). Two hundred cakes of, sent by Abigail to David (1Sa 25:18, 19-35). Dried and preserved (1Sa 30:12). Employed as a remedy (2Ki 20:7; Isa 38:21). Trade in (Ne 13:15).

FIG TREE In an allegory (Jdg 9:11). Jeremiah's parable of (Jer 24:1-10). Jesus' cursing of (Mt 21:18-22; Mk 11:12-14, 20-26). Barren, parable of (Lk 13:6-9; 21:29-31).

Figurative of signs of the end times (Mt 24:32; Rev 6:13).

FIGHT OF FAITH (1Ti 6:12; 2Ti 4:7; Heb 10:32; 11:32-34).

FIGURE See "Figurative" under principal topics throughout the work. *See also, Allegory; Pantomime; Parable; Symbols and Similitudes; Types.*

FILIGREE Ornate gold settings for the jewels of the ephod and breastpiece (Ex 28:13, 20; 39:6, 13, 16).

FINANCES Methods of raising money. *See Money; Temple; Tribute.*

FINE For personal injury (Ex 21:22, 30). For theft (Ex 22:4, 7-9; Pr 6:30-31). When sinning unknowingly (Lev 5:15-16; 22:14). For deception (Lev 6:2-6). Restitution for any wrongdoing (Nu 5:5-8).

See Damages and Compensations.

FINGER Used in priestly service (Ex 29:12; Lev 4:6, 17, 25, 30, 34). Six on one hand (2Sa 21:20; 1Ch 20:6).

FINGER OF GOD Anthropomorphism, indicating God's interaction with his creation. Creation (Ps 8:3). Miracles (Ex 8:19). Writing the tablets of the law (Ex 31:18; Dt 9:10). Exorcism (Lk 11:20). *See Anthropomorphisms.*

FINGERS, FINGERBREADTH A unit of measurement. The two bronze pillars of Solomon's temple were four fingers thick and hollow in the center (Jer 52:21). *See Measure.*

FINING POT *See Crucible.*

FIR TREE Wood of, used for building (SS 1:17).

FIRE Children sacrificed in (2Ki 16:3; 17:17). Used as a signal in war (Jer 6:1). Men were burned in a furnace (Jer 29:22; Heb 11:34). The threat of being thrown into a furnace is used by Nebuchadnezzar for all those who would not fall down and worship the image that he set up of (Da 3:6, 11, 15, 21).

Figurative:

Of judgments (Dt 4:24; 32:22; Isa 33:14; Jer 23:29; Am 1:4, 7, 10, 12, 14; 2:2; Mal 3:2; Lk 12:49; Rev 20:9), spiritual power (Ps 104:4; Jer 20:9; Mt 3:11; Lk 3:16), cleansing (Isa 6:6-7), of the destruction of the wicked (Mt 13:42, 50; 25:41; Mk 9:48; Rev 9:2; 21:8).

Everlasting fire (Isa 33:14; Mt 18:8; 25:41; Mk 9:48).

Miracles Connected With:

Miraculously descends upon and consumes Abraham's sacrifice (Ge 15:17), Elijah's (1Ki 18:38), David's (1Ch 21:26), Solomon's, at dedication of the temple (2Ch 7:1-3). Pillar of fire (Ex 13:21-22; 14:19, 24; 40:38; Nu 9:15-23).

Display of, at Elijah's translation (2Ki 2:11). Consumes, the conspirators with Korah, Dathan, and Abiram (Nu 16:35), the captains and their fifties (2Ki 1:9-15).

Torture by (Jer 29:22; Eze 23:25, 47; Da 3).

See Celestial Phenomena; Cloud, Pillar of.

Symbolic:

Of God's presence, with Abram in the covenant (Ge 15:17), in the burning bush (Ex 3:2), on Sinai (Ex 19:18).

Tongues of, on the disciples (Ac 2:3).

See Arson.

FIREBRAND Burning wood used for light (Jdg 7:16), torches used as weapons (Pr 26:18), a remnant of a burnt stick (Am 4:11). *See Torches.*

FIREPAN (*to rake together*). A vessel for carrying live coals (Ex 27:3; 38:3).

FIRKIN *See Gallon.*

FIRMAMENT *See Expanse.*

FIRST BEGOTTEN *See Firstborn.*

FIRST DAY OF THE WEEK *See Sunday.*

FIRSTBORN The first male born, whether man or animal, was reserved by God for himself (Ex 13:2, 12-16; 22:29-30; 34:19-20; Lev 27:26; Nu 3:13; 8:17-18; Dt 15:19-23; Ne 10:36).

Redemption of (Ex 13:13; 34:20; Lev 27:26-27; Nu 3:40-51; 18:15-17). Levites taken instead of firstborn of the families of Israel (Nu 3:12, 40-45; 8:16-18).

Birthright of:

Had precedence over other sons of the family (Ge 4:1, 5-7; Dt 21:15-17), a double portion of inheritance (Dt 21:15-17), royal succession (2Ch 21:3). Sold by Esau (Ge 25:29-34; 27:36; Ro 9:12-13; Heb 12:16). Set aside, that of Manasseh (Ge 48:15-20; 1Ch 5:1), Adonijah (1Ki 2:13-15), Hosah's son (1Ch 26:10). Forfeited by Reuben (Ge 49:3-4; 1Ch 5:1-2). Honorable distinction of (Ex 4:22; Ps 89:27; Jer 31:9; Ro 8:29; Col 1:15; Heb 1:6; 12:23; Rev 1:5).

See Birthright.

Jesus as Firstborn:

Among many brothers (Ro 8:29), over all creation (Col 1:15), from the dead (Col 1:18; Rev 1:5), God's firstborn (Heb 1:6).

FIRSTFRUITS

Offerings of:

First ripe of fruits, grain, oil, wine, and first of the fleece, required as an offering (Ex 22:29; Lev 2:12-16; Nu 18:12; Dt 18:4; 2Ch 31:5; Ne 10:35, 37, 39; Pr 3:9; Jer 2:3; Ro 11:16).

Offerings of, presented at the tabernacle (Ex 22:29; 23:19; 34:26; Dt 26:3-10), belonged to the priests (Lev 23:20; Nu 18:12-13; Dt 18:3-5), must be free from blemish (Lev 22:21; Nu 18:12). Freewill offerings of, given to the prophets (2Ki 4:42).

Offerings described:

Drink (Ge 35:14; Ex 29:40-41; 30:9; 37:16; Lev 23:13, 18, 37; Nu 4:7; Nu 6:15, 17; 15:5, 7, 10, 24; 28:7-31; 29:6, 11, 16, 18-39; Dt 32:38; 2Ki 16:13-15; 1Ch 29:21; 2Ch 29:35; Ezr 7:17; Isa 57:6; Jer 7:18; 19:13; 32:29; 44:17-25; 52:19; Eze 20:28; 45:17; Joel 1:9, 13; 2:14; Php 2:17; 2Ti 4:6). Freewill (Ex 35:29; 36:3; Lev 7:16; 22:18, 21, 23; 23:37-38; Nu 15:3; 29:39; Dt 12:6, 17; 16:10; 2Ch 31:14; Ezr 1:4, 6; 2:68; 3:5; 7:16; 8:28; Ps 54:6; Eze 46:12; Am 4:5). Burnt (Lev 1; 6:8-13). Grain (Lev 2; 6:14-23). Fellowship (Lev 3; 7:11-21). Sin (Lev 4-5:13; 6:24-30). Guilt (Lev 5:14-6:7; 7:1-10). Wave offering (Ex 29:22-26; 35:22; Lev 7:30; 23:10-14, 17).

To be offered as a thank offering upon entrance into the Land of Promise (Dt 26:3-10; 2Ch 29:31; 33:16; Ps 50:14, 23; 56:12; 107:22; 116:17; Jer 17:26; 33:11; Am 4:5).

Figurative: (Ro 8:23; 11:16; 1Co 15:20, 23; Jas 1:18).

See Offerings.

FIRSTLING *See Firstborn.*

FISH Creation of (Ge 1:20-22). Appointed for food (Ge 9:2-3). Clean and unclean (Lev 11:9-12; Dt 14:9-10). Broiled (Jn 21:9-13; Lk 24:42).

Caught with, spears (Job 41:7), nets (Ecc 9:12; Hab 1:14-17; Lk 5:2-6; Jn 21:6-8), hooks (Isa 19:8; Am 4:2; Hab 1:15; Mt 17:27). Sold by men from Tyre living in Jerusalem (Ne 13:16).

Figurative: (Eze 47:9-10).

Miracles Connected With:

Jonah swallowed by (Jnh 1:17; 2; Mt 12:40). The loaves and fishes (Mt 14:19; 15:36-38; Lk 9:13-17). Coin obtained from mouth of (Mt 17:27). Overflowing nets (Lk 5:6-7; Jn 21:6, 8, 11). Furnished for the disciples by Jesus after his resurrection (Lk 24:42; Jn 21:9-13).

FISH GATE An ancient gate on the E side of Jerusalem near Gihon where Tyrians held a fish market (2Ch 33:14; Ne 3:3; 12:39; 13:16; Zep 1:10).

FISH POOL *See Pool.*

FISH SPEAR *See Spear.*

FISHERMEN Certain apostles (Mt 4:18-21; Mk 1:16-20; Jn 21:2-3).

Figurative (Jer 16:16; Mt 4:19).

FISHHOOK *See Hooks.*

FITCH *See Caraway.*

FLAG *See Ensign; Reed.*

FLAGON *See Wine.*

FLATTERY Condemned and rebuked (Job 32:21-22; Ps 12:2-4; Pr 28:23; Lk 6:26). Deceives, self (Ps 36:2). The simple (Ro 16:18).

Practiced by enemies (Ps 12:2; Pr 26:28; 29:5; Jude 16). Against God (Ps 78:36). By seducing women (Pr 5:3; 6:24; 7:5, 21). Not practiced by Paul (1Th 2:4-6).

Instances of:

Jacob (Ge 33:10). Gideon (Jdg 8:1-3). Mephibosheth (2Sa 9:8). Woman of Tekoa (2Sa 14:17-20). Absalom (2Sa 15:2-6). Israel and Judah (2Sa 19:41-43). Adonijah (1Ki 1:42). Ahab (1Ki 20:4). False prophets (1Ki 22:1-13). Darius's officials (Da 6:1-9). Herodians (Lk 20:21). Tyrians (Ac 12:22). Tertullus flatters Felix (Ac 24:2-4). Paul flatters Felix (Ac 24:10). Agrippa (Ac 26:2-3).

FLAX In Egypt (Ex 9:31). In Palestine (Jos 2:6). Linen made from (Pr 31:13; Isa 19:9). *See Linen.*

FLEA (*mosquito*). (1Sa 24:14; 26:20).

FLEECE *See Prayer; Token, 1; Wool.*

FLESH

1. The physical part of the body of people or animals (Ge 17:13-14; 1Co 15:39).

2. Human nature, deprived of the Holy Spirit, and dominated by sin (Ro 7:5, ftn); usually "sinful [nature]" in the NIV.

See Body; Carnal Mindedness.

FLESHHOOK *See Meat Forks.*

F

FLIES Plague of (Ex 8:21-31; Ps 78:45; 105:31). Common sense analogy (Ecc 10:1). Figurative (Isa 7:18).

FLINT

1. Knives of flint used for circumcision (Ex 4:25; Jos 5:2-3).

2. Judah's heart had been inscribed with the point of a flint (Jer 17:1). The Israelites make their hearts harder than flint (Zec 7:12).

Figurative (Isa 5:28; 50:7; Jer 17:1; Eze 3:9; Zec 7:12).

See Hardest Stone; Minerals of the Bible, 1; Stones.

FLOCK A collection of sheep under the care of a shepherd, sometimes including goats as well (Ge 27:9; 30:32). Used figuratively of Christ's disciples (Lk 12:32; 1Pe 5:2-3).

FLOG, FLOGGING

Described:

The practice or system of punishment by repeated lashes or blows, usually with a rod or whip; or an instance of such punishment.

1. Beating is recognized as a legitimate form of punishment (Dt 25:1-3). According to Proverbs, hasty and poor judgments, like careless talk, often lead to strife; the settling of strife involves punishment for those who have been wrong, and it should be recognized that flogging (beating) is "for the back of fools" (Pr 19:29, w 18:6; 20:3).

It is permissible to discipline a child, and parents are encouraged to apply the rod of punishment to drive out folly (Pr 22:15) so that the child will not follow a path of destruction (Pr 19:18; 23:13-14).

The rod "imparts wisdom" (Pr 29:15) and promotes a healthy and happy family (Pr 29:17). Discipline is rooted in love not anger (Pr 3:11-12). *See Abuse.*

2. Elsewhere in the OT it is recognized that even the innocent may sometimes be scourged and crushed by evil individuals (Isa 52:13-53:12, esp 53:5). The suffering of the innocent, often at the hands of evildoers, is a common theme in the Psalms (13; 22; 28; 31:9-24; 35; 38; 41; 69; 71; 86; 102; 109).

3. Jesus warned certain of his disciples that they would be beaten in the synagogues if they continued to preach the gospel (Mk 13:9). According to Ac 5:40, the apostles were beaten by representatives of the Sanhedrin and ordered not to speak in the name of Jesus, but only after Gamaliel had pleaded with his fellow members not to put the defendants to death (Ac 5:33-39). Paul, who himself had beaten and imprisoned many Christians (Ac 22:19-20), was flogged with rods three times (2Co 11:25). In Ac 16:11-24, both Paul and Silas were involved.

Flogging of Jesus:

Prophesied (Isa 50:6). Described (Mt 20:19; 26:67-68; 27:26, 30; Mk 10:34; 15:15, 19; Lk 22:63-64; 23:16; Jn 18:22; 19:1).

See Assault and Battery; Bruise(s); Lashes; Scourging; Stoning; Stripes.

FLOOD Foretold (Ge 6:13, 17). History of (Ge 6-8). The promise that it should not recur (Ge 8:20-22; Isa 54:9). References to (Job 22:16; Mt 24:38-39; Lk 17:26-27; Heb 11:7; 1Pe 3:20; 2Pe 2:5).

See Meteorology.

FLOUR Finely crushed and sifted grain, generally wheat, rye, or barley (Jdg 6:19).

FLOWER *See Plants of the Bible.*

FLUTE A wind instrument (Da 3:5, 7, 10, 15). *See Music, Instruments of.*

FOAL *See Animals.*

FODDER (*mix, mingle*). Food for animals consisting of a mixture of grains (Ge 24:25, 32; 43:24; Jdg 19:19; Job 6:5; 24:6; Isa 30:24).

FOLLY *See Fool.*

FOOD

Articles of:

Bread (Ge 18:5-6; 1Sa 17:17), milk (Ge 49:12; Pr 27:27), vinegar (Nu 6:3; Ru 2:14), oil (Dt 12:17; Pr 21:17, 20; Eze 16:13, 18-19), butter (Ps 55:21; Pr 30:33), roasted grain (Ru 2:14; 1Sa 17:17; 25:18), cheese (1Sa 17:18; Job 10:10), dried fruit (1Sa 25:18; 30:12), meat (Pr 9:2), wine (Jn 2:3-10), fruit (2Sa 16:2), herbs (Ex 12:8; Nu 9:11; 2Ki 4:39; Job 30:4; La 3:15; Lk 11:42), honey (SS 5:1; Isa 7:15), fish (Mt 7:10; Lk 24:42).

From God (Ge 1:29-30; 9:3; Job 36:31; Ps 23:5; 104:14-15; 111:5; 136:25; 145:15; 147:9; Pr 30:8; Isa 3:1; Mt 6:11; Ac 14:17; Ro 14:14, 21; 1Ti 4:3-5).

Practices Concerning:
Men and women did not partake together (Ge 18:8-9; Est 1:3, 9). Prepared by females (Ge 27:9; 1Sa 8:13; Pr 31:15). A hymn sung after (Mt 26:30). Thanks given before (Mk 8:6; Ac 27:35).
Things prohibited as (Ex 22:31; Lev 11:4-8, 10-20, 41-42; 17:13-15). Peter's vision concerning (Ac 10:10-16). Paul's teaching concerning the eating of food offered to idols (Ro 14:2-23; 1Co 8:4-13; 10:18-32). Flesh unwarrantedly forbidden as (1Ti 4:3-4).
See Bread; Eating; Oven.

FOOL
In Scripture connotes conceit and pride, or deficiency in judgment rather than mental inferiority.

Described as:
Arrogant (Ps 5:5). Iniquitous (Ps 107:17; Tit 3:3). Atheistic (Ps 14:1; 53:1). A reproach (Ps 74:18, 22). Despising wisdom (Pr 1:7, 22; 18:2). Deceitful (Pr 1:14, 18). Contentious (Pr 1:18; 18:6-7; 29:9). Clamorous (Pr 9:13). An embarrassment to his father (Pr 10:1; 15:20; 17:25; 19:13). Excessively talkative (Pr 10:8, 10; 29:11; Ecc 10:12-14). A mocker (Pr 14:9). A dreamer (Pr 17:24). Quarrelsome (Pr 20:3). Wasteful (Pr 21:20). Idle (Ecc 4:5). Willful (Pr 1:7; 27:22). Lacking in understanding (Pr 9:13; 10:13; 15:21; 26:1, 3-12; Ecc 7:4-6). Deficient in conscience (Pr 10:23). Practice deception (Pr 14:8). Gullible (Pr 14:15). Unknowledgeable (Pr 15:7). Angry (Ecc 7:9). Unperceptive (Mt 7:26-27).

General:
Causes sorrow (Pr 10:1; 17:25; 19:13). To be forsaken (Pr 9:6). To be avoided (Pr 14:8). Some suffer affliction because of (Ps 107:17).

Parables of:
The foolish virgins (Mt 25:1-13). The rich fool (Lk 12:16-20).

FOOT
Washing the feet, of the disciples by Jesus (Jn 13:4-16), by disciples (1Ti 5:10). *See Purification; Washing.*
Figurative (Mt 18:8).
For footwear: *See Sandal.*

FOOTMAN
See Runner.

FOOTSTOOL
A literal support for the feet (2Ch 9:18), a figure of subjection (Ps 110:1; Isa 66:1; Mt 5:35).

FORD
(*pass over, through*). A shallow place in a stream where people and animals could cross on foot (Ge 32:22; Isa 16:2).

FOREHEAD
The part of the face above the eyes. Often revealing the character of the person— Shamelessness (Jer 3:3), courage (Eze 3:9), or godliness (Rev 7:3).

FOREIGNER
Among the Jewish people, anyone outside the nation was regarded as inferior (Ge 31:15) and possessed restricted rights.
He could not eat the Passover (Ex 12:43), intermarry on equal terms (Ex 34:12-16), become king (Dt 17:15), enter the sanctuary (Eze 44:9; Ac 21:28-29). They could be included in the nation by accepting the law and its requirements.
In the NT the word is applied to those who are not members of God's kingdom (Eph 2:19).

FOREKNOWLEDGE OF GOD
See God, Foreknowledge of, Wisdom of.

FOREMAN
See Master Craftsman.

FOREORDINATION
See Predestination.

FORERUNNER
Figurative of Christ, "who went before us" (Heb 4:14; 6:20).

FORESKIN
The fold of skin cut off in the process of circumcision (Ge 17:11, 14; Ex 4:25; 1Sa 18:25, 27; 2Sa 3:14). *See Circumcision.*

FORESTS

Described:
Abounded with wild honey (1Sa 14:25-26). Populated by wild beasts (Ps 50:10; 104:20; Isa 56:9; Jer 5:6; Mic 5:8). Undergrowth often in (Isa 9:18). Tracts of land covered with trees (Isa 44:14). Often afforded pasture (Mic 7:14).
Were places of refuge (1Sa 22:5; 23:16). Hereth (1Sa 22:5). Ephraim (2Sa 18:6, 8). Supplied timber for building (1Ki 5:6-8). Lebanon (1Ki 7:2; 10:17). Carmel (Isa 33:9; 35:1-2; Na 1:4). Often destroyed by enemies (2Ki 19:23; Isa 37:24; Jer 46:23). Jotham built towers in (2Ch 27:4). Owned by King Artaxerxes and kept by Asaph (Ne 2:8). The power of God extends over (Ps 29:9). The oaks of Bashan (Isa 2:13; Eze 27:6; Zec 11:2). Arabia (Isa 21:13). Called on to rejoice at God's mercy (Isa 44:23).

Illustrative:
Prophecies concerning the coming invasion of Jerusalem by Sennacherib, its failure to withstand the invasion, and the unbelief of the Jews. The moral change in the Jewish nation shall be as great as if the wooded Lebanon were to become a fruitful field and vice versa (Isa 29:17). These prophecies are illustrative of those accustomed to a life of self-indulgence, who because of the devastations of the enemy would now go without (Isa 32:15, 19). Illustrative of the sourthern kingdom (Eze 20:46-47).
Destruction of illustrates the destruction of the wicked (Isa 9:18; 10:17-18; Jer 21:14).

FORGERY
See Seal.

FORGETTING GOD
A characteristic of the wicked (Pr 2:17; Isa 65:11). Backsliders guilty of (Jer 2:32; 3:21).
Is forgetting his covenant (Dt 4:23; 2Ki 17:38), past deliverances (Jdg 8:34; Ps 78:42-43), what he has done (Ps 78:7, 11; 106:13), benefits (Ps 103:2), kindnesses (Ps 106:7), law (Ps 119:153, 176; Hos 4:6), Jerusalem (Ps 137:5), power to deliver (Isa 51:13-15), word of encouragement (Heb 12:5), Word of God (Jas 1:22-25).
Cautions against (Dt 6:12; 8:11). Prosperity leads to (Dt 8:11-20; Hos 13:6). Trials should not lead to (Ps 44:17-22). Exhortation to those guilty of (Ps 50:22). Resolve against (Ps 119:16, 93). Encouraged by false teachers (Jer 23:27).
Punishment of (Job 8:12-13; Ps 9:17; Isa 17:10-11; Eze 23:35; Hos 8:11-14), threatened (Ps 50:22).
See Apostasy; Backsliders; Forsaking God.

FORGIVENESS

Of Enemies:
By showing kindness to enemy's animal (Ex 23:4-5). By giving (Pr 25:21-22; Mt 5:39-41; Ro 12:20). Commanded (Pr 24:17; Mt 5:38-48; 18:21-35; Mk 11:25; Lk 6:27-37).
See Enemy.

Each Other:
(Lk 17:3-4; Eph 4:32; Col 3:13; Phm 10, 18). A condition of divine forgiveness (Mt 6:12-15; 18:21-35; Mk 11:25; Lk 11:4).
Spirit of, disallows rejoicing (Pr 24:17-18). Disallows retaliation (Pr 24:29; Ro 12:17, 19). Blesses (Ro 12:14; 1Co 4:12-13; 1Pe 3:9).

FORM
In religious service (1Ch 15:13-14; 2Ch 29:34). Irregularity in (2Ch 30:2-5, 17, 20; Mt 12:3-4).
See Church, The Body of Believers, State.

FORMALISM
Despised by God (Isa 1:11-15; 29:13-16; Ps 50:8-15; Jer 6:20; 14:12; Am 5:21-23; Mal 1:6-14; Lk 13:24-27; 2Ti 3:1-5). Empty (Mt 15:8-9; Ro 2:17-29; 1Co 7:19; Php 3:4-7).
Rejected by God for presenting sacrifices rather than, obedience (1Sa 15:22-23; Ecc 5:1; 1Co 7:19; 1Jn 2:3-11), thanksgiving (Ps 50:8-15; 69:30-31), repentance (Ps 51:16-17), mercy (Hos 6:6; Mic 6:6-8; Mt 9:13; 12:7), justice, mercy, and humility (Mic 6:6-8), a pure heart (Mt 15:8-9; Ro 2:17-29).

FORNICATION
Instructions concerning illicit sexual intercourse (Ac 15:20, 29; 21:25; 1Co 5:1; 6:13, 18; 7:2). More specifically and primarily unlawful intercourse of an unwed person (Mt 15:19; Mk 7:21; 1Co 6:9, 18; Gal 5:19). It was commonly associated with heathen worship (Jer 2:20; 3:6) and was used as a figure of disloyalty to God (Eze 16:3-22).
See Adultery; Prostitute.

FORSAKING GOD

Exemplified:
The wicked guilty of (Dt 28:20). Idolaters guilty of (1Sa 8:8; 1Ki 11:33). Backsliders guilty of (Jer 15:6).
Israelites (1Sa 12:10). Saul (1Sa 15:11). Ahab (1Ki 18:18). Amon (2Ki 21:22). Kingdom of Judah (2Ch 12:1, 5; 21:10; Isa 1:4; Jer 15:6). Kingdom of Israel (2Ch 13:11, w 2Ki 17:7-18). Many disciples (Jn 6:66). Phygelus and Hermogenes (2Ti 1:15). Balaam son of Beor (2Pe 2:15).

Condemned:
Forsaking the covenant (Dt 29:25; 1Ki 19:10; Jer 22:9; Da 11:30). Prosperity tempts to (Dt 31:20; 32:15). Provokes God to forsake people (Jdg 10:13; 2Ch 15:2; 24:20, 24). Resolve against (Jos 24:16; Ne 10:29-39).
Warnings against (Jos 24:20; 1Ch 28:9). His house (2Ch 29:6). His commandments (Ezr 9:10). Sin of, to be confessed (Ezr 9:10). Unreasonableness and ingratitude of (Jer 2:5-6). Leads men to follow their own devices (Jer 2:13). Wickedness of (Jer 2:13; 5:7). Trusting in man is (Jer 17:5). Curse pronounced upon (Jer 17:5). Brings confusion (Jer 17:13). Brings down his wrath (Ezr 3:12). Followed by remorse (Eze 6:9). The right way (2Pe 2:15).
See Forgetting God; Apostasy.

FORT, FORTIFICATION

A Military Defense:
Caves used for (Jdg 6:2; 1Sa 23:26). Field-made during military operations (Dt 20:19-20; 2Ki 25:1; Jer 6:6; 32:24; 33:4; Eze 4:2; 17:17; 26:8; Da 11:15). Defenses of cities (2Sa 5:9; 2Ch 11:10-11; 26:9, 15; Ne 3:8; 4:2; Isa 22:10; 25:12; 29:3; Jer 51:53; Na 3:14). Erected in, vineyards and herding grounds (Isa 5:2; Mt 21:33; Mk 12:1), the desert (2Ch 26:10).

Figurative:
Of God's care (2Sa 22:2-3, 47; Ps 18:2; 31:3; 71:3; 91:2; 144:2; Pr 18:10; Na 1:7).

FORTITUDE
See Courage.

FORTUNATUS
(*fortunate*). A Corinthian Christian, a friend of Paul (1Co 16:17).

FORTUNE
1. Changes of. See illustrated in lives of Joseph, from slave to prime minister. *See Joseph, 1.* Pharaoh's butler and baker (Ge 40). David, from shepherd boy to king, noting the changes (1Sa 15:3, 7-16:13; 2Sa 2:1-7). *See David; also Jeroboam; Haman; Mordecai; Esther; Job; Daniel.*
2. A pagan god (Isa 65:11).

FORTUNE-TELLING
See Sorcery.

FORTY
A significant number.

Days:
Of rain, at the time of the flood (Ge 7:17), of flood, before sending forth the raven (Ge 8:6). For embalming (Ge 50:3). Jesus in the desert (Mt 4:2; Mk 1:15; Lk 4:2), compare to Israel's forty years in the desert. Spies in the land of promise (Nu 13:25). Goliath challenged Israel (1Sa 17:16). Symbolic (Eze 4:6). Of probation, given to the Ninevites (Jn 3:4). Christ's stay after the Resurrection (Ac 1:3).

Days of fasting:
By Moses (Ex 24:18; 34:28; Dt 9:9, 25), Elijah (1Ki 19:8), Jesus (Mt 4:2).

Years:
Isaac's and Esau's age at time of marriages (Ge 25:20; 26:34). Wandering of the Israelites in the desert (Ex 16:35; Nu 14:34). Caleb's age when he spied out the land (Jos 14:7). Peace in Israel (Jdg 3:11; 5:31; 8:28). Eli as judge (1Sa 4:17), Saul as king (Ac 31:21), David as king (2Sa 5:4), Solomon (1Ki 11:42), Joash (2Ki 12:1). Egypt, to be desolated (Eze 29:11), to be restored after (Eze 29:13).

Lashes:
Administered as punishment for criminals (Dt 25:3; 2Co 11:24).

FORUM OF APPIUS
A place forty-three miles SE of Rome, where Paul was met by friends (Ac 28:15).

FOUNDATION
The lowest part of a building, and on which it rests (Lk 14:29; Ac 16:26).

Described:
Of stone (1Ki 5:17). Joined together by cornerstones (Ezr 4:12, w 1Pe 2:6, & Eph 2:20). Strongly laid (Ezr 6:3). Security afforded by (Mt 7:25; Lk 6:48). Deep laid (Lk 6:48).

Figuratively Applied to:
Kingdoms (Ex 9:18). The mountains (Dt 32:22). The heavens (2Sa 22:8). The earth (Job 38:4; Ps 104:5). The world (Mt 13:35). The ocean (Ps 104:8).

Illustrative of:
Hope of saints (Ps 87:1). The righteous (Pr 10:25). Christ (Isa 28:16; 1Co 3:11). Doctrines of the apostles (Eph 2:20). Decrees and purposes of God (2Ti 2:19). First principles of the gospel (Heb 6:1-2). Security of saints' inheritance (Heb 11:10).

Laid for:
Cities (Jos 6:26; 1Ki 16:34). Temples (1Ki 6:37; Ezr 3:10). Walls (Ezr 4:12; Rev 21:14). Houses (Lk 6:48). Towers (Lk 14:28-29).

FOUNDING
See Molding.

FOUNTAIN
Fountain of life (Ps 36:9; Pr 10:11; 13:14; 14:27; 16:22). Figurative of faithful wife (Pr 5:18; SS 4:12, 15).
Prophetic life-giving and cleansing fountain from the temple (Joel 3:18; Zec 13:1, w Rev 22:1-2).
See Fountain of Life; Spring; Wells.

FOUNTAIN GATE
A gate in the walls of Jerusalem (Ne 2:14; 3:15; 12:37).

FOUNTAIN OF LIFE
(Ps 36:9; Pr 13:14; 14:27; Jer 2:13; 17:13; Zec 13:1; Rev 7:17).

FOWL
See Birds.

FOWLER, FOWLER'S SNARE
A bird-catcher (Ps 91:3; 124:7).

Figurative:
1. Of the calamities and plots which await (Job 22:10; Ps 91:3; 124:7; Pr 22:5; Isa 24:17; Jer 48:43; Hos 9:8).
2. As the source or agent of calamity (Jos 23:13; Ps 69:22; Isa 8:14; Hos 5:1).

FOX
Samson uses, to burn the field of the Philistines (Jdg 15:4-5). Depreciations of (SS 2:15). Dens of (Mt 8:20; Lk 9:58).

Figurative: Of heretics (SS 2:15). Of unfaithful prophets (Eze 13:1-7). Of craftiness (Lk 13:32).
See Jackal.

FRACTURES
Treatment of (Eze 30:21).

Figurative: David calling for God to break the arm of the wicked man (Ps 10:15). David claiming that the power of the wicked will be broken (Ps 37:17). The strength of Moab is broken (Jer 48:25).

FRAGRANCE
Fragrant offerings (Lev 4:7; Nu 4:16). Metaphorical of acceptable service to God (2Co 2:14, 16; Eph 5:2; Php 4:18).

FRANKINCENSE
A fragrant gum resin consisting of small, white chunks and beads which are easily ground into a powder; this powder emits a sweet odor when burned. An ingredient of the sacred oil (Ex 30:34). Commerce in (Rev 18:11-13).

FRATERNITY
(*mutual, familial love*).

Commanded by:
Moses to the Israelites (Dt 15:7-15; Jos 1:14-15). David (Ps 22:22; 133:1-3). Malachi (Mal 2:10). Jesus (Ps 22:22; Mt 5:22-26; 18:15-18, 21-22, 35; 23:8; 25:40; Jn 13:34-35; 15:12-14; 21:17). Paul (Ro 12:10; 1Co 6:1-8; Gal 6:1-5; 1Th 4:9; 2Th 3:14-15). In Hebrews (Heb 13:1). Peter (1Pe 1:12; 2:17; 3:8; 2Pe 1:5, 7). John (1Jn 2:9-11).
Nazirites, vows of (Nu 6:1-21; La 4:7; Am 2:11-12; Ac 21:24-31). *See Nazirite(s), Nazarite(s).*
Unity (Ps 133:1-3). Broken (Zec 11:14). Incompatible with, pride of title (Mt 23:8). Indifference to another's conscience (1Co 8:1-13; 10:28-29). Selfishness (1Jn 3:17).

Exemplified:
By Abraham and Lot (Ge 13:8). By Jonathan and David (1Sa 18:1; 19:2-7; 20:17, 41-42; 23:16-18). By early Christians (Ac 2:42-47). By Paul (Ro 9:2-3; 10:1-4; 1Co 9:20-23). By James, Peter, and John (Gal 2:9). By Epaphroditus (Php 2:25-26). By the Thessalonian church (2Th 1:3).
See Brother; Church, The Body of Believers; Fellowship; Friendship; Love.

FRATRICIDE
One who kills or murders his own brother or sister. Instances of: Cain (Ge 4:8). Abimelech (Jdg 9:5). Absalom (2Sa 13:28-29). Solomon (1Ki 2:23-25). Jehoram (2Ch 21:4). *See Homicide; Murder.*

FRAUD
See Dishonesty.

FREEDMAN
A slave who has been granted his freedom (1Co 7:22), or a free man as contrasted with a slave (Gal 4:22-23), among Christians (Col 3:11).

FREEDMEN One of a number of synagogues at Jerusalem, conducted for Jews who spoke Greek rather than Aramaic, the latter being the native language of Palestinian Jews (Ac 6:9).
See Emancipation.

FREEDOM From servitude. *See Emancipation; Jubilee.*

FREEWILL *See Blessings, Spiritual, Contingent Upon Obedience.*

FREEWILL OFFERINGS In the category of gifts, freewill offerings were voluntary offerings prompted solely by the impulse of the donor (Lev 22:21, 23; 23:38; Nu 29:39; Dt 12:6, 17; 2Ch 31:14; Ezr 3:5; 7:16; 8:28; Ps 119:108; 2Co 8:1-15).
See Beneficence; Gift, Giving; Liberality; Offerings.

FRET The verb means to be irritated, angry, or nervous (Ps 37:1, 7-8; Pr 24:19).

FRIENDS

General:
Affectionate (Dt 13:6; 1Sa 18:1; 20:17; Jn 15:9-17). Sympathetic (Job 2:11; 6:14; Ps 35:14). Mercenary (Pr 14:20; 19:4, 6). Forsaken (Pr 17:9; 27:14). Faithful (Pr 17:17; 18:24; 27:6). Of mutual help (Pr 27:9, 19). Cause rejoicing (Pr 27:9). Not to forsake (Pr 27:10). *See Friendship.*
Jesus calls his disciples (Lk 12:4; Jn 15:14-15).

False: (Ps 41:9; 88:18; Zec 13:6).
Instances of: Pharaoh's chief cupbearer to Joseph (Ge 40:23). Delilah to Samson (Jdg 16:4-21). The wife of a Levite living in the hill country of Ephraim (Jdg 19:1-2). David, to Uriah (2Sa 11), to Joab (1Ki 2:5-6). Ahithophel to David (2Sa 15:12). Job's friends (Job 6:14-30; 19:13-22). David's friends to David (Ps 31:11-12; 35:11-16; 41:9; 55:12-14, 20-21; 88:8). Judas (Mt 26:48-49; Mk 14:43-50; Lk 22:47-48; Ac 1:16-17). Jesus' disciples (Mt 26:56, 58). Paul's friends (2Ti 4:16).
See Hypocrisy.

FRIENDSHIP

General:
Value of (Ecc 4:9-12). Faithfulness in (Ps 35:13-14; Pr 17:9, 17; 27:6, 9-10, 14, 17, 19). Trials growing out of (Dt 13:6-9; Pr 22:24-25).
Promoted by, sympathy (Job 6:14-15). Fidelity (Pr 11:13). Not wearing out one's welcome (Pr 25:17). Mutual understanding (Am 3:3).
See Friends.

Instances of:
Abraham and Lot (Ge 14:14-16). Ruth and Naomi (Ru 1:16-17). David and Jonathan (1Sa 18:1-4; 20; 23:16-18; 2Sa 1:17-27; 9:1-13). David and Abiathar (1Sa 22:23). David and Mephibosheth (2Sa 9). David and Nahash (2Sa 10:2). David and Ittai (2Sa 15:19-22). David and Hushai (2Sa 15:32-37; 16; 17:1-22). David and Hiram (1Ki 5:1). Joram and Ahaziah (2Ki 8:28-29; 9:16). Jehu and Jehonadab (2Ki 10:15-27). Job and his three friends (Job 2:11-13). Daniel and his three companions (Da 2:49).
The Marys, and Joseph of Arimathea, for Jesus (Mt 27:55-61; 28:1-8; Lk 24:10; Jn 20:11-18). Mary, Martha, and Lazarus, and Jesus (Lk 10:38-42; Jn 11:1-46). Luke and Theophilus (Ac 1:1). Paul and his nephew (Ac 23:16). Paul, Priscilla, and Aquila (Ro 16:3-4). Paul, Timothy, and Epaphroditus (Php 2:19-20, 22, 25).

FRINGES *See Tassel(s).*

FROGS Plague of (Ex 8:2-14; Ps 78:45; 105:30).
Symbolic (Rev 16:13).

FRONTLETS A leather band worn on the forehead (Ex 13:6-16; Dt 6:1-8; 11:18). *See Phylactery.*

FROST Appeared in winter on the high elevations in Bible lands (Job 37:10; 38:29).

FROWARDNESS *See Disobedience to God.*

FRUGALITY

General:
Diligent (Pr 12:27). Good (Pr 13:22). Wise (Pr 21:17; 21:20). Prudent (Pr 22:3). Industrious (Eph 4:28). The mark of a virtuous woman (Pr 31:27).
Admonition regarding (Pr 23:20-21). Commanded by Jesus (Jn 6:12).
Pretense of to cover greed (Mk 14:4-5).

Instances of:
The provisions made by the Egyptians against famine (Ge 41:48-54), the gathering of manna (Ex 16:17-18, 22-24). The gathering of bread and fish after the feeding of the multitudes (Mt 14:20; 15:37).
See Extravagance; Industry.

FRUIT TREES Planting and first harvest (Lev 19:23-25). Care for (Dt 20:19-20). In Ezekiel's vision, evergreen and with healing properties (Eze 47:12). *See Tree.*

FRUITS

Natural: Created (Ge 1:11-12, 27-29).
See the list of various fruit-producing trees at Tree.

Spiritual: (Gal 5:22-23). *See Righteousness, Fruits of; Sin, Fruits of; Holy Spirit, Fruit of.*

FRYING PAN *See Pan(s).*

FUEL Wood, charcoal, dried grass, and even the dung of animals and humans was used for fuel (Eze 4:12, 15; Mt 6:30; Jn 18:18).

FUGITIVES

From Servitude:
Not to be returned (Dt 23:15-16).

From Justice:
Moses (Ex 2:15), Absalom (2Sa 13:34-38).

From the Avenger of Blood:
See Avenger of Blood; Cities of Refuge.

From the Wrath of the King:
David (1Sa 21:10), Jeroboam (1Ki 11:40), Joseph, to Egypt (Mt 2:13-15).

Instances of:
From slavery, Shimei's servants (1Ki 2:39), Onesimus (Phm 10).
See Exodus.

FULLER NIV "launderer"; one who cleans or dyes cloth or garments. The word is also used at times for one who thickens and shrinks newly shorn wool and newly woven cloth after cleansing it of natural oils. He may also have traded in textiles (Mal 3:2; Mk 9:3). *See Soap.*

FULLER'S FIELD *See Washerman's Field.*

FULLNESS OF TIME The time appointed when God's purposes for mankind and history for a particular event have been fulfilled (Mk 1:15; Gal 4:4; Eph 1:10; 1Ti 2:6; Tit 1:3; Heb 9:26).

FUNERAL The ceremonies used in disposing of a dead human body. In Palestine the body was buried within a few hours after death in a tomb or cave. The body was washed, anointed with spices, and wrapped in cloths (Jn 12:7; 19:39-40). Refusal of proper burial was utter disgrace (Jer 22:19).

FURLONG *See Stadia.*

FURNACE Furnaces of the biblical period were made of brick or stone and were designed for different purposes, from small domestic types to large commercial smelters as those at Ezion Geber.

Figurative:
Of affliction (Dt 4:20; 1Ki 8:51; Ps 12:6; Isa 48:10; Jer 11:4). Of the Lord who refines the heart (Pr 17:3). Of lust (Hos 7:4). Of hell (Mal 4:1; Mt 13:42, 50; Rev 9:2).

Uses of:
For refining gold (Pr 17:3), silver (Eze 22:22; Mal 3:3). For melting lead and tin (Eze 22:20). For capital punishment, Shadrach, Meshach, and Abednego cast into by Nebuchadnezzar (Da 3:6-26).

FURNITURE The principle reference to furniture in the Bible concerns the articles in the tabernacle and temple. Common people had little furniture; kings had beds (Dt 3:11) and tables (Jdg 1:7).

FUTURE *See Immortality; Eschatology.*

FUTURE PUNISHMENT *See Punishment, Eternal.*

GAAL (*loathing*). Son of Ebed, who led the men of Shechem in a revolt against Abimelech, the son of Gideon (Jdg 9:26-41).

GAASH (*rumble, quake*). A foothill of Mt. Ephraim. Joshua's inheritance embraced (Jos 24:30). Joshua buried on the north side of (Jos 24:30; Jdg 2:9). Brooks of (2Sa 23:30).

GABA *See Geba.*

GABBAI (*collector*). A chief of Benjamin (Ne 11:8).

GABBATHA (possibly *height, ridge*). The place called "the Stone Pavement" (Jn 19:13), where Jesus was tried before Pilate.

GABRIEL (*[strong] man of God [El]*). A messenger of God. Appeared to Daniel (Da 8:16; 9:21), to Zechariah (Lk 1:11-19), to Mary (Lk 1:26-29).

GAD, GADITES (*fortune*).
1. Jacob's seventh son (Ge 30:11; 35:26; Ex 1:4). Children of (Ge 46:16; Nu 26:15-18; 1Ch 5:11). Prophecy concerning (Ge 49:19).
2. A tribe of Israel. Blessed by Moses (Dt 33:20). Enumeration of, at Sinai (Nu 1:14, 24-25), in the plains of Moab (Nu 26:15-18), in the reign of Jotham (1Ch 5:11-17). Place of, in camp and march (Nu 2:10, 14, 16). Wealth of, in cattle, and spoils (Nu 32:1; Jos 22:8). Petition for their portion of land E of the Jordan (Nu 32:1-5; Dt 3:12, 16-17; 29:8). Boundaries of territory (Jos 13:24-28; 1Ch 5:11). Aid in the conquest of the region W of the Jordan (Nu 32:16-32; Jos 4:12-13; 22:1-8). Erect a monument to signify the unity of the tribes E of the Jordan with the tribes W of the river (Jos 22:10-14).
Disaffected toward Saul as king and joined the faction under David in the wilderness of Hebron (1Ch 12:8-15, 37-38). Join the Reubenites in the war against the Hagrites (1Ch 5:10, 18-22). Smitten by the king of Syria (2Ki 10:32-33). Carried into captivity to Assyria (1Ch 5:26). Land of, occupied by the Ammonites, after the tribe is carried into captivity (Jer 49:1). Reallotment of territory to, by Ezekiel (Eze 48:27, 29).
3. A prophet of David (2Sa 24:11). Requests David leave Adullam (1Sa 22:5). Bears the divine message to David offering choice between three evils, for his presumption in numbering Israel (2Sa 24:11-14; 1Ch 21:9-13). Requests David build an altar on threshing floor of Araunah (2Sa 24:18-19; 1Ch 21:18-19). Assists David in organizing temple service (2Ch 29:25). Writings of (1Ch 29:29).

GADARENES The region around the city of Gadara is six miles SE of the S end of the Sea of Galilee (Mt 8:28). Mark and Luke identify the region by the capital city Gerasa, located about thirty-five miles southeast of the Sea (Mk 5:1; Lk 8:26 and ftns).
See Gerasenes.

GADDAH *See Hazar Gaddah.*

GADDI (*my fortune*). A chief of Manasseh. One of the twelve spies who explored Canaan (Nu 13:11).

GADDIEL (*God [El] is my fortune* BDB; *[pagan god] Gad is [my] god* KB). A chief of Zebulun. One of the twelve spies (Nu 13:10).

GADER *See Beth Gader.*

GADI (*my fortune*). Father of Menahem, a king of Israel (2Ki 15:14-20).

GAHAM (*burning brightly*). A son of Nahor by his concubine Reumah (Ge 22:24).

GAHAR (*[born in the] year of little rain*). One of the temple servants (Ezr 2:47; Ne 7:49).

GAIUS
1. A Macedonian and companion of Paul. Seized at Ephesus (Ac 19:29).
2. A man of Derbe. Accompanied Paul from Macedonia (Ac 20:4).
3. A Corinthian, whom Paul baptized (Ro 16:23; 1Co 1:14).
4. Man to whom 3 John was addressed (3Jn 1).

GALAL (possibly *tortoise* IDB; *roll away* KB).
1. A Levite (1Ch 9:15).
2. Son of Jeduthun (1Ch 9:16; Ne 11:17).

GALATIA A province of Asia Minor. Its churches visited by Paul (Ac 16:6; 18:23). Collection taken in, for Christians at Jerusalem (1Co 16:1). Peter's address to (1Pe 1:1). Churches in (Gal 1:1-2). *See Galatians, Epistle to the.*

GALATIANS, EPISTLE TO THE

Author: The apostle Paul

Date:
If the letter was addressed to churches located in north-central Asia Minor (Pessinus, Ancyra and Tavium), Galatians was written between A.D. 53 and 57.
If the letter was addressed to churches in the southern area of the Roman province of Galatia (Antioch, Iconium, Lystra and Derbe), Galatians was written A.D. 48 or 49.

Outline:
I. Introduction (1:1-9).
A. Salutation (1:1-5).
B. Denunciation (1:6-9).
II. Personal: Authentication of the Apostle of Liberty and Faith (1:10-2:10).
A. Paul's Gospel Was Received by Special Revelation (1:10-12).
B. Paul's Gospel Was Independent of the Jerusalem Apostles and the Judean Churches (1:13-2:21).
1. Evidenced by his early activities as a Christian (1:13-17).
2. Evidenced by his first post-Christian visit to Jerusalem (1:18-24).
3. Evidenced by his visit to Jerusalem fourteen years later (2:1-10).
4. Evidenced by his rebuke of Peter at Antioch (2:11-21).
III. Doctrinal: Justification of the Doctrine of Liberty and Faith (chs. 3-4).
A. The Galatians' Experience of the Gospel (3:1-5).
B. The Experience of Abraham (3:6-9).
C. The Curse of the Law (3:10-14).
D. The Priority of the Promise (3:15-18).
E. The Purpose of the Law (3:19-25).
F. Sons, Not Slaves (3:26-4:11).
G. Appeal to Enter Into Freedom From Law (4:12-20).
H. The Allegory of Hagar and Sarah (4:21-31).
IV. Practical: Practice of the Life of Liberty and Faith (5:1-6:10).
A. Exhortation to Freedom (5:1-12).
B. Life by the Spirit, Not by the Flesh (5:13-26).
C. Call for Mutual Help (6:1-10).
V. Conclusion (6:11-18).

GALBANUM A fragrant gum used in the sacred oil (Ex 30:34).

GALEED (*heap of [stones that are a] witness*). The name given by Jacob to the heap of stones which he and Laban raised as a memorial of their compact (Ge 31:47-48).

GALILEAN A native of Galilee (Mt 26:69; Jn 4:45; Ac 1:11; 5:37).

GALILEE (*ring, circle,* hence *region*). The northern district of Israel. A city of refuge in (Jos 20:7; 21:32; 1Ch 6:76). Cities in, given to Hiram (1Ki 9:11-12). Taken by king of Assyria (2Ki 15:29). Prophecy concerning (Isa 9:1; Mt 4:15). Called Galilee of the nations (Isa 9:1). Herod, tetrarch of (Mk 6:21; Lk 3:1; 23:6-7). Jesus resides in (Mt 17:22; 19:1; Jn 7:1, 9). Teaching and miracles of Jesus in (Mt 4:23, 25; 15:29-31; Mk 1:14, 28, 39; 3:7; Lk 4:14, 44; 5:17; 23:5; Jn 1:43; 4:3, 43-45; Ac 10:37). People of, receive Jesus (Jn 4:45, 53). Disciples were chiefly from (Ac 1:11; 2:7). Women from, ministered to Jesus (Mt 27:55-56; Mk 15:41; Lk 23:49, 55). Jesus appeared to his disciples in, after his resurrection (Mt 26:32; 28:7, 10, 16-17; Mk 14:28; 16:7; Jn 21).
Routes from, to Judea (Jdg 21:19; Jn 4:3-5). Dialect of (Mk 14:70). Called Gennesaret (Mt 14:34; Mk 6:53). Churches in (Ac 9:31).

GALILEE, SEA OF Also called the Lake of Gennesaret (Lk 5:1), the Sea of Kinnereth (Nu 34:11, ftn; Dt 3:17), and the Sea of Tiberias, because Herod's capital was on its shores (Jn 6:1; 21:1). The lake is thirteen miles long and eight miles wide, filled with fresh and clear water, and full of fish. Because it was located in a pocket in the hills, it was subject to sudden violent storms. *See Gennesaret, 2; Kinnereth, 3; Tiberias.*

GALL
1. The secretion of the human gall bladder (Job 16:13).
2. The poison of serpents (Job 20:14).
3. A bitter and poisonous herb (Jer 9:15; Hos 10:4; Am 6:12), perhaps used to deaden pain (Mt 27:34).
Figurative of the bitter end of immorality (Pr 5:4).

GALLERY A balcony of the temple in Ezekiel's vision (Eze 41:16; 42:3, 5-6).

GALLEY *See Ship.*

GALLIM (*heaps*). A town of Benjamin (Isa 10:30; 1Sa 25:44).

GALLIO Proconsul of Achaia. Dismisses complaint of Jews against Paul (Ac 18:12-17).

GALLON A unit of liquid measure. Six gallons is equal to the biblical measure known as a bath. Four quarts (one gallon), which is one sixth of a bath, is known as a hin. John records that the water jars used to hold water for ceremonial washing would hold twenty to thirty gallons of water; Jesus used this water to replenish the wine supply at the marriage celebration at Cana in Galilee (Jn 2:6).

GALLOWS Used for execution of criminals (Est 2:23; 5:14; 6:4; 7:9-10; 9:13, 25). Reproach of being hanged upon (Gal 3:13). *See Punishment.*

GAMALIEL (*recompense of God [El]*).
1. Chief of tribe of Manasseh (Nu 1:10; 2:20; 10:23).
2. An eminent Pharisee and teacher of the law, the teacher of Paul (Ac 22:3). He was broadminded and tolerant toward early Christians (Ac 5:34-39).

GAMBLING *See Betting; Lot, The.*

GAMES Footraces (1Co 9:24, 26; Gal 2:2; Php 2:16; Heb 12:1). Gladiatorial (1Co 4:9; 9:26; 15:32; 2Ti 4:7).

Figurative:
Of the Christian life (1Co 9:24, 26; Gal 5:7; Php 2:16; 3:14; Heb 12:1). Of a successful ministry (Gal 2:2; Php 2:16). Fighting wild beasts, of spiritual conflict (1Co 4:9; 9:26; 15:32; 2Ti 4:7).

GAMMAD (probably *valiant men*). Men of in the watchtowers of Tyre (Eze 27:11).

GAMUL (*weaned*). The head of the twenty-second course of priests (1Ch 24:17).

GANGRENE Perhaps in a running or festering sore (Ex 9:9-10; Lev 21:20, 22:22; Dt 28:27; Job 7:5). False teaching spreads like gangrene (2Ti 2:17).

GANNIM *See En Gannim.*

GARDEN A cultivated piece of ground planted with flowers, vegetables, shrubs, or trees, fenced with a mud or stone wall (Pr 24:31) or with thorny hedges (Isa 5:5). Gardens were sometimes used for burial places (Ge 23:17; 2Ki 21:18, 26; Jn 19:41). The future state of the saved is figuratively represented by a garden (Rev 22:1-5).

GARDENER *See Occupations and Professions.*

GAREB (*scabby*).
1. One of David's warriors (2Sa 23:38; 1Ch 11:40).
2. A hill near Jerusalem (Jer 31:39).

GARLAND A crown or wreath for the head; figurative of the rewards of wisdom (Pr 1:9; 4:9). *See Crown.*

GARLIC (Nu 11:5).

GARMENT Of righteousness (Isa 61:10; Mt 22:11; 2Co 5:3; Rev 3:18; 7:14; 16:15; 19:8). *See Dress; Robe.*

GARMITE (*bone, bony*). A title applied to Keilah (1Ch 4:19).

GARNER *See Barn; Granary; Storehouse.*

GARRISON A fortress manned by soldiers, used chiefly for the occupation of a conquered country (1Sa 10:5; 13:3; 14:1, 6; 2Sa 8:6, 14). *See Fort.*

GASHMU *See Geshem.*

GATAM Grandson of Esau (Ge 36:11, 16; 1Ch 1:36).

GATE, INSPECTION Name of one of the gates of Jerusalem (Ne 3:31).

GATEKEEPERS Guards at the city gates, the doors of the king's palace, and doors of the temple (1Ch 9:17-32; 2Ch 34:13; 35:15). Lodged round about the temple in order to be present for opening the doors (1Ch 9:27). One-third were gatekeepers of the temple (2Ch 23:4), one-third were gatekeepers of the king's house (2Ch 23:5), one-third were gatekeepers of the gate of the foundation (2Ch 23:5). They served, also, as gatekeepers of the gates of the walls (Ne 12:25). They served in twenty-four courses (1Ch 26:13-19). Their posts were determined by lot (1Ch 24:31; 26:13-19).

GATES Of cities (Dt 3:5; Jos 6:26; 1Sa 23:7; 2Sa 18:24; 2Ch 8:5). Made of iron (Ac 12:10), wood (Ne 1:3), bronze (Ps 107:16; Isa 45:2). Double doors (Isa 45:1; Eze 41:24).
The open square of, a place for idlers (Ge 19:1; 1Sa 4:18; Ps 69:12; Pr 1:21; Jer 17:19-20). Religious services held at (Ac 14:13). The law read at (Ne 8). Place for the transaction of public business, announcement of legal transactions (Ge 23:10, 16), conferences on public affairs (Ge 34:20), holding courts of justice (Dt 16:18; 21:19; 22:15; Jos 20:4; Ru 4:1; 2Sa 15:2; Pr 22:22; Zec 8:16). Place for public concourse (Ge 23:10; Pr 1:21; 8:3; Jer 14:2; 22:2). Thrones of kings at (1Ki 22:10; 2Ch 18:9; Jer 38:7; 39:3). Punishment of criminals outside of (Dt 17:5; Jer 20:2; Ac 7:58; Heb 13:12). Closed at night (Jos 2:5, 7), on the Sabbath (Ne 13:19). Guards at (2Ki 7:17; Ne 13:19, 22). Jails made in the towers of (Jer 20:2). Bodies of criminals exposed to view at (Jos 8:2-9; 2Ki 10:8).

Figurative:
Of the people of a city (Isa 3:26). Of the gospel (Isa 60:11). Of the powers of hell (Mt 16:18). Of death (Job 38:17; Ps 9:13; Isa 38:10). Of the grave (Isa 38:10). Of righteousness (Ps 118:19). Of salvation (Ge 28:17; Ps 24:7; 118:19-20; Isa 26:2). Narrow gate, of the way to life (Mt 7:13-14).

Symbolic: (Rev 21:12-13, 21, 25).
See Jerusalem, Gates of.

GATH (*winepress*). One of the five chief cities of the Philistines (Jos 13:3; 1Sa 6:17; Am 6:2; Mic 1:10). Anakites, a race of giants, inhabitants of (Jos 11:22). Goliath dwelt in (1Sa 17:4; 1Ch 20:5-8). Obed-Edom belonged to (2Sa 6:10). The ark taken to (1Sa 5:8). Inhabitants of, called Gittites (Jos 13:3). David takes refuge at (1Sa 21:10-15; 27:2-7). Band of Gittites, attached to David (2Sa 15:18-22). Taken by David (1Ch 18:1). Shimei's servants escape to (1Ki 2:39-41). Fortified by Rehoboam (2Ch 11:8). Taken by Hazael (2Ki 12:17). Recovered by Jehoash (2Ki 13:25). Besieged by Uzziah (2Ch 26:6). Called Metheg Ammah (2Sa 8:1).

GATH HEPHER (*winepress water pit*). A town on the border of Zebulun (Jos 19:12-13) and birthplace of Jonah the prophet (2Ki 14:25).

GATH RIMMON (*winepress of pomegranate*).
1. A city of Dan on the Philistine plain (Jos 19:45).
2. A town of Manasseh, W of Jordan, assigned to Levites (Jos 21:25).

GAULANITIS A province NE of the Sea of Galilee, ruled by Herod Antipas. It encompassed the region of OT Golan. *See Golan.*

GAZA (*strong*).
1. A city of the Philistines (Jos 13:3; Jer 25:20). One of the border cities of the Canaanites (Ge 10:19). A city of the Avvim and Anakim (Dt 2:23; Jos 11:22). Allotted to Judah (Jos 15:47; Jdg 1:18). A temple of Dagon, situated at (Jdg 16:23). Samson dies at (Jdg 16:21-31). On the western boundary of the kingdom of Israel in the time of Solomon (1Ki 4:24). Smitten by Pharaoh (Jer 47:1). Prophecies relating to (Am 1:6-7; Zep 2:4; Zec 9:5). Desert of (Ac 8:26-39).
2. A city of Ephraim (Jdg 6:4; 1Ch 7:28).

GAZATHITES, GAZITES NIV "[people of] Gaza" (Jos 13:3; Jdg 16:2). *See Gaza, 1.*

GAZELLE *See Animals.*

GAZER *See Gezer.*

GAZEZ (possibly *sheep shearer* IDB; possibly *one born at the time of shearing* KB). The name of the son and of the grandson of Ephah (1Ch 2:46).

GAZZAM (*some kind of bird or insect*). One of the temple servants (Ezr 2:48; Ne 7:51).

GE HARASHIM It may be the broad valley between Lod and Ono (1Ch 4:14, ftn; Ne 11:35).

GEBA (*hill*). A town in the territory of Benjamin (Jos 18:24; Ezr 2:26; Ne 7:30), assigned to the Levites (Jos 21:17). Jonathan defeated the Philistines at Geba (1Sa 13:3). Asa fortified the city (1Ki 15:22), and in Hezekiah's time it was the northern most city of Judah (2Ki 23:8). Men from Geba returned after the Exile (Ezr 2:26).

GEBAL (possibly *border* BDB; *hill* KB).
1. A seaport of Phoenicia N of Sidon, also known as Byblos. Modern Jebeil, twenty-five miles N of Beirut. The land of the Gebalites is mentioned (Jos 13:5-6). The town was renowned for its expert stonemasons (1Ki 5:17-18) and for shipbuilding (Eze 27:9).
2. A land between the Dead Sea and Petra (Ps 83:6-8).

GEBALITES The inhabitants of Gebal or Byblos (Jos 13:5). *See Gebal.*

GEBER (*[strong young] man*).
1. One of Solomon's suppliers in Ramoth Gilead (1Ki 4:13). Called Ben-Geber.
2. The son of Uri (1Ki 4:19).

GEBIM (*ditches*). A place near Anathoth (Isa 10:31).

GECKO (Lev 11:30). *See Animals, Names of.*

GEDALIAH (*great is Yahweh*).
1. Governor appointed by Nebuchadnezzar after carrying the Israelites into captivity (2Ki 25:22-24). Jeremiah committed to the care of (Jer 39:14; 40:5-6). Warned of the conspiracy of Ishmael by Johanan and the captains of his army (Jer 40:13-16). Slain by Ishmael (2Ki 25:25-26; Jer 41:1-10).
2. A musician (1Ch 25:3, 9).
3. A priest, who divorced his Gentile wife after the Exile (Ezr 10:18).
4. Ancestor of Zephaniah (Zep 1:1).
5. A prince who caused imprisonment of Jeremiah (Jer 38:1).

GEDEON *See Gideon.*

GEDER (*wall [of stones]*). An ancient city of Canaan (Jos 12:13). Possibly identical with Gedor, 2 or 3.

GEDERAH (*stone pen, sheep corral*). Located between the valleys of Sorek and Aijalon in the hills of Judah (Jos 15:36). Often identified as modern Jedirah, though others identify it with Khirbet Judraya.

GEDEROTH (*stone pens, sheep corrals*). A city in the plain of Judah (Jos 15:41; 2Ch 28:18).

GEDEROTHAIM (*two stone pens, two sheep corrals*). A city in the plain of Judah (Jos 15:36).

GEDI *See En Gedi.*

GEDOR (*wall* BDB; *pock-marked* KB).
1. A city in mountains of Judah (Jos 15:58).
2. The town of Jeroham (1Ch 12:7). Possibly identical with Geder. *See Geder.*
3. Valley of, taken by Simeonites (1Ch 4:39). *See Geder.*
4. An ancestor of Saul (1Ch 8:31; 9:37).
5. Either a place or a person, authorities disagree (1Ch 4:4, 18).

GEHAZI (possibly *valley of vision*). The servant of Elisha (2Ki 4:8-37; 5:1-27; 8:4-6). He was punished for greed by becoming a leper.

GEHENNA (*valley of Hinnom*). *See Ben Hinnom; Hell.*

GELILOTH (*region*). A place mentioned (Jos 18:17), as marking the boundary of Benjamin. Gilgal is substituted (Jos 15:7).

GEMALLI (*my reward* KB). Father of Ammiel, and one of the twelve spies (Nu 13:12).

GEMARIAH (*Yahweh has accomplished*).
1. Son of Shaphan the scribe and friend of Jeremiah (Jer 36:10-25).
2. A son of Hilkiah, sent as ambassador to Nebuchadnezzar (Jer 29:3).

GENEALOGY (*account of one's descent*). (Nu 1:18; 2Ch 12:15; Ezr 2:59; Ne 7:5; Heb 7:3). Of no spiritual significance (Mt 3:9; 1Ti 1:4; Tit 3:9).
From Adam to Noah (Ge 4:16-22; 5; 1Ch 1:1-4; Lk 3:36-38), to Abraham (Ge 11:10-32; 1Ch 1:4-27; Lk 3:34-38), to Jesus (Mt 1:1-16; Lk 3:23-38). Of the descendants of Noah (Ge 10), of Nahor (Ge 22:20-24), of Abraham, by his wife Keturah (Ge 25:1-4; 1Ch 1:32-33), of Ishmael (Ge 25:12-16; 1Ch 1:28-31), of Esau (Ge 36; 1Ch 1:35-54), of Jacob (Ge 35:23-26; Ex 1:5; 6:14-27; Nu 26; 1Ch 2-9), of Perez to David (Ru 4:18-22). Of the Jews who returned from the Captivity (Ezr 7:1-5; 8:1-15; Ne 7; 11:12). Of Joseph (Mt 1; Lk 3:23-38).

GENEALOGY OF JESUS CHRIST Two genealogies are given in the NT (Mt 1:1-17; Lk 3:23-28). Matthew traces the descent of Jesus from Abraham and David, and divides it into three sets of fourteen generations. He omits three generations after Joram, namely Ahaziah, Joash, and Amaziah (1Ch 3:11-12). Contrary to Hebrew practice, he names five women: Tamar, Rahab, Ruth, Bathsheba, and Mary. The sense of "became the father of" in Hebrew genealogies is not exact; it indicated immediate or remote descent, an adoptive relation, or legal heirship. Luke's genealogy moves from Jesus to Adam, agreeing with the accounts in 1 Chronicles between Abraham and Adam (1Ch 1:1-7, 24-28). From David to Abraham he agrees with Matthew; from Jesus to David he differs from Matthew. Perhaps Matthew gives the line of legal heirship, while Luke gives the line of physical descent.

GENERAL LETTERS The seven letters following Hebrews—James; 1 and 2 Peter; 1, 2, and 3 John and Jude—have often been designated as the General Letters. This term goes back to the early church historian Eusebius (c. A.D. 265-340), who in his *Ecclesiastical History* (2.23-25) first referred to these seven letters as Catholic Letters, using the word "catholic" to mean "universal."
The letters so designated may be said to be, for the most part, addressed to general audiences rather than to specific persons or localized groups. 2 and 3 John, the two letters that seem most obviously addressed to individuals, have long been viewed as appendages of 1 John, which is clearly general in its address. However, when compared with Paul's letters, all these letters except 3 John are clearly general in nature. By contrast, Paul addresses his letters to such recipients as the saints at Philippi, or the churches of Galatia, or Timothy or Titus.
As Eusebius noted long ago, one interesting fact connected with the General Letters is that most of them were at one time among the disputed books of the NT. James, 2 Peter, 2 John, 3 John, and Jude were all questioned extensively before being admitted to the canon of Scripture.

GENERALS Roman military leaders (Rev 6:15; 19:18). *See Captain.*

GENERATION A period of time (Ex 3:15; Da 4:3; Lk 1:50), or all the people living in a given period (Jdg 2:10; Mt 11:16), or a class of people having a certain quality (Dt 32:5, 20; Mt 8:38), or a company gathered together (Ps 49:19).

GENERATION, EVIL (Dt 32:5; Pr 30:12; Mt 3:7; 12:39, 45; Lk 9:41; Ac 2:40).

GENEROSITY *See Beneficence; Giving; Liberality.*

GENESIS (*beginning*).

Author: Historically, Jews and Christians alike have held that Moses was the author/compiler of the first five books of the OT.

Date: c. 1446 to 1406

Outlines:

Literary Outline:
I. Introduction (1:1-2:3).
II. Body (2:4-50:26).
A. "The account of the heavens and the earth" (2:4-4:26).
B. "The written account of Adam's line" (5:1-6:8).
C. "The account of Noah" (6:9-9:29).
D. "The account of Shem, Ham and Japheth" (10:1-11:9).
E. "The account of Shem" (1:10-26).
F. "The account of Terah" (11:217-25:11).
G. "The account of Abraham's son Ishmael" (25:12-18).
H. "The account of Abraham's son Isaac" (25:19-35:29).
I. "The account of Esau" (36:1-37:1).
J. "The account of Jacob" (37:2-50:26).

Thematic Outline:
I. Primeval History (1:1-11:26).
A. Creation (1:1-2:3).
1. Introduction (1:1-2).
2. Body (1:3-31).
3. Conclusion (2:1-3).
B. Adam and Eve in Eden (2:4-25).
C. The Fall and Its Consequences (3:1-24).
D. The Rapid "Progress" of Sin (4:1-16).
E. Two Genealogies (4:17-5:32).
1. The genealogy of pride (4:17-24).
2. The genealogy of death (4:25-5:32).
F. The Extent of Sin Before the Flood (6:1-8).
G. The Great Flood (6:9-9:29).
1. Preparing for the Flood (6:9-7:10).
2. Judgment and redemption (7:11-8:19).
a. The rising of the waters (7:11-24).
b. The receding of the waters (8:1-19).
3. The flood's aftermath (8:20-9:29).
a. A new promise (8:20-22).
b. New ordinances (9:1-7).
c. A new relationship (9:8-17).
d. A new temptation (9:18-23).
e. A final word (9:24-29).
H. The Spread of the Nations (10:1-11:26).
1. The diffusion of nations (10:1-32).
2. The confusion of tongues (11:1-9).
3. The first Semitic genealogy (11:10-26).
II. Patriarchal History (11:27-50:26).
A. The Life of Abraham (11:27-25:11).
1. Abraham's background (11:27-32).
2. Abraham's land (12:1-14:24).
3. Abraham's people (15:1-24:67).
4. Abraham's last days (25:1-11).
B. The Descendants of Ishmael (25:2-18).
C. The Life of Jacob (25:19-35:29).
1. Jacob at home (25:19-27:46).
2. Jacob abroad (28:1-30:43).
3. Jacob at home again (31:1-35:29).
D. The Descendants of Esau (36:1-37:1).
E. The Life of Joseph (37:2-50:26).
1. Joseph's career (37:2-41:57).
2. Jacob's migration (42:1-47:31).
3. Jacob's last days (48:1-50:14).
4. Joseph's last days (50:15-26).

GENIUS Mechanical, a divine inspiration (Ex 28:3; 31:2-11; 35:30-35; 36:1). *See Inspiration.*

GENNESARET
1. "The land of Gennesaret" is a plain on the NW shore of the Sea of Galilee (Mt 14:34; Mk 6:53).
2. "The Lake of Gennesaret" is the same as the Sea of Galilee (Lk 5:1). *See Galilee, Sea of.*

GENTILES (*nation, people*). Usually meaning non-Israelite people. *See Heathen.*

General:
Ways of, condemned (Jer 10:2-3; Eph 4:17-19). God's forbearance toward (Ac 14:16). Impartiality toward (Ro 2:9-11). Ignorant worship practices of (Mt 6:7-8, 31-32; Ac 17:4, 16, 22-27; 1Co 10:20; 12:2). Wicked practices of (Ro 1:18-32; Gal 2:15; Eph 5:12; 1Th 4:5; 1Pe 4:3-4). Moral responsibility of (Ro 2:14-15).
See Idolatry; Missions.

Prophecies of the Conversion of:
(Ge 12:3; 22:18; 49:10; Dt 32:21; Ps 2:8; 22:27-31; 46:4, 10; 65:2, 5; 66:4; 68:31-32; 72:8-11, 16, 19; 86:9; 102:15, 18-22; 145:10-11; Isa 2:2-4; 9:2, 6-7; 11:6-10; 18:7; 24:16; 35:1-2, 5-7; 40:5; 42:1-12; 45:6, 8, 22 24; 49:1, 5-6, 18-23; 54:1-3; 55:5; 56:3, 6-8; 60:1-14; 65:1; 66:12, 19, 23; Jer 3:17; 4:2; 16:19-21; Da 2:35, 44-45; 7:13-14; Hos 2:23; Joel 2:28-32; Am 9:11-12; Mic 4:3-4; Hag 2:7; Zec 2:10-11; 6:15; 8:20-23; 9:1, 10; 14:8-9, 16; Mal 1:11; Mt 3:9; 8:11; 12:17-21; 19:30; Mk 10:31; Lk 13:29-30; 21:24; Jn 10:16; Ac 9:15).
See Church, The Body of Believers, Prophecies Concerning.

Conversion of:
(Ac 10:45; 11:1-8; 13:2, 46-48; 14:27; 15:7-31; 18:4-6; 26:16-18; 28:28; Ro 1:5-7; 9:22-30; 10:19-20; 11:11-13, 17-21; 15:9-12; Gal 1:15-16; 2:2; 3:14; Eph 3:1-8; Col 3:11; 1Th 2:16; 1Ti 3:16; 2Ti 1:11; Rev 11:15; 15:4).
See Jesus the Christ, Kingdom of.

GENTILES, COURT OF THE The part of Herod's temple which the Gentiles could enter (not mentioned in the Bible). In the temple of Revelation (Rev 11:2).

GENTILES, INCLUSION OF *See Catholicity.*

GENTLENESS

Of Christ: (Isa 40:11; Mt 11:29; 2Co 10:1).
See Jesus the Christ, Compassion of, Humility of, Meekness of.

Of God: (2Sa 22:36; Ps 18:35; Isa 40:11).
See God, Compassion of, Longsuffering of.

Of Paul: (1Th 2:7).

Exhortations to:
A fruit of the Spirit (Gal 5:22; Jas 3:17). Required in the Lord's servants (2Ti 2:24-26). Required in all Christians (Tit 3:1-2).
See Humility; Kindness; Meekness; Patience.

GENUBATH (*thief*). A son of Hadad the Edomite (1Ki 11:20).

GEOLOGY Origin, in God (Ge 1:9-10; 1Sa 2:8; 2Sa 22:16; Job 12:8-9; Ps 18:15; 24:1-2; 104:5; 136:6; Pr 30:4; 2Pe 3:5-7). Control, by God (Job 28:9-11; Ps 104:5-13; Pr 30:4; Hab 3:9). Infinity of (Jer 31:37). Destruction of (2Pe 3:5-7).
See Astronomy; Creation; Earth; Hot Springs; Meteorology.

GERA (perhaps *sojourner*). A name common to the tribe of Benjamin.
1. A son of Benjamin (Ge 46:21).
2. A grandson of Benjamin (1Ch 8:3, 5).
3. The father of Ehud (Jdg 3:15).
4. A son of Ehud (1Ch 8:7).
5. Father of Shimei (2Sa 16:5).

GERAH A weight equal about 1/20 of a shekel or 1/2 gram (Ex 30:13; Lev 27:25; Nu 3:47). *See Measure.*

GERAR (*circle, region*).
1. A city of the Philistines (Ge 10:19). Abimelech, king of (Ge 20:1; 26:6). Visited by Abraham (Ge 20:1), by Isaac (Ge 26:1; 2Ch 14:13-14).
2. A valley (Ge 26:17-22).

GERASENES The region around Gerasa, one of the cities of the Decapolis near the SE end of the Sea of Galilee, in which the demoniacs lived whom Jesus healed (Mt 8:28, ftn; Mk 5:1; Lk 8:26, 37). *See Gadarenes.*

GERGESENES A variant reading probably harmonizing Gadarenes and Gerasenes, the region in which Jesus exorcized demons (Mt 8:28; Mk 5:1; Lk 8:26, ftns). *See Gadarenes; Gerasenes.*

GERIZIM Mount of blessing (Dt 11:29; 27:12; Jos 8:33). Jotham addresses the Shechemites from, against the conspiracy of Abimelech (Jdg 9:7). Samaritans worship at (Jn 4:20).

GERSHOM (*traveler there*).
1. Son of Moses (Ex 2:22; 18:3; 1Ch 23:15-16; 26:24).
2. *See Gershon.*
3. A descendant of Phinehas (Ezr 8:2).
4. A Levite (Jdg 18:30).

GERSHON, GERSHONITES Also called Gershom. Son of Levi (Ge 46:11; Ex 6:16-17; Nu 3:17-26; 4:22-28, 38; 7:7; 26:57; Jos 21:6; 1Ch 6:1, 16-17, 20, 43, 62, 71; 15:7; 23:6).
Descendants of Gershon (Nu 3:25; 4:24, 38; 7:7).

GERUTH KIMHAM (*lodging place of Kimham*). An unidentified place near Bethlehem, at which Ishmael and his fellow assassins stopped during their flight to Egypt (Jer 41:17).

GESHAN A descendant of Caleb (1Ch 2:47).

GESHEM (*rain shower*). An Arab who opposed the work of Nehemiah (Hebrew *Gashmu*, a variant of *Geshem*) (Ne 2:19; 6:1-2, 6, ftn).

GESHUR, GESHURITES (*bridge*).
1. District E of the sources of the Jordan. The inhabitants of, not subdued by the Israelites (Dt 3:14; Jos 12:5; 1Ch 2:23). David marries a princess of (2Sa 3:3; 1Ch 3:2). Absalom takes refuge in, after the murder of Amnon (2Sa 13:37-38; 15:8).
2. A people living S of the Philistines near Sinai. Their land was not taken at the time of the Conquest (Jos 13:2-13). Inhabitants of one of the villages of, exterminated, and the spoils taken by David (1Sa 27:8).

GETHER The third son of Aram (Ge 10:23; 1Ch 1:17).

GETHSEMANE (*olive oil press*). A garden near Jerusalem. Jesus betrayed in (Mt 26:36-50; Mk 14:32-46; Lk 22:39-49; Jn 18:1-2).

GEUEL (*splendor of God [El]*). A representative from the tribe of Gad sent to spy out Canaan (Nu 13:15).

GEZER (possibly *pieces*). A Canaanite royal city perhaps also called Gob (2Sa 21:18 w 1Ch 20:4). The king of, defeated by Joshua (Jos 10:33; 12:12). Canaanites not all expelled from, but made to pay tribute (Jos 16:10; Jdg 1:29). Allotted to Ephraim (Jos 16:10; 1Ch 7:28). Assigned to Levites (Jos 21:21). Battle with Philistines at (1Ch 20:4; 2Sa 21:18). Struck by David (2Sa 5:25; 1Ch 14:16). Fortified by Solomon after Pharaoh, king of Egypt, drives out Canaanites, making Gezer a dowry for Pharaoh's daughter (1Ki 9:15-17). Pharaoh Shishak, invaded the land in Rehoboam's fifth year as king. He launched an attack from Gezer, and was able to threaten and plunder Jerusalem from there (1Ki 14:25-28; 2Ch 12:1-12). Gezer was twelfth on a list of 156 cities captured by Shishak in his twentieth year. This record is found on a huge relief in the Egyptian stele at Karnak. Shishak's raids went as far N as the Sea of Galilee.

GHOR, THE The Arabic name for the Jordan Valley, biblical Arabah. *See Arabah.*

GHOST An apparition (Isa 29:4); Jesus mistaken for (Mt 14:26; Mk 6:49; Lk 24:37:39). KJV "give up the ghost," means to breathe one's last, to die (Ge 25:8; 35:29; 49:33; Job 11:20; Mt 27:50; Jn 19:30). KJV "Holy Ghost" is NIV "Holy Spirit." *See Holy Spirit; Spirit.*

GIAH (*bubbling spring*). A place on the way to the wilderness of Gibeon (2Sa 2:24).

GIANTS People of exceptional height and strength, such as Og, king of Bashan (Jos 12:4; 13:12), and Goliath, whom David killed (1Sa 17). The Nephilim and descendants of Anak were giants to the Israelites (Ge 6:4; Nu 13:33) as were the Rephaites (Dt 2:11, 20; 3:11). *See Anakites; Nephilim; Rephaites.*

GIBBAR (*[young vigorous] man, hero*). A man whose children returned from captivity with Zerubbabel (Ezr 2:20).

GIBBETHON (*mound, hill*). A city of Dan (Jos 19:44). Allotted to the Levites (Jos 21:23). Besieged by Israel, while in possession of Philistines (1Ki 15:27; 16:15, 17).

GIBEA (*mound, hill*). A Judah ite (1Ch 2:49).

GIBEAH (*mound, hill*).
1. Of Judah (Jos 15:57).
2. Of Saul. Also called Gibeah of Benjamin. The people's wickedness (Jdg 19:12-30; Hos 9:9; 10:9). Destroyed by the Israelites (Jdg 20). The city of Saul (1Sa 10:26; 15:34; 22:6). The ark of the covenant conveyed to, by the Philistines (1Sa 7:1; 2Sa 6:3). Deserted (Isa 10:29).
3. Another town in Benjamin, also called Gibeah (Jos 18:28).
4. Gibeah in the field (Jdg 20:31). Probably identical with Geba. *See Geba.*

GIBEATH HAARALOTH (*hill of foreskins*). Place where the Israelites were circumcised after the wilderness wanderings (Jos 5:3.).

GIBEATHITE (*of Gibeah*). Shemaah, two of whose sons were among David's warriors (1Ch 12:3).

GIBEON (*mound, hill*).
1. A city of the Hivites (Jos 9:3, 17; 2Sa 21:2). The people of deceive Joshua into a treaty (Jos 9). Made servants by the Israelites when their deception was discovered (Jos 9:27). The sun stands still over, during Joshua's battle with the five confederated kings (Jos 10:12-14). Allotted to Benjamin (Jos 18:25). Assigned to the Aaronites (Jos 21:17). The tabernacle located at (1Ki 3:4; 1Ch 16:39; 21:29; 2Ch 1:2-3, 13). Smitten by David (1Ch 14:16). Seven sons of Saul slain at, to avenge the inhabitants of (2Sa 21:1-9). Solomon worships at, and offers sacrifices (1Ki 3:4), God appears to him in dreams (1Ki 3:5; 9:2). Abner slays Asahel at (2Sa 2:18-32; 3:30). Ishmael, the son of Nethaniah, defeated at, by Johanan (Jer 41:11-16).
2. Pool of (2Sa 2:13; Jer 41:12).

GIBEONITE(S) (*people from Gibeon*). Descended from the Hivites and Amorites (Jos 9:3, 7, w 2Sa 21:2). A mighty and warlike people (Jos 10:2). Cities of (Jos 9:17).
Israel deceived by (Jos 9:4-13), made a league with (Jos 9:15). Spared on account of their oath (Jos 9:18-19). Appointed woodcutters (Jos 9:20-27). Attacked by the kings of Canaan (Jos 10:1-5). Delivered by Israel (Jos 10:6-10).
Saul sought to destroy (2Sa 21:2). Israel plagued for Saul's cruelty to (2Sa 21:1). Effected the destruction of the remnant of Saul's house (2Sa 21:4-9). The office of the temple servants probably originated in (1Ch 9:2, ftn). Part of, returned from the captivity (Ne 7:25).

GIBLITES *See Gebalites.*

GIDDALTI (*I pronounce [God as] Great* ISBE; *I reared up* KB). A son of Heman (1Ch 25:4, 29).

GIDDEL (*big*).
1. One of the temple servants (Ezr 2:47; Ne 7:49).
2. One of Solomon's servants (Ezr 2:56; Ne 7:58).

GIDEON (*one who cuts, hacks*). Call of, by an angel (Jdg 6:11, 14). His excuses (Jdg 6:15). Promises of the Lord to (Jdg 6:16). Angel attests the call to, by miracle (Jdg 6:21-24). He destroys the altar of Baal and builds one to the Lord (Jdg 6:25-27). Tests God's word with a fleece (Jdg 6:36-40). Leads an army against and defeats the Midianites (Jdg 6:33-35; 7; 8:4-12). Ephraimites rebuke, for not inviting them to join in the campaign against the Midianites (Jdg 8:1-3). Avenges himself upon the people of Succoth (Jdg 8:14-17). Israel desires to make him king; he refuses (Jdg 8:22-23). Makes an ephod which becomes a snare to the Israelites (Jdg 8:24-27). Had seventy sons (Jdg 8:30). Death of (Jdg 8:32). Faith of (Heb 11:32).

GIDEONI (*one who cuts, hacks*). Father of Abidan (Nu 1:11; 2:22; 7:60, 65; 10:24).

GIDOM (*a cutting off, stop pursuit*). Limit of pursuit after battle of Gibeah (Jdg 20:45).

GIER EAGLE *See Birds; Osprey.*

GIFT, GIVING A gift can be a blessing (1Sa 25;27), given to gain a favor (Ge 34:12), as an act of submission (Ps 68:29), an offering (Ex 28:38), a bribe (Pr 18:16). In the NT, anything given (Lk 21:1; Jas 1:17), a present (Mt 7:11), special spiritual endowment (Ro 1:11; 1Ti 4:14). *See Gifts From God.*

GIFTS FROM GOD

Himself:
In Christ, the Savior (Isa 42:6; 55:4; Jn 3:16; 4:10; 6:32-33), in the Holy Spirit, the Comforter. *See Holy Spirit.*

Temporal:
Food and clothing (Mt 6:25, 33). Rain and fruitful seasons (Ge 8:22; 27:28; Lev 26:4-5; Isa 30:23). Wisdom (2Ch 1:12). Peace (Lev 26:6; 1Ch 22:9). Gladness (Ps 4:7). Strength and power (Ps 29:11; 68:18). Wisdom and knowledge (Ecc 2:26; Da 2:21-23; 1Co 1:5-7). Talents, figurative of gifts and abilities (Mt 25:14-30).
All good things (Ps 21:2; 34:10; 84:11; Isa 42:5; Eze 11:19; Jn 16:23-24; Ro 8:32; 1Ti 6:17; Jas 1:17; 2Pe 1:3).
To be used and enjoyed (Ecc 3:13; 5:19-20; 1Ti 4:4-5). Should cause us to remember God (Dt 8:18). All creatures partake of (Ps 136:25; 145:15-16). Prayer for (Zec 10:1; Mt 6:11). *See Presents.*

Spiritual:
Of the Spirit (Ro 11:29; 12:6-8; 1Co 7:7; 12:4-11; 13:2; Eph 4:7; 1Pe 4:10). Life, eternal (Isa 42:5; Eze 11:19; Jn 3:16-17, 36; 6:27; Ro 5:16-18; 6:23). Grace (Jas 4:6). Wisdom (Pr 2:6; Jas 1:5). Repentance (Ac 11:28). Faith (Eph 2:8; Php 1:29). Rest (Mt 11:28). Glory (Jn 17:22).
See Blessings, Spiritual, From God; Charism, Charisma, Charismata; Miracles, Miraculous Gifts of the Spirit; Tongues, Gift of.

GIHON (*to gush forth*).
1. A river in Egypt (Ge 2:13).
2. Pools near Jerusalem (1Ki 1:33, 38, 45). Hezekiah brings the waters of the upper pool by an aqueduct into the city of Jerusalem (2Ch 32:4, 30; 33:14; Ne 2:13-15; 3:13-16; Isa 7:3; 22:9-11; 36:2).

GILALAI A priest and musician (Ne 12:36).

GILBOA (*bubbling*). A hill S of Jezreel, where Saul was defeated by the Philistines and died (1Sa 28:4; 31:1-8; 1Ch 10:1-8).

GILEAD (perhaps *monument of stones*).
1. A region E of the Jordan allotted to the tribes of Reuben and Gad and the half tribe of Manasseh (Nu 32:1-30; Dt 3:13; 34:1; 2Ki 10:33). Reubenites expel the Hagrites from (1Ch 5:9-10, 18-22). Ammonites make war against; defeated by Jephthah (Jdg 11; Am 1:13). The prophet Elijah a native of (1Ki 17:1). David retreats to, at the time of Absalom's rebellion (2Sa 17:16, 22, 24). Pursued into, by Absalom (2Sa 17:26). Absalom defeated and slain in the forests of (2Sa 18:9).
Hazael, king of Syria, attacks the land of (2Ki 10:32-33; Am 1:3). Invaded by Tiglath-Pileser, king of Syria (2Ki 15:29). A grazing country (Nu 32:1; 1Ch 5:9). Exported spices, balm, and myrrh (Ge 37:25; Jer 8:22; 46:11).
Figurative of prosperity (Jer 22:6; 50:19).
2. A mountain (Jdg 7:3; SS 4:1; 6:5).
3. A city (Hos 6:8; 12:11).
4. Grandson of Manasseh (Nu 26:29-30; 27:1; 36:1; Jos 17:1, 3; 1Ch 2:21, 23; 7:14, 17).
5. Father of Jephthah (Jdg 11:1-2).
6. A chief of Gad (1Ch 5:14).

GILGAL (*circle of stones*).
1. Place of the first encampment of the Israelites W of the Jordan (Jos 4:19; 9:6; 10:6, 43; 14:6). Monument erected in, to commemorate the passage of the Jordan by the Israelites (Jos 4:19-24). Circumcision renewed at (Jos 5:2-9). Passover kept at (Jos 5:10-11). Manna ceased at, after the Passover (Jos 5:12). Quarries at (Jdg 3:19). Eglon, king of Moab, resides and is slain at (Jdg 3:14-26). A judgment seat, where Israel, in that district, came to be judged by Samuel (1Sa 7:16). Saul proclaimed king over all Israel at (1Sa 11:15; 13:4-15; 15:6-23). Agag, king of the Amalekites, slain at, by Samuel (1Sa 15:33). Tribe of Judah assembles at, to proceed to the E side of the Jordan to conduct King David back after the defeat of Absalom (2Sa 19:14-15, 40-43). A school of the prophets at (2Ki 4:38-40).
Prophecies concerning (Hos 4:15; 9:15; 12:11; Am 4:4; 5:5).
2. A royal city in Canaan. Conquered by Joshua (Jos 12:23).

GILOH A town near Hebron in the western foothills of Judah (Jos 15:51; 2Sa 15:12).

GILONITE Ahithophel, one of David's counselors from the town of Giloh (2Sa 15:12; 23:34).

GIMZO (*place of sycamore trees*). A town off the Jerusalem Highway, three miles SW of Lydda (2Ch 28:18).

GIN *See Snare; Trap.*

GINATH (*protector*). The father of Tibni (1Ki 16:21).

GINNETHO *See Ginnethon.*

GINNETHON A priest who returned to Jerusalem with Zerubbabel (Ne 10:6; 12:4).

GIRDLE *See Belt; Sash.*

GIRGASHITES A Canaanite people (Ge 10:15). Land of given to Abraham and his descendants (Ge 15:21; Dt 7:1; Jos 3:10; Ne 9:8). Driven out before the Israelites (Jos 24:11).

GIRZITES (*people from Gezer*). A tribe named with the Geshurites and the Amalekites (1Sa 27:8).

GISHPA (*listener*). An overseer of the temple servants (Ne 11:21).

GITTAH-HEPHER *See Gath Hepher.*

GITTAIM (*two winepresses*). A town of Benjamin to which the Beerothites fled (Ne 11:31, 33; 2Sa 4:3). The site is unknown.

GITTITE(S) (*of Gath*). Natives of Gath (Jos 13:1-3; 2Sa 6:8-11; 15:18; 21:19).

GITTITH In the titles of Psalms 8, 81, 84. It may denote a musical instrument imported from Gath or may be the title of a tune.

GIVING Rules for: Without ostentation (Mt 6:1-4). Regularly (1Co 16:2). Liberally (2Co 9:6-15). Cheerfully (2Co 8:11-12; 9:7).
See Alms; Beneficence; Liberality.

GIZONITE The title of the sons of Hashem, among David's bodyguards (1Ch 11:34).

GLADIATOR One who contends with wild beasts (1Co 15:32). *See Games.*

GLADNESS *See Joy.*

GLASS Was manufactured as early as 2500 B.C. by the Egyptians, and later by the Phoenicians, who promoted its commercial use, especially in jewelry. In the KJV, the glass mentioned by Paul (2Co 3:18) and by James (Jas 1:23-24) was a mirror of polished bronze. *See Mirror.* The references in Revelation to the sea of glass (Rev 4:6; 15:2) and the new Jerusalem (Rev 21:18, 21) emphasize the purity and clarity of crystal.

GLEAN, GLEANING

Laws concerning
The Hebrew custom of allowing the poor to follow the reapers, and to gather the grain or grapes that remained after the harvest (Lev 19:9-10; 23:22; Dt 24:19-20). *See Orphan; Strangers; Widow.*

Figurative:
(Jdg 8:2; Isa 17:6; Jer 49:9; Mic 7:1).

Instances of:
Ruth in the field of Boaz (Ru 2:2-3).

GLEDE *See Red Kite.*

GLORIFIED SAINTS Great cloud of witnesses (Heb 12:1), righteous people made perfect (Heb 12:23; Rev 6:11), 144,000 (Rev 14:1-5). Under the altar (Rev 6:9), before the throne (Rev 14:3). Sing song of redemption (Rev 14:3), of worship (Rev 15:2-4).

GLORIFYING GOD Commanded (1Ch 16:28; Ps 22:23; Isa 42:12). Due to him (1Ch 16:29) for his holiness (Ps 99:9; Rev 15:4), mercy and truth (Ps 115:1; Ro 15:9), faithfulness and truth (Isa 25:1), wondrous works (Mt 15:31; Ac 4:21), judgments (Isa 25:3; Eze 28:22; Rev 14:7), deliverances (Ps 50:15), grace to others (Ac 11:18; 2Co 9:13; Gal 1:24).

Accomplished by:
Relying on his promises (Ro 4:20), praising him (Ps 50:23), doing all to glorify him (1Co 10:31), dying for him (Jn 21:19), suffering for Christ (1Pe 4:14, 16), glorifying Christ (Ac 19:17; 2Th 1:12), bringing forth fruits of righteousness (Jn 15:8; Php 1:11), patience in affliction (Isa 24:1-3, 15), faithfulness (1Pe 4:11). Required in body and spirit (1Co 6:20). Shall be universal (Ps 86:9; Rev 5:13).

Believers:
Should resolve on (Ps 69:30; 118:28), unite in (Ps 34:3; Ro 15:6), persevere in (Ps 86:12). All the blessings of God are designed to lead to (Isa 60:21; 61:3). The holy example of the believers may lead others to (Mt 5:16; 1Pe 2:12).
All, by nature, fail in (Ro 3:23). The wicked averse to (Da 5:23; Ro 1:21). Punishment for not (Da 5:23, 30; Mal 2:2; Ac 12:23; Ro 1:21). Heavenly hosts engaged in (Rev 4:11).

Exemplified:
By David (Ps 57:5), the multitude (Mt 9:8; 15:31), the virgin Mary (Lk 1:46), the angels (Lk 2:14), the shepherds (Lk 2:20), by Jesus (Jn 17:4), the paralyzed man (Lk 5:25), the woman with infirmity (Lk 13:13), the leper whom Jesus healed (Lk 17:15), the blind man (Lk 18:43), the centurion (Lk 23:47), the church at Jerusalem (Ac 11:18), the Gentiles at Antioch (Ac 13:48), Abraham (Ro 4:20), Paul (Ro 11:36).
See Praise.

GLORY Concerning God, the exhibition of his divine attributes and perfections (Ps 19:1) or the radiance of his presence (Lk 2:9). Concerning people, the manifestation of their commendable qualities, such as wisdom, righteousness, self-control, ability, etc. Glory is destiny of believers (Php 3:21; Ro 8:21; 1Co 15:43).

Spiritual:
Is given by God (Ps 84:11), is the work of the Holy Spirit (2Co 3:18).

Eternal:
Secured by the death of Christ (Heb 2:10), accompanies salvation by Christ (2Ti 2:10), inherited by believers (1Sa 2:8; Ps 73:24; Pr 3:35; Col 3:4; 1Pe 5:10), believers called to (2Th 2:14; 1Pe 5:10), enhanced by afflictions (2Co 4:17), present afflictions not worthy to be compared with (Ro 8:18), of the church shall be rich and abundant (Isa 60:11-13), the bodies of believers shall be raised in (1Co 15:43; Php 3:21), believers shall be glory of their ministers (1Th 2:19-20), afflictions of ministers are glory to believers (Eph 3:13).

Temporal:
Is given by God (Da 2:37), passes away (1Pe 1:24). The devil tries to seduce by (Mt 4:8). Of hypocrites turned to shame (Hos 4:7). Seek not, from man (Mt 6:2; 1Th 2:6). Of the wicked is in their shame (Php 3:19). Ends in destruction (Isa 5:14).

Of God:
Exhibited in Christ (Jn 1:14; 2Co 4:6; Heb 1:3). Ascribed to God (Gal 1:5).
Exhibited in his name (Dt 28:58; Ne 9:5), his majesty (Job 37:22; Ps 93:1; 104:1; 145:5, 12; Isa 2:10), his power (Ex 15:1, 6; Ro 6:4), his works (Ps 19:1; 111:3), his holiness (Ex 15:11).
Described as great (Ps 138:5), eternal (Ps 104:31), rich (Eph 3:16), highly exalted (Ps 8:1; 113:4).
Exhibited to Moses (Ex 34:5-7, w 33:18-23). Stephen (Ac 7:55), his church (Dt 5:24; Ps 102:16).
Enlightens the church (Isa 60:1-2; Rev 21:11, 23). Believers desire to behold (Ps 63:2; 90:16). God is jealous of (Isa 42:8). The earth is full of (Isa 6:3). The knowledge of, shall fill the earth (Hab 2:14).

GLOWING METAL
1. *Glowing metal* used to describe the color of divine glory (Eze 1:4, 27; 8:2).
2. *Bronze glowing in a furnace* used in John's description of the King of Glory (Rev 1:15).
See Amber; Minerals of the Bible, 1; Stones.

GLUTTONY

General:
Impoverishes (Pr 23:21). Deadens moral sensibilities (Am 6:4-7; Lk 12:19-20, 45-46; Php 3:19). Loathsome (Pr 30:21-22).
Warnings against (Pr 30:21-22; Lk 21:34; Ro 13:13-14; 1Pe 4:2-3). Punished, by death (Dt 21:20-21), plagues (Nu 11:32-33).
Associated with drunkenness (Dt 21:20-21; Pr 23:21; Ecc 10:17; Lk 12:45-46; Ro 13:13; 1Pe 4:3). Proverb relating to (Isa 22:13; 1Co 15:32).

Instances of:
Israelites (Ex 16:20-21; Nu 11:4, 32-35; Ps 78:18). Sons of Eli (1Sa 2:12-17). Belshazzar (Da 5:1). Jesus falsely accused of (Mt 11:19; Lk 7:34).
See Pleasure, Worldly.

GNASH To grind the teeth together as an expression of rage (Job 16:9), hatred (Ps 37:12), frustration (Ps 112:10). In the NT it expresses anguish and failure rather than anger (Mt 8:12; 13:42, 50; 25:30).

GNASHING OF TEETH Of the enemy, in maliciousness (Job 16:9; Ps 35:16; 37:12; 112:10; La 2:16). Of the lost, from anguish of spirit (Mt 8:12; 13:42; 22:13; 24:51; 25:30; Lk 13:28).

GNAT Plague of (Ex 8:16-19; Ps 105:31). *See Insects.*

GNOSTICISM A second-century heresy that was a mixture of Judaism, Christianity, and Greek mystery religions. Its forerunners are seen in the errors refuted in the books of Colossians, 1 and 2 Timothy, 2 Peter, and 1 John. Some of its major tenets were:
1. The human body is matter, and therefore is evil. It is to be contrasted with God, who is wholly spirit and therefore good.
2. Salvation is the escape from the body, achieved not by faith in Christ but by special knowledge (the Greek word for "knowledge" is *gnosis*, from which comes Gnosticism).
3. Christ's true humanity was denied in two ways: (1) Some said that Christ only seemed to have a body, a view called Docetism, and (2) others said that the divine Christ joined the man Jesus at baptism and left him before he died, a view called Cerinthianism, after its most prominent spokesman, Cerinthus. This view is the background of much of 1 John (see 1Jn 1:1; 2:22; 4:2-3).
4. Since the body was considered evil, it was to be treated harshly. This ascetic form of Gnosticism is the background of part Colossians (Col 2:21-23).
5. Paradoxically, this dualism also led to immorality. Since matter (and not the breaking of God's law) was considered evil, breaking his law was of no moral consequence.

GOAD An instrument for prodding animals (1Sa 13:21; Ac 26:14). Six hundred men slain with by Shamgar, a judge of Israel (Jdg 3:31). *See Oxgoad.*
Figurative of mental incentive (Ecc 12:11).

GOAH A place near Jerusalem (Jer 31:39).

GOAT Designated as one of the clean animals to be eaten (Lev 11:1-8; Dt 14:4). Used for food (Ge 27:9; 1Sa 16:20), for the passover feast (Ex 12:5; 2Ch 35:7), as a sacrifice by Abraham (Ge 15:9), by Gideon (Jdg 6:19), Manoah (Jdg 13:19).
Milk of, used for food (Pr 27:27). Hair of, used for clothing (Nu 31:20), pillows (1Sa 19:13), curtains of the tabernacle (Ex 26:7; 35:23; 36:14). Used for tents. *See Curtains; Tabernacle.* Mosaic law required that a kid should not be killed for food before it was eight days old (Lev 22:27), nor should it be boiled in its mother's milk (Ex 23:19). Numerous (Dt 32:14; SS 4:1; 6:5; 1Sa 25:2; 2Ch 17:11). Wild, in Israel (1Sa 24:2; Ps 104:18).

GOATS' HAIR (Ex 25:4; 26:7; 35:6; 36:14; Nu 31:20).

GOB (*cistern*). Site of two of David's battles with the Philistines (2Sa 21:18-19).

GOBLET *See Cup.*

GOD

Access to:
Israel (Dt 4:7). The pure of heart (Ps 24:3-4). The thirsty (Isa 55:3). Gentiles (Ac 14:27). Enemies of God (Col 1:21-22). Believers (Heb 4:16; 1Pe 1:17). The cleansed (Jas 4:8).
Through hope (Ps 27:4; 43:2), fear (Ps 145:18-19; 1Pe 1:17), prayer (Mt 6:6; Heb 4:10), faith (Heb 11:6), love (1Jn 4:16), Christ (Jn 10:7, 9; 14:6; Ro 5:2; Eph 2:13, 18; 3:12; Col 1:21-22; Heb 7:19, 25; 10:19, 22; 1Pe 1:17). Satisfying (Ps 65:4).

Anger of: *See Anger of God.*

Appearance of:
To Adam (Ge 3:8-21). To Abraham (Ge 17:1; 18:2-33). To Jacob, at Peniel (Ge 32:30), at Bethel (Ge 35:7, 9). To Moses, in the burning bush (Ex 3:2; Dt 33:16; Mk 12:26; Lk 20:37; Ac 7:30), at Sinai (Ex 19:16-24; 24:10; 33:18-23). To Moses and Joshua (Dt 31:14-15). To princes of Israel, at Sinai (Ex 24:9-11). To Gideon (Jdg 6:11-24). To Solomon (1Ki 3:5; 9:2; 11:9; 2Ch 1:7-12; 7:12-22). To Isaiah (Isa 6:1-5). To Ezekiel (Eze 1:26-28).

Compassion of: *See below, Longsuffering of; Mercy of.*

Condescension of:
(Ps 113:5-6). Manifested: In reasoning, with Noah (Ge 6:11-13), with Moses (Ex 4:2-17), with sinners (Isa 1:18-20). In entering into a covenant with Abraham (Ge 15:1-21; 18:1-22). In indulging Abraham's intercession for Sodom (Ge 18:2-33). In indulging Moses' prayer to behold his glory (Ex 33:18-23). In indulging

Gideon's tests (Jdg 6:36-40). In his care of man (Ps 8:4-6; 144:3). In redemption (Jn 3:16; Ro 5:8; Heb 6:17-18).

Creator:

(Ps 148:3-5; Pr 16:4; Isa 45:7; 66:2; Jer 51:19; Am 4:13; Mk 13:19; Ac 7:50; Ro 1:20; 1Co 11:12; Heb 2:10; 3:4; Rev 4:11). Of the earth (Ge 1:1-2, 9-10; 2:1-4; Ex 20:11; 1Sa 2:8; 2Ki 19:15; Ne 9:6; Job 38:4, 7-10; Ps 24:1-2; 89:11; 90:2; 95:5; 102:25; 104:2-3, 5-6, 24, 30; 119:90; 121:2; 124:8; 136:5-9; 146:5-6; Pr 3:19; 8:26-29; Isa 37:16; 40:28; 42:5; 44:24; 45:12, 18; 48:13; 51:13, 16; Jer 10:12; 27:5; 32:17; 51:15; Jnh 1:9; Ac 4:24; 14:15; 17:24-25; Rev 10:6; 14:7). Of the heavens (Ge 1:1, 6-8; 2:1-4; Ex 20:11; 2Ki 19:15; 1Ch 16:26; Ne 9:6; Job 9:8-9; 37:16, 18; Ps 8:3; 19:1, 4; 96:5; 102:25; 104:2-3, 5-6, 24, 30; 121:2; 124:8; 136:5; 146:5-6; Pr 3:19; 8:26-28; Isa 37:16; 42:5; 44:24; 45:18; Jer 32:17; Am 5:8; Ac 4:24; 14:15; Rev 10:6; 14:7). Of the sun, moon, and stars (Ge 1:14-19; Ps 136:7-9). Of the seas (Ge 1:9-10; Ex 20:11; Ne 9:6; Ps 95:5; 146:5-6; Pr 8:26-29; Jnh 1:9; Ac 4:24; 14:15; Rev 10:6; 14:7). Of vegetation (Ge 1:11-12). Of animals (Ge 1:20-25; Job 12:7-9; Jer 27:5).

Creator of mankind (Ge 1:26-28; 2:7; 5:1-2; 9:6; Ex 4:11; Dt 4:32; 32:6, 15, 18; Job 10:3, 8-9, 11-12; 31:15; 33:4; 34:19; Ps 94:9; 95:6; 100:3; 119:73; 149:2; Pr 20:12; 22:2; Ecc 7:29; 12:1; Isa 17:7; 42:5; 43:1, 7, 15; 44:2, 24; 45:12; 51:13; 64:8; Jer 27:5; Zec 12:1; Mal 2:10; Mk 10:6; Ac 17:24-29; 1Co 12:18, 24-25; Heb 12:9; 1Pe 4:19). Through Christ (Ro 11:36; 1Co 8:6; Eph 3:9; Heb 1:1-2). *See Jesus the Christ, Creator.* By his word (Ps 33:6-7, 9; 2Co 4:6; Heb 11:3; 2Pe 3:5). By his will (Rev 4:11).

Dissertations on:

His works and providence (Job 5:8-20). The administration of his government (Job 9:2-35; 10:1-22). His sovereignty (Job 12:7-20; 26:1-14). His providence and grace (Job 33:4-30; Ps 107). His righteousness (Job 34:10-30; 35:1-16; Na 1:2-9). His majesty and justice (Job 36:30-33). His majesty and works (Ps 104:10-15).

Dwells With the Righteous:

(Ex 25:8; 29:45; Lev 26:11-12; 1Ki 6:13; Eze 37:26-27; 2Co 6:16; Rev 21:3).

Eternity of:

(Ge 21:33; Ex 3:15; 15:18; Dt 32:40; 33:27; 1Ch 16:36; 29:10; Ne 9:5; Job 36:26; Ps 9:7; 41:13; 90:1-2, 4; 92:8; 93:2; 102:12, 24-27; 145:13; 146:10; Isa 40:28; 44:6; 57:15; 63:16; Jer 10:10; La 5:19; Da 4:3, 34; Hab 1:12; Ro 1:20; 16:26; Eph 3:21; 1Ti 1:17; 6:15-16; 2Pe 3:8; Rev 4:8-10; 11:17).

Faithfulness of:

(Ge 9:16; 28:15; Lev 26:44-45; Dt 4:31; Jdg 2:1; 1Sa 12:22; Isa 42:16; 44:21; 49:7, 14-16; Jer 29:10; 31:36-37; 32:40; 33:14, 20-21, 25-26; Eze 16:60; Hos 2:19-20; Ro 3:3-4; Heb 6:10, 13-19). Confidence in (Nu 23:19; Dt 32:4; 2Sa 7:28; 1Ch 28:20; Ne 1:5; Ps 36:5; 40:10; 89:1-2, 5, 8, 14, 24, 28, 33, 34; 92:1-2, 15; 94:14; 105:8, 42; 111:5, 7-9; 119:90-91; 132:11; Isa 25:1; La 3:23; Da 9:4; Mic 7:20; 1Co 1:9; 10:13; 2Co 1:18-20; 1Th 5:24; 2Th 3:3; 2Ti 2:13, 19; Tit 1:2; Heb 10:23; 11:11; 1Pe 4:19; 2Pe 3:9; 1Jn 1:9).

Exemplified (Ge 21:1; 24:27; Ex 2:24; 6:4-5; Dt 7:8-9; 9:5; Jos 21:45; 23:14; 1Ki 8:15, 20, 23-24, 56; 2Ki 8:19; 13:23; 2Ch 6:4-15; 21:7; Ne 1:5; 9:7-8; Ps 98:3; Hag 2:5; Lk 1:54-55, 68-70, 72-73; Ac 13:32-33; Heb 6:10, 13-19).

Fatherhood of:

Taught in the Old Testament (Ex 4:22; Dt 14:1; 32:5-6; 2Sa 7:14; 1Ch 28:6; 29:10; Ps 68:5; 89:26; Isa 1:2; 9:6; 63:16; 64:8; Jer 3:19; Hos 1:10; 11:1). Taught by Jesus (Mt 5:45; 6:4, 8-9; 7:11; 10:20, 29, 32-33; 11:25-27; 12:50; 13:43; 15:13; 16:17, 27; 18:10, 14, 19; 20:23; 26:29, 39; Mk 8:38; 11:25; 13:32; Lk 2:49; 10:21-22; 11:2; 11:13; 22:29; 23:46; 24:49; Jn 1:14, 18; 2:16; 4:21, 23; 5:17-23, 36-37, 43; 6:27, 32, 44-46; 8:19, 27, 38, 41-42, 49; 10:15, 29-30, 32-33, 36-38; 12:26-28, 50; 13:1, 3; 14:2, 6-13, 20-21, 23-24, 26, 31; 15:8-10, 16, 23-24, 26; 16:3, 10, 15, 23, 25-28; 17:1, 5, 11, 21, 24; 20:17, 21). Taught by the apostles (Ac 1:4; 2:33; Ro 1:3-4, 7; 8:14-16; 1Co 1:3; 8:6; 15:24; 2Co 1:3; 6:18; Gal 1:1, 3-4; 4:4-7; Eph 1:2-3, 17; 2:18; 3:14; 4:6; 5:20; 6:23; Php 1:2; Col 1:2-3, 12; 3:17; 1Th 1:1, 3; 3:11, 13; 2Th 1:1-2; 2:16; 1Ti 1:2; 2Ti 1:2; Tit 1:4; Heb 1:5-6; 12:9; Jas 1:17, 27; 3:9; 1Pe 1:2-3, 17; 1Jn 1:2; 2:1, 13, 15, 22-24; 3:1; 4:14; 2Jn 3-4, 9; Jude 1; Rev 1:5-6; 3:5; 14:1). *See Adoption, Spiritual Adoption.*

Favor of: *See below, Grace of.*

Foreknowledge of:

(Ac 15:18). Of contingencies (1Sa 23:10-12). Of future events (Isa 42:9; 44:7; 45:11; 46:9-10; 48:5-6; Jer 1:5; Da 2:28-29; Ac 2:23). Of human needs (Mt 6:8). Of the day of judgment (Mt 24:36; Mk 13:32). Of the redeemed (Ro 8:29; 11:2; 1Pe 1:2).

Glory of:

(Ps 24:8-10; 57:5, 11; 72:18-19; Isa 40:5; Php 1:11). Described (Eze 1:26-28; Hab 3:3-6). Transcendent (Ps 113:4). Shall endure forever (Ps 104:31). Ascribed by angels (Lk 2:14). To be ascribed by people (Ps 29:2; Ro 11:36).

Manifested in the burning bush (Ex 3:2). In Mount Sinai (Ex 19:18; 20:18-19; 24:10, 17; 33:18-23; 34:5, 29-35; Dt 4:11-12, 33, 36; 5:5, 24-25; Heb 12:18-21). In the tabernacle (Ex 40:34-35). In the heavens (2Sa 22:10-15; Ps 18:9-14; 19:1). In his sovereignty (Ps 97:2-6; 145:5, 11-12; Isa 6:1-5; 24:23; Jude 24-25). In the church (Isa 35:2; 60:1-2, 19-21; 61:3; Eph 3:21). In Christ (Jn 13:31-32; 14:13; 17:1). To Ezekiel (Eze 3:12, 23; 8:4). To Stephen (Ac 7:55)

Goodness of:

(Ex 33:19; Dt 30:9; Ps 25:8-10; 31:19; 33:5; 36:7; 86:5; 100:5; 106:1; 119:68; Na 1:7; Mt 5:45; Ac 14:17; Jas 1:17). Enduring (Ps 52:1). Leads to repentance (Ro 2:4). Gratefully acknowledged (1Ch 16:34; 2Ch 5:13; 7:3; Ps 68:19; 107:8-9, 43; 118:29; 135:3; 136:1; 145:7, 9; Isa 63:7).

Manifested: In gracious providence (Mt 7:11). To the righteous (Ps 31:19; La 3:25; Ro 11:22). To the wicked (Lk 6:35).

Grace of:

Unmerited favor (Dt 7:7-8; 2Ch 30:9; Eph 1:6; Tit 2:11; Heb 4:16). Divine help (Ps 84:11; 1Co 10:13; 2Co 1:12; 12:9; 1Pe 1:5). No warrant for sinful indulgence (Ro 6:1, 15). Intercessory prayer for (Jn 17:11-12, 15; 1Th 1:1; 3:20; 2Pe 1:2). Exhortation against rejecting (2Co 6:1-2). Exemplified with respect to Jacob and Esau (Ro 9:10-16).

Manifested: In drawing men to Christ (Jn 6:44-45), in redemption (Eph 1:5-9, 11-12), in justification (Ge 15:6; Ro 3:22-24; 4:4-5, 16; 5:2, 6-8, 15-21; Tit 3:7). In passing over transgression (Nu 23:20-21; Ne 9:17; Ro 3:25). In salvation (Ro 11:5-6; Eph 2:8-9; 2Ti 1:9), in calling to service (Gal 1:15-16), in spiritual growth (Eph 3:16). In spiritual gifts (1Co 1:4-8; Eph 4:7, 11).

Manifested: In character and conduct (2Co 1:12; Php 2:13), in the character and conduct of the righteous (1Co 15:10; 2Co 1:12; Php 2:13), in sustaining the righteous (1Ch 17:8; 2Co 12:9; 1Pe 1:5; Jude 24), in sustaining in temptation (1Co 10:13; Rev 3:10).

Manifestation of: To Enoch (Ge 5:24). To Noah (Ge 6:8, 17-18). To Abraham (Ge 12:2; 21:22). To Ishmael (Ge 21:20). To Isaac (Ge 26:24). To Jacob (Ge 46:3-4; 48:16). To Joseph (Ge 39:2-3, 23). To Moses (Ex 3:12; 33:12-17). To Israel (Dt 4:7). To Naphtali (Dt 33:23). To Joshua (Jos 1:5, 9). To Job (Job 10:12). To David (1Sa 25:26, 34; 2Sa 7:8-16). To Jeremiah (Jer 15:20). To the righteous (Ps 5:12; Ac 4:33).

Guidance of:

(Ge 12:1; 24:27; Ps 23:2-3; 48:14; 73:24; Pr 3:6; Jer 3:4; 32:19; Lk 1:79; Jn 10:3-4). By pillars of cloud and fire (Ex 13:21; Ne 9:19). By his presence (Ex 15:13; 33:13-15; Dt 32:10, 12; Ps 78:52; 80:1; 107:7). By the ark of the covenant (Nu 10:33). By his counsel (2Sa 22:29; Ps 5:8; 25:9; Isa 48:17). By his Spirit (Jn 16:13). Prayed for (Ps 25:5; 27:11; 31:3; 61:2). Promised (Ps 32:8; Isa 40:11; 42:16; 58:11).

Holiness of:

(Jos 24:19; 1Sa 6:20; 1Ch 16:10; Job 6:10; 15:15; 25:5; Ps 11:7; 22:3; 36:6; 47:8; 60:6; 89:35; 98:1; 105:3; 111:9; 119:142; 145:17; Pr 9:10; Isa 5:16; 6:3; 29:19, 23; 41:14; 43:14-15; 45:19; 47:4; 49:7; 52:10; 57:15; Eze 36:21-22; 39:7, 25; Da 4:8; Hos 11:9; Hab 1:12-13; Lk 1:49; Jn 17:11; Ro 1:23; 1Jn 2:20; Rev 4:8; 6:10; 15:4).

Incomparable (Ex 15:11; 1Sa 2:2; Job 4:17-19). Without iniquity (Dt 32:4; 2Ch 19:7; Job 34:10; 36:23; Ps 92:15; Jer 2:5; La 3:38; Mt 19:17; Mk 10:18; Lk 18:19; Jas 1:13).

A reason for personal holiness (Lev 11:44; 19:2; 20:26; 21:8; 2Ch 19:7; Mt 5:48; 1Pe 1:15-16). A reason for thanksgiving (Ps 30:4; 99:3, 5, 9; Isa 12:6). A reason for reverent approach to God (Ex 3:5; Jos 5:15).

Light, figurative of. *See below, Light.*

See Sin, Separates from God; below, God, Perfections of, Righteousness of.

Human Forms and Appearances of: *See Anthropomorphisms.*

Immanence of:

(Ge 26:24; 28:15; Ex 3:12; Dt 4:7; Jos 3:7; Ac 17:27-28).

Immutable:

(Nu 23:19-20; 1Sa 15:29; Ps 102:27; Isa 40:28; Jas 1:17). In purpose (Job 23:13; Ps 33:11; Pr 19:21; Ecc 3:14; 7:13; Isa 31:2; Heb 6:17-18). In faithfulness (Ps 119:89-91). In mercy (Isa 59:1; Hos 13:14; Mal 3:6; Ro 11:29).

Impartial:

(Dt 10:17). Despises none (Job 36:5). Does not show favoritism (2Ch 19:7; Job 34:19; 37:24; Ac 10:34-35; Ro 2:6, 11; Eph 6:8-9; Col 3:25; 1Pe 1:17).

Incomparable:

(Ex 16:11; Dt 33:26; 2Sa 7:22; 1Ki 8:23; Ps 35:10; 71:19; 89:6-8; 113:5; Mic 7:18).

Incomprehensible:

(Job 15:8; 37:1-24; Isa 40:12-31; 55:8-9; Mt 11:27; 1Co 2:16).

Infinite:

(1Ki 8:27; 2Ch 2:6; 6:1, 18; Ps 147:5; Jer 23:24).

Invisible:

(Ex 20:21; 33:20; Dt 4:11-12; 4:15; 5:22; 1Ki 8:12; 2Ch 6:1; Job 9:11; 23:8-9; Ps 18:11; 97:2; Jn 1:18; 5:37; 6:46; Ro 1:20; Col 1:13-15; 1Ti 1:17; 6:16; Heb 11:27; 1Jn 4:12).

Jealous:

(Ex 20:5, 7; 34:14; Dt 4:24; 5:9, 11; 6:15; 29:20; 32:16, 21; Jos 24:19; 2Ch 16:7-9; Isa 30:1-2; Eze 23:25; 36:5; 39:25; Joel 2:18; Na 1:2; Zec 1:14; 1Co 10:22).

Judge:

(Ge 16:5; Jdg 11:27; 1Sa 2:3, 10; 24:12, 15; 1Ch 16:33; Job 21:22; Ps 11:4-5; 26:1-2; 35:24; 43:1; 50:4, 6; 58:11; 75:7; 76:8-9; 82:8; 94:1-2; 135:14; Pr 16:2; 29:26; Ecc 3:17; 11:9; 12:14; Isa 3:13-14; 28:17, 21; 30:18, 27; 33:22; Jer 32:19; Da 7:9-10; Na 1:3; Mal 3:5; Ac 17:31; 1Co 5:13; Heb 10:30-31; 12:22-23; Rev 6:16-17; 11:18; 16:5; 18:8).

Just Judge (Ge 18:21, 25; Nu 16:22; Dt 32:4; Ne 9:33; Job 4:17; 8:3; 34:10-12; Ps 7:9, 11; 9:4, 7-8; 67:4; 96:10, 13; 98:9; Isa 26:7; 45:21; Jer 32:19; Ro 2:2, 5-16; 3:4-6, 26; 11:22, 23; Eph 6:8-9; 1Pe 1:17; Rev 19:2). Incorruptible Judge (Dt 10:17; 2Ch 19:7; Job 8:3; 34:19).

Justice of:

(Dt 32:4; 2Sa 22:25; 1Ki 8:32; Job 31:13-15; Ps 51:4; 62:12; 89:14; 97:2; 145:17; Pr 21:2-3; 24:12; Isa 61:8; Jer 9:24; 11:20; 20:12; 32:19; 50:7; Eze 14:23; 18:25, 29-30; 33:7-19; Da 9:7, 14; Na 1:3, 6; Zep 3:5; Ac 17:31; Ro 2:2, 5-16; Heb 6:10; 1Pe 1:17; 2Pe 2:9; 1Jn 1:9; Jude 6; Rev 11:18; 15:3).

Knowledge of:

(Ge 6:5; 1Sa 2:3; Job 12:13, 22; 21:22; 22:13-14; 26:6; 28:23-24; 36:4-5; 37:16; Ps 147:4-5; Pr 3:19-20; Isa 40:13-14, 26-28; 46:9-10; Mt 24:36; Mk 13:32; Ro 11:33-34; 1Co 1:25; 1Jn 1:5).

Knows the human state and condition (Ge 16:13; Ex 3:7; Dt 2:7; 2Ki 19:27; 2Ch 16:9; Job 23:10; 31:4; 34:21, 25; Ps 1:6; 11:4; 33:13-15; 37:18; 38:9; 66:7; 69:19; 103:14; 119:168; 139:1-4, 6, 12, 14-16; 142:3; Pr 5:21; 15:3, 11; Isa 29:15-16; 37:28; 66:18; Jer 23:24; 32:19; Am 9:2-4; Mt 10:29-30; 1Co 8:3).

Knows the human heart (Ge 20:6; Dt 31:21; 1Sa 16:7; 2Sa 7:20; 1Ki 8:39; 1Ch 28:9; 29:17; 2Ch 6:30; Job 11:11; Ps 7:9; 44:21; 94:9-11; Pr 15:11; 16:2; 17:3; 21:2; 24:12; Jer 11:20; 16:17; 17:10; 20:12; Eze 11:5; Am 4:13; Mt 6:4, 8, 18, 32; Lk 16:15; Ac 1:24; 15:8; 1Co 3:20; 1Th 2:4; Heb 4:13; 1Jn 3:20). *See above, Foreknowledge of; below, Wisdom of.*

Light:

(Da 2:22; Jas 1:17; 1Jn 1:5).

Longsuffering:

(Ge 6:3; 15:16; Ex 34:6; Nu 14:18; Ps 86:15; 103:8-10; Isa 5:1-4; 30:18; 48:9, 11; 57:16; Jer 7:13, 23-25; 9:24; Eze 20:17; Joel 2:13; Hab 1:2-4; Mt 21:33-41; Mk 12:1-9; Lk 20:9-16; Ac 14:16; Ro 3:25; 15:5; 1Pe 3:20).

Abused by people (Ne 9:28-31; Pr 1:24-27; 29:1; Ecc 8:11; Isa 5:1-4; Jer 7:13, 23-25; Mt 24:48-51). *See below, Mercy of.*

Manifested in deferring judgments (Mic 7:18; Lk 13:6-9; Ac 17:30; Ro 9:22-23; 2Pe 3:9, 15). In giving time for repentance (Jer 11:7; Mt 23:37; Lk 13:34; Ro 2:4).

Love of:

(Dt 4:37; 7:7-8, 13; 10:15, 18; 23:5; 33:3, 12; 2Sa 12:24; Job 7:17; Ps 42:8; 47:4; 69:16; Hos 11:1; Mal 1:2; 2Co 13:11, 14; 1Jn 3:1; 4:12, 16, 19; Jude 21). Everlasting (2Ch 20:21; Jer 31:3). Better than life (Ps 63:3).

For the wicked (Mt 18:12-14; Lk 15:4-7, 11-27; Ro 5:8; Eph 2:4-5). For the righteous (Ps 103:13; 146:8; Pr 15:9; Jn 14:21, 23; 16:27; 17:10, 23, 26; Ro 1:7; 9:13; 11:28; 2Th 2:16). For the cheerful giver (2Co 9:7).

Exemplified (Ex 19:4-6; Lev 20:24, 26; Dt 32:9-12; 2Sa 7:23-24; Ps 48:9, 14; Isa 43:1-4; 49:13-16; 54:5-6, 10; 62:4-5; 63:7-9; 66:13; Jer 3:14-15; Eze 16:8; Hos 2:19-20, 23; Zec 2:8). In forgiveness of sins (Isa 38:17; Tit 3:4-5). In the gift of his Son (Jn 3:16; 1Jn 4:8-10). In chastisements (Heb 12:6).

Mercy of:

(Ex 20:2, 6; Dt 5:10; Ex 33:19; Dt 4:31; 7:9; 1Ki 8:23; 2Ch 30:9; Ezr 9:9; Ps 18:50; 25:6, 8; 31:7; 32:10; 36:5; 57:10; 62:12; 69:16; 98:3; 108:4; 111:4; 116:5; 117:2; 119:64, 156; 138:2; 146:7-8; Isa 60:10; Jer 9:24; 31:20; 32:18; Da 9:4; Hos 2:23; Zec 10:6; Lk 6:36; Ac 17:30; Ro 9:15; 11:32; 15:9; 2Co 1:3; Heb 4:16; 1Pe 1:3; 2Pe 3:9). Everlasting (1Ch 16:34, 41; 2Ch 5:13; 7:3, 6, 14; Ezr 3:11; Ps 89:1-2, 28; 100:5; 103:17; 106:1; 107:1; 118:1-4, 29; 136:1-26).

Manifested: In withholding punishment (Ge 8:21; 18:26, 30-32; Ex 32:14; Nu 16:48; 2Sa 24:14, 16; 2Ki 13:23; Ezr 9:13; Job 11:6; Isa 12:1; 54:9; Eze 16:6, 42, 63; 20:17; Hos 11:8-9; Joel 2:13, 18; Jnh 4:2, 10-11; Mal 3:6). In rescuing from destruction (Ge 19:16; Nu 21:8; Jdg 2:18; 2Ki 14:26-27; Ne 1:10; 9:17-20, 27-31). In leading his people (Ex 15:13). In comforting the afflicted (2Co 12:9). In hearing prayer (Ex 22:27; Heb 4:16). In desire to save sinners (Dt 5:29; 32:29; Jdg 10:16; 2Ch 36:15; Isa 65:2, 8; Jer 2:9; 7:25; Eze 18:23, 31-32; 33:11; Mt 18:12-14; Lk 15:4-7; 1Ti 2:4, 6). In forbearance toward sinners (2Ch 24:18-19; Ps 145:8-9; La 3:22-23, 31-33; Da 4:22-27; Na 1:3). In granting forgiveness (Ex 34:6-7; Nu 14:18-20; 2Sa 12:13; 2Ch 7:14; Job 33:14-30; Ps 32:1-2, 5; 65:3; 78:38-39; 85:2-3; 86:5, 13, 15; 99:8; 103:3, 8-14; 130:3-4; 130:7-8; Pr 16:6; 28:13; Isa 55:7-9; Jer 3:12, 22; 31:20, 34; 33:8, 11; 36:3; 50:20; Eze 36:25; Da 9:9; Hos 14:4; Mic 7:18-19; Mt 6:14; 18:23-27; Lk 1:50, 77-78; Ac 3:19; 26:18; Ro 10:12-13; 2Co 5:19; Eph 1:6-8; 2:4-7; 1Ti 1:13; Tit 3:5; Heb 8:12; 1Jn 1:9).

Symbolized: In the atonement cover (Ex 25:17-22; 37:6-9; Lev 16:1-14; Nu 7:89; Heb 9:5).

Name of:

To be revered (Ex 20:7; Dt 5:11; 28:58; Ps 111:9; Mic 4:5; 1Ti 6:1). To be praised (Ps 34:3; 72:17). Not to be profaned (Ex 20:7; Lev 18:21; 19:12; 20:3; 21:6; 22:2, 32; Dt 5:11; Ps 139:20; Isa 52:5; Ro 2:24; Rev 16:9). Profaned (Ps 139:20).

Names of:

In the ancient world a name was not merely a label but the meaning of the name was virtually equivalent to whoever or whatever bore it (1Sa 25:25). Giving a name to anyone or anything was tantamount to owning or controlling it (Ge 1:5, 8, 10; 2:19-20; 2Sa 12:28). Changing a name could signify a promotion to a higher status (Ge 17:5; 32:28) or a demotion (2Ki 23:34-35; 24:17), and blotting out or cutting off the name of a person or thing meant that that person or thing was destroyed (2Ki 14:27; Isa 14:22; Zep 1:4; cf. Ps 83:4).

The name and being of God are often used in parallelism with each other (Ps 18:49; 68:4; 74:18; 86:12; 92:1; Isa 25:1; Mal 3:16), which stresses their essential identity. Believing in Jesus' name (Jn 3:18) is therefore the same as believing in Jesus himself. Prayer in his name would be prayer in concert with his character, mind, and purpose.

The name Jesus is the Greek form for the Hebrew Joshua or "*salvation of Yahweh.*" As Yahweh's Savior his name accurately describes his work and purpose (Mt 1:21).

El and its compounds—

El is the generic Semitic name for "God" or "deity." *El* is one of the oldest designations for deity in the ancient world. The word is found in several Semitic languages such as, Akkadian, Phoenician, and South Arabic. Even though the derivation of the word is uncertain, the root meaning is "power and authority" (Ge 1:1; Ps 19:1).

El Berith means "god of the covenant" (Jdg 9:46) and is an alternate form of the name *Baal-Berith* (Jdg 8:33; 9:4). These are names of pagan gods and not the God of Israel. The remains of the Canaanite temple to Baal-Berith at Shechem, has been recovered.

El Bethel means "God of Bethel," but is a place name, not a name of God. God directs Jacob to return to Bethel and build an altar there (Ge 35:1, 6-7).

El Elohe Israel means "God [El], the God of Israel" or "mighty is the God of Israel." Though a statement about God, it is actually the name of an altar, also associated with the travels of Jacob (Ge 33:18-20).

El Elyon; See below Elyon.

El Olam means "God the Everlasting One" or "God of Eternity." While living among the Philistines, Abraham calls upon the name of Yahweh, the Eternal God (Ge 21:33). Isaiah quotes God as saying, "The LORD is the everlasting God, the Creator of the ends of the earth" (Isa 40:28). The Psalmist expresses that, "from

G

everlasting to everlasting you are God" (Ps 90:1-2; cf 93:2; Isa 26:4).

El Roi means "God who sees me." As Hagar wandered in the desert, the angel of the LORD appeared to her (Ge 16:7-12). After his appearance she gave Yahweh this name saying, "You are the One who sees me." The well at that place was named "Beer Lahai Roi," which means "well of the Living One who sees me" (Ge 16:14).

El Shaddai appears seven times (Ge 17:1; 28:3; 35:11; 43:14; 48:3; Ex 6:3; Eze 10:5). It probably means "God the Mountain," similar to "God the Rock" (Dt 32:4). Older etymology defined it as "God the Provider," understanding *Shaddai* to be derived from the word for "breast." *See below Shaddai.*

Eloah—

Eloah is thought to be a singular form of "Elohim." It is used primarily in Job (42 times) as a way to refer to God, but without referring to him as the "God of Israel." In other references it is usually synonymous in meaning with *Elohim* (Ps 50:22-23), or *Yahweh* (Ps 139:19, 21), or *Adonay* (Ps 114:7). It also appears in the exilic and postexilic periods (2Ch 32:15; Ne 9:17; Da 11:37-39).

Elohim ***(and its compounds) and*** *Theos—*

Elohim, the plural form of *El, Eloah* is used as a plural to refer to the many gods of the nations. But *Elohim* is used in a singular sense in the great majority of instances, and is thus referred to as "plural of majesty." In the singular sense *Elohim* is sometimes applied to the god of another people as in Chemosh, the god of the Amorites (Jdg 11:24), or Ashtoreth (Ishtar), the goddess of Sidon (1Ki 11:5), or Baal-Zebub, the god of Ekron (2Ki 1:2), but is used overwhelmingly (over 2300 times) in the OT to refer to Israel's God, meaning "the true God."

Theos is the NT counterpart of *Elohim* (Mt 22:32 w Ex 3:6). It usually refers to the true God, but can refer to pagan deities (Ac 17:18, 23; 1Co 8:5).

Yahweh, Yah, ***and Compounds—***

Yahweh is the personal covenant name of Israel's God, the most common name for God in the OT (6829 times). *Yah* is its shortened form. The NIV consistently renders Yahweh as LORD. The name sounds like and may be derived from the Hebrew for the word "I AM" (Ex 3:14-15). The basic meaning of his name is "He who is" or "He who is truly present." or "I will be to you all that I am." For Israel, Yahweh is not merely one god among many; he is the Creator and Ruler of heaven and earth, who is worthy of and demands the exclusive homage of his people. It is important to understand that this is God's intensely personal name. The respect with which it was treated bears witness to the national feeling of Israel and also their fear of the God who is among them. This was recognized by the scribes who even avoided pronunciation of the name. They would use circumlocutions and alternate names where possible. *See below on Adonay.* In the NT, John records that Jesus made seven self-descriptions (Jn 6:35; 8:12 w 9:5; 10:7, 9; 10:11, 14; 11:25; 14:6; 15:1, 5), each one being introduced by "I am." The Greek text makes this statement solemnly emphatic and echoes God's self-revelation to Moses (Ex 3:14). In a similar fashion, Jesus expressed the eternity of his being and his oneness with the Father by saying, "I tell you the truth," Jesus answered, "before Abraham was born, I am!" (Jn 8:58). The people listening knew exactly what he meant by what he said: I AM GOD. The penalty for such blasphemy was stoning (Lev 24:16), which they fully intended to carry out (Jn 8:59).

Yahweh Nissi means "Yahweh is my banner or standard." This was the name given to the altar which Moses erected to commemorate the defeat of the Amalekites at Rephidim (Ex 17:8-15).

Yahweh Rapha. At Marah, on the way to Sinai, the LORD promised Israel that if they fully obeyed him, he would not bring on them the diseases he brought on Egypt. His name of assurance means "[I am] Yahweh who heals you" (Ex 15:26).

Yahweh Shalom means "Yahweh is peace." The angel of the LORD appeared to Gideon to commission him to liberate Israel from the Midianites (Jdg 6:1-22). The LORD greeted him with peace, so Gideon built an altar and named it "The LORD is Peace" (Jdg 6:23-24).

Yahweh Shammah means "The LORD is There." Not a name of God, this is the name given to the restored Jerusalem (Eze 48:35). The glory of God will return and Messiah will rule from New Jerusalem forever (Eze 43; cf. Rev 21). God's name is inseparably linked with Jerusalem.

Yahweh Tsabbaoth means "LORD of Hosts" and is consistently translated "LORD Almighty" in the NIV (e.g., 1Sa 1:3, 11). "Hosts" can refer to, human armies (Ex 7:4; Ps 44:9), celestial bodies (Ge 2:1; Dt 4:19; Isa 40:26), or heavenly creatures such as angels (Jos 5:14; 1Ki 22:19; Ps 148:2). This title is probably best understood as a general reference to the sovereignty of God over all powers in the universe. In the NT *Tsabbaoth* is twice transliterated by the Greek "Sabaoth" (Ro 9:29; Jas 5:4), but is usually *Pantokrator* (2Co 6:18; Rev 1:8; 4:8).

Yahweh Tsidkenu means "Yahweh our Righteousness." This is the designation of the future king who will rise up from the line of David to rule over Israel (Jer 23:5-6). Righteousness is the divine attribute of the Messiah who imputes his righteousness to his followers and therefore is able to reconcile them to God (2Co 5:21). In a second reference, Jeremiah directs attention to Jerusalem, the capital of the King, which because of her intimate relationship to Messiah, will be given the same name and nature of the righteous monarch (Jer 33:15-16).

Yahweh Yireh means "Yahweh will provide," "Yahweh will see [to it]." *Yireh* comes from the same Hebrew root as *Moriah*, the name of the region to which God sent Abraham to sacrifice Isaac (Ge 22:2; 2Ch 3:1). Both words are place names that confess Yahweh as the provider of a substitutionary sacrifice (Ge 22:14, cf. v. 8).

Adon, Adonay, ***and*** *Kurios*

Adon or *Adonay* is a title for God that emphasizes his sovereignty, that is "Lord." *Adon* is basically a title of honor. Out of respect one might address a superior with this title in the same way that we would say "sir" or "your honor." It would be used by a subject addressing a king (1Sa 24:8), a wife to her husband (Ge 18:12), a daughter or son to their father (Ge 31:35), a slave to his master (Ge 24:12; Ex 21:5), a subordinate to his leader (Nu 11:28). It therefore refers to one's position of authority and prestige (Ge 23:6; 45:8). The special spelling *Adonay* belongs preeminently to Yahweh, because he alone is the "Lord of the earth" (Jos 3:11, 13; Ps 97:5; Mic 4:13; Zec 4:14; 6:5). In the years after the Exile (after 538 B.C.), with reverence for the name of God increasing, the name *Yahweh* began to be pronounce as *Adonay* in the reading of the Scriptures. The LXX translators, out of fear of profaning the name of God, were led to translate *Yahweh* as *kurios* or "Lord." The Massoretic pronunciation of the Hebrew text continued this tradition by using the vowels of *Adonay* with the consonants of *Yahweh* as a signal that the proper name of God should be pronounced as *Adonay.* The misreading of this convention led to the misunderstanding of the name of God as *Jehovah.*

Kurios is the NT counterpart of both *Adonay* (Mt 22:44 w Ps 110:1) and *Yahweh* (Mt 4:10 w Dt 6:13). It is used as a term of respect (Mt 13:27) and submission (Jn 13:16; 15:20) as well as the title "Lord" (Mt 1:20, 22).

Shaddai—

Shaddai is used forty-eight times as a name of God, thirty-two times in Job (Job 5:17; 6:4, 14; etc.), seven times in the compound name *El Shaddai. See above EL.* It probably means "[God] the Mountain," similar to "God the Rock" (Dt 32:4). Older etymology defined it as "[God] the Provider," understanding *Shaddai* to be derived from the word for "breast." The NIV consistently translates *Shaddai* as "Almighty" (Ge 17:1; Ps 91:1).

Elyon ***and*** *Hupsistos—*

Elyon means "the Most High" or "the exalted One" (Ge 14:17-20; Ps 18:13; Isa 14:13-14). The NT Greek uses the form *hupsistos* meaning "highest," or "most exalted." Jesus was known as, and called, the Son of the Most High God (Mk 5:7; Lk 1:32-33; 6:28). The Holy Spirit is the power of the Most High (Lk 1:35). John the Baptist would be known as a prophet of the Most High God (Lk 1:76). Jesus taught his disciples to "love your enemies, do good to them, and lend to them without expecting to get anything back," because in so doing, their reward will be great and they will prove that they are "sons of the Most High, because he is kind to the ungrateful and wicked" (Lk 6:35). The Most High God is far too great and magnificent to be limited to houses made by men (Ac 7:48-50). The early apostles were known as servants of the Most High God (Ac 16:17). Melchizedek was king of Salem and priest of the Most High God (Heb 7:1 w Ge 14:17-20).

Other descriptive titles—

The Ancient of Days (Da 7:9, 13, 22). Deliverer (2Sa 22:2; Ps 18:2). Father (Ps 89:26; Mt 16:17; Mk 14:36; Lk 22:29; Jn 5:17; 8:54; 10:29; 14:23; Ro 8:15; Gal 4:6), Everlasting Father (Isa 9:6). The First and the Last (Isa 44:6; 48:12; Rev 1:17; 2:8; 22:13). God of gods (Dt 10:17; Ps 136:2; Da 2:47; 11:36), the God of heaven and earth (Ge 24:3, 7). The Holy One (Isa 41:14; 43:14-15; 48:17), a God whose name is Holy (Isa 57:15). A Jealous God (Ex 34:14). Judge (Ge 18:25; Dt 32:36; Jdg 11:26). King of kings (1Ti 6:15; Rev 17:14; 19:16). The Living God (Jer 10:10; Da 6:26; Hos 1:10; Mt 16:16). Lord of lords (Dt 10:17; Ps 136:3; 1Ti 6:15; Rev 17:14; 19:16). Lord of kings (Da 2:47). The Mighty One (Isa 49:26; 60:16), Mighty God (Isa 9:6; 10:21; Lk 22:69). Prince (Ac 5:31), Prince of Peace (Isa 9:6). Redeemer (Job 19:25; Ps 19:14; 78:35; Isa 41:14; 43:14; 44:6; Jer 50:34). Righteous One (1Sa 45:21; Ps 4:1; 7:9). Rock appears five times in the Song of Moses (Dt 32:4, 15, 18, 30, 31), and several times in the Psalms (Ps 18:2, 31, 46; 19:14; 28:1; 78:35; 89:26), Isaiah (Isa 17:10; 26:4; 30:29; 44:8), and Habakkuk (Hab 1:12); in the NT Paul says that the Rock of Israel was Christ (1Co 10:4). The blessed and only Ruler (1Ti 6:15). Savior (Dt 32:15; 1Ch 16:35; Ps 89:26; Isa 43:3; Jn 4:42; Lk 1:47; Ac 5:31; 1Ti 1:1; 2:3; 4:10; Tit 1:3). Shield (Ps 3:3; 18:30). Strength (Ps 22:19). A Warrior (Ex 15:3). Wonderful Counselor (Isa 9:6).

Omnipotent:

(Ge 17:1; 18:14; Job 42:2; Ac 26:8; Rev 19:6; 21:22). *See below, Power of.*

Omnipresent:

(Ge 28:16; 1Ki 8:27; 2Ch 2:6; Ac 7:48-49; Ps 139:3, 5, 7-10; Jer 23:23-24; Ac 17:24, 27-28). *See below, Presence of.*

Omniscient: *See above, Knowledge of; below, Wisdom of.*

Perfection of:

(Dt 32:4; 2Sa 22:31; Ps 18:30; Mt 5:48; Ro 12:2; Jas 1:17; 1Jn 1:5; Rev 15:3). *See above, Holiness of; below, Righteousness of.*

Personality of: *See below, Unity of.*

Power of:

(Ex 9:16; 15:6-7, 11-12; Nu 11:23; Dt 7:21; 11:2; Job 37:1-23; Ps 21:13; 29:3-9; 62:11; 68:34-35; 74:13, 15; 77:14, 16, 18; 78:12-51; 79:11; 89:8, 13; 93:1, 4; 105:26-41; 106:8; 111:6; 135:6, 8-12; 147:5, 16-18; Isa 26:4; 40:12, 22, 24, 26, 28; 51:10, 15; 63:12; Jer 5:22; 27:5; 32:17, 27; Da 2:20; Mt 19:26; Mk 10:27; 14:36; Lk 1:49, 51; 18:27; 22:29; 1Co 6:14; Rev 19:1).

Supreme (Dt 32:39; Jos 4:24; 1Sa 2:6-7; 14:6; 1Ch 29:11-12; 2Ch 14:11; 25:8-9; Job 5:9; 23:13-14; 26:7-14; 36:5, 22, 27-33; 38:8, 11; 40:9; 42:2; Ps 104:7, 9, 29-30, 32; Da 4:35).

Irresistible (Dt 32:39; Job 10:7; 1Sa 2:10; 2Ch 20:6; Job 9:4-7, 10, 12-13, 19; 11:10; 12:14-16; 14:20; 41:10-11; Ps 66:3, 7; 76:7; Isa 14:24, 27; 31:3; 43:13, 16-17; 46:10-11; 50:2-3; Na 1:3-6). Incomparable (Dt 3:24; Job 40:9; Ps 89:8). Omnipotent (Ge 18:14; Jer 32:27; Mt 19:26). Everlasting (Ro 1:20).

Creation by (Jer 10:12). The resurrection of Christ by (1Co 6:14; 2Co 13:4). The resurrection of believers by (1Co 6:14).

Manifested in behalf of believers (Dt 33:26-27; 2Ch 16:9; Ezr 8:22; Ne 1:10; Jer 20:11; Da 3:17). Manifested in his works (Dt 3:24; Ps 33:9; 107:25, 29; 114:7-8; Pr 30:4; Isa 48:13; Jer 10:12-13; 51:15; Ro 1:20). *See above, Omnipotent.*

Presence of:

(Ge 16:13; 28:16; Ex 20:24; 29:42-43; 30:6; 33:14; Dt 4:34-36, 39; 1Ki 8:27; Ps 139:3, 5, 7-10; Isa 57:15; 66:1; Jer 23:23-24; 32:18-19; Jnh 1:3-4; Ac 17:24, 27-28; 1Co 12:6).

Manifested above the atonement cover. *See Shekinah.*

Preserver:

(Ne 9:6; Job 33:18; Ps 3:3; 12:7; 17:7; 68:6; 73:23; Isa 27:3; 49:8; Jer 2:6; Da 5:23; Mt 10:29-31; Lk 12:6-7; 21:18; Jn 17:11, 15; 1Pe 3:12-13; 2Pe 2:9).

Of the righteous (Ge 15:1; 28:15; 49:24-25; Ex 8:22-23; 9:26; 11:7; 12:13, 17, 23; 15:2, 13, 16-17; 19:4; 23:20-31; Dt 1:30-31; 32:10; 33:12, 25-28; Jos 23:10; 1Sa 2:9; 2Sa 22:1-51; 2Ch 16:9; Job 1:10; 5:11, 18-24; 10:12; Ps 9:9; 18:14; 23:1-6; 31:20, 23; 32:6, 8; 34:7, 15, 17, 19-22; 37:17, 23-24, 28, 32-33; 41:1-3; 46:1, 7; 50:15; 84:11; 91:1, 3-4, 7, 9-10, 14-15; 102:19-20; 103:2-5; 107:9-10, 13; 116:6; 118:13; 121:3-4, 7-8; 125:1-3; 145:14, 19-20; 146:7-8; Pr 2:7-8; 10:3, 30; Isa 25:4; 30:21, 26; 33:16; 40:11, 29, 31; 42:16; 43:2; 46:3-4; 52:12; 58:11; 63:9; Jer 31:9-10, 28; Eze 11:16; 34:11-16, 22, 31; Da 3:27-28; Joel 2:18; Zec 2:5, 8; Mt 4:6; 1Co 10:13; 2Ti 4:17-18; 2Th 3:3; Jas 4:15).

His Preserving Care Exemplified—

To Noah and his family, at the time of the flood (Ge 6:8, 13-21; 7; 8:1, 15-16). To Abraham and Sarah, in Egypt (Ge 12:17), in Gerar (Ge 20:3). To Lot, when Sodom was destroyed (Ge 19). To Hagar, when Abraham cast her out (Ge 21:17, 19). To Jacob, when he fled from home (Ge 35:3), when he fled from Laban, his father-in-law (Ge 31:24, 29), when he met Esau (Ge 33:3-10), as he journeyed in the land of Canaan (Ge 35:3). To Joseph, in Egypt (Ge 39:2, 21). To Moses, in his infancy (Ex 2:1-10).

To the Israelites: In bringing about their deliverance from bondage (Ex 1:9-12; 2:23-25; 3:7-9). In exempting the land of Goshen from the plague of flies (Ex 8:22). In preserving their cattle from the plague (Ex 9:4-7). In exempting the land of Goshen from the plague of darkness (Ex 10:21-23). In saving the firstborn, when the plague of death destroyed the firstborn of Egypt (Ex 12:13, 23). In deliverance from Egypt (Ex 13:3, 17-22; 14; 19:4; Lev 26:13). In the wilderness (Ex 40:36-38; Nu 9:17-23; 10:33; 22:12; 23:8; Dt 1:31; 23:5; 26:7-9).

In victories under Joshua, over the Canaanites (Jos 6-11; 24:11-13), under Othniel (Jdg 3:9-11), under Ehud (Jdg 3:15-30), under Shamgar (Jdg 3:31), under Deborah (Jdg 4:5), under Gideon (Jdg 7; 8:1-23), under Jephthah (Jdg 11:29-40), under David (1Sa 17:45-49), under Ahab (1Ki 20). In delivering the kingdom of Israel from Syria (2Sa 8). In delivering Israel by Jeroboam II (2Ki 14:26-27), by Abijah (2Ch 13:4-18). In delivering from the oppressions of the king of Syria (2Ki 13:2-5). To the kingdom of Judah: In delivering from Egypt (2Ch 12:2-12), from the Ethiopians (2Ch 14:11-14). In giving peace with other nations (2Ch 17). In delivering them from the army of the Assyrians (2Ki 19). To David (1Sa 17:32, 45-47; 2Sa 7; 1Ch 11:13-14). To Hezekiah (2Ki 19). To Job (Job 1:9-12; 2:6). To Jeremiah and Baruch (Jer 36:26). To Daniel and the three Hebrew captives (Da 2:18-23; 3:27-28; 6). To Jonah (Jnh 1:17).

To the wise men of the east (Mt 2:12). To Jesus and his parents (Mt 2:13, 19-22). To Peter (Ac 12:3-17). To Paul and Silas (Ac 16:26-39). To Paul (Ac 27:24; 28:5-6, w Mk 16:18). *See below, Providence of; See Poor, God's Care.*

Providence of:

(Ge 24:7, 40-50, 56; 26:24; Lev 26:4-6, 10; Dt 8:18; 11:12-15; 15:4-6; 32:11-14; 1Sa 2:6-9; 1Ki 11:14-40; 1Ch 29:14, 16; Ps 23:1-6; 34:7, 9-10; 71:6-7, 15; Ps 107:1-43; 127:1-5; 136:5-25; 144:12-15; 147:8-9, 13-14; Pr 16:33; Ecc 2:24; 3:13; 5:19; Isa 46:4; 51:2; 55:10; Eze 36:28-38; Joel 2:18-26; Mt 5:45; Ro 8:28; Jas 4:15).

In providing for temporal necessities (Ge 1:29-30; 2:16; 8:22; 9:1-3; 28:20-21; 48:15-16; 49:24-25; Ex 16:15; Lev 25:20-22; Dt 2:7; 7:13-15; 8:4; 10:18; 28:2-13; 29:5; Ru 1:6; Ne 9:24-25; Job 5:8-11; 22:18, 25; Ps 36:6-7; 37:3, 19, 22, 25, 34; 65:9-13; 67:6; 85:12; 104:10-15; 111:5; 136:25; 145:15-16; Isa 43:20; 48:21; Jer 5:24; 27:6; Hos 2:8; Jnh 4:6; Zec 10:1; Mt 6:26, 30-33; 10:29-31; Lk 12:6-7, 24-28; 22:35; Jn 6:31; Ac 14:17; 2Co 9:10).

In sending prosperity (Ps 75:7; 127:1-2; Isa 48:14-15; 54:16-17; Eze 29:19-20). In sending adversity (1Sa 2:6-9; 2Sa 17:14; Ps 75:7; Ecc 3:10). In saving from adversity (Ge 7:1; Ex 9:26; 15:26; 23:25-26; Ps 103:3-5; 116:1-15; 118:5-6, 13-14; 146:7-9; Da 6:20-22).

In delivering from enemies (Ge 14:20; Ex 3:17; 6:7; 14:29-30; 23:22; 34:24; Dt 20:4; 23:14; 30:4, 20; 31:3, 8; 2Ki 20:6; 2Ch 20:3-30; 32:8; Ezr 8:22-23; Ps 18:17, 27; 44:1-3; 61:3; 78:52-55; 97:10; 105:14-45; Ac 7:34-36; 12:1-12; Pr 16:7). In thwarting evil purpose (Ge 37:5-20, w 45:5-7 & Ps 105:17 & Ac 7:9-10; Ex 14:4; Nu 23:7-8, 23, w 22:12-18; 24:10-13; Ezr 5:5; Ne 6:16; Est 7:10, w 6:1-12 & 9:25; Job 5:12-13, w Isa 8:9-10; Ps 33:10; Ac 5:38-39). In turning the curse into blessing (Dt 23:4, 6; Php 1:12, 19). In exalting the lowly (2Sa 7:8-9; 1Ch 17:7-8; Ps 68:6; 113:7-8). In leading people to repentance (Am 4:7-12).

In punishing evildoers (Dt 2:30; Jos 10:10-11, 19; Jdg 9:23-24; 1Ch 5:26; Isa 41:2, 4). In punishing rulers (Da 5:18, 22). In punishing nations (Dt 9:4-5; Job 12:23; Eze 29:19-20). In ordaining instruments of discipline (Isa 13:3-5). In using the Gentiles to execute his purpose (Ezr 6:22; Isa 44:28; 45:1-6, 13).

In fulfilling prophecy (1Ki 12:15; 2Ch 10:15; 36:22-23; Ezr 1:1; Ac 3:17-18).

In nature (Job 12:7-20; 37:6-24; 38:25-27, 41; 39:5-6; Ps 104:16-19, 24-30; 135:7; Jer 10:13; 51:16; 14:22; 31:35).

Instances of—

Saving Noah (Ge 7:1; 2Pe 2:5). The call of Abraham (Ge 12:1). Protecting Abraham, Sarah, and Abimelech (Ge 20:3-6). Deliverance of Lot (Ge 19). Care of Isaac (Ge 26:2-3), of Jacob (Ge 31:7). The mission of Joseph (Ge 37:5-10; 39:2-3, 21, 23; 45:7-8; 50:20; Ps 105:17-22). Warning Pharaoh of famine (Ge 41).

Delivering the Israelites (Ex 3:8; 11:3; 13:18; Ac 7:34-36). The pillar of cloud (Ex 13:21; 14:19-20). Dividing the Red Sea (Ex 14:21). Delaying and destroying Pharaoh (Ex 14:25 30). Purifying the waters of Marah (Ex 15:25). Supplying manna and quail (Ex 16:13-15; Nu 11:31-32). Supplying water at Meribah (Nu 20:7-11; Ne 9:10-25). Protection of homes while at feasts (Ex 34:24). In the conquest of Canaan (Ps 44:2-3). Saving David's army (2Sa 5:23-25). The revolt of the ten tribes (1Ki 12:15, 24; 2Ch 10:15). Fighting the battles of Israel (2Ch 13:12, 18; 14:9-14; 16:7-9; 20:15, 17; 22; 23; 32:21-22). Restoring Manasseh after his conversion (2Ch 33:12-13). Feeding Elijah and the widow (1Ki 17; 19:1-8). In prospering Hezekiah (2Ki 18:6-7; 2Ch 32:29), and Asa

(2Ch 14:6-7), and Jehoshaphat (2Ch 17:3, 5; 20:30), and Uzziah (2Ch 26:5-15), and Jotham (2Ch 27:6), and Job (Job 1:10; 42:10, 12), and Daniel (Da 1:9).

In turning the heart of the king of Assyria to favor the Jews (Ezr 6:22). In rescuing Jeremiah (La 3:52-58; Jer 38:6-13). Restoration of the Jews (2Ch 36:22-23; Ezr 1:1). Rescuing the Jews from Haman's plot (Esther). Rebuilding the walls of Jerusalem (Ne 6:16).

Warning Joseph in dreams (Mt 1:20; 2:13, 19-20), and the wise men of the east (Mt 2:12-13). Deliverance of Paul (2Co 1:10). Restoring Epaphroditus (Php 2:27). Banishment of John to Patmos (Rev 1:9).

Mysterious and Misinterpreted—
The silence of God (Job 33:13). The adversity of the righteous (Ecc 7:15; 8:14). The prosperity of the wicked (Job 12:6; 21:7; 24:1; Ps 73:2-5, 12-17; Ecc 7:15; 8:14; Jer 12:1-2; Mal 3:14-15). Likeness in the lot of the righteous and the wicked (Ecc 9:2, 11). Permitting the violence of the wicked toward the righteous (Job 24:1-12; Hab 1:2-3, 11, 13-14).

Rejected:
By Israel (1Sa 8:7-8; Isa 65:12; 66:4). By Saul (1Sa 15:26). *See Jesus the Christ, Rejected.*

Repentance Attributed to:
(Ge 6:6-7; Ex 32:14; Jdg 2:18; 1Sa 15:35; 2Sa 24:16; 1Ch 21:15; Ps 106:45; Jer 26:19; Am 7:3; Jnh 3:10). *See Anthropomorphisms; Relent.*

Righteousness of:
(Ge 18:25; Jdg 5:11; Ps 7:9; 72:1; 88:12; 89:16; 119:40; 143:1; Isa 41:10; 56:1; Jer 4:2; 9:24; Mic 7:9; Ac 17:31).

Ascribed by people (Ex 9:27; Ezr 9:15; Job 36:3; Ps 5:8; 48:10; 71:15, 19; 89:14; 97:2; 116:5; 145:7, 17; Jer 12:1; Da 9:7, 14; 2Ti 4:8). Ascribed by Jesus (Jn 17:25). Ascribed by the angel (Rev 16:5). Revealed in the heavens (Ps 50:6). Revealed in the gospel (Ro 1:17; 3:4-6, 21-22; 10:3-4; 2Pe 1:1).

Endures forever (Ps 119:142, 144; Isa 51:8). *See above, Holiness of, Perfection of.*

Savior:
(Ex 6:6-7; Ps 3:8; 18:30; 28:8; 31:5; 33:18-19; 34:22; 37:39-40; 74:12; 76:8-9; 85:9; 96:2; 98:2-3; 111:9; 118:14; 121:7; 149:4; Isa 26:1; 33:22; 35:4; 43:3, 11-12, 14; 45:15, 17, 21-22; 46:12-13; 49:25; 50:2; 59:1; 60:16; 63:8, 16; Jer 3:23; 14:8; 33:6; Eze 37:23; Hos 1:7; 13:4; Joel 3:16; Jnh 2:9; Lk 1:68; Jn 3:16-17; Ro 8:30-32; 1Ti 2:3-4; 4:10; Tit 1:2-3; 2:10-11; 3:4-5; 1Jn 4:9-10).

Called Redeemer (Ps 19:14; Isa 41:14; 47:4; 48:17; Jer 50:34). Salvation (Ps 27:1; 62:1-2; 62:6-7; Isa 12:2). God of salvation (Ps 25:5; 65:5; 68:19-20; 88:1). Rock of salvation (Dt 32:15, 31). Shield (Dt 33:29).

Salvation from national adversity (Ex 15:2; Isa 25:4, 9; 52:3, 9-10), from sin (Job 33:24, 27-30; 44:22-24; Ro 1:16), through Christ (2Ti 1:9).

Self-Existent:
Has life in himself (Jn 5:26). Is the I am that I am (Ex 3:14). Is the first and the last (Isa 44:6). Is the living God (Jer 10:10). Lives forever (Dt 32:40). Needs nothing (Ac 17:24-25).

Sovereign:
(Ex 20:3; Job 25:2; 33:13; 41:11; Ps 44:4; 47:8; 59:13; 74:12; 82:1, 8; 83:18; 93:1-2; 95:3-5; 96:10; 97:1, 5, 9; 98:6; 103:19; 105:7; 113:4; 115:3, 16; 136:2-3; Isa 24:23; 33:22; 40:22-23; 43:15; 44:6; 52:7; 66:1; La 3:37; Mic 4:7, 13; Mal 1:14; Jn 10:29; 19:11; Ac 7:49; Ro 9:19; 11:36; Eph 4:6; 1Ti 6:15-16; Heb 1:3; Jas 4:12; Rev 4:11; 19:6).

Over heaven (2Ch 20:6). Over earth (Ex 9:29; Jos 3:11; Ps 24:1, 10; 47:2, 7-8; 50:10-12; Isa 54:5; Jer 10:10; 10Co 10:26). Over heaven and earth (Ge 14:18-20, 22; 24:3; Ex 19:5; Dt 4:39; 10:14, 17; Jos 2:11; 2Ki 19:15; 1Ch 29:11-12; Ne 9:6; Ps 89:11; 135:5-6; Mt 6:10; 11:25; Lk 10:21; Ac 17:24-26; Rev 11:4, 13, 17).

Over the spirits of all mankind (Nu 27:16; Dt 32:39; Job 12:9-10, 16-17; Ps 22:28-29; Ecc 9:1; Isa 45:23; Jer 18:1-23; Eze 18:4; Ro 14:11). In human affairs (Ps 75:6-7; Jer 27:5-7; 32:27-28; Eze 16:50; 17:24; Da 2:20-21, 47; 4:3, 17, 25, 34-35, 37; 5:18, 26-28).

Everlasting (Ex 15:18; Ps 10:16; 29:10; 66:7; 145:11-13; 146:10; La 5:19; Da 6:26).

Spirit:
(Jn 4:24; Ac 17:29). *See Holy Spirit.*

Teacher:
(Job 36:22; Ps 94:10, 12; 119:135, 171; Isa 28:26; 54:13; Jn 6:45; 1Th 4:9).

Truth:
(Ge 24:27; Ex 34:6; Nu 23:19; 1Sa 15:29; Ps 25:10; 31:5; 33:4; 43:3; 57:3, 10; 71:22; 86:11, 15; 89:14; 108:4; 132:11; 138:2; Isa 25:1; 65:16; Da 4:37; Jn 8:26; Ro 3:4, 7; Tit 1:2; Rev 6:10; 15:3).

Endures to all generations (Ps 117:2; 146:6).

Ubiquitous: *See above, Omnipresent.*

Unchangeable: *See above, Immutable.*

Unity of:
(Dt 4:35; 6:4; 2Sa 7:22; Isa 42:8). Taught by Jesus (Mk 12:29, 32; Jn 17:3). Taught by Paul (1Co 8:4, 6; Gal 3:20; Eph 4:6; 1Ti 2:5). Disbelieved in by Syrians (1Ki 20:28). Believed in by demons (Jas 2:19).

Unsearchable:
Dt 29:29; Job 5:8-9; 9:10; 11:7-9; 26:9, 14; 36:26; 37:5, 23; 77:19; 139:6; 145:3; Pr 30:4; Ecc 3:11; 11:5; Isa 40:28; 45:15; 55:8-9; Ro 11:33-34; 1Co 2:10-11, 16).

Symbolized by darkness (Ex 20:21; Dt 4:11; 5:22; 1Ki 8:12; Ps 18:11; 97:2). By the cloud upon the atonement cover (Lev 16:2).

Name of, secret (Jdg 13:18). Dwells in thick darkness (1Ki 8:12; Ps 97:2). Known only to Christ, and to those to whom Christ reveals him (Mt 11:27)

See Mysteries.

Voice of: *See Anthropomorphisms.*

Wisdom of:
(Ezr 7:25; Job 9:4; 12:13, 16; Isa 31:2; Da 2:20-22, 28; Ro 11:33; 16:27; 1Co 1:24-25). Infinite (Ps 147:5). Manifold (Eph 3:10). Ascribed by angels (Rev 7:12). Works made in (Ps 104:24; 136:5; Pr 3:19-20; Jer 10:12). *See above, Knowledge of.*

Works of:
In creation (Job 9:8-9; Ps 8:3-5; 89:11; 136:5-9; 139:13-14; 148:4-5; Ecc 3:11; Jer 10:12). Good (Ge 1:10, 18, 21, 25). Faithful (Ps 33:4). Wonderful (Ps 26:7; 40:5). Incomparable (Ps 86:8). In his overruling providence in the human affairs (Ps 26:7; 40:5; 66:3; 75:1; 111:2, 4, 6; 118:17; 145:4-17). *See Creation.*

GODLESSNESS

Described as:
Destitute of the love of God (Jn 5:42, 44). Forgetting God (Job 8:11-13; Ps 9:17; 50:22; Isa 17:10; Jer 2:32). Ignoring God (Job 35:10; Ps 28:5; 52:7; 53:2-3; 54:3; 55:19; 86:14; Isa 5:12; 22:11; 30:1; 31:1; Hos 7:2-4). Forsaking God (Dt 32:15). Despising God (1Sa 2:30; Ps 36:1; Pr 14:2; Jn 15:23-25). Loving deceit (Isa 30:9-11). Devoid of understanding (Ps 14:2-3; 53:4; Isa 1:3; Ro 1:21-22; 3:11; Eph 4:18).

Rebellious (Ps 2:2; Isa 30:2; Da 5:23). Haters of God (Dt 7:10). Enemies of God (Col 1:21; Jas 4:4). Sinfulness (Ro 8:6-8). Impugning God's justice (Eze 33:17-20; Mal 2:17). Atheistic; rejecting God (Ps 10:4; 14:1; 53:1). Willfully sinning (Heb 10:26-27).

See Impenitence; Obduracy; Prayerlessness; Reprobacy; Unbelief; Wicked.

GODLINESS *See Holiness; Righteousness.*

GODLY *See Righteous.*

GODS *See Idol; Idolatry; Image.*

GOG (*precious golden object*).
1. A Reubenite (1Ch 5:4).
2. A Scythian prince. Prophecy against (Eze 38; 39; Rev 20:8).

GOIIM (*nations, Gentiles*). A people who, led by King Tidal, along with three Eastern kings, Amraphel king of Shinar, Arioch king of Ellasar, and Kedorlaomer king of Elam, went to war against Bera king of Sodom, Birsha king of Gomorrah, Shinab king of Admah, Shemeber king of Zeboiim, and the king of Bela (that is, Zoar) (Ge 14:1-2, 9). This latter group of kings joined forces in the Valley of Siddim (the Salt Sea, which is the Dead Sea) (Ge 14:3).

The Goiim may have been non-Semitic tribes who lived to the N. They have been identified with the Hittites because of the resemblance of the name Tidal to the royal Hittite name Tudhaliash, and less reasonably to the Guti (in NE Mesopotamia). Goiim may be the generic Hebrew term for "nations." *See Goyim.*

GOLAN A town in Bashan. Given to Manasseh as a city of refuge (Dt 4:43; Jos 20:8). A Levitical city (Jos 21:27; 1Ch 6:71). *See Gaulanitis.*

GOLD Exported from Havilah (Ge 2:11-12). From Ophir (1Ki 9:28; 10:11; 1Ch 29:4; 2Ch 8:18; Job 22:24), Tarshish (1Ki 22:48), Parvaim (2Ch 3:6), Sheba (1Ki 10:10; 2Ch 9:9; Ps 72:15), Uphaz (Jer 10:9).

Refined (Job 28:19; 31:24; Pr 8:19; 17:3; 27:21; Zec 13:9; Mal 3:3).

Used in the Arts:
Beaten work (2Ch 9:15), made into wire threads and wrought into embroidered tapestry (Ex 39:3), apparel (Ps 45:9, 13), in ornamenting the priests' garments (Ex 39), modeled into forms of fruits (Pr 25:11), into ornaments (Ge 24:22; Ex 3:22; 11:2; 28:11; Nu 31:50-51; SS 1:10; 5:14; Eze 16:17), crowns made of (Ex 25:25; 37:2-11; 39:30; Est 8:15; Ps 21:3; Zec 6:11), lampstands made of, for the tabernacle (Ex 25:31-38; 37:17-24), shields of (1Ki 10:16-17), overlaying with (Ex 25:11, 13, 24, 28; 26:27, 29; 30:5; 36:34, 36, 38; 37:2, 4, 11, 15; 1Ki 6:20-22; 28, 30, 32, 35), beds made of (Est 1:6). Wedge of (Jos 7:21; Isa 13:12)

Used as money (Ge 44:1, 8; 1Ch 21:25; Ezr 8:25-28; Isa 13:17; 60:9; Eze 7:19; 28:4; Mt 2:11; 10:9; Ac 3:6; 20:33; 1Pe 1:18). Solomon rich in (1Ki 10:2, 14, 21).

Vessels and utensils made of, for the tabernacle (Ex 25:26, 29, 38-39; 37:16), for the temple (1Ch 18:11; 22:14, 16; 29:2-7). Altar, lamps, and other articles made of (1Ki 7:49-51; 2Ki 25:15; Jer 52:19; Ezr 8:27; Da 5:3). *See above, Overlaying with.*

Belongs to God (Eze 16:17).

Figurative: (Ecc 12:6; Jer 51:7; La 4:1; 1Co 3:12).

Symbolic: (Da 2:32-45; Rev 21:18, 21).
See Goldsmith.

GOLDEN CANDLESTICK *See Lampstand.*

GOLDEN RULE (Mt 7:12; Lk 6:31; also Lev 19:18; Ro 13:9; Gal 5:14). *See Love.*

GOLDSMITH (2Ch 2:7, 14; Ne 3:8, 31-32; Isa 40:19; 41:7; 46:6).

GOLGOTHA (*skull*). The place of the crucifixion of Christ, located outside of Jerusalem (Mt 27:33; Mk 15:22) on the public road (Jn 19:20).

GOLIATH (*exile*). A giant champion of Gath. Defied the armies of Israel and is slain by David (1Sa 17; 21:9; 22:10). His sons (2Sa 21:15-22; 1Ch 20:4-8).

GOMER (*complete*).
1. Son of Japheth (Ge 10:2-3; 1Ch 1:5-6).
2. A people descended from Gomer (Eze 38:6).
3. Wife of Hosea (Hos 1:3).

GOMORRAH (*to overwhelm with water*). One of the "cities of the plain" (Ge 10:19; 13:10). Its king defeated by Kedorlaomer (Ge 14:2, 8-11). Wickedness of (Ge 18:20). Destroyed (Ge 19:24-28; Dt 29:23; 32:32; Isa 1:9-10; 13:19; Jer 23:14; 49:18; 50:40; Am 4:11; Zep 2:9; Mt 10:14-15; Mk 6:11; Lk 9:5; Ro 9:29; 2Pe 2:6; Jude 7). *See Cities of the Plain.*

GONORRHEA Possibly among the bodily discharges of Lev 15. *See Discharge, Bodily; Disease.*

GOOD AND EVIL Choice between, by Adam and Eve (Ge 3). Exhortation to choose between (Jos 24:15). Conflict between (Rev 16:13-21). Subjective conflict between (Ro 7:9-25).

GOOD FOR EVIL Injunctions by Christ concerning (Mt 5:44-48; Lk 6:27-36).

Instances of: Abraham, to Abimelech (Ge 20:14-18). David, to Saul (1Sa 24:17; 26), to his enemies (Ps 35:12-14). Elisha, to the Syrians (2Ki 6:22-23). Jesus, to his crucifiers (Lk 23:34). Stephen (Ac 7:60).

See Golden Rule; Evil for Good; Nonresistance.

GOOD NEWS (Pr 15:30; 25:25). *See Gospel.*

GOPHER WOOD *See Cypress Wood.*

GOSHEN (*mound of earth*).
1. A district in Egypt especially adapted to herds and flocks. Israelites dwelt in (Ge 45:10; 46:28; 47). Exempted from plagues (Ex 8:22; 9:26).
2. A town and district of Judah (Jos 10:41; 11:16; 15:51).

G

GOSPEL (*good news*). From God (Jn 17:7-8, 14; 2Th 2:14). Contrasted with the law (Lk 16:16; Jn 1:16-17; Ac 12:24; 19:20; 2Co 3:6-11). Called the New Covenant (Jer 31:31-34; Heb 7:22; 8:6-13; 9:8-15; 10:9; 12:22-24).

Described as:
Dispensation of grace (Eph 3:2). Doctrine according to godliness (1Ti 6:3). Everlasting gospel or eternal good tidings (Rev 14:6). The faith (Jude 3). Glorious gospel (1Ti 1:11). Pattern of sound teaching (2Ti 1:13). Gospel of the glory of Christ (2Co 4:4). Good tidings or good news (Isa 40:9; 41:27; 52:7; 61:1; Mt 11:5; Lk 7:22; Ac 13:32-33; 1Pe 1:25). Gospel, of Christ (Ro 1:16; 1Co 9:12, 18; Gal 1:7; Php 1:27; 1Th 3:2), of God (Ro 1:1; 15:16; 1Th 2:8; 1Pe 4:17), of grace of God (Ac 20:24), of Jesus Christ (Mk 1:1), of the kingdom (Mt 4:23; 24:14), of peace (Eph 6:15), of salvation (Eph 1:13).

The kingdom of God (Lk 16:16). The law of liberty (Jas 1:25). Ministration of the Spirit (2Co 3:8). Mystery, of Christ (Eph 3:4), of the gospel (Eph 6:19). Power of God (Ro 1:16; 1Co 1:18). Preaching of Jesus Christ (Ro 16:25). Word of Christ (Col 3:16), of faith (Ro 10:8), of God (1Th 2:13; 1Pe 1:23), of life (Php 2:16), of the Lord (1Pe 1:25), of reconciliation (2Co 5:19), of salvation (Ac 13:26), of truth (Eph 1:13). Words of this life (Ac 5:20).

Likened to:
A mustard seed (Mt 13:31-32; Mk 4:30-33; Lk 13:18-19), good seed (Mt 13:24-30, 36-43), yeast (Mt 13:33), a pearl of great price (Mt 13:45-46; Lk 13:20-21), a treasure hidden in a field (Mt 13:44), a householder (Mt 20:1-16), a feast (Lk 14:16-24).

Dissemination of (Ac 14:3; 16:17; 20:24), commanded (Mt 24:14; 28:18-20; Mk 13:10; 16:15; Ac 5:20; Ro 10:15-18; 16:25-26; 1Co 1:18, 21, 24-25; 9:16-18; Eph 3:8-11). Desired by prophets, righteous, kings (Mt 13:17; Lk 23:34). Hid from the lost (2Co 4:3-4). Comes in power, word, assurance (1Th 1:5).

Proclaimed to Abraham (Gal 3:8), by angels (Lk 2:10-11; Rev 14:6). Preached by Jesus (Mt 4:23; Mk 1:14-15), by Peter (Ac 10:36), by Paul (Ac 13:32-33; 20:24; Ro 15:29; 1Co 9:16-18; Gal 2:2; Col 1:5-6, 23), to the Gentiles (Gal 2:2; Eph 3:8; Col 1:23, 26-29), to both Jews and Gentiles (Ro 1:16; 1Co 1:24), to the poor (Mt 11:4-6; Lk 7:22), to the dead (1Pe 3:19; 4:6), to every nation (Lk 2:10-11; Ro 16:26; Rev 14:6).

Life and immortality brought to light in (2Ti 1:10). Salvation through (Ro 1:16-17; 1Co 15:1-2; Eph 1:13-14; Jas 1:21; 1Pe 1:23).

Prophecies concerning:
(Isa 2:3-5; 4:2-6; 9:2, 6-7; 25:7-9; 29:18, 24; 32:3-4; 35:5-10; 40:9; 41:27; 42:6-7; 46:13; 49:13; 51:4-6; 52:7; 55:1-5; 60:1-22; 61:1-3; Jer 31:31-34; Eze 34:23-31; 47:1-12; Joel 2:28-32; Mic 4:1-7; Mt 24:14; Lk 1:67-79; 2:12-14, 34). Fulfilled by Christ (Lk 4:18-19).

See Church, The Body of Believers, Prophecies Concerning; Jesus the Christ, Kingdom of, Mission of; Kingdom of God, of Heaven; Synoptic Gospels, The.

GOSSIP Proverbs concerning (Pr 11:13; 16:28; 17:9; 26:20).
Forbidden (Lev 19:16; Ps 50:20; Pr 11:3; 20:19; Eze 22:9).
See Slander; Speaking, Evil; Talebearer.

GOURD Carvings of decorated the temple (1Ki 6:18) and its cast metal Sea (1Ki 7:24). Elisha purifies stew made with poisonous gourds (2Ki 4:38-41).

GOUT Perhaps Asa's disease in the feet (2Ch 16:12). *See Disease.*

GOVERNMENT Paternal functions of (Ge 41:25-57). Civil service school provided by (Da 1:3-20). Maintains a system of public instruction (2Ch 17:7-9).

Constitutional:
It was provided in the law of Moses that in the event of the establishment of a monarchy a copy of the law of Moses should be made and the king should be required to study this law all the days of his life and conform his administration to it (Dt 17:18-20). This constituted the fundamental law and had its likeness to the constitution of modern governments. When David was crowned king of all Israel he made a league in the nature of a constitution which was a basis of good understanding between himself and the people (2Sa 5:3). When Joash was enthroned a covenant was made between him and the people (2Ch 23:3, 11). This no doubt refers to the law of Moses (Dt 17:18-20), which had been preserved by Jehoiada, the priest. Zedekiah made a covenant with the people proclaiming liberty (Jer 34:8-11). That the king of the Medes and

Persians was restricted by a constitution "which cannot be annulled," is evident from Da 6:12-15.

See Constitution; Israel, Israelites; Judge; Kings; Nation.

Corruption in: (1Ki 21:5-13; Pr 25:5; Mic 3:1-4, 9-11).

Instances of Corruption in: Pilate, in delivering Jesus to death to please the noisy crowd (Mt 27:24; Jn 19:12-16). Felix, who hoped for money from Paul (Ac 24:26).

See Court, Of Law, Corrupt; Church, The Body of Believers, Evil Conditions of; Corrupt; Rulers, Wicked.

Duty of Citizens to:

To pay taxes (Mt 22:17-21; Lk 20:22-25). To render obedience to civil authority (Ro 13:1-7; Tit 3:1; 1Pe 2:13-17).

God in:

(2Ch 22:7; Jer 18:6; Eze 21:25-27; 29:19-20). In appointment of Saul as king (1Sa 9:15-17; 10:1). In Saul's rejection (1Sa 15:26-28; Ac 13:22). In appointment of David (1Sa 16:1, 7, 13; 2Sa 7:13-16; Ps 89:19-37; Ac 13:22), of Solomon (1Ki 2:13-15). In counseling Solomon (1Ki 9:2-9). In magnifying Solomon (1Ch 29:25). In reproving Solomon's wickedness (1Ki 11:9-13). In raising adversaries against Solomon (1Ki 11:14, 23). In tearing the nation of Israel in two (1Ki 11:13; 12:1-24; 2Ch 10:15; 11:4). In blotting out the house of Jeroboam (1Ki 14:7-16; 15:27-30). In appointment of kings (1Ki 14:14; 16:1-2; 1Ch 28:4-5; Da 2:20-21, 37; 4:17; 5:18-23). In destruction of nations (Jer 25:12-17; Am 9:8; Hag 2:22).

Relation of God to: (Ps 22:28; Pr 8:15-16; Isa 9:6-7; Jer 1:9-10; 18:6-10; 25:12-17; Eze 21:25-27; 29:19-20; Da 2:20-21, 37; 4:17; 5:18-28; 10:13; Hos 8:4; Am 9:8; Hag 2:21-22; Jn 19:10-11).

See God, Sovereign; Jesus the Christ, Kingdom of.

Mosaic:

Administrative and judicial system (Ex 18:13-26; Nu 11:16-17, 24-25; Dt 1:9-17).

Popular Government, by a National Assembly, or Its Representatives—

Accepted the law given by Moses (Ex 19:7-8; 24:3, 7; Dt 29:10-15). Refused to make conquest of Canaan (Nu 14:1-10). Chose, or ratified, the chief ruler (1Sa 10:24; 8:4-22; 11:14-15; 2Sa 3:17-21; 5:1-3; 1Ch 29:22; 2Ch 23:3). Possessed veto power over king's purposes (1Sa 14:44-45). Constituted the court in certain capital cases (Nu 35:12, 24-25).

Delegated, Council of Elders—

Closely associated with Moses and subsequent leaders (Ex 3:16, 18; 4:29-31; 12:21; 17:5-6; 18:12; 19:7-8; 24:1, 14; Lev 4:15; 9:1; Nu 11:16-17, 30; 16:25; Dt 1:13-15; 5:23; 27:1; 29:10-15; 31:9, 28; Jos 7:6; 8:10, 32-33; 23:2-3, 6; 24:1, 24-25; Jdg 21:16-25; Ac 5:17-18, 21-41).

Miscellaneous Facts Relating to the Council—

Demands a king (1Sa 8:4-10, 19-22). Saul pleads to be honored before (1Sa 15:30). Chooses David as king (2Sa 5:3; 1Ch 11:3). Closely associated with David (2Sa 12:17; 1Ch 15:25; 21:16). Joins Absalom in his usurpation (2Sa 17:4). David rebukes (2Sa 19:11). Assists Solomon at the dedication of the temple (1Ki 8:1-3; 2Ch 5:2-4). Counsels King Rehoboam (1Ki 12:6-8, 13). Counsels King Ahab (1Ki 20:7-8). Josiah assembles, to hear the law of the Lord (2Ki 23:1; 2Ch 34:29-30).

Legislates with Ezra in reforming certain marriages with the heathen (Ezr 9:1; 10:8-14). Legislates in later times (Mt 15:2, 7-9; Mk 7:1-13). Sits as a court (Jer 26:10-24). Constitutes, with priests and scribes, a court for the trial of both civil and ecclesiastical causes (Mt 21:23; 26:3-5, 57-68; 27:1-2; Mk 8:31; 14:43, 53-65; 15:1; Lk 22:52-54, 66-71; Ac 4:1-21; 6:9-15). Unfaithful to the city (La 1:19). Seeks counsel from prophets (Eze 8:1; 14:1; 20:1, 3). Corrupt (1Ki 21:8-14; Eze 8:11-12; Mt 26:14-15, w Mt 27:3-4).

A similar council existed among the Egyptians (Ge 50:7) and among the Midianites and Moabites (Nu 22:4, 7, and Gibeonites (Jos 9:11).

Executive officers of tribes and cities, called princes or nobles, members of the national assembly (Nu 1:4-16, 44; 7:2-3, 10-11, 18, 24, 54, 84; 10:4; 16:2; 17:2, 6; 27:2; 31:13-14; 32:2; 34:18-29; 36:1; Jos 9:15-21; 17:4; 22:13-32; 1Ki 21:11-14; Ne 3:9, 12, 16, 18-19).

The Mosaic judicial system. *See Court, Of Law; Judge; Levites; Priest; Rulers; Sanhedrin; Synagogue.*

Ecclesiastical: *See Church, The Body of Believers, Government of; Church, The Body of Believers, State; Priest.*

Imperial: (Ge 14:1; Jos 11:10; 1Ki 4:21; Est 1:1; Da 4:1; 6:1-3; Lk 2:1).

Monarchical:

Tyranny in: By Pharaoh (Ex 1:8-22; 2:23-24; 3:7; 5:1-10). By Saul (1Sa 22:6, 12-19). By David (2Sa 11:14-17). By Solomon (1Ki 2:23-25, 28-34, 36-46). By Rehoboam (1Ki 12:1-16). By Ahab and Jezebel (1Ki 21:7-16). By Jehu (2Ki 10:1-14). By Xerxes (Est 1:11-12, 19-22; 3:6-15; 8:8-13). By Nebuchadnezzar (Da 1:10; 2:5-13; 5:19). By Herod (Mk 6:27-28).

Municipal:

Based on a local council and executive officers (Dt 19:12; 21:2-8, 18-21; 22:13-21; 25:7-9; Jos 20:4; Jdg 8:14-16; 11:5-11; Ru 4:2-11; 1Sa 11:3; 16:4; 30:26; 1Ki 21:8-14; 2Ki 10:1-7; Ezr 10:8, 14; Ne 3:9, 12, 16, 18-19; La 5:14).

Patriarchal: (Ge 27:29, 37).

Provincial:

(Ezr 4:8-9; 5:3, 6; 6:6; 8:36; Ne 2:7, 9; 5:14; Da 6:1-3; Mt 27:2; 28:14; Lk 2:2; 3:1; Ac 24:1).

Representative:

(Dt 1:13-15; Jos 9:11). *See above, Delegated, Council of Elders.*

Theocratic:

(Ex 19:3-8; Dt 26:16-19; 29:1-13; Jdg 8:23; 1Sa 8:6-7; 10:19; 12:12; Isa 33:22).

See God, Sovereign; Jesus the Christ, Kingdom of.

GOVERNOR A provincial or city ruler (1Ki 4:7; 10:15; Ezr 2:63; Jn 18:28). Joseph (Ge 42:6), Zebul (Jdg 9:30), Gedaliah (2Ki 25:23). Tattenai (Ezr 5:3, 6). Sheshbazzar (Ezr 5:14). Nehemiah (Ne 7:65, 70; 8:9; 10:1; 12:26).

GOYIM (*nations, Gentiles*). A people, where the king of Goyim in Gilgal, was among those defeated by Joshua (Jos 12:23). Goyim may be the generic Hebrew word for "nations." *See Goiim.*

GOZAN A city in NE Mesopotamia on the Habor River, to which the Israelites were deported by the Assyrians (2Ki 17:6; 18:11; 19:12; 1Ch 5:26).

GRACE A term employed by the Biblical writers with a wide variety of meaning: charm, sweetness, loveliness (Ps 45:2), the attitude of God toward men (Tit 2:11), the method of salvation (Eph 2:5), the opposite of legalism (Gal 5:4), the impartation of spiritual power or gifts (1Co 2:6; 2Ti 2:1), the liberty which God gives to men (Jude 4).

Before meals. *See Prayer, Thanksgiving, and Before Taking Food.*

GRACE OF GOD Unmerited favor (Dt 7:7-8; 2Ch 30:9; Eph 1:6; Tit 2:11; Heb 4:16). Abundant (1Ti 1:14). Divine help (Ge 20:6; Job 10:12; Ps 84:11; 94:17-19; 138:3; 1Co 10:13; 2Co 1:12; 12:9; 1Pe 1:5).

Growth in (Ps 84:7; Pr 4:18; Php 1:6, 9-11; 3:12-15; Col 1:10-11; 2:19; 1Th 3:10, 12-13; 2Th 1:3; Heb 6:1-3; 1Pe 2:1-3; 2Pe 3:18). Believers to be stewards of (1Pe 4:10). Intercessory prayer for (Ps 143:11; Da 9:18; Jn 17:11-12, 15; 1Th 1:1; 5:28; 2Pe 1:2). No warrant for sinful indulgence (Ro 6:1, 15). Exhortation against rejecting (2Co 6:1-2). With respect to Jacob and Esau (Ro 9:10-16).

Manifested:

In drawing people to Christ (Jn 6:44-45). In redemption (Eph 1:5-9, 11-12). In justification (Ge 15:6; Ro 3:22-24; 4:4-5, 16; 5:2, 6-8, 15-21; Tit 3:7). In passing over transgressions (Nu 23:20-21; Ne 9:17; Ro 3:25). In salvation (Ro 11:5-6; Eph 2:8-9; 2Ti 1:9). In calling to service (Gal 1:15-16). In spiritual growth (Eph 3:16). In spiritual gifts (1Co 1:4-8; Eph 4:7, 11).

In the character and conduct of the righteous (1Co 15:10; 2Co 1:12; Php 2:13). In sustaining the righteous (1Ch 17:8; Da 10:18-19; 2Co 12:9; 1Pe 1:5; 5:10; Jude 24). In sustaining in temptation (Ge 20:6; 1Co 10:13; Rev 3:10).

Manifested to:

Enoch (Ge 5:24). Noah (Ge 6:8, 17-18). Abraham (Ge 12:2; 21:22). Ishmael (Ge 21:20). Isaac (Ge 26:24). Jacob (Ge 46:3-4; 48:16). Joseph (Ge 39:2-3, 23). Moses (Ex 3:12; 33:12-17). Israel (Dt 4:7). Naphtali (Dt 33:23). Joshua (Jos 1:5, 9). Job (Job 10:12). David (1Sa 25:26, 34; 2Sa 7:8-16). Daniel (Da 10:18-19). Jeremiah (Jer 15:20). The righteous (Ps 5:12; Ac 4:33).

See God, Grace of.

GRACES Christian (Mt 5:3-11; Ro 5:3-5; 1Co 13:1-8, 13; Gal 5:22-23; 1Pe 1:5-9).

See Beatitudes; Character; Charitableness; Courage; Gentleness; Hope; Kindness; Knowledge; Longsuffering; Love; Meekness; Mercy; Patience; Peace; Perseverance; Purity; Righteousness, Fruits of; Stability; Temperance; Wisdom.

GRAFT A horticultural process by which the branches of a cultivated tree may be inserted into the trunk of a wild tree. Figurative of Gentiles partaking of Israel's covenants and blessings (Ro 11:17ff.).

GRAIN In valleys (Ps 65:13; Mk 4:28). A product of Egypt (Ge 41:47-49), Israel (Dt 33:28; Eze 27:17). Roasted (Ru 2:14; 1Sa 17:17; 25:18; 2Sa 17:28). Ground (2Sa 17:19). Eaten by the Israelites (Jos 5:11-12). Shocks of, burnt (Jdg 15:5). Mosaic laws concerning (Ex 22:6; Dt 23:25).

Individual heads of grain (Ge 41:5-7, 22-27; Lev 23:14; Ru 2:2; Job 24:24; Isa 17:5; Mk 4:26-29). Grain that is ripe but soft, which is roasted and eaten (Lev 2:14). The poor may pick what they can eat on the spot; refers to grain rubbed between the hands (Dt 23:25). Picked by Christ's disciples (Mt 12:1; Mk 2:23; Lk 6:1). Newly ripened heads of grain (2Ki 4:42).

Figurative: (Ps 72:16; Hos 14:7; Jn 12:24).

Symbolic: (Ge 41:5).

See Barley; Barn; Bread; Firstfruits; Glean, Gleaning; Harvest; Plants of the Bible; Reaping; Rye; Threshing; Tithes; Wheat.

GRANARY A storehouse for grain and other dry crops (Ex 22:29; Jer 50:26; Joel 1:17).

See Barn; Storehouse.

GRANDFATHER Called Father (Ge 10:21).

GRAPE Cultivated in vineyards, by Noah (Ge 9:20), Canaanites (Nu 13:24; Dt 6:11; Jos 24:13), Edomites (Nu 20:17), Amorites (Nu 21:22; Isa 16:8-9), Philistines (Jdg 15:5). Grown, at Baal Hamon (SS 8:11), Carmel (2Ch 26:10), En Gedi (SS 1:14), Jezreel (1Ki 21:1), Lebanon (Hos 14:7), Samaria (Jer 31:5), Shechem (Jdg 9:27), Shiloh (Jdg 21:20-21), Timnath (Jdg 14:5).

Culture of (Lev 25:3, 11; Dt 28:39; 2Ch 26:10; SS 6:11; Isa 5:1; Jer 31:5).

Wine made of (Jer 25:30). Wine of, forbidden to Nazirites (Nu 6:4). *See Nazirite(s).*

See Vine; Vineyards; Wine.

Figurative (Dt 32:32; Ps 128:3; Jer 2:21; Eze 15; Hos 10:1; Rev 14:18-20).

Fable of (Jdg 9:12-13). Parables of the vine (Ps 80:8-14; Eze 17:6-10; 19:10-14; Jn 15:1-5). Proverb of (Eze 18:2).

See Vine; Vineyards; Wine.

GRASS Created on the third creative day (Ge 1:11). Mown (Ps 72:6). God's care of (Mt 6:30; Lk 12:28). On roofs of houses (Ps 129:6).

Figurative (Ps 90:5-6; Isa 40:6; 1Pe 1:24; Jas 1:10-11).

GRASSHOPPER (Nu 13:33; Ecc 12:5; Isa 40:22; Na 3:17).

See Locust.

GRATE A copper network, placed under the top of the great altar, to hold the sacrifice while burning (Ex 27:4; 35:16; 38:4-5).

GRATITUDE *See Thankfulness.*

GRAVE Prepared by Jacob (Ge 50:5). Defilement from touching (Nu 19:16, 18). Weeping at (2Sa 3:32; Jn 11:31; 20:11). Of parents, honored (2Sa 19:37). Welcomed (Job 3:20-22).

Resurrection From:

Of Lazarus (Jn 11:43-44; 12:17), of Jesus (Mt 28:5-6; 1Co 15:12-20), of believers after Jesus' resurrection (Mt 27:52-53), of all the dead foretold (Jn 5:28; 1Co 15:22-54).

See Burial; Sheol; Tomb.

GRAVE CLOTHES Preparatory to burial, the body was washed and anointed with spices, then wrapped in a winding sheet, bound with strips of cloth, and the head wrapped in a square cloth (Jn 11:44; 19:40).

GRAVEL Figurative of food gained by fraud (Pr 20:17), of judgment (La 3:16).

GRAVEN IMAGE NIV "carved image" or "idol" of wood, stone, or metal (Dt 7:5; Isa 44:9-17; 45:20). *See Carving; Groves; High Places; Iconoclasm; Idol; Idolatry.*

GRAVING *See Engraving.*

GREAT OWL *See Birds.*

GREAT SEA *See Mediterranean Sea.*

GREATER SIDON *See Sidon.*

GREATNESS Of God (Dt 3:24; Ps 77:13; 95:3; 104:1; 135:5; 145:3; Isa 12:6; Jer 32:18; Mal 1:11). Of Christ (Isa 53:12; 63:1; Mt 12:6; Lk 11:31; Php 2:9-10).

GREAVES Leg armor worn below the knee (1Sa 17:6).

GREECE Inhabitants of, called Gentiles (Mk 7:26; Jn 7:35; Ro 2:10; 3:9; 1Co 10:32; 12:13), desire to see Jesus (Jn 12:20-23), marry among the Jews (Ac 16:1), accept the Messiah (Ac 17:2-4, 12, 34), persecute the early Christians (Ac 6:9-14; 9:29; 18:17). Gentiles called Greeks (Ro 10:12; Gal 3:28; Col 3:11).

Schools of philosophy in Athens (Ac 19:9). Philosophy of (1Co 1:22-23). Poets of (Ac 17:28).

See Asceticism; Athens; Epicureans; Stoicism; Stoics.

GREED

Described:

Greed is idolatry (Col 3:5). Insatiable (Pr 1:19; 21:26; Ecc 1:8; 4:8; 5:10-11; Isa 56:11). Root of evil (1Ti 6:9-11). Tends to poverty (Pr 11:24, 26; 22:16). Gains of, unstable (Job 20:15; Pr 23:4-6; Jer 17:11). Disqualifies from sacred office (Ex 18:21; 1Ti 3:3; Tit 1:7, 11; 1Pe 5:2). Disqualifies from kingdom of God (Mt 19:23-24; 22:25; Lk 18:24-25; 1Co 6:10; Eph 5:3, 5; Php 3:18-19). Denounced (Ps 10:3; Pr 1:19; Isa 5:8; Jude 11).

Forbidden:

Warnings against (Dt 15:9-10; Pr 1:19; 15:27; Hos 4:18; Hab 2:5-9; Mt 6:19-21, 24-25, 31-33; 13:22; 16:26; Mk 4:19; 7:21-23; Lk 8:14; 12:16-21; Jn 6:26-27; 1Co 5:11; 1Th 2:5; 1Ti 6:5-8; 2Ti 3:2, 5; Heb 13:5; Jas 4:2; 1Jn 2:15-17). Commandments against (Ex 20:17; Dt 5:21; Ro 13:9; Col 3:2; 1Ti 3:8). Prayer against (Ps 119:36).

Reproof for (Ne 5:7; Isa 1:23; Jer 6:13; 22:17; Eze 33:31; Hos 10:1; Mic 2:2; 3:11; 7:3; Hag 1:6; Ro 1:29). Punishment for (Ex 18:21; Job 31:24-25, 28; Isa 57:17; Jer 8:10; 51:13; Eze 22:12-13; Col 3:5-6; 2Pe 2:3, 14-17).

See Avarice; Greed; Rich, The; Riches; Worldliness.

Instances of:

Eve, in desiring the forbidden fruit (Ge 3:6). Lot, in choosing the plain of the Jordan (Ge 13:10-13). Laban, in giving Rebekah to be Isaac's wife (Ge 24:29-51), in deceiving Jacob when he served him seven years for Rachel (Ge 29:15-30), in deceiving Jacob in wages (Ge 31:7, 15, 41-42). Jacob, in defrauding Esau of his father's blessing (Ge 27:6-29), in defrauding Laban of his flocks and herds (Ge 30:35-43), in buying Esau's birthright (Ge 25:31). Balaam, in loving the wages of unrighteousness (2Pe 2:15, w Nu 22).

Achan, in hiding the treasure (Jos 7:21). Eli's sons, in taking the flesh of the sacrifice (1Sa 2:13-17). Samuel's sons, in taking bribes (1Sa 8:3). Saul, in sparing Agag and the booty (1Sa 15:8-9). David, of Bathsheba (2Sa 11:2-5). Ahab, in desiring Naboth's vineyard (1Ki 21:2-16). Gehazi, in taking a gift from Naaman (2Ki 5:20-27). Israelites, in exacting usury of their brothers (Ne 5:1-11), in keeping back the portion of the Levites (Ne 13:10), in building fine houses while the house of the Lord lay waste (Hag 1:4-9), in following Jesus for the loaves and fishes (Jn 6:26).

Money changers in the temple (Mt 21:12-13; Lk 19:45-46; Jn 2:14-16). The rich young ruler (Mt 19:16-22). The rich fool (Lk 12:15-21). Judas, in betraying Jesus for thirty pieces of silver (Mt 26:15-16; Mk 14:10-11; Lk 22:3-6; Jn 12:6). The unjust steward (Lk 16:1-8). The Pharisees (Lk 16:14).

Simon Magus, in trying to buy the gift of the Holy Spirit (Ac 8:18-23). The sorcerers, in filing complaint against Paul and Silas (Ac 16:19). Demetrius, in raising a riot against Paul and Silas (Ac 19:24, 27). Felix, in hoping for a bribe from Paul (Ac 24:26). Demas, in forsaking Paul for love of the world (2Ti 4:10).

See Avarice; Bribery; Covetousness; Rich, The; Riches.

GREEK LANGUAGE Was a branch of the Indo-European family from which most of the languages of Europe are descended. The Attic dialect spoken in Athens and its colonies on the Ionian coast was combined with other dialects in the army of Alexander the Great and was spread by his conquests through the East. A kind of "Jewish Greek," influenced by semitic thought and culture, was widely spoken in Israel and became the chief language of the early church (Ac 21:37).

GREEK VERSIONS There were several early translations of the Hebrew OT into Greek. Some of the major versions were:
1. The Septuagint, originating in Alexandria in the third and second centuries B.C.. This was the Bible of the early church.
2. The version of Aquila in the early second century A.D. 125) was a word-for-word rendering of the Hebrew produced for the Jewish people when Christians took over the Septuagint.
3. The version of Theodotion, a late second-century revision of the Septuagint.
4. The version of Symmachus, an idiomatic translation probably of the second century.

GREETINGS Antiquity of (Ge 18:2; 19:1).

Given:
By brothers to each other (1Sa 17:22). By inferiors to their superiors (Ge 47:7). By superiors to inferiors (1Sa 30:21). By all passersby (1Sa 10:3-4; Ps 129:8). On entering a house (Jdg 18:15; Mt 10:12; Lk 1:40-41, 44). Often sent through messengers (1Sa 25:5, 14; 2Sa 8:10). Often sent by letter (Ro 16:21-23; 1Co 16:21; Col 4:18; 2Th 3:17). Denied to persons of bad character (2Jn 10). Persons in haste excused from giving or receiving (2Ki 4:29; Lk 10:24).

Expressions Used as:
"You are welcome at my house" (Jdg 19:20).
"Long life to you! Good health to you and your household! And good health to all that is yours" (1Sa 25:6).
"Peace to this house" (Lk 10:5).
"The LORD be with you! The LORD bless you!" (Ru 2:4).
"The blessing of the LORD be upon you; we bless you in the name of the LORD" (Ps 129:8).
"The LORD bless you! I have carried out the [LORD's] instructions" (1Sa 15:13).
"God be gracious to you my son" (Ge 43:29).
"How are you, my brother?" (2Sa 20:9).
"Greetings, Rabbi!" (Mt 26:49).
"Greetings, you who are highly favored! The Lord is with you" (Lk 1:28).
"Greetings" (Mt 28:9).
Sometimes insincere (2Sa 20:9; Mt 26:49). Given to Christ in derision (Mt 27:29, w Mk 15:18).

Often Accompanied by:
Embracing and kissing (Ge 33:4; 45:14-15; Lk 15:20). Taking hold of the beard with the right hand (2Sa 20:9). Bowing frequently to the ground (Ge 33:3). Embracing and kissing the feet (Mt 28:9; Lk 7:38, 45). Touching the hem of the garment (Mt 14:36). Falling prostrate on the ground (Est 8:3; Mt 2:11; Lk 8:41). Kissing the dust (Ps 72:9; Isa 49:23). The Jews are condemned for giving only to their own countrymen (Mt 5:47). The Pharisees condemned for seeking, in public (Mt 23:7; Mk 12:38).

GREYHOUND NIV "strutting rooster" (Pr 30:31). *See Animals.*

GRIEF Attributed to the Holy Spirit (Eph 4:30; Heb 3:10, 17).
See Affliction; Sorrow.

GRIND To pulverize grain between two millstones (Mt 24:41; Lk 17:35). *See Mill; Millstone.*

GROUND Man made from (Ge 2:7; 3:19, 23; Job 4:19; 33:6). Animals from (Ge 2:19). Vegetables from (Ge 2:9).
Cursed (Ge 3:17; 5:29).

GROVES
1. Groups of fruit trees (Dt 6:11; Ecc 2:6). *See Tree.*
2. NIV "Asherah [poles]"; an image of the Canaanite goddess Asherah. *See Asherah, 2; High Places; Idolatry.*

GROWTH *See Conformity; Discipleship; Grace of God, Growth in; Holiness; Sanctification.*

GRUMBLING

Condemned:
Forbidden (1Co 10:10; Php 2:14*; Jas 5:9*). Rebuked (Job 15:11-13*; Ecc 7:10*; La 3:39*; Ro 9:19-20*). Punishment for (Nu 14:26-37*; 17:10-11). Foolish (Pr 19:3*).

Against God:
Cain (Ge 4:13-14). Moses (Ex 5:22-23*; Nu 11:11-15). Israelites (Ex 16:8*, 12*; 17:2-3; Nu 11:1-10; 14; 16:41; 20:2-5; 21:5-6; Dt 1:26-28; Ps 44:9-26*; 106:24-26; Mal 3:14*). Korah (Nu 16:8-11). Job (Job 3; 6; 7; 9:10; 13; 16:6-14; 19:7-20; 30; 33:12-13*). David (2Sa 6:8; Ps 116:10-11). The psalmist (Ps 73:13-22*). Elijah (1Ki 19:4, 10). Jonah (Jnh 4). Jews, against Jesus (Jn 6:41-43, 52).

Against Moses:
By the Israelites (Ex 5:21; 14:11-12; 15:24; 16:2-3; 17:2-3; Nu 14; 16:2-3, 14, 41; 20:2-5).

Against Others:
Rachel (Ge 30:1). Asaph (Ps 73:3). Solomon (Ecc 2:17-18). Hezekiah (Isa 38:10-18). Jeremiah (Jer 20:14-18; La 3). Martha (Lk 10:40*). Prodigal's brother (Lk 15:29-30).
See Doubt; Envy; Ingratitude; also Contentment; Resignation.

GUARD Imperial guard (Ge 37:36; 2Ki 25:8; Da 2:14), runner, trusted messengers of a king (1Ki 14:27-28), bodyguard (2Sa 23:23), executioner (Mk 6:27), Roman guard (Mt 27:65).

GUDGODAH (*cleft*). A station of the Israelites in the wilderness (Dt 10:7), probably identical with Hor Haggidgad (Nu 33:32-33).

GUEST Greetings to (Ge 18:2). Abraham's hospitality to. *See Hospitality.*
Rules for the conduct of (Pr 23:1-3, 6-8; 25:6-7, 17; Lk 10:5-7; 14:7-11; 1Co 10:27). *See Hospitality.*

GUEST ROOM According to Jewish custom an extra or upper room was offered to those who had come to Jerusalem to celebrate the Passover (Mk 14:14; Lk 22:11).

GUIDANCE *See God, Guidance of.*

GUILE *See Conspiracy; Deceit; Hypocrisy.*

GUILELESSNESS Truthfulness; without deceit. Commanded (Ps 34:13; 1Pe 2:1; 3:10). Of Jesus (1Pe 2:22). Of Nathanael (Jn 1:47). A grace of the righteous (Ps 32:2). *See Truthfulness.*

GUILT The deserving of punishment because of infraction of a law. Guilt could be the result of unconscious sin (Lev 5:17) or could be incurred by the group for the sin of an individual (Jos 7:10-15). There are degrees of guilt (Lk 12:47-48; Ac 17:30), but in the sight of God all people are guilty of sin (Ro 3:19).
See Conviction, of Sin.

GUILT OFFERING Sacrifice of a ram for the purpose of expiation of sins against others; in addition to the sacrifice, restitution had to be made (Lev 5:16-19; 6:5-18; 7:1-10; Nu 5:7-8). Of the Servant's self-sacrifice (Isa 53:10 w Mt 20:28; Mk 10:45). *See Offerings.*

GULL A bird. Forbidden as food (Lev 11:16; Dt 14:15).

GUM RESIN Fragrant ingredient used in incense (Ex 30:34). *See Aromatic Resin; Incense.*

GUNI (*spotted sand grouse*).
1. Son of Naphtali (Ge 46:24; 1Ch 7:13) and his clan (Nu 26:48).
2. Father of Abdiel (1Ch 5:15).

GUR Place where Jehu slew Ahaziah (2Ki 9:27).

GUR BAAL (*sojourn of Baal*). A town probably located S of Beersheba (2Ch 26:7).

GUTTER Of the temple in Ezekiel's vision (Eze 43:13, 14, 17).

H

HAAHASHTARI (*the Ahashtarites*). Son of Naarah (1Ch 4:6).

HAARALOTH *See Gibeath Haaraloth.*

HABAIAH *See Hobaiah.*

HABAKKUK (*garden plant* KB). Prophet of the book which bears his name; wrote when the temple was still standing (Hab 2:20; 3:19), between c. 605-587 B.C., probably during the reign of the Judean king Jehoiakim.

HABAKKUK, BOOK OF (*garden plant* KB).

Author: Habakkuk

Date: Close to the battle of Carchemish (605 B.C.)

Outline:
I. Title (1:1).
II. Habakkuk's First Complaint: Why Does the Evil in Judah Go Unpunished? (1:2-4).
III. God's Answer: The Babylonians Will Punish Judah (1:5-11).
IV. Habakkuk's Second Complaint: How Can a Just God Use Wicked Babylon to Punish a People More Righteous Than Themselves? (1:12-2:1).
V. God's Answer: Babylon Will Be Punished, and Faith Will Be Rewarded (2:2-20).
VI. Habakkuk's Prayer: After Asking for Manifestations of God's Wrath and Mercy (as in the Past), He Closes With Confession of Trust and Joy in God (ch. 3).
See Prophets, The Minor.

HABAZZINIAH (possibly *exuberant in Yahweh*). Head of the family of Recabites (Jer 35:3).

HABERGEON NIV "(coat of) armor," "javelin." *See Armor; Breastplate; Coat of Mail.*

HABIRU A people mentioned in Mari, Nuzi, and Amarna tablets; fundamental meaning seems to be "wanderers"; of mixed racial origin, including both Semites and non-Semites. Connection with Hebrews is obscure.

HABIT (Ex 21:29, 36; Nu 22:30; Jer 13:23; 22:21; Mic 2:1; 1Ti 5:13; Heb 10:25).

HABOR A river of Mesopotamia (2Ki 17:6; 18:11; 1Ch 5:26).

HACALIAH (*dark*). Father of Nehemiah (Ne 1:1; 10:1).

HACHILAH *See Hakilah.*

HACMONI, HACMONITE (*wise*). Father of Jehiel and Jashobeam (2Sa 23:8, ftn; 1Ch 11:11; 27:32). *See Tahkemonite.*

HADAD (*thunderer [Semitic storm god]*).
1. Grandson of Abraham (Ge 25:15).
2. A king of Edom (Ge 36:35-36; 1Ch 1:46-47).
3. Another king of Edom (Ge 36:39, ftn; 1Ch 1:50-51).
4. A member of the royal house of Edom who escaped to Egypt when David conquered Edom and then later returned to his homeland to revolt against Solomon (1Ki 11:14-25). The Hebrew actually reads "Adad" for the first "Hadad" in 1Ki 11:17, and it has been conjectured that 1Ki 11:14ff. combines two accounts, one of Hadad the Edomite and the other of Adad the Midianite. Convincing reasons have been given for identifying this Hadad with 3 above.
5. The ancient Semitic storm god who as the great Baal of the Ugaritic pantheon figured in the struggle of the religion of Israel against Canaanite religion.

HADAD RIMMON A place in the valley of Megiddo (Zec 12:11).

HADADEZER (*[pagan god] Hadad is a help*). Son of Rehob, king of Zobah, vanquished by David (2Sa 8:3-13; 10:15-19; 1Ki 11:23; 1Ch 18:3-10; 19:6-19).

HADAR (*thunderer, Semitic storm god*).
1. Son of Ishmael (Ge 25:15 KJV). *See Hadad, 1.*
2. King of Edom (Ge 36:39, ftn.). *See Hadad, 3.*

HADAREZER *See Hadadezer.*

HADASHAH (*new*). A town in Judah (Jos 15:37).

HADASSAH (*myrtle* BDB and KB; possibly *myrtle* or *bride* IDB). The Hebrew name of Esther (Est 2:7). *See Esther.*

HADATTAH *See Hazor Hadattah.*

H

HADES (*the underworld*). The unseen world (Mt 11:23; 16:18; Lk 10:15; 16:23; Ac 2:27, 31; Rev 1:18; 6:8; 20:13-14). The realm (or state) of the dead is usually expressed in Hebrew by *sheol* and in Greek by *hades* (2Sa 22:6; Job 26:5; Ps 6:5; 17:15; 30:9; 49:15; 86:13; 88:10-12; 115:17; 116:3; Pr 15:24; 21:16; 27:20; Ecc 9:4-6; Isa 5:14; Jnh 2:2; Lk 23:42-43; Jn 8:22; 2Co 12:4).
See Grave; Hell; Immortality; Paradise; Righteous, Promises to; Sheol; Spirit; Wicked, Punishment of.

HADID (*sharp*). A city of Benjamin. Captive of, returned from Babylon (Ezr 2:33; Ne 7:37; 11:34).

HADLAI (*resting* ISBE; *fat* IDB; *be stout* KB). Father of Amasa (2Ch 28:12).

HADORAM (*Hadad is exalted*).
1. Descendant of Shem (Ge 10:27; 1Ch 1:21).
2. Son of Tou (1Ch 18:10). Called Joram (2Sa 8:10).
3. Hebrew *Adoram* (2Sa 20:24, ftn) or *Hadoram* (2Ch 10:18, ftn), a variant of *Adoniram*. An officer in charge of forced labor during the reigns of David and then Solomon. He then held the same office under Rehoboam, Solomon's son. *See Adoniram.*

HADRACH A district of Syria (Zec 9:1).

HAELEPH A town of Benjamin, near Jerusalem (Jos 18:28).

HAGAB (*locust*). Ancestor of the temple servants who returned with Zerubbabel (Ezr 2:46).

HAGABA, HAGABAH (*locust*). One of the temple servants (Ezr 2:45; Ne 7:48).

HAGAR (*emigration, flight*). A servant of Abraham and handmaid of Sarah. Given by Sarah to Abraham to be his wife (Ge 16). Descendants of (Ge 25:12-15; 1Ch 5:10, 19-22; Ps 83:6, ftn). Allegorically identified with slavery to the law (Gal 4:24-25).

HAGARENES *See Hagar.*

HAGARITES, HAGERITES *See Hagrite(s).*

HAGGAI (*festal* BDB; *born on the feast day* KB). Haggai was a prophet who, with Zechariah, encouraged the returned exiles to rebuild the temple (Ezr 5:1-2; 6:14). The prophet's name ("festal, ") may indicate he was born during one of the three pilgrimage feasts (Unleavened Bread, Pentecost or Weeks, and Tabernacles; cf. Dt 16:16). Based on 2:3 Haggai may have witnessed the destruction of Solomon's temple. If so, he must have been in his early 70s during his ministry.

HAGGAI, BOOK OF

Author: Haggai

Date:
The messages of Haggai were given during a four-month period in 520 B.C., the second year of King Darius. The first message was delivered on the first day of the sixth month (Aug. 29), the last on the 24th day of the ninth month (Dec. 18).

Outline:
I. First Message: The Call to Rebuild the Temple (1:1-11).
A. The People's Lame Excuse (1:1-4).
B. The Poverty of the People (1:5-6).
C. The Reason God Has Cursed Them (1:7-11).
II. The Response of Zerubbabel and the People (1:12-15).
A. The Leaders and Remnant Obey (1:12).
B. The Lord Strengthens the Workers (1:13-15).
III. Second Message: The Temple to Be Filled With Glory (2:1-9).
A. The People Encouraged (2:1-5).
B. The Promise of Glory and Peace (2:6-9).
IV. Third Message: A Defiled People Purified and Blessed (2:10-19).
A. The Rapid Spread of Sin (2:10-14).
B. Poor Harvests Because of Disobedience (2:15-17).
C. Blessing to Come as the Temple Is Rebuilt (2:18-19).
V. Fourth Message: The Promise to Zerubbabel (2:20-23).
A. The Judgment of the Nations (2:20-22).
B. The Significance of Zerubbabel (2:23).
See Prophets, The Minor.

HAGGAN *See Beth Haggan.*

HAGGEDOLIM (*the great ones*). The father of Zabdiel, a priest (Ne 11:14).

HAGGI, HAGGITE (*festal* BDB; *born on the feast day* KB). Son of Gad (Ge 46:16) and his clan (Nu 26:15).

HAGGIAH (*feast of Yahweh*). A Levite (1Ch 6:30).

HAGGIDGAD *See Hor Haggidgad.*

HAGGITH (*festal* BDB; *born on the feast day* KB). Wife of David. Mother of Adonijah (2Sa 3:4; 1Ki 1:5, 11; 2:13; 1Ch 3:2).

HAGGOYIM *See Harosheth Haggoyim.*

HAGIOGRAPHA (*holy writings*). The third division of the Hebrew OT: Psalms, Proverbs, Job, Song of Solomon, Ruth, Lamentations, Ecclesiastes, Esther, Daniel, Ezra, Nehemiah, 1 and 2 Chronicles.

HAGRI (*wanderer*). Father of Mibhar (2Sa 23:36; 1Ch 11:38).

HAGRITE(S) (possibly *people from Hagar*). Descendants of Hagar, mother of Ishmael with whom Saul made war (1Ch 5:10, 19-21; 27:31; Ps 83:6, ftn).

HAHIROTH *See Pi Hahiroth.*

HAI *See Ai.*

HAIL (Job 38:22; Hag 2:17). Plague of, in Egypt (Ex 9:18-29; Ps 78:48; 105:32). Destroys army of the Amorites (Jos 10:11).

Figurative: (Isa 28:2; Rev 8:7; 11:19; 16:21).

HAIR Numbered (Mt 10:30; Lk 12:7). Worn long by women (Isa 3:24; Lk 7:38; 1Co 11:5-6, 15; 1Ti 2:9; 1Pe 3:3; Rev 9:8), by Absalom (2Sa 14:26). Worn short by men (1Co 11:14). Symbolic dividing of (Eze 5:1-2).

See Baldness; Leprosy; Mourning; Nazirite(s), Nazarite(s).

HAKILAH A hill in Judah where David and his followers hid from Saul (1Sa 23:19; 26:3).

HAKKATAN (*the small one*). Father of Johanan (Ezr 8:12).

HAKKEREM *See Beth Hakkerem.*

HAKKORE *See En Hakkore.*

HAKKOZ (*the thorn*).

1. The eponym of a family of priests in David's time (1Ch 24:10). Members of this family were among those unable to document their claim to priestly rank after the Exile and so were suspended from office (Ezr 2:61; Ne 7:63).

2. Ancestor of Meremoth, who helped repair the wall of Jerusalem (Ne 3:4, 21).

HAKUPHA (*crooked*). One of the temple servants (Ezr 2:51; Ne 7:53).

HALAH A place to which Israelite captives were transported (2Ki 17:6; 18:11; 1Ch 5:26).

HALAK, MOUNT OF (*bare, bald*). A mountain, the southern limit of Joshua's conquests (Jos 11:17; 12:7).

HALF-HOMER *See Homer; Measure.*

HALF-TRIBE *See Manasseh, 2.*

HALHUL A city in Judah (Jos 15:58).

HALI (*adornment*). A border town of Asher (Jos 19:25).

HALL

1. Court of the high priest's palace (Lk 22:55).

2. Official residence of a Roman governor (Mt 27:27; Mk 15:16).

HALLEL (*praise*). Two liturgical collections of Psalms read at Passover. Psalms 113-118 called the "Egyptian Hallel"; Psalm 136, "the Hallel"; Psalms 120-136 are often called the "Great Hallel." *See Passover.*

HALLELUJAH (*praise Yahweh*). Liturgical exclamation urging all to praise Yahweh. Occurs at the beginning of Psalms 106, 111-113, 117, 135, 146-150 and at the close of 104-106, 113, 115-117, 135, 146-150. *See Praise.*

HALLOHESH (*the whisperer*). Father of Shallum (Ne 3:12). Sealed the covenant with Nehemiah (Ne 10:24).

HALLOW, HALLOWED (*to render as holy*). To set apart for sacred use; to hold sacred; to reverence as holy (Ex 20:11; Mt 6:9).

HAM

1. Son of Noah (Ge 5:32; 9:18, 24; 1Ch 1:4). Provokes Noah's wrath, resulting in curse on Ham's son Canaan (Ge 9:18-27). His children (Ge 10:6-20; 1Ch 1:8-16).

2. Family name of the descendants of Ham (1Ch 4:40; Ps 78:51; 105:23, 27; 106:22).

3. Place where Kedorlaomer killed the Zuzites (Ge 14:5).

HAMAN Prime minister of Xerxes, king of Persia (Est 3:1, 10; 7:7-10).

HAMATH, HAMATHITES (*fortress*). A city of upper Syria; the N border of the ideal limits of the Promised Land (Nu 13:21; 34:8; Jos 13:5; Eze 47:16). Solomon's kingdom extended from the Wadi of Egypt to the entrance of Hamath (1Ki 8:65), and the kingdom of Israel at the time of Jeroboam reached northward to the entrance of Hamath (2Ki 14:25; Am 6:14).

Inhabited by Canaanites (Ge 10:18). Prosperity of (Am 6:2). David receives gifts of gold and silver from Tou, king of (2Sa 8:9-10; 1Ch 18:3, 9-10). Conquest of, by Jeroboam (2Ki 14:25, 28), by the Chaldeans (2Ki 25:20-21). Israelites taken captive to (Isa 11:11). Prophecy concerning (Jer 49:23). Solomon builds store cities in (2Ch 8:4).

HAMATH ZOBAH (*fortress of Zobah*). A town on the border of Israel. Subdued by Solomon (2Ch 8:3).

HAMMAHLEKOTH *See Sela Hammahlekoth.*

HAMMATH (*hot springs*).

1. Fortified city of Naphtali, c. one mile S of Tiberias (Jos 19:35).

2. Founder of Recabites (1Ch 2:55).

HAMMEDATHA (*given by the moon [god]*). Father of Haman (Est 3:1, 10; 8:5; 9:10, 24).

HAMMELECH NIV "the king" (Jer 36:26; 38:6).

HAMMER A tool used for a variety of purposes: Smoothing metals (Isa 41:7), driving tent pins (Jdg 4:21), forging (Isa 44:12). Sometimes used figuratively for any crushing power (Jer 23:29; 50:23).

HAMMOLEKETH (*the queen*). Daughter of Makir (1Ch 7:17-18).

HAMMON (*hot springs*).

1. A city of Asher (Jos 19:28).

2. A Levitical city of Naphtali (1Ch 6:76). Possibly identical with Hammath and Hammoth Dor.

HAMMOTH DOR (*hot spring of Dor*). Naphtali (Jos 21:32). Possibly identical with Hammath (Jos 19:35). Called Hammon (1Ch 6:76).

HAMMUEL (*God [El] of Ham* KB). A Simeonite (1Ch 4:26).

HAMMURABI King of Babylon (c. 1704-1662 B.C.). Not the same as Amraphel (Ge 14:1-12). He was a great builder and lawgiver (Code of Hammurabi). *See Texts, Ancient Near Eastern Non-Biblical Texts Relating to the Old Testament.*

HAMON *See Baal Hamon; Hamon Gog.*

HAMON GOG, VALLEY OF (*multitude of Gog*). Prophetic name for place E of Dead Sea where the "multitude of Gog" will be buried (Eze 39:11-15).

HAMONAH (*multitude*). Prophetic name of city near which Gog is defeated (Eze 39:16).

HAMOR (*male donkey*). Father of Shechem. Jacob buys ground from (Ge 33:19; Jos 24:32; Jdg 9:28). Murdered by the sons of Jacob (Ge 34:26; 49:6). Called Hamor (Ac 7:16).

HAMSTRING Disabling an animal by cutting the large tendon at the back of the knee, usually to render it useless for military service. Of horses (Jos 11:6, 9; 2Sa 8:4; 1Ch 18:4). Of oxen (Ge 49:6).

HAMUL, HAMULITE (*pitied*). Son of Perez (Ge 46:12; 1Ch 2:5) and his clan (Nu 26:21).

HAMUTAL (*my husband's father is like dew*). Wife of Josiah. Mother of Jehoahaz and Zedekiah (2Ki 23:31; 24:18; Jer 52:1).

HANAMEL (*God [El] is gracious*). Cousin of Jeremiah, to whom he sold a field in Anathoth (Jer 32:7-12).

HANAN (*gracious*).

1. Son of Shashak (1Ch 8:23).

2. Son of Azel (1Ch 8:38; 9:44).

3. One of David's mighty men (1Ch 11:43).

4. One of the temple servants (Ezr 2:46; Ne 7:49).

5. A Levite (Ne 8:7; 10:10). Probably identical with the one mentioned in Ne 13:13.

6. A chief who sealed the covenant with Nehemiah (Ne 10:22, 26).

7. An officer in the temple (Jer 35:2-10).

HANANEL, TOWER OF (*God [El] is gracious*). Name of a tower forming part of the wall of Jerusalem (Ne 3:1; 12:39; Jer 31:38; Zec 14:10).

HANANI (*gracious*).

1. Son of Heman (1Ch 25:4, 25).

2. A prophet who rebuked Asa, king of Judah (2Ch 16:7).

3. Father of Jehu the prophet (1Ki 16:1, 7; 2Ch 19:2; 20:34). Possibly identical with 2.

4. A priest (Ezr 10:20).

5. A brother of Nehemiah and keeper of the gates of Jerusalem (Ne 1:2; 7:2).

6. A priest and musician (Ne 12:36).

HANANIAH (*Yahweh is gracious*).

1. Son of Heman (1Ch 25:4, 23).

2. A captain of Uzziah's army (2Ch 26:11).

3. Father of Zedekiah (Jer 36:12).

4. A prophet of Gibeon who uttered false prophecies in the temple during the reign of Zedekiah (Jer 28).

5. Grandfather of Irijah (Jer 37:13).

6. Son of Shashak (1Ch 8:24).

7. Hebrew name of Shadrach. *See Shadrach.*

8. Son of Zerubbabel (1Ch 3:19, 21).

9. Son of Bebai (Ezr 10:28).

10. A priest (Ne 3:8).

11. Son of Shelemiah (Ne 3:30).

12. A keeper of the gates of Jerusalem (Ne 7:2).

13. One who sealed the covenant (Ne 10:23).

14. A priest in time of Jehoiakim (Ne 12:12, 41).

HAND

Ceremonial:

Laying on of hands (Heb 6:2), in consecration (Ge 48:14; Ex 29:10, 15, 19; Lev 1:4; 3:2, 8, 13; 4:15, 24, 33; 16:21), in ordaining the Levites (Nu 8:10-11), Joshua (Nu 27:18-23; Dt 34:9), Timothy (1Ti 4:14; 2Ti 1:6), in healing (Mk 6:5; 7:32; 16:18; Lk 4:40; Ac 28:8), in blessing children (Mt 19:13; Mk 10:16); in solemnizing testimony (Lev 24:14). Lifted up in benediction (Lev 9:22; Lk 24:50), in prayer. *See Hands, Laying on of; Prayer, Attitudes in.*

Ceremonial washing of (Mt 15:2; Mk 7:2-5). *See Washings; Cleanliness.*

Symbolic:

Symbolic of righteousness (Job 17:9). Washing of, a symbol of innocence (Dt 21:6; Mt 27:24).

Clasping of, in token of contract (Ezr 10:19; Pr 6:1; 17:18; Eze 17:18), of friendship (2Ki 10:15; Job 17:3). Right hand lifted up in swearing (Ge 14:22; Ps 106:26; Isa 62:8), symbol of power (Isa 23:11; 41:10), place of honor (Ps 45:9; 80:17).

Figurative:

(Mt 5:30; 18:8; Mk 9:43).

Anthropomorphic Use of:

Hand of the Lord considered limited in power (Nu 11:23), is mighty (Jos 4:24), was heavy (1Sa 5:6), against the Philistines (1Sa 7:13), on Elijah (1Ki 18:46), not limited in power (Isa 59:11), was with the early Christians (Ac 11:21). *See Anthropomorphisms.*

HANDBREADTH A measure, about four inches (Ex 25:25; 1Ki 7:26; 2Ch 4:5; Ps 39:5; Isa 48:13; Eze 40:5, 43; Jer 52:21). *See Fingers, Fingerbreadth; Span.*

HANDKERCHIEF Sometimes translated "cloth," used for a variety of purposes (Lk 19:20-23; Jn 11:44; 20:7; Ac 19:12).

HANDLE Door knob (SS 5:5).

HANDMAID, HANDMAIDEN Female slave or servant. *See Maid(s), Maidservant(s); Servant.*

HANDS, LAYING ON OF Ceremony having the idea of transference, identification, and devotion to God (Ex 29:10, 15, 19; Lev 16:21; Ac 8:14-17; 2Ti 1:6). *See Hand.*

HANDSTAFF NIV "war clubs" (Eze 39:9). *See Club.*

HANES A place in Egypt (Isa 30:4).

HANGING Not a form of capital punishment in Bible times. Where used, except 2Sa 17:23; Mt 27:5, it refers to the suspension of a body from a tree or post after the criminal had been put to death (Ge 40:19, 22; Dt 21:22).

HANGINGS Material hung in the tabernacle so as to preserve the privacy and sacredness of that which was within (Ex 27:9-19; Mt 27:51).

HANIEL *See Hanniel, 2.*

HANNAH (*favor*). Mother of Samuel. Her trials, prayer, and promise (1Sa 1:1-18). Samuel born to, dedicates him to God, leaves him at the temple (1Sa 1:19-28). Her hymn of praise (1Sa 2:1-10). Visits Samuel at the temple(annually Sa 2:18-19). Children of (1Sa 2:20-21).

HANNATHON A city of Zebulun (Jos 19:14).

HANNIEL (*favor of God [El]*).

1. A son of Ephod, appointed by Moses to divide the land among the several tribes (Nu 34:23).

2. A son of Ulla (1Ch 7:39).

HANOCH, HANOCHITE (*initiation*).

1. Grandson of Abraham by Keturah (Ge 25:4; 1Ch 1:33).

2. Son of Reuben (Ge 46:9; Ex 6:14; 1Ch 5:3) and his clan (Nu 26:5).

HANUKKAH (*dedication*). The Feast of Rededication. After Judas Maccabeus had cleansed the temple from the pollution of pagan worship (c. 165 B.C.), the twenty-fifth of Kislev (December) was kept annually in memory of this.

See Dedication; Feasts; Kislev; Maccabees; Month, 9.

HANUN (*favored*).

1. King of Ammon who provoked David to war (2Sa 10:1-5; 1Ch 19:1-5).

2. Two men who helped repair wall of Jerusalem (Ne 3:13, 30).

HAPHARAIM, HAPHRAIM (*place of two trenches*). A city of Issachar (Jos 19:19).

HAPPINESS

Of the Wicked:

Limited to this life (Ps 17:14; Lk 16:25), short (Job 20:5), uncertain (Lk 12:20), vain (Ecc 2:1; 7:6).

Is derived from their wealth (Job 21:13; Ps 52:7), their power (Job 21:7; Ps 37:35), their worldly prosperity (Ps 17:14; 73:3-4, 7), gluttony (Isa 22:13; Hab 1:16), drunkenness (Isa 5:11; 56:12), vain pleasure (Job 21:12; Isa 5:12), successful oppression (Hab 1:15). Marred by jealousy (Est 5:13), often interrupted by judgments (Nu 11:33; Job 15:21; Ps 73:18-20; Jer 25:10-11). Leads to sorrow (Pr 14:13). Leads to recklessness (Isa 22:12). Sometimes a stumbling block to saints (Ps 73:3, 16; Jer 12:1; Hab 1:13). Saints often permitted to see the end of (Ps 73:17-20), envy not (Ps 37:1). Woe against (Am 6:1; Lk 6:25).

Illustrated (Ps 37:35-36; Lk 12:16-20; 16:19-25).

Exemplified: Israel (Nu 11:33). Haman (Est 5:9-11). Belshazzar (Da 5:1). Herod (Ac 12:21-23).

Of the Righteous:
In the Lord, through abundance (Ps 36:8; Ecc 2:24-26; 3:12-13, 22). In chastisement (Job 5:17-27). In fellowship (Ps 133:1). In good works (Pr 14:21; Ecc 3:12; Mt 5:3-9). In hope (Ro 5:2). In obedience (Ps 40:8; 128:1-2; 144:15; 146:5; Pr 16:20; 28:14; 29:18). In peace (Php 4:7). In persecution (Mt 3:10-11; 2Co 12:10; 1Pe 3:14; 4:12). In protection (Dt 33:29; Isa 12:2-3). In satisfaction (Ps 63:5). Trust (Pr 16:20). In wisdom (Pr 3:13-18).
Beatitudes (Mt 5:3-12).
See Joy; Peace; Praise.

HAPPIZZEZ A governor of the temple (1Ch 24:15).

HARA (*hill, highland*). Place in Assyria to which Israelites were exiled by Assyrians (1Ch 5:26).

HARADAH (*place of fear*). One of the camps of Israel (Nu 33:24-25).

HARAM *See Beth Haram.*

HARAN (earlier *mountaineer*, but perhaps *sanctuary*).
1. Father of Lot and brother of Abraham (Ge 11:26-31).
2. Son of Caleb (1Ch 2:46).
3. A Levite (1Ch 23:9).
4. A place in Mesopotamia to which Terah and Abraham migrated (Ge 11:31; 12:4-5; Ac 7:2, 4). Death of Terah at (Ge 11:32). Abraham leaves, by divine command (Ge 12:1-5). Jacob flees to (Ge 27:43; 28:7; 29), returns from, with Rachel and Leah (Ge 31:17-21). Conquest of, by king of Assyria (2Ki 19:12). Merchants of (Eze 27:23). Idolatry in (Jos 24:2, 14; Isa 37:12).

HARARITE (*mountain dweller*). A place or family name (2Sa 23:11, 33; 1Ch 11:34).

HARASHIM *See Ge Harashim.*

HARBONA (*donkey driver*). Eunuch of Xerxes (Est 1:10; 7:9).

HARD, HARD-HEARTED *See Obduracy.*

HARDEST STONE The Lord makes Ezekiel's forehead harder than "the hardest stone" (Eze 3:9). *See Adamant; Diamond; Flint; Minerals of the Bible, 1; Stones.*

HARE *See Animals; Rabbit.*

HAREM The wives and concubines of a king (Ecc 2:8; Est 2:3, 13-14).

HAREPH (*autumn*, or *sharp* IDB; *scornful* ISBE). Son of Caleb (1Ch 2:51).

HARESETH *See Kir Hareseth.*

HARHAIAH Father of Uzziel (Ne 3:8).

HARHAS Grandfather of the husband of Huldah, the prophetess (2Ki 22:14). Called Hasrah (2Ch 34:22).

HARHUR (possibly *fever* BDB; possibly *raven* IDB; *one born during his mother's fever* KB). Head of a family that returned with Zerubbabel (Ezr 2:51; Ne 7:53).

HARIM (*consecrated [to Yahweh]*).
1. Priest (1Ch 24:8).
2. Family that returned with Zerubbabel (Ezr 2:39; Ne 7:35).
3. Family of priests (Ezr 2:39; 10:21; Ne 7:42; 12:15).
4. Family that married foreign wives (Ezr 10:31).
5. Father of a worker on the wall (Ne 3:11).
6. A man who sealed the covenant (Ne 10:27).

HARIPH (*one born at harvest time*).
1. One of the exiles (Ne 7:24). Probably the same as Jorah (Ezr 2:18).
2. One who sealed the covenant (Ne 10:19).

HARLOT *See Adultery; Prostitute..*

HARLOTRY *See Adultery; Prostitute.*

HARMON Possibly a place name (Am 4:3, ftn.).

HARNEPHER (*[pagan god] Horus is merciful*). Asherite (1Ch 7:36).

HAROD, HARODITE (*trembling*). Spring beside which Gideon encamped (Jdg 7:1). Family name of Shammah and Elika (2Sa 23:25).

HAROEH (*the seer*). Grandson of Caleb (1Ch 2:52).

HARORITE Shammoth, one of David's mighty men (1Ch 11:27).

HAROSHETH HAGGOYIM (*Harosheth of the nations*). Town in N Israel c. sixteen miles NW of Megiddo; home of Sisera (Jdg 4.2, 13, 16).

HARP A stringed instrument of music (Isa 38:20; Eze 33:32; Hab 3:19). With three strings (1Sa 18:6), ten strings (Ps 33:2; 92:3; 144:9; 150:4). Originated with Jubal (Ge 4:21). Made of almugwood (1Ki 10:12). David skillful in playing (1Sa 16:16, 23). Used in worship (1Sa 10:5; 1Ch 16:5; 25:1-7; 2Ch 5:12-13; 29:25; Ps 33:2; 43:4; 49:4; 57:8; 71:22; 81:2; 93:3; 98:5; 108:2; 147:7; 149:3; 150:3). Used, in national jubilees, after the triumph over Goliath (1Sa 18:6), over the armies of Ammon and Moab (2Ch 20:20-29), when the new walls of Jerusalem were dedicated (Ne 12:27, 36). Used in festivities (Ge 31:27; Job 21:11-12; Isa 5:12; 23:16; 24:8; 30:32; Eze 26:13; Rev 18:22), in mourning (Job 30:31). Discordant (1Co 14:7). Hung on the willows by the captive Israelites (Ps 137:2). Heard in heaven, in John's apocalyptic vision (Rev 5:8; 14:2; 15:2). The symbol used in the Psalms to indicate when the harp was to be introduced in the music was *neginah* or *neginoth. See titles of Pss 4; 6; 54; 55; 61; 67; 76.*
See Music, Instruments of, Symbols Used in.

HARROW Instrument for dragging or leveling off a field (Job 39:10), "breaking up the soil" (Isa 28:24; Hos 10:11). *See Picks, Iron.*

HARSHA (*deaf*). One of the temple servants (Ezr 2:52; Ne 7:54).

HART *See Deer.*

HARUM (*consecrated*). A descendant of Judah (1Ch 4:8).

HARUMAPH (*disfigured nose*). Father of Jedaiah (Ne 3:10).

HARUPHITE (*sharp* or *autumn*). Designation of Shephatiah (1Ch 12:5).

HARUZ (perhaps *gold*, or *eager*). Father-in-law of King Manasseh (2Ki 21:19).

HARVEST Sabbath to be observed in (Ex 34:21). Sabbath desecrated in (Ne 13:15-22).
Of wheat at Pentecost, in Israel (Ex 34:22; Lev 23:15-17), and before vintage (Lev 26:5). Of barley, before wheat (Ex 9:31-32).
Celebrated with joy (Jdg 9:27; Isa 9:3; 16:10; Jer 48:33). Promises of plentiful (Ge 8:22; Jer 5:24; Joel 2:23-24).
Figurative: (Job 24:5; Ps 10:5; Jer 8:20; Joel 3:13; Mt 9:37; 13:39; Lk 10:2; Rev 14:15).
See Pentecost, 1; Tabernacles, Feast of; Firstfruits; Reaping; Glean, Gleaning.

HASADIAH (*Yahweh is faithful*). Son of Zerubbabel (1Ch 3:20).

HASENUAH See *Hassenuah.*

HASHABIAH (*Yahweh has reckoned*).
1. Ancestor of Ethan (1Ch 6:45).
2. Ancestor of Shemaiah (1Ch 9:14; Ne 11:15).
3. Son of Jeduthun (1Ch 25:3).
4. Civil official in David's time (1Ch 26:30).
5. Overseer of tribe of Levi (1Ch 27:17).
6. Chief of Levites (2Ch 35:9).
7. Levite teacher (Ezr 8:19).
8. Chief priest (Ezr 8:24).
9. Worker on the wall (Ne 3:17).
10. Priest (Ne 12:21).
11. Ancestor of Uzzi (Ne 11:22).
12. Chief of Levites (Ne 3:17; 12:24).

HASHABNAH (probably *Yahweh has considered me*). Man who sealed covenant with Nehemiah (Ne 10:25).

HASHABNEIAH (probably *Yahweh has considered me*).
1. Father of Hattush (Ne 3:10).
2. A Levite (Ne 9:5).

HASHBADDANAH (probably *Yahweh has considered me*). A man who stood by Ezra as he read the law (Ne 8:4).

HASHEM Father of several members of David's guard (1Ch 11:34).

HASHMONAH A camp of the Israelites (Nu 33:29-30).

HASHUBAH (*consideration*). A descendant of King Jehoiakim (1Ch 3:20).

HASHUM (*broad-nosed*).
1. Family which returned from the Exile (Ezr 2:19; 10:33; Ne 7:22).
2. Priest who stood at side of Ezra when he read the law (Ne 8:4).
3. Chief of people who sealed the covenant (Ne 10:18). May be the same as 2.

HASHUPHA *See Hasupha.*

HASMONEANS *See Maccabees.*

HASRAH Grandfather of Shallum (2Ch 34:22), "Harhas" (2Ki 22:14).

HASSENAAH Father of sons who built fish gate in Jerusalem (Ne 3:3).

HASSENUAH (*the hated women*). A Benjamite and the father of Judah, a governor of Jerusalem (1Ch 9:7; Ne 11:9).

HASSHUB (*considerate*).
1. Son of Pahath-Moab (Ne 3:11).
2. One of the Captivity who assisted in repairing the wall of Jerusalem (Ne 3:23).
3. Head of a family (Ne 10:23).
4. A Levite (1Ch 9:14; Ne 11:15)

HASSOPHERETH (*the scribes*). May have once been an official title (Ezr 2:55).

HASTE In judgment, by Moses and the Israelites (Nu 32:1-19; Jos 22:10-34). *See Rashness.*

HASUPHA Family that returned from exile with Zerubbabel (Ezr 2:43; Ne 7:46).

HAT *See Dress; Headdress; Turbans.*

HATHACH (*good*). A eunuch in the court of Xerxes (Est 4:5-6, 9-10).

HATHATH (possibly *terror* BDB and KB; possibly *weakness* IDB). A son of Othniel (1Ch 4:13).

HATIPHA (*taken captive*). One of the temple servants (Ezr 2:54; Ne 7:56).

HATITA A gatekeeper of the temple (Ezr 2:42; Ne 7:45).

HATRED Is blinding (1Jn 2:9, 11). Carnal (Gal 5:19-20). Murderous (1Jn 3:15). Unforgiving (Mt 6:15). Leads to deceit (Pr 26:24-26). Opposite of love (Pr 15:17). Prevents from loving God (1Jn 4:20). Produces strife (Pr 10:12).
Toward the righteous (Ps 25:19; 35:19; Mt 10:22; Jn 15:18-19, 23-25; 17:14).
Forbidden (Eph 4:31; Col 3:8). Toward a brother (Lev 19:17). Toward an enemy (Mt 5:43-44).
Justified against iniquity (Ps 97:10; 101:3; 119:104, 128, 163; 139:21-22). Of God (Ps 5:5; 45:7; Isa 61:8; Mal 2:16).
See Envy; Jealousy; Malice; Revenge.

HATTAAVAH *See Kibroth Hattaavah.*

HATTIL (*talkative*). A returned exile (Ezr 2:57; Ne 7:59).

HATTIN, HORNS OF (*hollows*). Hill near village of Hattin on which, tradition says, Christ delivered the Sermon on the Mount.

HATTUSH
1. Descendant of Zerubbabel (1Ch 3:22).
2. Man who returned from Babylon (Ezr 8:2).
3. Worker on the wall (Ne 3:10). May be the same as 2.
4. Man who sealed the covenant (Ne 10:4). May be the same as 2 or 3.
5. Priest who returned with Zerubbabel (Ne 12:2).

HAUGHTINESS *See Pride.*

HAURAN (*black*). Plateau E of the Jordan and N of Gilead (Eze 47:16, 18). Called Bashan in ancient times; in the time of the Romans, Auranites.

HAVENS *See Fair Havens.*

HAVILAH (*stretch of sand*).
1. Son of Cush (Ge 10:7; 1Ch 1:9).
2. Son of Joktan (Ge 10:29; 1Ch 1:23).
3. Land encompassed by Pishon River (Ge 2:11-12).
4. One of the boundaries of the Ishmaelites (Ge 25:18; 1Sa 15:7).

HAVVOTH JAIR (*villages of Jair*). A group of unwalled towns in the NW part of Bashan (Nu 32:41; Dt 3:14; Jos 13:30; Jdg 10:4).

HAWK A carnivorous and unclean bird (Lev 11:16; Dt 14:15; Job 39:26).

HAY (Pr 27:25; Isa 15:6; 1Co 3:12).

HAZAEL (*God [El] sees*). King of Syria. Anointed king by Elijah (1Ki 19:15). Conquests by (2Ki 8:28-29; 9:14; 10:32-33; 12:17-18; 13:3, 22; 2Ch 22:5-6). Conspires against, murders, and succeeds to the throne of Ben-Hadad (2Ki 8:8-15). Death of (2Ki 13:24).

HAZAIAH (*Yahweh sees*). A man of Judah (Ne 11:5).

HAZAR (*a settlement*). Often prefixed to descriptive place names. Also used for encampments of nomads.

HAZAR ADDAR (*settlement of Addar*). Also called Addar, a place on the southern boundary of Canaan (Nu 34:4; Jos 15:3).

HAZAR ENAN (*settlement of Enan*). The NE boundary point of the promised land (Nu 34:9-10; Eze 47:17; 48:1).

HAZAR GADDAH (*settlement of [pagan god] Gad*). A town in the southern district of Judah (Jos 15:27).

HAZAR HATTICON *See Hazer Hatticon.*

HAZAR SHUAL (*settlement of Shual [jackal]*). Town in S Judah (Jos 15:28; 19:3; 1Ch 4:28; Ne 11:27).

HAZAR SUSAH, HAZAR SUSIM (*settlement of Susah [horse]*). A city of Judah (Jos 19:5; 1Ch 4:31).

HAZARMAVETH (*village of [pagan god] Maveth*). Son and descendants of Joktan (Ge 10:26; 1Ch 1:20).

HAZAZON TAMAR (*Hazazon of the palm trees*). The ancient name of En Gedi, a town on W coast of Dead Sea (Ge 14:7; 2Ch 20:2).

HAZEL *See Almond.*

HAZER HATTICON (*place of Hatticon*). A place on the boundary of Hauran, probably E of Damascus (Eze 47:16).

HAZERIM (*unwalled settlements*). A district in the S of Canaan (Dt 2:23).

HAZEROTH (*settlements*). A station in the travels of the Israelites (Nu 11:35; 12:16; 33:17-18; Dt 1:1).

HAZEZON-TAMAR *See Hazazon Tamar.*

HAZIEL (*vision of God [El]*). A Levite (1Ch 23:9).

HAZO A son of Nahor (Ge 22:22).

HAZOR (*an enclosure*).
1. City c. five miles W of waters of Merom, ruled by Jabin (Jos 11:1, 10), conquered by Joshua and, later, by Deborah and Barak

(Jdg 4; 1Sa 12:9), fortified by Solomon (1Ki 9:15), its inhabitants taken into exile by Assyria (2Ki 15:29).
2. Town in S of Judah (Jos 15:23).
3. Another town in S Judah (Jos 15:25).
4. Town N of Jerusalem (Ne 11:33).
5. Region in S Arabia (Jer 49:28-33).

HAZOR HADATTAH (*new Hazor*). Probably an adjective qualifying Hazor, making it equivalent to New Hazor. A city of Judah (Jos 15:25).

HAZZELELPONI Daughter of Etam (1Ch 4:3).

HAZZOBEBAH Daughter of Koz (1Ch 4:8).

HAZZURIM *See Helkath Hazzurim.*

HEAD Shaven when vows were taken (Ac 21:24). Diseases of (Isa 3:17). Anointed (Lev 14:18, 29).

HEAD OF THE CHURCH Christ, who gives the church life, direction, strength (Eph 1:22; 5:23; Col 1:18).

HEADBANDS Head coverings worn by priests (Ex 28:40; 29:9; Lev 8:13), by women (Isa 3:18, 20). Used in disguise (1Ki 20:38-41). *See Dress; Turban.*

HEADSTONE *See Cornerstone.*

HEALING

In the Old Testament:
The LORD the healer (Ge 20:17; Ex 15:26; Ps 6:2; 30:2; 103:3; Ac 4:30).
In answer to prayer (Jas 5:14-16), of Miriam (Nu 12:10-15), of Jeroboam (1Ki 13:1-6), of Hezekiah (2Ki 20:1-7). By Elisha, of Naaman (2Ki 5:1-14).

By Jesus:
The nobleman's son (Jn 4:46-53). The disabled man (Jn 5:2-9). A leper (Mt 8:2-4; Mk 1:40-45; Lk 5:12-13). Peter's mother-in-law (Mt 8:14-15). Paralyzed man (Mt 9:2-8; Mk 2:1-12; Lk 5:17-26). The man with the withered hand (Mt 12:9-13; Mk 3:1-5; Lk 6:6-10). The centurion's servant (Mt 8:5-13; Lk 7:1-10). Demoniacs (Mt 8:28-34, w Mk 5:1-20, & Lk 8:26-36; Mt 12:22; 17:14-18; Mk 9:14-27; Lk 9:38-42; 11:14). Blind and mute (Mt 9:27-33; 12:22; 20:30-34; Mk 8:22-25; 10:46-52; Lk 18:35-43). Woman with issue of blood (Mt 9:20-22; Mk 5:25-34; Lk 8:43-48). Many sick (Mt 8:16; 9:35; 14:14, 35-36; 15:30-31; 19:2; Mk 6:5, 53-56; Lk 4:40; 9:11). Daughter of the Syrian Phoenician woman (Mt 15:22-28; Mk 7:25-30). Woman with an infirmity (Lk 13:10-13). Ten lepers (Lk 17:12-14). *See Miracles, of Jesus.*
Power of, given to the apostles (Mt 10:1, 8; Mk 3:13-15; 6:7, 13; Lk 9:1-2, 6), to the Seventy (Lk 10:9, 17), to all believers (Mk 16:18). Special gifts of (1Co 12:9, 28, 30).

By the Apostles:
The lame man, in Jerusalem (Ac 3:2-10), in Lystra (Ac 14:8-10). Sick, in Jerusalem (Ac 5:15-16), on the island of Malta (Ac 28:8-9). Aeneas (Ac 9:34).

Figurative:
Healing of disease a metaphor for forgiving of sins (Ps 103:3; Hos 7:1).
See Miracles.

HEALTH Health was a promised blessing of the Old Covenant (Ex 15:26; Dt 7:12-16), as diseases were part of its curse (Lev 26:14-16; Dt 28:20-29, 58-63). Health can be affected by sin (Ps 38:3, 7), but not all disease is the result of sin (Jn 9:1-3).
The wish for health and wholeness (Hebrew *shalom*) was part of standard greetings (Ge 29:6; 43:27, 28; 1Sa 25:4-6; 3Jn 2). The fear of the LORD brings health (Pr 3:7-8), words of wisdom (Pr 4:20-22), good news (Pr 15:30).
See Healing.

HEAR *See Obedience.*

HEARERS Unresponsive (Eze 33:30-32; Mt 7:26-27; 13:14-15, 19-22; Lk 6:49; 8:11-14; Ro 2:13; Jas 1:22-24).
Obedient (Mt 7:24-25; 13:23; Lk 6:47-48; 8:15; Jas 1:25).

HEART Seat of affection and source of action (Dt 5:29; 6:5-6; 2Ch 12:14; Ps 57:7; 112:7; Pr 4:23; 14:30; 15:13-15; 16:1; Mt 9:4; 12:33, 35; 15:18-20; 23:26; Mk 7:21-23). Lives forever (Ps 22:26). Of the Gentiles, taught of God (Ro 2:14-16).

Changed:
(Ps 51:10). Instances of: Saul (1Sa 10:9), Solomon (1Ki 3:11-12), Paul (Ac 9:1-18).

Hardening of:
Forbidden (Heb 3:8, 15; 4:7). Instances of: Pharaoh (Ex 4:21; 7:3, 13, 22; 8:15, 32; 9:12, 35; 10:1; 14:8), Sihon (Dt 2:30), king of Canaan (Jos 11:20), Philistines (1Sa 6:6).

Known to God:
(Dt 31:21; 1Sa 16:7; 2Sa 7:20; 1Ki 8:39; 1Ch 28:9; 2Ch 6:30; Job 11:11; 16:19; 31:4; Ps 1:6; 44:21; 51:10; 94:11; 139:1-12; Pr 5:21; 16:2; 21:2; Isa 66:18; Jer 12:13; 17:10; Eze 11:5, 19-21; 36:25-26; Lk 16:15; Ac 1:24; 15:8; Ro 8:27; 1Co 3:20; Heb 4:12; Rev 2:23).
To Christ (Ro 8:27; Rev 2:23).

Regenerate:
Is penitent (Ps 34:18; 51:10, 17; 147:3; Pr 15:3). Renewed (Dt 30:6; Ps 51:10; Eze 11:19; 18:31; 36:26; Jn 3:3, 7; Ro 2:29; Eph 4:22-24; Col 3:9-10; Heb 10:22; Jas 4:8). Pure (Ps 24:4; 66:18; Pr 20:9; Mt 5:8; 2Ti 2:22; 1Pe 3:15). Enlightened (2Co 4:6). Established (Ps 57:7; 108:1; 112:7-8; 1Th 3:13). Refined by affliction (Pr 17:3). Tried or tested (1Ch 29:17; Ps 7:9; 26:2; Pr 17:3; Jer 11:20; 12:3; 20:12; 1Th 2:4; Heb 11:17; Rev 2:2, 10). Strengthened (Ps 27:14; 112:8; 1Th 3:13). Graciously affected of God (1Sa 10:26; 1Ch 29:18; Ezr 6:22; 7:27; Pr 16:1; 21:1; Jer 20:9; Ac 16:14).

Should Render to God:
Obedience (Dt 10:12; 11:13; 26:16; 1Ki 2:4; Ps 119:1, 12; Eph 6:6). Faith (Ps 27:3; 112:7; Ac 8:37; Ro 6:17; 10:10). Trust (Pr 3:5). Love (Dt 6:5-6; Mt 22:37). Fear (Ps 119:161; Jer 32:40). Fidelity (Ne 9:8). Zeal (2Ch 17:16; Jer 20:9). Seeking God (2Ch 19:3; 30:19; Ezr 7:10; Ps 10:17; 84:2).

Should Be:
Joyful (1Sa 2:1; Ps 4:7; 97:11; Isa 65:14; Zec 10:7). Perfect (1Ki 8:61; Ps 101:2). Upright (Ps 97:11; 125:4). Clean (Ps 51:10; 73:1). Pure (Ps 24:4; Pr 22:11; Mt 5:8; 1Ti 1:5; 2Ti 2:22; Jas 4:8; 1Pe 1:22). Sincere (Lk 8:15; Ac 2:46; Eph 6:5; Col 3:22; Heb 10:22). Repentant (Dt 30:2; Ps 34:18; 51:17). Devout (1Sa 1:13; Ps 4:4; 9:1; 27:8; 77:6; 119:10, 69, 145). Wise (1Ki 3:9, 12; 4:29; Job 9:4; Pr 8:10; 10:8; 11:29; 14:33; 23:15). Tender (1Sa 24:5; 2Ki 22:19; Job 23:16; Ps 22:14; Eph 4:32). Holy (Ps 66:18; 1Pe 3:15). Compassionate (Jer 4:19; La 3:51). Lowly (Mt 11:29).

The Unregenerate Heart:
Is full of iniquity (Ge 6:5; 8:21; 1Sa 17:28; Pr 6:14, 18; 11:20; Pr 20:9; Ecc 8:11; 9:3; Jer 4:14, 18; 17:9; Ac 8:21-23; Ro 1:21). Loves evil (Dt 19:18; Ps 95:10; Jer 17:5). A fountain of evil (Mt 12:34-35; Mk 7:21). *See Depravity.* Wayward (2Ch 12:14; Ps 101:4; Pr 6:14; 11:20; 12:8; 17:20; Jer 5:23; Heb 3:10). Blind (Ro 1:21; Eph 4:18). *See Blindness, Spiritual.* Is double (1Ch 12:33; Ps 12:2; Pr 28:14; Isa 9:9; 10:12; 46:12; Hos 10:2; Jas 1:6, 8). *See Instability.* Is hard (Ps 76:5; Eze 2:4; 3:7; 11:19; 36:26; Mk 6:52; 10:5; 16:14; Jn 12:40; Ro 1:21; 2:5). *See Impenitence; Obduracy.* Is deceitful (Jer 17:9). Proud (2Ki 14:10; 2Ch 25:19; Ps 101:5; Pr 18:12; 28:25; Jer 48:29; 49:16). *See Pride.* Is subtle (Pr 7:10). *See Hypocrisy.* Is sensual (Eze 6:9; Hos 13:6; Ro 8:7). *See Lasciviousness.* Is worldly (2Ch 26:16; Da 5:20; Ac 8:21-22). Judicially hardened (Ex 4:21; Jos 11:20; Isa 6:10; Ac 28:26-27). Malicious (Ps 28:3; 140:2; Pr 24:2; Ecc 7:26; Eze 25:15). *See Malice.* Is impenitent (Ro 2:5). *See Impenitence.* Is diabolical (Jn 13:2; Ac 5:3). Is covetous (Jer 22:17; 2Pe 2:14). *See Covetousness.* Is foolish (Pr 12:23; 22:15; Ecc 9:3). Under the wrath of God (Ro 1:18-19, 31; 2:5-6).
See Regeneration; Sanctification.

HEARTH Of an altar (Lev 6:9; Isa 30:14; Eze 43:15-16). Figurative (Isa 29:2).

HEAT Jonah overcome with (Jnh 4:8). *See Sunstroke.*

HEATH *See Bush.*

HEATHEN Gentiles, pagans. Under this head are all who are not descendants of Abraham, Isaac and Jacob.

Described:
Cast out of Canaan (Lev 18:24-25; Ps 44:2) and their land given to Israel (Ps 78:55; 105:44; 135:12; 136:21-22; Isa 54:1-3). Excluded from the temple (La 1:10).
Wicked practices of. *See Idolatry.*

Divine Revelations Given to:
Abimelech (Ge 20:3-7), Nebuchadnezzar (Da 4:1-18), Belshazzar (Da 5:5, 24-29), Cyrus (2Ch 36:23; Ezr 1:1-4), the Magi (Mt 2:1-11), the centurion (Mt 8:5-13; Lk 7:2-9), Cornelius (Ac 10:1-7).

Pious People Among:
(Isa 65:5; Ac 10:35). Melchizedek (Ge 14:18-20). Abimelech (Ge 20). Balaam (Nu 22). Jethro (Ex 18). Cyrus (Ezr 1:1-3). Eliphaz (Job 4). Bildad (Job 8). Zophar (Job 11). Elihu (Job 32). Nebuchadnezzar, after his restoration (Da 4). The Ninevites (Jnh 3:5-10). The Magi (Mt 2:1-12). The centurion of Capernaum (Mt 8:5-13; Lk 7:2-9), of Caesarea (Ac 10). Believed in Christ (Mt 8:5-13; Lk 7:2-9).
See Gentiles.

HEAVE OFFERING *See Offerings.*

HEAVE SHOULDER *See Offerings.*

HEAVEN

God's Dwelling Place:
(Dt 26:15; 1Ki 8:30, 39, 43, 49; 1Ch 16:31; 21:26; 2Ch 2:6; 6:21, 27, 30, 33, 35, 39; 7:14; 30:27; Ne 9:27; Job 22:12, 14; Ps 2:4; 11:4; 20:6; 33:13; 102:19; 103:19; 113:5-6; 123:1; 135:6; Ecc 5:2; Isa 57:15; 63:15; 66:1; Jer 23:24; La 3:41, 50; Da 5:23; Zec 2:13; Mt 5:34, 45; 6:9; 10:32-33; 11:25; 12:50; 16:17; 18:10, 14; Mk 11:25-26; 16:19; Ac 7:49, 55-56; Ro 1:18; Heb 8:1; Rev 8:1; 12:7-9; 21:22-27; 22:1-5).

Figurative:
Of divine government (Mt 16:19; 18:18; 23:22). Of God (Mt 21:25).

The Future Home of the Righteous:
(2Ki 2:11; Mt 5:12; 13:30, 43; Lk 16:22; Jn 12:8, 26; 13:36; 17:24; 2Co 5:1; Php 3:20; Col 1:5-6, 12; 3:9; 1Th 4:17; Heb 10:34; 11:10, 16; 12:22; 1Pe 1:4; Rev 2:7; 3:21).

Called:
A city (Heb 11:10, 16), a garden (Mt 3:12), a house (Jn 14:2-3; 2Co 5:1), a kingdom (Mt 25:34; Lk 12:32; 22:29-30), the kingdom of Christ and of God (Eph 5:5), a heavenly country (Heb 11:16), a rest (Heb 4:9; Rev 14:13), glory (Col 3:4), paradise (Lk 23:43; 2Co 12:2, 4; Rev 2:7).
Everlasting (2Co 5:1; Heb 10:34; 13:14; 1Pe 1:4; 2Pe 1:11). Allegorical representatives of (Rev 4:1-11; 5:1-14; 7:9-17; 14:1-3; 15:1-8; 21; 22:1-5). No marriage in (Mt 22:30; Lk 20:34-36). Names of the righteous written in (Lk 10:20; Heb 12:22-24). Treasures in (Mt 6:20; 19:21; Lk 12:33). Joy in (Ps 16:11; Lk 15:6-7, 10). Righteousness dwells in (2Pe 3:13). No sorrow in (Rev 7:16-17; 21:4). The wicked excluded from (Gal 5:21; Eph 5:5; Rev 22:15).
See Righteous, Promises to.

HEAVEN OPENED (Mt 3:16; Ac 7:56; 10:11; Rev 19:11).

HEAVENLY PLACES (Eph 1:3, 20; 2:6; 3:10).

HEAVENS, NEW To be created (Isa 65:17; 66:22; 2Pe 3:13; Rev 21:1-4).

HEAVENS, PHYSICAL (Ge 1:1; 2Ch 2:6; 6:18; Job 38:31-33; Ps 19:1; 50:6; 68:33; 89:29; 103:11; 113:4; 115:16; 136:5; Jer 31:37; Eze 1:1; Mt 24:29-30; Ac 2:19-20).
Created by God (Ge 1:1; 2:1; Ex 20:11; 1Ch 16:26; 2Ch 2:12; Ne 9:6; Job 9:8; Ps 8:3; 19:1; 33:6, 9; 102:25; 148:4-6; Pr 8:27; Isa 37:16; 40:22; 42:5; 45:12, 18; Jer 10:12; 32:17; 51:15; Ac 4:24; 14:15; Heb 1:10; Rev 10:6; 14:7). *See Creation; God, Creator; Heavens, New.*
Destruction of (Job 14:12; Ps 102:25-26; Isa 51:6; Mt 5:18; 24:35; Heb 1:10-12; 2Pe 3:10-12; Rev 6:12-14; 20:11; 21:1, 4). Figurative of divine judgment (Isa 34:4).
See Sky.

HEAVING AND WAVING *See Offerings.*

HEBER, HEBERITE (*associate*).
1. An Asherite, the son of Beriah; great-grandson of Jacob (Ge 46:17; Nu 26:45; 1Ch 7:31-32).
2. Kenite whose wife Jael killed Sisera (Jdg 4:11-21; 5:24).
3. A Judahite, the father of Soco and son of Ezrah (1Ch 4:18).
4. A Benjamite and son of Elpaal (1Ch 8:17).

HEBREW A word supposed to be a corruption of the name of Eber, who was an ancestor of Abraham (Ge 10:24; 11:14-26). *See Genealogy.* Applied to Abraham (Ge 14:13) and his descendants (Ge 39:14; 40:15; 43:32; Ex 2:6; Dt 15:12; 1Sa 4:9; 29:3; Jnh 1:9; Ac 6:1; 2Co 11:22; Php 3:5). Used to denote the language of the Jews (Jn 5:2; 19:20; Ac 21:40; 22:2; 26:14; Rev 9:11).
See Israel, Israelites; Jews.

HEBREW LANGUAGE The NW branch of the Semitic language family; has close affinity to Ugaritic, Phoenician, Moabitic, and the Canaanite dialects; sister languages include Arabic, Akkadian, and Aramaic. Except for a few Aramaic passages in Ezra, Daniel, and Jeremiah, it is the language of the OT.

HEBREW OF THE HEBREWS A Jew of pure blood, very strict in observing the law (Php 3:4-6).

HEBREWS, EPISTLE TO THE

Author: Anonymous. Historical speculations as to authorship include Paul, Barnabas, Apollos, and Priscilla.

Date: Before the destruction of Jerusalem and the temple in A.D. 70

Outline:
I. Prologue: The Superiority of God's New Revelation (1:1-4).
II. The Superiority of Christ to Leaders of the Old Covenant (1:5-7:28).
A. Christ Is Superior to the Angels (1:5-2:18).
1. Scriptural proof of superiority (1:5-14).
2. Exhortation not to ignore the revelation of God in his Son (2:1-4).
3. Further Scriptural proof of superiority over the angels (2:5-18).
B. Christ Is Superior to Moses (3:1-4:13).
1. Demonstration of Christ's superiority (3:1-6).
2. Exhortation to enter salvation-rest (3:7-4:13).
C. Christ Is Superior to the Aaronic Priests (4:14-7:28).
1. Exhortation to hold fast (4:14-16).
2. Qualifications of a priest (5:1-10).
3. Exhortation to abandon spiritual lethargy (5:11-6:12).
4. Certainty of God's promise (6:13-20).
5. Christ's superior priestly order (ch. 7).
III. The Superior Sacrificial Work of Our High Priest (chs. 8-10).
A. A Better Covenant (ch. 8).
B. A Better Sanctuary (9:1-12).
C. A Better Sacrifice (9:13-10:18).
D. Exhortations (10:19-39).
IV. Final Plea for Persevering Faith (chs. 11-12).
A. Examples of Past Heroes of the Faith (ch. 11).
B. Encouragement for Persevering Faith (12:1-11).
C. Exhortations for Persevering Faith (12:12-17).
D. Motivation for Persevering Faith (12:18:29).
V. Conclusion (ch. 13).
A. Practical Rules for Christian Living (13:1-17).
B. Request for Prayer (13;18-19).
C. Benediction (13:20-21).
D. Personal Remarks (13:22-23).
E. Greetings and Final Benediction (13:24-25).

HEBRON (*association*).
1. For Jos 19:28 *See Abdon, 1.*
2. A city of Judah, S of Jerusalem. When built (Nu 13:22). Fortified (2Ch 11:10). Also called Kiriath Arba (Ge 23:2; 35:27; Jos 15:13). Abraham dwells and Sarah dies at (Ge 23:2). Hoham, king of, confederated with other kings of the Canaanites against Joshua (Jos 10:3-39). Children of Anakim dwell at (Nu 13:22; Jos 11:21). Conquest of, by Caleb (Jos 14:6-15; Jdg 1:10, 20). A city of refuge (Jos 20:7; 21:11, 13). David crowned king of Judah at (2Sa 2:1-11; 3), of Israel (2Sa 5:1-5). The burial place of Sarah (Ge 23:2), Abner (2Sa 3:32), Ish-Bosheth (2Sa 4:12). The conspirators against Ish-Bosheth hanged at (2Sa 4:12). Absalom made king at (2Sa 15:9-10). Jews of the Babylonian captivity dwell at (Ne 11:25). Pool of (2Sa 4:12).
3. Son of Kohath (Ex 6:18; Nu 3:19; 1Ch 6:2, 18; 23:12, 19).
4. The family name of Mareshah (1Ch 2:42-43; 15:9).

HEDGE Protecting a vineyard (Isa 5:5). Of thorns (Mic 7:4; Mk 12:1). Figurative of divine protection (Job 1:10), of divine entrapment (Job 3:23). *See Fence.*

HEEDFULNESS Commanded (Ex 23:13; Pr 4:25-27).
Necessary: In the care of the soul (Dt 4:9). In the house and worship of God (Ecc 5:1). In what we hear (Mk 4:24). In how we hear (Lk 3:18). In keeping God's commandments (Jos 22:5). In conduct (Eph 5:15). In speech (Pr 13:3; Jas 1:19). In worldly company (Ps 39:1; Col 4:5). In giving judgment (2Ch 19:6-7).

Against sin (Heb 12:15-16). Against unbelief (Heb 3:12). Against idolatry (Dt 4:15-16). Against false Christs, and false prophets (Mt 24:4-5, 23-24). Against false teachers (Php 3:2; Col 2:8; 2Pe 3:16-17). Against presumption (1Co 10:12).

Promises to (1Ki 2:4; 1Ch 22:13).

See Obedience.

HEGAI Eunuch in charge of Xerxes' harem (Est 2:3, 8, 15).

HEIFER When used as sacrifice, must be without blemish and must not have come under the yoke (Nu 19:2; Dt 21:3). An atonement for murder (Dt 21:1-9). The red heifer used for the water of separation (Nu 19; Heb 9:13).

Used for plowing (Jdg 14:18), for treading out wheat (Hos 10:11). Tractable (Hos 10:11). Intractable (Hos 4:16).

See Cattle; Offerings.

Figurative: Of backsliders (Hos 4:16). Of the obedient (Hos 10:11).

HEIFER, RED *See Animals.*

HEIR

Literal:

Mosaic law relating to inheritance of (Nu 27:8-11; 36:1-8; Jos 17:3-6). Prescribing right of, to redeem alienated land (Lev 25:25; Ru 4:1-12). To inherit slaves (Lev 25:45-46). Firstborn son to have double portion (Dt 21:15-17). Children of wives and concubines are (Ge 15:3; 21:10; 25:5-6; Gal 4:30). All possessions left to (Ecc 2:18-19). Minor, under guardians (Gal 4:1-2).

See Birthright; Firstborn; Inheritance; Orphan; Will.

Figurative:

Of spiritual adoption (Ro 8:14-17; Gal 3:29; 4:6-7; Tit 3:7; Jas 2:5). *See Adoption.*

HELAH (*necklace* IDB; *rust* KB). A wife of Asher (1Ch 4:5).

HELAM Place in Syrian desert E of Jordan where David defeated forces of Hadadezer (2Sa 10:16-17).

HELBAH (*a fertile region*). A town of Asher (Jdg 1:31).

HELBON (*fertile*). A village near Damascus, noted for fine wines (Eze 27:18).

HELDAI (*mole*).

1. The Netophathite. One of David's heroes (1Ch 27:15). Heled is a variant spelling (2Sa 23:29; 1Ch 11:30).

2. A leader among those returned from the Exile (Zec 6:10, 14).

HELECH Possibly Cilicia, an area in SE (modern day) Turkey (Eze 27:11).

HELED *See Heldai, 1.*

HELEK, HELEKITE (*portion, lot*). Son of Gilead (Jos 17:2) and his clan (Nu 26:30).

HELEM (*health*).

1. A descendant of Asher (1Ch 7:35).

2. Probably the same as Heldai (Zec 6:10, 14).

HELEPH (possibly *sharp, cutting*). A town of Naphtali (Jos 19:33).

HELEZ (*vigor* BDB).

1. One of David's mighty men (2Sa 23:26; 1Ch 11:27; 27:10).

2. A man of Judah (1Ch 2:39).

HELI (*ascent [to God]*). Father of Joseph, the husband of Mary (Lk 3:23), or perhaps the father of Mary, the mother of Jesus.

HELIOPOLIS (*sun [god] city*). City near S end of the Nile Delta called "On" in the Bible (Ge 41:45; 46:20; Isa 19:18, ftn).

See City of Destruction.

HELKAI (*Yahweh is [my] portion*). A priest (Ne 12:15).

HELKATH (*portion*). A Levitical town (Jos 19:25; 21:31), also spelled Hukok (1Ch 6:75). *See Hukok.*

HELKATH HAZZURIM (possibly *portion [field] of rock*, or *swords* IDB; *portion [field] of snare* KB). Plain near pool of Gibeon where soldiers of Joab and Abner fought (2Sa 2:12-16).

HELL In the NIV, "hell" usually translates the Greek *geena* and *hades*, but is conceptually the same as the Hebrew *Sheol*, usually rendered "grave," the unseen world and abode of the dead (Ge 37:35; 42:38; 44:29, 31; Dt 32:22; 1Sa 2:6; 2Sa 22:6; 1Ki 2:6, 9; Job 7:9; 11:8; 14:13; 17:13; 21:13; 24:19; 26:6; Ps 9:17; 16:10; 18:5; 55:15; 86:13; 116:3; 139:8; Pr 5:5; 7:27; 9:18; 15:11, 24; 23:14; 27:20; Isa 5:14; 14:9, 15; 28:15, 18; 57:9; Eze 31:16-17; 32:21, 27; Am 9:2; Jnh 2:2; Hab 2:5). In the NT hell is the unseen world (Mt 11:23; 16:18; Lk 10:15; 16:23; Ac 2:27, 31; Rev 1:18; 6:8; 20:13-14), a place of torment (Mt 5:22, 29-30; 10:28; 18:9; 23:15, 33; Lk 12:5; Jas 3:6) and of captivity for fallen angels (2Pe 2:4).

Figurative:

Of divine judgments (Dt 32:22; Eze 31:15-17).

The Future State, or Abode, of the Wicked:

(Ps 9:17; Pr 5:5; 9:18; 15:24; 23:14; Isa 30:33; 33:14; Mt 3:12; 5:22, 29-30; 7:13; 8:11-12; 10:28; 13:30, 38-42, 49-50; 16:18; 18:8-9, 34-35; 22:13; 25:30, 41, 46; Mk 9:43-48; Lk 3:17; 16:23-28; Ac 1:25; 2Th 1:9; 2Pe 2:4; Jude 6, 23; Rev 2:11; 9:1-2; 11:7; 14:10-11; 19:20; 20:10, 15; 21:8).

See Grave; Hades; Sheol; Wicked, Punishment of.

HELLENISTS NIV "Grecian Jews"; Jews of the Dispersion who spoke Greek and followed some aspects of Greek culture (Ac 6:1; 9:29).

HELM *See Rudder(s).*

HELMET A defensive headgear worn by soldiers (1Sa 17:5, 38; 2Ch 26:14; Jer 46:4; Eze 23:24).

Figurative: (Isa 59:17; Eph 6:17; 1Th 5:8).

HELON (*strength, power*). Father of Eliab (Nu 1:9; 2:7; 7:24, 29; 10:16).

HELPER Woman created as a helper suitable for man (Ge 2:18, 20). Yahweh is the helper of Israel (Dt 33:29; Hos 13:9), of the fatherless (Ps 10:14), of David (Ps 27:9). Eliezer means "God is my helper" (Ex 18:4, ftn.).

HELPMEET *See Helper.*

HELPS One of the gifts of the Spirit, probably the ability to perform helpful works in a gracious manner (1Co 12:7-11, 28-31).

HEM OF A GARMENT Fringes or tassels on the borders of the Israelite outer garment (Nu 15:38-39).

HEMAM *See Homam.*

HEMAN (*faithful*).

1. A man noted for wisdom, to whom Solomon is compared (1Ki 4:31; 1Ch 2:6).

2. "The Singer," a chief Levite, and musician (1Ch 6:33; 15:17, 19; 16:41). The king's seer (1Ch 25:5). His sons and daughters temple musicians (1Ch 6:33; 25:1-6). "Maskil of," title of Psalm 88. *See Maskil.*

HEMATH

1. *See Hamath.*

2. *See Hammath, 2.*

HEMDAN (*desirable*). Son of Dishon (Ge 36:26).

HEMLOCK A poisonous and bitter plant (Hos 10:4; Am 6:12). *See Gall, 3; Plants of the Bible; Poison.*

HEMORRHAGE Menstruation (Lev 15:19; Mt 9:20; Lk 8:43). A woman subject to bleeding for twelve years (Mk 5:25-29; Mk 5:24-34; Lk 8:). *See Bleeding, Subject to; Menstruation.*

HEMORRHOIDS NIV "tumors" (Dt 28:27); a disease with which the Philistines were afflicted (1Sa 5:6, 12; 6:4; 5:11). *See Disease; Tumor.*

HEN (proper name: *gracious*).

1. Son of Zephaniah (Zec 6:14).

2. Hen protecting her chicks figurative of Jesus' desire for Jerusalem (Mt 23:37; Lk 13:34).

HENA (*[pagan god] Anath*). A city on the Euphrates (2Ki 18:34; 19:13; Isa 37:13).

HENADAD (*favor of Hadad [pagan god]*). A Levite (Ezr 3:9; Ne 3:18, 24; 10:9).

HENNA BLOSSOMS A shrub of Israel (perhaps the cypress) with tightly clustered, aromatic blossoms (SS 1:14; 4:13).

HENOCH *See Enoch.*

HEPHER, HEPHERITE (perhaps *help*).

1. Son of Gilead, and ancestor of Zelophehad (Nu 26:32-33; 27:1; Jos 17:2-3).

2. Son of Naarah (1Ch 4:6).

3. One of David's heroes (1Ch 11:36).

4. A city W of the Jordan (Jos 12:17; 1Ki 4:10).

HEPHZIBAH (*my pleasure is in her*).

1. Wife of Hezekiah (2Ki 21:1).

2. Symbolic name given to Zion (Isa 62:4).

HERALD (Isa 40:3; Da 3:4). Signified by the word "preacher" (1Ti 2:7; 2Ti 1:11; 2Pe 2:5).

HERBS Given for food (Ge 1:29-30; Pr 15:17). *See Vegetation.*

HERD Herds of cattle were used in plowing, threshing, and sacrifice (Ge 18:7; Job 1:3; 42:12).

HERDSMAN Person in charge of cattle (Ge 13:7) or pigs (Mt 8:33), despised in Egypt (Ge 46:34) but honored in Israel (Ge 47:6; 1Ch 27:29).

HEREDITY Like gives birth to like (Ge 5:3; Job 14:4; Jn 3:6-7).

Results of:

Natural, depravity (Job 21:19; Ps 51:5; 58:3; Isa 48:8; Jn 9:2; Ro 5:12; Eph 2:3).

Judicial, ordained consequences of parental conduct (Ex 20:5-6; 34:7; Nu 14:18, 33; Dt 5:9; Ps 37:28; Isa 14:20-21; 65:6-7; Jer 32:18; Ro 5:12; 1Co 15:22). Does not determine moral status (Jer 31:29-30; Eze 18:1-32; Mt 3:9).

HERES (*sun*).

1. District around Aijalon (Jdg 1:35).

2. Place E of the Jordan (Jdg 8:13).

3. Egyptian city, translated "city of destruction" (Isa 19:18), undoubtedly Heliopolis.

HERESH (*deaf, silent*). A Levite (1Ch 9:15).

HERESY Propagandism of, forbidden under severe penalties (Dt 13; Tit 3:10-11; 2Jn 10-11). Teachers of, among early Christians (Ac 15:24; 2Co 11:4; Gal 1:7; 2:4; 2Pe 2; Jude 3-16; Rev 2:2). Paul and Silas accused of (Ac 16:20-21, 23). Paul accused of (Ac 18:13). Disavowed by Paul (Ac 24:13-17). *See Teachers, False.*

HERETH A forest in which David found refuge from Saul (1Sa 22:5).

HERMAS Friend of Paul in the church at Rome (Ro 16:14).

HERMES (possibly *rock, cairn*).

1. Greek god (messenger), the same as Mercury in Latin. Paul mistaken for (Ac 14:12).

2. Friend of Paul in the church at Rome (Ro 16:14).

HERMOGENES (*born of Hermes*). A Christian who deserted Paul (2Ti 1:15).

HERMON, MOUNT (*consecrated place*). Mountain marking S end of Anti-Lebanon range; thirty miles SW of Damascus; 9000 ft. above sea level; marks N boundary of Israel; has three peaks. Has borne several names: the Amorites call it "Senir," (Dt 3:9), the Sidonians call it "Sirion" (Dt 3:9), "Siyon," (Dt 4:48). Probably the Mount of Transfiguration (Mt 17:1). Seat of Baal worship (Jdg 3:3). Modern Jebel es-Sheikh.

HEROD Idumean rulers of Israel (37 B.C. to A.D. 100). Line started with Antipater, whom Julius Caesar made procurator of Judea in 47 B.C.

1. Herod the Great, first procurator of Galilee, then king of the Jews (37-4 B.C.); built Caesarea, temple at Jerusalem; slaughtered children at Bethlehem (Mt 2:1-18). At his death his kingdom was divided among his three sons: Archelaus, Herod Antipas, and Philip.

2. Archelaus ruled over Judea, Samaria, and Idumea (4 B.C. to A.D. 6), and was removed from office by the Romans (Mt 2:22).

3. Herod Antipas ruled over Galilee and Perea (4 B.C. to A.D. 39); killed John the Baptist (Mt 14:1-12); called "fox" by Jesus (Lk 13:32).

4. Philip, tetrarch of Batanaea, Trachonitis, Gaulanitis, and parts of Jamnia (4 B.C. to A.D. 34). Best of the Herods.

5. Herod Agrippa I; grandson of Herod the Great; tetrarch of Galilee; king of Israel (A.D. 37-44); killed James the apostle (Ac 12:1-23).

6. Herod Agrippa II. King of territory E of Galilee (A.D. 50-100); Paul appeared before him (Ac 25:13-26:32).

HERODIANS They are mentioned as enemies of Jesus once in Galilee, and again at Jerusalem (Mt 22:15-22; Mk 3:6; 12:13-17; Lk 20:20-26). The Pharisees were ardent nationalists, opposed to Roman rule, while the hated Herodians, as their name indicates, supported the Roman rule of the Herods. Now, however, the Pharisees enlisted the help of the Herodians to trap Jesus in his words. After trying to put him off guard with flattery, they sprang their question: "Is it right to pay taxes to Caesar or not?" (Mt 22:17). If he said "no," the Herodians would report him to the Roman governor and he would be executed for treason. If he said "yes," the Pharisees would denounce him to the people as disloyal to his nation.

HERODIAS (feminine form of Herod). Granddaughter of Herod the Great who had John the Baptist put to death (Mt 14:3-6, Mk 6:17; Lk 3:19).

HERODION A Roman Christian (Ro 16:11).

HERON Large aquatic bird Israelites could not eat (Lev 11:19; Dt 14:18).

HESED *See Ben-Hesed.*

HESHBON (*reckoning*). A city of the Amorites (Nu 21:25-35; Dt 1:4). Built by Reuben (Nu 32:37). Allotted to Gad (Jos 21:38-39). Pools at (SS 7:4). Prophecy concerning (Isa 16:8; Jer 48:2, 34-35; 49:1-3).

HESHMON A town in the S of Judah (Jos 15:27).

HETH Son of Canaan and ancestor of the Hittites (Ge 10:15; 23:3, ftn, 5, 7, 10, 16, 18; 27:46; 49:32; 1Ch 1:13). *See Hittite(s).*

HETHLON A place on the northern frontier of Israel (Eze 47:15; 48:1).

HEXATEUCH (*six books*). A term referring to the Pentateuch and Joshua as though it were a literary unit.

HEZEKIAH (*Yahweh is [my] strength*)

1. King of Judah (2Ki 16:20; 18:1-2; 1Ch 3:13; 2Ch 29:1; Mt 1:9). Religious zeal of (2Ch 29; 30; 31). Purges the nation of idolatry (2Ki 18:4; 2Ch 31:1; 33:3). Restores the true forms of worship (2Ch 31:2-21). His piety (2Ki 18:2, 5-6; 2Ch 29:2; 31:20-21; 32:32; Jer 26:19). Military operations of (2Ki 18:19; 1Ch 4:39-43; 2Ch 32; Isa 36; 37). Sickness and restoration of (2Ki 20:1-11; 2Ch 32:24; Isa 38:1-8). His psalm of thanksgiving (Isa 38:9-22). His lack of wisdom in showing his resources to commissioners of Babylon (2Ki 20:12-19; 2Ch 32:25-26, 31; Isa 39). Prospered of God (2Ki 18:7; 2Ch 32:27-30). Conducts the Brook Gihon into Jerusalem (2Ki 18:17; 20:20; 2Ch 32:4, 30; 33:14; Ne 2:13-15; 3:13, 16; Isa 7:3; 22:9-11; 36:2). Scribes of (Pr 25:1). Death and burial of (2Ki 20:21; 2Ch 32:33). Prophecies concerning (2Ki 19:20-34; 20:5-6, 16-18; Isa 38:5-8; 39:5-7; Jer 26:18-19).

2. One of the exiles (Ezr 2:16; Ne 7:21; 10:17).

3. An ancestor of the prophet Zephaniah (Zep 1:1).

4. *See Hizkiah, 1.*

HEZION (*vision* BDB; *one with floppy ears* IDB). Grandfather of Ben Hadad (1Ki 15:18)

HEZIR (*boar*).

1. A Levite (1Ch 24:15).

2. A prince of Judah (Ne 10:20).

HEZRAI *See Hezro.*

HEZRO Also called Hezrai. A Carmelite (2Sa 23:35; 1Ch 11:37).

HEZRON, HEZRONITE (*enclosure*).

1. A son of Perez (Ge 46:12). Ancestor of the Hezronites (Nu 26:6). An ancestor of Jesus (Mt 1:3; Lk 3:33).

2. A son of Reuben (Ge 46:9; Ex 6:14; 1Ch 4:1; 5:3). Ancestor of the Hezronites (Nu 26:21).

HIDDAI One of David's heroes (2Sa 23:30). Called Hurai (1Ch 11:32).

HIDDEKEL *See Tigris.*

HIEL (*God [El] lives*). Rebuilder of Jericho (1Ki 16:34). In him was fulfilled the curse pronounced by Joshua (Jos 6:26).

HIERAPOLIS (*[pagan] sacred city*). Ancient Phrygian city near Colosse (Col 4:13).

HIEROGLYPHICS *See Writing.*

HIGGAION A musical term probably meaning "solemn sound" or "meditation." It occurs in Ugaritic as with the meaning "to utter." According to Gesenius, it signifies the murmuring tone of a harp and therefore should be rendered in a melancholy manner (Ps 92:3). Combined with *Selah*, it may have been intended to indicate a pause in the vocal music while the instruments played an interlude (Ps 9:16, ftn). Mendelssohn translates it "meditation, thought" (Ps 19:14). Therefore, the music was to be rendered in a mode to promote devout meditation.
See Music, Symbols Used in.

HIGH PLACES A term used to describe places of worship (Ge 12:8; 22:2, 14; 31:54; 1Sa 9:12; 2Sa 24:25; 1Ki 3:2, 4; 18:30, 38; 1Ch 16:39; 2Ch 1:3; 33:17). Signify a place of idolatrous worship (Nu 22:41; 1Ki 11:7; 12:31; 14:23; 15:14; 22:43; 2Ki 17:9, 29; Jer 7:31). Licentious practices at (Eze 16:24-43). The idolatrous, to be destroyed (Lev 26:30; Nu 33:52). Asa destroys (2Ch 14:3), Jehoshaphat (2Ch 17:6), Hezekiah (2Ki 18:4), Josiah (2Ki 23:8).
See Groves; Idolatry; Shrine.

HIGH PRIEST *See Priest.*

HIGHWAYS (*a built up road*). From, Gibeon to Beth Horon (Jos 10:10), Bethel to Shechem (Jdg 21:19), Judea to Galilee, by way of Samaria (Jn 4:3-5, 43). To Bethel (Jdg 20:31), to Gibeah (Jdg 20:31), to cities of refuge (Dt 19:3). Built by rulers (Nu 20:17; 21:22).
Figurative (Pr 16:17; Isa 11:16; 35:8-10; 40:3-4; Mt 3:3; 7:13-14).
See Roads.

HILEN A city of Judah. Assigned to the priests (1Ch 6:58). Called Holon (Jos 15:51; 21:15).

HILKIAH (*Yahweh is [my] portion*).
1. Father of Eliakim (2Ki 18:18).
2. Merarite Levite (1Ch 6:45).
3. Merarite Levite (1Ch 26:11).
4. High priest who found book of the Law and sent it to Josiah (2Ki 22-23; 2Ch 34:14).
5. Priest who returned with Zerubbabel (Ne 12:7).
6. Father of Jeremiah (Jer 1:1).
7. Father of Gemariah who stood by Ezra at Bible reading (Ne 8:4).

HILL COUNTRY Any region of hills and valleys, but in Scripture generally the higher part of Judea (Lk 1:39, 65).

HILLEL (*he has praises*). Father of Abdon (Jdg 12:13, 15).

HILLS Perpetual (Ge 49:26; Hab 3:6).

HIN A measure for liquids, and containing one-sixth or one-seventh of a bath. Probably equivalent to about four quarts (Ex 29:40; Lev 19:36; 23:13). *See Measure.*

HIND *See Deer.*

HINGE A fitting enabling a door or window to swing in its place (1Ki 7:50), often used figuratively for something of great importance.

HINNOM, VALLEY OF A valley W and SW of Jerusalem (Jos 15:8; 18:16; 2Ki 23:10; Ne 11:30). Children offered in sacrifice in (2Ch 28:3; 33:6; Jer 7:31-32; 19:2, 4, 6; 32:35). Possibly valley of vision identical with (Isa 22:1, 5).
See Ben Hinnom; Topheth, Tophet.

HIP AND THIGH Hebrew idiom denoting thoroughness with which Samson slew Philistines (Jdg 15:8, KJV).

HIPPOPOTAMUS *See Behemoth.*

HIRAH An Adullamite (Ge 38:1, 12).

HIRAM (*[my] brother is elevated*). Hiram (Hebrew *Huram*, a variant of *Hiram*), was a Phoenician king who was the first to accord the newly established King David international recognition. It was vital to him that he have good relations with the king of Israel since Israel dominated the inland trade routes to Tyre, and Tyre was dependent on Israelite agriculture for much of its food. A close relationship existed between these two realms until the Babylonian invasions. Builds a palace for David (2Sa 5:11; 1Ch 14:1; 2Ch 2:3). Aids Solomon in building the temple (1Ki 5; 2Ch 2:3-16). Dissatisfied with cities given by Solomon (1Ki 9:11-13). Makes presents of gold and seamen to Solomon (1Ki 9:14, 26-28; 10:11).

HIRE Law concerning hired property (Ex 22:14-15).
See Employer; Master; Servant; Wages.

HIRED SERVANT Jacob (Ge 29:15; 30:26), re-employed (Ge 30:27-34; 31:6-7, 41). Laborers for a vineyard (Mt 20:1-15). The prodigal (Lk 15:15-19). Kindness to (Ru 2:4). Treatment of, more considerate than that accorded slaves (Lev 25:53).

Rights of:
To receive wages (Mt 10:10; Lk 10:7; Ro 4:4; 1Ti 5:18; Jas 5:4), daily (Lev 19:13; Dt 24:15). To share in spontaneous products of land in Sabbatic year (Lev 25:6). Wages of, paid in portion of flocks or products (Ge 30:31-32; 2Ch 2:10), or in money (Mt 20:2, 9-10). Oppression of, forbidden (Dt 24:14; Col 4:1). Oppressors of, punished (Mal 3:5).
Mercenary (Job 7:2). Unfaithful (Jn 10:12-13).
See Employee; Master; Servant; Wages.

HIRELING *See Hired Servant.*

HISTORY (Job 8:8-10). *See Genesis; Joshua; Judges; Ruth; Samuel, 1 and 2; Kings, 1 and 2; Chronicles, 1 and 2; Ezra; Nehemiah; Esther; Israel, Israelites; Jesus the Christ, History of.*

HITTITE(S) (*descendants of Heth*). A tribe of Canaanites. Sons of Heth (Ge 10:15; 23:3, ftn, 5, 7, 10, 16, 18). Sell a burial site to Abraham (Ge 23). Esau intermarries with (Ge 26:34; 36:2). Dwelling place of (Ge 23:17-20; Nu 13:29; Jos 1:4; Jdg 1:26). Their land given to the Israelites (Ex 3:8; Dt 7:1; Jos 1:4). Conquered by Joshua (Jos 9:1-2; 10; 11; 12; 24:11). Intermarry with Israelites (Jdg 3:5-7; Ezr 9:1). Solomon intermarries with (1Ki 11:1; Ne 13:26). Pay tribute to Solomon (1Ki 9:20-21). Retain their own kings (1Ki 10:29; 2Ki 7:6; 2Ch 1:17). Officers from, in David's army (1Sa 26:6; 2Sa 11:3; 23:39).

HIVITE(S) A tribe of Canaanites (Ge 10:17; 1Ch 1:15). Shechemites and Gibeonites were families of (Ge 34:2; Jos 9:7; 11:19). Esau intermarries with (Ge 26:34; 36:2). Dwelling place of (Jos 11:3; Jdg 3:3; 2Sa 24:7). Their land given to the Israelites (Ex 23:23, 28; Dt 20:17; Jdg 3:5). Conquered by Joshua (Jos 9:1; 12:8; 24:11). Pay tribute to Solomon (1Ki 9:21; 2Ch 8:8).

HIZKI (*Yahweh is [my] strength*, or *my strength*). A Benjamite (1Ch 8:17).

HIZKIAH (*Yahweh is [my] strength*).
1. A son of Neariah (1Ch 3:23).
2. *See Hezekiah, 3.*

HIZKIJAH *See Hezekiah, 2.*

HOBAB (*beloved*, possibly *deceit*). Brother-in-law of Moses (Nu 10:29; Jdg 4:11).

HOBAH A place N of Damascus (Ge 14:15).

HOBAIAH (*Yahweh has hidden*). Priest whose descendants were excluded from priesthood (Ezr 2:61; Ne 7:63).

HOD (*grandeur*). A son of Zophah (1Ch 7:37).

HODAVIAH (*give thanks to Yahweh*).
1. Chief in Manasseh (1Ch 5:24).
2. Benjamite (1Ch 9:7).
3. Levite whose descendants returned with Zerubbabel (Ezr 2:40; 3:9; Ne 7:43).
4. Son of Elioenai (1Ch 3:24).

HODESH (*new moon*). Wife of Shaharaim (1Ch 8:9).

HODEVAH *See Hodaviah, 3.*

HODIAH (*grandeur is Yahweh*).
1. Wife of Ezra (1Ch 4:19).
2. A Levite (Ne 8:7; 9:5; 10:10, 13).
3. An Israelite chief (Ne 10:18).

HODSHI *See Tahtim Hodshi.*

HOGLAH (*partridge*). A daughter of Zelophehad (Nu 26:33; 27:1; 36:11; Jos 17:3).

HOHAM Amorite king who entered a league against Joshua (Jos 10:3).

HOLIDAY (*a good day*). For rest. *See Sabbath.* One year in seven (Lev 25:2-7). *See Jubilee.*

HOLINESS

Defined:
Sin and holiness, sinful man and the holy Yahweh, are the dominant ideas in the Mosaic law. The supreme purpose of the system of Mosaic ordinances was to impress Israel as a separated people and through Israel to impress all people for all time that a holy God can be pleased by none but holy people. This is a central truth of the true religion. The student must, therefore, seek for this spiritual purpose through all the ordinances of the law. Defilement and uncleanness, exclusion of the unclean from the congregation atonements and atoning sacrifices, washings and purifications, whole burnt offerings, unblemished priests and unblemished offerings, typifying unblemished and uncorrupted motives in worship and service— all these were ordained as object lessons to teach that there is a difference between unholiness and holiness and thus to exalt holiness as the supreme lesson of life.
As in the books of the Mosaic law, so throughout the Holy Scriptures, the attainment of holiness is a dominant theme.

Attribute of God:
(Jos 24:19; 1Sa 6:20; Job 6:10; Ps 22:3; 47:8; 60:6; 89:35; 111:9; 145:17; Isa 5:16; 6:3; 29:19, 23; 41:14; 43:14-15; 47:4; 49:7; 57:15; Eze 36:21-22; 39:7, 25; Hos 11:9; Hab 1:12-13; Lk 1:49; Jn 17:11; Ro 1:23; Rev 4:8; 6:10; 15:4).

Described:
(Ro 14:17). As walking in uprightness (Isa 57:2). As a highway (Isa 35:8). As departing from evil (Ps 34:14; 37:27). As satisfying (Jn 6:35). As crucifying the sinful nature (Gal 5:24). As a new creature (Gal 6:15). As a new self (Eph 4:24; Col 3:10). As a rest (Heb 4:3, 9). As pure, peaceable, gentle (Jas 3:17).

Commanded:
(Ge 17:1; Ex 22:31; Lev 10:8-10; 11:44-45; 19:2; 20:7, 26; Nu 15:40; Dt 13:17; 18:13; Jos 7:13; 2Ch 20:21; Job 5:24; Ps 4:4; 97:10; Isa 52:1, 11; Mic 6:8; Zep 2:3; Mt 5:19-30, 48; 12:33; Jn 5:14; Ro 6:1-23; 1Co 3:16; 5:7; 15:34; 2Co 6:14-17; 7:1; Eph 1:4; 5:1, 3, 8-11; 1Th 4:3-4, 7; 5:22-23; 2Th 2:13; 1Ti 4:12; 5:22; 6:11-12; 2Ti 2:19, 21-22; 1Pe 1:5; 2Pe 1:5-8; 1Jn 2:1, 5, 29; 2Jn 4; Rev 18:4).
Commanded upon Israel (Ex 19:6; 22:31; Dt 7:6; 26:19; 28:9; Isa 4:3; 52:1, 11; 60:1, 21; Zec 8:3; 14:20-21).
Commanded upon the church (2Co 11:2; 1Pe 2:5, 9; Rev 19:8).

Exhortations to:
(Mt 5:30; Jn 5:14; Ro 6:13, 19; 12:1-2; 13:12-14; 1Co 6:13, 19-20; 10:31; 2Co 13:7-8; Eph 4:22-24; Col 3:5, 12-15; 1Th 2:12; 3:13; 1Ti 4:12; Tit 2:9-10, 12; 1Pe 4:1; 2Pe 3:11-12, 14; 3Jn 11).

Motives to:
God's holiness (Ge 17:1; Lev 11:44-45; 19:2; 20:26; Isa 6:1-8; Mt 5:48; 1Pe 1:15-16). God's mercies (Ro 12:1).

Taught:
By figures (Isa 61:9-11; Mt 12:33; 1Co 3:17; Eph 2:21). By inscriptions (Ex 28:36; Zec 14:20).
By disfellowship: Of the uncircumcised (Ge 17:14). Of those who violated the law, of unleavened bread (Ex 12:15), of sacrifices (Lev 17:9; 19:5-7), of purification (Nu 19:20). Of those who were defiled (Lev 7:25, 27; 13:5, 21, 26; 17:10; 18:29; 19:8; 20:3-6; Nu 5:2-3; 19:13). Of those who were guilty of blasphemy (Nu 15:31).
As a condition of fellowship: (Heb 12:14).

Typified:
In unblemished offerings (Ex 12:5; Lev 1:3, 10; 3:1, 6; 4:3, 23; 5:15; 6:6; 9:2-3; 22:19, 21; Nu 28:3, 9, 11, 19, 31; 29:2, 8, 13, 17, 20, 23, 26, 29, 32, 36). In washing of offerings (Lev 1:9, 13). In washing of priests (Ex 29:4; Lev 8:6; 1Ch 15:14). In washing of garments (Lev 11:28, 40; 13:6, 34; 14:8-9, 47; 15:5-13; Nu 19:7-8, 10, 19, 21). In purifications (Lev 12:4, 6-8; 15:16-18, 21-22, 27; 16:4, 24, 26, 28; 17:15-16). By differentiating between clean and unclean animals (Lev 11:1-47; 20:25; Dt 14:3-20).
See God, Holiness of; Sanctification.

HOLM NIV "cypress" (Isa 44:14, RSV). *See Cypress Wood.*

HOLON (perhaps *sandy*).
1. Levitical city in hill country of Judah (Jos 15:51), called Hilen (1Ch 6:58).
2. Moabite town (Jer 48:21).

HOLY *See Holiness; Sanctification.*

HOLY DAY *See Holiday.*

HOLY GHOST *See Holy Spirit.*

HOLY OF HOLIES Most holy place, in the tabernacle (Lev 4:6), in the temple (1Ki 6:16). Separated from the holy place by the veil (Ex 26:33; Heb 9:3). Contained atonement cover and ark of the testimony (Ex 26:34; 40:20-21; 1Ki 8:6), the cherubim (Ex 25:18-20; 26:34; 37:7-9; Heb 9:3-5).
Divine dwelling place (Ex 25:8, 21-22; 26:34; Lev 16:2). Entered by the high priest on the Day of Atonement (Ex 26:34; Lev 16:12-13; Heb 9:6-7). Atonement made for (Ex 26:34; Lev 16:15-17, 33).
See Holy Place; Tabernacle.

HOLY PLACE In the tabernacle and the temple. Separated from the most holy place by the veil (Ex 26:33).
Contents of: Altar of incense (Ex 30:1-6; 40:5, 26), the table of the bread of the Presence (Ex 40:4, 24; Heb 9:2), the lampstand (Ex 26:35; 40:4, 24; Heb 9:2). *See various items by name.*
Priests, ministered in (Ex 29:30; 39:1, 41; Heb 9:6), required to eat sin offering in (Lev 6:25-26; 10:17).
See Sanctuary; Tabernacle; Temple.

HOLY SPIRIT (Ge 1:2; Ps 51:11; Mt 1:18, 20; Gal 3:2-3, 14; 6:8; Col 1:8; Heb 6:4).

Activities:
Convinces of sin (Ge 6:3; Jn 16:8-11). Comforts (Jn 14:16-17, 26; 15:26; 16:7-14; Ac 9:31). Guides (Jn 16:13; Ac 13:2-4; 15:8, 28; 16:6-7; Ro 8:4, 14; Gal 5:16, 18, 25). Helps our infirmities (Ro 8:26). Regenerates (Jn 3:5-6; 2Co 3:3, 18; Tit 3:5-6). Sanctifies (Ro 15:16; 1Co 6:11; 2Th 2:13; 1Pe 1:2). Dwells in believers (Ro 8:11). Invites to salvation (Rev 22:17). Communion with (2Co 13:14; Php 2:1).
Given to every Christian (1Co 12:7). Given in answer to prayer (Lk 11:13; Ac 8:15), through laying on of hands (Ac 8:17-19; 19:6).
Access to the Father by (Eph 2:18). Prayer in (Eph 6:18; Jude 20). Wisdom and strength from (Ne 9:20; Zec 4:6; Eph 3:16). Liberty from (2Co 3:17). Love of God given by (Ro 5:5).
Ministers commissioned by (Ac 20:28). Christian baptism in the name of, with the name of Father and son (Mt 28:19). Gospel preached in power of (1Co 2:4, 10; 1Th 1:5; 1Pe 1:12). Word of God, sword of (Eph 6:17). Water, a symbol of (Jn 7:38-39). Demons cast out by (Mt 12:28). Power to bestow, not for sale (Ac 8:18-20).
Poured Upon: Israel (Isa 32:15; Eze 39:29). The Gentiles (Ac 10:19-20, 44-47; 11:15-16). All people (Joel 2:28-29; Ac 2:17).

Jesus and the Spirit:
Immaculate conception of Jesus by (Mt 1:20; Lk 1:35). Jesus anointed and led by (Isa 61:1; Mt 3:16; 4:1; Mk 1:10; Lk 3:22; 4:18; Jn 1:32-33; Ac 10:38; Heb 9:14). Sent in Jesus' name (Jn 14:15-17; 15:26).

Christians:
Are temples of (1Co 3:16; 6:19). Are filled with (Ac 2:4, 33; 4:8, 31; 6:5; 8:17; 11:24; 13:9, 52; Eph 5:18; 2Ti 1:14). Have fellowship with (Ro 8:9, 11; 1Co 3:16; 6:19; 2Co 13:14; Php 2:1). Receive deposit of (2Co 1:22; 5:5; Eph 1:13-14). Are sealed with (2Co 1:22; Eph 1:13; 4:30). Have righteousness, peace, and joy in (Ro 14:17; 15:13; 1Th 1:6). Are unified by (1Co 12:13). Testify that Jesus is Lord by (Jn 15:26; 16:14; 1Co 12:3).

Baptism of:
(Mt 3:11; Mk 1:8; Lk 3:16; Jn 1:33; 20:22; Ac 1:5; 11:16; 19:2-6; 1Jn 2:20, 27).

Deity of: See Trinity, Holy.

Fruit of: (Ro 8:23; Gal 5:22-23).

Gifts of:
Foretold (Isa 44:3; Joel 2:28-29). Of different kinds (1Co 12:4-6, 8-10, 28). Bestowed for the confirmation of the gospel (Ro 15:19; Heb 2:4). *See Gifts From God.*

Inspiration of:
(Mt 10:20; Mk 13:11; Lk 12:12; 1Co 2:4, 10-14; 1Ti 4:1).

Instances of : Joseph (Ge 41:38). Bezalel (Ex 31:3; 35:31). The seventy elders (Nu 11:17). Balaam (Nu 24:2). Judges Othniel (Jdg 3:10), Gideon (Jdg 6:34), Jephthah (Jdg 11:29). King Saul (1Sa 11:6). King David (1Ch 28:11-12). The prophets (2Pe 1:21). Azariah (2Ch 15:1). Zechariah (2Ch 24:20).

Zechariah (Lk 1:67). Elizabeth (Lk 1:41). Simeon (Lk 2:25-26). John the Baptist (Lk 1:15). The disciples (Ac 6:3; 7:55; 8:29; 9:17; 10:45).

Intercession of: (Ro 8:26-27).

Power of:
Promised (Lk 24:49; Ac 1:8; 2:38). On Christ (Mt 12:28; Lk 4:14). On ministers (Ac 2:4; Ro 15:19). On the righteous (Ro 15:13; Eph 3:16).

Revelations from:
(Mk 12:36; Lk 2:26-27; Jn 16:13; 1Co 2:10-11; Eph 3:5; 1Ti 4:1; Heb 3:7; 2Pe 1:21; Rev 2:7, 11, 29; 14:13).

Sin Against:
(Ac 8:18-22; 1Jn 5:16). By grieving (Isa 63:10-11, 14; Eph 4:30). By resisting (Ac 5:9; 7:51; Eph 4:30; 1Th 5:19; Heb 10:29). By blaspheming (Mt 12:31-32; Mk 3:29; Lk 12:10). By lying to (Ac 5:3).

Withdrawn From Unrepentant Sinners:
(Ge 6:3; Dt 32:30; Jer 7:29; Hos 4:17-18; 9:12; Ro 1:24, 26, 28).

Instances of: Antediluvians (Ge 6:3-7). Israelites (Dt 1:42; 28:15-68; 31:17-18). Saul (1Sa 16:14; 18:12; 28:15-16; 2Sa 7:15).

Witness of:
(Ac 5:32; Ro 8:15-16; 9:1; 2Co 1:22; 5:5; Gal 4:6; Eph 1:13-14; Heb 10:15; 1Jn 3:24; 4:13; 5:6-8).

Emblems of:

Water—
(Jn 3:5; 7:38-39). Fertilizing (Ps 1:3; Isa 27:3; 44:3-4; 58:11). Refreshing (Ps 46:4; Isa 41:17-18). Freely given to those who are thirsty (Isa 55:1; Jn 4:14; Rev 22:17). Cleansing (Eze 16:9; 36:25; Eph 5:25-27; Heb 10:22). Abundant (Jn 7:37-38).

Fire—
As a guiding light as the Israelites traveled at night (Ex 13:21; Ps 78:14). Purifying (Isa 4:4; Mal 3:2-3). Searching (Zep 1:12, w 1Co 2:10).

Wind—
Powerful (1Ki 19:11, w Ac 2:2). Reviving (Eze 37:9-10, 14). Independent (Jn 3:8). The coming of the promised Holy Spirit at Pentecost (Ac 2:2).

Oil—
Consecrating (Isa 61:1). Comforting (Isa 61:3; Heb 1:9). Illuminating (Mt 25:3-4; 1Jn 2:20, 27). Healing (Lk 10:34; Jas 5:14).

Rain and Dew—
Blessing (Ps 133:3; Hos 14:5). Righteousness (Hos 10:12).

A Dove—
(Mt 3:16).

A Voice—
Guiding (Isa 30:21, w Jn 16:13). Speaking through the Twelve as they were to go out (Mt 10:20). Warning (Heb 3:7-11).

A Seal—
(Rev 7:2). Authenticating (Jn 6:27; 2Co 1:22). Securing (Eph 1:13-14; 4:30).

Tongues of Fire—
(Ac 2:3-4, 6-11).
See Titles and Names, Titles and Names of the Holy Spirit.

HOLY TRINITY *See God; Jesus the Christ; Holy Spirit; Trinity, Holy.*

HOMAGE Rendered, to Joseph (Ge 41:43), to kings (1Ki 1:16, 23, 31), to princes (Est 3:2, 5), to Mordecai (Est 6:11), to Daniel (Da 2:46). Refused, by Peter (Ac 10:25-26), by Paul and Barnabas (Ac 14:11-18), by the angel seen by John in his vision (Rev 10:10; 22:8-9).
See Worship.

HOMAM An Edomite and a son of Lotan (Hebrew *Hemam*, a variant of *Homam*) (Ge 36:22, ftn, 1Ch 1:39).

HOME *See Family.*

HOMELESS (Job 24:8; La 4:5; Lk 9:58; 1Co 4:11).

HOMER (*the load a donkey can carry*). A measure. *See Measure.*

HOMESTEAD Mortgaged (Ne 5:3). When alienable, and when inalienable (Lev 25:25-34). *See Land.*

HOMICIDE

Accidental:
(Ex 21:13; Nu 35:11-15, 22-28, 32; Dt 4:41-43; 19:1-10; Jos 20:1-9). *See Cities of Refuge.*

Murder:
(Job 24:14; Ps 10:8; 38:12; 94:3, 6; Pr 12:6; 28:17; Isa 59:3; Jer 2:34; 7:9-10; 19:4; Eze 22:9; Hos 4:1-3; Hab 2:10, 12). God's abhorrence of (Ps 5:6; 9:12; Pr 6:16-17).

Forbidden (Ex 20:13; Dt 5:17; Pr 1:15-16; Jer 22:3; Mt 5:21; 19:18; Mk 10:19; Lk 18:20; Ro 13:9; 1Ti 1:9; Jas 2:11; 1Pe 4:15; 1Jn 3:12, 15).

Through conspiracy (Ps 37:32; Pr 1:11-12). In hearts of the wicked (Mt 15:19; Mk 7:21). Impenitence for (Rev 9:21). Penitence for (Ps 51:1-17). Inquest over suspected (Dt 21:1-9).

Instances of:
Cain (Ge 4:8). Lamech (Ge 4:23-24). Simeon and Levi (Ge 34:25-31). Pharaoh (Ex 1:16, 22). Moses (Ex 2:12). Ehud (Jdg 3:16-23). Abimelech (Jdg 9:5, 18, 56). Joab (2Sa 3:24-27; 20:9-10; 1Ki 2:5). Solomon (1Ki 2:23-46). Recab and Baanah (2Sa 4:5-8). David (2Sa 11:14-17; 12:9). Absalom (2Sa 13:22-29). Baasha (1Ki 15:27-29). Zimri (1Ki 16:9-11). Ahab and Jezebel (1Ki 21:1024). Hazael (2Ki 8:15). Jehu (2Ki 9:24-37). Athaliah (2Ki 11:1). Of Joash by his servants (2Ki 12:20-21). Menahem (2Ki 15:16). Of Sennacherib, by his sons (2Ki 19:37; Isa 37:38). Manasseh (2Ki 21:16; 24:4). Of Amon, by his servants (2Ki 21:23). Jehoram (2Ch 21:4). Joash (2Ch 24:21). Amaziah's soldiers (2Ch 25:12). Nebuchadnezzar (Jer 39:6). Ishmael (Jer 41:1-7).

Herod the Great (Mt 2:16). Herod the tetrarch (Mt 14:10; Mk 6:27). Barabbas (Mk 15:7; Ac 3:14).

Punishment for:
(Lev 24:17; Dt 19:11-13; Ps 55:23). By a curse (Ge 4:9-12; 49:7; Dt 27:24-25). By death (Ge 9:5-6; Ex 21:12, 14; Nu 35:16-21, 30-33; Dt 17:6; 1Ki 21:19; Eze 35:6; Hos 1:4). By everlasting punishment (Rev 21:8; 22:15).

Instances Of Punishment For—
Cain (Ge 4:11-15). The murderer of Saul (2Sa 1:15-16). David (2Sa 12:9-18). Joab (1Ki 2:31-34). Haman (Est 7:10). The murderers of Ish-Bosheth (2Sa 4:11-12), of Joash (2Ki 14:5).

HOMOSEXUAL Sexual activity between members of the same sex is universally condemned in Scripture. Male homosexuality forbidden by law and punished by death (Lev 18:22; 20:13). Male and female homosexuality condemned (Ro 1:26). With other sexually immoral persons excluded from the kingdom of God (1Co 6:9-11). Male shrine prostitution was practiced even in the temple (1Ki 14:24; 15:12; 2Ki 23:7). Male prostitutes also translates the derogatory term "dog" (Dt 23:17-18; possibly Rev 22:15). *See Dog.*

Instances of: the men of Sodom (Ge 19:4-5; Jude 7) and Gibeah (Jdg 19:22).

HONESTY

General:
Prayer of (Ps 7:3-4). Promises for (Ps 15:5; 24:4). Pleases God (Pr 11:1; 12:22). Proceeds from God (Pr 16:11; 20:10). Golden rule of (Mt 7:12; Lk 6:31).

Commanded:
(Lev 19:35-36; Dt 16:20; 25:13-16; Pr 4:25; Eze 45:10; Mk 10:19; Lk 3:12-13; Ro 13:13; Php 4:8; Col 3:22; 1Th 4:11-12; 1Ti 2:2; 1Pe 2:11-12).

Instances of:
Jacob, returning money placed in sacks (Ge 43:12). Samuel, incorruptible in his judicial duties (1Sa 12:3-5). Overseers of temple repairs, with whom no reckoning was kept (2Ki 12:15; 22:4-7). Treasurers of the temple (Ne 13:13).

Paul, in all his actions (Ac 24:16; 2Co 4:1-2; 7:2; 8:21). The writer of Hebrews (Heb 13:18).
See Integrity; Righteousness; Dishonesty.

HONEY (Ex 16:31; 2Sa 17:29; Pr 25:27; SS 4:11; Isa 7:15; Mt 3:4). Not to be offered with sacrifices (Lev 2:11). Found in rocks (Dt 32:13; Ps 81:16), upon the ground (1Sa 14:25). Samson's riddle concerning (Jdg 14:14). Sent as a present by Jacob to Egypt (Ge 43:11). Plentiful in Israel (Ex 3:8; Lev 20:24; Dt 8:8; Eze 20:6), in Assyria (2Ki 18:32). An article of merchandise from Israel (Eze 27:17).

HOOD NIV "tiaras" (Isa 3:23). *See Crown.*

HOOF Parting of, one of the physical marks used for distinguishing clean and unclean animals (Lev 11:3-8; Dt 14:3-8).

HOOKS For tabernacle, made of gold (Ex 26:32, 37; 36:36), silver (Ex 27:10; 38:10-12, 17, 19). In the temple, seen in Ezekiel's vision (Eze 40:43). Used for catching fish (Eze 29:4). For pruning (Isa 2:4; 18:5; Joel 3:10). *See Meat Forks.*

Figurative: (Ex 38:4).

HOOPOE A bird forbidden as food (Lev 11:19; Dt 14:18). *See Birds.*

HOPE

Godly:
In God (Ps 31:24; 33:22; 38:15; 39:7; 43:5; 71:5, 14; 78:7; 130:7; 146:5; Jer 17:7; La 3:21, 24, 26; 1Pe 1:21). A helmet (1Th 5:8). An anchor (Heb 6:18-19). Joy in (Pr 10:28; Ro 5:2; 12:12; Heb 3:6).

Of God's calling (Eph 1:18; 4:4). Of eternal life (Col 1:5-6, 23, 27; Tit 1:2; 2:13; 3:7; 1Pe 1:3, 13; 1Jn 3:3). Of the resurrection (Ac 23:6; 24:14-15; 26:6-7; 28:20). Deferred (Pr 13:12).

Of wicked shall perish (Job 8:13; 11:20; 27:8; Pr 10:28; 11:7, 23).

Grounds of:
God's Word (Ps 119:74, 81; Ro 15:4). God's mercy (Ps 33:18). Jesus Christ (1Th 1:3; 1Ti 1:1).

Instances of:
(Job 31:24, 28; Ps 9:18; 16:9; 119:116; Pr 14:32; 23:18, 22; 24:14; Hos 2:15; Zec 9:12; Ro 4:18; 5:3-5; 15:13; 1Co 13:13; 2Co 3:12; Gal 5:5; Eph 2:12; Php 1:20; 2Th 2:16; Heb 6:11; 1Pe 3:15).
See Faith.

HOPHNI (*tadpole*). Son of Eli (1Sa 1:3). Sin of (1Sa 2:12-36; 3:11-14). Death of (1Sa 4:4, 11, 17).

HOPHRA A pharoah who ruled Egypt from 589-570 B.C. (Jer 44:30).

HOR (perhaps *mountain*). Mountain on which Aaron died (Nu 20:22-29; 21:4; 33:38-39; 34:7-8; Dt 32:50).

HOR HAGGIDGAD (*cavern of the Gidgad*). Israelite encampment (Nu 33:32-33), called Gudgodah (Dt 10:7).

HORAM (*height* ISBE). King of Gezer (Jos 10:33).

HOREB (*dry, desolate*). A range of mountains of which Sinai is chief (Ex 3:1; 17:6; 33:6; Dt 1:2, 6, 19; 4:10, 15; 5:2; 9:8; 29:1; 1Ki 8:9; 19:8; 2Ch 5:10; Ps 106:19; Mal 4:4). *See Sinai, Mount of, Desert of.*

HOREM (*consecrated*). A fortification in Naphtali (Jos 19:38).

HORESH A stronghold in the Desert of Ziph (1Sa 23:15-19).

HORI (*cave-dweller*).
1. Son of Lotan (Ge 36:22, 30; 1Ch 1:39).
2. A Simeonite (Nu 13:5).

HORITE(S) People conquered by Kedorlaomer (Ge 14:6), may be the same as the Hivites (Ge 34:2; Jos 9:7), thought to be Hurrians, from highlands of Media.

HORMAH (*consecration*). A city SW of the Dead Sea (Nu 14:45; 21:1-3; Dt 1:44). Taken by Judah and Simeon (Jdg 1:17; Jos 12:14). Allotted to Simeon (Jos 19:4; 1Ch 4:30). Within the territory allotted to Judah (Jos 15:30; 1Sa 30:30).

HORN Used to hold the anointing oil (1Sa 16:1; 1Ki 1:39). Used for a trumpet. *See Trumpet.*

Figurative:
Of divine protection (2Sa 22:3). Of power (1Ki 22:11; Ps 89:24; 92:10; 132:17).

Symbolic:
(Da 7:7-24; 8:3-9, 20; Am 6:13, ftn.; Mic 4:13; Zec 1:18-21; Rev 5:6; 12:3; 13:1, 11; 17:3-16).

HORNET (*depression, discouragement*). A hornet or wasp (Ex 23:28; Dt 7:20; Jos 24:12).

HORON *See Beth Horon.*

HORONAIM (*twin hollows, twin caves*). A town of Moab (Isa 15:5; Jer 48:3, 5, 34).

HORONITE (*citizen of Horonaim*, or more probably *of Beth Horon*). Sanballat the Horonite, who opposed Nehemiah in the restoration of Jerusalem (Ne 2:10, 19; 13:28).

HORSE

Description of:
Great strength (Job 39:19-25), swifter than eagles (Jer 4:13), snorting and neighing of (Isa 5:28; Jer 8:16), a vain thing for safety (Ps 33:17; Pr 21:31).

Used by the Egyptians in war (Ex 14:9; 15:19), the Israelites (1Ki 22:4). Used for cavalry (2Ki 18:23; Jer 47:3; 51:21). Egypt famous for (Isa 31:1). Forbidden to kings of Israel (Dt 17:16). Hamstrung by Joshua (Jos 11:6, 9), David (2Sa 8:4). Israel reproved for keeping (Isa 2:7; 3:1; Eze 17:15; Hos 14:3). Exported from Egypt (1Ki 10:28-29; 2Ch 9:25, 28), from Babylon (Ezr 2:66; Ne 7:68). Bits for (Jas 3:3), bells for (Zec 14:20), harness for (Jer 46:4). Commerce in (Rev 18:13). *See above, Exported.* Dedicated to religious uses (2Ki 23:11).

Symbolic:
(Zec 1:8; Rev 6:2-8; 9:17; 19:11-21).

HORSE GATE One of the gates of Jerusalem (Ne 3:28-32; Jer 31:38-40).

HORSE LEECH *See Leech.*

HORTICULTURE Encouraged (Lev 19:23-25; Dt 20:19-20). *See Agriculture; Graft; Pruning.*

HOSAH (*refuge*).
1. A city of Asher (Jos 19:29).
2. A Levite (1Ch 16:38; 26:10-11).

HOSANNA (*save now*). Originally a prayer, "O LORD, save us" (Ps 118:25), chanted when Jesus entered Jerusalem (Mt 21:9-15; Mk 11:9-10; Jn 12:13).

HOSEA (*salvation*).

Author: Hosea son of Beeri

Date: About the middle of the eighth century B.C.

Outline:
I. Superscription (1:1).
II. The Unfaithful Wife and the Faithful Husband (1:2-3:5).
   A. The Children as Signs (1:2-2:1).
   B. The Unfaithful Wife (2:2-23).
      1. The Lord's judgment of Israel (2:2-13).
      2. The Lord's restoration of Israel (2:14-23).
   C. The Faithful Husband (ch. 3).
III. The Unfaithful Nation and the Faithful God (chs. 4-14).
   A. Israel's Unfaithfulness (4:1-6:3).
      1. The general charge (4:1-3).
      2. The cause declared and the results described (4:4-19).
      3. A special message to the people and leaders (ch. 5).
      4. A sorrowful plea (6:1-3).
   B. Israel's Punishment (6:4-10:15).
      1. The case stated (6:4-7:16).
      2. The judgment pronounced (chs. 8-9).

3. Summary and appeal (ch. 10).
C. The Lord's Faithful Love (chs. 11-14).
1. The Lord's fatherly love (11:1-11).
2. Israel's punishment for unfaithfulness (11:12-13:16).
3. Israel's restoration after repentance (ch. 14).
See Prophets, The Minor.

HOSHAIAH (*Yahweh has saved*).
1. One of the returned exiles (Ne 12:32).
2. A distinguished Israelite captive (Jer 42:1; 43:2).

HOSHAMA (*Yahweh has heard*). Son of Jehoiachin, king of Judah (1Ch 3:18).

HOSHEA (*salvation*).
1. The original name of Joshua (Nu 13:8, 16; Dt 32:44). *See Joshua.*
2. A chief of Ephraim (1Ch 27:20).
3. King of Israel. Assassinates Pekah and usurps the throne (2Ki 15:30). Evil reign of (2Ki 17:1-2). Becomes subject to Assyria (2Ki 17:3). Conspires against Assyria and is imprisoned (2Ki 17:4). Last king of Israel (2Ki 17:6; 18:9-12; Hos 10:3, 7).
4. A Jewish exile (Ne 10:23).

HOSPITALITY Unselfish (Lk 14:12-14). Deceitful guise of (Pr 9:1-5; 23:6-8). Parable of (Mt 22:2-10).

Commanded:
(Isa 58:6-7; Mt 25:34-39; Ro 12:13; 1Ti 3:2; 5:10; Tit 1:7-8; Heb 13:2; 1Pe 4:9-11; 3Jn 5-8). Toward strangers (Ex 22:11; 23:9; Lev 19:10, 33-34; 24:22; Dt 10:18-19; 26:12-13; 27:19).

Instances of:
Pharaoh to Abraham (Ge 12:16). Melchizedek to Abraham (Ge 14:18). Abraham to angels (Ge 18:1-8). Lot to an angel (Ge 19:1-11). Abimelech to Abraham (Ge 20:14-15). Hittites, to Abraham (Ge 23:3, ftn, 6, 11). Laban, to Abraham's servant (Ge 24:31-33), to Jacob (Ge 29:13-14). Isaac to Abimelech (Ge 26:30). Joseph to his brothers (Ge 43:31-34). Pharaoh to Jacob (Ge 45:16-20; 47:7-12). Jethro to Moses (Ex 2:20). Rahab to the spies (Jos 2:1-16). Man of Gibeah to the Levite (Jdg 19:16-21). Pharaoh to Hadad (1Ki 11:17, 22). Jeroboam to the prophet of Judah (1Ki 13:7). The widow of Zarephath to Elijah (1Ki 17:10-24). The Shunammite to Elisha (2Ki 4:8). Elisha to the Syrian spies (2Ki 6:22). Job to strangers (Job 31:32). David to Mephibosheth (2Sa 9:7-13). King of Babylon to Jehoiachin (2Ki 25:29-30). Nehemiah to rulers and Jews (Ne 5:17-19).
Martha to Jesus (Lk 10:38; Jn 12:1-2). Pharisees to Jesus (Lk 11:37-38). Zacchaeus to Jesus (Lk 19:1-10). Disciples to Jesus (Lk 24:29). The tanner to Peter (Ac 10:6, 23). Lydia to Paul and Silas (Ac 16:15). Barbarians to Paul (Ac 28:2). Publius to Paul (Ac 28:7). Phoebe to Paul (Ro 16:2). Onesiphorus to Paul (2Ti 1:16). Gaius (3Jn 5, 8).

Rewarded:
Rahab (Jos 6:17, 22-25). Widow of Zarephath (1Ki 17:10-24).
See Feasts; Guest; Inhospitableness; Strangers.

HOST (*army*). Army (Ge 21:22), angels (Ps 103:21; Jos 5:14). Heavenly bodies (Dt 4:19), creation (Ge 2:1). LORD of hosts (1Sa 17:45). *See Almighty; God, Names of, Yahweh Tsabbaoth..* One who shows hospitality (Ro 16:23; Lk 10:35). *See Hospitality.*

HOSTAGES (2Ki 14:14; 2Ch 25:24).

HOSTILITY To the Righteous (Mic 7:6; Mt 10:21, 35-36; Mk 13:12; Lk 12:53).

HOT SPRINGS (Ge 36:24).

HOTHAM (*signet ring, seal*).
1. Son of Heber an Asherite (1Ch 7:32).
2. An Aroerite and father of two of David's mighty men (1Ch 11:44).

HOTHAN *See Hotham, 2.*

HOTHIR (*one who remains*). Son of Heman (1Ch 25:4, 28).

HOUGHING *See Hamstring.*

HOURS A division of time. Twelve, in the day (Jn 11:9; Mt 20:3-12; 27:45-46), in the night (Ac 23:23).
Symbolic (Rev 8:1; 9:15).

HOUSE Built of stone (Lev 14:40-45; Isa 9:10; Am 5:11), brick (Ge 11:3; Ex 1:11-14; Isa 9:10), wood (SS 1:17; Isa 9:10). Built into city walls (Jos 2:15).
Used for worship (Ac 1:13-14; 12:12; Ro 16:5; 1Co 16:19; Col 4:15; Phm 2).
"A man's castle" (Dt 24:10-11).

Architecture of:
Foundations of stone (1Ki 5:17; 7:9; Ezr 6:3; Jer 51:26). Figurative (Ps 87:1; Isa 28:16; 48:13; Ro 15:20; 1Co 3:11; Eph 2:20; 1Ti 6:19; Heb 6:1; Rev 21:14). Cornerstone (Job 38:6; Ps 144:12). Figurative (Ps 118:22; Isa 28:16; Eph 2:20; 1Pe 2:6).
Porches (Jdg 3:23; 1Ki 7:6-7), courts (Est 1:5), summer apartment (Jdg 3:20, w Am 3:15; 1Ki 17:19), inner chamber (1Ki 22:25), chambers (Ge 43:30; 2Sa 18:33; 2Ki 1:2; 4:10; Ac 1:13; 9:37; 20:8), guest chamber (Mk 14:14), pillars (Pr 9:1), with courts (Ne 8:16), lattice (Jdg 5:28), windows (Jdg 5:28; Pr 7:6), walls plastered (Da 5:5), hinges (Pr 26:14).
Roofs, flat (Jos 2:6; Jdg 16:27; 1Sa 9:25; 2Sa 11:2; 16:22; Isa 15:3; 22:1; Mt 24:17; Lk 12:3), battlements required in Mosaic law (Dt 22:8). Prayer on (Ac 10:9). Altars on (2Ki 23:12; Jer 19:13; 32:29; Zep 1:5). Booths on (Ne 8:16), used as place to sleep (Jos 2:8; Ac 10:9), as dwelling place (Pr 21:9; 25:24).
Painted (Jer 22:14; Eze 8:10, 12). Windows of (Hos 13:3). Laws regarding sale of (Lev 25:29-33; Ne 5:3). Dedicated (Dt 20:5; Ps 30 [title]).

Figurative:
(2Sa 7:18; Ps 23:6; 36:8; Jn 14:2; 2Co 5:1; 1Ti 3:15; Heb 3:2).

HOUSE OF GOD A place of prayer (Mt 21:13; Mk 11:17; Lk 19:46). Holy (Ecc 5:1; Isa 62:9; Eze 43:12; 1Co 3:17).
See Synagogue; Tabernacle; Temple.

HOUSEHOLD GODS Used by Laban, stolen by Rachel (Ge 31:19, 30-35), by Micah, stolen by the Danites (Jdg 17:5; 18:14, 17-20). Condemned and disposed of by Jacob (Ge 35:2-4, w Ge 31:35-39). Destroyed by Josiah (2Ki 23:24). *See Idol.*

HOUSETOPS As places of resort (Jos 2:6; 1Sa 9:25; Ne 8:16; Pr 21:9; Mt 10:27; 24:17; Lk 5:19; Ac 10:9).

HUBBAH (*God has hidden [someone from danger]*). An Asherite (1Ch 7:34).

HUKKOK A place on the boundary line of Naphtali (Jos 19:34).

HUKOK The name of a Levitical city in Asher (1Ch 6:75), a variant spelling of Helkath (Jos 31:21). *See Helkath.*

HUL Son of Aram (Ge 10:23; 1Ch 1:17).

HULDAH (*weasel*). A prophetess. Foretells the destruction of Jerusalem (2Ki 22:14-20; 2Ch 34:22-28).

HUMAN SACRIFICE *See Offerings, Human Sacrifices.*

HUMILIATION AND SELF-AFFLICTION
Commanded (Lev 16:29-31; 23:26-32; Ezr 8:21-23; 2Ch 7:14). *See Fasting; Humility.*

HUMILITY (Ps 51:17; 69:32; 138:6; Pr 3:34; 11:2; 12:15; 16:19; Isa 57:15; 66:2; Lk 10:21; 2Co 7:6; Gal 6:14; Jas 4:6).

Commanded:
(Dt 15:15; Pr 25:6-7a; 27:2; 30:32; Ecc 5:2; Jer 45:5; Mic 6:8; Mt 18:2-4; 20:26-27; Mk 9:33-37; 10:43-44; Lk 9:46-48; 14:10; 17:10; 22:24-27; Jn 13:14-16; Ro 11:18-20, 25; 12:3, 10, 16; 1Co 3:18; 4:6; 10:12; Gal 5:26; Eph 4:1-2; 5:21; Php 2:3-11; Col 3:12; Jas 1:9-10; 4:10; 1Pe 5:3, 5-6).
Feigned, forbidden (Col 2:18-23).

Rewards of:
(Job 5:11; 22:29; Ps 138:6; Pr 15:33; 18:12; 22:4; 29:23; Mt 5:3; 23:12; Lk 1:52; 14:11; 18:13-14).

Exemplified in:
Abraham (Ge 18:27, 32). Jacob (Ge 32:10). Joseph (Ge 41:16). Moses (Ex 3:11; 4:10). David (1Sa 18:18-23; 23:14; 26:20; 2Sa 7:18-20; 1Ch 17:16-18; 29:14). The Psalmist (Ps 8:3-4; 73:22; 131:1-2; 141:5; 144:3). Solomon (1Ki 3:7; 2Ch 1:10; 2:6). Mephibosheth (2Sa 9:8). Ahab (1Ki 21:29). kings and princes of Israel (2Ch 12:6-7, 12). Josiah (2Ki 22:18-19; 2Ch 34:26, 27). Job (Job 7:17-18; 9:14-15; 40:4-5; 42:2-6). Elihu (Job 32:4-7; 33:6). Ezra (Ezr 9:13, 15). Agur (Pr 30:2-3). Isaiah (Isa 6:5). Hezekiah (Isa 38:15). Jeremiah (Jer 1:6; 10:23-24). Daniel (Da 2:30). Ezra and the Jews (Ezr 8:21, 23).
Elizabeth (Lk 1:43). John the Baptist (Mt 3:14; Mk 1:7; Lk 3:16; Jn 1:27; 3:29-30). Jesus (Mt 11:29; 13:4-16). Woman of Canaan (Mt 15:27). The righteous (Mt 25:37-40). The tax collector (Lk 18:13). Centurion (Mt 8:8; Lk 7:6-7). Peter (Ac 2:12). Paul (Ac 20:19; Ro 7:18; 1Co 2:1-3; 15:9-10; 2Co 3:5; 11:30; 12:5-12; Eph 3:8; Php 3:12-13; 4:12; 1Ti 1:15).

HUMTAH (*an [unclean] reptile*). A city of Judah (Jos 15:54).

HUNGER

General:
"Man does not live on bread alone" (Dt 8:3; Mt 4:4; Lk 4:3). Labor excites (Pr 16:26). Source of temptation (Ge 25:29-34; Ex 16:2-3; Heb 12:16). An occasion of the temptation of Jesus (Mt 4:3-4; Lk 4:2-3). Of an enemy, an opportunity for good works (Pr 25:21-22; Ro 12:20).
Experienced by Jesus (Mt 21:18; Mk 11:12). Endured, by Jesus during his temptation (Mt 4:2-4; Lk 4:2-4), by Paul for Christ's sake (1Co 4:11). Foretold as a judgment upon the Israelites (Isa 8:21; 9:20).

Figurative:
Of spiritual desire (Ps 107:9; Pr 2:3-5; Isa 55:1-2; Am 8:11-13; Mt 5:6; Lk 1:53; 6:21; Jn 6:35; 1Pe 2:2).
See Appetite; Famine; Desire, Spiritual; Thirst.

HUNTING Authorized in the Mosaic law (Lev 17:13). By Nimrod (Ge 10:9). By Esau (Ge 27:3, 5, 30, 33). By Ishmael (Ge 21:20). Of lion (Job 10:16). Fowling (1Sa 26:20; Ps 140:5; 141:9-10; Pr 1:17; Ecc 9:12; La 3:52; Am 3:5).
Figurative: (Jer 16:16).

HUPHAM, HUPHAMITE Son of Benjamin and his clan (Nu 26:39).

HUPPAH (*canopy*, hence *protection*). Priest in David's time (1Ch 24:13).

HUPPIM, HUPPITES (*coast people*). Descendants of Benjamin (Ge 46:21; 1Ch 7:12, 15).

HUR (perhaps *child*).
1. An Israelite who assisted in supporting Moses' hands during battle (Ex 17:10, 12; 24:14).
2. A son of Caleb (Ex 31:2; 35:30; 38:22; 1Ch 2:19-20; 2Ch 1:5).
3. A king of Midian (Nu 31:8; Jos 13:21).
4. Called Ben-Hur, an officer of Solomon's commissary (1Ki 4:8).
5. Father of Caleb (1Ch 2:50; 4:4).
6. A son of Judah (1Ch 4:1).
7. A ruler (Ne 3:9).

HURAI One of David's heroes (1Ch 11:32). Also called Hiddai (2Sa 23:30).

HURAM, HURAM-ABI (*brother of the exalted one*).
1. Benjamite (1Ch 8:5).
2. King of Tyre (2Ch 2:3, ftn, 11-12). Usually called Hiram (Hebrew *Huram*, a variant of *Hiram*). *See Hiram.*
3. Tyrian craftsman whose full name is Huram-Abi, is sent by King Hiram to execute the artistic work of the interior of the temple (1Ki 7:13-45; 2Ch 2:13; 4:11-16).

HURI (*linen weaver* ISBE). Father of Abihail (1Ch 5:14).

HURRIANS *See Horite(s), Horim.*

HUSBAND

Relation to His Wife:
In general (Ge 2:23-24; Mt 19:5-6; Mk 10:7; 1Co 7:3-5). Love for (Eph 5:22-33; Col 3:19). Headship of (1Co 11:3). Chastity of (Pr 5:15-20; Mal 2:14-16). Rights of (1Co 7:3, 5). Sanctified in the wife (1Co 7:14, 16).
May give wife certificate of divorce (Dt 24:1-4). Law relating to, in cases where wife's virtue is questioned (Nu 5:11-31; Dt 22:13-21). Exemptions for (Dt 24:5).
Duties of (Ecc 9:9; Col 3:19; 1Pe 3:7). Family provider (Ge 30:30; 1Ti 5:8).

Examples:
Faithful: Isaac (Ge 24:67), Joseph (Mt 1:19-20). Unreasonable and oppressive (Est 1:10-22).

Figurative:
(Isa 54:5-6; Jer 3:14; 31:32; Hos 2:19-20).
See Family; Marriage.

HUSBANDMAN *See Agriculture; Farmer.*

HUSBANDRY *See Agriculture; Animals; Farmer.*

HUSHAH (perhaps *haste*). Son of Ezer (1Ch 4:4). Probably called Shuah (1Ch 4:11).

HUSHAI An Arkite. A counselor of David who overthrew counsels of Ahithophel (2Sa 15:32, 37; 16:16-18; 17:5-15; 1Ch 27:33).

HUSHAM A Temanite (Ge 36:34-35; 1Ch 1:45-46).

HUSHATHITE Family name of Sibbecai, one of David's heroes (2Sa 21:18; 1Ch 11:29; 20:4; 27:11).

HUSHIM
1. Son of Dan (Ge 46:23). Also called Shuham (Nu 26:42). *See Shuham, Shuhamite.*
2. Wife of Shaharaim (1Ch 8:8, 11).

HUSHITES Benjamites; descendants of Aher (1Ch 7:12).

HUSK The skin or heads of grain (Nu 6:4; 2Ki 4:42). *See Pods.*

HUZ Son of Nahor (Ge 22:21). *See Uz.*

HUZOTH *See Kiriath Huzoth.*

HYACINTH *See Colors, Figurative and Symbolic.*

HYBRIDIZING Forbidden (Lev 19:19).

HYENA A scavenging wild dog that roams the desert (Isa 13:22; 34:14; Jer 50:39). *See Animals.*

HYGIENE (1Co 6:18; 9:25). *See Sanitation and Hygiene.*

HYKSOS A W Semitic people who ruled an Egyptian empire embracing Syria and Palestine; the core of their rule over Egypt was from 1648-1540.

HYMENAEUS (*of [pagan god] Hymen*). Apostate Christian excommunicated by Paul (1Ti 1:19-20; 2Ti 2:16-18).

HYMN *See Psalms; Song.*

HYPOCRISY (*pretender, pretentious*).

Described:
(Job 31:33-34; Ps 5:6, 9; 52:4; 78:34-37; Isa 29:13; 32:5-6; 48:1-2; 58:2-5; Jer 12:2; 17:9; Eze 33:30-32; Hos 6:4; 10:1, 4; Zec 7:5-6; Mt 15:3-9; 21:28-32; Mk 7:5-13; 9:50; 14:34-35; Lk 18:11-12; Ro 9:6-7; 1Co 5:8; 13:1; 2Co 4:2; 1Jn 1:6, 10; 2:4, 9, 19; 4:20; Rev 3:1).
Betrays friends (Ps 55:12-14, 20-23; Pr 11:9; 25:19; Ob 7; Zec 13:6).
Hypocrisy of prostitutes (Pr 7:10-21), of false teachers (Mic 3:11; Ro 16:17-18; 2Pe 2:1-3, 17, 19), of dishonest buyers (Pr 20:14).

Condemned:
Abhorred by God (Job 13:16; Ps 50:16-17; Pr 15:8; 21:27; Isa 1:9-15; 9:17; 10:6; 58:2-5; 61:8; 65:2-5; 66:3-5; Jer 5:2; 6:20; 7:4, 8-10; Eze 5:11; 20:39; Hos 8:13; 9:4; 11:12; Am 5:21-27; Zec 7:5-6; Mal 1:6-14; 2:13).
Rebuked by Jesus (Mt 3:7-8; 7:7-8; 9:13; 15:7-9; 16:3; 23:2-33; Lk 6:46; 11:39, 42, 44; 12:54-56; 13:13-17; Jn 6:26, 70; 7:19; 15:2, 6; Rev 2:9; 3:9).
Exposed by Paul (Ro 2:1, 3, 17-29; 2Co 5:12; Gal 6:3; Php 3:2, 18-19; 1Ti 4:2; 2Ti 3:5, 13; Tit 1:16).
Warning to (Job 15:31, 33-34; 17:8; 20:4-5; 27:8-10; 34:30). Warning against (Pr 23:6-8; 26:18-19, 23-26; Jer 9:8; Mic 7:5; Mt 6:1-2, 5, 16, 24; 7:5, 15, 21-23; 16:6; 23:14; Mk 8:15; 12:38-40; Lk 12:1-2; 13:26-27; 16:13, 15; 20:46-47; Jas 1:8, 22-24, 26; 3:17; 4:8; 1Pe 2:1, 16; Jude 12-13).
Punishment for (Job 8:13-15; 36:13-14; Ps 55:23; 101:7; Isa 29:15-16; 33:14; 42:21-22; Eze 5:11; 14:3-4, 7-8; Hos 8:13; 9:4; Mt 22:12-13; 24:50-51; 25:41-45; Ro 1:18).
See Deceit; Deception.

Instances of:
Jacob, in impersonating Esau and deceiving his father (Ge 27). Jacob's sons, in deception of their father concerning Joseph (Ge 37:29-35). Joseph's deception of his brothers (Ge 42-44). Pharaoh (Ex 8:15, 28-29, 32; 9:27-35; 10:8-29). Balaam (Jude 11, w Nu

22-24). Delilah, the wife of Samson (Jdg 16). Jael (Jdg 4:8-21). Ehud (Jdg 3:15-25). The Assyrian field commander (2Ki 18:17-37). Ahaz (Isa 7:12, w 17-25). Johanan (Jer 42:1-12, 20, 22). Ishmael (Jer 41:6-7). The false prophets (Eze 13:1-23).

Herod (Mt 2:8). Judas (Mt 26:25, 48; Jn 12:5-6). Pilate (Mt 27:24). Pharisees (Mt 15:1-9; 22:18; Mk 12:13-14; Jn 8:4-9; 9:24; 19:15). The ruler (Lk 13:14-17). Spies sent to entrap Jesus (Lk 20:21). Priests and Levites (Lk 10:31-32). Chief priests (Jn 18:28). Ananias and Sapphira (Ac 5:1-10). Simon (Ac 8:18-23). Peter and others at Antioch (Gal 2:11-14). Judaizing Christians in Galatia (Gal 6:13). False teachers at Ephesus (Rev 2:2).

See Conspiracy; Treachery.

HYSSOP A plant indigenous to western Asia and northern Africa (1Ki 4:33).

Ceremonial Use:

The Israelites used, in sprinkling the blood of the Passover lamb upon the frames of their doors (Ex 12:22), in sprinkling blood in purifications (Lev 14:4, 6, 51-52; Heb 9:19). Used in the sacrifices of separation (Nu 19:6). Used in giving Jesus vinegar on the cross (Jn 19:29).

Figurative of spiritual cleansing (Ps 51:7).

I

I AM WHO I AM A name of God (Ex 3:14; Rev 1:4, 11, 17). *See God, Names of, Yahweh; Yahweh.*

IBEX Probably a species of antelope (Dt 14:5).

IBHAR (*he chooses*). Son of David (2Sa 5:15; 1Ch 3:6; 14:5).

IBLEAM A town given to the tribe of Manasseh (Jos 17:11). Ahaziah slain there (2Ki 9:27). Generally identified with Bileam (1Ch 6:70).

IBNEIAH (*Yahweh built*). A Benjamite (1Ch 9:8).

IBRI (*Hebrew*). A Levite (1Ch 24:27).

IBSAM (*fragrance*). Son of Tola (1Ch 7:2).

IBZAN (*swift*). The tenth judge of Israel (Jdg 12:8-10), had thirty sons and thirty daughters.

ICE (Job 6:16; 37:10; 38:29; Ps 147:17; Eze 1:22).

ICHABOD (*where is the glory?*). Son of Phinehas, Eli's son (1Sa 4:18-22).

ICONIUM A city of Asia Minor. Paul preaches in (Ac 13:51; 14:21-22; 16:2), is persecuted by the people of (Ac 14:1-6; 2Ti 3:11).

ICONOCLASM Idols to be destroyed (Ex 23:24; 34:13; Nu 33:52; Dt 7:5, 25-26; 12:1-4; Jdg 2:2; Jer 50:2). Destroyed by, Jacob (Ge 35:2-4), Moses (Ex 32:19-20), Gideon (Jdg 6:28-32), David (2Sa 5:21; 1Ch 14:12), Jehu (2Ki 10:26-28), Jehoiada (2Ki 11:18), Hezekiah (2Ki 18:3-6), Josiah (2Ki 23:4-20), Asa (2Ch 14:3-5; 15:8-16), Jehoshaphat (2Ch 17:6; 19:3), Jews (2Ch 30:14), Manasseh (2Ch 33:15).

See Idolatry.

IDALAH A town of Zebulun (Jos 19:15).

IDBASH (*honey*). A descendant of Judah (1Ch 4:3).

IDDO (probably *Yahweh has adorned*).

1. Father of Ahinadab (1Ki 4:14).
2. A descendant of Gershom (1Ch 6:21).
3. A son of Zechariah (1Ch 27:21).
4. A prophet (2Ch 9:29; 12:15; 13:22).
5. Ancestor of Zechariah (Ezr 5:1; 6:14; Zec 1:1, 7).
6. A priest (Ne 12:4, 16).
7. The chief of the Jews established at Casiphia (Ezr 8:17).

IDENTIFICATION With Jesus, price of (Mt 4:19; 8:22; 9:9; 16:24; 19:21; Mk 2:14; 8:34; 10:21; Lk 5:27; 9:23; 18:22; Jn 15:14, 18-19; 16:2). Indication of (Jn 10:27; 12:26; Ac 11:26). *See Discipleship.*

IDLENESS Comparisons regarding (Pr 15:19; 18:9; 22:13; 26:13-16; Ecc 4:5). Poverty from (Pr 6:6-11; 10:4-5; 12:9, 24, 27; 13:4; 14:23; 19:15; 20:4, 13; 23:21; 24:30-34; Ecc 10:18). Denounced (Pr 21:25-26; Isa 56:10; Lk 19:20-24; 2Th 3:10-11; 1Ti 5:13).

A sin of Sodom (Eze 16:49). Other instances of (Mt 20:6-7; Ac 17:21).

See Laziness; Slothfulness; Industry.

IDOL (*image*).

Manufacture of (Ex 20:4; 32:4, 20; Dt 4:23; Isa 40:19-20; 44:9-12, 17; Hab 2:18; Ac 19:24-25). Manufacture of forbidden (Ex 20:4; 34:17). Made of gold (Ex 32:3-4; Ps 115:4-7; 135:15-17; Isa 2:20; 30:22; 31:7; Hos 8:4), silver (Isa 2:20; 30:22; 31:7; Hos 8:4), wood and stone (Lev 26:1; Dt 4:28; 2Ki 19:18; Isa 37:19; 41:6; 44:13-19; Eze 20:32). Coverings of (Isa 30:22).

Prayer to, unanswered (1Ki 18:25-29). Falls down before the ark of Yahweh (1Sa 5:1-5). Used by Michal to save the life of David (1Sa 19:13-17). Derided (Ps 115:4-8; 135:15-18; Isa 44:9-17). To be abandoned (Isa 2:20). To be destroyed (Dt 12:3). Things offered to, not to be eaten (Ex 34:15). Paul's instructions concerning eating things offered to (1Co 8; 10:25-33).

See Iconoclasm; Idolatry.

IDOLATRY (*image*).

Wicked Practices of:

Human sacrifices (Lev 18:21; 20:2-5; Dt 12:31; 18:10; 2Ki 3:26-27; 16:3; 17:17-18; 21:6; 23:10; 2Ch 28:3; 33:6; Ps 106:37-38; Isa 57:5; Jer 7:31; 19:4-7; 32:35; Eze 16:20-21; 20:26, 31; 23:37, 39; Mic 6:7), practices of, relating to the dead (Dt 14:1), licentiousness of (Ex 32:6, 25; Nu 25:1-3; 1Ki 14:24; 15:12; 2Ki 17:30; 23:7; Eze 16:17; 23:1-44; Hos 4:12-14; Am 2:8; Mic 1:7; Ro 1:24, 26-27; 1Co 10:7-8; 1Pe 4:3-4; Rev 2:14, 20-22; 9:20-21; 14:8; 17:1-6).

Other Customs of:

Offered burnt offerings (Ex 32:6; 1Ki 18:26; Ac 14:13), libations (Isa 57:6; 65:11; Jer 7:18; 19:13; 32:29; 44:17, 19, 25; Eze 20:28), of wine (Dt 32:38), of blood (Ps 16:4; Zec 9:7), meat offerings (Isa 57:6; Jer 7:18; 44:17; Eze 16:19), peace offerings (Ex 32:6).

Incense burned on altars (1Ki 12:33; 2Ch 30:14; 34:25; Isa 65:3; Jer 1:16; 11:12, 17; 44:3; 48:35; Eze 16:18; 23:41; Hos 11:2). Prayers to idols (Jdg 10:14; Isa 44:17; 45:20; 46:7; Jnh 1:5). Praise (Jdg 16:24; Da 5:4).

Singing and dancing (Ex 32:18-19). Music (Da 3:5-7). Cutting the flesh (1Ki 18:28; Jer 41:5). Kissing (1Ki 19:18; Hos 13:2; Job 31:27). Bowing (1Ki 19:18; 2Ki 5:18). Tithes and gifts (2Ki 23:11; Da 11:38; Am 4:4-5).

Annual Feasts:

(1Ki 12:32; Eze 18:6, 11-12, 15; 22:9; Da 3:2-3).

Objects of:

Sun, moon, and stars (Dt 4:19; 2Ki 17:16; 21:3, 5; 2Ch 33:3, 5; Job 31:26-28; Jer 7:17-20; 8:2; Eze 8:15-16; Zep 1:4-5; Ac 7:42). Images of angels (Col 2:18), animals (Ro 1:23). Gods of Egypt (Ex 12:12). Golden calf (Ex 32:4). Bronze serpent (2Ki 18:4). Net and dragnet (Hab 1:16). Pictures (Nu 33:52; Isa 2:16). Pictures on walls (Eze 8:10). Earrings (Ge 35:4).

See Artemis; Shrine.

Folly of:

(Dt 4:28; 32:37-38; Jdg 6:31; 10:14; 1Sa 5:3-4; 12:21; 1Ki 18:25-29; 19:18; 2Ch 25:15; Ps 106:19-20; 115:4-5, 8; 135:15-18; Isa 37:19; 44:9-20; 45:20; 46:1-2, 6-7; Jer 2:28; 11:12; 16:19-20; 48:13; 51:17; Hos 8:5-6; Zec 10:2; Ac 14:13, 15; 17:22-23, 29; Ro 1:22-23; 1Co 8:4; 10:5; 12:2; Gal 4:8; Rev 9:20).

Illustrated by contrast of idols with the true God (Ps 96:5; Isa 40:12-26; 41:23-29; Jer 10:5; 14:22; Da 5:23; Hab 2:18-20). Exemplified in the ruin of Israel (2Ch 28:22-23).

Denounced:

(Dt 12:31; 27:15; Job 31:26-28; Ps 44:20-21; 97:7; Isa 42:17; 45:16; Jer 3:1-11; 32:34-35; Eze 16:16-63; 43:7-9; Hos 1:2; 2:2-5; 4:12-19; 5:1-3; 9:10; 13:2-3; Jnh 2:8; Am 4:4-5; Hab 1:16; Ac 17:16-29; Ro 1:25; 1Co 6:9-10).

Forbidden:

(Ge 35:2; Ex 20:3-6, 23; 23:13, 24, 32-33; 34:14, 17; Lev 19:4; 26:1, 30; Dt 4:15-28; 5:7-9; 7:2-5, 16; 11:16-17; 16:21-22; Ps 81:9; Eze 8:8-18; 14:1-8; 16:15-63; 20:7-8, 16, 18, 24, 27-32, 39; 23:7-49; Ac 15:20-29; 1Co 10:14, 20-22; 1Jn 5:21).

Prophecies Relating to:

(Isa 46:1-2). Its punishments (Nu 33:4; Dt 31:16-21, 29; Isa 21:9; Jer 51:44, 47, 52). Its end (Isa 2:8, 18, 20; 17:7-8; 27:9; Jer 10:11, 15; Hos 10:2; 14:8; Mic 5:13-14; Zep 2:11; Zec 13:2).

Punishment of:

(Dt 8:19; 11:28; 13:6-9; 17:2-5; 28:14-18; 30:17-18; 32:15-26; Jdg 2:3; 1Ki 9:6-9; Ne 9:27-37; Ps 16:4; 59:8; 78:58-64; 106:34-42; Isa 1:29-31; 2:6-22; 30:22; 65:3-7; Jer 1:15-16; 5:1-17; 7; 8:1-2, 19; 13:9-27; 16; 17:1-6; 18:13-17; 19; 22:5-9; 44; Eze 6; 8:8-18; 9; 14:1-8; 16:15-63; 20:7-8, 24-39; 22:4; 23:9-10, 22-49; 44:10-12; Hos 8:5-14; 10; 13:14; 5:5; Mic 1:1-9; 5:12-14; 6:16; Zep 1; Mal 2:11-13; Rev 21:8; 22:15).

See Groves; High Places; Iconoclasm; Idol; Prostitute.

IDUMEA (*[land of] Edom*). Greek and Roman name for Edom (Mk 3:8).

IEZER, IEZERITE (*my [father] is help*). Chief in the tribe of Manasseh (Nu 26:30). Also called Abiezer (Jos 17:2). *See Abiezer, 1.*

IFS OF THE BIBLE *See Blessings, Spiritual, Contingent Upon Obedience.*

IGAL (*he redeems*).

1. Spy of Issachar (Nu 13:7).
2. One of David's heroes (2Sa 23:36).
3. Descendant of Jehoiachin (1Ch 3:22).

IGDALIAH (*Yahweh is great*). Father of Hanan (Jer 35:4).

IGEAL (*he redeems*). Son of Shemaiah (1Ch 3:22).

IGNORANCE

Characteristic of Mankind:

(Job 8:9; 28:12-13, 20-21; Pr 8:5; 19:2; Ecc 7:23-24; Jer 10:23; Hos 4:14; Jn 13:7).

Concerning God (1Sa 3:7; Job 11:7-8, 12; 36:26, 29; 37:5, 15-16, 19, 23; Ps 139:6; Pr 30:3-4; Ac 17:23, 30), his works (Ecc 3:11; 8:17; 11:5), his wisdom (1Co 2:7-10).

Concerning the Holy Spirit (Ac 19:2).

Concerning the Scripture (Mt 22:29; Mk 12:24; Jn 20:9; 1Ti 1:7).

Concerning the future (Pr 27:1; Ecc 8:6-7; Ac 1:7; 1Co 13:9, 12).

Concerning snares of the wicked (Pr 7:6-23; 9:14-18; 22:3; 27:12).

Remedy for (Jas 1:5-6).

Sins of:

Sacrifices for: Unintentional sin by the anointed priest (Lev 4:1-12), by the whole community of Israel (Lev 4:13-21; Nu 15:22-26), by a leader (Lev 4:22-26), by a member of the community (Lev 4:27-35; 5:1-19; Nu 15:27-29; Eze 45:20).

Forgiven (1Ti 1:12-13; Heb 5:2). Forgiven on account of reparation (Ge 20:1-7).

Evil consequences of:

(Isa 5:13; Hos 4:6). Alienates from God (Eph 4:18-19). Darkens understanding (Lk 23:34; Jn 16:2-3; 1Co 2:8).

Punishment of:

(Eze 3:18; 33:6, 8; Lk 12:48). By fines (Lev 22:14).

Instances of: Pharaoh (Ge 12:11-17). Abimelech (Ge 20:1-18).

See Knowledge; Wisdom.

IIM (*heaps, ruins*).

1. For KJV Nu 33:45, *See Iyim.*
2. A town in the extreme S of Judah (Jos 15:29).

IJE-ABARIM *See Iye Abarim.*

IJON (*place of heaps [of stone]*). A town of Naphtali (1Ki 15:20; 2Ki 15:29; 2Ch 16:4).

IKKESH (*crooked, perverted*). Father of Iri (2Sa 23:26; 1Ch 11:28; 27:9).

ILAI One of David's heroes (1Ch 11:29), called Zalmon (2Sa 23:28).

ILLEGITIMATE Excluded from the assembly of the Lord to the tenth generation (Dt 23:2). Had no claim to paternal care or the usual privileges and discipline of legitimate children.

Instances of:

Ishmael (Ge 16:3, 15; Gal 4:22), Moab and Ammon (Ge 19:36-37), Jephthah (Jdg 11:1), David's child by Bathsheba (2Sa 11:2-5). Jesus slanderously accused of being (Jn 8:41).

Figurative: (Heb 12:8).

ILLYRICUM Also called Dalmatia. Visited, by Paul (Ro 15:19), by Titus (2Ti 4:10). Now part of Yugoslavia.

IMAGE

Manufactured Images: *See Idol; Idolatry.*

Figurative:

Mankind created in, of God (Ge 1:26-27; 5:1; 9:6; Jas 3:9). Regenerated into (Ps 17:15; Ro 8:29; 2Co 3:18; Eph 4:24; Col 3:10; 1Jn 3:1-3). Christ, of God (Col 1:15; Heb 1:3). *See Image of God.*

IMAGE, NEBUCHADNEZZAR'S Symbolic figure seen by Nebuchadnezzar in a dream, the meaning of which Daniel interpreted (Da 2).

IMAGE OF GOD Mankind is created in God's image (Ge 1:26-27; 5:1, 3; 9:6; 1Co 11:7; Eph 4:24; Col 3:10; Jas 3:9). The image is not corporeal but rational, spiritual, and social. The fall of man destroyed, but did not obliterate the image. Restoration of the image begins with regeneration.

IMAGE WORSHIP *See Idol.*

IMAGINATION Of mankind: Evil (Ge 6:5; 8:21; Dt 29:19-20; Pr 6:16-18). Vain (Ro 1:21). An abomination to God (Pr 6:16-18). Condemned, as equal to act (Mt 5:28).

Known by God (1Ch 28:9). To be subjected (2Co 10:3-5).

IMLAH (*fullness*). Father of Micaiah the prophet (1Ki 22:8-9; 2Ch 18:7-8).

IMMANENCE OF GOD *See Condescension of God.*

IMMANUEL (*God with us*). Isaiah foretold the birth of this child, a sign to Ahaz that God would come near in judgment (Isa 7:14-25). Isaiah's son is called Immanuel (Isa 8:8, 10) and might be the immediate fulfillment. The prophecy is applied to Jesus, whose name means "Yahweh is salvation." He is God come near to save (Mt 1:22-23). *See Jesus the Christ, Prophecies Concerning; Messianic Hope.*

IMMER (*lamb* KB).

1. A family of priests (1Ch 9:12; Ezr 2:37; 10:20; Ne 7:40; 11:13).
2. Head of a division of priests (1Ch 24:14).
3. Name of a man or town (Ezr 2:59; Ne 7:61).
4. Father of Zadok (Ne 3:29).
5. Father of Pashhur (Jer 20:1-2).

IMMORTALITY The biblical concept of immortality is not simply the survival of the soul after bodily death, but the self-conscious continuance of the whole person, body and soul together, in a state of blessedness, due to the redemption of Christ and the possession of "eternal life." The Bible nowhere attempts to prove this doctrine but everywhere assumes it as an undisputed postulate. The condition of believers in their state of immortality is not a bare endless existence but a communion with God in eternal satisfaction and blessedness.

Exemption from death and annihilation. *See Annihilation.*

Apparently Understood:

By David (2Sa 12:23; Ps 21:4; 22:26; 23:6; 37:18, 27; 86:12; 133:3; 145:1-2). By Nehemiah (Ne 9:5). By Job (Job 14:13). By the psalmists (Ps 49:7-9; 73:26; 121:8). By Moses (Ex 3:6; Mt 22:32; Mk 12:26-27; Lk 20:36-38; Ac 7:32). By Abraham (Heb 11:10).

Implied:

In the translation of Enoch (Ge 5:24; Heb 11:5). In the translation of Elijah (2Ki 2:11). In redemption from Sheol (Ps 16:10-11). In the spirit returning to God (Ecc 3:21; 12:7). In the soul surviving the death of the body (Mt 10:28). In the appearance of Moses and Elijah at the transfiguration of Jesus (Mt 17:2-9; Mk

9:2-10; Lk 9:29-36). In the abolition of death (Isa 25:8). In the Savior's promise to his disciples (Jn 14:2-3). In the resurrection (Isa 26:19; Da 12:2-3; Jn 6:40; 1Co 15:12-25; 1Th 4:13-18; 5:10). In eternal inheritance (Ac 20:32; 26:18; Heb 9:15; 1Pe 1:3-5). In the everlasting punishment of the wicked (2Th 1:7-9). In the Judgment (2Pe 3:7).

Taught:
By Christ (Mt 16:26; 19:16-17; 25:46; Mk 10:30; Lk 9:25; 10:25-28; Jn 3:14-16, 36; 5:39-40; 6:39-40, 44, 47, 50-58; 10:28; 11:25-26; 14:19; 17:2-3; Rev 3:4). By Paul (Ro 2:7; 6:22-23; 1Co 15:12-25; 2Co 5:1; Gal 6:8; Col 1:5-6; 2Th 2:16; 1Ti 4:8; 6:12, 19; 2Ti 1:9-10; Tit 1:2; 3:7). By John (1Jn 2:17, 25; 5:13; Rev 1:7; 22:5). By Jude (Jude 21). In Hebrews (Heb 9:15; 10:34; 11:5, 10, 13-16; 13:14).
See Eternal Life; Resurrection; Righteous, Promises to; Judgment; Wicked, Punishment of.

IMMUTABILITY (*not changeable*). The perfection of God by which he is devoid of all change in essence, attributes, consciousness, will, and promises (Mal 3:6; Ps 33:11; 102:26).

IMNA (possibly *he is withheld* BDB; *luck, fortune* IDB). Son of Helem (1Ch 7:35).

IMNAH, IMNITE (*good fortune*).
1. Firstborn of Asher (Ge 46:17; Nu 26:44; 1Ch 7:30).
2. A Levite (2Ch 31:14).

IMPENITENCE Leads to destruction (Mt 24:38-39, 48-51; Lk 13:3; 13:5; Rev 16:9-21).

Admonitions Against:
(Ps 95:8; Jer 6:16-19; 2Co 12:21; Heb 3:8; Rev 2:5, 16, 21-22; 3:3).

Judgments:
Denounced against (Lev 23:29; 26:22-43; Dt 29:19-21; 1Sa 15:23; Ps 7:11-13; 50:17, 21; 68:21; 81:11-12; 107:11-12; Pr 1:24-31; 11:3; 15:10, 32; 19:16; 28:13-14; 29:1; Eze 3:19, 26; 33:4-5, 9; Hos 7:13-14; Mt 11:16-21; 12:41-42; 13:15; 23:37-38; Lk 7:35; 10:13; 13:34; Ro 2:4-5).
Denounced against Israel's (Isa 65:12, 15; 66:4; Jer 12:11; 13:17, 27; 14:10; 15:6-7; 19:15; 26:4-6; Eze 3:19, 26; 20:8, 13, 21; Da 9:13; Zec 7:11-13; Mal 2:2).

Reason Given for Impenitence:
Evil company (Jer 2:25). Hypocrisy (Jer 3:10). Idolatry (Isa 46:12-13; Jer 44:17; Eze 20:8; Hos 4:17; 11:2, 7; Rev 9:20-21). Lack of understanding or spiritual blindness (Job 33:14; Ps 32:9; 82:5; Pr 26:11; Hos 5:4). Leniency (Ecc 8:11; Isa 26:10). Material abundance (Ps 52:1; Isa 32:9-11). Obstinacy (Isa 48:4, 8; Jer 8:5-7; Eze 2:4; Ac 7:51). Rebellion (Job 9:2, 4; 24:13; Ps 10:3; 50:7; 78:8; Pr 21:29; Isa 57:11; Jer 5:21-24; 6:10, 16-19; 44:10; Eze 2:4-5; 12:2; 22:8, 13, 21). Refusal to listen (Ps 58:3-5; 106:24-25; Isa 28:12; 42:22-25; Jer 6:16-19; 7:13-14, 24, 28; 11:8; 16:12; 17:23; 22:21; 25:4; 26:4-6; 29:19; 32:33; 35:14-17; 44:16-17; Eze 3:5-7; 20:8; Zec 1:4; 7:11-13; Mt 13:15; Lk 16:31). Seeming lack of hope (Jer 2:25; 18:12).

Instances of:
Pharaoh (Ex 9:30, 34; 10:27; 14:5-9). Israelites (Nu 14:22-23; 2Ki 17:14; 2Ch 24:19; 36:16-17; Ne 9:16-17, 29-30; Jer 36:31). Eli's sons (1Sa 2:25). Amaziah (2Ch 25:16). Manasseh (2Ch 33:10). Amon (2Ch 33:23). Zedekiah (2Ch 36:12-13; Jer 37:2). Jehoiakim and his servants (Jer 36:22-24). Belshazzar (Da 5:22-23). The rich young man (Mt 19:22). Jews who opposed Jesus (Mt 27:4, 25; Mk 3:5).
See Affliction, Of the Wicked; Backsliders; Blindness, Spiritual; Infidelity; Obduracy; Unbelief; Reprobates.

IMPORTS

Of Israel:
From Egypt: Horses, chariots, and linen (1Ki 10:28-29; 2Ch 1:16).
From Gilead: Spices, balm, and myrrh (Ge 37:25).
From Ophir: Gold (1Ki 10:11; 22:48; 1Ch 29:4).
From Tarshish: Gold, silver, ivory, apes, and baboons (1Ki 10:22; 2Ch 9:21), silver, iron, tin, lead, bronze, and slaves (Eze 27:12-13).
From Arabia: Sheep and goats (Eze 27:21).

Of Egypt:
From Gilead: Spices, balm, and myrrh (Ge 37:25).

Of Tyre:
All commodities from and of the trade world (Eze 27:12-25).

IMPORTUNITY *See Prayer.*

IMPOSTORS Deceivers who lead others astray (2Co 6:8); a general word for evil men, cheaters, who also lead others astray (2Ti 3:13).

IMPRECATION Instances of: Ruth (Ru 1:17). Samuel (1Sa 3:17). David (2Sa 1:21; 3:28-29). Shimei (2Sa 16:5, 13).

IMPRECATORY PSALMS 35, 58, 69, 70, 83, 109, 137, 140, among others. These contain expressions of an apparent vengeful attitude towards enemies. For some people these psalms constitute one of the "moral difficulties" of the OT. In his covenant with Abraham, God promises to curse those who curse his people (Ge 12:3). *See Curse; Psalms.*

IMPRISONMENT
Of Joseph (Ge 39:20). Jeremiah (Jer 38:6). John the Baptist (Mt 11:2; 14:3). Apostles (Ac 5:18). Paul and Silas (Ac 16:24). Peter (Ac 12:4).
Debtors (Mt 5:26; 18:30).
See Prison; Prisoners; Punishment.

IMPUTATION *See Impute.*

IMPUTE To attribute something to a person, or reckon something to the account of another.

Aspects of the Doctrine Found in the NT:
1. The imputation of Adam's sin to his posterity.
2. The imputation of the sin of man to Christ.
3. The imputation of Christ's righteousness to the believer (Ge 2:3; Ro 3:24; 5:15; Gal 5:4; Tit 3:7; 1Pe 2:24).

IMRAH (*he rebels*). A chief of the tribe of Asher (1Ch 7:36).

IMRI (*Yahweh spoke*).
1. A man of Judah (1Ch 9:4).
2. Father of Zaccur (Ne 3:2).

INCARNATION (*taking on flesh*). The doctrine that the eternal son of God became human, and that he did so without in any manner or degree diminishing his divine nature (Jn 1:4; Ro 8:3; 1Ti 3:16). *See Jesus the Christ, Incarnation of.*

INCENDIARISM *See Arson.*

INCENSE

General:
Formula for compounding (Ex 30:34-35). Uses of (Ex 30:36-38; Lev 16:12; Nu 16:17, 40, 46; Dt 33:10). Compounded by Bezalel (Ex 37:29), by priests (1Ch 9:30). Offered, morning and evening (Ex 30:7-8; 2Ch 13:11), on the golden altar (Ex 30:1-7; 40:5, 27; 2Ch 2:4; 32:12), in making atonement (Lev 16:12-13; Nu 16:46-47; Lk 1:10). Unlawfully offered by Nadab and Abihu (Lev 10:1-2), Korah, Dathan, and Abiram (Nu 16:16-35), by Uzziah (2Ch 26:16-21). Offered in idolatrous worship (1Ki 12:33; Jer 41:5; Eze 8:11). Presented by the wise men to Jesus (Mt 2:11).
See Altar of Incense.

Figurative:
Of prayer (Ps 141:2). Of praise (Mal 1:11). Of an acceptable sacrifice (Eph 5:2).

Symbolic:
Of the prayers of saints (Rev 5:8; 8:3-4).

INCEST

Defined and Forbidden:
(Lev 18:6-18; 20:11-12, 17-21; Dt 22:30; 27:20-23; Eze 22:11; 1Co 5:1).

Instances of:
Lot with his daughters (Ge 19:31-36). Abraham (Ge 20:12-13). Nahor (Ge 11:29). Reuben (Ge 35:22; 49:4). Amram (Ex 6:20). Judah (Ge 38:16-18; 1Ch 2:4). Amnon (2Sa 13:14). Absalom (2Sa 16:21-22). Israel (Am 2:7). Herod (Mt 14:3-4; Mk 6:17-18; Lk 3:19).

Instances of Marriage of Near Relatives:
Abraham with Sarah (Ge 20:11-13). Isaac with Rebekah (Ge 24:15, 67). Jacob with Leah and Rachel (Ge 29:23, 30). Rehoboam (2Ch 11:18).

INCINERATION *See Cremation.*

INCOMPARABILITY OF GOD *See God, Incomparable; None Like God.*

INCONSISTENCY Hypocritical (Mt 7:3-5; 23:3-4). Inexcusable (Ro 2:1, 21-23).
Instances of: Jehu (2Ki 10:16-31). The Jews, in oppressing the poor (Ne 5:8-9), in accusing Jesus of violating the Sabbath (Jn 7:22-23). Peter and the other disciples, in requiring of the Gentiles that which they did not require of themselves (Gal 2:11-14).
See Deceit; Deception; Hypocrisy.

INDECISION About God (1Ki 18:21; Hos 10:2; Mt 6:24). About ethics (Mt 26:41; Jas 1:8; 4:17; Rev 3:15).
See Decision; Instability; Lukewarmness.
Instances of: Moses at the Red Sea (Ex 14:15). Joshua at Ai (Jos 7:10). Esther (Est 5:8). Rulers, who believed in Jesus (Jn 12:42). Felix (Ac 24:25).

INDIA Probably the eastern limit of the kingdom of Xerxes (Est 1:1; 8:9).

INDICTMENTS

Instances of:
Naboth on charge of blasphemy (1Ki 21:13, w 21:1-16). Jeremiah of treasonable prophecy, but of which he was acquitted (Jer 26:1-24), a second indictment (Jer 37:13-15). Three Hebrew captives on the charge of resistance to authority (Da 3:12, w 3:1-28; 6:13, w 6:1-24).
Jesus, under two charges, first, of blasphemy (Mt 26:61, w Mk 14:58; Mt 26:63-65, w Mk 14:61-64; Lk 22:67-71; Jn 19:7), second, of treason (Mt 27:11, 37; Mk 15:2, 26; Lk 23:2-3, 38; Jn 18:30, 33; 19:12, 19-22).
Stephen for blasphemy (Ac 6:11, 13). Paul (Ac 17:7; 18:13; 24:5; 25:18-19, 26-27). Paul and Silas (Ac 16:20-21).
Indictment rejected (Ac 18:14-16).

INDIGESTION Of Timothy (1Ti 5:23). *See Disease.*

INDUSTRY Brings prosperity (Pr 10:4-5; 12:11, 24, 27; 13:4, 11; 21:5; 22:29; 28:19). Commanded (Ge 2:15; Ex 23:12; 35:2; Dt 5:13; Pr 20:13; 27:23-27; Ecc 9:10; 11:4, 6; Ro 12:11; Eph 4:28; 1Th 4:11-12; 2Th 3:10-12; 1Ti 5:8). Instigated (Pr 16:26). Profitable (Pr 14:4, 23). Reflections concerning (Ecc 1:3; 2:10-11, 17-22).

Exemplified:
By ants and conies (Pr 30:25-26). By prudent wife (Pr 31:13-27).

Instances of:
Jeroboam (1Ki 11:28). Paul (Ac 18:3; 20:33-34; 1Co 4:12; 1Th 2:9; 2Th 3:8).
See Frugality; Idleness; Labor; Slothfulness; Work.

INFANTICIDE The killing of children. Commanded by Pharaoh (Ex 1:15-16; Ac 7:19); by God concerning Midianite boys (Nu 31:17); by Herod (Mt 2:16-18).

INFANTS *See Children.*

INFERTILITY *See Barrenness.*

INFIDELITY

Relating to God:
Disbelief in God (Nu 15:30-31; 2Ch 32:14-19; Isa 29:16). Prosperity tempts to (Dt 32:15). Arguments against (Job 12:7-25; Ps 94:8-9; Isa 10:15; 19:16; 45:9, 18; Ro 1:20; 9:20-21).

Exemplified—
In mocking God (Ps 14:1, 6; 50:21; Isa 57:4-11; Eze 36:2; Da 3:15; Ac 17:18; 2Pe 3:3-4; Jude 18-19). In mocking God's servants (1Ki 22:24; 2Ki 2:23; 2Ch 30:6, 10; 36:16; Jer 17:15; 43:2; Eze 20:49; Ac 2:13).
In rejecting God (Ex 5:2; Job 15:25-26; 21:14-15; Ps 14:1; 53:1; 106:24-25; Jer 2:31). In rejecting Christ (Mt 12:24; 27:39-44; Mk 3:22; Lk 11:15; 19:14, 27). By Antichrist (Da 7:25; 8:25; 11:36-37).
In doubting God's help (Ex 17:7; Ps 3:2; 78:19-20, 22; 107:11-12). In impugning God's holiness (Job 35:3; Ps 10:11, 13; Eze 18:2, 29; Mal 1:7; 3:14), God's knowledge (Job 22:13-14, 17; Ps 59:7; 64:5; 73:11; Isa 29:15; Eze 8:12), God's mercy (Ps 42:3), God's righteousness (Eze 18:2, 29).

Punishment for—
(Nu 15:30-31; Dt 29:19-21; Ps 12:3-4; Pr 3:34; 9:12; 19:29; 24:9; Isa 3:8; 5:18-19, 24-25; 28:9-10, 14-22; 47:10-11; Jer 5:12, 14; 48:42; 50:24, 29; Eze 9:9-10; 32:20; Hos 7:5, 13, 15; Am 5:18; 7:16-17; Mic 7:10; Zep 1:12; Lk 19:14, 27; Heb 10:28-29; 2Pe 2:1).

Relating to Friends:
(Ps 41:9; Mt 26:14-16, 47-50; Mk 14:10-11, 43-46; Lk 22:3-6, 47-48; Jn 13:18; 18:2-5).
See Presumption; Skepticism; Unbelief.

INFINITY *See God, Infinite.*

INFIRMITY Physical (Ecc 12:3). Of Isaac (Ge 27:1). Of Jacob (Ge 48:10). Moses exempt from (Dt 34:7). Caleb exempt from (Jos 14:11). Of Eli (1Sa 3:2). Of Barzillai (2Sa 19:32).
See Affliction; Blindness; Deafness; Lameness; Old Age; Taste.

INFLAMMATION Disease brought as a curse for unfaithfulness to Yahweh (Dt 28:22). *See Disease.*

INFLUENCE

Intercession in Behalf of Friends:
Of Jonathan for David (1Sa 19:1-6; 20:4-9). Solicited, Bathsheba for Adonijah (1Ki 2:13-18). Offered, Elisha for Shunammite woman (2Ki 4:12-13). Of nobles of Judah in behalf of Tobiah (Ne 6:17-19). Of mother of Zebedee's children for sons (Mt 20:20-24). Of Blastus for Tyre and Sidon (Ac 12:20).

Good Influences:
Injunctions concerning (Mt 5:13-16; Mk 4:21-22; Lk 8:16; 11:33-36; Jn 7:38; 1Co 7:14, 16; Php 2:15; 1Th 1:7-8; 1Ti 6:1; Heb 11:4; 1Pe 2:11-12; 3:1-2, 15-16).

Instances of—
David over his successors (1Ki 3:3; 2Ki 18:3; 22:2; 2Ch 29:2; 34:2). Asa over Jehoshaphat (1Ki 22:42-43). Joash over Amaziah (2Ki 14:3). Amaziah over Azariah (2Ki 15:1-3). Uzziah over Jotham (2Ki 15:34). Josiah, in religious zeal (2Ki 22; 23:1-25; 2Ch 34:33). Hezekiah, for religious reform (2Ch 29-31). Ezra, against marriage with idolaters (Ezr 10:1, 9). Nehemiah, during the rebuilding of the walls of Jerusalem (Ne 4:7-23; 5).

Evil Influences:
Of ruler over servants (Pr 22:12). Of wicked parents over children (Jer 17:1-2). Of wicked priest and people (Hos 4:9). Warnings against (Pr 22:24-25; Lk 12:1; 1Co 5:6-8; Gal 5:7-9; 2Ti 2:14, 17-18; Heb 12:15). Parable of (Mt 13:24-25).

Instances of—
Eve over Adam (Ge 3:6). Solomon's wives (1Ki 11:3-4). The young men over Rehoboam (1Ki 12:8-14; 2Ch 10:8-14). Rehoboam over Abijah (1Ki 15:3). Jeroboam over Nadab (1Ki 15:25-26). Jezebel over Ahab (1Ki 21:4-16, 25). Ahab over Ahaziah (1Ki 22:52-53; 2Ki 8:25-27). Ahab over Jehoram (2Ki 8:16, 18; 2Ch 21:5-6; 22:3-5). Jeroboam over Israel (2Ki 17:21-22). Manasseh over Judah (2Ki 21:9; 2Ch 33:9). Manasseh over Amon (2Ki 21:20-21). Jehoiakim over Jehoiachin (2Ki 24:9).

Political Influence:
(1Ki 2:13-18; 2Ki 4:12-13; Ne 6:17-19; Pr 19:6; 29:26; Da 5:10-12; Mt 20:20-24; Ac 12:20).
See Example; Politics.

INGATHERING, FEAST OF *See Tabernacles, Feast of.*

INGRAFTING *See Graft.*

INGRATITUDE

To God:
(Ro 1:21; 2Ti 3:2). Prosperity tempts (Dt 6:10-12; 8:12-14; 32:6, 13, 15, 18; 2Ch 26:15-16; Jer 5:7-9, 24; Hos 13:6). Punishment for (Dt 28:47-48; 1Ki 16:1-3; 2Ch 32:25; Ps 78:16-17, 27-32, 42-68; Da 5:18, 20-21).

Instances of—
(Nu 16:9-10). Israel (Dt 31:16; Jdg 2:10-12; 8:34-35; 10:11, 13-14; 1Sa 8:7-8; 10:19; Ne 9:25-26, 35; Ps 106:7, 21; Isa 1:2; Jer 2:6-9, 17, 31; 4:7; 7:13, 19; 11:1, 3; Am 3:1-2; Mic 6:3-4). Saul (1Sa 15:17, 19). David (2Sa 12:7-9). Baasha (1Ki 16:1-2). Jerusalem (Eze 16:17). Humanity (Ro 1:21; 2Ti 3:2).

Ingratitude to Jesus:
The nine lepers (Lk 17:12-18). His own people (Jn 1:11).

Ingratitude of Person to Person:
(Pr 17:13; 2Ti 3:2).

Instances of—
Laban to Jacob (Ge 31). Pharaoh's cupbearer to Joseph (Ge 40:23). Israelites to Moses (Ex 16:3; 17:2-4; Nu 16:12-14), to Gideon (Jdg 8:35). Shechemites (Jdg 9:17-18). Men of Keilah to David (1Sa 23:5-12). Saul to David (1Sa 24). Nabal (1Sa 25:21). David to Joab (1Ki 2:5-6), with the history of Joab's services to David. *See Joab.* David to Uriah (2Sa 11:6-17). David's companions to David (Ps 35:11-16; 38:20; 41:9; 109:4-5). Citizens (Ecc 9:14-16). Joash (2Ch 24:22). Jeremiah's enemies (Jer 18:20).

INHERITANCE Of children (Ge 24:36; 25:5; 2Ch 21:3). Of children of concubines (Ge 15:3; 21:9-11; 25:6). Of children of polygamous marriages (Dt 21:15). Of daughters (Nu 27:8; Job 42:15). Of all mankind (Ecc 2:18-19). Of servants (Pr 17:2). Of real estate inalienable (1Ki 21:3; Jer 32:6-8; Eze 46:16-18).
Law concerning (Nu 27:6-11). Lesson concerning, of prodigal (Lk 15:12, 25-31). Proverbs concerning (Pr 17:2; 20:21).
Instance of Israel to Joseph (Ge 48:21-22).
Figurative: Spiritual (Mt 25:34; Ac 20:32; 26:18; Ro 8:16-17; Gal 4:7; Eph 1:11-14; Col 3:24; Tit 3:7; Heb 1:14; 9:15-17).
See Firstborn; Heir; Testament; Will.

INHOSPITABLENESS Instances of: Toward the Israelites: Edom (Nu 20:1, 18-21), Sihon (Nu 21:22-23), Ammonites and Moabites (Dt 23:3-6). Men of Gibeah toward a Levite (Jdg 19:15). Nabal toward David (1Sa 25:10-17). Samaritans toward Jesus (Lk 9:53). *See Hospitality.*

INIQUITIES, OUR (Job 14:17; Ps 40:12; 90:8; 130:3; Isa 59:2; 64:6; Jer 2:22; Mic 7:10). *See Sin.*

INIQUITY General references to (Job 15:16; Ps 41:6; 53:1; Isa 5:18; Jer 30:14; Eze 9:9; Hos 14:1; Mic 2:1; Mt 23:28; 24:12; Ro 6:19). *See Sin.*

INJUSTICE An abomination to God (Pr 17:15). To the righteous (Pr 29:27).
In civil administration (Ps 82:2; Ecc 5:8; La 3:34-36). In gains, unstable (Pr 28:8; Am 5:11-12). Judged (Pr 11:7; Ecc 3:16; Lk 16:10; 1Th 4:7; Rev 22:11). Practiced by the wicked (Isa 26:10), without shame (Zep 3:5). Protection from, given (Ps 12:5), interceded (Ps 43:1).
God innocent of (2Ch 19:7; Eze 18:25-29; Ro 3:5-8; 9:14-18; Heb 6:10). Job innocent of (Job 16:16-17; 31:13-15).

INK Any liquid used with pen or brush to form written characters (Jer 36:18; 2Co 3:3; 2Jn 12; 3Jn 13).

INKHORN *See Writing Kit.*

INN A lodging place for travelers. Inns in the modern sense were not very necessary in ancient times, since travelers found hospitality the rule (Ex 2:20; Jdg 19:15-21; 2Ki 4:8; Ac 28:7; Heb 13:2). Ancient inns were usually mere shelters for man and beast, although often strongly fortified.

INNOCENCE Signified by washing the hands (Dt 21:6; Ps 26:6; Mt 27:24). Found in Daniel (Da 6:22), Jeremiah (Jer 2:35). Professed by Pilate (Mt 27:24). Contrasted with guilt (Ge 2:25; 3:7-11).

INNOCENT Not to suffer for guilty (Dt 24:16; 2Ki 14:6; 2Ch 25:4; Jer 31:29-30; Eze 18:20).

INNOCENTS, SLAUGHTER OF The slaughter, by Herod the Great, of children in Bethlehem (Mt 2:16-18). *See Infanticide; Murder.*

INNUENDO (Ps 35:19; Pr 6:13; 10:10). *See Accusation, False.*

INQUEST Into an unsolved murder (Dt 21:1-9).

I.N.R.I The initials of the Latin superscription on the cross of Jesus, standing for IESUS NAZARENUS, REX IUDAEORUM, "Jesus of Nazareth, King of the Jews" (Mt 27:37; Mk 15:26; Lk 23:38; Jn 19:19).

INSANITY (Pr 26:18). Sent as a judgment from God (Dt 28:28; Zec 12:4).
Feigned by David (1Sa 21:13-15). Nebuchadnezzar's (Da 4:32-34). Jesus accused of (Mk 3:21; Jn 10:20). Paul (Ac 26:24-25). Cured by Jesus (Mt 4:24; 17:15).

Demonic:
Saul (1Sa 16:14; 18:10).

False accusation of:
Against Jesus (Mk 3:21; Jn 10:20), against Paul (Ac 26:24-25; 2Co 5:13).
See Demons, Possession by.

INSCRIPTIONS On gravestones (2Ki 23:17). On the turban of the high priest (Ex 28:36). On the sacred diadem (Ex 39:30). On the bells of horses (Zec 14:20).
Over Jesus at the Crucifixion (Mt 27:37; Mk 15:26; Lk 23:38; Jn 19:19). Precepts written on the doorframes and gates and worn on the hand and forehead (Dt 6:6-9; 11:18-20; Isa 57:8).

INSECTS Created by God (Ge 1:24-25). Fed by God (Ps 104:25, 27; Ps 145:9, 15).

Divided Into:
Clean and fit for food (Lev 11:21-22). Unclean and abominable (Lev 11:23-24).

Mentioned in Scripture:
Ant (Pr 6:6; 30:25). Bee (Jdg 14:8; Ps 118:12; Isa 7:18). Cricket (Lev 11:22). Flea (1Sa 24:14). Fly (Ex 8:22; Ecc 10:1; Isa 7:18). Gnat (Ex 8:16; Ps 105:31; Mt 23:24). Grasshopper (Lev 11:22; Jdg 6:5; Job 39:20; Ps 78:46; Isa 33:4; Na 3:15-16). Hornet (Dt 7:20). Katydid (Lev 11:22). Locust (Ex 10:12-13; Joel 1:4; 2:25). Maggot (Ex 16:20). Moth (Job 4:19; 27:18; Isa 50:9). Spider (Job 8:14; Isa 59:5). Worm (Job 25:6; Mic 7:17)

INSINCERITY *See Hypocrisy.*

INSINUATION *See Innuendo.*

INSOMNIA Instances of: Xerxes (Est 6:1). Nebuchadnezzar (Da 6:18).

INSPECTION GATE One of the gates of Jerusalem (Ne 3:31). *See Miphkad.*

INSPIRATION (*breathed into*).

Claims that the Scriptures are Inspired:
(2Ti 3:16; 1Ki 13:20; 2Ch 33:18; 36:15; Ne 9:30; Job 33:14-16; Isa 51:16; Jer 7:25; 17:16; Da 9:6, 10; Hos 12:10; Joel 2:28; Am 3:7-8; Zec 7:12; Lk 1:70; Ac 3:18; Ro 1:1-2; 1Co 12:7-11; Heb 1:1; 2Pe 1:21; Rev 10:7; 22:6, 8).

Instances of People Inspired by God:
Enoch (Jude 14). Joseph (Ge 40:8; 41:16, 38-39). Moses (Ex 3:14-15; 4:12, 15, 27; 6:13, 29; 7:2; 19:9-19; 24:16; 25:22; 33:9, 11; Lev 1:1; Nu 1:1; 7:8-9; 9:8-10; 11:17, 25; 12:6-8; 16:28-29; Dt 1:5-6; 5:4-5, 31; 34:10-11; Ps 103:7). Aaron (Ex 6:13; 12:1). The tabernacle workers (Ex 28:3; 31:3, 6; 35:31; 36:1). The seventy elders (Nu 11:16-17, 24-25). Eldad and Medad (Nu 11:26-29). Balaam (Nu 23:5, 16, 20, 26; 24:2-4, 15-16). Joshua (Dt 34:9; Jos 4:15).
Samuel (1Sa 3:1, 4-10, 19-21; 9:6, 15-20; 15:16). Saul (1Sa 10:6-7, 10-13; 19:23-24). Messengers of Saul (1Sa 19:20, 23). David (2Sa 23:2-3; 1Ch 28:19; Mk 12:36). Nathan (1Ki 14:5). Elijah (1Ki 17:1, 24; 19:15; 2Ki 10:10). Micaiah (1Ki 22:14, 28; 2Ch 18:27). Elisha (2Ki 2:9; 3:11-12, 15; 6:8-12, 32; 15:8). Jahaziel (2Ch 20:14). Azariah (2Ch 15:1-2). Zechariah, the son of Jehoiada (2Ch 24:20; 26:5). Isaiah (2Ki 20:4; Isa 6:1-9; 8:11; 44:26; Ac 28:25). Jeremiah (2Ch 26:12; Jer 1:9; 2:1; 7:1; 11:1, 18; 13:1-3; 16:1; 18:1; 20:9; 23:9; 24:4; 25:3; 26:1-2, 12; 27:1-2; 29:30; 33:1; 34:1; 42:4, 7; Da 9:2). Ezekiel (Eze 1:1, 3; 2:1-2, 4-5; 3:10-12, 14, 16-17, 22, 24, 27; 8:1; 11:1, 4-5, 24; 33:22; 37:1; 40:1; 43:5-6). Daniel (Da 2:19; 7:16; 8:16; 9:22; 10:7-9). Hosea (Hos 1:1-2). Joel (Joel 1:1). Amos (Am 3:7-8; 7:14-15). Obadiah (Ob 1). Jonah (Jnh 1:1; 3:1-2). Micah (Mic 1:1; 3:8). Habakkuk (Hab 1:1). Haggai (Hag 1:13). Zechariah (Zec 2:9; 7:8).
Elizabeth (Lk 1:41). Zechariah (Lk 1:67). Simeon (Lk 2:26-27). Disciples (Mt 10:19; Mk 13:11; Lk 12:11; Lk 12:12; 21:14-15; Ac 21:4). The apostles (Ac 2:4). Philip (Ac 8:29). Agabus (Ac 11:28; 21:10-11). John the apostle (Rev 1:10-11).
See Genius; Prophecy; Prophets; Revelation; Word of God, Inspiration of.

INSTABILITY

Warnings Against:
(Pr 24:21-22; 27:8; Mt 6:24; 8:19-22; 12:25; 13:20-21; Mk 4:16-17; Lk 8:13; 9:57-62; Eph 4:14; Heb 13:9; Jas 1:6-8; 4:8; 2Pe 2:14; Rev 2:4; 3:2).

Instances of:
Reuben (Ge 49:4). Pharaoh (Ex 8:15, 32; 9:34; 10:8-11, 16-20; 14:5). Israel (Ex 19:8; 24:3, 7; 32:8-10; Jdg 2:17; 1Ki 18:21; Ps 106:12-13; Jer 2:36). Saul in his feelings toward David (1Sa 18:19). David, in yielding to lust (2Sa 11:2-4). Solomon, in yielding to his idolatrous wives (1Ki 11:1-8). Ephraim and Judah (Hos 6:4). Jews (Hos 6:4-5; Jn 5:35). Lot's wife (Lk 17:32). Disciples (Jn 6:66). Mark (Ac 15:38). Galatians (Gal 1:6; 4:9-11).
See Backsliding; Hypocrisy; Indecision.

INSTINCT Of animals (Pr 1:17; Isa 1:3). Of birds (Jer 8:7). *See Animals; Birds.*

INSTRUCTION Provision for, made by the state (2Ch 17:7-9; Da 1:3-5, 17-20). Sought (Ps 90:12; 119:12; 143:8, 10). Paying attention to, commanded (Pr 4:1-2, 10, 13, 20; 5:1-2; 22:17; 23:12, 23). Lack of (2Ch 15:3; Pr 24:30-34). Hatred (Ps 50:17; Pr 1:29-30; 5:12-13; Jer 32:33; Lk 20:1-2). From nature (Pr 24:30-34; Ecc 1:13-18; 3; 4:1; Mt 6:25-30). From the study of human nature (Ecc 3-12).

In religion:
(Ex 24:12; Lev 10:11; Dt 24:8; 27:14-26; 31:9-13; 33:10; 2Ch 17:8-9; 35:3; Ne 8:7-13; Mal 2:6-7). By means of the law (Dt 27:1-26; Ro 2:18; Gal 3:24-25). By means of proverbs (Pr 1:1-6, 20-30). By means of the song of Moses (Dt 31:19; 32:1-44). By priests (Ezr 7:10; Mal 2:7). By Jesus (Mt 5:1-2; Mk 6:2; 12:35; Lk 4:16-21; 19:47; 20:1-8; 21:37-38; 24:27; Jn 7:14; 8:2). By preachers (Ro 10:14; 1Co 12:28-29; Eph 4:11; Col 1:2, 8). By teachers (2Ki 23:2; Ne 8:7-8; 1Co 12:28-29; Eph 4:11).
By symbols. *See Symbols and Similitudes.* By parables. *See Parable.* Inscriptions on doors and gates (Dt 11:20-21), on monuments (Jos 8:30-35). The public reading of the law (Dt 31:9-13; Jos 8:34-35; Ne 8:2-3).

By Object Lessons:
Passover feast (Ex 12:26-27). Dedication of firstlings (Ex 13:14-16). Phylacteries (Ex 13:9, 16). Inscriptions (Ex 28:36; 39:30; Dt 6:6-9; 11:18-20; Zec 14:20; Mt 27:37). The pot of manna, a reminder of God's care (Ex 16:32). The sacred oil, a symbol of holiness (Ex 30:31). The pillar of twelve stones at the fords of the Jordan (Jos 4:7, 19-24). Tassels on the borders of garments (Nu 15:38-39). The garment torn in pieces (1Ki 11:30-32). The symbolic wearing of sackcloth and going barefoot (Isa 20:2-3). The linen belt (Jer 13:1-11). Potter's vessel (Jer 19:1-12). Basket of figs (Jer 24). Bonds and yokes (Jer 27:2-11; 28). By stones being put in a brick pavement (Jer 43:8-13). Illustrations on a tile (Eze 4:1-3). Lying on one side in public view for a long period (Eze 4:4-8). Eating bread baked with dung (Eze 4:9-17). Shaving the head (Eze 5). Moving household goods (Eze 12:3-16). Eating and drinking sparingly (Eze 12:18-20). Sighing (Eze 21:6-7). The boiling pot (Eze 24:1-14). Widowhood (Eze 24:16-27). Two sticks joined together (Eze 37:16-22).

Of Children:
By parents, commanded (Ex 10:2; 12:26-27; 13:8-10, 14-16; Dt 4:9-10; 6:6-9; 11:18-19; Ps 78:5-8; Pr 22:6; Isa 38:19; Eph 6:4). Law concerning (Dt 31:9-13; Jos 8:35). Exemplified (Ps 34:11; Pr 20:7; Ac 22:3; 2Ti 3:15).
See Children.

By Types:
See Washings; Blemish; Defilement; Disfellowship; Types. See Firstborn; Holiness; Passover; Pillar; Purification.

INSTRUMENTALITY *See Agency.*

INSTRUMENTS, MUSICAL *See Music.*

INSURGENTS Army of, David's (1Sa 22:1-2).

INSURRECTION (Ps 64:2). Described by David (Ps 55). Led by Bicri (2Sa 20), Absalom. *See Absalom.* Barabbas (Mk 15:7).

INTEGRITY

General:
Essential (Ex 18:21; Lk 16:10; 2Co 8:21). Commanded (Dt 16:19-20; Pr 4:25-27; Isa 56:1; Mic 6:8; Zec 7:9; Lk 3:13-14; 6:31; 11:42; Ro 13:5; 14:5, 14, 22; Eph 6:6; Php 4:8; Col 3:22-23; 1Ti 1:5; 3:9; Tit 1:7-8; 1Pe 2:12; 3:16).
Rewards of (2Sa 22:21; Ps 15:1-5; 18:20; 24:3-5; Pr 10:9; 20:7; 28:20; Isa 26:7; 33:15-16; Jer 7:5, 7; Eze 18:5, 7-9).
Proverbs concerning (Pr 2:2, 5, 9; 3:3-4; 4:25-27; 10:9; 11:3, 5; 12:22; 14:30; 15:21; 16:11; 19:1; 20:7; 21:3, 15; 22:11; 28:6, 20).

Instances of:
Pharaoh, when he learned that Sarah was Abraham's wife (Ge 12:18-20). Abraham, in instructing his family (Ge 18:19). Abimelech, when warned of God that the woman he had taken into his household was Isaac's wife (Ge 26:9-11). Jacob, in the care of Laban's property (Ge 31:39). Joseph, in resisting Potiphar's wife (Ge 39:8-12), in his innocence of the charge on which he was cast into the dungeon (Ge 40:15). Moses, in taking nothing from the Israelites in consideration of his services (Nu 16:15). Samuel, in exacting nothing from the people on account of services (1Sa 12:4-5). Workmen, who repaired the temple (1Ki 12:15; 22:7).
Priests who received the offerings of gold and other gifts for the renewing of the temple under Ezra (Ezr 2:24-30, 33-34). Nehemiah, in his reforms and in receiving no compensation for his own services (Ne 5:14-19). Job (Job 1:8; 10:7; 13:15; 16:17; 27:4-6; 29:14; 31:1-40). The psalmist (Ps 7:3-5, 8; 17:3; 26:1-3; 69:4; 73:15; 119:121). The Recabites, in keeping the Nazirite vows (Jer 35:12-19). Daniel, in maintaining uprightness of character (Da 6:4). The three Hebrews, who refused to worship Nebuchadnezzar's idol (Da 3:16-21, 28). Levi, in his life and service (Mal 2:6).
Joseph, the husband of Mary, in not jealously accusing her of immorality (Mt 1:19). Zacchaeus, in the administration of his wealth (Lk 19:8). Nathanael, in whom was no guile (Jn 1:47). Joseph, a counselor (Lk 23:50-51). Peter, when offered money by Simon (Ac 8:18-23). Paul and Barnabas (Ac 14:12-15). Paul (Ac 23:1; 24:16; Ro 9:1; 2Co 4:2; 5:11; 7:2; 1Th 2:4). The author of Hebrews (Heb 13:18).
See Character; Dishonesty; Honesty; Justice; Righteousness.

INTEMPERANCE *See Abstinence; Drunkard; Drunkenness; Temperance; Wine.*

INTERCESSION

Of People With God:
(Jer 27:18). Priestly (Ex 28:12, 29-30, 38; Lev 10:17). For spiritual blessing (Nu 6:23-26; 1Sa 12:23; Job 1:5; 42:8-10). To avert judgment (Ge 20:7; Ex 32:9-14; Nu 14:11-21; 16:45-50; Dt 9:18-29; Isa 65:8). For deliverance from enemies (1Sa 7:5-9; Isa 37:4). For healing of disease (Jas 5:14-16). For stubborn sinners, unavailing (Jer 7:16; 11:14; 14:11).

Commanded—
(Jer 29:7; Joel 2:17; Mt 5:44; Eph 6:18; 1Ti 2:1-2; 1Jn 5:16).

Examples of—
(Ge 48:16; Ex 32:31-32; 34:9; Nu 10:35-36; 27:16-17; Jos 7:8-9; Jdg 5:31; Ru 2:12; 1Sa 1:17; 12:23; 2Sa 24:17; 1Ki 8:29, 38-39, 44-45; 1Ch 29:18-19; 2Ch 6:40-41; 30:18-19; Ps 7:9; 12:1; 20:1-4; 25:22; 28:9; 36:10; 51:18; 80:1-2, 14-19; 122:7-8; 125:4; 132:9-10; 134:3; 141:5; Isa 62:1; 63:17-19; 64:8-12; Jer 18:20; Eze 9:8; 11:13; Da 9:3-19; Joel 2:17; Mic 7:14; Mt 5:44; 6:10; Ac 7:60; 8:15; Ro 1:9; 10:1; 1Co 1:3; 2Co 9:10, 14; 13:7; Gal 1:3; 6:16; Eph 1:15-19; 3:14-19; Php 1:3-5, 9; Col 1:3-4, 9; 2:1-2; 4:12; 1Th 1:2; 3:10, 12-13; 5:23; 2Th 1:11; 2:16-17; 3:5, 16; 2Ti 1:3; 4:16; Phm 4, 6; Heb 13:20-21; 1Pe 5:10).

Instances of—
Abraham, in behalf of Sodom (Ge 18:23-32), in behalf of Abimelech (Ge 20:17-18). Abraham's servant, in behalf of his master (Ge 24:12). Jacob, in behalf of his children (Ge 49). Moses, in behalf of Pharaoh (Ex 8:12-13, 30-31; 9:33; 10:18-19). Moses for Israel (Nu 16:20-22; 21:7; Dt 33:6-17; Ps 106:23), for Miriam (Nu 12:13-15). David, for Israel (2Sa 24:17). Solomon, for Israel (1Ki 8:29-53). Ezra, for Israel (Ezr 9:5-15). Nehemiah, in behalf of Judah and Jerusalem (Ne 1:4-9). Asaph, for the church (Ps 80-83). The "Sons of Korah," for the church (Ps 85:1-7). Jeremiah, for Israel (Am 7:2-6). Syrian Phoenician woman, for her daughter (Mt 15:22). Disciples, in behalf of Peter's wife's mother (Lk 4:38-39). Parents, for demon-possessed son (Mt 17:15; Mk 9:17-27). Others, who sought Jesus in behalf of the afflicted (Mt 12:22; 15:22, 30; 17:14-18; Mk 1:32; 2:3; Lk 5:18-20; Jn 4:47, 49). Paul for the church (Ac 20:32). Onesiphorus (2Ti 1:16, 18). For Paul, by the churches (Ac 14:26; 15:40).

Requested—
By Pharaoh, of Moses (Ex 8:8, 28; 9:28; 10:17; 12:32), and by the Israelites (Nu 21:7). By Israel, of Samuel (1Sa 12:19). By Jeroboam, of a prophet (1Ki 13:6). By Hezekiah, of Isaiah (2Ki 19:1-4). By Zedekiah, of Jeremiah (Jer 37:3), and by Johanan (Jer 42:1-6). By Daniel, of Shadrach, Meshach, and Abednego (Da 2:17-18). By Darius, of the Jews (Ezr 6:10). By Simon the sorcerer, of Peter (Ac 8:24). By Paul, of the churches (Ro 15:30-32; 2Co 1:11; Eph 6:19-20; 1Th 5:25; 2Th 3:1; Heb 13:18).

Answered—
Of Moses in behalf of Pharaoh, for the plague of frogs to be ended (Ex 8:12, 15), the plague of flies (Ex 8:30-32), the plague of rain,

thunder, and hail (Ex 9:27-35), plague of locusts (Ex 10:16-20), plague of darkness (Ex 10:21-23); for the Israelites, during the battle with the Amalekites (Ex 17:11-14), after the Israelites had made the golden calf (Ex 32:11-14, 31-34; Dt 9:18-29; 10:10; Ps 106:23), after the murmuring of the people (Ex 33:15-17), when the fire of the Lord consumed the people (Nu 11:1-2), when the people murmured on account of the report of the spies (Nu 14:11-20), that the poisonous snakes might be taken away (Nu 21:4-9); that Miriam's leprosy might be healed (Nu 12:13); in behalf of Aaron, on account of his sin in making the golden calf (Dt 9:20). Of Samuel, for deliverance from the oppressions of the Philistines (1Sa 7:5-14). The prophet of Israel, for the restoration of Jeroboam's shriveled hand (1Ki 13:1-6). Of Elijah, for the raising from the dead the son of the hospitable widow (1Ki 17:20-23). Of Elisha, for the raising from the dead the son of the Shunammite woman (2Ki 4:33-36). Of Isaiah, in behalf of Hezekiah and the people, to be delivered from Sennacherib (2Ki 19).

Intercessional Influence of the Righteous—
(Ge 18:26-32; 19:22; 26:4-5, 24; 1Ki 11:12-13, 34; 15:4; 2Ki 8:19; 2Ch 21:7; Ps 103:17-18; Isa 37:35; Jer 5:1; Eze 14:14, 16, 18, 20; Mt 24:22; Ro 11:27-28; Rev 5:8; 8:3-4).

Intercession of People With Jesus: *See Mediation.*

Intercession of People with People:
Instances of: Reuben for Joseph (Ge 37:21-22). Judah for Joseph (Ge 37:26-27). Judah with Joseph (Ge 44:18-34). Pharaoh's chief baker for Joseph (Ge 41:9-14). Rahab for her people (Jos 2:12-13). Aaron for Miriam (Nu 12:12). Jonathan for David (1Sa 19:1-7). Abigail for Nabal (1Sa 25:23-35). Joab for Absalom (2Sa 14:1-24). Bathsheba, for Solomon (1Ki 1:11-22, 28-31), for Adonijah (1Ki 2:13-25). Esther for her people (Est 7:2-6). Ebed-Melech for Jeremiah (Jer 38:7-13). Elisha offers to see the king for the Shunammite (2Ki 4:13). The king of Syria for Naaman (2Ki 5:6-8). Paul for Onesimus (Phm 10-21).

Intercession of Jesus:
(Lk 22:31-32; 23:33-34; Jn 14:16; 17:9, 11, 15-17, 20-22; Ro 8:34; Heb 7:25; 9:24; 1Jn 2:1-2). *See Jesus the Christ, Mediation of.*

See Children, Of the Righteous, Blessed of God; Prayer, Intercessory.

INTEREST Income from lending money.

Charging Interest:
From a poor Israelite, forbidden (Ex 22:25; Lev 25:36-37; Dt 23:19). From a stranger, authorized (Dt 23:20). Unprofitable (Pr 28:8). Rebuked (Ne 5:1-13; Eze 22:12).

Charging No Interest:
Rewarded (Ps 15:5; Eze 18:8-9, 17). Lender and borrower equal before God (Isa 24:2).

See Borrowing; Debt; Debtor; Lending; Money; Usury.

INTERMARRY The patriarchs did not allow marriage outside their clan: Abraham (Ge 24:3), Jacob (Ge 28:1). Exceptions: Esau (Ge 26:34-35), Judah and his sons (Ge 38), Joseph (Ge 41:45, 50), Moses (Nu 12:1). Aaron and Miriam judged for criticizing Moses' intermarriage (Nu 12:1-15).

Israel was forbidden to intermarry with the Canaanites for religious reasons, not racial (Dt 7:1-6; Jos 23:12-13). Negative results of (Jdg 3:6-7), Solomon (1Ki 11:1-6), returned exiles (Ezr 9:14-15).

There are no racial barriers in the church (Col 3:11). Even marriage between believers and unbelievers does not have to end in divorce (1Co 7:12-16), though is not recommended (2Co 6:14-18). *See Marriage.*

INTERMEDIATE STATE Period of time which elapses between death and the resurrection. For the righteous it is one of blessedness (2Co 5:8); for the wicked it is one of conscious suffering (Lk 16:19-31).

INTERPRETATION Of dreams. *See Dream.* Of foreign tongues (1Co 14:9-19). *See Tongues, Gift of.*

INTERPRETER Of dreams (Ge 40:8; 41:16; Da 2:18-30). Of languages (Ge 42:23; 2Ch 32:31; Ne 8:8; Job 33:23). In Christian churches (1Co 12:10, 30; 14:5, 13, 26-28).
Figurative (Job 33:23).

INTOLERANCE

Religious:
Exemplified by Cain (Ge 4:8), Joshua (Nu 11:24-28), James and John (Mk 9:38-39; Lk 9:49), the Jews, in persecuting Jesus. *See Jesus the Christ, Rejected.*

History of:
In persecuting the disciples (Ac 4:1-3, 15-21; 17:13), Stephen (Ac 6:9-15; 7:57-59; 8:1-3), Paul (Ac 13:50; 17:5; 18:13; 21:28-31; 22:22-23; 23:2).

Of Idolatrous Religions:
Taught by Moses (Ex 22:20; Dt 13; 17:1-7).
Exemplified by: Elijah (1Ki 18:40), Jehu (2Ki 10:18-31), by the Jews, at the time of the religious revival under the leadership of Azariah (2Ch 15:12-13).
See Persecution.

INTOXICANTS *See Beer; Fermented Drink; Wine.*

INTOXICATION *See Abstinence; Drunkenness.*

INTRIGUE *See Conspiracy.*

INVECTIVE *See Satire.*

INVENTION Of musical instruments: By Jubal (Ge 4:21), by David (1Ch 23:5; 2Ch 7:6; 29:26; Am 6:5).
The use of metals (Ge 4:22). Machines of war (2Ch 26:15).

INVESTIGATION By Solomon, into nature and design of things (Ecc 1:13-18; 2:1-12; 7:25; 8:17; 12:9-14).

INVITATIONS The "Comes" of God's Word (Ge 7:1; Nu 10:29; Isa 1:18; 55:1; Mt 11:28; 22:4; Lk 14:17; Rev 22:17). Divine pleading (Pr 1:24; Isa 1:18; 55:1; Eze 18:31; Mic 6:3; Mt 23:37; Ro 10:21; 2Co 5:20).

Divine call: To repentance (Jer 35:15; Eze 33:11; Hos 6:1; Mt 22:3; 2Co 5:20; Rev 3:20). To leadership (Ge 12:1; Ex 3:10; Jdg 6:14; 1Ki 19:19; Isa 6:8; Ac 26:16). Universality of (Isa 45:22; 55:1; Mt 22:9; Jn 7:37; Ro 10:12; 1Ti 2:4; Rev 22:17).

Refused by people (Ps 81:11; Isa 65:12; Jer 7:13; Hos 9:17; Mt 22:3; Jn 5:40; Ro 10:21). Warnings (Ge 19:17; Dt 29:20; Jos 24:20; 1Sa 12:15; Isa 28:14; Jer 13:16; Jnh 3:4; Heb 12:25; 2Pe 3:17).

IPHDEIAH (*Yahweh redeems*). A Benjamite (1Ch 8:25).

IPHTAH (*he opens*). A city of Judah (Jos 15:43).

IPHTAH EL (*God [El] opens*). A valley in Zebulun (Jos 19:14, 27).

IR (possibly *stallion donkey*). A Benjamite (1Ch 7:12).

IR NAHASH (*city of Nahash*). Whether a man or a town is not clear (1Ch 4:12, ftn). *See Nahash.*

IR SHEMESH (*city of Shemesh*). A city of Dan (Jos 19:41).

IRA (possibly *stallion donkey*).
1. The Jairite, David's priest (2Sa 20:26).
2. The Ithrite, one of David's heroes (2Sa 23:38; 1Ch 11:40).
3. From Tekoa, one of David's heroes (2Sa 23:26; 1Ch 11:28; 27:9).

IRAD Son of Enoch (Ge 4:18).

IRAM A chief of Edom (Ge 36:43; 1Ch 1:54).

IRI (perhaps *donkey's colt*). A son of Bela (1Ch 7:7).

IRIJAH (*Yahweh sees*). A captain of the guard who imprisoned the prophet Jeremiah (Jer 37:13-14).

IRON
1. First recorded use of (Ge 4:22). Ore of (Dt 8:9; Job 28:2). Melted (Eze 22:20). Used in the temple (1Ch 22:3; 29:2, 7).

Articles Made of—
Ax (2Ki 6:6; 2Ch 18:10; Ecc 10:10; Isa 10:34), bed (Dt 3:11), breastplate (Rev 9:9), chariot (Jos 17:16, 18; Jdg 1:19; 4:3), fetters (Ps 105:18; 107:10, 16; 149:8), file (Pr 27:17), furnace (Dt 4:20; 1Ki 8:51; Jer 11:4), gate (Ac 12:10), harrow (2Sa 12:31), horn (1Ki 22:11; 2Ch 18:10; Mic 4:13), idols (Da 2:33; 5:4, 23), pans (Eze 4:3; 27:19), pen (Job 19:24; Jer 17:1), pillars (Jer 1:18), rods (Ps 2:9; Rev 2:27; 12:5; 19:15), threshing instruments (Am 1:3), tools (1Ki 6:7), vessels (Jos 6:24), weapons (Nu 35:16; 1Sa 17:7; Job 20:24; 41:7), yokes (Dt 28:48; Jer 28:13-14).
See Steel.
Figurative (2Sa 23:7; Jer 15:12; 1Ti 4:2).
2. A city of Naphtali (Jos 19:38).

IRONY Instances of: Michal to David (2Sa 6:20). Elijah to the priests of Baal (1Ki 18:27). Job to his accusers (Job 12:2). Ezekiel to the prince of Tyre (Eze 28:3-5). Micaiah (1Ki 22:15). Amos to the Samaritans (Am 4:4). Jesus to Pharisees (Mk 2:17). Pharisees and Herodians to Jesus (Mt 22:16). Roman soldiers to Jesus (Mt 27:29; Mk 15:17-19; Lk 23:11; Jn 19:2-3). Pilate, calling Jesus king (Mk 15:19; Jn 19:15). Superscription of Pilate over Jesus (Mt 27:37; Mk 15:26; Lk 23:38; Jn 19:19). Agrippa to Paul (Ac 26:28).
See Sarcasm; Satire.

IRPEEL (*God [El] heals*). A city of Benjamin (Jos 18:27).

IRRIGATION Of gardens (Dt 11:10; Pr 21:1; Ecc 2:6; Isa 58:11).
Figurative (1Co 3:6, 8).

IRU Eldest son of Caleb (1Ch 4:15).

ISAAC (*he laughs, he will laugh,* some contexts *mock;* other contexts *El [God] laughs*).
1. Miraculous son of Abraham (Ge 17:15-19; 18:1-15; 21:1-8; Jos 24:3; 1Ch 1:28; Gal 4:28; Heb 11:11). Ancestor of Jesus (Mt 1:2). Offered in sacrifice by his father (Ge 22:1-19; Heb 11:17; Jas 2:21). Is provided a wife from among his kindred (Ge 24; 25:20). Abrahamic covenant confirmed in (Ge 26:2-5; 1Ch 16:15-19). Dwells in the south country at the well Beer Lahai Roi (Ge 24:62; 25:11). With Ishmael, buries his father in the cave of Machpelah (Ge 25:9). Esau and Jacob born to (Ge 25:19-26; 1Ch 1:34; Jos 24:4). Dwells in Gerar (Ge 26:7-11). Prospers (Ge 26:12-14). Possesses large flocks and herds (Ge 26:14). Digs wells, and is defrauded of them by the herdsmen of Abimelech (Ge 26:15, 21). Removes to the valley of Gerar, afterward called Beersheba (Ge 26:22-33). His old age, last blessing upon his sons (Ge 27:18-40). Death and burial of (Ge 35:27-29; 49:31). His filial obedience (Ge 22:9). His peaceableness (Ge 26:14-22). Was a prophet (Ge 27:28-29, 39-40; Heb 11:20). Has devoutness (Ge 24:63; 25:21; 26:25; Mt 8:11; Lk 13:28). Prophecies concerning (Ge 17:16-21; 18:10-14; 21:12; 26:2-5, 24; Ex 32:13; 1Ch 16:16; Ro 9:7).
2. A designation of the ten tribes (Am 7:9).

ISAIAH, BOOK OF

Author: Isaiah son of Amoz

Date: Between c. 701 and 681 B.C.

Outline:

Part 1: The Book of Judgment (chs. 1-39):
I. Messages of Rebuke and Promise (chs. 1-6).
  A. Introduction: Charges Against Judah for Breaking the Covenant (ch. 1).
  B. The Future Discipline and Glory of Judah and Jerusalem (chs. 2-4).
    1. Jerusalem's future blessings (2:1-5).
    2. The discipline of Judah (2:6-4:1).
    3. The restoration of Zion (4:2-6).
  C. The Nation's Judgment and Exile (ch. 5).
  D. Isaiah's Unique Commission (ch. 6).
II. Prophecies Occasioned by the Aramean and Israelite Threat Against Judah (chs. 7-12).
  A. Ahaz Warned Not to Fear the Aramean and Israelite Threat (chs. 7).
  B. Isaiah's Son and David's Son (8:1-9:7).
  C. Judgment Against Israel (9:8-10:4).
  D. The Assyrian Empire and the Davidic Kingdom (10:5-12:6).
    1. The destruction of Assyria (10:5-34).
    2. The establishment of the Davidic king and his kingdom (ch. 11).
    3. Songs of joy for deliverance (ch. 12).
III. Judgment Against the Nations (chs. 13-23).
  A. Against Assyria and Its Ruler (13:1-14:27).
  B. Against Philistia (14:28-32).
  C. Against Moab (chs. 15-16).
  D. Against Aram and Israel (ch. 17).
  E. Against Cush (ch. 18).
  F. Against Egypt and Cush (chs. 19-20).
  G. Against Babylon (21:1-10).
  H. Against Dumah (Edom) (21:11-12).
  I. Against Arabia (21:13-17).
  J. Against the Valley of Vision (Jerusalem) (ch. 22).
  K. Against Tyre (ch. 23).
IV. Judgment and Promise (the Lord's Kingdom) (chs. 24-27).
  A. Universal Judgments for Universal Sin (ch. 24).
  B. Deliverance and Blessing (ch. 25).
  C. Praise for the Lord's Sovereign Care (ch. 26).
  D. Israel's Enemies: Punished but Israel's Remnant Restored (ch. 27).
V. Six Woes: Five on the Unfaithful in Israel and One on Assyria (chs. 28-33).
  A. Woe to Ephraim (Samaria)—and to Judah (ch. 28).
  B. Woe to David's City, Jerusalem (29:1-14).
  C. Woe to Those Who Rely on Foreign Alliances (29:15-24).
  D. Woe to the Obstinate Nation (ch. 30).
  E. Woe to Those Who Rely on Egypt (chs. 31-32).
  F. Woe to Assyria—but Blessing for God's People (ch. 33).
VI. More Prophecies of Judgment and Promise (chs. 34-35).
  A. The Destruction of the Nations and the Avenging of God's People (ch. 34).
  B. The Future Blessings of Restored Zion (ch. 35).
VII. A Historical Transition From the Assyrian Threat to the Babylonian Exile (chs. 36-39).
  A. Jerusalem Preserved From the Assyrian Threat (chs. 36-37).
    1. The siege of Jerusalem by Sennacherib and the Assyrian army (ch. 36).
    2. The Lord's deliverance of Jerusalem (ch. 37).
  B. The Lord's Extension of Hezekiah's Life (ch. 38).
  C. The Babylonian Exile Predicted (ch. 39).

Part 2: The Book of Comfort (chs. 40-66):
VIII. The Deliverance and Restoration of Israel (chs. 40-48).
  A. The Coming of the Victorious God (40:1-26).
  B. Unfailing Strength for the Weary Exiles (40:27-31).
  C. The Lord of History (41:1-42:9).
  D. Praise and Exhortation (42:10-25).
  E. The Regathering and Renewal of Israel (43:1-44:5).
  F. The Only God (44:6-45:25).
  G. The Lord's Superiority over Babylon's Gods (ch. 46).
  H. The Fall of Babylon (ch. 47).
  I. The Lord's Exhortations to His People (ch. 48).
IX. The Servant's Ministry and Israel's Restoration (chs. 49-57).
  A. The Call and Mission of the Servant (49:1-13).
  B. The Repopulation of Zion (49:14-26).
  C. Israel's Sin and the Servant's Obedience (ch. 50).
  D. The Remnant Comforted Because of Their Glorious Prospect (51:1-52:12).
  E. The Sufferings and Glories of the Lord's Righteous Servant (52:13-53:12).
  F. The Future Glory of Zion (ch. 54).
  G. The Lord's Call to Salvation and Covenant Blessings (55:1-56:8).
  H. The Condemnation of the Wicked in Israel (56:9-57:21).
X. Everlasting Deliverance and Everlasting Judgment (chs. 58-66).
  A. False and True Worship (ch. 58).
  B. Zion's Confession and Redemption (ch. 59).
  C. Zion's Peace and Prosperity (ch. 60).
  D. The Lord's Favor (ch. 61).
  E. Zion's Restoration and Glory (62:1-63:6).
  F. Prayer for Divine Deliverance (63:7-64:12).
  G. The Lord's Answer: Mercy and Judgment (ch. 65).
  H. Judgment for False Worshipers and Blessing for True Worshipers (ch. 66).

ISAIAH (*Yahweh saves*).

The Prophet:
Son of Amos (Isa 1:1). Prophecies in the days of Uzziah, Jotham, Ahaz, and Hezekiah, kings of Judah (Isa 1:1; 6:1; 7:1, 3; 14:27; 20:1; 36:1; 38:1; 39:1), at the time of the invasion by the Assyrian supreme commander (Isa 20:1). Symbolically wears sackcloth, and walks barefoot, as a sign to Israel (Isa 20:2-3). Comforts and encourages Hezekiah and the people in the siege of Jerusalem by Sennacherib, king of Assyria (2Ki 18; 19; Isa 37:6-7). Comforts Hezekiah in his affliction (2Ki 20:1-11; Isa 38). Performs the miracle of the returning shadow to confirm Hezekiah's faith (2Ki 20:8-11). Reproves Hezekiah's folly in exhibiting his resources to the commissioners from Babylon (2Ki 20:12-19; Isa 39). Is chronicler of the times of Uzziah and Hezekiah (2Ch 26:22; 32:32).

The Prophecies:
Foretells punishment of the Jews for idolatry, and reproves self-confidence and distrust of God (Isa 2:6-20). Foretells the destruction of the Jews (Isa 3). Promises to the remnant restoration of divine favor (Isa 4:2-6; 6). Delineates in the parable of the

vineyard the ingratitude of the Jews, and reproves it (Isa 5:1-10). Denounces existing corruption (Isa 5:8-30).

Foretells the ill success of the plot of the Israelites and Syrians against Judah (Isa 7:1-6). Pronounces calamities against Israel and Judah (Isa 7:16-25; 9:2-6). Foretells prosperity under Hezekiah, and the manifestation of the Messiah (Isa 9:1-7). Pronounces vengeance upon the enemies of Israel (Isa 9:8-12). Denounces the wickedness of Israel, and foretells the judgments of God (Isa 9:13-21). Pronounces judgments against false prophets (Isa 10:1-4). Foretells the destruction of Sennacherib's armies (Isa 10:5-34), the restoration of Israel and the triumph of the Messiah's kingdom (Isa 11).

The burden of Babylon (Isa 13; 14:1-28). Denunciation against the Philistines (Isa 14:9-32). Burden of Moab (Isa 15-16). Burden of Damascus (Isa 17). Obscure prophecy, supposed by some authorities to be directed against the Assyrians, by others against the Egyptians, and by others against the Ethiopians (Isa 18). The burden of Egypt (Isa 19-20). Denunciations against Babylon (Isa 21:1-10). Prophecy concerning Seir (Isa 21:11-12), Arabia (Isa 21:13-17), concerning the conquest of Jerusalem, the captivity of Shebna, and the promotion of Eliakim (Isa 22:1-22), the overthrow of Tyre (Isa 23), the judgments upon the land, but that a remnant of the Jews would be saved (Isa 25-27).

Reproves Ephraim for his wickedness, and foretells the destruction by Shalmaneser (Isa 28:1-5). Declares the glory of God upon the remnant who are saved (Isa 28:5-6). Exposes the corruption in Jerusalem and exhorts to repentance (Isa 28:7-29). Foretells the invasion of Sennacherib, the distress of the Jews and the destruction of the Assyrian army (Isa 29:1-8). Denounces the hypocrisy of the Jews (Isa 29:9-17). Promises a reformation (Isa 29:18-24). Reproves the people for their confidence in Egypt, and their contempt of God (Isa 30:1-17; 31:1-6). Declares the goodness and patience of God toward them (Isa 30:18-26; 32-35).

Reproves the Jews for their spiritual blindness and infidelity (Isa 42:18-25). Promises ultimate restoration of the Jews (Isa 43:1-13). Foretells the ultimate destruction of Babylon (Isa 43:14-17; 47). Exhorts the people to repent (Isa 43:22-28). Comforts the church with promises, exposes the folly of idolatry, and their future deliverance from captivity by Cyrus (Isa 44; 45:1-5; 48:20). Foretells the conversion of the Gentiles, and triumph of the gospel (Isa 45:5-25). Denounces the evils of idolatry (Isa 46). Reproves the Jews for their idolatries and other wickedness (Isa 48). Exhorts to sanctification (Isa 56:1-8). Foretells calamities to Judah (Isa 57-58; 59:9-12).

Foreshadows the person and the kingdom of the Messiah (Isa 32-35; 42; 45; 49-56; 59:15-21; 60-66).

ISCAH Daughter of Haran and sister of Lot (Ge 11:29).

ISCARIOT (*man of Kerioth* or *of the assassins*). *See Judas.*

ISHBAH (*he boasts, congratulates*). Father of Eshtemoa (1Ch 4:17).

ISHBAK Son of Abraham and Keturah (Ge 25:2; 1Ch 1:32).

ISHBI-BENOB A giant warrior slain by Abishai (2Sa 21:16).

ISH-BOSHETH (*man of shame*). Son of Saul. Called Esh-Baal (1Ch 8:33; 9:39). Made king by Abner (2Sa 2:8-10). Deserted by Abner (2Sa 3:6-12). Restores Michal, David's wife, to David (2Sa 3:14-16). Assassinated (2Sa 4:5-8). Avenged by David (2Sa 4:9-12).

ISHHOD (*man of grandeur*). One of the tribe of Manasseh (1Ch 7:18).

ISHI (*God has saved*).

1. A play on the two Hebrew words for husband. In this verse the first is "husband"; the second is "master" which is identical with the name of the god Baal. There will be such a vigorous reaction against Baal worship that this Hebrew word for "master" will no longer be used of the Lord (Hos 2:16, ftn).
2. A son of Appaim (1Ch 2:31).
3. A descendant of Judah (1Ch 4:20).
4. A Simeonite (1Ch 4:42).
5. One of the heads of Manasseh (1Ch 5:24).

ISHIAH *See Isshiah.*

ISHIJAH (*Yahweh forget*). One of the sons of Harim (Ezr 10:31).

ISHMA (*desolate* ISBE; *God [El] he heard* KB). A descendant of Judah (1Ch 4:3).

ISHMACHIAH *See Ismakiah.*

ISHMAEL (*God [El] he heard*).

1. Son of Abraham (Ge 16:11, 15-16; 1Ch 1:28). Prayer of Abraham for (Ge 17:18, 20). Circumcised (Ge 17:23-26). Promised to be the father of a nation (Ge 16:11-12; 17:20; 21:12-13, 18). Sent away by Abraham (Ge 21:6-21). With Isaac buries his father (Ge 25:9). Children of (Ge 25:12-18; 1Ch 1:29-31). Daughter of, marries Esau (Ge 28:9; 36:2-3). Death of (Ge 25:17-18).
2. Father of Zebadiah (2Ch 19:11).
3. A son of Azel (1Ch 8:38, 9.44).
4. One of the captains of hundreds (2Ch 23:1).
5. A priest of the Exile (Ezr 10:22).
6. A son of Nethaniah. Assassinated Gedaliah, governor of Judah under king of Babylon, and takes captive many Jews (Jer 40:8-16; 41:1-11; 2Ki 25:23-25). Defeated by Johanan and put to flight (Jer 41:12-15).

ISHMAELITE(S) (*one from Ishmael*). Descended from Abraham's son, Ishmael (Ge 16:15-16; 1Ch 1:28). Divided into twelve tribes (Ge 25:16). Heads of tribes of (Ge 25:13-15; 1Ch 1:29-31).

Original possessions of (Ge 25:18). Governed by kings (Jer 25:24). Dwelt in tents (Isa 13:20). Rich in cattle (1Ch 5:21). Wore ornaments of gold (Jdg 8:24). Were the merchants of the east (Ge 37:25; Eze 27:20-21). Traveled in large companies or caravans (Ge 37:25; Job 6:19). Waylaid and plundered travelers (Jer 3:2). Often confederate against Israel (Ps 83:6).

Called:

Hagrites, either Ishmaelites (descendants of Hagar; Ge 16) or a group mentioned in Assyrian inscriptions as an Aramean confederacy (1Ch 5:10, 19-22; 27:31), are named among the enemies of Israel (Ps 83:6). Arabs (Isa 13:20).

Overcome by:

Gideon (Jdg 8:10-24). Reubenites and Gadites (1Ch 5:10, 18-20). Uzziah (2Ch 26:7). Sent presents to Solomon (1Ki 10:15; 2Ch 9:14). Sent flocks to Jehoshaphat (2Ch 17:11).

Prophecies Concerning:

To be numerous (Ge 16:10; 17:20). To be wild and savage (Ge 16:12). To be warlike and predatory (Ge 16:12). To be divided into twelve tribes (Ge 17:20). To continue independent (Ge 16:12). To be a great nation (Ge 21:13, 18). To be judged with the nations (Ge 25:23-25). Their glory to be diminished (Isa 21:13-17). Their submission to Christ (Ps 72:10, 15). Probably preached to by Paul (Gal 1:17).

ISHMAIAH (*Yahweh heard*).

1. Gibeonite (1Ch 12:4).
2. Chief of Zebulunites (1Ch 27:19).

ISHMEELITE *See Ishmaelite(s).*

ISHMERAI (*Yahweh guards*). A chief Benjamite (1Ch 8:18).

ISHOD *See Ishhod.*

ISHPAH (*he judged*). A Benjamite (1Ch 8:16).

ISHPAN (possibly *may God judge*). Son of Shashak (1Ch 8:22).

ISHTAR Semitic goddess worshiped in Phoenicia, Canaan, Assyria, and Babylonia, and sometimes even by the Israelites. Some identify her with Ashtoreth or Ashtaroth (Jdg 2:13; 10:6; 1Ki 11:5; 2Ki 23:13).

ISHTOB (*man of Tob*). *See Tob, 2.*

ISHUAH *See Ishvah.*

ISHUAI *See Ishvi, Ishvite.*

ISHVAH (*he will level*). Son of Asher (Ge 46:17; 1Ch 7:30).

ISHVI, ISHVITE

1. Son of Asher (Ge 46:17; 1Ch 7:30) and his clan (Nu 26:44).
2. Son of Saul (1Sa 14:49).

ISLAND, ISLE

1. Dry land, as opposed to water (Isa 42:15).
2. Body of land surrounded by water (Jer 2:10).
3. Coastland (Ge 10:5; Isa 20:6).
4. The farthest regions of the earth (Isa 41:5; Zep 2:11).

ISMAIAH *See Ishmaiah.*

ISMAKIAH (*Yahweh sustains*). Overseer of the temple (2Ch 31:13).

ISPAH *See Ishpah.*

ISRAEL, ISRAELITES (*he struggles with God [El]*).

1. A name given to Jacob (Ge 32:24-32; 2Ki 17:34; Hos 12:3-4).
2. A name of the Christ in prophecy (Isa 49:3).
3. A name given to the descendants of Jacob, a nation. Also called Israelites and Hebrews (Ge 43:32; Ex 1:15; 9:7; 10:3; 21:2; Lev 23:42; Jos 13:6; 1Sa 4:6; 13:3, 19; 14:11, 21; Php 3:5).

Tribes of:

Tribes of Israel were named after the sons of Jacob. In lists usually the names Levi and Joseph, two sons of Jacob, do not appear. The descendants of Levi were consecrated to the rites of religion, and the two sons of Joseph, Ephraim and Manasseh, were adopted by Jacob in Joseph's stead (Ge 48:5; Jos 14:4), and their names appear in the lists of tribes instead of those of Levi and Joseph, as follows: Asher, Benjamin, Dan, Ephraim, Gad, Issachar, Judah, Manasseh, Naphtali, Reuben, Simeon, Zebulun.

Names of, seen in John's vision, on the gates of the New Jerusalem (Rev 21:12).

Prophecies, concerning (Ge 15:5, 13; 25:23; 26:4; 27:28-29, 40; 48:19; 49; Dt 33), of the multitude of (Ge 13:16; 15:5; 22:17; 26:4; 28:14), of their captivity in Egypt (Ge 15:13-14; Ac 7:6-7).

Divided into families, each of which had a chief (Nu 25:14; 26; 36:1; Jos 7:14; 1Ch 4-8).

Number of, who went into Egypt (Ge 46:8-27; Ex 1:5; Dt 10:22; Ac 7:14). Number of, at the time of the Exodus (Ex 12:37-38, w Ge 47:27; Ex 1:7-20; Ps 105:24; Ac 7:17). Number of, fit for military service when they left Egypt (Ex 12:37), at Sinai, by tribes (Nu 1:1-50), after the plague (Nu 26), when David numbered (2Sa 24:1-9; 1Ch 21:5-6; 27:23-24), after the Captivity (Ezr 2:64; Ne 7:66-67), in John's apocalyptic vision (Rev 7:1-8).

Early History:

Dwelt in Goshen (Ge 46:28-34; 47:4-10, 27-28). Dwelt in Egypt 430 years (Ge 15:13; Ex 12:40-41; Ac 7:6; Gal 3:17). Were enslaved and oppressed by the Egyptians (Ex 1-2; 5; Ac 7:18-36). Their groaning heard by God (Ex 2:23-25). Moses commissioned as deliverer (Ex 3:2-22; 4:1-17). The land of Egypt plagued on their account. *See Egypt.* Exempt from the plagues (Ex 8:22-23; 9:4-6, 26; 10:23; 11:7; 12:13). Children were spared when the firstborn of Egypt were slain (Ex 12:13, 23). Instituted the Passover (Ex 12:1-28). Borrowed jewels from the Egyptians (Ex 11:2-3; 12:35-36; Ps 105:37). Urged by the Egyptians to depart (Ex 12:31-39). Journey from Rameses to Succoth (Ex 12:37-39). Made the journey by night (Ex 12:42). The day of their deliverance to be a memorial (Ex 12:42; 13:3-16). Led of God (Ex 13:18, 21-22). Providentially cared for (Dt 8:3-4; 29:5-6; 34:7; Ne 9:21; Ps 105:37). *See Manna; Cloud, Pillar of.*

Journey from Succoth, to Etham (Ex 13:20), to Pi Hahiroth (Ex 14:2; Nu 33:5-7). Pursued by the Egyptians (Ex 14:5-31). Pass through the Red Sea (Ex 14:19-22; Dt 11:4; Ps 78; 105-107; 136). Order of march (Nu 2). Journey to Marah (Ex 15:23; Nu 33:8). Murmur on account of the bitter water (Ex 15:23-25); water of sweetened (Ex 15:25). Journey to Elim (Ex 15:27; Nu 33:9). The itinerary (Nu 33).

Murmured for food (Ex 16:2-3). Provided with manna and quails (Ex 16:4-36). Murmured for want of water at Rephidim (Ex 17:2-7), water miraculously supplied from the rock at Meribah (Ex 17:5-7). Defeat the Amalekites (Ex 17:13; Dt 25:17-18). Arrive at Sinai (Ex 19:1; Nu 33:15). At the suggestion of Jethro, Moses' father-in-law, they organize a system of government (Ex 18:25; Dt 1:9-18). The message of God to them, requiring that they shall be obedient to his commandments, and as a reward they would be to him a holy nation, and their reply (Ex 19:3-8). Sanctify themselves for receiving the law (Ex 19:10-15). The law delivered to (Ex 20-23; 24:1-4; 25-31; Lev 1-25; 27; Dt 5; 15:16). The people receive it and covenant obedience to it (Ex 24:3, 7). Idolatry of (Ex 32; Dt 9:17-21). The anger of the Lord in consequence (Ex 32:9-14). Moses' indignation; breaks the tables of stone; enters the camp; commands the Levites; three thousand slain (Ex 32:19-35). Visited by a plague (Ex 32:35). Obduracy of (Ex 33:3; 34:9; Dt 9:12-29). God withdraws his presence (Ex 33:1-3). The mourning of, when God refused to lead them (Ex 33:4-10). Tablets renewed (Ex 34). Pattern for the tabernacle and its furnishings, and forms of worship to be observed (Ex 25-31). Gifts consecrated for the creation of the tabernacle (Ex 35; 36:1-7; Nu 7). The building of the tabernacle; the manufacture of its furnishings, including the garments of the priests; and their sanctification (Ex 36:8-38; 37-40). First sacrifice offered by under the law (Lev 8:14-36; 9:8-24). Second Passover observed (Nu 9:1-5).

March out of the wilderness (Nu 10:11-36). Itinerary (Nu 33). Order of camp and march (Nu 2). Arrive at the border of Canaan (Nu 12:16). Send twelve spies to view the land (Nu 13; 32:8; Dt 1:22, 25; Jos 14:7). Return with a majority and minority report (Nu 13:26-33; 14:6-10). Murmuring over the report (Nu 14:1-5). The judgment of God upon them in consequence of their unbelief and murmuring (Nu 14:13-39). Reaction, and their purpose to enter the land; are defeated by the Amalekites (Nu 14:40-45; Dt 1:41-45). Stay at Kadesh (Dt 1:46). Return to the wilderness, where they remain thirty-eight years, and all die except Joshua and Caleb (Nu 14:20-39). Rebellion of Korah, Dathan, and Abiram (Nu 16:1-40; Dt 11:6). Murmur against Moses and Aaron; are plagued; 14, 700 die; plague stayed (Nu 16:41-50). Murmur for want of water in Meribah; the rock is struck (Nu 20:1-13). Are refused passage through the country of Edom (Nu 20:14-21). The death of Aaron (Nu 20:22, 29; 33:38-39; Dt 10:6).

Defeat the Canaanites (Nu 21:1-3). Are scourged with serpents (Nu 21:4-9). Defeat Sihon, king of the Amorites (Nu 21:21-32; Dt 2:24-35), and Og, the king of Bashan (Nu 21:33-35; Dt 3:1-17). Arrive in the plains of Moab, at the fords of the Jordan (Nu 22:1; 33:48-49). Commit idolatry with the people of Moab (Nu 25:1-5). Visited by a plague in consequence; 24,000 die (Nu 25:6-15; 26:1). The people numbered for the allotment of the land (Nu 26). The daughters of Zelophehad sue for an inheritance (Nu 27:1-11; Jos 17:3-6). Conquest of the Midianites (Nu 31). Nations dread (Dt 2:25). Renew the covenant (Dt 29). Moses dies, and people mourn (Dt 34). Joshua appointed leader (Nu 27:18-23; Dt 31:23). *See Joshua, 1.*

All who were numbered at Sinai perished in the wilderness except Caleb and Joshua (Nu 26:63, 65; Dt 2:14-16). Piety of those who entered Canaan (Jos 23:8; Jdg 2:7-10; Jer 2:2-3). Men chosen to allot the lands of Canaan among the tribes and families (Nu 34:17-29). Remove from Shittim to Jordan (Jos 3:1). Cross Jordan (Jos 4). Circumcision observed and Passover celebrated (Jos 5). Jericho taken (Jos 6). Ai taken (Jos 7-8). Make a covenant with the Gibeonites (Jos 9). Defeat the five Amorite kings (Jos 10). Conquest of the land (Jos 21:43-45, w Jdg 1). The land allotted (Jos 15-21).

Two-and-a-half tribes return from west side of the Jordan; erect a memorial to signify the unity of the tribes; the memorial misunderstood; the controversy which followed; its amicable adjustment (Jos 22). Joshua's exhortation immediately before his death (Jos 23). Covenant renewed, death of Joshua (Jos 24; Jdg 2:8-9). Religious fidelity during the life of Joshua (Jos 24:31; Jdg 2:7).

Under the Judges:

Public affairs administered 450 years by the judges (Jdg 2:16-19; Ac 13:20). The original inhabitants not fully expelled (Jdg 1:27-36; 3:1-7). Reproved by an angel for not casting out the original inhabitants (Jdg 2:1-5). People turn to idolatry (Jdg 2:10-23). Delivered for their idolatry to the king of Mesopotamia during eight years; their repentance and deliverance (Jdg 3:8-11). Renew their idolatry, and are put under tribute to the king of Moab during eighteen years; repent and are delivered by Ehud; eighty years of peace follow (Jdg 3:12-30). Shamgar resists a foray of the Philistines and delivers Israel (Jdg 3:31). People again do evil and are put under bonds for twenty years to the king of Syria (Jdg 4:1-3). Delivered by Deborah, a prophetess, and judged (Jdg 4-5). Seven years of bondage to the Midianites; delivered by Gideon (Jdg 6-7; 8:1-28). *See Gideon.* Return to idolatry (Jdg 8:33-34).

Abimelech foments an intertribal war (Jdg 9). Judged, by Tola twenty-three years (Jdg 10:1-2), by Jair twenty-two years (Jdg 10:3-4). People backslide, and are given over to the Philistines for discipline eighteen years; repent and turn to the Lord; delivered by Jephthah (Jdg 10:6-18; 11). Ephraimites go to war against other tribes; defeated by Jephthah (Jdg 12:1-7). Judged, by Ibzan seven years (Jdg 12:8-10), by Elon ten years (Jdg 12:11-12), by Abdon eight years (Jdg 12:13-15). Backslide again and are disciplined by the Philistines forty years (Jdg 13:1). Judged by Samson twenty years (Jdg 15:20, w Jdg 13-16). Scandal of the Bethlehemite's concubine, and the consequent war between the Benjamites and the other tribes (Jdg 19-21). Judged by Eli forty years (1Sa 4:18, w 1Sa 1-4). Smitten by the Philistines at Ebenezer (1Sa 4:1-2, 10-11). Demand a king (1Sa 8:5-20; Hos 13:10).

The United Kingdom:

Saul anointed king (1Sa 10; 11:12-15; 12:13). Ammonites invade Israel, are defeated (1Sa 11). Philistines smitten (1Sa 14). Amalekites defeated (1Sa 15). David anointed king (1Sa 16:11-13).

Goliath slain (1Sa 17). Israel defeated by the Philistines, and Saul and his sons killed (1Sa 31). *See Saul.* David defeats the Amalekites (1Sa 30; 2Sa 1:1), made king (2Sa 2:4, 11). Ish-Bosheth made king (2Sa 2:8-10).

The conflict between the two political factions (2Sa 2:12-32; 3:1).

David made king over all Israel (2Sa 5:1-5). Conquests of David (2Sa 8), Absalom's rebellion (2Sa 15-18). *See David.*

Solomon anointed king (1Ki 1:32-40). Temple built (1Ki 6). Solomon's palace built (1Ki 7). Solomon's death (1Ki 11:41-43). *See Solomon.*

The Revolt of the Ten Tribes:

Foreshadowing circumstances indicating the separation: Disagreement after Saul's death (2Sa 2; 1Ch 12:23-40; 13). Lukewarmness of the ten tribes, and zeal of Judah for David in Absalom's rebellion (2Sa 19:41-43). The rebellion of Sheba (2Sa 20). The two factions are distinguished as Israel and Judah during David's reign (2Sa 21:2). Providential (Zec 11:14).

Revolt consummated under Rehoboam, son and successor of Solomon (1Ki 12). The ten tribes that revolted from the house of David also called Ephraim (Hos 7:8, 11), Jacob (Hos 12:2).

Israel (The Ten Tribes):

War continued between the two kingdoms all the days of Rehoboam and Jeroboam (1Ki 14:30), and between Jeroboam and Abijah (1Ki 15:7), and between Baasha and Asa (1Ki 15:16, 32). Famine prevails in the reign of Ahab (1Ki 18:1-6). Israel, also called Samaria, invaded by, but defeats, Ben-Hadad, king of Syria (1Ki 20). Moab rebels (2Ki 1:1; 3). Army of Syria invades Israel, but peacefully withdraws through the tact of the prophet Elisha (2Ki 6:8-23). Samaria besieged (2Ki 6:24-33; 7), city of, taken, and the people carried to Assyria (2Ki 17). The land repopulated (2Ki 17:24).

The remnant that remained after the able-bodied were carried into captivity associated with the kingdom of Judah (2Ch 30:18-26; 34:6; 35:18).

The Kings of Israel

	Names	Ruled	Dates B.C.
1.	Jeroboam I	22 years	930-909
2.	Nadab	2 years	909-908
3.	Baasha	24 years	908-886
4.	Elah	2 years	886-885
5.	Zimri	7 days	885
6.	Omri	12 years	885-874
7.	Ahab	22 years	874-853
8.	Ahaziah	2 years	853-852
9.	Joram	12 years	852-841
10.	Jehu	28 years	841-814
11.	Jehoahaz	17 years	814-798
12.	Jehoash	16 years	798-782
13.	Jeroboam II	41 years	793-753
14.	Zechariah	6 months	753
15.	Shallum	1 month	752
16.	Menahem	10 years	752-742
17.	Pekahiah	2 years	742-740
18.	Pekah	20 years	752-732
19.	Hoshea	9 years	732-722

Note: Some kings, such as Jehoash and Jeroboam II, had overlapping reigns.

See also the chart at Kings; each king by name.

Prophecies Concerning—

Of captivity, famine, and judgments (1Ki 14:15-16; 17:1; 20:13-28; 2Ki 7:1-2, 17; 8:1; Isa 7:8; 8:4-7; 9:8-21; 17:3-11; 28:1-8; Hos 1:1-9; 2:1-13; 4-10; 11:5-6; 12:7-14; 13; Am 2:6-16; 3-9).

Of restoration (Hos 2:14-23; 11:9-11; 13:13-14; 14:8). Of the reunion of the ten tribes and Judah (Jer 3:18; Eze 37:16-22).

Judah:

The nation composed of the tribes of Judah and Benjamin, called Judah (Isa 11:12-13; Jer 4:3), and Jews ruled by the descendants of David. *See Jews.*

In the historical books of the Kings and the Chronicles the nation is called Judah, but in the prophecies it is frequently referred to as Israel (Isa 8:14; 49:7).

Rehoboam succeeds Solomon. In consequence of his arbitrary policy ten tribes rebel (1Ki 12). Other circumstances of his reign (1Ki 14:21-31; 2Ch 10-12). Death of Rehoboam (1Ki 14:31). Abijah's wicked reign (1Ki 15:1-8; 2Ch 13), Asa's good reign (1Ki 15:9-24; 2Ch 14-16). Asa makes a league with Ben-Hadad, king of Syria , to make war against Israel (1Ki 15:16-24). Jehoshaphat succeeds Asa (1Ki 15:24; 2Ch 17-20; 21:1), joins Ahab against the king of Syria (1Ki 22). *See Jehoshaphat.* Jehoram, also called Joram, reigns in the place of his father, Jehoshaphat (2Ki 8:16-24; 2Ch 21). Edom revolts (2Ki 8:20-22). Ahaziah also called Azariah (2Ch 22:6) and Jehoahaz (2Ch 21:17; 25:23), succeeds Jehoram (2Ki 8:24-29; 2Ch 22); slain by Jehu (2Ki 9:27-29; 2Ch 22:8-9); Athaliah, his mother, succeeds him (2Ki 11:1-16; 2Ch 22:10-12; 23:1-15).

The Kings (and Queen) of Judah

	Name	Ruled	Dates B.C.
1.	Rehoboam	17 years	930-913
2.	Abijah	3 years	913-910
3.	Asa	41 years	910-869
4.	Jehoshaphat	25 years	872-848
5.	Jehoram	8 years	848-841
6.	Ahaziah	1 year	841
7.	Queen Athaliah	6 years	841-835
8.	Joash	40 years	835-796
9.	Amaziah	29 years	796-767
10.	Uzziah / Azariah	52 years	792-740
11.	Jotham	16 years	750-735
12.	Ahaz	16 years	732-715
13.	Hezekiah	29 years	715-686
14.	Manasseh	55 years	697-642
15.	Amon	2 years	642-640
16.	Josiah	31 years	640-609
17.	Jehoahaz	3 months	609
18.	Jehoiakim	11 years	609-598
19.	Jehoiachin	3 months	598-597
20.	Zedekiah / Mattaniah	11 years	597-586

Note: Some kings, such as Uzziah and Jotham, had overlapping reigns.

See also the chart at Kings; each king by name.

Jehoash, also called Joash, succeeds Athaliah (2Ki 11:21; 12:1-21; 2Ch 24). The temple repaired (2Ki 12). Amaziah reigns, and Judah is invaded by the king of Israel; Jerusalem is taken and the sacred things of the temple carried away (2Ki 14:1-20; 2Ch 25). Azariah, also called Uzziah, succeeds him (2Ki 14:21-22; 15:1-7; 2Ch 26). Jotham succeeds Uzziah (2Ki 15:7, 32-38; 2Ch 27). Rezin, king of Syria, invades Judah (2Ki 15:37). Jotham is succeeded by Ahaz (2Ki 16:1; 2Ch 28). Judah is invaded by kings of Samaria and Syria; Ahaz hires the king of Assyria to make war on the king of Syria (2Ki 16:5-9). Ahaz changes the fashion of the altar in the temple (2Ki 16:10-18). Hezekiah succeeds Ahaz (2Ki 16:19-20; 2Ch 29-32). His good reign (2Ki 18:1-8). He revolts from the sovereignty of the king of Assyria (2Ki 18:7). King of Assyria invades Judah and blasphemes the God of Judah; his army overthrown (2Ki 18:9-37; 19). Hezekiah's sickness and miraculous restoration (2Ki 20). Succeeded by Manasseh (2Ki 20:21; 2Ch 33:1-20). Manasseh's wicked reign (2Ki 21:1-18). Amon succeeds Manasseh on the throne (2Ki 21:18-26; 2Ch 33:20-25).

Josiah succeeds Amon; the temple is repaired; the Book of the Law recovered; religious revival follows; and the king dies (2Ki 22; 23:1-30; 2Ch 34-35). Josiah is succeeded by Jehoahaz, who reigns three months, is dethroned by the king of Egypt, and the land put under tribute (2Ki 23:30-35; 2Ch 36:1-3). Jehoiakim is elevated to the throne; becomes tributary to Nebuchadnezzar for three years; rebels; is conquered and carried to Babylon (2Ki 24:1-6; 2Ch 36:4-8). Jehoiachin is made king, suffers invasion, and is carried to Babylon (2Ki 24:8-16; 2Ch 36:9-10). Zedekiah is made king by Nebuchadnezzar; rebels; Nebuchadnezzar invades Judah, takes Jerusalem, and carries the people to Babylon, despoiling the temple (2Ki 24:17-20; 25; 2Ch 36:11-21). The poorest of the people are left to occupy the country and are joined by fragments of the army of Judah, the dispersed Israelites in other lands, and the king's daughters (2Ki 25:12, 22-23; Jer 39:10; 40:7-12; 52:16). Gedaliah appointed governor over (2Ki 25:22). His administration favorable to the people (2Ki 25:23-24; Jer 40:7-12). Conspired against and slain by Ishmael (2Ki 25:25; Jer 40:13-16; 41:1-3). Ishmael seeks to betray the people to the Ammonites (Jer 41:1-18). The people take refuge in Egypt (2Ki 25:26; Jer 41:14-18; 42:13-18).

Captivity of Judah—

Great wickedness the cause of their adversity (Eze 5-7; 16; 23:22-44). Dwell in Babylon (Da 5:13; 6:13; Jer 52:28-30) by the Kebar River (Eze 1:1; 10:15). Patriotism of (Ps 137). Plotted against, by Haman (Est 3). Are saved by Esther (Est 4-9). Cyrus decrees their restoration (2Ch 36:22-23; Ezr 1:1-4). Cyrus directs the rebuilding of the temple and the restoration of the vessels that had been carried to Babylon (2Ch 36:23; Ezr 1:3-11). Proclamation renewed by Darius and Artaxerxes (Ezr 6:1-14). Ezra returns with 1, 754 of the captives to Jerusalem (Ezr 2). Temple rebuilt and dedicated (Ezr 3-6). Artaxerxes issues proclamation to restore the temple service (Ezr 7). Priests and Levites authorized to return (Ezr 8). Corruption among the returned captives; reform (Ezr 9-10).

Nehemiah leads 49, 942 captives back to the land (Ne 2; 7:5-67; Ps 85; 87; 107; 126). Wall of Jerusalem rebuilt and dedicated (Ne 2-6; 12). The law read and expounded (Ne 8). Solemn feast is kept, priests are purified; and the covenant sealed (Ne 8-10). One-tenth of the people, to be determined by lot, volunteer to dwell in Jerusalem, and the remaining nine parts dwell in other cities (Ne 11). Catalog of the priests and Levites who came up with Zerubbabel (Ne 12). Nehemiah reforms various abuses (Ne 13). Expect a Messiah (Lk 3:15). Many accept Jesus as the Christ (Messiah) (Jn 2:23; 10:42; 11:45; 12:11; Ac 21:20). Reject Jesus. *See Jesus the Christ, Rejected.*

Rejected by God (Mt 21:43; Lk 20:16).

Prophecies Concerning Israel and Judah:

Of their rejection of the Messiah (Isa 8:14-15; 49:5, 7; 52:14; 53:1-3; Zec 11; 13; Mt 21:33; 22:1).

Of war and other judgments (Dt 28:49-57; 2Ki 20:17-18; 21:12-15; 22:16-17; 23:26-27; Isa 1:1-24; 3; 4:1; 5; 6:9-13; 7:17-25; 8:14-22; 9; 10:12; 22:1-14; 28:14-22; 29:1-10; 30:1-17; 31:1-3; 32:9-14; Jer 1:11-16; 4:5-31; 6; 7:8-34; 8; 9:9-26; 10:17-22; 11:9-23; 13:9-27; 14:14-18; 15:1-14; 16; 17:1-4; 18:15-17; 19; 20:5; 21:4-7; 22:24-30; 25:8-38; 28; 34; 37; 38:1-3; 42:13-22; 43-45; La 5:6; Eze 4-5; 11:7-12; 12; 15-17; 19; 22:13-22; 23:22-35; 24; 33:21-29; Da 9:26-27; Joel 2:1-17; Am 2:4-5; Mic 2:10; 3; 4:8-10; Hab 1:6-11; Zep 1; Zec 11; 14:1-3; Mal 4:1; Mt 21:33-34; 23:35-38; 24:2, 14-42; Mk 13:1-13; Lk 13:34-35; 19:43-44; 21:5-25; 23:28-31; Rev 1:7).

Dispersion of (Isa 24:1; Jer 9:16; Hos 9:17; Joel 3:6, 20; Am 9:9; Eze 4:13; 5:10, 12; 20:23; 36:19; Da 9:7; Jn 7:35; Ac 2:5).

Of blessing and restoration (Isa 1:25-27; 2:1-5; 4:2-6; 11:11-13; 25; 26:1-2, 12-19; 27:13; 29:18-24; 30:18-26; 32:15-20; 33:13-24; 35; 37:31-32; 40:2, 9; 41:27; 44; 49:13-23; 51; 52:1-12; 60; 61:4-9; 62; 66:5-22; Jer 3:14-18; 4:3-18; 12:14-16; 23:3; 24:1-7; 29:1-14; 30:3-22; 32:36-44; 33; 44:28; Eze 14:22-23; 16:60-63; 20:40-41; 36:1-38; 37:12, 21; Da 11:30-45; 12:1; Joel 3; Am 9:9-15; Ob 17-21; Mic 2:12-13; 5:3; Zep 2:7; Zec 1:14-21; 2:8; 10:5-12; 12:1-14; 13; 14:3-21; Mal 3:4; Ro 11; 2Co 3:16; Rev 7:15).

ISRAELITES *See Israel, Israelites.*

ISSACHAR (*there is reward, Ge. 30:18; may [God] show mercy* IDB; *hired hand* KB).

1. Fifth son of Jacob (Ge 30:18; Ex 1:3; 1Ch 2:1). Jacob's prophetic benedictions upon (Ge 49:14-15). In the time of David (1Ch 7:1-5).

2. Tribe of. Descended from Jacob's son (Ge 30:17-18). Prophecies concerning (Ge 49:14-15; Dt 33:18-19).

Persons selected from to number the people (Nu 1:8), to spy out the land (Nu 13:7). To divide the land (Nu 34:26). Strength of, on leaving Egypt (Nu 1:28-29; 2:6). Encamped under the standard of Judah east of the tabernacle (Nu 2:5). Next to and under the standard of Judah in the journeys of Israel (Nu 10:14-15). Offering of, at the dedication (Nu 7:18-23). Families of (Nu 26:23-24). Strength of, on entering Canaan (Nu 26:25). On Gerizim said amen to the blessings (Dt 27:12). Bounds of their inheritance (Jos 19:17-23). Assisted Deborah against Sisera (Jdg 5:15). Officers of, appointed by David (1Ch 27:18), appointed by Solomon (1Ki 4:17). Some of, at David's coronation (1Ch 12:32). Number of warriors belonging to, in David's time (1Ch 7:2, 5). Many of, at Hezekiah's Passover (2Ch 30:18). Remarkable persons of (Jdg 10:1; 1Ki 15:27).

ISSHIAH (*Yahweh forgets*).

1. Man of Issachar (1Ch 7:3).

2. A disaffected Israelite who joined David at Ziklag; one of David's heroes (1Ch 12:6).

3. A Kohathite Levite (1Ch 23:20).

4. A Levite (1Ch 24:21).

ISSUE OF BLOOD *See Bleeding, Subject to; Hemorrhage.*

ISUAH *See Ishvah.*

ISUI *See Ishvi.*

ITALIAN REGIMENT Cohort of Italian soldiers stationed in Caesarea when Peter preached to Cornelius (Ac 10:1).

ITALY (Ac 27:1; Heb 13:24). Aquila and Priscilla expelled from (Ac 18:2).

ITCH A skin disease (Lev 13:30-37; 14:54; Dt 28:27). *See Disease; Scall.*

ITHAI One of David's valiant men (2Sa 23:29; 1Ch 11:31).

ITHAMAR (possibly *[is]land of palms* BDB; *[father] of Tamar* KB). Son of Aaron (Ex 6:23; 28:1; 1Ch 6:3). Entrusted with money of the tabernacle (Ex 38:21). Charged with duties of the tabernacle (Nu 4:28; 7:8). Forbidden to lament the death of his brothers, Nadab and Abihu (Lev 10:6-7). Descendants of (1Ch 24:1-19).

ITHIEL (*God [El] is with me*).
1. A Benjamite (Ne 11:7).
2. An unidentified person (Pr 30:1).

ITHLAH (*hanging, lofty place*). A city of Dan (Jos 19:42).

ITHMAH (*fatherless* KB; *purity* ISBE). A Moabite (1Ch 11:46).

ITHNAN A town in the extreme S of Judah (Jos 15:23).

ITHRA (*abundance* BDB; *what remained* KB). Hebrew Ithra is a variant of Jether (2Sa 17:25, ftn). Father of Amasa (2Sa 17:25; 1Ch 2:17). *See Jether, 3.*

ITHRAN (*what is over, profit* KB; *excellent* ISBE).
1. Son of Dishon (Ge 36:26; 1Ch 1:41).
2. Son of Zophah (1Ch 7:37).

ITHREAM (*remainder of the people*). Son of David (2Sa 3:5; 1Ch 3:3).

ITHRITE(S) (*excellence*, or *preeminence* ISBE; *remainder* KB). Family of two of David's heroes (2Sa 23:38; 1Ch 11:40).

ITINERARY Of the Israelites (Nu 33; Dt 10:6-7). *See Israel, Israelites.*

ITTAH-KAZIN *See Eth Kazin.*

ITTAI (possibly *with me* BDB).
1. Gittite who became a loyal follower of David (2Sa 15:18-22; 18:2, 5).
2. *See Ithai.*

ITUREA (*pertaining to Jetur*). Region NE of Israel; its people descended from Jetur, son of Ishmael, and from whom the name Iturea is derived (Ge 25:15), ruled by Philip (Lk 3:1).

IVAH *See Ivvah.*

IVORY (SS 5:1, 4; 7:4; Eze 27:15). Exported from, Tarshish (1Ki 10:22; 2Ch 9:21), the coasts of Cyprus, the Hebrew is Kittim (Eze 27:6).
Ahab's palace made of (1Ki 22:39). Other houses made of (Ps 45:8; Am 3:15). Other articles made of: Stringed instruments (Ps 45:8), thrones (1Ki 10:18; 2Ch 9:17), benches (Eze 27:6), beds (Am 6:4), vessels (Rev 18:12).

IVVAH District in Babylon conquered by the Assyrians (2Ki 18:34; 19:13; Isa 37:13).

IYE ABARIM (*heaps of Abarim [regions beyond]*). One of the places where Israel camped in the desert (Nu 21:11; 33:44). Also called Iyim (Nu 33:45, ftn).

IYIM (Nu 33:45). *See Iye Abarim.*

IYYAR *See Month, 2; Ziv.*

IZHAR, IZHARITES (*the shining one*). Son of Kohath (Ex 6:18, 21; 1Ch 6:2, 18, 38; 23:12, 18) and his descendants (Nu 3:27; 1Ch 24:22; 26:23, 29).

IZLIAH (*long living, eternal* IDB; *Yahweh delivers* ISBE). A Benjamite son of Elpaal (1Ch 8:18).

IZRAHIAH (*Yahweh, he shines*). Grandson of Tola (1Ch 7:3).

IZRAHITE (*shining*). Family name of Shamhuth (1Ch 27:8).

IZRI (*Yahweh designs*). Perhaps the same as Zeri. Leader of the fourth division of Levitical singers (1Ch 25:11).

IZZIAH (*may Yahweh sprinkle [in atonement]* BDB; *Yahweh unites* ISBE). An Israelite of the Parosh family who marries an idolatrous wife (Ezr 10:25).

J

JAAKAN, JAAKANITES Son of Ezer (Ge 36:20-21, 27; Dt 10:6; 1Ch 1:42). A Horite (1Ch 1:42), and the same as Akan (Ge 36:27). *See Akan; Bene Jaakan.*

JAAKOBAH (*may [deity] protect* IDB). Descendant of Simeon (1Ch 4:36).

JAALA One of the servants of Solomon returned from exile (Ezr 2:56; Ne 7:58).

JAALAM *See Jalam.*

JAAN *See Dan Jaan.*

JAANAI *See Janai.*

JAAR An alternate name for Kiriath Jearim (Ps 132:6, ftn). *See Kiriath Jearim.*

JAARE-OREGIM Father of Elhanan, who slew the giant brother of Goliath (2Sa 21:19). Spelled Jair (1Ch 20:5).

JAARESHIAH (*Yahweh plants*). Son of Jeroham (1Ch 8:27).

JAASAU *See Jaasu.*

JAASIEL (*God [El] does*). One of David's warriors (1Ch 11:47). Son of Abner (1Ch 27:21).

JAASU Of the family of Bani (Ezr 10:37).

JAAZANIAH (*Yahweh listens*).
1. Also called Jezaniah (Jer 40:8, ftn). A Maacathite captain who joined Gedaliah at Mizpah (2Ki 25:23; Jer 42:1).
2. A Recabite (Jer 35:3).
3. An idolatrous zealot (Eze 8:11).
4. A wicked prince of Judah (Eze 11:1-13).

JAAZER *See Jazer.*

JAAZIAH (*may Yahweh nourish* IDB). A descendant of Merari (1Ch 24:26-27).

JAAZIEL (*God [El] strengthens* ISBE). A Levite musician (1Ch 15:18).

JABAL Son of Lamech. A shepherd (Ge 4:20).

JABBOK (*flowing*). A stream on the E of the Jordan, the northern boundary of the possessions of the Ammonites (Nu 21:24; Jdg 11:13), of the Reubenites and the Gadites (Jos 12:2; Dt 3:16). The northern boundary of the Amorites (Jdg 11:22).

JABESH (*dry*).
1. Father of King Shallum (2Ki 15:8-13).
2. Short term for Jabesh-Gilead (1Ch 10:12).

JABESH GILEAD (*dry Gilead*). A city E of the Jordan (Jdg 21:8-15). Besieged by the Ammonites (1Sa 11:1-11). Saul and his sons buried at (1Sa 31:11-13; 2Sa 2:4; 1Ch 10:11-12). Bones of Saul and his son removed from, by David, and buried at Zela (2Sa 21:12-14).

JABEZ (*to grieve*).
1. A city of Judah (1Ch 2:55).
2. The head of a family (1Ch 4:9-10).

JABIN (*perceptive*).
1. King of Hazor, defeated and slain by Joshua (Jos 11).
2. Another king of Hazor, defeated by Barak (Jdg 4; 1Sa 12:9; Ps 83:9).

JABNEEL (*God [El] will build*).
1. Town in N border of Judah, just S of Joppa (Jos 15:11), modern Yebna. Called Jabneh (2Ch 26:6). Later called Jamnia.
2. Frontier town of Naphtali (Jos 19:33), modern Tell en-Naam.

JABNEH A Philistine city (2Ch 26:6). *See Jabneel, 1.*

JACAN A Gadite (1Ch 5:13).

JACHIN, JACHINITES *See Jakin.*

JACINTH (*hyacinth*). A precious stone in the high priest's breastpiece (Ex 28:19; 39:12), in the foundation of New Jerusalem (Rev 21:20). *See Minerals of the Bible, 1; Stones.*

JACKAL A carnivorous scavenger, inhabiting the desert. Often translated "dragon" in the KJV (Job 30:29; Ps 44:19; Isa 13:21, 22; Jer 9:11; Mal 1:3).

JACKAL WELL Named only in Ne 2:13; possibly En Rogel or the Pool or Siloam. *See En Rogel; Siloam, Pool of.*

JACOB (*follower, replacer, one who follows the heel*). Son of Isaac and twin brother of Esau (Ge 25:24-26; Jos 24:4; 1Ch 1:34; Ac 7:8). Ancestor of Jesus (Mt 1:2). Given in answer to prayer (Ge 25:21). Obtains Esau's birthright for a bowl of stew (Ge 25:29-34; Heb 12:16). Fraudulently obtains his father's blessing (Ge 27:1-29; Heb 11:20). Esau seeks to kill, escapes to Paddan Aram (Ge 27:41-46; 28:1-5; Hos 12:12). His vision of the stairway (Ge 28:10-22). God confirms the covenant of Abraham to (Ge 28:13-22; 35:9-15; 1Ch 16:13-18).

Lives in Haran with his uncle, Laban (Ge 29; 30; Hos 12:12). Serves fourteen years for Leah and Rachel (Ge 29:15-30; Hos 12:12). Sharp practice of, with the flocks and herds of Laban (Ge 30:32-43). Dissatisfied with Laban's treatment and returns to the land of Canaan (Ge 31). Meets angels of God on the journey and calls the place Mahanaim (Ge 32:1-2). Dreads to meet Esau; sends him presents; wrestles with an angel (Ge 32). Name of, changed to Israel (Ge 32:28; 35:10). *See Israel.* Reconciliation of, with Esau (Ge 33:4). Journeys to Succoth (Ge 33:17), to Shechem where he purchases a parcel of ground from Hamor, and erects an altar (Ge 33:18-20). His daughter, Dinah, raped and avenged (Ge 34).

Returns to Bethel, where he builds an altar and dedicates a pillar (Ge 35:1-7). Deborah, Rebekah's nurse, dies, and is buried at Bethel (Ge 35:8). Journeys to Ephrath; Benjamin is born to; Rachel dies, and is "buried on the way to Ephrath (that is, Bethlehem)" (Ge 35:16-19; 48:7). Erects a monument at Rachel's grave (Ge 35:20). The incest of his son, Reuben, and his concubine, Bilhah (Ge 35:22). List of the names of his twelve sons (Ge 35:23-26). Returns to Kiriath Arba, the city of his father (Ge 35:27). Lives in the land of Canaan (Ge 37:1).

His partiality for his son, Joseph, and the consequent jealousy of his other sons (Ge 37:3-4). Joseph's prophetic dream concerning (Ge 37:9-11). His grief over the loss of Joseph (Ge 37:34-35). Sends into Egypt to buy grain (Ge 42:1-2; 43:1-14). His grief over the detention of Simeon and the demand for Benjamin to be taken into Egypt (Ge 42:36). His love for Benjamin (Ge 43:14; 44:29). Hears that Joseph still lives (Ge 45:26-28).

Moves to Egypt (Ge 46:1-7; 1Sa 12:8; Ps 105:23; Ac 7:14-15). List of his children and grandchildren who went down into Egypt (Ge 46:8-27). Meets Joseph (Ge 46:28-34). Pharaoh receives him and is blessed by Jacob (Ge 47:1-10). The land of Goshen assigned to (Ge 47:11-12, 27). Lives in Egypt seventeen years (Ge 47:28). Exacts promise from Joseph to bury him with his fathers (Ge 47:29-31). His benediction upon Joseph and his two sons (Ge 48:15-22). Gives the land of the two Amorites to Joseph (Ge 48:22; Jn 4:5).

His final prophetic benedictions upon his sons: Reuben (Ge 49:3-4), Simeon and Levi (Ge 49:5-7), Judah (Ge 49:8-12), Zebulun (Ge 49:13), Issachar (Ge 49:14-15), Dan (Ge 49:16-18), Gad (Ge 49:19), Asher (Ge 49:20), Naphtali (Ge 49:21), Joseph (Ge 49:22-26), Benjamin (Ge 49:27). Charges his sons to bury him in the field of Machpelah (Ge 49:29-30). Death of (Ge 49:33). Body of, embalmed (Ge 50:2). Forty days mourning for (Ge 50:3). Burial of (Ge 50:4-13). Descendants of (Ge 29:31-35; 30:1-24; 35:18, 22-26; 46:8-27; Ex 1:1-5; 1Ch 2-9).

Prophecies concerning himself and descendants (Ge 25:23; 27:28-29; 28:10-15; Ge 31:3; 35:9-13; 46:3; Dt 1:8; Ps 105:10-11). His wealth (Ge 36:6-7). Well of (Jn 4:5-30).

JACOB'S WELL Well near base of Mt. Gerizim where Jesus talked with a Samaritan woman (Jn 4).

JADA (*shrewd one* BDB; *[God] has cared* IDB). A Judahite, son of Onam (1Ch 2:26, 28).

JADAH (*honeycomb*). Most Hebrew manuscripts have Jarah. Descendant of Gibeon (1Ch 9:42, ftn), Jehoaddah (1Ch 8:36).

JADAU *See Jaddai.*

JADDAI An Israelite who married a foreign woman during the Captivity (Ezr 10:43).

JADDUA (*one known*).
1. Prince who sealed covenant (Ne 10:21).
2. Son of Jonathan; priest who returned from Babylon (Ne 12:11).

JADON (*frail one* or *Yahweh rules* IDB). One who helped in rebuilding of Jerusalem wall (Ne 3:7).

JAEL (*mountain goat*). Wife of Heber and killer of Sisera (Jdg 4:17-22; 5:6, 24).

JAGUR A town of Judah (Jos 15:21).

JAHATH (*snatch up*).
1. Grandson of Judah (1Ch 4:1-2).
2. Great-grandson of Levi (1Ch 6:16-20).
3. Levite (1Ch 23:10-11).
4. Levite (1Ch 24:22).
5. Merarite Levite (2Ch 34:8-12). *See Merari.*

JAHAZ (perhaps *a trodden* or *open place*). Also called Jahzah. A Levitical city in Reuben, taken from the Moabites (Jos 13:18; 21:36; Isa 15:4; Jer 48:21). Sihon defeated at (Nu 21:23; Dt 2:32; Jdg 11:20).

JAHAZIAH *See Jahzeiah.*

JAHAZIEL (*God [El] will see*).
1. A disaffected Israelite who joined David at Ziklag (1Ch 12:4).
2. A priest (1Ch 16:6).
3. Son of Hebron (1Ch 23:19; 24:23).
4. A Levite, and prophet (2Ch 20:14).
5. A chief, or the father of a chief, among the exiles, who returned from Babylon (Ezr 8:5).

JAHDAI (*Yahweh lead*). A descendant of Caleb (1Ch 2:47).

JAHDIEL (*God [El] gives joy*). Head of a family of Manasseh (1Ch 5:24).

JAHDO (*[God] gives joy*). Son of Buz (1Ch 5:14).

JAHLEEL, JAHLEELITE (*wait for God [El]* BDB; possibly *may God [El] show himself friendly* IDB). Son of Zebulun (Ge 46:14; Nu 26:26).

JAHMAI (*protect*). Son of Tola (1Ch 7:2).

JAHZAH A city of Reuben (1Ch 6:78). *See Jahaz.*

JAHZEEL, JAHZEELITE (*God [El] apportions*). A son of Naphtali and his clan (Nu 26:48). Also spelled Jahziel (Ge 46:24; 1Ch 7:13).

JAHZEIAH (*Yahweh sees*). Israelite who opposed Ezra in the matter of divorcing wives (Ezr 10:15).

JAHZERAH (possibly *prudent*). A priest (1Ch 9:12).

JAHZIEL *See Jahzeel.*

JAILER Of Philippi, converted (Ac 16:27-34).

JAIR, JAIRITE (*he gives light*).
1. Son of Manasseh. Founder of twenty-three cities in Gilead (Nu 32:41; Dt 3:14; Jos 13:30; 1Ki 4:13; 1Ch 2:22-23).
2. A judge of Israel (Jdg 10:3-5).
3. A Benjamite (Est 2:5).
4. Father of Elhanan (1Ch 20:5).

JAIRUS (*he gives light*). A ruler of the synagogue in Capernaum (Mt 9:18). Daughter of, restored to life (Mt 9:18, 23-26; Mk 5:22-43; Lk 8:41-56).

JAKAN *See Akan; Jaakan, Jaakanites.*

JAKEH (*prudent*). Father of Agur, a writer of proverbs (Pr 30:1).

JAKIM (*he will establish*).
1. A Benjamite (1Ch 8:19).
2. Head of a priestly division in the tabernacle service (1Ch 24:12).

JAKIN, JAKINITE (*he establishes*).
1. Son of Simeon (Ge 46:10; Ex 6:15; Nu 26:12). Called Jarib (1Ch 4:24).
2. One of Solomon's bronze pillars erected at the temple. It stood on the right (south) side of the porch (1Ki 7:21; 2Ch 3:17). *See Boaz, 2.*
3. A priest who returned from exile to Jerusalem (1Ch 9:10; Ne 11:10).
4. A priest, head of one of the courses (1Ch 24:17).

JALAM Son of Esau (Ge 36:5, 14, 18; 1Ch 1:35).

JALON Son of Ezra (1Ch 4:17).

JAMBRES An Egyptian magician (Ex 7:11; 2Ti 3:8).

JAMES (*follower, replacer, one who follows the heel*; same as Jacob).
1. An apostle. Son of Zebedee and Salome (Mt 4:21; 27:56). *See Salome.* Brother of John, and a fisherman (Lk 5:10). Called to be an apostle (Mt 4:21-22; 10:2; Mk 1:19-20; Lk 6:14; Ac 1:13). Surnamed Boanerges by Jesus (Mk 3:17).
A close companion of Jesus, and present at the large catch of fish (Lk 5:10), the healing of Peter's mother-in-law (Mk 1:29), the raising of Jairus' daughter (Mk 5:37; Lk 8:51), the transfiguration of Jesus (Mt 17:1; Mk 9:2; Lk 9:28), in Gethsemane (Mt 26:37; Mk 14:33), at the sea of Tiberias when Jesus revealed himself to the disciples after his resurrection (Jn 21:2; 1Co 15:7). Asks Jesus concerning his second coming (Mk 13:3). Bigotry of (Lk 9:54). Civil ambitions of (Mt 20:20-23; Mk 10:35-41). Martyred (Ac 12:2).
2. The younger, an apostle. Son of Alphaeus (Mt 10:3; Mk 3:18; 15:45; Lk 12:17).
3. Brother of Jesus (Mt 13:55; Mk 6:3; Gal 1:19; 2:9, 12). The brother of Judas (Jude) and Joseph (Mt 13:55; Mk 6:3; Jude 1). A witness of Christ's resurrection (1Co 15:7). Addresses the council at Jerusalem in favor of liberty for the Gentile converts (Ac 15:13-21). Disciples sent by, to Antioch (Gal 2:12). Hears of the success attending Paul's ministry (Ac 21:18-19). Epistle of (Jas 1:1).
4. Father of apostle Judas (not Iscariot) (Lk 6:16; Ac 1:13).

JAMES, EPISTLE OF

Author: James, brother of Jesus. *See James, 3.*

Date: In the early 60s, possibly before A.D. 50

Outline:
I. Greetings (1:1).
II. Trials and Temptations (1:2-18).
A. The Testing of Faith (1:2-12).
B. The Source of Temptation (1:13-18).
III. Listening and Doing (1:19-27).
IV. Favoritism Forbidden (2:1-13).
V. Faith and Deeds (2:14-26).
VI. Taming the Tongue (3:1-12).
VII. Two Kinds of Wisdom (3:13-18).
VIII. Warning Against Worldliness (ch. 4).
A. Quarrelsomeness (4:1-3).
B. Spiritual Unfaithfulness (4:4).
C. Pride (4:5-10).
D. Slander (4:11-12).
E. Boasting (4:13-17).
IX. Warning to Rich Oppressors (5:1-6).
X. Miscellaneous Exhortations (5:7-20).
A. Concerning Patience in Suffering (5:7-11).
B. Concerning Oaths (5:12).
C. Concerning the Prayer of Faith (5:13-18).
D. Concerning Those Who Wander from the Truth (5:19-20).
See General Letters.

JAMES THE YOUNGER, THE LESS *See James, 2.*

JAMIN, JAMINITE (possibly *right hand* BDB; *south, an indication of [good] fortune* KB).
1. Son of Simeon (Ge 46:10; Ex 6:15; Nu 26:12; 1Ch 4:24).
2. Descendants of Hezron (1Ch 2:27).
3. A priest who expounded the law to the exiles who returned to Jerusalem (Ne 8:7).

JAMLECH (*he will reign*). Descendant of Simeon (1Ch 4:34).

JANAI (*he will answer*). A Gadite chief (1Ch 5:12).

JANIM A city of Judah (Jos 15:53).

JANNAI (*he will answer?*). Ancestor of Joseph (Lk 3:24).

JANNES An Egyptian magician (Ex 7:11; 2Ti 3:8).

JANOAH (*resting place*).
1. Town of Naphtali (2Ki 15:29).
2. Town on boundary of Ephraim (Jos 16:6-7).

JANUM *See Janim.*

JAPHETH (*enlarge*). Son of Noah (Ge 5:32; 6:10; 7:13; 10:21); had seven sons (Ge 10:2), descendants were maritime peoples (Ge 10:5); blessed by Noah (Ge 9:20-27).

JAPHIA (perhaps *may the deity shine*).
1. King of Lachish killed by Joshua (Jos 10:3).
2. Son David (2Sa 5:15; 1Ch 3:7).
3. City in E border of Zebulun (Jos 19:12).

JAPHLET (*he delivers* IDB; possibly *he escapes* ISBE). Grandson of Beriah (1Ch 7:33).

JAPHLETITES (*of Japhlet*). Clan on W border of Ephraim (Jos 16:1-3).

JAPHO *See Joppa.*

JAR(S) For holding water (Ge 24:14-26; Ru 2:9; Jn 2:6-7), flour (1Ki 17:10-16). Containing manna, kept in the ark (Ex 16:33; Heb 9:4). Figurative of fragile human body in which believers minister the New Covenant (2Co 4:7).

JARAH (*honeycomb*). *See Jadah.*

JAREB NIV "great king" of Assyria (Hos 5:13; 10:6).

JARED (*servant* KB).
1. A descendant of Seth (Ge 5:15-16, 18-20; 1Ch 1:2).
2. An ancestor of Jesus (Lk 3:37).
3. Son of Mahalalel (1Ch 1:2).

JARESIAH *See Jaareshiah.*

JARHA Egyptian slave of Sheshan (1Ch 2:34-35).

JARIB (*Yahweh contends*).
1. Son of Simeon (1Ch 4:24).
2. A chief among the Captivity (Ezr 8:16).
3. A priest who married an idolatrous wife (Ezr 10:18).

JARKON *See Me Jarkon.*

JARMUTH (*height*).
1. City of Judah sixteen miles W by S of Jerusalem (Jos 15:35), modern Tell Yarmuk.
2. Levite city of Issachar (Jos 21:28-29). Ramoth (1Ch 6:73), Remeth (Jos 19:21).

JAROAH (*soft, delicate*). A descendant of Gad (1Ch 5:14).

JASHAR, BOOK OF (*upright, straight*). Author of book quoted (Jos 10:13; 2Sa 1:18), in LXX version (1Ki 8:53).

JASHEN (possibly *asleep*). Father of some of David's heroes (2Sa 23:32), Hashem (1Ch 11:34).

JASHER, BOOK OF *See Jashar, Book of.*

JASHOBEAM (*the people return*).
1. Hero who joined David at Ziklag (1Ch 12:6).
2. One of David's leaders (1Ch 11:11), Adino the Eznite in Hebrew and Septuagint (2Sa 23:8, ftn).
3. Hacmoni (1Ch 27:2-3). *See above, 2.* May be the same.

JASHUB, JASHUBITE (*he returns*).
1. Son of Issachar (Ge 46:13; Nu 26:24).
2. Shear-Jashub, a son of Isaiah (Isa 7:3).
3. Man who married foreign wife (Ezr 10:29).

JASHUBI LEHEM (*[they] returned to Lehem*). A descendant of Shelah (1Ch 4:22).

JASIEL *See Jaasiel.*

JASON (*to heal*). A Christian at Thessalonica (Ac 17:5-7, 9) and possibly Paul's relative (Ro 16:21).

JASPER A precious stone set in the high priest's breastplate (Ex 28:20; 39:13; Job 28:18; Eze 28:13; Rev 4:3; 21:11, 18-19). *See Minerals of the Bible, 1; Stones.*

JATHNIEL (*God [El] hires* BDB; *God [El] is forever* KB). Son of Meshelemiah (1Ch 26:2).

JATTIR (possibly *preeminence* IDB). A Levitical city (Jos 15:48; 21:14; 1Sa 30:27; 1Ch 6:57).

JAVAN
1. A son of Japheth. Father of Elishah, Tarshish, Kittim, and Rodanim (Ge 10:4; 1Ch 1:7). Javan is same as Greek Ionia, with whom the Hebrews traded (Isa 66:19; Joel 3:4-6).
2. A city in Arabia in which the Phoenicians traded (Eze 27:13, 19).

JAVELIN A heavy lance (Eze 39:9), used by Goliath (1Sa 17:6), by Saul (1Sa 18:11; 19:9-10).

JAZER (*he helps*).
1. Taken from the Amorites (Nu 21:32; 32:1, 3, 35). Ammonite stronghold E of the Jordan, probably c. fourteen miles N of Heshbon; assigned to Gad (Jos 13:24-25), later given to Levites; a city of refuge E of the Jordan (Jos 21:39).
2. Sea of (Jer 48:32).

JAZIZ Overseer of David's flocks (1Ch 27:31).

JEALOUSY (Pr 6:34; 27:4; Ecc 4:4; SS 8:6). Law concerning, when husband is jealous of his wife (Nu 5:12-31). Image of (Eze 8:3-4). Forbidden (Ro 13:13).
Attributed to God (Ex 20:5; 34:13-14; Nu 25:11; Dt 29:20; 32:16, 21; 1Ki 14:22; Ps 78:58; 79:5; Isa 30:1-2; 31:1, 3; Eze 16:42; 23:25; 36:5-6; 38:19; Zep 1:18; 3:8; Zec 1:14; 8:2; 1Co 10:22).
See Anthropomorphisms.
A desire to emulate (Ro 10:19; 11:11).
See Emulation; Envy.

Figurative: (2Co 11:2).

Instances of:
Cain, of Abel (Ge 4:5-6, 8). Sarah, of Hagar (Ge 16:5). Joseph's brothers, of Joseph (Ge 37:4-11, 18-28). Saul, of David (1Sa 18:8-30; 19:8-24; 20:24-34). Joab, of Abner (2Sa 3:24-27). Nathan, of Adonijah (1Ki 1:24-26). Ephraimites, of Gideon (Jdg 8:1), of Jephthah (Jdg 12:1). The brother of the prodigal son (Lk 15:25-32). Sectional, between Israel and the tribe of Judah (2Sa 19:41-43).

JEALOUSY, WATER OF *See Water of Bitterness.*

JEARIM (*timberlands*). Hill on N border of Judah (Jos 15:10).

JEATHERAI Descendant of Gershom (1Ch 6:21).

JEBEREKIAH (*Yahweh blesses*). Father of Zechariah (Isa 8:2).

JEBUS Name of Jerusalem when in possession of Jebusites (Jos 15:63; Jdg 19:10), taken by Israelites (Jdg 1:8), but stronghold not captured until David's time (2Sa 5:7-8).

JEBUSITE(S) (*of Jebus*). One of the tribes of Canaan (Dt 7:1). Land of, given to Abraham and his descendants (Ge 15:21; Ex 3:8, 17; 23:23-24; Dt 20:17; Ex 33:2; 34:10-11). Conquered by Joshua (Jos 10-12; 24:11), by David (2Sa 5:6-9). Jerusalem within the territory of (Jos 18:28). Not exterminated, but intermarry with the Israelites (Jdg 3:5-6; Ezr 9:1-2; 10:18-44). Pay tribute to Solomon (1Ki 9:20-21).

JECAMIAH *See Jekamiah.*

JECOLIAH (*Yahweh is able*). Mother of King Uzziah (2Ch 26:3; 2Ki 15:2).

JECONIAH Variant of Jehoiachin (Jer 22:24, 28; 37:1). *See Jehoiachin.* King of Judah, captured by Nebuchadnezzar (2Ki 24:1-12).

JEDAIAH (*Yahweh has favored* IDB, or *Yahweh knows*).
1. Descendant of Simeon (1Ch 4:37).
2. A returned exile (Ne 3:10).
3. A priest of the Captivity (1Ch 9:10; 24:7; Ezr 2:36; Ne 7:39).
4. A priest who lived at Jerusalem after the return of the Captivity (Ne 11:10; 12:6, 19; Zec 6:10, 14).
5. Another priest, who returned from Babylon with Nehemiah (Ne 12:7, 21).

JEDIAEL (*known of God [El]*).
1. Son of Benjamin (1Ch 7:6, 10-11).
2. Son of Shimri (1Ch 11:45).
3. A Manassite chief who joined David at Ziklag (1Ch 12:20).
4. Son of Meshelemiah (1Ch 26:2).

JEDIDAH (*beloved* BDB; *lovely, beloved* KB). Mother of King Josiah (2Ki 22:1).

JEDIDIAH (*beloved of Yahweh*). Name that Nathan gave to Solomon (2Sa 12:24-25).

JEDUTHUN A musician of the temple (1Ch 16:41; 25:1). Called Ethan (1Ch 6:44; 15:17). *See titles of Psalms 39, 62, 77.*

JEEZER, JEEZERITES *See Abiezer, 1; Iezer.*

JEGAR SAHADUTHA (*witness heap*). Name given by Laban to heap of stones set up as memorial of covenant between him and Jacob; called Galeed by Jacob (Ge 31:47-48).

JEHALLELEL (*he shall praise God [El]* BDB; *God [El] shines forth* IDB).
1. Descendant of Judah (1Ch 4:16).
2. Merarite Levite (2Ch 29:12).

JEHATH Son of Gershon (1Ch. 6:20).

JEHDEIAH (*Yahweh rejoices [in his works]*).
1. Descendant of Moses (1Ch 24:20).
2. Man in charge of David's donkeys (1Ch 27:30).

JEHEZKEL (*God [El] gives strength*). Priest in David's time (1Ch 24:16).

JEHIAH (*Yahweh lives*). A Levite, and doorkeeper of the ark (1Ch 15:24).

JEHIEL (*God [El] lives*).
1. A Levite gatekeeper (1Ch 15:18). Probably identical with Jehiah. *See Jehiah.*
2. A Gershonite Levite (1Ch 23:8; 29:8).
3. A companion of David's sons (1Ch 27:32).
4. Son of Jehoshaphat (2Ch 21:2).
5. Son of Heman (2Ch 29:14).
6. A Levite overseer in the temple (2Ch 31:13).
7. A priest who gave extraordinary offerings for the Passover (2Ch 35:8).
8. Father of Obadiah (Ezr 8:9).
9. Father of Shecaniah (Ezr 10:2).
10. Name of two priests who married idolatrous wives (Ezr 10:21, 26).

JEHIELI (*of Jehiel*). Son of Ladan (1Ch 26:21-22).

JEHIZKIAH (*Yahweh gives strength*). Israelite chief in days of Ahaz, king of Judah (2Ch 28:12).

JEHOADDAH Descendant of King Saul (1Ch 8:36), Jadah (1Ch 9:42).

JEHOADDIN (probably *Yahweh is delight*). Wife of King Joash of Judah (2Ch 25:1), Jehoaddin (2Ki 14:2).

JEHOAHAZ (*Yahweh holds*).
1. Son of Jehu and king of Israel (2Ki 10:35; 13:1-9).
2. Son of Jehoram, king of Judah (2Ch 21:17). *See Ahaziah.*
3. Also called Shallum. King of Judah and successor of Josiah (2Ki 23:30-31; 1Ch 3:15; 2Ch 36:1; Jer 22:11). Wicked reign of (2Ki 23:32). Pharaoh Neco, king of Egypt, invades the kingdom of, defeats him, and takes him captive to Egypt (2Ki 23:33-35; 2Ch 36:3-4). Prophecies concerning (Jer 22:10-12).

JEHOASH, JOASH (*Yahweh bestows* ISBE; *man of Yahweh* KB).
1. Grandson of Benjamin (1Ch 7:8).
2. Descendant of Judah (1Ch 4:22).
3. Father of Gideon (Jdg 6:12).
4. Keeper of David's supply of oil (1Ch 27:28).

5. Israelite who joined David at Ziklag (1Ch 12:3).
6. Son of King Ahab (1Ki 22:26).
7. King of Judah (2Ki 11-13; 2Ch 24-25).
8. King of Israel (2Ki 13:10-13; 14:8-16; 2Ch 25:17-24).

JEHOHANAN (*Yahweh has been gracious*).
1. A gatekeeper of the tabernacle (1Ch 26:3).
2. A military chief under Jehoshaphat, whose corps consisted of 280,000 men (2Ch 17:15). Probably identical with a captain of a hundred (2Ch 23:1).
3. Son of Bebai (Ezr 10:28).
4. A priest among the exiles who returned from Babylon (Ne 12:13).
5. A choir member in the temple (Ne 12:42).

JEHOIACHIN (*Yahweh supports*). (Jer 22:24; 37:1). King of Judah and successor to Jehoiakim (2Ki 24:6-8; 1Ch 3:16; 2Ch 36:8-9; Jer 24:1). Wicked reign of (2Ki 24:9; 2Ch 36:9). Nebuchadnezzar invades his kingdom, takes him captive to Babylon (2Ki 24:10-16; 2Ch 36:10; Est 2:6; Jer 27:20; 29:1-2; Eze 1:2). Confined in prison thirty-seven years (2Ki 25:27). Released from prison by Evil-Merodach and promoted above other kings, and honored until death (2Ki 25:27-30; Jer 52:31-34). Prophecies concerning (Jer 22:24-30; 28:4). Sons of (1Ch 3:17-18). Ancestor of Jesus, called Jeconiah (Mt 1:11, 12).

JEHOIADA (*Yahweh has known*).
1. Father of Benaiah, one of David's officers (2Sa 8:18).
2. A high priest. Overthrows Athaliah, the usurping queen of Judah, and establishes Jehoash upon the throne (2Ki 11; 2Ch 23). Salutary influence of, over Joash (Hebrew *Jehoash*, a variant of *Joash*) (2Ki 12:2, ftn; 2Ch 24:2, 22). Directs the repairs of the temple (2Ki 12:4-16; 2Ch 24:4-14). Death of (2Ch 24:15-16).
3. A priest who led 3, 700 priests armed for war (1Ch 12:27).
4. Son of Benaiah (1Ch 27:34).
5. A returned exile (Ne 3:6).
6. A priest mentioned in Jeremiah's letter to the captive Israelites (Jer 29:26).

JEHOIAKIM (*Yahweh lifts up, establishes*). Also called Eliakim. King of Judah (1Ch 3:15). Wicked reign and final overthrow of (2Ki 23:24-37; 24:1-6; 2Ch 36:4-8; Jer 22:13-19; 26:22-23; 36; Da 1:1-2). Dies and is succeeded by his son, Jehoiachin (2Ki 24:6).

JEHOIARIB (*Yahweh argues [for me]*).
1. Priest in days of David (1Ch 24:7).
2. Priest who returned from exile (1Ch 9:10). *See Joiarib.*

JEHONADAB *See Jonadab, 2.*

JEHONATHAN (*Yahweh has given*).
1. Overseer of David's property (1Ch 27:25).
2. Levite (2Ch 17:8).
3. Priest (Ne 12:18).

JEHORAM (*Yahweh exalts*).
1. King of Judah (1Ki 22:50; 2Ki 8:16; 1Ch 3:11; 2Ch 21:5). Ancestor of Jesus (Mt 1:8). Marries Athaliah, whose wicked counsels influence his reign for evil (2Ki 8:18-19; 2Ch 21:6-13).
Slays his brothers to strengthen himself in his sovereignty (2Ch 21:4, 13). Edom revolts from (2Ki 8:20-22; 2Ch 21:8-10). Philistines and Arabs invade his territory (2Ch 21:16-17). Death of (2Ch 21:18-20; 2Ki 8:24). Prophecy concerning (2Ch 21:12-15).
2. A son of Ahab. *See Joram.*
3. A priest commissioned to go through Israel and instruct the people in the law (2Ch 17:8).

JEHOSHABEATH *See Jehosheba.*

JEHOSHAPHAT (*Yahweh has judged*).
1. David's recorder (2Sa 8:16; 20:24; 1Ki 4:3; 1Ch 18:15).
2. One of Solomon's district officers (1Ki 4:17).
3. King of Judah. Succeeds Asa (1Ki 15:24; 22:41; 1Ch 3:10; 2Ch 17:1; Mt 1:8). Strengthens himself against Israel (2Ch 17:2). Inaugurates a system of public instruction in the law (2Ch 17:7-9). His wise reign (1Ki 22:43; 2Ch 17:7-9; 19:3 11). His system of tribute (2Ch 17:11). His military forces and armament (2Ch 17:12-19). Joins Ahab in an invasion of Ramoth Gilead (1Ki 22; 2Ch 18). Rebuked by the prophet Jehu (2Ch 19:2). The allied forces of the Amorites, Moabites, and other tribes invade his territory and are defeated by (2Ch 20). Builds ships for commerce with Tarshish; ships are destroyed (1Ki 22:48-49; 2Ch 20:35-37). Joins Jehoram, king of Israel, in an invasion of the land of Moab, and defeats the Moabites (2Ki 3). Makes valuable gifts to the temple (2Ki 12:18). Death of (1Ki 22:50; 2Ch 21:1). Religious zeal of (1Ki 22:43, 46; 2Ch 17:1-9; 19; 20:1-32; 22:9). Prosperity of (1Ki 22:45, 48; 2Ch 17-20). Bequests of, to his children (2Ch 21:2-3).
4. Father of Jehu (2Ki 9:2, 14).
5. A priest who assisted in bringing the ark from Obed-Edom (1Ch 15:24).

JEHOSHAPHAT, VALLEY OF (*valley of Yahweh's judgment*). Symbolic name for a valley where all nations will be gathered by Yahweh for judgment (Joel 3:2, 12), also called "the valley of decision" (Joel 3:14).

JEHOSHEBA (*Yahweh is an oath* ISBE; *Yahweh gives plenty, satisfies* KB). Daughter of King Jehoram; wife of high priest Jehoiada; hid Joash from Athaliah (2Ki 11:2). Also spelled Jehoshabeath (1Ch 22:11, ftn).

JEHOSHUA, JEHOSHUAH *See Joshua, 1.*

JEHOVAH A misreading of the name of God, Yahweh. Hebrew was originally written using only consonants. The pronunciation (and vowels) of the Hebrew Bible was handed down orally. When the vowels were eventually added to the Hebrew text, the name Yahweh was no longer pronounced. Instead, out of reverence, the title *Adonay* (Lord) was substituted. In keeping with this oral tradition, the Jewish scribes inserted into Yahweh the vowels for Adonay, resulting in the spelling Yehowah, though the name was still pronounced Adonay in oral reading. In c. 1520 the Christian scholar Petrus Galatinus introduced the hybrid spelling Jehovah, which became widely used in English versions, literature, and hymns. In the NIV, Yahweh is represented by LORD.
See God, Names of; Yahweh.

JEHOVAH-JIREH *See God, Names of, Yahweh Yireh.*

JEHOVAH-NISSI *See God, Names of, Yahweh Nissi.*

JEHOVAH-RAPAH *See God, Names of, Yahweh Raphah.*

JEHOVAH-SHALOM *See God, Names of, Yahweh Shalom.*

JEHOVAH-SHAMMAH *See God, Names of, Yahweh Shammah.*

JEHOVAH-TSIDKENU *See God, Names of, Yahweh Tsidkenu.*

JEHOZABAD (*Yahweh endows*).
1. Son of Shomer, and one of the assassins of King Jehoash (2Ki 12:21; 2Ch 24:26).
2. Son of Obed-Edom (1Ch 26:4).
3. A Benjamite chief who commanded 180,000 men (2Ch 17:18).

JEHOZADAK (*Yahweh is just*). Also called Jozadak. A priest of the Exile (1Ch 6:14-15; Hag 1:1, 12, 14; 2:2, 4; Zec 6:11).

JEHU (*Yahweh is he*).
1. The prophet who announced the wrath of Yahweh against Baasha, king of Israel (1Ki 16:1, 7, 12; 2Ch 19:2; 20:34).
2. Son of Nimshi, king of Israel (1Ki 19:16; 2Ki 9:1-4). Religious zeal of, in killing idolaters (2Ki 9:14-37; 10:1-28; 2Ch 22:8-9). His territory invaded by Hazael, king of Syria (2Ki 10:32-33). Prophecies concerning (1Ki 19:17; 2Ki 10:30; 15:12; Hos 1:4). Death of (2Ki 10:35).
3. Son of Obed (1Ch 2:38).
4. Son of Joshibiah (1Ch 4:35).
5. A Benjamite (1Ch 12:3).

JEHUBBAH *See Hubbah.*

JEHUCAL (*Yahweh is capable*). Man sent by King Zedekiah to Jeremiah for prayers (Jer 37:3). Prince who put Jeremiah in prison (Hebrew *Jucal*, a variant of *Jehucal*) (Jer 38:1, ftn).

JEHUD (*declare*). Town in Dan, c. seven miles E of Joppa (Jos 19:45).

JEHUDI (*Jew*). Prince in Jehoiakim's court (Jer 36:14, 21).

JEHUDIJAH NIV "Judean" wife of Mered (1Ch 4:18).

JEHUSH *See Jeush, 4.*

JEIEL (*God [El] has preserved* IDB; possibly *God [El] sweeps up* KB).
1. Also called Jehiel. A Reubenite (1Ch 5:7).
2. A Benjamite (1Ch 9:35).
3. One of David's heroes (1Ch 11:44).
4. A Levite and singer in the tabernacle service (1Ch 15:18, 21; 16:5).
5. A Levite, ancestor of Jahaziel, who encouraged Judah against their enemies (2Ch 20:14).
6. A scribe during the reign of Uzziah (2Ch 26:11).
7. A Levite who cleansed the temple (2Ch 29:13).
8. A chief of the Levites who gave, with other chiefs, "five thousand Passover offerings and five hundred head of cattle for the Levites" for sacrifice (2Ch 35:9).
9. A son of Adonikam, an exile who returned to Jerusalem with Ezra (Ezr 8:13).
10. A priest who was defiled by marriage to an idolatrous woman (Ezr 10:43).

JEKABZEEL (*God [El] gathers*). A city in the S of Judah (Ne 11:25).

JEKAMEAM (*[my] kinsman establishes*). Son of Hebron (1Ch 23:19; 24:23).

JEKAMIAH (*Yahweh will establish*).
1. Judahite (1Ch 2:41).
2. Son of King Jehoiachin (Jehoiachin) (1Ch 3:18).

JEKUTHIEL (*God [El] will nourish*). Son of Ezra (1Ch 4:18).

JEMIMAH (*dove*). Daughter of Job born after restoration from affliction (Job 42:14).

JEMUEL Son of Simeon (Ge 46:10; Ex 6:15). Also called Nemuel (Nu 26:9, 12; 1Ch 4:24). *See Nemuel, 1.*

JEPHTHAH (*Yahweh opens, frees*). A judge of Israel. Illegitimate and therefore not entitled to inherit his father's property (Jdg 11:1-2). Escapes the violence of his half-brothers, lives in the land of Tob (Jdg 11:3). Recalled from the land of Tob by the elders of Gilead (Jdg 11:5). Made captain of the host (Jdg 11:5-11) and made head of the land of Gilead (Jdg 11:7-11). His message to the king of the Ammonites (Jdg 11:12-28). Leads the host of Israel against the Ammonites (Jdg 11:29-33). His rash vow concerning his daughter (Jdg 11:31, 34-40). Falsely accused by the Ephraimites (Jdg 12:1). Leads the army of the Gileadites against the Ephraimites (Jdg 12:4). Judges Israel six years, dies, and is buried in Gilead (Jdg 12:7). Faith of (Heb 11:32).

JEPHUNNEH (perhaps *may he [God] turn* or *turned*).
1. Father of Caleb (Nu 13:6).
2. Son of Jether (1Ch 7:38).

JERAH (*moon [god?]*). Son of Joktan (Ge 10:26; 1Ch 1:20).

JERAHMEEL, JERAHMEELITE (*God [El] will have compassion*).
1. Son of Hezron (1Ch 2:9).
2. Son of Kish (1Ch 24:29).
3. An officer of Jehoiakim, king of Judah (Jer 36:26).

JERASH *See Gerasenes.*

JERED (*rose* IDB; *servant* KB). A Judahite (1Ch 4:18).

JEREMAI (possibly *fat*). Of the family of Hashum (Ezr 10:33).

JEREMIAH, BOOK OF

Author: Jeremiah, son of Berekiah

Date: Between 626 and 586 B.C.

Outline:
I. Call of the Prophet (ch. 1).
II. Warnings and Exhortations to Judah (chs. 2-35).
A. Earliest Discourses (chs. 2-6).
B. Temple Message (chs. 7-10).
C. Covenant and Conspiracy (chs. 11-13).
D. Messages Concerning the Drought (chs. 14-15).
E. Disaster and Comfort (16:1-17:18).
F. Command to Keep the Sabbath Holy (17:19-27).
G. Lessons from the Potter (chs. 18-20).
H. Condemnation of Kings, Prophets and People (chs. 21-24).
I. Foretelling the Babylonian Exile (chs. 25-29).
J. Promises of Restoration (chs. 30-33).
K. Historical Appendix (chs. 34-35).
III. Suffering and Persecutions of the Prophet (chs. 36-38).
A. Burning Jeremiah's Scroll (ch. 36).
B. Imprisoning Jeremiah (chs. 37-38).
IV. The Fall of Jerusalem and Its Aftermath (chs. 39-45).
A. The Fall Itself (ch. 39).
B. Accession and Assassination of Gedaliah (40:1-41:15).
C. Migration to Egypt (41:16-43:13).
D. Prophecy Against Those in Egypt (ch. 44).
E. Historical Appendix: Promise to Baruch (ch. 45).
V. Judgment Against the Nations (chs. 46-51).
A. Against Egypt (ch. 46).
B. Against Philistia (ch. 47).
C. Against Moab (ch. 48).
D. Against Ammon (49:1-6).
E. Against Edom (49:7-22).
F. Against Damascus (49:23-27).
G. Against Kedar and Hazor (Arabia) (49:28-33).
H. Against Elam (49:34-39).
I. Against Babylon (chs. 50-51).
VI. Historical Appendix (ch. 52).

JEREMIAH (*Yahweh loosens [the womb]* BDB; *Yahweh lifts up* IDB; possibly *Yahweh shoots, establishes* KB). One of the greatest Hebrew prophets (c. 640-587 B.C.); born into priestly family of Anathoth, two-and-a-half miles NE of Jerusalem; called to prophetic office by a vision (Jer 1:4-10), and prophesied during last five kings of Judah (Josiah, Jehoahaz II, Jehoiakim, Jehoiachin, Zedekiah), probably helped Josiah in his reforms (2Ki 23), warned Jehoiakim against Egyptian alliance, prophetic roll destroyed by king (Jer 36), persecuted by nobility in days of the last king (Jer 36-37), Nebuchadnezzar kind to him after the destruction of Jerusalem (Jer 39:11-12), compelled to go to Egypt with Israelites who slew Gedaliah, and there he died (Jer 43:6-7).
Six other Jeremiahs are briefly mentioned in the OT:
1. Benjamite who came to David at Ziklag (1Ch 12:4).
2. A Gadite (1Ch 12:10).
3. A Gadite (1Ch 12:13).
4. A Manassite (1Ch 5:24).
5. Father of the wife of King Josiah (2Ki 23:30-31).
6. A Recabite (Jer 35:3).

JEREMOTH (*swollen* or *obese*).
1. A Benjamite (1Ch 7:8).
2. A Benjamite (1Ch 8:14)
3. Descendant of Elam who put away foreign wife (Ezr 10:26).
4. Descendant of Zattu who put away foreign wife (Ezr 10:27).
5. Descendant of Bani who put away foreign wife (Ezr 10:29).

JERIAH (*Yahweh founds*). A descendant of Hebron (1Ch 23:19; 24:23; 26:31).

JERIBAI (*Yahweh pleads*). A valiant man of David's guard (1Ch 11:46).

JERICHO (*moon city*).
1. A city E of Jerusalem and near the Jordan (Nu 22:1; 26:3; Dt 34:1). Called the City of Palm Trees (Dt 34:3). Situation of, pleasant (2Ki 2:19). Rahab the harlot lived in (Jos 2; Heb 11:31). Joshua sees the "captain of the host" of the Lord near (Jos 5:13-15). Besieged by Joshua seven days; fall and destruction of (Jos 6; 24:11). Situated within the territory allotted to Benjamin (Jos 18:12, 21). The Kenites lived at (Jdg 1:16). King of Moab makes conquest of, and establishes his capital at (Jdg 3:13). Rebuilt by Hiel (1Ki 16:34). Company of "the sons of the prophets," lived at (2Ki 2:4-5, 15, 18). Captives of Judah, taken by the king of Israel, released at, on account of the denunciation of the prophet Obed (2Ch 28:7-15). Inhabitants of, taken captive to Babylon, return to, with Ezra and Nehemiah (Ezr 2:34; Ne 7:36), assist in repairing the walls of Jerusalem (Ne 3:2). Blind men healed at, by Jesus (Mt 20:29-34; Mk 10:46; Lk 18:35). Zacchaeus lived at (Lk 19:1-10).
2. Plain of (2Ki 25:5; Jer 52:8).
3. Waters of (Jos 16:1). Purified by Elisha (2Ki 2:18-22).

JERIEL (*founded of God [El]* BDB; *God [El] will see* IDB). Son of Tola (1Ch 7:2).

JERIJAH *See Jeriah.*

J

JERIMOTH (*swollen* or *obese*). *See also Jeremoth.*
1. Son of Bela (1Ch 7:7).
2. A disaffected Israelite, who denounced Saul and joined David at Ziklag (1Ch 12:5).
3. Son of Mushi (1Ch 23:23; 24:30).
4. Son of Heman (1Ch 25:4, 22).
5. A ruler of the tribe of Naphtali (1Ch 27:19).
6. A son of David (2Ch 11:18).
7. A Levite (2Ch 31:13).

JERIOTH (*tents*). Wife of Caleb. Probably identical with Azubah (1Ch 2:18).

JEROBOAM (*the people increase* BDB).
1. First king of Israel after the revolt. Promoted by Solomon (1Ki 11:28). Ahijah's prophecy concerning (1Ki 11:29-39; 14:5-16). Flees to Egypt to escape from Solomon (1Ki 11:26-40). Recalled from Egypt by the ten tribes on account of disaffection toward Rehoboam, and made king (1Ki 12:1-20; 2Ch 10:12-19). Subverts the religion of Moses (1Ki 12:25-33; 13:33-34; 14:9, 16; 16:2, 26, 31; 2Ch 11:14; 13:8-9). Hand of, paralyzed (1Ki 13:1-10). His wife sent to consult the prophet Ahijah concerning her child (1Ki 14:1-18). His wars with Rehoboam (1Ki 14:19, 30; 15:6; 2Ch 11:1-4). His war with Abijah (1Ki 15:7; 2Ch 13). Death of (1Ki 14:20; 2Ch 13:20).
2. King of Israel. Successor to Jehoash (2Ki 14:16, 23). Makes conquest of Hamath and Damascus (2Ki 14:25-28). Wicked reign of (2Ki 14:24). Prophecies concerning (Am 7:7-13). Death of (2Ki 14:29). Genealogies written during his reign (1Ch 5:17).

JEROHAM (*he will be compassionate*).
1. A Levite, and grandfather of Samuel (1Sa 1:1; 1Ch 6:27, 34).
2. A chief of the tribe of Benjamin (1Ch 8:27).
3. A descendant of Benjamin (1Ch 9:8).
4. A priest, and father of Adaiah, who lived in Jerusalem after the Exile (1Ch 9:12; Ne 11:12).
5. Father of two Israelites who joined David at Ziklag (1Ch 12:7).
6. The father of Azarel (1Ch 27:22).
7. Father of Azariah (2Ch 23:1).

JERUB-BAAL (*Baal contends*). *See Gideon.*

JERUB-BESHETH (*Shame [Baal] contends*). *See Gideon.*

JERUEL (*God [El] is a foundation*). A wilderness in the S of Judah (2Ch 20:16).

JERUSALEM (*foundation of Shalem [peace]*).

Called:
Jebus (Jos 18:28; Jdg 19:10), Zion (1Ki 8:1; Zec 9:13), City of David (2Sa 5:7; Isa 22:9), Salem (Ge 14:18; Ps 76:2), Ariel (Isa 29:1), City of God (Ps 46:4), City of the Great King (Ps 48:2), City of Judah (2Ch 25:28), The Perfection of Beauty, The Joy of the Whole Earth (La 2:15), The Throne of the Lord (Jer 3:17), Holy Mountain (Da 9:16, 20), Holy City (Ne 11:1, 18; Mt 4:5), City of our festivals (Isa 33:20), City of Truth (Zec 8:3), to be called "The LORD Our Righteousness" (Jer 33:16), Yahweh Shammah (Eze 48:35), *See God, Names of: Yahweh Shammah.* New Jerusalem (Rev 21:2, 10-27).
Situation and appearance of (Ps 122:3; 125:2; SS 6:4; Mic 4:8). Walls of (Jer 39:4).

Gates of:
Benjamin Gate (Jer 37:13; 38:7; Zec 14:10). Corner Gate (2Ki 14:13; 2Ch 25:23; 26:9; Jer 31:38; Zec 14:10). Dung Gate (Ne 2:13; 3:13, 14; 12:31). East Gate (1Ch 26:14; 2Ch 31:14; Ne 3:29). Ephraim Gate (2Ki 14:13; 2Ch 25:23; Ne 8:16; 12:39). First Gate (Zec 14:10). Fish Gate (2Ch 33:14; Ne 3:3; 12:39; Zep 1:10). Fountain Gate (Ne 2:14; 3:15; 12:37). Foundation Gate (2Ch 23:5). Gate of Joshua (2Ki 23:8). Gate of the guards (2Ki 11:19). Horse Gate (2Ch 23:15; Ne 3:28; Jer 31:40). Inspection Gate (Ne 3:31). Jeshanah [Old] Gate (Ne 3:6; 12:39). King's Gate (1Ch 9:18). Middle Gate (Jer 39:3). New Gate (Jer 26:10; 36:10). North Gate (1Ch 26:14). Potsherd Gate (Jer 19:2). Shalleketh Gate (1Ch 26:16). Sheep Gate (Ne 3:1, 32; 12:39; Jn 5:2). South Gate (1Ch 26:15). Sur Gate (2Ki 11:6). Upper Gate (2Ki 15:35; 2Ch 23:20; 27:3). Upper Gate of Benjamin (Jer 20:2). Valley Gate (2Ch 26:9; Ne 2:13, 15; 3:13). Water Gate (Ne 3:26; 8:1, 3, 16; 12:37). West Gate (1Ch 26:16).
Gates of the twelve tribes in Ezekiel's vision (Eze 48:31-34). Measurement of (Eze 45:6).

Buildings:
High priest's palace (Jn 18:15). Barracks (Ac 21:34). Stairway of Ahaz (2Ki 20:11). Stairs (Ne 9:4).

Squares and Streets:
Square on the east side (2Ch 29:4). Square before the house of God (Ezr 10:9). Square before the Water Gate (Ne 8:1, 3, 16), by the Gate of Ephraim (Ne 8:16). Street of the bakers (Jer 37:21). Streets of Jerusalem (Jer 5:1; 7:17, 34; 11:6, 13; 14:16; 33:10; 44:6, 9, 17, 21; Zec 8:4).

Towers:
See Beth Millo; Hananel, Tower of; Meah; Ophel; Siloam, Tower of.

Places in and Around:
Moriah (2Ch 3:1). The tomb of Jesus (Jn 19:41). *See Gethsemane; Golgotha; Jehoshaphat, Valley of; Olives, Mount of; Topheth, Topheth.*

History of:
Melchizedek ancient king and priest of (Ge 14:18). King of, confederated with the four other kings of the Amorites, against Joshua and the hosts of Israel (Jos 10:1-5). Confederated kings defeated, and the king of Jerusalem slain by Joshua (Jos 10:15-26). Fell to Benjamin in the allotment of the land of Canaan (Jos 18:28). Conquest of, made by David (2Sa 5:7). The inhabitants of, not expelled (Jos 15:63; Jdg 1:21). Conquest of Mount Zion in, made by David (1Ch 11:4-6). The citadel of Mount Zion, occupied by David, and called the City of David (2Sa 5:5-9; 1Ch 11:7). Ark brought to, by David (2Sa 6:12-19). The threshing floor of Araunah within the citadel of (2Sa 24:16). David purchased and built an altar upon it (2Sa 24:16-25). The city built around the citadel (1Ch 11:8). The capital of David's kingdom by divine appointment (1Ki 15:4; 2Ki 19:34; 2Ch 6:6; 12:13).
Fortified by Solomon (1Ki 3:1; 9:15). The temple built within the citadel. *See Temple.*
The chief Levites lived in (1Ch 9:34). The high priest lived at (Jn 18:15). Annual feasts kept at (Eze 36:38, w Dt 16:16, & Ps 122:3-5; Lk 2:41; Jn 4:20; 5:1; 7:1-14; 12:20; Ac 18:21). Prayers of the Israelites made toward (1Ki 8:38; Da 6:10). Beloved (Ps 122:6; 137:1-7; Isa 62:1-7). *See Country, Love of; Patriotism.* Oaths taken in the name of (Mt 5:35).
Captured and pillaged by: Shishak, king of Egypt (1Ki 14:25-26; 2Ch 12:9), Jehoash, king of Israel (2Ki 14:13-14; 2Ch 25:23-24), Nebuchadnezzar, king of Babylon (2Ki 24:8-16; 25:1-17; 2Ch 36:17-21; Jer 1:3; 32:2; 39; 52:4-7, 12-24; La 1:5-8). Walls of, restored and fortified by: Uzziah (2Ch 26:9-10), Jotham (2Ch 27:3), Manasseh (2Ch 33:14). Water supply brought in from the Gihon by Hezekiah (2Ki 18:17; 20:20; 2Ch 32:3-4, 30; Ne 2:13-15; Isa 7:3; 22:9-11; 36:2). Besieged by: Pekah (2Ki 16:5), the Philistines (2Ch 21:16-17), Sennacherib (2Ki 18:13-37; 19:20-37; 2Ch 32). Rebuilding of ordered by proclamation of Cyrus (2Ch 36:23; Ezr 1:1-4). Rebuilt by Nehemiah under the direction of Artaxerxes (Ne 2-6). Wall of, dedicated (Ne 12:27-43). Temple restored. *See Temple.*
Roman rulers resided at: Herod I (Mt 2:3), Pontius Pilate (Mt 27:2; Mk 15:1; Lk 23:1-7; Jn 18:28-29), Herod III (Ac 12:1-23).
Life and miracles of Jesus connected with: *See Jesus the Christ, History of.*
Gospel preached first preached at (Mic 4:2; Lk 24:47; Ac 1:4; 2:14). Day of Pentecost at (Ac 2). Stephen martyred at (Ac 6:8-7:60). Disciples persecuted and dispersed from (Ac 8:1-4; 11:19-21).
For personal incidents occurring there: *See biographies of individuals; Israel, Israelites.*

Prophecies Concerning:
Prophecies against (Isa 3:1-8; Jer 9:11; 19:6, 15; 21:10; 26:9, 11; Da 9:2, 27; Mic 1:1; 3:12); of pestilence, famine, and war in (Jer 34:2; Eze 5:12; Joel 3:2-3; Am 2:5); of the destruction of (Jer 7:32-34; 26:18; 32:29, 31-32; Da 9:24-27). Destruction of, foretold by Jesus (Mt 23:37-38; 24:15; Mk 13:14-23; Lk 13:35; 17:26-37; 19:41-44; 21:20-24).
Prophecies of the rebuilding of (Isa 44:28; Jer 31:38-40; Eze 48:15-22; Da 9:25; Zec 14:8-11). Of final restoration of (Joel 3:20-21; Zec 2:2-5; 8).

Sins of:
Wickedness (Lk 13:33-34). Catalog of abominations in (Eze 22:3-12, 25-30; 23; 33:25-26). Led Judah to sin (Mic 1:5).

JERUSALEM, NEW City of God referred to as coming down out of heaven from God (Rev 3:12; 21:2). Described as the mother of believers (Gal 4:26).

JERUSHA (*possession*). Wife of King Uzziah and mother of King Jotham (2Ki 15:33; 2Ch 27:1).

JESARELAH Ancestral head of a course of musicians (1Ch 25:14, ftn). Also called Asarelah (1Ch 25:2).

JESHAIAH (*Yahweh saves*).
1. Grandson of Zerubbabel (1Ch 3:21).
2. Son of Jeduthun (1Ch 25:3, 15).
3. Grandson of Eliezer (1Ch 26:25).
4. A Jew of the family of Elam, who returned from exile (Ezr 8:7).
5. A Levite who joined Ezra to return to Jerusalem (Ezr 8:19).
6. A Benjamite, detailed by lot to live in Jerusalem after the Exile (Ne 11:7).

JESHANAH (*old*).
1. A city on the N of Benjamin (2Ch 13:19).
2. Gate in NW corner of Jerusalem in Nehemiah's time (Ne 3:6).

JESHEBEAB (*father lives*). Priest, and head of the fourteenth course (1Ch 24:13).

JESHER (perhaps *the deity shows himself just*). Son of Caleb (1Ch 2:18).

JESHIMON (*a waste, a desert*).
1. A place in the Sinai peninsula, E of the Jordan (Nu 21:20; 23:28).
2. A place in the desert of Judah (1Sa 23:24; 26:1).

JESHIMOTH *See Beth Jeshimoth.*

JESHISHAI (*aged*). A Gadite (1Ch 5:14).

JESHOHAIAH (possibly *Yahweh humbles*). A descendant of Simeon (1Ch 4:36).

JESHUA (*Yahweh saves*).
1. A priest, head of the ninth course (1Ch 24:11). Nine hundred and seventy-three of his descendants returned from Babylon (Ezr 2:36; Ne 7:39).
2. A Levite, had charge of the tithes (2Ch 31:15). His descendants returned with Ezra from Babylon (Ezr 2:40; Ne 7:43).
3. Also called Joshua. A priest who accompanied Zerubbabel from Babylon (Ezr 2:2; Ne 7:7; 12:1). Descendants of (Ne 12:10). He rebuilt the altar (Ezr 3:2). Assisted Zerubbabel in restoring the temple (Ezr 3; 4:1-6; 5; Hag 1:1, 12-14; 2:2). Contended with those who sought to defeat the rebuilding (Ezr 4:1-3; 5:1-2). Symbolic of the restoration of Israel (Zec 3; 6:9-15).
4. Father of Jozabad (Ezr 8:33).
5. Son of Pahath-Moab (Ezr 2:6; Ne 7:11).
6. Father of Ezer (Ne 3:19).
7. A Levite who explained the law to the people when Ezra read it (Ne 8:7; 12:8).
8. A Levite who sealed Nehemiah's covenant (Ne 10:9).
9. A city of Judah (Ne 11:26).

JESHURUN (*upright*). A name used poetically for Israel (Dt 32:15; 33:5, 26; Isa 44:2).

JESIAH *See Isshiah, 2 & 3.*

JESIMIEL (*God [El] will establish*). A descendant of Simeon (1Ch 4:36).

JESSE Father of David (Ru 4:17; 1Sa 17:12). Ancestor of Jesus (Mt 1:5-6). Samuel visits, under divine command, to select from his sons a successor to Saul (1Sa 16:1-13). Saul asks, to send David to become a member of his court (1Sa 16:19-23). Sons in Saul's army (1Sa 17:13-28). Lives with David in Moab (1Sa 22:3-4). Descendants of (1Ch 2:13-17).

JESTING Foolish, forbidden (Eph 5:4; Mt 12:36).

JESUI, JESUITES *See Ishvi, 1; Ishvites.*

JESUS THE CHRIST (*Yahweh Saves, Anointed One*).

History of:

Birth and Childhood—
Genealogy of (Mt 1:1-17; Lk 3:23-38).
The angel Gabriel appears to Mary (Lk 1:26-38). Mary visits Elizabeth (Lk 1:39-56). Mary's *magnificat* (Lk 1:46-55). An angel appears to Joseph concerning Mary (Mt 1:18-25).
Birth of (Lk 2:1-7). Angels appear to the shepherds (Lk 2:8-20). Magi visit (Mt 2:1-12). Circumcision of (Lk 2:21). Is presented in the temple (Lk 2:21-38). Flight into, and return from, Egypt (Mt 2:13-23). Disputes with the doctors in the temple (Lk 2:41-52).

Ministry—
Is baptized by John (Mt 3:13-17; Mk 1:9-11; Lk 3:21-23). Temptation of (Mt 4:1-11; Mk 1:12-13; Lk 4:1-13). John's testimony concerning him (Jn 1:1-18). Testimony of John the Baptist concerning (Jn 1:19-34). Disciples adhere to (Jn 1:35-51).
Miracles at Cana of Galilee (Jn 2:1-12). Drives the money changers from the temple (Jn 2:13-25). Nicodemus comes to (Jn 3:1-21). Baptizes (Jn 3:22; 4:2). Returns to Galilee (Mt 4:12; Mk 1:14; Lk 4:14; Jn 4:1-3). Visits Sychar, and teaches the Samaritan woman (Jn 4:4-42). Teaches in Galilee (Mt 4:17; Mk 1:14-15; Lk 4:14-15; Jn 4:43-45). Heals a nobleman's son of Capernaum (Jn 4:46-54). Is rejected by the people of Nazareth, lives at Capernaum (Mt 4:13-16; Lk 4:16-31). Chooses Peter, Andrew, James, and John as disciples, miracle of the catch of fishes (Mt 4:18-22; Mk 1:16-20; Lk 5:1-11).
Preaches throughout Galilee (Mt 4:23-25; Mk 1:35-39; Lk 4:42-44). Heals a demoniac (Mk 1:21-28; Lk 4:31-37). Heals Peter's mother-in-law (Mt 8:14-17; Mk 1:29-34; Lk 4:38-41). Heals a leper in Galilee (Mt 8:2-4; Mk 1:40-45; Lk 5:12-16). Heals a paralytic (Mt 9:2-8; Mk 2:1-12; Lk 5:17-26). Calls Matthew (Mt 9:9; Mk 2:13-14; Lk 5:27-28). Heals an invalid at the pool of Bethesda on the Sabbath day, is persecuted, and makes his defense (Jn 5:1-47). Defines the law of the Sabbath on the occasion of his disciples picking the heads of grain (Mt 12:1-14; Mk 3:1-6; Lk 6:6-11). Withdraws from Capernaum to the Sea of Galilee, where he heals many (Mt 12:15-21; Mk 3:7-12).
Goes up onto a mountain, and calls and ordains twelve disciples (Mt 10:2-4; Mk 3:13-19; Lk 6:12-19). Delivers the "Sermon on the Mount" (Mt 5-7; Lk 6:20-49). Heals the centurion's servant (Mt 8:5-13; Lk 7:1-10). Raises from the dead the son of the widow of Nain (Lk 7:11-17). Receives the message from John the Baptist (Mt 11:2-19; Lk 7:18-35). Rebukes the unbelieving cities about Capernaum (Mt 11:20-30). Anointed by a sinful woman (Lk 7:36-50). Preaches in the cities of Galilee (Lk 8:1-3).
Heals a demoniac, and denounces the scribes and Pharisees (Mt 12:22-37; Mk 3:19-30; Lk 11:14-20). Replies to the scribes and Pharisees who seek a sign from him (Mt 12:38-45; Lk 11:16-36). Denounces the Pharisees and other hypocrites (Lk 11:37-54). Discourses to his disciples (Lk 12:1-59). Parable of the barren fig tree (Lk 13:6-9). Parable of the sower (Mt 13:1-23; Mk 4:1-25; Lk 8:4-18). Parable of the weeds, and other teachings (Mt 13:24-53; Mk 4:26-34).
Crosses the Sea of Galilee, and stills the tempest (Mt 8:18-27; Mk 4:35-41; Lk 8:22-25). Casts out the legion of demons (Mt 8:28-33; Mk 5:1-21; Lk 8:26-40). Returns to Capernaum (Mt 9:1; Mk 5:21; Lk 8:40). Eats with tax collectors and sinners, and speaks on fasting (Mt 9:10-17; Mk 2:15-22; Lk 5:29-39). Raises to life the daughter of Jairus, and heals the woman who has the issue of blood (Mt 9:18-26; Mk 5:22-43; Lk 8:41-56). Heals two blind men and casts out a mute spirit (Mt 9:27-34). Returns to Nazareth (Mt 13:53-58; Mk 6:1-6). Teaches in various cities in Galilee (Mt 9:35-38).
Instructs his disciples and empowers them to heal diseases and cast out unclean spirits (Mt 10; Mk 6:6-13; Lk 9:1-6). Herod falsely supposes him to be John, whom he had beheaded (Mt 14:1-2, 6-12; Mk 6:14-16, 21-29; Lk 9:7-9). The Twelve return; he goes to the desert; multitudes follow him; he feeds five thousand (Mt 14:13-21; Mk 6:30-44; Lk 9:10-17; Jn 6:1-14). Walks on the water (Mt 14:22-36; Mk 6:45-56; Jn 6:15-21). Teaches in the synagogue in Capernaum (Jn 6:22-65). Disciples forsake him (Jn 6:66-71).
He justifies his disciples in eating without washing their hands (Mt 15:1-20; Mk 7:1-23). Heals the daughter of the Syrian Phoenician woman (Mt 15:21-28; Mk 7:24-30). Heals a mute man (Mt 15:29-31; Mk 7:31-37). Feeds four thousand (Mt 15:32-39; Mk 8:1-9). Refuses to give a sign to the Pharisees (Mt 16:1-4; Mk 8:10-12). Cautions his disciples against the yeast of hypocrisy (Mt 16:4-12; Mk 8:13-21). Heals a blind man (Mk 8:22-26). Foretells his death and resurrection (Mt 16:21-28; Mk 8:31-38; 9:1; Lk 9:21-27).
Is transfigured (Mt 17:1-13; Mk 9:2-13; Lk 9:28-36). Heals a demoniac (Mt 17:14-21; Mk 9:14-29; Lk 9:37-43). Foretells his death and resurrection (Mt 17:22-23; Mk 9:30-32; Lk 9:43-45). Miracle of tribute money in the fish's mouth (Mt 17:24-27). Reproves the ambition of his disciples (Mt 18:1-35; Mk 9:33-50; Lk 9:46-50). Reproves the intolerance of his disciples (Mk 9:38-39; Lk 9:49-50).
Journeys to Jerusalem to attend the Feast of Tabernacles, passing through Samaria (Lk 9:51-62; Jn 7:2-11). Commissions the Seventy (Lk 10:11-19). Heals ten lepers (Lk 17:11-19). Teaches in

Jerusalem at the Feast of Tabernacles (Jn 7:14-53; 8). Answers a lawyer, who tests his wisdom with the question, "What must I do to inherit eternal life?" by the parable of the good Samaritan (Lk 10:25-37). Hears the report of the Seventy (Lk 10:17-24). Teaches in the house of Mary, Martha, and Lazarus, in Bethany (Lk 10:38-42).

Teaches his disciples to pray (Lk 11:1-13). Heals a blind man, who, because of his faith in Jesus, was excommunicated (Jn 9). Teaches in Jerusalem (Jn 9:39-41; 10:1-21). Teaches in the temple at Jerusalem, at the Feast of Dedication (Jn 10:22-39). Goes across the Jordan to escape violence from the rulers (Jn 10:40-42; 11:3-16).

Returns to Bethany and raises Lazarus from the dead (Jn 11:1-46). Escapes to the city of Ephraim from the conspiracy led by Caiaphas, the high priest (Jn 11:47-54). Journeys toward Jerusalem to attend the Passover; heals many who are diseased and teaches the people (Mt 19:1-2; Mk 10:1; Lk 13:10-35). Dines with a Pharisee on the Sabbath (Lk 14:1-24). Teaches the multitude the conditions of discipleship (Lk 14:25-35).

Tells the parables of the lost sheep, the lost piece of silver, prodigal son, unjust steward (Lk 15:1-32; 16:1-13). Reproves the hypocrisy of the Pharisees (Lk 16). Tells the parable of the rich man and Lazarus (Lk 16:19-31). Teaches his disciples concerning offenses, meekness, and humility (Lk 17:1-10). Teaches the Pharisees concerning the coming of his kingdom (Lk 17:20-37). Tells the parables of the unjust judge, and the Pharisee and tax collector praying in the temple (Lk 18:1-14).

Interprets the law concerning marriage and divorce (Mt 19:3-12; Mk 10:2-12). Blesses little children (Mt 19:13-15; Mk 10:13-16; Lk 18:15-17). Receives the rich young ruler, who asks what he must do to inherit eternal life (Mt 19:16-22; Mk 10:17-22; Lk 18:18-24). Tells the parable of the vineyard (Mt 20:1-16). Foretells his death and resurrection (Mt 20:17-19; Mk 10:32-34; Lk 18:31-34). Listens to the mother of James and John in behalf of her sons (Mt 20:20-28; Mk 10:35-45). Heals two blind men at Jericho (Mt 20:29-34; Mk 10:46-50; Lk 18:35-43). Visits Zacchaeus (Lk 19:1-10). Tells the parable of the pounds (Lk 19:11-28).

Final Week in Jerusalem—

Goes to Bethany six days before the Passover (Jn 12:1-9). Triumphal entry into Jerusalem, while the people throw palm branches in the way (Mt 21:1-11; Mk 11:1-11; Lk 19:29-44; Jn 12:12-19). Enters the temple (Mt 21:12; Mk 11:11; Lk 19:45). Drives the money changers out of the temple (Mt 21:12-13; Lk 19:45-46). Heals the sick in the temple (Mt 21:14). Teaches daily in the temple (Lk 19:47-48).

Performs the miracle of causing the barren fig tree to wither (Mt 21:17-22; Mk 11:12-14, 20-22). Tells the parable of the two sons (Mt 21:28-31), the parable of the wicked farmers (Mt 21:33-46; Mk 12:1-12; Lk 20:9-19), of the marriage (Mt 22:1-14; Lk 14:16-24). Tested by the Pharisees and Herodians and enunciates the duty of the citizen to his government (Mt 22:15-22; Mk 12:13-17; Lk 20:20-26). Tried by the Sadducees concerning the resurrection of the dead (Mt 22:23-33; Mk 12:18-27; Lk 20:27-40) and by a lawyer (Mt 22:34-40; Mk 12:28-34). Exposes the hypocrisies of the scribes and Pharisees (Mt 23; Mk 12:38-40; Lk 20:45-47).

Extols the widow who casts two small copper coins into the treasury (Mk 12:41-44; Lk 21:1-4). Verifies the prophecy of Isaiah concerning the unbelieving Jews (Jn 12:37-50). Foretells the destruction of the temple and of Jerusalem (Mt 24; Mk 13; Lk 21:5-36). Laments over Jerusalem (Mt 23:37; Lk 19:41-44). Tells the parables of the ten virgins and of the talents (Mt 25:1-30). Foretells the scenes of the Day of Judgment (Mt 25:31-46).

Anointed with precious ointment (Mt 26:6-13; Mk 14:3-9; Jn 12:1-8). Last Passover, and institution of the Lord's Supper (Mt 26:17-30; Mk 14:12-25; Lk 22:7-20). Washes the disciples' feet (Jn 13:1-17). Foretells his betrayal (Mt 26:23; Mk 14:18-21; Lk 22:21; Jn 13:18). Accuses Judas of his betrayal (Mt 26:21-25; Mk 14:18-21; Lk 22:21-23; Jn 13:21-30). Teaches his disciples, and comforts them with promises, including the gift of the Holy Spirit (Jn 14-16). Last prayer (Jn 17).

Arrest, Crucifixion, Resurrection—

Moves to Gethsemane (Mt 26:30, 36-46; Mk 14:26, 32-42; Lk 22:39-46; Jn 18:1). Is betrayed and apprehended (Mt 26:47-56; Mk 14:43-54, 66-72; Lk 22:47-53; Jn 18:2-12).

Trial of, before Caiaphas (Mt 26:57-58, 69-75; Mk 14:53-54, 66-72; Lk 22:54-62; Jn 18:13-18, 25-27). Led by the council to Pilate (Mt 27:1-2, 11-14; Mk 15:1-5; Lk 23:1-5; Jn 18:28-38). Arraigned before Herod (Lk 23:6-12). Tried before Pilate (Mt 27:15-26; Mk 15:6-15; Lk 23:13-25; Jn 18:39-40; 19:1-16). Mocked by the soldiers (Mt 27:27-31; Mk 15:16-20). Is led away to be crucified (Mt 27:31-34; Mk 15:20-23; Lk 23:26-32; Jn 19:16-17).

Crucified (Mt 27:35-56; Mk 15:24-41; Lk 23:33-49; Jn 19:18-30). Taken from the cross and buried (Mt 27:57-66; Mk 15:42-47; Lk 23:50-56; Jn 19:31-42).

Arises from the dead (Mt 28:2-15; Mk 16:1-11; Lk 24:1-12; Jn 20:1-18). Is seen by Mary Magdalene (Mt 28:1-10; Mk 16:9; Jn 20:11-17), by Peter (Lk 24:34; 1Co 15:5). Appears to two disciples who journey to Emmaus (Mk 16:12-13; Lk 24:13-35). Appears in the midst of the disciples, when Thomas is absent (Mk 16:14-18; Lk 24:36-49; Jn 20:19-23), when Thomas was present (Jn 20:26-29), at the Sea of Galilee (Mt 28:16; Jn 21:1-14), to the apostles and five hundred believers on a mountain in Galilee (Mt 28:16-20, w Ac 10:40-42; 13:31; 1Co 15:6-7). Appears to James, and also to all the apostles (Ac 1:3-8; 1Co 15:7).

Ascension and Additional Appearances—

Ascends to heaven (Mk 16:19-20; Lk 24:50-53; Ac 1:9-12). Appears to Paul (Ac 9:3-17; 18:9; 22:14, 18; 23:11; 26:16; 1Co 9:1; 15:8). Stephen's vision of (Ac 7:55-56). Appears to John on Patmos (Rev 1:10-18).

Miscellaneous Facts Concerning:

Was with the Israelites in the wilderness (1Co 10:4, 9; Heb 11:26; Jude 5).

Brothers of (Mt 13:55; Mk 6:3; 1Co 9:5; Gal 1:19). Sisters of (Mt 13:56; Mk 6:3).

Appearances of, After His Resurrection:

To Mary Magdalene and other women (Mt 28:1-10; Mk 16:9; Lk 24:1-10; Jn 20:11-17). To Peter (Lk 24:34; 1Co 15:5). To two disciples who journey to Emmaus (Mk 16:12-13; Lk 24:13-31). In the midst of the disciples, when Thomas is absent, in Jerusalem (Jn 20:19-23), when Thomas is present (Mk 16:14-18; Lk 24:36-49; Jn 20:26-29; 1Co 15:5). To certain disciples, Sea of Galilee (Jn 21:1-14). To the eleven disciples, mountain in Galilee (Mt 28:16). To upwards of five hundred, Galilee (1Co 15:6). To James, and also all the apostles, Jerusalem (Ac 1:3-8; 1Co 15:7). To Paul (Ac 9:3-6; 23:11; 26:13-18; 1Co 9:1; 15:8).

In Stephen's vision (Ac 7:55-56). To John, in a vision, on Patmos (Rev 1:10-18).

Ascension of:

(Mk 16:19; Lk 24:50-51; Jn 14:2-4; Ac 1:9; 3:21; Eph 1:20; 4:8-10; 1Ti 3:16; Heb 1:3; 4:14; 9:24). Foretold (Ps 47:5; 68:18; Lk 24:26, 50; Jn 1:51; 6:62; 7:33; 14:2-3, 12, 28; 16:5, 7, 10, 16, 28; 17:13; 20:17).

Atonement by:

(Ro 3:24-26; 5:11, 15; 1Th 1:10; Heb 13:12; 1Jn 2:2; 3:5; 4:10; Rev 5:6, 9; 13:8).

Made once for all (Heb 7:27; 9:24-28; 10:10, 12, 14; 1Pe 3:18). Vicarious (Isa 53:4-12; Mt 20:28; Jn 6:51; 11:49-51; Gal 1:4; 3:13; Eph 5:2; 1Th 5:9-10; Heb 2:9; 1Pe 2:24).

Through his blood (Lk 22:20; 1Co 1:23; Eph 2:13-15; Heb 9:12-15, 25-26; 12:24; 13:12, 19-21; 1Jn 5:6; Rev 1:5; 5:9; 7:14; 12:11).

For reconciliation (Ro 5:1-21; 2Co 5:18-19, 21; Eph 2:6-17; Col 1:20-22; Heb 2:17).

For remission of sins (Zec 13:1; Mt 26:28; Lk 24:46-47; Jn 1:29; Ro 4:25; 1Co 15:3; Gal 1:3-4; Eph 1:7; Col 1:14; Heb 1:3; 10:1-20; 1Jn 1:7; 3:5).

Atonement Typified—

(Ex 29:36-37; 30:10, 15-16; Lev 1:4; 5:6, 16, 18; 6:7; 8:34; 9:2-3, 7; 10:17; 12:7-8; 14:18-20, 31, 53; 15:14-15, 29-30; 16:6, 10-11, 16-18, 24, 27, 30, 32-34; 17:11; 23:27-28; 25:9; Nu 8:19, 21; 16:46; 25:13; 28:22, 30; 29:5; 31:50).

Atoning blood (Mt 26:28; Mk 14:24; Lk 22:20; Eph 1:7; 2:13; Heb 9:14; 10:19; 1Jn 1:7). Atoning blood of, typified (Ex 12:7, 13, 22-23; 24:6, 8; 29:12, 15, 20-21; 30:10; Lev 1:5, 10-11; 3:2, 8, 13; 4:5-7, 17-18, 25, 30, 34; 5:8-9; 6:30; 7:2; 8:2, 15, 19, 23-24, 30; 9:9, 18; 14:6, 14-15, 25; 16:14-15, 18-19, 27; 17:6, 11; Nu 18:17; 19:2-4; Dt 12:27; 2Ki 16:13, 15; 2Ch 29:22; 30:16; 35:11; Eze 43:20; 45:19-20; 1Pe 1:19).

Benevolence of:

Manifested in his companionship with sinners (Mt 9:10-12; Mk 2:14-17; Lk 5:30; 15:2; 19:10-12). *See below, Compassion of; Love of.*

Compassion of:

For those who were in spiritual distress (Isa 42:3; Mt 9:36; 12:20; 18:12-13; 23:37; Mk 1:41; 6:34; Lk 7:13; 13:34; 15:4-9, 20-24; 19:41-42; Jn 11:33-38; 18:8-9; 2Co 8:9; Heb 4:15; 5:2). For those who were in temporal adversity (Isa 53:4; 63:9; Mt 8:3, 16-17; 14:14; 15:32; 20:34; Mk 8:2-3). For his sheep (Isa 40:11; Mk 6:34).

Condescension of:

(Lk 22:27; Jn 13:5, 14; 2Co 8:9; Php 2:7-8; Heb 2:11).

Confessing: *See Confession, of Christ; Testimony, Religious.*

Creator:

(Jn 1:3, 10; 1Co 8:6; Eph 3:9; Col 1:16-17; Heb 1:2, 10; Rev 3:14).

Death of:

(Jn 12:32-33; Ac 5:30; 7:52; Heb 2:14; 12:2, 24; Rev 5:12; 13:8).

Death foretold by God (Ge 3:15; Heb 2:14). By the psalmist (Ps 22:1, 17-18; Mt 27:46; Mk 15:34; Ps 22:17; Mt 27:36; Lk 23:35; Ps 22:18; Mt 27:35; Mk 15:24; Lk 23:34; Jn 19:23-24; Ps 34:20; Jn 19:36; Ps 69:21; Mt 27:34, 48; Mk 15:36; Lk 23:36; Jn 19:28-30). By Isaiah (Isa 52:14; 53:7-12). By Zechariah (Zec 13:7; Mt 26:31). By Jesus himself (Mt 12:40; 16:4, 21; 17:12-13, 22-23; 20:17-19; 21:33-39; 26:2, 12, 18; Mk 8:31; 9:31; 10:32-34; 14:8-9; Lk 9:22, 44; 12:50; 17:25; 18:31-33; 22:15, 21, 37; Jn 2:19, 21; 10:11, 15, 17-18; 12:7, 24, 32-34; 14:19; 18:11).

Paul's testimony concerning Jesus' death (Ac 17:3; 26:22-23; 1Co 1:17-18, 23-24; 2:2; 15:3-4; 2Co 4:10-11; 13:4; Gal 3:1; 1Th 2:15; 4:14).

See above, History of, for Circumstances of the Death of.

Purpose of His Death—

To make reconciliation (Ro 5:6-11; Eph 2:13-16).

To redeem (Isa 53:4-6, 8, 10-12; Mt 20:28; 26:28; Mk 10:45; 14:24; Jn 6:51; 10:11, 17; 11:49-52; Ac 20:28; 26:23; Ro 3:24-25; 8:3, 32; 1Co 5:7; 6:20; 8:11; 15:3; Gal 1:4; 3:13; 4:4-5; Eph 1:6-7; 5:2, 25-27; Col 1:14, 20, 22; 2:14-15; 1Th 1:10; 2:6; Tit 2:14; Heb 2:9-10, 14-15, 18; 7:27; 9:12-17, 25-26, 28; 10:10, 12, 14, 17-20; 1Pe 1:18-19; 2:21, 24; 3:18; 1Jn 2:2; 3:16; 4:10; Rev 1:5-6; 5:9-10; 13:8).

To purge sins (Zec 13:1; Lk 24:46-47; Jn 1:29; Heb 1:3; 13:11-12; 1Jn 1:7; Rev 7:14-15).

To secure forgiveness (Ac 5:30-31; Ro 4:25).

To save (Jn 3:14-17; Ro 6:3-5, 9-10; 14:9, 15; 2Co 5:14-15, 19, 21; 8:9; Gal 2:20; 1Th 5:9-10).

Vicarious Death of—

(Isa 53:4-12; Mt 20:28; Jn 6:51; 11:49, 51; Gal 3:13; Eph 5:2; 1Th 5:9-10; Heb 2:9; 1Pe 2:24).

Vicarious death of, typified (Ex 29:11, 15-16, 20; 29:38-42; Lev 1:5, 11, 15; 3:2, 8, 13; 4:4, 15, 24, 29; 6:25; 7:2; 8:15, 19; 9:8, 15, 18-19, 23-24; 14:13, 19, 25; 2Ch 29:22, 24; 30:15; 35:1).

See Atonement; Redemption.

Voluntary Death of—

(Isa 50:6; 53:12; Lk 9:51; 12:50; 22:15, 42; Jn 10:17-18; 18:5, 8, 11; Php 2:8; Heb 7:27; 9:26; 1Jn 3:16).

Divine Sonship of:

Testified to—

By God, at his baptism (Mt 3:17; Mk 1:11; Lk 3:22), at the transfiguration (Mt 17:5; Mk 9:7; Lk 9:35; 2Pe 1:17), in his commandment to believe in (1Jn 3:23).

By Jesus himself (Mt 11:27; Mt 26:63-64; 27:43; Mk 14:61-62; Lk 10:22; 22:70; Jn 3:16-18, 34-36; 6:27, 40, 46, 57; 9:35-37; 11:4; 19:7).

By the disciples (Mt 14:33; 1Jn 4:14), unclean spirits (Mt 8:29; Mk 3:11; 5:7, w Lk 8:28; Lk 4:41), Mark (Mk 1:1), John the Baptist (Jn 1:34), John the apostle (Jn 1:14, 18; 1Jn 1:7; 2:22-24; 3:8, 23; 4:9, 10, 14; 5:5, 9-13, 20; 2Jn 3; Rev 2:18), Nathanael (Jn 1:49), Martha (Jn 11:27), the centurion (Mt 27:54; Mk 15:39), Peter (Ac 3:13; 13:33), Paul (Ro 1:3-4, 9; 8:3, 29, 32; 1Co 1:9; 15:24, 27-28; 2Co 1:3, 19; Gal 1:16; 4:4; Eph 1:3; Col 1:3; 1Th 1:10), the author of Hebrews (Heb 1:1-3, 5; 4:14; 5:5, 8; 6:6; 7:3; 10:29).

Other Evidences—

Declared God to be his Father (Mt 15:13; 18:10, 19; 20:23; 26:53, 63-64; Lk 10:22; 22:29; Jn 5:19-21, 23, 26-27, 30, 36-37; 8:16, 19, 26-29, 38, 49, 54; 10:15, 17-18, 29-30, 36-38; 11:41; 12:49-50; 13:3; 14:7, 9-11, 13, 16, 20-21, 23-24, 28, 31; 15:1, 8-10, 15, 23-24; 16:15, 27-28, 32; 17:1-26; 20:17, 21).

Peter's confession of (Mt 16:15-17).

Prophecies concerning (Ps 2:7; Lk 1:32, 35).

Worshiped by the disciples as the Son of God (Mt 14:33).

See below, Deity of; Relation of, to the Father; Son of God; Son of Man.

Deity of:

Indicated by the Titles Ascribed to Him—

Immanuel (Isa 7:14, w Mt 1:23). First and Last (Rev 1:17; 22:13). God (Ps 102:24-27, w Heb 1:10-13; Jn 1:1; 20:28; Ro 9:5; 1Jn 5:20-21), God and Savior Jesus Christ (2Pe 1:1). God our Savior (Tit 2:13). Holy One (Ac 3:14). Lord of lords and King of kings (Rev 17:14). Lord (Ps 110:1 w Mt 22:42-45; Isa 40:3 w Mt 3:3; Ac 20:28). Lord Almighty (Isa 8:13-14; 1Pe 2:8). My Lord and My God (Jn 20:28). Lord of all (Ac 10:36; Ro 10:12). Mighty God (Isa 9:6). Only born of the Father (Jn 1:14, 18; 3:16, 18; 1Jn 4:9), Son of God (Mt 26:63-67; Mk 1:1; 15:39; 1Co 1:9; 2Co 1:19; Gal 2:20; Eph 4:13; Heb 1:2; 2Pe 1:17; 1Jn 1:2-3; 3:23; 5:10, 12-13, 20), Son of Man (Da 7:13-14; Mt 11:19; 12:8). *See above, Divine Sonship of; below, Son of God; Son of Man.*

***Addressed as Yahweh** (LORD)—*

(Isa 40:3 w Mt 3:3). King or LORD of glory (Ps 24:7, 10; 1Co 2:8; Jas 2:1). The LORD our righteousness (Jer 23:5-6; 1Co 1:30), The LORD all (Ps 97:9; Jn 3:31), The First and the last, the Alpha and the Omega (Isa 44:6, w Rev 1:17; Isa 48:12-16, w Rev 22:13). Yahweh's fellow and equal (Zec 13:7; Php 2:6). LORD Almighty (Isa 6:1-3 w Jn 12:41; Isa 8:13-14 w 1Pe 2:8). LORD (Ps 110:1; Mt 22:42-45). Yahweh the Shepherd (Isa 40:10-11; Heb 13:20). LORD, for whose glory all things were created (Pr 16:4; Col 1:16). Lord the messenger of the covenant (Mal 3:1; Lk 7:27). Invoked as LORD (Joel 2:32; 1Co 1:2).

Equality With God—

As the eternal God and Creator (Ps 102:24-27; Heb 1:8, 10-12). The Mighty God (Isa 9:6), the great God and Savior (Hos 1:7, w Tit 2:13), God over all (Ro 9:5), God the Judge (Ecc 12:14, w 1Co 4:5; 2Co 5:10; 2Ti 4:1), Immanuel (Isa 7:14, w Mt 1:23), Lord of lords and King of kings (Da 10:17, w Rev 1:5; 17:14), the Holy and Righteous One (1Sa 2:2, w Ac 3:14).

The Lord from heaven (1Co 15:47). Lord of the Sabbath (Ge 2:3, w Mt 12:8), Lord of all (Ac 10:36; Ro 10:11-13). Son of God (Mt 26:63-67), the only born Son of the Father (Jn 1:14, 18; 3:16, 18; 1Jn 4:9). His blood is called the blood of God (Ac 20:28). One with the Father (Jn 10:30, 38; 12:45; 14:7-10; 17:10). As sending the Spirit equally with the Father (Jn 14:16, w Jn 15:26). As unsearchable equally with the Father (Pr 30:4; Mt 11:27). As Creator of all things (Isa 40:28; Jn 1:3; Col 1:16), supporter and preserver of all things (Ne 9:6, w Col 1:17; Heb 1:3). Acknowledged by Old Testament saints (Ge 17:1, w 48:15-16; 32:24-30, w Hos 12:3-5; Jdg 6:22-24; 13:21-22; Job 19:25-27).

Is one with the Father (Jn 5:17-18, 23; 10:30, 33, 38; 12:45; 14:7-11; 17:11, 21-22). Sends the Holy Spirit equally with the Father (Jn 14:16). Identical with the Adonay (Lord) of the Old Testament (Jn 12:40-41, w Isa 6:8-11), and the Yahweh (LORD) of the Old Testament (Jn 19:37, w Zec 12:10).

Has power to forgive sins (Mt 1:21; 9:6; Mk 2:5; Lk 5:20; Col 3:13). Paul's apostleship from (Gal 1:1). Invoked with the Father and the Spirit in benedictions (Ro 1:7; 1Co 1:3; 2Co 1:2; Gal 1:3; Eph 1:2; 6:23-24; 1Th 1:1; 3:11; 2Th 1:1-2; 2:16-17; 2Ti 1:2). All power given to (Mt 28:17-18). Eternity ascribed to (Jn 1:1-2; 1Jn 1:1). *See below, Eternity of.* Is judge (2Co 5:10). *See below, Judge.*

Testimony Concerning His Deity—

By the Father (Jn 5:32, 34, 37; 6:27; 8:18; Ac 13:33; 1Jn 5:9), at his baptism (Mt 3:16-17; Mk 1:11; Lk 3:22), at his transfiguration (Mt 17:5; Mk 9:7; Lk 9:35; 2Pe 1:17).

By Jesus concerning himself (Jn 5:18, 31, 36; 8:18, 42; 10:33, 36, 38; 12:45; 14:11-13; 16:27-28; 17:5, 8, 24-25; 19:7), to Peter and other disciples (Mt 16:16-17; Mk 8:29-30; Lk 9:20-21), to the Jews (Mt 22:43-44; Jn 5:23; 10:30, 33, 36, 38; 12:45), to his disciples (Jn 16:27-28), to the restored blind man (Jn 9:35-37), to Philip (Jn 14:7-11, 20), to Caiaphas (Mt 26:63-64; Mk 14:61-62; Lk 22:67-70), to Pilate (Jn 18:36-37; 1Ti 6:13).

By the angel, to Joseph (Mt 1:23), to Mary (Lk 1:32, 35). John the Baptist (Jn 1:29-34; 5:33). John, the apostle (Jn 1:14, 18; 13:3; 1Jn 2:22-24). The disciples (Jn 16:30). Paul (Ac 9:20). The author of the epistle to the Hebrews (Heb 11:26). The Scriptures (Jn 5:39). Thomas (Jn 20:28). Demons (Mt 8:29; Mk 1:23-24; 3:11; 5:6-7; Lk 4:34, 41).

Eternity of:

Called everlasting Father (Isa 9:6). Was before creation (Jn 1:1-2, 15; 17:5, 24; Col 1:17; 2Ti 1:9). Was from the beginning (1Jn 2:13). Was from everlasting (Mic 5:2). Continues forever (Ps 102:24-27 w Heb 1:10-13; Ps 110:4; Eph 3:21; Heb 7:16, 24-25; Rev 5:13-14). The same yesterday and today and forever (Heb 13:8).

J

Exaltation of:
(Ps 2:8-9; 68:18; Eph 4:8). In glory (Mt 26:64; Mk 16:19; Lk 22:69; 24:26; Jn 7:39; Ac 2:33-34; 3:20-21; 7:55-56; Ro 8:17, 34; Eph 1:20-22; 4:10; Col 3:1; 1Ti 3:16; Heb 1:3; 10:12-13; 12:2; 1Pe 3:22; Rev 3:21). As Lord of heaven and earth (Php 2:9-11; Col 2:15). As Savior (Ac 5:31). As priestly mediator (Heb 4:10, 14; 6:20; 7:26; 8:1; 9:24).

An Example:
Claimed himself (Mt 11:29; 20:28; Mk 10:43-45; Lk 22:26-27; Jn 10:4; 13:13-15, 34; 17:14, 18, 21-22; Rev 3:21). Referred to by Paul (Ro 8:29; 13:14; 15:2-7; 2Co 4:10; 8:9; 10:1; Gal 3:27; 6:2; Eph 4:13, 15, 24; 5:2; 6:9; Php 2:5-8; Col 3:10-11, 13; 1Th 1:6). Referred to by other apostles (Heb 3:1; 12:2-4; 1Pe 1:15; 2:21-24; 3:17-18; 1Jn 2:6; 3:1-3, 16; 4:17).

Faith in: *See Faith in Christ; Salvation, Conditions of.*

Faithfulness of:
(Isa 11:5; Lk 4:43; Jn 7:18; 8:29; 9:4; 14:3; 17:8; Heb 3:2; Rev 1:5; 3:14). In mediation (Heb 2:17).

Genealogy of: *See above, History of.*

Glorification of:
(Jn 7:39; 12:16; 17:1; Ac 7:55-56; Heb 8:1).

Head of the Church:
(Ps 118:22-23, w Mt 21:42-43, & Mk 12:10; Isa 28:16, w Eph 2:2-22, & 1Pe 2:6; Lk 20:17-18, w 1Pe 2:7; Jn 15:1-8; 1Co 3:11; Eph 1:22-23; 4:15; 5:23-32; Col 1:18; 2:10, 19; 3:11; Rev 2:2-28; 3:1, 7; 22:16).

Holiness of:
Foretold (Ps 45:7; Isa 11:4-5; Jer 23:5; Zec 9:9). Professed by himself (Jn 5:30; 7:18; 8:46; 14:30; Rev 3:7).

Testified to: By the angel to his mother (Lk 1:35). By demons (Mk 1:24; Lk 4:34). By the centurion at the Crucifixion (Lk 23:47). By Stephen (Ac 7:52). By Peter (Jn 6:69; Ac 3:14; 4:27-30; 1Pe 1:19; 2:22). By John (1Jn 2:1, 29; 3:5). By Paul (Ac 13:35; 2Co 5:21). By the author of Hebrews (Heb 1:9; 4:15; 7:26-28; 9:14).

Humanity of:
(Ps 22:22; Jn 1:14). Took on himself human nature (Php 2:7-8; Heb 2:9-10, 14-18). Was born of flesh (Isa 9:6; Mt 1:18-25; Lk 2:11-14; 1Jn 4:2; 2Jn 7).

Called: Seed of the woman (Ge 3:15; Gal 4:4), son of David (Mt 20:30-31; 21:9; 22:42; Mk 12:35; Lk 18:38), a prophet like Moses (Dt 18:15-19; Ac 3:22-23; 7:37).

Humility of:
(2Co 8:9; Php 2:7-8). Became a servant (Lk 22:27; Jn 13:5, 14). *See below, Meekness of.*

Impeccability of: *See above, Holiness of; below, Temptation of.*

Incarnation of:
(Jn 16:28; 1Ti 3:16). Foretold (Ge 3:15; Dt 18:15-18; Ps 2:7; Isa 7:14-16; 9:6; 11:1; Jn 7:42; Ac 13:33; Heb 1:5). Accomplished through the generation of the Holy Spirit (Mt 1:1, 16-18, 23; Lk 1:26-56). Was made a little lower than the angels (Heb 2:9, 14). Was made flesh (Lk 24:39; Jn 1:14; 20:27; Ro 8:3; 1Co 15:47; 2Co 5:16; Gal 4:4; Php 2:7-8; Heb 1:3, 6; 2:9-18; 10:5; 1Jn 1:1-3; 4:2; 2Jn 7). Came in the lineage of Judah (Heb 7:14). Was of the seed of David (Mt 22:45; Ro 1:3; 9:5; Rev 22:16). Was the son of Mary (Mt 13:55; Lk 2:1-21).

See above, Humanity of; below, Relation of, to the Father.

Intercession of: *See below, Mediation of.*

Judge:
(Mt 3:12 w Lk 3:17; Mt 25:31-34; Ac 10:42; Ro 2:16; 1Co 4:4-5; 2Co 5:10; 2Ti 4:1, 8; Rev 2:23). Prophecy concerning (Isa 2:4 w Mic 4:3; Isa 11:3-4; Mic 5:1). Ordained of God (Jn 5:22; Ac 17:31). Righteous (2Ti 4:8).

Justice of:
(2Sa 23:3; Zec 9:9; Mt 27:19; Jn 5:30; Ac 3:14; 22:14).

King:
Prophecies concerning (Ge 49:10; 1Sa 2:10; 2Sa 7:12 w Ac 2:30; Ps 2:6; 18:43-44; 45:3-7; 72:5, 8, 11; 89:3-4, 19-21, 23, 27, 29, 36-37; 110:1-2; 132:11, 17-18; Isa 9:6-7; 22:22; 32:1; 52:7, 13; Jer 23:5; 30:9; 33:17; Eze 37:24-25; Da 2:35, 44; 7:13-14; Hos 3:5; Mic 5:2, 4; Zec 6:12-13; 9:9-10; Mt 2:2, 6; 21:5; 22:42-45; Lk 1:32-33; Ac 2:30). Appointed by the Father as King (Lk 22:29-30; Ac 2:30, 36 w 2Sa 7:12; Ac 5:31; Eph 1:20-22; Heb 2:7-8).

Authority of Jesus as King (Mk 2:28; Jn 5:27). Universal kingdom (Mt 11:27 w Lk 10:22; Mt 28:18; Lk 19:27; Jn 3:31, 33; 13:3; 17:2; Ro 9:5; 10:12; 14:9; Col 2:10; Heb 1:2-13; 2:7-8; 1Pe 3:22; Rev 3:7, 14, 21).

Dominion of Jesus, universal (Ac 10:36; 1Co 15:23-28; Eph 1:20-22; Php 2:9-11; Rev 1:5-7, 18; 11:15). Future glory of Jesus as King (Mt 19:28; 25:31-34; 26:64; Mk 14:62; Lk 22:69; Heb 10:12-13; Rev 5:13).

Kingship of: Avowed by himself (Mt 21:5; 27:11; Lk 23:2; Jn 18:36-37). Ascribed, by disciples (Lk 19:38; Jn 1:49; 12:13, 15; Ac 17:7). In superscription on the cross (Jn 19:12, 19). Symbolic statements concerning (Rev 5:5, 12; 6:2, 15-17; 14:14; 17:14; 19:11-12, 15-16).

See below, Lordship of.

Kingdom of:
Brings joy and gladness (Ps 46:4; Isa 25:6; 35; 52:9; 55:12). Brings peace (Ps 46:9; Isa 11:6-9). Is within us (Lk 17:21). Truth (Jn 18:37). Is not of this world (Jn 18:36).

Keys of (Mt 16:19). Glad tidings of (Lk 8:1). Mysteries of (Lk 8:10). Is not meat and drink (Ro 14:17).

Likened to—
A man who sowed good seed (Mt 13:24-30, 38-43; Mk 4:26-29). A mustard seed (Mt 13:31-32; Mk 4:30-31; Lk 13:18-19). Yeast (Mt 13:33; Lk 13:21). A treasure (Mt 13:44). A pearl (Mt 13:45). A net (Mt 13:47-50). A king who called his servants to account (Mt 18:23-35). A landowner (Mt 20:1-16). A king who made a marriage feast for his son (Mt 22:2-14; Lk 14:16-24). Ten virgins (Mt 25:1-13). A man who entrusted property to his servants (Mt 25:14-30; Lk 19:12-27).

Prophecies Concerning—
Its character: To enlighten (Jer 31:34; Heb 8:11). To bring peace (Ps 46:9; Isa 65:25; Mic 4:3-7). To bring salvation (Isa 62:11). To bring joy (Isa 25:6; 35:1-10; 42:1-7, 18-21; Lk 2:10). Shall be a river of salvation (Eze 47:1-12; Zec 14:8-9, 16, 20-21).

Will be forever (Isa 51:6, 8; Lk 1:33; Heb 1:8; 2Pe 1:11). Transforms (Isa 35:1-10; 55:12-13; 65:17-25). Future glory and greatness (Isa 49:22-23; Hag 2:7-9; Rev 21:9-27).

Universality of the kingdom (Ge 12:3; 22:18; 49:10; Ps 72:5, 8-11, 16-17, 19; 89:1-37; 113:3; Isa 9:6-7; 40:4-11; 42:1-7; 49:1-26; 52:10; 54:1-3; 59:19-21; Jer 3:14-19; Da 2:35, 44; 7:13-14, 18, 22, 27; Hab 2:14; Zec 9:1, 10; Mt 8:11; Lk 13:29-30; Rev 14:6). Unity of the kingdom (Jn 10:16).

Growth of the kingdom (Mt 13:31-33; Lk 13:21). Ends of earth shall turn to him (Ps 66:4; 86:9; Isa 2:2-4; 45:14; 60:1-9; Jer 3:17; 16:19-21; 33:16; Eze 17:22-23; Mic 4:1-4; Zep 2:11; Zec 2:10-11; 6:15; 8:20-23). Shall include all nations (Ps 2:8; 68:31-32; 110:4-6; Hos 2:23; Am 9:11-12; Mal 1:11).

Final triumph of the kingdom (Ge 3:15; Ps 2:9; Isa 11:1-13; Da 2:44; 7:9-14, 27; Mt 16:18; Ac 2:34-35; 1Co 15:24-28; Eph 1:10; Php 2:10-11; Heb 10:13; 12:23-24, 27-28; Rev 5:9-10, 13-14; 6:2; 11:15; 12:10; 19:11-21; 20:1-3).

Secular notions concerning: To restore the kingdom of Israel (Mk 11:9-10; Jn 6:14-15; Ac 1:6-7). Rank of princes in the kingdom of (Mt 20:20-23; Mk 10:35-40; Lk 9:46-48).

Love of:
(Ps 69:9; Rev 3:9, 19). Jesus' love compels us (2Co 5:13-14), surpasses knowledge (Eph 3:17-19).

Jesus' love for his disciples (Jn 10:3-4, 11, 14-16; 13:1, 23; 14:1-3, 18, 21, 27; 15:9-13, 15; 17:6-26; Ro 8:35, 37-39; 2Th 2:13). For children (Mt 19:13-15; Mk 10:13-14, 16; Lk 18:15-16). For his mother (Jn 19:26-27). For the lost (Isa 40:11; Mt 18:12-13; Mk 8:12; Lk 13:34).

Jesus' love exemplified: In renunciation (2Co 8:9; Php 2:6-8). In compassion (Isa 42:3; Mt 9:36; 14:14; 15:32; Lk 7:13; 22:31-32; Jn 11:5, 33-36; Ac 10:38; Heb 4:15). In his heart for others (Mt 23:37; Lk 23:28, 34; Jn 18:8-9). In his sacrifice (Gal 2:20; Eph 5:2, 25, 29-30; 1Jn 3:16; Rev 1:5). In his vicarious suffering (Isa 53:4; Mt 8:17; Ro 15:3). In redemption (Ps 72:14; Isa 63:9).

Lordship of:
The sovereignty of the Messiah, as conceived by Old Testament writers, seems best described by the word "King," but New Testament writers use the word "Lord." *See above, King.* Jesus said of himself, the Son of Man is Lord even of the Sabbath (Mt 12:8; Mk 2:28).

The student will find suggestions for profitable reflection in a study of the various forms of expression used by the authors of the epistles in which they attribute Lordship to our Savior (Mt 12:8; Ac 2:36; Ro 1:7; 5:1, 11, 21; 6:23; 7:25; 8:39; 10:9; 13:14; 14:14; 15:6, 30; 16:20; 1Co 1:2-3, 7-10; 5:4; 6:11; 8:6; 9:1; 11:25; 12:3; 15:31, 57; 16:23; 2Co 1:2-3, 14; 4:5, 14; 8:9; 11:31; 13:14; Gal 1:3; 6:14, 18; Eph 1:2-3, 17; 3:11; 5:20; 6:23-24; Php 1:2, 11; 2:19; 3:20; 4:23; Col 1:3; 2:6; 3:17, 24; 1Th 1:1, 3; 4:1; 5:10, 24, 28; 2Th 1:1-2, 7, 12; 2:1, 8, 15-16; 3:6, 12, 18; 1Ti 1:2, 12; 6:3, 14; 2Ti 1:2; Phm 1, 3, 5, 25; Jas 1:1; 2:1; 1Pe 1:3; 3:15; 2Pe 1:2, 8, 14, 16; 2:20; 3:18; Jude 4, 18, 21, 25).

Mediation of:
(Jn 14:6, 14; 16:23-24, 26; 20:31; Ro 1:8; 5:1-2; 6:23; 1Co 6:11; 15:57; 2Co 1:20; Eph 3:12; 4:32; 5:20; Col 3:17; 1Ti 2:1, 3, 5; Heb 9:11-28; 13:15; 1Pe 2:5; 1Jn 2:1-2, 12).

As a priest (Ps 110:4; Zec 6:13; Heb 2:17; 3:1-2; 4:14-15; 5:5-6, 10; 6:19-20; 7:1, 3, 19, 21, 24-28; 8:1-2, 6; 9:11; 10:19-21). Through his sacrifice (Eph 2:13-18; Heb 10:11-12; 12:24).

Exemplified in his intercession (Isa 53:12; Lk 13:8-9; 22:31-32; 23:33-34; Jn 14:16; 17:9, 11, 15-17, 19-22; Ro 8:34).

See below, Priesthood of.

Meekness of:
(Mt 11:29; Mk 14:60-61; 15:3-5; 2Co 10:1; Php 2:8). Prophecies concerning (Ps 45:4; Isa 42:1-3; 50:5-6; 52:1, 14; 53:7; Mt 12:19-20; 21:5; Ac 8:32).

Exemplified in not resenting false accusation (Mk 2:6-11). In submitting to enemies (Mt 26:47-63; 27:12-14; Jn 8:48-50; Heb 12:2-3; 1Pe 2:23). In praying for enemies (Lk 23:34). In becoming a servant (Php 2:7).

See above, Humility of; Meekness.

Messiah:
Messianic Psalms (Ps 2:1-12; 67:1-7; 68:1-35; 69:1-36; 72:1-20; 96:1-13; 98:1-9; 110:1-7). Prophecies concerning the Messiah (Da 9:25-26; Ac 3:18-20).

Simeon's testimony to the Messiah (Lk 2:28-32). Andrew's belief in the Messiah (Jn 1:41, 45). Peter's confession of the Messiah (Mt 16:15-16; Mk 8:29; Lk 9:20; Jn 6:69). Was proclaimed as Messiah by apostles (Ac 9:22; 13:27; 17:2-3; 26:6-7, 22-23; 28:23; Ro 1:1-3; 1Co 15:3; 1Pe 1:10-11; 2Pe 1:16-18; 1Jn 5:6-9).

Jesus' own testimony to his messiahship (Mt 11:3-6; 26:63-64; Lk 24:27; Jn 4:25-26, 29, 42; 5:33, 36-37, 39, 46; 6:27; 8:14, 17-18, 25, 28, 56; 13:19).

Was called David's son (Mt 22:42-45; Mk 12:35-37; Lk 20:41-44). Is the anointed of God (Ps 2:2; Ac 4:26-27).

See above, King; Lordship of; below, Son of Man. See also, Messianic Hope.

Miracles of:
Water made wine (Jn 2:1-11).
First miraculous catch of fishes (Lk 5:1-11).
Demoniac in the synagogue healed (Mk 1:23-26; Lk 4:33-36).
Heals Simon's wife's mother (Mt 8:14-15; Mk 1:29-31; Lk 4:38-39).
Heals diseases in Galilee (Mt 4:23-24; Mk 1:34).
Miracles at Jerusalem (Jn 2:23).
Cleanses the leper (Mt 8:1-4; Mk 1:40-45; Lk 5:12-16).
Heals the paralytic (Mt 9:1-8; Mk 2:1-12; Lk 5:17-26).
Heals the crippled man (Jn 5:1-16).
Restores the withered hand (Mt 12:9-13; Mk 3:1-5; Lk 6:6-11).
Heals multitudes from Judah, Jerusalem, and coasts of Tyre and Sidon (Lk 6:17-19).
Heals the centurion's servant (Mt 8:5-13; Lk 7:1-10).
Heals demoniacs (Mt 8:16-17; Lk 4:40-41).
Raises the widow's son (Lk 7:11-16).
Heals in Galilee (Lk 7:21-22).
Heals a demoniac (Mt 12:22-37; Mk 3:20-30; Lk 11:14-15, 17-23).
Stills the tempest (Mt 8:23-27; Mk 4:35-41; Lk 8:22-25; Mt 14:32).
Healing of the diseased in the land of Gennesaret (Mt 14:34-36).
The demoniacs in Gadarenes healed (Mt 8:28-34; Mk 5:1-20; Lk 8:26-39).
Raises Jairus' daughter (Mt 9:18-19, 23-26; Mk 5:22-24, 35-43; Lk 8:41-42, 49-56).
Heals the woman with the issue of blood (Mt 9:20-22; Mk 5:25-34; Lk 8:43-48).
Opens the eyes of two blind men in the house (Mt 9:27-31).
A demon cast out and a mute man cured (Mt 9:32-33).
Five thousand fed (Mt 14:15-21; Mk 6:35-44; Lk 9:12-17; Jn 6:5-14).
Heals sick in Galilee (Mt 14:14).
Walking on the sea (Mt 14:22-33; Mk 6:45-52; Jn 6:14-21).
The daughter of the Syrian Phoenician healed (Mt 15:21-28; Mk 7:24-30).
Healing of the lame, blind, mute, and maimed, near the Sea of Galilee (Mt 15:30).
Four thousand fed (Mt 15:32-39; Mk 8:1-9).
One deaf and mute cured (Mk 7:31-37).
One blind cured (Mk 8:22-36).
Child healed (Mt 17:14-21; Mk 9:14-29; Lk 9:37-43).
Piece of money in the fish's mouth (Mt 17:24-27).
The ten lepers cured (Lk 17:11-19).
Opening the eyes of one born blind (Jn 9).
Raising of Lazarus (Jn 11:1-54).
Woman with the spirit of infirmity cured (Lk 13:10-17).
The dropsy cured (Lk 14:1-6).
Two blind men cured near Jericho (Mt 20:29-34; Mk 10:46-52; Lk 18:35-43).
The fig tree blighted (Mt 21:17-22; Mk 11:12-14, 20-24).
Healing of Malchus's ear (Lk 22:49-51).
Second catch of fishes (Jn 21:6).
Not particularly described (Mt 4:23-24; 14:14; 15:30; Mk 1:34; Lk 6:17-19; 7:21-22; Jn 2:23; 3:2). Resurrection (Mt 28:6; Mk 16:6; Lk 24:6; Jn 20:1-18). Holds the vision of his disciples, that they should not recognize him (Lk 24:16, 31, 35). His appearances and disappearances (Lk 24:15, 31, 36-45; Jn 20:19, 26). Opening the understanding of his disciples (Lk 24:45). His Ascension (Lk 24:51; Ac 1:9).

See Miracles.

Mission of:
(Isa 42:7; Mt 18:12-14; Lk 12:49-53; Jn 4:25, 34; 18:37). To fulfill the Law and the Prophets (Mic 5:2; Mt 5:17; Ro 10:4). To be Lord of all (Ro 14:9; 15:8-9; 2Co 5:15; Eph 4:10). To glorify the Father (Jn 17:4).

To preach the gospel (Isa 61:1; Mt 4:23; 9:13; Mk 1:38; Lk 4:18-19, 43; 5:31-32; 8:1). To preach repentance (Lk 5:30-32; 24:47; Ac 3:26; 5:31). To bring life (Jn 6:51; 10:10; 2Co 5:14, 21). To give light (Isa 9:2; 42:6; Lk 1:78-79; 2:30-32, 34; Jn 1:1-9; 9:39; 12:46-47).

To condemn sin (Ro 8:3-4). To die for sinners (Ro 5:6-8). To be propitiation for sin (Mt 20:28; Mk 10:45; Lk 24:26, 46; Jn 6:51; Ac 26:23; Ro 4:24-25; 5:6-8; 2Co 5:18; Gal 1:3-4; 4:4-5; Heb 2:9, 14; 9:26; 1Jn 3:5, 8; 4:8, 10). To purge sins (Zec 13:1; Mal 3:2-3). To give remission of sins (Ac 10:43; Ro 4:25). To destroy the works of the devil (Ge 3:15; Jn 3:8).

To bring salvation (Mt 1:21; 15:24; 18:12-14; Lk 19:10; Jn 3:13-17; Ro 14:15; 1Ti 1:15). To deliver from fear of death (Heb 2:15). To deliver from temptation (Heb 2:18). To comfort the contrite (Isa 61:1-3). To baptize with the Holy Spirit and with fire (Mt 3:11-12; Lk 3:16). To preach to spirits in prison (1Pe 3:19; 4:6, cf. Eph 4:9).

Names, Appellations, and Titles of:
Adam (1Co 15:45). Advocate (1Jn 2:1). Almighty (Rev 1:8). Alpha and Omega (Rev 22:13). Amen (Rev 3:14). Angel (Ge 48:16; Ex 23:20). Angel of his presence (Isa 63:9). Anointed (Ps 2:2). Apostle (Heb 3:1). Arm of the Lord (Isa 51:9-10). Atoning sacrifice (1Jn 2:2). Author of life (Ac 3:15). Author of salvation (Heb 2:10). Author and perfecter of our faith (Heb 12:2).

Banner for the peoples (Isa 11:10). Beginning and End (Rev 22:13). Blessed and only Ruler (1Ti 6:15). Branch (Jer 23:5; Zec 3:8). Bread of life (Jn 6:48). Bridegroom (Mt 9:15). Bright Morning Star (Rev 22:16).

Capstone (Mt 21:42). Carpenter (Mk 6:3). Carpenter's son (Mt 13:55). Chief Shepherd (1Pe 5:4). Child (Isa 9:6; Lk 2:27). Chosen one (Isa 42:1). Chosen by God (1Pe 2:4). Chosen and precious cornerstone (1Pe 2:6). Christ (Mt 1:16). The Christ (Mt 16:20; Mk 14:61, 62; Lk 9:20). Christ, a king (Lk 23:2). Christ Jesus (Ro 3:24; 8:1; 1Co 1:2, 30). Christ Jesus our Lord (1Ti 1:12; Ro 8:39). Christ of God (Lk 9:20). Christ of God, the Chosen One (Lk 23:35). Christ the Lord (Lk 2:11). Christ the power of God and the wisdom of God (1Co 1:24). Christ, the Son of God (Jn 11:27). Christ, the Son of the Blessed One (Mk 14:61). Commander (Isa 55:4). Commander of the LORD's army (Jos 5:14). Consolation of Israel (Lk 2:25). Cornerstone (Eph 2:20). Counselor (Isa 9:6). Covenant for the people (Isa 42:6).

David (Jer 30:9). Deliverer (Ro 11:26). Desired of all nations (Hag 2:7). Doctor (Mt 9:12). Eternal life (1Jn 5:20). Everlasting Father (Isa 9:6). Exact representation of God's being (Heb 1:3).

Faithful and True (Rev 19:11). Faithful witness (Rev 1:5). Faithful and true witness (Rev 3:14). The First and the Last (Rev 1:17; 2:8; 22:13). Firstborn (Heb 1:6). Firstborn from the dead (Rev 1:5). Foundation (Isa 28:16). Fountain (Zec 13:1). Friend of tax collectors and sinners (Mt 11:19).

Gate (Jn 10:7). Gift of God (Jn 4:10). Glorious Lord Jesus Christ (Jas 2:1). Glory of Israel (Lk 2:32). God (Jn 20:28). God and Savior of Israel (Isa 45:15). God of all the earth (Isa 54:5). God over all, forever praised (Ro 9:5). God the One and Only (Jn 1:18). God with us (Mt 1:23). Good Shepherd (Jn 10:11, 14). Good Teacher (Mk 10:17). Great God and Savior (Tit 2:13). Great high priest

(Heb 4:14). Great Shepherd of the sheep (Heb 13:20). Guarantee (Heb 7:22).

Head of every man (1Co 11:3). Head of the body, the church (Col 1:18). Head of the church (Eph 5:23). Heir of all things (Heb 1:2). High priest (Heb 4:15). Holiness (1Co 1:30). Holy One (Ps 16:10). Holy One of God (Mk 1:24). Holy One of Israel (Isa 41:14; 54:5). Holy and Righteous One (Ac 3:14). Holy servant Jesus (Ac 4:30). Our Hope (1Ti 1:1). Horn of salvation (Lk 1:69).

I am (Jn 8:58). Immanuel (Isa 7:14; Mt 1:23). Indescribable gift (2Co 9:15). Innocent man (Mt 27:19). Israel (Isa 49:3).

Jesus (Mt 1:21). Jesus Christ (Mt 1:1; Jn 1:17; 17:3; Ac 2:38; 4:10; 9:34; 10:36; 16:18; Ro 1:6; 2:16; 5:15, 17; 1Co 2:2; 2Co 1:19; 4:5; Gal 2:16; Php 1:11; 2:11; 2Ti 2:8; Heb 13:8; 1Jn 1:3; 2:1). Jesus Christ our Lord (Ro 5:21; 7:25; 1Co 1:9; Jude 25). Jesus Christ our Savior (Tit 3:6). Jesus of Nazareth (Mk 1:24; Lk 24:19). Jesus of Nazareth, King of the Jews (Jn 19:19). Jesus, the King of the Jews (Mt 27:37). Jesus the Son of God (Heb 4:14). Jesus, the Son of Joseph (Jn 6:42). Judge (Ac 10:42).

King (Mt 21:5). King of Israel (Jn 1:49). King of kings (1Ti 6:15; Rev 17:14). King of glory (Ps 24:7-10). King of the ages (Rev 15:3). King of the Jews (Mt 2:2). King over the whole earth (Zec 14:9).

Lamb (Rev 5:6, 8; 6:16; 7:9-10, 17; 12:11; 13:8; 14:1, 4; 15:3; 17:14; 19:7, 9; 21:9, 14, 22-23, 27). Lamb of God (Jn 1:29). Lawgiver (Isa 33:22). Leader (Isa 55:4). Life (Jn 14:6). Light, everlasting (Isa 60:20). Light of the world (Jn 8:12). Light for the Gentiles (Isa 42:6). Light, true (Jn 1:9). Living bread (Jn 6:51). Living Stone (1Pe 2:4). Lion of the tribe of Judah (Rev 5:5). Lord (Jn 20:28). Lord Almighty (Jas 5:4). Lord of all (Ac 10:36; Ro 10:12). Lord of lords (Rev 17:14; 19:16). LORD Our Righteousness (Jer 23:6). Lord God Almighty (Rev 15:3). Lord and Savior Jesus Christ (2Pe 1:11; 3:18). Lord Christ (Col 3:24). Lord Jesus (Ac 7:59; Col 3:17; 1Th 4:2). Lord Jesus Christ (Ac 11:17; 15:26; 28:31; Ro 5:1, 11; 13:14). LORD mighty in battle (Ps 24:8). Lord of the dead and the living (Ro 14:9). Lord of the Sabbath (Mk 2:28). Lord's Christ (Lk 2:26). LORD, your holy one (Isa 43:15). LORD, your redeemer (Isa 43:14).

Man Christ Jesus (1Ti 2:5). Man of sorrows (Isa 53:3). Man who is close to me [the LORD] (Zec 13:7). Master (Mt 23:8). Mediator (1Ti 2:5). Messenger of the covenant (Mal 3:1). Messiah (Jn 1:41). Mighty God (Isa 9:6). Mighty One of Israel (Isa 1:24). Mighty one of Jacob (Isa 49:26). Mighty to save (Isa 63:1). Morning star (2Pe 1:19; Rev 22:16).

Nazarene (Mt 2:23).

Offspring of David (Rev 22:16). Offspring of the woman (Ge 3:15). The One and Only (Jn 1:14). One and only Son (Jn 3:16, 18). One he [the Father] loves (Eph 1:6). Only God our Savior (Jude 25). Overseer (1Pe 2:25).

Passover lamb (1Co 5:7). Perfecter of faith (Heb 12:2). Power of God (1Co 1:24). Physician (Lk 4:23). Precious cornerstone (Isa 28:16). Priest (Heb 7:17). Prince (Ac 5:31). Prince of Peace (Isa 9:6). Prophet (Dt 18:15, 18; Mt 21:11; Lk 24:19).

Rabbi (Jn 1:49). Rabboni (Jn 20:16). Radiance of God's glory (Heb 1:3). Ransom (1Ti 2:6). Redeemer (Isa 59:20). Resurrection and life (Jn 11:25). Redemption (1Co 1:30). Righteous Branch (Jer 23:5). Righteous Judge (2Ti 4:8). Righteous One (Ac 7:52; 22:14). Righteous servant (Isa 53:11). Righteousness (1Co 1:30). Rising sun (Lk 1:78). Rock (1Co 10:4). Rock that makes them fall (1Pe 2:8). Root of David (Rev 5:5; 22:16). Root of Jesse (Isa 11:10). Rose of Sharon (SS 2:1). Ruler (Mt 2:6; 1Ti 6:15). Ruler of God's creation (Rev 3:14). Ruler of the kings of the earth (Rev 1:5). Ruler over Israel (Mic 5:2).

Sacrifice (1Jn 2:2). Salvation (Lk 2:30). Sanctuary (Isa 8:14). Savior (Lk 2:11). Savior, Christ Jesus (2Ti 1:10). Savior Jesus Christ (Tit 2:13; 2Pe 1:1). Savior of the body (Eph 5:23). Savior of the world (1Jn 4:14). Scepter (Nu 24:17). Second man from heaven (1Co 15:47). Seed of Abraham (Gal 3:16). Servant (Isa 42:1). Servant of rulers (Isa 49:7). Serves in the sanctuary (Heb 8:2). Shepherd (Mk 14:27). Shepherd and Overseer of souls (1Pe 2:25). Shepherd, Chief (1Pe 5:4). Shepherd, good (Jn 10:11). Shepherd, great (Heb 13:20). Shepherd of Israel (Ps 80:1). Shiloh (Ge 49:10, ftn). Son he [God] loves (Col 1:13). Son of Abraham (Mt 1:1). Son of David (Mt 9:27). Son of the Father (2Jn 3). Son of God. *See Jesus the Christ, Son of God.* Son of Man. *See Jesus the Christ, Son of Man.* Son of the Blessed One (Mk 14:61). Son of the Most High (Lk 1:32). Star (Nu 24:17). Stone (Mt 21:42). Stone that causes men to stumble (1Pe 2:8). Sun of righteousness (Mal 4:2). Sure foundation (Isa 28:16).

Teacher (Jn 3:2). Tested stone (Isa 28:16). True God (1Jn 5:20). True vine (Jn 15:1). Truth (Jn 14:6).

Vine (Jn 15:1).

Way (Jn 14:6). Who is, who was, and who is to come (Rev 1:4). Wisdom (Pr 8:12). Wisdom of God (1Co 1:24). Witness (Isa 55:4; Rev 1:5). Wonderful Counselor (Isa 9:6). Word (Jn 1:1). Word of God (Rev 19:13). Word of life (1Jn 1:1).

Yahweh. *See in list above: I am, Lord, and* LORD.

In His Name—

(1Co 6:11; Php 2:9; Col 3:17; Rev 19:16). Baptism (Mt 28:19; Ac 2:38). Life (Jn 20:31). Miracles performed (Ac 3:6; 4:10; 19:13). Prayer (Jn 14:13; 16:23-24, 26; Eph 5:20; Col 3:17; Heb 13:15). Preaching (Lk 24:47). Faith (Mt 12:21; Jn 1:12; 2:23). Remission of sins (Lk 24:47; Ac 10:43; 1Jn 2:12). Salvation (Ac 4:12; 10:43). Those who use his name must turn away from wickedness (2Ti 2:19).

See above, Intercession of; below, Priesthood of.

Obedience of:

Foretold (Ps 40:8; Isa 11:5-6, Heb 10:7 9). To his parents (Lk 2:51). To God (Lk 2:49; Jn 4:34; 5:30, 36; 6:38; 8:29, 46, 55; 9:4; 14:31; 15:10; 17:4).

Exemplified: In his baptism (Mt 3:15). Sufferings (Mt 26:39, 42; Mk 14:36; Lk 22:42; Heb 5:8). Death (Jn 19:30; Php 2:8).

Omnipotence of:

(Ps 45:3-5; 110:3; Isa 9:6; 40:10; 50:2-3; 63:1; Mt 6:7; 12:13, 28-29; 28:18; Mk 3:27; Lk 5:17; 9:1; 11:20-22; Jn 2:10; 5:21, 28-29; 10:17-18, 28; Php 3:20-21; Col 1:17; 2Th 1:9; 1Ti 6:16; Heb 1:3; 7:25; 2Pe 1:16; Rev 1:8; 3:7; 5:12).

Omnipresence of:

(Mt 18:20; 28:20; Jn 3:13; Eph 1:23).

Omniscience of:

(Col 2:3; Rev 2:18, 23; 5:5, 12). Manifested in his knowledge, of the Father (Mt 11:27; Jn 7:29). Knowledge of human hearts (Mt 9:4; 12:25; 17:27; 22:18; Mk 2:8; Lk 5:22; 6:8; 9:46-48; 11:17; 22:10-12 w Mk 14:13-15; Jn 1:48; 2:24-25; 4:16-19, 28-29; 5:42; 6:64; 13:11; 21:17). Knowledge of future events (Mt 24:25; Jn 13:1, 3, 10; 16:30, 32; 18:4; 21:6). The coin in the fish's mouth (Mt 17:27), the presence of schools of fish (Lk 5:4-7; Jn 21:6).

Our example:

(Jn 10:4; Heb 3:1-2; 1Jn 2:6; Rev 14:4). In meekness (Mt 11:29; Heb 12:2-4; 1Pe 2:21-24). Humility (Lk 22:26-27; Jn 13:13-15, 34; 2Co 10:1; Php 2:5-8). Ministering (Mt 20:28; Mk 10:43-45; 2Co 8:9, w 8:5-11; Gal 6:2). Loving others (Jn 13:34; Eph 5:2). Character (Ro 8:29; 15:2-3, 5, 7; 1Pe 1:15-16; 1Jn 3:1-3, 16; 4:17). Enduring suffering (1Pe 3:17-18).

Parables of:

The wise and foolish builders (Mt 7:24-27; Lk 6:47, 49).
Two debtors (Lk 7:41-47).
The rich fool (Lk 12:16-21).
The servants waiting for their lord (Lk 12:35-40).
Barren fig tree (Lk 13:6-9).
The sower (Mt 13:3-9, 18-23; Mk 4:1-9, 14-20; Lk 8:5-8, 11-15).
The weeds (Mt 13:24-30, 36-43).
Seed growing secretly (Mk 4:26-29).
Mustard seed (Mt 13:31-32; Mk 4:30-32; Lk 13:18-19).
Yeast (Mt 13:33; Lk 13:20-21).
Hid treasure (Mt 13:44).
Pearl of great price (Mt 13:45-46).
Fishing net (Mt 13:47-50).
Unmerciful servant (Mt 18:23-35).
Good Samaritan (Lk 10:30-37).
Friend at midnight (Lk 11:5-8).
Good shepherd (Jn 10:1-16).
Great supper (Lk 14:15-24).
Lost sheep (Mt 18:12-14; Lk 15:3-7).
Lost piece of money (Lk 15:8-10).
The prodigal and his brother (Lk 15:11-32).
The unjust steward (Lk 16:19-31).
Rich man and Lazarus (Lk 16:19-31).
Importunate widow (Lk 18:1-8).
Pharisee and tax collector (Lk 18:9-14).
Laborers in the vineyard (Mt 20:1-16).
The pounds (Lk 19:11-27).
The two sons (Mt 21:28-32).
Wicked farmers (Mt 21:33-44; Mk 12:1-12; Lk 20:9-18).
Marriage of the king's son (Mt 22:1-14).
Fig tree in leaf (Mt 24:32; Mk 13:28-29).
Man taking a far journey (Mk 13:34-37).
Ten virgins (Mt 25:1-13).
Talents (Mt 25:14-30).
The vine (Jn 15:1-5).

Passion of: *See below, Sufferings of.*

Possibility of Sinning: *See below, Temptation of.*

Perfections of:

(Col 2:3). Is the image of God (2Co 4:4; Col 1:15). All the fullness of the Father lived in him (Col 1:19; 2:9). Righteous (Isa 11:5; Jn 7:18; 2Co 1:19). Without deceit (Isa 53:9). Sinless (Mt 27:3-4; Ac 13:28; 2Co 5:21). Faithful (2Th 3:3; 2Ti 2:13; Heb 3:2). Full of grace and truth (Jn 1:14, 18; Col 2:3). Just in judgment (Jn 5:30).

Perfected through sufferings (Heb 2:10).

Perfections of typified (Lev 21:17-21).

Persecutions of: *See Persecution.*

Popularity of:

(Mt 4:24; 8:1; 13:2; 14:13, 35; 19:1-2; 21:8-11; Mk 1:33; 2:2; 3:7, 20; 5:21; 6:33, 55-56; 10:1; 11:8-10; 12:37; Lk 4:14-15, 42; 5:1; 9:11; 12:1; 19:35-38; Jn 6:15; 12:12-13, 19).

Power of:

(Ps 110:3; 1Co 1:24). Called Mighty God (Isa 9:6). Has all power (Mt 28:18; Jn 10:17-18, 28; 17:2; Php 3:20-21; 2Th 1:9; 1Ti 6:16; 2Pe 1:16; Rev 3:7; 5:12).

Manifested: In creation (Jn 1:3, 10; Col 1:16). Salvation of men (Heb 7:25). Upholding all things (Col 1:17; Heb 1:3). In forgiving sins (Mt 9:2, 6; Mk 2:5, 10; Lk 5:20, 24; Col 3:13). In healing diseases (Mt 8:3, 16; 9:6-7; 12:13; Mk 5:27-34; Lk 5:17; 6:19; Ac 10:38). Casting out demons (Mt 8:16; 12:28-29; Mk 3:27; Lk 11:20-22). Stilling the tempest (Mt 8:27). Giving the apostles power to heal (Mt 10:1; Mk 6:7; Lk 9:11). Resurrection (Jn 2:19; 10:17-18).

Prayers of:

(Mt 11:25-26; Lk 3:21; 11:1). In secret (Mt 14:23; Mk 1:35; 6:46; Lk 5:16; 6:12; 9:18, 28-29). At the grave of Lazarus (Jn 11:41-42). For Peter (Lk 22:32). For believers (Jn 17:1-26). In Gethsemane (Mt 26:36-39; Mk 14:32-35; Lk 22:42-44; Heb 5:7). On the cross (Mt 27:46; Lk 23:34, 46).

Preexistence of:

Was in the beginning (Jn 1:1-3; 1Jn 2:13-14; Rev 3:14). Came from heaven (Jn 3:13; 6:62; Php 2:5-7). Came from the Father (Jn 13:3; 16:28). Was before creation (Jn 17:5, 24; 2Ti 1:9; 1Jn 1:1-2; 1Pe 1:20). Maker of all things (Jn 1:3; 1Co 8:6; Col 1:15-17; Heb 1:1-2, 8-12; Rev 4:11). Was before Abraham (Jn 8:56-58). With the Israelites in the wilderness (1Co 10:4, 9; Jude 5).

Prescience of: *See above, Omniscience of.*

Priesthood of:

Appointed and called by God (Heb 3:1-2; 5:4-5), after the order of Melchizedek (Ps 110:4; Heb 5:6; 6:20; 7:15-17), superior to Aaron and the Levitical priests (Heb 7:11, 16, 22; 8:1-2, 6). Consecrated with an oath (Heb 7:20-21). Has an unchangeable priesthood (Heb 7:23, 28). Is of unblemished purity (Heb 7:26, 28), faithful (Heb 3:2). Needed no sacrifice for himself (Heb 7:27).

Offered himself as a sacrifice (Heb 9:14, 26). His sacrifice superior to all others (Heb 9:13-14, 23). Offered sacrifice but once (Heb 7:27). Made reconciliation (Heb 2:17). Obtained redemption for us (Heb 9:12). Entered into heaven (Heb 4:14; 10:12). Sympathizes with saints (Heb 2:18; 4:15). Intercedes (Heb 7:25; 9:24). Blesses (Nu 6:23-26; Ac 3:26). On his throne (Zec 6:13). Appointment of, an encouragement to steadfastness (Heb 4:14).

Typified: Melchizedek (Ge 14:18-20). Aaron and his sons (Ex 40:12-15).

Promises of, to his disciples:

Of everlasting life (Mt 19:28; Mk 10:29-30; Lk 18:29-30; 23:43; Jn 5:25-29; 6:54, 57-58; 12:25-26). Of power (Lk 24:49; Jn 7:38-39; Ac 1:4-8). Of the Counselor (Jn 14:16, 26; 15:26-27; 16:7-14). Of his mediatorship (Jn 16:23-24, 26).

Prophecies Concerning:

(Ge 18:18; 22:18; 26:4; 28:14; Isa 53:2-12; Mt 8:17; Gal 3:8, 16).

Described in Prophecy as—

The branch (Isa 11:1; Jer 23:5-6; 33:15; Zec 3:8; Ro 15:12). Capstone and Cornerstone (Ps 118:22; Isa 28:16). Banner for the peoples (Isa 11:10). Fountain for sin (Zec 13:1). King (Zec 9:9). Leader and commander (Isa 55:4-5). Light to the Gentiles (Isa 42:6-7; 49:6; 52:10, 15; Lk 2:31-32). Lord (Isa 40:3, 5; 35:2; Jer 31:34; Mal 3:1-3; Lk 3:4). God's chosen one (Isa 42:1). Priest (Ps 110:4). Prophet (Dt 18:15, 18; Ac 3:22-24). Redeemer (Isa 59:20). Ruler over Israel (Mic 5:2). Savior (Isa 62:10-11; Mt 1:21; Lk 1:31). Seed of woman (Ge 3:15). Shepherd (Isa 40:11; Eze 34:23). Son of man (Da 7:13-14).

Future Glory and Power—

(Rev 19:11-12, 15). To have universal dominion (Ps 72:5, 8-11, 17, 19; Isa 2:2-4; 9:6-7; 60:1-9; Da 2:35, 44; 7:18, 22, 27; Mic 4:1-4). To be King of kings (Ps 72:5, 8-11, 17, 19; Rev 1:5-7; 11:15; 12:10; 17:14; 19:16; 20:4, 6). To sit at right hand of God (Mk 14:62; 1Pe 3:22). To be judge (Jude 14-15; Rev 2:23; 6:16-17; 14:14-16).

Prophet:

(Dt 18:15, 18; Mt 21:11, 46; Lk 7:16; 13:33; 24:19; Jn 4:19; 6:14; 7:40; 9:17; Ac 3:22-23; 7:37). Foretold (Isa 52:7; Na 1:15).

Anointed with the Holy Spirit (Isa 42:1; 61:1, w Lk 4:18; Jn 3:34). Reveals God (Mt 11:27; Jn 3:2, 13, 34; 17:6, 14, 26; Heb 1:1-2). Declared his doctrine to be that of the Father (Jn 8:26, 28; 12:49-50; 14:10, 24; 15:15; 17:8, 26). Foretold things to come (Mt 24:3-35; Lk 19:41-44). Faithful (Lk 4:43; Jn 17:8; Heb 3:2; Rev 1:5; 3:14). Abounded in wisdom (Lk 2:40, 47, 52; Col 2:3). Mighty in deed and word (Mt 13:54; Mk 1:27; Lk 4:32; Jn 7:46). Humble in his teaching (Isa 42:2; Mt 12:17-20). God commands us to hear (Dt 18:15; Ac 3:22). God will severely visit neglect of (Dt 18:15, 18-19; Ac 3:23; Heb 2:3).

Received:

Crowds attend his ministry (Mt 8:1; 13:2; 14:13, 35; 19:1-2; Mk 1:37, 45; 2:2, 15; 3:7, 20-21; 4:1; 5:21; 10:1; 11:18; 12:37; Lk 9:11; 12:1; 19:48; 21:38; Jn 6:2; 8:2).

Many believe on him (Mt 4:24; 21:8-11, 15; Mk 2:12; 6:55-56; 11:8-10; Lk 6:17-19; 7:16-17; 19:36-38, 47-48; 23:27; Jn 2:11, 23; 4:45; 8:30; 10:41-42; 11:45-48; 12:9, 11-13, 18-21, 42).

Authority of his teaching confessed (Mk 1:22; Lk 4:32; Jn 3:2; 7:46).

With astonishment and gladness (Mt 9:8, 27-28, 33; 13:54; 15:31; Mk 1:27; 2:12; 5:42; 7:37; Lk 4:36-37, 42; 5:26; 13:17; 18:43; Jn 7:31, 40-44; 9:17, 24-25, 29-30, 33; 11:37).

Instances of his being received: By Matthew (Mt 9:9), by Peter and other fishermen (Mk 1:16-20; Lk 5:3-11), by Philip (Jn 1:43, 45), by Nathanael (Jn 1:45-50), by Zacchaeus (Lk 19:1-10), by thief on the cross (Lk 23:40-42), by three thousand at Pentecost (Ac 2:41; 4:4).

Redeemer: *See below, Savior. See Redemption.*

Rejected:

(Lk 9:26; 10:16; 11:23; Heb 6:4-6; 1Pe 2:4, 7-8; 1Jn 2:22-23; 4:3; 2Jn 7).

Rejected by the Jews (Mt 13:54-58 w Isa 6:9-10; Mt 23:37; Mk 6:3-6; Lk 7:34; 13:34; 19:27, 42; 22:67; Jn 1:11; 5:38, 40, 43; 7:3-5, 12-13, 15, 25-27; 8:13, 21-22, 24, 45-47, 53; 9:16-17, 24; 10:20-21, 24, 33; 11:46-48; 12:37, 48; Ac 13:46; 18:5-6; 22:18; 28:24-25, 27; Ro 3:3; 9:31-32; 10:16, 21; 1Co 1:8). By Gadarenes or Gerasenes (Mt 8:34; Mk 5:17; Lk 8:37). By Gentiles (1Co 1:23). By followers (Jn 6:36, 60-66).

Prophecies concerning his rejection (Ps 2:1-3; 118:22; Isa 53:1-4; Lk 9:44). Foretold by himself (Mt 11:16-19; Mk 9:12; Lk 4:23-29; 7:31-35; 17:25; Jn 15:18, 20, 24). In the parable of the feast (Lk 14:16-24 w Mt 22:2-14). In the parable of the house built on the sand (Mt 7:26; Lk 6:46-49).

Punishment for rejection of, foretold (Mt 8:12; 10:14-15, 33; 12:38-45; Mk 12:1-12; 16:16; Lk 20:9-18; 2Ti 2:12; Heb 6:6; 10:29; 2Pe 2:1).

Relation of, to the Father:

(Ps 110:1; Mt 11:27; 1Th 5:18; Heb 2:9).

Called God his Father (Mt 20:23; 26:39; Mk 13:32; Rev 2:27).

With God in the beginning (Jn 1:1-2, 14). Was sent by God (Jn 3:34-35; 4:34; 6:27, 32-33, 38-40, 44-46; 7:16, 28-29, 33; 8:16, 19, 28-29, 38, 40, 42, 49, 54-55; 9:4; 11:41-42; 12:44, 49-50; 17:1-10, 24-26; 1Co 1:30; Heb 3:2; 1Pe 2:4, 23; 1Jn 4:9-10, 14). Endued with the Holy Spirit (Isa 42:1; 61:1; Mic 5:4; Ac 10:38).

Is the Son of God (Jn 5:19-26, 37, 45; Ro 8:32; 15:6; Heb 1:2-3; 5:5-10; 2Pe 1:17). Is one with the Father (Jn 10:18, 25, 30, 32-33, 36-38; 14:7, 9-14, 20, 24; 15:23-26). Is subject to the Father (Ps 110:1; Mk 10:40; Jn 20:17; Ac 2:22, 33, 36; 3:13, 26; 4:27; 1Co 15:24, 27-28). Is the image of God (2Co 4:4, 6; Php 2:6; Col 1:15, 19).

God raised him from the dead (Ac 13:37; Ro 1:4; Eph 1:17, 20-22; 1Pe 1:21). Ascended to the Father (Lk 24:51; Jn 16:5, 10, 28; Ac 1:9-11; Rev 3:12, 21).

See above, Deity of; Humanity of; Divine Sonship of.

Resurrection of:

Prophecies concerning (Ps 2:7; 16:9-10; Isa 55:3; Ac 13:13-34). Foretold by himself (Mt 12:40; 16:4, 21; 17:23; 20:19; 26:32; 27:52-53, 63; Mk 8:31; 9:9-10; 10:34; 14:58; Lk 9:22; 18:33; 24:7, 46; Jn 2:19, 21-22).

Certified by angels (Mt 28:6-7; Mk 16:6-7; Lk 24:5-7). Mary Magdalene (Mt 28:1-8; Mk 16:10; Lk 24:10; Jn 20:18). Clopas and his fellow disciple on the road to Emmaus (Mk 16:12-13; Lk

24:13-35). Luke (Ac 1:3, 22). Peter (Ac 2:24, 31-32 w Ps 16:9-10; Ac 3:15; 4:10, 33; 5:30-32; 10:40-41; 1Pe 1:3, 21; 3:18, 21). Paul (Ac 13:30-34 w Ps 2:7; Ac 17:2-3, 31; 26:23; 26:26; Ro 1:4; 4:24-25; 5:10; 6:4-5, 9-10; 8:11, 34; 1Co 6:14; 15:3-8, 12-19; 15:20-23; 2Co 4:10-11, 14; 5:15; 13:4; Gal 1:1; Eph 1:20; Php 3:10; Col 1:18; 2:12; 1Th 1:10; 4:14; 2Ti 2:8). The author of Hebrews (Heb 13:20). John (Rev 1:5, 18). Appeared to the eleven apostles after his resurrection (Mk 16:14; Lk 24:36-51; Jn 20:19-29).

Rose for our justification (Ro 4:25). Rose for our salvation (Ro 5:10; 10:9). An earnest of the general resurrection (Ro 6:5; 1Co 6:14; 15:21-23; 2Co 4:14; 1Th 4:14; 1Pe 1:3). The theme of apostolic preaching (Ac 2:24, 31-32; 3:15; 4:10, 33; 5:30-32; 10:40-41; 17:2-3).

See Resurrection.

Reticence of:

(Isa 53:7; Mt 26:63; 27:12, 14; Mk 14:61; 15:4-5; Jn 19:9; 1Pe 2:23).

Revelation by:

Concerning his kingdom (Mt 8:11-12; 10:23, 34; 13:24-50; 16:18, 28; 21:43-44; 24:14; Mk 9:1; 16:17-18; Lk 9:27; 12:40-53; 13:24-35; 17:20-37; Jn 4:21, 23; 5:25-29; 6:39, 54; 12:35; 13:19; 14:29; 16:4). His rejection by the Jews (Mt 21:33-44; Lk 17:25). His betrayal (Mt 26:21, 23-25). His crucifixion (Jn 3:14; 8:28; 12:32, w Lk 24:6-7). Judgments upon the Jews (Mt 23:37-39). The destruction of the temple, and Jerusalem (Mt 24; Mk 13; Lk 19:41-44). The destruction of Capernaum (Mt 11:23; Lk 10:15).

Concerning persecutions of Christians (Mt 23:34-36). His being forsaken by his disciples (Jn 16:32). Lazarus (Jn 11:4, 11, 23, 40). Peter (Jn 21:18-23). Fame of the woman who anointed his head (Mt 26:13; Mk 14:8-9). False Christs (Mt 24:4-5, 23-26; Mk 13:5-6, 21-23; Lk 17:23-24; 21:8). Things to come (Rev 1:1).

Concerning his death and resurrection (Mt 12:39-40; 16:21; 17:12, 22-23; 20:18-19; 21:33-39; 26:2, 18, 21, 23-24, 45-46; 27:63; Mk 8:31; 9:31; 10:32-34; Lk 9:22-24; 17:25; 18:31-33; 22:15, 37; Jn 2:19; 10:15, 17; 12:7, 23, 32; 13:18-27; 14:19; 16:20, 32). His ascension (Jn 7:33-34; 8:21; 13:33; 16:10, 16).

Righteousness of: *See above, Holiness of.*

Salvation by: *See Salvation.*

Savior:

(Mt 1:21; Ac 5:31; 13:23, 38-39, 47; 15:11; 16:31; 1Co 1:30; 15:57; Eph 5:23; Php 3:20; 1Ti 1:1, 15; 2Ti 1:9-10, 12; 2:10; 3:15; Tit 1:4; Heb 2:3; 5:9; 2Pe 1:11; 2:20; 1Jn 3:5; 4:9, 14; 5:11-13).

Savior through his death (Ro 3:25; 4:25; 5:1, 6, 8-10; Gal 1:4; 2:20; Eph 2:13-18, 20; 5:2, 25-26; Col 1:12-14; 1Th 1:10; 5:9-10; Tit 2:13-14; 1Pe 1:18-19; 3:18; 1Jn 4:10). Through his resurrection (Ac 3:26; Ro 10:9; 1Co 15:17; 1Pe 3:21).

Savior by his intercession (Heb 7:22, 25). By redemption (Ro 3:24). By reconciliation (Ro 5:15, 17-19, 21; 2Co 5:18-19, 21; Eph 2:7, 13-18, 20; Heb 2:17).

The only Savior (Ac 4:12; 1Co 3:11).

Prophecies concerning him as Savior (Ps 72:4, 12-14, 17; Isa 42:6-7; 49:6, 8-9, 16-17; 59:20; 61:1-3; Zec 9:9; Mal 4:2; Lk 1:68-77; 4:18-19).

Illustrated: By parables of lost sheep and lost coin (Mt 18:12-13; Lk 15:1-10).

Testified to by angels (Lk 2:11). By Simeon (Lk 2:30-32). By himself (Mt 9:12-13; Lk 5:31-32; 19:10; Jn 5:33-34, 40; 6:27, 32-33, 35, 37, 39, 51, 53-58; 7:37-39; 8:12; 9:5, 39; 10:7, 9-11, 14-16, 27-28; 11:25-26; 12:47; 14:6; 17:2-3, 12). By John (Jn 1:29). By the people of Sychar (Jn 4:42). By the heavenly host (Rev 5:5-14).

See above, Death of; Purpose of His Death.

Second Coming:

(Mt 26:64; Jn 14:28-29; 21:22; Ac 1:11; 3:20-21; 1Co 11:26; Php 3:20-21; 1Th 1:10; 2:19; 3:13; 4:15-17; 2Th 2:1-5; 2:8; 1Ti 6:14-15; Tit 2:13; 2Pe 3:3-4).

At an unexpected time (Mt 24:3, 27, 30-31, 36-39, 42-44; 25:6, 10, 13, 19; Mk 13:1-37; Lk 12:37-40; 17:22-30; 21:5-35; 1Th 5:2-3, 23; 2Pe 3:8-14; Rev 16:15; 22:20).

Coming in heavenly glory (Mt 16:27; 25:31; Mk 8:38; 13:26-27; 14:62; Lk 9:26; 21:27).

Coming to judge the world (Mt 16:27; 25:31-46; Lk 19:12-13, 15; 1Co 1:7-8; 4:5; 2Th 1:7-10; 2Ti 4:1; Rev 22:12).

Coming to receive his saints (Jn 14:3, 18; 1Co 15:23; Col 3:4; 2Th 1:10; 2Ti 4:8; Heb 9:28; 1Pe 5:4; 1Jn 3:2).

Exhortations in view of his coming (Jas 5:7-9; 1Pe 1:7, 13; 4:13; 1Jn 2:28; Rev 3:11).

Shepherd:

Jesus the true shepherd: Foretold (Ge 49:24; Isa 40:11; Eze 34:23; 37:24). The chief (1Pe 5:4). The good (Jn 10:11, 14). The great (Mic 5:4; Heb 13:20).

His sheep he knows (Jn 10:14, 27). He calls (Jn 10:3). He gathers (Isa 40:11; Jn 10:16). He guides (Ps 23:3; Jn 10:3-4). He feeds (Ps 23:1-2; Jn 10:9). He cherishes tenderly (Isa 40:11). He protects and preserves (Jer 31:10; Eze 34:10; Zec 9:16; Jn 10:28). He laid down his life for (Zec 13:7; Mt 26:31; Jn 10:11, 15; Ac 20:28). He gives eternal life to (Jn 10:28).

Typified: David (1Sa 16:11).

Son of God:

Acclaimed by God (Ps 2:4 w Ac 13:13; Ps 89:26-27; Mt 3:17; 17:5; Mk 1:11; 9:7; Lk 3:22; 9:35; 2Pe 1:17).

Proclaimed by angels (Lk 1:32, 35; Rev 2:18).

Claimed by Christ (Mt 10:40; 11:27; 15:13; 18:10, 19; 20:23; 21:37; 26:53, 63-64; 27:43; Mk 14:61-62; Lk 10:22; 20:13; 22:29, 70; Jn 5:17-37; 6:27, 38, 40, 46, 57, 69; 7:17, 28-29; 8:16, 19, 26-29, 38-42, 49, 54; 9:35-37; 10:15-18, 29-30, 36-38; 11:4, 27, 41; 12:49-50; 14:7-13, 16, 20, 24, 28, 31; 15:1, 8-10, 23-24; 16:5, 15, 27-28, 32; 17:1; 20:17, 21, 31). As equality with the Father (Mt 10:40; 11:27; Lk 10:22; Jn 1:1-2; 8:16, 19; 10:15-18, 29-30, 36-38; 14:7-13, 16, 20, 24, 28, 31; 15:23-24; 16:15).

Sonship recognized by the disciples (Mt 14:33; 16:15-17). By Peter (Mt 16:15-17). By the centurion (Mt 27:54; Mk 15:39). By Nathanael (Jn 1:49-50). By Martha (Jn 11:27). By Satan, who tempted him (Mt 4:3, 6; Lk 4:3, 9). By demons (Mk 3:11; 5:7; Lk 4:41; 8:28).

Claim to sonship recognized by the Jews (Mt 27:43; Jn 19:7). By the high priest (Mk 14:61-62).

Testified to by Mark (Mk 1:1). By Luke (Ac 3:13). By John (Jn 1:1-2, 14, 18, 34; 3:16-18, 34-36; 13:3; 1Jn 1:7; 2:22-24; 3:8, 23; 4:9-10, 14; 5:5, 9-10, 13, 20; 2Jn 3). By Paul (Ro 1:3-4, 9; 8:3, 29, 32; 1Co 1:9; 15:24, 27-28; 2Co 1:3, 19; Gal 1:16; 4:4; Eph 1:3; 3:14; Col 1:3, 15, 19; 3:17; 1Th 1:10). In Hebrews (Heb 1:1-3, 5; 4:14; 5:5, 8; 6:6; 7:3; 10:29).

Belief in, basis of eternal life (Jn 1:1-2, 12; 3:16-18, 34-36; 6:40; 20:31; 1Jn 2:22-24; 3:23; 5:5, 9-10, 13, 20), for growth and purity (Jn 15:1, 8-10; 1Jn 1:7).

Denial of, basis of antichrist (1Jn 2:22-24).

See above, Deity of; Relation of, to the Father. See Son of God.

Son of Man:

Used in a messianic sense (Da 7:13-14).

Used by Jesus: Of himself (Mt 11:19, 27; 16:13; Mk 14:21, 41; Lk 6:22; 7:34; 18:31; Jn 1:51; 3:13). In a messianic sense, of his coming (Mt 10:23; 16:27-28; 24:27, 30, 37, 44; 25:13, 31; Mk 13:26; Lk 9:26; 12:40; 17:22, 24, 26, 30; 18:8; 21:27), his kingdom (Mt 16:28; 19:28; Mk 8:38; 14:62), his judgment (Mt 24:29-30; Mk 8:38; Lk 9:26; 12:8, 10; 21:36), his lordship or deity (Mt 12:8; 13:37, 41; 16:13, w 16:16, 27-28; 19:28; 24:27; Mk 2:28; Lk 6:5; 12:8, 10; 17:22, 24; 21:36; 22:69; Jn 12:23; 13:31), his suffering and death (Mt 12:40; 17:9, 12, 22; 20:18, 28; 26:2, 24-25; Mk 8:31; 9:9, 12, 31; 10:33-34, 45; 14:21, 41; Lk 9:22, 44; 11:30; 17:22-26; 18:31; 22:22, 48; 24:7; Jn 3:14; 8:28; 12:23; 13:31), his resurrection (Mt 12:40; 17:9, 22-23; 20:18-19; Mk 8:31; 9:9, 31; 10:33-34; Jn 6:62; 12:23; 13:31).

Of himself, as the supreme human (Mt 8:20; 12:32), a servant of mankind (Mt 20:28; Mk 10:45; Lk 9:56, 58), the forgiver of sins (Mt 9:6; Mk 2:10; Lk 5:24; 12:10), the Redeemer (Mt 18:11; 20:28; Lk 12:8; 19:10; 6:27, 53).

Used by the angel at the empty tomb, in quoting Christ (Lk 24:7); Stephen, in his vision of Jesus (Ac 7:56); John, in his vision of Jesus (Rev 1:13; 14:14).

Synonymous with *Christ*, as used by, Caiaphas the high priest (Mt 26:63, w 26:65; Mk 14:61-62), the religious leaders (Lk 22:70, w 22:66-71, & 23:35), the people in questioning him (Jn 12:34).

The title is a reference to the human nature of Jesus, designating him as the God-Man (Mt 8:20; 12:32).

See Son of Man.

Sovereignty of: *See above, King; Lordship of.*

Sufferings of:

Foretold: By the psalmist (Ps 22:6-8, 11-13, 17-21, w Mt 27:35 & Mk 15:24 & Lk 23:34 & Jn 19:23-24; Ps 69:7-9, 20), by prophets (Isa 50:6; 52:13-14; 53:1-12, w Mt 26:67 & 27:26 & Lk 22:37 & Jn 12:38; Mic 5:1; Zec 11:12-13; Lk 24:26, 46; 1Pe 1:11), by himself (Mt 16:21; 17:12, 22-23; 20:17-19; Mk 8:31; 9:12; 10:32-34; Lk 9:22; 18:31-33; Jn 3:14; 13:21).

In Gethsemane (Mt 26:38-45; Mk 14:34-39; Lk 22:42-44; Jn 18:11). In Pilate's judgment hall (Mt 27:24-30; Mk 15:15-20; Jn 19:16-18). At his crucifixion (Mt 27:31-50; Mk 15:34, 36; Lk 23:33-46; Jn 19:28).

Apostolic teaching concerning his suffering (Ac 3:18; 17:3; 2Co 1:5; Php 2:8; 3:10; Heb 2:9; 4:15; 5:7-8; 12:2-3; 1Pe 1:11; 2:21-23; 3:18; 4:1, 13; Rev 5:6; 19:13).

See above, Death of.

Sympathy of: *See above, Compassion of, Love of.*

Teacher:

(Mt 5:1-2; Jn 7:46; Ac 1:1). From God (Jn 3:2).

Taught with authority (Mt 7:29; 23:8; Mk 1:22). Without respect of persons (Mt 22:16; Mk 12:14; Lk 20:21). By the lake shore (Mk 4:1). In cities and villages (Mt 11:1; Mk 6:6; Lk 23:5). In synagogues (Mt 4:23; Mk 1:21; Lk 4:15; 6:6). In the temple (Mt 21:23; 26:55; Mk 12:35; Lk 21:37; Jn 8:2). In the wilderness (Mk 6:34).

Temptation of:

(Lk 22:28). By the devil (Mt 4:1-11; Mk 1:12-13; Lk 4:1-13). In all points as we are (Heb 4:15).

Typified:

In offerings (Ge 4:4; 8:20; 22:13; Ex 12:5-7; 24:5; 29:36-37; Lev 1:4, 10-12; 3:6, 12; 4:3-7, 14-18, 20, 23-25, 28-30, 32-34; 5:6-11, 16, 18; 6:6-7; 7:2; 8:14-15, 18-19, 22-24; 9:2, 7-9, 18; 12:6-8; 14:12-14, 25, 30-31; 15:15, 29-30; 16:3, 5, 9, 11, 14-16, 21-22; 19:21-22; 22:18-19; 23:12, 18-19, 27-28; Nu 6:10-11, 14, 16-17; 8:8, 12; 15:24-25, 27; 28:3-4, 9, 11, 15, 19, 22-23, 27, 30; 29:5, 8, 11, 13, 16-34, 38; 1Ch 29:21; 2Ch 7:5; 29:21-24; Ezr 6:17, 20; 8:35; Eze 43:18-27; 45:15, 18-23).

In the Passover (Ex 12:3, 5; Nu 28:16). In the cornerstone (Isa 28:16; Mk 12:10-11).

In David (Eze 34:23-24; 37:24-25; Hos 3:5). Solomon (Ps 72). Hezekiah (Isa 32:1).

Unchangeable: (Heb 13:8).

Union of, With the Righteous: *See Righteous, Union of, with Christ.*

Wisdom of:

(Mk 6:2; Lk 2:40, 46-47, 52; Jn 7:15). *See above, Omniscience.*

Worship of:

(1Co 1:2; 2Co 12:8-9; Php 2:10-11). John's vision of (Rev 5:8-9, 12-14; 7:10).

Worship commanded (Jn 5:23; Heb 1:6).

Instances of: By the wise men (Mt 2:2). By a certain ruler (Mt 9:18). By the disciples (Mt 14:33). By the Canaanite woman (Mt 15:25). By a leper (Mt 8:2). By women after his resurrection (Mt 28:9). By the eleven disciples after his resurrection (Mt 28:17; Lk 24:52). By the multitudes (Mk 11:9-10 w Mt 21:9). By Simon Peter (Lk 5:8). By the blind man whom Jesus healed (Jn 9:38). By evil spirits (Mk 3:11). By a demon-possessed man (Mk 5:6-7). By Stephen (Ac 7:59-60). By Paul (1Ti 1:12; 2Pe 3:18).

Zeal of:

For God's house (Lk 2:49; Jn 2:17; Ps 69:9). In obedience to God (Jn 4:32, 34; 9:4; Ro 15:3). In doing good (Ac 10:38). In preaching the gospel (Mt 4:23; 9:35; Mk 6:6; Lk 4:43 w Mk 1:38; 8:1). In giving himself as a sacrifice (Lk 9:51; 12:50; 13:32-33; 1Ti 6:13).

JESUS, JUSTUS *See Justus, 3.*

JETHER (*abundance*).

1. Jethro is the father-in-law of Moses (Ex 4:18).
2. Gideon's eldest son (Jdg 8:20-21).
3. Father of Amasa (2Sa 17:25; 1Ch 2:17).
4. Judahite (1Ch 2:32).
5. Judahite (1Ch 4:17).
6. Asherite, same as Ithran (1Ch 7:37, w 7:38).

JETHETH Edomite chieftain (Ge 36:40; 1Ch 1:51).

JETHLAH *See Ithlah.*

JETHRO

(*remainder* KB). A priest of Midian and father-in-law of Moses (Ex 3:1), personal name probably Reuel (Ex 2:18; 3:1), father of Zipporah, whom Moses married (Ex 3:1-2), advised Moses (Ex 18:14-24).

JETUR

Son of Ishmael and descendants (Ge 25:15; 1Ch 1:31), Itureans of NT times.

JEUEL (*God [El] has preserved*).

1. Judahite (1Ch 9:6).
2. Levite (2Ch 29:13).
3. Leader in Ezra's company (Ezr 8:13).

JEUSH (perhaps *may God aid*).

1. Son of Esau (Ge 36:5).
2. Benjamite (1Ch 7:10).
3. Gershonite Levite (1Ch 23:10-11).
4. Descendant of Jonathan (1Ch 8:39).
5. Son of Rehoboam (2Ch 11:19).

JEUZ

(*he comes to help* BDB; possibly *encouraged* IDB). Head of a Benjamite family (1Ch 8:10).

JEWEL, JEWELRY

Articles of jewelry in OT times: diadems, bracelets, necklaces, anklets, rings for fingers, gold nets for hair, pendants, amulets and pendants with magical meanings, jeweled perfume and ointment boxes, crescents for camels; used for personal adornment and utility and for religious festivals. Not much said about jewelry in NT; most condemnatory (1Ti 2:9; Jas 2:2). The New Jerusalem is adorned with jewels (Rev 21:19).

See Minerals of the Bible, 1; Stones.

JEWS

(*from Judah*). A corrupted form of Judah, and applied to the people of the kingdom of Judah and Benjamin (2Ki 16:6; 25:25; 2Ch 32:18). After the dissolution of the kingdom of Israel, the name was applied to all Israelites as well as to those of the two tribes (Mt 27:11; Ac 2:5).

Sins that led to the Captivity of (Isa 1:4-25; 2:6-10; 3:9; 59:2-15; 65:2-7; Jer 5:1; 6:21-28; 44:1-3; Eze 5:6; 12:2; 16:2, 15-47, 57-63). See the book of Jeremiah, which deals chiefly with the sins of and the corrective judgments of God to be inflicted upon.

Captive in Babylon (2Ki 24:1-20; 25:1, 21). Haman's plot against (Est 3:6-15). Feast of Purim instituted to commemorate their deliverance from Haman's plot (Est 9:26-32).

The proclamation of Cyrus authorizing their return to the land of Canaan (2Ch 36:22-23; Ezr 1:2-4), and of Artaxerxes (Ezr 7:11-26).

After the Captivity:

Return from Babylon (Ezr 7:1-9; 8:31-32). Lists of those who returned from Babylon (Ezr 2:1-67; 8:1-20; Ne 7:6-69; 12:1-21). Rebuild the temple (Ezr 3:8-13). Rebuilding suspended during the reign of Artaxerxes (Ezr 4:1-24). Resumption of the rebuilding interfered with by Tattenai, governor of the province, by protest followed by a letter to Darius (Ezr 5). Darius' reply to Tattenai authorizing the rebuilding of the temple; temple completed (Ezr 6:1-15).

Vessels of the temple, that were taken to Babylon by Nebuchadnezzar, returned by command of Cyrus (Ezr 1:7-11; 6:5). Liberality of Artaxerxes toward the temple (Ezr 7:14-23).

Made marriages among the Canaanites: Ezra instituted reforms (Ezr 10). Rebuilt the walls of Jerusalem under proclamation of Artaxerxes (Ne 2; 3; 4; 5; 6). Walls dedicated (Ne 12:27-43).

Mission of Jesus to (Mt 10:5-6; 15:24; Mk 7:27). Some accept Jesus (Jn 2:23; 10:42; 11:45; 12:11; Ac 21:20). Others disbelieve in Jesus (Mt 13:5-8; Jn 5:38, 40, 43; 6:36; 12:37). Reject Jesus (Lk 13:34; 17:25; Jn 1:11). Crucify Jesus. *See Crucifixion.* Devout, among them (Ac 2:5). Spurned Paul's preaching (Ac 13:46; 18:5-6; 28:24-27). Persecuted Paul (Ac 9:22-23; 13:50; 20:3, 19; 23:12-30; 2Co 11:24). Entrusted with the oracles of God (Ac 7:38; Ro 3:1-2).

Prophecies Concerning:

Their rejection of the Messiah (Isa 49:5, 7; 52:14; 53:1-3; Zec 13; Mt 21:33-39; 22:1-5).

War and other judgments (Isa 3; 4:1; 5; 6:9-13; 7:17-25; 8:14-22; 10:12; 22:1-14; 28:14-22; 29:1-10; 30:1-17; 31:1-3; 32:9-14; Jer 1:11-16; 4:5-31; 6; 7:8-34; 8; 9:9-26; 10:17-22; 11:9-23; 13:9-27; 14:14-18; 15:1-14; 16; 17:1-4; 18:15-17; 19; 20:5; 21:4-7; 22:24-30; 25:8-38; 28; 34; 37; 38:1-3; 42:13-22; 43-45; La 5:6; Eze 4; 5; 11:7-12; 12; 15:17; 19; 22:13-22; 23:22-35; 24; 33:21-29; Da 9:26-27; Joel 2:1-17; Am 2:4-5; Mic 3; 4:8-10; Hab 1:6-11; Zep 1; Zec 14:1-3; Mal 4:1; Mt 21:33-45; 23:35-38; 24:2, 14-42; Mk 13:1-13; Lk 13:34-35; 19:43-44; 21:5-25; 23:28-31; Rev 1:7).

Dispersion of (Isa 24:1; Jer 9:16; Hos 9:17; Joel 3:6, 20; Am 9:9; Eze 4:13; 5:10, 12; 20:23; 36:19; Da 9:7).

Blessing and restoration of (Isa 1:25-27; 2:1-5; 4:2-6; 11:11-13; 25; 26:1-2, 12-19; 27:13; 29:18-24; 30:18-26; 32:15-20; 33:13-24; 35; 37:31-32; 40:2, 9; 41:27; 44; 49:13-23; 51; 52:1-12; 60; 61:4-9; 62; 66:5-22; Jer 3:14-18; 4:3-18; 12:14-16; 23:3; 24:1-7; 30:3-22; 32:36-44; 33; 44:28; Eze 14:22-23; 16:60-63; 20:40-41; 36:1-38; 37:12, 21; Da 11:30-45; 12:1; Joel 3; Am 9:9-15; Ob 17-21; Mic 2:12-13; 5:3; Zep 2:7; Zec 1:14-21; 2; 8; 10:5-12; 12:1-14; 13; 14:3-21; Mal 3:4; Ro 11).

See Israel, Israelites; Judah.

JEZANIAH (*Yahweh gives ear*). Also known as Azariah (Jer 42:1, ftn), as was King Uzziah (2Ki 14:21, ftn; 2Ch 26:1, ftn). *See also, Jaazaniah, 1.*

JEZEBEL (possibly *unexalted, unhusbanded* BDB). Daughter of Ethbaal, a Sidonian, and wife of Ahab (1Ki 16:31). Worshiped idols and persecuted the prophets of God (1Ki 18:4, 13, 19; 2Ki 3:2, 13; 9:7, 22). Vowed to kill Elijah (1Ki 19:1-3). Wickedly accomplishes the death of Naboth (1Ki 21:5-16). Death of, foretold (1Ki 21:23; 2Ki 9:10). Death of, at the hand of Jehu (2Ki 9:30-37).

Figurative (Rev 2:20).

JEZER, JEZERITE (*formed, fashioned*). Son of Naphtali (Ge 46:24; Nu 26:49; 1Ch 7:13).

JEZIAH *See Izziah.*

JEZIEL A disaffected Israelite who joined David at Ziklag (1Ch 12:3).

JEZLIAH *See Izliah.*

JEZOAR *See Zohar, 3.*

JEZRAHIAH (*Yahweh will arise* or *shine*).
1. Descendant of Issachar called Izrahiah (1Ch 7:3).
2. Musician (Ne 12:42).

JEZREEL, JEZREELITE (*God [El] will sow* or *scatter*).
1. A city in the S of Judah (Jos 15:56; 1Sa 25:43; 27:3; 29:1, 11).
2. A city of Issachar (Jos 19:18; 2Sa 2:9). Ahab's residence in (1Ki 18:45-46; 21:1). Naboth's vineyard in (1Ki 21:1). Joram's residence in (2Ki 8:29). Jehu kills King Ahab, his wife, and friends at (2Ki 9:15-37; 10:11). Prophecies concerning (Hos 1:4-5, 11).
3. A valley (Jos 17:16). Place of Gideon's battle with the Midianites (Jdg 6:33). Place of the defeat of the Israelites under Saul and Jonathan (1Sa 29:1, 11; 31:1-6; 2Sa 4:4).
4. A descendant of Etam (1Ch 4:3).
5. Figurative of Israel (Hos 1:4-5, 11).

JIBSAM *See Ibsam.*

JIDLAPH (*he weeps*). Son of Nahor (Ge 22:22).

JIMNA, JIMNAH *See Imnah.*

JIPHTAH *See Iphtah.*

JIPHTHAH-EL *See Iphtah El.*

JOAB (*Yahweh is father*).
1. Son of David's sister (1Ch 2:16). Commander of David's army (2Sa 8:16; 20:23; 1Ch 11:6; 18:15; 27:34). Dedicated spoils of his battles (1Ch 26:28). Defeated the Jebusites (1Ch 11:6). Defeats and slays Abner (2Sa 2:13-32; 3:27; 1Ki 2:5). Destroys all the males in Edom (1Ki 11:16). *See Psalm 60, title.* Defeats the Ammonites (2Sa 10:7-14; 1Ch 19:6-15). Captures Rabbah (2Sa 11:1, 15-25; 12:26-29; 1Ch 20:1-2).

Secures the return of Absalom to Jerusalem (2Sa 14:1-24). Barley field of, burned by Absalom (2Sa 18). Rebukes David for lamenting the death of Absalom (2Sa 19:1-8). Replaced by Amasa as commander of David's army (2Sa 17:25; 19:13). Kills Amasa (2Sa 20:8-13; 1Ki 2:5). Causes Sheba to be put to death (2Sa 20:16-22). Opposes the numbering of the people (2Sa 24:3; 1Ch 21:3). Numbers the people (2Sa 24:4-9; 1Ch 21:4-5; 27:23-24). Supports Adonijah as successor to David (1Ki 1:7; 2:28). Slain by Benaiah, under Solomon's order (1Ki 2:29-34).
2. A grandson of Kenaz (1Ch 4:14).
3. An Israelite (or the name of two Israelites) whose descendants returned from Babylon to Jerusalem (Ezr 2:6; 8:9; Ne 7:11).
4. "House of Joab" (1Ch 2:54). Probably identical with 1. *See Atroth Beth Joab.*

JOAH (*Yahweh is brother*).
1. Son of Asaph (2Ki 18:18, 26; Isa 36:3, 11, 22).
2. A descendant of Gershom (1Ch 6:21; 2Ch 29:12).
3. A son of Obed-Edom (1Ch 26:4).
4. A Levite, who repaired the temple (2Ch 34:8).

JOAHAZ (*Yahweh grips*). Father of Joah, recorder of King Josiah (2Ch 34:8).

JOANAN An ancestor of Jesus (Lk 3:27).

JOANNA (probably feminine form of *John*). Wife of Cuza, the steward of Herod Agrippa, and a disciple of Jesus (Lk 8:3; 24:10).

JOASH (*Yahweh has bestowed*).
1. Son of Beker (1Ch 7:8).
2. Keeper of the stores of oil (1Ch 27:28).
3. Father of Gideon (Jdg 6:11, 29, 31; 7:14; 8:13, 29-32).
4. Son of Ahab, king of Israel (1Ki 22:26; 2Ch 18:25).
5. Also called Jehoash. *See Jehoash, Joash.* Son of Ahaziah and king of Judah. Saved from his grandmother by Jehosheba, his aunt, and hidden for six years (2Ki 11:1-3; 2Ch 22:11-12). Anointed king by the priest, Jehoiada (2Ki 11:12-21; 2Ch 23). Righteousness of, under influence of Jehoiada (2Ki 12:2; 2Ch 24:2). Repaired the temple (2Ki 12:4-16; 2Ch 24:4-14, 27). Wickedness of, after Jehoiada's death (2Ch 24:17-22). Secured peace from Hazael, king of Syria, by gift of dedicated treasures from the temple (2Ki 12:17-18; 2Ch 24:23-24). Prophecy against (2Ch 24:19-20). Put Jehoiada's son to death (2Ch 24:20-22; Mt 23:35). Diseases of (2Ch 24:25). Conspired against and slain (2Ki 12:20-21; 2Ch 24:25-26).
6. A king of Israel. *See Jehoash, Joash.*
7. A descendant of Shelah (1Ch 4:22).
8. One of David's officers (1Ch 12:3).

JOATHAM *See Jotham, 3.*

JOB (*where is my father*, or perhaps *where is my father, O God?*).
1. A man who lived in Uz (Job 1:1). Righteousness of (Job 1:1, 5, 8; 2:3; Eze 14:14, 20). Riches of (Job 1:3). Trial of, by affliction of Satan (Job 1:13-19; 2:7-10). Fortitude of (Job 1:20-22; 2:10; Jas 5:11). Visited by Eliphaz, Bildad, and Zophar as comforters (Job 2:11-13). Complaints of, and replies by his three friends (Job 3-37). Replied to by God (Job 38-41). Submission of, to God (Job 40:3-5; 42:1-6). Later blessings and riches of (Job 42:10-16). Death of (Job 42:16-17).
2. *See Jashub.*

JOB, BOOK OF

Author: Anonymous

Date: Anytime from the reign of Solomon to the Exile.

Outline:
- I. Prologue (chs. 1-2).
  - A. Job's Happiness (1:1-5).
  - B. Job's Testing (1:6-2:13).
    - 1. Satan's first accusation (1:6-12).
    - 2. Job's faith despite loss of family and property (1:13-22).
    - 3. Satan's second accusation (2:1-6).
    - 4. Job's faith during personal sufferings (2:7-10).
    - 5. The coming of the three friends (2:11-13).
- II. Dialogue-Dispute (chs. 3-27).
  - A. Job's Opening Lament (ch. 3).
  - B. First Cycle of Speeches (chs. 4-14).
    - 1. Eliphaz (chs. 4-5).
    - 2. Job's reply (chs. 6-7).
    - 3. Bildad (ch. 8).
    - 4. Job's reply (chs. 9-10).
    - 5. Zophar (ch. 11).
    - 6. Job's reply (chs. 12-14).
  - C. Second Cycle of Speeches (chs. 15-21).
    - 1. Eliphaz (ch. 15).
    - 2. Job's reply (chs. 16-17).
    - 3. Bildad (ch. 18).
    - 4. Job's reply (ch. 19).
    - 5. Zophar (ch. 20).
    - 6. Job's reply (ch. 21).
  - D. Third Cycle of Speeches (chs. 22-26).
    - 1. Eliphaz (ch. 22).
    - 2. Job's reply (chs. 23-24).
    - 3. Bildad (ch. 25).
    - 4. Job's reply (ch. 26).
  - E. Job's Closing Discourse (ch. 27).
- III. Interlude on Wisdom (ch. 28).
- IV. Monologues (29:1-42:6).
  - A. Job's Call for Vindication (chs. 29-31).
    - 1. His past honor and blessing (ch. 29).
    - 2. His present dishonor and suffering (ch. 30).
    - 3. His protestations of innocence and final oath (ch. 31).
  - B. Elihu's Speeches (chs. 32-37).
    - 1. Introduction (32:1-5).
    - 2. The speeches themselves (32:6-37:24).
      - a. First speech (32:6-33:33).
      - b. Second speech (ch. 34).
      - c. Third speech (ch. 35).
      - d. Fourth speech (chs. 36-37).
  - C. Divine Discourses (38:1-42:6).
    - 1. God's first discourse (38:1-40:2).
    - 2. Job's response (40:3-5).
    - 3. God's second discourse (40:6-41:34).
    - 4. Job's repentance (42:1-6).
- V. Epilogue (42:7-17).
  - A. God's Verdict (42:7-9).
  - B. Job's Restoration (42:10-17).

JOBAB (*howl*).
1. Son of Joktan (Ge 10:29; 1Ch 1:23).
2. Second king of Edom (Ge 36:33; 1Ch 1:44-45).
3. King of Madon (Jos 11:1; 12:19).
4. Benjamite (1Ch 8:9).
5. Benjamite (1Ch 9:18).

JOCHEBED (*Yahweh is glorious*). Mother of Miriam, Aaron, and Moses (Ex 6:20; Nu 26:59). Nurses Moses when he is adopted by Pharaoh's daughter (Ex 2:1-9).

JODA An ancestor of Joseph, the father (so it was thought) of Jesus (Lk 3:26).

JOED (*Yahweh is witness*). A Benjamite (Ne 11:7).

JOEL (*Yahweh is God [El]*).
1. Son of Samuel (1Sa 8:2; 1Ch 6:33; 15:17).
2. A Simeonite (1Ch 4:35).
3. A Reubenite (1Ch 5:4, 8).
4. A Gadite (1Ch 5:12).
5. A Kohathite Levite (1Ch 6:36).
6. Descendant of Issachar (1Ch 7:3).
7. One of David's valiant men (1Ch 11:38). Called "Igal son of Nathan" (2Sa 23:36).
8. Name of two Gershonites (1Ch 15:7, 11; 23:8; 26:22).
9. Prince of Manasseh (1Ch 27:20).
10. A Kohathite who assisted in the cleansing of the temple (2Ch 29:12).
11. One of Nebo's family (Ezr 10:43).
12. Son of Zicri (Ne 11:9).
13. One of the twelve minor prophets, probably lived in the days of Uzziah (Joel 1:1; Ac 2:16).

JOEL, BOOK OF

Author: Joel

Date: As early as the ninth century B.C. to as late as the postexilic period (sixth century), after Haggai and Zechariah. In either case, its message is not significantly affected by its dating.

Outline:
- I. Title (1:1).
- II. Judah Experiences a Foretaste of the Day of the Lord (1:2-2:17).
  - A. A Call to Mourning and Prayer (1:2-14).
  - B. The Announcement of the Day of the Lord (1:15-2:11).
  - C. A Call to Repentance and Prayer (2:12-17).
- III. Judah Is Assured of Salvation in the Day of the Lord (2:18-3:21).
  - A. The Lord's Restoration of Judah (2:18-27).
  - B. The Lord's Renewal of His People (2:28-32).
  - C. The Coming of the Day of the Lord (ch. 3).
    - 1. The nations judged (3:1-16).
    - 2. God's people blessed (3:17-21).

See Prophets, The Minor.

JOELAH (*let him help*). One of David's recruits at Ziklag (1Ch 12:7).

JOEZER (*Yahweh is help*). A Korahite, who joined David at Ziklag (1Ch 12:6).

JOGBEHAH (*height*). City in Gilead assigned to Gad (Nu 32:35; Jdg 8:11).

JOGLI (perhaps *may God reveal*). A prince of Dan (Nu 34:22).

JOHA
1. A Benjamite (1Ch 8:16).
2. One of David's valiant men (1Ch 11:45).

JOHANAN (*Yahweh is gracious*).
1. Jewish leader who tried to save Gedaliah from plot to murder him (Jer 40:13-14), took Jews, including Jeremiah, to Egypt (Jer 40-43).
2. Son of King Josiah (1Ch 3:15).
3. Son of Elioenai (1Ch 3:24).
4. Father of Azariah, high priest in Solomon's time (1Ch 6:9-10).
5. Benjamite; joined David at Ziklag (1Ch 12:4).
6. Gadite; warrior in David's army (1Ch 28:12).
7. Ephraimite chief (2Ch 28:12).
8. Exile who left Babylon with Ezra (Ezr 8:12).
9. Son of Tobiah, who married a Jewess in days of Nehemiah (Ne 6:18).
10. Son of Eliashib (Ezr 10:6).
11. High priest, grandson of Eliashib (Ne 12:22).

JOHN (*Yahweh is gracious*).
1. John the Baptist. *See John the Baptist.*
2. The apostle, the son of Zebedee, and brother of James. *See John, the Apostle.*
3. John Mark. *See Mark.*
4. Father of Simon Peter (Jn 1:42; 21:15, 17).
5. Jewish religious dignitary who called Peter and John to account for their preaching about Jesus (Ac 4:6).
6. Father of Mattathias (1Mc 2:1).
7. Eldest son of Mattathias (1Mc 9:36).
8. Father of Eupolemus (2Mc 4:11).
9. John Hyrcanus, son of Simon (1Mc 13:53; 16:1).
10. Jewish envoy (2Mc 11:17).

JOHN, 1, 2 and 3

Author: The apostle John, son of Zebedee

Date: Between A.D. 85 and 95

Outline of 1 John:
- I. Introduction: The Reality of the Incarnation (1:1-4).
- II. The Christian Life as Fellowship With the Father and the Son (1:5-2:28).
  - A. Ethical Tests of Fellowship (1:5-2:11).
    - 1. Moral likeness (1:5-7).
    - 2. Confession of sin (1:8-2:2).
    - 3. Obedience (2:3-6).
    - 4. Love for fellow believers (2:7-11).
  - B. Two Digressions (2:12-17).
  - C. Christological Test of Fellowship (2:18-28).
    - 1. Contrast: apostates versus believers (2:18-21).
    - 2. Person of Christ: the crux of the test (2:22-23).
    - 3. Persistent belief: key to continuing fellowship (2:24-28).
- III. The Christian Life as Divine Sonship (2:29-4:6).
  - A. Ethical Tests of Sonship (2:29-3:24).
    - 1. Righteousness (2:29-3:10a).
    - 2. Love (3:10b-24).
  - B. Christological Tests of Sonship (4:1-6).
- IV. The Christian Life as an Integration of the Ethical and the Christological (4:7-5:12).
  - A. The Ethical Test: Love (4:7-5:5).
    - 1. The source of love (4:7-16).
    - 2. The fruit of love (4:17-19).
    - 3. The relationship of love for God and love for one's spiritual brother (4:20-5:1).
    - 4. Obedience: the evidence of love for God's children (5:2-5).
  - B. The Christological Test (5:6-12).
- V. Conclusion: Great Christian Certainties (5:13-21).

See General Letters.

Outline of 2 John:
- I. Salutation (1-3).
- II. Commendation (4).
- III. Exhortation and Warning (5-11).
- IV. Conclusion (12-13).

See General Letters.

Outline of 3 John:
- I. Salutation (1-2).
- II. Commendation of Gaius (3-8).
- III. Condemnation of Diotrephes (9-10).
- IV. Exhortation to Gaius (11).
- V. Example of Demetrius (12).
- VI. Conclusion (13-14).

See General Letters.

JOHN MARK *See Mark, John.*

JOHN, THE APOSTLE Son of Zebedee and Salome, and brother of James (Mt 4:21; 27:56; Mk 15:40; Ac 12:1-2), lived in Galilee, probably in Bethsaida (Lk 5:10; Jn 1:44), fisherman (Mk 1:19-20), became disciple of Jesus through John the Baptist (Jn 1:35), called as an apostle (Mk 1:19-20; Lk 5:10), one of three apostles closest to Jesus (the others are Peter and James), at raising of Jairus' daughter (Mk 5:37; Lk 8:51), transfiguration (Mt 17:1; Mk 9:2; Lk 9:28), Gethsemane (Mt 26:37; Mk 14:33), asked Jesus to call fire down on Samaritans, and given name Boanerges (sons of thunder) (Mk 3:17; Lk 9:54), mother requested that John and James be given places of special honor in coming kingdom (Mk 10:35), helped Peter prepare Passover (Lk 22:8), lay close to Jesus' breast at Last Supper (Jn 13:25), present at trial of Jesus (Jn 18:15-16), witnessed crucifixion of Jesus (Jn 19:26-27), recognized Jesus at Sea of Galilee (Jn 21:1-7), active with Peter in apostolic church (Ac 3:1-4:22; 8:14-17). Lived to an old age; fourth Gospel, three letters and Revelation attributed to him. *See John, 1, 2 and 3; John, the Gospel of; Revelation.*

JOHN THE BAPTIST Forerunner of Jesus; son of Zechariah and Elizabeth, both of priestly descent (Lk 1:5-25, 56-58), lived as Nazirite in desert (Lk 1:15; Mt 11:12-14, 18), began ministry beyond Jordan in the fifteenth year of Tiberias Caesar (Lk 3:1-3), preached baptism of repentance in preparation of coming of Messiah (Lk 3:4-14), baptized Jesus (Mt 3:13-17; Mk 1:9-10; Lk 3:21; Jn 1:32), bore witness to Jesus as Messiah (Jn 1:24-42), imprisoned and put to death by Herod Antipas (Mt 14:6-12; Mk 6:17-28), praised by Jesus (Mt 11:7-14; Lk 7:24-28), disciples loyal to him long after his death (Ac 18:25).

JOHN, THE GOSPEL OF

Author: The apostle John, son of Zebedee

Date: Traditionally toward the end of the first century, c. A.D. 85 or later. More recently, some scholars have suggested a date as early as the 50s and no later than 70.

Outline:
I. Prologue (1:1-18).
II. Beginnings of Jesus' Ministry (1:19-51).
  A. The Ministry of His Forerunner (1:19-34).
  B. Jesus' Introduction to Some Future Disciples (1:35-51).
III. Jesus' Public Ministry: Signs and Discourses (chs. 2-11).
  A. Changing Water to Wine (2:1-11).
  B. Cleansing the Temple (2:12-25).
  C. Interview with Nicodemus (3:1-21).
  D. Parallel Ministry With John the Baptist (3:22-4:3).
  E. Journey Through Samaria: The Woman at the Well (4:4-42).
  F. Healing of the Official's Son (4:43-54).
  G. To Jerusalem for an Annual Feast (ch. 5).
  H. The Feeding of the 5000 and the Sermon on the Bread of Life (ch. 6).
  I. Jesus at the Feast of Tabernacles (chs. 7-8).
  J. Healing of the Man Born Blind (ch. 9).
  K. Parable of the Good Shepherd (10:1-21).
  L. Debating at the Feast of Dedication (10:22-39).
  M. Ministry in Perea (10:40-42).
  N. The Raising of Lazarus (ch. 11).
IV. The Passion Week (chs. 12-19).
  A. The Anointing of Jesus' Feet (12:1-11).
  B. The Triumphal Entry (12:12-19).
  C. The Coming of the Greeks (12:20-36).
  D. Continued Jewish Unbelief (12:37-50).
  E. Farewell Discourses (chs. 13-17).
    1. Discourse at the Last Supper (chs. 13-14).
    2. Discourse on the way to Gethsemane (chs. 15-16).
    3. Jesus' prayer of intercession (ch. 17).
  F. Jesus' Betrayal and Arrest (18:1-12).
  G. The Trials of Jesus (18:13-19:15).
  H. The Crucifixion and Burial (19:16-42).
V. The Resurrection (20:1-29).
VI. The Statement of Purpose (20:30-31).
VII. Epilogue (ch. 21).
  See Synoptic Gospels, The.

JOIADA (*Yahweh knows*).
1. Repaired walls of Jerusalem (Ne 3:6).
2. Son of Eliashib (Ne 12:10; 13:28).

JOIAKIM (*Yahweh lifts up*). Father of Eliashib (Ne 12:10, 12, 26).

JOIARIB (*Yahweh contends, pleads [your case]*).
1. A returned exile (Ezr 8:16).
2. A descendant of Judah (Ne 11:5).
3. A priest who returned from Babylon (Ne 12:6, 19). *See Jehoiarib.*

JOKDEAM A city in Judah (Jos 15:56).

JOKIM (*Yahweh lifts up*). A descendant of Shelah (1Ch 4:22).

JOKMEAM (*let the people arise*). A Levitical city of Ephraim (1Ch 6:68).

JOKNEAM A Levitical city of Zebulun (Jos 12:22; 19:11; 21:34). *See Jokmeam.*

JOKSHAN Son of Abraham, by Keturah (Ge 25:2-3, 6; 1Ch 1:32).

JOKTAN (*smaller*). Son of Eber (Ge 10:25-26, 29; 1Ch 1:19-20, 23).

JOKTHEEL
1. A city of Judah (Jos 15:38).
2. A name given by Amaziah to Sela, stronghold of Edom (2Ki 14:7; 2Ch 25:11-12). *See Sela.*

JONA *See Jonah.*

JONADAB (*Yahweh is generous, noble*).
1. The son of Shimeah, David's brother (2Sa 13:3). His complicity with Amnon in his rape of Tamar (2Sa 13:3-5). Comforts David on death of Amnon (2Sa 13:32-35).
2. A Kenite who helped Jehu abolish Baal worship (temporarily) in Samaria (2Ki 10:15-27). *Jonadab* is spelled "Jehonadab" in this passage (2Ki 10:15-23). He was also a leader of a conservative movement that was characterized by various practices of a settled agricultural society, including the building of houses, the sowing of crops, and the use of wine. *See Nazirite(s).*
His followers still adhered to these principles nearly 250 years later and were known as Recabites (Jer 35:5-10, 16-19). *See Recabite(s).*

JONAH (*dove*). Prophet of Israel; son of Amittai; predicted victory over Syria through Jeroboam II, who reigned c. 793-753 B.C.; author of book of Jonah (2Ki 14:25; Jnh 1:1).

JONAH, BOOK OF

Author: Traditionally the prophet Jonah

Date: Before the fall of Samaria in B.C. 722-721

Outline:
I. Jonah Flees His Mission (chs. 1-2).
  A. Jonah's Commission and Flight (1:1-3).
  B. The Endangered Sailors' Cry to Their Gods (1:4-6).
  C. Jonah's Disobedience Exposed (1:7-10).
  D. Jonah's Punishment and Deliverance (1:11-2:1; 2:10).
  E. Jonah's Prayer of Thanksgiving (2:2-9).
II. Jonah Reluctantly Fulfills His Mission (chs. 3-4).
  A. Jonah's Renewed Commission and Obedience (3:1-4).
  B. The Endangered Ninevites' Repentant Appeal to the Lord (3:5-9).
  C. The Ninevites' Repentance Acknowledged (3:10-4:4).
  D. Jonah's Deliverance and Rebuke (4:5-11).
  See Prophets, The Minor.

JONAM (*Yahweh is gracious*). An ancestor of Christ (Lk 3:30).

JONAN *See Jonam.*

JONAS *See Jonah; John, 4.*

JONATH-ELEM-RECHOKIM NIV "To [the tune of] A Dove on Distant Oaks" (Ps 56:T). Probably the melody to which Ps 56 was sung. *See Music, Symbols Used in.*

JONATHAN (*gift of Yahweh*).
1. A Levite of Bethlehem, who becomes a priest for Micah, accepts idolatry, joins the Danites (Jdg 17:7-13; 18:1-30).
2. Son of Saul (1Sa 14:49). Victory of, over the Philistine garrison of Geba (1Sa 13:3-4, 16), over Philistines at Micmash (1Sa 14:1-18). Under Saul's curse pronounced against any who might take food before he was avenged of his enemies (1Sa 14:24-30, 43). Rescued by the people (1Sa 14:43-45). Love of, for David (1Sa 18:1-4; 19:1-7; 20; 23:16-18). Killed in battle with Philistines (1Sa 31:2, 6; 2Sa 21:12-14; 1Ch 10:2). Buried by inhabitants of Jabesh Gilead (1Sa 31:11-13). Mourned by David (2Sa 1:12, 17-27). Son of, cared for by David (2Sa 4:4; 9; 1Ch 8:34).
3. Son of Abiathar (2Sa 15:27). Acts as spy for David (2Sa 15:27-28; 17:17-22). Informs Adonijah of Solomon's succession to David (1Ki 1:42-48).
4. Nephew of David, slays a giant and becomes one of David's chief warriors (2Sa 21:21; 1Ch 20:7).
5. One of David's heroes (2Sa 23:32; 1Ch 11:34).
6. A son of Jada (1Ch 2:32-33).
7. Secretary of the cabinet of David (1Ch 27:32).
8. Father of Ebed (Ezr 8:6).
9. Son of Asahel (Ezr 10:15).
10. Also called Johanan. A descendant of Jeshua (Ne 12:11-12).
11. Name of two priests (Ne 12:14, 35).
12. A scribe (Jer 37:15, 20; 38:26).
13. Son of Kareah (Jer 40:8).

JOPPA (*beautiful*). An ancient walled town on coast of Israel, c. thirty-five miles NW of Jerusalem; assigned to Dan; mentioned in Amarna letters; seaport for Jerusalem. In NT times Peter raised Dorcas to life there (Ac 9:36ff) and received the vision of a sheet filled with animals (Ac 10:1ff; 11:5ff). Modern Jaffa.

JORAH (*one born during harvest*). Family which returned with Zerubbabel (Ezr 2:18). Also called Hariph (Ne 7:24).

JORAI (possibly *Yahweh sees* IDB; *whom Yahweh teaches* ISBE). A Gadite (1Ch 5:13).

JORAM (*Yahweh is exalted*). Short form of Jehoram. *See Jehoram.*
1. Son of king of Hamath (2Sa 8:10).
2. Levite (1Ch 26:25).
3. Son of Ahab, king of Israel (2Ki 8:29).
4. King of Judah (2Ki 8:21-24; 11:2; 1Ch 3:11; Mt 1:8).
5. Priest (2Ch 17:8).

JORDAN (*descent*).

River of:
A river in Israel. Empties into the Dead Sea (Jos 15:5). Fords of (Ge 32:10; Jos 2:7; Jdg 3:28; 7:24; 8:4; 10:9; 12:5-6; 2Sa 2:29; 17:22, 24; 19:15, 31; 1Ch 19:17). Swelling of, at harvest time (Jos 3:15; Jer 12:5), and in the early spring (1Ch 12:15). The waters of, miraculously separated for the passage of the Israelites (Jos 3; 4; 5:1; Ps 114:3), of Elijah (2Ki 2:6-8), of Elisha (2Ki 2:14). Crossed at a ford (2Sa 19:18). Naaman washes in, for the healing of his leprosy (2Ki 5:10-14). John the Baptist baptizes in (Mt 3:6; Mk 1:5), baptizes Jesus in (Mt 3:13; Mk 1:19).

Plain of:
(Ge 13:10-12). Israelites camped in (Nu 22:1; 26:3, 63). Solomon's foundry in (1Ki 7:46; 2Ch 4:17).

JORIM Ancestor of Jesus (Lk 3:29).

JORKEAM Descendant of Caleb (1Ch 2:44).

JOSABAD *See Jozabad, 1.*

JOSAPHAT *See Jehoshaphat.*

JOSE *See Joshua, 5.*

JOSECH Father of Semein; ancestor of Jesus (Lk 3:26).

JOSEDECH *See Jozadak.*

JOSEPH (*he will add*).
1. Son of Jacob (Ge 30:24). Personal appearance of (Ge 39:6). His favorite child (Ge 33:2; 37:3-4, 35; 48:22; 1Ch 5:2; Jn 4:5). His father's partiality for, excites the jealousy of his brothers (Ge 37:4, 11, 18-28; Ps 105:17; Ac 7:9). His prophetic dreams of his fortunes in Egypt (Ge 37:5-11). Sold into Egypt (Ge 37:27-28). Is falsely reported to his father as killed by wild beasts (Ge 37:29-35). Is bought by Potiphar, an officer of Pharaoh (Ge 37:36). Is prospered of God (Ge 39:2-5, 21, 23). Is falsely accused, and cast into prison; is delivered by the friendship of another prisoner (Ge 39; 40; Ps 105:18). Is an interpreter of dreams: of the two prisoners (Ge 40:5-23); of Pharaoh (Ge 41:1-37). His name is changed to Zaphenath-Paneah (Ge 41:45). Is promoted to authority next to Pharaoh at thirty years of age (Ge 41:37-46; Ps 105:19-22). Takes as his wife the daughter of the priest of On (Ge 41:45). Provides against the years of famine (Ge 41:46-57). Exports the produce of Egypt to other countries (Ge 41:57). Sells the stores of food to the people of Egypt, exacting of them all their money, flocks and herds, lands and lives (Ge 47:13-26). Exempts the priests from the exactions (Ge 47:22, 26).
His father sends down into Egypt to buy grain (Ge 42-44). Reveals himself to his brothers, sends for his father, provides the land of Goshen for his people, and sustains them during the famine (Ge 45; 46; 47:1-12). His two sons (Ge 41:50, 52; Dt 33:13-17). *See Ephraim; Manasseh, 1.* Mourns the death of his father (Ge 50:1-14). Exacts a pledge from his brothers to convey his remains to Canaan (Ge 50:24-25; Heb 11:22, w Ex 13:19; Jos 24:32; Ac 7:16). Death of (Ge 50:22-26).
Kindness of heart (Ge 40:7-8). His integrity (Ge 39:7-12), humility (Ge 41:16; 45:7-9), wisdom (Ge 41:33-57), piety (Ge 41:51-52), faith (Ge 45:5-8). Was a prophet (Ge 41:38-39; 50:25; Ex 13:19). God's providence with (Ge 39:2-5; Ps 105:17-22). Descendants of (Ge 46:20; Nu 26:28-37).
2. Father of Igal the spy (Nu 13:7).
3. Of the sons of Asaph (1Ch 25:2, 9).
4. A returned exile (Ezr 10:42).
5. A priest (Ne 12:14).
6. Husband of Mary (Mt 13:55; Mk 6:3; Mt 1:18-25; Lk 1:27). His genealogy (Mt 1:1-16; Lk 3:23-38). An angel appears and testifies to the innocency of his betrothed (Mt 1:19-24). Lives at Nazareth (Lk 2:4). Belongs to the city of Bethlehem (Lk 2:4). Goes to Bethlehem to be enrolled (Lk 2:1-4). Jesus born to (Mt 1:25; Lk 2:7). Presents Jesus in the temple (Lk 2:22-39). Returns to Nazareth (Lk 2:39). Warned in a dream to escape to Egypt in order to save the child's life (Mt 2:13-15). Warned in a dream to return to Nazareth (Mt 2:19-23). Attends the annual feast at Jerusalem with his family (Lk 2:42-51).
7. Of Arimathea. Requests the body of Jesus for burial in his own tomb (Mt 27:57-60; Mk 15:42-47; Lk 23:50-56; Jn 19:38-42).
8. Three ancestors of Joseph, 6 (Lk 3:24, 26, 30).
9. One of the brothers of Jesus (Mt 13:55; Mk 6:3).
10. Also called Barsabbas and Justus. One of the two persons nominated in place of Judas (Ac 1:21-23).
11. A Levite, called Barnabas by the apostles (Ac 4:36). *See Barnabas.*
12. A designation of the ten tribes of Israel (Am 5:6).

JOSES
1. Son of Mary, 2; brother of the younger James (Mt 27:56; Mk 15:40, 47).
2. *See Joseph, 9.*
3. *See Joseph, 11.*

JOSHAH (*gift of Yahweh*). A descendant of Simeon (1Ch 4:34).

JOSHAPHAT (*Yahweh judges*).
1. One of David's mighty men (1Ch 11:43).
2. Priest (1Ch 15:24).

JOSHAVIAH (*Yahweh places*). One of David's bodyguards (1Ch 11:46).

JOSHBEKASHAH (*one sitting in request [prayer?]*). Leader of the seventeenth course of musicians (1Ch 25:4, 24).

JOSHEB-BASSHEBETH (*one sitting in the seat*). A Tahkemonite, who was the chief of the Three; one of David's mighty men (2Sa 23:8). This is probably a corruption of Jashobeam, a Hacmonite (1Ch 11:11).

JOSHIBIAH (*Yahweh places*). A Simeonite (1Ch 4:35).

JOSHUA (*Yahweh saves*).
1. Also called Hoshea (Nu 13:8). Son of Nun (1Ch 7:27). Intimately associated with Moses (Ex 24:13; 32:17; 33:11). A religious zealot (Nu 11:28). Sent with others to view the promised land (Nu 13:8). Makes favorable report (Nu 14:6-10). Rewarded for his courage and fidelity (Nu 14:30, 38; 32:12). Commissioned, ordained, and charged with the responsibilities of Moses' office (Nu 27:18-23; Dt 1:38; 3:28; 31:3, 7, 23; 34:9). Divinely inspired (Nu 27:18; Dt 34:9; Jos 1:5, 9; 3:7; 8:8). His life miraculously preserved when he made a favorable report of the land (Nu 14:10). Promises to (Jos 1:5-9). Leads the people into the land of Canaan (Jos 1-4; Ac 7:45; Heb 4:8). Renews circumcision of the Israelites; reestablishes the Passover; has a vision of the angel of God (Jos 5). Besieges and takes Jericho (Jos 6). Takes Ai (Jos 7-8). Makes a league with the Gibeonites (Jos 9:3-27). The kings of the six nations of the Canaanites confederate against him (Jos 9:1-2), make war upon the Gibeonites, are defeated and slain (Jos 10). Defeats seven

other kings (Jos 10:28-43). Makes conquest of Hazor (Jos 11). Completes the conquest of the whole land (Jos 11:23). List of the kings whom Joshua killed (Jos 12). Allots the land (Jos 13-19). Sets the tabernacle up in Shiloh (Jos 18:1). Sets apart cities of refuge (Jos 20), forty-eight cities for the Levites (Jos 21). Exhortation of, before his death (Jos 23-24). Survives the Israelites who refused to enter Canaan (Nu 26:63-65). His portion of the land (Jos 19:49-50). Death and burial of (Jos 24:29-30). Esteem in which he was held (Jos 1:16-18). Faith of (Jos 6:16). Military genius of, as exhibited at the defeat of the Amalekites (Ex 17:13), at Ai (Jos 8), in Gibeon (Jos 10), at Hazor (Jos 11). Age of, at death (Jdg 2:8).

2. An Israelite (1Sa 6:14, 18).
3. A governor of Jerusalem (2Ki 23:8).
4. The postexilic high priest. *See Joshua, 3.*
5. An ancestor of Jesus (Lk 3:29).

JOSHUA, BOOK OF

Author: Traditionally Joshua the son of Nun

Date: Traditionally before 1375 B.C.

Outline:

I. The Entrance into the Land (1:1-5:12).
  A. The Exhortations to Conquer (ch. 1).
  B. The Reconnaissance of Jericho (ch. 2).
  C. The Crossing of the Jordan (chs. 3-4).
  D. The Consecration at Gilgal (5:1-12).
II. The Conquest of the Land (5:13-12:24).
  A. The Initial Battles (5:13-8:35).
    1. The victory at Jericho (5:13-6:27).
    2. The failure at Ai because of Achan's sin (ch. 7).
    3. The victory at Ai (8:1-29).
    4. The covenant renewed at Shechem (8:30-35).
  B. The Campaign in the South (chs. 9-10).
    1. The treaty with the Gibeonites (ch. 9).
    2. The long day of Joshua (10:1-15).
    3. The southern cities conquered (10:16-43).
  C. The Campaign in the North (ch. 11).
  D. The Defeated Kings of Canaan (ch. 12).
III. The Distribution of the Land (chs. 13-21).
  A. Areas Yet to Be Conquered (13:1-7).
  B. The Land East of the Jordan for Reuben, Gad and Half of Manasseh (13:8-33).
  C. The Lands Given to Judah and "Joseph" at Gilgal (chs. 14-17).
  D. The Lands Given to the Remaining Tribes at Shiloh (chs. 18-19).
    1. The tabernacle at Shiloh (18:1-10).
    2. The allotments for Benjamin, Simeon, Zebulun, Issachar, Asher, Naphtali, and Dan (18:1-10).
    3. The town given to Joshua (19:49-51).
  E. The Cities Assigned to the Levites (chs. 20-21).
    1. The six cities of refuge (ch. 20).
    2. The forty-eight cities of the priests (ch. 21).
IV. Epilogue: Tribal Unity and Loyalty to the Lord (chs. 22-24).
  A. The Altar of Witness by the Jordan (ch. 22).
  B. Joshua's Farewell Exhortation (ch. 23).
  C. The Renewal of the Covenant at Shechem (24:1-28).
  D. The Death and Burial of Joshua and Eleazar (24:29-33).

JOSIAH *(let or may Yahweh give)*.

1. King of Judah (2Ki 21:24-26; 22:1; 1Ch 3:14; 2Ch 33:25). Ancestor of Jesus (Mt 1:10-11). Slain in battle with Pharaoh Neco (2Ki 23:29-30; 2Ch 35:20-24). Lamentations for (2Ch 35:25). Piety of, exemplified in his repairing the temple (2Ki 22:3-7; 2Ch 34:1-4). Anxiety, when the copy of the law was discovered and read to him (2Ki 22:8-20; 2Ch 34:14-33), in keeping a solemn Passover (2Ki 23:21-23; 2Ch 35:1-19). Prophecies concerning (1Ki 13:1-3). Destroys the altar and high places of idolatry (2Ki 23:3-20, 24-25).

2. Son of Zephaniah (Zec 6:10).

JOSIAS *See Josiah.*

JOSIPHIAH *(Yahweh will add)*. Ancestor of family which returned with Ezra (Ezr 8:10).

JOT NIV "the smallest letter" of the Hebrew alphabet (Mt 5:17-18). Used figuratively to emphasize the importance of the smallest details of the law.

JOTBAH *(good, pleasant)*. A place in Judah (2Ki 21:19). Possibly the same as Jotbathah (Dt 10:7).

JOTBATHAH *(good, pleasant)*. The twentieth encampment of Israel (Nu 33:33-34; Dt 10:7). Possibly the same as Jotbah (2Ki 21:19).

JOTHAM *(Yahweh completes)*.

1. Son of Gideon; speaker of the first biblical parable (Jdg 9:5-57).
2. Judahite (1Ch 2:47).
3. Eleventh king of Judah; son of Uzziah, whose regent he was for a time; successful, righteous king (2Ki 15:5-38; 2Ch 27); contemporary of Isaiah (Isa 1:1), Hosea (Hos 1:1), Micah (Mic 1:1), ancestor of Jesus (Mt 1:9).

JOURNEY, SABBATH DAY'S Three thousand feet (Ac 1:12).

JOY (Ps 30:5; Ps 30:11; Ps 33:21; Ps 97:11; Ps 132:16; Pr 29:6).

General:

From God (Ecc 2:26; Ro 15:13). In the Lord (Ps 9:2; 104:34; Isa 9:3; 29:19; 41:16; 61:10; Lk 1:47; Ro 5:11). In Christ (Php 3:3; 4:4; 1Pe 1:8). In the word of God (Ps 19:8; 119:14, 16, 111, 162; Jer 15:16). In worship (2Ch 7:10; Ezr 6:22; Ne 12:43; Ps 42:4; 43:4; 71:23; Isa 56:7; Zep 3:14; Zec 2:10; 9:9).

A fruit of the Spirit (Gal 5:22; Eph 5:18-19). For salvation (Ps 13:5; 20:5; 21:1, 6; 35:9; Isa 12:2-3; 25:9; 35:1-2, 10; 55:12; Ro 5:2; 14:17). On account of a good conscience (2Co 1:12). Over a sinner's repentance (Lk 15:6-10, 22-32).

Under adversity (Ps 126:5-6; Isa 61:3; Mt 5:12; Ac 5:41; 2Co 6:10; 7:4; 8:2; 12:10; Col 1:11; 1Th 1:6; Heb 10:34; Jas 1:2; 1Pe 4:13). Fullness of (Ps 16:11; 36:8; 63:5; Jn 15:11; 16:24; Ac 2:28; 1Jn 1:4). Everlasting (Isa 51:11; 61:7). In heaven (Mt 25:21; Lk 15:7, 10).

Attributed to God (Dt 28:63; 30:9; Jer 32:41).

Commanded:

(Dt 12:18; Ne 8:10; Ps 2:11; 5:11; 32:11; 68:3; 97:12; 100:1-2; 105:3, 43; 149:2, 5; Joel 2:23; Lk 2:10; 6:23; 10:20; Ro 12:12; 1Th 5:16).

Instances of:

Moses and the Israelites, when Pharaoh and his army were destroyed (Ex 15:1-22). Deborah and the Israelites, when Sisera was overthrown (Jdg 5). Jephthah's daughter, when he returned from his victory over the Ammonites (Jdg 11:34). Hannah, when Samuel was born (1Sa 2:1-11). Naomi, when Boaz showed kindness to Ruth (Ru 2:20; 4:14). David, over the offerings of the princes and people for the house of God (1Ch 29:10-19). Jews, over the hanging of Haman (Est 8:15-16, w Est 7:10).

The Israelites: When Saul was presented as their king (1Sa 10:24), when David killed Goliath (1Sa 18:6-7), when they repaired to David to Hebron to make him king (1Ch 12:40), when they took the ark from Kiriath Jearim (1Ch 13:8), when they brought the ark from the house of Obed-Edom to Jerusalem (1Ch 15:16, 25, 28), when they made gifts to the house of God (1Ch 29:9), when they turned away from idolatry (2Ch 15:14-15; 23:18, 21; 29:30, 36; 30:21, 23, 26), when the foundation of the second temple was laid (Ezr 3:11-13), when they kept the dedication of the temple, and the feast of tabernacles under Ezra (Ezr 6:16, 22), after hearing again the word of God (Ne 8:9-18). when the Wall of Jerusalem was dedicated (Ne 12:43).

Elizabeth, when Mary visited her (Lk 1:5-44). Mary, when she visited Elizabeth (Lk 1:46-56). Zechariah, when John was born (Lk 1:67-79). The angels, when Jesus was born (Lk 2:13-14). The shepherds when they saw the infant Jesus (Lk 2:20). The Magi (Mt 2:10). Simeon, when Jesus was presented in the temple (Lk 2:28-32).

The disciples, because the demons were subject to them (Lk 10:17). The father, when his prodigal son returns (Lk 15:20-32). The angels, when sinners repent (Lk 15:7, 10). The disciples, when Jesus triumphantly entered Jerusalem (Mt 21:8-9; Mk 11:8-9; Mk 11:8-10). The women who returned from the Lord's tomb (Mt 28:8). The disciples, after the resurrection of Jesus (Lk 24:41), in the temple after the Ascension of Jesus (Lk 24:53), in the temple because they had received the gift of the Holy Spirit (Ac 2:46-47).

The crippled man, healed by Peter (Ac 3:8). Paul, when he went up to Jerusalem (Ac 20:22-24). Paul and Silas, in the jail at Philippi (Ac 16:25). Rhoda, when she heard Peter at the gate (Ac 12:14). The disciples at Jerusalem, when Peter told them about the conversion of Cornelius and other Gentiles (Ac 11:18). Barnabas, when he saw the success of the gospel at Antioch (Ac 11:22-23).

Paul and the Corinthians, because the excommunicated member repented (2Co 1:24; 2:3). Paul and Titus, because of the hospitality of the Corinthians (Ro 15:32; 1Co 16:18 2Co 7:13, w 2Co 8:6). The Macedonians, when he prayed for the Philippians (Php 1:4). The Thessalonians, when they believed Paul's gospel (1Th 1:6). Paul, rejoicing over his converts (1Th 2:19-20; 3:9; Phm 7). Early Christians, when they believed in Jesus (1Pe 1:8-9).

See Happiness; Praise; Thanksgiving.

Of the Wicked:

Short (Job 20:5). Meaningless (Ecc 2:10; 7:6; 11:8-9). Shallow (Pr 14:13; 15:21). Overshadowed by impending judgment and sorrow (Pr 14:13; Ecc 11:8-9; Isa 16:10; Jas 4:10).

JOZABAD *(Yahweh bestowed)*.

1. One of the two servants of Joash, who killed him in Millo (2Ki 12:21).
2. Gederathite; joined David at Ziklag (1Ch 12:4).
3. Two Manassites who also joined David (1Ch 12:20).
4. Levites (2Ch 31:13).
5. Chief Levite (2Ch 35:9).
6. Levite who assisted Ezra (Ezr 8:33).
7. Man who put foreign wife away (Ezr 10:22).
8. Another such man (Ezr 10:23).
9. Levite who helped Nehemiah (Ne 8:7).
10. Chief Levite in Nehemiah's time (Ne 11:16).

JOZACHAR *(Yahweh remembered). See Jehozabad, 1; Jozabad, 1; Zabad, 4.*

JOZADAK *(Yahweh is righteous)*. Father of Jeshua the high priest who returned with Zerubbabel (Ezr 3:2, 8; 5:2; 10:18; Ne 12:26). Called Jehozadak in Haggai and Zechariah. *See Jehozadak.*

JUBAL Son of Lamech. Inventor of harp and flute (Ge 4:21).

JUBILEE Called: Year of the Lord's favor (Isa 61:2). The year of freedom (Eze 46:17).

Laws concerning: (Lev 25:8-55; 27:17-24; Nu 36:4).
See Emancipation; Sabbatic Year.

JUBILEES, BOOK OF Jewish apocalyptic book written in intertestamental period.

JUCAL *See Jehucal.*

JUDA *See Judah.*

JUDAEA *See Judea.*

JUDAH *(praised)*.

1. Son of Jacob (Ge 35:23). Intercedes for Joseph's life when his brothers were about to slay him, and proposes that they sell him to the Ishmaelites (Ge 37:26-27). Takes two wives (Ge 38:1-6). Lives at Kezib (Ge 38:5). His incest with his daughter-in-law (Ge 38:12-26). Goes down into Egypt for grain (Ge 43:1-10; 44:14-34; 46:28). Prophetic benediction of his father upon (Ge 49:8-12). The ancestor of Jesus (Mt 1:2-3; Rev 5:5).

2. Tribe of: Prophecies concerning (Ge 49:10). Enrollment of the military forces of, at Sinai (Nu 1:26-27; 2:4), at Bezek (1Sa 11:8; 2Sa 24:9), in the plain of Moab (Nu 26:22). Place of, in camp and march (Nu 2:3, 9; 10:14). By whom commanded (Nu 2:3). Moses' benediction upon (Dt 33:7). Commissioned of God to lead in the conquest of the promised land (Jdg 1:1-3, w Jdg 1:4-21). Make David king (2Sa 2:1-11; 5:4-5). Rebuked by David for lukewarmness toward him after Absalom's defeat (2Sa 19:11-15). Accused by the other tribes of stealing the heart of David (2Sa 19:41-43). Loyal to David at the at the time of the insurrection led by Sheba (2Sa 20:1-2). Is accorded the birthright forfeited by Reuben (1Ch 5:1-2; 28:4; Ps 60:7). Loyal to the house of David at the time of the revolt of the ten tribes (1Ki 12:20). Inheritance of (Jos 15; 18:5; 19:1, 9).

3. Name of two exiled priests (Ezr 10:23; Ne 12:8).
4. A Benjamite (Ne 11:9).
5. A prince or priest who assisted in the dedication of the walls of Jerusalem (Ne 12:34, 36).

JUDAISM

1. The religion of the Jews in NT times (Gal 1:13-14).
2. "Converts to Judaism" (Ac 2:11; 6:5; 13:43). Gentiles who adopted the religious beliefs and customs of the Jews.

JUDAS (Greek for *Judah*).

1. Surnamed Iscariot. Chosen as an apostle (Mt 10:4; Mk 3:19; Lk 6:16; Ac 1:17). Treasurer of the disciples (Jn 12:6; 13:29). His greed exemplified by his protest against the breaking of the box of ointment (Jn 12:4-6), by his bargain to betray Jesus for a sum of money (Mt 26:14-16; Mk 14:10-11; Lk 22:3-6; Jn 13:2). His apostasy (Jn 17:12). Betrays the Lord (Mt 26:47-50; Mk 14:43-45; Lk 22:47-49; Jn 18:2-5; Ac 1:16-25). Returns the money to the rulers of the Jews (Mt 27:3-10). Hangs himself (Mt 27:5; Ac 1:18). Prophecies concerning (Mt 26:21-25; Mk 14:18-21; Lk 22:21-23; Jn 13:18-26; 17:12; Ac 1:16, 20, w Ps 41:9; 109:8; Zec 11:12-13).

2. One of the brothers of Jesus (Mt 13:55; Mk 6:3) and writer of the epistle of Jude (Jude 1).
3. Brother of James (Lk 6:16; Ac 1:13).
4. An apostle, probably identical with Lebbaeus, or Thaddaeus (Jn 14:22).
5. Of Galilee, who stirred up a sedition among the Jews soon after the birth of Jesus (Ac 5:37).
6. A disciple who entertained Paul (Ac 9:11).
7. Surnamed Barsabbas. A Christian sent to Antioch with Paul and Barnabas (Ac 15:22-32).

J

JUDE *(Judah)*. The writer of the last of the NT epistles. The brother of James (Jude 1:1), probably brother of Jesus (Mk 6:3).

JUDE, EPISTLE OF

Author: Jude the brother of Jesus and James

Date: Probably c. A.D. 65

Outline:

I. Salutation (1-2).
II. Occasion for the Letter (3-4).
  A. The Change of Subject (3).
  B. The Reason for the Change: The Presence of Godless Apostates (4).
III. Warning Against the False Teachers (5-16).
  A. Historical Examples of the Judgment of Apostates (5-7).
    1. Unbelieving Israel (5).
    2. Angels who fell (6).
    3. Sodom and Gomorrah (7).
  B. Description of the Apostates of Jude's Day (8-16).
    1. Their slanderous speech deplored (8-10).
    2. Their character graphically portrayed (11-13).
    3. Their destruction prophesied (14-16).
IV. Exhortation to Believers (17-23).
V. Concluding Doxology (24-25).
  See General Letters.

JUDEA *(land of the Judahites, Jews)*.

1. Greek spelling of Judah. The southern division of Israel. It extended from the Jordan and Dead Sea to the Mediterranean, and from Shiloh on the N to the wilderness on the S (Mt 4:25; Lk 3:17, Jn 4:47, 54). The term is applied to all of Israel (Lk 1:5). The term is applied to the territory E of Jordan (Mt 19:1; Mk 10:1; Lk 23:5).

2. Wilderness of. Called Beth Arabah (Jos 18:22). John the Baptist preaches in (Mt 3:1; Lk 3:3).

JUDGE

Character of and Precepts Relating to:

Must be righteous (Ex 18:21-22; Lev 19:15; Dt 16:18-20; 1Ki 3:9; Ps 58:1-2; 72:1-2, 4), intelligent (Dt 1:12-13; Isa 28:6). Must judge righteously (Dt 1:16-17).

Jurisdiction of as judge (1Sa 2:25). Inferior and superior judges (Dt 17:8-11). Held circuit courts (1Sa 7:16). Rules for guidance of (Ex 18:22; Dt 19:16-19; 25:1-3; 2Ch 19:5-10; Pr 24:23; Eze 44:24; Jn 7:24).

Kings and other rulers as (2Sa 8:15; 15:2; 1Ki 3:16-28; 10:9; 2Ki 8:1-6; Ps 72:1-4; Mt 27:11-26; Ac 23:34-35; 24; 25:11-12). Priests and Levites as (Dt 17:9; 1Ch 23:4; 2Ch 19:8; Eze 44:23-24; Mt 26:57-62). Women as: Deborah (Jdg 4:4).

Persian government provided (Ezr 7:25).

Corrupt:

(1Sa 8:3; Ps 82:2-4; Isa 5:22-23; Da 9:12; Mic 7:3; Zep 3:3).

Instances of: Eli's sons (1Sa 2:12-17, 22-25). Samuel's sons (1Sa 8:1-5). The judges of Jezreel (1Ki 21:8-13). Pilate (Mt 27:24, 26; Mk 15:15, 19 24). Felix (Ac 24:26-27)

Of Israel:

Executives and leaders of the nation. During the time when the land was ruled by judges (Jdg 2:16-19; Ac 13:20).

Othniel (Jdg 3:9-11). Ehud (Jdg 3:15, 30). Shamgar (Jdg 3:31). Deborah (Jdg 4:4-5). Gideon (Jdg 6:11-40; 7:8). Abimelech (Jdg 9:1-54). Tola (Jdg 10:1-2). Jair (Jdg 10:3-5). Jephthah (Jdg 12:7). Ibzan (Jdg 12:8-10). Elon (Jdg 12:11-12). Abdon (Jdg 12:13-14). Samson (Jdg 15:20; 16:31).

Eli (1Sa 4:18). Samuel (1Sa 7:6, 15-17). The sons of Samuel (1Sa 8:1-5).

See Court, Of Law; God, Judge; Justice; Witness.

JUDGES, BOOK OF

Author: Anonymous; traditionally Samuel

Date: Possibly between 1040 and 1000 B.C.

Outline:

I. Prologue: Incomplete Conquest and Apostasy (1:1-3:6).
 A. First Episode: Israel's Failure to Purge the Land (1:1-2:5).
 B. Second Episode: God's Dealings with Israel's Rebellion (2:6-3:6).
II. Oppression and Deliverance (3:7-16:31).
 Major Judges (A-F) *Minor Judges* (1-6)
 A. Othniel Defeats Aram Naharaim (3:7-11).
 B. Ehud Defeats Moab (3:12-30).
  1. Shamgar (3:31).
 C. Deborah Defeats Canaan (chs. 4-5).
 D. Gideon Defeats Midian (chs. 6-8).
  (Abimelech, the anti-judge, ch. 9).
  2. Tola (10:1-2).
  3. Jair (10:3-5).
 E. Jephthah Defeats Ammon (10:6-12:7).
  4. Ibzan (12:8-10).
  5. Elon (12:11-12).
  6. Abdon (12:13-15).
 F. Samson Checks Philistia (chs. 17-21).
III. Epilogue: Religious and Moral Disorder (chs. 17-21).
 A. First Episode (chs. 17-18; see 17:6; 18:1).
  1. Micah's corruption of religion (ch 17).
  2. The Danites' departure from their tribal territory (ch. 18).
 B. Second Episode (chs. 19-21; see 19:1; 21:25).
  1. Gibeah's corruption of morals (ch. 19).
  2. The Benjamites' removal from their tribal territory (chs. 20-21).

JUDGING *See Uncharitableness.*

JUDGMENT

General:

Forewarned (Ecc 11:9; 12:14; Mt 8:29 w 2Pe 2:4 & Jude 6; Mt 13:30, 40-43, 49-50; Mt 25:31-46; Mk 8:38; Ac 24:25; 2Th 1:7-8; Heb 6:2).

Fierce and fiery (Mt 3:12; 10:15; 11:22; 12:36-42; Lk 3:17; 10:10-14; 11:31-32; 13:24-29; Ac 2:19-20).

According to opportunity and works (Ge 4:7; 1Sa 26:23; Job 34:11-12; Ps 62:12; Pr 12:14; 24:11-12; Isa 3:10-11; 59:18; Jer 17:10; 32:19; Eze 7:3-4, 27; 18:4-9; 18:19-32; 33:18-20; Hos 4:9; 12:2; Zec 1:6; Mt 25:1-30; Lk 12:47-48; 13:6-9; 19:12-27; Jn 3:19-20; Ro 2:5-12; 1Co 3:8, 12-15; 2Co 11:15; Gal 6:7-8; Eph 6:7-8; Col 3:25; Heb 10:26-30; 12:25; Jas 2:13; 1Pe 1:17; 2Pe 2:20-21; Rev 2:23; 20:12-13).

Design of:

To exhibit a basis for rewards and punishments (2Co 5:10; 2Ti 4:8; Rev 11:18; 22:12). To reveal secrets (Ecc 12:14; Lk 12:2-3; Ro 2:16; 1Co 3:13).

Who Will Be the Judge:

God as Judge (1Ch 16:33; Ps 9:7; 50:4, 6; 96:13; 98:9; Ecc 12:14; Da 7:9-10; Ro 2:5, 16; 3:6; 2Ti 4:8; Heb 10:30; 12:23; 13:4; 1Pe 4:5; Rev 20:11-15).

Jesus Christ as Judge (Mt 7:22-23; 13:30, 40-43, 49-50; 16:25, 27; 25:31-46; Mk 8:38; Jn 5:22; 12:48; Ac 10:42; 17:31; Ro 2:16; 14:10; 1Co 4:5; 2Co 5:10; 2Th 1:7-8; 2Ti 4:1; 2Pe 2:9; 3:10; Rev 1:7; 6:15-17).

The saints as judges (Mt 19:28; 1Co 6:2; Jude 14).

Time of:

Appointed (Mt 13:30; Ac 17:31; Heb 9:27; 2Pe 3:7, 10-12). Known to God only (Mk 13:32).

Who Will Be Judged:

The righteous and wicked (Ecc 3:17; Mt 25:31-46; Jude 14-15; Rev 11:18). The wicked (Job 21:30; Eze 18:20-28; 2Pe 2:9; 3:7). The living and the dead (Ac 10:42; 2Ti 4:1; 1Pe 4:5). All must be made manifest (Mk 4:22; Ac 17:31; 2Co 5:10). Kings and princes, slaves and freemen (Rev 6:15-16). Fallen angels (2Pe 2:4; Jude 6).

See God, Judge; Jesus the Christ, Judge; Punishment, According to Deeds.

JUDGMENT, HALL OF *See Praetorium.*

JUDGMENT SEAT (Mt 27:19; Ac 18:12; 25:10). Of Christ (Ro 14:10).

JUDGMENTS Denounced against Solomon (1Ki 11:9-14, 23), Jeroboam (1Ki 14:7-15), Ahab and Jezebel (1Ki 21:19-24), Ahaziah (2Ch 22:7-9), Manasseh (2Ch 33:11). Against disobedience (Lev 26:14-39; Dt 28:15-68; 29:1-29; 32:19-43).

Design of:

To correct (Dt 30:1-2; 1Ki 8:33-34; 2Ch 7:13; Job 5:17; 23:10; 34:31-32; Ps 94:12-13; 107:10-14, 17; Pr 3:11; Isa 9:13-14; 26:9; Jer 24:5; 30:11; La 1:5, 12; Eze 20:37, 43; Hos 2:6-7; 5:15; 1Co 11:32; Heb 12:5-11). To humble (2Co 12:7).

Misunderstood:

(Jer 16:10; Joel 2:17). No escape from (Ex 20:7; 34:7; Isa 2:10, 12-19, 21; Eze 14:13-14; Am 5:16-20; 9:1-4; Mt 23:33; Heb 2:1-3; 10:28-29; 12:25; Rev 6:16-17). *See Escape.* Executed by human instrumentality (Jer 51:2). Delayed (Ps 10:6; 50:21; 55:19). *See Punishment, Delayed.*

Instances of:

On the serpent (Ge 3:14-15), Eve (Ge 3:16), Adam (Ge 3:17-19), Cain (Ge 4:11-15), the Antediluvians (Ge 6-7), Sodomites (Ge 19:23-25).

Egyptians, the plagues and overthrow (Ex 7-13; 14:1-31). Nadab and Abihu (Lev 10:1-3). Miriam (Nu 12:1-15).

Upon the Israelites: For worshiping Aaron's calf (Ex 32:35), for murmuring (Nu 11:1, 33-34; 14:22-23, 32, 35-37; 21:6; 25:4-5, 9). The forty years wandering, a judgment (Nu 14:26-39; 26:63-65; Dt 2:14-17), delivered into the hands of the Assyrians (2Ki 17:6-41), Chaldeans (2Ch 36:14-21).

Upon the Canaanites: (Lev 18:25; Dt 7; 12:29-32), with the conquest of, by Joshua. *See Canaanite(s).*

Upon Abimelech (Jdg 9:52-57), Uzzah (2Sa 6:7), Eli's house (1Sa 2:27-36, w 1Sa 4:10-22), the prophet of Judah, for disobedience (1Ki 13:1-24), Zimri (1Ki 16:18-19), Gehazi (2Ki 5:27), Sennacherib (2Ki 19:35-37), Hananiah, the false prophet (Jer 28:15, 17).

See Chastisement, From God; Punishment; Sin, Punishment of.

JUDITH (*Jewess* or *Judahite*).
1. Wife of Esau (Ge 26:34).
2. Heroine of the apocryphal book of Judith.

JULIA (*of Julian [the family of Julius Caesar]*). A Christian woman in Rome (Ro 16:15).

JULIUS (*of Julian [the family of Julius Caesar]*). Roman centurion to whom Paul was entrusted (Ac 27:1, 3).

JUNIAS A relative or countryman of Paul (Ro 16:7). Possibly a feminine name and an apostle.

JUNIPER *See Broom Tree.*

JUPITER Latin for the god Zeus. *See Zeus.*

JURISDICTION *See Church, The Body of Believers, State.*

JURY Of ten elders (Ru 4:2). Of seventy elders (Nu 11:16-17, 24-25).

JUSHAB-HESED (*loyal love will be returned*). Son of Zerubbabel (1Ch 3:20).

JUST, THE *See Righteous.*

JUST SHALL LIVE BY FAITH (Hab 2:4; Ro 1:17; Gal 3:11; Heb 10:38).

JUSTICE From God (Ps 72:1-2; Pr 29:26).

Commanded (Ex 23:1-3, 6-8; Lev 19:13-15; Dt 16:18-20; 25:1-4; Ps 82:3-4; 106:3; Pr 18:5; Isa 1:17; Jer 7:5, 7; La 3:35-36; Mic 6:8; Zec 7:9; 8:16; Jn 7:24, 51).

Must be impartial (Pr 24:23; 28:21). Can be perverted (Ecc 3:16; 5:8; Isa 59:14-15; Jer 22:3; Am 5:7, 11-12; Mic 7:3; Hab 1:4; Mt 12:7). Will be rewarded (Jer 22:4, 15-16; Eze 18:5-9).

Of God: *See God, Justice of.*

See Court, Of Law; Injustice; Judge.

JUSTIFICATION The act of divine grace which restores the sinner to the relationship with God that he would have had if he had not sinned; pardon of sin. The word is used also to denote the state of the sinner after he is restored to divine favor.

Not imputing guilt to the sinner (Ps 32:2; Isa 53:11; Zec 3:4; Jn 5:24; Ro 4:6; 8:1).

Comes from God (Isa 45:24-25; 50:8; 54:17; 61:10; Ro 3:25; 8:30, 33; 2Co 5:19, 21; Tit 3:7). Achieved through Christ (Isa 53:11; Jer 23:6; Ac 13:39; Ro 3:20-25; 5:9, 11, 16-18, 21; 1Co 1:30; 6:11; Col 2:13-14). Is based on his righteousness (Ps 71:16; 89:16; Isa 42:21; 46:12-13; 51:5-6; 56:1; Ro 1:16-17; Gal 5:4-6).

Is not by the law (Ro 3:20; Gal 2:16; 3:11; 5:4-6). Is by faith (Ge 15:6; Hab 2:4; Ro 1:16-17; 3:20-22, 24, 28, 30; 4:2-25; 5:1; 9:30-32; 10:4, 6, 8-11; Gal 2:14-21; 3:6, 8-9, 21-22, 24; 5:4-6; Php 3:8-9; Heb 11:4, 7; Jas 2:20-23, 26).

Fruits of: Peace (Ro 5:1). Holiness (Ro 6:22).

Example of: Abraham (Ge 15:6; Ro 4:3).

See Adoption; Forgiveness; Regeneration; Sanctification; Sin, Confession of, Forgiveness of.

JUSTUS (*just*).
1. A disciple nominated with Matthias to succeed Judas Iscariot (Ac 1:23).
2. A believer in Corinth (Ac 18:7).
3. Also called Jesus. A disciple in Rome (Col 4:11).

JUTTAH (*extended, inclined*). A Levitical city in Judah (Jos 15:55; 21:16).

K

KAB *See Cab; Measure.*

KABZEEL (*God [El] collects*). A city of Judah (Jos 15:21; 2Sa 23:20; 1Ch 11:22).

KADESH (*sacred place*). Also known as En Mishpat (Ge 14:7). A place c. seventy miles S of Hebron, in the vicinity of which Israel wandered for thirty-seven years (Dt 1:46; Nu 33:37-38; Dt 2:14). Miriam died there (Nu 20:1), Moses sent spies to Israel from there (Nu 13:21-26; Dt 1:19-25), Moses displeased God there by striking the rock instead of speaking to it (Nu 20:2-13). Often called Kadesh Barnea (Nu 32:8; Dt 2:14).

KADESH BARNEA (*sacred place of Barnea*). *See Kadesh.*

KADMIEL (*[stand] before God [El]*).
1. A Levite (Ezr 2:40; 3:9; Ne 7:43; 12:8, 24).
2. A Levite who assisted in leading the worship of the people (Ne 9:4-5; 10:9).

KADMONITES (*easterners*). Ancient Arab tribe between Egypt and Euphrates (Ge 15:18-21).

KAIN (*smith*).
1. Town in Judah (Jos 15:57).
2. Tribal name (Nu 24:22; Jdg 4:11). *See Kenite(s).*

KALLAI (*swift*). A priest (Ne 12:20).

KAMAI *See Leb Kamai.*

KAMON Place where Jair was buried (Jdg 10:5).

KANAH (*reed*).
1. Brook flowing between Ephraim and Manasseh into the Mediterranean (Jos 16:8; 17:9).
2. City c. eight miles SE of Tyre, near boundary of Manasseh (Jos 19:28).

KAREAH (*bald head*). Father of Johanan, governor of Judah in the time of Gedaliah (2Ki 25:23; Jer 40:8, 13; 41:11, 13-14, 16).

KARKA (*floor, ground*). A city of Judah (Jos 15:3).

KARKOR Place E of Jordan where Gideon defeated Midianites (Jdg 8:10). Exact location unknown.

KARNAIM (*horns*). A city conquered by Israel (Am 6:13).

KARTAH (*city*). A city of Zebulun (Jos 21:34).

KARTAN A Levitical city in Naphtali (Jos 21:32).

KATTATH A city in Zebulun (Jos 19:15).

KATYDID An insect permitted as food (Lev 11:22). *See Insects.*

KAZIN *See Eth Kazin.*

KEBAR A river of Mesopotamia (Eze 1:1, 3; 3:15, 23; 10:15, 22; 43:3).

KEDAR (*mighty*).
1. Son of Ishmael (Ge 25:13; 1Ch 1:29).
2. A nomadic clan of the Ishmaelites (Ps 120:5; SS 1:5; Isa 21:16; 42:11; 60:7; Jer 49:28). Flocks of (Isa 60:7; Jer 49:28). Princes and commerce of (Eze 27:21).

KEDEMAH (*east*). Son of Ishmael (Ge 25:15; 1Ch 1:31).

KEDEMOTH (*east*). A city of Moab, allotted to Reuben and the Merarite Levites (Jos 13:18; 1Ch 6:79). Encircled by a wilderness of same name (Dt 2:26).

KEDESH (*sacred place*).
1. A city of Judah (Jos 15:23). Possibly identical with Kadesh Barnea.
2. Called also Kishion and Kishon. A Canaanite city taken by Joshua (Jos 12:22; 19:20; 21:28; 1Ch 6:72).
3. Called also Kedesh in Naphtali. A city of refuge (Jos 20:7; 21:32). Home of Barak and Heber (Jdg 4:6, 9, 11). Captured by Tiglath-Pileser (2Ki 15:29).

KEDESH NAPHTALI (*sacred place of Naphtali*). *See Kedesh, 3.*

KEDORLAOMER (*servant of [the deity] Lagamar*). King of Elam (Ge 14:1-16).

KEDRON *See Kidron.*

KEEPERS Of the prison (Ge 39:22; Ac 5:23; 12:6; 16:27, 36).

KEHELATHAH (*assembly*). An encampment of Israel (Nu 33:22-23).

KEILAH
1. One of a group of nine cities in the southern part of Israel allotted to Judah (Jos 15:44). Philistines make a predatory excursion against, after harvest (1Sa 23:1). David rescues (1Sa 23:2-13). Rulers of, aid in restoring the wall of Jerusalem after the Captivity (Ne 3:17-18).
2. A descendant of Caleb (1Ch 4:19).

KELAIAH (perhaps *Yahweh has dishonored*). Called also Kelita. A Levite who divorced his Gentile wife after the Captivity and assisted Ezra in expounding the law (Ezr 10:23; Ne 8:7; 10:10).

KELAL (*perfection, completeness*). Son of Pahath-Moab (Ezr 10:30).

KELITA *See Kelaiah.*

KELUB (*basket*).
1. A descendant of Caleb (1Ch 4:11).
2. Father of Ezri (1Ch 27:26).

KELUBAI *See Caleb, 1.*

KELUHI Son of Bani (Ezr 10:35).

KEMUEL (*God's [El's] mound* ISBE).
1. Son of Nahor; uncle of Laban and Rebekah (Ge 22:21).
2. Prince of Ephraim (Nu 34:24).
3. Father of Hashabiah, leading Levite (1Ch 27:17).

KENAANAH (*toward Canaan*).
1. Father of the false prophet Zedekiah (1Ki 22:11, 24; 2Ch 18:10, 23).
2. Brother of Ehud (1Ch 7:10).

KENAN Great-grandson of Adam (1Ch 1:2). Enosh is the father of Kenan (Ge 5:9-14).

KENANI (*Yahweh strengthens*). A Levite (Ne 9:4).

KENANIAH (*Yahweh strengthens*).
1. A Levite (1Ch 15:22, 27).
2. An Izharite (1Ch 26:29).

KENATH (*possession*). Amorite city in region of Bashan in kingdom of Og (Nu 32:42; 1Ch 2:22-23).

KENAZ (*hunting*).
1. Grandson of Esau (Ge 36:11, 15; 1Ch 1:36).
2. A chief of Edom (Ge 36:42; 1Ch 1:53).
3. Brother of Caleb (Jos 15:17; Jdg 1:13; 3:9, 11; 1Ch 4:13).
4. Grandson of Caleb (1Ch 4:15).

KENITE(S) (*of the [copper] smiths*).
1. A Canaanite tribe whose country was given to Abraham (Ge 15:19; Nu 24:21-23).
2. The descendants of Jethro, a Midianite, father-in-law of Moses. Joined the Israelites and lived at Jericho (Jdg 1:16; 4:11; 1Ch 2:55), later in the wilderness of Judah (Jdg 1:16-17). Jael, one of the, betrayed and killed Sisera (Jdg 4:17-21).

KENIZZITE(S) Descendants of Kenaz (Ge 15:19). Caleb (Nu 32:12) and Othniel (Jos 15:17) were Kenizzites.

KENOSIS (*emptying*). A term applied to Christ's taking the form of a servant in the Incarnation (Php 2:7).

KEPHAR AMMONI (*village of Ammonites*). A town of Benjamin (Jos 18:24).

KEPHIRAH (*village*). A city of the Hivites (Jos 9:17; 18:26; Ezr 2:25; Ne 7:29).

KERAMIM *See Abel Keramim.*

KERAN A Horite (Ge 36:26; 1Ch 1:41).

KERCHIEF *See Handkerchief.*

KEREN-HAPPUCH (*horn of [cosmetic] eyeshadow;* i.e., *cosmetic case*). Youngest daughter of Job (Job 42:14).

KERETHITE(S) (possibly *Cretans* BDB KB; *executioners* ISBE). A Philistine tribe, which allied with David and, with the Pelethites, formed his bodyguard (1Sa 30:14, 16; 2Sa 8:18, 15:18; 20:7, 23; 1Ki 1:38, 44; 1Ch 18:17; Eze 25:16; Zep 2:5). Solomon's escort at his coronation (1Ki 1:38).

KERIOTH, KERIOTH HEZRON (*town of Hezron*).
1. A city of Judah (Jos 15:25).
2. A city of Moab (Jer 48:24, 41; Am 2:2).

KERITH (*cut off, perish*). A brook near Jericho (1Ki 17:3-7).

KEROS Ancestor of the temple servants who returned with Zerubbabel (Ezr 2:44; Ne 7:47).

KERUB Name of a place or person (Ezr 2:59; Ne 7:61).

KESALON A landmark in the N boundary of Judah (Jos 15:10).

KESED (*Chaldean [Babylonian]*). Son of Nahor (Ge 22:22).

KESIL A town in the S of Israel (Jos 15:30). Probably identical with Bethul (Jos 19:4), and Bethuel (1Ch 4:30).

KESULLOTH (*loins or flanks [of Mt. Tabor]* BDB). A city of Issachar (Jos 19:18). Probably identical with Kisloth Tabor (Jos 19:12) and Tabor (1Ch 6:77).

KETTLE Cooking vessel or basket (1Sa 2:14).

KETURAH (*incense, scented one*). Abraham's second wife. Mother of six sons, ancestors of Arabian tribes (Ge 25:1-6; 1Ch 1:33).

KEY (Jdg 3:25). A symbol of authority (Isa 22:22; Mt 16:19; Rev 1:18; 3:7; 9:1; 20:1). *See Binding and Loosing.*
Figurative: key of knowledge (Lk 11:52).

KEZIAH (*cassia [cinnamon]*). Second daughter of Job (Job 42:14).

KEZIB (*deceit*). Birthplace of Shelah (Ge 38:5), probably identical with Cozeba (1Ch 4:22), and Aczib (Jos 15:44).

KEZIZ *See Emek Keziz.*

KIBROTH HATTAAVAH (*graves of lust, greed*). A station where the Israelites were miraculously fed with quail (Nu 11:31-35; 33:16-17; Dt 9:22).

KIBZAIM A Levitical city in Ephraim (Jos 21:22).

KID *See Animals; Goats.*

KIDNAPPING Forbidden (Ex 21:16; Dt 24:7).
Instance of (Jdg 21:20-23).

KIDNEY Used with surrounding fat as a burnt offering (Ex 29:13, 22; Lev 3:4, 10, 15; 4:9). Regarded as the seat of the emotions; usually translated "heart" (Ps 7:9; 16:7).

KIDON Place where Uzzah was stricken to death because he had put his hand on the ark (1Ch 13:9-11). Called Nacon's threshing floor (2Sa 6:6).

KIDRON Brook of, running S under the eastern wall of Jerusalem between Jerusalem and the Mount of Olives (1Ki 2:37; Ne 2:15; Jer 31:40). David flees from Absalom across (2Sa 15:23). Destruction of idols at, by Asa, Josiah, and the Levites (1Ki 15:13; 2Ki 23:6, 12; 2Ch 29:16). Source of, closed by Hezekiah (2Ch 32:1-4). Jesus crossed, on the night of his agony (Jn 18:1).

KILEAB A son of David (2Sa 3:3). Also called Daniel (1Ch 3:1).

KILION (*annihilation*). Son of Elimelech and Naomi, married Orpah (Ru 1:2-5; 4:9-10).

KILLING *See Homicide.*

KILMAD Merchants of (Eze 27:23).

KIMHAM A Gileadite (2Sa 19:37-38, 40; Jer 41:17).

KINAH (*lament, dirge*). A city of Judah (Jos 15:22).

KINDNESS
Commanded: (Zec 7:9-10; Mt 5:42; Lk 6:30; 6:34-35; Ac 20:35; Ro 12:15; 15:1-2; Gal 6:1-2, 10; Eph 4:32; Col 3:12; 1Pe 3:8-9; 1Jn 3:17-18). To enemies (Ex 23:4-5; Lk 6:34-35). To strangers (Lev 19:34). To a brother (Dt 22:1).
Inspired by love (1Co 13:4-7). Commends ministers (2Co 6:6). Rewards of (Pr 14:21; Mt 5:7; 25:34-35).
Of God (Lk 6:35). Of good women (Pr 31:26; 1Ti 5:9-10). Of good men (Ps 112:5; Heb 5:2). Of Jesus. *See Jesus the Christ, Compassion of.*

Instances of:
Hittites to Abraham (Ge 23:6, 11). Keeper of the prison to Joseph (Ge 39:21-23). Pharaoh to Jacob (Ge 45:16-20; 47:5-6). Pharaoh's daughter to Moses (Ex 2:6-10). Moses to Jethro's daughters (Ex 2:17, 19). Jethro to Moses (Ex 2:20). Rahab to the spies (Jos 2:4-16). Boaz to Ruth (Ru 2:8-16; 3:15). David to Nabal (1Sa 25:15-16). Abigail to David (1Sa 25:14-35). David to Mephibosheth (2Sa 9:1-13). Joab to Absalom (2Sa 14:1-24). Obadiah to the prophets of the Lord (1Ki 18:4). Ahab to Ben-Hadad (1Ki 20:32-34). The Shunammite woman to Elisha (2Ki 4:8-10). Elisha to the Shunammite woman (2Ki 4:13-17, 28-37; 8:1). Evil-Merodach to Jehoiachin (2Ki 25:28-30). Jehosheba to Joash (2Ch 22:11). Nehemiah and the nobles to the people (Ne 5:8-19). Mordecai to Esther (Est 2:7). Ebed-Melech to Jeremiah (Jer 38:7-13). Nebuchadnezzar to Jeremiah (Jer 39:11-12).
Joseph to Mary (Mt 1:19, 24). Centurion to his servant (Lk 7:2-6). Jews to Mary and Martha (Jn 11:19, 33). John to Mary (Jn 19:27). Felix to Paul (Ac 24:23). Julius to Paul (Ac 27:3, 43). Barbarians to Paul (Ac 28:2, 7). Onesiphorus to Paul (2Ti 1:16-18).

KINE *See Cattle.*

KINGDOM OF GOD, OF HEAVEN The sovereign rule of God manifested in Christ to defeat His enemies, creating a people over whom He reigns, and issuing in a realm or realms in which the power of His reign is experienced. All they are members of the kingdom of God who voluntarily submit to the rule of God in their lives. Entrance into the kingdom is by the new birth (Jn 3:3-5); two stages in the kingdom of God; present and future in an eschatological sense; Jesus said that his ability to cast out demons was evidence that the kingdom of God had come among men (Mt 12:28). "Kingdom of heaven" is used exclusively in Matthew (33 times). Likened to, a man who sowed good seed (Mt 13:24-30, 38-43; Mk 4:26-29), a grain of mustard seed (Mt 13:31-32; Mk 4:30-31; Lk 13:18-19), leaven (Mt 13:33; Lk 13:21), a treasure (Mt 13:44), a pearl (Mt 13:45), a net (Mt 13:47-50), a king who called his servants to a reckoning (Mt 18:23-35), a house owner (Mt 20:1-16), a king who made a marriage feast for his son (Mt 22:2-14; Lk 14:16-24), ten virgins (Mt 25:1-13), a man traveling into a far country, who called his servants, and delivered to them his goods (Mt 25:14-30; Lk 19:12-27).
"My kingdom is not of this world" (Jn 18:36).
Children of the (Mt 18:3; 19:14; Mk 10:14; Lk 18:16). Rich cannot enter (Mt 19:23-24; Mk 10:23-25; Lk 18:24-25, 29-30). Keys of (Mt 16:19). Glad tidings of (Lk 8:1). Mysteries of (Lk 8:10). Is not eating and drinking (Ro 14:17).
See Church, The Body of Believers; Jesus, Kingdom of.

KINGDOM OF ISRAEL *See Israel.*

KINGDOM OF JUDAH *See Judah.*

KINGDOM OF SATAN The realm of Satan's influence (Mt 12:26; Lk 11:18).

KINGS

In Israel:
Israel warned against seeking (1Sa 8:9-18). Sin of Israel in seeking (1Sa 12:17-20). Israel in seeking, rejected God as their king (1Sa 8:7; 10:19). Israel asked for, that they might be like the nations (1Sa 8:5, 19-20). First given to Israel in anger (Hos 13:11). God reserved to himself the choice of (Dt 17:14-15; 1Sa 9:16-17; 16:12). When first established in Israel, not hereditary (Dt 17:20, w 1Sa 13:13-14; 15:28-29). Rendered hereditary in the family of David (2Sa 7:12-16; Ps 89:35-37). Of Israel not to be foreigners (Dt 17:15). Laws for the government of the kingdom by, written by Samuel (1Sa 10:25).
Forbidden to accumulate: Horses (Dt 17:16). Wives (Dt 17:17). Treasure (Dt 17:17).
Required to write and keep a copy of the divine law (Dt 17:18-20). Had power to make war and peace (1Sa 11:5-7). Often exercised power arbitrarily (1Sa 22:17-18; 2Sa 1:15; 4:9-12; 1Ki 2:23, 25, 31). Sometimes nominated their successors (1Ki 1:33-34; 2Ch 11:22-23). Punished for transgressing the divine law (2Sa 12:7-12; 1Ki 21:18-24).
Called the Lord's anointed (1Sa 16:6; 24:6; 2Sa 19:21).

Ceremonies at Inauguration of:
Anointing (1Sa 10:1; 16:13; Ps 89:20). Crowning (2Ki 11:12; 2Ch 23:11; Ps 21:3). Proclaiming with trumpets (2Sa 15:10; 1Ki 1:34; 2Ki 9:13; 11:14). Enthroning (1Ki 1:35, 46; 2Ki 11:19). Strapping on the sword (Ps 45:3). Putting into their hands the books of the law (2Ki 11:12; 2Ch 23:11). Covenanting to govern lawfully (2Sa 5:3). Receiving homage (1Sa 10:1; 1Ch 29:24). Shouting "Long live the King!" (1Sa 10:24; 2Sa 16:16; 2Ki 11:12). Offering sacrifice (1Sa 11:15). Feasting (1Ch 12:38-39; 29:22). Attended by a bodyguard (1Sa 13:2; 2Sa 8:18; 1Ch 11:25; 2Ch 13:10). Dwelt in royal palaces (2Ch 9:11; Ps 45:15). Arrayed in royal apparel (1Ki 22:30; Mt 6:29). Names of, often changed at their accession (2Ki 23:34; 24:17).

Officers of:
Prime minister (2Ch 19:11, w 2Ch 28:7). First Counselor (1Ch 27:33). Confident or king's special friend (1Ki 4:5; 1Ch 27:33). Comptroller of the household (1Ki 4:6; 2Ch 28:7). Scribe or secretary (2Sa 8:17; 1Ki 4:3). Captain of the host (2Sa 8:16; 1Ki 4:4). Captain of the guard (2Sa 8:18; 20:23). Recorder (2Sa 8:16; 1Ki 4:3). Providers for the king's table (1Ki 4:7-19). Master of the wardrobe (2Ki 22:14; 2Ch 34:22). Treasurer (1Ch 27:25). Storekeeper (1Ch 27:25). Overseer of, the tribute (1Ki 4:6; 12:18), royal farms (1Ch 27:26), royal vineyards (1Ch 27:27), royal plantations (1Ch 27:28), royal herds (1Sa 21:7; 1Ch 27:29), royal camels (1Ch 27:30), royal flocks (1Ch 27:31). Armor-bearer (1Sa 16:21). Cupbearer (1Ki 10:5; 2Ch 9:4). Approached with greatest reverence (1Sa 24:8; 2Sa 9:8; 14:22; 1Ki 1:23). Presented with gifts by strangers (1Ki 10:2, 10, 25; 2Ki 5:5; Mt 2:11). Right hand of, the place of honor (1Ki 2:19; Ps 45:9; 110:1). Attendants of, stood in their presence (1Ki 10:8; 2Ki 25:19). Exercised great hospitality (1Sa 20:25-27; 2Sa 9:7-13; 19:33; 1Ki 4:22-23, 28).

Their Revenues Derived From:
Voluntary contributions (1Sa 10:27, w 1Sa 16:20; 1Ch 12:39-40). Tribute from foreign nations (1Ki 4:21, 24-25; 2Ch 8:8; 17:11). Tax on produce of the land (1Ki 4:7-19). Tax on foreign merchandise (1Ki 10:15). Their own flocks and herds (2Ch 32:29). Produce of their own lands (2Ch 26:10).

Conspiracies Against:
Absalom against David (2Sa 15:10). Adonijah against Solomon (1Ki 1:5-7). Jeroboam against Rehoboam (1Ki 12:12, 16). Baasha against Nadab (1Ki 15:27). Zimri against Elah (1Ki 16:9-10). Omri against Zimri (1Ki 16:17). Jehu against Joram (2Ki 9:14). Shallum against Zechariah (2Ki 15:10). Menahem against Shallum (2Ki 15:14). Pekah against Menahem (2Ki 15:25).

The Kings of Israel and Judah:
See chart on the following page. *See also each king by name and the outlines of the books of Kings and Chronicles.*

Relation to God:
God chooses (Dt 17:15; 1Ch 28:4-6). God ordains (Ro 13:1). God anoints (1Sa 16:12; 2Sa 12:7). Set up by God (1Sa 12:13; Da 2:21). Removed by God (1Ki 11:11; Da 2:21). Christ is the Prince of (Rev 1:5). Christ is the King of (Rev 17:14). Reign by direction of Christ (Pr 8:15). Supreme judges of nations (1Sa 8:5). Resistance to, is resistance to the ordinance of God (Ro 13:2). Able to enforce their commands (Ecc 8:4). Numerous subjects the honor of (Pr 14:28). Not saved by their armies (Ps 33:16). Dependent on the earth (Ecc 5:9). Throne of, established by righteousness and justice (Pr 16:12; 29:14).

Should:
Fear God (Dt 17:19). Serve Christ (Ps 2:10-12). Keep the law of God (1Ki 2:3). Study the Scriptures (Dt 17:19). Promote the interests of the Church (Ezr 1:2-4; 6:1-12). Nourish the Church (Isa 49:23). Rule in the fear of God (2Sa 23:3). Maintain the cause of the poor and oppressed (Pr 31:8-9). Investigate all matters (Pr 25:2). Not pervert judgment (Pr 31:5). Prolong their reign by hating greed (Pr 28:16).

Specially Warned Against:
Impurity (Pr 31:3). Lying (Pr 17:7). Listening to lies (Pr 29:12). Intemperance (Pr 31:4-5). The gospel to be preached to (Ac 9:15; 26:27-28). Without understanding, are oppressors (Pr 28:16). Often reproved by God (1Ch 16:21). Judgments upon, when opposed to Christ (Ps 2:2, 5, 9).

When Good:
Regard God as their strength (Ps 99:4). Speak righteously (Pr 16:10). Love righteous lips (Pr 16:13). Abhor wickedness (Pr 16:12). Reject evil (Pr 20:8). Punish the wicked (Pr 20:26). Favor the wise (Pr 14:35). Honor the diligent (Pr 22:29). Befriend the good (Pr 22:14). Are pacified by submission (Pr 16:14; 25:15). Evil counselors should be removed from (2Ch 22:3-4; Pr 25:5).
Good exemplified: David (2Sa 8:15). Asa (1Ki 15:11). Jehoshaphat (1Ki 22:43). Amaziah (2Ki 15:3). Uzziah (2Ki 15:34). Hezekiah (2Ki 18:3). Josiah (2Ki 22:2).

Should Be:
Honored (Ro 13:7; 1Pe 2:17). Feared (Pr 24:21). Revered (1Sa 24:8; 1Ki 1:23, 31). Obeyed (Ro 13:1, 5; 1Pe 2:13). Prayed for (1Ti 2:1-2). Folly of resisting (Pr 19:12; 20:2). Punishment for resisting the lawful authority of (Ro 13:2). Guilt and danger of stretching out the hand against (1Sa 26:9; 2Sa 1:14). Curse not, even in thought (Ex 22:28; Ecc 10:20). Speak no evil of (Job 34:18; 2Pe 2:10). Pay tribute to (Mt 22:21; Ro 13:6-7). Be not presumptuous before (Pr 25:6). Wicked despise (2Pe 2:10; Jude 8).

KING'S GARDEN Near the Pool of Siloam (2Ki 25:4; Jer 39:4; 52:7; Ne 3:15).

KING'S HIGHWAY Ancient N and S route E of the Jordan through Edom and Moab (Nu 20:17; 21:22). The road is still in use.

KING'S VALLEY Valley of Shaveh E of Jerusalem (Ge 14:17; 2Sa 18:18).

KINGS, 1 and 2

Author: Anonymous; Jewish tradition credits Jeremiah

Date: Between 562 B.C. and 538

Outline:

I. The Solomonic Era (1:1-12:24).
  A. Solomon's Succession to the Throne (1:1-2:12).
  B. Solomon's Throne Consolidated (2:13-46).
  C. Solomon's Wisdom (ch. 3).
  D. Solomon's Reign Characterized (ch. 4).
  E. Solomon's Building Projects (5:1-9:9).
    1. Preparation for building the temple (ch. 5).
    2. Building the temple (ch. 6).
    3. Building the palace (7:1-12).

4. The temple furnishings (7:13-51).
5. Dedication of the temple (ch. 8).
6. The Lord's response and warning (9:1-9).
F. Solomon's Reign Characterized (9:10-10:29).
G. Solomon's Folly (11:1-13).
H. Solomon's Throne Threatened (11:14-43).
I. Rehoboam's Succession to the Throne (12:1-24).
II. Israel and Judah From Jeroboam I/Rehoboam to Ahab/Asa (12:25-16:34).
A. Jeroboam I of Israel (12:25-14:20).
B. Rehoboam of Judah (14:21-31).
C. Abijah of Judah (15:1-8).
D. Asa of Judah (15:9-24).
E. Nadab of Israel (15:25-32).
F. Baasha of Israel (15:33-16:7).
G. Elah of Israel (16:8-14).
H. Zimri of Israel (16:15-20).
I. Omri of Israel (16:21-28).
J. Ahab of Israel (16:29-34).
III. The Ministries of Elijah and Elisha and Other Prophets From Ahab/Asa to Joram/ Jehoshaphat (17:1-2Ki 8:15).
A. Elijah (and Other Prophets) in the Reign of Ahab (17:1-22:40).
1. Elijah and the drought (ch. 17).
2. Elijah on Mount Carmel (ch. 18).
3. Elijah's flight to Horeb (ch. 19).
4. A prophet condemns Ahab for sparing Ben-Hadad (ch. 20).
5. Elijah condemns Ahab for seizing Naboth's vineyard (ch. 21).
6. Micaiah prophesies Ahab's death; its fulfillment (22:1-40).
B. Jehoshaphat of Judah (22:41-50).
C. Ahaziah of Israel; Elijah's Last Prophecy (22:51-2Ki 1:18).
D. Elijah's Translation; Elisha's Inauguration (2Ki 2:1-18).
E. Elisha in the Reign of Joram (2:19-8:15).
1. Elisha's initial miraculous signs (2:19-25).
2. Elisha during the campaign against Moab (ch. 3).
3. Elisha's ministry to needy ones in Israel (ch. 4).
4. Elisha heals Naaman (ch. 5).
5. Elisha's deliverance of one of the prophets (6:1-7).
6. Elisha's deliverance of Joram from Aramean raiders (6:8-23).
7. Aramean siege of Samaria lifted, as Elisha prophesied (6:24-7:20).
8. The Shunammite's land restored (8:1-6).
9. Elisha prophesies Hazael's oppression of Israel (8:7-15).
IV. Israel and Judah From Joram/Jehoram to the Exile of Israel (2Ki 8:16-17:41).
A. Jehoram of Judah (8:16-24).
B. Ahaziah of Judah (8:25-29).
C. Jehu's Revolt and Reign (chs. 9-10).
1. Elisha orders Jehu's anointing (9:1-13).
2. Jehu's assassination of Joram and Ahaziah (9:14-29).
3. Jehu's execution of Jezebel (9:30-37).
4. Jehu's slaughter of Ahab's family (10:1-17).
5. Jehu's eradication of Baal worship (10:18-36).
D. Athaliah and Joash of Judah; Repair of the Temple (chs. 11-12).
E. Jehoahaz of Israel (13:1-9).
F. Jehoash of Israel; Elisha's Last Prophecy (13:10-25).
G. Amaziah of Judah (14:1-22).
H. Jeroboam II of Israel (14:23-29).
I. Azariah of Judah (15:1-7).
J. Zechariah of Israel (15:8-12).
K. Shallum of Israel (15:13-16).
L. Menahem of Israel (15:17-22).
M. Pekahiah of Israel (15:23-26).
N. Pekah of Israel (15:27-31).
O. Jotham of Judah (15:32-38).
P. Ahaz of Judah (ch. 16).
Q. Hoshea of Israel (17:1-6).
R. Exile of Israel; Resettlement of the Land (17:7-41).
V. Judah From Hezekiah to the Babylonian Exile (2Ki 18-25).
A. Hezekiah (chs. 18-20).
1. Hezekiah's good reign (18:1-8).
2. The Assyrian threat and deliverance (18:9-19:37).
3. Hezekiah's illness; alliance with Babylon (ch. 20).
B. Manasseh (21:1-18).
C. Amon (21:19-26).
D. Josiah (22:1-23:30).
1. Repair of the temple; discovery of the Book of the Law (ch. 22).
2. Renewal of the covenant; end of Josiah's reign (23:1-30).
E. Jehoahaz Exiled to Egypt (23:31-35).
F. Jehoiakim: First Babylonian Invasion (23:36-24:7).
G. Jehoiachin: Second Babylonian Invasion (24:8-17).
H. Zedekiah (24:18-20).
I. Babylonian Exile of Judah (25:1-21).
J. Removal of the Remnant to Egypt (25:22-26).
K. Elevation of Jehoiachin in Babylon (25:27-30).

K

The Kings of the United Kingdom

	Name	Ruled	Dates B.C.	Biblical References
1.	Saul	40 years	1050–1010	1Sa 11:15,31; 1Ch 10
2.	David	40 years	1010–970	2Sa 2:4; 1Ki 2:11; 1Ch 11–29
3.	Solomon	40 years	970–930	1Ki 1:39; 11:43; 2Ch 1–9

The Kings (and Queen) of Judah

	Name	Ruled	Dates B.C.	Biblical References
1.	Rehoboam	17 years	930–913	1Ki 12:1–24; 14:21–31; 2Ch 10:1–17; 12
2.	Abijah	3 years	913–910	1Ki 15:1–8; 2Ch 13
3.	Asa	41 years	910–869	1Ki 15:9–24; 2Ch 14; 16:14
4.	Jehoshaphat	25 years	872–848	1Ki 22:41–50; 2Ch 17; 21:1
5.	Jehoram	8 years	848–841	2Ki 8:16–24; 21
6.	Ahaziah	1 year	841	2Ki 8:25–29; 9:16–29; 2Ch 22:1–9
7.	Queen Athaliah	6 years	841–835	2Ki 11:1–3; 2Ch 22:10–12
8.	Joash	40 years	835–796	2Ki 11:4; 12; 2Ch 23–24
9.	Amaziah	29 years	796–767	2Ki 14:1–20; 2Ch 25
10.	Uzziah / Azariah	52 years	792–740	2Ki 14:21–22; 15:1–7; 2Ch 26
11.	Jotham	16 years	750–735	2Ki 15:32–38; 2Ch 27
12.	Ahaz	16 years	732–715	2Ki 16; 2Ch 28
13.	Hezekiah	29 years	715–686	2Ki 18–20; 2Ch 29–32
14.	Manasseh	55 years	697–642	2Ki 21:1–18; 2Ch 33:1–20
15.	Amon	2 years	642–640	2Ki 21:19–26; 2Ch 33:21–25
16.	Josiah	31 years	640–609	2Ki 22; 23:1–30; 2Ch 34–35
17.	Jehoahaz	3 months	609	2Ki 23:31–33; 2Ch 36:1–4
18.	Jehoiakim	11 years	609–598	2Ki 23:34–37; 24:1–6; 2Ch 36:5–8
19.	Jehoiachin	3 months	598–597	2Ki 24:8–16; 2Ch 36:9–10
20.	Zedekiah / Mattaniah	11 years	597–586	2Ki 24:17–20; 25:1–7; 2Ch 36:11–21

The Kings of Israel

	Name	Ruled	Dates B.C.	Biblical References
1.	Jeroboam I	22 years	930–909	1Ki 12:20,25; 14:20
2.	Nadab	2 years	909–908	1Ki 15:25–27,31
3.	Baasha	24 years	908–886	1Ki 15:28–34; 16:1–7
4.	Elah	2 years	886–885	1Ki 16:8–14
5.	Zimri	7 days	885	1Ki 16:11–12,15–20
6.	Omri	12 years	885–874	1Ki 16:23–28
7.	Ahab	22 years	874–853	1Ki 16:29–22:40
8.	Ahaziah	2 years	853–852	1Ki 22:51–53; 2Ki 1
9.	Joram	12 years	852–841	2Ki 3–9:26
10.	Jehu	28 years	841–814	2Ki 9:3–10; 36
11.	Jehoahaz	17 years	814–798	2Ki 13:1–9
12.	Jehoash	16 years	798–782	2Ki 13:10–25; 14:8–16
13.	Jeroboam II	41 years	793–753	2Ki 14:23–29
14.	Zechariah	6 months	753	2Ki 15:8–12
15.	Shallum	1 month	752	2Ki 15:13–15
16.	Menahem	10 years	752–742	2Ki 15:16–22
17.	Pekahiah	2 years	742–740	2Ki 15:23–26
18.	Pekah	20 years	752–732	2Ki 15:27–31; 16:5
19.	Hoshea	9 years	732–722	2Ki 17:1–6

Note: Some kings, such as Jehoash and Jeroboam II, had overlapping reigns.

KINNERETH (*zithers, lyres*).
1. A district in the N of Israel (Jos 11:2; 1Ki 15:20).
2. A city in Naphtali (Jos 19:35).
3. The sea of (Nu 34:11; Jos 12:3; 13:27). *See Galilee, Sea of.*

KINSMAN Family or friends (Job 19:14), of same tribe (1Ch 12:2, 29; 2Ch 29:34; Ezr 8:17), fellow Israelites (2Ch 28:8). Figurative of wisdom (Pr 7:4). *See Kinsman-Redeemer.*

KINSMAN-REDEEMER A close relative responsible for protecting the interests of needy members of the extended family. To provide an heir for a brother who had died (Ge 38:6-11; Dt 25:5-10; Ru 3-4). *See Levirite Marriage.* To redeem land that a poor relative had sold outside the family (Lev 25:25-28). To redeem a relative who had been sold into slavery (Lev 25:47-49). To avenge the killing of a relative (Nu 35:19-21). *See Avenger of Blood.*

KIOS An island W of Smyrna (Ac 20:15).

KIR (*walled enclosure*). The inhabitants of Damascus carried into captivity to, by the king of Assyria (2Ki 16:9). Prophecies concerning (Isa 22:6; Am 1:5; 9:7).

KIR HARESETH (*walled [city] of pottery fragments*). A city of Moab (2Ki 3:25; Isa 16:7, 11; Jer 48:31, 36). Called Kir of Moab (Isa 15:1).

KIR OF MOAB *See Kir.*

KIRIATH (*city of*). City of Benjamin (Jos 18:28).

KIRIATH ARBA (*city of four*). Ancient name for Hebron (Ge 23:2; Jos 14:15; 15:54; 20:7).

KIRIATH BAAL *See Kiriath Jearim.*

KIRIATH HUZOTH (*city of Huzoth [outside spaces]*). A residence of Balak (Nu 22:39).

KIRIATH JEARIM (*city of timberlands*). Called also Baalah, one of the four cities of the Gibeonites. Inhabitants of, not destroyed, on account of the covenant made by the Israelites with the Gibeonites, but put under servitude (Jos 9:17, w Jos 9:3-27).

In the territory allotted to Judah (Jos 15:9, 60; 18:14). The Philistines bring the ark to (1Sa 6:21, w 1Sa 6:1-21), ark remains twenty years at (1Sa 7:1-2; 1Ch 13:5-6). David brings the ark from (2Sa 6:1-11; 1Ch 13:5-8; 2Ch 1:4). Inhabitants of, who were taken into captivity to Babylon, returned (Ezr 2:25; Ne 7:29). Uriah, the prophet, an inhabitant of (Jer 26:20).

KIRIATH SANNAH (*city of Sannah*). A city of Judah (Jos 15:49); also called Kiriath Sepher and Debir. *See Debir; Kiriath Sepher.*

KIRIATH SEPHER (*city of scribe*). A city of Judah (Jos 15:15-16); also called Kiriath Sannah; Debir. *See Debir; Kiriath Sannah.*

KIRIATHAIM (*two cities*).
1. Town in Moab N of Arnon. Assigned to Reuben (Nu 32:37; Jos 13:19).
2. City of Gershonite Levites in Naphtali (1Ch 6:76). Called Kartan (Jos 21:32).

KIRIOTH *See Kerioth, Kerioth Hezron.*

KIRJATH-ARIM *See Kiriath Jearim.*

KISH (*bow, power*).
1. Father of Saul (1Sa 9:1-3; 10:21; 2Sa 21:14). Called Kish (Ac 13:21).
2. A Benjamite (1Ch 8:30; 9:36).
3. A Levite (1Ch 23:21-22; 24:29).
4. A Levite (2Ch 29:12).
5. Great-grandfather of Mordecai (Est 2:5).

KISHI (possibly *gift* IDB; *snarer* ISBE). Also called Kushaiah. Father of Ethan, a chief assistant in the temple music (1Ch 6:44; 15:17).

KISHION City of Issachar (Jos 19:20). Also called Kedesh (1Ch 6:72).

KISHON (*cunning*). A river of Israel emptying into the Mediterranean near the northern base of Mount Carmel. Sisera defeated here, and his army destroyed (Jdg 4:7, 13; 5:21; Ps 83:9). Prophets of Baal destroyed by Elijah at (1Ki 18:40).

KISLEV Month nine in sacred sequence, month three in civil sequence (Ezr 10:9; Jer 36:9, 22; Zec 7:1). The rainy season (November-December); the season for planting. The Feast of Dedication (Jn 10:22).
See Dedication; Feasts; Hanukkah; Maccabees; Month, 9.

KISLON (*slow* IDB; *strength* ISBE). Father of Eldad (Nu 34:21).

KISLOTH TABOR A place on the border of Zebulun (Jos 19:12). Called Tabor (1Ch 6:77). Probably the same as Kesulloth (Jos 19:18).

KISS Of affection (Ge 27:26-27; 31:55; 33:4; 48:10; 50:1; Ex 18:7; Ru 1:14; 2Sa 14:33; 19:39; Lk 15:20; Ac 20:37). The feet of Jesus kissed by the penitent woman (Lk 7:38).
Deceitful (Pr 27:6), of Joab, when he killed Amasa (2Sa 20:9-10), of Judas, when he betrayed Jesus (Mt 26:48; Lk 22:48).
Holy (Ro 16:16; 2Co 13:12; 1Th 5:26; 1Pe 5:14).

KITE A bird forbidden as food (Lev 11:14; Dt 14:13).

KITLISH Town in lowlands of Judah (Jos 15:40), site unknown.

KITRON (*incense, [sacrificial] smoke*). A city of Zebulun (Jdg 1:30).

KITTIM
1. Descendants of Javan (Ge 10:4; 1Ch 1:7).
2. The Hebrew name for Cyprus; probably inhabited islands of the Mediterranean (Isa 23:1, 12; Jer 2:10; Eze 27:6).
3. Prophecies concerning (Nu 24:24; Da 11:30).

KNEADING TROUGH Shallow vessel for kneading dough with hands (Ex 8:3; 12:34).

KNEE Bowing the knee or kneeling as an act of reverence (Ge 41:43; 2Ki 1:13), and subjection (Isa 45:23; Php 2:10).

KNIFE An edged tool used by Abraham in offering Isaac (Ge 22:6, 10). Of flint, used in circumcision (Ex 4:25; Jos 5:2, 3). Used for pruning (Isa 18:5), by scribes (Jer 36:23).

KNOB *See Capital.*

KNOWLEDGE Of good and evil (Ge 2:9, 17; 3:22). Is power (Pr 3:20; 24:5). Desire for (1Ki 3:9; Ps 119:66; Pr 2; 3; 12:1; 15:14; 18:15). Rejected (Hos 4:6). Those who reject are destroyed (Hos 4:6). Fools hate (Pr 1:22, 29). A divine gift (1Co 12:8). Is pleasant (Pr 2:10). Shall be increased (Da 12:4).
The earth shall be full of (Isa 11:9). Fear of the Lord is the beginning of (Pr 1:7). Of more value than gold (Pr 8:10). The priest's lips should keep (Mal 2:7).
Of salvation (Lk 1:77). Key of (Lk 11:52). Now we know in part (1Co 13:9-12). Of God more than burnt offering (Hos 6:6). Of Christ (Php 3:8).
See God, Knowledge of; Jesus the Christ, Omniscience of; Wisdom.

KOA People E of Tigris, between Elam and Media (Eze 23:23).

KOHATH Second son of Levi (Ge 46:11; Ex 6:16). Grandfather of Moses, Aaron, and Miriam (Nu 26:58-59). Father of the Kohathites, one of the divisions of the Levites (Ex 6:18; Nu 3:19, 27).
See Levites.

KOLAIAH (*Yahweh's voice*).
1. A Benjamite and ancestor of Sallu (Ne 11:7).
2. Father of the false prophet Ahab (Jer 29:21).

KORAH, KORAHITE(S) (*shaven, bald*).
1. Son of Esau (Ge 36:5, 14, 18; 1Ch 1:35).
2. Grandson of Esau (Ge 36:16).
3. Descendant of Caleb (1Ch 2:43).
4. Levite from whom the Korahites were descended (Ex 6:24; 1Ch 6:22).

KORAZIN Denunciation against (Mt 11:21; Lk 10:13).

KORE (*proclaimer*).
1. A Korahite (1Ch 9:19; 26:1).
2. A Levite, keeper of the East Gate (2Ch 31:14).

KORHITE(S) *See Korah, Korahite(s), 4; Levites.*

KOZ (*thorn*). The father of Anub and Hazzobebah (1Ch 4:8).

KUE Probably Cilicia in SE Asia Minor (1Ki 10:28; 2Ch 1:16).

KUSHAIAH Merarite Levite (1Ch 15:17). Also called Kishi (1Ch 6:44).

L

LAADAH (perhaps *having a fat neck or throat*). Son of Shelah (1Ch 4:21).

LAADAN *See Ladan.*

LABAN (*white*).
1. Son of Bethuel (Ge 28:5). Brother of Rebekah (Ge 22:23; 24:15, 29). Receives the servant of Abraham (Ge 24:29-33). Receives Jacob and gives him his daughters in marriage (Ge 29:12-30). Jacob becomes his servant (Ge 29:15-20, 27; 30:27-43). Outwitted by Jacob (Ge 30:37-43; 31:1-21). Pursues Jacob, overtakes him in hill country of Gilead, and covenants with him (Ge 31:22-55).
2. Place in Plains of Moab (Dt 1:1).

LABOR Honorable (Ps 128:2; Pr 21:25; 1Th 4:11). Laborers protected by laws (Dt 24:14). Creative work of God described as labor (Ge 2:2). Difficult labor the result of the curse (Ge 3:17-19). Sleep of labor sweet (Ecc 5:12).
Labor commanded (Ge 3:19; Ex 20:9-11; 23:12; 34:21; Lev 23:3; Lk 13:14; Ac 20:35; Eph 4:28; 1Th 4:11; 2Th 3:10-12).
Compensation for (Lev 19:13; Dt 25:4; 1Co 9:9; 1Ti 5:18; Jer 22:13; Mal 3:5; Mt 20:1-15; Lk 10:7; Jas 5:4). Of servants must not be oppressive (Dt 24:14-15).
Paul, an example (2Th 3:8-13).
See Capital and Labor; Employee; Employer; Idleness; Industry; Master; Servant.

LACE Cord used to bind high priest's breastplate to the ephod (Ex 28:28, 37; 39:21, 31).

LACHISH Canaanite royal city and Judean border fortress, occupying a strategic valley twenty-five miles SW of Jerusalem. It is identified with Tell ed-Duweir (Tell Lakhish). Joshua captured it (Jos 10:31-33); destroyed by Nebuchadnezzar along with Jerusalem (2Ki 24-25; Jer 34:7), resettled after the Exile (Ne 11:30). Lachish Letters (ostraca) from the time of Jeremiah reveal much about the city.

LACHRYMATORY A container for holding the tears of mourners (Ps 56:8, ftn).

LADAN
1. A descendant of Ephraim (1Ch 7:26).
2. A Levite, called also Libni (1Ch 6:17; 23:7-9; 26:21).

LADDER (Ge 28:12, ftn). *See Stairs.*

LAEL (*[belonging] to God [El]*). Father of Eliasaph (Nu 3:24).

LAHAD (perhaps *slow, indolent*). A descendant of Judah (1Ch 4:2).

LAHAI-ROI *See Beer Lahai Roi.*

LAHMAS Town in Judean Shephelah (Jos 15:40). Probably modern Khirbet el-Lahm.

LAHMI Brother of Goliath. Slain by Elhanan (2Sa 21:19; 1Ch 20:5).

LAISH (*lion*).
1. A Sidonian city at the N. extremity of Israel (Jdg 18:7, 14, 27, 29). Called also Leshem (Jos 19:47), and afterwards Dan. *See Dan, 3; Leshem.*
2. A native of Gallim; a Benjamite, whose son became the husband of Michal, David's wife (1Sa 25:44; 2Sa 3:15).
3. *See Laishah.*

LAISHAH (*lion*). A town near Jerusalem (Isa 10:30).

LAKE OF FIRE Place of final judgment (Rev 19:20; 20:10, 14-15; 21:8).

LAKKUM Town of Naphtali (Jos 19:33), location unknown.

LAMA SABACHTHANI *See Eloi, Eloi, Lama Sabachthani.*

LAMB Used, for food (Dt 32:14; Am 6:4), for sacrifices (Ge 4:4; 22:7), especially at Passover (Ex 12:3-5). Sacrificial lambs typical of Christ (Jn 1:29; Rev 5:6, 8).
Offering of (Lev 3:7; 5:6; 22:23; 23:12; Nu 7:15, 21; 28:3-8), at the daily morning and evening sacrifices (Ex 29:38-42). Offering of, at the Feast of Passover (Ex 12:15), Pentecost (Lev 23:18-20), Tabernacles (Nu 29:13-40), the New Moon (Nu 28:11), trumpets (Nu 29:2). Offering of, on the Sabbath day (Nu 28:9), at purifications (Lev 12:6; 14:10-25), by the Nazirite (Nu 6:12), for sin of ignorance (Lev 4:32).

Figurative:
The wolf living with, a figure of Messiah's reign (Isa 11:6; 65:25). A type of young believers (Jn 21:15).
A name given to Christ (Jn 1:29, 36; Rev 5:6, 8, 12-13; 6:1, 16; 7:9-10, 14; 12:11; 13:8; 14:4, 10; 17:14; 19:7, 9; 21:9, 14, 22-23, 27; 22:1, 3). Jesus compared to (Isa 53:7; Ac 8:32; 1Pe 1:19).

LAMB OF GOD A title of Jesus (Jn 1:29; Rev 6:16; 7:9-10, 14, 17; 12:11; 13:8; 14:1, 4; 15:3; 17:14; 19:7; 21:9, 14, 22-23, 27; 22:1, 3).

LAME *See Disease.*

LAMECH
1. Father of Jabal, Jubal, and Tubal-Cain (Ge 4:18-24).
2. Son of Methuselah, and father of Noah, lived 777 years (Ge 5:25-31; 1Ch 1:3). Ancestor of Jesus (Lk 3:36).

LAMENESS Disqualified priest from exercising the priestly office (Lev 21:18). Disqualified animals for sacrificial uses (Dt 15:21). Hated by David (2Sa 5:8). Healed by Jesus (Mt 11:5; 15:31; 21:14; Lk 7:22), by Peter (Ac 3:2-11).

LAMENTATIONS Of David (Ps 60:1-3). Of Jeremiah (La 1-5). Of Ezekiel (Eze 19; 28:12-19). *See Elegy.*

LAMENTATIONS, BOOK OF

Author: Anonymous, traditionally Jeremiah

Date: Shortly after the fall of Jerusalem in 586 B.C.

Outline:
I. Jerusalem's Misery and Desolation (ch. 1).
II. The Lord's Anger Against His People (ch. 2).
III. Judah's Complaint—and Basis of Consolation (ch. 3).
IV. The Contrast Between Zion's Past and Present (ch. 4).
V. Judah's Appeal for God's Forgiveness (ch. 5).

LAMP
Figurative: Of joy (Jer 25:10). Life (Job 18:5-6; 21:17; Pr 13:9; 20:20). The word of God (Ps 119:105; Pr 6:23; 2Pe 1:19). Spiritual illumination (Mt 6:22). Religious influence (Mt 5:15; Mk 4:21; Lk 8:16; 11:33). Jesus is the lamp of the New Jerusalem (Rev 21:23).
Symbolic (Rev 4:5; 8:10).
See Lampstand.

LAMPSTAND

Of the Tabernacle:
Made of gold after divine pattern (Ex 25:31-40; 37:17-24; Nu 8:4), burned olive oil (Ex 27:20). Place of (Ex 26:35; 40:24-25; Heb 9:2). Furniture of (Ex 25:38; 37:23; Nu 4:9-10). Burned every night (Ex 27:20-21). Trimmed every morning (Ex 30:7). Carried by Kohathites (Nu 4:4, 15). Called the lamp of God (1Sa 3:3).

Of the Temple:
Ten branches of (1Ki 7:49-50). Of gold (1Ch 28:15; 2Ch 4:20). Taken with other spoils to Babylon (Jer 52:19).
Symbolic (Zec 4:2, 11; Rev 1:12-13, 20; 2:5; 11:4).

LANCE *See Javelin; Spear.*

LAND Appeared on third creative day (Ge 1:9). Original title to, from God (Ge 13:14-17; 15:7; Ex 23:31; Lev 25:33). Bought and sold (Ge 23:3-18; 33:19; Ac 4:34; 5:1-8).
Sale and redemption of, laws concerning (Lev 25:15-16, 23-33; 27:17-24; Nu 36:4; Jer 32:7-16, 25, 44; Eze 46:18). Conveyance of, by written deeds and other forms (Ge 23:3-20; Ru 4:3-8, 11; Jer 32:9-14), witnessed (Ge 23:10-11; Ru 4:9-11; Jer 32:9-14).
Sold for debt (Ne 5:3-5). Rights in, alienated (2Ki 8:1-6). Leased (Lk 20:9-16; Mt 21:33-41).
Priest's part in (Ge 47:22; Eze 48:10). King's part in (Eze 48:21). Widow's share in (Ru 4:3-9). Unmarried woman's rights in (Nu 27:1-11; 36:1-11).
To rest every seventh year for the benefit of the poor (Ex 23:11). Products of, for all (Ecc 5:9). Monopoly of (Ge 47:20-26; Isa 5:8; Mic 2:1-2). *See Mortgage.*
Rules for apportioning Canaan among the tribes (Eze 47:22). *See Canaan.*

LANDMARKS (*border*). Protected from fraudulent removal (Dt 19:14; 27:17; Job 24:2; Pr 22:28; 23:10; Hos 5:10). *See Boundary Stones.*

LANES Country lanes (Lk 14:21). *See Streets.*

LANGUAGE Unity of (Ge 11:1, 6). Confusion of (Ge 11:1-9; 10:5, 20, 31). Dialects of the Jews (Jdg 12:6; Mt 26:73). Many spoken at Jerusalem (Jn 19:20; Ac 2:8-11).
Gift of (Mk 16:17; Ac 2:7-8; 10:46; 19:6; 1Co 12:10; 14). *See Tongues, Gift of.*

Mentioned in Scripture:
Aramaic (2Ki 18:26; Ezr 4:7; Da 2:4). Of Ashdod (Ne 13:24). Babylonian [or Chaldean] (Da 1:4). Canaanite (Isa 19:18). Egyptian (Ac 2:10; Ps 81:5). Greek (Jn 19:20; Ac 21:37). Hebrew (Rev 9:11; 16:16). Of Judah (Ne 13:24). Latin (Jn 19:20). Lycaonia (Ac 14:11). Parthia and other lands (Ac 2:9-11).

LANTERN (Jn 18:3).

LAODICEA A Phrygian city. Paul's concern for (Col 2:1). Epaphras' zeal for (Col 4:13). Epistle to the Colossians to be read in (Col 4:15-16). Message to, through John (Rev 1:11; 3:14-22).

LAODICEA, CHURCH AT *See Laodicea.*

LAODICEANS, EPISTLE TO Letter mentioned by Paul (Col 4:16). This is probably a letter of Paul that was not preserved for the canon. Some theorize it may be the letter to the Ephesians as a circular letter. An apocryphal epistle to the Laodiceans exists in Latin.

L

LAPIDARY One who cuts precious stones (Ex 31:5; 35:33).

LAPPED A Hebrew verb used to indicate alertness (Jdg 7:5-7) and disgust (1Ki 21:19; 22:38).

LAPPIDOTH (*flames*). Husband of Deborah (Jdg 4:4).

LAPWING *See Hoopoe.*

LARCENY *See Theft.*

LASCIVIOUSNESS Unbridled lust, licentiousness, wantonness.

Condemned:
Forbidden (Col 3:5; 1Th 4:3-6). Warnings against (Pr 2:16-18; 5:3-5, 8-13; 7:6-27; 9:13-18; 30:18-20; 31:3; Ro 13:13; 1Co 6:13, 15-18; 1Pe 4:2-3; Jude 4, 7).
Sinful practices in (Joel 3:3; Ro 1:22-29). Proceeds from unregenerate heart (Mk 7:21-23; Gal 5:19; Eph 4:17-19). Impenitence in (2Co 12:21). Excludes from the kingdom of God (1Co 6:9-10, 13, 15-18; 9:27; Gal 5:19, 21; Eph 5:5).
Lascivious practices in idolatrous worship. *See Idolatry, Wicked practices of.*
See Adultery; Homosexual; Incest; Lust; Prostitute; Rape; Sensuality.

Figurative: (Eze 16:15-59). *See Prostitute.*

Instances of:
Sodomites (Ge 19:5). Lot's daughters (Ge 19:30-38). Judah (Ge 38:15-16). The Gibeahites (Jdg 19:22-25). Eli's sons (1Sa 2:22). David (2Sa 5:13; 11:2-27). Amnon (2Sa 13:1-14). Solomon (1Ki 11:1-3). Rehoboam (2Ch 11:21-23). Persian kings (Est 2:3, 13-14, 19).

LASEA Seaport on S coast of Crete. Visited by Paul (Ac 27:8).

LASHA Place near Sodom and Gomorrah (Ge 10:19). Site not identified.

LASHARON (*[belonging to] Sharon*). King of, killed by Joshua (Jos 12:18).

LASHES
1. Beating could subject the culprit to abuse, so the law kept the punishment from becoming inhumane (Dt 25:2-3). Solomon uses hyperbole to illustrate that a rebuke has greater influence on a wise man than a hundred lashes will have on a fool (Pr 17:10). Compare Paul's experience (2Co 11:24). *See Stripes.*
2. A figurative description of Jerusalem experiencing the wrath of God finally being rebuilt into the Holy City, the New Jerusalem (Isa 54:11-12, w Rev 21:10, 18-21).
See Assault and Battery; Bruise(s); Flog, Flogging; Scourging; Stoning.

LAST First and last: a title of Yahweh (Isa 44:6; 48:12), of Jesus (Rev 1:17; 2:8; 22:13). *See Titles and Names.*
The first will be last and the last first (Nu 24:20; Mt 19:30; 20:16; Mk 9:35; 10:31; Lk 13:30).

LAST DAYS The days before the final judgment (Jn 12:48), when God's kingdom is established on earth (Isa 2:2-4; Mic 4:1-8), and Israel is restored to her God (Hos 3:5). Began with the coming of Jesus and of the Spirit (Ac 2:16-21; Heb 1:2; 1Pe 1:20). The time of the resurrection (Jn 6:39-44, 54; 11:24). A time of great trouble and deception (1Ti 3:1-17; 2Pe 3:3-17; Jude 18-19), culminating in the Second Coming of Christ (1Pe 1:5). *See Day of the Lord; Eschatology.*

LATCHET *See Thong.*

LATIN The language of the Roman Empire, used in Israel in NT times (Jn 19:20).

LATRINE Temple of Baal used as (2Ki 10:27).

LATTICE Latticework used for privacy, ventilation, decoration (Jdg 5:28; 2Ki 1:2; Pr 7:6).

LAUGHTER Used to express joy (Ge 21:6; Lk 6:21), derision (Ps 2:4), disbelief (Ge 18:13).

LAUNDERER *See Fuller.*

LAVER *See Bronze Basin; Bronze Sea.*

LAW
1. Ten Commandments given to Moses (Ex 20:3-17; Dt 5:6-21), summarizing God's requirements of mankind.
2. The Torah, first five books of OT (Mt 5:17; Lk 16:16).
3. The whole OT (Jn 10:34; 12:34).
4. God's will in words, acts, precepts (Ex 20:1-17; Ps 19:1-14).

The Purpose of the Law—
Under the old covenant, believers manifested their faith in Yahweh by observing the law for their own good (Dt 6:4-9; 10:12-13; 30:1-16). Christ fulfilled the law; respected, loved it, and showed its deeper significance (Mt 5:17-48). The law prepared the way for the coming of Christ (Gal 3:24). The law could not bring victory over sin (Ro 3-8; Gal).
Jesus' summary of the law: It demands perfect love for God, and love for one's neighbor comparable to that which one has for oneself (Mt 22:35-40).
Made for the lawless (1Ti 1:8-10). Must be obeyed (Mt 22:21; Lk 20:22-25).

Law of God:
(Ps 119:1-8; Jas 1:25). Spiritual (Ro 7:14). Must be obeyed (1Jn 5:3). Love, the fulfilling of (Ro 13:10; 1Ti 1:5).
See Litigation; Commandments and Statutes, Of God; Duty, Of People to God.

Law of Moses:
Contained in the books of Exodus, Leviticus, Numbers, and Deuteronomy. Divine authority for (Ex 19:16-24; 20:1-2; 24:12-18; 32:15-16; 34:1-4, 27-28; Lev 26:46; Dt 4:10-13, 36; 5:1-22; 9:10; 10:1-5; 33:2-4; 1Ki 8:9; Ezr 7:6; Ne 1:7; 8:1; 9:14; Ps 78:5; 103:7; Isa 33:22; Mal 4:4; Ac 7:38, 53; Gal 3:19; Heb 9:18-21).
Given at Sinai (Ex 19; Dt 1:1; 4:10-13, 44-46; 32:2; Hab 3:3). Received by the disposition of angels (Dt 32:2; Ps 68:17; Ac 7:53; Gal 3:19; Heb 2:2). Was given because of transgression until the Messiah came (Gal 3:19). Engraved on stone (Ex 20:3-17; 24:12; 31:18; 32:16; 34:29; 40:20; Dt 4:13; 5:4-22; 9:10), on monuments (Dt 27:2-8; Jos 8:30-35),
See Tablets of the Law; Commandments and Statutes, Of God.
Preserved in the ark of the covenant (Ex 25:16; Dt 31:9, 26). To be written on doorframes (Dt 6:9; 11:20) and as a symbol on the forehead and a sign on the hand (Ex 13:9, 16; Dt 6:4-9; 11:18-21), meaning the law was to govern society, home, personal thoughts and actions. Children instructed in. *See Children; Instruction.*
Expounded by priests and Levites (Lev 10:11; Dt 33:10; 2Ch 35:3), by princes, priests, and Levites (Ezr 7:10; Ne 8:1-18), from city to city (2Ch 17:7-10), in synagogues (Lk 4:16; Ac 13:14-52; 15:21, w Ac 9:20, & 14:1; 17:1-3; 18:4, 26). Expounded to the assembled nation at the feast of tabernacles in the sabbatic year (Dt 31:10-13). Rehearsed by Moses, with many admonitions (Dt 4:44-46; 5-34).
Obedience to, commanded (Dt 4:40; 5:32; 6:17; 7:11; 8:1, 6; 10:12-13; 11:1, 8, 32; 13:4; 16:12; 27:1; 30:16; 32:46; Jos 1:7; 22:5; 1Ki 2:3; 8:61; 2Ki 17:37). Found by Hilkiah in the house of the Lord (2Ki 22:8; 2Ch 34:14).
Blessings and curses of, responsively read by Levites and people at Ebal and Gerizim (Dt 27:12-26; Jos 8:33-35).
Formed a constitution on which the civil government of the Israelites was founded, and according to which rulers were required to rule (Dt 17:18-20; 2Ki 11:12; 2Ch 23:11). *See Constitution; Government.*
Was given because of transgressions until the coming of the Messiah (Gal 3:19). Was committed to the Jews (Ro 3:1-2). Brings the knowledge of sin (Ro 3:20; 7:7).
Prophecies in, of the Messiah (Lk 24:44; Jn 1:45; 5:46; 12:34; Ac 26:22-23; 28:23; Ro 3:21-22). *See Jesus the Christ, Prophecies Concerning.*
Epitomized by Jesus (Mt 22:40; Mk 12:29-33; Lk 10:27).
Temporary (Jer 3:16; Da 9:27; Heb 10:1-18). Weakness of the law (Ro 8:3, 6).
Fulfilled by Christ (Mt 5:17-45; Ac 6:14; 13:39; Ro 10:3-4; Eph 2:15; Heb 8:4-13; 9:8-24; 10:3-9).
Superseded by the gospel (Lk 16:16-17; Jn 1:17; 4:20-24; 8:35; Gal 4:30-31; Ac 10:28; 15:1-20; 21:20-25; Ro 7:1-6; 2Co 3:7-14; Gal 2:3-9, 19; 4:4-31; 5:1-18; Col 2:14-23; Heb 7:5-9).

LAW OF MOSES *See Law.*

LAWGIVER God is the only absolute lawgiver (Jas 4:12), instrumentally, Moses bears this description (Jn 1:17; 7:19).

LAWSUITS To be avoided (Pr 25:8-10; Mt 5:25-26; 1Co 6:1-8).
See Actions at Law; Adjudication at Law; Arbitration; Compromise; Court, Of Law; Justice.

LAWYER One versed in the law of Moses. Test Jesus with questions (Mt 22:35; Lk 10:25-37). Jesus' satire against (Lk 11:45-52). Tertullus presents case against Paul (Ac 24:1-2). Zenas (Tit 3:13). *See Litigation.*

LAYING ON OF HANDS Symbolic act signifying impartation of inheritance rights (Ge 48:14-20), gifts and rights of an office (Nu 27:18, 23), dedication of animals (Lev 1:4), priests (Nu 8:10), people for special service (Ac 6:6; 13:3).

LAZARUS (*one whom God helps*).
1. Brother of Martha and Mary; raised from the dead by Jesus (Jn 11:1-12:19).
2. Beggar who died and went to Abraham's side (Lk 16:19-31). *See Abraham's Side.*

LAZINESS (Pr 12:27; 18:9; 19:24; 21:25; 22:13; 26:13-16).
Brings adversity (Pr 12:24; Ecc 10:18), destruction (Pr 13:4; 19:15; 20:4; 23:21; 24:30-34).
Admonitions against (Pr 6:6-11; 10:4-5, 26; 15:19). Denounced (Mt 25:26-27). Of ministers, denounced (Isa 56:10). Forbidden (Ro 12:11; Heb 6:12).
See Idleness; Slothfulness.

LEAD A mineral (Ex 15:10). Purified by fire (Nu 31:22; Jer 6:29; Eze 22:18, 20). Used in making inscriptions on stone (Job 19:24). Refining (Jer 6:29; Eze 22:18, 20). Trade in (Eze 27:12). Used for weighing (Zec 5:7-8).

LEADERSHIP Instances of: Abraham, Moses, Joshua, Gideon, Deborah. *See each under its own entry.*

LEAF Leaf of a tree, page of a book, leaf of a door. Metaphorically, green leaves symbolize prosperity, and dry leaves ruin and decay (Ps 1:3; Pr 11:28; Job 13:25; Isa 1:30).

LEAGUE *See Alliances; Treaty.*

LEAH (possibly *wild cow* BDB; *wild cow, gazelle* IDB; *cow* KB [cf. Rachel = *ewe*]). Daughter of Laban (Ge 29:16). Married to Jacob (Ge 29:23-26). Children of (Ge 29:31-35; 30:9-13, 17-21). Flees with Jacob (Ge 31:4, 14, 17; 33:2-7). "Built up the house of Israel" (Ru 4:11).

LEANNOTH (*the suffering of affliction*, NIV; *sickness or suffering poem*, JB). *See Music, Symbols Used in.*

LEARNING *See Instruction; Knowledge.*

LEASE *See Land; Renting.*

LEASING An obsolete word for falsehood (Ps 4:2; 5:6).

LEATHER (*skin*). Designates the tanned hide of animals. Skins were used for rough clothing as well as for armor, bags, sandals, and writing materials (Lev 13:48; Eze 16:10; Mt 3:4; Heb 11:37).

LEAVEN (*piece of fermented dough*). For bread (Ex 12:34, 39; Hos 7:4; Mt 13:33). Leavened bread used with peace offering (Lev 7:13; Am 4:5), with wave offering (Lev 23:15-17). Leavened bread forbidden with meat offerings (Lev 2:11; 6:17; 10:12; Ex 23:18; 34:25), at the Passover (Ex 12:19-20; 13:3-4, 7; 23:18), with blood (Ex 23:18; 34:25).
A type of sin (1Co 5:6-8).

Figurative:
Of the hypocrisy of the Pharisees (Mt 16:6-12; Mk 8:15; Lk 12:1). Of other evils (1Co 5:6-8; Gal 5:9). Parable of (Mt 13:33; Lk 13:21).

LEB KAMAI (*the heart of my attackers*). A cryptogram (hidden code) for Babylon (Jer 51:1 ftn). *See Babylon.*

LEBANA, LEBANAH (*white*). Ancestor of a family which returned from the Exile (Ezr 2:45; Ne 7:48).

LEBANON (*white, snow*). A mountain range. Northern boundary of the land of Canaan (Dt 1:7; 3:25; 11:24; Jos 1:4; 9:1). Early inhabitants of (Jdg 3:3). Snow of (Jer 18:14). Streams of (SS 4:15). Cedars of (Jdg 9:15; 2Ki 19:23; 2Ch 2:8; Ps 29:5; 104:16; Isa 2:13; 14:8; Eze 27:5). Other trees (2Ki 19:23; 2Ch 2:8). Flower of (Na 1:4). Beasts of (Isa 40:16). Fertility and productiveness of (Hos 14:5-7). "Palace of the Forest of," (1Ki 7:2-5). Valley of (Jos 11:17; 12:7). Tower of (SS 7:4). Solomon had store cities (1Ki 9:19). Figurative: (Isa 29:17; Jer 22:6).

LEBAOTH (*lionesses*). Town in S Judah (Jos 15:32), also called Beth Lebaoth (Jos 19:6), and probably Beth Biri (1Ch 4:31).

LEBBAEUS (*[one near to] my heart*). An alternate reading in some mss for Thaddaeus, one of Christ's apostles (Mt 10:3). *See Thaddaeus.*

LEBO HAMATH (*the entrance to Hamath*). A city located on the Orontes River of Northern Syria, though it might be "the entrance to Hamath" rather than a named city (Nu 13:21; 34:8 and ftns). *See Hamath.*

LEBONAH (*frankincense*). A city on the highway from Bethel to Shechem (Jdg 21:19).

LECAH (*to you*). A town or person in Judah (1Ch 4:21).

LEECH Bloodsucking parasite, personifying greed (Pr 30:15). *See Animals.*

LEEK A herb of the lily family, similar in flavor to the onion (Nu 11:5).

LEES (*something preserved*). Sediment of wine (Isa 25:6). Also used figuratively to describe blessings of messianic times, spiritual lethargy, inevitability of God's judgment (Jer 48:11; Ps 75:8).

LEFT Used with a variety of meanings. Simple direction; North (Ge 14:15). Lesser blessing (Ge 48:13-19). Characteristic of Benjamites (Jdg 3:15, 21; 20:16).

LEFT-HANDED Characteristic of Benjamites (Jdg 3:15; 20:16; 1Ch 12:2).

LEGALISTIC Seeking God's favor by keeping the letter of the law without keeping its spirit (Mt 23:23-24). Legalists in the early church required circumcision for salvation (Ac 15:1-29). Paul's first letter, Galatians, was written to combat legalistic teaching about the Christian life (Gal 3:2, 10-14; 4:9-11).
The Christian lives a life of grace, not works (Eph 2:8-9) and is not judged by ritual observance of special diet or holy days (Ro 14:1-18; Col 2:16-19; Heb 13:9). *See Commandments and Statutes, Of Men; Grace.*

LEGENDS *See Inscriptions.*

LEGION (*military company*).
1. Largest unit in the Roman army, including infantry and cavalry.
2. Vast number (Mt 26:53; Mk 5:9).

LEGISLATION Class, forbidden (Ex 12:49; Lev 24:22; Nu 9:14; 15:15, 29; Gal 3:28). Supplemental, concerning Sabbath-breaking (Nu 15:32-35), inheritance (Nu 27:1-11). *See Government; Law.*

LEGS Of the crucified broken (Jn 19:31-32).

LEHABITES Descendants of Mizraim (Ge 10:13; 1Ch 1:11).

LEHEM *See Jashubi Lehem.*

LEHI (*jawbone*). Place where Samson killed a thousand Philistines with a jawbone of a donkey (Jdg 15:9, 14).

LEMUEL (*[belonging] to God [El]*). A king, otherwise unknown, to whom his mother taught the maxims in Pr 31:1-9.

LENDING

To the Poor, Commanded:
(Lev 25:35; Dt 15:7, 11). Commanded by Christ (Mt 5:42; Lk 6:34-35). Encouraged (Ps 112:5; Pr 19:17). God, the merciful Lender (Ps 37:25-26). Borrower to be released in the year of release (Dt 15:1-6).

Things Forbidden as Security of Loans:
Millstones (Dt 24:6). Widow's cloak (Dt 24:17).

Lender:
Forbidden to take interest from poor Hebrews (Ex 22:25-27; Lev 25:36-37; Dt 23:19-20). Forbidden to enter debtor's house for

security (Dt 24:10-11). Forbidden to keep overnight clothing left in pledge (Dt 24:12-13).

Oppression of borrower (Ne 5:1-13). Is master of borrower (Pr 22:7). Lender and borrower will be equal (Isa 24:1-2). Wicked, punished (Pr 28:8; Eze 18:13).

See Borrowing; Interest; Money.

LENTIL(S) (Ge 25:34; 2Sa 17:28; 23:11; Eze 4:9).

LEOPARD A carnivorous animal (SS 4:8). Fierceness of (Jer 5:6; 13:23; Hos 13:7; Hab 1:8).

Figurative: (Da 7:6). Taming of, the triumph of the gospel (Isa 11:6).

LEPROSY The word is used for various diseases affecting the skin—not necessarily leprosy (Hansen's disease).

General:

Law concerning (Lev 13-14; 22:4; Nu 5:1-3; 12:14; Dt 24:8; Mt 8:4; Lk 5:14; 17:14). Entailed (2Ki 5:27). Isolation of lepers (Lev 13:46; Nu 5:2; 12:14; 2Ki 15:5; 2Ch 26:21). Separate burial (2Ch 26:23).

Sent as a judgment. On Miriam (Nu 12:1-10), Gehazi (2Ki 5:27), Azariah/Uzziah (2Ki 15:5; 2Ch 26:20-21). Other instances: Four lepers outside Samaria (2Ki 7:3), Simon (Mk 14:3).

Healed:

Miriam (Nu 12:13-14), Naaman (2Ki 5:8-14), by Jesus (Mt 8:3; Mk 1:40-42; Lk 5:13; 17:12-14). Disciples empowered to heal (Mt 10:8).

LESBIAN Sexual activity between females is condemned (Ro 1:26). *See Homosexual.*

LESHEM (*lion*). City renamed Dan, at extreme N of Israel (Jos 19:47), variant of Laish. *See Dan, 3; Laish.*

LETHEK About 10 bushels (330 liters) (Hos 3:2). *See Measure.*

LETTER Designates an alphabetical symbol, rudimentary education (Jn 7:15), written communication, the external (Ro 2:27, 29), Jewish legalism (Ro 7:6; 2Co 3:6). In ancient times correspondence was privately delivered. Archaeology has uncovered many different kinds of letters. *See Writing.*

LETTERS Written by David to Joab (2Sa 11:14), king of Syria to king of Israel (2Ki 5:5-6), the field commander to Hezekiah (Isa 37:9-14), king of Babylon to Hezekiah (Isa 39:1), Sennacherib to Hezekiah (2Ki 19:14). Of Artaxerxes to Nehemiah (Ne 2:7-9). Open letter from Sanballat to Nehemiah (Ne 6:5). Luke to Theophilus, the books of Luke and Acts (Ac 1:1). Claudius Lysias to Felix (Ac 23:25-30). Letter of intercession by Paul to Philemon in behalf of Onesimus (Phm 1), of recommendation (2Co 3:1). In the NT, the books of Romans through Jude and Rev 1-3. *See Writing.*

LETUSHITES (*sharpened*). Descendants of Dedan, grandson of Abraham (Ge 25:3).

LEUMMITES (perhaps *peoples* or *hordes*). Descendants of Dedan (Ge 25:3).

LEVI (perhaps *wild cow* or *person pledged for a debt or vow*). Son of Jacob (Ge 29:34; 35:23; 1Ch 2:1). Avenges the seduction of Dinah (Ge 34; 49:5-7). Jacob's prophecy regarding (Ge 49:5-7). His age at death (Ex 6:16). Descendants of, made ministers of religion. *See Levites.*

LEVIATHAN (*coiled one [like a serpent]*). Possibly a crocodile (Job 41; Ps 104:26). A sea monster figurative of forces of chaos opposed to Yahweh (Job 3:8; Ps 74:14; Isa 27:1). *See Dragon; Serpent.*

LEVIRATE MARRIAGE Jewish custom according to which when an Israelite died without male heirs, his nearest relative married the widow, and their firstborn son became the heir of the first husband (Dt 25:5-10; Ru 3-4). *See Kinsman-Redeemer.*

LEVITES (*of Levi*). The descendants of Levi. Set apart as ministers of religion (Nu 1:47-54; 3:6-16; 16:9; 26:57-62; Dt 10:8; 1Ch 15:2). Substituted in the place of the firstborn (Nu 3:12, 41-45; 8:14, 16-18; 18:6). Religious zeal of (Ex 32:23-28; Dt 33:9-10; Mal 2:4-5). Consecration of (Nu 8:6-21). Sedition among, led by Korah, Dathan, Abiram, and On, on account of jealousy toward Moses and Aaron (Nu 16, w 4:19-20).

Three Divisions of:

Each having the name of one of its progenitors. Gershon, Kohath, and Merari (Nu 3:17). Gershonites and their duties (Nu 3:18-26; 4:23-26; 10:17). Ruling chief over the Gershonites was the second son of the ruling high priest (Nu 4:28). Kohathites, consisting of the families of the Amramites, Izharites, Hebronites, Uzzielites (Nu 3:27; 4:18-20). Of the Amramites, Aaron, and his family were set apart as priests (Ex 28:1; 29:9; Nu 3:38; 8:1-14; 17; 18:1), the remaining families appointed to take charge of the ark, table, lampstand, altars and vessels of the sanctuary, the hangings, and all the service (Nu 3:27-32; 4:2-15). The chief over the Kohathite was the oldest son of the ruling high priest (Nu 3:32; 1Ch 9:20). Merarites (Nu 3:20, 33-37; 4:31-33, 7:8, 10:17; 1Ch 6:19, 29-30; 23:21-23). The chief over the Merarites was the second son of the ruling high priest (Nu 4:33).

Place of, in camp and march (Nu 1:50-53; 2:17; 3:23-35). Cities assigned to, in the land of Canaan (Jos 21). Lodged in the chambers of the temple (1Ch 9:27, 33; Eze 40:44). Resided also in villages outside of Jerusalem (Ne 12:29).

Age of, when inducted into office (Nu 4:3, 30, 47; 8:23-26; 1Ch 23:3, 24, 27; Ezr 3:8), when retired from office (Nu 4:3, 47; 8:25-26).

Functions of:

Had charge of the tabernacle in camp and on the march (Nu 1:50-53; 3:6-9, 21-37; 4:1-15, 17-49; 8:19, 22; 18:3-6), and of the temple (1Ch 9:27-29; 23:2-32; Ezr 8:24-34).

Bore the ark of the covenant (Dt 10:8; 1Ch 15:2, 26-27). Ministered before the ark (1Ch 16:4). Custodians and administrators of the tithes and other offerings (1Ch 9:26-29; 26:28; 29:8; 2Ch 24:5, 11; 31:11-19; 34:9; Ezr 8:29-30, 33; Ne 12:44). Prepared the bread of the Presence (1Ch 23:28-29). Assisted the priests in preparing the sacrifice (2Ch 29:12-36; 2Ch 35:1-18). Killed the Passover for the children of the Captivity (Ezr 6:20-21). Teachers of the law (Dt 33:10; 2Ch 17:8-9; 30:22; 35:3; Ne 8:7-13; Mal 2:6-7). Were judges (Dt 17:9; 1Ch 23:4; 26:29; 2Ch 19:8-11; Ne 11:16). *See Judge.*

Were scribes of the sacred books. *See Scribe.* Pronounced the blessings of the law in the responsive service at Mount Gerizim (Dt 27:12; Jos 8:33). Were gatekeepers of the temple. *See Gatekeepers.* Were overseers in building and the repairs of the temple (1Ch 23:2-4; Ezr 3:8-9). Were musicians of the temple service. *See Music.* Supervised weights and measures (1Ch 23:29).

List of those who returned from the Captivity (Ezr 2:40-63; 7:7; 8:16-20; Ne 7:43-73; 12). Sealed the covenant with Nehemiah (Ne 10:9-28).

Privileges of:

In lieu of landed inheritance, forty-eight cities with suburbs were assigned to them (Nu 35:2-8, w 18:24 & 26:62; Dt 10:9; 12:12, 18-19; 14:27-29; 18:1-8; Jos 13:14; 14:3; 18:7; 1Ch 6:54-81; 13:2; 2Ch 23:2; Eze 34:1-5). Assigned to, by families (Jos 21:4-40). Suburbs of their cities were inalienable for debt (Lev 25:32-34). Tithes and other offerings (Nu 18:24, 26-32; Dt 18:1-8; 26:11-13; Jos 13:14; Ne 10:38-39; 12:44, 47). Firstfruits (Ne 12:44, 47). Spoils of war, including captives (Nu 31:30, 42-47). *See Tithes.* Tithes withheld from (Ne 13:10-13; Mal 3:10). Pensioned (2Ch 31:16-18). Owned lands (Dt 18:8, w 1Ki 2:26). Land allotted to, by Ezekiel (Eze 48:13-14).

Enrollment of, at Sinai (Nu 1:47-49; 2:33; 3:14-39; 4:2-3; 26:57-62; 1Ch 23:3-5). Degraded from the Levitical office by Jeroboam (2Ch 11:13-17; 13:9-11). Loyal to the ruler (2Ki 11:7-11; 2Ch 23:7).

Intermarry with Canaanites (Ezr 9:1-2; 10:23-24). Exempt from enrollment for military duty (Nu 1:47-54, w 1Ch 12:26). Subordinate to the sons of Aaron (Nu 3:9; 8:19; 18:6).

Prophecies Concerning:

(Jer 33:18; Eze 44:10-14; Mal 3:3), of their repentance of the crucifixion of the Messiah (Zec 12:10-13). John's vision concerning (Rev 7:7).

LEVITICUS (*relating to the Levites*).

Author: Moses

Date: Between 1445 and 1406 B.C.

Outline:

I. The Five Main Offerings (chs. 1-7).
 A. Their Content, Purpose and Manner of Offering (1:1-6:7).
 B. Additional Regulations (6:8-7:38).
II. The Ordination, Installation and Work of Aaron and His Sons (chs. 8-10).
III. Laws of Cleanness—Food, Childbirth, Infections, etc. (chs. 11-15).
IV. The Day of Atonement and the Centrality of Worship at the Tabernacle (chs. 18-20).
V. Moral Laws Covering Incest, Honesty, Thievery, Idolatry, etc. (chs. 18-20).
VI. Regulations for the Priests, the Offerings and the Annual Feasts (21:1-24:9).
VII. Punishment for Blasphemy, Murder, etc. (24:10-23).
VIII. The Sabbath Year, Jubilee, Land Tenure and Reform of Slavery (ch. 25).
IX. Blessings and Curses for Covenant Obedience and Disobedience (ch. 26).
X. Regulations for Offerings Vowed to the Lord (ch. 27).

LEVY A tribute imposed by a conquering king (2Ki 23:33; 2Ch 36:3).

LEX TALIONIS *See Retaliation.*

LIARS All people are liars (Ps 116:11). Satan the father of lies (Jn 8:44, 55). Ungodly (1Ti 1:10). Characterisitc of Cretans (Tit 1:12). Eternally punished (Rev 21:8).

God cannot lie (Nu 23:19; Tit 1:2; Heb 6:18).

See Deceit; Deception; False Witness; Falsehood; Hypocrisy.

LIBATION (*pour [as an offering]*). Pouring out of wine or some other liquid as an offering to a deity as an act of worship (Ex 29:40-41; Jer 44:17-25). *See Offerings, Drink.*

LIBERALITY

Commanded:

(Ex 22:29-30; 23:15; 34:20; Lev 23:22; 25:35-43; Dt 12:11-12, 17-19; Pr 3:27-28; Mt 5:42; Ac 20:35; Ro 12:8; 2Co 8:7, 9, 11-14, 24; 1Ti 6:18; Heb 13:16).

In offerings, for tabernacle (Ex 25:1-8; 35:4-29; 36:3-6; 38:8). For the temple (Hag 1:8). With the Levites (Dt 12:11-12, 17-19; 18:1-8). For the temple commanded by Cyrus (Ezr 1:2-4). In offerings for sacrifice (2Sa 24:24).

In paying tithes (Dt 14:27-29). In gifts to God (Ps 76:11).

In gifts to the poor (Dt 15:7-11; 24:19-22; Ne 8:10; Ps 41:1-3; Isa 58:6-7; Mt 19:21-22, Mk 10:21; Lk 3:10-11; Ro 12:13; 15:27; 2Co 9:6-15; Gal 2:10; Eph 4:28; 1Ti 5:16; 6:17-19; Jas 2:15-16; 1Jn 3:17-18). By the noble woman (Pr 31:20). In gifts to liberated Hebrew slaves (Dt 15:12-18).

Giving according to ability (Nu 35:8; Dt 16:10, 17; 1Co 16:1-3; 2Co 8:12). Giving without a show (Mt 6:1-4). Giving of freewill (Lev 19:5; 22:9; 1Ch 29:5; Pr 21:26; 2Co 8:12; 9:1-6; Phm 14). Giving with love (1Co 13:3).

Rewards for giving (Ps 112:5, 9; Pr 3:9-10; 11:24-25; 13:7; 14:21; 19:6, 17; 22:9; 28:27; Ecc 11:1-2; Isa 32:8; 58:10-12; Eze 18:7-16; Mal 3:10-12; Mt 5:42; 25:34-40, 46; Lk 6:30-38; 12:33-34; Heb 6:10).

See Alms; Beneficence; Charitableness; Giving; Minister; Poor, Duty to; Rich, The; Riches; Tithes.

Instances of:

King of Sodom to Abraham (Ge 14:21). Jacob, consecrating the tenth of his income (Ge 28:22). Pharaoh to Joseph's people (Ge 45:18-20). Israelites at the building of the tabernacle (Ex 35:21-29; 36:3-7; 38:8; Nu 7; 31:48-54; Jos 18:1). Reubenites (Jos 22:24-29). David (Ps 132:1-5; 2Sa 7:2; 1Ch 17:1; 2Sa 8:11; 1Ki 7:51; 8:17-18; 1Ch 21:24; 22; 26:26; 28:2; 29:2-5, 17). Barzillai and others to David (2Sa 17:27-29; 19:32). Araunah for sacrifice (2Sa 24:22-23). Joab to David (2Sa 12:26-28).

Israelites' offerings for the temple 1Ch 29:6-9, 16-17). Samuel (1Ch 26:27-28). Solomon (1Ki 4:29; 5:4-5; 2Ch 2:1-6; 1Ki 6; 7:51; 8:13). Queen of Sheba to Solomon (1Ki 10:10). Asa and Abijah (1Ki 15:15). Elisha toward Elijah (1Ki 19:21). Jehoshaphat (2Ki 12:18). Joash and his people (2Ki 12:4-14; 2Ch 24:4-14). David (1Ch 16:3). Hezekiah (2Ch 29; 30:1-12; 31:1-10, 21). Manasseh (2Ch 33:16). Josiah (2Ki 22:3-6; 2Ch 34:8-13; 35:1-19).

Jews after the Captivity (Ezr 1:5-6; 2:68-69; 3:2-9; 5:2-6; 6:14-22; 8:25-35; Ne 3; 4:6; 6:3; 7:70-72; 10:32-39; 13:12, 31; Hag 1:12-19). Cyrus (Ezr 1:2-4, 7-11; 3:7; 5:13-15; 6:3). Darius (Ezr 6:7-12). Artaxerxes (Ezr 7:13-27; 8:24-36).

The Magi (Mt 2:11). Centurion (Lk 7:4-5). Mary Magdalene (Lk 8:2-3). The good Samaritan (Lk 10:33-35). Poor widow (Lk 21:2-4). Christians in Jerusalem (Ac 2:44-45; 4:32-37), in Antioch (Ac 11:29), at Philippi (Php 4:18), Corinth (2Co 8:19; 9:1-13), Macedonia (2Co 8:1-4). People of Malta to Paul (Ac 28:10).

LIBERTINES *See Freedman.*

LIBERTY Freedom, whether physical, moral, or spiritual. Israelites who had becomes slaves were freed in the Year of Jubilee (Lev 25:8-17). Through Christ's death and resurrection the believer is free from sin's dominion (Jn 1:29; 8:36; Ro 6-7), Satan's control (Ac 26:18), the law (Gal 3), fear, the second death, future judgment.

Of Hebrew Servants:

In the seventh year (Ex 21:2; Dt 15:12; Jer 34:14), in Year of Jubilee (Lev 25:10, 40).

Political: (Ac 22:28).

Religious: In Rome (Ac 28:31).

Spiritual: (Ps 119:45; Isa 61:1; Lk 4:18; Jn 8:32-33, 36; Ro 6:6, 22; 8:1-2; 1Co 7:22; 2Co 3:17; Gal 2:4; 1Pe 2:16).

Figurative: Of the gospel (Jas 1:25; 2:12).

LIBNAH (*white*).

1. A station of the Israelites in the desert (Nu 33:20).

2. A city of Judah, captured by Joshua (Jos 10:29-32, 39; 12:15). Allotted to the priests (Jos 21:13; 1Ch 6:57). Sennacherib besieged; his army defeated near (2Ki 19:8, 35; Isa 37:8-36).

L

LIBNATH *See Shihor Libnath.*

LIBNI, LIBNITE(S) (*[descendant of] Libni* or *white*).

1. Son of Gershon (Ex 6:17; Nu 3:18; 1Ch 6:17, 20). Descendants called Libnites (Nu 3:21; 26:58).

2. Grandson of Merari (1Ch 6:29).

LIBRARIES Libraries, both public and private, were not uncommon in ancient times in the Oriental, Greek, and Roman worlds. The Dead Sea Scrolls are one example of an ancient library that has survived to modern times.

LIBYA, LIBYANS A people of N Africa, W of Egypt, who were allies of Egypt (2Ch 12:3; 16:8; Eze 30:5; 38:5; Da 11:43; Ac 2:10). Also called Put. *See Put, 2.*

LICE *See Gnat.*

LICENTIOUSNESS *See Adultery; Lasciviousness.*

LIEUTENANTS *See Satrap; Secretary.*

LIFE Breath of (Ge 2:7). Called breath of God (Job 27:3). Tree of (Ge 2:9; 3:22, 24; Pr 3:18; 13:12; Rev 2:7). Sacredness of, an inference from what is taught in the law concerning murder. *See Homicide.* Meaninglessness of (Ecc 1-7).

Length of:

Long life promised (Ge 6:3; Ps 91:16), to Solomon (1Ki 3:11-14), to the wise (Pr 3:16; 9:11), to the obedient (Dt 4:40; 22:7; Pr 3:1-2), to those who honor parents (Ex 20:12; Dt 5:16), to those who show kindness to animals (Dt 22:7), given to those who fear God (Pr 10:27; Isa 65:20).

See Longevity.

Brevity of (Ge 47:9; Job 10:9, 20-21; 13:12, 25, 28; Ps 89:47-48; 90:10; 146:4; Isa 2:22). Compared, to a shadow (1Ch 29:15; Job 8:9; 14:1-2; Ps 102:11; 144:3; 144:4; Ecc 6:12). To a weaver's shuttle (Job 7:6-10). To a courier (Job 9:25-26). To a handbreadth (Ps 39:4-5, 11). To a wind (Ps 78:39). To grass (Ps 90:3, 5-6, 9-10; 102:11; 103:14-16; Isa 40:6-8, 24; 51:12; Jas 1:10-11; 1Pe 1:24). To a leaf (Isa 64:6). To a vapor (Jas 4:14).

Weary of: Job (Job 3; 7:1-3; 10:18-19). Jeremiah (Jer 20:14-18), Elijah (1Ki 19:1-4), Jonah (Jnh 4:8), Paul (Php 1:21-24).

See Suicide.

Hated (Ecc 2:17). To be hated for Christ's sake (Lk 14:26). What shall a man give in exchange for (Mt 16:26; Mk 8:37). He that loses it for Christ's sake shall save it (Mt 10:39; 16:25-26; Lk 9:24; Jn 12:25).

Uncertainty of (1Sa 20:3; Job 4:19-21; 17:1; Pr 27:1; Lk 12:20). End of, certain (2Sa 14:14; Ps 22:29; Ecc 1:4; Isa 38:12).

See Death, Physical.

Comes From God:

(Ge 2:7; Dt 8:3; 30:20; 32:39; 1Sa 2:6; Job 27:3; Ps 30:3; 104:30; Ecc 12:7; Isa 38:16; Ac 17:25, 28; Ro 4:17; 1Ti 6:13; Jas 4:15).

Spiritual Life:

(Dt 8:3). From Christ (Jn 1:4; 6:27, 33, 35; 10:10; 17:2-3; Ro 6:11; 8:10; Col 3:4). Through faith (Jn 3:14-16; 5:24-26, 40; 6:40, 47; 11:25-26; 20:31; Gal 2:19-20). Signified, in figure of new birth

(Jn 3:3-8; Tit 3:5). In figure of death, burial, and resurrection (Ro 6:4-8).

Everlasting Life:
(Ps 21:4; 121:8; 133:3; Isa 25:8; Da 12:2; Mt 19:16-21, 29; 25:46; Mk 10:17-21, 29-30; Lk 18:18-22, 29-30; 20:36; Jn 3:14-16, 36; 4:14; 5:24-25, 29, 39; 6:27, 40, 47, 50-58, 68; 10:10, 27-28; 12:25, 50; 17:2-3; Ac 13:46, 48; Ro 2:7; 5:21; 6:22-23; 1Co 15:53-54; 2Co 5:1; Gal 6:8; 1Ti 1:16; 4:8; 6:12, 19; 2Ti 1:10; Tit 1:2; 3:7; 1Jn 2:25; 3:15; 5:11-13, 20; Jude 21; Rev 1:18).
See Immortality.

LIFE, THE BOOK OF Figurative expression denoting God's record of those who inherit eternal life (Php 4:3; Rev 3:5; 21:27).

LIGHT

Physical:
Created (Ge 1:3-5; Ps 74:16; Isa 45:7; 2Co 4:6). Miraculous (Ex 13:21; Dt 1:33; Mt 17:2; Mk 9:3; Lk 9:29; Ac 9:3; 12:7; 26:13).

Figurative:
(1Ki 11:36). Of the Lord (Ps 27:1; Isa 60:19-20; Jas 1:17; 1Jn 1:5, 7; 2:8-10). Of the Lord's word (Ps 119:105; Pr 6:23). Of personal influence for righteousness (Mt 5:14-16; Mk 4:21; Lk 8:16). Of the righteous (Lk 16:8; Eph 5:8, 14; Php 2:15; 1Th 5:5). Of John the Baptist (Jn 5:35). Of spiritual understanding (Isa 8:20; Lk 1:33-36; 2Co 4:6). Of the gospel (2Co 4:4, 6). Of spiritual wisdom (Ps 119:130; Isa 2:5; 2Pe 1:19). Of righteousness (Mt 5:16; Ac 26:18; 1Pe 2:9). Of heavenly glory (Rev 21:23).

Of Christ's heavenly glory (1Ti 6:16). Of Christ's kingdom (Isa 58:8). Of the Savior (Isa 49:6; Mal 4:2; Mt 4:16; Lk 2:32; Jn 1:4-5, 7-9; 3:19-21; 8:12; 9:5; 12:35-36, 46; Rev 21:23).

LIGHTNING (Job 28:26; 37:3; 38:25, 35; Ps 18:14; 77:18; 78:48; 97:4; 135:7; 144:6; Jer 10:13; 51:16; Eze 1:13-14; Da 10:6; Na 2:4; Zec 9:14; 10:1; Mt 24:27; 28:3; Lk 10:18; Rev 4:5; 8:5; 11:19; 16:18). Plague of, sent upon Egypt (Ex 9:23; Ps 77:18; 78:48; 105:32).

LIGN ALOES *See Aloes.*

LIGURE *See Jacinth.*

LIKHI (*take, marry*). Manassite (1Ch 7:19).

LILY The principal capitals of the temple ornamented with carvings of (1Ki 7:19, 22, 26). Molded on the rim of the bronze Sea in the temple (1Ki 7:26; 2Ch 4:5). Lessons of trust gathered from (Mt 6:28-30; Lk 12:27).
Figurative of the lips of the beloved (SS 5:13).

LIME (Isa 33:12; Am 2:1).

LINE Usually a measuring line (2Sa 8:2; Ps 78:55), a portion (Ps 16:6), sound made by a musical chord (Ps 19:4).

LINE OF JUDGMENT The divine (2Ki 21:13; Isa 28:17; 34:11; La 2:8; Am 7:8).

LINEN Exported from Egypt (1Ki 10:38; Eze 27:7), from Syria (Eze 27:16). Curtains of the tabernacle made of (Ex 26:1; 27:9). Robes of priests made of (Ex 28:5-8, 15, 39-42), of royal households made of (Ge 41:42; Est 8:15). Garments for men made of (Ge 41:42; Eze 9:2; Lk 16:19), for women (Isa 3:23; Eze 16:10-13). Bedding made of (Pr 7:16). Mosaic law forbade its being mingled with wool (Lev 19:19; Dt 22:11). The body of Jesus wrapped in (Mk 15:46; Jn 20:5).

Figurative:
Pure and white, of righteousness (Rev 15:6; 19:8, 14).

LINTEL Horizontal beam forming the upper part of the doorway (Ex 12:22-23).

LINUS A Christian at Rome (2Ti 4:21).

LION

General:
King of beasts (Mic 5:8). Fierceness of (Job 4:10; 28:8; Ps 7:2; Pr 22:13; Jer 2:15; 49:19; 50:44; Hos 13:8). The roaring of (Ps 22:13; Pr 20:2). Strength of (Pr 30:30; Isa 38:13; Joel 1:6). Instincts of, in taking prey (Ps 10:9; 17:12; La 3:10; Am 3:4; Na 2:12). Lair of, in the jungles (Jer 4:7; 25:38).

Kept in captivity (Da 6). Sent as judgment upon the Samaritans (2Ki 17:25-26). Slain by Samson (Jdg 14:5-9), David (1Sa 17:34, 36), Benaiah (2Sa 23:20), saints (Heb 11:33). Disobedient prophet slain by (1Ki 13:24-28), an unnamed person slain by (1Ki 20:36). Used for the torture of criminals (Da 6:16-24; 7:12; 2Ti 4:17).

The bases in the temple ornamented by moldings of (1Ki 7:29, 36). Twelve statues of, on the stairs leading to Solomon's throne (1Ki 10:19-20). Samson's riddle concerning (Jdg 14:14, 18). Proverb of (Ecc 9:4). Parable of (Eze 19:1-9).

Figurative:
Of a ruler's wrath (Pr 19:12; Jer 5:6; 50:17; Hos 5:14), of Satan (1Pe 5:8), of divine judgments (Isa 15:9).

Symbolic:
(Ge 49:9; Isa 29:1; Eze 1:10; 10:14; Da 7:4; Rev 4:7; 5:5; 9:8, 17; 13:2).

LITIGATION To be avoided (Mt 5:25; Lk 12:58; 1Co 6:1-8). *See Actions at Law; Adjudication at Law; Arbitration; Compromise.*

LITTER *See Wagon.*

LITTLE EVILS So called (Pr 6:10; Ecc 10:1; SS 2:15; 1Co 5:6).

LITTLE OWL *See Birds.*

LIVER Considered center of life and feeling (Pr 7:23), used especially for sacrifice (Ex 29:13) and divination (Eze 21:21).

LIVERY *See Dress; Land, Conveyance of.*

LIVING CREATURES Possibly identical with cherubim (Eze 1:5-22; 3:13; Rev 4:6-9).

LIVING GOD Title emphasizing the reality and existence of the true God (Dt 5:26; Jos 3:10; 1Sa 17:26; Ps 42:2; 84:2; Isa 37:17; Jer 23:36; Da 6:26; Mt 26:63; Ac 14:15; 1Th 1:9; Heb 10:31; Rev 7:2).

LIZARD Unclean; not permitted as food (Lev 11:29-30; Pr 30:28).

LO-AMMI (*not my people*). Symbolic naming for Hosea's third child to represent a break in the covenant relationship between the Lord and Israel (Ex 6:7; Jer 7:23). This break would later be restored (Hos 1:9-10, ftn; 2:1, 23). The warnings became more severe in moving from the first to the third child. *See Lo-Ruhamah; Ruhamah.*

LO DEBAR (*no pasture*). A city in Manasseh (2Sa 9:4-5; 17:27). Home of Mephibosheth, the lame son of Jonathan (2Sa 9:3-5).

LOAVES Miracle of the five (Mt 14:15-21; 16:9; Mk 6:37-44; Lk 9:12-17; Jn 6:5-13), of the seven (Mt 15:34-38; 16:10; Mk 8:1-10). *See Bread.*

LOBBYING To frustrate rebuilding the temple (Ezr 4:4-5).

LOCK Beams of wood or iron used for fastening gates or doors (SS 5:5; Lk 11:7).

LOCUST Authorized as food (Lev 11:22), used as (Mt 3:4; Mk 1:6). Plague of (Ex 10:1-19; Ps 105:34-35). Devastation by (Dt 28:38; 1Ki 8:37; 2Ch 7:13; Isa 33:4; Joel 1:4-7; Rev 9:7-10). Sun obscured by (Joel 2:2, 10). Instincts of (Pr 30:27).
See Grasshopper.
Figurative (Jer 46:23).
Symbolic (Rev 9:3-10).

LOD A city in Benjamin (1Ch 8:12; Ezr 2:33; Ne 7:37; 11:35). Called Lydda (Ac 9:38).

LODGE Temporary shelter built in a garden for a watchman guarding ripening fruit (Isa 1:8).

LOFT *See Upper Chamber, Upper Room.*

LOG A measure for liquids, holding about a pint (Lev 14:10, 12, 15, 24).

LOGIA Greek word for the nonbiblical sayings of Christ, such as those in the so-called Gospel of Thomas discovered in 1945.

LOGOS Usually rendered "word," in the Johannine writings it also appears as a title of Jesus: "The Word" (Jn 1:1ff; 1Jn 1:1; Rev 19:13). In the OT God creates by the word (Ge 1:3; Ps 33:9). In the Judaism of NT times, "word" was used as a way of referring to God himself. In Greek philosophy, "word" refers to the dynamic principle of reason operating in the world and forming a medium of communion between God and man. *See Jesus the Christ, Names, Appellations, and Titles of; Logos.*

LOIN Part of the body between the ribs and thighs (Lev 3:4, 10, 15), vulnerable (Dt 33:11), a seat of strength (Job 40:16).

LOIS (perhaps *more desirable, better*). Grandmother of Timothy, commended by Paul for her faith (2Ti 1:5).

LONGEVITY (Ge 6:3; Ps 90:10).

Promised:
To the obedient under the old covenant (Ex 20:12; Dt 4:40; 22:7). To the righteous (Job 5:26; Ps 21:4; 34:11-13; 91:16; Pr 3:2, 16; 9:11; 10:27; Isa 65:20; 1Pe 3:10-11). To Solomon (1Ki 3:11-14).

Instances of:
Adam, 930 years (Ge 5:5). Seth, 912 years (Ge 5:8). Enos, 905 years (Ge 5:11). Kenan, 910 years (Ge 5:14). Mahalalel, 895 years (Ge 5:17). Jared, 962 years (Ge 5:20). Enoch, 365 years (Ge 5:23). Methuselah, 969 years (Ge 5:27). Lamech, 777 years (Ge 5:31). Noah, 950 years (Ge 9:29). Shem (Ge 11:11). Arphaxad (Ge 11:13). Shelah (Ge 11:15). Eber (Ge 11:17). Peleg (Ge 11:19). Reu (Ge 11:21). Serug (Ge 11:23). Nahor (Ge 11:25). Terah, 205 years (Ge 11:32). Sarah, 127 years (Ge 23:1). Abraham, 175 years (Ge 25:7). Isaac, 180 years (Ge 35:28). Jacob, 147 years (Ge 47:28). Joseph, 110 years (Ge 50:26). Amram, 173 years (Ex 6:20). Aaron, 123 years (Nu 33:39). Moses, 120 years (Dt 31:2; 34:7). Joshua, 110 years (Jos 24:29). Eli, 98 years (1Sa 4:15). Barzillai, 80 years (2Sa 19:32). Job, 140 years (Job 42:16). Jehoiada, 130 years (2Ch 24:15). Anna, 84 years (Lk 2:36-37). Paul (Phm 9).
See Life; Old Age.

LONGSUFFERING (1Ti 1:16). A Christian grace (1Co 13:4, 7; 2Co 6:4-6; Gal 5:22; Col 1:11; 2Ti 3:10; 4:2). Commanded (Eph 4:2; Col 3:12-13).
See Charitableness; God, Longsuffering of; Patience.

LOOKING BACKWARD Toward the old life (Ge 19:17, 26; Nu 11:5; 14:4; Lk 9:62).

LOOKING GLASS *See Mirror.*

LORD A term applied to both men and God, expressing varied degrees of honor, dignity, and majesty; applied also to idols (Ex 22:8; Jdg 2:11, 13), used of Jesus as Messiah (Ac 2:36; Php 2:9-11; Ro 1:4; 14:8). *See God, Names of; Titles and Names; Yahweh.*

LORD'S DAY The day especially associated with the Lord Jesus Christ; a day consecrated to the Lord; the first day of the week, commemorating the resurrection of Jesus (Jn 20:1-25; Rev 1:10) and the pouring out of the Spirit (Ac 2:1-41), set aside for worship (Ac 20:7).

LORD'S PRAYER Prayer taught by Jesus as a model of how his disciples should pray (Mt 6:9-13; Lk 11:2-4).

LORD'S SUPPER Instituted by Christ on the night of his betrayal immediately after the Passover Feast to be a memorial of his death and a visible sign of the blessings of the new covenant.

Variously called: Body and blood of Christ (Mt 26:26, 28), communion of the body and blood of Christ (1Co 10:16), bread and cup of the Lord (1Co 11:27), breaking of bread (Ac 2:42; 20:7), Lord's Supper (1Co 11:20).
Not to be observed unworthily (1Co 11:27-32).
See Eucharist.

LO-RUHAMAH (*no compassion*). Symbolic name given to Hosea's daughter (Hos 1:6, 8; 2:4, 23). The naming represents a reversal of the love (compassion) that God had earlier shown to Israel (Ex 33:19; Dt 7:6-8) but was later promised again (Hos 2:23). *See Lo-Ammi; Ruhamah.*

LOST SHEEP Parable of (Mt 18:12-13; Lk 15:4-7).

LOST, THE *See Wicked, Punishment of.*

LOT The son of Haran. Accompanies Terah from Ur of the Chaldeans to Haran (Ge 11:31). Migrates with Abraham to the land of Canaan (Ge 12:4). Accompanies Abraham to Egypt; returns with him to Bethel (Ge 13:1-3). Rich in flocks, herds, and servants; separates from Abraham and locates in Sodom (Ge 13:5-14). Taken captive by Kedorlaomer; rescued by Abraham (Ge 14:1-16). Providentially saved from destruction in Sodom (Ge 19; Lk 17:28-29). Righteous (2Pe 2:7-8). Disobediently protests against going to the mountains, and chooses Zoar (Ge 19:17-22). His wife disobediently longs after Sodom, and becomes a pillar of salt (Ge 19:26; Lk 17:32). Commits incest with his daughters (Ge 19:30-38). Descendants of. *See Ammonite(s); Moabite(s).*

LOT, THE (Pr 16:33; 18:18; Isa 34:17; Joel 3:3). The scapegoat chosen by (Lev 16:8-10).

The land of Canaan divided among the tribes by (Nu 26:55; Jos 15; 18:10; 19:51; 21; 1Ch 6:61, 65; Eze 45:1; 47:22; 48:29; Mic 2:5; Ac 13:19). Saul chosen king by (1Sa 10:20-21). Priests and Levites designated by, for sanctuary service (1Ch 24:5-31; 26:13; Ne 10:34; Lk 1:9). Used after the Captivity (Ne 11:1). An apostle chosen by (Ac 1:26). Achan's guilt discovered by (Jos 7:14-18), Jonathan's (1Sa 14:41-42), Jonah's (Jnh 1:7). Used to fix the time for the execution of condemned persons (Est 3:7; 9:24). The garments of Jesus divided by (Ps 22:18; Mt 27:35; Mk 15:24; Jn 19:23-24).
For Feast of, *See Casting Lots; Purim.*

LOTAN (*of Lot*). Son of Seir (Ge 36:20, 22, 29).

LOTS, CASTING *See Casting Lots; Lot, The.*

LOTUS A water plant (Job 40:21-22). *See Plants of the Bible.*

LOVE (1Co 13; 14:1; Col 1:8; 2:2; 1Th 1:3; 5:8; 1Ti 6:11; 2Ti 1:7; Phm 5; Heb 10:24; 1Jn 4:7, 16-18).

The theme of the Song of Songs, and often allegorized representing the love of God for Israel, of the Messiah for the church and of his church for the Messiah (SS 1-8). *See Church, Loved.*

Love of Person for Person:
(Ro 5:7; Jas 1:27). Defined (1Co 13:1-13). In the parable of the good Samaritan (Lk 10:25-37). Is edifying (1Co 8:1). Is precious (Pr 15:17). Is unquenchable (Pr 17:17; SS 8:6-7). Is a fruit of the Spirit (Gal 5:22). Promotes peace (Pr 10:12; 17:9). A proof, of discipleship of Jesus (Jn 13:34-35), of regeneration (1Jn 3:14, 19).

Commanded—
(Lev 19:18; Mt 5:40-42; 7:12; 19:19; 22:39-40; Mk 12:30-33; Lk 6:30-38; Ro 12:9, 15; 13:8-10; 1Co 10:24; 16:14; Gal 6:1-2, 10; Eph 4:2, 32; 5:2; Php 1:9; Col 3:14; 1Th 3:12; 1Ti 1:5; 4:12; 6:11; 2Ti 2:22; Jas 2:8; 2Pe 1:7; 1Jn 4:20-21). Toward strangers (Lev 19:34; Dt 10:19). Toward enemies (Pr 24:17; Mt 5:43-48; Lk 6:35; Ro 12:14, 20). Toward fellow Christians (Jn 13:14-15, 34-35; 15:12-13, 17; Ro 12:9-10, 15-16; 14:19, 21; 15:1-2, 5, 7; 16:1-2; 1Co 14:1; 2Co 8:7-8; Gal 5:13-14; 6:1-2, 10; Eph 4:2, 32; Php 2:2; Col 2:2; 3:12-14; 1Th 3:12; 5:8, 11, 14; 1Ti 6:2; Phm 16; Heb 10:24; 13:13; 1Pe 1:22; 2:17; 3:8-9; 4:8; 2Pe 1:7; 1Jn 3:11, 14, 16-18, 19, 23; 4:7, 11-12, 20-21; 2Jn 5). Demonstrated by obedience (1Jn 5:1-2).
Rewards of (Mt 10:41-42; 25:34-40, 46; Mk 9:41; 1Jn 2:10).

Instances of—
Abraham for Lot (Ge 14:14-16). Moses for Israel (Ex 32:31-32). David and Jonathan (1Sa 18:1; 20:17). Israel for David (1Sa 18:16). David's subjects for David (2Sa 15:30; 17:27-29). Hiram for David (1Ki 5:1). Obadiah for the prophets (1Ki 18:4). Nehemiah for Israelites (Ne 5:10-18). Job's friends (Job 42:11). Centurion for his servant (Lk 7:2-6). Good Samaritan (Lk 10:29-37). Stephen (Ac 7:60). Roman Christians for Paul (Ac 28:15). Priscilla and Aquila for Paul (Ro 16:3-4).

Exemplified by Paul (Ac 26:29; Ro 1:11-12; 9:1-3; 1Co 4:9-16; 8:13; 2Co 1:3-6, 14, 23-24; 2:4; 3:2; 4:5; 6:4-6, 11-13; 7:1-4; 11:2; 12:14-16, 19-21; 13:9; Gal 4:19-20; Eph 3:13; Php 1:3-5, 7-8, 23-26; 2:19; 4:1; Col 1:3-4, 24, 28-29; 2:1, 5; 4:7; 1Th 2:7-8, 11-12, 17-20; 3:5, 7-10, 12; 2Th 1:4; 2Ti 1:3-4, 8; 2:10; Tit 3:15; Phm 9, 12, 16).
See Brother; Fraternity; Friendship; Golden Rule.

Love of Man for Woman:
Isaac for Rebekah (Ge 24:67). Jacob for Rachel (Ge 29:20, 30). Shechem for Dinah (Ge 34:3, 12). Boaz for Ruth (Ru 2-4).

Love of People for God:
Defined (1Jn 5:3; 2Jn 6). Incompatible with love of the world (1Jn 2:15), with hatred of brother (1Jn 4:20-21), with guilty fear (2Ti 1:7; 1Jn 4:18). Reasons for (Ps 116:1; 1Jn 4:19).

The gift of God (Dt 30:6; 2Ti 1:7). Through the Holy Spirit (Ro 5:5).

Commanded (Dt 6:5; 10:12; 11:1, 13, 22; 19:9; 30:16, 19-20; Jos 22:5; 23:11; Ps 31:23; Pr 23:26; Mt 22:37-38; Mk 12:29-30, 32-33; Lk 11:42; 2Th 3:5; Jude 21). Tested (Dt 13:3). Obedience proof of (1Jn 2:5; 5:1-2; 2Jn 6).

Leads to generosity (1Jn 3:17-18), hate of evil (Ps 97:10), love from God (Ps 8:1-8). Rewards of (Ex 20:6; Dt 5:10; 7:9; Ps 37:4; 69:35-36; 91:14; 145:20; Isa 56:6-7; Jer 2:2-3; Ro 8:28; 1Co 8:3).

Exemplified (Ps 18:1; 63:5-6; 73:25-26; 103).

Love of People for Jesus:

Commanded (Mt 10:37-38; Jn 15:9; 1Co 16:22). Love of God produces (Jn 8:42). Obedience results from (Jn 14:15, 21, 23; 2Co 5:6, 8, 14-15).

Rewards of (Mt 25:34-40, 46; Mk 9:41; Lk 7:37-50; Jn 16:27; Eph 6:24; 2Ti 4:8; Heb 6:10; Jas 1:12; 2:5).

Instances of—

Mary (Mt 26:6-13; Lk 10:39; Jn 12:3-8). Peter (Mt 17:4; Jn 13:37; 18:10; 20:3-6; 21:15-17). The healed demoniac (Mk 5:18; Lk 8:38). Thomas (Jn 11:16). The disciples (Mk 16:10; Lk 24:17-41; Jn 16:27; 20:20). Mary Magdalene and other disciples (Mt 27:55-56, 61; 28:1-9; Lk 8:2-3; 23:27, 55-56; 24:1-10; Jn 20:1-2, 11-18). Joseph of Arimathea (Mt 27:57-60). Nicodemus (Jn 19:39-40). Women of Jerusalem (Lk 23:27). Paul (Ac 21:13; Php 1:20-21, 23; 3:7-8; 2Ti 4:8). Philemon (Phm 5). Early Christians (1Pe 1:8; 2:7), lost that love (Rev 2:4).

Of Children for Parents: *See Children.*

Of God: *See God, Love of.*

Of Jesus: *See Jesus the Christ, Love of.*

Of Money:

A root of all kinds of evil (1Ti 6:10). *See Avarice; Riches.*

Of Parents for Children: *See Parents.*

LOVE FEAST (*agape feast*). A common meal eaten by early Christians in connection with the Lord's Supper to express and deepen brotherly love (1Co 11:18-22, 33-34; Jude 12).

LOVERS

Instances Within or Resulting in Marriage:

Isaac and Rebekah (Ge 24:67). Jacob and Rachel (Ge 29:20, 30). Boaz and Ruth (Ru 2-4). The beloved and her lover (SS 1-8).

Instances Outside of Marriage:

Shechem and Dinah (Ge 34:3, 12). Gomer and her lovers (Hos 1-3).

Figurative of Disloyalty to Yahweh:

Israel and pagan gods (Jer 3:1-2; Hos 2). Jerusalem and political allies (La 1:2; Eze 16:33-42; 23).

LOVING-KINDNESS The kindness and mercy of God toward people (Ps 17:7; 26:3).

LOYALTY Commanded (Ex 22:28; Nu 27:20; Ezr 6:10; 7:26; Job 34:18; Pr 24:21; Ecc 8:2; 10:4; Ro 13:1; Tit 3:1). Enforced (Ezr 10:8; Pr 17:11). Disloyalty (2Pe 2:10). *See Patriotism.*

Instances of:

Israelites (Jos 1:16-18; 2Sa 3:36-37; 15:23, 30; 18:3; 21:17; 1Ch 12:38). David (1Sa 24:6-10; 26:6-16; 2Sa 1:14). Uriah (2Sa 11:9). Ittai (2Sa 15:21). Hushai (2Sa 17:15-16). David's soldiers (2Sa 18:12-13; 23:15-16). Joab (2Sa 19:5-6). Barzillai (2Sa 19:32). Jehoiada (2Ki 11:4-12). Mordecai (Est 2:21-23).

LUBIM(S) *See Libya, Libyans; Put, 2.*

LUCAS *See Luke.*

LUCIFER Latin for "morning star" (Isa 14:12); a title of the king of Babylon, often understood as a reference to the devil. *See Devil; Satan.*

LUCIUS

1. A Christian at Antioch (Ac 13:1).
2. A relative of Paul (Ro 16:21).

LUD A son of Shem (Ge 10:22; 1Ch 1:17).

LUDITES Descendants of Mizraim (Ge 10:13; 1Ch 1:11). Perhaps the same as the Lydians. *See Lydia, Lydians.*

LUHITH A city of Moab (Isa 15:5; Jer 48:5).

LUKE A disciple. A physician (Col 4:14). Wrote to Theophilus (Lk 1:1-4; Ac 1:1-2). Accompanies Paul in his tour of Asia and Macedonia (Ac 16:10-13; 20:5-6), to Jerusalem (Ac 21:1-18), to Rome (Ac 27:28; 2Ti 4:1; Phm 24).

LUKE, GOSPEL OF

Author: Traditionally Luke, the companion of Paul

Date: The two most commonly suggested periods for dating the Gospel of Luke are: (1) A.D. 59-63, and (2) the 70s or the 80s.

Outline:

I. The Preface (1:1-4).
II. The Coming of Jesus (1:5-2:52).
  A. The Annunciations (1:5-56).
  B. The Birth of John the Baptist (1:57-80).
  C. The Birth and Childhood of Jesus (ch. 2).
III. The Preparation of Jesus for His Public Ministry (3:1-4:13).
  A. His Forerunner (3:1-20).
  B. His Baptism (3:21-22).
  C. His Genealogy (3:23-38).
  D. His Temptation (4:1-13).
IV. His Ministry in Galilee (4:14-9:9).
  A. The Beginning of the Ministry in Galilee (4:14-41).
  B. The First Tour of Galilee (4:42-5:39).
  C. A Sabbath Controversy (6:1-11).
  D. The Choice of the Twelve Apostles (6:12-16).
  E. The Sermon on the Plain (6:17-49)
  F. Miracles in Capernaum and Nain (7:1-18).
  G. The Inquiry of John the Baptist (7:19-29).
  H. Jesus and the Pharisees (7:30-50).
  I. The Second Tour of Galilee (8:1-3).
  J. The Parables of the Kingdom (8:4-21).
  K. The Trip Across the Sea of Galilee (8:22-39).
  L. The Third Tour of Galilee (8:40-9:9).
V. His Withdrawal to Regions Around Galilee (9:10-50).
  A. To the Eastern Shore of the Sea of Galilee (9:10-17).
  B. To Caesarea Philippi (9:18-50).
VI. His Ministry in Judea (9:51-13:21).
  A. Journey Through Samaria to Judea (9:51-62).
  B. The Mission to the Seventy (10:1-24).
  C. The Lawyer and the Parable of the Good Samaritan (10:25-37).
  D. Jesus at Bethany With Mary and Martha (10:38-42).
  E. Teachings in Judea (11:1-13:21).
VII. His Ministry in and Around Perea (13:22-19:27).
  A. The Narrow Door (13:22-30).
  B. Warning Concerning Herod (13:31-35).
  C. At a Pharisee's House (14:1-23).
  D. The Cost of Discipleship (14:24-35).
  E. The Parables of the Lost Sheep, the Lost Coin and the Prodigal Son (ch. 15).
  F. The Parable of the Shrewd Manager (16:1-18).
  G. The Rich Man and Lazarus (16:19-31).
  H. Miscellaneous Teachings (17:1-10).
  I. Ten Healed of Leprosy (17:11-19).
  J. The Coming of the Kingdom (17:20-37).
  K. The Persistent Widow (18:1-8).
  L. The Pharisee and the Tax Collector (18:9-14).
  M. Jesus and the Children (18:15-17).
  N. The Rich Young Ruler (18:18-30).
  O. Christ Foretells His Death (18:31-34).
  P. A Blind Beggar Given His Sight (18:35-43).
  Q. Jesus and Zacchaeus (19:1-10).
  R. The Parable of the Ten Minas (19:11-27).
VIII. His Last Days: Sacrifice and Triumph (19:28-24:53).
  A. The Triumph Entry (19:28-44).
  B. The Cleansing of the Temple (19:45-48).
  C. The Last Controversies With the Jewish Leaders (ch. 20).
  D. The Olivet Discourse (ch. 21).
  E. The Last Supper (22:1-38).
  F. Jesus Praying in Gethsemane (22:39-46).
  G. Jesus' Arrest (22:47-65).
  H. Jesus on Trial (22:66-23:25).
  I. The Crucifixion (23:26-56).
  J. The Resurrection (24:1-12).
  K. The Post-Resurrection Ministry (24:13-49).
  L. The Ascension (24:50-53).

See Acts of the Apostles; Synoptic Gospels, The.

LUKEWARMNESS Instances of: The Reubenites and other tribes, when Deborah called on them to assist Sisera (Jdg 5:16-17). Israel (Hos 10:2). The Jews (Ne 3:5; 13:11; Hag 1:2-11). The church, at Pergamum (Rev 2:14-16), Thyatira (Rev 2:20-24), Sardis (Rev 3:1-3), Laodicea (Rev 3:14-16).

See Backsliding; Blindness, Spiritual; Complacency.

LUNACY *See Insanity; Demons.*

LUST (*evil desires*). Sinful (Job 31:9-12; Mt 5:28). Worldly (1Jn 2:16-17). Chokes the word (Mk 4:19). Tempts to sin (Ge 3:6; Jas 1:14-15; 2Pe 2:18).

Forbidden (Ex 20:17; Pr 6:24-25; Ro 13:14; Eph 4:22; Col 3:5; 1Th 4:5; Tit 2:12; 1Pe 2:11). Warnings against (1Co 10:6-7; 2Ti 2:22).Wicked under power of (Jn 8:44; Ro 1:24, 26-27; 1Ti 6:9; Jas 4:1-3; 1Pe 4:3; 2Pe 3:3; Jude 16, 18). Of Israelites (Ps 106:13-14).

The righteous restrain (1Co 9:27).

See Adultery; Covetousness; Homosexual; Incest; Lasciviousness; Sensuality.

LUTE Stringed instrument used to accompany songs of praise (1Sa 18:6; 2Ch 20:28). *See Music, Instruments of.*

LLUZ (*almond tree*).

1. Town on N boundary of Benjamin (Jos 16:2; 18:13).
2. Hittite town (Jdg 1:26).

LYCAONIA A province of Asia Minor. Paul visits towns of (Ac 14:6-21; 16:1-2).

LYCIA A province of Asia Minor. Paul visits (Ac 27:5).

LYDDA Called also Lod. A city of Benjamin (1Ch 8:12; Ezr 2:33; Ne 11:35). Peter heals Aeneas in (Ac 9:32-35).

LYDIA, LYDIANS

1. A woman of Thyatira, who with her household, was converted through the preaching of Paul (Ac 16:14-15). Entertains Paul and Silas (Ac 16:15, 40).

2. A country and people in the N Africa or Asia Minor; mercenary warriors (Isa 66:19; Jer 46:9; Eze 27:10; 30:5). Perhaps the same as the Ludites. *See Ludites.*

LYING Lying spirit from God (1Ki 22:21-23; 2Ch 18:20-22). *See Falsehood; Hypocrisy; Liars.*

LYRE Used in religious services (2Sa 6:5; 1Ch 13:8; 16:5; 25:1, 5-6; 2Ch 29:25; Ps 33:2; 57:8; 71:22; 81:2; 92:3; 108:2; 144:9; 150:3). At the dedication of the new wall when the captives returned (Ne 12:27). Used in idolatrous worship (Da 3:5, 7, 10, 15).

See Music, Instruments of.

LYSANIAS A tetrarch (Lk 3:1).

LYSIAS Chief captain of Roman troops in Jerusalem (Ac 24:7, ftn; 24:22). *See Claudius Lysias.*

LYSTRA A city of Lycaonia to which Paul and Barnabas fled from persecutions in Iconium (Ac 14:6-23; 2Ti 3:11). Church of, elders ordained for, by Paul and Barnabas (Ac 14:23). Timothy a resident of (Ac 16:1-4).

M

MAACAH (perhaps *dull, stupid*).

1. Son of Nahor (Ge 22:24).
2. Mother of Absalom (2Sa 3:3; 1Ch 3:2).
3. Father of Achish, king of Gath (1Sa 27:2). Possibly the same as Maoch. (1Ki 2:39).
4. Mother of Abijah and grandmother of Asa (1Ki 15:2, 10-13; 2Ch 11:20-23; 15:16). Also called Micaiah (2Ch 13:2, ftn).
5. Wife of Makir (1Ch 7:15-16).
6. Concubine of Caleb (1Ch 2:48).
7. Wife of Jeiel (1Ch 8:29; 9:35).
8. Father of Hanan (1Ch 11:43).
9. Father of Shephatiah (1Ch 27:16).
10. A small kingdom E of Bashan. *See Maacathite(s).*

MAACATHITE(S) People of the nation of Maacah, in the region of Bashan (Dt 3:14; Jos 12:5; 13:11; 2Sa 10:6, 8; 23:34; 1Ch 4:19; 19:6-7).

MAADAI (*ornaments*). Israelite who married a foreign woman (Ezr 10:34).

MAADIAH *See Moadiah.*

MAAI (*to be compassionate*). Priest who blew trumpet at dedication of wall (Ne 12:36).

MAALEH-ACRABBIM *See Scorpion Pass.*

MAARATH (*barren*). A city of Judah (Jos 15:59).

MAASAI (*work of Yahweh*). Priestly family after the Exile (1Ch 9:12).

MAASEIAH, MAHSEIAH (*Yahweh is a refuge*).

1. Levite musician (1Ch 15:18, 20).
2. Army captain who assisted Jehoiada in overthrowing Athaliah (2Ch 23:1).
3. Officer of Uzziah (2Ch 26:11).
4. Son Ahaz, king of Judah (2Ch 28:7).
5. Governor of Jerusalem in Josiah's reign (2Ch 34:8).
6. A priest who married a foreigner (Ezr 10:18).
7. A priest who married a foreigner (Ezr 10:21).
8. A priest who married a foreigner (Ezr 10:22).
9. Israelite who married a foreigner (Ezr 10:30).
10. Father of Azariah (Ne 3:23).
11. Priest; assistant of Ezra (Ne 8:4).
12. Man who explained law to people (Ne 8:7).
13. Chief who sealed covenant with Nehemiah (Ne 10:25).
14. Descendant of son of Baruch (Ne 11:5).
15. Benjamite (Ne 11:7).
16. Priest who blew trumpet at dedication of temple (Ne 12:41).

MAATH (*to be small*). An ancestor of Jesus (Lk 3:26).

MAAZ (perhaps *angry* or *wrath*). A son of Ram (1Ch 2:27).

MAAZIAH (*Yahweh is a refuge*).

1. A priest (1Ch 24:18).
2. A priest who sealed the covenant with Nehemiah (Ne 10:8).

MACBANNAI (*clad with a cloak*). A Gadite warrior (1Ch 12:13).

MACBENAH (*bond*). A descendant of Caleb (1Ch 2:49). "Father of" may mean "founder of" or "leader of" a city.

MACCABEES (*hammer*). Hasmonean Jewish family of Modein (or Modin) that led revolt against Antiochus Epiphanes, king of Syria, and won freedom for the Jews. The family consisted of the father, Mattathias, an aged priest, and his five sons: Johanan, Simon, Judas, Eleazar, and Jonathan. The name Maccabee was first given to Judas, perhaps because he inflicted sledgehammer blows against the Syrian armies, and later was also used for his brothers. The revolt began in 168 B.C. The temple was recaptured and sacrifices were resumed in 165 B.C. The cleansing of the temple and resumption of sacrifices have been celebrated annually ever since in the Feast of Dedication. The Maccabees served as both high priests and kings. The story of Maccabees is told in two books of the Apocrypha, I and II Maccabees.

The following were the most prominent of the Maccabees: Judas (166-160 B.C.), Jonathan (160-142 B.C.), Simon (142-134 B.C.), John Hyrcanus (134-104 B.C.), Aristobulus (104-103 B.C.), Alexander Jannaeus (103-76 B.C.), Alexandra (76-67 B.C.), Aristobulus II (66-63 B.C.). In 63 B.C. the Romans took over when Pompey conquered the Israelites.

See Dedication; Feasts; Hanukkah; Kislev; Month, 9; Testaments, Time Between.

MACEDONIA A province in N Greece. Paul has a vision concerning (Ac 16:9), preaches in, at Philippi (Ac 16:12), revisits (Ac 20:1-6; 2Co 2:13; 7:5). Church at, sends contributions to the poor in Jerusalem (Ro 15:26; 2Co 8:1-5). Timothy visits (Ac 19:22). Disciples in (Ac 19:22; 27:2).

MACEDONIAN EMPIRE, THE Called the kingdom of Greece (Da 11:2).

Illustrated by the:
Bronze part of the image in Nebuchadnezzar's dream (Da 2:32, 39). Leopard with four wings and four heads (Da 7:6, 17). Shaggy goat with notable horn (Da 8:5-8, 21). Philippi the chief city of (Ac 16:12).

Predictions Respecting:
Conquest of the Medo-Persian kingdom (Da 8:6-7; 11:2-3). Power and greatness of Alexander its last king (Da 8:8; 11:3). Division of it into four kingdoms (Da 8:8, 22). Divisions of it ruled by strangers (Da 11:4). History of its four divisions (Da 11:4-29). The little horn to arise out of one of its divisions (Da 8:8-12). Gospel preached in, by God's desire (Ac 16:9-10). Liberality of the churches of (2Co 8:1-5).

MACHAERUS Fortress stronghold built by Alexander Janneus (c. 90 B.C.) and used as a citadel by Herod Antipas; located on E of Dead Sea; John the Baptist was put to death there (Mt 14:3ff).

MACHI *See Maki.*

MACHIR *See Makir.*

MACHPELAH (*double [cave]*). The burying place of Sarah, Abraham, Isaac, Rebekah, Leah, and Jacob (Ge 23:9, 17-20; 25:9; 49:30-31; 50:13; Ac 7:16).

MACNADEBAI (possibly *possession of Nebo*). Israelite who divorced foreign wife (Ezr 10:40).

MADAI (*Medes*). People descended from Japheth (Ge 10:2; 1Ch 1:5).

MADMANNAH (*dung place*).
1. Town in S Judah eight miles S of Kiriath Sepher (Jos 15:31).
2. Grandson of Caleb (1Ch 2:48-49).

MADMEN (sounds like *be silenced*).
1. A place (Jer 48:2).
2. A maniac, of insane persons (1Sa 21:15). *See Insanity.*

MADMENAH (*dunghill*). City of Benjamin (Isa 10:31).

MADNESS *See Insanity; Madmen.*

MADON (*contention*). Canaanite city near modern Qarn Hattin (Jos 11:1; 12:19).

MAGADAN Town on the NW shore of Sea of Galilee, three miles N of Tiberias. Also called Magdala, the home of Mary Magdalene (Mt 15:39). Mark (8:10) has "Dalmanutha." *See Dalmanutha.*

M

MAGBISH (perhaps *thick*). Name of man or place (Ezr 2:30).

MAGDALA *See Dalmanutha; Magadan.*

MAGDALENE (*of Magdala*). *See Mary, 3.*

MAGDIEL (*choice gift of God [El]*). Chief of Edom (Ge 36:43; 1Ch 1:54).

MAGGOT Infested leftover manna (Ex 16:20, 24). Synonymous with "worm" (Job 25:6). *See Animals.*

MAGI Originally a religious caste among the Persians; devoted to astrology, divination, and interpretation of dreams. Later the word came to be applied generally to fortune-tellers and exponents of esoteric religious cults throughout the Mediterranean world (Ac 8:9; 13:6, 8). Nothing is known of the Magi of the Nativity story (Mt 2); they may have come from S Arabia.

MAGIC The art or science of influencing or controlling the course of nature, events, and supernatural powers through occult science of mysterious arts (Ge 41:8; Ex 7:11, 22; 8:7, 18; Ac 19:19). Includes necromancy, exorcism, dreams, shaking arrows, inspecting entrails of animals, divination, sorcery, astrology, soothsaying, divining by rods, witchcraft (1Sa 28:8; Eze 21:21; Ac 16:16).

MAGICIAN A person who claims to understand and explain mysteries by magic (Da 1:20). Failed to interpret Pharaoh's dreams (Ge 41:8, 24), Nebuchadnezzar's (Da 2:2-13; 4:7). Worked apparent miracles (Ex 7:11-12, 22; 8:7, 18).

MAGISTRATE(S) An officer of civil law (Jdg 18:7; Ezr 7:25; Lk 12:11, 58; Ac 16:20, 22, 35, 38). Obedience to, commanded (Tit 3:1).
See Government; Rulers.

MAGNA CARTA *See Constitution.*

MAGNANIMITY Instances of: Joshua and the elders of Israel to the Gibeonites who had deceived the Israelites (Jos 9:3-27). Of Moses. *See Moses.* David to Saul (1Sa 24:3-11). Ahab to Ben-Hadad (1Ki 20:32-34).
See Charitableness.

MAGNIFICAT Song of praise by Mary (Lk 1:46-55).

MAGOG (perhaps *land of Gog*).
1. Son of Japheth (Ge 10:2; 1Ch 1:5).
2. Land of God.
Various identifications: Scythians, Lydians, Tartars of Russia. Used symbolically for forces of evil (Rev 20:7-9).

MAGOR-MISSABIB (*terror on every side*). A symbolic name given by Jeremiah to Pashhur (Jer 20:3-6).

MAGPIASH (*moth killer*). Israelite who sealed covenant with Nehemiah (Ne 10:20).

MAGUS, SIMON *See Simon, 8.*

MAHALAH *See Mahlah, 2.*

MAHALALEL (*praise of God [El]*).
1. Son of Kenan (Ge 5:12-17; 1Ch 1:2; Lk 3:37).
2. A man of Judah (Ne 11:4).

MAHALATH (*the suffering of affliction* NIV; *sickness or suffering poem, JB*).
1. Daughter of Ishmael (Ge 28:9).
2. Wife of Rehoboam (2Ch 11:18).
3. Musical term in the titles of Pss 53 and 88. Possibly the name of a tune. The Hebrew appears to be the word for "suffering" or "sickness." Perhaps the Hebrew phrase indicates here that the psalm is to be used in a time of affliction, when the godless mock. *See Music, Symbols Used in.*

MAHALI *See Mahli, 1.*

MAHANAIM (*double camp*). The place where Jacob had the vision of angels (Ge 32:2). The town of, allotted to Gad (Jos 13:26, 30). One of the Levitical cities (Jos 21:38). Ish-Bosheth establishes himself at, when made king over Israel (2Sa 2:8-12). David lodges at, during Absalom's rebellion (2Sa 17:27-29; 1Ki 2:8).

MAHANEH DAN (*camp of Dan*).
1. Place between Zorah and Eshtaol (Jdg 13:25).
2. Place W of Kiriath Jearim (Jdg 18:12).

MAHARAI (*impetuous* ISBE). One of David's warriors (2Sa 23:28; 1Ch 11:30; 27:13).

MAHATH (perhaps *tough*).
1. Kohathite; ancestor of Heman (1Ch 6:35).
2. Levite who helped Hezekiah (2Ch 29:12; 31:13).

MAHAVITE (*villagers*). Family name of Eliel, one of David's warriors (1Ch 11:46).

MAHAZIOTH (*visions*). Son of Heman (1Ch 25:4, 30).

MAHER-SHALAL-HASH-BAZ (*quick to the plunder, swift to the spoil*). Symbolic name Isaiah gave his son (Isa 8:1, 3).

MAHLAH (perhaps *weak one*).
1. Daughter of Zelophehad (Nu 26:33; 27:1ff; 36; Jos 17:3ff).
2. Grandson of Manasseh (1Ch 7:18).

MAHLI (perhaps *shrewd, cunning*).
1. Son of Merari (Ex 6:19; 1Ch 6:19; Ezr 8:18).
2. Son of Mushi (1Ch 6:47; 23:23; 24:30).

MAHLITE(S) Descendant of Mahli, son of Merari (Nu 3:33; 26:58; 1Ch 23:22).

MAHLON (*sick*). Son of Naomi and first husband of Ruth (Ru 1:2, 5; 4:9-10).

MAHOL (*place of round-dancing*). Father of Heman, Calcol, and Darda (1Ki 4:31).

MAID(S), MAIDSERVANT(S)
1. Female slave or servant (Ge 12:16; 16:1; Lk 12:45).
2. Female personal servant or attendant (Ge 24:61; 1Sa 25:42; Est 2:9).
See Servant.

MAIDEN(S)
1. Young woman (Ps 68:25; 148:12).
2. Young woman of marriageable age, probably a virgin (Ge 24:43; Ps 78:63; Isa 62:5; Jer 2:32).

MAIL
1. Sending of letters (2Sa 11:14-15; 1Ki 21:8-11; 2Ki 5:5-7; Est 3:13; 8:10; 2Pe 3:16). *See Letter; Letters.*
2. Armor (1Sa 17:5). *See Armor.*

MAIMED Not acceptable as sacrifices (Lev 22:22). *See Disease.*

MAJESTY Name of God (Heb 1:3; 8:1). *See God.*

MAJORITY AND MINORITY REPORTS Of the spies (Nu 13:26-33; 14:6-10).

MAKAZ A place in Judah (1Ki 4:9).

MAKHELOTH (*assemblies*). An encampment of Israel (Nu 33:25-26).

MAKI (perhaps *reduced* or *bought*). Gadite; father of Geuel, one of 12 spies (Nu 13:15).

MAKIR, MAKIRITE (*bought*).
1. One of the sons of Manasseh (Ge 50:23). Father of the Makirites (Nu 26:29; 36:1). The land of Gilead allotted to (Nu 32:39-40; Dt 3:15; Jos 13:31). Certain cities of Bashan given to (Jos 13:31; 17:1).
2. A man of Lo Debar who took care of Jonathan's lame son, Mephibosheth (2Sa 9:4-5; 17:27).

MAKKEDAH (*locality of shepherds*). A city in Judah, conquered by Joshua (Jos 10:28; 12:16). Five kings of the Amorites hide in a cave of, and are slain by Joshua (Jos 10:5, 16-27).

MAKTESH (*mortar*). A district where merchants traded (Zep 1:11, ftn). *See Agora; Market.*

MALACHI (*my messenger* or *messenger of Yahweh*). Prophet of Judah who lived c. 450-400 B.C.; author of OT book which bears his name; nothing known of him beyond what is said in his book; contemporary of Nehemiah (Mal 2:11-17; Ne 13:23-31).

MALACHI, BOOK OF

Author: The prophet Malachi

Date: c. 433 to 400 B.C.

Outline:
I. Title (1:1).
II. Introduction: God's Covenant Love for Israel Affirmed (1:2-5).
III. Israel's Unfaithfulness Rebuked (1:6-2:16).
A. The Unfaithfulness of the Priests (1:6-2:9).
1. They dishonor God in their sacrifices (1:6-14).
2. They do not faithfully teach the law (2:1-9).
B. The Unfaithfulness of the People (2:10-16).
IV. The Lord's Coming Announced (2:17-4:6).
A. The Lord Will Come to Purify the Priests and Judge the People (2:17-3:5).
B. A Call to Repentance in View of the Lord's Coming (3:6-18).
1. An exhortation to faithful giving (3:6-12).
2. An exhortation to faithful service (3:13-18).
C. The Day of the Lord Announced (ch. 4).
See Prophets, The Minor.

MALCAM (*their king* ISBE KB; or *[servant of] Malk [pagan god]*).
1. A Benjamite (1Ch 8:9).
2. Either Molech, a god of the Moabites and Ammonites (Jer 49:1, 3; Am 1:15; Zep 1:5, ftns) or their king; maybe both. *See Molech.*

MALCHIAH, MALCHIJAH *See Malkijah.*

MALCHIEL *See Malkiel.*

MALCHIJAH *See Malkijah, 2, 3, 4, 7, 11, 12.*

MALCHIRAM *See Malkiram.*

MALCHI-SHUA *See Malki-Shua.*

MALCHUS (*king*). Servant of the high priest; Peter assaults in Gethsemane; healed by Jesus (Mt 26:51; Mk 14:47; Lk 22:50-51; Jn 18:10).

MALEFACTOR *See Criminals.*

MALELEEL *See Mahalalel, 1.*

MALFEASANCE IN OFFICE Illustrated in the Parables of Jesus: The tenants of the vineyard (Mk 12:1-8; Lk 20:9-15). The rich man's manager (Lk 16:1-7).

MALICE

Characteristics:
Outgrowth of original sin (Ge 3:15). Is hated by God (Pr 6:16-19). Reacts (Job 15:35; Ps 7:15-16; 10:7, 14; Jer 20:10). Blinds those possessed of (1Jn 2:9-11; 4:20). Is murderous (1Jn 3:13-15). Preludes divine forgiveness (Mt 6:15; 18:28-35).
Is forbidden (Lev 19:14, 17-18; 2Ki 6:21-22; Pr 20:22; 24:17-18, 29; Zec 7:10; 8:17; Mt 5:38-41; Lk 6:29; Ro 12:19; 1Co 5:8; 14:20; Eph 4:31; Col 3:8; 1Th 5:15; 1Pe 2:1; 3:9). The wicked filled with (Dt 32:32-33; Ps 10:7-10, 14; Pr 4:16-17; 6:14; 21:10; 30:14; Isa 59:4-6; Mt 13:25, 28; Jn 8:44; Ro 1:29-32; Gal 5:19-21; Tit 3:3; 3Jn 10). Punishment for (Dt 27:17-18; Pr 6:14-15; 17:5; 28:10; Isa 29:20-21; 32:6; Eze 18:18; 26:2-3; 28:3, 6-7, 12-17; Am 1:11; Mic 2:1; Mt 26:52; Jas 2:13).
Proverbs concerning (Pr 4:16-17; 6:14-16, 18-19; 10:6, 12; 11:17; 12:10; 14:17, 22; 15:17; 16:30; 17:5; 20:22; 21:10; 24:8, 17-18, 29; 26:2, 27; 28:10; 30:14).

Instances of:
Cain toward Abel (Ge 4:8; 1Jn 3:12). Ishmael toward Sarah (Ge 21:9). Sarah toward Hagar (Ge 21:10). Philistines toward Isaac (Ge 26:12-15, 18-21). Esau toward Jacob (Ge 27:41-42). Joseph's brothers toward Joseph (Ge 37:2-28; 42:21; Ac 7:9-10). Potiphar's wife toward Joseph (Ge 39:14-20). Ammonites toward the Israelites (Dt 23:3-4). Saul toward David (1Sa 18:8-29; 19; 20:30-33; 22:6-23; 23:7-28; 26:1-2, 18). David toward Michal (2Sa 6:21-23), toward Joab (1Ki 2:5-6), toward Shimei (1Ki 2:8-9). Shimei toward David (2Sa 16:5-8). Ahithophel toward David (2Sa 17:1-3). Jezebel toward Elijah (1Ki 19:1-2). Ahaziah toward Elijah (2Ki 1:7-15). Jehoram toward Elisha (2Ki 6:31). Samaritans toward the Jews (Ezr 4; Ne 2:10; 4:6). Haman toward Mordecai (Est 3:5-15; 5:9-14). Not practiced by Job (Job 31:29-30). The psalmist's enemies (Ps 22:7-8; 35:15-16, 19-21; 38:16, 19; 41:5-8; 55:3; 56:5-6; 57:4, 6; 59:3-4, 7; 62:3-4; 64:2-6; 69:4, 10-12, 26; 86:14; 102:8; 109:2-5, 16-18; 140:1-4); the psalmist demands retribution (Ps 10:7-10, 14; 70:2-3; 71:10-13, 24). Jeremiah's enemies (Jer 26:8-11; 38:1-6). Nebuchadnezzar toward Zedekiah (Jer 52:10-11). Daniel's enemies (Da 6:4-15).
Herodias toward John (Mt 14:3-11; Mk 6:24-28). James and John toward the Samaritans (Lk 9:54). Enemies of Jesus (Ps 22:11; Mt 27:18, 27-30, 39-43; Mk 12:13; 15:10-11, 16-19, 29-32; Lk 11:53-54; 23:10-11, 39; Jn 18:22-23). Paul's enemies (Ac 14:5, 19; 16:19-24; 17:5; 19:24-35; 21:27-31, 36; 22:22-23; 23:12-15; 25:3; Php 1:15-17).
See Conspiracy; Hatred; Homicide; Jealousy; Persecution; Retaliation; Revenge.

MALINGERING Instances of: David feigning madness (1Sa 21:13-15), the sluggard (Pr 6:9-11).

MALKIEL, MALKIELITE (*God [El] is [my] king*). An Asherite; son of Beriah (Ge 46:17; Nu 26:45; 1Ch 7:31).

MALKIJAH (*Yahweh is [my] king*).
1. Gershonite (1Ch 6:40).
2. Ancestor of Adaiah (1Ch 9:12; Ne 11:12).
3. Priest (1Ch 24:9).
4. Israelite who married a foreigner (Ezr 10:25).
5. Another who married a foreigner (Ezr 10:25).

6. Another who married a foreigner (Ezr 10:31).
7. Son of Harim (Ne 3:11).
8. Son of Recab (Ne 3:14).
9. Goldsmith (Ne 3:31).
10. Man who assisted Ezra (Ne 8:4).
11. Israelite who sealed covenant with Nehemiah (Ne 10:3).
12. Priest (Ne 12:42). May be same as 11.
13. Father of Pashhur who helped arrest Jeremiah (Jer 21:1; 38:1).

MALKIRAM (*[my] king is exalted*). Son of Jehoiachin (1Ch 3:18).

MALKI-SHUA (*[my] king saves*). Son of King Saul (1Sa 14:49; 31:2; 1Ch 8:33; 9:39; 10:2).

MALLOTHI (*my expression*). Son of Heman, a singer (1Ch 25:4, 26).

MALLOWS *See Salt Herbs.*

MALLUCH (*counselor* ISBE; *king* KB).
1. Levite; ancestor of Ethan (1Ch 6:44).
2. Man who married foreign woman (Ezr 10:29).
3. Another such man (Ezr 10:32).
4. Priest who returned with Zerubbabel (Ne 10:4; 12:2).
5. Chief of people who sealed covenant (Ne 10:27).
6. Head of a priestly family (Ne 12:14).

MALTA An island in the Mediterranean. Paul shipwrecked there (Ac 28:1-10).

MAMMON (*wealth*). Aramaic word for riches (Mt 6:24; Lk 16:11, 13).

MAMRE (*strength*).
1. A plain near Hebron. Abraham resides in (Ge 13:18; 14:13), entertains three angels and is promised a son (Ge 18:1-15). Isaac lives in (Ge 35:27).
2. An Amorite and confederate of Abraham (Ge 14:13, 24).

MAN *See Mankind.*

MAN OF SIN *See Antichrist(s).*

MAN, SON OF A phrase used by God in addressing Daniel (Da 8:17) and Ezekiel (over eighty times), by Daniel in describing a person he saw in a night vision (Da 7:13-14), and many times by Jesus when referring to himself, undoubtedly identifying himself with the Son of Man of Daniel's prophecy and emphasizing his union with mankind (Lk 9:26; 19:10; 22:48; Jn 6:62).
See Jesus the Christ, Son of Man; Son of Man.

MANAEN (*comforter*). An associate of Herod in his youth, and a Christian teacher (Ac 13:1).

MANAHATH (*resting place*).
1. Son of Shobal (Ge 36:23; 1Ch 1:40).
2. A city in Benjamin (1Ch 8:6).

MANAHATHITES (*of Manahath*).
1. Descendants of Shobal, son of Caleb (1Ch 2:52).
2. Descendants of Salma, son of Caleb (1Ch 2:54).

MANASSEH (*one that makes to forget*).
1. Son of Joseph and Asenath (Ge 41:50-51; 46:20), adopted by Jacob on his deathbed (Ge 48:1, 5-20).
2. Tribe of. Descendants of Joseph. The two sons of Joseph, Ephraim and Manasseh, were reckoned among the primogenitors of the twelve tribes, taking the places of Joseph and Levi.
Adopted by Jacob (Ge 48:5). Prophecy concerning (Ge 49:25-26). Enumeration of (Nu 1:34-35; 26:29-34). Place of in camp and march (Nu 2:18, 20; 10:22-23). Blessing of Moses on (Dt 33:13-17). Inheritance of one-half of the tribe E of the Jordan (Nu 32:33, 39-42). One-half of the tribe W of the Jordan (Jos 16:9; 17:5-11). The eastern half assist in the conquest of the country W of the Jordan (Dt 3:18-20, Jos 1:12 15; 4:12-13). Join the other eastern tribes in erecting a monument to testify to the unity of all Israel; misunderstood; makes satisfactory explanation (Jos 22). Join Gideon in war with the Midianites (Jdg 6-7). Malcontents of, join David (1Ch 12:19, 31). Smitten by Hazael (2Ki 10:33). Return from the Captivity (1Ch 9:3). Reallotment of territory to, by Ezekiel (Eze 48:4). Affiliate with the Israelites in the reign of Hezekiah (2Ch 30). Incorporated into kingdom of Judah (2Ch 15:9; 34:6-7). 144,000 from (Rev 7:6).
See Israel, Tribes of.
3. The father of Gershom (Jdg 18:30).
4. King of Judah. History of (2Ki 21:1-18; 2Ch 33:1-20; Mt 1:10).
5. Two Jews who put away their Gentile wives after the Captivity (Ezr 10:30, 33).

MANASSES *See Manasseh.*

MANASSITES (*forgetting*). Descendants of Joseph's son Manasseh (Ge 41:51).

MANDRAKE (Ge 30:14-16; SS 7:13).

MANEH *See Mina.*

MANGER Stall or trough for feeding livestock (Job 39:9; Pr 14:4; Isa 1:3; Lk 2:7-16).

MANKIND

Created:
Male and Female (Ge 1:26-27; 2:7; 5:1-2; Dt 4:32; Job 4:17; 10:2-3, 8-9; 31:15; 33:4; 34:19; 35:10; 36:3; Ps 8:5; 100:3; 119:73; 138:8; 139:14-15; Ecc 7:29; Isa 17:7; 42:5; 43:7; 45:12; 64:8; Jer 27:5; Zec 12:1; Mal 2:10; Mt 19:4; Mk 10:6; Heb 2:7).
A little lower than the angels (Job 4:18-21; Ps 8:5; Heb 2:7-8), than God (Ps 8:5). Above other creatures (Mt 10:31; 12:12).

Design of:
To have dominion over all creation (Ge 1:26, 28; 2:19-20; 9:2-3; Ps 8:6-8; Jer 27:6; 28:14; Da 2:38; Heb 2:7-8; Jas 3:7). For the glory and pleasure of God (Pr 16:4; Isa 43:7).
Equality of all people (Job 21:26; 31:13-15; Ps 33:13-15; Pr 22:2; Mt 20:25-28; 23:8-10; 23:11; Mk 10:42-44; Ac 10:28, 34-35; 17:26). Equality under the gospel (Gal 3:28). *See Race, 1.*
Mortal (Job 4:17; Ecc 2:14-15; 3:20; 1Co 15:21-22; Heb 9:27). *See Immortality.* Insignificance of (Ge 6:3; 18:27; Job 4:18-19; 7:17; 15:14; 22:2-5; 25:2-6; 35:2-8; 38:4, 12-13; Ps 8:3-4; 78:39; 144:3-4).
A spirit (Job 4:19; 14:10; 32:8; Ps 31:5; Pr 20:27; Ecc 1:8; 3:21; 12:7; Isa 26:9; Zec 12:1; Mt 4:4; 10:28; 26:41; Mk 14:38; Lk 22:40; 23:46; 24:39; Jn 3:3-8; 4:24; Ac 7:59; Ro 1:9; 2:29; 7:14-25; 1Co 2:11; 6:20; 7:34; 14:14; 2Co 4:6-7, 16; 5:1-9; Eph 3:16; 4:4; 1Th 5:23; Heb 4:12; Jas 2:26).
See Duty; Ignorance; Neighbor; Women; Young Men.

MANNA (*What is it?; possibly food*). Miraculously given to Israel for food in the wilderness (Ex 16:4, 15; Ne 9:15).

Called:
God's manna (Ne 9:20). Bread of heaven (Ps 105:40). Bread from heaven (Ps 78:24). Angel's food (Ps 78:25). Spiritual food (1Co 10:3). Previously unknown (Dt 8:3, 16).

Described as:
Like coriander seed (Ex 16:31; Nu 11:7). White (Ex 16:31). Like in, color to resin (Nu 11:7), taste to wafers made with honey (Ex 16:31), taste to oil (Nu 11:8). Like frost (Ex 16:14). Fell after the evening dew (Nu 11:9). None fell on the Sabbath (Ex 16:26-27). Gathered every morning (Ex 16:21). An omer of, gathered for each person (Ex 16:16). Two portions of, gathered the sixth day on account of the Sabbath (Ex 16:5, 22-26). He that gathered much or little had sufficient and nothing left over (Ex 16:18). Melted away by the sun (Ex 16:21).

Given:
When Israel murmured for bread (Ex 16:2-3). In answer to prayer (Ps 105:40). Through Moses (Jn 6:31-32). To exhibit God's glory (Ex 16:7). As a sign of Moses' divine mission (Jn 6:30-31). For forty years (Ne 9:21). As a test of obedience (Ex 16:4). To teach that man does not live by bread only (Dt 8:3, w Mt 4:4). To humble and prove Israel (Dt 8:16). If kept longer than a day (except on the Sabbath) began to spoil (Ex 16:19-20).

The Israelites:
At first covetous of (Ex 16:17). Ground, made into cakes and baked in pans (Nu 11:8). Counted, inferior to food of Egypt (Nu 11:4-6). Loathed (Nu 21:5). Punished for despising (Nu 11:10-20). Punished for loathing (Nu 21:6). Ceased when Israel entered Canaan (Ex 16:35; Jos 5:12).

Illustrative of:
Christ (Jn 6:32-35). Blessedness given to saints (Rev 2:17). A golden pot of, laid up in the holiest for a memorial (Ex 16:32-34; Heb 9:4).

MANNERS Polite social customs. Obeisance to strangers (Ge 18:2; 19:1). Standing while guests eat (Ge 18:8), in presence of superiors (Ge 31:35; Job 29:8), of the aged (Lev 19:32). Courteousness commanded (1Pe 3:8). Rule for guests (Pr 23:1-2; 1Co 10:27). *See Salutations.*

MANOAH (*rest*). A Danite of Zorah and father of Samson (Jdg 13:2-24).

MANSERVANT *See Servant.*

MANSIONS Spacious homes of the rich that offer no protection from God's judgment (Ps 49:14; Isa 5:9; Am 3:15; 5:11).

MANSLAUGHTER *See Fratricide; Homicide; Infanticide; Regicide.*

MANSLAYER A person who has killed another human being accidentally; the manslayer could find asylum in cities of refuge (Nu 35; Dt 4:42; 19:3-10; Jos 20:3). *See Cities of Refuge.*

MANTLE Torn in token of grief (Ezr 9:3; Job 1:20; 2:12). Of Elijah (1Ki 19:19; 2Ki 2:8, 13-14). *See Dress.*

MANURE Used as fertilizer (Isa 25:10; Lk 13:8; 14:34-35).

MANUSCRIPTS, DEAD SEA *See Dead Sea Scrolls.*

MAOCH (*a poor one*). The father of Achish, king of Gath, who protected David (1Sa 27:2; 29:1-11). Possibly the same as Maacah, 2. *See Maacah, 2.*

MAON (*dwelling*).
1. Descendant of Caleb (1Ch 2:42-45).
2. Town S of Hebron (1Sa 23:24-28; 25:1-3).

MAONITES Enemies of Israel (Jdg 10:11-12), possibly from Maon 2, also called Meunim or Meunites. *See Meunim, Meunites.*

MARA (*bitter*). Name Naomi called herself (Ru 1:20).

MARAH (*bitter*). The first station of the Israelites, where Moses made the bitter waters sweet (Ex 15:22-25; Nu 33:8-9).

MARALAH A landmark on the boundary of Zebulun (Jos 19:11).

MARANATHA (*our Lord has come* or *our Lord, come!*). An expression of greeting and encouragement, marking the desire of Christians for the Lord's return (1Co 16:22).

MARBLE (*marble* or *alabaster*). In the temple (1Ch 29:2). Pillars of (Est 1:6; SS 5:15). Merchandise of (Rev 18:12). Mosaics of (Est 1:6).

MARCABOTH *See Beth Marcaboth.*

MARCHESHVAN *See Bul; Month, 8.*

MARCUS *See Mark, John.*

MARDUK Marduk, the chief god of the Babylonians (Jer 50:2).

MARESHAH (perhaps *head place*).
1. A city of Judah (Jos 15:44; 2Ch 11:8; 14:9-10). Birthplace of Eliezer the prophet (2Ch 20:37). Prophecy concerning (Mic 1:15).
2. Father of Hebron (1Ch 2:42).
3. A son of, or possibly a city founded by, Laadah (1Ch 4:21).

MARI Ancient city of Euphrates Valley, discovered in 1933 and subsequently excavated. Twenty thousand cuneiform tablets have been found, throwing much light upon ancient Syrian civilization. Mari kingdom was contemporary with Hammurabi of Babylon and the Amorite tribes of Canaan, ancestors of the Hebrews.

MARINER (1Ki 9:27; 2Ch 8:18; Isa 42:10; Eze 27:27). Perils of (Ps 107:23-30; Jnh 1:5; Ac 27:17-44). Cowardice of (Ac 27:30). *See Commerce; Ship.*

MARK A word with various meanings: a special sign of ownership (Eze 9:4, 6; Rev 7:2-8), signature (Job 31:35), a target (1Sa 20:20), a form of tattooing banned by the Lord (Lev 19:28), a goal to be attained (Php 3:14), a particular brand denoting the nature or rank of men (Rev 13:16).
See Mark, John.

MARK, GOSPEL OF

Author: Anonymous, traditionally John Mark

Date : Possibly in the 50s or early 60s A.D.

Outline:
I. The Beginnings of Jesus' Ministry (1:1-13).
A. His Forerunner (1:1-8).
B. His Baptism (1:9-11).
C. His Temptation (1:12-13).
II. Jesus' Ministry in Galilee (1:14-6:29).
A. Early Galilean Ministry (1:14-3:12).
1. Call of the first disciples (1:14-20).
2. Miracles in Capernaum (1:21-34).
3. A tour of Galilee (1:21-34).
4. Ministry in Capernaum (2:1-22).
5. Sabbath controversy (2:23-3:12).
B. Later Galilean Ministry (3:13-6:29).
1. Selection of the twelve apostles (3:13-19).
2. Teachings in Capernaum (3:20-35).
3. Parables of the kingdom (4:1-34).
4. Trip across the Sea of Galilee (4:35-5:20).
5. More Galilee miracles (5:21-43).
6. Unbelief in Jesus' hometown (6:1-6).
7. Six apostolic teams tour Galilee (6:7-13).
8. King Herod's reaction to Jesus' ministry (6:14-29).
III. Withdrawals From Galilee (6:30-9:32).
A. To the Eastern Shore of the Sea of Galilee (6:30-52).
B. To the Western Shore of the Sea of Galilee (6:53-7:23).
C. To Phoenicia (7:24-30).
D. To the Region of the Decapolis (7:31-8:10).
E. To the Vicinity of Caesarea Philippi (8:11-9:32).
IV. Final Ministry in Galilee (9:33-50).
V. Jesus' Ministry in Judea and Perea (ch. 10).
A. Teaching Concerning Divorce (10:1-12).
B. Teaching Concerning Divorce (10:13-16).
C. The Rich Young Man (10:17-31).
D. Prediction of Jesus' Death (10:32-34).
E. A Request of Two Brothers (10:35-45).
F. Restoration of Bartimaeus's Sight (10:46-52).
VI. The Passion of Jesus (chs. 11-15).
A. The Triumphal Entry (11:12-19).
B. The Cleansing of the Temple (11:12-19).
C. Concluding Controversies With Jewish Leaders (11:20-12:44).
D. The Olivet Discourse Concerning the End of the Age (ch. 13).
E. The Anointing of Jesus (14:1-11).
F. The Arrest, Trial and Death of Jesus (14:12-15:47).
VII. The Resurrection of Jesus (ch. 16).
See Synoptic Gospels, The.

MARK, JOHN (Mark [Latin] *large hammer*, John [Hebrew] *Yahweh is gracious*). Author of the second Gospel. John was his Jewish name, Mark (Marcus) his Roman; called John (Ac 13:5, 13), Mark (Ac 15:39), "John, also called Mark" (Ac 12:12), relative of Barnabas (Col 4:10), accompanied and then deserted Paul on first missionary journey (Ac 12:25; 13:13), went with Barnabas to Cyprus after Paul refused to take him on his second missionary journey (Ac 15:36-39), fellow-worker with Paul (Phm 24), recommended by Paul to church at Colosse (Col 4:10), may have been the young man of Mark 14:51-52. Early tradition makes him the "interpreter" of Peter in Rome and founder of the church in Alexandria.

MARKET A place for general merchandise. Held at gates. *See Gates.* Judgment seat at (Ac 16:19). Trade of, in Tyre, consisted of horses, horsemen, mules, horns, ivory, and ebony, emeralds, purple, embroidered wares, linen, coral, agate, honey, balm, wine, wool, oil, cassia, calamus, charioteers' clothing, lambs, rams, goats, precious stones, and gold, spices, and costly apparel (Eze 27:13-25). *See Agora.*

MAROTH (*bitterness*). A city of Judah (Mic 1:12).

MARRIAGE

General:
Divine institution of (Ge 2:18, 20-24; Mt 19:4-6; Mk 10:7-8; 1Co 6:16; Eph 5:31). Based on principle of creation (1Co 11:11-12; Ge 2:18).
Unity of husband and wife in (Ge 2:23-24; Mt 19:5-6; Mk 10:2-10; 1Co 6:16; Eph 5:31, 33). Obligations under, inferior to duty to God (Dt 13:6-10; Mt 19:29; Lk 14:26). Indissoluble except

M

for adultery (Mal 2:13-16; Mt 5:31-32; Mk 10:11-12; Lk 16:18; Ro 7:1-3; 1Co 7:39-40). Dissolved by death (Mt 22:29-30; Mk 12:24-25; Ro 7:1-3).

Commended (Pr 18:22; Heb 13:4). Commanded of exiled Israelites (Jer 29:6). Commanded because of immorality (1Co 7:1-7).

None in the resurrection state (Mt 22:29-30; Mk 12:24-25). Levirate (the brother required to marry a brother's widow) (Ge 38:8, 11; Dt 25:5-10; Ru 4:5; Mt 22:24-27; Mk 12:19-23; Lk 20:28-33).

Mosaic Laws Concerning:

Of priests (Lev 21:1, 7, 13-15). Captives (Dt 21:10-14). Divorced persons (Dt 24:1-5). A virgin, not pledged to be married, who has been seduced (Ex 22:16-17). Within tribes (Nu 36:8). Incestuous, forbidden (Lev 18:6-18 w Dt 22:30; Lev 20:14, 17, 19-21; Mk 6:17-18).

Among antediluvians (Ge 6:2). Among relatives, Abraham and Sarah (Ge 11:29; 12:13; 20:2, 9-16), Isaac and Rebekah (Ge 24:3-4, 67), Jacob and his wives (Ge 28:2; 29:15-30). Levirate (the brother required to marry a brother's widow) (Ge 38:8, 11; Dt 25:5-10; Ru 4:5; Mt 22:24-27; Mk 12:19-23; Lk 20:28-33).

Intermarriage. *See Intermarry.*

Various Principles:

Parents contract for their children: Hagar selects a wife for Ishmael (Ge 21:21). Abraham for Isaac (Ge 24). Laban arranges for his daughters' marriage (Ge 29). Samson asks his parents to procure him a wife (Jdg 14:2). Parents' consent required in the Mosaic law (Ex 22:17). Presents given to parents to secure their favor (Ge 24:53; 34:12; 1Sa 18:25). Nuptial feasts (Ge 29:22; Jdg 14:12; Est 2:18; Mt 22:11-12). Jesus present at (Jn 2:1-5). Ceremony attested by witnesses (Ru 4:1-11; Isa 8:1-3). Bridegroom exempt one year from military duty (Dt 24:5). Bridal ornaments (Isa 49:18; Jer 2:32). Bridal presents (Ge 24:53). Herald preceded the bridegroom (Mt 25:6). Wedding robes adorned with jewels (Isa 61:10). Festivities attending (Jer 7:34; 16:9; 25:10; Rev 18:23).

Wives obtained by purchase (Ge 29:20, 27-29; 31:41; Ru 4:10; 2Sa 3:14; Hos 3:2; 12:12), by kidnapping (Jdg 21:21-23). Given by kings (1Sa 17:25; 18:17, 27). Daughters given in, as rewards of valor (Jdg 1:12; 1Sa 17:25; 18:27).

Wives taken by edict (Est 2:2-4, 8-14). David gave 100 foreskins for a wife (2Sa 3:14).

Wives among the Israelites must be Israelites (Ex 34:16; Dt 7:3-4; Ezr 9:1-2, 12; Ne 10:30; 13:26-27; Mal 2:11). Betrothal a quasi-marriage (Mt 1:18; Lk 1:27).

Discouraged among the Corinthians (1Co 7:1, 8-9, 25-40). Celibacy deplored (Jdg 11:38; Isa 4:1). Unhappiness in (Pr 21:9, 19).

Marriage of widows (Ro 7:1-3; 1Co 7:39-40; 1Ti 5:14). Marriage of ministers (Lev 21:7-8, 13-14; Eze 44:22; 1Co 9:5; 1Ti 3:2, 12).

Prophecies concerning the forbidding of (1Ti 4:1, 3).

Figurative:

(Isa 54:5; 62:4-5; Jer 3:14; 31:32; Eze 16:8; Hos 2:19-20; Eph 5:23-32; Rev 19:7-9) Parables of (Mt 22:2-10; 25:1-10; Mk 2:19-20; Jn 3:29; 2Co 11:2).

See Bride; Bridegroom; Divorce; Husband; Intermarry; Wife.

M

MARROW Heart of the bone (Job 21:24), used figuratively of good things (Ps 63:5; Isa 25:6).

MARS HILL *See Areopagus.*

MARSENA Counselor of King Xerxes (Est 1:10-14).

MARSH Swamp lands (Eze 47:11).

MARTHA (*a lady, [female] lord*). Sister of Mary and Lazarus (Jn 11:1). Ministers to Jesus (Lk 10:38-42; Jn 12:2). Beloved by Jesus (Jn 11:5).

See Lazarus; Mary, 4.

MARTYR (*witness*). One who dies to bear witness to a cause (Ac 22:20; Rev 17:6).

MARTYRDOM Of prophets (Mt 23:34; Lk 11:50; Rev 16:6). Followers of Jesus exposed to (Mt 10:21-22, 39; 23:34; 24:9; Mk 13:12; Lk 21:16-17). Spirit of, required by Jesus (Mt 16:25; Lk 9:24; Jn 12:25). Possessed by the righteous (Ps 44:22; Ro 8:36; Rev 12:11). Must be based on love (1Co 13:3).

Prophetic reference to (Rev 6:9-11; 11:7-12; 17:6).

See Persecution.

Instances of:

Abel (Ge 4:3-8). Prophets slain by Jezebel (1Ki 18:4, 13). Zechariah (2Ch 24:21-22). John the Baptist (Mk 6:18-28). Jesus. *See Jesus the Christ, Death of.* Stephen (Ac 7:58-60). James the apostle (Ac 12:2). The prophets (Mt 22:6; 23:35; Ro 11:3; 1Th 2:15; Heb 11:32-37).

MARY (perhaps *fat one; See Miriam*).

1. *See Mary, The Virgin.*

2. Mother of James and Joses (Mt 27:56; Mk 15:40; Lk 24:10), probably the wife of Clopas (Jn 19:25), witnessed Crucifixion and visited grave on resurrection morning (Mt 27:56; 28:1).

3. Mary Magdalene; Jesus cast seven demons out of her (Mk 16:9; Lk 8:2), appears at Jesus' crucifixion (Mt 27:55-56; Mk 15:40-41; Jn 19:25), followed body of Jesus to grave (Mt 27:61) and was first to learn of the Resurrection (Mt 28:1-8; Mk 16:9; Lk 24:1-12; Jn 20:1-9, 18). *See Dalmanutha; Magadan.*

4. Mary of Bethany; sister of Lazarus and Martha; lived in Bethany (Jn 11:1), commended by Jesus (Lk 10:42), anointed feet of Jesus (Jn 12:3).

5. Mother of John Mark; sister of Barnabas (Col 4:10), home in Jerusalem meeting place of Christians (Ac 12:12).

6. Christian at Rome (Ro 16:6).

MARY, THE VIRGIN (perhaps *fat one; See Miriam*). Wife of Joseph (Mt 1:18-25), relative of Elizabeth, the mother of John the Baptist (Lk 1:36), of the seed of David (Ac 2:30; Ro 1:3; 2Ti 2:8), mother of Jesus (Mt 1:18, 20; Lk 2:1-20), attended to ceremonial purification (Lk 2:22-38), fled to Egypt with Joseph and Jesus (Mt 2:13-15), lived in Nazareth (Mt 2:19-23), took twelve-year-old Jesus to temple (Lk 2:41-50), at wedding in Cana of Galilee (Jn 2:1-11), concerned for Jesus' safety (Mt 12:46; Mk 3:21, 31ff; Lk 8:19-21), at the cross of Jesus (Jn 19:25ff) where she was entrusted by Jesus to the care of John (Jn 19:25-27), in the Upper Room (Ac 1:14).

Distinctive Roman Catholic doctrines about Mary: Perpetual Virginity, Intercession, Immaculate Conception (1854), and Assumption of Mary (1950).

MASCHIL *See Maskil.*

MASH Variant spelling of Meshech, son of Aram (Ge 10:22-23, ftn). *See Meshech.*

MASHAL Also called Mishal (Jos 19:26; 21:30). *See Mishal.* A Levitical city in Asher (1Ch 6:74).

MASKIL Occurs in the titles of several psalms (Pss 32; 42; 44-45; 52-55; 74; 78; 88-89; 142). The Hebrew word perhaps indicates that these psalms contain instruction in godliness (14:2; 53:2, "any who understand"; 41:1, "he who has regard"; 47:7, ftn).

See Music, Symbols Used in.

MASKING *See Disguises.*

MASON A trade in the time of David (2Sa 5:11), of later times (2Ki 12:12; 22:6; 1Ch 14:1; Ezr 3:7).

MASREKAH (perhaps *vineyard*). Royal city of King Samlah, in Edom (Ge 36:31, 36-37; 1Ch 1:47-48).

MASSA (*burden, oracle*). Tribe descended from Ishmael near Persian Gulf (Ge 25:14; 1Ch 1:30).

MASSACRE Authorized by Moses (Dt 20:13, 16). Decree to destroy the Jews (Est 3).

Instances of: Inhabitants of Heshbon (Dt 2:34), of Bashan (Dt 3:6), of Ai (Jos 8:24-26), of Hazor (Jos 11:11-12), of the cities of the seven kings (Jos 10:28-40). Midianites (Nu 31:7-8). Prophets of Baal (1Ki 18:40). Worshipers of Baal (2Ki 10:18-28). Sons of Ahab (2Ki 10:1-8). Royal family of Athaliah (2Ki 11:1). Inhabitants of Tiphsah (2Ki 15:16). Edomites (2Ki 14:7).

See Captive.

MASSAH (*test, try*). Site of rock in Horeb from which Moses drew water (Ex 17:1-7; Dt 6:16; 9:22), connected with Meribah (Dt 33:8).

MASTER Yahweh called (Jer 31:32, ftn; Hos 2:16). *See Baali.* Jesus called (Mt 8:19; 10:25; 23:8; 26:18, 25, 49; Mk 14:45; Lk 8:24; Jn 13:13-14). Jesus spoke against abuse of the title (Mt 23:8). *See Lord.*

MASTER, OF SERVANTS

Duties to Servants:

Must allow Sabbath rest (Dt 5:14). Compensate (Jer 22:13; Ro 4:4; Col 4:1; 1Ti 5:18). Pay promptly (Lev 19:13; Dt 24:15; Jas 5:4). Forbidden to oppress (Lev 19:13; 25:43; Dt 24:14; Job 31:13-14; Pr 22:16; Mal 3:5). Forbidden to threaten (Eph 6:9). Exhorted to show kindness (Phm 10-16). Exhorted to show wisdom (Pr 29:12, 21).

See Employer; Employee; Hired Servant; Servant.

Good Masters:

Abraham (Ge 18:19). Job (Job 31:13-15). The centurion (Lk 7:2).

Unjust Masters:

Instances of: Sarah to Hagar (Ge 16:6). Laban to Jacob (Ge 31:7). Potiphar's wife to Joseph (Ge 39:7-20). Violent, to be punished (Ex 21:20-21, 26-27).

MASTER CRAFTSMAN Instances of: Tubal-Cain (Ge 4:22), Bezalel (Ex 31:2-11; 35:30-35), Huram or Huram-Abi (1Ki 7:13-50; 2Ch 2:13-14; 4:11-18), Wisdom (Pr 8:30), Paul (1Co 3:10). *See Art.*

MATERIALISM Love of possessions.

Love of money:

A root of all kinds of evil (1Ti 6:10). Insatiable (Ecc 4:7-8; 5:10-11). Forbidden in overseer (1Ti 3:2-3; Tit 1:7). Materialists do not love God (Mt 6:24; 1Jn 2:15-17; 3:17).

Treasures in Heaven Versus Materialism:

(Mt 6:19-21; 1Ti 6:17-19).

See Avarice; Greed; Love, Of Money; Rich, The; Riches.

MATHUSALA *See Methuselah.*

MATRED (perhaps *spear*). Mother of Mehetabel, wife of Hadad (Ge 36:39), who is called "Hadad" (1Ch 1:50).

MATRI (*rainy*). Head of Benjamite family (1Sa 10:21).

MATTAN (*gift*).

1. A priest of Baal slain in the idol temple at Jerusalem (2Ki 11:18; 2Ch 23:17).

2. Father of Shephatiah (Jer 38:1).

MATTANAH (*gift*). Encampment of Israel in wilderness (Nu 21:18-19).

MATTANIAH (*gift of Yahweh*).

1. Original name of King Zedekiah (2Ki 24:17).
2. Chief choir leader and watchman (Ne 11:17; 12:8, 25).
3. Levite (2Ch 20:14).
4. Son of Elam (Ezr 10:26).
5. Son of Zattu (Ezr 10:27).
6. Son of Pahath-Moab (Ezr 10:30).
7. Son of Bani (Ezr 10:37).
8. Grandfather of Hanan (Ne 13:13).
9. Son of Heman; head musician (1Ch 25:4-5, 7, 16).
10. Levite who assisted Hezekiah (2Ch 29:13).

MATTATHA An ancestor of Jesus (Lk 3:31).

MATTATHAH *See Mattattah.*

MATTATHIAS (*gift of Yahweh*).

1. Assistant of Ezra, spelled Mattithiah (Ne 8:4).
2. Name borne by two ancestors of Christ (Lk 3:25-26).
3. Priest; founder of Maccabee family (1Mc 2). *See also, 1Mc 11:70; 16:14-16; 2Mc 14:19.*

MATTATTAH (*gift*). One of the family of Hashum (Ezr 10:33).

MATTENAI (*gift*).

1. Two Israelites who put away their Gentile wives after the Captivity (Ezr 10:33, 37).
2. A priest in the time of Joiakim (Ne 12:19).

MATTHAN (*gift*). Grandfather of Joseph, Mary's husband (Mt 1:15).

MATTHAT (*gift of God*).

1. Father of Heli, ancestor of Joseph (Lk 3:23).
2. Father of Jorim, and ancestor of Joseph (Lk 3:29).

MATTHEW (*gift of Yahweh*). Son of Alphaeus (Mk 2:14), tax collector, also called Levi (Mk 2:14; Lk 5:27), called by Jesus to become disciple (Mt 9:9; Mk 2:14; Lk 5:27) and gave feast for Jesus; appointed apostle (Mt 10:3; Mk 3:18; Lk 6:15; Ac 1:13).

MATTHEW, GOSPEL OF

Author: Anonymous, traditionally the apostle Matthew

Date: Probably in the late 60s A.D.

Outline:

I. The Birth and Early Years of Jesus (chs. 1-2).
  A. His Genealogy (1:1-17).
  B. His Birth (1:18-2:12).
  C. His Sojourn in Egypt (2:13-23).
II. The Beginnings of Jesus' Ministry (3:1-4:11).
  A. His Forerunner (3:1-12).
  B. His Baptism (3:13-17).
  C. His Temptation (4:1-11).
III. Jesus' Ministry in Galilee (4:12-14:12).
  A. The Beginning of the Galilean Campaign (4:12-25).
  B. The Sermon on the Mount (chs. 5-7).
  C. A Collection of Miracles (chs. 8-9).
  D. The Commissioning of the Twelve Apostles (ch. 10).
  E. Ministry Throughout Galilee (chs. 11-12).
  F. The Parables of the Kingdom (ch. 13).
  G. Herod's Reaction to Jesus' Ministry (14:1-12).
IV. Jesus' Withdrawals From Galilee (14:13-17:20).
  A. To the Eastern Shore of the Sea of Galilee (14:13-15:20).
  B. To Phoenicia (15:21-28).
  C. To the Decapolis (15:29-16:12).
  D. To Caesarea Philippi (16:13-17:20).
V. Jesus' Last Ministry in Galilee (17:22-18:35).
  A. Prediction of Jesus' Death (17:22-23).
  B. Temple Tax (17:24-27).
  C. Discourse on Life in the Kingdom (ch. 18).
VI. Jesus' Ministry in Judea and Perea (chs. 19-20).
  A. Teaching Concerning Divorce (19:1-12).
  B. Teaching Concerning Little Children (19:13-15).
  C. The Rich Young Man (19:16-30).
  D. The Parable of the Workers in the Vineyard (20:1-16).
  E. Prediction of Jesus' Death (20:17-19).
  F. A Mother's Request (20:20-28).
  G. Restoration of Sight at Jericho (20:29-34).
VII. Passion Week (chs. 21-27).
  A. The Triumphal Entry (21:1-11).
  B. The Cleansing of the Temple (21:12-17).
  C. The Last Controversies With the Jewish Leaders (21:18-23:39).
  D. The Olivet Discourse Concerning the End of the Age (chs. 24-25).
  E. The Anointing of Jesus' Feet (26:1-13).
  F. The Arrest, Trials and Death of Jesus (26:14-27:66).
VIII. The Resurrection (ch. 28).

See Synoptic Gospels, The.

MATTHIAS (*gift of Yahweh*). Apostle chosen by lot to take place of Judas (Ac 1:15-26), had been follower of Christ (Ac 1:21-22).

MATTITHIAH (*gift of Yahweh*).

1. A Levite who had charge of the baked offerings (1Ch 9:31).
2. A Levite musician (1Ch 15:18, 21; 16:5).
3. A chief of the fourteenth division of temple musicians (1Ch 25:3, 21).
4. An Israelite who divorced his Gentile wife after the Captivity (Ezr 10:43).
5. A prince who stood by Ezra when he read the law to the people (Ne 8:4).

MATTOCK (*cut in, plow*). Single-headed farming tool with point on one side and broad edge on other side (1Sa 13:20-21; Isa 7:25).

MAUL *See Club.*

MAW One of the stomachs of a ruminating animal (Dt 18:3).

MAZZAROTH *See Constellations.*

ME JARKON (*waters of Jarkon [greenish?]*). A city in Dan (Jos 19:46).

MEADOW

1. Place where reeds grow (Ge 41:2, 18).

2. Pastureland (Jdg 20:33).

MEAH NIV "Hundred" (Ne 3:1; 12:38). *See Tower, Of the Hundred.*

MEAL *See Grain.*

MEAL OFFERING *See Offerings.*

MEANINGLESS *See Vanity, 1.*

MEARAH (*cave*). *See Arah, 4.*

MEASURE

False and Just:
Just (Lev 19:35-36; Dt 25:13-16; Pr 16:11).
False (Hos 12:7-9). An abomination (Pr 11:1; 20:10, 23; Mic 6:10-12). *See Dishonesty; Integrity.*

Table of Measures:
See chart to the right.

MEAT *See Food.*

MEAT FORKS Used in the tabernacle (Ex 27:3; 38:3; Nu 4:14; 1Sa 2:13-14). Made of gold (1Ch 28:17), of bronze (2Ch 4:16).

MEAT OFFERING *See Offerings, Meat.*

MEBUNNAI (*well built*). One of David's bodyguards (2Sa 23:27), called Sibbecai (2Sa 21:18).

MECHANIC *See Art; Master Craftsman.*

MECHERATHITE *See Mekerathite.*

MECONAH (*foundation*). A city in Judah (Ne 11:28).

MEDAD (*beloved*). One of the seventy elders who did not go to the tabernacle with Moses, but prophesied in the camp (Nu 11:26-29).

MEDAN (*dissension*). Son of Abraham and Keturah (Ge 25:2; 1Ch 1:32).

MEDDLING *See Busybody; Talebearer.*

MEDEBA A city of Moab (Nu 21:30). An idolatrous high place (Isa 15:2). Allotted to Reuben (Jos 13:9, 16). David defeats army and the Ammonites at (1Ch 19:7-15).

MEDES Inhabitants of Media. Israelites distributed among, when carried to Assyria (2Ki 17:6; 18:11). Palace in the Babylonian province of (Ezr 6:2). An essential part of the Medo-Persian Empire (Est 1:1-19). Supremacy over the Babylonian Empire (Da 5:28, 31; 9:1; 11:1).

MEDIA *See Medes.*

MEDIATION

Between People and God:
(Ex 18:19; Job 9:33; Gal 3:19). Solicited by Israel (Ex 20:19-20; Dt 5:27).
Instances of: By Moses (Ex 32:11-13; 34:9; Nu 14:13-19; 27:5; Dt 5:5; 9:18-20, 25-29). Aaron (Nu 16:47-48). Joshua (Jos 7:6-9). Samuel (1Sa 8:10, 21). David (2Sa 24:17).

Between People and Jesus:
In behalf of the afflicted (Mt 12:22; 15:30; Mk 1:32). The four friends for the paralytic (Mt 2:3-12; 9:2-8; Lk 5:18-20). Jairus (Mt 9:18; Mk 5:23; Lk 8:41). The nobleman for his son (Jn 4:47, 49). The father of the demoniac for his son (Mt 17:15; Mk 9:17-18). The Syrian Phoenician woman for her daughter (Mt 15:22; Mk 7:24-26). The disciples for Peter's mother-in-law (Mk 1:30; Lk 4:38-39).

Between Persons:
Reuben for Joseph (Ge 37:21-22). Judah for Joseph (Ge 37:26-27). Pharaoh's chief baker for Joseph (Ge 41:9-13, w 40:14). Jonathan for David (1Sa 19:1-7). Abigail for Nabal (1Sa 25:23-35). Joab for Absalom (2Sa 14:1-24). Bathsheba for Solomon (1Ki 1:15-31), for Adonijah (1Ki 2:13-25). Ebed-Melech for Jeremiah (Jer 38:7-13). Elisha offers to see the king for the Shunammite (2Ki 4:13). The king of Syria for Naaman (2Ki 5:6-8). Paul for Onesimus (Phm 10-21).
See Intercession; Jesus, Mediation of.

MEDICINE Used (Isa 38:21; Lk 10:34; 1Ti 5:23). *See Disease; Physician.*
Figurative (Pr 17:22; Isa 1:6; Jer 8:22; 30:13; 46:11; 51:8-9; Eze 47:12; Rev 22:2).

MEDITATION On the Lord (Ps 63:5-6; 104:34; 139:17-18). On the law of the Lord (Ps 1:2; 19:14; 49:3; 119:11, 15-16, 23, 48, 55, 59, 78, 97-99, 119:148). Commanded (Jos 1:8). On the works of the Lord (Ps 77:10-12; 143:5).
Instances of: Isaac (Ge 24:63). David (Ps 4:4; 39:3).

MEDITERRANEAN SEA Mentioned in Scripture as: The Sea (Nu 34:5; Ps 80:11). The Great Sea (Nu 34:6-7; Jos 1:4; 9:1; 15:12, 47; 23:4; Eze 47:10, 15, 20; 48:28). Sea of the Philistines (Ex 23:31). The western sea (Dt 11:24; Joel 2:20; Zec 14:8).

MEDIUM A spiritist; one who consults the dead (Lev 19:31; 20:6; Dt 18:9-13; Isa 8:19-22). Punished by death in the law (Lev 20:27). Saul and the medium at Endor (1Sa 28:3-25; 1Ch 10:13-14). *See Necromancer, Necromancy; Sorcery; Spiritists.*

MEEKNESS

Described:
Advantageous (Ps 25:9; Pr 14:29; 17:1; 19:11; Ecc 7:8; 10:4; Am 3:3; 1Co 13:4-5, 7). Honorable (Pr 20:3). Potent (Pr 15:1, 18; 16:32; 25:15; 29:8). A fruit of the Spirit (Gal 5:22-23, 26).

Biblical Weights and Measures and Approximate Equivalents					
Dry Capacity:					
1.	Cor or homer	10 ephahs	6 bushels	220 liters	1Ki 4:22; 5:11; 2Ch 2:10; 27:5; Ezr 7:22
2.	Lethek	5 ephahs	3 bushels	110 liters	Hos 3:2
3.	Ephah	10 omers	3/5 bushel	22 liters	Ex 16:36; Lev 5:11; Nu 5:15; Jdg 6:19; Ru 2:17; 1Sa 1:24; Isa 5:10; Eze 45:10-11,13,24; Am 8:5
4.	Seah	1/3 ephah	7 quarts	7.3 liters	Ge 18:6; 1Sa 25:18; 1Ki 18:32; 2Ki 7:1,16,18
5.	Omer	1/10 ephah	2 quarts	2 liters	Ex 16:16,18,22,32-33,36
6.	Cab	1/18 ephah	1 quart	1 liter	2Ki 6:25
Liquid Capacity:					
1.	Bath	1 ephah	6 gallons	22 liters	1Ki 7:26,38; 2Ch 2:10; 4:5; Ezr 7:22; Isa 5:10; Eze 45:10-11,14; Lk 16:6
2.	Hin	1/6 bath	4 quarts	4 liters	Ex 29:40; 30:24; Lev 19:36; 23:13; Nu 15:4-10; 28:5,7,14; Eze 4:11; 45:24; 46:5,7,11,14
3.	Log	1/72 bath	1/3 quart	0.3 liter	Lev 14:10,12,14,21,24
Weight:					
1.	Talent	60 minas	75 pounds	34 kilograms	Ex 25:39; 38:27
2.	Mina	50 shekels	1.25 pounds	0.6 kilogram	1Ki 10:17; Ezr 2:69; Da 5:26-28
3.	Shekel	2 bekas	2/5 ounce	11.5 grams	Ge 20:16; Eze 45:12
4.	Pim	2/3 shekel	1/3 ounce	7.6 grams	1Sa 13:21, ftn
5.	Beka	10 gerahs	1/5 ounce	5.5 grams	Ge 24:22; Ex 38:26
6.	Gerah	1/20 shekel	1/50 ounce	0.6 gram	Ex 30:13; Lev 27:25
Length:					
1.	Cubit		18 inches	0.5 meter	Ge 6:15-16; Rev 21:17
2.	Span		9 inches	23 cm.	Ex 28:16; 1Sa 17:4; Isa 40:12; La 2:20; Eze 43:13
3.	Handbreadth		3 inches	8 centimeters	Ex 25:25; 1Ki 7:26; 2Ch 4:5; Ps 39:5; Eze 43:13
4.	Finger		0.75 inch	1.85 cm.	Jer 52:21

Commanded (Zep 2:3; Mt 5:38-41 w Lk 6:29; Mt 11:29; Mk 9:50; Ro 12:14, 18; 14:19; 1Co 6:7; 7:15; 10:32; 2Co 13:11; Gal 6:1; Eph 4:1-2; Php 2:14-15; Col 3:12-13; 1Th 5:14-15; 1Ti 3:3; 6:11; 2Ti 2:24-25; Tit 2:2, 9; 3:2; Heb 10:36; 12:14; Jas 1:4, 19, 21; 3:13; 1Pe 2:18-23; 3:4, 11, 15; 2Pe 1:5-7).
Rewards of (Ps 22:26; 37:11; 76:8-9; 147:6; 149:4; Isa 29:19; Mt 5:5; 11:29).

Instances of:
God (La 3:22, 28-30)
Abraham (Ge 13:8-9). Isaac (Ge 26:20-22). Moses (Ex 16:7-8; 17:2-7; Nu 12:3; 16:4-11). Gideon (Jdg 8:2-3). Hannah (1Sa 1:13-16). Saul (1Sa 10:27). David (1Sa 17:29; 2Sa 16:9-14; Ps 38:13-14). Psalmist (Ps 120:5-7).
Jesus (Isa 11:4; 42:1-4; 53:7; La 3:28-30; Mt 11:29; 12:19-20; 26:47-54; 27:13-14; Mk 15:4-5; Lk 23:34; 2Co 10:1; 1Pe 2:21-23). *See Jesus the Christ, Humility of; Meekness of.* Stephen (Ac 7:60). Paul (Ac 21:20-26; 1Co 4:12-13; 2Co 12:10; 1Th 2:7; 2Ti 4:16). The Thessalonians (2Th 1:4). Job (Jas 5:11). The archangel (Jude 9).
See Humility; Kindness; Patience.

MEGIDDO (*place of troops*). City on the Great Road linking Gaza and Damascus, connecting the coastal plain and the Plain of Esdraelon or Megiddo (Jos 12:21; 17:11; Jdg 1:27; 5:19), fortified by Solomon (1Ki 9:15), wounded Ahaziah died there (2Ki 9:27), Josiah lost life there in battle with Pharaoh Neco (2Ki 23:29-30; 2Ch 35:20-27). Large-scale excavations have revealed a great deal of material of great archaeological value.

MEGIDDON *See Megiddo.*

MEHETABEEL *See Mehetabel, 2.*

MEHETABEL (*God [El] does good*).
1. Wife of Hadad (Ge 36:39; 1Ch 1:50).
2. A person whose grandson tried to intimidate Nehemiah (Ne 6:10).

MEHIDA (possibly *bought as slave*). A person whose descendants returned from Babylon (Ezr 2:52; Ne 7:54).

MEHIR (*hired hand*). Son of Kelub (1Ch 4:11).

MEHOLAH, MEHOLATHITE A city in Issachar, probably the same as Abel Meholah. Barzillai and his son Adriel lived there (1Sa 18:19; 2Sa 21:8). *See Abel Meholah.*

MEHUJAEL Descendant of Cain; father of Methushael (Ge 4:18).

MEHUMAN Eunuch of Xerxes, king of Persia (Est 1:10).

MEHUNIM *See Maonites; Meunim, Meunites, 2.*

MEKERATHITE (*one of Mekerath*). Description of Hepher (1Ch 11:36).

MEKONAH *See Meconah.*

MELAH *See Tel Melah.*

MELATIAH (*Yahweh sets free*). A Gibeonite who assisted in repairing the wall of Jerusalem (Ne 3:7).

MELCHESEDEC *See Melchizedek.*

MELCHI *See Melki.*

MELCHIAH *See Malkijah.*

MELCHISHUA, MELCHI-SHUA *See Malki-Shua.*

MELCHIZEDEK (*[my] king is Zedek [just]*). Priest and king of Salem (Jerusalem); blessed Abram in the name of Most High God and received tithes from him (Ge 14:18-20), type of Christ, the Priest-King (Ps 110:4; Heb 5:6-10; 6:20; 7).

MELEA Ancestor of Jesus (Lk 3:31).

MELECH (*king*). Son of Micah (1Ch 8:35; 9:41).

MELICU *See Malluch, 6.*

MELITA *See Malta.*

MELKI (*my king*).
1. Ancestor of Jesus (Lk 3:24).
2. Remote ancestor of Jesus (Lk 3:28).

MELODY *See Music.*

MELON (Nu 11:5).

MELZAR NIV "guard" (Da 1:11, 16). *See Guard.*

MEMBER Any feature or part of the body (Job 17:7; Jas 3:5).

MEMORIAL Passover (Ex 12:14). *See Passover.*
Firstborn set apart as a (Ex 13:12-16). Pot of manna (Ex 16:32-34). Feast of Tabernacles (Lev 23:43). Shoulder stones of the ephod (Ex 28:12). Atonement money (Ex 30:16). The twelve stones of Jordan (Jos 4:1-9).
The Lord's Supper (Lk 22:19; 1Co 11:24-26).
See Pillar.

MEMPHIS Capital city of Egypt, on W bank of Nile, c. twenty miles S of modern Cairo; its destruction foretold (Isa 19:13; Jer 2:16; 44:1; 46:14, 19; Eze 30:13, 16).

MEMUCAN One of the seven nobles of Xerxes who counseled the king to divorce Queen Vashti (Est 1:14-21).

MENAHEM (*comforter*). Sixteenth king of Israel; evil; slew his predecessor, Shallum (2Ki 15:13-22).

MENAN *See Menna.*

MENE, MENE, TEKEL, PARSIN Four Aramaic words, probably meaning "numbered, numbered, weighed, and divided," which suddenly appeared on the walls of Belshazzar's banquet hall (Da 5:25-28).

MENI *See Destiny, 2.*

MENNA An ancestor of Jesus (Lk 3:31).

MENSES *See Menstruation.*

MENSTRUATION Law relating to (Lev 15:19-30; 20:18; Eze 18:6). Cessation of, in old age (Ge 18:11). Immunities of women during (Ge 31:35). Uncleanness of (Isa 30:22).
Figurative (Isa 30:22; La 1:17; Eze 36:17).
See Bleeding, Subject to.

MEON *See Baal Meon; Beth Baal Meon; Beth Meon.*

MEONENIM *See Soothsayers' Tree.*

MEONOTHAI (*my dwellings*). Father of Ophrah (1Ch 4:14).

MEPHAATH (*splendor*). A Levitical city in Reuben (Jos 13:18; 21:37; 1Ch 6:79; Jer 48:21).

MEPHIBOSHETH (*from the mouth of shame* [a derogatory term for Baal]).
1. Son of Saul, whom David surrendered to the Gibeonites to be slain (2Sa 21:8-9).
2. Son of Jonathan (2Sa 4:4). Also called Merib-Baal (1Ch 8:34; 9:40). Was lame (2Sa 4:4). David entertains him at his table (2Sa 9:1-7; 21:7). Property restored to (2Sa 9:9-10). His ingratitude to David at the time of Absalom's usurpation (2Sa 16:1-4; 19:24-30). Property of, confiscated (2Sa 16:4; 19:29-30).

MERAB (*abundant*). Daughter of King Saul (1Sa 14:49). Betrothed to David by Saul (1Sa 18:17-18), but given to Adriel as his wife (1Sa 18:19).

MERAIAH (*loved by Yahweh*). A priest (Ne 12:12).

MERAIOTH (*rebellious*).
1. High priest (1Ch 6:6-7).
2. Priest; ancestor of Hilkiah (1Ch 9:11).
3. Another priestly ancestor of Helkai (Ne 12:15). May be same as "Meremoth" (Ne 12:3).

MERARI, MERARITE(S) (*bitter*). Youngest son of Levi; progenitor of Merarites (Nu 3:17, 33-37; Jos 21:7, 34-40).

MERATHAIM (*double rebellion*). Symbolic name for Babylon (Jer 50:21).

MERCENARIES *See Soldiers.*

MERCHANDISE *See Commerce.*

MERCHANT (Ge 23:16; 37:28; 1Ki 10:15, 28; 2Ch 9:14; Ne 3:32; 13:20; Job 41:6; SS 3:6; Isa 23:2; 47:15; Eze 17:4; 27:13, 17, 21-36; 38:13; Hos 12:7; Na 3:16; Mt 13:45; Rev 18:3, 11, 23). *See Commerce.*

MERCURIUS, MERCURY *See Hermes, 1.*

MERCY (Ps 85:10; Pr 20:28; Hos 4:1; Jas 2:13).
A grace of the godly (Ps 37:25-26; Pr 11:17; 12:10; 14:22, 31; Ro 12:8). Iniquity atoned by (Pr 16:6). Of the wicked, cruel (Pr 12:10).
Commanded (Pr 3:3; Hos 12:6; Mic 6:8; Mt 9:13; 12:7; 23:23; Lk 6:36; Col 3:12-13). To be shown with cheerfulness (Ro 12:8).
Rewards of (2Sa 22:26; Ps 18:25; 37:25-26; Pr 14:21; 21:21; Mt 5:7).
See God, Mercy of; Kindness.
Instances of: The prison keeper, to Joseph (Ge 39:21-23). Joshua to Rahab (Jos 6:25). The Israelites to the man of Bethel (Jdg 1:23-26). David to Saul (1Sa 24:10-13, 17).

MERCY SEAT *See Atonement Cover; Tabernacle.*

MERED (*rebel*). Son of Ezra (1Ch 4:17-18).

MEREMOTH (*elevations*).
1. Priest who returned from the Exile (Ne 12:3).
2. Another priest who returned from the Exile (Ezr 8:33; Ne 3:4, 21).
3. Man who divorced foreign wife (Ezr 10:36).
4. Priest who signed covenant with Nehemiah (Ne 10:5).

MERES (*worthy*). One of the princes of Persia (Est 1:14).

MERIBAH (*to strive, contend*).
1. Place NW of Sinai where God gave Israelites water from a rock (Ex 17:1-7).
2. Place near Kadesh Barnea where God also gave Israelites water from a rock. Because of Moses' loss of temper God did not permit him to enter the Promised Land (Nu 20:1-13). Also called Meribah Kadesh (Nu 27:14; Dt 32:51).

MERIBAH KADESH *See Meribah, 2.*

MERIB-BAAL (*Baal contends*). Son of Jonathan (1Ch 8:34; 9:40). *See Mephibosheth, 2.*

MERIT Personal. *See Grace.*

MERODACH *See Marduk.*

MERODACH-BALADAN (*Marduk has given a son*). Twice king of Babylon (722-710; 703-702 B.C.), invited Hezekiah to join conspiracy against Assyria (2Ki 20:12-19; Isa 39:1-8).

MEROM (*high place*). Place near headwaters of Jordan river where Joshua defeated N coalition (Jos 11:5, 7). Possibly identified with Tell el-Khirba.

MERON *See Shimron Meron.*

MERONOTH, MERONOTHITE A place near Gibeon (Ne 3:7) and its inhabitants (1Ch 27:30).

MEROZ A place N of Mount Tabor. Deborah and Barak curse the inhabitants of, in their song of triumph (Jdg 5:23).

MESECH *See Meshech.*

MESHA
1. Place in S Arabia (Ge 10:30).
2. Benjamite (1Ch 8:9).
3. Descendant of Judah (1Ch 2:42).
4. King of Moab in days of Ahab, Ahaziah, and Jehoram (2Ki 3:4).

MESHACH (perhaps *I have become weak*). His Hebrew name was Mishael. He was taken as a captive to Babylon with Daniel, Hananiah, and Azariah, where each one was given a Babylonian name (Da 1:6-20; 2:17, 49; 3:12-30). Mishael was given the Akkadian name Meshach.
Shadrach, Meshach, and Abednego were chosen to learn the language and the ways of the Babylonians so that they could enter the king's service (Da 1:3-5, 17-20), c. 605 B.C. These three were eventually thrown into Nebuchadnezzar's furnace because they refused to bow down and worship the huge golden image that he had made (Da 3:1, 4-6, 8-30).

MESHECH
1. Son of Japheth (Ge 10:2; 1Ch 1:5).
2. Son of Shem (Ge 10:23; 1Ch 1:17).
3. A tribe (Ps 120:5; Eze 27:13; 32:26; 38:2-3); descendants of 1.

MESHELEMIAH (*Yahweh repays*). Father of Zechariah (1Ch 9:21; 26:1-2, 9), "Shelemiah" (1Ch 26:14).

MESHEZABEL (*God delivers*).
1. Ancestor of Meshullam (Ne 3:4).
2. Covenanter with Nehemiah (Ne 10:21).
3. Judahite (Ne 11:24).

MESHILLEMITH (*restitution*). A priest (1Ch 9:12).

MESHILLEMOTH (*restitution*).
1. Father of an Ephraimite who protested against the attempt of the Israelites to enslave their captive brothers (2Ch 28:12-13).
2. A priest (Ne 11:13).

MESHOBAB A Simeonite (1Ch 4:34).

MESHULLAM (*restitution* KB).
1. Grandfather of Shaphan (2Ki 22:3).
2. Son of Zerubbabel (1Ch 3:19).
3. Leading Gadite (1Ch 5:13).
4. Chief Benjamite (1Ch 8:17).
5. Father of Sallu (1Ch 9:7).
6. Benjamite of Jerusalem (1Ch 9:8).
7. Priest (1Ch 9:11; Ne 11:11).
8. Ancestor of priest (1Ch 9:12).
9. Kohathite (2Ch 34:12).
10. Israelite who returned with Ezra (Ezr 8:16).
11. Opposed divorcing foreign wives (Ezr 10:15).
12. Divorced foreign wife (Ezr 10:29).
13. Son of Berekiah; helped rebuild Jerusalem wall (Ne 3:4, 30; 6:18).
14. Another repairer of wall (Ne 3:6).
15. Helper of Ezra (Ne 8:4).
16. Priest (Ne 10:7).
17. Priest who sealed covenant (Ne 10:20).
18. Benjamite (Ne 11:7).
19. Priest (Ne 12:13).
20. Possibly the same man (Ne 12:33).
21. Another priest (Ne 12:16).
22. Levite (Ne 12:25).

MESHULLEMETH (*restitution*). Wife of Manasseh and mother of Amon (2Ki 21:19).

MESOBAITE *See Mezobaite.*

MESOPOTAMIA (*[land] between rivers*). The country between the Tigris and the Euphrates. Abraham a native of (Ac 7:2). Nahor lived in (Ge 24:10). People who lived in, called Syrians (Ge 25:20). Balaam from (Dt 23:4). The Israelites subjected to, eight years under the judgments of God (Jdg 3:8), delivered from, by Othniel (Jdg 3:9-10). Chariots hired from, by the Ammonites (1Ch 19:6-7). People of, present at Pentecost (Ac 2:9).
See Babylon; Chaldea.

MESS Any dish of food sent to the table (Ge 43:34; 2Sa 11:8; Heb 12:16).

MESSENGER (*send*). Figurative (Hag 1:13; Mal 2:7; 3:1; 4:5-6; Mt 11:10; Mk 1:2; Lk 7:27). Of Satan (2Co 12:7).

MESSIAH (*anointed*). The basic meaning of the Hebrew *mashiah* and the Greek *christos* is "anointed one."
In the OT the word is used of prophets, priests, and kings who were consecrated to their office with oil. The expression "the Lord's anointed" and its equivalent is not used as a technical designation of the Messiah, but refers to the king of the line of David ruling in Jerusalem and anointed by the Lord through the priest. With the possible exception of Da 9:25-26, the title "Messiah" as a reference to Israel's eschatological king does not occur in the OT. It appears in this sense later in the NT, where he is almost always called "the Christ." The OT pictures the Messiah as one who will put an end to sin and war and usher in universal righteousness and through his death will make vicarious atonement for the salvation of sinful people.
The NT concept of the Messiah is developed directly from the teaching of the OT. Jesus of Nazareth is the Messiah; he claimed to be the Messiah (Mt 23:63-64; Mk 14:61-62; Lk 22:67-70; Jn 4:25-26) and the claim was acknowledged by his disciples (Mt 16:16; Mk 8:29; Lk 9:20; Ac 4:27; 10:38).
See Jesus the Christ, Messiah.

MESSIANIC HOPE (Mt 13:17; Jn 8:56; Ac 9:22; Heb 11:13; 1Pe 1:10-12). Created by prophecy (Ge 49:10; Nu 24:17; 1Sa 1:10; 2Sa 7:12-13; Isa 9:6-7; 11:1-9; 33:17; 40:3-5; 55:3-5; 62:10-11; Jer 23:5-6; 33:15-17; Da 2:44; 7:13-14; 9:24-27; Mic 5:2; Zec 9:9; Mal 3:1-3; Ac 13:27), by the covenant with David to establish his throne forever (2Sa 7:12-16; 1Ch 17:11-14; 22:10; 28:7), by the messianic psalms (Pss 2; 16; 21; 22; 45; 72; 87; 89; 96; 110; 132:11, 17-18).
Confirmed in the vision of Mary (Lk 1:30-33). Exemplified, by the priest Zechariah (Lk 1:68-79), by the prophet Simeon (Lk 2:25, 29-32), by the prophetess Anna (Lk 2:36-38), by the wise men of the East (Mt 2:1-12), by John the Baptist (Mt 11:3), by the people (Jn 7:31, 40-42; 12:34), by Caiaphas (Mt 26:63; Mk 14:61), by Joseph of Arimathea (Mk 15:43; Lk 23:51), by the disciples on the way to Emmaus (Lk 24:21), by Paul (Ac 26:6-7).
See Jesus the Christ, Prophecies Concerning.

MESSIAS *See Messiah.*

METAL *See Bronze; Copper; Gold; Iron; Lead; Silver; Tin.*

METAPHOR A figure of speech that describes by comparison without using the word "like" or "as." Used extensively in the Song of Songs, for example "How beautiful you are, my darling! Oh, how beautiful! Your eyes are doves" (SS 1:15). Jesus spoke in metaphors (Mt 5:13-16). *See Parable.*

METEOROLOGY

Weather Described:
Controlled by God (Ge 2:5-6; 27:39; Job 9:7; 26:7-8, 11; Ps 19:2-6; 104:2-3, 7, 13, 19-20; 107:25; Ecc 11:3; Isa 13:13; 24:18; 50:3; Jer 4:11-12; 10:13; 51:16; Da 2:21; Hos 8:7; Joel 2:30-31; Am 9:6; Na 1:3; Mt 24:27; 24:29; 21:25; Jn 3:8; Ac 2:19-20; 2Pe 2:17; Jude 12). Tempest stilled by Jesus (Mt 8:24-27; Lk 8:22-25).
Weather, affected by godly prayers (1Sa 12:16-18; 1Ki 18:41-45; Isa 5:5-6; Jas 5:17-18). Forecast of weather (Mt 16:2-3; Lk 12:54-56).
Weather in the land of Uz (Job 27:20-21; 28:24-27; 29:19; 36:27-33; 37:6-22; 38:8-11, 22, 24-37). Weather in Israel (Ps 18:10-15; 29:3-10; 48:7; 65:8-12; 133:3; 135:6-7; 147:7-8; 148:7-8; Pr 25:23; 26:1; 30:4; Ecc 1:6-7; Hos 6:4; 13:15). The autumnal storms of the Mediterranean (Ac 27:9-20, 27).

Phenomena of:
The deluge (Ge 7:8). Fire from heaven on the cities of the plain (Ge 19:24-25). Plagues of hail, thunder, and lightning in Egypt (Ex 9:22-29; Ps 78:17-23), of darkness (Ex 10:22-23). East wind that divided the Red Sea (Ex 14:21), that brought the quails (Nu 11:31-32; Ps 78:26-28). Pillar of cloud and fire. *See Pillar.* Sun stood still (Jos 10:12-13). Dew on Gideon's fleece (Jdg 6:36-40). Stars in their courses fought against Sisera (Jdg 5:20). Stones from heaven (Jos 10:11). Fire from heaven at Elijah's command (2Ki 1:10-14). The whirlwind which carried Elijah to heaven (2Ki 2:1, 11).
Wind under God's control (Ps 107:25). East wind (Ps 48:7). Rain, formation of (Ps 135:6-7). Dew, copious (Ps 133:3). Rain in answer to Samuel's prayer (1Sa 12:16-18), Elijah's prayer (1Ki 18:41-45). Rain discomfits the Philistine army (1Sa 7:10). Wind destroyed Job's children (Job 1:18-19). Darkness at the Crucifixion (Mt 27:45; Lk 23:44-45).
See Astronomy; Celestial Phenomena; Dew; Hail; Rain; Weather.

Symbolic:
Used in the Revelation (Rev 6:12-14; 7:1; 8:3-12; 9:1-2, 17-19; 10:1-6; 11:6; 12:1-4, 7-9; 14; 15:1-4; 16:8, 17-21; 19:11-18; 20:11; 21:1).

METEYARD Archaic word for "measures of length" (Lev 19:35).

METHEG AMMAH (*the bridle of the metropolis*). A town David took from the Philistines (2Sa 8:1).

METHUSAEL *See Methushael.*

METHUSELAH (*man of the javelin*). Son of Enoch and grandfather of Noah (Ge 5:21-27; 1Ch 1:3).

METHUSHAEL (perhaps *man of God*). Father of Lamech (Ge 4:18).

MEUNIM, MEUNITES (*the people of Maon*).
1. People conquered by the Simeonites (1Ch 4:41); fought against Jehoshaphat (2Ch 20:1) and Uzziah (2Ch 26:7).
2. Counted among the temple servants (Ezr 2:50; Ne 7:52). May be the descendants of 1.
See Maonites.

ME-ZAHAB (*waters of gold*). Grandfather of Mehetabel (Ge 36:39; 1Ch 1:50).

MEZOBAITE Name of place otherwise unknown (1Ch 11:47).

MIAMIN *See Mijamin.*

MIBHAR (*choice*). One of David's valiant men (1Ch 11:38).

MIBSAM (*sweet odor*).
1. Son of Ishmael (Ge 25:13; 1Ch 1:29).
2. Son of Shallum (1Ch 4:25).

MIBZAR (*bastion*). Chief of Edom (Ge 36:42; 1Ch 1:53).

MICA (*who is like Yahweh?*).
1. Grandson of Jonathan (2Sa 9:12). *See Micah, 3.*
2. A Levite; descendant of Asaph (1Ch 9:15; Ne 11:17, 22).
3. A Levite covenanter (Ne 10:11), possibly the same as 2.

MICAH (*who is like Yahweh?*).
1. Ephraimite whose mother made an image for which he secured a priest; both image and priest were later stolen by the tribe of Dan (Jdg 17-18).
2. Reubenite (1Ch 5:5).
3. Grandson of Jonathan (1Ch 8:34; 9:40). *See Mica, 1.*
4. Levite (1Ch 23:20).
5. Father of Abdon, one of Josiah's officers (2Ch 34:20). *See Micaiah, 2.*
6. Prophet Micah, the Moreshethite; prophesied in the reigns of Jotham, Ahaz, and Hezekiah (Mic 1:1; Jer 26:18).

MICAH, BOOK OF
Author: The prophet Micah of Moresheth
Date: Sometime between 750 and 686 B.C.
Outline:
I. Superscription (1:1).
II. Judgment Against Israel and Judah (1:2-3:12).
A. Introduction (1:2).
B. The Predicted Destruction (1:3-7).
C. Lamentation for the Destruction (1:8-16).
D. Corruption in Micah's Society (2:1-11).
E. Hope in the Midst of Gloom (2:12-13).
F. The Leaders Condemned (ch. 3).
III. Hope for Israel and Judah (chs. 4-5).
A. The Coming Kingdom (ch. 4).
B. The Coming King (5:1-5a).
C. Victory for the People of God (5:5b-15).
IV. The Lord's Case Against Israel (ch. 6).
A. The Lord's Accusation (6:1-8).
B. The Coming Judgment (6:9-16).
V. Gloom Turns to Triumph (ch. 7).
A. Micah Laments the Corruption of His Society (7:1-6).
B. Micah's Assurance of Hope (7:7).
C. A Bright Future for God's People (7:8-13).
D. Victory for God's Kingdom (7:14-20).
See Prophets, The Minor.

MICAIAH (*who is like Yahweh?*).
1. A prophet living in Samaria who predicted the death of King Ahab (1Ki 22; 2Ch 18).
2. Father of Acbor, one of Josiah's officers (2Ki 22:12-14). *See Micah, 5.*
3. Daughter of Uriel of Gibeah (2Ch 13:2).
4. Offical of Jehoshaphat; a teacher (2Ch 17:7).
5. Ancestor of priest in Nehemiah's time (Ne 12:35).
6. Priest (Ne 12:41).
7. Grandson of Shaphan (Jer 36:11-13).
8. *See Maacah, 4.*

MICE *See Rat(s).*

MICHA *See Mica.*

MICHAEL (*who is like God [El]?*).
1. An Asherite (Nu 13:13).
2. Two Gadites (1Ch 5:13-14).
3. A Gershonite Levite (1Ch 6:40).
4. A descendant of Issachar (1Ch 7:3).
5. A Benjamite (1Ch 8:16).
6. A captain of the thousands of Manasseh who joined David at Ziklag (1Ch 12:20).
7. Father of Omri (1Ch 27:18).
8. Son of Jehoshaphat. Slain by his brother, Jehoram (2Ch 21:2-4).
9. Father of Zebadiah (Ezr 8:8).
10. The archangel. His message to Daniel (Da 10:13, 21; 12:1). Contention with the devil (Jude 9). Fights with the dragon (Rev 12:7).

MICHAH *See Micah.*

MICHAIAH *See Micaiah.*

MICHAL (*who is like God [El]?*). Daughter of Saul. Given to David as a reward for slaying Goliath (1Sa 18:22-28). Rescues David from death (1Sa 19:9-17). Saul forcibly separates them, and she is given in marriage to Paltiel (1Sa 25:44). David recovers her to himself (2Sa 3:13-16). Ridicules David on account of his religious zeal (2Sa 6:16, 20-23).

MICHMASH *See Micmash.*

MICHRI *See Micri.*

MICHTAM *See Miktam.*

MICMASH (perhaps *hidden place*). A place in Benjamin c. eight miles NE of Jerusalem; Jonathan led Israelites to victory over Philistines there (1Sa 14:31; Ne 11:31).

MICMETHATH A city between Ephraim and Manasseh (Jos 16:6; 17:7).

MICRI A Benjamite (1Ch 9:8).

MIDDIN A city in Judah in the wilderness just W of the Dead Sea (Jos 15:61).

MIDDLE WALL *See Dividing Wall.*

MIDIAN Son of Abraham by Keturah (Ge 25:2, 4; 1Ch 1:32-33).

MIDIANITE(S) Descendants of Midian, son of Abraham by Keturah (Ge 25:1-2, 4; 1Ch 1:32-33). Called Ishmaelites (Ge 37:25, 28; Jdg 8:24). Were merchants (Ge 37:28). Buy Joseph and sell him to Potiphar (Ge 37:28, 36). Defeated by the Israelites under Phinehas; five of their kings slain, the women taken captives, their cities burned, and rich spoils taken (Nu 31). Defeated by Gideon (Jdg 6-8). Owned multitudes of camels and large quantities of gold (Isa 60:6). A snare to the Israelites (Nu 25:16-18). Prophecies concerning (Isa 60:6; Hab 3:7).

MIDNIGHT Scenes at (Ex 11:4; Mt 25:6; Ac 16:25; 20:7).

MIDWIVES Assist in childbirth (Ge 35:17; 38:28). Save Israelite boys in Egypt (Ex 1:15-21).

MIGDAL EDER *See Eder, 1.*

MIGDAL EL (*tower of God [El]*). A city of Naphtali (Jos 19:38).

MIGDAL GAD (*tower of Gad*). A city of Judah (Jos 15:37).

MIGDOL (*tower*).
1. A place near the Red Sea where the Israelites encamped (Ex 14:2; Nu 33:7-8).
2. A city on the NE border of lower Egypt (Jer 44:1; 46:14).

MIGRON (*precipice*). A city in Benjamin. Saul encamps near, under a pomegranate tree (1Sa 14:2). Prophesy concerning (Isa 10:28).

MIJAMIN (*from the right hand*).
1. Priest in David's time (1Ch 24:9).
2. A man who divorced his foreign wife (Ezr 10:25).
3. Covenanter priest (Ne 10:7).
4. Priest who returned from the Exile (Ne 12:5).

MIKLOTH (*rods*).
1. A Benjamite of Jerusalem (1Ch 8:32; 9:37-38).
2. A ruler in the reign of David (1Ch 27:4).

MIKNEIAH (*Yahweh acquires*). A doorkeeper of the temple and musician (1Ch 15:18, 21).

MIKTAM The term always stands in the superscription of Davidic prayers occasioned by great danger (Ps 16, 56-60). Variously related to words for "golden," "inscription," and "atonement." *See Music, Symbols Used in.*

MILALAI A priest who took part in the dedication of the walls of Jerusalem (Ne 12:36).

MILCAH (*queen*).
1. Wife of Nahor and mother of Bethuel (Ge 11:29; 22:20-23; 24:15, 24, 47).
2. Daughter of Zelophehad. Special legislation in regard to the inheritance of (Nu 26:33; 27:1-7; 36:1-12; Jos 17:3-4).

MILCOM *See Molech.*

MILDEW (*yellow, pale*). Fungus growth destructive of grains and fruits (Dt 28:22; 1Ki 8:37; Am 4:9; Hag 2:17).

MILE Equal to about 3, 500 cubits or 8.6 stadia (Eze 45:3; Mt 5:41; Lk 24:13).

MILETUS A seaport in Asia Minor. Paul visits (Ac 20:15), and sends to Ephesus for the elders of the church, and addresses them here (Ac 20:17-38). Trophimus left sick at (2Ti 4:20).

MILITARY INSTRUCTION Of children (2Sa 1:18). *See Armies.*

MILK Used for food (Ge 18:8; Jdg 4:19; SS 5:1; Eze 25:4; 1Co 9:7). Of goats (Pr 27:27), sheep (Dt 32:14; Isa 7:21-22), camels (Ge 32:15), cows (Dt 32:14; 1Sa 6:7, 10). Churned (Pr 30:33). Kid not to be cooked in its mother's milk (Ex 23:19; Dt 14:21).
Figurative (Ex 3:8, 17; 13:5; 33:3; Nu 13:27; Dt 26:9, 15; Isa 55:1; 60:16; Jer 11:5; 32:22; Eze 20:6; Joel 3:18; 1Co 3:2; Heb 5:12-13; 1Pe 2:2).

MILL (Jer 25:10). Upper and lower stones of (Dt 24:6; Job 41:24; Isa 47:2). Used in Egypt (Ex 11:5). Operated by women (Mt 24:41), and captives (Jdg 16:21; La 5:13). Manna ground in (Nu 11:8). Sound of, to cease (Rev 18:22). *See Grind; Millstone.*

MILLENNIUM The Latin for a thousand years, from (Rev 20:1-15).
It refers to a period when Christ rules and Satan is bound; when Jesus shall have triumphed over all forms of evil (1Co 15:24-28; 2Th 2:8; Rev 14:6-18; 19:11-16). At the restoration of all things (Ac 3:21). When the creation shall be delivered from the corruption of evil (Ro 8:19-21). When the Son of Man shall sit on the throne of his glory (Mt 19:28; Lk 22:28-30), and the righteous shall be clothed with authority (Da 7:22; Mt 19:28; Lk 22:28-30; 1Co 6:2; Rev 2:5), and possess the kingdom (Mt 25:34; Lk 12:32; 22:29).
Christ rules from his throne in Zion or Jerusalem (Isa 65:17-25; Zep 3:11-13; Zec 9:9-10; 14:16-21). Christ fulfills the promise of the kingdom of God on earth (Mt 16:18-19; 26:29; Mk 14:25; Heb 8:11).
Amillenialists believe Jesus is reigning now. *Premillenialists* believe Jesus will literally reign on earth for a thousand years after his second coming. *Postmillenialists* believe the Church will Christianize the world for a long period of time after which Christ will return.
See Church, The Body of Believers, Prophecies Concerning; Jesus the Christ, Kingdom of; Second Coming of.

MILLET (Eze 4:9).

MILLO *See Beth Millo.*

MILLSTONE Not to be taken in pledge (Dt 24:6). Probably used in executions by drowning (Mt 18:6; Mk 9:42; Lk 17:2). Abimelech killed by one being hurled upon him (Jdg 9:53). Figurative of the hard heart (Job 41:24). *See Grind; Mill.*

MINA In the sexagesimal system (based on the number 60) that originated in Mesopotamia, there were 60 shekels in a mina and 60 minas in a talent. A shekel, which was about two-fifths of an ounce of silver, was the average wage for a month's work. Thus a mina would be the equivalent of five years' wages, and a talent would be 300 years' wages (1Ki 10:17, ftn, w 2Ch 9:16, ftn; Ezr 2:69; Ne 7:71-72, ftn). *See Measure.*

MINCING (*to go like a little child, i.e., to trip along*). To speak, walk, or behave in an affectedly elegant, dainty, or nice manner. Used of the haughty women of Zion (Isa 3:16).

MIND In Scripture it often means "heart" or "soul." In the NT it is often used in an ethical sense (Ro 7:25; Col 2:18).

MINERALS OF THE BIBLE The science of mineralogy is a recent one, and did not exist in ancient times. It is often impossible to be certain that when a mineral name is used in the Bible, it is used with the same meaning as that attached in modern mineralogy. The following minerals are mentioned in the Bible:

Precious Stones:
Agate (Ex 28:19; 39:12), amethyst (Ex 28:19; 39:12; Rev 21:20), aromatic resin or resin (Ge 2:12; Nu 11:7), beryl (Ex 28:17; 39:10; Eze 28:13; Rev 21:20), carnelian (Rev 4:3; 21:20), chalcedony (Rev 21:19), chrysolite (Da 10:6; Rev 21:20), chrysoprase (Rev 21:20), coral (Job 28:18; Eze 27:16), crystal (Job 28:17; Rev 4:6; 21:11; 22:1), emerald (Ex 28:18; 39:11), glowing metal (Eze 1:4, 27; 8:2; Rev 1:15), hardest stone (Eze 3:9; Zec 7:12), jacinth (Ex 28:19; 39:12; Rev 9:17), jasper (Ex 28:20; 39:13; Job 28:18; Eze 28:13; Rev 4:3; 21:11, 18, 19), onyx (Ge 2:12; Ex 25:7; 28:9, 20; 35:9, 27; 39:6, 13; 1Ch 29:2; Job 28:16; Eze 28:13), pearl (Rev 21:21), ruby (Ex 28:17; 39:10; Job 28:18; Eze 28:13, 16), sapphire (Ex 24:10; 28:18; 39:11; Eze 1:26; 10:1; 28:13; Rev 21:19), sardonyx (Rev 21:20), sparkling jewels (Isa 54:12), topaz (Ex 28:17; 39:10; Job 28:19; Eze 28:13; Rev 21:20), turquoise (Ex 28:18; Eze 27:16).

Metals:
Gold (Ge 2:11-12), silver (Mt 10:9), iron (Nu 31:22), bronze (Ge 4:22; Ezr 8:27), lead (Ex 15:10), tin (Nu 31:22), glowing metal (Eze 1:4, 27; 8:2), dross (Ps 119:119; Pr 25:4; Isa 1:22, 25; Eze 22:18-19).

Common Minerals:
Alabaster (Mt 26:7; Mk 14:3; Lk 7:37), flint (Isa 5:28; 50:7; Jer 17:1; Eze 3:9; Zec 7:12), marble (1Ch 29:2; Est 1:6; SS 5:15; Rev 18:12), soda (Pr 25:20; Jer 2:22), sulfur (Ge 19:24; Dt 29:23; Job 18:15; Ps 11:6; Isa 30:33; 34:9; Eze 38:22; Lk 17:29; Rev 9:17-18; 14:10; 19:20; 20:10; 21:8), water.
See Stones.

MINES, MINING An ancient occupation; described in (Job 28:1-11; Dt 8:9; 1Ki 7:13-50).

MINGLED PEOPLE Non-Israelite people who left Egypt with the Israelites (Ex 12:38). The term is also used for the mixed blood of certain of Israel's enemies (Jer 25:20; 50:37).

MINIAMIN (*from the right, good fortune*).
1. Levite (2Ch 31:15).
2. Head of a family of priests (Ne 12:17).
3. A priest in Nehemiah's time (Ne 12:41).

MINISTER (*servant*).
1. An officer in civil government. Joseph (Ge 41:40-44), Iri (2Sa 20:26), Zabud (1Ki 4:5), Ahithophel (1Ch 27:33), Zebadiah (2Ch 19:11), Elkanah (2Ch 28:7), Haman (Est 3:1), Mordecai (Est 10:3, w Est 8; 9), Daniel (Da 2:48; 6:1-3).
See Cabinet.
2. A sacred teacher.

Good Ministers:
Likened to sowers (Ps 126:6; Mt 13:3-8; Mk 4:3-8; Lk 8:5-8). Teachers of schools (1Sa 19:20; 2Ki 2:3, 5, 15; 4:38; 2Ch 15:3; 17:7-9; Ac 13:1).
Hired (Jdg 17:10; 18:4). Exempt from taxation (Ezr 7:24). In politics (2Sa 15:24-27). In war (2Ch 13:12-14).
Influential in public affairs (1Sa 12:6-10), designate kings (1Sa 9:15-16; 10:1; 16:1-13), recommend civil and military appointments (2Ki 4:13).

M

In vigorous opposition with rulers: Samuel with Saul (1Sa 13:11-14; 15:10-31), Nathan with David (2Sa 12:1-4), Elijah with Ahab (1Ki 18:17-18).

Recreation for (Mk 6:31-32). Take leave of congregations (Ac 20:17-38). Personal bearing of (Tit 2:7-8). Preach with ecclesiastical authority (Gal 1:15-24; 2:1-9). Work of, will be tried (1Co 3:12-15). Responsibility of (Eze 3:17-21; 33:8; Mt 10:14-40; Ac 18:6; 20:26-27; 1Co 1:23; 2Co 2:15-17; 5:11, 18-19; 1Ti 6:20). Speaking evil of, forbidden (Jude 8, 10). Clothed with authority (1Th 5:12; Tit 1:13-14; 2:15; 3:1-2, 8-9; Heb 13:6-7, 17). *See the epistles to Timothy and Titus in their entirety.* Clothed with salvation (2Ch 6:41). Exhorted to grow in grace (1Ti 6:11; 2Ti 2:22).

Marriage of (Lev 21:7-15; Mt 8:14; Mk 1:30; 1Co 9:5; 1Ti 3:2, 12; Tit 1:5-7).

Incorruptible: Balaam (Nu 22:18, 37-38; 23:8, 12; 24:12-14, w 2Pe 2:15-16), Micaiah (1Ki 22:13-14), Peter (Ac 8:18-23). Patience of (Jas 5:10). Inconsistent (Mt 27:3-7).

Love of, for the church, exemplified by Paul (Php 1:7; 1Th 1:2-4; 2:8, 11). Kindness to, Ebed-Melech to Jeremiah (Jer 38:7-13). Fear of (1Sa 16:4). Example to the flock (Php 3:17; 2Th 3:9; 1Ti 4:12; Tit 2:1, 7-8; 1Pe 5:3). Intolerance of (Mt 15:23; 19:13; Mk 10:13; Lk 18:15). Message of, rejected (Jer 7:27; Eze 33:30-33). God's care of (1Ki 17:1-16; 19:1-8; Mt 10:29-31; Lk 12:6-7). Their calling, glorious (2Co 3:7-11). Discouragements of (Isa 30:10-11; 53:1; Eze 3:8-9, 14; Hab 1:2-3; Mt 13:57; Mk 6:3-4; Lk 4:24; Jn 4:44).

Defended (Jer 26:16-24; Ac 23:9). Beloved (Ac 20:37-38; 21:5-6).

Sent out in teams of two: Disciples (Mk 6:7), Paul and Barnabas (Ac 13:2-3), Judas and Silas (Ac 15:27), Barnabas and Mark (Ac 15:37, 39), Paul and Silas (Ac 15:40), Paul and Titus (2Co 8:19, 23), Timothy and Erastus (Ac 19:22), Titus and a companion (2Co 12:18).

Call of—

(Am 2:11; Mt 9:38; Ro 10:14-15; Eph 4:11-12; Heb 5:4). Aaron and his sons (Ex 28:1; 1Ch 23:13; Heb 5:4). Levites (Nu 3:5-13; 16:5, 9). Samuel (1Sa 3:4-10). Elisha (1Ki 19:16, 19). Isaiah (Isa 6:8-10). Jeremiah (Jer 1:5). Jonah (Jnh 1:1-2; 3:1-2).

The twelve apostles (Mt 4:18-22 w Mk 1:17-20; Mt 9:9; Mk 2:14; Lk 5:27 w Mt 10:1-5; Jn 1:43). The seventy-two disciples (Lk 10:1-2). Paul (Ac 13:2-3; 20:24; 22:12-15; 26:14-18; Ro 1:1; 1Co 1:1, 27-28 w 2Co 1:1 & Col 1:1; 1Co 9:16-19; 2Co 5:18-20; Gal 1:15-16; Eph 3:7-8; Col 1:25-29; 1Ti 1:11; Tit 1:5). Barnabas (Ac 13:2-3). Archippus (Col 4:17).

See Call, Personal; Excuses.

Character and Qualifications of—

(Lev 10:3-11). Blameless (1Ti 3:2-4, 7-13; Tit 1:5-9). Compassionate (Heb 5:2). Consecrated (Nu 16:9-10). Consistent (Php 2:21-23). Courageous (Jer 1:7-8, 17-19; Ac 20:22, 24; 2Ti 1:7). Diligent (2Ch 29:11; 1Co 15:10). Eager to serve (Isa 6:8). Endued with power (Lk 24:49; Ac 1:8; 4:8, 31; Gal 2:8). Gentle (2Ti 2:24-25). A good example (Tit 2:1, 7-8, 15; Jas 3:1, 13, 16-18). Holy (Lev 21:6; Isa 6:7; 52:11; Mal 2:6; Jn 17:17; 1Co 9:27; 2Ti 2:21; Tit 1:5-9). Humble (Mt 20:25-28; 23:8, 10-11; Lk 22:27; Jn 13:13-17; 15:20; 2Co 4:5). Meek (1Co 4:12-13; 2Co 10:1). Patient (Jas 5:10). Persevering (Mt 10:22-24; 2Co 4:1, 8-10). Prepared (Ezr 7:10). Responsible (1Pe 4:10-11). Saved (2Ch 6:41). Sincere (2Co 4:1-2). Strong (2Ti 2:1). Tactful (1Co 9:18-23; 10:23, 28-33; 2Co 6:3; 12:16). Willing to suffer hardship (2Ti 2:3; 4:5). Wise (Mal 2:7; Pr 11:30; Mt 10:16; Lk 6:39; 2Co 4:6; 2Ti 2:7; 3:14, 16-17).

Not quarrelsome (2Ti 2:14, 23-24; Tit 3:9). Not of the world (Jn 15:19; 17:16). Not entangled with the world (2Ti 2:4-5).

Zealous (Jer 20:9; Eze 34:1-31; 2Ti 1:6-8; 4:2). *See Zeal.* Instances of: Titus (2Co 8:16-17), Epaphroditus (Php 2:25-30), Epaphras (Col 4:12-13), John, in his vision (Rev 5:4-5).

Faithful (1Sa 2:35; Mt 24:45; Lk 12:42-44; Ac 20:22, 24; 1Co 2:2; 2Co 6:4-7). Instances of: Moses (Dt 4:26; 30:19; Heb 3:2, 5), Micaiah (2Ch 18:12-13), Azariah (2Ch 26:16-20), Balaam (Nu 22:18, 38; 23:8, 12; 24:12-14), Nathan (2Sa 12:1-14), Isaiah (Isa 22:4-5; 39:3-7), Jeremiah (Jer 17:16; 26:1-15; 28; 37:9-10, 16-18), John the Baptist (Mt 3:2-12; Mk 6:18; Lk 3:7-19), the apostles (Ac 4:19-20, 31; 5:21, 29-32), Peter (Ac 2:14-40; 3:12-26; 4:8-12; 8:18-23), Paul (Ac 15:25-26; 17:16-17; 19:8; 20:26-27), Tychicus (Col 4:7).

See the epistles to Timothy and Titus in their entirety.

Described as—

Administering God's grace (1Pe 4:10). Ambassadors for Christ (2Co 5:20; Eph 6:20). Angels of the church (Rev 1:20; 2:1, 8, 12, 18; 3:1, 7, 14). Apostles (Lk 6:13; Rev 18:20). Apostles of Jesus Christ (Tit 1:1). Defenders of the gospel (Php 1:7). Elders (1Ti 5:17; 1Pe 5:1). Entrusted with God's work (Tit 1:7), with the secret things of God (1Co 4:1). Evangelists (Eph 4:11; 2Ti 4:5). Fishers of men (Mt 4:19; Mk 1:17). God's fellow workers (1Th 3:2). Lights (Jn 5:35). Men of God (Dt 33:1; 1Ti 6:11). Messengers of the Church (2Co 8:23), of the LORD Almighty (Mal 2:7). Ministers of God (Isa 61:6), before the LORD (Joel 2:17), of Christ (Ro 15:16; 1Ti 4:6), of a new covenant (2Co 3:6), in the Sanctuary (Eze 45:4).

Overseers (Ac 20:28). Pastors (Eph 4:11). Preachers (Ro 10:14; 1Ti 2:7), of righteousness (2Pe 2:5). Servants of the Church (2Co 4:5), of God (Tit 1:1; Jas 1:1), of the gospel (Eph 3:7; Col 1:23), of Jesus Christ (Php 1:1; Jude 1), of the Lord (2Ti 2:24), of the Word (Lk 1:2). Shepherds (Jer 23:4). Soldiers of Christ (Php 2:25; 2Ti 2:3-4). Stars (Rev 1:20; 2:1). Teachers (Isa 30:20; Eph 4:11). Watchmen (Isa 62:6; Eze 33:7). Witnesses (Ac 1:8; 5:32; 26:16). Workers (Mt 9:38; Phm 1), together with God (2Co 6:1).

Duties of—

(Eph 4:11-12). To preach (Mt 10:7; Ro 1:14-15). To preach the unsearchable riches of Christ (Eph 3:8-12). To admonish (Isa 58:1; 62:6-7). To exhort (2Co 5:20; 1Ti 4:13; 6:17-18; 2Pe 1:12-16). To warn (Jer 7:25; Eze 33:1-9). To reprove (Eze 6:11; 34; Jnh 1:2; 2Co 7:8). *See Reproof.* To teach (Lev 10:11; 2Ki 17:27-28; 2Ch 15:3; Ezr 7:10; Jer 26:2; Eze 44:23; Mt 10:7, 27; 28:19-20; Mk 10:43-45; Ac 5:20; 6:4; 16:4; 18:9-10; 26:16-18; Ro 1:15; 12:6-7; 2Co 10:8; Eph 3:8-10; 4:11-12; 1Ti 2:7; 4:13-16; 2Ti 2:2, 14-15, 24-25; 4:1-2, 5). To teach the lordship of Jesus (2Co 4:5). To serve (Mt 20:25-28; Mk 10:43-45; 2Co 4:5). To make disciples of Christ (Mt 28:19-20). To win souls (Pr 11:30; Jn 4:35-38; 2Co 5:18, 20). To witness for Christ (Lk 24:48; Jn 15:27; Ac 1:22; 10:42; 22:15). To do the work of an evangelist (2Ti 4:5). To give himself continually to prayer (Ac 6:4). To lament over the worldliness and sins of the church (Joel 1:13-15; 2:17). To speak boldly (Eph 6:20). To minister to all without respect of persons or races (Ro 1:14-15). To exercise authority in the church (Mt 16:19; 18:18; 1Co 4:19-21; 2Co 7:8-9, 12, 15; 13:2-3; 13:10; 2Th 3:4; 1Ti 1:3-4, 11, 18; 5:19-22; 1Pe 5:1-3). To feed the flock (Jer 3:15; 23:4, 22, 28; Jn 21:15-17; Ac 20:28; 1Co 14:1-33; 1Pe 5:2-4). To strengthen the discouraged (Lk 22:32). To comfort the people (Isa 40:1-2, 9, 11; 1Th 3:2).

Charges delivered to: (Nu 18:1-7; 27:18-23; Dt 31:7-8, 14-23; Jos 1:1-9; Jer 1:18-19; Eze 3:4). Jesus to the twelve (Mt 10:5-42), to the seventy-two (Lk 10:1-16). Paul charges Timothy (1Ti 1:18-20; 2; 3; 4; 5; 6; 2Ti 1:6-13; 2; 3; 4).

Duty of the Church to—

To esteem (1Th 5:12-13). To pray for (Heb 13:18; 2Ch 6:41; Ps 132:9; Mt 9:37-38; Ac 4:29; 12:5; Ro 15:30-32; 2Co 1:11; Eph 6:18-20; Php 1:19; Col 4:2-4; 1Th 5:25; 2Th 3:1-2; Phm 22; Heb 13:19). To imitate the example of (1Co 11:1; Php 3:17; 2Th 3:7; Heb 13:7). To submit to the authority of (1Co 11:2; 16:16; 1Th 5:12-13; 2Th 3:4; Heb 13:7, 17). To provide for the support, of priest and Levite (Nu 18:20-21; Dt 10:9; 14:27; 18:1-4; Jos 13:14; 18:7; Jer 31:14; Eze 44:28), of the twelve apostles (Mt 10:9-10; Mk 6:8; Lk 22:35), of the seventy-two disciples (Lk 10:7-8), of Christian preachers (1Co 9:3-4, 7-14; Gal 6:6; Php 4:10-18; 1Ti 5:18). Right of support, waived by Paul (Ac 20:33-35; 1Co 9:15-18; 2Co 11:7-10; 12:13-18; 1Th 2:5-6, 9; 2Th 3:7-9).

See Church, The Body of Believers, Responsibilities and Duties.

Hospitality to—

Woman of Zarephath to Elijah (1Ki 17:10-16). The Shunammite to Elisha (2Ki 4:8-10). The barbarians to Paul (Ac 28:1-10). Simon the tanner to Peter (Ac 9:43). The Philippian jailer (Ac 16:33-34). Aquila and Priscilla to Paul (Ac 18:3), to Apollos (Ac 18:26). Justus to Paul (Ac 18:7). Philip the evangelist to Paul (Ac 21:8-10).

Joys of—

(Jn 4:36-38; 2Co 2:14; 7:6-7; Php 2:16; 1Th 2:13, 19-20; 3:8-9; 2Jn 4; 3Jn 4).

Ordination of—

Matthias (Ac 1:26), seven deacons (Ac 6:5-6), Paul and Barnabas (Ac 13:3), Timothy (1Ti 4:14).

See Levites; Priest.

Prayer for—

Commanded (Mt 9:37-38; Lk 10:2; Ro 15:30-32; 2Co 1:11; Eph 6:18-20; Php 1:19; Col 4:2-4; 1Th 5:25; 2Th 3:1-2; Phm 22; Heb 13:18-19). Exemplified (2Ch 6:41; Ps 132:9; Ac 1:24-25; 4:29; 6:6; 12:5; 14:23).

Precepts for Guidance of—

(Jer 1:7-8, 17-19; Eze 2:6-8; Mt 7:6; 10:7-8, 11-13, 16, 25-28; Lk 10:1-11; Col 4:17; 1Ti 1:3-4, 11, 18-19; 4:6-7, 12-16; 5:1-3, 7-11, 19-22; 6:3-4, 10-14, 17-21; 2Ti 1:6-8; 2:2-7, 14-16, 23-25; 4:1-2, 5; 1Pe 5:1-4; 2Pe 1:12-16).

Promises to—

(2Sa 23:6-7; Ps 126:5-6; Jer 1:7-10, 17-19; 15:20-21; 20:11; Da 12:3; Mt 10:28-31; 28:20; Lk 10:19; 12:11-12; 24:49; Jn 4:36-38; Ac 1:4-5, 8; 18:9-10; 1Co 3:8; 9:9-10; 2Co 2:14-16; 7:6-7; Php 2:16; 1Th 2:13, 19-20; 3:8-9; 1Pe 5:4; 3Jn 4). *See Righteous, Promises to.*

Success Attending—

Jonah (Jnh 1:5-6, 9, 14, 16; 3:4-9). Apostles (Ac 2:1-4, 41). Philip (Ac 8:6, 8, 12). Peter (Ac 9:32-35). Paul (Ac 13:16-43; 1Co 4:15; 9:2; 15:11; 2Co 3:2-3; 12:12; 13:4; Php 2:16; 1Th 1:5). Apollos (Ac 18:24-28). *See Revivals.*

Trials and Persecutions of—

Foretold (Mt 10:16-27 w Jn 13:16; Mt 23:34). Rehearsed (Mt 23:34).

Instances of: Elijah (1Ki 22:24-27; 2Ch 18:23-26). Hanani (2Ch 16:10). Zechariah (2Ch 24:20-22, 25; Mt 23:35; Lk 11:51). Isaiah (Isa 20:2-3). Jeremiah (Jer 11:19-21; 15:10, 15; 17:15-18; 18:18-23; 20:1-3, 7-18; 32:2-3; 33:1; 37:15-21; 38:6-13; 39:15; 43:1-7; La 3:53-55). Ezekiel (Eze 3:24-25; 24:15-18). Hosea (Hos 1:2). Amos (Am 5:10; 7:10-17). The apostles (Ac 5:17-42). Peter (Ac 12:3-19). Paul (Ac 9:23-25, 29-30; 14:4-6, 11-20; 16:16-24; 17:5-10, 13-14; 18:12-13; 20:3; 21:27-40; 22:22-30; 23:10-35; 24:26-27; 27:9-44; 1Co 2:1-4; 4:9-13; 2Co 6:4-10; 7:5; 11:23-33; 12:7-10; Eph 3:1, 13; 2Ti 1:8, 16; 2:9; 4:16-17).

See Paul, Persecutions of; also, Accusation, False; Persecution.

Zealous—

Titus (2Co 8:16-17). Epaphroditus (Php 2:25-30). Epaphras (Col 4:12-13). Tychicus (Col 4:7). John, in his vision (Rev 5:4-5). *See Zeal.*

False and Corrupt:

(1Ki 12:31; Ne 13:29; Jer 2:8; 6:13-14; 8:10-11; 12:10; La 2:14; Eze 22:25, 28; 44:8, 10; Hos 9:7-8; Zep 3:4; Mal 1:6-10; 2Ti 4:3). Mercenary (Isa 8:3; Isa 56:11; Mic 3:11). Presumptuous (Dt 18:20-22; Jn 5:43). Insincere (Php 1:15-16). Senseless (Jer 10:21). Adulterous (1Sa 2:22; Jer 23:14; Hos 6:9). Murderous (Hos 6:9). Pervert the truth (2Co 2:17; 11:3-4, 13-15; Gal 1:6-8; 1Ti 4:1-3, 7). Lead the people astray (Isa 3:12; Jer 50:6). Addicted to alcohol (Isa 28:7; 56:12). Indifferent to good and evil (Isa 56:10; Eze 22:26). Desired by the wicked (Isa 30:10-11; Jer 5:13-14, 30-31; Am 2:11-12; Mic 2:11).

Condemned—

Denunciations against false ministers (Isa 5:20; Jer 23:11-40; La 4:13-14; Eze 13:1-23; 34:1-10, 16-22; Mt 23:4-7, 13-14, 36; 2Pe 2:1-22).

Warnings against false ministers (Dt 13:1-4; Isa 8:19-20; Jer 14:13-16; 27:9-18; Mt 5:19; 7:15-23; 15:9, 13-14 w Lk 6:39; Mt 23:3-4, 13; 24:4-5, 11, 24, 26, 48-51; Mk 13:21-22; Lk 21:8; Jn 10:1, 5, 8, 10, 12-13; Ac 20:20, 30; Eph 4:14; Php 3:2; Col 2:4, 8, 18-19; 1Ti 1:3-7; 6:3-5; 2Ti 2:17-18; Tit 1:10-14; 1Jn 2:18-19, 22-23, 26; 4:1-3, 5; 2Jn 7, 10-11; Rev 2:12, 14-15, 18, 20-23).

Judgments upon false ministers (Isa 29:10-11; Hos 5:1; Gal 5:10).

Punishment of false ministers (Dt 13:1, 5; 18:20; Isa 43:27-28; Jer 14:15; 23:1-2, 11, 15, 21; 27:9-18; La 4:13-14; Eze 14:9-10; Hos 4:5-6, 8-13; Mic 3:5-7; Zec 10:3; 13:2-5; Mal 2:1-3, 8-9; Lk 12:45-46; 2Pe 2:3; Jude 4, 11).

Instances of—

Nadab and Abihu (Lev 10:1-2). Korah, Dathan, and Abiram (Nu 16:1-40). Eli's sons (1Sa 2:12-17, 22, 25, 29, 34; 3:13; 4:11). Samuel's sons (1Sa 8:1-3). The old prophet of Bethel (1Ki 13:11-32). Jonathan (Jdg 17:7-13; 18). Noadiah (Ne 6:14). Priests under, Jehoash (2Ki 12:7; 2Ch 24:5-6), Hezekiah (2Ch 30:3, 5). Priests and Levites (Ezr 2:61-62; 9:1-2; 10:18-24; Ne 13:4-9, 28-29; Zec 7:5-6). Hananiah (Jer 28). Jonah (Jnh 1:1-6). Scribes and Pharisees (Mt 23:15-16), Caiaphas (Mt 26:2-3, 57, 63-65; Jn 11:49-51; 18:14). Judas (Mt 26:14-16, 21-25, 47-50; 27:3-5; Jn 12:4-6; Ac 1:18). Judaizing Christians (Gal 3:1-2; 4:17; 6:12-13). Hymenaeus (1Ti 1:20; 2Ti 2:17-18). Alexander (1Ti 1:20). Philetus (2Ti 2:17-18).

MINNI

A district of Armenia (Jer 51:27).

MINNITH

A place E of the Jordan (Jdg 11:33; Eze 27:17).

MINOR PROPHETS, THE

See Prophets, The Minor.

MINORITY REPORT

See Reports.

MINORS

Legal status of (Gal 4:1-2). *See Orphan; Young Men.*

MINSTREL

NIV "harpist" (1Sa 16:23); "flute players" (Mt 9:23). *See Flute; Harp.*

MINT

(*sweet odor*). (Mt 23:23; Lk 11:42).

MIPHKAD

See Gate, Inspection.

MIRACLES

General:

Called: Marvelous things (Ps 78:12), marvelous works (Ps 105:5; Isa 29:14), signs and wonders (Jer 32:21; Jn 4:48; 2Co 12:12).

Performed through the power of God (Jn 3:2; Ac 14:3; 15:12; 19:11), of the Holy Spirit (Mt 12:28; Ro 15:19; 1Co 12:9-10, 28-30), in the name of Christ (Mk 16:17; Ac 3:16; 4:30). Faith required in those who perform (Mt 17:20; 21:21; Jn 14:12; Ac 3:16; 6:8). Faith required in those for whom they were performed (Mt 9:28; Mk 9:22-24; Ac 14:9). Power to work, given the disciples (Mk 3:14-15; 16:17-18, 20). Demanded by unbelievers (Mt 12:38-39; 16:1; Lk 11:16, 29; 23:8).

Alleged miracles performed by magicians (Ex 7:10-12, 22; 8:7), by other impostors (Mt 7:22). Performed through the powers of evil (2Th 2:9; Rev 16:14). Done in support of false religions (Dt 13:1-2), by false Christs (Mt 24:24), by false prophets (Mt 24:24; Rev 19:20), by the medium of Endor (1Sa 28:7-14), by Simon (Ac 8:9-11). Not to be regarded (Dt 13:3). Deceive the ungodly (2Th 2:10-12; Rev 13:14; 19:20). A mark of apostasy (2Th 2:3, 9; Rev 13:13).

List of Miracles and Supernatural Events:

In the Old Testament—

Creation (Ge 1). Flood (Ge 7-8). Confusion of tongues (Ge 11:1-9). Fire on Abraham's sacrifice (Ge 15:17). Conception of Isaac (Ge 17:17; 18:12; 21:2). Destruction of Sodom (Ge 19). Lot's wife turned to salt (Ge 19:26). Closing of the wombs of Abimelech's household (Ge 20:17-18). Opening of Hagar's eyes (Ge 21:19). Conception of Jacob and Esau (Ge 25:21). Opening of Rachel's womb (Ge 30:22).

Burning bush (Ex 3:2). Transformation of Moses' rod into a serpent (Ex 4:3-4, 30; 7:10, 12). Moses' leprosy (Ex 4:6-7, 30). Plagues in Egypt. *See Plague.* Pillar of cloud and fire (Ex 13:21-22; 14:19-20). Passage of the Red Sea (Ex 14:22). Destruction of Pharaoh and his army (Ex 4:23-30). Sweetening the waters of Marah (Ex 15:25). Manna (Ex 16:4-31). Quail (Ex 16:13). Defeat of Amalek (Ex 17:9-13). Transfiguration of the face of Moses (Ex 34:29-35). Water from the rock (Ex 17:5, 7). Thundering and lightning on Sinai (Ex 19:16-20; 24:10, 15-17; Dt 4:33). Miriam's leprosy (Nu 12:10-15). Judgments by fire (Nu 11:1-3). Destruction of Korah (Nu 16:31-35; Dt 11:6-7). Plague (Nu 16:46-50). Aaron's rod buds (Nu 17:1-9). Waters from the rock in Kadesh (Nu 20:8-11). Plague of serpents (Nu 21:6-9). Destruction of Nadab and Abihu (Lev 10:1-2). Balaam's donkey speaks (Nu 22:23-30). Preservation of Moses (Dt 34:7).

Jordan divided (Jos 3:14-17; 4:16-18). Fall of Jericho (Jos 6:20). Midianites destroyed (Jdg 7:16-22). Hail on the confederated kings (Jos 10:11). Sun and moon stand still (Jos 10:12-14).

Dew on Gideon's fleece (Jdg 6:37-40). Samson's strength (Jdg 14:6; 16:3, 29-30). Samson supplied with water (Jdg 15:19).

Fall of Dagon (1Sa 5:7-14). Tumors (1Sa 5:9-12; 6:1-18). Destruction of the people of Beth Shemesh (1Sa 6:19-20). Thunder (1Sa 12:16-18). Destruction of Uzzah (2Sa 6:1-8). Plague in Israel (1Ch 21:14-26).

Fire on the sacrifices of Aaron (Lev 9:24), of Gideon (Jdg 6:21), of Manoah (Jdg 13:19-20), of Solomon (2Ch 7:1), of Elijah (1Ki 18:38).

Jeroboam's hand withered (1Ki 13:3-6). Appearance of blood (2Ki 3:20-22). Panic of the Syrians (2Ki 7:6-7). Elijah is fed by ravens (1Ki 17:6), by an angel (1Ki 19:1-8), increases the widow's meal and oil (1Ki 17:9-16; Lk 4:26), raises the widow's son (1Ki 17:17-24). Rain in answer to Elijah's prayer (1Ki 18:41-45). Elijah brings fire on Ahaziah's army (2Ki 1:10-12), divides Jordan (2Ki 2:8). Elijah's translation (2Ki 2:11).

Elisha divides Jordan (2Ki 2:14), sweetens the waters of Jericho (2Ki 2:19-22), increases a widow's oil (2Ki 4:1-7), raises the Shunammite's child (2Ki 4:18-37), renders the poisoned stew harmless (2Ki 4:38-41), feeds one hundred men (2Ki 4:42-44), cures Naaman (2Ki 5:1-19), strikes Gehazi with leprosy (2Ki 5:26-27), causes the ax to float (2Ki 6:6), reveals the counsel of the king of Syria (2Ki 6:12), causes the eyes of his servant to be opened (2Ki 6:17), strikes with blindness the army of the king of Syria (2Ki 6:18), the dead man restored to life (2Ki 13:21).

M

Destruction of Sennacherib's army (2Ki 19:35; Isa 37:36), return of the shadow on the stairway (2Ki 20:9-11), Hezekiah's cure (Isa 38:21), deliverance of Shadrach, Meshach, and Abednego (Da 3:23-27), of Daniel (Da 6:22), the sea calmed on Jonah being cast into it (Jnh 1:15), Jonah in the fish's belly (Jnh 1:17; 2:10), his plant (Jnh 4:6-7).

Surrounding the Birth of Jesus—
Conception by Elizabeth (Lk 1:18, 24-25). The incarnation of Jesus (Mt 1:18-25; Lk 1:26-80). The appearance of the star of Bethlehem (Mt 2:1-9). The deliverance of Jesus (Mt 2:13-23).

Of Jesus—
Water changed into wine (Jn 2:1-11). Heals the nobleman's son (Jn 4:46-54). Catch of fish (Lk 5:1-11). Heals the demoniac (Mk 1:23-26; Lk 4:33-36). Heals Peter's mother-in-law (Mt 8:14-17; Mk 1:29-31; Lk 4:38-39). Cleanses the leper (Mt 8:1-4; Mk 1:40-45; Lk 5:12-16). Heals the paralytic (Mt 9:1-8; Mk 2:1-12; Lk 5:17-26). Heals the crippled man (Jn 5:1-16). Restores the withered hand (Mt 12:9-13; Mk 3:1-5; Lk 6:6-11). Restores the centurion's servant (Mt 8:5-13; Lk 7:1-10). Raises the widow's son to life (Lk 7:11-16). Heals a demoniac (Mt 12:22-37; Mk 3:11; Lk 11:14-15). Stills the tempest (Mt 8:23-27; 14:32; Mk 4:35-41; Lk 8:22-25). Casts demons out of two men of Gadara (Mt 8:28-34; Mk 5:1-20; Lk 8:26-39). Raises from the dead the daughter of Jairus (Mt 9:18-19, 23-26; Mk 5:22-24, 35-43; Lk 8:41-42, 49-56). Cures the woman with the issue of blood (Mt 9:20-22; Mk 5:25-34; Lk 8:43-48). Restores two blind men to sight (Mt 9:27-31). Heals a demoniac (Mt 9:32-33). Feeds five thousand people (Mt 14:15-21; Mk 6:35-44; Lk 9:12-17; Jn 6:5-14). Walks on the sea (Mt 14:22-33; Mk 6:45-52; Jn 6:16-21). Heals the daughter of the Syrian Phoenician woman (Mt 15:21-28; Mk 7:24-30). Feeds four thousand people (Mt 15:32-39; Mk 8:1-9). Restores one deaf and mute (Mk 7:31-37). Restores a blind man (Mk 8:22-26). Restores a possessed child (Mt 17:14-21; Mk 9:14-29; Lk 9:37-43). Tribute money obtained from a fish's mouth (Mt 17:24-27). Restores ten lepers (Lk 17:11-19). Opens the eyes of a man born blind (Jn 9). Raises Lazarus from the dead (Jn 11:1-46). Heals the woman with the spirit of infirmity (Lk 13:10-17). Cures a man with dropsy (Lk 14:1-6). Restores two blind men near Jericho (Mt 20:29-34; Mk 10:46-52; Lk 18:35-43). Curses a fig tree (Mt 21:17-22; Mk 11:12-14, 20-24). Heals the ear of Malchus (Lk 22:49-51). Second catch of fish (Jn 21:6).

Of the Disciples of Jesus—
By the seventy-two (Lk 10:17-20), by other disciples (Mk 9:39; Jn 14:12), by the apostles (Ac 3:6, 12-13, 16; 4:10, 30; 9:34-35; 16:18). Peter cures the sick (Ac 5:15-16), Aeneas (Ac 9:34), raises Dorcas (Ac 9:40), announces the death of Ananias and Sapphira (Ac 5:5, 10). Peter and John cure a lame man (Ac 3:2-11). Peter and other apostles delivered from prison (Ac 5:19-23; 12:6-11; 16:26). Philip carried away by the Spirit (Ac 8:39). Paul strikes Elymas with blindness (Ac 13:11), heals a cripple (Ac 14:10), casts out evil spirits and cures sick (Ac 16:18; 19:11-12; 28:8-9), raises Eutychus to life (Ac 20:9-12), shakes a viper off of his hand (Ac 28:5). Paul cured of blindness (Ac 9:3-6, 17-18).

Convincing Effect of, on:
The Israelites (Ex 4:28-31; 14:31; Nu 17:1-13). Pharaoh's servants (Ex 10:7). Pharaoh (Ex 10:16-17; 12:31-32). Egyptians (Ex 12:33; 1Sa 6:6). The Canaanites (Jos 2:9-11; 5:1). Gideon (Jdg 6:17-22, 36-40; 7:1). People who witnessed Elijah's (1Ki 18:24, 37-39). Naaman (2Ki 5:14-15). Nebuchadnezzar (Da 2:47; 3:28-29; 4:2-3). Darius (Da 6:20-27).

Simon Peter (Lk 5:4-11). Disciples of Jesus (Jn 2:11, 22-23; 20:30-31). The nobleman whose child Jesus healed (Jn 4:48-53). People who witnessed Christ's (Jn 7:31; 11:43-45; 12:10-11). People who witnessed Philip's (Ac 8:6). People who witnessed Peter's (Ac 9:32-42). Sergius Paulus, the deputy (Ac 13:8-12). Gentiles (Ro 15:18-19).

Resisted by the hard-hearted (Ne 9:17; Ps 78:10-32; Jn 9:24-28; 15:24-25).

Design of:
To reveal God (Ex 7:5, 17; 8:8-10, 22; 9:4-16, 29; 10:1-2; 14:4, 18; Dt 4:33-39; Jos 4:23-24; 1Ki 18:24, 37-39; Jer 32:20). Produce faith in God (Ex 14:31; Nu 14:11; Jos 3:7-17; 2Ch 7:1-3; Ps 106:9-12). Produce the fear of God (1Sa 12:17-18; Da 6:20-27; Jnh 1:14-16). Encourage obedience (Ex 16:4-6; 19:4-5; Dt 11:1-8; 29:1-9; Jdg 2:7; Ps 78:10-32). Glorify God (Lk 5:26; Jn 11:4; Ac 4:21-22). Testify to the messiahship of Jesus (Mt 11:2-5 w Lk 7:19-22; Mk 2:9-12; Lk 5:24-26; 18:42-43; Jn 2:11; 4:48; 5:36; 11:4, 40-42; 14:11; 15:24). Glorify Jesus (Ac 3:1-10, 12-13). Testify to God's servants (Ex 4:2-9; 19:9; Nu 16:28-35; 1Sa 12:17-18; Zec 2:9; Ac 2:22; Heb 2:4). Preserve the righteous (Da 3:28-29; 6:20-27). Change wicked purposes (Ex 3:19-20; 9:16-17; 10:16-17; 11:1-10; 12:29-33; 14:24-25).

Miraculous Gifts of the Spirit:
Foretold (Isa 35:4-6; Joel 2:28-29). Of different kinds (1Co 12:4-6). Enumerated (1Co 12:8-10, 28). Christ was endued with (Mt 12:28). Poured out on Pentecost (Ac 2:1-4). Communicated on preaching the gospel (Ac 10:44-46), by laying on of the apostles' hands (Ac 8:17-18; 19:6), for the confirmation of the gospel (Mk 16:20; Ac 14:3; Ro 15:19; Heb 2:4), for the edification of the church (1Co 12:7; 14:12-13). To be sought after (1Co 12:31; 14:1). Temporary nature of (1Co 13:8). Not to be neglected (1Ti 4:14; 2Ti 1:6), or despised (1Th 5:20), or purchased (Ac 8:20).
See Gifts From God, Spiritual.

MIRE Figurative of distress (Ps 40:2; 69:2).

MIRIAM (variously *bitterness, plump one, the wished-for child, one who loves* or *is loved*).
1. Sister of Aaron and Moses; saved life of the baby Moses (Ex 2:4, 7-8), prophetess (Ex 15:20), criticized Moses for his marriage (Nu 12), buried at Kadesh (Nu 20:1).
2. Judahite (1Ch 4:17).

MIRMAH (*deceit*). A Benjamite (1Ch 8:10).

MIRROR Ancient mirrors were made of polished metal (Ex 38:8; Job 37:18; 1Co 13:12; 2Co 3:18; Jas 1:23). *See Glass.*

MISCARRY Of people, a judgment of God (Hos 9:14). Lack of in people and in animals, a sign of God's blessing (Ge 31:38; Ex 23:25-26; Job 21:10). *See Abortion.*

MISCEGENATION *See Intermarry.*

MISER (Ecc 4:7-8).

MISGAB NIV "stronghold"; a place otherwise unknown (Jer 48:1).

MISHAEL (*who belongs to God [El]?*).
1. A son of Uzziel, helps carry the bodies of Nadab and Abihu out of the camp (Ex 6:22; Lev 10:4).
2. A Jew who stood by Ezra when he read the law to the people (Ne 8:4).
3. Also called Meshach. *See Meshach.*

MISHAL Levitical city in Asher (Jos 19:26; 21:30), also called Mashal (1Ch 6:74). *See Mashal.*

MISHAM Son of Elpaal (1Ch 8:12).

MISHMA (*rumor*).
1. Son of Ishmael (Ge 25:14; 1Ch 1:30).
2. Of the tribe of Simeon (1Ch 4:25-26).

MISHMANNAH (*fatness*). A Gadite who joined David at Ziklag (1Ch 12:10).

MISHPAT *See En Mishpat.*

MISHRAITES Clan of Kiriath Jearim in Judah (1Ch 2:53).

MISJUDGMENT Instances of: Of the Reubenites and Gadites (Nu 32:1-33; Jos 22:11-31). Of Hannah (1Sa 1:14-17).
See Accusation, False; Uncharitableness.

MISPAR (*number*). Coworker of Zerubbabel (Ezr 2:2). "Mispereth" (Ne 7:7).

MISPERETH Also called Mizpar. A Jew who returned with Zerubbabel from Babylon (Ezr 2:2; Ne 7:7).

MISREPHOTH MAIM (*waters of Misrephoth [lime burning]*). Place near Sidon and Tyre (Jos 11:8; 13:6).

MISSIONARY JOURNEYS OF PAUL
I. The First Missionary Journey, c. A.D. 46-48 (Ac 13:1-14:28).
A. Barnabas and Saul are Sent From Antioch (13:1-3).
B. Ministry at Cyprus (13:4-13).
1. Preaching in the synagogues (13:4-5).
2. Controversy with Bar-Jesus (13:6-13).
C. Ministry at Antioch (13:14-50).
1. Paul preaches on first Sabbath (13:14-43).
2. Paul preaches on second Sabbath (13:44-50).
D. Ministry at Iconium (13:51-14:5).
E. Ministry at Lystra (14:6-20).
1. A lame man is healed (14:6-10).
2. Paul and Barnabas are deified (14:11-18).
3. Paul is stoned (14:19-20).
F. Ministry on the Return Trip (14:21-25).
G. Report on the First Missionary Journey (14:26-28).
II. The Jerusalem Council (15:1-35).
A. Debate Over Gentiles Keeping the Law (15:1-5).
B. Peter Preaches Salvation Through Grace (15:6-11).
C. Paul and Barnabas Testify (15:12).
D. James Proves Gentiles are Free From the Law (15:13-21).
E. The Council Sends an Official Letter (15:22-29).
F. Report to Antioch (15:30-35).
III. The Second Missionary Journey, c. A.D. 49-52 (Ac 15:36-18:22).
A. Contention Over John Mark (15:36-41).
B. Derbe and Lystra: Timothy is Circumcised (16:1-5).
C. Troas: Macedonian Call (16:6-10).
D. Philippi: Extensive Ministry (16:11-40).
1. Lydia is converted (16:11-15).
2. Spirit of divination is cast out (16:16-24).
3. Philippian jailer is converted (16:25-34).
4. Paul is released from prison (16:35-40).
E. Thessalonica: "Turn the World Upside Down" (17:1-9).
F. Berea: Many Receive the Word (17:10-15).
G. Athens: Paul's Sermon on Mars' Hill (17:16-34).
H. Corinth: One-and-a-Half Years of Ministry (18:1-17).
1. Paul works with Aquila and Priscilla (18:1-3).
2. Jews reject Paul (18:4-6).
3. Crispus, the Gentile, is converted (18:7-11).
4. Gallio will not try Paul (18:12-17).
I. Return Trip to Antioch (18:18-22).
IV. The Third Missionary Journey, c. A.D. 53-57 (Ac 18:23-21:16).
A. Galatia and Phrygia: Strengthening the Disciples (18:23).
B. Ephesus: Three Years of Ministry (18:24-19:41).
1. Apollos teaches effectively (18:24-28).
2. Disciples of John receive the Holy Spirit (19:1-7).
3. Paul teaches in Tyrannus' school (19:8-10).
4. Miracles are performed at Ephesus (19:11-20).
5. Timothy and Erastus are sent to Macedonia (19:21-22).
6. Demetrius causes uproar at Ephesus (19:23-41).
C. Macedonia: Three Months of Ministry (20:1-5).
D. Troas: Eutychus Falls From Loft (20:6-12).
E. Miletus: Paul Bids Farewell to Ephesian Elders (20:13-38).
F. Tyre: Paul is Warned About Jerusalem (21:1-6).
G. Caesarea: Agabus's Prediction (21:7-16).
V. The Trip to Rome, c. A.D. 57-59 (Ac 21:17-28:31).
A. Paul Witnesses in Jerusalem (21:17-23:33).
1. Paul conforms to Jewish customs (21:17-26).
2. Paul's arrest (21:27-39).
3. Paul's defense before the crowd (21:40-22:23).
4. Paul's defense before the centurion (22:24-29).
5. Paul's defense before the Sanhedrin (22:30-23:11).
6. Jews' plan to kill Paul (23:12-22).
7. Paul's rescue (23:23-33).
B. Paul's Witnesses in Caesarea (23:34-28:31).
1. Paul is tried before Felix (23:34-24:27).
2. Paul is tried before Festus (25:1-22).
3. Paul is tried before Agrippa (25:23-26:32).
C. Paul Witnesses in Rome (27:1-28:31).
1. Paul's witness during the shipwreck (27:1-44).
2. Paul's witness on Malta (28:1-15).
3. Paul's witness in Rome (28:16-31).
VI. The Fourth Missionary Journey, c. A.D. 62-68.

It is clear from Ac 13:1-21:17 that Paul went on three missionary journeys. There is also reason to believe that he made a fourth journey after his release from the Roman imprisonment recorded in Ac 28. The conclusion that such a journey did indeed take place is based on: (1) Paul's declared intention to go to Spain (Ro 15:24, 28), (2) Eusebius's implication that Paul was released following his first Roman imprisonment (*Ecclesiastical History*, 2.22.2-3) and (3) statements in early Christian literature that he took the gospel as far as Spain (Clement of Rome, *Epistle to the Corinthians*, ch. 5; *Actus Petri Vercellenses*, chs. 1-3; Muratorian Canon, lines 34-39).

The places Paul may have visited after his release from prison are indicated by statements of intention in his earlier writings and by subsequent mention in the Pastoral Letters. The order of his travel cannot be determined with certainty, but the itinerary that follows seems likely.
1. Rome: released from prison in c. A.D. 62.
2. Spain: c. A.D. 62-64 (Ro 15:24, 28).
3. Crete: c. A.D. 64-65 (Tit 1:5).
4. Miletus: c. A.D. 65 (2Ti 4:20).
5. Colosse: c. A.D. 66 (Phm 22).
6. Ephesus: c. A.D. 66 (1Ti 1:3).
7. Philippi: c. A.D. 66 (Php 2:23-24; 1Ti 1:3).
8. Nicopolis: c. A.D. 66-67 (Tit 3:12).
9. Rome: c. A.D. 67.
10. Martyrdom: c. A.D. 67/68.
See Paul; Pastoral Epistles.

MISSIONS Spreading the good news throughout the world.

General:
Religious propagandism (2Ki 17:27-28; 1Ch 16:23-24). Commanded (Ps 96:3, 10; Mt 28:19; Mk 16:15; Lk 24:47-48). Prophecy concerning (Mt 24:14; Mk 13:10). Peter's vision concerning (Ac 10:9-20).

Ordained by Jesus (Mt 24:14; 28:19; Mt 16:15-16; Lk 24:47-49). Saul and Barnabas ordained for (Ac 13:2-4, 47). Paul appointed to (Ac 26:14-18; 1Co 16:9). Practiced by the psalmist (Ps 18:49). Practiced by Jonah (Jnh 3:1-9). Symbolized by the flying angel (Rev 14:6-7).

Missionary hymn (Ps 96).

The first to do homage to the Messiah were Gentiles (Mt 2:11).
See Gentiles, Conversion of; Heathen; Jesus the Christ, King; Jesus the Christ, Kingdom of.

Missionaries, All Christians Should Be:
After the example of Christ (Ac 10:38). Women and children as well as men (Ps 8:2; Pr 31:26; Mt 21:15-16; Php 4:3; 1Ti 5:10; Tit 2:3-5; 1Pe 3:1). The zeal of idolaters should provoke to (Jer 7:18). The zeal of hypocrites should provoke to (Mt 23:15). An imperative duty (Jdg 5:23; Lk 19:40). The principle on which (2Co 5:14-15). However weak they may be (1Co 1:27). From their calling as saints (Ex 19:6; 1Pe 2:9). As faithful stewards (1Pe 4:10-11).

In youth (Ps 71:17; 148:12-13). In old age (Dt 32:7; Ps 71:18). In the family (Dt 6:7; Ps 78:5-8; Isa 38:19; 1Co 7:16; 1Pe 2:12). In first giving their own selves to the Lord (2Co 8:5). In declaring what God has done for them (Ps 66:16; 116:16-19). In hating one's life for Christ (Lk 14:26). In openly confessing Christ (Mt 10:32). In following Christ (Lk 14:27; 18:22). In preferring Christ above all relations (Lk 14:26; 1Co 2:2). In joyfully suffering for Christ (Heb 10:34). In forsaking all for Christ (Heb 10:34). In a holy example (Mt 5:16; Php 2:15; 1Th 1:7). In holy conduct (1Pe 2:12). In holy boldness (Ps 119:46). In dedicating themselves to the service of God (Jos 24:15; Ps 27:4). In devoting all property to God (1Ch 29:2-3, 14, 16; Ecc 11:1; Mt 6:19-20; Mk 12:44; Lk 12:33; 18:22, 28; Ac 2:45; 4:32-34).

In holy conversation (Ps 37:30, w Pr 10:31; Pr 15:7; Eph 4:29; Col 4:6). In talking of God and his works (Ps 71:24; 77:12; 119:27; 145:11-12). In showing forth God's praises (Isa 43:21).

In inviting others to embrace the gospel (Ps 34:8; Isa 2:3; Jn 1:46; 4:29). In seeking the edification of others (Ro 14:19; 15:2; 1Th 5:11). In admonishing others (1Th 5:14; 2Th 3:15). In reproving others (Lev 19:17; Eph 5:11). In teaching and exhorting (Ps 34:11; 51:13; Col 3:16; Heb 3:13; 10:25). In interceding for others (Col 4:3; Heb 13:18; Jas 5:16). In aiding ministers in their labors (Ro 16:3, 9; 2Co 11:9; Php 4:14-16; 3Jn 6). In giving a reason for their faith (Ex 12:26-27; Dt 6:20-21; 1Pe 3:15). In encouraging the weak (Isa 35:3-4; Ro 14:1; 15:1; 1Th 5:14). In visiting and relieving the poor and sick (Lev 25:35; Ps 112:9, w 2Co 9:9; Mt 25:36; Ac 20:35; Jas 1:27). With a willing heart (Ex 35:29; 1Ch 29:9, 14). With great generosity (Ex 36:5-7; 2Co 8:3).

Encouragement to (Pr 11:25, 30; 1Co 1:27; Jas 5:19-20). Blessedness of (Da 12:3). Illustrated (Mt 25:14; Lk 19:13).
See Minister.

MIST
1. Steamy vapor rising from the ground (Ge 2:6).
2. Dimness of vision (Ac 13:11).
3. Description of false teachers (2Pe 2:17).

MITE(S) *See Money; Penny.*

MITHCAH (*sweetness*). An encampment of the Israelites (Nu 33:28-29).

MITHNITE Family name of Joshaphat (1Ch 11:43).

MITHRAISM Cult of Mithras, Persian sun-god, widely disseminated in the Roman Empire in the first century A.D.

MITHREDATH (*gift to [pagan deity] Mithra*).
1. Treasurer of Cyrus (Ezr 1:8).

2. A Persian officer who joined in writing a letter hostile to the Jews (Ezr 4:7).

MITRE *See Turban.*

MITYLENE Capital of Lesbos. Paul visits (Ac 20:14-15).

MIXED MARRIAGE *See Intermarry.*

MIXED MULTITUDE Non-Israelites who traveled and associated with the Israelites (Nu 11:4-6; Ne 13:3).

MIZAR (*small*). A hill near Mt. Hermon (Ps 42:6).

MIZPAH (*lookout point*).

1. A city allotted to Benjamin (Jos 18:26). The Israelites assemble at (Jdg 20:1-3), and decree the penalty to be executed upon the Benjamites for their mistreatment of the Levite's concubine (Jdg 20:10). Assembled by Samuel that he might reprove them for their idolatry (1Sa 7:5). Crown Saul king of Israel at (1Sa 10:17-25). A judgment seat of Samuel (1Sa 7:16). Walled by Asa (1Ki 15:22; 2Ch 16:6). Temporarily the capital of the country after the Israelites had been carried away captive (2Ki 25:23, 25; Jer 40:6-15; 41:1-14). Captivity returned to (Ne 3:7, 15, 19).

2. A valley near Lebanon (Jos 11:3, 8).

3. A city in Moab. David gives his parents to the care of the king of (1Sa 22:3-4).

4. A city in the lowland of Judah (Jos 15:38).

5. A town in Gilead (Jos 10:17; Jdg 11:34). May be the location of a treaty between Jacob and Laban (Ge 31:48-49).

MIZPAR *See Mispar.*

MIZPEH *See Mizpah.*

MIZRAIM (Hebrew word for *Egypt*). Son of Ham (Ge 10:6, 13; 1Ch 1:8, 11), progenitor of the Egyptians, a people of N Africa, Hamitic people of Canaan.

MIZZAH (*terror*). Son of Reuel (Ge 36:13, 17; 1Ch 1:37).

MNASON A native and Christian of Cyprus who entertained Paul (Ac 21:16).

MOAB (*seed*).

1. Son of Lot (Ge 19:37).

2. Plains of. Israelites come in (Dt 2:17-18). Military forces numbered in (Nu 26:3, 63). The law rehearsed in, by Moses (Nu 35-36; Dt 29-33). The Israelites renew their covenant in (Dt 29:1). The land of promise allotted in (Jos 13:32).

MOABITE STONE Black basalt stele, two by four feet, inscribed by Mesha king of Moab, with thirty-four lines in the Moabite language (practically a dialect of Hebrew), giving his side of the story (2Ki 3).

M

MOABITE(S) Descendants of Lot through his son Moab (Ge 19:37). Called the people of Chemosh (Nu 21:29). The territory E of Jordan, bounded on the N by the Arnon River (Nu 21:13; Jdg 11:18). Israelites commanded not to distress the Moabites (Dt 2:9). Refuse passage of Jephthah's army through their territory (Jdg 11:17-18). Balak was king of (Nu 22:4), calls for Balaam to curse Israel (Nu 22-24; Jos 24:9; Mic 6:5). Are a snare to the Israelites (Nu 25:1-3; Ru 1:4; 1Ki 11:1; 1Ch 8:8; Ezr 9:1-2; Ne 13:23). Land of, not given to the Israelites as a possession (Dt 2:9, 29). David takes refuge among, from Saul (1Sa 22:3-4). David conquers (2Sa 8:2; 23:20; 1Ch 11:22; 18:2-11). Israelites had war with (2Ki 3:5-27; 13:20; 24:2; 2Ch 20). Prophecies concerning judgments upon (Jer 48).

MOADIAH (perhaps *Yahweh assembles* or *Yahweh promises*). A chief priest who returned from the Exile with Zerubbabel at the time of Joiakim (Ne 12:5, 17).

MOB At Thessalonica (Ac 17:5), Jerusalem (Ac 21:28, 30), Ephesus (Ac 19:29-40).

MOCKING Ishmael mocks Sarah (Ge 21:9). Elijah mocks the priests of Baal (1Ki 18:27). Zedekiah mocks Micaiah (1Ki 22:24). Children mock Elisha (2Ki 2:23). The tormentors of Job mock (Job 15:12; 30:1). The persecutors of Jesus mock him (Mt 26:67-68; 27:28-31, 39-44; Mk 10:34; 14:65; 15:17-20, 29-32; Lk 23:11; Jn 19:2-3, 5; 1Pe 2:23). The Ammonites mock God (Eze 25:3). Tyre mocks Jerusalem (Eze 26:2). The wicked mock (Isa 28:15, 22; 2Pe 3:3).

See Scoffing.

Figurative (Ecc 7:16; 1Co 7:31).

MODESTY Of women (1Ti 2:9).

Instances of: Moses (Nu 12:3). Saul (1Sa 9:21). Vashti (Est 1:11-12). Elihu (Job 32:4-7).

See Humility.

MOLADAH (*generation*). Town c. ten miles E of Beersheba (Ne 11:26).

MOLDING (*wreath* or *border*). (Job 28:2; Eze 24:11). The decorative ledge of gold around the ark of the covenant (Ex 25:11; 37:2), the table (Ex 25:24-25; 37:11-12), and the incense altar (Ex 30:3-4; 37:26-27). Of images (Ex 32:4, 8; 34:17; Lev 19:4; Dt 9:12), pillars (1Ki 7:15), bronze Sea (1Ki 7:23), done in the plain of Jordan (1Ki 7:46; 2Ch 4:17), mirrors (Job 37:18).

MOLECH (*"shameful" king*) Molech is the deliberate misvocalization of the name of a pagan god. The consonants for the word king, *melek*, are combined with the vowels for shame, *bosheth*.

An idol of the Ammonites (Ac 7:43). Worshiped by the wives of Solomon, and by Solomon (1Ki 11:1-8). Children sacrificed to (2Ki 23:10, w Jer 32:35; 2Ki 16:3; 21:6; 2Ch 28:3; Isa 57:5; Jer 7:31; Eze 16:20-21; 20:26, 31; 23:37, 39, w Lev 18:21; 20:2-5). *See Malcam, 2.*

MOLE(S) NIV "chameleon" (Lev 11:30), "rodent" (Isa 2:20). *See Animals; Chameleon.*

MOLID (*descendant*). A descendant of Judah, the son of Abishur and his wife Abihail (1Ch 2:29).

MOLTEN IMAGE *See Tabernacle.*

MONARCHY Described by Samuel (1Sa 8:11-18). *See Government; Kings.*

MONEY Silver used as (Ge 17:12-13, 23, 27; 20:16; 23:9, 13; 31:15; 37:28; 42:25-35; 43:12-23; 44:1-8; 47:14-18; Ex 12:44; 21:11, 21, 34-35; 22:7, 17, 25; 30:16; Lev 22:11; 25:37, 51; 27:15, 18; Nu 3:48-51; 18:16; Dt 2:6, 28; 14:25-26; 21:14; 23:19; Jdg 5:19; 16:18; 17:4; 1Ki 21:2, 6, 15; 2Ki 5:26; 12:4, 7-16; 15:20; 22:7, 9; 23:35; 2Ch 24:5, 11, 14; 34:9, 14, 17; Ezr 3:7; 7:7; Ne 5:4, 10-11; Est 4:7; Job 31:39; Ps 15:5; Pr 7:20; Ecc 7:12; 10:19; Isa 43:24; 52:3; 55:1-2; Jer 32:9-10, 25, 44; La 5:4; Mic 3:11; Mt 25:18, 27; 28:12, 15; Mk 14:11; Lk 9:3; 19:15, 23; 22:5; Ac 7:16; 8:20).

Gold used as (Ge 13:2; 24:35; 44:8, w 44:1; 1Ch 21:25; Ezr 8:25-27; Isa 13:17; 46:6; 60:9; Eze 7:19; 28:4; Mt 2:11; 10:9; Ac 3:6; 20:33; 1Pe 1:18).

Copper used as (Mt 10:9; Mk 6:8; 12:42; Lk 21:2).

Weighed (Ge 23:16; 43:21; Job 28:15; Jer 32:9-10; Zec 11:12). Image on (Mt 22:20-21). Conscience (Jdg 17:2; Mt 27:3, 5). Ransom atonement (Ex 30:12-16; Lev 5:15-16). Sin offering (2Ki 12:16). Value of, varied corruptly (Am 8:5). Love of, the root of evil (1Ti 6:10). *See Materialism.*

See Daric; Drachma; Gerah; Penny; Pound; Shekel; Silver; Talent.

MONEY CHANGERS Those who changed foreign currency into sanctuary money at a profit (Mt 21:12; Mk 11:15; Jn 2:14-15).

MONITOR LIZARD Unclean for food (Lev 11:30). *See Animals.*

MONOPOLY Of lands (Isa 5:8; Mic 2:2), by Pharaoh (Ge 47:19-26), of food (Pr 11:26).

MONOTHEISM (*one God*). Belief that there is but one God.

MONSTERS *See Animals; Behemoth; Leviathan; Serpent.*

MONTH Sun and moon for signs and seasons (Ge 1:14). The beginning and ending of the Flood (Ge 7:11; 8:4).

Twelve months reckoned to a year (1Ki 4:7; 1Ch 27:1-15; Est 2:12). Time computed by months (Ge 29:14; Nu 10:10; Jdg 11:37; 1Sa 6:1; Ps 81:3; Rev 22:2). Months in prophecy (Rev 11:2).

1. Abib (Post-Exilic name: **Nisan**)
March-April

Month 7 in civil sequence. The Jewish calendar began with (Ex 12:2; 13:4; Dt 16:1). Passover instituted and celebrated in (Ex 12:1-28; 23:15). Israelites left Egypt in (Ex 13:4). Tabernacle set up in (Ex 40:2, 17). Israelites arrive at Zin in (Nu 20:1). Cross Jordan in (Jos 4:19). Jordan overflows in (1Ch 12:15). After the Captivity called Nisan (Ne 2:1; Est 3:7). Decree to put the Jews to death in (Est 3:12). The death of Jesus in (Mt 26:27).

Season: Spring; Later rains.
Agriculture: Barley and flax harvest begin.
Feasts: 14th, Passover (Ex 12:18; Lev 23:5); 15-21st, Unleavened Bread (Lev 23:6); 16th, Firstfruits (Lev 23:10f).

2. Ziv (Post-Exilic name: **Iyyar**) **April-May**

Month 8 in civil sequence. Israel numbered in (Nu 1:1, 18). Passover to be observed in, by the unclean and others who could not observe it in the first month (Nu 9:10-11). Israel departed from the wilderness of Zin in (Nu 10:11). Temple begun in (1Ki 6:1; 2Ch 3:2). An irregular Passover celebrated in (2Ch 30:1-27). Rebuilding of the temple begun in (Ezr 3:8).

Season: Dry season begins.
Agriculture: Barley harvest.
Feasts: 14th, Later Passover (Nu 9:10-11).

3. Sivan (Post-Exilic name) **May-June**

Month 9 in civil sequence. Asa renews the covenant of himself and people in (2Ch 15:10).

Agriculture: Early figs ripen; Wheat harvest.
Feasts: 6th, Pentecost or Feast of Weeks (Lev 23:15ff); Harvest.

4. Tammuz (Post-Exilic name) **June-July**

Month 10 in civil sequence. The number only appears in the Bible. Jerusalem taken by Nebuchadnezzar in (Jer 39:2; 52:6-7).

Agriculture: Tending vines.
Feasts: None.

5. Ab (Post-Exilic name) **July-August**

Month 11 in civil sequence. Number only mentioned. Aaron died on the first day of (Nu 33:38). Temple destroyed in (2Ki 25:8-10; Jer 1:3; 52:12-30). Ezra arrived at Jerusalem in (Ezr 7:8-9).

Agriculture: Ripening of grapes, figs, and olives.
Feasts: None.

6. Elul (Post-Exilic name)
August-September

Month 12 in civil sequence. Wall of Jerusalem finished in (Ne 6:15). Temple built in (Hag 1:14-15).

Agriculture: Processing grapes, dates, summer figs, and olives.
Feasts: None.

7. Ethanim (Post-Exilic name: **Tishri**)
September-October

Month 1 in civil sequence. Feasts held in (Lev 23:24, 27; Ne 8:13-15). Jubilee proclaimed in (Lev 25:9). Solomon's temple dedicated in (1Ki 8:2). Altar rebuilt and offerings renewed in (Ezr 3:1, 6).

Season: Autumn (early) rains begin.
Agriculture: Plowing.
Feasts: 1st, Trumpets (Nu 29:1; Lev 23:24); 10th, Atonement (Lev 16:29ff; 23:27ff); 15-21st, Tabernacles or Booths (Lev 23:34ff); 22nd, Solemn assembly (Lev 23:36).

8. Bul (Post-Exilic name: **Marcheshvan**)
October-November

Month 2 in civil sequence. The temple finished in (1Ki 6:38). Jeroboam's idolatrous feast in (1Ki 12:32-33; 1Ch 27:11).

Season: Plowing.
Agriculture: Winter figs; sowing of wheat and barley.
Feasts: None.

9. Kislev (Post-Exilic name)
November-December

Month 3 in civil sequence.

Agriculture: Sowing.
Feasts: 25th, Hanukkah or Dedication (1Mc 4:52f; Jn 10:22).

10. Tebeth (Post-Exilic name)
December-January

Month 4 in civil sequence. Nebuchadnezzar besieges Jerusalem in (2Ki 25:1; Jer 52:4). Esther chosen queen (Est 2:16).

Season: Winter rains begin (snow on high ground).
Agriculture: None.
Feasts: None.

11. Shebat (Post-Exilic name)
January-February

Month 5 in civil sequence. Moses probably died in (Dt 1:3).

Agriculture: None.
Feasts: None.

12. Adar (Post-Exilic name)
February-March

Month 6 in civil sequence. Second temple finished in (Ezr 6:15). Feast of Purim (Est 9:1-26).

Agriculture: Almond trees bloom; citrus fruit harvest.
Feasts: Purim.

13. Adar Sheni (not in Bible)

Second Adar is an intercalary month added about every three years so the lunar calendar would correspond to the solar year.

See Calendar; Time. See also each month by name.

MONUMENT *See Pillar.*

MOON Created by God (Ge 1:16; Ps 8:3; 136:7-9). Its light (Job 31:26; Ecc 12:2; SS 6:10; Jer 31:35; 1Co 15:41). Its influences (Dt 33:14; Ps 121:6). Seasons of (months) (Ps 104:19). Joseph's dream concerning (Ge 37:9). Stand still (Jos 10:12-13; Hab 3:11). Worship of, forbidden (Dt 4:19; 17:3). Worshiped (2Ki 23:5; Job 31:26-27; Jer 7:18; 8:2; 44:17-19, 25). No light of, in eternity (Rev 21:23).

Figurative:

Shining of (Isa 30:26; 60:19; Rev 21:23). Darkening of (Job 25:5; Isa 13:10; 24:23; Eze 32:7; Joel 2:10, 31; 3:15; Mt 24:29; Mk 13:24; Lk 21:25; Ac 2:20; Rev 6:12; 8:12).

Symbolic: (Rev 12:1).

Feast of the New Moon:

(Nu 10:10; 28:11-15; 1Ch 23:31; 2Ch 31:3; Ezr 3:5). Trade at time of, prohibited (Am 8:5).

MORAL AGENCY *See Contingencies.*

MORAL LAW *See Law.*

MORALITY *See Duty of People to People; Integrity; Neighbor.*

MORASTHITE *See Moresheth.*

MORDECAI (*pagan Babylonian god Marduk*). A Jewish captive in Persia (Est 2:5-6). Foster father of Esther (Est 2:7). Informs Xerxes of a conspiracy against his life, and is rewarded (Est 2:21-23; 6:1-11). Promoted in Haman's place (Est 8:1-2, 15; 10:1-3). Intercedes with Xerxes for the Jews; establishes the festival of Purim in commemoration of their deliverance (Est 8-9).

MOREH (*[place of] instructor*).

1. A plain near Shechem and Gilgal (Ge 12:6; Dt 11:30).

2. A hill in the plain of Jezreel where the Midianites encamped (Jdg 7:1, 12).

MORESHETH (*possession of Gath*). Hometown of Micah; probably Moresheth Gath (Jer 26:18; Mic 1:1).

MORESHETH GATH (*possession of Gath*). Town c. five miles W of Gath in the Shephelah (Mic 1:14). *See Moresheth.*

MORIAH Place to which Abraham to offer up Isaac (Ge 22:2). Solomon built temple on Mt. Moriah (2Ch 3:1), but it is not certain whether it is the same place.

MORNING The second part of the day at the Creation (Ge 1:5, 8, 13, 19, 23, 31). The first part of the natural day (Mk 16:2). Ordained by God (Job 38:12). Began with first dawn (Jos 6:15; Ps 119:147). Continued until noon (1Ki 18:26; Ne 8:3). Dawning of calls for rejoicing (Ps 65:8).

The Jews:

Generally rose early in (Ge 28:18; Jdg 6:28). Eat but little in (Ecc 10:16). Went to the temple in (Lk 21:38; Jn 8:2). Offered a part of the daily sacrifice in (Ex 29:38-39; Nu 28:4-7). Devoted a part of to prayer and praise (Ps 5:3; 59:16; 88:13). Gathered the manna in (Ex 16:21). Began their journeys in (Ge 22:3). Held courts of justice in (Jer 21:12; Mt 27:1). Contracted covenants in (Ge 26:31). Transacted business in (Ecc 11:6; Mt 20:1). Was frequently cloudless (2Sa 23:4). A red sky in, a sign of bad weather (Mt 16:3). Ushered in by the morning stars (Job 38:7).

Illustrative:

Of the resurrection day (Ps 49:14). Breaking forth, of the glory of the church (SS 6:10; Isa 58:8). Star of, of the glory of Christ (Rev 22:16). Star of, of reward of saints (Rev 2:28). Clouds in, of the short-lived profession of hypocrites (Hos 6:4). Wings of, of rapid movements (Ps 139:9). Spread upon the mountains, of heavy calamities (Joel 2:2).

MORNING SACRIFICE *See Offerings.*

MORNING STAR Figurative of the glory of the king of Babylon (Isa 14:12). Of Jesus (2Pe 1:19; Rev 2:26; 22:16).

MORSEL A choice bit of food (Pr 18:8; 26:22).

MORTAL, MORTALITY A mortal is a being subject to death (Ro 8:11; 1Co 15:53-54).

MORTAR

1. An instrument for crushing grain (Nu 11:8; Pr 27:22). *See Grinding; Mill.*

2. A cement (Ex 1:14). Tar used as, in building tower of Babel (Ge 11:3). Used to plaster houses (Lev 14:42-45). Untempered, not enduring (Eze 13:10-15; 22:28). To be trodden to make firm (Na 3:14).

Figurative (Isa 41:25).

MORTGAGE (*take on pledge, give in pledge, exchange*). On land (Ne 5:3). *See Land.*

MORTIFICATION (*self-denial*). Instances of: David's ambassadors, sent to Hanun (2Sa 10:1-5). Judas (Mt 27:3-5). *See Humility.*

MOSAIC Picture or design made by setting tiny squares or cones of varicolored marble, limestone, or semiprecious stones in some medium such as plaster to tell a story or to form a decoration (Est 1:6).

MOSERAH (*possession*). An encampment of the Israelites where Aaron died (Dt 10:6). Probably identical with Moseroth, below.

MOSEROTH (*possession*). An encampment of the Israelites (Nu 33:30-31).

MOSES (*drawn out* Ex 2:10; Egyptian for *son*).

Personal History:

A Levite and son of Amram (Ex 2:1-4; 6:20; Ac 7:20; Heb 11:23). Hidden in an basket (Ex 2:3). Discovered and adopted by the daughter of Pharaoh (Ex 2:5-10). Learned in all the wisdom of Egypt (Ac 7:22). His loyalty to his race (Heb 11:24-26). Takes the life of an Egyptian; flees from Egypt; finds refuge among the Midianites (Ex 2:11-22; Ac 7:24-29). Joins himself to Jethro, priest of Midian; marries Jethro's daughter Zipporah; has two sons (Ex 2:15-22; 18:3-4). Is herdsman for Jethro in the desert of Horeb (Ex 3:1). Has the vision of the burning bush (Ex 3:2-6). God reveals to him his purpose to deliver the Israelites and bring them into the land of Canaan (Ex 3:7-10). Commissioned as a leader of the Israelites (Ex 3:10-22; 6:13). His rod miraculously turned into a serpent, his hand made leprous, and each restored (Ex 4:1-9, 28). With his wife and sons leaves Jethro to perform his mission (Ex 4:18-20). His controversy with his wife on account of circumcision (Ex 4:20-26). Meets Aaron in the wilderness (Ex 4:27-28).

With Aaron assembles the leaders of Israel (Ex 4:29-31). With Aaron goes before Pharaoh, in the name of Yahweh demands the liberties of his people (Ex 5:1). Rejected by Pharaoh; hardships of the Israelites increased (Ex 5). People murmur against Moses and Aaron (Ex 5:20-21; 15:24; 16:2-3; 17:2-3; Nu 14:2-4; 16:41; 20:2-5; 21:4-6; Dt 1:12, 26-28). *See Israel.* Receives comfort and assurance from the land (Ex 6:1-8). Unbelief of the people (Ex 6:9). Renews his appeal to Pharaoh (Ex 6:11). Under divine direction brings plagues upon the land of Egypt (Ex 7-12). Secures the deliverance of the people and leads them out of Egypt (Ex 13). Crosses the Red Sea; Pharaoh and his army are destroyed (Ex 14). Composes a song for the Israelites on their deliverance from Pharaoh (Ex 15). Joined by his family in the wilderness (Ex 18:1-12).

Institutes a system of government (Ex 18:13-26; Nu 11:16-30; Dt 1:9-18). Receives the law and ordains various statutes. *See Law of Moses.* Face of, transfigured (Ex 34:29-35; 2Co 3:13). Sets up the tabernacle. *See Tabernacle.* Reproves Aaron for making the golden calf (Ex 32:22-23), for irregularity in the offerings (Lev 10:16-20). Jealousy of Aaron and Miriam toward (Nu 12). Rebellion of Korah, Dathan, and Abiram against (Nu 16). Appoints Joshua as his successor (Nu 27:22-23; Dt 31:7-8, 14, 23; 34:9).

Not permitted to enter Canaan, but views the land from the top of Pisgah (Nu 27:12-14; Dt 3:17; 3:23-29; 32:48-52; 34:1-8). Death and burial of (Nu 31:2; Dt 32:50; 34:1-6). Body of, disputed over (Jude 9). 120 years old at death (Dt 31:2). Mourning for, thirty days in the plains of Moab (Dt 34:8). His virility (Dt 31:2; 34:7).

Present with Jesus on the Mount of Transfiguration (Mt 17:3-4; Mk 9:4; Lk 9:30).

Type of Christ (Dt 18:15-18; Ac 3:22; 7:37).

Benedictions of:

Upon the people (Lev 9:23; Nu 10:35-36; Dt 1:11). Last benediction upon the tribes (Dt 33).

Character of:

Murmurings of (Ex 5:22-23; Nu 11:10-15). Impatience of (Ex 5:22-23; 6:12; 32:19; Nu 11:10-15; 16:15; 20:10; 31:14). Respected and feared (Ex 33:8). Faith of (Nu 10:29; Dt 9:1-3; Heb 11:23-28). Called the man of God (Dt 33:1). God spoke to, as a man to his friend (Ex 33:11). Magnified of God (Ex 19:9; Nu 14:12-20; Dt 9:13-29, w Ex 32:30). Magnanimity of, toward Eldad and Medad (Nu 11:29). Meekness of (Ex 14:13-14; 15:24-25; 16:2-3, 7-8; Nu 12:3; 16:4-11). Obedience of (Ex 7:6; 40:16, 19, 21). Unaspiring (Nu 14:12-20; Dt 9:13-29, w Ex 32:30).

Intercessory Prayers of: *See Intercession, Instances of; Intercession, Solicited; Intercession, Answered,* .

Miracles of: *See Miracles.*

Prophecies of:

(Ex 3:10; 4:5, 11-12; 6:13; 7:2; 17:16; 19:3-9; 33:11; Nu 11:17; 12:7-8; 36:13; Dt 1:3; 5:31; 18:15, 18; 34:10, 12; Hos 12:13; Mk 7:9-10; Ac 7:37-38).

MOSES, ASSUMPTION OF Pseudonymous Jewish apocalyptic book, probably written early in the early first century A.D.; gives prophecy of future of Israel. Possibly quoted in Jude 9.

MOSES, LAW OF *See Law.*

MOST HIGH Title of God (Ge 14:18-19, 20, 22; Ps 7:17). *See God, Names of, Elyon.*

MOST HOLY PLACE *See Holy of Holies.*

MOTE *See Speck.*

MOTH An insect (Job 4:19; 27:18; Ps 39:11). Destructive of garments (Job 13:28; Isa 50:9; 51:8; Hos 5:12). Figurative (Mt 6:19-20; Jas 5:2).

MOTHER

Relationship With:

Reverence for, commanded (Ex 20:12; Lev 19:3; Dt 5:16; Pr 23:22; Mt 15:4; 19:19; Mk 7:10; 10:19; Lk 18:20; Eph 6:2). To be obeyed (Dt 21:18; Pr 1:8; 6:20). Love for (1Ki 19:20). Must be subordinate to love for Christ (Mt 10:37).— Dishonoring of, to be punished (Ex 21:15; Lev 20:9; Pr 20:20; 28:24; 30:11, 17; Mt 15:4-6; Mk 7:10-12). Incest with, forbidden (Lev 18:7).

Sanctifying influence of (1Co 7:14; 2Ti 1:5). Wicked (Ge 27:6-17; 2Ki 11:1-3).

Love of:

(Isa 49:15; 66:13). Exemplified by: Hagar (Ge 21:14-16). The mother of Moses (Ex 2:1-3). Hannah (1Sa 1:20-28). Rizpah (2Sa 21:8-11). Bathsheba (1Ki 1:16-21). The mother whose child was brought to Solomon (1Ki 3:16-26). The woman whose sons were to be taken for debt (2Ki 4:1-7). The Shunammite (2Ki 4:18-37). Mary the mother of Jesus (Lk 2:41-50). The bereaved mothers of Bethlehem (Mt 2:16-18). The Syrian Phoenician woman (Mt 15:21-28; Mk 7:24-30).

Grieves over wayward children (Pr 10:1; 19:26; 29:15). Rejoices over good children (Pr 23:23-25).

MOTHER-IN-LAW Not to be defiled (Lev 18:17; 20:14; Dt 27:23). Conflict with (Mic 7:6; Mt 10:35). Beloved by Ruth (Ru 1:14-17). Peter's, healed by Jesus (Mk 1:30-31).

MOTIVE Ascribed to God (Ps 106:8; Eze 36:21-22, 32). Right, required (Mt 6:1-18). Sinful, illustrated by Cain (Ge 4:7; 1Jn 3:12).

Misunderstood: The tribes of Reuben and Gad, in asking inheritance E of Jordan (Nu 32:1-33), when they built the memorial (Jos 22:9-34). David's, by King Hanun (2Sa 10:2-3; 1Ch 19:3-4). The king of Syria, in sending presents to the king of Israel by Naaman (2Ki 5:5-7). Job in his righteousness (Job 1:9-11; 2:4-5).

MOTTO *See Inscriptions.*

MOUNT EPHRAIM *See Ephraim.*

MOUNT OF BEATITUDES Site of the Sermon on the Mount (Mt 5-7), exact location unknown. *See Beatitudes; Hattin, Horns of; Sermon on the Mount.*

MOUNTAIN Melted (Ps 97:5; Dt 4:11; 5:23; Jdg 5:5; Isa 64:1-3; Mic 1:4; Na 1:5). Overturning and removing of (Job 9:5; 14:18; 28:9; Eze 38:20), by faith (Mt 17:20; 21:21; Mk 11:23). Abraham offers Isaac upon Mount Zion, the site of the temple (Ge 22:2). *See Zion.* Horeb appointed as a place for the Israelites to worship (Ex 3:12). Signals from (Isa 13:2; 18:3; 30:17). Used for idolatrous worship (Dt 12:2; 1Sa 10:5; 1Ki 14:23; Jer 3:6; Hos 4:13).

Jesus tempted upon (Mt 4:8; Lk 4:5). Jesus preaches from (Mt 5:1). Jesus goes up into, for prayer (Mt 14:23; Lk 6:12; 9:28), is transfigured upon (Mt 17:1-9; Mk 9:2-10; Lk 9:28-36), meets his disciples on, after his resurrection (Mt 28:16-17).

Burning mountains. *See Volcanoes.*

MOURNING

For the Dead:

Head uncovered (Lev 10:6; 21:10), lying on the ground (2Sa 12:16), personal appearance neglected (2Sa 14:2), cutting the flesh (Lev 19:28; 21:1-5; Dt 14:1; Jer 16:6-7; 41:5), lamentations (Ge 50:10; Ex 12:30; 1Sa 30:4; Jer 22:18; Mt 2:17-18), fasting (1Sa 31:13; 2Sa 1:12; 3:35). Priests prohibited, except for nearest of kin (Lev 21:1-11). For Nadab and Abihu forbidden (Lev 10:6). Sexes separated in (Zec 12:12, 14).

Hired mourners (2Ch 35:25; Ecc 12:5; Jer 9:17; Mt 9:23).

Abraham mourned for Sarah (Ge 23:2), Egyptians, for Jacob seventy days (Ge 50:1-3), Israelites, for Aaron thirty days (Nu 20:29).

David's lamentations over the death of Saul and his sons (2Sa 1:17-27), the death of Abner (2Sa 3:33-34), the death of Absalom (2Sa 18:33).

Jeremiah and the singing men and singing women lament for Josiah (2Ch 35:25).

For Calamities and Other Sorrows:

Tearing the garments (Ge 37:29, 34; 44:13; Nu 14:6; Jdg 11:35; 2Sa 1:2, 11; 3:31; 13:19, 31; 15:32; 2Ki 2:12; 5:8; 6:30; 11:14; 19:1; 22:11, 19; Ezr 9:3, 5; Job 1:20; 2:12; Isa 37:1; Jer 41:5; Mt 26:65; Ac 14:14). Wearing mourning dress (Ge 38:14; 2Sa 14:2). *See Sackcloth.* Cutting or plucking off the hair and beard (Ezr 9:3; Jer 7:29). *See Baldness.* Covering the head and face (2Sa 15:30; 19:4; Est 6:12; Jer 14:3-4), and the upper lip (Lev 13:45; Eze 24:17, 22; Mic 3:7). Laying aside ornaments (Ex 33:4, 6). Walking barefoot (2Sa 15:30; Isa 20:2). Laying the hand on the head (2Sa 13:19; Jer 2:37). Ashes put on the head (Eze 27:30). Dust on the head (Jos 7:6). Dressing in black (Jer 14:2). Sitting on the ground (Isa 3:26).

Caused ceremonial defilement (Nu 19:11-16; 31:19; Lev 21:1). Prevented offerings from being accepted (Dt 26:14; Hos 9:4).

See Elegy.

MOUSE *See Rat(s).*

MOUTH Has various connotations: literal mouth, language, opening; sometimes personified (Ps 119:108; Pr 15:14; Rev 19:15).

MOWING This was done by hand with a short sickle—originally of flint, later of metal (Ps 72:6; Jas 5:4). The king's share were the portion of the harvest taken as taxes (Am 7:1).

MOZA (*sunrise*).

1. A son of Caleb (1Ch 2:46).
2. A Benjamite (1Ch 8:36-37; 9:42-43).

MOZAH A Benjamite city (Jos 18:26).

MUFFLER *See Veil.*

MULBERRY TREE (Lk 17:6).

MULE Uses of: For royal riders (2Sa 13:29; 18:9; 1Ki 1:33, 38), by saints in Isaiah's prophetic vision of the kingdom of Christ (Isa 66:20), as pack animals (2Ki 5:17; 1Ch 12:40). Tribute paid in (1Ki 10:25). Used in barter (Eze 27:14), by the exiles returning from Babylon (Ezr 2:66; Ne 7:68), in war (Zec 14:15).

MULTITUDE FED Miraculously (Ex 16:13; Nu 11:31; 2Ki 4:43; Mt 14:21; 15:38).

MUMMIFICATION *See Embalming.*

MUNITIONS Fortifications (Na 2:1).

MUPPIM Son or descendant of Benjamin (Ge 46:21). Called Shupham (Nu 26:39) and Shuppim (1Ch 7:12, 15). Shephuphan may be the same person (1Ch 8:5).

MURDER Forbidden on penalty of death (Ge 9:4-6; Ex 21:14; Lev 24:17; Dt 19:11-13), a murdered man's nearest relative had the duty to pursue the slayer and kill him (Nu 35:19), but the slayer could flee to a city of refuge, where he would be tried and then either turned over to the avenger or be protected (Nu 35:9-34; Dt 19:1-10). *See Homicide; Infanticide; Regicide.*

MURMURING *See Grumbling.*

MURRAIN A plague of Egypt (Ex 9:3, 6; Ps 78:50).

MUSHI, MUSHITE(S) Merarite Levite; progenitor of Mushites (Ex 6:19; Nu 3:20; 26:58; 1Ch 6:19, 47; 23:21, 23).

MUSIC

Used:

At the crowning of kings (1Ki 1:39-40; 2Ch 23:13, 18). In national triumphs (Ex 15:1-21; Nu 21:17-18; Jdg 5:1-31; Jdg 11:34; 1Sa 18:6-7). In worship (1Ch 6:31-32; 15:16-22, 24, 27-28; 16:4-42; 23:5; 25:1-7; 2Ch 5:12-13; 20:19, 21-22, 28; 29:25-30; 35:15; Ezr 2:64-65; 3:10-11; Ne 12:27-47; Ps 33:1-3; 68:4, 25-26, 32; 81:1-3; 87:7; 92:1-3; 95:1-2; 98:1-8; 104:33; 105:2; 135:1-3; 144:9; 149:1-3, 6; 150:1-6; Mk 14:26; 1Co 14:15; Eph 5:19; Col 3:16; Heb 2:12). At the offering of sacrifices (2Ch 29:27-28). In idolatrous worship (Da 3:4-7, 10, 15). For dancing (Mt 11:17). In joy (Ge 31:27; 2Sa 19:35; Job 21:12; Ecc 2:8; Isa 5:12). In revelry (Am 5:12; 6:5). In mourning (2Ch 35:25). In preparing for funerals (Mt 9:23).

Refrained from in sorrow (Job 30:31; Pr 25:20; Isa 16:10; 24:8-9; Eze 26:13; Rev 18:22). Captive Jews refrained from (Ps 137:1-4).

Teachers of (1Ch 15:22; 25:7-8; 2Ch 23:13). Physical effect of, on people (1Sa 16:15-16, 23; Eze 33:32). Choir director (Ne 12:42). Chief musician (Ne 12:42; Hab 3:19). Chambers for musicians in the temple (Eze 40:44). In heaven (Rev 5:8-9; 14:2-3; 15:2-3).

Allegorical (Rev 5:8-9; 14:2-3; 15:2-3; 18:22). Symbolic of judgment (Isa 23:16). Of God's emotions (Isa 30:29, 32; Jer 31:4).

Instruments of:

Invented by Jubal (Ge 4:21), David (1Ch 23:5; 2Ch 7:6; 29:26, Am 6:5). Made by Solomon (1Ki 10:12; 2Ch 9:11; Ecc 2:8), Tyrians (Eze 28:13).

Kinds—

Horn (Da 3:5, 7, 10). *See Trumpet.* Cymbal (1Ch 15:19, 28; 1Co 13:1). *See Cymbal.* Flute (Ge 4:21; Da 3:5, 7, 10, 15). Gittith, possibly a stringed instrument (Ps 8; 81; 84, T). Harp (1Sa 10:5; 16:16, 23; 1Ch 16:5). *See Harp.* Lyre (1Ch 16:5). *See Lyre.* Pipe (1Sa 10:5; Isa 30:20; Da 3:5, 10, 15). *See Pipe.* Sistrum (2Sa 6:5). Tambourine (Ex 15:20). *See Tambourine.* Trumpet (Jos 6:4). *See Trumpet.* Zither (Da 3:5, 7, 10, 15).

Symbols Used in:

Many of psalm titles contain terms that may indicate the tunes of songs popular at the time of the psalmists. This practice of setting new words to an old tune is common to the hymnology of every age.

Aijeleth Shahar, NIV "To [the tune of] The Doe of the Morning" (Ps 22:T). This is probably a tune designation.

Alamoth (1Ch 15:20; Ps 46:T). The Hebrew word means "maidens." It may refer to "maidens playing tambourines" to accompany the music.

Al-taschith, NIV "[To the tune of] Do Not Destroy" (Titles of Ps 57-59; 75). The phrase also occurs in Isa 65:8, leading some to deduce it is the name of a vintage or wine-making song.

Gittith (Titles of Pss 8; 81; 84). This may mean a Gittite lyre or the name of a tune.

Higgaion (Ps 9:16). The word is also translated "meditation" (Ps 19:14), "melody" (Ps 92:3), and "mutter" (La 3:62). Combined with "Selah," it may have been intended to indicate a pause in the vocal music while the instruments played an interlude, a time for devout meditation.

Jonath-elem-rechokim, NIV "To [the tune of] A Dove on Distant Oaks" (Ps 56:T). This is probably a tune designation.

Mahalath (Ps 53:T), *Mahalath Leannoth* (Ps 88:T). The Hebrew appears to be the word for "suffering" or "sickness." Perhaps it indicates that the psalms are to be used in a time of affliction, such as when the godless mock.

Maskil (Titles of Pss 32; 42; 44; 45; 52; 53; 54; 55; 74; 79; 88; 89; 142). Related to a word meaning "to instruct" or "to become wise by instruction," it may indicate a psalm that instructs or that is skillfully made.

Miktam (Titles of Pss 16; 56-60). Variously related to words for "golden," "inscription," and "atonement."

Muth-Labben, NIV "To [the tune of] The Death of the Son" (Ps 9:T). This may be a variant of *alamoth* or a funeral song.

Neginah and *Neginoth,* NIV "stringed instruments" (Titles of Pss 4; 54-55; 61; 67; Hab 3:19). This seems to indicate that the song should be accompanied by stringed instruments.

Nehiloth, NIV "flutes" (Ps 5:T). This seems to indicate accompaniment (perhaps exclusively) by wind instruments (Ps 5).

Selah. This term appears seventy-one times in the Psalms and in Hab 3:3, 9, 13. Its meaning is not clear. Possibly it signified a pause in the vocal music while an instrumental interlude played.

Sheminith. (1Ch 15:21; Ps 6:T; 12:T). Related to the word for "eighth," this may have indicated an octave or accompaniment by a eight-stringed instrument.

Shiggaion (Ps 7:T) and *Shigionoth* (Hab 3:1). These could be tune designations or literary categories.

Shoshannim NIV "To [the tune of] Lilies" (Ps 45; 69:T) and *Shushan-eduth,* NIV "To [the tune of] The Lily of the Covenant" (Ps 60:T; 80:T). Again, these are probably tune designations.

MUSTARD SEED Kingdom of heaven compared to (Mt 13:31-32; Mk 4:31-32; Lk 13:19). Faith compared to (Mt 17:20).

MUSTER Of troops (1Sa 14:17; 2Sa 20:4; 1Ki 20:26; 2Ki 25:29; Isa 13:4). *See Armies.*

MUTE Stricken of God (Ex 4:11; Lk 1:20, 64), miraculous healing of, by Jesus (Mt 9:32-33; 12:22; 15:30-31; Mk 7:37; 9:17, 25-26). *See Deafness.*

MUTH-LABBEN NIV "To [the tune of] The Death of the Son" (Ps 9:T). Probably name of the tune to which the psalm was sung. *See Music, Symbols Used in.*

MUTILATORS Sarcastic term for Judaizers who required circumcision for salvation (Php 3:2). *See Circumcision.*

MUTINY Israelites against Moses (Nu 14:4). *See Conspiracy; Rebellion.*

MUZZLE Mosaic law forbade muzzling of oxen when they were treading out the grain (Dt 25:4).

MYRA A city of Lycia. Paul visits (Ac 27:5-6).

MYRRH A fragrant gum. A product of the land of Canaan (SS 4:6, 14; 5:1). One of the compounds in the sacred anointing oil (Ex 30:23). Used as a perfume (Est 2:12; Ps 45:8; Pr 7:17; SS 3:6; 5:13). Brought by wise men as a present to Jesus (Mt 2:11). Offered to Jesus on the cross (Mk 15:23). Used for embalming (Jn 19:39). Trade in (Ge 37:25; 43:11).

N

MYRTLE (Ne 8:15; Isa 41:19; 55:13; Zec 1:8). *See Plants of the Bible; Tree.*

MYSIA District occupying NW end of Asia Minor bounded by the Aegean, the Hellespont, the Propontis, Bithynia, Phrygia, and Lydia. In 133 B.C. it fell to the Romans and they made it a part of the province of Asia. Traversed by Paul (Ac 16:7-8).

MYSTERIES

Of God (Dt 29:29; Job 15:8; Ps 25:14; Pr 3:32; Am 3:5; Heb 5:11).

Of redemption (Mt 11:25; 13:11, 35; Mk 4:11; Lk 8:10; Ro 16:25-26; 1Co 2:7-10; 2Co 3:12-18; Eph 1:9-10; 3:3-5, 9, 18-19; 6:19; Col 1:25-27; 2:2; 4:3; 1Ti 3:9, 16; 1Pe 1:10-12; Rev 10:7).

Of regeneration (Jn 3:8-12).

Of iniquity (2Th 2:7).

MYSTERY RELIGIONS Greco-Roman religious movement that thrived from c. 700 B.C. to A.D. 400. To gain access to the divine mysteries, specially appointed priests carefully prepared individuals through stages of initiation, instruction, and secret revelation. The enlighted were then joined with the divine and could receive healing, success, and immortality. Though the word "mystery" is used in the NT (Ro 11:25; 16:25; 1Co 15:51; Eph 3:3-9), the openness of the preaching of the gospel makes it clear that Christianity is not a mystery religion. *See Mysteries.*

MYTHS Untrue stories or speculations about religion that are contrary to sound doctrine and godliness (1Ti 1:4; 4:7; 2Ti 4:4; Tit 1:14).

N

NAAM (*pleasant*). Son of Caleb (1Ch 4:15).

NAAMAH (*pleasant*).

1. Daughter of Lamech and Zillah (Ge 4:22).
2. Wife of Solomon; mother of Rehoboam (1Ki 14:21, 31).
3. Town in Judah (Jos 15:41), site unknown.

NAAMAN, NAAMITE (*pleasantness*).

1. Son of Benjamin (Ge 46:21).
2. Son of Bela and his clan (Nu 26:40; 1Ch 8:4).
3. Son of Ehud (1Ch 8:7).
4. A Syrian general healed of leprosy by Elisha (2Ki 5:1-23; Lk 4:27).

NAAMATHITE (*of Naamath*). Designation of Zophar (Job 2:11; 11:1; 20:1; 42:9).

NAARAH (*[young] woman*).

1. Wife of Ashhur (1Ch 4:5f).
2. Place on border of Ephraim (Jos 16:7).

NAARAI (*young man of Yahweh*). Also called Paarai. One of David's heroes (1Ch 11:37).

NAARAN A city in the eastern limits of Ephraim (1Ch 7:28).

NAARATH *See Naarah, 2.*

NAASHON, NAASSON *See Nahshon.*

NABAL (*fool*). Rich shepherd of Maon in Judah who insulted David and was saved from vengeance by his wife Abigail, who after Nabal's death became David's wife (1Sa 25:1-42).

NABATEA, NABATEANS Arabian tribe named in the Apocrypha but not in Bible. Their king, Aretas IV, controlled Damascus when Paul was there (2Co 11:32). Capital was Petra. *See Petra; Sela.*

NABONIDAS, NABONIDUS (*[pagan god] Nabu is wonderful*). Last ruler of Neo-Babylonian Empire (556-539 B.C.), his son Belshazzar (Da 5; 7:1; 8:1) was coregent with him from the third year of his reign.

NABOPOLASSAR (*[pagan god] Nabu protect the son!*). First ruler of the Neo-Babylonian Empire (626-605 B.C.). Allied with Medes and Scythians, he overthrew the Assyrian Empire, destroying Nineveh in 612 B.C., as prophesied (Zep 2:13-15).

NABOTH (*a sprout*). A Jezreelite. His vineyard forcibly taken by Ahab; stoned at the instigation of Jezebel (1Ki 21:1-19). His murder avenged (2Ki 9:21-36).

NACHOR *See Nahor, 1.*

NACON (*established*). Benjamite at whose threshing floor Uzzah was killed for touching the ark (2Sa 6:6). Also called Kidon (1Ch 13:9, ftn). The place was subsequently called Perez Uzzah. *See Perez Uzzah.*

NADAB (*volunteer, free will offering*).

1. Son of Aaron (Ex 6:23). Called to Mount Sinai with Moses and Aaron to worship (Ex 24:1, 9-10). Set apart to priesthood (Ex 28:1, 4, 40-43). Offers unauthorized fire to God and is destroyed (Lev 10:1-2; Nu 3:4; 26:61). Buried (Lev 10:4-5). His family forbidden to mourn (Lev 10:6-7).
2. Son and successor of Jeroboam (1Ki 14:20). His wicked reign; murdered by Baasha (1Ki 15:25-31).
3. Great-grandson of Jerahmeel (1Ch 2:28, 30).
4. A Benjamite (1Ch 8:30; 9:36).

NAGGAI An ancestor of Jesus (Lk 3:25).

NAGGING Proverbs concerning (Pr 19:13; 21:9, 19; 25:24; 26:21; 27:15). Jezebel's destroys Samson (Jdg 16:16).

NAHALAL (*watering place*). Also spelled Nahalol (Jdg 1:30). A Levitical city within Zebulun's territory (Jos 19:15; 21:35; Jdg 1:30).

NAHALIEL (*wadi of God [El]*). A station of the Israelites (Nu 21:19).

NAHALOL, NAHALLAL *See Nahalal.*

NAHAM (*repent, console*). Descendant of Judah through Caleb (1Ch 4:19).

NAHAMANI (*Yahweh has consoled*). A Jewish exile (Ne 7:7).

NAHARAI Beerothite, Joab's armor-bearer (2Sa 23:37).

NAHARAIM *See Aram Naharaim.*

NAHASH (*viper* or *copper*).

1. Ammonite king defeated by Saul (1Sa 11:1-2; 12:12).
2. Ammonite king whose son insulted David's messengers, and David avenged the insult (2Sa 10; 1Ch 19).
3. Father of Abigail and Zeruiah (2Sa 17:25).

See also Ir Nahash.

NAHATH (*descent;* possibly *rest*).

1. Son of Reuel (Ge 36:13, 17; 1Ch 1:37).
2. A Levite, grandson of the Kohathite Elkanah (1Ch 6:26); probably the same as Tohu (1Sa 1:1), and Toah (1Ch 6:34).
3. A Levite and overseer of the sacred offerings in the time of Hezekiah (2Ch 31:13).

NAHBI (perhaps *hidden* or *timid*). A leader of Naphtali and one of the twelve spies (Nu 13:14).

NAHOR (apparently from Assyrian place name Til-Nahiri, *the mound of Nahuru*).

1. Grandfather of Abraham (Ge 11:22-26; 1Ch 1:26). In the lineage of Christ (Lk 3:34).
2. Brother of Abraham (Ge 11:26; Jos 24:2). Marriage and descendants of (Ge 11:27, 29; 22:20-24; 24:15, 24).

NAHSHON (*small viper*). A captain of Judah's host (Ex 6:23; Nu 1:7; 2:3; 7:12, 17; 10:14). In the lineage of Christ (Mt 1:4; Lk 3:32).

NAHUM (*comfort*).

1. Author of book of Nahum; native of Elkosh; prophesied 663-612 B.C. (Na 1:1; 3:8-11).
2. An ancestor of Jesus (Lk 3:25).

NAHUM, BOOK OF

Author: The prophet Nahum

Date: Between 663 and 612 B.C.

Outline:

I. Title (1:1).

II. Nineveh's Judge (1:2-15).

A. The Lord's Kindness and Sternness (1:2-8).

B. Nineveh's Overthrow and Judah's Joy (1:9-15).

III. Nineveh's Judgment (ch. 2).

A. Nineveh Besieged (2:1-10).

B. Nineveh's Desolation Contrasted With Her Former Glory (2:11-13).

IV. Nineveh's Total Destruction (ch. 3).

A. Nineveh's Sins (3:1-4).

B. Nineveh's Doom (3:5-19).

See Prophets, The Minor.

NAIL

1. Fingernail (Dt 21:12; Da 4:33; 7:19).
2. Tent peg (Jdg 4:21-22; 5:26), peg driven into wall to hang things on (Ezr 9:8; Isa 22:23-25).
3. Nails of metal: iron, bronze, gold (1Ch 22:3; 2Ch 3:9).

NAIN (*pleasant, delightful*). A city in Galilee. Jesus restores to life a widow's son in (Lk 7:11).

NAIOTH (*dwellings*). Place in or near Ramah of Benjamin where Samuel lived with a band of prophets (1Sa 19:18-20:1).

NAKED

1. Without any clothing (Ge 2:25; 3:7-11).
2. Poorly clad (Job 22:6).
3. Without an outer garment (Jn 21:7). Often used figuratively for spiritual poverty (Rev 3:17) and a lack of power (Ge 42:9).

NAME Value of a good (Pr 22:1; Ecc 7:1). A new name given, to persons who have spiritual adoption (Isa 62:2), to Abraham (Ge 17:5), Sarah (Ge 17:15), Jacob (Ge 32:28), Peter (Mt 16:18), Paul (Ac 13:9). Intercessional influence of the name of Jesus. *See Jesus the Christ, In His Name.*

Symbolic (Hos 1:3-4, 6, 9; 2:1), of prestige (1Ki 1:47).

NAMES OF GOD *See God, Names of; Titles and Names.*

NAMES OF JESUS *See Jesus the Christ, Names, Appellations, and Titles of; Titles and Names.*

NANNAR (*lightgiver*). Name given at Ur to Babylonian moon-god Sin.

NAOMI (*my joy*). Wife of Elimelech; mother-in-law of Ruth; lived in Moab; returns to Bethlehem; kinswoman of Boaz (Ru 1-4).

NAPHISH (*refreshed*). The eleventh son of Ishmael; progenitor of a tribe, probably the Nephussim (Ge 25:15; 1Ch 1:31; 5:19).

NAPHOTH (*heights*). A town assigned to Manasseh, also called Dor and Naphoth Dor (Jos 17:11, ftn). Conquered by Joshua (Jos 11:2; 12:23). *See Dor; Naphoth Dor.*

NAPHOTH DOR (*heights of Dor*). A town assigned to Manasseh, also called Dor and Naphoth (Jos 17:11, ftn). *See Dor; Naphoth.*

NAPHTALI, NAPHTALITES (*wrestling*).

1. Son of Jacob and Bilhah (Ge 30:7-8; 35:25). Jacob blesses (Ge 49:21). Sons of (Ge 46:24; 1Ch 7:13).
2. Tribe of. Census of (Nu 1:42-43; 26:48-50). Position assigned to, in camp and march (Nu 2:25-31; 10:25-27). Moses' benediction on (Dt 33:23). Inheritance of (Jos 19:32-39; Jdg 1:33; Eze 48:3).

Defeat Sisera (Jdg 4:6, 10; 5:18). Follow Gideon (Jdg 6:35; 7:23). Aid in conveying the ark to Jerusalem (Ps 68:27). Military operations of (1Ch 12:34, 40), against (1Ki 15:20; 2Ki 15:29; 2Ch 16:4).

Prophecies concerning (Isa 9:1-2; Rev 7:6).

NAPHTUHITES The inhabitants of central Egypt (Ge 10:13; 1Ch 1:11).

NAPKIN Cloth for wiping perspiration off (Lk 19:20; Jn 11:44; 20:7).

NARCISSUS A believer at Rome (Ro 16:11).

NARD An aromatic plant (SS 4:13-14). *See Perfume; Plants of the Bible.*

NATHAN (*gift*).

1. Prophet during reigns of David and Solomon; told David that not he but Solomon was to build the temple (2Sa 7; 1Ch 17), rebuked David for sin with Bathsheba (2Sa 12:1-25), helped get throne for Solomon (1Ki 1:8-53), wrote chronicles of reign of David (1Ch 29:29) and Solomon (2Ch 9:29), associated with David in arranging musical services for house of God (2Ch 29:25).
2. Son of David (2Sa 5:14; 1Ch 14:4).
3. Father of Igal (2Sa 23:36).
4. Judahite (1Ch 2:36).
5. Israelite who returned from the Exile (Ezr 8:16).
6. Man who put away his foreign wife (Ezr 10:39).

NATHANAEL (*gift of God [El]*). Disciple of Jesus (Jn 1:45-51), identified commonly with Bartholomew. Church Fathers use the two names interchangeably.

NATHAN-MELECH (*gift of king* or *gift of Melek, Molech, Malk [pagan god]*). Officer of Josiah (2Ki 23:11).

NATION People divided into nations after the Flood (Ge 10:1-32). Ordained of God (Ac 17:26). Righteousness exalts (Pr 14:34).

Peace of:

(Job 34:29; Ps 33:12; 89:15-18). Promises of peace to (Lev 26:6; 1Ki 2:33; 2Ki 20:19; 1Ch 22:9; Ps 29:11; 46:9; 72:3, 7; 128:6; Isa 2:4; 14:4-7; 60:17-18; 65:25; Jer 30:10; 50:34; Eze 34:25-28; Hos 2:18; Mic 4:3-4; Zec 1:11; 3:10; 8:4-5; 9:10; 14:11). Prayer for peace (Jer 29:7; 1Ti 2:1-2). Peace given by God (Jos 21:44; 1Ch 22:18; 23:25; Ps 147:13-14; Ecc 3:8; Isa 45:7). Instances of national peace (Jos 14:15; Jdg 3:11, 30; 1Ki 4:24-25). *See War.*

Sins of:

Involved in sins, of rulers (Ge 20:4, 9; 2Sa 24:10-17; 1Ki 15:26, 30, 34; 2Ki 24:3; 1Ch 21:7-17; Jer 15:4), of other individuals, as Achan (Jos 7:1, 11-26).

Atonement made for (2Ch 29:21). Penitent, promises to (Lev 26:40-42; Dt 4:29-31; 5:29; 30:1-10; 2Ch 7:13-14; Jer 3:22).

In adversity, prayer of (Jdg 6:7; 10:10; 21:2-4; 2Ch 7:13-14; Ps 74; Jer 3:21; 31:18; Joel 2:12), prayer for (Ezr 9:6-15; Ne 1:4-11; Ps 74; 84:1-7; Isa 63:7-19; Jer 6:14; 8:11, 20-21; 9:1-2; 14:7, 20; La 2:20-22; Da 9:3-21). *See Sin, National.*

Judgments Against:

Chastisement of (Lev 18:24-30; 26:28; Dt 11:2; 2Ch 6:24, 26, 28; 7:13-14; Ps 106:43; Isa 14:26-27; Jer 2:30; 5:29; 18:6-10; 25:12-33; 30:14; 31:18-20; 46:28; Eze 2:3-5; 39:23-24; Da 7:9-12; 9:3-16; La 1:5; Hos 7:12; 10:10; Joel 1:1-20; Am 9:9; Zep 3:6, 8; Hag 2:17). Perish (Ps 9:17; Isa 60:12).

Judgments denounced against, on account of its unrighteousness (Dt 9:5; Ps 9:17; Isa 3:4-8; 14:24-27; 19:4; 59:1-15; 60:12; Jer 2:19, 35-37; 5:6-29; 6; 9:7-26; 12:14, 17; 18:6-10; 25:12-33; 50:45-46; 51; Eze 2:9-10; 7; 22:12-31; 24:6-24; 33:25-29; Hos 4:1-10; 7:12-13, 16; 13; Am 2; 3; 5; 9:8-10; Mic 6:13-16; Zep 3:8).

Instances of punishment of: The Canaanites (Dt 9:5). The Sodomites (Ge 19:24-25, 28-29; La 4:6). The Egyptians (Ex 7-11; 12:1-36; 14). The Israelites (2Sa 21:1; 24:14-16; 2Ki 24:2-4, 20; 2Ch 28:1, 5-8, 16-19; 29:8-9; 30:7; 36:16-20; Ezr 9:7; Ne 9:36-37; Jer 2:15-16; 30:11-15; La 1:3, 8, 14; Eze 36:16-20; 39:17-24; Joel 1:1-20; Am 4:6-11).

See Government; Kings; Rulers.

NATIONAL RELIGION Supported by taxes (Ex 30:11-16; 38:26). Ministers of, supported by state (1Ki 18:19; 2Ch 11:13-15). Subverted by Jeroboam (1Ki 12:26-33; 2Ch 11:13-15). Idolatrous, established by Jeroboam (1Ki 12:26-33).

NATIONS BLESSED BY ABRAHAM (Ge 12:2; 18:18; 22:18; 26:4; Ac 3:25; Gal 3:8).

NATURAL Natural death (Nu 16:29; 19:16, 18), sleep (Jn 11:13), physical relations (Ro 1:26-27), body (1Co 15:44, 46), instincts (Jude 1:19).

NATURAL RELIGION *See Religion, Natural.*

NATURALIZATION Giving rights of citizenship to aliens (Ac 22:28).

Figurative (Eph 2:12-13, 19).

NATURE The entire compass of one's life (Jas 3:6). The inherent character of a person or thing (Ro 1:26; 2:14; 11:21-24). Disposition (2Pe 1:4). Sinful nature (Ro 7:18, 25; 1Co 5:5; Gal 5:13).

Laws of, uniform in operation: In the vegetable kingdom (Ge 1:11, 12; Mt 7:16-18; Lk 6:43-44; 1Co 15:36-38; Gal 6:7; Jas 3:12), animal kingdom (Ge 1:21, 24-25; Jer 13:23), succession of seasons (Ge 8:22), succession of day and night (Ge 8:22; Jer 33:20).

NAUGHTINESS *See Sin.*

NAUM *See Nahum.*

NAVE *See Rim.*

NAVEL "Belly button" (SS 7:2).

NAVIGATION Sounding in (Ac 27:28). *See Commerce; Mariner; Navy.*

NAVY Solomon's (1Ki 9:26), Hiram's (1Ki 10:11), of Kittim (Da 11:30, ftn, 40).

See Commerce; Mariner.

NAZARENE (possibly *sprout, branch*).

1. Inhabitant of Nazareth (Mt 2:23); possibly a wordplay on the Hebrew *nezer,* "branch," a messianic title (cf. Isa 11:1). *See Branch.*

2. A Christian (Ac 24:5).

NAZARETH (possibly *sprout, branch* or *watchtower*). A village in Galilee. Joseph and Mary live at (Mt 2:23; Lk 1:26-27, 56; 2:4, 39, 51). Jesus from (Mt 21:11; Mk 1:24; 10:47; Lk 4:34; 18:37; 24:19). People of, reject Jesus (Lk 4:16-30). Its name infamous (Jn 1:46).

NAZARETH DECREE An inscription on a slab of white marble, dating c. A.D. 40-50, by Claudius Caesar, found in Nazareth, decreeing capital punishment for anyone disturbing graves and tombs.

NAZIRITE(S) (*one under sacred vow*). An Israelite who consecrated himself or herself and took a vow of separation and self-imposed abstinence for the purpose of some special service. The Nazirite vow included a renunciation of wine, prohibition of the use of the razor, and avoidance of contact with a dead body. The period of time for the vow was anywhere from 30 days to a lifetime (Nu 6:1-21; Jdg 13:5-7; Am 2:11, 12).

Instances of: Samson (Jdg 13:5, 7; 16:17). Samuel (1Sa 1:11). Recabites (Jer 35). John the Baptist (Mt 11:18; Lk 1:15; 7:33).

See Abstinence; Wine.

NEAH A border town in Zebulun (Jos 19:13). The site is unknown.

NEAPOLIS (*new city*). A seaport of Macedonia. Paul visits (Ac 16:11).

NEARIAH (*[young] man of Yahweh*).

1. Son of Shemaiah (1Ch 3:22-23).

2. A Simeonite leader (1Ch 4:42).

NEBAI (*thrive*). Signer of the covenant with Nehemiah (Ne 10:19).

NEBAIOTH Son of Ishmael (Ge 25:13; 28:9; 36:3; 1Ch 1:29). Prophecies concerning (Isa 60:7).

NEBALLAT A town occupied by the Benjamites after the Captivity (Ne 11:34).

NEBAT (*look to, regard [approvingly]*). Father of Jeroboam (1Ki 11:26; 12:2).

NEBO (*height* or *Mount of Nabu [Nebo]*).

1. A city allotted to Reuben (Nu 32:3, 38; 1Ch 5:8). Prophecies concerning (Isa 15:2; Jer 48:1, 22).

2. A mountain range E of the Jordan. Moses views Canaan from (Dt 32:49-50), dies on (Dt 34:1).

3. A city in Judah (Ezr 2:29; Ne 7:33).

4. The ancestor of certain Jews (Ezr 10:43).

5. A Babylonian idol (Isa 46:1).

NEBO-SARSEKIM A prince of Nebuchadnezzar who entered Jerusalem when it fell (Jer 39:3, ftn).

NEBUCHADNEZZAR (*Nebo protect my boundary stone* BDB and IDB; *Nebo protect my son!* KB).

1. The fourth Dynasty ruler of the Old Babylonian Empire (c. 1140 B.C.).

2. Ruler of the Neo-Babylonian Empire (605-562 B.C.); son of Nabopolassar; conquered Pharaoh Neco at Carchemish (605 B.C.); destroyed Jerusalem and carried Israelites into captivity (587 B.C.) (2Ki 25:1-21); succeeded by son Evil-Merodach. Often mentioned in OT (1Ch 6:15; 2Ch 36; Ezr 1:7; 2:1; 5:12, 14; 6:5; Ne 7:6; Est 2:6; Jer 21:2; 52:4; Da 1-5).

NEBUSHAZBAN (*Nebo [Nabu] save me!*). Chief officer of Nebuchadnezzar (Jer 39:11-14).

NEBUZARADAN (*Nebo [Nabu] has given seed [offspring]*). Nebuchadnezzar's general when the Babylonians besieged Jerusalem (2Ki 25:1, 11-12, 20; Jer 52:12ff), conducted captives to Babylon.

NECK Term often used in Bible with literal and figurative meanings (Ex 32:9; Dt 9:13; Ps 75:5; Ac 7:51).

NECKLACE Ornamental chain worn around the neck (Isa 3:19).

NECO Pharaoh of Egypt (609-595 B.C.); defeated Josiah at battle of Megiddo (2Ki 23:29; 2Ch 35:20ff); defeated by Nebuchadnezzar at battle of Carchemish (2Ki 24:7; Isa 10:9; Jer 46:2).

NECROMANCER, NECROMANCY Consulting with the dead; forbidden by Mosaic law (Dt 18:10-11), King Saul consulted with the medium of Endor (1Sa 28:7-25). Judgment upon (Isa 8:19; 29:4).

See Medium; Sorcery; Witchcraft.

NEDABIAH (*Yahweh volunteers*). A son of Jehoiachin (1Ch 3:18).

NEEDLE'S EYE Figure used by Jesus (Mt 19:24; Mk 10:25; Lk 18:25). Jesus does not say that salvation is threatened by possessing riches but that those who are wealthy will have great difficulty subordinating their riches to the will of God; in addition, a wealthy man will not enter the kingdom of God based on his riches, but only on the saving grace of God and the finished work of Jesus Christ (Mt 19:25-26).

NEEDLEWORK Art of working in with the needle various kinds of colored threads in cloth (Jdg 5:30; Ps 45:14).

NEESING NIV "snorting" (Job 41:18).

NEGEV (*dry [land],* hence *south country*). The desert region lying to the S of Judea, sometimes translated "the south" (Ge 12:9; 13:1; 20:1; Nu 13:29; 1Sa 27:5-6).

NEGINAH *See Music, Symbols Used in.*

NEGINOTH *See Music, Symbols Used in.*

NEHELAMITE (perhaps *of Nehelam* or a play on the word for *dream*). Designation of Shemaiah, a false prophet (Jer 29:24, 31-32).

NEHEMIAH (*Yahweh has comforted*).

1. Leader of Jews who returned with Zerubbabel (Ezr 2:2; Ne 7:7).

2. Son of Azbuk; helped rebuild walls of Jerusalem (Ne 3:16).

3. Son of Hacaliah; governor of Persian province of Judah after 444 B.C.; cupbearer to King Artaxerxes of Persia (Ne 1:11; 2:1); rebuilt walls of Jerusalem (Ne 1:4-6); cooperated with Ezra in numerous reforms (Ne 8); nothing known of the end of his life.

NEHEMIAH, BOOK OF

Author: Nehemiah

Date: c. 430 B.C.

Outline:

I. Nehemiah's First Administration (chs. 1-12).
  A. Nehemiah's Response to the Situation in Jerusalem (ch. 1).
    1. News of the plight of Jerusalem (1:1-4).
    2. Nehemiah's prayer (1:5-11).
  B. Nehemiah's Journey to Jerusalem (ch. 2).
    1. The king response (2:1-8).
    2. The journey itself (2:9-10).
    3. Nehemiah's nocturnal inspection of the walls (2:11-16).
    4. His exhortation to rebuild (2:17-18).
    5. The opposition of Sanballat, Tobiah and Geshem (2:19-20).
  C. List of the Builders of the Wall (ch. 3).
    1. The northern section (3:1-7).
    2. The western section (3:8-13).
    3. The southern section (3:14).
    4. The eastern section (3:15-32).
  D. Opposition to Rebuilding the Wall (ch. 4).
    1. The derision of Sanballat and Tobiah (4:1-5).
    2. The threat of attack (4:6-15).
    3. Rebuilding the wall (4:16-23).
  E. Social and Economic Problems (ch. 5).
    1. The complaints of the poor (5:1-5).
    2. The cancellation of debts (5:6-13).
    3. Nehemiah's unselfish example (5:14-19).
  F. The Wall Rebuilt Despite Opposition (ch. 6).
    1. Attempts to snare Nehemiah (6:1-9).
    2. The hiring of false prophets (6:10-14).
    3. The completion of the wall (6:15-19).
  G. List of Exiles (7:1-73a).
    1. Provisions for the protection of Jerusalem (7:1-3).
    2. Nehemiah's discovery of the list of returnees (7:4-5).
    3. The returnees delineated (7:6-72).
    4. Settlement of the exiles (7:73a).
  H. Ezra's Preaching and the Outbreak of Revival (7:73b-10:39).
    1. The public exposition of the Scriptures (7:73b-8:12).
    2. The Feast of Tabernacles (8:13-18).
    3. A day of fasting, confession and prayer (9:1-5a).
    4. A recital of God's dealings with Israel (9:5b-31).
    5. Confession of sins (9:32-37).
    6. A binding agreement (9:38).
    7. A list of those who sealed it (10:1-29).
    8. Provisions of the agreement (10:30-39).
  I. New Residents of Judah and Jerusalem (ch. 11).
    1. New residents for Jerusalem (11:1-24).
      a. Introductory remarks (11:1-4a).
      b. Residents from Judah (11:4b-6).
      c. From Benjamin (11:7-9).
      d. From the priests (11:10-14).
      e. From the Levites (11:15-18).
      f. From the temple staff (11:25-36).
    2. New residents for Judah (11:25-36).
      a. Places settled by those from Judah (11:25-30).
      b. Places settled by those from Benjamin (11:31-35).
      c. Transfer of Levites from Judah to Benjamin (11:36).
  J. Lists of Priests and the Dedication of the Wall (ch. 12).
    1. Priests and Levites from the first return (12:1-9).
    2. High priests and Levites since Joiakim (12:10-26).
    3. Dedication of the wall of Jerusalem (12:27-43).
    4. Regulation of the temple offerings and services (12:44-47).
II. Nehemiah's Second Administration (ch. 13).
  A. Abuses During His Absence (13:1-5).
    1. Mixed marriages (13:1-3).
    2. Tobiah's occupation of the temple quarters (13:4-5).
  B. Nehemiah's Return (13:6-9).
    1. His arrival (13:6-7).
    2. His expulsion of Tobiah (13:8-9).
  C. Reorganization and Reforms (13:10-31).
    1. Offerings for the temple staff (13:10-14).
    2. The abuse of the Sabbath (13:15-22).
    3. Mixed marriages (13:23-29).
    4. Provisions of wood and firstfruits (13:30-31).

NEHILOTH *See Music, Symbols Used In.*

NEHUM (*comfort*). Chief of Judah who returned with Zerubbabel; also called "Rehum" (Ezr 2:2; Ne 7:7).

NEHUSHTA (*[strong as* or *color of] bronze*). Wife of Jehoiakim, king of Judah, and mother of Jehoiachin (2Ki 24:6, 8).

NEHUSHTAN (combination of *bronze* and *viper*). The bronze serpent (2Ki 18:4).

NEIEL A landmark on the boundary of Asher (Jos 19:27).

NEIGHBOR Defined (Lk 10:25-37). Duty to, defined in the Golden Rule (Mt 7:12).

Love does no harm to (Ro 13:10). Love for, commanded (Lev 19:18; Mt 19:19; 22:39; Mk 12:31-33; Lk 10:25-37; Ro 13:9-10; Gal 5:14; Jas 2:8-9). Kindness to, commanded (Ex 23:4-5; Dt 22:1-4; Isa 58:6-7; Gal 6:10). Charitableness toward, commanded (Ro 15:2). Benevolence toward, commanded (Pr 3:28-29). Righteous treatment of, commanded (Zec 8:16-17). Honesty toward, commanded (Lev 19:13). Kindness to, rewarded (Isa 58:8-14; Mt 25:34-46). Righteous treatment of, rewarded (Ps 15:1-3).

False witness against, forbidden (Ex 20:16; Lev 19:16). Hatred of, forbidden (Lev 19:17). Oppression of, denounced (Jer 22:13). Penalty for violation of the rights of (Lev 6:2-5).

See Duty; Mankind.

NEKEB *See Adami Nekeb.*

NEKODA Head of a family of temple servants who could not prove Israelite descent (Ne 7:50, 62; Ezr 2:60).

N

NEMUEL, NEMUELITE
1. Brother of Dathan and Abiram (Nu 26:9).
2. Son of Simeon (Nu 26:12; 1Ch 4:24). Also called Jemuel (Ge 46:10; Ex 6:15). *See Jemuel.*

NEPHEG (*sprout, shoot*).
1. Brother of Korah, Dathan, and Abiram (Ex 6:21).
2. Son of David (2Sa 5:15; 1Ch 3:7; 14:6).

NEPHEW Grandson (Jdg 12:14), descendant (Job 18:19; Isa 14:22), grandchild (1Ti 5:4).

NEPHILIM (*ones falling [upon]*, hence *violent ones*, possibly *giants*). Antediluvians (Ge 6:4), aboriginal dwellers in Canaan (Nu 13:32-33), not angelic fallen beings (Dt 1:28).

NEPHISH *See Naphish.*

NEPHISHESIM *See Nephussim.*

NEPHTHALIM, NEPTHALIM *See Naphtali.*

NEPHTOAH (*an opening*). Spring and town on the border of Judah and Benjamin (Jos 15:9; 18:15), two miles NW of Jerusalem; modern Lifta.

NEPHUSSIM A family of the temple servants (Ezr 2:50; Ne 7:52).

NEPOTISM Of Joseph (Ge 47:11-12). Of Saul (1Sa 14:50). Of David (2Sa 8:16; 19:13). Of Nehemiah (Ne 7:2).

NER (*lamp*).
1. Father of Abner (1Sa 14:50; 26:14).
2. Grandfather of King Saul (1Ch 8:33).

NEREUS (*pagan Greek deity*). A Christian at Rome (Ro 16:15).

NERGAL (*pagan deity*). Babylonian deity of destruction (2Ki 17:30).

NERGAL-SHAREZER (*Nergal protect the prince!*). The name of princes of Babylon (Jer 39:3, 13).

NERI (*lamp of Yahweh*). An ancestor of Jesus (Lk 3:27).

NERIAH (*lamp of Yahweh*). Father of Baruch (Jer 32:12).

NERIGLISSAR *See Nergal-Sharezer.*

NERO (*family name*). The fifth Roman emperor (A.D. 54-68); killed many Christians when Rome burned in A.D. 64; called "Caesar" (Ac 25:11; Php 4:22).

NEST Bird's (Nu 24:21; Mt 8:20). Birds stir up (Dt 32:11).

NET Of interwoven chains (1Ki 7:17). Hidden in a pit (Ps 35:7-8). Set for birds (Pr 1:17), wild animals (Isa 51:20). Fish caught in (Mt 4:18-21; 13:47; Lk 5:4; Jn 21:6-11).
See Snare.
Figurative: (Job 18:8; 19:6; Ps 9:15; 10:9; 25:15; 31:4; 35:7-8; 57:6; 66:11; 140:5; 141:10; Pr 12:12; 29:5; Ecc 7:26; 9:12; Isa 19:8; Eze 26:5, 14; 47:10; Hos 7:12).

NETAIM Residence of Judahite potters (1Ch 4:23).

NETHANEL (*God [El] has given*).
1. The prince of Issachar. Numbers the tribe (Nu 1:8). Captain of the host of Issachar (Nu 2:5; 10:15). Liberality of, for the tabernacle (Nu 7:18-23).
2. A priest and doorkeeper for the ark (1Ch 15:24).
3. A Levite (1Ch 24:6).
4. Son of Obed-Edom and gatekeeper of the temple (1Ch 26:4).
5. A prince sent by Jehoshaphat to teach the law in the cities of Judah (2Ch 17:7).
6. A Levite (2Ch 35:9).
7. A priest who divorced his Gentile wife (Ezr 10:22).
8. A priest (Ne 12:21).
9. A Levite and musician (Ne 12:36).

NETHANIAH (*Yahweh has given*).
1. Father of Ishmael (2Ki 25:23, 25; Jer 40:8, 14-15; 41:1-2, 6-7, 9-12).
2. A singer and chief of the temple musicians (1Ch 25:2, 12).
3. A Levite appointed by Jehoshaphat to accompany the princes who were to teach the law in Judah (2Ch 17:8).
4. Father of Jehudi (Jer 36:14).

NETHINIM *See Temple Servants.*

NETOPHAH, NETOPHATHITE(S) (*trickle, drip*). Village of Judah and its inhabitants; c. three miles S of Jerusalem (2Sa 23:28-29; 1Ch 2:54; 9:16; Ne 12:28).

NETTLES A stinging plant (Pr 24:31; Isa 34:13).
Figurative (Job 30:7; Hos 9:6; Zep 2:9).

NETWORK White cloth (Isa 19:9), ornamental carving upon pillars of Solomon's temple (1Ki 7:18, 42), a grate for the great altar of burnt offerings at the tabernacle (Ex 27:4; 38:4).

NEW BIRTH The corruption of human nature requires (Jn 3:6; Ro 8:7-8). None can enter heaven without (Jn 3:3). Is of the will of God (Jas 1:18). Is of the mercy of God (Tit 3:5). Is for the glory of God (Isa 43:7).

Effected by:
God (Jn 1:13; 1Pe 1:3). Christ (1Jn 2:29). The Holy Spirit (Jn 3:6; Tit 3:5). By means of: The word of God (Jas 1:18; 1Pe 1:23). The resurrection of Christ (1Pe 1:3). The ministry of the gospel (1Co 4:15).

Described as:
A new creation (2Co 5:17; Gal 6:15; Eph 2:10). Newness of life (Ro 6:4). A spiritual resurrection (Ro 6:4-6; Eph 2:1, 5; Col 2:12; 3:1). A new heart (Eze 36:26). A new spirit (Eze 11:19; Ro 7:6). Putting on the new man (Eph 4:24). The inward man (Ro 7:22; 2Co 4:16). Circumcision of the heart (Dt 30:6, w Ro 2:29; Col 2:11). Partaking of the divine nature (2Pe 1:4). The washing of regeneration (Tit 3:5). All saints partake of (Ro 8:16-17; 1Pe 2:2; 1Jn 5:1).

Produces:
Likeness to God (Eph 4:24; Col 3:10). Likeness to Christ (Ro 8:29; 2Co 3:18; 1Jn 3:2). Knowledge of God (Jer 24:7; Col 3:10). Hatred of sin (1Jn 3:9; 5:18). Victory over the world (1Jn 5:4). Delight in God's law (Ro 7:22).

Evidenced by:
Faith in Christ (1Jn 5:1). Righteousness (1Jn 2:29). Brotherly love (1Jn 4:7). Connected with adoption (Isa 43:6-7; Jn 1:12-13). Literalistic objection to (Jn 3:4). Manner of effecting illustrated (Jn 3:8). Preserves from Satan's devices (1Jn 5:18).

NEW COVENANT *See Covenants, Major in the Old Testament.*

NEW CREATION *See Regeneration.*

NEW MOON Feast of (Nu 10:10; 28:11-15; 1Ch 23:31; 2Ch 31:3). Commerce at time of, suspended (Am 8:5).

NEW TESTAMENT A collection of twenty-seven documents regarded by the church as inspired and authoritative, consisting of four Gospels, the Acts of the Apostles, twenty-one letters, and the book of Revelation. All were written during the apostolic period, either by apostles or by men closely associated with the apostles. The Gospels tell the story of the coming of the Messiah, God in the flesh, to become the Savior of the world. Acts describes the beginnings and growth of the church. The letters set forth the significance of the person and work of Christ and rules for the Church. Revelation tells of the consummation of all things in Jesus Christ. The formation of the NT canon was a gradual process, the Holy Spirit working in the church and guiding it to recognize and choose those Christian books God wanted brought together to form the Christian counterpart of the Jewish OT. By the end of the fourth century, the NT canon was basically settled.

NEW THINGS (Isa 42:9; 43:19; 48:6; 65:17; 2Co 5:17; Rev 21:5).

NEW YEAR *See Feasts; Trumpets, Feast of.*

NEZIAH (*director [of worship]*). One of the temple servants (Ezr 2:54; Ne 7:56).

NEZIB (*pillar, garrison*). A city in Judah (Jos 15:43).

NIBHAZ An idol (2Ki 17:31).

NIBSHAN A city of Judah (Jos 15:62).

NICANOR (*victor*). A deacon of the church at Jerusalem (Ac 6:5).

NICODEMUS (*victor over people*). Pharisee; member of the Sanhedrin; came to Jesus at night for conversation (Jn 3); spoke up for Jesus before the Sanhedrin (Jn 7:25-44); brought spices for burial of Jesus (Jn 19:39-42).

NICOLAITANS (*follower of Nicolas*). A heretical sect with immoral practices (Rev 2:6, 15).

NICOLAS (*victor over people*). A proselyte of Antioch and deacon of the church at Jerusalem (Ac 6:5-6).

NICOPOLIS (*victory city*). City in Epirus in NW Greece, founded by Augustus Caesar (Tit 3:12).

NIGER (*black*). Surname of Simeon, leader of the church at Antioch (Ac 13:1-3).

NIGHT (Ge 1:5, 16, 18). Meditations in (Ps 19:2; 77:6; 119:148; 139:11). Worship in (Ps 134:1). Jesus prays all night (Lk 6:12). No night in heaven (Rev 21:25; 22:5). Divided into hours (Ac 23:23). Used figuratively (Isa 15:1; 21:11-12; Jn 9:4; Ro 13:12; 1Th 5:5).

NIGHT HAWK *See Screech Owl.*

NILE The main river of Egypt and of Africa, 4,050 miles long; it begins at Lake Victoria and flows northward to the Mediterranean; the annual overflow deposits sediment which makes N Egypt one of the most fertile regions in the world. Moses was placed on the Nile in a basket of papyrus (Ex 2:3); the turning of the Nile into blood was one of the ten plagues (Ex 7:20-21); on its bank grows the reed from which the famous papyrus writing material is made. *See River of Egypt.*

NIMRAH (*spotted leopard* BDB; *basin of limpid [clear] water* KB). A city of Gad (Nu 32:3).

NIMRIM, WATERS OF (*limpid [clear] waters* KB; *wholesome waters* BDB; possibly *waters of leopards* IDB). Waters on the borders of Gad and Moab (Isa 15:6; Jer 48:34).

NIMROD (perhaps *to rebel*, or *the Arrow, the mighty hero*). Son of Cush. "A mighty hunter before the LORD" (Ge 10:8-9; 1Ch 1:10). Founder of Babylon. *See Babylon.*

NIMRUD Ancient Calah in Assyria, founded by Nimrod (Ge 10:11, 12).

NIMSHI Father of Jehu (2Ki 9:2, 20).

NINEVEH A capital of the Assyrian Empire (Ge 10:11-12). Nineveh and its surrounding region had a population of upwards of 120,000 when Jonah preached (Jnh 4:11). Extent of (Jnh 3:4). Sennacherib in (2Ki 19:36-37; Isa 37:37-38). Jonah preaches to (Jnh 1:1-2; 3). Nahum prophesies against (Na 1-3). Zephaniah foretells the desolation of (Zep 2:13-15).

NISAN Babylonian name for Abib (Ne 2:1; Est 3:7). *See Abib; Month, 1.*

NISROCH An idol (2Ki 19:36-37; Isa 37:37-38).

NITRE *See Soda.*

NO *See Thebes.*

NOADIAH (*meet with Yahweh*).
1. Levite who returned to Jerusalem after the Exile (Ezr 8:33).
2. False prophetess who tried to terrorize Nehemiah (Ne 6:14).

NOAH (*rest, comfort*).
1. Son of Lamech (Ge 5:28-29), righteous in a corrupt age (Ge 6:8-9; 7:1; Eze 14:14), warned people of the Flood 120 years (Ge 6:3), built an ark (Ge 6:12-22), saved from the Flood with wife and family, together with beasts and fowl of every kind (Ge 7:8), repopulated earth (Ge 9:10), lived 950 years.
God establishes a covenant with (Ge 9:8-17). *See Covenants, Major in the Old Testament.*
2. Daughter of Zelophehad (Nu 26:33; 27:1; 36:11; Jos 17:3).

NOB A city of Benjamin (Ne 11:31-32). Called "the town of the priests" (1Sa 22:19). Home of Ahimelech the priest (1Sa 21:1; 22:11). Probable seat of the tabernacle in Saul's time (1Sa 21:4, 6, 9). David flees to, and is aided by Ahimelech (1Sa 21:1-9; 22:9-10). Destroyed by Saul (2Sa 22:19). Prophecy concerning (Isa 10:32).

NOBAH (*barking*).
1. Manassite; took Kenath from Amorites (Nu 32:42).
2. Town near which Gideon defeated the Midianites (Jdg 8:11).

NOBAI *See Nebai.*

NOBLE A word which is used to describe people who were renowned for deeds performed or in some other way were distinguished for skills or genius; people of high rank, position, title, or one well born (Jdg 5:13; Ezr 4:10; Est 6:9; Pr 17:26; Lk 19:12-27; 1Co 1:26), persons who possess high moral qualities or ideals (Ps 16:3; Isa 32:5; Ac 17:11), anything having qualities of a very high order (Eze 17:8, 23; 1Ti 3:1; Lk 21:5).
A nobleman supports and defends his community. He has a generous heart (Ex 35:5, 22; 2Ch 29:31; Nu 21:18; 1Ch 28:21). He is one belonging to a king (Jn 4:46-53). The noble wife is praised in Pr 31:10-31.

NOD (*wandering*). Region E of Eden to which Cain went (Ge 4:16).

NODAB Tribe of Arabs, probably Ishmaelites E of the Jordan (1Ch 5:19).

NOE *See Noah.*

NOGAH (*joy, splendor*). Son of David (1Ch 3:7; 14:6).

NOHAH (*rest*). Son of Benjamin (1Ch 8:2).

NOLLE PROSEQUI The complaint against Paul (Ac 18:12-17).

NON *See Nun.*

NONCONFORMITY *See Church, The Body of Believers, State; Form; Formalism.*

NONE LIKE GOD (Ex 8:10; 15:11; Dt 33:26; 2Sa 7:22; 1Ki 8:23; 1Ch 17:20; Ps 89:6; Isa 40:18; Mk 12:32).

NONRESISTANCE Commanded (Mt 5:38-41; Ro 12:17-21; 1Th 5:15; 1Pe 2:19-23). Forgive those who wrong you (Mt 18:15, 21-35; Lk 6:36-37; Eph 4:32; Jas 2:13; 1Pe 3:9). Love your enemies (Ex 23:4-5; Job 31:29-30; Pr 25:21-22; Mt 5:43-48; 6:14-15; Lk 6:27-36; 10:30-37; Ro 12:17-21; 13:10; 1Jn 3:10-11). Return good for evil (Pr 15:1; 25:21-22; Mt 5:38-41; 6:14-15; Ro 12:17-21; 1Th 5:15; 1Pe 3:9). Seek peace (Ps 34:14; 133:1-3; Mt 5:9; 18:15; 2Co 13:11; Gal 5:22; Col 3:12-13; Heb 12:14; Jas 3:17-18; 1Pe 3:11). Suffer gladly for Christ (Mt 5:10-12; Lk 6:22-23; Jn 15:20; Ac 5:41; Ro 12:14; 1Co 4:12-13; 13:7; Gal 5:22; Col 3:12-13; 1Pe 2:19-23; 3:14). Christ, our example (Lk 23:34; 1Pe 2:19-23; 1Jn 2:6). Exemplified by Stephen (Ac 7:60).
See Revenge; Good for Evil; Evil for Good.

NOON (Dt 28:29; Job 11:17; Ps 55:17; 91:6; Isa 58:10; Ac 22:6).

NOPH *See Memphis.*

NOPHAH A city of Sihon (Nu 21:30).

NORTH Often merely as a point of the compass; but sometimes a particular country, usually Assyria or Babylonia (Jer 3:18; 46:6; Eze 26:7; Zep 2:13).

NORTHEASTER A hurricane-force E wind the Mediterranean; shipwrecked Paul (Ac 27:14).

NOSE Jewels for (Pr 11:22; Isa 3:21; Eze 16:12). Mutilated (Eze 23:25).

NUBIANS An African people (Da 11:43).

NUCLEAR WAR Some see a reference to nuclear war in predictions of the fiery destruction of the earth (Zep 1:18; 2Pe 3:7, 10) and in the seven trumpets of Revelation (Rev 8:5-9:19).

N

NUMBERS Hebrews did not use figures to denote numbers. They spelled numbers out in full; from second century B.C. they used Hebrew letters of the alphabet for numbers. Numbers were often used symbolically; some had special religious significance (Ge 2:2; Ex 20:3-17; Dt 6:4), especially 1, 3, 7, 10, 12, 40, 70, 666, 1000.

NUMBERS, BOOK OF

Author: Traditionally ascribed to Moses

Date: 1445 to 1406 B.C.

Outline:

I. Israel at Sinai, Preparing to Depart for the Promised Land (1:1-10:10).
 A. The Commands for the Census of the People (chs. 1-4).
  1. The numbers of men from each tribe mustered for war (ch. 1).
  2. The placement of the tribes around the tabernacle and their order for march (ch. 2).
  3. The placement of the Levites around the tabernacle, and the numbers of the Levites and the firstborn of Israel (ch. 3).
  4. The numbers of the Levites in their tabernacle service for the Lord (ch. 4).
 B. The Commands for Purity of the People (5:1-10:10).
  1. The test for purity in the law of jealousy (ch. 5).
  2. The Nazirite vow and the Aaronic benediction (ch. 6).
  3. The offerings of the twelve leaders at the dedication of the tabernacle (ch. 7).
  4. The setting up of the lamps and the separation of the Levites (ch. 8).
  5. The observance of the Passover (9:1-14).
  6. The covering cloud and the silver trumpets (9:15-10:10).
II. The Journey From Sinai to Kadesh (10:11-12:16).
 A. The Beginning of the Journey (10:11-36).
 B. The Beginning of the Sorrows: Fire and Quail (ch. 11).
 C. The Opposition of Miriam and Aaron (ch. 12).
III. Israel at Kadesh, the Delay Resulting From Rebellion (14:1-20:13).
 A. The Twelve Spies and Their Mixed Report of the Good Land (ch. 13).
 B. The People's Rebellion Against God's Commission, and Their Defeat (ch. 14).
 C. A Collection of Laws on Offerings, the Sabbath and Tassels on Garments (ch. 15).
 D. The Rebellion of Korah and His Allies (ch. 16).
 E. The Budding of Aaron's Staff: A Sign for Rebels (ch. 17).
 F. Concerning Priests, Their Duties and Their Support (ch. 18).
 G. The Red Heifer and the Cleansing Water (ch. 19).
 H. The Sin of Moses (20:1-13).
IV. The Journey From Kadesh to the Plains of Moab (20:14-22:1).
 A. The Resistance of Edom (20:14-21).
 B. The Death of Aaron (20:22-29).
 C. The Destruction of Arad (21:1-3).
 D. The Bronze Snake (21:4-9).
 E. The Song of the Well (21:10-20).
 F. The Defeat of Sihon and Og (21:21-30).
 G. Israel Enters Moab (21:31-22:1).
V. Israel on the Plains of Moab, in Anticipation of Taking the Promised Land (22:2-32:42).
 A. Balak of Moab Hires Balaam to Curse Israel (22:2-41).
 B. Balaam Blesses Israel in Seven Oracles (chs. 23-24).
 C. The Baal of Peor and Israel's Apostasy (ch. 25).
 D. The Second Census (ch. 26).
 E. Instructions for the New Generation (chs. 27-30).
  1. The inheritance for women (27:1-11).
  2. The successor to Moses (27:12-23).
  3. Commands regarding offerings (28:1-15).
  4. Commands regarding festivals (28:16-29:40).
  5. Commands regarding vows (ch. 30).
 F. The War Against Midian (ch. 31).
 G. The Settlement of the Transjordan Tribes (ch. 32).
VI. Appendixes Dealing With Various Matters (chs. 33-36).
 A. The Stages of the Journey (ch. 33).
 B. The Land of Inheritance (chs. 34-35).
 C. The Inheritance for Women (ch. 36).

NUN (*fish* hence *fertile, productive*). Father of Joshua (Ex 33:11).

NURSE (Ge 24:59; 35:8; Ex 2:7; Ru 4:16; 2Ki 11:2; Isa 60:4; 1Th 2:7). Careless (2Sa 4:4).

NUT Pistachio and almond (Ge 43:11), perhaps walnut (SS 6:11).

NYMPHA A Christian of Laodicea. House of, used as a place of worship (Col 4:15).

O

OAK A tree. Grew in Israel (Ge 35:4). Absalom hung in the boughs of (2Sa 18:9, 14). Deborah buried under (Ge 35:8). Oars made of (Eze 27:6).
 Figurative (Am 2:9).

OAR For propelling boats (Isa 33:21; Eze 27:6, 29).

OATH A solemn and binding promise.

Used In Solemnizing Covenants:
 Between Abraham and the king of Sodom (Ge 14:22-23), and Abimelech (Ge 21:22-23), between Isaac and Abimelech (Ge 26:26-29, 31). Abraham requires oath of his servant Eliezer (Ge 24:2-3, 9). Esau confirms the sale of his birthright by (Ge 25:33). Jacob confirms the covenant between him and Laban by (Ge 31:53), requires Joseph to swear that he would bury Jacob with his fathers (Ge 47:28-31). Joseph requires a like oath (Ge 50:25). Rahab requires an oath from the spies (Jos 2:12-14; 6:14). The Israelites confirm the covenant with the Hivites (Jos 9:3-20). Moses covenants with Caleb by (Jos 14:9). The elders of Gilead confirm their pledge to Jephthah by (Jdg 11:10). The Israelites swear in Mizpah (Jdg 21:5). Ruth swears to Naomi (Ru 1:17). Boaz swears to Ruth (Ru 3:13). Saul swears to Jonathan (1Sa 19:6). Jonathan and David confirm a covenant by (1Sa 20:3, 13-17). David swears to Saul (1Sa 24:21-22; 2Sa 21:7). Saul swears to the medium of Endor (1Sa 28:10). David swears not to eat until the sun goes down (2Sa 3:35). Joab confirms his word by (2Sa 19:7). David swears to Bathsheba that Solomon confirms his word by (1Ki 2:23), so also does Shimei (1Ki 2:42). Elisha seals his vow to follow Elijah by (2Ki 2:2). King of Samaria confirms his word with an (2Ki 6:31). Gehazi confirms his lie by (2Ki 5:20). Jehoiada requires an oath from the rulers (2Ki 11:4). Zedekiah violates (2Ch 36:13). Ezra requires, of the priests and Levites (Ezr 10:5, 19), so also does Nehemiah (Ne 5:12-13). Zedekiah swears to Jeremiah (Jer 38:16). Gedaliah confirms his word by (Jer 40:9).
 Peter confirms his denial of Jesus by (Mk 14:71). Used to cast out demons (Ac 19:13); used by Gadarene demoniac in an attempt to keep Jesus from casting out the legion (Mk 5:7).
 Used in solemnizing testimony (Ex 22:10-11; Nu 5:19-24; Dt 6:13; 10:20; 1Ki 8:31-32; Ps 15:1-4; Heb 6:16). Used in confirming allegiance to sovereigns (Ecc 8:2). Used as a result of returning to God (Jer 4:2).
 Attributed to God (Ge 22:16; Ps 89:35; 95:11; 105:9; 132:11; Isa 14:24; 45:23; Jer 11:5; 22:5; 49:13; 51:14; Lk 1:73; Heb 3:11, 18; 4:3; 6:13-14, 17; 7:21, 28; Rev 10:6).
 Christ's teachings concerning (Mt 23:18-22). Required of Christ (Mt 26:63).
 Paul confirms certain statements by (2Co 1:23; Gal 1:20).
 Written in the law of Moses (Da 9:11). Mosaic law concerning (Ex 23:1). Samuel affirms his honesty of administration by (1Sa 12:5).
 Heard, in Daniel's vision (Da 12:7). In John's vision (Rev 10:5-6).

Profane and Wicked:
 Forbidden (Ex 20:7; Lev 19:12; Dt 5:11; Mt 5:33-37; Jas 5:12). Unrighteous, forbidden (Lev 19:12; Hos 4:15). Punishment for (Lev 6:2-5).
 Made by Israelites (Isa 48:1; Jer 5:2, 7; 7:8-9). By Herod (Mt 14:7, 9; Mk 6:23, 26). By enemies of Paul (Ac 23:12-14).

Idolatrous: (Jer 12:16).
 See Covenant; False Witness; God, Name of; Perjury.

OBADIAH (*servant [worshiper] of Yahweh*).
 1. Governor of Ahab's household (1Ki 18:3-16).
 2. Judahite (1Ch 3:21).
 3. Chief of Issachar (1Ch 7:3).
 4. Son of Azel (1Ch 8:38).
 5. Levite who returned from captivity (1Ch 9:16). Also called Abda (Ne 11:17).
 6. Gadite soldier (1Ch 12:9).
 7. Father of Ishmaiah, prince of Zebulun (1Ch 27:19).
 8. Prince of Judah (2Ch 17:7).
 9. Merarite Levite (2Ch 34:12).
 10. Jew who returned from captivity (Ezr 8:9).
 11. Priestly covenanter with Nehemiah (Ne 10:5).
 12. Gatekeeper in Jerusalem (Ne 12:25).
 13. A prophet who wrote the book of Obadiah.

OBADIAH, BOOK OF

Author: The prophet Obadiah

Date:
 If Obadiah relates to the invasion of Jerusalem by Philistines and Arabs during the reign of Jehoram (853-841 B.C.) (2Ki 8:20-22; 2Ch 21:8-20), the prophet would be a contemporary of Elisha.
 If Obadiah relates to the Babylonian attacks on Jerusalem (605-586), the prophet would be a contemporary of Jeremiah. This alternative seems more likely.

Outline:

I. Title and Introduction (1).
II. Judgment on Edom (2-14).
 A. Edom's Destruction Announced (2-7).
  1. The humbling of her pride (2-4).
  2. The completeness of her destruction (5-7).
 B. Edom's Destruction Reaffirmed (8-14).
  1. Her shame and destruction (8-10).
  2. Her crimes against Israel (11-14).
III. The Day of the Lord (15-21).
 A. Judgment on the Nations but Deliverance for Zion (15-18).
 B. The Lord's Kingdom Established (19-21).
 See Prophets, The Minor.

OBAL Called also Ebal. A son of Joktan (Ge 10:28; 1Ch 1:22).

OBDURACY Callousness, hardness. Angers God (Ps 78:31; Isa 57:17). Warnings against (Ps 95:8-11; Heb 3:8, 15; 4:7). Punishment for (Lev 26:23-25; Ps 78:31-32; Pr 1:24-31; 29:1; Jer 3:2; Am 4:6-11).
 Instances of: The antediluvians (Ge 6:3, 5, 7). Sodomites (Ge 19:14). Pharaoh (Ex 7:14, 22-23; 8:15, 19, 32; 9:7, 12, 35; 10:20, 28; 11:10; 14:5-8). Israelites (Nu 14:22; Ne 9:28-29; Ps 78:32; Isa 9:13-14; Jer 2:20; 5:3; Am 4:6-12; Zec 7:11-12). Sons of Eli (1Sa 2:22-25). Brothers of a rich man (Lk 16:31). Mankind in the last days (Rev 9:20-21).
 See Afflictions, Of the Wicked; Impenitence; Reprobacy.

OBED (*servant [worshiper]*).
 1. Son of Boaz and grandfather of David (Ru 4:17-22; 1Ch 2:12; Mt 1:5; Lk 3:32).
 2. Son of Ephlal and grandson of Zabad (1Ch 2:37-38).
 3. One of David's heroes (1Ch 11:47).
 4. Son of Shemaiah. A gatekeeper of the temple (1Ch 26:7).
 5. Father of Azariah (2Ch 23:1).

OBED-EDOM (*servant [worshiper] of Edom*).
 1. A Korahite Levite. Doorkeeper of the ark (1Ch 15:18, 24; 26:4-8). David leaves the ark with (2Sa 6:10; 1Ch 13:13-14). Ark removed from (2Sa 6:12; 1Ch 15:25). Appointed to sound with harps (1Ch 15:21). Appointed to minister before the ark (1Ch 16:4-5, 37-38).
 2. A doorkeeper of the temple (1Ch 16:38).
 3. A caretaker of the vessels of the temple in time of Amaziah (2Ch 25:24).

OBEDIENCE

General:
 Better than sacrifice (1Sa 15:22; Ps 40:6-9; Pr 21:3; Jer 7:22-23; Hos 6:6; Mic 6:6-8; Mt 9:13; 12:7; Mk 12:33; Heb 10:8-9).
 Commanded (Ge 17:9; Ex 23:22; Lev 19:19, 36-37; 20:8, 22; 22:31; Nu 15:38-40; 30:2; Dt 4:1-40; 5:1-33; 6:1-25; 8:1-6, 11-20; 10:12-13; 11:1-3, 8-9, 13-28, 32; 13:4; 26:16-18; 27:1-10; 32:46; Jos 22:5; 23:6-7; 24:14-15; 1Sa 12:14, 20, 24; 15:22; 2Ki 17:37-38; 1Ch 16:15; 28:9-10, 20; Ezr 7:23; Ps 76:11; Pr 7:1; Ecc 12:13; Jer 26:13; 38:20; Da 7:27; Mal 4:4; Eph 6:6-8; Php 2:12; 1Ti 6:14, 18; Jas 1:22-25; 2:10-12; 1Pe 1:2, 14).
 Proof of love (Jn 14:15, 21; 1Jn 2:5-6; 5:2-3; 2Jn 6, 9), under Mosaic law (Lev 18:5; Eze 20:11, 13, 21; Lk 10:28; Ro 10:5; Gal 3:10, 12). Proof that we know God (1Jn 2:3-4).
 Vows of (Ex 24:7; Jos 24:24; Ps 119:15, 106, 109). Prayer for guidance in (Ps 143:10).
 Cannot be rendered to two masters (Mt 6:24).

Rewards:
 (Ge 18:19; Lev 26:3-13; Nu 14:24; Dt 7:12-15; 28:1-15; Jos 14:6-14; 2Ki 21:8; Isa 1:19).
 Rewarded by: Prosperity (Dt 7:9, 12-15; 15:4; Jos 1:8; 1Ki 2:3-4; 9:3-5; 1Ch 22:13; 28:7-8; 2Ch 26:5; 27:6; Job 36:11; Pr 28:7; Jer 7:3-7; 11:1-5; 22:16; Mal 3:10-12; 1Jn 3:22). Long life (Dt 4:1, 40; 32:47; 1Ki 3:14; Pr 3:1-2; 19:16). Victory over enemies (Ex 23:22; Pr 16:7). Triumph over adversities (Mt 7:24-25; Lk 6:46-48). Divine favor (Ex 19:5; 20:6; Dt 5:10; 11:26-27; 12:28; 1Ki 8:23; Ne 1:5; Ps 25:10; 103:17-18, 20; 112:1; 119:2; Pr 1:33; Jer 7:23; 11:4; Mt 5:19; 25:20-23; Lk 11:28; 12:37-38; Jn 12:26; 13:17; Jas 1:25; Rev 22:7). Fellowship with Christ (Mt 12:50; Mk 3:35; Lk 8:21; Jn 14:23; 15:10, 14; 1Jn 3:24). Everlasting life (Mt 19:17, 29; Jn 8:51; 1Jn 2:17; Rev 2:10).

Exemplified:
 (Dt 33:9; Ps 1:2; 103:1-22; 1Th 1:9; Rev 2:19). Noah (Ge 6:9, 22; 7:5; Heb 11:7). Abraham (Ge 12:1-4; 17:23; 18:19; 21:4; 22:12, 18; 26:3-5; Ne 9:8; Ac 7:3-8; Heb 11:8-17; Jas 2:21). Bethuel and Laban (Ge 24:50). Jacob (Ge 35:1, 7). Laban (Ge 31:29). Moses (Nu 27:12-22; Heb 3:2-3). Moses and Aaron (Ex 7:6; 40:16, 21, 23, 32). Israelites (Ex 12:28; 32:25-29; 39:42-43; Nu 9:20-21, 23; Dt 33:9; Jos 22:2; Jdg 2:7; Ps 99:7). Israelites under the preaching of Haggai (Hag 1:12). Caleb (Nu 14:24; Dt 1:36, Jos 14:6-14). Joshua (Jos 10:40; 11:15). Reubenites (Jos 22:2-3). Gibeon (Jdg 6:25-28). David (1Ki 11:6, 34; 15:5; 2Ch 29:2; Ac 13:22). Elijah (1Ki 17:5).
 The psalmist (Ps 17:3; 26:3-6; 119:30-31, 40, 44, 47-48, 51, 55-56, 59-60, 67, 69, 100, 102, 105-106, 110, 112, 119, 166-168). Elisha (1Ki 19:19-21). Hezekiah (2Ki 18:6; 20:3; 2Ch 31:20-21; Isa 38:3). Josiah (2Ki 22:2; 23:24-25). Asa (2Ch 14:2). Jehoshaphat (2Ch 17:3-6; 20:32; 22:9). Uzziah (2Ch 26:4-5). Jotham (2Ch 27:2). Levites (2Ch 29:34). Cyrus (Ezr 1:1-4). Ezra (Ezr 7:10). Hanani (Ne 7:2). Job (Job 1:8). The three Hebrews (Da 3). Jonah (Jnh 3:3). Ninevites (Jnh 3:5-10).
 Zechariah (Lk 1:6). Simeon (Lk 2:25). Joseph (Mt 1:24; 2:14). Mary (Lk 1:38). Jesus (Mt 3:15; 26:39, 42; Lk 22:42; Jn 4:32, 34; 5:30; 6:38; 8:28-29; 9:4; 12:49-50; 14:31; 17:4; Php 2:8; Heb 3:2). By, John the Baptist (Mt 3:15). John and James (Mk 1:19-20). Matthew (Mt 9:9). Simon and Andrew (Mk 1:16-18). Levi (Mk 2:14). The rich young man (Mt 19:20; Mk 10:20; Lk 18:21). The disciples (Jn 17:6; Ac 4:19-20; 5:29). Cornelius (Ac 10:2). Paul (Ac 23:1; 24:17; 26:4-5; Php 3:7-14; 2Ti 1:3). Paul and Timothy (2Co 1:12; 6:3). Paul, Timothy, and Silas (1Th 2:1). The Christians at Rome (Ro 6:17).
 To Civil Law. *See Citizens.*
 Filial. *See Children.*
 See Blessings, Spiritual, Contingent Upon Obedience; Commandments and Statutes, Of God; Duty; Faithfulness; Law.

OBEISANCE The act of bowing low or of prostrating oneself in token of respect or submission (Ge 43:28; Ex 18:7; 2Sa 1:2). *See Worship, Attitudes in.*

OBIL (*camel driver*). An Ishmaelite. Camel-keeper for David (1Ch 27:30).

OBJECT TEACHING *See Instruction.*

OBLATION *See Offerings.*

OBLIGATION A motive of obedience (Dt 4:32-40; 6-11; 26:16; 32:6; 1Sa 12:24; 1Ch 16:12; Ro 2:4; 2Co 5:15). Acknowledgment of (Ps 116:12-14, 17). *See Duty.*

OBLIQUITY *See Depravity.*

OBOTH (*fathers*). A camping place of Israel in the forty years' wandering (Nu 21:10-11; 33:43-44).

OBSEQUIOUSNESS *See Tact.*

OBSTETRICS (Eze 16:4). *See Midwives.*

OCCULTISM *See Sorcery.*

OCCUPATIONS AND PROFESSIONS Artisan—a worker with any materials, as carpenter, smith, engraver, etc.—author; baker; barber; beggar; carpenter; clerk; coppersmith; counselor; cupbearer, doctor; diviner, dyer; farmer; fisherman; gatekeeper; herdsman; hunter; judge; launderer; lawyer; magician;

mason; medium; musician; nurse; perfumer; physician; plowman; potter; preacher; priest; prophet; rabbi; recorder; robber; ruler; sailor; scribe; seer; servant; sheepshearer; shepherd; silversmith; singer; slave; smith; soldier; sorcerer; spinner; steward; tanner; taskmaster; tax collector; teacher; tentmaker; tiller; town clerk; treasurer; watchman; weaver; witch; writer.
See each occupation by name.

OCRAN (*trouble*). An Asherite and the father of Pagiel who numbered Israel (Nu 1:13; 2:27; 10:26).

ODED (*restorer*).
1. A prophet in Samaria (2Ch 28:9).
2. Father of the prophet Azariah (2Ch 15:1).

ODOR Pleasant or unpleasant smell (Ge 8:21; Lev 1:9-17; Jn 11:39). Also used figuratively (Ro 5:8).

OFFENSE Used in a variety of ways: Injury, hurt, damage, occasion of sin, stumbling block, infraction of the law, sin, transgression, state of being offended.

OFFERINGS Holy (Lev 2:3; 6:17, 25, 27, 29; 7:1, 6; 10:12; Nu 18:9-10). Offered at door of the tabernacle (Lev 1:3; 3:2; 17:4, 8-9), of the temple (1Ki 8:62; 12:27; 2Ch 7:12).

All animal sacrifices, must be eight days old or over (Lev 22:27), must be without blemish (Ex 12:5; 29:1; Lev 1:3, 10; 22:18-25; Dt 15:21; 17:1; Eze 43:23; Mal 1:8, 14; Heb 9:14; 1Pe 1:19). *See Bruise(s), 2,* must be salted (Lev 2:13; Eze 43:24; Mk 9:49), accompanied with leaven (Lev 7:13; Am 4:5), without leaven (Ex 23:18; 34:25), eaten (1Sa 9:13). Ordinance relating to scapegoat (Lev 16:7-26). Atonement for sin made by. *See Atonement.*

Figurative:
(Ps 51:17; Jer 33:11; Ro 12:1; Php 4:18; Heb 13:15).

Animal Sacrifices:
A type of Christ (Ps 40:6-8, w Heb 10:1-14; Isa 53:11-12, w Lev 16:21; Jn 1:29; 1Co 5:7; 2Co 5:21; Eph 5:2; Heb 9:19-28; 10:1, 11-12; 13:11-13; Rev 5:6).

Burnt:
(Lev 9:2). Its purpose was to make an atonement for sin (Lev 1:4; 7). Ordinances concerning (Ex 29:15-18; Lev 1; 5:7-13; 6:9-13; 17:8-9; 23:18, 26-37; Nu 15:24-25; 19:9; 28:26-31; 29). Accompanied by other offerings (Nu 15:3-16). Skins of, belonged to priests (Lev 7:8). Offered daily, morning and evening (Ge 15:17; Ex 29:38-42; Lev 6:20; Nu 28; 29:6; 1Ch 16:40; 2Ch 2:4; 13:11; Ezr 3:3; Eze 46:13-15). Music with (Nu 10:10).

Offered, by Noah (Ge 8:20), in idolatrous worship (Ex 32:6; 1Ki 18:26; 2Ki 10:25; Ac 14:13). For cleansing leprosy (Lev 14).

Daily:
Sacrificial (Ex 29:38-42; Lev 6:20; Nu 28:3-8; 29:6; 1Ki 18:29; 1Ch 16:40; 2Ch 2:4; 13:11; Ezr 3:3-6; 9:4-5; Ps 141:2; Eze 46:13-15; Da 9:21, 27; 11:31).

Drink:
Libations of wine offered with the sacrifices (Ge 35:14; Ex 29:40-41; 30:9; Lev 23:13, 18; Nu 6:17; 15:24; 28:5-15, 24-31; 29:6-11, 18-40; 2Ki 16:13; 1Ch 29:21; 2Ch 29:35; Ezr 7:17).

Fellowship:
Laws concerning (Ex 20:24; 24:5; Lev 3:6; 7:11-18; 9:3-4, 18-22; 19:5; 23:10; Nu 6:14; 10:10). Offered, by the tribal leaders (Nu 7:17, 23, 29, 35, 41, 47, 53, 59, 65, 71, 77, 83, 88), by Joshua (Jos 8:31), by David (2Sa 6:17; 24:25).

Offered in idolatrous worship (Ex 32:6). Offered by harlots (Pr 7:14).

Free Will:
(Lev 23:38; Nu 29:39; Dt 12:6; 2Ch 31:14; Ezr 3:5). Must be perfect (Lev 22:17-25). To be eaten, at tabernacle (Dt 12:17-18), by priests (Lev 7:16-17). With meat and drink offerings (Nu 15:1-16). Obligatory (Dt 16:10), when signified in a vow (Dt 23:23).

Guilt:
Ordinances concerning (Lev 5; 6:1-7; 7:1-7; 14:10-22; 15:15, 29-30; 19:21-22; Nu 6:12; Ezr 10:19). To be eaten by the priests (Lev 7:6-7; 14:13; Nu 18:9-10). Offered by idolaters (1Sa 6:3, 8, 17-18). *See below, Sin.*

Heave: *See below, Presentation or Wave.*

Human Sacrifices:
Forbidden (Lev 18:21; 20:2-5; Dt 12:31). Offered by Abraham (Ge 22:1-19; Heb 11:17-19), by Canaanites (Dt 12:31), Moabites (2Ki 3:27), Israelites (2Ki 16:3; 2Ch 28:3; 2Ki 23:10; Isa 57:5; Jer 7:31; 19:5; 32:35; Eze 16:20-21; 20:26, 31; 23:37, 39), by the Sepharvites to idols (2Ki 17:31). To demons (Ps 106:37-38), to Baal (Jer 19:5-6).

Meat:
Ordinances concerning (Ex 29:40-41; 30:9; 40:29; Lev 2; 5:11-12; 6:14-23; 7:9-13, 37; 9:17; 23:13, 16-17; Nu 4:16; 5:15, 18, 25-26; 8:8; 15:3-16, 24; 18:9; 28:5, 9, 12-13, 20-21, 26-31; 29:3-4, 14). To be eaten in the Holy Place (Lev 10:13; Nu 18:9-10). Offered with animal sacrifices (Nu 15:3-16). Not mixed with leaven (Lev 2:4, 11; 6:14-18; 10:12-13; Nu 6:15, 17). Storerooms for, in the temple (Ne 12:44; 13:5-6), provided for in the vision of Ezekiel (Eze 42:12).

Peace: *See above, Fellowship.*

Presentation or Wave:
Given to the priests' families as part of their share (Lev 10:14; Nu 5:9; 18:10-19, 24). Consecrated by being elevated by the priest (Ex 29:27). Consisted of the right thigh or hindquarter (Ex 29:27-28; Lev 7:12-14, 32, 34; 10:15), spoils, including captives and other articles of war (Nu 31:29, 41). When offered (Lev 7:12-14; Nu 6:20; 15:19-21). In certain instances this offering was brought to the tabernacle, or temple (Dt 12:6, 11, 17-18). To be offered on taking possession of the land of Canaan (Nu 15:18-21).

Sin:
Ordinances concerning (Ex 29:10-14, w Heb 13:11-13; Lev 4; 5; 6:1-7, 26-30; 9:1-21; 12:6-8; 14:19, 22, 31; 15:30; 23:19; Nu 6:10-11, 14, 16; 8:8, 12; 15:27; 28:15, 22-24, 30; 29:5-6, 11, 16-38). Temporary (Da 11:31; Heb 9-10).

Special Sacrifices:
In consecration of the altar. *See Altar.* Of priests. *See Priest.* Of the temple. *See Temple, Solomon's.* For leprosy. *See Leprosy.* For defilement. *See Defilement.*

Thank:
Ordinances concerning (Lev 7:11-15; 22:29; Dt 12:11-12).

Trespass: *See above, Guilt.*

Vow:
(Lev 7:16-17; 22:17-25; Dt 23:21-23).

Wave:
Ordinances concerning (Ex 29:22, 26-28; Lev 7:29-34; 8:25-29; 9:19-21; 10:14-15; 23:10-11, 17, 20; Nu 5:25; 6:19-20). Belonged to the priests (Ex 29:26-28; Lev 7:31, 34; 8:29; 9:21; 23:20; Nu 18:11, 18). To be eaten (Lev 10:14-15; Nu 18:11, 18-19, 31).

Wood:
Fuel for the temple (Ne 10:34; 13:31).

Insufficiency of:
(Heb 8:7-13; 9:1-15; 10:1-12, 18-20). Unavailing, when not accompanied by piety (1Sa 15:22; Ps 40:6; 50:8-14; 51:16-17; Pr 21:3, 27; Isa 1:11-14; 66:3; Jer 6:20; 7:21-23; 14:12; Hos 6:6; 8:13; Am 5:21-24; Mic 6:6-8; Mt 9:13; 12:7; Mk 12:33).

OFFICER

Civil:
Chosen by the people (Dt 1:13-16), appointed by kings (2Sa 8:16-18; 20:23-26; 1Ki 4:1-19; 9:22; Ezr 7:25). *See Government; Judge; Rulers.*

Ecclesiastical: *See Priest; Levites; Apostle; Elders; Deacon; Minister.*

OFFSCOURING Term of contempt; NIV "scum" (La 3:45; 1Co 4:13).

OG King of Bashan. A man of gigantic stature (Nu 21:33; Dt 3:11; Jos 12:4; 13:12). Defeated and slain by Moses (Nu 21:33-35; Dt 1:4; 3:1-7; 29:7; 31:4; Jos 2:10; 9:10; Ps 135:10-11; 136:18-20). Land of, given to Gad, Reuben, and Manasseh (Nu 32:33; Dt 3:8-17; 4:47-49; 29:7-8; Jos 12:4-6; 13:12, 30-31; 1Ki 4:19; Ne 9:22; Ps 136:20-21).

OHAD Son of Simeon (Ge 46:10; Ex 6:15).

OHEL (*[skin] tent*). Son of Zerubbabel (1Ch 3:20).

OHOLAH (*she who has a tent*). In God's parable to Ezekiel (ch. 23), Oholah is a woman representing Samaria, who with her sister Oholibah (Jerusalem) was accused of being unfaithful to Yahweh. Imaginary characters, figurative of idolatry (Eze 23:4-5, 36, 44).

OHOLIAB (*tent of [my] Father*). A craftsman of the tabernacle (Ex 31:6; 35:34; 36:1-2; 38:23).

OHOLIBAH (*my tent is in her*). *See Oholah.*

OHOLIBAMAH (*[my] tent is a high place*).
1. One of Esau's three wives (Ge 36:2, 18, 25). Also called Judith the daughter of Beeri (Ge 26:34).
2. An Edomite chief (Ge 36:41; 1Ch 1:52), probably so named from the district of his possession.

OIL Sacred (Ex 30:23-25; 31:11; 35:8, 15, 28; 37:29; 39:38; Nu 4:16; 1Ch 9:30). Compounded by Bezalel (Ex 37:1, 29). Punishment for profaning (Ex 30:31-33). Used for idols (Eze 23:41). Illuminating, for tabernacle (Ex 25:6; 27:20; Lev 24:2-4). Of olives (Ex 25:6).

For domestic use (Mt 25:3). Used for food (Lev 2:4-5; 14:10, 21; Dt 12:17; 1Ki 17:12-16; Job 29:6; Pr 21:17; Eze 16:13; Hos 2:5). For the head (Ps 23:5; 105:15; Lk 7:46). For anointing kings (1Sa 10:1; 16:1, 13; 1Ki 1:39).

Tribute paid in (Hos 12:1). Commerce in (2Ki 4:1-7).
See Anointing; Ointment.

OIL TREE *See Plants of the Bible.*

OINTMENT (Job 41:31). Used in care of newborns (Eze 16:9).

OLD AGE Wise (1Ki 12:6-8; 2Ch 10:6-8; Job 12:12). Devout (Lk 2:37). Exemplary, commanded (Tit 2:2-3). Deference toward (Lev 19:32; Job 32:4-9). Righteous, is glorious (Pr 16:31). Wasted, is bitter (Ge 47:9; Ecc 6:3, 6; 12:1-7).

Promised to the righteous (Ge 15:15; Job 5:26; Ps 34:12-14; 91:14, 16; Pr 3:1-2). God's care in (Isa 46:4). Psalmist prays not to be forsaken in (Ps 71:9, 18). David enjoys (1Ch 29:28). Paul, the aged (Phm 9).

Infirmities in (2Sa 19:34-37; Ps 90:10). Vigor in (Dt 34:7; Ps 92:12-14). Join in praise to the Lord (Ps 148:12-13).
See Longevity; Infirmity.

OLD GATE *See Jeshanah, 2.*

OLD TESTAMENT In Protestant Bibles, thirty-nine books from Genesis to Malachi: Five of law, twelve of history, five of poetry, five of major prophets, and twelve of minor prophets. In the Hebrew Bible, the same contents are organized into twenty-four books from Genesis to Chronicles: Five of law, eight of the prophets, and eleven of miscellaneous writings. All of these books were regarded by Israelites as Scripture, inspired and authoritative, before the first century A.D. (Mt 5:17-20; Lk 24:44; Jn 17:17; 2Ti 3:16). They appeared over a period of c. 1000 years. The authors of many of them are unknown.

OLIVE A fruit tree. Branch of, brought by the dove to Noah's ark (Ge 8:11). Common to the land of Canaan (Ex 23:11; Dt 6:11; 8:8), Israelites commanded to cultivate in the land of promise (Dt 28:40). Branches of, used for booths (Ne 8:15). Produces blooms (Job 15:33). Precepts concerning gleaning the fruit of (Dt 24:20; Isa 17:6). Cherubim made of the wood of (1Ki 6:23, 31-33). Fable of (Jdg 9:8).

Figurative:
Of prosperity (Ps 128:3). The wild, a figure of the Gentiles; the cultivated, of the Jews (Ro 11:17-21, 24).

Symbolic: (Zec 4:2-12; Rev 11:4).

Fruit of:
Oil extracted from, used as illuminating oil in the tabernacle (Ex 39:37; Lev 24:2; Zec 4:12).
See Oil.

OLIVES, MOUNT OF A ridge, c. one mile long, with four identifiable summits, E of Jerusalem, beyond the Valley of Jehoshaphat, through which flows the Kidron stream. Gethsemane, Bethphage, and Bethany are on its slopes (2Sa 15:30; Zec 14:4; Mt 21:1; 24:3; 26:30; Mk 11:1; 13:3; 14:26; Lk 19:29, 37; 22:39; Jn 8:1; Ac 1:12).

OLIVET *See Olives, Mount of.*

OLYMPAS A believer at Rome (Ro 16:15).

OMAR (*speaker*). Son of Eliphaz, grandson of Esau (Ge 36:11, 15; 1Ch 1:36).

OMEGA Alpha and Omega, a title of Christ, meaning he is the beginning and end of all things (Rev 1:8, 11; 21:6; 22:13). *See Jesus the Christ, Names of; Titles and Names.*

OMER One-tenth part of an ephah. A dry measure containing, according to the Rabbis, two quarts, but according to Josephus, three and one-half quarts (Ex 16:16-18, 36).

OMNIPOTENCE (*all power*). The attribute of God which describes his ability to do whatever he wills. He cannot do anything contrary to his nature as God, such as to ignore sin, to sin, or to do something absurd or self-contradictory. God is not controlled by his power, but has complete control over it; otherwise he would not be a free being. Although the word "omnipotence" is not found in the Bible, the Scriptures clearly teach the omnipotence of God (Job 42:2; Jer 32:17; Mt 19:26; Lk 1:37; Rev 19:6).
See God, Omnipotent; Jesus the Christ, Power of.

OMNIPRESENCE (*all presence*). The attribute of God by virtue of which he fills the universe in all its parts and is present everywhere at once. Not a part, but the whole of God is present in every place. The Bible teaches the omnipresence of God (Ps 139:7-12; Jer 23:23-24; Ac 17:27-28). This is true of all three members of the Trinity.
See God, Omnipresent.

OMNISCIENCE (*all knowing*). The attribute by which God perfectly and eternally knows all things which can be known, past, present, and future. God's omniscience is clearly taught in Scripture (Ps 147:5; Pr 15:11; Isa 46:1).
See God, Knowledge of; Jesus the Christ, Omniscience of.

OMRI (*thrive, live long* ISBE).
1. King of Israel. Was commander of the army of Israel, and was proclaimed king by the army upon news of the assassination of King Elah (1Ki 16:16). Defeats his rival, Tibni, and establishes himself (1Ki 16:17-22). Surrendered cities to the king of Syria (1Ki 20:34). Wicked reign and death of (1Ki 16:23-28). Denounced by Micah (Mic 6:16).
2. Son of Beker, grandson of Benjamin (1Ch 7:8).
3. A descendant of Perez (1Ch 9:4).
4. Son of Michael, and ruler of tribe of Issachar in time of David (1Ch 27:18).

ON (*sun [god] city*).
1. Capital of lower Egypt (Ge 41:45; 46:20).
2. A leader of the Reubenites who rebelled against Moses (Nu 16:1).

ONAM (*intense, strong*). A son of Shobal (Ge 36:23; 1Ch 1:40).

ONAN (*powerful, intense*). Son of Judah. Slain for his refusal to raise seed to his brother (Ge 38:4, 8-10; 46:12; Nu 26:19; 1Ch 2:3).

ONE AND ONLY A title applied to Jesus by John (Jn 1:14, 18; 3:16, 18; 1Jn 4:9), and once in Hebrews (Heb 11:17). It emphasizes the unique relationship of Jesus to God the Father. In ancient mss of Jn 1:18, Jesus is called God the One and Only, a clear reference to his deity.

ONE ANOTHER Responsibilities of fellow believers to (1Pe 4:7-10). All believers members of (Ro 12:5; Eph 4:25).

Commanded to:
Admonish (Ro 15:14; Col 3:16, w 2Th 3:15). Assemble together with (Heb 10:24). Bear burdens of (Gal 6:2). Comfort (1Th 4:18; 5:11, w 14). Confess faults to (Jas 5:16). Consider above self (Heb 10:24). Be courteous (1Pe 3:8). Edify (Ro 14:18; 1Th 5:11). Encourage (Heb 10:24). Equality with (Ro 12:16; 15:5, 7; 1Co 11:33; 12:25; Php 2:3). Exhort daily (Heb 3:13). Have fellowship with (1Jn 1:7). Forgive (Eph 4:32; Col 3:13). Do good to (1Th 5:15). Be hospitable to (1Pe 4:9), in greeting (Ro 16:16; 1Co 16:20; 2Co 13:12; 1Pe 5:5). Be kind to (Eph 4:32). Love (Jn 13:34-35; 15:12, 17; Ro 12:10; 13:8; 1Co 12:25; Gal 5:13; Eph 4:2, 32; 1Th 3:12; 4:9; 1Pe 1:22; 2:17; 3:8; 1Jn 3:11, 23; 4:7, 11-12; 2Jn 5). Minister to (1Pe 4:10). Be patient with (Eph 4:2; Col 3:13). Be at peace with (Mk 9:50; 1Th 5:13). Pray for (Jas 5:16). Prefer (Ro 12:10; Php 2:3; 1Ti 5:21). Provoke to love and good works (Heb 10:24). Serve (Gal 5:13; 1Pe 4:10), by washing feet of (Jn 13:14). Be subject to (1Pe 5:5), husband and wife, each to be subject to (Eph 5:21). Teach (Col 3:16). Wait for (1Co 11:33).

Love of, exemplified (2Th 1:3).

Commanded Not to:
Deceive (1Co 7:5), devour and consume (Gal 5:15), do evil to (1Th 5:5), envy (Gal 5:26), grudge (Jas 5:9), judge (Ro 14:13), lie to (Lev 19:11; Col 3:9), owe anything to (Ro 13:8), provoke (Gal 5:26), speak evil of (Jas 4:11).

ONE GOD (Dt 4:35; 6:4; 32:39; 2Sa 7:22; 1Ch 17:20; Ps 83:18; 86:10; Isa 43:10; 44:6; 45:18; Mk 12:29; 1Co 8:4; Eph 4:6; 1Ti 2:5; 1Jn 5:7). That God is one (Dt 6:4) does not deny the doctrine of the Trinity, for the same word is used of husband and wife as "one flesh" (Ge 2:24).

ONESIMUS (*useful*). Runaway slave of Philemon of Colosse; converted through Paul, who wrote the letter to Philemon in his behalf (Col 4:9; Phm).
See Philemon, Epistle to.

ONESIPHORUS (*one bringing usefulness*). A Christian of Ephesus (2Ti 1:16-17; 4:19).

ONION Enjoyed by Israel in Egypt (Nu 11:5).

ONLY-BEGOTTEN *See One and Only.*

ONO (*strong*). Town in Benjamin, c. six miles SE of Joppa (1Ch 8:12; Ne 6:2; 11:35).

ONYCHA A component of the sacred perfume, made from the shells of a species of mussel, possessing an odor (Ex 30:34).

ONYX Exported from Havilah (Ge 2:12). Contributed by Israelites for the priests' garments (Ex 25:7; 35:9). Used in the breastplate (Ex 28:9-12, 20; 39:6, 13). Used in building the temple (1Ch 29:2). Precious stone (Job 28:16; Eze 28:13). Seen in the foundations of the city of the New Jerusalem in John's apocalyptic vision (Rev 21:20).
See Minerals of the Bible, 1; Stones.

OPHEL (*mound, hill*). A gate in the wall of the city and the temple (2Ch 27:3; 33:14; Ne 3:26-27).

OPHIR
1. Son of Joktan (Ge 10:29; 1Ch 1:23).
2. A country celebrated for its gold and other valuable merchandise. Products of, used by Solomon and Hiram (1Ki 9:28; 10:11; 2Ch 8:18; 9:10). Jehoshaphat sends ships to, which are wrecked (1Ki 22:48). Gold of, proverbial for its fineness (1Ch 29:4; Job 22:24; 28:16; Ps 45:9; Isa 13:12).

OPHNI A town of the Benjamites (Jos 18:24).

OPHRAH (*young gazelle*).
1. A city in Benjamin (Jos 18:23; 1Sa 13:17). Possibly identical with Ephron (2Ch 13:19) and Ephraim (Jn 11:54).
2. A city in Manasseh, home of Gideon (Jdg 6:11, 24; 8:27, 32; 9:5).
3. Son of Meonothai and descendant of Judah through Kenaz and Othniel (1Ch 4:14).

OPINION

Public:
Kings influenced by. *See Kings.* Jesus inquires about (Mt 16:13; Lk 9:18). Feared by Nicodemus (Jn 3:2), Joseph of Arimathea (Jn 19:38), the parents of the man who was born blind (Jn 9:21-22), rulers who believed in Jesus but feared the Pharisees (Jn 12:42-43), chief priests who feared to answer the questions of Jesus (Mt 21:26; Mk 11:18, 32; 12:12), and to further persecute the disciples (Ac 4:21; 5:26).

Concessions to:
By Paul in circumcising Timothy (Ac 16:3). James and the Christian elders who required Paul to observe certain rites (Ac 21:18-26). Disciples who urged circumcision (Gal 6:12). Peter and Barnabas with others (Gal 2:11-14).
See Prudence.

Corrupt Yielding to:
By Herod, in the case of John the Baptist (Mk 6:26), of Peter (Ac 12:3), by Peter, concerning Jesus (Mt 26:69-75), by Pilate (Mt 27:23-27; Mk 15:15; Lk 23:13-25; Jn 18:38-39; 19:4-16), by Felix and Festus, concerning Paul (Ac 24:27; 25:9).

OPPORTUNITY Providential (1Co 16:9; 2Co 2:12). Neglected (Lk 12:47). Spurned (Pr 1:24-25; Mt 23:34-38; Lk 14:16-24). Lost (Nu 14:40-43; Pr 1:28; Jer 8:20; Hos 5:6; Mt 24:50-51; 25:1-10, 24-28; Lk 19:20-24; 13:25-28). Terrible consequences of neglecting (Eze 3:19; Mt 25:3-13, 24-30, 41-46).
Terrible consequences of spurning (Pr 1:24-32; Mt 10:14-15; 11:20-24).
The measure of responsibility (Pr 1:24-30; Jer 8:20; Eze 3:19; 33:1-17; Hos 5:6; Mt 10:14-15; 11:20-24; Mt 23:34-38; 25:1-46 w Lk 19:20-24; Lk 12:47; 13:25-28; 14:16-24).
See Judgment, According to Opportunity and Works; Responsibility.

OPPRESSION Seeming hopelessness under (Ecc 4:1). Proverbs concerning (Pr 3:31; 14:31; 22:16, 22; 28:3; 30:14; Ecc 4:1; 5:8; 7:7).

God:
A refuge from (Ps 9:9; 12:5). Promises aid against (Ps 12:5; 72:4, 14; Isa 58:6; Jer 50:34). God will judge (Ps 10:17-18; 103:6; Ecc 5:8; Isa 10; Jer 21:12; 22:17; Eze 22:7; Am 4:1; Mic 2:2; Hab 2:5-11; Mal 3:5; Jas 5:4). God will reward those who fight against (Isa 33:15-16).

National:
God judges (Ac 7:7), relieved (Ex 3:9; 12:30-39; Dt 26:7-8; Jdg 2:14; 6-8; 10-11; 2Ki 13; Isa 52:4). Prayer for deliverance from (Ps 17:8-9; 44:24; 74:21; 119:121, 134; Isa 38:14).

Oppressors:
Punished (Job 27:13-23; Ps 72:4; 103:6; Isa 10). Oppression forbidden (Ex 22:21-24; Dt 23:15-16; 24:14-15; Pr 22:22; Zec 7:10). Oppression warned against (Ps 62:10; Eze 45:9; Jas 2:6). Command to relieve the oppressed (Isa 1:17).

Instances of:
Hagar, by Sarah (Ge 16:6). Jacob, by Laban (Ge 31:39). Israelites, by Egyptians (Ex 1:10-22; 5), by Assyrians (Isa 52:4). Rehoboam resolves to oppress the Israelites (1Ki 12:14). Strangers and the poor and needy, by Israelites (Eze 22:29; Am 5:11-12; 8:4-6). Of people, by the scribes and Pharisees (Mt 23:2-4).

ORACLE (*speak*). Utterance of prophecy. KJV "burden," (Isa 14:28; 15:1; Eze 12:10; Na 1:1) or "parable" (Nu 23:7, 18; 24:3, 4, 15, 16, 20, 21, 23) or "prophecy" (Pr 30:1; 31:1).

ORACLES NIV "words" of God. Scriptures called (Ac 7:38; Ro 3:2; Heb 5:12; 1Pe 4:11).

ORATOR A public speaker. Instances of: Judah (Ge 44:18-34). Aaron (Ex 4:14-16). Moses (Dt 1-4:40). Jonah (Jnh 3:4-10). Peter (Ac 2:14-40; 3:12-26; 4:8-12; 10:34-48; 11:4-17). Stephen (Ac 7:2-60). Paul and Barnabas (Ac 14:14-17). Paul (Ac 13:16-41; 17:22-31; 22:1-21; 24:10-21; 26:1-29; 27:21-25). James (Ac 15:13-21). Apollos (Ac 18:24-28). Herod (Ac 12:21). The city clerk (Ac 19:35-41). Tertullus (Ac 24:1).

ORDAIN, ORDINATION An act of conferring a sacred office upon someone, as: Deacons (Ac 6:6), missionaries (Ac 13:3), elders (Ac 14:23). OT priests were ordained to office (Ex 28:41; 29:9).
Instances of: Priests (Ex 29:1-9, 19-35; 40:12-16; Lev 8:6-35; Heb 7:21). Apostles (Mk 3:14). Ministers: the seven (Ac 6:5-6), Paul and Barnabas (Ac 13:2-3), Timothy (1Ti 4:14).

ORDINANCE A decree of the Law (Ex 12:14, 24, 43; 13:10; 15:25; Nu 9:14; 10:8; 15:15; 18:8; Isa 24:5; Mal 4:4; Ro 13:2; 1Pe 2:13).
Insufficiency, in salvation (Isa 1:10-17; Gal 5:6; 6:15; Eph 2:15; Col 2:14, 20-23; Heb 9:1, 8-10).
See Form; Formalism.

OREB (*raven*).
1. A prince of Midian, overcome by Gideon and killed by the Ephraimites (Jdg 7:25; 8:3; Ps 83:11).
2. A rock E of the Jordan, where Oreb was slain (Jdg 7:25; Isa 10:26).

OREN (*fir or cedar* BDB IDB; *laurel* KB). Son of Jerahmeel (1Ch 2:25).

ORGAN *See Flute; Music, Instruments of.*

ORION The constellation of (Job 9:9; 38:31; Isa 13:10; Am 5:8).

ORNAN *See Araunah.*

ORONTES The chief river of Syria, c. 400 miles long, rises in Anti-Lebanon range and flows N for most of its course.

ORPAH (*neck, the girl with a full mane[?],* or *rain cloud*). Daughter-in-law of Naomi (Ru 1:4, 14).

ORPHAN To be visited (Jas 1:27). Beneficent provision for (Dt 14:28-29; 16:10-11, 14; 24:19-22; 26:12-13). Kindness toward (Job 29:12-13; 31:16-18, 21). God the friend of (Ex 22:22-24; Dt 10:18; Ps 10:14; 10:17-18; 27:10; 68:5; 146:9; Pr 23:10-11; Jer 49:11; Hos 14:3; Mal 3:5). Justice to, required (Dt 24:17-22; 27:19; Ps 82:3; Isa 1:17, 23; Jer 7:6-7; 22:3). Oppressed (Job 6:27; 22:9; 24:3, 9; Isa 10:1-2; Jer 5:28).
See Adoption; Children; Widow.
Instances of: Lot (Ge 11:27-28). Daughters of Zelophehad (Nu 27:1-5). Jotham (Jdg 9:16-21). Mephibosheth (2Sa 9:3). Joash (2Ki 11:1-12). Esther (Est 2:7). A type of Zion in affliction (La 5:3).

OSEE *See Hosea.*

OSHEA *See Joshua.*

OSNAPPAR *See Ashurbanipal.*

OSPRAY *See Vulture.*

OSPREY A carnivorous bird. Forbidden as food (Lev 11:13; Dt 14:12).

OSSIFRAGE *See Vulture.*

OSTENTATION In prayer and almsgiving (Mt 6:1; Pr 25:14; 27:2). *See Boasting.*

OSTIA The port of Rome on the Tiber, some sixteen miles from the city.

OSTRACA Inscribed fragments of pottery, or potsherds. Some important ancient documents have come down to us in this form, i.e., the Lachish Letters.

OSTRICH A large, flightless bird that does not take care of its young well (Job 39:13-18; La 4:3).

OTHNI Son of Shemaiah (1Ch 26:7).

OTHNIEL Son of Kenaz and nephew of Caleb. Conquers Kiriath Sepher, and as reward secures Caleb's daughter as his wife (Jos 15:16-20; Jdg 1:12-13). Becomes deliverer and judge of Israel (Jdg 3:8-11). Death of (Jdg 3:11). Descendants of (1Ch 4:13-14).

OUCHES *See Filigree.*

OUTCASTS General references to (Isa 11:12; 16:3; 27:13; Jer 30:17).

OVEN Ancient ovens were primitive, often a hole in the ground coated with clay and in which a fire was made. The dough was spread on the inside and baked. Sometimes ovens were made of stone, from which the fire was raked when the oven was very hot and into which the unbaked loaves were placed (Ex 8:3; Lev 2:4; 7:9; 11:35; 26:26; Hos 7:4-7).
Figurative (Ps 21:9; Mal 4:1; Mt 6:30; Lk 12:28).

OVERCOMING *See Perseverance.*

OVERSEER Ruler (Pr 6:7). Office of church leadership, traditionally "bishop," (Ac 20:28; Php 1:1; 1Ti 3:1-7) same as an elder (Tit 1:5-9; 1Pe 5:1-4). A title of Christ (1Pe 2:25). *See Elders.*

OVERWEIGHT *See Corpulency.*

OWL Several kinds of carnivorous birds (Isa 14:23; 34:11; Zep 2:14). Unclean for food (Lev 11:16-18; Dt 14:15-17). Lives in the desert (Job 30:29; Ps 102:6; Isa 13:21; 34:11-15; 43:20; Jer 50:39; Mic 1:8).

OWNER OF A SHIP Usually captained his ship or contracted to state service (Ac 27:11).

OX *See Bull; Cattle; Wild Ox.*

OXGOAD A pointed stick used to prod the ox on to further effort. Used by Shamgar to kill six hundred Philistines (Jdg 3:31).

OZEM
1. Son of Jesse (1Ch 2:15).
2. Son of Jerahmeel (1Ch 2:25).

OZIAS *See Uzziah, 1.*

OZNI, OZNITE (*my ear, my hearing*). Son of Gad and his clan (Nu 26:16).

P

PAARAI (*devotee of Peor*). One of David's valiant men (2Sa 23:35). Called Naarai (1Ch 11:37).

PACK ANIMALS Used for transporting army supplies (1Ch 12:40).

PADDAN ARAM (*plain of Aram*).
1. Region near the head of the fertile crescent; sometimes called simply "Paddan," (Ge 48:7, ftn). Another name for Aram Naharaim (Ge 24:10). Literally "Aram of the two rivers"—the Euphrates and the Tigris. Naharaim was the northern part of the area called later by the Greeks "Mesopotamia"—literally "between the rivers." It was located NE of Canaan, the area known today as Syria.
2. A town near Shechem (Ge 33:18, ftn).

PADON (*ransom*). One of the temple servants (Ezr 2:44; Ne 7:47).

PAGIEL (perhaps *fortune of God* or *God is entreated,* less probably *God has met his worshiper*). Son of Ocran and leader of the tribe of Asher at the time of the Exodus (Nu 1:13; 2:27; 7:72, 77; 10:26).

PAHATH-MOAB (*supervisor of Moab*). The ancestor of an influential family of Judah, which returned to Jerusalem from the Captivity (Ezr 2:6; 10:30; Ne 3:11; 7:11).

PAI *See Pau.*

PAIN Experienced on earth (Job 14:22; 30:17-18; La 3:5; Rev 16:10). Chastens (Job 33:19). None in Heaven (Rev 21:4).
See Afflictions.

PAINTING Around the eyes, to enhance their appearance (2Ki 9:30; Jer 4:30; Eze 23:40). Of rooms (Jer 22:14). Of portraits (Eze 23:14).

PALACE For kings (1Ki 21:1; 2Ki 15:25; Jer 49:27; Am 1:12; Na 2:6). Of David (2Sa 7:2). Of Solomon (1Ki 7:1-12). At Babylon (Da 4:29; 5:5; 6:18). At Susa (Ne 1:1; Est 1:2; 7:7; Da 8:2).
Archives kept in (Ezr 6:2). Proclamations issued from (Am 3:9).
Figurative of a government (Am 1:12; 2:2; Na 2:6).

PALAL (*he has judged*). Son of Uzai. One of the workmen in rebuilding the walls of Jerusalem (Ne 3:25).

PALE HORSE Symbol of death (Rev 6:8).

PALESTINE The name is derived from Philistia, an area along the S seacoast occupied by the Philistines (Ps 60:8). The original name was Canaan (Ge 12:5); after the Conquest it came to be known as Israel (1Sa 13:19), and in the Greco-Roman period, Judea, Samaria, and Galilee. The land was c. seventy miles wide and 150 miles long, from the Lebanon mountains in the N to Beersheba in the S. The area W of the Jordan was 6000 miles; E of the Jordan, 4000 miles. In the N, from Acco to the Sea of Galilee was twenty-eight miles. From Gaza to the Dead Sea in the S, fifty-four miles.
Physically, the land is divided into five parts: the Plain of Sharon and the Philistine Plain along the coast; adjoining it, the Shephelah, or foothills region; then the central mountain range; after that the Jordan valley; and E of the Jordan the Transjordan plateau.
The varied configuration of Palestine produces a great variety of climate. The Maritime Plain has an annual average temperature of 57 degrees at Joppa; Jerusalem averages 63 degrees; while Jericho

and the Dead Sea area have a tropical climate. As a result, plants and animals of varied latitudes may be found.

Before the Conquest the land was inhabited by Canaanites, Amorites, Hittites, Horites, and Amalekites. These were conquered by Joshua, the judges, and the kings. The kingdom was split in 931 B.C.; the N kingdom was taken into captivity by the Assyrians in 722 B.C.; the S kingdom by the Babylonians in 587 B.C. From 587 B.C. to the time of the Maccabees the land was under foreign rule by the Babylonians, Persians, Alexander the Great, Egyptians, and Syrians. In 63 B.C. the Maccabees lost control of the land to the Romans, who held it until the time of Mohammed.

In NT times Palestine W of the Jordan was divided into Galilee, Samaria, and Judea; and E of the Jordan into the Decapolis and Perea.

See Philistia; Philistines.

PALLU, PALLUITE (*wonderful*). Son of Reuben (Ge 46:9; Ex 6:14; Nu 26:5, 8; 1Ch 5:3).

PALM SUNDAY *See Triumphal Entry of Jesus.*

PALM TREE Deborah judged Israel under (Jdg 4:5). Wood of, used in the temple (1Ki 6:29, 32, 35; 2Ch 3:5). In the temple seen in the vision of Ezekiel (Eze 40:16; 41:18). Branches of, thrown in the way when Jesus made his triumphal entry into Jerusalem (Jn 12:13). Jericho was called the City of Palm Trees (Dt 34:3).

Figurative: Of the prosperity of the righteous (Ps 92:12). Used as a symbol of victory (Rev 7:9).

PALMER WORM *See Locust.*

PALMS, CITY OF *See Jericho.*

PALSY *See Paralysis.*

PALTI (*[God (El)] is [my] deliverance*).
1. Spy from Benjamin (Nu 13:9),
2. *See Paltiel, 2.*

PALTIEL (*God [El] is [my] deliverance*).
1. Prince of Issachar (Nu 34:26).
2. Son-in-law of Saul (1Sa 25:44; 2Sa 3:15).

PALTITE (*delivered*). One of David's mighty men (2Sa 23:26), "Pelonite" (1Ch 11:27; 27:10).

PAMPHYLIA A province in Asia Minor. Men of, in Jerusalem (Ac 2:10). Paul goes to (Ac 13:13-14; 14:24). John, surnamed Mark, in (Ac 13:13; 15:38). Sea of (Ac 27:5).

PAN(S) Clay pan for cooking the grain offering (Lev 2:7; 7:9). For baking bread (2Sa 13:9). Silver pans of the temple (Ezr 1:9). Iron (Eze 4:3).

PANIC In armies (Lev 26:17; Dt 32:30; Jos 23:10; Ps 35:5). From God (Ge 35:5; Ex 15:14-16; Jdg 7:22; 1Sa 14:15-20; 2Ki 7:6-7; 2Ch 20:22-23).

See Armies.

PANNAG *See Confection.*

PANTOMIME By Isaiah (Isa 20:2-3). By Ezekiel (Eze 4:1-8; 12:18). Agabus (Ac 21:11).

PAPER (2Jn 12). *See Parchment.*

PAPHOS A city of Cyprus. Paul blinds a sorcerer in (Ac 13:6-13).

P

PAPS NIV "breasts" (Lk 23:28) or "chest" (Rev 1:13). *See Breast.*

PAPYRUS (*reed plant*). A reed which grows in swamps and along rivers or lakes, especially along the Nile; from eight to twelve feet tall; used to make baskets, sandals, boats, and especially paper, the most common writing material of antiquity (Job 8:11; Isa 18:2). The NT books were undoubtedly all written on papyrus. Moses' basket of (Ex 2:3).

PARABLE (*to be similar, to be comparable*).

Defined:
1. Proverbial saying used in wisdom and prophetic discourse (Ps 78:2; Pr 1:6).
2. A story in which things in the spiritual realm are compared with events that could happen in the temporal realm; or, an earthly story with a heavenly meaning (Eze 17; 24; Mt 13; Lk 15). Differs from a fable, myth, allegory, or proverb. A characteristic teaching method of Jesus.

Listing of:
Of the trees (Jdg 9:8-15). Of the lamb (2Sa 12:1-6). Of the woman of Tekoa (2Sa 14:5-12). Of the garment torn to pieces (1Ki 11:30-32). Of the prisoner of war (1Ki 20:39-42). Of the thistle and cedar (2Ki 14:9). Of a vine of Egypt (Ps 80:8-16). Of the vineyard (Isa 5:1-7; 27:2-3). Of the farmer (Isa 28:23-29). Of the skins filled with wine (Jer 13:12-14). Of the two eagles (Eze 17). Of lions' cubs (Eze 19:1-9). Of Oholah and Oholibah (Eze 23). The boiling pot (Eze 24:3-5). The plant (Jnh 4:10-11).

The sheet let down from heaven in Peter's vision (Ac 10:10-16). The two covenants (Gal 4:22-31). The mercenary soldier (2Ti 2:3-4). Husbandman (2Ti 2:6). Furnished house (2Ti 2:20-21). The athlete (2Ti 2:5). Mirror (Jas 1:23-25).

See Jesus the Christ, Parables of; Symbols and Similitudes; Types.

PARACLETE (*comforter, exhorter*). One who pleads another's cause. Used by Christ of the Holy Spirit in John's Gospel (Jn 14:16, 26; 15:26; 16:7), and of Christ (1Jn 2:1).

PARADISE (*park* or *garden*). Park (Ecc 2:5), forest (Ne 2:8), orchard (SS 4:13), home of those who die in Christ (Lk 23:43).

PARADOX Of wealth (Pr 13:7). Wisdom (1Co 3:18). Life (Mt 10:39; 16:25; Mk 8:35; Lk 17:33; Jn 12:25). Christian life (2Co 6:4, 8-10; 12:4, 10-11; Eph 3:17-19; Php 3:7). New Jerusalem (Rev 21:18, 21).

PARAH (*cow*). A Benjamite city (Jos 18:23).

PARALLELISM A characteristic of OT Hebrew poetry. Rather that rhyming words as in English poetry, Hebrew poetry rhymes thoughts by comparison and contrast of two or three lines. Two major categories of parallelism are "synonymous," in which the parallel lines echo similar ideas, and "antithetical," in which the parallel lines contrast. In the NIV, parallelism is shown by identation: the indented line is parallel to the preceding line.

Examples of Synonymous Parallelism—
1 Why do the nations conspire
  and the peoples plot in vain?
2 The kings of the earth take their stand
  and the rulers gather together
against the LORD
  and against his Anointed One.
3 "Let us break their chains," they say,
  "and throw off their fetters."
4 The One enthroned in heaven laughs;
  the Lord scoffs at them. (Ps 2:1-4)

Examples of Antithetical Parallelism—
For the LORD watches over the way of
    the righteous,
  but the way of the wicked will perish. (Ps 1:6)
The fear of the LORD is the beginning of
    knowledge,
  but fools despise wisdom and discipline.
    (Pr 1:7)
See Poetry; Psalms.

PARALYSIS (*lame*). Cured by Jesus (Mt 4:24; 8:6, 13; 9:2, 6), by Philip (Ac 8:7), by Peter (Ac 9:33-34).

PARAMOUR *See Lovers.*

PARAN, MOUNT PARAN, DESERT OF PARAN (*plain*). Desert or wilderness of (Ge 21:21; Nu 10:12; 12:16; 13:3, 26; Dt 1:1). Mountains of (Dt 33:2; Hab 3:3). Israelites encamp in (Nu 12:16). David takes refuge in (1Sa 25:1). Hadad flees to (1Ki 11:17-18).

PARBAR NIV "the court to the west" of the temple (1Ch 26:18).

PARCHED LAND Symbolic of loss of strength or blessing (Job 30:1; Ps 143:6). Changed to flowing springs, symbolic of blessing (Ps 107:35; Isa 35:1).

PARCHMENT Writing material made of animals skins, probably copies of books of the OT in 2Ti 4:13.

PARDON Forgiveness. God demands a righteous ground for pardoning the sinner—the atoning work of Christ (Ex 34:9; 1Sa 15:25-26; Isa 55:7). *See Atonement; Forgiveness.*

PARENTAL BLESSINGS Very important in OT times; often prophetic of a child's future (Ge 27:4, 12, 27-29).

PARENTS

General:
To be revered (Ex 20:12; Lev 19:3; Dt 5:16; Mt 15:4; 19:19; Mk 7:10; 10:19; Lk 18:20). Obeyed (Pr 1:8; 6:20; 23:22; Eph 6:1; Col 3:20).

Covenant blessings of, entailed upon children (Ge 6:18; Ex 20:6; Ps 103:17). Curses upon, entailed upon children (Ex 20:5; Lev 20:5; Isa 14:20; Jer 9:14; La 5:7). Involved in children's wickedness (1Sa 2:27-36; 4:10-18). Cursing of, to be punished (Ex 21:17; Lev 20:9).

Beloved:
By Joseph (Ge 46:29). Rahab (Jos 2:12-13). Ruth (Ru 1:16-17). Elisha (1Ki 19:20).

Mother, beloved (Pr 31:28).

Duties of:
Fathers to direct household (Ge 18:19; Lev 20:9; Pr 3:12; 13:24; 19:18; 1Ti 3:4-5, 12; Tit 1:6; Heb 12:7). To govern with kindness (Eph 6:4; Col 3:21). A prerequisite to church leadership (1Ti 3:4-5, 12). To provide for children (2Co 12:14; 1Ti 5:8). To instruct children in righteousness (Ex 10:2; 12:27; 13:8, 14; Dt 4:9-10; 6:7, 20-25; 11:18-21; 32:46; Ps 78:5-6; Pr 22:6, 15; 27:11; Isa 38:19; Joel 1:3; Eph 6:4; 1Th 2:11). To discipline children (Pr 19:8; 22:6, 15; 23:13-14; 29:15, 17).

Indulgent:
Eli (1Sa 2:27-36; 3:13-14), David (1Ki 1:6).

Influence of:
Evil (1Ki 15:26; 22:52-53; 2Ki 8:27; 21:20; 2Ch 21:6; 22:3). Good (1Ki 22:43; 2Ki 15:3, 34). *See Influence.*

Love of:
Reflection of God's love (Ps 103:13; Pr 3:12; Isa 49:15; 66:13; Mt 7:9-11; Lk 11:11-13). Must be exceeded by love for Christ (Mt 10:37). To be taught (Tit 2:4).

Love Exemplified—
By Hagar (Ge 21:15-16), Rebekah's mother (Ge 24:55), Isaac and Rebekah (Ge 25:28), Isaac (Ge 27:26-27), Laban (Ge 31:26-28), Jacob (Ge 37:3-4; 42:4, 38; 43:13-14; 45:26-28; 48:10-11), Moses' mother (Ex 2), Naomi (Ru 1:8-9), Hannah (1Sa 2:19), David (2Sa 12:18-23; 13:38-39; 14:1, 33; 18:5, 12-13, 33; 19:1-6), Rizpah (2Sa 21:10), the mother of the infant brought to Solomon by the harlots (1Ki 3:22-28), Mary (Mt 12:46; Lk 2:48; Jn 2:5; 19:25), Jairus (Mk 5:23), father of the demoniac (Mk 9:24), nobleman (Jn 4:49).

Paternal Blessings:
Of Noah (Ge 9:24-27), Abraham (Ge 17:18), Isaac (Ge 27:10-40; 28:3-4), Laban (Ge 31:55), Jacob (Ge 48:15-20; 49:1-28), reproaches (Ge 9:24-25; 49:3-7).

Partiality of:
Isaac for Esau (Ge 25:28), Rebekah for Jacob (Ge 25:28; 27:6-17), Jacob for Joseph (Ge 33:2; 37:3; 48:22), for Benjamin (Ge 42:4). *See Partiality.*

Prayers in Behalf of Children:
Of Hannah (1Sa 1:27), David (2Sa 7:25-29; 1Ch 17:16-27; 2Sa 12:16; 1Ch 22:12; 29:19), Job (Job 1:5).

See Children, Instruction of.

PARLOR *See Upper Room.*

PARMASHTA (*the very first*). Son of Haman (Est 9:9).

PARMENAS (*steady, reliable*). One of seven men chosen for daily ministration to the poor (Ac 6:5).

PARNACH Father of Elizaphan (Nu 34:25).

PAROSH (*flea*). The ancestor of one of the families which returned to Jerusalem from captivity in Babylon (Ezr 2:3; 8:3; Ne 7:8; 10:14).

PAROUSIA (*presence, coming*). A Greek word frequently used in NT of our Lord's return (Mt 24:3; 1Co 15:23; 1Th 3:13; 4:15; 2Pe 1:16).

PARRICIDE One who murders his father, mother, or a close relative (2Ki 19:37; 2Ch 32:21; Isa 37:38).

PARSHANDATHA One of the ten sons of Haman (Est 9:7).

PARSIMONY Stinginess with money or resources. Of the Jews toward the temple (Hag 1:2, 4, 6, 9), toward God (Mal 3:8-9). Punishment of (Hag 1:9-11). *See Liberality.*

PARSIN Aramaic for "divided," symbolic of the division of Babylon between the Medes and Persians (Da 5:24-28).

PARTHIANS The inhabitants of Parthia, a country NW of Persia (Ac 2:9).

PARTIALITY Forbidden, among Christians (1Ti 5:21), by parents (Dt 21:15-17). Effects upon children (Ge 37:4). *See Parents.*

Instances of:
Of Brothers: Joseph for Benjamin (Ge 43:30, 34).

Of parents: Isaac for Esau (Ge 25:25), Rebekah for Jacob (Ge 25:28; 27:6-17), Jacob, for Joseph (Ge 33:2; 37:3-4; 48:22), for Benjamin (Ge 42:4).

Of husbands: Jacob for Rachel (Ge 29:30), Elkanah for Hannah (1Sa 1:4-5).

See Respect of Persons.

PARTICEPS CRIMINIS Participating in evil (2Jn 11). *See Collusion.*

PARTITION, MIDDLE WALL OF *See Dividing Wall.*

PARTNERSHIP With God (1Co 3:7, 9; 2Co 6:1; Php 2:13).

PARTRIDGE (1Sa 26:20; Jer 17:11).

PARUAH (*blooming* ISBE; *cheerful* KB). Father of Jehoshaphat (1Ki 4:17).

PARVAIM An unknown gold region (2Ch 3:6).

PAS DAMMIM (*place of blood*). A battle between David and the Philistines, fought at (1Ch 11:13). Called Ephes Dammim (1Sa 17:1).

PASACH (*to divide*). Son of Japhlet (1Ch 7:33).

PASCHAL LAMB *See Passover.*

PASEAH (*hobbling one*).
1. A son of Eshton (1Ch 4:12).
2. Ancestor of a family which returned to Jerusalem from captivity in Babylon (Ezr 2:49; Ne 7:51).
3. Father of Jehoiada, probably identical with preceding (Ne 3:6).

PASHHUR (perhaps *be quiet*, and *round about*).
1. A priest, son of Malkijah (1Ch 9:12). An influential man and ancestor of an influential family (Jer 21:1; 38:1; Ezr 2:38; 10:22; Ne 7:41; 10:3; 11:12).
2. Son of Immer and governor of the temple. Beats and imprisons Jeremiah (Jer 20:1-6).
3. Father of Gedaliah, who persecuted Jeremiah (Jer 38:1).

PASSAGE Ford of a river (Ge 32:23), mountain pass (1Sa 13:23), a crossing (Jos 22:11).

PASSENGERS *See Commerce.*

PASSION
1. Lust or desire (Hos 7:6; 1Co 7:9).
2. Often used as a technical term of the suffering of Jesus. *See Jesus the Christ, Sufferings of.*

PASSIVITY *See Nonresistance.*

PASSOVER (*pass over, spare*). Institution of (Ex 12:3-49; 23:15-18; 34:18; Lev 23:4-8; Nu 9:2-5, 13-14; 28:16-25; Dt 16:1-8, 16; Ps 81:3, 5). Design of (Ex 12:21-28). Special Passover, for those who were unclean, or on a journey, to be held in the second month (Nu 9:6-12; 2Ch 30:2-4). Lamb killed by Levites, for those who were ceremonially unclean (2Ch 30:17; 35:3-11;

Ezr 6:20). Strangers authorized to celebrate (Ex 12:48-49; Nu 9:14).

Observed at place designated by God (Dt 16:5-7), with unleavened bread (Ex 12:8, 15-20; 13:3, 6; 23:15; Lev 23:6; Nu 9:11; 29:17; Dt 16:3-4; Mk 14:12; Lk 22:7; Ac 12:3; 1Co 5:8). Penalty for neglecting to observe (Nu 9:13).

Reinstituted by Ezekiel (Eze 45:21-24).

Observation of, renewed by the Israelites on entering Canaan (Jos 5:10-11), by Hezekiah (2Ch 30:1), by Josiah (2Ki 23:22-23; 2Ch 35:1, 18), after return from captivity (Ezr 6:19-20). Observed by Jesus (Mt 26:17-20; Lk 22:15; Jn 2:13, 23; 13). Jesus in the temple at the time of (Lk 2:41-50). Jesus crucified at the time of (Mt 26:2; Mk 14:1-2; Jn 18:28). The lamb of, a type of Christ (1Co 5:7). Lord's supper ordained at (Mt 26:26-28; Mk 14:12-25; Lk 22:7-20).

Prisoner released at, by the Romans (Mt 27:15; Mk 15:6; Lk 23:16-17; Jn 18:39). Peter imprisoned at the time of (Ac 12:3).

Christ called our Passover (1Co 5:7).

See Feasts; Hallel.

PASSPORTS *See Safe-Conduct.*

PASTOR A leader of the church (Eph 4:11), possibly the same as elder and overseer. *See Elders; Overseer.*

PASTORAL EPISTLES A common title for 1 and 2 Timothy and Titus, which were written by the apostle Paul to his special envoys sent on specific missions in accordance with the needs of the hour. They give instruction to Timothy and Titus concerning the pastoral care of churches. Though some date the Pastorals within the framework of Acts, most scholars believe all three were written not long after the events of Ac 28. After his imprisonment in Rome (c. A.D. 60-62), Paul most likely began his fourth missionary journey. *See Missionary Journeys of Paul.*

First Timothy was written to Timothy at Ephesus while Paul was still traveling in the coastal regions of the Aegean Sea. Titus was written to Titus in Crete (c. A.D. 63-65), probably from Nicopolis or some other city in Macedonia. Second Timothy was written from Rome toward the end of Paul's second imprisonment shortly before he was executed (A.D. 67 or 68).

The epistles concern church organization and discipline, including such matters as the appointment of bishops and deacons, the opposition of heretical or rebellious members, and the provision for maintenance of doctrinal purity.

Certain themes and phrases recur throughout the Pastoral Letters: (1) *God the Savior.* Three times in 1 Timothy and three times in Titus God the Father is called Savior (1Ti 1:1; 2:3; 4:10; Tit 1:3; 2:10; 3:4). Once in 2 Timothy and three times in Titus Jesus is also called Savior (2Ti 1:10; Tit 1:4; 2:13; 3:6). (2) *Sound doctrine, faith, and teaching.* Correct teaching, in keeping with that of the apostles (1Ti 1:10; 6:3; 2Ti 1:13; 4:3; Tit 1:9). The teaching is called "sound" not only because it builds up in the faith, but because it protects against the corrupting influence of false teachers. (3) *Godliness.* A key word (along with "godly") in the Pastorals, occurring eight times in 1 Timothy (2:2; 3:16; 4:7-8; 6:3, 5-6, 11), once in 2 Timothy (3:5) and once in Titus (1:1), but nowhere else in the writings of Paul. (4) *Controversies.* Appearing in (1Ti 1:4; 6:4; 2Ti 2:23; Tit 3:9); (5) *Trustworthy sayings.* A clause found nowhere else in the NT but used five times in the Pastorals (1Ti 1:15; 3:1; 4:9; 2Ti 2:11; Tit 3:8).

The authorship of these letters has been disputed because of differences in vocabulary and style from the other epistles ascribed to Paul, and because their references to his travels do not accord with the itineraries described in Acts. The differences though real, have been exaggerated, and can be explained on the basis of a change of time, subject matter, scribes, and destination.

See also Church, New Testament Church, Qualifications for Elders/Overseers and Deacons; Timothy, 1 and 2; Titus.

PASTURE A place to graze sheep (Jn 10:9; Ge 29:7); essential for survival of flocks (Ge 47:4; 1Ch 4:39-41; Job 39:8; Isa 14:30; Jer 14:6); where David worked (2Sa 7:8; 1Ch 17:7); for cattle (1Ki 4:23); a figure of peace (Ps 23:2; Ps 37:3); a figure of God's flock (Ps 74:1; 79:13; 83:12; 95:7; 100:3; Jer 23:1-3; 50:7, 19; Eze 34:14); for camels (Eze 25:5). Pasturelands were the environs around towns and villages (Nu 35).

PATARA A Lycian city in Asia Minor. Visited by Paul (Ac 21:1-2).

PATHROS *See Upper Egypt.*

PATHRUSITES (*of Pathros*). A descendant of Mizraim and ancestor of the Philistines (Ge 10:14; 1Ch 1:12).

PATHS, RIGHT (Ps 16:11; 23:3; 25:10; 119:35; Pr 2:9; 4:11, 18; Isa 2:3; 26:7; Heb 12:13).

PATHWAY OF SIN General references to (Pr 2:15; 12:15; 13:15; 14:12; 15:9; Isa 49:8; Mt 7:13). Walking in (Dt 29:19; Jer 7:24; Eph 2:2; Php 3:18; 1Pe 4:3; 2Pe 2:10; 3:3; Jude 18).

PATIENCE Commended (Ecc 7:8-9; La 3:26-27). Commanded (Ps 37:7-9; Eph 4:2; Col 3:12-13; 1Th 5:14; 1Ti 6:11; 2Ti 2:24-25; Tit 2:2; Heb 12:1; Jas 5:7-8; 2Pe 1:5-6). A fruit of tribulation (Ro 5:3-4; Rev 1:9). A grace of the righteous (Lk 8:15; 21:19; Ro 2:7; 8:25; 12:12; 15:4-5; 1Co 13:4-5; 2Co 6:4-6; 12:12; Col 1:10-11; 1Th 1:3; 2Th 3:5; Heb 6:12; 10:36; Jas 1:3-4, 19; 1Pe 2:19-23; Rev 14:12). Prerequisite of a overseer (1Ti 3:2). Propagates peace (Pr 15:18). Possible because of God's righteousness (Rev 13:10).

Instances of: Isaac toward the people of Gerar (Ge 26:15-22). Moses (Ex 16:7-8). Job (Job 1:21; Jas 5:11). David (Ps 40:1). Simeon (Lk 2:25). Paul (2Ti 3:10). Prophets (Jas 5:10). The Thessalonians (2Th 1:4). The church at Ephesus (Rev 2:2-3) and Thyatira (Rev 2:19). John (Rev 1:9).

Of Jesus (1Pe 2:21-23; Rev 1:9). *See Jesus the Christ.*

See Longsuffering; Meekness.

PATMOS An island in the Aegean Sea. John an exile on (Rev 1:9).

PATRIARCHAL GOVERNMENT *See Government.*

PATRIARCHS, PATRIARCHAL AGE (*first father [of a nation, tribe]*). Name given in NT to those who founded the Hebrew race and nation: Abraham (Heb 7:4), sons of Jacob (Ac 7:8-9), David (Ac 2:29). The term is now commonly used to refer to the persons whose names appear in the genealogies and covenant-histories before the time of Moses (Ge 5, 11).

PATRICIDE Killing one's father. Of Sennacherib (2Ki 19:37; Isa 37:38; 1Ti 1:9).

PATRIOTISM Commanded (Ps 51:18; 122:6-7). Exhortation concerning (2Sa 10:12). Religious ceremony for the fostering of, commanded (Dt 26:1-11). Appealed to in battle (2Sa 10:12). Songs of: Deborah (Jdg 5:1-31), Israel (Ps 85:1-13; 137:1-6). Lack of, lamented (La 5:1-22).

Instances of:

Moses (Heb 11:24-26). Deborah and Barak (Jdg 4:5). The tribes of Zebulun and Naphtali (Jdg 5:18-20). Eli (1Sa 4:17-18). Phinehas' wife (1Sa 4:19-22). Joab (2Sa 10:12). Uriah (2Sa 11:11). The Psalmist (Ps 51:18; 85:1-13). Hadad (1Ki 11:21-22). The lepers of Samaria (2Ki 7:9). Israelite exiles (Ne 1:1-11; 2:1-20; Ps 137:1-6). Nehemiah (Ne 1:2, 4-11; 2:3). The Jews in public defense (Ne 2:3; 4:1-23). Isaiah (Isa 62:1). Jeremiah (Jer 8:11, 21-22; 9:1-2; La 5:1-22).

Lacking in:

The tribes of Reuben, Asher, and Dan (Jdg 5:15-17). Inhabitants, of Meroz (Jdg 5:23), of Succoth and Peniel (Jdg 8:4-17).

See Country, Love of.

PATROBAS (*father of existence*). A believer at Rome (Ro 16:14).

PATTERN Of the tabernacle (Heb 8:5-9:23). *See Tabernacle.*

PAU (*groaning, bleating*). A city of Edom (Ge 36:39; 1Ch 1:50).

PAUL (*little*).

Background and conversion:

Also called Saul (Ac 8:1; 9:1; 13:9). Of the tribe of Benjamin (Ro 11:1; Php 3:5). Personal appearance of (2Co 10:1, 10; 11:6). Born in Tarsus (Ac 9:11; 21:39; 22:3). Educated at Jerusalem in the school of Gamaliel (Ac 22:3; 26:4). A zealous Pharisee (Ac 22:3; 23:6; 26:5; 2Co 11:22; Gal 1:14; Php 3:5). A Roman (Ac 16:37; 22:25-28). Persecutes the Christians; present at and gives consent to the stoning of Stephen (Ac 7:58; 8:1, 3; 9:1; 22:4). Sent to Damascus with letters for the arrest and return to Jerusalem of Christians (Ac 9:1-2).

His vision and conversion (Ac 9:3-22; 22:4-19; 26:9-15; 1Co 9:11; 15:8; Gal 1:13; 1Ti 1:12-13). Is baptized (Ac 9:18; 22:16). Called to be an apostle (Ac 22:14-21; 26:14-21; 26:16-18; Ro 1:1; 1Co 1:1; 9:1-2; 15:9; Gal 1:1, 15-16; Eph 1:1; Col 1:1; 1Ti 1:1; 2:7; 2Ti 1:1, 11; Tit 1:1, 3). Preaches in Damascus (Ac 9:20, 22). Is persecuted by the Jews (Ac 9:23-24). Escapes by being let down from the wall in a basket; goes to Arabia (Gal 1:17), Jerusalem (Ac 9:25-26; Gal 1:18-19). Received by the disciples in Jerusalem (Ac 9:26-29). Goes to Caesarea and returns to Tarsus (Ac 9:30; 18:22).

Brought to Antioch by Barnabas (Ac 11:25-26). Teaches at Antioch one year (Ac 11:26). Brings the contributions of the Christians in Antioch to the Christians in Jerusalem (Ac 11:27-30). Returns with John to Antioch (Ac 12:25).

First Missionary Journey:

See Missionary Journeys of Paul. Sent to the Gentiles (Ac 13:2-3, 47-48; 22:17-21; Ro 11:13; 15:16; Gal 1:15-24). Visits Seleucia (Ac 13:4), Cyprus (Ac 13:4). Preaches at Salamis (Ac 13:5), at Paphos (Ac 13:6). Sergius Paulus the proconsul is converted (Ac 13:7-12). Contends with Elymas the sorcerer (Ac 13:6-12). Visits Perga in Pamphylia (Ac 13:13). John, a companion of, departs for Jerusalem (Ac 13:13). Visits Antioch in Pisidia and preaches in the synagogue (Ac 13:14-41). His message received gladly by the Gentiles (Ac 13:42, 49). Persecuted and expelled (Ac 13:50-51). Visits Iconium and preaches to the Jews and Greeks; is persecuted; escapes to Lystra; goes to Derbe (Ac 14:1-6). Heals an crippled man (Ac 14:8-10). The people attempt to worship him (Ac 14:11-18). Is persecuted by Jews from Antioch and Iconium and is stoned (Ac 14:19; 2Co 11:25; 2Ti 3:11). Escapes to Derbe, where he preaches the gospel, and returns to Lystra, Iconium, and to Antioch, encourages the disciples, and ordains elders (Ac 14:19-23). Revisits Pisidia, Pamphylia, Perga, Attalia, and returns to Antioch (Ac 14:24-28).

Contends with the Judaizing Christians against circumcision (Ac 15:1-2). Refers the question of circumcision to the apostles and elders at Jerusalem (Ac 15:2, 4). He declares to the apostles at Jerusalem the miracles and wonders God had done among the Gentiles by them (Ac 15:12). Returns to Antioch, accompanied by Barnabas, Judas, and Silas, with letters to the Gentiles (Ac 15:22, 25).

Second Missionary Journey:

See Missionary Journeys of Paul. Makes his second tour of the churches (Ac 15:36). Chooses Silas as his companion, and passes through Syria and Cilicia, confirming the churches (Ac 15:36-41). Visits Lystra; circumcises Timothy (Ac 16:1-5). Goes through Phrygia and Galatia; is forbidden by the Holy Spirit to preach in Asia; visits Mysia; desires to go to Bithynia, but is restrained by the Spirit; goes to Troas, where he has a vision of a man saying, "Come over into Macedonia, and help us"; he immediately proceeds to Macedonia (Ac 16:6-10). Visits Samothrace and Neapolis; comes to Philippi, the chief city of Macedonia; visits a place of prayer at the riverside; preaches the Word; the merchant, Lydia of Thyatira, is converted and baptized (Ac 16:11-15). Exorcizes a demon from a fortune-teller (Ac 16:16-18). Persecuted, beaten, and cast into prison with Silas; sings songs of praise in the prison; an earthquake shakes the prison; he preaches to the alarmed jailer, who believes and is baptized with his household (Ac 16:19-34). Is released by the civil authorities on the ground of his being a Roman citizen (Ac 16:35-39; 2Co 6:5; 11:25; 1Th 2:2). Is received at the house of Lydia (Ac 16:40). Visits Amphipolis, Apollonia, and Thessalonica; preaches in the synagogue (Ac 17:1-4). Is persecuted (Ac 17:5-9; 2Th 1:1-4). Escapes to Berea by night; preaches in the synagogue; many honorable women and men believe (Ac 17:10-12). Persecuted by the Jews who come from Thessalonica; is conducted by the brothers to Athens (Ac 17:13-15). Disputes on Mars' Hill with philosophers (Ac 17:16-34).

Visits Corinth; lives with Aquila and his wife, Priscilla, who were tentmakers; joins in their trade; reasons in the synagogue every Sabbath; is rejected by the Jews; turns to the Gentiles; stays there one year and six months, teaching the word of God (Ac 18:1-11). Persecuted by Jews, taken before the proconsul; accusation dismissed; takes his leave after many days, and sails to Syria, accompanied by Aquila and Priscilla (Ac 18:12-18). Visits Ephesus, where he leaves Aquila and Priscilla; enters a synagogue, where he reasons with the Jews; starts on his return journey to Jerusalem; visits Caesarea, and returns to Antioch (Ac 18:19-22).

Third Missionary Journey:

See Missionary Journeys of Paul. Returning to Ephesus, passes through Galatia and Phrygia, strengthening the disciples (Ac 18:18-23). Baptizes disciples of John in the name of the Lord Jesus; preaches in the synagogue, remains in Ephesus for two years; heals the sick (Ac 19:1-12). Jewish exorcists are beaten by a demon and many Ephesians believe, bringing their books of sorcery to be burned (Ac 19:13-20; 1Co 16:8-9). Sends Timothy and Erastus into Macedonia, but he himself remains in Asia for a period of time (Ac 19:21-22). The spread of the gospel through his preaching interferes with the idol-makers; he is persecuted, and a great uproar of the city is created; the city clerk appeases the people; dismisses the accusation against Paul, and disperses the people (Ac 19:23-41; 2Co 1:8; 2Ti 4:14).

Proceeds to Macedonia after encouraging the churches in those parts; comes into Greece and stays three months; returns through Macedonia, accompanied by Sopater, Aristarchus, Secundus, Gaius, Timothy, Tychicus, and Trophimus (Ac 20:1-6). Visits Troas; preaches until the break of day; restores to life Eutychus, who fell from the window (Ac 20:6-12). Visits Assos, Mitylene, Kios, Samos, and Miletus, hurrying to Jerusalem, to be there at Pentecost (Ac 20:13-16). Sends for the elders of the church of Ephesus; tells them of how he had preached in Asia, and of his tests and afflictions testifying repentance toward God; declares he was compelled by the Spirit to go to Jerusalem; exhorts them to watch over themselves and their flock; kneels down, prays, and departs (Ac 20:17-38). Visits Cos, Rhodes, Patara; takes a ship for Tyre; stays seven days; is brought on his way by the disciples to the outskirts of the city; kneels, prays, and leaves; comes to Ptolemais; greets the brothers and stays one day (Ac 21:1-7). Departs for Caesarea; enters the house of Philip the evangelist; is warned by Agabus not to go to Jerusalem; proceeds to Jerusalem (Ac 21:8-16).

Arrest and Trials:

See Missionary Journeys of Paul. Is received warmly by the brothers; talks of the things that had been done among the Gentiles by his ministry; enters the temple; the people are stirred against him by the Jews from Asia; an uproar is created; he is thrown out of the temple; the commander of the troops interposes and arrests him (Ac 21:17-33). His defense (Ac 21:33-40; 22:1-21). Is confined in the barracks (Ac 22:24-30). Is brought before the Sanhedrin; his defense (Ac 22:30; 23:1-5). Is returned to the barracks (Ac 23:10). Is encouraged by a vision, promising him that he must testify in Rome (Ac 23:11). Jews conspire against his life (Ac 23:12-15). Thwarted by his nephew (Ac 23:16-22). Is escorted to Caesarea by a military guard (Ac 23:23-33). Is confined in Herod's palace in Caesarea (Ac 23:35). His trial before Felix (Ac 24). Remains in custody for two years (Ac 24:27). His trial before Festus (Ac 25:1-12). Appeals to Caesar (Ac 25:10-12). His examination before Agrippa (Ac 25:13-27; 26).

Is taken to Rome in custody of Julius, a centurion, and guard of soldiers; boards the ship, accompanied by other prisoners, and sails along the coast of Asia; stops at Sidon and Myra (Ac 27:1-5). Transferred to a ship of Alexandria; sails past Cnidus, Crete, and Salmone to Fair Havens (Ac 27:6-8). Predicts loss of the ship; his advice not heeded, and the voyage resumed (Ac 27:9-13). The ship encounters a hurricane; Paul encourages and comforts the officers and crew; the soldiers advise putting the prisoners to death; the centurion interferes, and all 276 on board are saved (Ac 27:14-44). The ship is wrecked, and all on board take refuge on the island of Malta (Ac 27:14-44). Kind treatment by the inhabitants of the island (Ac 28:1-2). Is bitten by a viper and miraculously preserved (Ac 28:3-6). Heals the chief official's father and others (Ac 28:7-10). Is delayed in Malta three months; proceeds on the voyage; delays at Syracuse; sails by Rhegium and Puteoli; meets brothers who accompany him to Rome from the Forum of Appius; arrives at Rome and is permitted to live by himself in custody of a soldier (Ac 28:11-16). Calls the chief Jews together; states his situation; is kindly received; expounds the gospel; testifies to the kingdom of heaven (Ac 28:17-29). Lives two years in his own hired house, preaching and teaching (Ac 28:30-31).

Sickness of in Asia (2Co 1:8-11). Caught up to the third heavens (2Co 12:1-4). Has "a thorn in the flesh" (2Co 12:7-9; Gal 4:13-14). His independence of character (1Th 2:9; 2Th 3:8).

Persecutions of:

(Ac 9:16, 23-25, 29; 14:19; 16:19-25; 20:22-24; 21:13, 27-33; 22:22-24; 23:10, 12-15; Ro 8:35-37; 1Co 4:9, 11-13; 2Co 1:8-10; 4:8-9; 6:4-5, 8-10; 11:23-27, 32-33; 12:10; Gal 5:11; 6:17; Php 1:30; Col 1:24; 1Th 2:2, 14-15; 3:4; 2Ti 1:12; 2:9-10; 3:11-12; 4:16-17).

Character of:

(2Co 10:1, 10; 11:6; Gal 4:13). Cheerful in adversity (Ac 10:25; Ro 8:35-37; 2Co 4:8-10; 12:10; 2Ti 2:10; 3:11-12; 4:16-17). Courageous (Ac 9:29; 20:22-24; 21:13; Eph 6:20; 1Th 2:2). Purposeful, even when the Holy Spirit warns him not to go to Jerusalem (Ac 20:22-23; 21:4, 10-14). Indomitable (Ro 8:35-37; 1Co 4:9-13; 2Co 4:8-12; 6:4-10; 11:23-33; 12:10; 1Th 2:2; 2Ti 1:12; 3:11; 4:17). Joyous in suffering (Ac 16:25; Php 2:17; Col 1:24; 2Ti 2:9). Meek (1Co 4:12-13; 2Ti 4:16). Self-forgetful (1Co 4:9, 11-13). Self-supporting (Ac 18:3; 20:33-35; 2Co 11:7, 9; 1Th 2:9; 2Th 3:8). Tactful (1Co 9:19-22; 10:33; Phm 8-21). Zealous (Ro 9:3; 2Co 5:11-14; 6:4-10; 11:22-33; 12:10, 14-15; Php 3:6-16; Col 1:29). Ready for death (2Ti 4:6-8).

PAULUS, SERGIUS Roman proconsul of Cyprus; became a Christian through Paul (Ac 13:6-12).

PAVEMENT, STONE The courtyard outside the palace in Jerusalem where Pilate passed public sentence on Jesus (Jn 19:13).

PAVILION (*booth, tent*). Movable tent or canopy (1Ki 20:12; Jer 43:10). Figuratively of God's protection (Ps 27:5) or majesty (Job 36:29).

PAWN *See Surety.*

PAZZEZ *See Beth Pazzez.*

PEACE

From God:
(Nu 6:26; Ps 29:11; 85:8; Isa 26:12; 57:19; 1Co 14:33).

Social:
Beneficence of (Ps 133:1; Pr 15:17; 17:1, 14; Ecc 4:6). Honorable (Pr 20:3).
Commanded (Ge 45:24; Ps 34:14; Jer 29:7; Mk 9:50; Ro 12:18; 14:19; 2Co 13:11; Eph 4:3, 31-32; 1Th 5:13; 1Ti 2:2; 2Ti 2:22; Heb 12:14; 1Pe 3:10-11). Love of, commanded (Zec 8:19). Promised (Lev 26:6; Job 5:23-24; Isa 2:4; 11:6-9, 13; 60:17-18; Hos 2:18). The righteous assured of (Pr 16:7). Broken by the gospel (Mt 10:21-22, 34-36; Lk 12:51-53). Moses' efforts in behalf of, resented (Ex 2:13-14; Ac 7:26-29).
Promoters of peace promised: Joy (Pr 12:20). Adoption (Mt 5:9). Fruit of righteousness (Jas 3:17-18). God's favor (Lk 2:14).
Instances of promoters of peace: Abraham (Ge 13:8-9), Abimelech (Ge 26:29), Mordecai (Est 10:3). David (Ps 120:6-7).
See Charitableness; Nation, Peace of.

Spiritual:
Through Christ (Isa 2:4; 9:6-7; 11:6, 13; Mic 4:3, 5; Lk 1:79; Jn 7:38; 14:27; Ac 10:36; Ro 5:1; 10:15). To the world (Isa 2:4; 11:6-9; Lk 2:14). To God's children (Isa 54:10, 13).
From God (Job 34:29; Ps 29:11; 72:3, 7; 85:8; Jer 33:6; Eze 34:25; Hag 2:9; Mal 2:5; Ro 15:13, 33; 16:20; 1Co 1:3; 14:33; 2Co 1:2; Gal 1:3; Php 4:7, 9; 1Th 1:1; 5:23; 2Th 3:16; 1Ti 1:2; 2Ti 1:2; Tit 1:4; Phm ; Heb 13:20; Rev 1:4). From Christ (Mt 11:29; Jn 14:27; 16:33; 20:19; Eph 2:14-17; Col 3:15; Rev 1:4-5).
A fruit of the Spirit (Ro 14:17; Gal 5:22). A fruit of righteousness (Ro 2:10). Assured to the righteous (Ps 37:4, 11, 37; 125:1, 5; Pr 3:17, 24; Isa 26:3, 12; 32:2, 17-18; 55:2, 12; 57:1-2, 19; Ro 8:6).
Through the reconciliation of Christ (Isa 53:5; Jn 7:38; Ro 5:1; Col 1:20), acquaintance with God (Job 22:21, 26; Ps 4:8; 17:15; 73:25-26; Isa 12:1-2; 25:7-8; 28:12; Lk 2:29), loving God's law (Ps 1:1-2; 119:165), obedience (Ps 25:12-13; Isa 48:18; Jer 6:16).
No peace to the wicked (Isa 48:22; 57:21). To be made with God (Isa 27:5).
See Charitableness; Joy; Praise.

PEACE OFFERINGS *See Fellowship Offerings; Offerings.*

PEACOCK *See Baboons; Ostrich.*

PEARL (Rev 17:4; 18:12, 16). "Pearl of great price" (Mt 13:45-46). Ornaments made of (1Ti 2:9).

Figurative:
Teaching should be given in accordance with the spiritual capacity of the learners (Mt 7:6).

Symbolic:
The twelve gates of the Holy City, the New Jerusalem, are each made of a single pearl (Rev 21:21).
See Minerals of the Bible, 1; Stones.

P

PECULIAR PEOPLE *See Saints.*

PEDAHEL (*God [El] ransoms*). Chief of Naphtali (Nu 34:28).

PEDAHZUR (*the Rock ransoms*). Father of Gamaliel (Nu 1:10; 2:20; 7:54, 59; 10:23).

PEDAIAH (*Yahweh ransoms*).
1. Grandfather of Jehoiakim (2Ki 23:36).
2. Father of Zerubbabel (1Ch 3:18).
3. Father of Joel, chief of Manasseh (1Ch 27:20).
4. Man who helped build the wall of Jerusalem (Ne 3:25).
5. A Benjamite, the father of Joed (Ne 11:7).
6. Levite; temple treasurer (Ne 13:13).

PEEP NIV "chirp" of a bird (Isa 10:14); "whisper" of a medium supposed to come from the dead (Isa 8:19).

PEKAH (*he has opened*). The son of Remaliah the eighteenth king of Israel; murdered Pekahiah; reigned from 752-732 B.C. (2Ki 15:27); made a league with Damascus against Judah (2Ki 15:37-38); became subject to Assyria (2Ki 15:29); murdered by Hoshea (2Ki 15:25-31; 2Ch 28:5-15).

PEKAHIAH (*Yahweh opens*). Israel's seventeenth king; son of Menahem; wicked and idolatrous (2Ki 15:24); murdered by Pekah (2Ki 15:22-25).

PEKOD (*visitation*). Aramean tribe living to the E and near the mouth of the Tigris (Jer 50:21; Eze 23:23).

PELAIAH (*Yahweh is spectacular*).
1. Son of Elioenai (1Ch 3:24).
2. A Levite who assisted Ezra in instructing the people in the law (Ne 8:7; 10:10).

PELALIAH (*Yahweh intercedes in arbitration*). A priest; the father of Jeroham and Amzi (Ne 11:12).

PELATIAH (*Yahweh rescues*).
1. Grandson of Zerubbabel (1Ch 3:21).
2. A Simeonite military leader (1Ch 4:42).
3. A man who sealed a covenant with Nehemiah (Ne 10:22).
4. A prince of Israel; Ezekiel prophesied against him (Eze 11:2, 13).

PELEG (*water canal*). The son of Eber (Ge 10:25; 11:16-19; 1Ch 1:19, 25; Lk 3:35).

PELET (*rescue*).
1. Son of Jahdai (1Ch 2:47).
2. Son of Azmaveth (1Ch 12:3).

PELETH (perhaps *swift*, or *swiftness*).
1. A Reubenite (Nu 16:1).
2. Son of Jonathan (1Ch 2:33).

PELETHITES (*courier*). A part of David's bodyguard (1Ki 1:38; 2Sa 8:18; 20:7, 23; 1Ch 18:17). Absalom's escort (2Sa 15:18).

PELICAN *See Owl.*

PELLA A city E of the Sea of Galilee; one of the cities forming the Decapolis.

PELONITE(S) (*separates*). Designation of two of David's mighty men: Helez (1Ch 11:27; 27:10) and Ahijah (1Ch 11:36).

PELUSIUM An Egyptian city on the E arm of the Nile, KJV "Sin" (Eze 30:15-16).

PEN (Jdg 5:14; Ps 45:1; Isa 8:1; Jer 8:8; 3Jn 13). Made of iron (Job 19:24; Jer 17:1).

PENALTY

Vicariously assumed:
By Rebekah (Ge 27:13), Abigail (1Sa 25:24), the woman of Tekoa (2Sa 14:9), the persecutors of the Jews (Mt 27:25), Jesus for the human race (Gal 3:13). Paul desires to assume for Israel (Ro 9:3). *See Suffering, Vicarious.*
See Fine; Judgments; Punishment; Sin, Punishment of; Wicked, Punishment of. See also penalties under various crimes, such as Murder.

PENCE *See Money; Penny.*

PENDANTS Articles of jewelry (Jdg 8:26). *See Dress.*

PENIEL (*face of God [El]*). The place where Jacob wrestled with the angel of Yahweh (Ge 32:24-32), not far from Succoth (Jdg 8:8-9, 17). Also spelled Penuel (Ge 32:31; Jdg 8:8; 1Ki 12:25, ftns).

PENINNAH (possibly *pearls, coral branches* BDB; *woman with rich hair* KB). One of the wives of Elkanah (1Sa 1:2).

PENITENCE *See Repentance; Sin, Confession of.*

PENITENT

Promises to:
Of mercy (Lev 26:40-42; Dt 4:29-31; 30:1-10; 2Ki 22:19; 1Ch 28:9; Job 22:23-29; 33:26-28; Ps 6:8-9; 9:10; 22:26; 90:14-15; 145:18-19; 147:3; Isa 27:5; Mt 5:4; 7:7-11 w Lk 11:9-13; Mt 12:20, 31; Lk 12:10).
Of forgiveness (Ps 32:5-6; 34:18; 51:17; 86:5; Isa 55:7; Eze 18:21-23; 33:10-16; Mt 6:14-15; 11:28-30; Lk 6:37; 15:4-32 w Mt 18:12-14; Lk 18:10-14; Jn 6:37; Ac 13:38-39; 1Jn 1:9).
Of salvation (Ps 145:18-19; Lk 4:18; 19:10; Ro 10:9-13; Heb 7:25).
Of divine favor (Nu 5:6-7; Isa 66:2).
See Forgiveness; Repentance; Sin, Confession of. See also, Obduracy; Reprobacy.

PENKNIFE *See Knife.*

PENNY The smallest Roman copper coin (Mt 5:26; Mk 12:42; Lk 12:6, 59). *See Money.*

PENS
1. Walled enclosure for livestock (Nu 32:16, 24, 36; Jn 10:1, 16).
2. Instrument for writing (Ps 45:1; Isa 8:1; Jer 8:8; 3Jn 13).

PENSION Of Levites (2Ch 31:16-18).

PENTATEUCH, THE (*five books*, i.e., the *torah* or law). The first five books of the Bible; covers the period of time from the creation to the end of the Mosaic era; authorship is attributed to Moses in Scripture.

Outline:
1. Era of beginnings (Ge 1:1-11:32).
2. Patriarchal period (Ge 12:1-50:26).
3. Emancipation of Israel (Ex 1:1-19:2).
4. Religion of Israel (Ex 19:3-Lev 27:34).
5. Organization of Israel (Nu 1:1-10:10).
6. Wilderness wanderings (Nu 10:11-22:1).
7. Preparations for entering Canaan (Nu 22:2-36:13).
8. Retrospect and prospect (Dt 1-34).

PENTECOST (*fiftieth [day]*).
1. The Israelite Feast of Weeks (Ex 34:22; Dt 16:9-11), also called the Feast of Harvest (Ex 23:16) and the day of firstfruits (Nu 28:26), which fell on the fiftieth day after Passover. The feast originally celebrated the dedication of the firstfruits of the wheat harvest, the last crop to ripen. The ritual of the feast is described (Lev 23:15-21). Institution of (Ex 23:16; 34:22; Lev 23:15-21; Nu 28:26-31; Dt 16:9-12, 16). Called in the NT the Day of Pentecost (Ac 2:1; 20:16; 1Co 16:8). *See Annual Feasts; Feasts.*
2. The Christian Pentecost fell on the same day as the Israelite Feast of Weeks. The coming of the Holy Spirit (Ac 2) transformed the Israelite festival into a Christian anniversary, marking the beginning of the Christian church.

PENUEL (*face of God [El]*).
1. Son of Hur and chief of Gedor (1Ch 4:4).
2. Son of Shashak (1Ch 8:25).
3. Variant spelling of Peniel. *See Peniel.*

PENURIOUSNESS *See Parsimony.*

PEOPLE Common. Heard Jesus gladly (Mt 7:28; 9:8, 33; 13:54; Mk 6:2).

PEOR (*opening*).
1. A mountain in Moab near the town of Beth Peor (Dt 3:29).
2. Contraction for Baal Peor (Nu 25:18; 31:16; Jos 22:17). *See Baal Peor.*

PERAEA *See Perea.*

PERATH In Hebrew it has the same spelling as Euphrates (Jer 13:4-7, ftn). Some identify it with Wadi Farah (Parah, Jos 18:23) near Anathoth.

PERAZIM, MOUNT (*breaking out*). Usually identified with Baal Perazim, where David obtained a victory over the Philistines (2Sa 5:20; 1Ch 14:11).

PERDITION (*ruin, destruction*). In the NT the word refers to the final state of the wicked, one of loss or destruction (Jn 17:12; Php 1:28; 2Th 2:3; 1Ti 6:9).

PERDITION, SON OF A phrase used to designate Judas Iscariot (Jn 17:12) and the "man of lawlessness" who is the Antichrist (2Th 2:3).

PEREA (*beyond the Jordan*). The name given by Josephus to the region E of the Jordan; known in the Gospels as "across the Jordan" (Mt 4:15, 25; Mk 3:7-8).

PERES (*divided*). One of the words written on a wall for Belshazzar and interpreted by Daniel (Da 5:1-29).

PERESH (*offal eviscerated* BDB; *dung* ISBE; *contents of stomach [not intestine]* KB). Son of Makir (1Ch 7:16).

PEREZ, PEREZITE (*breaking out*). A son of Judah by Tamar (Ge 38:29; 1Ch 2:4), descendants of (Ge 46:12; Nu 26:20-21; 1Ch 2:5; 9:4), return from the Captivity (Ne 11:4, 6). In the lineage of David and Jesus (Ru 4:12; Mt 1:3; Lk 3:33).

PEREZ UZZAH (*breaking out of Uzzah*). The name of the place where Uzzah was struck dead for touching the ark of God (2Sa 6:8, ftn). Perez Uzzah means *outbreak against Uzzah;* the place name memorialized a divine warning that was not soon forgotten.
See Nacon.

PERFECTION Major idea: complete or whole, rather than without fault or shortcoming. None without sin (1Ki 8:46; 2Ch 6:36; Ecc 7:20).
From God (Ps 18:32; 1Pe 5:10). Through Christ (Col 1:21-22, 28; 2:9-11; Heb 10:14; 13:20-21; 1Pe 5:10; 1Jn 3:6-10). Through God's love (1Jn 4:12).

Ascribed to:
Noah (Ge 6:8-9), Jacob (Nu 23:21), David (1Ki 11:4, 6), Asa (1Ki 15:14), Job (Job 1:1), Zechariah and Elizabeth (Lk 1:6), Nathanael (Jn 1:47). The peaceful (Ps 37:31, 37). The wise (1Co 2:6). Man of God (2Ti 3:17). The self-controlled (Jas 3:2). Those who obey God's word (1Jn 2:5).

Blessings of:
(Ps 106:3; 119:1-3, 6; Mt 5:6). Reward of (Ps 37:31, 37; Pr 2:21; Lk 6:40; 1Jn 5:18).

Commanded:
(Ge 17:1; Dt 5:32; 18:13; Jos 23:6; 1Ki 8:61; 1Ch 28:9; Mt 5:48; 2Co 7:1; 13:11; Php 1:10; 2:15; Col 3:14; Jas 1:4). Requirements for (Dt 5:32; Jos 23:6; 1Ki 8:61; 1Ch 29:19; Mt 19:21; 2Co 7:1). Program for (Eph 4:11-13; Heb 6:1; 1Jn 2:5).

Desire for:
(Mt 5:6; 2Ti 3:17). In Job (Job 9:20-21). In David (Ps 101:2). In Paul (Php 3:12-15).

Prayer for:
(1Ch 29:19; 2Co 13:9; Col 4:12; 1Th 3:10, 13; Heb 13:20-21).

God is Perfect:
(Dt 32:4; 2Sa 22:31; Ps 18:30; 19:7; 50:2).
See God, Perfection of; Holiness; Sanctification.

PERFIDY *See Conspiracy; Hypocrisy; Treachery.*

PERFUME, PERFUMER
1. For personal use (Pr 7:17; 27:9; SS 1:12; 3:6; Isa 3:20, 24), burial (2Ch 16:14).
2. For sacred incense (Ex 30:34-38; 37:29).
See Nard.

PERGA The capital of Pamphylia. Paul preaches in (Ac 13:13-14; 14:25).

PERGAMUM A city of Mysia. One of the "seven churches" (Rev 1:11; 2:12-17).

PERIDA (*single, unique*). One of the servants of Solomon. Descendants of, returned to Jerusalem, from captivity in Babylon (Ne 7:57). Called Peruda (Ezr 2:55).

PERIZZITES (*villager*). One of the seven nations in the land of Canaan (Ge 13:7). Territory of, given to Abraham (Ge 15:20; Ex 3:8; 23:23). Doomed to destruction (Dt 20:17). Not all destroyed; Israelites marry among (Jdg 3:5-7; Ezr 9:1-2).
See Canaanite(s).

PERJURY (Isa 48:1; Jer 5:2; 7:9; 1Ti 1:9-10).

Condemned:
Forbidden (Lev 19:12; Zec 8:17; Mt 5:33). Penalty for (Lev 6:2-7). Judgments upon perjurers (Hos 10:4; Zec 5:3-4; Mal 3:5).

Instances of:
Zedekiah (2Ch 36:13). Witnesses against Naboth (1Ki 21:8-13), against David (Ps 35:11), against Jesus (Mt 26:59-61; Mk 14:56-59), against Stephen (Ac 6:11, 13-14). Peter, when he denied Jesus with an oath (Mt 26:74; Mk 14:71).
See Falsehood; False Witness; Oath.

PERSECUTION

Of Jesus:
(Ac 4:27; Heb 12:2-3; 1Pe 4:1). Meekly endured (Isa 50:6).
Foretold (Ge 3:15; Isa 49:7; 50:6; 52:14; 53:2-10; Mic 5:1; Zec 12:10; Mt 2:13). Typified, in the persecutions of Israel's kings (Ps 2:1-5; 22:1-2, 6-8, 11-21; 69:1-21; 109:25; Ro 15:3).
Persecution by the Jews (Mt 12:14; 22:15; 26:3-4; Mk 12:13; 15:14; Lk 6:11; 11:53-54; 20:20; 22:2-5, 52-53; 23:23; Jn 5:16; 7:1, 7, 19; 11:57; 15:18, 20-21; 18:22-23; 19:6, 15; Ac 2:23). In making false imputation (Mt 12:24; Mk 3:22; Lk 11:15; Jn 10:20). In bringing false accusation (Mt 11:19; Lk 7:34; Jn 8:29-30). In acts of violence (Lk 4:28-29; 22:63-65 w Mt 26:67; Mk 14:65). In seeking false testimony (Mt 26:59). In seeking his death (Mt 26:14-16; Mk 3:6, 21; 14:1, 48; 11:18; Lk 19:47; Jn 7:20, 30, 32; 8:37, 40, 48, 52, 59; 10:31). In crucifying him (Ac 3:13-15; 7:52; 13:27-29; 1Co 2:8).
Persecution by Herod (Lk 13:31; 23:11). Persecution by the Roman soldiers (Mt 27:25-30; Mk 15:15-20; Jn 19:2-3).
Forsaken by God (Mk 15:34).

Of the Righteous:
(Ge 49:23; Ps 11:2; 37:32; 38:20; 74:7-8; 119:51, 61, 69, 78, 85-87, 95, 110, 157, 161; Pr 29:10, 27; Isa 26:20; 29:20-21; 59:15; Jer 11:19; 15:10; 18:18; Am 5:10; Ro 8:35; 2Co 12:10; Gal 4:29; 6:17).
By mocking (Ps 42:3, 10; 69:9-12; 119:51; Jer 20:7-8). By violence (Ps 94:5; Jer 2:30; 50:7; Ac 5:29, 40-42; 7:52; Gal 6:12, 17; 1Th 2:2, 14-15; Jas 2:6). By ecclesiastical censure (Jn 9:22, 34; 12:42; 2Ti 4:16-17).
Divine permissions of, mysterious (Hab 1:13). The mode of divine chastisement (La 1:3). Done to church members (Ac 8:1, 4; 11:19-21; Php 1:12-14, 18). Powerless to separate from the love of Christ (Ro 8:17, 35-39).
Exhortations to courage under (Isa 51:12, 16; Heb 12:3-4; 13:13; 1Pe 3:14, 16-17; 4:12-14, 16, 19). Courageously endured (Jer 26:11-14; 1Co 4:9-13; 2Co 4:8-12; 6:4-5, 8-10; 11:23-27; 12:10; 2Th 1:4; 2Ti 1:8, 12; 2:9-10; Heb 11:25-27; 11:33-38; Jas 5:6, 10). Rejoicing under (Ro 5:3; Col 1:24; 1Th 1:6; Heb 10:32-34). Perseverance under (Ps 44:15-18, 22).
Prayer for deliverance from (Ps 70:1-5; 83:1; 140:1, 4; 142:6). Deliverance from (Ps 124; 129:1-2). John's vision concerning (Rev 2:3, 10, 13; 6:9-11; 7:13-17; 12:10-11; 17:6; 20:4).
Of Christians, foretold (Mt 20:22; 23:34-35; 24:8-10; Mk 13:9-13; Lk 21:12-19; Jn 15:18-21; 16:1-2; 2Ti 3:2-3, 12-13; 1Jn 3:1, 13). Christ offers consolation (Mk 8:38; 9:42; Lk 6:22-23; 17:33; Jn 17:14). Promises to those who endure (Mt 5:10-12; 10:16-18, 21-23, 28-31; Lk 6:22-23). Should provoke love (1Co 13:3).

Instances of:
Abel (Ge 4:8; Mt 23:35; 1Jn 3:12). Lot (Ge 19:9). Moses (Ex 2:15; 17:4). David (Ps 31:13; 56:5; 59:1-2). Prophets martyred by Jezebel (1Ki 18:4). Gideon (Jdg 6:28-32). Elijah (1Ki 18:10; 19; 2Ki 1:9; 2:23). Micaiah (1Ki 22:26; 2Ch 18:26). Elisha (2Ki 6:31). Hanani (2Ch 16:10). Zechariah (2Ch 24:21; Mt 23:35). Job (Job 1:9; 2:4-5; 12:4-5; 13:4-13; 16:1-4; 17:2; 19:1-5; 30:1-10). Jeremiah (Jer 11:19; 15:10, 15; 17:15-18; 18:18-23; 26; 32:2; 33:1; 36:26; 37; 38:1-6). Uriah (Jer 26:23). The prophets (2Ch 36:16; Mt 21:35-36; 1Th 2:15). The three Hebrews of the Captivity (Da 3:8-23). Daniel (Da 6). The Jews (Ezr 4; Ne 4).
John the Baptist (Mt 14:3-12). James (Ac 12:2). Simon (Mk 15:21). The disciples (Jn 9:22, 34; 20:19). Lazarus (Jn 9:22, 34; 12:10; 20:19). The apostles (Ac 4:3-16, 18; 5:18-42; 12:1-19; Rev 1:9). Stephen (Ac 6:9-15; 7:1-60). The church (Ac 8:1; 9:1-14; Gal 1:13). Timothy (Heb 13:23). John (Rev 1:9). Antipas (Rev 2:13). The church of Smyrna (Rev 2:8-10).
Paul (2Ti 2:9-10; 4:16-17; Ac 9:16, 23-25, 29; 16:19-25; 21:2-33; 22:22-24; 23:10, 12-15; 1Co 4:9, 11-13; 2Co 1:8-10; 4:8-12, 6:4-5, 8-10, 11:23-27, 32-33, Col 1:24, 1Th 2:2, 14-15, 2Ti 1:8, 12; 3:11-12). *See Paul.*

PERSEPOLIS Capital of Persia, thirty miles NE of modern Shiraz; founded by Darius I (521-486 B.C.); destroyed by Alexander the Great in 331 B.C.

PERSEVERANCE

From the Lord:
(Ps 37:24, 28; Ro 8:30, 33-35; 1Co 1:8-9; 2Co 1:21-22). Acknowledged (Ps 73:24; 138:8; Ro 8:37-39; Col 2:7; 2Ti 4:18). Promised (Jer 32:40; Jn 6:34-40; 10:28-29).

Commanded:
(1Ch 16:11; Hos 12:6; 1Th 5:21; 2Th 2:15-17; 2Ti 2:1, 3, 12; 3:14; Tit 1:9; Jas 1:4, 25; 1Pe 4:16; 5:8-9; Rev 22:11). Exhortations to (Ac 11:23; 13:43; 14:21-22; 1Co 15:58; 16:13; Gal 5:1, 10; Eph 4:14-15; 6:13, 18; Php 1:27; 3:16; 4:1; Col 1:10, 22-23; 1Th 3:8; 2Th 3:15; 2Ti 1:13; Heb 2:1; 6:1, 11-12, 15; 10:23, 35-36; 12:5-15; 13:9, 13; 2Pe 3:17-18; Rev 16:15).
A proof of discipleship (Jn 8:31-32). A condition of fruitfulness (Jn 15:4-5, 7, 9). Intercessory prayer for (Lk 22:31-32).

Motives to:
The example, of Moses (Heb 3:5). Of the prophets (Jas 5:10-11). Of Christ (Heb 3:6, 14; 12:2-4). The intercession of Christ (Heb 4:14). The heavenly witnesses (Heb 12:1). Acceptance by Christ (2Co 5:9, 15; 1Pe 1:4-7).
Rewards contingent upon (Gal 6:9; Jas 1:12; Rev 2:7, 10-11, 17, 25-28; 3:5, 11, 21; 14:12; 21:7). Eternal life contingent upon (Mt 10:22; 24:13; Mk 13:13; Ro 2:6-7; 2Pe 1:10-11).

Lacking in:
The wayside and other hearers (Mk 4:3-8). Churches of Asia (Rev 2:5; 3:1-3, 14-18).

Instances of:
Caleb and Joshua, in representing the land of promise (Nu 14:24, 38). The righteous (Job 17:9; Pr 4:18).
In prayer, Abraham in interceding for Sodom (Ge 18:23-32), Jacob (Ge 32:24-26), Elijah for rain (1Ki 18:42-45), Paul for the removal of the thorn in his flesh (2Co 12:7-9).
See Character; Instability; Stability.

PERSIA

In Biblical History:
An empire which extended from India to Ethiopia, comprising 127 provinces (Est 1:1; Da 6:1). Government of, restricted by constitutional limitations (Est 8:8; Da 6:8-12). Municipal governments in, provided with dual governors (Ne 3:9, 12, 16-18). The princes advisory in matters of administration (Da 6:1-7). Status of women in, queen sat on the throne with the king (Ne 2:6). Vashti divorced for refusing to appear before the king's courtiers (Est 1:10-22; 2:4).
Israel captive in (2Ch 36:20), captivity foretold (Hos 13:16). Men of in the Syrian army (Eze 27:10).

Rulers of:
Xerxes (Est 1:3). Darius (Da 5:31; 6; 9:1). Artaxerxes I (Ezr 4:7-24). Artaxerxes II (Ezr 7; Ne 2; 5:1). Cyrus (2Ch 36:22-23; Ezr 1; 3:7; 4:3; 5:13-14, 17; 6:3; Isa 41:2-3; 44:28; 45:1-4, 13; 46:11; 48:14-15). Princes of (Est 1:14).
System of justice (Ezr 7:25). Prophecies concerning (Isa 13:17; 21:1-10; Jer 49:34-39; 51:11-64; Eze 32:24-25; 38:5; Da 2:31-45; 5:28; 7; 8; 11:1-4).
See Babylon; Chaldea.

PERSIS (*female Persian*). A Christian woman in Rome (Ro 16:12).

PERSONAL CALL *See Call, Personal; Minister, Call of.*

PERSONIFICATION Of wisdom (Pr 1; 2:1-19; 8-9). Of the Israel and/or the Church, in allegorical interpretation (SS 1-8). *See Pantomime.*

PERUDA (*single, unique*). One of the servants of Solomon. Descendants of, return to Jerusalem from captivity in Babylon (Ezr 2:55). Called Perida (Ne 7:57).

PERVERSENESS (Pr 11:3; 12:8; 15:4; 28:6; Eze 9:9; Mt 17:17; Tit 3:5).

PESHITTA (*simple*, i.e., no marginal notes). Ancient Syriac translation of the Bible.

PESTILENCE Sent as a judgment (Lev 26:16, 25). Sent upon the Egyptians. *See Egypt; Plague.*

PESTLE An instrument used to grind in a mortar (Pr 27:22).

PETER, 1 and 2

1 Peter:

Author: The apostle Peter

Date: In the early 60s A.D.

Outline:
I. Salutation (1:1-2).
II. Praise to God for His Grace and Salvation (1:3-12).
III. Exhortations to Holiness of Life (1:13-5:11).
A. The Requirement of Holiness (2:4-12).
B. The Position of Believers (2:4-12).
1. A spiritual house (2:4-8).
2. A chosen people (2:9-10).
3. Aliens and strangers (2:11-12).
C. Submission to Authority (2:13-3:7).
1. Submission to rulers (2:13-17).
2. Submission to masters (2:18-20).
3. Christ's example of submission (2:21-25).
4. Submission of wives to husbands (3:1-6).
5. The corresponding duty of husbands (3:7).
D. Duties of All (3:8-17).
E. Christ's Example (3:18-4:6).
F. Conduct in View of the End of All Things (4:7-11).
G. Conduct of Those Who Suffer for Christ (4:12-19).
H. Conduct of Elders (5:1-4).
I. Conduct of Young Men (5:5-11).
IV. The Purpose of the Letter (5:12).
V. Closing Greetings (5:13-14).
See General Letters.

2 Peter:

Author: The apostle (Simon) Peter

Date: Probably between 65 and 68.

Outline:
I. Introduction (1:1-2).
II. Exhortation to Growth in Christian Virtues (1:3-11).
A. The Divine Enablement (1:3-4).
B. The Call for Growth (1:5-7).
C. The Value of Such Growth (1:8-11).
III. The Purpose and Authentication of Peter's Message (1:12-21).
A. His Aim in Writing (1:12-15).
B. The Basis of His Authority (1:16-21).
IV. Warning Against False Teachers (ch. 2).
A. Their Coming Predicted (2:1-3a).
B. Their Judgment Assured (2:3b-9).
C. Their Characteristics Set Forth (2:10-22).
V. The Fact of Christ's Return (3:1-16).
A. Peter's Purpose in Writing Restated (3:1-2).
B. The Coming of Scoffers (3:3-7).
C. The Certainty of Christ's Return (3:8-10).
D. Exhortations Based on the Fact of Christ's Return (3:11-16).
VI. Concluding Remarks (3:17-18).
See General Letters.

PETER, SIMON (*rock, stone*). Also called Simon and Cephas (Mt 16:16-19; Mk 3:16; Jn 1:42). Simeon (Ac 15:14, ftn). A fisherman (Mt 4:18; Lk 5:1-7; Jn 21:3). Call of (Mt 4:18-20; Mk 1:16-18; Lk 5:1-11). His wife's mother healed (Mt 8:14; Mk 1:29-30; Lk 4:38). An apostle (Mt 10:2; 16:18-19; Mk 3:16; Lk 6:14; Ac 1:13). An evangelist (Mk 1:36-37). Confesses Jesus as Christ (Mt 16:16-19; Mk 8:29; Lk 9:20; Jn 6:68-69). His presumption in rebuking Jesus (Mt 16:22-23; Mk 8:32-33), when the throng was pressing Jesus and the woman touched him (Lk 8:45), when Jesus foretold his persecution and death (Mt 16:21-23; Mk 8:31-33), in refusing to let Jesus wash his feet (Jn 13:6-11). Present at the healing of Jairus's daughter (Mk 5:37; Lk 8:51), at the transfiguration (Mt 17:1-4; Mk 9:2-6; Lk 9:28-33; 2Pe 1:16-18), in Gethsemane (Mt 26:36-46; Mk 14:33-42; Lk 22:40-46). Seeks the interpretation of the parable of the manager (Lk 12:41), of the law of forgiveness (Mt 18:21), of the law of defilement (Mt 15:15), of the prophecy of Jesus concerning his second coming (Mk 13:34). Walks upon the water of the Sea of Galilee (Mt 14:28-31). Sent with John to prepare the Passover (Lk 22:8). Calls attention to the withered fig tree (Mk 11:21). His failure foretold by Jesus, and his profession of fidelity (Mt 26:33-35; Mk 14:29-31; Lk 22:31-34; Jn 13:36-38). Cuts off the ear of Malchus (Mt 26:51; Mk 14:47; Lk 22:50). Follows Jesus to the high priest's palace (Mt 26:58; Mk 14:54; Lk 22:54; Jn 18:15). His denial of Jesus and his repentance (Mt 26:69-75; Mk 14:66-72; Lk 22:55-62; Jn 18:17-18, 25-27). Visits the tomb (Lk 24:12; Jn 20:2-6). Jesus sends message to, after the Resurrection (Mk 16:7). Jesus appears to (Lk 24:34; 1Co 15:4-5). Present at the Sea of Tiberias when Jesus appeared to his disciples; leaps into the sea, and comes to land when Jesus is recognized, is commissioned to feed the flock of Christ (Jn 21:1-23).
Remains in Jerusalem (Ac 1:13). His statement before the disciples concerning the death of Judas, and his recommendation that the vacancy in the apostleship be filled (Ac 1:15-22). Preaches at Pentecost (Ac 2:14-40). Heals the crippled man in the portico of the temple (Ac 3). Accused by the council; his defense (Ac 4:1-23). Foretells the death of Ananias and Sapphira (Ac 5:1-11). Imprisoned and scourged; his defense before the council (Ac 5:17-42). Goes to Samaria (Ac 8:14). Prays for the baptism of the Holy Spirit (Ac 8:15-18). Rebukes Simon, the sorcerer, who desires to purchase like power (Ac 8:18-24). Returns to Jerusalem (Ac 8:25). Receives Paul (Gal 1:18; 2:9). Visits Lydda; heals Aeneas (Ac 9:32-34). Visits Joppa; stays with Simon the tanner; raises Dorcas from the dead (Ac 9:36-43). Has a vision of a sheet containing clean and unclean animals (Ac 10:9-16). Receives the servant of the centurion; goes to Caesarea; preaches and baptizes the centurion and his household (Ac 10). Advocates, in the council of the apostles and elders, the preaching of the gospel to the Gentiles (Ac 11:1-18; 15:7-11). Imprisoned and delivered by an angel (Ac 12:3-19). Writes two letters (1Pe 1:1; 2Pe 1:1).
Miracles of. *See Miracles, Of the Disciples of Jesus.*

PETHAHIAH (*Yahweh opens*).
1. A priest in the reign of David (1Ch 24:16).
2. A Levite who divorced his Gentile wife (Ezr 10:23).
3. A Levite, probably identical with 2 (Ne 9:5).
4. A counselor of Artaxerxes (Ne 11:24).

PETHOR A city in Mesopotamia. Home of the prophet Balaam (Nu 22:5; Dt 23:4).

PETHUEL (*God's opening*). Father of the prophet Joel (Joel 1:1).

PETITION Right of, recognized by Pharaoh (Ex 5:15-18), Israel (Nu 27:1-5; 32:1-5; 36:1-5; Jos 17:4, 14, 16; 21:1-2), David (1Ki 1:15-21), Rehoboam (1Ki 12:1-17; 2Ch 10), Jehoram (2Ki 8:3, 6).

P

PETRA (*rock, cliff, rock grotto*). OT Sela (Jdg 1:36; 2Ki 14:7; Isa 16:1). Capital city of the Nabateans. *See Nabatea, Nabateans; Sela.*

PEULLETHAI (*worker, wage earner*). A gatekeeper of the tabernacle (1Ch 26:5).

PHALEC *See Peleg.*

PHALLU *See Pallu.*

PHALTI *See Palti.*

PHALTIEL *See Paltiel.*

PHANUEL (*face of God [El]*). Father of Anna the prophetess (Lk 2:36).

PHARAOH (*the great house*).
1. King of Egypt at the time of Abraham (Ge 12:14-20; Ps 105:14).
2. Ruler of Egypt at the time of the famine. *See Egypt; Israel, Israelites.*
3. Ruler of Egypt at the time of the deliverance and exodus of the Israelites. *See Israel, Israelites.*
4. Father-in-law of Mered (1Ch 4:18).
5. Ruler of Egypt at the time of David (1Ki 11:17-22).
6. Father-in-law of Solomon (1Ki 3:1; 9:16).
7. At the time of Hezekiah (2Ki 18:21).
8. Pharaoh Neco. His invasion of Assyria, Josiah's death (2Ki 23:29-35; 24:7; 2Ch 35:20-24; 36:3-4; Jer 46:2; 47:1).
9. Pharaoh. (Jer 37:4-7, 44; Eze 17:15-17). Prophecies concerning (Jer 44:30; 46:25-26; Eze 29; 30:21-26).

PHARES, PHAREZ *See Perez.*

PHARISEES (*separate ones*). A sect of the Jews (Ac 15:5). Doctrines of (Mt 15:9), concerning the Resurrection (Ac 23:6, 8), association with tax collectors and sinners (Mt 9:11-13).
Traditions of, in regard to fasting (Mt 9:14; Lk 18:12), the washing of hands (Mt 15:1-3; Mk 7:1-15), the duties of children to parents (Mt 15:4-9), the Sabbath (Mt 12:2-8). Denounced by Jesus (Mt 23:2-36; Lk 11:39-44). Hypocrisy of, reproved by John (Mt 3:7-10), by Jesus (Mt 6:2-8, 16-18; 15:1-9; 16:1-12; 21:33-46;

23:2-33; Lk 11:14-54; 12:1; 15:1-9). Reject John (Lk 7:30), Christ (Mt 12:38-39; 15:12; Jn 7:48). Come to Jesus with questions (Mt 19:3; 22:15-22).

Minister to Jesus (Lk 7:36; 11:37; 14:1). Become disciples of Jesus (Jn 3:1; Ac 15:5; 22:5).

Paul a Pharisee (Ac 23:6; 26:5).

See Herodians; Sadducees; Testaments, Time Between.

PHAROSH *See Parosh.*

PHARPAR A river of Damascus. Referred to by Naaman (2Ki 5:12).

PHARZITES *See Perez, Perezite.*

PHASEAH *See Paseah.*

PHASELIS Rhodian colony in Lycia (1Mc 15:23).

PHASELUS Latinization of Phasael, the son of Antipater the Idumean, and brother of Herod the Great.

PHEBE *See Phoebe.*

PHENICE *See Phoenicia; Phoenix.*

PHENICIA *See Phoenicia.*

PHICOL Chief captain of the Philistines (Ge 21:22, 32; 26:26).

PHILADELPHIA (*love of brother, sister*). A city of Lydia. One of the seven churches (Rev 1:11; 3:7-13).

PHILANTHROPY *See Alms; Beneficence; Charitableness; Giving; Liberality; Neighbor; Poor.*

PHILEMON (*beloved*). Convert of Paul at Colosse; Epistle to Philemon written to him.

PHILEMON, EPISTLE TO

Author: The apostle Paul

Date: c. A.D. 60

Outline:

I. Greetings (1-3).
II. Thanksgiving and Prayer (4-7).
III. Paul's Plea for Onesimus (8-21).
IV. Final Request, Greetings and Benedictions (22-25).

PHILETUS (*beloved*). False teacher in the church at Ephesus (2Ti 2:17).

PHILIP (*horse lover*).

1. King of Macedonia; father of Alexander the Great; founder of city of Philippi in Macedonia (1Mc 1:1).
2. Philip V, king of Macedonia (1Mc 8:5).
3. Governor of Jerusalem under Antiochus, regent of Syria (2Mc 5:22).
4. Herod Philip. Married Herodias (Mt 14:3; Mk 6:17; Lk 3:19).
5. Herod Philip II, tetrarch of Batanaea, Trachonitis, Gaulanitis, and parts of Jamnia. Best of Herods (Lk 3:1).

PHILIP THE APOSTLE Native of Bethsaida, the same town as Andrew and Peter (Jn 1:44), undoubtedly first a disciple of John the Baptist (Jn 1:43), brought his friend Nathanael to Jesus (Jn 1:45), called to apostleship (Mt 10:3; Mk 3:18; Lk 6:14), faith tested by Jesus before feeding of the 5000 (Jn 6:5-6), brought Greeks to Jesus (Jn 12:20-23), asked to see the Father (Jn 14:8-12), in the Upper Room with 120 (Ac 1:13).

P

PHILIP THE EVANGELIST Chosen one of the seven (Ac 6:5). A Hellenist, or Greek-speaking Jew, preached in Samaria (Ac 8). Ethiopian eunuch converted through him (Ac 8:26-40). Paul stayed at his home in Caesarea, where he lived with his four unmarried daughters who were prophetesses (Ac 21:8-9).

PHILIPPI A city of Macedonia. Paul preaches in (Ac 16:12-40; 20:1-6; 1Th 2:1-2). Contributes to the maintenance of Paul (Php 4:10-18). Paul sends Epaphroditus to (Php 2:25). Paul writes a letter to the Christians of (Php 1:1).

PHILIPPIANS, EPISTLE TO

Author: The apostle Paul

Date: c. A.D. 61

Outline:

I. Salutation (1:1-2).
II. Thanksgiving and Prayer for the Philippians (1:3-11).
III. Paul's Personal Circumstances (1:12-26).
IV. Exhortations (1:27-2:18).
 A. Living a Life Worthy of the Gospel (1:27-30).
 B. Following the Servant Attitude of Christ (2:1-18).
V. Paul's Associates in the Gospel (2:19-30).
 A. Timothy (2:19-24).
 B. Epaphroditus (2:25-30).
VI. Warnings Against Judaizers and Antinomians (3:1-4:1).
 A. Against Judaizers or Legalists (3:1-16).
 B. Against Antinomians or Libertines (3:17-4:1).
VII. Final Exhortations, Thanks and Conclusion (4:2-23).
 A. Exhortations Concerning Various Aspects of the Christian Life (4:2-9).
 B. Concluding Testimony and Repeated Thanks (4:10-20).
 C. Greetings and Benediction (4:21-23).

PHILISTIA The seacoast in the W of Dan and Simeon (Ps 60:8; 87:4; 108:9).

PHILISTINES Descendants of Mizraim (Ge 10:14; 1Ch 1:12; Jer 47:4; Am 9:7). Called Kerethites (1Sa 30:14-16; Eze 25:16; Zep 2:5), Casluhites (Ge 10:14; 1Ch 1:12), Caphtor (Jer 47:4; Am 9:7). Territory of (Ex 13:17; 23:31; Dt 2:23; Jos 13:3; 15:47).

Rulers of (Jos 13:3; Jdg 3:3; 16:5, 30; 1Sa 5:8, 11; 6:4, 12; 7:7; 29:2, 6-7). Kings of: Abimelech I (Ge 20), Abimelech II (Ge 26), Achish (1Sa 21:10-15; 27:2-12; 28:1-2; 29).

Allowed to remain in Canaan (Jdg 3:3-4). Shamgar slays six hundred with an oxgoad (Jdg 3:31). For their history during the leadership of Samson (Jdg 13-16). Defeat the Israelites; take the ark; suffer plagues, and return the ark (1Sa 4-6). Army of (1Sa 13:5). Defeated by Samuel (1Sa 7), by Saul and Jonathan (1Sa 9:16; 13-14). Their champion, Goliath, slain by David (1Sa 17). David slays two hundred (1Sa 18:22-30). David finds refuge among (1Sa 27). Defeat the Israelites and slay Saul and his sons (1Sa 31; 1Ch 10:1). Defeated by David (2Sa 5:17-25; 23:9-16; 1Ch 14:8-16). Pay tribute to Jehoshaphat (2Ch 17:11). Defeated by Hezekiah (2Ki 18:8).

Prophecies against (Isa 9:11-12; 14:29-31; Jer 25:17-20; 47; Eze 25:15-17; Am 1:6-8; Zep 2:4-7; Zec 9:5-7).

PHILOLOGUS (*lover of words [education]*). Christian in Rome to whom Paul sent a salutation (Ro 16:15).

PHILOSOPHY (*lover of discernment, lover of wisdom*). The nature of things (Ecc 1-7). A philosophical discourse on wisdom (Job 28). Philosophical inductions and deductions relating to God and his providence (Job 5:8-20; 9; 10:2-21; 12:6-24; 33:12-30; 37). Reveals the mysteries of providence (Pr 25:2; Ro 1:19-20). Is not sufficient for an adequate knowledge of God (1Co 1:21-22), or of salvation through the atonement of Jesus Christ (1Co 2:6-10). Employment of, was not Paul's method of preaching the gospel (1Co 1:17, 19, 21; 2:1-5, 13). Greek schools of (Ac 17:18). Rabbinical (Col 2:8, 16-19; 1Ti 6:20).

See Aratus; Asceticism; Epicureans; Gnosticism; Stoicism; Stoics; Reasoning; Wisdom.

PHINEHAS (*the Negro*).

1. Son of Eleazar and grandson of Aaron (Ex 6:25; 1Ch 6:4, 50; 9:20; Ezr 7:5; 8:2), who slew Zimri and Cozbi at God's command (Nu 25:6-15; Ps 106:30).

God establishes a covenant with (Nu 25:10-13). *See Covenants, Major in the Old Testament.*

2. Son of Eli; sinful priest (1Sa 1:3; 2:12-17, 22-25, 27-36; 3:11-13). He and his brother were killed by Philistines (1Sa 4).
3. Father of Eleazar who returned from exile (Ezr 8:33).

PHLEGON (*burning*). A disciple in Rome (Ro 16:14).

PHOEBE (*radiant*). A deaconess of the church at Cenchrea (Ro 16:1).

PHOENICIA (*land of purple [dye for trading]*, possibly *land of date palms*). Country along Mediterranean coast, c. 120 miles long, extending from Arvad (Arados, 1Mc 15:23) to Dor, just S of Carmel. The Semitic name for the land was Canaan. The term Phoenicia is from a Greek word meaning "purple-red," perhaps because the Phoenicians were the discoverers of the crimson-purple dye derived form the murex shellfish. The people were Semites who came in a migration from the Mesopotamian region during the second millennium B.C. They became great seafarers, establishing colonies at Carthage and Spain, and perhaps even reached England. Inhabitants of, descended from Canaan (Ge 10:15, 18-19). Called Sidonians (Jdg 18:7; Eze 32:30). They were famous shipbuilders (Eze 27:9) and carpenters (1Ki 16:31; 18:19). Hiram, one of their kings was friendly with David and Solomon (2Sa 5:11; 1Ki 5:1-12; 2Ch 2:3-16), and another Hiram helped Solomon in the building of the temple in Jerusalem (1Ki 7:13-47; 2Ch 2:13-14). Jews from, hear Jesus (Mk 3:8). Jesus healed a Syrian Phoenician woman's daughter in its regions (Mk 7:24-30). Paul visited Christians there (Ac 15:3; 21:2-7; 27:3).

PHOENIX Town on the S coast of Crete (Ac 27:12).

PHRYGIA An inland province of Asia Minor. People from, in Jerusalem (Ac 2:10). Paul in (Ac 16:6; 18:23).

PHURAH *See Purah.*

PHUT *See Put.*

PHUVAH *See Puah.*

PHYGELUS (*fugitive*). A Christian in Asia. Turns from Paul (2Ti 1:15).

PHYLACTERY (*safeguard, means of protection*). A small box containing slips of parchment on which were written portions of the law (Ex 13:9, 16; Dt 6:4-9; 11:18). Worn ostentatiously on the forehead and left arm (Mt 23:5).

PHYSICIAN (2Ch 16:12; Mt 9:12; Mk 5:26; Lk 8:43). Proverbs about (Mk 2:17; Lk 4:23). Luke a physician (Col 4:14).

Figurative (Job 13:4; Jer 8:22; Lk 5:31).

PHYSIOGNOMY The art of discovering temperament and character from outward appearance. Character revealed in (Isa 3:9). *See Countenance; Face.*

PHYSIOLOGY The human body (Job 10:11; Ps 139:14-16; Pr 14:30). *See Hygiene.* Figurative of the Church (Eph 4:16; Col 2:19).

PI-BESETH (*temple [house] of Bastet [pagan goddess]*). *See Bubastis.*

PI HAHIROTH (*temple [house] of Hathor [pagan goddess]*; possibly *mouth of canals*). The place on the W shore of the Red Sea where Pharaoh overtook the Israelites (Ex 14:2, 9; Nu 33:7-8).

PICKS, IRON An instrument of iron used by prisoners of war (2Sa 12:31; 1Ch 20:3), who were used by victorious kings as menial laborers in royal building projects (1Ki 9:20-21; cf. also Ex 1:11).

PICTURES *See Idol; Idolatry.*

PIECE OF SILVER *See Silver.*

PIERCING THE EAR A token of servitude for life (Ex 21:6; Dt 15:17; Ps 40:6).

PIETY Religious duty.

PIG An unclean animal (Lev 11:7; Dt 14:8; Isa 65:4; 66:3, 17). Possessed by demons (Mt 8:30-33). *See Animals.*

PIGEON (*young bird*). Used as sacrifice (Ge 15:9; Lev 1:14; 5:7; 12:8; 14:22; Lk 2:24). *See Dove.*

PILATE, PONTIUS (*family name*). Roman governor of Judea (Mt 27:2; Lk 3:1). Causes slaughter of certain Galileans (Lk 13:1). Tries Jesus and orders his crucifixion (Mt 27; Mk 15; Lk 23; Jn 18:28-40; 19; Ac 3:13; 4:27; 13:28; 1Ti 6:13). Allows Joseph of Arimathea to take Jesus' body (Mt 27:57-58; Mk 15:43-45; Lk 23:52; Jn 19:38).

PILDASH (*steely* ISBE; *spider* KB). Son of Nahor (Ge 22:22).

PILEHA *See Pilha.*

PILGRIM *See Sojourners.*

PILGRIMAGE

1. Jews were expected to make pilgrimages to the temple in Jerusalem for the great feasts (Ps 120-134; Ac 2:5-11).
2. The NT describes Christians as pilgrims or aliens (Heb 11:13; 1Pe 2:11).

PILHA (*millstone* IDB; *plowman* ISBE; *harelip* KB). One of those who sealed the covenant with Nehemiah (Ne 10:24).

PILLAR Of Solomon's temple (1Ki 7:13-22; 2Ki 25:17). Broken and carried to Babylon (2Ki 25:13; Jer 52:17, 20-21). Of Solomon's palaces (1Ki 7:6). Pillar of salt, Lot's wife turned to (Ge 19:26; Lk 17:32).

Used to mark roads (Jer 31:21).

Monuments erected to commemorate events: By Jacob, his vision of angels (Ge 28:18, w 31:13; 35:14), his covenant with Laban (Ge 31:45); by Moses, the covenant between Yahweh and Israel (Ex 24:4); by Joshua, the passing over Jordan (Jos 4:1-9, w Dt 27:2-6; Jos 8:30), at Shechem (Jos 24:25-27, w Jdg 9:6); by Samuel, the discomfiture of the Philistines (1Sa 7:12); by Absalom, to keep his name in remembrance (2Sa 18:18). As a boundary (Jos 15:6, w 18:17), a marker (1Sa 20:19), a landmark (2Sa 20:8; 1Ki 1:9). Prophecy of one in Egypt (Isa 19:19). Monuments of idolatry, to be destroyed (Dt 12:3).

Figurative (Rev 3:12).

PILLAR OF CLOUD AND FIRE God guided Israel out of Egypt and through the wilderness by a pillar of cloud by day and fire by night (Ex 13:21-22). The pillar of cloud rested over the tent of meeting outside the camp whenever the Lord met Moses there (Ex 33:7-11). The cloud and fire were divine manifestations. *See Celestial Phenomena.*

PILLOW

1. A support for the head (Ge 28:11, 18; 1Sa 26:7, 11, 16).
2. NIV "magic charms" (Eze 13:18, 20).

PILOT Captain or operator of a ship (Ac 27:11; Jas 3:4).

PILTAI (*Yahweh rescues*). A priest who returned to Jerusalem from captivity in Babylon (Ne 12:17).

PIM *See Measure.*

PIN Tent peg (Jdg 4:21; 5:26), stick for beating wool in the loom (Jdg 16:13-14). KJV "crisping pins" (Isa 3:22) are NIV "purses."

PINE A tree (Ne 8:15; Isa 41:19; 60:13).

PINING AWAY (Lev 26:39; La 4:9; Eze 4:17; 24:23; 33:10).

PINNACLE (*sun*, or *a little wing*). On a building, a turret, battlement, pointed roof or peak. Satan tried to get Jesus to throw himself down from the pinnacle of the temple (Mt 4:5-6; Lk 4:9).

PINON (*darkness* ISBE; name related to *famous copper mines* KB). Chief of Edom of the family of Esau (Ge 36:40-41; 1Ch 1:52).

PIPE A wind instrument of music. Used in religious services (1Sa 10:5; Isa 30:29). *See Music, Instruments of.*

PIRAM (possibly *wild donkey* IDB; *indomitable* ISBE; possibly *zebra* KB). A king of the Amorites. Overcome and slain by Joshua (Jos 10:3, 16-18, 24-27).

PIRATHON, PIRATHONITE A place in the land of Ephraim (Jdg 12:15). Men of (Jdg 12:13; 2Sa 23:30; 1Ch 11:31; 27:14).

PISGAH A ridge or mountain E of the Jordan, opposite to Jericho. The Israelites come to (Nu 21:20). The water courses flowing from Mount Pisgah were a boundary of the country assigned to the Reubenites and Gadites (Dt 3:17; 4:49; Jos 12:3). Balaam prophesies on (Nu 23:14-24). Moses views Israel from (Dt 3:27; 34:1-4).

PISHON One of the rivers of Eden (Ge 2:11).

PISIDIA A province in Asia Minor. Paul visits (Ac 13:14; 14:24).

PISIDIAN ANTIOCH *See Antioch, 2; Pisidia.*

PISON *See Pishon.*

PISPAH An Asherite (1Ch 7:38).

PISTACHIO Nuts, in a gift sent by Jacob to Joseph (Ge 43:11). *See Plants of the Bible; Tree.*

PIT Bitumen deposit "tar pits" (Ge 14:10), deep place (Ge 37:20-29; Mt 12:11), well or cistern (Jer 14:3; Lk 14:5), earthen vessel (Lev 11:33), death, grave, or Sheol (Job 33:18; Isa 14:15; Nu 16:30, 33).

PITCH
1. Pitch or tar (Ge 14:10; Ex 2:3). *See Caulkers; Tar.*
2. To encamp (Ge 12:8; 31:25; Ex 17:1; Nu 1:51; Jos 8:11).

PITCHER Jars for temple service and personal use (Ex 25:29; 37:16; 1Ch 28:17; Ecc 12:6; Mk 7:4).

PITHOM (*temple [house] of [pagan god] Atum*). Egyptian store city in a valley between the Nile and Lake Timsah; dedicated to the sun god Atum (Ex 1:11).

PITHON Son of Micah (1Ch 8:35; 9:41).

PITY Tender, considerate, compassionate feeling for others.
Commanded (Job 6:14; 1Pe 3:8). For the poor (Pr 19:17; 28:8). Forbidden, to Canaanites (Dt 7:16), to idolatrous proselytizers (Dt 13:8), to murderers (Dt 19:13), to false witnesses (Dt 19:21), to wife in certain situations (Dt 25:12).
Withholding of, from Jesus, prefigured in David (Ps 69:20). Of God (Ps 103:13; Isa 63:9; Joel 2:18; Jnh 4:11; Jas 5:11), withheld from reprobates (Jer 13:14; 21:7; Eze 5:11; 7:4; 8:18; 9:5, 10; Zec 11:6).
Required of believers (Isa 1:17; Mt 18:28-35).
See God, Mercy of; Jesus the Christ, Compassion of; Mercy.

PLACE OF ATONEMENT *See Atonement Cover.*

PLAGUE As a judgment on the Egyptians (Ps 105; 135:8-9; Ac 7:36). The plague of blood (Ex 7:14-25), frogs (Ex 8:1, 15), lice (Ex 8:16-19), flies (Ex 8:20). On cattle (Ex 9:1-7). Of boils and blains (Ex 9:8-12), hail (Ex 9:18-34), locusts (Ex 10:1-20), darkness (Ex 10:21-23). Death of the firstborn (Ex 11:4-7; 12:17, 29-30).
On the Israelites: On account of idolatry (Ex 32:35), after eating quail (Nu 11:33), after refusing to enter the promised land (Nu 14:37), after murmuring on account of the destruction of Korah (Nu 16:41-50), of serpents (Nu 21:6), for the sin of Peor (Jos 22:17), on account of David's sin (2Sa 24:10-25).
On the Philistines (1Sa 6:4-5).
Denounced as a judgment (Lev 26:21; Dt 28:59). Foretold (Rev 11:6; 15:1, 6-8; 16; 22:18-19).
See Judgments; Pestilence.

PLAIN Broad stretch of level land (Ge 11:2; Eze 3:22).

PLAN OF SALVATION *See Jesus the Christ, Mission of; Redemption; Salvation.*

PLANE A tool (Isa 44:13). *See Tools.*

PLANE TREE Possibly a chestnut tree (Ge 30:37; Eze 31:8).

PLANET *See Astronomy; Stars.*

PLANTS OF THE BIBLE The following plants are mentioned in the Bible. Some of them are not identifiable with certainty.
Acacia tree (Ex 25:10ff), algum tree (2Ch 2:8; 9:11), almond (tree) (Ge 30:37; Ex 25:33-36; Ecc 12:5; Jer 1:11), almugwood (1Ki 10:11, 12; 2Ch. 2:8, 9:10 ftn.), aloes (Nu 24:6; Ps 45:8; Pr 7:17; SS 4:14; Jn 19:39), apple tree (SS 2:3; 8:5; Joel 1:12).
Balm (Ge 37:25; 43:11; 2Ch 28:15; Jer 8:22; 46:11; Eze 27:17), barley (Hos 3:2), beans (2Sa 17:28; Eze 4:9), brambles (Isa 34:13; Jdg 9:14-15), briers (Jdg 8:7, 16; Job 31:40; Isa 5:6, 7:23; Eze 28:24), broom tree (1Ki 19:3-4; Job 30:4; Ps 120:4), bush (burning bush) (Ex 3:2-3).
Calamus (SS 4:14; Isa 43:24; Jer 6:20; Eze 27:19), caraway (Isa 28:25-27), cassia (Ex 30:22-25; Ps 45:8; Eze 27:19), cedar (Lev 14:4, 6, 49; Nu 19:6; 2Sa 5:11; 1Ki 5:8), cedars of Lebanon (1Ki 4:33; Eze 31:3, 5), cinnamon (Ex 30:23; Pr 7:17; SS 4:14; Rev 18:13), citron wood (Rev 18:12), coriander (Ex 16:31; Nu 11:7), crocus (Isa 35:1), cucumber (Nu 11:5), cummin (Isa 28:26-27; Mt 23:23), cypress (Ge 6:14; Isa 41:19, 44:14, 60:13; Eze 27:6).
Date (Nu 33:9), dill (Mt 23:23), ebony (Eze 27:15), fig (Ge 3:6-7; Dt 8:8; Jdg 9:10-11; 1Ki 4:25), fir (Isa 41:19; 60:13), flax (Ex 9:31; Jos 2:6; Jdg 15:14), frankincense (Ex 30:34; Rev 18:13), galbanum (Ex 30:34-36), garlic (Nu 11:5), gourd (1Ki 6:18; 7:24; 2Ki 4:39), grain (Lev 23:14), grape (Ge 40:10-11), green tree (Ps 37:35), gum resin (Ex 30:34).
Henna blossoms (SS 1:14; 4:13), herbs, bitter herbs (Ex 12:8), hyssop (Ex 12:22; Lev 14:4; Ps 51:7; 1Ki 4:33), leeks (Nu 11:5), lentils (Ge 25:29-30, 34; 2Sa 17:28), lilies (1Ki 7:19, 22, 26; SS 5:13; Mt 6:28; Lk 12:27), linen (Est 1:5-6).
Mandrakes (Ge 30:14-16; SS 7:13), melon (Nu 11:5; Isa 1:8; Jer 10:5), millet (Eze 4:9; 27:17), mint (Mt 23:23; Lk 11:42), mulberry tree (Lk 17:6), mustard (Mt 13:31-32; 17:20; Mk 4:31; Lk 13:19), myrrh (Ge 37:25-27, 43:11; Est 2:12; Pr 7:17; SS 1:13; Mt 2:11), myrtle (Isa 41:19, 55:13; Zec 1:7-10), nettles (Isa 34:13), nut trees (SS 6:11), nuts [pistachio] (Ge 43:11).
Oak (Ge 35:4; Zec 11:2), olive tree (Jdg 9:8; Job 15:33; Ps 52:8; Isa 17:6; Isa 41:19), onion (Nu 11:5), onycha (Ex 30:34-35), palm (Nu 33:9), pine tree (1Ki 5:10; Isa 60:13), plane tree (Ge 30:37; Eze 31:8), poisonous weeds (Hos 10:4), pomegranate (Dt 8:8; 1Sa 14:2), poplars (Ge 30:37; Lev 23:40; Job 40:22; Ps 137:2; Isa 15:7, 44:4), reed (Job 40:15, 20-22), reeds (Ex 2:3; Job 8:11), resin (Ge 2:12; Nu 11:6-7), rose of Sharon (SS 2:1-2), rue (Lk 11:42), rush (Isa 9:6).
Saffron (SS 4:14), salt herbs (Job 30:1, 3-4), seaweed (Jnh 2:5), seed pods (2Ki 6:25, ftn.), spelt (Ex 9:32; Isa 28:5; Ezr 4:9), spices (Ge 37:25; 43:11; Ex 25:6; Mt 23:23), sycamore (1Ki 10:27; 1Ch 27:28; 2Ch 1:15; Am 7:14; Lk 19:4), terebinth (Isa 6:13; Hos 4:13), thistles (Ge 3:18; 2Ki 14:9; Heb 6:8), thorns (Isa 7:19; Mt 27:29; Mk 15:17; Jn 19:5), tumbleweed (Ps 83:13; Isa 17:13), vine (Ge 9:20, 40:9-11; Jnh 4:5-7), weeds (Job 31:40; Pr 24:31; Mt 13:25), wheat (Ge 30:14; Dt 8:8), wild vine (2Ki 4:39; Jer 2:21), willow (Eze 17:5), wormwood (Rev 8:11).
See Tree.

PLASTER In Egypt stone buildings, even the finest granite, were plastered, inside and out, to make a smooth surface for decoration (Dt 27:2, 4). The poor used a mixture of clay and straw. In Israel an outside clay coating would have to be renewed after the rainy season.

PLASTER, MEDICINAL A cake of figs applied to a boil (Isa 38:21).

PLATE, PLATTER Dedicated to the tabernacle (Nu 7:13, 19, 25, 31, 37, 43, 49, 55, 61, 67, 73, 79, 84-85). John the Baptist's head carried on (Mt 14:8, 11).

PLEADING (Dt 17:8). Of the guilty (Jos 7:19-21). Jesus declined to plead (Mt 26:62; Mk 15:2; Lk 23:3; Jn 18:33-34). Prisoners required to plead (Ac 7:1). *See Defense.*

PLEASANT LAND The land of Israel (Ps 106:24; Zec 7:14; cf. Jer 3:19; 12:10; Dt 8:7-9). *See Israel.*

PLEASING AROMA Of sacrifices (Ge 8:21; Ex 29:18, 25, 41; Lev 1:9, 13, 17; 2:2, 9, 12; 3:5, 16; 4:31; 6:15, 21; 8:21, 28; 17:6; 23:13, 18; 26:31; Nu 15:3, 7, 10, 13, 14, 24; 18:17; 28:2, 6, 8, 13, 24, 27; 29:2, 6, 8, 13, 36; Eze 6:13; 16:19; 20:28, 41). Of Christian service (2Co 2:15; Eph 5:2; Php 4:18). *See Offerings.*

PLEASURE, WORLDLY Unfulfilling (Job 21:12-13; Ecc 1:17; 2:1-13; 1Ti 5:6). Proverbs and parables concerning (Pr 9:17; 15:21; 21:17; Lk 8:14).
Rejected and judged by God (Job 20:12-16; Isa 5:11-12; 22:12-13; 47:8-9; Am 6:1; Ro 1:32; 2Th 2:12). Rejected by Moses (Heb 11:25-26), by Paul (2Ti 3:4; Tit 3:3), by Peter (2Pe 2:13).
See Gluttony; Happiness; Joy; Worldliness.

PLEDGE
1. Personal property of a debtor held to secure a payment (Ge 38:17-18). Law of Moses was concerned with protection of the poor. A pledged outer garment had to be restored at sunset for a bed covering (Ex 22:26-27), a widow's clothing could not be taken (Dt 24:17), a handmill or its upper millstone could not be taken (Dt 24:6).
2. In marriage *See Betrothal.*

PLEIADES (*heap, group [of stars]*). Stars in the constellation Taurus (Job 9:9; 38:31).

PLINY Gaius Plinius Caecilius Secundus, called "the Younger," Roman governmental official, famous as the author of literary letters covering all types of subjects, one of which contains a description of the Christian church in Bithynia, a province which Pliny governed in A.D. 112. The letter, together with the reply of the emperor Trajan are important evidence for the official attitude towards the Christians.

PLOTTING General references to (Est 3:9; Ps 36:4; 37:12; Pr 6:14; Isa 32:7; Mic 2:1). Against Christ (Mt 12:14; 26:4; 27:1; Lk 6:11; 19:47; 22:4; Jn 5:16; 11:47, 53).
General examples of (Ge 37:18; Nu 16:3; Jdg 9:1; 2Ki 12:20; 14:19; Da 6:4; Mt 12:14; Ac 23:13).

PLOW The ancient plow consisted of a forked stick, the trunk hitched to the animals which drew it, the branch braced and terminating in the share, which was at first the sharpened end of the branch, later a metal point. It was ordinarily drawn by a yoke of oxen (Job 1:14; Am 6:12). Such a plow did not turn over the soil; it did little more than scratch the surface.
Figurative of afflictions (Ps 129:3).

PLOWSHARE (*the blade of a plow*). To beat swords into plowshares was symbolic of an age of peace (Isa 2:4), to beat plowshares into swords portended coming war (Joel 3:10).

PLUMB LINE A cord with a weight, the plummet, tied to one end; used in testing whether a wall is perpendicular (Am 7:7-9; 2Ki 21:13; Isa 28:17).

PLUMMET *See Plumb Line.*

POCHERETH *See Pokereth-Hazzebaim.*

PODS Seed pods eaten in famine (2Ki 6:24). Perhaps carob, eaten by the prodigal son and the pigs (Lk 15:16). *See Plants of the Bible.*

POET (*doer,* or *a maker*). Paul quotes from pagan poets (Ac 17:28; 1Co 15:32; Tit 1:12). A great deal of the OT is written in the form of poetry.

POETRY

Acrostic:
(Ps 25; 34; 37; 111; 112; 119; 145; Pr 31:10-31; La 1-5).

Didactic:
Moses' song (Dt 32). The book of Job, the Proverbs, the Song of Songs, much of the books of prophecy. *See Psalms, Topically Arranged.*

Elegy:
On the death of Saul (2Sa 1:19-27). Of Abner (2Sa 3:33-34). *See Elegy.*

Epic:
Moses' song (Ex 15:1-19). Miriam's song (Ex 15:21). Deborah's song (Jdg 5) David's song of praise (2Sa 22).

Lyrics, Sacred:
Moses' and Miriam's songs (Ex 15). Hannah's song (1Sa 2:1-10). The song of Elizabeth (Lk 1:42-45). Of Mary (Lk 1:46-55). Of Zechariah (Lk 1:68-79). The Psalms. *See Psalms.*
See Parallelism

POETS, PAGAN, QUOTATIONS FROM Paul quotes pagan poets in arguments. Examples include: Cleanthes (Ac 17:28), Epimenides (Tit 1:12), Menander (1Co 15:33).

POISON A substance producing a deadly effect, like the venom of reptiles (Dt 32:24, 33; Job 20:16; Ps 58:4). Vegetable poisons were known in antiquity: poisonous weeds (Hos 10:4), wild gourd (2Ki 4:39-40). A poisoned drink is referred to in Mark (Mk 16:18).

POKERETH-HAZZEBAIM (*pitfall of gazelles,* i.e., *gazelle hunter*). The ancestor of a family which returned to Jerusalem from captivity in Babylon (Ezr 2:57; Ne 7:59).

POLE Used to carry the ark (Ex 24:13-15), the table of the bread of the Presence (Ex 25:27-28), the bronze altar (Ex 27:6-7), the incense altar (Ex 30:4-5). Standard on which the bronze serpent was displayed (Nu 21:8-9).

POLICY *See Diplomacy.*

POLITARCH City magistrate of Thessalonica (Ac 17:6, 8). Sixteen epigraphical inscriptions with the word have been discovered.

POLITICS Statecraft.

Corruption in:
(Ps 12:8), in the court of Xerxes (Est 3), of Darius (Da 6:4-15).

Instances of:
Absalom, electioneering for the throne (2Sa 15:2-6). Pilate, condemning Jesus to gratify popular clamor (Mt 27:23-27; Mk 15:15; Lk 23:13-25; Jn 18:38-39; 19:4-13).

Ministers:
Zadok the priest, a partisan of David (2Sa 15:24-29). Nathan the prophet influences the selection of David's successor (1Ki 1:11-40).

Women in:
The wise woman of Abel, who saved the city through diplomacy (2Sa 20:16-22). Bathsheba, in securing the crown for Solomon (1Ki 1:15-21). Herodias, in influencing the administration of Herod (Mt 14:3-11; Mk 6:17-28). Mother of Zebedee's children, in seeking favor for her sons (Mt 20:20-23).
Influence in. *See Influence, Political.*
See Diplomacy; Government.

POLL TAX *See Tax.*

POLLUTION Ceremonial or moral defilement, profanation, and uncleanness (Ex 20:25; 2Pe 2:20). *See Corruption; Defilement; Unclean, Uncleanness; Sanitation and Hygiene.*

POLLUX With Castor, one of the twin gods, sons of Zeus and patrons of sailors (Ac 28:11).

POLYGAMY (*many marriages*). Forbidden (Dt 17:17; Lev 18:18; Mal 2:14-15; Mt 19:4-5; Mk 10:2-8; 1Ti 3:2, 12; Tit 1:6). Authorized (2Sa 12:8).

Examples of:
Tolerated (Ex 21:10; 1Sa 1:2; 2Ch 24:3). Practiced by, (Job 27:15), Lamech (Ge 4:19), Abraham (Ge 16), Esau (Ge 26:34; 28:9), Jacob (Ge 29:30), Ashhur (1Ch 4:5), Gideon (Jdg 8:30), Elkanah (1Sa 1:2), David (1Sa 25:39-44; 2Sa 3:2-5; 5:13; 1Ch 14:3), Solomon (1Ki 11:1-8), Rehoboam (2Ch 11:18-23), Abijah (2Ch 13:21), Jehoram (2Ch 21:14), Joash (2Ch 24:3), Ahab (2Ki 10:1), Jehoiachin (2Ki 24:15), Belshazzar (Da 5:2, w 1Ch 2-8), Hosea (Hos 3:1-2). Mosaic law respecting the firstborn in (Dt 21:15-17).
Sought by women [polyandry] (Isa 4:1).

The Evil Effects of:
Husband's favoritism in (Dt 21:15-17), Jacob's (Ge 29:30; 30:15), Elkanah's (1Sa 1:5), Rehoboam's (2Ch 11:21). Domestic infelicity, in Abraham's family (Ge 16; 21:9-16), Jacob's (Ge 29:30-34; 30:1-23), Elkanah's (1Sa 1:4-7). Upon Solomon (1Ki 11:4-8).
See Concubinage; Marriage.

POLYTHEISM (Ge 31:19; 35:2, 4; Jos 24:2, 23; Jdg 2:13; 3:7; 10:16; 17:5; Jer 2:28; 11:13; Da 4:8; 1Co 8:5).

POMEGRANATE A fruit. Abounded in the land of Canaan (1Sa 14:2). Brought by the spies to show the fruitfulness of the land of Canaan (Nu 13:23). Figures of the fruits of, were embroidered on the ephod (Ex 28:33-34; 39:24), carved on the pillars of the temple (1Ki 7:18, 20, 42; Jer 52:22-23). Wine made of (SS 8:2).

POMMEL *See Capital.*

PONTIUS PILATE *See Pilate, Pontius.*

PONTUS (*sea*). A province of Asia Minor (Ac 2:9; 1Pe 1:1). Aquila lived in (Ac 18:2).

POOL Of Gibeon (2Sa 2:13; Jer 41:12). Of Hebron (2Sa 4:12). Of Samaria (1Ki 22:38). Of Heshbon (SS 7:4).
Of Jerusalem: Upper pool (2Ki 18:17; Isa 36:2), lower pool (Isa 22:9), Siloam (Jn 9:7, 11), called Siloam (Ne 3:15, ftn), and probably identical with the king's pool (Ne 2:14).

POOR

Proverbs Concerning:
(Ps 37:16 w Isa 29:19; Pr 10:15; 13:7-8, 23; 18:23; 19:1, 4, 7, 17, 22; 20:13; 21:13; 22:2, 9; 23:21; 24:20-21, 31; 28:6, 8, 11, 19; 29:14; Ecc 4:6, 13; 6:8; 9:15-16). Always part of the society (Mt 26:11; Mk 14:7; Jn 12:8).

Attitudes toward:
Job (Job 30:25). Jesus and the poor widow (Mk 12:43-44). Lazarus (Lk 16:20-21). Judas (Jn 12:6). James (Jas 1:9-10).

Duty to:
(Ex 22:25-27; 23:11; Lev 19:9-10; 25:25-28, 35-43; Dt 14:28-29; 15:2-14; 24:12-21; 26:12-13; Ne 8:10; Ps 37:21, 26;

41:1-3; 112:4-5, 9; Pr 28:27; 29:7; 31:9, 20; Isa 1:7; 16:3-4; 58:7, 10; Eze 18:7; Da 4:27; Zec 7:10; Mt 5:42; 19:21; 25:35-36; Mk 14:7; Lk 3:11; 6:30; 11:41; 12:33; 14:12-14; 18:22; 19:8; Ac 20:35; Ro 12:8, 13, 20; 1Co 13:3; 16:1-2; 2Co 6:10; 8:9; 9:5-7; Gal 2:10; 6:10; Eph 4:28; 1Ti 5:9-10, 16; Heb 13:3; Jas 1:27; 2:2-9, 15-16; 5:4; 1Jn 3:17-19).

God's care of:

(1Sa 2:7-8; Job 5:15-16; 31:15; 34:18-19, 28; 36:6, 15; Ps 9:18; 10:14; 12:5; 14:6; 34:6; 35:10; 68:10; 69:33; 72:2, 4, 12-14; 74:21; 102:17; 107:9, 36, 41; 109:31; 113:7-8; 132:15; 140:12; 146:5, 7; Pr 22:2, 22-23; 29:13; Ecc 5:8; Isa 11:4; 14:30, 32; 25:4; 29:19; 41:17; Jer 20:13; Zep 3:12; Zec 11:7; Mt 11:5; Lk 4:18; 7:22; 16:22; Jas 2:5).

See God, Goodness of, Providence of.

The Poor, Without Friends:

(Pr 14:20; 19:4, 7). Wisdom of, despised (Ecc 9:15-16).

Warning against neglect of (Pr 20:13; 21:13; 22:16; Eze 16:49). Neglect of, by the disciples (Ac 6:1-6). Neglect of, denounced (Mt 25:42, 45).

Kindness to:

Commanded (Ne 8:10, 12). Rewarded (Ps 41:1-3; Isa 58:10; Lk 14:12-14).

Righteous treatment of, required (Ps 82:3-4; Pr 22:22; 31:9; Isa 1:17). Rewarded (Pr 29:14; Jer 22:16; Eze 18:7, 16-17; Da 4:27). Compassion toward (Job 30:25; Pr 14:21; 29:7; Heb 13:3; Jas 1:27).

Liberality to (Pr 31:20; Isa 58:7; Mt 5:42, w Lk 6:30; Lk 3:11; 19:8; Ro 12:8, 13, 20; 1Co 13:3; 16:1-2; 2Co 9:1-15; Gal 2:10; Eph 4:28; 1Ti 5:9-10, 16; Jas 2:15-16; 1Jn 3:17). Liberality to, rewarded (Pr 19:17; 22:9; 28:27; Ps 112:9; Mt 19:21; 25:34-36; Lk 6:35; 12:33; 18:22; Ac 20:35).

Instances of Kindness—

Ruth, to Naomi (Ru 2:2, 11). Boaz, to Ruth (Ru 2:8-16; 3:15). Elijah, to the widow of Zarephath (1Ki 17:12-24). Elisha, to the prophet's widow (2Ki 4:1-7). The Jews (Est 9:22). Job (Job 29:11-17; 31:16-22, 38-40). The Temanites (Isa 21:14). Nebuzaradan (Jer 39:10).

The good Samaritan (Lk 10:33-35). Zacchaeus (Lk 19:8). Dorcas (Ac 9:36). Cornelius (Ac 10:2, 4). Christian church, at Jerusalem (Ac 6:1), at Antioch (Ac 11:29-30). Churches of Macedonia and Achaia (Ro 15:25-26; 2Co 8:1-5). By Paul (Ro 15:25).

Oppression of:

(Ne 5:1-13; Job 20:19-21; 22:6-7, 9-11; 24:4, 7-12; Ps 10:2, 8-10; 37:14; 109:16; Pr 14:31; 17:5; 19:7; 22:7, 16; 28:3, 15; 30:14; Ecc 5:8; Isa 3:14-15; 10:1-2; 32:6-7; Eze 18:12; 22:29; Am 2:6; 4:1; 5:11-12; 8:4-6; Hab 3:14; Jas 2:6; 5:4). Oppression forbidden (Dt 24:14; Zec 7:10).

Instances of oppression of (2Ki 4:1; Ne 5:1-5).

Mosaic laws concerning:

Atonement money of, must be uniform with that of the rich (Ex 30:15). Inexpensive offerings authorized for (Lev 5:7; 12:8; 14:21-22).

Discrimination, in favor of, forbidden (Ex 23:3; Lev 19:15); against, forbidden (Ex 23:6; Jas 2:2-9).

Exactions of interest from, forbidden (Ex 22:25; Lev 25:35-37). Garments of, taken in pledge, to be restored (Ex 22:26; Dt 24:12-13). To participate triennially in the tithes (Dt 14:28-29; 26:12-13). Gleanings reserved for (Lev 19:9-10; 23:22; Dt 24:19-21). To share the products of the land in the seventh year (Ex 23:11). To be released from servitude, in seventh year (Dt 15:12), in Jubilee (Lev 25:39-43). Alienated lands of, to be restored in Jubilee (Lev 25:25-28).

Figurative:

Poor in spirit (Isa 66:2; Mt 5:3; Lk 6:20).

See Alms; Beneficence; Creditor; Debtor; Employee; Employer; Liberality; Orphans; Poverty; Rich, The; Riches; Servants; Wages; Widow.

POPLAR (*white*). A tree (Ge 30:37; Hos 4:13).

POPLARS, RAVINE OF A brook, probably on the boundary between Moab and Edom (Isa 15:7).

POPULARITY Instances of: David (2Sa 3:36). Absalom (2Sa 15:2-6, 13). Job (Job 29).

POPULARITY OF JESUS (Mt 4:24; 8:1; 13:2; 14:13, 35; 19:1-2; 21:8-9; Mk 1:33; 2:2; 3:7, 20; 5:21; 6:33, 55-56; 10:1; 11:8-10; 12:37; Lk 4:14-15, 42; 5:1; 9:11; 12:1; 19:35-38; Jn 6:2, 15; 12:12-13, 19).

PORATHA Son of Haman (Est 9:8).

PORCH An area with a roof supported by columns: colonnade (1Ki 7:6ff), porch (Jdg 3:23, ftn), place before a court (Mk 14:68), gateway (Mt 26:71).

PORCIUS *See Festus, Porcius.*

PORPHYRY A purple stone used in mosaics (Est 1:6).

PORPOISE *See Sea Cow.*

PORTERS *See Gatekeepers.*

PORTION A part; less than the whole of anything; share (Nu 31:30, 47; Ne 8:10, 12).

POST

1. Of the tabernacle (Ex 26:32, 37; 27:1-17). Of a city gate (Jdg 16:3).

2. Of a watchman (Ne 7:3; 13:11; Ecc 10:4; Isa 62:6).

POSTERITY PROMISED (Ge 15:5, 18; 17:20; 22:17; 26:14; Lev 26:9; Dt 7:13; Ro 4:18).

POT Utensil of metal of clay for holding liquids or other substances (2Ki 4:38).

POTENTATE *See Rulers.*

POTIPHAR (*he whom [pagan god] Ra gives*). An officer of Pharaoh. Joseph's master (Ge 37:36; 39:1).

POTIPHERA (*he whom [pagan god] Ra gives*). A priest of On. Joseph's father-in-law (Ge 41:45, 50; 46:20).

POTSHERD A fragment of earthenware (Job 2:8; Isa 45:9).

POTTAGE *See Stew.*

POTTER *See Occupations and Professions.*

POTTER'S FIELD Piece of ground which the priests bought with the money Judas received for betraying our Lord (Mt 27:7).

POTTER'S GATE Of Jerusalem (Jer 19:2).

POTTERY One of the oldest crafts in the Bible lands. The place where potter's clay was dug was called "potter's field" (Mt 27:7). Pottery was shaped by hand on a potter's wheel, powered by foot or by an apprentice (Jer 18:3-6), then dried and baked in a kiln.

Many different items were made: basins, bowls, cups, dishes, flasks, jars, lamps, ovens, pots. Thousands of objects have been found by the archaeologists. Careful study has been made of the historical development of pottery styles, so that experts can date and place pottery with considerable accuracy.

POUND A talent equaled about seventy-five pounds (Ex 25:39, ftn), a mina about 1.25 pounds (1Ki 10:17, ftn), forty shekels about one pound (Ge 3:15, ftn). *See Measure.*

POVERTY (1Sa 2:7). Destructive (Pr 10:15). A source of temptation (Pr 30:8-9). To be preferred over wealth, with trouble (Pr 15:16), without right (Pr 16:8; Ecc 4:6). *See Poor.*

Caused, by laziness (Pr 6:11; 20:13; 24:33-34), by drunkenness (Pr 23:21), by evil associations (Pr 28:19).

POWER

Of Christ:

As the Son of God, is the power of God (Jn 5:17-19; 10:28-30), as man, is from the Father (Ac 10:38).

Described as supreme (Eph 1:20-21; 1Pe 3:22), unlimited (Mt 28:18), over all flesh (Jn 17:2), over all things (Jn 3:35; Eph 1:22), glorious (2Th 1:9), everlasting (1Ti 6:16). Is able to subdue all things (Php 3:21).

Exemplified in, creation (Jn 1:3, 10; Col 1:16), upholding all things (Col 1:17; Heb 1:3), salvation (Isa 63:1; Heb 7:25), His teaching (Mt 7:28-29; Lk 4:32), working miracles (Mt 8:27; Lk 5:17), enabling others to work miracles (Mt 10:1; Ac 5:31), giving spiritual life (Jn 5:21, 25-26), giving eternal life (Jn 17:2), raising the dead (Jn 5:28-29), rising from the dead (Jn 2:19; 10:18), overcoming the world (Jn 16:33), overcoming Satan (Col 2:15; Heb 2:14), destroying the works of Satan (1Jn 3:8), ministers should make known (2Pe 1:16).

Saints made willing by (Ps 110:3), aided by (Heb 2:18), strengthened by (Php 4:13; 2Ti 4:17), preserved by (2Ti 1:12; 4:18), bodies of, shall be changed by (Php 3:21), rests upon saints (2Co 12:9). Present in the assembly of saints (1Co 5:4). Shall be specially manifested at his second coming (Mk 13:26; 2Pe 1:16). Shall subdue all power (1Co 15:24). The wicked shall be destroyed by (Ps 2:9; Isa 11:4; 63:3; 2Th 1:9).

See Jesus the Christ, Omnipotence of; Power of.

Of God:

One of his attributes (Ps 62:11).

Expressed by the voice of God (Ps 29:3, 5; 68:33), finger of God (Ex 9:3, 15; Isa 48:13), arm of God (Job 40:9; Isa 52:10), thunder of his power (Job 26:14).

Described as, great (Ps 79:11; Na 1:3), strong (Ps 89:13; 136:12), glorious (Ex 15:6; Isa 63:12), mighty (Job 9:4; Ps 89:13), everlasting (Isa 26:4; Ro 1:20), sovereign (Ro 9:21), effectual (Isa 43:13; Eph 3:7), irresistible (Dt 32:39; Da 4:35), incomparable (Ex 15:11-12; Dt 3:24; Job 40:9; Ps 89:8), unsearchable (Job 5:9; 9:10), incomprehensible (Job 26:14; Ecc 3:11).

All things possible to (Mt 19:26). Nothing too hard for (Ge 18:14; Jer 32:27). Can save by many or by few (1Sa 14:6). Is the source of all strength (1Ch 29:12; Ps 68:35).

Exemplified, in the creation (Ps 102:25; Jer 10:12), in establishing and governing all things (Ps 65:6; 66:7), in the miracles of Christ (Lk 11:20), in the resurrection of Christ (2Co 13:4; Col 2:12), in the resurrection of saints (1Co 6:14), in making the gospel effectual (Ro 1:16; 1Co 1:18, 24), in delivering his people (Ps 106:8), in the destruction of the wicked (Ex 9:16; Ro 9:22).

Saints, long for exhibitions of (Ps 63:1-2), have confidence in (Jer 20:11), receive increase of grace by (2Co 9:8), strengthened by (Eph 6:10; Col 1:11), upheld by (Ps 37:17; Isa 41:10), supported in affliction by (2Co 6:7; 2Ti 1:8), delivered by (Nu 1:10; Da 3:17), exalted by (Job 36:22), kept by, for salvation (1Pe 1:5). Exerted in behalf of saints (1Ch 16:9). Works in and for saints (2Co 13:4; Eph 1:19; 3:20). The faith of saints stands in (1Co 2:5).

Should be acknowledged (1Ch 29:11; Isa 33:13), pleaded in prayer (Ps 79:11; Mt 6:13), feared (Jer 5:22; Mt 10:28), magnified (Ps 21:13; Jude 25). Efficiency of ministers is through (1Co 3:6-8; Gal 2:8; Eph 3:7). Is a ground of trust (Isa 26:4; Ro 4:21).

The wicked do not know (Mt 22:29), have it against them (Ezr 8:22), shall be destroyed by it (Lk 12:5).

The heavenly host magnified (Rev 4:11; 5:13; 11:17).

See God, Omnipotent, Power of.

Of the Holy Spirit:

Is the power of God (Mt 12:28, w Lk 11:20). Christ worked his miracles (Mt 12:28).

Exemplified in creation (Ge 1:2; Job 26:13; Ps 104:30), the conception of Christ (Lk 1:35), raising Christ from the dead (1Pe 3:18), giving spiritual life (Eze 37:11-14, w Ro 8:11), working miracles (Ro 15:19), making the gospel efficacious (1Co 2:4; 1Th 1:5), overcoming all difficulties (Zec 4:6-7). Promised by the Father (Lk 24:49). Promised by Christ (Ac 1:8).

Saints upheld by (Ps 51:12), strengthened by (Eph 3:16), enabled to speak the truth boldly by (Mic 3:8; Ac 6:5, 10; 2Ti 1:7-8), helped in prayer by (Ro 8:26), abound in hope by (Ro 15:13). Qualifies ministers (Lk 24:49; Ac 1:8-9). God's word the instrument of (Eph 6:17).

See Holy Spirit.

Spiritual:

From God (Isa 40:29-31; Lk 24:49; 1Co 1:24-28; Php 2:13; 2Ti 1:7). From Christ (2Co 12:9; Eph 1:19-20). From the Holy Spirit (Jn 7:38-39; Ac 1:8; 2:2-4). On believers (Ac 6:8, 10; 1Co 4:19-20; Heb 6:5). In the spirit of Elijah (Lk 1:17).

In preaching (Ac 4:33; 6:10; 1Th 1:5), of Christ (Lk 4:32). Through prayer (Ge 32:28; Mk 9:29; Lk 24:49; Ac 1:14; 2:1; 2:2-4).

PRAETOR Originally the highest Roman magistrate; later, officials elected to administer justice; under the principate the office declined in prestige, power, and functions.

PRAETORIAN GUARD (*residence of the Praetor [leader]*). Guard of imperial palace or provincial governor; NIV "palace guard" (Php 1:13) and "Caesar's household" (Php 4:22).

PRAETORIUM (*residence of the Praetor [leader]*). In the Gospels it refers to the temporary palace or headquarters of the Roman governor while in Jerusalem (Mt 27:27; Mk 15:16), the palace of Herod at Caesarea (Ac 23:35).

PRAISE

Examples of:

(Ps 7:17; 22:22-23; 28:6-7; 32:11; 34:1-3; 41:13; 42:4; 51:15; 65:1; 71:8, 14-15; 75:1; 79:13; 81:1; 84:4; 86:12; 89:95; 104:33-34; 109:30; 113:1-2; 115:18; 118:15; 140:13; 145:1-21; 146:1-10; 148:1-14; 149:1-9; 150; Isa 24:15-16; 25:1; 35:10; 38:19; 43:21; 49:13; 51:3; 52:7-10; Jer 31:7; Ro 11:36; 16:27; 1Co 15:57; Eph 3:20-21; Heb 2:12; Jude 25; Rev 1:6; 14:7).

With music (Ps 33:2-3; 43:3-4; 47:1, 6-7; 57:7-9 w 108:1-3; 66:1-2, 4; 67:4; 68:4, 32-34; 69:30; 71:22; 81:1; 92:1-3; 95:1-2; 98:4-6; 104:33; 144:9; 149:2-3; 150:3-5; Jas 5:13).

Daily (1Ch 23:30; Ps 92:1-2; 145:2). In the night (Ps 42:8; 63:5-6; 77:6; 92:1-3; 119:62; 134:1; 149:5; Ac 16:25). Seven times a day (Ps 119:164).

Congregational (Ps 22:22; 26:12; 68:26; 111:1; 116:18-19; 134:1-2; 135:2; 149:1).

For God's goodness and mercy (Ps 13:6; 63:3-6; 100:5; 101:1; 106:1, 48; 107:8-9, 15, 21, 31; 117:2; 118:29; 136; 138:2; 144:1-2; 145:7-9, 14-21; 146:7-9; Isa 12:1-6; Jer 33:11). For God's greatness (Ps 48:1; 145:3, 10-12; 147:1-20; Isa 24:14). For God's holiness (Ps 99:2, 5, 9). For God's works (Ps 9:1-2; 107:8-9, 15, 21, 31-32; 145:4-6, 10-13; 147:12-18; 150:2). For deliverance from enemies (Ge 14:20; Ps 44:7-8; 54:6-7; 69:16). For salvation (Isa 61:3).

Commanded:

(Dt 8:10; Ps 9:11; 30:4; 32:11; 33:1-3; 69:34; 70:4; 95:1-2, 6-7a; 96:1-4, 7-9; 97:12; 100:1-5; 105:1-5; 117:1; 134:1-2; 135:1-3, 19-21; Isa 42:10-12; Eph 5:19; Heb 13:15; 1Pe 4:11; 5:11). All nations to praise God (Ps 69:34; 103:22; 148:1-14).

Angels exhorted to (Ps 103:20-21; 148:2). In heaven (Ne 9:6; Job 38:7; Ps 103:20-21; 148:2-4; Isa 6:3; Eze 3:12; Lk 2:13-14; 15:7, 10; Rev 1:6; 4:8-11; 5:9-14; 7:9-12; 11:16-17; 14:2-3; 15:3-4; 19:1-6).

Instances of:

Song of Moses, after the passage of the Red Sea (Ex 15:1-19). Miriam (Ex 15:21). Deborah, after defeating the Canaanites (Jdg 5:1-31). Hannah (1Sa 2:1-10). David, celebrating his deliverance from the hand of Saul (2Sa 22 w Ps 18). On bringing the ark to Zion (1Ch 16:8-36). At the close of his reign (1Ch 29:10-19). The choir when Solomon brought the ark into the temple (2Ch 5:13). Israelites (2Ch 7:2-3; Ne 9:5-6). Daniel (Da 2:20, 23). Nebuchadnezzar (Da 4:37). Jonah (Jnh 2:9).

Mary (Lk 1:46-55). Shepherds (Lk 2:20). The leper (Lk 17:15). Jesus and his disciples (Mt 26:30; Mk 14:26). Disciples (Ac 2:46-47; 4:24). Paul and Silas, in prison (Ac 16:25).

Psalms of:

For God's goodness to Israel (Pss 46; 48; 65:66; 68; 76; 81; 85; 98; 105; 124; 126; 129; 135; 136). For God's goodness to the righteous (Pss 23; 34; 36; 91; 100; 103; 107; 117; 121). For God's goodness to individuals (Pss 9; 18; 22; 30; 40; 75; 103; 108; 116; 118; 138; 144). For God's attributes (Pss 8; 19; 22; 24; 29; 33; 47; 50; 65-66; 76-77; 92-93; 95-99; 104; 111; 113-115; 134; 139; 147-148; 150).

See Glorifying God; Hallelujah; Prayer; Thankfulness.

PRAYER (Ps 17:1, 6; 22:1-2, 19; 28:1-2; 35:22; 55:1-2, 16-17; 57:2; 61:1-2; 70:5; 102:1-2; 130:1-2; 141:1-2; 142:1-2).

General:

Attitudes in: *See Worship.*

Boldness in: Commanded (Heb 4:16). Exemplified by Abraham in his inquiry concerning Sodom (Ge 18:23-32), by Moses, supplicating for assistance in delivering Israel (Ex 33:12, 18). Secret (Ge 24:63; Mt 6:6). Silent (Ps 5:1). Weeping in (Ezr 10:1). In a loud voice, satirized by Elijah (1Ki 18:27).

Long: Of Pharisees (Mt 23:14), scribes (Mk 12:40; Lk 20:47). Profuse, to be avoided (Ecc 5:2; Mt 6:7). Vain repetitions of, to be avoided (Mt 6:7).

Daily: In the morning (Ps 5:3; 88:13; 143:8; Isa 32:2). Morning and evening (Ps 92:2). Twice daily (Ps 88:1). Three times a day (Ps 55:17; Da 6:10). In the night (Ps 119:55, 62). All night (Lk 6:12). Without ceasing (1Th 5:17).

Disbelief in: (Job 21:15).

Family: By Abraham (Ge 12:7-8; 13:4, 8). By Jacob (Ge 35:3, 7). Cornelius (Ac 10:2).

Hypocritical, forbidden (Mt 6:5). Discreet (Ecc 5:2; Mt 6:6).

"Lord's prayer": A model taught to the disciples (Mt 6:9-12; Lk 11:2-4). *See below, Of Jesus.*

Of the righteous, acceptable: (Pr 15:8, 29). Spirit of, from God (Zec 12:10). Divine help in (Ro 8:26).

Postures in: Bowing (Ge 24:26, 48, 52; Ex 4:31; 34:8-9; 2Ch 29:29). Kneeling (1Ki 8:54; 2Ch 6:13; Ezr 9:5; Ps 95:6; Da 6:10;

Lk 22:41; Ac 20:36; 21:5). Hands uplifted (1Ki 8:22; 2Ch 6:12-13; Ezr 9:5; Isa 1:15; La 3:41; 1Ti 2:8). Standing (Lk 18:11, 13).

Power of (Mk 9:28-29; Jas 5:16-18). Accompanied by works (Ne 4:9). Kept in divine remembrance (Rev 5:8; 8:3-4).

Prayer contest: Proposed by Elijah (1Ki 18:24-39).

Public, should edify (1Co 14:14-15). Social (Mt 18:19; Ac 1:13-14; 16:16, 25; 20:36; 21:5). Held in private houses (Ac 1:13-14; 12:12), in the temple (Ac 2:46; 3:1). Perseverance in (Ro 12:12; Eph 6:18). Evils averted by (Jer 26:19).

Private commanded (Mt 6:6). Exemplified by Lot (Ge 19:20), Eliezer (Ge 24:12), Jacob (Ge 32:9-12), Gideon (Jdg 6:22, 36, 39), Hannah (1Sa 1:10), David (2Sa 7:18-29), Hezekiah (2Ki 20:2), Isaiah (2Ki 20:11), Manasseh (2Ch 33:18-19), Ezra (Ezr 9:5-6), Nehemiah (Ne 2:4), Jeremiah (Jer 32:16-25), Daniel (Da 9:3, 19), Jonah (Jnh 2:1), Habakkuk (Hab 1:2), Anna (Lk 2:37), Jesus (Mt 14:23; 26:36, 39; Mk 1:35; Lk 9:18, 29), Paul (Ac 9:11), Peter (Ac 9:40; 10:9), Cornelius (Ac 10:30).

Rebuked: Of Moses, at the Red Sea (Ex 14:15), when he prayed to see Canaan (Dt 3:23-27). Of Joshua (Jos 7:10).

Submissiveness in: Exemplified by Jesus (Mt 26:39; Mk 14:36; Lk 22:42), David (2Sa 12:22-23), Job (Job 1:20-21).

Signs asked for, as assurance of answer: By Abraham's servant (Ge 24:14, 42-44). By Gideon (Jdg 6:36-40).

Answer to:

Promised—

(Ex 33:17-20; 1Ki 8:22-53; 1Ch 28:9; 2Ch 6; Job 8:5-6; 12:4; 22:27; 33:26; Ps 10:17; 81:10; Pr 10:24; 15:8, 29; 16:1; Isa 58:9; 65:24; Eze 36:37; Mt 6:5-8; 18:19-20; 21:22; Mk 11:24-25; Lk 11:9-13; 18:6-8; 21:36; 4:10, 23-24; Jn 16:23-27; Ro 8:26; 10:12-13; Eph 2:18; 3:20; Heb 4:16; 10:22-23; Jas 1:5-7; 1Jn 3:22; 5:14-15).

Promised to those in adversity (Ex 6:5-6 w Ac 7:34; Ex 22:23, 27; Ps 9:10, 12; 18:3; 32:6; 34:15, 17; 37:4-5; 38:15; 50:15; 55:16-17; 56:9; 65:2, 5; 69:32-33; 86:7; 91:15; 102:17-20; Isa 19:20; 30:19; 31:9; Joel 2:18-19, 32; Zec 10:1, 6; 13:9). Promised to those who diligently seek God (2Ch 7:14; Ps 145:18-19; Pr 2:3, 5-6; Isa 55:6; Jer 29:12-13; 33:3; La 3:25; Am 5:4-6; Zep 2:3; Zec 13:9; Mt 7:7-11; Jn 9:31; 15:7, 16; Heb 11:6; Jas 4:8, 10; 5:16). Promised to the meek (Mk 11:25). Promised to the penitent (Dt 4:30-31; 2Ch 7:13-15).

Delayed—

(Ps 22:1-2; 40:1; 80:4; 88:14; Jer 42:2-7; Hab 1:2; Lk 18:7).

Withheld: Of Balaam (Dt 23:5; Jos 24:10). Of Job (Job 30:20, w 42:12). Of the Israelites, when attacked by the Amorites (Dt 1:45). The prayer of Jesus, "Let this cup pass" (Mt 26:39, 42, 44, w 45-75 & Mt 27).

Differs From Request—

Exceeds petition (Eph 3:20). Solomon asked wisdom; the answer included wisdom, riches, honor and long life (1Ki 3:7-14; 2Ch 1:7-12). Disciples prayed for Peter, the answer included Peter's deliverance (Ac 12:15, w v.5).

Moses asked to see God's face; God revealed his goodness (Ex 33:18-20). Moses asked to be permitted to cross the Jordan; the answer was permission to view the land of promise (Dt 3:23-27). Martha and Mary asked Jesus to come and heal their brother Lazarus; Jesus delayed, but raised Lazarus from the dead (Jn 11). Paul asked that the thorn in the flesh be removed; the answer was a promise of grace to endure it (2Co 12:8-9).

Answered—

(Job 34:28; Ps 3:4; 4:1; 6:8-9; 18:6; 21:2, 4; 22:4-5, 24; 28:6; 30:2-3; 31:22; 34:4-6; 40:1; 66:19-20; 77:1-2; 81:7; 99:6-8; 106:44; 107:6, 13; 116:1-8; 118:5, 21; 119:26; 120:1; 138:3; La 3:57-58; Hos 12:4; Jnh 2:1-2, 7; Lk 23:42-43; Ac 4:31; 2Co 12:8-9; Jas 5:17-18).

Instances of—

Cain (Ge 4:13-15). Abraham, for a son (Ge 15), entreating for Sodom (Ge 18:23-33), for Ishmael (Ge 17:20), for Abimelech (Ge 20:17). Hagar, for deliverance (Ge 16:7-13). Abraham's servant, for guidance (Ge 24:12-52). Rebekah, concerning her pains in pregnancy (Ge 25:22-23). Jacob, for deliverance from Esau (Ge 32:9-32; 33:1-17).

Moses, for help at the Red Sea (Ex 14:15-16), at the waters of Marah (Ex 15:25), at Horeb (Ex 17:4-6), in the battle with the Amalekites (Ex 17:8-14), concerning the murmuring of the Israelites for flesh (Nu 11:11-35), in behalf of Miriam's leprosy (Nu 12:13-15). Moses, Aaron, and Samuel (Ps 99:6).

Israelites: For deliverance from bondage (Ex 2:23-25; 3:7-10; Ac 7:34), from Pharaoh's army (Ex 14:10-30), from the king of Mesopotamia (Jdg 3:9, 15), Sisera (Jdg 4:3, 23-24; 1Sa 12:9-11), Ammon (Jdg 10:6-18; 11:1-33), for God's favor under the reproofs of Azariah (2Ch 15:1-15), from Babylonian bondage (Ne 9:27).

Gideon, asking the token of dew (Jdg 6:36-40). Manoah, asking about Samson (Jdg 13:8-9). Samson, asking for strength (Jdg 16:28-30). Hannah, asking for a child (1Sa 1:10-17, 19-20). David, asking whether Keilah would be delivered into his hands (1Sa 23:10-12), and Ziklag (1Sa 30:8), whether he should go into Judah after Saul's death (2Sa 2:1), whether he should go against the Philistines (2Sa 5:19-25). David, in adversity (Ps 118:5; 138:3). Solomon, asking wisdom (1Ki 3:1-13; 9:2-3).

Elijah, raising the widow's son (1Ki 17:22), asking fire on his sacrifice (1Ki 18:36-38), rain (1Ki 17:1; 18:1, 42-45; Jas 5:17). Elisha, leading the Syrian army (2Ki 6:17-20). Jabez, asking for prosperity (1Ch 4:10). Abijah, for victory over Jeroboam (2Ch 13:14-18). Asa, for victory over Zerah (2Ch 14:11-15). The people of Judah (2Ch 15:15). Jehoshaphat, for victory over the Canaanites (2Ch 18:31; 20:6-7). Jehoahaz, for victory over Hazael (2Ki 13:4). Priests and Levites, when blessing the people (2Ch 30:27). Hezekiah and Isaiah, for deliverance from Sennacherib (2Ki 19:14-20; 2Ch 32:20-23), to save Hezekiah's life (2Ki 20:1-7, 11; 2Ch 32:24). Manasseh, for deliverance from the king of Babylon (2Ch 33:13, 19). Reubenites, for deliverance from the Hagrites (1Ch 5:20). The Jews, returning from the Captivity (Ezr 8:21, 23). Ezekiel, to have the baking of his bread of affliction changed (Eze 4:12-15). Daniel, for the interpretation of Nebuchadnezzar's dream (Da 2:19-23), interceding for the people (Da 9:20-23), in a vision (Da 10:12).

Zechariah, for a son (Lk 1:13). The leper, for healing (Mt 8:2-3; Mk 1:40-43; Lk 5:12-13). Centurion, for his servant (Mt 8:5-13; Lk 7:3-10; Jn 4:50-51). Peter, asking that Tabitha be restored (Ac 9:40). The disciples, for Peter (Ac 12:5-17). Paul, to be restored to health (2Co 1:9-11).

Confession in:

(Lev 26:40; Ezr 10:1; Lk 15:21; 16:13). Commanded (Lev 5:5; Nu 5:6-7; Jer 3:13, 25). A condition of forgiveness (1Ki 8:47, 49-50; Pr 28:13; 1Jn 1:9).

Instances of—

(Jdg 10:10, 15; 1Sa 12:10; Ne 9:2-3, 33-35; Ps 31:10; 32:5; 38:4, 18; 40:11-12; 41:4; 51:2-5; 69:5; 106:6; 119:176; 130:3). Moses for Israel (Ex 32:31-32; 34:9). Ezra confesses for Judah (Ezr 9:6-15). Nehemiah confesses for Judah (Ne 1:4-11). Isaiah confesses for Judah (Isa 14:20-21; 59:12-15; 64:5-7). Jeremiah confesses for Judah (Jer 14:7, 20; La 1:18, 20; 3:42). Daniel confesses for Judah (Da 9:5-15).

Commanded:

(1Ch 16:11, 35; Ps 105:3-4; Isa 55:6; La 3:1; Lk 18:1; Eph 1:18; Php 4:6; Col 4:2; 1Th 5:17-18; 1Ti 2:8; Heb 4:16).

Exemplified:

By Eliezer (Ge 24:12). Jacob (Ge 32:9-12). Gideon (Jdg 6:22, 36, 39). Hannah (1Sa 1:10, 13). David (2Sa 7:18-29). Solomon at the dedication of the temple (1Ki 8:23-53; 2Ch 6:14-42). Hezekiah (2Ki 20:2). Isaiah (2Ki 20:11). Manasseh (2Ch 33:18-19). Ezra (Ezr 9:5-15). Nehemiah (Ne 2:4). Jeremiah (Jer 32:16-25). Daniel (Da 9:3-19). Jonah (Jnh 2:1-9). Habakkuk (Hab 1:2). Anna (Lk 2:37). Jesus (Mt 14:23; 26:36, 39; Mk 1:35; 6:46; Lk 5:16; 6:12; 9:18, 28-29). Paul (Ac 9:11). Peter (Ac 9:40; 10:9). Cornelius (Ac 10:30).

Persistence in:

(Ps 17:1-6; 22:1-2, 19; 28:1-2; 35:22-23; 55:1-2, 16-17; 57:2; 61:1-2; 70:5; 86:3, 6; 88:1-2, 9, 13; 102:1-28; 119:145-147; 130:1-2; 141:1-2; 142:1-2; Isa 62:7; Hos 12:4; Lk 11:5-8; 18:1-7).

Instances of—

Abraham (Ge 18:23-32). Jacob (Ge 32:24-30). Moses (Ex 32:32; 33:12-16; 34:9; Dt 9:18, 25). Gideon (Jdg 6:36-40). Samson (Jdg 16:28). Hannah (1Sa 1:10-11). Elijah (1Ki 18:24-44; Jas 5:17-18). Hezekiah (2Ki 19:15-19; Isa 38:2-3). Asa (2Ch 14:11). Ezra (Ezr 9:5). Nehemiah (Ne 1:4-11; 9:32). Isaiah (Isa 64:12). Daniel (Da 9:3, 17-19). Sailors (Jnh 1:14). Habakkuk (Hab 1:2).

Two blind men of Jericho (Mt 20:30-31; Mk 10:48; Lk 18:39). The Syrian Phoenician woman (Mt 15:22-28; Mk 7:25-30). The centurion (Mt 8:5; Lk 7:3-4). Jesus (Mt 26:39, 42; Mk 14:36, 39; Lk 22:42-44; Heb 5:7). Paul (2Co 12:8). Believers (Ro 8:26; Eph 6:18).

Imprecatory:

Asking for vengeance against enemies (Nu 16:15; 22:6-11; 23:7-8; 24:9-10; Dt 11:29-30; 27:11-13; 33:11; Jos 8:33-34; Jdg 16:28; 2Sa 16:10-12; Ne 4:4-5; 5:13; Job 3:1-10; 27:7, Ps 5:10, 6:10; 9:20; 10:2, 15; 25:3; 28:4; 31:17-18; 35:4, 8, 26; 40:14-15; 54:5; 55:9, 15; 56:7; 58:7; 59:5, 11, 15; 68:1-2; 69:23-24, 27-28; 70:2 3; 71:13; 79:10, 12; 83:13-17; 94:2; 109:7, 9-20, 28-29, 119:78, 84; 129:5; 140:9-10; 143:12; 144:6; Jer 11:20; 12:3; 15:15; 17:18; 18:21-23; 20:12; La 1:22; 3:64-66; Gal 1:8-9; 2Ti 4:14-15). *See Imprecation.*

In Adversity:

By Jacob (Ge 43:14). Moses (Ex 32:32). The Israelites (Nu 20:16; Dt 26:7; Jdg 3:9). David (2Sa 22:7). Hezekiah (2Ki 19:16, 19). Jehoshaphat (2Ch 20:4-13). Manasseh (2Ch 33:12-13). The Psalmist (Ps 5:1-12; 7:1-2, 6-7; 13:1-4; 22:1-21; 25:2, 16-19, 22; 27:11-12; 28:1; 31:1-4, 9, 14-18; 35:1-28; 38:1-22; 43:1-5; 44:4, 23-26; 54:1-3; 55:1-17; 56:1-13; 57:1-2; 59:1-17; 64:1-2; 69:1-36; 70:1-5; 71:1-24; 74:1-23; 79:1-13; 94:1-23; 102; 108:6, 12; 109:1-2, 21, 26-28; 120:2; 140:1-13; 142:1-2, 5-7; 143:1-12). Jeremiah (Jer 15:15). Jonah (Jnh 2:1-9). Stephen (Ac 7:59-60). Paul and Silas (Ac 16:25).

In Behalf of the Nations: *See Nation, Sin of.*

Intercessory:

(Ge 20:7; Jer 27:18; 29:7; Mt 5:44; Eph 6:18-19; 1Ti 2:1; Heb 13:20-21; Jas 5:14-16).

Priestly (Ex 28:12, 29-30, 38; Lev 10:17). For spiritual blessing (Nu 6:23-26; 1Sa 12:23; Job 1:5; 42:8-10). To avert judgments (Ge 20:7; Ex 32:9-14; Nu 14:11-21; 16:45-50; Dt 9:18-20, 25-29; Isa 65:8). For deliverance from enemies (1Sa 7:5-9; Isa 37:4). For healing disease (Jas 5:14-16).

For the unrepentant, unavailing (Jer 7:16; 11:14; 14:11).

Of Moses for Israel (Ex 32:11-14, 31-32; 34:9; Nu 14:19; 21:7; Dt 9:18, 20, 24-29). Of Joshua for Israel (Jos 7:6-7). Of Boaz for Ruth (Ru 2:12). Of Eli for Hannah (1Sa 1:17). Of Samuel for Israel (1Sa 7:9; 12:23). Of David, for Israel (2Sa 24:17; 1Ch 29:18), for Solomon (1Ch 29:19). Of Solomon (1Ki 8:31-53; 2Ch 6:22-42). Of Hezekiah for transgressors (2Ch 30:18-19). Of Job for his three friends (Job 42:8-10). Of the Psalmist for the righteous (Ps 7:9; 28:9; 36:10; 80:14-15). Of Daniel for Israel (Da 9:3-19). Of Jesus for his murderers (Lk 23:34). Of Stephen for his murderers (Ac 7:60). Of Peter and John for Samaritan believers (Ac 8:15). Of the recipients of bounty for Corinthian donors (2Co 9:14).

Of Paul, for unbelieving Jews (Ro 10:1), for Roman Christians (Ro 1:9), for Ephesian Christians (Eph 1:15-19; 3:14-19), for Philippian Christians (Php 1:3-5, 9), for Colossian Christians (Col 1:3, 9), for Thessalonian Christians (1Th 1:2; 3:10, 12-13; 5:23; 2Th 1:11-12; 2:16-17; 3:5, 16), for Onesiphorus (2Ti 1:16, 18), for Philemon (Phm 4). Of Philemon for Paul (Phm 22).

See Intercession; Jesus the Christ, Mediation of; Mediation.

Requested (Nu 21:7; Ro 15:30-32; 2Co 1:11; Eph 6:19; Col 4:3; 1Th 5:25; 2Th 3:1; Heb 13:18). *See Intercession, Solicited.*

Of Jesus:

(Mt 6:9-13; 11:25-26; Lk 3:21; Lk 11:1-4; Jn 12:27-28). Before day (Mk 1:35). In secret (Mt 14:23; Mk 1:35; 6:46; Lk 5:16; 6:12; 9:18, 28-29). In a mountain (Mt 14:23; Mk 6:46; Lk 6:12; 9:28). In the wilderness (Lk 5:16). Thanksgiving before eating (Mt 14:19; 15:36; 26:26-27; Mk 6:41; 8:6; 1Co 11:24). In distress (Jn 12:27; Heb 5:7). In blessing children (Mt 19:13, 15; Mk 10:16). At the grave of Lazarus (Jn 11:41-42). For Peter (Lk 22:31-32). For believers (Jn 17:1-26). For the Comforter, the Holy Spirit (Jn 14:16). In Gethsemane (Mt 26:36-44; Mk 14:32-35; Lk 22:41-44; Heb 5:7). On the cross (Mt 27:46; Lk 23:34, 46). Present ministry, at the right hand of the Father (Heb 7:25), Of his apostles (Ac 1:24-25).

See Jesus the Christ, Prayers of.

Of the Wicked, Not Heard:

(Dt 1:45; 2Sa 22:42; Job 35:12-13; Ps 18:41; 66:18; Pr 1:24-28; 15:8, 29; 21:13, 27; 28:9; Isa 1:15; 45:19; 59:2; Jer 11:11; 14:12; 15:1; 18:17; La 3:8, 44; Eze 8:18; 20:8, 31; Hos 5:6; Mic 3:4; Zec 7:12-13; Mal 2:11-13; Jn 9:31; Jas 1:6-7; 4:3). *See Wicked, Prayers of.*

To idols (1Ki 18:26-29). *See Idolatry.*

Penitential:

Of David (Ps 51:1-17), the tax collector (Lk 18:13). *See above, Confession in; See Sin, Confession of.*

Pleas Offered in:

(Ex 33:13; Nu 14:13-19; 16:22; Dt 3:24-25; 9:26-29; Jos 7:7-9; 2Sa 7:25-29; 2Ki 19:15-19; 2Ch 14:11; Ne 9:32; Ps 9:19-20; 38:16; 71:18; 74:10-11, 18, 20-23; 79:10-12; 83:1-2, 18; 119:42, 73, 146, 149, 153; 143:11-12; Isa 37:15-20; 63:17-19; La 3:56-63; Joel 2:17).

Pleas based on God's mercy (Ps 69:13, 16; 109:21, 26-27; 115:1; 119:124). God's providence (Ps 4:1; 27:8). God's promises (Ge 32:9-12; Ex 32:13; 1Ki 8:25-26, 59-60; Ne 1:8-9; Ps 89:49-51; 119:43, 49, 116; Jer 14:21). Personal consecration (Ps 119:94). Personal righteousness (Ps 86:1-2, 4-5, 17; 119:38, 145, 173-176; Jer 18:20).

Thanksgiving, and Before Taking Food:

(Jos 9:14; 1Sa 9:13; Ro 14:6; 1Co 10:30-31; 1Ti 4:3-5).

See Praise; Thankfulness.

Exemplified—

By Jesus (Mt 14:19; 15:36; 26:26-27; Mk 6:41; 8:6-7; 14:22-23; Lk 9:16; 22:19; Jn 6:11, 23; 1Co 11:24). By Paul (Ac 27:35).

PRAYERFULNESS

Commanded (Ro 12:12; Col 4:2; 1Th 5:17). Spirit of, from God (Zec 12:10).

Exemplified by: The psalmist (Ps 5:1-3; 42:8; 109:4; 116:2). Daniel (Da 6:10). Anna (Lk 2:37). The apostles (Ac 6:4). Cornelius (Ac 10:2). Peter (Ac 10:9). Paul (Ro 1:9; Eph 1:15-16; Col 1:9; 1Th 3:10; 2Ti 1:3). Widows (1Ti 5:5).

See Prayer; Prayerlessness.

PRAYERLESSNESS

(Jos 9:14; Job 15:4; 21:14-15; Ps 14:4; 53:4; 79:6; Isa 43:22; 64:7; Jer 10:21, 25; Da 9:13; Hos 7:7; Jnh 1:6; Zep 1:6). *See Prayer.*

PREACHING

The act of exhorting, prophesying, reproving, teaching.

General:

Noah called preacher (2Pe 2:5). Solomon called preacher (Ecc 1:1, 12). Sitting while (Mt 5:1; Lk 4:20; 5:3). Moses slow to (Ex 4:10-12).

Appointed and practiced by Jesus as the method of promulgating the gospel (Mt 4:17; 11:1; Mk 16:15, 20; Lk 4:18-19, 43). Attested to by Paul (Tit 1:3). Grave responsibility of (2Co 2:14-17).

Repentance, the subject, of John the Baptist's (Mt 3:2; Mk 1:4, 15; Lk 3:3), of Christ's (Mt 4:17; Mk 1:15), the apostles' (Mk 6:12). The gospel of the kingdom of God, the subject of Christ's (Mk 1:14-15; 2:2; Lk 8:1). Christ crucified and risen, the burden of Paul's (Ac 17:3).

Jesus preaches to the spirits in prison (1Pe 3:19; 4:9, w Eph 4:9).

Preaching Should:

Edify (1Co 14:1-25). Be skillful (2Ti 2:15-16). Be in power (1Th 1:5). Be with boldness (Ac 13:46; 2Co 3:12-13). Not be, with mere human strategy (Mt 26) with deceit or flattery (1Th 2:3-6).

Effective Preaching:

By Azariah (2Ch 15:1-15), Jonah (Jnh 3), Haggai (Hag 1:7-12), Peter (Ac 2:14-41), Philip (Ac 8:5-12, 27-38), Paul (Ac 9:20-22; 13:16-43). *See Revivals.*

Impenitence Under:

Asa (2Ch 16:7-10), Ahab (2Ch 18:7-26), the Jews (Ac 13:46). *See Obduracy.*

See Minister; Call, Personal.

PRECEPTS

See Commandments and Statutes, Of God; Law.

PRECIOUS STONES

In the breastpiece of the high priest the stones were set, probably, in the order of the tribes of the Israelites. The first stone, ruby, was probably the tribal stone for Reuben; topaz for Simeon; beryl for Levi; turquoise for Judah; sapphire for Issachar; emerald for Zebulun; jacinth for Dan; agate for Naphtali; amethyst for Asher; chrysolite for Gad; onyx for Joseph; jasper for Benjamin (Ex 28:9-21; 39:6-14). Voluntary offerings of, by the Israelites for the breastpiece and ephod (Ex 35:27). Exported, from Sheba (1Ki 10:2, 10; 2Ch 9:1, 9; Eze 27:22), from Ophir (1Ki 10:11; 2Ch 9:10).

Partial catalog of (Eze 28:13). Seen in the foundation of the New Jerusalem in John's apocalyptic vision (Rev 21:19-21). In kings' crowns (2Sa 12:30; 1Ch 20:2).

Figurative (Isa 54:11-12).

See Stones; Agate; Amethyst; Beryl, 1; Carbuncle; Crystal; Diamond; Emerald; Jasper; Ruby; Sapphire; Sardis; Topaz.

PREDESTINATION

According to the purpose of grace (Ex 33:19; Isa 44:1-2, 7; Mal 1:2-3; Ac 13:48; Ro 8:28-30, 33; 9:11-29; 11:5, 7-8; 1Co 1:26-29; Eph 1:4-5, 9-11; 3:11; 2Th 2:13; 2Ti 1:9; Tit 1:1-2; 1Pe 1:2, 20).

Of prosperity to Abraham (Ge 21:12; Ne 9:7-8). Of Joseph's mission to Egypt (Ge 45:5-7; Ps 105:17-22). Of Israel as a nation (Ge 21:12; Dt 4:37; 7:7-8; 10:15; 32:8; 1Sa 12:22; Ps 33:12; 135:4). Of Ishmael as a nation (Ge 21:12-13; 25:12-18). Of famine in Egypt (Ge 41:30-32). Of judgment to Pharaoh (Ex 9:16). Of David as king (2Ch 6:6; Ps 78:67-68, 70-72). Of Jehu's dynasty (2Ki 10:30; 15:12). Of the dividing of Solomon's kingdom (1Ki 11:11-12, 31-39; 12:15). Of mercy to the widow at Sidon (Lk 4:25-27).

P

Of the destruction of the Canaanites (Jos 11:20), of Ben-Hadad (1Ki 20:42), of Ahaziah (2Ch 22:7), of Amaziah and the idolatrous Israelites (2Ch 25:20).

Acknowledged by Job (Job 23:13-14). Of agent to execute divine judgments (2Ki 19:25; 2Ch 22:7; Hab 1:12). Of Jeremiah as prophet (Jer 1:4-5). Of revelation to a chosen people (Mt 11:25-26; Lk 8:10; 1Co 2:7).

Of the death of Jesus (Mt 26:24; Mk 14:21; Lk 22:22; 24:26-27; Ac 2:23; 3:18; 4:28; Rev 13:8).

Of Paul to the ministry (Ac 9:15; Gal 1:15-16; 1Ti 2:7).

Of the times and bounds of nations (Ac 17:26). Of times and seasons (Ac 1:7).

Of the standard of righteousness (Eph 2:10). Of the kingdom prepared for the righteous (Mt 25:34).

Of salvation and election (Mt 20:16; 20:23; 24:22, 40; Mk 13:20, 22; Lk 10:20; 17:34-36; 18:7; Jn 6:37, 39, 44-45; 15:16, 19; 17:2, 6, 9; Ac 2:39, 47; 13:48; 22:14; Ro 1:6; 8:28-30, 33; 11:5, 7-8; 1Co 1:26-29; Eph 1:9-11; Col 3:12; 1Th 1:4; 2:12-13; 2Ti 1:9; Tit 1:1-2; Jas 1:18; 1Pe 1:2, 20; 2Pe 1:10).

Of the wicked, to the day of evil (Pr 16:4), to condemnation (Jude 4). Of the day of judgment (Ac 17:31).

See Election.

PREJUDICE *See Respect of Persons.*

PREPAREDNESS
(Mt 24:44; 25:1-13; Mk 13:32-37; Lk 12:35-48; 19:41-44). *See Faithfulness.*

PRESBYTERY *See Elders.*

PRESCIENCE *See God, Foreknowledge of.*

PRESENTS
To Abraham, by Pharaoh (Ge 12:16), by Abimelech (Ge 20:14). To Rebekah (Ge 24:22). To Esau (Ge 32:13-15). To prophets (1Ki 14:3; 2Ki 4:42). To those in adversity (Job 42:10-11).

Betrothal (Ge 24:53). Marriage (Est 2:18). Propitiatory (Ge 32:20; 33:8-11; 1Sa 25:27-35; Pr 21:14). To confirm covenants (Ge 21:28-30; 1Sa 18:3-4). Rewards of service (Da 5:7). Kings to kings (2Sa 8:10; 1Ki 10:10, 13; 15:18-19).

To corrupt courts, forbidden (Ex 23:8; Dt 16:19; 27:25; Isa 5:23). *See Bribery; Liberality.*

PRESIDENTS *See Administrators.*

PRESS
Crowd (Mk 2:4; Lk 8:19).

PRESSVAT
NIV "wine vat" (Hag 2:16). *See Wine.*

PRESUMPTION
(Dt 29:19-20; Ps 10:6; 19:13; 73:8-9).

Admonitions Against:
(Pr 25:6-7; Lk 14:7-11). Warning against (1Co 10:9-12). Excommunication for (Nu 15:30). Proverbs concerning (Pr 18:12-13; 25:6-7a). Punishment for (Jer 23:34).

Sins of:
The self-righteous (Isa 65:5; Lk 18:11-12). The selfish rich, in forgetting God (Lk 12:18-20). Temptation to (Dt 6:16; Mt 4:5-7; Lk 4:9-11).

In ignoring God (Isa 10:15; 29:16; 37:23-25; Ro 9:23-25, 20-21; Jas 4:13-15). Questioning God's righteousness (Isa 58:3; Ro 9:20-21). Defying God (Job 15:25; Ps 94:7; Isa 5:18-25; 14:13-14; 28:14-18, 22; 29:15-16, 20; 40:27; 45:9-10; Ro 1:32; 9:20-21; 2Th 2:3). Reviling God's prophet (1Ki 22:24). Despising the lordship of Christ, and the authority of the Church (2Pe 2:10-11).

Instances of:
Satan, when he said to Eve, "You will not surely die" (Ge 3:1-5). Builders of Babel (Ge 11:4). Abraham, in questioning about Sodom (Ge 18:23-32). Pharaoh (Ex 5:2). Moses, in scolding Yahweh (Nu 11:11-15, 22). Nadab and Abihu (Lev 10:1-2). Israelites, in ascending to the top of the hill against the Amalekites (Nu 14:44-45, w Dt 1:43). Murmuring (Ex 14:11-12; 17:2, 7; Nu 16:41; 21:5; 1Co 10:9-12). In reviling God (Mal 1:6-7, 12; 3:7-8, 13). Korah, Dathan, and Abiram (Nu 16:3).

Saul, in sacrificing (1Sa 13:8-14), sparing the Amalekites (1Sa 15:3, 9-23). Men of Beth Shemesh (1Sa 6:19). Uzzah, in steadying the ark (2Sa 6:6-7). David's anger at Uzzah's death (2Sa 6:8). David, in numbering Israel (2Sa 24:1-17). Jeroboam (1Ki 13:4). Ben-Hadad (1Ki 20:10). The Syrians, in limiting the sovereignty of God (1Ki 20:23, 28). Zedekiah (1Ki 22:24-25; 2Ch 18:23-24). Uzziah (2Ch 26:16). Sennacherib (2Ki 19:22; 2Ch 32:13-14; Isa 37:23-25). Job, in cursing the day of his birth (Job 3), reproved by Eliphaz (Job 4:5). Jonah (Jnh 4:1-8).

Peter, in objecting to Jesus' statement that he must be killed (Mt 16:21-23; Mk 8:32), in reflecting on his knowledge when he asked, amid a throng, who touched him (Lk 8:45), in objecting to Jesus washing his feet (Jn 13:8), in asking Jesus, "What shall this man do?" (Jn 21:20-22). The disciples, in rebuking those who brought little children to Jesus (Mt 19:13; Mk 10:13-14; Lk 18:15), in their indignation at the anointing of Jesus (Mt 26:8-9; Mk 14:4-5; Jn 12:5), reproving Jesus (Jn 7:3-5). The brothers of Jesus (Jn 7:3-5). James and John, in desiring to call down fire on the Samaritans (Lk 9:54). Those who reviled Jesus (Mt 27:42-43; Mk 15:29-32). Theudas (Ac 5:36). Sons of Sceva (Ac 19:13-14). Diotrephes (3Jn 9).

See Blasphemy; Mocking; Pride.

PRETORIUM *See Praetorium.*

PRICK *See Goad; Thorn.*

PRIDE

Condemned:
Admonitions against (Dt 8:11-14, 17-20; Ps 49:11; 75:4-6; Jer 9:23; Mt 23:5-7; Lk 14:8-9; 20:46-47; Ro 11:17-21, 25; 12:3, 16; 1Co 4:6-8, 10; 5:2, 6; 8:1-2; 10:12; 13:4; 14:38; 2Co 10:5, 12, 18; Gal 6:3; Eph 4:17; Php 2:3; 1Ti 2:9; 6:3-4, 17; 2Ti 3:2, 4; 1Pe 5:3; Rev 3:17-18).

Prayer regarding (Ps 9:20; 10:2-6, 11). Prevented by divine discipline (2Co 12:7). Proceeds from the carnal mind (Mk 7:21-22; 1Jn 2:16). Leads, to strife (Pr 13:10; 28:25), to destruction (Pr 15:25; 16:18; 17:19; 18:11-12; Isa 14:12-16; 26:5; 28:3; Da 11:45; Zep 3:11; Mal 4:1; 1Ti 3:6; Rev 18:7-8).

Rebuked (1Sa 2:3-5; 2Ki 14:9-10; 2Ch 25:18-19; Job 12:2; Jer 13:9, 15, 17; Hab 2:4-5, 9). Repugnant to God (Job 37:24; Ps 12:3; 18:27; 31:23; 101:5; 138:6; Pr 6:16-17; 8:13; 16:5; Jer 50:31-32; Lk 1:51; Jas 4:6).

The proud shall be humbled (Lev 26:19; Ps 52:6-7; Pr 11:2; Isa 2:11-17; 3:16-26; 5:13; 13:11; 22:16, 19; 23:7, 9; 24:4, 21; Jer 49:4, 16; Da 4:37; Ob 3-4; Mt 23:12; Mk 10:43; Lk 1:52; 9:46; 18:14; Rev 18:7-8).

Pride discussed with Job (Job 11:12; 12:2-3; 13:2, 5; 15:1-13; 18:3-4; 21:31-32; 32:9-13; 37:24). Proverbs concerning (Pr 3:34; 6:16-17; 8:13; 10:17; 11:2, 12; 12:9, 15; 13:10; 14:21; 15:5, 10, 12, 25, 32; 16:5, 18-19; 17:19; 18:11-12; 21:4, 24; 25:14, 27; 26:5, 12, 16; 27:2; 28:11, 25; 29:8, 23; 30:12-13). Cited by the psalmists (Ps 10:2-6, 11; 49:11; 52:7; 73:6, 8-9; 119:21, 69-70, 78).

See Rich, The.

Instances of:
Pharaoh (Ex 7-11; 12:29-36; 14). Ahithophel (2Sa 17:23). Naaman (2Ki 5:11-13). Hezekiah (2Ki 20:13; 2Ch 32:25-26, 31; Isa 39:2). Uzziah (2Ch 26:16-19). Haman (Est 3:5; 5:11, 13; 6:6; 7:10).

Moab (Isa 16:6-7; Jer 48:7, 14-29; Zep 2:9). Israel (Isa 9:9-10; Hos 5:5; 7:10). Assyria (Isa 10:5-16; Eze 31:10-11). Jerusalem (Eze 16:56). Tyre (Eze 28:2-9, 17). Egypt (Eze 30:6). Nebuchadnezzar (Da 4:30-34; 5:20). Moab and Ammon (Zep 2:9). Nineveh (Zep 2:15).

The Scribes and Pharisees (Mt 20:6; 23:6-8, 11-12; Mk 10:43; 12:38-39; Lk 9:46; 11:43; 18:14; 20:45-47). Herod (Ac 12:21-23).

See Ambition.

PRIEST

Before the Mosaic Covenant:
Melchizedek (Ge 14:18; Heb 5:6, 10-11; 6:20; 7:1-21). Jethro (Ex 2:16). Priests in Israel before the giving of the law (Ex 19:22, 24).

Mosaic:
(Ex 28:1-4; 29:9, 44; Nu 3:10; 18:7; 1Ch 23:13). Hereditary descent of office (Ex 27:21; 28:43; 29:9). Consecration of (Ex 29:1-9, 19-35; 40:12-16; Lev 6:20-23; 8:6-35; Heb 7:21). Is holy (Lev 21:6-7; 22:9, 16). Washings of (Ex 40:30-32; Lev 16:24). Must be without blemish (Lev 21:17-23). Vestments of (Ex 28:2-43; 39:1-29; Lev 6:10-11; 8:13; Eze 44:17-19). Put on vestments in the temple (Eze 42:14; 44:19). Atonement for (Lev 16:6, 24; Eze 44:27). Defilement and purification of (Eze 44:25-26). Marriage of (Lev 21:7-15; Eze 44:22). Chambers for, in the temple (Eze 40:45-46). Exempt from tax (Ezr 7:24). Armed and organized for war at the time of the disaffection toward Saul (1Ch 12:27-28). Beard and hair of (Eze 44:20).

Twenty-four courses of (1Ch 24:1-19; 28:13, 21; 2Ch 8:14; 31:2; 35:4-5; Ezr 2:36-39; Ne 13:30). Chosen by lot (Lk 1:8-9, 23),

Usurpations of the office of (Nu 3:10; 16; 18:7; 2Ch 26:18). Jeroboam appointed priests who were not of the sons of Levi (1Ki 12:31; 13:33).

See Levites; Minister.

Compensation for—
No part of the land of Canaan allowed to (Nu 18:20; Dt 10:9; 14:27; 18:1-2; Jos 13:14, 33; 14:3; 18:7; Eze 44:28). Provided with cities and suburbs (Lev 25:32-34; Nu 35:2-8; Jos 21:1-4, 13-19, 41-42; 1Ch 6:57-60; Ne 11:3, 20; Eze 45:1-6; 48:8-20). Own lands sanctified to the Lord (Lev 27:21). Tithes of the tithes (Nu 18:8-18, 26-32; Ne 10:38). Part of the spoils of war, including captives (Nu 31:25-29). Firstfruits (Lev 23:20; 24:9; Nu 18:12-13, 17-18; Dt 18:3-5; Ne 10:36). Redemption money (Lev 27:23), of the firstborn (Nu 3:46-51; 18:15-16). Things devoted (Lev 27:21; Nu 5:9-10; 18:14). Fines (Lev 5:16; 22:14; Nu 5:8). Trespass money and other trespass offerings (Lev 5:15, 18; Nu 5:5-10; 18:9; 2Ki 12:16). The bread of the Presence (Ex 25:30; Lev 24:5-9; 2Ch 2:4; 13:11; Ne 10:33; Mt 12:4; Heb 9:2). *See Bread, Consecrated.* Portions of sacrifices and offerings (Ex 29:27-34; Lev 2:2-3, 9-10; 5:12-13, 16; 6:15-18, 26; 7:6-10, 31-34; 10:12-14; 14:12-13; Nu 6:19-20; 18:8-19; Dt 18:3-5; 1Sa 2:13-14; Eze 44:28-31; 45:1-4; 1Co 9:13; 10:18).

Regulations by Hezekiah concerning compensation (2Ch 31:4-19). Portion of the land allotted to, in redistribution in Ezekiel's vision (Eze 48:8-14). For sustenance of their families (Lev 22:11-13; Nu 18:11, 19).

Duties of—
To offer sacrifices (Lev 1:4-17; 2:2, 16; 3:5, 11, 13, 16; 4:5-12, 17, 25-26, 30-35; 1Ch 16:40; 2Ch 13:11; 29:34; 35:11-14; Ezr 6:20; Heb 10:11). *See Offerings.* To offer the first fruits (Lev 23:10-11; Dt 26:3-4). To pronounce benedictions (Nu 6:22-27; Dt 21:5; 2Ch 30:27). Teach the law (Lev 10:11; Dt 24:8; 27:14; 31:9-13; 33:10; Jer 2:8; Mal 2:7). Light the lamps in the tabernacle (Ex 27:20-21; 2Ch 13:11; Lev 24:3-4). Keep the sacred fire always burning (Lev 6:12-13). To furnish a quota of wood for the sanctuary (Ne 10:34). Responsible for the sanctuary (Nu 4:5-15; 18:1, 5, 7). To act as scribes (Ezr 7:1-6; Ne 8:9). Be present at and supervise the tithing (Ne 10:38). Sound the trumpet in calling assemblies and in battle (Nu 10:2-10; 31:6; Jos 6; 2Ch 13:12). Examine lepers. *See Leprosy.* Purify the unclean (Lev 15:31). *See Defilement.* Value things devoted (Lev 27:8, 12). Officiated in the holy place (Heb 9:6). Chiefs of Levites (Nu 3:9, 32; 4:19, 28, 33; 1Ch 9:20). To act as magistrates (Nu 5:14-31; Dt 17:8-13; 19:17; 21:5; 2Ch 19:8; Eze 44:23-24). To encourage the army on the eve of battle (Dt 20:2-4). Bear the ark through the Jordan (Jos 3; 4:15-18), in battle (1Sa 4:3-5).

Figurative (Ex 19:6; Isa 61:6; 1Pe 2:9; Rev 1:6; 5:10; 20:6).

High Priest:
Moses did not designate Aaron chief or high priest. The function he served was superior to that of other priests. The title appears after the institution of the office (Lev 21:10-15; Nu 3:32). Qualifications of, consecration of, etc. *See above, Mosaic.*

Clothing of (Ex 28:2-43; 39:1-31; Lev 8:7-9). Respect due to (Ac 23:5).

Duties of—
Had charge of the sanctuary and altar (Nu 18:2, 5, 7). To offer sacrifices (Heb 5:1; 8:3). To designate subordinate priests for duty (Nu 4:19; 1Sa 2:36). To officiate in consecrations of the Levites (Nu 8:11-21). To have charge of the treasury (2Ki 12:10; 22:4; 2Ch 24:6-14; 34:9). To light the lamps of the tabernacle (Ex 27:20-21; 30:8; Lev 24:3-4; Nu 8:3). To burn incense (Ex 30:7-8; 1Sa 2:28; 1Ch 23:13). To place bread of the Presence on the table every Sabbath (Lev 24:8). To offer for his own sins of ignorance (Lev 4:3-12).

On the Day of Atonement (Ex 30:10; Lev 16; Heb 5:3; 9:7, 22-23).

Judicial (Nu 5:15; Dt 17:8-13; 1Sa 4:18; Hos 4:4; Mt 26:3, 50, 57, 62; Ac 5:21-28; 23:1-5). To number the people (Nu 1:3). Officiate at the choice of the ruler (Nu 27:18-19, 21). To distribute the spoils of war (Nu 31:26-29).

Compensation of. *See above, Compensation for.*

A second priest, under the high priest (Nu 3:32; 4:16; 31:6; 1Ch 9:20; 2Sa 15:24; 2Ki 25:18; Lk 3:2).

Miscellaneous Facts Concerning:
Priestly office performed by prophets (1Sa 16:5). Loyal to Rehoboam at the time of the revolt of the ten tribes (2Ch 11:13). Zeal of (1Ch 9:10-13), in purging the temple (2Ch 29:4-17). Wickedness of (2Ch 36:14). Taken with the captives to Babylon (Jer 29:1). Return from the Captivity (Ezr 1:5; 2:36-39, 61, 70; 3:8; 7:7; 8:24-30; Ne 7:39-42, 63-73; 10:1-8; 12:1-7). Polluted by marrying idolatrous wives (Ezr 9:1-2; 10:5, 18-19; Ne 10:28). Restore the altar and offer sacrifices (Ezr 3:1-7). Supervise the building of the temple (Ezr 3:8-13). Inquire of John the Baptist whether he was the Christ (Jn 1:19). Conspire to destroy Jesus (Mt 26:3-5, 14-15, 47, 51; Mk 14:10-11, 43-47, 53-66; 15:1; Lk 22:1-6, 50, 54, 66-71; 23:1-2; Jn 11:47; 19:15-16, 18). Try and condemn Jesus (Mt 26:57-68; 27:1-2; Mk 14:53-65; Lk 22:54-71; 23:13-24; Jn 18:15-32). Incite the people to ask that Barabbas be released and Jesus destroyed (Mt 27:20; Mk 15:11; Lk 23:18). Persecute the disciples (Ac 22:5). Reprove and threaten Peter and John (Ac 4:6-21; 5:17-41). Try, condemn, and stone Stephen (Ac 6:12-15; 7). Paul brought before (Ac 22:30; 23:1-5). Many converts among (Ac 6:7).

Corrupt:
(Jer 23:11-12; Eze 22:26; Lk 10:31). Instances of: Eli's sons (1Sa 2:12-17, 22), of the returned exiles (Ezr 9:1-2; 10:18-22; Ne 13:4-9, 13, 28-29).

Idolatrous (1Ki 12:32; 2Ki 10:19; 11:18; 23:5; 2Ch 23:17; 34:4-5; Jer 48:35; Hos 10:5; Zep 1:4).

PRIMOGENITURE *See Birthright; Firstborn.*

PRINCE OF PEACE *See Jesus.*

PRINCE, PRINCESS
A prince is a leader, an exalted person clothed with authority. A princess is the daughter or wife of a chief or king. The prince may be the head of a family or tribe, a ruler, governor, magistrate, satrap, or royal descendant (Nu 22:8; 1Sa 18:30). He may also be a spiritual ruler (Isa 9:6) or the ruler of demons (Mt 9:34).

PRINCIPALITIES
1. Rule; ruler (Eph 1:21; Tit 3:1).

2. Order of powerful angels and demons (Ro 8:38; Eph 3:10; 6:12). *See Demons.*

PRINT
A mark made by pressure (Lev 19:28; Jn 20:25).

PRISCILLA, PRISCA
Priscilla (diminutive of Prisca) was the wife of the Jewish Christian Aquila, with whom she is always mentioned in the NT; tentmakers; had a church in their house; taught Apollos; assisted Paul (Ac 18:2, 26; Ro 16:3; 1Co 16:19; 2Ti 4:19).

PRISON
Prisoners were often put in dry wells or cisterns (Ge 37:24; Jer 38:6-13), or dungeons which were part of a palace (1Ki 22:27). The Herods and the Romans had royal prisons (Lk 3:20; Ac 12:4; 23:10, 35). Jesus foretells imprisonment for his disciples (Lk 21:12). Disobedient spirits are now in prison (1Pe 3:19). Satan will be imprisoned (Rev 20:7).

PRISONERS

General:
Required to labor (Jdg 16:21). Kept on bread and water of affliction (1Ki 22:27; 2Ch 18:26; Isa 30:20), in chains (Ac 12:6), in stocks (Pr 7:22; Jer 29:26; Ac 16:24).

Confined in the court of the palace (Jer 32:2), house of the scribe (Jer 37:15), house of captain of the guard (Ge 40:3). Visited by friends (Mt 11:2; Ac 24:23). Bound to soldiers (Ac 12:6-7).

Severe hardships of, mitigated (Jer 37:20-21). Cruelty to (Jer 38:6; La 3:53-54). *See Captive.* Keepers responsible for (Ac 12:18-19). Tortured to extort self-incriminating testimony (Ac 22:24). Flogged (Mt 27:26; Mk 15:15; Ac 16:23, 33; 2Co 6:5; 11:23-24). *See Flog, Flogging; Scourging.* Permitted to make defense (Ac 24:10; 25:8, 16; 26:1; 2Ti 4:16).

Kindness to: By the prison keeper to Jeremiah (Jer 38:7-28), by Philippian jailer to Paul (Ac 16:33), by Felix (Ac 24:23), by Julius, the centurion (Ac 27:1, 3; 28:16, 30-31). To be visited and ministered to (Mt 25:35-46). Released at feasts (Mt 27:15-17; Mk 15:6; Lk 23:17; Jn 18:39).

Of War:
Put to death (Jos 10:16-27; 1Sa 15:33; 27:11; 2Sa 12:31; 2Ki 25:7; 1Ch 20:3; Hos 13:16; Am 1:13; La 3:34), by divine command (Nu 31:9, 17). Thumbs and toes cut off (Jdg 1:6-7). Blinded (2Ki 25:7). *See Captive.*

Consolations for (Ps 69:33; 79:11; 102:19-20; 146:7).

See Captive; Imprisonment.

Examples of:
Joseph (Ge 39:20-23; 40; 41:44). Jeremiah (Jer 38:6-28; 39:14). John the Baptist (Mt 11:2; 14:3-12; Mk 6:17; Lk 3:20). Jesus (Mt 26:47-75; 27; Mk 14:43-72; 15; Lk 22:47-71; 23; Jn 18:3-40; 19). Apostles (Ac 5:17-42). Peter (Ac 12:3-19). Paul (Ac 16:19-40; 21:27-40; 22-28). Silas (Ac 16:19-40).

Figurative: (Isa 61:1; Lk 4:18).

PRIVILEGE *See Judgment, According to Opportunity and Works; Responsibility.*

PRIZE A reward of competition according to the rules (1Co 9:24-27), figurative of living the Christian life by faith (Php 3:14; Col 2:18).

PROBATION A period of critical examination and evaluation (Ro 5:3-4).

Adam on (Ge 2:15-17; 3:3). Amorites (Ge 15:16). Solomon (1Ki 3:14; 9:4-9, w 11:9-12). Taught in parables of the talents and minas (Mt 25:14-30; Lk 19:12-27), the fig tree (Lk 13:6-9), embezzling steward (Lk 16:1-12). Taught by the author of Hebrews (Heb 6).

None after death (Mt 12:32; 25:10-13; 26:4).

See Perseverance.

PROCHORUS *See Procorus.*

PROCLAMATION Imperial (2Ch 30:1-10; Est 1:22; 6:9; 8:10-14; Isa 40:3, 9; Da 3:4-7; 4:1; 5:29). Emancipation (2Ch 36:23; Ezr 1:1-4).

PROCONSUL (*for the consul*). Roman official who served as deputy consul in a Roman province; term of the office was usually one year; Sergius Paulus and Gallio were proconsuls (Ac 13:7; 18:12).

PROCORUS An early Christian deacon (Ac 6:5).

PROCRASTINATION (Eze 11:2-3; 12:22, 27-28). Rebuked (Mt 8:21-22; Lk 9:59, 61). Admonition against (1Th 5:2-3). Forbidden (Ex 22:29). Warning against (Heb 3:7-19).

Parables of: Evil servant (Mt 24:48-51). The five foolish virgins (Mt 25:2-13).

See Excuses.

Instances of: Pharaoh (Ex 8:10). Elisha (1Ki 19:20-21). Esther (Est 5:8). Disciple of Christ whose father died (Mt 8:21; Lk 9:59, 61). Felix (Ac 24:25).

PROCURATOR The governor of a Roman province appointed by the emperor; often subject to the imperial legate of a larger political area. Pilate, Felix, and Festus were procurators (Mt 27:2; Ac 23:24; 26:30).

PRODIGAL SON Parable of (Lk 15:11-32).

PRODIGALITY *See Extravagance; Frugality; Industry.*

PROFANATION Of God's name (Lev 20:3; Pr 30:9), forbidden (Ex 20:7; 18:21; 19:12; 21:6; 22:2-3; Dt 5:11).

Instances of: (Ps 139:20; Isa 52:5; Ro 2:24). Of the Sabbath (Ne 13:15-22; Eze 20:12-13, 16; 22:8; 23:38). Of the house of God (2Ch 33:7; Ne 13:7; Jer 7:11; Mt 21:13; Mk 11:17; Lk 19:46). Of holy things: Forbidden (Lev 22:15).

See Profane; Profanity.

PROFANE (*unloose, set free*). To desecrate or defile (Ex 31:14; Lev 19:8, 12; Eze 22:26; Mt 12:5), common as opposed to holy (Eze 28:16; 42:20), godless, unholy (Heb 12:16). *See Sacrilege.*

PROFANITY Of the name of God. *See God, Name of.* Of the Sabbath. *See Sabbath.*

See Blasphemy; Oath.

PROFESSION False (Pr 20:6; Hos 8:2). Of faith in Jesus. *See Confession; Testimony, Religious.*

PROGNOSTICATION By astrologers (Isa 47:13). *See Prophecy; Prophets.*

PROHIBITION Of the use of intoxicating beverages. To priests on duty (Lev 10:9). To Nazirites (Nu 6:3-4).

See Abstinence; Commandments and Statutes, Of God; Drunkenness.

PROMISCUITY Punished by death under the law (Dt 22:20-21).

Figurative of Israel's alliances with the nations and their gods (Eze 16; 23).

See Adultery; Bestiality; Fornication; Homosexual; Prostitute.

PROMISE First promise of the Redeemer (Ge 3:15), promise repeated to Abraham (Ge 12:2, 7), promise made to David that his house would continue forever (2Sa 7:12-13, 28). Jesus' promise of the Spirit fulfilled at Pentecost. There are hundreds of promises made to believers (Jas 2:5; 1Ti 4:8; 2Pe 3:9).

PROMISES To the afflicted. *See Afflictions, Consolation Under.* To backsliders. *See Backsliders.* To children. *See Children.* To orphans. *See Orphans.* To the righteous. *See Righteous.* To seekers. *See Seekers.*

PROMISES, OR GROUND OF ASSURANCE

General:

(Heb 6:12; Jas 2:5; 2Pe 1:4; 3:13). Against the recurrence of universal flood (Ge 9:11). Of answer to prayer (2Ch 7:14; Job 22:27; Ps 2:8; 145:19; Isa 58:9; 65:24; Jer 29:12; 33:3; Mt 6:6; 7:7-8, 11; 17:20; 18:19; 21:22; Mk 11:24; Lk 11:13; Jn 14:13-14; 15:7, 16; 16:23-24; Jas 1:5; 5:15-16; 1Jn 5:14-15). Of blessings upon worshipers (Ex 20:24; Isa 40:31). Of comfort in sorrow (Ps 46:1; 50:15; 146:8; 147:3; Isa 43:2; Lk 6:21; 2Co 1:3-4; 7:6). Of spiritual enlightenment (Isa 29:18, 24; 35:5-6; 42:16; Mt 10:19; Lk 21:14-15; Jn 7:17; 8:12, 32; Heb 8:10). Of God's presence (Ex 3:12; Dt 31:8; 1Sa 10:7). Of Christ's presence with believers (Mt 18:20; 28:20). Of forgiveness (Ps 130:4; Isa 1:18; 43:25; 55:7; Jer 31:34; 33:8; Mt 6:14; 12:31-32; Mk 3:28; Lk 12:10; Ac 10:43; 13:38-39; Jas 5:15-16; 1Jn 1:9). Of healing (Jas 5:15). Of the Holy Spirit (Joel 2:28; Lk 11:13; 24:49; Jn 7:38-39; 14:16-17, 26; 15:26; 16:7; Ac 2:38). Of spiritual adoption (Lev 26:12; 2Co 6:17-18; Heb 8:10). Of victory of the Messiah over Satan (Ge 3:15).

Given:

To believers (Jer 17:7-8; Mk 16:16-18; Jn 3:15-16; 5:24; 6:35, 40, 47; 7:38; 11:25; 14:12-14; Ro 9:33; 10:9, 11). Backsliders (Lev 26:40-42; Dt 30:1-3; 2Ch 30:9; Jer 3:12-15; Hos 14:4; Mal 3:7). Children (Ex 20:12; Dt 5:16; Mt 19:14; Mk 10:14; Lk 18:15-16; Eph 6:3).

To the burdened (Mt 11:28-29). The afflicted (Job 33:24-28; 36:15; Ps 9:9; 12:5; 18:27; 41:3; La 3:31). Orphans and widows (Dt 10:18; Ps 68:5; 146:9; Pr 15:25; Jer 49:11).

To seekers (Dt 4:29; 1Ch 28:9; 2Ch 15:2; Ezr 8:22; Ps 34:10; 145:18; Jer 29:13; Mt 5:6; 6:33; Lk 6:21; Jn 6:37; Ro 10:13; Heb 11:6).

To the faithful (Mt 25:21, 23; Lk 12:42-44; 19:16-19; Ro 2:7, 10; Rev 2:10). The forgiving, of divine forgiveness (Mt 6:14; Mk 11:25; Lk 6:37). The humble (Isa 57:15; Mt 5:3; 18:4; 23:12; Lk 6:20; 14:11; 18:14; Jas 4:6; 1Pe 5:5-6). The compassionate giver (Ps 41:1-3; 112:9; Pr 3:9-10; 11:25; 22:9; 28:27; Ecc 11:1; Isa 58:10-11; Mt 6:4; Lk 6:38; 2Co 9:6, 8). The meek (Ps 10:17; 22:26; 25:9; 37:11; 147:6; 149:4; Pr 29:23; Isa 29:19; Mt 5:5). The merciful (2Sa 22:26; Ps 18:25; 41:1-3; Mt 5:7). Ministers (Ps 126:5-6; Jer 1:8; 20:11; Da 12:3; Mt 28:20; Jn 4:36-37; 1Pe 5:4).

To the obedient (Ex 15:26; 19:5-6; 20:6, w Dt 5:11; Ex 23:22, 25-26; Dt 4:40; 6:2-3; 12:28; 28:1-6; 30:2-10; 1Ki 3:14; Ne 1:5; Ps 1:1, 3; 25:10; 103:17-18; 119:1-2; Pr 1:33; Isa 1:19; Jer 7:23; Eze 18:19; Mal 3:10-11; Mt 5:19; 12:50; Mk 3:35; Lk 8:21; 11:28; Jn 8:51; 12:26; 14:21, 23; 15:10; 1Jn 2:5, 17; 3:24).

To those who fear the Lord (Ps 34:7; 103:11-13, 17; 112:1; 115:13; 128:1-6; 145:19; Pr 10:27; 19:23; Ecc 7:18; 8:12). Those who have spiritual desire (Isa 55:1; Mt 5:6; Lk 6:21). Those who endure to the end (Mt 10:22; 24:13; Mk 13:13; Rev 2:7, 11, 17, 26-28; 3:5, 12, 21; 21:7). Those who love their enemies (Mt 5:44-45). Those who rebuke the wicked (Pr 24:25). Those who confess Christ (Mt 10:32; Ro 10:9; 1Jn 2:23; 4:15). Peacemakers, of sonship (Mt 5:9). Penitents (Lev 26:40-42; Dt 4:20-31; 2Ch 7:14; 30:9; Ps 34:18; 147:3; Isa 1:18; 55:7; Mt 5:4). The poor (Ex 22:27; Job 36:15; Ps 12:5; 35:10; 69:33; 72:2, 4, 12-14; 109:31; 132:15; Pr 22:22-23; Isa 41:17). The pure in heart (Mt 5:8). Persecuted saints (Mt 5:10-11; Lk 6:22-23; 21:12-18; 1Pe 4:14).

To the righteous (Job 17:9; 36:11; Ps 1:1-3; 34:7, 22; 37:4-5; 55:22; 119:1, 105; 138:8; 145:20; 146:8; Pr 25:22; Isa 58:8; Jer 17:7; Mt 6:30, 33; 10:22, 42; 24:13; Lk 6:35; 18:6-8; Ro 5:9; 8:30-31; 1Co 2:9; 3:21-22; Gal 6:9; Php 4:7; 2Th 3:3; Rev 2:17, 26, 28; 3:5; 14:13). The wise of heart (Pr 2:10-21).

Concerning:

Answer to prayer (Pr 15:29; Mk 11:23-24; Jn 14:13-14; Ac 10:4; 1Pe 3:12; 1Jn 3:22). Blessings upon their children (Ps 103:17; 112:2-3; Isa 59:21). Comfort (Isa 25:8; 66:13-14; Mt 5:4; Jn 14:16-18; Rev 21:4).

Deliverance, from temptation (1Co 10:13; Jas 4:7; 2Pe 2:9), from trouble (Job 5:19-24; Ps 33:18-19; 34:15, 17; 50:15; 97:10-11; Pr 3:25-26; Isa 41:10-13; 43:2). Divine help (Ps 55:22; Isa 41:10-11, 13; 2Co 12:9; Php 4:19; Heb 13:5-6). Divine guidance (Ps 25:12; 32:8; 37:23-24; 48:14; 73:24; Pr 3:5-6; 58:11). Divine mercy (Ps 32:10; 103:17-18; Mal 3:17). Divine presence (Ge 26:3, 24; 28:15; 31:3; Ex 33:14; Dt 31:6, 8; Jos 1:5; 1Ki 6:13; Hag 1:13; 2:4-5; Mt 18:20; 28:20; Jn 14:17, 23; 2Co 6:16; 13:11; Php 4:9; Heb 13:5; Jas 4:8; Rev 21:3). Divine likeness (1Jn 3:2). The ministry of angels (Heb 1:14).

Peace (Isa 26:3; Jn 16:33; Ro 2:10). Providential care (Ge 15:1; Ex 23:22; Lev 26:5-6, 10; Dt 33:27; 1Sa 2:9; 2Ch 16:9; Ezr 8:22; Job 5:15; Ps 34:9-10; 37:23-26; 121:2-8; 125:1-3; 145:19-20; Pr 1:33; 2:7; 3:6; 10:3; 16:7; Isa 49:9-11; 65:13-14; Eze 34:11-17, 22-31; Lk 12:7; 21:18; 1Pe 5:7). Overruling providence (Ro 8:28; 2Co 4:17). Spiritual enlightenment (Isa 2:3; Jn 8:12). Seeing God (Mt 5:8). Spiritual blessings (Isa 64:4; 1Co 2:9).

Refuge in adversity (Ps 33:18-19; 62:8; 91:1, 3-7, 9-12; Pr 14:26; Na 1:7). Strength in adversity (Ps 29:11). Security (Ps 32:6-7; 84:11; 121:3-8; Isa 33:16). Temporal blessings (Lev 25:18-19; 26:5; Dt 28:1-13; Ps 37:9; 128:1-6; Pr 2:21; 3:1-4, 7-10; Mt 6:26-33; Mk 10:30; Lk 18:29-30). Wisdom (Jas 1:5).

The rest of faith (Heb 4:9). Heavenly rest (Heb 4:9). Eternal life (Da 12:2-3; Mt 19:29; 25:46; Mk 10:29-30; Lk 18:29-30; Jn 3:15-16, 36; 4:14; 5:24, 29; 6:40; 10:28; 12:25; 17:2; Ro 2:7; 6:22-23; Gal 6:8; 1Th 4:15-17; 1Ti 1:16; 4:8; Tit 1:2; 1Jn 2:25; 5:13; Rev 22:5). Living with Christ (Jn 14:2-3; 17:24; Col 3:4; 1Th 4:17; 5:10). Everlasting remembrance (Ps 112:6). Names written in heaven (Lk 10:20).

Resurrection (Jn 5:29; 1Co 15:48-57; 2Co 4:14; 1Th 4:16). Future glory (Mt 13:43; Ro 8:18; Col 3:4; 2Ti 2:10; 1Pe 1:5; 5:4; Rev 7:14-17). Treasure in heaven (Mt 10:21; Lk 18:22). Inheritance (Mt 25:34; Ac 20:32; 26:18; Col 1:12; 3:24; Tit 3:7; Heb 9:15; Jas 2:5; 1Pe 1:4). Heavenly reward (Mt 5:12; 13:43; 2Ti 4:8; Heb 11:16; Jas 1:12; 2Pe 1:11; Rev 2:7, 10; 22:5, 12, 14). Reigning forever (Rev 22:5, w 1Co 4:8; Rev 5:10; 11:15).

See Blessings, Spiritual; God, Goodness of; Jesus the Christ, Compassion of, Love of.

PROMOTION (Ps 75:6-7; 78:70-71; 113:7-8). As a reward of merit (1Ch 11:6).

Instances of: Abraham (Ge 12:2). Joseph, from imprisoned slave to prince (Ge 41:1-45). Moses, from exile to lawgiver. *See Moses.* Aaron, from slave to high priest. *See Aaron.* Saul, from obscurity to a scepter. *See Saul.* David, from shepherd to throne. *See David.* Jeroboam, from slave to the throne (1Ki 11:26-35). Baasha, "out of dust" to the throne (1Ki 16:1-2). Daniel, from captive to premier (Da 2:48). *See Daniel.* Shadrach, Meshach, and Abednego (Da 3:30).

PROPAGATION Of species, commanded (Ge 1:11-12, 21-25, 28; 9:1, 7). *See Barrenness.*

PROPERTY

In Real Estate:

(Ge 23:17-18; 26:20). Rights in, violated (Ge 21:25-32; 26:18-22). Dedicated (Lev 27:16-25). *See Land.*

Dwellings:

Alienated for debt (Lev 25:14-15). Confiscation of Naboth's vineyard (1Ki 21:15-16). Priests exempt from taxes (Ge 47:22). Restriction of to lineal descendants (Nu 27:1-11; 36:1-9). Inherited (Ecc 2:21). Landmarks of, not to be removed (Dt 19:14; 27:17).

Personal:

Rights in, sacred (Ex 20:17; Dt 5:21). Laws concerning trespass of, and violence to (Ex 21:28-36; 22:9; Dt 23:25). Strayed, to be returned to owner (Lev 6:3-4; Dt 22:1-3). Hired (Ex 22:14-15), or loaned (Ex 22:10-15). Sold for debt (Pr 22:26-27), rights of redemption of (Jer 32:7). Dedicated to God, redemption of (Lev 27:9-13, 26-33). In slaves (Ex 21:4).

PROPHECY (*speak before*). Concerning the Church. *See Church, The Body of Believers, Prophecies Concerning.* Relating to various countries, nations, and cities. *See under their respective names.* Respecting individuals. *See individuals by name.*

Concerning Jesus the Messiah:

The first messianic prophecy (Ge 3:15), concerns the announcement of the victor over Satan, the victor described as "the seed of the woman."

Messianic Prophecies and Fulfillments

Prophecy	Fulfillment
Ge 12:3; 18:18; 22:18	Ac 3:25; Gal 3:8
Ge 17:7, 19; 22:16-17	Lk 1:55, 72-74
Dt 18:15, 18	Ac 3:22-23
Ps 2:1-2	Ac 4:25-26
Ps 2:7	Ac 13:33; Heb 1:5; 5:5
Ps 8:2	Mt 21:16
Ps 8:4-6	Heb 2:6-8
Ps 16:8-11	Ac 2:25-28, 31
Ps 16:10	Ac 13:35
Ps 22:1	Mt 27:46; Mk 15:34
Ps 22:18	Mt 27:35; Mk 15:24; Lk 23:34; Jn 19:24
Ps 22:22	Heb 2:12
Ps 31:5	Lk 23:46
Ps 41:9	Jn 13:18; Ac 1:16
Ps 45:6-7	Heb 1:8-9
Ps 68:18	Eph 4:8-13
Ps 69:21	Mt 27:34, 48; Mk 15:23, 36; Lk 23:36; Jn 19:28-29
Ps 69:25; 109:8	Ac 1:20
Ps 78:2	Mt 13:35
Ps 95:7-11	Heb 3:7-11; 4:3, 5-7
Ps 102:25-27	Heb 1:10-12
Ps 110:1	Mt 22:43-44; Mk 12:36-37; Lk 20:42-44; Ac 2:34-36; Heb 1:13
Ps 110:4	Heb 5:6; 7:15-17, 21
Ps 118:22-23	Mt 21:42; Mk 12:10-11; Lk 20:17; Ac 4:11; Eph 2:20; 1Pe 2:7
Ps 118:25-26	Mt 21:9; Mk 11:9; Lk 13:35; Jn 12:13
Ps 132:11, 17	Lk 1:69; Ac 2:30
Isa 7:14	Mt 1:23
Isa 9:1-2	Mt 4:15-16
Isa 9:7; Da 7:14, 27	Lk 1:32-33
Isa 11:10	Ro 15:12

P

Isa 25:8	1Co 15:54-55
Isa 28:16	Ro 9:33; 10:11; 1Pe 2:6
Isa 40:3-5	Mt 3:3; Mk 1:3; Lk 3:4-6; Jn 1:23
Isa 42:1-4	Mt 12:17-21
Isa 49:6	Lk 2:32; Ac 13:47-48; 26:23
Isa 53:1	Jn 12:38; Ro 10:16
Isa 53:3-6	Ac 26:22-23
Isa 53:4-6, 11	1Pe 2:24-25
Isa 53:4	Mt 8:17
Isa 53:9	1Pe 2:22
Isa 53:12	Mk 15:27-28; Lk 22:37
Isa 54:13	Jn 6:45
Isa 55:3	Ac 13:34
Isa 59:20-21	Ro 11:26-27
Jer 31:31-34	Heb 8:8-12; 10:16-17
Hos 1:10	Ro 9:26
Hos 2:23	Ro 9:25; 1Pe 2:10
Joel 2:28-32	Ac 2:16-21; Ro 10:13
Am 9:11-12	Ac 15:16-17
Mic 5:2	Mt 2:5-6; Jn 7:42
Hab 1:5	Ac 13:40-41
Hag 2:6	Heb 12:26
Zec 9:9	Mt 21:4-5; Jn 12:14-15
Zec 11:13	Mt 27:9-10
Zec 12:10	Jn 19:34
Zec 13:7	Mt 26:31, 56; Mk 14:27, 50
Mal 3:1	Mt 11:10; Mk 1:2; Lk 7:27
Mal 4:5-6	Mt 11:13-14; 17:10-13; Mk 9:11-13; Lk 1:16-17

See Jesus the Christ, Prophecies Concerning; Jesus the Christ, King, Prophecies Concerning.

General:

Inspired (Isa 28:22; Lk 1:70; 2Ti 3:16; 2Pe 1:21). "The word of the Lord came to," Elijah (1Ki 17:8; 21:17, 28), Isaiah (Isa 2:1; 8:5; 13:1; 14:28; 38:4), Jeremiah (Jer 1:4; 7:1; 11:1; 13:8; 16:1; 18:1; 25:1-2; 26:1; 27:1; 29:30; 30:1, 4; 32:1, 6, 26; 33:1, 19, 23; 34:12; 35:12; 36:1; 37:6; 40:1; 43:8; 44:1; 46:1; 49:34; 50:1), Ezekiel (Eze 3:16; 6:1; 7:1; 11:14; 12:1, 8, 17, 21; 13:1; 14:12; 15:1; 16:1; 17:1, 11; 18:1; 20:45; 21:1, 8, 18; 22:1, 17, 23; 23:1; 24:1, 5, 20; 25:1; 26:1; 27:1; 28:1, 11, 20; 29:1, 17; 30:1, 20; 31:1; 32:1, 17; 33:1, 23; 34:1; 35:1; 36:16; 37:15; 38:1), Amos (Am 7:14-15), Jonah (Jnh 3:1), Haggai (Hag 2:1, 10, 20), Zechariah (Zec 1:7; 4:8; 6:9; 7:1, 4, 8; 8:1, 18).

Publicly proclaimed (Jer 11:6). Exemplified in pantomime (Eze 4; 5:1-4; Ac 21:11). Written, by an amanuensis (Jer 45:1), in books (Jer 45:1; 51:60).

Proof of God's foreknowledge (Isa 43:9). Sure fulfillment of (Eze 12:22-25, 28; Hab 2:3; Mt 5:18; 24:35; Ac 13:27, 29). Cessation of (La 2:9).

Of apostasy (1Jn 2:18; Jude 17-18), false teachers (2Pe 2:3). Tribulations of the righteous (Rev 2:10).

Miscellaneous, Fulfilled:

The birth and zeal of Josiah (1Ki 13:2; 2Ki 23:1-20). Death of the prophet of Judah (1Ki 13:21-22, 24-30). Extinction of Jeroboam's house (1Ki 14:5-17), of Baasha's house (1Ki 16:2-3, 9-13). Concerning the rebuilding of Jericho (Jos 6:26; 1Ki 16:34). The drought, foretold by Elijah (1Ki 17:14). Destruction of Ben-Hadad's army (1Ki 20:13-30). The death of a man who refused to kill a prophet (1Ki 20:35-36). The death of Ahab (1Ki 20:42; 21:18-24; 22:31-38). The death of Ahaziah (2Ki 1:3-17). Elijah's translation (2Ki 2:3-11). Cannibalism among the Israelites (Lev 26:29; Dt 28:53; 2Ki 6:28-29; Jer 19:9; La 4:10). The death of the Samaritan lord (2Ki 7:2, 19-20). The end of the famine in Samaria (2Ki 7:1-18). Jezebel's tragic death (1Ki 21:23; 2Ki 9:10, 33-37). The killing of Syria by Joash (2Ki 13:16-25). Conquests of Jeroboam (2Ki 14:25-28). Four generations of Jehu to sit upon the throne of Israel (2Ki 10:30, w 15:12). Destruction of Sennacherib's army, and his death (2Ki 19:6-7, 20-37). The captivity of Judah (2Ki 20:17-18; 24:10-16; 25:11-21).

Concerning Christ. *See Jesus the Christ, Prophecies Concerning. See above, Concerning Jesus the Messiah.*

Concerning John (Mt 3:3). Rachel weeping for her children (Jer 31:15; Mt 2:17-18). Deliverance of Jeremiah (Jer 39:15-18). Invasion of Judah by the Chaldeans (Hab 1:6-11), fulfilled (2Ki 25; 2Ch 36:17-21), betrayal of Jesus by Judas, prophecy (Ps 41:9), fulfillment (Jn 13:18; 18:1-9), Judas' self-destruction (Ps 69:25; Ac 1:16, 20), fulfilled (Mt 27:5; Ac 1:16-20). Outpouring of the Holy Spirit (Joel 2:28-29), fulfilled (Ac 2:16-21). Spiritual blindness of the Israelites (Isa 6:9; 29:13), fulfilled (Mk 7:6-7; Ac 28:25-27). Mission of Jesus (Ps 68:18), fulfilled (Eph 4:8, 10). *See Jesus the Christ, Mission of.* Captivity of the Israelites (Jer 25:11-12; 29:10, 14; 32:3-5; Da 9:2, w 2Ki 25:1-8; Ezr 1). Of the destruction of the ship in which Paul sailed (Ac 27:10, 18-44). *See Prophetesses; Prophets.*

PROPHETESSES (*speak before*). Miriam (Ex 15:20). Deborah (Jdg 4:4). Huldah (2Ki 22:14). False (Eze 13:17-19). Isaiah's wife (Isa 8:3). All the daughters of Israel (Joel 2:28-29). Noadiah (Ne 6:14). Elizabeth (Lk 1:41-45). Anna (Lk 2:36-38). Daughters of Philip (Ac 21:9). Jezebel (Rev 2:20).

See Women.

PROPHETS (*speak before*).

General:

Called seers (1Sa 9:19; 2Sa 15:27; 24:11; 2Ki 17:13; 1Ch 9:22; 29:29; 2Ch 9:29; 12:15; 29:30; Isa 30:10; Mic 3:7). Schools of (1Ki 20:35; 2Ki 2:3-15; 4:1, 38; 9:1). Kept the chronicles or records (1Ch 29:29; 2Ch 9:29; 12:15). Not honored in their own country (Mt 13:57; Lk 4:24-27; Jn 4:44). Officiate at installation of kings (1Ki 1:32-35). Counselors to kings (1Ki 22:6-28; 2Ki 6:9-12; Isa 37:2-3; Jer 27:12-15).

Inspired by angels (Zec 1:9, 13-14, 19; Ac 7:53; Gal 3:19; Heb 2:2). Persecutions of (2Ch 36:16; Am 2:12). Martyrs (Jer 2:30; Mt 23:37; Mk 12:5; Lk 13:34; 1Th 2:15; Heb 11:37; Rev 16:6).

Compensation of: Presents (1Sa 9:7-8; 1Ki 14:3; 2Ki 4:42; 8:8-9; Eze 13:19). Presents refused by (Nu 22:18; 1Ki 13:7-8; 2Ki 5:5, 16).

Inspiration of: (1Ki 13:20; 2Ch 33:18; 36:15; Ne 9:30; Job 33:14-16; Jer 7:25; Da 9:6, 10; Hos 12:10; Joel 2:28; Am 3:7-8; Zec 7:12; Lk 1:70; Ac 3:18; Ro 1:1-2; 1Co 12:7-11; Heb 1:1; 2Pe 1:21; Rev 10:7; 22:6, 8).

Examples of Prophets:

Enoch (Jude 14). Joseph (Ge 40:8; 41:16, 38-39). Moses (Ex 3:14-15; 4:12, 15, 27; 6:13, 29; 7:2; 19:9-19; 24:16; 25:22; 33:9, 11; Lev 1:1; Nu 1:1; 7:89; 9:8-10; 11:17, 25; 12:6-8; 16:28-29; Dt 1:5-6; 5:4-5, 31; 34:10-11; Ps 103:7). Aaron (Ex 6:13; 12:1), Eleazar (Nu 26:1). Balaam (Nu 23:5, 16, 20, 26; 24:2-4, 15-16). Joshua (Jos 4:15).

Samuel (1Sa 3:1, 4-10, 19-21; 9:6, 15-20; 15:16). Saul (1Sa 10:6-7, 10-13; 19:23). Saul's men (1Sa 19:20). David (2Sa 23:2-3; Mk 12:36). Nathan (2Sa 7:3-4; 2Sa 7:8). Gad (2Sa 24:11). Ahijah (1Ki 14:5). Elijah (1Ki 17:1, 24; 19:15; 2Ki 10:10). Micaiah (1Ki 22:14, 28; 2Ch 18:27). Elisha (2Ki 2:9; 3:11-12, 15; 5:8; 6:8-12, 32). Jahaziel (2Ch 20:14). Azariah (2Ch 15:1-2). Zechariah, the son of Jehoiada (2Ch 24:20; 26:5).

Isaiah (2Ki 20:4; Isa 6:1-9; 8:11; 44:26; Ac 28:25). Jeremiah (2Ch 36:12; Jer 1:1-19; 2:1; 7:1; 11:1, 18; 13:1-3; 16:1; 18:1; 20:9; 23:9; 24:4; 25:3; 26:1-2, 12; 27:1-2; 29:30; 33:1; 34:1; 42:4, 7; Da 9:2). Ezekiel (Eze 1:1, 3; 2:1-2, 4-5; 3:10-12, 14, 16-17, 22, 24, 27; 8:1; 11:1, 4-5, 24; 33:22; 37:1; 40:1; 43:5-6). Daniel (Da 2:19; 7:16; 8:16; 9:22; 10:7-9). Hosea (Hos 1:1-2). Joel (Joel 1:1). Amos (Am 3:7-8; 7:14-15). Obadiah (Ob 1). Jonah (Jnh 1:1; 3:1-2). Micah (Mic 1:1; 3:8). Habakkuk (Hab 1:1). Haggai (Hag 1:13). Zechariah, the son of Berekiah (Zec 2:9; 7:8).

Elizabeth (Lk 1:41). Zechariah (Lk 1:67). Simeon (Lk 2:26-27). John the Baptist (Lk 3:2). The apostles (Ac 2:4). Philip (Ac 8:29). Agabus (Ac 11:28; 21:10-11). Disciple at Tyre (Ac 21:4), John the apostle (Rev 1:10-11).

See Revelation; Word of God, Inspiration of.

False:

(Dt 18:21-22; 1Ki 13:18; Ne 6:12; Jer 23:16-27, 30-32; La 2:14). Warnings against (Dt 13:1-3; Mt 24:5, 23-24, 26; Mk 13:6, 21-22; Lk 21:8). Denunciations against (Dt 18:20; Jer 14:15). Punishment of (Dt 18:20; Jer 14:13-16; 20:6; 28:16-17; 29:32; Zec 13:3). Drunken (Isa 28:7).

Instances of—

Noadiah (Ne 6:14), four hundred in Samaria (1Ki 22:6-12; 2Ch 18:5), Pashhur (Jer 20:6), Hanani (Jer 28; Ro 15:16).

Idolatrous—

(1Ki 18:19, 22, 25-28, 40).

See Minister, False and Corrupt.

PROPHETS, THE MINOR Also known as "The Book of the Twelve." In Ecclesiasticus (an Apocryphal book written c. 190 B.C.), Jesus ben Sirach spoke of "the twelve prophets" (Sir 49:10) as a unit parallel to Isaiah, Jeremiah and Ezekiel. He thus indicated that these twelve prophecies were at that time thought of as a unit and were probably already written together on one scroll, as is the case in later times. Josephus (*Against Apion*, 1.8.3) also was aware of this grouping. Augustine (*The City of God*, 18.25) called them the "Minor Prophets," referring to the small size of these books by comparison with the major prophetic books and not at all suggesting that they are of minor importance.

In the tradition of Jewish canon these works are arranged in what was thought to be their chronological order:

(1) the books that came from the period of Assyrian power (Hosea, Joel, Amos, Obadiah, Jonah, Micah),

(2) those written about the time of the decline of Assyria (Nahum, Habakkuk, Zephaniah) and

(3) those dating from the postexilic era (Haggai, Zechariah, Malachi).

On the other hand, their order in the Septuagint (the earliest Greek translation of the OT) is: Hosea, Amos, Micah, Joel, Obadiah, Jonah, Nahum, Habakkuk, Zephaniah, Haggai, Zechariah, Malachi (the order of the first six was probably determined by length, except for Jonah, which is placed last among them because of its different character).

In any event, it appears that within a century after the composition of Malachi the Jews had brought together the twelve shorter prophecies to form a book (scroll) of prophetic writings, which was received as canonical and paralleled the three major prophetic books of Isaiah, Jeremiah and Ezekiel. The great Greek manuscripts Alexandrinus and Vaticanus place the minor prophets before the major prophets, but in the traditional Jewish canon and in all modern versions they appear after them.

PROPITIATION (*to cover*). To appease the wrath of God so that his justice and holiness will be satisfied and he can forgive sin. Propitiation does not make God merciful; it makes divine forgiveness possible. An atonement must be provided; in OT times, animal sacrifices; now, the death of Christ for man's sin. Through Christ's death propitiation is made for man's sin (Ro 3:25; 5:1, 10-11; 2Co 5:18-19; Col 1:20-22; 1Jn 2:2; 4:10; Heb 9:5).

See Atonement.

PROSELYTE A person of Gentile origin who had accepted the Jewish religion, whether living in Israel or elsewhere (Mt 23:15; Ac 2:10; 6:5; 13:43). A distinction was apparently made between uncircumcised proselytes, i.e., those who had not fully identified themselves with the Jewish nation and religion; and circumcised proselytes, those who identified themselves fully with Judaism. *See Converts.*

PROSPERITY From God (Ge 33:11; 49:24-26; Ps 127:1; 128:1-2). Design of (Ecc 7:14). Promised to the righteous (Job 22:23-27).

Evil effects of: Pride in (2Ch 32:25). Forgetfulness of God in (2Ch 12:1; 26:16; Hos 4:7). The prosperous despise the unfortunate (Job 12:5). Dangers of (Dt 8:10-18; 31:20; 32:15; Jer 5:7; Hos 13:6).

Instances of wisdom in: Joseph and Daniel as deduced from their general conduct. *See Joseph, 1; Daniel.*

See Blessings, Temporal; Rich, The; Riches.

PROSTITUTE Forbidden (Lev 19:29; Dt 23:17). Punishment of (Lev 21:9). Shamelessness of (Pr 2:16; 7:11-27; 9:13-18). Schemes of (Pr 7:10; 9:14-17; Isa 23:15-16; Hos 2:13). To be shunned (Pr 5:3-20; 7:25-27).

In ancient heathen worship a special class of prostitutes was connected with shrines and temples (Ge 38:15, 21, 22), male (1Ki 14:24; 15:12). *See Shrine.* Their earnings were not to be received at the temple (Dt 23:17-18). The term is often used in the OT to refer to religious unfaithfulness (Ex 34:15-16; Isa 1:21; Jer 2:20; Eze 23).

Rahab (Jos 2:3-6; 6:17, 23, 25; Heb 11:31). Jephthah, the son of (Jdg 11:1). Gomer (Hos 1:2-3; 3:3). Babylon (Rev 17).

PROSTRATION *See Obeisance; Worship, Attitude in.*

PROTRACTED MEETINGS (1Ki 8:65; 2Ch 7:8-10; 30:23). *See Revivals.*

PROUD *See Pride.*

PROVENDER *See Fodder.*

PROVERB Pithy saying, comparison or question expressing a familiar or useful truth (Ge 10:9; 1Sa 10:12; Proverbs). Design of (Pr 1:1-4). Written and compiled by Solomon (Pr 1:1; 25:1).

Miscellany of:

(1Sa 10:12; 24:13-14; 2Sa 3:8; 20:18; 1Ki 20:11; Pr 1:17; Eze 12:22-23; 16:44; 18:2-4, w Jer 31:29; Hos 4:9; Mt 12:33, w Lk 6:44; Lk 4:23; 14:34; Jn 1:46; 1Co 15:33; Gal 6:7).

See Proverbs, The Book of Proverbs Arranged Topically.

PROVERBS, BOOK OF

Authors: Although the book begins with a title ascribing the proverbs to Solomon, it is clear from later chapters that he was not the only author of the book. Pr 22:17 and 24:23 refer to the "sayings of the wise." Ch. 30 is attributed to Agur son of Jakeh and 31:1-9 to King Lemuel.

Date: If Solomon is granted a prominent role in the book, most of Proverbs would stem from the tenth century B.C. The role of Hezekiah's men (25:1) indicates that important sections of Proverbs were compiled and edited from 715 to 686 B.C. Perhaps it was also at this time that the sayings of Agur (ch. 30) and Lemuel (31:1-9) and the other "sayings of the wise" (22:17-24:22; 24:23-34) were added to the Solomonic collections.

Outline:

I. Prologue: Purpose and Theme (1:1-7).
II. The Superiority of the Way of Wisdom (1:8-9:18).
  A. Appeals and Warnings Confronting Youth (1:8-33).
    1. Enticements to secure happiness by violence (1:8-19).
    2. Warnings against rejecting wisdom (1:20-33).
  B. Commendation of Wisdom (chs. 2-4).
    1. Benefits of accepting wisdom's instructions (ch. 2).
    2. Wisdom's instructions and benefits (3:1-20).
    3. Wisdom's instructions and benefits (3:21-35).
    4. Challenge to hold on to wisdom (ch. 4).
  C. Warnings Against Folly (chs. 5-7).
    1. Warning against adultery (ch. 5).
    2. Warning against perverse ways (6:1-19).
    3. Cost of committing adultery (6:20-35).
    4. Warning against the enticements of an adulteress (ch. 7).
  D. Appeals Addressed to Youth (chs. 8-9).
    1. Wisdom's appeal (ch. 8).
    2. Invitations of wisdom and folly (ch. 9).
III. The Main Collection of Solomon's Proverbs (10:1-22:16).
IV. The Thirty Sayings of the Wise (22:17-24:22).
V. Additional Sayings of the Wise (24:23-34).
VI. Hezekiah's Collection of Solomon's Proverbs (chs. 25-29).
VII. The Words of Agur (ch. 30).

VIII. The Words of King Lemuel (31:1-9).
IX. Epilogue: The Ideal Wife (31:10-31).

The Book of Proverbs Arranged Topically:

Introduction to Wisdom—

The call of Wisdom (8:1-36; 9:1-6). Benefits of following Wisdom (2:1-22; 3:13-24). Dangers of rejecting Wisdom (1:20-33; 9:13-18). Solomon' personal plea (4:1-27).

Proverbs of Solomon and Sayings of the Wise—

Value of wise sayings (22:17-21). Purpose of the Proverbs (1:1-7).

Preeminence of God: Fear of the Lord (9:10-12; 10:27; 14:2, 26-27; 15:33; 19:23; 28:14). Trust in God or self (3:5-8; 14:12, & 16:25; 16:3, 20; 18:2, 4, 10; 19:3; 20:24; 21:22; 26:12; 28:26; 29:25). Divine providence (15:3; 16:1, 4, 9, 33; 19:21; 21:30-31; 22:12; 27:1).

Insight and Ignorance: Wisdom and folly (13:14; 14:24; 15:24; 16:22; 17:12; 24:7, 13-14). Dealing with fools (26:4-11; 27:22; 29:9). Discernment and understanding (10:13, 23; 13:15; 14:6, 8, 15, 33; 15:21; 16:16; 17:24; 19:8; 20:5; 20:12). Knowledge (10:14; 13:16; 14:18; 15:14; 18:15; 19:2; 20:15; 21:11-12; 23:3-4).

Sharing and Responding to Wisdom: Advice and rebuke (3:1-2; 9:7-9; 10:8; 12:15; 13:1; 13:13; 15:31; 17:10; 19:16, 20, 25, 27; 23:9; 25:12; 27:5-6; 27:17; 29:1). Value of Advisors (11:14; 15:22; 20:18; 24:5-6). Discipline (3:11-12; 10:17; 12:1; 13:18, 24; 15:5, 10, 12, 32; 19:18; 20:30; 22:6, 15; 23:13-14; 29:15, 17, 19, 21). Lawkeeping (28:4, 7, 9; 29:18). Repentance (14:9; 28:13).

Good and Evil: Righteousness and wickedness (10:6-7, 16, 28-30; 11:5-10, 18-20, 23; 12:2-3, 5-8, 12, 21, 28; 13:9, 21, 25; 14:11, 19, 23; 15:6, 9; 20:7; 21:18; 24:15-16; 28:12, 28; 29:2, 16, 27). Integrity and perversion (10:9; 13:6; 15:26; 21:8; 24:8-9; 28:18; 29:10). Appropriate consequences (3:33-35; 10:3, 22; 10:24-25; 11:21, 27, 30-31; 14:14, 22; 16:7; 17:13; 18:3; 19:29; 21:12, 16, 21; 22:8; 26:1, 3, 27).

Sincere Motivation: Motive and the heart (15:11; 16:2; 17:3; 20:11, 27; 21:2; 27:19). False worship (15:8, 29; 21:3, 27). Duplicity (6:12-15; 10:10-11; 11:3; 16:30; 20:14; 23:6-8; 26:23-26).

Concern for others: Love and faithfulness (3:3-4; 16:6; 20:6; 25:19). Love, hatred, and compassion (10:12; 15:17; 17:5; 24:17-18; 25:21-22). Kindness and mercy (11:16-17; 12:10, 25; 21:10). Overstaying welcome (25:16-17).

Concern for Self: Pride and humility (11:2; 12:9; 13:7, 10; 15:25; 16:5, 18-19; 18:12; 19:10; 20:9; 21:4, 24; 22:4; 25:27; 26:16; 27:2; 27:21; 29:23). Selfishness (18:1). Jealousy (27:4). Envy (14:30; 24:19-20). Greed (28:25).

Control of Self: Self-control (25:28; 29:11). Rashness (20:25; 21:5; 25:8; 29:20). Temper and patience (12:16; 14:16-17, 29; 15:18; 16:32; 19:11, 19; 22:24-25; 29:8, 22). Drunkenness and gluttony (20:1; 23:19-21; 23:29-35). Adultery (5:1-23; 6:20-35; 7:1-27; 22:14). Prostitution (23:26-28; 29:3).

Control of the Tongue: Wise and foolish talk (14:3; 15:2, 7; 16:23; 18:6-7; 19:1; 23:15-16). Righteous and wicked talk (10:20-21, 31-32; 11:11; 12:13-14; 13:2; 15:28; 17:4). Appropriate speech (15:23; 16:21, 24; 25:11; 27:14). Maintaining silence (10:19; 12:23; 13:3; 17:28; 18:13; 21:23). Controlled speech (15:1; 17:27; 25:15). Flattery (26:28; 28:23; 29:5). Slander and gossip (10:18; 11:13; 16:28; 17:9; 18:8, & 26:22; 20:19; 26:20). Hurtful talk (11:12; 12:18; 15:4; 16:27; 25:23; 26:2). Quarreling (17:14, 19; 20:3; 22:10; 26:21). Lying (12:19, 22; 17:20; 19:5, 22; 21:6). Power of tongue (18:20-21).

Disharmony and Strife: Solicitation to evil (1:10-19; 16:29; 25:26; 27:3; 28:10). Violence (3:31-32; 21:7; 21:29). Murderers (28:17). Causing others harm (3:29-30). Revenge (20:22; 24:28-29). Dissension and strife (6:16-19; 17:1; 18:18-19). Meddling (26:17).

Honesty: Truthfulness (12:20; 13:5; 24:26; 26:18-19). Accurate weights (11:1; 16:11; 20:10, 23). Boundary stones (22:28; 23:10-11). Wrongfully obtained gains (10:2; 13:11; 20:17, 21). Bribery (15:27; 17:8, 23; 21:14).

Justice: False witnesses (12:17; 14:5, 25; 19:9, 28; 21:28; 25:18). Open-mindedness (18:17). Judicial justice (17:15, 26; 18:5; 21:15; 24:11-12, 23-25; 28:5; 29:26).

Economic Well-Being: Wealth and poverty (3:9-10; 10:15; 11:4, 28; 13:8; 14:20; 15:16; 17:16; 18:11, 23; 19:4, 6-7; 22:2, 7; 23:4-5; 27:7; 28:6, 8, 11, 20-22). Benevolence and generosity (3:27-28; 11:24-26; 13:22; 14:21; 18:16; 19:17; 21:13; 22:9; 25:14; 28:27). Oppression of the poor (13:23; 14:31; 15:15; 16:8; 22:16, 22-23; 29:7, 13). Industriousness (6:6-11; 10:4-5, 26; 12:11, 24, 27; 13:4; 14:4, 23; 15:19; 16:26; 18:9; 19:15; 19:24, & 26:15; 20:4, 13, 17; 21:25-26; 22:29; 24:27, 30-34; 26:14; 27:18, 23-27; 28:19). Conservation (21:20). Surety for another (6:1-5; 11:15; 17:18; 20:16, & 27:13; 22:26-27).

Persons and Attributes: Parents and children (1:8-9; 10:1; 11:29; 15:20; 17:2, 6, 21, 25; 19:26; 20:20; 23:22-25; 28:24). The elderly (16:31; 20:29). Women and wives (11:22; 12:4; 14:1; 18:22; 19:13-14; 21:9, & 25:24; 21:19; 27:15-16). Kings and rulers (14:28, 35; 16:10, 12-15; 17:7, 11; 19:12; 20:2, 8, 26, 28; 21:1; 22:11; 23:1-3; 24:21-22; 25:2-7; 28:2-3; 28:15-16; 29:4, 12, 14). Messengers (13:17; 25:13). Companions (12:26; 13:20; 14:7; 17:17; 18:24; 24:1-2; 27:8-10; 29:24).

Various Concerns: Caution (16:17; 22:3, & 27:12; 22:5). Reputation (22:1; 25:9-10). Courage (3:25-26; 14:32; 22:13; 24:10; 26:13; 28:1). Hope (13:12; 13:19; 23:17-18).

Various Observations: Joy and grief (14:10, 13; 15:13; 17:22; 18:14; 25:20; 27:11; 29:6). Good news (15:30; 25:25). Curiosity (27:20).

The sayings of Agur son of Jakeh (30:1-33).
The sayings of King Lemuel (31:1-9).
A wife of noble character (31:10-31).

PROVIDENCE The universal sovereign reign of God; God's preserving and governing all his creatures, and all their actions (Job 9:5-6; 28:25; Ps 104:10-25; 145:15; 147:9; Mt 4:4; 6:26-28; Lk 12:6-7; Ac 17:25-28). General providence includes the government of the entire universe, especially the affairs of men. Special providence is God's particular care over the life and activity of the believer (Ro 8:28).

See God, Providence of.

PROVINCE Unit of an empire, like those of the Roman Empire. In Persia they were called satrapies. Rome's provinces were divided into two categories: imperial, those requiring a frontier army, and ruled by a legate appointed by the emperor; senatorial, those presenting no major problems and ruled by someone appointed by the Senate—a proconsul (Ac 13:7).

PROVOCATION Any cause of God's anger at sin (1Ki 15:30; 21:22; Eze 20:28; Ne 9:18, 26).

PROXY In priest's service (2Ch 30:17). *See Substitution; Suffering, Vicarious.*

PRUDENCE

General:

(Job 34:3-4; Ps 112:5; Hos 14:9; Mt 7:6).

In restraining speech (Ps 39:1; Pr 12:8; 21:23; 23:9; 26:4; 29:11; Am 5:13). In heeding counsel (Pr 15:5; 20:18). In restraining appetite (Pr 23:1-2). In avoiding strife (Pr 25:8-10; 29:8). In refraining from making a guarantee (Pr 6:1-2).

Proverbs concerning (Pr 8:12; 11:13, 15, 29; 12:8, 16, 23; 13:16; 14:8, 15-16, 18; 15:5, 22; 16:20-21; 17:2, 18; 18:15-16; 19:2; 20:5, 16, 18; 21:5, 20, 23; 22:3, 7, 26-27; 23:1-3, 9; 24:6, 27; 25:8-10; 26:4-5; 27:12; 29:8, 11; Ecc 7:16-17; 8:2-3; 10:1, 10). Illustration of (Lk 14:28-32). Injunctions concerning (Ro 14:16; 1Co 6:12; 8:8-13; 10:25-33; Col 4:5; Jas 1:19).

See Diplomacy; Gentleness; Wisdom.

Instances of:

Jacob, in his conduct toward Esau (Ge 32:3-21), toward his sons, after Dinah's defilement (Ge 34:5, 30). Joseph, in the affairs of Egypt (Ge 41:33-57). Jethro's advice to Moses (Ex 18:17-23). The Israelites, in the threatened war with the two-a-one-half tribes (Jos 22:10-34). Saul, in not slaying the Jabesh Gileadites (1Sa 11:13). David, in his overthrowing Ahithophel's counsel (2Sa 15:33-37). Abigail, in averting David's wrath (1Sa 25:18-31). Achish, in dismissing David (1Sa 29). Elijah, in his flight from Jezebel (1Ki 19:3-4). Rehoboam's counselors (1Ki 12:7). Jehoram, in suspecting a Syrian stratagem (2Ki 7:12-13). Nehemiah, in conduct of affairs at Jerusalem (Ne 2:12-16; 4:13-23). Daniel (Da 1:8-14). Certain elders of Israel (Jer 26:17-23).

Jesus, in charging those who were healed not to advertise his miracles (Mt 9:30; 16:20; Mk 3:12; 5:43; 7:36; 8:30; 9:9), going to the feast secretly (Jn 7:10), in restricting his public appearances (Jn 11:54; 12:36), in avoiding his enemies (Mt 12:14-16; Mk 3:7; Jn 11:47-54). Joseph, in his conduct toward Mary (Mt 1:19). Peter, in escaping Herod (Ac 12:17). Paul, in circumcising Timothy (Ac 16:3), in performing temple rites (Ac 21:20-26), in setting the Jewish sects on each other (Ac 23:6), avoiding suspicion in administering the gifts of the churches (2Co 8:20), his lack of, in his persistence in going to Jerusalem despite the warnings of the Spirit and his friends (Ac 20:22-25, 37-38; 21:10-14), Paul and Barnabas, in escaping persecution (Ac 14:6), Paul and Silas, in escaping from Berea (Ac 17:10-15). The town clerk of Ephesus, in averting a riot (Ac 19:29-41).

See Diplomacy; Tact.

PRUNING To care for and increase productivity of vines (Lev 25:3-4; Isa 5:6; 18:5). Pruning hook (Isa 2:4; 18:5; Joel 3:10; Mic 4:3). Figurative of discipline (Jn 15:2-6).

PSALMODY *See Music.*

PSALMS

Psalms Outside the Book of:

Of Moses celebrating the deliverance at the Red Sea (Ex 15:1-19). Didactic songs composed by Moses, celebrating the providence, righteousness, and judgments of God (Dt 32:1-43; Ps 90). Song of Deborah, celebrating Israel's victory over Sisera (Jdg 5). Of Hannah, in thankfulness for a son (1Sa 2:1-10). Of David, celebrating his deliverance (2Sa 22), on the occasion of removing the ark (1Ch 16:7-36), at the close of his reign (2Sa 23:2-7; 1Ch 29:10-19). Of Isaiah (Isa 12; 25-26). Of Hezekiah, celebrating deliverance from death (Isa 38:9-20). Of Mary (Lk 1:46-55). Elizabeth (Lk 1:42-45). Zechariah (Lk 1:68-79).

Book of Psalms:

Collection and Structure—

The Hebrew Psalter is divided into five books:

1. Psalms 1-41.
2. Psalms 42-72.
3. Psalms 73-89.
4. Psalms 90-106.
5. Psalms 107-150.

The formation of psalters probably goes back to the early days of the first (Solomon's) temple or even to the time of David. The Psalter was put into its final form by postexilic temple personnel, who completed it probably in the third century B.C.

Topically Arranged—

Psalms of affliction (Ps 3-5; 11; 13; 16-17; 22; 26-28; 31; 35; 41-42; 44; 54-57; 59-64; 69-71; 74; 77; 79-80; 83-84; 86; 88-89; 102; 109; 120; 123; 129; 137; 140-143). Didactic psalms (Ps 1; 5; 7; 9-12; 14-15; 17; 24-25; 32; 34; 36-37; 39; 49; 50; 52-53; 58; 73; 75; 82; 84; 90-92; 94; 101; 112; 119; 121; 125; 127-128; 131; 133). Historical psalms (Ps 78; 105-106). Imprecatory psalms. *See Prayer, Imprecatory.* Intercessional psalms (Ps 20; 67; 122; 132; 144). Messianic Psalms. *See Jesus the Christ, Messiah, Messianic Psalms.* Penitential psalms (Ps 6; 25; 32; 38; 51; 102; 130; 143). Psalms of praise (Ps 8; 19; 24; 29; 33; 47; 50; 65-66; 76-77; 93; 95-97; 99; 104; 111; 113-115; 134; 139; 147-148; 150). Prophetic psalms (Ps 2; 16; 22; 40; 68-69; 72; 87; 97; 110; 118).

Psalms of thanksgiving: For God's goodness to Israel (Ps 21; 46; 48; 65-66; 76; 81; 85; 98; 105; 124; 126; 129; 135-136; 149). For God's goodness to good people (Ps 23; 34; 36; 91; 100; 103; 107; 117; 121; 145-146). For God's mercies to individuals (Ps 9; 18; 30; 34; 40; 75; 103; 108; 116; 138; 144).

Superscriptions and authorship—

Of the 150 psalms, only 34 lack superscriptions of any kind (only 17 in the Septuagint). If the superscriptions refer to authorship, authors include Moses (Ps 90), David (Ps 3-9; 11-32; 34-41; 51-65; 68-70; 86; 101; 103; 108-110; 122; 124; 131; 133; 138-145), Solomon (Ps 72; 127), Asaph (Ps 50; 73-83), sons of Korah (Ps 42; 44-49; 84-85; 87-88), Heman (Ps 88), Ethan (Ps 89). Many of the psalm titles include musical terms in Hebrew, some designating ancient melodies, others preserving musical instructions. The meaning of some of these terms is uncertain or unknown. *See Music, Symbols Used in.*

PSALMS OF SOLOMON One of the pseudepigrapha, consisting of 18 psalms in imitation of the canonical psalms, probably written between 64 and 46 B.C.

PSALTERY *See Harp; Lyre.*

PSEUDEPIGRAPHA (*writing under a false name*). Books not in the Hebrew canon or the Apocrypha, ascribed to earlier biblical authors. They were written chiefly during the intertestamental, apostolic, and post-apostolic periods.

PTOLEMAIS A seaport in Asher, formerly called Acco. Paul visits (Ac 21:7).

See Acco.

PTOLEMY Common name of the fifteen Macedonian kings of Egypt whose dynasty extended from the death of Alexander the Great in 323 B.C. to the murder of Ptolemy XV, son of Julius Caesar and Cleopatra in 30 B.C.; Ptolemy I, Soter (323-285 B.C.); Ptolemy II, Philadelphus (285-246 B.C.); LXX translated, Golden Age of Ptolemaic Egypt; Ptolemy III (c. 246-221 B.C.); Ptolemy IV, Philopator (221-203 B.C.); Ptolemy V, Epiphanes (203-181 B.C.); Ptolemy VI, Philometor (181-146 B.C.); Ptolemy VII, Neos Philopator (146-117 B.C.); Ptolemy XI was the last of the male line of Ptolemy I, killed by Alexandrians; Ptolemy XII (51-47 B.C.) fled to Rome; Ptolemy XIII had Cleopatra as his wife.

See Testaments, Time Between.

PUAH (perhaps from the Ugaritic meaning *girl*).

1. Son of Issachar (Ge 46:13; Nu 26:23, ftn; 1Ch 7:1).
2. A Hebrew midwife (Ex 1:15).
3. Father of Tola (Jdg 10:1).

PUBLIC OPINION Jesus inquires about (Mt 16:13; Mk 8:27; Lk 9:18).

Feared By:

Nicodemus (Jn 3:2), by Joseph of Arimathea (Jn 19:38), by the parents of the man who was born blind (Jn 9:21-22), by rulers who believed in Jesus but feared the Pharisees (Jn 12:42-43), by Herod (Mt 14:5), by chief priests (Mt 21:26; Mk 11:18, 32; Lk 12:12; 20:6), by those who feared to further persecute the disciples (Ac 4:21; 5:26).

Kings Influenced By:

Saul (1Sa 14:45; 15:24), David (2Ch 20:21), Hezekiah (2Ch 30:2), Zedekiah (Jer 38:19, 24-27), Herod (Mt 14:5; Ac 12:2-3), Pilate (Jn 19:6-13).

Concessions to:

By Paul in circumcising Timothy (Ac 16:3). By James and the Christian elders who required Paul to observe certain rites (Ac 21:18-26). By disciples who urged circumcision (Gal 6:12). By Peter and Barnabas with others (Gal 2:11-14).

Corrupt Yielding to:

By Herod in the case of John the Baptist (Mk 6:26), Peter (Ac 12:3). By Peter concerning Jesus (Mt 26:69-75; Mk 14:66-72; Lk 22:54-62). By Pilate (Mt 27:23-27; Mk 15:15; Lk 23:13-25; Jn 18:38-39; 19:4-16). By Felix and Festus concerning Paul (Ac 24:27; 25:9).

PUBLICANS *See Tax Collectors.*

PUBLIUS (*first*). Chief man in the island of Malta. Father of, healed by Paul (Ac 28:7-8).

PUDENS (*modest*). A Christian in Rome (2Ti 4:21).

PUHITES *See Puthites.*

PUITE The descendants of Puah, of the tribe of Issachar (Nu 26:23, ftn, 1Ch 7:1). *See Puah.* The Masoretic Text has "through Puvah, the Punite."

PUL

1. King of Assyria. Forced tribute from Menahem, king of Israel (2Ki 15:19; 1Ch 5:26).
2. A place or tribe in Africa (Isa 66:19).

PULPIT NIV "platform" used primarily as a position from which to speak (Ne 8:4).

PULSE NIV "lentils" (2Sa 17:28) and "vegetables" (Da 1:12, 16). *See Vegetarians; Vegetation.*

PUNISHMENT Assumed for others (Ge 27:13; 1Sa 25:24; 2Sa 14:9; Mt 27:25).

See Affliction; Afflictions; Chastisement, From God; Fine; Judgments; Penalty; Retaliation; Wicked, Punishment of.

Death Penalty:

Shall not be remitted (Nu 35:31). In the Mosaic law the death penalty was inflicted for murder (Ge 9:5-6; Nu 35:16-21, 30-33; Dt 17:6), adultery (Lev 20:10; Dt 22:24), incest (Lev 20:11-12, 14), bestiality (Ex 22:19; Lev 20:15-16), sodomy (Lev 18:22; 20:13), promiscuity (Dt 22:21-24), rape of an engaged virgin (Dt 22:25), perjury (Zec 5:4), kidnapping (Ex 21:16; Dt 24:7), a priest's daughter who became a prostitute (Lev 21:9), witchcraft (Ex 22:18), offering human sacrifice (Lev 20:2-5), striking or cursing father or mother (Ex 21:15, 17; Lev 20:9), disobedience to parents (Dt 21:18-21), theft (Zec 5:3-4), blasphemy (Lev 24:11-14, 16, 23), Sabbath desecration (Ex 35:2; Nu 15:32-36), prophesying falsely or propagating false doctrines (Dt 13:1-10), sacrificing to false gods (Ex 22:20), refusing to abide by the decision of a court (Dt 17:12), treason (1Ki 2:25; Est 2:23), sedition (Ac 5:36-37).

P

Modes of execution of Death Penalty—
Burning (Ge 38:24; Lev 20:14; 21:9; Jer 29:22; Eze 23:25; Da 3:19-23), stoning (Lev 20:2, 27; 24:14; Nu 14:10; 15:33-36; Dt 13:10; 17:5; 22:21, 24; Jos 7:25; 1Ki 21:10; Eze 16:40), hanging (Ge 40:22; Dt 21:22-23; Jos 8:29), beheading (Mt 14:10; Mk 6:16, 27-28), crucifixion (Mt 27:35, 38; Mk 15:24, 27; Lk 23:33), the sword (Ex 32:27-28; 1Ki 2:25, 34, 46; Ac 12:2). Executed by the witnesses (Dt 13:9; 17:7; Ac 7:58), by the congregation (Nu 15:35-36; Dt 13:9).

Not inflicted on testimony of less than two witnesses (Nu 35:30; Dt 17:6; 19:15).

Minor Offenses:
Punishable by scourging (Lev 19:20; Dt 22:18; 25:2-3; Pr 17:10; 19:29; 20:30; Mt 27:26; Mk 15:15; Lk 23:16; Jn 19:1; Ac 22:24, 29), imprisonment (Ge 39:20; 40). *See Prison.* Confinement within limits (1Ki 2:26, 36-38).

By God:
According to deeds (Job 34:11; Ps 62:12; Pr 12:14; 24:12; Isa 59:13; Jer 17:10; Eze 7:3, 27; 16:59; 39:24; Zec 1:6; Mt 5:22; 16:27; 25:14-30; Mk 12:40; Lk 12:47-48; 2Pe 3:7).

See Judgment, According to Opportunity and Works.

See parables of the vineyard (Isa 5:1-7), landowner (Mt 21:33-41), talents (Mt 25:14-30), servants (Lk 12:47-48).

Imposed on children (Ex 34:7; Jer 31:29; La 5:7). Not imposed on children (Dt 24:16; 2Ch 25:4).

Delayed (Ps 50:21; 55:19; Pr 1:24-31; Ecc 8:11-13; Hab 1:2-4).

Design of, to secure obedience (Ge 2:17; Ex 20:3-5; Lev 26:14-39; Dt 13:10-11; 17:13; 19:19-20; 21:21-22; Pr 19:25; 21:11; 26:3). *See Judgments, Design of.*

No escape from (Ge 3:7-19; 4:9-11; Job 11:20; 34:21-22; Pr 1:24-31; 11:21; 16:5; 29:1; Isa 10:3; Jer 11:11; 15:1; 25:28-29; Eze 7:19; Am 2:14-16; 9:1-4; Zep 1:18; Mt 10:28; 23:33; Ro 2:3; 1Th 5:2-3; Col 3:25; Heb 2:3; 12:25-26; Rev 6:15-17).

Eternal (Isa 34:8-10; Da 12:2; Mt 3:12; 10:28; 18:8; 25:41, 46; Mk 3:29; Lk 3:17; Jn 5:29; Heb 6:2; 10:28-31; Rev 14:10-11; 19:3; 20:10).

See Wicked, Punishment of.

PUNISHMENT, EVERLASTING Is taught in Scripture for those who reject God's love revealed in Christ (Mt 25:46; Da 12:2). The final place of everlasting punishment is called the "lake of fire" (Rev 19:20; 20:10, 14-15), also called "the second death" (Rev 14:9-11; 20:6). "Hell" in Scripture translates the word *Hades*, the unseen realm where the souls of all the dead are. *Gehenna* is the place of punishment of *Hades; paradise* is the place of blessing of *Hades* (Lk 16:19-31). The reason for eternal punishment is man's rejection of God's provision for the forgiveness of sin through the life and work of Jesus Christ, God's Son (Jn 3:16-18).

See Hades; Hell.

PUNITE *See Puite.*

PUNON A city of Edom. A camping ground of the Israelites, in their forty years' wandering (Nu 33:42-43).

PUR (*lots*). Lot cast to destroy Jews in the time of Esther (Est 3:7; 9:24, 26). Feast of Purim is a Jewish festival commemorating the deliverance of the Jews from mass murder by Haman. *See Lot, The; Purim.*

PURAH (*branch* ISBE; *imposing* KB). A servant of Gideon (Jdg 7:10-11).

PURIFICATION In studying the Mosaic law relating to purifications, it must be kept in mind that sin defiles. To keep this great truth constantly before the mind of the Israelites, specific ordinances concerning purifications were given to Moses; the purpose being, by this object lesson, to teach that sin defiles and only the pure in heart can see God. Therefore, certain incidents, such as eating that which had died of itself, touching the dead, etc., were signified as defiling, and definite ceremonies were prescribed for persons who were defiled. During the period of defilement, and when performing the ceremonies required of them, the defiled were expected to contemplate the defilement of sin and the need of purification of the heart.

Required:
Sanitary and symbolic (Ex 19:10, 14; Heb 9:10). For women after childbirth (Lev 12:6-8; Lk 2:22). After menstruation (Lev 15:19-33; 2Sa 11:4). After intercourse (Lev 15:16-18). For a discharge (Lev 15:4-18). For those cleansed of leprosy (Lev 14:8-9). For eating that which died of itself (Lev 17:15). For those who had slain in battle (Nu 31:19-24).

Of priests (Ex 29:4; 30:18-21; 40:12, 30-32; Lev 8:6; 16:4, 24, 26, 28; 22:3; Nu 19:7-8; 2Ch 4:6). Of Levites (Nu 8:6-7, 21). Of lepers. *See Leprosy.* Of the Jews before the Passover (Jn 11:55).

By fire, for things that resist fire (Nu 31:23). By blood (Ex 24:5-8; Lev 14:6-7; Heb 9:12-14, 19-22). By abstaining from sexual intercourse (Ex 19:15). By washing in water, parts of animal sacrifices (Lev 1:9, 13; 9:14; 2Ch 4:6).

Penalty to be imposed upon those who do not observe the ordinances concerning (Lev 7:20-21; 22:3; Nu 19:13, 20).

Water of (Nu 19:17-21; 31:23). Washing hands in water, symbolic of innocence (Dt 21:6; Ps 26:6). Traditions of the elders concerning (Mt 15:2; Mk 7:2-5, 8-9; Lk 11:38).

See Washing; Defilement; Sanitation and Hygiene; Spiritual Purification.

Practiced by:
Jacob (Ge 35:2). Moses (Ex 19:10, 14). Aaron (Ex 29:4; 30:18-21; 40:12, 30-32; Lev 8:6). Paul, to show his fidelity to the law (Ac 21:24, 26).

Figurative:
(Ps 26:6; 51:7; Eze 36:25). *See Spiritual Purification.*

PURIM (*lots*). A feast instituted to commemorate the deliverance of the Jews from the plot of Haman (Est 9:20-32). *See Annual Feasts; Lot, The; Pur.*

PURITY A Christian virtue (1Ti 4:12; 5:22; Tit 1:15). Word of God pure (Ps 12:6; 19:8; 119:140).

Of the human heart (Ps 24:3-5; 65:3; Pr 15:26; 20:9; 21:8; 30:12; Isa 1:18, 25; 6:7; Mic 6:11; 1Ti 1:5; 2Ti 2:21-22; Heb 10:2).

Blessedness of (Mt 5:8). Prayer for (Ps 51:7; Da 12:10; Heb 9:13-14). Through divine discipline (Mal 3:2-3; Jn 15:2), the blood of Christ (Heb 9:13-14).

Commanded (1Ti 3:9; 5:22; 2Ti 1:3; 2:21-22; Jas 4:8; 1Pe 1:22). Meditation upon, commanded (Php 4:8).

Jesus our pattern in (1Jn 3:3). Exemplified by Paul (2Ti 1:3).

See Holiness; Sanitation and Hygiene; Spiritual Purification.

For symbolisms of purity, *See Colors, Figurative and Symbolic, White; Defilement; Purification; Washings.*

PURPLE A color highly esteemed in ancient times; because of its costliness, it became a mark of distinction to wear robes of purple. Royalty was so dressed. The color included various shades between crimson and violet (Ex 25:4; 26:36; 28:15; 35:6; Jdg 8:26; 2Ch 2:14).

See Colors, Figurative and Symbolic.

PURSE A bag for holding money (Pr 1:14; 7:20; Hag 1:6; Lk 10:4).

PURTENANCE Entrails (Lev 1:9).

PURVEYOR Those providing supplies to Solomon (1Ki 4:7-19, 27).

PUT
1. Son of Ham (Ge 10:6; 1Ch 1:8).
2. The descendants of Put, or the country inhabited by them; Put has also been taken to signify Egypt and is often associated with the Libyans (Isa 66:19, ftn; Eze 27:10; 30:5; 38:5; Jer 46:9; Na 3:9). *See Libya.*

PUTEOLI (Latin *rotten [sulfur] smell* or *well, spring*). Seaport of Italy, eight miles W of Naples; nearest harbor to Rome (Ac 28:13-14).

PUTHITES (*simple*). Family descended from Caleb (1Ch 2:50, 53).

PUTIEL (*he whom God [El] gives*). The father-in-law of Eleazar the priest (Ex 6:25).

PUVAH *See Puah.*

PYGARG *See Ibex.*

PYRAMIDS (possibly *pointed* [like a flame tongue, or a wheat tip]). Tombs with superstructures of triangular form made for the interment of royalty in Egypt. About eighty survive. *See Ziggurat.*

PYRRHUS (*fiery red*). Father of Sopater (Ac 20:4).

Q

QUAIL Miracle of, in the wilderness of Sin (Ex 16:13), Kibroth Hattaavah (Nu 11:31-32; Ps 105:40).

QUARANTANIA The mountain where according to tradition Satan tempted Jesus to worship him (Mt 4:8-10), Tell el-Sultan, a short distance W of OT Jericho.

QUARANTINE For prevention of the spread of disease. *See Sanitation and Hygiene.*

QUARRIES A place to remove building stone (Jos 7:5; 1Ki 5:17, 6:7; Ecc 10:9; Isa 51:1).

QUARTUS (*fourth [born]*). A Christian in Corinth (Ro 16:23).

QUATERNION (*four*). A squad of four soldiers (Ac 12:4).

QUEEN The wife of a king (1Ki 11:19). Crowned (Est 1:11; 2:17). Divorced (Est 1:10-22). Sits on the throne with the king (Ne 2:6). Makes feasts for the women of the royal household (Est 1:9). Exerts an evil influence in public affairs. *See Jezebel.* Counsels the king (Da 5:10-12). Queen of Sheba visits Solomon (1Ki 10:1-13). Candace, of Ethiopia (Ac 8:27).

Queen Athaliah was the only independent female ruler of Israel or Judah. *See Athaliah.*

Queen of Heaven (Jer 7:18; 44:7-19, 25). *See Idolatry; Queen of Heaven.*

QUEEN OF HEAVEN Probably Ishtar, Babylonian female deity (Jer 7:18; 44:17-25). *See Idolatry.*

QUICKENING Coming to life. Of the church: By the Father (Ps 71:20; 80:18; Ro 4:17; 8:11; Eph 2:1; 1Ti 6:13), by the Holy Spirit (Jn 6:63; Ro 8:11; 2Co 3:6; 1Pe 3:18). *See Life; Regeneration; Resurrection.*

QUICKSANDS NIV "sandbars" (Ac 27:17). *See Sandbars.*

QUIRINIUS Governor of Syria A.D. 6-9. His census of A.D. 6 at the request of the emperor Augustus is referred to in Ac 5:37. Another census, in which Joseph and Mary were registered, is mentioned in Lk 2:2. This may indicate Quirinius served an earlier term as governor of Syria and Luke mentions his "first" (NIV) and otherwise unknown census. Or the verse may be translated "This was *before* the census that took place while Quirinius was governor of Syria."

QUIVER (from a root meaning *to hang, suspend*). For arrows (Ge 27:3; Isa 22:6).

R

RA Egyptian sun-god. Joseph married a daughter of the priest of On, center of the cult of Ra (Ge 41:45, 50). The plague of darkness was an insult against (Ex 10:21-23).

RAAMAH
1. Son of Cush (Ge 10:7; 1Ch 1:9).
2. A place in Arabia (Eze 27:22).

RAAMIAH (*Yahweh has thundered*). An Israelite who returned from captivity with Zerubbabel (Ne 7:7).

RAAMSES *See Rameses.*

RABBAH (*chief, capital [city]*).
1. A town in Judah (Jos 15:60), not now identifiable.
2. Capital of Ammon, represented today by Amman, the capital of Jordan, twenty-two miles E of Jordan (Jos 13:25; 2Sa 11:1; 12:27-29; 1Ch 20:1; Jer 49:2-3). Subsequently captured by Ptolemy Philadelphus (285-247 B.C.), who changed its name to Philadelphia; became one of the cities of the Decapolis. Twice spelled "Rabbath" (Dt 3:11; Eze 21:20).

RABBATH-AMMON (*chief city of Ammon*). *See Rabbah.*

RABBI, RABBONI (*[my] great one, [my] master*). The title of a teacher (Mt 23:7-8; Jn 3:2). Ostentatiously used by the Pharisees (Mt 23:7). Used in addressing John the Baptist (Jn 3:26), in addressing Jesus (Mt 26:25, 49; Mk 9:5; 10:51; 11:21; 14:45; Jn 4:31; 9:2; 11:8 Jn 1:38, 49; 3:2; 6:25). Jesus called "Rabboni" (Jn 20:16). Forbidden by Jesus as a title to his disciples (Mt 23:8).

RABBIM *See Bath Rabbim.*

RABBIT Forbidden as food (Lev 11:6; Dt 14:7). *See Animals.*

RABBITH (*great*). A city in Issachar (Jos 19:20).

RABBLE (Ex 12:38; Nu 11:4; Mt 26:47; Ac 16:22; 17:5).

RABBONI (*[my] great one, [my] master*). Variant of Rabbi, the Aramaic word for Teacher (Jn 20:16).

RABMAG NIV "high official"; the Babylonian title of Nergal-Sharezer (Jer 39:3, 13).

RABSARIS NIV "chief officer"; a title used of Assyrian (2Ki 18:17) and Babylonian officials (Jer 39:3, 13).

RABSHAKEH NIV "field commander"; a title of a Assyrian officer sent by Sennacherib against Jerusalem. He speaks publicly in Hebrew to cause disloyalty to Hezekiah and a surrender of the city (2Ki 18:17-37; 19:4, 8; Isa 36; 37:4, 8).

RACA (*empty [headed]*). A term of contempt and scorn (Mt 5:22).

RACAL (*trade*). A city in Judah (1Sa 30:29).

RACE
1. Human. Unity of (Ge 3:20; Mal 2:10; Ac 17:26). *See Mankind.*
2. Foot race. Figurative: (Ps 19:5; Ecc 9:11; 1Co 9:24; Gal 5:7; Php 2:16; Heb 12:1-2).

RACHAB *See Rahab.*

RACHAL *See Racal.*

RACHEL (*ewe*). Daughter of Laban and wife of Jacob. Meets Jacob at the well (Ge 29:9-12). Jacob serves Laban fourteen years to secure her for his wife (Ge 29:15-30). Sterility of (Ge 29:31). Her grief in consequence of her sterility; gives her maid to Jacob in order to secure children in her own name (Ge 30:1-8, 15, 22-34). Later fertility of; becomes the mother of Joseph (Ge 30:22-25), of Benjamin (Ge 35:16-18, 24). Steals the household images of her father (Ge 31:4, 14-19, 33-35). Her death and burial (Ge 35:18-20; 48:7; 1Sa 10:2).

RADDAI (possibly *beating down* ISBE; *Yahweh rules* KB). Son of Jesse (1Ch 2:14).

RAGAU *See Reu.*

RAGUEL *See Jethro; Reuel, 2.*

RAHAB (*spacious, broad*).
1. A prostitute of Jericho who hid Israelites spies (Jos 2:1), mother of Boaz; great-grandmother of King David (Mt 1:5; Ru 4:18-21), shining example of faith (Heb 11:31).
2. Mythical monster of the deep; enemy of Yahweh (Job 9:13; Ps 89:10), applied to Egypt (Ps 87:4; Isa 30:7; 51:9).

RAHAM (*compassion*). Son of Shema (1Ch 2:44).

RAHEL *See Rachel.*

RAIL Taunts of the enemy (Ps 102:6). *See Slander; Speaking or Speech, Evil.*

RAIMENT *See Cloth; Clothing; Dress; Garment; Robe.*

RAIN Forty days of, at the time of the Flood (Ge 7:4, 10-12, 17-24). The plague of, upon Egypt (Ex 9:22-26, 33-34). Miraculously caused by Samuel (1Sa 12:16-19), by Elijah (1Ki 18:41-45). David delivered by (2Sa 5:17-21; Isa 28:21). North wind unfavorable to (Pr 25:23). Withheld as judgment (Dt 11:17; 28:24; 1Ki 8:35; 2Ch 7:13; Jer 3:3; Am 4:7; Zec 14:17). The earth shall no more be destroyed by (Ge 9:8-17). Sent by God (Dt 11:13-14; Job 37:6; Isa 30:23; Jer 5:24; 14:22). Contingent upon obedience (Lev 26:3-4; Dt 11:13-14). Prayer for (1Ki 8:35-36; 2Ch 6:26-27). Answer to prayer for, promised (2Ch 7:13-14; Zec 10:1). Withheld, in answer to prayer (Jas 5:17-18).

In Israel the rainy season extends from October to April; the dry season, from May to September. The early rain occurs in October and November (Ps 84:6; Isa 30:23; Jer 5:24), the latter rain in March and April (Job 29:23; Pr 16:15; Jer 3:3; 5:24; Zec 10:1). Crops are therefore planted so that they will grow during the rainy season.

"Rain" is often used in the OT in a figurative sense. An abundance of rain denotes the rich blessing of Yahweh upon his people (Dt 28:12), lack of rain is a sign of God's displeasure (Dt 28:23-24). In Canaanite religion, Baal was conceived of as the god of rain, and was therefore ardently worshiped.

RAINBOW A token that the earth shall never again be destroyed by flooding (Ge 9:8-16; Eze 1:28). *See Meteorology.*
Symbolic (Rev 4:3; 10:1).

RAISIN Preserved grapes. Given by Abigail to David (1Sa 25:18). Given to the famished Egyptian to revive him (1Sa 30:12). Given by Ziba to David (2Sa 16:1). Given to David at Ziklag (1Ch 12:40).

RAISING From the dead. *See Dead; Resurrection.*

RAKEM (*weaver, embroider*). A descendant of Makir, son of Manasseh (1Ch 7:16).

RAKKATH (*narrow place*). A fortified city in Naphtali (Jos 19:35), probably near the Sea of Galilee on the site of Tiberias.

RAKKON (*narrow place*). A city in Dan (Jos 19:46).

RAM (As a proper name *high, exalted*).
1. The son of Hezron and an ancestor of Jesus (Ru 4:19; 1Ch 2:9-10). Called Aram (Mt 1:3-4; Lk 3:33).
2. The son of Jerahmeel (1Ch 2:25, 27).
3. An ancestor, probably of Elihu (Job 32:2).
4. A sheep. Skins of, used for the roof of the tabernacle (Ex 26:14; 39:34). Seen in Daniel's vision (Da 8:3, 20). Used in sacrifice. *See Offerings.*
Trumpets made of the horns of. *See Horn; Trumpet.*
5. A weapon used to break down doors and gates. *See Battering Ram.*

RAMAH (*elevated spot*).
1. A city allotted to Benjamin (Jos 18:25; Jdg 19:13). Attempted fortification of, by King Baasha; destruction of, by Asa (1Ki 15:17-22; 2Ch 16:1-6). People of, return from the Babylonian Captivity (Ezr 2:26; Ne 7:30; 11:33). Jeremiah imprisoned in (Jer 40:1). Prophecies concerning (Isa 10:29; Jer 31:15; Hos 5:8; Mt 2:18).
2. A city of S Judah allotted to the tribe of Simeon (Jos 19:8).
3. A city of Asher (Jos 19:29).
4. A city of Naphtali (Jos 19:36).
5. Also called Ramathaim. A city in the hill country of Ephraim (Jdg 4:5; 1Sa 1:1). Home of Elkanah (1Sa 1:1, 19; 2:11), and of Samuel (1Sa 1:19-20; 7:17; 8:4; 15:34; 16:13). David flees to (1Sa 19:18). Samuel dies and is buried in (1Sa 25:1; 28:3).
See Ramoth Gilead.

RAMATH *See Ramah, 2.*

RAMATH LEHI (*height [hill] of Lehi*). The place where Samson killed a thousand Philistines with the jawbone of a donkey (Jdg 15:17).

RAMATH MIZPAH (*height [hill] of Mizpah [watch tower]*). Northern boundary line of Gad (Jos 13:26). Also called Mizpah, Galeed, and Jegar Sahadutha (Ge 31:47-49).

RAMATHAIM-ZOPHIM, RAMATHAIM ZUPHIM (*two heights of Zophim*). *See Ramah, 5.*

RAMATHITE (*of Ramah*). Designation of Shimei, King David's overseer in charge of the vineyards (1Ch 27:27).

RAMESES (*Ra [pagan sun god] created him*).
1. Egyptian store city built by Israelites (Ex 1:11), possibly the modern San el-Habar in the NE part of the Delta.
2. The name of eleven Egyptian pharaohs, of whom Rameses II (c. 1301-1234 B.C.) was the most famous, many scholars holding that he was the pharaoh of the Exodus. Some of these pharaohs must have had at least an indirect influence on Israelite life, but none of them is mentioned in the OT.

RAMIAH (*Yahweh is exalted*). An Israelite in the time of Ezra who married a foreign wife (Ezr 10:25).

RAMOTH (*height*).
1. Ramoth in Gilead. *See Ramoth Gilead.*
2. Ramoth Negev. A place probably in the south of Simeon (Jos 19:8; 1Sa 30:27). *See Ramah, 2.*
3. A city of Issachar, allotted to the Levites (1Ch 6:73).
4. *See Jeremoth, 6.*

RAMOTH GILEAD (*heights in Gilead*). A city of Gad, and a city of refuge (Dt 4:43; Jos 20:8; 1Ch 6:80). One of Solomon's district governors at (1Ki 4:13). In the possession of the Syrians (1Ki 22:3). Besieged by Israel and Judah; Ahab slain at (1Ki 22:29-36; 2Ch 18). Recovered by Joram; Joram wounded at (2Ki 8:28-29; 9:14-15; 2Ch 22:5-6). Elisha anoints Jehu king at (2Ki 9:1-6).

RAMS' HORNS *See Shofar; Trumpet.*

RAMS' SKINS Skins of sheep; used for clothing of shepherds and covering for the tabernacle (Ex 25:5).

RANSOM Of a human life (Ex 21:30; 30:12; Job 36:18; Ps 49:7-8; Pr 6:35; 13:8; Hos 13:14).
Jesus as (Mt 20:28; Mk 10:45; 1Ti 2:5-6; Heb 9:15).
Figurative (Job 33:24; Isa 35:10; 51:10).
See Jesus the Christ, Redeemer; Savior, Saviour; Redemption.

RAPACITY Of the wicked (Lk 11:39; 20:14, 47; Jn 10:12; Ac 20:29; Gal 5:15; Jas 4:2; 1Pe 5:8). *See Greed; Wicked.*

RAPE Law imposes death penalty for (Dt 22:25-27). Captives afflicted with (Isa 13:16; La 5:11; Zec 14:2).
Instances of: Dinah by Shechem (Ge 34:1-2). The servant of a Levite by Benjamites; tribe of Benjamin nearly exterminated by the army of the other tribes as punishment for (Jdg 19:22-30; 20:35). Tamar by Amnon; avenged in the death of Amnon at the hand of Absalom, Tamar's brother (2Sa 13:6-29, 32-33).

RAPHA, RAPHAH (possibly *one healed*).
1. Son of Benjamin (1Ch 8:2).
2. A descendant of Jonathan also called Rephaiah (1Ch 9:43) and Raphah (1Ch 8:37). *See Rephaiah, 4.*
3. An ancestor of certain Philistine warriors (2Sa 21:16, 20, 22; 1Ch 20:4, 6, 8). *See Rephaites.*

RAPHU (*healed*). The father of Palti, who was sent from the tribe of Benjamin to spy out the land of Canaan (Nu 13:9).

RAPTURE Theological term not used in the Bible. The imminent translation or removal from earth of the Church at the second coming of Christ (Mt 24:36-42; Mk 13:32; Ac 1:7, 11; 1Co 15:50-52; 1Th 4:14-18; Tit 2:13; 1Pe 3:12; Rev 1:7). Includes both living and dead (1Co 15:50-52; Php 3:20-21; 1Th 4:13-17; 1Jn 3:2). Followed by the marriage of the Church to Christ (Mt 25:1-10; 2Co 11:2; Eph 5:23, 32; Rev 19:6-9), believers being rewarded (Mt 25:19; 1Co 3:12-15; 2Co 5:10; 2Ti 4:8; 1Pe 5:2).
See Second Coming of Christ, The.

RAS SHAMRA (*fennel mound*). The modern name of the mound marking the site of the ancient city of Ugarit, located on the Syrian coast opposite the island of Cyprus; an important commercial center; destroyed by Sea Peoples who overran the area c. 1200 B.C.; reached the peak of prosperity in 1500-1200 B.C. Several hundred clay tablets, forming part of a scribal library, were found from 1929 through 1936; personal and diplomatic correspondence; business, legal, and governmental records; veterinary texts, and most importantly, religious literature. These throw a great deal of light upon Canaanite religion and culture, and Hebrew literary style; they show striking similarities between Canaanite and Hebrew systems of worship. They clarify our knowledge of the world in which Israel developed. *See Texts, Ancient Near Eastern Non-Biblical Texts Relating to the Old Testament.*

RASH Regulations for determining whether clean or unclean (Lev 13-14). *See Disease.*

RASHNESS (Ps 116:11; Pr 19:2). Admonitions against (Pr 25:8; Ecc 5:2; 7:9). Folly of (Pr 14:29; 29:20). Leads to poverty (Pr 21:5).

Instances of:
Moses, in slaying the Egyptian (Ex 2:11-12; Ac 7:24-25), when he struck the rock (Nu 20:10-12). Jephthah's vow (Jdg 11:31-39). Israel's vow to destroy the Benjamites (Jdg 21:1-23). Uzzah, in steadying the ark (2Sa 6:6-7). David, in his generosity to Ziba (2Sa 16:4, w 19:26-29). Rehoboam, in forsaking the counsel of the old men (1Ki 12:8-15). Josiah, in fighting against Neco (2Ch 35:20-24). Naaman, in refusing to wash in the Jordan (2Ki 5:11-12).
Peter, in cutting off the ear of Malchus (Mt 26:51; Mk 14:47, Lk 22:50). James and John, in desiring to call down fire on the Samaritans (Lk 9:54). Paul, in persisting to go to Jerusalem against the repeated admonitions of the Holy Spirit (Ac 21:4, 10-15). The centurion, in rejecting Paul's counsel (Ac 27:11).

RAT(S) Forbidden as food (Lev 11:29), used as food (Isa 66:17). Images of (1Sa 6:4-5, 11, 18).

RAVEN (*crow, raven*). A black carnivorous bird (Pr 30:17; SS 5:11). Forbidden as food (Lev 11:15; Dt 14:14). Preserved by Noah in the ark (Ge 8:7). Fed Elijah (1Ki 17:4-6). Cared for by divine providence (Lk 12:24).

RAVISHMENT *See Rape.*

RAZOR (*any instrument of iron*). Priests of Israel were not permitted to cut their beard (Lev 21:5). Nazirites could not use the razor as long as they were under vows (Nu 6:5).

READING Taught (Dt 6:9; 11:20).

READINGS, SELECT
Judah's Defense (Ge 44:18-34). Joseph Revealing His Identity (Ge 45:1-15). The Deliverance of the Israelites From Pharaoh (Ex 14:5-30). Song of Moses When Pharaoh and His Army Were Overthrown (Ex 15:1-19). David's Lament Over Absalom (2Sa 18:19-33). Lights and Shadows (Ru 1:1-22). Elijah's Miraculous Preservation (1Ki 17:1-16). Elisha and the Widow's Oil (2Ki 4:1-7). Naaman the Leper (2Ki 5:1-14). Esther's Triumph (Est 4:1-17; 7:1-10).
The Brevity of Life (Job 14:1-10). Nature's Testimony (Job 28:1-28). God's Challenge to Job (Job 38). The Beasts of the Field (Job 39).
The Righteous and the Wicked in Contrast (Ps 1). The Triumphant King (Ps 2). Mankind in Nature (Ps 8). Mankind in Extremity (Ps 18:1-19). Confidence in God (Ps 23). The King of Glory (Ps 24). The Glory of God (Ps 29). Our Refuge (Ps 46). The Majesty of God (Ps 77:13-20). The Joy of the Righteous (Ps 84). The State of the Glory (Ps 91). The New Song (Ps 98). The Majesty and Providence of God (Ps 104). In Captivity (Ps 137). The Omnipresence of God (Ps 139). Old Age (Ecc 12:1-7).
Christ's Kingdom Foreshadowed (Isa 35:1-10). The Omnipotence and Incomparableness of God (Isa 40:1-30). The Wrath of God (Am 9:1-6). The Majesty of God (Hab 3:3-13).
Mary's Magnificat (Lk 1:46-56). The Prophetic Blessing of Zechariah (Lk 1:67-80). The Beatitudes (Mt 5:1-16). God's Providence (Mt 6:26-34). Wise and Foolish Builders (Mt 7:21-27). The Good Samaritan (Lk 10:25-37). The Prodigal Son (Lk 15:11-32). The Raising of Lazarus (Jn 11:1-45). The Betrayal (Lk 22:47-62). The Resurrection (Lk 24:1-12).
Peter at Pentecost (Ac 2:1-36). Stephen's Defense (Ac 7). Paul and Silas in Prison (Ac 16:16-40). Paul on Mars' Hill (Ac 17:22-31). Paul Before Felix (Ac 24:1-27). Paul Before Agrippa (Ac 26:1-32). Love (1Co 13). The New Heaven and the New Earth (Rev 21:1-7). The River of Life (Rev 22:1-21).

REAIA *See Reaiah, 2.*

REAIAH (*Yahweh has seen*).
1. A man of Judah, son of Shobal (1Ch 4:2). Apparently called Haroeh (1Ch 2:52).
2. Son of Micah, a Reubenite (1Ch 5:5).
3. Ancestor of a family that returned to Jerusalem from captivity in Babylon (Ezr 2:47; Ne 7:50).

REAPING In ancient times done either by pulling up grain by roots or cutting with a sickle. The stalks are then bound into bundles and taken to threshing floor (Ps 129:7).
Laws concerning gleaning at the time of reaping (Lev 19:9-10; 23:22; Dt 24:19-20).
Figurative (Ps 126:6; Hos 10:12-13; Jn 4:35-38), of deeds that produce own harvest (Pr 22:8; Hos 8:7; 1Co 9:11; Gal 6:7-8).

REASONING With God (Job 13:3, 17-28). God reasons with people (Ex 4:11; 20:5, 11; Isa 1:18; 5:3-4; 43:26; Hos 4:1; Mic 6:2).
Natural understanding (Da 4:36). To be applied to religion (1Co 10:15; 1Pe 3:15). Not a sufficient guide in human affairs (Dt 12:8; Pr 3:5; 14:12). Of the Pharisees (Lk 5:21-22; 20:5). Of Paul from the Scriptures (Ac 17:2; 18:4, 19; 24:25). The gospel cannot be explained by human wisdom (1Co 1:18-2:14).
See Investigation; Philosophy; Wisdom.

REBA (*fourth part*). A king of Midian. Slain by the Israelites (Nu 31:8; Jos 13:21).

REBECCA *See Rebekah.*

REBEKAH (possibly *choice calf*). Daughter of Bethuel, grand-niece of Abraham (Ge 22:20-23). Becomes Isaac's wife (Ge 24:15-67; 25:20). Mother of Esau and Jacob (Ge 25:21-28; Ro 9:10). Passes as Isaac's sister (Ge 26:6-11). Displeased with Esau's wives (Ge 26:34-35). Prompts Jacob to deceive Isaac (Ge 27:5-29). Sends Jacob to Laban (Ge 27:42-46). Burial place of (Ge 49:31).

REBELLION Treasonable (Pr 17:11).
Instances of: Absalom (2Sa 15-18). Sheba (2Sa 20). Revolt of the ten tribes (1Ki 12:16-20; 2Ch 10; 13:5-12).
See Sin.

REBUKE Cain rebukes God (Ge 4:13-14). Pharaoh rebukes Abraham for calling his wife his sister (Ge 12:18-19). Abimelech rebukes Abraham for a like offense (Ge 20:9-10). Abimelech rebukes Isaac for similar conduct (Ge 26:9-10). Isaac and Laban rebuke each other (Ge 31:26-42). Jacob rebukes Simeon and Levi for killing Hamor and Shechem (Ge 34:30). Reuben rebukes his brothers for their treatment of Joseph (Ge 42:22). Israelites rebuke Moses and tempt God (Ex 17:7). Deborah rebukes Israel in her poem (Jdg 5:16-23). David rebukes Joab for killing Abner (2Sa 3:28-31). Joab rebukes David for lamenting the death of Absalom (2Sa 19:5-7).
Jesus rebukes his disciples because of their unbelief (Mt 8:26; 14:31; 16:8-11; 17:17; Mk 4:40; Lk 8:25), for slowness of heart (Mt 15:16; 16:8-9, 11; Mk 7:18; Lk 24:25; Jn 14:9), for sleeping in Gethsemane (Mt 26:40; Mk 14:27), for forbidding children to be brought to him (Mt 19:14; Mk 10:14; Lk 18:16).
David prays to escape Yahweh's rebuke (Ps 6:1; 38:1). Do not rebuke a mocker (Pr 9:8), an older man (1Ti 5:1).

RECAB (probably *rider* or *horseman*, from *to mount, ride*).
1. Son of Rimmon. Murders Ish-Bosheth, son of Saul; put to death by David (2Sa 4:5-12).
2. Father of Jehonadab (2Ki 10:15, 23; 1Ch 2:55; Jer 35:6, 8, 16, 19). Ancestor of the Recabites (Jer 35).
3. Father of Malkijah (Ne 3:14).

RECABITE(S) A family of Kenites descended from Recab, through Jonadab (1Ch 2:55; Jer 35:6). Commanded by Jonadab to drink no wine (Jer 35:6); perpetuation of the family promised as a reward (Jer 35).
See Abstinence; Nazirite(s).

RECAH Unknown place in tribe of Judah (1Ch 4:12).

RECHAB *See Recab.*

RECHABITE(S) *See Recabite(s).*

RECHAH *See Recah.*

RECIPROCITY Returning good for good (Ro 15:27; 1Co 9:11; Gal 6:6). *See One Another.*

RECONCILIATION

Between People:
(Mt 5:23-26). Between Esau and Jacob (Ge 33:4, 11). Between Saul and David (1Sa 19:7). Between Pilate and Herod (Lk 23:12).

Between God and People:
Through atonement of animal sacrifices (Lev 8:15; Eze 45:15). After the seventy weeks of Daniel's vision (Da 9:24).
Through Christ (Ro 5:1, 10; 11:15; 2Co 5:18-21; Eph 2:15-18; Col 1:20-22; Heb 2:17).
See Atonement; Jesus the Christ, Mission of; Propitiation; Redemption.

RECONNAISSANCE Of Jericho (Jos 2:1-24), Bethel (Jdg 1:23), Laish (Jdg 18:2-10). *See Spies.*

RECORDER *See Occupations and Professions.*

RECREATION *See Rest.*

RED Bloodlike or blood-red color (Ex 25:5; 26:14; 35:7; Zec 1:8; Rev 6:4).

RED HEIFER Ashes of red heifer were used for removal of certain types of ceremonial uncleanness (Nu 19:9).

RED KITE A carnivorous bird, unclean for food (Dt 14:13).

RED SEA "Sea of Reeds" in NIV ftns. The locusts that devastated Egypt destroyed in (Ex 10:19). Israelites cross; Pharaoh and his army drowned in (Ex 14; 15:1, 4, 11, 19; Nu 33:8; Dt 11:4; Jos 2:10; 4:23; 24:6-7; Jdg 11:16; 2Sa 22:16; Ne 9:9-11; Ps 66:6; 78:13, 53; 106:7-11, 22; 136:13-15; Isa 43:16-17; Ac 7:36; 1Co 10:1-2; Heb 11:29). Israelites camp by (Ex 14:2, 9; Nu 14:25; 21:4; 33:10-11; Dt 1:40; 2:1-3). Boundary of the promised land (Ex 23:31). Solomon builds ships on (1Ki 9:26).

REDEEMED, THE (Isa 35:9; 51:11; Mt 8:11; Rev 5:9; 7:9; 14:4; 19:6).

REDEEMER *See Jesus the Christ, Savior; Redemption.*

REDEMPTION (*to tear loose; a ransom*). Deliverance from the enslavement of sin and release to a new freedom by the sacrifice of the Redeemer, Jesus Christ. The death of Christ is the redemptive price. The word contains both the ideas of deliverance and the price of that deliverance, or ransom (Ro 3:24; Gal 3:13; Eph 1:7; 1Pe 1:18-19).

Of Person or Property:
(Ex 13:13; Lev 25:25-34; 27:2-33; Ro 4:3-10). Redemption money paid to priests (Nu 3:46-51). Of the firstborn (Ex 13:13; 34:20; Lev 27:27; Nu 3:40-51; 18:15-17).

Of Land:
(Lev 27:19-20; Jer 32:7). In Hebrew society, any land that was forfeited through economic distress could be redeemed by the nearest of kin. If not so redeemed, it returned to its original owner in the Year of Jubilee (Lev 25:24-34).

Of Our Souls:
(Ps 111:9; 130:7). Through Christ (Mt 20:28; Mk 10:45; Lk 2:38; Ac 20:28; Ro 3:24-26; 1Co 1:30; 6:20; 7:23; Gal 1:4; 2:20; 4:4-5; Eph 1:7; 5:2; Col 1:14, 20-22; 1Ti 2:6; Tit 2:14; Heb 9:12, 15; 1Pe 1:18-19; Rev 5:9-10).
See Atonement; Ransom; Redeemer.

REED A water plant (Isa 19:6-7; 35:7; Jer 51:32). Used as a measuring device of six cubits (Eze 40:3-8; 41:8; 42:16-19; 45:1; Rev 11:1; 21:15-16). Mockingly given to Jesus as a symbol of royalty (Mt 27:29). Jesus struck with (Mt 27:30; Mk 15:19).
Figurative of weakness (1Ki 14:15; 2Ki 18:21; Isa 36:6; 42:3; Eze 29:6; Mt 11:7; 12:20).

REEDS, SEA OF *See Red Sea.*

REELAIAH A returned captive from Babylon (Ezr 2:2).

REFINING The process of eliminating by fire the dross of metals. Of gold (1Ch 28:18). Of silver (1Ch 29:4). Of wine (Isa 25:6).
Figurative: Of the corrective judgments of God (Isa 1:25; 48:10; Jer 9:7; Zec 13:9; Mal 3:2-3). Of the purity of the word of God (Ps 18:30; 119:140).

REFUGE, CITIES OF *See Cities of Refuge.*

REFUGEE SLAVES Laws concerning (Dt 23:15-16). Onesimus (Phm 1). *See Servant.*

REGEM (*friend*). Son of Jahdai (1Ch 2:47).

REGEM-MELECH (*friend of king,* possibly *chief of troops of the king*). A captive sent as a messenger from the Jews in Babylon to Jerusalem (Zec 7:2).

REGENCY *See Deputy.*

REGENERATION The new birth, the inner recreating of fallen human nature by the gracious working of the Holy Spirit. It changes human disposition from godlessness, lawlessness, rebellion, self-seeking, and unbelief to a desire to love and serve God.
Necessity of (Jer 13:23; Mt 12:33-35; 18:3; Mk 10:15; Lk 18:17; Jn 3:3, 5; Tit 3:5-6).
Parables of (Mt 13:23, 33; Mk 4:20, 26-29; Lk 13:21).

Also Called:
Born again or born from above (Jn 3:3-8; 1Pe 1:2-3, 22-23). Born of God (Jn 1:12-13, 16; Jas 1:18; 1Jn 2:27, 29; 3:9, 14; 4:7; 5:1, 4-5, 11-12, 18). Born by the Spirit (Jn 3:5-6; Gal 4:29), through the Holy Spirit (Eze 12:10; Jn 3:5-8; 1Co 12:13; 2Th 2:13; 1Pe 1:2-3, 22-23).
Circumcision of the heart (Dt 29:4; 30:6; Eze 44:7, 9; Ro 2:28; Col 2:11-13). Change of heart (Ps 51:2, 7, 10; Jer 24:7; 31:33-34 w Heb 8:10-11; Jer 32:28-40; Eze 11:19-20; 18:31; 36:26-27, 29; Ro 12:2). New creature (2Co 5:17; Gal 6:15; Eph 4:22-24; Col 3:9-10). Spiritual cleansing (Jn 15:3; Ac 15:9; 1Co 6:11). Spiritual illumination (Jn 6:44-45; 8:12; Ac 26:18; 1Co 2:11-16; 2Co 4:6; Eph 5:14; Heb 10:16). To make spiritually alive (Heb 6:21). Spiritual resurrection (Jn 5:24; Ro 6:3-23; 8:2-4; Gal 2:20).

Other Scriptures Related to:
(1Ki 8:58; Ps 36:9; 65:3; 68:18; 110:3; Pr 4:23; 12:28; 14:27; Isa 1:16-17, 25; 4:4; 12:3; 26:12; 32:3-4, 15, 17; 35:5-6; 42:16; 43:7; 44:3-5; 55:1-3; Jer 17:13-14; 24:7; 31:3; 33:6; Eze 16:9; Lk 1:16-17; Jn 4:10, 14; 10:9-10; 13:8; 17:2; Ac 2:38, 47; 3:26; 11:17, 21; 16:14; Ro 7:6, 24; 15:16; 1Co 1:9, 24, 30; 3:6-7, 9; 15:10; 2Co 1:21-22; 3:3, 18; Php 1:6; Heb 4:12; Jas 5:19-20; 1Pe 2:3, 9; 2Pe 1:3-4).
See Atonement; Conversion; Reconciliation; Redemption; Righteous; Salvation; Sanctification; Sin, Forgiveness of.

REGICIDE (*murder of a king.*) Of Ehud (Jdg 3:16-23). Of Saul (2Sa 1:16). Of Ish-Bosheth (2Sa 4:5-8). Of Nadab (1Ki 15:27-29). Of Elah (1Ki 16:9-11). Of Joram (2Ki 9:24). Of Ahaziah (2Ki 9:27). Of Joash (2Ki 12:20-21). Of Amaziah (2Ki 14:19-20). Of Zechariah (2Ki 15:10). Of Shallum (2Ki 15:14). Of Pekahiah (2Ki 15:25). Of Pekah (2Ki 15:30). Of Sennacherib (2Ki 19:36-37; Isa 37:37-38).
See Homicide.

REGISTRATION Of citizens (Isa 4:3). *See Census.*

REHABIAH (*Yahweh has enlarged*). Son of Eliezer (1Ch 23:17; 24:21; 26:25).

REHOB (*broad, wide [place, market]*).
1. Father of Hadadezer, king of Zobah (2Sa 8:3, 12).
2. A Levite who sealed the covenant with Nehemiah (Ne 10:11).
3. A town in northern Israel. The limit of the investigation made by the twelve spies (Nu 13:21). Possessed by the Syrians (2Sa 10:6, 8). Called Beth Rehob (2Sa 10:6).
4. A town of Asher (Jos 19:28).
5. A Levitical city of Asher (Jos 19:30; 21:31; 1Ch 6:75). Canaanites not driven from (Jdg 1:31).

REHOBOAM (*[my] people will enlarge, expand*). Successor to Solomon as king (1Ki 11:43; 2Ch 9:31). Refuses to reform abuses (1Ki 12:1-15; 2Ch 10:1-15). Ten tribes, under the leadership of Jeroboam, who successfully revolt from (1Ki 12:16-24; 2Ch 10:16-19; 11:1-4). Builds fortified cities; is temporarily prosperous (2Ch 11:5-23). Invaded by the king of Egypt and despoiled (1Ki 14:25-28; 2Ch 12:1-12). Death of (1Ki 14:31; 2Ch 12:16). Genealogy and descendants of (1Ch 3; Mt 1:7).

REHOBOTH (*broad, wide [places, markets]*).
1. A city built by Asshur (Ge 10:11).
2. A city of the Edomites (Ge 36:37; 1Ch 1:48).
3. The name given to a well dug by Isaac (Ge 26:22).

REHUM (*[he] is compassionate*).
1. A captive who returned to Jerusalem from Babylon (Ezr 2:2). Called Nehum (Ne 7:7).
2. An official who wrote a letter to Artaxerxes, influencing him against the Jews (Ezr 4:8-9, 17, 23).
3. A Levite who repaired part of the wall of Jerusalem (Ne 3:17).
4. A Jew of the Exile who signed the covenant with Nehemiah (Ne 10:25).
5. A priest who returned to Jerusalem from the Captivity in Babylon (Ne 12:3).

REI (*friendly* or *[my] friend*). An Israelite loyal to David at the time of the usurpation of Adonijah (1Ki 1:8).

REINS KJV word for internal parts; kidneys as the seat of the emotions (Ps 7:9; 26:2; Jer 17:10; Job 19:27). *See Heart; Kidney.*

REJECTION Of God (1Sa 8:7; 10:19; 2Ki 17:15; Lk 7:30). *See God, Rejected.*
Of Israel by God (Nu 14:12, 26-37; 2Ki 17:20; Jer 6:30; 7:29; 14:19; La 5:22). Of Saul by God (1Sa 15:23, 26).
Of Jesus. *See Jesus the Christ, Rejected.*

REKEM (*friendship*).
1. A king of the Midianites, slain by the Israelites (Nu 31:8; Jos 13:21).
2. A son of Hebron (1Ch 2:43-44).
3. A city in Benjamin (Jos 18:27).

RELEASE Year of: *See Jubilee; Sabbatic Year.*

RELENT God relents, or changes his mind, in response to change in his people (Jer 18:5-10; 26:1-6, 12-13, 17-19). In response to the intercession of Moses, when Israel sinned with the golden calf (Ex 32:11-14); of Amos (Am 7:1-6). Because of his covenant love (Ps 106:44-45; Joel 2:13-14; Jnh 3:8-4:2).
Requests for God to relent (Job 6:29; Ps 90:13-16).
God will not relent when his people deserve his judgment (Jer 4:27-28; Eze 24:14).
See Repentance.

RELIGION

False: (Dt 32:31-33).
See Idolatry; Intolerance; Teachers, False.

Family: *See Family.*

National:
Supported by taxes (Ex 30:11-16; 38:26). Priests supported by the state (1Ki 18:19; 2Ch 11:13-15). Subverted by Jeroboam (1Ki 12:26-33; 2Ch 11:13-15). Idolatrous established by Jeroboam (1Ki 12:26-33).

Natural:
(Job 12:7-16; 37:1-24; Ps 8:1-9; 19:1-6; Ac 14:17; 17:23-28; Ro 1:18-20; 10:16-18). *See Revivals.*

True, As Presented By:
Jesus (Mt 22:36-40). In the "Sermon on the Mount": True blessedness (Mt 5:2-16), fulfillment of the law (Mt 5:17-48), "acts of righteousness" (Mt 6:1-18), service and treasure (Mt 6:19-21), judgment (Mt 7:1-6), asking (Mt 7:7-11), the "golden rule" (Mt 7:12), wholehearted commitment to God (Mt 7:13-29; Mt 22:26-35).
Paul (Ro 8:18; 10:1-13; 12:1-21; 1Co 13:1-13; Gal 5:22-25; 1Th 5:15-23). James (Jas 1:27; 2:8-26). Peter (1Pe 2:5-9). Jude (Jude 20-21).
See Blessings, Spiritual; Commandments and Statutes, Of God; Duty; Graces; Regeneration; Repentance; Sanctification; Sin, Forgiveness of.

Instances of Properly Religious Persons:
Abel (Ge 4:4-8; Heb 11:4). Noah (Ge 6-9). Abraham (Ge 12:1-8; 15; 17; 18:22-33). Jacob (Ge 28:10-22; 32:24-32). Moses (Ex 3:2-22; Dt 32-32). Jethro (Ex 18:12). Joshua (Jos 1). Gideon (Jdg 6-7). Samuel (1Sa 3). David. *See Psalms.* Solomon (1Ki 5:3-5; 2Ch 6). Jehu (2Ki 10:16-30). Hezekiah (2Ki 18:3-7; 19:14-19). Jehoshaphat (2Ch 17:3-9; 19-20). Jabez (1Ch 4:9-10). Asa (2Ch 14-15). Josiah (2Ki 22-23). Daniel (Da 6:4-22). The three Hebrews (Da 3). Zechariah (Lk 1:13, 67-79). Simeon (Lk 2:25-35). Anna the prophetess (Lk 2:36-37). The centurion (Lk 7:1-10). Cornelius (Ac 10). Eunice and Lois (2Ti 1:5).
See for additional instances John, Paul, Peter, Simon, Stephen, and other apostles and disciples, also each of the prophets.

RELIGIOUS

Coercion:
(Ex 22:20; 2Ch 15:12-15; Da 3:2-6; 6:26-27). *See Intolerance.*

Revivals:
(Zec 8:20-23). Prayer for (Hab 3:2). Prophecies concerning (Isa 32:15; Joel 2:28; Mic 4:1-8). *See Revivals.*

Testimony:
(Ps 18:49; 22:22; 26:12; 34:8-9; Isa 45:24; 1Co 13:1; Rev 12:11). *See Testimony, Religious.*

REMALIAH (*Yahweh has adorned*). Father of Pekah, king of Israel (2Ki 15:25, 27, 30; 16:1, 5; 2Ch 28:6; Isa 7:1, 4; 8:6).

REMETH (*heights*). A city in Issachar (Jos 19:17-21), probably, Ramoth (1Ch 6:73), and Jarmuth (Jos 21:29).

REMMON *See Rimmon, 2.*

REMMON-METHOAR *See Rimmon, 3.*

REMNANT
1. People who survived political or military crises (Jos 12:4; 13:12).
2. Spiritual core of Israel who would survive God's judgment and become the seed of the new people of God (Isa 10:20-23; 11:11-12; Jer 32:38-39; Zep 3:13; Zec 8:12).

REMORSE (Pr 1:25-27). Of the promiscuous (Pr 5:7-13). Of the lost (Lk 13:28). Of the wicked (Pr 28:1; Isa 2:19; 57:20-21; Eze 7:16-18, 25-26). Of Israelites (Eze 33:10). Of believers (1Jn 3:20).
Instances of: David (Ps 31:10; 38:2-6; 51:1-19). Isaiah (Isa 6:5). Jeremiah (La 1:20). Peter (Mt 26:75). Judas (Mt 27:3-5). The Jews (Ac 2:37). Paul (Ac 9:6).
See Conviction, of Sin; Penitent; Repentance; Sin, Confession of.

REMPHAN *See Rephan.*

RENDING Of garments, a token of affliction (Ge 37:29, 34; 44:13; Nu 14:6; Jdg 11:35; 2Sa 1:2, 11; 3:31; 13:19, 31; 15:32; 2Ki 2:12; 5:8; 6:30; 11:14; 19:1; 22:11, 19; Ezr 9:3, 5; Job 1:20; 2:12; Isa 36:22; 37:1; Jer 41:5; Mt 26:65; Ac 14:14).
Figurative (Joel 2:13). Symbol of dividing of a kingdom (1Sa 15:27-28).

RENTING Land (Mt 21:33-41; Lk 20:9-16). Houses (Ac 28:30).

RENUNCIATION (Php 3:7-8). Of self for others, exemplified, by Moses (Ex 32:32), Jesus (Php 2:7), Paul (Ro 9:3; 2Co 13:7). Of self for Christ (Mt 16:25; Lk 14:26-33; 17:33; Jn 12:25). Of business for Christ (Mt 4:20; 9:9; Mk 1:18-20; 2:14; Lk 5:27-28).
Of possessions for Christ (Mt 19:21-29; Mk 10:21-30; Lk 18:22-30). Of one's all for Christ, illustrated by parable (Mt 13:44-46).
Of the will, to the Father, exemplified by Jesus (Mk 14:36; Lk 22:42; Jn 5:30; 6:38).
See Self-Denial.

REPENTANCE (Ps 34:14, 18; Isa 22:12).

Exhortations to:
(Pr 1:22-23; Jer 6:16-18; 7:3; 26:3; Hos 6:1; 14:1-3; Am 5:4-6; Mt 3:2).
Commanded (Dt 32:29; 2Ch 30:6-9; Job 36:10; Isa 22:12; 31:6; 44:22; 55:6-7; Jer 3:4, 12-14, 19, 22; 18:11; 25:5-6; 26:13; 35:15; Eze 12:1-5; 14:6; 18:30-32; 33:10-12, 14-16, 19; Da 4:27; Hos 10:12; 14:1-2; Joel 1:14; 2:12-13, 15-17; Am 4:12; Jnh 3:8-9; Hag 1:7; Zec 1:3; Mt 4:17; Mk 1:4, 15; 6:12; Lk 3:3; Ac 2:38; 3:19; 8:22; 17:30; Rev 2:5, 16; 3:2-3, 19).

Source:
Gift of God (2Ti 2:25). Gift of Christ (Ac 5:31). Goodness of God leads to (Ro 2:4). Tribulation leads to (Dt 4:30; 30:1-3; 1Ki 8:33-50; 2Ch 6:36-39; Job 34:31-32).

Condition:
Of forgiveness (Lev 26:40-42; Dt 4:29-31; 30:1-3, 8; 1Ki 8:33-50; 2Ch 6:36-39; 7:14; Ne 1:9; Job 11:13-15; 22:23; Ps 34:18; Pr 28:13; Isa 55:7; Jer 3:4, 12-14, 19; 7:5-7; 18:7-8; 36:3; Eze 18:21-23, 27-28, 30-31; Am 5:6; Mal 3:7; Mt 5:4; Lk 13:1-5; 1Jn 1:9). Of divine favor (Lev 26:40-42; 2Ch 7:14; Isa 57:15).

Foretold:
Of Israel (Jer 50:4-5; Eze 11:18-20; Hos 3:5; Zec 12:10). Universal (Ps 22:27; Ro 14:11).

Rewards of:
(Isa 59:20; Pr 1:23; Jer 7:3, 5, 7; 24:7; Eze 18:21-23, 27-28).

Preached by:
John the Baptist (Mt 3:2, 7-8; Mk 1:4, 15; Lk 3:3). Jesus (Mt 4:17; Mk 1:15; Lk 5:32). Peter (Ac 2:38, 40; 3:19; 8:22). Paul (Ac 17:30; 20:21; 26:20). The apostles (Mk 6:12).
To be preached to all nations (Lk 24:47). Joy in heaven over (Lk 15:1-10).
Unavailing, to Israel (Nu 14:39-45), to Esau (Heb 12:16-17).

Attributed to God:
God relents, or changes his mind, in response to change in his people (Ge 6:6-7; Ex 32:14; Dt 32:36; Jdg 2:18; 1Sa 15:11, 35; 2Sa 24:16; 1Ch 21:15; Ps 106:45; 110:4; 135:14; Jer 15:6; 18:1-10; 26:3; 42:10; Joel 2:13; Am 7:3, 6; Jnh 3:9-10). *See Relent.*
God will not repent (Nu 23:19; 1Sa 15:29; Ps 110:4; Ro 11:29).

Exemplified:
By Job (Job 7:20-21; 9:20; 13:23; 40:4; 42:5-6), David (Ps 32:5; 38:3-4, 18; 40:12; 41:4; 51:1-4, 7-17), the Israelites (Nu 21:7; 2Ch 29:6; Jer 3:21-22, 25; 14:7-9, 20; 31:18-19; La 3:40-41), Daniel for the Jews (Da 9:5-7; 10:12), the prodigal son (Lk 15:17-20).

Instances of:
Joseph's brothers, for their ill treatment of Joseph (Ge 42:21; 50:17-18). Pharaoh, for his hardness of heart (Ex 9:27; 10:16-17). Balaam, for his spiritual blindness (Nu 22:34, w 22:24-35). Israelites, for worshiping the golden calf (Ex 33:3-4), for their murmuring on account of the lack of bread and water, when the plague of fiery serpents came upon them (Nu 21:4-7), when rebuked by an angel for not expelling the Canaanites (Jdg 2:1-5), for their idolatry, when afflicted by the Philistines (Jdg 10:6-16; 1Sa 7:3-6), for asking for a king (1Sa 12:16-20), in the time of Asa, under the preaching of Azariah (2Ch 15:1-15), under the preaching of Oded (2Ch 28:9-15), under the influence of Hezekiah (2Ch 30:11). Achan, for his theft (Jos 7:19-21). Saul, at the reproof of Samuel for not destroying the Amalekites (1Sa 15:24, w 15:6-11). Job (Job 42:6).
David, at the rebuke of Nathan, the prophet (2Sa 12:11, 13, w 12:7-14; Ps 32:5; 38:3-4, 18; 40:12; 41:4; 51:1-4, 7-17), for numbering Israel (2Sa 24:10, 17). The psalmist (Ps 106:6; 119:59-60, 176; 130:1-3). *See Psalms, Topically Arranged.*
Rehoboam, when his kingdom was invaded, and Jerusalem besieged (2Ch 12:1-12). Isaiah (Isa 6:5). Hezekiah, for his pride (Isa 38:15), at the time of his sickness (2Ch 32:26), when reproved by the prophet Micah (Jer 26:18-19). Ahab, when reproved by Elijah for his idolatry (1Ki 21:27). Jehoahaz (2Ki 13:4). Josiah, when he heard the law which had been discovered in the temple (2Ki 22:11-20). Manasseh, when he was carried captive to Babylon by the king of Assyria (2Ch 33:12-13). Jonah, after his punishment (Jnh 2:2-9). The Ninevites, at the preaching of Jonah (Jnh 3:5, 9-10).
The Jews of the Exile, at the dedication of the temple (Ezr 6:21; 9:4, 6, 10, 13-14), for their idolatrous marriages (Ezr 10), for their oppressive usury (Ne 5:1-13), after hearing the law expounded by Ezra (Ne 9:1-3), under the preaching of Haggai (Hag 1).
The Jews under the preaching of John the Baptist (Mt 3:6). The woman who anointed Jesus with oil (Lk 7:37-48). The disobedient son (Mt 21:29). The prodigal son (Lk 15:17-21). The tax collector (Lk 18:13). Peter, of his denial of Jesus (Mt 26:75; Mk 14:72; Lk 22:62). The Ephesians, under the preaching of Paul (Ac 19:18).
See Conviction, of Sin; Penitence; Remorse; Sin, Confession of; Sin, Forgiveness of.

REPETITION In Prayers: *See Babbling; Prayer, Persistence in.*

REPHAEL (*God [El] heals*). A gatekeeper of the temple in the time of David (1Ch 26:7).

REPHAH (possibly *rich* IDB; *easy [life]* KB). A grandson of Ephraim (1Ch 7:25).

REPHAIAH (*Yahweh heals*).
1. A descendant of David (1Ch 3:21).
2. A Simeonite captain (1Ch 4:42).
3. Son of Tola, of the tribe of Issachar (1Ch 7:2).
4. A descendant of Jonathan (1Ch 9:43). Also called Raphah (1Ch 8:37).
5. Governor over half of Jerusalem in the time of Nehemiah (Ne 3:9).

REPHAIM *See Rephaites.*

REPHAIM, VALLEY OF (*sunken, powerless ones [giants]* BDB; possibly *shades, ghosts of the dead [giants]* KB). Fertile plain S of Jerusalem, three miles from Bethlehem (Jos 15:8; 18:16; 2Sa 5:18, 22; 23:13; 1Ch 11:15; 14:9; Isa 17:4-5).

REPHAITES (*mighty*). Giant people who lived in Canaan even before Abraham's time (Ge 14:5; 15:20; Dt 2:11, 20; 3:11, 13; Jos 12:4; 13:12; 17:15; 1Ch 20:4). *See Giants.*

REPHAN A pagan god noted in Ac 7:43 quoting the LXX (Am 5:26, ftn). In Am 5:26, the NIV translates the Hebrew word "pedestal," though the ftn offers the proper name "Kaiwan." The Egyptain *repa* and the Assyrian "Kaiwan" both refer to the planet Saturn, which may harmonize the two texts. *See Chiun.*

REPHIDIM (possibly *supports, rests* BDB; *resting place* KB). Encampment of Israelites in the wilderness; there Moses struck a rock to secure water (Ex 17:1-7; 19:2), battle with Amalekites took place there (Ex 17:8-16).

REPORTS Majority and minority, of spies (Nu 13:26-33; 14:6-10).

REPROBACY Admonitions against (2Co 13:5-7; Heb 3:10-12, 17-19; 6:4-9; 12:15-17). Curses denounced against (Dt 28:15-68; 31:17-18; Isa 65:12; Hos 9:12; Mk 3:29; Heb 10:26-31).
See Reprobates.

REPROBATE Moral corruption, unfitness, disqualification, disapproved (Ro 1:28; 1Co 9:27). *See Reprobacy; Reprobates.*

REPROBATES (Jer 6:30; Ro 1:21-32; 2Ti 3:8; 1Jn 5:16; Jude 4-13; Rev 22:4).

Described as:
Men of corrupt minds (2Ti 3:8), vessels of wrath (Ro 9:22). Moral insensibility of (Isa 22:12-14; 28:13; 29:9-12; Mt 13:14-15; 15:14; Ro 11:7-8). Rejected of God (Ps 81:11-12; Pr 1:24-28; Jer 6:30; 7:16; 15:1; Hos 5:6; Mt 15:14; 25:8-13; Lk 13:24-28; 14:24; Jn 10:26; Ro 1:21-26, 28; 2Th 2:10-11; Heb 3:10-12, 17-19; 6:4-8; 10:26-31).
Admonitions against (Heb 12:15-17).

Instances of:
Antediluvians (Ge 6:5-7). Sodomites (Ge 13:13; 19:13; Jude 7). Jannes and Jambres (2Ti 3:8). Eli's house (1Sa 3:14). Saul (1Sa 15:23; 16:14; 18:12; 28:15). Judas (Jn 17:12). Angels (Jude 6). Antichrist (2Th 2:7-12).
In Israel (Nu 14:26-48; Dt 1:42; Isa 6:9-10; Heb 3:10-12, 17-19; Jude 5). In the Church (2Co 13:5-7; Heb 3:10-12, 17-19; 6:4-9; Jude 4-13).
See Obduracy; Reprobacy.

REPRODUCTION *See Propagation.*

REPROOF, REPROVE

Commanded:
(Lev 19:17; Ps 141:5; Pr 9:7-8; 10:17; 26:5; Mt 18:15-17; Lk 17:3-4; Eph 5:11; 1Th 5:14, 20; 2Ti 4:2; Tit 1:13; Heb 3:13).
Of elders, forbidden (1Ti 5:1-2).

Profitable:
(Pr 13:18; 15:5, 31-32; 27:5-6; 28:23; Ecc 7:5). Wise profit by (Pr 17:10; 19:25; 21:11; 25:12).

Needed in the Church:
(Eph 4:15; Php 3:1; 1Th 5:14; 1Ti 5:1-2, 20; 2Ti 4:2; Tit 1:13; Heb 3:13).

Hated:
(Pr 10:17; 12:1; 15:10, 12; Am 5:10; Jn 7:7; Gal 4:16). By the Israelites (Nu 14:9-10; Jer 26:11). By Ahab (1Ki 18:17; 21:20; 22:8). By Asa (2Ch 16:10). By Herodias (Mk 6:18-19). By people of Nazareth (Lk 4:28-29). Jews (Ac 5:33; 7:54).

Faithfulness in:
Instances of: Moses, of Pharaoh (Ex 10:29; 11:8), of the Israelites (Ex 16:6-7; 32:19-30; Nu 14:41; 20:10; 32:14; Dt 1:12, 26-43; 9:16-24; 29:2-4; 31:27-29; 32:15-18), of Eleazar (Lev 10:16-18), of Korah (Nu 16:9-11). Israelites, of the two-a-one-half tribes (Jos 22:15-20), of the tribe of Benjamin (Jdg 20.12-13).
Samuel, of Saul (1Sa 15:14-35). Jonathan, of Saul (1Sa 19:4-5). Nathan, of David (2Sa 12:1-9). Joab, of David (2Sa 19:1-7; 24:3; 1Ch 21:3). The prophet Gad, of David (2Sa 24:13). Shemaiah, of Rehoboam (2Ch 12:5). A prophet of Judah, of Jeroboam (1Ki 13:1-10; 2Ch 13:8-11). Elijah, of Ahab (1Ki 18:18-21; 21:20-24), of Ahaziah (2Ki 1). Micaiah, of Ahab (1Ki 22:14-28). Elisha, of Jehoram (2Ki 3:13-14), of Gehazi (2Ki 5:26), of Hazael (2Ki 8:11-13), of Jeroboam (2Ki 13:19).
Amos, of the Israelites (Am 7:12-17). Isaiah, of Hezekiah (2Ki 20:17). Jehoash, of Jehoiada (2Ki 12:7). Azariah, of Asa (2Ch 15:2), of Uzziah (2Ch 26:17-18). Hanani, of Asa (2Ch 16:7-9). Jehu, of Jehoshaphat (2Ch 19:2). Zechariah, of the princes of Judah (2Ch 24:20). Oded, of the people of Samaria (2Ch 28:9-11). Jeremiah, of the cities of Judah (Jer 26:8-11). Ezra, of the men of Judah and Benjamin (Ezr 10:10). Nehemiah, of the Jews (Ne 5:6-13), of the corruptions in the temple, and of the violation of the Sabbath (Ne 13). Daniel, of Nebuchadnezzar (Da 4:27), of Belshazzar (Da 5:17-24).
Jesus, of the Jews: When Pharisees and Sadducees came to him desiring a sign (Mt 16:1-4; Mk 8:11-12), of the scribes and Pharisees (Mt 23; Lk 11:37-54), of the Pharisees (Lk 16), when they brought the woman to him who was caught in adultery (Jn 8:7).
Jesus, in his parables: Of the king's feast (Lk 14:16-24), of the two sons (Mt 21:28-32), of the vineyard (Mt 21:33-46; Mk 12:1-12; Lk 20:9-20), of the barren fig tree (Lk 13:6-9), the withering of the fig tree (Mt 21:17-20; Mk 11:12-14).
John the Baptist, of the Jews (Mt 3:7-12; Lk 3:7-9), of Herod (Mt 14:3; Mk 6:17; Lk 3:19-20). Peter, of Simon, the sorcerer (Ac 8:20-23). Stephen, of the high priest (Ac 7:51-53). Paul, of Elymas, the sorcerer (Ac 13:9-11), of Ananias, the high priest (Ac 23:3). Paul and Silas, of the magistrates of Philippi (Ac 16:37-40).
See One Another; Reprobacy.

REPTILES (1Ki 4:33; Ac 10:12; 11:6; Ro 1:23). Adder (Job 20:16). Cobra (Isa 11:8). Chameleon (Lev 11:30). Frog (Ex 8:2). Gecko (Lev 11:30). Lizards (Lev 11:29-30). Serpent (Job 20:14, 16). Skink (Lev 11:30). Snake (Ex 7:9-12). Viper (Ge 49:17; Isa 59:5). *See Animals.*

REPUTATION, GOOD (Pr 3:4; 22:1; Ecc 7:1). Of Mordecai (Est 9:4). Of overseers (1Ti 3:7). *See Character; Name.*

RESEN A town founded by Nimrod (Ge 10:8-12), between Nineveh and Calah.

RESERVOIR A place where water is collected and kept for use when wanted, chiefly in large quantities. Because most of W Asia was subject to periodic droughts, and because of frequent sieges, reservoirs and cisterns were a necessity (2Ch 26:10; 18:31; Ecc 2:6).

RESHEPH (*flame, flash of fire*). Grandson of Ephraim (1Ch 7:25).

RESIGNATION

Commanded:
(Ps 4:4; 46:10; Lk 21:19; Ro 12:12; Php 2:14; Col 1:10-11; Jas 1:9-10; 4:7; 1Pe 4:12-13, 19). Under chastisement and afflictions (Job 5:17; Pr 3:11; 18:14; Jer 51:50; La 3:39; Mic 6:9; 1Th 3:3; 2Ti 2:3; 4:5; Heb 2:6-12; 12:5, 9; Jas 5:11, 13; 1Pe 1:6). Under bereavement (1Th 4:13-18).

Exemplified by:
Aaron (Lev 10:1-3). The Israelites (Jdg 10:15). Eli (1Sa 3:18). David (2Sa 12:23; 15:26; 16:10-11; 24:14). The Shunammite (2Ki 4:26). Hezekiah (2Ki 20:19; Isa 39:8). Nehemiah (Ne 9:33). By Esther (Est 4:16). Job (Job 1:13-22; 2:9-10; 34:31; Jas 5:11). The psalmists (Ps 39:9; 103:10; 119:75). Jeremiah (Jer 10:19; La 1:18). Daniel (Da 9:14). Micah (Mic 7:9).
Jesus (Mt 26:39; Mk 14:36; Lk 22:42; Jn 18:11). The thief on the cross (Lk 23:40-41). Stephen (Ac 7:59-60). Agabus, Luke, and others when Paul insisted on going to Jerusalem (Ac 21:14). Paul (Ro 5:3-5; 2Co 6:4-10; 7:4; Php 1:20-24; 4:11-12; 2Ti 4:6). Paul and Silas (Ac 16:25). Thessalonian believers (2Th 1:4). Hebrew believers (Heb 10:34).
See Afflicted Believers; Affliction; Afflictions, Made Beneficial.

RESIN *See Aromatic Resin; Gum Resin.*

RESPECT To the aged (Lev 19:32). To rulers (Pr 25:6). To a host (Lk 14:10). To one another (Ro 12:10; Php 2:3; 1Pe 2:17).

RESPECT OF PERSONS Favoritism (Pr 24:23; 28:21; Jas 2:1-9). God does not have (Dt 10:17; 2Ch 19:7; Job 31:13-15; 34:19; Ac 10:34; 15:9; Ro 2:11-12; 10:12; Eph 6:8-9; Col 3:25; 1Pe 1:17). *See God, Justice of; Justice.*

RESPONSIBILITY Attempts to shift: Adam (Ge 3:12-13), Eve (Ge 3:13), Sarah (Ge 16:5, w 16:2), Esau (Ge 27:36, w Ge 25:29-34), Aaron (Ex 32:22-24), Saul (1Sa 15:20-21), Pilate (Mt 27:24). Assumed by the Jews for the death of Jesus (Mt 27:25).
Personal (Eze 14:14-20; 18:20, 30; Mt 12:37; Jn 9:41; 15:22-24; Ro 14:12; 1Co 3:8, 13-15; Gal 6:5; 1Pe 4:5; Rev 2:23).
According to privilege (Eze 18:1-30; 33:1-19; Mt 10:11-15; 11:20-24; 12:41-42; 23:31-35; 25:14-30; Mk 6:11; Lk 9:5; 10:10-15; 11:31-32, 49-51; 13:6-9; 19:12-27; 21:1-4; Jn 3:18-19; 12:48; 15:22, 24; Ac 17:30-31; Ro 12:3, 6-8; Eph 4:7; 1Ti 6:20).
See Judgment, According to Opportunity and Works.

RESPONSIVE RELIGIOUS SERVICE Reciting the curses of the covenant (Dt 27:14-26). In worship (Ps 48; 118:2-4; 124:1; 129:1). At the dedication of the wall of Jerusalem (Ne 12).

REST Divine institution for. *See Sabbath.* Commanded (Ex 16:23; 20:10; 23:12; 31:15; 34:21; 35:2; Dt 5:12, 14).
The annual feasts added rest days: First and last days of feasts of Passover and Tabernacles (Ex 12:16; Lev 23:5-8, 39-40; Nu 28:18, 25; 29:12, 35), Pentecost (Nu 28:26), Trumpets (Lev 23:24-25; Nu 29:1), Atonement (Lev 16:29-31; 23:27-28; Nu 29:7). In seventh year (Ex 23:11; Lev 25:1-4). In the Year of Jubilee (Lev 25:11-12).
Recommended by Jesus (Mk 6:31-32; 7:24, w Mt 8:18, 24). Heavenly (2Th 1:7). Spiritual (Mt 11:29; Heb 4:1-11).
See Peace, Spiritual; Resignation.

RESTITUTION To be made for injury to life, limb, or property (Ex 21:30-36; Lev 24:18), for theft (Ex 22:1-4; Pr 6:30-31; Eze 33:15), for dishonesty (Lev 6:2-5; Nu 5:7; Job 20:18; Eze 33:15; Lk 19:8).

RESTORATION Of the Jews. *See Israel; Israelites.* Of all things (Ac 3:21; Rev 21:1-5).

RESURRECTION

In the Old Testament:
As understood by Job (Job 14:12-15; 19:25-27). By the psalmists (Ps 16:9-10; 17:15; 49:15). By the prophets (Isa 25:8; 26:19; Da 12:2-3, 13; Hos 13:14).

In the New Testament:
Debated by the Pharisees and Sadducees (Ac 23:6, 8; 24:14-15; 26:6-8; Mt 22:23-32).
Taught by Jesus (Mt 22:30-32; 24:31; Mk 12:25-27; Lk 14:14; 20:27-38; Jn 5:21, 25, 28-29; 6:39-40, 44, 54; 11:23-25). By the apostles (Ac 4:1-2; 17:18, 31-32; 23:6-8; 24:14-15; 26:6-8; Ro 4:16-21; 8:10-11, 19, 21-23; 1Co 6:14; 15:12-57; 2Co 4:14; 5:1-5; Php 3:10-11, 21; Rev 20:5-6; Heb 6:2; 11:35).
Error in the early church (2Ti 2:18; 1Co 15:12-58).

Of Jesus:
Typified by Isaac (Ge 22:13; Heb 11:19), by Jonah (Jnh 2:10, w Mt 12:40). Foretold (Ps 16:9-10), by himself (Mt 16:21; 17:9, 23; 20:19; 26:61; 27:63; Mk 8:31; 9:9-10, 31; 10:34; Lk 9:22; 18:33; 24:7, 46; Jn 2:19-21; 10:17-18; 14:19).
Appearances after the resurrection (Mt 27:53; 28:2-15; Mk 16:1-11; Lk 24:1-12; Jn 20:1-18; Rev 1:18). Denied by the Jews (Mt 28:12-15).
Raised by the power of God (Ac 2:24, 32; 3:15, 26; 4:10; 5:30; 10:40; 15:20, 30, 33-34, 37; 17:31; Ro 4:24; 8:11; 10:9; 1Co 6:14; 15:15; 2Co 4:14; Gal 1:4; Eph 1:20; Col 2:12; 2Ti 1:10; 1Pe 1:21), for our justification (Ro 4:25; 1Pe 3:21). Guarantee of general resurrection (1Co 15:12-15; 1Pe 1:3).
The theme of apostolic preaching (Ac 2:24, 31-32; 3:15; 4:10, 33; 5:30-32; 10:40-41; 17:2-3, 18).
See Grave; Jesus the Christ, Resurrection of.

Special Resurrections:
Of saints after Christ's resurrection (Mt 27:52-53). The two witnesses (Rev 11:11).
See Dead, Raised to Life.

At Christ's Second Coming:
(1Th 4:14, 16). The first resurrection (Rev 20:4-6). Of all the dead (Jn 5:28-29; Ac 24:15; 1Co 15:20-21; Rev 20:13).

Figurative:
Of the restoration of Israel (Eze 37:1-14). Of regeneration (Ro 6:4; Eph 2:1, 5-6; Col 2:12; 3:1).

RETALIATION (Ps 10:2). Judicial, ordained in Mosaic law (Ex 21:23-25; Lev 24:17-22; Dt 19:19-21). Malicious, forbidden (Lev 19:18; Pr 20:22; 24:29; Mt 5:38-44; 7:1-2; Lk 9:54; Ro 12:17, 19; 1Co 6:7-8; 1Th 5:15; 1Pe 3:9). Warning against (Pr 26:27; Isa 33:1; Mt 7:1-2).
See Avenger of Blood; Hatred; Malice; Revenge.
Instances of: Israelites on the Amalekites (Dt 25:17-19, w 1Sa 15:1-9). Gideon on the princes of Succoth (Jdg 8:7, 13-16), kings of Midian (Jdg 8:18-21), Peniel (Jdg 8:8, 17). Joab on Abner (2Sa 3:27, 30). David upon Michal (2Sa 6:21-23), on Joab (1Ki 2:5-6), Shimei (1Ki 2:8-9). Jews on their enemies (Est 9).

RETICENCE OF JESUS (Isa 53:7; Mt 26:63; 27:12, 14; Mk 14:61; 15:4-5; Jn 19:9; 1Pe 2:23). *See Jesus the Christ, Reticence of.*

RETRIBUTION *See Sin, Punishment of.*

REU (*friend [of God]*). Son of Peleg and ancestor of Abraham and of Jesus (Ge 11:18-21; 1Ch 1:25; Lk 3:35).

REUBEN (*see, a son!* [Ge. 29:32]; *substitute a son* IDB). Son of Jacob (Ge 29:32; 1Ch 2:1). Brings mandrakes to his mother (Ge 30:14). Commits incest with one of his father's concubines, and, in consequence, forfeits the birthright (Ge 35:22; 49:4; 1Ch 5:1). Tactfully seeks to save Joseph from the conspiracy of his brothers (Ge 37:21-30; 42:22). Offers to become surety for Benjamin (Ge 42:37). Jacob's prophetic benediction upon (Ge 49:3-4). His children (Ge 46:9; Ex 6:14; 1Ch 5:3-6; Nu 16:1).

REUBENITE(S) (*of Reuben*). The descendants of Reuben. Military enrollment of, at Sinai (Nu 1:20-21), in Moab (Nu 26:7). Place of, in camp and march (Nu 2:10). Standard of (Nu 10:18). Have their inheritance east of the Jordan (Nu 32; Dt 3:1-20; Jos 13:15-23; 18:7). Assist the other tribes in conquest of the region west of the Jordan (Jos 1:12-18; 22:1-6). Unite with the other tribes in building a monument to signify the unity of the tribes on the east of the Jordan with the tribes on the west of the river; monument misunderstood; the explanation and reconciliation (Jos 22:10-34). Reproached by Deborah (Jdg 5:15-16). Taken captive into Assyria (2Ki 15:29; 1Ch 5:26).
See Israel.

REUEL (*friend of God [El]*).
1. Son of Esau (Ge 36:4, 10).
2. Father-in-law of Moses (Ex 2:16-22), probably the same as Jethro (Ex 3:1). *See Jethro.*
3. The father of Eliasaph (Nu 2:14). Called Deuel (Nu 1:14).
4. Benjamite (1Ch 9:8).

REUMAH A concubine of Nahor (Ge 22:24).

REVELATION The doctrine of God's making himself and relevant truths known to mankind. Revelation is of two kinds: general and special. General revelation is available to all people, and is communicated through nature, conscience, and history. Special revelation is revelation given to particular people at particular times (although it may be intended for others as well), and comes chiefly through the Bible and Jesus Christ.
God reveals himself to Moses (Ex 3:1-6, 14; 6:1-3). The law is revealed (Ex 20-35; Lev 1-7). The pattern of the temple (1Ch 28:11-19). The sonship of Jesus (Mt 3:17; 16:17; 17:5). The nature of the Father through the Son (Jn 1:18; 14:8).
See Inspiration; Prophecy; Prophets; Word of God, Inspiration of.

REVELATION, BOOK OF THE

Author: The apostle John

Date: Probably in the latter part of Nero's reign (A.D. 54-68) or the latter part of Domitian's reign (81-96).

Outline:
I. Introduction (1:1-8).
A. Prologue (1:1-3).
B. Greetings and Doxology (1:4-8).
II. Jesus Among the Seven Churches (1:9-20).
III. The Letters to the Seven Churches (chs. 2-3).
A. Ephesus (2:1-7).
B. Smyrna (2:8-11).
C. Pergamum (2:12-17).
D. Thyatira (2:18-29).
E. Sardis (3:1-6).
F. Philadelphia (3:7-13).
G. Laodicea (3:14-22).
IV. The Throne, the Scroll and the Lamb (chs. 4-5).
A. The Throne in Heaven (ch. 4).
B. The Seven-Sealed Scroll (5:1-5).
C. The Lamb Slain (5:6-14).
V. The Seven Seals (6:1-8:1).
A. First Seal: The White Horse (6:1-2).
B. Second Seal: The Red Horse (6:3-4).
C. Third Seal: The Black Horse (6:5-6).
D. Fourth Seal: The Pale Horse (6:7-8).
E. Fifth Seal: The Souls Under the Altar (6:9-11).
F. Sixth Seal: The Great Earthquake (6:12-17).
G. The Sealing of the 144,000 (7:1-8).
H. The Great Multitude (7:9-17).
I. Seventh Seal: Silence in Heaven (8:1).
VI. The Seven Trumpets (8:2-11:19).
A. Introduction (8:2-5).
B. First Trumpet: Hail and Fire Mixed With Blood (8:6-7).
C. Second Trumpet: A Mountain Thrown in the Sea (8:8-9).
D. Third Trumpet: The Star Wormwood (8:10-11).
E. Fourth Trumpet: A Third of the Sun, Moon and Stars Struck (8:12-13).
F. Fifth Trumpet: The Plague of Locusts (9:1-12).
G. Sixth Trumpet: Release of the Four Angels (9:13-21).
H. The Angel and the Little Scroll (ch. 10).
I. The Two Witnesses (11:1-14).
J. Seventh Trumpet: Judgments and Rewards (11:15-19).
VII. Various Personages and Events (chs. 12-14).
A. The Woman and the Dragon (ch. 12).
B. The Two Beasts (ch. 13).
C. The Lamb and the 144,000 (14:1-5).
D. The Harvest of the Earth (14:6-20).
VIII. The Seven Bowls (chs. 15-16).
A. Introduction: The Song of Moses and the Seven Angels with the Seven Plagues (ch. 15).
B. First Bowl: Ugly and Painful Sores (16:1-2).
C. Second Bowl: Sea Turns to Blood (16:3).
D. Third Bowl: Rivers and Springs of Water Become Blood (16:4-7).
E. Fourth Bowl: Sun Scorches People With Fire (16:8-9).
F. Fifth Bowl: Darkness (16:10-11).
G. Sixth Bowl: Euphrates River Dries Up (16:12-16).
H. Seventh Bowl: Tremendous Earthquake (16:17-21).
IX. Babylon: The Great Prostitute (17:1-19:5).
A. Babylon Described (ch. 17).
B. The Fall of Babylon (ch. 18).
C. Praise for Babylon's Fall (19:1-5).
X. Praise for the Wedding of the Lamb (19:6-10).
XI. The Return of Christ (19:11-21).
XII. The Thousand Years (20:1-6).
XIII. Satan's Doom (20:7-10).
XIV. Great White Throne Judgment (20:11-15).
XV. New Heaven, New Earth, New Jerusalem (21:1-22:5).
XVI. Conclusion (22:6-21).

REVELING Any extreme intemperance and lustful indulgence, usually accompanying pagan worship (Gal 5:21; 1Pe 4:3).

REVENGE Forbidden (Lev 19:18; Pr 24:29; Ro 12:17, 19; 1Th 5:15; 1Pe 3:9). Jesus an example of forbearing (1Pe 2:23). Rebuked by Jesus (Lk 9:54-55). Inconsistent with a Christian spirit (Lk 9:55). Proceeds from a spiteful heart (Eze 25:15). Punishment for (Eze 25:15-17; Am 1:11-12).

Exemplified:
By Simeon and Levi (Ge 34:25). By Samson (Jdg 15:7-8; 16:28-30). By Joab (2Sa 3:27). By Absalom (2Sa 13:23-29). By Jezebel (1Ki 19:2). By Ahab (1Ki 22:27). By Haman (Est 3:8-15). By the Edomites (Eze 25:12). By the Philistines (Eze 25:15). By Herodias (Mk 6:19-24). By James and John (Lk 9:54). By the chief priests (Ac 5:33). By the Jews (Ac 7:54-59; 23:12).
See Retaliation; Vengeance.

REVENUE Solomon's (2Ch 9:13-14).
See Tax.

REVERENCE For God (Ge 17:3; Ex 3:5; 19:16-24; 34:29-35; Isa 45:9). *See Fear of God.* For God's house (Lev 19:30; 26:2). For ministers (1Sa 16:4; Ac 28:10; 1Co 16:18; Php 2:29; 1Th 5:12-13; 1Ti 5:17; Heb 13:7, 17). *See Minister.* For Kings (1Sa 24:6; 26:9, 11; 2Sa 1:14; 16:21; Ecc 10:20; 1Pe 2:17). *See Rulers.* For magistrates (Ex 22:28; 2Pe 2:10; Jude 8). *See Rulers.* For parents (Ex 20:12; Lev 19:3; Isa 45:10). *See Parents.* For the aged (Lev 19:32; Job 32:4-7).

REVILE, REVILING To revile is to address or speak of someone abusively; to reproach (Ex 21:17; Zep 2:8; Mk 15:32; 1Co 6:10).

REVIVALS

Religious:
(Zec 8:20-23). Prayer for (Hab 3:2). Prophecies concerning (Isa 32:15; Joel 2:28; Mic 4:1-8; Hab 3:2).

Instances of:
Under Joshua (Jos 5:2-9), Samuel (1Sa 7:1-6), Elijah (1Ki 18:17-40), Jehoash and Jehoiada (2Ki 11-12; 2Ch 23-24), Hezekiah (2Ki 18:1-7; 2Ch 29-31), Josiah (2Ki 22-23; 2Ch 34-35), Asa (2Ch 14:2-5; 15:1-14), Manasseh (2Ch 33:12-19). In Nineveh (Jnh 3:4-10). At Pentecost and post-Pentecostal times (Ac 2:1-42, 46-47; 4:4; 5:14; 6:7; 9:35; 11:20-21; 12:24; 14:1; 19:17-20).
See Religion.

REVOLT Of the ten tribes (1Ki 12:1-24).

REWARD (Isa 40:10-11). In Moses' choice (Heb 11:26). For bravery (1Sa 17:25; Jdg 1:13).

A Motive:
To repentance (Lev 26:40-45; Isa 1:16-20; Ac 26:18). To obedience (Ex 20:6; Lev 25:18-19; 26:3-13; Dt 4:40; 6:3, 18; 11:13-16, 18-21, 26-29; 27:12-26; Jos 8:33; Isa 1:16-20; 3:10; Eph 6:1-3; Heb 12:28). To faithfulness (Mt 24:45-47; 25:14-33; Lk 12:42-44; 19:12-27; 1Co 3:8; Rev 2:10; 22:12). To righteous conduct (Ro 2:10; 1Pe 3:9-12). To patience (Heb 10:36). To perseverance (Mt 10:22; 24:13; Mk 13:13; Ro 2:6-7; Gal 6:9; Rev 2:17, 25-27; 3:5, 11-12, 21; 21:7). To honesty (Dt 25:15).
To follow Christ (Mt 10:32; 16:24-27; 20:1-16; 25:34-46; Mk 10:21; Lk 12:8; 2Pe 1:10-11). To endure persecution (Lk 6:22-23; Heb 10:34). To endure tribulation (Rev 2:7, 10; 7:17). To love enemies (Lk 6:35). To deliver the oppressed (Jer 17:24-26; 22:3-4). To honor parents (Ex 20:12; Eph 6:1-3). To honor the Sabbath (Jer 17:24-26). To give generously (Dt 15:9-11; 24:19). To show kindness to animals (Dt 22:6-7).
See Blessings, Spiritual, Contingent Upon Obedience; Punishment; Righteous, Promises to; Sin, Separates From God; Wicked, Punishment of.

REZEPH (*heated stones, live coals*). A city destroyed by the Assyrians (2Ki 19:12; Isa 37:12).

REZIA *See Rizia.*

REZIN
1. A king of Syria who harassed the kingdom of Judah (2Ki 15:37; 16:5-9). Prophecy against (Isa 7:1-9; 8:4-8; 9:11).
2. A returned Babylonian captive (Ezr 2:48; Ne 7:50).

REZON (*prince* IDB; *high official* KB). King of Damascus. An adversary of Solomon (1Ki 11:23-25).

RHEGIUM A city of Italy. Touched by Paul on the way to Rome (Ac 28:13).

RHESA An ancestor of Jesus (Lk 3:27).

RHODA (*rose*). A servant or slave girl in the home of Mary, John Mark's mother (Ac 12:13).

RHODES (*rose*). An island on the SW tip of Asia Minor; commercial center until crippled by Rome is 166 B.C.; famous for Colossus, a statue of Helios; Paul stopped off there (Ac 21:1).

RIBAI (*opponent*). A Benjamite. The father of Ittai (2Sa 23:29; 1Ch 11:31).

RIBBON Ribbon used in poetic imagery (SS 4:3). Tassels of thread on the corners of garments; NIV "cord" (Nu 15:38).

RIBLAH
1. A city on the boundary of Canaan and Israel, N of the Sea of Galilee (Nu 34:11).
2. An important town on the E bank of the Orontes River fifty miles S of Hamath. There Pharaoh Neco (609 B.C.) put King Jehoahaz II of Judah in chains. Also in this place, Nebuchadnezzar killed the sons of King Zedekiah of Judah (587 B.C.) and put out his eyes. Following this, Zedekiah was carried off in chains to Babylon (2Ki 25:6f; Jer 39:5-7). It is possible that the two Riblahs may be the same.

RICH, THE

Admonitions to:
(Jer 9:23; 1Ti 6:17-19; Jas 1:9-11). Not to trust riches for divine favor (Ps 49:16-18; Ecc 7:19; Zep 1:18).

Characteristics of:
Wicked (Job 21:7-15; Ps 73:3-9; Pr 28:8, 20, 22; Jer 5:27-28; Lk 12:15-21; 16:19-31; Jas 2:6-7). Immoral (Jer 5:7-8). Deluded (Pr 11:28; 13:7; 18:11). Conceited (Pr 28:11). Proud (Ps 73:3, 6, 8-9; Eze 28:5). Arrogant (Ps 73:8). Oppressive (Ne 5:1-13; Mic 6:10-13; Jas 2:6). Cruel to the poor (Pr 18:23). Envied (Ps 73:3-22). Hated (Job 27:19, 23). Denounced (Isa 5:8; Jer 17:11; 22:13-15; Am 6:1-6; Lk 6:24-25; Jas 5:1-4).
Have many friends (Pr 14:20; 19:9). Made so by God (Ecc 5:19-20). Difficult to enter the kingdom (Mt 19:24; Mk 10:17-27; Lk 18:24-25). Unscrupulous methods of (Jer 5:26-28). Discrimination in favor of, in the church, forbidden (Jas 2:1-9). Divine judgments against (Job 27:13-23; Ps 52:1-7; 73:18-20).

Instances of Righteous Rich:
Abraham (Ge 13:2; 24:35). Isaac (Ge 26:12-14). Solomon (1Ki 10:23; 2Ch 9:22). Jehoshaphat (2Ch 18:1). Hezekiah (2Ki 20:12-13). Job (Job 1:3; 31:24-25, 28). Joseph of Arimathea (Mt 27:57). Zacchaeus (Lk 19:2).
See Riches.

RICHES (1Sa 2:7; Ps 37:16; 52:7; Pr 11:4; 14:24; 15:6, 16-17; 16:8; 19:4; Ecc 4:8; 5:11-14; 6:1-2; 7:11-12; 10:19; Isa 5:8; Jer 48:36). Delusive (Pr 11:28; Lk 12:16-21). Unstable (Pr 23:5; 27:24).
Unsatisfying to the covetous (Ecc 5:10-12). A snare (Dt 6:10-12; 8:7-17; 31:20; 32:15; Pr 30:8-9; Jer 5:7-8; Hos 12:8; Mt 13:22; 19:16-24; Mk 4:19; 10:17-25; Lk 16:19-26; 18:18-25; 1Ti 6:9-11, 17).
Worthless in the day of calamity (Eze 7:17, 19; Zep 1:18). Fraudulently gotten, unprofitable (Pr 10:2; 21:6; 28:8; Jer 17:11). Admonitions against the desire for (Pr 23:4; 28:20, 22; 1Ti 6:9-11, 17). The heart not to be set upon (Ps 62:10; Mt 6:19-21).
Liberality with (Pr 13:7-8). Benevolent use of, required (1Jn 3:17).
Figurative (Rev 3:17-18).
See Covetousness; Rich, The.

RIDDLE (*hidden saying, proverb*). Any "dark saying" of which the meaning is not immediately clear and must be found by shrewd thought (Nu 12:8; Pr 1:6). It may be a parable (Ps 49:4), or something for men to guess (Jdg 14:12-19), or just a hard question (1Ki 10:1; 2Ch 9:1).

RIGHTEOUS

Compared with:
The sun (Jdg 5:31; Mt 13:43), stars (Da 12:3), lights (Mt 5:14; Php 2:15). Mount Zion (Ps 125:1-2), Lebanon (Hos 14:5-7). Treasure (Ex 19:5; Ps 135:4), treasured possession (Mal 3:17). Gold (Job 23:10; La 4:2), vessels of gold and silver (2Ti 2:20), stones of a crown (Zec 9:16), living stones (1Pe 2:5).
Babies (Mt 11:25; 1Pe 2:2), little children (Mt 18:3; 1Co 14:20), obedient children (1Pe 1:14), members of the body (1Co 12:20, 27), soldiers (2Ti 2:3-4), runners in a race (1Co 9:24; Heb 12:1), wrestlers (2Ti 2:5), good servants (Mt 25:21), strangers and pilgrims (1Pe 2:11).
Sheep (Ps 78:52; Mt 25:33; Jn 10), lambs (Isa 40:11; Jn 21:15), calves of the stall (Mal 4:2), lions (Pr 28:1; Mic 5:8), eagles (Ps 103:5; Isa 40:31), doves (Ps 68:13; Isa 60:8), thirsty deer (Ps 42:1), good fish (Mt 13:48).
Dew and showers (Mic 5:7), watered gardens (Isa 58:11), unfailing springs (Isa 58:11), vines (SS 6:11; Hos 14:7), branches of a vine (Jn 15:2, 4-5), pomegranates (SS 4:13), good figs (Jer 24:2-7), lilies (SS 2:2; Hos 14:5), poplars by flowing streams (Isa 44:4), trees planted by rivers (Ps 1:3), cedars in Lebanon (Ps 92:12), palm trees (Ps 92:12), green olive trees (Ps 52:8; Hos 14:6), fruitful trees (Ps 1:3; Jer 17:8), grain (Hos 14:7), wheat (Mt 3:12; 13:29-30), salt (Mt 5:13).

Relation to God:
(Lev 20:24-26). Access to God (Ps 31:19-20; Isa 12:6). Few (Mt 7:14; 22:14). Righteous and wicked, circumstances of, contrasted (Job 8; Ps 17:14-15). *See below, Contrasted With the Wicked.*
At the judgment. *See Judgment.*
Fellowship of. *See Fellowship.*

Hatred toward. *See Persecution.*
Joy of. *See Joy.*
Perseverance of. *See Perseverance.*

Contrasted With the Wicked:
(Ps 1:1-6; 11:5; 17:14-15; 32:10; 37:17-22, 37-38; 73:1-28; 75:10; 91:7-8; Pr 2:21-22; 3:32-33; 4:16-19; 10:3, 6, 9, 11, 16, 20-21, 23-25, 28-32; 11:3, 5-6, 8-11, 18-21, 23, 31; 12:3, 5-7, 10, 12-13, 21, 26; 13:5-6, 9, 17, 21-22, 25; 14:2, 11, 19, 22-32; 15:6, 8-9, 28-29; 22:5, 8-9; 24:16; 28:1, 4-5, 13-14, 18; 29:2, 6-7, 27; Isa 32:1-8; 65:13-14; Ro 2:7-10; Eph 2:12-14; Php 2:15; 1Th 5:5-8; Tit 1:15; 1Pe 4:17-18; 1Jn 3:3-17).
See Wicked, Contrasted With the Righteous; Described as.

Described:
(Ps 1:1-3; 15:1-5; 24:3-5; 37:26, 30-31; 84:7; 112:1-10; 119:1-3; Isa 33:15-16; 51:1; 62:12; 63:8; Jer 17:7-8; 31:12-14, 33-34; Eze 18:5-9; Zec 3:2, 7-8). As dead to sin (Ro 6:2, 11; Col 3:3). Freed from sin (Ro 6:7, 18, 22; 1Jn 3:6, 9).
Good (Lk 6:45). Pure (Mt 5:8; 1Jn 3:3; 2Ti 2:21-22). Holy (Dt 7:6; Eph 1:4; 4:24; Col 1:22; 3:12; 1Pe 1:15; 2Ti 2:19; Heb 3:1). Sanctified (1Co 1:2; 6:11). Godly (Ps 4:3; 2Pe 2:9). Wise (Ps 37:30; Pr 2:9-12). Faithful (Mt 24:45; 25:21, 23; Lk 19:17; Eph 1:1; Col 1:2; Rev 17:14). Merciful (Mt 5:7). Meek (Mt 5:5; 2Ti 2:25). Industrious (Eph 4:28; 2Jn 9). Stable (Mt 7:24-27; Eph 4:14). Saved (Ac 2:47). Saints (Ro 1:7; 1Co 1:2; Eph 1:1). Chosen (1Pe 2:9; Rev 17:14). Spotless (Jas 1:27). Separate (Ex 33:16). Obedient (Mt 12:50; Jn 15:14; 1Jn 2:3, 5). New creature (2Co 5:17; Eph 2:10; 4:23-24; Col 3:9-10). Spiritually minded (Ro 8:4, 6). Patient, long-suffering, joyful (Col 1:11; 1Th 1:3). Peaceful, meek, gentle, patient (2Ti 2:21-25). Blameless, harmless, and without blemish (Eph 1:4; Php 2:15). Kind, tenderhearted, forgiving (Eph 4:32).
Servants of Christ (Eph 6:6). Servants of righteousness (Ro 6:19). Children of light (1Th 5:5). Children of God (Ro 8:14, 16; 1Jn 3:2). A temple of God (2Co 6:16). Beloved of God (Ro 1:7). Poor in spirit (Mt 5:3). Hungering and thirsting after righteousness (Mt 5:6). Growing in grace (Ps 84:7; Eph 4:13). Imitators of Christ (1Pe 4:1-2; 1Jn 2:6). Salt of the earth (Mt 5:13). City set on a hill (Mt 5:14). Led by the spirit (Ro 8:14; Gal 5:18). Filled with goodness and knowledge (Ro 15:14; Col 1:9-13). Grounded in love (Eph 3:17). Following Christ (Mt 10:38; 16:24; Mk 8:34; Lk 9:23). Rooted in Christ (Col 2:7).
Hating falsehood (Pr 13:5), abhorring wickedness (Ps 101:3-4), having renounced dishonesty (2Co 4:2). Without bitterness, wrath, anger, clamor, evil speaking, malice (Eph 4:31). Grieved by the wickedness of the wicked (Ps 119:158; Ac 17:16; 2Pe 2:7-8).

Happiness of:
(Job 5:17-27; Pr 3:13-18; 16:20; Mt 4:3-12). Satisfying (Ps 36:8; 63:5). Under fiery trials (1Pe 4:12-13). Under persecution (Mt 5:10-12).

Promises to and Comfort of:
Deliverance from temptation (1Co 10:13; 2Pe 2:9). Deliverance from trouble (Job 5:19-24; Ps 34:15, 17; 50:15; 91:15; 97:10-11; Pr 3:25-26; Isa 41:10-13; 43:2). Refuge in adversity (Ps 33:18-19; 62:8; 91:1-15; Pr 14:26; Na 1:7). Strength in adversity (Ps 29:11). Security (Ps 32:6-7; 84:11; 121:3-8; Isa 33:16). Providential care (Ge 15:1; Ex 23:22; Lev 26:5-6, 10; Dt 33:27; 1Sa 2:9; 2Ch 16:9; Ezr 8:22; Job 5:15; Ps 34:9-10; 125:1-3; 145:19-20; Pr 1:33; 2:7; 3:6; 10:3; 16:7; Isa 49:9-11; 65:13-14; Eze 34:11-17, 22-31; Lk 12:7, 32; 21:18; 1Pe 5:7). Overruling providence (Ro 8:28; 2Co 4:17).
Answer to prayer (Pr 15:29; Mk 11:23-24; Jn 14:13-14; Ac 10:4; 1Pe 3:12; 1Jn 3:22). Temporal blessings (Lev 25:18-19; 26:5; Dt 28:1-13; Ps 37:9; 128:1-6; Pr 2:21; 3:1-4, 7-10; Mt 6:26-33; Mk 10:30; Lk 18:29-30). Blessings upon their children (Ps 103:17; 112:2-3).

Righteous Receive—
Comfort in tribulation (Isa 25:8; 66:13-14; Mt 5:4; Jn 14:16-18; Rev 21:4). Joy (Isa 35:10; 51:11). Spiritual enlightenment (Isa 2:3; Jn 8:12). Peace (Isa 26:3; Ro 2:10). Seeing God (Mt 5:8). Inconceivable spiritual blessings (Isa 64:4; 1Co 2:9). The rest of faith (Heb 4:9). Wisdom (Jas 1:5). Divine help (Ps 55:22; Isa 41:10-13; Heb 13:5-6). Divine guidance (Ps 25:12; 32:8; 37:23-24; 48:14; 73:24; Pr 3:5-6). Divine mercy (Ps 32:10; 103:17-18; Mal 3:17). The divine presence (Ge 26:3, 24; 28:15; 31:3; Ex 33:14; Dt 31:6, 8; Jos 1:5; 1Ki 6:13; Hag 1:13; 2:4-5; Mt 28:20; Jn 14:17, 23; 2Co 6:16; 13:11; Php 4:9; Heb 13:5; Jas 4:8; Rev 21:3). The divine likeness (1Jn 3:2). The ministry of angels (Heb 1:14). Dwelling with Christ (Jn 14:2-3; Col 3:4; 1Th 4:17; 5:10). Everlasting remembrance (Ps 112:6). Having names written in heaven (Lk 10:20).
Resurrection (Jn 5:29; 1Co 15:48-57; 2Co 4:14; 1Th 4:16). Future glory (Ro 8:18; Col 3:4; 2Ti 2:10; 1Pe 5:4). Inheritance (Mt 25:34; Ac 20:32; 26:18; Col 1:12; 3:24; Tit 3:7; Heb 9:15; Jas 2:5; 1Pe 1:4). Heavenly reward (Mt 5:12; 13:43; 2Ti 4:8; Heb 11:16; Jas 1:12; 2Pe 1:11; Rev 2:7, 10; 22:5, 12, 14). Eternal life (Da 12:2-3; Mt 19:29; 25:46; Mk 10:29-30; Lk 18:29-30; Jn 3:15-18, 36; 4:14; 5:24, 29; 6:39-40; 10:28; 12:25-26; Ro 2:7; 6:22-23; Gal 6:8; 1Th 4:15-17; 1Ti 1:16; 4:8; Tit 1:2; 1Jn 2:25; 5:13; Rev 7:14-17).
Contingent upon perseverance (Heb 10:36; Rev 2:7, 10-11, 17, 26-28; 3:4-5, 10, 12, 21; 21:7).
See Adoption; Affliction, Comfort in; God, Preserver, Providence of.
Promises in specific areas. *See the specific topic.*

Union of:
With God (1Jn 3:24; 4:13, 15-16; 2Jn 9).
With Christ (Jn 6:51-58; 14:20, 15:1-11; 17:21-23, 26; Ro 8:1; 12:5; 1Co 6:13-20; 10:16; 2Co 13:5; Gal 2:20; Col 1:27; 2:6-7; 1Jn 2:6, 24, 28; 3:6, 24; 5:12, 20; 2Jn 9).
See Adoption; Communion; Fellowship, with Christ.

RIGHTEOUSNESS (Ps 15:1-5; 24:3-5; 106:3; Pr 11:5-6, 18, 30; Hos 10:12; Mt 5:20; Lk 1:75; Jn 16:8, 10; Ro 6:19-22; 8:4; Eph 4:24; Jas 1:27).

Required:
(Isa 28:17; Hos 10:12; Mic 6:8; Zec 7:9-10; 8:16-17; Mal 3:3; Mt 5:20; 23:23; Lk 3:10-14; 13:6-9; Ro 6:19-22; 7:4-6; 8:4; 14:17-19; 2Ti 2:22; 1Jn 3:10). Commanded in official administration (Jer 22:3, 6).

Imputed:
On account of obedience (Rev 6:25; Ps 106:31; Eze 18:9), on account of faith (Ge 15:6; Ro 4:3, 5, 9, 11, 13, 20, 22, 24; Gal 3:6; Jas 2:23). Proof of regeneration (1Jn 2:29). Exalts a nation (Pr 14:34). Safeguards life (Pr 10:2, 16; 11:19; 12:28; 13:6). Winning others to, rewarded (Da 12:3).

Fruits of:
(Ps 1:3; Mt 7:16-18; 12:35; Lk 6:43; Jn 15:4-8; 2Co 9:10; Gal 5:22-23; Php 1:11; Col 3:12-15; 1Th 1:3; Tit 2:2-6, 11-12; 1Pe 3:8-14; 2Pe 1:5-8; 1Jn 3:7). Generosity (Ac 11:29). Peace (Isa 32:17; Jas 3:8).

Symbolized:
(Eze 47:12; Rev 22:2). Figuratively described as a garment (Job 29:14; Isa 61:10; Zec 3:4; Mt 22:11-14; Rev 6:11; 7:9; 19:8).

Of God: *See God, Righteousness of.*

Of Jesus: *See Jesus the Christ, Holiness of, Righteousness of.*
See also, Sin, Fruits of; Works, Good.

RIM The rim of a wheel (1Ki 7:33; Eze 1:18).

RIMMON (*pomegranate*, or *Rimmon [pagan thunder, storm god]*).
1. Father of the murderers of Ish-Bosheth (2Sa 4:2, 5, 9).
2. A city S of Jerusalem (Zec 14:10). Allotted to Judah (Jos 15:32; Ne 11:29), afterward to Simeon (Jos 19:7; 1Ch 4:32). Also called En Rimmon (Ne 11:29).
3. A city of Zebulun (Jos 19:13). Also called Rimmono (1Ch 6:77).
4. A rock in Benjamin (Jdg 20:45, 47; 21:13).
5. A Syrian idol (2Ki 5:18).

RIMMON-METHOAR *See Rimmon, 3.*

RIMMON PEREZ (*pomegranate pass [breach]*). A camping place of the Israelites (Nu 33:19-20).

RIMMON, ROCK OF (*pomegranate rock*). The fortress to which 600 Benjamites fled after escaping slaughter (Jdg 20:45, 47; 21:13), near Gibeah.

RIMMONO *See Rimmon, 3.*

RING Of gold (Nu 31:50). Worn as a sign of office (Ge 41:42). Given as a token (Est 3:10, 12; 8:2-10). Worn in the nose (Pr 11:22; Isa 3:21). Offerings of, to the tabernacle (Ex 35:22; Nu 31:50).

RINGSTRAKED *See Streaked.*

RINNAH (*ringing cry [of joy] to Yahweh*). A son of Shimon (1Ch 4:20).

RIOT To squander in evil ways (Pr 23:20; 28:7), waste (Tit 1:6; 1Pe 4:4), revelry (Ro 13:13), luxury (2Pe 2:13).

RIPHATH A son of Gomer (Ge 10:3; 1Ch 1:6).

RISING

Early:
(Pr 31:15). For devotions (Ps 5:3; 59:16; 63:1; 88:13; SS 7:12; Isa 26:9). Practiced by the wicked (Pr 27:14; Mic 2:1; Zep 3:7), by drunkards (Isa 5:11). Illustrates spiritual diligence (Ro 13:11-12).

Instances of:
Lot (Ge 19:23). Abraham (Ge 19:27; 21:14; 22:3). Isaac (Ge 26:31). Abimelech (Ge 20:8). Jacob (Ge 28:18; 32:31). Laban (Ge 31:55). Moses (Ex 8:20; 9:13). Joshua (Jos 3:1; 6:12, 15; 7:16). Gideon (Jdg 6:38). Elkanah (1Sa 1:19). Samuel (1Sa 15:12). David (1Sa 17:20). Mary (Mk 16:2; Lk 24:1). Apostles (Ac 5:21).
See Industry.

Late:
Consequences of (Pr 6:9-11; 24:33-34).
See Idleness; Slothfulness.

RISSAH (*dew* ISBE). Encampment of Israelites in the wilderness (Nu 33:21-22), site unknown.

RITHMAH (*[place of] broom plants*). A camping place of the Israelites (Nu 33:18-19).

RIVER May refer to large streams (Ge 2:10-14), the Nile (Ge 41:1; 2Ki 19:24), a winter torrent, the bed of which is dry during summer (Am 6:14), fountain stream (Ps 119:136).
Figurative: Of salvation (Ps 36:8; 46:4; Isa 32:2; Eze 47:1-12; Rev 22:1-2). Of grief (Ps 119:136; La 3:48).

RIVER OF EGYPT
1. The Brook or Wadi of Egypt on the SW border of Israel, flowing into the Mediterranean Sea (Ge 15:18; Nu 34:5; 2Ki 24:7; Isa 27:12), probably modern Wadi el-Arish, though some identify it with the Nile.
2. The Nile (Am 8:8; 9:5).
See Egypt; Nile.

RIVERS Names of: Abana (2Ki 5:12). Arnon (Dt 2:36). Kebar (Eze 1:1). Euphrates (Ge 2:14). Gozan (2Ki 17:6; 1Ch 5:26). Jordan. *See Jordan.* Kanah (Jos 16:8). Kishon (Jdg 5:21). Of Egypt (Ex 1:22). Pharpar (2Ki 5:12). Pishon (Ge 2:11). Tigris (Ge 2:14). Ulai (Da 8:16).

RIZIA (possibly *pleasant one* KB). An Asherite (1Ch 7:39).

RIZPAH (*heated stones, live coals*). Concubine of Saul (2Sa 3:7). Guards the bodies of her sons hanged by command of David (2Sa 21:8-11).

ROADS May refer to paths or highways; hundreds of allusions to roads in the Bible; road robbers quite common (Mt 11:10; Lk 10:30), Romans built highways throughout the empire, some of which are still in use; used by traders, travelers, and armies; Paul used Roman roads on his missionary journeys; the statement "All roads lead to Rome" shows how well provided the Roman empire was with roads. *See Highways.*

ROBBERS (Pr 1:11-16). Dens of (Jer 7:11). Bands of (Hos 6:9; 7:1).

ROBBERY
Illegal seizure of another's property; forbidden by law (Lev 19:13); highways unsafe (Jdg 5:6; Lk 10:30; 2Co 11:26); houses built to resist robbers; even priests sometimes turned to pillage (Hos 6:9); denounced by prophets (Isa 61:8; Eze 22:29); withholding tithes and offerings from God's storehouse regarded as robbery (Mal 3:8). *See Theft.*

ROBE Of righteousness (2Ch 6:41; Isa 61:10; Rev 6:11; 7:9, 13). Parable of the man who was not dressed in a wedding garment (Mt 22:11).
See Dress.

ROBINSON'S ARCH The remains of ancient Jerusalem masonry, named for the American archaeologist Edward Robinson, who discovered it in 1838. Giant stones, projecting from the SW wall of the temple enclosure are evidently part of an arch that in Herod's time supported a monumental stairway.

ROBOAM *See Rehoboam, 2.*

ROCK Struck by Moses for water (Dt 8:15; Ps 78:15-16, 20). Houses in (Jer 49:16; Ob 3; Mt 7:24-25). Oil from (Job 29:6; Dt 32:13). Name of deity (Dt 32:4). *See God, Names of.*
Figurative (2Sa 22:32, 47; 23:3; Ps 18:2; 31:2; 40:2; Isa 17:10; 32:2; Mt 16:18; 1Co 10:4).

ROD Branch, stick, staff; symbol of authority (Ex 4:2, 17, 20; 9:23; 14:16), discipline symbolized by rod (Mic 5:1), messianic ruler (Isa 11:1), affliction (Job 9:34).

ROD OF AARON (Ex 7:9-10, 12, 15, 19-20; 8:5, 16-17; Nu 17:6, 8, 10; Heb 9:4).

ROD OF CORRECTION (Ps 89:32; Pr 10:13; 13:24; 22:15; 23:14; 26:3; 29:15; La 3:1).

ROD OF MOSES (Ex 4:2, 17, 20; 7:19; 8:16; 9:23; 10:13; 14:16; 17:5, 9).

RODANIM (*people of Rhodes*). The son of Javan; most manuscripts of the Masoretic Text have *Dodanim* (Ge 10:4, ftn). Tribe descended from Javan, son of Japheth (1Ch 1:7).

RODENTS (Isa 2:20). *See Animals; Rat(s).*

ROE DEER Permitted as food (Dt 14:5). *See Deer.*

ROGELIM (*[place of] treaders, fullers [one who cleans clothes by kneading with no soap]*). A town near Mahanaim whose citizens assisted David (2Sa 17:27, 29; 19:31).

ROHGAH Son of Shomer (1Ch 7:34).

ROI *See Beer Lahai Roi.*

ROLL Sheets of papyrus or parchment (made of skin) sewn together to make a long sheet of writing material which was wound around a stick to make a scroll (Isa 34:4; Jer 36; Eze 3:1-3; Rev 5; 10:1-10).

ROLLER NIV "splint" (Eze 30:21).

ROMAMTI-EZER (*[he is my] highest help*). Son of Heman (1Ch 25:4, 31).

ROMAN EMPIRE City of Rome founded in 753 B.C.; a monarchy until 509 B.C.; a republic from 509 to 31 B.C.; the empire began in 31 B.C., fell in the fifth century A.D. Rome extended its hold over all Italy and eventually over the whole Mediterranean world, Gaul, half of Britain, the Rhine-Danube rivers, and as far as Parthia.
Augustus, the first Roman emperor, divided the Roman provinces into senatorial districts, which were ruled by proconsuls (Ac 13:7; 18:12; 19:38), and imperial districts ruled by governors (Mt 27:2; Lk 2:2; Ac 23:24). Moral corruption was among the causes of the decline and fall of the Roman Empire. Roman reservoirs, aqueducts, roads, public buildings, statues survive.
Many Roman officials are referred to in the NT, including the emperors Augustus (Lk 2:1), Tiberius (Lk 3:1), Claudius (Ac 11:28), and Nero (Ac 25:11-12).

ROMANS, EPISTLE TO THE

Author: The apostle Paul

Date: Probably written in the early spring of A.D. 57

Outline:
I. Introduction (1:1-15).
II. Theme: Righteousness From God (1:16-17).
III. The Unrighteousness of All Mankind (1:18-3:20).
  A. Gentiles (1:18-32).
  B. Jews (2:1-3:8).
  C. Summary: All People (3:9-20).
IV. Righteousness Imputed: Justification (3:21-5:21).
  A. Through Christ (3:21-26).
  B. Received by Faith (3:27-4:25).
    1. The principle established (3:27-31).
    2. The principle illustrated (ch. 4).
  C. The Fruits of Righteousness (5:1-11).
  D. Summary: Man's Unrighteousness Contrasted With God's Gift of Righteousness (5:12-21).
V. Righteousness Imparted: Sanctification (chs. 6-8).
  A. Freedom From Sin's Tyranny (ch. 6).
  B. Freedom From the Law's Condemnation (ch. 7).

C. Life in the Power of the Holy Spirit (ch. 8).
VI. God's Righteousness Vindicated: The Problem of the Rejection of Israel (chs. 9-11).
A. The Justice of the Rejection (9:1-29).
B. The Cause of the Rejection (9:30-10:21).
C. Facts That Lessen the Difficulty (ch. 11).
1. The rejection is not total (11:1-10).
2. The rejection is not final (11:11-24).
3. God's ultimate purpose is mercy (11:25-36).
VII. Righteousness Practiced (12:1-15:13).
A. In the Body—the Church (ch. 12).
B. In the World (ch. 13).
C. Among Weak and Strong Christians (14:1-15:13).
VIII. Conclusion (15:14-33).
IX. Commendation and Greetings (ch. 16).

ROME The capital of the Roman Empire. The Jews were excluded from Rome by Claudius (Ac 18:2). Paul's visit to Rome. *See Paul.* Visited by Onesiphorus (2Ti 1:16-17). Paul desires to preach in (Ro 1:15). Abominations in (Ro 1:18-32). Christians in (Ro 16:5-17; Php 1:12-18; 4:22; 2Ti 4:21).

ROOF
See House, Architecture of.

ROOM
1. Chamber in a house (Ac 1:13). Used as a place for private prayer (Mt 6:6).
2. Place or position in society (Mt 23:6; Lk 14:7-8; 20:46).

ROOSTER Stately in its stride (Pr 30:31). Its crowing a sign of Peter's denial of Jesus (Mt 26:34, 74-75; Mk 13:35; 14:30, 68, 72).

ROOT Usually used in a figurative sense.
1. Essential cause of something (1Ti 6:10).
2. Foundation or support of something (2Ki 19:20; Job 5:3).
3. Injured roots means loss of life or vitality (Job 31:12; Isa 5:24).
4. Root of Jesse and Root of David, messianic titles (Isa 11:10; Ro 15:12; Rev 5:5; 22:16). *See Titles and Names, Of Jesus.*

ROPE Threefold (Ecc 4:12). Worn on the head as an emblem of servitude (1Ki 20:31-32). Used in casting lots (Mic 2:5).
Figurative: Of love (Hos 11:4). Of affliction (Job 36:8). Of temptations (Ps 140:5; Pr 5:22).

ROSE Or "crocus" (SS 2:1; Isa 35:1).

ROSETTA STONE Inscribed basalt slab, found on Rosetta branch of the Nile in 1799, with text in hieroglyphics, demotic (a cursive Egyptian language), and Greek. It furnished the key for the decipherment of hieroglyphics.

ROSH (*head, leader*).
1. Son of Benjamin (Ge 46:21).
2. Chief of three nations that are to invade Israel during the latter days (Eze 38:2; 39:1).

ROW, ROWERS *See Ship.*

RUBY A precious stone (Job 28:18; Pr 20:15; 31:10; La 4:7; Eze 27:16). In the priestly breastplate (Ex 28:17; 39:10). In the Garden of Eden (Eze 28:13).
See Minerals of the Bible, 1; Sardius; Stones.

RUDDER(S) Used to steer a ship (Ac 27:40; Jas 3:4).

RUDDY Red or fair complexion (1Sa 16:12).

RUDE (*untrained, ignorant of rules*). Technically not trained (2Co 11:6).

RUDIMENTS (*first principles or elements of anything*). Elements (Gal 4:3, 9; 2Pe 3:10, 12), first principles (Heb 5:12), physical elements of the world (2Pe 3:10, 12).

RUE (Lk 11:42).

RUFUS (*red haired*).
1. Brother of Alexander and son of Simon of Cyrene who bore the cross (Mk 15:21).
2. Friend of Paul (Ro 16:13).

S

RUHAMAH (*pitied*). A symbolic name of Israel used to indicate the return of God's mercy (Hos 2:1; cf Ro 9:25-26; 1Pe 2:10). A play on words is involved, for the second child of Gomer, wife of Hosea, was called Lo-Ruhamah, denoting a time when God had turned his back on Israel because of her apostasy. The NT references apply to Gentiles coming into the Church (Ro 9:25-26; 1Pe 2:10).
See Lo-Ammi; Lo-Ruhamah.

RULERS

General:
Appointed and removed by God. *See Government, God in.*
Chastised (Da 4). *See Nation.*
Monarchical. *See Kings.*
Patriarchal (Ge 27:29, 37). Instances of: Nimrod (Ge 10:8-10). Abraham (Ge 14:13-24; 17:6; 21:21-32). Melchizedek (Ge 14:18). Isaac (Ge 26:26-31). Judah (Ge 38:24). Heads of families (Ex 6:14). Ishmael (Ge 17:20). Esau and the chiefs of Edom (Ge 36).
Theocratic. *See Government.*
Ordained of God (2Ch 9:8; Ro 13:1-2, 4; 1Pe 2:14). Appointed by God (1Sa 9:15-17; 10:1; 15:17; 16:1, 7, 13; 2Sa 7:13-16; 1Ki 14:14; 16:1-4; 1Ch 28:4-5; 29:25; Ps 89:19-37; Da 2:21, 37; 5:21; Ac 13:22). Accountable to God (2Ch 19:6-7).
Servants of the people (1Ki 12:7; 2Ch 10:7; Eze 34:2-4). Loyalty to, commanded (Eze 7:26). Must not be reviled (Ex 22:28; 2Sa 16:9; 19:21; Ecc 10:20; Ac 23:5; 2Pe 2:10-11; Jude 8).
Righteous, beloved (Pr 29:2, 14). A terror to evildoers (Pr 14:35; Ro 13:3). Incompetent, oppress (Pr 28:16). Corrupted, by evil counselors (Pr 25:5), by gifts (Pr 29:4; Isa 1:23; Am 5:11-12; Mic 7:3).
Mosaic law concerning atonement for sins of (Lev 4:22-26).

Character and Qualifications of:
(Nu 27:16-17; 2Sa 23:4; Pr 20:8, 26, 28). Diligent (Ro 12:8). Wise (Ge 41:33; Dt 1:13; Ps 2:10; Pr 20:26; 28:2). Merciful (Isa 16:5; Zec 7:9).
Required to know the law (Jos 1:8; Ezr 7:25), to fear the Lord (Ps 2:11), to be truthful (Pr 17:7), to be righteous (Ex 18:21; Dt 16:19; 27:19; 2Sa 23:3-4; Pr 16:10, 12), to judge justly (Ex 18:16, 20-21; 23:3, 6-7, 9; Lev 19:15; 24:22; Dt 1:16-17; 25:1; 2Ch 9:8; Ps 82:2-4; Pr 31:9; Isa 16:5; 58:6; Jer 22:2-3; Zec 7:9-10; 8:16).
Should not drink wine (Pr 31:4-5). Forbidden to take bribes (Ex 23:8; Dt 16:19), to show partiality (Lev 19:15; Dt 1:17; 16:19; Pr 24:23).

Duties of:
To rule in righteousness (Isa 58:6; Jer 22:1-3). To be judges (2Ch 9:8). To judge according to law (Dt 17:18-19; Jos 1:7-8). In judicial functions to make thorough investigations (Dt 19:18-19).

Righteous, Instances of:
Pharaoh, in his treatment of Abraham (Ge 12:15-20). Abimelech, in his treatment of Abraham (Ge 20), of Isaac (Ge 26:6-11). Joseph, in his conduct of the affairs of Egypt (Ge 41:37-57). Pharaoh, in his treatment of Jacob and his family (Ge 47:5-10; 50:1-6). Moses, in his administration of the affairs of the Israelites (Nu 16:15). *See Government, Mosaic.* Samuel, in not taking reward for judgment (1Sa 12:3-4). Saul, after the defeat of the Ammonites (1Sa 11:12-13).
Solomon, in his judgment between the two women who claimed the same child (1Ki 3:16-28), according to the testimony of the queen of Sheba (1Ki 10:6-9). Asa, in abolishing sodomy and other abominations of idolatry (1Ki 15:11-15; 2Ch 14:2-5). Jehoshaphat, in walking in the ways of the Lord (1Ki 22:41-46; 2Ch 17:3-10; 19; 20:3-30). Hezekiah, in his fear of the Lord (2Ki 18:3; 20:1-11; 2Ch 30; 31). Josiah, in repairing the temple and in other good works (2Ki 22; 23; 2Ch 34; 35). Cyrus, in emancipating the Jews (Ezr 1). Darius, in advancing the rebuilding of the temple (Ezr 6:1-12). Artaxerxes, in commissioning Ezra to restore the forms of worship at Jerusalem (Ezr 7; Ne 2; 5:14). Nehemiah (Ne 4; 5). Daniel. *See Daniel.* King of Nineveh, in repenting and proclaiming a fast (Jnh 3:6-9).

Wicked:
(Ne 9:34-37; Ps 58:1-2; 82:2; 94:20-21; Ecc 3:16-17; 5:8; Isa 5:7; 28:14-15; Hos 7:3). Oppress the people (Ex 3:9; 1Sa 8:10-18; Job 35:9; Pr 28:15-16; Am 4:1; 5:11-12). Pervert justice (Dt 27:19). Cause people to mourn (Pr 29:2; Ecc 4:1). A public calamity (Ecc 10:16; Isa 5:22-23). An abomination to God (Pr 17:15). Abhorred by men (Pr 21:24; 29:2).
Admonitions to (Eze 34:2-4, 7-10; 45:9). Denounced (Eze 34:2-4, 7-10; Am 4:1-2; Mic 3:1-3, 9-11; Zep 3:3). Divine judgment upon (Isa 3:14-15; 10:1-3; 30:33; 40:23; Jer 5:28-29; Eze 21:25-26; Hos 5:10; Am 5:11-12; Zep 1:8).

Instances of—
Potiphar, putting Joseph into prison (Ge 39:20, w 40:15). Pharaoh, oppressing the Israelites (Ex 1-11). Adoni-Bezek, torturing seventy kings (Jdg 1:7). Abimelech, slaying his seventy brothers (Jdg 9:1-5). Eli's sons, desecrating the sacrifices (1Sa 2:12-17), debauching themselves and the worshipers (1Sa 2:22). Samuel's sons, taking bribes (1Sa 8:1-5).
Saul, sparing Agag and the best of the booty (1Sa 15:8-35), in jealousy plotting against David (1Sa 18:8-29), seeking to slay David (1Sa 19), slaying Ahimelech and the priests (1Sa 22:7-19), Hanun, mistreating David's servants (2Sa 10:4; 1Ch 19:2-5). David, numbering Israel and Judah (2Sa 24:1-9; 1Ch 21:1-7; 27:23-24). Solomon, luxurious and idolatrous (1Ki 11:1-13), oppressing the people (1Ki 12:4; 4:7-23). Rehoboam, making the yoke heavy (1Ki 12:8-11; 2Ch 10:1-15).
Jeroboam, perverting the true worship (1Ki 12:26-33; 13:1-5; 14:16), exalting wicked persons to the priesthood (1Ki 12:31; 13:33; 2Ki 17:32; 2Ch 11:14-15; Eze 44:7, w Nu 3:10). Abijah, walking in the sins of Rehoboam (1Ki 15:3). Nadab, walking in the ways of Jeroboam (1Ki 15:26). Baasha, walking in the ways of Jeroboam (1Ki 15:33-34). Asa, imprisoning the seer and oppressing the people (2Ch 16:10). Zimri, walking in the ways of Jeroboam (1Ki 16:19). Omri, walking in the ways of Jeroboam (1Ki 16:25-29). Ahab, serving Baal (1Ki 16:30-33; 21:21-26), confiscating Naboth's vineyard (1Ki 21, w 1Sa 8:14; 1Ki 22:38; 2Ki 9:26). Jehoram, following the sins of Jeroboam (2Ki 3:2-3). Hazael, committing atrocities (2Ki 8:12; 10:32; 12:17; 13:3-7). Jehoram, walking in the ways of the kings of Israel (2Ki 8:18; 2Ch 21:13). Jehu, did not depart from the sins of Jeroboam (2Ki 10:29). Jehoahaz, in following the sins of Jeroboam (2Ki 13:1-2). Jehoash, in following the wicked example of Jeroboam (2Ki 13:10-11). Jeroboam II, not departing from the sins of Jeroboam (2Ki 14:23-24). Zechariah, Menahem, Pekahiah, and Pekah, following the sins of Jeroboam (2Ki 15:9, 18, 24, 28), conspiring against and slaying Pekahiah (2Ki 15:25). Hoshea, who conspired against Pekah (2Ki 15:30), in permitting Baal worship (2Ki 17:1-2, 7-18). Ahaz, burning his children in idolatrous sacrifice (2Ki 16:3; 2Ch 28:2-4).
Manasseh, who committed the abominations of the heathen (2Ki 21:1-17; 2Ch 33:2-7). Amon, who followed the evil example of Manasseh (2Ki 21:19-22). Jehoahaz, who followed in the ways of his fathers (2Ki 23:32). Jehoiakim, in walking in the ways of his fathers (2Ki 23:37), and Jehoiachin (2Ki 24:9). Zedekiah, following the evil example of Jehoiakim (2Ki 24:19; 2Ch 36:12-13) and persecuting Jeremiah (Jer 38:5-6). Joash, killing Zechariah (2Ch 24:2, 17-25). Ahaziah, doing evil like the house of Ahab (2Ch 22:1-9). Amaziah, worshiping the gods of Seir (2Ch 25:14). Uzziah, invading the priest's office (2Ch 26:16).
Xerxes and Haman, decreeing the death of the Jews (Est 3). Nebuchadnezzar, commanding to destroy the wise men (Da 2:1-13), and committing the three Hebrews to the furnace (Da 3:1-23). Belshazzar, in drunkenness and committing sacrilege (Da 5:22-23). Darius, in deifying himself (Da 6:7, 9). The princes, conspiring against Daniel (Da 6:1-9).
Herod the Great, slaying the children in Bethlehem (Mt 2:16-18). Herod Antipas, in beheading John the Baptist (Mt 14:1-11), in craftiness and tyranny (Lk 13:31-32; 23:6-15). Herod Agrippa, persecuting the church (Ac 12:1-19). Pilate, delivering Jesus for crucifixion (Mt 27:11-26; Mk 15:15). Chief priests, elders, and all the council, seeking false witness against Jesus (Mt 26:59). Ananias, commanding that Paul be struck (Ac 23:2).
See Government; Judge; Kings.

RUMAH (*height*). Home of Pedaiah, whose daughter Zebidah bore Jehoiakim to Josiah, king of Judah (2Ki 23:36), perhaps Arumah near Shechem, or Rumah in Galilee.

RUNNER A bodyguard running before kings and princes (1Sa 8:11; 2Sa 15:1; 1Ki 1:5). An athlete (Job 9:25; 1Co 9:24). *See Army; Games.*

RUSH A water plant (Isa 19:6). *See Plants of the Bible; Reed.*

RUTH (*friendship* BDB; *refreshed [as with water]* IDB; possibly *comrade, companion* ISBE). A Moabitess who married a son of Elimelech and Naomi of Bethlehem (Ru 1:1-4), ancestor of Christ (Mt 1:5), the Book of Ruth is about her.

RUTH, BOOK OF

Author: Anonymous, Jewish tradition points to Samuel

Date: During the period of the monarchy

Outline:
I. Introduction: Naomi Emptied (1:1-5).
II. Naomi Returns From Moab (1:6-22).
A. Ruth Clings to Naomi (1:6-18).
B. Ruth and Naomi Return to Bethlehem (1:19-22).
III. Ruth and Boaz Meet in the Harvest Fields (ch. 2).
A. Ruth Begins Work (2:1-7).
B. Boaz Shows Kindness to Ruth (2:8-16).
C. Ruth Returns to Naomi (2:17-23).
IV. Ruth Goes to Boaz at the Threshing Floor (ch. 3).
A. Naomi Instructs Ruth (3:1-5).
B. Boaz Pledges to Secure Redemption (3:6-15).
C. Ruth Returns to Naomi (3:16-18).
V. Boaz Arranges to Marry Ruth (4:1-12).
A. Boaz Confronts the Unnamed Kinsman (4:1-8).
B. Boaz Buys Naomi's Property and Announces His Marriage to Ruth (4:9-12).
VI. Conclusion: Naomi Filled (4:13-17).
VII. Epilogue: Genealogy of David (4:18-22).

RYE *See Spelt.*

S

SABACHTHANI *See Eloi, Eloi, Lama Sabachthani.*

SABAEANS *See Sabeans; Seba.*

SABAOTH, LORD OF (*Yahweh of [angelic] armies*). Regularly translated "LORD Almighty" in the NIV. *See Almighty; God, Names of; Yahweh Tsabbaoth.*

SABBATH (*cease, rest*).

A Time of Rest:
(Ge 2:2-3; Lev 23:25; 26:34-35). Holy (Ex 16:23; Ex 20:8, 11; 31:14; 35:2; Dt 5:12; Ne 9:14; Isa 58:13-14; Eze 44:24). A sign (Ex 31:13, 16-17; Eze 20:12-13, 16, 20-21, 24). The Lord is represented as resting on (Ge 2:2-3; Ex 31:17; Heb 4:4).
Rest on, commanded (Ex 16:28-30; 23:12; 31:15; 34:21; 35:2-3; Lev 6:29-31; 19:3, 30; 23:1-3, 27-32; 26:2; Dt 5:12-15; 2Ch 36:21; Jer 17:21-22, 24-25, 27; Lk 23:56), of servants and animals (Ex 16:5, 23-30; 20:10; Mk 16:1; Lk 23:56).

Observation of:
Offerings prescribed for (Lev 24:8; Nu 28:9-10; 1Ch 9:32; 23:31; 2Ch 2:4; Eze 46:4-5). Song for (Ps 92:1-15; 118:24). Preparation for (Ex 16:5, 22; Mt 27:62; Mk 15:42; Lk 23:54; Jn 19:31). Religious usages on (Ge 2:3; Mk 6:2; Lk 4:16, 31; 6:6; 13:10; Ac 13:14).
Worship on (Eze 46:1, 3; Ac 15:21; 16:13). Commanded (Eze 46:1, 3). Religious instruction on (Mk 6:2; Lk 4:16, 31; 6:6; 13:10; Ac 13:14, 27, 42, 44; 15:21; 17:2; 18:4). Apostles taught on (Ac 13:14-43, 44-48; 17:2; 18:4). Hypocritical observance, provokes divine displeasure (Isa 1:13; La 2:6; Eze 20:12-13, 16, 21, 24; Am 8:5). Rewards for observance of (Isa 56:2, 4-7; 58:13-14; Jer 17:21-22, 24-25).
Observed by: Moses (Nu 15:32-34). Nehemiah (Ne 13:15, 21). The women preparing to embalm the body of Jesus (Lk 23:56). Paul (Ac 13:14). The disciples (Ac 16:13). John (Rev 1:10).

Violations of:
Punished, by death (Ex 35:2; Nu 15:32-36), by judgments (Jer 17:27). Instances of: Gathering manna (Ex 16:27). Gathering sticks (Nu 15:32). By men from Tyre (Ne 13:16). Inhabitants of Jerusalem (Jer 17:21-23). Profanation of (Ex 16:27-28; Nu 15:32-36; Ne 10:31; 13:15, 21; Jer 17:21-23; Eze 22:8; 23:38).

Christ's Interpretation of:
(Mt 12:1-8, 10-13; Lk 6:1-10; Mk 2:23-28; 13:10-17; 14:1-5; Jn 7:21-24; 9:14). Christ is Lord of (Mt 12:8; Mk 2:28; Lk 6:5). Christ performed miracles on (Mt 12:10-13; Mk 3:1-5; Lk 6:1-10; Lk 13:10-17; Jn 5:5-14; 7:21-24). Christ taught on (Mk 1:21-22; 6:2; Lk 4:16, 31; 6:6; 13:10-17).

The Christian and the Sabbath:
Christian not to be judged regarding (Col 2:16; Ro 1:1-12).

The first day of the week is called the Lord's day (Mt 28:1, 5-7; Mk 16:9; Jn 20:1, 11-16, 19, 26; Ac 20:7; 1Co 16:2; Rev 1:10).

SABBATH, COVERT FOR THE NIV "Sabbath canopy" (2Ki 16:18).

SABBATH, DAY AFTER THE The waving of the sheaf in Lev 23:11 may be on the day after the ordinary weekly Sabbath or after the first day of the Passover.

SABBATH DAY'S JOURNEY A limited journey (c. 3000 feet) which Rabbinic scholars thought a Jew might travel on the Sabbath without breaking the law (Ac 1:12; cf. Ex 16:29; Nu 35:5; Jos 3:4).

SABBATIC YEAR A rest recurring every seventh year. Called the Year of Release (Dt 15:9; 31:10). Ordinances concerning (Ex 23:9-11; Lev 25). Israelite servants set free in (Ex 21:2; Dt 15:12; Jer 34:14). Creditors required to release debtors in (Dt 15:1-6, 12-18; Ne 10:31). Ordinances concerning instruction in the law during (Dt 31:10-13; Ne 8:18). Punishment to follow a violation of the ordinances concerning (Lev 26:34-35, w 32-41; Jer 34:12-22). *See Jubilee.*

SABBEUS *See Shemaiah, 17.*

SABEANS One of the Sabean monarchs was the famous Queen of Sheba (1Ki 10:1, 4, 10, 13; 2Ch 9:1, 3, 9, 12). *See Sheba, 7.* The Sabeans were a merchant people from Sheba who in early times lived in SW Arabia (modern Yemen) in a region bordering Ophir and Havilah (Isa 45:14; Eze 23:42 cf. Eze 27:20-22). Romans called it *Arabia Felix.* Sabean raiders invaded the land of Uz and killed Job's flocks and servants (Job 1:15; Isa 43:3). Prophecies concerning (Isa 43:3; Joel 3:8). Giants among (Isa 45:14). Proverbial drunkards (Eze 23:42, ftn). They were slave traders (Joel 3:8). *See Seba.*

SABTA, SABTAH A son of Cush (Ge 10:7; 1Ch 1:9), perhaps also a place in S Arabia.

SABTECA A son of Cush (Ge 10:7; 1Ch 1:9).

SACAR (*reward [given by God]*, possibly *hired hand*).
1. Father of Ahiam (1Ch 11:35), "Sharar" (2Sa 23:33, ftn). *See Sharar.*
2. Son of Obed-Edom (1Ch 26:4).

SACKBUT *See Lyre.*

SACKCLOTH A symbol of mourning (1Ki 20:31-32; Job 16:15; Isa 15:3; Jer 4:8; 6:26; 49:3; La 2:10; Eze 7:18; Da 9:3; Joel 1:8). Worn by Jacob when it was reported to him that Joseph had been devoured by wild beasts (Ge 37:34). Animals covered with, at the time of national mourning (Jnh 3:8).
See Mourning.

SACRAMENT (*something obligated [to do]*). A symbolic rite instituted by Christ setting forth the central truths of the Christian faith: death and resurrection with Christ and participation in the redemptive benefits of Christ's mediatorial death. The Roman Catholic Church has seven sacraments; the Protestant Church has two, often called ordinances: baptism and the Lord's Supper.

SACRED PLACES (Dt 12:5, 11; 14:23; 15:20; 16:2; 17:8; Jos 9:27; 18:1; 1Ch 22:1; 2Ch 7:15; Ps 78:68). *See Tabernacle; Temple.*

SACRIFICES

Figurative:
(Isa 34:6; Eze 39:17; Zep 1:7-8; Ro 12:1; Php 2:17; 4:18). Of self-denial (Php 3:7-8). Of praise (Ps 116:17; Jer 33:11; Hos 14:2; Heb 13:15). "Fruit of the lips" signifies praise (Hos 14:2).
See Bruise(s), 2; Offerings.

SACRILEGE (*stealing*, hence, *profaning something sacred*). Profaning holy things. Forbidden (Lev 19:8; 1Co 3:17; Tit 1:11; 1Pe 5:2).

Instances of:
Esau sells his birthright (Ge 25:33). Nadab and Abihu offer unauthorized fire (Lev 10:1-7; Nu 3:4). Of Uzzah (2Sa 6:6-7). Of Uzziah (2Ch 26:16-21). Of Korah and his company (Nu 16:40). Of the people of Beth Shemesh (1Sa 6:19). Of Ahaz (2Ch 28:24). Of money changers in the temple (Mt 21:12-13; Lk 19:45; Jn 2:14-16). Of those who profaned the Lord's Supper (1Co 11:29).

SADDLE (*to ride, riding seat*). Getting a beast ready for riding (Ge 22:3; Nu 22:21; Jdg 19:10; 2Sa 16:1; 17:23). Donkeys were not ridden with saddles; when carrying heavy burdens they had a thick cushion on their backs.

SADDUCEES (*followers of Zadok;* possibly *righteous*). A Jewish religious sect in the time of Christ. Beliefs: Acceptance only of the Law and rejection of oral tradition; denial of the Resurrection, immortality of the soul, and the spirit world (Mk 12:18; Lk 20:27; Ac 23:8); they supported the Maccabeans; a relatively small group, but generally held the high priesthood; they were denounced by John the Baptist (Mt 3:7-8) and Jesus (Mt 16:6, 11-12); they opposed Christ (Mt 21:12f; Mk 11:15f; Lk 19:47) and the apostles (Ac 5:17, 33). *See Testaments, Time Between.*

SADOC *See Zadok.*

SAFE-CONDUCT Letters or passports provided to Nehemiah (Ne 2:7).

SAFFRON *See Plants of the Bible.*

SAHADUTHA *See Jegar Sahadutha.*

SAIL *See Ship.*

SAILORS *See Mariner; Occupations and Professions.*

SAINTS (*unique, consecrated, holy ones*).
1. A member of God's covenant people Israel, whether a layman (Ps 34:9; 79:1; 85:8), or a leader (2Ch 6:41; Ps 16:3).
2. A NT believer (Ac 9:13; 2Co 1:1). The saints are the Church (2Co 1:1), people called out of the world to be God's own people. Throughout the Bible the saints are urged to live lives befitting their position (Eph 4:1; Col 1:10), for even saints can sin (1Jn 1:10-2:2). *See Sanctification; Holiness.*

SAKIA (possibly *one who looks to Yahweh* KB). Son of Shaharaim (1Ch 8:10).

SALAH, SALA (*missile* or *petition* ISBE; possibly *javelin* KB). *See Shelah, 1.*

SALAMIS (*peace*). A city of Cyprus. Paul and Barnabas preach in (Ac 13:4-5).

SALATHIEL *See Shealtiel, 2.*

SALECAH A city on the NE boundary of Bashan (Dt 3:10; Jos 12:5; 13:11; 1Ch 5:11); possibly identified with Salkhad.

SALEM (*peace*). Name of a city of which Melchizedek was king (Ge 14:18; Ps 76:2; Heb 7:1-2), probably Jerusalem.

SALIM A place near Aenon W of Jordan (Jn 1:28; 3:23, 26; 10:40).

SALLAI (possibly *God had restored*).
1. A Benjamite dwelling in Jerusalem (Ne 11:8).
2. *See Sallu.*

SALLU (possibly *he restores*).
1. A Benjamite dwelling in Jerusalem (1Ch 9:7; Ne 11:7).
2. A priest who returned to Jerusalem with Zerubbabel (Ne 12:20).

SALMA (*little spark* KB).
1. A son of Caleb (1Ch 2:51, 54).
2. *See Salmon.*

SALMON (*little spark* KB). The father of Boaz, the husband of Ruth (Ru 4:20-21; 1Ch 2:11). In the lineage of Joseph (Mt 1:4-5; Lk 3:32). Also spelled Salma (Ru 4:20, ftn).

SALMONE A promontory of Crete (Ac 27:7).

SALOME (*peaceful, prosperous one*).
1. The wife of Zebedee and the mother of James and John (Mt 27:56; Mk 15:40; 16:1), ministered to Jesus (Mk 15:40-41), present at the crucifixion of Jesus (Mt 27:56), came to the tomb to anoint the body of Jesus (Mk 16:1).
2. The daughter of Herodias; as a reward for her dancing she obtained the head of John the Baptist (Mt 14:3-11; Mk 6:17-28). Her name is not given in the Gospels, but in Josephus.

SALT Lot's wife turned into a pillar of (Ge 19:26). The city of Salt (Jos 15:62). The valley of salt (2Sa 8:13; 2Ki 14:7). Salt sea (Ge 14:3; Nu 34:12; Dt 3:17; Jos 3:16; 12:3; 15:2). Salt pits (Zep 2:9). All animal sacrifices were required to be seasoned with (Lev 2:13; Ezr 6:9; Eze 43:24; Mk 9:49). Used in ratifying covenants (Nu 18:19; 2Ch 13:5). Elisha casts, into the pool of Jericho, to purify it (2Ki 2:20-21).
Symbolic: Of fidelity (Nu 18:19; 2Ch 13:5), of barrenness and desolation (Dt 29:23; Jdg 9:45; Jer 17:6; Zep 2:7).
Figurative: Of the saving efficacy of the church (Mt 5:13; Mk 9:49-50; Lk 14:34). Of wise conversation (Col 4:6).

SALT, CITY OF A city in the wilderness of Judah, between Nibshan and En Gedi (Jos 15:62), the site of which is uncertain; possibly Qumran.

SALT, COVENANT OF A covenant confirmed with sacrificial meals at which salt was used (Lev 2:13; Nu 18:19).

SALT HERBS A plant that grows in harsh terrain (Job 30:4).

SALT SEA *See Dead Sea.*

SALT, VALLEY OF A valley between Jerusalem and Edom in which great victories were won over the Edomites (2Sa 8:13; 2Ki 14:7; 2Ch 25:11).

SALU (*restored* IDB). Father of Zimri (Nu 25:14).

SALUTATIONS *See Greetings.*

SALVATION

Call to:
(Dt 30:19-20; Isa 55:1-3, 6-7; Lk 3:6; Ac 16:31; Heb 2:3).

Signifying:
Gracious providence (Dt 32:15; Ps 68:19-20; 91:16; 95:1; 116:13; 149:4; Isa 12:2-3). Personal deliverance from enemies (2Sa 22:36; Ps 3:8; 18:2; 37:39; Isa 1:18; 32:1-4). National deliverance from enemies (Ex 15:2; 1Ch 16:35; Ps 98:2-3; 106:8; Isa 46:12-13; Jer 3:23). A divine standard of righteousness (Isa 56:1), the saving power of divine truth (Isa 45:17), the light and glory of Zion (Isa 62:1). The promised Messiah (Jn 4:22). Personal righteousness (2Ch 6:41; Ps 132:16). Eternal life (1Th 5:8-9; 1Pe 1:5, 9; 1Jn 5:11). Everlasting (Isa 45:17; 52:10). Liberty (Isa 61:1-3; Mt 11:28-30).
To be developed (Php 2:12; 1Th 5:8-10; Jude 3).

From God:
(Ps 3:8; 36:8-9; 37:39; 68:18-20; 91:16; 98:2-3; 106:8; 121:1-8; Isa 46:12-13; 51:4-5; 63:9; Jer 3:23; 21:8; Eze 18:32; Joel 2:32; 1Pe 1:5; 1Jn 2:25).

Through Christ—
(Isa 61:10; Mt 1:21; Lk 19:10; 24:46-47; Jn 3:14-17; 11:51-52; Ac 4:12; 13:26, 38-39, 47; 16:30-31; Ro 5:15-21; 7:24-25; 9:30-33; 1Co 6:11; Gal 1:4; 3:13-14; Eph 1:9-10, 13; 2Ti 1:9-10; 2:10; Tit 3:5-7; Heb 2:3, 10; 5:9; 7:25; 1Jn 4:9-10; 5:11; Jude 3; Rev 3:20; 5:9).

By—
The atonement (1Co 1:18, 21, 24-25; Gal 1:4; 3:8, 13-14, 21, 26-28; Col 1:20-23, 26-27; 1Ti 2:6; Rev 5:9), the Resurrection (Ro 5:10), the gospel (Ro 1:16; Jas 1:21), the grace of God (Eph 2:8-9; Tit 2:11; 2Pe 3:15), the word of God (Jas 1:21), the power of God (1Co 1:18).

Message of:
Foretold by the prophets (Isa 29:18-19, 24; 35:8; Lk 2:31-32; 1Pe 1:10). By angels (Lk 2:9-14). From the seed of Abraham (Ge 12:13). Proclaimed by Christ (Lk 19:10; Jn 12:32). Preached by the apostles (Ac 11:17-18; 16:17). Wisdom for, derived from the Scriptures (2Ti 3:15). Praise for, ascribed to God and the Lamb (Rev 7:9-10).

For:
Israel (Isa 45:17; 46:12-13; Ac 13:26, 38-39, 47; Ro 1:16).
The Gentiles (1Ki 8:41-43; Isa 52:10, 15; 56:1, 6-8; Mt 21:31; 24:14; Jn 10:16; Ac 11:17-18; 15:7-9, 11; 28:28; Ro 11:11-12; 15:9, 16; Gal 3:8, 14; Eph 3:6, 9).
All people (Mt 18:14; 22:9-10; 22:14; Lk 2:10, 31 32; 3:6; 13:29; Gal 3:28; Eph 2:14, 17; Col 3:11; 1Ti 2:3-4; 4:10; 2Pe 3:9; Rev 5:9; 7:9-10; 14:6; 22:17).
Experienced by Moses (Ex 15:2). Priests clothed with (2Ch 6:41; Ps 132:16).

From:
From sin (Mt 1:21; Mk 2:17; Lk 5:31-32). From spiritual hunger and thirst (Jn 4:14; 6:35; 7:37-38).
See Adoption; Redemption; Regeneration; Sanctification.

Conditions of:
Repentance (Mt 3:2; Mk 1:4; Lk 3:8; Ac 2:38; 3:19; 2Co 7:10). Faith in Christ (Mk 16:15-16; Jn 3:14-18; 5:24; 6:47; 9:35; 11:25-26; 12:36; 20:31; Ac 2:21; 16:30-31; 20:21; Ro 1:16-17; 3:21-30; 4:1-25; 5:1-2; 10:4, 8-13; Gal 2:16; 3:8, 26-28; Eph 2:8; Php 3:9; 2Th 2:13; 1Ti 1:15-16; Heb 4:1-2; 1Pe 1:9). Supreme love to Christ (Lk 14:25-27). Renunciation of the world (Mt 19:16-21; Lk 14:33; 18:18-26). Choice (Dt 30:19-20; Ps 65:4; Eph 1:4-5). Seeking God (Am 5:4). Fear of God (Pr 14:27; 15:23; 16:6; Mal 4:2).
Not by works (Ro 3:28; 4:1-25; 9:30-33; Ro 11:6; Gal 2:16; Eph 2:8-9; 2Ti 1:9-10; Tit 3:5-7).
See Blessings, Spiritual, Contingent Upon Obedience; Faith; Obedience; Perseverance; Repentance.

Plan of:
(Jn 17:4; Heb 6:17-20). Foreordained (Eph 1:4-6; 3:11). Described as a mystery (Mt 13:11; Mk 4:11; Lk 8:10; Ro 16:25-26; 1Co 2:7-9; Eph 1:9-10, 13; 3:9-10; 6:19; Col 1:26-27; 1Ti 3:16; Rev 10:7).

Includes—
The incarnation of Christ (Gal 4:4-5). The atonement by Christ (Jn 18:11; 19:28-30; Ac 3:18; 17:3; Ro 16:25-26; 1Co 1:21-25; 2:7-9; Eph 1:7-11; 3:18; 6:19; Col 1:26-27; Heb 2:9-18; 10:10). Initial grace (Jn 6:37, 44-45, 65; Eph 2:5; Tit 2:11). The election of grace (2Th 2:13-14; 2Ti 1:9-10). Inheritance (Heb 1:14). Regeneration (Jn 3:3-12).

Sets Forth—
Reconciliation to God through Christ (2Co 5:18-19; Col 1:9, 19-23; Heb 2:14-18). Righteousness by faith in the atonement of Christ, as opposed to righteousness by works (Ro 10:3-9; 16:25-26; Eph 2:6-10).

Offered and Rejected—
(Dt 32:15; Mt 22:3-13; 23:37; Lk 14:16-24; Jn 5:40).

Parables of: (Lk 15:2-32).

Illustrated by:
A horn (Ps 18:2; Lk 1:69), a tower (2Sa 22:51), a helmet (Isa 59:17; Eph 6:17), a shield (2Sa 22:36), a lamp (Isa 62:1), a cup (Ps 116:13), clothing (2Ch 6:41; Ps 132:16; 149:4; Isa 61:10), wells (Isa 12:3), walls and bulwarks (Isa 26:1; 60:18), chariots (Hab 3:8), a victory (1Co 15:57).
Typified by the bronze snake (Nu 21:4-9, w Jn 3:14-15).
See Atonement; Jesus the Christ, Mission of; Redemption; Regeneration; Sanctification; Sin, Forgiveness of.

SAMARIA (*belonging to clan of Shemer, 1Ki. 16:24, BDB*).
1. City of, built by Omri (1Ki 16:24). Capital of the kingdom of the ten tribes (1Ki 16:29; 22:51; 2Ki 13:1, 10; 15:8). Besieged by Ben-Hadad (1Ki 20; 2Ki 6:24-33; 7). The king of Syria is led into, by Elisha, who miraculously blinds him and his army (2Ki 6:8-23). Ahab ruled in. *See Ahab; Jezebel.* Besieged by Shalmaneser, king of Assyria, three years; taken; the people carried away to Halah and Habor, cities of the Medes (2Ki 17:5-6; 18:9-11). Idolatry of (1Ki 16:32; 2Ki 13:6). Temple of, destroyed (2Ki 10:17-28; 23:19). Paul and Barnabas preach in (Ac 15:3). Visited by Philip, Peter, and John (Ac 8:5-25).
2. Country of (Isa 7:9). Foreign colonies distributed among the cities of, by the king of Assyria (2Ki 17:24-41; Ezr 4:9-10). Roads through, from Judea into Galilee (Lk 17:11; Jn 4:3-8). Jesus journeys through (Jn 4:1-42), heals lepers in (Lk 17:11-19). The good Samaritan from (Lk 10:33-35). No dealings between the Jews and the inhabitants of (Jn 4:9). Expect the Messiah (Jn 4:25). Disciples made from the inhabitants of (Jn 4:39-42; Ac 8:5-8, 4-17, 25). Jesus forbids the apostles to preach in the cities of (Mt 10:5).

SAMARITAN PENTATEUCH *See Samaritan(s), 2.*

SAMARITAN(S) (*of Samaria*).
1. The inhabitants of the region of Samaria (2Ki 17:26; Mt 10:5; Lk 9:52; 10:33; Jn 4:9, 30, 40; Ac 8:25). After the captivity of the N kingdom colonists from Babylonia, Syria, Elam, and other Assyrian territories (2Ki 17:24-34), intermarried with remnants of Jews in Samaria; held in contempt by the Jews (Ne 4:1-3; Mt 10:5; Jn 4:9-26).
2. The sect which derived its name from Samaria, a term of contempt with the Jews (Jn 8:48). Religion of the Samaritans was based on the Pentateuch alone.

S

SAMGAR, SAMGAR-NEBO Depending on word division, Samgar is the city of Nergal-Sharezer, a Babylonian official at the siege of Jerusalem, or Samgar-Nebo is himself an official (Jer 39:3 and ftn).
See Nebo-Sarsekim.

SAMLAH (*a garment*). One of the ancient kings of Edom (Ge 36:36-37; 1Ch 1:47-48).

SAMOS (*heights, lofty place*). An island in the Aegean Sea. Visited by Paul (Ac 20:15).

SAMOTHRACE (*Thracian Samos*). An island in the Aegean Sea. Visited by Paul (Ac 16:11).

SAMSON (*little one of Shemesh [pagan sun god]* or *sunny* IDB KB; *strong*, Josephus *Antiq.* 5.8.4). A judge of Israel (Jdg 16:31). A Danite, son of Manoah; miraculous birth of; a Nazirite from his mother's womb; the mother forbidden to drink wine or strong drink, or to eat any unclean thing during gestation (Jdg 13:2-7, 24-25). Desires a Philistine woman for his wife; slays a lion (Jdg 14:1-7). His marriage feast and the riddle propounded (Jdg 14:8-19). Wife of, estranged (Jdg 14:20; 15:1-2). Is avenged for the estrangement of his wife (Jdg 15:3-8). His great strength (Jdg 15:7-14; Heb 11:32). Slays a thousand Philistines with the jawbone of a donkey (Jdg 15:13-17). Miraculously supplied with water (Jdg 15:18-19). Consorts with Delilah, a harlot; her plots with the Philistines to overcome him (Jdg 16:4-20). Is blinded by the Philistines and confined to hard labor in prison; pulls down the pillars of the temple, killing himself and many Philistines (Jdg 16:21-31; Heb 11:32).

SAMUEL (*his name is God [El]* BDB IDB ISBE; *heard of God*, KD; *the unnamed god is El* KB).
1. Last of the judges (1Sa 7:15), and first of the prophets after Moses (2Ch 25:18; Jer 15:1). A seer (1Sa 9:9) and priest (1Sa 2:18, 27, 35). The son of Elkanah and Hannah (1Sa 1:19-20), birth the result of special providence. Brought up by Eli (1Sa 3), anointed Saul (1Sa 10) and David (1Sa 16:13). Traditional author of biblical books which bear his name, died at Ramah (1Sa 25:1).
2. Descendant of Issachar (1Ch 7:2).

SAMUEL, 1 and 2

Author: Anonymous, some have suggested Zabud, son of Nathan the prophet, who is referred to in 1Ki 4:5 as the "personal adviser" to King Solomon.

Date: Probably shortly after Solomon's death (930 B.C.)

Chronology of the Books of Samuel
(all dates B.C.):
1105: Birth of Samuel (1Sa 1:20).
1080: Birth of Saul.
1050: Saul anointed to be king (1Sa 10:1).
1040: Birth of David.
1025: David anointed to be Saul's successor (1Sa 16:1-13).
1010: Death of Saul and beginning of David's reign over Judah in Hebron (2Sa 1:1; 2:1, 4, 11).
1003: Beginning of David's reign over all Israel and capture of Jerusalem (2Sa 5).
997-992: David's wars (2Sa 8:1-14).
991: Birth of Solomon (2Sa 12:24; 1Ki 3:7; 11:42).
980: David's census (2Sa 24:1).
970: End of David's reign (2Sa 5:4-5; 1Ki 2:10-11).

Outline:
I. Historical Setting for the Establishment of Kingship in Israel (1Sa 1-7).
A. Samuel's Birth, Youth and Calling to Be a Prophet; Judgment on the House of Eli (1Sa 1-3).
B. Israel Defeated by the Philistines, the Ark of God Taken and the Ark Restored; Samuel's Role as Judge and Deliverer (1Sa 4-7).
II. The Establishment of Kingship in Israel Under the Guidance of Samuel the Prophet (1Sa 8-12).
A. The People's Sinful Request for a King and God's Intent to Give Them a King (1Sa 8).
B. Samuel Anoints Saul Privately to Be King (1Sa 9:1-10:16).
C. Saul Chosen to Be King Publicly by Lot at Mizpah (1Sa 10:17-27).
D. The Choice of Saul as King Confirmed by Victory Over the Ammonites (1Sa 11:1-13).
E. Saul's Reign Inaugurated at a Covenant Renewal Ceremony Convened by Samuel at Gilgal (1Sa 11:14-12:25).
III. Saul's Kingship a Failure (1Sa 13-15).
IV. David's Rise to the Throne; Progressive Deterioration and End of Saul's Reign (1Sa 16:1-2Sa 5:5).
A. David Is Anointed Privately, Enters the Service of King Saul and Flees for His Life (1Sa 16-26).
B. David Seeks Refuge in Philistia, and Saul and His Sons Are Killed in Battle (1Sa 27-31).
C. David Becomes King Over Judah (2Sa 1-4).
D. David Becomes King Over All Israel (2Sa 5:1-5).
V. David's Kingship in Its Accomplishments and Glory (2Sa 5:6-9:12).
A. David Conquers Jerusalem and Defeats the Philistines (2Sa 5:6-25).
B. David Brings the Ark to Jerusalem (2Sa 6).
C. God Promises David and Everlasting Dynasty (2Sa 7).
D. The Extension of David's Kingdom Externally and the Justice of His Rule Internally (2Sa 8).
E. David's Faithfulness to His Covenant With Jonathan (2Sa 9).
VI. David's Kingship in Its Weaknesses and Failures (2Sa 10-20).
A. David Commits Adultery and Murder (2Sa 10-12).
B. David Loses His Sons Amnon and Absalom (2Sa 13-20).
VII. Final Reflections on David's Reign (2Sa 21-24).

SANBALLAT (*Sin [pagan moon god] has given life*). A very influential Samaritan who tried unsuccessfully to defeat Nehemiah's plans for rebuilding the walls of Jerusalem (Ne 4:1ff; 6:1-14; 13:28).

SANCTIFICATION Separated, set apart, made holy: For God (Ex 33:16; Dt 7:6). From iniquity (2Ti 2:21).

By:
God (Ex 29:44; 31:13; Lev 20:8; 21:8, 15, 23; 22:9, 16; Jer 1:5; Eze 20:12; 37:28). In Christ (1Co 1:2, 30; 6:11; Eph 5:25-27; Heb 2:11; 10:10, 14; 13:12). By the Holy Spirit (Ro 15:16; 2Th 2:13-14; 1Pe 1:2).
By the blood of Christ (Heb 9:14; 13:12). By faith in Christ (Ac 26:17-18). By the truth (Jn 17:17, 19). By confession of sin (1Jn 1:9). By intercessory prayer for (1Th 5:23). Sanctification is the will of God (1Th 4:3-4).

Instances of:
The altar sanctifies the gift (Ex 29:37; 30:29; Mt 23:19).
The Sabbath (Ge 2:3; Dt 5:12; Ne 13:22). Mount Sinai (Ex 19:23). The tabernacle (Ex 29:43-44; 30:26, 29; 40:34-35; Lev 8:10; Nu 7:1). The furniture of the tabernacle (Ex 30:26-29; Nu 7:1). The altar of burnt offerings (Ex 29:36-37; 40:10-11; Lev 8:11, 15; Nu 7:1). The basin (Ex 30:23; Lev 8:11). The temple (2Ch 29:5, 17, 19).
Houses (Lev 27:14-15). Land (Lev 27:16-19, 22). Offerings (Ex 29:27). Material things by anointing (Ex 40:9-11).
The firstborn of Israelites (Ex 13:2; Lev 27:26; Nu 8:17; Dt 15:19). Eleazar to get the ark (1Sa 7:1). Jesse to offer a sacrifice (1Sa 16:5). Job's children, by Job (Job 1:5).
Of Levites (1Ch 15:12, 14; 2Ch 29:34; 30:15), commanded (1Ch 15:12; 2Ch 29:5). Of priests (1Ch 15:14; 2Ch 5:11; 30:24), commanded (Ex 19:22). Of Aaron and his sons (Ex 28:41; 29:33, 44; 40:13; Lev 8:12, 30). Of Israel (Ex 29:10, 14)], commanded (Ex 19:10; Lev 11:44; 20:7; Nu 11:18; Jos 3:5; 7:13; Joel 2:16).
Of the Corinthian Christians (1Co 1:2; 6:11; 7:14). Of the church (Eph 5:26; 1Th 5:23; Jude 24).
See Holiness; Purity; Sin, Forgiveness of; Spiritual Purification.

SANCTUARY (*sacredness, apartness, place apart, sacred place, holy place*).
1. The tabernacle or temple, where God established his earthly abode.
2. Judah (Ps 114:2).
3. Place of asylum (1Ki 2:28f).
4. In plural, idolatrous shrines (Am 7:9).
5. Earthly sanctuary a type of the heavenly sanctuary, in which Christ is high priest and sacrifice (Heb 10:1-18).

SAND Found in the desert and on the shores of large bodies of water; symbolic of numberlessness, vastness (Ge 22:17; Jer 33:22; 1Ki 4:29), weight (Job 6:3), and instability (Mt 7:26).

SANDAL Taken off on holy ground (Ex 3:5; Jos 5:15; Ac 7:33), in mourning (Eze 24:17), in token of refusal to observe the Levirate marriage (Dt 25:9; Ru 4:7-8). Of the Israelites did not wear out (Dt 29:5). Poor sold for a pair of (Am 2:6; 8:6). Made of leather (Eze 16:10), thong of (Ge 14:23; Isa 5:27; Mk 1:7), untying of, a humble service (Lk 3:16).
See Dress.

SANDBARS Off the shores of N Africa S of Crete; site of Paul's shipwreck (Ac 27:17, 41).

SANHEDRIN (*sit together*). Highest Jewish tribunal during Greek and Roman periods; its origin is unknown; lost its authority when Jerusalem fell to the Romans in A.D. 70; in the time of Jesus it had authority only in Judea, but its influence was recognized even in the Diaspora (Ac 9:2; 22:5; 26:12). Composed of seventy members, plus the president, who was the high priest; members drawn from chief priests, scribes, and elders (Mt 16:21; 27:41; Mk 8:31; 11:27; 14:43, 53; Lk 9:22); the secular nobility of Jerusalem; final court of appeal for all questions connected with the Mosaic law; could order arrests by its own officers of justice (Mt 26:47; Mk 14:43; Ac 4:3; 5:17f; 9:2); did not have the right of capital punishment in the time of Christ (Jn 18:31-32). *See Elders, Council of.*

SANITATION AND HYGIENE

Relating to:
Carcasses (Lev 5:2; 10:4-5; 11:24-40; 22:4, 6; Nu 9:6, 10; 19:11-16; 31:19; Dt 21:22-23). Childbirth (Lev 12:3; Eze 16:4). Circumcision. *See Circumcision.* Contagion (Lev 5:2-3; 7:19, 21; 11:24-40; Nu 9:6, 10; 19:11-16, 22; 31:19-20). Infectious skin diseases (Lev 13-14; Nu 5:2-4; Dt 24:8). Bodily discharges (Lev 15:2-33; 22:4-8).

For Prevention of the Spread of Disease:
By washing (Lev 13:6, 34, 53-54, 58-59; 14:8-9, 46, 48, 54-57; 15:2-28; Nu 31:19-20, 22-24; Dt 23:10-11). By burning (Lev 7:19; 13:51-52, 55-57; Nu 31:19-20, 22-23). By isolation, *i.e.*, quarantine (Lev 13:2-5, 31-33, 45-50; 14:34-38; 15:19; Nu 5:2-3; 12:10, 14-15; 2Ki 7:3; 15:5; 2Ch 26:21; Lk 17:12). By demolishing infected houses (Lev 14:39-45).

Food:
Acceptable: Animals with split hoof that chew cud (Lev 11:2-3; Dt 14:6). Aquatic animals having fins and scales (Lev 11:9; Dt 14:9). Certain insects (Lev 11:22).
Forbidden: Fat (Lev 3:17; 7:23-25). Blood (Lev 3:17; 7:26-27; 17:10-14; 19:26; Dt 12:16, 20-25; 15:22-23). Meat that touched anything unclean (Lev 7:19). Meat of fellowship and thank offerings remaining until the second day (Lev 7:15; 22:30). Meat of vow or voluntary offerings left until the third day (Lev 7:16, 18; 19:5-8). Animals that only chew cud or only have a split hoof (Lev 11:4, 8, 26; Dt 14:7-8). Aquatic animals without fins and scales (Lev 11:10-12; Dt 14:10). Animals dying of themselves or torn by beasts (Ex 22:31; Lev 17:15; 22:8; Dt 14:21). Certain insects (Lev 11:23). Certain creatures that move on the ground (Lev 11:20-21, 28-31, 41). Certain birds (Lev 11:13-18).

Waste Products:
Disposition (Ex 29:14, 34; Lev 4:11-12, 21; 6:30; 7:17, 19; 8:17, 32; 9:11; 16:27-28; 19:6; Dt 23:12-13; Heb 13:11).

Women in Childbirth: (Lev 12:2, 4-5).

Penalties Concerning:
(Dt 28:15, 21-22, 27, 35, 45, 59-62).
See Defilement; Leprosy; Purification; Unclean, Uncleanness; Washings.

SANNAH *See Kiriath Sannah.*

SANSANNAH (*a palm branch*). A city of Judah (Jos 15:31).

SAPH (*a basin, threshold*). A Philistine giant, slain by one of David's heroes (2Sa 21:18; 1Ch 20:4).

SAPHIR *See Shaphir.*

SAPPHIRA (*beautiful*). The wife of Ananias; struck dead at Peter's feet because she lied (Ac 5:1-10).

SAPPHIRE
1. A precious stone (Ex 24:10; Eze 28:13).
2. Set in the priestly breastplate (Ex 28:18; 39:11).

Symbolic:
Throne of God (Ex 24:10; Eze 1:26; 10:1). Seen in the foundation of the Holy City, the New Jerusalem in John's apocalyptic vision (Rev 21:19).

Figurative:
Ezekiel uses imagery of the Creation and the Fall to picture the career of the king of Tyre; unlike Adam, who was naked, the king is pictured as a fully clothed priest, ordained to guard God's holy place; the nine stones listed are among the twelve worn by the priest (Eze 28:13).
See Minerals of the Bible, 1; Stones.

SARAH, SARAI (*princess*).
1. The wife of Abraham (Ge 11:29-31; 12:5). Near of kin to Abraham (Ge 12:10-20; 20:12). Abraham represents her as his sister, and Abimelech, king of Gerar, takes her; she is restored to Abraham by means of a dream (Ge 20:1-14). Is sterile; gives her maid, Hagar, to Abraham as a wife to bear his child (Ge 16:1-3). Her jealousy of Hagar (Ge 16:4-6; 21:9-14). Her miraculous conception of Isaac (Ge 17:15-21; 18:9-15). Name changed from Sarai to Sarah (Ge 17:15). Gives birth to Isaac (Ge 21:3, 6-8). Death and burial of (Ge 23; 25:10). Character of (Heb 11:11; 1Pe 3:5-6).
2. The daughter of Asher (Ge 46:17; Nu 26:46; 1Ch 7:30).

SARAPH (*burning one, serpent*). A descendant of Shelah (1Ch 4:22).

SARCASM

Instances of:
Cain's self-justifying argument when God asked him where Abel was (Ge 4:9). Israelites reproaching Israel (Nu 11:20; Jdg 10:14). Balak reproaching Balaam (Nu 24:11). Joshua to descendants of Joseph (Jos 17:15). By Jotham (Jdg 9:7-19), Samson (Jdg 14:18). The men of Jabesh to Nahash (1Sa 11:10). Eliab to David (1Sa 17:28). Elijah to the priests of Baal (1Ki 18:27). David's reply to Michal's irony (2Sa 6:21). Ahab's reply to Ben-Hadad (1Ki 20:11). Jehoash to Amaziah (2Ki 14:9-10; 2Ch 25:18-19). The field commander to Hezekiah (2Ki 18:23-24). Sanballat's address to the army of Samaria (Ne 4:2-3). Zophar to Job (Job 11:12). Job to Zophar (Job 12:2-3). Of Solomon (Pr 26:16). The persecutors of Jesus (Mt 27:28-29; Lk 23:11; Jn 19:2-3, 5, 15). Paul (1Ti 4:7). Agrippa to Paul (Ac 26:28).
See Irony; Satire.

SARDINE *See Carnelian; Minerals of the Bible.*

SARDIS Chief city of Lydia; famous for arts and crafts; patron of mystery cults (Rev 1:11; 3:1-6).

SARDITE *See Sered, Seredite.*

SARDIUS *See Carnelian; Minerals of the Bible, 1; Ruby; Stones.*

SARDONYX A precious stone seen in the foundation of the Holy City, the New Jerusalem (Rev 21:20). *See Minerals of the Bible, 1; Stones.*

SAREPTA *See Zarephath.*

SARGON (*firm, faithful king* BDB; *the king is legitimate* IDB).
1. Sargon I, king and founder of early Babylonian Empire (2400 B.C.). Not referred to in the Bible.
2. Sargon II (722-705 B.C.), an Assyrian king (Isa 20:1), successor of Shalmaneser who captured Samaria (2Ki 17:1-6), defeated Egyptian ruler So (2Ki 17:4), destroyed the Hittite Empire; succeeded by his son Sennacherib.

SARID (*survivor*). A village on the boundary of Zebulun (Jos 19:10, 12); modern Tel Shadud, N of Megiddo.

SARON *See Sharon.*

SARSECHIM *See Nebo-Sarsekim.*

SARUCH *See Serug.*

SASH A belt or waistband. Worn by the high priest (Ex 28:4, 39; 39:29; Lev 8:7; 16:4), by other priests (Ex 28:40; 29:9; Lev 8:13), by women (Isa 3:18-24), by Jesus in John's vision (Rev 1:13). Commerce in (Pr 31:24). *See Belt; Dress.*

SATAN (*hostile opponent*).
1. As a common noun; enemy or adversary (1Sa 29:4; 1Ki 5:4; 11:14; Ps 38:20; 109:6).
2. As a proper noun; the chief of the fallen spirits, the grand adversary of God and man (Jn 1:6, 12; 2:1; Zec 3:1), hostile to everything good. Not an independent rival of God, but is able to go only as far as God permits (Job 1:12; 2:6; Lk 22:31). Basically evil; story of his origin not told, but he was originally good; fell as

S

a star out of heaven because of pride (possibly Isa 14:12; Eze 29:12-19; Lk 10:18; 1Ti 3:6). Ruler of a powerful kingdom standing in opposition to God (Mt 12:26; Lk 11:18); continually seeks to defeat the divine plans of grace toward mankind (1Pe 5:8); defeated by Christ at Calvary (Ge 3:15; Jn 3:8).

Sterilizes the heart (Mt 13:19, 38-39; Mk 4:15; Lk 8:12). Causes spiritual blindness (2Co 4:4), physical infirmities (Lk 13:16).

Devices of (2Co 2:11; 12:7; Eph 6:11-12, 16; 1Th 2:18; 1Ti 3:6-7).

Hymenaeus and Alexander delivered to (1Ti 1:20). Contends with Michael (Jude 9). Ministers of, masquerade as apostles of Christ (2Co 11:15).

To be resisted (Eph 4:27; Jas 4:7; 1Pe 5:8-9). Resistance of, effectual (1Jn 2:13; 5:18). Gracious deliverance from the power of (Ac 27:18; Col 1:13). Persecutes the church (Rev 2:10, 13-14).

Christ accused of being (Mt 9:34; Mk 2:22-26; Lk 11:15, 18). Paul accuses Elymas the sorcerer of being (Ac 13:10).

Called:

Beelzebub (Mt 12:24; Mk 3:22; Lk 11:15). Belial (2Co 6:15). The devil (Mt 4:1; 13:39; Lk 4:2-6; Rev 20:2). Satan (1Ch 21:1; Job 1:6; Zec 3:1; Lk 22:31; Jn 13:27; Ac 5:3; 26:18; Ro 16:20). Possibly Apollyon (Rev 9:11) and Lucifer (Isa 14:12, KJV). *See Titles and Names, Of the Devil.*

Character of:

Accuser (Job 1:6-7, 9-12; 2:3-7). Adversary (Lk 22:31, 53; 1Pe 5:8). Deceiver of the whole world (Rev 12:9). Murderer and liar (Jn 8:44; Ac 5:3). Sinned from the beginning (1Jn 3:8). Subtle (Ge 3:1; 2Co 11:3). Tempter (Mt 4:3; 1Co 7:5; 1Th 3:5; 1Ti 5:15). Transforms himself into an angel of light (2Co 11:14).

Described as:

Accuser of our brothers (Rev 12:10). Ancient serpent (Rev 12:9; 20:2). Angel of the bottomless pit (Rev 9:11). Enemy (Mt 13:29). Father of lies (Jn 8:44). Great dragon (Rev 12:9). Evil one (Mt 13:19, 38). Power of darkness (Col 1:13). Prince of this world (Jn 12:31; 14:30; 16:11), of demons (Mt 12:24), of the power of the air (Eph 2:2). Ruler of the darkness of this world (Eph 6:12). Spirit that works in the children of disobedience (Eph 2:2). The god of this world (2Co 4:4).

Instances of Temptations of:

Eve (Ge 3:1, 4-5, 14-15; 2Co 11:3). Job (Job 1:13-22; 2:7-10). David (1Ch 21:1). Jesus (Mt 4:1-11; Mk 1:13; Lk 4:1-13; Jn 14:30). Judas (Jn 13:2, 27).

Kingdom of:

Called gates of hell (Mt 16:18). To be destroyed (Ge 3:15; Mt 13:30; Ro 16:20; 1Jn 3:8).

Symbolized:

By the serpent (Ge 3:13; 2Co 11:3). By the dragon (Rev 12:3-4).

Synagogue of: (Rev 2:9; 3:9).
See Demons.

Destiny of:

A conquered enemy of believers (Jn 12:31; 16:9-10; 1Jn 3:8; Col 2:15). Judged already (Jn 16:11). Under perpetual curse (Ge 3:14; Isa 65:25). To be cast out of this world (Jn 12:31), bound (Rev 20:1-3), cast into the lake of fire (Mt 25:41; Rev 20:10).

SATIRE Hannah's song of exultation over Peninnah (1Sa 2:1-10, w 1:5-10). Of Jesus against hypocrites (Mt 23:2-33; Mk 12:13-40; Lk 11:39-54). *See Irony; Sarcasm.*

SATRAP (*protector of the land*). An official in the Persian Empire who ruled several small provinces (satraps), each having its own governor. (Ezr 8:36; Est 3:12; 8:9; 9:3; Da 3:2-3, 27; 6:1-7).

SATYR NIV "goat idols" (Lev 17:7; 2Ch 11:15); "wild goats" (Isa 34:14).

SAUL (*asked,* possibly *dedicated to God*).

1. Also called Shaul. King of Edom (Ge 36:37-38; 1Ch 1:48-49)

2. King of Israel. A Benjamite, son of Kish (1Sa 9:1-2). Sons of (1Ch 8:33). His personal appearance (1Sa 9:2; 10:23). Made king of Israel (1Sa 9; 10; 11:12-15; Hos 13:11). Dwells at Gibeah of Saul (1Sa 14:2; 15:34; Isa 10:29). Defeats the Philistines (1Sa 13; 14:46, 52). Kills the Amalekites (1Sa 15). Is reproved by Samuel for usurping the priestly functions (1Sa 13:11-14), for disobedience in not slaying the Amalekites; the loss of his kingdom foretold (1Sa 15). Dedicates the spoils of war (1Sa 15:21-25; 1Ch 26:28). Sends messengers to Jesse, asking that David be sent to him as musician and armor-bearer (1Sa 16:17-23). Defeats the Philistines after Goliath is slain by David (1Sa 17). His jealousy of David; gives his daughter, Michal, to David to be his wife; becomes David's enemy (1Sa 18). Tries to slay David; Jonathan intercedes and incurs his father's displeasure; David's loyalty to him; Saul's repentance; prophesies (1Sa 19). Hears Doeg against Ahimelech and slays the priest and his family (1Sa 22:9-19). Pursues David to the wilderness of Ziph; the Ziphites betray David to (1Sa 23). Pursues David to En Gedi (1Sa 24:1-6). His life saved by David (1Sa 24:5-8). Saul's contribution for his bad faith (1Sa 24:16-22). David is again betrayed to, by the Ziphites; Saul pursues him to the hill of Hakilah; his life spared again by David; his confession and his blessing upon David (1Sa 26). Slays the Gibeonites; crime avenged by the death of seven of his sons (2Sa 21:1-9). His kingdom invaded by Philistines; seeks counsel of the medium of Endor, who foretells his death (1Sa 28:3-25; 29:1). Is defeated and with his sons is slain (1Sa 31), their bodies exposed in Beth Shan; rescued by the people of Jabesh and burned; bones of, buried under a tree at Jabesh (1Sa 31, w 2Sa 1; 2; 1Ch 10). His death a judgment on account of his sins (1Ch 10:13).

3. Of Tarsus. *See Paul.*

SAVIOR (*deliverer*). One who saves, delivers, or preserves from any evil or danger, whether physical or spiritual, temporal or eternal; term applied both to people (Jdg 3:9, 15; 2Ki 13:5; Ne 9:27; Ob 21) and to God (Ps 44:3, 7; Isa 43:11; 45:21; 60:16; Jer 14:8; Hos 13:4). In NT it is never applied to people, but only to God and Christ (Lk 1:47; 1Ti 1:1; 2:3; 4:10; Tit 1:3). Savior is preeminently the title of the Son (2Ti 1:10; Tit 1:4; 2:13; 3:6; 2Pe 1:1; 1Jn 4:10).
See God, Savior; Jesus the Christ, Savior.

SAVOR Taste (Mt 5:13; Lk 14:34), smell (Joel 2:20). Also used metaphorically (2Co 2:14; Eph 5:2; Php 4:18).

SAVORY MEAT NIV "tasty food." Meals made by Jacob and Esau for their father Isaac prior to receiving his blessings (Ge 27:4, 9, 14, 17, 31).

SAW Used as an instrument of torture (Heb 11:37), for cutting stone (2Sa 12:31; 1Ki 7:9).
Figurative (Isa 10:15).

SCAB Disease of the skin (Lev 13:2, 6-8; 14:56; 21:20; 22:22; Dt 28:27; Isa 3:17).
See Disease; Sanitation and Hygiene.

SCAFFOLD NIV "platform" (2Ch 6:13).

SCALE

1. Only fish having fins and scales were permitted as food for Hebrews (Lev 11:9-12).

2. Instrument for weighing (Isa 40:12; Pr 16:11; 20:23).

SCALL NIV "itch," an infectious skin disease (Lev 13:30-37; 14:54; Dt 28:27). *See Disease; Leprosy; Sore.*

SCAPEBIRD (Lev 14:4-7, 53).

SCAPEGOAT The second of two goats for which lots were cast on the Day of Atonement (Lev 16:8, 10, 26). The first was sacrificed as a sin offering, but the second had the people's sins transferred to it by prayer and was then taken into the wilderness and released.
See Azazel.

SCARLET Probably a bright rich crimson. Scarlet cloth was used for the hangings of the tabernacle (Ex 25:4), high priest's vestments (Ex 39:1), royal or expensive apparel (2Sa 1:24). Sins are "as scarlet" (Isa 1:18).
See Colors, Figurative and Symbolic.

SCEPTER (*royal staff*). A staff used by kings to signify favor or disfavor to those who desired audience (Est 5:2; 8:4). A symbol of authority (Nu 24:17; Isa 14:5). Made of gold (Est 4:11), of iron (Ps 2:9; Rev 2:27; 12:5).
Figurative (Ge 49:10; Nu 24:17; Isa 9:4).

SCEVA Chief priest living in Ephesus whose seven sons were exorcists (Ac 19:14-17).

SCHISM (*division*). A formal division inside a religious group (1Co 12:25). *See Divisions.*

SCHOOL Company of the prophets at Naioth (1Sa 19:20), Bethel (2Ki 2:3), Jericho (2Ki 2:5, 15), Gilgal (2Ki 4:38), Jerusalem, probably (2Ki 22:14; 2Ch 34:22). Crowded attendance at (2Ki 6:1). In the home (Dt 4:9-10; 6:7, 9; 11:19-20; Ps 78:5-8). Assembly to hear public reading of the law (Dt 31:10-13).

State (2Ch 17:7-9; Da 1:3-21). Of Gamaliel (Ac 5:34; 22:3). Of Tyrannus (Ac 19:9).
See Instruction; Psalms, Topically Arranged; Sons of the Prophets.

SCIENCE Observations of, and deductions from, facts (Job 26:7-14; 28; Ecc 1:13-17). The key of knowledge (Lk 11:52; Ro 2:20). *See Astronomy; Geology; Philosophy.*

SCOFFER One who derides, mocks (2Pe 3:3).

SCOFFING

By:

The people of Israel (2Ch 30:6-10; 36:16; Ps 78:19-20; 107:11-12; Hos 7:5). Unbelievers (Ps 42:3, 10; 73:8-9, 11-12; Pr 1:22, 25; Jer 17:15; 43:2; La 1:7; Eze 8:12; 9:9; 12:22; 2Pe 3:3-4). The Wicked, at God's requirements (Job 21:14-15; Isa 10:15; 57:4; Eze 11:2-3; 33:20).

Against:

Christ (Mt 12:24; Mk 3:22; Lk 4:23; 11:15; 16:14). The first Christians (Ac 2:13). Paul (Ac 13:45; 17:18, 32).

Proverbs Concerning:

(Pr 1:22, 25; 3:34; 9:12; 13:1; 14:6, 9; 19:29; 21:11, 24; 22:10; 24:9).

Punishment for:

(Pr 3:24; 9:12; 19:29; Isa 5:18-19, 24-25; 29:20; Heb 10:29).
See Hatred; Malice; Unbelief.

Instances of:

Ishmael (Ge 21:9). Children at Bethel (2Ki 2:23). Ephraim and Manasseh (2Ch 30:10). Chiefs of Judah (2Ch 36:16). Sanballat (Ne 4:1). Enemies of Job (Job 30:1, 9). Enemies of David (Ps 35:15-16). Rulers of Israel (Isa 28:14). Ammonites (Eze 25:3). Tyrians (Eze 26:2). Heathen (Eze 36:2-3). Soldiers (Mt 27:28-30; Lk 23:36). Chief priests (Mt 27:41). Pharisees (Lk 16:14). The men who held Jesus (Lk 22:63-64). Herod (Lk 23:11). People and rulers (Lk 23:35). Some of the multitude (Ac 2:13). Athenians (Ac 17:32).

SCORNERS (Ps 1:1; Pr 9:12; 21:11, 24). An abomination (Pr 24:9). Admonitions to (Pr 1:22-23). Punishment of (Pr 19:29; Isa 29:20). Warnings against (Pr 3:34; 13:1; 14:6; 19:29; 22:10; 29:8).
See Mocking; Scoffing.

SCORPION A venomous insect common in the wilderness through which the Israelites journeyed (Dt 8:15). Power over, given to the seventy-two (Lk 10:19). Unfit for food (Lk 11:12). Sting of in the tail (Rev 9:10).

Symbolic (Rev 9:3, 5, 10).

Figurative: Of enemies (Eze 2:6). Of cruelty (1Ki 12:11, 14).

SCORPION PASS A chain of hills in the south of Israel (Nu 34:4; Jdg 1:36). Area assigned to tribe of Judah (Jos 15:3).

SCOURGING Corporal punishment by stripes. Prescribed in the Mosaic law for fornication (Lev 19:20; Dt 22:18), for other offenses (Dt 25:2). Forty stripes the maximum limit (Dt 25:3). Fatal (Job 9:23), of servants avenged (Ex 21:20). Foretold by Jesus as a persecution of the Christians (Mt 10:17).

Of children. *See Children, Correction and Punishment; Punishment.*

Instances of:

Of Jesus (Mt 20:19; 27:26; Mk 15:15; Jn 19:1). Of Paul and Silas (Ac 16:23). Of Paul (Ac 21:32; 22:24; 2Co 11:24-25). Of Sosthenes (Ac 18:17).

Figurative:

Of the oppressions of rulers (1Ki 12:11). Of the evil tongue (Job 5:21).
See Assault and Battery; Bruise(s); Lashes; Stoning; Stripes.

SCREECH OWL Forbidden as food (Lev 11:16; Dt 14:15). *See Birds.*

SCRIBE (*write, copy*). A writer and transcriber of the law (2Sa 8:17; 20:25; 1Ki 4:3; 2Ki 12:10; 18:37; 19:2; 1Ch 24:6; 27:32; Ne 13:13; Jer 36:12). King's secretary (2Ki 12:10-12; 22:1-14; Est 3:12; 8:9). Mustering officer of the army (2Ki 25:19; 2Ch 26:11). Instructors in the law (Mt 7:29; 13:52; 17:10; 23:2-3). *See Levites.* Test Jesus with questions, bringing to Jesus a woman taken in adultery (Jn 8:3). Members of the council (Mt 2:4). Conspire against Jesus (Mt 26:3, 57; 27:41; Mk 14:1; Lk 22:66). Hypocrisy of, reproved by Jesus (Mt 15:20; 9:3; 12:38; 15:1; 16:21; 20:18; 21:15).

SCRIPTURES (*writing*). The Word of God (Jer 30:2). Interpreted by doctors (Jn 3:10; 7:52). Inspired (2Ti 3:16).
See Word of God.

SCROLL A document made of papyrus or smoothed skins of animals sewn together to make a long strip which was wound around sticks at both ends (Isa 34:4; Jer 36; Eze 3:1-3; Rev 5; 10:1-10). They varied in length from a few feet to thirty-five feet. The codex form of a book was not used until the second century A.D.

SCROLLS, DEAD SEA *See Dead Sea Scrolls.*

SCULPTURE *See Art.*

SCURVY *See Disease; Scab; Sore.*

SCYTHIAN A nomadic people, savage and uncivilized, living N and E of the Black Sea (Col 3:11).

SEA Creation of (Ge 1:9-10; Ps 95:5; 148:4-5). Limits of established by God (Ge 1:9; Job 26:10; 38:8; Ps 33:7; Jer 5:22). Calmed by Jesus (Mt 8:24-26; Mk 4:37-39). Jesus walked on (Mt 14:25-31). Dead, to be given up by, at the Resurrection (Rev 20:13).

Symbolic:

In Daniel's vision (Da 7:2-3). In John's apocalyptic vision (Rev 4:6; 8:8-9; 10:2, 5-6, 8; 13:1; 15:2; 16:3; 21:1).

Waves of:

Reuben is as turbulent as (Ge 49:3-4). God walks on (Job 9:8). God controls (Job 38:8, 11; Ps 65:7; 89:9; 93:3-4; Jer 5:22). The wicked are like (Isa 57:20-21; Jude 13). Jesus controls (Mt 8:23-26; 14:32; Mk 4:35-41). Jesus walks through on the surface of the sea of Galilee (Mt 14:22-33). When God's people are built up and become mature, attaining to the whole measure of the fullness of Christ, they will no longer be tossed back and forth by every deceitful doctrine and scheme like the waves of the sea (Eph 4:14). Doubters are like (Jas 1:6).

SEA, BRONZE The great basin in Solomon's temple where the priests washed their hands and feet preparatory to temple ministry (1Ki 7:23-26; 2Ch 4:2-6).

SEA COW Native to the Red Sea. Skins of, used for covering of tabernacle (Ex 25:5; 26:14; 35:7, 23; 36:19; 39:34; Nu 4:6, 8, 10-12, 14, 25). For sandals (Eze 16:10).

SEA MEW *See Birds.*

SEA MONSTER Figurative of forces of chaos opposed to God (Job 7:12; Ps 74:13; Isa 27:1; Eze 32:2). *See Dragon; Leviathan.*

SEA OF GALILEE Called Sea of Kinnereth (Nu 34:11; Dt 3:17; Jos 12:3; 13:27). Lake of Gennesaret (Lk 5:1). Sea of Tiberias (Jn 21:1). Jesus calls disciples on the shore of (Mt 4:18-22; Lk 5:1-11). Jesus teaches from a boat on (Mt 13:13). Miracles of Jesus on (Mt 8:24-32; 14:22-33; 17:27; Mk 4:37-39; Lk 5:1-9; 8:22-24; Jn 12:1-11).

SEA OF GLASS A crystalline pavement or basin before the throne of God (Rev 4:6; 15:2).

SEA OF JAZER Perhaps the Dead Sea (Jer 48:32).

SEAL

1. A stamp used for signifying documents. Given as a pledge (Ge 38:18). Engraved (Ex 28:11, 21, 36; 39:6, 14, 30; 2Ti 2:19). Decrees signified by (1Ki 21:8; Est 8:8).

Documents sealed with: Ahab's letter, under false pretenses (1Ki 21:8), covenants (Ne 9:38; 10:1; Isa 8:16), decrees (Est 8:8; Da 6:9), deeds (Jer 32:10). Treasures secured by (Dt 32:34). Lion's den made sure by (Da 6:17), tomb of Jesus (Mt 27:66).

Circumcision a seal of righteousness (Ro 4:11).

Figurative: Of secrecy (Da 12:9; Rev 5:1). Of certainty of divine approval (Jn 6:27; 2Co 1:22; Eph 1:13; 4:30; Rev 7:3-4). In John's vision (Rev 6; 8:1; 10:4).

2. An amphibious animal. Skins of were used as a covering of the tabernacle (Ex 25:5; 26:14; 35:7, 23; 36:19; 39:34; Nu 4:25).

SEAMEN *See Mariner.*

SEASONS (Ge 1:14; 8:22; Ps 104:19; Jer 33:20; Da 2:21; Mt 21:41; 24:32; Mk 12:2; Ac 1:7; 1Th 5:1).

SEAT Chair, stool, throne (1Sa 20:18; Lk 1:52).

SEBA
1. Son of Cush (Ge 10:7; 1Ch 1:9).
2. A region in Ethiopia (Ps 72:10; Isa 43:3).
See Sabeans; Sheba.

SEBAM (*sweet smell*). A town in Reuben (Nu 32:3), also called Sibmah (Nu 32:38), E of the Dead Sea, but the exact location is unknown.

SEBAT *See Shebat.*

SECACAH (*thicket, cover*). A village in the wilderness of Judah (Jos 15:61), location unknown.

SECHU *See Secu.*

SECOND ADAR This intercalary month (not in the Bible) was added about every three years so the lunar calendar would correspond to the solar year.
See Adar Sheni; Month, 13.

SECOND COMING OF CHRIST

Called the:
Times of refreshing from the presence of the Lord (Ac 3:19). Times of restitution of all things (Ac 3:21, w Ro 8:21). Last time (1Pe 1:5). Appearing of Jesus Christ (1Pe 1:7). Revelation of Jesus Christ (1Pe 1:13). Glorious appearing of the great God and our Savior (Tit 2:13). Coming of the day of God (2Pe 3:12). Day of our Lord Jesus Christ (1Co 1:8).

Foretold by:
Prophets (Da 7:13; Jude 14). Jesus (Mt 25:31; Jn 14:3). Apostles (Ac 3:20; 1Ti 6:14). Angels (Ac 1:10-11). Signs preceding (Mt 24:3).
The time of, unknown (Mt 24:36; Mk 13:32).

The Manner of:
In clouds (Mt 24:30; 26:64; Rev 1:7). In the glory of his Father (Mt 16:27). In his own glory (Mt 25:31). In flaming fire (2Th 1:8). With power and great glory (Mt 24:30). As he ascended (Ac 1:9, 11). With a shout and the voice of the archangel (1Th 4:16). Accompanied by angels (Mt 16:27; 25:31; Mk 8:38; 2Th 1:7). With his saints (1Th 3:13; Jude 14). Suddenly (Mk 13:36). Unexpectedly (Mt 24:44; Lk 12:40). As a thief in the night (1Th 5:2; 2Pe 3:10; Rev 16:15). As the lightning (Mt 24:27). The heavens and earth shall be dissolved (2Pe 3:10, 12). They who shall have died in Christ shall rise first at (1Th 4:16). The saints alive at, shall be caught up to meet him (1Th 4:17). Is not to make atonement (Heb 9:28, w Ro 6:9-10; Heb 10:14).

The Purposes of:
To complete the salvation of saints (Heb 9:28; 1Pe 1:5). Be glorified in his saints (2Th 1:10). Be marveled at among those who believe (2Th 1:10). Bring to light the hidden things of darkness (1Co 4:5). Judge (Ps 50:3-4, w Jn 5:22; 2Ti 4:1; Jude 15; Rev 20:11-13). Reign (Isa 24:23; Da 7:14; Rev 11:15). Destroy death (1Co 15:25-26). Every eye shall see him at (Rev 1:7). Should be always considered as at hand (Ro 13:12; Php 4:5; 1Pe 4:7). Blessedness of being prepared for (Mt 24:46; Lk 12:37-38).

The Saints:
Assured of (Job 19:25-26). Love (2Ti 4:8). Look for (Php 3:20; Tit 2:13). Wait for (1Co 1:7; 1Th 1:10). Speed its coming (2Pe 3:12). Pray for (Rev 22:20). Should be ready for (Mt 24:44; Lk 12:40). Should watch for (Mt 24:42; Mk 13:35-37; Lk 21:36). Should be patient unto (2Th 3:5; Jas 5:7-8). Shall be preserved unto (Php 1:6; 2Ti 4:18; 1Pe 1:5; Jude 24). Shall not be ashamed at (1Jn 2:28; 1Jn 4:17). Shall be blameless at (1Co 1:8; 1Th 3:13; 5:23; Jude 24). Shall be like him at (Php 3:21; 1Jn 3:2). Shall see him as he is (1Jn 3:2). Shall appear with him in glory at (Col 3:4). Shall receive a crown of glory at (2Ti 4:8; 1Pe 5:4). Shall reign with him at (Da 7:27; 2Ti 2:12; Rev 5:10; 20:6; 22:5). Faith of, will be praised at (1Pe 1:7).

The Wicked:
Scoff at (2Pe 3:3-4). Presume upon the delay of (Mt 24:48). Shall be surprised by (Mt 24:37-39; 1Th 5:3; 2Pe 3:10). Shall be punished at (2Th 1:8-9). The man of sin to be destroyed at (2Th 2:8). Illustrated (Mt 25:6; Lk 12:36, 39; 19:12, 15).
See Jesus the Christ, Second Coming.

SECOND DEATH (Rev 19:20; 20:14; 21:8). Righteous exempt from (Rev 2:11). *See Punishment, Eternal; Wicked, Punishment of.*

SECRET Alms to be given in (Mt 6:4). Prayer to be offered in (Mt 6:6). Of others not to be divulged (Pr 25:9; Mt 18:15).
Belong to God (Dt 29:29; Ps 25:14). God knows secrets of the heart (Dt 31:21; 1Sa 16:7; 2Sa 7:20; 2Ki 19:27; Ps 44:21; 90:8; Heb 4:12-13).
Shall be revealed and judged (Ecc 12:14; Da 2:28, 47; Am 3:7; Mk 4:22; Lk 8:16-17; Ro 2:16; 1Co 4:5).
See Mysteries.

SECRETARY (2Sa 8:17; 20:24; 1Ki 4:3; 2Ki 12:10-12; 18:18, 37; 22:1-14; 1Ch 27:32; Est 3:12; 8:9). Military (2Ki 25:19; 2Ch 26:11). *See Amanuensis; Scribe.*

SECT (*sect, party, school*). Religious group with distinctive doctrine: Sadducees (Ac 5:17), Pharisees (Ac 15:5; 26:5), Christians (Ac 24:5; 28:22).

SECU (*lookout point*). Village near Ramah (1Sa 19:22).

SECUNDUS (*second*). A Thessalonian Christian. Accompanies Paul from Corinth (Ac 20:4-6).

SECURITY

In Salvation:
The theological teaching which maintains the certain continuation of the salvation of those who are saved; also known as the perseverance of the saints (Jn 10:28; Ro 8:38-39; Php 1:6; 2Th 3:3; 1Pe 1:5).

False:
From the evils of sin. Promises peace and long life (Job 29:18). Is ignorant of God and truth (Ps 10:4; 50:21). Trusts in lies (Isa 28:15; Rev 3:17). Is inconsiderate and forgetful (Isa 47:7). Relies on earthly treasures (Jer 49:4, 16). Is deceived by pride (Ob 3; Rev 18:7). Puts off the evil day (Am 6:3). Leads to increased guilt (Ecc 8:11). Its refuge will be swept away (Isa 28:17). Ruin shall overtake it (Isa 47:9; Am 9:10). God is against it (Jer 21:13; Eze 39:6; Am 6:1).
See Confidence, False; Self-Deception; Self-Delusion.

For Debt:
A guarantee to pay: not to be taken if essential to life (garments) or livelihood (millstones) (Ex 22:26; Dt 24:6, 6, 17); not to be used as unreasonable leverage upon the disadvantaged (Job 22:6; 24:3, 9; Eze 18:16; Am 2:8).
Instances of: Judah (Ge 43:9; 44:32); fields and vineyards (Ne 5:3).
Warnings against: (Pr 6:1; 11:15; 17:18; 20:16).
See Debt.

SEDITION Charged against Paul (Ac 24:5). How punished (Ac 5:36-37).

SEDUCER *See Impostors.*

SEDUCTION (2Ti 3:6, 13). Laws concerning (Ex 22:16-17; Dt 22:23-29). *See Rape.*
Instances of: Of Dinah (Ge 34:2). Tamar (2Sa 13:1-14).

SEED Every herb, tree, and grass, yields its own (Ge 1:11-12, 29). Each kind has its own body (1Co 15:38). Not to be mingled in sowing (Lev 19:19; Dt 22:9).
Parables concerning (Mt 13; Lk 8).
Illustrative (Ecc 11:6; Hos 10:12; 2Co 9:6; Gal 6:7-8).
Sowing of, type of burial of the body (1Co 15:36-38).

SEEDTIME *See Agriculture.*

SEEKERS

Must:
Have faith (Heb 11:6). Remember God's mercies (Isa 51:1). Count the cost (Lk 14:26-33).

Seeking God:
Commanded (1Ch 16:11; 22:19; Ps 105:4; Isa 26:8-9; Hos 10:12; Joel 2:12-13; Am 5:4-6, 8, 14; Zep 2:3; Mt 6:33; Jas 4:8; Rev 22:17). For salvation (Ge 49:18). To sacrifice (2Ch 11:16). The result of adversity (Ps 78:34; 83:16; Hos 5:15). Prophesied (Jer 50:4; Hos 3:5; Zec 8:20-23). Punishment for not seeking (2Ch 15:13; Isa 8:19). Not of self (Ro 3:11). By unrepentant sinners, vain (Am 8:12; Lk 13:24).
See Seeking God.

Promises:
(Jn 6:37). Of finding God (Dt 4:29; 1Ch 28:9; 2Ch 15:2, 12; Pr 8:17, 34-35; Isa 45:19, 22; Jer 29:13; Ac 17:27). Of pardon (2Ch 30:18-19; Ps 69:32; Isa 55:6-7; Eze 18:21-23; Ac 2:21). Of salvation (Heb 9:28). Of providential care (2Ch 26:5; Ezr 8:22; Ps 34:4; 81:10; 145:19; Isa 49:9-12, 23; Mt 6:33). Of spiritual blessings (Job 8:5-6; Ps 9:10; 22:26; 24:3-6; 40:1-4; 63:1-8; 70:4-5; 119:2; 145:18-19; Pr 2:3-5; 28:5; Isa 44:3-4; 45:19, 22; 55:6-7; 61:1-3; La 3:25-26, 41; Mt 5:6; 6:33; 7:7-11; Lk 6:21; 11:9-13; Ac 2:21; Ro 10:12-13; Heb 7:25; Rev 3:20; 21:6).

Instances of:
Asa (2Ch 14:7). Jehoshaphat (2Ch 17:3-4). Uzziah (2Ch 26:5). Hezekiah (2Ch 31:21). Josiah (2Ch 34:4). Ezra (Ezr 7:10). Job (Job 5:8). David (Ps 17:1-2; 25:5, 15; 27:4, 8; 34:4; 40:1-2; 63:1-8; 143:6). The psalmists (Ps 33:20; 42:1-4; 77:1-9; 84:2; 119:10; 130:5-6). The beloved for her lover (SS 3:1-4). Daniel (Da 9:3-4). The Magi (Mt 2:1-2). Cornelius, the Centurion (Ac 10:7, 30-33).
See Backsliders; Penitent; Sin, Confession of; Sin, Forgiveness of; Zeal.

SEEKING GOD Commanded (Isa 55:6; Mt 7:7).

Includes Seeking:
His name (Ps 83:16). His Word (Isa 34:16). His strength (1Ch 16:11; Ps 105:4). His commandments (1Ch 28:8; Mal 2:7). His precepts (Ps 119:45, 94). His kingdom (Mt 6:33; Lk 12:31). His righteousness (Mt 6:33). Christ (Mal 3:1; Lk 2:15-16). Honor which comes from him (Jn 5:44). Justification by Christ (Gal 2:16-17). The city which God has prepared (Heb 11:10, 16; 13:14). By prayer (Job 8:5; Da 9:3). In his house (Dt 12:5; Ps 27:4).

Should Be:
Immediate (Hos 10:12). Evermore (Ps 105:4). While he may be found (Isa 55:6). With the heart (Dt 4:29; 1Ch 22:19). In the day of trouble (Ps 77:2).

Ensures:
His being found (Dt 4:29; 1Ch 28:9; Pr 8:17; Jer 29:13). His favor (La 3:25). His protection (Ezr 8:22). His not forsaking us (Ps 9:10). Life (Ps 69:32; Am 5:4, 6). Prosperity (Job 8:5-6; Ps 34:10). Being heard by him (Ps 34:4). Understanding all things (Pr 28:5). Gifts of righteousness (Hos 10:12). Imperative upon all (Isa 8:19). Afflictions designed to lead to (Ps 78:33-34; Hos 5:15). None, by nature, are found to be engaged in (Jas 4:2, w Ro 3:11; Lk 12:23, 30).

The Saints:
Specially exhorted to (Zep 2:3). Desirous of (Job 5:8). Purpose, in heart (Ps 27:8). Prepare their hearts for (2Ch 30:19). Set their hearts to (2Ch 11:16). Engage in, with the whole heart (2Ch 15:12; Ps 119:10). Early in (Job 8:5; Ps 63:1; Isa 26:9). Earnest in (SS 3:2, 4). Characterized by (Ps 24:6). Is never in vain (Isa 45:19). Blessedness of (Ps 119:2). Leads to joy (Ps 70:4; 105:3). Ends in praise (Ps 22:26). Promise connected with (Ps 69:32). Shall be rewarded (Heb 11:6).

The Wicked:
Are gone out of the way of (Ps 14:2-3, w Ro 3:11-12). Do not prepare their hearts for (2Ch 12:14). Refuse, through pride (Ps 10:4). Not led to, by affliction (Isa 9:13). Sometimes pretend to (Ezr 4:2; Isa 58:2). Rejected, when too late in (Pr 1:28). They who neglect are denounced (Isa 31:1). Punishment of those who neglect (Zep 1:4-6).

Exemplified:
Asa (2Ch 14:7). Jehoshaphat (2Ch 17:3-4). Uzziah (2Ch 26:5). Hezekiah (2Ch 31:21). Josiah (2Ch 34:3). Ezra (Ezr 7:10). David (Ps 34:4). Daniel (Da 9:3-4).

SEER An older term for prophet (1Sa 9:9). *See Prophets.*

SEGUB (*exalted*).
1. Son of Hiel, the rebuilder of Jericho (1Ki 16:34).
2. Grandson of Judah (1Ch 2:4-5, 21-22).

SEIR (*hairy, shaggy, covered with trees* BDB IDB; possibly *the place of the goats* or *the place of Esau* [Ge 25:25, BDB]; *small forest, rich forest* KB). A Horite; an ancestor of the inhabitants of the land of Seir (Ge 26:20; 1Ch 1:38).

SEIR, LAND OF and MOUNT

1. Alternate names for the region occupied by the descendants of Edom or Esau. Originally called the land of Seir (Ge 32:3), later called Edom (Ge 36:8-9), extends S from Moab on both sides of the Arabah c. one hundred miles; mountainous; in the Greek period it was called Idumea. Mt. Seir c. 3, 500 feet high. "Seir" also used for people who lived in Mt. Seir (Eze 25:8).
2. Region on the border of Judah W of Kiriath Jearim (Jos 15:10).

SEIRAH (*place of the goats* BDB possibly *woody hills* IDB KB; *shaggy forest* ISBE). A town in Ephraim, probably in the SE part (Jdg 3:26).

SEIZING Of property. *See Land.*

SEIZURES An affliction resulting from demon possession (Mt. 4:24; 17:5). Some feel this is a reference to epilepsy. *See Disease.*

SELA (*rocky crags, cliffs*). An Edomite city (Isa 16:1; 42:11), also called Joktheel (2Ki 14:7). *See Joktheel.* Later the capital of the Nabateans, called Petra by the Greeks. *See Nabatea, Nabateans; Petra.*

SELA HAMMAHLEKOTH (*slippery rock* BDB). A cliff in the wilderness of Maon (1Sa 23:28).

SELAH This term appears seventy-one times in the Psalms and in Hab 3:3, 9, 13. Its meaning is not clear. Possibly it signified a pause in the vocal music while an instrumental interlude played.
See Music, Symbols Used in.

SELED (*jump for joy*). A descendant of Jerahmeel (1Ch 2:30).

SELEUCIA A seaport of Syrian Antioch, founded by Seleucus I in 300 B.C. (Ac 13:4).

SELEUCIDS A dynasty of rulers of the kingdom of Syria (it included Babylonia, Bactria, Persia, Syria, and part of Asia Minor), descended from Seleucus I, a general of Alexander the Great. It lasted from 312 to 64 B.C., when the Romans took it over. One of them, Antiochus Epiphanes, precipitated the Maccabean War by trying forcibly to Hellenize the Jews. *See Testaments, Time Between.*

SELF-CONDEMNATION (1Ki 8:31-32; Job 9:20; Pr 5:12-13; Mt 23:31; Ro 2:1; 1Jn 3:20; Rev 1:7).
Parables of (Mt 21:33-41; 25:24-27; Mk 12:1-12; Lk 19:21-22).
Instances of: Achan (Jos 7:19-25). David (1Sa 24:1-15; 26:1-20; 2Sa 12:5-7; 24:17). Ahab (1Ki 20:39-42). Jonah (Jnh 1:12). Those who condemned the woman (Jn 8:9).
See Self-Incrimination; Remorse; Repentance.

SELF-CONFIDENCE *See Confidence, False.*

SELF-CONTROL

A Virtue:
Without self-control temptation and evil may freely assault a person (Pr 25:28). Of Saul (1Sa 10:27). Of David (1Sa 24:1-15; 26:1-20). Of Jesus (Mt 26:62-63; 27:12-14).
Paul instructed concerning self-control in relation to righteousness (Ac 24:25), the marriage bed (1Co 7:5); as a fruit of the Spirit (Gal 5:23); in contrast to the godlessness of the last days (1Th 5:8; 2Ti 3:3; 2Th 1:6). Overseers and deacons must have a life that is characterized by self-control (1Ti 3:2; Tit 1:8). Taught by leaders and exemplified by older believers (Tit 2:2, 5-6); taught by the grace of God (Tit 2:12).
Peter lists self-control as one of the qualities of a godly life (2Pe 1:6). A believer should continually be prepared for Christ's return, exhibiting a self-controlled life (1Pe 1:13; 4:7). Be self-controlled and prepared for the devil, who prowls about looking for those who have a false sense of security which therefore make them prime candidates for his trap in the world's system (1Pe 4:7).

Sexual Self-control:
Vow of (Job 31:1). Commanded (Mt 5:27-28; Ro 13:13; 1Co 7:1-9, 25-29, 36-38; Col 3:5; 1Ti 4:12; 5:1-2).

Instances of—
Joseph (Ge 39:7-12). Uriah (2Sa 11:8-13). Boaz (Ru 3:6-13). Joseph, husband of Mary (Mt 1:24-25). Eunuchs (Mt 19:12). Paul (1Co 7:8; 9:27). Believers (Rev 14:1, 4-5).
See Abstinence; Chastity; Discipline; Graces, Christian; Patience; Rashness; Self-Discipline; Tact.

S

SELF-DECEPTION (Jas 1:26). *See Confidence, False; Security, False.*

SELF-DEFENSE Accused heard in (Mt 27:11-14; Mk 15:2-5; Lk 23:3; Jn 7:51; Ac 2:37-40; 22; 23; 24:10-21; 26). *See Defense.*

SELF-DELUSION A characteristic of the wicked (Ps 49:18). Prosperity frequently leads to (Ps 30:6; Hos 12:8; Lk 12:17-19). Obstinate sinners often given up to (Ps 81:11-12; Hos 4:17; 2Th 2:10-11).

Exhibited In Thinking That:
Our own ways are right (Pr 14:12), we should adhere to established wicked practices (Jer 44:17), we are pure (Pr 30:12), we are better than others (Lk 18:11), we are rich in spiritual things (Rev 3:17), we may have peace while in sin (Dt 29:19), we are above adversity (Ps 10:6), gifts entitle us to heaven (Mt 7:21-22), privileges entitle us to heaven (Mt 3:9; Lk 13:25-26), God will not punish our sins (Jer 5:12), Christ will not come to judge (2Pe 3:4), our lives will be prolonged (Isa 56:12; Lk 12:19; Jas 4:13).
Frequently persevered in to the last (Mt 7:22; 25:11-12; Lk 13:24-25). Fatal consequences of (Mt 7:23; 24:48-51; Lk 12:20; 1Th 5:3).

Exemplified:
Ahab (1Ki 20:27, 34). Israelites (Hos 12:8). Jews (Jn 8:33, 41). Church of Laodicea (Rev 3:17).
See Confidence, False; Security, False.

SELF-DENIAL (Lk 21:2-4; 1Co 6:12; 9:12, 15, 18-19, 23, 25-27; 10:23-24; 2Co 6:3; Php 2:4-8; 3:7-9; 2Ti 2:4; Tit 2:12; Heb 13:13; Rev 12:11).

In Respect to:
Appetite (Pr 23:2; Da 10:3). Sinful pleasures (Mt 5:29-30; 18:8-9; Mk 9:43). Carnality (Ro 6:6; 8:12-13, 35-36; 13:14; 1Co 9:27; Gal 5:16-17, 24; Col 3:5; Tit 2:12; 1Pe 2:11-12, 14-16).

Required of Christ's Disciples:
(Mt 8:19-22; 10:37-39; 16:24-25; 19:12, 21; Mk 2:14; 8:34-35; 10:29; Lk 5:11; 9:23-24, 57-58; 12:33; 14:26-27, 33; 18:27-30; Jn 12:25; 2Ti 2:4; Heb 13:13; 1Pe 4:1; 3Jn 7). For a brother's sake (Ro 14:1-22; 15:1-5; 1Co 8:10-13; 10:23-24; Php 2:4). For the sake of the ministry (2Co 6:3). Christ's teachings concerning (Mk 12:43-44; Lk 21:2-4).

Parables of:
(Mt 13:44-46; 18:8-9; Mk 9:43).

Instances of:
Abraham, when he accorded to Lot his preference for the grazing lands of Canaan (Ge 13:9; 17:8), in offering Isaac (Ge 22:12). Moses, in choosing suffering over pleasure (Heb 11:25), in taking no compensation from the Israelites (Nu 16:15). Samuel, in his administration of justice (1Sa 12:3-4). The widow of Zarephath, in sharing with Elijah the last of her sustenance (1Ki 17:12-15).
David, in paying for the threshing floor (2Sa 24:24). The psalmist (Ps 132:3-5). Daniel, in refusing royal food (Da 1:8), in refusing rewards from Belshazzar (Da 5:16-17). Esther, in risking her life for her people (Est 4:16). The Recabites, in refusing wine or fermented drink, or even to plant vineyards (Jer 35:6-7).
Peter and other apostles, in abandoning their vocations to follow Jesus (Mt 4:20; 9:9; Mk 1:16-20; 2:14; Lk 5:11, 27-28), in forsaking all (Mt 19:27; Mk 10:28; Lk 5:28). The widow, who cast all into the treasury (Lk 21:4). The early Christians, in having everything in common (Ac 2:44-45; 4:34). Joseph, in selling his possessions and giving all to the apostles (Ac 4:36-37).
Paul (1Co 10:23-24; Gal 2:20; 6:14), in not counting even his life valuable to himself (Ac 20:24; 21:13; Php 3:7-8), in laboring for his own support while he taught (Ac 20:34-35; 1Co 4:12; 10:33), in not exercising his authority (1Co 6:12; 9:12, 15, 18-19, 23-27).
See Cross; Humility.

SELF-DISCIPLINE Needed: Not to give in to sin (Ro 6:12-14); to "run the race" of life according to the rules (1Co 9:24-27; 2Ti 2:1-7). Contrasted to timidity (2Ti 1:7). *See Self-Control.*

SELF-EXALTATION Christian attitude toward (2Co 10:5, 17-18). Christ's teaching concerning (Mk 12:38). Parables of (Lk 14:7-11).
Self-deception of (Isa 5:21; 1Co 3:18; 8:2; Gal 6:3). Punishment for (Eze 31:10-14; Ob 3-4).
Instances of: Job (Job 12:3). Pharaoh (Ex 9:17). Korah, Dathan, and Abiram (Nu 16:1-11). Sennacherib (2Ch 32:9-19). Prince of Tyre, making himself God (Eze 28:2, 9-10). Nebuchadnezzar (Da 4:30; 5:20). Belshazzar (Da 5:22-23). Simon the sorcerer (Ac 8:9-11). Herod, when deified by the people (Ac 12:20-23). The man of lawlessness (2Th 2:4).
See Pride; Self-Righteousness.

SELF-EXAMINATION

Commanded:
(Ps 4:4; Hag 1:7; 1Co 11:28, 31; 2Co 13:5; Gal 6:4). By inference (Jer 17:9).
Conversion as a result of (Ps 119:59; La 3:40).

Exemplified by:
Job (Job 13:23). David (Ps 19:2; 26:2; 139:23-24). The psalmist (Ps 77:6; 119:59). The disciples (Mt 26:22; Mk 14:19).
See Meditation; Repentance; Sin, Confession of.

SELF-INCRIMINATION Under ancient customs, accused persons were required to give self-incriminating testimonies of guilt of the offense charged and were, on occasions, scourged to force self-incriminating testimony whether guilty or innocent (Nu 5:11-27; 2Sa 1:10, 16; 1Ki 8:31-32; 2Ch 6:22; Ac 22:24). Instances of: Achan (Jos 8:19-25). *See Self-Condemnation.*

SELF-INDULGENCE Instances of: Solomon (Ecc 2:10). The rich fool (Lk 12:16-20). The rich man as contrasted to Lazarus (Lk 16:19). *See Gluttony; Idleness; Slothfulness; also, Self Denial.*

SELFISHNESS

Denounced:
Admonitions against (Lk 6:32-34; Ro 14:15; 15:1-3; 1Co 10:24; Gal 6:2; Php 2:4). Christ's example against (Ro 15:3; 2Co 5:15; Php 2:5-8). Judged (Pr 18:17; 24:11-12; Hag 1:4, 9-10).

Exemplified by:
Corrupt officials (Mic 3:11). Corrupt priests and prophets (Eze 34:18; Zec 7:6). Those who accumulate too much (Pr 11:26; Isa 5:8; Mt 19:21-22). The self-indulgent (Ro 14:15; 2Ti 3:2-4). Those unsympathetic with the unfortunate (Pr 28:27; Jas 2:15-16; 1Jn 3:17). Cain (Ge 4:9). The Gadites and Reubenites (Nu 32:6). David's friends (Ps 38:11). The Israelites (Hag 1:4; Mal 1:10). Early Christians (Php 2:20-21).
See Liberality; Poor; Unselfishness.

SELF-RIGHTEOUSNESS

Described as:
Assertive (Pr 20:6; Mt 7:22-23). Delusive (Pr 12:15; 16:2; 21:2; 28:26; Isa 28:20; 50:11; 64:6; Hos 12:8; Mt 7:22-23; 22:12-13; Gal 6:3).

Denounced:
(Job 12:2; Pr 25:14, 27; 26:12; 30:12-13; Isa 5:21; 65:3-5; Jer 2:13, 22-23, 34-35; 8:8; Eze 33:24-26; Am 6:13; Mt 9:10-13; Mk 2:16; 8:15; Lk 5:30; 16:14-15; 18:9-14; 22:12-13; 23:29-31; Ro 11:19-21).
Admonitions against (Dt 9:4-6; 1Sa 2:9; Pr 27:2, 21; Jer 7:4; Hab 2:4; 2Co 1:9; 10:17-18).
Judgments against (Pr 14:12; Isa 28:17; 50:11; Jer 8:8; 49:4, 16; Zep 3:11).
Proverbs concerning (Pr 12:15; 14:12; 16:2; 20:6; 21:2; 25:14, 27; 26:12; 27:2, 21; 28:13, 26; 30:12-13).
Parables concerning (Lk 7:36-50; 10:25-37; 15:25-32; 18:9-14).
Paul's instruction regarding (Ro 2:17-20; 3:27; 10:3; 11:19-21; 2Co 1:9; 10:17-18; Gal 6:3).

Instances of:
Job accused of (Job 11:4; 32:1-2; 33:8-9; 35:2, 7-8). Israelites (Nu 16:3; Ro 2:17-20; 10:3). Saul (1Sa 15:13-21). The wicked (Ps 10:5-6).
Pharisees (Mt 9:10-13; Mk 2:16-17; Lk 5:30; 7:39; 15:2; 16:14-15; 18:9-14; Jn 9:28-41). The rich young ruler (Mt 19:16-22; Mk 10:17-22; Lk 18:18-23). The lawyer (Lk 10:25-29). Church of Laodicea (Rev 3:17-18).
See Hypocrisy; Self-Exaltation.

SELF-WILL Stubbornness.

Forbidden:
(2Ch 30:8; Ps 75:5). Ministers should be without (Tit 1:7), warn their people against (Heb 3:7-12), pray that their people may be forgiven for (Ex 34:9; Dt 9:27). Characteristic of the wicked (Pr 7:11; 2Pe 2:10). The wicked will not cease from (Jdg 2:19). Punishment for (Dt 21:21; Pr 29:1).

Proceeds From—
Unbelief (2Ki 17:14), pride (Ne 9:16, 29), an evil heart (Jer 7:24). God knows (Isa 48:4). Exhibited in refusing to listen to God (Pr 1:24), refusing to listen to the messengers of God (1Sa 8:19; Jer 44:16; Zec 7:11), refusing to walk in the ways of God (Ne 9:17; Isa 42:24; Ps 78:10), refusing to listen to parents (Dt 21:18-19), refusing to receive correction (Dt 21:18; Jer 5:3; 7:28), rebelling against God (Dt 31:27; Ps 78:8), resisting the Holy Spirit (Ac 7:51), walking in the counsels of an evil heart (Jer 7:24, w Jer 23:17), hardening the neck (Ne 9:16), hardening the heart (2Ch 36:13), going backward and not forward (Jer 7:24), heinousness of (1Sa 15:23).

Illustrated: (Ps 32:9; Jer 31:18).

Exemplified:
Simeon and Levi (Ge 49:6). Israelites (Ex 32:9; Dt 9:6, 13). Saul (1Sa 15:19-23). David (2Sa 24:4). Josiah (2Ch 35:22). Zedekiah (2Ch 36:13).
See Obduracy.

SELVEDGE NIV the "edge" of each of the two curtains which covered the boards of the tabernacle (Ex 26:4; 36:11).

SEM *See Shem.*

SEMAKIAH (*Yahweh sustains, consecrates*). The son of Shemaiah (1Ch 26:7).

SEMEI *See Shimei, 18.*

SEMEIN (*Yahweh has heard*). An ancestor of Christ (Lk 3:26).

SEMITES (*of Shem*). A diverse group of ancient peoples whose languages are related, belonging to the Semitic family of languages; their world was the Fertile Crescent. The principal Semitic peoples of ancient times: Akkadians—including Babylonians and Assyrians; Arameans; Canaanites—including Edomites, Ammonites, and Moabites; Hebrews; Arabs; Ethiopians (Ge 10:22-31).

SENAAH Descendants of Senaah (sometimes spelled Hassenaah), returned with Zerubbabel (Ezr 2:35; Ne 7:38).

SENATE *See Elders, Council of.*

SENATOR *See Elders; Occupations and Professions.*

SENEH (*thorny* BDB; possibly *[cliff shaped like] a tooth* IDB). A rock protecting the garrison of the Philistines at Micmash (1Sa 14:5).

SENIR The Amorite name of Mt. Hermon (Dt 3:9; 1Ch 5:23; SS 4:8; Eze 27:5).

SENNACHERIB (*[pagan moon god] Sin has increased the brothers* BDB ISBE; *Sin replace the [lost] brothers!* IDB). The king of Assyria (705-681 B.C.), the son and successor of Sargon II; a great builder and conqueror; invaded Judah in the time of Hezekiah, but his army was miraculously destroyed (2Ki 18; 19; Isa 36; 37). Accounts of his campaigns recorded on clay prisms survive.

SENSUALITY (Ecc 2:24; 8:15; 11:9).
Of the glutton (Isa 22:13). Of the drunkard (Isa 56:12). Of the selfish rich (Lk 12:19-20; 16:25). Epicurean Philosophy Justifies (Isa 22:13; 1Co 15:32).
Admonition against (Jas 5:5). Warning against (Jude 18-19).
See Adultery; Drunkenness; Fornication; Gluttony; Homosexual; Lasciviousness; Self-Indulgence; also, Abstinence; Continence; Self-Denial; Temperance.

SENTRY *See Watchman.*

SENUAH (*sons of the hated [rejected] woman, i.e., the poor class* BDB). *See Hassenuah.*

SEORIM (*one born at the time of the barley [harvest]*). A descendant of Aaron; head of the fourth course of priests (1Ch 24:1-8).

SEPHAR A mountain in Arabia (Ge 10:30).

SEPHARAD A place to which the inhabitants of Jerusalem were exiled (Ob 20); possibly Sardis or Sparta.

SEPHARVAIM An Assyrian city, from which the king of Assyria colonized Samaria (2Ki 17:24, 31; 18:34; 19:13; Isa 36:19; 37:13).

SEPHARVITES The people of Sepharvaim (2Ki 17:31).

SEPHER *See Kiriath Sepher.*

SEPTUAGINT (*seventy*). A translation of the OT into Greek, prepared in Alexandria in the second and third centuries B.C. *See Testaments, Time Between; Texts and Versions.*

SEPULCHRE *See Burial.*

SEPULCHRE, CHURCH OF THE HOLY One of two main sites identified as the tomb of Jesus; built by Constantine in A.D. 325.

SERAH (*one who explains, opens, extends* IDB; *abundance* ISBE KB). *See Sarah, 2.*

SERAIAH (*Yahweh persists* BDB ISBE; *Yahweh is prince* IDB; *Yahweh contends* KB).
1. David's secretary. Probably the same as Sheva, Shisha, and Shavsha. (2Sa 8:17; 20:25; 1Ki 4:3; 1Ch 18:16).
2. Chief priest at the time of the taking of Jerusalem (2Ki 25:18). Father of Ezra (Ezr 7:1). Slain by Nebuchadnezzar (2Ki 25:18-21; Jer 52:24-27).
3. An Israelite captain who surrendered to Gedaliah (2Ki 25:23; Jer 40:8).
4. The son of Kenaz (1Ch 4:13-14).
5. A Simeonite (1Ch 4:35).
6. A priest who returned from the Babylonian captivity (Ezr 2:2; Ne 12:1, 12). Called Azariah (Ne 7:7).
7. One who sealed the covenant with Nehemiah (Ne 10:2). Possibly identical with 6, above.
8. A ruler of the temple after the Captivity (Ne 11:11).
9. The son of Azriel. Commanded by King Jehoiakim to seize Jeremiah (Jer 36:26).
10. A servant of Zedekiah (Jer 51:59, 61).

SERAPHS (*burning ones, [winged] serpents*). Celestial beings whom Isaiah saw standing before the enthroned Lord (Isa 6:2-3, 6-7). Possibly the same as the "living creatures" (Rev 4:6-9).

SERED, SEREDITE The son of Zebulun and his descendants (Ge 46:14; Nu 26:26).

SERGEANTS NIV "officers." *See Occupations and Professions.*

SERGIUS PAULUS A Roman deputy and convert of Paul (Ac 13:7-12).

SERMON ON THE MOUNT
The Sermon on the Mount is the first of five great discourses in Matthew (chs. 5-7; 10; 13; 18; 24-25). It contains three types of material: (1) beatitudes, or declarations of blessedness (5:1-12), (2) ethical admonitions (5:13-20; 6:1-7:23) and (3) contrasts between Jesus' ethical teaching and Jewish legalistic traditions (5:21-48). The sermon ends with a short parable stressing the importance of practicing what has just been taught (7:24-27) and an expression of amazement by the crowds at the authority with which Jesus spoke (7:28-29).

S

Opinion differs as to whether the sermon is a summary of what Jesus taught on one occasion or a compilation of teachings presented on numerous occasions. Matthew possibly took a single sermon and expanded it with other relevant teachings of Jesus. Thirty-four of the verses in Matthew's account of the sermon occur in different contexts in Luke than the so-called "Sermon on the Plain" (Lk 6:17-49).
The Sermon on the Mount's call to moral and ethical living is so high that some have dismissed it as being completely unrealistic or have projected its fulfillment to the future kingdom. There is no doubt, however, that Jesus (and Matthew) gave the sermon as a standard for all Christians, realizing that its demands cannot be met in our own power. It is also true that Jesus occasionally used hyperbole to make his point. For example, Jesus is not teaching self-mutilation (Mt 5:29-30), for even a blind man can lust. The point is that we should deal as drastically with sin as necessary.

SERPENT Satan appears in the form of, to Eve (Ge 3:1-15; 2Co 11:3). Subtlety of (Ge 3:1; Ecc 10:8; Mt 10:16). Curse upon (Ge 3:14-15; 49:17). Metaphorically feeds on the dust (Ge 3:14; Isa 65:25; Mic 7:17). Unfit for food (Mt 7:10). Venom of (Dt 32:24, 33; Job 20:16; Ps 58:4; 140:3; Pr 23:31-32; Ac 28:5-6). The staff

of Moses transformed into (Ex 4:3; 7:15). Poisonous, sent as a plague upon the Israelites (Nu 21:6-7; Dt 8:15; 1Co 10:9); the wound of miraculously healed by looking upon the bronze image set up by Moses (Nu 21:8-9). Charming of (Ps 58:4-5; Ecc 10:11; Jer 8:17). Mentioned in Solomon's riddle (Pr 30:19). Constriction of (Rev 9:19). Sea serpent (Am 9:3). The seventy-two given power over (Lk 10:19). The apostles given power over (Mk 16:18; Ac 28:5).

Figurative (Pr 23:32; Isa 14:29).

See Adder; Cobra; Dragon; Viper.

SERUG (*descendant* i.e., *younger branch* BDB). An ancestor of Abraham (Ge 11:20-23; 1Ch 1:26). Called Serug (Lk 3:35).

SERVANT Distinguished as a bond servant (who was a slave) and hired servant.

Bond Servant:

Laws of Moses concerning (Ex 20:10; 21:1-11, 20-21, 26-27, 32; Lev 19:20-22; 25:6, 10, 35-55; Dt 5:14; 15:12, 14, 18; 24:7). Kidnapping and slave trading forbidden (Dt 21:10-14; 24:7; 1Ti 1:10; Rev 18:13).

Fugitive, not to be returned to master (Dt 23:15-16). David erroneously supposed to be a fugitive slave (1Sa 25:10). Instances of fugitive: Hagar, commanded by an angel to return to her mistress (Ge 16:9). Sought by Shimei (1Ki 2:39-41). Interceded for, by Paul (Phm 10-21).

Bought and sold (Ge 17:13, 27; 37:28, 36; 39:17; Lev 22:11; Dt 28:68; Est 7:4; Eze 27:13; Joel 3:6; Am 8:6; Rev 18:13). Captives of war made (Dt 20:14; 21:10-14; 2Ki 5:2; 2Ch 28:8, 10; La 5:13), captive bondservants shared by priests and Levites (Nu 31:28-47). Thieves punished by being made (Ge 43:18; Ex 22:3). Defaulting debtors made (Lev 25:39; Mt 18:25). Children of defaulting debtors sold for (2Ki 4:1-7).

Voluntary servitude of (Lev 25:47; Dt 15:16-17; Jos 9:11-21). Given as dowry (Ge 29:24, 29). Owned by priests (Lev 22:11; Mk 14:66). Slaves owned slaves (2Sa 9:10). The master might marry or give in marriage (Ex 21:7-10; Dt 21:10-14; 1Ch 2:34-35). Taken in concubinage (Ge 16:1-2, 6; 30:3, 9). Used as soldiers by Abraham (Ge 14:14). Rights of those born to a master (Ge 14:14; 17:13, 27; Ex 21:4; Pr 29:21; Ecc 2:7; Jer 2:14).

Must be circumcised (Ge 17:13, 27; Ex 12:44). Must enjoy religious privileges with the master's household (Dt 12:12, 18; 16:11, 14; 29:10-11). Must have rest on the Sabbath (Ex 20:10; 23:12; Dt 5:14).

Servitude threatened, as a national punishment, for disobedience of Israel (Dt 28:68; Joel 3:7-8). Degrading influences of bondage exemplified by cowardice (Ex 14:11-12; 16:3; Jdg 5:16-18, 23).

Social status of (Mt 10:24-25; Lk 17:7-9; 22:27; Jn 13:16). Equal status of, with other disciples of Jesus (1Co 7:21-22; 12:13; Gal 3:28; Eph 6:8).

Proverbs concerning (Pr 12:9; 13:17; 17:2; 19:10; 25:13; 26:6; 27:18, 27; 29:19, 21; 30:10, 21-23).

Parables of (Mt 24:45-51; Lk 12:35-48; 16:1-13).

Conspiracy by. *See Conspiracy.*

Cruelty to—

Hagar (Ge 16:1-21; Gal 4:22-31). Joseph (Ge 37:26-28, 36). The Israelites (Ex 1:8-22; 2:1-4; 5:7-9; Dt 6:12, 21; Ac 7:19, 34). Sick, abandoned (1Sa 30:13). Gibeonites (Jos 9:22-27). Canaanites (1Ki 9:21). Jews in Babylon (2Ch 36:20; Est 1:1-10), freeing of (2Ch 36:23; Ezr 1.1-4).

Admonitions against cruelty to (Jer 22:13).

Kindness to—

(Ps 123:2; Pr 29:21). Commanded (Lev 25:43; Eph 6:9). Exemplified by Job (Job 19:15-16; 31:13-14), by Boaz (Ru 2:4), by the centurion (Mt 8:8-13; Lk 7:2-10), by Paul (Phm 1-21).

Duties of—

To be faithful (1Co 4:2). Obedient (Mt 8:9; Eph 6:5-9; Col 3:22-25; Tit 2:9-10; 1Pe 2:18-20). To honor masters (Mal 1:6; 1Ti 6:1-2).

Warning to (Zep 1:9).

Figurative (Lev 25:42, 55; Ps 116:16; Isa 52:3; Mt 24:45, 51; Lk 12:35-48; 16:1-13; 17:7-9; Jn 8:32-35; Ro 6:16-22; 1Co 4:1-2; 7:21-23; Gal 5:13; 1Pe 2:16; 2Pe 2:19; Rev 7:3).

Good, Instances of—

Joseph (Ge 39:2-20; 41:9-57; Ac 7:10), Elisha (2Ki 2:1-6). Servants of Abraham (Ge 24), of Boaz (Ru 2:4), of Jonathan (1Sa 14:7), of Abigail (1Sa 25:14-17), of David (2Sa 12:18; 15:15, 21), of Ziba (2Sa 9), of Naaman (2Ki 5:2-3, 13), of Nehemiah (Ne 4:16, 23), of centurion (Mt 8:9), of Cornelius (Ac 10:7), Onesimus (Phm 11). Servants in the parable of the pounds and talents (Mt 25:14-23; Lk 19:12-19).

Redeemed (Ne 5:8). Freed (2Ch 36:23; Ezr 1:1-4; Jer 34:8-22; Ac 6:9; 1Co 7:21). Called Freedmen (Ac 6:9). Tact in management of (Ecc 7:21).

Wicked and Unfaithful, Instances of—

Jeroboam (1Ki 11:26), Gehazi (2Ki 5:20-27), Zimri (1Ki 16:9-10; 2Ki 9:31), Onesimus (Phm 11).

Servants of Abraham and Lot (Ge 13:7), of Abimelech (Ge 21:25), of Ziba (2Sa 16:1-4, w 2Sa 19:26-27), of Absalom (2Sa 13:28-29; 14:30), of Shimei (1Ki 2:39), of Joash (2Ki 12:19-21), of Amon (2Ki 21:23), of Job (Job 19:15-16). In the parable of the talents and pounds (Mt 25:24-30; Lk 19:20-26). In the parable of the vineyard (Mt 21:33-41; Mk 12:1-9).

See Employee; Employer; Master.

Hired Workers:

Jacob (Ge 29:15; 30:26), reemployed (Ge 30:27-34; 31:6-7, 41). Parable of laborers for a vineyard (Mt 20:1-15). Of the father of the prodigal son (Lk 15:17, 19), of the prodigal son (Lk 15:5-19).

Kindness to (Ru 2:4). Treatment of, more considerable than that accorded slaves (Lev 25:53). Await employment in the marketplace (Mt 20:1-3).

Mercenary (Job 7:2). Unfaithful (Jn 10:12-13).

Rights of—

Receive wages (Mt 10:10; Lk 10:7; Ro 4:4; 1Ti 5:18; Jas 5:4). Daily payment of wages (Lev 19:13; Dt 24:15). Share in spontaneous products of land in the seventh year (Lev 25:6). Wages of, paid in a portion of the flocks or products (Ge 30:31-32; 2Ch 2:10), or in money (Mt 20:2, 9-10).

Oppression of, forbidden (Dt 24:14; Col 4:1), punished (Mal 3:5).

See Master, of Servants; Wages.

SERVANT OF THE LORD Agent of the LORD such as the patriarchs (Ex 32:13), Moses (Nu 12:7f), and the prophets (Zec 1:6).

Used as a title for the Messiah in Isaiah 40-66. The NT applies Isaiah's Servant passages to Jesus (Isa 42:1-4; Mt 12:16-21).

See Jesus the Christ, Messiah; Obedience of.

SERVICE Refers to all sorts of work from the most inferior and menial to the most honored and exalted (Lev 23:7f; Nu 3:6ff).

SERVITOR *See Occupations and Professions; Servant.*

SETH (*determined, granted, Ge 4:25; restitution* KB).

1. The third son of Adam and Eve, born after the murder of Abel. Name is a play on "granted," Eve said, "God has granted me another child in place of Abel, since Cain killed him" (Ge 4:25). It was through Seth that the genealogy of Noah passed (Ge 4:25-26; 5:3, 8; 1Ch 1:1; Lk 3:38).

2. *See Sheth.*.

SETHUR (*concealed [by deity]* IDB). One of the twelve spies (Nu 13:13).

SEVEN Interesting facts concerning the number.

Days:

Week consists of (Ge 2:3; Ex 20:11; Dt 5:13-14). Noah in the ark before the Flood (Ge 7:4, 10), remains in the ark after sending out the dove (Ge 8:10-12). Mourning for Jacob lasted (Ge 50:10), of Job (Job 2:13). The plague of bloody waters in Egypt lasted (Ex 7:25). The Israelites circled Jericho (Jos 6:4). The Passover lasted (Ex 12:15). Saul directed by Samuel to wait at Gilgal for the prophet's command (1Sa 10:8; 13:8). The elders of Jabesh Gilead ask for a truce of (1Sa 11:3). Dedication of the temple lasted double (1Ki 8:65). Ezekiel sits by the Kebar River in astonishment (Eze 3:15). The Feast of Tabernacles lasted (Lev 23:34, 42). Consecration of priests and altars lasted (Ex 29:30, 35; Eze 43:25-26). Defilements lasted (Lev 12:2; 13:4). Fasts of (1Sa 31:13; 2Sa 12:16, 18, 22). The firstborn of flocks and sheep shall remain with the mother before being offered (Ex 22:30). The feast of Xerxes continued (Est 1:5). Paul stayed at Tyre (Ac 21:4), at Puteoli (Ac 28:14).

Weeks:

In Daniel's vision concerning the coming of the Messiah (Da 9:25). Ten times (Da 9.24-27). The period between the Passover and Pentecost (Lev 23:15).

Months:

Holy convocations in the seventh month (Lev 23:24-44; Nu 29; Eze 45:25).

Years:

Jacob serves for each of his wives (Ge 29:15-30). Of plenty (Ge 41:1-32, 53). Famine lasted in Egypt (Ge 41:1 32, 54-56), in Canaan (2Sa 24:13; 2Ki 8:1). Insanity of Nebuchadnezzar (Da 4:32). Seven times, the period between the Jubilees (Lev 25:8).

Miscellaneous Sevens:

Of clean beasts taken into the ark (Ge 7:2). Abraham gives Abimelech seven lambs (Ge 21.28). Rams and bulls required in sacrifices (Lev 23:18; Nu 23:1; 29:32; 1Ch 15:26; Eze 45:23). Blood sprinkling seven times (Lev 4:6; 14:7), oil (Lev 14:16). Seven cows and seven heads of grain in Pharaoh's vision (Ge 41:2-7). Israelites marched around Jericho seven times, on the seventh day sounding seven trumpets (Jos 6:4). Elisha's servant looked seven times for the appearance of rain (1Ki 18:43). Naaman was required to wash in the Jordan seven times (2Ki 5:10).

Seven steps in the temple seen in Ezekiel's vision (Eze 40:22, 26). The heat of Nebuchadnezzar's furnace intensified sevenfold (Da 3:19). The light of the sun intensified sevenfold (Isa 30:26). The threatened sevenfold punishment of Israel (Lev 26:18-21). Silver purified seven times (Ps 12:6). Worshiping seven times a day (Ps 119:164). Seven eunuchs at the court of Xerxes (Est 1:10), seven princes (Est 1:14). Seven counselors at the court of Artaxerxes (Ezr 7:14). Seven maidens given to Esther (Est 2:9). Symbolic of many sons (Ru 4:15; 1Sa 2:5; Jer 15:9), of liberality (Ecc 11:1-2). Seven wise men (Pr 26:16). Seven women shall seek polyandrous marriage (Isa 4:1). Seven shepherds to be sent forth against Assyria (Mic 5:5-6). Seven lamps and pipes (Zec 4:2).

See Seven Words From the Cross.

Seven ministers in the apostolic church (Ac 6:3). Seven churches in Asia (Rev 1:4, 20). Seven seals (Rev 5:1). Seven thunders (Rev 10:3). Seven heads and seven crowns (Rev 12:3; 13:1; 17:9). Seven kings (Rev 17:10). Seven stars (Rev 1:16, 20; 3:1; Am 5:8). Seven spirits (Rev 1:4; 3:1; 4:5; 5:6). Seven eyes of the Lord (Zec 3:9; 4:10; Rev 5:6). Seven golden lampstands (Rev 1:12). Seven angels with seven trumpets (Rev 8:2). Seven plagues (Rev 15:1). Seven horns and seven eyes (Rev 5:6). Seven angels with seven plagues (Rev 15:6). Seven golden bowls (Rev 15:7). Scarlet colored beast having seven heads (Rev 17:3, 7).

SEVEN WORDS FROM THE CROSS The seven statements Jesus made from the cross. No single Gospel account recounts them all:

"Father, forgive them, for they do not know what they are doing." (Lk 23:34).

"I tell you the truth, today you will be with me in paradise." (Lk 23:43).

"Dear woman, here is your son," and to the disciple "Here is your mother." (Jn 19:26-27).

"My God, my God, why have you forsaken me?" (Mt 27:46-47; Mk 15:34-36).

"I am thirsty." (Jn 19:28).

"It is finished." (Jn 19:30).

"Father, into your hands I commit my spirit." (Lk 23:46; cf.Mt 27:50; Mk 15:37).

SEVENTY Seventy descendants of Jacob in Egypt (Ex 1:5; Dt 10:22). The council of the Israelites composed of seventy elders (Ex 24:1, 9; Nu 11:16, 24-25). Seventy-two (KJV seventy) disciples sent forth by Jesus (Lk 10:1-17). The Jews in captivity in Babylon seventy years (Jer 25:11-12; 29:10; Da 9:2; Zec 1:12; 7:5). *See Israel.*

SEVENTY WEEKS, THE The name applied to a period of time (probably 490 years) referred to in Daniel (Da 9:24-27).

SEVENTY-TWO, THE Seventy-two (KJV seventy) disciples were sent on a preaching mission by Jesus (Lk 10:1-17).

SEXUAL PURITY *See Chastity; Self-Control.*

SEXUAL RELATIONS *See Adultery; Bestiality; Fornication; Homosexual; Incest; Prostitute; Rape.*

SHAALABBIN (*site of foxes*). Town between Ir Shemesh and Aijalon (Jos 19:42).

SHAALBIM (site of foxes). A town, probably in central Israel, won by Danites from Amorites (Jdg 1:35).

SHAALBONITE Designation of Eliahba, one of David's mighty men (2Sa 23:32; 1Ch 11:33).

SHAALIM, LAND OF (possibly *[land of] hollow depth* KB). A region probably near the N boundary of Benjamin's territory (1Sa 9:4).

SHAAPH

1. Son of Jahdai (1Ch 2:47).
2. Son of Caleb (1Ch 2:49).

SHAARAIM (*double gates*).

1. A town in Judah (Jos 15:36; 1Sa 17:52).
2. A town in Simeon (1Ch 4:31), "Sharuhen" (Jos 19:6), and "Shilhim" (Jos 15:32).

SHAASHGAZ A eunuch of Xerxes' court (Est 2:14).

SHABBETHAI (*one born at Sabbath* ISBE KB).

1. A Levite, assistant to Ezra (Ezr 10:15).
2. An expounder of the Law (Ne 8:7).
3. A chief Levite, attendant of the temple (Ne 11:16).

SHACHIA *See Sakia.*

SHACKLES Made of bronze (Jdg 16:21; 2Ki 25:7; 2Ch 33:11; 36:6; Jer 39:7; 52:11). Used for securing prisoners (2Ch 33:11; 36:6; Mk 5:4). *See Chains; Fetters.*

SHADDAI (*the Mountain One* IDB; other suggestions: 1. *mountain* 2. *maternal goddess of many breasts* 3. *self-sufficient* 4. *an Akkadian spirit, Shad* 5. *almighty, omnipotent* KB). *Shaddai* is used forty-eight times as a name of God, thirty-two times in Job (Job 5:17; 6:4, 14; etc.), seven times in the compound name *El Shaddai.* The NIV consistently translates *Shaddai* as "Almighty" (Ge 17:1; Ps 91:1).

See God, Names of, Shaddai.

SHADOW Used literally, figuratively (1Ch 29:15; Ps 17:8; Isa 30:3), theologically (Col 2:17; Heb 8:5; 10:1).

SHADOW OF DEATH *See Darkness.*

SHADRACH (*servant of [pagan moon god] Aku*). His Hebrew name was Hananiah. He was taken as a captive to Babylon with Daniel, Mishael, and Azariah, where each one was given a Babylonian name (Da 1:6-20; 2:17, 49; 3:12-30). Hananiah was renamed Shadrach.

Shadrach, Meshach, and Abednego were chosen to learn the language and the ways of the Chaldeans (Babylonians) so that they could enter the king's service (Da 1:3-5, 17-20), c. 605 B.C. These three were eventually thrown into Nebuchadnezzar's furnace because they refused to bow down and worship the huge golden image that he had made (Da 3:1, 4-6, 8-30).

SHAFT

1. Stem of the gold lampstand (Ex 25:31; 37:17).
2. Shaft of a spear (1Sa 17:7).
3. Water (2Sa 5:8) or mine shaft (Job 28:4).

SHAGEE (*wanderer, meanderer [like feeding sheep]*). The father of Jonathan, one of David's guard (1Ch 11:34).

SHAHAR *See Zereth Shahar.*

SHAHARAIM (*one born at early [reddish] dawn* KB). A Benjamite (1Ch 8:8).

SHAHAZUMAH (*elevated place*). A city in Issachar (Jos 19:22).

SHALEM (*peace or safe*). *See Paddan Aram, 2.*

SHALIM, LAND OF *See Shaalim, Land of.*

SHALISHA (*a third part*). A district bordering on the Mount Ephraim (1Sa 9:4).

SHALISHAH *See Baal Shalishah.*

SHALLEKETH (possibly *[gate of] sending forth* BDB). One of the gates of the temple (1Ch 26:16).

SHALLUM (*peace, well being, prosperity*).

1. The son of Naphtali (1Ch 7:13), "Shillem" (Ge 46:24; Nu 26:48-49). *See Shillem, Shillemite.*
2. The son of Shaul (1Ch 4:25).
3. The son of Sismai (1Ch 2:40-41).

4. The son of Korah chief of the gatekeepers (1Ch 9:17, 19, 31; Ne 7:45), "Meshelemiah" (1Ch 26:1), "Shelemiah" (1Ch 26:14).
5. The son of Zadok (1Ch 6:12f), "Meshullam" (1Ch 9:11; Ne 11:11).
6. A king of Israel (2Ki 15:10-15).
7. The father of Jehizkiah (2Ch 28:12).
8. Husband of the prophetess Huldah (2Ki 22:14).
9. The king of Judah (1Ch 3:15), better known as Jehoahaz II.
10. The uncle of Jeremiah (Jer 32:7).
11. The father of Maaseiah (Jer 35:4).
12. A Levite who divorced his foreign wife (Ezr 10:24).
13. A man who divorced his foreign wife (Ezr 10:42).
14. A ruler who helped build Jerusalem's walls (Ne 3:12).

SHALLUN (*recompense*). A Jew who repaired a gate of Jerusalem (Ne 3:15).

SHALMAI (perhaps *Yahweh is well-being*). An ancestor of the temple servants that returned with Zerubbabel (Ezr 2:46; Ne 7:48).

SHALMAN (abbreviation of *Shalmaneser* IDB ISBE). Either a contraction of Shalmaneser or the Moabite king Salamanu (Hos 10:14).

SHALMANESER (*the god Shulman is chief,* or *Sulmanu is leader*). The title of five Assyrian kings, of whom one is mentioned in the OT, another refers to an Israelite king.
1. Shalmaneser III (859-824 B.C.), the son of Ashurnasirpal; inscription left by him says that he opposed Ben-Hadad of Damascus and Ahab of Israel, and made Israel tributary.
2. Shalmaneser V (726-722 B.C.), the son of Tiglath-Pileser; received tribute from Hoshea; besieged Samaria and carried the N tribes of Israel into captivity (2Ki 17:3; 18:9), "Shalman" (Hos 10:14).

SHAMA (*one obedient [to Yahweh]*). One of David's heroes (1Ch 11:44).

SHAMARIAH *See Shemariah, 2.*

SHAMBLES NIV "meat market" (1Co 10:25).

SHAME Of Adam and Eve: no shame before the Fall (Ge 2:25), but after (Ge 3:10). Jesus is ashamed of those who deny him (Mk 8:38; Lk 9:26). Of believers who do not continue in Christ (1Jn 2:28). Of the cross (Heb 12:2).
Destitute of, the Israelites when they worshiped the golden calf (Ex 32:25), the unjust (Zep 3:5).

SHAMED *See Shemed.*

SHAMELESSNESS Of the wicked (Jer 6:15; 8:12; Zep 3:5).

SHAMER
1. *See Shemer.*
2. *See Shemer; Shomer, 2.*

SHAMGAR (*[the pagan Hurrian god] Shimke gave [a son]* IDB). The son of Anath; judge; killed 600 Philistines with an oxgoad (Jdg 3:31; 5:6).

SHAMHUTH (possibly *one born at a time of a horrible event* KB). David's fifth divisional army commander (1Ch 27:8). *See Shammah, 4.*

SHAMIR (possibly *thorny* or *emery [flint]*).
1. A town in Judah c. thirteen miles SW of Hebron (Jos 15:48).
2. A town in Ephraim; the home of Tola (Jdg 10:1f).
3. A temple attendant (1Ch 24:24).

SHAMMA (*astonishment*). The son of Zophah, an Asherite (1Ch 7:37).

SHAMMAH (*waste*).
1. The grandson of Esau (Ge 36:13, 17; 1Ch 1:37).
2. The brother of David (1Sa 16:9; 17:13), also called Shimea (1Ch 20:7) and Shimeah (2Sa 13:3, 32).
3. One of David's mighty men (2Sa 23:11), also called Shagee (1Ch 11:34).
4. Another of David's mighty men (2Sa 23:33), also called Shammoth (1Ch 11:27) and Shamhuth (1Ch 27:8). May be the same as 3.

SHAMMAI (*Yahweh has heard*).
1. The son of Onam (1Ch 2:28, 32).
2. The father of Maon (1Ch 2:44-45).
3. The son of Ezra (1Ch 4:17).

SHAMMOTH (*desolation*). One of David's mighty men (1Ch 11:27), apparently the same as Shammah, 4 (2Sa 23:25) and Shamhuth (1Ch 27:8).

SHAMMUA (possibly *[Yahweh] hears* KB; *rumor,* ZPEB).
1. The son of Zaccur; Reubenite spy (Nu 13:4).
2. The son of David and Bathsheba (2Sa 5:14; 1Ch 14:4).
3. A Levite; the father of Abda (Ne 11:17), also called Shemaiah (1Ch 9:16).
4. A priest (1Ch 24:14; Ne 12:6, 18).

SHAMMUAH *See Shammua, 2.*

SHAMSHERAI (a combination of *Shemesh [pagan sun god] and Shamar [guard]*). The son of Jeroham (1Ch 8:26).

SHAN *See Beth Shan.*

SHAPHAM A chief of Gad (1Ch 5:12).

SHAPHAN (*rock badger*).
1. A secretary of King Josiah (2Ki 22:3-14; 2Ch 34:8-20). The father of Gemariah (Jer 36:10-12).
2. The father of Ahikam and the grandfather of Gedaliah (2Ki 22:12; 25:22; 2Ch 34:20; Jer 26:24; 39:14; 40:5, 9, 11; 41:2; 43:6).
3. The father of Elasah (Jer 29:3).
4. The father of Jaazaniah (Eze 8:11).

SHAPHAT (*he judges*).
1. A Simeonite spy (Nu 13:5).
2. The father of Elisha the prophet (1Ki 19:16, 19).
3. A Gadite chief in Bashan (1Ch 5:12).
4. A herdsman of David (1Ch 27:29).
5. The son of Shemaiah (1Ch 3:22).

SHAPHER *See Shepher, Mount.*

SHAPHIR (*lovely*). A town probably in SW Israel (Mic 1:10-15).

SHARAI A descendant of Bani who divorced his Gentile wife (Ezr 10:40).

SHARAIM *See Shaaraim, 1.*

SHARAR (*firm*). The father of one of David's mighty men (2Sa 23:33), "Sacar" (1Ch 11:35). *See Sacar, 1.*

SHARE Plowshare (1Sa 13:20).

SHAREZER (*[pagan god] protect the king!*).
1. The son of the Assyrian king Sennacherib (2Ki 19:37; Isa 37:38).
2. Contemporary of Zechariah the prophet (Zec 7:2).

SHARON (*plain, level country*).
1. Israel coastal plain between Joppa and Mount Carmel (1Ch 27:29; Isa 35:2; Ac 9:35).
2. Suburbs of Sharon possessed by the tribe of Gad (1Ch 5:16).
3. *See Lasharon.*
4. Figurative of fruitfulness, glory, peace (Isa 35:2; 65:10).

SHARONITE (*of Sharon*). Shitrai, in charge of David's herds in Sharon (1Ch 27:29).

SHARUHEN A Simeonite town in Judah's territory (Jos 19:6). Apparently the same as Shilhim (Jos 15:32), and Shaaraim (1Ch 4:31); possibly identified with Tell el-Farah.

SHASHAI (*noble*). A descendant of Bani, who put away his Gentile wife (Ezr 10:40).

SHASHAK A Benjamite (1Ch 8:14, 25).

SHAUL, SHAULITE (*asked,* possibly *dedicated to God*).
1. The son of Simeon and his descendants (Ge 46:10; Ex 6:15; Nu 26:13; 1Ch 4:24).
2. An ancient king of Edom (Ge 36:37; 1Ch 1:48-49).
3. Son of Uzziah (1Ch 6:24)

SHAVEH KIRIATHAIM (*level plain of two towns*). The plain where Kedorlaomer defeated the Emites (Ge 14:5), probably on the E of the Dead Sea (Nu 32:37).

SHAVEH, VALLEY OF (*level valley*). The valley where, after rescuing his nephew Lot, Abraham met the king of Sodom (Ge 14:17).

SHAVING The priests and Nazirites were prohibited from shaving (Lev 21:5; Nu 6:5), Hebrews generally wore beards. Shaving was often done for religious reasons, as an act of contrition (Job 1:20), consecration for Levites (Nu 6:9; 8:7), cleansing for lepers (Lev 14:8f; 13:32ff), also as an act of contempt (2Sa 10:4).

SHAVSHA David's secretary (1Ch 18:16), also called Shisha (1Ki 4:3), Seraiah (2Sa 8:17), and Sheva (2Sa 20:25).

SHEAF A handful of grain left behind by the reaper, gathered and bound by women and children, and later taken to the threshing-floor (Jer 9:22; Ru 2:7, 15). Some sheaves were left behind for the poor (Dt 24:19).

SHEAL (*May God grant!, asking*). A descendant of Bani, who put away his Gentile wife (Ezr 10:29).

SHEALTIEL (*I have asked [him] of God [El]* BDB ISBE KB; possibly *God [El] is a shield, God [El] is a victor* IDB).
1. Father of Zerubbabel and an ancestor of Jesus (1Ch 3:17; Ezr 3:2, 8; 5:2; Ne 12:1; Hag 1:1, 12, 14; 2:2, 23).
2. A son of Jehoiachin, king of Judah (Mt 1:12), or of Neri (Lk 3:27). He may have been the real son of Neri, but only the legal heir of Jehoiachin.

SHEARIAH (possibly *Yahweh breaks*). The son of Azel; descendant of Jonathan (1Ch 8:38; 9:44).

SHEARING HOUSE *See Beth Eked.*

SHEAR-JASHUB (*a remnant will return*). The symbolic name of Isaiah's oldest son (Isa 7:3; 8:18).

SHEBA (*seven* or *oath*).
1. The son of Raamah (Ge 10:7; 1Ch 1:9).
2. The son of Joktan (Ge 10:28; 1Ch 1:22).
3. The son of Jokshan (Ge 25:3; 1Ch 1:32).
4. A Benjamite who led an insurrection against David (2Sa 20).
5. A Gadite (1Ch 5:13).
6. A city of Simeon (Jos 19:2).
7. Queen of, visits Solomon (1Ki 10:1-13; 2Ch 9:1-12). Kings of, bring gifts to Solomon (Ps 72:10). Rich in gold (Ps 72:15), incense (Jer 6:20). Merchandise of (Eze 27:22-23; 38:13). Prophecies concerning the people of, coming into the kingdom of Messiah (Isa 60:6).
See Sabeans; Seba.

SHEBAH *See Shibah.*

SHEBAM *See Sebam.*

SHEBANIAH
1. Trumpeter priest (1Ch 15:24).
2. Levite who signed covenant with Nehemiah (Ne 9:4-5; 10:10).
3. Another Levite who signed a covenant (Ne 10:12).
4. A priest who signed a covenant (Ne 10:4).
5. Priest (Ne 12:14).

SHEBARIM (*quarry*). A place, called the "stone quarries" in the NIV, near Ai to which Israelite soldiers were chased (Jos 7:5, ftn).
See Quarries; Stones.

SHEBAT (*[the month of] destroying [rain]*). Month eleven in sacred sequence (Zec 1:7), month five in civil sequence. Winter (January-February). *See Month, 11.*

SHEBER (possibly *lion* IDB; possibly *breaking* or *crushing* or *roughly broken grain* KB). The son of Caleb (not the Israelite spy of the land of Canaan) (1Ch 2:48).

SHEBNA (*[Yahweh] return now* IDB).
1. A scribe of Hezekiah (2Ki 18:18, 26, 37; 19:2; Isa 36:3, 11, 22; 37:2).
2. An official of the king (Isa 22:15-19).

SHEBUEL (possibly *captive of God [El]* or *God [El] restores*). *See Shubael.*

SHECANIAH (*Yahweh has taken up his abode*).
1. The head of the tenth course of priests in the days of David (1Ch 24:11).
2. Levite (2Ch 31:15).
3. Descendant of David (1Ch 3:21-22).
4. Man who returned with Ezra (Ezr 8:3).
5. Another man who returned with Ezra (Ezr 8:5).
6. Man who proposed to Ezra that foreign wives be put away (Ezr 10:2-4).
7. Keeper of E gate of Jerusalem in the time of Nehemiah (Ne 3:29).
8. The father-in-law of Tobiah the foe of Nehemiah (Ne 6:18).
9. The chief priest who returned with Zerubbabel (Ne 12:3).

SHECHEM, SHECHEMITE (possibly *shoulder [saddle of a hill]* BDB; *shoulders [and upper part of the back]* KB).
1. A district in the central part of the land of Canaan. Abraham dwells in (Ge 12:6). Jacob buys a piece of ground in, and builds an altar (Ge 33:18-20). The flocks and herds of Jacob kept in (Ge 37:12-14). Joseph buried in (Jos 24:32). Jacob buried in (Ac 7:16, w Ge 50:13).
2. Also called Sychar, a city of refuge in Mount Ephraim (Jos 20:7; 21:21; Jdg 21:19). Joshua assembled the tribes of Israel at, with all their elders, chiefs, and judges, and presented them before the Lord (Jos 24:1-28). Joshua buried at (Jos 24:30-32). Abimelech made king at (Jdg 8:31; 9). Rehoboam crowned at (1Ki 12:1). Destroyed by Abimelech (Jdg 9:45), rebuilt by Jeroboam (1Ki 12:25). Men of, slain by Ishmael (Jer 41:5). Jesus visits; disciples made in (Jn 4:1-42).
3. Son of Hamor; seduces Jacob's daughter; slain by Jacob's sons (Ge 33:19; 34; Jos 24:32; Jdg 9:28).
4. Descendant of Manasseh and his clan (Nu 26:31; Jos 17:2).
5. Son of Shemida (1Ch 7:19).

SHECHINAH *See Shekinah.*

SHEDEUR (*Shaddai is light,* or *Shaddai is fire*). Reubenite; father of Elizur (Nu 1:5; 2:10; 7:30; 10:18).

SHEEP Offered in sacrifice, by Abel (Ge 4:4), by Noah (Ge 8:20), by Abraham (Ge 22:13). *See Offerings.* Required in the Mosaic offerings. *See Offerings.*
The land of Bashan adapted to the raising of (Dt 32:14), Bozrah (Mic 2:12), Kedar (Eze 27:21), Nebaioth (Isa 60:7), Sharon (Isa 65:10). Jacob's management of (Ge 30:32-40). Milk of, used for food (Dt 32:14). Shearing of (Ge 31:19; 38:12-17; Isa 53:7), feasting at the time of shearing (1Sa 25:11, 36; 2Sa 13:23). First fleece of, belonged to priests and Levites (Dt 18:4). Tribute paid in (2Ki 3:4; 1Ch 5:21; 2Ch 17:11).

Figurative:
(1Ch 21:17; Ps 74:1; Jer 13:20). Of backsliders (Jer 50:6). Of lost sinners (Mt 9:36; 10:6). Of the righteous (Jer 50:17; Eze 34; Mt 26:31; Mk 14:27; Jn 10:1-16). Of the defenselessness of ministers (Mt 10:16).
Parable of the lost (Mt 18:11-13; Lk 15:4-7).

SHEEP GATE An ancient gate of Jerusalem (Ne 3:1, 32; 12:39; Jn 5:2).

SHEEP MARKET NIV "Sheep Gate" (Jn 5:2).

SHEEP PEN Enclosure for protection of sheep (Nu 32:16; Jdg 5:16; 1Sa 24:3; Jn 10:1, 16).

SHEEPMASTER *See Occupations and Professions; Shepherd.*

SHEEP-SHEARER *See Occupations and Professions.*

SHEERAH (*blood relationship* or *female relative* IDB; *remainder* KB). The daughter of Ephraim; the descendants built three villages (1Ch 7:24).

SHEET A large piece of linen (Ac 10:11; 11:5).

SHEHARIAH (*he seeks Yahweh*). The son of Jeroham; Benjamite (1Ch 8:26).

SHEKEL (*weight*). A weight, equal to twenty gerahs (Ex 30:13; Nu 3:47; Eze 45:12). Used to weigh silver (Jos 7:21; Jdg 8:26; 17:2-3). Fractions of, used in currency (Ex 30:13; 1Sa 9:8; Ne 10:32). Used to weigh gold (Ge 24:22; Nu 7:14, 20-86; Jos 7:21; 1Ki 10:16), cinnamon (Ex 30:23), hair (2Sa 14:26), iron (1Sa 17:7), myrrh (Ex 30:23), rations (Eze 4:10). Fines paid in (Dt 22:19, 29). Fees paid in (1Sa 9:8). Sanctuary revenues paid in (Ex 30:13; Ne 10:32).

Of different standards: Of the sanctuary (Ex 30:13), of the king's weight (2Sa 14:26). Corrupted (Am 8:5).

SHEKINAH Jewish term for the dwelling presence of God's glory (Ex 25:22; Lev 16:2; 2Sa 6:2; 2Ki 19:14-15; Ps 80:1; Isa 37:16; Eze 9:3; 10:18; Heb 9:5). Not used in the Bible.

SHELAH (*missile [a weapon], sprout* ISBE).

1. Son of Arphaxad and ancestor of Joseph (Ge 10:24; 11:12-15; 1Ch 1:18, 24; Lk 3:35).
2. Son of Judah (Ge 38:5, 11, 14, 26; 46:12; Nu 26:20; 1Ch 2:3; 4:21).
3. The father of Zechariah (Ne 11:5).

SHELANITE (*missile [a weapon], sprout* ISBE). Descendants of Shelah (Nu 26:20). *See Shelah, 2.* Apparently called Shilonites (1Ch 9:5). *See Shilonite(s), 2.*

SHELEMIAH (*Yahweh pays back,* possibly *restores peace offering of Yahweh*).

1. Doorkeeper of tabernacle (1Ch 26:14), in previous verses of this chapter he is called "Meshelemiah."
2. Son of Cushi (Jer 36:14).
3. Man sent to arrest Jeremiah (Jer 36:26).
4. Father of a man whom Zedekiah sent to Jeremiah to ask his prayers (Jer 37:3).
5. The son of Hananiah (Jer 37:13).
6. Two men who divorced foreign wives (Ezr 10:39, 41).
7. Father of Hananiah (Ne 3:30).
8. Priest; treasurer (Ne 13:13).

SHELEPH (*one plucked out, drawn out*). The son of Joktan (Ge 10:26; 1Ch 1:20).

SHELESH (*triplet* KB; possibly *obedient* or *gentle* IDB). The son of Helem (1Ch 7:35).

SHELISHIYAH *See Eglath Shelishiyah.*

SHELOMI (*at peace*). The father of Ahihud, Asherite prince (Nu 34:27).

SHELOMITH (*at peace*).

1. Daughter of Dibri; her son was killed for blasphemy (Lev 24:10-12, 23).
2. The daughter of Zerubbabel (1Ch 3:19).
3. Cousin of Moses (1Ch 23:18).
4. A descendant of Moses (1Ch 26:25).
5. Child of Rehoboam (2Ch 11:20).
6. An ancestor of a family that returned with Ezra (Ezr 8:10).

SHELOMOTH (*at peace*).

1. Gershonite Levite (1Ch 23:9).
2. Izharite Levite (1Ch 24:22).

SHELUMIEL (*God [El] is [my] peace*). The son of Zurishaddai and leader of Simeon in the time of Moses (Nu 1:6; 2:12; 7:36, 41; 10:19).

SHEM (*name, fame*). The son of Noah. Preserved in the ark (Ge 5:32; 6:10; 7:13; 9:18; 1Ch 1:4). His filial conduct (Ge 9:23-27). The descendants of (Ge 10:1, 21-31; 11:10-29; 1Ch 1:17-54). In genealogy of Jesus (Lk 3:36).

SHEMA (*he hears*).

1. A town in S Judah (Jos 15:26).
2. The son of Hebron (1Ch 2:43-44).
3. The son of Joel (1Ch 5:8).
4. A Benjamite (1Ch 8:13).
5. An assistant of Ezra (Ne 8:4).
6. The Hebrew name for, "Hear, O Israel: The LORD our God, the LORD is one" (Dt 6:4, ftn).

S

SHEMAAH (possibly *Yahweh hears*). The father of Ahiezer and Joash, soldiers of David (1Ch 12:3).

SHEMAIAH (*Yahweh hears*).

1. Simeonite prince (1Ch 4:37).
2. Reubenite (1Ch 5:4), possibly the same as Shema of (1Ch 5:8).
3. The chief Levite (1Ch 15:8, 11).
4. A Levite scribe (1Ch 24:6).
5. The son of Obed-Edom (1Ch 26:4, 6-7).
6. A prophet who forbade Rehoboam to war against Israel (1Ki 12:22-24).
7. A descendant of David (1Ch 3:22).
8. A Merarite Levite (1Ch 9:14; Ne 12:18).
9. A Levite who returned from exile (1Ch 9:16). Also called Shammua (Ne 11:17).
10. A Levite (2Ch 17:8).
11. A Levite who cleansed the temple (2Ch 29:14).
12. A Levite who assisted in the distribution of food (2Ch 31:15).
13. A Levite in the days of Josiah (2Ch 35:9).
14. A Levite who returned with Ezra (Ezr 8:13).
15. One whom Ezra sent back for ministers (Ezr 8:16), possibly the same as (Ezr 8:13).
16. A priest who divorced his foreign wife (Ezr 10:21).
17. Another priest who divorced his foreign wife (Ezr 10:31).
18-23. Men who played various roles in Nehemiah's rebuilding and in the dedication of the Jerusalem wall (Ne 3:29; 6:10ff; 10:8; 12:6, 18, 34, 35, 36, 42).
24. The father of Uriah the prophet (Jer 26:20).
25. A false prophet who fought against Jeremiah (Jer 29:24-32).
26. The father of Delaiah, a prince in the days of Jehoiakim (Jer 36:12).

SHEMARIAH (*Yahweh guards, preserves*).

1. One of David's mighty men (1Ch 12:5).
2. The son of Rehoboam, king of Judah (2Ch 11:19).
3. A man who put away his foreign wife (Ezr 10:32).
4. Another man who put away his foreign wife (Ezr 10:41).

SHEMEBER The king of Zeboiim, a city near the Dead Sea (Ge 14:2).

SHEMED (*destruction*). The son of Elpaal (1Ch 8:12).

SHEMER (possibly *watch* IDB; possibly *sediment of wine from which clear wine is made* KB). *See Shomer, 1, 3, 4.*

SHEMESH *See Beth Shemesh; En Shemesh; Ir Shemesh.*

SHEMIDA, SHEMIDAITE (possibly *the name knows* BDB KB; possibly *[pagan god] Eshmun has known* IDB). The son of Gilead; a family descended from Shemida (Nu 26:32; Jos 17:2; 1Ch 7:19).

SHEMINITH (*eight [strings]*). A musical term of uncertain meaning, possibly "octave" (1Ch 15:21; Ps 6; 12, titles).

See Music, Symbols Used in.

SHEMIRAMOTH (*heights, heavens* BDB; possibly *proper name of a pagan goddess* KB).

1. A Levite musician (1Ch 15:18, 20; 16:5).
2. A Levite sent by Jehoshaphat to instruct the people in the law (2Ch 17:8).

SHEMUEL (possibly *his name is God [El]* BDB IDB ISBE; *the unnamed god is El* KB; *heard of God [El]* KD).

1. A Simeonite leader (Nu 34:20).
2. *See Samuel, 2.*

SHEN (*tooth, crag [of rock]*). An unidentified site near which Samuel erected the stone "Ebenezer" (1Sa 7:12).

SHENAZZAR (*may [the moon god] Sin protect*). The son of Jehoiachin (1Ch 3:18).

SHENIR *See Senir.*

SHEOL (possibly *place of inquiry [of the dead]* BDB; *desolate place, no-country underworld* KB). The OT name for the place of departed souls, corresponding to the NT word "Hades." When translated "hell" it refers to the place of punishment, but when translated "grave" the reference is to the place of the dead in general. It often means the place or state of the soul between death and resurrection. The clearest indication of different conditions in Sheol is in Christ's parable of the rich man and Lazarus (Lk 16:19-31).

See Grave; Hades; Hell.

SHEPHAM (*nakedness*). A place in NE of Canaan, near Sea of Galilee (Nu 34:10-11).

SHEPHATIAH (*Yahweh has judged*).

1. The son of David (2Sa 3:4).
2. The son of Reuel (1Ch 9:8).
3. One of David's mighty men (1Ch 12:5).
4. A Simeonite prince (1Ch 27:16).
5. The son of King Jehoshaphat (2Ch 21:2).
6. The founder of a family which returned with Zerubbabel (Ezr 2:4).
7. One of the children of Solomon's servants whose descendants returned with Zerubbabel (Ezr 2:57).
8. One whose descendants returned with Ezra (Ezr 8:8). May be the same as (Ezr 2:57).
9. The son of Mahalalel (Ne 11:4).
10. The prince who wanted Jeremiah to be put to death for prophesying (Jer 38:1).

SHEPHELAH, THE (*lowland*). Hilly country between the mountains of Judah and the maritime plain S of the plain of Sharon, extending through the country of Philistia along the Mediterranean (Jos 12:8).

SHEPHER, MOUNT A mountain, camping place of the Israelites in the desert (Nu 33:23-24).

SHEPHERD

General:

One who cares for flocks (Ge 31:38-40; Ps 78:52-53; Jer 31:10; Am 3:12; Lk 2:8). David defends his flock against a lion and a bear (1Sa 17:34-35). Causes the flock to rest (Ps 23:2; SS 1:7; Jer 33:12). Numbers the flock (Lev 27:32; Jer 33:13). Knows his flock by name (Jos 10:3-5). Keeps the sheep and goats apart (Mt 25:32). Waters the flocks (Ge 29:2-10). Keeps the flocks in folds (Nu 32:16; 1Sa 24:3; 2Sa 7:8; Jn 10:1). Watch towers of (2Ch 26:10; Mic 4:8). Dogs of (Job 30:1). Was an abomination to the Egyptians (Ge 46:34). Angels appeared to (Lk 2:8-20).

Instances of:

Abel (Ge 4:2). Rachel (Ge 29:9). Daughters of Jethro (Ex 2:16). Moses (Ex 3:1). David (1Sa 16:11; 2Sa 7:8; Ps 78:70).

Figurative:

(Ge 49:24). Of prophets, priests, Levites, and civil authorities (Eze 34). Of Cyrus (Isa 44:28). Of Yahweh (Ps 23; Isa 40:11). Of Christ (Zec 13:7; Mt 26:31; Mk 14:27; Jn 10:1-16; Heb 13:20; 1Pe 2:25).

SHEPHI *See Shepho.*

SHEPHO (possibly *track, bare ways formed without human work by the traffic caravans* KB). Early descendant of Seir (Ge 36:23; 1Ch 1:40). Lesser known brother of Groucho, Harpo, and Chico.

SHEPHUPHAN (perhaps *serpent*). The son of Bela (1Ch 8:5).

SHERAH *See Sheerah.*

SHERD *See Potsherd*

SHEREBIAH (possibly *Yahweh has sent burning heat* BDB).

1. A prominent Levite in Ezra's time (Ezr 8:18, 24).
2. Covenanter with Nehemiah (Ne 10:12).
3. Levite who returned with Zerubbabel (Ne 12:8).
4. The chief Levite (Ne 12:24).

SHERESH (*root, rootstock, sucker [of a plant]*). The son of Makir (1Ch 7:16).

SHEREZER *See Sharezer.*

SHERIFF (Da 3:2-3). *See Magistrates.*

SHESHACH (cryptogram for *Babel [Babylon]*). Perhaps a cryptogram for "Babel" or "Babylon" (Jer 25:26, ftn; 51:41, ftn).

SHESHAI (possibly *sixth [child]*). The son of Anak (Nu 13:22; Jos 15:14; Jdg 1:10).

SHESHAN A descendant of Jerahmeel (1Ch 2:31, 34-35).

SHESHBAZZAR (*may [the pagan moon god named] Sin protect [the father]*). A Jewish official whom Cyrus made deputy governor of Judah and who helped lay the foundation of the temple (Ezr 1:8, 11; 5:14, 16). Some believe that Sheshbazzar and Zerubbabel were the same person for the following reasons:

1. Both were governors (Ezr 5:14; Hag 1:1; 2:2).
2. Both are said to have laid the foundation of the temple (Ezr 3:2-8; 5:16; Hag 1:14-15; Zec 4:6-10).
3. Jews in Babylon were often given "official" Babylonian names (cf. Da 1:7).
4. Josephus (*Antiq.*, 11.1.3) seems to identify Sheshbazzar with Zerubbabel.

Others point out, however:

1. The Apocrypha distinguishes between the two men (1Es 6:18).
2. Sheshbazzar was likely an elderly man at the time of the return, while Zerubbabel was probably a younger contemporary.
3. Sheshbazzar may have been viewed as the official governor, while Zerubbabel served as the popular leader (Ezr 3:8-11).
4. Whereas the high priest Jeshua is associated with Zerubbabel, no priest is associated with Sheshbazzar.
5. Although Sheshbazzar presided over the foundation of the temple in 536 B.C., so little was accomplished that Zerubbabel had to preside over a second foundation sixteen years later (Hag 1:14-15; Zec 4:6-10).

Others identify Sheshbazzar with Shenazzar (1Ch 3:18), the fourth son of King Jehoiachin. Zerubbabel would then have been Sheshbazzar's nephew (compare 3:2 with 1Ch 3:18). *See Zerubbabel.*

SHETH (*sons of tumult,* or *sons of pride, compensation*). A designation for Moab (Nu 24:17).

SHETHAR A prince of Persia (Est 1:14).

SHETHAR-BOZENAI (*delivering the kingdom*). Persian official who tried to hinder Jews (Ezr 5:3, 6).

SHEVA (*vanity, emptiness* IDB; *one who will emulate* IDB KB).

1. David's scribe (2Sa 20:25), perhaps the same as "Seraiah" (1Ch 2:49). *See Seraiah, 1.*
2. The son of Caleb (1Ch 2:49).

SHEWBREAD *See Bread, Consecrated.*

SHIBAH (possibly *seven* BDB ISBE; possibly *oath* BDB IDB; *plenty* KB). The name of the well dug by Isaac's servants. A town of Beersheba named from this well (Ge 26:31-33, ftn). Called Beersheba in NIV.

SHIBBOLETH (*flowing stream* BDB KB; or *ear of grain* IDB). A word differently pronounced on the two sides of the Jordan, and was used by the men of Gilead to determine whether the speaker was of Ephraim or not. Those who said "Sibboleth" instead of "Shibboleth" were killed. Forty-two thousand Ephraimites were killed at the fords of the Jordan at that time (Jdg 12:5-6).

SHIBMAH *See Sibmah.*

SHICRON *See Shikkeron.*

SHIELD

Defensive Armor:

Different kinds of (Ps 35:2; Eze 38:4). Used by Saul (2Sa 1:21), by the Benjamites (2Ch 14:8; 17:17). Uzziah equipped the Israelites with (2Ch 26:14). Made of bronze (1Ki 14:27), of gold (2Sa 8:7; 1Ki 10:16-17; 2Ch 9:15-16), of wood (Eze 39:9-10). Stored in armories (1Ki 10:17; 2Ch 11:12; 32:5, 27), in the tabernacle (2Ki 11:10; 2Ch 23:9). Covered when not in use (Isa 22:6). Painted red (Na 2:3). *See Armor.*

Figurative:

Of God's protection (Ge 15:1; Dt 33:29; 2Sa 22:3, 36; Ps 5:12; 18:2, 35; 33:20; 59:11; 84:9, 11; 89:18; Pr 30:5). Of God's truth (Ps 91:4). Of kings (Ps 47:9). Of an entire army (Jer 46:3).

SHIGGAION (*go astray, wander [i.e., a wild, passionate song, with rapid changes in rhythm]* BDB; possibly Akkadian for *dirge* KB). A musical term of unknown meaning found in the heading of (Ps 7).

See Music, Symbols Used in.

SHIGIONOTH (*go astray, wander [i.e., a wild, passionate song, with rapid changes in rhythm]* BDB; possibly Akkadian for *dirge* KB). The plural of *shiggaion.* The heading of Habakkuk's psalm (Hab 3:1).
See Music, Symbols Used in.

SHIHON *See Shion.*

SHIHOR (possibly *black water* BDB; Egyptian *Canal of [pagan god] Horus* KB). May refer to the Nile, a stream which separated Egypt from Israel, or a branch of the Nile (Jos 13:3; 1Ch 13:5; Isa 23:3; Jer 2:18).

SHIHOR LIBNATH A small stream on the S border of Asher (Jos 19:26).

SHIKKERON (possibly *drunkenness* IDB; *hog bean plant* IDB). A town on the N boundary of Judah (Jos 15:11).

SHILHI (possibly *[my] javelin [thrower?]* IDB KB). Father-in-law of Jehoshaphat, king of Judah (1Ki 22:42; 2Ch 20:31).

SHILHIM A city of Judah (Jos 15:32).

SHILLEM, SHILLEMITE (*recompense* BDB IDB; possibly *whole, healthy, complete* KB). The son of Naphtali (Ge 46:24; 1Ch 7:13), and his descendants (Nu 26:49).

SHILOAH A stream or pool (Isa 8:6). Probably identical with Siloah and Siloam. *See Siloam, Pool of.*

SHILOH
1. A city in Ephraim, c. twelve miles N and E of Bethel where the tabernacle remained from the time of Joshua to the days of Samuel (Jdg 21:19; 1Sa 4:3), Benjamites kidnapped wives (Jdg 21:15-24), residence of Eli and Samuel (1Sa 3:21), home of the prophet Ahijah (1Ki 14:3), a ruin in Jeremiah's time (Jer 7:12, 14).
2. A word of uncertain meaning regarded by many Jews and Christians as a reference to the Messiah; the NIV has "until he comes to whom it belongs" (Ge 49:10, ftn).

SHILONI *See Shelah, 3.*

SHILONITE(S) (*of Shiloh*).
1. A man of Shiloh (1Ki 12:15; 15:29; 2Ch 9:29; 10:15).
2. Apparently denotes a descendant of Shelah (1Ch 9:5). *See Shelanite.*

SHILSHAH (possibly *obedient* or *gentle* IDB; *third [part, child?], triplet* KB). An Asherite; the son of Zophah (1Ch 7:37).

SHIMEA (*he has heard* or *he is obedient*).
1. Brother of David (1Ch 20:7). Perhaps the same as "Shammah" (1Sa 16:9), "Shimeah" (2Sa 21:21).
2. The son of David and Bathsheba (1Ch 3:5).
3. A Merarite Levite (1Ch 6:30).
4. A Gershonite Levite (1Ch 6:39).

SHIMEAH (*he has heard* or *he is obedient*).
1. The brother of David (2Sa 13:3, 32; 21:21).
2. A Benjamite (1Ch 8:32), "Shimeam" (1Ch 9:38).

SHIMEAM *See Shimeah, 2.*

SHIMEATH (*guardian, watcher*). The mother of an assassin of King Joash (2Ki 12:21; 2Ch 24:26).

SHIMEATHITES A family of scribes (1Ch 2:55).

SHIMEI, SHIMEITES (*Yahweh has heard,* or *famous*).
1. Son of Gershon (Ex 6:17; Nu 3:18; 1Ch 6:17; 23:7, 10) and his descendants (Nu 3:21).
2. A Benjamite. Curses David; David's magnanimity toward (2Sa 16:5-13; 19:16-23, w 1Ki 2:36-46).
3. An officer of David (1Ki 1:8).
4. One of Solomon's district governors (1Ki 4:18).
5. A son of Jesse (1Ch 2:13).
6. The grandson of Jehoiachin (1Ch 3:19).
7. The son of Zaccur (1Ch 4:26-27).
8. A Reubenite. The son of Gog (1Ch 5:4).
9. A Merarite. The son of Libni (1Ch 6:29).
10. A Gershonite. The son of Jahath (1Ch 6:42).
11. The father of a family in Benjamin (1Ch 8:21).
12. A Levite (1Ch 23:9).
13. A leader of singers in the time of David (1Ch 25:17).
14. David's overseer of vineyards (1Ch 27:27).
15. A son of Heman (2Ch 29:14).
16. A Levite. The treasurer of tithes and offerings in the time of Hezekiah (2Ch 31:12-13).
17. A Levite who put away his Gentile wife (Ezr 10:23).
18. The name of two Israelites who put away Gentile wives (Ezr 10:33, 38).
19. A Benjamite. The grandfather of Mordecai (Est 2:5).
20. The ancestor of a family (Zec 12:13). Possibly identical with 1.

SHIMEON (possibly *offspring of hyena and wolf* BDB KB). An Israelite who divorced his Gentile wife (Ezr 10:31).

SHIMHI *See Shimei, 11.*

SHIMI *See Shimei, 1.*

SHIMMA *See Shimea, 1.*

SHIMON A man of Judah (1Ch 4:20).

SHIMRATH (*guardian, watchman*). The son of Shimei (1Ch 8:21).

SHIMRI (*Yahweh guards, preserves*).
1. The son of Shemaiah; a Simeonite (1Ch 4:37).
2. The father of Jediael and Joha, two of David's mighty men (1Ch 11:45).
3. A Merarite Levite doorkeeper (1Ch 26:10).
4. A Levite who assisted in cleansing the temple (2Ch 29:13).

SHIMRITH (*guardianess, watch woman*). A Moabitess; the mother of Jehozabad who helped kill Joash, king of Judah (2Ch 24:26), "Shomer" (2Ki 12:21).

SHIMROM *See Shimron, 1.*

SHIMRON, SHIMRONITE (*guardian, watchman*).
1. The son of Issachar (Ge 46:13; 1Ch 7:1) and his descendants (Nu 26:24).
2. A town in N Canaan whose king fought Joshua (Jos 11:1ff); probably Shimron Meron. *See Shimron Meron.*

SHIMRON MERON A city conquered by Joshua (Jos 12:20). Probably identical with Shimron, 2. *See Shimron, 2.*

SHIMSHAI (*one given to [pagan sun god] Shemesh*). A scribe who tried to hinder the Jews in rebuilding the temple (Ezr 4:8-9, 17, 23).

SHINAB (*[pagan god] Sin is his father*). The king of Admah. A Canaanite city, later destroyed (Ge 14:2).

SHINAR An alluvial plain of Babylonia in which lay the cities of Babel, Erech, Akkad, and Calneh (Ge 10:10), the Tower of Babel was built there (Ge 11:1-9), Amraphel, king of Shinar, invaded Canaan (Ge 14:1, 9). Elsewhere rendered Babylon(ia): Nebuchadnezzar transported the temple treasures to (Da 1:2, ftn), Jews exiled to (Zec 5:11, ftn).

SHION A town in Issachar near Nazareth (Jos 19:19).

SHIP Built, by Noah (Ge 6:13-22), by Solomon (1Ki 9:26; 2Ch 8:17), by Jehoshaphat (1Ki 22:48; 2Ch 20:35-36), of cypress wood (Ge 6:14), of fir wood (Eze 27:5), of papyrus (Isa 18:2), sealed with pitch (Ge 6:15).
Equipped with, rudder (Ac 27:40; Jas 3:4), rigging (Isa 33:23; Ac 27:19), sails (Isa 33:23; Ac 27:1, 9, 17, 40), embroidered sails (Eze 27:7), masts (Isa 33:23; Eze 27:5), oars (Jnh 1:13; Mk 6:48), figurehead (Ac 28:11), anchor (Ac 27:29-30, 40; Heb 6:19), lifeboats (Ac 27:30, 32).
Used, in commerce (Ac 21:3; 27:10), in commerce with Tarshish (1Ki 22:48; Isa 60:9; Jnh 1:3), with Ophir (1Ki 10:11; 2Ch 8:18), with Adramyttium (Ac 27:2), for passenger traffic (Isa 60:9; Jnh 1:3; Ac 20:13; 27:2, 37; 28:11).
Repaired by caulking (Eze 27:9).
Wrecked, at Ezion Geber (1Ki 22:48; 2Ch 20:35-37), at Malta (Ac 27:14-44).
Warships used by Kittim (Nu 24:24; Da 11:30).
See Mariner.

SHIPHI (*flowing abundance*). The father of Ziza (1Ch 4:37).

SHIPHMITE (*family name of Zabdi*). Vineyard overseer (1Ch 27:27).

SHIPHRAH (*beautiful, fair*). A Hebrew midwife who saved Hebrew boy babies (Ex 1:15-21).

SHIPHTAN (*he has judged*). The father of the representative of Ephraim on the committee which divided the promised land among the Israelites (Nu 34:24).

SHISHA The father of two of Solomon's secretaries (1Ki 4:3), may be identical with Seraiah (2Sa 8:17), Sheva (2Sa 20:25), and Shavsha (1Ch 18:16).

SHISHAK The first Egyptian Pharaoh mentioned by name in the Bible; the founder of the twenty-second dynasty (945-924 B.C.), gave refuge to Jeroboam (1Ki 11:40), invaded Jerusalem in the reign of Rehoboam (1Ki 14:25f).

SHITRAI (*scribe, officer*). A chief shepherd of David (1Ch 27:29).

SHITTAH *See Beth Shittah.*

SHITTAH TREE NIV "acacia." *See Acacia Wood; Plants of the Bible; Tree.*

SHITTIM (*acacia trees*).
1. Also called Abel Shittim (Nu 33:49). A camping place of Israel (Nu 25:1; 33:49). Joshua sends spies from (Jos 2:1). Valley of (Joel 3:18). Balaam prophesies in (Mic 6:5). *See Abel Shittim.*
2. Hebrew for acacia (Joel 3:18).
See Acacia Wood.

SHIZA A Reubenite. The father of one of David's mighty men (1Ch 11:42).

SHOA (*rich*). People mentioned in association with the Babylonians, Chaldeans, and Assyrians (Eze 23:23). May be Sutu of Amarna letters.

SHOBAB (*one who turns back, repents*).
1. The grandson for Hezron (1Ch 2:18).
2. The son of David (2Sa 5:14; 1Ch 3:5; 14:4).

SHOBACH The captain of the host of Hadadezer. Slain by David's army (2Sa 10:16, 18). Also called Shophach (1Ch 19:16, 18).

SHOBAI (possibly *captive* or *Yahweh returns*). A gatekeeper, whose descendants returned to Jerusalem with Zerubbabel (Ezr 2:42; Ne 7:45).

SHOBAL (perhaps a nickname *basket*).
1. Chief of the Horites (Ge 36:20, 23, 29).
2. Ephrathite; founder of Kiriath Jearim (1Ch 2:50, 52).
3. Grandson of Judah (1Ch 4:1-2).

SHOBEK (*victor* IDB). A Jew who sealed the covenant with Nehemiah (Ne 10:24).

SHOBI (possibly *captive* or *Yahweh returns*). The son of Nahash. Brought supplies to David in his flight from Absalom (2Sa 17:27).

SHOCHO *See Soco, 2.*

SHOE *See Sandal.*

SHOFAR (*ram horn*). A trumpet of ram's horn (Jos 6:4-6, 8, 13). *See Trumpet.*

SHOHAM (*carnelian [precious stone]*). A Merarite (1Ch 24:27).

SHOMER (*guardian, watchman*).
1. A man who sold the hill of Samaria to Omri, king of Israel (1Ki 16:24).
2. The father of Jehozabad, conspirator of Joash of Judah (2Ki 12:20-21).
3. A Merarite Levite (1Ch 6:46).
4. The great-grandson of Asher (1Ch 7:32, 34).

SHOPHACH A Syrian general slain by David (1Ch 19:16, 18), "Shobach" (2Sa 10:16).

SHOPHAN *See Atroth Shophan.*

SHORE Coast line or beach (Jos 15:2; Jdg 5:17; Mt 13:2).

SHOSHANNIM NIV "Lilies." *See Music, Symbols Used in.*

SHOULDER The shoulder of a sacrificed ox or sheep went to the priest as his portion (Dt 18:8), the sacred furniture of the tabernacle had to be carried upon the shoulders (Nu 7:6-9).

SHOULDER PIECE
1. Part of the ephod in which the front and the back were joined together (Ex 28:7-8).
2. A piece of meat taken from the shoulder of an animal (Eze 24:4).

SHOUTING In joy and praise (1Ch 15:28; 2Ch 15:12-14; Ezr 3:11-13; Ps 47:1; Isa 12:6; Lk 17:15; 19:37-41; Ac 3:8-9; Rev 5:12-14).
See Clap; Praise; Worship.
In battle (Jos 6:20; Jdg 7:18; 1Sa 17:20, 52; 2Ch 13:15).

SHOVEL A utensil in the tabernacle (Ex 27:3; 38:3; Nu 4:14), temple (1Ki 7:40; Jer 52:18).

SHOWBREAD *See Bread, Consecrated.*

SHRINE Places of idolatrous worship, often a high place (Eze 16:24-25, 31, 39). Frequented by temple prostitutes (Ge 38:21-22; Dt 23:17; Hos 4:14), including male prostitutes (1Ki 14:24; 15:12; 22:46; 2Ki 23:7; Job 36:14). A shrine also refers to an idolatrous symbol, certain small idol houses, made by the silversmith, Demetrius, and sold to the worshipers of the Temple of Diana (Ac 19:24).
See Artemis; Groves; High Places; Idolatry; Prostitute.

SHRIVELED HAND As a judgment (1Ki 13:4). Jesus heals on the Sabbath (Mt 12:10-13 w Mk 3:1-6; Lk 6:6-11). *See Disease.*

SHROUD A sheet to cover the dead (Isa 25:7).

SHRUB *See Plants of the Bible.*

SHUA (*prosperity* ISBE).
1. A Canaanite whose daughter became Judah's wife (Ge 38:2, 12).
2. Heber's daughter (1Ch 7:32).

SHUAH (*depression, lowland [an Aramean land on the Euphrates River]*).
1. The son of Abraham by Keturah (Ge 25:2; 1Ch 1:32).
2. *See Shua, 1.*
3. *See Shuhah.*

SHUAL (*fox* or *jackal*).
1. District near Micmash (1Sa 13:17).
2. The son of Zophah (1Ch 7:36).

SHUBAEL (possibly *captive of God [El],* or *God [El] restores*).
1. The son of Gershom son of Moses (1Ch 23:16; 26:24).
2. The son of Amram (1Ch 24:20).
3. A singer, the son of Heman (1Ch 25:4, 20).

SHUHAH (*pit, depression*). Kelub's brother (1Ch 4:11).

SHUHAM, SHUHAMITE The son of Dan and his clan (Nu 26:42-43); also called Hushim (Ge 46:23). *See Hushim, 1.*

SHUHITE (*of Shuah*). Bildad, one of Job's friends (Job 2:11; 8:1; 18:1; 25:1); possibly a descendant of Shuah, 1.

SHULAMMITE (*peaceful*). A designation of the beloved in the Song of Songs (SS 6:13); possibly the same as Shunammite.

SHUMATHITES (*garlic*). Family of Kiriath Jearim (1Ch 2:53).

SHUNAMMITE
1. A person from Shunem. Abishag, the woman who nourished David (1Ki 1:3), desired by Adonijah as wife (1Ki 2:13-25).
2. A woman who gave hospitality to Elisha and whose son he raised to life (2Ki 4:8-37).

SHUNEM A city of Issachar (Job 19:18), three-and-a-half miles N of Jezreel; the site of a Philistine encampment before battle (1Sa

28:4), the home of Abishag, David's nurse (1Ki 1:3), home of a woman who befriended Elisha (2Ki 4:8-37).

SHUNI, SHUNITE The son of Gad (Ge 46:16) and his clan (Nu 26:15).

SHUPHAM, SHUPHAMITE The son of Benjamin and progenitor of Shuphamites (Nu 26:39). May be the same as Shephuphan (1Ch 8:5).

SHUPPIM
1. A Levite (1Ch 26:16).
2. *See Shuppites.*

SHUPPITES Descendants of Ir (1Ch 7:12, 15).

SHUR (*wall*). A wilderness southwest of Israel (Ge 16:7; 20:1; 25:18; Ex 15:22; 1Sa 15:7; 27:8).

SHUSHAN *See Susa.*

SHUSHAN-EDUTH (*lily of testimony*). *See Music, Symbols Used in.*

SHUTHELAH, SHUTHALHITE
1. The son of Ephraim and his clan (Nu 26:35-36).
2. The son of Zabad; father of Ezer and Elead (1Ch 7:21).

SHUTTLE Part of a weaving loom; used as a figure of the shortness of life (Job 7:6).

SIA (*assembly*). Progenitor of the temple servants that returned with Zerubbabel (Ne 7:47), "Siaha" (Ezr 2:44).

SIAHA *See Sia.*

SIBBECAI One of David's mighty men, designated "Hushathite" (2Sa 21:18; 1Ch 11:29; 20:4; 27:11), killed the Philistine "Saph" (2Sa 21:18).

SIBBOLETH *See Shibboleth.*

SIBMAH A city of Reuben (Nu 32:38; Jos 13:19; Isa 16:8-9; Jer 48:32). Apparently also called Sebam (Nu 32:3).

SIBRAIM A place on the N boundary of Israel (Eze 47:16).

SICHEM *See Shechem, 1.*

SICILY An island lying off the "toe" of Italy, visited by Paul (Ac 28:12). *See Syracuse.*

SICK, THE Visiting (Ps 41:6). Visiting, a duty (Mt 25:36, 43; Jas 1:27). *See Afflicted; Affliction; Disease.*

SICKLE (*reaping hook*). A tool used for cutting grain, sometimes also for pruning (Dt 16:9; Joel 3:13; Mk 4:29). Used figuratively for God's judgment (Joel 3:13; Rev 14:14).

SICKNESS Figurative of sin and judgment (Isa 1:5-6; Hos 5:13). *See Affliction; Disease; Sick, The.*

SIDDIM, VALLEY OF (possibly *valley of furrows, valley of demons* BDB; *valley of bordering furrows* KB). Vale of, a valley of uncertain location. Scene of the king of Sodom (Ge 14:3, 8, 10).

SIDON (*fishery*).
1. The son of Canaan (Ge 10:15; 1Ch 1:13).
2. A city on the northern boundary of the Canaanites, twenty-two miles N of Tyre (Ge 10:19). Designated by Jacob as the border of Zebulun (Ge 49:13). Was on the northern boundary of Asher (Jos 19:28; 2Sa 24:6). Belonged to the land of Israel according to the promise (Jos 13:6). Inhabitants of lived in security (Jdg 18:7). Israelites failed to make the conquest of (Jdg 1:31; 3:3). The inhabitants of, contributed cedar for the first and second temple (1Ki 5:6; 1Ch 22:4; Ezr 3:7). Solomon marries a woman of (1Ki 11:1). Chief gods were Baal and Ashtoreth (1Ki 11:5, 33; 2Ki 23:13). Jezebel, wife of King Ahab, was a daughter of a king of Sidon (1Ki 16:31). People of, come to hear Jesus (Mk 3:8; Lk 6:17). Inhabitants of, offend Herod (Ac 12:20-23).
Commerce of (Isa 23:2, 4, 12). Seamen of (Eze 27:8). Prophecies concerning (Jer 25:15-22; 27:3-11; 47:4; Eze 28:21-23; 32:30; Joel 3:4-8). Jesus visits the region of, and heals the daughter of the Syrian Phoenician woman (Mt 15:21-28; Mk 7:24-31). Visited by Paul (Ac 27:3).

S

SIEGE An offer of peace must be made to the city before beginning (Dt 20:10-12). Conducted by erecting embankments parallel to the walls of the besieged city (Dt 20:19-20; Isa 29:3; 37:33). Battering rams used in. *See Battering Ram.* Distress of the inhabitants during (2Ki 6:24-29; 25:3; Isa 9:20; 36:12; Jer 19:9). Cannibalism in (2Ki 6:28-29).

Instances of:
Of Jericho (Jos 6). Rabbah (2Sa 11:1), Abel (2Sa 20:15), Gibbethon (1Ki 15:27), Tirzah (1Ki 16:17). Jerusalem, by the children of Judah (Jdg 1:8), by David (2Sa 5:6, 9), by Rezin, king of Syria, and Pekah, son of Remaliah, king of Israel (2Ki 16:5), by Nebuchadnezzar (2Ki 24:10-11; Da 1:1; 2Ki 25:1-3; Jer 52), by Sennacherib (2Ch 32:1-23). Samaria (1Ki 20:1; 2Ki 6:24; 17:5; 18:9-11).

SIEVE A sifting device for grain; made of reeds, horsehair, or strings (Isa 30:28; Am 9:9). Also used figuratively (Lk 22:31).

SIGN A miracle to confirm faith (Mt 12:38; 16:4; 24:30; Mk 8:11-12; 13:4; Jn 2:11; 3:2; 4:48). Asked for by, and given to Abraham (Ge 15:8-17), Moses (Ex 4:1-9), Gideon (Jdg 6:17, 36-40), Hezekiah (2Ki 20:8), Zechariah (Lk 1:18). Given to Jeroboam (1Ki 13:3-5).
A token of coming events (Mt 16:3-4; 24:3).
See Miracles.

SIGNAL Used in war (Isa 18:3).
See Armies; Ensign; Trumpet.

SIGNET *See Seal.*

SIHON King of the Amorites. His seat of government at Heshbon (Nu 21:26). The proverbial chant celebrating the victory of Sihon over the Moabites (Nu 21:26-30). Conquest of his kingdom by the Israelites (Nu 21:21-25; Dt 2:24-37; 3:2, 6, 8).

SIHOR *See Shihor.*

SILAS (*asked*, possibly *dedicated to God*). Also called Silvanus (1Th 1:1, ftn). Sent to Paul, in Antioch, from Jerusalem (Ac 15:22-34). Becomes Paul's companion (Ac 15:40-41; 2Co 1:19; 1Th 1:1; 2Th 1:1). Imprisoned with Paul in Philippi (Ac 16:19-40). Driven, with Paul, from Thessalonica (Ac 17:4-10). Left by Paul at Berea (Ac 17:14). Rejoins Paul at Corinth (Ac 17:15; 18:5). Carries Peter's epistle to Asia Minor (1Pe 5:12).

SILENT YEARS, FOUR HUNDRED *See Testaments, Time Between.*

SILK Wearing apparel made of (Pr 31:22; Eze 16:10, 13). Merchandise of (Rev 18:22). *See Linen.*

SILLA (*embankment*). A place of uncertain location (2Ki 12:20).

SILOAH *See Siloam.*

SILOAM, POOL OF (*sent*). A reservoir located within the city walls of Jerusalem at the S end of the Tyropean Valley; receives water through a 1, 780-foot tunnel from En Rogel (Ne 3:15; Lk 13:4; Jn 9:7, 11), constructed by Hezekiah in the late eighth century B.C. "Shiloah" (Isa 8:6). The pool today is called Birket Silwan and a nearby village is Silwan. *See Siloam, Village of.*

SILOAM, TOWER OF Probably part of the fortification system of the Jerusalem wall, near the pool of Siloam (Lk 13:4).

SILOAM, VILLAGE OF Not mentioned in the Bible; the modern village (Silwan) situated across the valley E of the Gihon Spring.

SILVANUS *See Silas.*

SILVER (*pale, white*). From Tarshish (Eze 27:12). Refining of (Pr 17:3; 25:4; 26:23; Eze 22:18-22; Jer 6:29-30; Zec 13:9; Mal 3:3). *See Refining.*
Used for money (Ge 13:2; 17:12; 20:16; 23:13-16; Am 8:6; Mt 10:9; 26:15; Mk 14:11; Ac 19:19). *See Money.* For ornamentation of, and in the manufacture of, the utensils for the tabernacle (Ex 26:19; 27:17; 35:24; 36:24; 38:25; Nu 7:13, 19, 25, 31, 37, 43, 49, 55, 61, 67, 73, 79, 85), of the temple (1Ch 28:14; 29:2-5; Ezr 5:14; 6:5; 8:26; Da 5:2). Cups made of (Ge 44:2), trumpets (Nu 10:2), cords (Ecc 12:6), chains (Isa 40:19), shrines (Ac 19:24), idols (Ex 20:23; Isa 30:22; Hos 13:2), baskets, or filigree (Pr 25:11), jewels (SS 1:11). *See Jewel, Jewelry.* Towers, figurative (SS 8:9). Vessels of (Nu 7:85; 1Ki 10:25; 2Sa 8:10; 2Ki 12:13; 1Ch 18:10; 2Ch 24:14; Ezr 1:6; 5:14; 6:5; 8:26; Da 5:2; 11:8).
Abundance of (1Ki 10:27; 1Ch 22:14; 29:2-7; 2Ch 1:15; Ecc 2:8; Isa 2:7). Dross from (Pr 25:4; 26:23). Rejected (Jer 6:30). Workers in (2Ch 2:14; Ac 19:24). *See Smith.*
Symbolic (Da 2:32, 35).

SILVERSMITH (Ac 19:24). *See Smith.*

SIMEON (*he has heard* or *obedient one*).
1. The son of Jacob (Ge 29:33; 35:23; Ex 1:1-2; 1Ch 2:1). With Levi avenges upon the Shechemites the seduction of Dinah (Ge 34; 49:5-7). Goes down to Egypt to buy grain; is bound by Joseph and detained (Ge 42:24, 36; 43:23). His sons (Ge 46:10; Ex 6:15; 1Ch 4:24-37). Descendants of (Nu 26:12-14).
See below, Tribe of.
2. Tribe of: Military enrollment of, at Sinai (Nu 1:22-23; 2:13), in the plains of Moab (Nu 26:14). Place of, in camp and march (Nu 2:12; 10:18-19). Inheritance allotted to (Jos 19:1-9; Jdg 1:3-17; 1Ch 4:24-43). Stood on Mount Gerizim to bless at the time of the rehearsal of the law (Dt 27:12). Joined with the people of Judah and Benjamin in the renewal of the Passover (2Ch 15:9, w 15:1-15). Idolatry of (2Ch 34:6, w 34:1-7).
See Israel.
3. A devout man in Jerusalem. Blesses Jesus in the temple (Lk 2:25-35).
4. An ancestor of Jesus (Lk 3:30).
5. A disciple. Also called Niger (Ac 13:1).
6. Hebrew name of Peter (Ac 15:14, ftn). *See Peter, Simon.*

SIMEONITE(S) (*of Simeon*). A member of the tribe of Simeon.

SIMILITUDE (*likeness*). Pattern, resemblance, similarity (Nu 12:8; 2Ch 4:3; Ps 106:20; Heb 7:15).

SIMON (*he has heard* or *obedient one*).
1. *See Peter, Simon.*
2. One of the twelve apostles. Called the Zealot (Mt 10:4; Mk 3:18; Lk 6:15; Ac 1:13). *See Zealot.*
3. A brother of Jesus (Mt 13:55; Mk 6:3).
4. A leper. Jesus dines with (Mt 26:6; Mk 14:3).
5. A man of Cyrene. Compelled to carry Jesus' cross (Mt 27:32; Mk 15:21; Lk 23:26).
6. A Pharisee. Jesus dines with (Lk 7:36-44).
7. The father of Judas Iscariot (Jn 6:71; 12:4; 13:2, 26).
8. A sorcerer. Converted by Philip; rebuked by Peter (Ac 8:9-13, 18-24).
9. A tanner. Peter lodges with (Ac 9:43; 10:6, 17, 32).

SIMON MACCABEUS Hasmonean ruler in Israel (143-134 B.C.).

SIMONY Ecclesiastical corruption, named after Simon the sorceror (Ac 8:9-19).

SIMPLE Naive; easily led into wrong-doing (Ps 19:7; 119:130; Pr 7:7).

SIMRI *See Shimri, 3.*

SIN

Adamic:
Original, of Adam (Ge 3:6; Hos 6:7; Ro 5:12, 15-19).

Sin Nature:
The inherited tendencies to evil (Mt 7:17-18; 12:33-35; Mk 7:20-23; Lk 6:45; Ro 6:6; 7:17, 20, 23, 25; 8:3, 5-7; Gal 5:16-17; Eph 2:3; Jas 1:14; 4:17).

Defined:
Transgressing the law (Hos 6:8; Mt 5:28; 1Co 8:12; Heb 12:15; Jas 2:10-11; 4:17; 1Jn 3:4; 5:17). Turning away from God (Dt 29:18; Ps 95:10). Not seeking God (2Ch 12:14). Foolish thoughts (Pr 24:8-9). Self-deception (Isa 42:20). That which is not of faith (Ro 14:23).
See Atonement; Conviction, of Sin; Depravity; Regeneration; Repentance; Reprobacy; Salvation; Sanctification; Wicked, Punishment of.
Against the body (Ecc 5:6). Against conscience (Ro 14:23). Against knowledge (Pr 26:11; Lk 12:47-48; Jn 9:41; 15:22; Ro 1:21, 32; 2:17-23; Heb 10:26; Jas 4:17; 2Pe 2:21-22). *See Ignorance, Sins of.* Attempts to cover, vain (Ge 3:10; Job 31:33; Isa 29:15; 59:6).
Christ's description of (Mt 5:2-20; Jn 8:34, 44).
Deceitful (Heb 3:13). Defiles (Ps 51:2, 7; Isa 1:18; Heb 12:15; 1Jn 1:7). *See Defilement.* Degrees in (Lk 7:41-47; 12:47-48). Dominion of (Ro 3:9). Enslaves (Jn 8:34; Ro 6:16; 2Pe 2:19).
From the heart (Isa 44:20; Jer 7:24; 17:9; Eze 20:16; Mt 5:28; 7:17-18; 12:33-35; 15:8, 11, 16-19; Lk 6:45). Of the tongue (Ecc 5:6). In thought (Pr 24:9). Fools mock at (Pr 14:9). Little sins (SS 2:15). Magnitude of (Job 22:5; Ps 25:11).
None in heaven (Rev 22:3-4).
Parable of (Mt 13:24-25, 33, 39). Paul's discussion of the responsibility for (Ro 2-9). Pleasures of (Jn 20:12-16; 21:12-13; Lk 8:14; Heb 11:25). *See Pleasure, Worldly.*
Reproach to God (2Sa 12:14).
Secret sins (Ps 19:12; 44:22; 64:2; 90:8; Ecc 12:14; Eze 8:12; 11:5; Mt 10:26; Lk 8:17; 12:2-3; Jn 3:20; Ro 2:16; Eph 5:12). Sinfulness of (Job 22:5; Ps 25:11; Isa 1:18; Ro 7:13).
To be hated (Dt 7:26; Ps 119:113).

Confession of:
(1Ki 8:47; Pr 28:13). Signified by placing hands on the head of the offering (Lev 3:2, 13; 4:4, 15, 24, 29, 33; 16:21; Nu 8:12). Illustrated in parables, of the prodigal son (Lk 15:17-21). Of the Pharisee and the tax collector (Lk 18:13).
To God, commanded (Lev 5:5-10; 16:21). Exemplified by Israel (Nu 14:40; Jdg 10:10; 1Sa 7:6), by Saul (1Sa 15:2, 4), by David (2Sa 12:13; 24:10, 17; 1Ch 21:17), by the psalmist (Ps 32:5; 38:3-4, 18; 40:11-12; 41:4; 51:2-5; 69:5; 73:21-22; 119:59-60, 176), by the Jews (2Ch 29:6; Ezr 9:4-7, 10-15; Ne 9:2-38; Ps 106:6; Isa 26:13; 59:12-15; 64:5-7; Jer 3:21-22, 25; 8:14-15; 14:7, 20; 31:18-19; La 3:40-42; Da 9:5-6, 8-11, 15), by Job (Job 7:20; 9:20; 13:23; 40:4; 42:5-6), by Isaiah (Isa 6:5), by Jeremiah (La 1:18-20), by Paul (1Co 15:9).
To believers, commanded (Jas 5:16; 1Jn 1:8-10).

Consequences of:
Look on the face (Isa 3:9). Guilty fear (Ge 3:7-10; Pr 10:24; 25:1). Depraved conscience (Pr 30:20). Judgment (Jer 5:25). Trouble (Isa 57:20-21; Jer 4:18).
Effects upon children (Ex 20:5; 34:7; Lev 26:39-40; Nu 14:33; Dt 5:9; Ps 21:10; 37:28; 109:9-10; Pr 14:11; Isa 14:20-22; 65:7; Jer 32:18; La 5:7; Ro 5:12-21). Attributed to Job's children because of Job's alleged wickedness (Job 5:4; 18:19; 21:19). Punishment for, not brought upon children (Dt 24:16; 2Ki 14:6; 2Ch 25:4; Jer 31:29-30; Eze 18:2-4, 20).
No escape from (Ge 3:8-19; Isa 28:18-22; Am 9:2-4; Mt 23:33; Heb 2:3). *See Punishment, No Escape From; Wicked.*

Conviction of:
Produced by dreams (Job 33:14-17), by visions (Ac 9:3-9), by afflictions (Job 33:18-20; La 1:20; Lk 15:17-21), by adversity (Ps 107:4-6, 10-14, 17-20, 23-30), by the gospel (Ac 2:37), by religious testimony (1Co 14:24-25), by the conscience (Jn 8:9; Ro 2:15), by the Holy Spirit (Jn 16:7-11). *See Conviction, of Sin; Repentance, Instances of.*

Forgiveness of:
(Ac 26:18; Eph 1:7). Promised (Ex 34:6-7; Lev 4:20, 26, 31, 35; 5:4-13; Nu 14:18; 15:25; Dt 4; Ps 130:4; Isa 1:6-18; 43:25-26; 44:21-22; 55:6-7; Jer 31:34; 33:8; Eze 18:21-22; 33:14-16; Mt 12:31; Mk 3:28; Heb 8:12; 10:17; Jas 5:15; 1Jn 1:7, 9). Blessedness of (Ps 32:1-2; Ro 4:7-8).

Instances of Forgiveness—
Israelites (Nu 14:20; Ps 85:2-3; 99:8; 103:12). David (2Sa 12:13; Ps 32:5). Isaiah (Isa 6:7). Paralytic (Mt 9:2, 6; Mk 2:5; Lk 5:20, 24). The prostitute (Lk 7:48; Jn 8:11). Believers (Col 2:13).

Conditions of Forgiveness—
Repentance (Mt 3:6; Lk 3:3; 13:3, 5; Ac 2:38; 3:19). Faith (Ac 10:36, 43; 13:38-39; 26:16-18). Confession of sins (1Jn 1:7, 9). Parable of (Mt 18:23-27).
Through the shedding of blood (Heb 9:22). The mission of Christ to secure (Mt 1:21; 26:28; Lk 24:47; 1Jn 2:1-2, 12; Rev 1:5).
Prayer for (Ps 19:12; 25:7, 11; 51:9; 79:9). Spirit of (Mt 6:12, 14-15; 18:35; Mk 11:25). Intercessory prayer for (1Ki 8:22-50). Apostolic (Jn 20:23).
See Atonement; Conviction, of Sin; Offerings; Repentance.

Fruits of:
(Dt 29:18; Mk 7:21-23; 1Co 3:3; 6:9-11; Gal 5:19-21; 1Pe 4:3; Jas 5:11). Fruits of original sin (Ge 3:7-24; 4:9-13; Ro 5:12-21). God's anger (Jer 7:19). Moral insensibility (Pr 30:20). No peace (Isa 57:20-21). Shame (Pr 3:35). Withholding of God's goodness (Jer 7:19).

Destruction and death (Ge 6:5-7; 1Ki 13:33-34; Job 5:2; Ps 5:10; 94.23, Pr 5:22-23; 10:24, 29-31; 11:18-19, 27, 29; Isa 3:9, 11; 9:18; 14:21; Jer 14:16; 21:14; Eze 11:21; 22:31; 23:31-35; Hos 12:14; 13:9; Ro 6:23).

The same as sown (Job 4:8; 13:26; 20:11; Ps 9:15-16; 10:2; 141:10; Pr 1:31; 11:5-7; 12:13, 14-21, 26; 22:8; Isa 50:11; Jer 4:18; 21:14; Eze 11:21; Hos 8:7; 10:13; Mic 7:13; Ro 7:5; Gal 6:7-8).

Proverbs concerning (Pr 1:31; 3:35; 5:22-23; 8:36; 10:24, 29-31; 11:5-7, 18-19, 27, 29; 12:13-14, 21, 26; 13:5-6, 15; 22:8; 28:1; 29:6; 30:20).

Known:

To God (Ge 3:11; 4:10; 18:13; Ex 16:8-9, 12; Nu 12:2; 14:26-27; Dt 1:34; 31:21; 32:34; Jos 7:10-15; 10:14; 11:11; 13:27; 14:16-17; 20:27; 24:23; 34:21-22, 25; Ps 44:20-21; 69:5; 90:8; 94:11; Ecc 5:8; Isa 29:15; Jer 2:22; 16:17; 29:23; Eze 21:24; Hos 5:3; 7:2; Am 5:12; 9:1-4, 8; Hab 2:11; Mal 2:14; Mt 10:26).

To Jesus (Mt 26:46; Lk 6:8; Jn 4:17-19; 5:42; 6:64; 13:11; Rev 2:23).

To the Holy Spirit (Ac 5:3-11).

See God, Omniscient; Jesus the Christ, Omniscience of.

Love of:

(Job 15:16; 20:12-13; Pr 2:14; 4:16-17; 10:23; 16:30; 26:11; Jer 14:10; Eze 20:16; Hos 4:8; 9:10; Mic 7:3; Jn 3:19-20; 12:43; 1Pe 3:19-20; 2Pe 2:22).

See Reprobacy; Wicked, Described As.

Moved to:

By the devil (Mt 13:24-25, 38-39; Jn 8:34, 44; Eph 2:1-2; 1Jn 3:6, 8-10, 15). By the fallen nature (Gal 5:16-17; Eph 2:3; Jas 1:14-15; 4:1-3).

National, Punishment of:

(Ge 6:5-7; 7:21-22; Lev 26:14-38; Dt 9:5; Job 34:29-30; Isa 19:4; Jer 12:17; 25:31-38; 46:28; Eze 16:49-50; Jnh 1:2).

See Government; Nation.

Instances of—

The Sodomites (Ge 18:20). Egyptians (Ex 7-14). *See Egypt.* Israelites (Lev 26:14-39; Dt 32:30; 2Sa 21:1; 24:1; 2Ki 24:3-4, 20; 2Ch 36:21; Ezr 9; Ne 9:36-37; Isa 1:21-23; 3:4, 8; 5; 59:1-15; Jer 2; 5; 6; 9; 23; 30:11-15; La 1:3, 8, 14; 4:6; Eze 2; 7; 22; 24:6-14; 28:18; 33:25-26; 36:16-20; 39:23-24; 44:4-14; Hos 4:1-11; 6:8-10; 7:1-7; 13; Am 2; 5; Mic 6; 7:2-6). Babylon (Jer 50:45-46; 51). *See Babylon; See also prophecies cited under Assyria; Damascus; Edom; Elam; Ethiopia; Philistines; Syria.*

Not imputed:

To righteous (Ps 32:2; Ro 4:6-8), to ignorant (Ro 4:15; 5:13), to redeemed (2Co 5:19).

Progressive:

(Dt 29:19; 1Ki 16:31; Ps 1:1; Isa 5:18; 30:1; Jer 9:3; 16:11-12; Hos 13:2; 2Ti 3:13; Jas 1:14-15). Progressiveness exemplified in Joseph's brothers, from jealousy (Ge 37:4), to conspiracy (Ge 37:18), to murder (Ge 37:20). *See also, Cain; Abel.* Retroactive (Ps 7:15-16; 9:15-16; 10:2; 94:23; Pr 1:31; 5:22-23; 8:36; 11:5-6, 27, 29; Isa 3:9, 11; Jer 2:19; 4:8; 7:19). A root of bitterness (Dt 29:18; Heb 12:15).

Punishment of:

(Ge 2:17; 3:16-19; 4:10-14; 6:5-7; 18:20; 19:13; Ex 32:33-34; 34:7; Lev 19:8; 26:14-21; Nu 15:30-31; 32:23; Dt 28:15-68; 1Ki 13:33-34; 1Ch 21:7-27; Job 21:17; Ps 95:10-11; Pr 1:24-32; Jer 44:2-6; Eze 18:4; Mt 25:41, 46; Ro 6:23).

See Punishment; Wicked, Punishment of.

Pollution of:

Typified, by the defilement caused by touching any unclean thing (Lev 5:2-3; 11:24-28, 31; 22:5), by eating any unclean thing (Lev 11:41-47), by touching a dead body (Lev 21:1; Nu 5:2; 9:6, 10; 19:11, 13, 16; 31:19), by skin diseases (Lev 13:3, 8, 11, 20, 25, 27, 30, 36, 44-46, 51, 55; 14:44; Nu 5:2-3), by sexual impurities (Lev 15:1-33; 22:4; Dt 23:10-11).

Repentance for:

Commanded (2Ch 30:7-9; Job 36:10; Ps 34:14; Pr 1:22-23; Isa 22:12; 31:6; 44:22; 55:6-7; Jer 3:4, 12-14, 19; 6:8, 16; 18:11; 25:5; 26:13; 35:15; Eze 14:6; 18:30-32; 33:10-12; Da 4:27; Hos 6:1; 10:12; 14:1-2; Joel 1:14; 2:12-13, 15-18; Am 4:12; Jnh 3:8-9; Zec 1:3; Mt 4:17; Mk 1:15; 6:12; Ac 2:38, 40; 3:19; 8:22; 17:30; 20:21; Jas 4:8-10; Rev 2:5, 16; 3:2-3, 19).

Gift, of God (2Ti 2:25), of Christ (Ac 5:31). Tribulation leads to (Dt 4:30; 1Ki 8:33-50; 2Ch 6:36-39; Ps 107:4-6, 10-14, 17-20, 23-30). Goodness of God leads to (Ro 2:4).

A condition of pardon (Lev 26:40-42; Dt 4:29-31; 30:1-3; 2Ch 7:14; Ne 1:9; Pr 28:13; Jer 7:5-7; 36:3; Eze 18:21-23, 27-28, 30-31; Mal 3:7; 1Jn 1:9).

Repugnant:

To God (Ge 6:6-7; Lev 18:24-30; Nu 22:32; Dt 25:16; 32:19; 2Sa 11:27; 1Ki 14:22; Ps 5:4-6; 10:3; 11:5; 78:59; 95:10; 106:40; Pr 3:32; 6:16-19; 11:20; 15:8-9, 26; 21:27; Isa 43:24; Jer 25:7; 44:4, 21-22; Hab 1:13; Zec 8:17; Lk 16:15). *See God, Holiness of.*

To Christ (Rev 2:6, 15).

To the righteous (Ge 39:7-9; Dt 7:26; Job 1:1; 21:16; 22:18; Ps 26:5, 9; 84:10; 101:3-4, 7; 119:104, 113, 128, 163; 120:2, 5-7; 139:19-22; Pr 8:13; 29:27; Jer 9:2; Ro 7:15, 19, 23-24; 2Pe 2:7-8; Jude 23; Rev 2:2). *See Holiness.*

Separates From God:

(Dt 31:17-18; Jos 7:12; 2Ch 24:20; Ps 78:59-61; Isa 59:1-2; 64:7; Eze 23:18; Hos 9:12; Am 3:2-3; Mic 3:4; Mt 7:23; 25:41; Lk 13:27; Ro 8:7; Heb 12:14). *See God, Holiness of; Wicked, Punishment of.*

Works spiritual death (Ro 5:12, 21; 6:21, 23; 7:13; Eph 2:1; Jas 1:15).

By the righteous, dishonors God (2Sa 12:14), a reproach (2Sa 12:14).

Against the Holy Spirit, unpardonable (Mt 12:31; Mk 3:29; Lk 12:10; 1Jn 5:16-17).

Typified:

The design of the Mosaic ordinances was to impress the Israelites, and through them the consciences of all people for all time, with the offensiveness of sin. To produce this effect the Mosaic law contained numerous types of sin, the design of which was to teach that sin is repugnant to God, and that it separates from God and from the righteous. Hence, we find many object lessons about uncleanness and defilement, blemishes, separation from the congregation, atonements from the congregation, atonements and atoning sacrifices, washings and purifications; all of which were designed to typify the corruption of sin and the necessity, in order to please a holy Yahweh, that sin must be purged and the heart purified.

By blemishes that disqualified animals for sacrifices (Ex 12:5; Lev 1:10; 3:1, 6; 4:3, 23; 5:15; 6:6; 9:2-3; 22:19-22; Nu 28:3, 9, 11, 19, 31; 29:2, 8, 13, 17, 20, 23, 26, 29, 32, 36). By blemishes of priests, disqualifying them from performing sacred offices (Lev 21:17-23). By unclean animals (Lev 11:1-47; 20:25; Dt 14:3-20).

Its effect, in separating the wicked from God and from the righteous, by excluding the defiled and unclean from the congregation (Lev 7:20, 25, 27; 13:5, 26, 33; 15:19; 17:9-10, 15; 18:29; 19:8; 20:3-6; Nu 5:2-3; 19:20; Dt 23:10-11).

Words for:

Missing the mark (Ro 5:12). Overstepping the boundary, or trespassing (Ro 4:15). Blunder, or offense (Ro 5:15). Disobedience, or disregard (Ro 5:19). Unrighteousness (Ro 1:18). Ungodliness (Ro 1:18). Lawlessness (Tit 2:14).

SIN, CITY OF *See Pelusium.*

SIN, DESERT OF (*desert of clay* or possibly *desert of Sin [pagan moon god]*). The wilderness through which the Israelites passed; between Elim and Mount Sinai (Ex 16:1; 17:1; Nu 33:11-12).

SIN MONEY NIV "money from ... sin offerings" (2Ki 12:16). *See Blood Money.*

SINA *See Sinai.*

SINAI, MOUNT OF; DESERT OF (*Sin [pagan moon god]; glare [from white chalk]* ISBE).

1. A mountain in the peninsula E of the Red Sea. Israelites arrive at in their wanderings in the wilderness (Ex 19:2; Dt 1:2). The law delivered to Moses upon (Ex 19:3-25; 20; 24:12-18; 32:15-16; 34:2-4; Lev 7:38; 25:1; 26:46; 27:34; Nu 3:1; Dt 4:15; 5:26; 29:1; 33:2; Ne 9:13; Ps 68:8, 17; Mal 4:4; Ac 7:30, 38).

God establishes a covenant (Ex 19-24). *See Covenants, Major in the Old Testament.*

Figurative of the law (Gal 4:24-25).

See Horeb; Israel, Israelites.

2. Desert of. Israelites journeyed in (Nu 10:12), kept the Passover in (Nu 9:1-5), numbered in (Nu 26:64).

SINCERITY Does not exempt from guilt (Ge 20). *See Ignorance, Sins of.* Forgiveness of enemies must be sincere (Mt 18:35). Servants must render honest service (Eph 6:5-7). Whatever is done must be in (1Co 10:31). Jesus was an example of (1Pe 2:22). Ministers should be examples of (Tit 2:7). Opposed to human wisdom (2Co 1:12).

Should characterize our love to God (2Co 8:8, 24), our love to Jesus (Eph 6:24), our service to God (Jos 24:14), our faith (1Ti 1:5), our love to one another (Ro 12:9; 1Pe 1:22; 1Jn 3:18), our whole conduct (2Co 1:12), the preaching of the gospel (2Co 2:17; 1Th 2:3-5).

A characteristic of the doctrines of the gospel (1Pe 2:2). The gospel sometimes preached without (Php 1:16). The wicked devoid of (Ps 5:9; 55:21). Exhortations to (1Co 5:8; 1Pe 2:1). Blessedness of (Ps 32:2).

Exemplified:

By men of Zebulun (1Ch 12:33). By Hezekiah (Isa 38:3). By Nathanael (Jn 1:47). By Paul (2Co 1:12). By Timothy (2Ti 1:5). By Lois and Eunice (2Ti 1:5).

SINEW Tendon, in contrast to bone structure (Ge 32:32; Job 40:17; Eze 37:6-8).

SINFULNESS Universal (1Ki 8:46; 2Ch 6:36; Ps 14:3; Ecc 7:20; Ro 3:23; 11:32; 1Jn 1:8, 10). *See Depravity; Sin.*

SINGERS *See Music.*

SINGLE EYE NIV "good eye"; connotes generosity (Mt 6:22). *See Eye.*

SINIM *See Aswan.*

SINITES A tribe of Canaanites (Ge 10:17; 1Ch 1:15).

SINLESSNESS (Ps 119:3). The believer's goal (Php 1:9-11; 1Th 3:13; 5:23; 1Pe 4:1-2; 1Jn 3:6, 9; 5:18). Impossible to attain (1Jn 1:8, 10).

SINNER *See Wicked.*

SIN OFFERING

Offered:

For sins of ignorance (Lev 4:2, 13, 22, 27). At the consecration of priests (Ex 29:10, 14; Lev 8:14). At the consecration of Levites (Nu 8:8). At the expiration of a Nazirite's vow (Nu 6:14). On the Day of Atonement (Lev 16:3, 9). Was a most holy sacrifice (Lev 6:25, 29). Probable origin of (Ge 4:4, 7).

Consisted of:

A young bull for priests (Lev 4:3; 9:2, 8; 16:3, 6). A young bull or he-goat for the congregation (Lev 4:14; 16:9; 2Ch 29:23). A male goat for a ruler (Lev 4:23). A female goat or female lamb for a private person (Lev 4:28, 32). Sins of the offerer transferred to, by laying on of hands (Lev 4:4, 15, 24, 29; 2Ch 29:23). Was killed in the same place as the burnt offering (Lev 4:24; 6:25).

The blood of:

For a priest or for the congregation, brought by the priest into the tabernacle (Lev 4:5, 16). For the priest or for the congregation, sprinkled seven times before the Lord, outside the veil, by the priest with his finger (Lev 4:6, 17). For a priest or for the congregation, put upon the horns of the altar of incense (Lev 4:7, 18). For a ruler or for a private person put upon the horns of the altar of burnt offering by the priest with his finger (Lev 4:25, 30). In every case poured at the foot of the altar of burnt offering (Lev 4:7, 18, 30; 9:9). Fat, kidneys, etc. burned on the altar of burnt offering (Lev 4:8-10, 19, 26, 31; 9:10).

When for a priest or the congregation, the skin, carcass, burned without the camp (Lev 4:11-12, 21; 6:30; 9:11). Was eaten by the priests in a holy place when its blood had not been brought into the tabernacle (Lev 6:26, 29, w 30). Aaron rebuked for burning and not eating that of the congregation, its blood not having been brought into the tabernacle (Lev 10:16-18, w 9:9, 15). Whatever touched the flesh of, was rendered holy (Lev 6:27). Garments sprinkled with the blood of, to be washed (Lev 6:27). Laws respecting the vessels used for boiling the flesh of (Lev 6:28). Was typical of Christ's sacrifice (2Co 5:21; Heb 13:11-13).

SION *See Siyon, Mount; Zion.*

SIPHMOTH A city of Judah (1Sa 30:28).

SIPPAI A Philistine giant (1Ch 20:4). Called Saph (2Sa 21:18).

SIRACH, SON OF The author of Ecclesiasticus also known as the Wisdom of Jesus ben Sirach; wrote c. 190-170 B.C. *See Apocrypha.*

SIRAH A well, c. one mile N of Hebron (2Sa 3:26).

SIRION (*coat of mail*). A Sidonian name of Mount Hermon (Dt 3:9; Ps 29:6). *See Hermon, Mount; Siyon, Mount.*

SISAMAI *See Sismai.*

SISERA

1. Captain of the army of Jabin, king of Hazor; defeated in battle by Barak; slain by Deborah (Jdg 4:5; 1Sa 12:9; Ps 83:9).

2. Ancestor of the temple servants who returned with Zerubbabel (Ezr 2:53; Ne 7:55).

SISMAI (possibly *belonging to Sisam [pagan god]*). The son of Eleasah (1Ch 2:40).

SISTER

1. A full or half-sister (Ge 20:12; Dt 27:22).
2. Wife (SS 4:9).
3. A woman of the same country or tribe (Nu 25:18).
4. Blood relatives (Mt 13:56; Mk 6:3).
5. Female fellow Christian (Ro 16:1; 2Jn 15).

SISTRUMS Percussion instruments (2Sa 6:5). *See Music, Instruments of.*

SITHRI (possibly *Yahweh is my hiding place*). Kohathite Levite; cousin of Aaron and Moses (Ex 6:22).

SITNAH (*hostility*). A well dug by Isaac between Gerar and Rehoboth (Ge 26:21).

SIVAN Month three in sacred sequence (Est 8:9), month nine in civil sequence. Time of the wheat harvest (May-June) and the Feast of Weeks or Pentecost (Dt 16:9-12). *See Month, 3.*

SIYON, MOUNT A name of Mount Hermon (Dt 4:48, ftn w 3:9). *See Hermon, Mount; Sirion.*

SKEPTICISM (Job 21:15; 22:17; Ps 14:1; 53:1; Zep 1:12; Mal 3:14). Of Pharaoh (Ex 5:2). Of Thomas (Jn 20:25-28). *See Unbelief.*

SKILL Examples of (Ex 28:3; 31:3; 35:35; 38:23; 1Ki 7:14; 1Ch 22:15; 2Ch 2:13; 26:15).

SKIN Clothes of (Ge 3:21). For covering the tabernacle (Ex 25:5; Nu 4:8-14). Diseases of (Lev 13:38-39; Dt 28:27, 35; Job 7:5). *See Boil; Leprosy.*

SKINK Unclean for food (Lev 11:30). *See Animals.*

SKIRT *See Dress.*

SKULL *See Golgotha.*

SKY Clouds, firmament; also used figuratively (Dt 33:26).

SLANDER

Characteristics of:

Comes from the evil heart (Lk 6:45). Often arises from hatred (Ps 109:3). Idleness leads to (1Ti 5:13).

The wicked addicted to (Ps 50:20). Hypocrites addicted to (Pr 11:9). A characteristic of the devil (Rev 12:10). The wicked love (Ps 52:4). They who indulge in, are fools (Pr 10:18).

Women warned against (Tit 2:3). Ministers' wives should avoid (1Ti 3:11).

Christ was exposed to (Ps 35:11; Mt 26:60). Rulers exposed to (Jude 8). Ministers exposed to (Ro 3:8; 2Co 6:8). The nearest relations exposed to (Ps 50:20). Saints exposed to (Ps 38:12; 109:2; 1Pe 4:4).

Saints should, keep their tongues from (Ps 34:13, w 1Pe 3:10), lay aside (Eph 4:31), be warned against (Tit 3:1-2), give no occasion for (1Pe 2:12; 3:16), return good for (1Co 4:13), blessed in enduring (Mt 5:11), characterized as avoiding (Ps 15:1, 3).

Should not be listened to (1Sa 24:9). Causes anger (Pr 25:23). A fruit of wickedness (Ro 1:29-30; 2Co 12:20; 2Pe 2:10).

Forbidden (Ex 23:1; 1Ti 3:11; Tit 2:3; 3:2; Jas 4:11; 1Pe 2:1). Punishment for (Dt 19:16-21; 22:13-19; Ps 101:5; 1Co 6:10).

Instances of:

Joseph, by Potiphar's wife (Ge 39:14-18). Land of Canaan misrepresented by the spies (Nu 14:36). Of Mephibosheth, by Ziba (2Sa 16:3; 19:24-30). Of David, by his enemies (Ps 31:13; 35:21; 41:5-9; 64:3; 140:3). Of Naboth, by Jezebel (1Ki 21:9-14). Of

S

Jeremiah, by the Jews (Jer 6:28; 18:18). Of the Jews, of one another (Jer 9:4).

Of Jesus, by the Jews falsely charging that he was a drunkard (Mt 11:19), that he blasphemed (Mk 14:64; Jn 5:18), that he had a demon (Jn 8:48, 52; 10:20), that he was seditious (Lk 22:65; 23:5), that he was a king (Lk 23:2; Jn 18:37, w 19:1-5). Of Paul. *See Paul.*

Effects of:

Separating friends (Pr 16:28; 17:9), deadly wounds (Pr 18:8; 26:22), strife (Pr 26:20), discord among brothers (Pr 6:19), murder (Ps 31:13; Eze 22:9). End of, is wicked madness (Ecc 10:13). People shall give account for (Mt 12:36).

The Tongue:

(Job 5:21). Is venomous (Ps 140:3; Ecc 10:11), is destructive (Pr 11:9).

See Accusation, False; Backbiting; False Witness; Falsehood; Speaking or Speech, Evil.

SLAVE, SLAVERY Both the OT and the NT included regulations for societal situations such as slavery and divorce (Dt 24:1-4), which were the results of the hardness of hearts (Mt 19:8). Such regulations did not encourage or condone such situations but were divinely given, practical ways of dealing with the realities of the day.

See Servant.

SLAYER, THE NIV "one accused of murder" (Nu 35:11-28; Dt 4:42; 19:3-6; Jos 20:3). *See Cities of Refuge.*

SLEEP From God (Ps 127:2). Of the sluggard (Pr 6:9-10). Of Jesus (Mt 8:24; Mk 4:38; Lk 8:23). A symbol of death (Job 14:12; Mt 9:24; Mk 5:39; Lk 8:52; Jn 11:11-12; 1Th 4:14). *See Death, Physical.*

SLIME Slime pit (Job 9:31; Ps 40:2). *See Caulkers; Pitch; Tar.*

SLING Used for throwing stones (Pr 26:8). David slays Goliath with (1Sa 17:40-50). Dexterous use of (Jdg 20:16; 2Ki 3:25; 2Ch 26:14).

SLIP A cutting from a plant (Isa 17:10).

SLOTHFULNESS Characteristic of the sluggard (Pr 10:4-5, 26; 13:4; 15:19; 18:9; 19:15, 24; 20:4; 21:25; 22:13; 23:21; 24:30-34; 26:13-16; Isa 56:10).

Results in: poverty (Pr 10:4-5; 12:24, 27; 13:4; 15:19; 18:9; 19:15, 24; 20:4; 21:25; 23:21; 24:30-34; 26:13-16; Ecc 10:18), condemnation (Mt 25:26-27).

Condemned: The ant, an example against (Pr 6:6-11). Christians are not to be lazy (Ro 12:11; 2Th 3:10-12; Heb 6:12).

See Idleness; Industry.

SLOW TO ANGER (Ne 9:17; Ps 103:8; 145:8). *See God, Longsuffering; Longsuffering.*

SLUG Melting away (Ps 58:8). *See Animals.*

SLUGGARD *See Idleness; Laziness; Slothfulness.*

SMITH A worker in metals. Tubal-Cain (Ge 4:22). Bezalel (Ex 31:1-11). The Philistines (1Sa 13:19). Jewish, carried captive to Babylon (2Ki 24:14; Jer 24:1). The manufacturers of idols (Isa 41:7; 44:12). Genius of, from God (Ex 31:3-5; 35:30-35; Isa 54:16).

SMITING *See Assault and Battery.*

SMITING AND SCOURGING OF JESUS *See Flog, Flogging.*

SMOKE Rising from destruction (Ge 19:28; Jos 8:20; Rev 19:3).

Figurative of God's presence (Ex 19:18; Isa 6:4; Rev 15:8), of short-lived humanity (Ps 37:20; 68:2; 102:3; Hos 13:3).

SMYRNA An ancient seaport on the W coast of Asia Minor forty miles N of Ephesus; the seat of an important Christian church (Rev 1:11; 2:8-11).

SNAIL NIV "skink" (Lev 11:30), "slug" (Ps 58:8). *See Animals.*

SNAKE *See Serpent.*

SNARE A device for catching birds and animals (Ps 124:7), also used figuratively (Ps 91:3).

SNIFF Smelling the wind (Jer 2:24). Showing contempt for God's sacrifices (Mal 1:13).

SNOUT Long projecting nose of a beast, as of a pig (Pr 11:22).

SNOW Falls in elevated areas of Israel in January and February, but soon melts; Mt. Hermon covered with snow even in summer; used for cooling purposes. Used figuratively for righteousness and purity (Isa 1:18; Ps 51:7; Mt 28:3; Rev 1:14).

SNUFF *See Sniff.*

SNUFFDISHES NIV "trays" for the lamps of the tabernacle and temple. *See Wick Trimmers.*

SNUFFERS *See Wick Trimmers.*

SO A king of Egypt with whom Hoshea, king of Israel, made an alliance, so bringing down the wrath of Assyria upon Israel (2Ki 17:4), possibly Oskoron.

SOAP In a modern sense was unknown in OT times, but launderers made a cleansing material compounded from vegetable alkali (Jer 2:22; Mal 3:2). *See Soda.*

SOBERMINDEDNESS Commanded (Ro 12:3; 1Pe 1:13; 4:7; 5:8), to women (1Ti 3:11; Tit 2:4-5), to men (Tit 2:2, 6), to ministers (1Ti 3:2; Tit 1:8).

SOBRIETY Commanded (1Pe 1:13; 5:8). The gospel designed to teach (Tit 2:12). With watchfulness (1Th 5:6). With prayer (1Pe 4:7). Required in ministers (1Ti 3:2-3; Tit 1:8), wives of ministers (1Ti 3:11), aged men (Tit 2:2), young men (Tit 2:6), young women (Tit 2:4), all saints (1Th 5:6, 8). Women should exhibit in dress (1Ti 2:9). We should estimate our character and talents with (Ro 12:3). We should live in (Tit 2:12). Motive for (1Pe 4:7; 5:8).

See Temperance; Drunkenness; Self-Control.

SOCO (perhaps *thorny place*).

1. Son of Heber (1Ch 4:18).
2. A city in Judah, built by Rehoboam (2Ch 11:7; 28:18).

SOCOH (possibly *thorny place* IDB).

1. A town in Judah (Jos 15:35; 1Sa 17:1; 1Ki 4:10), NW of Adullam; identified with Khirbet Shuweikeh.
2. Another city by this name ten miles SW of Hebron (Jos 15:48).

SODA A mixture of washing and baking sodas found in deposits around alkali lakes of Egypt. Used to make soap (Job 9:30; Pr 25:20; Jer 2:22). *See Soap.*

SODI (*Yahweh confides*). The father of a Zebulun spy (Nu 13:10).

SODOM Situated in the plain of the Jordan (Ge 13:10). The southeastern limit of the Canaanites (Ge 10:19). Lot dwells at (Ge 13:12). The king of, joins other kings of the nations resisting the invasion of Kedorlaomer (Ge 14:1-12). Wickedness of the inhabitants of (Ge 13:13; 19:4-13; Dt 32:32; Isa 3:9; Jer 23:14; La 4:6; Eze 16:46, 48-49; Jude 7). Abraham's intercession for (Ge 18:16-33). Destroyed on account of the wickedness of the people (Ge 19:1-29; Dt 29:23; Isa 13:19; Jer 49:18; 50:40; La 4:6; Am 4:11; Zep 2:9; Mt 10:15; Lk 17:29; Ro 9:29; 2Pe 2:6).

Figurative of wickedness (Dt 23:17; 32:32; Isa 1:10; Eze 16:46-56).

SODOMITES (*of Sodom*). Inhabitants of Sodom. Wickedness of (Ge 19:4-14). Destroyed by fire as a judgment (Ge 19:24-25). To be judged according to opportunity (Mt 11:24; Lk 10:12). *See Homosexual.*

SODOMY *See Homosexual.*

SOJOURNERS Temporary residents (Ge 12:10; 20:1; 21:34; 47:4; Lev 18:26; 20:2; 25:40; Nu 15:15; Dt 26:5; Jdg 17:7; Ru 1:1; Heb 11:9).

SOLDER *See Welding.*

SOLDIERS Military enrollment of Israel in the wilderness of Sinai (Nu 1; 2), in the plains of Moab (Nu 26). Levies of, in the ration of one man to ten subject to duty (Jdg 20:10). Dressed in scarlet (Na 2:3). Cowards, excused from duty as (Dt 20:8; Jdg 7:3). Others exempt from service (Dt 20:5-9; 24:5). Come to John (Lk 3:14). Mock Jesus (Mt 27:27-31; Mk 15:16-20; Lk 23:11, 36-37). Officers concerned in the betrayal of Jesus (Lk 22:4). Crucified Jesus (Mt 27:27, 31-37; Mk 15:16-24; Jn 19:23-24). Guard the tomb (Mt 27:65; 28:11-15). Guard prisoners (Ac 12:4-6; 28:16). Maintain the peace (Ac 21:31-35). Their duty as sentinels (Ac 12:19). Perform escort duty (Ac 21:31-33, 35; 22:24-28; 23:23, 31-33; 27:1, 31, 42-43; 28:16).

Figurative: Of the divine protection (Isa 59:16-17). Of the Christian (Eph 6:11-17; 2Ti 2:3). *See Armies.*

SOLOMON (*peace, well being*). Son of David by Bathsheba (2Sa 12:24; 1Ki 1:13, 17, 21). Named Jedidiah, by Nathan the prophet (2Sa 12:24-25). Ancestor of Joseph (Mt 1:6). Succeeds David to the throne of Israel (1Ki 1:11-48; 2:12; 1Ch 23:1; 28; Ecc 1:12). Anointed king a second time (1Ch 29:22). His prayer for wisdom and his vision (1Ki 3:5-14; 2Ch 1:7-12). Covenant renewed in a vision after the dedication of the temple (1Ki 9:1-9; 2Ch 7:12-22). His rigorous reign (1Ki 2).

Builds the temple (1Ki 5; 6; 9:10; 1Ch 6:10; 2Ch 2; 3; 4; 7:11; Jer 52:20; Ac 7:45-47). Dedicates the temple (1Ki 8; 2Ch 6). Renews the courses of the priests and Levites and the forms of service according to the regulations of David (2Ch 8:12-16; 35:4; Ne 12:45).

Builds his palace (1Ki 3:1; 7:1, 8; 9:10; 2Ch 7:11; 8:1; Ecc 2:4), his house of the forest of Lebanon (1Ki 7:2-7), for Pharaoh's daughter (1Ki 7:8-12; 9:24; 2Ch 8:11; Ecc 2:4). Ivory throne of (1Ki 7:7; 10:18-20). Porches of judgment (1Ki 7:7). Builds Millo, the wall of Jerusalem; the cities of Hazor, Megiddo, Gezer, Beth Horon, Baalath, Tadmor; store cities and cities for chariots and for cavalry (1Ki 9:15-19; 2Ch 9:25). Provides an armory (1Ki 10:16-17). Plants vineyards and orchards of all kinds of fruit trees; makes pools (Ecc 2:4-6), imports apes and baboons (1Ki 10:22). Drinking vessels of his houses (1Ki 10:21; 2Ch 9:20). Musicians and musical instruments of his court (1Ki 10:12; 2Ch 9:11; Ecc 2:8). The splendor of his court (1Ki 10:5-9, 12; 2Ch 9:3-8; Ecc 2:9; Mt 6:29; Lk 12:27).

Commerce of (1Ki 9:28; 10:11-12, 22, 28-29; 2Ch 1:16-17; 8:17-18; 9:13-22, 28). Presents received by (1Ki 10:10; 2Ch 9:9, 23-24). Is visited by the queen of Sheba (1Ki 10:1-13; 2Ch 9:1-12). Wealth of (1Ki 9; 10:10, 14-15, 23, 27; 2Ch 1:15; 9:1, 9, 13, 24, 27; Ecc 1:16). Has seven hundred wives and three hundred concubines (1Ki 11:3, w Dt 17:17); their influence over him (1Ki 11:3). Marries one of Pharaoh's daughters (1Ki 3:1). Builds idolatrous temples (1Ki 11:1-8; 2Ki 23:13). His idolatry (1Ki 3:3-4; 2Ki 23:13; Ne 13:26).

Extent of his dominions (1Ki 4:21, 24; 8:65; 2Ch 7:8; 9:26). Receives tribute (1Ki 4:21; 9:21; 2Ch 8:8). Officers of (1Ki 2:35; 4:1-19; 2Ch 8:9-10). His suppliers (1Ki 4:7-19). Divides his kingdom into subsistence departments; the daily subsistence rate for his court (1Ki 4:7-23, 27-28).

Military equipment of (1Ki 4:26, 28; 10:16-17, 26, 28; 2Ch 1:14; 9:25, w Dt 17:15-16). Cedes certain cities to Hiram (1Ki 9:10-13; 2Ch 8:2). Wisdom and fame of (1Ki 4:29-34; 10:3-4, 8, 23-24; 1Ch 29:24-25; 2Ch 9:2-7, 22-23; Ecc 1:16; Mt 12:42). Piety of (1Ki 3:5-15; 4:29; 8). Beloved of God (2Sa 12:24). Justice of, illustrated in his judgment of the two harlots (1Ki 3:16-28). Oppressions of (1Ki 12:4; 2Ch 10:4).

Reigns forty years (2Ch 9:30). Death of (2Ch 9:29-31).

Prophecies concerning (2Sa 7:12-16; 1Ki 11:9-13; 1Ch 17:11-14; 28:6-7; Ps 132:11).

A type of Christ (Ps 45:2-17; 72).

SOLOMON, SONG OF *See Song of Solomon, Song of Songs.*

SOLOMON'S POOLS Three pools near Jerusalem from which water was brought by means of aqueducts to Jerusalem (Ecc 2:6). They are still in use.

SOLOMON'S PORCH Colonnade built by Solomon on the E side of the temple area (Jn 10:23; Ac 3:11; 5:12).

SOLOMON'S SERVANTS Slaves used by Solomon in his temple for menial tasks; their descendants returning from Babylon under Zerubbabel (Ezr 2:55, 58; Ne 7:57, 60; 11:3).

SOLOMON'S TEMPLE *See Temple.*

SON

1. A direct male offspring (Ge 4:25, 26).
2. A male descendant generations removed (Mt 1:1).
3. The member of a guild or profession (1Ki 20:35).
4. Spiritual son (1Ti 1:18).
5. Address to a younger man (1Sa 3:6).
6. Adopted son (Ex 2:10).
7. Native (La 4:2).
8. Possessor of a quality (Jn 12:36).
9. Used of Jesus in a unique sense. *See One and Only; Son of God; Son of Man.*

SON OF GOD A title of Jesus referring to his equality, eternity, and consubstantiality with the Father and the Spirit in the eternal Triune Godhead (Jn 5:18, 23, 36). Christ claimed to be eternal, equal and of the same substance as the Father. He is uniquely God's son. *See Jesus the Christ, Son of God; One and Only.*

SON OF MAN

1. A human being (Eze 2:1, 3, 8ff; Ps 8:4).
2. Used in a messianic sense (Da 7:13-14). Jesus applies the term to himself many times in the Gospels (Mt 8:20; 9:6; 10:23; 11:19; 12:8, etc). Sometimes he uses it in connection with his earthly mission, but he also uses it when describing his final triumph as Redeemer and Judge (Mt 16:27f; 19:28; 24:30; 25:31). The phrase identifies him with humanity (cf. Heb 2:14-18) and with the heavenly Son of Man (Da 7:13-14). *See Jesus the Christ, Son of Man.*

SONG Sung at the Passover (Mt 26:30; Mk 14:26). Didactic (Dt 32). *See Psalms, Topically Arranged.* Personification of the church (SS 1-8). Of Moses (Ex 15:1-19). Of Deborah and Barak (Jdg 5). Of Hannah (1Sa 2:1-10). Of David (2Sa 22:2-51; 23:1-7). Of Mary (Lk 1:46-55). Of Moses and the Lamb (Rev 15:3-4). New (Ps 33:3; 40:3). Prophetic. *See Psalms, Topically Arranged.* Spiritual, singing of, commanded (Eph 5:19; Col 3:16). Of praise. *See Poetry; Praise; Psalms, Topically Arranged; Thankfulness.* Of redemption (Rev 5:9-10). Of the redeemed (Rev 14:2-5). Of thanksgiving. *See Psalms, Topically Arranged; Thankfulness.* War (Ex 15:1-21; Nu 21:27-30; Jdg 5; 2Sa 1:19-27; 22). Solomon wrote one thousand and five (1Ki 4:32).

See Poetry; Praise; Psalms, Topically Arranged.

SONG OF DEGREES *See Ascents, Songs of; Music.*

SONG OF SOLOMON, SONG OF SONGS

Author: Verse 1 appears to ascribe authorship to Solomon

Date: In the tenth century B.C. during Solomon's reign

Outline:

I. Title (1:1).
II. First Meeting (1:2-2:7).
III. Second Meeting (2:8-3:5).
IV. Third Meeting (3:6-5:1).
V. Fourth Meeting (5:2-6:3).
VI. Fifth Meeting (6:4-8:4).
VII. Literary Climax (8:5-7).
VIII. Conclusion (8:8-14).

SONG OF THE THREE HEBREW CHILDREN An addition to the book of Daniel found in the OT Apocrypha. Anonymous; written before 100 B.C.

SON-IN-LAW Unjust, Jacob (Ge 30:37-42). Faithful, Peter (Mk 1:29-30; Lk 4:38).

SONS OF GOD, CHILDREN OF GOD Any personal creatures of God: angelic beings (Job 1:6; 2:1; 38:7), the entire human race (Ac 17:28), the regenerate as distinguished from the unregenerate (1Jn 3:10). The "sons of God" (Ge 6:1-4).

SONS OF THE PROPHETS NIV usually "company of the prophets." Members of prophetic guilds or schools; gathered around great prophets like Samuel and Elijah for common worship, united prayer, religious fellowship, and instruction of the people (1Sa 10:5, 10; 2Ki 4:38, 40). In the times of Elijah and Elisha they lived together at Bethel, Jericho, and Gilgal (2Ki 2:3, 5; 4:38). *See School.*

SOOTHSAYER, SOOTHSAYING One claiming power to foretell future events (Jos 13:22; Jer 27:9), interpret dreams (Da 4:7), and reveal secrets (Da 2:27).

SOOTHSAYERS' TREE A pagan shrine near Shechem (Jdg 9:37), possibly the great tree of Moreh (Ge 12:6).

SOP NIV "piece of bread" used to dip food from a common platter (Jn 13:26-27).

SOPATER (*saving one's father*). Berean Christian; companion of Paul (Ac 20:4).

SOPHERETH (*scribe*). A servant of Solomon, whose descendants returned from captivity to Jerusalem (Ne 7:57).
See Hassophereth.

SORCERY Divination by an alleged assistance of evil spirits. Forbidden (Lev 19:26-28, 31; 20:6; Dt 18:9-14). Denounced (Isa 8:19; Mal 3:5).
Practiced: By, the Egyptians (Isa 19:3, 11-12), the magicians (Ex 7:11, 22; 8:7, 18), Balaam (Nu 22:6; 23:23, w 22; 23), Jezebel (2Ki 9:22), the Ninevites (Na 3:4-5), the Babylonians (Isa 47:9-13; Eze 21:21-22; Da 2:2, 10, 27), Belshazzar (Da 5:7, 15), Simon the sorceror (Ac 8:9, 11), Elymas (Ac 13:8), the young woman at Philippi (Ac 16:16), vagabond Jews (Ac 19:13), sons of Sceva (Ac 19:14-15), astrologers (Jer 10:2; Mic 3:6-7), false prophets (Jer 14:14; 27:9; 29:8-9; Eze 13:6-9; 22:28; Mt 24:24).
To cease (Eze 12:23-24; 13:23; Mic 5:12).
Messages of, false (Eze 21:29; Zec 10:2; 2Th 2:9). Diviners shall be confounded (Mic 3:7). Belongs to the works of the flesh (Gal 5:20). Wickedness of (1Sa 15:23). Vainness of (Isa 44:25). Punishment for (Ex 22:18; Lev 20:27; Dt 13:5). Divining by familiar spirits (Lev 20:27; 1Ch 10:13; 2Ch 33:6; Isa 8:19; 19:3; 29:4), by entrails (Eze 21:21), by images (2Ki 23:24; Eze 21:21), by rods (Hos 4:12).
Saul consulted the medium of Endor (1Sa 28:7-25).
Books of, destroyed (Ac 19:19).

SORE Laws to determine whether clean or unclean (Lev 13). Festering sores disqualified from priesthood (Lev 21:20) or acceptable offering (Lev 22:22). Figurative of judgment for sin (Jer 30:13). *See Disease.*

SOREK, VALLEY OF (*[blood red grapes]*; hence, *choice vines*). A valley in the Philistine territory c. eight-and-a-half miles S of Joppa (Jdg 16:4).

SORROW God takes notice of Hagar's (Ge 21:17-20), Israelites (Ex 3:7-10).
For sin (2Co 7:10-11). *See Repentance; Sin, Confession of.*
No sorrow in heaven (Rev 21:4). "Sorrow and sighing will flee away" (Isa 35:10).
Of Hannah (1Sa 1:15). Of David for Absalom (2Sa 18:33; 19:1-8). Of Mary and Martha (Jn 11:19-40). Jeremiah (La 1:12). Jesus (Isa 53:11; Mt 26:37-44; Mk 14:34-42; Lk 22:42-44).
From bereavement: Of Jacob for Joseph (Ge 37:34-35), for Benjamin (Ge 43:14).
Of the lost (Mt 8:12; 13:42, 50; 22:13; 24:51; 25:30; Lk 13:28; 16:23). *See Wicked, Punishment of.*
See Affliction, Consolation Under; Suffering.

SOSIPATER (*saving ones father*). Kinsman of Paul (Ro 16:21).

SOSTHENES
1. Chief ruler of the synagogue in Corinth (Ac 18:17).
2. A Christian with whom Paul wrote the first letter to the Corinthians (1Co 1:1).

SOTAI A servant of Solomon whose descendants returned from captivity to Jerusalem (Ezr 2:55; Ne 7:57).

SOUL The immortal, nonmaterial part of a human being (Mt 10:28; Rev 6:9; 20:4). Can represent the whole person (Jdg 5:21) or one's life (Job 33:18; Ps 26:9). Used with heart to represent the will and emotions (Dt 4:29; 6:4). *See Immortality; Mankind, A Spirit; Spirit.*

SOUNDING In navigation (Ac 27:28).

SOUTH
1. A direction of the compass (Ge 13:14).
2. The Negev, an indefinite area lying between Israel and Egypt (Ge 12:9; 13:1; 1Sa 27:8-12; 2Ch 28:18).

SOVEREIGNTY OF GOD The supreme authority of God. He is not subject to any power or law which could be conceived as superior to or other than himself (Isa 45:9; Ro 9:20-21).
See God, Sovereign; Jesus the Christ, King.

SOWER Parable of the (Mt 13:3-8; Mk 4:3-20; Lk 8:5-8). Sowing (Ecc 11:4; Isa 28:25).
Figurative (Ps 126:5; Pr 11:18; Isa 32:20; Hos 8:7; 10:12; Gal 6:7-8).

SPAIN The westernmost peninsula of Europe. Paul hoped to visit this Roman province (Ro 15:24, 28).

SPAN About nine or ten inches (Ex 28:16; 39:9).

SPARROW Nests of (Ps 84:3). Two sold for a penny (Mt 10:29; Lk 12:6).

SPEAKING OR SPEECH

Evil:
(Ps 10:8; 52:2-4; Isa 32:6-7; Jer 20:10; Jude 8, 10). Causes strife (Pr 15:1; 16:27-28; 17:9; 25:23). Excludes from kingdom of heaven (1Co 6:10). Hated by God (Pr 6:16-19; 8:13).
Characteristic of mankind (Ro 1:29-30; 3:13-14). Not characteristic of a Christian (Eph 4:25, 29, 31; 5:4; Tit 3:2; Jas 1:26; 3:5-6, 8-10; 4:11; 1Pe 2:1; 3:9-10).
Forbidden (Ex 22:28; Ps 34:13; Pr 4:24; 6:16-19; Mt 5:22, 37; 12:34-37; Ac 23:5; Eph 4:25, 29, 31; Tit 3:2; Jas 1:26; 3:5-6, 8-10; 4:11; 1Pe 2:1; 3:9-10). Punishment for (Ps 12:3-4; 52:1-4).
Proverbs concerning (Pr 4:24; 6:16-19; 8:13; 10:11, 19, 31-32; 11:11; 12:5-6, 13, 17-19; 13:3; 14:25; 15:1, 4, 28; 16:27-28; 17:4, 9, 20; 18:8, 21, 23; 19:1, 22-23; 24:2; 25:23; 26:20-23, 28; Ecc 10:11, 20).
Prayers for deliverance from curse of (Ps 64:2-5; 70:3; 120:1-7).
Self-accusation: Solomon (Ecc 7:22). Isaiah (Isa 6:5). Paul (Ac 23:5)

Instances of—
Against Job (Job 19:18). Against Lot, those of Sodom (2Pe 2:7-8, 10). Against Moses (Ps 106:33). Against the psalmists (Ps 35:21; 41:5-9; 69:12, 26; 102:8; 119:23). Against the church, those of the circumcision (Tit 1:10-11). False teachers (Jude 8, 10).
See Accusation, False; Blasphemy; Busybody; Falsehood; Flattery; Slander; Talebearer; Uncharitableness.

Foolish:
(Job 13:5; 16:3-4; 38:2). Accountable to God (Mt 12:36-37). Forbidden (Pr 30:18). Not characteristic of a Christian (Eph 5:4).
Proverbs concerning (Pr 10:14; 12:23; 13:3; 14:3; 15:2, 7, 14; 18:6-7, 13; 26:4, 7, 9; 29:11, 20; 30:10; Ecc 5:3, 5; 10:13-14).
See Fool.

Wise:
(Job 16:5; 27:4; Am 5:13; Zep 3:13; Zec 8:16; Rev 14:17). As good as nails (Ecc 12:11). Precious as jewels (Pr 20:16).
Edifying (Eph 4:29). Rewards of (Ps 15:1-3; 50:23; Pr 14:3; 22:11).
Of the noble woman (Pr 31:26).
Admonitions concerning, to believers (Eph 4:22, 25, 29; Php 1:27; Col 4:6; Jas 1:19, 26; 3:2, 13; 1Pe 2:12; 3:15-16). Christ's words concerning (Mt 12:35, 37; Lk 6:45).
Of psalmists (Ps 37:30; 39:1; 77:12; 119:13, 27, 46, 54, 172; 141:3; 145:5-7, 11-12).
Proverbs concerning (Pr 10:11, 13, 19-21, 31-32; 11:12-14; 12:6, 14, 16-20, 23; 13:2-3; 14:3; 15:1-2, 4, 7, 23, 26, 28; 16:21, 23-24; 17:7, 27-28; 18:4, 20; 19:1; 20:15; 21:23; 22:11; 24:6; 25:11, 15; 26:5; 29:11; 31:26; Ecc 3:7; 9:17; 10:12; 12:9-11).
Prayer concerning (Ps 141:3).
See Wisdom.

SPEAR Spears and javelins differed in weight and size but had similar uses.
An implement of war (2Ki 11:10; Ne 4:13). Goliath's (1Sa 17:7). Saul's (1Sa 18:10-11). Stored in the temple (2Ch 23:9). To be changed into pruning hooks (Isa 2:4; Mic 4:3). Pruning hooks to be beaten into (Joel 3:10). Thrust into Jesus' side (Zec 12:10; Jn 19:34; 20:27; Rev 1:7). For catching fish (Job 41:7, 26). *See Armory.*

SPECK Particle of dust or splinter of wood in one's eye, figurative of improper judgment (Mt 7:3-5; Lk 6:41-42). *See Judgment.*

SPECKLED Mottled in color (Ge 30:25-43). *See Streaked.*

SPELT A small grain grown in Egypt (Ex 9:32). Cultivated in Canaan (Isa 28:25). Used in bread (Eze 4:9).

SPERMATORRHEA A disease of the genitals (possibly Lev 15:16).

SPICES In the formula for the sacred oil (Ex 25:6; 35:8). Stores of (2Ki 20:13). Used in the temple (1Ch 9:29). Exported from Gilead (Ge 37:25). Sent as a present by Jacob to Joseph (Ge 43:11). Presented by the queen of Sheba to Solomon (1Ki 10:2, 10). Sold in the markets of Tyre (Eze 27:22). Used in the embalming of Asa (2Ch 16:14). Prepared for embalming the body of Jesus (Mk 16:1; Lk 23:56; 24:1; Jn 19:39-40).

SPIDER Web of, figurative of the hope of the hypocrite (Job 8:14; Isa 59:5).

SPIES (Ge 42:9). Sent to investigate Canaan (Nu 13), Jazer (Nu 21:32), Jericho (Jos 2:1). Used by David (1Sa 26:4), at the court of Absalom (2Sa 15:10; 17:1-17). Pharisees acted as (Lk 20:20). In the church of Galatia (Gal 2:4). *See Reconnaissance.*

SPIKENARD *See Nard; Perfume, 2.*

SPINDLE Implement used in spinning (Ex 35:24; Pr 31:19).

SPINNING By hand (Ex 35:25; Pr 31:19).

SPIRIT (*breath, wind, spirit*). The immortal, nonmaterial part of a human being, similar to the soul (Job 7:11). Represents one's lifeforce or strength (Ge 45:27; Jas 2:26), character (Nu 14:24; Dt 2:30; 1Pe 3:4), desire (2Sa 13:39), heart or emotions (Ps 73:21; 77:6). The self is often called "spirit" when the direct relationship of the individual to God is the point of emphasis (2Ti 4:22; Phm 25). *See Ghost; Immortality; Mankind, A Spirit; Soul.*

SPIRIT, HOLY *See Holy Spirit.*

SPIRITISTS Divination by means of communication with the spirit of the dead (necromancy) was known and practiced in the ancient Near East.

Consulting of:
Forbidden (Lev 19:31; 20:6, 27; Dt 18:10-11), vain (Isa 8:19; 19:3). Those who consulted, to be cut off (Lev 20:6, 27).

Instances of Consulting of:
Saul (1Sa 28:3-25; 1Ch 10:13-14). Manasseh (2Ki 21:6; 2Ch 33:6). A slave girl (Ac 16:16-18).
See Demons; Medium; Necromancer, Necromancy; Sorcery; Witchcraft.

SPIRITS IN PRISON Those who in the days of Noah refused his message (1Pe 3:18-20; 4:6). The exact interpretation of this passage is strongly debated.

SPIRITS *See Demons.*

SPIRITUAL ADOPTION *See Adoption, Spiritual.*

SPIRITUAL BLESSINGS *See Blessings, Spiritual; Holy Spirit; Sanctification.*

SPIRITUAL BLINDNESS Blindness, Spiritual.

SPIRITUAL BOASTING (Ro 11:18-21). Incompatible, with faith (Ro 3:27; Eph 2:8-10), with humility (1Co 1:20, w 1:17-31; 4:6-7; 2Co 10:12-16). In the Lord, approved (Jer 9:24; 2Co 10:17-18; Gal 6:14).
See Boasting, Spiritual.

SPIRITUAL DEATH Alienation from the life of God; a state of condemnation (Ro 7:9, 11; 8:5-6, 13; Eph 4:18). Making alive from (Jn 5:24-26; Ro 5:12, 15; Eph 2:1, 5-6; 5:14; Col 2:13).
See Death, Physical; Second Death.

SPIRITUAL DESIRE *See Desire, Spiritual.*

SPIRITUAL DILIGENCE *See Zeal.*

SPIRITUAL GIFTS Extraordinary gifts of the Spirit given to Christians to equip them for the service of the Church (Ro 11:29; 12:6-8; 1Co 12:4-11, 28-30; Eph 4:7-11; 1Pe 4:10-11).
See Charism, Charisma, Charismata; Holy Spirit; Tongues, Gift of.

SPIRITUAL HUNGER *See Hunger, Figurative.*

SPIRITUAL PEACE (Isa 27:5; 54:1, 10, 13; 55:2, 12; 57:19; Eze 34:25; Lk 2:14, 29; Ro 5:1; 1Co 14:33). Christ's kingdom, a kingdom of (Isa 9:6; 11:6-9, 13; Mic 5:5; Lk 1:79; Ac 10:36).
See Peace, Spiritual.

SPIRITUAL PURIFICATION (Ps 65:3; 73:1; Pr 20:9; Jn 13:8-9). By corrective judgments (Isa 4:3-4). By mercy and truth (Pr 16:6). By the Holy Spirit (1Co 6:11; Tit 3:5-6). By the blood of Christ (Heb 1:3; 9:14; 2Pe 1:9; 1Jn 1:7; Rev 1:5; 7:14).
Of the Church (Eph 5:26).
Commanded (Isa 1:16; Mt 23:26; Ac 22:16; 1Co 5:7; 2Co 7:1; Heb 10:22; Jas 4:8).
Promised (Isa 1:18; Jer 33:8; Eze 36:25; Da 12:10; Zec 13:1; 1Jn 1:9). Prayer for (Ps 51:2, 7; 79:9).
See Purification; Sanctification.

SPIRITUAL UNDERSTANDING (Mt 13:23; Lk 10:21-22; Jn 7:17). Of apostles (Mt 13:16-17; Lk 8:10; 10:23-24). Of Peter (Mt 16:16-17). Of Mary (Lk 10:39, 42).
Lacking, in disciples (Mt 15:15-16; Lk 24:25), in Jews (Mt 13:11-16; Jn 6:26, 41, 52; 9:28-29, 39-41; 12:27-40; Ac 28:24-27).

Commanded:
Concerning, the importance of preaching (Mt 11:13-15), the importance of parables (Mt 13:9, 43; Lk 8:8), the character of the disciples of Jesus (Lk 14:33-35), the Holy Spirit's message to the churches (Rev 2:7).
See Wisdom, Spiritual.

SPIRITUALISM *See Necomancer; Sorcery.*

SPIRITUALITY Described as the great and enduring good (Lk 10:42), as love and devotion to God (Dt 6:5; Jos 22:5; 1Ki 8:23; Ps 1:2; 51:6).
Brings peace (Isa 26:3; Jer 33:6; Ro 8:6; 14:17), indifference to worldly good (1Co 7:29-31; Col 3:1-3), thirst for heavenly blessings (Mt 5:6; Jn 6:27).
Is produced by the indwelling of the Holy Spirit (Jn 14:16-17; Ro 8:4).

SPITTING In the face, as an indignity (Nu 12:14; Dt 25:9; Job 30:10; Mt 26:67; 27:30). Jesus used spittle in healing (Mk 7:33; 8:23).

SPOILS Of war (Ge 14:11-12; Nu 31:9-10; Dt 2:35). Divided between the combatants and noncombatants of the Israelites, including priests and Levites (Nu 31:25-54; 1Sa 30:24). Dedicated to the Lord (1Sa 15:15; 1Ch 26:27; 2Ch 15:11).

SPOKES Rods connecting the rim of a wheel with the hub. Basins for washing of sacrifices were set on bases moving upon wheels. The spokes were part of these wheels (1Ki 7:27-33).

SPONGE (Mt 27:48; Mk 15:36; Jn 19:29).

SPOONS Of the tabernacle (Ex 25:29; Nu 4:7; 7). Of the temple (1Ki 7:50; 2Ch 4:22).

SPOT Blemish, blot (SS 4:7; Job 11:15; Lev 24:19ff; Pr 9:7; Jude 23).

SPOUSE *See Bride; Marriage.*

SPREAD Scatter, disperse (Mt 21:8; Mk 1:28).

SPRING
1. Of water. Hot (Ge 36:24).
Figurative: muddied or salty (Pr 25:26; Jas 3:11).
See Wells.
2. Season of, promised annual return of (Ge 8:22). Described (Pr 27:25; SS 2:11-13).

SPRINKLING Of blood (Lev 14:7, 51; 16:14; Heb 9:13, 19, 21; 11:28; 1Pe 1:2). *See Blood.* Of water (Nu 8:7; Eze 36:25; Heb 9:19; 10:22).

STABILITY Of character (Ps 57:7; 108:1; 112:7).
Commanded (1Co 7:20; 15:58; 2Th 2:15; Heb 10:23; 13:9; Jas 1:23-25; Rev 22:11). Rewarded (Mt 10:22; 24:13; Mk 4:20; 2Th 3:3).
See Character; Decision; Perseverance.

STABLE *See Pasture.*

STACHYS (*head of grain*). A Christian in Rome (Ro 16:9).

STACTE *See Gum Resin.*

STADIA Plural of *stadion,* about 202 yards (Rev 14:20; 21:16).

STAFF Used as weapons (Mt 27:30; Mk 15:19).
Symbolic (Zec 11:7-14).

S

See Rod.

STAIRS Steps leading to an upper chamber (1Ki 6:8; Ac 21:40), or some other elevated place (Ne 9:4; Eze 40:6; 43:17). Jacob's vision of a stairway from earth to heaven (Ge 28:10-22). The sign to Hezekiah on the stairway of Ahaz (1Ki 20:1-12).

STAKE Tent pin or tent pole (Ex 27:19; Isa 33:20).

STALL A place for care of livestock or compartment in a stable for one animal (2Ch 32:28). Solomon's barns provided stalls for 4000 horses (2Ch 9:25).

STAMMERING (Isa 32:4; 33:19). Of Moses (Ex 4:10).

STANDARD An ensign used by each of the tribes of Israel in camp and march (Nu 1:52; 2:2). Banners used as (Ps 20:5; SS 6:4, 10). Used in war (Jer 4:21). Used to signal the route to defended cities (Jer 4:6), to call attention to news (Jer 50:2; 51:12).
See Armies; Banner; Ensign.
Figurative (Isa 49:22; 62:10; Jer 4:6).

STARS Created by God (Ge 1:16; Job 26:13; Ps 8:3; 33:6; 136:7, 9; Am 5:8). Differ in splendor (1Co 15:41). Worship of, forbidden (Dt 4:19). Worshiped (2Ki 17:16; 21:3; 23:5; Jer 19:13; Am 5:26; Zep 1:5; Ac 7:42-43). Constellations of (Isa 13:10), Orion (Job 9:9; Am 5:8), serpent (Job 26:13). Planets (2Ki 23:5), the morning star (Job 38:7; Rev 2:28; 22:16). Darkening of (Job 9:7; Ecc 12:2; Isa 13:10; 34:4; Joel 2:10; 3:15; Rev 8:11-12). Comets (Jude 13). Falling of (Da 8:10; 9:1; 12:4). Guides the wise men (Mt 2:2, 7, 9-10).

Figurative:
Of the deliverer (Nu 24:17). Seven stars of the seven churches (Rev 1:16, 20). Crown of twelve stars (Rev 12:1). Of Jesus (Rev 22:16).

STATE *See Church, The Body of Believers, State; Government.*

STATECRAFT Wisdom in (Pr 28:2). School in (Da 1:3-5). Skilled in.
Instances of: Joseph (Ge 47:15-26), Samuel (1Sa 11:12-15), Nathan (1Ki 1:11-14), Jeroboam (1Ki 12:26-33), Daniel. *See Daniel.*
See Government; Kings; Rulers.

STATURE Natural height of an animal body (2Sa 21:20; Isa 45:14; Lk 19:3).

STAVES *See Staff.*

STEADFASTNESS (Ps 57:7; 108:1; 112:7; Ro 14:4; 1Th 3:8; Col 1:23; Jas 1:25).
Commanded (1Co 7:20; 15:58; 16:13; Gal 6:1; Eph 6:11, 13-14; Php 1:27; 4:1; 1Th 5:21; 2Th 2:15; 3:13; Heb 10:23; 13:9; Jas 1:25; 1Pe 5:9).
Rewards of (Mt 10:22; 24:13; Mk 13:13; Rev 2:7, 10-11, 17, 25-28; 3:5, 11-12, 21; 21:17).
See Decision; Perseverance; Stability.

STEALING *See Theft.*

STEEL Steel is not mentioned in the Bible. *See Bronze.*

STELE (*erect block* or *shaft*). Narrow, upright slab of stone with an inscription cut on it to commemorate an event, mark a grave, or give a votive likeness of a deity. Prevalent especially in Egypt and Greece.

STEPHANAS (*victor's wreath*). A Christian in Corinth, whose household Paul baptized (1Co 1:16; 16:15, 17).

STEPHEN (*victor's wreath*). A Christian martyr. Appointed one of the committee of seven to oversee power of (Ac 6:5, 8-10). False charges against (Ac 6:11-15). Defense of (Ac 7). Stoned (Ac 7:54-60; 8:1; 22:20). Burial of (Ac 8:2). Gentle and forgiving spirit of (Ac 7:59-60).

STERILITY Of women. *See Barrenness.*

STEW Soup of vegetables and meat (Ge 25:29-30, 34; 2Ki 4:38-39).

S

STEWARD (Ge 15:2; 43:19; 1Ch 28:1; Lk 8:3). Must be faithful (1Co 4:1-2; Tit 1:7; 1Pe 4:10).
Figurative: The faithful steward described (Lk 12:35-38, 42). The unfaithful, described (Lk 16:1-8). The parable of the pounds (Lk 19:12-27), of the talents (Mt 25:14-30).

STEWARDSHIP Of the gospel (1Co 9:17; Gal 2:7; Col 1:25; 1Th 2:4; 1Ti 1:11; Tit 1:3).

STICKS Used as cymbals (Eze 37:16).

STIFF-NECKED *See Impenitence; Obduracy.*

STOCK
1. Wooden idol worshiped by apostate Israel (Isa 44:19; Jer 2:27).
2. Family (Lev 25:47; Isa 40:24; Ac 13:26; Php 3:5).
3. Instrument of punishment in which head, hands, and feet were fastened (2Ch 16:10; Jer 20:2; Job 13:27).

STOICISM A Grecian philosophy, inculcating doctrines of severe morality, self-denial, and inconvenient services.
Scripture analogies to: John the Baptist, wears camel's hair and subsists on locusts and wild honey (Mt 3:4), comes "neither eating nor drinking" (Mt 11:18; Lk 7:33). Jesus requires self-denial and crosses (Mt 10:38-39; 16:24; Mk 8:34-35; Lk 9:23-26; 14:27), the subordination of natural affection (Mt 10:37; Lk 14:26). Paul teaches that the "law of my mind" is at war with the "law of sin at work within my members" (Ro 7:23, w 7:14-24), that the body must be kept under (1Co 9:27), advises celibacy (1Co 7:1-9, 25-26, 32-33, 39-40).
School of, at Athens (Ac 17:18).
See Aratus; Asceticism; Cleanthes.

STOICS (*[learners on the painted] porch*). *See Aratus; Asceticism; Cleanthes; Stoicism.*

STOMACHER NIV "fine clothing" (Isa 3:24).

STONES Commandments engraved upon (Ex 24:12; 31:18; 34:1-4; Dt 4:13; 5:22; 9:9-11; 10:1-3). The law of Moses written upon (Jos 8:32). Houses built of (Isa 9:10; Am 5:11). Temple built of (1Ki 5:17-18; 7:9-12; Mt 24:2; Lk 19:44; 21:5-6). Prepared in the quarries (1Ki 6:7). Hewn (Ex 34:1; Dt 10:1; 1Ki 5:17; 6:36; 7:9; 2Ki 12:12; 22:6; 1Ch 22:2; 2Ch 34:11; La 3:9). Sawn (1Ki 7:9). Stonemasons (1Ki 5:18; 2Ki 12:12; 1Ch 22:15).
City walls built of (Ne 4:3). Memorial pillars of (Ge 28:18-22; 31:45-52; Jos 4:2-9, 20-24; 24:25; 1Sa 7:12). Great, as landmarks, Abel (1Sa 6:18), Ezel (1Sa 20:19), Zoheleth (1Ki 1:9).
Cast upon accursed ground (2Ki 3:19, 25). Used in building altars (Jos 8:31), for weighing (Lev 19:36), for closing tombs (Mt 27:60; Mk 15:46; 16:3). Tombs cut in (Mt 27:60; Mk 15:46; 16:3). Idols made of (Dt 4:28; 28:36, 64; 29:17; 2Ki 19:18; Isa 37:19; Eze 20:32).
Great, in Solomon's temple (1Ki 5:17-18; 7:9-12). Magnificent, in Herod's (Mk 13:1). Skill in throwing (Jdg 20:16; 1Ch 12:2). *See Sling.*
See Adamant; Chalcedony; Marble; Onyx; Pillar. See below, Precious.

Figurative—
(Ge 49:24; Zec 3:9). Of temptation, "a stone that causes men to stumble" (Isa 8:14; Ro 9:33; 1Pe 2:8). Of Christ, "a tested stone, a precious cornerstone for a sure foundation" (Isa 28:16), of Christ's rejection, the rejected corner stone (Ps 118:22; Mt 21:42-44; Mk 12:10; Lk 20:17-18; Ac 4:11; 1Pe 2:4), the true foundation (Isa 28:16; Mt 16:18; 1Co 3:11; Eph 2:20; Rev 21:14). Of Christ, the source of spiritual water (1Co 10:4). Of the impenitent heart (Eze 36:26). Of the witness of the Spirit, the white stone (Rev 2:17).

Symbolic—
Of the kingdom of Christ (Da 2:34, 45).

Precious:
In the breastplate and ephod (Ex 28:9-21; 39:6-14). Voluntary offerings of, by the Israelites for the breastplate and ephod (Ex 35:27). Exported from Sheba (1Ki 10:2, 10; 2Ch 9:9-10; Eze 27:22), Ophir (1Ki 10:11). Partial catalog of (Eze 28:13). Seen in the foundation of the New Jerusalem in John's apocalyptic vision (Rev 21:19-20).
In kings' crowns (2Sa 12:30; 1Ch 20:2).

Figurative: (Isa 54:11-12).
See Adamant; Agate; Amber; Amethyst; Bdellium; Beryl; Carbuncle; Carnelian; Chalcedony; Chrysolite; Chrysoprase; Coral; Crystal; Diamond; Emerald; Flint; Glowing Metal; Hardest Stone; Jacinth; Jasper; Minerals of the Bible, 1; Onyx; Pearl; Ruby; Sapphire; Sardius; Sardonyx; Topaz; Turquoise.

STONING The ordinary form of capital punishment prescribed by Hebrew law (Lev 20:2) for blasphemy (Lev 24:16), idolatry (Dt 13:6-10), desecration of the Sabbath day (Ex 31:15; 35:2; Nu 15:32-36), human sacrifice (Lev 20:2), occultism (Lev 20:27).
Unlike unintentional sins, for which there are provisions of God's mercy, one who sets his hand defiantly to despise the word of God and to blaspheme his name must be punished. The one who sins defiantly (literally "with a high hand"), whether in the case of the willful blasphemer (Ex 20:7; 22:28; Lev 24:11-16), or the Sabbath-breaker (Ex 31:12-15; 35:2), was guilty of high-handed rebellion and was judged with death (Nu 15:30-31, 32-36).
Execution took place outside city (Lev 24:14; 1Ki 21:10, 13; Ac 7:58).
See Assault and Battery; Bruise(s); Flog, Flogging; Lashes; Scourging; Stripes.

STOOL
1. Delivery stool (Ex 1:16).
2. Footstool. Figurative: Of the earth (Isa 66:1; Mt 5:35; Ac 7:49), temple (1Ch 28:2; La 2:1), sanctuary (Ps 99:5; 132:7), enemies of Jesus (Ps 110:1; Mt 22:44; Mk 12:36; Lk 20:43; Ac 2:35; Heb 1:13). *See Footstool.*

STORE CITIES Supply depots for provisions and arms (1Ki 9:15-19; 2Ch 8:4-6; 16:4).

STOREHOUSE Place for keeping treasures, supplies, and equipment (Dt 28:8; 1Ch 29:16; 2Ch 31:10; Mal 3:10). *See Barn; Granary.*

STORK (*kindly, loyal one*). Forbidden as food (Lev 11:19). Nest of, in fir trees (Ps 104:17). Migratory (Jer 8:7).
Figurative (Zec 5:9).

STOVE Household stoves usually made of clay; were small and portable, burning charcoal; the well-to-do had metal stoves or braziers (Jer 36:22ff).

STRAIGHT Name of a street in Damascus (Ac 9:11).
Figurative of righteousness, "straight paths" (Isa 40:3-4; Mt 3:3; Heb 12:13).

STRAIT GATE *See Gates, Figurative.*

STRAKES Archaic word for:
1. "White stripes" (Ge 30:37). *See Stripes, 4.*
2. "Greenish or reddish depressions" (Lev 14:37).

STRANGERS Mosaic law relating to: Authorized bondservice of (Lev 25:44-45), usury of (Dt 15:3; 23:20), sale to, of flesh of animals that had died (Dt 14:21), forbid their being made kings over Israel (Dt 17:15), their eating the Passover (Ex 12:43, 48), their eating things offered in sacrifice (Ex 29:33; Lev 22:10, 12, 25), their blaspheming (Lev 24:16), their approaching the tabernacle (Nu 1:51), their eating blood (Lev 17:10), injustice to (Ex 12:49; Lev 24:22; Nu 9:14; Dt 1:16; Jer 22:3), oppression of, forbidden (Ex 22:21; Lev 23:9; Dt 24:14, 17; 27:19; Jer 22:3). Instances of oppression of (Eze 22:29; Mal 3:5).
Required to observe the Sabbath (Ex 20:10; 23:12). Might offer sacrifices (Lev 17:8; 22:18-19). Were buried in separate burial places (Mt 27:7).
Kindness to, required (Lev 19:33-34). Love of, commanded (Dt 10:18-19). Abhorrence of, forbidden (Dt 23:7). Marriage with, forbidden (Dt 25:5). Hospitality to. *See Hospitality.*
See Alms; Foreigner; Heathen; Proselyte.

STRANGLE To deprive of life by choking. Israelites were forbidden to eat flesh from strangled animals (Lev 17:12). At the Jerusalem council even Jewish Christians were forbidden to eat such meat (Ac 15:20).

STRATEGY In war (Ge 14:14-15; 32:7-8; Jos 8:3-25; Jdg 7:16-23; 20:29-43; 2Sa 15:32-34, w 17:7-14; Ne 6; Isa 15:1; Jer 6:5).
See Ambush; Armies.

STRAW Used for feed (Ge 24:32; Isa 65:25), for brick (Ex 5:7).

STRAY Animals straying to be returned (Ex 23:4; Dt 22:1-3). Instances of animals straying, Kish's (1Sa 9).

STREAKED Mottled or blotchy of color, characterizing Laban's sheep (Ge 30:35; 31:8, 12). *See Speckled.*

STREAM OF EGYPT *See River of Egypt.*

STREETS (Pr 1:20; Na 2:4; Mk 6:56; Lk 14:21; Ac 9:11).

STRENGTH A title given Yahweh (1Sa 15:29). Spiritual. *See Power, Spiritual.*

STRIFE

General:
(Ps 55:9; 80:6). Domestic (Pr 19:13; 21:19; 25:24). Hated by God (Isa 58:4; Hab 1:3).
Christ brings (Mt 10:34-36; Lk 12:51-53, 58-59).
Caused by: Busybodies (Pr 26:20). Perversity (Pr 16:28). Hatred (Pr 10:12). Lusts (Jas 4:1-2). Pride (Pr 13:10). Scornfulness (Pr 22:10). Wrath (Pr 15:18; 29:22; 30:33). Excessive indulgence in intoxicating drinks (Pr 23:29-30).
Destructive (Mt 12:25; Mk 3:24-25; Lk 11:17).

Exhortations against:
(Ge 13:8; 45:24; Ps 31:20; Pr 3:30; 17:14; 25:8; Mt 5:25, 39-41; Ro 12:18; 13:13; 14:1, 19, 21; 16:17-18; 1Co 4:6-7; 2Co 12:20; Gal 5:15, 20; Php 2:3, 14-15; 1Ti 3:2-3; 6:3-5, 20-21; 2Ti 2:14, 23-25; Tit 3:1-3, 9; Jas 3:14-16).
Punishment for (Isa 41:11-12; Ro 2:8-9). Correction of (Mt 18:15-17).
Abstinence from, honorable (Pr 20:3).
Prayers concerning (Ps 55:9; 1Ti 2:8).
Proverbs concerning (Pr 3:30; 6:12-14, 16-19; 10:12; 13:10; 15:18; 17:1, 14, 19; 18:6, 19; 19:13; 20:3; 21:19; 22:10; 23:29-30; 25:8, 24; 26:17, 20-21; 27:15; 28:25; 29:22; 30:33).
See Anger; Envy; Jealousy; Malice.

Instances of:
Between Abraham and Lot's herdsmen (Ge 13:6-7), Abimelech's (Ge 21:25), Isaac's and those of Gerar (Ge 26:20-22). Laban and Jacob (Ge 31:36). Israelites (Dt 1:12). Jephthah and his brothers (Jdg 11:2), and Ephraimites (Jdg 12:1-6). Israel and Judah, about David (2Sa 19:41-43).
Disciples, over who might be the greatest (Mk 9:34; Lk 22:24). Jews, concerning Jesus (Jn 10:19). Christians at Antioch, about circumcision (Ac 15:2). Paul and Barnabas, about Mark (Ac 15:38-39). Pharisees and Sadducees, concerning the Resurrection (Ac 23:7-10). Christians, at Corinth (1Co 1:10-12; 3:3-4; 6:1-7; 11:16-21). At Philippi (Php 1:15-17).

STRIKER
See Violence.

STRINGED INSTRUMENTS *See Music.*

STRIPES
1. Wounds inflicted by scourges for punishment (Ex 21:25). *See Bruise(s), 1.*
2. Authorized by Jewish law for certain offenses (Dt 25:2-3). *See Lashes, 1.*
3. Practiced also by Romans (Mt 27:26 & Jn 19:1, w Isa 53:5). Roman floggings were so brutal that sometimes the victim died before crucifixion. *See Flog, Flogging.*
4. The Hebrew terms for the words "poplar" and "white stripes" are puns on the name Laban. As Jacob had gotten the best of Esau (whose other name, Edom, means "red") by means of red stew (Ge 25:30), so he now tries to get the best of Laban (whose name means "white") by means of white branches (Ge 30:37). *See Strakes, 1.*
See also, Assault and Battery; Scourging; Stoning.

STRIVING WITH GOD Folly of (Job 9:3; 33:13; 40:2; Isa 45:9; Ro 9:20).

STRONG DRINK *See Beer; Fermented Drink; Wine.*

STUBBLE Figurative of the wicked (Ex 15:7; Job 21:18; Ps 83:13; Isa 5:24; 40:24; 41:2; 47:14; Jer 13:24; Joel 2:5; Na 1:10; Mal 4:1).

STUBBORNNESS *See Obduracy.*

STUDENTS Poverty of (2Ki 4:1). In state school (Da 1). In schools of the prophets (1Sa 19:20; 1Ki 20:35; 2Ki 2:2-3, 5, 7, 15; 4:1). *See Instruction; School.*

STUMBLING Causes of (Ps 69:6). Stone of (Isa 8:14; Ro 9:32-33; 1Pe 2:8). Stumbling block (Lev 19:14; Ps 119:165; Isa

57:14; Jer 6:21; Eze 3:20; 7:19; 14:3-4, 7; Zep 1:3; Lk 11:52; Ro 11:9; 14:13; 1Co 1:23; 8:9-13; Rev 2:14).
See Temptation.

SUAH (possibly *offal, dung, viscera*). An Asherite. The son of Zophah (1Ch 7:36).

SUBJECTS *See Citizens; Government; Patriotism; Rulers.*

SUBMISSION To authority: Jesus an example of (Mt 26:39, 42; Mk 14:36; Lk 22:42; Heb 5:8).
Of Paul (1Co 16:7).
See Obedience.

SUBSTITUTION (Ge 22:13; Ex 28:38). The offering for the offerer (Lev 1:4; 16:21-22). The Levites for the firstborn of the Israelites (Nu 3:12, 41, 45; 8:18). The life of Ahab for that of Ben-Hadad (1Ki 20:42).
Of Christ for us (Isa 53:4-6; 1Co 5:7; 2Co 5:21; Gal 3:13; 1Pe 2:24).
See Suffering, Vicarious.

SUBURB *See Pasture.*

SUCATHITES One of three clans of scribes who lived at Jabez (1Ch 2:55).

SUCCESSION Of priests, irregularity in (Heb 7:1-28). *See Priest.* Of kings. *See Kings.*

SUCCOTH (*booths*).
1. A city probably east of the Jordan. Jacob builds a house in (Ge 33:17). Allotted to Gad (Jos 13:27). People of, punished by Gideon (Jdg 8:5-8, 14-16). Located near the Jordan (1Ki 7:46; 2Ch 4:17; Ps 60:6; 108:7).
2. First camping place of the Israelites on leaving Rameses (Ex 12:37; 13:20; Nu 33:5-6).

SUCCOTH BENOTH A pagan idol brought into Samaria after Assyria had captured it (2Ki 17:24-30).

SUCHATHITES *See Sucathites.*

SUDDEN EVENTS (Ecc 9:12; Mal 3:1; Mt 24:27; Mk 13:36; Lk 2:13; Ac 2:2; 9:3; 16:26).

SUETONIUS A Roman writer (c. A.D. 69-140), famous for his *Lives of the Caesars.*

SUFFERING

For Christ:
Promised by Christ (Mt 10:34-36; Lk 12:51-53, 58-59; Ac 9:16). Fellowship with Christ on account of (Php 3:10). Conditions of joint heirship with Christ (Ro 8:17-22, 26). A privilege (Php 1:29). Rejoicing in (Ac 5:41; Col 1:24).
Motives for patient enduring of. Future glory (Ro 8:17-18, 2Co 4:8-10; 2Co 4:11-12, 17-18; 1Pe 4:13-14). Reigning with Christ (2Ti 2:12; Rev 22:5).
Consolations in (2Co 1:7; Php 2:27-30; 2Ti 2:12; 1Pe 5:10). Patience in (1Co 4:11-13; 2Th 1:4-5; Jas 5:10; 1Pe 4:14).
See Affliction; Persecution.

Of Christ:
Purpose of his coming (Lk 24:46-47; Jn 6:51; 10:11, 15; 11:50-52). Reason for his coming (Ro 4:25; 5:6-8; 14:15; 1Co 1:17-18, 23-24; 15:3; 2Co 5:14-15; Gal 1:4; 2:20-21; Eph 5:2, 25; 1Th 5:9-10; Heb 2:9-10, 14, 18; 5:8-9; 9:15-16, 28; 10:10, 18-20; 1Pe 2:21, 24; 3:18; 4:1; 1Jn 3:16).
See Atonement; Jesus the Christ, Death of; Purpose of His Death; Sufferings of.

Vicarious:
(Ex 9:13-16; Jn 15:13; Ro 9:3; 1Pe 2:21-24; 1Jn 3:16).
See Jesus the Christ, Sufferings of; Penalty, Vicariously Assumed; above, Suffering, Of Christ.
Instance of: Goliath, for the Philistines (1Sa 17).

SUICIDE (Am 9:2; Rev 9:6). Temptation to, of Jesus (Mt 4:5-6; Lk 4:9-11). Of the Philippian jailer (Ac 16:27). *See Death, Physical, Desired.*
Instances of: Samson (Jdg 16:29-30). Saul and his armor bearer (1Sa 31:4-5; 1Ch 10:4-5). Ahithophel (2Sa 17:23). Zimri (1Ki 16:18). Judas (Mt 27:5; Ac 1:18).

SUING (Mt 5:40). *See Creditor; Debtor.*

SUKKITES Mercenary soldiers, possibly Libyan, who joined Shishak in his invasion of Judah (2Ch 12:3).

SUKKOTH *See Succoth.*

SULFUR Fire and, rained upon Sodom (Ge 19:24; Lk 17:29). In Israel (Dt 29:23). Figurative of God's judgment (Job 18:15; Ps 11:6; Isa 30:33; Eze 38:22; Rev 9:17-18; 14:10; 19:20; 21:8). *See Minerals of the Bible.*

SUMER One of two political divisions, Sumer and Akkad, originally comprising Babylonia.

SUMMER Season of, promised while the earth remains (Ge 8:22). Cool rooms for (Jdg 3:20, 24; Am 3:15). Fruits of (2Sa 16:1-2; Isa 16:9; 28:4; Jer 40:10, 12; 48:32; Am 8:1-2; Mic 7:1). Drought of (Ps 32:4). Given by God (Ps 74:17). The time for labor and harvest (Pr 6:6-8; 10:5; 30:25; Jer 8:20). Snow in (Pr 26:1). Threshing in (Da 2:35). Approach of (Mt 24:32; Mk 13:28; Lk 21:30).
Figurative (Jer 8:20).

SUMMER HOUSE, SUMMER PALACE The wealthy had separate residences for hot and cold seasons. Called a "summer house" (Am 3:15), a "summer palace" (Jdg 3:20, ftn). *See Winter Apartment, Winter House.*

SUN Created (Ge 1:14-18; Ps 74:16; 136:7; Jer 31:35). Rising and setting of (Ecc 1:5). Diurnal motion of (Ps 19:4, 6). Worship of, forbidden (Dt 4:19; 17:3). Worshiped (Job 31:26-28; Jer 8:2; Eze 6:4, 6; 8:16). Kings of Judah dedicate horses to (2Ki 23:11).
Miracles concerning: Darkening of (Ex 10:21-23; Isa 5:30; 24:23; Eze 32:7; Joel 2:10, 31; 3:15; Am 8:9; Mic 3:6; Mt 24:29; 27:45; Mk 13:24; 15:33; Lk 21:25; 23:44-45; Ac 2:20; Rev 6:12; 8:12; 9:2; 16:8). Stands still (Jos 10:12-13; Hab 3:11). Shadow of, goes back on Ahaz's stairway (2Ki 20:11; Isa 38:8).
Light of, not needed in eternity (Rev 21:23).
Figurative (Ps 84:11; Mal 4:2; Jdg 5:31; Isa 30:26; 60:19-20; Jer 15:9; Rev 1:16; 12:1; 19:17).

SUN, WORSHIP OF Worship of the sun found varied forms in the ancient world. Even the Israelites at times worshiped sun images (Lev 26:30; Isa 17:8). Shamash was a great sun god of the ancient Middle East. Phoenicia worshiped a sun Baal, Baal Hamon. In Egypt the center of sun worship was On, or Heliopolis, where the sun was called Re.

SUNDAY The first day of the week, commemorating the resurrection of Jesus (Jn 20:1-25), and the Day of Pentecost (Ac 2:1-41). For a time after the Ascension of Jesus the Christians met on the seventh and the first days of the week, but as the Hebrew Christian churches declined in influence, the tendency to observe the Hebrew Sabbath slowly passed. The disciples at Troas worshiped on the first day (Ac 20:7). Paul admonished the Corinthians to lay by in store as God had prospered them, doing it week by week on the first day (1Co 16:2). The term "Lord's Day" occurs (Rev 1:10).

SUN-DIAL NIV "stairway" (2Ki 20:11; Isa 38:8). *See Stairs.*

SUNSTROKE (2Ki 4:19).

SUPER-APOSTLES Paul's critics (2Co 11:5; 12:11).

SUPEREROGATION The doctrine of excessive and meritorious righteousness (Eze 33:12-13; Lk 17:10).

SUPERSCRIPTION (*inscription*).
1. The wording on coins (Mt 22:20).
2. Words written on a board attached to the cross naming the crime of which the condemned was accused (Mk 15:26; Lk 23:38; Jn 19:19-20).
3. Titles of the Psalms. *See Music, Symbols Used in; Psalms.*

SUPERSTITION (Ac 25:19).

Instances of:
Israelites in supposing that their defeat in battle with the Philistines was due to their not having brought the ark of the covenant with them (1Sa 4:3, w 4:10-11), attributing their calamities to having stopped offering sacrifices to the Queen of Heaven (Jer 44:17-19). Philistines in refusing to step on the threshold where the image of Dagon had repeatedly fallen (1Sa 5:5).
The belief of the Syrians concerning the help of the gods (1Ki 20:23). Nebuchadnezzar in supposing that the spirit of the gods was upon Daniel (Da 4:8-9). The sailors who threw Jonah into the sea (Jnh 1:4-16). The disciples in supposing they saw a spirit when Jesus came walking upon the sea (Mt 14:26; Mk 6:49-50). Herod in imagining that John the Baptist had risen from the dead (Mk 6:14, 16).
The Gadarenes on account of Jesus casting demons out of the demoniac (Mt 8:34). The disciples who were frightened at the appearance of Peter (Ac 12:14-15). The Ephesians in their sorceries (Ac 19:13-19). The people of the island of Malta in imagining Paul to be a god (Ac 28:6).
See Idolatry; Sorcery.

SUPERSTITIOUS NIV "very religious" (Ac 17:22), could either commend or criticize the Athenians.

SUPH, SUPHAH (*reeds, rushes*). "The Red Sea" is used for these words (Nu 21:14; Dt 1:1). Suph is an unidentified region E of the Jordan; Suphah, is probably the region of the Red Sea.

SUPPER *See Feasts; Eucharist.*

SUPPER, LORD'S *See Lord's Supper.*

SUPPLICATION *See Prayer.*

SUPREME COMMANDER Commander-in-chief of the Assyrian army (Isa 20:1; 2Ki 18:17).

SUR The gate of the temple (2Ki 11:6).

SURETY *See Security, For Debt; Debt.*

SURFEITING Overindulgence of food or drink; dissipation (Lk 21:34).

SUSA
1. Capital of the Medo-Persian Empire (Est 1:2-3; 8:15).
2. King's palace at (Ne 1:1; Est 1:2, 5; 2:5, 8; 4:8, 16; 8:14-15; 9:11, 15).

SUSAH *See Hazar Susah.*

SUSANCHITES NIV "of Susa" (Ezr 4:9). *See Susa.*

SUSANNA (*lily*).
1. Woman who ministered to Christ (Lk 8:1-3).
2. Heroine of *The History of Susanna*, in the OT Apocrypha.

SUSI (*[my] horse*). A Manassite (Nu 13:11).

SUSIM *See Hazar Susah.*

SUSPICION *See Accusation, False.*

SWADDLING BAND Bands of cloth in which a newborn baby was wrapped (Lk 2:7, 12). Used figuratively (Job 38:9).

SWALLOW Builds its nest in the sanctuary (Ps 84:3). Chattering of, figurative of the mourning of the afflicted (Isa 38:14). Migration of (Jer 8:7).

SWAN *See White Owl.*

SWEARING *See Blasphemy; God, Name of; Oath.*

SWEAT (Ge 3:19). An offense in the sanctuary (Eze 44:18). Of blood (Lk 22:44).

SWEAT, BLOODY Physical manifestation of the agony of Jesus in Gethsemane (Lk 22:44). Christ's sweat most likely did not become bloody, but "his sweat was like great drops of blood falling to the ground" as if from an open wound.

SWEET INCENSE Made of spices (Ex 25:6). *See Incense.*

SWEET SAVOR *See Pleasing Aroma.*

SWELLING Usually "pride"; or means the flooding of the Jordan in the spring (Jer 12:5; 49:19; 50:44). It refers to the tumult of a stormy sea (Ps 46:3).

SWIFT An amphibious bird (Isa 38:14; Jer 8:7).

SWINE *See Animals; Pig.*

SWORD, THE Probable origin of (Ge 3:24). Was pointed (Eze 21:15). Frequently had two edges (Ps 149:6).

Described as:
Sharp (Ps 57:4). Bright (Na 3:3). Glittering (Dt 32:41; Job 20:25). Oppressive (Jer 46:16). Hurtful (Ps 144:10). Carried in a sheath or scabbard (1Ch 21:27; Jer 47:6; Eze 21:3-5). Suspended from the belt (1Sa 17:39; 2Sa 20:8; Ne 4:18; Ps 45:3).

Was Used:
By the patriarchs (Ge 34:25; 48:22). By the Jews (Jdg 7:22; 2Sa 24:9). By heathen nations (Jdg 7:22; 1Sa 15:33). For self-defense (Lk 22:36). For destruction of enemies (Nu 21:24; Jos 6:21). For punishing criminals (1Sa 15:33; Ac 12:2). Sometimes for self-destruction (1Sa 31:4-5; Ac 16:27). Hebrews early acquainted with making of (1Sa 13:19). In time of war, plowshares made into (Joel 3:10). In time of peace, made into plowshares (Isa 2:4; Mic 4:3). Sharpened and furbished before going to war (Ps 7:12; Eze 21:9). Was brandished over the head (Eze 32:10). Was thrust through enemies (Eze 16:40). Often threatened as a punishment (Lev 26:25, 33; Dt 32:25). Often sent as a punishment (Ezr 9:7; Ps 78:62). Was one of God's four sore judgments (Eze 14:21). Those slain by, communicated ceremonial uncleanness (Nu 19:16).

Illustrative:
Of the Word of God (Eph 6:17, w Heb 4:12). Of the word of Christ (Isa 49:2, w Rev 1:16). Of the justice of God (Dt 32:41; Zec 13:7). Of the protection of God (Dt 33:29). Of war and contention (Mt 10:34). Of severe and heavy calamities (Eze 5:2, 17; 14:17; 21:9). Of deep mental affliction (Lk 2:35). Of the wicked (Ps 17:13). Of the tongue of the wicked (Ps 57:4; 64:3; Pr 12:18). Of persecuting spirit of the wicked (Ps 37:14). Of the end of the wicked (Pr 5:4). Of false witnesses (Pr 25:18). Of judicial authority (Ro 13:4). Drawing of illustrative of war and destruction (Lev 26:33; Eze 21:3-5). Putting into its sheath illustrative of peace and friendship (Jer 47:6). Living by illustrative of violence (Ge 27:40). Not departing from one's house illustrative of perpetual calamity (2Sa 12:10).

SYCAMINE NIV "mulberry tree" (Lk 17:6).

SYCAMORE-FIG A tree. Abundant in the land of Canaan (1Ki 10:27; 2Ch 1:15; 9:27; Isa 9:10). Groves of, cared for (1Ch 27:28). Destroyed by frost (Ps 78:47). Care of (Am 7:14). Zacchaeus climbs into (Lk 19:4).

SYCHAR A village one half mile N of Jacob's well, on the E slope of Mt. Ebal (Jn 4:5).

SYCHEM *See Shechem, 1.*

SYENE *See Aswan.*

SYMBOLS, AND SIMILITUDES

General
Almond tree branch (Jer 1:11). Altar split apart (1Ki 13:3, 5). Basket for measuring (Zec 5:6-11). Belt (Jer 13:1-7; Ac 21:11). Blood sprinkled (Ex 24:8). Book cast into Euphrates (Jer 51:63). Bow shot (1Sa 20:21-37; 2Ki 13:15-19). Bread (Mt 26:26; Mk 14:22; Lk 22:19). Breaking of clay jar (Jer 19). Change of residence (Eze 12:3-11). Childlike (Mt 18:3; Mk 10:14-15; Lk 18:16-17). Circumcision, of the covenant of Abraham (Ge 17:11; Ro 4:11). Cooking (Jer 1:13; Eze 4:9-15; 24:3-5). Curtain of the temple torn in two (Mt 27:51; Mk 15:38; Lk 23:45). Darkness (Ex 20:21; Lev 16:2; 1Ki 8:12; Ps 18:11; 97:2; Heb 12:18-19). Death [without mourning] (Eze 24:16-19). Deeds of land (Jer 32:1-16). Eating food with anxiety (Eze 12:17-20). Figs [basket of good and bad] (Jer 24). Fish [Jonah in the] (Mt 16:4; Lk 11:29-30). Food (2Ki 19:29; Isa 37:30). Fruit [basket of] (Jer 24:1-3; Am 8:1-2).
Handwriting on the wall (Da 5:5-6, 16-28). Harvest (2Ki 19:29). Invitation by enemy to approach (1Sa 14:8-12). Isaiah's children (Isa 8:18). Manna [in the desert] (Jn 6:31-58). Marrying a prostitute (Hos 1:2-9; 3:1-4). Men meeting Saul (1Sa 10:2-7). Mosaic rites [system of] (Heb 9:9-10, 18-23). Mute (Eze 3:26-27; 24:27; 29:21; 33:22; Lk 1:20-22, 62-64). Nakedness (Isa 20:2-4). Passover [of the sparing of the firstborn] (Ex 12:3-28). Passover [atonement made by Christ] (1Co 5:7). Pillar of cloud (Ex 13:21-22; 14:19-20; 19:9, 16). Plumb line (Am 7:7-8). Posture [lie on side] (Eze 4:4-8). Pot for cooking (Eze 24:1-5). Praying toward the temple (1Ki 8:29; Da 6:10). Rainbow (Ge 9:12-13).

Sacrificial animals (Ge 15:8-11; Jn 1:29, 36). Salt [gracious words] (Col 4:6). Salt, Covenant of (Nu 18:19). Scroll flying (Zec 5:2-4). Shadow on Ahaz's stairway (2Ki 20:8-11; Isa 38:7-8). Shaving head and beard (Eze 5:1-4). Siege (Eze 4:1-3). Snake of bronze [lifted up, of Christ] (Nu 21:8-9; Jn 3:14). Spiritual rest [Canaan] (Heb 3:11-12; 4:5). Star in the east (Mt 2:2). Sticks and staffs (Eze 37:16-17; Zec 11:7, 10-11, 14). Striken rock [of Christ] (Ex 17:6; 1Co 10:4). Tabernacle and sanctuary (Ps 15:1; Eze 37:27; Heb 8:2, 5; 9:1-12, 23-24). Thunder and lightning on Mount Sinai (Ex 19:9, 16). Thunder and rain (1Sa 12:16-18). Trees of life and knowledge (Ge 2:9, 17; 3:3, 24; Rev 22:2). Unclean food [preparing of] (Eze 4:9-17). Vine (Eze 15:2; 19:10-14). Water [lapping of] (Jdg 7:4-8). Water to drink [drawing of in hospitality of] (Ge 24:13-15, 42-44). Waving and ritual offering (Ex 29:24-28; Lev 8:27-29; 9:21). Wine (Jer 25:15-17; Mt 26:27; Mk 14:23; Lk 22:17). Wine [of the atoning blood] (Mt 26:27-29; Mk 14:23-25; Lk 22:17-18, 20). Wineskins (Jer 13:12; 19:1-2, 10). Wounding (1Ki 20:35-40). Yokes (Jer 27:2-3; 28:10).

Of the Holy Spirit:

Water (Jn 3:5; 7:38-39): cleansing by (Eze 16:9; 36:25; Eph 5:26; Heb 10:22), making prosperous (Ps 1:3; Isa 27:3, 6; 44:3-4; 58:11).

Fire (Mt 3:11): refining (Isa 4:4; Mal 3:2-3), guiding (Ex 13:21; Ps 78:14), searching (Zep 1:12, w 1Co 2:10). Flame shaped like tongues (Ac 2:3, 6, 11).

Wind (SS 4:16): incomprehensible (Jn 3:8; 1Co 12:11), powerful (1Ki 19:11, w Ac 2:2), quiet but present (Jn 3:8), reviving, life giving (Eze 37:9-10, 14).

Oil (Ps 45:7): healing (Isa 1:6; Lk 10:34; Rev 18:13), joy causing (Isa 61:3; Heb 1:9), illuminating (Zec 4:2-3, 11-13; Mt 25:3-4; 1Jn 2:20, 27), consecrating (Ex 29:7; 30:30; Isa 61:1).

Rain and dew (Ps 72:6): enriching and fertilizing (Eze 34:26-27; Hos 6:3; 10:12; 14:5), refreshing (Ps 68:9; Isa 18:4), abundant (Ps 133:3), imperceptible (2Sa 17:12, w Mk 4:26-28).

Dove (Mt 3:16).

Voice (Isa 6:8): speaking (Mt 10:20), guiding (Isa 30:21, w Jn 16:13), warning (Heb 3:7-11).

Seal (Rev 7:2): impressing (Job 38:14, w 2Co 3:18), guarantee (Eph 1:13-14; 4:30; 2Co 1:22).

See Holy Spirit, Emblems of.

Washings, a symbol of purity. *See Washings; Purification.* For symbolisms of color, *See Colors, Figurative and Symbolic.*

See also, Allegory; Instruction, By Object Lessons; By Types; In Religion.

SYMEON *See Simeon.*

SYMPATHY
(Ecc 7:2). Commanded (Ro 12:15; Jas 1:27; 1Pe 3:8). In Christ (Php 2:1-2).

Instances of:

David with Hanun (2Sa 10:2). The Jewish maid with Naaman (2Ki 5:1-4). Job's friends (Job 2:11-13), turned against Job (Job 6:14; 22:29). Ebed-Melech with Jeremiah (Jer 38:7-13). Nebuchadnezzar with Daniel (Da 6:18-23).

The four friends with the crippled man whom they took to Jesus (Mk 2:3-4). Others with the helpless whom they brought to Jesus (Mt 4:24). The good Samaritan with the man who fell among robbers (Lk 10:33-35). The Jews with Martha and Mary (Jn 11:19, 31, 33). The people of Malta with the shipwrecked mariners (Ac 28:1-2).

See Afflicted; Afflictions; Jesus the Christ, Compassion of; Kindness; Pity; Poor.

SYNAGOGUE
(*place of gathering*).

1. Primarily an assembly (Ac 13:43; Jas 2:2). Constitutes a court of justice (Lk 12:11; Ac 9:2). Had powers of criminal courts (Mt 10:17; Mt 23:34; Ac 22:19; 26:11), of ecclesiastical courts (Jn 9:22, 34; 12:42; 16:2).

2. Place of assembly. Scriptures read and expounded in (Ne 8:1-8; 9:3, 5; Mt 4:23; 9:35; 13:54; Mk 1:39; Lk 4:15-33; 13:10; Jn 18:20; Ac 9:20; 13:5-44; 14:1; 15:21; 17:2, 10; 18:4, 19, 26).

In Jerusalem (Ac 6:9), Damascus (Ac 9:2, 20), other cities (Ac 14:1; 17:1, 10; 18:4). Built by Jairus (Lk 7:5), Jesus performed healing in (Mt 12:9-13; Lk 13:11-14). Alms given in (Mt 6:2).

Of Satan (Rev 2:9; 3:9).

See Church, Place of Worship; Testaments, Time Between.

SYNAGOGUE, MEN OF THE GREAT
Or of the Great Assembly, a college of learned men supposedly organized by Nehemiah after the return from exile (Ne 8-10), to which Jewish tradition attributed the origination and authoritative promulgation of many ordinances and regulations.

SYNOPTIC GOSPELS, THE
A careful comparison of the four Gospels reveals that Matthew, Mark, and Luke are noticeably similar, while John is quite different. The first three Gospels agree extensively in language, in the material they include, and in the order in which events and sayings from the life of Christ are recorded. (Chronological order does not appear to have been rigidly followed in any of the Gospels, however). Because of this agreement, these three books are called the Synoptic Gospels (*syn,* "together with"; *optic,* "seeing"; thus "seeing together"). For an example of agreement in content see Mt 9:2-8; Mk 2:3-12; Lk 5:18-26. An instance of verbatim agreement is found in Mt 10:22a; Mk 13:13a; Lk 21:17. A mathematical comparison shows that 91 percent of Mark's Gospel is contained in Matthew, while 53 percent of Mark is found in Luke. Such agreement raises questions as to the origin of the Synoptic Gospels. Did the authors rely on a common source? Were they interdependent? Questions such as these constitute what is known as the Synoptic Problem. Several suggested solutions have been advanced:

1. *The use of oral tradition.* Some have thought that tradition had become so stereotyped that it provided a common source from which all the Gospel writers drew.

2. *The use of an early Gospel.* Some have postulated that the Synoptic authors all had access to an earlier Gospel, now lost.

3. *The use of written fragments.* Some have assumed that written fragments had been composed concerning various events from the life of Christ and that these were used by the Synoptic authors.

4. *Mutual dependence.* Some have suggested that the Synoptic writers drew from each other with the result that what they wrote was often very similar.

5. *The use of two major sources.* The most common view currently is that the Gospel of Mark and a hypothetical document, called *Quelle* (German for "source") or *Q,* were used by Matthew and Luke as sources for most of the materials included in their Gospels.

6. *The priority and use of Matthew.* Another view suggests that the other two Synoptics drew from Matthew as their main source.

7. *A combination of most of the above.* This theory assumes that the authors of the Synoptic Gospels made use of oral tradition, written fragments, mutual dependence on other Synoptic writers or on their Gospels, and the testimony of eyewitnesses.

SYNTYCHE
(*coincidence, success*). Christian woman at Philippi (Php 4:2).

SYRACUSE
A city of Sicily. Paul visits (Ac 28:12).

SYRIA
Highlands lying between the Euphrates river and the Mediterranean Sea. Called Aram, from the son of Shem (Ge 10:22-23; Nu 23:7; 1Ch 1:17; 2:23). In the time of Abraham it seems to have embraced the region between the rivers Tigris and Euphrates (Ge 24:10, w 25:20), including Paddan Aram (Ge 25:20, ftn; 28:5).

Minor kingdoms within the region: Aram Zobah, also called Zobah (1Sa 14:47; 2Sa 8:3; 10:6, 8; 1Ki 11:23; 1Ch 18:5, 9; 19:6; Ps 60, title), Geshur (2Sa 15:8), Aram Rehob, also called Beth Rehob (2Sa 10:6, 8), Damascus (2Sa 8:5-6; 1Ch 18:5-6), Hamath (2Sa 8:9-10).

Conquest of: By David (2Sa 8:3-13), by Jeroboam (2Ki 14:25, 28), by Tiglath-Pileser, king of Assyria (2Ki 16:7-9; 18:33-34). People of, colonized in Samaria by the king of Assyria (2Ki 17:24). Confederate with Nebuchadnezzar (2Ki 24:2; Jer 39:5).

The Roman province of, included the land of Canaan (Lk 2:2-3), and Phoenicia (Mk 7:26; Ac 21:3). The fame of Jesus extended over (Mt 4:24).

Paul goes to, with letters to apprehend the Christians; is converted and begins his evangelistic ministry (Ac 9:1-31). *See Paul.*

Paul preaches in (Ac 15:41; 18:18; 21:3; Gal 1:21). Damascus, the capital of. *See Damascus.*

Wars between, and the kingdoms of Judah and Israel. *See Israel.* Prophecies concerning (Isa 7:8-16; 8:4-7; 17:1-3; Jer 1:15; 49:23-27; Am 1:3-5; Zec 9:1).

SYRIAC *See Aramaic.*

SYRIAC VERSIONS *See Texts and Versions.*

SYRIA-MAACHAH *See Aram Maacah.*

SYRIAN
The people of Syria (Lk 4:27). *See Aram, 6; Aramaic; Syria.*

SYRIAN PHOENICIAN
The nationality of a woman whose daughter was cured by Jesus (Mt 15:21-28; Mk 7:24-30).

SYRTIS
Banks of quicksand off the coast of Libya (Ac 27:17).

T

TAANACH
A city conquered by Joshua (Jos 12:21). Allotted to Manasseh (Jos 17:11; 1Ch 7:29). Canaanites not driven from (Jos 17:12; Jdg 1:27). Assigned to the Levites (Jos 21:25). The scene of Barak's victory (Jdg 5:19). One of Solomon's district governors at (1Ki 4:12).

TAANATH SHILOH
(possibly *approach to Shiloh* IDB). Town on the NE border of Ephraim (Jos 16:6), c. ten miles E of Shechem.

TABALIAH
(*Yahweh has dipped*). The son of Hosah (1Ch 26:11).

TABBAOTH
(*[ornamental or signet] ring*). A family of temple servants who returned with Zerubbabel (Ezr 2:43; Ne 7:46).

TABBATH
(possibly *good*). A place probably E of the Jordan between Jabesh Gilead and Succoth (Jdg 7:22).

TABEAL *See Tabeel, 2.*

TABEEL
(*God [El] is good*).

1. A Persian official in Samaria (Ezr 4:7).

2. The father of one whom the kings of Syria and Israel sought to make king in Judah instead of Ahaz (Isa 7:6).

TABERAH
(*burning*). An encampment of Israel in the wilderness where fire of the Lord consumed some complainers (Nu 11:1-3; Dt 9:22), the site is unidentified.

TABERNACLE
One existed before Moses received the pattern authorized on Mount Sinai (Ex 33:7-11). The one instituted by Moses was called Sanctuary (Ex 25:8), Tent of Meeting (Ex 27:21; 33:7; 2Ch 5:5), Tabernacle of the Testimony (Ex 38:21; Nu 1:50), Tent of the Testimony (Nu 17:7-8; 2Ch 24:6), Temple of the Lord (1Sa 1:9; 3:3), House of the Lord (Jos 6:24).

The pattern of, revealed to Moses (Ex 25:9; 26:30; 39:32, 42-43; Ac 7:44; Heb 8:5). Materials for, voluntarily offered (Ex 25:1-8; 35:4-29; 36:3-7). Value of the substance contributed for (Ex 38:24-31). Workmen who constructed it were inspired (Ex 31:1-11; 35:30-35).

Description of: Frame (Ex 26:15-37; 36:20-38). Outer covering (Ex 25:5; 26:7-14; 36:14-19). Second covering (Ex 25:5; 26:14; 35:7, 23; 36:19; 39:34). Curtains of (Ex 26:1-14, 31-37; 27:9-16; 35:15, 17; 36:8-19, 35, 37). Court of (Ex 27:9-17; 38:9-16, 18; 40:8, 33).

Holy Place of (Ex 26:31-37; 40:22-26; Heb 9:2-6, 8). The Most Holy Place (Ex 26:33-35; 40:20-21; Heb 9:3-5, 7-8).

Furniture of (Ex 25:10-40; 27:1-8, 19; 37; 38:1-8). *See Altar; Ark; Atonement Cover; Bread, Consecrated; Lampstand; Cherubim.*

Completed (Ex 39:32). Dedicated (Nu 7). Sanctified (Ex 29:43; 40:9-16; Nu 7:1). Anointed with holy oil (Ex 30:25-26; Lev 8:10; Nu 7:1). Sprinkled with blood (Lev 16:15-20; Heb 9:21, 23). Filled with the cloud of glory (Ex 40:34-38).

How prepared for removal during the travels of the Israelites (Nu 1:51; 4:5-15). How and by whom carried (Nu 4:5-33; 7:6-9). Strangers forbidden to enter (Nu 1:51). Duties of the Levites concerning. *See Levites.* Defilement of, punished (Lev 15:31; Nu 19:13, 20; Eze 5:11; 23:38). Duties of the priests in relation to. *See Priest.* Israelites worship at (Nu 10:3; 16:19, 42-43; 20:6; 25:6; 1Sa 2:22; Ps 27:4). Offerings brought to (Lev 17:4; Nu 31:54; Dt 12:5-6, 11-14).

Tribes encamped around, while in the wilderness (Nu 2). All males required to appear before, three times each year (Ex 23:17). Tabernacle tax (Ex 20:11-16).

Carried in front of the Israelites in the line of march (Nu 10:33-36; Jos 3:3-6). The Lord reveals himself at (Lev 1:1; Nu 1:1; 7:89; 12:4-10; Dt 31:14-15).

Pitched at Gilgal (Jos 4:18-19), at Shiloh (Jos 18:1; 19:51; Jdg 18:31; 20:18, 26-27; 21:19; 1Sa 2:14; 4:3-4; Jer 7:12, 14), at Nob (1Sa 21:1-6), at Gibeon (1Ch 21:29). Renewed by David and pitched on Mount Zion (1Ch 15:1; 16:1-2; 2Ch 1:4). Solomon offers sacrifice at (2Ch 1:3-6). Brought to the temple by Solomon (2Ch 5:5, w 1Ki 8:1, 4-5).

Symbol of spiritual things (Ps 15:1; Heb 8:2, 5; 9:1-12, 24).

See Levites; Priest; Temple.

TABERNACLES, FEAST OF
Also called the Feast of Ingathering. Instituted (Ex 23:16; 34:22; Lev 23:34-43; Nu 29:12-40; Dt 16:13-16). Design of (Lev 23:42-43). The law read in connection with, every seventh year (Dt 31:10-12; Ne 8:18). Observance of, after the captivity (Ezr 3:4; Ne 8:14-18), by Jesus (Jn 7:2, 14). Observance of, omitted (Ne 8:17). Penalty for not observing (Zec 14:16-19).

Jeroboam institutes an idolatrous feast to correspond to, in the eighth month (1Ki 12:32-33; 1Ch 27:11).

TABITHA
(*gazelle*). A Christian woman in Joppa; befriended poor widows; raised from dead by Peter (Ac 9:36-43).

TABLE
1. Table for food (Jdg 1:7; 1Ki 2:7).

2. Lord's table = Lord's Supper (1Co 10:21).

3. "Wait on tables" (Ac 6:2) refers to distribution of food, etc., to the Christian poor.

4. Tabernacle and temple were provided with various tables (Ex 25:23-30).

TABLE OF CONSECRATED BREAD
Twelve loaves of consecrated, unleavened bread were placed on a table in the Holy Place in the tabernacle and temple (Ex 25:30; Lev 24:5-9).

TABLET
1. Stone or clay tablets for writing (Ex 24:12; Eze 4:1; Lk 1:63). Metaphorical (2Co 3:3). *See Tablets of the Law.*

2. *See Dress.*

TABLETS OF THE LAW
Stone tablets on which Moses wrote the Ten Commandments (Ex 31:18; 32:15-16; Dt 4:13; 5:22). *See Commandments and Statutes, Of God.*

TABOR
1. A mountain on the border of Issachar (Jos 19:22; Jdg 8:18; Ps 89:12; Jer 46:18; Hos 5:1). Assembling place of Barak's army (Jdg 4:6, 12, 14).

2. A plain located by the great tree of Tabor (1Sa 10:3).

3. A Levitical city in Zebulun (1Ch 6:77).

See Kisloth Tabor.

TABRET *See Tambourine.*

TABRIMMON
(*[pagan god] Rimmon is good*). The father of Ben-Hadad, king of Syria (1Ki 15:18).

TACHE *See Clasp.*

TACHMONITE *See Tahkemonite.*

TACKLE
The masts and rigging of a ship (Isa 33:23; Ac 27:19).

TACT
(Pr 15:1; 25:15). In preaching (1Co 9:19-22; 2Co 12:6). Of Gideon (Jdg 8:1-3). Of Saul, in managing malcontents (1Sa 10:27; 11:7, 12-15). Nabal's wife (1Sa 25:18-37). In David's popular methods: In mourning for Abner (2Sa 3:28-37), in organizing the temple music (1Ch 15:16-24), in securing popular consent to bringing the ark to Jerusalem (1Ch 13:1-4). Mephibosheth (2Sa 9:8). Joab's trick in obtaining David's consent to the return of Absalom (2Sa 14:1-22). The woman of Tekoa (2Sa 14:4-20). The wise woman of Abel (2Sa 20:16-22). Solomon, in arbitrating between the harlots (1Ki 3:24-28).

Mordecai, in concealing Esther's nationality (Est 2:10). Esther, in placating the king (Est 5-7). Paul, in circumcising Timothy (Ac 16:3), in turning the preaching of adversaries to account (Php 1:10-22), in stimulating benevolent giving (2Co 8:1-8; 9:1-5), in

arraying the two religious factions of the Jews against each other when he was in trouble (Ac 23:6-10). The town clerk of Ephesus (Ac 19:35-41). The church council at Jerusalem (Ac 21:20-25).
See Wisdom.

TACTICS *See Armies; Strategy.*

TADMOR (*palm tree*). A city in the desert NE of Damascus (1Ki 9:18; 2Ch 8:4), a fabulously rich trade metropolis later called Palmyra. Magnificent ruins have been excavated.

TAHAN, TAHANITE (possibly *grace, favor*).
1. The son of Ephraim and his clan (Nu 26:35).
2. A descendant of Ephraim (1Ch 7:25).

TAHAPANES *See Tahpanhes.*

TAHASH (*a species of dolphin*). The son of Nahor and Reumah (Ge 22:24).

TAHATH (*compensation*).
1. Camping place of the Israelites (Nu 33:26-27).
2. A Kohathite (1Ch 6:24, 37).
3. The name of two Ephraimites (1Ch 7:20).

TAHKEMONITE The family of David's chief captain (2Sa 23:8); also spelled Hacmonite (1Ch 11:11).

TAHPANHES (*the fortress of Penhase [the Black Man]*). A fortress city at the E edge of the Nile Delta to which Israelites fled after the fall of Jerusalem (Jer 2:16; 43:7-9; 44:1; 46:14; Eze 30:18).

TAHPENES (title *wife of the king*). A queen of Egypt (1Ki 11:19-20).

TAHREA (possibly *clever one* BDB). The grandson of Mephibosheth (1Ch 9:41), also spelled Tarea (1Ch 8:35).

TAHTIM HODSHI A place E of Jordan in the land of the Hittites (2Sa 24:6).

TAILORING (Ex 31:2-3, 6, 10; 39:1).

TALEBEARER (*The vice of repeating damaging reports, either true or false*). (Ps 15:1-3; Pr 11:13; 20:19).
Separates friends (Pr 16:28; 17:9). Causes strife (Pr 26:20), tension (Pr 18:8).
Is forbidden (Lev 19:16; 1Ti 5:11, 13).
See Busybody; Gossip; Slander; Speaking, Evil.
Instances of: Joseph (Ge 37:2). Israelites (2Sa 3:23). Tobiah (Ne 6).
See Backbiting; Slander.

TALENT A weight equal to sixty minas or about seventy-five pounds (1Ki 9:14, 28; 10:10, 14; Ex 25:39; 38:27). Parables of the (Mt 18:23-34; 25:15-30). *See Measure.*

TALES Avoid myths and old wives' tales (1Ti 4:7). *See Myths.*

TALITHA KOUM Aramaic for "Little girl, get up!" (Mk 5:41).

TALKING With God. *See Communion.*

TALMAI (possibly *[my] furrow maker*).
1. A son of Anak (Nu 13:22; Jos 15:14; Jdg 1:10).
2. King of Geshur (2Sa 3:3; 13:37; 1Ch 3:2).

TALMON (perhaps *brightness*). A gatekeeper of the temple (1Ch 9:17). Family of, returned from captivity with Zerubbabel (Ezr 2:42; Ne 7:45; 11:19; 12:25).

TALMUD (*education, instruction*). A collection of Jewish tradition of the early Christian centuries; The two forms: Palestinian and Babylonian.

TAMAH *See Temah.*

TAMAR (*date palm*).
1. The wife of Er, then of Onan; mother of Perez and Zerah (Ge 38; Mt 1:3).
2. Daughter of David; abused by his half brother Amon (2Sa 13:1-33).
3. The daughter of Absalom (2Sa 14:27).
4. Unidentified borderland site in restored Israel (Eze 47:19; 48:28).
5. A city in Syria, more commonly known as Tadmor, later Palmyra.

TAMARISK A tree (1Sa 22:6; 31:13), planted by Abraham (Ge 21:33). *See Tree.*

TAMBOURINE Used by Miriam (Ex 15:20), by Jephthah's daughter (Jdg 11:34). Used in religious service (2Sa 6:5; 1Ch 13:8; Ps 68:25; 81:2; 149:3; 150:4). Used in dances (Job 21:12). *See Music, Instruments of.*

TAMIR *See Tadmor.*

TAMMUZ
1. Month four in sacred sequence, month ten in civil sequence. Not mentioned by name in the Bible. Ezekiel called in the fourth month (Eze 1:1); Nebuchadnezzar breaks through the wall of Jerusalem (Jer 39:1). The time for tending vines (June-July). *See Month, 4.*
2. The fertility god worshiped in Mesopotamia, Syria, and Israel; corresponded to Osiris in Egypt and Adonis of the Greeks (Eze 8:14).

TANACH *See Taanach.*

TANHUMETH (*comfort*). The father of Seraiah (2Ki 25:23; Jer 40:8).

TANIS *See Zoar.*

TANNER, TANNING Tanning is the conversion of skin into leather by removing the hair and soaking it in tanning solution (Ex 25:5; 26:14; Ac 10:6).

TANTALIZING NIV "provoking" (1Sa 1:6-7); "taunt" (1Ki 18:27).

TAPESTRY (Pr 7:16; 31:22). Of the tabernacle (Ex 26:1-14, 31-37; 27:9-17; 36:8-18). Gold thread woven in (Ex 39:3). In palaces (Est 1:6; SS 1:5). In groves (2Ki 23:7). *See Curtains; Embroidery; Veil.*

TAPHATH (possibly *little child*). The daughter of Solomon (1Ki 4:11).

TAPPUAH (*apple*).
1. A city of Judah (Jos 12:17; 15:34).
2. A city in Ephraim (Jos 16:8; 17:8).
3. A city near Tirzah in Samaria (2Ki 15:16); a variant reading for Tiphsah. *See Tiphsah, 2.*
4. The son of Hebron (1Ch 2:43).

TAR A flammable substance, asphalt (Ge 14:10). Lumps of asphalt are often seen even today floating in the southern end of the Dead Sea. Used as mortar in building the Tower of Babel (Ge 11:3), and in setting the burnt brick which formed the outer layers of the ziggurat of Ur. It was used by Moses' mother to caulk the papyrus basket (Ex 2:3), as for the rafts and reed boats on the Euphrates.
See Caulkers; Pitch.

TARAH *See Terah, 2.*

TARALAH A city of Benjamin between Irpeel and Zelah (Jos 18:28).

TAREA A son of Micah (1Ch 8:35). Called Tahrea (1Ch 9:41).

TARES *See Weeds, 2.*

TARGET A defensive article of armor. Made of bronze (1Sa 17:6), of gold (1Ki 10:16; 2Ch 9:15). Used by spearmen (2Ch 14:8).
See Shield.

TARIFF *See Duty, 1.*

TARPELITES *See Tripolis.*

TARSHISH (possibly *[precious stone] yellow jasper* BDB; possibly *greedy one* IDB; *foundry, refinery* KB).
1. The son of Javan (Ge 10:4).
2. A place in the W Mediterranean, perhaps in Spain or Tunisia (2Ch 9:21; 20:36-37; Ps 72:10; Jn 1:3).
3. "Ships of Tarshish", large, seagoing trade ships (1Ki 9:26; 10:22; 22:48; 2Ch 9:21).
4. Great-grandson of Benjamin (1Ch 7:10).
5. Persian prince (Est 1:14).

TARSUS Capital of Cilicia, in Asia Minor. Paul's birthplace (Ac 9:11; 21:39; 22:3). Paul sent to, from Jerusalem, to avoid assassination (Ac 9:30). Paul brought from, by Barnabas (Ac 11:25-26).

TARTAK A god worshiped by Avvites, colonists in Samaria (2Ki 17:31).

TARTAN *See Supreme Commander.*

TASKMASTER One who burdens another with labor: overseer (Ex 1:11; 3:7; 5:6, 10, 13).

TASSEL(S) Prescribed for garments worn by the Israelites, to remember God's commands (Nu 15:38-41; Dt 22:12). Made long by the Pharisees (Mt 23:5).

TASTE The sense of, lost (2Sa 19:35). Figurative (Job 27:2; Ps 34:8; 119:103; Heb 6:4-5; 1Pe 2:3); taste death (Mt 16:28; Mk 9:1; Lk 9:27; Jn 8:52; Heb 2:9). *See Savor; Savory Meat.*

TATTENAI The Persian governor ordered to assist the Jews in rebuilding the temple (Ezr 5:3, 6; 6:6, 13).

TATTLER *See Gossip; Talebearer.*

TATTOO Pagan custom; forbidden (Lev 19:28). *See Mark.*

TAVERNS, THREE A place, c. thirty-three miles SE of Rome where Paul met Roman Christians (Ac 28:15).

TAX Census (Ex 30:11-16; 38:26; Ne 10:32; Lk 2:1). Jesus pays (Mt 17:24-27).
Land (Ge 41:34, 48; 2Ki 23:35). Land mortgaged for (Ne 5:3-4). Priests exempted from (Ge 47:26; Ezr 7:24). Paid in grain (Am 5:11; 7:1), in provisions (1Ki 4:7-28).
Personal (1Ki 9:15; 2Ki 15:19-20; 23:35). Resisted by Israelites (1Ki 12:18; 2Ch 10:18). Worldwide, levied by Caesar.
Collectors of *See Tax Collectors.*

TAX COLLECTORS Disreputable (Isa 33:18; Da 11:20; Mt 5:46-47; 9:11; 11:19; 18:17; 21:31; Lk 18:11). Repent under the preaching of John the Baptist (Mt 21:32; Lk 3:12; 7:29). Matthew, the collector of Capernaum, becomes an apostle (Mt 9:9; 10:3; Mk 2:14; Lk 5:27). Parable concerning (Lk 18:9-14). Zacchaeus, chief among, receives Jesus into his house (Lk 19:2-10).

TEACHERS Samuel, head of school of the prophets (1Sa 19:20). Elisha, head of, at Gilgal (2Ki 4:38).
Itinerant (2Ch 17:7-9). Of public assemblies (Ne 8:1-8, 13, 18). Should receive compensation (Gal 6:6).
See Instruction; Jesus, Teacher; Minister, Duties of.

False:
Admonition against (Dt 13:1-3; Mt 5:19; 7:15; 15:2-20; 23:2-33; Lk 11:38-52).
See Heresy; Minister, False and Corrupt.

TEACHING *See Instruction; Minister, Duties of.*

TEAR *See Rending.*

TEARS (Ps 6:6; 39:12; 42:3). Wash Jesus' feet (Lk 7:38, 44). Observed by God (Ps 56:8; Isa 38:3-5). Wiped away (Rev 7:17). None in heaven (Rev 21:4). Figurative (Ps 80:5).

TEBAH (possibly *one born at the time or place of slaughtering* KB IDB).
1. The son of Nahor (Ge 22:24).
2. A city of Zobah, E of Anti-Lebanon Mountains (1Ch 18:7-9, ftn); a city belonging to Hadadezer, Hebrew Betah (2Sa 8:8, ftn).

TEBALIAH *See Tabaliah.*

TEBETH Month ten in sacred sequence, month four in civil sequence (December-January). Esther taken to King Xerxes (Est 2:16). *See Month, 10.*

TECHNICALITIES Legal (Mt 12:2, 10; Lk 6:2, 7).

TEETH (Pr 10:26). Gnashing of (Ps 112:10; La 2:16; Mt 8:12; 13:42, 50; 22:13; 24:51; 25:30; Mk 9:18; Lk 13:28).

TEHAPHNEHES *See Tahpanhes.*

TEHINNAH (*supplication for favor*). The son of Eshton (1Ch 4:12).

TEIL TREE *See Terebinth.*

TEKEL Weighed (Da 5:25, 27).

TEKOA, TEKOITE
1. The son of Ashhur (1Ch 2:24; 4:5). Some authorities interpret these passages to mean that Ashhur colonized the town of Tekoa.
2. A city in Judah (2Ch 11:6). Home of the woman who interceded for Absalom (2Sa 14:2, 4, 9). Rebuilt by Rehoboam (2Ch 11:6). Desert of (2Ch 20:20). People of, work on the new wall of Jerusalem (Ne 3:5, 27). Prophecy concerning (Jer 6:1). Home of Amos (Am 1:1).

TEKOAH *See Tekoa, 2.*

TEL A mound or hill that marks the site of an ancient city. Composed of accumulated debris, usually covering a number of archaeological or historical periods and showing numerous building levels or strata (Dt 13:16; Jer 30:18). In the following four place names.

TEL ABIB (*mound of barley* ISBE; Akkadian *mound of storm tide* KB; *mound of flood* IDB). A place on the Kebar River where Ezekiel lived (Eze 3:15).

TEL ASSAR (*ruined city mound of Assar*). A city or district conquered by the Assyrians (2Ki 19:12; Isa 37:12).

TEL HARSHA (*the ruined city mound of the deaf mute*). A place in Babylonia (Ezr 2:59; Ne 7:61).

TEL MELAH (*ruined city and mound of salt*). Babylonian town, probably not far N of Persian Gulf (Ezr 2:59; Ne 7:61).

TELAH (*fissure, split, fracture*). The son of Rephah (1Ch 7:25).

TELAIM (*lambs*). The place where Saul mustered an army against Amalek (1Sa 15:4), may be the same as Telem in Judah (Jos 15:24).

TELEM (*brightness*).
1. A city of Judah (Jos 15:24).
2. A gatekeeper who put away his Gentile wife (Ezr 10:24).

TELL EL AMARNA *See Amarna, Tell El; Ras Shamra.*

TEMA (*on the right side,* hence *south country*).
1. The son of Ishmael (Ge 25:15; 1Ch 1:30).
2. A people of Arabia, probably descended from Tema, Ishmael's son (Job 6:19; Isa 21:14; Jer 25:23).

TEMAH One of the temple servants (Ezr 2:53; Ne 7:55).

TEMAN (*on the right side,* hence *south country*).
1. The grandson of Esau (Ge 36:11).
2. Edomite chief (Ge 36:42).
3. A city in NE Edom (Jer 49:7).

TEMANI, TEMANITE(S) (*on the right side, southern*). Inhabitant of Teman (Ge 36:34). Of Eliphaz, one of Job's friends (Job 2:11; 4:1).

TEMENI (*one from the right,* hence *southerner*). The son of Ashhur (1Ch 4:6).

TEMPER *See Anger; Malice; Self-Control.*

TEMPERANCE (Php 4:5; Tit 1:8; 2Pe 1:6). In eating (Pr 23:1-3; 25:16). In the use of wine (1Ti 3:8; Tit 2:3).
Commanded (Ro 13:14; 1Th 5:6-8; 1Ti 3:2; Tit 2:2-3, 12; 2Pe 1:5-6).
Practiced: By athletes (1Co 9:25, 27). By Daniel (Da 1:8, 12-16).
See Abstinence; Drunkenness; Self-Control; Wine.

TEMPLE

Solomon's:

Described—
Also called Father's House (Jn 2:16). Glorious Temple (Isa 60:7). Holy Mountain (Isa 27:13). Holy and Glorious Temple (Isa 64:11). Holy Temple (Ps 79:1; 1Ch 29:3). House of Prayer (Isa 56:7; Mt 21:13). House of God (1Ch 29:2). House of the God of Jacob (Isa 2:3). House of the Lord (Jer 28:5). Mountain of the Lord's Temple (Isa 2:2). Palatial structure (1Ch 29:1, 19). Sanctuary (2Ch 20:8; 2Ch 36:17). Temple of the Lord (2Ki 11:10; 2Ch 23:9). Temple for Sacrifice (2Ch 7:12). Tent of the Testimony (2Ch 24:6). Zion (Ps 20:2; 48:12; 74:2; 87:2; Isa 2:3).

Greatness of (2Ch 2:5-6). Beauty of (Isa 64:11). Holiness of (1Ki 8:10; 9:3; La 1:10; Mt 23:17; Jn 2:14-16).

History—
David undertakes the building of (2Sa 7:2-3; 1Ch 22:7; 28:2; Ps 132:2-5; Ac 7:46), forbidden of God because he was a warrior (2Sa 7:4-12; 1Ki 5:3; 1Ch 22:8; 28:3). Not asked for by God (2Sa 7:7). The building of, committed to Solomon (2Sa 7:13). David makes preparations of (1Ch 22; 28:14-18; 29:1-5; 2Ch 3:1; 5:1).

Solomon builds (Ac 7:47; 2Sa 7:13). Solomon conscripts laborers for the building of (1Ki 5:13-16; 2Ch 2:2, 17-18). Materials for, furnished by Hiram (1Ki 5:8-18). Pattern and building of (1Ki 6; 7:13-51; 1Ch 28:11-19; 2Ch 3; 4; Ac 7:47). Time when begun (1Ki 6:1, 37; 2Ch 3:2), finished (1Ki 6:38). Site of (1Ch 21:28-30; 22:1; 2Ch 3:1), where Abraham offered Isaac (Ge 22:2, 4).

Materials prepared for (1Ki 5:17-18). No tools used on temple site (1Ki 6:7). Foundations of (1Ki 5:17-18; Lk 21:5).

Destroyed by Nebuchadnezzar, and the valuable contents carried to Babylon (2Ki 24:13; 25:9-17; 2Ch 36:7, 19; Ps 79:1; Isa 64:11; Jer 27:16, 19-22; 28:3; 52:13, 17-23; La 2:7; 4:1; Ezr 1:7). Vessels of, used by Belshazzar (Da 5:2-3). Destruction of, foretold (Isa 66:6; Jer 27:18-22; Eze 7:22, 25; Mt 24:2; Mk 13:2).

Restoration of, ordered by Cyrus (Ezr 1:7-11).

Areas and Furnishings of—
Inner Sanctuary (1Ki 6:19-20; 8:6). Called the Most Holy Place (2Ch 3:8), innermost room (1Ki 6:27).

Most Holy Place: Description of (1Ki 6:16, 19-35; 2Ch 3:8-14; 4:22). Contents of the Most Holy Place: Ark (1Ki 6:19; 8:6; 2Ch 5:2-10), cherubim (1Ki 6:23-28; 2Ch 3:10-13; 5:7-8). Called Holy Place (1Ki 8:8, 10), the main hall (2Ch 3:5). Description of (1Ki 6:15-18; 2Ch 3:3, 5-7, 14-17). *See Ark; Atonement Cover; Cherubim; Curtains; Veil.*

Holy Place (1Ki 8:8, 10). Contents of the holy place: The Golden table of the Bread of Presence (1Ki 7:48; 2Ch 29:18). *See Bread, Consecrated.* Other tables of gold and silver (1Ch 28:16; 2Ch 4:18-19). Lampstands and their utensils (1Ki 7:49-50; 1Ch 28:15; 2Ch 4:7, 20-22). *See Lampstand.* Altar of incense and its furniture (1Ki 6:20; 7:48, 50; 1Ch 28:17-18; 2Ch 4:19, 22). *See Altar of Incense.*

Porch of, called Porch of the Lord (2Ch 15:8). Dimensions of (1Ki 6:3; 2Ch 3:4). Doors of (2Ch 29:7). Overlaid with gold (2Ch 3:4). Pillars of (1Ki 7:15-22; 2Ki 11:14; 23:3; 25:17; 2Ch 3:15-17; 4:12-13).

Structure around (1Ki 6:5-10; 2Ki 11:2-3). Offerings brought to (Ne 10:37-39). Treasuries in. *See Treasure.*

Courts of: Of the priests (2Ch 4:9), inner (1Ki 6:36), surrounded by rows of stones and cedar beams (1Ki 6:36; 7:12). Contents of the courts: Altar of burnt offering (2Ch 15:8). *See Altar.* The Sea of cast metal (1Ki 7:23-37, 44, 46; 2Ch 4:2-5, 10), ten basins (1Ki 7:38-46; 2Ch 4:6). Large court of (2Ch 4:9; Jer 19:14; 26:2).

Sabbath canopy and royal entryway (2Ki 16:18).

Gates of: Upper Gate (2Ki 15:35). New Gate (Jer 26:10; 36:10). Gate facing east (Eze 46:1, 12). Gifts received at (2Ch 24:8-11).

Uses of—
A dwelling place of the Lord (1Ki 8:10-11, 13; 9:3; 2Ki 21:7; 1Ch 29:1; 2Ch 5:13-14; 7:1-3, 16; Eze 10:3-4; Mic 1:2), to contain the ark of the covenant (1Ki 8:21), for the offering of fragrant incense (2Ch 2:4), for the regular offering of consecrated bread and the burnt offerings (2Ch 2:4), for prayer and worship (1Ki 8; 2Ki 19:14-15; 2Ch 30:27; Isa 27:13; 56:7; Jer 7:2; 26:2; Eze 46:2-3, 9; Zec 7:2-3; 8:21-22; Mk 11:17; Lk 1:10; 2:37; 18:10; Ac 3:1; 22:17), prayer made toward (1Ki 8:38; Da 6:10; Jnh 2:4), for weapon storage (2Ki 11:10; 2Ch 23:9-10), for refuge (2Ki 11:15; Ne 6:10-11).

Facts About—
Dedication of (1Ki 8; 2Ch 5-7), services in, organized by David (1Ch 15:16; 23:24). Sacking and pillaging by Shishak (1Ki 14:25-26), by Jehoash, king of Israel (2Ki 14:14). Repaired by Jehoash, king of Judah (2Ki 12:4-14; 2Ch 24:7-14), by Josiah (2Ki 22:3-7; 2Ch 34:8-13). Ahaz changes the detailed plans (2Ki 16:10-17). Purified by Hezekiah (2Ch 29:15-19). Converted into an idolatrous shrine by Manasseh (2Ki 21:4-7; 2Ch 33:4-7).

Treasures of, used in the purchase of peace: By Asa, from Ben-Hadad (1Ki 15:18), by Jehoash, king of Judah, from Hazael (2Ki 12:18), by Hezekiah, from the king of Assyria (2Ki 18:15-16). Jews swore by (Mt 23:16-22).

Ezekiel's Vision: (Eze 37:26, 28; 40-48).

The Second:
Rebuilt by Zerubbabel (Ezr 1; 2:68-69; 3:2-13; 4; 5:2-17; 6:3-5; Ne 7:70-72; Isa 44:28; Hag 2:3). Building of, suspended (Ezr 4), resumed (Ezr 4:24; 5; 6; Hag 1:2-9; 2:15; Zec 8:9), finished (Ezr 6:14-15), dedicated (Ezr 6:15-18). Artaxerxes' favorable action toward (Ezr 7:11-28; 8:25-34).

Prophecies of its restoration (Isa 44:28; Da 8:13-14; Hag 1; 2; Zec 1:16; 4:8-10; 6:12-15; 8:9-15; Mal 3:1).

Herod's—
Forty-six years in building (Jn 2:20). Massive and beautiful stones of (Mk 13:1; Lk 21:5). Magnificence of (Mt 24:1). Beautiful gate of (Ac 3:10). Solomon's Colonnade (Jn 10:23; Ac 3:11; 5:12). Treasury of (Mk 12:41-44). Zechariah receives promise of a son (Lk 1:5-23, w 1:57-64). Jesus the infant brought to, according to the law and custom (Lk 2:21-39), Simeon blesses Jesus in (Lk 2:25-35), Anna the prophetess never left (Lk 2:36-37).

Jesus in, when a youth (Lk 2:46), taken to the highest point of, in his temptation (Mt 4:5-7; Lk 4:9-12), teaches in (Mk 11:27-33; 12:35-44; 14:49; Jn 5:14-47; 7:14-28; 8; 10:23-38; 18:20), performs miracles in (Mt 21:14-15), drives money changers from (Mt 21:12-13; Mk 11:15-17; Lk 19:45-46; Jn 2:15-16).

Officer of temple guard (Lk 22:52; Ac 4:1; 5:24, 26). Judas threw the money into (Mt 27:5). Veil of, torn at the time of the crucifixion (Mt 27:51).

The disciples worship in, after the resurrection (Lk 24:53; Ac 2:46; 3:1). Peter heals the crippled man at the gate of (Ac 3:1-16). Disciples preach in (Ac 5:20-21, 42). Paul's vision in (Ac 22:17-21). Paul observes the rights of (Ac 21:26-30), is arrested in (Ac 21:33).

Prophecies concerning its destruction, by Daniel (Da 8:11-15; 11:30-31). Jesus predicts the destruction of (Mt 24; Mk 13:2; Lk 21:6).

Figurative:
Of the body of Jesus (Mt 26:61; 27:40; Jn 2:19). Of the indwelling of God (1Co 3:16-17; 2Co 6:16). Of the church (Eph 2:21; 2Th 2:4; Rev 3:12). Of the kingdom of Christ (Rev 11; 14:15, 17). Of Christ, the head of the church, sending forth the forces of righteousness against the powers of evil (Rev 15:5-8; 16:1-17).

Idolatrous:
Of Dagon, at Ashdod (1Sa 5:2), of the calves, at Bethel (1Ki 12:31, 33), of Rimmon, at Damascus (2Ki 5:18), of Baal, at Samaria (2Ki 10:21, 27), at Babylon (2Ch 36:7; Da 1:2), of Diana, at Ephesus (Ac 19:27).

Trophies stored in (1Sa 31:10; 1Ch 10:9-10; Da 1:2).

See Tabernacle.

TEMPLE SERVANTS
Large group of servants who performed menial tasks in the temple (1Ch 9:2; Ezr 2:43-58; 8:17-20; Ne 7:46-56), probably descended from Midianites (Nu 31:47), Gibeonites (Jos 9:23), and other captives. Usually listed with the priests, Levites, singers, and gatekeepers (Ezr 2:70).

TEMPORAL BLESSINGS
See Blessings.

TEMPTATION
(*trial, proof*). Has two meanings: Any attempt to entice or tempt into evil; a testing which aims at an ultimate spiritual good.

Temptation to Evil:
(Pr 12:26; Ro 8:35-39). Called snares of death (Pr 13:14; 14:27).

The way of escape from (1Co 10:13). Christ gives help in (Heb 2:18; 4:15; Rev 3:10). The Lord delivers from (2Pe 2:9).

Benefits of: (Jas 1:2-4, 12; 1Pe 1:6-7).

Leading into:
To be avoided (Mt 5:29-30; 6:9; Mk 9:42-48; Lk 17:1; Ro 14:13, 15, 21; 1Co 7:5; 8:9-13; 10:28-32). Prayer against being led into (Mt 6:13; 26:41; Mk 14:38; Lk 11:4; 22:40, 46). Not to lead others into (Ro 14:13-15, 21; 1Co 7:5; 8:9-13; 10:28-32).

Instances of—
Abraham, of Pharaoh (Ge 12:18-19), of Abimelech (Ge 20:9). Rebekah, of Jacob (Ge 27:6-14). Balak, of Balaam (Nu 22:5-7, 16-17; 23:11-13, 25-27). Eli's sons, of Israel (1Sa 2:24-25). Gideon, of Israel (Jdg 8:27). The old prophet of Bethel, of the prophet of Judah (1Ki 13:15-19). Jeroboam, of Israel (1Ki 15:30, 34).

Resistance to:
Commanded (Dt 7:25-26; Pr 1:10-19; 4:14-15; 5:3, 8; 19:27; Mt 24:42-44; 25:13; 26:41; Mk 13:21-22; 13:33-37; 14:37-38; Ro 6:12-14; 12:21; Eph 6:11, 13-17; Jas 4:7; 1Pe 5:8-9; 1Jn 4:4). Source of resistance (Ps 17:4; 73:2-25; 94:17-18).

Rewards to those who resist (Isa 33:15-16; Jas 1:12; Rev 3:10).

Instances of—
Joseph (Ge 39:7-12). Balaam (Nu 22:7-18, 38; 23:7-12, 18-24). David (1Sa 26:5-25). The prophet of Judah (1Ki 13:7-9). Micaiah (1Ki 22:13-28). The people of Jerusalem (2Ki 18:30-36). Job (Job 1:6-21; 2:4-10; 31:1, 5-17, 19-34, 38-40). Recabites (Jer 35:5-9). Nehemiah (Ne 4:9).

Jesus (Mt 4:1-11; 26:38-42; Lk 4:1-3; Heb 4:15; 12:3-4).

Sources of:
Cherished pleasures (Mt 5:29-30; 18:7-9; Mk 9:43-45). Evil company (Ex 34:13-16; Pr 2:10-16). Adultery and sexual desires (Pr 5:1-20; 6:24-29; 7:1-27; 9:15-18; Ecc 7:26). Sinful desires (Ro 7:5; Gal 5:17; Jas 1:13-15; 2Pe 2:18; 1Jn 2:16-17). False teachers (Mt 18:6-7; Lk 17:1; 1Jn 2:26; 4:1-3; Rev 2:20). Persecutions (Jn 16:1-2). Prosperity (Dt 8:10-17; Lk 12:16-21). Riches (Mt 19:16-24; Mk 10:17-30; 1Ti 6:9-10). Cares, riches and pleasures (Mt 13:22; Lk 8:13-14; 21:34-38).

Satan (Ge 3:1-5; 1Ch 21:1; Mk 4:15, 17; Lk 22:3, 31-32; 2Co 2:11; 11:3, 14-15; 12:7; Gal 4:14; Eph 4:27; 6:11, 13-17; 1Th 3:5; 1Ti 5:15; Jas 4:7; 1Pe 5:8-9; Rev 12:10-11, 17).

Wicked people (Pr 16:29; 28:10; Hos 7:5; Am 2:12; Mt 5:19; 2Ti 3:13).

See Demons; Faith, Trial of; Satan.

Warnings Against Yielding to:
(Ex 34:12-16; Dt 8:11-20; Pr 2:10-16; 5:1-21; 6:27-28; 7:1-27; 9:15-18; Ecc 7:26; Jer 2:25; Mt 26:31, 41; Mk 14:37-38; Lk 21:34-36; 22:40; 1Co 16:13; Eph 6:11, 13-17; Heb 12:3-4; 1Pe 4:7; 5:8-9; 2Pe 3:17; Rev 3:2-3).

Instances of—
Adam and Eve (Ge 3:1-19). Sarah, to lie (Ge 12:13; 18:13-15; 20:13). Isaac, to lie (Ge 26:7). Jacob to defraud Esau (Ge 27:6-13). Balaam (Nu 22:15-22; 2Pe 2:15). Achan (Jos 7:21). David, to commit adultery (2Sa 11:2-5), to number Israel (1Ch 21). Solomon, to become an idolater through the influences of his wives (1Ki 11:4; Ne 13:26). The prophet of Judah (1Ki 13:11-19). Hezekiah (2Ki 20:12-20; Isa 39:1-4, 6-7). Peter (Mt 26:69-74; Mk 14:67-71; Lk 22:55-60).

Of Jesus:
(Lk 22:28). In all points as we are (Heb 4:15). By the devil (Mt 4:1-11; Mk 1:12-13; Lk 4:1-13). Before his crucifixion (Mt 26:38-42).

Test of God:
Design of, a test (Ps 66:10-13; 119:101, 110; Da 12:10; Zec 13:9; 1Pe 1:6-7; 4:12). Of fidelity (Dt 13:1-3; 2Ch 32:31; Job 1:8-22; 2:3-10). Of obedience (Ge 22:1-14; Dt 8:2, 5; Heb 11:17).

Benefits of (Jas 1:2-4, 12; 1Pe 1:6-7). Rewards of (Isa 33:15-16; Lk 12:35-38; Jas 1:12; 1Jn 4:4).

See Affliction; Afflictions; Faith, Trial of.

TEN
Used for an indefinite number (Ge 31:7; Lev 26:26; Nu 14:22; Zec 8:23).

TEN COMMANDMENTS
See Commandments and Statutes, Of God; Decalogue.

TENANTS
Evicted (Mt 21:41; Mk 12:9; Lk 20:16).

TENONS
NIV "projections" on tabernacle boards to hold the boards in place (Ex 26:17).

TENSION
See Anxiety.

TENT
Used for dwelling (Ge 4:20), by Noah (Ge 9:21), by Abraham (Ge 12:8; 13:18; 18:1), by Lot (Ge 13:5), by Moses (Ex 18:7), by Israelites (Nu 24:5-6; 2Sa 20:1; 1Ki 12:16), by the Midianites (Jdg 6:5), by Cushites (Hab 3:7), by Arabs (Isa 13:20), by shepherds (Isa 38:12; Jer 6:3). Women had tents apart from men (Ge 24:67; 31:33). Used for cattle (2Ch 14:15). Manufacture of (Ac 18:3). Used as a place of worship. *See Tabernacle.*

TERAH
1. The son of Nahor (Ge 11:24-25), father of Abraham, Nahor, Haran (Ge 11:26), idolater (Jos 24:2), went as far as Haran with Abraham (Ge 11:24-32).

2. The encampment of the Israelites in wilderness (Nu 33:27-28).

TERAPHIM
See Household Gods; Idolatry.

TEREBINTH
A small tree (Isa 6:13; Hos 4:13).

TERESH
(perhaps *desire*). A Persian eunuch. Plotted against Xerxes (Est 2:21-23; 6:2).

TERRACE
Steps leading up to the temple (2Ch 9:11).

TERROR
Extreme fear or dread; or sometimes the one who causes such agitation (Ge 35:5; Ps 55:4; 2Co 5:11).

TERTIUS
(*third*). Paul's amanuensis in writing the book of Romans (Ro 16:22).

TERTULLUS
(*third*). Diminutive of Tertius; lawyer employed by the Jews to state their case against Paul before Felix (Ac 24:1).

TESTAMENT
1. A covenant. *See Covenant.*

2. Testamentary disposition or will. *See Will, A Testament.*

3. Divisions of the English Bible. *See New Testament, Old Testament.*

TESTAMENTS OF THE TWELVE PROPHETS
A pseudepigraphal document that claims to report the last words of the twelve sons of Jacob; probably written c. second century A.D.

TESTAMENTS, TIME BETWEEN
A time of the realignment of traditional power blocs and the passing of a Near Eastern cultural tradition that had been dominant for almost 3000 years.

In biblical history, the approximately 400 years that separate the time of Nehemiah from the birth of Christ are known as the intertestamental period (c. 432-5 B.C.). Sometimes called the "silent" years, they were anything but silent. The events, literature and social forces of these years would shape the world of the NT.

History:
With the Babylonian captivity, Israel ceased to be an independent nation and became a minor territory in a succession of larger empires. Very little is known about the latter years of Persian domination because the Jewish historian Josephus, our primary source for the intertestamental period, all but ignores them.

With Alexander the Great's acquisition of Israel (332 B.C.), a new and more insidious threat to Israel emerged. Alexander was committed to the creation of a world united by Greek language and culture, a policy followed by his successors. This policy, called Hellenization, had a dramatic impact on the Jews.

At Alexander's death (323 B.C.) the empire he won was divided among his generals. Two of them founded dynasties—the Ptolemies in Egypt and the Seleucids in Syria and Mesopotamia—that would contend for control of Israel for over a century.

The rule of the Ptolemies was considerate of Jewish religious sensitivities, but in 198 B.C. the Seleucids took control and paved the way for one of the most heroic periods in Jewish history.

The early Seleucid years were largely a continuation of the tolerant rule of the Ptolemies, but Antiochus IV Epiphanes (whose title means "God made manifest" and who ruled 175-164 B.C.) changed that when he attempted to consolidate his fading empire through a policy of radical Hellenization. While a segment of the Jewish aristocracy had already adopted Greek ways, the majority of Jews were outraged.

Antiochus's atrocities were aimed at the eradication of Jewish religion. He prohibited some of the central elements of Jewish practice, attempted to destroy all copies of the Torah (the Pentateuch), and required offerings to the Greek god Zeus. His crowning outrage was the erection of a statue of Zeus and the sacrificing of a pig in the Jerusalem temple itself.

Opposition to Antiochus was led by Mattathias, an elderly villager from a priestly family, and his five sons: Judas (Maccabeus), Jonathan, Simon, John, and Eleazar. Mattathias destroyed a Greek altar established in his village, Modein, and killed Antiochus's emissary. This triggered the Maccabean revolt, a 24-year war

T

(166-142 B.C.) that resulted in the independence of Judah until the Romans took control in 63 B.C.

The victory of Mattathias's family was Pyrrhic, however. With the death of his last son, Simon, the Hasmonean dynasty that they founded soon evolved into an aristocratic, Hellenistic regime sometimes hard to distinguish from that of the Seleucids. During the reign of Simon's son, John Hyrcanus, the orthodox Jews who had supported the Maccabees fell out of favor. With only a few exceptions, the rest of the Hasmoneans supported the Jewish Hellenizers. The Pharisees were actually persecuted by Alexander Janneus (103-76 B.C.).

The Hasmonean dynasty ended when, in 63 B.C., an expanding Roman empire intervened in a dynastic clash between the two sons of Janneus, Aristobulus II and Hyrcanus II. Pompey, the general who subdued the East for Rome, took Jerusalem after a three-month siege of the temple area, massacring priests in the performance of their duties and entering the Most Holy Place. This sacrilege began Roman rule in a way that Jews could neither forgive nor forget.

Literature:

During these unhappy years of oppression and internal strife, the Jewish people produced a sizable body of literature that both recorded and addressed their era. Three of the more significant works are the Septuagint, the Apocrypha and the Dead Sea Scrolls.

Septuagint—

Jewish legend says that seventy-two scholars, under the sponsorship of Ptolemy Philadelphus (c. 250 B.C.), were brought together on the island of Pharos, near Alexandria, where they produced a Greek translation of the OT in seventy-two days. From this tradition the Latin word for seventy, "Septuagint," became the name attached to the translation. The Roman numeral for seventy, LXX, is used as an abbreviation for it.

Behind the legend lies the probability that at least the Torah (the five books of Moses) was translated into Greek c. 250 B.C. for the use of the Greek-speaking Jews of Alexandria. The rest of the OT and some noncanonical books were also included in the LXX before the dawning of the Christian era, though it is difficult to be certain when.

The Septuagint quickly became the Bible of the Jews outside Israel who, like the Alexandrians, no longer spoke Hebrew. It would be difficult to overestimate its influence. It made the Scriptures available both to the Jews who no longer spoke their ancestral language and to the entire Greek-speaking world. It later became the Bible of the early church. Also, its widespread popularity and use contributed to the retention of the Apocrypha by some branches of Christendom.

Apocrypha—

Derived from a Greek word that means "hidden," Apocrypha has acquired the meaning "false," but in a technical sense it describes a specific body of writings. This collection consists of a variety of books and additions to canonical books that, with the exception of 2 Esdras (c. A.D. 90), were written during the intertestamental period. Their recognition as authoritative in Roman and Eastern Christianity is the result of a complex historical process.

The canon of the OT accepted by Protestants today was very likely established by the dawn of the second century A.D., though after the fall of Jerusalem and the destruction of the temple in 70. The precise scope of the OT was discussed among the Jews until the Council of Jamnia (c. 90). This Hebrew canon was not accepted by the early church, which used the Septuagint. In spite of disagreements among some of the church fathers as to which books were canonical and which were not, the Apocryphal books continued in common use by most Christians until the Reformation. During this period most Protestants decided to follow the original Hebrew canon while Rome, at the Council of Trent (1546) and more recently at the First Vatican Council (1869-70), affirmed the larger "Alexandrian" canon that includes the Apocrypha.

The Apocryphal books have retained their place primarily through the weight of ecclesiastical authority, without which they would not commend themselves as canonical literature. There is no clear evidence that Jesus or the apostles ever quoted any Apocryphal works as Scripture (Jude 14). The Jewish community that produced them repudiated them, and the historical surveys in the apostolic sermons recorded in Acts completely ignore the period they cover. Even the sober, historical account of 1 Maccabees is tarnished by numerous errors and anachronisms.

There is nothing of theological value in the Apocryphal books that cannot be duplicated in canonical Scripture, and they contain much that runs counter to its teachings. Nonetheless, this body of literature does provide a valuable source of information for the study of the intertestamental period.

Dead Sea Scrolls—

In the spring of 1947 an Arab shepherd chanced upon a cave in the hills overlooking the southwestern shore of the Dead Sea that contained what has been called "the greatest manuscript discovery of modern times."

The documents and fragments of documents found in those caves, dubbed the "Dead Sea Scrolls," included OT books, a few books of the Apocrypha, apocalyptic works, pseudepigrapha (books that purport to be the work of ancient heroes of the faith), and a number of books peculiar to the sect that produced them.

Approximately a third of the documents are Biblical, with Psalms, Deuteronomy and Isaiah—the books quoted most often in the NT—occurring most frequently. One of the most remarkable finds was a complete 24-foot-long scroll of Isaiah.

The Scrolls have made a significant contribution to the quest for a form of the OT texts most accurately reflecting the original manuscripts; they provide copies a thousand years closer to the originals than were previously known. The understanding of Biblical Hebrew and Aramaic and knowledge of the development of Judaism between the Testaments have been increased significantly. Of great importance to readers of the Bible is the demonstration of the care with which OT texts were copied, thus providing objective evidence for the general reliability of those texts.

Social Developments:

The Judaism of Jesus' day is, to a large extent, the result of changes that came about in response to the pressures of the intertestamental period.

Diaspora—

The Diaspora (dispersion) of Israel begun in the Exile accelerated during these years until a writer of the day could say that Jews filled "every land and sea."

Jews outside Israel, cut off from the temple, concentrated their religious life in the study of the Torah and the life of the synagogue (see below). The missionaries of the early church began their Gentile ministries among the Diaspora, using their Greek translation of the OT.

Sadducees—

In Israel, the Greek world made its greatest impact through the party of the Sadducees. Made up of aristocrats, it became the temple party. Because of their position, the Sadducees had a vested interest in the status quo.

Relatively few in number, they wielded disproportionate political power and controlled the high priesthood. They rejected all religious writings except the Torah, as well as any doctrine (such as the Resurrection) not found in those five books.

Synagogue—

During the Exile, Israel was cut off from the temple, divested of nationhood and surrounded by pagan religious practices. Her faith was threatened with extinction. Under these circumstances, the exiles turned their religious focus from what they had lost to what they retained—the Torah and the belief that they were God's people. They concentrated on the law rather than nationhood, on personal piety rather than sacramental rectitude, and on prayer as an acceptable replacement for the sacrifices denied to them.

When they returned from the Exile, they brought with them this new form of religious expression, as well as the synagogue (its center), and Judaism became a faith that could be practiced wherever the Torah could be carried.

The emphases on personal piety and a relationship with God, which characterized synagogue worship, not only helped preserve Judaism but also prepared the way for the Christian gospel.

Pharisees—

As the party of the synagogue, the Pharisees strove to reinterpret the law. They built a "hedge" around it to enable Jews to live righteously before God in a world that had changed drastically since the days of Moses. Although they were comparatively few in number, the Pharisees enjoyed the support of the people and influenced popular opinion if not national policy. They were the only party to survive the destruction of the temple in A.D. 70 and were the spiritual progenitors of modern Judaism.

Essenes—

An almost forgotten Jewish sect until the discovery of the Dead Sea Scrolls, the Essenes were a small, separatist group that grew out of the conflicts of the Maccabean age. Like the Pharisees, they stressed strict legal observance, but they considered the temple priesthood corrupt and rejected much of the temple ritual and sacrificial system. Mentioned by several ancient writers, the precise nature of the Essenes is still not certain, though it is generally agreed that the Qumran community that produced the Dead Sea Scrolls was an Essene group.

Because they were convinced that they were the true remnant, these Qumran Essenes had separated themselves from Judaism at large and devoted themselves to personal purity and preparation for the final war between the "Sons of Light and the Sons of Darkness." They practiced an apocalyptic faith, looking back to the contributions of their "Teacher of Righteousness" and forward to the coming of two, and possibly three, Messiahs. The destruction of the temple in A.D. 70, however, seems to have delivered a death blow to their apocalyptic expectations.

Attempts have been made to equate aspects of the beliefs of the Qumran community with the origins of Christianity. Some have seen a prototype of Jesus in their "Teacher of Righteousness," and both John the Baptist and Jesus have been assigned membership in the sect. There is, however, only a superficial, speculative base for these conjectures.

TESTIMONY

Commandments:

Those revealed to Moses (Ex 25:16; Dt 4:44-45; 1Ki 2:3). Kept in the ark (Ex 25:16, 21). Engraved on tablets (Ex 31:18; 32:15; 38:21). Atonement cover was over (Ex 26:34; 30:6; 40:20).

Ark, called ark of (Ex 25:22; 26:34; 40:3, 5, 20-21). Tabernacle called tabernacle of (Nu 1:50, 53; 9:19; 10:11). *See Ark; Tabernacle.*

See Commandments and Statutes, Of God; Decalogue.

Legal: *See Evidence; Witness.*

Religious:

(Ps 18:49; 22:22; 26:12; 34:1-4, 8-9; 77:12; 119:13, 26-27, 46, 67, 71; Isa 43:10; 44:8; 45:24; 1Co 1:5-6; 12:3; 15:15).

Required of the righteous (1Ch 16:8-9; Ps 9:11; Isa 12:4-6; 43:10; 44:8; Jer 51:10; Mt 4:21; 5:15-16, 19-20; Mk 4:21; 5:19-20; Lk 8:16, 39; 24:48; Jn 15:27; Ac 1:8, 22; 3:15; 5:32; 13:31; Ro 10:9-10; Eph 5:19; 2Ti 1:8; 1Pe 3:15; 5:12).

Concerning God's, faithfulness (Ps 73:23-26, 28; 89:1), glory (Ps 145:11-12), merciful providence (Ps 40:1-3; 54:7; 91:2-13; Da 4:2-3; Ac 14:15-17), righteousness (Ps 35:28; 71:16), salvation (Ps 30:1-6; 40:1-3; 62:1-2; 66:16-20; 71:15, 18; Gal 2:20; Php 3:4-14; Tit 3:3-7; Heb 2:3, 12), words (Ps 119:172), works (Ps 71:17, 24; 145:4-7, 10-12; Jer 51:10; Ac 2:11).

Concerning confidence in God (Ps 16:5-9; 18:2-3, 35-36; 23:1-6; 26:6-7; 27:1-6, 13; 28:6-8; 30:1-6). Rewards of (Mt 10:32; Lk 12:8). Victory by (Rev 12:11).

Exemplified by:

Job (Job 19:25-27). The psalmist (Ps 35:28; 40:1-3, 9; 57:7-9; 116:1-19). Nebuchadnezzar (Da 4:34-37). The woman of Sychar (Jn 4:28-30, 39, 41-42). The blind man whom Jesus healed (Jn 9:17, 30-33). The apostles to the resurrection of Jesus (Ac 4:33; 1Jn 1:1-4). The disciples at Pentecost (Ac 2:4-11). Peter (Ac 4:18-20; 1Pe 5:1, 12; 2Pe 1:16). John (Ac 4:18-20; 1Jn 1:1-4). Paul's conversion (Ac 22:1-16; 26:12-23), devotion to Christ (1Co 13:1; Php 3:4-14), confidence in Christ (2Co 4:13-14; 5:1; 2Ti 1:12), hope of the crown of righteousness (2Ti 4:7-8), hope of eternal life (Tit 1:1-2).

TETRARCH Ruler of a fourth part of a region (Mt 14:1; Lk 3:1; 9:7; Ac 13:1).

TEXTS, ANCIENT NEAR EASTERN NON-BIBLICAL TEXTS RELATING TO THE OLD TESTAMENT

Major representative examples of ancient Near Eastern non-biblical documents that provide parallels to or shed light on various OT passages.

Amarna Letters: [Canaanite Akkadian]—*fourteenth century B.C. Hundreds of letters, written primarily by Canaanite scribes, illuminate social, political and religious relationships between Canaan and Egypt during the reigns of Amenhotep III and Akhenaten.*

Amenemope's Wisdom: [Egyptian]—*early first millennium B.C. Thirty chapters of wisdom instruction are similar to Pr 22:17-24:22 and provide the closest external parallels to OT wisdom literature.*

Atrahasis Epic: [Akkadian]—*early second millennium B.C. A cosmological epic depicts Creation and early human history, including the Flood (cf. Ge 1-9).*

Babylonian Theodicy: [Akkadian]—*early first millennium B.C. A sufferer and his friend dialogue with each other (cf. Job).*

Cyrus Cylinder: [Akkadian]—*sixth century B.C. King Cyrus of Persia records the conquest of Babylon (cf. Da 5:30; 6:28) and boasts of his generous policies toward his new subjects and their gods.*

Dead Sea Scrolls: [Hebrew, Aramaic, Greek]—*third century B.C. to first century A.D. Several hundred scrolls and fragments include the oldest copies of OT books and passages.*

Ebal Tablets: [Sumerian, Eblaite]—*mid-third millennium B.C. Thousands of commercial, legal, literary, and epistolary texts describe the cultural vitality and political power of a prepatriarchal civilization in northern Syria.*

Elephantine Papyri: [Aramaic]—*late fifth century B.C. Contracts and letters document life among Israelites who fled to southern Egypt after Jerusalem was destroyed in 586 B.C.*

Enuma Elish: [Akkadian]—*early second millennium B.C. Marduk, the Babylonian god of cosmic order, is elevated to the supreme position in the pantheon. The seven-tablet epic contains an account of creation (cf. Ge 1-2).*

Gezer Calendar: [Hebrew]—*tenth century B.C. A schoolboy from west-central Israel describes the seasons, crops and farming activity of the agricultural year.*

Gilgamesh Epic: [Akkadian]—*early second millennium B.C. Gilgamesh, ruler of Uruk, experiences numerous adventures, including a meeting with Utnapishtim, the only survivor of a great deluge (cf. Ge 6-9).*

Hammurapi's Code: [Akkadian]—*eighteenth century B.C. Together with similar law codes that preceded and followed it, the Code of Hammurapi exhibits close parallels to numerous passages in the Mosaic laws of the OT.*

Hymn to the Aten: [Egyptian]—*fourteenth century B.C. The poem praises the beneficence and universality of the sun in language somewhat similar to that used in Ps 104.*

Ishtar's Descent: [Akkadian]—*first millennium B.C. The goddess Ishtar temporarily descends to the netherworld, which is pictured in terms reminiscent of OT descriptions of Sheol.*

Jehoiachin's Ration Dockets: [Akkadian]—*early sixth century B.C. Brief texts from the reign of Nebuchadnezzar II refer to rations allotted to Judah's exiled king Jehoiachin and his sons (cf. 2Ki 25:27-30).*

King Lists: [Sumerian]—*late third millennium B.C. The reigns of Sumerian kings before the Flood are described as lasting for thousands of years, reminding us of the longevity of the pre-Flood patriarchs in Ge 5.*

Lachish Letters: [Hebrew]—*early sixth century B.C. Inscriptions on pottery fragments vividly portray the desperate days preceding the Babylonian siege of Jerusalem in 588-586 B.C. (cf. Jer 34:7).*

Lamentation Over the Destruction of Ur:

[Sumerian]—*early second millennium B.C. The poem mourns the destruction of the city of Ur at the hands of the Elamites (cf. the OT book of Lamentations).*

Ludlul Bel Nemeqi: [Akkadian]—*late second millennium B.C. A suffering Babylonian nobleman describes his distress in terms faintly reminiscent of the experience of Job.*

Mari Tablets: [Akkadian]—*eighteenth century B.C. Letters and administration texts provide detailed information regarding customs, language, and personal names that reflect the culture of the OT patriarchs.*

Merneptah Stele: [Egyptian]—*thirteenth century B.C. Pharaoh Merneptah figuratively describes his victory over various peoples in western Asia, including "Israel."*

Mesha Stele (*Moabite Stone*)**:** [Moabite]—*ninth century B.C. Mesha, king of Moab (see 2Ki 3:4), rebels against a successor of Israel's king Omri.*

Murashu Tablets: [Akkadian]—*fifth century B.C. Commercial documents describe financial transactions engaged in by Murashu and Sons, a Babylonian firm that did business with Jews and other exiles.*

Mursilis's Treaty with Duppi-Tessub:

[Hittite]—*mid-second millennium B.C. King Mursilis imposes a suzerainty treaty on King Duppi-Tessub. The literary outline of this and other Hittite treaties is strikingly paralleled in OT covenants established by God with his people.*

Nabonidus Chronicle: [Akkadian]—*mid-sixth century* B.C. *The account describes the absence of King Nabonidus from Babylon. His son Belshazzar is therefore the regent in charge of the kingdom (cf. Da 5:29-30).*

Nebuchadnezzar Chronicle: [Akkadian]—*early sixth century* B.C. *A chronicle from the reign of Nebuchadnezzar II includes the Babylonian account of the siege of Jerusalem in 597* B.C. *(2Ki 24:10-17).*

Nuzi Tablets: [Akkadian]—*mid-second millennium* B.C. *Adoption, birthright sale and other legal documents graphically illustrate OT patriarchal customs current centuries earlier.*

Pessimistic Dialogue: [Akkadian]—*early first millennium* B.C. *A master and his servant discuss the pros and cons of various activities (cf. Ecc 1-2).*

Ras Shamra Tablets: [Ugaritic]—*fifteenth century* B.C. *Canaanite deities and rulers experience adventures in epics that enrich our understanding of Canaanite mythology and religion and of OT poetry.*

Sargon Legend: [Akkadian]—*first millennium* B.C. *Sargon I (the Great), ruler of Akkad in the late third millennium* B.C. *claims to have been rescued as an infant from a reed basket found floating in a river (cf. Ex 2).*

Sargon's Display Inscription: [Akkadian]— *eighth century* B.C. *Sargon II takes credit for the conquest of Samaria in 722/721* B.C. *and states that he captured and exiled 27, 290 Israelites.*

Sennacherib's Prism: [Akkadian]—*early seventh century* B.C. *Sennacherib vividly describes his siege of Jerusalem in 701* B.C., *making Hezekiah a prisoner in his own royal city (but cf. 2Ki 19:35-37).*

Seven Lean Years Tradition: [Egyptian]—*second century* B.C. *Egypt experiences seven years of low Nile levels and famine, which, by a contractual agreement between Pharaoh Djoser (twenty-eighth century* B.C.*) and a god, will be followed by prosperity (cf. Ge 41).*

Shalmaneser's Black Obelisk: [Akkadian]—*ninth century* B.C. *Israel's king Jehu (or his servant) presents tribute to Assyria's king Shalmaneser III. Additional Assyrian and Babylonian texts refer to other kings of Israel and Judah.*

Shishak's Geographical List: [Egyptian]— *tenth century* B.C. *Pharaoh Shishak lists the cities that he captured or made tributary during his campaign in Judah and Israel (cf. 1Ki 14:25-26).*

Siloam Inscription: [Hebrew]—*late eighth century* B.C. *A Judahite workman describes the construction of an underground conduit to guarantee Jerusalem's water supply during Hezekiah's reign (cf. 2Ki 20:20; 2Ch 32:30).*

Sinuhe's Story: [Egyptian]—*twentieth to nineteenth centuries* B.C. *An Egyptian official of the twelfth dynasty goes into voluntary exile in Syria and Canaan during the OT patriarchal period.*

Tale of Two Brothers: [Egyptian]—*thirteenth century* B.C. *A young man rejects the amorous advances of his older brother's wife (cf. Ge 39).*

Wenamun's Journey: [Egyptian]—*eleventh century* B.C. *An official of the Temple of Amun at Thebes in Egypt is sent to Byblos in Canaan to buy lumber for the ceremonial barge of his god.*

TEXTS AND VERSIONS

Old Testament

Major Hebrew texts—

1. The oldest copies of the Hebrew OT are the famous Dead Sea Scrolls, dating from 250 B.C. to c. A.D. 70. *See Dead Sea Scrolls; Testaments, Time Between.*

2. Portions of the OT text include the Nash Papyrus (second century B.C.) and the Cairo Genizah fragments (sixth to ninth centuries A.D.).

3. The Masoretes preserved and standardized the Hebrew text between the sixth and tenth centuries A.D.. The oldest examples of this text type include the Cairo Codex of the Prophets (895), the Aleppo Codex (c. 900-925) and the Leningrad Codex (1008).

4. The Samaritan Pentateuch (eleventh century A.D.).

Major versions—

1. Greek: Septuagint (250-100 B.C.); second century A.D. versions by Aquila, Theodotion, and Symmachus; by Origen c. A.D. 240.

2. Aramaic (first to fifth century A.D.).

3. Syriac (second or third century A.D.).

4. Latin: Old Latin (second century A.D.), Jerome's Vulgate (383-405 A.D.).

New Testament:

Major Greek texts—

Greek manuscripts of portions or of the whole of the NT total nearly 5000. Of these, c. 70 are papyri, 250 uncials, 2, 500 minuscules, and 1800 lectionaries.

1. Fragments and books on papyrus date back to the second century A.D., such as Bodmer Papyrus p^{66} of John.

2. Codex Sinaiticus (fourth century) contains the entire NT.

3. Codicies Alexandrinus (fifth century) and Vaticanus are nearly complete.

4. Quotations from the early church fathers also provide an ancient witness to the NT.

Major versions—

1. Latin (second to fourth centuries).

2. Syriac (second to sixth centuries).

3. Coptic (second and third centuries).

THADDAEUS

(possibly *breast nipple*). One of the twelve apostles (Mt 10:3; Mk 3:18). This name does not appear in (Lk 6:16; Ac 1:13), the name "Judas son of James" occurs instead. Little is known about him.

See Lebbaeus.

THAHASH

See Tahash.

THAMAH

See Temah.

THAMAR

See Tamar, 1.

THANK OFFERINGS

See Offerings.

THANKFULNESS

To God:

Commanded or required (Ge 35:1; Ex 12:14, 17, 42; 13:3, 8-10, 14-16; 16:32; 34:26; Lev 19:24; 23:14; Dt 12:18; 16:9-15; 26:10; Jdg 5:11; Ps 50:14-15). Commanded (Ps 48:11; 106:1; Pr 3:9-10; Ecc 7:14; Isa 48:20; Joel 2:26; Ro 2:4; 15:27; Eph 1:16; 5:4, 19-20; Php 4:6; Col 1:12; 2:7; 3:15-17; 4:2; 1Th 5:18; Heb 13:15; Jas 1:9). Exhorted (Ps 98:1; 105:1, 5, 42-45; 107:1-2, 15, 22, 42-43; 118:1, 4; Col 3:15; 1Ti 2:1; 4:3-5).

Jesus set an example of (Mt 11:25; 15:36; 26:27; Mk 8:6-7; 14:23; Lk 22:17, 19; Jn 6:11, 23; 11:41).

Should Be Offered—

To God (Ps 30:4; 50:14; 75:1; 92:1; 97:12; 106:1; 118:1; 2Co 9:11; Eph 5:4, 19-20; Php 4:6; Col 1:12; 2:7; 3:15-17; 4:2; 1Th 5:18; 1Ti 2:1; Heb 13:15), through Christ (Ro 1:8; Col 3:17; Heb 13:15), in the name of Christ (Eph 5:20), in behalf of ministers (2Co 1:11), in private worship (Da 6:10), in public (1Ch 23:30; 25:3; Ne 11:17; Ps 35:18), in everything (1Th 5:18), upon the completion of great undertakings (Ne 12:31, 40), before taking food (Mt 14:19; Mk 8:9; Lk 24:30; Jn 6:11; Ac 27:35), always (Eph 1:16; 5:20; 1Th 1:2), as the remembrance of God's holiness (Ps 30:4; 97:12).

For—

The goodness and mercy of God (Ps 68:19; 79:13; 89:1; 100:4; 106:1; 107:1; 116:12-14, 17; 136:1-3; Isa 63:7), the gift of Christ (2Co 9:15), Christ's power and reign (Rev 11:17), the reception and effectual working of the word of God in others (1Th 2:13), deliverance, from adversity (Ps 31:7, 21; 35:9-10; 44:7-8; 54:6-7; 66:8-9, 12-16, 20; 98:1), through Christ, from indwelling sin (Ro 7:23-25), providential deliverance (Ex 12:14, 17, 42; 13:3, 8-10, 14-16; Jdg 5:11; Ps 105:1-45; 107:1-2, 15, 22, 42-43; 136:1-26; Joel 2:26), victory over death and the grave (1Co 15:57), wisdom and might (Da 2:23), the triumph of the gospel (2Co 2:14), the conversion of others (Ro 6:17), faith exhibited by others (Ro 1:8; 2Th 1:3), love exhibited by others (2Th 1:3), the grace bestowed on others (1Co 1:4; Php 1:3-5; Col 1:3-6), the zeal exhibited by others (2Co 8:16), nearness of God's presence (Ps 75:1), appointment to the ministry (1Ti 1:12), willingness to offer our property for God's service (1Ch 29:6-14), the supply of our bodily wants (Ro 14:6-7; 1Ti 4:3-4), all men (1Ti 2:1), all things (2Co 9:11; Eph 5:20), temporal blessings (Ro 14:6-7; 1Ti 4:3-5).

By—

Ministers appointed to offer, in public (1Ch 16:4, 7; 23:30; 2Ch 31:2).

Saints, exhorted to (Ps 105:1; Col 3:15), resolve to offer (Ps 18:49; 30:12), habitually offer (Da 6:10), offer sacrifices of (Ps 116:17), abound in the faith with (Col 2:7), magnify God by (Ps 95:2), come before God with (Ps 95:2), should enter God's gates with (Ps 100:4). Of hypocrites, full of boasting (Lk 18:11). The wicked averse to (Ro 1:21).

The heavenly host (Rev 4:9; 7:11-12; 11:16-17).

Accompanied By—

Should be accompanied by intercession for others (1Ti 2:1; 2Ti 1:3; Phm 4). Should always accompany prayer (Ne 11:17; Php 4:6; Col 4:2). Should always accompany praise (Ps 92:1; Heb 13:15). Expressed in psalms (1Ch 16:7).

Cultivated, by the Feast of Tabernacles (Dt 16:9-15), by thank offerings (Ex 34:26; Lev 19:24; 23:14; Dt 12:18; 26:10; Pr 3:9-10), by songs (1Ch 16:7-36; Ps 95:2; 100).

Instances of—

Eve (Ge 4:1, 25). Noah (Ge 8:20). Melchizedek (Ge 14:20). Lot (Ge 19:19). Abraham (Ge 12:7). Sarah (Ge 21:6-7). Abraham's servant (Ge 24:27). Isaac (Ge 26:22). Leah (Ge 29:32-35). Rachel (Ge 30:6). Jacob (Ge 32:10; 35:3, 7; 48:11, 15-16). Joseph (Ge 41:51-52).

Moses (Ex 15:1-18). Miriam (Ex 15:19-21). Jethro (Ex 18:10). Israel (Ex 4:31; 15:1-18; Nu 21:17; 31:49-54; 1Ch 29:22). Deborah (Jdg 5). Hannah (1Sa 1:27-28; 2:1-10). Samuel (1Sa 7:12).

David (2Sa 6:21; 1Ch 29:13). Solomon (1Ki 8:15, 56; 2Ch 6:4). Queen of Sheba (1Ki 10:9). Hiram (2Ch 2:12). Jehoshaphat's army (2Ch 20:27-28). The psalmist (Ps 9:1-2, 4; 13:6; 22:23-25; 26:7; 28:7; 30:1, 3, 11-12; 31:7, 21; 35:9-10, 18; 40:2-3, 5; 41:11-12; 44:7-8; 54:6-7; 56:12-13; 59:16-17; 66:8-9, 12-16, 20; 68:19; 71:15, 23-24; 79:13; 89:1; 92:1-2, 4; 98:1; 100:4; 102:18-20; 104:1; 116:12-14, 17; 119:65, 108; 136).

Isaiah (Isa 63:7). Daniel (Da 2:23; 6:22). Nebuchadnezzar (Da 4:2, 34). The mariners (Jnh 1:16). Jonah (Jnh 2:9). Ezra (Ezr 7:27). The Levites (2Ch 5:12-13; Ne 9:4-38). The Jews (Ne 12:31, 40, 43).

The shepherds (Lk 2:20). Simeon (Lk 2:28). Anna (Lk 2:38).

Those whom Jesus healed: The paralyzed man (Lk 5:25), the demoniac (Lk 8:39), the woman bent with infirmity (Lk 13:13), one of the ten lepers (Lk 17:15-16), blind Bartimaeus (Lk 18:43), the centurion for his son (Jn 4:53).

The lame man healed by Peter (Ac 3:8). Early Christians (Ac 2:46-47). Paul (Ac 27:35; 28:15; Ro 1:8; 6:17; 1Co 1:4; 2Co 2:14; Php 1:3-5; Col 1:3-6; 2Th 1:3; 1Ti 1:12).

See Joy; Praise; Psalms; Worship.

Of Person to Person:

The Israelites, to Joshua (Jos 19:49-50). The spies, to Rahab (Jos 6:22-25). Saul, to the Kenites (1Sa 15:6). Naomi, to Boaz (Ru 2:19-20). David, to the men of Jabesh Gilead (2Sa 2:5-7), to Hanun (2Sa 10:2), to Barzillai (1Ki 2:7). Paul, to Phoebe (Ro 16:1-4), to Onesiphorus (2Ti 1:16-18). The people of Malta, to Paul (Ac 28:10).

THANKSGIVING

By Jesus (Mt 11:25; 15:36; 26:27; Mk 8:6-7; 14:23; Lk 22:17, 19; Jn 6:11, 23; 11:41).

For food, commonly called "grace" (1Sa 9:13; Mt 14:19; 15:36; Mk 6:41; 8:6-7; Lk 9:16; 24:30; Jn 6:11, 23; Ac 27:35; Ro 14:6; 1Co 10:30-31; 1Ti 4:3-5).

Instances of: Jesus (Mt 14:19; Mk 8:6-7). Paul (Ac 27:35).

See Praise; Prayer, Thanksgiving; Thankfulness.

THARA

See Terah, 2.

THARSHISH

See Trade and Travel; Tarshish, 2, 4.

THEATER

A place for dramatic and musical performances (Ac 19:29, 31).

THEBES

(*town, village*). Capital of Egypt during the eighteenth dynasty (KJV "No"); on the E bank of the Nile; famous for temples; cult center of the god Amon (Jer 46:25), denounced by prophets (Jer 46:25; Eze 30:14-16).

THEBEZ

A city in Ephraim about halfway from Beth Shan to Shechem; Abimelech, the son of Gideon, slain there (Jdg 9:50; 2Sa 11:21).

THEFT

(Na 3:1; Mt 6:19-20; 15:19; Mk 7:21-22; Ro 2:21; Rev 9:21).

Forbidden:

(Ex 20:15; Lev 19:11, 13; Dt 5:19; 23:24-25; Ps 62:10; Mt 19:18; Lk 18:20; Ro 13:9; Eph 4:28; Tit 2:10; 1Pe 4:15). Penalty for (Ex 21:16; 22:1-4, 10-15; Lev 6:2-5; Pr 6:30-31; Zec 5:3; Mt 27:38, 44; Mk 15:27). Restitution for things stolen required of the penitent (Eze 33:15).

Instances of:

Rachel, of the household gods (Ge 31:19, 34-35). Achan (Jos 7:11). Micah (Jdg 17:2). The spies of Laish (Jdg 18:14-27). Israelites (Eze 22:29; Hos 4:1-2). Judas (Jn 12:6).

See Dishonesty; Robbery; Thief, Thieves.

THELASAR

See Tel Assar.

THEOCRACY

(*rule of God*). Established (Ex 19:8; 24:3, 7; Dt 5:25-29; 33:2-5; Jdg 8:23; 1Sa 12:12). Rejected by Israel (1Sa 8:7, 19; 10:19; 2Ch 13:8).

See God, Sovereign; Government.

THEOLOGY

See God.

THEOPHANY

(*appearance of God*). Visible appearance of God, generally in human form (Ge 3:8; 4; 28:10-17).

THEOPHILUS

(*friend of God*). A man to whom the Gospel of Luke and Acts of the Apostles are addressed (Lk 1:3; Ac 1:1). Nothing is known of him.

THESSALONIANS, 1 and 2

1 Thessalonians:

Author: the apostle Paul

Date: c. A.D. 51

Outline:

I. The Thanksgiving for the Thessalonians (ch 1).
- A. The Grounds for the Thanksgiving (1:1-4).
- B. The Genuineness of the Grounds (1:5-10).

II. The Defense of the Apostolic Actions and Absence (chs. 2-3).
- A. The Defense of the Apostolic Actions (2:1-16).
- B. The Defense of the Apostolic Absence (2:17-3:10).
- C. The Prayer (3:11-13).

III. The Exhortations to the Thessalonians (4:1-5:22).
- A. Primarily Concerning Personal Life (4:1-12).
- B. Concerning the Coming of Christ (4:13-5:11).
- C. Primarily Concerning Church Life (5:12-22).

IV. The Concluding Prayer, Greetings and Benediction (5:23-28).

2 Thessalonians:

Author: the apostle Paul

Date: c. A.D. 51 or 52

Outline:

I. Introduction (ch. 1).
- A. Salutation (1:1-2).
- B. Thanksgiving for Their Faith, Love and Perseverance (1:3-10).
- C. Intercession for Their Spiritual Progress (1:11-12).

II. Instruction (ch. 2).
- A. Prophecy Regarding the Day of the Lord (2:1-12).
- B. Thanksgiving for Their Election and Calling (Their Position) (2:13-15).
- C. Prayer for Their Service and Testimony (Their Practice) (2:16-17).

III. Injunctions (ch. 3).
- A. Call to Prayer (3:1-3).
- B. Charge to Discipline for the Disorderly and Lazy (3:4-15).
- C. Conclusion, Greeting and Benediction (3:16-18).

THESSALONICA

A city of Macedonia. Paul visits (Ac 17:1; Php 4:16). People of, accompany Paul (Ac 20:4; 27:2). Paul writes to Christians in (1Th 1:1; 2Th 1:1). Demas goes to (2Ti 4:10).

THEUDAS

(*gift of God*). A Jew who led a rebellion against Rome (Ac 5:36-37).

THICKET

(1Sa 13:6; Jer 4:7).

THIEF, THIEVES

In Mosaic law, punishment of thieves was very severe (Ex 22:1-4).

Penalty for (Dt 24:7; Pr 6:30-31; Eze 18:10, 13; Zec 5:3; Mt 27:38, 44; Mk 15:27).

Collusion with (Ps 50:18). Excluded from the kingdom of God (1Co 6:10). Desecrated the temple (Mt 21:13; Mk 11:17; Lk 19:45-46). Disgraceful (Jer 2:26). Worship of, offensive to God (Jer 7:9-10).

Christ's coming again as unexpected as (Rev 3:3).

Figurative (Ob 5; Jn 10:1).
See Theft.

THIGH To put one's hand under the thigh of another was to enhance the sacredness of an oath (Ge 24:2, 9; 47:29).

THIMNATHAH *See Timnah.*

THIRST Figurative of the ardent desire of the devout mind (Ps 42:1-4; 63:1; 143:6; Isa 55:1; Am 8:11-13; Mt 5:6; Jn 4:14-15; 7:37; Rev 21:6; 22:17).
See Desire, Spiritual; Diligence; Hunger, Figurative; Zeal.

THISTLE Exists in many varieties in Israel. Used figuratively for trouble, desolation, judgment, wickedness (Nu 33:55; Pr 24:31; 15:19; Isa 5:6; 2Co 12:7).

THOMAS (*twin*). Called Didymus. One of the twelve apostles (Mt 10:3; Mk 3:18; Lk 6:15). Present at the raising of Lazarus (Jn 11:16). Asks Jesus the way to the Father's house (Jn 14:5). Absent when Jesus first appeared to the disciples after the Resurrection (Jn 20:24). Skepticism of (Jn 20:25). Sees Jesus after the Resurrection (Jn 20:26-29; 21:1-2). Lives with the other apostles in Jerusalem (Ac 1:13-14). Loyalty of, to Jesus (Jn 11:16; 20:28).

THOMAS, GOSPEL OF A Gnostic gospel consisting entirely of sayings attributed to Jesus; dated c. A.D. 140; found at Nag Hammadi in Egypt in 1945.

THONG Strap to fasten a sandal to the foot. Used figuratively of something small and insignificant (Ge 14:23; Isa 5:27). Untying of, an act of humble service (Mk 1:7; Lk 3:16).

THORN The ground cursed with (Ge 3:18). Used as an awl (Job 41:2), for fuel (Ps 58:9; 118:12; Ecc 7:6). Hedges formed of (Hos 2:6; Mic 7:4). Crown of, mockingly put on Jesus' head (Mt 27:29; Mk 15:17; Jn 19:2, 5).

Figurative:
Of afflictions (Nu 33:55; 2Co 12:7). Of the adversities of the wicked (Pr 22:5). Of the evils that spring from the heart to choke the truth (Mt 13:7, 22).

THORN IN THE FLESH Paul's description of a physical ailment from which he prayed to be relieved (2Co 12:7). What it was is not known.

THOUGHTS, GOD'S (Ps 40:5, 17; 139:17; Isa 55:9; Jer 29:11).

THOUSAND Often used symbolically in the Bible. In the OT sometimes means "many" (1Sa 21:11; 2Ch 15:11), "family" (Nu 10:4).

THOUSAND YEARS As a day to the Lord (Ps 90:4; 2Pe 3:8). Satan bound (Rev 20:1-3). The reign of Christ (Rev 20:4-6). *See Millennium.*

THRACE Kingdom and later a Roman province, in SE Europe, E of Macedonia (2Mc 12:35).

THREAD (Ge 14:23; Jdg 16:21; SS 4:3).

THREATENINGS Of God against the wicked (Lev 26:16; Jos 23:15; 1Sa 12:25; 1Ki 9:7; Ps 7:12; Isa 14:23; 66:4; Mal 3:5).

THREE HOLY CHILDREN, SONG OF Apocryphal additions to the OT book of Daniel; probably written in the first century B.C.

THREE TAVERNS A town in Italy. Roman Christians meet Paul in (Ac 28:15).

THRESHING By beating (Ru 2:17), by treading (Dt 25:4; Isa 25:10; Hos 10:11; 1Co 9:9; 1Ti 5:18). With instruments of wood (2Sa 24:22), of iron (Am 1:3), with a cart wheel (Isa 28:27-28). Floors for (Ge 50:10-11; Jdg 6:37; Ru 3:2-14; 1Sa 23:1; 2Sa 6:6; Hos 9:2; Joel 2:24). Floor of Araunah bought by David for a place of sacrifice (2Sa 24:16-25). Floor for, in barns (2Ki 6:27).

THRESHING FLOOR A place where grain was threshed, usually clay soil packed to a hard, smooth surface (Dt 25:4; Isa 28:27; 1Co 9:9).

THRESHOLD A piece of wood or stone at the bottom of a door, which has to be crossed on entering a house.

THRONE (*judgment seat*). Of Pharaoh (Ge 41:40; Ex 11:5). Of David (1Ki 2:12, 24; Ps 132:11-12; Isa 9:7; Jer 13:13; 17:25; Lk 1:32). Of Solomon (1Ki 2:19; 2Ch 9:17-19). Of ivory (1Ki 10:18-20). Of Solomon, called the throne of the LORD (1Ch 29:23). Of Herod (Ac 12:21). Of Israel (1Ki 8:20; 10:9; 2Ch 6:10).
Abdicated by David (1Ki 1:32-40).

Figurative:
Anthropomorphic use of: Of God (2Ch 18:18; Ps 9:4, 7; 11:4; 47:8; 89:14; 97:2; 103:19; Isa 6:1; 66:1; Mt 5:34; 23:22; Heb 8:1; 12:2; Rev 14:3, 5), of Christ (Mt 19:28; 25:31; Ac 2:30; Rev 1:4; 3:21; 4:2-10; 7:9-17; 19:4; 21:5; 22:3).

THRUSH A bird (Isa 38:14; Jer 8:7). *See Birds.*

THUMB Blood put on, in consecration (Ex 29:20; Lev 8:23), in purification (Lev 14:14, 25). Oil put on (Lev 14:17, 28). Of prisoners cut off (Jdg 1:6-7). *See Hand.*

THUMMIM *See Urim and Thummim.*

THUNDER Sent as a plague upon the Egyptians (Ex 9:3-24), the Philistines, in battle with the Israelites (1Sa 7:10). Sent as a judgment (Isa 29:6). On Sinai (Ex 19:16; Ps 77:18; Heb 12:18-19). A token of divine anger (1Sa 12:17-18). A manifestation of divine power (Job 26:14; Ps 77:18). Sons of Zebedee called sons of (Mk 3:17).

THUNDER, SONS OF A title given James and John by Jesus (Mk 3:17).

THUTMOSE (*[Egyptian god] Thoth is born*). The name of four kings of Egypt of the eighteenth dynasty, centering in Thebes. Under their rule, Egypt attained her greatest power. Thutmose III may have been the Pharaoh who enslaved the Hebrews (Ex 1:8).

THYATIRA A city in the Roman province of Asia; on the boundary of Lydia and Mysia; noted for weaving and dyeing (Ac 16:14; Rev 2:18-29).

THYINE *See Citron Wood.*

TIARAS (Isa 3:23). *See Crown; Jewel, Jewelry.*

TIBERIAS A city on the W shore of the Sea of Galilee; built by Herod Antipas and named for the emperor Tiberius; a famous health resort; after A.D. 70 it became a center of rabbinic learning. Modern Tabariya.

TIBERIAS, SEA OF *See Sea of Galilee.*

TIBERIUS The second Roman emperor (A.D. 14-37); reigning emperor at the time of Christ's death (Lk 3:1).

TIBHATH *See Tebah, 2.*

TIBNI The son of Ginath; unsuccessful competitor for the throne of Israel (1Ki 16:21).

TIDAL King of Goiim; confederate of Kedorlaomer (Ge 14:1-17).

TIGLATH-PILESER (*my trust is in the son of [the temple] Esharra*). A famous Assyrian king (745-727 B.C.); great conqueror; received tribute from King Azariah of Judah and King Menahem of Samaria (2Ki 15:19-20), Ahaz secured his help against Pekah of Israel and Rezin of Syria; deported Trans-Jordanian Israelites (1Ch 5:6, 26), Ahaz gave tribute to him (2Ch 28:20-21).

TIGRIS (*arrow*). One of the two great rivers of the Mesopotamian area; 1, 150 miles long (Ge 2:14; Da 10:4).

TIKVAH (*hope*).
1. Father-in-law of the prophetess Huldah (2Ki 22:14). *See Tokhath.*
2. Father of Jahzeiah (Ezr 10:15).

TILE Ceiling tiles (Lk 5:19).

TILGATH-PILNESER *See Tiglath-Pileser.*

TILON The son of Shimon (1Ch 4:20).

TIMAEUS (*precious, valuable*). The father of Bartimaeus (Mk 10:46).

TIMBREL *See Tambourine.*

TIME In the early biblical period, time was marked by sunrise and sunset, phases of the moon, seasons, and years (Ge 1:14). *See Calendar.*
Ancient people had no method of reckoning long periods of time. They dated from great and well-known events, like the Exodus, the Babylonian Exile, the earthquake (Am 1:1), and especially the reigns of kings (1Ki 15:1; Hag 1:1). The year was lunar (354 days, 8 hours, 38 seconds), divided into twelve lunar months, with seven intercalary months added over nineteen years. The Hebrew month began with the new moon. Early Hebrews gave the months names; later they used numbers; and after the Exile they used Babylonian names. *See Month.*
Months were divided by the Jews into weeks of seven days, ending with the Sabbath (Ex 20:11; Dt 5:14-15). Days were divided into twenty-four hours of sixty minutes of sixty seconds. The Roman day began at midnight and had twelve hours (Jn 11:9), the Hebrew day was reckoned from sunset. Night was divided into watches. At first the Hebrews had three watches; in the time of Christ there were four. *See Day; Watches of the Night.*

TIMES, OBSERVER OF A person who has a superstitious regard for days regarded as lucky or unlucky, as decided by astrology (Dt 18:8-14).

TIMNA (*lot, portion*).
1. Concubine of Eliphaz (Ge 36:12).
2. Sister of Lotan (Ge 36:22).
3. Chieftain of Edom (Ge 36:40).
4. Son of Eliphaz (1Ch 1:36).

TIMNAH (*lot, portion*).
1. A town about two-and-a-half miles west of Beth Shemesh (Ge 38:12-14; 2Ch 28:18).
2. A town on the border of Judah approximately three miles SW of Beth Shemesh (Jos 15:10), possibly modern Tell Batash.
3. A town in the hill country of Judah (Jos 15:57), possibly the same as 1.
4. A Philistine town (Jdg 14:1-5), possibly the same as 1.

TIMNATH *See Timnah.*

TIMNATH HERES (*place of the sun [worship]*). A city in the hill country of Ephraim (Jdg 2:9).

TIMNATH SERAH (*place of the sun [worship]*). Given to Joshua (Jos 19:50). Joshua buried in (Jos 24:30). Modern Khirbet Tibnah.

TIMNITE A native of Timnah (Jdg 15:3-6).

TIMON (*precious, valuable*). One of seven ministers (Ac 6:5).

TIMOTHEUS *See Timothy.*

TIMOTHY (*precious one of God*). Parentage of (Ac 16:1). Reputation and Christian faith of (Ac 16:2; 1Co 4:17; 16:10; 2Ti 1:5; 3:15). Circumcised; becomes Paul's companion (Ac 16:3; 1Th 3:2). Left by Paul at Berea (Ac 17:14). Rejoins Paul at Corinth (Ac 17:15; 18:5). Sent into Macedonia (Ac 19:22). Rejoined by Paul; accompanies Paul to Asia (Ac 20:1-4). Sent to the Corinthians (1Co 4:17; 16:10-11). Preaches to the Corinthians (2Co 1:19). Sent to the Philippians (Php 2:19, 23). Sent to the Thessalonians (1Th 3:2, 6). Sent by Paul in Ephesus (1Ti 1:3). Joins Paul in the Epistle to the Philippians (Php 1:1), to the Colossians (Col 1:1-2), to the Thessalonians (1Th 1:1; 2Th 1:1), to Philemon (Phm 1).
Zeal of (Php 2:19-22; 1Ti 6:12). Power of (1Ti 4:14; 2Ti 1:6). Paul's love for (1Co 4:17; Php 2:22; 1Ti 1:2, 18; 2Ti 1:2-4). Paul writes to (1Ti 1:1-2; 2Ti 1:1-2).

TIMOTHY, 1 and 2

1 Timothy:

Author: the apostle Paul

Date: c. A.D 63-65

Outline:
I. Salutation (1:1-2).
II. Warning Against False Teachers (1:3-11).
A. The Nature of the Heresy (1:3-7).
B. The Purpose of the Law (1:8-11).
III. The Lord's Grace to Paul (1:12-17).
IV. The Purpose of Paul's Instructions to Timothy (1:18-20).
V. Instructions Concerning the Administration of the Church (chs. 2-3).
A. Public Worship (ch. 2).
1. Prayer in public worship (2:1-8).
2. Women in public worship (2:9-15).
B. Qualifications for Church Officers (3:1-13).
1. Overseers (3:1-7).
2. Deacons (3:8-13).
C. Purpose of These Instructions (3:14-16).
VI. Methods of Dealing With False Teaching (ch. 4).
A. False Teaching Described (4:1-5).
B. Methods of Dealing With It Explained (4:6-16).
VII. Methods of Dealing With Different Groups in the Church (5:1-6:2).
A. The Older and Younger (5:1-2).
B. Widows (5:3-16).
C. Elders (5:17-25).
D. Slaves (6:1-2).
VIII. Miscellaneous Matters (6:3-19).
A. False Teachers (6:3-5).
B. Love of Money (6:6-10).
C. Charge to Timothy (6:11-16).
D. The Rich (6:17-19).
IX. Concluding Appeal (6:20-21).

2 Timothy:

Author: the apostle Paul

Date: c. A.D. 66-67

Outline:
I. Introduction (1:1-4).
II. Paul's Concern for Timothy (1:5-14).
III. Paul's Situation (1:15-18).
IV. Special Instructions to Timothy (ch. 2).
A. Call for Endurance (2:1-13).
B. Warning About Foolish Controversies (2:14-26).
V. Warning About the Last Days (ch. 3).
A. Terrible Times (3:1-9).
B. Means of Combating Them (3:10-17).
VI. Paul's Departing Remarks (4:1-8).
A. Charge to Preach the Word (4:1-5).
B. Paul's Victorious Prospect (4:6-8).
VII. Final Requests and Greetings (4:9-22).
See Church, The Body of Believers, Qualifications for Elders/Overseers and Deacons; Missionary Journeys of Paul; Pastoral Epistles.

TIN (Nu 31:22; Eze 22:18, 20; 27:12).

TINKLING The sound of small bells worn by women on chain fastened to anklets (Isa 3:16).

TIPHSAH
1. City on Euphrates (1Ki 4:24).
2. A town, apparently not far from Tirzah in Samaria (2Ki 15:16); some versions have Tappuah. *See Tappuah, 3.*

TIRAS The son of Japheth (Ge 10:2; 1Ch 1:5).

TIRATHITES A family of scribes in Jabez (1Ch 2:55).

TIRE (*headdress*). Ornamental headdress (Eze 24:17, 23; Isa 3:20; 61:10).

TIRHAKAH An Egyptian king, third of the twenty-fifth dynasty; defeated by Sennacherib (2Ki 19:9; Isa 37:9), and later by Esarhaddon and Ashurbanipal.

TIRHANAH The son of Caleb and Maacah (1Ch 2:48).

TIRIA The son of Jehallelel (1Ch 4:16).

TIRSHATHA *See Governor.*

TIRZAH (*pleasant one* or *compensation*).
1. A daughter of Zelophehad (Nu 26:33; 36:11; Jos 17:3). Special legislation in regard to the inheritance of (Nu 27:1-11; 36; Jos 17:3-4).
2. A city of Canaan. Captured by Joshua (Jos 12:24). Becomes the residence of the kings of Israel (1Ki 14:17; 15:21, 33; 16:6, 8-9, 15, 17, 23). Royal residence moved from (1Ki 16:23-24). Base of military operations of Menahem (2Ki 15:14, 16). Beauty of (SS 6:4).

T

TISHBE, TISHBITE The designation of Elijah (1Ki 17:1), probably to be identified with modern el-Istib, little W of Mahanaim.

TISHRI *See Ethanim; Month, 7.*

TITHES (*a tenth*). Paid by Abraham to Melchizedek (Ge 14:20; Heb 7:2-6). Jacob vows a tenth of all his property to God (Ge 28:22).

Mosaic laws instituting (Lev 27:30-33; Nu 18:21-24; Dt 12:6-7, 17, 19; 14:22-29; 26:12-15). Customs relating to (Ne 10:37-38; Am 4:4; Heb 7:5-9). Tithe of tithes for priests (Nu 18:26; Ne 10:38). Stored in the temple (Ne 10:38-39; 12:44; 13:5, 12; 2Ch 31:11-12; Mal 3:10).

Payment of, resumed in Hezekiah's reign (2Ch 31:5-10). Under Nehemiah (Ne 13:12). Withheld (Ne 13:10; Mal 3:8).

Customary in later times (Mt 23:23; Lk 11:42; 18:12). Observed by idolaters (Am 4:4-5).

See Alms; Beneficence; Giving; Liberality; Tax.

TITLE To real estate. *See Land.*

TITLES AND NAMES

Of God: *See God, Names of.*

Titles and Names of Christ:

Adam, Last (1Co 15:45). Almighty (Rev 1:8). Alpha and Omega (Rev 1:8; 22:13). Amen (Rev 3:14). Angel of his presence (Isa 63:9). Angel of the Lord (Ex 3:2; Jdg 13:15-18). Angel (Ge 48:16; Ex 23:20-21). Anointed One (Da 9:25; Jn 1:41). Apostle (Heb 3:1). Arm of the Lord (Isa 51:9; 53:1). Author of life (Ac 3:15). Author and Perfecter of our faith (Heb 2:10; 12:2).

Blessed and only Ruler (1Ti 6:15). Branch (Jer 23:5; Zec 3:8; 6:12). Bread of Life (Jn 6:35, 48).

Chief Shepherd (1Pe 5:4). Chief Cornerstone (Eph 2:20; 1Pe 2:6). Chosen One of God (Isa 42:1). Christ of God (Lk 9:20). Commander of the Lord's army (Jos 5:14-15). Commander (Isa 55:4). Consolation of Israel (Lk 2:25). Counselor (Isa 9:6).

David (Jer 30:9; Eze 34:23). Defender (1Jn 2:1). Deliverer (Ro 11:26). Door (Jn 10:7).

Eternal life (1Jn 1:2; 5:20). Everlasting Father (Isa 9:6).

Faithful witness (Rev 1:5; 3:14). First and Last (Rev 1:17; 2:8). Firstborn of the dead (Rev 1:5). Firstborn of all creation (Col 1:15).

Glory of the Lord (Isa 40:5). God over all (Ro 9:5). God (Isa 40:9; Jn 20:28). Good Shepherd (Jn 10:14). Great High Priest (Heb 4:14). Guarantee (Heb 7:22).

Head of the Church (Eph 5:23; Col 1:18). Heir of all things (Heb 1:2). Holy One of God (Mk 1:24). Holy One (Ps 16:10, w Ac 2:27, 31). Holy One of Israel (Isa 41:14). Horn of salvation (Lk 1:69).

I Am (Ex 3:14, w Rev 1:8; 22:13). Immanuel (Isa 7:14, w Mt 1:23). Israel's Ruler (Mic 5:1).

Jesus (Mt 1:21; 1Th 1:10).

King of the Jews (Mt 2:2). King of Israel (Jn 1:49). King of Kings (1Ti 6:15; Rev 17:14). King of the ages (Rev 15:3). King (Zec 9:9, w Mt 21:5).

Lamb of God (Jn 1:29, 36). Lamb (Rev 5:6, 12; 13:8; 21:22; 22:3). Lawgiver (Isa 33:22). Leader (Isa 55:4). Life (Jn 14:6; Col 3:4; 1Jn 1:2). Light of the world (Jn 8:12). Lion of the tribe of Judah (Rev 5:5). Lord of all (Ac 10:36). Lord of glory (1Co 2:8). Lord our righteousness (Jer 23:6). Lord God Almighty (Rev 15:3). Lord God of the prophets (Rev 22:6).

Mediator (1Ti 2:5). Mighty One of Jacob (Isa 60:16). Mighty God (Isa 9:6). Morning Star (Rev 22:16).

Nazarene (Mt 2:23).

One and Only (Jn 1:14). One Before Us (Heb 6:20). Our Passover (1Co 5:7).

Prince of peace (Isa 9:6). Prophet (Lk 24:19; Jn 7:40).

Ransom (1Ti 2:6). Redeemer (Job 19:25; Isa 59:20; 60:16). Resurrection and life (Jn 11:25). Righteous One (Ac 7:52). Rock (1Co 10:4). Root of Jesse (Isa 11:10). Root of David (Rev 22:16). Root and Offspring of David (Rev 22:16). Ruler of the kings of the earth (Rev 1:5). Ruler of the creation of God (Rev 3:14). Ruler over Israel (Mic 5:2). Ruler (Mt 2:6).

Savior (2Pe 2:20; 3:18). Servant (Isa 42:1; 52:13). Shepherd and Overseer of Souls (1Pe 2:25). Son of the Most High (Lk 1:32). Son of man (Jn 5:27; 6:37). Son of David (Mt 9:27). Son of God (Lk 1:35; Jn 1:49). Son of the Blessed One (Mk 14:61). Star (Nu 24:17). Sun of righteousness (Mal 4:2).

The desired of all nations (Hag 2:7). True Light (Jn 1:9). True Vine (Jn 15:1). True God (1Jn 5:20). Truth (Jn 14:6).

Way (Jn 14:6). Wisdom (Pr 8:12). Witness (Isa 55:4). Wonderful (Isa 9:6). Word of Life (1Jn 1:1). Word (Jn 1:1; 1Jn 5:7). Word of God (Rev 19:13).

Titles and Names of the Church:

Assembly of the saints (Ps 89:7). Assembly of the saints (Ps 149:1). Body of Christ (Eph 1:22-23; Col 1:24). Bride of Christ (Rev 21:9). Church of the Firstborn (Heb 12:23). Church of the firstborn (Heb 12:23). Church of the Living God (1Ti 3:15). Church of God (Ac 20:28). City of the Living God (Heb 12:22). Council of the upright (Ps 111:1). Dwelling of God (Eph 2:22).

Family in heaven and on earth (Eph 3:15). Flock of God (Eze 34:15; 1Pe 5:2). Flock of Christ (Jn 10:16). God's field (1Co 3:9). God's inheritance (Joel 3:2; 1Pe 5:3). God's building (1Co 3:9). Golden lampstand (Rev 1:20). Holy City (Rev 21:2). House of the God of Jacob (Isa 2:3). House of Christ (Heb 3:6). House(hold) of God (1Ti 3:15; Heb 10:21; Eph 2:19). Inheritance (Ps 28:9; Isa 19:25). Israel of God (Gal 6:16). Lamb's bride (Rev 19:7; 21). Mount Zion (Ps 2:6; Heb 12:22). Mountain of the Lord's house (Isa 2:2).

New Jerusalem (Rev 21:2). Pillar and foundation of the truth (1Ti 3:15). Portion of the Lord (Dt 32:9). Princess (Ps 45:13). Sanctuary of God (Ps 114:2). Shoot of God's Planting (Isa 60:21). Sought After, the City no longer Deserted (Isa 62:12). Spiritual house (1Pe 2:5). Temple of the Living God (2Co 6:16). Temple of God (1Co 3:16-17). Vineyard (Jer 12:10; Mt 21:41).

Titles and Names of the Devil:

Abaddon (Rev 9:11). Accuser of our brothers (Rev 12:10). Ancient serpent (Rev 12:9; 20:2). Angel of the Abyss (Rev 9:11). Apollyon (Rev 9:11). Beelzebub (Mt 12:24). Belial (2Co 6:15). Coiling serpent (Isa 27:1). Dominion of darkness (Col 1:13). Dragon (Isa 27:1; Rev 20:2). Enemy (Mt 13:39; 1Pe 5:8). Evil one (Mt 13:19, 38). Evil spirit (1Sa 16:14; Mt 12:43).

Father of lies (Jn 8:44). Gliding serpent (Isa 27:1). God of this age (2Co 4:4). Leviathan (Isa 27:1). Liar (Jn 8:44). Lying spirit (1Ki 22:22). Murderer (Jn 8:44). Powers of this dark world (Eph 6:12). Prince of demons (Mt 12:24). Prince of this world (Jn 14:30). Red dragon (Rev 12:3). Ruler of the kingdom of the air (Eph 2:2). Satan (1Ch 21:1; Job 1:6). Serpent (Ge 3:4, 14; 2Co 11:3). Spirit that works in those disobedient (Eph 2:2). Tempter (Mt 4:3; 1Th 3:5).

Titles and Names of the Holy Spirit:

Breath of the Almighty (Job 33:4). Counselor (Jn 14:16, 26; 15:26). Eternal Spirit (Heb 9:14). God (Ac 5:3-4). Good Spirit (Ne 9:20; Ps 143:10). Holy Spirit (Ps 51:11; Lk 11:13; Eph 1:13; 4:30). Power of the Most High (Lk 1:35).

Sevenfold Spirit (Rev 1:4 ftn). Spirit of fear of the Lord (Isa 11:2). Spirit of knowledge (Isa 11:2). Spirit of understanding (Isa 11:2). Spirit of power (Isa 11:2). Spirit of truth (Jn 14:17; 15:26). Spirit of holiness (Ro 1:4). Spirit of glory (1Pe 4:14). Spirit of fire (Isa 4:4). Spirit of judgment (Isa 4:4; 28:6). Spirit of revelation (Eph 1:17). Spirit, The (Mt 4:1; Jn 3:6; 1Ti 4:1). Spirit of counsel (Isa 11:2). Spirit of Christ (Ro 8:9; 1Pe 1:11). Spirit of the Father (Mt 10:20). Spirit of God (Ge 1:2; 1Co 2:11; Job 33:4). Spirit of the Lord (Isa 11:2; Ac 5:9). Spirit of wisdom (Isa 11:2; Eph 1:17). Spirit of his Son (Gal 4:6). Spirit of sonship (Ro 8:15). Spirit of life (Ro 8:2; Rev 11:11). Spirit of prophecy (Rev 19:10). Spirit of grace (Zec 12:10; Heb 10:29). Willing Spirit (Ps 51:12).

Titles and Names of Ministers:

Administers of the grace of God (1Pe 4:10). Ambassadors for Christ (2Co 5:20). Apostles of Jesus Christ (Tit 1:1). Apostles (Lk 6:13; Eph 4:11; Rev 18:20). Deacons (Ac 6:1ff; 1Ti 3:8; Php 1:1). Elders (1Ti 5:17; 1Pe 5:1). Entrusted with the secrets of God (1Co 4:1). Entrusted with God's work (Tit 1:7). Evangelists (Eph 4:11; 2Ti 4:5). Fellow workers with God (2Co 6:1). Fishers of men (Mt 4:19; Mk 1:17). Messengers of the Church (Rev 1:20; 2:1 ftn). Messenger of the Lord Almighty (Mal 2:7).

Ministers of the New Covenant (2Co 3:6). Ministers in the sanctuary (Eze 45:4). Ministers of the Lord (Joel 2:17). Ministers of Christ (Ro 15:16; 1Co 4:1). Overseers (Ac 20:28; Php 1:1; 1Ti 3:1; Tit 1:7). Pastors (Jer 3:15; Eph 4:11). Preachers (Ro 10:14; 1Ti 2:7). Representatives of the Church (2Co 8:23).

Servant of the Church (Col 1:24-25). Servant of this gospel (Eph 3:7; Col 1:23). Servants of the word (Lk 1:2). Servants of the Church (2Co 4:5). Servants of righteousness (2Co 11:15). Servants of God (2Co 6:4). Servants of God (Tit 1:1; Jas 1:1). Servants of the Lord (2Ti 2:24). Servants of Jesus Christ (Php 1:1; Jude 1). Shepherds (Jer 23:4). Soldiers of Christ (Php 2:25; 2Ti 2:3). Stars (Rev 1:20; 2:1). Teachers (Isa 30:20; Eph 4:11). Watchmen (Isa 62:6; Eze 33:7). Witnesses (Ac 1:8; 5:32; 26:16). Workers (Mt 9:38, w Phm 1; 1Th 2:2).

Titles and Names of Saints:

Believers (Ac 5:14; 1Ti 4:12). Blessed by the Father (Mt 25:34). Blessed by the Lord (Ge 24:31; 26:29). Brothers (Mt 23:8; Ac 12:17). Brothers of Christ (Lk 8:21; Jn 20:17). Called to belong to Jesus Christ (Ro 1:6).

Children of Abraham (Gal 3:7). Children (Jn 13:33; 1Jn 2:1). Children of the free woman (Gal 4:31). Children of promise (Ro 9:8; Gal 4:28). Children of the Lord (Dt 14:1). Children of the resurrection (Lk 20:36). Children of God (Jn 1:12; Php 2:15; 1Jn 3:1-2). Children of God (Jn 11:52; 1Jn 3:10). Chosen instrument (Ac 9:15). Chosen ones (1Ch 16:13). Chosen people (1Pe 2:9). Chosen of God (Col 3:12; Tit 1:1). Christians (Ac 11:26; 26:28). co-heirs with Christ (Ro 8:17). Dear brothers (1Co 15:58; Jas 2:5). Dearly loved children (Eph 5:1). Disciples of Christ (Jn 8:31; 15:8).

Faithful brothers in Christ (Col 1:2). Faithful in the land, The (Ps 101:6). Faithful, The (Ps 12:1). Fellow citizens with God's people (Eph 2:19). Fellow servants (Rev 6:11). Freedman (1Co 7:22). Friends of God (2Ch 20:7; Jas 2:23). Friends of Christ (Jn 15:15). Glorious ones (Ps 16:3). Godly, The (Ps 4:3; 2Pe 2:9). Guests of the bridegroom (Mt 9:15). Heirs with you of the gracious gift of life (1Pe 3:7). Heirs of God (Ro 8:17; Gal 4:7). Heirs together with Israel (Eph 3:6). Heirs of promise (Heb 6:17; Gal 3:29). Holy brothers (Heb 3:1). Holy people (Dt 26:19; Isa 62:12). Holy nation (Ex 19:6; 1Pe 2:9). Holy priesthood (1Pe 2:5). Inheritors of salvation (Heb 1:14). Inheritors of the kingdom (Jas 2:5). Instrument for noble purposes (2Ti 2:21).

Kingdom of priests (Ex 19:6). Kings and priests to serve God (Rev 1:6). Lambs (Isa 40:11; Jn 21:15). Letter from Christ (2Co 3:3). Light of the world (Mt 5:14). Living stones (1Pe 2:5). Loved of God (Ro 1:7). Man of God (1Ti 6:11; 2Ti 3:17). Members of Christ (1Co 6:15; Eph 5:30). Oaks of righteousness (Isa 61:3). Obedient children (1Pe 1:14). Objects of mercy (Ro 9:23).

People close to God's heart (Ps 148:14). People of God (Heb 4:9; 1Pe 2:10). People saved by the Lord (Dt 33:29). People of Zion (Ps 149:2; Joel 2:23). Pillars in the temple of God (Rev 3:12). Ransomed of the Lord (Isa 35:10; Isa 51:11). Righteous, The (Hab 2:4). Royal priesthood (1Pe 2:9). Salt of the earth (Mt 5:13). Sheep of Christ (Jn 10:1-16; 21:16). Slaves of Christ (1Co 7:22; Eph 6:6). Slaves to Righteousness (Ro 6:18).

Sons of the Living God (Ro 9:26). Sons of Jacob (Ps 105:6). Sons of the Most High (Lk 6:35). Sons of light (Lk 16:8; Eph 5:8; 1Th 5:5). Sons of the day (1Th 5:5). Sons of the Father (Mt 5:45). Sons of the kingdom (Mt 13:38). Treasured possession (Ex 19:5; Dt 14:2; Tit 2:14; 1Pe 2:9). Witnesses for God (Isa 44:8).

Titles and Names of the Wicked:

Accursed brood (2Pe 2:14). Base and nameless brood (Job 30:8). Brood of rebels (Isa 57:4). Brood of evildoers (Isa 1:4; 14:20). Brood of vipers (Mt 3:7; 12:34). Child of the devil (Ac 13:10; 1Jn 3:10). Children unwilling to hear the Lord's instruction (Isa 30:9). Children unfaithful (Dt 32:20). Children given to corruption (Isa 1:4). Clasp hands with Pagans (Isa 2:6). Corrupt generation (Ac 2:40). Crooked and depraved generation (Php 2:15).

Deceitful children (Isa 30:9). Disobedient ones (Eph 2:2; Col 3:6). Enemies of God (Ps 37:20; Jas 4:4). Enemies of the cross of Christ (Php 3:18). Enemies of everything right (Ac 13:10). Evil men (Ps 37:1; Pr 4:14; 2Ti 3:13). Evil generation (Dt 1:35). Evildoer (Ps 101:8; Pr 17:4; Ps 28:3; 36:12). Evildoers (Hos 10:9). Failers of a test (2Co 13:5-7). Fools (Pr 1:7; Ro 1:22). Foreigners (Ps 144:7). God-haters (Ps 81:15; Ro 1:30). Hardened rebels (Jer 6:28). Invent ways of doing evil (Ro 1:30). Men of this world (Ps 17:14). Mockers (Ps 1:1). Natural children (Ro 9:8).

Objects of wrath (Ro 9:22; Eph 2:3). Obstinate children (Eze 2:4; Isa 30:1; 65:2). Offspring of liars (Isa 57:4). Offspring of the wicked (Ps 37:28; Isa 14:20). Opposers of the Lord (1Sa 2:10). People loaded with guilt (Isa 1:4). People of this world (Lk 16:8). Perverse generation (Dt 32:20; Mt 17:17). Proud, The (Job 41:34). Rebellious people (Isa 30:9). Rebellious house (Eze 2:5, 8; 12:2). Senseless children (Jer 4:22). Sinful generation (Mk 8:38). Sinners (Ps 26:9; Pr 1:10; Ps 37:38). Slaves to sin (Jn 8:34; Ro 6:20). Slaves of Depravity (2Pe 2:19). Snakes (Mt 23:33). Son of hell (Mt 23:15). Sons of the evil one (Mt 13:38). Stubborn and rebellious generation (Ps 78:8). Transgressors (Ps 51:13).

Warped and crooked generation (Dt 32:5). Wicked men (Dt 13:13; 2Ch 13:7). Wicked traitors (Ps 59:5). Wicked generation (Mt 12:45; 16:4). Wicked servants (Mt 25:26). Wicked and adulterous generation (Mt 12:39). Wicked of the earth (Ps 75:8). Wicked people (2Sa 7:10). Worthless servants (Mt 25:30). Wrongdoers (1Pe 2:14). *See also Wicked, Compared With.*

TITTLE NIV "the least stroke of a pen"; figurative of the smallest details of the law (Mt 5:18; Lk 16:17).

TITUS A Greek companion of Paul. Paul's love for (2Co 2:13; 7:6-7, 13-14; 8:23; Tit 1:4). With Paul in Macedonia (2Co 7:5-6). Affection of, for the Corinthians (2Co 7:15). Sent to Corinth (2Co 8:6, 16-22; 12:17-18). Character of (2Co 12:18). Accompanies Paul to Jerusalem (Gal 2:1-3, w Ac 15:1-29). Left by Paul in Crete (Tit 1:5), to rejoin him in Nicopolis (Tit 3:12). Paul writes to (Tit 1:1-4). With Paul in Rome; goes to Dalmatia (2Ti 4:10).

TITUS, EPISTLE TO

Author: the apostle Paul

Date: Probably between A.D. 63 and 65

Outline:

I. Salutation (1:1-4).
II. Concerning Elders (1:5-9).
  A. Reasons for Leaving Titus in Crete (1:5).
  B. Qualifications of Elders (1:6-9).
III. Concerning False Teachers (1:10-16).
IV. Concerning Various Groups in the Congregations (ch. 2).
  A. The Instructions to Different Groups (2:1-10).
  B. The Foundation for Christian Living (2:11-14).
  C. The Duty of Titus (2:15).
V. Concerning Believers in General (3:1-8).
  A. Obligations as Citizens (3:1-2).
  B. Motives for Godly Conduct (3:3-8).
VI. Concerning Response to Spiritual Error (3:9-11).
VII. Conclusion (3:12-15).

See Church, The Body of Believers, Qualifications for Elders/Overseers and Deacons; Missionary Journeys of Paul; Pastoral Epistles.

TITUS, FLAVIUS VESPASIANUS A Roman emperor (A.D. 79-81); captured and destroyed Jerusalem in A.D. 70.

TITUS JUSTUS *See Justus.*

TIZITE The designation of Joha, one of David's soldiers (1Ch 11:45).

TOAH An ancestor of Samuel (1Ch 6:34), probably the same as "Nahath" (1Ch 6:26), and perhaps "Tohu" (1Sa 1:1). *See Nahath, 2; Tohu.*

TOB (*good*).

1. A district in Syria, extending NE from Gilead, to which Jephthah fled (Jdg 11:3, 5).

2. Place in Israel which supplied Ammonites with soldiers against David (2Sa 10:6, 8).

TOB-ADONIJAH (*good is [my] lord Yahweh*). A Levite sent by Jehoshaphat to instruct the people in the law (2Ch 17:8).

TOBIAH (*Yahweh is good*).

1. An ancestor of a family of Babylonian captives (Ezr 2:60; Ne 7:62).

2. An enemy of the Jews in the time of Nehemiah. Opposes the rebuilding of the wall of Jerusalem (Ne 2:10, 19; 4:3, 7-8). Conspires to injure and intimidate Nehemiah (Ne 6:1-14, 19). Subverts nobles of Judah (Ne 6:17-18). Allies himself with Eliashib, the priest (Ne 13:4-9).

TOBIJAH (*Yahweh is good*).

1. A Levite chosen by Jehoshaphat to instruct the people in the law (2Ch 17:8).

2. A captive in Babylon (Zec 6:10, 14).

TOBIT, BOOK OF *See Apocrypha.*

TOCHEN *See Token, 2.*

TOE Anointed in consecration (Ex 29:20; Lev 8:23-24), in purification (Lev 14:14, 17, 25, 28). Of prisoners of war cut off (Jdg 1:6-7). Six, on each foot (2Sa 21:20; 1Ch 20:6).

TOGARMAH Son of Gomer (Ge 10:3; 1Ch 1:6). Descendants of (Eze 27:14; 38:6).

TOHU An ancestor of Samuel (1Sa 1:1), probably the same as "Nahath" (1Ch 6:26), and perhaps "Toah" (1Ch 6:34). *See Nahath, 2; Toah.*

TOI *See Tou.*

TOKEN (*measure*).

1. A sign (Ex 3:12). Sun and moon for time and seasons (Ge 1:14). The mark of Cain (Ge 4:15). Rainbow, that the world might no more be destroyed by a flood (Ge 9:12-17). Circumcision, of the covenant of Abraham (Ge 17:11). Presents (Ge 21:27, 30).

Miracles of Moses, of the divine authority of his missions (Ex 4:1-9). Blood of the Passover lamb (Ex 12:13). The Passover (Ex 13:9). Consecration of the firstborn (Ex 13:14-16). The Sabbath (Ex 31:13, 17), a fringe (Nu 15:38-40). Scarlet thread (Jos 2:18, 21). Cover of the altar (Nu 16:38-40). Aaron's rod (Nu 17:10). Memorial stones (Jos 4:2-9). Dew on Gideon's fleece (Jdg 6:36-40). Prayer for tokens of mercy (Ps 86:17).

See Miracles.

2. A city in Simeon (1Ch 4:32).

TOKHATH Father-in-law of Huldah the prophetess; also called Tokhath (2Ch 34:22, ftn). *See Tikvah.*

TOLA, TOLAITE (*worm of scarlet*).

1. The son of Issachar (Ge 46:13).
2. Judged Israel twenty-three years (Jdg 10:1-2).

TOLAD City of Simeon (1Ch 4:29).

TOLERANCE Religious (Mic 4:4-5; Mk 9:38-40; Lk 9:49-50; Ac 17:11; 28:31; Ro 14; 1Co 10:28-32). *See Intolerance.*

TOLL *See Tribute; Tax.*

TOMB A burial place. Most Hebrew burying sites were unmarked; some kings were buried in a vault in Jerusalem (2Sa 2:32; Ne 2:3). Tombs of NT times were natural or man-made caves, sealed with circular stones weighing from one to three tons (Lk 24:2; Jn 20:1). *See Grave; Pillar; Tombstone.*

TOMBSTONE At the tomb of the man of God from Judah (2Ki 23:17). A pillar at Rachel's grave (Ge 35:20). *See Pillar.*

TONGS Used to tend the lamps in the temple (1Ki 7:49). In Isaiah's vision (Isa 6:6). *See Wick Trimmers.*

TONGUE Language (Ge 10:5, 20; Isa 66:18; Rev 7:9). Confusion of (Ge 11:1-9). Gift of (Ac 2:1-18, 33; 10:46; 19:6; 1Co 12:10, 28, 30; 14).

Chattering (Pr 10:8, 19). Restrained by wisdom (Pr 17:27; 21:23; Ecc 3:7). Hasty (Pr 29:20).

An evil. *See Speaking, Evil; Slander.*

TONGUES, CONFUSION OF Punishment by God for arrogant attempt to build tower reaching to heaven (Ge 11:1-9).

TONGUES, GIFT OF A spiritual gift (Mk 16:17; Ac 2:1-13; 10:44-46; 19:6; 1Co 12; 14). The gift appeared on the day of Pentecost with the outpouring of the Holy Spirit on the assembled believers (Ac 2:1-13). The phenomenon appeared again in the home of Cornelius (Ac 10:44-11:17), at Ephesus (Ac 19:6), and in the church at Corinth (1Co 12; 14). Instruction regarding the use of tongues in worship (1Co 12-14).

TONGUES OF FIRE One of the phenomena that occurred at the outpouring of the Holy Spirit on the Day of Pentecost. Symbolic of the Holy Spirit who came in power on the church (Ac 2:3).

TOOLS The following kinds are mentioned in the Bible: cutting, boring, forks and shovels, carpentry, drawing, measuring, tilling, metalworking, stoneworking.

TOOTH Both human and animal teeth are mentioned (Nu 11:33; Dt 32:24), figurative use is common: cleanness of teeth, famine (Am 4:6), gnashing of teeth, rage and despair (Job 16:9), oppression (Pr 30:14), plenty (Ge 49:12).

TOPAZ

1. A precious stone (Eze 28:13; Rev 21:20).
2. In the priestly breastplate (Ex 28:17; 39:10).

Figurative:

Topaz cannot compare to the price of wisdom (Job 28:19).

Symbolic:

Seen in the foundation of the Holy City, the New Jerusalem (Rev 21:20).

See Minerals of the Bible, 1; Stones.

TOPHEL (*cement*). A place in the wilderness where Moses addressed the Israelites (Dt 1:1), possibly modern el-Tafila, fifteen miles SE of the Dead Sea.

TOPHETH A place in the valley of the sons of Hinnom or Ben Hinnom (2Ki 23:10). Israelite children burned in sacrifice to Molech there (2Ki 23:10; Jer 7:31-32; 19:6, 11-14; 32:35; cf. 2Ch 28:3; 33:6). Destroyed by Josiah (2Ki 23:10). Horror of (Isa 30:33).

See Ben Hinnom; Hinnom, Valley of.

TOPOGRAPHY Of Canaan (Jos 13:15-33; 15; 18:9).

TORAH Divine law (Ex 13:9); instruction (Ex 16:4, 28); the Law of Moses (1Ki 2:3); the Book of the Law (Dt 28:61); the entire Jewish Scriptures (Jn 10:34). *See Law.*

TORCHES (Jdg 7:16; 15:4; Na 2:3; Jn 18:3).

TORMENTOR Conquerors of Israel (Ps 137:3; Isa 51:23). Abusive jailers (Mt 18:34).

TORMENTS Of the wicked (Lk 16:23-28; Rev 14:10-11).

See Wicked, Punishment of.

TORTOISE *See Lizard.*

TOTAL ABSTINENCE *See Abstinence.*

TOU King of Hamath who congratulated David for victory over Hadadezer (2Sa 8:9-11; 1Ch 18:9-10).

TOW NIV "thong, tinder, wick." Short fibers of flax or hemp (Jdg 16:9; Isa 1:31; 43:17).

TOWEL A cloth for wiping and drying (Jn 13:4-5).

TOWER Of Babel (Ge 11:1-9). Of Eder (Ge 35:21). Peniel (Jdg 8:8-9, 17). Of Shechem (Jdg 9:46, 49). Of the Hundred (Ne 3:1; 12:39). Of Hananel (Ne 3:1; 12:39; Jer 31:38; Zec 14:10). Of David (SS 4:4). Of Aswan (Eze 29:10). Of Siloam (Lk 13:4). In the walls of Jerusalem (2Ch 26:9; 32:5; Ne 12:38-39). Of other cities (2Ch 14:7).

In the desert (2Ch 26:10). For watchmen or sentinels (2Ki 9:17; 18:8). As fortress (Mt 21:33).

Parable of (Lk 14:28-29).

See Fortification; Ziggurat.

Figurative of divine protection (2Sa 22:3, 51; Ps 18:2; 61:3; 144:2; Pr 18:10).

TOWN In ancient times, large cities had towns or villages surrounding them for protection (Nu 21:25, 32; Jos 15:45-47), sometimes it means an unwalled town (Dt 3:5; 1Sa 16:4).

TOWNCLERK *See City Clerk.*

TRACONITIS (*rough, stony district*). An area of c. 370 sq. miles S of Damascus; tetrarchy of Philip (Lk 3:1).

TRADE AND TRAVEL

Trade in the OT:

Ur of the Chaldeans a trading port; Egypt, from earliest times, a great trading nation (Ge 37:25). First organized commerce of Hebrew people was under Solomon, who formed a partnership with the great mercantile cities of Tyre and Sidon (1Ki 9:27-28; 10:11); after the death of Solomon, Israel again became an agricultural nation.

Trade in the NT:

Jewish trade and commerce have small place in the Gospels. Through the NT times, trade, in the wider sense of the word, was in the hands of Rome and of Italy.

Travel:

Motives for travel: Trade, colonization, exploration, migration, pilgrimage, preaching, courier service, exile. Travel had serious hazards (Ac 27-28; 2Co 11:25-27); was facilitated by wonderful Roman roads, some of which still are used. Regular passenger service by land or sea was unknown.

TRADE GUILDS Societies of tradesmen organized chiefly for the purpose of social interaction (Ac 19), not trade unions in the modern sense.

TRADERS *See Commerce; Merchant.*

TRADITION The decisions and minor precepts taught by Paul (1Co 11:2; 2Th 2:15; 3:6).

Commandments of men (Mt 12:1-8; 15:2-6; Mk 7:3-9; Lk 6:1-11; Col 2:8; 1Pe 1:18). Not authoritative (Mt 15:3-20; 1Ti 1:4; 4:7). *See Commandments and Statutes, of Men.*

TRAFFIC Commerce suspended on the Sabbath (Ne 13:15-22).

TRAIN

1. Retinue of a monarch (Ps 68:18).
2. Skirt of a robe (Isa 6:1).
3. To educate or discipline (2Sa 22:35; Pr 22:6).

TRAITOR Judas (Mt 26:14-16, 46-50; Mk 14:10-11, 43-45; Lk 22:3-6, 21-23, 47-48; Jn 13:2, 27-30; 18:2-8, 13).

See Treason.

TRAMP NIV "bandit" (Pr 6:11).

TRANCE (*a throwing of the mind out of its normal state*). A mental state in which the senses are partially or wholly suspended and the person is unconscious of his environment while he contemplates some extraordinary object (Ac 10:9-16; 22:17-21).

TRANS-EUPHRATES The region beyond the Euphrates; from the Persian perpective it included Israel and its neighbors (Ezr 4:10-20; 5:6; 6:6).

TRANSFIGURATION Of Moses (Ex 34:29-35). Of Jesus (Mt 17:2-9; Mk 9:2-10; Lk 9:29-36; 2Pe 1:16-18). Of Stephen (Ac 6:15). *See Translation.*

TRANSGRESSION Breaking of a law (Pr 17:19; Ro 4:15). *See Sin.*

TRANSJORDAN (*beyond [East of] the Jordan*). A large plateau E of Jordan, comprised in modern Hashemite Kingdom of Jordan; in the NT times, the Perea and the Decapolis; in OT times, Moab, Ammon, Gilead, and Bashan. Associated with Moses; Joshua; the tribes of Reuben, Gad, and Manasseh; David; Nabateans.

TRANSLATION Removal from earth to heaven. Of Enoch (Ge 5:24; Heb 11:5). Of Elijah (2Ki 2:1-12). Of Jesus (Mk 16:19; Lk 24:51; Ac 1:9-11). Desired by Paul (2Co 5:4).

TRANSLATIONS OF THE BIBLE Ancient: *See Texts and Versions.*

TRANSPORTATION In ancient times done chiefly by camels, donkeys, horses, and boats.

TRAP (Jos 23:13; Job 18:10; Jer 5:26).

TRAVAIL Pangs of childbirth (Ge 35:16; 38:27; 1Sa 4:19), trouble (Isa 23:4; 54:1), to be weak or sick (Jer 4:31), weariness (Ex 18:8).

TRAVEL *See Trade and Travel.*

TREACHERY (Jer 9:8). Of Rahab to her people (Jos 2). Of the man of Bethel (Jdg 1:24-25). Of Jael (Jdg 4:18-21). Of Shechemites (Jdg 9:23). Of Joab (2Sa 3:26-27). Of Baanah and Recab (2Sa 4:6). Of David to Uriah (2Sa 11). Of Joab to Amasa (2Sa 20:9-10). Of Jehu (2Ki 10:18-28). Of the enemies of Nehemiah (Ne 6).

See Conspiracy; Treason.

TREASON

Instances of:

Of Aaron and Miriam against Moses (Nu 12:1-11). Of Korah, Dathan, and Abiram against Moses and Aaron (Nu 16:1-33). Of Rahab against Jericho (Jos 2). Of the betrayer of Bethel (Jdg 1:24-25). Of the Shechemites against Abimelech (Jdg 9:22-25). Of the Ephraimites against Jephthah (Jdg 12:1-4). Of the Israelites against Saul (1Sa 10:27), against Rehoboam (1Ki 12:16-19). Of the Egyptian servant against the Amalekites (1Sa 30:15-16). Of Abner against Ish-Bosheth (2Sa 3:6-21). Of Jehoiada against Athaliah (2Ki 11:14-16). Of Absalom against his father. *See Absalom.*

Death penalty for (Est 2:23).

Jesus falsely accused of (Mt 27:11, 29-30; Lk 23:2-3, 38; Jn 19:12, 14-15, 19). Paul falsely accused of (Ac 17:7).

David's amnesty of the traitors (2Sa 19:16-23), to Amasa (2Sa 19:13).

See Conspiracy; Treachery.

TREASURE A thing of highly estimated value. Money (Ge 42:25, 27-28, 35; 43:23, w 43:18, 21-22). Valuables of the temple and royal residence (1Ki 14:26; 2Ki 20:13).

Cannot save life (Job 20:20). Jesus forbids the hoarding of (Mt 6:19; 19:21; Lk 12:33). Hidden (Mt 13:44).

Figurative:

Of God's people (Ex 19:5; Dt 7:6). Of wisdom (Pr 2:4; 24:4; Col 2:3). Of spiritual understanding (Mt 13:52; Col 2:3), spiritual calling (2Co 4:6-7).

Treasures in heaven (Mt 6:19-21; 19:21; Lk 12:33-34). Gospel called (2Co 4:7). Parables of (Mt 13:44, 52).

TREASURE CITIES NIV "store cities" for Pharaoh (Ex 1:11).

TREASURE HOUSE *See Treasury.*

TREASURER One trusted with charge of the treasury. *See Treasury.* Of the temple (2Ki 12:5, 7). Of Persia (Ezr 1:8; 7:21). Of Babylon (Da 3:2, 3).

TREASURY Of kings (2Ki 14:14; 2Ch 32:27-28; Ezr 1:7-8; Est 3:9). Records preserved in (Ezr 6:1). *See Archives.* Treasurer in charge of (Ezr 7:20-21). *See Treasurer.*

Tabernacle used for (Jos 6:19, 24). Solomon's temple used for (1Ki 7:51; 2Ki 12:4-14, 18; 22:4-5; 1Ch 28:11-12; Mt 27:6; Mk 12:41, 43; Lk 21:1; Jn 8:20). Under the charge of the Levites (1Ch 26:20). Storerooms provided in the temple for various kinds of offerings (Ne 10:38-39; 13:5, 9, 12; Mal 3:10). Priests and Levites in charge of (1Ch 9:26; 26:20-28; Ne 12:44; 13:13). Pagan temples used for (Da 1:2).

TREATY Between nations: Israelites and Gibeonites (Jos 9:3-15), Judah and Syria (1Ki 15:19). Cession of territory by (1Ki 9:10-14; 20:34). Sacredness of (Jos 9:16-21, w 2:8-21).

Reciprocity (1Ki 5:1-12). With idolatrous nations forbidden (Ex 34:12, 15).

See Covenant.

TREE Israel in ancient times was far more wooded than today. Over 25 different kinds of trees have been identified as having grown in the Holy Land. Trees were venerated by heathen people; Hebrews forbidden to plant a tree near a sacred altar (Dt 16:21). Known by its fruit (Mt 7:17-19; Lk 6:43-44).

Specific Trees:

Acacia tree (Ex 25:10ff). Algum tree (2Ch 2:8; 9:11). Almond tree (Ge 30:37; Ex 25:33-36; Ecc 12:5; Jer 1:11). Almug tree (1Ki 10:11, 12; 2Ch. 2:8, 9:10 ftn). Apple tree (SS 2:3; 8:5; Joel 1:12). Balsam trees (2Sa 5:23-24). Broom tree (1Ki 19:3-4; Job 30:4; Ps 120:4). Cedar Wood (Lev 14:4, 6, 49, 51, 52; 2Sa 5:11; 2Sa 7:2; 1Ki 4:33). Citron Wood (Rev 18:12). Cypress Wood (Ge 6:14; Isa 44:14, 60:13; Eze 27:6). Fig tree (Dt 8:7). Fir (Isa 41:19; 60:13; SS 1:17. Fruit trees (Ge 1:29; Lev 19:23). Incense tree (SS 4:14). Mulberry tree (Lk 17:6). Mustard tree (Mt 13:32; Lk 13:18). Myrtle tree (Ne 8:15). Nut trees (SS 6:11). Oak (Ge 35:4; Zec 11:2; Eze 6:13). Olive tree (Jdg 9:8; Job 15:33; Ps 52:8; Isa 17:6; Isa 41:19). Palm trees (Ex 15:27). Pine tree (1Ki 5:10; Ps 104:17 ;Isa 60:13). Pistachio (Ge 43:11). Plane tree (Ge 30:37; Eze 31:8). Pomegranate (Dt 8:8; 1Sa 14:2). Poplars (Ge 30:37; Lev 23:40; Job 40:22; Ps 137:2; Isa 15:7, 44:4). Sycamore-fig tree (1Ki 10:27; 1Ch 27:28; 2Ch 1:15; Am 7:14; Lk 19:4). Tamarisk tree (Ge 21:33; 1Sa 22:6; 31:13). Terebinth (Isa 6:13; Hos 4:13).

Generic and Symbolic Trees:

Bad tree (Mt 7:18; 12:33; Lk 6:43). Eden trees (Eze 31:9, 18). Execution tree (Dt 21:23; Ac 5:30; 10:39; 13:29). Field trees (Isa 55:12). Forest trees (1Ch 16:33; Ps 96:12). Good tree (2Ki 3:19, 25; Mt 7:17, 12:33; Lk 6:43). Great trees (Ge 13:18; 14:13; Jos 19:33). Great tree (Ge 12:6). Green tree (Ps 37:35; Lk 23:30). Tree of Knowledge (Ge 2:9). Leafy tree (Eze 20:28). Tree of Life (Ge 3:22-24; Pr 3:18, 11:30, 13:12; 15:4; Rev 2:7; 22:2, 19). Lofty trees (Isa 10:33). Shade tree (Ne 8:15). Spreading tree (Dt 12:2; 1Ki 14:23; 2Ki 16:4, 17:10). Wild olive tree (Ro 11:24). Of Nebuchadnezzar (Da 4:1-27).

See Plants of the Bible; Tree of Knowledge; Tree of Life.

TREE OF KNOWLEDGE A special tree in the garden of Eden, set apart by the Lord as an instrument to test the obedience of Adam and Eve (Ge 2:9, 17; 3:3-6, 11-12, 17).

TREE OF LIFE Another special tree in the Garden of Eden; its fruit conferred immortality on persons eating it (Ge 2:9; 3:22, 24; Rev 22:2).

TRENCH Rampart, entrenchment (2Sa 20:15; 1Sa 17:20; 26:5).

TRES TABERNAE *See Three Taverns.*

TRESPASS (Ex 22:9). Of an ox (Ex 21:28-36). Of a brother (Mt 18:15-18; Lk 17:3-4). Creditor shall not enter a debtor's house to take a pledge (Dt 24:10). *See Sin.*

TRESPASS OFFERING *See Guilt Offering; Offerings.*

TRIAL Before court (Lev 24:10-14). Right of (Jn 7:51; Ac 16:37-39; 22:25-30). *See Court, Of Law; Justice; Prisoners.*

TRIAL OF JESUS Betrayed by Judas into the hands of the Jewish religious leaders, Jesus was first brought before Annas, former high priest, and father-in-law of the current high priest Caiaphas, for a brief examination (Jn 18:13); then before dawn he appeared before the Sanhedrin in the palace of Caiaphas, where he was questioned and insulted (Mk 14:60-65; Lk 22:63-64); at dawn he appeared before the Sanhedrin again and was condemned to death (Lk 22:66-70); next he was brought by the Sanhedrin before Pilate, who after an examination pronounced him innocent (Jn 18:33-38), but the Jews would not hear of his being released.

Pilate therefore sent him to Herod Antipas, who was also present for the Passover, on the plea that he belonged to Herod's jurisdiction. Herod; however, merely mocked Jesus and returned him to Pilate uncondemned (Lk 23:2-12); Pilate then gave the Jews the opportunity of choosing for release either Barabbas or Jesus, and the Jews chose Barabbas; another attempt by Pilate to have Jesus released met with failure, for the Jews threatened him if he did not carry out their wishes; after the Roman soldiers flogged and mocked Jesus, he was crucified (Mk 15:16-20).

See Jesus, History of.

TRIBE, TRIBES The tribes of Israel were descended from the twelve sons of Jacob, with Joseph's sons, Ephraim and Manasseh forming two, while no tribal territory was allotted to Levi (Ge 48:5; Nu 26:5-51; Jos 13:7-33; 15-19). The leaders of the tribes are called by various names: princes, rulers, heads, chiefs (Ex 34:31; Nu 1:16; Ge 36:1ff); before the Israelites entered the promised land two tribes, Reuben and Gad, and half of Manasseh chose to settle on the E side of the Jordan (Nu 32:33). During the period of the Judges in Israel, the tribes were each one a law to themselves. When David became king over the whole land the 12 tribes were unified. He appointed a captain over each tribe (1Ch 27:16-22). The captivities wiped out tribal distinctions.

TRIBULATION, GREAT A period of suffering sent from God upon the earth at the end time because of its awful wickedness (Da 12:1; Mt 24:21).

TRIBUTE From conquered nations (Jos 16:10; Jdg 1:30-33; 2Ki 15:19; 23:35; Mt 17:24-27; 22:15-22; Lk 2:1-5). By Arabs to Solomon (2Ch 9:14), to Jehoshaphat (2Ch 17:11). *See Duty; Levy; Tax.*

TRIMMERS, WICK *See Wick Trimmers.*

TRINITY, HOLY (*triad, union of three*). The word "trinity" is not used in the Bible. Plurality in the unity of God is implied in the OT; Father, Son, and Spirit are all called "God" in the NT.

Implied in the Old Testament:

God speaks of self in the plural (Ge 1:26; 3:22; Isa 6:3, 8). LORD, Servant, and Spirit (Isa 11:2-3; 42:1 w Mt 12:48; Isa 48:16). Tri-holiness of God suggests (Isa 6:3; Rev 4:8).

Implied in the NT:

Father, Son, and Spirit (Mt 28:19; Lk 3:22 w Mt 3:16; Jn 3:34-35; 14:16-17, 26; 15:26; 16:7, 13-15; Ac 1:2, 4-5; 2:33; 10:36-38; Ro 1:3-4; 8:9-11, 26-27; 1Co 12:3-6; 2Co 1:21-22; 5:5; 13:14; Gal 4:4, 6; 2Th 2:13-14, 16; 1Ti 3:16; Tit 3:4-6; Heb 9:14; 1Pe 1:2; 3:18; 1Jn 5:6-7). Tri-holiness of God suggests (Isa 6:3; Rev 4:8).

Relationships Within the Godhead:

The Father and the Son (Mt 11:27; Lk 9:26; Jn 3:35; 5:19-27; 6:27; 10:36; 17:1; Ac 13:33; Heb 1:5; 5:5; 2Pe 1:17; 1Jn 1:3; 2:22-24).

The Father and the Holy Spirit (Isa 42:1; 48:16; 63:9-10; 1Co 2:10-11; 6:19).

Jesus and the Holy Spirit (Isa 61:1-3; Lk 4:18; Mt 1:18, 20; 12:28; 28:19; Lk 1:35; 4:1, 14; Jn 1:32-33; 7:39; 20:22; 1Co 8:6; 2Co 3:17; Php 1:19; Col 2:2).

See Angel [of the Lord]; God; Holy Spirit; Jesus the Christ, Deity of.

TRIPOLIS People sent as colonists to Samaria by the Assyrians (Ezr 4:9-10).

T

TRIUMPH (*to lead in triumph*). In Roman times a magnificent procession in honor of a victorious general (2Co 2:14; Col 2:15).

TRIUMPHAL ENTRY OF JESUS Into Jerusalem (Ps 118:26; Zec 9:9; Mt 21:5, 8-10; Mk 11:7-11; Lk 19:35-38; Jn 12:12-13).

TROAS A chief city and port of the Roman Province of Asia, on the Aegean coast, c. ten miles from the ruins of ancient Troy; known as Alexandria Troas (Ac 16:8; 20:5; 2Co 2:12).

TROGYLLIUM A promontory thrusting SW from the Asian mainland N of Miletus, opposite the island of Samos (Ac 20:15, KJV).

TROPHIES Goliath's head and armor (1Sa 17:54; 21:9), Saul's (1Sa 31:8-10). Placed in temples. *See Temple.*

TROPHIMUS (*nourished [child]*). An Ephesian companion of Paul. Accompanies Paul from Greece to Asia (Ac 20:4). With Paul in Jerusalem; made the occasion of an attack on Paul (Ac 21:27-30). Left ill at Miletus (2Ti 4:20).

TROUBLE Being anxious, forbidden (Mt 6:25-34; Php 4:6). Remedy for anxiety (Jn 16:6-7; 1Pe 5:7).

See Affliction; Anxiety; Suffering.

Instances of:

Israelites at the Red Sea (Ex 14:10-12), about water (Ex 15:23-25; 17:2-3; Nu 20:1-13), food (Ex 16:2-3; Nu 11:4-33). When Moses remained on Mount Sinai (Ex 32:1). When the spies brought their adverse report (Nu 13:28-29, 31-33; 14:1-4, w 14:4-12). Elijah, under the broom tree and in the cave (1Ki 19:4-15). The disciples, as to how the multitude could be fed (Mt 14:15; Mk 6:37), in the tempest, when Jesus was asleep in the ship (Mt 8:23-26; Mk 4:36-39; Lk 8:22-24), when Jesus was crucified (Lk 24:4-9, 24-31, 36-40). Mary at the tomb (Jn 20:11-17). The people in the shipwreck (Ac 27:22-25, 30-36).

TRUCE In battle (2Sa 2:26-31).

TRUMPET Made of ram's horn (Jos 6:4-6, 8, 13), of silver (Nu 10:2).

Uses of:

Prescribed by Moses (Nu 10:1-10). Used in war (Job 39:24-25; Jer 4:19; 6:1, 17; 42:14; 51:27; Eze 7:14; Am 2:2; 3:6; Zep 1:16; 1Co 14:8). To summon soldiers, by Phinehas (Nu 31:6), by Ehud (Jdg 3:27), by Gideon (Jdg 6:34), by Saul (1Sa 13:3), by Joab (2Sa 2:28; 18:16; 20:22), by Absalom (2Sa 15:10), by Sheba (2Sa 20:1), by Nehemiah (Ne 4:18, 20). Gideon's soldiers (Jdg 7:8-22). In war, of Abijah (2Ch 13:12, 14). In the siege of Jericho (Jos 6:4-20).

Sounded in time of danger (Eze 33:3-6; Joel 2:1).

Used at Sinai (Ex 19:13-19; 20:18; Heb 12:19), on the Day of Atonement (Isa 27:13), at the Jubilee (Lev 25:9), at the bringing up of the ark (2Sa 6:5, 15; 1Ch 13:8; 15:28), the anointing of kings (1Ki 1:34, 39; 2Ki 9:13; 11:14), dedication of Solomon's temple (2Ch 5:12-13; 7:6), in worship (1Ch 15:24; 16:42; 25:5; Ps 81:3-4), at Jehoshaphat's triumph (2Ch 20:28), at the foundation of the second temple (Ezr 3:10-11), at the dedication of the wall (Ne 12:35, 41).

Figurative:

(Isa 27:13; Eze 33:3; Joel 2:1; Zec 9:14; Mt 6:2).

Symbolic:

(Mt 24:31; 1Co 15:52; 1Th 4:16; Rev 1:10; 4:1; 8; 9:1-14; 10:7; 11:15).

See Horn; Music, Instruments of.

TRUMPETS, FEAST OF When and how observed (Lev 23:24-25; Nu 29:1-6). Celebrated after the captivity with joy (Ne 8:2, 9-12).

See Feasts.

TRUST *See Faith.*

TRUSTEE Mosaic law concerning (Ex 22:7-13; Lev 6:2-7). The parable of the pounds (Mt 25:14-28; Lk 19:12-27).

See Steward.

TRUTH Truth and faithful(ness) are translated from the same Hebrew and Greek words. *See Faithfulness.*

Characteristics of:

(Ps 85:10-11). Precious (Pr 23:23). Preserves (Ps 46:11; 61:7; 91:4; Pr 20:28). Purifies (Pr 16:6; 1Pe 1:22). Sanctifies (Jn 17:17, 19; 2Th 2:13). Brings freedom (Jn 8:32).

Reaches to the clouds (Ps 57:10; 108:4). Endures forever (Ps 100:5; 117:2). Ways of the Lord in (Ps 25:10).

The foundation of which Christ is the cornerstone (Eph 2:20). Came by Jesus Christ (Jn 1:17; 8:45; 14:6; 18:37-38; Eph 2:20). Revealed to the righteous (Ps 57:3; 86:11).

Word of God called the word of (Jn 17:17; Eph 1:13; Col 1:5; 2Ti 2:15; Jas 1:18). Scripture of (Da 10:21).

Acceptance of, necessary to salvation (2Th 2:12-13; 1Ti 2:4; 2Ti 2:25; 3:7; Heb 10:26). Rejection of, brings condemnation (2Th 2:10-12; Tit 1:14).

To be taught by parents to children (Isa 38:19). Church is the pillar of (1Ti 3:15).

Believers should worship God in (Jn 4:24, w Ps 145:18), serve God in (Jos 24:14; 1Sa 12:24), walk before God in (1Ki 2:4; 2Ki 20:3), keep religious feasts with (1Co 5:8), value as inestimable (Pr 23:23), love (Zec 8:19), rejoice in (1Co 13:6), speak to one another (Zec 8:16; Eph 4:25), execute judgment with (Zec 8:16), meditate upon (Php 4:8), bind about the neck (Pr 3:3), write upon the tables of the heart (Pr 3:3).

The fruit of the light (Eph 5:9). They who speak, show righteousness (Pr 12:17), are the delight of God (Pr 12:22), will be established forever (Pr 2:1).

The wicked are destitute of truth (Isa 59:14-15; Da 9:13; Hos 4:1; 1Ti 6:5). The wicked resist (2Ti 3:8; 4:4), turn away from (2Ti 4:4), speak not (Jer 9:5), plead not for (Isa 59:4), are not valiant for (Jer 9:3), punished for lack of (Jer 9:5, 9; Hos 4:1, 3). *See Wicked.*

The Gospel As:

Came by Christ (Jn 1:17). Is in Christ (1Ti 2:7). John bore witness to (Jn 5:33). Is according to godliness (Tit 1:1). Is sanctifying (Jn 17:17, 19). Is purifying (1Pe 1:22). Is part of the Christian armor (Eph 6:14). Revealed abundantly to saints (Jer 33:6). Abides continually with saints (2Jn 2).

Should be acknowledged (2Ti 2:25). Should be believed (2Th 2:12-13; 1Ti 4:3). Should be obeyed (Ro 2:8; Gal 3:1). Should be loved (2Th 2:10). Should be manifested (2Co 4:2). Should be rightly divided (2Ti 2:15). The church is the pillar and ground of (1Ti 3:15).

The devil is devoid of (Jn 8:44).

Of the Gospel:

(2Ti 4:3-4; Tit 1:1, 14; 2:1; Jas 1:18, 21, 23, 25; 2:13; 5:19; 1Pe 1:22-25; 2:2, 8; 3:1; 5:12; 2Pe 1:12). *See God, Truth.*

Of God:

Is one of his attributes (Dt 32:4; Isa 65:16). Often linked with his mercy (Ps 85:10-11; 93:3; 100:5).

He keeps, forever (Ps 146:6), abundant (Ex 34:6), inviable (Nu 23:19; Tit 1:2), enduring to all generations (Ps 100:5). Exhibited in his ways (Rev 15:3), works (Ps 33:4; 111:7; Da 4:37), judicial statutes (Ps 19:9), word (Ps 119:160; Jn 17:17), fulfillment of promises in Christ (2Co 1:20), fulfillment of His covenant (Mic 7:20), dealings with saints (Ps 25:10), deliverance of saints (Ps 57:3), punishment of the wicked (Rev 16:7). Is a shield and buckler to saints (Ps 91:4).

Believers should confide in (Ps 31:5; Tit 1:2). Plead in prayer (Ps 89:49). Pray for its manifestation to ourselves (2Ch 6:17). Pray for its exhibition to others (2Sa 2:6). Make known, to others (Isa 38:19). Magnify (Ps 71:22; 138:2).

Is denied by the devil (Ge 3:4-5), the self-righteous (1Jn 1:10), unbelievers (1Jn 5:10).

Attribute:

Of God (Ex 34:6; Dt 32:4; Ps 31:5; 40:10-11; 71:22; 86:15; 89:14; 115:1; 117:2; 138:2; 146:6; Isa 25:1; 65:16; Jer 4:2; 5:3). Exhibited in His government (Ps 119:151), in His judgments (Ps 96:13; Ro 2:2), in His word (Jn 17:19), in His works (Ps 111:7-8; Da 4:37).

Of Christ (Jn 1:14; 14:6).

Of the Holy Spirit (Jn 14:17; 16:13; 1Jn 5:7-8).

Of the Righteous (Ps 51:6; Pr 3:3; Jn 3:21; 3Jn 3).

Righteous, should be prepared with (Eph 6:14), should know (1Ti 4:3; 1Jn 2:21; 3:19; 4:6), should love (Zec 8:19; 2Th 2:10), should rejoice in (1Co 13:6), should meditate upon (Php 4:8).

TRUTHFULNESS Commended (Pr 12:17, 19). Commanded (Zec 8:16; Eph 4:25; Col 3:9). Magistrates should be men of (Ex 18:21). Fearlessness in (2Co 12:6; Gal 4:16). Of Job (Job 27:4; 36:4).

Wicked, lack (Jer 9:5). Satan, devoid of (Jn 8:44). *See Satan; Wicked.*

TRYPHENA (*dainty*). A Christian woman friend of Paul's in Rome (Ro 16:12).

TRYPHOSA (*delicate*). A Christian woman friend of Paul's in Rome (Ro 16:12).

TUBAL The son of Japheth (Ge 10:2; 1Ch 1:5). Descendants of, become a nation (Isa 66:19; Eze 27:13; 32:26; 38:2-3; 39:1).

TUBAL-CAIN The son of Lamech and Zillah; worker in bronze and iron (Ge 4:22).

TUMBLEWEED Symbolic of wicked blown away in judgment (Ps 83:13; Isa 17:13). *See Plants of the Bible.*

TUMOR A disease with which the Philistines were afflicted (1Sa 5:6, 9, 12; 6:4-5, 11, 17). *See Disease; Hemorrhoids.*

TUNIC A shirtlike garment worn by men and women under other clothes in Bible times. Worn by priests (Ex 28:4, 39-40). Saul offers his to David (1Sa 17:38-39), as does Jonathan (1Sa 18:4). *See Dress.*

TURBAN Headcovering. Worn by the high priest (Ex 28:3, 37-39), by other priests (Eze 44:18), by royalty (Eze 21:26). *See Headbands.*

TURQUOISE In the high priest's breastpiece (Ex 28:18; 39:11), in the temple (1Ch 29:2). Commerce in (Eze 27:16). *See Minerals of the Bible; Stones.*

TURTLE, TURTLEDOVE *See Dove, Turtle.*

TUTOR (2Ki 10:1; Ac 22:3; Gal 4:1-2).

TWELVE, THE *See Apostles.*

TWILIGHT (1Sa 30:17; 2Ki 7:5; Job 3:9; Eze 12:6).

TWINS Jacob and Esau (Ge 25:24-26). Perez and Zerah (Ge 38:27-30). *See Castor and Pollux.*

TWO-AND-A-HALF TRIBES Reuben, Gad, and half of Manasseh settled in the Trans-Jordan (Jos 14:3).

TYCHICUS (*good fortune*). An Asian companion of Paul. Accompanies Paul from Greece to Asia (Ac 20:4). With Paul in Nicopolis (Tit 3:12), in Rome (Eph 6:21-22; Col 4:7-8). Sent to Ephesus (Eph 6:21-22; 2Ti 4:12), to Colosse (Col 4:7-8).

TYPES

Miscellaneous:

Bride, a type of the church (Rev 21:2, 9; 22:17). The sanctuary a type of the heavenly sanctuary (Ex 40:2, 24; Heb 8:2, 5; 9:1-12). The saving of Noah and his family, of the salvation through the gospel (1Pe 3:20-21).

Defilement a type of sin. *See Defilement; Purification.* Leaven a type of sin. *See Leaven.* Washings a type of purification. *See Washings.*

See Allegory; Parable; Symbols and Similitudes.

Of Sin: *See Blemish; Defilement; Leaven.*

Of the Savior:

(Col 2:17; Heb 9:7-15, 18-28; 10:1-10). High priest, typical of the mediatorship (Ex 28:1, 12, 29-30, 38; Lev 16:15; Zec 6:12-13, w Heb 5; 8:2; 10:21). The institutions ordained by Moses (Mt 26:54; Lk 24:25-27, 44-47; Col 2:14-17; Heb 10:1-14). The sacrifices (Lev 4:2-3, 12; Heb 9:7-15, 18-25; 10:1-22, 29; 13:11-13; 1Pe 1:19; Rev 5:6). The morning and evening sacrifice (Jn 1:29, 36). The red heifer (Nu 19:2-6, w Heb 9:13-14). The Passover lamb (1Co 5:7). The bronze altar (Ex 27:1-2, w Heb 13:10). The bronze basin (Ex 30:18-20, w Zec 13:1; Eph 5:26-27). Atonement cover (Ex 25:17-22, w Heb 4:16). The veil (Ex 40:21; 2Ch 3:14, w Heb 10:20). Manna (Jn 6:32-35; 1Co 10:3). Cities of refuge (Nu 35:6, w Heb 6:18). Bronze snake (Nu 21:9; Jn 3:14-15). Tree of life (Ge 2:9, w Jn 1:4; Rev 22:2).

Adam (Ro 5:14; 1Co 15:45). Abel (Ge 4:8, 10, w Heb 12:24). Noah (Ge 5:29, w 2Co 1:5). Melchizedek (Heb 7:1-17). Moses (Dt 18:15, 18; Ac 3:20, 22; 7:37; Heb 3:2-6). David (2Sa 8:15; Ps 89:19-20; Eze 37:24; Php 2:9). Eliakim (Isa 22:20-22; Rev 3:7). Jonah (Jnh 1:17, w Mt 12:40).

TYRANNUS (*ruler*). A Greek teacher in whose school Paul preached after he was expelled from the synagogue (Ac 19:9).

TYRANNY (Pr 28:16; Isa 54:11-14). *See Government.*

TYRE, TYRIANS (*rocky place*).
1. Kingdom of; Hiram, king of (1Ki 5:1-2; 2Ch 2:3). Sends material to David for his palace (2Ch 2:3). Men and materials sent from, to Solomon, for the building of the temple and palaces (1Ki 5:1-11; 9:10-11; 2Ch 2:3-16).
See Hiram.
2. City of. Situated on the shore of the Mediterranean. On the northern boundary of Asher (Jos 19:29). Pleasant site of (Hos 9:13). Fortified (Jos 19:29; 2Sa 24:7). Commerce of (1Ki 9:26-28; 10:11; Isa 23; Eze 27; 28:1-19; Zec 9:2; Ac 21:3). Merchants of (Isa 23:8). Antiquity of (Isa 23:7). Riches of (Isa 23:8; Zec 9:3). Besieged by Nebuchadnezzar (Eze 26:7; 29:18).
Jesus goes to the coasts of (Mt 15:21). Heals the daughter of the Syrian Phoenician woman near (Mt 15:21-28; Mk 7:24-31). Multitudes from, come to hear Jesus and to be healed of their diseases (Mk 3:8; Lk 6:17). Herod's hostility toward (Ac 12:20-23). Paul visits (Ac 21:3-7).
To be judged according to its opportunity and privileges (Mt 11:21-22; Lk 10:13-14).
Prophecies relating to (Ps 45:12; 87:4; Isa 23; Jer 25:22; 27:1-11; 47:4; Eze 26-28; Joel 3:4-8; Am 1:9-10; Zec 9:2-4).

TYROPEON VALLEY (*valley of the cheese makers*). A valley in Jerusalem separating W and E hills and joining Kidron and Hinnom valleys on the S.

U

UCAL (possibly *I am consumed*, or *I cease*). An obscure word; usually taken as son or pupil of Agur (Pr 30:1).

UEL (possibly *will of El [God]* BDB KB). An Israelite who divorced his Gentile wife (Ezr 10:34).

UGARIT *See Amarna, Tell El; Ras Shamra; Texts, Ancient Near Eastern Non-Biblical Texts Relating to the Old Testament.*

ULAI A river in Elam near Susa on whose bank Daniel saw a vision (Da 8:2, 16).

ULAM (*first, leader*).
1. The son of Sheresh (1Ch 7:16-17).
2. The son of Eshek (1Ch 8:39-40).

ULLA An Asherite (1Ch 7:39).

UMMAH A city of Asher (Jos 19:30).

UNBELIEF

Characteristics of:
Caused by spiritual blindness (Isa 6:9-10; Mt 13:13-15, 58; Lk 13:34; 19:41-42; Jn 12:37, 39-40, 47). Hardens the heart (Ps 95:8-11; Heb 3:12; 3:16-19; Ac 19:9). Rejects Christ (Isa 53:1-3; Jn 12:38; Mk 6:3, 6; Jn 1:11; 5:38, 40, 44, 46-47; 10:25-26). Displeases God (Ps 78:19-22; Heb 11:6). Makes God a liar (1Jn 5:10). Does not nullify God's faithfulness (Ro 3:3-4). Allows God to extend his mercy (Ro 11:20, 30-32). Characteristic of all mankind (Ro 11:20, 30-32; 2Th 3:2).
Illustrated (Ro 10:6-7, 16; 2Pe 3:4). Parable of (Mk 4:24-25; Lk 8:12, 18; 14:16-24).
At Christ's second coming (Lk 18:8). The spirit of the antichrist (1Jn 2:22-23; 4:3).
Used as an excuse by Moses (Ex 4:1).

Condemned:
Leads to: Defeat (Isa 7:9). Destruction (Ro 11:20; 2Th 2:12). Reproof (Jn 16:8-9). Condemnation (Ro 14:23). Rejection (1Pe 2:7-8). Instability (Jas 1:6-7).
Admonitions against (Ac 13:40-41; 2Co 6:14-16; Heb 3:12, 16-19; 4:1-3, 6, 11; 12:25).

UNBELIEVERS Are spiritually blind (Jn 14:17; 1Co 2:14; 2Pe 3:4-7). Are impure (Tit 1:15). Make God a liar (1Jn 5:10). Will not be convinced (Lk 16:31; 22:67; Jn 4:48; 12:37-40). God's forbearance toward (Ro 10:16, 21). Shall be destroyed (Jer 5:12-14; Mt 10:14-15; Lk 12:46; Jn 8:24; 12:48; Ac 13:41; 1Co 1:18; 2Th 2:11-12; Jude 5-7; Rev 21:8). Tongues a sign to (1Co 14:22).

Instances of:
Eve (Ge 3:4-6). Moses (Nu 11:21-23) and Aaron (Nu 20:12). Israelites (Dt 9:23; 2Ki 17:14; Ps 78; 106:7, 24; Isa 58:3; Mal 1:2, 7). Naaman (2Ki 5:12). Samaritan lord (2Ki 7:2).
Disciples (Mt 17:17; Lk 24:11, 25). Zechariah (Lk 1:20). Chief priests (Mt 21:32; Lk 22:67). The Jews (Mt 11:16-19; Mk 1:45; 2:6-11; 8:11-12; 15:29-32; Lk 7:31-35; Jn 5:38, 40, 43, 46-47; Ac 22:18; 28:24). Disciples (Mt 17:20; Mk 4:38, 40; 16:14, 16; Lk 24:11, 21, 25-26, 36-45; Jn 6:36, 60-62, 64, 66, 70-71). The father of a child possessed with a spirit confesses (Mk 9:24). Brothers of Christ (Jn 7:5). Thomas (Jn 20:25). Jews of Iconium (Ac 14:2). Thessalonian Jews (Ac 17:5). Jews in Jerusalem (Ro 15:31). Ephesians (Ac 19:9). Saul (1Ti 1:13). People of Jericho (Heb 11:31).

UNBELIEVING ISRAELITES Destroyed (Nu 14:11, 13-39; 32:11; Dt 1:34-35; Ps 95:11; 106:26; 1Co 10:5, 10; Heb 3:17; Jude 5).

UNBLEMISHED Offerings must be (Ex 12:5; Lev 22:21; Eph 5:27; 1Pe 1:19).

UNCHARITABLENESS (Isa 29:21).

Admonitions Against:
(Mt 7:1-5; Lk 6:37-42; 12:57; Jn 7:24; 8:7; Ro 2:1; 14:1-15; 1Co 4:3-5, 7; 13:1-6). Forbidden (Jas 4:11-12).
See Accusation, False; Charitableness; Judgment; Slander; Speaking, Evil; Talebearer.

Instances of:
The Israelites toward Moses, charging him with having made them abhorred by the Egyptians (Ex 5:21), charging him with bringing them out of Egypt to die (Ex 14:11-12), in murmuring against Moses. *See Murmuring, Instances of.*
The tribes west of Jordan toward the two and a half tribes (Nu 32:1-33; Jos 22:11-31). Of Eli toward Hannah (1Sa 1:14-17).
Eliab toward David, charging him with presumption, when he offered to fight Goliath (1Sa 17:28). Princes of Ammon toward David, when he sent commissioners to convey his sympathy to Hanun (2Sa 10:3). Bildad toward Job (Job 8). Eliphaz toward Job (Job 15; 22; 42:7-8). Zophar toward Job (Job 11:1-6; 20). Nathanael, when he said, "Can any good thing come out of Nazareth" (Jn 1:46). The Jews, charging Paul with teaching contrary to the law and against the temple (Ac 21:28).

UNCIAL LETTERS A style of handwriting that uses capitals for most letters. Early Greek manuscripts of the NT were written in uncials.

UNCIRCUMCISED
1. One who has not submitted to the Jewish rite of circumcision.
2. Gentiles (Ge 34:14; Jdg 14:3; Ro 4:9).
3. One whose heart is not open to God (Jer 4:4; 6:10; Ac 7:51).

UNCLE
1. Brother of one's father or mother (2Ki 24:17).
2. Any kinsman on father's side (Lev 10:4; Am 6:10).

UNCLEAN, UNCLEANNESS
1. Two kinds of uncleanness: Moral and ceremonial.
2. Foods regarded as unclean in the OT: Animals that did not chew the cud and have a split hoof; animals and birds that eat blood or carrion; anything strangled or that died of itself (Lev 11:1-8, 26-28); water creatures without scales and fins (Lev 11:9-12); insects without hind legs for jumping (Lev 11).
3. Other forms of ceremonial uncleanness; contact with the dead (Lev 11:24-40; 17:15; Nu 19:16-22), leprosy (Lev 13; 14; Nu 5:2), sexual discharge (Lev 15:16-33), childbirth (Lev 12:6-8). In Christianity uncleanness is moral, not ceremonial.
See Purification.

UNCLOTHED Figurative (Mt 22:11; 2Co 5:3; Rev 3:17; 16:15).

UNCTION *See Anointing.*

UNDEFILED Any person or thing not tainted with moral evil (Ps 119:1; Heb 7:26; 13:4; 1Pe 1:4).

UNDERGARMENTS For the priests (Ex 28:42; 39:28; Lev 6:10; 16:4; Eze 44:18). Of Jesus (Jn 19:23). *See Dress.*

UNDERSETTERS NIV "supports" for the movable stands in Solomon's temple (1Ki 7:30, 34).

UNFAITHFULNESS

Characteristics of:
Unfaithful in little, unfaithful in much (Lk 16:10). Brings spiritual bankruptcy (Mt 13:12; 25:29). Brings destruction (Jn 15:2). Brings condemnation (Lk 19:12-27; Mt 25:41-46). God deals with accordingly (Pr 24:11-12; Mt 25:8-13, 24-30, 41-46).

Denounced:
In the parables of the vineyard (Isa 5:1-7; Mt 21:33-43; Mk 12:1-9). In the parable of the empty vine (Hos 10:1-2). In the parable of the slothful servant (Mt 25:24-30; Lk 19:20-27).

Illustrated:
By the unfruitful tree (Mt 3:10; Mk 11:13-14). By the unfruitful branch (Jn 15:2, 4, 6). By blindness (2Pe 1:8-9).
See Sin, Fruits of; Unfruitfulness; also, Righteousness, Fruits of.
Of friends: *See Friends, False.*

UNFRUITFULNESS Punished (Isa 5:1-10; Mt 3:10 w Lk 3:9; Mt 7:19; 13:3-7 w Mk 4:3-7, 14-19 & Lk 8:4-14; Mt 21:19-20; Mk 11:13; Lk 3:9; 13:6-9; Jn 15:2, 4; 15:6).
See Sin, Fruits of; Unfaithfulness; also, Righteousness, Fruits of.

UNGODLY To be avoided (Ps 1:1). Seem to materially prosper (Ps 73:11). Judged (Ps 1:6; 3:7; 2Pe 3:7). Christ died for (Ro 5:6), therefore God justifies (Ro 4:5). Law made for (1Ti 1:9).
See Wicked.

UNICORN *See Wild Ox.*

UNION Advantages of (Pr 15:22; Ecc 4:9-12).
Of the righteous: *See Unity, Of the Righteous; Righteous, Union of, with Christ.*

UNITY

Of the Godhead: *See God, Unity of.*

Of the Righteous:
(Ps 133:1; Isa 52:8; Ac 4:32). Advantages of (Pr 15:22; Ecc 4:9-12). Fraternal (Mt 23:8).
Commanded among Christians (Ro 12:16; 14:19; 15:5-6; 1Co 1:10; 2Co 13:11; Eph 4:3; Php 1:27; 2:2; 3:16-17; 1Pe 3:8). Christ's prayer for, of the church (Jn 17:11, 21-23).
See Communion; Fellowship; One Another.

UNKNOWN GOD Inscription on an altar at Athens dedicated to an unknown god that worshipers did not want to overlook (Ac 17:23).

UNKNOWN TONGUE KJV "unknown" is a translator's insertion (in italics) for the term normally rendered simply "tongues" (1Co 14:2, 4, 13-14, 19, 27). *See Tongues, Gift of.*

UNLEARNED Illiterate (Ac 4:13; 2Pe 3:16), nonprofessional (1Co 14:16, 23f).

UNLEAVENED Unmixed with yeast (1Co 5:7-8).

UNLEAVENED BREAD Bread made without yeast (Ex 12:8).

UNLEAVENED BREAD, FEAST OF *See Feasts.*

UNNI (*Yahweh has answered*).
1. A Levite; musician (1Ch 15:18, 20).
2. A Levite; musician (Ne 12:9).

UNPARDONABLE SIN Blasphemy against the Holy Spirit (Mt 12:31-32; Mk 3:28-29; Lk 12:10); either attributing to Satan the work of the Holy Spirit through Jesus, or rejecting the testimony of the Holy Spirit regarding the person and work of Jesus Christ. Possibly the same as the sin that leads to death (1Jn 5:16-17).
Instances of unpardoned sin: Israel (Nu 14:26-45), Eli's house (1Sa 3:14).

UNSELFISHNESS

Commanded:
In the royal law (Jas 2:8). In the church (Ro 12:10; 15:1; 1Co 10:24; Gal 6:2; Php 2:3-4).

Inspired by:
Love (1Co 13:4-5). Jesus' love (2Co 5:14-15).

Instances of:
Abraham (Ge 13:9; 14:23-24). King of Sodom (Ge 14:21). Hittites (Ge 23:6, 11). Judah (Ge 44:33-34). Moses (Nu 11:29; 14:12-19). Gideon (Jdg 8:22-23). Saul (1Sa 11:12-13). Jonathan (1Sa 23:17-18). David (1Sa 24:17; 2Sa 15:19-20; 23:16-17; 1Ch 21:17; Ps 69:6). Araunah (2Sa 24:22-24). Nehemiah (Ne 5:14-18). Jews (Est 9:15). Daniel (Da 5:17). Jonah (Jnh 1:12-13).
Joseph (Mt 1:19). Jesus (Ro 15:3; 2Co 8:9). The disciples (Ac 4:34-35). Priscilla and Aquila (Ro 16:3-4). Paul (1Co 10:33; Php 1:18; 4:17; 2Th 3:8). Philemon (Phm 13-14). Onesiphorus (2Ti 1:16-18).
See Charitableness; Fellowship; Fraternity; Selfishness.

UNTEMPERED MORTAR *See Whitewash.*

UNWORTHINESS (Mt 10:37; 22:8; Ac 13:46).

UPHARSIN *See Parsin.*

UPHAZ A place where gold was obtained (Jer 10:9; Da 10:5), location unknown. Perhaps "Ophir" should be read. *See Ophir, 2.*

UPPER CHAMBER, UPPER ROOM A room built on the wall or roof of a house (1Ki 17:19; Ac 20:9); scene of the Lord's Last Supper (Mk 14:15; Lk 22:12).

UPPER EGYPT Pathros; southern Egypt. Israelite captives in (Isa 11:11, ftn; Jer 44:1, 15; Eze 29:14). Prophecy against (Eze 30:14). *See Egypt.*

UPRIGHTNESS *See Righteousness.*

UR (*flame, light*). Father of Eliphal (1Ch 11:35). Possibly the same as Ahasbai (2Sa 23:34). *See Ahasbai.*

UR OF THE CHALDEANS A city in S Mesopotamia, c. 140 miles SE of old Babylon; the early home of Abraham (Ge 11:28, 31; 15:7; Ne 9:7).

URBANUS (*refined, elegant*). A Roman Christian (Ro 16:9).

URI (*Yahweh is [my] flame, light*).
1. The father of Bezalel (Ex 31:2; 35:20; 38:22; 1Ch 2:20; 2Ch 1:5).
2. The father of Geber (1Ki 4:19).
3. The temple gatekeeper who divorced his foreign wife (Ezr 10:24).

URIAH (*Yahweh is [my] flame, light*).
1. A Hittite; the husband of Bathsheba (2Sa 11:3).
2. High priest during the reign of Ahaz of Judah, for whom he built a pagan altar in the temple (2Ki 16:10-16).
3. A priest who aided Ezra (Ne 8:4).
4. The father of Meremoth (Ezr 8:33; Ne 3:4).
5. The son of Shemaiah, a prophet of Kiriath Jearim, in the time of Jehoiakim. Prophesies against Judah (Jer 26:20). Fled to Egypt; taken; slain by Jehoiakim (Jer 26:21-23).

URIEL (*God [El] is [my] flame, light*).
1. A Kohathite Levite (1Ch 6:24).
2. A chief of the Kohathites who assisted in bringing the ark from the house of Obed-Edom (1Ch 15:5, 11).
3. The father of Maacah, wife of Rehoboam (2Ch 13:2, ftn).

URIJAH *See Uriah.*

URIM AND THUMMIM (*lights and perfections*). Signifying light and perfection. In the breastplate (Ex 28:30; Lev 8:8). Eleazar to ask counsel for Joshua, after the judgment of (Nu 27:21). Priests only might interpret (Dt 33:8; Ezr 2:63; Ne 7:65). Israelites consult (Jdg 1:1; 20:18, 23). Withheld answer from King Saul (1Sa 28:6).

USURPATION

Of Political Functions:
By Absalom (2Sa 15:1-12). By Adonijah (1Ki 1:5-9). By Baasha (1Ki 15:27-28). By Zimri (1Ki 16:9-10). By Jehu (2Ki 9:11-37). By Athaliah (2Ki 11:1-16). By Shallum (2Ki 15:10). *See Rebellion.*

In Ecclesiastical Affairs:
By Saul, in assuming priestly functions (1Sa 13:8-14). By Solomon, in thrusting Abiathar out of the priesthood (1Ki 2:26-27). By Uzziah, in assuming priestly offices (2Ch 26:16-21). By Ahaz (2Ki 16:12-13).
See Church, The Body of Believers, State; Government, Ecclesiastical.

Of Executive Power:
In ordering Naboth's death and confiscation of his vineyard (1Ki 21:7-19). In the scheme of Joseph to dispossess the Egyptians of their real and personal property (Ge 47:13-26). Of Pharaoh, making bondservants of the Israelites (Ex 1:9-22). Moses accused of (Nu 16:3).

USURY Interest, not necessarily unreasonable exaction, but all income from loans. Forbidden (Ex 22:25; Lev 25:35-37; Dt 23:19; Ps 15:5; Pr 28:8; Jer 15:10; Eze 18:8, 13, 17; 22:12). Exaction of, rebuked (Ne 5:1-13). Authorized, of strangers (Dt 23:20). Exacted by the Jews (Eze 22:12). Just men innocent of the vice of requiring (Eze 18:8).
See Interest; Money.

UTHAI (possibly *superiority of Yahweh* IDB; possibly *[my] restoration* KB).
1. The son of Ammihud (1Ch 9:4).
2. A man who returned with Ezra (Ezr 8:14).

UZ
1. The son of Nahor (Ge 22:21).
2. The son of Aram (Ge 10:23; 1Ch 1:17).
3. The son of Dishan (Ge 36:28).
4. The country in which Job lived (Job 1:1); the site is uncertain.

UZAI (*Yahweh has given ear, listened*). Father of Palal (Ne 3:25).

UZAL
1. The son of Joktan (Ge 10:27; 1Ch 1:21).
2. A region, perhaps Yemen or the area between Haran and the Tigris (Eze 27:19).

UZZA (*strength*).
1. The son of Shimei (1Ch 6:29).
2. The son of Ehud (1Ch 8:7).
3. The owner or caretaker of a garden in which Manasseh and Amon were buried (2Ki 21:18, 26).
4. One whose children returned under Zerubbabel (Ezr 2:49; Ne 7:51).

UZZA, GARDEN OF A garden in which Manasseh and his son were buried (2Ki 21:18, 26).

UZZAH (*strong, fierce one*). The son of Abinadab; slain for touching the ark to steady it when the oxen carrying it stumbled (2Sa 6:3-8; 1Ch 13:6-11).

UZZEN SHEERAH (perhaps *ear of Sheerah*). A town built by Ephraim's daughter Sheerah (1Ch 7:24).

UZZI (*Yahweh is [my] strength*).
1. Descendant of Aaron (1Ch 6:5, 51; Ezr 7:4).
2. The grandson of Issachar (1Ch 7:2-3).
3. A Benjamite (1Ch 7:7).
4. The father of Elah (1Ch 9:8).
5. An overseer of the Levites (Ne 11:22).
6. A priest in the family of Jedaiah (Ne 12:19).

UZZIA (*[my] strength* or *Yahweh is [my] strength*). One of David's mighty men (1Ch 11:44).

UZZIAH (*Yahweh is [my] strength*).
1. Also called Azariah. The king of Judah (2Ki 14:21; 15:1-2; 2Ch 26:1, 3). Rebuilds Elath (2Ki 14:22; 2Ch 26:2). Reigns righteously (2Ki 15:3; 2Ch 26:4-5). Defeats the Philistines (2Ch 26:6-7). Takes tribute from the Ammonites; strengthens the kingdom (2Ch 26:8). Strengthens the fortifications of Jerusalem (2Ch 26:9). Promotes cattle raising and agriculture (2Ch 26:10). Military establishment of (2Ch 26:11-15). Is presumptuous in burning incense; stricken with leprosy; quarantined (2Ch 26:16-21; 2Ki 15:5). Jotham regent during quarantine of (2Ki 15:5; 2Ch 26:21). Death of (2Ki 15:7; 2Ch 26:23). History of, written by Isaiah (2Ch 26:22; Isa 1:1). Earthquake in the reign of (Am 1:1; Zec 14:5). An ancestor of Jesus and listed in Matthew's record of Jesus' genealogy (Mt 1:8-9).
2. The son of Uriel (1Ch 6:24).
3. The father of Jonathan (1Ch 27:25).
4. A priest who divorced his Gentile wife (Ezr 10:21).
5. The father of Athaiah (Ne 11:4).

UZZIEL, UZZIELITES (*God [El] is [my] strength*).
1. A Kohathite Levite (Ex 6:18, 22; Lev 10:4).
2. The son of Ishi; Simeonite (1Ch 4:42).
3. Head of Benjamite family (1Ch 7:7).
4. The son of Heman (1Ch 25:4), also known as Azarel (1Ch 25:18). *See Azarel, 2.*
5. A Levite who helped in cleansing the temple (2Ch 29:14-19).
6. The son of Harhaiah (Ne 3:8). Anyone descended from Uzziel, the Levite, was known as an Uzzielite (Nu 3:27; 1Ch 15:10; 26:23).

V

VAGABOND NIV "wanderer, wandering." A word used in a curse pronounced upon Cain (Ge 4:12, 14), in an imprecatory prayer of David (Ps 109:10), and of professional exorcists (Ac 19:13).

VAIL *See Curtains; Veil.*

VAIN REPETITIONS *See Babbling.*

VAIZATHA (possibly *given of the best one* BDB). The son of Haman (Est 9:9).

VALLEY Low-lying ground; plain, ravine, gorge, a wadi (Dt 34:6; Jos 10:40; Lk 3:5).

Mentioned in Scripture:
Achor (Jos 7:24; Isa 65:10; Hos 2:15). Aijalon (Jos 10:12). Baca (Ps 84:6). Beracah (2Ch 20:26). Bokim (Jdg 2:5). Craftsmen (1Ch 4:14, ftn). Elah (1Sa 17:2; 21:9). Emek Keziz (Jos 18:21). Eshcol (Nu 32:9; Dt 1:24). Gad (2Sa 24:5). Gerar (Ge 26:17). Gibeon (Isa 28:21). Hebron (Ge 37:14). Ben Hinnom or Tophet (Jos 18:16; 2Ki 23:10; 2Ch 28:3; Jer 7:32). Hamon Gog (Eze 39:11). Iphtah El (Jos 19:14, 27). Jehoshaphat or decision (Joel 3:2, 14). Jericho (Dt 34:3). Jezreel (Hos 1:5). King's Valley (Ge 14:17; 2Sa 18:18). Lebanon (Jos 11:17). Megiddo (2Ch 35:22; Zec 12:11). Moab, where Moses was buried (Dt 34:6). Rephaim (Jos 15:8; 18:16; 2Sa 5:18; Isa 17:5). Salt (2Sa 18:13; 2Ki 14:17). Shaveh (Ge 14:17; 2Sa 18:18). Shittim (Joel 3:18). Siddim (Ge 14:3, 8, 10). Sorek (Jdg 16:4). Succoth (Ps 60:6). Zeboim (1Sa 13:18; Ne 11:34). Zephathah (2Ch 14:10). Zered (Nu 21:12).

VALLEY GATE A gate in the Jerusalem walls (Ne 2:13; 3:13; 12:31, 38), location uncertain.

VALOR *See Courage.*

VANIAH (possibly *worthy of love* IDB). A man who divorced his foreign wife (Ezr 10:36).

VANITY
1. Archaic word meaning "temporary" or "meaningless":
"Temporary, a breath." Every human is but a breath (Ps 39:5, 11; 62:9; 144:4). Beauty is fleeting (Ps 39:11; Pr 31:30). Wealth acquired by lies (Pr 21:6).
"Futile, meaningless, in vain, worthless." A consequence of the Fall (Ro 8:20). Human life (Job 7:16; Ecc 6:12), youth and vigor (Ecc 11:10), thoughts (Ps 94:11), help (Ps 60:11; La 4:17). Worldly wisdom (Ecc 2:15, 21; 1Co 3:20), pleasure (Ecc 2:1-3, 10-11), activity (Ps 39:6; 127:2), achievement (Ecc 2:11; 4:4), possessions (Ecc 2:4-11). Accumulating wealth (Ecc 2:26; 4:8), love of wealth (Ecc 5:10; 6:2). Everything (Ecc 1:2). Foolish controversies (1Ti 1:6-7; 6:20; 2Ti 2:14, 16; Tit 3:9). The conduct of the ungodly (1Pe 1:18). The religion of hypocrites (Isa 1:13; Jas 1:26), pagans (Mt 6:7). Faith without works is (Jas 2:14).
The wicked, especially characterized by (Job 11:11). Fools follow those given to (Pr 12:11), leading to poverty (Pr 28:19). Saints hate the thoughts of (Ps 119:113), pray to be kept from (Ps 119:37; Pr 30:8), avoid (Ps 24:4), avoid those given to (Ps 26:4).
2. *See Pride.*

VASHNI KJV Samuel's firstborn (1Ch 6:28). NIV follows the LXX and supplies "Joel" as the firstborn (cf. 1Sa 6:33; 8:2; 15:17), rendering *vashni* as "the second." *See Joel, 1.*

VASHTI (*one beautiful, desired*). The wife of Xerxes; queen of Persia; divorced (Est 1:19).

VEDAN A place whose merchants traded with Tyre (Eze 27:19, NRSV). Translated as the Hebrew conjunction *vav* and the proper name Danites/Dan in the NIV and KJV. *See Dan, 2.*

VEGETARIANS Persons who eat no meat. Daniel chooses to eat only vegetables (Da 1:11-16). Christians are not to judge or be judged by diet (Ro 14).

VEGETATION Created the third day (Ge 1:11; 2:5). For food (Ge 1:29-30).

VEIL
1. Scarf used for concealment or for protection against the elements (Ge 24:65; 1Co 11:4-16). Worn by Rebekah (Ge 24:65), by Tamar (Ge 38:14, 19), by Moses, to screen his face when he descended from Mount Sinai (Ex 34:33, 35). Metaphoric of failing to understand the gospel (2Co 3:14-18; 4:3-4).
2. *See Curtains.*

VEIN NIV "mine" for silver (Job 28:1). *See Mines, Mining.*

VENERATION For parents (Ge 48:15-16). *See Old Age; Parents; Reverence.*

VENGEANCE Any punishment meted out in the sense of retribution (Jdg 15:7; Jer 11:20; 20:12). It belongs to God (Dt 32:35-36; Ps 94:1; Lk 18:7-8; Ro 12:19; 2Th 1:6; Heb 10:30; Rev 6:10).
Instance of: Sons of Jacob on Hamor and Shechem (Ge 34:20-31).
See Judgments; Revenge; Retaliation.

VENISON NIV "(wild) game," taken in hunting (Ge 25:28; 27:5-33).

VENTRILOQUISM Possibly a trick of mediums and spiritists (Isa 29:4).

VERDICT Against Jesus (Mt 26:66; 27:24-26; Mk 15:15; Lk 23:24; Jn 19:16). *See Court, Of Law.*

VERMILION *See Red.*

VERSIONS OF THE BIBLE Ancient: *See Texts and Versions.*

VESSEL Any material thing which may be used for any purpose, whether a tool, implement, weapon, or receptacle (Isa 22:24; 52:11; 66:20). A ship (Isa 2:16).
KJV "earthen vessels" is NIV "jars of clay" (2Co 4:7). *See Jar(s).* KJV "weaker vessel" is NIV "weaker partner" (1Pe 3:7). *See Women.*

VESTMENTS Of priests. *See Priest.*

VESTRY *See Wardrobe.*

VESTURE An archaic word for garments (Ge 41:42; Dt 22:12; Ps 22:18). Sometimes used metaphorically (Ps 102:26; Heb 1:12).
See Cloak; Clothing; Dress; Robe.

VIA DOLOROSA The traditional route which our Lord traveled on the day of his crucifixion from the judgment seat of Pilate to the place of his crucifixion (Mt 27:26, 31, 33).

VIAL *See Bowl.*

VICARIOUS DEATH The ram for Isaac (Ge 22:13). Jesus for sinners. *See Jesus the Christ, Death of; Mission of; Savior; Sufferings of; also, Atonement; Suffering, Vicarious.*

VICEGERENCY Imputed authority. Of Elisha, in miraculously rewarding the Shunammite (2Ki 4:16-17), in cursing Gehazi (2Ki 5:27). Of the apostles (Mt 16:19; 18:18; Jn 20:23).

VICTORIES In battle, from God (Ps 55:18; 76:5-6). Celebrated in song (Jdg 5; 2Sa 22), by women (1Sa 18:6-7; 2Sa 1:20).
See Armies; War.

VICTUAL Food.

VIGILANCE Instances of: The LORD in the Exodus (Ex 12:42). King of Jericho (Jos 2:1-3).
See Watchman.

VILLAGE Villages were usually grouped around a fortified town to which the people could flee in a time of war (2Ch 8:18).

VINE Degeneracy of (Jer 2:21). Fable of (Jdg 9:12-13). Pruned (Isa 5:6; Jn 15:1-5). Parables of (Ps 80:8-14; Eze 17:6-10; 19:10-14). *See Vineyards.*
Symbolic (Jn 15:1-5).

VINEGAR A sour wine. Forbidden to the Nazirites (Nu 6:3). Used with food (Ru 2:14; Ps 69:21; Pr 10:26; 25:20). Offered to Christ on the cross (Mt 27:34, 48; Jn 19:29, w Mk 15:23).

VINEYARDS Origin and antiquity of (Ge 9:20). The design of planting (Ps 107:37; 1Co 9:7). Frequently walled or fenced with hedges (Nu 22:24; Pr 24:31; Isa 5:2, 5). Cottages built in, for the keepers (Isa 1:8). Provided with the apparatus for making wine (Isa 5:2; Mt 21:33). The stones carefully gathered out of (Isa 5:2).

Laws Respecting:
Not to be planted with different kinds of seed (Dt 22:9). Not to be cultivated during the sabbatical year (Ex 23:11; Lev 25:4). The spontaneous fruit of, not to be gathered the sabbatical or jubilee year (Lev 25:5, 11). Compensation in kind to be made for injury done to (Ex 22:5). Strangers entering, allowed to eat the fruit of, but not to take any away (Dt 23:24).
The gleaning of, to be left for the poor (Lev 19:10; Dt 24:21). The fruit of new, not to be eaten for three years (Lev 19:23), to be holy to the Lord in the fourth year (Lev 19:24), to be eaten by the owners from the fifth year (Lev 19:25).
Planters of, not liable to military service till they had eaten of the fruit (Dt 20:6). Frequently rented out to tenant farmers (SS 8:11; Mt 21:33). Rent of, frequently paid by part of the fruit (Mt 21:34). Were often mortgaged (Ne 5:3-4). Estimated rent of (SS 8:11; Isa 7:23). Estimated profit arising from, to the cultivators (SS 8:12). The poor engaged in the culture of (2Ki 25:12; Isa 61:5). Members of the family often wrought in (SS 1:6; Mt 21:28-30). Mode of hiring and paying laborers for working in (Mt 20:1-2). Of the kings of Israel superintended by officers of state (1Ch 27:27).

The Vintage or Ingathering of:
Was a time of great rejoicing (Isa 16:10). Sometimes continued to the time of sowing seed (Lev 26:5). Failure in, occasioned great grief (Isa 16:9-10). Of red grapes particularly esteemed (Isa 27:2). The produce of, was frequently destroyed by enemies (Jer 48:32). The whole produce of, often destroyed by insects (Dt 28:39; Am 4:9). In unfavorable seasons produced but little wine (Isa 5:10; Hag 1:9, 11). The wicked judicially deprived of the enjoyment of (Am 5:11; Zep 1:13). The Recabites forbidden to plant (Jer 35:7-9). Of the slothful man neglected and laid waste (Pr 24:30-31).

Illustrative:
Of Israel (Isa 5:7; 27:2; Jer 12:10; Mt 21:23).

VINEYARDS, PLAIN OF THE *See Abel Keramim.*

VINTAGE (Lev 26:5; Jdg 8:2; Isa 16:10; 24:13; 32:10; Jer 48:32; Mic 7:1). *See Vine; Vineyards.*

VIOL *See Lyre; Music, Instruments of.*

VIOLENCE A cause of the Flood (Ge 6:11-13). Prayer for deliverance from (2Sa 22:49; Ps 7:9; Hab 1:2-3). Divorce (Mal 2:16). An overseer must not be (1Ti 3:3; Tit 1:7).

VIPER A poisonous snake (Dt 32:24; Isa 59:5). Fastens on Paul's hand (Ac 28:3).

Figurative (Ge 49:17; Ps 140:3; Pr 23:32; Mt 3:7; 23:33; Lk 3:7).

See Adder; Cobra; Serpent.

VIRGIN

General:

Proofs of (Dt 22:13-21). Dowry of (Ex 22:17). Character of, to be protected (Dt 22:17-21, 23-24). Betrothal of, a quasi-marriage (Dt 22:23-24). Distinguishing apparel of (2Sa 13:18). Priests might marry none but (Lev 21:14). Mourn in the temple (La 1:4; 2:10). Virginity of, bewailed (Jdg 11:37-39).

Parable of the wise and foolish (Mt 25:1-13). Advised by Paul not to marry (1Co 7).

Mother of Jesus (Isa 7:14; Mt 1:23; Lk 1:27). *See Virgin Birth.*

Figurative:

Of the Church (Isa 62:5; Jer 14:17; 31:4, 13; 2Co 11:2). Of personal purity (1Co 7:25, 37; Rev 14:4).

VIRGIN BIRTH The NT teaching that Jesus Christ became a human being without the mediation of an earthly father, not born by means of sexual intercourse, but as a result of the supernatural overshadowing of the Holy Spirit (Mt 1:18-25; Lk 1:26-2:7).

VIRGINITY *See Virgin.*

VIRTUE Positive character traits (Col 3:12-14). *See Character.*

VISION A mode of revelation (Nu 12:6; 1Sa 3:1; 2Ch 26:5; Ps 89:19; Pr 29:18; Jer 14:14; 23:16; Da 1:17; Hos 12:10; Joel 2:28; Ob 1; Hab 2:2; Ac 2:17).

Examples of:

Of Abraham, concerning his descendants (Ge 15:1-17). Of Jacob, of the stairway with ascending and descending angels (Ge 28:12), at Beersheba (Ge 46:2). Of Job, of a spirit (Job 4:12-16). Of Moses, of the burning bush (Ex 3:2), of the glory of God (Ex 24:9-11; 33:18-23). Of the Israelites, of the manifestation of the glory of God (Ex 24:10, 17; Heb 12:18-21). Of Balaam, in a trance. *See Balaam.* Of Joshua, of the captain of the Lord's host (Jos 5:13-15).

Of David, of the angel of the Lord by the threshing floor of Araunah (1Ch 21:15-18, ftn v.15). *See Araunah.* Of Elisha, at the translation of Elijah (2Ki 2:11). Of Elisha's servant, of the chariots of the Lord (2Ki 6:17). Of Micaiah, of the defeat of the Israelites; of the Lord on his throne; and of a lying spirit (1Ki 22:17-23; 2Ch 18:16-22).

Of Isaiah, of the Lord and his glory in the temple (Isa 6), of the valley of vision (Isa 22). Of Jeremiah, of an almond rod (Jer 1:11), of the boiling pot (Jer 1:13). Of Ezekiel, of the glory of God (Eze 1:3, 12-14; 3:23), of the scroll (Eze 2:9), of the man of fire (Eze 8-9), of the coals of fire (Eze 10:1-7), of the dry bones (Eze 37:1-14), of the city and temple (Eze 40-48), of the waters (Eze 47:1-12). Of Daniel, of the four beasts (Da 7), of the Ancient of Days (Da 7:9-27), of the ram and the goat (Da 8), of the angel (Da 10).

Of Amos, of grasshoppers (Am 7:1-2), of fire (Am 7:4), of a plumb line (Am 7:7-8), of summer fruit (Am 8:1-2), of the temple (Am 9:1). Of Zechariah, of horses (Zec 1:8-11), of horns and carpenters (Zec 1:18-21), of the high priest (Zec 3:1-5), of the golden lampstand (Zec 4), of the flying scroll (Zec 5:1-4), of the mountains and chariots (Zec 6:1-8).

Of Zechariah, in the temple (Lk 1:13-22). Of John the Baptist, at the baptism of Jesus (Mt 3:16; Mk 1:10; Lk 3:22; Jn 1:32-34). Peter, James, and John, of the transfiguration of Jesus and the appearance of Moses and Elijah (Mt 17:1-9; Lk 9:28-36). Of the people, of the tongues of fire at Pentecost (Ac 2:2-3). Of Stephen, of Christ (Ac 7:55-56).

Of Paul, of Christ, on the way to Damascus (Ac 9:3-6; 1Co 9:1), of Ananias (Ac 9:12), of a man of Macedonia, saying, "Come over to Macedonia and help us" (Ac 16:9), in Corinth (Ac 18:9-10), in a trance (Ac 22:17-21), of paradise (2Co 12:1-4). Of Ananias, of Christ (Ac 9:10-12). Of Cornelius, the centurion, of an angel (Ac 10:3). Of Peter, of the sheet let down from heaven (Ac 10:9-18).

Of John on the Isle of Patmos—

Of Christ and the golden lampstands (Rev 1:10-20), the open door (Rev 4:1), a rainbow and throne (Rev 4:2-3), twenty-four elders (Rev 4:4), seven lamps (Rev 4:5), sea of glass (Rev 4:6), four living creatures (Rev 4:6-8), book with seven seals (Rev 5:1-5), golden bowls (Rev 5:8), of the six seals (Rev 6), four horses (Rev 6:2-8), earthquake and celestial phenomena (Rev 6:12-14).

Four angels (Rev 7:1), sealing of the 144, 00 (Rev 7:2-8), of the seventh seal and seven angels (Rev 8-11), of the censer (Rev 8:5), hail and fire (Rev 8:7), mountain cast into the sea (Rev 8:8-9), falling star (Rev 8:10-11; 9:1), the third part of sun and moon and stars darkened (Rev 8:12), bottomless pit (Rev 9:2), locusts (Rev 9:3-11), four angels loosed from the Euphrates (Rev 9:14), army of horsemen (Rev 9:16-19), angel having a book (Rev 10:1-10), seven thunders (Rev 10:3-4), measurement of the temple (Rev 11:1-2), two witnesses (Rev 11:3-12), court of the Gentiles (Rev 11:2), two olive trees and two lampstands (Rev 11:4), the beast out of the bottomless pit (Rev 11:7), fall of the city (Rev 11:13), second and third woes (Rev 11:14), a woman clothed with the sun and the birth of the male child (Rev 12), a red dragon (Rev 12:4-17), war in heaven (Rev 12:7-9), the beast rising out of the sea (Rev 13:1-10), the beast coming out of the earth (Rev 13:11-18).

The Lamb on Mount Zion (Rev 14:1-5), the angel having the everlasting gospel (Rev 14:6-7), the angel proclaiming the fall of Babylon (Rev 14:8-13), the Son of man with a sickle (Rev 14:14-16), an angel reaping the harvest (Rev 14:14-20), angel coming out of the temple (Rev 14:17-19), an angel having power over fire (Rev 14:18), the vine and the winepress (Rev 14:18-20), angels with the seven last plagues (Rev 15), sea of glass (Rev 15:2), temple opened (Rev 15:5), the plague upon the people who had the mark of the beast (Rev 16:2), sea turned into blood (Rev 16:3), the seven angels with the seven bowls of the wrath of God (Rev 16-17), destruction of Babylon (Rev 18), of the multitude praising (Rev 19:1-9), of him who is faithful and true riding a white horse (Rev 19:11-16), an angel in the sun (Rev 19:17-21).

Satan bound a thousand years (Rev 20:1-3), thrones of judgment, and the resurrection, and the freeing of Satan (Rev 20:1-10), the great white throne (Rev 20:11), opening of the Book of Life (Rev 20:12), death and hell (Rev 20:14), New Jerusalem (Rev 21), river of life (Rev 22:1), Tree of Life (Rev 22:2). *See Revelation, Book of.*

VISITATION A divine visit for purpose of rewarding or punishing people for their deeds (Jer 10:15; Lk 19:44; 1Pe 2:12).

VISITORS *See Guest.*

VOICE, OF GOD (Eze 1:24, 28; 10:5; Jn 5:37; 12:28-30; Ac 7:31; 9:4, 7; 26:14-15). *See Anthropomorphisms.*

VOLCANOES Smoking or flaming mountains symbolic of God's presence (Dt 4:11; 5:23; Jdg 5:5; Ps 97:5; 104:32; 144:5; Isa 34:9-10; 64:1-3; Jer 51:25; Mic 1:4; Na 1:5-6).

See Earthquakes; Mountain.

VOLUPTUOUSNESS *See Lasciviousness; Sensuality.*

VOPHSI The father of Nahbi (Nu 13:14).

VOWS A part of Israel's worship (Ps 22:25; 61:8; 65:1). Heard by God (Ps 61:5). Obligatory (Nu 30:2; Dt 23:21-23; Job 22:27; Ps 50:14; 56:12; 66:13-14; 76:11; Ecc 5:4-5; Na 1:15). In affliction (Ps 116:14-19).

Mosaic Laws Concerning:

Must be voluntary (Lev 22:18-25; 23:37-38; Nu 15:2-16; 29:39).

Must be performed (Lev 5:4-13; Nu 30:2-16). *See above, Obligatory.* Estimation of the redemption price of things offered in vows, to be made by the priest, according to age and gender of the person making the offering (Lev 27:1-13). The redemptive price of the offering of real estate, to be valued by the priest (Lev 27:14-15), of a field (Lev 27:16-25).

Of women (Nu 30:3-16). Of Nazirites (Nu 6:1-21). Unintentional (Lev 5:4-5). Offerings devoted under (Lev 5:6-13; 7:16-18; 27:1-25; Nu 15:2-16). Things offered in, must be perfect (Lev 22:18-25).

Edible things offered in, to be eaten the same day they were offered (Lev 7:16-18). Things offered in, to be brought to the tabernacle or temple (Dt 12:6, 11, 17-18, 26), belonged to the priests (Nu 18:14).

Things forbidden to pay a vow (Dt 23:18).

Traditions that invalidate vows (Mk 7:11-13).

See Contract; Covenant.

Rash Vows:

(Pr 20:25; Ecc 5:6). By Jephthah (Jdg 11:29-40), by Israelites (Jdg 20:7-11).

Instances of:

Of Jacob (Ge 28:20-22). Of the mother of Micah, in the dedication of silver for the making of an idol (Jdg 17:2-3). Of Hannah, to consecrate to the Lord the child for which she prayed (1Sa 1:11, w 1:27-28). Of Elkanah (1Sa 1:21). Of Absalom (2Sa 15:7-8). Of Job, not to entertain thoughts of fornication (Job 31:1). Of David (Ps 132:2).

Of Jephthah, and of the Israelites. *See above, Rash Vows.*

Of Ananias and Sapphira, in the dedication of the proceeds of the sale of their land (Ac 5:1-11). Of the Jews, to kill Paul (Ac 23:12-15).

See Nazirite(s).

VULTURE The name given to several kinds of large birds of prey, usually feeding on carrion; unclean for food (Lev 11:13; Dt 14:12; Mic 1:16; Hab 1:8).

WADI (*ravine, valley*). A valley which forms the bed of a stream during the winter, but which dries up in the summer (Ge 26:19).

WADI OF EGYPT *See River of Egypt.*

WAFERS Thin cakes (Ex 16:31; 1Ch 23:29).

WAGES Of Jacob (Ge 29:15-30; 30:28-34; 31:7, 41).

Laborer entitled to (Dt 25:4; Mt 10:10; Lk 10:7; Ro 4:4). Must be just (Col 4:1). Must be paid promptly (Lev 19:13; Dt 24:15). Withholding of, denounced (Jer 22:13; Mal 3:5; Jas 5:4). Wasting of, denounced (Hag 1:6). Contentment with, commanded (Lk 3:14).

Parable concerning (Mt 20:1-15).

Figurative (Ro 6:23).

WAGON Used to carry supplies (Isa 66:20; Eze 23:24; 26:10). *See Cart(s).*

WAHEB If this is a proper noun then it is an unknown place in Moab. Its meaning is uncertain (Nu 21:14).

WAIL In ancient funeral processions wailing relatives and hired mourners and musicians preceded body to grave (Jer 9:17-21; Am 5:16; Mt 9:23). Of the wicked (Mt 13:42).

WAITING

Upon God:

As the God of providence (Jer 14:22), as the God of salvation (Ps 25:5), as the giver of all temporal blessings (Ps 104:27-28; 145:15-16).

Is good (Ps 52:9). God calls us to (Zep 3:8). Exhortations and encouragements to (Ps 27:14; 37:7; Hos 12:6).

For—

Mercy (Ps 123:2), pardon (Ps 39:7-8), the consolation of Israel (Lk 2:25), salvation (Ge 49:18; Ps 62:1-2), guidance and teaching (Ps 25:5), protection (Ps 33:20; 59:9-10), the fulfillment of his word (Hab 2:3), the fulfillment of his promises (Ac 1:4), hope of righteousness by faith (Gal 5:5), coming of Christ (1Co 1:7; 1Th 1:10).

Attitudes in Waiting—

Should be with the soul (Ps 62:1, 5), with earnest desire (Ps 130:6), with patience (Ps 37:7; 40:1), with resignation (La 3:26), with hope in his word (Ps 130:5), with full confidence (Mic 7:7), continually (Hos 12:6), all the day (Ps 25:5), specially in adversity (Ps 59:1-9; Isa 8:17), in the way of his judgments (Isa 26:8).

Those Who Wait Upon God—

They who engage in, wait upon him only (Ps 62:5), are heard (Ps 40:1), are blessed (Isa 30:18; Da 12:12), experience his goodness (La 3:24-26), shall not be ashamed (Ps 25:3; Isa 49:23), shall renew their strength (Isa 40:31), shall inherit the earth (Ps 37:9), shall be saved (Pr 20:22; Isa 25:9), shall rejoice in salvation (Isa 25:9), shall receive the glorious things prepared by God for them (Isa 64:4).

Saints resolve on (Ps 52:9; 59:9). Saints have expectation from (Ps 62:5). Saints plead, in prayer (Ps 25:21; Isa 33:2). The patience of saints often tried in (Ps 69:3).

Predicted of the Gentiles (Isa 42:4; 60:9). Illustrated (Ps 123:2; Lk 12:36; Jas 5:7).

Exemplified:

Jacob (Ge 49:18), David (Ps 39:7), Isaiah (Isa 8:17), Micah (Mic 7:7), Joseph (Mk 15:43).

Faith; Hope.

WALKING

With God—a Godly Lifestyle:

According to his commands (Dt 5:33; Ps 1; Jer 7:23); in his ways (Dt 28:9; Jos 22:5); in the old paths (Jer 6:16); as taught by him (1Ki 8:36; Isa 2:3; 30:21); uprightly (Pr 2:7); in his statutes and judgments (Eze 37:24); in newness of life (Ro 6:4); not after the flesh, but after the Spirit (Ro 8:1; Gal 5:16); honestly, as in the day (Ro 13:13); by faith, not by sight (2Co 5:7); in love, following Christ (Eph 5:2); worthy of the Lord (Col 1:10); in Christ (Col 2:6); by the gospel rule (Php 3:16); in the light, as God is (1Jn 1:7); in white clothing (Rev 3:4); in the light of heaven (Rev 21:24).

Instances of: Enoch (Ge 5:24), Noah (Ge 6:9).

WALLED CITIES Settlements were enclosed with walls for protection against invasion (Lev 25:29-31; 1Ki 4:13). *See Walls.*

WALLS Of the cities: Of Bashan, destroyed by the Israelites (Dt 3:5-6). Of Jericho (Jos 2:15; 6). Of Jerusalem. *See Jerusalem.* Of Babylon (Jer 51:44), broad (Jer 51:58). Of Beth Shan (1Sa 31:10). Of Rabbah (2Sa 11:20). Of Abel (2Sa 20:15, 21).

Houses built upon (Jos 2:15). Double (2Ki 25:4; Isa 22:11). Sentinels on. *See Watchman.*

Figurative of the New Jerusalem (Rev 21:12, 14, 17-21).

WAR Divine approval of (2Sa 22:35). Civil (Jdg 12:1-6; 20; 2Sa 2:12-31; 3:1; 20; 1Ki 14:30; 16:21; Isa 19:2), forbidden (2Ch 11:4), averted (Jos 22:11-34). Enemy harangued by general of opposing side (2Ki 18:19-36; 2Ch 13:4-12). Of extermination (Nu 31:7-17; Dt 2:33-34; 3:6; 20:13-18; Jos 6:21, 24; 8:24-25; 10:2-40; 11:11-23; 1Sa 15:3-9; 27:8-11).

Tumult of (Am 2:2). Slain in, neglected (Isa 14:19; 18:6). Evils of (2Sa 2:26; Ps 46:8; 79:1-3; 137:9; Isa 3:5, 25-26; 5:29-30; 6:11-12; 9:5, 19-21; 13:15-16; 15; 16:9-10; 18:6; 19:2-16; 32:13-14; 33:8-9; 34:7-15; Jer 4:19-31; 5:16-17; 6:24-26; 7:33-34; 8:16-17; 9:10-21; 10:20; 13:14; 14:18; 15:8-9; 19:7-9; 25:33; 46:3-12; 47:3; 48:28, 33; 51:30-58; La 1-5; Eze 33:27; 39:17-19; Hos 10:14; 13:16; Joel 2:2-10; Am 1:13; 6:9-10; 8:3; Na 2:10; 3:3, 10; Zec 14:2; Lk 21:20-26; Rev 19:17-18).

To cease (Ps 46:9; Isa 2:4; Mic 4:3).

Wars and rumors of (Mt 24:6; Mk 13:7; Lk 21:9).

God and War—

God in (Ex 14:13-14; Dt 1:30; 3:21-22; 7:17-24; 20:1, 4; 31:6-8, 23; 32:29-30; Jos 1:1, 5-7, 9; Jdg 1:2; 6:16; 7:9; 11:29; 1Sa 17:45-47; 19:5; 30:7-8; 2Sa 5:22-24; 22:18; 1Ki 20:28; Ps 18:34; 76:3; Jer 46:15; Am 5:8-9; Zec 10:5). God uses, as a judgment (Ex 23:24; Lev 26:17, 31-39; Dt 28:25-68; 32:30; Jdg 2:14; 2Ki 15:37; 1Ch 5:22, 26; 21:12; 2Ch 12:1-12; 15:6; 24:23-24; 33:11; 36; Job 19:29; Ps 44:9-16; 60:1-3; 105:25; Isa 5:1-8, 25-30; 9:8-12; 13:3-4, 9; 19:2; 34:2-6; 43:28; 45:7; Jer 12:7, 12; 46:15-17, 21; 47:6-7; 48:10; 49:5; 50:25; Eze 23:22-25; Am 3:6; 4:11; Zep 1:7-18; Zec 8:10; 14:2).

Repugnant to God (1Ch 22:8-9; Ps 68:30; 120:6-7; Rev 13:10). God sends panic in (Ex 15:14-16), threatens defeat in (Dt 32:25; 1Sa 2:10; 2Ch 18:12-16; Isa 30:15-17; Eze 15:6-8; 21:9-17), inflicts defeat in (Jos 7:12-13; 2Ch 12:5-8; 24:23-24; Ps 48:4-7; Pr 11:14; 20:18). Wisdom required in (Pr 21:22; 24:6; Ecc 9:14-18; Lk 14:31-32).

See Armies; Armor; Fort; Soldiers; Strategy; Tower; Watchman.

Figurative:

Warfare of Saints—

Is not after the flesh (2Co 10:3). Is a good warfare (1Ti 1:18-19). Called the good fight of faith (1Ti 6:12).

Is against the devil (Ge 3:15; 2Co 2:11; Eph 6:12; Jas 4:7; 1Pe 5:8; Rev 12:17), the flesh (Ro 7:23; 1Co 9:25-27; 2Co 12:7; Gal 5:17; 1Pe 2:11), enemies (Ps 38:19; 56:2; 59:3), the world (Jn 16:33; 1Jn 5:4-5), death (1Co 15:26, w Heb 2:14-15).

Often arises from the opposition of friends or relatives (Mic 7:6; Mt 10:35-36). To be carried on under Christ, as our Captain (Heb

2:10), under the Lord's banner (Ps 60:4), with faith (1Ti 1:18-19), with a good conscience (1Ti 1:18-19), with steadfastness in the faith (1Co 16:13; 1Pe 5:9, w Heb 10:23), with earnestness (Jude 3), with watchfulness (1Co 16:13; 1Pe 5:8), with sobriety (1Th 5:6; 1Pe 5:8), with endurance of hardness (2Ti 2:3, 10), with self-denial (1Co 9:25-27), with confidence in God (Ps 27:1-3), with prayer (Ps 35:1-3; Eph 6:18), without earthly entanglements (2Ti 2:4). Mere professors do not maintain (Jer 9:3).

Saints are all engaged in (Php 1:30), must stand firm in (Eph 6:13-14), exhorted to diligence in (1Ti 6:12; Jude 3). Encouraged in (Isa 41:11-12; 51:12; Mic 7:8; 1Jn 4:4), helped by God in (Ps 118:13; Isa 41:13-14), protected by God in (Ps 140:7), comforted by God in (2Co 7:5-6), strengthened by God in (Ps 20:2; 27:14; Isa 41:10), strengthened by Christ in (2Co 12:9; 2Ti 4:17), delivered by Christ in (2Ti 4:18), thank God for victory in (Ro 7:25; 1Co 15:57).

Armor for—

A belt of truth (Eph 6:14), the breastplate of righteousness (Eph 6:14), readiness from the gospel (Eph 6:15), shield of faith (Eph 6:16), helmet of salvation (Eph 6:17; 1Th 5:8), sword of the Spirit (Eph 6:17). Called armor of God (Eph 6:11), weapons of righteousness (2Co 6:7), armor of light (Ro 13:12), not weapons of the world (2Co 10:4). Mighty through God (2Co 10:4-5), the whole is required (Eph 6:13), must be put on (Ro 13:12; Eph 6:11), to be on the right hand and the left (2Co 6:7).

Victory in—

Is from God (1Co 15:57; 2Co 2:14), through Christ (Ro 7:25; 1Co 15:57; 2Co 12:9; Rev 12:11), by faith (Heb 11:33-37; 1Jn 5:4-5), over the devil (Ro 16:20; 1Jn 2:14), over the flesh (Ro 7:24-25; Gal 5:24), over the world (1Jn 5:4-5), over all that exalts itself (2Co 10:5), over death and the grave (Isa 25:8; 26:19; Hos 13:14; 1Co 15:54-55), triumphant (Ro 8:37; 2Co 10:5).

They who overcome in, shall eat of the hidden manna (Rev 2:17), eat of the tree of life (Rev 2:7), be clothed in white garments (Rev 3:5), be pillars in the temple of God (Rev 3:12), sit with Christ in his throne (Rev 3:21), have a white stone and on it a new name written (Rev 2:17), have power over the nations (Rev 2:26), have the name of God written upon them by Christ (Rev 3:12), have God as their God (Rev 21:7), have the morning star (Rev 2:28), inherit all things (Rev 21:7), be confessed by Christ before God the Father (Rev 3:5), be sons of God (Rev 21:7), not be hurt by the second death (Rev 2:11), not have their names blotted out of the book of life (Rev 3:5).

Symbolized by a red horse (Rev 6:4).

In Heaven:

Symbolic (Rev 12:7).

WAR SONGS Celebrating the destruction of Pharaoh's army (Ex 15:1-21); victory over Sihon, king of the Amorites (Nu 21:24-30); victory over Sisera (Jdg 5); David's victories over his enemies and his deliverance from Saul (2Sa 22). David's lament over the defeat of Saul (2Sa 1:19-27).

WARDROBE Place where royal or ceremonial garments were kept (2Ki 10:22; 22:14; 34:22). *See Dress.*

WARFARE *See War, Figurative; In Heaven.*

WARNING *See Wicked, Warned.*

WARRIORS (Nu 32:17; Jos 4:13; 1Ch 8:40; 12:2, 8, 21; 2Ch 14:8; 17:18; 25:5; 26:13).

WARTS Unacceptable on a sacrificial animal (Lev 22:22).

WASHERMAN'S FIELD A field outside Jerusalem where fullers or launderers washed the cloth that they were processing (2Ki 18:17; Isa 7:3; 36:2).

WASHINGS (Ex 19:10, 14; Mt 15:2; Mk 7:2-5, 8-9; Lk 11:38; Heb 9:10).

General:

Of priests (Ex 29:4; 30:18-21; 40:12, 31-32; Lev 8:6; 16:4, 24, 26, 28; Nu 19:7-10, 19; 2Ch 4:6).

Of burnt offerings (Lev 1:9, 13; 9:14; 2Ch 4:6). Of the dead (Ac 9:37). Of infants (Eze 16:4). Of the face (Mt 6:17). Of feet (Ge 18:4; 19:2; 24:32; 43:24; Ex 30:19, 21; 40:31; Jdg 19:21; 2Sa 11:8; SS 5:3; Lk 7:38, 44; Jn 13:5; 1Ti 5:10). Of hands (Ex 30:18-21; 40:30-32), as a token of innocency (Dt 21:6; Ps 26:6; Mt 27:24).

For defilement of, lepers (Lev 14:8-9), those having bloody issue (Lev 15:5-13), those having eaten that which died (Lev 17:15-16).

Traditions of, not observed by Jesus (Lk 11:38-39).

Figurative:

Of baptism (Ac 22:16). Of believers (1Co 6:11; Tit 3:5; Heb 1:3; 9:14; 2Pe 1:9; 1Jn 1:7, 9). Of bodies (Heb 10:22). Of the Church (Eph 5:26). Of conscience (Heb 9:14; 10:22). Of hands (Ps 73:13; Jas 4:8). Of leaven (1Co 5:7). Of robes (Rev 7:14; 22:14).

Of regeneration (Ps 51:7; Pr 30:12; Isa 1:16; 4:4; Zec 13:1; 1Co 6:11; Eph 5:26; Tit 3:5).

Of sin: Corporate (Ps 79:9; Isa 1:16, 18; 4:3-4; Da 12:10; Zec 13:1; Jn 13:8; 2Co 7:1; Rev 1:5). General (Pr 16:6). Personal (Ps 51:2; 65:3; Pr 20:9; Jn 13:8; 2Pe 1:9; 1Jn 1:7, 9).

By Christ, work and blood of (Eph 5:26; Tit 3:5-6; Heb 1:3; 9:14; 1Jn 1:7; Rev 1:5; 7:14).

See Defilement; Fuller; Purification; Regeneration; Soap.

WASTE PLACES Restored (Isa 35:1; 41:19; 44:26; 49:19; 51:3; 52:9; 58:12; 61:4; Eze 36:10).

WATCH A man or group of men set to guard a city, crops, etc. (Ne 4:9; Mt 27:62-66).

WATCHES OF THE NIGHT Divisions into which hours of the night were divided. Jews had a threefold division; Romans, fourfold (Jdg 7:19; Mk 6:48). *See Time.*

WATCHFULNESS (Ps 102:7; Hab 2:1; 1Co 9:27).

In Prayer:

(Ne 4:9; Mt 26:41; Mk 13:33; Eph 6:18; Col 4:2; 1Pe 4:7).

Commanded:

(Dt 4:15; 6:17; Jos 22:5; 23:11; 1Ki 2:3-4; 8:25; 2Ch 19:7; Job 36:18-21; Pr 8:34; 16:17; Na 2:1; Mt 18:10; 24:42-51; 25:13; Mk 4:24; 13:32-37; Lk 8:18; 11:35; 12:35-40; 17:3; 21:34-36; Ro 11:20; 1Co 10:12; 11:28; 16:13; Gal 6:1; Eph 5:15; Col 2:8; 1Th 5:4, 6, 21; Heb 2:1; 1Pe 5:8; 2Pe 1:19; 1Jn 5:18).

Upon: Israel (Dt 27:9). Young men (Ps 119:9; Pr 4:23-27). Married men (Mal 2:15). Ministers (Ac 20:28-31; 1Co 3:10; Col 4:2; 1Ti 4:16; 2Ti 4:5).

Over: Motives (Mt 6:1-5). Conscience (Lk 11:35). The heart (Pr 4:23; 28:26). The tongue (Ps 39:1; 141:3; Jas 3:5-8).

Against: Hypocrisy (Mt 16:6). Apostasy (2Jn 8). Lethargy (Ro 13:11; 1Pe 1:13, 17). Backsliding (Dt 4:9, 23; Heb 3:12; 12:15; Jude 20-21; Rev 3:2-3, 11). Worldliness (1Co 7:29-31). Covetousness (Mt 24:42-47; Mk 13:33-37; Lk 12:15, 35-40). Idolatry (Ex 23:13; Dt 4:23; 11:16; 12:13). Evil associations (Ex 34:12; Php 3:2; 2Pe 3:17). False teachers (Mt 7:15; Mk 13:22-23; Ac 20:28-31; 1Jn 4:1). Deceivers (Mt 24:4).

See Temptation.

WATCHMAN A sentinel. On the walls of cities (SS 3:3; 5:7), of Jerusalem (2Sa 13:34; 18:24-25; Ne 4:9; 7:3; Isa 52:8; 62:6), of Babylon (Jer 51:12). On towers (2Ki 9:17; 2Ch 20:24; Isa 21:5-12; Jer 31:6). At the gates of the temple (2Ki 11:6-7). Alarm of, given by trumpets (Eze 33:3-6). Unfaithfulness in the discharge of duty of, punished by death (Eze 33:6; Mt 28:14; Ac 12:19). *See Guard.*

WATER

General:

Creation of (Ps 148:4-5). Covered the whole earth (Ge 1:9). Daily allowance of (Eze 4:11). City waterworks (2Ki 20:20). Vision of, by Ezekiel (Eze 47:1-5). Of separation (Nu 19:2-22). Libation of (1Sa 7:6). Irrigation with. *See Irrigation.*

Miraculously supplied to the Israelites (Ex 17:1, 6; Nu 20:11), to Samson (Jdg 15:19), to Jehoshaphat's army (2Ki 3:16-20). Purified by Elisha (2Ki 2:19-22). Red Sea divided (Ex 14:21-22), the Jordan River (Jos 3:14-17; 2Ki 2:6-8, 14). Jesus walks on (Mt 14:25). Changed to wine (Jn 2:1-11), to blood (Rev 16:3-5).

Figurative:

Water of life (Jn 4:14; 7:37-39; Rev 21:6; 22:17). Of affliction (2Sa 22:17; Ps 69:1; Isa 30:20; 43:2). Of salvation (Isa 12:3; 49:10; 55:1; Eze 36:25; Jn 4:10; 7:38). Domestic love (Pr 5:15).

Symbolic:

(Isa 8:7; Rev 8:11; 12:15; 16:4; 17:1, 15).

WATER JAR Clay or stone jars for carrying or holding water (Ru 2:9; Jn 2:6-7; 4:28). *See Jar(s).*

WATER OF BITTERNESS Water mingled with dust which a woman suspected of unfaithfulness was expected to drink to prove her innocence (Nu 5:12-31).

WATER OF SEPARATION Water for removal of impurity (Nu 19:9, 13, 20-21; 31:23).

WATERSPOUT NIV "waterfalls" (Ps 42:7).

WATERWAY *See Aqueduct.*

WAVE OFFERING Sacrificial portion waved before the Lord (Ex 29:24-27; Lev 7:30; 8:27-29). *See Offerings.*

WAVES *See Sea, Waves of.*

WAX (Ps 22:14; 68:2; 97:5; Mic 1:4).

WAY

Figurative:

Of holiness (Ps 16:11; Isa 35:8-9; Jer 6:16; Hos 14:9). Of righteousness, narrow (Mt 7:14). Of sin, broad (Mt 7:13). Jesus the (Jn 14:6; Heb 9:8). Doctrines taught by Christ (Ac 9:2; 19:23; 22:4; 24:14, 22).

WAYFARING MAN Traveler (Jdg 19:17; 2Sa 12:4; Isa 33:8; 35:8).

WAYS OF GOD Perfect (Ps 18:30), righteous or just (Ps 145:17; Da 4:37; Hos 14:9; Rev 15:3), higher than human ways (Isa 55:9), eternal (Hab 3:6).

WEAK Duty of the strong to (Job 4:3-4; Isa 35:3-7; Mt 25:35, 40; Ro 14:1-23; 15:1-3; 1Co 8:7-13; 9:22; 2Co 11:29; Gal 6:1-2; Jas 5:19-20). *See Kindness.*

WEALTH Abundance of possessions, whether material, social, or spiritual. In early history of Israel, wealth consisted largely of flocks and herds, silver and gold, bronze, iron, and clothing (Jos 22:8). God taught Israel that he was the giver of their wealth (Dt 8:18), taught them to be generous (Pr 11:24). Jesus did not condemn wealth but stressed the difficulty of the rich in entering the kingdom of God (Mt 19:24; Lk 16:19-31).

WEANING To wean is to accustom a child to depend upon other food than its mother's milk; celebrated by a feast (Ge 21:8), and with an offering (1Sa 1:24).

WEAPONS *See Armor.*

WEASEL A small, carnivorous animal, allied to the ferret; for Israelites, unclean (Lev 11:29).

WEATHER There is no Hebrew word corresponding to "weather, " but the Israelites were keenly aware of weather phenomena. The great topographical diversity of Israel assures a variety of weather on a given day: on the top of Mt. Hermon (9, 232 feet above sea level) there is snow on the ground the year round; while at Jericho (800 feet below sea level) the heat is oppressive in summer, and the region around the Dead Sea (1, 290 feet below sea level) is intolerable in summer. On the coast even the hottest summer day is made bearable by refreshing breezes from the Mediterranean. Signs of (Mt 16:2-3). Sayings concerning (Job 37:9, 17, 22). *See Meteorology.*

WEAVING (Isa 19:9; 38:12). Bezalel skilled in (Ex 35:35). Wrought by women (2Ki 23:7). Of the ephod (Ex 28:32; 39:22). Of coats (Ex 39:27).

Weaver's shuttle (Job 7:6), beam (Jdg 16:14; 2Sa 21:19; 1Ch 11:23).

WEDDING A joyous occasion, celebrated with music, feasting, drinking of wine, joking; after the Exile written contracts were drawn up and sealed; bridegroom went to the bride's home with friends and escorted her to his own house (Mt 25:7); festive apparel expected of guests; festivities lasted one or two weeks (Ge 29:27; Jdg 14:12).

WEDGE A bar of gold (Jos 7:21, 24).

WEEDING (Mt 13:28).

WEEDS

1. A general term for obnoxious plants (Job 31:40).

2. Probably bearded darnel, a poisonous plant resembling wheat (Mt 13:25-30).

WEEK *See Calendar; Time.*

WEEKS, FEAST OF Pentecost, celebrated fifty days after the sheaf waving on the sixteenth of Nisan (Ex 34:18-26).

See Annual Feasts; Feasts; Pentecost.

WEEPING (Ro 12:15; 1Co 7:30). In perdition, the outer darkness (Mt 8:12; 22:13; 24:51; 25:30). None in heaven (Rev 7:17). Penitential (Jer 50:4; Joel 2:12).

Instances of Penitential:

The Israelites (Jdg 2:4-5). Peter (Mt 26:75; Mk 14:72; Lk 22:62). While doing good (Ps 126:5-6). For others (Jer 9:1). On account of tribulation (Jer 22:10; Am 5:16-17).

Instances of:

Of Abraham for Sarah (Ge 23:2). Of Esau (Ge 27:38). Of Jacob and Esau (Ge 33:4). Of Jacob (Ge 37:35). Of Joseph (Ge 42:24; 43:30; 45:2, 14; 46:29; 50:1, 17). Of Hannah (1Sa 1:7). Of Jonathan and David (1Sa 20:41). Of David (2Sa 1:17; 3:32; 13:36; 15:23, 30; 18:33). Of Hezekiah (2Ki 20:3; Isa 38:3). Of Jesus, over Jerusalem (Lk 19:41), at the grave of Lazarus (Jn 11:35). Of Mary, when she washed the feet of Jesus (Lk 7:38; Jn 11:2, 33). Of Mary Magdalene (Jn 20:11). Of Paul (Ac 20:19; Php 3:18).

WEIGHTS AND MEASURES Balances were used for scales (Lev 19:36; Pr 16:11), and stones for weights (Lev 19:36). For biblical weights and measures, *See Measure.*

WELDING A process used to join metals together (Isa 41:7).

WELLS The occasion of feuds: between Abraham and Abimelech (Ge 21:25-30), between Isaac and Abimelech (Ge 26:15-22, 32-33). Of Jacob (Jn 4:6). Of Solomon (Ecc 2:6). Of Uzziah (2Ch 26:10). Of Hezekiah. *See Gihon.* At Haran (Ge 24:16).

Figurative: Of salvation (Isa 12:3; Jn 4:14). Without water (Jer 15:18; 2Pe 2:17).

See Spring.

WEN *See Warts.*

WEST Used figuratively with "east" to denote great distance (Ps 103:12).

WHALE *See Fish; Sea Monster.*

WHEAT (Rev 6:6). Grown in Israel (1Ki 5:11; Ps 81:16; 147:14). Offerings of (Nu 18:12). Prophecy of the sale of a measure of, for a penny (Rev 6:6). Parables of (Mt 13:25; Lk 16:7). Winnowing of (Mt 3:12; Lk 3:17). Ground in a mortar (Pr 27:22). Chaff of (Jer 23:28; Mt 3:12; Lk 3:17). Growth of, figurative of vicarious death (Jn 12:24).

Figurative: Of God's mercy (Ps 81:16; 147:14). Of self-righteousness (Jer 12:13).

WHEEL Potter's (Jer 18:3).

Figurative (Pr 20:26; Ecc 12:6).

Symbolic (Eze 1:15-21; 3:13; 10:9-19; 11:22).

WHELP *See Cub.*

WHIP (1Ki 12:11; Pr 26:3; Na 3:2).

WHIRLWIND Destructive (Pr 1:27). From the south in the land of Uz (Job 37:9), in the valley of the Euphrates (Isa 21:1), in the land of Canaan (Zec 9:14). From the north (Eze 1:4). Elijah translated in (2Ki 2:1, 11). God answered Job in (Job 38:1).

See Meteorology.

Figurative:

Of the judgment of God (Jer 23:19; 30:23). Of the fruits of unrighteousness (Hos 8:7). Of divine judgments (Eze 1:4).

WHISPER *See Busybody; Slander; Talebearer.*

WHISPERER A slanderer (Ro 1:29; 2Co 12:20). *See Slander; Speaking, Evil.*

WHITE *See Colors, Figurative and Symbolic.*

WHITE OWL Forbidden as food (Lev 11:18; Dt 14:16). *See Owl.*

WHITEWASH Used to "repair" a flimsy wall (Eze 13:10-16). Whitewashed tomb or wall a picture of hypocrisy (Mt 23:27-28; Ac 23:3).

WHOEVER
Of condemnation (Ex 32:33; Dt 18:19; Mt 5:22; Jn 8:34; Ro 2:1; 1Jn 2:23; 3:4, 10, 15; 2Jn 9)

Of salvation (Lk 12:8; Jn 4:14; Ac 10:43; 1Jn 5:1; Rev 22:17).

WHORE, WHOREDOM
See Adultery; Idolatry; Fornication; Prostitute.

WHOREMONGER
See Adultery; Sensuality.

WICK TRIMMERS
Used to trim and adjust the wicks of the lamps in the temple and the tabernacle (Ex 37:23; Nu 4:9; 1Ki 7:50; 2Ki 12:13; 25:14; 2Ch 4:22; Jer 52:18).

WICKED

General:
God is angry with (Ps 5:5-6; 7:11; Ro 9:13; 1Co 10:5). Spirit of God withdrawn from (Ge 6:3; Hos 4:17-19; Ro 1:24, 26, 28). Hate the righteous (Mt 5:11-12; Lk 6:22-23). Worship of, offensive to God (Ps 50:16-17; Isa 1:10-15).

God's mercy to (Job 33:14-30), love for (Dt 5:29; 32:29; Mt 18:11-14; Jn 3:16-17; Ro 5:8; 1Jn 3:16; 4:9-10). Gospel invitation to, illustrated by the parables of the householder (Mt 20:1-16), and marriage supper (Mt 22:1-14).

Prosperity of (Job 5:3-5; 12:6; 15:21-23, 27, 29; 20:5, 22; 21:7-13; Ps 37:1, 35-36; 49:10-15; 73:3-22; 92:6-7; Ecc 8:12-13; Jer 12:1-2; Hab 1:3-4, 13-17; Mal 3:15). Hate reproof (1Ki 22:8; 2Ch 18:7). Dread God (Job 18:11).Temporal punishment of (Job 15:20-35; 18:5-21; 20:5-29; 21:7-33; 24:2-24; 27:13-23; Jer 5:25; Eze 11:10; 12:19-20; Zec 14:17-19). False hope to (Job 8:13-18).

Warned (Jer 7:13-15, 23-25; 25:4-6; 26:2-7, 12-13; 29:17-19; Eze 33:8; Da 4:4-27; 5:4-29; Zep 2:1-2; Lk 3:7-9; 1Co 10:11; Jude 4-7; Rev 3:1-3, 16-19). Terrors of, at the judgment (Rev 1:7). Death of (Ps 49:14; 73:4).

Compared With:
Ashes under the feet (Mal 4:3), bad fish (Mt 13:48), bad trees (Lk 6:43), beasts (Ps 49:12; 2Pe 2:12), the blind (Zep 1:17; Mt 15:14), bronze and iron (Jer 6:28; Eze 22:18), briers and thorns (Isa 55:13; Eze 2:6), bulls of Bashan (Ps 22:12), burning thorns (Ps 118:12), bushes in the wastelands (Jer 17:6), chaff (Job 21:18; Ps 1:4; Mt 3:12).

Clouds without rain (Jude 12), corpses trampled underfoot (Isa 14:19), deaf cobras (Ps 58:4), dogs (Pr 26:11; Mt 7:6; 2Pe 2:22), dross (Ps 119:119; Eze 22:18-19), early dew that passes away (Hos 13:3), earthenware coated with glaze (Pr 26:23), fading leaves (Isa 1:30), fiery furnace (Ps 21:9; Hos 7:4), fools building upon sand (Mt 7:26), fuel for the fire (Isa 9:19).

Garden without water (Isa 1:30), goats (Mt 25:32), grass that withers (2Ki 19:26; Ps 37:2; 92:7), green plants that die away (Ps 37:2), horses charging into the battle (Jer 8:6), idols (Ps 115:8), lions hungry for prey (Ps 17:12), melting wax (Ps 68:2), morning mist (Hos 13:3), moth-eaten garments (Isa 50:9; 51:8), pigs (Mt 7:6), poor figs (Jer 24:8), rejected branches (Isa 14:19), rejected silver (Jer 6:30), rocky places (Mt 13:5).

Scorpions (Eze 2:6), serpents (Ps 58:4; Mt 23:33), smoke through a window (Hos 13:3), sows (2Pe 2:22), springs without water (2Pe 2:17), storms sweeping by (Pr 10:25), straw before the wind (Job 21:18), stubble (Mal 4:1), tossing sea (Isa 57:20), tumbleweeds (Ps 83:13), visions of the night (Job 20:8), wandering stars (Jude 13), wayward children (Mt 11:16), weeds (Mt 13:38), whitewashed tombs (Mt 23:27), wild waves of the sea (Jude 13), wild donkey's colts (Job 11:12).

See Base Fellows; Impenitence; Obduracy; Penitence; Reprobate; Reprobacy; Seekers; Sin, Confession of.

Contrasted With the Righteous:
(Ps 1:1-6; 11:5; 17:14-15; 32:10; 37:17-22, 37-38; 73:1-28; 75:10; 91:7-8; 107:33-38; 125:5; Pr 2:21-22; 3:32-33; 4:16-19; 10:3, 6, 9, 11, 16, 20-21, 23-25, 28-32; 11:3, 5-6, 8-11, 18-21, 23, 31; 12:2-3, 5-7, 10, 12-13, 21, 26; 13:5-6, 9, 17, 21-22, 25; 14:2, 11, 19, 22, 32; 15:6, 8-9, 28-29; 21:15, 18, 26, 29; 22:5, 8-9; 24:16; 28:1, 4-5, 13-14, 18; 29:2, 6-7, 27; Isa 32:1-8; 65:13-14; Mal 3:18; Ro 2:7-10; Eph 2:12-14; Php 2:15; 1Th 5:5-8; Tit 1:15; 1Pe 4:17-18; 1Jn 1:6-7; 3:3-17).

Present and future state of the wicked and righteous contrasted (Job 8; Ps 49). *See below.*

Described as:
(Job 8:13-17; 15:16, 20-35; Ps 10:4-11; 36:1-4; 73:4-12; Isa 59:2-8; Jer 2:22-25). Abomination (Pr 13:9; 15:9; Hos 9:10). Alienated (Col 1:21). Beasts (Ps 49:20). Dogs (Ps 59:6; 2Pe 2:22; Rev 22:15). Horse rushing into battle (Jer 8:6).

Blind (Eze 12:2). Carnal (Ro 8:5, 7-8; 9:8). Children of the devil (Jn 8:44; Ac 13:10; 1Jn 3:10). Perverse (Jer 9:6; Ro 1:21; 2:4-5; Php 2:15). Despising God (Job 21:14; Ro 11:28). Contentious (Ro 2:8). Corrupt (Ps 53:1; 73:8; Isa 59:3; Jer 2:22; Eze 16:47; 20:16; Mic 7:2-4; Tit 1:15). Loving darkness (Jn 3:19-20). Dead in sin (Eph 2:1-3; 1Jn 3:14). Delighting in lies (Ps 62:4), in perversity (Pr 2:13-19).

Defiled (Tit 1:15-16). Depraved (Isa 1:4-6; Jer 17:9; 30:12-15; Ro 1:20-32; 3:10-18; 1Ti 1:9-10; 2Ti 3:2-9, 13; Tit 3:2; Pe 2:10, 12-19; Jude 12-13). Destitute of faithfulness (Ps 5:9). Destitute of the love of God (Jn 5:42). Devilish (1Jn 3:8). Devisers of evil (Ps 52:1-4; 64:3-6; Pr 4:16; 6:12-15; 10:23; Isa 32:6-7; Jer 4:22). Enemies (Ro 5:10; Col 1:21). Filthy (Ezr 9:11). Full of bitterness (Ac 8:23).

Uncircumcised (Isa 52:1; Jer 6:10; Eze 28:10; 31:18; 32:19-32). Uncircumcised of heart (Lev 26:41; Eze 44:7; Ac 7:51), of lips (Ex 6:12). Disobedient (Jer 11:8; Tit 1:16). Alienated from God (Col 1:21). Full of bitterness and venom (Dt 32:32-33; Ps 58:3-5). Grievous sinners (Ge 13:13; 18:20; Job 22:5; Isa 1:4-6).

Hating: Correction (Pr 15:10; Am 5:10). Instruction (Ps 50:17; Pr 1:29-30). The light (Jn 3:20).

Being in moral darkness (Mt 4:16; 6:23; Lk 1:79; Eph 4:17-18). Not knowing the way of the Lord (Jer 5:4). Lewd (Jer 11:15). Lost (Lk 19:10). Loving wickedness (Ps 7:14; Jer 14:10; Hos 4:8; Mic 3:2). Malicious toward the righteous (Ps 37:12; 94:3-8; 140:9). Mocking sin (Pr 14:9). Obdurate (Ps 10:4, 11; Pr 1:29-30; Isa 26:10-11; Eze 3:7). Outsiders (Mk 4:11). Past feeling (Eph 4:19). Progressing in wickedness (Isa 30:1, 10-11; Jer 9:3; 2Ti 3:13). Rebellious (Dt 9:24).

Sensual (Php 3:19; Jude 19). Servants of sin (Jn 8:34). Shameful (Eph 5:11-12). Shameless (Jer 6:15; 8:12; Zep 3:5). Unscrupulous (Job 24:2-24; Ps 10:4-10; Isa 5:18-23; Jer 5:26-28; 9:2-6). Sold to work iniquity (1Ki 21:20). Stiff-necked (Dt 9:13; Ac 7:51). Under condemnation (Jn 3:18-19). Unclean (Ezr 9:11; Job 14:4; Hag 2:14). Ungodly (Ro 5:6), without strength (Ro 5:6). Vomit (Lev 18:25). Wretched, miserable, poor, blind, naked (Rev 3:17-18).

Happiness of:
Sensual (Isa 22:13; 56:12). Limited to this life (Lk 16:25). Ends suddenly (Job 21:12-13; Lk 12:19-20).

Hope of:
Shall perish (Job 8:13; 11:20; 27:8; Pr 10:28).

Prayers of:
Abominable to God (Pr 15:8, 29; 21:27; 28:9).

Not answered (Dt 1:45; 1Sa 28:6; 2Sa 22:42; Job 27:9; 35:12-13; Ps 18:41; 66:18; Pr 1:24-28; 21:13, 27; Isa 1:15; 59:2; Jer 11:11; 14:12; 18:17; La 3:8, 44; Eze 8:18; 20:3, 31; Hos 5:6; Mic 3:4; Zec 7:13; Mal 1:9; 2:11-13; Jn 9:31; Jas 1:6-7; 4:3; 1Pe 3:7).

On behalf of, not answered (Dt 3:26; Jer 15:11).

Prosperity of:
(Job 12:6; 21:7-13; Ps 73:3-12; Jer 12:1-2; Mal 3:15). Brief (Job 5:3-5; 15:21, 23, 27, 29; 20:5, 22-23; 21:17-18; 24:24; Ps 37:35-36; 49:10-14; 73:18-19; 92:7; Ecc 8:12-13).

Punishment of:
(Ge 4:7; Ex 20:5; 34:7; Nu 32:23; 1Sa 3:11-14; 2Sa 3:39; 7:14; 22:27-28; 23:6-7; 1Ki 21:20-21; Job 8:20, 22; 11:20; 18:5-21; 19:29; 21:7 33; 27:13-23; 36:12, 17; Ps 3:7; 5:5; 18:14, 26-27; 36:12; 37:1-2, 9-10, 17, 20, 22, 34-38; 64:7-8; 73:18-20, 27; 91:8; 97:3; 107:17, 33-34; 119:21, 118-119, 155; 129:4; 146:9; 147:6; Pr 3:33; 10:3, 6-8, 14, 24-25, 27-31; 11:3, 5-8, 19, 21, 23, 31; 13:2, 5-6, 9, 21, 25; 14:12, 19, 32; 16:4-5; 22:5, 23; Ecc 8:12-13; Isa 3:11; 26:21; Jer 21:14; 36:31; La 3:39; Eze 3:18-20; 18:1-32; 33:7-20; Hos 14:9; Am 3:2; Mic 2:3; 6:13; Mt 15:13; Ro 1:18; 2:5, 8-9; Col 3:25; 1Th 1:10; 1Pe 3:12; 2Pe 2:3-9, 12-17; Jude 5-7; Rev 14:10-11).

By—
Chastisements (Ps 89:32; 1Co 5:5; 1Ti 1:20). Judgments (Ex 32:35; Lev 26:14-39; Dt 11:26-28; 28:15-68; 30:15, 18-19; Job 20:5-29; Ps 11:6; 21:9-10; 39:11; 75:8; 78:49-51; Isa 5:11-14, 24; 9:18; 10:3; 13:9, 11, 14-22; 24:17-18; 28:18-22; 65:12-15; Jer 5:25; 8:12-14, 20-22; 14:10, 12; 25:31; 44:2-14, 23-29; 49:10; La 3:39; 4:22; 5:16-17; Eze 5:4, 8-17; 9:5-7, 10; 20:8; 22:14, 20-21, 31; 24:13-14; Hos 2:9-13; 5:4-6, 9; 9:7, 9, 15; Joel 2:1-2; 3:13-16; Am 5:18-20; Lk 12:46; 1Co 10:5-11; 1Ti 5:24; Heb 10:26-31; 1Pe 4:17-18).

Sorrow (Ge 3:16-19; Job 15:20-24; Ps 32:10; Ecc 2:26; Isa 50:11). Trouble (Isa 48:22; 57:20-21). Being rejected of the Lord (1Ch 28:9; 2Ch 15:2; Mt 10:33; Mk 8:38; Lk 9:26; 13:27-28; Mt 7:23; Jn 8:21; 2Ti 2:12-13; Heb 6:8). Being excluded from the kingdom of heaven (1Co 6:9-10; Gal 5:19-21; Eph 5:5; Rev 21:27; 22:19). Being blotted from God's book (Ex 32:33).

Destruction (Ge 6:3, 7, 12-13; Nu 15:31; Dt 7:9-10; 1Sa 12:25; 1Ch 10:13-14; Job 4:8-9; 31:3; Ps 2:9; 7:11-13; 9:5, 17; 34:16, 21; 52:5; 55:19, 23; 92:7, 9; 94:13, 23; 101:8; 104:35; 106:18, 43; 145:20; Pr 2:22; 12:7; 21:12, 15-16; 24:20; Isa 11:4; 13:8; 64:5-7; Jer 13:14, 16, 22; Eze 25:7; Hos 7:12-13; Am 8:14; Na 1:2, 8-10; Zep 1:12-18; Zec 5:2-4; Mal 4:1; Mt 3:10, 12 w Lk 3:17; Mt 7:13, 19; 10:28 w Lk 12:4-5; Mt 21:41, 44 w Mk 12:1-9 & Lk 20:16, 18; Mt 24:50-51; Lk 9:24-25 w Mt 16:26 & Mk 8:36; Lk 19:27; Jn 5:29; Ac 3:23; Ro 2:12; 9:22; 1Co 3:17; Php 3:19; 1Th 5:3; 2Th 2:8-10). Sudden destruction (Pr 6:15; 24:22; 28:18; 29:1). Everlasting destruction (2Th 1:9). Everlasting contempt (Da 12:2). Everlasting fire (Isa 28:18-22; Mt 18:8-9; 25:41; Mk 9:43; Rev 20:15; 21:8).

Death (Ge 2:17; Ps 1:4-6; Pr 16:25; 19:16; Hos 13:1, 3; Am 9:1-5, 10; Ro 5:12, 21; 6:16, 21; 8:2, 6, 13; 1Co 15:21-22; 2Co 7:10; Gal 6:8; 1Jn 3:14-15; Jas 1:15; 5:20; Rev 2:22-23). The second death (Rev 21:8).

Condemnation to hell (Mt 23:33; Mk 16:16; Jn 3:15-16, 18, 36). Being cast into outer darkness (Mt 8:12; 22:13; 25:30). The last judgments (Rev 6:15-17; 9:4-6, 15, 18; 11:18; 16:2-21; 18:5; 19:15, 17-21; 20:10, 15; 21:8, 27; 22:19). Everlasting (Mt 25:46; Rev 14:10-11; 20:10). Degrees in (Mt 10:15; 11:22, 24; Mk 12:40). No escape from (Job 34:22; 1Th 5:3; Heb 2:3).

God has no pleasure in the death of (Eze 18:23; 33:11).

Punishment Illustrated in Parables—
The weeds (Mt 13:24-30, 38-42, 49-50). The talents (Mt 25:14-30). The barren fig tree (Lk 13:6-9). The man who built his house on the sand (Mt 7:26-27; Lk 6:49). Lazarus and the rich man (Lk 16:22-28).

Woes Against the Wicked:
(Isa 5:8, 11, 18-23; Mt 26:24; Mk 14:21; Lk 11:52; 17:1-2; 22:22; Jude 11).

Warned:
(Jer 7:13-15, 23-25; 25:4-6; 26:2-7, 12-13; 29:17-19; Eze 33:8; Da 4:4-27; 5:4-29; Zep 2:1-2; Lk 3:7-9; 1Co 10:11; Rev 3:1-3, 16-19).

See Hell; Judgments; Punishment.

WIDOW

Mosaic Laws Concerning:
High priest forbidden to marry (Lev 21:14). Supported by father, when daughter of priest (Lev 22:13). Vows of, binding (Nu 30:9). Entitled to glean in the orchards and harvest fields (Dt 24:19-21). Levirate marriage of (Dt 25:5-10).

Care of commanded (Dt 14:28-29; 16:11, 14; Isa 1:17; Jer 7:6-7).

Widow's dowry. *See Dowry.*

In the Church:
Remarriage of, authorized (Ro 7:3; 1Co 7:39; 1Ti 5:14). Remarriage of, discouraged (1Co 7:8-9).

Qualifications for widows in 1Ti 5:3-16 may indicate a church office.

Kindness to:
Exemplified by Job (Job 29:13; 31:16, 22). God, the friend of (Dt 10:18; Ps 68:5; 146:9; Pr 15:25; Jer 49:11). Care of in the church (Ac 6:1; 1Ti 5:3-6, 9-12, 16; Jas 1:27).

Oppression of:
(Job 22:9; 24:3, 21; Ps 94:6; Isa 1:23; Eze 22:7; Mk 12:40; Lk 20:47).

Oppression of, forbidden (Ex 22:22-24; Dt 24:17; 27:19; Isa 10:2; Jer 22:3; Zec 7:10; Mal 3:5).

Instances of:
Naomi (Ru 1:3). Ruth (Ru 1-4). The widow of Zarephath, who sustained Elijah during a famine (1Ki 17). The woman whose sons Elisha saved from being sold for debt (2Ki 4:1-7). Anna (Lk 2:36-37). The woman who gave two mites in the temple (Mk 12:41-44; Lk 21:2), of Nain, whose only son Jesus raised from the dead (Lk 7:11-15).

See Levirate Marriage; Marriage; Women.

WIFE

Described:
Called a helper (Ge 2:18, 20), desire of the eyes (Eze 24:10). Compared to a fruitful vine (Ps 128:3).

Beloved, by Isaac (Ge 24:67), by Jacob (Ge 29:30). Hated (Ge 29:31-33).

Contentious (Pr 19:13; 21:9, 19; 25:24). Instances of: Zipporah (Ex 4:25), Peninnah (1Sa 1:6-7).

Loyal, Jacob's (Ge 31:14-16).

Unfaithful (Nu 5:12-31). Instances of: Potiphar's (Ge 39:7), Bathsheba (2Sa 11:2-5).

Prudent (Pr 19:14). Tactful: Abigail (1Sa 25:3, 14-34), Esther (Est 5:5-8; 7:1-4). Virtuous (Pr 12:4; 31:10-12). Incorruptible or strong-willed: Vashti (Est 1:10-12). Wise (Pr 14:1).

Marrying of:
Commended (Pr 18:22; 1Co 7:2; 1Ti 5:14).

Bought (Ge 29:18-30; 31:41; Ex 21:7-11; Ru 4:10). Obtained by kidnapping (Jdg 21:21). Procured (Ge 24; 34:4-10; 38:6).

Duty:
Husband to wife (1Co 7:2-5, 27; Eph 5:25, 28, 31, 33; Col 3:19; 1Pe 3:7).

Wife to husband: To be obedient (1Co 14:34-35; Eph 5:22, 24; Col 3:18; Tit 2:5; 1Pe 3:1, 6). To be affectionate (Tit 2:4). To be faithful (Tit 3:11).

Relation of, to the husband (Ge 2:18, 23-24; 1Co 7:2-5, 10-11, 13, 39; 11:3, 8-9, 11-12).

Domestic duties of (Ge 18:6; Pr 31:13-27).

Vows of (Nu 30:6-16). *See Vow.*

Instances of Evil Influence of:
Eve (Ge 3:6, 12). Solomon's wives (1Ki 11:1-8; Ne 13:26). Jezebel (1Ki 21:25; 2Ki 9:30-37). Haman's (Est 5:14). Herodias (Mt 14:3, 6-11; Mk 6:17, 24-28).

See Husband; Marriage; Parents; Widow; Women.

WILD OX
A powerful animal (Nu 23:22; 24:8; Ps 92:9); two-horned (Dt 33:17); wild and difficult to catch (Job 39:9-12; Ps 29:6); KJV "unicorn." *See Animals.*

WILDERNESS
Wandering of the Israelites in. *See Israel.* Typical of the sinner's state (Dt 32:10). Jesus' temptation in (Mt 4:1; Mk 1:12-13; Lk 4:1).

See Deserts.

WILL

The Mental Faculty:
Freedom of, recognized by God (Ge 4:6-10; Dt 5:29; 1Ki 20:42; Isa 1:18-20; 43:26; Jer 36:3, 7; Jn 7:17).

See Blessings, Spiritual, Contingent Upon Obedience; Choice; Contingencies.

Of God:
Defined: God's purpose (2Ti 1:9, w Eph 1:9), God's plan (1Co 12:11; 2Co 1:15; Jas 3:4), God's will (Ac 27:12; Eph 1:11).

The supreme rule of duty (Mt 6:10; 12:50 w Mk 3:35; Mt 26:39, 42; Mk 14:36; Lk 22:42; Jn 4:34; 5:30; 6:38-40; Ro 12:2; Eph 5:17). Plans of the righteous subject to (Ac 18:21; Ro 1:10; 15:32; 1Co 4:19; 16:7; Heb 6:3; Jas 4:15).

"Lord's prayer" concerns (Mt 6:10; Lk 11:2). *See Agency.*

Reasons for Wanting to Know—
Love for God (Jn 14:15, 21, 23-24), desire to please God (1Jn 3:22). Blessings in this life (1Pe 3:10-12), rewards in the future life (1Co 3:10-15; 2Ti 4:8; Heb 10:35). Avoid discipline (1Co 3:16-17; 11:31-32; 1Pe 4:17). Good example to other believers (1Co 4:16; 1Th 1:7; 2Th 3:9; Heb 13:7). Will not be ashamed at the Second Coming (1Jn 2:28). Glorify God (1Co 10:31; Col 3:17, 23; Heb 12:10; 2Pe 1:4). Obligation to know (Eph 5:15-17).

How God Reveals—
Through his Word (Ps 119:105; 2Ti 3:16-17). Through control of thoughts, indirectly (2Co 7:8-11; 12:7; 1Pe 1:6-7; 4:12-13; Jas 1:2-4), directly (Pr 16:1, 9; 21:1; Eph 2:13), through Satan (Job 1:12; 2:6). Through the control of circumstances (Pr 16:9; 20:24; Ac 2:23; 4:28; Eph 1:11). Until revelation is complete, through dreams (Ge 20:3, 6; 31:11, 24; 1Ki 3:5; Mt 2:12-13) and visions (Ge 15:1; Zec 1:7-8; Ac 10:10-11).

Prerequisites: Spiritual maturity (Isa 55:8-9; 1Co 2:7; Eph 4:14; Col 1:9; 1Ti 3:6; Heb 5:13-14; 13:21), through the teaching ministry of the Holy Spirit (Jn 16:13-14; 1Co 2:12-14; 1Jn 2:27), through application in testings (Php 3:15; Heb 5:14; 12:7, 11; Jas 1:2-5). Yieldedness or self-denial (Ro 6:13, 19; 12:1; 1Pe 2:9; Rev 1:6), discipleship (Mt 16:24; Mk 8:34; Lk 9:23). Desire to know God's will (Jn 7:17), to do it (Mk 4:24-25; Ac 10:22, 35, 44, 47; 1Jn 2:11). Willingness to obey daily (Mt 16:24; Mk 8:34; Lk 9:23; Ro 6:16; Php 2:13; 2Pe 2:19). Faith (Ps 37:5; Pr 3:5-6; Ro 14:23; 2Co 5:7; Php 2:13; Heb 11:17, 27). Patience (Ps 37:7; Jas 1:5-6). Common sense (Tit 2:12). Peace of God (Col 3:15). A clear conscience (Ro 14:23).

A Testament:
Of Abraham (Ge 25:5-6). Jacob (Ge 48:49). David (1Ki 2:1-9). Jehoshaphat (2Ch 21:3). May not be annulled (Gal 3:15). In force after death only (Heb 9:16-17). *See Testament; Wills.*

WILLFULNESS *See Obduracy; Self-Will.*

WILLOW A type of tree growing along the brook or near water; several species in Israel; symbol of joy (Lev 23:40; Job 40:22), sorrow (Ps 137:2).

WILLOWS, BROOK OF THE *See Poplars, Ravine of.*

WILLS
Statements, oral or written in a form, to which law courts give effect, by which property may be disposed of after death (Heb 9:16-17). *See Covenant; Will, A Testament.*

WIMPLE *See Cloak.*

WIND

Characterized:
Blasting (2Ki 19:7, 35).
East: Hot and blasting in Egypt (Ge 41:6), in the valley of the Euphrates (Eze 19:12), in Canaan (Hos 13:15; Lk 12:55), at Nineveh (Jnh 4:8), tempestuous in Uz (Job 27:21).
West: Took away the plague of locusts from the land of Egypt (Ex 10:19).
North: Free from humidity in Canaan (Pr 25:23).
South: Soothing (Job 37:17), tempestuous (Job 37:9), purifying (Job 37:21).

Figurative:
(Hos 4:19). Of the judgments of God (Jer 22:22; Hos 13:15; Mt 7:25). Of the Spirit (Jn 3:8). Of heresy (Eph 4:14).

WINDOW An opening in a wall (Ge 6:16; 26:8; Jos 2:15, 21; 1Ki 6:4; Eze 40:16-36; Ac 20:9).

WINE

General
Made from grapes (Ge 49:11; Jer 40:10, 12), from pomegranates (SS 8:2). Kept in wineskins (Jos 9:4, 13; Job 32:19; Jer 13:12; Mt 9:17; Lk 5:37-38), in jars (Jer 48:12), in vats (1Ch 27:27), in buildings (2Ch 32:28). Commerce in (Rev 18:13). Banquets of (Est 5:6). Plentiful in Canaan (Dt 33:28; 2Ki 18:32).
Fermented (Lev 10:9; Nu 6:3; Dt 14:26; 29:6). New wine, a staple (Hos 2:8, 22; 7:14; Joel 2:24; Hag 1:11; Mk 2:22; Lk 5:37-39). Aged wine, a delicacy (Isa 25:6; Jer 48:11). Old wine (Lk 5:39).

Positive Use of:
Offered with sacrifices (Ex 29:40; Lev 23:13; Nu 15:5, 10; 18:12; 28:7, 14; Dt 14:23; Ne 10:39).
For enjoyment (Ps 4:7; 104:15; Pr 31:6-7; Ecc 2:3; Isa 25:6; Zec 9:17; 10:7).
Recommended by Paul to Timothy (1Ti 5:23).
Given by Melchizedek to Abraham (Ge 14:18). Used at meals (Mt 26:27-29; Mk 14:23). Made by Jesus at the marriage feast in Cana (Jn 2:9-10). Used in the Lord's Supper (Mt 26:27-29; Lk 22:17-20). Given to Jesus at the Crucifixion, possibly as a pain killer (Mt 27:48; Mk 15:23; Lk 23:36; Jn 19:29).

Negative Use of:
Drunkenness condemned (Pr 20:1; Isa 5:11, 22; 24:9; 28:1, 3, 7; 56:12; Jer 23:9; Hos 4:11; Joel 1:5; Am 6:6; Hab 2:5; Eph 5:18; 1Ti 3:8; Tit 2:3). Addiction and craving condemned (Pr 21:17; 23:29-32; Joel 1:5). Children sold for (Joel 3:3).

Instances of drunkenness—
Noah (Ge 9:21), Lot (Ge 19:32), Joseph and his brothers (Ge 43:34), Nabal (1Sa 25:36), Amnon (2Sa 13:28-29), Xerxes (Est 1:10), kings of Israel (Hos 7:5). Falsely charged against Jesus (Mt 11:19; Lk 7:34) and the disciples (Ac 2:13).

Abstinence From:

Required—
Of Levites while on duty (Lev 10:9; Eze 44:21). Of Nazirites during their vow (Nu 6:3). Of Samson's mother during her pregnancy (Jdg 13:4-5). *See Nazirite(s).* Required of kings and rulers (Pr 31:4-5). Of John the Baptist (Lk 1:15).

Chosen—
By Daniel to avoid defilement (Da 1:8-20), in mouring (Da 10:3). By the Recabites to honor a vow (Jer 35:6, 8, 14, 16). With bread, denied to the Israelites in the desert (Dt 29:6). Temperance allowed the quests at Xerxes' banquet (Est 1:8).
For the sake of the weaker brother (Ro 14:21). Possibly abstained from by Timothy (1Ti 5:23).

Figurative:
Of, the divine judgments (Ps 60:3; 75:8; Jer 51:7; Rev 14:10; 16:19), the joy of wisdom (Pr 9:2, 5), the joys of religion (Isa 25:6; 55:1; Joel 2:19), abominations (Rev 14:9; 17:2; 18:3).

Symbolic:
Of the blood of Jesus (Mt 26:28; Mk 14:23-24; Lk 22:20; Jn 6:53-56).
See Abstinence; Drunkenness; Vine; Vineyards.

WINEBIBBER *See Drunkard; Drunkenness; Wine.*

WINEPRESS (Nu 18:27, 30; Dt 15:14; Jdg 6:11). In vineyards (Isa 5:2; Mt 21:33; Mk 12:1).
Figurative: Treading the winepress of the judgments of God (Isa 63:2-3; La 1:15; Rev 14:19-20).

WINESKIN Made of tanned whole skins of animals (Mt 9:17). *See Wine.*

WING Often used figuratively (Ps 18:10; 55:6; 68:13; Pr 23:5; Mt 23:37).

WINNOWING Separating kernels of threshed grain from chaff; done by shaking bunches of grain into air so that the kernels fall to the ground, while the chaff is blown away by the wind (Ru 3:2).

Figurative:
Of Israel in destroying its enemies (Isa 41:15-16). God's judgment separating evil people from good (Jer 15:7; 51:2; Mt 3:12; Lk 3:17). The character of a good king, not all kings (Pr 20:8; 20:26).

WINTER Annual return of, shall never cease (Ge 8:22). Plowing in, in Canaan (Pr 20:4). Rainy season in, in Canaan (SS 2:11). Shipping suspended in, on the Mediterranean Sea (Ac 27:12; 28:11). Paul remains for one, at Nicopolis (Tit 3:12). Summer and winter houses (Jer 36:22; Am 3:15).
See Meteorology.

WINTER APARTMENT, WINTER HOUSE The wealthy had separate residences for hot and cold seasons. Called a "winter apartment" (Jer 36:22), a "winter house" (Am 3:15).
See Summer House, Summer Palace.

WISDOM (Job 32:9; Ps 2:10; 90:12; Pr 2:1-20; 4:18-20; 7:4; 9:1-6; 10:13, 21, 23; 12:1, 8, 15; 13:14-16; 14:6-8, 16, 18, 33; 15:2, 7, 14, 33; 16:16, 20-24; 17:10, 24; 18:15; 19:8, 20; 21:11; Ecc 8:1, 5; 9:13-18; 10:12; 12:11; Isa 11:9; 29:24; Mt 11:19; Lk 1:17; 7:35; 21:15; Jas 1:5).

Spiritual:
(Dt 32:29; Job 5:27; 8:8, 10; 12:2-3, 7-13, 16-17, 22).
The fear of the Lord is the beginning of (Ps 111:10; Pr 1:7; 9:10; Isa 33:6). Is revealed to the obedient (Ps 107:43; Pr 28:5, 7; 29:3; Ecc 8:5; Da 12:3-4, 10; Hos 6:3, 6; 14:9; Mt 6:22-23; Lk 11:34-36; Jn 7:17; 10:4, 14; 1Co 2:6-10; 8:3; 1Jn 4:6). Exemplified (Ps 9:10; 76:1; Pr 1:5; 11:12; Mt 7:24-25; 25:1-13; Mk 12:32-34; Ac 6:10; Ro 15:14; 1Co 13:11; Php 3:7-8, 10; 1Th 5:4-5; Jas 3:13).

Commended—
(Pr 3:13-26; 24:3-7; Ecc 7:11-12, 19; 10:1, 12). Is above value (Job 28:12-19; Pr 3:13-15; 16:16). Exhortations to attain to (Pr 2:1-20; 4:4-13, 18-20; 22:17-21; 23:12, 19; 23:23; 24:13-14; Ro 16:19; 1Co 8:3; 14:20; 2Co 8:7; Eph 5:15-17; Col 3:10, 16; 2Pe 3:18).
Parable of (Mt 25:1-13).
Personified (Pr 1:20-33; 8; 9:1-18).
See Knowledge; Speaking or Speech, Wise.

From God—
(Ex 4:12; 8:4, 10; Dt 4:5-6, 35-36; 29:4; 1Ch 22:12; Ne 9:20; Job 4:3; 11:5-6; 22:21-22; 28:20-28; 32:7-8; 33:16; 35:10-11; 36:22; 38:36-37; Ps 16:7; 19:1-2; 25:8-9, 12, 14; 32:8; 36:9; 51:6; 71:17; 94:12; 112:4; 119:130; Pr 1:23; 2:6-7; 3:5-6; Ecc 2:26; Isa 2:3; 11:1-3; 30:21; 42:6-7, 16; 48:17; 54:13; Jer 9:23-24; 24:7; Da 1:17; 2:21-23; 11:32-33; Mt 11:25-27; 13:11; 16:16-17; Lk 1:76-79; 12:11-12; 21:15; 24:32, 45; Jn 1:1, 4-5, 7-9, 17; 6:45; 8:12, 31-32; 9:5, 39; 12:46; 14:7; 16:13-14; 17:3, 6-8, 25-26; 18:37; Ro 1:19-20; 1Co 1:30; 2:9, 11-14; 12:8; 2Co 3:15; 4:6; Gal 4:9; Eph 4:11-13; Php 3:15; Col 1:26-28; 1Ti 2:4; 2Ti 1:7; 3:15; Jas 3:17; 2Pe 1:2-5, 8, 12; 3:18; 1Jn 2:20, 27; 5:20). *See God, Wisdom of.*

Exemplified—
Of Joseph (Ge 41:16, 25-39; Ac 7:10). Of Moses (Ac 7:22). Of Bezalel (Ex 31:3-5; 35:31-35; 36:1). Of Oholiab (Ex 31:6; 35:34-35; 36:1), of other skilled artisans (Ex 36:2), of women (Ex 35:26). Of Hiram (1Ki 7:14; 2Ch 2:14). Of Solomon (1Ki 3:12, 16-28; 4:29-34; 5:12; 10:24). Of Ethan, Heman, Calcol, and Darda (1Ki 4:31). Of the princes of Issachar (1Ch 12:32). Of Ezra (Ezr 7:25). Of Daniel (Da 1:17; 5:14). Of Paul (2Pe 3:15). Of the Magi (Mt 2:1-12).
Prayer for (Nu 27:21; Jdg 20:18, 23, 26-28; 1Ki 3:7, 9; 8:36; 2Ch 1:10; Job 34:32; Ps 5:8; 25:4-5; 27:11; 31:3; 39:4; 43:3; 86:11; 90:12; 119:12, 18-19, 26-27, 33-34, 66, 68, 73, 80, 124-125, 135, 144, 169, 171; 139:24; Eph 1:16-19; 3:14-19; 6:18-20; Php 1:9; Col 1:9-10; 2:1-3; 4:2-4; 2Ti 2:7; Jas 1:5).
To be possessed in humility (Jer 9:23-24; Jas 3:13). *See Desire, Spiritual.* Solomon's prayer for. *See Solomon.*
Promised (Jn 8:22). Opportunity to obtain, forfeited (Pr 1:24-31). Shall become universal.

Worldly:

Condemned—
(Job 4:18-21; 5:13; 11:2, 12; 37:24). Desired by Eve (Ge 3:6-7). Misleading (Pr 21:30; Isa 47:10; 1Co 8:1-2). Ending in death (Pr 16:25). Folly of (Ecc 2:1-26; 7:11-13, 16-25; 8:1, 16-17; Jer 8:7-9; 49:7; Mt 6:23; Ro 1:21-23). Increases sorrow (Ecc 1:18; Isa 47:10-11).
Denounced (2Co 1:12). Woe denounced against (Isa 5:21). Shall perish (Isa 29:14-16). Illustration of (Mt 7:24-27; Lk 16:8).
Admonitions against (Pr 3:7; Col 2:8; 1Ti 6:20-21). Admonitions against glorying in (Jer 9:23-24).
Heavenly things not discerned by (Mt 11:25; Lk 10:21). Gospel not to be preached with (1Co 1:17-26; 2:1-14). To be renounced in order to attain spiritual wisdom (1Co 3:18-20).

Commended—
Council of others commanded (Pr 15:22; 20:18; 24:3-7). Wise application of, profitable (Ecc 10:10; Isa 28:24-29).

Of God: *See God, Wisdom of.*

Of Jesus: *See Jesus the Christ, Wisdom of.*

WISDOM OF JESUS, SON OF SIRACH *See Apocrypha.*

WISDOM OF SOLOMON *See Apocrypha.*

WISE MEN
1. Men of understanding and skill in ordinary affairs (Pr 1:5; Job 15:2; Ps 49:10), came to be recognized as a distinct class, listed with priests and prophets (Jer 18:18), and also found outside Israel (Ge 41:8; Ex 7:11; Da 2:12-5:15).
2. The Magi (Mt 2:1-12), astrologers who came from the East. Their number and names are not given in Scripture. *See Magi.*

WITCH One (usually a woman) in league with evil spirits who practices witchcraft, sorcery, and divination; condemned by law (Ex 22:18; Dt 18:9-14; 1Sa 28:3, 9; 2Ki 23:24; Isa 8:19; Ac 19:18-19). *See Divination; Medium; Sorcery; Spiritists; Witchcraft.*

WITCHCRAFT Detestable to God (Dt 18:9-13; 2Ki 9:22; 2Ch 33:6; Na 3:4; Gal 5:19). To be destroyed (Mic 5:12).
See Divination; Sorcery; Spiritists; Witch.

WITHE NIV "thong" (Jdg 16:7-9).

WITHERED HAND Hand wasted away through some form of atrophy (Mk 3:1-6).

WITNESS (Lev 5:1; Pr 18:17). Qualified by oath (Ex 22:11; Nu 5:19, 21; 1Ki 8:31-32), by laying hands on the accused (Lev 24:14). Two necessary to establish a fact (Nu 35:30; Dt 17:6; 19:15; Mt 18:16; Jn 8:17; 2Co 13:1; 1Ti 5:19; Heb 10:28). Required to cast the first stone in executing sentence (Dt 13:9; 17:5-7; Ac 7:58).
To the transfer of land (Ge 21:25-30; 23:11, 16-18; Ru 4:1-9; Jer 32:9-12, 25, 44). To marriage (Ru 4:10-11; Isa 8:2-3). Incorruptible (Ps 15:4). Corrupted by money (Mt 28:11-15; Ac 6:11, 13).
Figurative of instruction in righteousness (Rev 11:3).
See Court, Of Law; Evidence; Falsehood; False Witness; Holy Spirit; Testimony, Religious.

WITNESS OF THE SPIRIT Direct, personal communication by the Holy Spirit that we are children of God (Ro 8:15-16), or some other truth (Ac 20:23; 1Ti 4:1).

WITNESSING FOR CHRIST (Lk 2:17, 38; 24:48; Ac 1:8; 10:39; 22:15; 23:11; 26:22). Of John the Baptist (Jn 1:15; 3:26). Of the apostles (Jn 15:27; 19:35; Ac 10:39-43; 1Jn 1:1-5), to his resurrection (Ac 1:22; 2:32; 3:15; 4:33; 5:32; 1Co 15:3-8).

WIZARD *See Spiritists.*

WOLF Ravenous (Ge 49:27; Jer 5:6; Eze 22:27; Zep 3:3; Jn 10:12).
Figurative: Of the enemies of the righteous (Mt 7:15; 10:16; Jn 10:12; Ac 20:29). Of the reconciling power of the gospel (Isa 11:6).

WOMEN

General:
Creation of (Ge 1:27; 2:21-22). Named (Ge 2:23). Fall of and curse upon (Ge 3:1-16; 2Co 11:3; 1Ti 2:14). Promise to (Ge 3:15).
Took part in ancient worship (Ex 15:20-21; 38:8; 1Sa 2:22), in choir (1Ch 25:5-6; Ezr 2:65; Ne 7:67). Served at the entrance to the Tent of Meeting (Ex 38:8; 1Sa 2:22). Consecrated jewels to tabernacle (Ex 35:22), mirrors (Ex 38:8). Required to attend the reading of the law (Dt 31:12; Jos 8:35). Ministered in the tabernacle (Ex 38:8; 1Sa 2:22). Religious privileges of, among early Christians (Ac 1:14; 12:12-13; 1Co 11:5; 14:34; 1Ti 2:11).
Purifications of after menstruation (Lev 15:19-33; 2Sa 11:4), childbirth (Lev 12; Lk 2:22). Difference in ceremonies made between male and female children (Lev 12). Vows of (Nu 30:3-16).
Had their own tents (Ge 24:67; 31:33). Domestic duties of (Ge 18:6; Pr 31:15-19; Mt 24:41). Cooked (Ge 18:6). Spun (Ex 35:25-26; 1Sa 2:19; Pr 31:19-24). Embroidered (Pr 31:22). Made garments (1Sa 2:19; Ac 9:39). Gleaned (Ru 2:7-8, 15-23). Kept vineyards (SS 1:6). Tended flocks and herds (Ge 24:11, 13-14, 19-20; 29:9; Ex 2:16). Worked in fields (Isa 27:11; Eze 26:6, 8). Doorkeeper (Mt 26:69; Jn 18:16-17; Ac 12:13-14). Did not serve in army (Isa 19:16; Jer 50:37; 51:30; Na 3:13).
Veiled the face (Ge 24:65), *See Veil.* Forbidden to wear men's clothing (Dt 22:5). Ornaments of (Isa 3:16-23; Jer 3:32). Wore hair long (1Co 11:5-15). Commended for modesty in dress (1Ti 2:9-10; 1Pe 3:3-6).
Compassionate to her children (Isa 49:15), rejoice with dancing (Jdg 11:34; 21:21; Jer 31:13), courteous to strangers (Ge 24:17-20), wise (1Sa 25:3; 2Sa 20:16-22), weaker partner but co-heir (1Pe 3:7).
Property rights of: In inheritance (Nu 27:1-11; 36; Jos 17:3-6; Job 42:15), to sell real estate (Ru 4:3-9).
First to sin (Ge 3:6). Last at the cross (Mt 27:55-56; Mk 15:40-41). First at the tomb (Mk 15:46-47; 16:1-6; Lk 23:27-28, 49, 55-56; 24:1-10). First to whom the risen Lord appeared (Mk 16:9; Jn 20:14-18). Converted by preaching of Paul (Ac 16:14-15; 17:4, 12, 34).
Virtuous, held in high esteem (Ru 3:11; Pr 11:16, 22; 12:4; 14:1; 31:10-30). *See below, Good.*
Zealous in promoting superstition and idolatry (Jer 7:18; Eze 13:17, 23). Active in instigating iniquity (Nu 31:15-16; 1Ki 21:25; Ne 13:26). Guilty of lesbianism (Ro 1:26). *See below, Wicked.*
Could not marry without consent of parents, father (Ge 24:3-4; 34:6; Ex 22:17; Jos 3:16-17; 1Sa 17:25; 18:17-27). Not to be given in marriage considered a calamity (Jdg 11:37; Ps 78:63; Isa 4:1). When charged with infidelity, guilt or innocence was determined by trial (Nu 5:12-31). Sold for husband's debts (Mt 18:25). Taken captive (Nu 31:9, 15, 17-18, 35; La 1:18; Eze 30:17-18).
Punishment to be inflicted on men for seducing, when betrothed (Dt 22:23-27). Punishment for seducing, when not betrothed (Ex 22:16-17; Dt 22:28-29). Protected during menstruation (Lev 18:19; 20:18). Treated with cruelty in war (Dt 32:25; La 2:21; 5:11).

In Leadership:

Rulers of nations—
Deborah, judge and prophetess (Jdg 4:4); Athaliah, queen of Judah (2Ki 11:1-16; 2Ch 22:2-3, 10-12; 23:1-15); Jezebel, queen of Israel (1Ki 16:31); as rulers in Israel (Isa 3:12); Queen of Sheba (1Ki 10:1-13; 2Ch 9:1-9, 12); Esther, queen of Persia (Est 2:17); Candace, queen of Ethiopia (Ac 8:27).

Patriots—
Miriam (Ex 15:20), Deborah (Jdg 4:4-16; 5), women of Israel (1Sa 18:6), of Thebez (Jdg 9:50), of Abel (2Sa 20:16-22), Esther (Est 4:4-17; 5:1-8; 7:1-6; 8:1-8), of the Philistines (2Sa 1:20). Aid in defensive operations (Jdg 9:53).

W

Influential in public affairs—

The wise woman from Tekoa (2Sa 14:1-21), Bathsheba (1Ki 1:15-21), Jezebel (1Ki 21:7-15, 25), Athaliah (2Ki 11:1, 3; 2Ch 21:6; 22:3), Huldah (2Ki 22:14-20; 2Ch 34:22-28), the queen of Babylon (Da 5:9-13), Pilate's wife (Mt 27:19).

In business (1Ch 7:24; Pr 31:14-18, 24).

Poets—

Miriam (Ex 15:21), Deborah (Jdg 5), Hannah (1Sa 2:1-10), Elizabeth (Lk 1:42-45), Mary (Lk 1:46-55).

Prophets—

Miriam (Ex 15:20-21; Mic 6:4), Deborah (Jdg 4:4-5), Huldah (2Ki 22:14-20; 2Ch 34:22-28), Anna (Lk 2:36-38), Philip's daughters (Ac 21:9).

False prophets and mediums—

The medium at Endor (1Sa 28:7-25), false prophets (Eze 13:17-23), Noadiah the prophetess (Ne 6:14).

In the church—

Present at the selection of Matthias (Ac 1:13-26), present at Pentecost (Ac 2:1-18), churches met in women's homes (Ac 12:12; 16:40; Ro 16:3-5; 1Co 1:11; 16:19; Col 4:15; 2Jn), teachers (Ac 18:26; Tit 2:3-5), deaconesses or wives of deacons (Ro 16:1-2; 1Ti 3:11), and if Junias was a woman, apostles (Ro 16:7). Widow may have been a church office (1Ti 5:1-16).

Social Status of:

In Persia (Est 1:10-22; Da 5:1-12). In Roman empire (Ac 24:24; 25:13, 23; 26:30).

Paul's precepts concerning women in the church (Gal 3:28; 1Co 11:5-15; 14:34-35; Eph 5:22-24; Col 3:18; 1Ti 2:9-12; 3:11; 5:1-16; Tit 2:3-5).

See Widow; Wife. See also, Husbands; Parents.

Good:

Good wife, from the Lord (Pr 12:4; 18:22; 19:13-14; 31:10-31; 1Ti 2:9-10; 3:11; 5:3-16; Tit 2:3-5). Virtuous (Ru 3:11; Pr 11:16, 22; 12:4; 14:1). Affectionate (2Sa 1:26), to offspring (Isa 49:15). Illustrated by the five wise virgins (Mt 25:1-10).

Instances of—

Deborah, a judge, prophetess, and military leader (Jdg 4:5). Mother of Samson (Jdg 13:23). Naomi (Ru 1:2; 3:1; 4:14-17). Ruth (Ru 1:4, 14-22, & Ru 2-4). Hannah, the mother of Samuel (1Sa 1:9-18, 24-28). Widow of Zarephath, who fed Elijah during the famine (1Ki 17:8-24). The Shunammite, who gave hospitality to Elisha (2Ki 4:8-38). Vashti (Est 1:11-12). Esther (Est 4:15-17; 5:1-8; 7:1-6; 8:1-8).

Mary (Lk 1:26-38). Elizabeth (Lk 1:6, 41-45). Anna (Lk 2:37). The widow who cast her mite into the treasury (Mk 12:41-44; Lk 21:2-4). Mary and Martha (Mk 14:3-9; Lk 10:42; Jn 11:5). Mary Magdalene (Mk 16:1; Lk 8:2; Jn 20:1-2, 11-16). Pilate's wife (Mt 27:19). Dorcas (Ac 9:36). Lydia (Ac 19:14). Priscilla (Ac 18:26). Phoebe (Ro 16:1-2). Julia (Ro 16:15). Mary (Ro 16:6). Lois and Eunice (2Ti 1:5). Philippians (Php 4:3). The chosen lady (2Jn).

Figurative—

Of the church of Christ (Ps 45:2-15; Gal 4:26; Rev 12:1). Of saints (Mt 25:1-4; 2Co 11:2; Rev 14:4).

Wicked:

(2Ki 9:30-37; 23:7; Jer 44:15-19, 25; Eze 8:14; Ro 1:26). Zeal of, in licentious practices of idolatry (2Ki 23:7; Hos 4:13-14), in promoting superstition and idolatry (Jer 7:18; Eze 13:17, 23). Careless (Isa 32:9-11). Contentious (Pr 27:15-16). Fond of self-indulgence (Isa 32:9-11), of ornaments (Jer 2:32). Guilty of lesbianism (Ro 1:26). Subtle and deceitful (Pr 6:24-29, 32-35; 7:6-27; Ecc 7:26). Weak-willed (2Ti 3:6).

Active in instigating iniquity (Nu 31:15-16; 1Ki 21:25; Ne 13:26). Idolatrous (Nu 31:15-16; 2Ki 23:7; Ne 13:26; Jer 7:18). Gossips (1Ti 5:11-13). Haughty and vain (Isa 3:16). Odious (Pr 30:23). Guileful and licentious (Pr 2:16-19; 5:3-20; 6:24-29, 32-35; 7:6-27; Ecc 7:26; Eze 16:32; Ro 1:26). Commits forgery (1Ki 21:8). Subtle and deceitful (Pr 6:24-29, 32-35; 7:6-27; Ecc 7:26). Illustrated by the five foolish virgins (Mt 25:1-12).

Instances of Wicked—

Eve, in yielding to temptation and seducing her husband (Ge 3:6; 1Ti 2:14). Sarah, in her jealousy and malice toward Hagar (Ge 21:9-11, w 21:12-21). Lot's wife, in her rebellion against her situation, and against the destruction of Sodom (Ge 19:26; Lk 17:32). The daughters of Lot, in their incestuous lust (Ge 19:31-38). Rebekah, in her partiality for Jacob and her actions to secure for him Isaac's blessing (Ge 27:11-17). Rachel, in her jealousy of Leah (Ge 30:1), in stealing images (Ge 31:19, 34). Leah in her imitation of Rachel in the matter of children (Ge 30:9-18). Tamar, in her adultery (Ge 38:14-24). Potiphar's wife, in her lust and slander against Joseph (Ge 39:7-20).

Miriam, in her sedition with Aaron against Moses (Nu 12). Rahab, in her harlotry (Jos 2:1). Delilah, in her conspiracy against Samson (Jdg 16:4-20). Peninnah, the wife of Elkanah, in her jealous taunting of Hannah (1Sa 1:4-8). The Midianite woman in the camp of Israel, taken in adultery (Nu 25:6-8).

Michal, in her derision of David's religious zeal (2Sa 6:16, 20-23). Bathsheba, in her adultery and in becoming the wife of her husband's murderer (2Sa 11:4-5, 27; 12:9-10). Solomon's wives, in their idolatrous and wicked influence over Solomon (1Ki 11:1-11; Ne 13:26). Jezebel, in her persecution and destruction of the prophets of the Lord (1Ki 18:4, 13); in her persecution of Elijah (1Ki 19:2), ;in her conspiracy against Naboth to despoil him of his vineyard (1Ki 21:1-16); in her evil influence over Ahab (1Ki 21:25, w 21:17-27, & 2Ki 9:30-37). The cannibal mothers of Samaria (2Ki 6:28-29). Athaliah, in destroying the royal household and usurping the throne (2Ki 11:1-16; 2Ch 22:10, 12; 23:12-15).

Noadiah, a false prophetess, in troubling the Jews when they were restoring Jerusalem (Ne 6:14). Haman's wife, in counseling him to hang Mordecai (Est 5:14; 6:13). Job's wife, in counseling him to curse God (Job 2:9; 19:17). The idolatrous wife of Hosea (Hos 1:2-3; 3:1).

Herodias, in her incestuous marriage with Herod (Mt 14:3-4; Mk 6:17-19; Lk 3:19) and causing the death of John the Baptist (Mt 14:6-11; Mk 6:24-28). The daughter of Herodias, in her complicity with her mother in causing the death of John the Baptist (Mt 14:8; Mk 6:18-28). Sapphira, in her blasphemous falsehood (Ac 5:2-10).

Figurative—

Of backsliding (Jer 6:2; Rev 17:4, 18). Of the wicked (Isa 32:9, 11; Mt 25:1-13).

Symbolic—

Of wickedness (Zec 5:7-8; Rev 17; 19:2).

See Widow; Wife.

WONDERFUL

The acts of God (1Ch 16:9; Ps 26:7; 107:8, 15, 21, 24, 31). The name of God is (Jdg 13:18, ftn). A name of the Messiah (Isa 9:6).

See Jesus the Christ, Names of; Titles and Names.

WOOL

Used for clothing (Lev 13:47-52, 59; Pr 31:13; Eze 34:3; 44:17). Prohibited in the priest's temple dress (Eze 44:17). Mixing of, with other fabrics forbidden (Lev 19:19; Dt 22:11). Fleece of (Jdg 6:37). First fleece of, belonged to the priests (Dt 18:4).

WORD

A title of Jesus (Jn 1:1, 14; 1Jn 5:7; Rev 19:13). *See Jesus the Christ, Names of; Logos.*

WORD OF GOD

Written Word; the Bible:

Psalms of (Ps 19; 119).

Called—

Book (Ps 40:7; Rev 22:19). Book of the Lord (Isa 34:16). Book of the Law (Ne 8:3; Gal 3:10). Holy Scriptures (Ro 1:2; 2Ti 3:15). Law of the Lord (Ps 1:2; Isa 30:9). Oracles (Zec 9:1; 12:1; Mal 1:1). Scriptures (1Co 15:3). Scriptures of Truth (Da 10:21). Sword of the Spirit (Eph 6:17).

The Word (Jas 1:21-23; 1Pe 2:2). Word of God (Lk 11:28; Heb 4:12). Good Word of God (Heb 6:5). Word of Christ (Col 3:16). Word of Life (Php 2:16). Word of Truth (Pr 22:21; Eph 1:13; 2Ti 2:15; Jas 1:18).

Compared to—

A lamp (Ps 119:105; Pr 6:23). Fire (Jer 23:29). Seed (Mt 13:38, 18-23, 37-38; Mk 4:3-20, 26-32; Lk 8:5-15). To a two-edged sword (Heb 4:12).

To Be—

Publicly read (Ex 24:7; Dt 31:11-13; Jos 8:33-35; 2Ki 23:2; 2Ch 17:7-9; Ne 8:1-8, 13, 18; Isa 2:3; Jer 36:6; Ac 13:15, 27; Col 4:16; 1Th 5:27). Instruction of, to be desired (Ps 119:18-19). The people stood and responded saying "Amen" (Ex 24:7; Dt 27:12-26; Ne 8:5-6).

Publicly expounded (Ne 8:8), by Jesus (Lk 4:16-27; 24:27, 45; Jn 2:22), by the apostles (Ac 2:16-47; 8:32, 35; 17:2; 28:23).

Searched (Ac 17:11). Searching of, commanded (Isa 34:16; Jn 5:39; 7:52). To be studied (2Ti 2:15; 1Pe 2:2-3). Various portions to be compared (2Pe 2:20). Studied by rulers (Dt 17:18-19; Jos 1:8). Taught to children (Dt 6:7; 11:19; 21:12-13; Ps 78:5).

Obeyed (Dt 4:5-6; 29:29; Ps 78:1, 7; Isa 34:16; Eze 44:5; Hab 2:2; Mt 7:24-25; Lk 6:47-49; 11:28; Ro 16:26; 1Co 11:2; 1Th 4:1-2; 2Th 2:14-15; Heb 2:1-3; Jas 1:25; 2Pe 3:1-2; Jude 3, 17; Rev 1:3). Believed (Mk 1:15; 1Jn 5:11, 13). Longed for (Ps 119:20, 131; Am 8:11-13). Walked after (Ps 119:30).

In the heart (Dt 30:11-14; Job 22:22; Ps 37:31; 40:8; 119:11; Pr 6:20-21; Isa 51:7; Eze 3:10; Ro 10:6-8). Meditated upon (Jos 1:8; Ps 1:2; 119:15, 23, 48, 78, 97, 99, 148). Worn on the hand and forehead (Ex 13:9; Dt 6:8; 11:18). Written on the doorframes (Dt 6:9; 11:20). In public places (Dt 27:2-3, 8; Jos 8:32). Placed inside of the ark of the covenant (Ex 40:20), beside the ark (Dt 31:26), read in public assemblies (Dt 31:11), *See above, In Public Places.* Taught in the Psalms (Dt 31:19, 21; Ps 119:54). Used for teaching and admonishing one another (1Co 10:11; Col 3:16). Instruction (2Ti 3:16-17).

Not To Be—

Added to nor taken from (Dt 4:2; 12:32; Pr 30:6; Rev 22:18-19). Handled deceitfully (2Co 4:2). Broken (Jn 10:35).

Nature of—

Comforting (Ps 119:28, 50, 52, 76, 83, 92). Delight of the righteous (Job 23:12; Ps 1:2; 119:16, 24, 35, 77, 103, 143, 162, 174). Desired more than gold (Ps 119:72, 127). Edifying (Ps 119:98, 99, 104, 130; Ac 20:32; Ro 4:23-24; 15:4; 1Ti 4:6; 1Jn 2:7-8, 12, 14, 21). Effective (Isa 55:11). Enduring forever (Ps 119:89, 160, 152; Isa 40:8; Mk 13:31; Lk 16:17; 1Pe 1:23-25). Full of hope (Ps 119:81; Col 1:5). Full of joy (Jer 15:16; 1Jn 1:4).

Inspired (Ex 19:7; 20:1; 24:3-4, 12; 31:18; 32:16; 34:27, 32; Lev 26:46; Dt 4:5, 10, 14; 2Ki 17:13; 2Ch 33:18; Ps 99:7; 147:19; Isa 34:16; 59:21; Jer 30:2; 36:1-2, 27-28, 32, 59-64; Eze 11:25; Da 10:21; Hos 8:12; Zec 7:12; Ac 1:16; 28:25; Ro 3:1-2; 1Co 2:12-13; 14:37; Eph 6:17; 1Th 2:13; 2Ti 3:16-17; Heb 1:1-2; 3:7-8; 4:12; 2Pe 1:21; 3:2, 15; Rev 1:1-2, 11, 17-19; 2:7; 22:6-8).

Life giving (Ps 119:25, 93; Jas 1:18; 1Pe 1:23). Living (Heb 4:12). Loved (Ps 119:47-48, 70, 97, 111, 113, 119, 159, 163, 167). Part of the Christian armor (Eph 6:17). Perfect (Ps 19:7; Jas 1:24). Powerful (Lk 1:37; Heb 4:12). Praiseworthy (Ps 56:4). Pure (Ps 12:6; 19:8; 119:140; Pr 30:5). Restraining (Ps 17:4; 119:11). Revered (Ps 119:161; 138:2).

Sanctifying (Jn 15:3; 17:17, 19; Eph 5:26; 1Ti 4:5). Spirit and life (Jn 6:63). Spiritual food, bread (Dt 8:3; Mt 4:4). Standard of righteous (Ps 119:138, 144, 172; Isa 8:20). Trustworthy (Ps 19:7, 9; 33:4, 6; 93:5; 111:7-8; 119:86). Truth (Ps 119:142, 151, 160; 1Th 2:13; Jas 1:18). Wonderful (Ps 119:129).

Bears the test of criticism and experience (2Sa 22:31; Ps 18:30). Cleanses life of youth (Ps 119:9). Convicts of sin (2Ki 22:9-13; 2Ch 17:7-10; 34:14-33). Gives peace (Ps 119:165). Inspires faith (Ro 10:17; Heb 11:3). Makes free (Ps 119:45; Jn 8:32). Makes wise (Ps 119:99; 2Ti 3:15). Rejoices the heart (Ps 119:111; Jer 15:16). Spirit of, gives life (2Co 3:6). Standard of judgment, the world to be judged by (Jn 12:48; Ro 2:16). Works salvation (1Th 2:13; 1Pe 1:23).

Fulfilled by Jesus (Mt 5:17; Lk 24:27; Jn 19:24). Testify of Jesus (Jn 5:39; 20:31; Ac 10:43; 18:28; 1Co 15:3; Heb 10:7). *See Jesus the Christ, Prophecies Concerning.*

Ignorance of—

(Mt 22:29; Mk 12:24).

Disbelief in (Lk 16:31; 24:25; Jn 5:46-47; 8:37; 2Ti 4:3-4; 1Pe 2:8; 2Pe 3:15-16).

Rejected by the wicked (Ps 50:16-17; Pr 1:29; 13:13; Isa 5:24; 28:9-14; 30:9-11; 53:1; Jer 6:10; 8:9; Hos 8:12; Am 2:12; Mic 2:6; Mk 7:9, 13; Lk 16:31; 24:25; Jn 3:20; 5:46-47; 8:37, 45; Ac 13:46; 1Co 1:18, 22-23; 2Ti 4:3-4; 1Pe 2:8; 2Pe 3:15-16; Rev 22:19).

See Commandments and Statutes, Of God.

Jesus, the Living Word:

(Jn 1:1, 14; 1Jn 5:7; Rev 19:13). *See Jesus the Christ, Names of; Logos.*

WORDS

Of Jesus:

Gracious (Lk 4:22), spirit and life (Jn 6:63), eternal life (Jn 6:68), shall judge (Jn 12:47-48).

Of the Wise:

As goads, and as nails well fastened (Ecc 12:11), gracious (Ecc 10:12). Spoken in season (Pr 15:23; Isa 50:4). Fitly spoken, like apples of gold in settings of silver (Pr 25:11). Of the perfect man, gentle (Jas 3:2). Of the teacher, should be plain (1Co 14:9, 19).

Should be acceptable to God (Ps 19:14).

Unwise:

Unprofitable, to be avoided (2Ti 2:14). Unspeakable, heard by Paul in paradise (2Co 12:4). Vain, not to be regarded (Ex 5:9; Eph 5:6), like a tempest (Job 8:2). Without knowledge, darken counsel (Job 38:2). Idle, account must be given for in the day of judgment (Mt 12:36-37).

Hasty, folly of (Pr 29:20). In a multitude of, is sin (Pr 10:19). Fool known by the multitude of (Ecc 5:3), will swallow himself (Ecc 10:12-14). Seditious, deceive the simple (Ro 16:18). Deceitful, are a snare to him who utters them (Pr 6:2). Of the hypocrite, softer than oil (Ps 55:21). Of the talebearer, wounds to the soul (Pr 18:8).

See Busybody; Slander; Speaking, Evil; Talebearer.

WORK

See Industry; Labor.

WORKS, GOOD

General:

(2Co 9:8; Eph 2:10; Php 2:13; Col 1:10; 1Th 1:3, 7-8; 2Th 2:17, 21; Jas 1:22-27; 3:17-18).

Under the Law (Lev 18:5; Eze 20:11, 13, 20; Lk 10:28; Ro 10:5; Gal 3:12). In humanitarian service (Eze 18:7-8; Mt 10:42; 25:35-46; Jas 1:27). Hypocritical (Mt 6:1-4).

Jesus an example of (Jn 10:32; Ac 10:38). Ministers should be patterns of (Tit 2:7). Ministers should exhort to (1Ti 6:17-18; Tit 3:1, 8, 14). Holy women should manifest (1Ti 2:10; 5:10). Manifest faith (Ps 37:3; Mt 19:16-21; Ro 2:13; Gal 6:4; Jas 2:14-26). Scriptures given for (Tit 2:14).

God is glorified by (Mt 25:34-46; Jn 15:2-8, 14; 1Co 3:6-9; Php 1:11; Heb 13:21). Designed to lead others to glorify God (Mt 5:16; 1Pe 2:12). A blessing attends (Jas 1:25). God remembers (Dt 6:25; 24:13; Ps 106:30-31; Jer 22:15-16; Eze 18:5-9; Mt 6:1-4; 18:5; 25:34-36; Jn 15:2-8, 14; Ac 10:14, 38; Heb 6:9-10; Rev 14:13; 22:14).

Of the righteous, are manifest (1Ti 5:25). God remembers (Ne 13:14; Heb 6:9-10). Shall be brought into judgment (Ecc 12:14, w 2Co 5:10). In the judgment, will be an evidence of faith (Mt 25:34-40, w Jas 2:14-20).

Parables relating to: The talents and pounds (Mt 25:14-29; Lk 19:12-27), the laborers in the vineyard (Mt 20:11-15), the two sons (Mt 21:28-31), the barren fig tree (Lk 13:6-9).

Commanded:

(Ps 37:3; Mt 3:8; Jn 14:2-8, 14) To ministers (Tit 2:7), women professing godliness (1Ti 2:10), widows (1Ti 5:10). To Christians (Mt 5:16; Col 3:13; Tit 3:1-2, 8, 14; Heb 10:24; Jas 1:22-27; 3:13; 1Pe 2:12). To the rich (1Ti 6:18). To be done without a show (Mt 6:1-4). Following the example of the faithful (Heb 10-14). Zeal in (Tit 2:14).

Insufficient for Salvation:

(Ps 49:7-8; 127:1-2; Ecc 1:14; Isa 13:14; 57:12; 64:6; Eze 7:19; 33:12-19; Da 9:18; Mt 5:20; Lk 17:7-10; 18:9-14; Ac 13:39; Ro 3:20-21; 4:1-25; 8:3; 9:16, 31-32; 11:6; 1Co 13:1-3; Gal 2:16, 21; 3:10-12, 21; 4:9-11; 5:2, 4, 6, 18; 6:15; Eph 2:8-9; Php 3:3-9; Col 2:20-23; 2Ti 1:9; Tit 3:4-5; Heb 4:3-10; 6:1-2; 9:1-14; Jas 2:10-11).

WORKS OF GOD

In creation (Job 9:8-9; Ps 8:3-5; 89:11; 136:5-9; 139:13-14; 148:4-5; Ecc 3:11; Jer 10:12), good (Ge 1:10, 18, 21, 25). Faithful (Ps 33:4). Wonderful (Ps 26:7; 40:5). Incomparable (Ps 86:8). In his overruling providence in human affairs (Ps 26:7; 40:5; 66:3; 75:1; 111:2, 4, 6; 118:17; 145:4-17).

See also, God, Works of.

WORLD

1. Universe (Jn 1:10).
2. Human race (Ps 9:8; 96:13; Ac 17:31).
3. Unregenerate humanity (Jn 15:18; 1Jn 2:15).
4. Roman Empire (Lk 2:1).

WORLDLINESS

Described:

(Ecc 1:8; 8:15; Isa 56:12; Jn 15:19; Tit 3:3; 2Pe 2:12-15, 18-19). Proverbial theme (Isa 22:13; Lk 12:19; 1Co 15:32). Tends to poverty (Pr 21:17; Hag 1:6). Fatal to spirituality (Gal 6:8; Php 3:19; 1Ti 5:6). Chokes the Word (Mt 13:22; Mk 4:19; Lk 8:14).

Leads to: The rejection of the gospel (Mt 22:2-6; Lk 14:17-24). The rejection of Christ (Jn 5:44; 12:43). Moral insensibility (Isa 22:13; 32:9-11; 47:7-9). Death (Pr 14:12-13).

Prosperity of is short-lived (Job 20:4-29; 21:11-15; Ps 49:16-18; Isa 24:7-11; 28:4).

Prayer regarding (Ps 73:2-22). Parables of (Lk 16:1-13, 19-25). Vanity of (Ecc 2:1-12; 6:11-12).

Admonitions Against:

(Pr 23:20-21; 27:1, 7; Ecc 7:2-4; 11:9-10; Hos 9:1, 11, 13; Am 6:3-7; 8:10; Mic 2:10; 6:14, 19, 24; Mt 6:25-34; 16:26; 24:28;

Mk 8:36-37; Lk 17:26-29, 33; 21:34; Jn 12:25; Ro 12:2; 1Co 7:29-31; 10:6; Col 3:2, 5; 2Ti 2:4, 22; 3:2-9; Tit 2:12; Jas 2:1-4; 4:4, 9; 5:5; 1Pe 1:14, 24; 2:11; 4:1-4; 1Jn 2:15-17). Denounced (Isa 5:11-12; 47:8-9; Jude 11-13, 16, 19).

Moses' choice against (Heb 11:24-26).

Instances of:

Antediluvians (Mt 24:38-39; Lk 17:26-27). Sodomites (Lk 17:28-29). Esau (Ge 25:31-34; Heb 12:16). Jacob (Ge 25:31-34; 27:36; 30:37-43). Judah (Ge 37:26-27). Israelites (1Sa 8:19-20). Balaam (2Pe 2:15; Jude 11, w Nu 22; 23; 24). Eli's sons (1Sa 2:12-17). Gehazi (2Ki 5:20-27).

Herod (Mt 14:6-7). The disciples (Mt 18:1-4; Mk 9:34; Lk 9:46-48). The rich fool (Lk 12:16-21). Dives (Lk 16:19-25). The worldly steward (Lk 16:1-13). Cretans (Tit 1:12).

See Worldly Pleasure.

WORLDLY CARE *See Anxiety.*

WORLDLY PLEASURE (Job 20:12; Ecc 7:4; Isa 22:13; 2Ti 3:4; Tit 3:3). Rejected by Moses (Heb 11:25). To be rejected by the righteous (1Pe 4:3-4). Brings poverty (Pr 21:17). Chokes righteousness (Lk 8:14). Leads to suffering (Isa 47:8-9; 2Pe 3:13), spiritual death (1Ti 5:6). Denounced (Isa 5:11-12; Jas 5:5). Folly of (Ecc 1:17; 2:1-13).

See Worldliness.

WORLDLY WISDOM Desired by Eve (Ge 3:6-7). Misleading (Isa 47:10). Increases sorrow (Ecc 1:18). Shall perish (Isa 29:14). Heavenly things not discerned by (Mt 11:25; Lk 10:21). Gospel not to be preached with (1Co 1:17-26; 2:1-14). To be renounced in order to attain spiritual wisdom (1Co 3:18-20). Admonitions against (Col 2:8; 1Ti 6:20-21). Admonitions against glorying in (Jer 9:23-24).

See Wisdom.

WORM Low form of life (Ex 16:24; Isa 51:8; Ac 12:23), used metaphorically of mankind's insignificance (Job 25:6; Isa 41:14).

WORMWOOD Bitter plant that grows in wastelands; name of a star that turns water bitter (Rev 8:11).

WORSHIP

General:

To be rendered to God only (Ex 20:3; Dt 5:7; 6:13; Mt 4:10; Lk 4:8; Ac 10:26; 14:15; Col 2:18; Rev 19:10; 22:8). Not needed by God (Ac 17:24-25).

Divine presence in (Ex 29:42-43; 40:34-35; Lev 19:30; Nu 17:4; 1Ki 8:3-11; 2Ch 5:13-14; Ps 77:13; 84:4; Isa 56:7; Mt 18:20; Ac 2:1-4; Heb 10:25).

Origin of (Ge 4:26). Of Jesus. *See Jesus the Christ, Worship of.* Acceptable to God (Ge 4:4; 8:21). Of the wicked, rejected (Ge 4:5, 7). *See Prayer, of the Wicked.* "Iniquity of the holy things" (Ex 28:38).

Sanctuary instituted for (Ex 25:8, 22; 29:43; 40:34-35; Nu 17:4).

Attitudes in: Bowing (Ex 34:8; 2Ch 20:18). Prostration (Ge 17:3; Mk 3:11).

Prayer in. *See Prayer.*

Benedictions pronounced. *See Benedictions.*

With music (2Ch 5:13-14; Ezr 3:10-11; Ps 100:1-2; 126:1-3; Isa 30:29; 38:20). Rendering praise (Ps 22:22; 138:2; 149:1). Thanksgiving (Ps 35:18; 100:4; 116:17).

In spirit and in truth (Jn 4:23-24; 1Co 14:15; Php 3:3). Renews strength (Isa 40:31). Loved by God's people (Ps 27:4; 84:1-4; 84:10; Zec 8:21). Reward of (Ps 65:4; 92:13-14; 122:1).

Preparation for (Ex 19:10-13, 21-24; 20:24-25; 30:19, 21; Lev 10:3; Ps 26:6; Isa 56:6-7; Zep 3:18; Mal 3:3-4). Requirements of (Ps 24:3-6; 51:18-19).

Proprieties in (Ecc 5:1-2; 1Co 11:13, 20-22; 14:2-19). Reverence in (Ex 3:5; 19:10-12, 21-24; 24:1-2; Ecc 5:1; Hab 2:20). Private (Mt 6:6; 14:23; Lk 6:12).

At night (Isa 30:29; Ac 16:25). Jesus prays at night (Lk 6:12). In the temple (Jer 26:2; Lk 18:10; 24:53; Ac 3:1). In the heavenly temple (Rev 11:1). In private homes (Ac 1:13-14; 5:42; 12:12; 20:7-9; Ro 16:5; 1Co 16:19; Col 4:15; Phm 2). Anywhere (Jn 4:21-24). To become universal (Isa 45:23; Ro 14:11; Php 2:10).

Of hypocrites, despised by God (Isa 1:11-15; 29:13-16; Hos 6:6; Am 5:21-24). Of the wicked, rejected (Ge 4:5, 7).

Of angels, forbidden (Rev 19:10; 22:8-9).

Commanded:

(Ge 35:1; Ex 15:1; 23:17-18; 34:23; Dt 12:5-7, 11-12; 16:6-8; 31:11-13; 33:19; 2Ki 17:36; 1Ch 16:29; Ne 10:39; Ps 29:2; 45:11; 76:11; 96:8-9; 97:7; 99:5; Isa 12:5-6; 49:13; 52:9; Jer 31:11-12; Joel 1:14-15; 2:15-17; Na 1:15; Hag 1:8; Zec 14:16-18; Mt 8:4; Mk 1:44; Lk 4:8; 5:14; 1Ti 2:8; Heb 10:25; 12:28; Rev 14:7; 19:10).

Summons to (Ps 95:6; Isa 2:3; Mic 4:2).

Family:

(Dt 16:11, 14). Of Abraham (Ge 12:7-8; 13:4, 18). Of Jacob (Ge 35:2-3). Of Job (Job 1:5). Of the Philippian jailer (Ac 16:34).

National:

(Rev 15:4). The whole nation required to assemble for, including men, women, children, servants, and strangers (Dt 16:11; 31:11-13), in Mount Gerizim and Mount Ebal (Jos 8:32-35). The word of God read in public assemblies (Ex 24:7; Dt 27:12-26; 31:11-13; Jos 8:33-35; 2Ki 23:1-3; Ne 8:1-8, 13-18; Mt 21:23; Lk 4:16-17).

See Affliction, Prayer Under; Blasphemy; Children; Church, The Body of Believers; Consecration; Dedication; Idolatry; Instruction, in Religion; Levites; Minister; Music; Offerings; Praise; Prayer; Preaching; Priest; Psalms; Religion; Sacrilege; Servant; Strangers; Tabernacle; Temple; Thanksgiving; Women; Word of God; Young Men.

Instances of:

Israel (Ex 15:1-2; Ps 107:6-8, 32). Moses (Ex 34:8). Solomon (2Ch 7:1). Priests and Levites (2Ch 30:27). Psalmists (Ps 5:7; 42:4; 48:9; 55:14; 63:1-2; 66:4, 13-14; 89:7; 93:5; 103:1-4; 116:12-14, 17; 119:108; 132:7, 13-14). Isaiah (Isa 49:13; 52:9).

WORSHIPERS Examples of (Ge 22:5; 24:26; Ex 34:8; Jos 5:14; Jdg 7:15; 1Sa 1:28; 2Sa 12:20; 2Ch 7:3; Ne 8:6; Job 1:20; Rev 4:10; 7:11; 11:16).

WOUNDS Treatment of (Pr 20:30; Isa 1:6; Lk 10:34). By Jesus' wounds we are healed (Isa 53:5; 1Pe 2:24).

WRATH

1. Anger of people (Ge 30:2; 1Sa 17:28), may be evil (2Co 12:20), or a reaction to evil (1Sa 20:34), or a work of the flesh (Gal 5:20). *See Anger.*

2. Anger of God—reaction of a righteous God against sinful people and evil in all forms (Dt 9:7; Isa 13:9; Ro 1:18; Eph 5:6; Rev 14:10, 19). *See Anger of God.*

WREATHS Decorating the tabernacle and temple (Ex 28:14; 1Ki 7:17; 2Ch 4:12).

WRESTLE To contend by grappling with an opponent (Ge 32:24-25), used figuratively (Ge 30:8; Eph 6:12).

WRITING Discovered to be in use in Mesopotamia as early as 3200 B.C., its development credited to the Sumerians. They had a primitive, nonalphabetic linear writing, not phonetic but pictographic, ideas being recorded by means of pictures of sense-symbols, rather than by sounds-symbols. The next stage in the history of writing was the introduction of the phonogram, or the type of sign which indicates a sound, and afterward came alphabetic scripts. The Egyptians first developed an alphabetic system of writing. Hebrews derived their alphabet from Phoenicians. Semitic writing dating between 1900 and 1500 B.C. has been found at Serabit el-Khadim in Sinai. Greeks received their alphabet from Phoenicians and Arameans.

Writing mentioned in Bible (Ex 17:14). Ten Commandments written with the finger of God (Ex 31:18; 32:15-16). Ancient writing materials: clay, wax, wood, metal, plaster (Dt 27:2-3; Jos 8:32; Lk 1:63), later, parchment (2Ti 4:13), and papyrus (2Jn 12). Instruments of writing: reed on papyrus and parchment; stylus on hard material (Ex 32:4).

See Book; Engraving; Ink; Letters; Pen; Tablet, 1.

WRITING KIT

In Ezekiel's vision (Eze 9:2-3, 11).

XERXES

1. Xerxes is a transliteration of the Greek form of the Persian name Khshayarshan; KJV Ahasuerus. The king of Persia mentioned in the book of Esther and Ezr 4:6. Xerxes succeeded his father Darius I the Great and reigned from 486 to 465 B.C.

2. Father of Darius the Mede (Da 9:1).

YAHWEH (*He who is [I am]* or *He who causes to be*) . The Hebrew personal name for God, Yahweh, is translated in the KJV and NIV as LORD, and sometimes also in the KJV as GOD. God revealed his name as "I AM WHO I AM," his eternal covenant name implying self-existence and saving presence (Ex 3:14-17).

YHWH is often called the "tetragrammaton," referring to the "four letters" or consonants of Yahweh.

See God, Names of, Yahweh; Jehovah.

YARMUK, WADI EL Stream six miles SE of Sea of Galilee flowing into Jordan, marked S boundary of Bashan.

YARN

1. Blue, purple, and scarlet yarn used to embroider the tabernacle and priestly garments (Ex 25:4; 26:1; 28:5), in the temple (1Ch 2:7, 14; 3:14). Used in cleansing sacrifices (Lev 14:4, 6, 49, 51-52).

2. *See Kue.*

YAUDI A place in N Aram or the same as Judah (2Ki 14:28, ftn).

YEAR (Ge 1:14). Divided into months (Ex 12:2; Nu 10:10; 28:11). *See Month.*

Annual feasts (Lev 25:5). *See Feasts.*

Redemption of houses sold, limited to one (Lev 25:29-30). Land to rest one, in seven (Lev 25:5). Of release (Dt 15:9).

Age computed by: of Abraham (Ge 25:7), of Jacob (Ge 47:9). *See Longevity.*

A thousand, with the Lord as one day (Ps 90:4; 2Pe 3:8). Satan to be bound a thousand (Rev 20:2-4, 7).

See Jubilee; Millennium; Time.

YEAST *See Leaven.*

YHWH *See Lord; Yahweh.*

YOKE Wooden frame for joining two draft animals; a wooden bar held on neck by thongs around neck (Nu 19:2; Dt 21:3). Yoke of oxen is a pair (1Sa 14:14; Lk 14:19).

Figurative of:

Oppression (Lev 26:13; 1Ki 12:4; 2Ch 10:4, 9-11; Isa 9:4; 10:27; Jer 28:2, 4, 10; 30:8), the bondage of sin (La 1:14), burdensome ordinances (Ac 15:10; Gal 5:1), discipleship to Christ (Mt 11:29-30), discipline (La 3:27).

Removal of, figurative of deliverance (Ge 27:40; Jer 2:20; Mt 11:29-30).

YOKEFELLOW (*yoked together*). Person united to another by close bonds, as in marriage or labor (Php 4:3, ftn).

YOM KIPPUR Hebrew for "Day of Atonement." *See Feasts.*

YOUNG MEN, WOMEN *Note:* In the proverbs throughout this entry, "son" can be read as an inclusive term for both male and female children.

Wise and Foolish:

Wise, exemplified in Moses' wise choice (Ex 24:3-5; Heb 11:24-26). A comfort to parents (Pr 10:1; 15:20; 29:3). Glory of (Pr 20:29).

Foolish, a sorrow to parents (Pr 10:1; 17:25; 19:13, 26; 28:7).

Wise and foolish, contrasted (Pr 10:1; 13:1; 15:20). *See below, Folly of.*

Admonitions to:

(Pr 3:1-5; 4:20-27; 6:1-5, 20-25; 19:27; 23:15-26; 24:1-12, 15-34; 27:11). Against lust (2Ti 2:22-23). Against drunkenness (Pr 23:20-21; 23:29-35). Against loving the world (1Jn 2:13-17). Against the snares of the adulteress (Pr 5:3-14; 6:24-35; 7:1-27; 23:27-28; 31:1-3). Against the enticements of sinners (Pr 1:10-16). Against evil companions (Pr 2:12-15; 4:14-15; 24:1-2).

Exhortations to:

Be sober-minded (Tit 2:6). Be an example of piety (1Ti 4:12). Keep the heart with all diligence (Pr 4:23). Paying attention to God's word (Ps 119:9). Seek wisdom (Pr 2:1-8; 3:13-23; 4:5-13; 24:13-14). Obey parents (Pr 6:20-23; 23:22-26). Obey the Lord (Pr 3:5-12). Praise the Lord (Ps 148:12-13).

Instances of Religious: *See Joseph, 1; Joshua; Samuel; David; Solomon; Uriah.*

Foolish, Exemplified:

Esau (Ge 25:31-34; Heb 12:16-17), Rehoboam's counselors (1Ki 12:8-11). Rehoboam (1Ki 12:13-14). The rich young ruler (Mt 19:16-22; Mk 10:17-22; Lk 18:18-23). The prodigal son (Lk 15:11-32).

See also, Children; Parents.

Z

ZAANAIM *See Zaanannim.*

ZAANAN A place of uncertain location (Mic 1:11).

ZAANANNIM A plain near Kedesh (Jos 19:33; Jdg 4:11).

ZAAVAN (possibly *trembling, terror*). A son of Ezer (Ge 36:27; 1Ch 1:42).

ZABAD (*he bestows*).

1. Son of Nathan (1Ch 2:36-37).
2. An Ephraimite (1Ch 7:21).
3. One of David's valiant men (1Ch 11:41).
4. An assassin of King Joash (2Ch 24:26). Also called Jozabad (2Ki 12:21). *See Jozabad, 1.*
5. Three Israelites who divorced their Gentile wives (Ezr 10:27, 33, 43).

ZABBAI (perhaps *God has given*).

1. Son of Bebai (Ezr 10:28).
2. Father of Baruch (Ne 3:20).

ZABBUD *See Zaccur, 5.*

ZABDI (*Yahweh bestows*).

1. Father of Carmi (Jos 7:1, 17-18, ftn). *See Zimri, 3.*
2. A Benjamite (1Ch 8:19).
3. A Shiphmite in charge of David's wine vats (1Ch 27:27).
4. Son of Asaph (Ne 11:17).

ZABDIEL (*God [El] bestows*).

1. Father of Jashobeam (1Ch 27:2).
2. An chief officer of 128 able men who lived in Jerusalem (Ne 11:14).

ZABUD (*[he has] bestowed upon*). A chief officer of Solomon (1Ki 4:5).

ZABULON *See Zebulun.*

ZACCAI (*Yahweh has remembered,* or perhaps *Yahweh remember*). A Jew whose descendants returned from the Exile (Ezr 2:9; Ne 7:14).

ZACCHAEUS (*righteous, pure one*). Chief tax collector; climbed sycamore tree to see Jesus and became his disciple (Lk 19:8).

ZACCUR *(remembering).*
1. Father of Reubenite spy, Shammua (Nu 13:4).
2. Simeonite (1Ch 4:26).
3. Son of Merari (1Ch 24:27).
4. Son of Asaph; musician (1Ch 25:1-2; Ne 12:35).
5. A returned exile (Ezr 8:14).
6. Son of Imri who helped rebuild walls of Jerusalem (Ne 3:2).
7. Man who sealed covenant with Nehemiah (Ne 10:12).
8. Father of Hanan (Ne 13:13).

ZACHARIAH *See Zechariah, 1 & 15.*

ZACHARIAS *See Zechariah, 30 & 31.*

ZACHER *See Zeker.*

ZADOC *See Zadok, 10.*

ZADOK *(righteous one).*
1. High priest in time of David's reign (2Sa 19:11; 20:25; 1Ch 15:11; 16:39). Removes the ark from Jerusalem at the time of Absalom's usurpation; returns with it at David's command (2Sa 15:24-36; 17:15, 17-21). Stands aloof from Adonijah at the time of his attempted usurpation (1Ki 1:8, 26). Summoned by David to anoint Solomon (1Ki 1:32-40, 44-45). Performs the function of high priest after Abiathar was deposed by Solomon (1Ki 2:35; 1Ch 29:22).
2. Father of Jerusha (2Ki 15:33; 2Ch 27:1).
3. Son of Ahitub (1Ch 6:12).
4. A man of valor (1Ch 12:28).
5. Son of Baana (Ne 3:4).
6. A priest (Ne 3:29).
7. A returned exile (Ne 10:21).
8. Son of Meraioth (Ne 11:11).
9. A treasurer of the temple (Ne 13:13).
10. Descendant of Zerubbabel and an ancestor of Jesus (Mt 1:14).

ZAHAM *(putrid, loathsome).* Grandson of Solomon (2Ch 11:19).

ZAHAR An area NW of Damascus (Eze 27:18); modern Sahra.

ZAIR *(small, insignificant,* hence *narrow pass).* Village E of Dead Sea where Jehoram NIV, broke through the lines of the Edomites (2Ki 8:21).

ZALAPH *(low, prickly shrub [caper plant]).* Father of man who helped Nehemiah repair walls (Ne 3:30).

ZALMON *(in his image, a copy; black hill).*
1. Forest near Shechem (Jdg 9:48).
2. One of David's mighty men (2Sa 23:28), called "Ilai the Ahohite" (1Ch 11:29).

ZALMONAH *(dark, gloomy, shaded place).* Encampment of Israelites in wilderness, SE of Edom (Nu 33:41-42).

ZALMUNNA *(protection refused).* King of Midian (Jdg 8:5-21; Ps 83:11).

ZAMZUMMITES *(babblers).* Ammonite name for Rephaites (Dt 2:20), lived E of Jordan. May be same as Zuzites (Ge 14:5). *See Rephaites; Zuzites.*

ZANOAH *(rejected).*
1. A city of W Judah (Jos 15:34; Ne 3:13; 11:30).
2. A city of E Judah (Jos 15:56).
3. A descendant of Caleb (1Ch 4:18).

ZAPHENATH-PANEAH *(the [pagan] god speaks and he [the newborn] lives).* Name given to Joseph by Pharaoh (Ge 41:45).

ZAPHON (possibly *North* or *[proper name of a god], Zephon).* Territory E of Jordan assigned to Gad (Jos 13:27); possibly modern Amateh.

ZARA, ZARAH *See Zerah.*

ZAREAH A city of Judah (Ne 11:29). *See Zorah.*

ZAREATHITES *See Zorathites.*

ZARED *See Zered.*

ZAREDA *See Zeredah.*

ZAREPHATH (possibly *smelting place* BDB; *place of pigmenting, staining* KB). A city between Tyre and Sidon. Elijah performs two miracles in (1Ki 17:8-24; Lk 4:26).

ZARETHAN Place in Ephraim or Manasseh near Beth Shan and Adam (Jos 3:16; 1Ki 4:12), and near Succoth (1Ki 7:46; 2Ch 4:17). Exact site not known.

ZARETH-SHAHAR *See Zereth Shahar.*

ZARHITES *See Zerahite(s).*

ZARTANAH, ZARTHAN *See Zarethan.*

ZATTU
1. One whose descendants returned with Zerubbabel (Ezr 2:8; 10:27; Ne 7:13).
2. One who sealed the covenant with Nehemiah (Ne 10:14). Probably the same as 1.

ZAVAN *See Zaavan.*

ZAZA *(a form of a shortened nickname; term of endearment).* Son of Jonathan (1Ch 2:33).

ZEAL *(zeal, jealousy).*

General:
Without love, unprofitable (1Co 13:3). Without knowledge (Nu 11:27-28; Jdg 11:30-31, 34-35; Ecc 7:16; Mt 8:19-20; Lk 9:57-58; Jn 16:2; Ac 21:20; Ro 10:2-3; Gal 1:13-14).
Wisdom of (Pr 11:30).
Required (Isa 62:6-7; Mt 5:13-16; Mk 4:21-22; Lk 8:16-17; Ac 10:42; 1Co 15:58; Tit 2:14; 3:1). Commanded (Jos 24:15-16; Ezr 7:23; Ps 60:4; 96:2; Ecc 9:10; Isa 60:1, Hag 2:4; Ro 12:11; 1Co 7:29-35; Gal 6:9; Eph 5:15-16; 6:10-20; Php 1:27-28; Col 4:5; 2Th 3:13; Heb 12:1-2; 13:13-15; 1Pe 2:2; 2Pe 1:10-11; 3:14; Jude 3, 22-23; Rev 3:19).
Expected (Hab 2:2; Zec 14:20-21; 2Co 4:8-10, 13, 16-18; Gal 4:18; Php 2:15).
Rewards of (Da 12:3; Mt 25:21, 23; Lk 19:17-19; Jas 5:20).

Exemplified in:
Moses (Ex 2:12; 11:8; 32:19-20, 31-32; Nu 10:29; 11:29; Dt 9:18-19). Phinehas (Nu 25:7-13; Ps 106:30). Joshua (Nu 11:27-29; Jos 7:6; 24:14-16). Gideon (Jdg 6:11-32). Jephthah (Jdg 11:30-31, 34-39). Samuel (1Sa 12:23; 15:11, 35; 16:1).
David (1Sa 17:26; 2Sa 6; 7:2; 8:11-12; 24:24; 1Ch 29:17; Ps 40:8-10; 42:1-2; 51:13; 69:7-9; 71:17-18). Solomon (1Ki 8:31-53; 2Ch 6:22-42). Elijah (1Ki 19:10). Obadiah (1Ki 18:3-4). Micaiah (1Ki 22:14). Jehu (2Ki 9:10). Jehoiada (2Ki 11:4-17; 2Ch 23:1-17). Asa (1Ki 15:11-15; 2Ch 14:1-5, 15). Israelites (2Ch 15:15; Eze 9:4). Jehoshaphat (2Ch 17:3-10, 19).
Isaiah (Isa 6:8; 62:1). Hezekiah (Isa 37:1). Josiah (2Ki 22:11-13; 2Ch 34:3-7, 29-33). Priests (Eze 44:15). Ezra (Ezr 7:10; 9:10; Ne 8:1-6, 13, 18). Nehemiah (Ne 4; 5; 13:7-9, 15-28). Job (Job 16:19). Psalmist (Ps 119:53, 126, 136, 139, 158). Jeremiah (Jer 9:1-3; 13:17; 18:20; 20:9; 25:3-4; 26:12-15). Three Hebrews (Da 3:17-18). Habakkuk (Hab 1:2-4). Old Testament faithful (Heb 11).
Jesus (Mt 23:27; Lk 19:41; Jn 4:34-35; 9:4). Anna (Lk 2:38). Andrew and Philip (Jn 1:41-46). Apostles (Mk 16:20; Ac 4:31, 33; 5:21, 25, 29-32, 41-42; 8:4, 25, 30, 35, 40; 11:19-20, 24, 26). Two blind men proclaiming the miracle of healing, contrary to the injunction of Jesus (Mt 9:30-31). The restored leper (Mk 1:44-45). Man delivered of demons (Mk 5:19-20).
Peter (Mt 16:22; Mk 14:29-31; Lk 22:33; Ac 2:14-40; 3:12-26; 4:2, 8-12, 18-20; 5:29-32; 2Pe 1:12-15). Samaritan woman (Jn 4:28-30, 39).
Paul and Barnabas (Ac 14:14-15).
Timothy (Php 2:22). Phoebe (Ro 16:1-2). Epaphroditus (Php 2:26, 30). Corinthians (1Co 14:12; 2Co 7:11; 9:2). Thessalonians (1Th 1:2-8). Ephesians (Rev 2:2-3, 6). Christian Jews (Heb 10:34). John (Ac 4:8-13, 18-20; 3Jn 4; Rev 5:4).

Paul—
For the evangelization of the Jews (Ro 9:1-3; 10:1; 11:14).
In his ministry (Ac 9:21-29; 14:1-28; 15:25-26; 17:16-17, 22-31; 19:8-10; 20:18-24, 26-27, 31, 33-34; 21:13; 24:14-25; 26:1-18; Ac 26:19-29; 28:23, 30-31; Ro 1:1, 8-9, 14-32; 1Co 4:1-21; 9:12-27; 2Co 1:12, 17-19; 5:9, 11, 13-14, 20; 6:3-11; 11:16-33; 12:10-21; Gal 1:15-16; 2:2; 4:19; Eph 6:20; Php 1:18, 20, 24-25, 27; 2:16-17; 3:4-16; Col 1:28-29; 2:1, 5; 1Th 1:5-6; 2:2-11; 2Th 3:7-9; 2Ti 1:3, 7, 11-13).
In his piety (1Co 4:12; 10:33; 15:31; 2Co 4:8-18; 11:22-33; 12:10; Php 3:4-16; 4:11-12, 17; 2Ti 3:10-11).
In providing self-support (Ac 20:33-34; 1Co 4:12; 2Co 11:7-12; 2Th 3:7-9).
In suffering for Christ (Ac 21:13; 2Co 6:4-5, 8-10; 11:22-33; 12:10, 14-15, 21; 2Ti 2:9-10; 3:10-11).

In Punishing the Wicked:
Moses and Levites (Ex 32:20, 26-29). Phinehas (Nu 25:11-13; Ps 106:30-31). Israelites (Jos 22:11-20; Jdg 20). Samuel (1Sa 15:33). David (2Sa 1:14; 4:9-12). Elijah (1Ki 18:40). Jehu (2Ki 10:15-28). Jehoiada (2Ki 11:18). Josiah (2Ki 23:20).

In Reproving Iniquity: *See Reproof, Faithfulness in.*

ZEALOT Member of Jewish patriotic party started to resist Roman rule over Israel; violent; fanatical.

ZEALOT, SIMON THE An apostle (Mt 10:4; Mk 3:18; Lk 6:15; Ac 1:13), was known either for religious zeal or for membership in the party of the Zealots. *See Simon, 2; Zealot.*

ZEBADIAH *(Yahweh bestows).*
1. Benjamite (1Ch 8:15).
2. Another Benjamite (1Ch 8:17).
3. Ambidextrous Benjamite soldier of David (1Ch 12:1-2, 7).
4. Korahite gatekeeper (1Ch 26:2).
5. Son of Asahel (1Ch 27:7).
6. Levite sent by Jehoshaphat to teach law to residents of Judah (2Ch 17:8).
7. Son of Ishmael; head of Jehoshaphat's affairs (2Ch 19:11).
8. Son of Michael; returned with Ezra (Ezr 8:8).
9. Son of Immer; priest who divorced foreign wife (Ezr 10:20).

ZEBAH *(sacrifice).* King of Midian defeated and slain by Gideon (Jdg 8:10, 12, 18, 21; Ps 83:11).

ZEBAIM *See Pokereth-Hazzebaim.*

ZEBEDEE *(Yahweh bestows).* Father of James and John (Mt 4:21; 20:20; 27:56; Mk 1:20).

ZEBIDAH *(given).* Wife of Josiah, king of Judah (2Ki 23:36).

ZEBINA *(one bought, purchased).* Son of Nebo (Ezr 10:43).

ZEBOIIM, ZEBOIM *(hyenas).*
1. Called Zeboiim: One of the cities in the valley of Siddim (Ge 10:19; 14:2, 8; Dt 29:23; Hos 11:8).
2. Called Zeboim: A city and valley in Benjamin (1Sa 13:18; Ne 11:34).

ZEBUDAH *See Zebidah.*

ZEBUL *(elevation, height, lofty [temple]).* An officer of Abimelech (Jdg 9:28-41).

ZEBULONITES *See Zebulun.*

ZEBULUN, ZEBULUNITE *(honor* Ge. 30:20 ISBE).
1. Son of Jacob and Leah (Ge 30:20; 35:23; 46:14; 49:13; Ex 1:3; 1Ch 2:1). Descendants of (Ge 46:14; Nu 26:26-27).
2. Tribe of. Place of, in march and camp (Nu 2:3, 7; 10:14, 16). Territory awarded to (Ge 49:13; Jos 19:10-16; Mt 4:13). Aboriginal inhabitants of the territory of, not expelled (Jdg 1:30). Levitical cities of (Jos 21:34-35; 1Ch 6:77). Moses' benediction upon (Dt 33:18-19).
Loyalty of, in resisting the enemies of Israel: With Barak against Sisera (Jdg 4:6, 10; 5:14, 18), with Gideon against the Midianites (Jdg 6:35), with David when made king over Israel (1Ch 12:33, 38-40). Joins with Hezekiah in renewing the Passover (2Ch 30:11, 18). Conquest of, by Tiglath-Pileser; carried to Assyria into captivity (2Ki 15:29; Isa 9:1). Jesus lived in the land of (Mt 4:15). Twelve thousand sealed (Rev 7:8).
See Israel.

ZECHARIAH *(Yahweh remembers).*
1. Son of Jeroboam II, and last of the house of Jehu, whose reign lasted six months (2Ki 10:30; 14:29; 15:8-12).
2. Reubenite chief (1Ch 5:7).
3. Korahite, son of Meshelemiah (1Ch 9:21; 26:2, 14).
4. Benjamite (1Ch 9:37).
5. Levite; musician (1Ch 15:20; 16:5).
6. Priest; trumpeter (1Ch 15:24).
7. Levite (1Ch 24:25).
8. Merarite Levite (1Ch 26:11).
9. Manassite chief; father of Iddo (1Ch 27:21).
10. Prince who taught in cities of Judah (2Ch 17:7).
11. Father of prophet Jahaziel (2Ch 20:14).
12. Son of Jehoshaphat; killed by Jehoram (2Ch 21:2 4).
13. Son of Jehoiada, the high priest; stoned (2Ch 24:20-22).
14. Prophet in reign of Uzziah (2Ch 26:5).
15. Grandfather of Hezekiah and father of Abijah, wife of Ahaz (2Ki 18:2; 2Ch 29:1).
16. Levite; son of Asaph (2Ch 29:13).
17. Kohathite who assisted in repair of temple in days of Josiah (2Ch 34:12).
18. Temple ruler (2Ch 35:8).
19. Man who returned with Ezra (Ezr 8:3).
20. Another man who returned with Ezra (Ezr 8:11).
21. Adviser of Ezra (Ne 8:4; Ezr 8:15-16).
22. Man who divorced foreign wife (Ezr 10:26).
23. Judahite (Ne 11:4).
24. Another Judahite (Ne 11:5).
25. Son of Pashhur; aided rebuilding of walls (Ne 11:12).
26. Son of Iddo; priest (Ne 12:16).
27. Priest; son of Jonathan; trumpeter (Ne 12:35, 41).
28. Son of Jeberekiah (Isa 8:2).
29. Prophet; son of Berekiah and grandson of Iddo (Zec 1:1), returned with Zerubbabel; contemporary with Haggai.
30. Father of John the Baptist (Lk 1:5), righteous priest; angel announced to him he would have a son (Lk 1:5-80).
31. Son of Berekiah; slain between altar and temple (Mt 23:35; Lk 11:51)

ZECHARIAH, BOOK OF

Author: Zechariah son of Berekiah

Dates (correlated with Haggai and Ezra):
1. Haggai's first message (Hag 1:1-11; Ezr 5:1): Aug. 29, 520 B.C.
2. Resumption of the building of the temple (Hag 1:12-15; Ezr 5:2): Sept. 21, 520
3. Haggai's second message (Hag 2:1-9): Oct. 17, 520
4. Beginning of Zechariah's preaching (1:1-6): Oct./Nov., 520
5. Haggai's third message (Hag 2:10-19): Dec. 18, 520
6. Haggai's fourth message (Hag 2:20-23): Dec. 18, 520
7. Tattenai's letter to Darius concerning the rebuilding of the temple (Ezr 5:3-6:14).: 519-518
8. Zechariah's eight night visions (1:7-6:8): Feb 15, 519
9. Joshua crowned (6:9-15): Feb 16 (?), 519
10. Repentance urged, blessings promised (chs. 7-8).: Dec. 7, 518
11. Dedication of the temple (Ezr 6:15-18): Mar. 12, 516
12. Zechariah's final prophecy (chs. 9-14): After 480 (?)

Outline.

Part I (chs. 1-8):
I. Introduction (1:1-6).
  A. The Date and the Author's Name (1:1).
  B. A Call to Repentance (1:2-6).
II. A Series of Eight Night Visions (1:7-6:8).
  A. The Horseman among the Myrtle Trees (1:7-17).
  B. The Four Horns and the Four Craftsmen (1:18-21).
  C. A Man with a Measuring Line (ch. 2).
  D. Clean Garments for the High Priest (ch. 3).
  E. The Gold Lampstand and the Two Olive Trees (ch. 4).
  F. The Flying Scroll (5:1-4).
  G. The Woman in a Basket (5:5-11).
  H. The Four Chariots (6:1-8).
III. The Symbolic Crowning of Joshua the High Priest (6:9-15).
IV. The Problem of Fasting and the Promise of the Future (chs. 7-8).
  A. The Question by the Delegation from Bethel (7:1-3).
  B. The Rebuke by the Lord (7:4-7).
  C. The Command to Repent (7:8-14).
  D. The Restoration of Israel to God's Favor (8:1-17).
  E. Kingdom Joy and Jewish Favor (8:18-23).

Part II (chs. 9-14):
V. Two Prophetic Oracles: The Great Messianic Future and the Full Realization of God's Kingdom (chs. 9-14).
  A. The First Oracle: The Advent and Rejection of the Messiah (chs. 9-11).
    1. The advent of the Messianic King (chs. 9-10).
    2. The rejection of the Messianic Shepherd-King (ch. 11).
  B. The Second Oracle: The Advent and Reception of the Messiah (chs. 12-14).
    1. The deliverance and conversion of Israel (chs. 12-13).
    2. The Messiah's coming and his kingdom (ch. 14).
See Prophets, The Minor.

ZEDAD (*a siding*). A place near Hamath (Nu 34:8; Eze 47:15).

ZEDEKIAH (*Yahweh is [my] righteousness*).
1. Made king of Judah by Nebuchadnezzar (2Ki 24:17-18; 1Ch 3:15; 2Ch 36:10; Jer 37:1). Breaks his allegiance to Nebuchadnezzar (2Ki 24:20; 2Ch 36:13; Jer 52:3; Eze 17:12-21). Forms an alliance with the king of Egypt (Eze 17:11-18). The allegiance denounced by Jeremiah (2Ch 36:12; Jer 21; 24:8-10; 27:12-22; 32:3-5; 34; 37:7-10, 17; 38:14-28), by Ezekiel (Eze 12:10-16; 17:12-21). Imprisons Jeremiah on account of his denunciations (Jer 32:2-3; 37:15-21; 38:5-28). Seeks the intercession of Jeremiah with God in his behalf (Jer 21:1-3; 37:3; 28:14-27). Wicked reign of (2Ki 24:19-20; 2Ch 36:12-13; Jer 37:2; 38:5, 19, 24-26; 52:2). Nebuchadnezzar destroys the city and temple, takes him captive to Babylon, blinds his eyes, slays his sons (2Ki 25:1-10; 2Ch 36:17-20; Jer 1:3; 32:1-2; 39:1-10; 51:59; 52:4-30).
2. Grandson of Jehoiakim (1Ch 3:16).
3. A chief prince of the exiles who returned to Jerusalem (Ne 10:1).
4. A false prophet (Jer 29:21-23).
5. A prince of Judah (Jer 36:12).
6. A false prophet. Prophesies to Ahab victory over the Syrians, instead of defeat (1Ki 22:11; 2Ch 18:10). Smites Micaiah, the true prophet (1Ki 22:24; 2Ch 18:23).

ZEEB (*wolf*). A prince of Midian (Jdg 7:25; 8:3; Ps 83:11).

ZEKER (*memorial*). Son of Jeiel (1Ch 8:31), called Zechariah (1Ch 9:37). *See Zechariah, 4.*

ZELA (*side, slope*). Saul buried in (2Sa 21:14).

ZELAH (*side, slope*). A city in Benjamin (Jos 18:28).

ZELEK (*cry aloud* KB). An Ammonite (2Sa 23:37; 1Ch 11:39).

ZELOPHEHAD (*shadow of dread, terror* [i.e., *protection from dread and terror*]). Grandson of Gilead. His daughters petition for his inheritance (Nu 27:1-11; 36; Jos 17:3-6; 1Ch 7:15).

ZELOTES *See Zealot.*

ZELZAH A city of Benjamin (1Sa 10:2).

ZEMARAIM (possibly *double peak* KB).
1. Town c. four miles N of Jericho assigned to tribe of Benjamin (Jos 18:22).
2. Mountain in Ephraim upon which King Abijah rebuked King Jeroboam (2Ch 13:4).

ZEMARITES (*[snow, wool] white;* possibly *peak, height*). A tribe descended from Canaan (Ge 10:18; 1Ch 1:16).

ZEMIRAH (possibly *song [with instrumental accompaniment]* KB; possibly *Yahweh has helped* IDB). Grandson of Benjamin (1Ch 7:8).

ZENAN (*place of flocks*). A city of Judah (Jos 15:37).

ZENAS (*gift of Zeus*). A Christian believer and lawyer (Tit 3:13).

ZEPHANIAH (*Yahweh has hidden [to shelter]* or *Yahweh has hidden [as a treasure]*).
1. Ancestor of prophet Samuel (1Ch 6:36).
2. Author of book of Zephaniah (Zep 1:1), of royal descent; principal work done in Josiah's reign; contemporaries were Nahum and Habakkuk.
3. Priest, son of Maaseiah (2Ki 25:18-21; Jer 21:1),
4. Father of a Josiah to whom God sent the prophet Zechariah (Zec 6:10).

ZEPHANIAH, BOOK OF

Author: The prophet Zephaniah

Date: Probably between 640 and 627 B.C.

Outline:
I. Introduction (1:1-3).
A. Title: The Prophet Identified (1:1).
B. Prologue: Double Announcement of Total Judgment (1:2-3).
II. The Day of the Lord Coming on Judah and the Nations (1:4-18).
A. Judgment on the Idolaters in Judah (1:4-9).
B. Wailing throughout Jerusalem (1:10-13).
C. The Inescapable Day of the Lord's Wrath (1:14-18).
III. God's Judgment on the Nations (2:1-3:8).
A. Call to Repentance (2:1-3).
B. Judgment on Philistia (2:4-7).
C. Judgment on Moab and Ammon (2:8-11).
D. Judgment on Cush (2:12).
E. Judgment on Assyria (2:13-15).
F. Judgment on Jerusalem (3:1-5).
G. Jerusalem's Refusal to Repent (3:6-8).
IV. Redemption of the Remnant (3:9-20).
A. The Nations Purified, the Remnant Restored, Jerusalem Purged (3:9-13).
B. Rejoicing in the City (3:14-17).
C. The Nation Restored (3:18-20).
See Prophets, The Minor.

ZEPHATH (*watchtower* IDB). A Canaanite city c. twenty-two miles SW of S end of Dead Sea; destroyed by tribes of Judah and Simeon and renamed "Hormah" (Jdg 1:17, ftn).

ZEPHATHAH (*watchtower* IDB). Valley near Mareshah in W part of Judah (2Ch 14:10).

ZEPHI *See Zepho.*

ZEPHO (possibly *gaze* BDB ISBE). The grandson of Esau (Ge 36:11, 15; 1Ch 1:36).

ZEPHON, ZEPHONITE (possibly *gaze* BDB; possibly *look out [tower], watch* KB). A son of Gad and his descendants (Ge 46:16; Nu 26:15).

ZER A city in Naphtali (Jos 19:35).

ZERAH (*dawning, shining,* or *flashing [red or scarlet] light* KB).
1. Son of Reuel (Ge 36:13, 17; 1Ch 1:37).
2. Father of Jobab (Ge 36:33; 1Ch 1:44).
3. Son of Judah and Tamar (Ge 38:30; 46:12; Nu 26:20; 1Ch 2:4, 6).
4. Son of Simeon (Nu 26:13; 1Ch 4:24).
5. A Gershonite (1Ch 6:21).
6. A Levite (1Ch 6:41).
7. King of Ethiopia, possibly Pharaoh Osorkon I (2Ch 14:9-15).

ZERAHIAH (*Yahweh shines brightly [red or scarlet]; Yahweh has risen [like the sun]* BDB).
1. Levite in ancestry of Ezra (1Ch 6:6, 51).
2. Leader of 200 who returned with Ezra (Ezr 8:4).

ZERAHITE(S) (*those who shine*).
1. Descendants of Zerah, son of Judah (Nu 26:20; Jos 7:17; 1Ch 27:11, 13).
2. Descendants of Zerah, son of Simeon (Nu 26:13).

ZERED, VALLEY OF, BROOK OF (*valley of [some kind of] plant*). Valley between Moab and Edom; encampment of Israel in wilderness wanderings (Nu 21:12; Dt 2:13-14).

ZEREDAH A city or district on the N of Mount Ephraim, but in Manasseh, and the birthplace of Jeroboam (1Ki 11:26).

ZEREDATHAH *See Zarethan.*

ZERERAH Part of Valley of Jezreel to which Midianites fled from Gideon (Jdg 7:22).

ZERESH (possibly *[pagan goddess] Kirisha* BDB IDB; *gold* ISBE; *mop-head* KB). Wife of Haman the Agagite (Est 5:10, 14; 6:13).

ZERETH (*splendor*). Son of Ashhur (1Ch 4:7).

ZERETH SHAHAR (*the glory of dawn*). A city in Reuben (Jos 13:19).

ZERI (*balsam* IDB). The son of Jeduthun (1Ch 25:3).

ZEROR (*money bag, pouch,* or possibly *pebbles* KB). Benjamite; great-grandfather of King Saul (1Sa 9:1).

ZERQA *See Jabbok.*

ZERUAH (*one with skin disease*). Mother of Jeroboam (1Ki 11:26).

ZERUBBABEL (*offspring [seed] of Babylon* BDB ISBE KB; *scion* i.e., *one grafted into the [plant] of Babylon* IDB). Directs the rebuilding of the altar and temple after his return from captivity in Babylon (Ezr 3:2-8; 4:2-3; 5:2; Hag 1:12-14). Leads the freed Jews back from Babylon (Ezr 2; Ne 12). Appoints the Levites to inaugurate the rebuilding of the temple (Ezr 3:2-8). Prophecies relating to (Hag 2:2; Zec 4:6-10). In the genealogy of Joseph (Mt 1:12; Lk 3:27).
Possibly the same as Sheshbazzar (Ezr 1:8, 11; 5:14, 16). *See Sheshbazzar.*

ZERUIAH (*perfumed resin* IDB KB). Sister of David (1Ch 2:16). Mother of three of David's great soldiers (1Ch 2:16; 2Sa 2:18; 3:39; 16:9-11; 17:25).

ZETHAM (possibly *olive tree*). A son of Ladan (1Ch 23:8; 26:22).

ZETHAN (*olive tree* or *one who deals in olives*). Son of Bilhan (1Ch 7:10).

ZETHAR (possibly *conqueror* BDB; *slayer* KB). Chamberlain of Xerxes (Est 1:10).

ZEUS (*shine, bright*). Chief of Greek gods, corresponding to Roman Jupiter (Ac 14:12-13).

ZIA (possibly *trembler* IDB). A Gadite (1Ch 5:13).

ZIBA (*gazelle*). Member of Saul's household staff (2Sa 9:2), appointed by David to work for Mephibosheth; slandered Mephibosheth (2Sa 19:24-30).

ZIBEON (*hyena*).
1. A Hivite (Ge 36:2, 14).
2. Son of Seir (Ge 36:20, 24, 29; 1Ch 1:38, 40).

ZIBIA (*gazelle*). Early descendant of Benjamin (1Ch 8:9).

ZIBIAH (*gazelle*). Woman of Beersheba who married King Ahaziah; mother of King Joash (2Ki 12:1; 2Ch 24:1).

ZICRI (*Yahweh remembers* IDB).
1. A Levite; son of Izhar, cousin of Aaron and Moses (Ex 6:21).
2. Three Benjamites (1Ch 8:19, 23, 27).
3. A Levite; ancestor of Mattaniah who returned from captivity (1Ch 9:15), "Zabdi" (Ne 11:17).
4. Two chiefs in the days of David; a descendant of Eliezer (1Ch 26:25), father of Eliezer, a Reubenite (1Ch 27:16).
5. Father of Amasiah; a soldier (2Ch 17:16).
6. Father of Elishaphat (2Ch 23:1).
7. An Ephraimite; killed the son of Ahaz (2Ch 28:7).
8. Father of Joel, the overseer of the Benjamites (Ne 11:9).
9. A descendant of Abijah; a priest (Ne 12:17).

ZIDDIM (*place on the sides or flanks [of the hill]*). A city in Naphtali (Jos 19:35).

ZIDKIJAH *See Zedekiah, 3.*

ZIDON *See Sidon.*

ZIDONIANS *See Sidon.*

ZIF *See Ziv.*

ZIGGURAT (*pinnacle*). Temple tower of the Babylonians, consisting of a lofty structure in the form of a pyramid, built in successive stages, with staircases on the outside and a shrine at the top. The tower of Babel may have been a ziggurat (Ge 11:1-9). *See Pyramids; Tower.*

ZIHA
1. Head of family of temple servants that returned with Zerubbabel (Ezr 2:43; Ne 7:46).
2. Leader of the temple servants (Ne 11:21).

ZIKLAG A city within the territory allotted to the tribe of Judah (Jos 15:31). Reallotted to the tribe of Simeon (Jos 19:5). David lives at (1Sa 27:5-6; 2Sa 1:1; 1Ch 12:1). Amalekites destroy (1Sa 30). Inhabited by the returned exiles of Judah (Ne 11:28).

ZIKRI *See Zicri.*

ZILLAH (*[God is my] shadow* [i.e., *protection*]). Wife of Lamech (Ge 4:19, 22-23).

ZILLETHAI (*shadow of Yahweh*).
1. A Benjamite (1Ch 8:20).
2. A captain of Manasseh (1Ch 12:20).

ZILPAH (*short-nosed person* KB). Leah's handmaid (Ge 29:24). Mother of Gad and Asher by Jacob (Ge 30:9-13; 35:26; 37:2; 46:18).

ZIMMAH (*consider, plan* ISBE).
1. A son of Jahath (1Ch 6:20).
2. Two Gershonites (1Ch 6:42; 2Ch 29:12).

ZIMRAN (*wild goats, sheep* ISBE). Son of Abraham (Ge 25:2; 1Ch 1:32).

ZIMRI (*wild goats, sheep* ISBE; possibly *awe of Yahweh* IDB).
1. Prince of Simeon; slain by Phinehas, grandson of Aaron, for committing adultery with Midianite woman (Nu 25:14).
2. The fifth king of N kingdom; murdered King Elah; ruled seven days (c. 885 B.C.); overthrown by Omri (1Ki 16:8-20).
3. Son of Zerah; grandson of Judah (1Ch 2:6). *See Zabdi, 1.*
4. Benjamite; father of Moza (1Ch 8:36; 9:42).
5. Unknown tribe in East (Jer 25:25).

ZIN A desert S of Judah (Nu 13:21; 20:1; 27:14; 33:36; 34:3-4; Dt 32:51; Jos 15:1, 3).

ZINA (possibly *dry place*). *See Ziza.*

ZION (*citadel*). Taken from the Jebusites by David (2Sa 5:6-9; 1Ch 11:5-7). Called thereafter "the city of David" (2Sa 5:7, 9; 6:12, 16; 1Ki 8:1; 1Ch 11:5, 7; 15:1, 29; 2Ch 5:2). Ark of the covenant placed in (2Sa 6:12, 16; 1Ki 8:1; 1Ch 15:1, 29; 2Ch 5:2). Removed from to Solomon's temple on Mount Moriah (1Ki 8:1; 2Ch 5:2, w 2Ch 3:1).
Collectively, the place, the forms, and the assemblies of Israelite worship (2Ki 19:21, 31; Ps 9:11; 48:2, 11-12; 74:2; 132:13; 137:1; Isa 35:10; 40:9; 49:14; 51:16; 52:1-2, 7-8; 60:14; 62:1, 11; Jer 31:6; 50:5; La 1:4; Joel 2:1, 15; Mt 21:5; Jn 12:15; Ro 9:33; 11:26; 1Pe 2:6). Name of, applied to Jerusalem (Ps 87:2, 5; 149:2; SS 3:11; Isa 33:14, 20; Jer 9:19; 30:17; Zec 9:13). Called the city of God (Ps 87:2-3; Isa 60:14). Restoration of, promised (Isa 51:3, 11, 16; 52:1-2, 7-8; 59:20; 60:14; Ob 17, 21; Zep 3:14, 16; Zec 1:14, 17; 2:7, 10; 8:2-3; 9:9, 13). Name of, applied to the city of the redeemed (Heb 12:22; Rev 14:1).
See Church, Place of Worship; Jerusalem.

ZIOR (*small, insignificant*). Town in S Judah probably near Hebron (Jos 15:54).

ZIPH
1. City in Negev, probably c. four miles S by E from Hebron (Jos 15:55).
2. Wilderness named from above city where David hid (1Sa 23:14-24; 26:1-2).
3. City in W Judah (2Ch 11:8).
4. Calebite family name (1Ch 2:42).
5. Judahite (1Ch 4:16).

ZIPHAH A son of Jehallelel (1Ch 4:16).

ZIPHIMS *See Ziphites.*

ZIPHION (possibly *gaze* BDB ISBE; possibly *place of the lookout, tower* KB). *See Zephon.*

ZIPHITES Inhabitants of Ziph (1Sa 23:19; 26:1-5; Ps 54:T).

ZIPHRON A place in the N of Israel (Nu 34:9).

ZIPPOR (*bird, swallow*). Father of Balak (Nu 22:2, 4, 10, 16; 23:18; Jos 24:9).

ZIPPORAH (*bird, swallow*). Wife of Moses (Ex 2:16-22). Reproaches Moses (Ex 4:25-26). Separates from Moses, is brought again to him by her father (Ex 18:2-6). May have been a Cushite (Nu 12:1).

ZITHER A stringed instrument (Da 3:5, 7, 10, 15). *See Music, Instruments of.*

ZITHRI *See Sithri.*

ZIV (*bright [as in colorful flowers]*). Month two in sacred sequence, month eight in civil sequence. Also called Iyyar (not in the Bible). Time of the barley harvest (April May); the dry season begins. Solomon begins building the temple (1Ki 6:1, 37). The later Passover is celebrated (Nu 9:10-11). *See Month, 2.*

ZIZ (possibly *ascent where the flowers grow*). Cliff near W side of Red Sea on way from En Gedi to Tekoa (2Ch 20:16).

ZIZA (a childish duplicated abbreviation, like "mama, " as a name of endearment, IDB ISBE).
1. Simeonite; son of Shiphi (1Ch 4:37-41).
2. Son of Rehoboam and brother of Abijah, kings of Judah (2Ch 11:20).
3. A son of Shimei (1Ch 23:10-11, ftn).

ZIZAH *See Ziza, 3.*

ZOAN A city in Egypt. Built seven years after Hebron in the land of Canaan (Nu 13:22). Prophecies concerning (Eze 30:14). Wise men from, were counselors of Pharaoh (Isa 19:11, 13). Princes of (Isa 30:4).

ZOAR (*small, insignificant*). A city of the Moabites near the Jordan (Ge 13:10). Territory of (Dt 34:3; Isa 15:5; Jer 48:34). King of, fought against Kedorlaomer (Ge 14:2, 8). Not destroyed with Sodom and Gomorrah (Ge 19:20-23, 30).

ZOBAH Also called Aram Zobah; Hamath Zobah. A kingdom in the N of Israel (1Sa 14:47). Conquest of, by David (2Sa 8:3-8, 12; 1Ki 11:23-24; 1Ch 18:2-9). Its inhabitants mercenaries of the Ammonites against David (2Sa 10:6-19; 1Ch 19:6-19). David writes a psalm after the conquest of (Ps 60, title). Invaded by Solomon (2Ch 8:3).
See Aram Maacah; Aram Naharaim.

ZOBEBAH (*one who slithers [like a lizard]* or *one born in a covered wagon*). *See Hazzobebah.*

ZODIAC *See Constellations; Mazzaroth.*

ZOHAR (*one yellowish red, tawny*).
1. Hittite; father of Ephron from whom Abraham purchased field of Machpelah (Ge 23:8; 25:9).
2. Son of Simeon, second son of Jacob (Ge 46:10; Ex 6:15); "Zerah" (Nu 26:13; 1Ch 4:24).
3. A son of Helah, wife of Ashhur (1Ch 4:7).

ZOHELETH (*serpent*). Stone or ledge by En Rogel (1Ki 1:9).

ZOHETH (*proud*). Son of Ishi (1Ch 4:20).

ZOPHAH (*bellied jug*). Son of Helem (1Ch 7:35-36).

ZOPHAI (*[dripping, full] honeycomb*). Ancestor of Samuel the prophet (1Ch 6:26), also called Zuph (1Ch 6:35).

ZOPHAR (possibly *peep, twitter [as a bird]* KB). One of Job's three friends (Job 2:11; 11; 20; 42:7-9).

ZOPHIM (*watchers, lookouts*).
1. A place on the top of Pisgah (Nu 23:14).
2. A city on Mount Ephraim (1Sa 1:1).

ZORAH A city of Dan or Judah (Jos 15:33; 19:41). The city of Samson (Jdg 13:2, 24-25; 16:31). Representatives of the tribe of Dan sent from, to spy out the land with a view to its conquest (Jdg 18). Fortified by Rehoboam (2Ch 11:10). Repopulated after the Captivity (Ne 11:29).

ZORATHITES Inhabitants of Zorah (1Ch 2:53).

ZOREAH *See Zorah.*

ZORITES Judahite family, descendants of Salma (1Ch 2:54).

ZOROBABEL *See Zerubbabel.*

ZUAR (*little one*). Father of Nethanel (Nu 1:8; 2:5; 7:18, 23; 10:15).

ZUPH, ZUPHITE (*honeycomb*).
1. Ancestor of the prophet Samuel (1Sa 1:1; 1Ch 6:35), also called Zophai (1Ch 6:26).
2. District in Benjamin, near N border (1Sa 9:5), Location unknown.

ZUR (*rock*).
1. King of Midian slain by Israel (Nu 25:15; 31:8).
2. Son of Jeiel (1Ch 8:29, ftn; 8:30).

ZURIEL (*God [El] is [my] rock*). Son of Abihail, prince of Merarite Levites in wilderness (Nu 3:35).

ZURISHADDAI (*Shaddai is [my] rock*). Father of Shelumiel (Nu 1:6; 2:12; 7:36, 41; 10:19).

ZUZITES (*strong nations* ISBE; *babblers* KB). A people defeated by Kedorlaomer and his allies (Ge 14:5). May be the same as Zamzummites. *See Rephaites; Zamzummites.*

ADDITIONAL FEATURES

MAJOR SOCIAL CONCERNS IN THE MOSAIC COVENANT

1. Personhood Everyone's person is to be secure (Ex 20:13; Dt 5:17; Ex 21:16-21,26-31; Lev 19:14; Deut 24:7; 27:18).	**9. Fruit of the Ground** Everyone is to share the fruit of the ground (Ex 23:10-11; Lev 19:9-10; 23:22; 25:3-55; Deut 14:28-29; 24:19-21).
2. False Accusation Everyone is to be secure against slander and false accusation (Ex 20:16; Deut 5:20; Ex 23:1-3; Lev 19:16; Deut 19:15-21).	**10. Rest on Sabbath** Everyone, down to the humblest servant and the resident alien, is to share in the weekly rest of God's sabbath (Ex 20:8-11; Deut 5:12-15; Ex 23:12).
3. Woman No woman is to be taken advantage of within her subordinate status in society (Ex 21:7-11,20,26-32; 22:16-17; Deut 21:10-14; 22:13-30; 24:1-5).	**11. Marriage** The marriage relationship is to be kept inviolate (Ex 20:14; Deut 5:18; see also Lev 18:6-23; 20:10-21; Deut 22:13-30).
4. Punishment Punishment for wrongdoing shall not be excessive so that the culprit is dehumanized (Deut 25:1-5).	**12. Exploitation** No one, however disabled, impoverished or powerless, is to be oppressed or exploited (Ex 22:21-27; Lev 19:14,33-34; 25:35-36; Deut 23:19; 24:6,12-15,17; 27:18).
5. Dignity Every Israelite's dignity and right to be God's freedman and servant are to be honored and safeguarded (Ex 21:2,5-6; Lev 25; Deut 15:12-18).	**13. Fair Trial** Everyone is to have free access to the courts and is to be afforded a fair trial (Ex 23:6,8; Lev 19:15; Deut 1:17; 10:17-18; 16:18-20; 17:8-13; 19:15-21).
6. Inheritance Every Israelite's inheritance in the promised land is to be secure (Lev 25; Num 27:5-7; 36:1-9; Deut 25:5-10).	**14. Social Order** Every person's God-given place in the social order is to be honored (Ex 20:12; Deut 5:16; Ex 21:15,17; 22:28; Lev 19:3,32; 20:9; Deut 17:8-13; 21:15-21; 27:16).
7. Property Everyone's property is to be secure (Ex 20:15; Deut 5:19; Ex 21:33-36; 22:1-15; 23:4-5; Lev 19:35-36; Deut 22:1-4; 25:13-15).	**15. Law** No one shall be above the law, not even the king (Deut 17:18-20).
8. Fruit of Labor Everyone is to receive the fruit of his labors (Lev 19:13; Deut 24:14; 25:4).	**16. Animals** Concern for the welfare of other creatures is to be extended to the animal world (Ex 23:5,11; Lev 25:7; Deut 22:4,6-7; 25:4).

OLD TESTAMENT SACRIFICES

Sacrifice	OT References	Elements	Purpose
Burnt Offering	Lev 1; 6:8–13; 8:18–21; 16:24	Bull, ram or male bird (dove or young pigeon for the poor); wholly consumed; no defect	Voluntary act of worship; atonement for unintentional sin in general; expression of devotion, commitment and complete surrender to God
Grain Offering	Lev 2; 6:14–23	Grain, fine flour, olive oil, incense, baked bread (cakes or wafers), salt; no yeast or honey; accompanied burnt offering and peace offering (along with drink offering)	Voluntary act of worship; recognition of God's goodness and provisions; devotion to God
Peace Offering	Lev 3; 7:11–34	Any animal without defect from herd or flock; variety of breads	Voluntary act of worship; thanksgiving and fellowship (it included a communal meal)
Sin Offering	Lev 4:1—5:13; 6:24–30; 8:14–17; 16:3–22	1. Young bull: for high priest and congregation 2. Male goat: for leader 3. Female goat or lamb: for common person 4. Turtledove or pigeon: for the poor 5. Tenth of an ephah of fine flour: for the very poor	Mandatory atonement for specific unintentional sin; confession of sin; forgiveness of sin; cleansing from defilement
Guilt Offering	Lev 5:14—6:7; 7:1–6	Ram or lamb	Mandatory atonement for unintentional sin requiring restitution; cleansing from defilement; make restitution; pay 20% fine

When more than one kind of offering was presented (as in Num 7:16,17), the procedure was usually as follows: (1) sin offering or guilt offering, (2) burnt offering, (3) peace offering and grain offering (along with a drink offering). This sequence furnishes part of the spiritual significance of the sacrificial system. First, sin had to be dealt with (sin offering or guilt offering). Second, the worshiper committed himself completely to God (burnt offering and grain offering). Third, fellowship or communion between the Lord, the priest and the worshiper (peace offering) was established. To state it another way, there were sacrifices of expiation (sin offerings and guilt offerings), consecration (burnt offerings and grain offerings) and communion (peace offerings—these included vow offerings, thank offerings and freewill offerings).

HEBREW CALENDAR AND SELECTED EVENTS

NUMBER OF MONTH		HEBREW NAME	MODERN EQUIVALENT	BIBLICAL REFERENCES	AGRICULTURE	FEASTS
1 Sacred sequence begins	7	Abib; Nisan	March–April	Ex 12:2; 13:4; 23:15; 34:18; Dt 16:1; Ne 2:1; Est 3:7	Spring (later) rains; barley and flax harvest begins	Passover; Unleavened Bread; Firstfruits
2	8	Ziv (Iyyar)*	April–May	1Ki 6:1, 37	Barley harvest, dry season	
3	9	Sivan	May–June	Est 8:9	Wheat harvest	Pentecost (Weeks)
4	10	(Tammuz)*	June–July		Tending vines	
5	11	(Ab)*	July–August		Ripening of grapes, figs and olives	
6	12	Elul	August–September	Ne 6:15	Processing grapes, figs and olives	
7	Civil 1 sequence	Ethanim (Tishri)*	September–October	1Ki 8:2	Autumn (early) rains begin; plowing	Trumpets; Atonement Tabernacles (Booths)
8	2	Bul (Marcheshvan)*	October–November	1Ki 6:38	Sowing of wheat and barley	
9	3	Kislev	November–December	Ne 1:1; Zec 7:1	Winter rains begin (snow in some areas)	Hanukkah ("Dedication")
10	4	Tebeth	December–January	Est 2:16		
11	5	Shebat	January–February	Zec 1:7		
12	6	Adar	February–March	Ezr 6:15; Est 3:7, 13; 8:12; 9:1, 15, 17, 19, 21	Almond trees bloom; citrus fruit harvest	Purim
		(Adar Sheni)* Second Adar	This intercalary month was added about every three years so the lunar calendar would correspond to the solar year.			

** Names in parentheses are not in the Bible.*

OLD TESTAMENT FEASTS AND OTHER SACRED DAYS

Name	Old Testament References	OT Time	Modern Time
Sabbath	Ex 20:8–11; 31:12–17; Lev 23:3; Dt 5:12–15	7th day	Same
Sabbath Year	Ex 23:10–11; Lev 25:1–7	7th year	Same
Year of Jubilee	Lev 25:8–55; 27:17–24; Nu 36:4	50th year	Same
Passover	Ex 12:1–14; Lev 23:5; Nu 9:1–14; 28:16; Dt 16:1–3a, 4b–7	1st month (Abib) 14	Mar.–Apr.
Unleavened Bread	Ex 12:15–20; 13:3–10; 23:15; 34:18; Lev 23:6–8; Nu 28:17–25; Dt 16:3b, 4a, 8	1st month (Abib) 15–21	Mar.–Apr.
First fruits	Lev 23:9–14	1st month (Abib) 16	Mar.–Apr.
Weeks (Pentecost) (Harvest)	Ex 23:16a; 34:22a; Lev 23:15–21; Nu 28:26–31; Dt 16:9–12	3rd month (Sivan) 6	May–June
Trumpets (Later: Rosh Hashanah)	Lev 23:23–25; Nu 29:1–6	7th month (Tishri) 1	Sept.–Oct.
Day of Atonement (Yom Kippur)	Lev 16; 23:26–32; Nu 29:7–11	7th month (Tishri) 10	Sept.–Oct.
Booths (Tabernacles) (Ingathering)	Ex 23:16b; 34:22b; Lev 23:33–36a, 39–43; Nu 29:12–34; Dt 16:13–15; Zec 14:16–19	7th month (Tishri) 15–21	Sept.–Oct.
Holy Convocation	Lev 23:36b; Nu 29:35–38	7th month (Tishri) 22	Sept.–Oct.
Purim	Est 9:18–32	12th month (Adar) 14, 15	Feb.–Mar.

On Kislev 25 (mid-December) Hanukkah, the feast of dedication or festival of lights, commemorated the purification of the temple and altar in the Maccabean period (165/4 B.C.). This feast is mentioned in John 10:22.

Description	Purpose	New Testament References
Day of rest; no work	Rest for people and animals	Mt 12:1–14; 28:1; Lk 4:16; Jn 5:9; Ac 13:42; Col 2:16; Heb 4:1–11
Year of rest; fallow fields	Rest for land	
Canceled debts; liberation of slaves and indentured servants; land returned to original family owners	Help for poor; stabilize society	
Slaying and eating a lamb, together with bitter herbs and bread made without yeast, in every household	Remember Israel's deliverance from Egypt	Mt 26:17; Mk 14:12–26; Jn 2:13; 11:55; 1Co 5:7; Heb 11:28
Eating bread made without yeast; holding several assemblies; making designated offerings	Remember how the Lord brought the Israelites out of Egypt in haste	Mk 14:1; Ac 12:3; 1Co 5:6–8
Presenting a sheaf of the first of the barley harvest as a wave offering; making a burnt offering and a grain offering	Recognize the Lord's bounty in the land	Ro 8:23; 1Co 15:20–23
A festival of joy; mandatory and voluntary offerings, including the first fruits of the wheat harvest	Show joy and thankfulness for the Lord's blessing of harvest	Ac 2:1–4; 20:16; 1Co 16:8
An assembly on a day of rest commemorated with trumpet blasts and sacrifices	Present Israel before the Lord for his favor	
A day of rest, fasting and sacrifices of atonement for priests and people and atonement for the tabernacle and altar	Cleanse priests and people from their sins and purify the holy place	Ro 3:24–26; Heb 9:7; 10:3, 19–22
A week of celebration for the harvest; living in booths and offering sacrifices	Memorialize the journey from Egypt to Canaan; give thanks for the productivity of Canaan	Jn 7:2, 37
A day of convocation, rest and offering sacrifices	Commemorate the closing of the cycle of feasts	
A day of joy and feasting and giving presents	Remind the Israelites of their national deliverance in the time of Esther	

In addition, new moons were often special feast days (Nu 10:10; 1Ch 23:31; Ezr 3:5; Ne 10:33; Ps 81:3; Isa 1:13-14; 66:23; Hos 5:7; Am 8:5; Col 2:16).

WEIGHTS, LENGTHS AND MEASURES OF THE BIBLE

	Biblical Unit	Approximate American Equivalent	Approximate Metric Equivalent
Weights	talent (60 minas)	75 pounds	34 kilograms
	mina (50 shekels)	1 1/4 pounds	0.6 kilogram
	shekel (2 bekas)	2/5 ounce	11.5 grams
	pim (2/3 shekel)	1/3 ounce	1/3 ounce
	beka (10 gerahs)	1/5 ounce	5.5 grams
	gerah	1/50 ounce	0.6 gram
Length	cubit	18 inches	0.5 meter
	span	9 inches	23 centimeters
	handbreadth	3 inches	8 centimeters
	Capacity		
Dry Measure	cor [homer] (10 ephahs)	6 bushels	220 liters
	lethek (5 ephahs)	3 bushels	110 liters
	ephah (10 omers)	3/5 bushel	22 liters
	seah (1/3 ephah)	7 quarts	7.3 liters
	omer (1/10 ephah)	2 quarts	2 liters
	cab (1/18 ephah)	1 quart	1 liter
Liquid Measure	bath (1 ephah)	6 gallons	22 liters
	hin (1/6 bath)	4 quarts	4 liters
	log (1/72 bath)	1/3 quart	0.3 liter

The figures of the table are calculated on the basis of a shekel equaling 11.5 grams, a cubit equaling 18 inches and an ephah equaling 22 liters. The quart referred to is either a dry quart (slightly larger than a liter) or a liquid quart (slightly smaller than a liter), whichever is applicable. The ton referred to in the footnotes is the American ton of 2,000 pounds.

This table is based upon the best available information, but it is not intended to be mathematically precise; it merely gives approximate amounts and distances. Weights and measures differed somewhat at various times and places in the ancient world. There is uncertainty particularly about the ephah and the bath; further discoveries may shed more light on these units of capacity.

THE KINGS OF THE UNITED KINGDOM

	Name	Ruled	Dates B.C.	Biblical References
1.	Saul	40 years	1050–1010	1Sa 11:15,31; 1Ch 10
2.	David	40 years	1010–970	2Sa 2:4; 1Ki 2:11; 1Ch 11–29
3.	Solomon	40 years	970–930	1Ki 1:39; 11:43; 2Ch 1–9

THE KINGS (AND QUEEN) OF JUDAH

	Name	Ruled	Dates B.C.	Biblical References
1.	Rehoboam	17 years	930–913	1Ki 12:1–24; 14:21–31; 2Ch 10:1–17; 12
2.	Abijah	3 years	913–910	1Ki 15:1–8; 2Ch 13
3.	Asa	41 years	910–869	1Ki 15:9–24; 2Ch 14; 16:14
4.	Jehoshaphat	25 years	872–848	1Ki 22:41–50; 2Ch 17; 21:1
5.	Jehoram	8 years	848–841	2Ki 8:16–24; 21
6.	Ahaziah	1 year	841	2Ki 8:25–29; 9:16–29; 2Ch 22:1–9
7.	Queen Athaliah	6 years	841–835	2Ki 11:1–3; 2Ch 22:10–12
8.	Joash	40 years	835–796	2Ki 11:4; 12; 2Ch 23–24
9.	Amaziah	29 years	796–767	2Ki 14:1–20; 2Ch 25
10.	Uzziah / Azariah	52 years	792–740	2Ki 14:21–22; 15:1–7; 2Ch 26
11.	Jotham	16 years	750–735	2Ki 15:32–38; 2Ch 27
12.	Ahaz	16 years	732–715	2Ki 16; 2Ch 28
13.	Hezekiah	29 years	715–686	2Ki 18–20; 2Ch 29–32
14.	Manasseh	55 years	697–642	2Ki 21:1–18; 2Ch 33:1–20
15.	Amon	2 years	642–640	2Ki 21:19–26; 2Ch 33:21–25
16.	Josiah	31 years	640–609	2Ki 22; 23:1–30; 2Ch 34–35
17.	Jehoahaz	3 months	609	2Ki 23:31–33; 2Ch 36:1–4
18.	Jehoiakim	11 years	609–598	2Ki 23:34–37; 24:1–6; 2Ch 36:5–8
19.	Jehoiachin	3 months	598–597	2Ki 24:8–16; 2Ch 36:9–10
20.	Zedekiah / Mattaniah	11 years	597–586	2Ki 24:17–20; 25:1–7; 2Ch 36:11–21

THE KINGS OF ISRAEL

1.	Jeroboam I	22 years	930–909	1Ki 12:20,25; 14:20
2.	Nadab	2 years	909–908	1Ki 15:25–27,31
3.	Baasha	24 years	908–886	1Ki 15:28–34; 16:1–7
4.	Elah	2 years	886–885	1Ki 16:8–14
5.	Zimri	7 days	885	1Ki 16:11–12,15–20
6.	Omri	12 years	885–874	1Ki 16:23–28
7.	Ahab	22 years	874–853	1Ki 16:29–22:40
8.	Ahaziah	2 years	853–852	1Ki 22:51–53; 2Ki 1
9.	Joram	12 years	852–841	2Ki 3–9:26
10.	Jehu	28 years	841–814	2Ki 9:3–10; 36
11.	Jehoahaz	17 years	814–798	2Ki 13:1–9
12.	Jehoash	16 years	798–782	2Ki 13:10–25; 14:8–16
13.	Jeroboam II	41 years	793–753	2Ki 14:23–29
14.	Zechariah	6 months	753	2Ki 15:8–12
15.	Shallum	1 month	752	2Ki 15:13–15
16.	Menahem	10 years	752–742	2Ki 15:16–22
17.	Pekahiah	2 years	742–740	2Ki 15:23–26
18.	Pekah	20 years	752–732	2Ki 15:27–31; 16:5
19.	Hoshea	9 years	732–722	2Ki 17:1–6

Note: Some kings, such as Jehoash and Jeroboam II, had overlapping reigns.

A HARMONY OF THE GOSPELS

	MATTHEW	MARK	LUKE	JOHN
A Preview of Who Jesus Is				
Luke's purpose in writing a gospel			1:1–4	
John's prologue: Jesus Christ, the preexistent Word incarnate				1:1–18
Jesus' legal lineage through Joseph and natural lineage through Mary	1:1–17		3:23b-38	
The Early Years of John the Baptist				
John's birth foretold to Zacharias			1:5–25	
Jesus' birth foretold to Mary			1:26–38	
Mary's visit to Elizabeth and Elizabeth's song			1:39–45	
Mary's song of joy			1:46–56	
John's birth			1:57–66	
Zacharias's prophetic song			1:67–79	
John's growth and early life			1:80	
The Early Years of Jesus Christ				
Circumstances of Jesus' birth explained to Joseph	1:18–25			
Birth of Jesus			2:1–7	
Praise of the angels and witness of the shepherds			2:8–20	
Circumcision of Jesus			2:21	
Jesus presented in the temple with the homage of Simeon and Anna			2:22–38	
Visit of the magi	2:1–12			
Escape into Egypt and murder of boys in Bethlehem	2:13–18			
Return to Nazareth	2:19–23		2:39	
Growth and early life of Jesus			2:40	
Jesus' first Passover in Jerusalem			2:41–50	
Jesus' growth to adulthood			2:51–52	
The Public Ministry of John the Baptist				
His ministry launched		1:1	3:1–2	
His person, proclamation, and baptism	3:1–6	1:2–6	3:3–6	
His messages to the Pharisees, Sadducees, crowds, tax collectors, and soldiers	3:7–10		3:7–14	
His description of Christ	3:11–12	1:7–8	3:15–18	
The End of John's Ministry and the Beginning of Christ's Public Ministry				
Jesus' baptism by John	3:13–17	1:9–11	3:21–23a	
Jesus' temptation in the wilderness	4:1–11	1:12–13	4:1–13	
John's testimony about himself to the priests and Levites				1:19–28
John's testimony to Jesus as the Son of God				1:29–34
Jesus' first followers				1:35–51
Jesus' first miracle: water becomes wine				2:1–11
Jesus' first stay in Capernaum with His relatives and early disciples				2:12
First cleansing of the temple at the Passover				2:13–22
Early response to Jesus' miracles				2:23–25
Nicodemus's interview with Jesus				3:1–21
John superseded by Jesus				3:22–36
Jesus' departure from Judea	4:12	1:14a	3:19–20; 4:14a	4:1–4
Discussion with a Samaritan woman				4:5–26
Challenge of a spiritual harvest				4:27–38
Evangelization of Sychar				4:39–42
Arrival in Galilee				4:43–45

	MATTHEW	MARK	LUKE	JOHN
The Ministry of Christ in Galilee				
Opposition at Home and a New Headquarters				
Nature of the Galilean ministry	4:17	1:14b-15	4:14b-15	
Child at Capernaum healed by Jesus while at Cana				4:46–54
Ministry and rejection at Nazareth			4:16–31a	
Move to Capernaum	4:13–16			
Disciples Called and Ministry Throughout Galilee				
Call of the four	4:18–22	1:16–20	5:1–11	
Teaching in the synagogue of Capernaum authenticated by healing a demoniac		1:21–28	4:31b-37	
Peter's mother-in-law and others healed	8:14–17	1:29–34	4:38–41	
Tour of Galilee with Simon and others	4:23–25	1:35–39	4:42–44	
Cleansing of a man with leprosy, followed by much publicity	8:2–4	1:40–45	5:12–16	
Forgiving and healing of a paralytic	9:1–8	2:1–12	5:17–26	
Call of Matthew	9:9	2:13–14	5:27–28	
Banquet at Matthew's house	9:10–13	2:15–17	5:29–32	
Jesus defends His disciples for feasting instead of fasting with three parables	9:14–17	2:18–22	5:33–39	
Sabbath Controversies and Withdrawals				
Jesus heals an invalid on the Sabbath				5:1–9
Effort to kill Jesus for breaking the Sabbath and saying He was equal with God				5:10–18
Discourse demonstrating the Son's equality with the Father				5:19–47
Controversy over disciples' picking grain on the Sabbath	12:1–8	2:23–28	6:1–5	
Healing of a man's withered hand on the Sabbath	12:9–14	3:1–6	6:6–11	
Withdrawal to the Sea of Galilee with large crowds from many places	12:15–21	3:7–12		
Appointment of the twelve and Sermon on the Mount				
Twelve apostles chosen		3:13–19	6:12–16	
Setting of the Sermon	5:1–2		6:17–19	
Blessings of those who inherit the kingdom and woes to those who do not	5:3–12		6:20–26	
Responsibility while awaiting the kingdom	5:13–16			
Law, righteousness, and the kingdom	5:17–20			
Six contrasts in interpreting the law	5:21–48		6:27–30, 32–36	
Three hypocritical "acts of righteousness" to be avoided	6:1–18			
Three prohibitions against avarice, harsh judgment, and unwise exposure of sacred things	6:19–7:6		6:37–42	
Application and conclusion	7:7–27		6:31, 43–49	
Reaction of the crowds	7:28–8:1			
Growing Fame and Emphasis on Repentance				
A centurion's faith and the healing of his servant	8:5–13		7:1–10	
A widow's son raised at Nain			7:11–17	
John the Baptist's relationship to the kingdom	11:2–19		7:18–35	
Woes upon Chorazin and Bethsaida for failure to repent	11:20–30			
Christ's feet anointed by a sinful but contrite woman			7:36–50	
First Public Rejection by Jewish Leaders				
A tour with the twelve and other followers			8:1–3	
Blasphemous accusation by the scribes and Pharisees	12:22–37	3:20–30		
Request for a sign refused	12:38–45			
Announcement of new spiritual kinship	12:46–50	3:31–35	8:19–21	
Secrets About the Kingdom Given in Parables				
To the Crowds by the Sea				
The setting of the parables	13:1–3a	4:1–2	8:4	
The parable of the soils	13:3b-23	4:3–25	8:5–18	
The parable of the seed's spontaneous growth		4:26–29		
The parable of the tares	13:24–30			

	MATTHEW	MARK	LUKE	JOHN
The parable of the mustard tree	13:31–32	4:30–32		
The parable of the leavened loaf	13:33–35	4:33–34		
To the Disciples in the House				
The parable of the tares explained	13:36–43			
The parable of the hidden treasure	13:44			
The parable of the valuable pearl	13:45–46			
The parable of the dragnet	13:47–50			
The parable of the head of a household	13:51–53			
Continuing Opposition				
Crossing the lake and calming the storm	8:18, 23–27	4:35–41	8:22–25	
Healing the Gerasene demoniacs and resultant opposition	8:28–34	5:1–20	8:26–39	
Return to Galilee, healing of a woman who touched Jesus' garment, and raising of Jairus's daughter	9:18–26	5:21–43	8:40–56	
Three miracles of healing and another blasphemous accusation	9:27–34			
Final visit to unbelieving Nazareth	13:54–58	6:1–6a		
Final Galilean Campaign				
Shortage of workers	9:35–38	6:6b		
Commissioning of the twelve	10:1–42	6:7–11	9:1–5	
Workers sent out	11:1	6:12–13	9:6	
Antipas's mistaken identification of Jesus	14:1–2	6:14–16	9:7–9	
Earlier imprisonment and beheading of John the Baptist	14:3-12	6:17–29		

The Ministry of Christ Around Galilee

	MATTHEW	MARK	LUKE	JOHN
Lesson on the Bread of Life				
Return of the workers		6:30	9:10a	
Withdrawal from Galilee	14:13–14	6:31–34	9:10b-11	6:1–3
Feeding the five thousand	14:15–21	6:35–44	9:12–17	6:4–13
A premature attempt to make Jesus king blocked	14:22–23	6:45–46		6:14–15
Walking on the water during a storm on the lake	14:24–33	6:47–52		6:16–21
Healings at Gennesaret	14:34–36	6:53–56		
Discourse on the true bread of life				6:22–59
Defection among the disciples				6:60–71
Lesson on the Leaven of the Pharisees, Sadducees, and Herodians				
Conflict over the tradition of ceremonial uncleanness	15:1–3a, 7–9b, 3b–6, 10–20	7:1–23		7:1
Ministry to a believing Greek woman in Tyre and Sidon	15:21–28	7:24–30		
Healings in Decapolis	15:29–31	7:31–37		
Feeding the four thousand in Decapolis	15:32–38	8:1–9a		
Return to Galilee and encounter with the Pharisees and Sadducees	15:39–16:4	8:9b-12		
Warning about the error of the Pharisees, Sadducees, and Herodians	16:5–12	8:13–21		
Healing a blind man at Bethsaida		8:22–26		
Lesson of Messiahship Learned and Confirmed				
Peter's identification of Jesus as the Christ and first prophecy of the church	16:13–20	8:27–30	9:18–21	
First direct prediction of the rejection, crucifixion, and resurrection	16:21–26	8:31–37	9:22–25	
Coming of the Son of Man and judgment	16:27–28	8:38–9:1	9:26–27	
Transfiguration of Jesus	17:1–8	9:2–8	9:28–36a	
Discussion of resurrection, Elijah, and John the Baptist	17:9–13	9:9–13	9:36b	
Lessons on Responsibility to Others				
Healing of demoniac boy and unbelief rebuked	17:14–20	9:14–29	9:37–43a	
Second prediction of Jesus' death and resurrection	17:22–23	9:30–32	9:43b-45	
Payment of temple tax	17:24–27			
Rivalry over greatness in the kingdom	18:1–5	9:33–37	9:46–48	
Warning against causing believers to sin	18:6–14	9:38–50	9:49–50	
Treatment and forgiveness of a sinning brother	18:15–35			

	MATTHEW	MARK	LUKE	JOHN
Journey to Jerusalem for the Feast of Booths				
Complete commitment required of followers	8:19–22		9:57–62	
Ridicule by Jesus' half-brothers				7:2–9
Journey through Samaria			9:51–56	7:10
The Later Judean Ministry of Christ				
Ministry Beginning at the Feast of Booths				
Mixed reaction to Jesus' teaching and miracles				7:11–31
Frustrated attempt to arrest Jesus				7:32–52
Jesus' forgiveness of a woman caught in adultery				7:53–8:11
Conflict over Jesus' claim to be the light of the world				8:12–20
Jesus' relationship to God the Father				8:21–30
Jesus' relationship to Abraham, and attempted stoning				8:31–59
Healing of a man born blind				9:1–7
Response of the blind man's neighbors				9:8–12
Examination and excommunication of the blind man by the Pharisees				9:13–34
Jesus' identification of Himself to the blind man				9:35–38
Spiritual blindness of the Pharisees				9:39–41
Allegory of the good shepherd and the thief				10:1–18
Further division among the Jews				10:19–21
Private Lessons on Loving Service and Prayer				
Commissioning of the seventy			10:1–16	
Return of the seventy			10:17–24	
Story of the good Samaritan			10:25–37	
Jesus' visit with Mary and Martha			10:38–42	
Lesson on how to pray and parable of the bold friend			11:1–13	
Second Debate with the Scribes and the Pharisees				
A third blasphemous accusation and a second debate			11:14–36	
Woes to the Pharisees and the scribes while eating with a Pharisee			11:37–54	
Warning the disciples about hypocrisy			12:1–12	
Warning about greed and trust in wealth			12:13–34	
Warning against being unprepared for the Son of Man's coming			12:35–48	
Warning about the coming division			12:49–53	
Warning against failing to discern the present time			12:54–59	
Two alternatives: repent or perish			13:1–9	
Opposition from a synagogue ruler for healing a woman on the Sabbath				13:10–21
Another attempt to stone or arrest Jesus for blasphemy at the Feast of Dedication				10:22–39
The Ministry of Christ in and Around Perea				
Principles of Discipleship				
From Jerusalem to Perea				10:40–42
Question about salvation and entering the kingdom			13:22–30	
Anticipation of Jesus' coming death and His sorrow over Jerusalem			13:31–35	
Healing of a man with dropsy while eating with a prominent Pharisee on the Sabbath, and three parables suggested by the occasion			14:1–24	
Cost of discipleship			14:25–35	
Parables in defense of association with sinners			15:1–32	
Parable to teach the proper use of money			16:1–13	
Story to teach the danger of wealth			16:14–31	
Four lessons on discipleship			17:1–10	
Sickness and death of Lazarus				11:1–16
Lazarus raised from the dead				11:17–44
Decision of the Sanhedrin to put Jesus to death				11:45–54
Teaching While on Final Journey to Jerusalem				
Healing of ten lepers while passing through Samaria and Galilee			17:11–21	

	MATTHEW	MARK	LUKE	JOHN
Instructions regarding the Son of Man's coming			17:22–37	
Two parables on prayer: the persistent widow, and the Pharisee and the tax collector			18:1–14	
Conflict with Pharisaic teaching on divorce	19:1–12	10:1–12		
Example of little children in relation to the kingdom	19:13–15	10:13–16	18:15–17	
Riches and the kingdom	19:16–30	10:17–31	18:18–30	
Parable of the landowner's sovereignty	20:1–16			
Third prediction of Jesus' death and resurrection	20:17–19	10:32–34	18:31–34	
Warning against ambitious pride	20:20–28	10:35–45		
Healing of blind Bartimaeus and his companion	20:29–34	10:46–52	18:35–43	
Salvation of Zacchaeus			19:1–10	
Parable to teach responsibility while the kingdom is delayed			19:11–28	
The Formal Presentation of Christ to Israel and the Resulting Conflict				
Triumphal Entry and the Fig Tree				
Arrival at Bethany				11:55–12:1, 9–11
Triumphal entry into Jerusalem	21:1–3, 6–7, 4–5, 8–11, 14–17	11:1–11	19:29–44	12:12–19
Cursing of the fig tree having leaves but no figs	21:18–19a	11:12–14		
Second cleansing of the temple	21:12–13	11:15–18	19:45–48	
Request of some Greeks to see Jesus and necessity of the Son of Man's being lifted up				12:20–36a
Different responses to Jesus and Jesus' response to the crowds				12:36b-50
Withered fig tree and the lesson on faith	21:19b-22	11:19–25	21:37–38	
Official Challenge to Christ's Authority				
Questioning of Jesus' authority by the chief priests, teachers of the law, and elders	21:23–27	11:27–33	20:1–8	
Jesus' response with His own question and three parables	21:28–22:14	12:1–12	20:9–19	
Attempts by Pharisees and Herodians to trap Jesus with a question about paying taxes to Caesar	22:15–22	12:13–17	20:20–26	
Sadducees' puzzling question about the resurrection	22:23–33	12:18–27	20:27–40	
A Pharisee's legal question	22:34–40	12:28–34		
Christ's Response to His Enemies' Challenges				
Christ's relationship to David as son and Lord	22:41–46	12:35–37	20:41–44	
Seven woes against the scribes and Pharisees	23:1–36	12:38–40	20:45–47	
Jesus' sorrow over Jerusalem	23:37–39			
A poor widow's gift of all she had		12:41–44	21:1–4	
Prophecies in Preparation for the Death of Christ				
The Olivet Discourse: Jesus Speaks Prophetically About the Temple and His Own Second Coming				
Setting of the discourse	24:1–3	13:1–4	21:5–7	
Beginning of birth pains	24:4–14	13:5–13	21:8–19	
Abomination of desolation and subsequent distress	24:15–28	13:14–23	21:20–24	
Coming of the Son of Man	24:29–31	13:24–27	21:25–27	
Signs of nearness but unknown time	24:32–41	13:28–32	21:28–33	
Five parables to teach watchfulness and faithfulness	24:42–25:30	13:33–37	21:34–36	
Judgment at the Son of Man's coming	25:31–46			
Arrangements for Betrayal				
Plot by the Sanhedrin to arrest and kill Jesus	26:1–5	14:1–2	22:1–2	
Mary's anointing of Jesus for burial	26:6–13	14:3–9		12:2–8
Judas's agreement to betray Jesus	26:14–16	14:10–11	22:3–6	
The Last Supper				
Preparation for the Passover meal	26:17–19	14:12–16	22:7–13	

	MATTHEW	MARK	LUKE	JOHN
Beginning of the Passover meal and dissension among the disciples over greatness	26:20	14:17	22:14–16, 24–30	
Washing the disciples' feet				13:1–20
Identification of the betrayer	26:21–25	14:18–21	22:21–23	13:21–30
Prediction of Peter's denial	26:31–35	14:27–31	22:31–38	13:31–38
Conclusion of the meal and the Lord's Supper instituted (1Co 11:23–26)	26:26–29	14:22–25	22:17–20	
Discourse and Prayers from the Upper Room to Gethsemane				
Questions about His destination, the Father, and the Holy Spirit answered				14:1–31
The vine and the branches				15:1–17
Opposition from the world				15:18–16:4
Coming and ministry of the Spirit				16:5–15
Prediction of joy over His resurrection				16:16–22
Promise of answered prayer and peace				16:23–33
Jesus' prayer for His disciples and all who believe				17:1–26
Jesus' three agonizing prayers in Gethsemane	26:30, 36–46	14:26, 32–42	22:39–46	18:1
The Death of Christ				
Betrayal and Arrest				
Jesus betrayed, arrested, and forsaken	26:47–56	14:43–52	22:47–53	18:2–12
Trial				
First Jewish phase, before Annas				18:13–14, 19–23
Second Jewish phase, before Caiaphas and the Sanhedrin	26:57, 59–68	14:53, 55–65	22:54a, 63–65	18:24
Peter's denials	26:58, 69–75	14:54, 66–72	22:54b-62	18:15–18, 25–27
Third Jewish phase, before the Sanhedrin	27:1	15:1a	22:66–71	
Remorse and suicide of Judas Iscariot (Ac 1:18–19)	27:3–10			
First Roman phase, before Pilate	27:2, 11–14	15:1b-5	23:1–5	18:28–38
Second Roman phase, before Herod Antipas			23:6–12	
Third Roman phase, before Pilate	27:15–26	15:6–15	23:13–25	18:39–19:16a
Crucifixion				
Mockery by the Roman soldiers	27:27–30	15:16–19		
Journey to Golgotha	27:31–34	15:20–23	23:26–33a	19:16b-17
First three hours of crucifixion	27:35–44	15:24–32	23:33b-43	19:18, 23–24, 19–22, 25–27
Last three hours of crucifixion	27:45–50	15:33–37	23:44–45a, 46	19:28–30
Witness of Jesus' death	27:51–56	15:38–41	23:45b, 47–49	
Burial				
Certification of Jesus' death and procurement of His body	27:57–58	15:42–45	23:50–52	19:31–38
Jesus' body placed in a tomb	27:59–60	15:46	23:53–54	19:39–42
The tomb watched by the women and guarded by the soldiers	27:61–66	15:47	23:55–56	
The Resurrection and Ascension of Christ				
The Empty Tomb				
The tomb visited by the women	28:1	16:1		
The stone rolled away	28:2–4			
The tomb found to be empty by the women	28:5–8	16:2–8	24:1–8	20:1
The tomb found to be empty by Peter and John			24:9–12	20:2–10
The Post Resurrection Appearances				
Appearance to Mary Magdalene		16:9–11		20:11–18
Appearance to the other women	28:9–10			
Report of the soldiers to the Jewish authorities	28:11–15			
Appearance to the two disciples traveling to Emmaus		16:12–13	24:13–32	
Report of the two disciples to the rest (1Co. 15:5a)			24:33–35	
Appearance to the ten assembled disciples		16:14	24:36–43	20:19–25
Appearance to the eleven assembled disciples (1Co. 15:5b)				20:26–31

	MATTHEW	MARK	LUKE	JOHN
Appearance to the seven disciples while fishing				21:1–25
Appearance to the Eleven in Galilee (1Co. 15:6)	28:16–20	16:15–18		
Appearance to James, Jesus' brother (1Co. 15:7)				
Appearance to the disciples in Jerusalem (Ac 1:3–8)			24:44–49	
The Ascension				
Christ's parting blessing and departure (Ac 1:9–12)		16:19–20	24:50–53	

PROPHECIES OF THE MESSIAH FULFILLED IN JESUS

OT Text	NT Text	Subject
Ge 3:15	Lk 22:53	Satan against Jesus
Ge 3:15	Heb 2:14; 1Jn 3:8	Jesus' victory over Satan
Ge 12:3	Ac 3:25; Gal 3:8	Gentiles blessed through Christ as the offspring of Abraham
Ge 13:15	Gal 3:15–16, 19	Messiah as the seed of Abraham
Ge 14:18–20	Heb 7	Jesus' priesthood according to the likeness of Melchizedek
Ge 18:18	Ac 3:25; Gal 3:8	Gentiles blessed through Christ as the offspring of Abraham
Ge 22:18	Ac 3:25; Gal 3:8	Gentiles blessed through Christ as the offspring of Abraham
Ge 49:10	Lk 1:32–33	Coming ruler from Judah
Ex 12:1–14, 46	Jn 19:31–36; 1Co 5:7; 1Pe 1:19	The Messiah as the Passover Lamb
Ex 16:4	Jn 6:31–33	Messiah to give true bread from heaven
Ex 24:8	Heb 9:11–28	The Messiah's blood to be shed as sacrifice
Lev 15:15–17	Ro 3:25; Heb 9:1–14, 24; 1Jn 2:2	Atoning sacrifice of blood
Nu 21:8–9	Jn 3:14–15	Life through looking at one on a cross
Nu 24:17	Lk 1:32–33	Coming ruler from Jacob
Nu 24:17	Rev 22:16	Coming star out of Jacob
Dt 18:17	Jn 6:14; 12:49–50; Ac 3:22–23	Coming prophet sent from God
Dt 21:23	Gal 3:13	Messiah cursed for hanging on a tree
Dt 30:12–14	Ro 10:6–8	Jesus is God's word near to us
2Sa 7:14	Heb 1:5	Messiah to be God's Son
2Sa 7:16	Lk 1:32–33; Rev 19:11–16	David's Son as eternal king
1Ch 17:13	Heb 1:5	Messiah to be God's Son
1Ch 17:14	Lk 1:32–33; Rev 19:11–16	David's Son as eternal king
Ps 2:7	Mt 3:17; 17:5; Mk 1:11; 9:7; Lk 3:22; 9:35; Ac 13:33; Heb 1:5	God's address to his Son
Ps 2:9	Rev 2:27	Messiah to rule the nations with power
Ps 8:2	Mt 21:16	Children to praise God's Son
Ps 8:4–5	Heb 2:6–9	Jesus lower than the angels

OT Text	NT Text	Subject
Ps 8:6	1Co 15:27–28; Eph 1:22	Everything subject to God's Son
Ps 16:8–11	Ac 2:25–32; 13:35–37	David's Son to be raised from the dead
Ps 22:1	Mt 27:46; Mk 15:34	God–forsaken cry by the Messiah
Ps 22:7–8	Mt 27:29, 41–44; Mk 15:18, 29–32; Lk 23:35–39	Messiah mocked by a crowd
Ps 22:18	Mt 27:35; Mk 15:24; Lk 23:34; Jn 19:24	Casting lots for Jesus' clothes
Ps 22:22	Heb 2:12	Jesus to declare his name in the church
Ps 31:5	Lk 23:46	Messiah to commit his spirit to God
Ps 34:20	Jn 19:31–36	Messiah to have no broken bones
Ps 35:19	Jn 15:25	Messiah experiencing hatred for no reason
Ps 40:6–8	Jn 6:38; Heb 10:5–9	Messiah to do God's perfect will
Ps 41:9	Jn 13:18	The Messiah's betrayal by a friend
Ps 45:6–7	Heb 1:8–9	Characteristics of the coming King
Ps 68:18	Eph 4:7–11	Ascension and giving gifts to humans
Ps 69:4	Jn 15:25	Messiah experiencing hatred for no reason
Ps 69:9	Jn 2:14–22	The Messiah's zeal for God's house
Ps 69:21	Jn 19:29	The thirst of the suffering Messiah
Ps 69:25	Ac 1:20	Judgment on the Messiah's persecutor
Ps 78:2	Mt 13:34–35	Messiah to speak in parables
Ps 102:25–27	Heb 1:10–12	Characteristics of the coming King
Ps 110:1	Ac 2:34–35; 1Co 15:25; Eph 1:20–22; Heb 1:13; 10:12–13	Jesus exalted in power at God's right hand
Ps 110:1	Mt 22:41–45; Mk 12:35–37; Lk 20:41–44	Jesus as Son and Lord of David
Ps 110:4	Heb 5:6; 7:11–22	Jesus' priesthood after Melchizedek
Ps 118:22–23	Mt 21:42–44; Mk 12:10; Lk 20:17–19; Ac 4:10–11; 1Pe 2:7–8	Rejected stone to become capstone
Ps 118:26	Mt 21:9; Mk 11:9; Lk 19:38; Jn 12:13	Messiah to come in the name of the Lord
Isa 6:9–10	Mt 13:14–15; Mk 4:12; Lk 8:10; Jn 12:37–41	Hearts to be closed to the gospel
Isa 7:14	Mt 1:18–23; Lk 1:26–35	Virgin birth of the Messiah

OT Text	NT Text	Subject
Isa 8:14	Ro 9:32-33; 1 Pe 2:7–8	A stone over which people stumble
Isa 9:1–2	Mt 4:13-16; Mk 1:14–15; Lk 4:14-15	Ministry to begin in Galilee
Isa 9:6–7	Lk 1:32-33	David's Son as eternal king
Isa 9:7	Jn 1:1, 18	The Messiah to be God
Isa 9:7	Eph 2:14–17	The Messiah to be a man of peace
Isa 11:1–2	Mt 3:16; Mk 1:16; Lk 3:21–22	Branch of Jesse (David) to receive the Spirit)
Isa 11:10	Lk 1:32-33	Root of Jesse (David) as coming ruler
Isa 11:10	Ro 15:12	Salvation to be available for Gentiles
Isa 22:22	Rev 3:7	Jesus to receive the key of David
Isa 25:8	1Co 15:54	Death to be swallowed up in victory
Isa 28:16	Ro 9:32–33; 1Pe 2:6	Messiah to be the chief cornerstone
Isa 35:5–6	Mt 11:4–6; Lk 7:22	Messiah to be a mighty worker of miracles
Isa 40:3–5	Mt 3:3; Mk 1:3; Lk 3:4; Jn 1:23	Jesus' forerunner, a voice in the desert
Isa 42:1–4	Mt 12:15–21	Messiah as the chosen servant of the Lord
Isa 45:23	Ro 14:11; Php 2:10	Every knee to bow before the Messiah
Isa 49:6	Ac 13:46–47	Messiah as a light to the Gentiles
Isa 50:6	Mt 27:26–30; Mk 14:65; 15:15, 19; Lk 22:63; Jn 19:1, 3	Beating God's servant
Isa 50:6	Mt 26:67; Mk 14:65	Spitting on God's servant
Isa 53:1	Jn 12:38; Ro 10:16	Israel not to believe in the Messiah
Isa 53:3	Jn 1:11	Messiah to be rejected by his own people
Isa 53:4–5	Mt 8:16–17; Mk 1:32–34; Lk 4:40–41; 1Pe 2:24	Healing ministry of God's servant
Isa 53:7–8	Jn 1:29, 36; Ac 8:30–35; 1Pe 1:19; Rev 5:6, 12	Suffering Lamb of God
Isa 53:9	Heb 4:15; 1Pe 2:22	The sinless servant of God
Isa 53:9	Mt 27:57–60	Messiah to be buried in a rich man's grave
Isa 53:12	Mt 27:38; Mk 15:27–28; Lk 22:37; 23:33; Jn 19:18	God's servant numbered with transgressors
Isa 55:3	Lk 22:20; 1Co 11:25	Everlasting covenant through the Messiah
Isa 55:3	Ac 13:33	Blessings of David given to the Messiah

OT Text	NT Text	Subject
Isa 59:20–21	Ro 11:26–27	Israel's Deliverer to come from Zion
Isa 60:1–3	Mt 2:11; Ro 15:8–12	Gentiles coming to worship the Messiah
Isa 61:1–2	Mt 4:16; Mk 1:10; Lk 4:18–21	The Messiah anointed by the Holy Spirit
Isa 65:1	Ro 10:20	Gentiles would believe in the Messiah
Isa 65:2	Ro 10:21	Israel would reject the Messiah
Jer 23:5	Lk 1:32–33	David's Son to be a great King
Jer 23:6	Mt 1:21	David's Son to be Savior
Jer 23:6	1Co 1:30	Messiah to be named "Our Righteousness"
Jer 31:5	Mt 2:16–18	Rachel weeping when God's Son is born
Jer 31:31–34	Lk 22:20; 1Co 11:25; Heb 8:8–12; 10:15–18	Jesus and the new covenant
Jer 32:40	Lk 22:20; 1Co 11:25	Everlasting covenant through the Messiah
Jer 33:15	Lk 1:32–33	David's Son to be a great King
Jer 33:16	Mt 1:21	David's Son to be Savior
Jer 33:16	1Co 1:30	Messiah to be named "Our Righteousness"
Eze 21:26–27	Lk 1:32–33	A rightful crown for the Messiah
Eze 34:23–24	Jn 10:11, 14, 16; Heb 13:20; 1Pe 5:4	The coming good shepherd
Eze 37:24–25	Lk 1:32–33	Messiah to be David's son and a king
Eze 37:24–25	Jn 10:11, 14, 16; Heb 13:20; 1Pe 5:4	The coming good shepherd
Eze 37:26	Lk 22:20; 1Co 11:25	Messiah's everlasting covenant of peace
Da 7:13–14	Mt 24:30; 26:64; Mk 13:26; 14:62; Lk 21:27; Rev 1:13; 14:14	The coming of the Son of Man
Da 7:27	Rev 11:15	The coming everlasting kingdom of the Messiah
Da 9:24–26	Gal 4:4	Timetable for the Messiah's coming
Hos 11:1	Mt 2:14–15	Jesus to return from Egypt
Joel 2:28–32	Ac 2:14–21	God's Spirit to be poured out
Am 9:11–12	Ac 15:13–18	Gentiles would believe in the Messiah
Jnh 1:17	Mt 12:39–40	Messiah to be three days and nights in grave
Mic 5:2	Mt 2:1–6	The Messiah to be born in Bethlehem
Mic 5:2	Lk 1:32–33	The Messiah as an eternal king
Mic 5:4	Jn 10:11, 14	The coming shepherd of God's flock

OT Text	NT Text	Subject
Mic 5:5	Eph 2:14–17	The Messiah to be a man of peace
Zec 9:9	Mt 21:1–9; Mk 11:1–10; Lk 19:28–38; Jn 12:12–16	The coming ruler on a donkey
Zec 11:12–13	Mt 27:1–10	Thirty pieces of silver for a potter's field
Zec 12:10	Jn 19:37; Rev 1:7	Looking on the pierced Messiah
Zec 13:7	Mt 26:31; 26:55–56; Mk 14:27; 14:48–50	Striking the coming shepherd; the sheep flee
Mal 3:1	Mt 11:7–10; Mk 1:2–4; Lk 7:24–27	The forerunner to the Messiah
Mal 4:5–6	Mt 11:14; 17:11–13; Mk 9:11–13; Mk 9:11–13; Lk 1:16–17	The forerunner as Elijah returned

PARABLES OF JESUS

Parable	Matthew	Mark	Luke
Lamp under a basket	5:14–15	4:21–22	8:16; 11:33
Wise and foolish builders	7:24–27		6:47–49
New cloth on an old garment	9:16	2:21	5:36
New wine in old wineskins	9:17	2:22	5:37–38
Sower and the soils	13:3–8, 18–23	4:3–8, 14–20	8:5–8, 11–15
Tares	13:24–30, 36–43		
Mustard seed	13:31–32	4:30–32	13:18–19
Leaven	13:33		13:20–21
Hidden treasure	13:44		
Valuable pearl	13:45–46		
Dragnet	13:47–50		
Head of a household	13:52		
Lost sheep	18:12–14		15:4–7
Unmerciful slave	18:23–34		
Laborers in the vineyard	20:1–16		
Two sons	21:28–32		
Vine-growers	21:33–44	12:1–11	20:9–18
Wedding feast	22:2–14		
Fig tree	24:32–35	13:28–29	21:29–31
Faithful and sensible slave	24:45–51		12:42–48
Ten virgins	25:1–13		
Talents (minas)	25:14–30		19:12–27
Sheep and goats	25:31–46		
Growing seed		4:26–29	
Watchful slaves		13:35–37	12:35–40

Parable	Matthew	Mark	Luke
Moneylender			7:41–43
Good Samaritan			10:30–37
Friend in need			11:5–8
Rich fool			12:16–21
Unfruitful fig tree			13:6–9
Lowest seat at the feast			14:7–14
Big dinner			14:16–24
Cost of discipleship			14:28–33
Lost coin			15:8–10
Lost (prodigal) son			15:11–32
Shrewd manager			16:1–8
Rich man and Lazarus			16:19–31
Master and his slave			17:7–10
Persistent widow			18:2–8
Pharisee and tax collector			18:10–14

MIRACLES OF JESUS

Healing Miracles	**Matthew**	**Mark**	**Luke**	**John**
Man with leprosy	8:2–4	1:40–42	5:12–13	
Roman centurion's servant	8:5–13		7:1–10	
Peter's mother–in–law	8:14–15	1:30–31	4:38–35	
Two men from Gadara	8:28–34	5:1–15	8:27–35	
Paralyzed man	9:2–7	2:3–12	5:18–25	
Woman with bleeding	9:20–22	5:25–29	8:43–48	
Two blind men	9:27–31			
Mute, demon–possessed man	9:32–33			
Man with a withered hand	12:10–13	3:1–5	6:6–10	
Blind, mute, demon–possessed man	12:22		11:14	
Canaanite woman's daughter	15:21–28	7:24–30		
Boy with a demon	17:14–18	9:17–29	9:38–43	
Two blind men (including Bartimaeus)	20:29–34	10:46–52	18:35–43	
Deaf mute		7:31–37		
Possessed man in synagogue		1:23–26	4:33–35	
Blind man at Bethsaida		8:22–26		
Crippled woman			13:11–13	
Man with dropsy			14:1–4	
Ten men with leprosy			17:11–19	
The high priest's servant			22:50–51	
Official's son at Capernaum				4:46–54
Sick man at pool of Bethesda				5:1–9
Man born blind				9:1 7

Miracles showing power over nature	**Matthew**	**Mark**	**Luke**	**John**
Calming the storm	8:23–27	4:37–41	8:22–25	
Walking on water	14:25	6:48–51		6:19–21
Feeding of the 5,,000	14:15–21	6:35–44	9:12–17	6:6–13
Feeding of the 4,,000	15:32–38	8:1–9		
Coin in fish	17:24–27			
Fig tree withered	21:18–22	11:12–14, 20–25		
Large catch of fish			5:4–11	
Water turned into wine				2:1–11
Another large catch of fish				21:1–11
Miracles of raising the dead				
Jairus's daughter	9:18–19, 23–25	5:22–24, 38–42	8:41–42, 49–56	
Widow's son at Nain			7:11–15	
Lazarus				11:1–44

OLD TESTAMENT CHRONOLOGY (FROM ABRAHAM)

Abram born	2166 B.C.
Abraham dies	1991
Jacob and family in Egypt	1876
Moses born	1526
The Exodus	1446
Moses dies; Israelites enter Canaan	1406
The Judges	1375–1050
Saul as king	10501010
David as king	1010–970
Solomon as king	970–930
Northern kingdom of Israel	930–722
Southern kingdom of Judah	930–586
Exile	586–538
First return under Zerubbabel	538
Temple rebuilt	536–516
Second return under Ezra	458
Wall of Jerusalem rebuilt	445
Third return under Nehemiah	432
Close of OT history and prophecy	c. 400

NEW TESTAMENT CHRONOLOGY

Birth of Jesus	7–5 B.C.
Baptism of Jesus	A.D. 26
Crucifixion of Jesus	30
Conversion of Saul	34/35
Death of Herod Agrippa I	44
James written	before 50 (?)
First Missionary Journey	46–48
Galatians written	48/49
Jerusalem Conference	49/50
Second Missionary Journey	50–52
Paul at Corinth	50–52
1 and 2 Thessalonians written	51

Arrival of Gallio as Proconsul	52
Third Missionary Journey	53–57
Paul at Ephesus	54–57
1 and 2 Corinthians written	55
Romans written	57
Paul's Arrest in Jerusalem	57
Imprisonment at Caesarea	57–59
On Island of Malta	59
Arrival at Rome	59
Roman Imprisonment	59–61/62
Colossians, Philemon, Ephesians written	60
Philippians written	61
Paul's Release and Further Work	62–67
1 Timothy and Titus written	63–65
Synoptic Gospels and Acts written	before 67
1 and 2 Peter written	67/68
Peter's Death at Rome	67/68
Paul's Second Roman Imprisonment	67/68
2 Timothy written	67/68
Paul's Death at Rome	67/68
Jude written	c. 65–80
Writings of John	c. 90–100
Death of John	c. 100

TABLE OF NATIONS

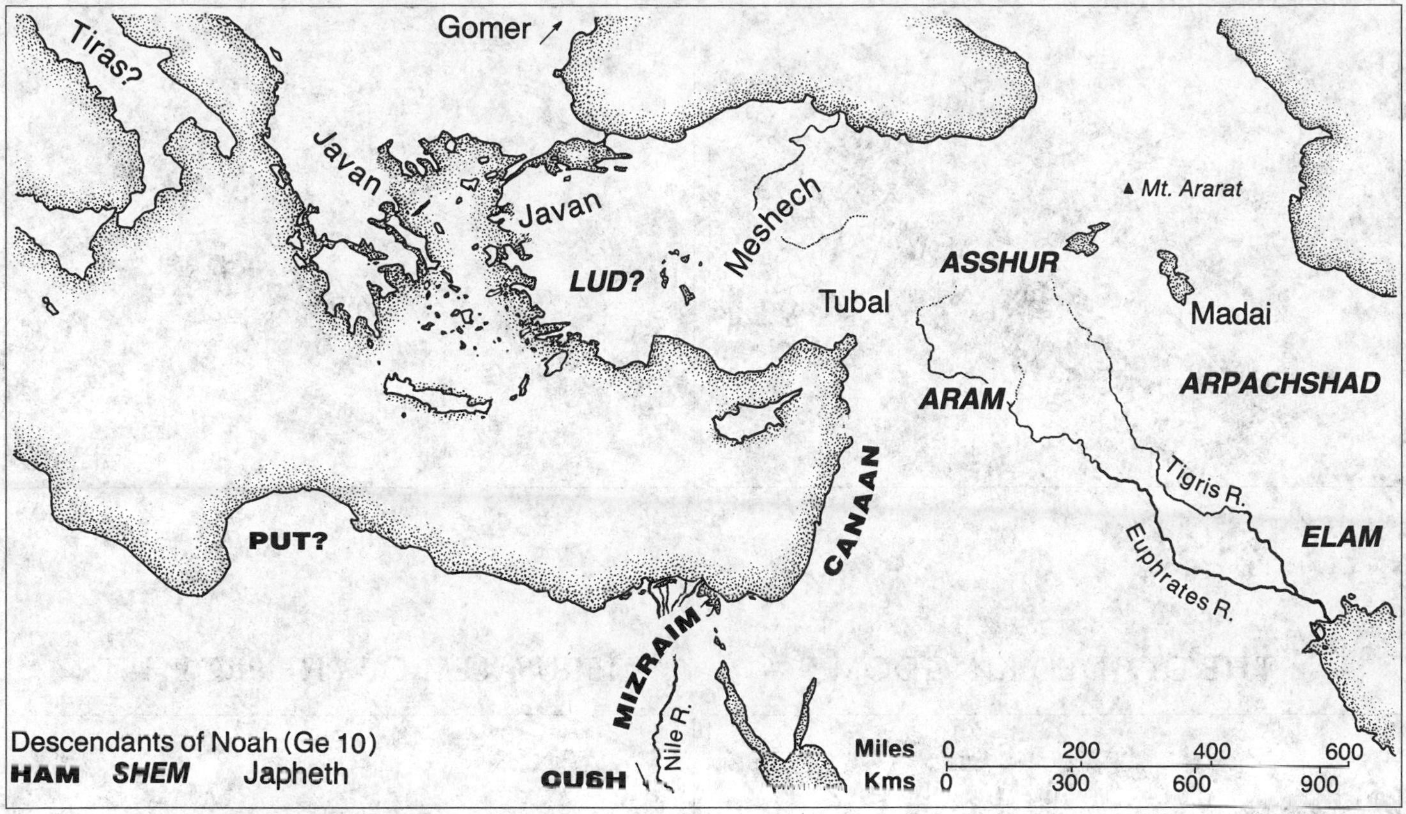

Gomer
Tiras?
Javan
Javan
LUD?
Meshech
Tubal
Mt. Ararat
ASSHUR
Madai
ARPACHSHAD
ARAM
Tigris R.
Euphrates R.
ELAM
PUT?
CANAAN
MIZRAIM
Nile R.
CUSH
Descendants of Noah (Ge 10)
HAM SHEM Japheth
Miles 0 200 400 600
Kms 0 300 600 900

THE EXODUS

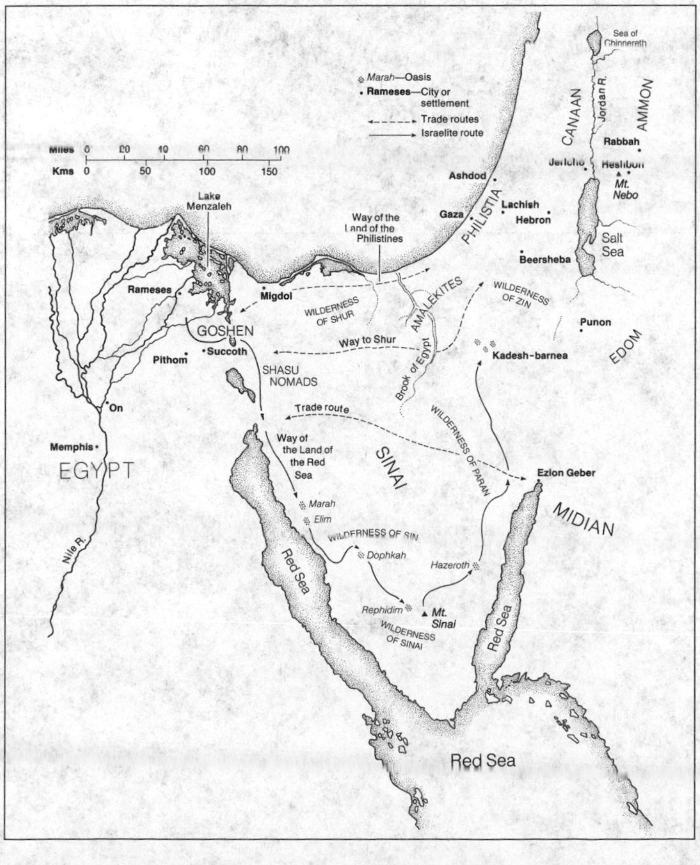

Marah—Oasis
Rameses—City or settlement
Trade routes
Israelite route
Miles 0 20 40 60 80 100
Kms 0 50 100 150
Sea of Chinnereth
CANAAN
Jordan R.
AMMON
Rabbah
Jericho
Heshbon
Mt. Nebo
Ashdod
Lake Menzaleh
Way of the Land of the Philistines
Gaza
PHILISTIA
Lachish
Hebron
Salt Sea
Beersheba
Rameses
Migdol
WILDERNESS OF SHUR
AMALEKITES
WILDERNESS OF ZIN
GOSHEN
Punon
Way to Shur
Pithom
Succoth
Kadesh-barnea
EDOM
SHASU NOMADS
Brook of Egypt
On
Trade route
WILDERNESS OF PARAN
Memphis
Way of the Land of the Red Sea
SINAI
EGYPT
Ezion Geber
Marah
Elim
MIDIAN
WILDERNESS OF SIN
Nile R.
Dophkah
Hazeroth
Red Sea
Rephidim
Mt. Sinai
WILDERNESS OF SINAI
Red Sea
Red Sea

CITIES OF REFUGE

Kedesh
Acco
Golan
Dor
Ramoth
Beth-shan
Peniel
Shechem
Gezer
Gibeon
Bezer
Heshbon
Hebron
The six cities of refuge are shown in bold type.
Beersheba
Miles 10 5 0 10 20
Kms 10 5 0 10 20 30

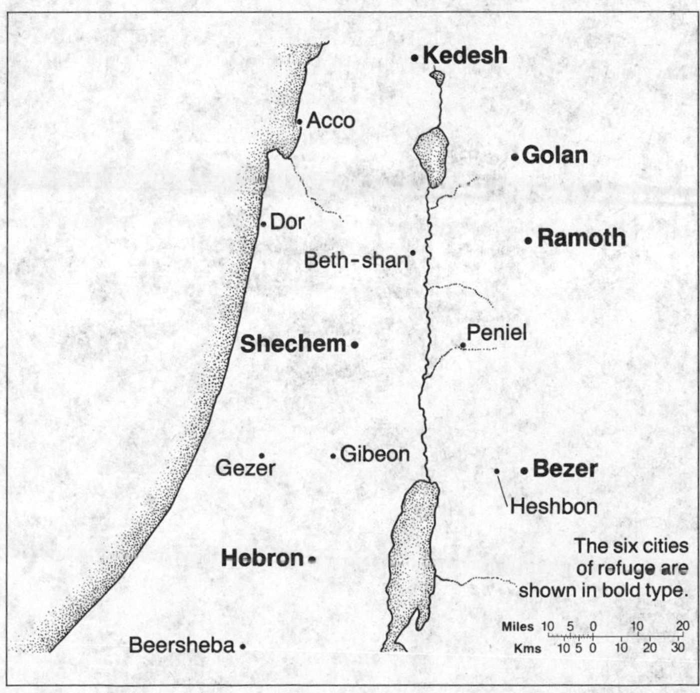

DAVID'S JERUSALEM

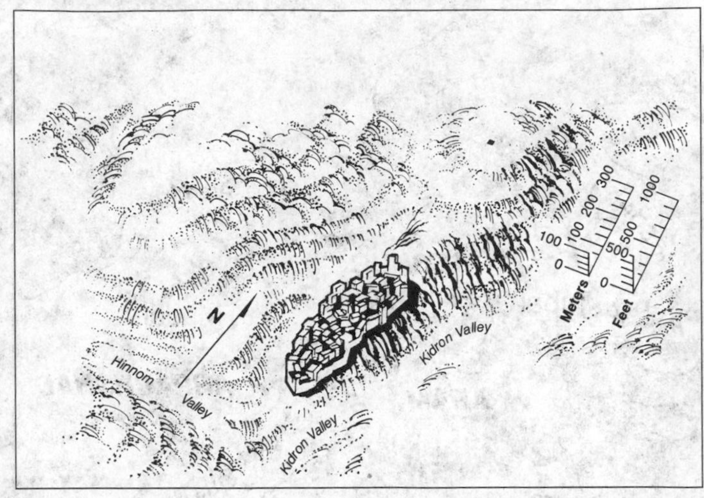

SOLOMON'S JERUSALEM

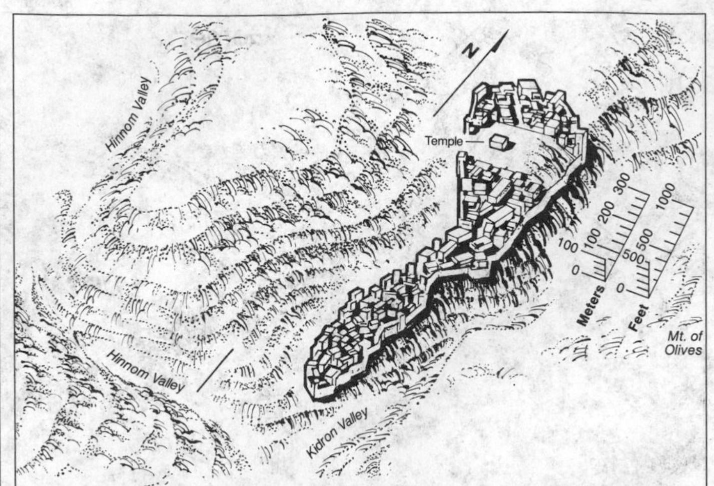

THE DIVIDED KINGDOM

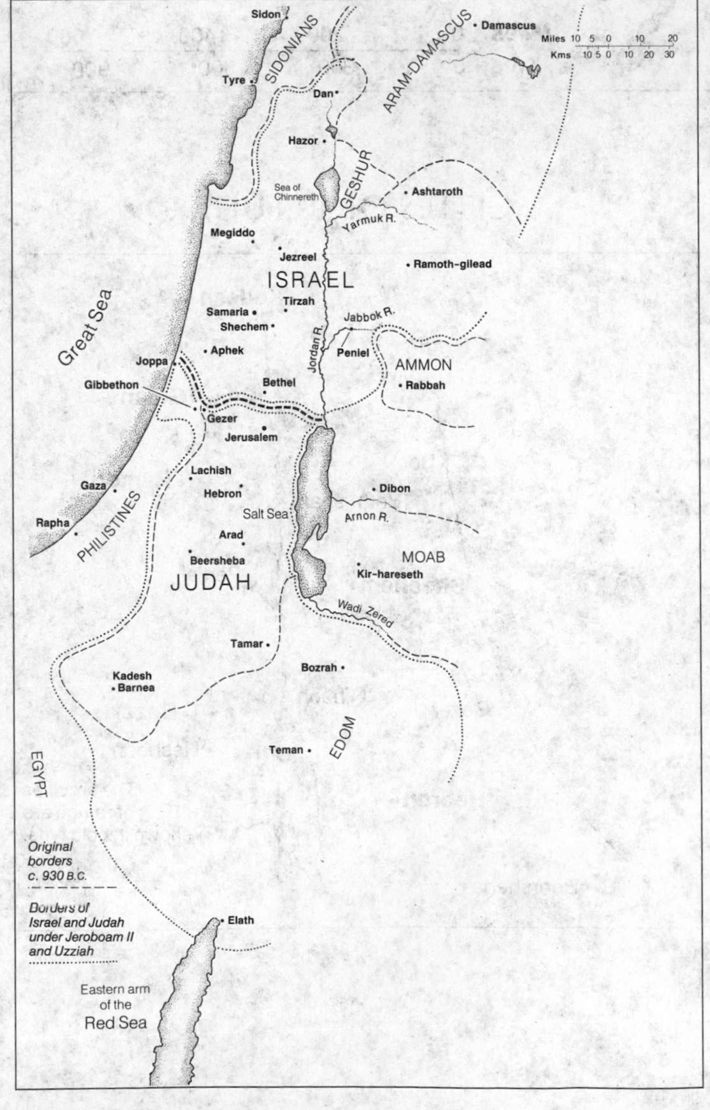

JERUSALEM OF THE PROPHETS

EXILE OF THE NORTHERN KINGDOM

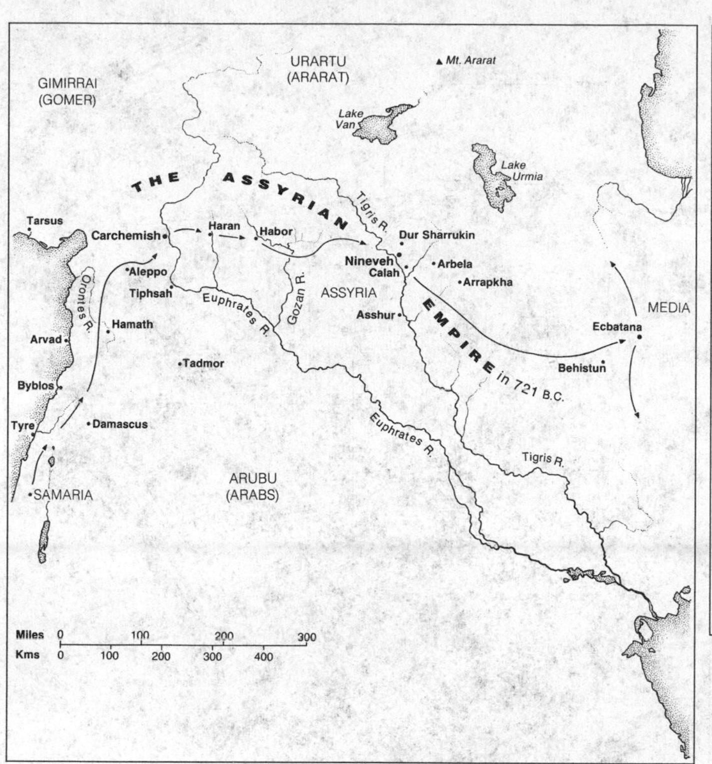

EXILE OF THE SOUTHERN KINGDOM

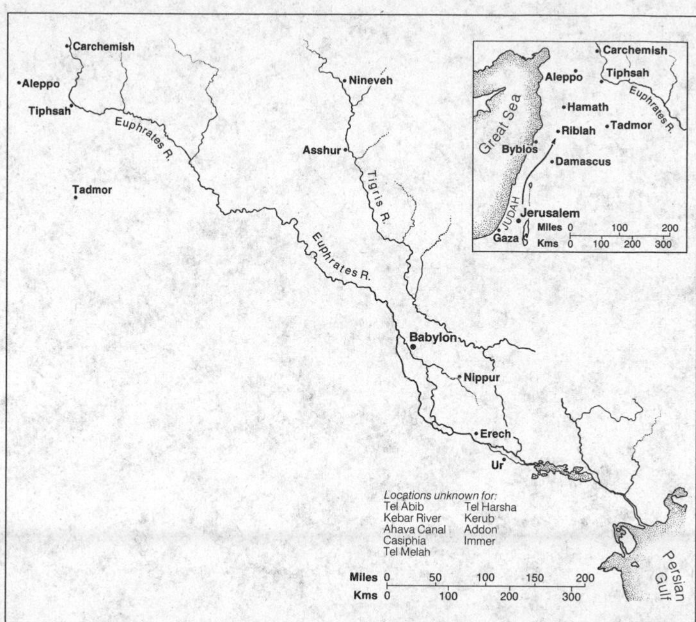

RETURN FROM EXILE

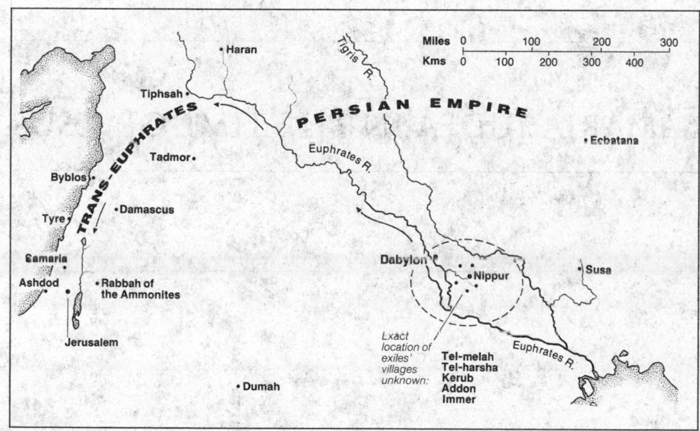

JERUSALEM OF THE RETURNED EXILES

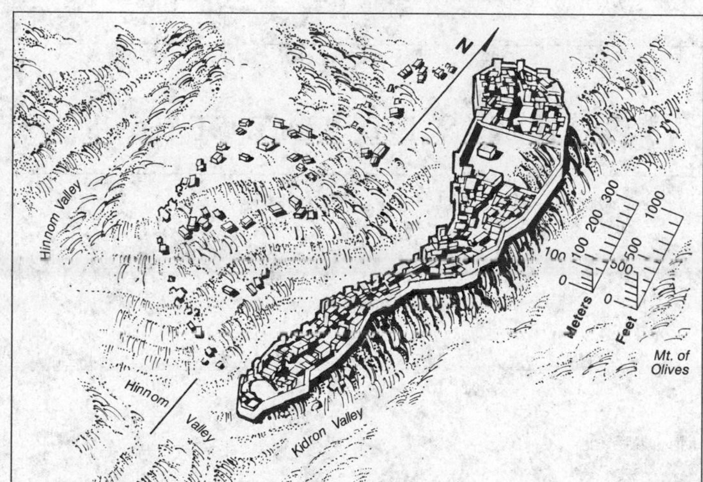

THE KINGDOM OF HEROD

Fortress cities of Herod
General location of boundaries of Herod's kingdom
Indefinite boundary (desert, etc.)
Mountain

ITUREA
Abana R.
Sidon
ABILENE
Damascus
Leontes R.
Mt. Hermon
Pharpar R.
PHOENICIA
Tyre
Caesarea Philippi
TRACHONITIS
Lake Semechonitis
GAULANITIS
Mt. Meiron
Chorazin
Bethsaida
Capernaum
Raphana
BATANEA
Acco (Ptolemais)
Sea of Galilee
Tiberias
Dion
Mt. Carmel
GALILEE
Nazareth
Mt. Tabor
Nain
Yarmuk R.
AURANITIS
The Great Sea (Mediterranean)
Dor
Caesarea
Scythopolis
Pella
DECAPOLIS
SAMARIA
Samaria
Mt. Ebal
Mt. Gerizim
Sychar
ARABIA
Jabbok R.
Antipatris
Alexandrium
Joppa
Arimathea
Phasaelis
PEREA
Jordan R.
Lydda
Ephraim
Philadelphia
Jamnia
Ramah
JUDEA
Jericho
Ashdod
Azotus
Jerusalem
Qumran
Mt. Nebo
Bethlehem
Ashkelon
Herodium
Machaerus
Dead Sea
Hebron
Gaza
Arnon R.
ARABIA
IDUMEA
Masada
Beersheba
NABATEAN KINGDOM
Miles 10 5 0 10 20
Kms 10 0 10 20 30

JERUSALEM IN THE TIME OF JESUS

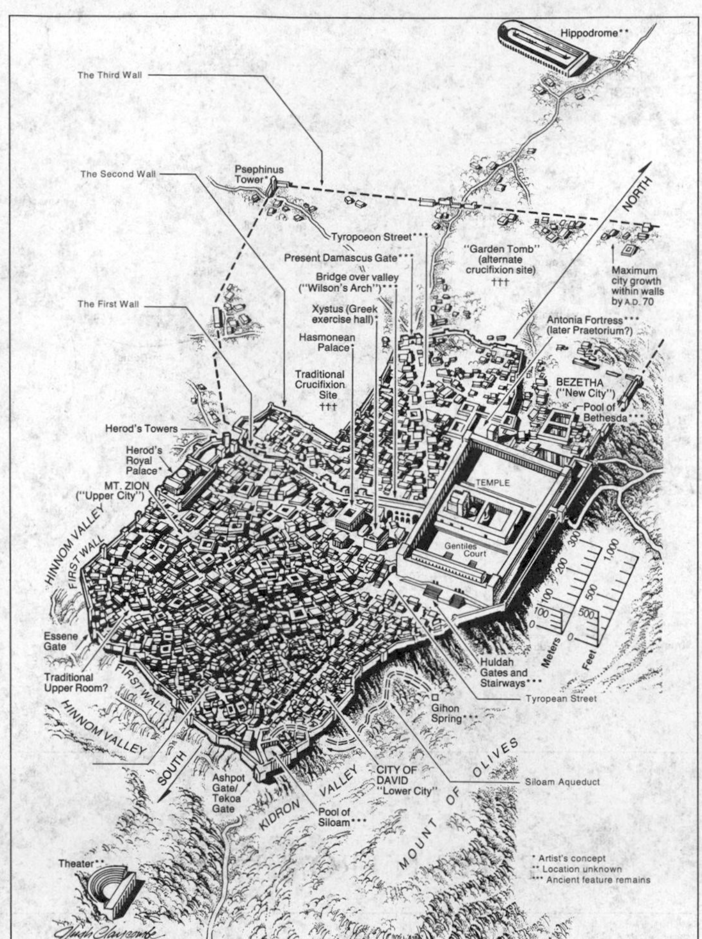

GALILEE IN THE TIME OF JESUS

Lake Semechonitis
Ptolemais
Chorazin
Bethsaida
Mediterranean Sea
Capernaum
Magdala
Sea of Galilee
Tiberias
Mt. Carmel
Kishon R.
Cana
Nazareth
Mt. Tabor
Yarmuk R.
Nain
Jordan R.
Miles 10 5 0 10
Kms 10 5 0 10
Scythopolis
Caesarea

SAMARIA-JUDEA IN THE TIME OF JESUS

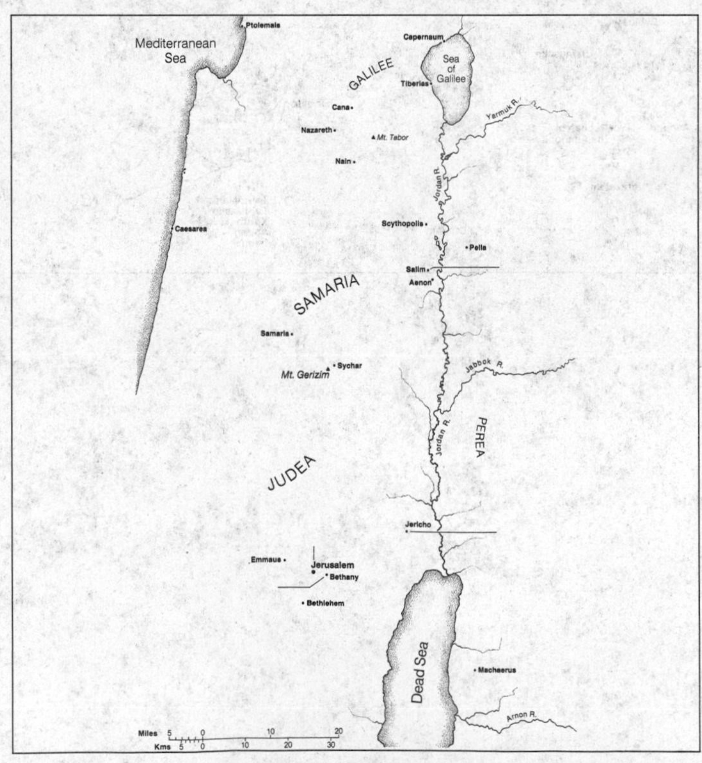

PAUL'S FIRST MISSIONARY JOURNEY

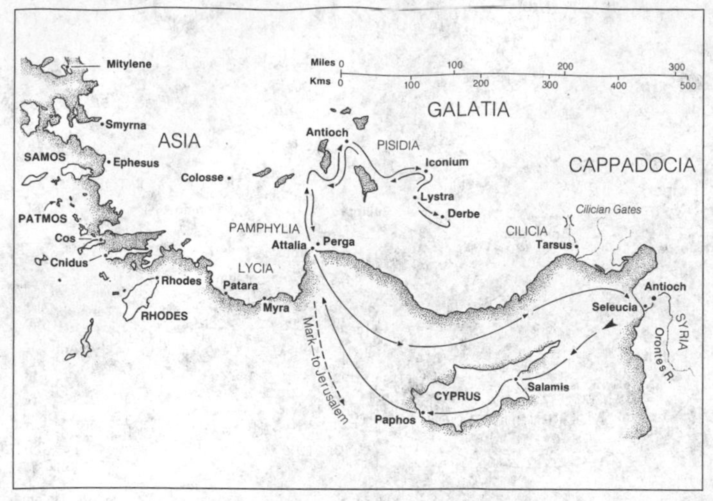

PAUL'S SECOND MISSIONARY JOURNEY

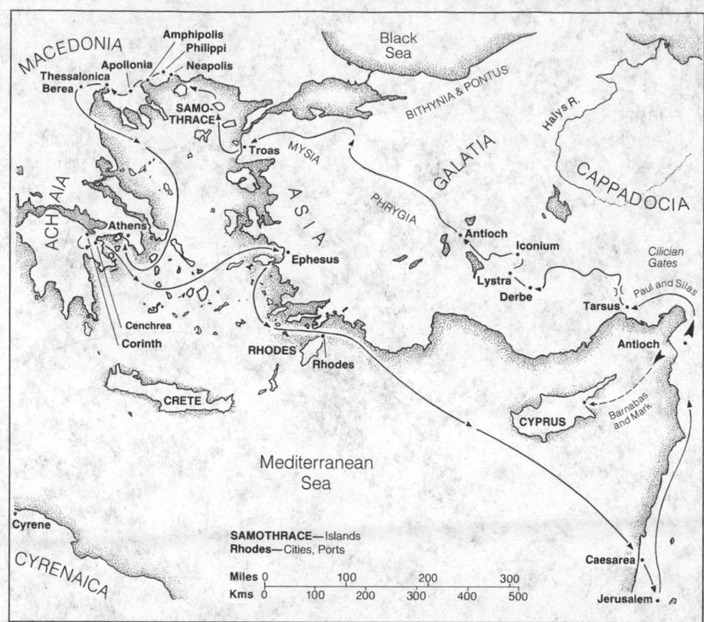

PAUL'S THIRD MISSIONARY JOURNEY

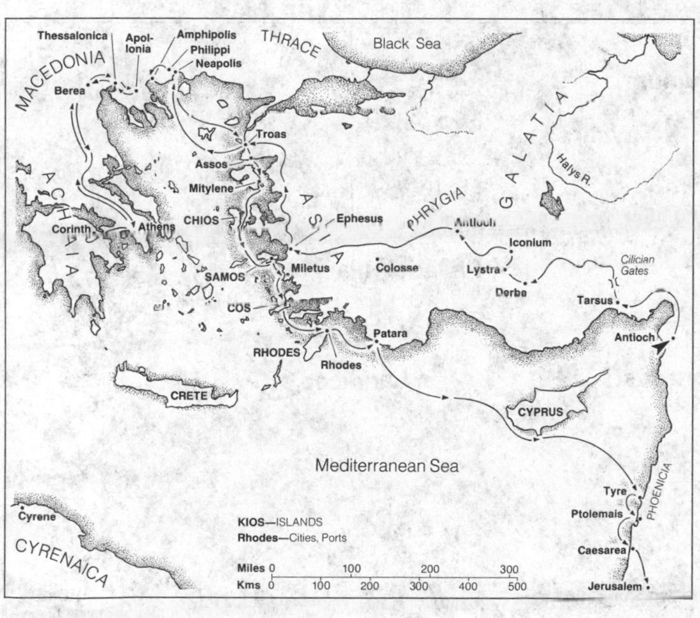

PAUL'S JOURNEY TO ROME

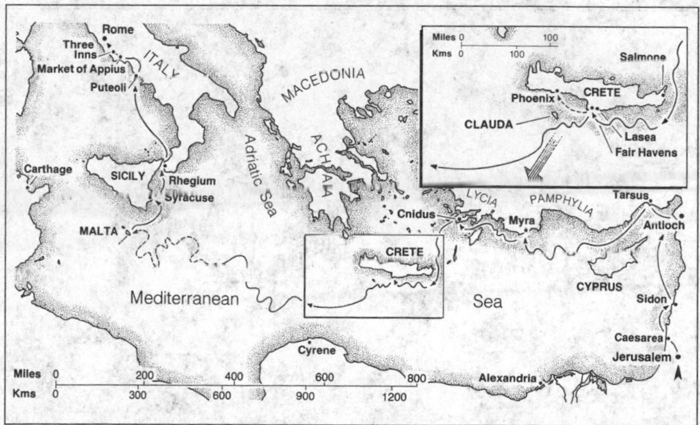

PAUL'S FOURTH MISSIONARY JOURNEY

GALLIA
Atlantic Ocean
HISPANIA
Massilia
Tarraco
Toletum
CORSICA
SARDINIA
Carthage Nova
Gades
Tingis
Carthage
ITALIA
Rome
Neapolis
SICILY
Syracuse
ILLYRICUM
Adriatic Sea
Brundisium
MACEDONIA
Nicopolis
ACHAIA
Athens
THRACE
Philippi
Byzantium
Nicomedia
Black Sea
BITHYNIA & PONTUS
GALATIA
Troas
Pergamum
Ephesus
Colosse
Miletus
CAPPADOCIA
Tarsus
CILICIA
Antioch
CYPRUS
Mediterranean Sea
CRETE
Jerusalem
Cyrene
Alexandria
Memphis
EGYPT
Nile River
Thebes
Miles 0 200 400 600
Kms 0 200 400 600 800

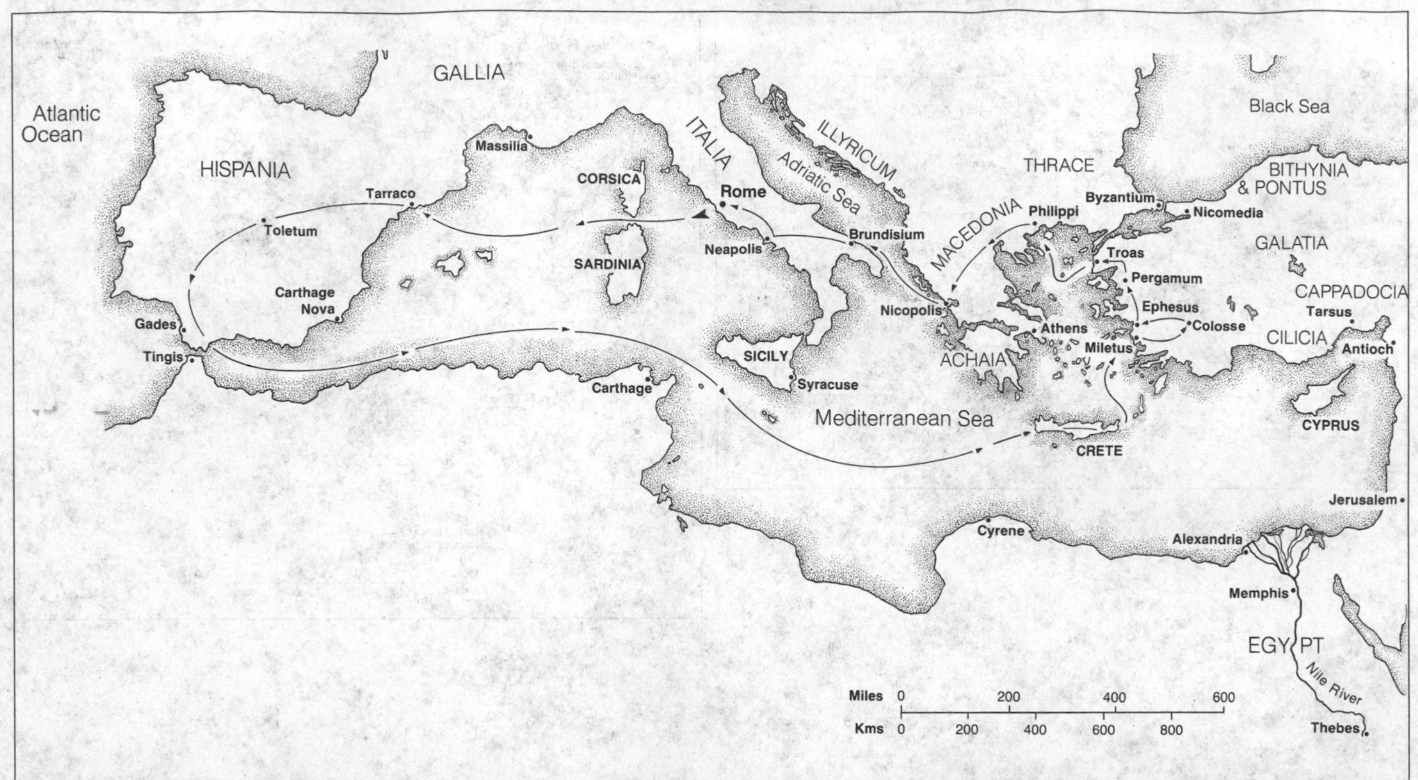

THE SEVEN CHURCHES OF REVELATION

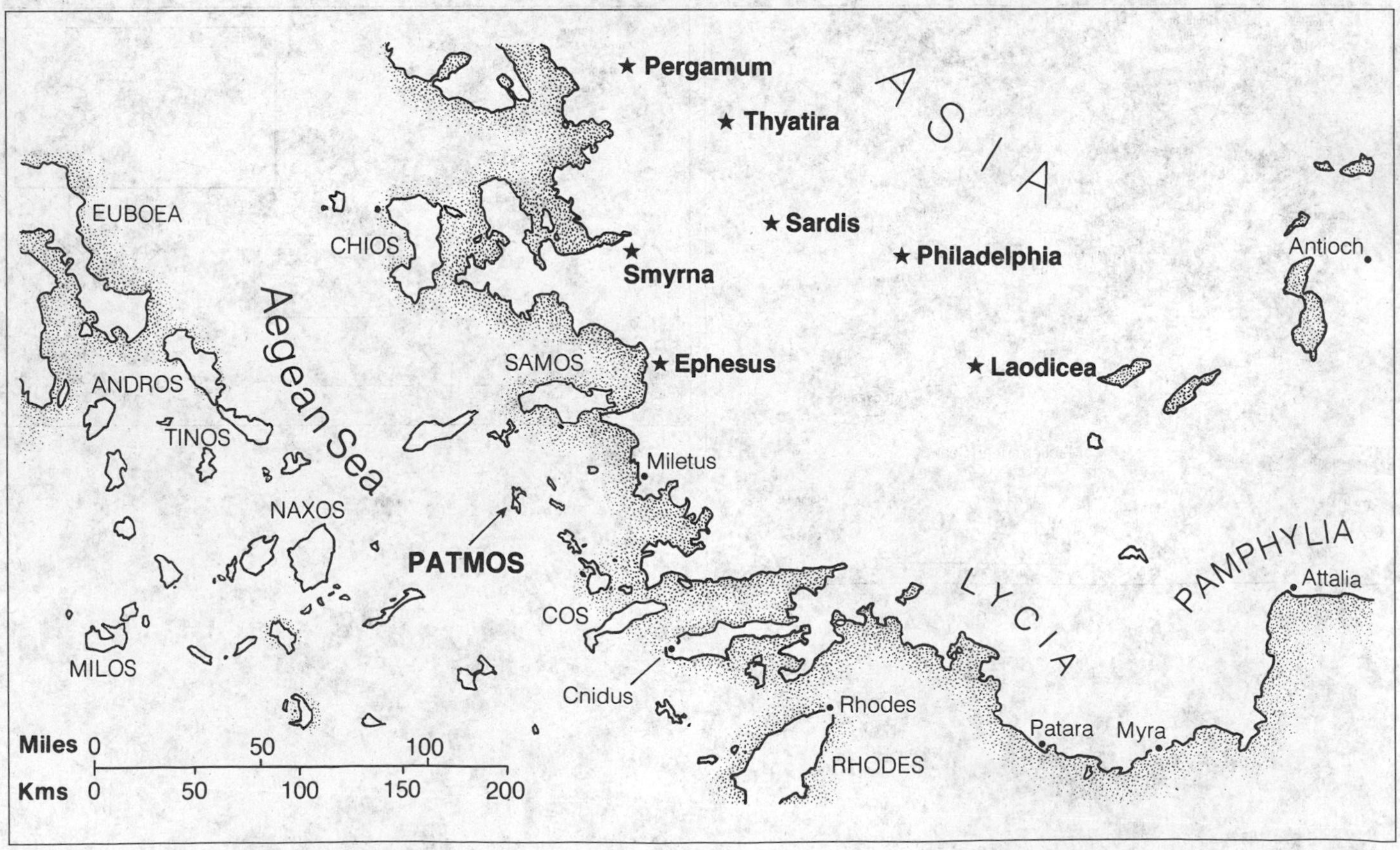

★ Pergamum
★ Thyatira
ASIA
★ Sardis
★ Philadelphia
★ Smyrna
★ Ephesus
★ Laodicea
EUBOEA
CHIOS
Aegean Sea
SAMOS
ANDROS
TINOS
NAXOS
Miletus
PATMOS
COS
MILOS
Cnidus
Rhodes
RHODES
LYCIA
PAMPHYLIA
Attalia
Antioch
Patara
Myra
Miles 0 50 100
Kms 0 50 100 150 200